Facts On File Five-Year Index 1976-1980

THE INDEX OF WORLD EVENTS

DOROTHY KATTLEMAN, Managing Editor
MARJORIE B. BANK, Assistant Managing Editor

RICHARD SPOHN, SUSAN GINZBURG, KURT ROTH, Associate Editors

Published by **Facts On File, Inc.**
460 Park Avenue South, New York, N.Y. 10016

Library of Congress Catalog Card Number 42-24704

ISBN 0-87196-071-0

US ISSN 0014-6641

Printed in the United States of America

FOREWORD

The 1976-1980 Five-Year Index is the seventh volume in the series of Facts On File master news indexes covering the 35 years beginning in 1946.

Subscribers to Facts On File, familiar with the service's cumulative news index and with the annual index found in Facts On File Yearbooks, will find the series an invaluable addition to their research and reference collections. Those who have not previously used Facts On File indexes will find the 1976-1980 edition a comprehensive yet simple-to-use guide to the 200,000 most significant events of the period.

The Five-Year Index is designed for use in exactly the same way as a book or periodical index. It incorporates some special features to speed the researcher's task, whether he or she is spot-checking a key date or constructing the chronology of a complex political event involving several countries.

- The five vertical columns each contains a full year's index entries for the headings covered on the page.
- Parallel alphabetization of the headings in each column gives the researcher five years of information on a subject with a single scan of the page.
- Every event covered is indexed or cross-referenced names by subject, country or organization and personal names. This means, for example, that the researcher seeking information on the 1979 takeover of the U.S. Embassy in Iran would find the event indexed under IRAN—U.S. Embassy Takeover.
- Index entries give a brief description of the event, followed by the date it occurred and the page, column and marginal letter for locating the more detailed Facts On File report in the yearbook concerned. Additional information usually can be found in newspapers of the day following the date of the event.

Used together with the library of bound Facts On File Yearbooks, published since 1941, the seven volumes of Five-Year Indexes are a powerful aid to rapid research on the events of the recent past. This new edition is one more step in a forty-year tradition of recording and indexing the news—a tradition that has placed Facts On File in newsrooms, libraries, schools and research centers throughout the world.

DOROTHY KATTLEMAN
Index Managing Editor

Editor's note: For U.S. Government agencies, see under U.S. GOVERNMENT; for United Nations agencies, see UNITED Nations; for U.S. foreign relations, see foreign country names; for foreign cities, see country names.

The bold stars (*) refer to corrections in the Facts On File news text. Errata will be found on the last pages of this volume.

Facts On File
Five Year Index
1976-80

A

1976

A-Plane Series—*See ARMAMENTS–Aircraft*
AALTO, Alvar
Dies 5-11, 404E1
AARON, Betsy
Interviews Reagan 3-12, 197A1
AARON, David
At Carter Meeting 11-29, 898C3
AARON, Henry
Drives in 3 in opener 4-8, 272B2
AASLING, Nils
Named to Swedish Cabt 10-8, 794C2
ABAT, Brig. Gen. Fortunato
Named PI army commander 3-27, 255B3
ABBAS, Maj. Gen. Khaled Hassan (ret.)
Sudan health min 2-10, 502C1
ABBATUCCI, Joseph
Linked to Libya binocular fraud 12-30, 1107C1
ABBOTT, Anthony
Sworn consumer affairs min 9-15, 692F1
ABBOTT Laboratories
SEC lists forgn paymts 5-12, 726A2
Scores FDA cyclamate ban 10-4, 876F1
Signs Sovt pact 12-8, 948C2
ABBOTT, George
Wins Tony award 4-18, 460F2
ABC—*See AMERICAN Broadcasting Co.*
ABDALA, Carlos
Shot 6-8, dies 6-9, 542D3
ABDEL-Kerim, Tayeh
Vs Saudis on oil price hike 12-18, 975A3
ABDNOR, Rep. James (R, S.D.)
Reelected 11-2, 830A4
ABDUL Gassim, Maj. Mohamed Ibrahim
Named SSU secy gen, Khartoum comr 8-9, 857E2
ABDULLAH, Emad
Chrgd as blast suspect 8-9, 588G2
ABEL, I. W.
USW conv backs policies 8-30—9-3, 669A3
ABELIN, Pierre
Out as French cooperatn min 1-12, 49B2
ABERCROMBIE & Fitch Co.
Swaebe named chief exec 8-6, 984E3
Bankruptcy plea granted 8-9, 984D3
ABERNATHY, Rev. Ralph David
Carter gets endorsmt 4-13, 261C2
Asks new King death probe 4-29, 344G1

ABORTION
Pope vs legalizatn 1-4, 32D3
US bishops challenge '73 Sup Ct ruling 1-7, 32C3
Vatican stand protested 1-17, Pope scores 1-21, 124C2
Canada Appeals Ct upholds MD's acquittal 1-20, 72G1

1977

A-Plane Series—*See ARMAMENTS—Aircraft*
AARON, Henry
Oh breaks HR record 9-3, comments 9-5, 748E2
AARON, Dr. Henry
Named HEW asst secy 1-19, 53B1
AASE, Don
Traded to Angels 12-8, 990F1
AAU (Amateur Athletic Union)—*See specific sport (e.g., TRACK & Field)*
ABA—*See AMERICAN Bar Association*
ABAL, Sir Tei
Loses gov-gen electn 2-18, 203B2
ABAL Medina, Juan Manuel
Mex asks safe-conduct 1-18, 66D2
ABBAS, Abul
Factions clash 2-10—2-11, 106F2
Forces fight Syrians 4-23—4-26, 316D2
ABBOT, Brig. Henry L.
On Pretoria township arrests 11-10, 887F2
ABBOTT, Anthony Chisholm
Canada small business min 9-16, 725B3
ABBOTT Laboratories
Saccharin ban scored 3-9, 176F3
DNA research statemt 3-9, 184D2
ABC—*See AMERICAN Broadcasting Cos.*
ABDALLAHI Ould Daddah
Rptd replaced 3-18, 394E3
ABDEL-Amin, Ahmed Tarek
Police seek 7-11, 542C2
ABDELAZIZ, Mohamed
Warns forgn natls 5-21, 440D3
ABDESSALEM, Belaid
Algeria light indus min 4-23, 470B2
Econ priorities shifted 12-4, 963F1
ABDULAHI Hassan Mohamed
On Ogaden fighting 5-24, 428G2
ABDUL Gassim, Maj. Mohamed Ibrahim
Replaced as party ldr 2-9, 117G2
ABDUL-Jabbar, Kareem
NBA final standings 4-10, 331C3, E3
Named NBA MVP 5-23, top all-star 6-13, 584F3
Punches player 10-18, fined $5000 10-20, 870E1
Teammate injures rival 12-9, 990D3
ABDULLAH, Sheik Mohammed
Party wins Kashmir electn 6-30, 7-3, 544F1
ABDULLAH Egal Mur
OKs US, UK arms aid 7-28, 608A2
ABDULLAHI Yousuf
Assassinated 7-30, 649C1
ABEL, I. W.
McBride leads USW pres vote 2-8, 130B3
Steel contract talks open 2-14, 130F3
Steel contract OKd 4-9, 273C3
ABEL, Rudolf
Francis Gary Powers dies 8-1, 696E3
ABELA, Joseph
Presents budget 1-31, 136E2
ABEL Co., A. S.
Trust suit settled 5-26, 504B2
ABERCROMBIE & Fitch Co.
Closing planned 11-12, stores rptd closed 12-14, 980D3
ABERNATHY, Rev. Ralph David
Loses US House race 3-15, 192B1
ABERNATHY, Roy
Dies 2-28, 164B2
ABILAMAH, Farouk
Named security chief 4-11, 297A3
ABLONDI, Italo H.
Vs shoe import curbs 1-6, 248B3
ABM (antiballistic missiles)—*See ARMAMENTS—Missiles*
ABOOD v. Detroit Board of Education
Agency shops upheld 5-23, 444D1

ABORTION
Reagan gets Electoral Coll vote 1-6, 14G2
Califano backs Medicaid fund bar 1-13, 34F3
Packwood votes vs Califano 1-24, 52F2
Sup Ct affirms Ind rule on minors 1-25, 80F2

1978

A-Plane Series—*See ARMAMENTS—Aircraft*
AAA—*See AMERICAN Automobile Association*
AABA (All-America Basketball Alliance) (defunct)—*See BASKETBALL—Professional*
AABERG, Dennis
Big Wednesday released 7-27, 969D3
AALEM, Maj. Abdullah Abdel
Tied to Ghashmi slaying 6-25, 499D2
AANTJES, Willem
Quits Dutch posts re SS link 11-7, 871G3
AARON, David
Visits Ethiopia 2-17—2-18, 137A2
Clark mtg on rebel aid plan rptd, Carter denies knowledge 5-24, 383B2, 443D1
AARON, Paul
Different Story released 6-13, 619E1
AASLING, Nills
Rpts shipyd closings 6-17, 691A1
AAU (Amateur Athletic Union)—*See specific sport (e.g., TRACK & Field)*
ABA—*See AMERICAN Bar Association*
ABA (American Basketball Association) (defunct)—*See BASKETBALL—Professional*
ABALONE Alliance
Diablo Canyon A-plant protested 8-6—8-7, 609D3
ABAUNZA Salinas, Rodolfo
Shuns Chamorro death probe panel 4-6, 376C2
ABBAS, Abul
Chrgs PLO rivalry re Beirut bldg blast, denied 8-14, 637G2
ABBAS Ghaboush, Philip
Disbands party 7-3, 595C1
ABBOTT, Anthony Chisholm
On Canada Econ Dvpt Bd 11-24, 921B3
ABBOTT, George
Winning Isn't Everything opens 12-3, 1031C3
ABBOTT Laboratories
Depakene OKd for epilepsy 2-28, 231B2
ABC—*See AMERICAN Broadcasting Cos.*
ABC Evening News—*See AMERICAN Broadcasting Cos.*
ABDALLAH, Ahmed (Comoro Islands head of state)
To lead new Comoro govt 5-23, 445B3
Mercenary quits Comoros 9-27, 798B3
Const draft OKd 10-1; Ahmed quits 10-3, 885C2
ABDALLAH Mohamed Kamil (Djibouti premier; replaced Sept. 21)
Names Cabt 2-5, 115F2
Replaced in Cabt shuffle 9-21, 840E3
ABDELMOUNINE, Moulaye
Ousted as Mauritania health min 1-26, 95D1
ABDNOR, Rep. James (R, S.D.)
Reelected 11-7, 852C2, 855C1
ABDUL Gassim, Maj. Mohamed Ibrahim
Chad peace plan OKd 2-24, 130B2
ABDUL-Jabbar, Kareem
NBA scoring, field-goal ldr 4-9, 271D2, E2
ABDUL-Karim, Tayeh
Backs OPEC price hike, cites purchasing power drop 6-18, 465E1
ABE, Shintaro
Vs Sovt protest on China 121G3
ABEDI, Agha Hasan
SEC chrgs 3-18, settles 3-19, 204A2, E2
ABERNATHY, Rev. Ralph David
Testifies on King assassinatn, scores FBI 8-14, 641B1
Israel frees US Arab 10-18, 783D2
ABEX Corp.—*See under IC Industries Inc.*
ABORIGINES—*See under AUSTRALIA*
ABORTION
HEW issues rules 1-26, 116D1
Carter vs fed funding 2-17, 123G2-A3
Akron (O) ordinance passed 2-28, 744A1
Catholic views polled 3-2, 295C1
Clinic firebombings, vandalism rptd up 3-7, 5-17, 744A2

1979

A-Plane Series—*See ARMAMENTS–Aircraft*
AAA—*See AMERICAN Automobile Association*
A'ALAM, Dr. Jamshid
Executed 9-24, 814B3
AARON, David
USSR dissident-spy swap talks rptd 4-27, 317D1
AARON, Henry (Hank)
Mays in Baseball HOF 8-5, 618E3
Assails baseball racism 8-15, 1003D1
Yastrzemski gets 3000th hit 9-12, 1002D3
AARON, Henry J.
Soc Sec chngs urged 12-7, 946F2
AARON v. SEC
Case accepted by Sup Ct 10-15, 848B1
AASE, Don
Angels lose AL pennant 10-6, 797F2
AAU(Amateur Athletic Union)—*See specific sport(e.g., TRACK & Field)*
ABA—*See AMERICAN Bar Association*
ABA al-Khayl, Sheik Muhammad
Warns IMF-World Bank on oil prices 10-3, 779B3
Sees Miller on assets freeze 11-25, 896B3
On Saudi money reserves 12-18, 968F3
ABBAS Mohri, Hojatoeslam Haj Seyyed
Kuwait ousts 9-26, 752A3
ABBOTT, Anthony Chisholm
In India 57A3
ABC—*See AMERICAN Broadcasting Cos.*
ABDELGHANI, Mohamed Ben Ahmed (Algerian premier)
Named Algeria premier 3-8, 215E2
ABDEL-Shafi, Haidar
Dayan contacts 8-29, comments 8-30, 9-4, 658D3-659B1
Son arrested 9-7, 676G3
ABDEL-Shafi, Tarik Haidar
Arrested as Gaza terrorist 9-7, 676G3
ABDUL-Jabbar, Kareem
Chamberlain interview scores 3-21, 291C1
NBA scoring, field-goal, rebound, block shot ldr 4-8, 290E2, F2, A3
ABDULLAH, Taha Ibrahim
Iraq planning min 7-16, 544E3
ABDULLAH, Col. Tareq Hamed
Iraq Cmnd Cncl secy 7-28, 583F1
ABDULLAH al-Kahtani, Mohammed
Leads Mecca mosque takeover 11-20, role disputed 11-30, 898C3, 899F1
ABEDI, Agha Hasan
Cited re Lance '78 oil deal influence chrg 4-9, 306A1
ABELS, Rev. Paul
Methodists uphold apptmt 11-1, 931G3
ABERDEEN, Robert
Deadly Deillah opens 7-6, 711D2
ABKO Realty Corp.
Chrysler unit purchased 8-22, 663D2
ABLAH, George
Abko buys Chrysler unit 8-22, 663D2
ABM (antiballistic missile)—*See ARMAMENTS–Missiles*
ABORIGINES—*See under AUSTRALIA*

ABORTION
Pa control law voided by Sup Ct 1-9, 14A1
NJ Medicaid paymts ordrd 1-9, 315D1
Tex record access case declined by Sup Ct 1-22, 54A2
Legalized abortn anniv marked in DC, NY 1-22, 63C2

1980

A-Plane Series—*See ARMAMENTS--Aircraft*
AARON, David
Dem platform backs MX 6-24, 479D3
FBI, CIA probes re Trigon arrest rptd 9-22, 754B1
Rptd cleared in spy leak 12-5, 940A3
AARON, Henry
Boycotts awards ceremony, chrgs racism 1-28, 637F1
AARON & Co., E.L. (defunct)
SEC fraud intent proof required by Sup Ct 6-2, 512C3
AARON v. SEC
Case decided by Sup Ct 6-2, 512A3
ABA—*See AMERICAN Bar Association*
ABA al-Khayl, Sheik Muhammad
In US oil talks 3-1—3-4, 165C3
ABBESZADEH, Mohamad
Protests Canada cultural exhibitn bar, Egypt pavillion rental 7-3, 520G3-521B1
ABBEY Road (recording)
Lennon slain 12-8, 934E3
ABBEY v. Control Data Corp.
Case refused by Sup Ct 1-7, 16A1
ABBOTT Laboratories
Cyclamate ban rptd upheld by FDA 2-7, 317D2, A3
Interferon productn rptd up 3-5, 317D3
US sets tranquilizer warnings 7-11, 584G1
ABBOUD, A. Robert
Ousted in First Chicago shakeup 4-28, 456A2
Named Occidental pres, chief operating officer 8-4, 702A1
ABC—*See AMERICAN Broadcasting Cos.*
ABC v. Vegod
Case refused by Sup Ct 10-6, 782F2
ABDEL Aziz, Prince Sawaz ibn (Saudi Arabia)
Resignatn as Mecca gov cited 1-1, 22E1
ABDELGHANI, Mohamed Ben Ahmed (Algerian premier)
Loses interior post 1-13, 55G3
ABDNOR, Rep. James (R, S.D.)
Wins Sen primary 6-3, 439B3
Elected to US Sen 11-4, 840C3, 843F2, 845A2
ABDUL Aziz, Prince Sultan ibn (Saudi Arabia)
France naval aid set 10-14, 790D1*
Mediates Syria-Jordan feud 11-30—12-2, 911G2
Syria-Jordan border troops withdraw 12-10—12-11, 931A3
ABDUL-Jabbar, Kareem
NBA scoring, field-goal, block shot ldr 3-30, 278C3, D3, G3
Lakers win NBA title 5-16, 432A1
Named NBA MVP 5-29, 656A3
On NBA all-league team 6-2, 656D3
Airplane released 7-2, 675G1
ABECASSIS, Snu
Dies in Lisbon plane crash 12-4, 923E1
ABERNATHY, Rev. Ralph David
Endorses Reagan 10-16, 802B2
Visits Reagan 12-9, 956A2
ABI-Ackel, Ibrahim
Orders RC priest expelled 10-30, 870E3
ABILOV, Ismail
Wins Olympic medal 7-31, 624E3
ABORIGINES—*See under AUSTRALIA*

ABORTION
Anti-abortionists vs 'test-tube baby' clinic 1-8, 24E1, A2
'78 data rptd 1-9, 23F2
Fetal skin disease test rptd 1-10, 64E1
US rpts smoking-health risks 1-14, 40C2
Medicaid aid ban voided 1-15, 35A3

1976

Swiss referendum rptd backed 1-25, 104E1
Sup Ct bars Mo Medicaid rule review 1-26, 87B3
Sup Ct bars pvt hosp rule review 3-1, 170C1
Canada Sup Ct upholds MD's acquittal 3-15, 537B3
Canada law review urged 3-25, 250D3
Italy Parlt OKs limited amendmt 4-1, dispute flares 4-2—4-7, 254A1
Italy referendum set 4-16, 333B3
Sen tables anti-abortn amendmt 4-28, 346G1-A2
Sen kills anti-abortn amendmt 4-28, 883D3
Baptists affirm stand 6-15—6-18, 951E2
Sup Ct extends women's rights; voids spousal, parental consent 7-1, 518E2
Rev Franzoni defrocked 8-4, 951B2
Ford at intl RC cong 8-8, 596A3
Italy therapeutic abortns rptd, church scores 8-13—8-25, 840D3
3d Canada MD acquittal 9-18; chrgs dropped 12-10, 946C1
Medicaid fund curb overridden 9-30, 726F2, G3
Ct voids Medicaid fund curb 10-22, Sup Ct bars stay 11-8, 848F1
World populatn growth down 10-28, 863A2
US Bishops Conf backs Vatican stand 11-8—11-11, 859G1
'72-74 IUD deaths rptd 11-18, 931E2
Sup Ct upholds MD office abortns 11-29, 900C3
Presidential Campaign Issue—*See also McCORMACK, Ellen*
Ford backs limited abortns 2-3, 88A1
US Dem platform plank 6-15, 432F3
Dem platform text 6-15, 472A2
NY Dem conv protests 7-12—7-15, 513D1
Carter proposes progrm 8-3, 564B3
Reagan: Schweiker compatible 8-4, 564D1
Reagan asks platform abortn ban 8-8, 583C1
GOP platform com OKs plank 8-13, 582E3
US GOP platform adopted 8-18, 600B3, 601D1; text 604D3, 605F2
Indep Party platform plank 8-27, 666F1
Carter sees RC bishops 8-31, 645C2
Carter Phila church mtg shifted; Scranton protests 9-7, 664A1
Ford backs state regulatn 9-8, 665D1
Carter defends policy stand 9-9, 664D3
Bishops review Ford stand 9-10, assert neutrality 9-16, 686D1-B2
Ford, Carter debate 10-22, 802C1
Dole campaigns vs abortn 10-31, 827A3
Reagan electoral vote rptd 12-13, 979B1
ABOUREZK, Sen. James (D, S.D.)
Scores arms aid bill 2-17, 151G3
Udall 2d in SD 6-1, 390A1
Scores Letelier murder, asks probe 9-21, 710E2
Gets Sadat peace bid 11-14 878B1
ABRAHAM, Claude
Testifies for Concorde 1-5, 5F2
ABRAM, Morris B.
Accuses Paraguay, asks US aid cutoff 4-5, 403E2
ABRAMOWITZ, Morton I.
Rpts on Korean crisis 9-1, 641E1
ABRAMS, Robert
Bayh quits '76 race 3-4, 165D2
ABSARI, Hushang
Meets US energy aide 5-9, 340C1
ABU Basha, Gen. Hassan
Chrgs Libya re bombing 8-8, 588G2
ABU Dhabi—*See also UNITED Arab Emirates*
French Mirage purchase cited 1-16, 36C2
Sadat visits, gets aid vow 2-27, 162E1
Total IMF oil loan rptd 4-1, 340F2
ABU Zeid, Maj. Maamoun Awad (ret.)
Sudan interior min 2-10, 502C1
ABZUG, Rep. Bella S. (D, N.Y.)
Lauds pub works-urban aid vote 1-29, 94B1
Scores privacy abuses 2-12, 151A3
Hills on SEC boycott rules 6-4, 747E2
Women get Carter rights pledge 7-12, 513A1
Loses Sen primary 9-14, vows Moynihan support 9-15, 687E2
Electn results 11-2, 820D2, 821F2
ACADEMY Awards—*See 'Awards' under MOTION Pictures*

ACCIDENTS (number in parenthesis: total killed)
US health rpt issued 1-12, 32C1
'74 death rates rptd 2-3, 123G3
Italy ski-lift (42) 3-9, 384E1
Colo ski-lift (4) 3-26, 384F1
Pak bldg collapses (140) 9-13, 816E1
Aviation
Middle East 707 in Saudi (82) 1-1, 79G3
'74 Eastern NC crash damages awarded 1-19, 80A2
'74 TWA Va crash rpt 1-21, 80A1
'75 US death toll 124 1-24, 736B2
Gulf of Mex copter crash (12) 4-23, 736G2
St Thomas crash (37) 4-27, 335F2, A3 ★
'75 Eastern crash rpt 5-1, 736D2
Iranian 747 in Spain (17) 5-9, 404B3
Air Manila crash in Guam (46) 6-4, 736A2
Thomas Atlantic balloon flight 7-1, 640E3
Czech crash (70) 7-28, 560G3
Littons' pvt plane in Mo (6) 8-3, 565C2

1977

Carter budget revision 2-22, 125G3
Carter affirms oppositn 5-17, 381C3
Conn minor requiremt voided 5-23, 444C3
'76 figures rptd 6-1, 787B1
NY contraceptive curbs voided 6-9, 501C2
House bars HEW funds 6-17, 478B1, A2
Sup Ct upholds state fund curbs 6-20, 516C2
NYS, SD rulings vacated; NJ case refused 6-27, 538G3
Sen OKs eased funding curb 6-29, 515E2, G3
'76 Hyde Amendmt stay vacated 6-29, 557B3
Carter backs Sup Ct decisns 7-12, 533B1, F2-534A1
US proposes adoptn subsidy alternative 7-12, 628A3
Carter aides protest fed funds ban 7-15, 786E2
Family planning groups urge alternatives, teenage rates rptd 7-19, 786C3
Bell extends Hyde Amendmt scope 7-27, 786C2
Hyde Amendmt stay lifted, Califano bans fed subsidies 8-4, 786G1
Dissident Episcs form new church 9-14—9-16, 731D2
Sen bars Eagleton amendmt 9-16, 738C1
Cong funding debate delays HEW-Labor bill 10-1, Califano urges passage 10-11, 786C2
ACLU sets '78 rights drive 10-6, 786A3
State funding rptd 10-12, 786F3
Natl Women's Conf backs, conservatives rally vs 11-19—11-21, 917A3, G3
Funding curb clears Cong 12-7, 958C2; signed 12-9, 1001F2
LSC aid in suits barred 12-28, 1002D2
Foreign Developments
Israel law OKd 1-31, 135D2
Canada backs clinics 3-4, 237A3
Italy legalizatn bill defeated 6-7, 527F2
Israel vows more curbs 6-9, 474B3
Canadian Anglicans drop debate 8-18, 732D2
Dutch coalitn talks halted 8-25, 656B1
Dutch parties heal rift 9-2, 729F2
Swiss reform referendum fails 9-25, 766C3
ABORTION Rights Action League, National
Abortn funding curb scored 12-7, 958B3
ABOUREZK, Sen. James (D, S.D.)
Visits Cuba 4-4—4-8, 282C3
Filibusters vs gas deregulatn 9-22—10-3, 757G2
ABRAHAM, Eric
Flees to Botswana 1-5, 3D3
ABRAHAMSEN, Dr. David
Berkowitz fit for trial 10-21, 848C3
ABRIL Martorell, Fernando
Spain 3d deputy premier 7-5, 545G1
ABU Dhabi—*See UNITED Arab Emirates*
ABU Gharbiyah, Bahjat
Loses race for Palestine post 3-13, 208D1
ABULOC, Ernesto H.
Kills 7 in theft plot 3-31, 312F3
ABUSAID, Carlos
Slain in kidnap attempt 11-3, 1011A2
ABZUG, Bella S.
Declines Carter Admin post 2-19, 140B3
Koch wins mayoral primary 9-8, 723B2
Natl Women's Conf meets 11-19—11-21, 917A3
ACADEMY Awards—*See MOTION Pictures—Awards*

ACCIDENTS (number in parenthesis: total killed)
Black life expectancy linked 12-13, 962D3
Aviation
Uganda plane in Sudan 1-30, 102C3
RAAF Mirage jet (1) 2-2, 113F2
Jordan queen in copter (4) 2-9, 87D1
Pa offcls pvt plane (9) 2-24, 204D3
Pilot chrgd in '76 St Thomas crash 3-6, 312G1
Pan Am, KLM in Canary I (577) 3-27, 244C1
Canary I crash suits filed in US 3-31—4-6; probe begun 4-4; 2 survivors die 4-19, 311F2, B3-312C1
Southern Air jet in Ga (70) 4-4, 286A3
Guterma pvt plane in NYC (7) 4-5, 286E3
'74 Turk jet crash setlmt 4-14, 312C1
Israel mil copter (54) 5-10, 396E2
US '76 death toll 5-12, 412G2
NY Airways copter (5) 5-16, 412A3
Yugo air controller sentncd in '76 crash 5-16, 497A3

1978

March of Dimes halts genetic disease grants 3-8, 744B2
Ill law struck down 4-13, 744A1
Calif MD mistrial in '77 death 5-5, 369C2
'75, '76 US data compared 5-24, 8-10, 744C1
Teen contraceptive survey rptd 6-7, 598B2
House votes funding curb 6-13, 445D3
State funding, other state dvpts 6-20, 743A3
Mil fund curb passes US House 8-9, 604F2
ABA backs Medicaid funds 8-9, 626B3
'72-77 opinion polls rptd 8-9, 744F1
Ky cnty cuts off funding, sets curbs 8-22, 743G2
Ky woman acquitted of self-abortn 8-30, 743B2
La law delayed by ct 9-7, 743D3-744A1
Mo law ruled unconst 9-13, 744A1
Mil fund curb signed 10-13, 833F1
Ill control law appeal refused by Sup Ct 10-16, 789D2
State voters reject 11-7, 845F2
Clark loses US Sen reelectn 11-7, 854C2
Cleveland zoning ordinance case refused by Sup Ct 11-27, 937D2
Foreign Developments
Canada solicitor-gen resigns in scandal 1-30, 70B1; not chrgd 2-23, 166C2
NZ law in effect 4-1, repeal petitn rptd in Parlt 5-18, 498A2
Spain parlt OKs debate; 310,000 illegal abortns rptd 4-26, 576A3
Italy reform bill enacted 5-18, 375C1
Swiss voters rejct reform 5-28, 558E2
Amer Human Rights Conv vs 7-18, 829B1
New Pope elected, views cited 8-26, 658B1
Australia gays protest 'Right to Life' mtg 8-27, 686D1
Dutch Cabt OKs liberalized bill 11-16, 965F1-A2
NZ electn issue 11-25, 924A3
ABORTION Rights Action League, National
Rpts violence vs clinics 3-7, 5-17, 744A2
Mil abortn fund curb scored 8-9, 604G2 ★
ABOUREZK, Sen. James (D, S.D.)
Votes for Panama Canal neutrality pact 3-16, 177D2
Redwood Park bill passed 3-21, 218G1
Threatens vote vs 2d Canal pact 4-17; assured on gas deregulatn, votes for pact 4-18, 273B1, C2
Holds mock Carter energy plan fete 4-20, 304B3
Not standing for reelectn 6-6, 448A2
Ends filibuster vs energy tax measure 10-15, 787A1
Israel frees US Arab 10-18, 783D2
Pressler wins seat 11-7, 855B1
ABRAHAM, Arnold—*See GOODMAN, Lord*
ABRAHAMS, Alan H. (alias James A. Carr)
Arrested 1-10; flees, identity revealed 1-14, apprehended 1-24, 83B2-D3
Gets jail term on probatn violatn 4-20, 283C1
Indicted for fraud 8-3, 665C2
ABRASIMOV, Pyotr Andreevich
Lauds E Ger ties 1-31, 61G3
Hints neutron bomb tradeoff 4-4, 254A2
ABREU, Gen. Hugo de Andrade
Quits re Figueiredo pres bid 1-4, 6D3
Rpt scores Figueiredo bid 1-13, 165F3
Leads Figueiredo mil oppositn 5-29, 555E3
Jailed; Bentes protests 10-2, 771E3
Arrested 10-2; govt corruptn, tap chrgs corroborated 10-17, 836F2
ABRIL Martorell, Fernando
Named Spain dep premr for econ 2-24, 394F2
ABRUZZO, Ben
Crosses Atlantic by balloon 8-11—8-17, '77 attempt cited 652E3
ABU Dhabi—*See NONALIGNED Nations Movement, UNITED Arab Emirates*
ABU Dhabi Fund for Economic Development
Poor-natn aid rise rptd 4-9, 257G2
ABZUG, Bella S.
Loses US House nominatn 1-15, overturned 1-18; upset in electn 2-14, 108F1-B2
Women's group sees Carter 3-22, 218C2
Natl Advisory Com cancels Carter mtg 11-22, 915F1
ACADEMY Awards—*See MOTION Pictures—Awards*
ACCIDENTS (number in parenthesis: total killed)
Hartford arena roof collapses 1-18, 95A3; design deficiencies rptd 6-15, 460C1
W Va scaffold collapse (51) 4-27, OSHA issues rpt 6-8, 459F2
Tex church roof collapses (1) 5-21, 460F1
Pa 'tug-of-war' injures 70 6-13, 460G2
SC pool light electrocutn (4) 6-27, 636F3
Italy chem plant toxic cloud (3) 9-19, 724G2
Aviation
Air India 747 off Bombay (213) 1-1, 23F3-24A1
US '77 carrier deaths rptd 1-6, 24B1
Uruguay AF transport (31) 2-10, 270G3
Canada Pacific Westn jet (40) 2-11, 271A1
Delta '73 Boston crash suit review refused 2-21, 126A2
Venez airline in Carib (47) 3-3, 271A1

1979

Utah House OKs bill 2-16, 315F1
Minn Planned Parenthood funds ban upset 2-23, 310E2
Mo curb end backed by Sup Ct 3-5, 185A1
SC MD prosecutn ban voided by US Sup Ct 3-5, 185A1
Medicaid '78 decline rptd 3-8, 315A1
Edelin '75 convictn reversal cited 3-15, 272B1
Neb law revised 3-19, suspended 4-20, 315C1
Public views polled 4-22, 315F1
Prenatal hemophilia test rptd 4-26, 315E2
Death data rptd 4-29, 547C3
Mass Medicaid funds case refused by Sup Ct 5-14, 383D1
Mass sets strict law 6-12, 547G2
Mass consent law voided by Sup Ct 7-2, 559G1-D2
US House OKs anti-abortion amendmts 7-11, 514E3
Steinem cites as '80 electn issue 7-13–7-15, 578C3
Cong OKs '80 continuing funds resolutns 10-12, 11-16, 900F1, A2
Fla trust case declined by Sup Ct 10-29, 884D2
DC funds bill signed 10-30, 870A1
Public opinion poll rptd 11-11, 930A2
Funding cases accepted by Sup Ct 11-26, 919A2
NOW vs Carter reelectn bid 12-9, 961B3
Foreign Developments
Pope presents 1st encyclical 3-15, 216G3
World figures rptd 4-29, 547B3
Veil voted EC Parlt pres 7-17, 537E2
Pope in US, affirms oppositn 10-3–10-7, 758B3, 759B2, E2, G3
China access rptd 10-10, 790B1
Spain law protested 10-20–10-21, trial suspended 10-26, 875B3
Spain rally denounces 11-18, 952B2
France legalizes permanently 11-30, 949F1-A2
Spain sentences abortionist 12-11, 952D2
Israel tightens abortn law 12-25, 995B1
ABORTION Rights Action League, National
Low-income aid set 1-21, NOW conf OKd 1-22, 63G2
ABOU, Husni Mahmoud
Admits violence planned 9-7, 755A1
ABRAHAM, F. Murray
Teibele & Her Demon opens 12-16, 1007F2
ABRAHAM, Karl
On 3 Mile I A-accident 3-28, 242F2
On 3 Mile I shutdown 4-27, 322F1, A2
ABRAHAMS, Alan H. (alias James A. Carr)
5 Lloyd Carr offcls convicted 2-22, sentncd 3-19, 220E2
ABRAHAMS, Doris Cole
Once A Catholic opens 10-10, 956F3
ABRAMS, Mike
On Fla pres caucuses 10-14, 783E1
ABRAMS, Robert
Stays Woolworth takeover 4-20, 304C2
Chrgs AMA in chiropractors suit 7-5, 570F2
'78-79 Broadway season rptd successful 11-4, 956D2
ABU Dhabi—*See UNITED Arab Emirates*
ABZUG, Bella S.
Carter ousts as women's panel com head 1-12, controversy sparked 1-12–1-17, 30C2
Robb named women's panel head 5-9, 351A2
Speaks at NWPC conv 7-14, 578B3
ACADEMY Awards—*See MOTION Pictures—Awards*

ACCIDENTS (number in parenthesis: total killed)
Aviation
UK airline '72 crash case refused by Sup Ct 1-15, 32D1
NYC near-collisn 2-11, 206C2; rpt 4-9, 412C2
Japan Air '77 Alaska crash rpt 2-13, 412F1
Chinese jet transport (44) 3-14, 240G2
Jordanian jet in Qatar (45) 3-14, 240C3
Sovt airliner near Moscow (90) 3-17, 240B3
Quebecair turboprop (17) 3-29, 240D3
Kenya pvt plane (1) 4-3, 356F3
TWA 727 mid-air plunge, Detroit emergency landing 4-4, 412G1
2 US AF F-5Es (2) 4-12, 404A3
San Diego '78 collisn rpt 4-19, 412D2*
Amer DC-10 in Chicago (275) 5-25; inspectns ordrd, flaws rptd 5-29–5-31, 411C3-412E1; grounded 6-6, 420E2, ban lifted 7-13, 538F2 411C3-412E1

1980

Marshall stays Medicaid aid order 2-14, Sup Ct lifts stay, accepts case 2-19, 130F2-B3
Utah parental notificatn case accepted by Sup Ct 2-25, 187G3
Medicaid funding cases argued in Sup Ct 4-21, 306A2
DC Christian rally held 4-29, 348E3, 349A1
US Families Conf opens in Baltimore 6-5, 442C3; meets in Minn 6-19—6-21, LA 7-10—7-12, 601A2, E2
Medicaid funding limits upheld by Sup Ct; reactn 6-30, 491F2-492A2
Mass pro-abortionists win primary 9-16, 724C2
Medicaid funding review denied by Sup Ct 9-17, 703A3
US electn results; supporters defeated, rights threatened 11-4, 846E2, B3, 848C2, 850C1
Foreign Developments
UK demonstratn backs 2-8, 132F3-133B1
Pope in Africa, affirms oppositn 5-2—5-10, 363A3
Australia anti-abortn bill defeated 5-30, 428D2
W Ger RC bishops enter pol debate 9-13, 712D1
RC bishops family conf opens 9-26, 810D2
Pope in W Ger, affirms traditionalism 11-15—11-19, 905D1
Dutch parlt OKs liberal law 12-20, 996F3
U.S. Presidential Election (& Transition)
Reagan assails Bush 2-5, Bush explains stance 2-7, 128G2, A3
Reagan defends GOP focus in NH 2-20, 129B3
Dem platform drafted 6-24, 479G2, B3
GOP platform com debates 7-7—7-10; seeks US amendmt ban, Medicaid funds bar 7-9, 506B2-F2
Evangelical Christian pol actn profiled 7-11—9-15, 818E3, 819B1, B2, C2
Hooks asks GOP stand chng 7-15, 535B1
GOP platform adopted; text 7-15, 535A3, F3
ABA repudiates GOP plank 8-6, 744F1
Dem conv keynote speech 8-11, 612A2*, A3
Dem platform planks OKd 8-12; Carter disavows, conv adopts 8-13, 611B1, E1; text excerpts 614G3, 615D1
Anderson platform offered 8-30, 665C2
Reagan, Anderson TV debate 9-21, 721F2, 722A2
Reagan clarifies judicial apptmt stand 9-30, 738C3
Reagan reaffirms stand 11-6, 839C3
ABRAHAMS, Alan H. (alias James A. Carr)
Sentenced 6-20, 503C1
ABRAHAMS, Jim
Airplane released 7-2, 675G1
ABRAMKIN, Valery
Sentenced 10-11, 863B2
ABRAMSON, David
Fined 2-11, 134D3
ABRAMS v. Salla
Case declined by Sup Ct 4-21, 344C2
ABRASIMOV, Pyotr
Warns on new Cold War 2-7, 107A1
ABSALDOV, Saipulla
Wins Olympic medal 7-31, 624D3
ABSCAM Scandal—*See under U.S. GOVERNMENT--FEDERAL Bureau of Investigation*
ABU Dhabi—*See also UAE*
Financial Gen deal set 7-25, 600E3
US debates forgn bank takeovers 8-28, 9-17, 806A3
US OKs DC bank 10-1, 806F3
ABU Dhabi International Bank
US OKs DC branch 10-1, 806F3
ABUHAZIRA, Aharon
Indicted 12-1; police chief admits rights abuses 12-30, ousted 12-31, 994E3
ABUSHEV, Magomedgasan
Wins Olympic medal 7-29, 624D3
ABU-Wardeh, Mohammed
Slain in Gaza Strip 11-18, 880B1
ABZUG, Bella S.
At DC draft protest 3-22, 228A1
ACADEMY Awards—*See MOTION Pictures*

ACCIDENTS (number in parenthesis: total killed)
Colombia bullring collapse (222) 1-21, 80C3
Aviation
Private plane off Va (2) 1-11, 175A3
Iranian 727 near Tehran (128) 1-21, 80F3
'79 rate rise rptd 2-20, 347D1
Munson family files wrongful-death suit 2-27, 637E1
Polish jet near Warsaw (87) 3-14, 213E3; engine failure seen 3-31, 256B3
Brazilian airliner (54) 4-12, 527G3
UK jet in Canary I (146) 4-25, 392B1
Thai airliner near Bangkok (40) 4-27, 527G3
Bolivia pvt plane (3) 6-2, 728D1
Panama AF plane in El Salvador 6-15, 462C3
US DC-9 in Honolulu 6-15; FAA orders engine inspectns 7-16, 667B1
Gandhi's son in New Delhi (2) 6-23, 487A2

1976

USAF transport in UK (18) 8-28, 859B2
USAF transport in Greenland (21) 8-28, 859B2
Venez transport in Azores (68) 9-4, 696F3
Brit Airways, Yugo jet collisn (176) 9-10, 696B3
F-14 lost off carrier 9-14, recovered 11-11, 941D1
Turkish 727 hits Karakaya Mt (155) 9-19, 736F1-A2
Johnson & Johnson jet (11) 9-26, 840G2
AF tanker crash in Mich (15) 9-26, 840G3
Bombed Cuba jet in Carib (73) 10-6, 779A3
Indian Airlines in Bombay (95) 10-12, 840F2
Bolivia cargo jet (100) 10-13, 876G2
Colombia crash (32) 10-25, 876F2
US Skyhawk downed by Phantom 12-10, 941B3

Fires & Explosions—*See also other appropriate headings in this section; 'Arson' under CRIME*

Belgian cafe (15) 1-1, 80D1
Neb hotel blast (18) 1-10, 80E1
Ill nursing home (7) 2-4, 271B3
'75 Ala A-plant rpt issued 2-28, 171C3
Finn ammunitn factory (45) 4-13, 404C3
Italy chem factory 7-10, 560A3
Italy chem factory dvpts 8-11—10-11, 840B3; co pays damages 12-2, 932A1
La oil refinery blast (13) 8-12, 816A2
Washn A-waste cntr blast 8-30, 670D3
NYC gum factory blast 11-21, 969A2
Olympic Airways crash (50) 11-23, 912D2
Sovt Aeroflot crash (72) 11-28, 912C2
Fire destroys Australia navy planes 12-5, 922E3
Tanker explodes in LA harbor 12-17, 969F1
Eur forest fire losses rptd 12-31, 977E3

Marine

Norwegian freighter lost (30) 1-19, 79D3
Oil rig sinks (13) 4-15, 544D3
Spain oil tanker explodes (1) 5-12, 384C1
Shafer acquitted, Knull convicted re '75 warships collisn 5-12, 6-22, 941G2
St Lawrence oil barge spill 6-23, 859D2
Chem barge capsizes off Va 8-18, 796F2
US, Sovt ships collide in Ionian 8-28, 941B3
Japan tanker split 9-11, 796C2
F-14 sinks off carrier 9-14, recovered 11-11, 941D1
Kennedy, Bordelon collide 9-14, 941F2
Sovt ship bombed in US 9-17, 908A1
E Ger tanker sinks off France (13) 10-14, 912E2
US ship lost in Bermuda Triangle (37) 10-15, 912D1
Norwegian tanker, Miss ferry collide (71) 10-20, 876G1
Japan ship sinks off Hawaii (19) 11-11, 892D1
Liberia tanker grounded off Nantucket 12-15, 968D3; liability hearing 12-28—12-31, Coast Guard sinks 12-31, 1013E3
Liberia tanker explodes in LA harbor (4) 12-17, 969F1
Tanker grounded in Del R 12-27, 1014E1
Tanker grounded off PR 12-28, 1014A2

Mine

'75 India blast search ended 1-19, 80A2
1st female miner in Ky 1-27, 80E3
Ky Scotia Coal blasts (26) 3-9—3-11, 256A3
Ky Scotia Coal bodies removed 11-19, 892B1

Motor Vehicle—*For safety standards, see AUTOMOBILES*

'74 death rate rptd 2-3, 123G3
'66-73, '75 death rate rptd 2-23, 186F2
Taiwan rail collisn (40) 4-21, 404D3
Greek MP killed 5-1, 351D3
Yuba (Calif) HS bus (28) 5-21, 383G3; no chrgs filed 7-22, 595A3
'75 death rate rptd 7-31, 911F1
Vienna bridge collapse (4) 8-1, 796D2
Ind passenger suits bar stands 11-8, 882D3
French bus crash (17) 12-21, 969C2

Radiation—*See 'Environmental Hazards' under ATOMIC Energy; also ENVIRONMENT*

Rail

Chicago collisn (1) 1-9, 80G1
Taiwan bus collisn (40) 4-21, 404D3
Dutch commuter collisn (23) 5-4, 560E3
Belgium derailmt (11) 6-27, 560F3
Transvaal collisn (31) 9-6, 840E3
Mexico collisn (15-24), 10-10, 816G1
Polish crash (25) 11-3, 912B2
Kenya crash (14) 11-29, 912G1

ACCOUNTABILITY of Power, The (book)
Cited in Mondale blog 512G3

ACCOUNTING—*See also GENERAL Accounting Office under U.S. GOVERNMENT; company names*

Boston GSA audit rptd 1-20, 71D1
Merck panel scores Andersen 3-9, 361A2
Sup Ct rules on stock frauds 3-30, 262E1
IRS use of worksheets upheld 4-21, 331G2
Andersen Alaska pipe audit rptd 7-6, 690D3
SEC accuses Seidman 9-1, 984F2-B3
US sues Texas bd 11-18, 989A1

1977

Sovt jet in Cuba (66) 5-27, 604D1
Multilingual communicatns held unrelated 7-8, 561F3
Powers in Calif copter crash 8-1, 696E3
Japan jet in Malaysia (34) 9-27, 808B1
Rock band charter (6) 10-20, 888G3
Airline employe liability case review refused 10-31, 835C3
Portugal TAP crash (130) 11-19, 928G2
Argentine jet 11-20 (45), 992D2
Bulgarian jet in Libya (56) 12-2, 992E2
Hijacked Malaysian jet 12-4 (100), 992B2
La oil rig copter crash (17) 12-8, 1023F2
Ind team charter (29) 12-13, 1023C2
Swiss jet off Madeira (36) 12-18, 1023E2

Fires & Explosions—*See under 'F'*

Marine—*See also SHIPS—Safety Issues*

San Fran Bay oil spills 1-5, 2-10, 214F2, A3
Tampa Bay oil barge crash 1-9, 214F2
Panama tanker sinks off Cape Cod (38) 1-11, 104E3, 214D3
Spain freighter, US Navy launch collide (46) 1-17, 104A3
Greek tanker splits off Midway (3) 1-17, 214G2
Hudson R oil barge spill 2-4, 214G2
Ship hits Va bridge 2-24, 204F3
Liberian oil tanker off Honolulu (1) 2-24, 214A3
Kuwait tanker sinks off Taiwan 3-3, 214C3
Yugoslav ship '74 collisn cited; Italy salvage operatn starts 4-4, 284B3
Japan tanker, freighter collide 4-6, 1000A1
US '76 death toll 5-12, 412G2
Supertankers collide off S Africa 12-16, 999E3-1000A1

Mine

Pa coal mine fire 2-7—4-5, 396C2
Pa coal mine flooded (9) 3-1, 204C3
25 Japanese killed 5-11, 808D1
'76 Ky coal blasts laid to spark 6-13, 8-10; widows' suit dismissed 9-12, 900F3, 901A1
Mozambique coal blast (70) 8-2, 768E3
S Africa cave-ins (14) 9-3, 768G3

Motor Vehicle—*For safety standards, see AUTOMOBILES*

US '76 death toll 5-12, 412F2
Presley mourners in Memphis (2) 8-18, 696G1
UK rock star 9-16, 787G3
Fla truck-train collisn 10-2 (10), 992G2

Radiation—*See under 'R'*

Rail

Chicago collisn (11) 1-4, 104F2-A3; hearings 5-16—5-18, 412E3
Australia derailmt (82) 1-18, 104C3
US '76 death toll 5-12, 412G2
Indian train falls into river 5-30 (44), 992F2
E Ger express collisn (29) 6-27, 888C3
Fla truck-train collisn 10-2 (10), 992G2
India express crash (61) 10-10, 888B3
S Kor freight train blast (57) 11-11, 928B3

ACCOUNTING—*See also GENERAL Accounting Office under U.S. GOVERNMENT*

Sen subcom rpt scores Big 8 1-17, 78A3
FDIC suit vs Franklin auditors rptd 2-9, 155C3
Hamilton trustees sue auditors 2-11, 155A3
SEC sues Leidesdorf 2-16, 156C2
Sen subcom hearings 4-19—6-13, SEC urges self-policing 6-13, 519E2
Andersen OKs paymt in Mattel class-action suits 4-26, 519D3
SEC new rules rptd 4-29, 369A1
Equity Funding '73 suit settled 5-11, 409A1
Touche Ross, Lasser merge; big 8 firms ranked 8-22, 650E2

1978

Libya copter crash (11) 3-6, 228D1
Venez pvt plane (1) 3-16, 231A1
Bulgaria airline (73) 3-16, 271A1
Burma airline explosn (48) 3-25, 271B1
Auto Club charter (9) 4-23, 460E2
Clemente family case vs FAA declined by Sup Ct 5-1, 364D1
Fla '76 AF-pvt plane collisn damages awarded 5-5, 460E1
Natl jet in Fla bay (3) 5-8, 460C2
Egypt '76 jet crash in Thai laid to pilot 5-12, 460A1
Turkish jet '74 crash damages awarded 5-13, 460E1
Kenya ex-min in plane (4) 5-24, 479B1
Natl pilots fired re Fla bay crash 6-16, 636E3
Air Canada jet on Toronto takeoff (3) 6-26, 636D3
Va US Sen nominee in plane (1) 8-2, 645A3
Ind team '77 crash blame fixed 8-18, 758C3
USSR reconnaissance crash (7) 8-28, 820G1-F2
Pvt plane off Virgin I (1) 9-2, 777F3
Rhodesia jet shot down (48) 9-3, 740E3
Pa copter stalls (7) 9-4, 758A3
Malaysian '77 hijacked jet rpt 9-7, 888F1
Pl AF jet (33) 9-14, 758B3
PSA jet collides over San Diego (150) 9-25, 758D2; new air-safety rules proposed 12-27, 1006C3-1007B1
'57 AF jet wreckage identified 10-12, 843E3
Canary I '77 crash rpt 10-18, 888A2
Sovt TU-144 crash confrmd (3) 10-27, 1032B1
Va '74 crash claims setld 11-4, 908C2
Natl Fla bay crash rpt 11-9, 908F2 ★
Sri Lanka jet crash (183) 11-15, 908G1
Indian AF transport (78) 11-19, 908B2
Alaskan pvt jet (5) 12-4, 1032A1
US AF C-130 in Ky (5) 12-10, 984F2
Alitalia jet off Sicily (108) 12-23, 1031G3
United DC-8 in Oregon (10) 12-28, 1031D3

Fires & Explosions—*See FIRES & Explosions*

Marine—*See also SHIPS—Safety Issues*

Tanker oil, gas spills rptd 1-10—5-26, 524F1-C2
Supertanker breaks off French coast, '67 tanker spill cited 3-17, 201C3; France sues Amoco 3-19; wreckage spreads 3-23—3-29, 238B1, 749C1
L Superior '75 ore ship sinkage rpt 4-20, 460A1
Italy completes Yugo ship salvage operatn 4-25, 330E3
Norwegian tanker, Miss ferry '76 collisn rpt 5-17, 460B1
Canadian canoeists drown (13) 6-11, 460D2
Ky swimming pool chlorine leak 6-28, 636E3
Chesapeake Bay collisn (11) 10-20, 908C3

Motor Vehicle—*See also AUTOMOBILES—Safety Issues*

PR schl bus plunge (11) 2-15, 270F3
Argentina truck-train collisn (37) 2-25, 270E3
Cleveland '73 crash award 5-3, 460D1
US '77 motorcycle deaths rptd 6-29, 636A2
Pinto crashes in Pa (3) 7-6, 7-8, 569C3
US '77 death toll 7-11, 636F1
Egypt bus plunges into Nile (56) 7-17, 636B3
Canada bus plunges into lake (41) 8-4, 636A3
Italian Grand Prix crash (1) 9-11, 778A2
Pinto crash in Ind, Ford indicted (3) 9-13, 718F3-719A1

Radiation—*See ATOMIC Energy—Industrial*

Rail—*See also RAILROADS—Safety Issues*

Amtrak train stranded in Ind 1-25—1-26, 105B3
Tenn derailmt 2-23, propane tank car blast (12) 2-24, 196C1
Argentina truck-train collisn (37) 2-25, 270E3
Fla derailmt chlorine gas spill (8) 2-26, 196F1
'77 derailmts rptd 3-13, 196E1
Squaw Valley tram car falls (4) 4-15, 460A2
Italian trains collide (45) 4-15, 460B2
UK train fire (11) 7-6, 636F2
Calif freight train 8-13, 759B1
Va derailmt (6) 12-3, 972D1

ACCOUNTING—*See also U.S. GOVERNMENT—GENERAL Accounting Office*

Carter budgets oil indus audit 1-23, 46E2
Peat Marwick, Price Waterhouse, Andersen rpt '77 financial data, rankings 1-30, 84B1
Coopers & Lybrand named in Ford suit 5-16, 391A1
Methodists settle pensn fund fraud suit 5-21, 489F3
Ernst rpts Cleveland deficit 8-22, 663C3

1979

Mauritania army transport off Senegal (12) 5-27, 412E1
Dutch probe Canary I '77 crash 5-29, 412C2
Downeast commuter plane (17) 5-30, 412E2
Seaplane off Portugal (1) 6-28, 508D2
Chicago DC-10 crash rpt issued by FAA 7-10, findings disputed 7-12, 538E3-539E1
Indonesia airliner in N Sumatra (61) 7-11, 639F1
Prinair prop on St Croix (8) 7-24, 830G2
Munson jet in Ohio (1) 8-2, 671A3; pilot error blamed 9-16, 1002F3
Aeroflot jets over Ukraine (173) 8-17, 639D1
Air Canada DC-9 blowout, Boston emergency landing 9-17, 830D2
Westn Air DC-10 in Mex City (74) 10-31, 912B2; rpt blames crew 12-14, 996B3
'56 US B-47 at UK A-site rptd (4) 11-5, 845G1
Pak jet in Saudi (156) 11-26, 912F1
NZ DC-10 in Antarctica (257) 11-28, pilot error blamed 11-29, 912B1
Chicago DC-10 crash rpt issued by Safety Bd 12-21, 988F2

Fires & Explosions—*See FIRES & Explosions*

Marine—*See also SHIPS–Safety Issues*

Greek oil tanker off Spain (28) 1-1, 201A1
French oil tanker in Irish port (50) 1-8, 201C1
Chesapeake Bay '78 collisn rpts 1-20, 140F3; 2-26, 3-2, 240E3; Cuyohoga cmdr convicted 11-3, 887A3
Mex illegal aliens (8) 2-11, 127E2
Liberia '78 tanker wreckage rpt issued 3-8, 162C2, A3, 163A1
UK tanker off Nova Scotia 3-15, 201D1
N Orleans barges snap 3-15, 288F3
Italian cruise ship burns 3-30, 316B3
Rams owner drowns 4-2, 356G3
Oil platform collapses (8) 5-10, 472G3
Greek, Liberian tankers collide off Tobago (27) 7-19, 553G2; Greek tanker sinks 8-2, 592A3
Fastnet yacht race in Irish Sea (18) 8-14, 799F3; rpt issued 12-10, 955C1
'74-78, 1st 1/4 '79 oil spill data; tanker safety records rptd 8-15, 608A1
Miss R barge blast (3) 8-30, 800D1
Liberian freighter, tanker collide off Tex (15) 11-1, 954F3

Mine

Coalport (Pa) slide (1) 10-2, 860G2

Motor Vehicle

US Army truck in Canal Zone (16) 1-11, 140D3
State ct immunity curbed by Sup Ct 3-5, 185C1
Greek bus, Yugo gas truck collisn (30) 3-14, 240E3
Teen-age drinking data 4-16, 309F3
'78 deaths rptd 4-20, 309G1
Thai bus, truck collisn (52) 6-2, 639A2
Tanzania bus (60) 7-14, 639A2
USSR death rate rise rptd 10-10, 857B2
Mich RR crossing (3) 10-12, 800A2
Zimbabwe guerrilla ldr in Mozambique 12-29, 976A1

Radiation—*See ATOMIC Energy–Industrial Use*

Rail

Fla, NY, Pa, Ohio tank car derailmts 4-8, 5-3, 5-6, 472D3
Jan-Sept '78 tank car derailmts, evacuatns rptd 4-9, 472C3
Ivory Coast derailmt (15) 6-17, 639A2
Yugo collisn (60) 9-13, 800C2
Conrail freight trains collide (2) 10-1, 912G3
Amtrak crashes in Ill, Kan, Mich (7) 10-2, 10-12, 10-13, 800F1
Phila commuter trains collide 10-16, 912E3
Canada train derails 11-10—11-11, suburb evacuated 11-11—11-14, 871D3; evacuees compensated 11-19, 927C2

ACCOUNTING

Bell & Howell to reimburse home-study students 3-26, 308D3
Customer suits curbed by Sup Ct 6-18, 499C1
Peat Marwick elects chrmn 10-10, 851E3

1980

Italian jet in Tyrrhenian Sea (81) 6-28, 769A3
US copter off Gulf Coast (13) 8-9, 621F2
Saudi airliner burns at Riyadh (301) 8-19, 778B1*
Graiver family wins damages 10-15, 826G3
US news copter in Caribbean (4) 11-13, 869C3
US mil transport jet in Egypt (13) 11-13, 914B3
Portugal premr in Lisbon crash (9) 12-4, 923D1

Fires & Explosions—*See FIRES & Explosions*

Marine

Liberia supertanker off Senegal 1-17; Shell sues, chrgs fraud 2-7, 108D2
Coast Guard cutter, oil tanker collide off Fla (23) 1-28, suit rptd filed 2-3, hearing begins 2-6, 256D2
'79 cargo ship losses rptd 2-18, 108E3
Liberia tanker rams Fla bridge 3-8, 391A2
N Sea oil platform capsizes (123) 3-27, 256D1
Fla bridge collapses (35) 5-9; capt's safety record rptd 5-10, 391B1
Cuba refugee boat (14) 5-17, 380F1
China '79 oil rig collapse rptd (70) 7-6, 621E3
US aircraft carrier, Panamanian freighter off Pl (2) 7-29, 675D1
Liberian oil tanker runs aground off Gulf Coast 8-9, 621A3
Sovt A-sub off Japan (9) 8-20, 653B1
DR stowaways on Panama freighter (22) 9-5, 687C3
Dutch ocean liner fire off Alaska 10-4, 769B2
La lake 'swallowed' in salt-mine collapse; illus 11-20, 970C2, E2

Mine

S Africa elevator crash (31) 3-27, 256E3
Canada cave-in (8) 5-20, 603G1
La salt-mine collapse, lake 'swallowed'; illus 11-20, 970C2, E2

Motor Vehicle

Fla bus in Tampa Bay 5-9, 391C1
NBA player near Cleveland 5-23, 656A2
S Africa bus-train collisn (67); truck collisn (17) 6-7, 769B3
W Ger terrorist near Stuttgart (2) 7-25, 581C1

Radiation—*See ATOMIC Energy–Industrial Use*

Rail

Miss derailmt, gas blasts 2-13, 309C2
NC train collisn 4-2, 391F3
Somerville (Mass) tank car sideswiped 4-3, 392E1
S Africa bus-train collisn (67) 6-7, 769B3

ACCOUNTING

Bahamas bank looting case rptd 3-3, 229B1

1976

ACETO, Joseph
Indicted 7-14, pleads guilty 9-10, 796B3
ACHEAMPONG, Gen. Ignatius Kutu
Cancels Kissinger visit 4-28, 295G1
'75 plotters rptd on trial 5-20, 543E2
ACHILLE-Fould, Aymar
Dropped from French cabt 1-12, 49C2
ACKER, Gary
Angola sentences 6-28, 480B2, F2
ACKERMAN, I. W.
Asks press curbs 10-27, 927A3
ACKERMANN, Rosemarie
Wins Olympic medal 7-28, 576G1
ACN (acrylonitrile)—*See CHEMICALS*
ACOSTA Velasco, Jorge
Gets amnesty 1-22, 363F3
ACRA, Prof. Atim
Warns of Beirut epidemic 7-9, 514B3
ACRYLONITRILE (ACN)—*See CHEMICALS*
ACTIS, Gen. Omar (ret.)
Assassinated 8-19, 672B1
ACTURK, Barin
Named as Uganda hijacker 7-5, 486A1
ADAMS, Rep. Brock (D, Wash.)
Biographical sketch 936D3
Vs revenue sharing program 2-23, 149D3
Presents budget proposals 3-23, 231D1
Ford scores defns cuts 3-26, 231F3
Reelected 11-2, 831A2
Carter meets cong ldrs 11-17, 864B2
Carter names as Transport secy 12-14, 936C1
ADAMS, Sir Grantley
Son sworn as Barbados prime min 9-3, 673E1
ADAMS, Howard G.
Veneris US visit OKd 6-29, 484F2
ADAMS, James B.
FBI probe rptd 3-21, 248G1
Ford funds probe initiated 10-1, 723G2
ADAMS, J. M. G. (Tom)
Sworn Barbados prime min 9-3, 672F3
Americans deported re 'plot' 10-25, 962C1
ADAMS, John (1735-1826)
Ford quotes in acceptnc speech 8-19, 611G2
ADAMS Chronicles, The (book)
On best-seller list 12-5, 972D2
ADAMSON, Campbell
Knighted 1-1, 80F2
ADAMSON, Harold
On Toronto police brutality 7-28, 588B1
ADAMSON, John Harvey
Chrgd in Bolles murder 6-21, 483A3-G3
Rptrs probe crime 10-2, 849C2
Mistrial declared 10-21, 859E2
New judge, trial site set 11-19, 12-7, 971D3
ADB—*See ASIAN Development Bank*
ADDABBO, Rep. Joseph Patrick (D, N.Y.)
Angola aid cutoff passed 1-27, 69B1
S Korea payoffs probed 2-19, 171D1
S Korea probe rptd 10-30, 11-13, 900A2
Reelected 11-2, 830G1
ADDICTION Research Foundation (Ontario)
Alcoholism rpt published 8-8, 814E3
ADDISON-Wesley Publishing Co.
US files consent decree 7-27, 989G1
ADELEYE, R. A.
Nigeria industry min 3-15, 222B3
ADERS, Robert
Replaced in Labor post 5-12, 412G1
ADLER, Johan
On US visits to S Africa 8-25, 654F2
ADLER Prize, Isaac
Boyse wins 2-11, 272C1
ADNAC, Inc.
St. Charles Elevator Grain Co.
Fined 3-4, 247C2
ADOLF Hitler (book)
On best-seller list 12-5, 972D2
ADOLPHE, Rosalie
Named Tontons head 8-17, 1005E3
ADOPTION—*See CHILDREN*

1977

Fscl '75, '76 fed deficit rptd on accrual basis 11-7, 941G2
Vesco auditors scored, ICC suit vs urged 11-29, 980B3
Forgn paymts bill ordrs acctg reforms 12-7, 938C1
ACCOUNTING Standards Board, Financial
Sen subcom rpt scores 1-17, 78G3
ACDA—*See U.S. GOVERNMENT—ARMS Control & Disarmament*
ACHEAMPONG, Gen. Ignatius Kutu (Ghana head of state)
On civilian govt com 1-10, 48F1
Pledges civln rule 7-1, sets date 7-14, 598G1
Cedi devaluatn bar cited 7-1, 598E2
ACLU—*See AMERICAN Civil Liberties Union*
ACOMBA, David
Union bars forgn permit 8-31, 742F2
ACOSTA Caballero, German
Radical Lib pres candidate 10-21, 845B1
ACOSTA Velasco, Jaime
Pres bid rptd 8-26, 842G1
ACQUIN, Lorne J.
Charged 7-23, indicted 9-7, 712E1
ACQUISITIONS—*See MERGERS & Acquisitions*
ACREE, Vernon D.
On marijuana smuggling 3-14, 332E3
ACTION—*See under U.S. GOVERNMENT*
ACTION Grants—*See U.S. GOVERNMENT—HOUSING & Urban Development*
ACTION Industries Inc.
Sea-Land settles rebate case 1-5, 6C3
ACTION on Smoking and Health
Eastn to add no-smoking seats 6-14, 593A2
CAB votes airline cigar, pipe smoking ban 11-22, 900A2
ACZEL, Gyoergy
Meets with Graham 9-8, 732D1
ADA—*See AMERICANS for Democratic Action*
ADAIR, Paul (Red)
Team caps N Sea oil well 4-30, 336E1
ADAIR, Ross
Cited in Park indictmt 9-6, 688D1
ADAMI, Fenech
Elected Malta oppositn ldr 1-16, 136C2
ADAMO, Msgr. Salvatore
Fired 2-11, replaced 6-16, 471E1
ADAMS, Brockman (Brock)
Sen com OKs nominatn 1-19, confrmd 1-20, 34B1, B3
Tightens tanker safety rules 1-31, 214D2
Butchman confrmd 2-10, 148D3
Rpts personal finances 2-25, 147B3
Asks transit bill delay 2-25, 213A3
Backs mandatory air bags 3-21, 213B2
Amtrak 'Mountaineer' svc to end 5-3, 368E3
'76 campaign surplus rptd 5-3, 482B2
NY Concorde ruling backed 5-11, 368C2
Sets gas mileage standards 6-26, 522E1
Orders air bags on '82 cars 6-30, 521F3
Backs fed no-fault auto insurnc standards 7-15, 7-21, 594E3-595A1
Signs UK air svc pact 7-23, 593C1
Proposes expanded Concorde landing rights 9-23, 738B2
Backs mass-transit fund 10-12, 860B3
Black co alliance with S African co scored 10-15, 979G1
Nader scores NHTSA admin 11-30, 1008C1
ADAMS, Florrie
Vows evictn fight 7-24, 599E2
ADAMS, Sherman
Nixon version of firing disputed 5-4, 5-5, 367C1
ADAMS, Willy
Named to Canada Sen 4-5, 281A3
ADAMSON, John Harvey
Pleads guilty 1-15, testifies 1-26—1-27, 161D3
2 convctd of Bolles murder 11-6, 871C2
ADAMS-Schneider, Lance
On Sovt auto import plan 7-4, 638F2
ADB—*See ASIAN Development Bank*
ADDABBO, Rep. Joseph P. (D, N.Y.)
Anti-Concorde amendmt fails 6-8, 463C2
ADDAMS, Jane (1860-1935)
FBI surveillance rptd 6-19, 481D1
ADDERLEY, Paul
Retains Cabt posts 7-29, 675D1
ADDINSELL, Richard
Dies 11-15, 952A2
ADEN, Gulf of—*See GULF of Aden*
ADENAUER, Konrad (1876-1967)
Ludwig Erhard dies 5-5, 452A3
ADENINE Arabinoside (ara-A)—*See 'Diseases' under MEDICINE*
ADENOSIS—*See MEDICINE—Cancer*
ADERMANN, Evan
Australia N Territory min 12-19, 982A2
ADHAM, Sheik Kamal
CIA liaison role rptd 2-22, 124G2
ADL—*See B'NAI B'rith—Anti-Defamation League*
ADLEY, Ronald
Rescued from Pa coal mine 3-6, 204C3
ADOPTION—*See CHILDREN*
ADRIAN, Lord Edgar Douglas
Dies 8-4, 696B2

1978

ACDA—*See U.S. GOVERNMENT—ARMS Control & Disarmament Agency*
ACHEAMPONG, Gen. Ignatius Kutu (Ghanaian head of state)
Replaced as Ghana ldr 7-5, 515C2
Aides ousted 7-7, 596C2
Plotters freed 11-16, 1021F3
ACHOUR, Habib
Quits PSD pol bur 1-10, arrested 1-28, 74C1
Release sought 1-31, union suspends 2-2, 170D1
Rptd Masmoudi ally 2-5, 170G1
Coup plot chrgs cited 8-11, 671D1
Sentenced to 10 yrs 10-10, 872E3
ACKER, Jean
Dies 8-16, 708A2
ACKER, Brig. Gen. William P.
Sees AF volunteer shortage 12-12, 960C1-E1
ACKERMAN, Robert Allan
Prayer For My Daughter opens 1-17, 760B3
Fathers & Sons opens 11-16, 1031E1
ACKERMANN, Barbara
3d in primary for Mass gov 9-19, 736A3
ACLU—*See AMERICAN Civil Liberties Union*
ACOSTA Mejia, Gustavo
Honduras junta adviser 8-9, 691E3
ACQUISITIONS—*See MERGERS & Acquisitions*
ACRYLONITRILE—*See CHEMICALS*
ACT (Assure Competitive Transportation)
Formed, scores ICC chrmn 11-15, 1007A2
ACT, The (play)
Minnelli wins Tony 6-4, 579G2
ACTION—*See under U.S. GOVERNMENT*
ACTORS & Actresses—*See BROADCASTING, MOTION Pictures, THEATER; personal names*
ADA—*See AMERICANS for Democratic Action*
ADAMO Wrecking Co.
EPA curbed on asbestos rule 1-10, 13F2
ADAMO Wrecking Co. v. U.S.
EPA curbed on asbestos rule 1-10, 13B3
ADAMS, Brockman (Brock)
NE rail project offcls quit 1-30, 225D1
Issues transportatn policy statemt 2-8, 109B1
Backs more aid for Conrail 2-15, 224D3
On E Coast booms-Concorde link 3-15, 187D2
Hikes RR roadbed, track maintenance aid 4-15; advances tank-car safety deadlines 5-9, 365G2, E3
Proposes Amtrak route cutbacks 5-8, 366C1
Issues intl air policy outline 8-21, 640E1
Lowry wins US House seat 11-7, 857B3
Proposes trucking, rail deregulatn 11-13, 1007F1
Hails RR rate hike 11-24, 1007A3
ADAMS, Brooke
Days of Heaven released 9-13, 970A1
Invasn of Body Snatchers released 12-21, 1030A3
ADAMS, Gerard
Released by UK judge 9-6, 723B1
ADAMS, Lee
Broadway Musical opens 12-21, 1031A1
ADAMS, Paula
Held in Guyana murder probe 11-28, 911C1
ADAMS, Polly
Porch opens 11-14, 1031G2
ADAMSON, John H.
Bolles killers sentenced 1-10, 24B2
Sentenced 12-9, 992D2
ADASS, Chieck
Coup plot trial asked 1-22, 94B2
ADDABBO, Rep. Joseph Patrick (D, N.Y.)
Reelected 11-7, 851D3
ADDERLEY, Paul
In Bahamas Cabt com on investmt 3-6, 194A2
ADDLESTONE, David
On upgraded mil dischrg for gays 8-21, 683E2
ADDOU, Abdullahi
Scores US aid bar 1-18, 43A3
ADEN, Gulf of
US surveillnc flights from Israel Sinai base rptd 3-26, US denies 3-27, 215F1, G1
ADHAM, Sheik Kamal
Financial Gen sues 2-17, 204B3
SEC chrgs 3-18, settles 3-19, 204B2
Boeing payoff cited 7-28, 643B1
ADJANI, Isabelle
Barocco released 4-7, 618B3
Driver released 7-28, 970B1
ADL—*See B'NAI B'rith—Anti-Defamation League*
ADLER, James B.
'More' ceases publicatn, merges with Columbia Journalism Review 7-21, 672G1
ADLER, Lou
Up In Smoke released 9-22, 970C3
ADNAN, Hammad
Assassinated 8-3, 582B3
Iraq agents blamed for death 8-4; funeral held, revenge vowed 8-5, 602F2
ADOPTION—*See under CHILDREN*
ADORATION of the Golden Calf (painting)
Slashed 4-3, 335D1
ADOULA, Cyrille
Dies 5-24, 440D2
ADRIAN VI, Pope (Adrian Florensz) (1459-1523)
Non-Italian elected Pope 10-16, 781B1

1979

ACHEAMPONG, Gen. Ignatius Kutu
Executed 6-16, 468D3
ACKERMAN, Daniel
Legal immunity curbed by Sup Ct 12-4, 987E3
ACKERMAN, Robert Allan
Taken in Marriage opens 2-26, 292D3
ACKNER, Desmond
Curbs secondary picketing 1-26, 96B3
ACLI International Inc.
Chrgd re coffee price squeeze 3-13, 348A2
ACLU—*See AMERICAN Civil Liberties Union*
ACME Meat Co.
Settles '78 beef-price suit 10-22, 985E3
ACNE—*See MEDICINE & Health-Diseases*
ACOSTA, Ivan
El Super released 4-28, 528B2
ACQUIN, Lorne
Convicted in Conn mass murder 10-19, 819B2
Sentenced 11-30, 954A1
ACQUISITIONS—*See MERGERS*
ACT (Assure Competitive Transportation)
ICC sued over vacant seats 1-4, 111D3
ACTION—*See under U.S. GOVERNMENT*
ACTION on Smoking and Health (ASH)
PHS report scored 1-11, 23E1
ACTORS & Actresses—*See BROADCASTING, MOTION Pictures, THEATER; personal names*
ADA—*See AMERICANS for Democratic Action*
ADAIR, Paul (Red)
At Mex oil-well blowout 6-3–6-16, 462B2
ADAMS, Brockman (Brock)
Rail deregulatn plan rptd 1-15, 35C3
Backs '85 gas mileage standard 1-19, 87C3
Coast Guard safety training faulted 1-20, 140E3
Revises Amtrak route cutback plan 1-31, 129A1, C1
Outlines urban-aid policy 2-13, 129A2
'Car of the future' plan set, cites indus research spending level 5-18, 441C3
Auto role seen undiminished 6-18, 514A3
Sees Jordan on Cabt shuffle 7-19, resigns Transportatn post 7-20, 529C1, 530F1-B3
Goldschmidt named successor 7-27, 577D1
ADAMS, Brooke
Man, Woman & Bank released 9-28, 820A2
Cuba released 12-21, 1007B3
ADAMS, David C.
Salant NBC apptmt rptd 3-29, 335B1
ADAMS, James
FBI ex-agent's statemt in SWP trial sought 1-16, 92D2
ADAMS, John (1725-1826)
Stuart portrait goes to Natl Gallery 4-10, 375B1
ADAMS, Polly
Bedroom Farce opens 3-29, 711D1
ADAMS, Thomas A.
Liberia deal set 9-7, 720E3
ADAMS, Tony
10 released 10-5, 1008G1
ADAMS, Willis
In NFL draft 5-3, 335G1
ADAMSON, Terry
On King, JFK murder plot review 1-2, 4C1
On Paisley death probe 1-24, 55B1
Forgn student visa probe planned 1-29, 93G2
Rpts natl sec legis planned 2-8, 88G1
On Mex border fence end 4-26, 327A3
ADDINGTON, Frank
Mental hosp commitmt standard tightened by Sup Ct 4-30, 364E2
ADDINGTON v. Texas
Case decided by Sup Ct 4-30, 364E2
ADDONIZIO, Hugh J.
Subject to rejailing by Sup Ct 6-4, 438G3
Paroled 10-2, 891F1
ADL—*See B'NAI B'rith-Anti-Defamation League*
ADLER, Samuel
Dies 11-12, 932A2
ADMINISTRATIVE Office of the U.S. Courts—*See under U.S. GOVERNMENT-JUDICIARY*
ADOPTION—*See under CHILDREN*

1980

AC/DC (singing group)
Back in Black on best-seller list 12-3, 948C3
ACERBI, Msgr. Angelo
DR Emb siege ends, freed in Cuba 4-27, 335G1
ACID Rain—*See ENVIRONMENT--Air & Water*
ACKERMAN, Nathaniel H.
On Tieri indictmt 6-30, 502G3
ACKERMAN, Robert Allan
Salt Lake City opens 1-23, 136E3
ACKROYD, David
Hide & Seek opens 5-4, 392B3
ACLI International Inc.
Hunt silver debts rptd 5-2, 345C1
ACLU—*See AMERICAN Civil Liberties Union*
ACQUISITIONS—*See MERGERS*
ACT of Kindness, An (play)
Opens 9-11, 756A3
ACTORS Theater of Louisville (Ky.)
Wins Tony 6-8, 692C3
ACYL, Ahmat Alkabache
Joins Oueddi forces 3-31, 311F1
ADA—*See AMERICANS for Democratic Action*
ADACH, Kazimierz
Wins Olympic medal 8-2, 622F1
ADA County—*See IDAHO*
ADAMES, John
Gloria released 10-1, 836A3
ADAMS, Don
Nude Bomb released 5-9, 675B3
ADAMS Jr., Brig. Gen. F. Cecil
Cleared in recruiting scandal 3-6, 369C3
ADAMS, Gerald William
Murdered 8-4, Tekere chrgd 8-6, 621D1
Tekere freed 12-8, 946A2
ADAMS, Gerry
Claims hunger strike victory 12-19, 993F3
ADAMS, Jani
Cleared in murder case 5-30, 656A1
ADAMS, Jim
Wins Polk award 2-25, 692F3
ADAMS, K. S. (Bud)
Fires Phillips as Oilers coach, gen mgr 12-31, 999F1
ADAMS, Lane W.
Sees '80s cancer deaths rise 4-28, 356C3
ADAMS, Dr. Martin
Links stuttering, physical abnormalities 1-5, 63E3
ADAMS, Neil
Wins Olympic medal 7-25, 623C1
ADAMS, Philip
Getting of Wisdom released 8-5, 675G2
ADAMS, Rodney H.
On '79 univ endowmt earnings 3-24, 319F1
ADAMS, Rev. Theodore
Dies 2-27, 175C3
ADAMS Extract Co.
Mead rptd guilty of box price fixing 9-15, 917F1
ADAMSON, Harold
Dies 8-17, 675G3
ADAMSON, John H.
Bolles case convictns overturned 2-25, 214C3
Convicted in Bolles killing 10-17, 860F3
Sentenced to death 11-14, 926B3
ADAMSON, Joy
Found dead 1-3, 104D1
Suspect chrgd in slaying 2-2, 238B3
ADB—*See ASIAN Development Bank*
ADDABBO, Rep. Joseph Patrick (D, N.Y.)
House OKs '81 defns appropriatn, Maybank amendmt repealed 9-16, 741C3, E3
Reelected 11-4, 843D3
ADDERLEY, Herb
Enters Pro Football HOF 8-2, 999B2
ADDISON—*See ILLINOIS*
ADEGA Fresneda, Juan
Hijacks Delta jet to Cuba 9-17, returned to US for trial 9-18, 704B1, B2
ADHAM, Sheik Kamal
Financial Gen deal set 7-25, 600D3
ADIRONDACK Mountains
Acid rain lake peril rptd 2-2, 145B3
ADKINS, John
NRA endorses Reagan 11-1, 844F1
ADOLPH Coors Co. v. R.E. Spriggs Co. Inc.
Case declined by Sup Ct 2-19, 131D1
ADOPTION—*See CHILDREN--Adoption*
ADORNO Maldonado, Jose Juan
Murdered 8-11, 786B2

1976

ADRIATIC Sea
'75 Yugo-Albania clash rptd 2-6, 224D1
Yugo opens Belgrade RR link 5-28, 543D3
ADRIAZOLA, Gen. Oscar
Loses air force command 1-6, 26G3
ADRIKI, Maj. Gen. Mustapha
Freed 9-1; replaced as defns min 10-12, 874A2
ADULTERY—*See MARRIAGES*
ADVENTURES of Sherlock Holmes' Smarter Brother (film)
Top-grossing film 2-25, 208G3
ADVENTURES of the Wilderness Family, The (film)
Top-grossing film 1-28, 104F3
ADVERTISING
Canada ad tax agrmt rptd 2-3, 116G3
Firestone settles on safety ads 2-16, 186A3
ABA OKs lawyers' ads 2-17, 136D3
Canada ad tax OKd, Time halts editn 2-25, 188G2
Rollins admits Mex payoffs 3-3, 419D3
Louis Sissman dies 3-10, 316C1
Consumer leasing protectn bill signed 3-23, 234C1
Australia bans TV tobacco ads 3-23, 237G1
Cong curbs FDA vitamin rules 4-12, 282C3
Drug price ad ban voided 5-24, 393E1
Sup Ct bars review of FTC cigaret ad fines 6-1, 414A3
Merrill Lynch settles job bias suits 6-4, 414E1
Canada ends tax deductn for US TV 9-22, 771C3
Political Ads
FCC rules on Ill, Fla pol ads 3-4, 180E2-A3
Goldwater ad scores Reagan 5-8—5-9, 342B3
Carter scores Udall ads 5-28, 390F2
Ford ads vs Reagan stir controversy 6-5—6-6, 410G1, B2 ★
Ford defends ads 10-20, 784D3
Ford, Carter debate 10-22, 800F3
Carter spending rptd 11-17, 938B2
AEGEAN Sea
US, Greece letters exchng released 4-15, 259B2
Greece, Turkey oil dispute flares 6-27—7-13, 538D1
Greece, Turkey oil dispute grows; UN debates 7-23—8-16, 622D1, D2
Greek, Turkey feud continues 8-20—8-24; UN urges setlmt 8-25, 643D2
Turk ship returns, Greece alerts navy 9-1—9-25, 845A2
Caramanlis asks Turk talks 9-4; World Ct bars Greek injunctn plea 9-11; talks resume 11-2, 845A1-B2
Greece, Turk reach truce 11-11, 897G1
AEROFLOT (Soviet airline)
NY office bombed 3-8, 259E3
US indicts in rebate case 7-27, 908B1
Employe arrested in US 11-10, 907E3
2 Swiss chrgd as Sovt spies 11-24, 1011C3
Crash kills 72 11-28, 912C2
AERONUTRONIC Ford Corp. —*See under FORD Motor*
AEROSOLS—*See CHEMICALS*
AEROSPACE Industry—*See AVIATION*
AETNA Life & Casualty
Johnson resigns as pres 1-8, 80E2
AFANASYEV, Viktor
Communist Central Com head 3-5, 195A3
AFARS & Issas, French Territory of the (Djibouti) (formerly French Somaliland)
Policeman killed, demonstratns banned 1-3, 1-6, arrests rptd 1-14, 86A1
'75 Aref assassinatn attempt rptd 1-6, 86B1
Aref asks contd French mil role 1-8, 85E3
FLCS ldr rptd arrested in Somalia 1-14, 85G3
Aref in Paris; bars new electns, scores Socialists 1-23, 85F3
Immigrants expelled to Somalia 2-2, 86B1
FLCS hijacks schl bus 2-3, French troops kill 6 2-4, 85E2, G2
Cuba, Sovt Red Sea mil buildup rptd 4-5, 242B2
OAU backs independence 7-6, 487E3
13 die in tribal clash 7-10, 519E2
Ali Aref resigns 7-17, replaced 7-29, 696A2, C2 ★

1977

ADRIATIC Sea
Cavcat poison cargo recovery begun 4-4, 284B3
ADSIT, Boyd D.
'76 Redfearn case closed 1-6, 15F3
ADULTERY—*See MARRIAGES*
ADVANCE Investors Corp.
Carter to sell shares 1-4, 5A1
ADVANCE Transportation Co.
ICC sues 11-3, 861C1
ADVANI, L. K.
Released 1-18, 45E2
Lists political detainees 1-27, 71D2
India info min 3-26, 240A1
ADVERTISING
Canada ends ad deletns from US TV programs 1-21, 60G3
Vitamin ads to children barred 2-7, 217C1
Finland bans alcohol, tobacco ads 3-1, 182B2
Ogilvy & Mather forgn paymts rptd 3-30, 233D3
Dresser ad scores antiboycott bill 4-14, 323B3
FTC-Beneficial dispute review refused 4-25, 342B3
Miss State U gay ad case review refused 4-25, 342C3
FCC reverses pol ad stand 5-6, 376G1
Tennis tourn fee disclosures 5-7—5-20, FCC rpts probe 7-8, 548C2
Ford complaint vs FTC refused 5-16, 419D2
Porno trial role upheld 6-6, 478B3
NY contraceptive curbs voided 6-9, 501G1
TWA 'on-time' ads curbed 6-13, 463D2
Fairfax Cone dies 6-20, 532G2
Lawyers fee ads OKd 6-27, 538C3
Gen Foods sued on cereal ads 6-30, 613A2
FTC corrective ad rule upheld 8-2, 613F1-A2
ABA issues guidelines 8-10, 630F1
FTC challenges LA Times policy 8-17, 658C3
FCC acts on phone ads 8-26, White House backs curbs 10-21, 921A1
House subcom TV violence rpt scored 10-24, 921G1
Bryant Fla citrus contract renewed 11-16, 927G2
Canada TV deletn upheld 11-30, 946F1
John Crichton dies 12-28, 1024D1
ADVERTISING Agencies, American Association of
John Crichton dies 12-28, 1024D1
AEGEAN Sea
Greek, Turk mins meet 1-29, 1-31, 122D2
US envoy sees Greek, Turk ldrs 2-17—2-22, 122F1
Turkey halts oil drilling 6-20, 565C2
Greece rejcts US envoy 7-22, 598G2
Greece in NATO exercise 9-28, 957G1
AEGIS Anti-Aircraft System—*See ARMAMENTS—Missiles*
AEROFLOT (Soviet airline)
Ilyushin dies 2-9, 164B3
Matzos ban protested 2-25, 226C2
Cuba crash 5-27, 604D1
Jet hijacked to Finland 7-10—7-12, 537F1
Moscow bars Airbus, asks new French air accord 9-1, 736D1
AERONUTRONIC Ford Corp.—*See FORD Motor Co.—Ford Aerospace & Communications*
AEROPERU
US rebate case settled 2-18, 324G3
AEROSOLS—*See CHEMICALS*
AEROSPACE Industry—*See AVIATION*
AEORSPATIALE
US boycott called 2-4, Eastn to lease Airbus 5-24, 441D2, G2
AERO Systems Engineering Inc.
Questionable paymts rptd 3-11, 233E3
AFANASYEV, Viktor
On Carrillo speech ban 11-6, 865E3
AFARS & Issas, French Territory of the—*See DJIBOUTI*

1978

ADRIATIC Sea
Italy completes Cavcat poison cargo recovery 4-25, 330F3
ADRIEN Arpel's Three-Week Crash Makeover, Shapeover Beauty Program (book)
On best-seller list 4-30, 356A2
ADRISI, Mustafa
Rptd injured 4-19, flown to Egypt 4-24; Amin scores 4-28, 331B3
Presumed dead, army unrest cited 11-1, 830D3
ADULTERY
Saudi executns confrmd 2-1, 172G3
Spain punishmt ended 2-2, 136A3
Pub employe firing case declined by Sup Ct 12-11, 981A1
ADVERTISING
FTC complaint vs Safeway rptd setld 1-10, 348A1
FTC suit vs STP setld 2-9, 348C1
FTC proposes children's TV ad curbs 2-28, 4-28, Cong wary 4-26—5-2, 347G1, D2
Canada orders US TV statn dropped re ad policy 3-28, 226A2
FTC corrective ad rule review denied by Sup Ct 4-3, 280C3
'77 mail frauds cost $1 bln 4-3, 389G1
Trib ceases publicatn 4-5, 270B2
Burnett study compares black, white female consumers 4-12, 811G3-812D1
Anacin ads enjoined 5-2, 347F3
Carter scores attys 5-4, 320F3
Venez hires US experts for pol campaign 5-5, 395G1
Gannett plans Combined purchase 5-8, 345A3
Ray Rubicam dies 5-8, 440D3
Boone held liable for acne ads 5-11, 702F2-A3
Sears withdraws TV ads 5-12, 599C3
Rafshoon to join Carter staff 5-18, 386E3
Children excluded from porno rule by Sup Ct 5-23, 405G2
FTC adopts eyewear proposal 5-24, 434C1
Lawyer soliciting for profit barred by Sup Ct 5-30, 430C2
FCC 'fairness doctrine' case refused by Sup Ct 5-30, 430D3
Bede Aircraft OKs FTC trustee plan 6-13, 702C2
Coll cigaret smoking rptd down 7-5, 727D1
Anheuser-Busch halts Chelsea soft drink ads 7-22, 941F3-942A1
FCC to renew children's TV probe 7-28, 672B2
ABA backs lawyer TV ads 8-9, 626C3
US TV statns protest Canadian tax law 8-29, 686B3
Grey dental ad complaint rptd setld 8-31, 702E2
Book club settles FTC complaint 9-7, 702G1
Bridgestone Tire suit rptd settled 9-14, 942A1
Anacin ads ruled misleading 9-16, 769F3
FTC egg ad case declined by Sup Ct 10-2, 751D2
FTC injunctn halts acne ads 10-10, 942B1
FTC children's ad probe curbed 11-3; stay denied, probe affirmed 11-17, 941G2-C3
NY newspaper strike ends 11-6, 865A2
MD ad ban voided 11-29, AMA to appeal 11-30, 947D2
FTC tightens vocational schl rules 12-13, 963B1
AEGEAN Sea
Caramanlis OKs Ecevit talks 1-23, 2-9, 170E2
Greece-Turkey seabed, airspace talks 3-10—3-11, 216G2
Greece scores US on Turkish arms embargo end 4-4, 277A1
Turkey bars World Ct arbitratn 4-25, 398A3
Caramanlis, Ecevit meet 5-29, 398C3
Greece-Turkey seabed, airspace talks continue 7-4—7-6, 624A1
Greece protests Turkey boat sinking 11-1, 905B3
World Ct bars actn on Greece-Turkey dispute 12-19, 1000E3
AEPPLI, Oswald
Italy rpts lawsuit probe 1-10, 151C1
AER Lingus (Irish airline)
Strike ends 5-5, 393B1
AERO Mayflower Transit Inc.
ICC sues 7-6, 589B2
AEROSOLS—*See CHEMICALS*
AEROSPACE Industry—*See AVIATION*
AETNA Life & Casualty Co.
Exec pay curb pledged 5-31, 428A1
AFARS & Issas, French Territory of the—*See DJIBOUTI*

1979

ADRISI, Mustafa
Flight to Sudan rptd 6-8, 489B1
ADULTERY
Pak enacts Islamic law 2-10, 116F2
Frampton 'live-in-partner' suit dismissed 4-17, 289E1
Pope in US, affirms oppositn 10-5, 759B2, F2
ADVANCE Mortgage Corp.—*See under CITICORP*
ADVERTISING
Pan Am deceptn chrgd 1-10, 35F2
Alcoa false ad chrg settled 1-10, 91G2
HEW to step up TV anti-smoking drive 1-11, 23D1
ABC to cut children's TV ads 1-18, 78A3
Sony video recorder copyright trial opens 1-22, 120F2
Cigaret, ad cos ordrd to obey FTC subpoenas 1-25, 91C3
Litton deceptn chrgd 2-1, 91F3
Clorox settles '76 FTC complaint 2-19, 308G2
Professnal use of corp names curbed by Sup Ct 2-21, 128F2
Paramount resumes 'Warriors' ads 2-22, 174F1-A2
Washn Post TV viewing survey rptd 2-28, 3-1, 173G1
CAB adopts new charter rules 3-1, 166C3
Chrysler lures agency from Ford 3-1, 188B1
Nev real estate rule affirmed by Sup Ct 3-5, 184G3
Williams settles PVM chrg 3-6, 308B3
Calif hearing-aid case refused by Sup Ct 3-19, 203B3
Camel cigaret sales rptd 3-20, 218A3
ITT bread fiber chrg setld 3-25, 308C3
Bell & Howell to reimburse home-study students 3-26, 308D3
Thompson settles Sears dishwasher chrg 4-15, 308F3
Coll ads seen misleading 4-18, 282D2
Dental ad accord reached 4-27, 596D1
Rolling Stone, Look merge 5-7, 430F3
Colo land sale refunds set 5-8, 595G3
FTC backs nonprescriptn drug limits 5-22, 596G1
CPG settles FTC toy ad chrg 5-23, 596A2
Carter '76 campaign probed 5-25, 401A3; improprieties denied 6-22, 500B2
NAB sued over TV ad limit 6-14, 618G2
Pa jobs-wanted case declined by Sup Ct 6-18, 499E1
Kroger ads ruled deceptive 6-21, 596B2
Young & Rubicam, Marsteller merger set 6-27, 560E2
Acne ad refunds set 7-2, 596D2
AMF to produce bike safety ads 7-8, 595G2
CIA recruiting drive rptd 8-10, 610F3
Amer Express travelers check TV ad chngd 8-29, 903C1
Coming percolator recall set 9-4, 902E3
Radio deregulation proposed 9-6, 859A1
Mail fraud crackdown set 9-19, 921B3
ABC wins TV rights to '84 LA Olympics 9-25, 797F3
Horizon land sales scored by FTC 10-3, 903F1
Beckman runs ads to free 2 execs in El Salvador 10-10, 790D3
Bristol-Myers ads assailed by FTC 10-12, 902F3
Sears dishwasher ads faulted by FTC 10-16, 903A2
AMA ad ban ordrd ended 10-24, 902F2
Guatemala leftist ads run 10-26, 813E3
Ohio attys billbd case refused by Sup Ct 11-5, 884B3
Reagan pres bid aired 11-13, 866G2
Mobil exec joins Kennedy campaign 11-19, 962C2
FCC upholds Carter ad bid 11-20, 918G3
NYS utility ban case accepted by Sup Ct 11-26, 919A3
FTC mail-order case refused by Sup Ct 12-3, 964D2
Carter pol broadcast aired 12-4, 918A3, 919C1
Connally shifts strategy 12-15, 982A3, B3
AEA Investors Inc.
Bliss & Laughlin purchase bid rptd 8-10, 942B2
AEC—*See U.S. GOVERNMENT—ATOMIC Energy Commission*
AEGEAN Captain (Liberian tanker)
Collides off Tobago 7-19, oil spill rptd 553G2
AEGIS Anti-Aircraft System—*See ARMAMENTS—Missiles*
AER Lingus (Irish airline)
Workers strike 3-20, 211F3
AEROFLOT (Soviet airline)
US swaps Sovt spies, dissidents 4-27, 317C1
Sovt mid-air collisn kills 173 8-17, 639D1
Dancer detained in NY airport 8-24, leaves 8-27, 644G3
AERONAUTICS and Astronautics, American Institute of
Solar power satellites backed 1-10, 36C1
AEROPERU
Pilots, technicians strike 5-7, 411F2
AEROSOLS—*See CHEMICALS*
AEROSPACE Industry—*See AVIATION*
AFARS & Issas, French Territory of the—*See DJIBOUTI*

1980

ADRIATIC Sea
Venice aid vowed 3-8—3-9, 194C2
ADUBATO, Richie
Robertson replaces as Pistons coach 6-5, 656F3
ADULTERY
UK film on Saudi princess strains ties 4-10, 4-11, 294B1; 4-22—4-25, 313C2-B3
Australia bars Saudi film showing 4-15, 309E3
US broadcast of Saudi film protested 5-8, aired 5-12; cts rule on dispute 5-9, 5-12, 375E2-376A1
UK regrets Saudi film 5-22, 407A3
Nehru, Mountbatten affair alleged 9-27, 890A3
Swanson, Jos Kennedy affair alleged 10-13, 907E3
Pope in W Ger, affirms traditionalism 11-15—11-19, 905D1
ADVANI, L. K.
New Hindu party formed 4-6, 275C2
ADVERTISING
FCC lifts 3 RKO Gen licenses 1-24, 119A3
Mobil TV ad rejectn rptd 1-31, 120D1
Latham dies 2-21, 176B2
FTC chrgs misleading birth control ads, complaint setld 2-28, 358F2
TV rates rptd soaring, '79 top 10 advertisers listed 4-4, 376F1, A2
NBC hints revised Olympic coverage 4-14, 282F2
Mets fined for ad campaign 5-1, 637D1
NBC drops Olympic telecast, estimates loss 5-6, 379F3
Mobil protests Saudi film telecast 5-8, 375B3
FTC rules LaSalle Extensn U ads misleading 5-12, 703G1
Sears appliance performance claim order rptd 5-19, 703D2
FTC OKs food ad rules 5-21, 703D2
FTC unfair trade rules barred 5-28, 702F3
State ct legal immunity defined by Sup Ct 6-2, 512F3
Schl newspaper censorship power upheld 6-13, 583A1
FTC TV child ad probe case refused by Sup Ct 6-16, 511D3
Harper's to cease publicatn 6-17, 501B1
Utilities' free speech upheld by Sup Ct 6-20, 555G1-C2
Evangelical Christian direct mail use rptd 7-11—9-15, 819C2, E3
Benton & Bowles settles FTC bike chrg 7-31, 703E1
'Playing for Time' sponsor secrecy rptd 9-30, 835E3
Sun Maid model dies 10-14, 876F3
Ferrigno wins suit 11-3, 890E2
'Dallas' TV episode viewing record rptd 11-25, 905G3
ABC, CBS in cultural cable TV deals 12-2, 12-10, 1003A1, B1
Presidential Election (& Transition)
Kennedy broadcasts aired 1-14, 32B3; 1-28, 75A1
Bush denies '70 campaign gift coverup 2-7, 129C1
Carter '79 ad bid upheld by Appeals Ct 3-14, 221F3
Carter, Kennedy, Bush Pa campaigns cited 4-22, 304D1, D2, G2
Common Cause sues vs 'independnt' com spending 7-1, 493C1
Carter, Reagan budgets rptd 9-4, 665B3
AEGEAN Sea
Turkey, Greece end air dispute 2-22, 2-23, 150F2
Turkey, Greece talks omit 6-28, 500D2
Greece rejoins NATO mil wing 10-20, 800D1, F1
AEGIS Anti-Aircraft System—*See ARMAMENTS--Missiles*
AEROFLOT (Soviet airline)
US reduces flights 1-8, Australia bans 1-9, 9D1, E2
Kennedy flight boycotted, diverted to Montreal 1-11, 55C2
NYC office bombed 1-13, 55A2
Kennedy, Dulles flights delayed by Teamsters 1-18, 1-22, 45E1
Kennedy radar tampering probed 1-31; USSR to end flights 2-4, 114F3
Spain arrests Suranov 2-14, 141A3
Paris office bombed 2-24, 149F3; French arrest 11 7-1, 522A2
Frankfurt office bomb found 3-7, 236B1
Sovts misplace body of Chad envoy 6-7, 491C3
5 Cubans defect at Lisbon airport 10-18, 828E3
AEROLINEAS Argentinas
Jet hijacked, Martinez extortn fails 6-30—7-1, 519F2
AEROSPACE Industry—*See AVIATION*
AFFARS & Issas, French Territory of the—*See DJIBOUTI, Republic of*

1977

AFDC (Aid to Families With Dependent Children)—*See HEALTH, Education & Welfare under U.S. GOVERNMENT*
AFFIRMATIVE Action—*See EDUCATION—School Integration; LABOR—Job Bias; MINORITIES; U.S. GOVERNMENT—HEALTH, Education & Welfare—Affirmative Action Office*
AFFIRMED (race horse)
Named top 2-yr old colt 12-13, 970F3
AFGE—*See GOVERNMENT Employees, American Federation of*

1978

AFC (American Football Conference)—*See FOOTBALL—Professional*
AFDC (Aid to Families With Dependent Children)—*See U.S. GOVERNMENT—HEALTH, Education & Welfare*
AFFEL, Charles
Vietnam frees 1-5, 8E2
AFFIRMATIVE Action—*See EDUCATION—School Integration; LABOR—Job Bias; MINORITIES*
AFFIRMED (race horse)
Wins Triple Crown 6-10, 538G3-539A2
Loses Marlboro Cup 9-16, 1028D1
Named top horse, best 3-yr old 12-12, 1028B1, C1

1979

AFDC (Aid to Families With Dependent Children)—*See U.S. GOVERNMENT—HEALTH, Education & Welfare*
AFFIRMATIVE Action—*See EDUCATION—School Integration; LABOR—Job Bias; MINORITIES*
AFFIRMED (race horse)
Wins Santa Anita H'cap 3-4, 448C3
Withdrawn from Marlboro Cup 9-4; wins Woodward Stakes 9-23, Jockey Gold Cup 10-6, 876E2, A3, F3
Retired to stud 10-22, named top horse 12-11, 1005B1

1980

AFFATIGATO, Marco
Arrested 8-6, 620B1
AFFIRMATIVE Action—*See EDUCATION--School Integration, LABOR--Job Bias, MINORITIES*
AFFIRMED (race horse)
Spectacular Bid sets winnings mark 6-8, 447E3
AFFRIME, Mindy
Tell Me a Riddle released 12-17, 1003E2

AFGHANISTAN

1976

AFGHANISTAN—*See also ADB, NONALIGNED Nations Movement*
Listed as 'not free' nation 1-19, 20D3
UN Palestine com member 2-26, 162C1
Aide in bombed Cambodian town 3-2—3-4, 238B2

1977

AFGHANISTAN—*See also NONALIGNED Nations Movement*
UN Assemb member 3F3
Planning min assassinated 11-16, suspect seized 11-17, 969E2

1978

AFGHANISTAN—*See also NONALIGNED Nations Movement*
Islamic bank poor-natn aid rise rptd 4-9, 257F2
Oppositn offcl killed 4-17, CP figures arrested 4-26, 317D1
Pres, mins killed in coup 4-27; violence continues, 1000s rptd dead 4-28, 317A1
Taraki, Revolutionary Cncl hd new govt 4-30; neutrality pledged 5-4, 317B1
USSR extends recognitn 4-30, US: ties unbroken 5-1, 317C1
Govt makeup detailed 5-2, 5-6, 349D2
Taraki denies heavy coup toll, Sovt links; pledges Iran, Pak, US ties 5-6, 349C2, E2
US, UK, Iran, Pak affirm ties 5-6, 349A3
USSR denies coup role 5-7, 349A3
Civil servants purged 5-8, 349B3
Iran, Pak fear new govt, Sovt role in Baluchistan 5-19, 391D1
Jets bomb rebel tribesmen 5-31, 434F2
250 mil, religious ldrs flee to Pak 6-5, 434G2
US, India discuss new regime 6-13—6-15, 466G3
Ex-king loses citizenship 6-14, 538A1
USSR '54-76 credits cited 595F2
Pak border floods kill 122 7-9, 655C1
Nur named amb to US 7-10, 538A1
2 mins ousted, reassigned 7-10, 538A1 ★
UK cancels debts 7-31, 592D1
Coup attempt smashed 8-17, 671F1
S Korea ties cut 9-18, 738D2
UN Assemb member 713B3
Forgn plot rptd smashed 9-20, 738B2
Tribesmen flee to Pak 9-24, 738C2
US to renew econ aid to Pak 10-24, 840B1
Taraki in Moscow 12-4, pact signed 12-5, 943D2
Moslem rebels battle army 12-5, 943F2

1979

AFGHANISTAN—*See also NONALIGNED Nations Movement*
Foreign Relations (misc.)—*See also 'Soviet' and 'UN' below*
Rebels set up hq in Pak 1-7, 56F2
China vows to aid Pak vs 'aggressn' 1-22, 59D3
Pak denies mil aid to rebels 2-2, 147A3
Iran border incursn chrgd 3-18, 209A2
Pak, Iran, China rebel aid chrgd by USSR 3-18, 209D2
War refugees enter Pak, Iran 3-22, 232E3
Iran ousts Afghan aide 3-22, 233A1
Pak raid chrgd 4-8, denied 4-9; refugee exit data 4-10, 284A1
Iran, Pak rebel aid chrgd 4-22, 4-27, 368C2
War refugees rptd in Pak 7-20, 562E1
Pak, Iran linked to army mutiny 8-5, 599E2
Amin chrgs forgn rebel aid 8-9, 666F2
6 W Gers, Canadian slain 9-7, 9-8, 696C1
Amnesty Intl chrgs rights breach 9-19, 748E2
Pak, Iran linked to coup try 10-16, 810F3
W Eur heroin supply role cited 11-11, 972E3
Government & Politics—*See also other appropriate subheads in this section*
Freedom House lists as not free 13A1
Anti-govt fighting renewed 1-7, 56D2; **see 'Rebellion' below**
Amin named premr, Taraki stays pres 3-27, 233C1
Taraki, Amin kin flee to USSR 6-7, 443A1
Cabt shifted, Amin gets defns post 7-28, 580E2
Rebels establish govt 8-18, claim advances 8-20, 666C2
2 pro-Taraki mins ousted 9-14; Taraki replaced by Amin 9-16, rptd slain 9-18; violence detailed 9-14–9-19, 695C3
4 province govs rptd ousted 9-20, 696C1
Amin: Taraki alive 9-23, 748D2
Amin denounced in leaflets 9-26, 748E2
Amin commutes 2 death sentences 10-8, 787E2
Taraki death confirmed 10-9, 787D2
Amin ousted in coup, executed; Karmal assumes power 12-27, names Cabt 12-28, 973A1-G1
Amin govt prisoners, Taraki widow freed 12-29, 973C2
Rebellion—*See also 'Soviet' below*
Moslem rebels renew fighting 1-7, claim victories 1-10, 56D2; 1-27, 2-19, 147G2
Moslem rebel ldr flees to Pak 3-5, rebel clashes continue 3-14, 209E2
Rebel fighting spreads 3-22–3-28, 232E2
Refugees enter Pak, Iran 3-22, 232E3
Jalalabad troop mutiny crushed 4-3, 599G2
Pak refugee exit data rptd 4-10, 284B1
Rebels claim victories 4-11, 284C1
Rebellion spreads 4-22, 368A2; combat intensifies 6-7, 443B1
Kabul riots erupt, purge rptd 6-23–6-24, 521D2
Rebel groups listed, issues rptd 7-13, 521F2-D3
Rebel retreat from Herat, Jalalabad rptd 7-16; 3,000 prisoners rptd executed 7-22, 562C1-F1
Refugees rptd in Pak 7-20, 562E1
Kabul army mutiny crushed 8-5, 599D2
Rebels claim successes 9-2–10-30, 832C1
2 pro-Taraki mins ousted 9-14; Taraki replaced 9-16, rptd killed 9-18; violence detailed 9-14–9-19, 695C3
Amin offers refugee amnesty 9-20, 696C1
Army uprising crushed 10-15–10-16, 810F2
Rebellion seen at impasse 10-29, 832A1
Pak refugee data rptd 11-26, 12-6, 966G1
Fighting spreads 11-28, 12-6, 966E1
Rebels rpt Pakia prov offensive 11-29, successes noted 12-10, 966B1
Amin ousted in coup, executed; Sovts linked, troops invade 12-27, 973A1; see 'Soviet Military Intervention' below

1980

AFGHANISTAN—*See also ADB, NONALIGNED Nations*
Foreign Relations (misc.)—*See also 'Soviet Military Intervention', 'UN Policy' below*
World Bank freezes loans 1-14, 50B2
Islamic conf boycotted; ousted 1-29, 67G1
EC offers neutrality guarantee 2-19, 123F3
French CP issues rights rpt 2-20, 149E3
Soccer players defect to W Ger 3-26, 271A2
Canadian UN offcl freed 6-22, 486B2
Wrestlers defect to Pak 7-6, Olympic team denies defectn plans 7-21, 590B2
W Ger pol asylum rules rptd tightened 7-31, 581F2
Islamic League meets 11-10, 895A2
Government & Politics—*See also other appropriate subheads in this section*
Karmal asks people's support 1-2, 3D2
2,000 pol prisoners rptd freed 1-6, 3E2
Karmal on power assumptn 1-10, 27C3
Afghans storm jail to free kin 1-11, 46B1
Taraki death probe, 3 Amin aides face trial 1-14, 27B3
Amin tied to rebel ldr, CIA; Sovt coup role detailed 1-21, 44F1, B2
Govt shootout rptd 2-7; Karmal ouster denied 2-16, 123G2
Afghan aide defects to US 2-22, 139C1
Mil draft call announced 3-8, 205E3
Party ldrs on rebel death list 3-12, 205F3
CP takeover 2d anniv marked 4-29, 349E2
Mil draft rptd 6-4, 443D1
13 pro-Amin aides executed 6-8, 6-16, 475B2
2 Cabt mins slain 7-2, 602D1
Karmal asks purge 7-13, consolidates power 7-20, 561A1
2 more Cabt mins rptd slain 9-14, 727G2

1976

1977

1978

1979

Soviet Military Intervention
USSR role in death of US amb denied 2-16–2-19, US cable rebuts 2-22, 147G1-F2
US cuts Afghan aid 2-22, 147E2
USSR chrgs US, Pak, Iran, China rebel aid; USSR govt aid rptd 3-18, 209C2
US warns USSR on govt aid 3-23, 232F3
USSR rebel aid chrgs scored 4-2, govt role noted 4-11–4-17, 284E1
USSR personnel trap mutineers 4-3, 599D3
USSR naval activity cited 4-12, 313G3
USSR copter gunships to govt rptd 5-3, 368B2
USSR role protested in Iran 5-24, 407B3; 6-12, 445G3-446D1
USSR warns Pak re rebel aid 6-1; chrg China, Pak train rebels 6-11, 443C1
Taraki, Amin kin flee to USSR 6-7, 443A1
USSR role widens 6-11, 443B1
USSR chrgs US rebel aid, US denies 6-11, 443C1
USSR ask India role 6-14, 443D1
SALT II summit topic 6-15–6-18, 449D1
USSR seen unsure of Taraki ldrshp ability 6-24, 521E2
USSR linked to Cabt shift 7-28, broader govt base asked 8-1, 580E2
USSR warned by US 8-2, 580C2
USSR mil role bared 8-9, 8-21, 666E2
USSR chrgs Iran press distortn 8-22, 666G2
Sovts widen war role 11-28, 12-6, 12-10, Afghans concede presence 12-14,, 966A1
US rpts Sovt mil buildup 12-21, 12-26; USSR denies 12-23, 974D1
Amin ousted in coup; Sovts linked, troops invade 12-27, 973A1
USSR vows aid to new govt 12-28–12-30, admit mil interventn 12-30, 12-28, 973A2, D2
US warns Brezhnev 12-28, rpts Sovt coup role 12-31, 973G2-974D1
Intl protests 12-28–12-31, 974C2
Sovt troops control Kabul 12-29, battle Afghan army dissidents 12-31, 973E2
US assures Pak 12-30, India protests to US 12-31, 974G1-B2

1980

Soviet Military Intervention
Map of Afghanistan, surrounding areas 25A1
Pak, China, Egypt rebel training chrgd 1-1, 1D2
Afghan govt says Sovts asked in 1-1, 3D2
Sovt force rptd at 85,000; rebel resistance mounts 1-2—1-4, 3D1-A2
Sovt offcl rptd killed 1-3, 26B2
Rebel groups seek merger 1-4; army unit defectn rptd 1-5, 3A2
USSR accuses US, Pak on rebel arms 1-4, 1-7, 10D2
Sovt buildup continues, force forecast at 10,000 1-7; Afghan army rptd in major role 1-8, 10F1
Sovts fight Afghan army, Moslem rebels, civilns 1-9, 10C2
Sovt deploymt near Iran rptd heavy 1-10, 1-16, 26C1, E1
Rebels control 2 NE provs 1-10, 26D1
Sovt losses rptd at 900-1200 1-11, 26F1
Sovt, Afghan army clashes rptd 1-13, 26G1; 1-17, 44B1
Rebels rptdly get Iran Baluchi aid 1-15, 26B2
China rebel aid agrmt rptd 1-16, 31A2
Sovts airlift reinforcemts, mass near Iran border 1-19; poison gas use chrgd 1-23, 44A1, D1
Sovt offcl's missn rptd 1-21, 44B2; death rpts conflict 2-2, 123A3
Sovts rpt rebel resistance; claim China, Pak aid 1-25, 1-28, 67F2
Rebel sniper kills Sovt soldier in Kabul 1-25, 67G2
Rebels claim 'Free Islam Repub' set 1-25, 6 rebel groups merge 1-27, 67A3
More Sovt troops arrive 1-30, svc rotatn noted 1-31, 85A3
Rebel successes claimed 2-1—2-20, 123F1
US: Sovt losses 2,500 2-2, 85F2
'79 village massacre, Sovt role rptd 2-4; Sovts deny, US comments 2-5, 85G1-D2
Sovts reinforce tanks near Pak border 2-4, 85G2
Karmal: Sovts invaded 10 days before '79 coup 2-7, 85D2
US says Sovts mass near Iran 2-8; Iran confirms 2-9; Sovts deny 2-10, 123E2
Egypt says trains rebels 2-13, 123D1
US rptdly arms rebels 2-14, 2-15; US denies, Sovts score US 2-16, 122D3
Afghans ask volunteer force 2-18, 123D2
Sovts ignore US exit deadline, expand force; US lowers force estimate 2-20, 123D1
Kabul anti-Soviet strike; 300 die in clashes, US, Pak natls arrested 2-21—2-27; martial law imposed 2-22, 138B2-C3
US rpts Sovt setbacks 2-21, 139B1
Sovts reinforce 3 eastern provs 2-22, 138D3-139A1
Kabul-Peshawar (Pak) highway closed 2-23, 138C3
Shiite Moslems rounded up 2-26, 138B3
Kabul unrest subsides 2-28, troops thwart anti-govt rally 2-29; 240 rioters freed 3-4, 164G3
Rebels routed in Kunar prov 2-29—3-4, 164B3
Sovt jet intrudes over Pak 3-1, 164D3
Major rebel group bars Pak-based alliance 3-3, 5 other groups merge 3-4, 164E3
Sovt poison gas use rptd 3-4—3-5, 205G2-B3
More refugees flee to Pak 3-4—3-5; Pak invites camp inspectn 3-6, 205D3
Rebel group denied Kunar prov defeat 3-6, 205B3
Anti-rebel drive in Paktia rptd 3-10, 205E2
US says Sovts execute Afghans 3-28, 271G1
India rpts on Sovt Kunar drive 3-29, 271E1
Rebels kill 75 Afghan troops 3-31, 600 Sovts 4-3, 271D1
US rpts fighting impasse 4-4, 271A1
Sovt troop pact OKd, Karmal bars peace talks 4-5, 271F1
US estimates Sovt casualties 4-17, 349D3
Kabul students protest 4-21—5-1, 349D2
Hockey team rptd ambushed 5-3, 349F2
Pak rebel bldg bombed 5-3, 349G2
Afghan proposes Sovt troop exit terms 5-14; Pak vs, US doubtful 5-15, 361E2
Kabul protests vs Sovts renewed, Karmal denounced 5-15, 387E2
Afghan refugees total 800,000 5-17, 387G2
Kabul riots 5-18, US rpts 5-20—5-29; deaths total 140, US, China blamed 6-8, 442F2
Rebel-Sovt battle near Kabul rptd 6-7, 443A1
Rebels ambush Sovt column 6-11; Afghans from Pak join battle 6-15, 507F3
Afghan troops rebel at Sovt base 6-20, 508A1
Sovts set partial troop exit 6-22; divisn, 108 tanks to leave 475D1
Brezhnev calls success 6-23, 475F1
Sovts rejct further troop exit 6-27, 490B1
US rpts 5,000 troop exit completed 7-2, 507A3
Sovts restate exit conditns 7-2, 507B3
More Sovt troops rptd sent, long stay seen 7-3, 507F2

1976 1977 1978 1979 1980

Rebel-Sovt clashes near Kabul rptd 7-3—7-6, 7-9, 507D3
USSR bars US, French independnc day speeches 7-4, 7-14, 566B3
Sovts mine Afghan-Pak passes 7-7, 507F3
Rebels disrupt Sovt supply lines 7-12, kill 350 in Paktia 7-20, 561E1
Sovt raids level villages 7-14, 561C1
Sovt troops thwart coup 7-18, 602C1
Airline pres abducted, 12 employees seized 7-20, 561F1
Afghan troop mutiny 7-24; Sovt troops crush 8-3, 602B1
Sovt chem weapons use chrgd 8-7, 628D3
Fighting rptd intensified 8-10—8-26; rebels claim 1,200 civilians killed by Sovts 8-17, 649G2-650E1
Sovts claim 'bandits' delay exit 8-18, 650A2
Sovt chem weapon use disputed 8-21, 650F1-A2
Sovt-Afghan, rebel clashes 8-30—9-8; rebel ldr slain; US, Chinese, Pak arms seized 9-1, 686A1
Rebel factions clash 9-2, 686D1
Sovt use of dumdum bullets rptd 9-10, 727F2
Heavy clashes near Kabul 9-13, 9-15, 727D2
Non-Sovt troops rptd seen 9-15, 705B1
Afghan copters raid Pak border 9-26, 766A1
Sovt Kunar Valley drive rptd 10-2, 766C1
High Sovt losses hinted 10-8, 827C2
Sovt, Afghan army troops clash in Kabril 10-15; rebels step up raids 10-16, 827F1
Sovts open new drive near Pak border 10-23, 827E2
Pak refugee camps strafed 10-24, 900C1
Jalalabad airport hit by rebels 10-26, 900C1
Sovts annexing Wakhan salient 11-4, 900A1

Soviet Military Intervention (reaction)

USSR defends actns, scores US response 1-1—1-6, 1C2
W Eur, Japan, India reactns 1-1—1-6, 2D2, 11G3
Afghan exiles protest in Iran 1-1, 1-3, 1-6, in India 1-2, US 1-4, 2G2-3B1
US pres campaign topic 1-1—1-3, 5B1-B2; 1-5—1-10, 12G3, 13C1, B2, D2
US recalls amb, seeks SALT delay 1-2, 1B2
Gold prices soar 1-2—1-18, 30B3
Sakharov scores 1-2, 46A3
UN Cncl mtg sought 1-3—1-4; debate 1-5—1-6; Sovts veto res for pullout 1-7 2F1
W Eur, Moslem, E Eur reactns 1-4—1-10, 10F2-11B1
US ordrs econ, pol retaliatn 1-4, plans other moves 1-5, 51B1; for subsequent developments, see GRAIN—Soviet Embargo, SPORTS—Olympic Games
Italy CP condemns USSR 1-5; French CP backs 1-11, Soclsts score 1-12—1-13, 57G2, A3, F3
Refugees to Pak total 402,000 1-6, 3C2
US, China in mil talks 1-6—1-9, 11B2; US rpts China rebel aid agrmt 1-16, 31A2
Sadat, Begin discuss crisis 1-7—1-10, 12F1
Canada's Trudeau asks role on anti-USSR moves 1-7, Clark rejects 1-8, 38D1
US bars NY, Kiev consulates, tracks Sovt trawlers, cuts Aeroflot flights 1-8, suspends tech exports 1-9; ILA boycotts ships 1-8, 9A1
US-Egypt air exercises rptd 1-8, 11C1
Australia bars Sovt flights 1-9, 9E2
UN Cncl shifts invasn issue to Assemb 1-10; res demands pullout, Afghan votes vs 1-14, 25E1-26B1
Canada, Portugal set retaliatn 1-11, 1-15, 28A2
US rejects USSR tech export licenses 1-11, 28C2
Sovt airline boycotted in US 1-11, 55C2; 1-18, 1-22, 45E1
Brezhnev scores Carter 'lies'; US, internal divisn denied 1-12, 26C2
Pak gets US aid offer 1-12, 27A1; for subsequent developments, see PAKISTAN—Soviet-Afghan Issue
Iran backs rebels 1-14, 1-17, 27E2
Sovts explain Amin overthrow 1-14, 27G2
UK ships shifted to Medit 1-14, 46A2
NATO meets re anti-USSR steps 1-15, 28D1
India rebukes Sovts 1-16, 27G1
Iran assured, Ban-Sadr vs Sovt move 1-16, 27B2
US VP Mondale hits issue 1-16, 50G2
Australia, Japan score 1-16, 78F1
US newsmen ousted 1-17, 26A3
US to limit USSR ammonia imports 1-18, 45A2
US, Sovt, naval, air buildup in Persian Gulf, Indian Ocean rptd 1-18—1-22, 46D1
Iran bolsters border re Sovt massing 1-19; forgn min concerned 1-19, 1-22, 44D1
China cancels Sovt tie talks 1-19, 45G3-46A1
Reagan vs Carter retaliatn 1-19, 50C3
Israel sees no Palestinian link 1-20, 48F2
US to buy Sovt-bound chickens 1-21, 44C3

1976	1977	1978	1979	1980

1980

US cancels Kama R plant computer parts 1-21, 45F1
USSR links Canada spy ousters 1-22, 56A3
NZ sets anti-Sovt steps 1-22, 100D2
Carter warns USSR 1-23, 41A1, E1-C2, 42B1
Tass scores Carter warning 1-24, 43A3
US to sell China mil gear 1-24, 46B2
US pres candidates note 1-24—2-7, 91C2, E2, A3, B3
Japan, UK retaliate vs Sovts 1-25, 1-26, 67B3
Sovts end artist visits to US 1-28, 67D3
Egypt vs move, cuts Sovt emb staff 1-28, 69E1
Kennedy scores Carter 1-28, 74F2-A3, B3
Sakharov denounces 1-28, 86E1
Australia broadens trade curbs 1-28, 1-29, 116C1
US gen sees Sovt confidence gain 1-29, 65C2
Islamic conf scores 1-29, 67F1
US shipping boycott ends 1-29, 2-1, 169B1
US, India discuss 1-30—1-31; Gandhi fears Pak arms aid 1-30, 83A3
Gromyko seeks Rumania, India support 1-31—2-2, 108F3
US airport-Aeroflot dispute 1-31—2-4, 114G3-115E1
Detente backed by Brezhnev 2-4, 84F3
Khomeini scores invasn 2-4, 88A2; 2-11, 106A1
US, Saudi agree on significance 2-5, 83G1-A2
France, W Ger ask pullout 2-5, USSR sees US pressure 2-6, 84E2-C3
US issues rights rpt 2-5, 86A2, A3
France joins W Ger condemnatn 2-5, bars W Eur-US mtg 2-8, 106D2
China denounces at Geneva conf 2-5, 108B1
N Korea, Rumania bar support 2-6—2-7, 109A2
USSR urges W Eur anti-US stand 2-7, 106C3
US draft registratn plan issued 2-8, debated 2-12, 2-13, 110D1, C2, F2
Carter pol ads cited 2-10, 109E1
US Persian Gulf assault force dispatched 2-12, 106A2
Kennedy attacks Carter 2-12, 110G1-A2
Australia lifts trade curbs 2-12, 148A1, C1
Carter news conf stresses 2-13, 110B1
UN rights comm meets, US scores invasn 2-13; res adopted 2-14, 123F3
Italy CP scores USSR, US 2-17; CP govt role barred 2-21, 134D1, E1
EC offers UK-proposed neutrality plan re Sovt exit 2-19, 123F3
Australia sets defns spending hike 2-19, 132C1
AFL-CIO scores USSR 2-19, 146G3
USSR OKs US, Japan steel deal delay 2-19, 235F3
Vance sees Westn allies on policy coordinatn 2-20—2-21, 139G1
US businessman arrested 2-21—2-22, freed 3-27, 271E2
US bars Sovt scientists from 2 confs 2-22, 135F1
US, Pak natls arrested 2-22, 2-24, 138D2
Afghan aide defects, scores USSR 2-22, 139C1
Brezhnev offers pullout for neutrality vow 2-22; Carter asks exit first 2-25, 139E2, G2
US bars phosphates to USSR 2-25, 139D3
USSR pullout hints rptd, US skeptical 2-27, 165E1
USSR gets UK neutrality plan, US backs 2-28; USSR, China score 3-2, 165B1
Vance sees Dobrynin 2-29, 165E1
US ouster of Sovt bloc diplomats as spies rptd 2-29, 189E2
Reagan 'basic speech' cites invasn 2-29, 207B3
Carter, Schmidt meet, in close agrmt 3-5, 205B2
Connally cites in 'basic speech' 3-7, 184E3, 185E1
USSR W Ger consulate bombed, Aeroflot Frankfurt office bomb found 3-7, 236B1
Sovts vs UK neutrality plan 3-11, 3-14; US sees no setlmt 3-12, scores W Eur 3-18, 205A1
Rumania, UK vs Sovt invasn 3-14, 205G1
Carter hints SALT renunciatn, doubts ratificatn 3-14, 209E1
US tightens Sovt export curbs 3-18, 204E3
Arrested US natl called spy 3-19; on TV, scores CIA 3-26; accuses West, China 4-3, 271F2
W Ger, French stand scored 3-20, 236F3
Hungary backs USSR 3-24, 274G3
Soccer players defect to W Ger 3-26, 271A2
UK issues defense paper 4-2, 274A2
Japan forms defense panel 4-7, 314E3
Carter defends policy 4-10, 263G3
US sees Iran threatened 4-17, 281A2
E, W Ger offcls meet 4-17, 303B2
Anderson scores Carter 4-20, 328D1
Soviet-French talks held 4-24—4-25, 351E3, F3
Europn CPs meet 4-28—4-29, 327A3
Canada Cup hockey tourn cancelled 4-30, 488B3
USSR May Day parade boycotted 5-1, 354G2
Muskie scores Sovt policy 5-7, 343C1
NATO denounces USSR 5-14, 377B2

1976 1977 1978 1979 1980

Muskie, Gromyko meet 5-16, 378B1
Carter backs India uranium sale 5-16, 440D3
Alleged US spy freed 5-16, 443D1
Islamic Conf 5-17—5-22, Afghan rebel reps join 5-17; Iran scores 'aggressn' 5-19; talks proposed 5-22, 395F2, E3
Franco-Sovt summit held 5-19, US scores France 5-20, 378F2-379D1
Sovt trade blitz in W Eur rptd 5-22, 430G3-431A1
Sovt Jewish emigratn drop cited 5-24, 467G2
China, Japan discuss 5-27—6-1, 422B1
USSR-W Ger trade accord set 5-29, 411B2
Carter cites 'aggressn' 5-29, 423F3
Jones scores Carter defns budget 5-29, 424F2
UK Labor Party scores USSR, urges exit 5-31, 429F2
Vance urges SALT OK 6-5, 421D3
Sino-Sovt trade declines 6-6, 451F3
Saudi F-15 gear request considered by US 6-17, 450B2
Carter OKs uranium sale to India 6-19, 495A3
Italy-US communique vs 6-20, 474B2
Basketball players defect to Pak 6-20, 475D2
Venice summit seeks total troop exit 6-22, Carter scores USSR, backs Sovt-Eur ties 6-23, 473B1, F1
US doubts Sovt troop exit plan 6-22, 475B2
Schmidt USSR trip plans rptd 6-23, 474G1
Carter backs transitnal plan 6-24, USSR scores 6-25, 474F2-B3
US, Yugo back UN charter 6-25, 474B3
Portugal, US urge anti-USSR actn 6-26, 475C1
NATO condemns 6-26, 489E2
Schmidt in USSR, urges exit 6-30—7-1; econ pact signed 7-1, 489A1-D3
Carter issues draft registratn proclamatn 7-2, 494A1
Carter transitn plan scored by USSR 7-2, 507C3
China links Viet Thai raids 7-5, 508D2
Saudis press for US F-15 gear 7-9, 538C3
Carter, Hua meet 7-10, 506D1
Reagan pres nominatn acceptance speech 7-17, 533A1, 534G3
Canada lifts Sovt grain embargo 7-24, 577F3
Carter pres renominatn acceptance speech 8-14, 613B1
US-Sovt trade drop rptd 8-20, 711C2
Japan to aid refugees in Pak 9-1, 686F1
Afghan Emb aides in Turkey defect to US 9-6, 705C1
Hua scores interventn 9-7, 678B1
Muskie hints SALT ratificatn 9-7, 680A1
Commonwealth scores USSR 9-8, 680C1
CSCE prep talks begin 9-9, 679C3
China sees war danger 9-11, 706F3
Sovt soldier seeks US Emb asylum 9-15; Sovts ask release, US bars 9-16; US chrgs emb pressure 9-17, 704G2
Afghan airline employes defect to W Ger 9-15, 705A1
US union affirms shipping ban 9-18, 826D3
US protests Franco-Soviet steel deal 9-19, 728E3
Sovt soldier leaves US Emb 9-21, 727A2
Canada min scores USSR 9-22, 748G3-749B1
Carter quotes Reagan on Cuba blockade 9-23, 722D3
Portugal CP electn loss linked 10-5, 760E1
Muskie warns of Reagan's 'endless' wars 10-11, 776B3
Muskie urges SALT action 10-16, 776A2
Carter scores Reagan response 10-16, 802F2
Karmal in Moscow, Sovts vow contd aid 10-16; communique 10-19, 827B1
Food, medical shortage rptd 10-16, 827C2
Warsaw Pact communique issued 10-20, 800C2
EC to resume Sovt barley sales 10-23, 832B1
UNESCO delegate vs Sovt invasn, defects to W Ger, asks asylum 10-25, 827E2
China cites Sovt threat 10-30, 952D1
Sovts scored at CSCE mtg 11-12, 11-13, 863C1; 11-14—12-19, 950C2
US curbs French steel imports 11-17, 886C1
UN Assemb again votes Sovt exit 11-20; res scored by USSR 11-20, Afghan 11-21, 899F2-900A1
Schmidt condemns invasn 11-24, 904C2
Brezhnev to Gandhi: Sovt troops to stay 12-9, 930F2
Brezhnev scores intl arms buildup, denies Persian Gulf threat 12-10; US scores contd presence 12-11, 930A2
US scores USSR Persian Gulf peace plan 12-11, 930C2
Castro backs invasn 12-17, 12-20, 992E3
Rebels urge strike on invasn anniv 12-27; anti-govt, anti-Sovt rioting in Kabul 12-29, 991C1

Soviet Relations—*See also 'Soviet Military Intervention' above*

Sovt-backed gas field opened 1-27, 85B3
Afghan-Sovt trade pact rptd 2-5, 85D3
Afghans in Teheran, New Delhi protest Sovt invasn 12-27, USSR protests attack on Iran emb 12-28, 990G3

1979

UN Policy & Developments
Membership listed 695D2

U.S. Relations—*See also 'Soviet' above*
US amb Dubs kidnaped, killed; US protests Afghan, Sovt role 2-14, 106C2
USSR regrets Dubs death, denies blame 2-16—2-17, 147D2
Afghan rejcts US protest, denies Sovt role 2-19, 147E2
US cuts forgn aid 2-22, 147B1
US secret cable details Dubs death 2-22, 147E1
US rpts fighting spread 3-22; airlift increase 3-28, 232G2
US emb evacuatn set 7-23, 562A1
US air attache beaten 9-8, leaves 9-9, 696E1
Rebellion seen at impasse 10-29, 832A1
Evacuatns, travel curbs ordrd 11-26, 894A2

1980

Sports
Soccer players defect to W Ger 3-26, 271A2
Hockey team rptd ambushed 5-3, 349F2
Basketball players defect to Pak 6-20, 475D2
Wrestlers defect to Pak 7-6; Olympic team denies defectn plans 7-21, 590B2
Hockey team ambush detailed 7-15, 561G1-B2

UN Policy & Developments
Cncl mtg on Sovt invasn opens 1-5, Sovts veto res for pullout 1-7, 2F1
Cncl shifts invasn issue to Assemb 1-10; res demands pullout, Afghan votes vs 1-14, 25E1-26B1
Rights Comm meets 2-13, anti-Sovt res adopted 2-14, 123D3
USSR rptdly weighs peace force 2-27, 165F1
Yugo, US back UN Charter 6-25, 474B3
UNESCO conf delegate defects 10-25, 827E2
Assemb again votes Sovt exit 11-20; res scored by USSR 11-20, Afghan 11-21, 899F2-900A1

U.S. Relations—*See also 'Soviet Military Intervention' above*
Dubs official rpt released 2-20, 140B1
'79 terrorism deaths rptd 5-11, 365E3
CBS newsman denies gang slaying tie 8-4, 602D1

1976

AFL-CIO—*See AMERICAN Federation of Labor and Congress of Industrial Organizations*

AFONSO Cerqueira (Portuguese warship)
In Intl Naval Review 7-4, 488C3

AFRICA—*See also specific countries, organizations*
Cuba mil advisers rptd 1-10, 138F1
Freedom House survey rptd 1-19, 20B3
Algeria, Libya, Niger seek regional cooperatn 4-8, 372B1
Arab-African parley 4-19—4-22, 355G3
French-African summit 5-10—5-11, 355F2
WHO rejcts Israel rpt 5-17, 355G1
French pres visits US 5-17—5-22, 372A2
S Africa A-plant deal set 5-29, 387F1
Sovt, Cuban presence rptd 6-13, 467C1
Summer Olympics withdrawls rptd 7-21, 528G2
S Africa warns vs USSR role 8-13, 661C1
5 state heads meet in Tanzania 9-6—9-7, 661C3, E3★
Callaghan talks with Trudeau 9-16, 730B2
World Bank poverty data chart 778C1
USSR warned re southn Africa talks 10-29, 832B1
W Africa econ pact ratified 11-6, 974D2
UNESCO readmits Israel 11-22, 879A1

EC Relations
40-natns OK Lome conv 2-3, 164D3
Backs southn states independnc 2-23, 163A1
Sets Zaire, Zambia, Malawi aid 4-6, 276C2

Rhodesian Relations—*See under RHODESIA*

U.S. Relations—*See also specific country names*
Kissinger sees 37 ambs, sets visit 1-15, 16B2
Ford State of Union message 1-19, 38B3
Kissinger backs majority rule, warns Cuba 3-22, 3-23, 214D3, F3
Kissinger visits 4-24—4-29; policy speech on southn Africa 4-27, reactn 4-27—4-29; text excerpts 293A1-295A2
Issue at black Dem caucus 5-1, 5-2, 343B3, F3
Kissinger ends 6-natn tour 5-6, 317A1-318G3
Ford, Reagan exchng chrgs 6-5, 6-6, 410A2, C2
US rpts Sovt, Cuba troop presence 6-13, 467C1
Dem platform text cites 6-15, 477E2, 478A3
US vetoes Angola UN membership 6-23, 455C2
Kissinger on southern Africa problem 6-24, 446F2
Kissinger on detente, Sovt southn Africa role 6-25, 466D2
Schaufele begins 6-natn tour 7-7, 523A1
GOP platform com actn 8-13, 582B3
GOP platform text cites 8-18, 610E1, A2
Ford acceptnc speech cites 8-19, 612B1
Kissinger meets Vorster in Zurich 9-4—9-6, 660B2
Ford plans southn Africa mediatn effort 9-8, 665G1
Schaufele in Tanzania, Zambia briefings 9-8—9-9, 681F1
Kissinger on US goal 9-11; sees Tanzania, Zambia ldrs 9-15—9-16, 681A1

1977

AFI—*See AMERICAN Film Institute*

AFL-CIO—*See AMERICAN Federation of Labor and Congress of Industrial Organizations*

AFRAH, Hussein Kulmia
Kenya border pact set 7-20, 588C1

AFRICA—*See also specific countries, organizations*
Cuba black natlst aid rptd 1-9, 19A1
Sweden budgets black natlst aid 1-10, 23B1
Pan-Africa festival 1-15—2-12, 106B1
S Africa scores UN re southern Africa 1-21, 67B1
Mid-'75 populatn rptd 1-30, 123G2
Frelimo cong 2-3—2-7, 137D1
CIA paymts to Israel rptd 2-22, 124B2
Castro tours 8 natns 3-1—4-2, 249F1
Afro-Arab summit 3-7—3-9, 170D1-D2, 188B2
Church conf scores silence re Uganda archbp death 3-18, 308B3
Podgorny tours southn Africa 3-23—4-2, 247G2
E Ger black natlst backing cited 4-2, 249E3
WHO launches immunizatn drive 4-7, 287C3
USSR Horn of Africa strategy rptd 4-16, 328B1
French-African summit 4-20—4-21, 316C3
USSR role stressed at Sudan-French talks 5-17—5-19, 450D1
Sahel conf sets dvpt plan 5-30—6-1, 458D3
North-South conf backs aid 6-3, 437F2
Zaire warns of Cuba presence 6-9—6-10, 490E1
Giscard, Brezhnev conf 6-21, 495C1
Lutheran World Fed head named 6-24, 732E1
Djibouti independnc ends colonialism 6-27, 506B3
Horn of Africa alliances shift 7-6, 588E1
Giscard evaluates Sovt role 7-25, 551B1
E Ger Horn of Africa role noted 8-21, 684F3
Kaunda asks UN rebel aid 8-22, 661G2
UN desert conf 8-29—9-9, 770C1
Waldheim sees southn Africa deadlock 9-19, 713F1
New Sahel famine seen 9-19, 770G1-A2
Brezhnev backs colonial borders 9-28, 830D1
USSR '76 arms sales rptd 10-13, 949B2
Refugees pour into Portugal 11-6, 886G3
Amnesty Intl chrgs rights violatns 12-8, 956D2
French-UK summit re southn Africa 12-12—12-13, 1013G1
S Africa oil ban asked in UN 12-14, 1016A2

Rhodesian Relations *See RHODESIA*

U.S. Relations—*See also specific countries*
Pan-Africa festival 1-15—2-12, 106B1
Ford budgets Sahel aid 1-17, 31G1
Carter on Cuba role 3-5, 171B2
Carter backs majority rule 3-17, 186D1★
Rhodesian chrome imports banned 3-18, 191D1, F1
Carter seeks more VOA funds 3-22, 230A1
Carter, Sadat talks 4-4—4-5, 245C1
Young vs 'cold-war' policy 4-11, 271C3
US ambs confer 5-9—5-12, 398A3

1978

AFL-CIO—*See AMERICAN Federation of Labor and Congress of Industrial Organizations*

AFRICA—*See also country, organization names*
Sub-Sahara drought danger rptd 1-3, 24G1
Japan '77 aid sets record 1-3, 28F2
France seeks Afro-Eur 'solidarity pact' 1-11—1-15, 71B1
Colonial boundary commitmt cited 43B3
Sahel relief rptd sought 2-1, 3-8, 237F1
Virus to control cattle disease rptd 2-23, 334F1
6 W African natns meet, back ECOWAS 3-18; USSR scores 3-20, 237D1
Venez pres scores Cuba role 3-28, 233D1
Arab poor-state aid rise rptd 4-9, 257C2
Forsyth '72 plot chrgd 4-16, 335A3
French-African summit backs mil aid, opposes defns force 5-22—5-23; troop totals rptd 5-24, 382F2
USSR influence blamed on US 5-24, 488C1
China scores USSR, Cuba 5-29, 422A1; 6-7, 441D2
NATO summit debates USSR role 5-30—5-31, 397D1, 398A1
Saudi fears communist role 5-31, 441A2
Westn natns meet on pan-Africa force 6-5, 441E2
Locusts plague E Africa, aid sought 6-6—6-14, 465C2
Tanzania scores pan-Africa force; defends Cuba, USSR presence 6-8, 441G1
Pan-Africa force support rptd split 6-8, 442D1
Hungary backs Cuba, USSR; scores West 6-10, 534F2
China backs Spain policy 6-18, 576E2
Yugo scores US, USSR 6-20, 519F2
Forgn troops issue debated at OAU summit 7-18—7-22, 561A1-D2
Nonaligned score Cuba role 7-25—7-30, 583A2-A3
'64 papal visit cited 8-6, 601B2
Malaria rise rptd 8-6, 636A1
Somalia scores Cuba mil role 8-14—8-26, 676C2
China scores Sovt hegemony 8-16, 674E3
China, Yugo back African borders, vs forgn interventn 8-21—8-22, 8-25—8-27, 675E2, G2
Cuba troops block US-Cuba ties 8-31, 687D1
Southn Africa on UN Assemb agenda 9-19, 713G2
Comoros rptd shunned re Belgian mercenary 9-27, 798C3
USSR called racist by US amb 10-14, 821D1
WCC rebel aid protested 10-25—11-8, 906D3, 907B1
Uganda-Tanzania conflict seen violating OAU border stand 11-6, 860B2
Smallpox eradicatn countdown continues 11-7, 927F1, A2
Cuba troops hurt US-Cuba ties 11-13, 880F3
Pressure re Uganda exit from Tanzania cited 11-14, 870B2
USSR-US arms sales talks stalled 12-5—12-15, 996C3, F3

1979

AFL-CIO—*See AMERICAN Federation of Labor and Congress of Industrial Organizations*

AFL-CIO v. Kahn
Case refused by Sup Ct 7-2, 498C2

AFRA, Saad
Egypt-Israel pact in effect 4-25, 295A3

AFRICA—*See also DEVELOPING Nations; also country, organization names*
Westn-natn Guadeloupe summit discusses aid 1-5—1-6, 12G2
WCC retains grants program 1-10, 23F3
New hominid species claimed 1-18, 137F3
Amnesty Intl rpts '78 rights abuses 2-1, 85G2
UN rights comm condemns white-minority govts 2-21, 148F1
Refugee total estimated 2-22, 201E1
Baptism rites agrmt reached 3-31, 375F2
UK Tories set policy 4-11, 285B3
Illegal abortns rptd common 4-29, 547D3
France debt relief vow rptd 5-4, 371C3
Pan-African News Agency planned 5-9, 342C1
French-African summit backs Eur ties 5-21–5-22, 398B3
E Ger mil aid rptd, role detailed 5-23, 406E2
SALT II summit topic 6-15–6-18, 449D1; communique text 458A2
OAU summit; conflicts erupt, post-independnc econ dvpt rptd 7-17–7-21, 552D1, G2
Turkey sets trade hike 8-21, 637E2
Nonaligned natns debate Egypt, southn Africa rebels 8-28–9-1, 675B1, C1
IISS rpts largest armies 9-4, 825B3
'78 smoking rise rptd 11-22, 970F2
Amnesty Intl reviews '79 rights 12-9, 980A2, D2

Cuban Relations—*See CUBA–African Relations; also African country names*

Soviet Relations—*See USSR–African Relations; also African country names*

U.S. Relations—*See also specific countries*
Guadeloupe summit discusses aid 1-5–1-6, 12G2
SALT linkage to Cuba role sought by GOP 2-3, 86B1
US response to Sovt surrogates urged 2-8, 89B2
UN rights comm res vs white-minority govts opposed 2-21, 148G1
AID rpts refugee total 2-22, 201E1
Gov Brown on tour 4-7, 271E3
UK Tory policy cites 4-11, 285D3
US defends 'new diplomacy' 5-1, 347D2
US sen scores Sovt policy 6-12, 459F2
SALT II summit topic 6-15–6-18, 449D1; communique text 458A2
Carter addresses Cong on SALT II 6-18, 449E3, 459A3
Kissinger backs SALT linkage 7-31, 590B3
Young in 7-natn trade missn, urges Israel ties; trade data, deals rptd 9-5–9-21, 720F2-721C2
NAACP seeks closer ties 9-9, 677A2
US cigaret exports cited 11-22, 970G2

1980

AFL-CIO—*See AMERICAN Federation of Labor*

AFRICA—*See also country, organization names; also related headings (e.g., DEVELOPING Nations)*
Ex-EAC ldrs meet 1-2, 90E1
Rift Valley Fever epidemic rptd 3-2, 318F2-D3
French min's office attacked 3-18, 232A1
9 southn natns seek econ unity vs S Africa 4-1, 243C1
Pope in 6-natn tour 5-2—5-10, 363B1-364A1
French-Vatican talks 5-31, 476D3
Malaria outbreak rptd 5-31, 478B1
Black African summit in Zambia backs UN Namibia plan 6-2, 462C3
Venice summit notes refugees 6-22, 473D1
Food forecast gloomy 7-23, 573B2
World Bank '80 econ forecast grim 8-17, 628G2
PLO status in World Bank, IMF disputed 9-4—9-22, 719D3
France expels US journalist 10-3, 790B2
OPEC members vow oil exports 11-9, 864D2
UNESCO illiteracy study rptd 12-4, 953E1
Sovt '79 arms sales rptd 12-10, 933C2

U.S. Relations
Carter State of Union address 1-23, 42C3
A-blast mystery unsolved in US rpt 1-23, 49A3
Ali to promote Carter Olympic stand 1-31, 68G1
US issues rights rpt 2-5, 87E2
UN rejctn of Israel bid on Kenya complex protested 6-19, 476B2
US GOP platform adopted 7-15, 537A1
Reagan pres nominatn acceptance speech 7-17, 534G3
Moynihan warns of 'Sovt empire' 8-11, 612D3
'81 refugee quota rptd 9-19, 883B3
US journalist ousted from France 10-3, 790B2
'80 grain imports rptd 11-4, 855A2

1976

Kissinger sees 4 ldrs 9-20—9-23, 717G2
Carter backs southn Africa role 9-27, 724B2
Gromyko scores US southern role 9-28, Kissinger rebuts 9-30, 719B1
Scranton for Butz resignatn 10-3, 744C2
Ford, Carter debate 10-6, 741A1, C1, D2
US warns USSR re southn Africa talks 10-29, 832B1
2 share Rockefeller award 11-16, 911F3
US stresses majority rule 12-16, 936B3; 12-22, 955B1
AFRICAN-American Nationalist Committee
Scores CORE Angola policy 2-14, 163B3
AFRICAN Development Bank (Algeria, Benin, Botswana, Burundi, Cameroon, Central African Empire, Chad, Congo Republic, Egypt, Ethiopia, Gabon, Gambia, Ghana, Guinea, Ivory Coast, Kenya, Lesotho, Liberia, Libya, Malawi, Mali, Mauritania, Mauritius, Morocco, Niger, Nigeria, Rwanda, Senegal, Sierra Leone, Somalia, Sudan, Swaziland, Tanzania, Togo, Tunisia, Uganda, Upper Volta, Zaire, Zambia)
US Cong OKs fund authorzn 5-20, 392C3
AFRO-American Patrolmen's League
Wins Chicago job bias suit 1-5, 6C2
AFRO-Asian People's Solidarity Organization
Meets in Angola 2-2, 82F2
AGATHANGELOU, Ioannis
Arrested 12-16, 1004D2
AGCAOILI, Fidel
Arrested 638A3

AGED Persons
Anchorage anti-bias law passage rptd 1-3, 7D1
Neb hotel blast 1-10, 80F1
US health rpt issued 1-12, 32D1
'77 budget proposal 1-21, 62B3, 65F1
House votes library aid 2-17, 170E3
HEW frees food funds 4-2, 249G1
Sen OKs food-stamp reform 4-8, 283A1
Jobs program funded 4-15, 282C2
Butler wins Pulitzer 5-3, 352D3
Ford signs '77 food funds 7-12, 533C3
Eucharistic Cong meets 8-1—8-8, 596D2
Ford signs housing aid 8-3, 566F3
Soc svcs 'means tests' end 9-7, 689D1
Cong clears tax credits 9-16, 705D3
Flu immunizatn prgrms suspended 10-12—10-17, 795F1
Medicare—*See under MEDICINE*
Nursing Home Issues—*See 'Hospitals & Nursing Homes' under MEDICINE*
Pensions & Retirement—*See under 'P'*
Presidential Campaign Issue
Ford wins Fla primary 3-9, 179E2
Humphrey scores anti-DC talk 3-24, 233E1
Carter stresses commitmt 6-14, 433C1
Dem platform text 6-15, 469C2, 470B1, 471C3, 472G3, 473E2, F3, 474C2
GOP platform topic 6-21, 451E1
Carter acceptance speech 7-15, 510G2
GOP platform text 8-18, 604B3, 606B2
Mondale scores Ford 9-16, 687C2
Mondale, Dole debate 10-15, 782F2, 783C1
Social Security—*See SOCIAL Security under U.S. GOVERNMENT*

1977

Young tours 5-10—5-24, sees Mondale 5-15, 398A2, G2-400C1
Carter outlines policy 5-22, 397D1
Carter backs Young statemts 5-23, 444B1; 5-26, 6-6, 417E3
US links Cuba ties, troop exit 6-2; GOP ldrs score Cuba thaw 6-3, 6-5, 455D3, F3
Young warns vs 'race war' 6-3, 6-6, sees Carter 6-7, 443C3
Young to shift focus 6-10, 460E2
Vance vs US-USSR arms race 7-1, 535D3
Carter seeks arms sale curbs 7-28, 574B3
Southn Africa, Sahel aid authorizatns signed 8-4, 668D1, G1
US poll for Cuba exit 8-8, 654A2
Church sees Castro 8-10, 653G3
Carter cites US role 10-27, 813B3
US scores USSR, Cuba re Horn conflict 11-14, 875E1
US warns Cuba on mil buildup 11-17, 896C1
AFRICAN, The (book)
Haley accused of plagiarism 4-22, reissue set 4-25, 356E1
Courlander sues Haley 5-24, 643E1
AFRICAN Festival of Arts & Culture, World Black &—*See BLACK & African Festival, etc.*
AFRO-Americans—*See BLACK Americans*
AGA Khan
Daily Natn editor quits 5-3, 393F1

AGE and Aged Persons
CBO issues poverty rpt 1-13, 80E3
Exxon job bias judgemt reversed 1-30, 279A1
Flu shots resumed 2-8, 103G2
Hartford Fire job bias suit rptd 2-9, 279B1
Cong sets new '77 budget levels 3-3, 174E1
White House conf planned 4-18, 322B2
Rptr wins Pulitzer for series 4-18, 355F2
Job funds cleared by Cong 5-5, 365F2; Carter signs 5-13, 380D3
Intercity bus fare hiked 5-15, 423C2
Stimulus tax credit cleared 5-16, 381G3
AMC sued on job bias 5-20, 422A2
Carter welfare plan outlined 5-25, 445F2
Atlantic City low-income housing drive set 5-27, 424C1
Carter proposes welfare chngs 8-6, 608E3, 609A1
Amtrak redcap svc end blocked 9-12, 778A3
Energy tax credits OKd by Sen 10-31, 832A3
Test pilot bias case refused 11-28, 919D2
Bias chrg filing time extended 11-29, 919A2
Career guidance aid, anti-bias projects clears Cong 11-29, 959B2; signed 12-13, 1001G2
Govt job list drops age refs 12-17, 979G2
Medicare—*See under MEDICINE*
Pensions & Retirement—*See PENSIONS*
Social Security—*See U.S. GOVERNMENT—SOCIAL Security*

1978

Horn of Africa—*See DJIBOUTI, ETHIOPIA, SOMALI Republic*
Rhodesian Relations—*See RHODESIA*
U.S. Relations—*See also specific countries*
US mil edge over USSR seen 1-6, 5D3
Carter scores Sovt role 1-12, 12F1
Carter State of Union Message 1-19, 31G2
Carter urges USSR cooperatn 1-25, 43D3
Carter warns USSR, Tass scores 3-17, 202E1, G2
CIA spying on black radicals rptd 3-17, 243G2
Carter scores Cuba role 3-28, 4-1; visits Nigeria, Liberia 3-31—4-3, 233A1, D1, F2-234E1
Carter scores USSR interventn 5-5, 342E1
Carter orders aid curbs reviewed, scores Cong 5-16—5-23; Byrd, Young rebut, study authorized 5-20—5-22, 383A1
'77 arms bid rejctns rptd 5-19, 386G3
US-China concern re Sovts noted 5-22, 384A3
'77 mil, econ aid totals rptd 5-24, 421F1
IISS blames US re USSR Africa influence 5-24, 488C1
Carter scores Sovt, Cuba role; vs more Cong curbs 5-25; Cuba denies chrgs 5-30, 418C1, F1
US, USSR dispute Sovt aims; SALT seen affected 5-27—6-4, 422E1-C2
Brzezinski scores USSR 5-28, 399D1
Carter scores Sovt, Cuban role 5-30; Callaghan comments 5-31, 397E1, G1
Brezhnev scores US criticism 5-31, 423A2
US vs pan-Africa force 6-5, 441F2
Carter details US goals, scores USSR 6-7, 424B1
Tanzania scores US role 6-8, 442A1
House com asks Brzezinski 'hardline' clarified 6-8; Vance outlines policy, denies SALT 'linkage' 6-19, 490A3, C3
USSR scores policy 6-17, 464G3
Vance policy statemt 6-20, 487C1-B3
Yugo scores policies 6-20, 519F2
Carter addresses OAS, shuns Cuba Africa role 6-21, 489A3
Carter lauds Young 7-20, 549E2
OAU warns vs easing Rhodesia sanctns 7-22, 561C1
US sees Cuban troops blocking ties 8-31, 687D1
Carter signs southn Africa aid 9-26, 734G1
Cuba-US ties seen hurt by troops 11-13, 880F3
Vance sees contd problems 11-25, 925E1
USSR-US arms sales talks stalled 12-5—12-15, 996C3, F3
AFRICAN, The (book)
Alexander plagiarism suit vs Haley dismissed 9-21, 759B3
Courlander suit settled 12-14, 1029E3
AFRICAN Games—*See under SPORTS*
AFRO-Americans—*See BLACK Americans*
AFRO-Asian People's Solidarity Conference
Sebai slain in Cyprus, hostages seized 2-18, 117D1
AFSCME—*See STATE, County & Municipal Employes, American Federation of*
AFSHAR, Amir Khosrow
Named Iran forgn min 8-27, 668B1
AGARWAL, Bela
'Test-tube' daughter born 10-3, 824D3
AGARWAL, Durga
2d 'test-tube baby' 10-3, 824D3
AGARWAL, Pravat
'Test-tube' daughter born 10-3, 824D3

AGE & Aged Persons
Bias in govt programs rptd 1-10, 14C1
Carter State of Union Message 1-19, 30E2
Carter budgets SSI program 1-23, 47B1
Jury trials in job bias suits backed 2-22, 126F2
Carter seeks job-bias unit reorgn 2-23, 124A1
PR SSI benefits exclusn upheld 2-27, 143A1
New CPIs described 222D2
Cath laity pastoral role rptd 4-7, 294G3
AMC to end bus productn, fed rules cited 5-31, 665B2
Fire victim data rptd 10-8, 972C1
Carter cites US commitmt 11-27, 914C3
Kennedy vs Admin on budget 12-9, 956G1
Medicare—*See under MEDICINE*
Nursing Home Issues—*See MEDICINE—Hospitals & Nursing Homes*
Pensions & Retirement—*See PENSIONS*
Social Security—*See U.S. GOVERNMENT—SOCIAL Security*

1979

AFRIFA, Gen. Akwasi A.
Executed 6-26, 485E2
AFRO-Americans—*See BLACK Americans*
AFTERTONES of Infinity (musical composition)
Schwantner wins Pulitzer 4-16, 336G2
AGACHE-Willot
Korvettes-Shure Brothers patent case refused by Sup Ct 11-5, 884D3
AGAH, Ali
Pledges Javitses safety 5-23, 408G2
Pahlevi family oil revenue skimming rptd 11-26, 897F3
AGAPOVA, Ludmila
Sup Sovt candidacy set 2-2, 100E1
AGATHA (film)
Released 2-8, 174C2

AGE & Aged Persons
Carter aide warns Dems on 'new realities' 1-4, 3F2
Sears sues US on bias laws 1-24, 92D1
'77 health cost share rptd 2-24, 163E3
Hosp cost-control hearings open 3-9, 194E3
Ultraviolet impact rptd 3-20, 290G1
Pa, Mo boarding home fires kill 34 4-1, 4-2, 316F2
SSI COL hike rptd 4-26, 310G1
Beneficial Corp credit bias chrgd 5-8, 596F1
Kennedy offers natl health plan 5-14, 362D1
Sears suit vs US dismissed 5-15, 365B3
Flu vaccine progrm rptd underutilized 5-18, 471C1
State bias filings required by Sup Ct, time limit barred 5-21, 400C2
Carter seeks SSI food stamp plan chng 5-23, 384D1
Carter unveils natl health plan 6-12, 438D2
Mammal cloning advance rptd 7-28, 692F2
Mail fraud crackdown set 9-19, 921C3
Amtrak funding bill signed 9-29, 867G3
Oldest US citizen dies 10-5, 860E3
Oil industry protested 10-17, 831C2
Kennedy visits Chicago group 11-8, 962C1
Heating aid bill clears Cong 11-9, 883B2; Carter signs 11-27, 920C1
Ohio boarding home fire kills 14 11-11, 954D2

1980

AFRICAN Methodist Episcopal Church—*See under METHODISTS*
AFRO-Americans—*See BLACK Americans*
AFTER The Love Has Gone (recording)
Wins 2 Grammys 2-27, 296D3
AFXENTIOU, Afxentis
Cabt shuffled 9-9, 749F2
AGACHE-Willot
NY Mafia boss indicted for Korvettes conspiracy 6-30, 503B1
Korvettes financial dvpts, closings 8-22—10-9, 985C3
AGAINST The Wind (recording)
On best-seller list 4-2, 280F3; 4-30, 360A1; 6-4, 448F3; 7-9, 568F3
AGAR, Herbert
Dies 11-24, 928F1

AGE & Aged Persons
'79 church attendance rptd 1-4, 8A1
State of State messages 1-8, 1-10, 403D3, G3; 1-9, 1-10, 4-8, 483C1, D2, 484E2; 1-15, 269B2
Fed heating aid given despite lodging 1-9, 54D2
Carter budget proposals 1-28, 72F2, B3
108-yr-old war vet dies 3-10, 279E3
Fla property tax cut voted 3-11, 184G1
Senility, aluminum link rptd 4-19, 415G3
US median age at 30 yrs 6-21, 519E1
Midwest, South hit by heat wave, death toll rptd 6-23—8-15, 616D1
US, Canada data compared 7-16, 562A3
NJ hotel fire kills 23 7-26, 621B3
Enzyme-lifespan link rptd 8-21, 716E1
Midwest, South heat wave death toll final rpt 9-7, 857G1
107-yr-old immigrant votes 11-4, 890G2*
Medicare—*See under MEDICINE*
Nursing Home Issues—*See MEDICINE--Hospitals*
Pensions & Retirement—*See PENSIONS*
Presidential Election (& Transition)
Kennedy 'basic speech' excerpts 3-10, 183C1, B2
GOP plank scores Carter 7-10, 506A3
Reagan accepts nominatn 7-17, 531C2
Carter attacks GOP stands 7-17, 532E1
Dem conv keynote speech 8-11, 612A2*, A3
Kennedy Dem conv speech 8-12, 610B2, 613F3, 614A2
Dem platform planks adopted 8-13, 614D2, F2, F3
Carter accepts renominatn 8-14, 612G3, 613F1, B2

1976

AGEE, Philip B.
Spain rpts alleged CIA agents 1-14, 77C1 *
UK orders expulsn 11-17, 946B2
AGENCE France-Presse (news agency)
Developing natns OK press pool 7-13, 619A3
AGENT in Place (book)
On best-seller list 12-5, 972E2
AGHA Khan, Prince Sadruddin
Rpts Leb casualty toll 2-21, 145E2
Vs Iran return of Sovt defector 11-1, 854D2
AGNELLI, Giovanni
Libya buys into Fiat 12-1, sees Qaddafi in USSR 12-9, denies Sovt benefits 12-10, 964G3-965E1
AGNEW, Spiro T(heodore)
White linked to Pallotine investmts 6-18, 951B1
Cited in Ford biog sketch 614E1
AGOSTI, Brig. Orlando
In mil junta 3-24, 211E2
Junta takes final exec powers 3-25, 236C1

AGRICULTURE—*See also FOOD and other commodity names; also RURAL Affairs; also country, organization names*
Farms, populatn data 1-2, 1-12, 216C2
Ford addresses Farm Bur, plans estate-tax law chng 1-5, 3F1-B3
Environmental costs rptd 1-18, 45D1
Ford State of Union message 1-19, 37D3, G3, 39G1
Dec, '75 farm income rptd 1-19, 91E2
'77 budget proposals 1-21, 63F1, B3, 66G1-D2
West Coast drought ends 2-5, 271C3
Jan farm income rptd 2-17, 168F3
Feb farm income rptd down 3-17, 216A1
Fiscal '77 budget estimate tables 231B1, 358C2
Mar farm income rptd 4-15, 279D2
OPEC aids UN fund 5-11, 389F1
Ford urges regulatory reform 5-13, 346G3
French-UK talks end 6-24, 481E3
May export rise rptd 6-28, 494D3
Chile loans OKd 8-13, 10-22, 871D1
Sen OKs embargo ban 8-27, 746E2
Cong clears tax bill 9-16, 706B1
Cong sets '77 budget levels, table 9-16, 706B2
Sup Ct bars review of Calif labor organizing rule 10-4, 766E1
Farm populatn drop rptd 10-5, 10-18, 833F1
US delays Israel deal 10-16, 810G3
Vogel gets Science Medal 10-18, 858F3
Jobless benefits revisn signed 10-20, 788D1
US '75-76 Sovt imports up 10-27, 856F2
3d ¼ equipmt industry profits up 10-28, 866G2
Calif rejects organizing propositn 11-2, 825B1, E3
Deere & Co strike ends 11-9, 847D3
Strikes, Sept indl output linked 11-15, 866D3
Venez, UK pact signed 11-23, 929D3
Jan-Sept exports to USSR rptd 11-30, 947C3
US-Sovt soil expert exchng canceled 12-20, 1011E1
EC Developments—*See EUROPEAN Community*
Farm Price Issues—*See 'Price Issues' under FOOD*
Migrant Workers
EC pact with Tunisia, Morocco rptd 1-13; Algeria 1-21, 84A3, B3
Calif labor dispute continues 1-22—2-11, 153G1
Chavez speaks at Dem conv 7-14, 506E1
Chavez endorses Carter 9-25, 724D1
Sup Ct bars review of Calif organizing rule 10-4, 766E1
Dole scores Calif propositn 10-30, 827G2
Calif propositn rejected 11-2, 825B1, E3
Pesticides—*See under 'P'*
Presidential Campaign Developments
Ford seeks Ill farm vote 3-5—3-6, 179G3
Ford: US to stay on top 3-26, 231D3
Dem platform text 6-15, 469C2, 470B2-D2, 475B2-A3, 476F3
Chavez speaks at Dem convention 7-14, 506E1
Carter acceptance speech 7-15, 510F2
Mondale record cited 512G2, D3
Mondale scores GOP farm policy 7-31, 565C1
GOP platform text 8-18, 602G3
Ford acceptance speech 8-19, 612C2, E2-A3
Dole legis record cited 614C2
Dole cites farm ties 8-22, 631C2

1977

AGEE, Philip
UK confirms ouster 2-16, 134A2
US bars prosecutn 3-18, 212A2
Names CIA agents in Australia 5-17, 5-19, 410F1
Leaves UK under '76 deportatn order 6-3, 526C3
Rpts CIA agents in Greece 6-11, 618B1
Expelled from France, arrives Belgium 8-18; chrgs US pressure 8-19, 654D2
Asked to leave Holland 12-2, 986E1
AGENCE France-Presse (news agency)
Interviews King Khalid 1-24, 50A2
Czech police attack Debeusscher 3-3, 220D3
Ethiopia ousts rptr 4-25, 327C3
AGENCY for International Development (AID)—*See under U.S. GOVERNMENT—STATE*
AGGARWAL, Shivkumar
Arrested 8-23, 655F2
AGGREY, O. Rudolph
Replaced as amb to Senegal, Gambia 6-23, 626D2
AGHA Khan, Prince Sadruddin
Rpts Viet refugee flow up 3-25, 243E3
AGING, National Council on the
Mrs Carter addresses 4-18, 322B2
AGIP SpA—*See under ENTE Nazionale Idrocarburi*
AGNEW, Spiro T(heodore)
Jones sentenced 4-4, 312C3
Nixon-Frost interview 5-25, 419C3, G3
Prosecutn team member joins FBI probe 12-13, 979C3
AGOSTI, Lt. Gen. Orlando
Sees Vance 11-21, 912F2

AGRICULTURE—*See also FOOD and other commodity names; country, organization names*
US-Canada study vs ND irrigatn project 1-7, 60C3
Ford '78 budget proposals 1-17, 31F1, 32F2, A3
Midwest farm ponds rptd frozen 1-19, 54E2
Deere rpts forgn paymts 2-1, 94G1
Farm equipmt makers' '76 4th ¼ profits rptd 2-8, 301E1
Farm cooperatives OK merger 2-11, 408E3
UN rpts '76 raw material prices up 2-14, 146B1
'76 special interest campaign gifts rptd 2-15, 128A2, D2, F2
ND irrigatn project stalled 2-18, 133A1
Carter keeps Ford budget 2-22, 125B2
AFL-CIO seeks labor law chngs 2-22, 153B2
Pesticide use analyzed 2-22, 183E3
'71-75 St Louis productivity rptd 2-23, 184C1
Carter call-in topic 3-5, 171D1
Calif drought losses estimated 3-7, 244E2
US Sen backs water projcts 3-10, 174C2
UFW-Teamsters sign pact 3-10, 177D3
Farmland fund plan withdrawn 3-11, 195A1
UN Water Conf held 3-14—3-25, 250F1
Carter asks drought aid 3-23, 210B2
Bergland outlines Carter plan 3-23, 214C1
Giaimo proposes '78 budget 3-23, 228F3, 229A1
Tex High Plains drought rptd 3-24, 244F3
US drought aid signed 4-7, 273E1
Calif losses scaled down 4-9, Bergland rpts 4-18, 376D3
Carter outlines anti-inflatn plan 4-15, 299B1
Record Mar, 1st ¼ futures trading rptd 4-18, 301B2
Carter presents energy plan 4-20, 293B1
House OKs embargo amendmt 4-20, 323E3
House OKs strip-mining curbs 4-29, 365C3
'76 per-capita income rptd 5-10, 387B3
Sen panel eases Cuba embargo 5-10—5-11, 389D3
McGovern scores Carter 5-13, 381D2
Urban business confidence rptd 5-16, 385C1
Cong sets '78 budget target 5-17, 405A1
Carter energy plan scored 5-18, 443E2
Carter vs Sen farm bill 5-26, 417C1; O'Neill cautns vs veto 6-1, 459A3
'77 US exports drop seen 5-26, 445F1
Export control bill clears Cong 6-12, 460D1
Drought-related losses rptd 6-23—8-24, 659E3
June exports rptd down 7-27, 585D1
'78 funds bill signed 8-12, 688G2
Calif crop damage rptd 8-17, 747F2
Westn land holdings breakup sought 8-18, 8-22, 703G1, F2
Tenneco buys Phila Life 8-25, 650G3
Farm bill signed; target prices, dispute detailed 9-29, 736D2
Carter sees farm editors 10-2, 761E2
Carter visits Iowa 10-21, 817B1
'77 disaster aid ceiling lifted by Cong 10-25, 833B3; signed 11-8, 1001E2
Garst dies 11-5, 952D2
Ore vs irrigatn projct 11-8, 879B2
NZ prime min in US talks 11-9—11-10, 925F3

1978

AGEE, Philip
Dutch residency extensn rejctd, W Ger bar cited 1-25, 90E3
Chrgs CIA re Cuba ship blast 8-1, 831C1
AGENCY for International Development (AID)—*See under U.S. GOVERNMENT—STATE*
AGENT Orange—*See HERBICIDES*
AGENT Orange Victims International
Founder dies 12-14, 984E1
AGE-Scarpelle
Viva Italia released 7-9, 970D3
AGHA Khan, Prince Sadruddin
Quits UN refugee post 12-31-77, 62B1
AGLIETTA, Maria Adelaide
Red Brigades threaten 3-10, 191G1
AGNEW, Spiro T(heodore)
Justice Dept releases case papers 3-3, 164E3
AGOSTINHO, Joaquim
3d in Tour de France 7-23, 692C2
AGOSTO, Joseph V.
Deportatn trial backed by Sup Ct 6-6, 447F3
AGOSTO v. Immigration and Naturalization Service
Agosto deportatn trial backed by Sup Ct 6-6, 447F2
AGRICULTURAL and Industrial Chemicals, Inc.
Learsy elected Trib chrmn 1-17, 75D3

AGRICULTURE—*See also FOOD and other commodity names; also organization names*
Mondale tours Westn states 1-9—1-13, 34D1
Farmers rally in DC 1-18—1-21; meet Bergland 1-20, protest Sen testimony 1-24; see Carter 2-14, 163B2
Carter State of Union Message 1-19, 30F3
Carter budget proposals 1-23, 44F2, 48D1; table 45E2
Carter vs 100% parity price supports 1-30, 62C3
'53, '78 cong membership compared 1-30, 107F2
GOP attacks Carter budget 1-31, 63B1, C1
'77 environmental decline rptd 85C2
Grain acreage set-aside participatn rptd small 2-8, Bergland pelted on tour, tours 2-21, 163D2, E2
Ohio blizzard losses rptd 2-11, 105D3
Drought aid extensn signed 2-27, 218A2
New CPIs described 222C2
Parity explained 163A2
Calif A-plant voted down, water needs cited 3-8, 184D1
Carter backs emergency farm bill 3-13, 177A3
Farmers in DC protest 3-15, occupy USDA 3-16, 219F1
100% parity goal in Humphrey-Hawkins bill 3-16, 182B3
Prelim farm bill clears Sen; set-aside paymts, target prices set 3-21; reactn 3-21, 3-22, 218F2-219A1
Admin farm aid plan revised, '78 food inflatn forecast revisn linked 3-28, 219E2
Carter farm aid plan revised, Mondale warns cong bill veto 3-29, 219C1-D2
Farm bill controversy continues 4-6—4-10; Carter vows veto 4-6, 261B2
Carter reaffirms farm bill veto vow, cites export rise need 4-11, 259G3, 260G1
Carter denies Bergland rift 4-11, 260G3
Farm bill defeated in House 4-12, 261C1
1st ¼ '77, '78 equipmt mfrs profits rptd down 4-27, 403D2
Admin farm policy scored by Colo sen 5-2, 342B2
Farm bill compromise clears Cong 5-4, 343C1-A2
Cong '79 budget target cleared 5-17, 385E1
Carter plans budget cuts 5-25, 404A3
Calif property-tax cut voted 6-6, 425B2
Carter proposes natl water policy 6-6, 426C3
Price supports, inflatn linked 6-19, 427D2
US House OKs agri funds 6-22, 467D2-A3
'74 black, white-owned farm data 7-20, 811G2
'77-78 2d ¼ profit drop for farm-equipmt makers rptd 7-28, 642C3
Carter addresses farm assn in Mo 8-14, 626C1
July exports rptd down 8-29, 680D1
Farm groups pressed on gas compromise 9-1, 678A2
Truck joint rate expansn case declined by Sup Ct 10-10, 789C3
Land purchase registratn signed 10-14, 897B2
Tax-cut bill clears 10-15, 786E1
3d ¼ farm equipmt mfrs profits rptd down 10-30, 919G2
Calif voters OK vet farm loans 11-7, 915D2
EC Developments—*See EUROPEAN Community*

1979

Library outreach urged 11-15—11-19, 901G1
Medicare—*See under MEDICINE*
Nursing Home Issues—*See MEDICINE—Hospitals*
Pensions & Retirement—*See PENSIONS*
Social Security—*See under U.S. GOVERNMENT*
AGEE, Philip
CIA alleged agents abroad listed, '78 Cuba mtg cited 1-4, 17C3
US revokes passport 12-22, 991D2
Barred Iran tribunal role 12-23; CIA files-hostage exchng plan rejectd 12-27, 991E2
AGENCY for International Development—*See under U.S. GOVERNMENT-STATE*
AGENT Orange
Viet defoliant suit filed 2-1, 90B1
US Viet troop exposure rptd 11-24, Mass vets sue 5 mfrs 11-26, 904B2-A3
AGENT Orange Victims International
Mass vets sue 5 cos 11-26, 904G2
AGER, Milton
Dies 5-6, 432D2
AGE-Scarpelli
Teresa the Thief released 5-5, 528F3
AGHA, Ali
US orders emb staff cut 12-12, 933C1
AGOSTINHO, Joaquim
3d in Tour de France 7-22, 655F2

AGRICULTURE—*See also FOOD and other commodity names; also organization names*
Carter budget proposals 1-22, 45G3-46D1; table 42F2
Carter State of Union Message 1-23, 46F1, 47B1
Farm land rptd lost to dvpt 1-25, 90D2
Farmers protest in DC 2-5—2-6, 109C2
Equipmt mfrs '78 4th 1/4 profits rptd down 2-7, 201B3
Carter proposes Educ Dept 2-8, 110A3
Carter on farmers' DC protest 2-27, 149A3
Farm protesters' DC permit expires 2-28, 149D3
Equipmt mfrs 1st 1/4 profits rptd up 4-27, 385E1
Carter vows energy supplies 5-4, 346C3
Carter asks irrigatn cost-sharing 5-16, 365G2
Diesel fuel shortage seen 5-18, 361G2-D3; allocatn rules adopted 5-25, 395C2
EPA coal-use rules scored 5-25, 404A1
'78 state gas use rptd 5-27, 395E2, A3
NC PCB dumping chrgd 6-4—6-13, disposal disputed 6-5, 597C3
Ariz labor law restored by Sup Ct 6-5, 464A3
Truckers strike 6-7—6-15, 462G3; impact assessed 6-18—6-28; Carter ends diesel fuel allocatn rule, farmers score 6-22, 479A3, D3, 480A1
Solar heat tax credit proposed 6-20, 498E1
Farm gas allocatn limit set 7-16, 557A3
Energy conservatn measure clears House 8-1, 595F2
Diesel fuel allocatn vowed by Carter 8-22, 622A3
Coll test score rise rptd 10-4, 810D2
'80 Agri Dept funds clear Cong 10-26, 10-31, Carter signs 11-9, 920A1
Equipmt mfrs 3d 1/4 profits rptd up 10-31, 923C1
Milwaukee Rd embargoes westn track 11-1—11-5, 867A3
UFW field talk case refused by Sup Ct 11-5, 884C3
Kennedy scores Carter 11-12, 11-29, 962D1, E1
'79 farm acreage, other data rptd 12-31, 985D1
EC Developments—*See EUROPEAN Community*
Farm Income—*See INCOMES*
Farm Prices—*See FOOD—Price Issues*
Foreign Developments (including U.S. international news)
US loan to Poland set 1-6, 39B3
El Salvador, Bolivia migratn pact rptd 2-12, 235A2
US, Mex sign land dvpt pact 2-16, 124D3
USSR '78 US imports rptd 3-6, 172E1
Grenada US aid overtures rptd 3-24, 236D3
GATT pact signed, tariff cuts seen 4-12, 273A2, E2
India-Bangladesh irrigatn comm set 4-18, 328D2
Turkey sets new exchng rate 6-12, 447B1
Lome pact extension set 6-27, 512G3
FAO hunger conf held 7-13—7-20, 554B1
Bulgaria decentralizatn rptd 7-16, 741C3
Pope lauds rural life 10-4, 759B1, D1-A2
Lome pact extensn signed 10-31, 845F1
US bars Sovt ammonia import curbs 12-11, 939E2

1980

Carter scores Reagan on Soc Sec plan 9-3, 699B1
Reagan vows strong Soc Sec system 9-7, 699A3
Carter backs expanded Soc Sec, natl health insurnc 10-10, 778B3, C3, 779A2
Reagan vows to preserve Soc Sec 10-10, 780B1
Carter ridicules Reagan 'secret plan' 10-22, 802E3
Mondale hits Reagan record 10-26, 816G3
Carter chrgs Reagan 'flipflop' 10-27, 816B3
Social Security—*See under U.S. GOVERNMENT*
AGEE, Philip
US asks suit 2-5, ct OKs 4-1, 268E2
CIA alleged agents abroad listed 3-7, 189F2
Book profits seizure denied by Dist Ct 10-2, 990G2
Passport revocatn case accepted by Sup Ct 10-6, 782C3
AGEE, William M.
Cunningham resigns 10-9, 958E3
AGENCE France-Presse (news agency)
Iraq expels newsman 10-2, 775A1
3d World coverage study rptd 11-29, 914D1
AGENT Orange
Carter vetoes dioxins study 1-2, 17G2
Australian birth defects rptd 1-3, 6A1; study ordrd 1-8, 37E2
Ark dump suit filed 3-4, 190E3
New Australian rpt ordered 3-26, 252F2
AGES of Man (recording)
Wins Grammy 2-27, 296G3
AGINS v. City of Tiburon
Case decided by Sup Ct 6-10, 512F1
AGNEW, Spiro Theodore
Links resignatn to assassinatn fears 4-20, Dean discounts 4-23, 333C3, E3
Garrison sentenced 6-10, 460C1
Md papers placed on sale 7-10, 639B2
AGRICULTURE—*See also commodity names*
Small business defined 455D3
State of State messages 1-2, 1-14, 1-15, 269B1, B2, D2; 1-9, 1-15, 403A3, 404F1; 483G2, 484G1
Carter budget proposals 1-28, 73A2; table 70F1
Equipmt mfrs '79 4th 1/4 profits rptd up 2-7, 222G1
Allis-Chalmers pact set 3-15, 308A3
Children's work limited by Appeals Ct 3-20, 227C1
Water law compliance rptd 4-10, 308E1
Iowa farm cancer study rptd 4-15, 357A3
FRB farm loans increased 4-17, 286A2
Pollutn control benefits seen 4-21, 308B1
Mt St Helens erupts, impact rptd 5-22, 382E2; damage assessed 5-24—7-4, 503E3, G3
Standby gas rationing plan submitted by Carter 6-12, 552A1
Imperial Valley water rights upheld by Sup Ct 6-16, 511E2
Midwest, South hit by drought, damage rptd 6-23—8-15, 616C1-C2
Lindane use curbs sought 7-3, 519C3
Crop land loss forecast 7-23, 573B2
Carter orders grain price support increase 7-28, 575E1
Midwest, South drought damage final rpt 9-7, 857C2
Agri Act clears Cong 11-17, signed 12-3, 981G1
Farm appropriatns clears Cong 12-4, 954E3; signed 12-15 982B1
Farm Prices—*See FOOD—Price Issues*
Foreign Developments (including U.S. international news)
Australia '79 stock gains cited 1-18, 56D1
OECD warns on future 1-23, 49C3
French-Cuba accord rptd 4-1, 253A3
Yugo-EC trade pact signed 4-2, 365B3
China '79 econ rpt issued 5-1, 521D1
Canada drought damages crops 6-27, 520C2
USSR-US 1st 1/2 trade drop rptd 8-20, 711D2
Poland seeks US credits 8-27, 659B2
China '79, '80 output data 9-1, 678D1
Canada rejects Massey-Ferguson aid plea 9-4, 728D2
World Bank '80 loans rptd 9-22, 720C1
France to seek new mkts 10-1, 749F3
USSR shortfalls rptd, '81 targets set 10-21—10-23, 797B1, F2, 798F1
Islamic econ conf 11-4—11-6, 865C1
Polish '81 investmt rise seen 11-19, 878F2, G2
USSR sets 11th 5-yr plan 12-1, 945F2
Australia defers bank rate hikes 12-2, 964C1
Massey-Ferguson equity plan announced 12-13; '80 debt rptd 12-17, 992D1-B2
Polish farmers to form union 12-14, 976G1
U.S. Presidential Election (& Transition)
Crane scores Admin 1-5, 4E3
Kennedy on econ control exemptns 2-6, 91A1
Reagan dogged by parity issue 4-9, 288F2-A3
Reagan vs 'cheap food' policy 4-17, 4-18, 327E3-328A1
Reagan on farmer's plight 5-29, 424A1
Kennedy stresses issue 6-25, 480D1
Dem platform planks adopted 8-13, 614D2, 615A2
Carter accepts renominatn 8-14, 613B2
Bush visits Ill hog farm 9-9, 780E3

1976

Carter in Ia 8-24, 8-25; Dole scores grain policy 8-26, 631G2, G3-632E1, E2
Mondale visits Mo farm 9-8, 665A3
Carter at Minn Farm Fest 9-15, 686B3
Dole in farm belt 9-17—9-28, 724B3
Ford addresses credit bank execs 9-20, 703F3
Chavez endorses Carter 9-25, 724D1
Butz resigns, reassures farmers 10-4, 744D2, G2
Ford, Carter debate 10-6, 741E3
Dole, Mondale debate 10-15, 782C3, 783A3
Ford attacks Carter 10-15, 784G1
Dole campaigns 10-16—10-27, 804C1
Calif organizing referendum rejected 11-2, 825B1, E3

AGUADO, Nazario
Freed 5-25, 422F2

AGUILAR, Sgt. Henry
Charges dropped 8-18, 942B2

AGUSTSSON, Einar
In UK talks, signs cod pact 5-31—6-1, 389B3

AHALT, J. Dawson
On grain-support rates 10-12, 787E3

AHDAB, Brig. Gen. Abdel Aziz al-
Proclaims self mil gov; asks Karami, Franjieh quit 3-11, 3-12, asks Franjieh replaced 3-14, 209G1, F2
OKs amnesty 3-11, 209B2
Gets ultrarightist backing 3-12, 209C2
Forms cmnd council 3-21, 210B2
Resigns post 5-21, 369B2

AHLMARK, Per
Named to Swedish Cabt 10-8, 794B2

AHLQUIST, Dr. Raymond P.
Wins Lasker award 11-17, 910E3

AHMAD, Sabah al-
Seeks Syria, Egypt talk renewal 5-23, 370C2

AHMED, Abdul Aziz Haj
Deported 3-27, 227C2

AHMED, Eqbal
Discloses letter on Letelier 9-23, 710E3

AHMED, Fakhruddin Ali
Oppositn to boycott Parlt 1-4, 29A1
Opens Parlt session 1-5, 28E3
Signs rights curbs order 1-8, 28C3

AICHI, Kiichi
Newsman's '74 acquittal reversed 7-20, 539F1

AID, Foreign—*See FOREIGN Aid*

AIKENS, Joan D.
Renamed to FEC 5-17; confrmd 5-18, sworn 5-21, 391D3

AILES, Stephen
Named to intelligence bd 2-17, 127E1

AIR America
Sen com rpts CIA ownership 4-26, 299D2

AIR Bags—*See AUTOMOBILES—Safety Issues*

AIRBORNE Warning & Control Systems (AWACS)—*See 'Aircraft' under ARMAMENTS*

AIR Canada
Seeks fare hike 8-10, 587E2
Pilots ask bilingualism 8-12, 637B2
Court OKs bilingual pilots 9-7, 692C2
Language appeal rejected 9-22, 730D2
OKs spoken French 9-29, 790G1

1977

Clean-water bill revised 11-10, 900G2
Jobs bill support cited 11-14, 877B1
Farmers protest in Plains, seek 100% parity 11-25, 916D1; nationwide strike begins 12-14; Carter vs parity demand 12-24, 1002E3
US-Sovt talks 12-12—12-14, pact extended 12-13, 1017G2
Carter hikes export loans 12-20, 997B3
Carter cites campaign vow 12-28, 1002A1
Massey Ferguson admits overbilling 12-29, 1010G2
Polish credits OKd by Carter 12-30, 1001A2
EC Developments—*See EUROPEAN Community*
Farm Income—*See INCOMES*
Farm Price Issues—*See 'Prices' under FOOD*
Migrant Workers
Fla frost to cost jobs 1-24, 55C1
Mex stresses US exports 2-15, 136E3
AFL-CIO seeks labor law chngs 2-22, 153B2
UFW, Teamsters sign pact 3-10, 177E3
Helsinki review conf adjourns 12-22, 997D2
Pesticides—*See under 'P'*
Price Issues—*See under FOOD*

AGRICULTURE, Department of—*See under U.S. GOVERNMENT*

AGRICULTURE Movement, American
Strike threatened over parity prices 11-25, 11-27, 916F1

AGUDELO Villa, Hernando
Affirms '78 primary plan 8-17, 727E2

AGUERO Echeverria, Carlos
Rptd killed 4-9, 476C1

AGUILAR, Andres
Defends OAS rights com 6-17, 494C2

AGUIRRE Salinas, Osmin
Slain 7-12, 580B3

AHA—*See HOSPITAL Association, American*

AHEARNE, John
Vs A-plant licensing halt 10-3, 794D3
On spent A-fuel storage fee 10-18, 794B2

AHMAD, Datuk Ali
Killed in jet crash 12-4, 992D2

AHMED, Aziz
On French A-plant deal 1-3, 12B3
Signs Treaty of Izmir 3-12, 190C2
Pak forgn min 3-30, 258D3
Scores BBC role 4-28, 349A2

AHMED, Fakhruddin Ali
Dies 2-11, funeral 2-13, 116A1

AHMED, Ghafoor
Released 6-2, 450A3

AHMED, Nazir (d. 1972)
Bhutto tied to death 9-5, 707D2

AHMED, Viqar
Suspension rptd 545C1

AHSRAF, Mohammed
Released 6-3, 450A3

AHTISAARI, Martti
Rptd named UN Namibia comr 109D3

AHUMADA, Adolfo
On govt econ pkg 1-5, 46E2

AID—*See U.S. GOVERNMENT—STATE—Agency for International Development*

AID, Foreign—*See FOREIGN Aid*

AID to Families With Dependent Children—*See U.S. GOVERNMENT—HEALTH, Education & Welfare*

AIM—*See AMERICAN Indian Movement*

AIR Bags—*See AUTOMOBILES—Safety Issues*

AIRBORNE Warning & Control System (AWACS)—*See ARMAMENTS—Aircraft*

AIR Canada
Cuts services 1-12, 43C2
Pilots fined re '76 strike 2-16, 133E1
Domestic fares raised 2-24, 200E1
'76 loss rptd 4-20, 372F3
Domestic charters rptd OKd 12-7, 966A1

1978

Farm Income—*See INCOMES*
Farm Prices—*See FOOD—Prices*
Foreign Developments (including U.S. international news)—*For foreign domestic news, see country names*
Carter vs Mex migrant worker progrm renewal 1-30, 62D3
US farmers block Mex imports, 200 arrested 3-1, 3-3, 163F1-B2
USSR, Turkey sign trade pact 4-5, 477D1
US scientists visit China 7-6—7-10, 564C2-C3
US-Japan trade talks fail 9-5—9-7, '77 data cited 695B1
Viet, Thai cooperatn agreed 9-6—9-10, 696G1
Bergland ends China visit, sees grain, cotton sales rise 11-14, 901G3-902A1
US, forgn unions set Chile trade boycott 11-24; 1st effects felt 12-15, 1014G1
US-Japan pact signed 12-5, 988F2
US to continue Taiwan pacts 12-15, 12-17, 973C2, 975B1, G1, C2
Migrant Workers
Carter vs Mex program renewal 1-30, 62D3
UFW ends boycotts 1-31, 83F1
Rural health program planned 10-2, 770F1
Pesticides—*See PESTICIDES*

AGRICULTURE, Department of—*See under U.S. GOVERNMENT*

AGRICULTURE Movement, American
Hidalgo farmers block Mex imports 3-1, 3-3, 163G1-B2
DC protest 3-15, USDA occupied 3-16, Carter OKs farm aid plan 3-29, 219E1
House defeats farm bill 4-12, 261B2

AGUILAR, Andres
Scores Paraguay rights abuse 6-30, 505D3

AGUIRRE, Jesus
Marries Duchess of Alba 3-16, 420E2

AGULLA, Horacio
Murdered 8-28, 792F3

AGUSTSSON, Einar
On Iceland electns 6-25, 497C2

AHA—*See HOSPITAL Association, American*

AHERN, Maj. Gen. Timothy
On NATO U-2 use 8-22, 748B3

AHL (American Hockey League)—*See HOCKEY, Ice*

AHLMARK, Per
Quits Swedish govt 1-31, 93C1

AHMAD, Abdullah
Seized in Iraq consulate raid 8-2, 582D3

AHMED, Mohammed (Comoro Islands co-head; resigns Oct. 3)
To lead new Comoro govt 5-23, 445B3
Quits 10-3, 885C2

AHN, Philip
Dies 2-28, 196B2

AHOUA, Timouthee
Page Airways paymt chrgd 4-13, 449C2

AHRENS, Moshe
Warns Syrians in Leb 7-7, 521G2
Says US bars Israel aid to Leb Christns in Beirut 8-7, 638D2
Warns Syria on Leb 8-28, 674F1
Calls Camp David summit pacts risk 9-18, 712F3

AHRNE, Marianne
Near & Far Away released 3-24, 619B3

AHTISAARI, Martti
Arrives Namibia 8-6, 633D3
Leaves Namibia, no progress seen 8-23, 669E2
Waldheim Namibia rpt issued 8-30, 741G3
S Africa talks to reopen 10-19, 819E3, F3

AHUMADA, Adolfo
Panama govt, justice min 10-12, 884A2

AIAW—*See INTERCOLLEGIATE Athletics for Women, Association for*

AID—*See U.S. GOVERNMENT—STATE—Agency for International Development*

AID, Foreign—*See FOREIGN Aid*

AID to Families With Dependent Children (AFDC)—*See U.S. GOVERNMENT—HEALTH, Education & Welfare*

AIM—*See AMERICAN Indian Movement*

AIN'T Misbehavin' (play)
Opens 5-9, 760A1 *
Wins Tonys 6-4, 579G2, A3

AIO—*See ARAB Industries Organization*

AIR Anglia
UK-Scandinavia pact OKd 12-22, 1017B2

AIRBORNE Warning & Control System (AWACS)—*See ARMAMENTS—Aircraft*

AIRBUS—*See AVIATION—Foreign Developments*

AIRBUS Industrie
Eastern buys airbuses 4-6, 264B3
UAL orders Boeing jets 7-14, 570A1
Brit Airways 757 order scored 8-31, 684A2
UK role OKd by France 10-24, 10-25, 902A3

AIR Canada
Toronto runway crash kills 3 6-26, 636D3
Pilots contract setlmt reached 8-24, svc suspended in IAM dispute 8-25—9-5, 686B2

AIRCO Inc.
BOC purchase OKd, Martin Marietta withdraws 4-7, 403C3

AIR Conditioners—*See ELECTRIC & Electronics Industry*

AIRCRAFT—*See ARMAMENTS—Aircraft; AVIATION*

1979

'79 US farm exports rptd 12-31, 985C1
Migrant Workers—*See MIGRANT Workers*
Obituaries
Warren, Gertrude 9-6, 756F3

AGRICULTURE, Department of—*See under U.S. GOVERNMENT*

AGRICULTURE Movement, American
DC protest 2-5-2-6, 109D2

AGUIRRE, Alfredo Cesar
Managua svcs restored 7-27, 574D1

AHA—*See HOSPITAL Association, American*

AHART, Gregory J.
Scores FDA drug approval process 6-19, 572C2

AHEARNE, John
Backs Met Ed license 10-26, 826B2
On A-plant safety dispute 11-5, 849F1
Named temporary NRC chrmn 12-7, 940G1

AHERN Jr., Thomas L.
False Belgian passport chrgd 12-6, 914G2-A3

AHMED, Ali Salem
Slain 12-15, 980F1

AHTISAARI, Martti
Reopens Namibia talks 1-13, 171B2

AHUMADA, Cardinal Ernesto Corripio
Installed cardinal 6-30, 640B2

AIAW—*See INTERCOLLEGIATE Athletics for Women, Association for*

AID—*See U.S. GOVERNMENT-STATE-Agency for International Development*

AID, Foreign—*See FOREIGN Aid*

AID to Families With Dependent Children—*See U.S. GOVERNMENT-HEALTH, Education & Welfare*

AIELLO, Danny
Knockout opens 5-6, 712A1

AIKENS, Joan D.
Carter primary spending OKd 4-2, 265D1*
Succeeded as FEC chrmn 5-17, 401D3

AIKENS, Willie Mays
Traded to Royals 12-6, 1002F2

AIN'T Misbehavin' (play)
'78-79 Broadway success rptd 11-4, 956E2

AIN'T Misbehavin' Soundtrack (recording)
Wins Grammy 2-16, 336G3

AIRBORNE Warning & Control System (AWACS)—*See ARMAMENTS-Aircraft*

AIRBUS—*See AVIATION-Foreign Developments*

AIRBUS Industrie
Iran Air cancels Airbus deal 2-25, 144E3
New models rptd backed by Barre 6-18, 485C2

AIR Canada
Bilingual svcs scored 2-20, 168D3
US protests bargain fares 4-18-4-20, 329E2
DC-9 mid-air blowout, Boston emergency landing 9-17, 830D2

AIRCRAFT—*See ARMAMENTS-Aircraft; AVIATION*

1980

Reagan outlines policy 9-30, 738A3
Carter optimistic 10-12, 779D1
Reagan in Idaho, SD; pledges price supports 10-14, 780B1
Kennedy scores Reagan record 10-22, 817D1

AGRICULTURE, Department of—*See under U.S. GOVERNMENT*

AGRICULTURE Movement, American
Urges grain loan paymts 1-6, 10C1

AGROBULK Shipping Corp.
Jamaica sues US grain shippers 2-4, 99B3

AGUILAR Mawdsley, Andres
On UN comm to probe shah 2-17, 122B1
Sees Colombia DR Emb hostages 4-22, 311E3

AGUIRRE, Mark
Named top coll basketball player 3-21, 240E3

AHEARNE, John
Carnesale named NRC chrmn 7-9, 551B3

AHERN Jr., Thomas L.
Hostages' letters publshd 1-18—1-20, 47B3
Fellow hostage calls spy 4-9, 282C3

AHMANSON & Co., H. F.
Home Savings & Loan Association
Prime mortgage rate cut to 12.75% 5-7, 384F3
Fidelity Financial acquired 7-1, 557C2
Mortgage rate raised to 12.25% 7-23, 575B1
Mortgage rate raised to 13.5% 7-31—8-19, 631A1
Mortgage rate raised to 14% 9-25, 867C2
Mortgage rate hiked to 16% 12-15, 984A1*

AHUMADO, Cardinal Ernesto Corripto
Violence mars Romero funeral 3-30, 253C3

AID, Foreign—*See FOREIGN Aid*

AIELLO, Stephen R.
Named Carter aide 1-3, 5G3

AIKENS, Willie Mays
In World Series; sets homer mark 10-14—10-21, 811F2, 812G1

AIR Canada
Cuts fares 6-14, 461E3

AIRCRAFT—*See under ARMAMENTS; AVIATION*

1976

AIR Express International Corp.
Boycott rpts released 10-18—10-20, 786A1, C1, A2
AIR Force (magazine)
Rpts Latin defns budgets, mil forces 1-2, 60E3
Corsica separatists blow up jet 9-7, 693A2
AIR France
Kennedy flights barred 3-11, 378A3
Concorde runs to US begun 5-24, 378C2-C3
Jet hijacked 6-27, 462C3; **for subsequent developments, see 'Entebbe' under MIDDLE EAST—AVIATION Incidents**
Sets nonstop flights to Israel 7-2, 486B2
Rpts '76 deficit 11-18, 905B3
AIR India
Resumes Pak flights 7-21, 538G1 *
AIR Line Employes Association (ALEA) (AFL-CIO)
Natl Airlines pact 2-19, 153A3
AIR Line Pilots Association, International (AFL-CIO)
'74 TWA crash rpt scored 1-21, 80C1
St Thomas safety warnings cited 4-29, 335A3 *
Canada strike slows US flights 6-24, 481E2
AIRLINE Pilots Committee of 76
Seeks cockpit smoking ban 4-20, 308A2
AIRLINES—*See AVIATION*
AIR Manila
Guam crash kills 46 6-4, 736A2
AIR Music (musical composition)
Wins Pulitzer 5-3, 352D3
AIRPLANES—*See ACCIDENTS—Aviation; ARMAMENTS; AVIATION; ENVIRONMENT—Noise Abatement*
AIR Pollution—*See under ENVIRONMENT*
AIRPORTS—*See AVIATION*
AIR and Space Museum (Washington, D.C.)
Ford addresses opening 7-1, 488F3
AIR Transport Association, International (IATA)
N Atlantic, Concorde fares hiked 4-30, 378E3
Qantas admits price cutting 9-23, 749D3
OKs Australia fare rise 12-21, 997B3
AJMAN—*See UNITED Arab Emirates*
AKAKA, Daniel
Elected 11-2, 825C1, 829E2
AKENDENGUE, Herve
Named Labor min 10-19, 1003A2
AKOBO, M. T.
Nigeria econ min 3-15, 222B3
AKRON, O.—*See OHIO*
AKSENOV, Vladimir
Soyuz 22 launched 9-15, 684C1
AKUFFO, Brig. Frederick Kwasi
Acting chief of staff 11-14, 1003E2
AL—*Arabic names bearing this prefix are indexed by surname (e.g., ATIKI, Abdel Rahman al-)*
ALA Arab, Issam
Demands blockade lift 1-4, 1D1
ALABAMA
Primary date set 22B2
Wallace affirms record as gov 1-9, 22F2
Black RR workers win suit 1-9, 25D3
Prison reforms ordered 1-13, 25G2
'63 Birmingham bomb probe reopened 2-18, 159D3
EPA urges toxic chem law 2-26, 171C3
'75 A-plant fire rpt 2-28, 171G3
3 '57 murder suspects freed 4-14, 316D2
Primary results 5-4, 322E2, 323C2
Carter wins 2 runoff delegates 5-25, 373E3
Dem conv women delegates, table 508A2
Dem conv pres vote, table 7-14, 507A2
GOP pre-conv delegate count 8-14, 583A3
GOP conv pres, vp vote tables 8-18—8-19, 8-19, 599A1, A3
Carter with Wallace in Birmingham 9-13, 686C2
Fiscal '75 per capita income, tax burden rptd 9-15, 10-12, 959E1, C2
Ford campaigns 9-26, 723B3
Fiscal '76 bankruptcies rptd 10-20, 984C3
'Scottsboro Boy' pardoned 10-25, 859G3—860B1
Electn results 11-2; pres 818A1, 819B2; cong 821E3, 828F2
Sup Ct to review job physique rules 11-29, 901C1
Flu shot paralysis rptd 12-17, 950E1
Wallace Presidential Campaign—*See WALLACE, George C.*

1977

AIRCRAFT Carriers—*See ARMAMENTS-Ships*
AIR Egypt
Leb bomb blast 11-18, 890G2
AIR Force, Department of the—*See under U.S. GOVERNMENT*
AIR Force Academy, U.S.—*See under U.S. GOVERNMENT—AIR Force*
AIR France
Unions vs wage restraint 1-26—2-1, 159G2
Airbus use cited 4-28, 441F2
Amin Entebbe raid role rptd 6-8, 487A1
'76 losses rptd, govt blamed 6-27, 543G2
Soviets bar Airbus 9-1, 736F1
Concorde Developments—*See AVIATION—SST/Concorde*
AIR India
CAB acts on NY-London budget fare 9-9, 9-15, Carter overrules 9-26, 860E2
AIR Inter (French airline)
Jet hijacked, returned 9-30, 807C3
AIR Line Employes Association, International (AFL-CIO)
EEOC suit rptd 3-15, 279C2
AIR Line Pilots Association, International (AFL-CIO)
Canada unit OKs St Hubert bilingualism 2-15, 133F1
Canada unit fined re '76 strike 2-16, 133C1
EEOC suit rptd 3-15, 279C2
AIRLINE Pilots Associations, International Federation of (IFALPA)
Strike postponed 10-21, 868C3; called off 11-3, 852C3
AIRLINE Pilots Committee of '76
FAA rejects crew smoking ban 9-1, 778F3
AIRLINES—*See AVIATION*
AIRPLANES—*See ACCIDENTS—Aviation; ARMAMENTS; AVIATION*
AIR Pollution—*See under ENVIRONMENT*
AIRPORTS—*See AVIATION*
AIRPORT 77 (film)
Top-grossing film 4-6, 264E1; 4-27, 356E2
AIR Transport Association, International (IATA)
CAB actions 1-10—3-29, 324B3-325D1
3 airlines indicted 2-3, 93G2
US-UK air svc pact set 6-22, 500C2
AIR Vietnam
Jet hijacked to Singapore 10-29, 848C2
AITKEN, Max
Beaverbrook chain sold 6-30, 526F3
AJC—*See AMERICAN Jewish Congress*
AJMAN—*See UNITED Arab Emirates*
AKASHA, Zuhair Yousof (Capt. Mahmoud)
Hijacks W Ger jet 10-13, killed 10-18, 789A1, 790A1
Identified as Lufthansa hijacker 10-27, 868F2
AKE, Simon
Ivory Coast forgn min 7-30, 772B1
AKHUND, Iqbal A.
Lauds Sweden debt cancelatn 10-13, 904C1
AKL, Basil
Meets Scranton 6-24, US denies missn role 7-19, 550B2
AKSENOV, Vladimir
Soyuz 22 landing rptd 109G3
AL—*Arabic names bearing this prefix are indexed by surname (e.g. ASSAD, Hafez al-)*
ALABAMA
Legislature schedule rptd 6C2
Gas shortage forces textile layoffs 1-17, 37D2
Winter rptd worst in 100 yrs 1-22, 54D2
Birmingham rpts record low 2-6, 91D2
Tornadoes, floods hit 4-3—4-6, disaster areas declared 4-9, 311E2
Scottsboro figure denied compensatn 4-6, 396B3
'76 per-capita income table 5-10, 387E2
Shapp fund repaymt ordrd 5-12, 482C2
Ct aid bill signed 6-13, 464F3-465A1
UMW wildcat strikes 6-18—9-6, 690G2
Mitchell in Maxwell AF base jail 6-22, 483G2
TVA sued on air pollution 6-22, 521B3
Drought-related agri losses rptd 6-23, fed aid OKd 8-24, 659F3
Prison employe standards voided 6-27, 538E3
'Scottsboro' libel suit vs NBC dismissed 7-12, 643B1
Johnson named FBI dir 8-17, 626A2
Wallaces file for divorce 9-12, 9-15, 808C2
'76 per capita income, tax burden table 9-13, 10-18, 821D2
'58 Birmingham church bombing suspect surrenders 9-28, '63 bomber convicted 11-18, 907G2, D3
ERA econ boycott rptd 11-4, 918D1
TVA bias suit case review refused 12-5, 939D1
Scottsboro plant sale challenged 12-9, 1004F3

1978

AIRCRAFT Carriers—*See ARMAMENTS—Ships*
AIRCRAFT Owners and Pilots Association
Baker scores FAA air-safety proposals 12-27, 1007A1
AIRD, George (d. 1974)
Accused killers acquitted 5-24, 396C2
AIR Force, Department of the—*See under U.S. GOVERNMENT*
AIR Force Academy, U.S.—*See under U.S. GOVERNMENT—AIR Force*
AIR Force Association
Allen address rptd 9-23, 737G3
AIR India
747 crashes off Bombay 1-1, 23F3-24A1
AIRLIE Foundation (Warrenton, Va.)
Flood '71-73 influence-selling rptd 1-27, 3-9, exec dir denies 3-7, 240A2
AIRLINE Pilots Association, International (AFL-CIO)
Northwest struck 4-29—8-15, 680E3
Natl Fla bay crash pilots fired 6-16, 636E3
Mil pilot recruitmt denied 12-13, 984D2 *
AIRLINES—*See AVIATION; specific names*
AIR New Zealand
Natl Airways merged 4-1, 498D2
AIRPLANES—*See ACCIDENTS—Aviation; ARMAMENTS; AVIATION*
AIR Pollution—*See under ENVIRONMENT*
AIRPORTS—*See AVIATION*
AIR Rhodesia
ZAPU down civiln jet 9-3, 740E3
AIR Taxi Co.
US FRB nominee queried re Khatemi link 1-24—2-28; CIA, Defense info rptd 1-25, 2-17, 161G1-G2
AIR Transport Association, International (IATA)
Delta to end membership 11-11, 894C3
Structure revised 11-13, 894A3
AJAR, Emile
Madame Rosa released 3-19, 619A3
AJC—*See AMERICAN Jewish Congress*
AJMAN—*See NONALIGNED Nations Movement, UNITED Arab Emirates*
AJMANI, Jagdish
On Ananda Marga bombings 3-25, 225E2
AKAKA, Rep. Daniel K. (D, Hawaii)
Reelected 11-7, 850C3, 857C1
AKIHITO, Crown Prince (Japan)
Colombia terrorist plot rptd 2-18, 147D3
AKOVA, Enver
Named Turkey state min 1-5, 21D2
AKUFFO, Lt. Gen. Fred W. K. (Ghanaian head of state)
Named Ghana ldr 7-5, frees prisoners 7-6, 515C2
Ousts Acheampong aides 7-7, 596C2
Sets exile amnesty 7-10, 596C2
Sets state of emergency, bans strikes 11-7, 882B2
Frees plotters 11-16, 1021F3
AL—*Arabic names bearing this prefix are indexed by surname (e.g. ASSAD, Hafez al-)*
AL (American League)—*See BASEBALL*
ALABAMA
Legislature schedule rptd 14D3
Wallace divorce suit setld 1-4, 96A1
'67, '77 sales-tax rates rptd 1-5, 15D3
State govt tax revenue table 1-9, 84B2
Scottsboro lawyer dies 1-11, 96F2
Church-bond probes rptd 2-27, 295G3
Treasurer indicted 3-21, 379G3
Tornadoes hit 4-17—4-18, 5-1, 479G2, A3
Wallace quits US Sen race 5-16, 362G2
Death penalty law upheld 5-19, 388G3
Construction pact signed 5-22, 429D3
Treasurer convicted 5-24, 6-25, sentncd 6-8; ousted from office 6-9, 886F3
Sen Allen dies 6-1, widow named to seat 6-8, 432E1-G1
KKK informant for FBI rptd agent-provocateur 7-9, 7-11; Justice probes violence, cover-up 7-12, 527F3-528B2
Dallas Cnty ex-sheriff arrested on marijuana chrgs 7-14, 844G2; sentenced 12-1; chrgd with fraud in NY 10-27, 992G1-A2
Primary results, runoff set 9-5, 699E1
GM, UAW set plant accord 9-11, 699E3
KKK informant indicted for '65 Liuzzo slaying 9-20, 720D2
Primary runoff results 9-26, 769D1
Election results 11-7: cong 846E1, G1, 848C1, 849G2, 850A1; state 847C1, E1, 849F2, C3, 853D2, 915D2
Rabies epidemic declared 11-10, 992E2
Tuscaloosa govt power over Holt backed by US Sup Ct 11-28, 937A3

1979

AIRCRAFT Carriers—*See ARMAMENTS—Ships & Submarines*
AIR Force, Department of the—*See under U.S. GOVERNMENT*
AIR Force Academy, U.S.—*See under U.S. GOVERNMENT-AIR Force*
AIR France
Dallas-DC Concorde svc begins 1-12, 35A3
Entebbe hijack case declined by US Sup Ct 4-30, 364G3
US-France air svc pact rptd 5-12, 465B3
Concorde program ended, unsold jets allocated 9-21, 721F2
Workers strike 10-2, 11-8, 791D2, 872E3
Spain, France in air traffic talks 11-26—11-27, 952A2
AIR Holding Corp.—*See under SUMMA Corp.*
AIR-Launched Cruise Missile (ALCM)—*See ARMAMENTS-Missiles*
AIRLIE Foundation (Warrenton, Va.)
Head convicted 10-12, sentncd 10-24, 906D1
AIRLINE Executive (magazine)
'78 world's busiest airports listed 421D1
AIRLINE Passengers Association Inc.
DC-10s ordrd grounded by ct 6-5, 420A3
AIRLINES—*See AVIATION; specific lines*
AIR Lines Pilots Association
Controllers computer safety protest backed 11-20, 989A1
AIR New Zealand
Antarctica DC-10 crash kills 257 11-28, pilot error blamed 11-29, 912B1
AIR Panama
Cargo mgr indicted 5-14, 386E3
AIRPLANES—*See ACCIDENTS-Aviation; ARMAMENTS-Aircraft; AVIATION*
AIR Pollution—*See under ENVIRONMENT*
AIRPORTS—*See AVIATION*
AIR Rhodesia
Guerrillas down jet, 59 die 2-12, 136A3
Wankie flights ended 2-22, 170F2
AIR-To-Surface Ballistic Missile (ASBM)—*See ARMAMENTS-Missiles*
AIR Traffic Controllers Organization, Professional
Computer safety scored 11-20, 988F3-989A1
AIR Transport Association, International (IATA)
Jamaica conf opens, Pan Am ends membership 1-31, 112A1
Air fare hike set 4-3, 324D1
Members agree on fare hikes 7-30, 721F3
CAB grants limited trust immunity 9-10, 725G3-726A1
CAB ends probe 12-5, 989D1
AIR Transport Association of America
DC-10s grounded, travel chaos rptd 6-6, 420F3
AIR Transport Lodge v. Turner
Case declined by Sup Ct 6-4, 439G1
AIR West—*See SUMMA Corp.-Air Holdings*
AJMAN—*See UNITED Arab Emirates*
AKALAITIS, JoAnne
Southern Exposure opens 2-27, 292B3
AKHMADULINA, Bella
Metropole issued 1-18, 100C2
AKMANDOUR, Neset
Named Turkish defns min 1-14, 40F2
AKRON, O.—*See OHIO*
AKSYONOV, Vasily Pavlovich
Metropole issued 1-18, 100C2
Hints union resignatn 12-19, 980A3
AKUFFO, Gen. Fred W. K. (Ghanaian head of state; deposed June 4)
Ousted as Ghana head of state 6-4, 425F1
Acheampong executed 6-16, 468D3
Executed 6-26, 485E2
AL—*Arabic names bearing this prefix are indexed by surname (e.g., ASSAD, Hafez al-)*
ALABAMA
Med malpractice arbitratn rptd 1-28, 139E3
Single-sex alimony barred by US Sup Ct 3-5, 184C2
Pub schl cost share rptd 3-5, 282E3
Tenn R projct upheld 3-13, 188B3
NHL-WHA merger set 3-22, Birmingham team to fold 3-30, 355A3
Florence hit by tornado 4-11, 288B3
Selma, other floods 4-17, 288E3
Truckers strike shooting 6-12, 462F3; more violence 6-20, protests 6-28, 479C2, D2
Gulf of Mex oil, gas lease bids placed 7-31, accepted 8-28, 664E3
Army recruiting fraud probed 8-19, 649G2
Hurricane Frederic lashes Mobile 9-12; looting rptd, disaster aid OKd 9-14, 691C1
'78 per capita income rptd 9-16, 746F1, E2
Army guns rptd found 10-4, 852C1
Hurricane Frederic loss rptd 10-5, 954G2
US sues Sears re job bias 10-22, 885D3
Crime & Civil Disorders
Mitchell paroled from Maxwell AF Base prison 1-19, 176D1
Holman jail conditns scored by Amnesty Intl 2-1, 85F2
Prisons put in receivership, gov named agent 2-2, 112A3
KKK informant's extraditn OKd 2-7, 120C1
Evans death delay refused by Sup Ct 4-13, executn stayed 4-20, 400F1

1980

AIR Florida
Cuban refugees hijack jets to Havana 8-10, 8-13, 617A2
AIR Force, Department of the—*See under U.S. GOVERNMENT*
AIR Force Academy, U.S.—*See under U.S. GOVERNMENT--AIR Force*
AIR France
Braniff drops Dallas-DC Concorde svc 4-14, 346F3
Jet blown up in Guadeloupe 9-17, 769G1
AIR Line Pilots Association
O'Donnell abstains on Carter endorsemt 8-20, 647A3
AIRLINES—*See AVIATION*
AIRPLANE! (film)
Released 7-2, 675G1
Top-grossing film 8-6, 640C3
US summer boxoffice gross rptd 9-10, 732D2
AIRPLANES—*See ACCIDENTS--Aviation, ARMAMENTS--Aircraft, AVIATION*
AIR Pollution—*See ENVIRONMENT--Air & Water*
AIR Portugal
Pilots strike 6-23—7-14, 580F1
AIR Supply (singing group)
Lost In Love on best-seller list 4-30, 360A1; 6-4, 448F3
All Out of Love on best-seller list 9-10, 716E3; 10-8, 796B3
AJMAN—*See UAE*
AKA, Gen. Ghol
Sovts plan partial Afghan exit 6-22, 475G1-A2
AKAKA, Rep. Daniel (D, Hawaii)
Reelected 11-4, 842C3, 852C2
AKALAITIS, JoAnne
Dead End Kids opens 11-18, 1003A3
AKHMADULINA, Bella Akhatovna
Defends Sakharov 1-31, 86B1
AKRAM, Ahmed
Defects to US 9-6, 705C1
AKRON, Canton & Youngstown Railroad Co. et al v. ICC, et al
Case declined by Sup Ct 10-6, 782E2
AKSENOV, Vladimir
In space flight 6-5—6-9, 477B1
AKSYONOV, Vasily Pavlovich
Vs Sakharov exile 1-29, 86B1
Plans emigratn 4-17, 326B3
Leaves Moscow for US 7-22, 566E3
AL—*Arabic names bearing this prefix are indexed by surname (e.g., ASSAD, Hafez al-)*
ALABAMA
BN, Frisco RR merger OKd 4-17, 345F2
Anniston purposeful job bias case declined by Sup Ct 4-28, 369B2
Sears bias suit dropped 5-22, 485E1
Mobile ILA workers reject pact 9-18, 826F2
Gulf coast oil leasing bids set records 9-30, 785A2
Stevens, union come to terms 10-19, 805C1-D2
Atomic Energy & Safeguards
Brown's Ferry (Decatur) A-dump site planned 1-16, 54D1
Brown's Ferry A-plant FBI probe disclosed 3-7, 249F1-A2
Brown's Ferry shutdown fails 6-28; NRC orders GE reactors probed 7-7, 551G1-C3
Crime & Civil Disorders
Waterfront racketeers sentenced 1-11, 64B2
'58 Birmingham church bomber extradited 1-11, 55A3; sentncd 5-14, 405A1
'63 KKK Birmingham bombing prosecutn rpt blocked, FBI informant '65 murder probe cited 2-18, 227C2
FBI A-plant sabotage probe disclosed 3-7, 249F1-A2
Hines '78 rape convictn overturned 3-18, 215E2-A3
Radical group protests in Birmingham 3-20, 485A3
Black dist judge nominees accused 5-19; Clemon confrmd 6-26, Gray withdraws 9-17, 744F2
Nixon impeachmt lawyer sentenced 6-10, 460B1
Death penalty struck down by Sup Ct 6-20, 555C1
KKK assaulter convicted 10-2, 884F3
Death row inmates ordrd retried 10-15, 869A1
Anti-KKK suit filed 11-4, 884G3-885A1
Hines declared unfit for retrial 11-21, 927F1
FBI informant cleared re '65 murder 12-15, 990B1
Politics & Government—*See also other appropriate subheads in this section*
Legislature schedule rptd 18C1
2 blacks named dist judges 1-10; controversy ensues 5-19—9-17; Clemon confrmd 6-26, Gray withdraws 9-17, 744B2
Mobile at-large electns upheld by Sup Ct 4-22, 343B2
Mobile munic strike 7-14—7-24, 576D1
Primary results, runoff set 9-2, 682E2
Stewart loses primary runoff 9-23, 745F1
5th judicial circuit split 10-14, 918A3
Election results 11-4; cong 840B1, 842A1, 846A1, 849E1; state 845C2
'80 census rptd 12-31, 983D1
Presidential Election (& Transition)
Connally fund shortage rptd 2-20, 129D1
Carter, Reagan sweep primary 3-11, 182G3
Carter in Tuscumbia, Reagan notes Klan 'birthplace' 9-1, remark stirs furor, Reagan clarifies 9-2, 663E3, 664D2

1976

ALABAMA, University of (University)
'75 football rankings 1-2, 31B3
Wins Liberty Bowl 12-20, 1014G2
ALARCON Quesada, Ricardo
Chrgs China-CIA collusion in Angola 3-29, 228G2
ALASKA
Anchorage bias law passage rptd 1-3, 7D1
Sen votes natl park mining end 2-4, 135A2
Cong OKs wildlife refuges 2-4, 2-17, 152A3
Anchorage Daily wins Pulitzer 5-3, 352D3
Anchorage archbp named 5-4, 424D1
Sex chrg vs Gravel rptd 6-12, 434B1
9 indictd in Valdez 7-8, 816F2
Dem conv women delegates, table 508A2
Dem conv pres vote, table 7-14, 507A2
GOP pre-conv delegate count 8-14, 583A3
Reagan, Ford seek delegates at conv 8-16, 8-17, 601G2, A3, B3
GOP conv pres, vp vote tables 8-18—8-19, 8-19, 599A1, A3
GOP platform text 8-18, 605C3, 607A3
Ford park plan rptd 8-31, 644B3
Fscl '75 per capita income, tax burden rptd 9-15, 10-12, 959B1, G1, E2
Natl parks mining curbs signed 9-28, 834B2
Revenue sharing funds OKd 9-30, 764C3; Ford signs 10-13, 763A3
Ford, Carter debate 10-22, 801A3
Election results 11-2: pres 818A1, 819B1; cong 828G2; state 824E3
Capital shift to Willow OKd 11-2, 824E3
US-Canada hwy pact rptd 11-12, 945E3
Oil & Gas Developments
'77 budget proposal 1-21, 64E3
US-Canada pipeline treaty initialed 1-28, 116D3
US gas pipe proposal offered 2-26, 149G1
Cong orders North Slope exploratn 3-31, 246C3
Admin, House panel assess pipeline problems 5-21—9-10; Alyeska rpts repairs 7-15, 690F2-691B2
Pipeline cost estimate hiked 6-30, 691B2
Canada plans oil line 7-16, 587E3
Offshore lease bids accepted 8-26, 648F3
Transport study bill signed 10-22, 834D3
FEA vs surplus export 11-30, 991E3
Final pipeline sectn laid 12-5, 991F3 ★
FPC backs pipeline 12-7, 998A2

ALASSANE, Traore Moise
Upper Volta social min 2-9, 269E3
ALAWI, Youssef al-
Rpts S Yemen border clashes 1-9, 52B2
ALBANIA
Listed as 'not free' nation 1-19, 20D3
Shuns Balkan natns' mtg 1-26—2-5, 213E3
Ship captn death in '75 Yugo Adriatic clash rptd 2-6, 224D1
Boycotts Sovt CP Cong 2-24—3-5, 195B3
Name-chng decree rptd 2-26, 'Albanianism' held natl religion 3-17, 331G3
Aide in bombed Cambodian town 3-2—3-4, 238B2
Anti-China plot, purge revealed 4-30; US comment 5-4, 331C3
China-Albania metal combine opens 4-30, 331E3
Shuns E, W Eur CP conf 6-29—6-30, 461D2
China delegatn views Mao remains 9-13, 711E3
Myftire named dep prime min 10-13, 850B1
CP cong: Hoxha backs self-reliance, scores US, USSR 11-1—11-7, 849E3
Grain sufficiency rptd 11-1, 850A1
Hoxha on '73 purge 11-1, 850A1
Hoxha reelected 11-7, 850B1
Cabt shuffled 11-14, 949G1
Koleka named Presidium chrmn 12-30, 1012B2
Bars Westn, Sovt bloc pacts 12-30, 1012C2

1977

ALABAMA, University of (University)
'76 football rankings 1-2, 8E3
Antiviral drug rptd 8-10, 675G2
ALABAMA Power Co.—*See SOUTHERN Co.*
ALABAMA Power Co. v. Davis
Pension credit backed by Sup Ct 6-6, 478G2
ALAMEDA County, Calif.—*See CALIFORNIA*
ALAS, Rev. Jose Inocencio
Says tortured by rightists 7-21, 580C2
ALASKA
Legislature schedule rptd 6C2
Warm temp linked to wind shift 1-27, 77B1
Mondale trip stopover 69D1
'64 quake measure revised 2-14, 161C3
Pot law impact rptd 3-31, 332A3
Martin confrmd to US post 4-11, 272B3
Laetrile use cited 4-17, 375G3; 6-23, 508E1
'76 per-capita income table 5-10, 387G2, A3
Intl Inuit conf 6-13—6-17, 619D2
UK air svc pact set 6-22, 500A2
Forest fires rptd 7-8, 8-23, 660B2
'76 per capita income, tax burden table 9-13, 10-18, 821E1, F2-A3
Vast US parks plan proposed, ct challenge filed 9-14, 9-15, 739A3, C3
Anchorage landing rights for Concorde proposed 9-23, 738B2
Free abortions contd 10-12, 787A1
Sirica vs whaling ban 10-21; ruling reversed, Burger backs ban 10-24, 835A2
Air cargo deregulatn bill signed 11-9, 899B3
Natl Women's Conf OKs minority res 11-19—11-21, 917C3
Bowhead whale ban lifted 12-7, 936A3
Pot law detailed 12-11, 972D3
Oil & Gas Developments
Ford '78 budget proposal 1-17, 31D2
Canada pipeline pact signed 1-28, 82C2
'76-80 share of world supply estimated 1-28, 108B2
FPC judge backs pipeline 2-1, 82C2
Carter-Trudeau gas pipe talks 2-21—2-23, 132C3
Mex reserves compared 3-18, 240D3
New gasoline output process rptd 3-23, 278B2
Carter energy message 4-18, 294A3, C3
House OKs Japan oil export ban 4-20, 323E3
FPC splits on gas pipe route 5-2, 369C2
Canada asks US gas pipe delay 5-9, 372G1
Urban business confidence rptd 5-16, 385C1
Offshore oil sales delayed 5-17, 498F3
Oil pipeline rates disputed 6-1—6-7, 477G1
Oil export control bill clears Cong 6-12, 460D1
Intl Inuit conf 6-13—6-17, 619F2
Pipeline opens, cost estimated; map 6-20, 476A2, D2
Oil pipeline environmental damage rptd 6-20, 477B1
Subsidized ships OKd for oil transport 6-24, 498G1
ICC rejcts Alyeska rate bid 6-28, 497E3-498F1
Canada bd backs US gas pipe route 7-4, 525F1
Explosn closes oil pipeline, 1 killed 7-8; Alyeska comments 7-10; US orders probe 7-11, 537C3
US bars oil trade with Japan 7-10, 538B1
Pipeline resumptn OKd; 'human error' blamed re explosn 7-18, 558A3
Tractor hits pipeline 7-19, flow resumes 7-20, 558C3
Alyeska rpts on pipe blasts, damages 7-20; 3 arrested 7-26, 7-27, 627E3
US studies 2d Panama canal 7-21, 589E3
Canada issues gas pipe rpts 7-28, 8-2, 596E2-B3
Oil arrives Valdez 7-29, Cherry Pt (Wash) 8-5, 627F2
ICC price ceiling upheld 7-29, 628C1
Pipe constructn waste chrgd 8-7, 627G2
Canada Parlt OKs gas pipe 8-8, 616B2
Washington sues 10 oil cos 8-16, 691E3
Carter, Trudeau OK gas pipe 9-8, 687C1
Canada, US sign gas pipe pact 9-20, 725C3
Sup Ct OKs pipe interim rate rise 10-20, upholds order 11-14, 878D2
Alcan gas rte OKd by Cong 11-2, Carter signs 11-8, 856C3
Sup Ct accepts pipe rates case 11-28, 919E2
Tex oil pipe OKd by Interior Dept 12-2, 942D3
Carter to hike Prudhoe output 12-20, 997A3
ALASKAN Arctic Gas Pipeline Co.
FPC judge upholds pipeline 2-1, 82D2 ★
FPC splits on pipe route 5-2, 369D2
Canada rpt asks pipe delay 5-9, 372D2
Alcan pipeline route backed 7-4, 525F1
8 US cos back Alcan route 7-29, 596C3
ALASKA Slope Regional Corp.
ICC sets Alaska pipeline rates 6-28, 498D1
ALBANIA
UN Assemb member 3F3
CP scores China, rift seen 7-8, 540D3
Greek air link set 7-18, 595F1
China dispute continues, rift denied 7-26—8-2, 595C1
Tito scored, China dispute cited 9-2, 710C1
Anti-China govt purge rptd 9-9, 731A1
Not in UN Medit pollutn pact 10-21, 876B2

1978

ALABAMA, University of (University)
Wins Sugar Bowl 1-2, '77 rank rptd 1-3, 8G2, D3
2 in NFL draft 5-2, 336F3, G3
ALABAMA State University (Montgomery)
Hiring bias vs whites ruled 5-1, 348A3
ALAH, Zayed Hussein Ahmed
In Cyprus terror raid, hijacks jet 2-18; surrenders 2-19, 117D1
Trial starts 3-9, gets death sentnc 4-4, 236E3
Death sentnc commuted 11-14, 870G1
ALAMEDA County Jail (Santa Rita, Calif.)
Press data access curbed by Sup Ct 6-26, 566A3
ALARCON Monsanto, Carlos
Guatemala labor min 7-21, 722C3 ★
ALASKA
Legislature schedule rptd 14D3
No state sales taxes rptd 1-5, 15C3
Canada defends seal hunt 1-9, 35A3
State govt tax revenue table 1-9, 84B2
USSR satellite falls in Canada 1-24, 57F1
USSR admits satellite error 2-4, 103D1
USSR radar statn probe rptd 2-28, 298E1
Anchorage-London air fare agreed 3-17, 206D2
Anchorage '77 living costs rptd 4-26, 349E1
Plea bargaining rpt released 5-15, 396E1
Land bill OKd by US House 5-19, 386G1
Earthquake hits Aleutians 5-24, 480F1
'77 prison populatn rptd up 6-3, 440D1
Aleuts win mistreatmt claim 6-21, 569F1
US Sen ratifies UK tax pact 6-27, 588B3
US Sup Ct voting alignmt shift noted 7-3, 566C1
Fairbanks makes bad-air list 7-5, 513D1
Canada, US to study caribou 7-6, 531C3
Extended jobless aid rptd 7-10, 552A3; 8-4, 607D3
Bad-air list corrected 7-19, 644B2
Teamster fund scored 8-14, 625E1
Primary results 8-22, 682D3
Aleuts covered in US minority business contracts ruling 9-23, 811F2
Land bill dies 10-15, 785A1
Primary results final 10-20, 831D2
US, W Ger air svc pact expanded 10-25, 831F1
Election results 11-7: cong 846A2, 848C1, 850B1, 856B2; state 847D1, B3, 853D2, 856A2, 897D3, 915B2
US Sen campaign spending rptd 11-15, 898C1
RCA plans phone unit sale 11-30, 935B2
Carter transfers land to natl park system 12-1, 936F3
Anchorage jet crash kills Mrs Stevens, 4 others 12-4, 1032A1
Environmentalists laud Carter 12-20, 1009D1
Oil & Gas Developments
Canada gas purchase optn OKd 1-17, 53G2
Carter budgets exploratn 1-23, 47F2
Canada Parlt gets gas pipe legis 2-3, NEB sets specificatns 2-20, 130A1
US '77 output rptd up 2-14, 158E3
Pipeline sabotage spills oil 2-15, 108C3
Canada bars Kitimat oil depot 2-23, 130F1
Canada Parlt OKs gas pipe legis 4-4, US delay seen 8-16, 647F2
'77 crude oil output rise rptd 4-10, 282E1
Venez competitn rptd 4-16, 331G3
Jan-Mar import drop rptd 4-20, 282A2
Mar trade deficit narrowed 4-26, 344D2
US rpt forecasts domestic output 5-8, 366B2
'77 pipeline saboteur convicted 5-11, 380A2
Schlesinger vs Japan exports 5-26, 408F1
ICC pipe rates backed by Sup Ct 6-6, 447B2
New rules for Calif set 6-15, 470C3
Job preference law voided by US Sup Ct 6-22, 508F3
1st ½ oil imports rptd down 7-19, 590A1
June import drop, pipeline oil hike linked 7-26, 607C1
GAO vs oil exports to Japan 9-12, 702D1
Sen OKs natural gas bill 9-27, 733F1, E2
Calif voters OK Sohio lease 11-7, 857B1
ALASKA Coalition
Carter gets high rating 12-20, 1009F1
ALBA, Duchess of
Marries 3-16, 420E2
ALBANIA
Greek min visits; trade pact signed, ethnic areas toured 3-28—3-30, 374B2
Yugo dissident compares rights 6-6, 504B3
China ends aid 7-13, technicians exit set 7-16, 549A1
China gets letter detailing dispute 7-30, 635C1
China premr's visit to Rumania, Yugo scored; war plot chrgd 9-3, 674B3, 676B1
UN Assemb member 713B3

1979

KKK, blacks demonstrate in Decatur 5-26, 6-9; Decatur, Birmingham, Tuscaloosa, Montgomery KKK activity cited 7-22, 11-11, 865B1, G2, E3
Jewish inmate rights case refused by Sup Ct 6-4, 439F1
FBI sued over '65 civil rights death 7-5, 521E1
Birmingham police slaying protested 7-20, 869C3
200 KKK marchers arrested 8-12, 631A1
Legal counsel law case declined by Sup Ct 10-1, 768A2
Death row populatn rptd 11-25, 989F3
Politics & Government—*See also 'Crime' above*
Legislature schedule rptd 5C3
Regulatory bds rptd segregated 4-9, 307A2
Black pol conv in Birmingham 5-25—5-27, 423D1
Wallace upholds integratn 8-2, 650F1
Birmingham elects black mayor 10-30, 829B1
Kennedy campaigns 12-6, 962G1
ALABAMA, University of (University)
Wins Sugar Bowl 1-1, '78 rank rptd 1-2, 1-3, 8B2, E2
Female exertn tests rptd 3-8, 196D2
NIT results 3-21, 238E3, F3
Krauss, Lyons in NFL draft 5-3, 335F2
Faulty auto repairs study issued 5-7, 595B3
Wallace addresses Birmingham students 8-2, 650G1
ALADDIN Hotel Corp.
Owner convicted 3-13, Nev takes over casino 3-16 209B1
HCA to buy casino 6-12; licenses revoked 6-15, HCA drops bid 6-27, 520F1
Casino sale rejected 12-15, 965D1
Natl Kinney sets casino purchase 12-21, 992A2
ALASKA
Legislature schedule rptd 5C3
Med malpractice arbitratn rptd 1-28, 139E3
Fscl '78 tax revenue rptd 2-13, 152B2
Anchorage '77 air crash rpt issued 2-13, 412F1
Blumenthal stopover in Anchorage 2-23, 141D2
US House com OKs lands bill 3-1, 187E1
Pub schl cost share rptd 3-5, 282E3
US House OKs land bill 5-16, 366E3
State workers quit Soc Security 9-10, 726F3-727B1
Teachers' strikes rptd 9-12, 679B1
'78 per capita income rptd 9-16, 746C1, F1, G2
Anchorage '79 living costs ranked 12-28, 990F3
Oil & Gas Developments
Carter cuts exploratn budget 1-22, 45E3
Property tax expiratn cited 2-13, 152B2
US House com OKs lands bill 3-1, 187E1
Carter affirms Canada gas pipe plan 3-3, 168F1
Calif-Tex oil pipe canceled, oil swap seen 3-13, 183E1, A2
Trudeau offers oil pipe routes 4-10, 284E2
Sohio '78 sales gains, North Slope productn linked 5-7, 305A1
Forgn-flag tanker case refused by US Sup Ct 5-14, 383E1
US House OKs land bill 5-16, 366G3
Alcan pipe viability doubted 7-4, 522B2
US seeks gas pipe dvpt 7-8, 517F3
Calif LNG imports OKd 8-14, 9-27, 769C2
Sohio profits hike linked 9-6, 687A1
Beaufort Sea offshore lease sale held 12-11, 990D2
ALASKA Airlines Inc.
Alaska NW Properties divested 8-14; CAB blocks Wien Air stock ploy 8-28, judge backs 10-4, 830F1
Wien Air-HFC stock deal rptd, suit filed 11-20, 989A2
CAB rejcts Wien Air stock sale 12-20, 989F1
ALASKA Northwest Properties Inc.
Alaska Airlines spun off 8-14; CAB blocks Wien Air stock ploy 8-28, judge backs 10-4, 830F1
Wien Air-HFC stock deal rptd 11-20, 989A2
CAB rejcts Wien Air stock sale 12-20, 989F1
ALBANIA
US-China plot chrgd 1-27, 69C3
Iran leftists reject alignment 2-14, 125C1
China invasn of Viet scored 2-22, 122F2
Bible availability cited 3-13, 238F1
Quake kills 35 4-15, 316D3
UN membership listed 695D2
Iran takeover of US Emb backed 11-10, 878B3
Eur pollutn pact vetoed 11-13, 864B3
Taiwan trade bar affirmed 11-28, 952B3

1980

Tuscumbia KKK endorses Reagan 9-2, 664F1
Election results 11-4, 838A1, 839B2, D3
ALABAMA, University of (University)
Wins Sugar Bowl 1-1, '79 rank rptd 1-2, 22G3, 23C1
McNeal in NFL draft 4-29, 336G3
Woodard ties high jump record 6-7, 892A1
Mathews resigns 6-11, 638E2
ALABAMA A&M University (Normal)
3d in NCAA soccer 12-14, 1001C3
ALABAMA State University (Montgomery)
Loses NAIA basketball title 3-15, 240D3
ALABYEV, Anatoly
Wins Olympic medals 2-16, 2-19, 155D3
ALAM, John Shamsul
Bull Pen opens 6-12, 756C3
ALAMO (San Antonio, Tex.)
Radicals occupy 3-20, 485A2
ALASKA
Carter asks lands protectn 1-21, 43F3
US extends land protectn 2-12, 131F2-B3
Hunts bailout loan collateral listed 5-28, 425F3
Lands bill clears Sen 8-19, 631B2-A3; sent to Carter 11-12, 866E2-C3
Dutch ocean liner fire off Sitka 10-4, 769B2
Marubeni, Hitachi units convicted 11-5, 957C3
Lands bill signed, Hammond issues statemt 12-2, 915G3-916D1
Oil & Gas Developments
US OKs Alcan pipe sectn 1-10, westn sectn constructn to begin 1-22, 56F3, G3
Carter OKs Northern Tier oil pipe 1-18, 56B3
Sohio '79 profit rptd linked 1-25, 90D3
Tanker subsidies repaymt backed by Sup Ct 2-20, 170F2
Fscl '79 tax revenue rptd 2-20, 307A3
2d 1/4 gas use targets set 3-20, 250F3
Windfall oil profits tax bill exempts 4-2, 244B3
Income tax ended, wealth shared 4-15, 307B3
'79 tax collectn rptd 4-17, 307D2
Sohio 1st 1/4 profit rptd 4-23, 331A2
Alcan pipe eastn leg OKd 4-24, 331A1
Windfall profits tax suit filed 10-14, 960E2
Beaufort Sea leases upheld 10-14, 960B3
Royalty sharing plan backed by Ct 10-24, 960E2
Panama Canal clogged by trade shipmts 11-24, 895D3
US reserve pvt exploratn clears Cong 12-1, 954E2
Lands bill signed 12-2, 915G3-916D1
'81 Interior appropriatns signed 12-12, 982B1
Politics & Government—*See also other appropriate subheads in this section*
Legislature schedule rptd 18C1
State of State message 1-15, 268C3
Anchorage cancels bond issue 2-26, 186F1
Kennedy claims Dem caucus win 3-11, 209B1
Income tax break OKd 4-15, 307B3
US Sen primary results 8-26, 683E1-B2
Income tax break overturned 9-5, income tax repeal signed 9-24, 747A1
NRA endorses Reagan 11-1, 844G1
Election results 11-4: pres 838A1, 839B1, D3; cong 840C1, 842B1, 846A1, 852F1; state 845C2, 847A1
'80 census rptd 12-31, 983D1
ALASKA Interstate Co.
C&K Petroleum merger set 8-18, 745F3
ALBADALEJO, Francisco
Sentncd for '77 murders 3-4, 196C2
ALBANESE, Alfredo
Slain 5-12, death described 5-17, 408C1, A3
Sohio gas price hike order rescinded 5-1, 366B2
Prudhoe Bay oil stockpiling site studied 6-16, 552D2
Offshore leasing speedup OKd 6-17, 552F2
US vows '85 Alcan pipe completn 6-27—7-17, Canada OKs southn leg pre-bldg 7-17, 562F1-F2
Lease curbs lifted 7-3, 7-8; leases OKd 7-9, 552E3
Oil refiners paymt plan rptd, Sohio price hike cited 7-7, 553D2
Canada filibuster vs Alcan defeated 7-23, 577A3
Lands bill clears Sen 8-19, 631C2
Income tax break overturned 9-5, income tax repeal signed 9-24, 747A1
US Aug oil imports show record drop; Jan-Aug decline rptd 9-6, 785B3
Exxon Beaufort Sea find rptd 10-3, 785E2-A3
ALBANIA
IOC rpts Olympic boycott 3-28, 259F3
Cabt changes rptd; Yugo, Greece, Italy trade linked 5-2, 356E2
Medit pollutn pact signed 5-17, 381D3
IOC issues Olympic acceptance list 5-27, 420E3
CSCE conf absence cited 9-9, 679B3

1976

ALBANO-Garcia, Ester
Jailing protested 10-2, 751G3
ALBANY, N.Y.—*See NEW York State*
ALBANY (Ga.) Herald (newspaper)
Ford endorsement rptd 10-30, 827F3
ALBANY (N.Y.) Knickerbocker News (newspaper)
Carter endorsement rptd 10-30, 831G2
ALBERS, Joseph
Dies 3-25, 240C3
ALBERT, Rep. Carl (Bert) (D, Okla.)
Scores Ford Angola aid plea 1-27, 69D1
Ford warns vs Angola aid cutoff 1-27, 69E1
Dingell scores re gas bill 2-3, 109A1
Declines Ford probe aid 2-13, 151E1
Staff aide probed 2-19, 171E1
Names House reform task force 6-4, 551D2
Announces retirement 6-5, 434B3
Rpts Hays quits com post 6-18, 551F2
Marks Bicentennial 7-2, 489A2
Names assassinatn panel 9-21, 729G1
Scores Ford on HEW, Labor funds veto 9-29, 726G3
Full employmt bill not cleared 10-2, 884A1
Watkins wins seat 11-2, 822G2
Dems elect O'Neill 12-6, 919A1
ALBERTAZZIE, Ralph
Loses primary for gov 5-11, 342D3
ALBERTSON, Jack
Wins Emmy 5-17, 460B2
ALBRECHT, Ernst
Wins Lower Saxony electn 1-15, 77G1
Wins Lower Saxony revote 2-6, 157C2
ALBUQUERQUE, N.M.—*See NEW Mexico*
ALBUQUERQUE Tribune (newspaper)
Ford endorsement rptd 10-30, 831F2
ALBUQUERQUE Queiroz, Ayrton de
Arrest confirmed 3-9, 288B1
ALCAN Aluminium Ltd.
Guyana to buy Sprostons 1-6, 252F3
Sup Ct refuses import surchrg challng 11-29, 901A1
ALCOA—*See ALUMINUM Co. of America*
ALCOHOLIC Beverages & Alcoholism
Sup Ct to review Okla beer law 1-12, 24D1
HEW rpt scores excess use 1-12, 32A1
Peru cuts imports 1-12, 142B2
Algeria-EC pact rptd 1-21, 84B3
CIA expenditures rptd scored 1-26, 1-27, 93D1
Tunisia, Morocco chrg EC pact 'bias' 2-3, 164A3
Md food chain admits beer co paymt 2-13, 360G2
Beer mfr rptd testing plastic bottles 4-21, 308C2
Ga still operator's convictn reinstated 4-21, 331D1
Angola natlizes Portugal brewery 5-6, 371A2
SEC suit vs Emersons settled 5-11, 359D3, 360F2
Falstaff-Ballantine merger cited 5-11, 360F2
Anheuser-Busch strike ends 6-6, 436A2
Rand study released 6-9; scored 6-9, 6-10, 442F3-443E1
Blue Cross studies coverage 6-9, 443F1
US Dem platform text 6-15, 472E3
Liquor label deadline extended 7-1, 571D1
SEC sues Foremost-McKesson 7-7, 669D1
Rptd most abused drug 7-9, 524E1, B2
2d ¼ profits rptd 7-28, 708F3
Rand study backed 8-8, 814D3
US GOP platform text 8-18, 605A2
PepsiCo to up Sovt vodka imports 8-18, 679G2
PHS issues 5-yr plan 9-7, 680G1
Cong OKs Indian aid 9-16, 745F3; signed 9-30, 982G1
Australia Aborigine alcoholism rptd 10-7, 869F3
Scandinavia expels N Korea envoys 10-15—10-22, 799E2
S Africa hotel bar integratn rptd 11-20, 928E2
'60-75 consumer spending rptd 11-23, 959G2
Brandy duties raised 11-26, 976F2-C3
New alcoholism test rptd 12-3, 950C3
Margaux vineyard sold 12-18, 964F2-A3
Angola to curb stills 12-19, 995F3
Sup Ct bars Okla beer law 12-20, 960D1

France-Italy Wine Dispute

French growers seek Italy import ban 1-7, 1-14, violence flares 1-19—2-5, 138B3, F3-139A1
Agri mins meet, EC mediator named 1-20, 138E3
EC OKs Italy border tax 2-6, 163C3
EC mediates wine talks 2-24, 163D3
French clashes spread 3-1—3-4, 204A3
EC drafts pact 3-6, 276A3

Obituaries

Rosenstiel, Lewis 1-21, 80G3
Schoonmaker, Frank 1-11, 56F3
ALCOHOLICS Anonymous, General Service Board of
Norris vs Rand study 6-9, 443E1
ALCOHOLISM, National Council on
Scores Rand study 6-10, 442E3, 443D1
New alcoholism test rptd 12-3, 950E3

1977

ALBEDA, Willem
Dutch soc affairs min 12-19, 986A1
ALBERT, Carl (Bert)
House elects O'Neill 1-4, 5D3
Ex-aide rptd KCIA agent 6-5, 442B1
Thomson testifies on Korea lobbying 8-17, 8-25, 688G1
Korean probe subpoena rptd 12-1, 915F1
ALBERTA Gas Trunk Line Ltd.
FPC splits on Alaska pipe route 5-2, 369C3
ALBERTO-Culver Co.
Hair dye linked to cancer 10-17, 962G3
ALBRECHT, Ernst
On A-plant waste disposal 1-13, 117F3
ALBRECHT, Richard R.
Replaced as Treas gen counsel 8-2, 626B3
ALBRECHT, Susanne
Sought in Ponto slaying 7-30, 601B3
Linked to Baader atty 11-18, 969A1
ALBRECHT, Ted
In NFL draft 5-3, 353B2
ALBRIGHT, Tenley
Elected USOC secy 4-29, 491B3
ALBUQUERQUE, N.M.—*See NEW Mexico*
ALCAN Aluminium Ltd.
Quebec strike pact reached 1-31, 114D2
Revere sale challenged 12-9, 1004F3
ALCAN Pipeline Co.
FPC splits on pipe route 5-2, 369D2
Canada bd backs US route 7-4, 525E1-E2
Canada issues pipe rpts 7-28, 8-2, 596E2-B3
US cos back route 7-29, 596C3; Canada Parlt OKs 8-8, 616B2
Carter, Trudeau OK gas pipe 9-8, 687B1
Gas pipe pact signed 9-20, 725C3
US Cong OKs route 11-2, Carter signs 11-8, 856C3
ALCANTARA, Dick
Says econ min contacted IMF 7-12, 563B3
ALCOA—*See ALUMINUM Co. of America*
ALCOHOL, Drug Abuse & Mental Health Administration—*See under U.S. GOVERNMENT—PUBLIC Health Service*
ALCOHOLIC Beverages & Alcoholism
Ariz murder plot chrgd 1-27, 162E1
Bollinger dies 2-22, 164D2
Finland bans ads 3-1, 182B2
Carter concern cited 3-14, 332A2
Pa radio statn loses license 4-4, 395B3
HEW handicapped rules controversy 4-5, 301C3
Handicapped rules signed 4-28, 338B3
1st ¼ profits rptd up 4-28, 668F3
Pregnant women warned 5-31, 6-1, 472E1
VA rpts patient rise 6-7, 472A2
Carter drug-abuse message 8-2, 609A2
Calif nightclub license revocatn case review refused 10-17, 797F3
Natl Distillers, Emery plan merger 12-19, 1004B3

Payments Issues

ARA Svcs rpts rebates 1-28, 94E1
Natl Distillers kickbacks rptd 1-28, 215G1
Olympia questionable paymts rptd 2-4, 215D2
Amer Airlines gifts rptd 2-9, 112C1
Falstaff, Dixie bribery chrgd 2-16, 215D2
Foremost pleads no contest 3-7, 215E1
Amer Brands rpts Beam gifts 3-10, 215C2
Interstate United rebates rptd 3-16, 215F2
SEC sues Schlitz 4-7, Anheuser-Busch 5-19, 503D3, E3
NYS chrgs Schenley rebates 10-6, 860E1
Jacquin settles SEC rebates chrgs 10-17, 860E1
ALCOHOLICS Anonymous, General Service Board of
Inmate union curbs upheld 6-23, 539E2
ALCOHOLISM, National Council on
Pregnant women warned 5-31, 472G1

1978

ALBANY, N.Y.—*See NEW York State*
ALBECK, Andreas
Named United Artists pres 1-17, 75B3
ALBEE, Edward
At pro-Shcharansky, Ginzburg rally 7-10, 542B3
ALBERT, Carl (Bert)
Mitchell on FBI memo re Thomson link to KCIA 3-21, 203E2
ALBERTA (Canadian province)—*See CANADA*
ALBERTA Gas Trunk Line Co. Ltd.
Husky Oil stock purchased 6-23—6-26; announces takeover 6-27, reassures investors 6-29, 628E3, 629B2
ALBERTO, Carlos
On NASL All-Star team 8-20, named top defensive player 8-21, 707G2, A3
ALBOSTA, Donald J.
Wins US House seat 11-7, 851E1, 854B1
ALBRECHT, Ernst
Assumes Puvogel's duties 3-23, 477G2
ALBRECHT, Susanne
Rptd in Colombia 2-18, 147C3
ALBRIGHT & Wilson Ltd.
Tenneco purchase offered 5-23, 404F1
ALBUQUERQUE, N.M.—*See NEW Mexico*
ALCALA, Diego
Arguello KOs 6-3, 600F1
ALCAN Pipeline Co.
Canada gas purchase optn OKd 1-17, 53G2
Canada Parlt gets constructn legis 2-3, NEB sets specificatns 2-20, 130A1
Canada Parlt OKs constructn legis 4-4, US delay seen 8-16, 647F2
ALCATRAZ Island, Calif.—*See CALIFORNIA*
ALCOA—*See ALUMINUM Co. of America*
ALCOHOL, Drug Abuse & Mental Health Administration—*See under U.S. GOVERNMENT—PUBLIC Health Service*
ALCOHOLIC Beverages—*See also ALCOHOLISM*
Miller 'Lite' trademark case review barred 1-9, 13C1
USSR vodka-Pepsi deal expanded 1-10, 20D3
UFW ends Gallo boycott 1-31, 83F1
Distillers' '77 4th ¼ profits rptd down 2-7, 282E3
Schlitz sued re kickbacks, tax fraud 3-15, 223C2
Experimental fuel use backed in farm bill 3-21, 218A3
Anheuser-Busch fined re rebates 3-31, 449F2
Australia threatens EC brandy export curbs 4-6, talks delayed 4-14, 310D3
Farm bill gasohol provisn clears Cong 5-4, 343F1
Miller '77 sales, 'Lite' beer success cited 5-15, 364B3
Poland price hikes, consumptn data rptd 5-28, 535C2
Schlitz settles SEC chrgs 7-9, 642E3
Chelsea soft drink ads halted 7-22, 941G3
Hungary price hikes rptd 7-24, 691E3
Australia tax hike proposed 8-15, 628A2
US-Japan wine quota talks fail 9-5—9-7, 695B1
SEC sues Seagram, case setld 9-8, 961E3
Schlitz pleads no contest, fined 11-1, 877C1
Mich drinking age hiked 11-7, 854C1
Kan referendum results 11-7, 854G2
Greek EC entry terms set 12-21, 1017D3
ALCOHOLISM
Mrs Ford treated for alcoholism 4-10—5-5, 420A1
Carter asks fed ct load eased 5-4, 320B3
Saudis whip 2 UK workers 5-15; other natls rptd arrested, sentncd 6-15, 6-17, 515E3
Pilots blamed for '76 Miss R boat collisn 5-17, 460B1
Brain tissue regeneratn rptd 6-10, 1023C2
Joan Kennedy details alcoholism 6-20, 844F2
Synanon incidents 9-19—10-17; Calif probes 10-15, 10-17, 841G2-842B1
Carter rpts on Viet vets, urges progrm 10-10, 878D1, E1
Synanon founder arrested 12-2, 971G1
Mass drunk rights waiver ruling affirmed by Sup Ct 12-11, 980G3

1979

ALBANY, U.S.S. (cruiser)
Retirement announced 1-23, 89C3
ALBERT, Prince (Great Britain) (1819-61)
Victoria secret marriage alleged 5-22, 368F2
ALBERT, Eddie
Concorde Airport '79 released 8-3, 820A1
ALBERT, Michel
'81-86 natl plan presented 4-4, 267B2
ALBERTA (Canadian province)—*See CANADA*
ALBERTA Gas Trunk Line Co. Ltd.
Husky takeover set 5-13, 405F2
ALBERT Einstein College of Medicine (Bronx, N.Y.)
Heart failure pill rptd effective 5-8, 472C1
ALBERTO, Carlos
Named to NASL All-Star team 8-27, 776E1
Suspended in playoffs 8-31, 775F3
ALBERTON'S Inc.
PCB contaminated eggs destroyed 9-17, 704D3
ALBRECHT, Ernst
Blocks Gorleben A-reprocessing plant 5-16, 410E3
CDU-CSU alliance faces split 5-24, 5-28, 489E1
Strauss wins CDU support 7-2, 506A1
ALBUQUERQUE, N.M.—*See NEW Mexico*
ALBUQUERQUE Journal (newspaper)
Libel case refused by Sup Ct 12-3, 964B2
ALBUQUERQUE Tribune (newspaper)
Libel case refused by Sup Ct 12-3, 964B2
ALCAN Aluminum Ltd.
Queensland smelter studied 8-3, 600A1
ALCAN Pipeline Co.
US affirms constructn plan 3-3, 168F1
GAO doubts gas pipe viability 7-4, 522C2
ALCM (air-launched cruise missile)—*See ARMAMENTS—Missiles*
ALCOA—*See ALUMINUM Co. of America*
ALCOHOL & Alcoholic Beverages—*See also ALCOHOLISM*
Ingredient labeling proposed 2-1, 91G3
Darvon warning ordrd 2-15, 138A3
Schenley SEC setlmt rptd 2-16, 131E3
FTC brewer competitn study rptd 3-2, 305C2
UN rpts consumptn hike 3-9, 218B3
Moderate use linked to heart disease preventn 3-19, 219A1
Mass raises drinking age 4-16, 309E3
State-local '78 tax revenues up 5-16, 386C2
Mass driver license suspensn rule upheld by Sup Ct 6-25, 540G1
Distillers' 2d 1/4 profits rptd down 8-17, 628G2
Imperial Group to buy Howard Johnson 9-10, Calif bar seen 10-12, 942B3-E3
Cancer agents found in beer, warning urged 9-19, 9-22, 735E3-736B1
Seagram unit admits Pa bribery 9-27, 809E3
Distillers' 3d 1/4 profits rptd up 10-31, 923C1

Foreign Developments—*See also 'Fuel Use' below*

Hungary ups beer prices 1-8, 101B2
Canada air safety abuses rptd 2-8—2-14, 134D1
Pak enacts Islamic law 2-10, 116F2
UN rpts global consumptn up 3-9, 218B3
French wine mislabeling chrgd 4-25, 330A3
Poland bans sales for Pope's visit 6-1—6-4, 414C2
Brazil fuel use, gasohol experimts rptd 6-4, 430G1
Turkey hikes prices 6-12, 447D1
NZ plans tax hike 6-22, 566A3
USSR hikes beer price 7-2, 504E2
Australia fuel projct rptd 8-30, 666C3
Dutch plan tax hike 9-18, 730C3
Canada budgets price hike 12-12, defeated 12-13, 936D3

Fuel Use

Brazil use with special engines, gasohol experimts rptd 6-4, 430G1
Gasohol tax exemptn proposed 6-20, 498F1
Gasohol in Carter energy plan 7-15, 534B1
Gasohol sales tests set 8-10, 649F1
Brazil, car cos set dvpt plan 8-18; auto race held 9-7, 871C2
Gasohol supported by Carter 8-22, 622A3
Australia projct rptd 8-30, 666C3
Gasohol use backed by Pressler 9-25, 724G1
Brazil gets $1.2 bln loan 11-26, 907F2
ALCOHOL, Drug Abuse & Mental Health Administration—*See under U.S. GOVERNMENT—PUBLIC Health Service*
ALCOHOLISM
Genetic link rptd 1-5, 289C3
Carter budget proposals 1-22, 44B3
Sen Talmadge hospitalized 1-22, 176E1
Billy Carter hospitalized 3-7, 271A3
UN rpts global rise, urges measures 3-9, 218B3
Teen-age rise cited 4-16, 309F3
Mont homicide convictn reversed by Sup Ct 6-18, 499F1
Rep Bolling hospitalized 6-25, 527A3
USSR crime fight rptd 9-11, 857C2
Viet vet study reveals 9-25, 725D1
USSR male deaths linked 10-10, 857B2
Australia Aborigine health study ordrd 11-28, 906D3

1980

ALBANY (Ga.) Herald (newspaper)
Postell indicted in 'death row' escape 8-27, 712F2-D3
Postell cleared 11-12, 927A1
ALBECK, Andy
Named UA chrmn 12-12, 986A3
ALBECK, Stan
Hired as Spurs coach 6-11, 656G3
ALBEDA, Willem
Voluntary wage freeze urged 1-7, 21F1
ALBEE, Edward
Lady From Dubuque opens 1-31, 136C3
ALBERGER, Bill
Backs auto import probe speedup 7-18, 556G1
ALBERT, Eddie
Foolin' Around released 10-17, 836G2
ALBERTA (Canadian province)—*See CANADA*
ALBERTA Gas Truck Line Co. Ltd.
US OKs Alcan pipe sectn 1-10, westn sectn constructn to begin 1-22, 56F3, 57A1
Pipe extensn to Quebec OKd 5-16, 406G1
Canada gets US assurances on Alcan pipe completn 6-27—7-17, OKs southn leg pre-bldg 7-17, 562F1-F2
Canada filibuster vs Alcan defeated 7-23, 577A3
ALBERTO, Carlos
Cosmos win NASL title 9-21, 770B2
ALBOSTA, Rep. Donald (D, Mich.)
Reelected 11-4, 843F1
ALBRECHT, Silvia
Wins Olympic medal 2-17, 156B1
ALBUQUERQUE—*See NEW Mexico*
ALCOA—*See ALUMINUM Co. of America*
ALCOHOL, Drug Abuse & Mental Health *See under U.S. GOVERNMENT--PUBLIC Health Service*
ALCOHOL & Alcoholic Beverages
US issues dietary guidelines 2-4, 157A3
Sebastiani dies 2-16, 176C3
Miller 'Lite' trademark case refused by Sup Ct 2-19, 131A1
Coors Calif trust case declined by Sup Ct 2-19, 131D1
Calif brewers dual seniority system backed by Sup Ct 2-20, 146F2-B3
Calif wine pricing law held illegal by Sup Ct 3-3, 210E1
Petri dies 4-7, 360G2
State-local '79 tax collectns rptd 4-17, 307D2
3 Mile I health study rptd 4-17, 332B2
Credit fixing curbed by Sup Ct 5-27, 453G2
Cholesterol rpt scored 6-1, 432F3
US orders ingredient labeling 6-10, 485A3
Beer carcinogen levels rptd down 6-12, 526D3
Anderson, Reagan debate excise tax 9-21, 722E1
Calif winery strike ends 9-22, 747A3*

Foreign Developments (including U.S. international news)

Ireland plans levy hike 2-27, 150G3
French wine fraud re US exports disclosed 3-6, 193B2
UK plans tax hikes 3-26, 232E1
Zimbabwe hikes prices 4-20, 301B2
Canada plans tax hike 4-21, 310F2
Argentine vintner arrested 4-25, 350A1
Anheuser-Busch beer to be brewed in Canada 6-17, 486D2
France plans tax hike 9-20, 688D1
Norway sets tax hike 10-6, 792G3
W Ger wine scandal rptd; France, Luxembourg suspect 11-3, 11-18, 925C2
France consumptn rptd 12-10, 942G1

Fuel Use

State of State messages 1-7, 1-10, 403D2, E3
Carter sets productn goal 1-11, 33B2
Carter budget proposals 1-28, 72A1
Brazil promotn outlined 4-20, program delays rptd 6-3; US sales surge 6-10, 460G3-461A2
Synfuel bill clears Cong 6-19, 6-26, 479C2; Carter signs 6-30, 494G1-A2
GOP platform adopted 7-15, 537B1
Gasohol Competitn Act clears Cong 11-19, 953D2; signed 12-2, 982A1
US grain reserve authrzn clears Cong 11-17, signed 12-3, 981G1

Mergers & Acquisitions

Hiram Walker, Canada gas co merger set 1-9, 19D1; OKd 4-8, 310D3
Foremost-McKesson rejects investor group 2-6, 386C1
Seagram accepts Sun bid for Tex Pacific 4-11, 385B2
Imperial Group completes Howard Johnson deal 6-17, 557C3
Seagram unit, Sun merger complete 9-12, 985A1
Heublein, United Vintners divestiture order rptd overturned 10-15, 917C1
ALCOHOLISM
Maternity risks rptd 1-4, 23G3
Life span changes rptd 1-19, 62G3
Carter budget proposals 1-28, 72C3
2 baseball players rpt treatmt 3-4, 3-14, 637E1
On the Nickel released 5-4, 416D3
Mass prof indicted in fraud case 5-13, 414F3
Army cuts overseas duty time 6-6, 458B3
Heredity link rptd 6-7, 715G1
Sovt '71-76 infant mortality rise rptd 6-25, 525F2
Natl Cncl founder dies 7-22, 608D2
RFK's son arrested for drunk driving 7-27, 639C2
Rockefeller's grandson arrested 8-18, denied pub defender 9-22, 908B3

1976

ALCOREZA Melgarejo, Gen. Carlos
Loses army command 1-6, 26G3
ALDAMA, Andres
Wins Olympic medal 7-31, 574C1
ALEJO, Francisco Javier
'75 Spain overture rptd 1-8, 75F2
ALESSANDRI, Jorge
Accepts govt advisory role 1-4, 8D2
Anaconda anti-Allende offer rptd 12-23, 999B2
ALEXANDER, Donald C.
IRS-Justice probe agrmt issued 1-10, 41C3
Montoya IRS audit rptd 3-24, 247C1
Probes clear on 2 items; rpt Montoya audit irregularities 4-12, 283D3
ALEXANDER, Doyle
In World Series 10-16—10-21, 815C2
Contract rptd signed 12-5, 951E3
ALEXANDER, Eugene P.
Indicted 11-4, 886F3
ALEXANDER, Henry
Indicted in '57 murder 3-5, freed 4-14, 316E2
ALEXANDER, Herbert E.
Book excerpts published 4-25, 687G3 *
ALEXANDER Jr., Rep. William Vollie (Bill) (D, Ark.)
Reelected 11-2, 828G3
ALEXANDRIA, Va.—*See VIRGINIA*
ALEXANDROV, I.
USSR asks renewed border talks 4-28, 341A3
ALEXEYEV, Pyotr F.
Izvestia Central Com head 3-5, 195A3
ALEXEYEV, Vasily
Wins Olympic medal 7-27, 576F2
ALEXEYEVA, Lyudmila
In CSCE monitor group 5-13, 408B2
ALEYNIK, Vladimir
Wins Olympic medal 7-27, 575D3
ALFA Romeo S.p.A.
US ends car dumping probe 5-4, 321D2
Turin strike 10-8, 10-12, 10-13, 838D2
AL Fatah—*See 'Palestinian Developments' under MIDDLE EAST—ARAB Policies*
ALFEEVA, Lidiya
Wins Olympic medal 7-23, 576E1
ALFRED, Jean
Wins recount 12-1, 924D1
ALGER Hiss: the True Story (book)
Review published 3-18, 217E1, 218E1

ALGERIA—*See also AFRICAN Development Bank, ARAB League, NONALIGNED Nations Movement, OAU, OPEC*
'76 budget presented 1-2, 45E3
Bomb explodes 1-3, 3 arrested, admit link to France 1-8; France denies chrg 1-9, 1-11, 45B2-E3
Cuba troop training rptd 1-10, 138F1
Oil pact with N Viet signed 1-17, 46A1
Listed as 'not free' nation 1-19, 20D3
EC pact rptd 1-21, 84A3
Tunisia, Morocco protest EC pact 2-3, 164A3
At intl econ conf 2-11—2-20, 148B1
Australia names amb 2-18, 155B1
Offices in France bombed 2-20, 2-22, 455A1
US to curb gas imports 2-26, 149D2
7 sentncd as French-linked spies 3-3, 454F3-455A1
Morocco, Mauritania sever ties 3-7, 178A3
Castro visits 3-12—3-14, 251C3
Passports required of French natls 3-25, 455B1
Closer Libya, Niger ties set 4-8, 372A1
Giscard scores French Socialist ldr's visit 4-22, 312E3
Oil co gets Euro$ loan 5-6, 455D1
Private schools banned 5-12, 455C1
Voting age lowered 5-15, 455C1
Sovt mil presence rptd 6-13, 467C1
Nov const referendum set 6-24, natl charter OKd 6-27, 543G1
Bars Libyan hijacked jet 7-6, 539A2
Rpt planned '75 OPEC raid 7-15, 531F1
Canada foundry pact rptd 7-16, 902C2
Olympic withdrawal rptd 7-21, 528B3
$ securities issue rptd 7-27, 902B2
Friday rest day in effect 8-27, 902A2

1977

ALCON Laboratories Inc.
OKs Nestle bid 11-17; merger table 880D1, G1
ALCORN, Meade
Disputes Nixon re Adams firing 5-5, 367C1
ALCORTA, Alfredo
Freed 1-27, 'house arrest' chrgd 2-16, 167D3
ALDA, Alan
Wins Emmy 9-11, 1022A1
ALDREDGE, Theoni V.
Wins Tony 6-5, 452E1
ALDRIN—*See PESTICIDES*
ALECHINSKY, Pierre
Wins 1st Mellon prize 8-1, 808F2
ALEIXANDRE, Vicente
Wins Nobel Prize 10-6, 951F2
ALEKSEYEV, Vladimir I.
US ousts 2-5, 101C1
ALEMAYEHU Haile, Capt.
Dergue secy-gen 1-7, 62G3
Killed 2-3, 98D2
ALEXANDER Jr., Clifford L.
Named Army secy 1-19, 52F3
Confirmed 2-11, 148C3
Reprimands Gen Starry 6-17, 483A1
Denies Slovik appeal 8-13, 808F1
ALEXANDER, Donald C.
On IRS-Miami probe, intellignc curbs 1-6, 16E1
Bahama bank tax evidence barred 4-28, 395E3
ALEXANDER, Howard W.
Indicted 3-3, 204D1
ALEXANDER, John
Australia wins Davis Cup 12-4, 970F1, E2
ALEXANDER, Margaret Walker (Margaret Walker)
Sues Haley 4-22, 356D1
ALEXANDER & Allen Inc.
Principals indicted 3-3, 204D1
ALEXANDRAKIS, Menelas D.
Greece rejects US envoy 7-22, 598A3
ALEXEYEVA, Ludmila
Emigratn rptd 2-22, 137C3
ALFARO Castillo, Carlos
Killed by guerrillas 9-16, 747E1
AL Fatah—*See MIDDLE EAST—PALESTINIAN Developments*
ALFONSIN, Raul
Asks ct missing persons probe 4-11, 388C3
Defends pol parties 7-24, 615A2
ALFORD, Dr. Charles
Antiviral drug rptd 8-10, 675G2
ALFVEN, Hannes
Vs nuclear energy use 5-9, 403C1

ALGERIA—*See also ARAB League, NONALIGNED Nations Movement OAU, OPEC*
'77 budget presented 1-6, 24E1
Natl Assemb elected 2-25, 309E1
Cabt shuffled 4-23, 4-27, 470A2
'78 indl investmt cuts seen 9-5, 963B2
Econ priorities shifted, '76 farm output cited 12-4, 963E1
Arab-Israeli Conflict—*See MIDDLE EAST*
Foreign Relations (misc.)
UN Assemb member 3F3
Canary separatists blamed for airline blast 1-3, 22C3
De Broglie linked to black mkt 1-5, 44G1
France arrests Daoud 1-7, expels to Algeria 1-11; scores French police 1-12, 9A1, F1, D2
Daoud on release 1-14, 1-15, 27E3
'76 EC trade pact cited 1-18, 73E3
Malta scores security talks delay 2-10, 136A3
Israel boycott eased 2-18, 167F2
Castro visits 3-1, 3-31—4-2, 249F1, E3
Spain hijacked jet lands 3-14, 224B3
Iraqi Kurds free hostage 3-28, 256F3
Arab monetary fund created 4-18, 318C1
Venez pres visits 5-4—5-5, 362A1
N-S 'oil dialogue' opposed 6-3, 437D2
6 French natls amnestied 6-19, 566G3
Mediates Egypt-Libya clashes 7-24—7-25, 569F2
Japan jet hijackers give up 10-3; Japan dispute re extraditn 10-5, 756D3
Yugo pres visits, backs nonaligned natns 10-19—10-20, 844E2
UN pollutn conf ends, Medit pact reached 10-21, 876B2

1978

ALCOHOL, Tobacco & Firearms, Bureau of—*See under U.S. GOVERNMENT—TREASURY*
ALCON Laboratories
Natamycin OKd by FDA 11-1, 948A3
ALCOTT, Amy
Wins Amer Defender Classic 4-23, 356A1
2d in LPGA Champnshp 6-11, 580A3
LPGA top money winner 11-20, 990C3
ALDA, Alan
Same Time, Next Yr released 11-22, 970A3
ALDRICH, William
Great Chefs of Eur released 10-6, 970E3
ALEMAN, Jose
At JFK death hearing 9-27, cited 9-28, 750E1, G1
ALEMAN, Juan
Vs World Cup soccer spending 2-17, 310C3 *
Home bombed 6-22, 520F3
ALEMU Abebe
Defends terror campaign 2-8, 100C2
ALESSANDRI, Jorge
UN rights panel interviewed 7-27, 591E2
Chile land reform to end 10-6, 795B1
ALEUTIAN Islands—*See ALASKA*
ALEXANDER Jr., Clifford L.
OKs W Ger gun for XM-1 1-31, 81F3
Gen Singlaub resigns 4-28, 321G2
On Army 2-yr enlistmt 11-10, 895A3
Rpts Army MD shortage 11-27, 916D3
ALEXANDER, Eben Roy
Dies 10-30, 888D2
ALEXANDER, Eugene P.
Sentenced 9-21, 768B3
ALEXANDER, Gary
Traded to A's 3-15, 194G3
ALEXANDER, Jane
1st Monday in Oct opens 10-3, 1031G1
ALEXANDER, John
Loses Louisville Intl 7-30, Volvo Intl 8-6, 1027A2
ALEXANDER, Lamar
Wins Tenn gov primary 8-3, 606A2
Elected Tenn gov 11-7, 853C1, E3
ALEXANDER, Mayor Lee (Syracuse, N.Y.)
On Carter urban-aid plan 3-27, 3-28, 218C1
Urges Carter vs budget cuts 12-20, 980C2
ALEXANDER, Margaret Walker (Margaret Walker)
'Roots' suit dismissed 9-21, 759A3
ALEXANDER, Terry
Nongogo opens 12-3, 1031F2
ALEXANDER Jr., Rep. William Vollie (Bill) (D, Ark.)
Reelected 11-7, 850C1, 855A2
ALFARO, Jose Miguel
Rejcts Vesco citizenship bid 2-23, 152B2
ALFA Romeo Inc.
Milan exec wounded 2-16, 133D2
Italian showrooms bombed 4-22, 4-30, 330E1, G1; 5-22, 393F3
Cortesi, 3 execs sentenced 5-29, 454E2
Alfasud exec shot in Naples 6-22, 517A2
Exec wounded 9-29, 826G3
AL Fatah—*See MIDDLE EAST, subheads LEBANON and PALESTINIAN Developments*
ALFORD v. Florida
Secret evidence death convictn case declined by Sup Ct 5-30, 430C3

ALGERIA—*See also ARAB League, NON-ALIGNED Nations Movement, OAU, OPEC*
'78 budget set 1-17, 94D1
Econ dvpt plans rptd slowed 2-20, 122E1, A2
Boumedienne dies; facts on; Bitat sworn interim pres 12-27, 1012B2
Arab-Israeli Conflict—*See MIDDLE EAST*
Foreign Relations (misc.)—*See also 'Monetary, Trade, Aid & Investment' and 'UN' below*
Boumedienne visits Malta 1-3, 39B2
Cyprus jet hijackers denied landing 2-19, 117B2
Canary separatist ldr wounded 4-5, Spain blamed 4-20; 2 tried, sentncd 5-6—5-7, 576C3
Cuba Eritrea role rptd opposed 6-21, 584B3
Canada protests Maschino kidnaping 7-1, 7-4, 531D3
Japan Red Army hijackers expelled 7-3, 524D3
Egypt team attacked at games 7-22; Egypt athletes to boycott 7-24, 573C1
UK holds suspect in Iraq amb death try 8-2, 582F2
Iraq-PLO feud mediated 8-9—8-11, 8-23, 674A2
Castro visits 9-19, 776G3
Hardliners conf ends; Egypt ties severed, USSR contacts sought 9-24, 729F2
W Ger terrorist suspects refuge hinted, denied 11-18, 906B2
Monetary, Trade, Aid & Investment
French import cuts ordrd, trade deficit cited 1-11, 11C3
Islamic, Arab poor-natn aid rise rptd 4-9, 257F2

1979

Alcoholics Anonymous founder dies 12-6, 1008E3
ALCOHOL, Tobacco & Firearms, Bureau of—*See under U.S. GOVERNMENT-TREASURY*
ALCOTT, Amy
Wins Arden Classic 2-18, 220E3
Wins Peter Jackson Classic 7-29, 587F3
Wins United Va Bank Classic 10-14, Mizuno Classic 11-3, 970F1, B2
LPGA top money winner 11-30, 969G2
ALDA, Alan
Joe Tynan released 8-17, 820C3
Wins Emmy 9-9, 858E2
ALDA, Rutanya
When A Stranger Calls released 10-12, 1008A2
ALDERTON, John
All Things Bright & Beautiful released 3-8, 528B1
ALDREDGE, Tom
On Golden Pond opens 2-28, 712G1
ALDRICH, Robert
Frisco Kid released 7-6, 820C1
ALEKSANDROV, A. M.
Cited in SALT II summit communique 6-18, 457D1
ALEMANN, Juan
Escapes shooting 11-7, 887F3
ALESSANDRINI, Emilio
Killed 1-29, 98B1
ALEX, Eddie
Glorious Monster opens 7-10, 711D3
ALEXANDER, Charles
In NFL draft 5-3, 335F1
ALEXANDER Jr., Clifford L.
Scores Spanish language ban 2-7, 89E2
Rpts XM-1 tank engine problem 3-2, 207G2-A3
Disputes US draft need 3-13, 307A2
Army reserve recruiting failure rptd 8-23, 649D3
OKs E Coast oil refinery 10-4, 769G3-770F1
Ft Dix to stay open 10-10, 809D1
ALEXANDER, Doyle
Traded to Braves 12-7, 1002F2
ALEXANDER, Jane
Losing Time opens 9-30, 956C3
Kramer vs Kramer released 12-19, 1007F3
ALEXANDER, John
Loses Milan WCT 4-1, 391B3
Loses Atlanta Open 9-17, 734E2
ALEXANDER, Joyce London
Sworn US magistrate 8-7, 901F3
ALEXANDER, Gov. Lamar (R, Tenn.)
Installed gov, curbs convict releases 1-17, 36F1, B3
Blanton pardons still in dispute 1-19—1-31; orders audits 1-22, asks prison reform 2-14, 152E2
ALEXANDER, Lincoln
Canada labor min 6-4, 423F3
ALEXANDER'S Inc.
Sentncd re TV import rebates 3-29, 298C3
ALEXANDER v. HUD
Govt relocatn aid curbed by Sup Ct 4-17, 325G3
ALEXANDRA, Princess (Great Britain)
At St Lucia independnc rite 2-21, 181B2
ALFA Romeo SpA
Joint ventures stressed in survival plan 9-13, 709E1
AL Fatah—*See MIDDLE EAST-PALESTINIAN Developments*
ALFORD, Lamar
Second Thoughts opens 5-4, 712C2
ALGARD, Ole
Lauds Leb govt troop dispatch 4-26, 297A1
ALGEMENE Bank Nederland N.V. (Amsterdam)
Iran banks natlzd 6-7, compensatn vowed 6-10, 469B2
ALGERIA—*See also ARAB League, DISARMAMENT-Geneva Committee, NONALIGNED Nations Movement, OAU, OPEC*
Benjedid elected pres 2-7, 94B2
Benjedid names Cabt 3-8, 215E2
Liberalizatn moves rptd 5-11, 522A3
Ben Bella freed 7-4, 521E3
Revolutn marked 11-1, 842B2
Foreign Relations (misc.)—*See also 'Oil' and 'UN' below*
Mauritania ties restored 8-14, 626G3
Libya fete attended by Arab ldrs 9-1, 688C3
Iran premr visits 11-1, 842B2
Envoy sees US hostages in Iran 11-10, 862A2
Algiers archbishop in Iran 12-24—12-27, 975B1
Oil & Gas Developments—*See also OPEC*
24% price hike request rptd 3-5, 162D1
Sweden seeks LNG deal cancelatns 3-13, 213F3
Prices, surchrg hiked 3-27, 227C3
Prices hiked 13% 5-21, 396D2
Prices hiked again 6-28, 473F1
Spain '79 imports forecast 7-10, 546B2
Oil output cut rptd 7-30, 645D2
Prices hiked above OPEC limit 10-24, 864G1
Price per barrel rptd 12-21, 977A2
Sahara Conflict—*See SAHARA*
UN Policy & Developments
Membership listed 695D2
U.S. Relations
ISC paymts alleged 7-9, 541F3
US aide visits, sees Iran premr 11-1, 842D2
Envoy visits US hostages in Iran 11-10, 862A2

1980

Bauman, Talmadge lose reelectn 11-4, 846B2, 849G2
Pope in W Ger, warns vs abuse 11-15—11-19, 905G2
France sets anti-alcoholism effort 12-10, 942F1
ALCOHOLISM, National Council on
Marty Mann dies 7-22, 608D2
ALCORN State University (Lorman, Miss.)
Young in NFL draft 4-29, 336G3
ALCOTT, Amy
2d in Winners Circle 4-6, Women's Intl 5-4, Lady Michelob 5-11; wins Amer Defender 4-13, 412C3, F3, G3
2d in Boston 5 Classic 6-15, WUI 7-27; wins Mayflower 7-6, 715B1-E1
Wins US Women's Open 7-13, 714A3
Wins Inamori Classic 10-12, Pioneer Cup 11-2, Vare Trophy 12-9, 971D3, 972D2, F2
LPGA top money winner 10-12, 971F3
ALDAMA, Andres
Wins Olympic medal 8-2, 622G1
ALDERMANN, Evan
Ousted from Australia Cabt 11-2, 857F2
ALDREDGE, Theoni V.
Wins Tony 6-8, 692C3
ALEINIK, Vladimir
Wins Olympic medal 7-28, 623F3
ALEMAN v. U.S.
Cases declined by Sup Ct 3-24, 265C1
ALEVAR, Bishop Estevao
'79 attack rptd 1-11, 95C3
ALEX, Jane
2d in LPGA Team tourn 10-5, 972D2
ALEXANDER, Jane
Goodbye Fidel opens 4-23, 392G2
ALEXANDER, Matthew
Tricks of the Trade opens 11-16, 892G3
ALEXANDER Jr., Rep. William Vollie (D, Ark.)
Reelected 11-4, 842C1
ALEXANDER L. Keilland (oil platform)
Capsizes, 123 killed 3-27, 256D1
ALEXANDROV, Anatoly Petrovich
On A-plant constructn lag 1-25, 79G3
ALEXANDROV, Roumen
Wins Olympic medal 7-27, 624F2
ALEXANDRU, Constantin
Wins Olympic medal 7-22, 624G2
ALFA Romeo S.p.A.
Nissan project OKd 9-20, 751B3
AL Fatah—*See PALESTINIANS*

ALGERIA—*See also ARAB League, GENEVA Committee, NONALIGNED Nations, OAU, OPEC*
Cabt, staff shifted 1-13, 55F3
Econ chngs, more Arabic use planned; Arabic student unrest cited 1-14, 55F2
Berbers riot, chrg repressn 4-7—4-24, 334A1
Quakes hit 10-10; death toll rptd at 20,000 10-14, 775G3-776G1
Ben Bella freed from prison 10-30, 870E1
Foreign Relations (misc.)—*See also 'Oil & Gas', 'UN Policy' below*
Tunisia blames Libya re attack 1-28, 90B1
Syria says Israel plans attack 2-23, 140C3
Arab hardliners meet 4-14—4-15, 284F2
US, France, Morocco blamed for Berber riots 4-24, 334D1
Jamaica bauxite deal rptd 6-4, 465G1
Sahara dispute condemned by OAU, Polisario entry shelved 7-1—7-4, 509E1
Saudi urges holy war vs Israel 8-14, 627A3
Leb cleric kidnaper jailed 9-9, 709D1
Quake aid begins 10-11, 776E1
Palestinian rights, Israel exit from Jerusalem urged 11-28, 950F2
Sovt '79 arms sales rptd 12-10, 933A3
Spain recognizes Polisario 12-17, 995E3
Iran-U.S. Hostage Issue
Iran names as intermediary on US hostage release 11-2; Malik delivers terms 11-3, 853F2, B3
US offcls in Algiers 11-10—11-11; Iran gets response to hostage demands 11-12, 861A1
Hostage talks in US 11-26—11-27, Algiers 12-2—12-3; US rpts 12-4, 912E3-913A1

1976

Rpt Libya annexes border area 9-9, 696F2
New const OKd 11-19, 902E1
Boumedienne reelected 12-10, 1012C2
Guinea names amb 12-11, 1005A2
Iraq's Hussein visits 12-14, 954A1
Middle East Conflict—*See MIDDLE EAST*
Sahara—*See SAHARA*
UN Policy & Developments
UNESCO literacy drive fails 2-4, 85C2
Vs Israel, S Africa at UNCTAD conf 5-5, 320C2
ALI, Abu
Killed 7-3, named as hijacker 7-5, 485C1, F2
ALI, Lt.-Gen. Beshir Mohamed
Named Sudan defense min 8-9, 857F2
ALI, Muhammad
Carter, Artis get new trial 3-17, 256G3
Beats Young, Dunn 4-30, 5-25, 424B3
Decisns Norton 9-28, 756C2
ALI Aref Bourhan
'75 assassinatn attempt rptd 1-6, 86B1
Asks contd French mil role 1-8, 85E3
In Paris; bars new electns, scores Socialists 1-23, 85F3
13 die in tribal clash 7-10, 519F2 ★
Resigns 7-17, replaced 7-29, 696A2, C2 ★
ALIENS—*See IMMIGRATION & Refugees*
ALIER, Abel
Cabt shuffled 2-10, 502D1
Rpts mil plot crushed 4-12, 502B1
ALIYEV, Geidar A.
Politburo alternate member 3-5, 195D2
ALLAF, Mowaffak
Asks chng in UN resolutn 242 1-13, 18B2 ★
Scores US UN veto 1-26, 59F3 ★
Vs UN fact-finders to Mideast 3-4, 162A1
ALL Africa Conference of Churches
Ethiopia deposes patriarch 2-18, arrest rptd 3-1, 173D1
ALLANA, Ghulam Ali
Chile rights abuse chrgd 2-10, 310C1
ALLARD, Henry
Accepts Palme resignation 9-20, 714D1
ALLEGHENY County, Pa.—*See PENNSYLVANIA*
ALLEGHENY Ludlum Industries Inc.
Top steel makers hike prices 11-24—11-29, 897F2
Titanium price-fixing rptd 12-5, 988A2
ALLEN, Bruce
'72 campaign gift listed 4-25, 688D1
ALLEN, Charles
Malagasy ousts 9-23, 926A1
ALLEN, Rep. Clifford (D, Tenn.)
Reelected 11-2, 830B4
ALLEN, Ethel D.
Seconds Ford nominatn 8-18, 597G2
ALLEN, Sen. James B. (D, Ala.)
Sees food-stamp bill veto 4-8, 282E3
GOP conv vp vote table 8-19, 599F3
Sen OKs rights-suit fees bill 9-29, 788D2
ALLEN, John F.
Indicted 2-18, stiffer penalties asked 10-5, 886E1; sentncd 11-30, 921F2

1977

W Ger asks more Algiers airport security 10-23, Frankfurt flight canceled 11-8, 868D3, E3
France drops immigrant curb plan 10-30, 1013E1
Cuba med aides rptd 11-17, 896F1
Egypt recalls amb 12-4, cuts ties 12-5, 929A1, C2
Sahara—*See SAHARA*
U.S. Relations
US natl resentenced 1-25, 139D3
US gas imports set 2-4, 91B3
US FPC OKs gas imports 4-29, 370C1
Haynes confrmd US amb 5-9, 418E1
US to challenge USSR role 6-10, 460D2
ALI, Muhammad
Decisns Evangelista 5-16, 395A1
Decisions Shavers 9-29, 827C3
At Pele tribute 10-1, 827D2
Shavers match telecast probed 11-2, 949F3
Spinks decisns Righetti, '78 fight set 11-18, 970C2, D3 ★
WBC softens threat 12-1, 970B2
'77 boxing champion 12-17, 970A2, A3
ALI, Tariq
Chrgs Dobson bias 10-20, 864A1
ALIA, Queen (Jordan)
Killed in air crash 2-9, 87D1
ALI Abdul-Khail, Muhammad
On Saudi IMF loan plan role 5-3, 5-4, 363F1
ALI Aref Bourhan
Coalitn slate backing rptd 5-7, 363A3
ALIENS—*See IMMIGRATION & Refugees*
ALIER, Abel
Chrgs forgn role in coup try 2-6, 117D2
ALI Khan, Chief Justice Yakub
OKs Bhutto arrest petitn 9-20, ousted 9-22, 765A3
ALIM, Maj. Abdullah Abdul
In N Yemen ruling cncl 10-10, 784A1
ALIOTO, Joseph L.
Wins libel award 5-3, 532B2
ALI Youssouf, Ismael
Named Djibouti justice min 7-15, 583C2
ALLAF, Mouaffak el-
Scores Sadat, Egypt envoy walks out 11-22, 894G1
ALL Africa Council of Churches
Carr scores Uganda deaths 2-17, 2-19, 139A1
Scores Africa silence re Uganda deaths 3-18, 308B3
ALLEGED (race horse)
Wins Arc de Triomphe 10-2, 971G1-A2
ALLEGHENY Ludlum Industries Inc.
Steelworkers OK contract 4-9, 273G2
Wins Chemetron control 9-8, 880C2
ALLEN Jr., Charles
Group wins Irvine Co 5-20, 519C1, E1
ALLEN, Sen. James B. (D, Ala.)
Votes vs Marshall 1-26, 52B3
Anti-pay hike attempt fails 2-2, 127F2
Scores Panama Canal talks 7-29, 589G3
Canal wiretap hearings postponed 9-30, 756E1
Vs US-Panama aid pacts 10-28, for House Canal treaty vote 11-3, 912G1, B2
ALLEN, June
Va A-plant safety cover-up rptd 9-30, 838E1

1978

Zaire chrgs Shaba rebel aid 5-14, 359A2
Arab fund loan to Sudan rptd 8-17, 925F3
US rejcts natural gas imports 12-18, 983E3
Obituaries
Kaid, Ahmed 3-5, 252A3
Sahara—*See SAHARA*
Sports
Egypt team attacked at games, Egypt athletes to boycott 7-24, 573C1
UN Policy & Developments
Leb peace force support rptd 3-20, 198F2
Assemb member 713B3
U.S. Relations
CIA spying on Black Panthers rptd 3-17, 243G2
ITT paymts chrgd 11-2, 876C1
Carter lauds Boumedienne 12-27; Blumenthal at funeral 12-29, 1012C3
ALGORITHM—*See MATHAMATICS*
ALI, Prince (Jordan)
Named Hussein successor 6-8, 580C1
ALI, Lt. Gen. Kamel Hassan
Promoted 10-3, assumes office 10-5, 774A3
In Israel pact talks 10-12—10-18, 782C2
Recalled from Israel talks 11-21, 892E2
ALI, Moses
Amin scores 4-28, 331E3
Rpts '77 coffee productn 6-24, 616G2
Dismissal rptd 7-26, 616A3
ALI, Muhammad
Loses heavywgt title to Spinks 2-15, 171B1-C2
Asks Spinks rematch 3-4, fight set 3-8, 211C3-212C1
Spinks rematch plan protested 3-8, site shifted 3-9, 212E1
Spinks rematch contract signed 4-11, 378E3
Holmes wins WBC heavywgt title 6-9, 600C1, F1
Decisns Spinks for 3d heavywgt title 9-15, TV viewing mark rptd 9-20, 726B1, E2
Holmes KOs Evangelista 11-10, 969C1
At Boumedienne funeral 12-29, 1012C3
ALICE, Mary
Nongogo opens 12-3, 1031F2
ALIENS—*See IMMIGRATION & Refugees*
ALIERZA, Ali Abdallah
Denies Saudis favor PLO raid vs Israel 3-13, 176E1
ALIKHANIAN, Artemi I.
Dies 2-25, 196B2
ALIMONY—*See DIVORCE*
ALIOTO, Joseph
Rice dealer chrgd 5-26, 432G3
ALIOTO, Kathleen Sullivan
Loses Sen primary in Mass 9-19, 736B3
ALIQUIPPA, Pa.—*See PENNSYLVANIA*
ALITALIA Airlines
108 die in crash off Sicily 12-23, 1031G3
ALL-America Basketball Alliance (AABA) (defunct)—*See BASKETBALL—Professional*
ALLARD, Henry
Falldin submits resignatn 10-5, 764F2
ALLBRITTON, Joseph L.
FCC OKs WJLA, KOCO-TV exchng 1-12, Time rpts Washn Star purchase agrmt 2-3; FCC scores 2-13, 109F2, ★ D3 ★
WJLA-TV swap OKd again 3-9, halts deal 3-24, 270A3
Resigns as Washn Star publisher 5-31, 672D2
ALLEGHANY Corp.
Kirby-Murchison '60 proxy fight cited 3-24, 402A3
ALLEGHENY Airlines
Nader '73 'bumping' case award cut 1-10, 67F3-68A1
ALLEGHENY Ludlum Industries Inc.
Vice pres rptd in Muzorewa plea 5-2, 317E2
Drops Chemetron unit sale plan 10-24, 897E1
ALLEGHENY Power System Inc.
Monongahela W Va power plant scaffold collapses 4-27, 459G3
ALLEGRUCCI, Don
Wins Kan Cong primary 8-1, 606G1
ALLEN, Rep. Clifford R. (D, Tenn.)
Dies 6-18, 540D2
Boner wins seat 11-7, 853E1
ALLEN, Corey
Avalanche released 8-28, 969B3
ALLEN, George
Fired as Redskins coach, gen mgr 1-18; joins Rams 2-1, 171E2
Fired as Rams coach 8-13, 1024F2
ALLEN, Sen. James B. (D, Ala.)
Seeks Canal pact amendmts 2-8, procedural ploy defeated 2-22, 120E1, E3
Votes vs Canal neutrality pact 3-16, 177F2, 178G1
Votes vs 2d Canal pact 4-18, 273B1
Dies 6-1, widow named to seat 6-8, 432E1-G1
Widow faces primary runoff 9-5, 699F1
Widow loses runoff 9-26, 769E1
Stewart wins seat 11-7, 849A3
ALLEN Jr., Gen. Lew
Named AF Chief of Staff 4-5, 281A2
Rpts new US land-based missile plan 7-12, 528G3
MAP missile backing rptd 9-23, 737G3

1979

ALI, Kamel Hassan
In Israel, US talks on Sinai pullout 3-18—3-19, 198F1
Says Saudis made down paymt for US jets 360B1
Sees Weizman on Sinai exit 4-25—4-27, 320D1
Palestinian autonomy talks open 5-25, 394F1
Egypt, Israel, US Sinai pact set 9-18, 694D1
Lauds US arms shipments 10-6, 762D3
ALI, Muhammad
Retires from boxing 6-26, Tate wins WBA heavywgt title 10-20, 838F2-A3
ALI, Salamat
Arrested 11-14, sentncd 11-29, 951F1
ALIBRANDI, Antonio
Suspends bank offcl 4-17, 313D2
ALICE in Wonderland (book)
But Never Jam Today opens 7-31, 711G1
ALIEN (book)
On best-seller list 7-1, 548D3
ALIEN (film)
Released 5-24, 527G3
Top-grossing film 6-27, 548G3
ALIENS—*See IMMIGRATION & Refugees*
ALIMONY—*See DIVORCE*
ALIQUIPPA and Southern Railroad v. ICC
Case refused by Sup Ct 3-19, 203D2
ALITALIA (Italian airline)
Leb Moslems hijack jet 9-7, surrender in Iran 9-8, 677B3
ALKATH Corp.
Argent, Karat, Fremont units fined 8-23, 851A1
Argent sale completed 12-10, 965B1
ALLAN, Rasa
What the Devil opens 4-16, 712E3
ALLAN, Robert
Bent opens 12-2, 1007C2
ALLARD, Alain
Returns to Canada 12-23, chrgd re bombings 12-24, 992F3
ALLBRITTON, Louise
Dies 2-16, 176E2
ALLEGHENY Airlines Inc.
Name chng OKd 6-5, 465G2
Montreal flight cuts warned 8-24, 651C1
ALLEN, Al
Sentncd in GSA kickback scandal 3-28, 367A3
ALLEN, Bryan
Pedals aircraft across Eng Channel 6-12, 527F3
ALLEN, Charles J. (Jim)
Sentenced in GSA scandal 8-3, 964G3
ALLEN Jr., Maj. Gen. Frank A.
Dies 11-20, 932A2
ALLEN, Fred (1894-1956)
Minerva Pious dies 3-16, 272E3
ALLEN, Irwin
Beyond the Poseidon Adventure released 5-24, 528D1
ALLEN, Janis
Meatballs released 7-3, 820A2
ALLEN, Jimmie Lee
Chrgd in Bedford Hills (NY) slayings 7-19, 548F1
ALLEN, Maj. Gen. Levin C.
Dies 9-27, 756A2

1980

Iran demands US $10 bln deposit for hostage return 12-19, 973B1
Aide, Iran prelate visit hostages 12-25—12-26, 974E1
Algerians take new US hostage plan to Iran 12-31, 973E2
Oil & Gas Developments
Import limits, conservatn planned 1-14, 55G2
Oil price hike set 6-11, 435A3
France LNG deal rptd set 9-7; Dutch, W Ger plan canceled 9-11, 827A3, C3
Africa exports vowed 11-9, 864D2
UN Policy & Developments
Anti-Sovt Afghan abstentns 1-14, 25F2; 2-14, 123E3
Bedjaoui on comm to probe shah 2-17, 122C1
U.S. Relations—*See also 'Iran-U.S. Hostage Issue' above*
US blamed for Berber riots 4-24, 334D1
Iran ex-aide slain 7-22, assassin sought 7-23, 545D2
Quake aid rptd 10-11, 776E1
ALHEGELAN, Sheik Faisal
Protests 'Death of a Princess' telecast 5-8, 375F2
Vs US stand on F-15 gear 7-9, 538B3
Vs Carter F-15 gear stance 10-30, 821E1
ALI, Chaudhri Mohammed
Dies 12-1, 1003G3
ALI, Kamel Hassan
Offers US mil bases 1-7, 11F1
Rpts US '79 joint air exercises 1-8, 11D1
Says Egypt trains Afghan rebels 2-13, 123D1
Named forgn min, dep premr 5-15, 389A2
Autonomy talks renewal OKd 7-2—7-3, 539D1
Vs Israel vote on Jerusalem as capital 7-30, 572E3
Egypt seeks delay in autonomy talks, rejcts Israeli law on Jerusalem 8-3, 585C1
ALI, Muhammad
Named Athlete of Decade 1-13, announces comeback 3-3, 320G3
Amateur Club Olympic boycott vote rptd 1-18, 45D3
To promote Olympics boycott in Africa 1-31, 68F1
Rebuffed in Tanzania 2-3, 85C1
Holmes KOs 10-2, blames drug misuse 10-7, 771F3
With Carter in NY 10-20, 803B1
ALIBRANDI, Antonio
Orders loan fraud arrests 3-4, 173F1
ALIEN (film)
'79 top domestic rental film 2-6, 120G2
Wins Oscar 4-14, 296A2
ALIENS—*See IMMIGRATION & Refugees*
ALIKEN, Vladimir
Wins Olympic medal 2-19, 155D3
ALIMADI, Erifasi Otema
Confirms invasn 10-10, 794E2
ALLAN, Ted
Falling in Love Again released 11-21, 972D3
ALLARD, Alain
Sentenced 4-8, 310F3
ALLDER, Nick
Wins Oscar 4-14, 296A2
ALLEGHENY Ludlum Industries Inc.
USW contract settled 4-15, 289B2
Steel unit sale set 11-12, 985D2
ALLEN, James (d. 1978)
Denton wins US Sen seat 11-4, 849F1
ALLEN, Jay Presson
Just Tell Me released 2-8, 216A3
ALLEN, Karen
Cruising released 2-15, 216D2
Small Circle of Friends released 3-9, 216F3
ALLEN, Lewis
Billy Bishop opens 5-29, 756B3

1976

ALLEN, Richard V.
Nixon bid for Grumman donatn chrgd 9-13, denies 9-15, 979G1-D3
ALLEN, Timothy Charles
Arrested on drug chrg 8-24, 636A3
ALLEN, Ward P.
Dies 12-17, 1015A1
ALLENDE, Hortensia Bussi de (Mrs. Salvador)
Greets Mrs Torres in Mex 6-7, 456F2
Says junta killed Letelier 9-26, 781B1
ALLENDE, Jose Antonio
Scores Cordoba rightist terror 1-17, 96F1
Hendrix chrgd re ITT probe 11-5, 869G2

ALLENDE Gossens, Salvador (1908-73)
'70 CIA media manipulatn rptd 1-16, 92B3
Frei scored 1-21, 99D3
US aid rptdly continues 1-26, 99F2
Nephew in CR, Chile asks extraditn 2-2, 99G3
Nixon testimony released 3-11, 183G2
ITT rpts on '70 paymts 5-12, 361F1
Widow: junta killed Letelier 9-26, 781B1
Cuba exiles linked to Letelier murder 10-12, 780C3
'70 Anaconda offer rptd 12-23, 999A2
ALLERGAN Pharmaceuticals
Rpts foreign payoffs 3-19, 362E1
SEC lists forgn paymts 5-12, 726A2
ALLERGIES—*See 'Diseases' under MEDICINE*
ALLEYNE, Sidney Burnett
DLP bank payoffs alleged 8-28, 673B1
Seized re Barbados 'plot' 10-25, 962D1
ALLIANCE for Progress—*See under OAS*
ALLIED Chemical Corp.
Baltimore cancer deaths rptd 2-16, 224E3
Kepone poisoning probed 2-26, 171B3
Indicted re Kepone, other suits pending 5-7, 349A1
Barge capsizes off Va 8-18, 796F2
'75 tax paymt rptd 10-2, 847B2
Fined re Kepone 10-5, 767D3
US files consent decree 11-16, 989C1
Union Texas Petroleum
In Viet oil talks 4-24, 352B2
ALLIGATORS—*See WILDLIFE*
ALLIN, Bishop John Maury
Urges women's ordinatn compromise 9-11, 755C2
ALLISANDRATOS, A.D.
Defeated 11-2, 822D3
ALLMAND, W. Warren
Commons votes civiln death penalty end 7-14, 520G2
Sworn Indian affairs min 9-15, 692F1
ALL Nippon Airways Co. Ltd.
Denies Lockheed bribery chrgs 2-5, 2-16—2-17, 131F3, 132F1
Lockheed probes pressed, deals threatened 2-26, 3-1, 3-5, 190C3-E3, 191F1
3 seized in Lockheed case 6-22, 450A3
2 more seized in Lockheed case 7-7, 7-8, 497F2
Watanabe arrested 7-9, 3 execs indicted 7-13, 557A2
Tanaka arrested 7-27, 557F1
Wakasa, execs indicted 7-28, Aoki out on bail 8-17, 624A2, D2
Rep Sato arrested 8-20, 628C2
Govt Lockheed rpt omits Osano 10-15, 838B3
ALLON, Yigal
Meets Kissinger, says US vows UN veto vs PLO 1-7—1-9, 18E2, B3
Secret Zambia talks rptd leaked 35A1
Cabt OKs Avineri appointmt 2-15, 125G2
Vs Scranton UN speech 3-26, 227B3
Lauds Kadum closure 5-9, 338G1
Sees no Syria threat re Leb 6-13, 430C1
Vs Uganda re missing hostage 7-13, 515D3
Vs rpt on Galilee Arabs 9-13, 683F1, B2
Troop exit plan rptd 9-17, Cabt vs debate 9-21, 699D2
Offers peace plan at UN 10-7, 760B1
Meets Ford 10-11, 759A2
Scores US UN vote 11-12, 863B1
Doubts Sadat peace bid 11-16, 878E1
For Leb army border role 11-29, 894E2, A3
Lauds Sadat remark on Palestine 12-30, 973F1
ALLOWAY, Edward C.
Kills 7 in Calif, arrested 7-12, 860G1
ALLSTATE Insurance Co.—*See SEARS Roebuck*
ALLTRANSPORT Inc.
Boycott rpt released 10-18, 786A1
ALMEIDA, Cmdr. Julio (Juju) de
Sees MPLA victory 1-19, 35G3
On MPLA drive south 1-23, 57D1
ALMEIDA, Luis de
Lauds OAU Angola summit 1-13, 16F1
Confirms Cuba troop exit 5-25, 370D3
ALMEIDA e Costa, Cmdr. Vasco
Portugal interim premier 6-24, 482D3
ALMEYDA, Clodomiro
Greets Mrs Torres in Mex 6-7, 456F2
ALMON, John V.
Denver SWP break-in link rptd 7-30, 569A3
Rpt informts supervisn ends 8-11, 634A1

1977

ALLEN, Robert J.
Indicted 3-3, 204D1
ALLEN Associates, R.J.
Principals indicted 3-3, 204D1
ALLENDE, Beatriz
Dies 10-12, 871G3

ALLENDE Gossens, Salvador (1908-73)
CIA, US multinatls rptd vs '64 pres bid, bribes chrgd 1-9, 1-11, 18B2
Frei denies CIA paymt chrgs 2-21, 219C2
US aide regrets '73 coup role 3-8, repercussns 3-8—3-9, 218F3
Australia '72 coup role rptd 5-4, 372F1
Nixon-Frost interview 5-25, 419D3
Daughter dies 10-12, 871G3
Helms pleads no contest re '73 testimony 10-31, 838B3
ALL-England Lawn Tennis Championship (Wimbledon)—*See TENNIS*
ALLEN Township, O.—*See OHIO*
ALLIANCE for Energy Conservation—*See ENERGY Conservation, Alliance for*
ALLIED Chemical Corp.
Kepone fine cut, Va pollutn fund set 2-1, 95B1
Sup Ct backs EPA authority 2-23, 150A3
SEC sues re Kepone 3-4, 252E2
Va Kepone suits setld 10-13, 800C1
Allied-General Nuclear Services—*See separate listing*
ALLIED-General Nuclear Services
Carter bars SC A-plant aid 4-7, 267C3
ALLIN, Bishop John M.
Sees dissidents 8-16, 9-14—9-16, 731F2
Offers resignatn 9-30, bishops decline 10-5, 845G1
Fund drive scored 10-4, 845E2
ALLISON, Wilmer
Dies 4-20, 356F2
ALLMAND, W. Warren
Eskimos file new land claim 5-13, 411D1
Gets native prov plan 7-14, rejected 8-3; Trudeau scored 8-4, 616D2, G2
Backs Inuit in language dispute 8-31, 694A1
Canada consumer affairs min 9-16, 725A3
Opens Canada uranium cartel probe 10-3, 895G2
NDP bares '72 RCMP raid letter 11-2, 903F1
ALL Nippon Airways Co. Ltd.
Lockheed bribe trials open 1-27, 1-31, 83C2
ALLON, Yigal
On Sadat Jordan-Palestine plan 1-2, 10F1
Vs PLO contacts 1-3, 10G2
Vs Daoud release 1-11—1-13, 9F2, 27F2
Vs PLO at Geneva conf 1-19, 50E1
Warns Syria on troop moves 1-31, 72C1
Sends US protest on Syria 2-6, rpts troop pullback 2-13, 106B2
Vs UN peace role 2-7, 86B3
French ties reconciled 2-8, 87B1 ★
Signs EEC pact, scores terms 2-8, 146C1
Meets Waldheim 2-10, 86F2
Sees no Arab peace chng 2-11, 107F1
Vance visits 2-16—2-17, 121C1
Egypt scores Carter plan 3-10, 166E1
Defers premier bid 4-9, 267B2 ★
Warns Palestinians near border 4-12, 266F1
Sees Israel-US tensions 4-24, 316G1
US assures on ties 5-11, 360G3
Chrgs new US Mideast plan 5-29, 440B2
Sees US amb, vs Carter on UN resolutns 5-31, 440A2
Vs Begin peace plan 7-19, 549G2
Vs US-Sovt Geneva plan 10-2, 750D1
ALLRED, Rulon C.
Slain 5-10, 6 chrgd 9-27, 847F3
ALL the President's Men (film)
Wins Oscar 3-28, 264C1
ALL Things Wise and Wonderful (book)
On best-seller list 10-2, 808D3; 11-6, 872D3; 12-4, 1021G2
ALMEIDA, Sergio Cardosa de
Scores Geisel pol reforms 5-4, 523B3
ALMEYDA, Clodomiro
Sees Christopher 5-27, 493D1
ALMON, Bill
NL batting ldr 10-2, 926D3

1978

ALLEN, Acting Sen. Maryon Pittman (Mrs. James B.)
Husband dies 6-1, named to fill seat 6-8, 432F1
Faces primary runoff 9-5, 699F1
Loses runoff 9-26, 769D1
Stewart wins seat 11-7, 849A3
Gets low ADA rating 12-17, 981E2
ALLEN, Mel
Wins Frick broadcast award 8-8, 618A1
ALLEN, Melba Till
Indicted 3-21, 379G3
Convicted 5-24, 6-25, sentncd 6-8; ousted as Ala treas 6-9, 886F3
ALLEN, Nancy
Wanna Hold Your Hand released 4-21, 619E2
ALLEN, Woody
Wins Oscars 4-3, 315B3
Interiors released 8-2, 970F1

ALLENDE Gossens, Salvador (1908-73)
CIA press briefing detailed 1-4, 14B3
Battle of Chile released 1-12, 618C3
Letelier murder suspect linked 3-6, 188D3, F3
ITT execs sued, Helms plea cited 3-20, Korry, OPIC chrgs re CIA rptd 3-21, 206C3
Letelier murder suspect extraditn scored 4-21, 371C1
Chile land reform to end 10-6, 795B1
ITT Chile paymts chrgd 11-2, 876E2
ALL-England Lawn Tennis Championship (Wimbledon)—*See TENNIS*
ALLEN Motor Inn (Honesdale, Pa.)
Arson kills 11 11-5, 971C3
ALLENTOWN, Pa.—*See PENNSYLVANIA*
ALLERGIES—*See MEDICINE—Diseases*
ALLIANCE of Independent Telephone Unions—*See TELEPHONE Unions, Alliance of Independent*
ALLIED Chemical Corp.
In Dow Jones indl avg 66E2
ALLIED-General Nuclear Services
Barnwell (SC) A-plant protest 4-29—5-1, 347D1
ALLIED Printing Trades Council
NY strike ends 11-6, 865D1
ALLIED Structural Steel Co.
Minn pensn funds law voided by US Sup Ct 6-28, 567C1
ALLIED Structural Steel Co. v. Spannaus
Minn pensn funds law voided by US Sup Ct 6-28, 567B1
ALL in the Family (TV series)
Wins Emmy 9-17, 1030F1
ALLIS-Chalmers Corp.
Amer Air filter purchase set 7-28, 718F1
ALLISON, Bobby
Wins Daytona 500 2-19, 538A3
ALLMAND, W. Warren
RCMP '74 break-in bared 1-11, 35E2
RCMP '75 tap chrgd 2-22, called accident 2-27, 166G1
Held aware of RCMP illegalities 10-24, 837B2
ALL 'N' All (recording)
On best-seller list 2-4, 116G3
ALL-Nippon Airways Co. Ltd.
6 more tied to Lockheed scandal 1-30, 72D3
Nakasone cited in Lockheed case 10-26, 838F3
ALLON, Yigal
Vs Begin stand on Res 242 3-8, 156B3
Warns Syria on Leb 8-28, 674G1
ALL'S Well That Ends Well (play)
Opens 7-5, 760B1
ALL Things Wise And Wonderful (book)
On best-seller list 1-8, 24D3; 2-5, 116B3; 3-5, 195E3; 4-2, 272C3; 10-9, 800C3; 12-3, 971C1
ALMANN Ortiz, Fernando
Named CR econ min 3-4, 171A1
ALMOND, Lincoln
Nominated for RI gov 9-12, 716A3
Loses electn for RI gov 11-7, 847G3

1979

ALLEN, Rae
Father's Day opens 6-21, 711A3
ALLEN, Woody
Manhattan released 4-24, 528A3

ALLENDE Gossens, Salvador (1908-73)
Letelier murder trial begins 1-15, 58A1
US drops case vs ITT execs 2-8, 88D1; 3-7, 188A2
Turkish strikes banned 3-29, 333D2
Mass grave discovered at Yumbel 10-18, 789C1
ALL-England Lawn Tennis Championship (Wimbledon)—*See TENNIS*
ALLEN'S Creek: Unit 1—*See TEXAS–Atomic Energy*
ALLEREST—*See MEDICINE–Drugs*
ALLERGIES—*See MEDICINE–Diseases*
ALL-European Conference
'80 mtg backed in SALT II communique 6-18, 458A2
ALL Fly Home (recording)
Jarreau wins Grammy 2-16, 336E3
ALLIANCE for Safe Available Future Energy (ALLSAFE)
Sponsors pro-nuclear rally in Calif 10-13, 806D3
ALLIANZ-Versicherungs A.G.
Allianz of America Inc.
To buy N Amer Life 5-11, Fidelity Union 6-25, 942C2
ALLIED Artists Industries
Bankruptcy petitn filed 4-4, 430G3
ALLIED Chemical Corp.
In Dow Jones indl avg 72E1
Fluorocarbon suit settled 1-5, 56G1
Indicted on kickbacks 4-17, 985B3
Eltra purchase set 6-28, 560G1
Connor on Pay Advisory Com 10-16, 829E2
ALLIED Structural Steel Co. v. Spannaus
Case cited by Sup Ct 10-15, 847F3
ALLIED Van Lines Inc.
Fined by ICC 1-15, 92B1
ALLINSON, Sir Leonard
Bars Zambia raid compensatn 11-20; emb attacked 11-22–11-23, recalled 11-24, 899G2, A3
ALLISON, Bobby
Wins Carolina 500 3-4, 491B1
ALLISON, Donnie
Crashes in Daytona 500, NASCAR fines 2-20, 490F3
Crashes in Carolina 500 3-4, 491A1
ALLMAND, W. Warren
Admits knew of RCMP break-ins 4-3–4-5, 311D2
Dare on '72 APLQ break-in 7-4, 522B3
ALL 'N' All (recording)
Earth, Wind & Fire win Grammy 2-16, 336E3
ALLRED, Rulon C. (d. 1977)
4 acquitted in '77 death, 2 sought 3-20, 240B2
ALL-Round Reduced Personality, The (film)
Released 4-23, 528A1
ALLSTATE Insurance Co. v. Kelly
Case refused by Sup Ct 6-11, 478G3
ALL That Jazz (film)
Released 12-20, 1007F2
ALL The President's Men (book)
'Brethren' publicatn stirs controversy 12-2, 988B2
ALL Things Bright and Beautiful (film)
Released 3-8, 528A1
ALMENDROS, Nestor
Wins Oscar 4-9, 336A2
ALMOND, Lt. Gen. Edward (Ned) M.
Dies 6-11, 508D2
ALMOST Perfect Affair, An (film)
Released 4-26, 528B1

1980

ALLEN, Neil
NL pitching ldr 10-6, 926G2
ALLEN, Richard V.
At GOP platform hearings, vs intelligence curbs 1-15, 32A2
Conflict-of-interest chrgd 10-28, quits Reagan post 10-20, 817E3
Named Reagan forgn policy advisor 11-6, 839F2
Reagan backs Camp David process 12-1, 930C3
Warns Sovts vs Poland mil interventn 12-2, 910A3
Disavows Percy's stance on Palestine 12-7, 936E1
Named natl security aide 12-23, 980A2
ALLEN, Woody
Stardust Memories released 9-26, 836F3
Side Effects on best-sellers list 12-7, 948E3
ALLEN & Co.
Kerkorian, Columbia shareholders file suits 9-30, 10-7; Columbia dirs countersue 10-2, 10-20, 906D2
ALLENDE, Andres Pascal
Accused in army officer's death 7-15, 563A1

ALLENDE Gossens, Salvador (1908-73)
'75-78 Chile econ recovery detailed 1-14, 19G1
Grenada scores overthrow 6-20, 498F2
Nephew accused of leftist activities 7-15, 563A1
Pinochet rule scored 8-27, 9-2, 669F2
Chile to repay Soviet debt 11-26, 965A2
ALL-England Lawn Tennis Championship (Wimbledon)—*See TENNIS*
ALLEN v. McCurry
Case decided by Sup Ct 12-9, 937B1
ALLERGIES—*See MEDICINE--Diseases*
ALLERGY, American Academy of
Faster hay fever treatmt rptd 2-18, 159G3
ALLEY Theater (Houston)
Nina Vance dies 2-18, 176G3
ALLIED Chemical Corp.
In Dow Jones indl avg 76E1
La chem-dump suit names 7-15, 558G3
ALLIN, Michael
Flash Gordon released 12-5, 972E3
ALL-Indian Pueblo Council
Bush addresses 9-30, 781A2
ALLIS-Chalmers Corp.
UAW setlmt reached 3-15, 308A3
ALLISON, Bobby
2d in Daytona 500 2-17, 637D3
ALLMAND, W. Warren
RCMP tape rptd 4-24, 350F3
ALLODI, Federico
Chrgs Colombia rights harrassmt 1-17, 96F2
ALLON, Yigal
Dies 2-29, 175D3
ALL Out of Love (recording)
On best-seller list 9-10, 716E3; 10-8, 796B3
ALLRED, Gloria
Scores Navy lesbian probe 6-13, 517E3
ALLRED, Rulon C. (d. 1977)
Polygamist convicted of murder 5-28, sentenced 6-2, 502A3
ALL That Jazz (film)
Top-grossing film 2-27, 200G3; 4-23, 360B1
Wins Oscars 4-14, 296F1-A2
ALL You Need to Know About the IRS (book)
On best-seller list 4-6, 280B3; 5-4, 359E3
ALMADEN Vineyards Inc.
Winery strike ends 9-22, 747B3
ALMIRANTE, Giorgio
Naples advance rptd 7-22, 579E1
ALMOG, Zeev
On Israeli raids in Leb 5-8, 341A1

1976

ALOHA Airlines
CAB reporting penalty cited 12-29, 986G1
ALONSO Plaza, Fidel
Arrested 1-17, 54A3
Urges West support MPLA 1-30, 82B2
ALPKAYA, Gen. Emin
Quits AF post 3-5, denies Lockheed paymt 3-7, 192A2
Pleads innocent 4-7, 298G1
Acquitted 4-30, 322A3
ALSOGARAY, Alvaro
Asks Peron quit 2-10, 154E2
ALSOP, Judge Donald D.
Dismisses 3M chrgs 7-27, 566C2
ALSTON Jr., Philip H.
'70 Carter campaign donor 10-17, 804G3
ALSTON, Walter
Resigns 10-3, 816A1
ALTESOR, Alberto
'75 disappearance rptd 1-13, 55E3
ALTMANN, Klaus—*See BARBIE, Klaus*
ALTON Box Board Co.
Trust suit dvpts 2-18—10-5, 886F1, F2; Wolf sentncd 11-30, 921G2
ALTOONA, Pa.—*See PENNSYLVANIA*
ALUMINUM & Bauxite
US co sues Jamaica 1-13, 51G1
Brazil co starts operatns 1-16, 98F2
1st ¼ US profits rptd 4-29, 376C3
US-Jamaica conflict rptd 5-14, 522A2
Reynolds, Kaiser admit forgn paymts 6-2, 6-10, 690D1
French-Sovt aluminum plant deal set 7-3, 540E2
Alcoa discloses forgn paymts 7-9—7-19, 690C1-D2
Can co contracts extended 8-18, 670C1
Jamaica output, exports rptd down 10-1, 965F2
Dow drop, price hikes linked 11-10—12-31, 984D1
Alcoa, Reynolds up prices 11-29, 11-30; House plans hearings 12-2, 898F1, A2
Australia refinery set 12-9, 961G3
ALUMINUM Co. of America (ALCOA)
Kaiser, Reynolds admit forgn paymts 6-2, 6-10, 690D2
Discloses forgn paymts 7-9, US amb to Jamaica implicated 7-16, 7-19, 690C1-D2
Ford admits golf trip 9-28, 722D3
'75 tax paymt rptd 10-2, 847A2
Raises can-metal prices 11-29, 898F1
ALVAREZ, Frank G.
Arrested 5-15, 401D2
ALVAREZ, Santiago
Arrested 6-3, 459F1
Freed 8-4, 753G2
ALVAREZ, Sebastian
Scores Cuba exile indictmts 11-2, 843G3
ALVAREZ Penaranda, Gen. Raul
Bolivia army chief 1-6, 26G3
Scores Reque 5-15, Reque rebuts 5-17, 415E3
ALVARIZA, Carlos
Rptd tortured to death 3-5, 207D3
ALVEAR, Bishop Enrique
DINA abuse chrgs rptd 6-3, 465F1
ALVES, Maj. Vitor
FLA mars Azores visit 1-28, 143A3
ALVSNABBEN (Swedish warship)
In Intl Naval Review 7-4, 488C3
ALY, Koussai Said
Malagasy soc affairs min 8-20, 926C1
ALYESKA Pipeline Service Co.
Alaska pipeline problems assessed 5-21—9-10, repairs rptd 7-15, 690G2-691B2
Ups pipeline cost estimate 6-30, 691B2
AMALGAMATED Clothing and Textile Workers Union—*See CLOTHING and Textile, etc.*
AMALGAMATED Transit Union—*See TRANSIT Union, Amalgamated*
AMALRIK, Andrei
Arrested 2-21, seeks emigratn 4-8, chrgs harassmt 4-12, 313F3
Scores Uruguay rights abuse 5-10, 441A2
Emigrates to Netherlands 7-15, 540G2
AMALRIK, Gyusel
Emigrates to Netherlands 7-15, 540G2
AMATEUR Athletic Federation, International (IAAF)
Expels S Africa 7-22, 562B2

1977

ALSOP, Joseph
On CIA-link charge 9-12, 721A1, B1
ALSOP, Stewart
CIA link charged 9-12, 721A1
ALSTON Jr., Philip Henry
Named amb to Australia 4-7, confrmd 4-29, 418B1
Whitlam mtg on CIA role rptd 8-4, 632G3
ALSTON, Miller & Gaines
Spann installed ABA pres 8-10, 630A2
ALTERNATIVE, The (book)
Writer seized 8-23, 684F1
ALTHER, Lisa
Kinflicks on best-seller list 4-3, 264A2; 5-1, 356D2
ALTMEIER, Peter
Dies 8-28, 696B2
ALTUNIN, Gen. Alexander
Promoted 2-16, 306D3
ALUMINUM & Bauxite
EC, 3 Arab natns sign pact 1-18, 73G3
Alcan strike pact reached 1-31, 114D2
Jamaica buys Kaiser, Reynolds assets 2-2, 3-31; other deals planned 2-10, 257F2
NW hydroelec cuts asked 2-11, 244D3
New USW pacts reached 5-24, 421F3
Alcan expansn set 5-31, 425B1
Prices hiked, previous rise cited 6-14—6-21, Admin scores 6-14, 577F1
Australia refinery canceled 7-7, 523F1-A2
Guyana-E Ger dvpt pact rptd 7-11, 710C3
Drought-related job loss rptd 7-28, 659E3
Venez bauxite find rptd 8-22, 674F2
Venez to buy Jamaica aluminum 9-2, 884E3
US-USSR 1st ½ trade rptd 9-12, 766B2
CPSC sues elec wire makers 10-27, 900C3
Surinam plans econ expansn, bauxite dependence cited 10-31, 905F3
US Jamaican death plots rptd, denied 11-2, 884G1
10 natns set base bauxite price 12-7, 975D1
Revere sale to Alcan challenged 12-9, 1004E3
ALUMINUM Co. of America (ALCOA)
Hikes prices 3-25, 4-4, 6-17, 577F1
New USW pact reached 5-24, 422E1
Australia refinery canceled 7-7, 523F1-A2
ALVA Orlandini, Javier
Scorns pol, econ plan 2-25, 241C2
ALVAREZ, Elio
US beaten in Davis Cup 4-29—5-1, 353D3
ALVAREZ Arena, Lt. Gen. Felix
Aide fired re CP protest 4-20, 307B1
ALVAREZ Berla, Col. Oscar
Loses consumer post 6-15, business enmity rptd 7-1, 565F3
ALVAREZ Dominguez, Luis
Venez dvpt min 1-7, 23E2
ALVAREZ Geoffrey, Carlos
Kidnaped 8-11, freed 8-19, 710F2
ALVAREZ Icaza, Jose
Police raid rights group 7-7, anti-church campaign chrgd 8-4, 746F1
ALVAREZ Miranda, Fernando
Elected Spain Chamber ldr 7-13, 545D2
ALVAREZ Rojas, Federico
US science acad seeks info 4-27, 315A2
ALVAREZ Ruiz, Donaldo
Admits pol violence spreading 8-18, MLN seeks censure 8-23, 672G3
ALVAREZ Torres, Gen. Francisco
Venez defense min 1-7, 23E2
Replaced as defense min 7-15, 566C1
ALVAREZ Zalba, Brig. Gen. Manuel
Fired 4-20, 307A1
ALVES, Nito
Purged 5-21, rebellion backs 5-27, 424F1
Rebelln detailed 6-20, 484B2
Seeks UNITA union 6-26, 522D2
ALYESKA Pipeline Service Co.
FPC splits on gas pipe route 5-2, 369C3
Transport costs disputed 6-1—6-17, 477B1, G1
Pipeline opens, cost estimated; map 6-20, 476A2, D2
ICC rejcts rate bids 6-28, 497F3-498F1
Explosn, 1 killed 7-8; offcls comment 7-10, 537C3
US OKs reopening 7-18, 558C3
Rpts on pipe blasts, damages 7-20, 627E3
ICC price ceiling upheld 7-29, 628D1
Pipe constructn waste chrgd 8-7, 627A3
AMALRIK, Andrei
Protests French policy 2-23, 2-24, 143A1
AMANRICH, Gerard
Slays family 2-1, self 4-19, 312E3

1978

ALONTO, Abul Kair
Challenges Moslem rebel ldrshp 650A2
ALONZO, John A.
FM released 4-28, 619A2
ALOUABA, Kumbha
Run'ers' opens 5-3, 887A3
ALP, Orhan
Named Turkey indus min 1-5, 21F2
Forgn investmt invited 10-19, 10-26, 840F2
ALPER, Jonathan
Safe House opens 4-13, 760C3
ALT, Rev. Ernst
Convicted in exorcism death 4-21, 379E3
ALTAMIRANO Duque, Tomas
Panama housing min 10-12, 884B2
ALTEC Corp.
Garmon kills self 1-21, 96A2
ALTMAN, A. Arthur
Coolest Cat opens 6-23, 760F1
ALTMAN, Jean
Coolest Cat opens 6-23, 760F1
ALTMAN, Robert
Wedding released 9-29, 970D3
ALTO, Vincent R.
On GSA scandal 8-30, 685G1
Evaluates GSA probe 11-13, steps down 11-14, 899E1
Borowski named successor 11-13, 899B2
ALTOBELLI, Joe
Named NL top mgr 10-24, 928B2
ALTON, Ill.—*See ILLINOIS*
ALTON Box Board Co.
Indicted for price fixing 1-25, 67C2
Fined 10-13, 1005G2
ALUMINUM & Bauxite
NW productn resumed 1-10, 1-11, 24E1
Caricom dvpt plans fail; Venez-Jamaica deal, Trinidad smelter set 1-13, 100F2, A3
Jamaica to get Hungary aid; plans Mex, Venez sales 2-28, 194E2
Australia bauxite mine planned 3-22, 225E1
Sovt '77 top export to US 3-29, 229G3
Wire dispute refused by Sup Ct 10-2, 751E1
Australia export plan set 10-24, 836B1
Australia Alcoa plant expansn planned 12-14, 963G2
Guinea-USSR bauxite trade noted 12-20, 1018B1
ALUMINUM Co. of America (Alcoa)
In Dow Jones indl avg 66E2
Washn productn lines reopen 1-10, 24F1
Australia bauxite revenue tax proposed 7-20, 570F2
Australia plant expansn set 12-14, 963G2
ALUNNI, Corrado
Chrgd in Moro case, sought by police 6-6, 689C2
Arrested 9-13, sentncd 9-20, 733F3
ALVAREZ, Gen. Domingo
In Honduras mil junta 8-7, 614A3
ALVAREZ, Gen. Gregorio
Uruguay army chief 3-2, 292D1
Sees civiln pol consultatns 3-27, 537B3
Intelligence chief fired, arrested 6-25, 537A3
ALVAREZ, Dr. Luis Walter
Father dies 6-18, 540D2
ALVAREZ, Dr. Walter Clement
Dies 6-18, 540D2
ALVAREZ Bogaert, Fernando
Quits as DR vice pres nominee 5-5, 354F2
Loses sugar cncl post 8-25, 774C2
ALVAREZ Ruiz, Donaldo
Admits 'death squad' 6-30, 722G2 ★
Keeps Cabt post 7-21, 722C3 ★, D3 ★
ALVEAR, Bishop Enrique
Banned union workers backed 10-23, 1014G2
Rpts bodies in lime kiln 12-6; 27 rptd unearthed 12-12, 1013G3
ALVES, Nito
MPLA party purge rptd 1-30, 87C3
ALWORTH, Lance
Enters Pro Football HoF 7-29, 1025C1
ALYDAR (race horse)
Loses Triple Crown 6-10, 539A1-A2
ALYESKA Pipeline Service Co.
On pipeline blast spill 2-17, 108D3
AM (Amplitude Modulation)—*See BROADCASTING—Radio*
AMA—*See AMERICAN Medical Association*
AMADO, Jorge
Dona Flor released 2-26, 619F1
AMADO, Juan Jose
Panama indus, commerce min 10-12, 884B2
AMADOR, Salvador
Death rptd 11-6, 883A2
AMALGAMATED Insurance Agency Services Inc.
US sues to bar Teamster contract 10-16, 792E1
US Teamster suit rejctd 11-1, 11-7, 899D1
AMALGAMATED Sugar Co.
'74 trust chrgs settled 6-12, 511C1
AMALGAMATED Wireless Ltd.
ICAO picks US bad-weather landing system 4-19, 319C3
AMARILLO, Tex.—*See TEXAS*
AMATEUR Athletic Federation, International—*See TRACK & Field*

1979

ALPERT, Herb
Rise on best-seller list 10-3, 800E3; 11-7, 892E3
ALPHAND, Herve
Wife dies 2-15, 176E2
ALPHAND, Nicole (Mrs. Herve)
Dies 2-15, 176E2
ALSEA, Ore.—*See OREGON*
ALSOP, Judge Donald
Bars Planned Parenthood funds ban 2-23, 310D2
ALTAMIRANO, Carlos
'75 assassinatn plot cited 1-18, 58D1, G2
ALTMAN, Anatoly
Release cited 4-29, 317D2
ALTMAN, Robert
Quintet released 2-8, 174D3
Perfect Couple released 4-5, 528C3
ALTOBELLI, Joe
Fired as Giants mgr 9-6, 1002F1
ALUMINUM & Bauxite
Australia rejects bauxite floor price 1-9, 18D3
Alcoa false ad chrgs settled 1-10, 91G2
Alcoa price hike deferral rptd 3-15, 182A2
Australia plans smelter 4-20, 311D1
Iran industries natlzd 7-5, 503F2
Guyana strike prompts pol crisis, world supply data rptd 7-23—8-28, 687G1
Alusuisse acquires Maremont 7-30, 770G2
Alcan Australia smelter studied 8-3, 600A1
Jamaica bauxite output down, tax halved 10-9, 996D1
ALUMINUM Co. of America (Alcoa)
In Dow Jones indl avg 72E1
False ad chrgs settled 1-10, 91G2
Price hike deferral rptd 3-15, 182A2
ALUSUISSE—*See SCHWEIZERISCHE Aluminum*
ALVARADO, Trini
Rich Kids released 8-17, 820B3
ALVAREZ, Jose Antonio (Tony)
Indicted in arms plot 5-14, 386E3
ALVAREZ, Walter
Links dinosaur extinctn, extraterrestial event 5-28, 691B3
ALVAREZ Montalvan, Emilio
Proposed for Nicaragua junta 7-6, 504D1
ALVERTON (race horse)
Destroyed in Grand Natl 3-31, 448A3
ALZAGA, Raul
Death threats rptd 5-3, 350B3
AMA—*See AMERICAN Medical Association*
AMADO, Jorge
Sarava opens 2-11, 292F2
AMANA Refrigeration Inc.—*See RAYTHEON Co.*
AMATEUR Athletic Federation, International—*See specific sport (e.g., TRACK)*

1980

ALPERT, Herb
Wins Grammy 2-27, 296C3
ALSOP, Mary
Dies 10-14, 876A1
ALTER, Louis
Dies 11-3, 928G1
ALTMAN, Dr. Lawrence K.
Reagan interview publshd 6-11, 452E2
ALTMAN, Robert
Popeye released 12-12, 972F3
ALUMINUM & Bauxite
Alcoa suspends USSR smelter talks 1-3, 9G1
Australia projcts rptd 1-19, 56E1; 2-8, 95E1
France-India alumina pact set 1-28, 97B3
USSR buying noted 2-5, 85E1
Jamaican sales rptd up 4-7, 276F1
USW basic steel pact set 4-15, 289B2
Aluminum, senility link rptd 4-19, 416A1
Australia Aborigines protest mining 5-8, 371B1
Mex-Canada ventures agreed 5-27, 409D2
USW basic pact setld 5-30, 482D2*
Jamaica bauxite expansn, Algeria deal rptd 6-4, 465F1
Justice Dept aluminum trust suit rptd dropped 11-18, 916E3
Alusuisse buys Phelps Dodge Consolidated share 11-23, 985C2
ALUMINUM Co. of America (Alcoa)
In Dow Jones indl avg 76E1
USSR smelter talks suspended 1-3, 9G1
USW pact settled 5-30, 482F2
Jamaica bauxite expansn rptd 6-4, 465F1
ALUMINUM Workers International Union (AFL-CIO)
Basic contract setld 5-30, 482F2
ALUNNI, Corrado
Accused re Moro affair 1-2, 20G2
Escapes jail, recaptured 4-28, 353B1
Sentncd 6-22, 523C3
Alleged Front Line successor arrested 10-13, 791B3
ALUSUISSE
Phelps Dodge sells Consolidated Alum share 11-23, 985C2
ALVARADO Piza, Alejandro
Held hostage in El Salvador 1-11, freed 1-14, 38G3-39A1
CR Emb in El Salvador occupied 7-11, 563A3*
ALVAREZ, Choco
PR attends Moscow Olympics 6-29, 588B2
ALVAREZ, Luis
Proposes dinosaur extinctn theory 1-1, 415F1
ALVAREZ Cordoba, Enrique
Asks Mex support for leftists, scores US interventn 5-26, 444A3
Kidnaped, slain 11-27, 921E1
ALZAMORA Bejares, Cecilia
Kidnaped 7-26; freed, confrms rightist death squad 8-2, 603F2
Right-wing terrorists arrested 8-12, 618C3
AMA—*See AMERICAN Medical Association*
AMADEUS (play)
Opens 12-17, 1003G2
AMALFITANO, Joe
Hired as Cubs mgr 7-25, 926A2
AMALRIK, Andrei A.
Dies 11-11, 928G1
AMANTOVA, Ingrida
Wins Olympic medal 2-17, 156C1
AMARO da Costa, Adelino
Sworn Portugal defense min 1-3, 21E3
Dies in Lisbon plane crash 12-4, 923D1

1976

AMAX Inc.
Firm, chem unit indicted 6-29, 748E1
AMAYA, Mario Abel
Kidnaped 8-18, rescued 8-30, 672G1
Dies in jail 10-19, 996G1
AMBRO Jr., Rep. Jerome A. (D, N.Y.)
Reelected 11-2, 830F1
AMBROSIO, Giuseppe
Police free 6-16, 446B1
AMENDOLA, Georgia
Backs Italy NATO, EEC role 4-18, 297A1
AMERADA Hess Corp.
Indicted 6-1, 413D3, E3
Conn oil leak 12-28, 1014G1
AMERASINGHE, Hamilton Shirley
Elected UN Assemb pres 9-21, 718D3
Warns on world economy 12-22, 955A1
AMERICAN—*For organizations not listed below, see key words*
AMERICAN Academy of Arts & Letters—*See under ARTS & Letters, National Institute of*
AMERICAN Airlines, Inc.
Testifies at privacy comm probe 2-11—2-13, 151E2
St Thomas crash 4-27, 335F2
SEC lists paymts 5-12, 726B2
'74 zero tax paymt rptd 10-2, 847G1
Pregnancy bias ruling rptd 10-14, 943B3
Flagship Intl indicted 11-17, 989F2
CAB reporting penalty cited 12-29, 986G1
AMERICAN-Australian Association (N.Y.)
Hears Australia forgn min 3-17, 204A1
AMERICAN Bag & Paper Corp.
Indicted 10-29, 886C3
AMERICAN Bakeries Co.
Fortune rpts '75 stock mkt return 437E2
AMERICAN Ballet Theater
Blair dies 4-1, 484C3
AMERICAN Bankers Association (ABA)
Smith lobbying ties cited 2-17, 185F2
Volcker addresses 3-9, 185F3
Dole addresses 10-4, 743F1-A2
AMERICAN Bankshares Corp.
Rptd on FRB 'problem' list 1-22, 111C2
AMERICAN Bank & Trust Corp.
Rptd on FRB 'problem' list 1-22, 111C2
American Bank & Trust Co. (N.Y.)
Fails 9-15, sold 9-16; owners, money rptd missing 9-25, 940A1
AMERICAN Bank & Trust Co. (North Providence, R.I.)
Fails 11-16, 940F1

AMERICAN Bar Association (ABA)
Rosenberg unit formed 1-8, 70F2
Walsh backs judges' pay hike suit 2-13, 136F2
Conv: State of Judiciary message read 2-15, resolutns voted 2-16, 2-17, 136B3-137C1
Carter addresses 8-11, 585B2; disavows dumping memo 8-13, 616C3
Stanley named pres 8-11, 640G3
AMERICAN Beef Packers Inc.
Found guilty 1-21, 78B3
AMERICAN Brands Inc.
Bars boycott compliance 3-18, 747B2

AMERICAN Broadcasting Cos. Inc. (ABC)
US-Cuba baseball series barred 1-7, 23F1
Muskie rebuts Ford message 1-21, 40E1
Westin quits 1-26, 160E2
Polish joke case review denied 2-23, 169G3
Udall on Issues & Answers 3-7, 179A3
Hussein on Issues & Answers 4-4, 242F1
Walters signs $1 mln contract 4-22, 504A2
Rockefeller on Issues & Answers 5-2, 324E2
Wins Emmy sports awards 5-17, 460C2
Connally on Issues & Answers 8-8, 584E2
Frank Mariano dies 8-8, 892C3
Sees Ford nomination 8-17, 601E3
Anderson on Good Morning 8-17, 616G1
OKs debate coverage rules 9-19, 703C2
Airs 1st debate, summary; Reynolds on panel 9-23, 700E2-703A2
1st pres debate sound loss explained 9-24, 725F1
Walters moderates pres debate 10-22, 800A1
NBC, US in programming pact 11-17, 869B2
US asks FCC probe 11-23, 901E1

1977

AMATEUR Athletic Union (AAU)—*See specific sport (e.g., TRACK & Field)*
AMATO, Anthony
Loses Madison (Wis) mayoral race 4-5, 252F3
AMAURY, Emilien
Dies 1-2, 84E2
Parisien Libere strike ends 8-16, 654D3
AMAX Inc.
Montana coal lease revoked 1-13, 59A1
Price-fixing chrgs dismissed 6-10, 483D3, F3
US Metals unit struck 7-1, 558G1
FALN bomb found in NYC hq 8-8, 613G3
AMAYA, Mario Abel (d. 1976)
Solari exiled 5-1, 388E3
AMCHARI, Mahmoud el- (d. 1972)
Saleh slain 1-3, 9C1
AMERADA Hess Corp.
Alaska pipeline opens 6-20, 476B3
ICC sets Alaska pipeline rates 6-28, 498F1
Convicted 8-30, 691A3
Fined 9-16, 918F2
AMERICAN—*For organizations not listed below, see key words*
AMERICAN Academy of Arts and Letters—*See under ARTS and Letters, National Institute of*
AMERICAN Airlines, Inc.
'76 US air deaths rptd 1-13, 41G3
SEC paymts chrgs setld 2-9, 111F2
Pilot chrgd in '76 St Thomas crash 3-6, 312G1
CAB OKs 'Super-Saver' fares 3-15, 325D1
Flagship Intl fined 5-11, 504D2
CAB 'no-frills' rule review denied 5-16, 419C2
Mex slush fund rptd 5-17, 503A1
CAB procedures case review refused 10-3, 760B3
Stewardesses win pregnancy suit 10-3, 819B1
AMERICAN-Arab Association for Commerce and Industry
Hussein addresses 4-27, 316C1
Barnes dies 10-24, 872A1
AMERICAN Bag & Paper Corp.
No contest pleas cited 11-23, 918B3
AMERICAN Bank Note Co.
FALN bombs printing plant 3-21, 261A2
AMERICAN Bank & Trust Co.—*See BANK Leumi Trust Co.*

AMERICAN Bar Association (ABA)
Death penalty repeal resolutn rejctd 2-15, 594C3
Inmate rights rpt issued 4-26, 383C2
NYC conf hears Burger 5-27, 444C3
Sup Ct OKs legal fee ads 6-27, 538C3
Fed no-fault auto insurnc standards opposed 7-18, 595A1
Conv 8-4—8-11: Mondale, Bell address 8-8; grand jury chngs urged 8-9; ad rules set, pres installed 8-10, 629F3, 630A1-A2
Backs pot decriminalizatn 11-13, 972A3
AMERICAN Beef Packers Inc.
West convictn review denied 4-4, 341G3
'76 Fortune 500 list drops 341D1
AMERICAN Brands Inc.
Duffy-Mott ex-pres sentncd 1-26, 103B2
Beam liquor gifts rptd 3-10, 215C2

AMERICAN Broadcasting Cos., Inc. (ABC)
FCC sets probe 1-14, 119E1
Roots sets TV viewing record 1-23—1-30, 118C3
NBC gets Moscow Olympics 2-1; '76 ABC costs cited 2-3, 131A1
Sadat on Issues & Answers 2-27, 144G1
Suspends US Boxing Championships 4-16, issues report 9-3, 828B1
Carter energy plan poll rptd 4-23, 320B3
Riccardo on Issues & Answers 4-24, 320D1
Arledge to head news dept 5-2, budget hike set 5-10, 395G1
O'Neill on Issues & Answers 5-8, 364A3
Begin on Issues & Answers 5-22, 401G2
Rule, Goldenson pay rptd 5-23, 408D3
Castro TV interview 5-24, 427F1
Walters-Castro interview 6-9, 456E1-B2
Refutes TV job bias study 8-15, 642G3
CIA links charged, denied 9-12, 720B3, F3, 721C1
Brown on Issues & Answers 10-6, 857B3
CBS reorganizes 10-17, 846A2
NFL record TV pact rptd 10-26, 950F1-A2
House subcom probes TV sports 11-2, 949E3, 950A1

1978

AMATEUR Athletic Union (AAU)—*See also specific sport (e.g., TRACK & Field)*
Naber wins Sullivan Award 2-7, 780F2
NCAA rejoins USOC 4-15, 842D3
Cong OKs amateur sports bill 10-15, 842E2-C3; Carter signs 11-8, 1003B1
AMATEUR Wrestling News
Coll rankings rptd 3-13, 379A3
AMAX Inc.
Socal takeover bid rejctd 9-7, trading disclosures spur NYSE probe 9-8, 9-11, 700B2
China-Australia iron ore deal rptd 9-29, 754C2
AMAX Iron Ore Corp.—*See AMAX Inc.*
AMAZON River
Basin pact signed by 8 natns 7-3, 829B2
AMBAC Industries Inc.
United Tech purchase planned 3-2, 185C1
AMBEDKAR, Bhimaro R. (deceased)
Caste riots erupt 7-27, 631F3
AMBRO Jr., Rep. Jerome A. (D, N.Y.)
Reelected 11-7, 851C3
AMEN Corner (play)
Opens 4-22, 760B1
AMENDMENTS, U.S. Constitutional—*See CONSTITUTION, U.S.*
AMENDOLA, Maria
Pleads guilty to misdemeanor 8-31, 725E1
AMERASINGHE, Hamilton Shirley
Elected UN Sea Law Conf pres 4-6, 401C3
AMERICAN—*For organizations not listed below, see key words*
AMERICAN Air Filter Co. Inc.
Allis-Chalmers purchase set 7-28, 718F1
AMERICAN Air Filter Co. Inc. v. FTC
Case refused by Sup Ct 11-6, 873D3
AMERICAN Airlines, Inc.
'76 tax nonpaymt rptd 1-27, 65G2
More 'Super Saver' fares OKd 3-3, 206A3
Western, Continental merger set 8-31, 684B1
Begins 3-class svc 10-15, 812D2
3-class svc dropped 12-26, 1007E3
AMERICAN Automobile Association (AAA)
Gasoline price hike rptd 11-20, 939F1
'78 gas price rise rptd 12-19, 1010F1
AMERICAN Bag & Paper Corp.
Co, Schottland fined 9-21, 768G2, B3
AMERICAN Ballet Company
Baryshnikov joins NYC Ballet 4-26, 335E3
AMERICAN Bank & Trust Co.—*See BANK Leumi Trust Co.*

AMERICAN Bar Association (ABA)
Housing, zoning rules linked to segregatn 1-8, 13F3
N Orleans mtg: Burger defends trial lawyer criticism; Spann scores, Ill res defeated 2-10—2-13, 107F3
Carter addresses LA unit 5-4, 320A3
Burger: improve law students' skills 5-16, 388F2
AIM activists acquitted in Calif 5-24, 396D2
Conv 8-3—8-10: legal aid plan rejctd 8-7, US regulatory overhaul asked 8-8; Burger addresses, pres installed 8-9, 626G1-C3
AMERICAN Basketball Association (ABA) (defunct)—*See BASKETBALL—Professional*
AMERICAN Bell International—*See AMERICAN Telephone & Telegraph*
AMERICAN Brands Inc.
In Dow Jones indl avg 66E2

AMERICAN Broadcasting Cos. Inc. (ABC)
FCC OKs WJLA, KOCO-TV exchng 1-12, 109A3
Silverman to head NBC 1-20, replaced by Thomopoulos 2-1, 75D2
Lance becomes WXIA-TV commentator 2-6, 172F2
Carter poll rating low 3-30, 308B1
News show chngs set 4-19, Reasoner move to CBS set 5-12, 419A3, C3
FCC faults boxing tourn 4-25, 379D1
Ehrlichman interviewed 4-27, 320E2
Spinks-Ali rematch rights rptd sold 5-2, 378G3
Rule, Goldenson on '77 top-paid execs list 5-15, 364F3
Carter popularity poll rptd 5-24, 404C3
AAU suspends 4 track stars 6-23, 692F2
FBI informant accused on '20/20' 7-10, 720F2
Carter poll status still bleak, 8-27, 682B2
Indep news producers sue 9-11, 759G1
Pfeiffer named NBC chrmn, RCA dir 9-13, 759D3
Ali-Spinks bout 9-15, TV viewing record rptd 9-20, 726E2
Fla slayer loses TV violence suit 9-26, 759G2

1979

AMATEUR Athletic Union (AAU)—*See specific sport (e.g. TRACK)*
AMAX Inc.
Aborigine land drilling OKd 6-18, 467G1
Rosario Resources sought 10-22, 986D3
AMAYA, Victor
Loses Denver Grand Prix 2-25, 391G2
Wins World Invitatn 5-20, 570C2
AMBACH v. Norwick
Case upheld by Sup Ct 4-17, 325F3
AMBASSADOR College (Pasadena, Calif.)
Worldwide Church receivership lifted 3-17, 376C2
AMBROSE, David
5th Musketeer released 9-7, 820B1
AMDAHL Corp.
Comten bid matched, offer withdrawn 4-23, 440G3
Memorex bid rejctd, 10-28, talks end 11-20, 942D2
AMENDMENTS, U.S. Constitutional—*See CONSTITUTION, U.S.*
AMENDOLA, Giorgi
Defeated for EC Parlt pres 7-17, 537D2
AMERADA Hess Corp.
St Lucia dvpt program cited 2-21, 181E2
Price violatns chrgd 5-17, 385A2; 5-30, 396C1
July gas supplies rptd 6-27, 479F1
US overchrgs alleged 11-6, 849G2; 11-8, 11-14, 905F2-A3
Price violatns chrgd 12-13, 990G2
AMERICAN—*For organizations not listed below, see key words*
AMERICAN Airlines Inc.
$99 cross-country fares, new routes OKd 1-12, 35E2
NYC near-collisn 2-11, FAA updates radar improvemt 3-12, 206C2; rpt issued 4-9, 412C2
Chicago DC-10 crash kills 275 5-25; inspectns ordrd, flaws rptd 5-29—5-30, 411C3-412D1
FAA grounds DC-10s, travel chaos rptd 6-6, 420F2, E3, G3
Serbian hijacks jet 6-20, 491E2
Half-fare plan takes effect 7-1, 579A1
Chicago DC-10 crash rpt issued by FAA 7-10, findings disputed 7-12, 538E3-539E1
FAA lifts DC-10 flight ban 7-13, 538G2
Canada discount fares halted 8-30, 667F2
DC-10 safety fine paid 11-16, 988D3
Tex hijacker demands Iran flight 11-24, 898E2
Chicago DC-10 crash rpt issued by Safety Bd 12-21, 988G2
AMERICAN-Arab Relations Committee
Sirhan parole hearing denied 11-7, 953C3
AMERICAN Assembly—*See COLUMBIA University*
AMERICAN Atomics Corp.
Ariz radioactive tritium plant seized 9-26, decontamination begun 9-29; reorganizatn sought 10-6, 806C2
AMERICAN Automobile Association (AAA)
Gas statn closings rptd 6-23—6-24, 479C1
AMERICAN Ballet Company (ABT)
Baryshnikov named dir 6-20, 527E3
Godunov resigntn rptd 11-21, 1005E3
Dancers OK pact 12-20, 987G1-B2
AMERICAN Bank Note Co.
Food stamp probe rptd 2-2, 93C3
AMERICAN Bank & Trust Co.—*See BANK Leumi Trust Co.*
AMERICAN Bar Association (ABA)
Mid-winter mtg: Burger, Bell address; new disciplinary rules OKd; other actns 2-7—2-14, 130C1
UN observer scores Argentine justice 5-26, 467C1
Conv rejcts 3d party search limits, death penalty, prisoner rights; other actns rptd; pres installed 8-9—8-15, 768C3-769B1
Dallas conv, Powell comments on press closures 8-13, 630B3
AMERICAN Brands Inc.
In Dow Jones indl avg 72E1
FTC subpoena compliance ordrd 1-25, 91D3
FDS acquired 2-14, 132B2

AMERICAN Broadcasting Cos. Inc. (ABC)
Children's TV ad cuts set 1-18, 78A3
Wage-price compliance rptd 2-6, 128C1
O'Brien discloses Sup Ct rulings 4-16, 4-17, ct worker fired re leaks 4-20, 302G2
Pierce promoted to vp 4-30, 334F3
Rule on '78 top-paid execs list 5-14, 347F3
O'Brien leaks another Sup Ct ruling 5-18, 382A3
Stewart slain in Nicaragua 6-20, 461F2; suspect confesses 6-30, 512B3
Carter poll rating low 7-9, 514D1
TV network affiliates rptd on par with rivals 7-31, 588A2
Ex-newsman linked to KGB 8-11, 611E1
Carter denies Young wiretap 8-30, 661G2
TV rights to '84 LA Olympics won 9-25, 797C3
Macmillan offer accepted 10-16, talks ended 11-22, 942A3
FCC scores children's TV 10-30, NAB responds 11-1, 858C3, D3
'Jaws' viewed by 80 mln 11-4, 1006F3
Khomeini TV news interview 11-18, 877B2

1980

AMATO, Mario
Slain 6-23, 564G2
AMATO, Pino
Slain 5-19, 408E2
AMAX Inc.
Signs 2d agreemt to buy Rosario 2-4, 385D3
Aborigines protest mining 5-8, 371B1; 8-11, 617G2
Agrees to buy Borden unit 5-16, 746E1
Ford elected to bd 9-18, 959A3
USW copper strike drags on 10-24, 805B3
AMAYA, Victor
Australian Open results 1-2, 213F1
Loses Denver Grand Prix 2-24, 607F2
Wins French Open men's doubles 6-7, 606F3
Loses Western Open 8-17, 691C3
Dubai Golden results 11-23, 947F2
AMAZON River
Pope tours 7-11, 538E2
8 natns sign basin dvpt, ecology pact 10-28, 865B2
AMBARTSUMYAN, David
Wins Olympic medal 7-28, 623F3
AMBRO, Rep. Jerome (D, N.Y.)
Joins open-conv move 7-25, 7-28, 570F1, A2
Loses reelectn 11-4, 848C3
AMBROSE, David
Final Countdown released 8-1, 675E2
AMENDMENTS, U.S. Constitutional—*See CONSTITUTION, U.S.*
AMENDOLA, Giorgio
Dies 6-5, 528A1
AMERASINGHE, Hamilton S.
Dies 12-4, 1004A1
AMERICAN—*For organizations not listed below, see key words*
AMERICAN Airlines Inc.
FAA seeks DC-10 safety system chngs 1-12; no pylon defects found 1-23, 53C2-G2
LA flight hijacked to Cuba 4-9, 617A3
FAA ends DC-10 probe 5-16; ct holds immune from damages 5-23, 518D3-519A1
Coast-to-coast fares cut 6-6, hiked 7-1, 516B2, C2
Crandall named pres 7-16, 600F2
Ariz ex-football coach, employee indicted 7-24, 875B3
AMERICAN Ballet Company (ABT)
Fernandez dies 3-3, 279F2
AMERICAN Bankers Association
Bush addresses Chicago conv 10-15, 817F2

AMERICAN Bar Association (ABA)
Mid-winter mtg: Burger address; ethics code revisn unveiled; FBI charter backed; other actns 1-30—2-5, 114E2
Winberry found 'unqualified' for US judgeship 3-2, Sen panel rejects 3-4, 250F2
Va black dist judge nominee backed 4-9, 744G3
Ctroom cameras case accepted by Sup Ct 4-21, 344F1
Ala black dist judge nominees scored 5-19, 744C2, B3
Pretrial data secrecy rule support rptd 6-19, 632C1
Conv backs law schl minority 'opportunities', repudiates GOP plank; other actns rptd 7-31—8-6, 744C1-B2
Civiletti at Honolulu conv 8-7, 595E2
5th judicial circuit split, backing cited 10-14, 918D3
Del Law Schl libel case declined by Sup Ct 11-10, 868B3
AMERICAN Brands Inc.
In Dow Jones indl avg 76E1
AMERICAN Broadcasting Cos. Inc. (ABC)
Frost interviews shah 1-17, 47G1
'84 Winter Olympic rights won 1-24, 206F1
Mobil TV ad rejectn rptd 1-31, 120E1
Iran chrgs Jennings took gifts from shah 2-9, 122B3
Iran readmits newsmen 3-7, 178C2
Iran hostage film purchase rejected 4-10, 282C3
Liddy, Anderson on Good Morning Amer 333B3
'79-80 Nielsen ratings rptd, CBS regains lead; Acad Awards cited 4-22, 376A1
'Charlie's Angels' fraud probe rptd 5-1, 376G1, C3
CBS, US settle trust dispute 5-8, 501D3
Howard Tuckner dies 8-2, 676E3
Spelling-Goldberg ties rptd probed by SEC 8-7—8-8, 640B1
US trust suit setld 8-22, 732E1
Walters interviews Hoffman 9-2, 713E2
'Shogun' aired by NBC 9-15—9-19, top ratings rptd 9-24, 835B3
Appeals ct backs Abscam tapes broadcast 10-1; Sup Ct refuses stay, tapes aired 10-14, 781F2

1976

AMERICAN Cancer Society
Backs thermography use 7-28, 680B1
Breast X-ray curb urged 8-23, 679F3
Rpts tar, nicotine study 9-14, 875F3
Anti-smoking drive announced 10-15, 875D3
Rauscher named vp 11-1, 876D1
AMERICAN Can Co.
Trust suit dvpts 2-18—10-5, 886B1, F2; Wedin sentncd 11-30, 921A3
USW contracts extended 8-18, 670C1
AMERICAN Chicle Division—*See WARNER-Lambert*
AMERICAN City Bank & Trust Co.—*See AMERICAN Bankshares Corp.*
AMERICAN Civil Liberties Union (ACLU)
Harrises suit filed 1-5, 70G1
Scores clemency bd rpt 1-6, 4E1
'75 rpt on FBI-terrorist ties rptd 1-11, 42B1, F1
Hearst jury selectn plea rejctd 2-2, 113B3
Colby vs CIA budget disclosure 3-17, 217E1
Some church-college aid OKd 6-21, 452F3
Shattuck replaces Morgan as DC dir 9-6, 680F2 ★
On Sup Ct double jeopardy protectn rulings 11-12, 848F2
Gilmore executn stay rptd sought 11-12, 891E1
Sup Ct refuses Va oral sex case 11-29, 901B1
Vows fight vs Gilmore executn 12-15, 952G2
Calif bd vs marine KKK suit 12-16, 983B2
AMERICAN Color & Chemical Corp.
US files consent decree 11-16, 989C1
AMERICAN Company, An: The Tragedy of United Fruit (book)
Published 10-21, 844D3
AMERICAN Cyanamid Co.
SEC lists forgn paymts 5-12, 726B2
'69 trust suit ends in mistrial 8-17, 988B3
CDC blames polio vaccine shortage on Lederle, contract dispute settled 9-21, 776D1
Sup Ct bars review of trust case 10-4, 807B3
US files consent decree 11-16, 989C1
AMERICAN Electric Power Co.
Cook to quit, White named 1-27, 160E2
'74 zero tax paymt rptd 10-2, 847G1
Appalachian Power Co.
New River scenic system, dam project OKd 3-12, 3-24, 219A3
Dam bar signed 9-11, 689D1
AMERICAN Express Co.
Testifies at privacy comm hearings 2-11, shifts policy 2-13, 151C2
Algeria $ securities issue OKd 7-27, 902B2

AMERICAN Federation of Labor and Congress of Industrial Organizations (AFL-CIO)—*See also MEANY, George; affiliated unions*
Ford com members quit 1-8, 3F3
Usery named US Labor secy 1-22, 40G3
Meeting, summary 2-11—2-23, 148D3
AFSCME quits AFL-CIO dept 2-15, 154A1
Tonelli at Canada CLL Cong 5-18, 401D1
Warns on economy 5-19, 391C1
USSR scores labor delegatn visa denials 5-25—5-28, 408A1
Carter addresses Ohio unit 5-27, 390F1
Exec Cncl backs Carter 7-19, 532D2
Corbett endorses Carter 7-22, 551E1
Nathaniel Goldfinger dies 7-22, 656F3
Mondale at Seattle state conv 8-17, 617B3
Carter sees gen bd 8-31, 645B2
Carter addresses Mich conv 9-15, 686D3

1977

Wins Emmys 11-6, 1022B1
Begin speech text 11-20, 890A1
NBC trust accord OKd 12-1, 918C3
On most reliable govt news source list 12-10, 1009C1

AMERICAN Cancer Society
Breast X-rays curbed 5-10, 431C2
AMERICAN Can Co.
Carter shares put in trust 1-4, 5A1
Steelworkers OK new pact 10-31, 837D1

AMERICAN Civil Liberties Union (ACLU)
Sup Ct voids homosexual dismissal ruling 1-10, 57C1
Bell confrmatn hearings 1-11—1-18, 34F1
Wins Gilmore executn stay; Appeals Ct overturns, Sup Ct rejcts review 1-17, 40C2
On Viet pardon action 1-21, 51F2
Robert Dunn dies 1-21, 84G2
Religious deprogramming scored 2-5, 287E1
Backs FBI curbs 2-15, 157C3
Ind judge bars biology text 4-14, 471E3
FBI '20-42 surveillnc rptd 6-19, 481B1
Calls Carter record 'poor' 7-20, 575C2
FBI ties revealed 8-4, 628E1
FCC cable TV obscenity rule suspensn ordrd 9-1, 846C2
'78 abortn rights drive set 10-6, 786A3
AMERICAN Conservative Union
Begins mail, ad campaign vs Panama Canal pacts 8-21, 678G1
TV campaign vs Canal pacts begins 10-29, 912B1
AMERICAN Council for Nationalities Service
New Viet refugees arrive 9-20, 739G3
AMERICAN Criminal Law Review (magazine)
ABA inmate rights rpt issued 4-26, 383D2
AMERICAN Cyanamid Co.
Sup Ct backs EPA authority 2-23, 150G2
To promote S Africa equality 3-1, 160B3
AMERICAN Express Co.
Greek office rptd bombed 7-14, 618D1

AMERICAN Federation of Labor and Congress of Industrial Organizations (AFL-CIO)—*See also MEANY, George; also affiliated unions*
Exec Cncl vs Carter econ plan 1-10, 14D1
More pub works backed 2-1, 2-4, 98E2, F2
'76 cong contributns rptd 2-15, 128F1
Exec Cncl meets 2-21—2-27; legis drive planned 2-21; Bukovsky addresses 2-25, 142D3, 153G1-B3
Backs B-1 bomber funding 2-27, 153B3
Missing Nev ldr found slain 3-17, 261C3
Admin min wage plan scored 3-24, 229E2
Kirkland scores Carter re shoe imports 4-5, 248C2
USSR reps denied visas 4-16, 306G2
Carter energy plan study rptd 4-23, 320C2

1978

Wage-price poll rptd 10-24, 807B1
NBC drops fall TV lineup 11-29, 1030D1
Walters interviews Carter 12-14, 951B1, 979G2, F3
Issues & Answers
Bell 2-12, 108C1
Schultze 12-3, 962D2
Ullman 4-23, 306B1
AMERICAN Broadcasting Cos. Inc. v. Writers Guild of America, West Inc.
Unions curbed on supervisor discipline by Sup Ct 6-21, 509E1
AMERICAN Caesar: Douglas MacArthur 1880-1964 (book)
On best-seller list 10-9, 800B3; 11-6, 887G3; 12-3, 971B1
AMERICAN Can Co.
In Dow Jones indl avg 66E2
Outbids Interco for Fingerhut 8-14, 718D1
AMERICAN Chicle Division—*See WARNER-Lambert*

AMERICAN Civil Liberties Union (ACLU)
Carter intell reorgn, curbs scored 1-24, 49B3
Skokie Nazi defense causes split 1-27, 69B1
Criminal law revisn scored 1-30, 64A2
Tenn prison bldg ordrd closed 1-30, 440F1
Sen intell reorg bill evaluated 2-9, 107F1
FCC cable-TV access rules voided 2-24, 195G2
Sup Ct curbs NH gov on flag lowerings 3-24, 221A2
House OKs lobbying curbs 4-26, 323A2, B2
Skokie rally ordinances struck down 5-23; Nazi rally delay sought 6-9, Sup Ct denies stay 6-12, 447A3
Nonprofit lawyer soliciting backed by Sup Ct 5-30, 430D2
Skokie march canceled; Chicago rally OKd 6-20—7-7; rally, counter-demonstratns held 7-9, 529A2
Dorsen on Bakke ruling 6-28, 482G2
Navy sea duty rule hailed 7-27, 589E1
LA busing appeal won 9-6, 698E3
House curbs on natl security taps backed 9-7, 697B1
Scores Carter vets proposals 10-10, 878F1
95th Cong gains noted 10-20, 981A3
Natl security tap curbs signed 10-25, 863D1
CIA mail-opening damages upheld 11-9, 940E1
FBI mail scrutiny held unconst 11-29, 940B1
AMERICAN Cyanamid Co.
Forgn natn tetracycline suit OKd 1-11, 33E3
AMERICAN Electric Power Co.
Sporn dies 1-24, 96F3
Low '76 tax paymt rptd 1-27, 65A3
Coal strike billing audit rptd 5-10, 366F3
Ind & Mich wins Gen Atomic damages 5-16, 366B3
Ind & Mich trust suit rule refused by Sup Ct 5-22, 388C2
AMERICAN Export Lines Inc.
Farrell acquisitn cited 11-6, 888A3

AMERICAN Federation of Labor and Congress of Industrial Organizations (AFL-CIO)—*See also MEANY, George; affiliated unions*
Hal Davis dies 1-11, 96F1
Exec cncl meets 2-20—2-24; urges econ stimulus 2-20, trade law chngs 2-21, 141E3-142F1
New CPIs described 222A3
Italy CP labor group OKs ties 3-14, 191B3
House OKs lobbying curbs 4-26, 323C2
Meany, exec cncl see Carter; rejct wage-restraint plea 5-10; Bosworth backs stand 5-11, 361F2, D3
Southn constructn pact signed 5-22, 429D3
Fined $10,000 re pol spending 6-12, 509D3
Cotton dust rules challenged 6-19, 471F3

1979

Walters interviews shah 11-22, 897C3
Reagan tops GOP poll 11-25, 982E1
NBC Iran hostage interview scored 12-11, 934D3
Iran forgn min interviewed 12-16, 958D1
Issues & Answers
Muzorewa 4-29, 332C2
Udall 4-1, 245E1
Volcker 10-28, 940D3
Yigal 8-19, 644F3
AMERICAN Caesar: Douglas MacArthur 1880-1964 (book)
On best-seller list 1-7, 80C3; 2-4, 120C3; 3-4, 173E3

AMERICAN Cancer Society
Waxman wins House health subcom chair 1-30, 86E3
USC job hostility study rptd 2-10, 139A3
Blacks' cancer rate rptd up, educ drive set 2-16, 139E2
Filter cigarets rptd less perilous 2-22, 218A2
Mrs Bayh dies 4-24, 356B3
Nixon gift rptd 7-11, 527B3
AMERICAN Citizens for Honesty in Government—*See SCIENTOLOGY, Church of*
AMERICAN Civil Liberties Union (ACLU)
SWP wins funds rpt exemption 1-9, 13G3
Mil dischrg suits filed 1-19, 53C1
Va inmate gets rape setlmt 3-17, 316D2
Justice Dept admits H-bomb documt security error 6-8, ends effort to stop H-bomb article publicatn 9-17, 713E1
Navy recruiting bias chrgd 6-14, 519B3
FBI sued over '65 Liuzzo death 7-5, 521C1
FBI charter evaluated 7-31, 599B3
Phila, Iowa church-state suits filed 9-13, 9-24, 760D3
Bishop executn stay rejctd by Sup Ct 10-21, 817D2
Radio deregulatn pub review asked 11-5, 859C1
Iranian DC protest ban upheld 11-19, 879B1
NJ Iranian bus driver firings protested 11-22, 898C2
State death row figures rptd 11-25, 989F3
Viet vet drug dischrgs ordrd upgraded 11-28, 992F1
Iranian student probes ruled illegal 12-11, 935G2
AMERICAN Commodity Exchange (ACE)—*See under AMERICAN Stock Exchange*
AMERICAN Consumer Inc.
'Cross of Lourdes' refunds set 1-19, 91B3
AMERICAN Credit Corp.
Barclays purchase OKd 5-29, 440B3
AMERICAN Cyanamid Co.
W Va sterilizatn suit threatnd 1-4, 56A3
3-yrs' back-pay order upheld 2-10, 131A1
AMERICAN Export Lines Inc.—*See FARRELL Lines*
AMERICAN Express Co.
McGraw-Hill purchase sought 1-9, 15G3
McGraw-Hill rejcts bid 1-15; tender offer filed 1-16, suits 1-18, 1-19, 53B2-A3
McGraw-Hill scores Morgan Guaranty 1-22, 53A3
McGraw-Hill rejcts sweetened bid 1-31, proxy battle dropped 2-23, offer expires 3-1, 151B3
Woolworth suit compared 4-12, 304B1
Travelers check TV ad chngd 8-29, 903C1
Nicaraguan debt paymts in doubt 9-28, 753F2

AMERICAN Federation of Labor and Congress of Industrial Organizations (AFL-CIO)—*See also MEANY, George*
Chile unions offered more freedom by govt 1-3, 7A1
Carter meets with offcls 1-12, 13D3
SEC role in pensn plans barred by Sup Ct 1-16, 32D2
Exec cncl meets, maps plans 2-19—2-26, 148C2-149G1
Wage-guide suit filed 3-13, 182B2
Wage-guide ruling sought 5-2, hearing set 5-4, 345E1
Exec Cncl calls guidelines 'flop', sets oil decontrol fight 5-8, 345A2
Ct bars wage-guide contract denial 5-31; 399B3, E3
Clerks, meat cutters merge 6-6, 419F3
Appeals ct backs wage-guide contract denial 6-22, 480G2
Wage-price penalty upheld 6-22, case refused by Sup Ct 7-2, 498C2

1980

News copter missing in Carib 11-13, 869D3
LA DA ends 'Charlie's Angels' probe 12-2, 1002E2
Warner Amex cultural cable-TV deal set 12-2, 1002G3-1003C1
Issues & Answers
Anderson 7-20, 550B1
Baker 2-10, 110F3
Duncan 7-24, 553E1
Ghotbzadeh 3-30, 241G2
Kennedy 1-20, 50D2
Marshall 8-31, 659F3
Meese 11-30, 914F3
Miller 6-29, 492F3
Weinberger 11-23, 897G1
Presidential Campaign & Election
Pres poll rptd 3-9, 208B1
Carter ad bid upheld by Appeals Ct 3-14, 222B1
Wis pres primary poll rptd 4-1, 246G2
Pres poll rptd 5-6, 342G1
Reagan delegate majority rptd 5-20, 382F3
Pres poll taken 6-3, 423A1
Reagan takes poll lead 6-17, 452B2
Carter poll rating at new low 7-30, 570B2
Reagan equal-time bid rejctd 9-19, 723B1
Post-debate pres poll rptd 9-23, 739G2
Walters interviews Carter 10-8, 778B2
Reagan paid TV address 10-24, 817B2
Pres poll standings tighten, toss-up seen 10-27, 816A2
Walters on pres TV debate panel 10-28, 813F1
Pol airtime case accepted by Sup Ct 11-3, 856D2
Pres voting poll 11-4, 838G1
NBC early electn projectns scored 11-5, 866A1
AMERICAN Cancer Society
Interferon tests rptd 1-16, 62E3
Cancer risks chart 357B1
Fewer cancer tests urged 3-20, 316B3-317D1
'80s cancer deaths rise seen, '79 crusade funds rptd 4-28, 356D3
Interferon success rptd 5-28, 526D2
AMERICAN Can Co.
In Dow Jones indl avg 76E1
May named NYU business schl dean 3-18, 224E3
AMERICAN Civil Liberties Union (ACLU)
NM prison riot 2-2—2-3, 112B3
FBI Abscam tactics, disclosures scored 2-6, 2-8, 82F2, C3
Mass schl prayer stay denied 2-13, 156F1
Chicago strip search suit setld 3-26, 404D2
Itinerants registratn upset in La 5-13, 370A3
LA busing plan ordered 5-19, 426F3
Draft registratn plan sued 6-26, 478D3
Medicaid abortn funding limit scored 6-30, 492A2
Navy drops lesbian chrgs vs 4 8-21, 899A1
Lynch argues Nixon taps case in Sup Ct 12-8, 937B2
AMERICAN Clock, The (play)
Opens 11-20, 1003G2
AMERICAN Conservative Union (ACU)
Cong '79 voting survey rptd 1-18, 53B3
AMERICAN Continental Corp.
Keating named Connally campaign head 1-25, 91G3
AMERICAN Cyanamid Co.
Italy ct rules vs fibers 4-4, 294B3
EC textile duties rptd 5-6, 412A1
AMERICAN Electric Power Co.
Nader coalitn attacks 4-17, 308B2
AMERICAN Enterprise Institute (AEI)
US defense spending seen too low 1-25, 70D3
Sup Ct '79-80 term analyzed 7-2, 540G2
Baroody dies 7-29, 608B1
Kirkpatrick named to Reagan Cabt 12-22, 979F2
Anti-inflatn study issued 12-24, 980C3
AMERICAN Export Lines v. Alvez
Case decided by Sup Ct 5-12, 426D3
AMERICAN Express Co.
McGraw-Hill takeover case declined by Sup Ct 11-3, 856A2
ABC cultural cable-TV deal set 12-2, 1003A1
AMERICAN Express Handbook for Woman, The (book)
Author indicted 1-10, 216G1

AMERICAN Federation of Labor & Congress of Industrial Organizations (AFL-CIO)
George Meany dies 1-10, 14G2
Exec cncl meets 2-18—2-25; econ statemt issued 2-18, 146C3
Kirkland warns of wage-price guidelines breakdown 2-22, 144E2
Kirkland scores Carter budget revisns, econ policies 3-31, 244E1, 247A2
Carter denies Iran apology 4-1, 241G1
Kirkland meets Mondale, asks new job programs 5-2, 344B3
Kirkland: US guidelines no curb 5-6, 385E1
Exec cncl meets, backs natl accord 5-6, 385B2
Carter pressed on Haitian refugee plight 5-7, 340C1
Carter platform statemt 'acceptable' 8-13, 611A2

1976

UMW rejects affiliatn 9-27, 748G2
Mondale sees Cleveland unit 9-28, 725C1
Lobbying disclosure bill not cleared 10-2, 883D1
Campaign donatns rptd 10-22, 938C3
Kirkland named Carter aide 11-19, 881D3
Building & Construction Trades Department
Georgine vs Ford on bill veto 1-8, 4B1
USSR scores labor delegatn visa denials 5-25—5-28, 408A1
Committee for Political Education (COPE)
'75 Schweiker rating cited 7-26, 549E2
AMERICAN Financial Corp.
Bantam consent decree filed 7-27, 989G1
Bantam Books Inc.
90 Minutes at Entebbe publshd 7-26, 547F1
AMERICAN Fletcher Corp.
Rptd on FRB 'problem' list 1-22, 111D2
AMERICAN Home Products Corp.
Updates forgn payoffs rpt 3-9, 361C2
SEC lists forgn paymts 5-12, 726B2
Wyeth Laboratories
Swine-flu immunizatn delayed 9-1, 656C3
AMERICAN Hospital Supply Corp.
SEC sues, setlmt agreed 12-29, 986G1
AMERICAN Independent Party (AIP)
Maddox heads pres ticket, other conv dvpts 8-26—8-27, 666D1
Maddox threatens pres debate suit 9-2, 644F1
Maddox pres debate challenge rejctd 9-20, 703F2
Pres vote results 11-2, 818E2
Final pres vote tally 12-18, 979B2
AMERICAN Indian Movement (AIM)
Ariz BIA office threatened 1-1, 7F1
Russell Means shot 5-5, 384E2
Canada to extradite Peltier 12-17, 999B1
AMERICAN Indians—*See INDIANS, American*
AMERICAN Institute for Free Labor Development (AIFLD)
Cuba, China mil presence in Guyana rptd 3-10, 253F1
AMERICAN Institute of Aeronautics & Astronautics
CIA briefs on Israel A-bombs, Sovt space program 3-11; Kranish resignatn request rptd 3-19, 216F2
AMERICAN Institute of Public Opinion—*See GALLUP Poll*
AMERICAN Jewish Committee
Mondale at LA event 9-1, 665B3
AMERICAN Jewish Congress (AJC)
Rpts 22 cos bar boycott compliance 3-18, 747G1
Gets rpt on NASD boycott probe 8-11, 747E2
AMERICAN Legion
Pa conv 7-21—7-24, mystery disease kills 23 7-27—8-5, 573C2
Mystery disease probe continues 8-6—8-31, 656D2-A3
Carter addresses 8-24, Dole 8-25, 631F2, D3, 632B2
New disease probe set 9-30, 815D1
Pa conv hotel closes 11-18, disease probe scored 11-23—11-24, 911B2, F2

AMERICAN Medical Association (AMA)
Mental illness, econ linked 1-26, 159A3
New asthma drug rptd 2-17, 159F2
Ill MD wins malpractice suit 6-1, 1016C3
Morris Fishbein dies 9-27, 1015D1
Health manpower aid signed 10-13, 788D3
Campaign donatns rptd 10-22, 938C3, E3
'73-75 MD fees, malpractice rates linked 10-25, 1016F3
Backs natl health insurnc 12-7, 931C2
New rabies vaccine rptd 12-13, 972E3
AMERICAN Motors Corp.
Calif fines, bans 3 models 1-5, 5D3
'75 profits rptd 2-4, 215E3
Sales slump, layoff rptd 3-7, 280F2
US ends car dumping probe 5-4, 321D2
Suspends productn 6-10, rpts layoffs 7-14, 10-25, 885G1
UAW opens Big 3 talks 7-19, 570F1
EPA gas-econ ratings 9-22, 766G2-770B1
Car price hikes rptd 10-6, 747B3
Oct sales drop rptd 11-3, 885G2
Cuts '77 prices 11-4, offers rebates 11-9, 11-16, 885C1
Rpts 4th ¼ '76 losses 11-10, 885F1
Trade Act aid OKd 11-17, 885D2
Nov sales rptd up 12-3, 987G2
AMERICAN Museum of Natural History (N.Y.)
Archbold dies 8-1, 816D3
AM General Corp.
'75 arms sales listed 2-6, 147A3

1977

Exec Cncl scores Carter 5-4, 364B3
UAW OKs re-entry study 5-19, 408G1-E2
OSHA refocusing welcomed 5-19, 422A2
Energy tax plans scored 5-19, 443C2
House eases Hatch Act 6-7, 442C3
Carter backs $2.65 min wage 7-12, 534C1
Labor law reform backed 7-18, 555G2-B3
US eases visa curb 8-17, 667G2
Panama Canal pacts backed 8-29, 679B1; Laxalt scores 9-9, 698B3
House minimum wage bill scored 9-17, 758E3
UAW shelves reentry questn 10-5, 762D1
Labor reform bill OKd by House 10-6, 795B2
Sup Ct hears Bakke case arguments 10-12, 834D3
US quits ILO 11-1, 829B1
Sakharov rpts invitatns blocked 12-1, 955A3
Conv stresses protectionism; Meany reelected, other highlights 12-8—12-13, 960D3
US sues on pol spending 12-16, 980A1
Building & Construction Trades Department
Conv OKs Dem 'hit list', membership drive urged 11-30, 961A2
AMERICAN Film Institute (AFI)
Davis gets Achievemt Award 3-1, 354G1
AMERICAN Financial Corp.
Bantam Books Inc.
Roots plagiarism chrgd 4-22, reissues set 4-25, 356F1
AMERICAN Fund for Czechoslovak Refugees Inc.
New Viet refugees arrive 9-20, 739G3
AMERICAN General Insurance Co.
Richmond OKs Continental bid 4-12, 274D3
AMERICAN G. I. Forum
Sues Gen Foods on cereal ads 6-30, 613F2
AMERICAN Independent Oil Co.—*See under REYNOLDS Industries*
AMERICAN Indian Movement (AIM)
Peltier sentenced to life 6-2, 491G3
AMERICAN Indians—*See INDIANS, American*
AMERICAN Institute of Public Opinion—*See GALLUP Poll*
AMERICAN Jewish Committee
Boycott exemptns agreed 5-3, 460B1
Proselytism scored 5-13, 492E2
Kovadloff flees Argentina 6-28, office closed 7-8, 615C1
AMERICAN Jewish Congress (AJC)
Vs Bell confrmatn 1-11—1-18, 34A2
Scores Dixon anti-Nader slur 1-17, 96B1
Cancels French trips 1-18, 28D1
Boycott exemptns agreed 5-3, 460B1
AMERICAN Law Institute
Burger disputes critics 5-17, 419E2-B3
AMERICAN Legion
Legion fever bacterium found 1-18, 81E1
Scores Viet pardon action 1-21, 51E2
Ex-cmdr scores Panama rights, canal pact 9-16, 716D3
Legion fever widespread 9-23, 748D1
Cong vet dischrg review bill cleared 9-23, 759E2

AMERICAN Medical Association (AMA)
TV violence outcry rptd 2-9—2-18, 157F3
'76 cong gifts rptd 2-9—2-18, 157F3
Hosp drug deaths rptd 2-28, 224D2
Hysterectomies disputed 5-9, 732A3
Califano addresses 6-19, 479B1
Laetrile sale rejctd 6-21, 508D2
Pot decriminalizatn backed 11-13, 972A3
AMERICAN Motors Corp.
'76 productn, sales 1-3, 1-6, 38E3, 39A1
Rebate deadline extended 1-9, 39B1
Carter energy plan reactn 4-24, 320E1
'76 losses rptd 340C2
US sues on age bias 5-20, 422A2
Layoffs set 6-2, May sales 6-3, 463C3
Clean air bill amended 6-10, 461B1; enacted 8-8, 610F2
Air bag order scored 6-30, 522D1
Aug new-car sales rptd 9-6, 722A3
Egypt pact signed 863B2
'78 price changes 10-18, 859D2
Chapin quits, Meyers elected 10-21, 962C1
Nov sales rptd 12-5, 962C1

1978

Labor law revisn set back 6-22, 508G2
Meany scores Carter health plan 7-28, 586G1
8th-leading PAC fund-raiser 9-7, 753C2
Humphrey-Hawkins bill reactn 10-21, 808A2
Meany scores Carter wage-price, $ defns plans 10-31, 11-1, 11-5; Marshall, Kahn reactn 10-31, 11-5, 863G1-G2
Chile trade boycott backed 11-24, 12-10, 1014F1
CWA's Watts scores Meany 12-11, 960F3
Building & Construction Trades Department
A-plant constructn accord set 4-18, 281C3
AMERICAN Financial Corp.
Bantam Books Inc.
'Holocaust' sales data rptd 316D2
AMERICAN Friends Service Committee—*See under FRIENDS, Religious Society of*
AMERICAN Graffiti (film)
Top-grossing film 5-31, 460E3
AMERICAN Heritage (magazine)
Bruce Catton dies 8-28, 708C2
AMERICAN Hockey League (AHL)—*See HOCKEY, Ice*
AMERICAN Home Products Corp.
Anacin ads enjoined 5-2, 347G3
FDA '76 Inderal OK cited 8-7, 727E3
Anacin ads ruled misleading 9-16, 769F3
AMERICAN Hot Wax (film)
Released 3-16, 618A3
Top-grossing film 3-29, 272E3
AMERICAN Indian Movement (AIM)
'Longest Walk' 2-11—7-15, DC demonstratns 7-15—7-23; Bellecourt asks Carter mtg 7-18, 568D3
Calif bars Banks extraditn 4-19, 327E1
2 activists acquitted in Calif 5-24, 396B2
AMERICAN Indians—*See INDIANS, American*
AMERICAN Institute of Public Opinion—*See GALLUP Poll*
AMERICAN Institutes for Research
Bilingual educ rpt cited 5-9, 349A1
AMERICAN Insulated Wire Corp.
Sued re price-fixing 9-21, 769C1
AMERICAN-Israel Public Affairs Committee
Ribicoff vs Israel stand 3-13, 176D3
NCC stand on Israel cluster bombs scored 5-12, 358C3
US reassures on Mideast jet sale 5-15, 5-18, 358C1
AMERICAN Jewish Congress (AJC)
Nonprofit travel agents case refused by Sup Ct 3-27, 241B2
Rpts Jan-May, '75-77 USSR emigratn data 6-8, 504D1
AMERICAN Law Institute
Burger urges improved law student skills 5-16, 388D2
AMERICAN League (AL)—*See BASEBALL*
AMERICAN Legion
Va educ progrm shift opposed 4-14, 279B2
AMERICAN Lutheran Church—*See under LUTHERANS*

AMERICAN Medical Association (AMA)
Rural health conf rpts MD shortage 4-6—4-7, 577E3
Carter scores 5-5, 342C1
Conv; MD, hosp fee curbs asked 6-21, 578C1
Hosp cost lid rejectn lauded 7-18, 551A1
MD surplus seen 8-3, 597C2
Indus-funded study finds cigaret smoking harmful 8-5, 726D3
VD epidemic among homosexuals rptd 11-6, 992G2
FTC voids ad ban 11-29, appeal announced 11-30, 947D2
'71-77 state discipline vs MDs rptd up 12-1, 992D3
AMERICAN Medical Colleges, Association of
Applicants decline 4-13, 597D2
AMERICAN Medical Political Action Committee
4th-leading PAC fund-raiser 9-7, 753B2
AMERICAN Medicorp Inc.
Humana bid OKd, Hilton bid withdrawn 1-10, 66D2
AMERICAN Motors Corp. (AMC)
'77 sales drop rptd 1-5, 4D3
Ohio blizzard idles workers 1-26, 105E3
Renault plans joint productn, distributn 3-31, 283F3-284B1
EPA orders '76 cars recalled 5-10, 349B1
Recall extended to Calif 5-19, 409F2
Small-car prices hiked 5-26, 428A2
Bus productn rptd ending 5-31, 665B2
Sues to block FTC probe 9-11, 768C1
UAW 2-yr pact signed 9-25, 737G2-C3
Meyers named chrmn 10-20, 809G3
Nov sales drop rptd 12-6, 935E3
Cuts Spirit model price 12-14, 1004F1
AMERICAN Museum of Natural History (N.Y.)
Burden dies 11-14, 972F2
Margaret Mead dies 11-15, 972D3

1979

Rubber pact details rptd 6-23, 480F1
Weber case Sup Ct ruling backed 6-27, 477G2
Hackler trade post oppositn rptd 8-3, 647C1
Exec Cncl urges oil natlzn study 8-6, 629C2, D2*
Exec Cncl backs SALT pact 8-7, 591D1
Mex oil spill suit planned 9-18, 718C3
Meany to retire 9-28, 744D1
Pollard heads delegatn to Israel 10-14—10-17, 780C3
Kirkland on Pay Advisory Com 10-16, 829F2
Conv in DC: Meany bids farewell, Carter addresses 11-15; Kirkland elected new pres, Donahue, secy-treas 11-19, 877F2, 884G3-885D2
Building and Construction Trades Department
Carter addresses 10-11, 807E2
AMERICAN Financial Corp.
SEC chrg setld, Lindner repaymt set 7-2, 746A1
Bantam Books
Krantz paperback rights bought for record sum 9-12, 755D3
AMERICAN Friends Service Committee—*See under FRIENDS, Religious Society of*
AMERICAN Game, The (film)
Released 4-28, 528B1
AMERICAN General Insurance Co.
Southn Pacific to buy Ticor 3-28, 283E1
AMERICAN Heart Association
Smoking tied to birth perils 1-16, 63F3
AMERICAN Hoechst Corp.
Price violatn chrgd 5-17, 385A2
AMERICAN Home Products Corp.
DES banned in animal feed 6-28, 571B3
AMERICAN Hospital Association, Journal of
Hosp closings rptd 9-2, 970F3
AMERICAN Indian Movement (AIM)—*See AMERICAN Indian Movement*
FBI files preservatn sought 6-26, 521A1
AMERICAN Indians—*See INDIANS, American*
AMERICAN Institute in Taiwan
Taiwan relatns bill signed 4-10, 259A3
AMERICAN Institute of Public Opinion—*See GALLUP Poll*
AMERICAN Jet Industries
SEC sues Gulfstream re forgn paymts 1-3, case settled 1-4; '78 purchase cited 16D1
AMERICAN Jewish Committee
Black criticism rejctd 8-23, 661E3
Connally Mideast peace plan scored 10-11, 783D2
AMERICAN Jewish Congress (AJC)
Young resignatn pressure denied 8-16, 606B2; 8-19, 624F1
SCLC mtg on Young resignatn 8-21, 624D1
Black criticism rejctd 8-23, 661E3
Connally Mideast peace plan scored 10-11, 783D2
AMERICAN League—*See BASEBALL*
AMERICAN Legion
Carey lauds job-preferne ruling 6-5, 421C1
Annual conv held, SALT backed 8-22, 644C1
AMERICAN Lutheran Church—*See under LUTHERANS*
AMERICAN Maritime Association v. Blumenthal
Case refused by Sup Ct 5-14, 383F1

AMERICAN Medical Association (AMA)
Journal rpts vegetarian diet studies 2-22, 140G1
Unneeded surgery debate scored 3-19, 218F3
Dental ad accord reached 4-27, 596D1
NY files chiropractors trust suit 7-5, 570E2
FTC orders ad ban, other curbs ended 10-24, 902F2
Carter hosp cost-control bill defeated 11-15, 883C1
AMERICAN Motors Corp. (AMC)
Price cut wiped out 1-2, 5D1
'78 sales drop rptd 1-5, 5B1
Renault sales pact signed 1-10, 131E2
Renault-Mack Trucks deal rptd 3-20, 236F2
Price hike rptd 3-31, 305E2
Arab arms plant in Egypt to close 5-14, 359G3
'Car of the future' plan set 5-18, 441D3
Meyers backs Chrysler aid 9-18, 699G2
Dividend declared, '79 revenues cited 9-21, 784E3
Renault to buy interest, '78 car sales cited 10-12, 784F2
FTC challenge declined by Sup Ct 11-5, 884G2
Oct, Nov sales rptd up 11-6, 12-5, 963G2
AMERICAN Motors Corp. v. FTC
Case declined by Sup Ct 11-5, 884F2
AMERICAN Museum of Natural History (N.Y.)
Margaret Mead park dedicated 9-15, 892D2

1980

Exec cncl backs Carter, scores Reagan 8-20, 647F2
Kirkland urges Polish strike support 8-21, 627B1
Woman named to exec cncl 8-21, 647C3
Exec cncl backs reindustrializn bd, pensn investmt role 8-21, 647D3
Kirkland named to Econ Revitalizatn Bd 8-28, 663C2
Kirkland praises Polish workers 8-31, 'seed money' rptd planned 9-4, 659C3
Polish worker fund OKd 9-4; Warsaw protests 9-9—9-10, US disavows 9-11, 679F1-D2
Kirkland named to Synfuels Corp bd 9-13, Sen panel OKs 9-25, 725F2
Carter addresses Calif unit 9-22, 722A3
Kirkland named to interim Synfuels Corp bd 10-5, 786F2
Pol funds case declined by Sup Ct 11-10, 868C3
Early pol endorsements studied 12-5, 938F3
Building and Construction Trades Department
Carter addresses 4-1, 247B1
AMERICAN Financial Corp.
New Haven RR reorgn challenge refused by Sup Ct 12-15, 957D2
AMERICAN Footwear Corp.
'Bionic' trademark case declined by Sup Ct 3-31, 291D3
AMERICAN Gigolo (film)
Released 2-1, 216A2
Top-grossing film 2-27, 200G3
AMERICAN Health Foundation
Saccharin cancer risk study rptd 3-6, 317F1
AMERICAN Heart Association
Cholesterol rpt scored 6-1, 432F3
AMERICAN Historians, Organization of
Ex-pres denied Md faculty post 6-12, 638D3
AMERICAN Hoechst Corp.
La chem-dump suit names 7-15, 558G3
AMERICAN Home Products Corp.
FTC chrgs misleading birth control ads, complaint setld 2-28, 358F2
'79 top TV advertiser 4-4, 376A2
AMERICAN Immigration Reform, Federation for
Census postponemt denied by Sup Ct 3-17, 226B1
AMERICAN Industrial Health Council
OSHA job cancer rules scored 1-16, 36E1
AMERICAN Institute of Public Opinion—*See GALLUP Poll*
AMERICAN International Group
Iran assets damages backed by US ct 7-10, 546E1
AMERICAN Jewish Committee
US Nazi search deadline rptd set 1-16, 228D2
Mass schl prayer stay denied 2-13, 156F1
Tanenbaum vs evangelical Christian pol movemt 9-15, 819F2
Baptist ldr's prayer remark denounced 9-18, 811C1
TV evangelist reverses prayer stance 10-11, 811F1
AMERICAN Jewish Congress (AJC)
Redgrave TV role protested 1-13, 120D2
Carter assures US Jews re Israel 3-4, 164D1
NCC PLO support scored 11-6, 864F1
AMERICAN Law Institute
Burger warns vs ct systems 'merger' 6-10, 632D1
AMERICAN League—*See BASEBALL*
AMERICAN Legion
El Salvador rightist honored 7-1, 521E3
Pres candidates address conv 8-19—8-21, 629E1, D2, F3
AMERICAN Medical Association (AMA)
US dietary guidelines scored 2-4, 157E3
Journal rpts pot cancer use 3-24, 357G3
Chicago conv; ethics code, health plan res OKd 7-22—7-24, 583E2
AMERICAN Motors Corp. (AMC)
Prices hiked 1-2, 1-8, 14E2
'79 sales rptd down 1-4, 14C2
Jan sales rptd up 2-5, 127B3
Mar sales rptd up 4-3, 287B3
Jeep, Renault rebates offered 5-13, 384D2
Greathouse quits UAW post 6-4, 457B
May sales plunge rptd 6-5, 481E3
Worker layoffs rptd 6-21, 481F3
Renault loan set 7-1, 556B3
Prices hiked 7-3, 556E2
Canada May, June sales down 7-5, 520A3
June sales rptd down 7-6, 556D2
2d 1/4 losses rptd 7-24, 574A1, C1
Aug sales rptd down 9-4, 701G2
Worker layoffs rptd 9-11, 701A3
Workers strike 9-16, UAW pact set 9-17, 725B1
Renault increases share; rescue plan rptd, finance unit set 9-24, 724C3
Lepeu replaces Sick as up 9-29, 959E2
'Playing for Time' sponsored 9-30, 835F3
Sept sales rptd down 10-6, 784G2
Oct sales rptd down 11-4, 857B1
3d 1/4 loss rptd 11-7, 883B2
Renault aid rptd crucial, losses seen 11-19, 883C2
Credit agrmt set 12-11, 938G2

1976

AMERICAN Nazi Party (National Socialist White People's Party)
'Kill' list rptd 6-14—6-16, 453F1

AMERICAN Party
Conv nominates pres, vp 6-18—6-19, 490C3
Anderson pres debate suit rejctd 9-17, 703E2
Final pres vote tally 12-18, 979B2

AMERICAN Samoa (U.S. territory)
GOP platform text 8-18, 605E3
Standard Oil retrial bid eased 10-18, 867G2

AMERICAN Savings Insurance Co.
Miss S&Ls crisis 5-7—6-8, 438G1
Miss closes S&Ls 6-20; audit rptd, Tenn hearings set 7-7, 495A1, D1

AMERICAN Security Council
China ICBM projct rptd dropped 2-24, 190C1

AMERICANS for Constitutional Action (ACA)
Mondale rating cited 512D3
Dole rating cited 614F2

AMERICANS for Democratic Action (ADA)
Noel quits Dem com post 5-14, 357G3
Mondale, Humphrey ratings cited 512D3
Schweiker '75 rating cited 7-26, 549D2

AMERICAN Ship Building Co.
SEC lists paymts 5-12, 725G3, 726C2

AMERICAN Society of Composers, Authors and Publishers (ASCAP)
Edgar Leslie dies 1-22, 80E3

AMERICAN Standards Inc.
SEC lists forgn paymts 5-12, 726C2

AMERICANS United (organization)
Sup Ct refuses Mo tuitn case 12-13, 960A3

AMERICAN Telephone & Telegraph Co. (AT&T)
Lilley to quit, Lindholm named 1-21, 160D2
Testifies at privacy comm probe 2-12, 151E2
SEC notes paymts probe 5-12, 726C2
SEC lists Southn Bell paymts 5-12, 729B1
Reverse bias damages ordrd 6-9, 944G1
Affirmative action plan rptd upheld 8-27, 944B2
Rpts $1 bln Aug ¼ profit 9-15, 984F1
Cornfeld sentncd in Pacific Tel case 9-27, 860G2
Westn Elec '75 zero tax paymt rptd 10-2, 847F1
'75 US tax paymt rptd 10-2, 847A2
Westn Elec bias damages, quotas ordrd 10-22; co appeals 11-5, 943D2
Southn Bell takes blame for payoffs, exec chrgs dropped 10-25, 939C1
Justice Dept trust suit OKd 11-16, 886G3
Sup Ct refuses '74 FCC pvt equipmt ruling 12-13, 960F2
SW Bell loses tap suit 12-17, 995E1-A2

AMERICAN Trial Lawyers Association
Scored re no-fault bill defeat 3-31, 234D2

AMERICAN University (Wash., D.C.)
Sisco to become pres 2-23, 186E2

AMERIGO Vespucci (Italian sailing ship)
In Operation Sail 7-4, 488B3

AMES, Juanita
Bolles judge chng OKd 11-19, 971E3

AMESER, Capt. Santiago
Bolivia housing min 1-12, 27A1

AMES Research Center (Mountain View, Calif.)
Pollack rpts Martian sky color 7-21, 526C2

AMF Inc.
SEC lists forgn paymts 5-12, 726C2

AM General Corp.—*See under AMERICAN Motors*

AMIN, Ali
Press post ouster rptd 3-19, 333F1

AMIN, Mustafa
Press post ouster rptd 3-19, 333F1

AMIN, Samani Bin Mohammed
Arrested 6-22, 497G3

AMIN Dada, Maj. Gen. Idi
Lauds Angola summit 1-13, 16C1
Recognizes Angola MPLA 2-10, 105E2
Blocks oil to Rwanda 4-7, 502F2
Assassinatn try 6-10; denies purges, threatens BBC newsman 6-14, 502C2
Named pres for life 6-25, 523F1
Mediates in hijacking 6-28, 6-30, 463B1, F1
Opens OAU summit 7-2, 487G2, A3
On Israeli raid toll 7-4, 485D1
Israel chrgs hijacking role 7-4, 485G1-A2
Hints reprisals vs Israel, links Kenya 7-5, 486B1

1977

AMERICAN Natural Resources Co.
Mich unit Alaska pipe rule 5-2, 369B3

AMERICAN Nazi Party
Tape restraining order upheld 12-21, 1008A2

AMERICAN Palestine Committee
Accuses Israel re '67 US ship raid 9-18, 715A1

AMERICAN Samoa
Coleman elected gov 11-22, 943E3

AMERICANS for Democratic Action (ADA)
Vs Bell confrmatn 1-11—1-18, 34A2
McGovern scores Carter 5-7, 364E2
Albert Coolidge dies 8-31, 696E2

AMERICAN Soccer League (ASL)—*See SOCCER*

AMERICAN Spring Wire Corp.
Chrgs Japan, India dumping 10-17, 836C3
US probes dumping chrg 11-22, 933B3

AMERICAN Stock Exchange (Amex)
'68 NYS stock transfer tax amendmts ruled illegal 1-12, 57D2
Sen subcom rpt scores accountants 1-17, 79A1
CBOE options trade war rptd 2-17, 521F1
NYSE merger talks fail, options trading issue cited 5-19, 520F3
Asks SEC probe NYSE options plan 6-13, 521C2
Closed during NY blackout 7-14, 537A3
SEC limits option trading, begins probe 10-18, 859C3
Levitt elected chrmn 11-10, 859D3
SEC scores natl mkt move delay, ITS cited 12-1, 1004F1
'77 index gain rptd 12-30, 1003G3

AMERICAN Symphony Orchestra
Stokowski dies 9-13, 788A3

AMERICAN Telephone & Telegraph Co. (AT&T)
Sup Ct bars '76 trust case review 1-25, 80B2
Rpts record '76 earnings 2-1, 93B3
Stocks, debt outstanding rptd 2-14, 156C1
Hikes dividend 2-16, 156B1
Sup Ct bars Western Union dispute review 2-22, 150A1
FCC backs practices 2-23; reactn 2-23—2-24, 217C2
Adams rpts holdings 2-25, 147C3
Carter call-in 3-5, 171F3
Western Elec on '76 Fortune 500 list 340F1 *
Employe stock plan set 5-6, 409E1
Jobless aid for strikers upset 5-24, 463B1
FCC revokes '76 Telpak order 6-1, OKs pvt rates 6-1, 6-8, 465C1
ITT sues 6-10, 520C2
B Graham fund holding rptd 6-26, 732A1
Privacy panel asks safeguards 7-12, 632C1
To maintain Telpak service 7-21, FCC upheld on 'end-link' repricing 8-5, 631C3, F3
Southn Bell, 5 offcls indicted 8-2, 631A3
CWA pact reached 8-6, 613F2
NE, Mid-Atlantic job losses, Sunbelt gains seen 8-7, 629F2
SW Bell loses slander suit, AT&T acquitted 9-12, 724B2, D2
Pacific Telephone ordrd to pay refunds, cut rates 9-13, 839A2
3d ¼ profits top $1 bln mark 9-21, 918D2
FCC equipmt registratn order review refused 10-3, 760F3
Bell Labs laser finds cited 10-11, 860A1
Anderson of Bell Labs wins Nobel 10-11, 951G2
Sup Ct bars trust appeal 11-28, 919B2
Phone surveillnc ct orders backed 12-7, 939F1
SW Bell, Nazi tape restraining order upheld 12-21, 1008B2

AMERICAN Telephone & Telegraph Co. v. U.S.
Sup Ct bars appeal 11-28, 919D2

AMERICAN Television & Communications Corp.
Time Inc plans purchase 12-22, 1004C3

AMERICAN University (Washington, D.C.)
Kim Han Cho accused 6-5, 441F3

AMES, Bruce N.
Tris sterility peril warned 8-30, 820D2

AMES, Elizabeth
Dies 3-28, 264B2

AMEX—*See AMERICAN Stock Exchange*

AMF Inc.
Rpts paymts to SEC 2-8, 93G3

AMIN Dada, Maj. Gen. Idi (Ugandan President)
6th anniv fete 1-25, 102D3
Amnesty Intl rpts death total 2-6, 139G1
Denies purge, warns Luwum 2-14, 138E3
Luwum, 2 mins killed 2-16; denounced 2-17—2-21, 138B3-139E1
Mil dissidents rptd 139F1
Claims invasn threats 2-22—3-2, 141C2
Admits mil unrest 2-23, 141F2
Christian purge detailed 2-23, 2-25, 3-2, 141G2
Waldheim asks Luwum death probe 2-24, 142C1

1978

AMERICAN Natural Resources Co.
Coal gasificatn plant financing plan submitted 6-2, 471A3

AMERICAN Public Gas Assoc. v. Federal Energy Regulatory Commission
'76 natural gas rates review refused 2-27, 143C2

AMERICAN Samoa (U.S. territory)
House delegate bill clears Cong 10-13, signed 10-31, 1003A1

AMERICAN Security Council
Singlaub scores Carter Admin 6-2, 433C2
Pro-defns cong coalitn formed 8-8, 604B3
New China policy opposed 12-20, 976B1

AMERICANS for Democratic Action (ADA)
Conv hears McGovern vs Propositn 13 6-17, 526B1
Sen ratings issued, conservative shift seen 12-17, 981D2

AMERICAN Soccer League (ASL)—*See SOCCER*

AMERICAN Society of Travel Agents v. Blumenthal
Case refused by Sup Ct 3-27, 241C2

AMERICAN Stock Exchange (Amex)
'77 index gain cited 1-1, 66G3
11 optns traders indicted by NYS; Amex scores, '77 probe cited 1-5, 4F3-5A1
Occidental-Husky collusn chrg probed 6-19, 629G1
'78 index rptd up 12-29, 1004D2

AMERICAN Tax Reduction Movement
Jarvis announces formation 8-21, 735A3

AMERICAN Telephone & Telegraph Co. (AT&T)
In Dow Jones indl avg 66E2
Rate rise stay lifted 1-9, 13C2
MCI phone svc case review barred 1-16, 33A2
FCC OKs Telpak rate hike 1-18, 84F1
Low '76 tax paymt rptd 1-27, 65A3
'77, 4th ¼ record profits rptd 2-1; hikes dividend 2-15, 282G3
Southn Bell pleads guilty 2-13, fined 2-16, 116G2
SW Bell '76 tap rule overturned, slander suit appeal cited 2-16, 142E3
Women employes profiled 2-28, 565C3
ITT suit cited 3-1, 510D3
Southn Bell theater purchase foiled 3-5, 293A2
Craig dies 4-21, 356E2
US trust suit cited 4-26, 510D2
Electron beam use for biochem process study rptd by Bell Labs 5-5, 334F3
Bell Labs study finds antimatter in galaxy center 5-6, 653E3
Westn Elec on '77 Fortune 500 list 5-8, 325F1
MCI phone svc case stay denied by Sup Ct 5-22, 388A2
'73 consent decree impact rptd 5-22, 554G3
Exec pay curb, Westn Elec price freeze pledged 5-23, 427D3-428A1
Rate hike case declined by Sup Ct 6-5, 431D2
Bias case declined by Sup Ct 7-3, 551G3
Exec chngs announced 10-18, 808C3
Iran Amer Bell Intl workers harassed 11-13, 869F2
Centrex case refused by Sup Ct 11-13, 874D2
'77 documts order backed by Sup Ct 11-13, 874A3
MCI connectns case declined by Sup Ct 11-27, 937A2
SW Bell slander judgmt reversed 11-29, 963F1 *
Vows price compliance 12-1, 934B3
Calif Pacific Telephone refund case refused by US Sup Ct 12-11, 981E1

AMERICAN Telephone v. MCI Telecommunications
Phone svc case review barred 1-16, 33A2

AMEX—*See AMERICAN Stock Exchange*

AMFAC Inc.
Marshall Field to buy Liberty House stores 1-20, 185F1

AMIAMA Castillo, Cmdr. Francisco
Named DR navy staff chief 8-16, 648E2

AMIN, Hafizullah
Says plot smashed 9-20, 738B2

AMIN, Jamil Abdullah-al (H. Rap Brown)
Rpts conversn, name chng 6-15, 844D2

AMIN, Mustafa
Denies bigoted articles 1-24, 42B1

AMIN Dada, Maj. Gen. Idi (Ugandan President)
Kenyan smugglers rptd pardoned 1-31, 95C2
Police disciplined for smuggling 2-1, 95B2
Page Airways gift chrgd 4-13, 449B2
Takes Cabt posts 4-28, 5-3, 331A3
Envoy to Denmark loses libel suit 6-18, 688B1
US Sen OKs trade ban 7-28, 616E2
Tanzania invasn chrgd 10-12, 822F3
Army unrest tied to Tanzania invasn 11-1, 830C3

1979

AMERICAN Nazi Party
2 arrested in NC slayings 11-3, 864F3
22 arrested in NJ 11-24, 991C3

AMERICAN Nuclear Insurers
3 Mile I paymts detailed 4-5, 260F2-A3

AMERICANS for Constitutional Action (ACA)
Labor '78 cong campaign gifts rptd 6-13, 595B1
Baker rating cited 11-1, 828E3

AMERICANS for Democratic Action (ADA)
Carter firing of Abzug scored 1-13, 30B3
Carter budget deplored 1-26, 70C1
Schlesinger addresses conv 6-23, Kennedy pres bid backed 6-24, 482C2
Baker rating cited 11-1, 828E3

AMERICAN Soccer League—*See SOCCER*

AMERICAN Society of Anesthesiologists
'Laughing gas' peril rptd 10-24, 971B3

AMERICAN Standard Inc.
Marquard on '78 top-paid execs list 5-14, 347G3

AMERICAN Stock Exchange (Amex)
SEC asks options trading overhaul, scores surveillance 2-15; freeze end seen 2-22, 348B3-349A1, D1
Volume record set 10-10, 765C2

American Commodity Exchange (ACE)
CFTC OKs T-bill futures trading 6-19, 681B3

AMERICAN Stores Co.
Skaggs to take over 3-14, 283C1

AMERICAN Telephone & Telegraph Co. (AT&T)
In Dow Jones indl avg 72E1
ITT long-distance phone svc OKd 1-4, 15A2
Documts order review declined by Sup Ct 1-8, 14G3
Speedy trust trial date proposed, US refusal seen 1-11, 88A3
US clears on job-bias decree 1-17, 92F1
Sears sues US on bias laws 1-24, 92E1
Jobless pay for strikers upheld by Sup Ct 3-21, 231D1
Data access case declined by Sup Ct 3-26, 231A1
FCC OKs local access phone pact 4-12, 350G3
ITT offers long-distance phone svc 4-23, 350F3
Westn Elec on '78 Fortune 500 list 5-7, 304F1
Dow Jones index revised 6-28, 481A3
SW Bell hqs land purchase rptd 8-31, 887C2
FCC scores pvt line rates 9-20, 870D1
Southn Bell pol paymts scored by FCC 9-20, 870F1
Pacific Telephone refund stay refused by Sup Ct 10-1, 768D1; appeal denied by Sup Ct 10-15, 848B1
Westn Elec job bias case refused by Sup Ct 10-29, 884C2
'75 Saudi note purchase cited 12-27, 986A2

AMERICAN Telephone & Telegraph Co. v. U.S.
Case declined by Sup Ct 1-8, 15A1

AMERICUS, Ga.—*See GEORGIA*

AMERY, Julian
On Commonwealth Zimbabwe plan 8-7, 590F1
UK Tories endorse Zimbabwe policy 10-10, 791A3

AMF Inc.
Bike safety ads agreed 7-8, 595G2

AMHERST (Mass.) College
S Africa stock divestiture rptd 3-24, 271B1

AMIN, Hafizullah (Afghan president; executed Dec. 27)
Rejcts US protest re Dubs, denies Sovt role 2-19, 147E2
Named Afghan premier 3-27, 233C1
Warns Iran, Pak on aiding rebels 4-27, 368C2
Kin flees to USSR 6-7, 443A1
Gets defense post 7-28, 575E2
On Sovt mil role, chrgs forgn rebel aid 8-9, 666F2
Ousts 2 pro-Taraki Cabt mins 9-14; move fought, escapes ambush 9-14–9-15, 695D3, 696B1
Succeeds Taraki as pres 9-16, explains power seizure 9-17, 695C3, F3
Fires 4 province govs 9-20, 696C1
Claims Taraki alive 9-23, 748D2
Tactics scored in leaflets 9-26, 748E2
Ex-mins death sentncs commuted 10-8, 787E2
Confirms Taraki death 10-9, 787D2
Army uprising crushed 10-15–10-16, 810F2
Power shift hampers rebel defeat 10-29, 832B1
Overthrown, executed 12-27, 973A1
Carter on overthrow 12-28, 974A1
New govt frees prisoners 12-29, 973C2

AMIN Dada, Maj. Gen. Idi (Ugandan president; replaced April 11)
Obote asks ouster 1-12, 78G1
Chrgs Tanzania attack 1-25, 85C3
Uganda rebel group asks overthrow 2-5, 101B3
Tanzanian forces, Ugandan exiles advance on Kampala, ouster vowed 2-11–3-1, 146C3
Asks OAU mediatn, Nyerere issues demands 2-28, 146G3
Flees Kampala 3-25, denies defeat 4-11; rebels form new govt 4-11, 257B1, D1

1980

AMERICAN Natural Resources Co.
ND synfuels plant gets $1.5 bln fed loan 11-19, ct blocks projct 12-8, 962A1

AMERICAN Occupational Medical Association
UAW pres addresses 4-22, 356G3

AMERICAN Physical Society
Reines addresses 4-30, 416G1

AMERICANS, The (book)
On best-seller list 3-9, 200C3; 4-6, 280D3

AMERICAN Samoa (U.S. territory)
Carter sets econ plan 2-14; govs meet, set projcts 2-19—2-22, 495B1
N Marianas lose US citizenship 3-7, 495F1

AMERICAN Savings & Loan Association
Mortgage rate cut to 12.75% 5-16, 385A1

AMERICANS Concerned About Corporate Power
'Big Business Day' held 4-17, 308G1

AMERICAN Security Council
CBS 'dovish' complaint case refused by Sup Ct 1-7, 16B1
El Salvador rightist honored 7-1, 521E3

AMERICAN Security Council v. FCC
Case refused by Sup Ct 1-7, 16B1

AMERICANS for an Effective Presidency
Reagan funding drive upheld 8-28, 681A2

AMERICANS for Change
Named in Common Cause suit 7-1, 493D1
Reagan funding drive upheld 8-28, 681A2

AMERICANS for Democratic Action (ADA)
Kennedy addresses conv; support reaffirmed 6-14; Carter disaffectn seen 6-15, 480D1

AMERICAN Stock Exchange (AMEX)
Record 1-day loss follows Carter anti-inflatn plan 3-17, 203A3
SEC ends optns trading ban 3-26, 224B2
Index sets record loss, Hunt silver empire totters 3-27, 223B2
Financial Gen deal set 7-25, 600E3
Auto-Train trading halted 8-18, 958F2
Natl securities mkt failure scored 9-12, 806G1
New options issues banned 10-10, 986E2

American Commodities Exchange (ACE)
NYFE merger set 3-21, 224B1

AMERICAN Telephone & Telegraph Co. (AT&T)
In Dow Jones indl avg 76E1
RCA to rent satellite 2-20, 160C3
ITT trust chrgs setld 2-27, 240B1
Phone industry deregulatn set by FCC 4-7, 370G1
Westn Elec on '79 Fortune 500 list 5-5, 290F1
MCI wins $1.8 bln suit 6-13, 456B3
CWA, 2 other union contracts settled 8-9, 648B1
Equipmt suppliers trust setlmt reached 8-18, 917C2
Reorgn begun; managemt realigned, intl unit established, other measures ordrd 8-20, 648E1-A3
DeButts named to Synfuels Corp bd 9-13. Sen panel OKs 9-25, 725F2
Telecommunicatns bill tabled by Cong 9-30, 835E2
DeButts named to interim Synfuels Corp bd 10-5, 786F2
FCC OKs WATS line resales 10-21, 987B3
FCC revises phone deregulatn plan 10-28, 987A3
FCC seeks small cos regulatn end 12-16, 987D3

AMERICAN Telephone v. MCI Telecommunications
MCI wins $1.8 bln suit 6-13, 456B3

AMERICAN Textile Manufacturers Institute, et al v. Marshall
Case accepted by Sup Ct 10-6, 782C1

AMEX—*See AMERICAN Stock Exchange*

AMF Inc.
Benton & Bowles settles FTC bike ad chrg 7-31, 703E1

AMIN, Abdullah
Executed 6-8, 475D2

AMIN, Assadullah
Executed 6-8, 475D2

AMIN, Hafizullah (d. 1979)
Sovts link to CIA, Taraki death 1-3, 1F2
Paputin mtg rptd 1-3, 26C2
Karmal on overthrow 1-10, 27D3
Sovts explain overthrow 1-14, 27G2
Linked to rebels, CIA 1-21, 44F1
Paputin coup role disputed 2-2, 123B3
US issues rights rpt 2-5, 87A1
Karmal says Sovts invaded 10 days before coup 2-7, 85E2
French CP issues rights rpt 2-20, 149E3
13 aides, backers executed 6-8, 6-16, 475B2

AMIN Dada, Maj. Gen. Idi
Army group stages coup 5-11, 375A2
Obote scores 5-27, 446G1
Desires return to Uganda; scores Nyerere 6-3, 446C2
Backers invade Uganda 10-6, 794E2
Backers flee Uganda 10-15, 832F3

1976

UK amb meets on missing hostage 7-8—7-9; says hostage returned 7-9, 515G2
Rpt lauded Israeli raid 7-9, 515A2
Israel vetoed Dayan missn 7-10, 515D1
Rabin ties to hijackers 7-11, 515B2
Israeli raiders impersonatn rptd 7-12, 515E1
UK envoys ousted 7-13—7-22, UK cuts ties 7-28, 547F3, 548D1
Chrgs Kenya oil blockade; sees Zaire, Sudan, Rwanda ambs 7-16, 548F1
Bars Kenya attack, lauds UK role 7-20, 548D2
OKs hijacked jet release 7-21, plane returns to Paris 7-22, 547D1
Resumes Kenya threats 7-24, 7-28; asks UN, OAU mediatn 7-25, 548F2, A3
90 Minutes at Entebbe publshd 7-26, 547C2
Signs Kenya accord 8-7, 580E3
Denies students massacred 8-9, 10-8, 874G1
Frees Kenyans 8-10; vows better UK, Kenya ties 10-7, 874B1
Asks Israel Entebbe paymt 8-19, 663C3
Rpts Chile repressn continues 8-23, 711A1
Returns jet to Israel 9-6, 663A3
Gets rpt on Entebbe raid 11-16, 861C2

AMINOFF, Carl-Goeran
Sworn Finnish forgn trade min 9-29, 750D3

AMMERMAN, Joseph S.
Elected 11-2, 830F3

AMNESTY International (London)
Rpts on Sovt pol patients 1-1, 30A3
Rpts '75 Uruguay pol arrests 1-13, 55E3
Vs World Bank Chile loan 2-3, 99G2
Chrgs Uruguay rights abuse 2-18—3-11, 207E2
Tverdokhlebov sentncd 4-15, 292A2
Uruguay scored by USSR 5-10, US Cong panel 6-5, 441G1, A2
Tverdokhlebov appeal denied 5-12, 421G2
Scores Argentina, Chile, Uruguay 5-24, 399C2-D2 ★
Spain torture chrgs cited 501D2
Scores Haiti jail conditns 6-23, 1005F3
Asks India end emergency rule 6-24, 497A1
Chrgs Pl torture 6-26, govt to probe 6-27, 500D1
Rpts Morocco '73 plotters tried 7-8, 559F3
Guatemala killings rptd 7-23, 12-13, 1004G3
Kennedy: Cuba denies prison access 8-28, 791A2
Chrgs Pl torture 9-15, 751D3
US bans aid to Uruguay 10-1, 814F2
Quoted on Venez prisoners 10-1, 875B1
Rpts rise in Latin repressn 10-31, 975D1
Panel probes Argentine rights abuse 11-5—11-15, 996C2
Chrgs Iran torture 11-28, 925G2
Bukovsky press conf 12-19, 955G2

AMNESTY Issue—*See ARMED Forces under U.S. GOVERNMENT; country names*

AMOCO—*See STANDARD Oil Co. (Indiana)*

AMORN Sirikaya, Adm.
Heads internal affairs 10-8, 775B3

AMOUZEGAR, Jamshid
Meets US energy aide 5-9, 340C1

AMPEX Corp.
Sup Ct bars review of class-action ruling 10-4, 807B3

AMPHETAMINES—*See NARCOTICS & Dangerous Drugs*

AMSTER, Gerald
Sentenced in USSR 8-27, 655F1-A2
Loses appeal 10-26, 857F1

AMSTERDAM, Anthony G.
Vs death sentence 3-30, 3-31, 262B1

AMTRAK (National Railroad Passenger Corp.)
Ford budget proposals 1-21, 66A1
Subsidy enacted 3-30, 233G2

1977

Bars US natls exit, relents 2-25—3-1, 141A1
Bishops protest cited 3-5, 308C3
Asks US reopen embassy 3-6, 308F2
Denies atrocities 3-7, 3-8, 170D2
Atrocity rpts continue 3-9—4-2, 308D1
Jobless round-up decreed 3-12, 308F3
Warns UK, US natls vs lies 3-13, 308E2
Luwum replaced as archbp 3-19, 308G2
Chrgs CIA-church tie 3-26, 308G2
NZ prime min calls 'maniac' 3-31, 258C2
In Zaire; pledges aid, scores Angola 4-22, 317B2
Leaves for more Zaire talks 4-28, 394C1
Chrgs Tanzania plot 5-3, pardons invaders 5-11, 429A2
ICJ condemns killings 5-17, 429G1
Guatemala pres cites 5-20, 414B3
Threatens to 'crash' Commonwealth conf, curb UK natls 6-7—6-8, 486E3
Ex-min claims Bloch, Luwum deaths ordrd 6-8, 487A1
UK natls curbed 6-10, 508B1
Commonwealth conf condemns 6-15, 486B3
Assassinatn plot rptd 6-18, denied 6-23, 507E3
Lifts UK natls curbs 7-1, 600C3
At OAS mtg, confirms death plot 7-4, 512G1
Sees Canada rptr 7-10, chrgs Luwum arms smuggling 7-15, 600A3
Chrgs Army, civilns in plot 7-30, 641G1
Orders EAC employes home 7-30, 200 in Tanzania refuse 8-17, 641B2
7 executns rptd 8-6, 8-17, 641A2
Exile coup plot rptd 8-8, 641F1
On USSR envoy defectn 8-10, 606F2
Coma alleged 9-7, rptd well 9-15, 709G2
15 plotters executed 9-9, 709E2
Ousts Christian groups 9-20, 805D2
Repudiates EAC debts 10-9, 805B2

AMINOIL USA Inc.—*See under REYNOLDS Industries*

AMIT, Meir
Israel transport min 10-24, 827A2

AMNESTY—*See U.S. GOVERNMENT—ARMED Forces; country names*

AMNESTY, National Council for Universal and Unconditional
Scores Viet pardon actn 1-21, 51E2

AMNESTY International
Rpts 800 Brazil pol prisoners 1-1, 3B1
US rpts on Indonesia pol prisoners 1-1, 51B1
Dec '76 Uruguay arrests, deaths chrgd 1-27, 351F3
Chilean asked to end US visit 1-28, 219E2
Iran drops Dutch boycott threat 2-3, 250F1
Accuses Uganda, asks UN probe 2-6, 139F1
Guatemala disappearances, executns rptd 2-21, 168A3
Rpts 1500 Chileans missing 3-16, 493A2
Libya accused 3-24, executns rptd 4-12, 348A3
Ethiopia rights abuses chrgd 3-28, 238B3
S Africa denies Namibia torture chrg 4-4, 349G2
Turchin arrested 7-4, 551B3
Mex police raid rights group 7-7, 746E1
Nicaragua '76 peasant exterminatn chrgd 8-15, govt scores 8-16, 656B2
Drinan '76 Argentina harassmt cited 8-20, 670A2
Lists jailed, missing lawmakers 9-5, 753G1
'75 Panama rights rpt cited 9-8, 699E1
Rpts on Cuba prison abuses 9-17, 781E3
Rhodesia torture chrgd 9-21, 811D2
Rpts Irish police brutality 9-28, 782C3
E Ger pol prisoner chrgd 10-10, 782D1
Wins Nobel Peace Prize 10-10, 951D2
Turchin leaves USSR, Vladimov replaces 10-14, 812B2
W Ger plans terrorist autopsies 10-18, 790C3
Indonesia chrgd re prisoners 10-18, 805E3
Says Haiti abuses continue 10-21, 905G2
Paraguay campaign planned 10-28, 905B3
Morocco torture chrgd 10-31, 869B2
US prisoners probed 11-5, 942G3-943A1
Medical prisoners listed 11-28, 956E2
UN gets amnesty petitn 12-7, 956E2
UN natns rights violatns chrgd 12-8, 956B2
Indonesia prisoner release doubted 12-20, 984C3

AMOCO—*See STANDARD Oil Co. (Indiana)*

AMORN Chantaharasomboon
Arrested 3-30, 243D2

AMOS, John
Roots makes TV history 1-23—1-30, 118G3

AMOUZEGAR, Jamshid (Iranian premier)
Says oil agrmts honored 3-8, 227A3
Iran considers '78 oil price freeze 7-12, 552D2
Becomes Iran premier 8-7, 618E1
Indl expansn plans cut 8-18, 655G2-A3

AMPHETAMINES—*See NARCOTICS & Dangerous Drugs*

AMREP Corp.
Rio Rancho, ATC land sales convictns 1-24, 156A2; 4 sentncd 3-10, 203A3

AMRITRAJ, Vijay
Wins WCT doubles title 5-8, 430D2

AMSTAR Corp.
'76 sales drop rptd 340C1

AMTORG Trading Corp.
USSR ownership cited 10-31, 949G1

AMTRAK (National Railroad Passenger Corp.)
DOT issues future trends rpt 1-15, 58B3
Ford '78 budget proposals 1-17, 33E1
Carter budget revisions 2-22, 125D3

1978

Nyerere vows defeat 11-2; OAU rep sees 11-6, 860B1
Offers Tanzania exit 11-8, Nyerere rejects terms 11-9, 870C2
Says Tanzania exit ordrd, forgn pressure cited; Tanzania denies order 11-14, 870A2
Tanzania attack rptdly aids domestic popularity 11-15, 870B2

AMINI, Ali
In talks on lifting march ban 12-8, 953F2

AMIRZADA Khan
Purged 2-7, 113C1

AMIT, Meir
Quits Cabt, joins DMC group 9-13, 798F3

AMITYVILLE Horror, The (book)
On best-seller list 1-8, 24E3*; 2-5, 116C3; 3-5, 195E3; 9-4, 708D1; 10-9, 800D3

AMMERMAN, Rep. Joseph S. (D, Pa.)
Loses reelectn 11-7, 849E2

AMMON, Ander
Ransomed, kidnapers free 2-17, 133E3

AMMONIA—*See CHEMICALS*

AMMUNITION—*See ARMAMENTS—Firearms, FIREARMS*

AMNESTY International
S Africa torture chrgd 1-19, 39D1
Equatorial Guinea rights abuses rptd 1-25, 152A3
Tanzania '77 rpt cited 2-6, 169E3
Guatemala '77 pol deaths, kidnaps rptd 2-22, 168B3
Iran rights breach chrgd 2-28, 190D2
USSR '77 worker arrests rptd 3-6, 180D1
Torture conf held 3-10—3-11, 180B3
Chile pol prisoner rpt cited 4-5, 267C1
Ethiopia terror rpt cited 4-12, 372F3
Carter lauds Cambodia stand 4-21, 301B2
Uruguay torture probe asked, deaths rptd 5-3, 395G3
Ulster police brutality chrgd 6-1, inquiry set 6-8, 474E1
Uganda rpt to US Sen subcom 6-15, 616F2
Guinea prisoners rptd 6-21, 596D2
Equatorial Guinea prisoners rptd 7-25, 596G1
Tunisia workers rptd tortured 8-1, 671E1
On Argentina May-Aug kidnaps 9-8, 792F3
Amsterdam protest staged re terrorist suspects treatmt 10-9, 885E1
Chrgs Iran torture 12-11, 954E1

AMOCO Cadiz (Liberian supertanker)
Breaks off French coast 3-17, 201C3
Wreakage, oil spill spreads 3-23—3-29, 238B1
US warns Liberia on tanker safety 4-3, 234E1
Shell Brittany hq bombed 5-29, 474C1
French sen comm rpt issued 7-1—7-2, 524C1
Liberian inquiry bd ends hearings 7-1, 524D1
France sues Amoco 9-13, 749C1

AMOCO International Oil Co.—*See under STANDARD Oil Co. (Indiana)*

AMOCO Production Co.—*See under STANDARD Oil Co. (Indiana)*

AMORN Sirikaya, Adm.
Gets Thai Cabt post 8-13, 691B2

AMOS, Sharon
Found dead in Guyana with children 11-19, 890D3
Guyana arrests Beikman 11-25, holds cultists as witnesses 11-28, 910E2
Beikman hearing held 12-4, 955B2
Stephan Jones confesses 12-18, Guyana indicts 12-19, 1000B1

AMOUZEGAR, Jamshid (Iranian premier; replaced Aug. 27)
Bars '78 oil price rise 2-10, 158G2
Replaced 8-27, 667E3

AMRITRAJ, Ashok
Strings win WTT title 9-21, 1027F1

AMRITRAJ, Vijay
Strings win WTT title 9-21, 1027F1

AMSTAR Corp.
Settles 78 civil trust suits 7-28, 768G3

AMSTERDAM, Jack
Sentenced in trust case 2-3, 142E2

AMSTERDAM Kill, The (film)
Released 3-30, 618B3

AMTEL Inc.
'77 stockholder equity return rptd 5-8, 326A1

AMTRAK (National Railroad Passenger Corp.)
Carter budget proposal 1-23, 47C3
Blizzard strands train in Ind 1-25—1-26, 105B3

1979

Lule sworn 4-13, residence toured 4-14, 288A1, A2
Astles rptd arrested 4-18, 288E1
CIA-disputed article publshd 4-19, 309B3
Jinja falls 4-22, 314B3
Scored by USSR 4-29, forgn aid rptd 5-28, 429G1
E Ger aid rptd 5-23, 406A3
EC vows Uganda aid 5-24, 429F2
Locatn rpts vary 5-27, 429F1
Entebbe victim's body found 5-30, 429E1
Koboko taken, conquest rptd complete 6-2–6-3, 429B1
Adrisi rptd in Sudan 6-8, 489B1
Astles trial opens 6-11, 488G3
Confirmed in Libya 6-13, 489A1
Nimeiry scores Tanzania re invasn 7-17, 552C2
Reward for capture set 8-5, 637B3
Uganda pol prisoners freed 10-16, 998E2
Uganda rescinds Christianity ban 11-7, 998D2
Binaisa ousts defens min 11-19, 998B2
Uganda releases Libyan POWs 11-28, 998D2

AMINI, Ali
Bars Iran regency cncl apptmt 1-13, 25G1

AMINI-Afshar, Maj. Gen. Parviz
Executed 2-16, 125E1

AMISH—*See MENNONITES*

AMITYVILLE Horror, The (book)
On best-seller list 1-7, 80D3; 2-4, 120D3; 9-2, 672D3

AMITYVILLE Horror, The (film)
Released 7-26, 819D3
Top-grossing film 8-1, 620G3; 8-29, 672G3

AMMONIA—*See CHEMICALS*

AMMUNITION—*See ARMAMENTS–Firearms; FIREARMS*

AMNESTY International
'78 rpt cites rights violatns by US, others 2-1, 85C2
Rhodesia rebels free 4 whites 2-2, 99B1
Ulster police brutality chrgs backed 3-11, 190F1
CAE students rptd slain 5-14, 387F1
Argentine missing persons rptd 6-17, 467C1
Argentine rights groups harassmt scored 8-13, 611F3
Israel sentncs 2 W Gers for '76 jet plot 9-11, 677E2
Guatemala '78-79 pol deaths listed 9-12, 708D2
Afghan rights breach chrgd 9-19, 748E2
Czech dissident sentncd 10-23, 802D2
Syria torture, Jewish curbs chrgd 10-24, 857A3
'79 rpt cites increased repressn 12-9, 980G1

AMOCO Cadiz (Liberian supertanker)
Wreckage probe rpt issued 3-8, 162C2, A3, 163A1

AMOCO International Oil Co.—*See under STANDARD Oil Co. (Indiana)*

AMON Carter Museum of Western Art (Fort Worth, Tex.)
Johnson named Natl Gallery trustee 5-3, 375F1

AMOS, Sharon (d. 1978)
Jonestown radio message transcripts rptd 1-29, 118E1
S Jones retracts 'confessn' 2-2, 118A1

AMPHETAMINES—*See NARCOTICS & Dangerous Drugs*

AMPUTATION—*See MEDICINE–Surgery*

AMRAM, Avraham
Traded for PLO prisoners 3-14, 178G2

AMRITRAJ, Vijay
Wins Indian Grand Prix 11-25, 1003G3

AMSTUTZ, J. Bruce
Secret cable details Dubs death 2-22, 147F1

AMTRAK (National Railroad Passenger Corp.)
Carter budget proposals 1-22, 45C1
Route cutback plan revised; maps 1-31, 129A1, C1

1980

AMIRANTE, Sam
Gacy convicted 3-12, gets death sentence 3-13, 214F1

AMIS, Martin
Saturn 3 released 2-15, 216D3

AMITYVILLE Horror, The (film)
'79 top domestic rental film 2-6, 120G2
Jay Anson dies 3-12, 279C1

AMMONIA—*See CHEMICALS*

AMMUNITION—*See ARMAMENTS--Firearms, FIREARMS*

AMNESTY International
Colombia harrassmt chrgd 1-17, 96E2
Sakharov exile condemned 1-22, 46C3
2 Argentine ex-prisoners describe detentn 2-4, 95A1
Nigeria record cited 3-3, 354F1
Liberia pres slain in coup 4-12, 285A1
Colombia rpt issued 4-16, Turbay scores 4-20, 311F3, 335F2
USSR '75-79 dvpts rptd 4-29, 326A2
W Ger prisoner abuse chrgd, Bonn denies 5-28, 411E2, 446E3
Turkey torture chrgd 6-9, 445D3
Iran executns scored, hostage pleas cited 8-28, 671E2
Chile rpt issued, rights abuses protested 9-8, 749C1
2d Colombia rpt issued, torture chrgs documented 9-22, 749A2
Turkish torture, jail deaths chrgd 11-27, 923E3
'80 rpt issued 12-10, 978D2

AMOCO International Oil Co.—*See under STANDARD Oil Co. (Indiana)*

AMOS, Linda Sharon
Beikman sentenced 4-8, 313C3

AMOS, Sharon
Beikman chrgs rptd dropped 9-20, 751B1

AMOUDI, Sheik Mohammed al-
In Hunt silver-backed bond group 3-26, 223B1

AMPEX Corp.
Signal agrees to buy 2-19, 385F3-386A1
Signal merger revised 10-13, signed 10-29, 985F1

AMRAM, David
Harold & Maude opens 2-7, 136B3

AMRAN, Maj. Gen. Abdul-Majid
Saudi land forces cmdr 1-1, 22D1

AMRITRAJ, Vijay
Loses WCT Tourn of Champs 2-24, Milan WCT 3-30, 607F2, A3
Wins Hall of Fame championship 7-14, 691G2
Wins Bangkok Grand Prix 11-23, 947F2
Loses WCT Challenge Cup 12-14, 1002D2

AMTRAK (National Railroad Passenger Corp.)
Carter budget proposals 1-28, 73B1
NC train wreck injuries 100 4-2, 391F3
NE Corridor aid clears Cong 5-22, signed 5-30, 427E1

1976

To buy Boston-DC corridor 4-1, 235B2
Cong clears '77 funds 8-4, 646B2; signed 8-14, 982F1
Moot named Ford campaign com treas 8-24, 688B3
Boston-DC corridor buy set 8-29, 648G1
'77, '78 subsidy signed 10-19, 834D2
AMVETS—*See VETERANS of World War II, Korea and Vietnam, American*
ANACONDA Co.
'70 anti-Allende aid offer rptd 12-23, 999A2
ANAHEIM, Calif.—*See CALIFORNIA*
ANANDA Marga—*See PATH of Bliss*
ANAND Panyarachun
Ousted 10-24, 813G2
ANCHORAGE, Alaska—*See ALASKA*
ANCHORAGE Daily News (newspaper)
Wins Pulitzer Prize 5-3, 352D3
ANDA, Geza
Dies 6-13, 524C2
ANDEAN Group (Bolivia, Chile, Colombia, Ecuador, Peru, Venezuela)
Kissinger pledges US support 2-17, 177C2
Peru, Bolivia, Ecuador score IDB 5-18, 5-19, 465E3
Chile leaves 10-6, 999D1
ANDERS, Andy
Named in grain fraud 3-11, 247C3
ANDERS, William A.
Defends A-plant safety 2-10, 115A2
Amb to Norway 3-18; confrmd 4-1, 262B3
ANDERSEN & Co., Arthur
Merck panel scores 3-9, 361A2
Alyeska audit set 5-21, results 7-6, 690C3
ANDERSON, George Lee (Sparky)
Reds win World Series 10-21, 815G1
ANDERSON, Rep. Glenn M. (D, Calif.)
Reelected 11-2, 829D1
ANDERSON, Gregorio Villagran
Arrested 1-8, 45C2-B3, D3; sentncd 3-3, 454F3-455A1
ANDERSON, Jack
Rpts Noel interview 4-24, 357F3
Rpts GOP conv vote bribe chrg 8-17, 616G1
Rpts US Steel hosted Ford 9-21, 722F2
Resigns from bank bd 11-21, 899B2

ANDERSON, Rep. John B. (R, Ill.)
Backs Ford 5-11, 343E1
Vs Connally vp selectn 8-5, 584G2
Asks Butz dismissal 10-2, 744C2
Reelected 11-2, 829A3
GOP conf chairman 12-8, 981D3

1977

Sets fare hikes, "Mountaineer" service to end 5-3, 368D3
Fare hike set 8-31, redcap svc end blocked 9-12, '78 added funds sought 9-19, 778E2
Fla truck-train collisn 10-2, 992G2
Cong com votes '78 added funds, cuts canceled 11-3, 860E3
AMUR River
USSR, China reach accord 10-7, 853D2
AMVETS—*See VETERANS of World War II, Korea and Vietnam, American*
ANACONDA Co., The
'70 anti-Allende aid offer cited 1-9, 18G2
Arco completes merger 1-12, 55F2
Arco takeover cited in table 880F1
Aluminum output cut 2-16, 244E3
Copper price raised 3-18, 209C2
OPIC Chile claim setld 3-31, 449F1
Strike begins 7-1, 558G1
Cuts copper prices 7-2, 7-20, 577D2
ANASTASI Brothers Corp.
Govt bars contracts 8-25, 669F2
Govt reinstates 11-23, 979F2
ANCHORAGE, Alaska—*See ALASKA*
ANCHOR Hocking Corp.
Strike ends 10-14, 818F3
ANCHOVIES—*See FISH & Fishing*
ANDEAN Group (Bolivia, Colombia, Ecuador, Peru, Venezuela)
Chile revokes tariff, investmt rules 1-3, 18G1
Chile sets new forgn investmt law 3-18, 449A1
Peru seeks arms control pact 6-3, 455C1
ANDERS, William A.
Replaced as amb to Norway 7-13, 626A3
ANDERSEN, Knud
Danish forgn min 2-25, 373D1
ANDERSEN & Co., Arthur
Sen subcom rpt scores 1-17, 78C3, E3
Hamilton trustees sue 2-11, 155A3
OKs Mattel case paymt 4-26, 519D3
Earnings disclosure cited 5-10, 519D3
Rptd 2d largest acctg firm 8-22, 650G2
ANDERSON, Judge Aldon J.
Rejcts Gilmore stay 1-14, 40A2
ANDERSON, Bette Beasley
Named Treas undersecy 3-4, confrmd 3-29, 272E2
ANDERSON, Eddie (Rochester)
Dies 2-28, 164B2
ANDERSON, Edwin F.
Indicted 6-6, 504C1
ANDERSON, Jack
CIA surveillance rptd 5-4, 423A1
On Letelier death 9-8, 743F2

ANDERSON, Rep. John B. (R, Ill.)
On proposed King hearing 3-3, 149F1

1978

NE rail offcls resign 1-30; more funds allocated 2-11, projct delays rptd 2-24, 225B1
Reistrup resigns as pres 3-29, 284C2
Boyd named pres 4-25, 349A2
Route cutbacks proposed 5-8, 366C1
AMURRIO, Casiano
Bolivia pres nominatn rptd 5-30, 478G2
AMUSEMENT Parks—*See PARKS & Recreation Areas*
AMYGDALIN (Laetrile)—*See MEDICINE—Laetrile*
ANACIN—*See MEDICINE—Drugs*
ANACONDA Co., The (Atlantic Richfield subsidiary)
Strike ends at brass plants 4-3, 284C3
'77 sales rptd up 5-8, 325A2
US sues re price fixing 9-22, 769A1
ANAHEIM, Calif.—*See CALIFORNIA*
ANAYA, Toney
Unopposed in NM primary for US Sen 6-6, 448C2
Loses electn 11-7, 855D2
ANCHORAGE, Alaska—*See ALASKA*
ANDEAN Group (Bolivia, Colombia, Ecuador, Venezuela, Peru)
Colombia pres vows support 8-7, 629A3
ANDEH, Davidson
Wins World Amateur Boxing tourn 5-6—5-20, 600E2
ANDERSEN, Anar
Killed 6-27, 519E1
ANDERSEN, Anders
Named Danish econ min 8-30, 688A1
ANDERSEN & Co., Arthur
Issues '77 financial data 84D1
ANDERSON, Ind.—*See INDIANA*
ANDERSON, Christopher
Rhodesia law, order min 11-18, 912D2
ANDERSON, Craig
Da opens 3-13, 887E1
Winning Isn't Everything opens 12-3, 1031C3
ANDERSON, D. R.
Bistro Car opens 3-23, 887B1
ANDERSON, Frank
Cromwell opens 7-12, 887E1
ANDERSON, Fred
On Proposition 13 7-6, 526A1
ANDERSON, Rep. Glenn M. (D, Calif.)
Reelected 11-7, 850B2
ANDERSON, Jack
Suit vs Nixon, aides dismissed 4-4, 265B1
Rpts Bourne drug use, Bourne denies 7-20, 568C1
Vesco 'pol fix' chrg denied by Admin 9-10; revises column 9-11, 719D3, 720A1
ANDERSON, Jodi
Sets long jump mark 6-8—6-10, 600C3
ANDERSON, John
In NFL draft 5-2, 336G2

ANDERSON, Rep. John B. (R, Ill.)
Wins renomination 3-21, 207E1
Carter, GOP energy conferees meet 4-12, 304C2
Scores farm aid bill 5-4, 343A2
Cong electn funds rejected 7-19, 550G2
Reelected 11-7, 850E3
Reelected GOP conf chrmn 12-4, 958G1
Backs full China ties 12-16, 976A1

1979

Fare hike set 2-20, 167D1
Fares raised 7-15, 726C3
Carter backs 8-7, 592E3
6 trains ordrd cut 8-29, San Joaquin to continue operatn 8-31, 868A1
May-June record ridership rptd 9-8, 726G2-C3
Staff shake-up announced 9-26, 868E1
Fare hike set 9-27, 868E1
'80-82 authrzn clears Cong 9-25, 9-27, Carter signs 9-29, 867C3-868A1
Ill, Kan, Mich crashes kill 7 10-2, 10-12, 10-13, 800F1
'Superliner' unveiled 10-12, 868F1
'80 funds clear Cong 11-15, 11-19, Carter signs 11-30, 920E1
AMWAY Corp.
Price-fixing end ordrd 5-23, 985F3
AMYGDALIN (Laetrile)—*See MEDICINE-Laetrile*
ANACONDA Co., The (of Atlantic Richfield)
Chile copper exploratn set 5-10, 369B3
ANAMBAS Islands—*See INDONESIA*
ANASTASIO, Anthony
Indicted 1-17, 87A3
Convicted 11-15, 890D1
ANASTASIO, Anthony (Tough Tony) (d. 1963)
Scotto, others indicted 1-17, 87B3
Scotto, nephew convicted 11-15, 890D1
ANCHORAGE, Alaska—*See ALASKA*
ANCHOUEY, Michel
Lome pact talks collapse 5-26, 399B1
Lome pact extensn set 6-27, 512F3
ANCHOVIES—*See FISHING Industry*
ANDEAN Group (Bolivia, Colombia, Ecuador, Peru, Venezuela)
10th anniv mtg: Ct of Justice formed; expanded trade, econ dvpt planned 5-26—5-28, 398A2
Venez, Ecuador mins see Somoza, urge pol solutn 6-11, 446E3
Nicaragua rebels praised 6-17, 461B2
US seeks joint Nicaragua pol solutn 7-4—7-6, rebels rejct 7-5, 503E3-504E1
ANDERSEN & Co., Arthur
Regulatory costs rptd 3-14, 230F2
ANDERSON, Arthur B.
Asks US apology for A-cancer 1-13, 91C1
ANDERSON, Christopher
Zimbabwe justice min 5-30, 393E1
ANDERSON, Craig
Lovely Sunday opens 1-21, 292A2
On Golden Pond opens 2-28, 712G1
Ride A Cock Horse opens 3-18, 292E2
ANDERSON, David
Firing case declined by Sup Ct 6-4, 439A2
ANDERSON, Gordon
Loses North Amer squash tourn 1-14, 527A2
ANDERSON, Jack
Niehous' wife appeals to kidnapers 2-12, 192G3
Rpts CIA '63 Castro death plot confrmd 5-2, 367E3-368A1
Admin denies forgn spy aid rpt 8-9, 664C2
On E Timor famine, fighting 11-8, 856C1
ANDERSON, James R.
US mil spending inequities rptd 11-18, 904F1
ANDERSON, Jay
Amityville Horror on best-seller list 9-2, 672D3
ANDERSON, John
On diesel fuel supplies 5-18, 361C3
ANDERSON, Rep. John B. (R, Ill.)
House GOP Conf chrmn 71B1
Alaska land bill OKd 5-16, 367A1
Announces pres bid 6-8, 439C2
Pres campaign funds rptd 7-12, 594A1
Scores Carter energy speech 7-15, 534F2

1980

'81 Transport funds clear Cong 9-30, signed 10-9, 980E3
AMY, Jose
Errico convicted 5-19, 447B3
AMYGDALIN (Laetrile)—*See MEDICINE--Laetrile*
ANACONDA Co., The (of Atlantic Richfield)
2 Montana units to close 9-30, 825F2
USW copper strike continues 10-24, 805A3
USW copper strike ends 11-21, 987G3
ANAHEIM—*See CALIFORNIA*
ANASTASIO, Anthony
Sentenced 1-23, 64A3
ANATOMY Illustrated (book)
Wins Amer Book Award 5-1, 692C2
ANATOMY of an Illness (book)
On best-seller list 2-10, 120C3; 3-9, 200C3; 5-4, 359E3
ANCHORAGE—*See ALASKA*
ANDEAN Group (Bolivia, Colombia, Ecuador, Peru, Venezuela)
Cuban refugee resetlmt debated 4-9—4-10, US offers sanctuary 4-10, 261D2
Bolivia mil coup condemned 7-29, 577D1
Bolivia denounces members 8-6, 602F3
Bolivia debt paymts postponed 9-3, 686B3
Bolivia to boycott Santa Marta conf 12-10; threatns participatn end 12-18, 992A2
ANDERS, Karen
Manhattan Showboat opens 7-1, 756E3
ANDERS, Robert C.
Escapes Iran 1-28, 66E2
Details escape 2-1, 88D3; 2-12, 106E1
ANDERSCH, Alfred
Dies 2-21, 279C1
ANDERSEN, Terje
Wins Olympic medal 2-21, 156A1
ANDERSON, Eileen
Wins Honolulu mayoral primary 9-20, 745D1
ANDERSON, Glenn
Dies 6-25, 528A1
ANDERSON, Rep. Glenn M. (D, Calif.)
Reelected 11-4, 842B2
ANDERSON, Ian
Arrows win MISL title 3-23, 771B2
ANDERSON, Jack
Peace Corp volunteer freed 2-11, 117B1
Liddy book excerpts reveal death plot 4-21, 333A3, B3
Got B Carter Libya cables in '79 7-31, 570A1
Rpts US Iran invasion plan 8-16; says publicatn decision 'anguishing' 8-18, 635A1
Iran militants move US hostages, invasn plan discounted 8-25, 644A2, B2
ANDERSON, Jodi
Sets indoor 640-yd relay mark 2-29, 892E1
Wins US Olympic trials women's pentathlon 6-21; sets long jump mark, denies steroid chrg 6-28, 891D2

ANDERSON, Rep. John B. (R, Ill.)
In Ia GOP debate, backs USSR grain embargo, gas tax 1-5, 4F2, G2, E3
Ia poll results 1-11, 33F1, G1
6th in Iowa caucus vote 1-21, 50F1
Publicity problem rptd, strategy detailed 2-15, 129D2
NH gun control forum 2-18, GOP pres debate 2-20, 129B3, E3, G3
NH debate exclusn spurs controversy 2-23, 143D1
Wins 10% in NH primary 2-26, 142D3, G3, 143F1
2d in Mass, Vt primaries 3-4, 166C2-F3
Wins 9% in Fla, Ga primaries 3-11, 183C3
In Ill GOP forum 3-13, 206E2
2d in Ill primary 3-18, stresses Reagan oppositn 3-19, 206D2, G3
3d in Conn primary 3-25, 221E2, B3
Mulls over independent bid 3-25, 221E3
Gallup Poll results 3-31, 4-1, 246F3, 247B1
Wis, Kan primary results 4-1, 246G1, A2, A3
Addresses newspr eds, weighs independent pres bid 4-10, 264E3
Poll rating negative 4-18, 305A1
On rivals in Playboy interview 4-20, 328C1
Not in Pa primary 4-22, 304C2
Announces independent bid 4-24, 303D2
Garth named media consultant 4-24, campaign mgr 8-28, 665B3
Would drop bid if aided Reagan win 4-25, 328B1
Sears: could win 4-29, 328E1
Tex uncommitted vote cited 5-3, 342G2
Tenn, Ind, NC pres primary results 5-6, 342C1
Md, Neb primary results 5-13, 366F2, G2, C3
Poll results 5-19—6-23, 452A2
Mich, Ore vote results 5-20, 382G3-383E1
Kennedy warns Carter 5-21, 383F1
Ford sees House deciding electn 5-26, 399G2

1976

ANDERSON, John D.
Links unemploymt, inflatn 11-15, 869E3
ANDERSON, Martin
Seeks GOP platform compromise 8-17, 601B1
ANDERSON, Robert
Amb to Morocco 1-20; confrmd 1-28, 110A2
ANDERSON, Robert B.
Currie censured 3-16, 200B3
ANDERSON, Thomas J.
Amer Party pres candidate 6-18, 490C3
Pres debate suit rejctd 9-17, 703E2
Ill press endorsemt rptd 10-30, 827E3 ★
Final pres vote tally 12-18, 979B2
ANDERSON, Gov. Wendell R. (D, Minn.)
Platform hearings 5-17—5-20, 357G2, 358A1
Reserve Mining deadline set 7-7, 570F3
With Carter at Farm Fest 9-15, 686D3
Seeks Mondale Sen seat 11-10, 865B1
ANDERSSON, Bibi
Announces expatriatn 4-22, 368E3
ANDIEV, Soslan
Wins Olympic medal 7-31, 576E3
ANDLEMAN, David
Rpts Cambodia populatn shift 1-19, 46D2
ANDO, Kenkichi
Wins Olympic medal 7-19, 576D2
ANDORRA
Listed as 'partly free' 1-19, 20C3
ANDRAS, Robert K.
Sworn Treasury Bd pres 9-15, 692D1
To discipline strikers 10-19, 836D3
Sets audit rpt study comm 11-2, 904B1
ANDRE, Antonio
Loses Cabt post 9-7, 1005D3
ANDRE, Gen. Valerie
Named French gen 4-21, 316F1
ANDREAS, Dwayne O.
Ford donatn rptd 10-22, 938F3
ANDREOTTI, Giulio
Named CIA aid recipient 1-31, comments 2-2, 140C3, E3
Denies oil co payoffs 4-11, 267C2
Named premier 7-13, 539A1
US, W Eur loan ban rptd 7-16, 531C1
Sees oppositn party ldrs 7-22—7-23, CP Cabt role seen 7-24—7-27, 556E3, G3
Meets CP Cabt demand 7-29, 573C1
Sworn premier 7-30, 573B1, F1
Presents austerity plan 8-4, 573A2
Gets confidence vote 8-6, 8-11, 624C1

1977

ANDERSON, Ken
Tarkenton breaks passing record 11-13, 1019D3
ANDERSON, M. E.
Signs UFW pact 3-10, 177E3
ANDERSON, Marian
1st black DAR member rptd 12-3, 1021D2
ANDERSON, Philip W.
Wins Nobel Prize 10-11, 951G2
ANDERSON, Roy A.
Named Lockheed chrmn 9-29, 858D3
ANDERSON Clayton & Co.
Seeks Gerber takeover 4-18, ends bid 9-19, 799F1
Bid-cutting strategy cited 8-12, 799E1
ANDORRA (French-Spanish principality)
Gen Cncl asks financial review 1-5, 47G3
ANDRADE, Paes de
Asks MDB disband 7-1, 541A2
ANDRADE, Silva Pereira de
Seized in 'death squad' murders 8-31, 805A3
ANDRAS, Robert Knight
Issues civil svc bilingual rules 9-30, 763E2
ANDREOTTI, Giulio (Italian premier)
Wage curb plan rejctd 1-6, 8D2
Sees Schmidt in Bonn 1-17—1-18, 64F3
Mondale visits 1-26, 69C1
At 7-natn econ summit 5-7—5-8, 357C1
Sees Giscard in Paris 7-19, Carter in US 7-25—7-27, 581A2
Kappler jail escape delays Schmidt mtg 8-15, 638B1
Kappler escape stirs pol crisis 8-18—9-18; demotes Lattanzio 9-18, 728G3, 729C1
Accepts Zamberletti resignatn 9-1, 783E1
Testifies at '69 Milan bombing trial 9-15, 1014D3
Meets Schmidt in Verona 12-1, 1014G3
Canada A-pact rptd signed 12-15, 982A3

1978

ANDERSON, Knud B.
Quits Danish Cabt, sets parlt bid 6-2, 596E1
ANDERSON, Lindsay
Kingfisher opens 12-6, 1031B2
ANDERSON, M. E.
'76 earnings rptd 2-20, 365B2
ANDERSON, Marian
Receives Cong gold medal 10-17, 844F1
ANDERSON, Max
Crosses Atlantic by balloon 8-11—8-17, '77 attempt cited 652E3
ANDERSON, Sparky
NL wins All-Star game 7-11, 559C3
Fired as Reds mgr 11-28, 1026E1
ANDERSON, Warren M.
Role in NYC fiscal crisis 86C3
ANDERSON, Sen. Wendell (D, Minn.)
Votes for Panama Canal neutrality pact 3-16, 177D2
Votes for 2d Canal pact 4-18, 273B1
Wins primary 9-12, 716C1
Loses reelectn 11-7, 845E2, 846B1, 854A3
ANDERSON, Clayton & Co. v. U.S.
Corp earnings tax case refused by Sup Ct 6-5, 431F2
ANDRAS, Ferenc
Rain & Shine released 12-21, 1030D3
ANDRAS, Robert Knight
Details budget cuts 8-16, 666C2
Sets further spending cuts 9-8, 739B1
Vs PC mortgage tax relief 9-28, 755C2
To head Econ Dvpt Bd, replaced on Treas Bd 11-24, 921A3-D3
ANDRE, Armand
Confirms Baader gang suicides 1-23, 114G3
ANDREAS, Dwayne O.
Gartner bars resignatn re stock gift 6-28, 513A3
ANDREI, Stefan
In Hungary 2-16—2-19, 180D2
ANDREOTTI, Giulio (Italian premier)
Testifies at Miceli trial 1-9, 19G1
Submits govt resignatn 1-16, 37F3
Meets Sadat 2-13, 98B3
Rpts govt econ plans 3-10, 191B1
Forms Cabt with CP support 3-11, 190G2, 191B1

1979

ANDERSON, Kenneth C.
Vs AT&T speedy trust trial date 1-11, 88B3
ANDERSON, Martin
Reagan staff chng cited 11-14, 982E2
ANDERSON, Ottis
In NFL draft 5-3, 335F1
ANDERSON, Peggy
Nurse on best-seller list 11-4, 892D3
ANDERSON, Peter
Whitecaps win NASL title 9-8, 775A3
ANDERSON, Rick
Traded to Mariners 11-1, 1002C3
ANDERSON, Sparky
Hired as Tigers mgr 6-12, 619C2
ANDERSON, Wendell
Labor '78 campaign gifts rptd 6-13, 595D1
ANDERSON Clayton Inc.
Chrgd re coffee price squeeze 3-13, 348A2
ANDERSSON, Bibi
Quintet released 2-8, 174D3
ANDERS v. Floyd
SC abortn prosecutn ban voided by US Sup Ct 3-5, 185B1
AND Justice For All (film)
Released 10-19, 1007G2
Top-grossing film 10-31, 892G3
ANDINO, Mario
Joins El Salvador junta 10-17, 790F2
ANDRACA Roca, Manuel
Assassinated 2-14, 237E1
ANDRADE Fajardo, Antonio
Ecuador agri min 12-9, 967E3
ANDREAS, Christine
Oklahoma opens 12-13, 1007D2
ANDREAZZA, Mario
Brazil interior min designate 1-19, 95D1
Says Jari to be Brazil-run 7-12, 542B2
ANDREOTTI, Giulio (Italian premier; replaced Aug. 5)
Controversial state co heads nominated 1-8, 20F3
'79-81 econ plan revealed 1-15, 38C2
Stockbrokers score Pazzi apptmt, strike 1-17, 38F3
CP demands more influence 1-18, 38B3, C3
Resigns govt 1-31, 76E1, C2
Parlt probe of Moro kidnap sought 2-8, 98A1; OKd 2-9, 136B1

1980

Ida, Ky primary votes 5-27, 399D2, E2
Carter bars any debate, Reagan favors 5-27, 399A3
Pres polls rptd 6-3, 423B1, C1
Calif, NM, SD primary results 6-3, 423B2-G2
Scores Carter on economy 6-6, 437B3
Addresses Mayors Conf, urges urban aid progrm 6-9, 438F3
Registratn funding signed 6-12, 478D2
24 offcls protest Dem, GOP ballot moves 6-24, 493C2
Delegate count table 6-28, 506B2
Reaffirms pres bid 7-1, 493F1
Addresses NAACP 7-1, 515F2, G2
On Mideast, Eur tour 7-7—7-18, scores Reagan 7-20, 549F2
Crisp vs GOP platform 7-9, 506G2
Gets 37 votes at GOP conv 7-16, 529E1
PLO scores Israel stand 7-22, 572C2
2d in Calif poll 7-30, 570C2
Sees Kennedy, holds news conf 7-31, 570C2
Rpts '79 tax data 8-4, 596D3
Addresses Urban League, backs cities aid 8-4, 597E1
Assaulted in Denver 8-5, 596E3-597A1
Poll ratings 13%-15% 8-17, 8-19, 630B1
Presents defense views 8-19, 629F3-630A1
Clark asks pres race withdrawal 8-20, 682B1
Picks Lucey as running mate 8-25, 646B3
Carey vows Carter reelectn support 8-28, 663F2
Offers platform 8-30, 664F3
Campaign ruled eligible for fed funds, finances rptd 9-4, 665C2
Addresses B'nai B'rith; vows Israel support 9-4, 681G3
Poll sees vote shift in NY 9-5, gets Liberal Party endorsemt 9-6, 681D1
Carter rejcts 3-way debate 9-9, decisn scored 9-10, 680D2
Debates on TV with Reagan, notes Carter absence 9-21, 721C2-722E2
Deplores warmongering issue 9-23, 722C3
Post-debate poll findings 9-23—9-28, 739F2
2d debate plans falter 9-25, 739F3
Ballot access costly, 43 states gained 9-27, 818B2
Scolds fundamentalists 9-29, 739C2
Talks to black journalists 9-29, 739E2
Bank loan plan fails 10-2, abandoned 10-15, 818E1
Commoner uses vulgar radio ad 10-15, 818A3
Excluded from TV debate 10-21, 801F3
Poll rating at 9% 10-27, 816G1
Answers Carter, Reagan debate questns on cable TV 10-28, declares 'draw' 10-29, 815F3
Clark on 50 state ballots 10-28, 818E2
Press endorsemts rptd 11-1, 841E3, 844F1
Reagan favored by London gamblers 11-3, 844F3
Wins 7% pres vote 11-4, '84 run possible 11-5, 837F2, 838F3
Exit poll results 11-4, 838G1
Popular vote table 11-4, 838A2
Martin wins seat 11-4, 850D3
FEC paymt $4.1 mln 11-13, 866F1
ANDERSON, Ken
NFL '79 passing ldr 1-5, 8A2
ANDERSON, Kris
Crosses N Amer by balloon 5-12—5-15, 470E3
ANDERSON, Larry
NFL '79 kick return ldr 1-5, 8D3
Steelers win Super Bowl 1-20, 61D3-62C1
ANDERSON, Marjorie D.
Loses US House electn 11-4, 848C1
ANDERSON, Martin
Named Reagan domestic aide 12-23, 980A2
ANDERSON, Mary
At anti-US conf in Iran 6-2—6-5, 418D2, 419D1
ANDERSON, Maxie L.
Crosses N Amer by balloon 5-12—5-15, 470E3
ANDERSON, O. J. (Ottis Jerome)
NFL '79 rushing ldr 1-5, 8E3
Named NFL top rookie 1-9, 175B1
ANDERSON, Roar
USF wins NCAA soccer title 12-14, 1001D3
ANDERSON, Steve
Loses US House primary 5-20, 404C3
ANDERSON Hospital and Tumor Institute, M. D. (Houston, Tex.)
Interferon productn rptd up 3-5, 317C3
ANDIEV, Sosian
Wins Olympic medal 7-31, 624E3
ANDINO, Mario
Quits El Salvador junta 1-4, 19G3
AND I Worked at the Writer's Trade (book)
Wins Amer Book Award 5-1, 692C2
ANDRADE, Francisco
Jari project dispute rptd 10-16, 787A3
ANDRADE Manrique, Felio
Heads M-19 jail break probe 6-25, 521C2
ANDRE, Harvie
Scores US gas purchases 4-21, 334E3
ANDREATTA, Benjamino
Named Italy min without portfolio 4-4, 275F3
Named treas min 10-18, 809B1
ANDREI, Vasile
Wins Olympic medal 7-23, 624B3
ANDREOTTI, Giulio
Christian Dems bar CP Cabt posts 2-21, 134D1
Piccoli voted party secy 3-6, 194F2

1976

Denies Lockheed payoffs 8-31, letters publshd 9-1, 684B3
Rpts austerity measures 10-1, 751E2
Payoff probe dropped 10-13, 858A2
CP backs austerity plan 10-18, 838B2
Sees Venez pres 11-18, 929C3
Withdraws pay freeze 11-23, 947B2
Giscard asks econ summit 12-2, 964E1
Ends US visit 12-8, 947D1
ANDREWS, Rep. Ike F. (D, N.C.)
Reelected 11-2, 830E2
ANDREWS, Rep. Mark (R, N.D.)
Reelected 11-2, 823D3, 830F2
ANDRIANARAHINJAKA, Lucien Xavier Michel
Malagasy pres counselor 8-20, 926C1
ANDRIANOV, Nikolai
Wins Olympic medals 7-21, 7-23, 574B3-D3
ANDROPOV, Yuri V.
Named to Politburo 3-5, 195B2
ANDRUS, Gov. Cecil D. (D, Idaho)
Named Govs Conf chairman 7-6, 493B1
Named Interior secy 12-18, 956E1
Photo 956A3
Biographical sketch 957C1
ANER, Kerstin
Named to Swedish Cabt 10-8, 794C2
ANGEL and Big Joe (film)
Wins Oscar 3-29, 240B3
ANGELELLI, Bishop Enrique
Dies 8-4, foul play suspected 8-6, 9-2, 672E1
ANGELS (book)
On best seller list 1-25, 80C3; 2-29, 208F3; 12-5, 972B2
ANGHELOV, Stefan
Wins Olympic medal 7-24, 576G2
ANGLICANS—*See also EPISCOPAL Church, Protestant*
Coggan, Pope dispute female ordinatn 8-20, 756A1
Guyana govt takes over schools 10-1, 1005D2
Canada ordains women 11-29, 932C1
ANGLO-American Corp. of South Africa Ltd.
Chrysler-Illings merger set 11-3, 856D1
ANGLO-Ecuadorean Oilfields Ltd.
Yields oil installatns 1-16, 49F1

1977

ANDRESKI, Mitchell
Killed 1-20, 65G3
Killers seized 4-13—4-14, 528G3
ANDRETTI, Mario
Wins Calif Grand Prix 4-3, 2d in US Grand Prix 10-1; final standing 10-23, 870D3, E3
2d in Schaefer 500 6-26, 871D1
ANDREWS, Ammett
Joins AFL-CIO exec cncl 12-12, 961G1
ANDRIESSEN, Frans
Named Dutch finance min 12-19, 986B1
ANDRONIKOS, Manolis
Finds King Philip's tomb 11-24, 952D1
ANDROPOV, Yuri Vladimirovich
Scores dissidents as spies 9-9, 753E1
ANDRUS, Cecil D.
Sen com OKs nominatn 1-18, confrmd 1-20, 34B1, G3
On Western drought 2-15, 2-20, 152E3
Water projct cuts protested 2-23, 209E3
Rpts personal finances 2-25, 147C3
Ties oil lease renewal to productn 3-15, 195F3
Asks Redwood Pk expansn 4-19, 322G3
Delays offshore oil sales 5-17, explains 5-19, 6-3, 498F3
Cancels 2 offshore leases 6-8, 499C1
Orders Alaska pipe blast probe 7-11, 537F3
Alaska pipe resumptn OKd 7-18, 558B3
Seeks Westn land holdings breakup 8-22, 703G1
On E Coast offshore drilling 8-25, 650C1
Proposes Alaska parks plan 9-15, 739A3
Mendelsohn nominatn withdrawn 11-11, 877B2
ANGEL Dust—*See NARCOTICS*
'ANGEL of Death'—*See MENGELE, Josef*
ANGLICAN Church in America—*See ANGLICANS*
ANGLICAN Church of North America
Episc fellowship forms 9-14—9-16, 731C2
Episc secessn data 9-30, 845B2
Fla parish joins 10-2, 845G2-A3
US Episc bishops score 10-5, 845D2
ANGLICANS—*See also EPISCOPAL Church, Protestant*
RC papal primacy agrmt issued 1-18, 119D3
S Africa schls to desegregate 1-22, 67F1
Police accused in S Africa unrest 1-25, 100A3
Vatican scores female ordinatn 1-27, 119B3
Uganda archbp killed 2-16; Coggan, Brown score 2-17, 2-21, 138B3, 139D1
S Africa apartheid scored, priest sentncd 2-17, 145F1
Rumania Canterbury rep rptd held 3-3, 314E2
Uganda ousts white bishop 3-4; OAU, UN help sought 3-14, 308A3
Uganda archbp named 3-19, 308F2
Coggan sees Pope 4-28—4-29, 374F2
Coggan, E Orth ldr dispute ordinatn of women 5-1, 374D3
Canada synod meets; gets euthanasia rpt 8-17, drops abortn debate 8-18, 732G1
Uganda permits freedom 9-20, 805D2
Coggan, Russian Orth debate women priests 9-25, 845B3
Guyana sugar strikers' food rptd seized 11-4, 869G1
Anglican Church of North America—*See separate listing*
ANGLO-American Corp. of South Africa Ltd.
Coal miners protest 6-1, 469B2
Govt bars manganese deal 8-16, 657B2

1978

Moro kidnaped; adjourns Parlt, calls Cabt mtg 3-16, 199F2
At Moro guards' funeral 3-17, 199D3
Wins confidence vote 3-17, 200B2
Moro letter released 4-4, 246E3
Takes hard-line vs terrorism, bars talks 4-4, 246E3, 247F1
Addresses Parlt 5-10, fears electn rift 5-11, 338A1
Takes over Interior post 5-11, 393F2
Denies negligence in Moro death 5-23, Moro's widow scores 5-25, 689G2
Rognoni named Interior min 6-13, 558B2
Pertini elected pres 7-8, 558A1
At 7-natn Bonn econ summit 7-16—7-17, 543C2, 544B2
Moro characterizatn rptd 10-1, 817F1
Parlt backs wage policy 10-31, 882G3
Backs Italy EMS entry despite CP oppositn 12-12—12-13, 952D1
ANDRETTI, Mario
Wins world driving title 9-10, 968C3
ANDREW Albert Christian Edward, Prince (Great Britain)
Celebrates 18th birthday 2-19, 172D2
ANDREWS, E. F.
Plea to Muzorewa re govt split rptd 5-2, 317E2
ANDREWS, Emmet
Postal pact revised 9-15, 766A2
ANDREWS, Fred
Traded to Mets 3-23, 779C3
ANDREWS, Rep. Ike F. (D, N.C.)
Reelected 11-7, 851B3
ANDREWS, Rep. Mark (R, N.D.)
Vs FTC children's TV ad curbs 5-2, 347E2
Reelected 11-7, 851C3, 855A1
ANDRIESSEN, Frans
Presents '79 budget to parlt 9-19, 965B1
ANDRIEUX, Roger
Bonjour Amour released 6-11, 618D3
ANDRONICA, James
Nunzio released 5-13, 619C3
ANDROPOV, Yuri
Vs Hua trip to Rumania, Yugo 8-5, 675G3
ANDRUS, Cecil D.
Tours Westn states 1-9—1-13, 34E1
Lauds NJ offshore drilling OK 2-21, 125A3
Sees govs on water policy 2-26, 144G3
Okefenokee Refuge expanded 3-14, 186A3
Denies '76-77 gas withholding 4-27, 322C1
Haskell scores 5-2, 342B2
Names Mendelsohn asst secy 6-10, 446F3, 447B1
Sees Indian ldrs 7-18, 569A1
Evans unopposed in primary 8-8, 625D3
Offshore oil, gas leasing chngs clear Cong 8-22, 662B3
Vacations with Carters 8-22, 664E1
Evans elected Ida gov 11-7, 856A1
Alaska lands protected 11-16, 12-1, 937C1
ANDRUS v. Charlestone Stone Products
Water-based land claims barred by Sup Ct 5-31, 431F1
ANDY Warhol's Last Love (play)
Opens 6-30, 887A1
ANEMIA—*See MEDICINE—Diseases*
ANGEL (play)
Opens 5-10, 760C1
ANGELO State University (San Angelo, Tex.)
Wins NAIA Div I football title 12-16, 1025C2
ANGLICANS—*See also EPISCOPAL Church, Protestant*
Female canon preaches in Westminster 4-2, 294E2
Westminister mass protested 7-6, 557D3
Namibia rev ousted 7-14, 547B3
'66 papal mtg cited 8-6, 601C2
ANGLO-American Corp. of South Africa Ltd.
Africa gold mine riot crushed 5-21, 456C1

1979

La Malfa asked to form govt 2-22, 155F1
Makes new Cabt bid 3-7, 169B3
Announces new Cabt 3-20, 212A1
Loses confidence vote 3-31, parlt dissolved 4-2, 254E2
Opposes death penalty 5-3, 331E2
Army joins anti-terror effort 5-9, 372C1
Electns held; Christian Dems retain plurality 6-3-6-4, 426E1
At Tokyo energy summit 6-28-6-29, 493B1
Fails to form govt 7-2-7-7, 525G2, C3
Pandolfi asked to form govt 7-27, 583A3
Cossiga sworn premier 8-5, 602G3
ANDRESS, Ursula
5th Musketeer released 9-7, 820B1
ANDRETTA, Stephen
Indicted 2-22, 155G3
Sentenced 7-10, 548E1
ANDRETTA, Thomas
Indicted 2-22, 155G3
Sentenced 7-10, 548E1
ANDREWS, George
In NFL draft 5-3, 335G1
ANDREWS, Julie
10 released 10-5, 1008A2
ISANO, Gui
gs From the City Streets opens 4-9, 12E2
RUS, Cecil D.
Mass offshore oil-lease ban lifted 2-20, 187B1
On water projct cost-sharing 5-16, 365F2
ANDRUS v. Allard
Case upheld by Sup Ct 11-27, 919G3
ANDRUS v. Sierra Club
Case decided by Sup Ct 6-11, 478F3
ANDRUSYSHYN, Zenon
NFL '78 punting ldr 1-6, 80B2
ANDUEZA, Jose Guillermo
Venez justice min 3-10, 192C3
ANDUJAR, Joaquin
NL wins All-Star Game 7-17, 569A1
ANESTHESIOLOGISTS, American Society of—*See AMERICAN Society of Anesthesiologists*
ANGELES National Forest (Calif.)
Brush fires destroy 34,000 acres 9-13-9-23, 799G2
ANGELETTI, Pio
Till Marriage Do Us Part released 7-20, 820E3
ANGELI, Claude
Giscard tax rpt arrest made 10-12, 791C2
ANGLETON, James
Sovt spy chrg rejctd by CIA 2-27, 152D3
ANGLICANS—*See also EPISCOPAL Church, Protestant*
Baptism rites agrmt reached 3-31, 375G2
Women priests barred from US svcs 7-27, 640A3
Runcie named Archbp of Canterbury 9-7, 755E2
S Africa synod to defy apartheid 12-7, priest chrgd re ban violatn 12-10, 969D1
ANGLIM, Philip
Elephant Man opens 1-14, 292E1
ANGLIN, Ernie
Murdered 4-14, 309A3

1980

ANDRETTI, Mario
CART membership cited 6-30, 1002A2
ANDREWS, Dr. Gould A.
Dies 7-1, 608B1
ANDREWS, Rep. Ike E. (D, N.C.)
Reelected 11-4, 843B4
ANDREWS, Julie
Little Miss Marker released 3-21, 216C3
ANDREWS, Rep. Mark (R, N.D.)
Wins US Sen primary 9-2, 683C1
Elected to US Sen 11-4, 840F2, 845A3, 851A2
ANDREWS, V. C.
Petals on best-seller list 7-13, 568C3, 8-17, 640G3; 9-14, 716D3
ANDRIANOV, Nikolai
Wins Olympic medals, Dityatin breaks record 7-24, 7-25, 588F3, 622E3, F3
ANDRIESSEN, Frans
Quits Dutch Cabt post 2-20, 173C3
Van der Stee replaces 3-25, 276E3
ANDRON, Suzanne
Kate Smith estate feud setld 9-4, 908D2
ANDROSCH, Hannes
Denies hosp scandal chrgs 8-27, 667D3
Hosp scandal spurs Kreisky reforms proposal 9-2, reforms OKd, compliance seen 9-9, 705E2
Wins confidence vote 10-8, 870F3
Sets resignatn 12-11, 964A2
ANDRUS, Cecil D.
Extends Alaska land order 2-12, 131F2-B3
Suspends oil lease lottery 2-29, orders resumptn 4-7, 330B2
Plans Calif offshore lease sales 3-28, 330C3
Ousts Park Svc dir 4-24, 333A2
Imperial Valley water rights upheld by Sup Ct 6-16, 511F2
OKs offshore leasing speedup 6-17, 552E2
Carter names to Synfuels Corp bd 9-13, Sen panel OKs 9-25, 725E2
Omitted from interim Synfuels Corp bd 10-5, 786G2-A3
Calif desert plan issued 12-22, 986G3
ANDRUS v. Glover Construction Co.
Case decided by Sup Ct 5-27, 454B1
ANDRUS v. Idaho
Case decided by Sup Ct 4-16, 328D3
ANDRUS v. Indiana
Case accepted by Sup Ct 10-6, 782D1
ANDRUS v. Shell Oil
Case decided by Sup Ct 6-2, 513D1
ANDRUS v. Utah
Case decided by Sup Ct 5-19, 440A2
ANDRUS v. Virginia Surface Mining and Reclamation Association
Case accepted by Sup Ct 10-6, 782D1
ANGI Vera (film)
Released 1-9, 216B2
ANGLICANS
S Africa sentences priest 2-28, 195G2, A3
Runcie enthroned Archbp of Canterbury 3-25, 364D2
Runcie meets Pope 5-9, 363B3
Iran arrests 3 missionaries 8-8, 8-9, 671C3
Nicaragua mins deportatns seen 10-2, 792A2
ANGLO American Corp. of South Africa Ltd.
De Beers buys Consolidated Gold interest 2-12, 398A3
S Africa accident kills 31 3-31, 256G3

1976

ANGOLA—*See also NONALIGNED Nations Movement*
Tribal backing rptd 35C3
Luanda typhoid threat rptd 1-9, 16D3
Quibala strikes rptd 1-12, 16E3
Listed as 'not free' nation 1-19, 20D3
MPLA rejects Unita, FNLA coalitn 1-19, 35F3
Luanda press cntr set up 2-6, 105F2
Econ downfall seen 5-6, 371B2
Mil plan issued, Neto rescinds 5-21, 455G2
Neto policy speech stresses socialism 5-23, 455A3
Rpt govt takes over newsprs 7-3, 862A3
Neto named state head 10-29; Cabt OKd 11-27, 995B3
Newspaper closes 11-20, 995F3
Anti-crime units set 12-19, 995E3
Cabinda
FLEC raids from Zaire rptd 4-20, 5-12, Zaire shuts border 5-20, 480D3
Foreign Relations (misc.)—*See also 'Military Developments' and 'Refugees' below*
US mercenary training rptd 1-2, 1-3, 3B2
UK chrgs Sovt African bribe 1-3, USSR denies 1-6, 2E2
Ford scores Sovt role, bars grain sales as diplomatic tool 1-5, 2B2, 3F1

1977

ANGOLA—*See also NONALIGNED Nations Movement, OAU*
Guerrilla war continues; coffee output down, strikes rptd 1-8, 86D1
Coffee crop damage cited 74A3
2 soldiers executed 1-15, 86B2 ★
Cabinda rebels rpt offensive 5-4, 484E2
MPLA expels 2 5-21; rebelln crushed 5-27, arrests rptd 5-31, 424F1-A2
FNLA rpts victories 5-31, 484D2
Prov govts suspended 6-7, rebelln detailed 6-20, 484A2
2 arrested re rebelln 6-19, 522E2
Rebelln ldr seeks UNITA union 6-26, 522D2
UNITA town recapture rptd 6-27, 522A2
Amin on Neto death plot 7-4, 512A2
UNITA town recapture confrmd 7-21, 675B1
UNITA attacks rptd 7-26, 675A1
Finance min named 8-31, 772A1
Mine share natlztn set 9-1, 779B1
MPLA cong 12-4—12-11, 1009A2
UNITA rpts urban attacks 12-14, 1009B2
Foreign Relations (misc.)
UN Assemb member 3F3
S Africa details war role 1-3, 85B2
Civilians rptd seeking aid in Namibia 1-5, 48B1
Zaire, Gabon rebel aid rptd 1-8, 86A2

1978

ANGOLA—*See also NONALIGNED Nations Movement*
Freedom House lists as not free 44A2
RC radio rptd closed 1-27, 87D3
Religious affiliatns cited 87E3
MPLA purge rptd, '77 coup try cited 1-30, 87B3
RR damage cited 3-8, 170C1
Anti-UNITA offensive rptd 4-4, 265B2
Rebel attacks rptd up 5-20; anti-UNITA offensive launched 6-4, rptd repulsed 6-16, 645C3
Pol prisoners released 9-15, 925A3
Anti-UNITA offensive rptd 10-10, 925A3
UNITA blamed for Huambo bombings 11-11, 906C2
Econ problems, pvt business OK cited 12-9, 985E1
Foreign Relations (misc.)
Cuban mutiny rptd 1-25, death toll mounts 3-2; troop total cited 165A1, D1
UK rpts mercenary recruitmt 1-27, 87F3
Namibia rebel, army clash rptd 1-29, 114D1
France, Morocco troop raids chrgd 2-1, 87G3
Nigeria troop presence chrgd by UNITA 2-10, 165D1

1979

ANGOLA—*See also NONALIGNED Nations Movement, OAU*
Refugees total rptd high 2-22, 201E1
Neto dies, dos Santos named interim pres 9-10, 705A2
Dos Santos named offcl pres 9-20, 796F2
Foreign Relations (misc.)
UN Namibia plan falters 1-13-3-3; S Africa rejcts truce 3-5, raids SWAPO bases 3-6, 171E1-B3
Benguela RR rptd unusable 2-15, 137D3
Pretoria demands SWAPO bases control 3-19-3-22, 354D2
S Africa-SWAPO clashes rptd 4-27, 354A3
Zaire ends rocket tests 4-27, 411A3
E Ger mil aid rptd 5-23, 406G2
S Africa raids SWAPO camps 7-4-7-6, 585G1
S Africa '76-79 raid toll rptd 8-2, '78 gas use claimed 8-3, 617F2, A3
Cuba troop total rptd 9-12, 673E2
Young vs US Cuba 'fear' 9-16, 721B1
UN membership listed 695D2
S Africa raids chrgd 10-31, UN condemns 11-2, 875F1
Namibia demilitarized zone OKd by UN conf 11-16, 889C3

1980

ANGOLA—*See also NONALIGNED Nations, OAU*
Foreign Relations (misc.)
UN res vs Sovt Afghan invasn opposed 1-14, 25G1
At regional econ unity mtg 4-1, 243D1, E1
S Africa delays new Namibia talks 5-12, 374D2
S Africa bombers shot down 6-7; rpt denied 6-13, 466A3
S Africa troops raid SWAPO bases 6-13, 466F2-A3
S Africa raids protested 6-26, Pretoria denies civiln deaths, UN censures 6-27, 7-2; troop exit disputed 6-28, 7-1, 524D3
OAU scores S Africa raids 7-1, 509A2
UN women's conf racism motion withdrawn 7-28, 587G2
UN Namibia talks schedule agreed 11-24, 967B2
ANC guerrilla training cited 11-26, 968E1
Castro admits Cuban troop role 12-17, 12-20, 993B1
U.S. Relations
Reagan 'basic speech' cites Sovt-Cuba ties 2-29, 207B3

1976

US pres campaign issue 1-5, 1-8, 4D3, 5E1; 2-10, 109G2
USSR defends MPLA aid, rebuffs US interventn chrgs 1-6, 2B2
Tunney chrgs arms airlift 1-6, US denies 1-7, 2D2
Waldheim asks end to forgn role 1-6, 16C2
US scores Sovt warships presence 1-7, USSR denies 1-8, 2E1
Nigeria scores Ford letter, reaffirms MPLA stand 1-7; US rebuts 1-8, 2F2, D3 ★
UNITA issues Westn arms aid plea 1-7, 3E1
US bars Cuba baseball series 1-7, 23E1
OAU preparatory summit mtg 1-8, 3B1
OAU summit deadlocks 1-10—1-13; reactn 1-11—1-15, 15E2, 16C1
Cuba defies Azores refueling ban 1-10—1-15, US protests 1-19, 53C2
Senegal, Zaire warn Ethiopia vs MPLA ties 1-11, 1-13, 16A1
Nigeria anti-US demonstratns rptd 1-11, 16B2
FNLA scores US arms aid 1-11, 16F2
Cuba, Sovt, other forgn troop support rptd 1-11, 16D3
Cuba vows contd MPLA aid, admits June '75 entry 1-11, 1-15, 16E3, 138F1 ★
Javits: Cuba role 'aborted' US ties 1-11, 52F2
UNITA bars Westn newsmen 1-14, 16B3
Kissinger sets Moscow trip 1-14, 17A1
Ethiopia recognizes MPLA, denies US pressure 1-15, 15G3
Kissinger sees African ambs, sets visit 1-15, 16B2
Kissinger briefs NATO on FNLA losses 1-15, 16D2
Cuban, S African troop estimates rptd 1-16—1-20, 35C3
Zaire protests Dilolo raid to UN Cncl 1-16; warns USSR, Cuba 1-17, 1-19, 36A1
French, W Ger jets to Zaire rptd 1-16, 36C1
UNITA hints Zaire airlift aid 1-18, 35A3
Tanzania scores Ford letter; backs USSR, Cuba roles 1-18, 36C1
UK Tory leader scores USSR 1-19, 101D1
US aid irregularities chrgd 1-20, 92E1, D3
S Africa seeks mil stalemate 1-21, 35F2
US Sen aid bar noted 1-21, 40E2
Kissinger in Moscow 1-21—1-23, briefs NATO 1-23, 61F3
Cuba halts troop airlift 1-21; Azores, Canada refueling 1-28, 1-30, 106B2
US OAU summit econ pressure disputed 1-23, 1-28, 67E3
Venez, Carib natns score Cuba 1-24, 138G1
UNITA rpts S Africa troop exit, alert 1-25, 57F2
Rpt MPLA seeks better US ties 1-25, 82D2
S Africa confrms troop exit, defends role 1-26, 57G1
US House bars Angola aid 1-27, 69A1
Zambia invokes emergency powers; scores Sovt, Cuban roles 1-28, 77E3
UK mercenaries aid FNLA 1-28—2-3, 81E2
UNITA asks Westn aid 1-29, 57C1
Sierre Leone, Cameroon recognize MPLA 1-29, 2-2, 82G2
USSR hints pol compromise 1-29, scores Kissinger 2-1, 2-4, 82A3
US studies open Angola aid, Sovt confrontatn 1-29—1-30, 88B3
Zambia copper transit halted 1-30, 77G3
MPLA welcomes Westn ties 1-30, 82A2
UN censures S Africa 1-31, 103D2
E, W Ger mercenaries rptd 2-1, Dutch 2-2, 82B1
US denies mercenary role 2-2, 82E1
MPLA sets terms for Zaire ties; scores US, China 2-2, 82E2
Zaire bars mercenary transit 2-3, 82B1
UNITA asks black American aid 2-3, 82C1
Kissinger scores Cong aid bar 2-3, 88C2
S Africa buffer force rptd 2-3, 106G1
Canada prime min on Cuba trip 2-3, 116D2
Cuba domestic dissent rptd 2-4, 138C2
Kissinger scores Cuba role 2-5, 138C1
UK mercenaries rptd executed 2-8; UK sets probe, detains 44 2-10, 105F2
More UK mercenaries rptd recruited 2-8, 106D1
MPLA recognized by Uganda, Togo 2-10, Gabon, Upper Volta 2-12, 105E2
Ford scores Cong aid bar 2-10, 109G2-B3
US CORE recruits medics 2-10, 163A3
OAU recognizes, admits MPLA 2-11, 105C2
UK rules out mercenary chrgs 2-12, 163F2
MPLA offers S Africa guarantees 2-13, demands forces quit south 2-19, 162B3
African, Arab natns recognize MPLA 2-13—2-23; Zambia bars ties 2-18, chrgs copper seizure 2-20, 163E2
Kissinger, Latin ldrs discuss Cuba role 2-16—2-23, 177E2, 178B1, E1
EC, other Westn natns, Japan recognize MPLA 2-17—2-25, 162D3, 163D1, 178C1 ★
US Sen bars arms aid authorizatn 2-18, 151F3
US defers MPLA recognitn 2-18, OKs Gulf, Boeing contacts 2-21, 163D1
Brezhnev cites aid to MPLA 2-24, 194G1
Zaire recognizes MPLA; Neto, Mobutu in pact; Congo role cited 2-28, 163G1

1977

Cuba details war role 1-9, 18F3; Moss rpt disputes 1-31, 86A1
Sweden budgets aid 1-10, 23B1
Namibia bars refugees 1-12, 21E3
Cuba admits Canada spy recruiting 1-12, 42E3
2 executed for Portuguese death 1-15, 86B2 ★
Cabinda rebels blamed in Congo RR attack 1-17, 48E1
US Amb Young: Cuba troops brought stability 1-25; US clarifies 1-31, 2-2, 105F1
France ties set 1-31, 86B2
Young sees Neto in Nigeria 2-8, 105E1
Cuban troops rptd cut 2-15, US links ties 2-16, 110A1, G1, 180G2
CIA paymts to Roberto rptd 2-19, 124F1
200 flee to Namibia 2-21, 145C2
Zaire prov invaded 3-8, troop role chrgd 3-11; US confirms 3-18, 207A2, E3
Zaire border bombings chrgd 3-22, 260F3
Castro visits, vows unlimited aid 3-23—3-31; jt communique backs liberatn movemts 4-12, 249G1, A3
Kenya-Sovt talks 3-26, 247E3
US gen scores Cong meddling 3-27, 232A1
US-Cuba '74-75 secret talks rptd 3-28, 283D2
Southern Africa natlst ldrs visit 3-29, 249D3
S Africa rpts civiln deaths 3-30, refugees 4-13, 424B2
Nigeria mediatn on Zaire rejctd 4-1, 261B1
Cuba confrms troop cuts 4-8, 283B1
Zaire scores Cuba, Sovt role 4-9, 265C2
Neto scores Zaire aid; denies Cuba, Sovt roles 4-11, 265F2
Young defends Cuba statemt 4-11, 271F3
UK Secy Owen visits 4-17, 296E1
Morocco chrgs Cuban role in Zaire 4-18, 317G1
French-African summit held 4-20—4-21, 316E3
Zaire POWs claim Cuban training 4-20, 4-26, 317E1
Amin scores Zaire role 4-22, 317C2
S Africa border clashes rptd 4-26, 349F2
Zaire retakes border towns 5-20—5-26, 490F1
Carter cites USSR, Cuba role 5-22, 397F1
Ford links Cuba ties, troops 6-5, 456B1
Castro confrms troop exit halted 6-9, 456F1
UNITA rep backs S Africa aid, scores black natns stand 6-26, 522B2
S Africa, Zaire rebel aid rptd 7-25, 7-26, 675A1
S Africa rpts terrorists seized 7-28, 600C1
Namibia rebel clashes 8-3, 8-14, 639E3
US bars arms aid 8-4, 668B1
More Cuban troops rptd, total estimated at 20,000 9-11, 779A1
S Africa asks SWAPO confinemt to bases 9-22—9-26, 770F2
Neto in USSR 9-28, 830D1
Brazil gen scores ties 10-12, 840A1
US stand re intl agency loans set 10-19, 815A2-C2
S Africa rpts SWAPO clashes 10-27—10-29, 11-10, 876E1
Cuba buildup detailed 11-17, 896E1
Namibia contact group tours 11-21—12-7, 1016E3
US asks Cuba pullout, Castro rejects 12-5, 1011G2
Jamaica defends Cuba role 12-16, 1019G1
Rhodesian Relations—*See RHODESIA*

1978

Cuban troops, E Eur technicians rptd executed 2-28, 165C1
Eur mercenaries rptd with FNLA 3-1, 165C1
Zambia shipmt outlet curbed 3-8, 170C1
Zaire attack rptd repelled 3-24, 238B3
Westn indep plan for Namibia backed 3-26, 248G2
Cubans rptd in anti-UNITA drive 4-4, 265B2
Namibia rebels hijack bus 4-22, 299D2
S Africa raids SWAPO camps 5-4, UN Cncl condemns 5-6, 338A3
S Africa scores US re raid warning 5-12, 475E3
Zaire chrgs rebel aid 5-14, 359A2
Cubans rptd killed 5-17, 5-20; anti-UNITA drive launched 6-4, rptd repulsed 6-16, 645C3
Zambian pres urges pol solutn 5-19, 395A3
Zaire rebel retreat rptd 5-23, 381A2
Zambia troops, Zaire rebels clash 5-24, 417C3
Zaire role chrgd 5-25, 5-30, 418A1, G1
S Africa frees raid captives 5-27, 475E3
Martins expelled re Neto plot 5-31, 594D1
Morocco vows Zaire aid 6-2, 441B1
Zaire rebel camps rptd 6-2, 442F1
USSR role scored 6-7, 423C3
Tanzania defends Cuba role 6-8, 442B1
Zaire pan-Africa force rptd opposed 6-8, 442D1
Zaire rebels to be disarmed; Cuba, USSR aid denied 6-10, 441A2
Namibia rebels OK talks 6-11, 475D3
Castro denies Zaire role 6-13, 442F2
S Africa raid scored by UN refugee comr, WHO 6-16, 475D3
Zaire rpts rebel buildup 6-17, 478C2
Cuba Eritrea role rptd opposed 6-21, 584B3
USSR backs aid 6-22, 487C3
Tanzania lauds US Angola move 6-25, 487D3
Portugal cooperatn OKd 6-26, 562A2
Comecon observer 6-27—6-29, 504G3
Westn indep plan for Namibia OKd 7-12, 547F2
Zaire reconciliatn set 7-17, 562D1
Cuba death toll rptd 7-18, 603D3
Neto backs Cuban troops 7-21, US bars ties 7-22, 562G1
S Africa jails SWAPO reps again 7-26, 634A1
Zaire diplomatic ties OKd 7-29, 646A1
Refugees rptd returning from Portugal 8-10, 645E3
Neto in Zaire 8-19—8-21, 645G3
S Africa trades prisoners 9-2, 742A2
UN Assemb member 713B3
Benguela RR reopened 11-4, 1021D2
S Africa mil threat rptd 11-7, 925B3
Polisario recognitn cited 11-10, 999G2
S Africa 'undeclared war' chrgd 11-11, 906C2
Pro-West trend seen 12-10, 985C1
S Africa threat cited re Cuba troops 12-13, 985A1
Rhodesian Relations—*See RHODESIA*
U.S. Relations
CIA ex-agent scores '75 civil war role 5-8, Colby responds 5-14, 367A2-368F3
S Africa scores US re raid warning 5-12, 475E3
Carter scores Cong on rebel aid curbs 5-23, Admin proposals rptd rejctd 5-24, 383B1, A2, 443D1
Carter chrgs Zaire role 5-25, 5-30, 418A1, G1
CIA rpts Zaire rebel camps 6-2, 442F1
Carter scores USSR role 6-7, 423C3
Castro chrgs CIA aids UNITA 6-18, 645E3
Vance seeks aid re Zaire unrest 6-20, 487A3
McHenry visits 6-21—6-26, US-Angola contacts rptd 6-22, 487F3, 488B1
Tanzania lauds contact plan 6-25, 487D3
Carter unaware of CIA rebel aid 6-26, 491G1-A2
McHenry visit results rptd 7-8, 547G2 ★
Neto asks US recognitn 7-21, US bars 7-22, 562F1
US cites Zaire moves, releases aid 8-16, 652F2
US 'Pegasus' satellite falls off coast 9-17, 714G1
US econ aid authorzn signed 9-26, 734G1
US econ aid funds signed 10-18, 862E2
McGovern visits, sees US prisoners, pro-West trend cited 12-13, 985A1

1979

Cuba rptd training children 12-4, 12-10, 981B2
S Africa OKs Namibia proposal 12-5, 969G1
U.S. Relations
Texaco oil pact signed 9-4, 705G2
Neto lauded 9-11, 705G2
Young regrets lack of US ties, scores 'fear' re Cuba 9-16, 721B1
Israel says US 'lost' 9-18, 694B1
US abstains on S Africa UN vote 11-2, 875G1
Zimbabwe Rhodesian Relations—*See ZIMBABWE*

1980

US sues ex-CIA agent Stockwell 3-3, 268A3
Connally cites Sovt threat 3-7, 184E3
Stockwell settles suit 6-25, 516E3-517A1

1976	1977	1978	1979	1980

Ford calls Castro 'outlaw' 2-28, 165G2-A3
Angola aid offer to Namibia rptd 2-28—3-6, 206F1
Reagan scores US policy 3-4, 165G3
Tito lauds Cuba MPLA aid 3-6, 251B3
Guyana denies Cuba refueling stops 3-6, 253B2
UK, France deny US covert aid chrgs 3-9, 228D3
Kissinger warns USSR 3-11, 197D3
Gulf, Texaco pay '75 royalties 3-11, 3-17, Gulf Cabinda operatns to resume 4-5, 287E2
Austria vs Cuba, S Africa roles 3-13, 380E2
Sovt-UK talks 3-15—3-19, 3-25, 228G3, 229A1
Neto sees Castro, Cabral, Sekou Toure 3-15—3-16, 251E3
US halts Sovt joint comm talks 3-16, 196F1
UK, Sovt, UN mediatory roles re S Africa rptd 3-21, 3-25, 3-26, 228A1
Kissinger warns Cuba anew 3-22, 3-23, 214D3
UN Cncl meets, Angola defends Sovt, Cuba aid 3-26; S Africa censured 3-31, 228A2
US reaffirms non-recognition of MPLA 3-26, 228C3
US scores USSR, Cuba; cites 13,000 Cuba troops 3-31, 228C3
Reagan scores Ford policy 3-31, 232E3
EC sets Zaire, Zambia, Malawi aid 4-6, 276C2
S Africa pact on Cunene projct 4-6, 287C2
Zambia recognizes 4-15, 335E1
Cuba emb in Portugal bombed 4-22, 371F1
US Sen com cites US role 4-26, 298G3
Australia recognizes 4-28, 332D1
US links ties to Cuban exit 4-30, 318A2
Zaire cites Sovt arms buildup 4-30, 318A3
S Africa sets buffer zone 5-19, 386C1
Cuba sets troop exit rate, US urges speed-up 5-21—5-26, 370B3
Neto vows nonalignmt 5-23, 455A3
Nonaligned back membership 5-31, 455D3
Premr in USSR, mil aid vow rptd 5-31, 480F3
Australia scores Sovt role 6-1, 438D2
3 US, UK journalists expelled 6-9—6-16, 480B3
US, UK mercenary trial begins 6-11; 13 sentncd, 4 to die 6-28, 480E1
US rpts Sovt, Cuba mil presence; NATO sees no Cuba troop exit 6-13, 467D1
US Dem platform text cites 6-15, 475G3, 477E2, 478B3, E3
Rumsfeld-Zaire talks re Sovt, Cuba roles 6-17—6-19, 467B1
US vetoes UN membership 6-23, 455E1
China scores Sovt role 6-23, 455F1
Carter airs US policy view 6-24, 490B2
US bars aid 6-30, 533C1
At COMECON summit 7-7—7-9, 722D2
4 mercenaries executed despite US, UK protests 7-10, 519G2
Rumanian envoy rptd shot 7-12, 649F2
US mercenary's body returned 7-26, 559C3
Castro vows aid 7-26, Neto ends visit 7-29, 649E2
US journalist expelled 8-15, 649G2
US GOP platform text cites 8-18, 610A2, C2
Gulf rpts oil output rate 8-19, 649G2
Kaunda, Neto conf 8-21; envoy exchng, joint comm OKd 9-22, 862F2 ★
Israel aid to S Africa chrgd 8-22, 654A3
Netherlands ties set 8-30, 862F2
Neto in Tanzania conf on ANC 9-6—9-7, 661D3
US Rhodesia, Namibia rebel aid asked 9-14, 681C1
Cuba troop exit rptd 9-22, 862A2
Scores Rhodesia majority rule plan 9-26, 718D1
US scores Sovt-Cuba role 9-30, 719E1
Ford, Carter debate 10-6, 741D1, G2
Neto in USSR 10-7—10-13; signs treaty 10-8; statemt issued 10-14, 856C3
Castro Nov visit plan cited 10-15, 780F1
S Africa denies attack chrg 11-11, 862E2
Nkomo, Mugabe see reps 11-19, 879B2
UN Cncl backs entry; US abstains, protests Cuba role; China shuns 11-22, 879C1
UN Assemb votes entry 12-1, 895B3
S Africa attack seen 12-10, 995G3
Mercenary trial scored 12-21, 995E3
Zambia ousts UNITA 12-27, 995D3
Military Developments
MPLA takes Uige, southn region 1-5; UNITA issues aid plea 1-7, 3D1
Cuban battle role rptd, UNITA shows prisoners 1-7, 3A2
MPLA takes Ambriz, other northn cities; FNLA collapse feared 1-9, 1-15, 16C2
FNLA-UNITA clashes rptd 1-10—1-27, 58A1
FNLA attacks Quifangondo 1-12, 16F2
MPLA displays S Africa, Portugal mercenaries 1-12, 16G2-A3
S Africa battalion rptd at Cela 1-12, 16A3
MPLA attacks UNITA strongholds 1-13, 16A3
FNLA northn losses rptd 1-14—1-18, 35A3 ★
Cuba-backed MPLA raid Dilolo 1-15, 16C3
Fighting on southn front continues, MPLA takes Cela 1-15—1-23, 35A2
FNLA denies northn collapse 1-16, 35F2
Zaire jets strafe border town 1-16, 36B1
UNITA vows FNLA support 1-18, 35G2

1976

MPLA AF formed 1-22, 57F1
MPLA pushes south 1-23—1-26, UNITA quits Huambo 1-27, 57A1
MPLA claims Novo Redondo victory 1-23, UNITA disputes 1-25, 57E1, F1
Northern plunder laid to FNLA, Zaire 1-29, 58B1
Cela, Huambo clashes rptd 2-1—2-5, MPLA takes Lobito 2-2, 82G1
S Africa troops rptd at Huambo 2-1, 82A2
MPLA gains in Maquela do Zombo 2-2, 82F1
Sovt ships sighted off Lobito 2-5, Lobito shelled 2-11, 105D1
2 S Africans killed in south 2-7, 106B2
Huambo, other UNITA strongholds fall to Cuban-supported MPLA 2-8—2-12, 105A1
FNLA loses more ground in north 2-8, 2-9, 105B2
Unita vows guerrilla war 2-9, 105G1
Unita guerrilla war declaratn 2-12, 162G2
MPLA takes Luso, Benguela ry control 2-13, 162A3
S Africa troop exit ends 3-27, 227G3-228C1
FLEC raids on Cabinda rptd 4-20, 5-12, 480E3
UNITA attacks, Cuba troop massing rptd 6-3, 455C2
Neto chrgs S African attacks 7-10, Botha denies 11-11, 862D2
Neto named cmdr-in-chief 7-31; draft rptd set 8-4, 862G2
S Africa rpts 500 slain 9-28; denied 10-1, 734A3
Govt, Cuban, SWAPO drive vs UNITA rptd 10-29—11-10, 862F1
SWAPO asks aid 11-11, 862E2
Cuba denies drive vs Unita 11-14, 862A2

Portuguese Relations—*See also 'Refugees' below*
Cuba defies Azores refueling ban 1-10—1-15; Portugal, US protest 1-13, 1-19, 53C2
FNLA-UNITA clashes rptd 1-10, 58B1
Portugal suspends '75 pact 2-11, 105E2
Lisbon recognizes MPLA 2-22, 163B1
Angola closes Portugal office, suspends visas 4-26; cuts ties 5-19, 371D1
Angola OKs assets adoptn 5-3, 19 natlzns rptd 5-6, 371G1
Portugal to seek closer ties 7-19, 558F1
Ties restored 9-30, 812C2

Refugees
S Africa denies entry 1-13, 16B3
Portugal airlift resumes 1-22, 53F2
Portuguese flee from north, chrg plunder 1-29, 58B1
S Africa buffer force rptd 2-3, 106A2
S Africa deplores UN aid bar 2-12; UN stance rptd 3-25, 228F1
Luanda suspends Portugal visas 2-21, 163B1
Zaire, MPLA set exchng 2-28, 163C2
Evacuee, camp totals rptd 3-1, 3-12, 228D1
S Africa, Red Cross end aid 3-27, 228E1
Flight to Namibia rptd, return slated 3-27, 3-29, 228G1
Angola cuts Portugal ties 5-19, 371F1
Intl aid program rptd 8-6, 862G2
UN rpts refugee total 10-2, 862C2
Rpt 8000 to Namibia, some forced to return 11-12, 862B2
S Africa rpts shootings 12-10, 995F3

ANGUILLA (British territory)
Self-govt in effect 2-10, 270B3
Election results 3-15, 270C3
ANHEUSER-Busch Inc.
Long Teamster strike ends 6-6, 436A2
ANIMALS—*See LIVESTOCK, WILDLIFE*
ANISIMOVA, Tatyana
Wins Olympic medal 7-29, 576A2
ANKE, Hannelore
Wins Olympic medal 7-24, 575A3
ANKER, Irving
Scores HEW job bias chrgs 11-9, 922B1
ANN Arbor, Mich.—*See MICHIGAN*
ANN Arbor News, The (newspaper)
Newhouse buys Booth chain 11-8, 901B3
ANN Arbor Railroad Co.
Conrail begins operation, Mich purchase slated 4-1, 235E1
ANNENBERG, Walter
'72 campaign gift listed 9-25, 688B1
ANNUNZIO, Rep. Frank (D, Ill.)
Reelected 11-2, 829G2
AN Puong Mu
Sentence suspended 12-29, 1013G2
ANSARY, Hushang
Signs Occidental deal 6-20, 450C2
Signs US arms, trade pact 8-7, 581A2
Signs Iran-Krupp pact 10-19, 782C2
ANSELMI, Tina
Sworn Italy labor min 7-30, 573D1, G1
ANSQUER, Vincent
French quality of life min 8-27, 650G3

1977

ANGUILLA (British territory)
Webster loses confidence vote 2-1, replaced 2-2; backers riot 2-9, 190D2
Nevis votes to rejoin UK 8-18, 675D2
ANHEUSER-Busch Inc.
SEC sues, chrgs settled 5-19, 503D3
ANICK, Betty
Dies 3-22, 264C2
ANIKULAPO-Kuti, Fela
Home burned 2-18, rptr ousted 3-12, 258F1
ANIMAL Farm (book)
USSR bars entry 9-6, 765G3
ANIMAL Feed—*See LIVESTOCK*
ANIMALS—*See also LIVESTOCK, WILDLIFE*
New life form identified 11-2, 907G3
ANN Arbor, Mich.—*See MICHIGAN*
ANNE Elizabeth Alice Louise, Princess of Edinburgh (Great Britain)
Pregnancy rptd 4-8, 396A3
Son born 11-14, christened 12-22, 1021E2
ANNIE (play)
Wins Tony 6-5, 452C1
ANNIE Hall (film)
Top-grossing film 4-27, 356E2; 6-1, 452C2
AN Ping-sheng
Named Yunnan CP chief 2-12, 133G3
ANSARY, Hushang
Remains in Iran Cabt 8-7, 618F1
ANTAEUS Laboratory (Fayetteville, Ark.)
Richards sex test rejected 4-12, 354E1
ANTANAS Snechkus (Soviet ship)
US seizes 4-10, 270A1
US frees 4-14, 363B3

1978

ANHEUSER-Busch Inc.
Fined re rebates 3-31, 449F2
'77 top beer sales cited 5-15, 364C3
Halts Chelsea soft drink ads 7-22, 941F3-942A1
ANIMAL Feed—*See GRAIN*
ANIMALS—*See specific kinds (e.g., MONKEYS)*
ANKER, Irving
Suspends local schl bd 3-10, 264G1
ANNAPURNA One (Nepal)
Amer women climb 10-15, 2 killed 10-17, 843G2
ANNE Frank: The Diary of a Young Girl (book)
Drama revived 12-18, 1031D1
ANNIE (recording)
Wins Grammy 2-24, 316B1
ANNIE Hall (film)
Top United Artists execs quit 1-13, 1-16, 75B3
Wins Oscars 4-3, 315B3
Top-grossing film 4-26, 356C1
ANN-Margaret
Joseph Andrews released 4-13, 619F2
Magic released 11-18, 970A2
ANNUNZIO, Rep. Frank (D, Ill.)
Reelected 11-7, 850E3
ANSARI, Soraya
Sentenced 4-25, 353F3
ANSELMI, Tina
Named Italy health min 3-11, 191C1
ANSLINGER, Harry J. (1892-1975)
McCarthy called drug addict 11-19, 943A3
ANSON, Jay
Amityville on best-seller list 1-8, 24E3*; 2-5, 116C3; 3-5, 195E3; 9-4, 708D1; 10-9, 800D3
ANSONIA, Conn.—*See CONNECTICUT*
ANSPACH, Susan
Big Fix released 10-6, 969C3
ANTAR, Lt. Col. Ali
Takes power in S Yemen 6-27, 499C1

1979

ANIMAL Farm (book)
Seized by USSR 9-4, 690D1
ANIMALS—*See also specific kinds*
Hartz Mt settles FTC complaint 8-29, 903B1
ANNAKIN, Ken
5th Musketeer released 9-7, 820B1
ANNAPURNA One (Nepal)
2 climb 5-8, 392G2
ANN Arbor, Mich.—*See MICHIGAN*
ANNIE (play)
'78-79 success rptd 11-4, 956E2
ANN-Margaret
Villain released 7-20, 820E3
ANNUNZIO, Rep. Frank (D, Ill.)
Scores FHLBB re variable rate mortgage 5-30, 403G2
ANSETT Transport Industries
Murdoch gains control, named chief exec 12-18, 966E3
ANSON, Jay
Amityville Horror on best-seller list 1-7, 80D3; 2-4, 120D3
Amityville Horror released 7-27, 819D3
ANSPACH, Susan
Running released 11-2, 1008D1

1980

ANGOLA State Prison (La.)
Angolite wins Polk award 2-25, 692G3
ANGOLITE (magazine)
Wins Polk award 2-25, 692G3
ANGUILAR, Jose
Wins Olympic medal 8-2, 622F1
ANGUILLA
Webster electd prime min 5-28, 469E1
ANHEUSER-Busch Inc.
Beer to be brewed in Canada 6-17, 486D2
ANHIELO, Alfredo
NASL goalkeeping ldr 8-24, 770D3
ANIASI, Aldo
Italy health min 4-4, 275F3
ANIMALS
Bacteria gene differences rptd 1-23, 160B1
Rabies vaccine OKd 6-9, 526A3
Lindane use curbs sought 7-3, 519D3
Mammoth-elephant link rptd 7-11, 715F3
ANKER, Charlotte
Onward Victoria opens 12-14, 1003E3
ANNAUD, Jean-Jacques
Coup De Tete released 1-21, 216D2
ANNE, Princess (Anne Bowes-Lyon) (Denmark)
Dies 9-27, 755A2
ANNISTON—*See ALABAMA*
ANNUNZIO, Rep. Frank (D, Ill.)
Reelected 11-4, 842E3
ANOTHER Brick in the Wall (Part 2) (recording)
On best-seller list 3-5, 200E3; 4-2, 280E3; 4-30, 359G3
ANOTHER One Bites the Dust (recording)
On best-seller list 9-10, 716E3; 10-8, 796A3; 12-3, 948B3
ANSON, Jay
Dies 3-12, 279C1

1976

ANTARCTIC Regions
Mars soil sample comparison rptd 8-7, 595E1
USSR curbs whale catch 11-3, 1011C2
ANTHIMOS
Dies 9-19, 1015B1
ANTHONY, Dart
Loses Nev Cong primary 9-14, 705C1
ANTHONY, (John) Douglas
Devaluation rpts denied 1-5, 7B3
Australian govt ends uranium role 2-1, 97A1
Visits Japan 2-4—2-15, 137C3
In S Korean trade talks 3-23, 237A2
Mine financing policy revised 6-2, 415E1
Announces Sovt meat deal 8-3, 587C2
In UK; scores EC, Japan trade curbs 8-12, 623A2
Welcomes devaluatn 11-29, 896G1
ANTIBIOTICS—*See 'Drugs' under MEDICINE*
ANTI-Defamation League—*See under B'NAI Brith*
ANTIGUA (British associated state)—*See WEST Indies*
ANTIHISTAMINES—*See 'Drugs' under MEDICINE*
ANTIOCH College (Yellow Springs, O.)
Birenbaum elected pres 4-12, 504F2
ANTI-Semitism—*See JEWS*

1977

ANTARCTIC Regions
Chile renews claim 1-5, 18B3
Dufek dies 2-10, 164F2
NSF '78 authorizatn signed 8-15, 689E1
Ross Ice Shelf penetrated 12-9, 971F2
ANTHONY, (John) Douglas
On China wheat sale 3-8, 178G3
On Australia uranium mining 5-31, 465A3
On China wheat sale 6-6, 578G2
On NW Shelf gas dvpt 8-24, 704F3-705B1
Estimates uranium reserves 8-25, 693D3
On ACTU uranium motion 9-15, 740F2
On Dillingham compensatn offer 10-3, 762D2
Lauds Japan trade agrmts 10-30, 862B1
Australia dep prime min, trade min 12-19, 982A2
ANTHROPOLOGY
Loren Eiseley dies 7-9, 604A3
ANTIBALLISTIC Missiles (ABM)—*See ARMAMENTS—Missiles, DISARMAMENT*
ANTIBIOTICS—*See MEDICINE—Drugs*
ANTI-Defamation League—*See under B'NAI B'rith*
ANTIGUA (British associated state)—*See WEST Indies*
ANTI-Semitism—*See JEWS*

1978

ANTARCTIC Regions
Frederick Crockett dies 1-17, 96E1
Chile-Argentina territorial rights talks open 3-1, 216D1
Chile-Argentina Beagle Channel talks fail 5-22—11-2, 860F2
Australia urged to increase activities 9-17, 900G2
Australia panel urges whaling ban 12-18, 1012G3
ANTHONY Jr., Beryl F.
Wins US House seat 11-7, 850D1, 855A2
ANTHONY, (John) Douglas
Delays uranium export 1-6, 16E1
On Japan import agrmts 3-20, 208A3
Rpts Japan to import iron 5-25, 411D1
Uranium mining, export rules adopted 5-31, 434C3, F3
Signs Finland uranium accord 7-20, 590E1
China favored trade status set 10-11, 836A2
Bars Aborigine uranium dvpt veto 10-16, 812C3, D3 ★
Mineral export policy set 10-24, 836A1
Hails US coal deal 12-11, 963B2
ANTHROPOLOGY
Hominid tracks in Tanzania rptd 3-4, 334A2
Obituaries
Mead, Margaret 11-15, 972D3
ANTIBIOTICS—*See MEDICINE—Drugs*
ANTI-Defamation League—*See under B'NAI B'rith*
ANTIGUA (British associated state)—*See also CARIBBEAN Community*
Canada-S Africa arms deal rptd probed 11-7, 904F2
ANTI-Semitism—*See JEWS*
ANTISLAVERY Society
Morocco child labor rptd 5-29, 596F2

1979

ANTARCTIC Regions
US projects impact rpts ordrd 1-5, 16F3
US rpts unknown A-blast 10-25, 824B3
NZ DC-10 crash kills 257 11-28, 912B1
ANTHONY, (John) Douglas
Bauxite floor price rejected 1-9, 18E3
Ranger uranium accord signed 1-9, 36E2
Aborigine mining rights probed 1-24, 94B3
Cabt operatns streamlined 2-4, 113D2
Japan iron ore price rise set 3-6, 188E2
Japan gets coal price cut 3-13, 233B2
Canada wheat accord rptd 4-3, 253A1
Japan trade accord signed 4-6, 266B2
Mineral export compromise set 4-23, 328B1
BP to join mining projct 7-27, 580G2
Ranger share sale planned 8-7, 600D1
On Roxby Downs dvpt 9-16, 749D2
Sinclair quits Cabt post 9-27, 787G3
S Korea trade accord rptd 10-16, 788D1
Rpts new drug unit 11-6, 870D2
Peko to buy Ranger share 12-18, 992C2
ANTHONY, Susan B(rownell) (1820-1906)
$1 coin rptd shunned 9-25, 727B2
ANTHROPOLOGY
New hominid species claimed 1-18, Leakey disputes 2-17, 137F3-138D1
Ancient hominid footprints rptd 3-21, 691A2
Margaret Mead park dedicated 9-15, 892D2
ANTIBALLISTIC Missile (ABM)—*See ARMAMENTS—Missiles*
ANTI-Defamation League (ADL)—*See under B'NAI Brith*
ANTIGUA (British associated state)—*See also CARIBBEAN Community*
St Lucia diplomatic svc seen 2-19, 181A3
ANTIOBIOTICS—*See MEDICINE-Drugs*
ANTIOCH University (Yellow Springs, Ohio)
S Africa stock divestiture rptd 3-24, 271C1
Bankruptcy averted 6-4, 482G1
ANTIQUES
Monaco auction records rptd 6-27, 672F1
Cyprus icons seized 9-14, UN rep resigns 9-15, 751E2
ANTI-Semitism—*See JEWS*

1980

ANTARCTIC Regions
Finn Ronne dies 1-12, 104F3
Intl fishing pact set 5-20, 398D1; signed 9-11, 721B1
Acid rain rptd centuries old 9-18, 716E2
Beagle Channel accord proposed 12-12, 979A1
ANTHONY, (John) Douglas
Widens Sovt trade curbs 1-29, 116C1
EC steel accord rptd set 2-5, 132B1
On Sovt rutile embargo end 2-12, 141B1
French A-plant support rptd 3-3, 171B1
Vs Saudi princess film, Hayden scores 4-15, 309E3, 310A1
Japan coal projct bid barred 4-15, 334F1
UK tariff breaks to end 4-16, 309D3
China dep premr visits 5-7—5-11, 387G3
On coalitn rift 6-18, 486A1
EC sheepmeat talks founder 7-15, 561D3
Scores Sinclair 'persecutn' 8-14, 650F2
Airbus deal OKd 9-29, 748B1
ANTHONY Jr., Rep. Beryl F. (D, Ark.)
Reelected 11-4, 842D1
ANTHONY, John
Temperence Hill wins Belmont 6-7, 447A3
ANTHONY, Michael
Wins Olympic medal 8-2, 622E1
ANTHRAX—*See MEDICINE--Diseases*
ANTHROPOLOGY
Ape-human ancestor rptd discovered 2-7, 416E1
Obituaries
Ardrey, Robert 1-14, 104E1
Bateson, Gregory 7-4, 608D1
Farb, Peter 4-8, 360E1
Weltfish, Gene 8-2, 676F3
ANTIGUA (British associated state)
Bird reelected prime min 4-24, 411D3
Canada fines S Africa arms seller 8-14, 618A3

1976

ANTITRUST Actions
Shriver urges stricter enforcemt 1-7, 22G2
Sup Ct lets stand NYSE svc chrg rule 1-12, 24C1
Bechtel sued on Arab boycott issue 1-16, 44E2
Ford State of Union message 1-19, 37E3, 39C2
US comptroller scored re bank mergers 2-17, 3-1, 185D2, C3
Paperbd indictmts 2-18; cos fined 9-20, stiffer penalties asked 10-5, 885F3; offcls sentncd 11-30, 921D2
Goodyr, Firestone suits dropped 3-2, 988G2
Sup Ct bars Westn Air ruling review 3-8, 219B2
NY dismisses '74 chrgs vs 3 oil cos 3-10; case vs 7 rptd pending 3-11, 413B1
House OKs state attys suits 3-18, 246D3-247B1
FTC chrgs GM 3-22, 989E3
Sup Ct rules on drug sales to hosps 3-24, 218A3
9 steel firms fined 4-10, 988D3
FTC reveals Gen Tire probe 4-27, 360C2
Levi Strauss price-fixing chrgd 5-7, 989D3
US files Mid-Amer Dairymen consent decree 5-28, 989B2
7 oil cos indicted 6-1, 412C3
Dem platform text 6-15, 470F1, 471D2
8 potash producers indicted 6-29, 748A1
Sup Ct backs suits vs state-regulated elec cos 7-6, 569F1
FTC car rental suit setld 7-12, 989G2
Mondale record cited 512G2
FTC chrgs Gen Foods 7-16, 989B3
Carter backs 2 bills, vs oil industry breakup 8-9, 585A1, D1
'69 drug suit ends in mistrial 8-17, 988A3
GOP platform text 8-18, 603C2
Football draft ruled illegal 9-8, 736B3
Cong clears enforcemt bill 9-16, 728D1 ★; Ford signs 9-30, 982F1
Calif anti-boycott law signed 9-27, 987E1
Sup Ct bars review of NC drug case 10-4, 807B3
Ford cites Arab boycott actn 10-6, 742B1
Standard Oil retrial bid eased 10-18, 867G2
Paper-bag makers chrgd 10-29, 11-4, 886B3
Sup Ct bars review of judge removal in Olson Farms case 11-15, 882G2
AT&T trust suit OKd 11-16, 886G3
US files consent decree vs 9 dye cos 11-16, 989B1
NBC, US in programming pact 11-17, 869D1
Radiologists bar price-fixing, '75 MD agrmts cited 11-17, 988F3-989A1
9 hotel firms indicted 11-17, 989E2
Australia blocks US uranium actn 11-18, 997C2
6 coal cos indicted 11-19, 989C2
US asks jail terms for price-fixing 11-20, 885B3
FCC network probe asked 11-23, 901D1
Titanium price-fixing talks rptd 12-5, 988A2 ★

1977

ANTITRUST Actions
NY mag purchase probe rptd 1-6, 48E3
Gypsum cos' convictns overturned 1-6, 156E2
US, Bechtel settle 1-10, 78C2
Arco, Anaconda merger OKd 1-12, 55G2
TV network probe OKd 1-14, 119C1
Dental groups sued 1-14, 156G2
Sup Ct bars AT&T rule review 1-25, 80B2
Sup Ct voids Brunswick ruling 1-25, 80D2
3 airlines indicted 2-3, 93E2
NBC sued re Olympics 2-14, 131E1
Ill Podiatry Soc sued 2-15, 156B3
Paperbd execs sentences cut 2-17, 504D1
Sup Ct voids US Steel credit ruling 2-22, 149E2
Sup Ct refuses US Steel-Southn Concrete case 2-22, 149B3
Sup Ct bars review of newspaper agreemt ruling 2-22, 150G1
AT&T practices OKd 2-23, reactn 2-23—2-24, 217B2
'76 chrgs dismissed vs Potash Co of Amer 2-25, 5 others 6-10, 483C3
Joint media ownership barred 3-1, 216B1
Westinghouse dispute setld 3-3, 177A3
FTC vs Tenneco bid for Monroe 3-15, 274G3
6 coal cos fined 3-21; 2 indicted 6-2, 520G2
Sugar firms indicted 3-30, fined 5-19, 504G1-A2
Babcock sues to block United Tech purchase 4-4, 274B3
Double jeopardy protectn broadened 4-4, 341B3
Carter defends energy plan 4-22, 321E2
Canada uranium cartel, Gulf role rptd 4-25; NYS, US cong probes 6-9—6-17, 479A2-480F2
NFL labor pact challenged 4-25, 491F2
4 Hawaii hotels fined 5-11, 504C2
US probe of Japan TV mfrs rptd 5-20, 416F1
Baltimore papers settle suit 5-26, 504A2
3 steel firms indicted 6-6, 504B1
FTC accuses Sunkist 6-6, 520E2
Price-fixing suits curbed 6-9, 501E2
ITT sues AT&T 6-10, 520C2
US-Canada arbitratn com set, uranium dispute cited 6-18, 525G2
Brinks, Wells Fargo indicted 6-21, 520D3
'Schwinn doctrine' overturned, Sylvania rules upheld 6-23, 539E1
NHL-WHA 'expansion' proposed 6-24, 603E1
Norton Simon buys Avis shares 6-27, 519A2
Sup Ct OKs legal fee ads 6-27, 538D3
Cigar co merger blocked 6-28, 520E3
Vendo contract dispute award ordrd 6-29, 557D3
Kennecott sells Peabody 6-30, 520F1
United Tech's Babcock takeover blocked 7-5, 520D1
NY Nets' move to NJ set 7-26, 584C2, F2
ICC curbs rail grain-car deals 8-1, 613B1
Bell vows multinatl probes 8-8, 629E3
FTC asks Gulf-Kewanee merger delay 8-9, 612G2

1978

ANTITRUST Actions
US to drop suit vs Texaco 1-3, 67E2
Amer Medicorp OKs Humana bid 1-10, 66A3
Foreign natn suits OKd by Sup Ct 1-11, 33A3
IBM-Greyhound case review denied 1-16, 33E2
US, Canada frictn cited, US OKs new info-gathering policy 1-17, 53D3
Berkey wins suit vs Kodak 1-21, 67C1
Cardbd mfrs indicted 1-25, 67A2
Elec wiring device makers sentncd 2-3, 142F1
Film, TV industry probe rptd 2-4, 351E2
Carter Hawley drops Marshall Field bid 2-22, 185G1
Sachs takeover halted 2-23, 211B1
NOW boycott injunctn sought by Mo, Nev 2-28, 3-3, 494F2
Maritime Comm labor contract jurisdictn enlarged 3-1, 143G3
ITT wins GTE suit 3-1, 510A3
United Nuclear wins uranium cartel suit, impact on other Gulf suits seen 3-2, 144C1, B2
FCC to probe Western Union 3-9, 270D2
Gen Atomic damage determinatn stay denied by Sup Ct 3-20, 206D1
Berkey wins Kodak damages 3-22, 205A1
Cities liability upheld by Sup Ct 3-29, 280F1-E2
FTC suit vs BOC Airco purchase cited 4-7, 403D3
Du Pont pigment monopoly chrgd 4-10, 345G3
New United Nuclear case evidence rptd 4-20, 346F2-B3
Armored car firms fined 4-22, 5-4, 511D1
Engineers' fee code ruled illegal by Sup Ct 4-25, 323A1
Coke, Pepsi bottler curbs barred 4-25, 346B1
US rests case vs IBM 4-26, 510C2
Gulf chrgd by US re uranium cartel 5-9, 346D1-D2
Gulf sues Westinghouse 5-9, 346D2
Gen Atomic documts rule declined by Sup Ct 5-15, 387E3
Gen Atomic damages awarded United Nuclear, Ind & Mich 5-16, 366G2
Ind & Mich utility suit rule refused by Sup Ct 5-22, 388C2
Gen Atomic trial judge interference ruled by Sup Ct 5-30, 430A3
Australia adopts uranium rules 5-31, 434E3
US sues CBS, seeks Fawcett divestiture 6-1, 510E3
Gulf fined in uranium cartel case 6-2, 449G2-A3
SCM set back in Xerox suit 6-7, 510E1-C2
FCC cross-media ban backed by Sup Ct 6-12, 467B3
Poultry group denied immunity by Sup Ct 6-12, 468A1
Redskins liability case refused by Sup Ct 6-12, 468E1
Sugar refiners settle '74 chrgs 6-12, 511B1

1979

ANTITRUST Actions
AT&T documts order review declined by Sup Ct 1-8, 14G3
AT&T proposes speedy trial date, US refusal seen 1-11, 88A3
Mail delivery svc monopoly plea declined by Sup Ct 1-15, 32A1
Adams' rail deregulatn plan criticism rptd 1-15, 35F3
Natl comm rpt issued 1-16, 88C2
IBM case marks 10th yr 1-17, 88D3
Kennedy offers consumer suits bill 1-31, 308B2
United Tech-Carrier merger OKd 1-31, terms set 3-30, 349E3-350A1
Kennedy introduces trucking deregulatn bill 1-22, clashes with Cannon 2-7, 111A3
Carter State of Union Message 1-23, 46G3
Carter seeks price-fixing consumer suit bill 1-25, 70C2
FCC ends Westn Union telegram monopoly 1-25, 78A2
Kerr-McGee OKs oil-price refund 2-8, 112G3
ABA OKs cong testimony 2-13, 130A2
ERA conv boycott upheld 2-21, 128F1
A&P milk price actn backed by Sup Ct 2-22, 150F2
ICC clears Seaboard 2-22, 205G3
Braniff pays fine 2-23, 206D2
AFL-CIO urges US drive 2-24, 148F3
Monopoly intent case refused by Sup Ct 2-26, 164C3
Blue Shield drug plan trust rule upheld by Sup Ct 2-27, 165A1
ICC limits truckers' immunity 2-28, 166E3
FTC brewer competitn study rptd 3-2, 305C2
Auto insurnc wage rate ruling voided by Sup Ct 3-5, 184G3
Calif fuel price law challenge declined by Sup Ct 3-5, 185E1
AT&T data access case declined by Sup Ct 3-26, 231A1
FTC data disclosure to states OKd 3-28, 308D2
Kapp NFL damages case declined by Sup Ct 4-16, 302F3
Music license fee case remanded by Sup Ct 4-17, 326A1
Cardbd mfrs acquitted 4-29, civil setlmts revealed 5-1, 327B3
Fairchild rejcts Gould merger bids 5-4, 5-8, suits filed 5-8, 5-9, 350D1
Merger dangers seen by FTC chrmn 5-7, 349C2
GM car-radio suit settled 5-14, 441F3-442A1
Oil firm-shortage link probed 5-15, 361E2
FTC opens film industry probe 5-23, 430C3
7 shipping cos indicted 6-1, 423A2; fines levied 6-8, 442A2
Rail decontrol bill scored 6-6, 579E2
Consumers' right to sue protected by Sup Ct 6-11, 478D2
Schick sues Gillette 6-14, 481D3
NAB sued over TV ad limit 6-14, 618G2-A3

1980

ANTITRUST Actions
Real estate brokers ruled subject to suits by Sup Ct 1-8, 16C1
NCAA women's title tourn move scored 1-8, 103G3
Paper bag price fixing appeals declined by Sup Ct 1-14, 37E1
Md real estate convictn appeals declined Sup Ct 1-21, 93B3
Kennedy vs monopolies 1-28, 75A1; urges enforcemt 2-6, 91B1
Comsat direct satellite TV svc OKd 1-30, 240B1
Berkey appeal refused by Sup Ct 2-19, 130F3
Coors Calif case declined by Sup Ct 2-19, 131D1
NFL franchise move attempt sparks trust controversy 2-22—3-5, 175G1-C2
FTC procedure case accepted by Sup Ct 2-25, 187E3
IBM judge's ouster rejected 2-25, 266C2
Loews film productn OKd by Dist Ct 2-27, 229E1
AT&T, ITT settle lawsuits 2-27, 240B1
Calif wine pricing law held illegal by Sup Ct 3-3, 210E1
Gypsum price fixing case settled 3-3, 557E3
Schlumberger OKs Unitrode divestiture 3-4, 558A1
Phone industry deregulatn set by FCC 4-7, 370C2
Getty Oil pay-TV film venture probe set 4-24, 376F2
Mandatory civil jury case refused by Sup Ct 4-28, 369G1
CBS, US settle dispute 5-8, 501C3
FTC ends detergent indus probe 5-12, 703A2
Chattanooga (Tenn) papers partially join 5-12, Civiletti OKs 9-2, 732G2
FTC ends tuna indus probe 5-22, 703E2
Credit fixing curbed by Sup Ct 5-27, 453F2
FTC offcl resigns in protest 5-27, 703A1
MCI wins $1.8 bln AT&T suit 6-13, 456D3
Unpatented key ingredient monopolies backed by Sup Ct 6-27, 511C2
Borg-Warner, Bosch violatn rptd 7-11, 917F2
Bendix, Warner & Swasey chrgs rptd setld 7-14, 917E2
Oil cos absolved in '79 shortage 7-17, 552D1
Paint-resin price setlmt reached 7-22, 917D1
US Steel Ohio plant closings upheld 7-25, 575E2
McDermott bid for Pullman ruled OK 7-31, 784B3
Getty Oil pay-TV film plan draws suit 8-4, 639D3
ABC ties to Spelling-Goldberg rptd probed by SEC 8-7—8-8, 640B1
ICC curbs RR collective rate fixing 8-13, 616E3
AT&T, equipmt suppliers settle 8-18, 917C2
AT&T begins reorgn 8-20, 648B2
ABC settles US suit 8-22, 732E1
Mead rptd guilty of box price fixing 9-15, 917E1

1976

GE, Westinghouse suits dropped 12-10, 988C2
Coleman to OK superports 12-17, 992A1

ANTONELLI, Vittorio
Arrested 2-20, freed on bail 3-27, 298E1
ANTONIOZZI, Dario
Sworn Italy tourism min 7-30, 573G1
ANTONOPLIS, Lea
Beats Richards in Tennis Week Open 8-27, loses final 8-29, 716F1, A2
ANTONOVA, Elena
Wins Olympic medal 7-24, 575F1
ANTONSSON, Johannes
Named to Swedish Cabt 10-8, 794C2
ANZUS—*See AUSTRALIA, New Zealand, U.S. Treaty Organization*
AOKI, Hisayori
Arrested 6-22, 450B3
Indicted 7-13, 557B2
Freed on bail 8-17, 624A2
AP—*See ASSOCIATED Press*
A&P—*See GREAT Atlantic & Pacific Tea Co.*
APARTMENTS—*See HOUSING*
APEL, Hans
Mark revalued 10-17, cites Eur float protectn 10-18, 782A1
APEX Oil Co.
Sup Ct bars review of spill liability case 10-4, 807D3
APODACA, Gov. Jerry (D, N.M.)
Officeholders successn defeated 11-2, 824F2
APPALACHIA
Dem platform text 6-15, 475C1
NE aid plan urged 11-14, 864F3
APPALACHIAN Power Co.—*See under AMERICAN Electric Power*

1977

Calif forgn banks chrgd 8-9, 669A3
Braniff, Tex Intl sued 8-16, 629C3
Washington sues 10 oil cos 8-16, 691E3
Western land holding breakup sought 8-18, 8-22, 703C2
McDermott wins Babcock bidding war 8-25, 666F3
5 indep oil cos convicted 8-30, 691G2
Oil, gas firm acquisitn curbs rejctd 9-8, 702F3
Crane withdraws Chemetron bid 9-8, 880E2
NY Times, IHT, Intl Trib sued 9-13, 723D1
5 indep oil cos fined 9-16, 918F2
Canada opens uranium cartel probe 10-3, Denison scores 10-19, 895F2
Japan asks steel export exemptn 10-4, 775E1
Record fine levied on Medusa unit 10-5, 918D2
ITT, Lazard settle chrgs re Hartford 10-13, 980B3
NY sugar exchng chrgd 10-17, 818G2
Elec wiring device makers chrgd 10-27, 918G3-919A1
Paper-bag makers acquitted, convicted 11-1, 11-23, 918G2-B3
Merger activity, enforcemt fears linked 11-4, 879G3
US probes LTV, Lykes merger 11-4, 943A3
Champion Intl convictn review declined 11-7, 857B2
J P Stevens sued by union 11-10, 899B1
Inco allowed to keep ESB 11-11, 918E3
Eaton loses Carborundum to Kennecott 11-16, 880D1
TVA sues 13 uranium producers 11-18, 895C1
Sup Ct bars AT&T appeal 11-28, 919B2
NBC accord OKd 12-1, 918C3
UK denies Westinghouse Rio Tinto evidence 12-1, 1003D3, E3
Hunt oil suit case declined 12-5, 938E3
Satra drops suit vs NBC 12-9, 971D2
Revere sale to Alcan challenged 12-9, 1004E3
Marshall Field vs Carter Hawley bid 12-14, 1004B2

ANWAR ul-Haq
Heads Pak Supreme Ct 9-23, 765B3
ANYONA, George
Rptd held 9-5, 753B2
ANZUS—*See AUSTRALIA, New Zealand, U.S. Treaty Organization*
AP—*See ASSOCIATED Press*
A&P—*See GREAT Atlantic & Pacific Tea Co.*
APA—*See PODIATRY Association, American*
APALACHICOLA National Forest (Fla.)
Fire destroys 7,000 acres 5-23—5-26, 660D3
APALATEGUI, Miguel Angel
French detentn protested 8-18—8-24; vanishes after release 10-7, 826E2
APARICIO, Sergio
Freed 8-24, 784F2
APARTHEID—*See SOUTH Africa*
APARTHEID, World Conference for Action Against
Nigeria hosts 8-22—8-26, 661E2
APARTMENTS—*See HOUSING*
APEL, Hans
Says mark overvalued 12-6, 933A1
API—*See PETROLEUM Institute, American*

1978

Hosps denied cost containmt exemptn 6-13, 577C2
Md refiner-run gas statn ban upheld by Sup Ct 6-14, 491F3
Mt Hood award vs Greyhound curbed by Sup Ct 6-19, 492A3
Oil pipe ownership curb backed by Sen subcom 6-21, 471D1
Bell backs LTV-Lykes merger 6-21, 492C3
Gypsum price-fixing ruling upheld by Sup Ct 6-29, 567F2
Insurance co policyholder suits backed by Sup Ct 6-29, 567C3
Kodak award to Berkey cut 7-3, 808E2
IBM-Memorex case mistrial 7-5, 510F2
Van Dyk-Xerox trial begins 7-12, 664E3
Interco settles FTC chrgs 7-14, 768E3
SCM-Xerox verdicts 7-19, 7-11; damages set 8-9, 8-16, 664G2
NFL Rams plan '80 Anaheim move, LA Coliseum suit cited 7-25, 1023F3
ITT-Hartford settlemt cited 7-28, 767F1
Amstart settles 78 civil suits 7-28, 768G3
Beatrice-Tropicana challenge rejctd 8-2, cos merge 8-7, 767C2, D3
Mead vs Occidental takeover bid 8-18, 767D2-A3
Intl Paper settles '78, '76 chrgs 8-25, 10-1; 3 other '76 defendants settle 9-25, 10-2, 768C3
Justice Dept asks merger notificatn 9-5, probes set 10-4, 767B1
Indep news producers sue networks 9-11, 759F1
20th Century-Fox fined 9-12, 759D2
NHL compensatn clause ruled illegal 9-18, 990D3
'77 paper co defendants sentncd 9-21, 10-2, 768F2-B3
Copper wire producers sued 9-21, 769B1
Kodak lawyer pleads guilty 9-21, sentncd 10-17, 808C2
Elec cable makers sued 9-22, 768G3
Constructn cos, execs indicted 9-27, 769A1
Titanium cos, execs indicted 9-28, 768F1, C2
Elec fuse makers, execs chrgd 9-28, 769C1
Justice Dept sets voluntary disclosure plan; '74 law prosecutns, '78 convctns cited 10-4, 768E1-C2
Canada sugar refineries fined 10-6, 794F3
US sues vs Occidental-Mead merger 10-11, expands suit 10-25, 895A3
Cardbd mfrs fined 10-13, plead no contest 10-16, 10-25, 1005F2
Allegheny drops Chemetron unit sale plan 10-24, 897E1
Oreck damage award case refused by Sup Ct 10-30, 832G2
Rockwell Textron indicted on Singer disclosure 11-1, 935A3
Law firm dual-representatn case refused by Sup Ct 11-6, 873G3
ICC proposes trucking deregulatn; indus, cong ldrs leery 11-7—12-21, 1007D1, G1
EC Comm orders fiber cartel modificatn 11-9, 871B3
Lykes-LTV merger probe by FTC asked by Kennedy 11-9, FTC rejcts 11-21; shareholders OK merger 12-5, 935C2
AT&T Centrex case refused by Sup Ct 11-13, 874D2
AT&T documents order backed by Sup Ct 11-13, 874A3
IATA revises structure 11-13, 894B3
US sues vs United Tech-Carrier merger 11-13, 896D1
TV music licenses challenged 11-27, 1030A1
FTC probe of Shell rptd 11-28, 939C2
AMA ad ban voided 11-29, AMA to appeal 11-30, 947D2
Shell gas sale monopoly chrgd 11-30, 939D3
Calif auto franchise law upheld by US Sup Ct 12-5, 959E3
Occidental restrained by ct 12-9, ends Mead takeover effort 12-20, 1004C3
Carter vows actn vs oil indus abuses 12-12, 983E2
Cleveland Elec suit cited 1008A3
SCM Xerox award set aside 12-29, 1005D2

ANTONIOZZI, Dario
Named Italy culture min 3-11, 191C1
ANTONOVICH, Mike
Winnipeg wins WHA title 5-22, 458C2
ANTUNES, Carlos
Arrested in violence probe 6-22, 594E1
ANYONA, George
Freed 12-12, 968A2
AOKI, Isao
Wins World Match Play title 10-16, 990A2
AP—*See ASSOCIATED Press*
APARTHEID—*See SOUTH Africa*
APARTMENT Association of Los Angeles County
Calif voters OK Jarvis amendmt 6-6, 425F1
APARTMENTS—*See HOUSING*
APEL, Hans
Named W Ger defns min 2-3, 93D2, A3
Curbs W Ger armed forces reorganizatn 3-23, 354G1
Questns NATO maneuvers 9-23, affirms commitmt 9-27, 748E2-A3
API—*See PETROLEUM Institute American*
APODACA, Gov. Jerry (D, N.M.)
Primary results 6-6, 448C2
King elected successor 11-7, 855D2, F2
APPALACHIAN Region
Coal Policy Projct issues rpt 2-9, 184E2

1979

Ocean Spray action urged by FTC staff 6-20, 985G3-986B1
Berkey award reversed 6-25, 517C2-A3
United Tech-Carrier merger faulted 6-25, 541A3
Paperbd civil suit setld, criminal chrgs cited 6-28, 647G3
Tex offshore port OKd 7-2, 518F2
AMA chrgd in NY chiropractors suit 7-5, 570F2
Pan Am, TXI bids for Natl Airlines OKd by CAB 7-10; TXI quits race 7-28, Pan Am buys shares 8-2, 7-10, 579A1
IBM seeks judge's ouster 7-19, 610E2
Stevens '77 union suit dismissed 8-6, 598C3
Kerkorian case dismissed 8-14, 756C1
Bechtel suit cited 8-27, 648G2
Argus accuses Kodak, 2 others 8-28, 986B1
Hartz Mt settles FTC complaint 8-29, 903B1
CAB grants IATA limited immunity 9-10, 725G3-726A1
Du Pont pigment monopoly case dismissed 9-17, 810C1
NBC '77 setlmt challenge refused 10-1, 768C2
Flying Tiger-Seaboard merger ban sought 10-2, 830C2
Battle Creek sues FTC for environmt statemt 10-9, 809G3
IBM wins Transamerica suit 10-18, 851F2
Water-heater firms acquitted 10-22, 986E1
AMA ad ban ordrd ended 10-24, 902G2
Fla abortn case declined by Sup Ct 10-29, 884E2
Carter asks indl research rules clarified 10-31, 829G3
Renfrew '74 price-fix ruling cited 11-20, 946B3
Cincinnati papers joint pact OKd 11-26, 1007A2
Telex lawyer fee case declined by Sup Ct 12-3, 964C2
CAB ends IATA probe 12-5, 989D1
NBC '77 setlmt challenge refused again by Sup Ct 12-10, 988A2

Foreign Developments (including U.S. international news)

W Ger publishers fined 2-7, 101B1
EC '76 Hoffman-La Roche ruling upheld 2-13, 137B1
W Ger probes banks 5-17, 374E1
Denmark chrgs 10 in Unilever case 7-2, 563F3
OPEC suit dropped 8-23, 647C3
UK trust bill proposed, US law targeted 10-31, 855C3

ANTITRUST Laws and Procedures, National Commission for the Review of—*See under U.S. GOVERNMENT*

ANTON, Susan
Goldengirl released 6-15, 820C1
ANTONELLI, Laura
Wifemistress released 1-6, 174G3
Innocent released 1-11, 174G2
Till Marriage Do Us Part released 7-20, 820E3
Divine Nymph released 10-12, 1007C3
ANTOON, A. J.
Nasty Rumors opens 4-12, 712F1
ANTUOFERMO, Vito
Decisns Corro for world middlewgt title 6-30, 838E3
Draws with Hagler 11-30, 1004D3
ANZUS—*See AUSTRALIA, New Zealand, U.S. Treaty Organization*
AOKI, Isao
Loses World Match Play title 10-14, 970G1
AP—*See ASSOCIATED Press*
A&P—*See GREAT Atlantic & Pacific Tea Co.*
APARTHEID—*See SOUTH Africa*
APEL, Hans
AWACS deal threat rptd 8-1, 586A2
Rejects joint French A-force 9-21, 733C1
US rptd upset re defns spending 9-21, 733B2
Backs US A-missiles 11-14, 880B2
APES
Surviving hybrid rptd 7-21, 692B2
APLIN, Billy Joe
Killed 8-3, 660D1
APNEA (sleep breathing)—*See MEDICINE—Heart*
APOCALYPSE Now (film)
Released 8-15, 819D3
Top-grossing film 10-31, 892G3
APOSTOLIC United Brethren
4 acquitted in Allred '77 death, 2 sought 3-20, 240B2
APPALACHIAN Region
Malnutritn rptd down 4-30, 386A3

1980

Fine paper suits rptd setld 9-29, 12-3, 917A2, B2
McDonald's acquitted in franchise suit 9-29, 917B3
Telecommunicatns bill tabled by Cong 9-30, 835D2
Rockwell, Serck settle plug valve suit 10-1, 917G1
NOW Mo boycott case refused by Sup Ct 10-6, 782F1-A2
Greyhound-Mt Hood case declined by Sup Ct 10-6, 782C2
Xerox win in Van Dyk suit rptd upheld 10-6, 917D3
Beef pricing case refused by Sup Ct 10-14, 781G3
RR deregulatn bill signed 10-14, 784B1
Heublein, United Vintners divestiture order rptd overturned 10-15, 917C1
Paperbd setlmt case dismissed by Sup Ct 10-20, 807A3
Du Pont monopoly case dismissal upheld 10-27, 916F3
Trust damages liability sharing case accepted by Sup Ct 11-3, 856C2
Chattanooga papers' pact gets final OK 11-6, 907E1
US Steel Ohio plant suit ends 11-14, 917A1
Aluminum indus suit rptd dropped by Justice Dept 11-18, 916E3
NFL cross-ownership ban backed 11-18, 999A1
Levi win in Wrangler trademark suit rptd 11-19, 917B3
IBM win in Memorex suit rptd upheld 11-20, 917E3
Beatrice, Tropicana merger found illegal 11-28, 917F3
Levi retail price fixing suits rptd setld 12-2, 917G2
Oil cos FTC complaint challenge curbed by Sup Ct 12-15, 957D1
Goodrich settles US suit 12-15, 986C1
Cuisinarts fined 12-19, 986B1

Foreign Developments (including U.S. international news)

Canada convicts Valium producer 2-6, 116E2-B3
Indl Investmt vs Mitsui case declined by Sup Ct 2-25, 188B1
EC fines W Ger, French steelmakers 4-3, 262F2

ANTONOV, Alexei K.
Named Sovt dep premr 12-19, 996C2
ANTUOFERMO, Vito
Minter decisns for world middlewgt title, victory disputed 3-16, 320C2
ANTURANE (sulfinpyrazone)—*See MEDICINE--Drugs & Health-Care Products*
ANY Which Way You Can (film)
Released 12-17, 1003F1
ANZUS—*See AUSTRALIA, New Zealand, U.S. Treaty Organization*
AOKI, Isao
2d in US Open 6-15, 714E2
AP—*See ASSOCIATED Press*
APEL, Hans
Sworn W Ger defense min 11-5, 925F1
API—*See PETROLEUM Institute, American*
APOCALYPSE Now (film)
Wins Oscars 4-14, 296A2
APOLLO (U.S. spacecraft series)—*See ASTRONAUTICS--Manned Flight*
APPALACHIAN Spring (recording)
Davies, St Paul Chamber Orchestra win Grammy 2-27, 296F3

1976

APPAREL—See CLOTHING
APPELGATE, Douglas
Elected 11-2, 823F3, 830B3
APPIES, Leonardo
Detained 8-13, 624D3
APPLE Dumpling Gang (film)
'75 top rental film 1-7, 32F3
APPLETON, Wis.—See WISCONSIN
APPLIANCES, Electrical—See ELECTRIC & Electronic Industries
AQUINO Jr., Benigno S.
Arraigned 8-3, boycotts trial 8-11, 695D1
ARAB Boycott—See under BUSINESS
ARAB Countries—See also specific names; also organizations (e.g., ARAB League); for Arab-Israeli conflict, see MIDDLE EAST
Regional defns spending rptd 1-2, 60F3
Freedom House survey rptd 1-19, 20B3
1st IMF gold auction held 6-2, 430G2
World Bank chart on poverty data 778C1
4th IMF gold auction 10-29, 832E2
Economic Boycott—See 'Arab Boycott' under BUSINESS
ARAB Emirates, United—See UNITED Arab Emirates
ARABIAN American Oil Co. (Aramco)
On Saudi price cut 6-9, 407D3
ARABIAN Sea
UK to quit bases 7-19, 594F2
ARAB Information Center (Dallas, Tex.)
Cited re FBI burglary probe 8-17, 634A2
ARAB-Israeli Conflict—See MIDDLE EAST
ARAB League (Algeria, Bahrain, Egypt, Iraq, Jordan, Kuwait, Lebanon, Libya, Mauritania, Morocco, Oman, Palestine Liberation Organization, Qatar, Saudi Arabia, Somalia, Southern Yemen, Sudan, Syria, Tunisia, United Arab Emirates, Yemen Arab Republic)
Riad Sahara mediatn fails 3-2, 178C3
Conf 3-24—4-3, 242B1
Scores Vorster Israel trip 275F3
Arab-Africa mtg, Zionism scored 4-19—4-22, 356A1
Sets up monetary fund 4-26—4-27, 341C1
EC talks end 5-20, 529B3
Vs Air France hijacking 7-1, 486E1
To probe Libya role in Sudan coup 8-8, 592G2
Libya asks mtg on Egypt buildup 8-15, 629F3
PLO becomes 21st member 9-6, 663C2
Economic Boycott—See 'Arab Boycott' under BUSINESS
Lebanon Civil War—See under MIDDLE EAST—ARAB Policies
ARAFAT, Yasir
Vs raids on Leb camps 1-14, 17D2
Scores Karantina attack 1-18, 34C1
Backs Leb accord 1-22, 33F1
Khaddam vows Leb sovereignty 1-29, 83A2
Scores Saiqa on press raid 1-31, 83B1
Briefed on Syria-Leb talks 2-8, 107A2

1977

APPAREL—See CLOTHING
APPAREL Manufacturers Association, American
Tris recall cost sharing upheld 5-19, 483C2
APPLES—See FRUITS & Vegetables
APPLIANCES, Electrical—See ELECTRIC & Electronics Industries
APPLIED Digital Data Systems Inc.
Racal wins Milgo takeover 2-17, 275A1
APPLIED Systems Analysis, International Institute for
World petroleum resource rpt 4-26, 362F2
AQUINO Jr., Benigno S.
Chrgs views silenced 7-6, 619A1
Sanguyo slain 9-1, 746G3-747A1
Gets death sentnc 11-25; appeals, new trial ordrd 11-28, 947A1
ARA-A (adenine arabinoside)—See MEDICINE—Drugs
ARAB, Issam al-
Forces fight Syrians 4-23—4-26, 316D2
ARAB Americans
Dixon slurs Nader 1-17, regrets 2-1, 2-2, 96A1
ARAB-Americans, National Association of
Dixon regrets Nader slur 2-1, 96D1
ARAB Boycott—See under BUSINESS
ARAB Countries—See also specific names; also organizations (e.g., ARAB League); for Arab-Israeli conflict, see MIDDLE EAST
Arms industry group cited 10B3
US rpt scores arms sales 1-24, 70D2
Spain forgn min starts tour 1-27, 101D3
Afro-Arab summit 3-7—3-9, 170D1-D2, 188B2
Red Sea summit 3-22—3-23, 208D2
Arab fund created 4-18, 317F3
Dinar SDR link, $ value rptd 4-18, 318G1
UN desert conf protest 8-30, 770D1
Somalia arms offers rptd 9-1, 684G2; 9-14, 715A3
Cholera rptd widespread 9-26, 747G3-748C1
Economic Boycott—See BUSINESS—Arab Boycott
ARAB Development Bank
Intl consortium OKs Egypt aid 5-11—5-12, 390B3
ARAB Emirates, United—See UNITED Arab Emirates
ARAB Fund for Economic and Social Development (Algeria, Bahrain, Egypt, Iraq, Jordan, Kuwait, Lebanon, Libya, Morocco, Oman, PLO, Qatar, Saudi Arabia, Somalia, Sudan, Syria, Tunisia, United Arab Emirates, Yemen, Yemen Arab Republic)
Intl consortium OKs Egypt aid 5-11—5-12, 390B3
ARABIAN American Oil Co. (Aramco)
Price hikes rptd 1-5, 12D1
Saudi oil mktg plan rptd; Yamani scores rpt, cites consumer pact 2-15, 108C1-F1
Says Saudis to up output, Aramco figures cited 5-11, 362F1
Saudi pipe fire 5-11—5-12, sabotage suspected 5-12, 362B2
Saudi fire out 5-13, losses rptd 5-15, 5-19, 402B2
ARAB-Israeli Dispute—See MIDDLE EAST
ARAB-Latin American Bank
Peru govt seeks branch 8-17, 785B2
ARAB League (Algeria, Bahrain, Djibouti, Egypt, Iraq, Jordan, Kuwait, Lebanon, Libya, Mauritania, Morocco, North Yemen, Oman, Palestine Liberation Organization, Qatar, Saudi Arabia, Somalia, South Yemen, Sudan, Syria, Tunisia, United Arab Emirates)
EC '70-75 trade data rptd 1-18, 74A1
In EEC talks 2-10—2-12, 146G1
Afro conf preparatory mtgs 3-3—3-5, summit 3-7—3-9, 170D1-D2
Afars independnc vote observed 4-8, 363B2
Libya protests Egypt actns 4-13, 361F2
Kenya pro-Arab shift rptd 7-6, 588G1
Mediates Egypt-Libya feud 7-24—7-25, 570A1
Assad for Geneva conf PLO substitutn 8-26, 663A2
Forgn mins meet 9-3—9-6; OK Djibouti entry, delay Comoros; avoid Ethiopia-Somalia issue 9-4, 685A1
Forgn mins meet re Geneva problem, summit, Leb raids 11-12—11-14, 874F1
Libya asks Egypt ouster 11-18, 890A3
Tripoli conf sets debate on Egypt status 12-5, 929A2
Economic Boycott—See BUSINESS—Arab Boycott
Lebanon Developments—See LEBANON
ARAB Monetary Fund
Created 4-18, 317F3
ARAFAT, Yasir
At Saleh memorial rites 1-9, 9D2
Ivory Coast pres gets note 1-25, 86C3
Meets Waldheim 2-6—2-7, 86F2
Meets Syrians on Leb clashes 2-15, 106D3, 107B1
Waldheim sees PLO moderatn 2-16, 107E1

1978

APPAREL—See CLOTHING
APPLEGATE, Douglas
Wins US House seat 11-7, 851F3
APPLES on a Tablecloth (painting)
Stolen from Chicago museum 12-27, 1028F3
APPLETON Paper Co.
Occidental-Mead trust suit filed 10-11, expanded 10-25, 895F3
APPLIANCES, Electrical—See ELECTRIC & Electronic Industries
APPROACHING Zero (play)
Opens 11-30, 1030G3
AQABA, Gulf of
Begin notes Egypt navigatn rights agrmt 1-23, 41F2
Camp David summit pact affirms navigatn rights 9-17, 712B2
AQUACULTURE—See FISHING Industry
AQUINO Jr., Benigno
Loses PI Assemb electn race 4-7, 268B3
AQUINO, Maj. Heitor
Paymts from US billionaire rptd 1-13, 165G3
ARAB Boycott—See under BUSINESS
ARAB Countries—See also country, organization names; for Arab-Israel conflict, see MIDDLE EAST
Japan '77 aid sets record 1-3, 28F2
Venez loan rptd 1-17, oil competitn cited 4-16, 332A1, F1
Mauritania loan rptd 1-27, 95E1
Dvpt plans rptd slowed 2-20, 122D1-A2
Oil exporters' poor state aid rise rptd 4-9, 257B2
Rptd Rhodesia arms source 7-23, 616D2
Transkei loan rptd 8-22, 885G3
CORE Arab-financed NY housing dvpt plan cited 9-18, 810G1
Pressure re Uganda exit from Tanzania cited 11-14, 870B2
ARAB Emirates, United—See UNITED Arab Emirates
ARAB Fund for Economic and Social Development (Algeria, Bahrain, Egypt, Iraq, Jordan, Kuwait, Lebanon, Libya, Morocco, Oman, PLO, Qatar, Saudi Arabia, Somalia, Sudan, Syria, Tunisia, United Arab Emirates, Yemen, Yemen Arab Republic)
Poor-natn aid rise rptd 4-9, 257G2
Sudan loan rptd 8-17, 925F3
ARABIAN American Oil Co. (Aramco)
Jan exports rptd down 2-22, 158F2
ARABIAN Sea
Air India 747 jet crashes 1-1, 23F3-24A1
ARAB Industries Organization (AIO) (Egypt, Qatar, Saudi Arabia, United Arab Emirates)
France signs arms pact; US, UK deals cited 3-14, 237B1, C1 *
ARAB-Israeli Dispute—See MIDDLE EAST
ARAB League (Algeria, Bahrain, Djibouti, Egypt, Iraq, Jordan, Kuwait, Lebanon, Libya, Mauritania, Morocco, North Yemen, Oman, Palestine Liberation Organization, Qatar, Saudi Arabia, Somalia, South Yemen, Sudan, Syria, Tunisia, United Arab Emirates)
Cncl mtg, 5 states shun: sets summit on Leb; extends Leb peace force; vs USSR, Cuba in Ethiopia 3-27—3-29, 215A1
Meets, 7 members boycott 7-1—7-2; suspends ties with S Yemen re N Yemen pres death 7-2, 522F1
Hardliners ask Cairo hq shift 9-24, 730B1
Cncl mtg, 5 states shun; Leb force mandate extended, Egypt abstains 10-26, 803D1
Summit vs Camp David pact 11-2—11-5; Sadat shuns delegatn 11-4, Egypt press scores Hoss 11-5, 859B2
Economic Boycott—See BUSINESS—Arab Boycott
Lebanon Developments—See LEBANON under 'L' and under MIDDLE EAST
ARAB Revolutionary Army—See MIDDLE EAST
ARAFAT, Yasir
Vs US stand on Palestinians 1-1, 1-2, 3B1
Calls mtg on PLO Leb pullback 2-3, 79C3
14 PLO gunmen rptd sent to Cyprus airfield 2-19, Kyprianou disputes 2-21, 118F1

1979

APPAREL—See CLOTHING & Fashion
APPLE Dumpling Gang Rides Again, The (film)
Released 8-31, 819E3
APPLIANCES, Electrical—See ELECTRIC & Electronics Industries
APTED, Michael
Agatha released 2-8, 174C2
A&P v. FTC
A&P milk price actn backed by Sup Ct 2-22, 150G2
AQUINO Jr., Benigno
PI archbp asks release, Marcos vs 9-14, 710E1
AQUINO Garcia, Francisco
Army plot foiled 9-25—9-26, 751G3
ARAB-American University Graduates, Association of
$10,000 pledged to PUSH 10-13, 780G3
ARAB Bank for Economic Development in Africa (BADEA) (Algeria, Bahrain, Egypt, Iraq, Jordan, Kuwait, Lebanon, Libya, Mauritania, Morocco, Oman, PLO, Qatar, Saudi Arabia, Sudan, Syria, Tunisia, United Arab Emirates)
Egypt ouster rptd 4-27, 319E2*
ARAB Boycott—See under BUSINESS
ARAB Countries—See also country, organization names; for Arab-Israel conflict, see MIDDLE EAST
B Carter's rptd anti-Semitic remarks stir controversy 1-9—1-13, 31D2
UK queen tours 2-12—3-2, 190A1
Illegal abortns rptd common 4-29, 547D3
French pres asks closer ties 5-21, 398B3
Kissinger backs SALT linkage 7-31, 590B3
Canada envoy tours 9-9—10-20, 833C2
4 US natls killed in Turkey 12-14, 998D1
ARAB Emirates, United—See UNITED Arab Emirates
ARABIAN American Oil Co. (Aramco)
Saudi 1st 1/4 oil output rise seen 1-30, 69G3
ARABIAN Sea
Whaling banned, sanctuary set 7-11, 554C2
USSR scores naval maneuvers 12-5, 913F2
ARAB Investment Co.
Egypt ouster rptd 4-27, 319E2
ARAB-Israeli Dispute—See MIDDLE EAST
ARAB League (Algeria, Bahrain, Djibouti, Egypt, Iraq, Jordan, Kuwait, Lebanon, Libya, Mauritania, Morocco, North Yemen, Oman, PLO, Qatar, Saudi Arabia, Somalia, South Yemen, Sudan, Syria, Tunisia, United Arab Emirates)
Amin asks aid vs Tanzania 1-25, 85D3
N-S Yemen border missn asked 2-25, mediatn agreed 2-28, 144B2
Yemen truce patrol set 3-17, 199D2
Riad quits as secy gen 3-22, Egypt freezes ties 3-27, 248A3
Meets in Baghdad; Oman, Sudan shun 3-27—3-31; Egypt econ boycott imposed, ties cut 3-31; Egypt, US score 4-1, 4-2, 248B2-D3
Egypt recalls 7 envoys, bars hq shift 4-7, 278D1
Arab People's Cong meets 5-7—5-10, 341G2
Meets in Tunisia; Klibi named head, Leb force extended 6 mos 6-28, 475E2
Canada econ ties cut 6-29, 502C2
Tunis summit backs PLO in Leb; scores US, Israel; debates other issues, bars Iran emissaries 11-20—11-22, 916F1
Economic Boycott—See BUSINESS—Arab Boycott
Lebanon Developments—See MIDDLE EAST—LEBANON
ARAB Mining Co.
Egypt ouster rptd 4-27, 319E2
ARAB Monetary Fund (Algeria, Bahrain, Egypt, Iraq, Jordan, Kuwait, Lebanon, Libya, Mauritania, Morocco, North Yemen, Oman, Qatar, Saudi Arabia, Somolia, South Yemen, Sudan, Syria, Tunisia, United Arab Emirates)
Egypt suspended 4-18, 278B2
Canada deposits halted re Israel emb move 6-19, 467B3
ARAB Organization for Industrialization
To disband 5-14, 359E3
ARAB Organization of Administrative Sciences
Egypt ousted 4-18, 278B2
ARAB People's Congress
Meets; vows actn vs US, Arab 'reactionaries' 5-7—5-10, 341D2-A3
ARAFAT, Yasir
Asks more raids vs Israel 1-18, 50E2
Meets Leb premr, OKs shelling halt 1-23, 69A2
In Iran; gets Khomeini aid vow, Israel legatn bldg 2-17—2-19, 126A1
Iran vows Jerusalem 'liberatn' 2-26, 144F1

1980

APPAREL—See CLOTHING
APPLE Game, The (film)
Released 1-16, 216B2
APPLEGATE, Rep. Douglas (D, Ohio)
Reelected 11-4, 843F4
APPLE Records
Lennon slain 12-8, 934F3
APPLIANCES, Electrical—See ELECTRIC & Electronics
AQUARIAN Effort
D Kennedy drug therapy program rptd 1-22, 199F3
AQUATIC Exploration Co.
Hunts interest rptd 5-28, 426E1
AQUINO Jr., Benigno
Farm expropriated 5-7; freed, flies to US 5-8, 354D2
In US, speeches warn of anti-Marcos violence 8-4, 8-20, 672D3
Marcos scores US visit, bombing campaign 9-20, 752B3
Arrest warrant issued 10-20, 809G1
Urges restraint by Marcos foes 11-16, 902C3
AQUINO Jr., Mrs. Benigno S.
Family farm expropriated 5-7; husband freed, flies to US 5-8, 354E2
ARAB Boycott—See under BUSINESS
ARAB Countries—See also country, organization names; for Arab-Israeli conflict, see ARAB-Israeli Developments
Canada envoy issues rpt 2-29, 230C3
Japan trade deficit rptd 4-15, 314G3
Food forecast gloomy 7-23, 573B2
PLO status in World Bank, IMF disputed 9-4—9-22, 719D3
Syria, Libya merge 9-8; Syrian min tours 6 states re support 9-10, 697C1-C2
Yugo loans rptd 9-20, 833B2
Arab summit boycott, internal conflicts linked 11-25—11-27, 911C1
Sovt '79 arms sales rptd up 12-10, 933B2
U.S. Relations
US issues rights rpt 2-5, 87F2
US regrets Abscam term 2-12, 111A2
CIA rpts on '79 terrorism 5-11, 365F3
UN rejctn of Israeli constructn bid protested 6-19, 476B2
Abscam term redefined 8-20, 684E2
'80 grain imports rptd 11-4, 855G1
ARABIAN American Oil Co. (Aramco)
Offcls see US energy secy 3-1—3-4, 165C3
Mobil dividends tax backed by Sup Ct 3-19, 249F2
Mobil protests Saudi film telecast 5-8, 375C3
Saudi hikes prices 8% 5-14, 365B1
Saudi names 4 dirs 7-8; completes takeover, bd members listed 9-4, 661G3
OPEC pricing agrmt impact seen 9-18, 695B1
Saudi purchase lowers US net investmt income 9-18, 725A2
Saudi exec joins Mobil bd 12-1, 960D3
ARABIAN Sea
US assault force dispatched 2-12, 106G1
ARAB League (Algeria, Bahrain, Djibouti, Egypt, Iraq, Jordan, Kuwait, Lebanon, Libya, Mauritania, Morocco, North Yemen, Oman, PLO, Qatar, Saudi Arabia, Somalia, South Yemen, Sudan, Syria, Tunisia, United Arab Emirates)
Syria troop role in Leb extended 1-23, 89G2
Mtg re Libya-Tunisia dispute ends unresolved 2-28, comm named 2-29, 197B1
Waldheim addresses NY dinner 7-25, 572F2
Klibi backs Iraq in Iran war, mediatn effort cited 9-23, 719E2
Summit boycotted by Syria, 5 others 11-25—11-27, 911A1
ARAFAT, Yasir
Libya ends Al Fatah ties 1-5, 107G3
At Iran anniv rites 2-11, 106B1
Lauds Giscard stand on Palestinians 3-8, 180D1
Lauds Austria for PLO special status 3-15, 206A1
Visits India 3-28—3-29, 260E3

1976

Briefed on Leb reforms 2-14, 125D1
US sen rpts proposal for UN zone in W Bank, Gaza 2-28, 161A1
Gets Syria truce plea 3-30, 225A2
Meets Habash 3-30, 225C2
Warns US vs Leb fleet move 3-30, 242B1
Aided Leb truce 3-31, 4-1, 225A1, E2
Meets Assad, new Leb plan set; briefs Jumblat 4-16, 273A1, E1
Ends feud with Egypt 5-5, 319D2
Meets Assad, vs Leb electn delay 5-7, 337E1
Asks PLA quit Tripoli 5-14, force leaves 5-15, 354A3
In Leb mediation 5-17, 355C1
Meets Sarkis on peace moves 5-20, 369B2
Rabin on Syrian invasn of Leb 6-2, 385A2
Arab League meets on Leb 6-8, 405E1
Chrgs Syrian 'massacre' 6-8, 406C1
Syria troop oppositn scored 6-15, 429C2
In Leb crisis talks 6-21, 448F3
Asked to intervene in hijacking 486F2
Warns Egypt of Syria threat to Beirut 7-8, 514C3
Asks Arab aid vs Syria 7-11, 514F2
Gets Syria vow to quit Saida 7-12, denies exit 7-13, 514B2
USSR seeks to bar Leb defeat 7-13, 514D3
Sets Syria talks strategy 7-15, 528D1
Rpts Tel Zaatar shelling deaths 7-24, 546C2
Syria talks rptd 7-27, pact signed 7-29, 546F1, 547D1
Disavows Syria peace pact 7-30, 577G2
On Tel Zaatar 'massacre' 8-13, 618B1
In truce talks 9-17, 9-19, 698F2
Vows truce to aid Sarkis 9-23, 699G1
Fatah denies Damascus raid 9-27, 720E3
Syria pressures; asks Arabs block Syrian drive 9-28, 720D1
Syrians score 10-4, 737G1
Plea to Arabs vs Syria drive 10-13, 758D2
Asks Saudi aid vs Syria 10-14, 779D1
Saudis urge Leb truce 10-15, 779C1
At Riyadh peace conf 10-17—10-18, 778B3
Meets with Assad 10-20, 779E1
Rpt Syria seeks PLO replacemt 894E1
Meets Assad, OKs arms surrender 12-3, 913C1
US Sup Ct refuses Kelner case 12-13, 960E3

ARAGON, Joe
Voter-registratn drive opens 8-23, 631F2
ARAI, Masao
Wins Olympic medal 7-31, 576C3
ARALUCE y Villar, Juan Maria de
Assassinated 10-4, 774G2
ARAM, Bahran
Slain 11-16, 910F2
ARAMBURU, Juan Carlos Cardinal
Named cardinal 4-27, 336B2
Asks justice for priest killers 7-14, 571D2
ARAMBURU, Lt. Gen. Pedro Eugenio (1903-70)
Norma Arrostito killed 12-3, 996B2
ARAMCO—*See ARABIAN American Oil Co.*
ARAMIYA, Rev. Jose
Queried re Lockheed payoffs 3-5, 191E1
ARANA Osorio, Carlos
Rpt bribed PR members re Lopez vote 6-25, 1005D1
Rightist coalitn controls Cong 7-18, 1005C1
ARANCETA, Javier
Torture alleged 5-13, 422E2
ARAUJO Noguera, Alvaro
Colombia agri min 10-19, 925B1
ARAUZ Castex, Manuel
Ousts UK envoy 1-13, 26F1
Loses cabt post 1-15, replaced 1-16; dismissal scored 1-17, 71B2, A3
ARAYA, Bernardo
Among vanished detainees 8-7, 711C1
ARBATOV, Georgi
US slows detente 4-2, 277D2
ARBULU Galliani, Gen. Guillermo
Peru premr, war min, army cmdr 7-17, 590B3
ARBULU Ibanez, Gen. Luis
Peru agri min 7-17, 590C3
ARCE Larco, Jose
Lima magazine closed 7-3, 499D3
ARCHAEOLOGY
Spain Armada ships found 1-11, 124C3
Knossos tomb, Athens cemetery excavatns rptd 1-31, 160F1
Socrates' jail identified 2-1, 124A3
Ancient China laws rptd found 3-28, 265F3
New Bronze Age date set 5-13, 504E3
Mortimer Wheeler dies 7-23, 716G3
Ramses mummy in Paris for repairs 9-26, damage disputed 11-8, 912F2
Neil Judd dies 12-26, 1015F1
ARCHBOLD, Richard
Dies 8-1, 816D3
ARCHER, Rep. W. R. (Bill) (D, Tex.)
Reelected 11-2, 830C4
ARCHER-Daniels-Midland Co.
Fined 3-4, 247C2
Exec named in grain fraud 3-11, 247C3
Grain abuse plan cited 3-16, 248C1
Adnac, Inc.—*See separate listing*
ARCHERY
Olympic results 7-30, 573F3
ARCHITECTURE
Boston GSA contracting violatns rptd 1-20, 71D1, F1
Alvar Aalto dies 5-11, 404F1
Canada bans eastn drilling 7-27, 587F3
ARCTIC Gas Pipeline Co.
Rpt backs pipeline plan 12-7, 998A2

1977

OKs south Leb pullback pact 2-25, 143B2
Meets Hussein 3-8, 170C2
Vows Jumblat death reprisals 3-16, 188G1
For Palestine 'homeland,' secular state 3-17, 188A1
Reelected PLO head 3-20, 208C1
Plans drive vs Christns 4-3, 246D1
Visits Moscow 4-4—4-8, 297C2
Sees Assad on Leb clashes 4-9, truce call ignored 4-10, 266B3
Rpt OKs Israel recognition 360F2
Warns of Israeli clashes in S Leb 5-24, 401E3
New PLO army created 5-31, 6-1, 439C3
Asked to halt PLO massing near Israeli border 6-16, 510C2
Sees Assad, for hard line vs Israel 6-20, 496A2
Note to Carter rptd 7-20, 550B2
Mediates Egypt-Libya feud 7-22—7-24, 569E2
Sadat assures on Geneva conf 8-4, 588F2
PLO cncl meets 8-25—8-26, 663B1
In Moscow, vs US aims 8-30—8-31, 663C1
Lauds US call for Palestinian peace role 9-13, 697F1
Sees Arab ldrs on Leb fighting 9-16, 714E2
Meets Egypt ldrs on Geneva 10-18—10-19, 793B1
Vs PLO pullout from south Leb 11-6, 849D2
Reps greet Capucci in Rome 11-6, 850C3
Assad asks PLO pullback from south Leb 11-10; meets factns on Israeli attacks 11-11, 874G2
Sadat trip scored 11-17, 890F2
At Tripoli anti-Sadat mtg 12-2—12-5, 929B2
Sadat: Sovts sought to block '75 Sinai pact 12-6, 929E2
Vs Carter Palestine stand 12-31, 995B1

ARAGON, Joseph W.
Named Carter special asst 1-14, 35D3
Greets emigrants from Cuba 9-22, 781D2
ARAMCO—*See ARABIAN American Oil Co.*
ARA Services Inc.
Rpts forgn paymts, rebates 1-28, 94D1
ARAUTOFF, Peter
Hartwick wins NCAA soccer title 12-4, 1020F3
ARAUZ, Pedro
Killed 10-17, 802E2
ARAZOZA Rodriguez, Hector
Canada expels 1-12, 42G3
ARBATOV, Georgi A.
Warns US on rights stand 3-16, 226F1
Scores Carter policies 8-3, 590D1
ARBITRAGE—*See STOCKS*
ARBITRATION Association, American
Sweden to settle US-Sovt business disputes 1-11, 29F3
ARBULU Galliani, Guillermo (Peruvian prime minister; replaced Jan. 31)
Bans ONIS rights rpt 3-18, 241B3
To retire in Feb '78 10-4, 784B2
ARCATA National Corp.
Redwood Pk expansion asked 4-19, 323A1
ARCHAEOLOGY
Dead Sea scroll analyzed 11-12, 1022F3
King Philip's tomb found 11-24, 952D1
ARCHER, George
2d in Westchester Classic 8-21, 675G3
ARCHER, Jeffrey
Onassis quits Viking 10-13, 927B3
ARCHIBALD, Nate (Tiny)
Injures ankle 10-15, 870G2
ARCHITECTURE
CRS Design rpts forgn paymts 6-23, 503G2
Eliot Noyes dies 7-17, 604E3
Ross inducted into golf HOF 8-23, 675E3
ARCO—*See ATLANTIC Richfield Co.*
ARCOGRAPHITE (motor oil)
Arco to mkt 7-11, 558D3
ARCTIC Gas Study Group—*See ALASKAN Arctic Gas Pipeline Co.*
ARCTIC National Wildlife Range (Alaska)
FPC splits on gas pipe route 5-2, 369E3
ARCTIC Ocean
USSR sets 200-mi limit 3-1, 147E1
Norway declares Svalbard fishing zone 6-3, USSR disputes 11-11, 967F2
Intl Inuit conf 6-13—6-17, 619F2
Greenland, Denmark oil accord rptd 7-13, 672A2
Sirica vs bowhead whaling ban 10-21; ruling reversed, Burger backs ban 10-24; bowhead data cited 835A2

1978

Vs Sadat stand on Palestinians 2-24, 138D2
Egypt chrgs radical ties 2-27, 138B2
Visits Moscow 175D3
Abu Sayed slain 3-8, 157C2 ★
OKs raid on Israel 3-12, 175D3
Vows cooperatn with UN in Leb 3-28, 213B1
Waldheim says OKs Leb truce 3-28, 213D1
Vows Leb truce 3-31, 236G1, B2
Meets Waldheim on Leb truce 4-17, 274C2
Averts Fatah breakup 4-24, 300B2
Vs Leb militia curbs 4-25, 299G3-300A1
Orders crackdown vs Leb leftists 5-4, 340C1
Bars Leb truce, Unifil role 5-11, 383A3
Meets Unifil head on Leb infiltratn 5-16, 383G2
OKs PLO exit from Leb 5-24; PLO factns score, demand ldrship chng 5-24—5-28, 400G2
Waldheim says will obey Leb truce 6-14, 462B2
Scores Jerusalem terror role 6-30, 503G2
Fatah in dispute with Iraq 7-17, 546D3
Blamed re Iraq amb death try 8-3, 583A1
Vs Camp David summit pacts 9-19, 712E1; asks Hussein reject 9-22, 730C1
In Moscow, Camp David pact scored 10-29—11-1, 828C1
For UN force role in Palestine state; on Camp David, Israel-Egypt pact 11-19, 893B1
UN removes photo at PLO exhibit 11-29, 951G2

ARAMCO—*See ARABIAN American Oil Co.*
ARBATOV, Georgi A.
On SALT impasse 3-28, 297E2
Warns on US-China ties 12-16, 976G3
ARBER, Werner
Wins Nobel Prize 10-12, 886E2
ARBULU Galliani, Gen. Guillermo (Peruvian prime minister; replaced Jan. 31)
Retires from army, govt posts 1-30; replaced 1-31, 134G2
ARBUZOV, Aleksei
Somersaults opens 1-9, 760A2
Promise opens 3-8, 760B3
ARCHAEOLOGY
Israel Shiloh dig disputed 2-2, 2-5, 78A2, C2; 2-9, 97G2
Obituaries
Bieber, Margarete 2-25, 196C2
Kelso, James L 6-28, 540A3
Mallowan, Max 8-19, 708B3
ARCHER, Rep. W. R. (Bill) (R, Tex.)
Reelected 11-7, 852A3
ARCHER Daniels Midland Co.
Gartner bars resignatn re stock gift 6-28, 513A3
ARCHIBALD, Nate (Tiny)
Traded to Celtics 7-7, 655G2
ARCHITECTURE
Natl Galley additn opens 6-1, 578E2
Solar, other renewable energy loan aid signed 7-4, 512G1
Obituaries
Rich, Lorimer 6-2, 540F3
Stone, Edward Durell 8-6, 708E3
Wright, Lloyd 5-31, 440G3
ARCO—*See ATLANTIC Richfield Co.*
ARCO Pipe Lines Co. v. U.S.
ICC Alaska pipe rates backed by Sup Ct 6-6, 447B2

1979

Scores Egypt re Israel pact 3-11—3-13, 178C1-G1
Sees Hussein, vs Egypt-Israel treaty 3-17, 198C2
Meets Gromyko in Damascus 3-24—3-26, 222E2
Vows fight vs US interests 3-26, 222B2
At Arab League mtg 3-27—3-31; rebuffed on US boycott, walks out 3-28, 248F2
Libyan '75 A-bomb effort rptd 4-14, 299D3
Vows contd attacks vs Israel 5-8, 341C1
Moslem Gaza ldr slain 6-1, 414B3
Vows not to attack Israel from Leb 6-6, 415E1
Sees Kreisky, Brandt 7-6—7-8, 511A3
UN panel asks Israel halt setlmts 7-14, 551B2
PLO critic shot 7-25, dies 7-26, 552D1
Links Egypt to Mohsen death 7-26, 625E2
On Young resignatn from UN post 8-15, 606C2
Warns US vs blocking Palestinian state 8-20, 659A2
Kreisky mtg rptd 8-22, 625E1
Rumanian pres seeks Israel feud mediatn 8-31, 659D2
W Ger assures Israel on Brandt mtg 9-10, 677C1
Visits Spain 9-13—9-15, 694C3
Sees SCLC ldrs in Beirut 9-20, 694C2; US invite rptd, nonviolence plea rejctd 9-21, 763D2
Meets Jesse Jackson 9-29—9-30, 10-4, 763D1, F1
At E Ger celebratn 10-7, 761E2
SCLC withdraws invitatn 10-11, 780F3
Iran bars PLO role in US hostage release 11-8, 842C1
At Lisbon conf, tied to Israel Emb raid 11-13, 882C1
At Arab League summit; clashes with Leb pres, sees Iran emissaries 11-20—11-22, 916B2, E2
Qaddafi scores Israel policy 12-10, 937G3
Qaddafi chrgs 'insults' 12-11, 980E1
Aide slain in Cyprus 12-15, 980F1

ARAGON, Joseph W.
Replaced as pres spec asst 8-10, 608G2
ARAQI, Hessam
Slain 8-26, 653A3
ARAQI, Mehdi
Slain 8-26, 653A3
ARASKOG, Rand V.
Named ITT chief exec 7-11, 517A2
ARBER, Bobby
Gold wins ASL title, named game defensive MVP 9-16, 776D2
ARBITRAGE—*See STOCKS*
ARBITRATION Association, American
Med malpractice arbitratn rptd 1-28, 139C3
ARBOUR, Al
Named top NHL coach 6-12, 470E2
ARCE, Manuel
El Super released 4-28, 528B2
ARCHAEOLOGY
Spanish galleon treasure find rptd 1-1, 24E1
Ecuador frees alleged US smugglers 1-5, 62G2-A3
Viking artifact identified in Me 2-7, 138E1
Puritan site found in Cambridge 8-9, 631B3
ARCHITECTURE
5 US A-plants ordrd shut 3-13, 186A2
US no longer top DC area hirer 3-24, 232B2
Pei to design NYC Conv Cntr 4-21, 375B2
Fuller in Arts Institute 12-7, 1005A3
Obituaries
Nervi, Pier Luigi 1-9, 104E3
ARCO—*See ATLANTIC Richfield Co.*
ARCTIC Ocean
Canada, US draft Atlantic pact 1-23, 95E3

1980

At hard-line Arab summit 4-14—4-15, 284G2
Scores US hostage rescue try 4-27, 324D2
Vows W Bank setlmt raids 5-3, sees deported ldrs in Leb 5-7, 340G1, F2
Warns W Eur, France on pro-Israel stand 5-18, 418F1
Reelected Fatah head 5-31, 418C2
Tours Moscow Olympic Village 7-20, 590B1
Visits Nicaragua 7-21, PLO ties formalized 7-22, 565E3
Sees EC rep 8-4, Israel chrgs 'double talk' 8-5, 586A1
Visits Leb front, orders alert 8-19, 643D2
Iran-Iraq war mediatn effort cited 9-23, 719F2
Meets 2 Israeli CP Knesset members 9-25, 736D3
Addresses UNESCO conf, scores US, Israel 10-27, 821D3
Israel Labor Party proposes state plan 11-8, 863C3
US Sen Percy backs Palestine state role 12-5, 931D1, A2

ARAKAWA, Tetsuo
Asks US tariff rise delay 7-1, 599B2
ARAMCO—*See ARABIAN American Oil Co.*
ARATSILOV, Magomedhan
Wins Olympic medal 7-31, 624E3
ARBATOV, Georgi
Reactn to new arms talks rptd 12-15, 951A1
ARBITRAGE—*See STOCKS*
ARC Armored Services of Puerto Rico Inc.
15 steal $2.4 mln 11-21, terrorists suspected 11-24, 971G2
ARCE, Bayardo
Scores Sandanista oppositn 11-9, 874D1
ARCE Gomez, Col. Luis
US journalist rpts death threat 8-12, 668E1
Junta tied to drug trafficking 8-15, 668C1
Rpts Gueiler gets exit OK 9-15, 728A1
ARCHAEOLOGY
Jerusalem road project OKd 7-18, 573C1
Obituaries
Carpenter, Rhys 1-2, 104B2
Healey, Giles 2-29, 279D3
ARCHARAY Enterprises
Day arrested 1-2, 94B3
ARCHER, Anne
Hero at Large released 2-8, 216G2
ARCHER, Jeffery
Kane & Abel on best-seller list 8-17, 640E3
ARCHER, Rep. W. R. (Bill) (R, Tex.)
Reelected 11-4, 844E2
ARCHER Daniels Midland Co.
Jamaica names in grain fraud suit 2-4, 99D2
ARCHERY
Moscow Olympic results 8-2, 622C1
ARCHIBALD, Nate (Tiny)
NBA assist ldr 3-30, 278E3
ARCHIE Bunker's Place (TV series)
Stapleton to quit 4-2, 471B3
ARCHITECT'S Eye: American Architectural Drawings from 1799-1978, The (book)
Wins Amer Book Award 5-1, 692C2
ARCHITECTURE
Obituaries
Gruen, Victor 2-14, 176D1
ARCO—*See ATLANTIC Richfield Co.*
ARCOVERDE, Waldyr
Sabin polio drive stalled 4-16, 310A2

1976

ARCTIC Regions
Canada chrgs Sovt occupatn of ice islands 6-17, 456C3
ARECHIGA, John J.
5 reps accuse Agri Dept 1-29, 136E1
AREILZA, Jose Maria de
'75 Mex ties bid rptd 1-10, 75F2
Signs US defense pact 1-24, 76E1
Sees Portugal forgn min 2-12, 143C1
TV interview banned 4-12, 269A2
In US; for Spain in EEC, NATO 6-3, 459F2
Suarez named premr 7-3; Cabt post refusal rptd 7-5, 7-6, 500D3, F3, 523B2
ARELLANO Stark, Gen. Sergio
Quits mil post 1-3; replaced 1-6, 47C1
ARENA Stage (Washington, D.C.)
Wins Tony 4-18, 460F2
ARENDT, Walter
Cited re Focke resignatn 10-16, 857B3
Resigns, replaced 12-15, 968G1, A2
ARENS, Richard
Accuses Paraguay 4-5, 403A3
ARES, Roberto
Argentina interior min 1-15, 71C2
Sought for arrest 3-26, 236E3
ARGAN, Giulio Carlo
Named Rome mayor 8-8, 589A3

1977

ARCTIC Regions
Intl Inuit conf 6-13—6-17, 619F2
AREILZA, Jose Maria de
Center-right coalitn backed 1-21, 68B2
AREVALO, Antonio
Sentenced 2-10, 100B1
ARGAN, Giulio
Vatican ties scored 1-6, 8B3

1978

ARCTIC Regions
Sweden protests Sovt sub patrols 3-1, 291A3
Uemura reaches North Pole 5-1, 420A2
USSR icebreaker travels 5-25—6-12, 506A2
Canada grants Inuit hunting rights 7-14, 556B2
ARDIZZONE, Flora Pirri
Charged in Moro case 6-6, 689C2
AREBI, Youssef
Scores defeat of ILO anti-Israel res 6-27, 523E3
ARENA, Angelo
On Carter Hawley takeover bid 2-22, 185G1
ARENAS, Jesus
9th in Colombia pres vote 6-4, 443E2
ARENS, Moshe
On US Sen jet pkg OK 5-16, 358B2
AREN'T You Glad You're You (recording)
Wins Grammy 2-24, 316B1
ARGAN, Carlo Giulio
On Rome violence 1-9, 19F2
At Moro death rally 5-9, 337G1
ARGANA, Luis
Rejcts OAS rights abuse rpt 6-30, 505C3

1979

ARCTIC Regions
Canada gas find announced 5-15, 405B2
Petro-Canada breakup studied 9-5, 684G3
ARDALAN, Ali
Named Iran finance min 2-19, 125D1
ARDIS Publishers
Proffers denied USSR visa 8-29, 690B1
ARDIZZONE, Edward Jeffrey Irving
Dies 11-8, 932B2
AREILZA, Jose Maria de
Forms rightist coalitn 1-16, 61B2
ARGAN, Carlo Giulio
Palace of Sens bombed 4-20, 313A2
ARGENT Corp.—*See ALKATH Corp.*

1980

ARDEKANI, Shams
US walks out on UN speech 7-25, 572E2
ARDREY, Robert
Dies 1-14, 104E1
ARENS, Moshe
Vs defense min post 9-1, 712D2

ARGENTINA

1976

ARGENTINA—*See also IDB, DISARMAMENT—Geneva Committee, LAFTA, Nonaligned Nations Movement, OAS, SELA*
Aramburu named cardinal 4-27, 336B2
La Rioja bishop dies 8-4, foul play suspected 8-6, 9-2, 672E1

Economy & Labor (domestic)
'75 inflatn at 334.8% 1-5; unions warn 1-8, 7G2
'75 oil output down 4% 1-9, 96D3
Peso devalued 1-12, 26A2
Cordoba CGT, munic workers protest terrorism 1-17, 96F1
Drought damages corn, sorghum crops 1-17, 96B3
Labor ldrs score cabt shift 1-21, Miguel backs Peron 1-23, 71D2
18% wage hike scored; state workers win raise, others strike 1-22—1-30, 96C2
Peso devalued 1-26, 96G2
Jan price rise 14.6% 2-2, 154A3
Businessmen lockout set 2-3, lockout called 2-16, 154F1, F2
Subway workers strike for higher pay 2-3, 154G2
Econ, labor mins replaced 2-3, 154G2
'75 auto productn down 2-11, 212C3
Labor ldrs ask new cabt 2-20, 2-23, 154C2
Peso devalued 4.6% 2-23, 212E2
Annual inflatn at 423.6% 2-29, 211E3
'Emergency' plan set 3-5, protested 3-6—3-13, 212B2
Mil shuts unions, banks, seizes labor ldrs 3-24—3-25, 211G2
Union activities curbed 3-25, bank accts frozen 3-30, 236C3
Martinez de Hoz, econ team sworn 3-29, 236B1, F2
New govt details econ plan 3-31, 236F1
Strike promotn outlawed 4-1; metalworkers seized 4-17, 264A1
Indl productn rptd up 4-2, 236F2
Mil-labor pre-coup pact rptd 4-2, 236F2
Govt sets econ plan 4-2, 264D2
Peronist labor ldrs sentncd 4-8, 263D3
Labor corruptn probes set 4-21, 399C3
Wages, pension hikes set 5-9, 554D1
12-mo price hikes rptd 5-14, Mar-May CPI 6-22, June COL 7-4, 554C1
Herreras escape cited 5-15, 399D3
Labor unions dissolved 6-4, ldrs arrested 6-23, 519F3
'76 budget deficit set 7-9, 649F3
Oilfields opened to pvt dvpt 7-27, 554D1
Real wage fall rptd 8-13, 649G3
Stock market boom rptd 8-16, 650A1
Pub employmt data rptd 8-30, 649F3
Auto indus slowdown rptd 8-30, 650A1

Falkland (Malvinas) Dispute—*See FALKLAND Islands*

Foreign Economic Developments
Brazil tourism, wheat smuggling up 1-9, 96A3
Venez econ pact signed 1-14, 96C3
French Mirage purchase cited 1-16, 36C2
US banks set grain export credits 1-28, 96B3
Beef exports to Eur down 80% 2-2, 96C3
At intl econ conf 2-11—2-20, 148B1
Tourist influx continues 2-27, 212C3
IMF-approved plan protested 3-12, 212C2, B3
'51 Dutch bribes rptd 3-12, 254D3
Freer forgn investmt vowed 3-30; new investmt law planned 3-31, 236F1-E2
Total IMF oil loans rptd 4-1, 340B2
Forgn investmt incentives set 4-2, 264D2, G2
IMF OKs loan 4-2, 264C3
EC beef ban losses, Sovt sales rptd 4-9, 264C3
'75 Sovt trade rptd 5-5, 341A1
'75 paymts deficit rptd up 5-10, 466A1
Intl financing project rptd 7-23, 554B1
Forgn debt rptd renegotiated 7-25, 553G3
Oilfields opened to pvt dvpt 7-27, 554D1
Jan-June trade surplus rptd 8-2, 649C3
IMF OKs standby credit 8-6, 649A3
Liberal forgn investmt law issued 8-14, 649D3

1977

ARGENTINA—*See also DISARMAMENT—Geneva Committee, IDB, NONALIGNED Nations Movement, OAS*
Charter jet crashes 11-20, 992D2
Quake hits, toll near 100 11-23, 928D2

Atomic Energy & Safeguards
Canada A-sale agent tied to pol paymts 1-7, 43A1
Canada warned vs A-sale agent disclosure 1-25, contract cancelatn barred 2-3, 114C1
Canada presses for A-safeguards treaty OK 1-28, 190G1
Brazil A-deal backed 2-7, 3-11, 190C1, G1
A-technology lead rptd 259F1
Peru A-plant trade pacts signed 3-5, 259D1
Canada A-agency head fired 7-7, 541E3
Vance sees Montes, 3 junta members; Tlatelolco Treaty signing agreed 11-21, 912A3

Economy & Labor (domestic)—*See also 'Kidnapings' below*
Govt OKs 20% wage hike 1-1, 42G1
Union ldrs score govt policies 1-6, reprisals set 1-7, 17C1
'76 inflatn sets record 1-7, 17C1
Unions cancel protest mtg 1-12, 42A2
Real wages down in '76 1-14, 42F1
Labor law disclosed 1-21; workers protest, Smith kidnaped 1-24—3-4, 198D2
'76 GDP rptd down 2.9% 2-23, 199A1
Jan-Feb COL up 21.9% 3-2, 199B1
A-technology lead rptd 259F1
La Opinion offcls seized 4-1—4-16, guerrilla financing rptd 4-11, 345A2; **see 'Graiver Scandal' below**
Lanusse, ex-aides seized re aluminum deal 5-4, 371A1
'61-75 GDP variatns table 5-30, 439A1
Govt lifts price 'truce' 7-7; gas transport prices rise 7-29, 614C2
Monthly peso devaluatns rptd 7-8, 614D2
Real wages, worker purchasing power rptd down 7-15; constructn, consumer purchases up 7-22, 614B2, E2
Manufacturers assn abolished 7-22, 614G2
'76 jobless rate rptd steady 7-25, 614B3
Jan-July COL up 64% 8-10, 614A2
Pol ldrs seek open unionism 8-13—8-16, 670F1
Teachers ldr vanishes 9-8, arrest admitted 9-20, 922A2
Strikers demand higher pay 10-11—11-10, 981B1
Econ min scored 10-21, 11-6, 981C2
State co problems noted 11-10, 981B2
Real wages down since '60 11-11, 981A2
Jan-Oct inflatn at 125% 11-17, 981G1

Falkland Islands Dispute—*See FALKLAND Islands*

Foreign Relations (misc.)—*See also 'Atomic Energy' above; 'Kidnapings', 'Monetary, Trade & Aid' and 'Unrest' below*
UN Assemb member; Ruda on World Ct 3F3, 4G1
Land for Rhodesia emigrants set 1-17, 29F1
Spain arrests Cezarsky 3-2, infiltrates exile groups 3-5, 307F2
Videla visits Peru 3-3—3-6, 259D1
UN Water Conf held 3-14—3-25, 250D1
Videla visits Venez; protests staged 5-11—5-14, Panama canal claim backed 5-13, 547G1-F2
Chilean hijacked jet lands 6-21, 537C2
Nazi extraditn ordrd 7-4, W Ger reciprocity agrmt rptd 7-22, 614C3
Archbp Lefebvre visits 7-20, 620G1
Spain Soclst ldr backs Montoneros 7-23, 595B3
Nazi flees, rptd dead in Paraguay 8-11, 670D3
Videla at Panama Canal pact signing 9-7, 678C1
Uruguay expels newspaper editor 9-29, 905D1
Chile Beagle Channel islands settlement cited 11-4, 944C3

1978

ARGENTINA—*See also DISARMAMENT—Geneva Committee, GATT, IDB, NON-ALIGNED Nations Movement, OAS*
'77 quake deaths rptd 1-29, 480A2
Truck-train collisn kills 37 2-25, 270E3

Atomic Energy & Safeguards
Canada '74 A-sale paymts scored 2-27, 166A3
Plutonium processing plant planned 10-17, 840B3

Beagle Channel Dispute—*See BEAGLE Channel*

Economy & Labor (domestic)
Auto worker layoffs rptd 1-13; hint GM to quit mfg 2-24, 310B2
Buenos Aires expenses rated 1-14, 28A3
'77 GDP rptd up 4.8% 1-27, 310F2
Oct '77 low jobless rate rptd 2-3, 310C2
World Cup soccer costs scored 2-17, 310C3
RR strike averted by arrests 3-9, 310A2
Jan real wages rptd down, labor repressn cited 3-10, 310A2
'78 budget OK rptd 3-24, 310F2
Oil find rptd 3-27, 310B3
1st 1/4 inflatn rise rptd, Martinez upset 4-14, 310E1
Oil exploratn law enacted 4-17, 310A3
Radicals score govt policy 4-23, 611D3
Navy chief scores econ min 5-2, 611A3
Phone lines commandeered for World Cup 6-1—6-25, communicatns min resigns 6-25, 520G3
Union ldr Bravo moved to house arrest 6-18; 35 others seized 9-22, 793A1
World Cup soccer costs rptd $700 mln 6-25, 519G3
Peronist labor mtgs barred 7-3, mtgs continue 9-12, 793A2
Jan-June inflatn 69.5% 7-21, 793F2
GM sets pullout 8-4, govt policies scored 8-25, 793B2
Govt wage guidelines rptd 8-11, dockworkers get raise 8-18, 793G2
June '77-78 inflatn rate ranked world's worst 10-18, 914E1
Press criticism of policy allowed 10-27, 865D3
Martinez retained in Cabt shuffle 11-6, 865E2

Falkland Islands Dispute—*See FALKLAND Islands*

Foreign Relations (misc.)—*See also 'Atomic Energy' above, 'Monetary, Trade, Aid & Investment' below*
Guerrillas in Mex chrg murder threat 1-18, 208F1
French nuns' release sought 3-21, 286B1
Massera in France, sees Montoneros 4-9, 285E3
Anti-soccer tourn campaign by guerrillas chrgd 4-12, 285C3
Intl press linked to Timerman jail release 4-17, 286A1
Chile pol exile arrives 4-27, 351E2
Peru deports leftist ldrs 5-25, 475E1
Amer Human Rights Conv enacted 7-18, 829A1
Peruvian terrorists seen imitating AAA 8-29—9-15, 776B1
Videla in Italy, leftists protest 9-5, 689D3
UN Assemb Assemb member 713B3
Bolivia names Banzer amb 10-6, 823E2
OAS rights probe OKd 10-19, 792B2
Videla sees Bolivia pres, backs sea outlet 10-25, 860C3
Forgn min quits 10-27, 840G2
DR Sen rejects Beauchamp as amb 11-9, 881B1
Spain king visits 11-26—11-30, 967G2, D3

1979

ARGENTINA—*See also GATT, IDB, LAFTA, NONALIGNED Nations Movement, OAS*

Atomic Energy & Safeguards
W Ger, Swiss A-plant deals rptd; Canada installatn cited 10-1, 749C1
Canada scores A-sale loss 10-2—10-3, 788B3

Beagle Channel Dispute—*See BEAGLE Channel*

Economy & Labor
'78 inflatn world's highest 1-10, 40A3
Labor ldrs arrested, strike threat defused 4-23—4-27, 351B2
1st 1/4 econ recovery, inflatn rptd 6-2, 466F2-467A1
Terrorists bomb planning secy's home 9-27, 748G3-749C1
Treas secy escapes shooting 11-7, 887G3
Unions banned from pol activity 11-16, 887E2

Falkland Islands Dispute—*See FALKLAND Islands*

Foreign Relations (misc.)—*See also 'Atomic' above, 'Monetary' and 'UN' below*
Chile asks prisoner release 1-5, 51E3
Chile newsman disappears 40C3; freed 1-11, 117C1
Bolivia ex-pres ends exile 3-16, 233D2
Latin refugees occupy Swedish consulate in Rio, protest repressn 8-6; UN responds 8-8, 627D1, F1
Nazi fugitive asylum cited 8-8, 616F3
Nicaragua expels radicals 8-16, 636C2
Eur scores missing persons law 9-12, 728G1
Timerman gets Israel visa 9-25, 728B1
DR forgn min, OAS score rights abuse 10-24, 10-30, 824D2, F2
UK amb exchng set 11-16, 906C2
Campora granted safe passage from Mex Emb 11-20, 906A2
UK editor rpts death threat 12-4, leaves 12-16, 966E2

1980

ARGENTINA—*See also GATT, GENEVA Committee, IDB, NONALIGNED Nations, OAS*
Natl Museum art stolen 12-25, dir issues appeal 12-27, 991D1

Atomic Energy & Safeguards
Swiss heavy water plant deal opposed by US 3-10—3-11, contract signed 3-14, 229A2
Brazilians arrive for talks 3-18, bilateral agrmts with 7 other Latin natns cited 229C2
Brazil accord set 5-15—5-17, 405C2

Beagle Channel Dispute—*See BEAGLE Channel*

Economy & Labor
Major pvt bank closed 3-28, 252B2
Pvt banking system shaken by bankruptcies; govt assumes control, raises deposit guarantees 4-25, 349D3
Martinez's policies protested by hijacker 6-30—7-1, 519G2
Tax cuts, other fscl reforms proposed 7-11, 561B2

Foreign Relations (misc.)—*See also 'Atomic Energy' above, 'Monetary' below*
Colombia amb eludes DR emb raiders 2-27, 141C1
Cuban refugees offered asylum 4-16, 285C1
Moscow Olympic boycott joined 5-8, 379D2
Brazil pres visits, ties strengthened 5-15—5-17, 405B2
Italy arrests terrorist suspects 6-5, 523C3
Peru snubs Videla; intell operatns disclosed, probe seen 7-28, 580C1
Bolivia mil govt recognized 7-31, 577F1
Latin Anti-Communist Conf meets 9-3, 686E3
Somoza slain in Paraguay 9-17: Argentina terrorists sought, suspect slain 9-18, 697F2
Uruguayan hijacks plane to Buenos Aires 11-12, surrenders 11-13, 888C3

1976

EEC agri purchases seen 8-20, 649D3
'75-76 US bank loans cited 11-10, 915F1
Canada A-sale irregularities rptd 11-22, 904C1; hearings open 11-30, 923B3
Canada A-purchase probe under way 11-27, 997A2
Canada police to seek A-sale agent 12-15, 962A3
Canada A-pact delay rptd 12-22, 998G1

Foreign Relations (misc.)—*See also 'Kidnapings', 'UN Policy' and 'Unrest' below*
Chile OKs Frei book 1-23, 99B3
Carrio vs Chile rights abuse 3-5, 310F1
Lopez Rega extraditn from Spain asked 3-8, 211G3
ERP, Paraguay police clash 4-4—4-6, 403B2
Zileri returns to Peru 5-14, 500C1
Balbin at intl soc dems mtg 5-23—5-25, 449C3
Spain extraditn of Lopez Rega sought 10-25, 997F1

Government & Politics—*See also 'Unrest' and other appropriate subheads in this section*
'75 budget, mil forces rptd 1-2, 60F2
Peron testamt com named 1-5, testamt publshd 1-7, 26B2
Mil ldrs block provincial takeovers 1-8, 26E1
Peron reelectn bid barred 1-13, 1-20, 71B3
Cabt shuffled 1-15—1-16, pol ldrs score 1-16—1-27, 71A2
Listed as 'partly free' 1-19, 20C3
New electn date planned 1-26, 71C3
Pol ldrs ask Peron quit 2-10, 154E2
Peron closes Cong 2-16, bars reelectn bid 2-18; labor, mil ldrs seek resignatn, new cabt 2-19—2-23, 154E1
Peron fires defense min 2-23, 211F3
Peron impeachmt bid fails 2-26, 3-4, 211E3
Lopez Rega extraditn asked 3-8, 211G3
Mil seizes power 3-24; Peron, 800 others arrested 3-24—3-25, 211E2
Security laws tightened 3-24, 3-26, 263G2
Junta takes final exec power 3-25, 236C1
ERP, other leftists banned; judges, 'subversive' state employes removed 3-25, 236G2, C3
CP backs junta 3-27, 3-29, 236G2
Videla becomes pres, swears cabt 3-29; details plans, 3-30, 236A1 ★
Peron, Campora, other bank accts frozen 3-30, 236D3
Sup Ct sworn 4-1; 24 judges ousted 4-5, cts reopen 4-6, 263E3
Junta revises legis comm 4-2, names Cordoba AF chief 4-10, 264B1
3,000 ex-aides rptd held 4-10; corruptn probes set 4-21, 399C3
Peron, Gonzalez queried, Peron denies chrgs 4-30; prelim chrgs filed 5-6, 399E2
Campora chrgd 4-30; rptd in Mexico emb 5-20, 399E3
Univ pol activity barred 5-1, 264A1
Pre-coup watch rptd 5-15, 399C3
Pol activities banned 6-4; Peron, ex-offcls lose rights, ordrd arrested 6-23, 519F3
Peron funds misuse chrgs leaked 6-4, 6-18; Peron, ex-aides goods frozen 7-1, 520E1
Oscar Ivanissevich dies 6-5, 524G2
Death penalty restored 6-26, 496F1
Rights curbed in anti-corruptn drive 8-19, 672E2
Eva Peron buried 10-2, Juan 12-19, 997A2
Peron, aides indicted 10-25, 997B1
Hard-line gens retired 12-3, 996A3
Listed as not free 12-22, 977B3

Kidnapings
Rosario workers seized 1-7, found dead 1-8, 25G3
Cordoba abductns raise concern, army role asked 1-12, 26A1
Montoneros score Quieto abductn 1-13, 26C1
Cordoba abductns continue 1-17, 96E1
Exec killed in kidnap try 2-25, 212G1
30 civilians kidnaped 3-13—3-20, 212A1
Conti, Echegoyen, Pita seized 5-5, 5-30, 399A1
2 Uruguay exiles seized 5-18, found dead 5-20; forgn protests 5-21, 5-24; govt vows probe 5-24, 399E1-D2 ★
Liberoff seized 5-19, 399D2
Bolivia's Torres seized 6-1, found dead 6-2, 415D2
Forgn refugees seized 6-11, freed 6-12, 495G3
Echegoyen killed 7-10, 571G1
30 Uruguay refugees rptd seized 7-19, 571A3
Solari, Amaya seized 8-18; rescued 8-30, 672G1
Kraiselburd child seized 9-1, 996F3
Erb seized 9-15; in jail 10-2, 996E1
Koelliker, Fossatti rptd missing; Vacca freed 12-30, 996E3

Press & Censorship
Peron bans TV program, closes La Opinion 2-10, 154F2
Prior censorship imposed 3-24, lifted 3-25, 211A3
Media controls set 3-26; newsmen rptd seized 3-30, papers closed 4-8, 263F3-264A1
Rpts on pol violence barred 4-24, 399D1
Pol rptg banned 6-4, 520A1

1977

Sovt ship released 11-9, 982D1
Chile activists detained 11-23, 983F2
Backs Belize independnc at UN 11-28, 969A3

Government & Politics—*See also other appropriate subheads in this section*
Govt pol 'dialogue' plan doubted, UCR prosecutn seen 6-14—6-19, 522E2
Radicals cleared of pol chrg 7-2; UCR-govt feud continued 7-3—8-6, 615D1-C2
Videla '78 electn plan rptd 7-22, 595C2
Pol ldrs seek open 'dialogue' 8-13—8-16, 670F1
Trade min quits 10-21, 981D2

Graiver Scandal
Graiver rptd killed in '76 air crash 345D2
La Opinion offcls seized 4-1—4-16, Jara freed 4-23, 345C2, B3
Guerrilla financing scandal breaks 4-11, 15 arrested 4-14; Videla admits Graivers' role 4-19, 345A2
Orfila, govt officials meet 4-19, 371C3
Background, probe info rptd 4-22, 371C2
La Opinion owner protectn cited 4-22, 371E2
More arrests 4-23—4-29, 371A2
Orfila linked, denies illegal 4-23—4-29, 371A3
Bank accts frozen 4-26, 5-2; Graiver bank closed 5-3, 371B2
La Opinion vp seized 4-29, 371B2
Army rpts 'proof' 5-4, 371G1
Lanusse link rptd 5-5, 371D1
Lanusse, ex-aides freed 6-13, 522D3
Anti-Semitism linked 7-7, 614G3
Gelbard dies 10-4, Klein 10-8, 872A2, 922A3
8 to be tried re rebel ties 10-15, 922G2
La Opinion owner loses rights 11-10, 922E2
Graivers, employes sentncd 12-9, 981G3
Case witness rptd dead 12-10, 982C1

Kidnapings & Disappearances
Journalist disappears 1-9, 42D1
Prestes children seized 1-11, 42D1
Laborer found dead 1-13, 42C1
Smith seized 2-11, 198B3
Muniz Barreto, secy seized 2-16, 198B1
Eguren, Margarinos rptd seized 2-25, 198B1
2 magazine publishers held 3-1—3-7, 198B1
2 newsmen disappear 4-1; Ferreiros kidnaped 4-3, found dead 4-5, 345E3
Ct asked to probe disappearances 4-11, Journalists disappear 6-25—7-21, 595E2
6 attys seized 7-6—7-7; 1 killed, 3 freed 7-12, 595E2
Amb to Venez seized 7-18, 595G1
Pol newsletter scores amb kidnap 7-26, owner disappears 8-5, 670F2
Resnizky son seized 7-28, rescued 8-3, 670G2
Cartoonist, wife presumed seized 8-8, 670G2
100 protesters arrested 8-15, 670E1
Army lt seized 8-20, found dead 8-21, 670B3
Disappearances rptd up, govt vows probe 8-26, 670D2
2 mutilated corpses found 8-26, 670E2
Jews kidnaped, arrested 8-27—9-11; 30-50 rptd seized in '77 9-13, 922D2
Radical ldr rpts army torture 9-2, 922F1
Union ldr Bravo disappears 9-8, arrest admitted 9-20, 922G1-A2
Uruguay ex-editor rptd in hiding 10-3, 905B2
Women protest disappearncs 10-14, 922B1
Serrat seized 11-10, freed 11-11, 922G1, B2
US asks info on missing 11-21, 912F2
Rights activists seized 12-8, 981G2-B3
French nuns seized 12-8, 12-10; guerrillas claim responsibility 12-17, 981B3
Videla on disappearances 12-10, 981D3

Monetary, Trade, & Aid Issues (including all foreign economic developments)—*See also 'Atomic Energy' above*
US '77 arms aid rptd 1-1, 50C3
Boeing rpts consultant 1-5, ct backs secrecy 2-25, 215C3
'76 exports, trade surplus rptd 1-11, 42A2
US to cut aid re rights abuse 2-24; actn scored 2-25, 2-28, '78 mil credits rejctd 3-1, 142E1, B2
US modifies duty-free list 2-28, 189E3
'75-76 trade, paymts data; table 3-11, 189B1, A2 ★
'66-75 arms transfers table 4-8, 415A2, F2, C3
IWC cuts whaling quotas 6-24, 496G3
Monthly peso devaluatns rptd 7-8, 614D2
US delays police aid 7-17, 572F3
'76 trade surplus rptd; US, Japan deficits down, EC trade up 7-25, 614A3
'76 forgn investmt law ineffective 7-25, 614B3
US bars '78 arms aid 8-4, 668B1
IMF OKs $137 mln loan 9-19, 981F2
USSR, Bulgaria fishing boats seized 9-21—10-1, USSR protests 9-23, 10-8; attack seen reckless 11-4, 944F2
Hydroelec talks with Brazil, Paraguay 9-22—9-23, 794D3
US Cong bars mil training funds, credit sales 10-19, 815A3; bill signed 11-1, 834D1
Fraguio quits re Martinez' trade policy 10-21, 981D2
Chile territorial waters dispute cited 11-4, 944C3

1978

Government & Politics—*See also other appropriate subheads*
Mrs Peron convicted of embezzlemt 2-20, 208E2
Videla asks 'dialogue' with natl ldrs 3-29; Radicals welcome, score econ policy, ldrs detained 4-23; interior min vs pol parties' criticism 4-26, 611C3
Videla pres term extensn rptdly disputed by mil 4-21—4-23, 5-2; term extended 5-2, 611G2, F3
Radicals meet local ldrs, Balbin arrested 5-1, 611E3
Videla vows more dem govt 5-29, 8-1, 611G3
Videla quits army, junta; Viola succeeds 7-31, 611F2
Viola: next pres a mil man 8-23, 793C1
Mrs Peron moved to house arrest 8-28; ex-Cabt mins rptd freed 9-1, 793F1
Videla sees eventual democracy 9-5, 793B1
Mil pol plans rptd, AF asks pro-mil party 10-12, 10-15, 793D1
Forgn min quits 10-27, 840G2
Cabt shuffled; 2 civilns added 11-6, 865C2

Human Rights—*See 'Press' and 'Unrest' below*

Kidnapings & Disappearances—*See 'Unrest' below*

Monetary, Trade, Aid & Investment
'77 auto exports rptd down 1-13; GM unit pullout hinted 2-24, 310B2
Paraguay '77 timber exports cut 2-17, 292F3
Canada '74 A-sale paymts scored 2-27, 166A3
Spain grants $340-mln loan 3-8, 310B3
'77 trade surplus rptd 4-8, 310E2
US indicts Graiver for embezzlemt 4-12, 326C1
Forgn investmt return rptd, oil stressed 4-24, 310G2
China trade pact signed 6-9, 793G2
US blocks Eximbank hydro loan 7-19, OKs 9-26; bars mil sales 9-26, 792D2
GM sets pullout 8-4, Ford may hike investmts 8-17; govt policies scored 8-25, 793B2
Chrysler operatns cited 8-10, 623F2
Chile trade halted re Beagle Channel spat 860A3
Brazil, Paraguay hydroelec talks cited 10-20, 829B3
Spain king in meat, wheat trade talks 11-26—11-30, 967A3
Peso falls to 1,000 to US $ 12-7, 1021F2

1979

Government & Politics—*See also other appropriate subheads in this section*
Army chief sets retiremt, moderate named 12-7, 947E2
Democratic rule planned 12-19, 966B2

Human Rights—*See also 'Press' and 'Unrest' below*
Freedom House lists as not free 13A1
US rights rpt omits 2-10, 107A2
3 rights groups raided, files confiscated 8-10; Amnesty Intl scores 8-13, 611F2-612A1
Pol refugees occupy Swedish consulate in Rio, protest repressn 8-6; UN responds 8-8, 627D1, F1
OAS comm opens probe 9-6; sees Videla, detentn cntrs denied 9-7, 683D2
Missing persons law revised 9-12, 728E1
2-yr missing toll rptd 4-26, 351C2
US attys fault justice 5-26, 467B1
Amnesty Intl lists missing 6-17, 467C1
Canada speech, A-sale loss linked 10-2–10-3, 788D3
DR forgn min, OAS score abuses 10-24, 10-30, 824D2, F2

Monetary, Trade, Aid & Investment—*See also 'Atomic' above*
Wheat export ldrs rptd 4-3, 253C1
GATT pact signed 4-12, 273B1
1st 1/4, May reserves, devaluatns rptd 6-2, 466G2, 467A1
Ford Motor to invest $76 mln; sales, Chrysler-VW plans cited 7-20, 562F1
Nicaragua junta vs debt paymt 7-25, 574C1
Chrysler plans sale to VW 9-15, 699A2
Brazil, Paraguay dam accords signed 10-19, 845A1
Chrysler-VW deal rptd set 11-19, 887F2

1980

Government & Politics—*See also other appropriate subheads in this section*
Junta delays naming Videla successor, Lambruschini rift rptd 9-30, 747E2
Viola named Videla successor, junta rift resolved 10-3, 766E1-B2
Peron '76 arrest order lifted 12-24, 991F1

Human Rights—*See also 'Unrest' below*
2 ex-prisoners describe ordeal 2-4, 95A1
US issues rights rpt 2-5, 86A3, 87E1
OAS rpt issued, abuses chrgd 4-18; govt scores 4-19, 309D2
Intell operatns scandal disclosed, 3 exiles missing 7-28, 580D1
Perez awarded Nobel Peace Prize 10-13, 889A2
Graiver imprisonmt cited 10-15, 827A1
OAS debate stirs boycott threat, Carter rights policy scored 11-20; OAS cites poor record 11-27, 913C3, D3
Amnesty Intl scores 12-10, 978A3

Monetary, Trade, Aid & Investment
USSR grain sale increase barred 1-12, 27E3, 28B1
Sovt grain embargo cooperatn sought by US 2-5, 87G1
USSR signs trade deal; '79, 1st 1/4 data 4-15, 336F1
Brazil trade accords signed 5-15—5-17, 405E2
Forgn currency curbs lifted, import duties cut; '79 debt rise cited 7-11, 561D2
Bolivia mil econ aid seen 7-31, 577F1

1976

2 magazines rptd closed 7-23, 620C3
Nazi publicatns scored 8-15, 8-28, La Opinion bombed 8-27, 672A2
Kraiselburd child kidnaped 9-1, 996F3
Los Principios closed, newsmen arrested 9-13—9-18, 996G3-997A1
Anti-Semitic publicatns banned 9-14, 996G3
EFE bur chief held, freed 11-7, 997A1
Adepa asks arrest probes 12-30, 996D3

UN Policy & Developments
WHO rep found dead 1-21, 96A2
Refugee comr reassured re asylum 4-9, 264B2
Refugee comr protests kidnapings 6-12, asks Latin asylum 6-14, 495G3
Refugees protest 7-6—7-18, more kidnapings rptd 7-19, 571E2, A3
IAEA dir cites 9-21, 760F3

Unrest (including political prisoner and refugee issues)—*See also 'Economy & Labor' and 'Kidnapings' above*
2 killed in theater bombing, actress flees 1-2, 25G3
19 die in pol violence 1-3—1-9, 7D2
'75 death toll rptd 1-3, 7E2
Soldiers, cops kill 3 1-10, 26D1
Guerrillas attack arms depot 1-11, 26D1
UK files writ for prisoners 1-12, 26A2
Pol death toll mounts 1-15—2-1, 96A1
Russell ct scores rights abuse 1-17, 61D2, E2
Lopez Rega link to AAA rptd 2-4, 212B1
AAA arms rptdly smuggled from Paraguay 2-4, 212C1
Pol violence, killings mount 2-5—2-25, 3-13—3-20, 212A1
Actn on UK prisoners urged 2-27, 220F2
Venez detains natls 3-2, 208D2
Paraguay border clash re smuggling rptd 3-5, 205G3
2 die in CP hq gunfight 3-25, 236B3
Post-coup arrests, violence 3-26—3-31, 236D3
Pol death toll mounts 3-29—4-9, 1,000 arrests rptd 4-2, 264C1
Herreras gets Mex emb asylum in Uruguay 3-31, safe-conduct 4-9, 382B3
Forgn refugees ordrd to rpt 4-2; Chileans seized 4-3, contd asylum vowed 4-9, 264B2
Peruvian radical killed 4-3, 264F1
Pol refugees in Mex emb get safe-conduct 4-3, 264G1
UK couple freed 4-8, score police 4-11, 264A2
Pol death toll mounts 4-10—5-30, 398E3
ERP rpts Enriquez seized 4-10, 399B1
Fiat exec killed 5-4, 398G3
Army, police arrests rptd 5-17, 399C1
Campora in Mex emb 5-20, Ferreira in Austrian 5-24, 399D2, E3
Amnesty Intl chrgs exile abuse 5-24, 399D2 ★
Uruguay linked to Michelini, Gutierrez deaths 5-28, 441B2
Ferreira arrives France 5-31, 441B2
Pol, mil violence; death toll mounts 6-1—7-5, 495A3-496E1
Torres widow scores 6-8, 456G2
Forgn refugees list stolen 6-10, 496C1
Death penalty restored 6-26, 496F1
Forgn refugees stage protest 7-6—7-18; Canada, 4 W Eur natns OK visas 7-19, 571E2
Police chief replaced 7-6, SSF crisis rptd 7-9, 571B3
ERP lists seized 7-10; Santucho, other ldrs slain 7-19, 571E1
12 Chile refugees fly to Canada 7-15, 571G2
French priests murdered 7-21, 571B2
'76, July death tolls rptd 7-23, 7-30, 571A2
Rightist terror forces mag closings 7-23, 620D3
Leftist death toll mounts 8-2—9-4; pol reorganizatn rptd 8-6, 8-20, 671B3
Seminarians arrested 8-3; bishop dies 8-4, foul play suspected 8-6, 9-2, 672C1
Chilean seminarian seized 8-3, 672C1
Lanusse scores profs arrests 8-4, detained 8-6—8-11, 672F2-A3
Cuba emb aides vanish 8-9, 672F1
Anti-Semitic incidents rptd 8-15—8-30, 672A2
Eur soclsts score violence 8-26, 672C2
3 bodies found in River Plate 9-6, 814A3
Political killings continue 9-11—12-19, 996A1-B2
Chile exile harassmt rptd 9-21, 710B3
US warning re rights abuse rptd 10-5; Guzzetti scores US cong probe 10-6; US emb rpt access suit filed 12-19, 996E2
Irish priest tortured, expelled 10-11—12-3, 996B1
Castro chrgs CIA re missing emb aides 10-15, 780B2
'75-76 repressn rptd up 10-31, 975D1
Amnesty Intl probes rights abuse 11-5—11-15, 996C2
Spain newsman held, freed 11-7, 997A1
Gelbard extraditn asked 12-7, 997F1

U.S. Relations—*See also 'Foreign Economic Developments' above*
2 Bendix execs assassinated 1-29, 96A2
Talamante freed, deported 3-27, 236F3
Chrysler, Swift execs killed 4-14, 5-28, 398G3
Kennedy scores Uruguay exile murders 5-21, 399C2
Intl drug dealers arrested 5-27, 971B3
US rep indicted 6-2, 414C3
Ship in US Bicentennial event 7-4, 488A3
US priest arrested 8-3, expelled 8-19, 672C1

1977

World Bank OKs loan 11-10, 981F2
Paraguay vs elec grid frequency chng 11-11, 976C1
Jan-Sept trade surplus rptd 12-2, 981E2

Obituaries
Gainza Paz, Alberto 12-26, 1024F1
Gelbard, Jose Ber 10-4, 872A2; 922A3
Klein, Jose 10-8, 922B3

Press & Censorship—*See also 'Kidnapings' above*
Prensa Libre editor found dead 1-18, 197F3
Emanuelle banned 3-1, 198C1
Pro-Nazi press closed 3-3, 198D2
Uruguay seizes newspaper 3-24, 351E2
La Opinion offcls seized 4-1—4-16, Jara freed 4-23, 345C2-B3; **see 'Graiver Scandal' above**
Cox held 4-22—4-23, 345E3
La Prensa discounts pol 'dialogue' 6-14, 522G2
Uruguay expels editor 9-29, 905D1
La Opinion owner loses rights, detentn to continue 11-10, 922E2
Vance sees Jews 11-21, 912G2
La Prensa editor dies 12-26, 1024F1

Sports
Beats US in Davis Cup 4-29—5-1, 353E2
US vet indicted re horse-switch 12-2, 971A1
Australia wins Davis Cup 12-4, 970G1

Unrest (including political prisoner & refugee issues)—*See also 'Economy & Labor' and 'Kidnapings' above*
Pol prisoners rptd freed 1-1, 3A1
Guerrilla suspects killed 1-1—1-4; '76 losses rptd 1-3, 16C3
US chrgs rights abuse 1-1, 50E2, A3
AAA activities probed 1-4, 16E3
Pol violence continues 1-5—1-14, 42A1
Mex amb asks safe-conduct for Campora, others 1-18, 66B2, D2 ★
Arrests, executns by rt-wing commandos rptd 1-18—3-7, 197F3-198C1
Gonzalez shot 1-19; Jan-Mar terrorist death toll rptd 197E3
Videla escapes bomb blast 2-18, 197B3
Widespread torture, rights abuse rpts continue 2-21—3-3; UN comm bars probe 3-4, Videla denies abuses 3-15, 198C1
Videla Peru visit protested 3-3—3-6 259B2
La Opinion offcls seized 4-1—4-16, guerrilla financing rptd 4-11, 345A2; **see 'Graiver Scandal' above**
Unchrgd detainees rptd 4-14, 388D3
Rights activist seized 4-4, UN panel protests 6-20, 522G3
Army: Montoneros 'defeated' 4-19, 345D3
Orfila meets offcls re rights 4-19, 371C3
Montoneros rptdly to form new pol party 4-21, 345F3
Solari exiled at Venez behest 5-1, 388E3
Guerrillas wound forgn min 5-7, 388F2
Death toll put at 340 5-7, 388A3
Bishops score abuses 5-7, 388F3
Videla Venez visit protested 5-11—5-14, 547A2
Gen Vilas jailed 5-27, 522B3
Guerrilla ldr killed 5-29, 14 others 6-23—6-24, 522F3
Anti-Semitism rpts mount 6-28—7-8, 614F3
ERP offers peace terms, rpts new ldr 7-20, 595C3
6 guerrillas killed, death total rptd 7-21, 595A3
W Ger to extradite rebels 7-22, 614D3
Guerrillas killed 8-6, 8-16, 8-20; pol death toll hits 578 8-20, 670C3
US offcls see rights improvemt 8-7—8-30, 100 protestors seized 8-15, 670C1
Pres aide's home bombed 8-22, 670D3
Guerrilla ldrs killed 9-7, 9-12; army claims major victories 9-28, 9-30, death toll rptd 10-2, 921D3
Videla on rightist terror 9-9, actn pledged 9-12, 922C1
4,000 rptd jailed without ct access 9-22, 922B2
Guerrillas resume attacks 10-13—11-7, 921A3
Vance sees junta ldrs, rights activists, Jews 11-21, 912F2
Amnesty Intl lists jailed medical workers 11-28, 956G2
Chrysler exec's guards killed 12-2, 981F3
Videla plans arrests list; sees terror end 12-10, 981C3
Peugeot exec killed 12-16, 981F3
Pol violence death toll rptd 12-16, 981G3
US group scores rights abuse, rpts prisoner total 12-22, 1018E3
432 pol prisoners to be freed 12-26, 1018D3

U.S. Relations
US releases rights abuse rpt, contd mil aid backed 1-1, 50E2, A3
Boeing rpts consultant 1-5, ct backs secrecy 2-25, 215C3
US to cut aid re rights abuse 2-24; reactn 2-28—3-1, 142E1, B2; 3-2, 3-15, 198B2
US modifies duty-free list 2-28, 189E3
US A-arms concern rptd 259G1
US rpt sent to Cong 3-12, 187E1
'66-75 arms transfers table 4-8, 415A2, F2
Carter OAS speech reactn 4-17, 296C1
Science acad probes missing scientists 4-27, 315A2
Todman visit shelved 5-11, 414D1
US rights stand scored 6-1, 439D1

1978

Press & Censorship
80 newsmen rptd under arrest 3-17, 286A1
Newsprs closed re Videla pres term extensn rpt 4-21—4-23, 611F3
Journalists kidnaped 6-4, 7-23, 2 freed 8-26, 9-30, 792C3
US scores abuses 6-23, 6-24, 489G3, 490C1
Magazine dir killed 8-28, 792F3
Press persecutn scored 9-23, 10-9, 792B3
IAPA rpts press curbs, asks rptrs freed, La Opinion control returned 10-13, 829G1, B2
Press loses air-fare discount; actn scored, govt role in attacks chrgd 10-27, 865F2
Criticism of econ policy OKd, Videla warning cited 10-27, 865D3

Sports
World Cup soccer funds set, govt offcl scores 2-17, 310C3
Guerrillas vow no World Cup unrest 4-7, govt discredits 4-12, 285C3
World Cup soccer finals 6-1—6-25; team wins championship, photo 6-25, 519D3-520G3

Unrest (including political prisoners)—*See also 'Press' above*
Guerrillas in Mex chrg murder threat 1-18, 208F1
US ups pressure 1-29, cites contd disappearances 3-6, asks Timerman release 3-13, 207G3
2000 pol prisoners named in govt lists 2-3, 2-13, 2-19, 207B3
US rpt of 12,000-17,000 prisoners cited 2-13, 207E3
Non-Catholic sect registratn ordrd 2-14, 208E1
Relig sect members seized 2-15—2-19, 208C1
75 disappearances in Jan rptd 2-19, 208C1
RR union ldrs arrested 3-9, 310A2
55 die in prison riot 3-14, 207F2-B3
Church seeks prisoner release 3-21; Videla sees archbips 4-10, 286B1
Jehovah's Witnesses seized 3-21, 3-29, press scores 3-31, 286D1
Guerrillas vow no World Cup violence 3-25, 520A1
'Armed subversn' end seen 3-27, 285B3
Commuter lines blasted 3-28, police station 4-6, 285E3
Guerrillas vow no World Cup unrest 4-7, govt discredits 4-12, 285C3
Massera sees Montoneros in France 4-9, 285E3
Prisoner total, missing persons held rptd 4-9, 4-12, 286C1
Padilla killed 4-11, guerrilla campaign vs soccer tourn chrgd 4-12, 285A3
Timerman moved to house arrest 4-17; US encouraged 4-17, 285F3
Navy chief seeks rights progress 5-2, 611B3
Cop dies in bomb blast 5-10, 612D1
Videla vows chngs 5-29, 8-1, 611G3
Bravo moved to house arrest 6-18, 35 other union ldrs seized 9-22, 793A1
Treas secy's home bombed 6-22, 520F3
Peronist demonstratn smashed 7-1, 793A2
US blocks hydro loan 7-19, OKs 9-26; bars mil sales 9-26, 792D2
Timerman ordrd freed, still held 7-24, 792F3
Adm's daughter slain in blast 8-1; US scores 8-2, 612A1
Govt solves 201 disappearances 8-7, rights groups deny 8-8, 792G2
151 Jan-June disappearances rptd 8-8, 100 May-Aug kidnaps 9-8, 792F2, F3
Perosio kidnaped 8-8, 792G3
US aide scores rights abuse; forgn min, press rebuke 8-20, 792E2
AAA seen as Peruvian terrorist model 8-29—9-15, 776B1
Videla admits govt repressn 9-5, 793B1
13 pol prisoners rptd killed 9-8, 793B1
OAS rights probe OKd 10-19, 792B2
Release of jailed women asked 10-22, 840A3
Spain king gets pol prisoner aid pleas; king sees Videla, backs rights 11-27, 967E3
159 missing rptd found 12-14, 1021E2

U.S. Relations—*See also 'Monetary, Trade, Aid & Investment' and 'Unrest' above*
Graiver '76 death doubted 4-12, 4-13, 326C1
Freighter, US Coast Guard cutter collide 10-20, 908C3
US asks more Beagle Channel talks 12-12, cites peace role 12-15, 979B3

1979

Press & Censorship
Publisher vanishes 1-5, Chilean newsman 40B3; freed 1-11, 1-13, 117C1
Timerman wins Freedom Prize 6-17, 467E1
PEN scores on rights 7-21, 554B1
Timerman ordrd freed 9-18, expelled 9-25, 728A1
Editor rpts death threat 12-4, leaves 12-16, 966E2

Sports
Argentina Open tennis results 11-25, 1003G3

UN Policy & Developments
Refugee comr responds to Latin protests 8-8, 627F1
Membership listed 695D2
Severini chairs world radio conf 9-27-12-6, 1006B3

Unrest—*See also 'Press' above*
Unchrgd prisoners freed, exiled 1-5, 40C3
Graiver kin rptd jailed 1-8, 163E1
Forgn Min worker found dead 1-11, new autopsy ordrd 1-12, 117B1
Labor ldrs arrested, strike threat defused 4-23-4-27, 351B2
26 politicians detained 5-5, 351F2
Pol refugees occupy Swedish consulate in Rio, protest repressn 8-6; UN responds 8-8, 627D1, F1
3 rights groups raided, files confiscated 8-10, 611F2-612A1
Terrorists bomb econ offcl's home 9-27, 748G3
Army rebellion crushed 9-29, 748G2-F3
Treas secy escapes shooting 11-7, 887F3
Prominent exec killed 11-13, 906E2

U.S. Relations
NYS ct rules Graiver dead, dismisses chrgs 1-8, 163B1
'78 freighter collisn rpts issued 1-20, 140F3; 2-26, 3-2, 240E3; US cmdr convicted 11-3, 887B3
US rights rpt omits 2-10, 107A2
US attys score justice 5-26, 467B1
Ford Motor to invest $76 mln; sales, Chrysler plans cited 7-20, 562F1
US to challenge coastal sea claims 8-10, 646A3
Chrysler plans operatns sale 9-15, 699A2
Terrorist activity rptd up 11-15, 882A2

1980

Obituaries
Campora, Hector J 12-19, 1004B1
Farrell, Edelmiro S 10-31, 876E1
Galindez, Victor 10-26, 876E1
Sandrini, Luis 7-5, 608G2

Sports
Jones wins Gr Prix 1-13, 1002B1
Wins Davis Cup Amer Zone 3-9, 607F1
Moscow Olympic boycott joined 5-8, 379D2
Wins Nations Cup 5-12, 607G1
[illegible]s win Davis Cup 12-7, 946F3

[illegible]nrest
[illegible]sues rights rpt 2-5, 87E1
Aerolineas jet hijacked, Martinez extortn fails 6-30—7-1, 519F2

U.S. Relations
US issues rights rpt 2-5, 86A3, 87E1
Swiss A-plant deal oppositn rptd 3-10—3-11, 229B2
Graivers win '76 jet crash damages 10-15, 826G3

1976

US student kidnaped 9-15, in jail 10-2, 996E1
Argentina warned on rights abuse 10-5; Guzzetti scores cong probe 10-6; US emb rpt access suit filed 12-19, 996E2
US exec's daughter killed 10-20, 996A2
Judge asks Gelbard extraditn 12-7, 997F1

1977

Jewish ldr flees to US 6-28, 615D1
US delays police aid 7-17, 572F3
'76 US trade deficit rptd down 7-25, 614A3
US bars '78 arms aid 8-4, 668B1
US offcls visit, see rights improvemt 8-7—8-30, 670C1
Carter rptdly encouraged Radical oppositn 9-2, 922E1
Videla at Panama Canal pact signing 9-7, 678C1
Videla in US 9-9, rightist terror end pledged 9-12, 922E1
Bank of Amer in intl loan 9-19, 981G2
US Cong bars mil training funds, credit sales 10-19, 815A3; bill signed 11-1, 834D1
Castro new US amb 10-20, 817B2
Vance visits 11-20—11-22, 912E2
US vet indicted re horse switch 12-2, 971A1
Chrysler exec's guards killed 12-2, 981F3
US research group issues rights abuse rpt 12-22, 1018E3

1978

1979

1980

1976

ARGO Merchant (Liberian tanker)
Grounded, spills oil off Nantucket 12-15, 968D3
Oil spill liability hearing 12-28—12-31, suit delayed 12-30, 1013F3
Coast Guard sinks 12-31, 1014D1
ARGONAUT Insurance Co.
Hawaii malpractice rates hiked 9-1, 1016E3 ★
ARIAS, Arnulfo
Panama denounces 1-21, return barred 1-26, 1-29, 121D2, D3, F3
ARIAS Navarro, Carlos
Charges subversion 1-19, 54E3
EC trade talk ban lifted 1-20, 84E3
Announces mild pol reforms 1-28, 144A1
Resignatn asked 3-11, 3-12, 207B1
Bans Areilza TV interview 4-12, 269G1
Legis process speeded 4-24; govt struggle rptd 4-27, 314C2
Dismissed 7-1, 500A3
Reformists refuse Cabt posts 7-6, 10 mins remain 7-8, 523A2
ARISMENDI, Valentin
Uruguay econ min 8-27, 678B2
ARITA, Kazuhisa
In new party 6-25, 497B3
ARIZONA
Parker BIA office bomb threat 1-1, 7E1
Sen votes natl park mining end 2-4, 135A2
ERA fails ratificatn 3-1, 172E1
Methane ice on Pluto rptd 4-2, 443G2
Ford aide in Phoenix 4-5, 245E2
Sup Ct bars Church libel suit review 4-5, 262A2
Utah power projct dropped 4-14, 284E2
Bolles slain in Phoenix, land frauds cited 6-2—6-21, state reforms rptd spurred 6-22, 483G2
Bolles case dvpts 7-2—10-26, mistrial declared 10-21, 859E2
Ford suspends HEW father-son, mother-daughter ruling 7-7, 535E2
Dem conv women delegates, table 508A2
Dem conv pres vote, table 7-14, 507A2
GOP pre-conv delegate count 8-14, 583A3
GOP conv pres, vp vote tables 8-18—8-19, 8-19, 599A1, A3
US Sen primary results 9-7, 687G2
Carter in Phoenix 9-13—9-14, 686F2
18 indicted re land fraud 9-14, Curran arrested 9-17, 859D3
Fscl '75 per capita income, tax burden rptd 9-15, 10-12, 959D2
Natl parks mining curbs signed 9-28, 834B2
Press team opens crime probe 10-2, 849B2
Ehrlichman in Safford jail 10-28, 849F2
Election results 11-2: pres 818A1, 819B1; cong 820A1, D2, 824B1, 828B1, F3; state 824E1, 825B3
Bolles trial gets new judge, site 11-19, 12-7, 971C3
Flu shot paralysis rptd 12-17, 950E1
ARIZONA, University of (Tucson)
Gas clouds in space found 5-25, 443D2
Bolles wins Zenger award 12-9, 971G3
ARIZONA Public Service Co.
Utah project dropped 4-14, 284C2
ARIZONA Republic (newspaper)
Bolles hurt in bombing 6-2, dies 6-13, 1 chrgd 6-21, 483G2, 484E1; **for subsequent developments see BOLLES, Don**
Bolles wins press award 12-9, 971G3
ARIZONA State University (Tempe)
'75 football rankings 1-2, 31B3
ARJA, Jayel Al-
Killed 7-3, named as hijacker 7-5, 485C1, F2

1977

ARGUS (weekly)
Vorhees dies 2-6, 164F3
ARIAS Navarro, Carlos
To run for upper house 4-22, 331C1
ARIBIAH, Oberu
Nigeria works comr 3-15, 393D2
ARISTODOMOU, Chrystoforos—*See CHRYSOSTOMOS*
ARIYOSHI, Gov. George (D, Hawaii)
Fasi trial folds 12-27, 1008A2

ARIZONA
Legislature schedule rptd 6C2
US Sup Ct reverses '73 land ruling 1-12, 57C3
Bolles suspect pleads guilty 1-15, implicates others 1-15, 1-26—1-27, 161D3
Navajo ldr, ex-aide indicted 2-9, 162E3
Carter cuts water project $ 2-22, 126E1
Mafia ties probed 3-13—3-20, infiltratn rptd widespread 5-16, 568E1, G1
US water project hearing 3-21, 210F1
Phoenix archbp installed 3-22, 375G2
WHA Phoenix team folds 4-1, 262G3
Mex drug smuggling rptd 4-3, 4-8, 332D3-G3
Hughes property assessmt rptd 4-14, 354A3
Phoenix populatn growth rptd 4-14, 388C1
Carter backs water project 4-18, 299E3
'76 per-capita income table 5-10, 387F2
Tucson, Phoenix econ data table 5-16, 384F2, 385B1
Navajo fraud case dismissed 5-17, 492A1
'77 death row population rptd 6-7, 594C1
State abortn funding rptd 6-20, 787B1
Coronado Natl Forest Fire 6-22, 660G3
Laetrile legalization cited 6-23, 508E1
Lawyers fee ads OKd 6-27, 538C3
Wash sues 10 oil cos 8-16, 691E3
Oil cos settle fed suit 8-31, 691C3
State oil trust case merged 9-12, 691G3
'76 per capita income, tax burden table 9-13, 10-18, 821E2
GM cuts '78 Chevette price 9-15, 722F3
Judge's daughter found dead 9-20, 871F2
Bolin sworn gov 10-20, 817B2
Copper indus layoffs rptd 10-31, 859F1
Bolles murder convictns 11-6, 871B2
ERA econ boycott rptd 11-14, 918D1
ARIZONA, University of (Tucson)
Stockton weather research cited 2-21, 183D2
Move to Pac-8 conf cited 12-25, 1020C2
ARIZONA Republic, The (newspaper)
Bolles murder suspect pleads guilty 1-15, 161D3
Ariz Mafia ties probed 3-13—4-20, 568G1
Bolles murder convictns 11-6, 871B2
ARIZONA State University (Tempe)
800-mtr relay mark set 4-30, 603C1
Wins coll baseball title 6-18, 568A1
Loses Fiesta Bowl, move to Pac-8 conf cited 12-5, 1020B2

1978

ARGUELLO, Alexis
TKOs Escalera 1-28, 379A2
TKOs Tam 4-29, 379D2
KOs Alcala 6-3, 600F1
Decisns Leon 11-10, 969D1
ARGUELLO, Gustavo A.
Death in prison rtpd 9-14, 705A3
ARIAS (recording)
Baker wins Grammy 2-24, 316D1
ARIAS, Arnulfo
Returns to Panama, scores govt 6-10, 463C3
Liberals join govt pol comm 7-28, 632A2
Natl Assemb elected 8-6, Torrijos scores 8-7, 632E1
ARIAS Carrizosa, Juan Manuel
Colombia communicatns min 8-7, 629D3
ARISMENDI, Valentin
Rpts Jan-July inflatn up 23% 8-10, 692E1
ARIYOSHI, Gov. George R. (D, Hawaii)
Wins renomination 10-7, 791C3
Reelected 11-7, 853E2, 857B1
ARIZIN, Paul
In basketball HOF 5-1, 457D3
ARIZONA
Legislature schedule rptd 14D3
'67, '77 sales-tax rates rptd 1-5, 15D3
State govt tax revenue table 1-9, 84B2
Bolles killers sentenced 1-10, 24B2
Wilderness area clears Cong 2-9, 109D2; signed 2-24, 218A2
Rain floods drought areas 3-3—3-5, 207D2
Bolin dies, Babbitt sworn gov 3-4, 186F3
Ehrlichman freed from Swift Trail Prison 4-27, 320A2
'77 prison populatn rptd down 6-3, 440D1
Union insurnc scheme chrgd 6-15, 560B3
Cnty abortn funding rptd 6-20, 743C3
Murder scene search warrants backed, hosp interrogatns curbed by US Sup Ct 6-21, 509D2
TV actor found slain 6-29, 540E2
Phoenix makes bad-air list 7-5, 513D1
Bad-air list corrected 7-19, 644B2
Primary results 9-12, 736A2
US parks bill cleared 10-13, 834D3
Trade missn rptd in Japan 10-18, 798D1
Election results 11-7: cong 848C1, 850C1, 855F1; state 847C1, E1, 855D1, 897C3
Synanon founder arrested in Lake Havasu City 12-2, 971F1
Phoenix populatn ranked 12-6, 942F3
Bolles state witness jailed 12-9, 992D2
Extraditn probes barred by US Sup Ct 12-18, 981G1
Nev A-test claims filed 12-21, 1011G3
ARIZONA, University of (Tucson)
Oil study discounts shortage 6-5, 449E3 ★, G3
Sun vibratn rptd measured 8-3, 654F2
ARIZONA Republic, The (newspaper)
Bolles killers sentenced 1-10, 24B2
ARIZONA State University (Tempe)
AIAW swimming title won 3-18, 780G2
Jefferson in NFL draft 5-2, 336F3
Horner 1st pick in baseball draft 6-6, 779G3
Loses NCAA baseball title lost 6-8, 560F1
Wins Garden State Bowl 12-16, 1025B2

1979

ARGERSINGER v. Hamlin
Right-to-counsel doctrine clarified by Sup Ct 3-5, 185G1
ARGUELLO, Alexis
TKOs Escalera 1-29, 412D3
TKOs Limon 7-8, 839B1
ARGUELLO, Gen. Ariel
Killed 6-20, 461E2
ARGUELLO Hurtado, Roberto
Tribunals to try Somoza soldiers 7-22, 574E1
ARGUS Inc.
Sues vs Kodak, 2 others 8-28, 986B1
ARGYLL, Duke of
Iona rptd for sale 3-23, 268C2
Iona sold to Scottish millionaire 5-24, 407F1
ARIAS, Arnulfo
Crocamo coup plot fails 10-24, 836E3
ARIMORI, Kunio
Indicted 5-15, 389E2
ARIRI, Obed
SIU-Edwardsville wins NCAA soccer title 12-9, 1004A2
ARIYOSHI, Gov. George R. (D, Hawaii)
Announces strike setlmt 12-3, 922A3
ARIZONA
Legislature schedule rptd 5C3
Treas ex-secy discloses Sindona loan 1-9, 205D3
Phoenix freeway-aid policy cited 2-13, 129A3
Legis rejcts DC voting rep amendmt 3-7, 367E1
Calif grand jury transcript examinatn barred by Sup Ct 4-18, 346C2
Farm labor law restored by Sup Ct 6-5, 464A3
Fires destroy 76,200 acres 7-2, 572D3
Burger visits Flagstaff 8-8, 630A3
Tucson schl busing rptd set 9-2, 679E3
Cocaine trade growth rptd 9-5, 972G2
MX 'racetrack' deploymt sites studied 9-7, 677G3
'78 per capita income rptd 9-16, 746F2
Horizon land sales scored by FTC 10-3 903F1
Phoenix quake tremors 10-15, 799D2
Atomic Energy
Palo Verde A-plant delay seen 5-9, 382D1
Palo Verde A-plant additn canceled 7-16, 609E3
NM A-waste spill traces rptd 9-5, 744B1
Radioactive tritium plant seized 9-26, decontamination begun 9-29; Amer Atomics seeks reorganizatn 10-6, 806B2
ARIZONA, University of (Tucson)
Demic in NBA draft 6-25, 507A3
Stevens addresses 9-8, 745C1
Loses Fiesta Bowl 12-25, 1001A3
ARIZONA Public Service Co.
Palo Verde A-plant additn canceled; Calif, fed regulatn blamed 7-16, 609E3
ARIZONA Public Service Co. v. Snead
Case decided by Sup Ct 4-18, 346B2
ARIZONA State University (Tempe)
'78 football win over USC cited 1-2, 1-3, 8D2
Harris in NFL draft 5-3, 335F2
Fires Kush 10-13, Kush sues univ 11-9, 1001C3

1980

ARGO, Victor
Bull Pen opens 6-12, 756C3
ARGOV, Shlomo
Vs Irish stand on Leb clash 4-20, 302C3
ARGUE, Hazen
Canada wheat bd min 3-3, 171F1, B2
Lifts Sovt grain embargo 7-24, 577F3-578A1
Sovt grain embargo support ended, cites US-China pact 11-18, 900C2
ARGUELLO, Alexis
KOs Castillo 1-20, 320A3
Limon defends WBC super featherwgt title 12-11, 1001B1
ARIAS, Arnulfo
Torrijos party wins Panama cncl vote 9-28, 752D2
ARIYAK, Sarik
Slain 12-17, 991C2
ARIYOSHI, Gov. George R. (D, Hawaii)
Heads territorial islands econ planning group 2-19—2-22, 495D1

ARIZONA
Rainstorms hit 2-14—2-17, disaster declared 2-20, 213C3
DES in cattle rptd 4-24, 358F1
Central Ariz Project funds clears Cong 6-25, 9-10, Carter signs 10-1, 803E2
Forest fire damage rptd 6-29, 616C2
Crime & Civil Disorders
Bolles killers convictns overturned 2-25, 214G2
El Salvador aliens rescued in desert 7-4—7-5; search continues 7-7, arrests rptd 7-9, 518D2-C3; 4 held 7-11, 7-19, 560E2
Ariz U ex-football coach, others indicted 7-24, state probe asked 10-16, 875G2
Mex alien case mistrial declared 7-29, retrial sought 8-29, 713E2
Religious deprogrammer convicted for Tucson abductn 8-29, 727B1; sentncd 9-26, 857B3
Bonanno convicted 9-2, 712E3
Phoenix CBS-TV statn firebombed 9-30, 835D3
Bolles killer convicted 10-17, 860E3
El Salvador alien deportatn proceedings begin 10-18, 2 smugglers convicted 10-20, 825F3, G3
Ehrlichman parole ended 10-27, 890E1
3d El Salvador smuggler sentncd 11-4, 870B1
Bolles killer sentenced 11-14, 926B3
Methodists settle retiremt home fraud suit 12-10, 963D3
Politics & Government—*See also other appropriate subheads in this section*
Legislature schedule rptd 18C1
State of State message 1-14, 268G3-269B1
Reagan gains delegates 5-3, 342B3
Sen primary results 9-9, 700D2
Election results 11-4: pres 838A1, 839B1, D3; cong 840C1, 842B1, 845B3, 851A3; state 845C2, 847G2, C3
'80 census rptd, reapportmt seen 12-31, 983D1
Sports
ASL Phoenix Fire folds 4-19, 771D1
Ariz U ex-football coach, others indicted 7-24; state probe asked 10-16, 875G2
ARIZONA, University of (Tucson)
FDA OKs laetrile testing 1-3, 23F2
Wins NCAA baseball title 6-6, 796E2
Ex-football coach, others indicted for fraud 7-24, state probe asked 10-16, 875G2
Pac-10 transcript scandal penalties avoided 8-11, 875B2
ARIZONA Republic, The (newspaper)
Bolles killers convictns overturned 2-25, 214B3
Bolles killer convicted 10-17, 860E3; sentenced 11-14, 926B3,
ARIZONA State University (Tempe)
Fires Miller 1-3; hires Rogers as football coach 1-17, settles with Kush 1-29, 175D2
Transcript scandal spreads 1-23—5-23, 469B2
Malone in NFL draft 4-29, 336G3
Pac-10 punishes in transcript scandal 8-11, 875D1

1976

ARKANSAS
Primary date set 22C2
Little Rock area off US jobless list 5-5, 347D2
Reagan barnstorms 5-20, 374E1
Primary results 5-25, 373F1, G1, F2, B3, 374A2
Dem conv women delegates, table 508B2
Dem conv pres vote, table 7-14, 507A2
GOP pre-conv delegate count 8-14, 583B3
Reagan seeks conv delegates 8-16, 601G2
GOP conv pres, vp vote tables 8-18—8-19, 8-19, 599A1, A3
Fscl '75 per capita income, tax burden rptd 9-15, 10-12, 959E1, C2
US Sup Ct remands death penalty case 10-4, 746F1
Election results 11-2: pres 818A1, 819B2; cong 821F3, 828G3; state 820A3, 822A1, 831C1
10% get swine flu shots 12-2, 911B1
ARKANSAS, University of (Fayetteville)
Wins Cotton Bowl 1-1, '75 rank rptd 1-2, 31B3
ARKANSAS State University (State University)
Bell sets pole-vault mark 5-29, 424D3
ARLEN, Michael J.
Wins Natl Book Award 4-19, 292D3
ARLEN, Richard
Dies 3-28, 240C3
ARLINGTON, Va.—*See VIRGINIA*
ARLINGTON Heights, Ill.—*See ILLINOIS*

1977

ARKANSAS
Legislature schedule rptd 6C2
Coll integratn rules ordrd 1-17, 112B2
Schl desegregatn reviews ordrd 2-17, 156C3
Coll integratn rules reordrd 4-1, 446D1
Biology text barred in Ind 4-14, 471E3
'76 per-capita income chart 5-10, 387E2
Coll integratn plan issued 7-5, 630G2
'76 per capita income, tax burden table 9-13, 10-18, 821D2, F3
ERA econ boycott rptd 11-14, 918D1
Sen McClellan dies 11-27, 952A3
Hodges replaces McClellan 12-10, 1005A3
ARKANSAS, University of (Fayetteville)
3 football players suspended 12-21, 12-29, 1020D2
ARLEDGE, Roone
To head ABC News 5-2, 395G1
Defends TV sports coverage 11-2, 950A1
ARLINGTON County, Va.—*See VIRGINIA*
ARLINGTON Heights, Village of v. Metropolitan Housing Development Corp.
Ruling reversed, case remanded 1-11, 14G3

1978

ARKANSAS
'67, '77 sales-tax rates rptd 1-5, 15D3
State govt tax revenue table 1-9, 84B2
McDonnell Douglas Melbourne strike 1-13—4-16, 284A3
College integratn plan OKd 2-2, 85D1
Little Rock clean-air rating rptd 2-23, 144E3
FCC cable-TV access rules voided 2-24, 195G2
'Right-to-die' law rptd 3-18, 597F3
Robbery, rape convictns reversed by US Sup Ct 4-3, 309B1
Tornadoes hit 4-17—4-18, 479G2
Construction pact signed 5-22, 429D3
Primary results, Sen runoff set 5-30, 426G1
Pryor wins primary runoff 6-13, 467E1
Abortns rptd down 6-20, 743D3
Prison reform, atty fees backed by Sup Ct 6-23, 566D1
Pine Bluff nerve gas plant planned 10-19, 833G2
Electn results 11-7: cong 846G1, A3, 855G1; state 847C1, 853D2, 855F1
US Sen campaign spending rptd 11-15, 898D1
El Dorado hit by tornado 12-3, 972G1, A2
ARKANSAS, University of (Fayetteville)
Wins Orange Bowl 1-2, '77 rank rptd 1-3, 8G2, B3
Holtz named top coll football coach 1-21, 172A1
NCAA basketball tourn results 3-25, 3-27, 272A1
Little in NFL draft 5-2, 336F3
Brewer in NBA draft 6-9, 457F3
Football players suspended on rape complaint 12-14, 1025B3
Ties in Fiesta Bowl 12-25, 1025E2
ARKHIPOV, Ivan V.
Joint India projcts agreed 3-1—3-6, 169C1
ARLEDGE, Roone
ABC news show chngs set 4-19, 419A3
ARLINGTON Heights, Ill.—*See ILLINOIS*
ARLINGTON Heights v. Metropolitan Housing Development
Zoning case review barred 1-9, 13E2

1979

ARKANSAS
Legislature schedule rptd 5C3
Tornado hits Camden 4-9, Polk Cnty 4-11, 288B3, C3
Regulatory bds rptd segregated 4-9, 307A2
Pub worker grievance policy backed by US Sup Ct 4-30, 364D3
Gathings dies 5-22, 432G2
Truck strike violence 6-27, 6-28, 479B2, D2
'78 per capita income rptd 9-16, 746E2
Army BZ stockpile rptd 9-24, 727A2
Baker seeks '80 conv win 11-1, 828G3
Midwest quake threat rptd 11-15, 954C1
R Carter campaigns 12-8, 961D3
Atomic Energy
Ark Nuclear One (Russellville) A-plant safety study urged 4-1, 245F1
Ark Nuclear One A-plant shut by NRC 4-27, 322A1
A-protest rptd 4-28—4-29, 322F3
Ark Nuclear One protest 6-2, 416C2
ARKANSAS, University of (Fayetteville)
'78 rank rptd 1-2, 8E2
Frozen sperm study rptd 1-7, 64E2
NCAA basketball tourn results 3-26, 238A3
Hampton in NFL draft 5-3, 335E2
2d in NCAA baseball title 6-8, 569A3
Moncrief in NBA draft 6-25, 507A3
ARKANSAS Nuclear One—*See ARKANSAS—Atomic Energy*
ARKANSAS v. Sanders
Case decided by Sup Ct 6-20, 516C2
ARKIN, Alan
In-Laws released 6-15, 820D1
Magician of Lublin released 11-9, 1008A1
ARKUS, Leon A.
Sets Carnegie Museum retiremt 5-11, 375C2

1980

ARKANSAS
FBI Brilab probe rptd 2-8—2-9, 111C3
US files chem-dump suit 3-4, 190E3
108-yr-old war vet dies 3-10, 279E3
Tornadoes hit 4-7—4-8, 391G2
Drought, heat wave hit, poultry losses rptd 6-23—8-15, 616C1, A2, D2
Brothers rptd reunited 6-29, 638A3
L Bates dies 8-22, 676A1
Drought, heat wave damage final rpt 9-7, 857C2
Pine Bluff arsenal funds challenge defeated 9-16, 741D3
Levi trust case tentative setlmt award rptd 12-2, 917B3
Calif prison probe curbed by Sup Ct 12-8, 937D1
Atomic Energy & Safeguards
Babcock plant review ordrd 3-4, 169F2
Russellville A-plant accident 5-10, gas venting delay order defied 5-13, 441B1
A-missile silo blast kills 1 9-19, warhead removed 9-22; diagram 765E1
Politics & Government—*See also other appropriate subheads in this section*
Election results 11-4; cong 840C1, 842C1, 845A3, 849G1-B2; state 845D2, 847B1, F2 849A2
'80 census rptd 12-31, 983D1
Presidential Election (& Transition)
GOP caucus results 2-2, 92A1
More GOP delegates picked 2-16, 130F1
Primary results 5-27, 399B1-C2
Mondale at Dem state conv 9-19, 780E2
Reagan in Texarkana 10-30, 840A1, B1
Election results 11-4, 838A1, 839B2, D3
Refugee Issues
Cuban refugees fill Ft Chaffee 5-21, 380E1
Ft Chaffee processing cntr hit by unrest, 300 flee 5-26; Natl Guard called in 5-27, 396C1
Cubans riot at Ft Chaffee 6-1; processing suspended, troops enforce calm 6-2, 419G3-420D1
Carter orders criminals expelled 6-7; UN processing aid rptd 6-9, 435A1, A2
Ft Chaffee gays await processing 7-7, 514G2, C3
Ft Chaffee readied for 'hard-core' transfers, resetlmt problems grow 8-29, 685A1
Ft Chaffee gets 'hard-core' transfers 9-25, 725C3
Aid to states clears Cong 9-25, 10-1, signed 10-10, 785B1
ARKANSAS, University of (Fayetteville)
Loses Sugar Bowl 1-1, '79 rank rptd 1-2, 23C1
Wins Hall of Fame Bowl 12-27, 999D3
ARKANSAS Power & Light Co.
A-plant accident 5-10, gas venting delay order defied 5-13, 441B1
ARKHIPENKO, Vasily
Wins Olympic medal 7-26, 624A1
ARKHIPOV, Ivan
Sovt 1st dep premr 10-27, 832A1
Meets Polish aide 12-29, 976D3
ARKIN, Alan
Simon released 2-29, 216E3
ARLT, Lewis
Interview opens 4-24, 392D3
ARMACOST, Samuel H.
Named Bank America pres, chief exec 12-1, 959C1

ARMAMENTS

1976

ARMAMENTS—*Note: Weapon items are listed here. For defense issues, see country names. For arms control, see DISARMAMENT & Arms Control*
US arms to Morocco rptd 1-7, 36D2
Japan export ban end urged 1-9—2-1, 157F1-A2
US to resume Yugo sales 1-13, 1-14, 55B1
French arms sales disputed 1-15, 1-25, 126F2
'75 Swiss arms sales rptd up 1-22, 104D1
US-Spain defns pact signed 1-24, 77B1
US pledges more aid to Morocco 1-30, 107G2
France: Algeria deal possible 1-31, 107F2
Europn Independent Program Group meets 2-2, 2-9, 297B3
Argentina-Paraguay smuggling rptd 2-4, 212C1; clash 3-5, 205G3
US cos '75 forgn sales listed 2-6, 147A2
'75 US exports triple since '71 152B1
US Sen OKs aid authorizatn, export curbs 2-18, 151C3
US study finds world arms spending up 2-29, 182D3
US House votes arms aid, sales bill 3-3; appropriatn 3-4, 181G1-D2
India rpts Pak arms buildup 3-31, 278B3
US Cong com OKs Chile cash arms sales 3-31, 310A2
US House OKs '77 arms authorizatn 4-9, 283G1
Rpt US guns traded for Mex drugs 4-14, 420E1
US Cong OKs authorizatn 4-28, Ford vetoes 5-7, 344B3-345C1
Israel aid to Ethiopia rptd 5-18; Turk, Yugo, Czech aid rptd 5-19, 364G2
Iran seeks US arms relay to Morocco 5-22, 458C2
US Sen OKs '77 arms authorzn 5-26, 411B2

1977

ARMAMENTS—*See also DISARMAMENT & Arms Control. For defense issues, see country names*
Ford '78 budget requests 1-17, 30F2-31D1, G1
Brown proposes '78 budget cuts 1-25, 1-26, 2-2, 94E2
ASEAN arms standardizatn chrgd 2-24, 145D3
Carter presents aid program 3-17, 210D3
US chem warfare effort rptd 3-21, 232E1-A2
US House OKs '78 authorizatn 4-25, 323E3
US dvpt, procuremt consolidatn rptd 4-25, 343A3
Carter urges NATO standardizatn 5-10, 359A1
US plans spending cuts 5-10—6-1, 420D3
China arms Pl rebels 6-11, 468B3
US, USSR spending compared 6-30, 673E3
Canada sets modernizatn 7-13, 579D3
US Cong clears '78 authorizatn 7-14, 575D2, 576A2; signed 7-30, 592A2
IISS assesses E-W mil balance 9-2, 686D1
US Cong clears '78 funds 9-9, 704E2-B3
US '78 funds bill signed 9-21, 834D1
Brookings study on US needs, USSR buildup publshd 9-26, 858A1-E1
US supplemental authorizatn cleared 11-3, 856E1-A2
US plans contract competitn, feasibility studies 11-21, 942E1
Africa Issues—*See also other subheads in this section*
USSR shipmt to Ethiopia rptd 4-16, 328A1
US shipmts to Ethiopia halted 4-30, 390F3; Ethiopia scores 9-18, 715E2

1978

ARMAMENTS—*See also DISARMAMENT & Arms Control; for domestic defense issues, see country names*
Aircraft
USSR airlift to Ethiopia rptd halted 1-5, 3C3
Syria-Sovt deal rptd 1-11, 42C2
Carter budgets A, E, F-planes, AWACS, B-1, copters 1-23, 45C1, E1, A2, 46A1
Textron Iran, Nigeria paymts queried 1-24—2-28, 161F1-C2
Australia to review EC Mirage deal 1-26, 69B3
USSR danger to NATO seen in Brookings study 1-29, 81B3
Pentagon urges buildup; cites USSR bomber, tactical aircraft, copter edge 2-2, 81D1, C2
US F-planes sought by Egypt 2-6, 2-7, 78B1
Egypt, France rptd in Mirage talks 2-13, 98B3
US to sell F-planes to Egypt, Saudi, Israel 2-14; Israel deplores, other reactn 2-14—2-15, 97A1-E2
Israel vs US jets to Saudis, US reassures 2-16, 139G1
Carter defends Mideast sale 2-17, 123C2
US to bolster S Korea air power 2-18, 135G2
US affirms Asia commitmt; vows F-planes, AWACS, B-52 missile deploymt 2-20, 126D3
NATO, Warsaw Pact force compared 2-20, 162D3
Vance: Saudi transfer of US jets barred 2-21, 139E1
US blocks Libya plane sale 2-21, 139C2
US sees USSR Backfire threat 2-23, 127C2
USSR MiGs rptd deployed in Ethiopia 2-24, 137F1
US: jet sale to Egypt, Saudis, Israel pkg deal 2-24, 139B1

1979

ARMAMENTS—*See also DISARMAMENT; for domestic defense issues, see country names*
Aircraft
Rhodesia US copters ruled illegal 1-5, 7F3
China to buy UK Harrier jets 1-5, 12B3
US, USSR '74-77 sales compared 1-7, 13A2
Carter budgets A-, E-, F-, P-planes, AWACS, B-52s, copters; omits Harrier funds 1-22, 42A2-43B1, E2
US bombers rptd aging 1-25, 52F2
USSR interceptor jet '67-77 outlay rptd 1-25, 99C3
Iran cancels 160 F-16s, other orders 2-4, 82B2
US fuel price refund OKd by Kerr-McGee 2-8, 113B1
US vows F-5s to N Yemen, Sudan 2-11, 143C2
US concerned re Iran F-14 safety 2-12, 106D1
Israel asks F-16 delivery speedup 2-13, 143G2
Iraq, Syria MiG-23 buildup rptd 2-13, 143A3
Egypt asks US jets 2-16—2-18, 143C3
US OKs F-5Es to N Yemen 2-26, 144F2; offers Saudis aid 3-7, 158A1
US speeds F-5s to N Yemen 3-7; orders AWACS for Saudis 3-8, 2 sent 3-9, 179B1-D1
US aid agrmt with Egypt, Israel rptd 3-20, 198B2
Iran OKs F-14 return to US 3-27, 229A1
U-2 use for SALT verificatn seen 4-3, 258D2
SALT scored re Backfire omissn 4-5, 258F1
USSR Backfire bomber threat seen 4-11, 295E1, C2
US F-5E offer to Pak rptd 4-16, 277G2

1980

ARMAMENTS
Aircraft
US refuses Taiwan long-range fighters 1-3, 11A3
US OKs FX for export 1-4, 16B3
US asks Japan F-plane purchase 1-14, 31B2
US productn lag seen 1-25, 66A1
USSR '79 outlays estimated by CIA 1-27, 65E2
Carter budgets A-, C-, F-, KC-planes, AWACS, B-52s, copters 1-28, 71B1-D1, D2
Sovt Backfire threat seen 1-29, 65A2
Zambia announces MiG purchase 2-7, 119E1
French Mirage 2000 linked to Sovt spy discovery 2-9, 141F2
Australia seeks Mirage replacemts 2-19, 132E1
Egypt to buy US F-16s, defers F-15 buy 2-25, 140B2
Israel to build own jet fighter 2-25; cancel 100 US F-16s 2-29, 180E1
US A-6s grounded after crashes 2-27, flights resumed 3-4, 228F1
Tunisia gets US copters 2-29, 197C1
Reagan 'basic speech' cites B-1s, Sovt fighters in Cuba 2-29, 207F2, C3
Connally cites B-1 in 'basic speech' 3-7, 184D2
Peru-Soviet fighter deal rptd 3-12, 213D1
US F-14s, F-15s rptd grounded by parts shortage 3-30, 267A2
US jet fuel contract awarded to Mobil 4-1, 248C2
Italy cancels Iran copter deliveries 4-8, 282D1
France, UK, W Ger plan joint fighter 4-14, 303E1
Canada to buy US F-18As 4-16, 293C2
US outlay increase urged 5-9, 369B3

1976

US House panel bars aid to Uruguay 6-5, 441E1
US deals with Zaire, Kenya set 6-15—6-19, 466F3
US-Spain defns pact ratified 6-21, 7-23, 534F2, 541D3
S Africa seeks end to US embargoes 6-24, 446B3
'76, 77 US aid authorized; Cong oversight expanded 6-30, 532C3
'76 US aid funds signed 6-30, 533A2
US Cong clears '77 authorizatn 7-1, Ford signs 7-14, 516F2
NATO '77-82 goals rptd 7-1, 760C3
US '77 request, authorizatn table 517A2
US Sen com rpts on Iran arms sales 8-1, 578E2
US-Iran pact signed 8-7, 581A2
NATO tests new arms 9-20, 760D2
Ford signs '77 funds; table 9-22, 706F3
'77 US aid, credits signed, Uruguay aid banned 10-1, 806C3, 814C1
UN vetoes S Africa arms embargo 10-19, 781C3
Chile rejects US aid 10-19, 10-20, 871A1
US arms taken by N Viet rptd 11-11, 961D2
US sens ask NATO reinforcemts 11-14, 879E3
US cost estimate rptd hiked 11-16, 982C3
US Army overspending rptd 11-19, 982A3
Peru, Chile purchases cited 12-7, 975E2
US Latin sales curb urged 12-14, 975A1
US grant to Israel cited 12-22, 958E1
Libya binocular fraud rptd 12-25—12-30, 1006D3

Aircraft—*See also 'Aviation' under ACCIDENTS*
Pentagon employe wins award in C-5A costs case 1-1, 6F3
Rpt GAO scored repairs 1-12, 43G2
Yugo seeks US copters 1-13, 55D1
Morocco Mirage order rptd, other purchasers cited 1-15, 1-16, 36A2
French, W Ger jets to Zaire rptd 1-16, 36C1
Iran drops US F-14, may buy F-16s 1-17, 140B1
'77 US budget proposals 1-21, 63F3, 64A1, E1
Pentagon rpt to Cong issued, B-1 fund request scored 1-27, 68B2
Iran may drop F-19 purchase 2-4, 102E1
Brookings study opposes B-1 productn 2-8, 183F1
US-Morocco F-5E deal rptd 2-21, 458F2
US-Sovt strength listed 2-27, 182F2
Reps vs US AWACS planes sale to NATO 3-2, 183E2
Swiss OK US F-5, F-5E buy 3-16, 314F3
US F-4 Phantoms set for Turkey 3-26, 244A3
Canada-Lockheed P-3 Orion contract deferred 4-1, 250D2; signed 4-30, 332F2; deal fails 5-18, 362G3
S Africa denies Israel jet deal 4-9, 275F3
US House OKs '77 authorizatn 4-9, 283C2
Egypt-China pact signed; USAF comment 4-21, 275E2, B3
US Admin asks '77 STOL budget hike 5-4, 394D1
French Cabt OKs '77-82 defns budget 5-5, 417F2, G2
3 US cos in Iran barter talks 5-9, 5-11, 340A1
US sells Ethiopia F-5Es 5-14, 364G2
Sen defers B-1 funding 5-20, 392F3
Iran for US F-5A to Morocco 5-22, 458D2, F2
US Sen OKs '77 authorzn 5-26, 411D2-E2
NATO defers AWACS decisn 6-10—6-11, 449A2
W Ger aid to Portugal cited 6-10—6-11, 449D2
US F-5s to Kenya set 6-15—6-17, 467A1
Dem platform text cites B-1 6-15, 477E1
Lockheed-Australia C130-H sale rptd 7-1, 481F1
Rpt Libya transferred French Mirage jets to Uganda 7-9, 516A3
Ford OKs '77 authorizatn 7-14, 516G3, 517A1, B1
US '77 request, authorizatn table 517A2
Libya confrms Mirage transfer to Uganda 7-18, 548C2 ★
Canada-Lockheed revised deal signed 7-21, 554G3
Sovt Medit strength rptd 7-22, 558B3
US-Iran pact signed 8-7, 581D2
US threatens Pak jet sale bar 8-8—8-9, 581B3
Australia budgets US, French purchases 8-17, 636F3
GOP platform text cites 8-18, 608G3
Peru-USSR deal rptd 8-19, 652B3
Belgium-Pratt & Whitney accord 8-24, 734D3
'F-14' documentary televised 8-27, 979E3
Sovt MiG-25 pilot defects in Japan, asks US asylum 9-6; Japan experts examine plane 9-8, US aid seen 9-13, 695D3-696G1
US Sen panel hearings on F-16s to Iran 9-10, 9-16, 773F2
Sen subcom probes Japan, Iran sales 9-13—9-26, 979G1-G3
US '77 funds, B-1 delay signed; table 9-22, 707A1
Ford visits B-1 plant 10-7, 763A2
US experts rpt on MiG-25 10-7; USSR, Japan return talks begin 10-12, 839F2
France expels Sovt as spy 10-14, 852G2
US to send F-15s, F-111s to NATO 10-27; F-16 to get A-capacity 11-18, 879A3, 961G1

1977

UN conf asks S Africa embargo 5-21, 399G2
Tanzania asks S Africa embargo 8-6, 624B1
USSR shipmts to Somalia rptd 8-18, 649B1
E Ger aid rptd 8-21, 685A1
US, France, UK cancel Somalia sales; Arab aid rptd 8-31—9-2, 684F2
USSR-Ethiopia deal rptd 9-1, 684C3
Somalia vs USSR shipmt halt 9-7, 715B3
Somalia vs US on vows 9-19, 715D3
US bars S Africa spare parts 10-27, 851G3
UN votes S Africa ban, Pretoria condemns; text 11-4, 851C1

Aircraft
Sovt, French, US sales to Peru noted; Chile embargo cited 1-10, 2A3
Ford State of Union message 1-12, 13F3
B-1 backed in Ford State of Union 1-12, 13F3
Ford '78 budget requests 1-17, 30B3, D3, 31A1
NATO sets F-16 sale review 1-17, 70C3
Rumsfeld backs B-1, tactical buildup 1-18, 39E1, A2
Brown proposes '78 budget cuts 1-25, 1-26, 94C3
NATO defers AWACS purchase 1-27, 71B1
US Joint Chiefs claim bomber lead 1-30, 70B3
US bars Israel sale to Ecuador 2-7, 87A3
Jane's scores B-1 cancellatn; 2-7, 942B1
US flying cmnd post demonstrated 2-11, 110E3
Israel rues US jet sale bar 2-19, 121F1
Carter budget revisns 2-22, 125B1, F1
Egypt to get back 50 Sovt MiG-21s 2-27, 144F1
AFL-CIO backs B-1 funding 2-27, 153B3
US affirms Israel F-16 sale 3-7—3-8, 165A2
F-14 engine repair costs rptd 3-21, 343G2
UK rejcts AWACS, sets Nimrod dvpt; US scores 3-31, 360C1
Sovt MiG-21s to Uganda rptd 4-2, 308B2
Egypt seeks US F-5Es 4-5, 245B1
US OKs Sudan sale 4-7, 327G3
France rpts transports loaned to Morocco 4-10—4-12; US reactn 4-11, 265B1
US OKs C-130s to Zaire 4-12, 265F1
F-15, F-16, B-1 in House arms bill 4-25, 324B1
W Ger gets 21 F-15s 4-28, 360F1
NATO natns buy F-16s 5-5, 441A2
B-1 cost estimate hiked 5-18, 420F3
Sudan orders French copters, Mirage jets 5-23, 450F1
US pledges Sudan C-130s 5-24, 400G1
US bars A-7 sale to Pak 6-2, 450C3
Ecuador vs US Israel sale bar 6-2, 454C3
Carter kills B-1, backs cruise missile 6-30, 514C1
US reviews Israel Ecuador sale ban 7-5, repeats ban 7-6, 511C1
Guatemala buys Israel STOL jets 7-6, 553E2
Carter plans Iran AWACS sale 7-7, drops deal 7-28, 8-12, 611D2
Canada to buy Lockheed Orion anti-sub aircraft 7-13, 579E3
B-1, F-planes, copter funds authorized 7-14, 575G3-576G1; signed 7-30, 592A2
US OKs Israeli Cobra copter productn funds 7-22, 570C3
US backs Hercules, other plane sales to Egypt 7-26; Begin vs 7-27, 570G2-B3
US-ROK F-16 deal agreed 7-26, 572G1
USSR Backfire rptd in sub exercise 7-28, 591A2
USSR deploymt lag rptd 8-22, 673G2
Peru purchases from USSR cited 8-31, 785C1
USSR-Ethiopia deal rptd 9-1, 684C3
US-Sovt bombers compared 751A3
Warsaw Pact, NATO compared 9-2, 686F1, C2
B-1 cut from '78 funds 9-9, 704F2-A3
NATO tactical force discouraged 9-10, 700D1
US backs Egypt MiG-21 aid, other jet sales 9-15, 698C1
UK cites NATO contributn 9-16, 957E1
US copter sale to Nigeria set 10-17, 986B3
B-1 revival fails in US House 10-20, 795E3
FB-111H study bid by Admin cited re B-1 revival effort 796A1
B-52, FB-111H, F-14, wide-bodied transport supplemental authorizatn cleared 11-3, 856F1-A2; signed 11-15, 1001E2
S Africa purchases cited 851E2
US denies Israel F-16 co-productn 11-8, 850D3
Iran buys 7 US AWACS, 16 F-16S 11-8, 905A3; Cong debate cited 11-16, 897A2
USSR aid to Ethiopia cited 11-17, 896B2
US plans F-16 contract competitn 11-21, 942B2
Grumman-Iran F-14 comm settlemt rptd 12-15, 978B1
US OKs Sudan F-5 sale 12-23, 1019C2

Atomic Weapons & Tests—*See also specific subheads in this section; for safeguards issue, see ATOMIC ENERGY—Industrial Use; for banning or control, see DISARMAMENT*
Intl Inuit conf vs tests 6-13—6-17, 619G2
France bars A-weapons abroad 6-23, 1012F3

1978

Egypt said to order French jets 3-1, 139B2
US, USSR bombers combat aircraft compared 3-6, 162A3, F3
B-1 fund rescissn signed 3-7, 160F2
French govt to acquire Dassault stock 3-8, 313E1
Saudis press US F-16 sale, US sen sees no sale 3-14, 176G3
Saudis rptdly hired US pub relatns co 3-31, 236F3-237B1
Kenya gets US F-plane shipmt 3-31, 289E2
USSR jets, napalm rptd in Angola 4-4, 265C2
Peru rpts Sovt paymts rolled back 4-9, 352A2
US assurnc to Israel on F-15s to Saudi rptd 4-10, 257G1
US F-16 review urged by GAO 4-24, 407D2
Carter sees Mideast sale as pkg deal, vs legis delay 4-25, 307A1, B1
Dayan vs US pkg deal 4-27, 299F2
US gen scores B-1 cancellatn 4-27, resigns 4-28, 321F2
US vows Thai sales 5-5, 360F3
US proposal for cruise missiles in 747s, B-52s rptd 5-7, 5-26, 423B1
Textron Ghana bribe evidence rptd destroyed 5-8, 448G3
US pledges more Israel F-15 sales 5-9, Saudi curbs 5-10; other Admin lobbying efforts rptd 5-15, 357D1
US Sen com splits vote on Mideast pkg, refers issue to Sen 5-11, 357G2
Saudis vs US jet pkg terms 5-12, stress need for F-15s 5-13, 358D2
US Sen meets on Saudi security, OKs Mideast jet pkg; Carter lauds vote 5-15, 357A1, C2, 358A1
US reassures Mideast jet sale opponents 5-15—5-16, 5-18, 358B1
Israel scores US Sen jet pkg OK; Egypt, Saudis laud 5-16, 358G1
NATO Eurogroup OKs US F-16 training, Lynx copter program 5-17, 398G1
US '77 arms bid rejctns rptd 5-19, 386G3, 387A1
NATO nears AWACS pact 5-19, 398E1
F-planes, VSTOL bombers authorized by US House 5-24, 406F3
New USSR A-bomber rptd 6-19, 518E3
A-6 used in cruise missile test, B-1 cancellatn affirmed 6-21, 493A2, C2
Spain rpts Mirage jet purchase 6-26, 649B2
USSR Backfire bombers, anti-sub jets seen 6-27, 563E3
US bars Taiwan F-4 sale 6-30, 506C1
US OKs Israel Kfir jet fighters sale to Taiwan 7-2, 7-4; Taiwan rejcts 7-6, 524D2
F-18 authorized by US Sen 7-11, 526G2
US Cong clears '79 authrzn 8-4, **Carter vetoes** 8-17, 621D1, B2-G2; House upholds 9-7, 677A2
U-2 (TR-1) NATO missns rise rptd 8-22, 748A3
Japan procuremt studies set 9-3, 694E1
US OKs Yugo jet engine sale 9-28, 758D1
India to buy Anglo-French Jaguar 10-6, 10-7, 796G3-797B1
US F-5E deal with Pak rptd, US denies 10-6; rpt Pak vs bid 10-16, 797B1
Harrier B V/STOL funded, copter chngs dropped 10-13, 833E1
Saudis deny funds to Egypt for US jet sale 10-19, delivery delayed 10-20, 783B2
'79 revised authorzn signed 10-20, 833G1
Backfire dispute persists in SALT 10-22—10-23, 803D3, 804D1
Sovt MiGs rptd successful vs cruise missile 10-23, 877C2
USSR MiGs to Tanzania, Uganda cited 11-2, 860C1
US again bars F-4s to Taiwan; OKs more F-5s, Kfirs 11-6, 872E2-A3
USSR MiG-23s rptd in Cuba 11-14, 905F1
Cuba spy photo flights resumed by US 11-16; Carter: USSR assured re MiGs 11-20, 1016F1
China MiGs in Zambia rptd 11-20, 912D1
USSR Backfire affected by US spy satellite leaks 11-23, 940A3
NATO lists '79 purchases 12-4, 954C3
AWACS, Nimrods purchase OKd by NATO 12-5, 954A2
French Assemb OKs Dassault share 12-8, 987G2
US AF grounds C-130 fleet 12-11, 984E2
US probes Rhodesia copters, Cessnas 12-13, 955E3
Rhodesia admits US copters in use 12-14, 1019G3
Backfire agreemt in SALT talks rptd 12-21, 995G3
US rpts USSR look-down radar, discounts anti-cruise missile defns 12-26, 1020C3

Atomic Weapons & Tests—*See also 'Neutron Bomb' and other subheads in this section; for safeguards and radiation issues, see ATOMIC Energy—Industrial Use; for banning or control, see DISARMAMENT*
US '77 rpt sees USSR parity, scores limited strike 1-6, 5E2
Carter State of Union Message 1-19, 29B1, A3, 31D2
CIA '74 documt on Israel weapon possessn, other natns capability released 1-26, 61F1
USSR strategy shift seen in Brookings study 1-29, 81E3
Brown sees US-USSR balance 2-2, 81C1

1979

Turkey-US controversy re U-2 flights 5-7—5-29, 397B3
Saudi-US talks on Egypt plane funding rptd 5-8, 341D2
US, USSR bombers compared 338F3
Saudis seen reneging on Egypt-US jet deal, buying Mirages 5-12, 360A1
Taiwanese pilots to fly N Yemen jets 5-29, 395F1
Egypt to buy China MiGs 6-5, 415A3
SALT II Backfire dispute 6-16—6-17, 449A2; Backfire statemt 6-16; treaty text 6-18, 450C2-457A2
Carter addresses Cong on SALT II, cites Backfire 6-18, 459B1, F1
China-Egypt jet exchng rptd 6-22, 475C1
Turkey mil chief, premr vs U-2 flights 6-24, 6-27, 488B2
SALT II Backfire terms scored in US 6-27, 496D3
US delays F-5s to Egypt re Saudi finance halt, OKs F-4s 7-6, 512A1
Nicaragua vs Israel, Argentina paymt 7-25, 574C1
W Ger threat to NATO AWACS deal rptd 8-1, 586E1
Morocco arms aid studied 8-2, 592B2
Iran intends F-14s disposal 8-10, 634D3
US studies Pak F-16 sale 8-11, 607F3
US sens get Kosygin pledge re Backfire 8-30, 657E2
US drops U-2 plan for SALT 9-12, 762D1
B-1 abandonmt scored by Ford 9-26, 739F2
US resumes jet, cargo spare parts shipmts to Iran 10-5, 773B3
Syria to get more MiG-25s 10-15, 857F2
US, S Korea to assemble F-5Es, F-5Fs 10-19, 803E2*
US Admin OKs Morocco sale 10-22, 803F3
US F-15, F-16 engine trouble rptd 10-24, 852G1-A3
UK Harrier sales to China seen 11-1, 854G1
US Sen com defeats SALT II Backfire 'killer amendmt' 11-6, 864B1
US halts Iranian flight training 11-23, 898G1
US CX-plane budget rptd 12-5, 924A1

Atomic Weapons & Tests—*See also other subheads in this section; for safeguards and radiation issues, see ATOMIC Energy—Industrial Use; for banning or control, see DISARMAMENT*
A-scientists 'doomsday clock' unchngd 1-1, 13D1
Sovt beam-weapon threat discounted 1-10, 52F3
US A-target chng urged 1-13, 52A3
Utah A-cancer apology asked 1-13, 91C1
Sovt A-test rptd 1-17, Japanese protest 1-19, 52D1
Carter budget proposals 1-22, 42F1
Carter State of Union Message 1-23, 47F2, D3, 48E1
US A-test rptd 1-24, 52E1
USSR '67-77 outlay rptd 1-25, 99B3
US '57 A-test, cancer linked; high radiatn rptd 1-29, 2-1, 91E1
USSR '78 A-tests set record 1-31, 109B2
US '53 A-test radiatn liabilty appeal lost, notificatn suit OKd 2-9, 112C2
21 DC protesters arrested 2-12, 133A2-A3
Utah '50s sheep deaths, child cancer rates rptd 2-14, 112F1-C2
More Nev A-test claims filed 2-23, 208C1
NATO A-attack documts rptd in defector's possessn 3-6, 180G3
'78 underground tests rptd 3-6, 625D3
US H-bomb article blocked 3-9, 193C2-194A1; 3-26, 230A1
A-war survivors said to face grim future 3-23, 232D2
UK Labor bars A-weapon ban 4-6, 267F3
US sees Pak A-arms threat 4-6, Pak denies 4-8, 277B2

1980

NATO plans Eur mil buildup 5-14, 377F2
Nixon trial order petitn re C-5A dismissal case rejected by Sup Ct 5-19, 440G1
Dow chrgs EPA spying 5-25, 387A3
US OKs China mil gear sale 5-29, 397F3
Ethiopia gets Sovt combat copters 6-13, 509B2
Saudis seek extra gear for F-15s 6-16; US weighs request; Israel, Sen Church vs 6-17, 450F1-D2
Saudi-US talks on F-15 gear 6-26; US sens vs 7-8; Saudis score 7-9, 538G2
Turkey bars USSR consultatn re U-2 7-4, 526C1
Canada OKs F-18 deal 7-8; US discount offered; NORAD, NATO benefits seen 7-11, 543E3
Egypt F-4E problems rptd 7-8, US squadron deployed for joint war games 7-10, 548A2
US GOP platform adopted 7-15, 536F1
US OKs Australia fighter sales 7-24, 561G3
Peru vs Sovt fighter purchase 7-28, 580B1
Japan plans more US purchases 7-29, 579D2
Japan research, dvpt urged 8-5, 635D3
US 'stealth' fighter said to evade radar 8-20, 630B2
Carter's brother denies Libya C-130 talks 8-21, 647D1
US rpt finds Iran rescue missn flawed 8-23, 644C1
Reagan scores 'stealth' plane disclosure; Brown, Perry testify on leaks 9-4, 665D3
Sovt Backfire used in Warsaw Pact maneuvers 9-8—9-11, 696F1
CX, 'stealth' bomber authrzn signed 9-8, 765B1
Australia-US B-52 base talks set; Australia plans fighter squadron 9-9, 705D1
CX funds appropriatn rejected by House, 'stealth' bomber funds OKd 9-16, 741G3, 742A1
US sends 4 AWACS to Saudis 9-30, 734A3
US sends more aid to Saudis 10-5, offers aid to other Gulf states 10-7, 758A1
US AWACS rpt on Iran-Iraq war 10-8; US sends KC-135's to Saudi 10-11, 773E2, G2
Iran scores US AWACS to Saudi 10-17, US assures 10-17—10-19, 798E2, B3
France OKs '81 spending hike 10-23, 886F1-A2
Carter lauds Iran, Israel jet success 10-24, 816A3
Carter vs some Saudi F-15 gear 10-24, US says undecided 10-27; Saudi scores 10-30, 821A1-F1
US OKs Israeli jet sale to Mex, Venez, Colombia 10-31, 865A2
CX appropriatn clears Sen; Navy, AF procuremt funds OKd 11-21, 896D3, E3
CX appropriatn clears Cong 12-5, 935A3; signed 12-15, 982B1
US dispatches AWACS on Poland fears 12-9, 929F2
Japan rpts USSR backfire bomber coastal deploymt 12-11, 953C1

Atomic Weapons & Tests—*See also DISARMAMENT & Arms Control*
A-scientists 'doomsday clock' moved up 1-1, 12C3
UK plans uranium enrichmt plant 1-9, 39B3
'70-79 underground tests totaled 1-17, 31E3
'79 A-blast mystery off S Africa unsolved 1-23, 49A3
Calif quakes force Livermore lab evacuatn 1-24—1-27, 80G2
Kennedy attacks Carter policies 2-20, 130C2
Israel test linked to '79 S Africa blast; denied 2-21, 141E3
Pak progrm seen bar to US aid 2-27, 165F2
Vienna conf backs plutonium fuel 2-27, 220D3
Reagan cites neutron bomb in 'basic speech' 2-29, 207F2; Connally 3-7, 184D2
US delays India uranium fuel shipmts 3-13, 182A1
Italy A-aid to Iraq seen; US concern noted 3-17, disputed 3-18, 220A3
Eniwetok Atoll resetld 4-9, 349A3
Colo A-plant protests held 4-19—4-20, 441F1
Calif lab cancer cases rptd 4-22, 356E3
DC protests held 4-26—4-28, 441G1
NRC bars India uranium sale 5-16, 440E3
UK Laborites vs neutron bomb 5-31, 429F2
US computer errors trigger A-alerts 6-3, 6-6, failed component blamed 6-17; Brown discounts war 6-9, valid warnings detailed 6-15, 457C3-458C2
UK A-weapons protested 6-22, 487E1
French Soclsts back neutron bomb research 6-25, neutron bomb rptd 6-26, 486B3

1976

US sales to China scored 11-4, 880B1
US arms taken by N Viet rptd 11-11, 961F2
Japan returns Sovt MiG-25 11-12, 908D1
B-1 contracts awarded 12-2, 942B1
NATO defers AWACS decisn, UK system cited 12-6—12-10, 933D1

Angola Aid Issue—*See ANGOLA*

Atomic Weapons—*See specific subheads in this section; also 'Weapons' under ATOMIC Energy; for banning or control, see DISARMAMENT*

Middle East Issues—*See appropriate subheads under MIDDLE EAST—INTERNATIONAL Developments*

1977

Carter defers neutron bomb decisn 7-12, 533A1, E1; facts on bomb 534A2
Neutron bomb a Carter town mtg topic 7-21, 575B1
US neutron bomb funds OKd 7-25, 592C3 ★
US assures S Korea 7-26, 572F1
USSR scores US neutron bomb dvpt 8-3, 590G1
28 CPs ask US neutron bomb ban 8-8, USSR scores funding 8-9, 8-16, 640E2
S Africa warned vs A-tests 8-22, 656F3
Carter rpts S Africa reassurances 8-23, 649E2
S Africa test rptdly headed off by USSR, Westn natns 8-28—8-29, 663A3
IISS assesses US-USSR balance 9-2, 686B2
Reprocessed reactor-fuel bomb use rptd 9-14, 812D2-B3
Neutron bomb debated at NATO mtgs 10-11—10-12, 12-6—12-7, 956G2
Neutron-bomb protesters arrested at Carter church 10-16, 797G2
S Africa denies bomb ban vow 10-23, 825D2
ERDA authorizatn, neutron bomb provisn signed 11-15, 878A1
French Pacific tests rptd 11-23, 11-25, 1013B1
NATO sees West losing parity 12-8, 941F3
'57 Nev test, cancer link probed 12-13, 1022C3

Helicopters—*See 'Aircraft' above*

Latin Issues—*See also other subheads in this section*

Latin '66-75 purchases rptd 4-8, 415A2, D2
US delays Latin police sales 7-17, 572E3
Peru purchases cited 9-1, 785B1
US sales to Guatemala rptd resumed 9-7, 706A3
Nicaragua to buy US arms 9-30, 767G2
Nicaragua rebel ldr asks US end aid 10-26, 864G3

Middle East Issues—*See also other subheads in this section*

Israel arms sales rptd 1-6, 1-8, 1-15; US consults Israel 1-8, 1-14, Honduran deal OKd 1-17, 28G2
Israel estimates '76, '77 shipmts 1-14, 28F3
US sales cited re NATO shortages 1-24, 70D2
US reviews Israel bomb sales 2-8, 88A3
US drops concussn bomb sale to Israel, others 2-17, 121D1
Egypt '67, '73 Sovt shipmts admitted 2-19, 144D2
Egypt asks US aid 4-4—4-5, 245A1
Leb asks US arms aid 4-25, 316B3
US assures Israel 5-11, 5-12, 360G3, 361D1
Saudis assured re US sales 5-24, 402D1
Austria defns min quits re Syria arms shipmt 5-30, 424D3
Libya asks US C-130 delivery 6-12, 488C1
France bars Pluton abroad 6-23, 1012G3
Egypt rpts China parts deal 6-25, 496D2
Carter seeks $115 mln arms sale to Israel 6-25, 511G1
US-Saudi secret pact rptd 6-27, 474E1
Guatemala buys Israeli rifles 7-6, 553E2
US OKs $250 mln aid for Israel 7-22, 570B3
Egypt suspends Sovt debt paymt 10-26, 811F3
Iran warns US vs sales ban 11-16, 897A2
US, USSR OK ABM accord 11-21, 997E1
US chrgs USSR ABM violatns 11-23, 997C1

1978

Haldeman chrgs USSR sought '69 attack vs China; USSR, US deny 2-16, 124A2
US CIA calls USSR civil defns overrated, DIA offcl disputes 2-17, 126G3
Australia-US monitoring statn declassified 3-1, 145A2
A-material ban rptdly backed by Vance, Defense Dept oppositn rptd 4-3, 277B2
Bikini islanders relocatn set, '54 bomb test cited 4-12, 278C2-A3
India confirms rpt of US A-device loss 4-17, 288B2
Low-fallout (RRR) bomb rptd studied 4-30, 407F1
Colo A-arms plant protest 5-1, 347F1
USSR scores US deploymt in Eur 5-26, 421A2
Carter affirms A-parity with USSR 6-7, 424A1
US civil defns reorganizatn proposed 6-19, 466G2
'45 Hiroshima pilot dies 7-1, 620F2
CIA issues USSR civil defns study 7-19, 563F3
French A-test in Pacific 7-19, 649D2
US vet wins A-test cancer claim 8-1, 702E3
A-foes mark Hiroshima anniv 8-6—8-7, 609B3
US edge over USSR rptd by ACDA 8-29, 676G3
Bikini islanders leave for Kili 8-31, 685A3
E-W balance assessed by IISS 9-1, 676B3
Turkey OKs US base reopening 10-4, 776G1
Australia concerned re A-waste, UK denies '50s test negligence 10-5—10-10, 771G2
Brazil A-power program lags 10-15, 836D3
GAO links A-plants, arms productn 10-23, 900F1
S Korea A-arms effort rptd 11-1, 862D3
A-test ban effect on arms reliability questnd 11-3, 877F1-B2
'77 world fallout rise rptd, '76 China A-test linked 11-5, 1000G3
Australia waste monitoring centralized 11-9, 900C2
Carter plans civil defns spending hike 11-12, 895E1
UK Aldermaston safety study released 11-21, 964E3
China test rptd 12-14, radioactive debris over US 12-23, 1001A2
Nev A-test site '47 debate rptd 12-18, 1012B1
Nev A-test claims filed 12-21, 1011F3

Firearms

US M60 described 71D3
Olin indicted for S Africa sales 3-14, 193G2; fined 3-30, 249E2; 6-1, 632G3
US M60 cache found in Ulster 4-3, 268B2
US artillery modernizatn order rptd 4-7, 253B1
US Cong clears '79 authrzn 8-4, Carter vetoes 8-17, 621C1; House upholds 9-7, 677A2
US issues WWII secret documts 9-10—9-18, 744D3
US '61-79 sales to Yugo rptd 9-28, 758E1
'79 ammunitn funds signed 10-13, 833D1
'79 revised authorzn signed 10-20, 833G1
Canada-S Africa deal suspected 11-6—11-7, 904G2

Foreign Developments—*specific subheads in this section; for U.S. foreign developments, see 'U.S.' below*

Leb arms shipmt to IRA rptd seized in Belgium 1-4, 7F3
USSR airlift to Ethiopia rptd halted 1-5, 3C3
Syria-Sovt deal rptd 1-11, 42B2
Somali-Egypt deal rptd 1-24, 44B1
USSR scores China-EC trade pact 2-9, 102C3; 4-4, 302G3
Saudi arms mfg city rptd planned 2-18, 199G1
Syria gets more Sovt arms 2-24, Egypt scores 2-25, 139D2, G2
France signs AIO pact; US, UK deals cited 3-14, 237B1, C1 ★
USSR, Turkey sign trade pact 4-5, 477D1
Israel rpts Sovt arms capture in Leb 4-12, 256D3
UK, Australia resrch pact rptd 4-18, 391E2
USSR proposes Turkey aid 4-26, Cyprus reassured 5-5, 477D1
UN rpts S Africa embargo compliance lags 4-28, 377A2
Brezhnev urges restraint 5-2, 417C1
W Ger aid pledge to Turkey rptd 5-15, 398F2
Argentina, Chile hike purchases 5-22—11-2, 860G2
$400 bln rptd spent on arms 5-23, 421B1
Saudi, Egypt pledge Zaire aid 6-1, 6-7, 6-13, 441G1
USSR aid to Rhodesia rebels rptd 6-6, 455D2
USSR '77 poor natns trade rptd 6-28, 634E3
OAS sets spending cut talks 7-1, 505C2
Fatah chrgs Iraq seizes arms plant, China cargo 7-17, 546C3
Rhodesia fines 3 in arms swindle 7-20, 616G2-C3
'76 worldwide spending rptd 7-23, 585A2
E-W balance assessed by IISS 9-1, 676G2
Camp David summit pact sets limits 9-17, 711B2

1979

Sovt superiority seen by US ex-mil ldrs 4-11, 295B1
'71, '75 Libya A-bomb bids rptd 4-14, 299C3
India bars A-bomb 4-20, sees Pak threat 5-3, 323D3
Terrorist 'backpack' A-bomb said possible 4-25, 327D2
US rpts Pak A-bomb materials purchase 5-1, 323E3
French-W Ger plutonium dispute resolved 5-16, 380C1
US '53 A-test radiatn liability case refused by Sup Ct 5-21, 400A3
France A-weapon policy re NATO cited 5-31, 415G3
US admits H-bomb documt security error 6-8, judge continues to block H-bomb article publicatn 6-15, 713C1, E1
Radiological weapons agrmt cited in SALT II communique 6-18, 457G3
US seeks giant USSR blast info 6-27, 625E3
US H-bomb article hearing order denied by Sup Ct 7-2, 559A1
Joint Chief's chrmn seeks modernizatn 7-24, 643D3
US film stars' deaths tied to '53 A-test 8-4, 630B1
US seeks Pak A-projct halt 8-11, Pak fears covert actn 8-14, 607C3
India warns of Pak A-race 8-15, 646C1
France reaffirms priority 9-11, 686G1
US judge bans H-bomb letter publicatn 9-15, 2 papers defy ban 9-16, 9-18, 713B1, B2; text of H-bomb letter, diagram 714D1-717E3
US ends effort to stop H-bomb article publicatn 9-17, 713A1
3 US scientists deny H-bomb letter chrgs 9-17, 714B2
'50s fallout, SAT decline linked 9-17, 747A2
Pak denies A-arms plan 9-22, 794D2
Franco-German joint force rejected 9-24, 733C1
US-Pak talks 10-17—10-18, 794B2
US rpts A-blast off S Africa 10-25, S Africa denies 10-26, 10-27, 824B3
'50s Kissinger-FBI link cited 11-3, 870B3
'56 UK air crash rptd 11-5, 845G1
US A-war alert placed 11-9, USSR scores 11-10, 11-16, 869F2-B3, 882D2
NZ rpts A-blast fallout 11-13, rpt disputed 11-14, 882F2

Firearms

USSR '74-77 artillery sales rptd 1-7, 13A2
US rpts doubt NATO defns capability 2-17, 147F3
US indicts 5 in Panama plot 5-14, 386C3
US M-2s rptd found 10-4, 852B1
US indicts Iranian smugglers 11-26, 898F2
US cites NATO ammunitn shortages 12-11, 959D2

Foreign Developments—*See also specific subheads in this section; for U.S. foreign developments, see 'U.S.' below*

Iran to review contracts 2-4, 82C2
USSR mil airlift to Viet rptd 2-22, 122B1
Iran to seek new sources 3-27, 229B1
Arab arms plant in Egypt to close 5-14, 359E3
Tunisia intercepts PLO arms for Nicaragua 7-11, 512E2
France-Iraq agrmt rptd 7-11, 564F1
Nicaragua junta vs Israel, Argentina paymt 7-25, 574C1
Nicaragua to seek Eur, Latin aid 8-31, 689A3
IISS assesses '79-80 mil balance; notes Sovt, 3d World efforts 9-4, 825A2-C3
Israel S Africa embargo compliance cited 9-7, 720D3
Morocco gets Egypt arms 9-8, 697G1
'80s spending forecast by Castro 10-12, 778D3
'77 world spending rptd 10-13, 804E1
Nicaragua IMF loan misuse rptd 11-27, 909F3
W Ger bars Iran exports 12-7, 934B1

1980

A-weapons dvpt appropriatn clears Cong 6-25, 9-10; Carter signs 10-1, 803F2
W Ger backs French modernizatn 7-11, 539G3
'79 A-blast dispute continues 7-14, 548E2
US GOP platform adopted 7-15, 536E1
Iraq denies A-weapon plans 7-20—7-21, Israel vs French deal 7-28, 573A3
Brazil scores arms race 7-28, 605G2
US A-war strategy revised 8-5, 591D3
US reassures allies on A-strategy shift, Muskie not consulted 8-8; Sovts score 8-11, 615D2-616B1
Moynihan scores Sovt increase 8-11, 612D3
Muskie regrets A-strategy ommissn, sees enhanced role 8-13, 630E2
Brown outlines A-strategy, ICBM vulnerability seen 8-20, 630D1
Carter defends A-strategy shift 8-21, 629F2
Carter blasts Reagan on A-race 9-2, 664A3
Sovt A-test rptd 9-14, US protests 9-15, 730F1
Ark A-missile silo blast kills 1 9-19, warhead removed 9-22; diagram 765E1
US, Sovts trade missile force data 9-26, 776G3-777C1
Nigeria hints A-bomb dvpt 10-3, 792D2
Carter assails Reagan on A-superiority 10-16, 10-19, 802E2, A3
China conducts test 10-16, fallout hits US 10-20, 828A3
France OKs '81 spending hike 10-23, 886F1
Carter, Reagan TV debate 10-28, 814F2
Anderson answers TV debate questns 10-28, 815G3
Carter hits Reagan on A-arms 10-29, 816C2
US computer error A-alert rpt issued 10-29, 986B3
Carter plans spokesman role, on Reagan policy support 11-12, 865F2, A3
A-arms authrzn clears Cong 12-1, signed 12-17, 981B1
Pope issues social justice encyclical 12-2, 969G3

Firearms

US OKs Taiwan gun sale 1-3, 11G2
Turkey, US sign aid pact 3-29, 255F3
NATO OKs ammunitn buildup 5-14, 377E2
Panama denies El Salvador gunrunning 6-16, 462D3
S Africa displays SWAPO Sovt bloc equipmt 7-2, 525B1
US airlift to Thai starts, USSR scores 7-5, 508B1
Canada fines co for S Africa sales 8-14, 618F2
Small arms added funds rejected by House 9-16, 742B1
France OKs '81 spending hike 10-23, 886G1

Foreign Developments—*See also specific subheads in this section; for U.S. foreign developments, see 'U.S.' below*

China to hike Afghan rebel aid 1-16, 31A2
Sovts vow arms to Syria 1-27—1-29, 140D3
Egypt: Sovts use Saudi air space to ship S Yemen arms 1-28, 69A2
Cuban aid to El Salvador rebels rptd 3-27, 220C2
NATO plans Eur mil buildup 5-14, 377E2
India-Sovt pact 5-28, 398A1
UK Laborites back spending cuts 5-31, 429E2
W Ger seeks Eur mil balance 6-23, 474F1
UK lifts Chile arms embargo 7-22, Amnesty Intl protests 9-8, 749E1
Peru vows spending cuts 7-28, 580B1
Japan research, dvpt urged 8-5, 635B3
USSR rptdly denies Iraq request 9-21—9-22, 719D1
Sovt arms stockpiles rptdly sent to Iraq 10-6, 757C1
Iran seeks world arms purchase 10-7; N Korea sale rptd 10-8, 757F2
UN war rules accord endorsed 10-10, 777E1
UK vs arms to Iran, Iraq 11-4; Iraq seeks arms from USSR, 4 others 11-11—11-12, 879G2
Jordan seeks Westn arms speedup 12-1, 911B3
Kenya, Ethiopia urge Somali shipmt ban 12-4, 933A2
Sovt, E Eur, China '79 3d World sales rptd 12-10, 933A2

1976

Missiles & Rockets

Australia, UK SAM deal rptd 1-6, 7E3
Yugo seeks US TOWs 1-13, 55D1
Ford State of Union message 1-19, 38G2
'77 US budget proposals 1-21, 63F3, 64A1, B1
US Pacific, Indian O mil capabilities evaluated 1-25, 68G2
Pentagon rpt to Cong issued 1-27, 68B2
Pentagon backs cruise missile dvpt 2-6, 183F1
Brookings study backs cruise missiles for B-52s 2-8, 183A2
US-Sovt supplies, research compared 2-17—2-27, 182F2-C3
UK-Australia rocket range to close 2-18, 154C3
Australia rpts US frigate deal 2-18, 154C3
Navy, AF cruise missile tests vary 2-20, 2-24, 3-5, 183A1
China ICBM projct rptd dropped 2-24, 190C1
3 US sens back US, Sovt cruise missile test halt 2-25, Kissinger vs halt 2-26, 183D1
Covert Sovt arms sales to Chile rptd 2-25, 288E3
US, Sovt ICBMs, SLBMs compared 2-27, 182F2
India rpts Pak buildup 3-31, 278B3
SAM missiles in Somalia rptd 4-5, 242G1
US House OKs '77 authorizatn, rejcts MaRV test ban 4-9, 283D2
Reagan compares US-Sovt strength 4-10, 281B3
Ford seeks more Minuteman funds 4-26, 307C3
French Cabt OKs '77-82 defense budget 5-5, 417F2
US Sen OKs '77 authorzn 5-26, 411C2, G2-A3
USSR rocket aid to Mozambique rptd 6-12, 427B2
Ford OKs '77 authorizatn 7-14, 516F3, 517A1
US '77 request, authorizatn table 517A2
Sovt Medit strength rptd 7-22, 558C3
GOP platform text cites 8-18, 608G3
French-Egypt deal rptd set 8-27, 675A1
Sovt MIRV buildup cited 8-31, 739D1
Sovt arms in Libya parade 9-2, 682D3
US-Sovt balance rptd 9-3, 760B3
US '77 funds signed, table 9-22, 707B1, E1
US Sen com vs Saudi sale 9-24, 746B3
Rumsfeld on Sovt deploymt 9-27, 961F1
Sovt electronic lag rptd 10-5, 961C1
Pentagon offcl cited re Condor 10-14, 983A1
Sunken F-14 missile recovered 10-31, 941E1
US sens ask NATO reinforcemts 11-14, 879E3
NATO sees Sovt SS-20 threat 11-18, 879D2
UK, Iran deal signed 11-18, 906F1
Sovt aid to Rhodesia rebels rptd 11-18, 1009E3
US Army overspending rptd 11-19, 982A3
Sovt-built silos in Laos rptd 12-27, 1013C1

Political Payments Issues—*See under BUSINESS*

1977

Missiles & Rockets

US rpts Sovt ICBM dvpt 1-3, 39B3
Proxmire cites MIRV, Trident, cruise progrms 1-5, 40D1
Sovt sales to Peru cited 1-10, 2A3
Trident, M-X cruise funds authorized; Aegis carrier 7-14, 576A1, E1; signed 7-30, 592A2
2 seized in Fla re cruise info 7-20, 576A3
Carter on USSR dvpt, backs mutual cuts 7-21, 550C3
USSR scores cruise missile deploymt 8-3, 590G1; 8-16, 640E2
USSR ICBM tech lag rptd 8-22, 673G3
USSR-Ethiopia deal rptd 9-1, 684C3
US-Sovt ICBMs, SLBMs, MIRVs, Minuteman compared 751A3
Warsaw Pact, NATO compared 9-2, 686F1, C2
NATO cruise deploymt urged 9-10, 700D1
China tests A-tipped missile 9-12, 706B2
Women to be assigned to US sites 9-23, 777C3
US backs M-X dvpt, Minuteman vulnerability compared; arms control impact feared 10-6—10-8, 777A1
NATO fears cruise missile, SALT compromise 10-11—10-12, 956C3
Carter sees MIRV limit progress 10-27, 814A1
Cruise scored 10-29, Pentagon defends 11-1, 857C3
Cruise, M-X supplemental authorizatn cleared 11-3, 856E1; signed 11-15, 1001E2
S Africa purchases cited 851E2
Lance warhead productn authorizatn signed 11-15, 878C1
US plans cruise missile contract competitn 11-21, 942B2
Trident sub delay, cost overrun rptd 11-29, 919G3, 920A1 ★
Poseidons to carry Tridents 11-29, 920C1
Jane's vs cruise missile substitutn for B-1 12-7, 942C1

Payments Issues—*See under BUSINESS*

Sales—*See also other appropriate subheads in this section*

Carter for export controls 1-24, 51E3
NATO shortages rptd, US Mideast sales cited 1-24, 70C2
US bids France curb sales 1-29, 69F1, B2
US drops concussn bomb sales 2-17, 121E1
Carter sets arms-sales policy 5-19, 380D2
Carter seeks arms sale curbs 7-28, 574G2
France confrms Pak A-deal 9-8, 1013A1
NATO sales to Turkey rptd 9-25, 957F1
US sales to Taiwan scored by Peking 10-2, 10-4, 781A1
Carter backs curbs in UN speech 10-4, 752F1
US to hike Yugo sales 10-13, 785G3
US forgn mil credit funds OKd by Cong 10-19, 815F2; signed 11-1, 834D1
US '77 arms sales rptd 11-11, 920C1
France bars curbs 11-22, 1012E3
US, USSR discuss curbs 12-14—12-16, '77 data cited 996E3
Ford State of Union backs ICBM, Trident progrm 1-12, 13F3
Ford '78 budget requests 1-17, 30B3, E3-31D1
Rumsfeld backs M-X 1-18, 39F1
NATO shortages rptd 1-24, 70C2
Brown proposes '78 budget cuts 1-25, 1-26, 2-2, 94C3
Sovt edge denied 1-30, 70A3
W Ger OKs Turkey, Indonesia sales 2-2, 139E2
Carter asks US-USSR missile dvpt halt, notice of test launches 2-8, 88A2
Carter budget revisns 2-22, 125D1
2 US execs sentncd for Sovt sales 3-14, 203F2
USSR rejcts US SALT levels 3-30, 225B1, A2
Sovt-Kuwait aid pact signed 4-13, 394D3
US pullout from S Korea starts 4-14, 306A2
Cruise missiles set for SAC 4-24, 343F2
Sovt SAM-7s rptd in Mozambique 4-24, 456E3
House cuts cruise missile funds 4-25, 324B1
USSR antimissile beam rptd 5-2, US discounts, cites research 5-2, 5-3, 343D3
More Minuteman IIIs ordrd 5-3, 343B3
Cruise missile SALT role debated 5-6, 5-18, 401C1
US-UK mil info exchng OKd 5-16, 379G3
US, USSR OK SALT levels 5-20, 400G2-A3
US defends new Minuteman III warhead 6-1, 462B1
USSR SS-20 deploymt rptd 6-9, 530G1
Wernher von Braun dies 6-16, 532G3
Carter backs cruise missile 6-30, 514C1
Lance warhead decisn deferred 7-12, 534B2

1978

Syria gets more Sovt arms 10-5—10-6, 762C2
USSR warns vs China sales by W Eur 10-26, 814B1
UK sends arms to Zambia 10-27, 10-28, 829E3-830A1
USSR-France tensns re France-China deal cited 10-29, 830G3
Canada-S Africa deal suspected 11-6—11-7, 904E2
UN asks arms ban vs Israel 11-27, 931A3
NATO sets '79 arms list 12-4, 954B3

Helicopters—*See 'Aircraft' above*

Missiles

Syria-Sovt deal rptd 1-11, 42C2
Carter budgets Trident, cruise, M-X, Minuteman, others 1-23, 45C1, A2, 46A1
Israel A-warhead dvpt rptd in '74 CIA rpt 1-26, 61F1
Brown rpts Sovt ICBM, other advances; notes US M-X dvpt 2-2, 81D1, G1
US affirms Asia commitmt; vows Trident, cruise missile deploymt 2-20, 126D3
USSR SS-20 scored by UK 2-21; facts on 140F1
USSR SS-16 deploymt rptd 2-22, 298G1
Sweden protests USSR sub patrols 3-1, 291A3
US, USSR ICBMs, MIRVs, tactical missiles compared 3-6, 162F2-A3, B3
Carter warns USSR vs mil buildup 3-17, 202D1, C2
US short-range missile modernizatn order rptd 4-7, 253B1
NATO A-group concerned re US cruise missile dvpt 4-19; Haig resignatn threat rptd, denied 4-25, 298D2, F2
Vance reassures NATO on cruise missile 4-24, US-USSR talks rptd 4-25, 297D1
NATO multiple rocket launch system rptd 4-25, 299A1
Sen votes budget target res, M-X backing cited 4-26, 305C3
US proposal for cruise missiles in 747s, B-52s rptd 5-7, 5-26, 423B1
NATO Eurogroup OKs Swingfire program 5-17, 398A2
M-X delay backed by OMB, Trident option cited 5-24, 407B1
Brookings Inst sees threat to US land missiles 5-24, 407E1
USSR SS-20 deploymt scored by US 5-24, 421D1
US sees cruise missile defns edge 6-1, 407F2
Cruise missile tested in pub, Sovt SA-10 defns seen inadequate 6-21, 493A2
USSR SAMs seen, US cruise missile cited 6-27, 563E3
New US MAP land-based missile plan rptd 7-12, 528G3
MAP plan scored by USSR 7-23, Warnke defends 8-24, 747A3
US Cong clears '79 authrzn 8-4, **Carter vetoes** 8-17, 621D1, D2; House upholds 9-7, 677A2
US rpts laser use vs anti-tank missiles 8-23, 683E3-684A1
US edge over USSR rptd by ACDA 8-29, 677B1
E-W balance assessed by IISS 9-1, 676B3
China ICBM deploymt rptd possible 9-1, 676F3
US issues WWII documts on V2 rocket 9-10—9-18, 744D3
US reps protest MAP plan 9-22, AF chief backs 9-23, 737D3
US studies gen purpose missile as Trident, M-X replacemt 9-26, 738B1
Trident components funded 10-13, 833E1
Lance warhead parts productn ordrd 10-18, authorzn signed 10-25, 833D2
France to sell China anti-aircraft, antitank missiles 10-20, 814A1
'79 revised authorzn signed 10-20, 833G1
SALT cruise missile limit plan revised, MIRV, other issues discussed 10-22—10-23, 803D3-804D1
Sovt success vs cruise missile rptd, ships rptd armed 10-23, 877C2
Zambia gets UK Tigercats 10-27, 829E3-830A1
US sees cruise missile improvemts 11-14, 1020E3
M-X, Trident 2 in '79 suplmtl budget request 11-15, 916C3
USSR SS-20 affected by US spy satellite leaks 11-23, 940A3
Carter: no decisn on Trident 2, M-X 11-30, 916B3
NATO lists '79 purchases 12-4, 954C3
MAP backed by Nitze 12-14, 996B2
SALT agrmts, compromises on cruise missiles, MIRVs rptd, pact delayed 12-21—12-23, 995A3-G3
USSR A-data encoding limit rptd OKd 12-21, 995B3
US rpts look-down radar, discounts anti-cruise missile defns 12-26, 1020C3

Neutron Bomb

USSR warns NATO vs deploymt 1-23, 103C2
USSR seeks Austria aid 2-8, 110E2
UK scores Sovt campaign 2-21, 140D1
Dutch dispute 2-24—3-8, defns min resigns 3-4, 169D1-B2
US links defermt, Sovt arms restraint 3-10; USSR rejcts trade-off 3-11, hints talks 4-4, 254F1
Dutch forum, protest rally 3-18—3-19, 255C1
Carter cancellatn rumor sparks furor, senators protest 4-4—4-7, 253C1, G2
Carter defers productn, asks comparable Sovt restraint 4-7; NATO, W Ger deploymt issue cited 4-17, 253A1, E1

1979

Helicopters—*See 'Aircraft' above*

Missiles

Glossary of terms 450F3
US A-target chng urged 1-13, 52A3
Carter budgets Trident, cruise, MX, Minuteman, others 1-22, 42A2, 43C1-C2, E2
Carter State of Union Message cites Poseidon 1-23, 47D3, 48E1
US ICBMs rptd vulnerable, mobile missiles urged 1-25, 52F2
USSR warned re data encoding 1-31, 258F2
USSR long-range cruise tests rptd 2-1, 99E3
US concerned re Iran Phoenix safety 2-12, 106D1
US to equip Israel F-16s 2-13, 143A3
Egypt asks US Hawks 2-16–2-18, 143C3
USSR SS-20 threat seen, W Ger missile deploymt hinted 2-20, 148A1
Chinese rpt 7 Viet sites destroyed 2-27, 141E1
Boeing MX info leak alleged 3-1, 207D2
US to speed antitank missiles to N Yemen 3-7, 179C1
14-MIRV SS-18 '78 test rptd 3-13, 258G2
Israel Sinai exit schedule 249F2
Brown sees MX, cruise need re SALT 4-5, 258B1
Trident sub launch fails 4-10, 307B3
USSR ICBM, SS-20 threat seen 4-11, 295A1-F1
USSR tactical SS-21 deploymt rptd 4-23, 340E1
Carter concerned re vulnerability 4-25, 294G2
NATO A-arms modernizatn urged, Sovt capacity cited 4-25, 340A1
US spy satellite data rptd compromised 4-28, 318B3
US, USSR '79, '72 ICBMs, SLBMs, MIRVs compared 338E3
NATO error re USSR SS-21 deploymt rptd 5-23, 399E1
Carter on MX deploymt 5-29, 402D1
Brown sees USSR first strike ability, MX dvpt seen 5-30, 410A2
NATO unified policy re SALT III, A-modernization urged 5-30–5-31, 415E3
USSR SS-18, SS-19 warheads yields seen lower 5-31, 410C1
Carter OKs MX dvpt, Minuteman cited 6-8; Sovt, US reactn 6-9–6-11, 437E2-438D1
MX authorized by US Sen 6-13, 438E1
US gen sees Minutemen vulnerability in '80s 6-15, 460B2
Ballistic, cruise, MX missiles cited in SALT II pact text 6-18, 450E1-456G2
Carter addresses Cong on SALT II; cites ballistic, cruise, MX missiles 6-18, 459B1
SALT II terms scored in US 6-27, 496D3
MX scored by Gov Brown 6-29, 496G3
MX dvpt funds clear US Cong 7-17, 7-20, Carter signs 7-25, 700A2
Haig scores SALT II protocol re cruise deploymt ban 7-26, 643B3
USSR denies US 1st-strike capability, ICBM chrgs 8-2, 644F1
AFL-CIO seeks A-warheads curb 8-7, 591F1
India rocket assessed 8-11, 626B3
Carter chooses 'racetrack' MX deploymt plan; diagram 9-7, 677F2, 678A2
W Ger defns paper cites Sovt strength 9-24, 733E1
MX deploymt delay scored by Ford 9-26, 739F2
Carter cites '62 USSR-Cuban crisis 10-1, 738E2
SALT verificatn assessed by Sen com 10-5, 762A1
USSR offers Eur A-missile freeze 10-6; NATO, W Ger, US vs 10-7, 10-9, 761E1, A3-F3
USSR vs NATO A-missiles, offers cuts 10-13–11-6, 880F2
ICBM, Backfire, MX, cruise missiles cited in US Sen com SALT votes 10-15–10-31, 822C2-B3
US sen reassured by Carter on MX dvpt 10-25, 822C3
China premr backs NATO A-missiles 11-5, 854D2
USSR warns vs NATO A-missiles 11-7, 856F2
USSR SS-18 aided by US trade 11-8, 857B1
NATO group backs A-missiles 11-14, 880A2
USSR warns W Ger vs NATO A-missiles 11-21–11-24, 938A3
MX dvpt funds included in '80 mil constructn bill 11-30, 945G1
E Ger scores NATO A-missiles 12-5, 938D3
Dutch parlt rejects NATO A-missile plan, W Ger Soc Dems back 12-6, 938C2, E2
US seeks NATO A-missile plan support, SS-20 cited 12-7, 938D1

1980

Missiles

USSR rejects Eur A-missile talks 1-3, 4A3
US OKs Taiwan sale 1-3, 11G2
Cruise missile crashes rptd 1-7, 16F2
Turkey-US bases accord set 1-9, 22G2
UK A-weapon plans revealed 1-24, 79F1
USSR '79 outlays estimated by CIA, US ICBM spending compared 1-27, 65E2
Carter budgets Trident, cruise, MX, Patriot, others 1-28, 71E1-G1, D2
Australia-US missile frigate talks set 2-19, 132E1
Reagan 'basic speech' cites neutron warhead, cruise, MX, Trident 2-29, 207F2
Connally cites MX, Trident in 'basic speech' 3-7, 184D2
US tank detector system rptd 3-21, 267D1
Cruise missile contract to Boeing 3-25, 288D1
Gen Dynamics wins short-range cruise contract 4-2, 267B3
Europn CPs vs NATO A-missile deploymt 4-29, 327C3
MX deploymt rptd chngd 5-6, 369B2
US outlay increase urged 5-9, 369B3
China rpts ICBM test 5-18, 389A1
USSR vs NATO A-missile nondeploymt offer 5-19, 378B3
UK Laborites vs cruise missiles 5-31, 429F2
W Ger rpts USSR vs A-missile freeze 6-9; Schmidt gets Carter letter 6-16, seeks mtg 6-18, 450B3-451D1
USSR warns W Ger vs NATO A-missiles 6-12, 451D1
UK sets cruise missile sites 6-17, 486G3
US, Italy back NATO A-missile deploymt 6-20, W Ger seeks Eur balance 6-23, 474F1, C2
Dem platform backs MX 6-24, 479A3, C3
Schmidt, Brezhnev in A-missile talks, negotiatns seen 6-30—7-1; US comments 7-2, 489B1
S Africa displays SWAPO Sovt bloc equipmt 7-2, 525B1
Carter weighs Sovt talks proposal 7-5, 506A1
US GOP platform adopted; text 7-15, 536E1, D2
W Ger urges NATO A-deploymt 7-15, 540A1, C1
UK Trident acquisitns set 7-15, 544A2
US A-war strategy revised 8-5, 591F3
Dem plank on MX, Trident, cruise missile adopted 8-13, 611C2, 615B2
Anderson vs MX 8-19, 630A1
US Minuteman vulnerability seen 8-20, 630D1
Anderson platform offered 8-30, 665A2
Carter signs MX authrzn 9-8, 765B1
Sovt ABM system rptd updated 9-14, 730A3
MX deploymt funds stay rejected by House 9-16, 741D3
US rep chrgs Sovt SALT violatns, US denies 9-18, 730C2
Sovt ICBMs rptd accurate, said US threat 9-18, 730E3
Belgium OKs US A-missile deploymt 9-19, 737B2
Ark A-missile silo blast kills 1 9-19, warhead removed 9-22; diagram 765E1
Reagan, Anderson debate MX 9-21, 721E2, 722B1
US, Sovts trade force data 9-26, 776G3
MX need rptd distorted 10-5, 897B1
France OKs '81 spending hike 10-23, 886F1
Nev voters bar MX installatn 11-4, 847D3
MX sites chosen 11-18, 897A1
MX funds cut rejected by Sen 11-21, 896D3

1976

Ships & Submarines

Rpt allied A-ships offered Australia ports use 1-15, 26D2
House intellignc com rpt leaked 1-20, 93A3
'77 US budget proposals 1-21, 63F3, 64A1, A2
Australia sets A-ship rules for ports use 1-22, 46D1
US-Spain A-subs agrmt 1-24, 77A1
French sub gets H-bomb warheads 1-24, 139B2
US Pacific, Indian O mil capabilities evaluated 1-25, 68G2
Pentagon rpt to Cong issued 1-27, 68B2
US 600-ship fleet rptd abandoned 1-27, 68E2
Iran may drop US destroyer purchase 2-4, 102D1
Pentagon backs cruise missile dvpt 2-6, 183F1
Australia to OK US navigatn base 2-17, 137C2
Australia rpts US missile deal 2-18, 154C3
Navy, AF cruise missile tests vary 2-20, 2-24, 3-5, 183A1
3 US sens back US, Sovt cruise missile test halt 2-25, Kissinger vs halt 2-26, 183D1
US-Sovt figures rptd 2-27, 182F2-G2
Pacific Forum backs US presence 3-8—3-9, 179B2
US, Sovt naval strength compared 3-10—5-15, 394E1-D3
Australia OKs US base 3-23, 237D1
India rpts Pak gunboats 3-31, 278B3
Navy to pay shipyds 4-8, 309A2
US House OKs '77 authorizatn 4-9, 283A2, D2
Reagan compares US-Sovt strength 4-10, 281B3
US Admin asks '77 budget hike 5-4, 394B1
Navy shipyd overrun paymts disputed 5-4—6-10, 453D3
French Cabt OKs '77-82 defense budget 5-5, 417F2
US Sen OKs '77 authorzn 5-26, 411B2, E2-A3
Ford OKs '77 authorizatn 7-14, 516F3, 517A1, D1
US '77 request, authorizatn table 517A2
Mondale carrier stand cited 512C3
Sovt Medit strength rptd 7-22, 558B3
S Africa buys 2 French warships 7-31, 714C1
Australia budgets US purchase 8-17, 636F3
GOP platform text cites 8-18, 608G3
US A-ship in NZ spurs dock strike 8-27—9-2, 677E2
US frigate, Sovt sub collide 8-28, 941B3
US A-ship in Australia prompts dock strike 9-7, 691C3
Plane lost off Kennedy 9-14, recovered 11-11, 941E1
Kennedy, Bordelon collide 9-14, Bordelon decommissn set 12-3, 941E2
US '77 funds signed, table 9-22, 706G3, 707F1
Australia sets spending plan 11-4, 850A2
US arms taken by N Viet rptd 11-11, 961F2
W Eur navies scored, Sovt sub threat cited 11-15, 879B3
US A-carrier cost estimate cited 11-16, 982E3

Soviet Armaments (including U.S.-Soviet developments)—*See also specific subheads in this section*

Sovt arms aid to S Yemen rptd 1-14, 52A2
US-Sovt weapons study released 2-10, 182G2
US defense aide rpts on Sovt new weaponry, research 2-15, 2-26, 182A3
Cong gets Pentagon-CIA data on US, Sovt spending 2-27; data challenged 3-5, 3-7, 182F1-E2
US-Sovt weapons compared 2-27, 182F2
NATO on Sovt buildup 5-21, 353A1
Namibia, Rhodesia rebels Sovt arms use rptd 9-15, 681E1
CIA hikes Sovt spending estimate 10-5, 960E3

1977

Ships & Submarines

Proxmire cites Trident progrm 1-5, 40C1
UK sales to Peru cited 1-10, 2B3
Ford State of Union backs Trident progrm 1-12, 13F3
Ford '78 budget requests 1-17, 30B3, 31C1
Rumsfeld backs Trident, expanded fleet 1-18, 39E1, B2
Brown proposes '78 budget cuts 1-25, 1-26, 94C3
W Ger OKs Indonesia sub sale 2-2, 139E2
US Navy settles shipbldg cost claims 2-11, 3-8, 232A2
Carter budget revisns 2-22, 125B1, E1
Nimitz carrier, A-cruiser funds rescinded 3-15, 195C3
Litton unit indicted re overruns 4-6, 344A1
NATO standardizatn progress rptd 5-14, 359F3
US sells 2 warships to Pak 5-19, 450E3
Canada to buy Lockheed Orion anti-sub aircraft, 20 warships 7-13, 579E3
Trident, Nimitz, Aegis, other procuremt funds authorized; Seafarer 7-14, 576A1-F1; signed 7-30, 592A2
US funds Israeli boat productn 7-22, 570C3
USSR exercise rptd 7-28, 591E1
USSR deploymt lag rptd 8-22, 673G3
'77-78 Jane's rpts USSR sub superiority 8-25, 686E2
US-Sovt SLBMs compared 751A3
NATO forces scored 9-10, 700E1
UK cites NATO contributn 9-16, 957D1
US, USSR Indian O deploymt rptd 9-26, 992B2
Bodine wins United Tech suit 9-28, 860D1
US-Australia base pact OKd 10-19, 800F3
S Africa purchases cited 851E2
France cancels S Africa sales 11-8, 883B1; 934D2
French A-sub funds dropped 11-19, 924G1
Guinea seeks US patrol boats 11-19, 989G1
Nigeria gunboat purchases rptd 11-23, 986G2
Trident delay, cost jump rptd 11-29, 919G3, 920A1 ★
Poseidons to carry Trident missiles 11-29, 920C1
NATO sees Sovt hovercraft threat 12-8, 941D3
Mich backed for Seafarer 12-15, 977D3-978B1

1978

USSR calls deferral 'maneuver' 4-7, 4-8, 254C1
NATO wary on US deferral, EC silent 4-7; ldrs rptd concerned re Carter handling 4-8—4-9, 254B2, 258F1
Pub controversy detailed 4-9, 253G1
W Ger clarifies deploymt stand, warns US vs sudden policy shifts 4-12, 254A3
French test rptd 4-17, govt denies 4-24, 312G3
NATO A-group backs US decisn 4-19, 298A2
Australians protest French test 4-21, 311C1
USSR seeks US-USSR restraint, Carter vs USSR offer 4-25, 297A2, 307A2
Haig resignatn threat rptd, denied 4-25, 298E2-B3
US gen scores delay 4-27, resigns 4-28, 321F2
Brezhnev warns West vs deploymt 5-2, in W Ger 5-4—5-7, 417A1, C1
Gromyko scores at UN 5-26, 421A2
Schmidt reviews Carter talks 6-1, 519C2
US gen continues to score Carter on deferral 6-2, 433B2
US Sen com urges stockpile, cites NATO defns; Carter indecisn scored 6-11, 469A3
Carter orders parts productn 10-18, signs authorzn 10-25; USSR scores 8-26, 833B2, E2
USSR rpts early tests 11-17, 905D1

Ships & Submarines

US '77 rpt cited re naval expansn curb 1-6, 5G2
Carter budget proposals 1-23, 45G1, A3
Brown rpts Sovt sub missile advances; notes US Trident, other naval programs 2-2, 81D1, A2, D2
Portsmouth shipyd workers radiatn-cancer link probed 2-19, 2-28, 164E1, B3
US affirms Asia commitmt, vows Trident deploymt 2-20, 126D3
US debates nuclear vs oil-fueled carriers 2-21, 2-23, 127G1
US blocks patrol boats to Ethiopia 2-22, 137C2
US Navy sees Sovt sub threat 2-23, 127C2
Sweden protests USSR sub patrols 3-1, 291A3
US, USSR sub missiles, surface ships compared 3-6, 162A3, B3, F3
Gen Dynamics warns work stoppage on US A-subs 3-13, temporary accord reached 3-23, 224C1
Carter warns USSR vs mil buildup 3-17, 202C2
US shipbldg goals cut 3-24, 223F2
US Navy secy on carrier type, Admin shipbldg cuts 3-27, 223F3 ★
Litton overrun indictmt dismissal reversed 4-5, 368F1
Trident cost overruns seen by GAO 4-13, 407A2
UK, Australia resrch pact rptd 4-18, 391F2
Sen votes budget target res, expansn backing cited 4-26, 305C3
NATO Eurogroup OKs torpedo progrm 5-17, 398A2
US '77 arms bid rejctns rptd 5-19, 387A1
US arrests Sovt spies 5-20, 409A3, B3
A-carrier, Aegis authorized by US House 5-24, 406E3
Trident deploymt study urged by OMB 5-24, 407D1
US antisub edge asserted 5-24, 407B3
Carter threatens carrier authorizatn veto 6-8, 432A1
US to sell China detectn equipmt 6-9, 436E2
Gen Dynamics, Navy settle A-sub contract dispute 6-9, 469A1
US Navy sets sub cost study, seeks Trident, 688-attack sub alternatives 6-14, 469E2
Litton, Navy settle LHA, destroyer contract dispute 6-20, 469A2
Lockheed cleared on overbilling chrg 6-22, 493B3
China to review Zaire aid 6-24, 652G2
USSR anti-sub emphasis seen 6-27, 563D3
Proxmire scores Navy 'bailout' of Gen Dynamics, Litton 7-6, 528B3
UK Polaris workers strike 7-7—8-13, 650A1
A-carrier authorized by US Sen 7-11, 526E2
French test A-sub warheads 7-19, 649E2
US Navy settles Lockheed '71 claims 7-28, 665E3
US Cong clears '79 authrzn 8-4; **Carter vetoes, scores A-carrier funds** 8-17, 621A1-G2; veto upheld by House 9-7, 677A2
Carter dedicates USS Miss 8-5, 605F3
A-carrier funds pass US House 8-9, 604C2
Seychelles denies Sovt sub base offer 8-20, 692D1
E-W balance assessed by IISS 9-1, 676E3
US issues WWII documts 9-10—9-18, 744E2, A3
US studies gen purpose missile as Trident replacemt 9-26, 738D1
Litton overrun indictmt ruling refused by Sup Ct 10-2, 751A2
Turkey OKs US base reopening 10-4, 776G1
US A-sub theft plot foiled 10-4, 824F1; 2 convicted 12-14, 12-19, 992E1
Trident components funded 10-13, 833E1

1979

NATO OKs US Pershing II, cruise deploymt 12-12; USSR, E Ger score 12-13–12-17, 12-12, 959D1-B2, E2-A3
Carter cites MX, cruise dvpt 12-12, 963E1
USSR negative on US Eur A-missile reductn talks 12-13, 12-14, 12-16, 959F2
Dutch govt backed on NATO A-missiles 12-20, 959E2

Ships & Submarines

US, USSR '74-77 sales compared 1-7, 13A3
Carter budgets Trident, carrier, others 1-22, 42A2, 43B1, C2
Carter State of Union Message cites Poseidon 1-23, 47D3, 48E1
US Navy plans ship retiremt 1-23, 89B3
US subs rptd aging 1-25, 52F2
USSR '67-77 sub outlay rptd 1-25, 99B3
Cuba gets Sovt sub, torpedo boats 2-10, 109B3
USSR reinforces E China Sea fleet 2-21, 122B1
US sends warships to back Saudis in Yemen war 3-5, 157E2
US A-sub theft plot sentences 3-15, 3-20, 240E2
Cuba gets 2d Sovt sub 3-30, 334B1
Brown sees Trident need re SALT 4-5, 258B1
Trident sub launch fails 4-10, 307B3
USSR, US carriers rptd in Indian O 4-12, 4-16, 313E3-314A1
US, USSR '79, '72 SLBMs compared 338E3
USSR high-speed sub assessed by US 5-17, 390B2
SLBMs, SLCMs cited in SALT II pact text 6-18, 450B2-456G2
Carter addresses Cong on SALT II, cites sub missiles 6-18, 459B1
US Cong OKs destroyer purchase funds bill 7-17, 7-20, Carter signs 7-25, 700A2
USSR scores US re A-subs 8-2, 644A2
USSR steals US dummy torpedo 8-9, returns 8-10, 636F3
Navy settles '75 Tenneco unit A-cruiser dispute 8-29, 747C1
S Africa suggests Sovt sub mishap caused A-blast 10-27, 824E3
Carter cites Trident dvpt 12-12, 963E1
USSR A-powered carrier rptd, global navy capability seen 12-17, 997A3

1980

Ships & Submarines

UK links A-subs, uranium enrichmt plant plans 1-9, 39G2
Cuba gets 3d Sovt sub 1-17, 192E1
USSR scores Carter Persian Gulf warning 1-24, 43A3
UK Polaris plans revealed 1-24, 79F1
Carter budgets deploymt ships, Trident sub, carrier, others 1-28, 71C1, E1, G1
US AEGIS need re Sovt threat seen 1-29, 65A2
Australia-US missile frigate talks set 2-19, 132E1
Reagan 'basic speech' cites Trident, Sovt subs in Cuba 2-29, 207F2, C3
Connally cites Trident in 'basic speech' 3-7, 184D2
Turkey, US sign aid pact 3-29, 255F3
US outlay rise urged 5-9, 369B3
Mex-Sweden patrol boat deal studied 5-24, 409A3
Nimitz returns to Norfolk 5-26, 403G1-B2
UK Laborites vs A-sub force 5-31, 429E2
US sub reactor rptd lost 6-17, 458E2
US GOP platform adopted 7-15, 536F1
UK Trident acquisitns set 7-15, 544A2
W Ger lifts navy curbs 7-18, 540E1
Japan plans more US purchases 7-29, 579D2
Japan research, dvpt urged 8-5, 635D3
Canada to upgrade destroyers 8-8, 618D2
Dem plank on Trident adopted 8-13, 615B2
Sovt A-sub crippled off Japan 8-20; no A-leak rptd 8-24, 653B1
Sovt hover craft used in Warsaw Pact maneuvers 9-8—9-11, 696F1
Carter signs shipbldg authrzn 9-8, 765B1
Australia dvpt plans rptd 9-9, 705F1
French A-carriers rptd OKd 9-24, 750A2
US bars turbine engines to Iraq 9-25, 719B1
US, Sovts trade missile force data 9-26, 778A3
Navy carriers rptd unready, sub force rptd ready 9-30, 786E1
Navy sub vulnerability rptd distorted 10-5, 897B1
US deploys Persian Gulf cruiser 10-11, 773E2
US Navy sub total rptd at 13-yr low 10-11, 986D3
France OKs '81 spending hike 10-23, 886F1, G1
France sets Persian Gulf mine-sweeping force 10-28, 812D2
Navy procuremt appropriatn clears Sen 11-21, 896E3

1976

US denies Sovt laser use vs US surveillnc satellite 11-23; Sovt hunter-killer rptd 12-18, 961A2
Peru, Chile purchases cited 12-7, 975E2

Tanks

'77 US budget proposals 1-21, 64E1
US to consider German Leopard II 2-12, 183C2
Kuwait buys UK tanks 2-16, 126B2
US-Sovt strength listed 2-27, 182F2
Inner Mongolia tunnels rptd 3-2, 190F1
India rpts Pak buildup 3-31, 278B3
Reagan compares US-Sovt strength 4-10, 281B3
NATO OKs Canada W Ger Leopard buy 6-10—6-11, 449B2
Ford OKs '77 authorizatn 7-14, 517B1
US '77 request, authorizatn table 517B2
US XM-1, Leopard standardizatn set, Leopard NATO issue unresolved 8-4, 581D1
US-Iran pact signed 8-7, 581D2
GOP platform text cites 8-18, 609A1
Sovt tanks in Libya parade 9-2, 682D3
US '77 funds signed, table 9-22, 707F1, G1
US arms taken by N Viet rptd 11-11, 961E2
US picks Chrysler over GM; Ger Leopard still in contest 11-12, 941C3
Sovt aid to Rhodesia rebels rptd 11-18, 1009E3

U.S. Presidential Election

Reagan scores A-policy, Ford rebuts 2-10, 109A2, E2
Ford defends A-policy 3-5, 179C3
Reagan compares US-Sovt strength 4-10, 281B3
Dem platform plank 6-15, 432E3
Dem platform text 6-15, 476D3, 477A1, G1
Carter scores sales role 6-23, 451G3
Mondale carrier stand cited 512C3
Mondale pledges US policy shift 7-31, 565F1
US GOP platform text 8-18, 608G3
Mondale scores US sales 8-30, 645C3
Carter scores US sales 9-8; Ford, Dole rebut 9-9, 664C3, 665C2, 666B1
Ford, Carter debate 10-6, 740C3, 741A2, 742F2
Ford scores Carter on B-1 10-7, 763A2
Dole disputes Carter on Iran, Saudi sales 10-8, 764A1
Ford vs Carter on boycotts 10-20, 784A3
Dole scores Mondale 10-25, 804C2

1977

Tanks (& ground vehicles)

Sovt sales to Peru cited 1-10, 2A3
Ford '78 budget requests 1-17, 30G3
NATO shortages rptd 1-24, 70C2
W Ger OKs Turkey, Indonesia sales 2-2, 139E2
Egypt seeks US antitank weapons 4-5, 245B1
US firing problems rptd 4-10, 343D2
Sovt-Kuwait aid talks rptd 4-13, 394D3
USSR shipmt to Ethiopia rptd 4-16, 328A1
US vs tanks for Zaire 4-22, 317A3, 321B3
NATO Leopard standardizatn rptd 5-14, 359F3
Canada to buy Leopards 7-13, 579E3
XM-1, M-60, anti-tank copter funds authorized 7-14, 576C1; signed 7-30, 592A2
US funds Israeli Chariot productn 7-22, 570C3
USSR-Ethiopia deal rptd 9-1, 684C3
USSR displays T-72 11-7, 866A1
NATO sets anti-tank arms hike 12-7, 956E3
NATO sees Sovt tank threat 12-8, 941D3
New combat vehicle (IFV) faulted, XM-1 incompatibility detailed 12-15, 978G1

1978

'79 revised authorzn signed, Navy contract setlmt funded 10-20, 833G1-A2
Sovt SA-11 missiles rptd installed 10-23, 877C2
8 women rpt for US Navy duty 11-1, 877F2-A3
French Assemb budgets 6th A-sub 11-7, 882A1
UK diesel engines sale to China OKd by US 11-7, 901G3
USSR Pacific buildup rptd 11-9, 914G1-A2
Trident 2 in '79 suplmtl budget request 11-15, 916C3
Carter: no decisn on Trident 2 missile 11-30, 916B3
NATO lists '79 purchases 12-4, 954C3

Tanks (& other armored vehicles)

USSR airlift to Ethiopia rptd halted 1-5, 3C3
Syria-USSR deal rptd 1-11, 42C2
Carter budgets XM-1, M-60, 1-23, 45C1, 46A1
US OKs W Ger gun for XM-1, Army to purchase 7000 tanks 1-31, 81F3
US plans buildup, notes USSR increased productn 2-2, 81B2, D2
Somalia gets French-made tanks from Saudi 2-8, 100A1
W Ger Orion 80 spy convictns 2-13, 115D1
NATO, Warsaw Pact force compared 2-20, 162D3
USSR tanks rptd deployed in Ethiopia 2-24, 137F1
Egypt cites Syria '73 war losses 2-25, 139A3
US XM-1, USSR T-72, T-62 compared 3-6, 162E3
Neutron bomb controversy rptd 4-9, 253C2
NATO tanks withdrawn by UK 4-17, 298B3
Carter notes USSR strength 4-25, 307B2
US '77 arms bid rejctns rptd 5-19, 386G3, 387A1
US notes Sovt tank advantage 6-23, 493E2
China to review Zaire aid 6-24, 652G2
US Cong clears '79 authrzn 8-4, Carter vetoes 8-17, 621E2; House upholds 9-7, 677A2
US purchase bar rejctd by House 8-8, 604E2
US mil constructn funds clear Cong 8-21, 662A2
US rpts laser use vs anti-tank missiles 8-23, 683E3-684A1
E-W balance assessed by IISS 9-1, 676D3
US issues WWII secret documts 9-10—9-18, 744D3
'79 revised authorzn signed 10-20, 833G1
NATO lists '79 purchases 12-4, 954C3

U.S. Developments (including U.S.-foreign news)—*See also specific subheads in this section*

Carter scores Sovt role 1-12, 12F1
Carter State of Union Message 1-19, 31D2
Sadat seeks US arms 1-20, Syria scores 1-22, 41G1, 42E1
Carter budget proposals 1-23, 44G3-46B1
US imposes sales ceiling on non-allies 2-1, 106D2
Pentagon urges buildup to match Sovts 2-2, 81A1
Egypt seeks US aid 2-3—2-8, Begin scores 2-8, 77A1, G2-78D1
Cyprus scores US rights rpt 2-5, 148D1
US issues rights rpt, lists buyers 2-9, 101C3
Carter vows sales cut 2-17, 123D2
US plans '79 mil aid cut 2-22, 127C1
Korea aid bar by US Cong seen; Brown warns vs 2-22, 204D1
Israel seeks US arms 3-8, 176E3
US-Yugo deal rptd 3-8, 194C1
Vance links Turkey arms aid, Cyprus 3-9, Ecevit scores 3-10, 216C3
AIO deal cited 3-14, 237C1 ★
US moves to lift Turkish arms embargo 3-29—4-6; reactn 4-2—4-16, 276G1-277A2
US set back in moves to lift Turkish arms embargo 5-3, 5-11; reactn 5-12, 378B1
Carter scores USSR role in Africa 5-5, 342E1
US-Israel agrmt on cluster bomb use rptd 5-12, 354G2
US church group scores Israel on cluster bombs 5-12, 358B3
Carter orders Africa aid curbs reviewed, scores Cong 5-16—5-23; Admin proposal rptd rejctd 5-24, 383A1
'77 sales rejctns rptd, '78 rise seen 5-19, 386E3-387B1
Weapons '79 authrzn OKd by House 5-24, 406B3; Sen 7-11, 526A2; cleared 8-4, 622B1
US to sell China mil-related technology 6-9, 436G1
US vows aid to friendly Africans 6-20, 487D2
Turkey, USSR pacts strain US ties 6-21—6-23; West reassured 6-24, 6-30, 595G1
Turkey embargo end, US base reopening seen 6-28, 587C3
Sales policy assessed 7-16, 564F1
US '76 spending rptd 7-23, 585B2
Cong gives prelim OK to Turkey embargo end 8-1, reactn 8-2, 587D2-588B1
Defns budget cut rejctd by House 8-8, 604E2
Carter vetoes '79 authrzn 8-17, 621A1; House upholds 9-7, 677A2

1979

Tanks (& other armored vehicles)

US, USSR '74-77 sales compared 1-7, 13A2
Carter budgets XM-1, M-60 1-22, 42A2, 43D2
US vows N Yemen sales 2-11, 143C2
Egypt asks US equipmt 2-16–2-18, 143C3
US speeds N Yemen shipmts 2-26, 144F2; 3-7, 179B1
XM-1 engine problem rptd 3-2, 207G2-A3
US aid agrmt with Israel, Egypt rptd 3-20, 198B2
Swiss plan US purchases 4-11, 391B1
US OKs XM-1 productn 5-8, 386D1
US to sell Jordan M-60s 7-26, deal delayed 7-31, 574A3
USSR T-72 shipmt to Syria rptd, Israel arsenal compared 8-28, 643B2
IISS notes Sovt superiority 9-4, 825A3
USSR sets E Ger cut 10-6, 761D1
USSR T-72s in E Ger parade 10-7, 761D2
USSR offers Eur tank exit 10-13–10-16, 880G2
Syria to get more T-72s 10-15, 857F2
USSR seen aided by US 11-8, 856G3
XM-1 defects said solved 11-20, 925C1

U.S. Developments (including U.S. International news)—*See also specific subheads in this section*

China: would buy arms if offered 1-9, 27A1
US OKd Taiwan arms ban in China tie talks 1-12, 27D1
Carter backs existing Iran pacts 1-17, 26A2
Carter State of Union Message 1-23, 47F2
Iran cancels arms orders 2-4, 82G1
US vows Thai arms speedup 2-7, 84A2
Somalia vs US shipmts delay 2-7, 193A2
US, Saudi plan mil aid to N Yemen 2-8, 89D2
Nicaragua mil ties cut 2-8, 255C1, D1
Rights rpt on 115 natns issued 2-10, 107G1, A2
Cong rpts doubt NATO defns capability 2-17, 147F3
Intl arms exhibit spurs protests 2-18–2-19, 152F3
N Yemen arms shipmt speedup rptd 2-26, 2-28, 144D2; 3-7, 178B3, 179A1
US-Israel-Egypt mil talks 3-18–3-19, US details aid 3-19, 3-20, 198F1
US assures N Yemen delivery 3-19, 199E2
Iran arms sales policy scored 3-27, 229B1
'63 Utah land mines destroyed 3-27, 307C3
US-Taiwan relatns bill signed 4-10, 259B3
Egypt seeks US coproductn 6-5, 415C3
'80 authrzn OKd by Sen 6-13, 438E1
Iran arms role rift rptd 7-9, 525A2
Saudis to get more aid 7-13, 536B3
Jt Chiefs, Nunn, Amer Legion back budget, SALT linkage; Vance reaffirms budget hike vow 7-24–8-22, 643C3-644D1
Carter vs budget, SALT linkage 7-27; Kissinger backs 7-31, 8-2; US sens react 8-2, 8-3, 590G2-591D1
Citizens Party platform backs cuts 8-1, 595A1
Warsaw Pact purchase confrmd 8-1, 627A1
Ulster police sales suspended 8-2, 601F3
USSR denies mil spending hike, scores US budget plans 8-2, 644G1
El Salvador mil aid review rptd 8-2, 652C2
Israel '52 pact breach hinted 8-7, 592D1
Iran cancels deals 8-10, 634D3
Aid sanctns studied 8-11, 607F3
Nicaragua seeks aid 8-31, 689A3
Carter asks budget hike 9-11, 678D1
Nixon urges China aid 9-15, 751G1

1980

Tanks (& other armored vehicles)

XM-1 full-scale productn rptd OKd 1-21, 54E3
Carter budgets XM-1 1-28, 71C2
French, W Ger accord set 2-5, 84A3
Zambia announces USSR purchases 2-7, 119E1
Israel says PLO gets Sovt tanks 2-12, 107E3
Egypt to buy US M-60A3s 2-25, 140C2
W Ger-Turkey talks re Leopard 1 cited 2-25, 153F3
Tunisia gets US personnel carriers 2-29, 197C1
US tank detector system rptd 3-21, 267D1
US to sell 100 M-60s to Jordan 6-19, 450E1
UK sets armor purchases 7-14, 564E1
Japan research, dvpt urged 8-5, 635D3
Sovts T-72 used in Warsaw Pact maneuvers 9-8—9-11, 696G1
France OKs '81 spending hike 10-23, 886G1
Iraq awards Jordan 30 captured US tanks for backing vs Iran 12-9, 12-10, 931F3

U.S. Developments (including U.S. International news)—*See also specific subheads in this section*

India concerned re US sale to Pak 1-1, 2F2
USSR chrgs US plans Pak sale renewal 1-4, 10D2
India vs Pak aid 1-5, 12A1
Thais arms order rptd 1-5, 68G2
US to increase Pak arms aid 1-16, 31A2
China to buy US mil gear, no arms 1-24, 46B2
Reagan suggests Cuba blockade 1-27, seeks rearmamt 1-29, 91C3, D3
Clifford reassures India on Pak aid 1-30—1-31; India to get mil gear 2-1, 83C2, B3
Pak aid vs Sovt threat vowed 2-3, 83A1
USSR: spurs arms race 2-6, 84B3
USSR, India score Pak arms plan 2-13, 108G3
Zaire aid rptd diverted 2-28, 356C2
Reagan 'basic speech' excerpts 2-29, 207F3
Reagan links armamts, forgn policy 3-17, 208G1
US-Canada firm guilty of S Africa sales 3-25, 278F1
Turkey aid pact signed 3-29, 255B3, F3
Iran sanctns widened 4-17, 281C1
Oman, Kenya aid set 4-21, 303A1
US outlay increase urged 5-9, 369G2-C3
China mil gear sale OKd 5-29, 397D3
Carter vs Sovt buildup 7-10, 506C1
GOP platform adopted 7-15, 536E1, D2, 537A1
Carter pres renominatn acceptance speech 8-14, 612D1, F3, 613B1
Israel asks $1.76 bln aid 8-20, 662F3
Carter: US could compete 8-21, 629E2
Somalia pact signed 8-21, 645B3
Anderson platform offered 8-30, 665A2
Reagan scores Arab sales 9-3, 681B3
'81 arms authrzn signed 9-8, 764F3
Rockwell settles job bias suit 9-26, 746G3
US denies spare parts-hostage trade 10-16, Iraq repeats chrg 10-18, 799C2, 800B1
Jordan seeks arms speedup 12-1, 911B3

1976

ARMBRO Regina (race horse)
2d in Hambletonian 9-4, 716F2
ARMCO Steel Corp.
Fined 4-10, 988E3
Fined 5-4, 379F2
Ford sets steel quotas 6-7, 430F3
Defers planned price hike 8-26, 646D3
Hikes prices 6% 11-26, 897E2
Reserve Mining Co.—*See separate listing*
ARMENIAN Soviet Socialist Republic—*See 'Republics' under USSR*
ARMOR, Dr. David J.
Alcohol study scored 6-9, 6-10, 442F3-443E1
ARMS Control—*See DISARMAMENT*
ARMS Control Organization
Arms spending study released 2-29, 182G3
ARMSTRONG, Anne
Amb to UK 1-20; confrmd 1-27, 68B1
Rptd Ford vp prospect 8-10, 584D1
GOP vp poll rptd 8-11, 583F3
GOP conv vp vote table 8-19, 599E3
ARMSTRONG, Barbara
Dies 1-18, 56G2
ARMSTRONG, Dwight
Fine arrested 1-7, 32F2
ARMSTRONG, Karleton
Fine arrested 1-7, 32F2
ARMSTRONG, Michael
Sues Figueres 9-22, 1000A3
ARMSTRONG, Rep. William L. (R, Col.)
Reelected 11-2, 824E1, 829G1
ARMSTRONG-Jones, Antony—*See SNOWDON, Earl of*
ARMY, Association of the U.S.
Haig addresses 10-13, 879G3
ARNOLD, William H.
Dies 9-30, 1015B1
ARONSON, Boris
Wins Tony 4-18, 460E2
AROSEMENA, Carlos Julio
Gets amnesty 1-22, 363E3
Party to boycott const talks 10-11, 872F2
ARPELS, Louis
Dies 3-20, 240D3
ARRASATE, Jose Luis
Kidnaped 1-14, 55B1
ARRATA, Gen. Andres (ret.)
Ecuador defense min 1-14, 49B1
ARRIGHI, Pascal
Corsicans urge ouster 1-3, 50E2
ARROSTITO, Norma
Killed 12-3, 996B2
ARROW, Kenneth
Pleads for Sovt dissident 3-24, 421A3

1977

ARMCO Steel Corp.
Paymts total cited 1-21, 79G1
Steelworkers OK contract 4-9, 273G2
Price-fixing chrgd 6-6, 504B1
India seeks steel plant aid 8-24, 655C2
Chrgs Japan, India dumping 10-17; 11-3, 836F3
US probes Japan, India dumping chrgs 11-22, 933B3
Dumping chrgs vs UK filed 12-5, 932C1, 933A3
Backs US import plan, vows no new dumping chrgs 12-7, 932C1
Reserve Mining Co.—*See separate listing*
ARMED Forces, U.S.—*See under U.S. GOVERNMENT*
ARMED Forces of Puerto Rican National Liberation—*See FALN*
ARMENIAN Soviet Socialist Republic—*See 'Republics' under USSR*
ARMORED Cars
Brinks, Wells Fargo indicted 6-21, 520D3
ARMS Control—*See DISARMAMENT*
ARMS Control & Disarmament Agency—*See under U.S. GOVERNMENT*
ARMS Sales—*See ARMAMENTS—Sales*
ARMSTRONG, Anne
Replaced as amb to UK 4-29, 418C1
ARMSTRONG, Dwight Alan
Arrested 4-9, sentncd 6-8, 6-10, 492C1
ARMSTRONG, Joe
Jack Ford named asst 2-24, 345C2
ARMSTRONG, Michael
To probe boxing scandal 4-19, issues report 9-3, 828F1
ARMSTRONG, Tate
In NBA draft 6-10, 584B2
ARMSTRONG, Wally
2d in Western Open 6-26, 676F1
ARMSTRONG Rubber Co.
Tire-grading case review denied 3-21, 230E2
ARMY, Department of the—*See under U.S. GOVERNMENT*
ARNDT, Rudi
Resignatn cited 353B1
ARNELLO, Mario
Canada amb apptmt withdrawn 2-26, 219G2
ARNON, Yaakov
In Israel peace group 10E2
ARNS, Archbishop Paulo Evaristo Cardinal
Backs student protests 5-8, 5-19, 447G2
Honored in US 5-22, 447A3
Scores police raids on univ 9-25, 840A2
ARPELS, Claude
Indicted 3-3, fined 4-20, 312G2-A3
ARRIA, Diego
Venez informatn, tourism min 1-7, 23F2
ARRIAGA Bosque, Rafael
Killed 9-29, 805B3
ARRON, Henck
Coalitn wins electns 10-31, 844E1
Surinam econ problems cited 10-31, 905E3
ARROSTITO, Norma
Guerrillas rptd in disarray 1-3, 16G3

1978

Laser weapon use rptd by US 8-23, 683E3-684A1
US-Iranian sales cited 9-10, 693F2
'79 forgn aid, security funds authrzn cleared 9-12, signed 9-26; provisns include arms sales lid; Turkey, Rhodesia curbs end 734C1-G2
Argentina purchases blocked 9-26, 792D2
'61-79 sales to Yugo rptd 9-28, 758E1
'79 aid funds signed 10-18, 862C2
Nerve gas productn order rptd 10-19, 833F2-A3
'79 revised authorzn signed 10-20, 833F1-A2
Joint chiefs vs Sovt buildup, for budget hike 10-30, 833A3
West arms sales to China OKd 11-3, 11-9, 901D3
Carter cites '79 authorzn veto 11-6, 862D1
Canada-S Africa deal rptd probed 11-7, 904E2
'80 defns budget hike planned 11-9, 874E3, 875B2
Spy satellite leaks aids USSR 11-23, 940G2
Carter bars China, Sovt sales 11-30, 936F2
US, USSR clash on sales curbs, talks stalled 12-5—12-15; US rift rptd 12-19, 996A3

ARMANI, Giorgio
'78 high chic fashion rptd 8-4—8-11, 10-27—11-3, 1029C2
ARMCO, Inc.
Verity backs trigger prices 1-4, 3G2
'76 tax nonpaymt rptd 1-27, 65G2
Price hike undercuts US Steel 4-3, 263C1
Verity on Carter anti-inflatn plan 10-25, 806D3
Eur steel dumping chrgs withdrawn 12-28, 1006B1
Reserve Mining Co.—*See separate listing*
ARMED Forces, U.S.—*See under U.S. GOVERNMENT*
ARMED Forces Policy Council—*See under U.S. GOVERNMENT—DEFENSE*
ARMENIAN Soviet Socialist Republic—*See USSR—Republics*
ARMORED Vehicles—*See ARMAMENTS—Tanks*
ARMS Control—*See DISARMAMENT*
ARMS Control & Disarmament Agency—*See under U.S. GOVERNMENT*
ARMSTRONG, Edwin Howard (1891-1954)
Papers given to Columbia U 5-21, 844C2
ARMSTRONG, Neil
Gets space medal of honor 10-1, 861C2
ARMSTRONG, Neill
Named Bears coach 2-16, 171G2
ARMSTRONG, Scott
In Haldeman book scoop by-line 2-16, 124F2
ARMSTRONG, Rep. William L. (R, Colo.)
Wins US Sen primary in Colo 9-12, 736E2
Wins electn 11-7, 846C1, 848D1, 855F3
ARMY, Department of the—*See under U.S. GOVERNMENT*
ARNAUT, Antonio
Named Portugal soc affairs min 1-30, 91C3
ARNOLD, Judge William J.
Jascalevich curare case-press freedom controversy 6-30—8-30, 678E2
Jascalevich acquitted 10-24, 841G1
ARNS, Archbishop Paulo Evaristo Cardinal
Sees Carter in Rio 3-31, 233E2
Backs anti-inflatn petitn 10-13, 836G3
ARONOFF, Arnold
Indicted re fraud 10-10, 808F2
AROSEMENA, Carlos Julio
Pres bid barred, party scores 2-20, 148F1, B2
ARPEL, Adrien
3-week Crash Makeover on best-seller list 4-30, 356A2
ARRIA, Diego
Carter pollster hired 5-5, 395G1
Sets pres bid; scores AD, Copei 5-21, 395E1
4th in pres vote 12-3, returns incomplete 12-8, 952B3, 953B1
ARRIGHI, Mel
Unicorn in Captivity opens 11-15, 1031B3

1979

Carter cites 'special' USSR-Cuban ties 10-1, 738A3
Defns Dept for arms to China 10-3, Vance reaffirms ban 10-4, 789E1
Iran spare parts shipmts resumed 10-5, 773B3
US shipments to Egypt start, arms displayed 10-6, 762C3
'80s spending forecast by Castro 10-12, 778D3
'77 spending rptd 10-13, 804F1
NATO shortages cited 12-11, 959D2
UK, US discuss Ulster police sales 12-17, 968B2

ARMANI, Giorgio
'79 fashion roundup rptd 1006A2, B2
ARMED Forces—*See under U.S. GOVERNMENT*
ARMED Forces for Popular Resistance
Claims credit for US, PR bombings 10-17, Navy ambush 12-3, 786D2, 924C3
ARMED Forces of National Liberation—*See FALN*
ARMED Revolutionary Movement
PR ambush kills 2 US sailors 12-3, 924B3
ARMIJOS, Rafael
Bucaram alliance cited 11-29, 967C3
ARMINONE—*See MEDICINE-Drugs*
ARMORED Vehicles—*See ARMAMENTS-Tanks*
ARMS Control—*See DISARMAMENT*
ARMS Control & Disarmament Agency—*See under U.S. GOVERNMENT*
ARMSTRONG, Garner Ted
'78 break with father, '76 chrgs cited 1-3, 23C3-E3
ARMSTRONG, Herbert W.
Church sued, put in receivership; '78 break with son cited 1-3, 23G2
Church audit set 3-16, receivership lifted 3-17, 376B2
ARMSTRONG, Scott
'Brethren' publicatn stirs controversy 12-2, 988B2
ARMSTRONG, Sen. William L. (R, Colo.)
Vs SALT treaty 4-5, 258F1
Finances disclosed 5-18, 383E2
ARMY, Department of the—*See under U.S. GOVERNMENT*
ARNAZ, Lucie
They're Playing Our Song opens 2-11, 292E3
ARNDT, Arno R.
Indicted for IRS fraud 3-16, 240F1
ARNDT, Marlise R.
Indicted for IRS fraud 3-16, 240F1
ARNESON, Paul
Registers Pressler pres campaign com 8-2, 59 F2
ARNHEITER, Marcus A.
Libel cases declined by Sup Ct 10-29, 884G1
ARNHEITER Affair, The (book)
Libel cases declined by Sup Ct 10-29, 884A2
ARNHEITER v. Random House
Case declined by Sup Ct 10-29, 884A2
ARNHEITER v. Sheehan
Case declined by Sup Ct 10-29, 884A2
ARNOLD, Richard J.
Sentncd 3-13, 239C3
ARNOLD, Robert
On Met Ed fine 10-26, 826D2
ARNOLD & Porter
Rogers on Mex-Fla vegetable growers rift 7-19, 553E2
ARNS, Cardinal Paulo Evaristo
Backs Nicaragua, El Salvador prelates 2-12, 108F3
ARONOFF, Arnold
Pleads guilty to fraud 5-21, 656A1*
ARONSON, Jane
Nonpatent royalties upheld by Sup Ct 2-28, 165B2
ARONSON v. Quick Point Pencil Co.
Nonpatent royalties upheld by Sup Ct 2-28, 165B2
ARRATA de Sorroza, Ines
Ecuador welfare min 12-9, 967G3
ARRINGTON, Richard
Elected Birmingham mayor 10-30, 829B1

1980

ARMAS, Tony
AL batting ldr 10-6, 926E3
ARMCO Inc.
USSR OKs steel deal delay 2-19, 235F3
USW contract settled 4-15, 289B2
NN Corp merger set 8-20, 745G3
Verity on Carter econ renewal plan 8-28, 663B3
US protests Franco-USSR steel deal 9-19, 728D3
ARMED Forces—*See under U.S. GOVERNMENT*
ARMED Forces Journal (magazine)
Perry testifies on 'stealth' plane disclosure 9-4, 666A1
ARMED Forces of National Liberation—*See FALN*
ARMENIANS
Turkey amb to Switz attacked 2-6, other envoy deaths noted 2-28, terrorist groups described 3-1, 197A2
Turkey airline Rome office bombed 3-10, amb to Vatican attacked 4-17, 316G1-A2
Sovt emigratn rise rptd 5-24, 467E2
Turk diplomat attacks continue 7-31, 8-5, 606A1
Turkey offices in NY, Calif, London bombed 10-12, 794D1, G1*
Turkish consul, bodyguard slain in Australia 12-17, 991A2
ARMORED Vehicles—*See ARMAMENTS--Tanks*
ARMOUR v. Nix
Case decided by Sup Ct 5-12, 386C3
ARMS Control—*See DISARMAMENT*
ARMSTRONG, Anne
Addresses GOP conv 7-15, gets 1 vote as pres nominee 7-16, 529F1, 531D3
Named to Reagan com 7-22, 549A3
Bars Reagan Cabt apptmt 11-26, 935E2
ARMSTRONG, Gillian
My Brilliant Career released 2-1, 216C3
ARMSTRONG, Karleton
Parole rptd 1-1, 24F3
ARMSTRONG, Louis (Satchmo) (d. 1971)
Bignard dies 6-27, 528B1
ARMSTRONG, Scott
Brethren on best-seller list 1-13, 40B3; 2-10, 120C3; 3-9, 200B3; 4-6, 280C3
US atty named Abscam leaks prosecutor 2-11, 111C2
Powell refutes Sup Ct media image 5-1, 368A3
ARMSTRONG, Sen. William L. (R, Colo.)
Scores '81 budget res 11-20, 896C2
ARMY, Department of the—*See under U.S. GOVERNMENT*
ARNALDI, Eduardo
Commits suicide 4-19, 408G1
ARNAZ, Lucie
Jazz Singer released 12-19, 1003B2
ARNDT, Russell
Protests Sovt grain embargo 1-6, 10D1
ARNEZ, Gen. Antonio
Sworn Bolivia interior min 4-7, 272F1
ARNOLD, Elliot
Dies 5-13, 448B1
ARNOLD, John
NFL '79 punt return, kick return ldr 1-5, 8F3, G3
ARNOLD, Robert C.
Asks 3 Mile I cleanup aid 8-9, 649A3
ARNOTT, Mark
Return of the Secaucus 7 released 9-14, 836E3
ARONSON, Boris
Dies 11-16, 928B2
AROSEMENA Gomez, Otto
Shoots 2 in Ecuadoran cong 9-30, 789D2
ARRESE, Jaime
Slain 10-23, funeral 10-24, 832D2
ARRON, Henck A. E. (Surinamese premier; ousted Feb. 25)
Deposed in coup 2-25, 153G1
Surrender rptd 2-29, 174E3
Surinam pres ousted by mil 8-13, 653F2
ARROW, Jerry
5th of July opens 11-6, 892C3
ARROW, Kenneth J.
Cuts Sovt ties re dissidents 4-16, 326A3

1976

ARRUPE, Rev. Pedro
Scores Paraguay 5-10, 403D2
At Intl Eucharistic Cong 8-2, 596D2
ARSON—*See under CRIME*
ARTHRITIS—*See 'Diseases' under MEDICINE*
ARTIS, John
Gets new trial 3-17; released 3-19, 256D3
2d trial opens 10-12, reopens 11-11, 860B1
Found guilty 12-21, sentencing set 12-23, 1015C3
ARTS & Culture—*See also NATIONAL Foundation on the Arts & Humanitites under U.S. GOVERNMENT; also specific art, country names*
Southeby names 1st woman auctioneer 1-27, 272B1
Dem platform text 6-15, 473D1
GOP platform text 8-18, 608F1
Sup Ct bars review of rules re pub funds 10-18, 867A3
US issues Helsinki rpts 12-2, 934F1
ARTS & Letters, National Institute of
Admits Gwendolyn Brooks; presents awards 5-19, 504B3
American Academy of Arts and Letters
Presents Natl Book Awards 4-19, 292C3
ARTS & Sciences, American Academy of
Warns Unesco vs politics 1-5, 36B3
ARZAMENDIA, Mario
Torture death rptd 6-9, 557D3
ARZUMANYAN, Grigory
Dies 11-28, 932C3
ASBESTOS
Rptd in 5 water supplies 4-30, 349F1
Minn iron plant fined 5-4, 379E2
ASCHENBACH, Hans-Georg
Wins Olympic medal 2-7, 159E1
ASEAN—*See ASSOCIATION of Southeast Asian Nations*
ASGHAR Khan
Political foes jailed 10-30, 873C3
ASHBERY, John
Wins Natl Book Award 4-19, 292D3
Wins Pulitzer Prize 5-3, 352C3
ASHBROOK, Rep. John Milan (R, Ohio)
'72 primary spending rptd 4-25, 688A2
Scores Reagan vp choice 7-27, 550A2
Reelected 11-2, 830B3
ASHE, Arthur
Wins Rotterdam WCT tourn 2-29, 716D2
Loses Wimbledon 6-26, 504F1
ASHE, Derick
Returns to UK 1-19, 96D3
ASHLAND Oil Inc.
SEC lists paymts 5-12, 725G3, 726C2
Indicted 6-1, 412D3, E3
Colo oil-shale lease suspended, consortium breakup cited 8-23, 648G3, 649D1
ASHLEY, James H.
Wins SW Bell tap suit 12-17, 995F1
ASHLEY, Rep. Thomas Ludlow (D, O.)
Reelected 11-2, 830A3
ASHWORTH, Richard
Cited in Sen rpt on Callaway 10-5, 745C1

1977

ARSENIC
Canada contaminatn chrgd 1-16, 61E1
Canada probe rpt issued 6-6, 447E3
ARSON—*See FIRES & Explosions*
ARTAMONOV, Nikolai—*See SHADRIN, Nikolai*
ARTHUR, Beatrice
Wins Emmy 9-11, 1022A1
ARTIME, Manuel
Dies 11-18, 952B2
ARTIS, John
Sentenced 2-9, 140C1
ARTS, National Endowment for the—*See under U.S. GOVERNMENT—NATIONAL Foundation on the Arts and the Humanities*
ARTS & Culture—*See also specific art, country names*
'75 Ford Foundatn grants cited 1-11, 56E1
Pan-Africa festival 1-15—2-12, 106B1
Belgium-Zaire talks 1-17—1-24, 200A1
US-Cuba talks seen 2-15, 110F1
'76 business gifts rptd 5-12, 409C2
Alechinsky wins 1st Mellon prize 8-1, 808F2
US hosts Sovt exhibit 11-12, 988C2
Obituaries
Ames, Elizabeth 3-28 264B2
Finley, David 2-1 164G2
Wagner, Gerald 11-22, 952F3
ARTS & Humanities, National Foundation on the—*See U.S. GOVERNMENT—NATIONAL Foundation on the Arts and Humanities*
ARTS and Letters, National Institute of American Academy of Arts and Letters
Natl Book Awards presented 4-11, 355G1
ARUBA—*See NETHERLANDS Antilles*
ARUN Thavathasin, Gen.
Slain in coup try 3-26, 243F1
Slayers sentncd 4-21, 331E2
ARVEY, Col. Jacob M.
Dies 8-25, 696C2
ASAHI Corp.
Murayama dies 8-7, 696E3
ASAKA, Shizuo
Denies Boeing kickback chrg 2-14, 136F1
ASARCO Inc.
Copper price raised 3-20, 3-22, 209C2
Cuts copper prices 6-1, 7-20, 577D2
Strike begins 7-1, 558G1
ASBESTOS
Quebec natlzatn plan disclosed 1-25, 81G3, 82D1
Minn plant wins dump site 1-31, 95E2
Workers sue HEW 2-15, 422C2
Quebec plan eased 2-28, 254G2
ASCIONE, Justice Alfred M.
OKs Richards US Open play 8-17, 787C2
ASEAN—*See ASSOCIATION of Southeast Asian Nations*
ASGHAR Khan
Chrgs vote fraud 3-8, 202A1
Arrested 3-17, bars releases 3-21, 223C1
Released 6-3, 450A3
ASHBEE, Barry
Dies 5-12, 452D2
ASHBROOK, Rep. John M. (R, O.)
Amendmt bars Viet aid 5-4, 333F1
Amends Hatch Act bill 5-19, 442B3
ASHE, Arthur
Scores US Open racial remark 9-8, 787G2
On Biko death 9-25, 735E3
ASHESHOV, Nicholas
Peru police question 9-6, 784E2
ASHFORD, Evelyn
Wins 100-mtr dash, sets 200-mtr dash mark 6-9—6-11, 602A3, C3
ASHLAND Oil Inc.
Nigeria payoffs rptd 5-17, 503B1
Loop license signed 8-1, 724E3
Convicted 8-30, 691A3
Fined 9-16, 918F2
Commonwealth stock purchase OKd 9-22, 723B1
Helium dispute case declined 10-31, 11-28, 919F2
ASHLEY, James H.
Wins SW Bell slander suit 9-12, 724B2
ASHLEY, Rep. Thomas Ludlow (D, O.)
'76 spec interest gifts rptd 2-15, 128F2
Named energy panel head 4-21, 321D1
Scores Schlesinger comments on energy legis 11-22, reassured 11-23, 916E3, 917B1
ASHLEY National Forest (Utah)
Fire kills 3 7-16—7-19, 660A3

1978

ARSENIEV, Yuri
Dersu Uzala released 1-13, 619E1
ARSHI, Abdel Karim al-
Takes power in N Yemen 6-25, 499G1
ARSON—*See FIRES & Explosions*
ARTAUD, Antonin
Taudshow opens 3-24, 887D3
ARTIFICIAL Insemination—*See CHILDBIRTH*
ART Institute of Chicago
3 Cezanne paintings stolen 12-27, 1028E3
ART Metal-USA Inc. (Newark, N.J.)
Cited in GSA probe, denies kickbacks 9-19, 714G2
ARTS & Culture—*See also specific art; country names*
Pak, India in exchng agrmt 2-6—2-7, 113B1
Arts Institute honors 8 2-7, 316D1
Harvard revises curriculum 5-2, 348C2
Turkey, USSR sign cultural pact 6-21—6-23, 595G1, E2
Versailles bombed 6-26, 496C1
US blacks asks S Africa ban 7-6, 632E3
Indians protest in DC 7-15—7-23, 568E3
China, Iran sign pact 8-31, 675B3
Obituaries
Koussevitzky, Olga 1-5, 96E2
Zellerbach, Harold 1-29, 96G3
ARTS and Letters, American Academy and Institute of
Members elected 2-7, 316D1
'77 merger cited 2-7, 316F1
Publishers assn presents Natl Book Awards 4-10, 315C2
Rodgers gives $1 mln endowmt 5-1, 335E3 *
ARTS and Letters, American Academy of—*See ARTS and Letters, American Academy and Institute of*
ARTS and Letters, National Institute of—*See ARTS and Letters, American Academy and Institute of*
ARTS & the Humanities, National Foundation on the—*See under U.S. GOVERNMENT*
ARUM, Bob
Reveals Spinks-CBS pact 2-17, threatens suit vs WBC 3-16, 211E3, 212C1
Shifts Spinks-Ali rematch site 3-9, 212G1
Spinks-Ali rematch contract signed 4-11, 378F3
ARUTUNYAN, Eduard
Sentence rptd 12-5, 947F1
ARUTUNYAN, Shagin
Sentence rptd 12-5, 947F1
ASAT (antisatellite interceptor)—*See ASTRONAUTICS—Satellites*
ASBESTOS
EPA curbed on work rule 1-10, 13E2
Tex workers get $20 mln setlmt 2-8, 326C3
HEW to warn workers 4-26, 326F2
Southn constructn pact OKd 5-22, 429E3
EPA amends regulation 6-15, 512D3
Minn plant to continue 7-7, 553F2
Schl inspectns urged 12-21, 1009G1
ASBESTOSIS (white lung disease)—*See MEDICINE—Heart & Lung*
ASCAP—*See COMPOSERS, Authors and Publishers, American Society of*
ASCARRUNZ, Col. Ariel
Bolivia transport min 11-24, 913E1
ASCHKENASY, Ernest
Assesses JFK death shots 12-29, 1002F1, A2
ASCOLI, Max
Dies 1-1, 96C1
ASEAN—*See ASSOCIATION of Southeast Asian Nations*
ASENCIO, Diego
Signs Colombia-US anti-drug pact 9-29, 815B1
ASGHAR Khan
Says govt provokes riots 10-8, 775E2
ASHBROOK, Rep. John Milan (R, O.)
Reelected 11-7, 851F3
May join China policy suit 12-20, 975C3
ASHBY, Hal
Coming Home released 2-15, 619B1
ASHEVILLE, N.C.—*See NORTH Carolina*
ASHFORD, Evelyn
Sets 200-mtr dash mark 7-8, 692B3
ASHIOTIS, Costas
On Turkish Cypriot plan 4-21, 328G3
ASHLAND Oil Inc.
$52.1 mln refund sought 7-12, 610B3
ASHLEY, James H.
SW Bell '76 tap rule overturned, slander suit appeal cited 2-16, 142E3
SW Bell slander judgmt reversed 11-29, 963F1 *
ASHLEY, Rep. Thomas L. (D, Ohio)
Defends pvt energy conf com mtgs 4-13, 304G2-A3
Lauds energy bill, $ aid 10-15, 786B3
Reelected 11-7, 851E3
ASHQAR, Capt. Samir
Killed 11-1, forgn min ambush thwarted 11-2, 828B2
ASHRAF, Princess (Iran)
Shah curbs govt role 9-26, 740B2
ASHWORTH, Emily
Loses primary for Oregon gov 5-23, 406G2

1979

ARRUPE, Very Rev. Pedro
Says Jesuits seek China return 3-16, 218C1
Orders Jesuits to curb liberal theology 12-7, 999C3
ARSENIC
Australia prawn levels rptd high 2-20, 188E3
ARSON—*See FIRES*
ARTHUR, Robert Alan
All That Jazz released 12-20, 1007F2
ARTOM, Guido
Vs French knitwear import curbs 8-20, 668D3
ARTS & Culture—*See also specific art; country names*
Carter budget proposals 1-22, 46A3
Canada panel asks more prov power 1-25, 74E2
US-China pact signed 1-31, 65D1
USSR-Australia ties to be renewed 4-3, 253D1
US-Taiwan relatns bill signed 4-10, 259B3
B Carter '78 Libya visit linked 4-15, 310E1
Asian Society, NYC museum get Japan gifts 5-4, 375A2
US arts cncl sets business skills program 7-4, 672F2
Time, Control Data to sponsor shows 7-19, 672C2
US-China expanded pact signed 8-28, 644C2
China pacts with W Ger, UK, Italy OKd 10-24, 11-1, 11-6, 854D1, A2, D2
Mass arts lottery set 11-15, 892G2
Obituaries
Belmont, Eleanor 10-24, 860A2
Brown, John N 10-9, 860D2
ARTS & the Humanities, National Foundation on the—*See under U.S. GOVERNMENT*
ARTS & Letters, American Academy and Institute of
Tuchman elected pres 2-27, 176G1
New members elected 12-7, 1005A3
ARUM, Bob
Benitez decisns Palomino, chrgs fix 1-14, 79B3
ARZENO, Luis
Arrested 9-25, plot exposed 9-26, 751G3
ARZENO Regalado, Col. Luis
Arrested 9-25, plot exposed 9-26, 751F3
ARZNER, Doris
Dies 10-1, 860G1
ASARCO Inc.
Southern Peru Copper Co.—*See separate listing*
ASAT (antisatellite interceptor)—*See ASTRONAUTICS—Satellites*
ASBESTOS
Hair dryer recall sought 4-19, 308E2
Quebec plans expropriatn 5-2, 352D2
Hair dryer recall praised 5-17, 595F3
Quebec expropriatn law enacted, Asbestos Corp sues 6-21; takeover halted 6-27, 484F1
Asbestos Corp loses Quebec suit 7-25, 563A1
Quebec prepares US co takeover 10-4, 771D3
US co granted injunctn vs Quebec takeover 12-13, 948G3
ASBESTOS Corp.—*See GENERAL Dynamics*
ASBM (air-to-surface ballistic missile)—*See ARMAMENTS—Missiles*
ASCHKENASY, Ernest
JFK acoustics testimony reaffirmed 3-16, 205A1
ASEAN—*See ASSOCIATION of Southeast Asian Nations*
ASGHAR Khan
Detained 10-17, 794F1
ASHBROOK, Rep. John M. (R, Ohio)
Amends Educ Dept bill 7-11, 514E3
IRS tax power curb amendmt OKd 9-26, Carter signs 9-29, 883D1
ASHCROFT, John
ERA conv boycott upheld 2-21, 128F1
ASHCROFT v. Freiman
Mo abortn curb end backed by Sup Ct 3-5, 185A1
ASHDOD (Israeli freighter)
Sails through Suez Canal 4-30, 320E1
ASHE, Arthur
Australian Open results 1-3, 103D2
Loses Grand Prix Masters 1-14, 103A3
Loses US Pro Indoor 1-28, US Natl Indoor 3-4, 391F2, A3
Suffers heart attack 7-31, undergoes surgery 12-13, 1004A1
ASHFORD, Evelyn
Sets indoor 60-yd dash mark 2-23, 100-mdash mark 6-16, named AAU outdoor champ MVP 6-17, 911G1, A2, E2
ASHLAND Oil Inc.
July gas supplies rptd 6-25, 479E1
Ashland Exploration Inc.
Holdings sold 2-4, 560E3
ASHLEY, Rep. Thomas L. (D, Ohio)
Meets Teng in Peking 1-2, 2F1
ASHMAN, Howard
God Bless You Mr Rosewater opens 5-20, 711D3
ASHTON, Ken
Journalists strike ends 1-18, 38B2
ASHWORTH, Judge Clyde
Awards Davis divorce setlmt 4-20, 392D3

1980

ARROW Electronics Inc.
13 execs killed in NY hotel fire 12-4, 948C2
Waddell named chrmn, acting pres 12-8, 959F3
ARROZAL, Arnel
Kim decisns 6-29, 1000G3
ARRUPE, Very Rev. Pedro
Orders Drinan quit politics 5-4, Drinan complies 5-5, 341D2, A3
ARSENIC
Memphis area illness probed 4-2, 331B3
Medit pollutn pact signed 5-17, 381C3
Auto plant curbs to ease 7-8, 505E1
Anaconda to close 2 Montana units 9-30, 825A3
Chem clean-up bill signed 12-11, 936B1, C1
ARTHUR Taylor & Co.
RCTV wins BBC rights 12-11, 1002C3
ARTS and Letters, American Academy and Institute of
Members elected 12-5, 998C1
ARTS & Culture
US bans Sovt cultural exchngs for Afghan invasn 1-4, 1E1; Australia suspends 1-9, 9E2
Pacific orgn studied 1-20, 78B2
Sovts end visits to US 1-28, 67D3
US-Greek pact signed 4-22, 352E2
Australia-China pact signed 5-7—5-11, 338A1
Iran protests Canada exhibitn bar, Egypt pavillion rental 7-3, 520F3-521B1
Calif artist royalties case declined by Sup Ct 11-10, 868B2
Natl Endowmt authrzn clears Cong 11-20, 953F2; signed 12-4, 982A1
NATO studies Sovt exchng curb 12-12, 949G1
ARUBA Bonair Curacao & Trust Co.
International News Keyes Inc.
Berkeley Barb folds 7-3, 582F3
ARVIDSSON, Par
Sets US butterfly marks 3-28—3-29, 4-11; Berkeley wins NCAA title 3-29, 834F3, 835B1
Wins Olympic medal 7-23, 623F2
ASARCO Inc.
Idaho tax case remanded by Sup Ct 3-24, 265B2
USW copper strike drags on 10-24, 805B3
Bendix sells back shares 10-29, 985F2
USW copper strike ends 11-10, 987E3
ASARCO Inc. v. Idaho State Tax Commission
Case remanded by Sup Ct 3-24, 265B2
ASBESTOS
OSHA cites Va shipyd 2-27, 147E3
Minn plant ends Lake Superior dumping 3-16, 227B1
Quebec buys Turner & Newall units 5-8, 371D3
CPSC seeks use data 5-30, 703F2
ASCENSION, The (painting)
Sold for record sum 4-17, 472A3
ASEAN—*See ASSOCIATION of Southeast Asian Nations*
ASENCIO, Diego C.
Seized in Colombia DR Emb raid 2-27, 141B1
Emb raid ends, freed in Cuba 4-27, 335G1, B2
ASHBROOK, Rep. John Milan (R, Ohio)
Reelected 11-4, 843F4
ASHE, Arthur
Retires from tennis competitn 4-16, 607A2
Named Davis Cup captain 9-7, 692A1
McEnroe, Borg decline S Africa match offer 10-16, 947E1
ASHE, Robert
Viets capture 6-25, release 6-29, 508G2
ASHES (book)
Wins Amer Book Award 5-1, 692F2
ASHFORD, Emmett
Dies 3-1, 279D1
ASHLAND Oil Inc.
Gas refining advance unveiled 3-31, 251E1
Paint-resin price trust setlmt reached 7-22, 917E1
Wholesale gas prices cut 8-27, 666G2
Ashland-Warren Inc.
Bid-rigging indictmt rptd 7-5, 655B2
ASHLEY, Elizabeth
Windows released 1-18, 216G3
Hide & Seek opens 5-4, 392B3
ASHLEY, Ted
Retires from Warner Bros 12-1, 959E3
ASHLEY, Rep. Thomas L. (D, Ohio)
Loses reelectn 11-4, 837E1, 846F1, 851D2

1976

ASIA—*See also country, organization names*
Freedom House survey rptd 1-19, 20B3
Australia vows SE Asia aid 6-1, 438F2
Immigrants in UK attacked, 2 killed 6-2—6-21, 482B1
World Bank poverty data, chart 778C1
Australia sees SE Asia pol chng 11-4, 850B2
U.S. Relations
Ford State of Union message 1-19, 38B3
Marine Corps reorganizatn urged 2-2, 95C3
US Dem platform text cites 6-15, 477E2, 478C2
Kissinger on detente 6-25, 466D2
More SE Asia refugees arrive US, total rptd 8-16, 696A3
US GOP platform text cites 8-18, 609B2
ASIAN Americans
Carter sees LA group 10-7, 762D1
ASIAN Development Bank (ADB) (Afghanistan, Australia, Austria, Bangladesh, Belgium, British Solomon Islands, Burma, Cambodia, Canada, Denmark, Fiji, Finland, France, Great Britain, Hong Kong, India, Indonesia, Italy, Japan, Laos, Malaysia, Nationalist China, Nepal, Netherlands, New Zealand, Norway, Pakistan, Papua New Guinea, Philippines, Singapore, South Korea, Sri Lanka, Sweden, Switzerland, Thailand, Tonga, U.S., Vietnam, Western Samoa, West Germany)
Vietnam joins 9-23, 721E3
'77 US aid signed 10-1, 806E3
ASIAN Wall Street Journal, The (newspaper)
Faces Thai censorship 10-11, 775E3
ASKEW, John
Venez panel rpts Occidental bribe role 6-8, arrest ordrd 7-14, 593D1
Occidental chrgs dropped 11-16, 930E1
ASKREN, Dr. Edward
Testifies for Williams 8-23, 796F3
ASNER, Edward
Wins Emmy 5-17, 460A2
ASPEN (book)
On best seller list 2-29, 208F3
ASPIN, Rep. Les (D, Wis.)
Denies Angola UK mercenary executns 2-9, 106C1
Scores AWACS sale offer 3-2, 183E2
Challenges Pentagon Sovt arms spending data 3-5, 182G1-C2
On Navy overrun contracts 5-4, 454D1
On US, USSR naval spending 5-9, 394C2
Marine prosecutn data rptd 6-27, 493B3
On Marine recruit training 7-10, 587A1
Testifies in Schorr probe 7-20, 748F3
Reelected 11-2, 831A3
ASS, Iosif
Freed 11-15, 966D3

ASSAD, Hafez al-
Joint Jordan war games rptd 1-18, 35D1
Seeks Sahara setlmt 1-27, 1-29, 58C2
Gets Leb peace missn rpt 1-27, 59B2
Meets Franjieh 2-7; briefs PLO on talks 2-8, 107F1-A2
US Sen Stevenson rpts demand for Israeli exit 2-28, 161C1
Calls off Leb mediatn 3-11, 209F1
Confs with Franjieh 3-16, Karami 3-20, 210A1, D1
Jumblat vs truce 3-29, 225E1
Warns Leb vs war, airs Jumblat talks 4-12, 257F1
Meets Arafat, Leb peace plan set 4-16, 273A1
Sees Assad on Leb electns 4-26, 295G3
Meets Arafat 5-7, 337E1
Meets Jalloud 5-17—5-18, 355C1
Waldheim visits 5-25—5-27, 385G2
Meets with Kosygin 6-1—6-4, 385B2, 406F2
Nablus Arabs score 6-9, 406B3
Visits French pres 6-17—6-19, 448D3
May meet Sadat in summit 6-24, 449A1
Khalef warns on Tel Zaatar fall 7-3, 487B1
Rpt bodyguard unit fighting in Leb 514C1
Sovts ask to quit Lebanon 7-13, 514E3
PLO asks Sovt pressure 7-15, 528E1
Defends mil role in Leb 7-20, 528G1-B2
Ayoubi quits, Khleifawi named 8-1, 594F2
Rpt brother mapped Tripoli drive 8-23, 629G1
Meets Sarkis on ties 8-31, 662G3
USSR asks Leb exit 9-11, rejects 10-1, 10-5, 737G1
Scores Damascus raiders 9-26, 720F3, 721A1
Saudis urge Leb truce 10-15, 779C1
At Riyadh peace conf 10-17—10-18, 778A3
Meets with Arafat 10-20, 779E1
Arafat OKs arms surrender 12-3, 913C1
Meets Hussein on merger 12-7—12-8, 913A2
Meets Sadat, Egypt union set 12-18—12-21, 954D2
Sadat: talks backed final peace setlmt 12-30, 973E1
ASSAD, Kamal al-
Asks Franjieh resign 3-12, 209D2
Meets French mediator 4-10, 258D1
Sees Assad on electns 4-26, sets date 4-27, 295G3
Seeks new pres candidate 319C1
ASSAD, Lt. Col. Rifaat
Rpt mapped Tripoli drive 8-23, 629G1

1977

ASIA—*See also country, organization names*
Mid-'75 populatn rptd 1-30, 123G2
CP ldrs at Frelimo cong 2-3—2-7, 137D1
'76 econ growth rptd 2-16, 147A2
WHO launches immunizatn drive 4-7, 287C3
Indochina refugee flow up 6-12, 6-19, 497B1
Econ grouping seen 6-22, 504E2
Malaria upsurge rptd 9-4, 747D3
Canada min on tour 9-22—10-4, 780F2
Eur heroin use up 10-17—10-21, 971C3
Amnesty Intl chrgs rights violatns 12-8, 956D2
U.S. Relations
US stresses commitmt 2-1, 69G1, G2
Carter asks more VOA funds 3-22, 230A1
Carter vows cooperatn 5-22, 397F1
US vows active role 7-27, 572B2
US heroin flow rptd down 11-7, 972B1
ASIAN Americans
Natl Women's Conf OKs minority res 11-19—11-21, 917C3
ASIAN Development Bank (ADB) (Afghanistan, Australia, Austria, Bangladesh, Belgium, British Solomon Islands, Burma, Cambodia, Canada, Denmark, Fiji, Finland, France, Great Britain, Hong Kong, India, Indonesia, Italy, Japan, Laos, Malaysia, Nationalist China, Nepal, Netherlands, New Zealand, Norway, Pakistan, Papua New Guinea, Philippines, Singapore, South Korea, Sri Lanka, Sweden, Switzerland, Thailand, Tonga, U.S., Vietnam, Western Samoa, West Germany)
'78 funds cleared 10-19, 815F2; signed 11-1, 834D1
ASIA Society, The (N.Y.)
S Korea oppositn ldr addresses 3-7, 203A1
Vance speech 6-29, 513G3
ASKEW, Gov. Reubin (D, Fla.)
Declares weather emergency 1-22, 54G3; estimates storm damage 1-28, 76B1
Backs laetrile bill 5-2, 375G3
Asks drought aid 6-27, 659G3 ★
Replaced as Govs Assn chrmn 9-9, 719C2
ASL (American Soccer League)—*See SOCCER*
ASLAN, Dr. Ana
Gerovital authorized in Nev 5-20, 308C3
ASMAR, Sali al-
Slain by PLO 995F2
ASNAJ, Abdallah
Diplomatic corps shift announced 10-10, 784C1
ASPARTAME—*See SWEETENERS, Artificial*
ASPEN, Colo.—*See COLORADO*
ASPIN, Rep. Les (D, Wis.)
Visits Cuba 4-4—4-9, 282C3, 283B1
Mil pension amendmt fails 4-25, 324C1
S Africa sugar lobby gift alleged 7-20, 614F1
Rpts NATO sales to Turkey 9-25, 957F1
ASRI Haji Muda, Datuk
Quits Malaysia Cabt 11-8, 885A2
ASSAD, Hafez al- (Syrian president)
Meets Sarkis, cooperatn set 2-2, 72A2
Khaddam sees Sadat 2-3, pol cmnd formed 2-4, 87A1
Asked to ease Beirut camp siege 2-15, 106D3
Vance meets 2-20, 122A1
Adirsch slain 2-22, 457C3
OKs Palestinian south Leb exit 2-23, 143B2
Sudan joins Egypt-Syria cmnd 2-27—2-28, 143F2
Demands Leb Christns end Israel link 246F1
Sees Arafat on Leb clashes 4-9, 266B3
Visits Moscow 4-18—4-22, 297B2, 317C2
Backs demilitarized zones 5-5, 360E2
Meets Carter 5-9, 360G1-A3
US briefs Israel on Carter talks 5-11, 361A1
Sees Sadat, Khalid on Israel electn 5-19, 401D3
Takes hard stand on Israel recognitn 6-15, 496F1
Sees Arafat, backs hard line vs Israel 6-20, 496A2
Begin asks peace talks 6-21, 474C2
Begin asks UN aid on Syrian Jews 7-22, 571A1
Sees Vance; vs Israel-Arab forgn mins mtg plan 8-4, 588G2
Vs 'proximity talks' 8-12, 623D3
For Israel peace, vs ties 8-26, 663F1
For PLO at peace conf 9-26, 734D1
Vs US-Israel working paper 10-21, 831B2
Sees Sarkis on peace moves 11-5, 850C1
Meets Arafat, asks PLO pullback from south Leb 11-10, 874F2
Arab League delays Geneva decisn 11-12—11-14, 874B2
Begin to ask Israel 11-15, 873G1
Meets Sadat re Israel visit 11-16, 873A2
Scores Sadat trip 11-17, 890E2
Sees Jordan premr on Egypt rift 11-22, 894E1
Bars Sadat Cairo conf 11-28, 909A2
At Tripoli anti-Sadat mtg 12-2—12-5, 929D1
Iraq chrgs 'surrender' 12-5, 929F1
Sees Hussein on Egypt rift 12-7, 930C2
In Saudi, Kuwait, Bahrain, Qatar, UAE; seeks aid vs Cairo conf 12-8—12-11, 954F2
Meets Vance, vs Cairo conf 12-13, 954D1
Carter: PLO 'negative' 12-15, 954D3
ASSAD, Kamal al-
Vs Israel on Syria troop moves 1-28, 72D1

1978

ASIA—*See also country, organization names*
Japan '77 aid sets record 1-3, 28F2
Viet offcl ends SE Asia tour 1-12, 43B1
France urges detente in SE Asia 1-19, 71F1
Arab poor-state aid rise rptd 4-9, 257C2
Rumania, UK talks 6-13—6-16, 515D3
China chrgs Viet-Sovt plot to control SE Asia 7-12, 547G3; 9-6, 696D1
China scores Sovt hegemony 8-16, 674E3
China, Yugo talks rptd 8-21—8-22, 675E2
USSR warns West vs China arms deals 10-26, 814D1
Canada drug source 12-18, 1013E3
U.S. Relations
US troop presence rptd 1-2, 5D2
US '77 rpt warns vs mil cuts 1-6, 5E3
Carter State of Union Message 1-19, 31G2
US affirms mil commitmt 2-20, 126B3
Carter warns USSR vs mil buildup, interventn 3-17, 202F1
Japan says US confrms commitmt 5-4, 341C3
US '77 arms bid rejctns rptd 5-19, 386G3
US pledges A-weapon restraint 6-12, 445A2
ASIAN Americans—*See also CHINESE Americans*
Harvard admissions progrm described 483B2
Covered in US minority business contracts ruling 9-23, 811F2
ASIA Society (N.Y., N.Y.)
Rockefeller 3d dies 7-10, 620D3; art bequeathed 7-20, 628E1
ASKEW, Gov. Reubin (D, Fla.)
Graham elected Fla gov 11-7, 849C3
ASL (American Soccer League)—*See SOCCER*
ASNAJ, Abdallah
Rpts S Yemen fighting 10-21, 885E3
ASNER, Edward
Wins Emmy 9-17, 1030F1
ASPIN, Rep. Les (D, Wis.)
Urges lower mil recruiting standards 7-2, 528E3
Reelected 11-7, 852C4
ASPIRIN—*See MEDICINE—Drugs*

ASSAD, Hafez al- (Syrian president)
On anti-Sadat summit results 2-5, 78G2
Reelected 2-8, 136F3
In Moscow 2-21—2-22, to get more arms 2-24, 139D2
Sadat scores Sovt arms pledge 2-25, 139G2
Sees Sarkis on Israel invasn 3-15, 174D3
Opens border for aid to PLO in Leb 3-18, 198D2
Israeli Leb invasn protested 3-21, 198D3
Names Halabi premier 3-27, 269F3
OKs Leb troop role in south 5-31—6-1, 462C3
Meets Leb speaker 7-11; questns Sarkis on resignatn 7-12; Sarkis to stay on 7-15, 547B1
Warns Israel on Leb role 8-29, 674A2
Vs Camp David summit pacts 9-20, 712F1
Hardliners end conf, USSR contact sought 9-24, 730A1
Vance sees on summit pacts 9-24, 731C1
Asks Hussein, Saudis reject summit pact 9-26, 9-27, 730F1, A2
Carter lauds for Leb truce 9-30, 745F1
Sarkis seeks to prolong truce 10-1, 746A1
Vs French Leb peace plan 10-3, 745C2
Carter asks Leb truce role 10-5, 761C1
In Moscow, to get more Sovt arms 10-5—10-6, 762C3
Meets Sarkis re Leb truce 10-7—10-9, 761E1
Meets Sarkis on Leb peace plan 10-12, 783B1
Meets Bakr; Syria, Iraq to join forces 10-24—10-26, 803F1
ASSAD, Kamal al-
Asks Israel, PLO Leb exit, more Unifil troops 4-4, 236B1
Meets Syrian pres 7-11, Sarkis questnd on resignatn 7-12, 547C1
ASSAD, Kayed
Admits Iraqi ties 8-4, 602A3
Chrgd with PLO deaths 8-5, 602G2
ASSANTE, Armand
Paradise Alley released 10-10, 970F2

1979

ASIA—*See also DEVELOPING Nations; also country, organization names*
Viet, Cambodia sign friendship pact, SE ties stressed 2-18, 123C2
A-power programs to continue 4-6, 323B2
SALT II summit topic 6-15—6-18, 449D1; communique text 458B2
'78 smoking rise rptd 11-22, 970F2
Amnesty Intl reviews '79 rights 12-9, 980D2
U.S. Relations
US sees stability re China tie 1-15, 27C2
US plays down China invasn impact 2-20, 123A1
Blumenthal ends trip 3-5, 159G3-160D1
US defends 'new diplomacy' 5-1, 347D2
US health team dispatched 6-5, 550E2
SALT II summit topic 6-15—6-18, 449D1; communique text 458B2
Kissinger backs SALT linkage 7-31, 590B3
US cigaret exports cited 11-22, 970G2
ASIAN Americans
Sup Ct workforce data rptd 6-11, 464A2
Govt constructn grants case argued in Sup Ct 11-27, 945A1
ASIAN Development Bank (ADB) (Afghanistan, Australia, Austria, Bangladesh, Belgium, Burma, Cambodia, Cook Islands, Denmark, Fiji, Finland, France, Great Britain, Hong Kong, India, Indonesia, Italy, Japan, Kiribati, Laos, Malaysia, Maldives, Nepal, Netherlands, New Zealand, Norway, Pakistan, Papua New Guinea, Philippines, Singapore, Solomon Islands, South Korea, Sri Lanka, Sweden, Switzerland, Taiwan, Thailand, Tonga, U.S., Vietnam, Western Samoa, West Germany)
US to weigh S Korea loans 10-17—10-19, 803A3
ASIAN Society (N.Y., N.Y.)
Japan gifts presented 5-4, 375A2
ASKEW, Reubin
Named US immigratn policy comr 2-16, 127A1
Named Carter trade rep 8-8, 647B1*
Sworn trade rep 10-2, 803E1
ASLEEP At The Wheel (singing group)
Wins Grammy 2-16, 336F3
ASNAJ, Abdallah
Asks Arab League mtg on border clashes 2-25, 144C2
ASPIN, Rep. Les (D, Wis.)
On US arms aid to N Yemen 3-19, 199E2
Praises US intell on China-Viet war 3-25, 231F3
On N Korea mil buildup 6-11, 495G1
On U-2 SALT verificatn 7-1, 497C1
Scores mil pension reform plan 7-19, 628C2
Rebuts Young re PLO mtg rpt 10-28, 823D2

ASSAD, Hafez al- (Syrian president)
In Iraqi unity talks 1-28—1-30, 69F2
Warns vs Israel-Egypt pact 3-8, 157F1
Meets Sovt forgn min 3-24, Israel-Egypt pact scored 3-26, 222D2
Sadat notes Faisal warning 5-1, Saudi denies 5-2, 319A2
Meets Sarkis re Leb unrest 5-14—5-15, 378G2
Meets Bakr 6-17—6-18, joint pol cmnd set 6-19, 462D1
Egypt ties to Emb raid in Turkey 7-16, 536A3
Tied to Iraq plot 8-5, denies 8-6, 602A3
Rumanian pres seeks Israel feud mediatn 8-31, 659D2
Sunni resentment cited 754G3
Meets Jesse Jackson 10-2, 763E1
In USSR, gets arms vow 10-15—10-18, 857E2
Sees Iran emissaries at Arab League summit 11-21, 916E2
ASSANTE, Armand
Prophecy released 6-15 -2-19, 820A3

1980

ASIA—*See also country, organization names; also related headings (e.g., DEVELOPING Nations)*
Brezhnev backs detente 2-4, 84F3
Chile pres cancels Pacific tour 3-22, 230F3
Libyan students occupy embs 5-10, 373A3
Malaria outbreak rptd 5-31, 478B1
Food forecast gloomy 7-23, 573B2
World Bank '80 econ forecast grim 8-17, 628G2
UNESCO illiteracy study rptd 12-4, 953E1
USSR, India vs forgn interventn 12-11, 930D2
U.S. Relations
Carter State of Union address 1-23, 42C3
US issues rights rpt 2-5, 87C1, G1-C2
Carter asks draft registratn 2-8, 110G2
Moynihan warns of 'Soviet empire' 8-11, 612D3
US Dem platform plank adopted 8-13, 615C1
Carter accepts pres renominatn 8-14, 613C1
'81 refugee quota rptd 9-19, 883B3
ASIAN Americans
Govt constructn grants upheld by Sup Ct 7-2, 510C1
NY Times settles '74 job bias suit 9-17, 746B3
House electn results 11-4, 846B2, F3
ASIAN Development Bank (ADB) (Afghanistan, Australia, Austria, Bangladesh, Belgium, Burma, Cambodia, Cook Islands, Denmark, Fiji, Finland, France, Great Britain, Hong Kong, India, Indonesia, Italy, Japan, Kiribati, Laos, Malaysia, Maldives, Nepal, Netherlands, New Zealand, Norway, Pakistan, Papua New Guinea, Philippines, Singapore, Solomon Islands, South Korea, Sri Lanka, Sweden, Switzerland, Taiwan, Thailand, Tonga, U.S., Vietnam, Western Samoa, West Germany)
US pressures to cancel ROK loan 6-12, 467D1
ASKEW, Reubin O.
Japan to end US auto parts tariff 5-15, 482C1
Nissan exec asks tariff rise delay 7-1, 599C2
In Detroit re auto aid 7-7, 505A2
ASL (American Soccer League)—*See SOCCER*
ASNER, Ed
Wins Emmy 9-7, 692C1
ASPIN, Rep. Les (D, Wis.)
Asks CIA details re press, clergy, academics 2-25, 189A3
On Sovt anthrax cover-up 6-29, 500E1
Reelected 11-4, 844C4

ASSAD, Hafez al- (Syrian president)
Purges ldrship, reelected to posts 1-6, 22D2
Forms new Cabt 1-16, 102G1
Ordrs Beirut troop exit 2-4, defers 2-5, 89E2
Leb asks Syrians to stay in Beirut 2-13, 125G2
Daoudy on UN comm to probe shah 2-17, 122C1
Says Israel plans attack 2-23, 140C3
Vows arms for popular militia 212F3
Blames CIA, US for unrest 3-10, 3-16, 212F3
Gen strike in Aleppo, Hama 3-31, 295A2
At hard-line Arab summit 4-14—4-15, 284G2
Escapes death try 6-26; Moslem Brotherhood linked, curbs set 7-2, 7-3, 525F3-526B1
Bitar slain in Paris 7-21, 567C2
900 in Moslem Brotherhood accept amnesty 8-29, 674A1
Libya proposes Syria merger 9-1, OKs concept 9-2, 660E3
In Libya merger talks 9-8—9-9; unity OKd 9-10, 697D1
Begin cites isolatn 9-9, 697D2
Signs Syria-Sovt friendship pact 10-8, 759D2
Relative killed in Beirut 11-5, 873G3
Jordan gets terms in Syria feud 12-2, 911F2
To attend Jordan feud talks 12-5, 931A3
Meets Qaddafi, merger delayed 12-16—12-18, 978B2
Political ally slain 12-27, 996G2-A3
ASSAD, Rifaat al-
Keeps party post 1-6, 22E2
On Moslem Brotherhood search 7-2, 526B1

1976

ASSASSINATIONS, Political—*See 'Political Assassinations' under CRIME*
ASSOCIATED General Contractors of America
Ford addresses, gets award 3-9, 180C1
ASSOCIATED Press (AP)
'75 coll football rankings 1-2, 31B3
Rpts '75 Argentina death toll 1-3, 7E2
'75 athletes honored 1-13, 1-15, 31A3, F3
Hauser interviewed 3-1, 200E2
Lewine named to Gridiron Club 3-5, 272A1
Fuller named pres 5-3, 504F2
Denies Sovt spy chrg 5-25, 371A3
GOP delegate totals 6-19, 450G2
Developing natns OK press pool 7-13, 619A3
GOP conv delegate polls rptd 8-7—8-8, 616A2
Rpt Cuba aides 'desert' 8-16, 672F1
Sees Ford nominatn 8-17, 601E3
Carter interview 9-17, TV debate cites 9-23, 701B3, 703G2-B3
Butz story coverage cited 744B1
Mears on pres debate panel 10-15, 782B3
Pl bur chief ousted 11-2; chrgs denied 11-6, 855D1
ASSOCIATION—*For organizations not listed below, see key words*
ASSOCIATION for the Rights and Defense of Peoples
To replace Russell Tribunal 1-17, 61E2
ASSOCIATION of Southeast Asian Nations (Asean) (Indonesia, Malaysia, Philippines, Singapore, Thailand)
Australia sees ldrs 1-16—1-18, 46B1
Conf OKs amity pact 2-9—2-10, 108A2
Summit pact backs close ties 2-23—2-24, 148A2
Australia vows talks 10-10, 789B2
ASSOGBA, Nicolas
Sentenced 2-1—2-2, 404D1
ASTHMA—*See 'Heart & Lungs' under MEDICINE*

ASTRONAUTICS
'77 budget proposals 1-21, 62F1, 64C2
US CIA discounts Sovt progrms 3-11, 216F2
Fiscal '77 US budget estimate tables 231A1, 358B2
Cong OKs NASA funds 5-21, 411G3-412C1; Ford signs 6-4, 982F1
Ford OKs '77 ERDA progrm 7-12, 517G2

1977

ASSASSINATIONS—*Note: Initial incident only listed; for subsequent developments, see country, personal names*
US House com revived 2-2, 77C1; **see 'Assassinations, Select Committee on' under U.S. GOVERNMENT—HOUSE of Representatives**
Ethiopia prov min 2-2, 98F2
'72 Marcos plotters sentncd 2-10, 100A1
Rockefeller plot mistrial 3-10, 261F2
Sanjay Gandhi try foiled 3-14, 205F2
Leb Moslem ldr slain 3-16, 188C1
Congo ldr slain 3-18, Cardinal 3-23, 220A2, C2
Cuban exile sentenced 3-18, 288E3
N Yemen ex-premier 4-10, 284D3
El Salvador forgn min 5-10, 373B2
Turkish amb to Vatican 6-9, 656G1-A2
Syrian gen slain 6-18, 496E2
Haiti amb to Brazil 7-3, 583C2
Former Egypt min 7-4, 525E3
Colombian colonel 7-6, 636A1
Mauritania envoy 7-7, 543B2
Ethiopia offcls 8-4, 649C1
Ne Win plotters arrested 9-3, 779D2
Spain Basque ldr 10-8, 826B2
N Yemen pres, brother 10-10, 783F3; others rptd 10-12, 10-14, 824F1
UK foils Togo plot 10-13, 988F2
UAE state min 10-25, 811B3
Ethiopia ldrs 11-2, 11-13, 875E2
Afghan min 11-16, 969E2
ASSAULT & Battery
Ranger player slugs mgr 3-28, suspended 4-5, 310E3★; fined 7-28, 644G2
Dorsett chrgs dropped 8-18, 659C2
Ranger player sued by ex-mgr 9-21, 768D2
Youth sentncd in Fla TV trial 10-7, 907F3
NBA players fined 10-20, 870E1; 12-12, 990G2-G3
Yankee player acquitted 11-1, 927C2
Battered wife acquitted of murder 11-3, 928E1
Battered wife prgrms urged by Natl Women's Conf 11-19—11-21, 917D3
NL pres robbed 11-30, 990F2
ASSOCIATED General Contractors of America
Calif minority constructn quota challenged 10-31, 979A1
ASSOCIATED Milk Producers Inc.—*See MILK Producers Inc., Associated*
ASSOCIATED Newspapers Group Ltd.
Buys Esquire 8-26, 695A3
ASSOCIATED Press, The (AP)
'76 coll football rankings 1-3, 8E3
Tarver to be chrmn 1-18, 140E2
Carter interview 1-24, 51B3
USSR ousts Krimsky 2-4, 101C1
Rpts Carter-Washn Post mtg 2-25, 151G2
Uruguay curbs rptrs 3-24, 351E2
Zaire ousts Goldsmith 4-4, 261B1
2 win Pulitzers 4-18, 355F2, A3
Goldsmith held in CAE 7-14—8-15, 634E3
Uruguay detains Garces 7-20—7-21, 601B2
FCC '75 'end-link' order upheld 8-5, 632A1
Teng Hsiao-ping interview 9-6, 686D3
CIA links charged 9-12, 720B3, 721C1
Poll: Panama Canal pacts opposed 9-21, 755F2
Bergland interview 10-21, 814C2
Baseball top mgrs named 10-25, 10-26, 927A2
Argentina rptr kidnaped 11-10—11-11, 922G1, B2
JFK assassinatn files received 12-1, 943E1
Baughman details Rhodesia atrocities 12-2, 1015F3-1016C1
On most reliable govt news source list 12-10, 1009B1
ASSOCIATION—For organizations not listed below, see key words
ASSOCIATION of Southeast Asian Nations (ASEAN) (Indonesia, Malaysia, Philippines, Singapore, Thailand)
Australia sets review panel 1-20, sees wider trade ties 1-24, 60D2
Trade pact signed; US, Japan talks urged 2-24, 145F2
Sovt chrgs mil plans 2-24, 145C3
SEATO head wants merger 514B2
Westn econ ties urged 6-27—6-29, 537D1
Indochina ties backed 7-5—7-8, 537C1
Australia vs ASEAN trade criticism 7-9, 561A1
Summit conf sets reserve fund, urges Indochina ties; Viet, Cambodia score 8-4—8-5, 607C1
Mtg with Japan, Australia, NZ ldrs 8-6—8-7, 607A2
ASTHMA—*See MEDICINE—Diseases*
ASTIN, Patty Duke
Wins Emmy 9-11, 1022A1
ASTLES, Robert
On Amin US mtg order 2-27, 141G1
Amin rptd well 9-15, 709A3
ASTOR, Gerturude
Dies 11-9, 952B2
ASTRONAUTICS
Ford '78 budget proposals 1-17, 31D1, 32F2
Carter keeps Ford budget 2-22, 125B2
US, USSR OK cooperatn pact 5-18, 400A3
Wernher von Braun dies 6-16, 532G3
NASA '78 authorizatn signed 7-30, 688G3

1978

ASSASSINATION Information Bureau
JFK murder film assessed 11-26, 916G1, E2
House com asks JFK film review 12-30, 1002D1
ASSASSINATIONS—*Note: Initial incident only listed; for subsequent developments, see country, personal names*
Barcelona ex-mayor 1-25, 135G3
N Korea pres' son '77 try 2-5, 115E3
S Africa tribal health min 2-7, 114B1
Egypt newspaper editor 2-18, 117A1, C1
Hustler owner shot 3-6, 186G3
Qaddafi plot hinted 3-6, 228D1
PFLP's Sayed 3-8, 157C2★
Ankara prosecutor 3-24, 230G1
Argentina econ undersecy 4-11, 285A3
Uganda vp attempt suspected 4-19, 331B3
PLO aide in Kuwait 6-15, 489A2
N Yemen pres 6-24, 498F2
USSR Azerbaijan min 6-29, 518G3
Iraqi ex-premr Naif 7-10, 522E2
Carter threat rptd hoax 8-30, 664G1
Tito plot 12-1, 933C3
ASSAULT—*See under CRIME*
ASSEMBLIES of God
'76 membershp growth rptd 6-12, 907B3
ASSEYEV, Tamara
Wanna Hold Your Hand released 4-21, 619E2
ASSOCIATED Milk Producers Committee for Thorough Agricultural Political Education—*See MILK Producers, etc.*
ASSOCIATED Press, The (AP)
'77 coll football rankings 1-3, 8F2
Lee named top coll basketball player 3-13, 272D2
Baughman wins Pulitzer 4-17, 315F1, B2
Czechoslovakia ousts rptr 5-1, 439B3
Young interviewed 7-12, 542D3
Carter poll rating rptd low 8-10, 682C2
Poll rpts econ pessimism growing 8-13, 679E2
ERA poll rptd 8-16, 661B3
Baseball top mgrs named 10-24, 928C2
ASSOCIATION—For organizations not listed below, see key words
ASSN. of Motion Picture & Television Producers Inc. v. Writers Guide of America, West Inc.
Unions curbed on supervisor discipline by Sup Ct 6-21, 509E1
ASSOCIATION of Southeast Asian Nations (ASEAN) (Indonesia, Malaysia, Philippines, Singapore, Thailand)
Indonesia secy-gen Dharsono ousted 1-23, 72E1; formally quits, Umarjadi replaces 2-18, 122B2
In econ talks with US, common fund set 8-3—8-4 603F2-C3
Thai, Viet peace zone agrmt reached 9-10, 697B2
US ambs meet Holbrooke 10-25, 830G1
China lauds anti-Sovt role 11-6, 894B1
ASSURE Competitive Transportation—*See ACT*
ASTAIRE, Fred
Wins Emmy 9-17, 1030G1
ASTARITA, Marzio
Shot 5-11, 393D2
ASTLES, Maj. Robert
Rpts Tanzania attack repulsed 11-12, 870D2
ASTOR, Vincent (1892-1959)
Ex-wife M C Fosburgh dies 11-4, 972B3
ASTORGA, Lidia
Kills mil ldr 3-8, rptd in Mex emb 3-27, 376G1

ASTRONAUTICS
Carter budget proposals 1-23, 46C1; table 45D2
France, W Ger OK launcher constructn 2-7, 122B1
US Cong '79 budget target res cleared 5-17, 385E1
China dvpt plan outlined 5-28, 436F1

1979

ASSASSINATIONS
Al Fatah ldr 1-22, 51A1
Guatemala sen 1-25, 97E1
US amb to Afghanistan 2-14, 106C2
Spain army gen 3-5, 191E3
Israel honorary consul in El Salvador 3-21, 234B3
UK amb to Holland 3-22, 228E2-D3
Guatemala pol ldr 3-22, 237B1
UK Tory MP 3-30, 254E1
Iran armed forces ex-staff chief 4-23, 297C1
Iran Islam offcl 5-1, 321D1
Carter alleged plot probed 5-5—5-29, 404C1
El Salvador educ min 5-23, 387C3
Spain army personnel chief 5-25, 428D2
Swiss diplomat in El Salvador 5-30, 406A3
Guatemala Army staff chief 6-10, 445B3
Pan-Africa Cong UN rep 6-12, 476G3
Iran relig ldr 7-8, 525E1
Iran ayatollah escapes, Khomeini aide shot 7-15, 544G2, A3
PLO aide in France 7-26, 551G3
UK's Lord Mountbatten 8-27, 641A1
Spain mil gov 9-23, 754G1
Somoza's nephew 10-4, 793F3
Guyana educ min 10-24, 838B2
S Korean pres 10-26, 821A1
Shah's nephew in Paris 12-7, 935B1
Khomeini ally 12-18, 958F2
ASSAULT—*See under CRIME*
ASSELIN, Martial
Gets Canada Intl Dvpt Agency post 6-4, 423F3
ASSEYEV, Tamara
Norma Rae released 3-1, 174C3
ASSOCIATED Newspapers Group Ltd.
Esquire sale to Tenn firm rptd 5-1, 334D2
ASSOCIATED Press, The (AP)
'78 coll football rankings 1-3, 8B2
'Son of Sam' interviewed 2-22, 156G2
Bird named top coll basketball player 3-12, 290E3
Energy shortage poll rptd 5-4, 343F1-B2
4 US papers to open China offices 5-30, 406B2
Jaffe interviewed 8-11, 611G1
Iran closes Teheran office 9-4, 670G1
Carter job rating poll rptd 9-13, 680A2
UPI press partnership sale rptd 10-4, 859G2
Carter to videotape Vesco testimony 12-5, 943C2
ASSOCIATION of Southeast Asian Nations (ASEAN) (Indonesia, Malaysia, Philippines, Singapore, Thailand)
Australia air policy oppositn rptd 1-5, 6C1
Meets 1-12—1-13, demands Viets quit Cambodia 1-13, 28A2
Singapore scores Viet SE Asia policy 1-13, 28G1
China Viet invasn concern voiced 2-20, 123G1
USSR vetoes res on Viet, Cambodia conflicts 3-16, 200E1
Indochina refugee conf held 5-15—5-16, 379E1
Meets on Indochina refugees, bars more admissns 6-28—6-30, 495A2
Indochina refugee asylum asked by US, Japan to hike UN aid 7-2, 495E2
ANZUS backs Viet Cambodia exit 7-5, 495A3
UN urges Viet exit from Cambodia 11-14, 863F3
ASSURE Competitive Transportation—*See ACT*
ASTAIRE, Jarvis
Agatha released 2-8, 174C2
ASTLES, Maj. Robert
Kenya rpts arrest 4-18, 288E1
Returned to Uganda 6-8, trial opens 6-11, 488G3-489A1
ASTORGA, Nora
Named Nicaraga spec prosecuter 12-3, 950D3
ASTRODOME (Houston, Tex. stadium)
Astros sale OKd 5-16, 619D1

ASTRONAUTICS
CIA UFO probe detailed 1-12, 93A1
Carter budget proposals 1-22, 46E1; table 42F2
SALT II communique backs exploratn 6-18, 458D1
'80 NASA funds clear Cong 10-24, Carter signs 11-5, 883G2

1980

ASSASSINATIONS—*Note: Initial incident only listed; for subsequent developments, see country, personal names*
Syria Sunni Moslem clergyman 2-2, 154C2
El Salvador atty gen 2-23, 149G1
Chile pres plot foiled 3-23, 231D1
El Salvador archbishop 3-24, 220E1
Iraqi dep premr escapes 4-1, 261C1
Liberia pres 4-12, 284A3
India prime min escapes 4-14, 294A3
Guinea pres attempt foiled 5-14, 431E3
Grenada prime min escapes 6-19, 498B2
Syria pres Assad escapes 6-26, 525F3
Chile army officer 7-15, 563A1
Bakhtiar attempt fails 7-18, 545A1
Turkey ex-premr 7-19, 567B3
Syrian ex-premr in Paris 7-21, 567C2
Iran ex-attache in US 7-22, 545B1, B2
Baath Party offcl in Leb 7-28, 579A3
Leb press official 7-23, 579F2
Spain gen escapes 7-29, 605G3
US amb to Leb escapes 8-28, 643F3
Spain gen by GRAPO 9-2, 673G2
Cuban UN attache 9-11, 685A2
Somoza in Paraguay 9-17, 697F2
El Salvador human rights chief 10-26, 829C2
Gaza Arab ldr 11-18, 880B1
ASSAULT—*See CRIME--Assault & Battery*
ASSOCIATED Newspapers Ltd.
Evening News, Evening Standard to merge 10-1, 750D3
ASSOCIATED Press, The (AP)
'79 coll football rankings 1-2, 22G3
Ali named Athlete of Decade 1-13, 320G3
Iran invites 25 newsmen 2-27, 138G1
Aguirre named top coll basketball player, Meyer named top coach 3-21, 240E3, F3
Rptr, photographer seized in Leb 4-18, 302A3
Jankowski CBS resignatn hoax 5-23, 501B2
Pres polls rptd 6-3, 423A1; 8-19, 630B1
Post-debate pres poll rptd 9-26, 739B3
Reagan interviewed 9-30, 738C3, E3
Pres poll standings tighten, toss-up seen 10-27, 816A2
Top baseball mgrs named 11-17, 11-20, 926C1
3d World coverage study rptd 11-29, 914D1
ASSOCIATION of National Advertisers v. FTC
Case refused by Sup Ct 6-16, 511E3
ASSOCIATION of Southeast Asian Nations (ASEAN) (Indonesia, Malaysia, Philippines, Singapore, Thailand)
China, Japan discuss 5-27—6-1, 422B1
Meets 6-25—6-26; Viet Thai incursn scored 6-26, 508F1
US vows Thailand arms aid 6-27, 491C3
India-Cambodia ties assailed 7-7, 547G2
Australia, NZ in S Pacific islands trade pact 7-24, 576G3
Viet Cambodia-Thai DMZ plan opposed 8-1, 591E1
ASTIN, Alexander W.
On coll freshmen survey 1-20, 319E3

ASTRONAUTICS
Carter budget proposals 1-28, 71E2; table 70F1
US research backed; USSR, Japan, Eur efforts cited 2-16, 160E2
Carter revised budget proposals 3-31, 244E1

1976

US Space Exploratn Day proclaimed 7-19, 527A2
Cong sets '77 budget levels, table 9-16, 706B2
Wm Nordberg dies 10-3, 970G2
'60 Sovt disaster rptd 11-6, 948G3

Communication Projects
US House OKs educ broadcast funds 1-20, 94B2

Interplanetary Projects
US Uranus probe deferred 1-21, 64D2
US Viking I lands on Mars; atmosphere analyzed, seismometer, scoop fail 7-20—7-22; diagram, photo 525A1-527B2
Viking cost rptd 527B1
Viking I scoop fixed, soil tests begin; atmospheric, other data rptd 7-25—7-27, 548G3-549A3
Viking 2 landing site rptd set 7-28, 549B3
Viking I soil test data rptd 7-30—8-7; scoop fails again 8-3, repaired 8-7, 594A3, 595A1
Viking 1 tests continue 8-13—9-11, 683F3
Viking 2 lands; transmissn, scoop fail 9-3—9-13, 683C2

Manned Flight
China program gains rptd 1-7, 1-8, 78E1
'77 US budget proposals 1-21, 64C2
US CIA discounts Sovt program 3-11, 216F2
Cong OKs shuttle funds 5-21, 412A1
Sovt Salyut 5 orbited 6-22, 527B2
Mondale shuttle record cited 512C3
Cosmonauts return from Salyut 5 8-25, 684E1
Sovts set '78 E Eur role 9-14, 684D1
Sovt Soyuz 22 launched 9-15, 684C1
Soyuz 23 launched 10-14, aborted 10-16, 839C3

Moon Exploration
Sovt Luna 24 launched 8-9, returns 8-22, 684G1

Satellites, Earth
Cosmos 787 orbited 1-6, 56G2
'77 US budget proposals 1-21, 64D2
US CIA discounts program 3-11, 216F2
China orbits 6th satellite 8-30, 674D1
US denies Sovt laser use vs surveillnc craft 11-23; Sovt 'hunter-killers' rptd 12-18, 961A2
China launch cited 12-18, 961C2

1977

Communication Projects
Australia defends US facilities 1-25, 81C2
Indonesia probes Hughes Aircraft payoff chrgs 2-4, 182G2
ESA satellite launch postponed 6-16, aborted 9-13, 735G3
ESA-N Amer projct shelved 9-19, 736B1
Viacom-RCA pay-TV pact rptd 10-25, 921D1
Calif constructn dispute declined 11-7, 857E2

Interplanetary Projects
Relativity evidence rptd 1-7, 170E3
Ford '78 budget proposals 1-17, 31E1
Mars' moon photos taken 2-18, 170D3
Jupiter probe authorizatn signed 7-30, 689A1
Voyager 2 launched for Jupiter, Saturn 8-20, Voyager 1 delayed 8-29, 664A1
Voyager 1 launched 9-5, Voyager 2 OK 9-10, 731D1
Jupiter probe funds signed 10-4, 796E3

Manned Flight—*See also 'Space Shuttle' below*
Sovt Soyuz 22 landing rptd 109G3
Ford '78 budget proposals 1-17, 31E1
Sovt Soyuz 24 launched 2-7, 109E3; lands 2-25, 170E2
US-ESA venture planned 2-16, 170C3
Carter call-in topic 3-5, 171B1
Sovt Salyut 6 launched 9-29; Soyuz 25 fails docking 10-9—10-11, 771C3
Sovts launch Soyuz 26 12-10, docks with Salyut 12-11, permanent statn planned 12-26, 999D1

Moon Exploration
Data-collecting statns closed 9-30, 908E3

Satellites, Earth
Sovt immigrant seized as spy 1-7, 41C3
Ford '78 budget proposals 1-17, 31F1
Carter seeks arms accord 3-9, 172E3
US, USSR OK working group 3-30, 225A2
ESA missn postponed 6-16, aborted 9-13, 735G3
US: USSR can destroy some satellites 10-4, 777A2
Sun-earth study satellites launched 10-22, 908A3

Space Shuttle (Enterprise)
US shuttle test flight 2-18, 170A3
'78 shuttle authorizatn OKd 7-30, 688G3
Space shuttle flight test 8-12, 626G3
2d shuttle test goes well 9-13, 731A2
Passes crucial test flight 10-12, 771E3
Landing tests end, vibratn tests set 10-26, 908C3

1978

Carter affirms US space ldrshp, marks NASA anniv 10-1, 861A2
US sets 10-yr goals 10-11, 861F1

Communications Projects
FCC, Comsat settle dispute 5-9, 494C3
ESA satellite launched 5-12, 384D3
US '79 defns authrzn vetoed 8-17, 622A1

Interplantetary Projects
Carter budgets solar research 1-23, 46D1
Venus probe launched, 2d craft scheduled 5-20, 445C1
US launches Pioneer Venus 2 8-8, 623B1
USSR Venus launchings rptd 9-10, 9-15, 714D1
Apollo XI image OKd for $ coin 10-10, 788D2
Venus orbiter arrives 12-4, probes explore atmosphere 12-9—12-11, 968C2-B3
Sovt Venera probes land on Venus 12-21, 12-25, 1021F2

Manned Flight—*See also 'Space Shuttles' below*
Sovt Soyuz 27, Salyut 6 dock 1-11, 11B2, D2 ★
Sovt team returns after Salyut 6 docking 1-16, 157A3
Apollo 13 A-powered craft fall cited 57E1
Sovt Salyut 6 fueled by unmanned craft 2-2, 157C3
Czech, Sovt team launched 3-2, docks with Salyut 6 3-3, 157E2; return 3-10, 181B1
Sovt Soyuz crew breaks US space-stay record 3-4, 157D2; flight ends 3-16, 180D3
Soyuz 29, Salyut 6 dock 6-17, 505E3
Soyuz 30 docks with Salyut, Pole in crew 6-28, 506A1
Soyuz 30 lands 7-5, supply ship docks with Salyut 6 7-9; USSR sets space-stay record 8-2, 622C3
Soyuz 31 docks with Salyut 8-27, Soyuz 31 crew returns to Earth 9-3, 714A1
Space-stay record broken by USSR 9-20, 714C1
Salyut 6 crew returns to Earth in Soyuz 31 spacecraft 11-2, 860G3

Obituaries
Bushuyev, Konstantin D 10-26, 888F2
Keldysh, Mistislav 6-24, 540A3

Satellites, Earth
Facts on Cosmos 954 57C1
US, USSR meet on Cosmos fall 1-12, 1-17, 57B1, F2
US alerts NATO, other natns to Cosmos fall 57E1
US reorganizes intell agencies 1-24, 49F2
USSR Cosmos falls into Canada 1-24; radiatn detected, debris found 1-25—2-1, 57A1
US '64, '70 A-accidents cited 57D1, F2
Canada protests USSR policy 1-25; US, USSR defend cooperatn 1-27, 1-28, 57D2
France asks disarmamt verificatn system 1-25, 61A3
US rpts USSR ASAT advances, other weapons progrms 2-2, 81E2
Canada rpts Cosmos search cost 2-3, plans USSR paymt claim 2-13, 103E1
Canada retrieves Cosmos radioactive debris, Sovt scientist admits error 2-4, 103A1
US rpt on radiatn hazards issued 2-6, 103F1
USSR vetoes UN safety study, offers Canada damages 2-14, 238A2
Canada Cosmos search rptd ended 4-2, 238C2
W Ger testing site in Zaire rptd 4-29, 382G1
ESA launches communicatns unit 5-12, 384D3
USSR killer satellite test rptd 5-24, US-USSR talks held 6-8—6-16, 488E2
USSR satellites aid Arctic ship 5-25—6-12, 506A3
San Andreas Fault shift rptd 6-18, 480C1
Canada presses Cosmos 954 search 7-5, 514C3
US '79 defns authrzn vetoed 8-17, 622A1
CIA ex-aide arrested as spy 8-17, Sovt manual rptd missing 8-23, 645E2
HEAO-1 detects gas cloud in galaxy cluster 9-16, 1023G2
US Pegasus I falls 9-17, 714F1
USSR Barentsburg tracking statn rptd 9-28, 820D2
CIA ex-offcl's death, Sovt spy link denied 10-1—10-26, 835F3
Carter admits US spy satellites use 10-1, 861B2
Canada ends Cosmos 954 search 10-18, 1013G2
CIA ex-aide convicted 11-18, manual leaks said to help USSR 11-23, 940F1, G2; sentncd 12-22, 1011C3

Skylab Program (U.S. program for manned orbiting laboratory)
USSR breaks US space-stay record 3-4, 157E2; flight ends 3-16, 180E3
Skylab maneuvered to prevent fall, '79 shuttle missn planned 6-8—6-11, 444D1, 445A1
Skylab maneuvered again 7-25, 623D1
NASA '79 funds signed 9-30, 750G2

Space Shuttles
NASA names 35 astronauts; women, minorities included 1-16, 157E3-158A1
Carter budgets 4 shuttles 1-23, 46C1
Calif launching base OKd by House 5-22, 407B1

1979

Communications Projects
US, China sign satellite pact 1-31, 65C1
World radio conf held 9-27–12-6, 1006C3
Australia plans satellite system 10-18, 852B2
Postal Svc satellite leasing plan rejctd 10-18, 921F2
RCA loses Satcom III 12-10, 991D1

Interplanetary Projects
Carter budget proposals 1-22, 46F1
Venus chasm found by Pioneer orbiter 2-7, 290A1
Voyager I Jupiter photos 2-13, 3-4, 162D2
Voyager I makes close Jupiter approach 3-5, findings detailed 3-5–3-17, 215E3-216D3
Pioneer orbiter Venus findings described 5-29, 692A1
Voyager I hot cloud detectn rptd 6-9, 692G1
Mondale cites Apollo 7-8, 517C3
Voyager II flies by Jupiter, findings detailed 7-9, 552B3-553E1
Viking photo reveal Mars surface water 8-9, 692B3
Pioneer 11 flies by Saturn; findings listed 9-1, 696F1
Voyager data reveals 14th Jovian moon 10-17, 1000D2

Manned Flight—*See also 'Space Shuttles' below*
Sovt Soyuz 32 launched 2-25, docks with Salyut 6 2-26, 163F1
Sovt Soyuz 33 launched 4-10, Salyut linkup fails, returns to Earth 4-12, 279A2
USSR-French flight proposed 4-27, 323B3
USSR cosmonauts set space endurance record aboard Salyut 6 7-15, 553E1
USSR cosmonauts end record flight 8-19, 626D2
Apollo moonlanding press coverage cited 760F3

Satellites
Carter vows SALT monitors 1-23, 48D1
Canada bills USSR for Cosmos 954 search 1-23, 96D1
CIA ex-offcl's death, manual theft linked 1-24, 55C1
US, China sign communicatns pact 1-31, 65C1
US spy photo release urged 1-31, 89F2
US weather satellite rpts Great Lakes unnavigable 2-20, 176C2
Sovt spy case cited re SALT verificatn 4-11, 295D1
Canada sets research grant 4-17, 311C3
Cable TV 'superstatn' to expand programming 4-23, 334E3
US-USSR killer satellite talks inconclusive, Sovt test suspensn cited 4-23–7-15, 979C2
Zaire ends W Ger tests 4-27, 411A3
US spy satellite data rptd compromised 4-28, 318F2
SALT II communique backs ASAT agrmt 6-18, 457F3
Carter addresses Cong on SALT II 6-18, 459E1
SALT II verificatn methods sought 6-28, 497C1
Vance warns vs SALT rejectn 7-10, 510D2
CIA spying on antiwar activists rptd 7-16, 561A2
India launch fails 8-10, 626G2
USSR troops in Cuba rptd 8-31, 657C1
US Vela detects mystery A-blast 9-22, 824B3, F3
World radio conf held 9-27-12-6, 1006C3
Australia plans communicatns satellite 10-18, 852B2
RCA loses communicatns satellite 12-10, 991D1

Skylab Program (U.S. program for manned orbiting laboratory)
Skylab comes down on Australia, Indian O; no injuries rptd 7-11, 509A1-510C1

Space Shuttles
Carter budget proposals 1-22, 46E1
USSR asks shuttle ban, US rejcts 7-15, 979D2
Carter support affirmed despite delays 11-14, 883E3
'80 mil constructn bill signed 11-30, 945A2

1980

Communications Projects
Comsat direct TV svc OKd 1-30, 240A1
RCA to rent AT&T satellite, missing Satcom III cited 2-20, 160B3
Lloyd's Satcom liability cited 3-31, 266F1
US asks Iran Intelsat bar 4-17, 281E1
Getty Oil in satellite-TV film venture 4-22, Justice Dept to probe 4-24, 376D2
French-W Ger TV satellite pact signed 4-30, 356D1
CBS barred from Cuba broadcast 5-22, 397C1; cleared 6-1, 420G2
ESA rocket test fails 5-23, 397G2
Comsat broadcast satellite TV plan advances 10-2, 906D3
ABC, CBS in cultural cable-TV deals 12-2, 12-10, 1002G3-1003C1
FCC OKs launching of 20 satellites 12-4, 990C3

Interplanetary Projects
Voyager data reveals 15th Jovian moon 5-6, 416C1
Pioneer Venus I rpts surface data 5-28, 477F1
Voyager data reveals 16th Jovian moon 9-6, 716C2
Voyager 1 flies by Saturn, findings detailed 11-12, 932C2-933A1
Sovt Venus, Halley's comet missions rptd planned 11-23, 933C1

Manned Flight
Salyut 6 research cited 2-16, 160B3
Apollo 8 abort attempt rptd 3-3, 189A2
Sovt Soyuz 35 launched 4-9, docks with Salyut 4-10, 365G1
Soyuz 36 launched with Hungarian partner 5-26, docks with Salyut 5-27, 397B3
NASA ups astronaut corps 5-29, 477E1
Soyuz 36 returns 6-3; Soyuz T-2 launched 6-5, docks with Salyut 6-6, returns 6-9, 477B1
Soyuz 37 launched with Viet partner 7-23, docks with Salyut 7-24, 547F3
Viet-Sovt team lands 7-31, 592C1
Cuba-Soviet team launched, docks with Salyut 9-18—9-25, returns 9-26, 737D2
Popov-Ryumin team ends record flight 10-11, 777B3
Soyuz T-3 launched 11-27, docks with Salyut 6 11-28, 914G1
Soyuz T-3 team returns 12-10, 933B1

Obituaries
Powers, Shorty 1-1, 104E3

Satellites
US Vela-linked A-blast mystery unsolved 1-23, 49B3
US-China memo signed 1-24, 46D2
Comsat direct TV svc OKd 1-30, 240A1
US launches Solar maximum mission Observatory 2-14, 160C2
RCA to rent AT&T communications satellite, missing Satcom III cited 2-20, 160B3
Lloyd's Satcom liability cited 3-31, 266F1
US asks Iran Intelsat bar 4-17, 281E1
USSR Cosmos killer satellite test rptd 4-18, 365A2
Getty Oil in communications venture 4-22, Justice Dept to probe 4-24, 376D2
French-W Ger TV pact signed 4-30, 356D1
CBS barred from Cuba broadcast 5-22, 397C1; cleared 6-1, 420G2
ESA rocket test fails 5-23, 397G2
US Vela-linked A-blast dispute continues 7-14, 548B3
ESA plans comet probe 7-15, 548A1
India launches satellite 7-18, 547D3
Comsat broadcast satellite TV plan advances 10-2, 906D3
USSR to pay for '78 Canada crash 11-21, 920C3
ABC, CBS in cultural cable-TV deals 12-2, 12-10, 1002G2-1003C1
FCC OKs 20 launchings 12-4, 990C3

Space Shuttle
Launch target date moved back 1-29, 71F2
ESA rocket test fails 5-23, 397A3

1976

ASTRONOMY
US cncl cites cosmic radiatn 2-27, 171D2
Methane ice on Pluto rptd 4-2, 443G2-B3
China rpts meteorite shower 4-21, 443D3
US Cong OKs research funds 5-21, 412B1
NASA Jupiter symposium 5-24, 443C3
Gas clouds rptd in space 5-25, 443D2
Pickering gets science medal 10-18, 858F3
Donald Menzel dies 12-14, 1015B2
ASTURIAS (Spanish warship)
In Intl Naval Review 7-4, 488B3
ATAI, Ramzi Abbas
Sentenced 2-24, 156B3
ATAKA and Co.
Itoh 'affiliatn' rptd 2-17, 221F2
Newfndlnd refinery bankrupt 3-12, 221D2
ATAKA Textile
Off Arab blacklist 3-24—4-3, 242C1
ATASSI, Mahmoud al-
Says Sovt ties unchngd 6-10, 406E2
ATFIELD, Michael
Iran seeks re sugar deal 2-10, 156D3
ATHERTON Jr., Alfred L.
Briefs Arabs, Israel on UN stand 18F2
Censured for leak 3-12, 198D2
In talks on Leb crisis 6-22, 448B2
On Arab boycott bill, Saudi arms bar 9-27, 746A3
ATHLETES—*See SPORTS*
ATIKI, Abdel Rahman al-
'74 statemt on OPEC aid cited 15G1
ATIYEH, Victor
Seconds Ford nominatn 8-18, 598A1
ATKINS, Chet
Wins Grammy 2-28, 460C3
ATKINS, Susan
Denied new trial 8-13, 640C3
ATLANTA, Ga.—*See GEORGIA*
ATLANTA Constitution (newspaper)
Murphy abductor sentncd 9-17, 796E3
Chambers named '70 Carter campaign donor 10-17, 804G3
Carter endorsemt rptd 10-30, 831G2
ATLANTA Journal (newspaper)
Rpts Rockefeller remarks on Jackson staff 4-21, 305D3
Chambers named '70 Carter campaign donor 10-17, 804G3
Carter endorsement rptd 10-30, 831G2
ATLANTA Life Insurance Co.
Hill endorses Carter 4-13, 261C2
ATLANTIC City, N.J.—*See NEW Jersey*
ATLANTIC Monthly (magazine)
Louis Sissman dies 3-10, 316C1
ATLANTIC Ocean
'77 US budget proposal 1-21, 64E3
Thomas balloon flight fails 7-1, 640E3
NYC sewage-dump halt ordrd 7-23, 570F3
Offshore lease sale challenged 8-13—8-17, bids accepted 8-25, 648C2-F3
Yost sets balloon record 10-10, 892E2
Ford, Carter debate 10-22, 801E2
Nantucket oil spill 12-15, 968E3; hearing 12-28—12-31, suit delayed 12-30, 1013F3

1977

ASTRONOMY
Sunspots weather linked 2-21, 183C2
Rings around Uranus rptd 3-30, 908E2
NSF '78 authorizatn signed 8-15, 689E1
Rare meteorite awarded to Calif 9-7, 712G2
NASA gets orbital telescope funds 10-4, 796E3
'Mini-planet' rptd 11-8, 908B2
ATC Realty Co.—*See AMREP Corp.*
ATHERTON Jr., Alfred Leroy
US weighs Leb mil aid 6-30, 510C3
Says next move up to PLO 8-16, 623G2
Egypt MiG-21 aid backed 9-15, 698C1
Named Cairo conf envoy 11-30, 910C1, 913C2
At Cairo conf 12-14—12-15, 953E1
ATKINS, Judge C. Clyde
IRS Miami effort rptd cleared 1-6, 16B1
ATKINS, Ollie F.
Dies 1-9, 84F2
ATKINSON, George
Loses slander suit 7-22, 659C1
ATLANTA, Ga.—*See GEORGIA*
ATLANTA Constitution, The (newspaper)
Tarver rptd AP chrmn 1-18, 140E2
Rpts buyer for Lance stock 7-26, 574C2
ATLANTA Journal, The (newspaper)
Tarver rptd AP chrmn 1-18, 140E2
Rpts buyer for Lance stock 7-26, 574C2
ATLANTA Junior College
Young rpts net worth 2-25, 148F1
ATLANTA Newspapers Inc.
Chambers confrmd amb to Belgium 4-29, 418C1
ATLANTIC City, N.J.—*See NEW Jersey*
ATLANTIC Monthly (magazine)
Journalists' thoughts protected 11-7, 920G2
ATLANTIC Ocean
IWC cuts whaling quotas 6-24, 497A1
Carter for oil probes 7-22, 575A2
USSR sub exercise rptd 7-28, 591E1
LI sewage dumping upheld 9-19, 723G3
ESA-N Amer satellite plan shelved 9-19, 736B1

1978

Skylab maneuvered to prolong orbit, '79 missn planned 6-8—6-11, 444G1, 445A1
Orbital flight target date rptd set 9-26, 861C2
5-shuttle fleet signed 9-30, 750A3 ★ -B3
US sets 10-yr goals 10-11, 861F1
NASA drops rescue plan 12-18, 1021C3
ASTRONOMICAL Society of the Pacific
Black hole rptd in constellatn Scorpio 6-22, 654D2
ASTRONOMY
Young star sighting rptd 1-6, 11E2
'Germane' rptd part of Jupiter atmosphere 1-7, 293C2
Lightning rptd linked to cosmic rays 1-12, 293E2
Galaxy rptd surrounding BL Lacertae 1-15, 293D2
Volcanos rptd on Venus surface 1-26, 293F2
Gamma ray spectral line rptd 2-25, 293G2
Black hole at center of galaxies rptd 3-9, 4-13, 293E3
Asteroids near Earth rptd 3-12, 293D3
Planets in sun's galaxy estimated 4-21, 294B1
Antimatter rptd in Earth galaxy cntr 5-6, 653E3
Sulfuric acid in Venus atmosphere calculated 5-6, 654B1
Sun-Earth weather link studied 5-11, 654C1
9 Uranus rings rptd sighted 5-27, 654E1
Quasar found near Earth galaxy 6-8, 654F1
Black hole rptd in constellatn Scorpio 6-22, 654D2
Pluto moon discovered 7-7, 623G1
Sun vibratn rptd measured 8-3, 654F2
Gas cloud in galaxy cluster rptd 9-16, 1023G2
'79 NASA authorzn signed 9-30, 750C3
Gravity wave evidence rptd 12-14, 12-16, 1023D3
ASTROPHYSICAL Journal Letters (magazine)
Rpts galaxy surrounding BL Lacertae 1-15, 293D2
ASW (anti-submarine warfare)—*See ARMAMENTS—Ships*
ATCHISON, Topeka & Santa Fe Railroad—*See under SANTA Fe Industries*
ATCON Inc.
Freight-rate case refused by Sup Ct 12-4, 959B2
ATHERTON Jr., Alfred L.
Israel talks open in Jerusalem 1-20, 41C1
Briefs Hussein 1-27—1-28; in Egypt, ends mediation effort 1-30—2-1, 60D1
To press Mideast mediatn 2-5, 77G1
Begin backs mediation 2-13, 98G1
Seeks Israel backing of Res 242 2-21—3-6, 156E2, E3
Resumes Cairo-Jerusalem shuttle 2-21—3-6; Syria bars visit 2-27; in Amman 3-5, Hussein vs mediatn 3-6, 156D3
Weizman vs shuttle diplomacy 3-24, 214E2
In Cairo to press talks renewal 4-21—4-25, 299A3
Says PLO not terror group 6-27, 503B3
In Israel, Egypt 7-27—7-30, 581E2
Fahd says Israel blocks peace 582C1
ATHLETES In Action—*See CAMPUS Crusade for Christ*
ATHLETICS—*See SPORTS*
ATIYEH, Victor
Wins primary for Oregon gov 5-23, 406F2
Elected Ore gov 11-7, 853D3, 857A2
ATKINS, Roland J.
Loses US House electn 11-7, 849E2
ATKINSON, Eugene V.
Wins US House seat 11-7, 849F2, 852A2
ATKINSON, Richard C.
Univ of Wis protests secrecy order 5-11, 514B1
ATKINSON, Dr. Walter Sydney
Dies 1-6, 96C1
ATKINS v. U.S.
'73 judicial pay raise veto review barred 1-9, 13B1
ATLANTA, Ga.—*See GEORGIA*
ATLANTA Constitution (newspaper)
Murphy cites abductn 10-8, 824D1
ATLANTA Landmarks Inc.
Fox theater rescued 3-5, 293A2
ATLANTA & St. Andrews Bay Railroad—*See under INTERNATIONAL Paper Co.*
ATLANTIC City, N.J.—*See under NEW Jersey*
ATLANTIC Ocean
Sludge-dumping sites OKd 3-3, 164A1
Phila sued on sewage 5-24, 409A2
1st woman sails world solo 6-8, 653E2
2 British balloonists fail 7-30, 653C1
3 Amer balloonists cross, set records 8-11—8-17, 652D3
Angola-Zaire RR reopened 11-4, 1021D2
Beagle Channel Dispute—*See BEAGLE Channel*
Offshore Development—*See under PETROLEUM*
ATLANTIC Pepsi-Cola Bottling Co.
Liggett agrees to buy 11-16, 1005C2

1979

ASTRONOMY
Comet origin study rptd 1-4, 289D3
Uranus ring theory rptd 1-11, 289G3
Carter budgets research 1-22, 46G1
Venus chasm rptd 2-7, 290A1
Voyager I Jupiter photos 2-13, 3-4, 162D2
Voyager I Jupiter findings detailed 3-5–3-17, 215E3-216D3
Black hole at galaxy cntr seen 3-31, 290D1
Quasar sighting studied 5-17, 8-23, 691D2
Extraterrestial event, dinosaur extinctn linked 5-28, 691B3
Venus surface described 5-29, 692A1
Gas cloud around galaxy rptd 6-1, 692D1
Hot cloud rptd between Mars, Jupiter 6-9, 692G1
Voyager II Jupiter findings detailed 7-9, 552B3-553E1
Mars surface water rptd 8-9, 692B3
Pioneer 11 flies by Saturn 9-1, 696F1
14th Jovian moon rptd discovered 10-17, 1000D2
Obituaries
Payne-Gaposhkin, Cecelia 12-6, 1008D3
Velikovsky, Immanuel dies 11-17, 932F3
ASUKATA, Ichio
2d in Japan upper House vote 11-6, 844D3
ATANDIAN, Daria
Beggars Soap Opera opens 7-23, 711D1
ATATURK, Kemal (1881-1938)
Pope visits tomb 11-28, 930C3
AT Budokan (recording)
On best-seller list 5-2, 356B3; 5-30, 448F3; 7-4, 548F3; 8-1, 620F3
ATCHISON, Topeka & Santa Fe Railroad—*See SANTA Fe Industries*
ATHENAEUM, The (Boston library)
Stuart portraits sale halted 4-14, 374E3
ATHERTON Jr., Alfred L.
US seeks talk renewal 1-11; in Israel 1-16–1-24, Egypt 1-25, 51E1
Meets Egypt min 1-26–1-27; sees 'gap' in Egypt, Israel stands 1-27; mission fails 1-28, 69C1
Replaced as Mideast amb 4-24, 296A1
Named amb to Egypt 5-8, 347B3
ATHLETICS—*See SPORTS; sport name*
ATIYEH, Gov. Victor (R, Ore.)
Scores Calif gas hike 5-17, 361D2
Signs pot treatmt law 6-18, 492C3
ATKEY, Ronald
Indochina refugee admissns hiked 549E2
Canada employmt min 6-4, 423F3
ATKINS, Humphrey
UK Northn Ireland secy 5-5, 338G1
On Ulster police arms sales 8-2, 602D1
Plans US visit 8-7, 602E1
Lauds UK troops in Ulster 8-16, 614E2
On UK-Eire security accord 10-5, 792E3, 793B1
Plans Ulster home rule talks 10-25, 835B3
Offers Ulster home rule plans 11-20, defers talks 11-29, 927B3
ATKINS, Dr. Robert C.
Cleared of malpractice 1-16, 78F3
ATLANTA, Ga.—*See GEORGIA*
ATLANTA Constitution (newspaper)
Carter peanut loan scheme denied 3-11, 184E1
US, Israel deny Young-PLO talks bugged 8-16, 606D1
Murphy abductor parole rptd set 12-18, 1005E3
ATLANTICA S.p.A.
US fine rptd 10-31, 985G2
ATLANTIC City, N.J.—*See under NEW Jersey*
ATLANTIC Coast Line—*See SEABOARD Coast Line Industries*
ATLANTIC Container Line Ltd.
Indicted re price fixing 6-1, 423E2; pleads no contest, fined 6-8, 442B2
UK trust legis proposed 10-31, 855E3
ATLANTIC Empress (Greek tanker)
Collides off Tobago 7-19, oil spill rptd 7-21, 553G2
Sinks off Barbados 8-2, 592A3
ATLANTIC Monthly, The (magazine)
US confrms arms dvpt restraint, denies exec agrmt rpt 2-23, 258C2
'State of mind' libel queries backed by Sup Ct, '73 suit cited 4-18, 302B1
Fallows article vs Carter publshd 4-22, 300C3
2d Fallows article rptd 5-18, 627G2
ATLANTIC Ocean
US, Canada draft pact 1-23, 95D3
Phila sludge dumping suit setld 5-30, 704F2
US-Canada pact threatened 9-4, 667C2
US rpts unknown A-blast 10-25, 824B3
Beagle Channel Dispute—*See BEAGLE Channel*
Offshore Developments—*See under PETROLEUM*

1980

ASTRONOMY
Dinosaur extinctn theory rptd 1-1, 415F1
'Big Bang' remnants rptd 1-20, 415C2
Siberia '08 blast linked to meteorite 1-24, 160D3
Insteller gas cloud bubble rptd 1-26, 415G1
Contact binary X-rays rptd 3-20, 415E2
Immense quasar rptd 4-10, 415D3
Pluto moon theory rptd 4-22, 416D1
Sovts discount stellar civilizatns 4-25, 416A1
Neutron star, gamma ray link rptd 5-4, 416B1
15th Jovian moon rptd found 5-6, 416C1
Venus contour map released 5-28, 477F1
Quasar triple image rptd, 'gravitational lens' seen 6-26, 715A3
Stellar study questns planet presence 6-29, 715D2
ESA plans Halley's Comet probe 7-15, 548A1
Solar radiatn drop rptd 8-6, 716D1
Sunspots, gas motions rptd linked 8-7, 716A1
Galaxy formatn study rptd 8-14, 716B1
16th Jovian moon rptd found 9-6, 716C2
ASUKATA, Ichio
Chrgs govt corruptn 5-16, 381A1
Loses premr electn 7-17, 539G2
ATATURK, Kemal (1881-1938)
Ecevit affirms commitmt 10-30, 832E3
AT Fargo, 1940 (recording)
Ellington wins Grammy 2-27, 296E3
ATHERTON Jr., Alfred L.
Vs Begin E Jerusalem office move 6-26, 476A2
ATHERTON, William
American Clock opens 11-20, 1003A3
ATHLETICS—*See SPORTS*
ATKEY, Ronald
On PC electn loss 2-18, 121E1
ATKINS, Christopher
Blue Lagoon released 6-20, 675G1
ATKINS, Humphrey
Home rule talks adjourned 3-19, 232C3
Home rule plan offered 7-2, 523A1
Home rule talks renewed, stalemate rptd 9-22—9-23, 750F2
IRA hunger strike ends 12-18, 12-19, 993B3
ATKINS, Orin E.
Unveils new refining process 3-31, 251F1
ATKINS, Susan
Denied parole 7-29, 639D2
ATKINSON, Rep. Eugene V. (D, Pa.)
Reelected 11-4, 844A2
ATLANTA—*See GEORGIA*
ATLANTA Constitution (newspaper)
Connally Saudi bank connectns rptd 2-11, 129A2
Carter pres endorsemt rptd 11-1, 841G3
ATLANTIC Monthly, The (magazine)
Sale rptd 3-1, 239F1
Whitworth named editor 9-22, 908F2
ATLANTIC Monthly Co.
Sale rptd 3-1, 239F1
ATLANTIC Ocean
Quake hits Azores 1-1, 24E2
'79 A-blast mystery unresolved 1-23, 2-21, 7-14, 49A3, 141E3, 548A3
ESA rocket test fails 5-23, 397A3
Sailing record set 8-1, 907G3
Beagle Channel—*See BEAGLE Channel*
Offshore Developments—*See under PETROLEUM (& Petroleum Products)*

1976

ATLANTIC Richfield Co.
Testifies at privacy comm probe 2-11—2-13, 151E2
Petro-Canada buys unit 6-7, 417C1
Mesa rpts oil find off Scotland 8-19, 675F2
'75 oil-shale projct pullout cited 8-23, 649D1
Hanford A-cntr waste blast 8-30, 670G3
ATNAFU Abate, Lt. Col.
Eritrean offensive set 5-14, 364B1
March on Eritrea halted 6-19, 457B2

1977

ATLANTIC Richfield Co. (Arco)
Completes Anaconda merger 1-12, 55F2
Anaconda takeover cited in merger table 880F1
Denies Pertamina shakedown 2-2, 93D2
On '76 Fortune 500 list 340F1
Employee stock plan cited 5-6, 409G1
Alaska pipeline opens 6-20, 476B1, B3
ICC sets Alaska pipeline rates 6-28, 498F1
Announces new motor oil 7-11, 558D3
Washington sues 8-16, 691E3
Anaconda Co.—*See separate listing*
ATLAS (magazine)
Quincy Howe dies 2-17, 164A3
ATLAS Roofing Co.
Sup Ct backs OSHA penalties 3-23, 276F1
ATNAFU Abate, Lt. Col.
Teferi plot chrgd 2-3, 98E2
Govt role set 2-6, 98A3
Sets pro-Sovt policy 2-11, 238A3
Executed 11-13, 875C2
ATO, Inc.
Loses Red Sox sale dispute 12-6, 989A3
ATO Kefle Wodajo
Defectn rptd; replaced 3-11, 238E2

1978

ATLANTIC Richfield Co. (Arco)
States curbed on oil tanker regulatn 3-6, 161F3
On '77 Fortune 500 list 5-8, 325F1, A2
ICC Alaska pipe rates backed by Sup Ct 6-6, 447B2
Computer program patents curbed by Sup Ct 6-22, 509B1
Crude oil '73-77 price violatns chrgd 8-4, 610A2
Gas rationing rptd sought 12-3, 939C1
Anaconda Co.—*See separate listing*
ATLANTIC Sugar Ltd.
Fined record sum 10-6, 794F3
ATOMIC Bomb—*See ARMAMENTS—Atomic Weapons*

1979

ATLANTIC Richfield Co. (Arco)
US files overchrg suit 1-5, 17B1
Oil, gas allocatn planned 2-21, 126C2
US overchrg claims denied 5-2, 343B2
Arco Solar, Energy Conversn in solar dvpt accord 5-2, 419C1
On '78 Fortune 500 list 5-7, 304F1
July gas supplies rptd 6-25, 479E1
Dow Jones index revised 6-28, 481G2
Heating oil shortfall seen 6-28, 514G2
US overchrg claims denied 10-18—11-6, 849G2-F3
3d 1/4 oil profits rptd up 10-25, 804D3
US overchrgs alleged 12-19, 990E2
Anaconda Co.—*See separate listing*
ATOMIC Bomb—*See ARMAMENTS—Atomic Weapons*

1980

ATLANTIC Richfield Co. (Arco)
'79 profit rptd 1-31, 90F2
1st 1/4 profit rptd 4-28, 331D1, G1
On '79 Fortune 500 list 5-5, 290F1
Solar production rptd 5-5, 554D1
Exxon buys shale oil project 5-13, 553A3
Bressler named BN pres 5-19, 456F2
Phila refining tax dropped, 'contributn' set 6-10, 743F3
Foundatn buys Harper's 7-9, 582B3
Wholesale gas price cut rptd 8-8, 666D3
Gasoline prices cut 9-11, 786B1
USW copper strike continues 10-24, 805B3
US oil stockpiling rptd resumed 10-27, 826D1
ATLANTIC Richfield Foundation
Harper's purchased 7-9, 582B3
ATOMIC Bomb—*See ARMAMENTS--Atomic Weapons & Tests--See also other appropriate subheads*

ATOMIC ENERGY

1976

ATOMIC Energy—*See also ARMAMENTS, DISARMAMENT (for banning or control of nuclear weapons), ENERGY, UNITED Nations—International Atomic Energy Agency; also appropriate subheads under U.S. GOVERNMENT*
Environmental Hazards (including safety issues)
ERDA OKs breeder projct 1-2, 115G2
'77 US budget proposals 1-21, 64G2
Vt plant shut down 1-26, 115B2
US rpts India plant leak 1-30, India denies 2-7, 156D2
A-engineers quit over safety; utilities, NRC deny chrgs 2-3—2-10, 115A1
UN Medit pollutn pact signed 2-16, 126D3
'45-47 plutonium tests on humans rptd 2-22, 272B3
'75 Ala plant fire rpt issued 2-28, 171G3
AEC prisoner tests confrmd 2-28, 316B2
NRC OKs NJ offshore plant 4-9, 284G1-B2
Cong OKs '77 NRC funds 5-5, 5-10, 358F2
Sup Ct curbs EPA powers 6-1, 414B3
Calif safety bill enacted 6-3, 409E2
Calif voters ban A-plant curbs 6-8, 409D2
7-natn A-waste conf opens 7-12, 739G1 ★
A-plant hearings ordrd 7-21, 570B3
A-plant licensing moratorium set 8-13, 671E1
Washn A-cntr waste blast 8-30, 670D3
A-waste cntrs called major hazard 9-7, 671B1
Issue in Vt primary 9-14, 705A2
Ford, Carter debate 9-23, 702E2
NRC for environmt impact, plant license link 10-13, lifts moratorium 11-5, 849A1
Ford, Carter debate 10-22, 801A3
6 US states reject A-plant curbs 11-2, 824A1-F1, B2, 825A3
'58 Sovt A-waste explosn rptd 11-6, 948A3
Sup Ct bars Ind A-plant rule review 11-8, 882C3
W Ger waste project protested 11-11, violence 11-13, 931B1
China blast linked to thyroid cancer 12-27, 992F1
Industrial Use—*See also 'Environmental Hazards' above*
ERDA OKs breeder project 1-2, 115F2
Italy A-plant plans rptd OKd 1-5, 74B3
Ford State of Union message 1-19, 37G3, 39D2
Lilienthal urges export ban 1-19, 115B3
'77 US budget proposals 1-21, 64E2
A-plant growth down 63% 1-22, 115C2
NRC neutral on A-centers 1-22, 115E2
US-Spain A-plant credits set 1-24, 77B1
S Korea sets Canada reactor deal 1-26, 103C3
7 natns agree on export rules 1-27, 84A1
S Korea cancels French A-plant purchase 1-29, 1-31, 103G2
NRC petitioned for tighter security 2-2, 115A3
Westinghouse uranium pact set 2-3, 115E3
French-Australia info exchng planned 2-4, 116B2
UNECE rpt issued 2-10, 164A2
Canada, Pak talks on uranium fuel 2-23—2-25; suspended 3-2, 174G3
US vs French-Pak A-plant deal 2-23; IAEA OKs plant 2-24, 175C1
US OKs 7-natn export pact, cites French stance 2-23, 243G2
Ford message to Cong 2-26, 149F2
EC asks new A-plant study 2-26, 164B2
Cuba to build plants 3-2, 251G3
7 more to join 7-natn group 3-13, 4-1, 243F2
French, Pak A-plant pact signed 3-18, 581C3
France to build Libya plant 3-22, 239A3
USSR, W Ger drop Sovt plant plan 3-30, 243C2
'75 energy output share up 4-4, 285C1
Australia rpts purchase plan 4-8, 249B3
French export safeguards set 4-8, 372C3

1977

ATOMIC Energy—*See also ARMAMENTS, DISARMAMENT (for banning or control of nuclear weapons); also appropriate subheads under U.S. GOVERNMENT*
Environmental Hazards—*See 'Industrial Use' below*
Industrial Use
Australia uranium shipmt to W Ger blocked 1-2, 17B2
Australia scientists urge uranium ban 1-3, 7B1
Pak confrms French A-plant deal 1-3, 12B3
Canada sets water treatmt plant 1-5, 43G2
COMECON plans Cuba A-plant 1-6, 19D3
EPA sets radiatn limits 1-6, 95B2
Ford submits energy message 1-7, 14B3
Canada A-sale agent tied to pol paymt 1-7, 42G3
Australia uranium dvpt defended 1-11, 17C2
20th Century Fund, OECD urge greater use 1-11, 1-27, 169E3, 170C1
W Ger N Rhine plants banned 1-13, Bavaria plant shut 1-14, 117G2
Ford '78 budget proposals 1-17, 31D2-A3
Carter urges safeguards 1-24, 51D3
Mondale urges W Ger, France curb sales 1-25, 1-29, 69F1, B2
Canada warned vs A-sale agent disclosure 1-25, contract cancelatn barred 2-3, 114C1
Uranium collaboratn effort by US, Australia Canada 2-4—3-11; cartel aim denied by US, intl fuel bank sought 6-29, 624C3
US rptd vs Bonn-Brazil deal 2-7, curbs hinted 2-8, 118A1
Argentina backs Brazil A-deal 2-7, 190G1
Sweden rpts new waste disposal process 2-8, 470B1
S Africa reactor dvpt rptd 2-16, 160F1
US A-fuel sale to S Africa rptd 2-16, 160B2
Carter budget revisns 2-22, 124E3, 125B2, C2
US orders A-plant security tightened, rpts '76 threats 2-22, 197E1-B2
Vepco fined 2-23, 235A2
US, PI, EC press for Australia uranium deals 2-24—3-16, 218B1
US aid, Brazil safeguards linked 3-1; talks on Bonn deal fail 3-2, intl pressure rptd 3-11, 189F3
Westinghouse, 3 utilities settle uranium dispute 3-3, 177B2
Argentina, Peru sign A-plant pact 3-5, 259D1
Argentina Latin lead rptd 259F1
French Fessenheim reactor opened 3-7; French, Ger protests rptd 4-11, 391C3
'76 US use rptd 3-13, 196B2
Carter energy plan 3-17, 186C1, 191A1
Va Elec cancels 2 A-plants, other delays rptd 3-18, 235E1
US, Japan A-talks stalled 3-21—3-22, 209F2
Ford-Mitre study scores breeder, plutonium use 3-21; A-researchers dispute 3-26, 234A3, G3
Fraser rpts Carter A-safeguards exchng 3-23, 217F3
Australia cancels Japan uranium contracts 3-24, 218D1
Schlesinger vs plutonium use 3-25, 234C2
US OKs Japan spent-fuel export 3-28, 235D1
USSR warns vs S Africa sales 3-29, 248B1
Australia asks uranium safeguards 3-29, 253G2
Westinghouse dispute formally ends 3-30, 252G1-B2
UN Sri Lanka energy experiment rptd 3-30, 298E3
Japan vs Carter waste reprocessing ban 3-30, 4-2, 329C3
US presses W Ger on Brazil deal 3-31; W Ger honors agrmt 4-5, 268F2
Accident liability limit voided 3-31, 277C2
NRC halts NH A-plant constructn 3-31, A-plant foes protest 4-30—5-3, 344G2

1978

ATOMIC Energy—*See also ARMAMENTS, DISARMAMENT (for banning or control of nuclear weapons); also appropriate subheads under U.S. GOVERNMENT*
Environmental Hazards—*See 'Industrial Use' below*
Industrial Use (& safeguards issue)
US OKs India uranium sale, safeguard discord rptd 1-2—1-3, 1G2
Australia delays uranium export 1-6, 16E1
NH A-plant gets final NRC OK 1-7, EPA to reopen hearings 3-22, 242A3
UK-India talks, India sets safeguard terms 1-9, 37E1
'77 safeguard pact detailed 1-11, 11B1
NAACP backs A-power, breeder dvpt 1-11, 68D1
Japan plans US trade missn 1-13, 27A1
Westinghouse PI A-contract fee rptd 1-13, probe ordrd 1-16, 38D2
Dutch premr delays reactors 1-16, 90A3
Canada lifts EC uranium ban; UK, W Ger shipmts, inspectn set 1-16, 102D3
Australia to honor uranium contracts 1-16, 110B1
Carter budgets research, omits Clinch R breeder 1-23, 46G1, D2
US probes low-level radiatn effects 1-24—2-28, 164C1
Belgium A-plant leak disputed 1-25, 69F3
Canada, Japan initial uranium pact 1-26, 88F3
Dutch OK Brazil uranium sales, Urenco plant expansn OKd 2-1; Almelo protest 3-4, 169C2, F2
Australian uranium find rptd 2-3, 88A1
US A-export curbs clear Sen 2-7, 82E2
US research authrzn clears Cong 2-8, 107B2; signed 2-25, 218B2
US questns PI A-plant safety 2-8, 2-14, 134C3
S Africa sets enrichmt expansn 2-13, 135A1
Carter backs state role in A-dvpt 2-17, 123E2
US-USSR plant safety protocol rptd 2-22, 202B1
Australia joins A-supplier group 2-24, 129C2
US, UK researchers rpt safe A-fuel reprocessing technique 2-27, 144F2
Carter rpts waste-disposal plan, govs urge firmer commitmt 2-27, 145A1, B1
Canada A-sale probe rpt issued 2-27, 166G2
United Nuclear wins uranium cartel suit, impact on other Gulf suits seen 3-2, 144C1-F2
Brazil pres visits W Ger, US A-deal oppositn cited 3-6—3-10, 332D3
Clinch R breeder funds signed, Carter plans halt 3-7; GAO declares halt illegal 3-10, 160C3, 183D2
Kern Cnty (Calif) votes vs A-plant 3-7, 184B1
US A-export curbs signed 3-10, 183E1
US prelim waste study backs rock storage, N Mex test site; Nader group doubts safety 3-15, 183A3
NM worker wins mental health damages 3-15, 242F3
US licensing, constructn expeditn proposed by Admin, reactn 3-17, 205B2
Clinch R breeder compromise proposal rptd 3-17, 3-23, 241F3
FBI probes black-mkt uranium sale bid to Westinghouse 3-19, 242C2-A3
Gen Atomic damage determinatn stay denied by Sup Ct 3-20, 206D1
Australia seeks Japan treaty 3-20, 208B3
UK OKs Windscale reprocessing plant 3-22, 227G1
Carter stresses safeguards 3-29, W Ger A-deal oppositn scored 3-30, 233A2, C2
NRC sets Mo worker firing probe, GAO safety review sought 3-29, 242F1
Australia uranium exports protested 4-1, 243E3
US ct A-plant rulings curbed 4-3, 280E2
EC disputes US A-export renegotiatn 4-4—4-9, 258D1

1979

ATOMIC Energy—*See also ARMAMENTS, DISARMAMENT; also appropriate subheads under U.S. GOVERNMENT*
Environmental Hazards—*See 'Industrial Use' below*
Industrial Use & Safeguards Issue (domestic)
Wis, NC A-plant plans canceled 1-4, 2-27, 186C2
Nev A-waste storage studied 1-5, 54D3
Colo protesters sentncd 1-8, 17D3
NRC calls '75 safety rpt unreliable 1-19, 54B2
Carter budget proposals 1-22, 45D2-A3
UCS asks A-plant shutdown, NRC hedges 1-26, 90G2
2 unions ask HEW radiatn safety study 1-30, 90D3
Portsmouth shipyd cancer study begins 1-31, 91A1
GE worker chrgd in uranium theft 2-1, 119F3
21 DC protesters arrested 2-12, 133A2
Environmt cncl sees use cut 2-20, 132F2
US rpt sees low-level radiatn risks 2-27, 208A1
Colo radium waste sites rptd 3-5, 187F1
NH A-protesters arrested 3-9, 186E2
Schlesinger backs as oil substitute 3-12, 183E2
5 A-plants ordrd shut, quake danger cited 3-13, 186E1-C2
A-plant communities studied 3-17, 207D3
Carter proposes regulatory reform 3-25, 230A2
3 Mile Island accident 3-28; radiatn released; explosn, meltdown feared 3-28—4-3; Carter visits 4-1, 241A1-246C1
3 Mile I A-plant diagrams 242A1, 243A3
Facts on radiatn exposure 244C2
China Syndrome impact seen 3-29, 4-1, 246C3
3 Mile I accident protests sparked abroad, govt reactns vary 3-31—4-5, 246C1-C3
3 Mile I accident sparks protests, reassessmts 3-31—4-8, 261G2-262B1
NY, Calif, Mich utility shareholders bar A-power delays 4-3, 4-18, 4-23, 322F3
Colo A-plant dispute rptd settled 4-3, 344E2
3 Mile I errors, clean-up detailed; crisis declared over 4-4—4-9; Carter forms probe panel 4-5, poll publshd 4-10, 259D2-261G2
Carter vows 'full account' re 3 Mile I 4-5, 251A1
3 Mile I forgn reactn continues 4-6—4-13, 276E1-E2
Gallup A-power poll rptd 4-9, 323A1
Carter reaffirms commitmt; vows 3 Mile I panel apptmts, A-plant licensing reform 4-10, 263A3
NRC plans safety rules review 4-10, warns 34 A-plants 4-12; advisory com proposes chngs 4-17, 275F1
Carter names 3 Mile I comm 4-11; reactor shutdown starts, other dvpts 4-13—4-18; Met Ed rate hike suspended 4-19, 274E2-275F1
3 Mile I media treatmt in E Eur rptd 4-11, 323B1
3 Mile I NRC transcripts released 4-12, 275D2
'78 A-plant incidents, '77 shutdowns rptd 4-15; pipe leaks common 5-2, 322D2-D3
NRC plant shutdown case refused by Sup Ct 4-16, 303A1
Westinghouse settles 3 US uranium suits 4-16, 5-5, 5-15, 366C1
Maine A-plant unhurt by quake 4-17, 323E1
Gov Brown urges end to A-power use 4-24, 322G3
Carter shuns A-hecklers 4-25, 300C1
GPU cuts dividend, salaries 4-26, 322B2

1980

ATOMIC Energy
Industrial Use & Safeguards Issue (domestic)
Low-level waste bill clears Cong 12-13, signed 12-22, 981C1
Colo protesters arrested 1-1, 17G3
38 A-plants fail NRC safety rules 1-2, 16F3
NRC reactor licensing resumptn urged 1-9, 17B1
State of State messages 1-9, 404E1; 1-10, 1-15, 483A1, 484E1; 1-24, 1-25, 269C3, F3
CEA ex-chrmn urges use 1-14, 32F1
NAS backs A-power, fast-breeder reactor 1-14, 53D3
Tenn fuel plant reopens despite uranium loss 1-16, 54A1
Ala A-dump site planned 1-16, 54D1
Carter asks NRC reorganizatn, A-waste progrm 1-21, 43E3
Calif quakes force Livermore lab evacuatn 1-24—1-27, 80G2
Rogovin 3 Mile I study issued 1-24, Sen rpt released 7-2, 550F3
Carter budget proposals 1-28, 71F3
Kennedy seeks A-plant moratorium 2-2, 91D1
Brown Maine support linked 2-10, 109C1
3 Mile I radioactive water leaks 2-11, 128E1
Carter outlines waste storage plan, names advisory panel 2-12, 127D3, 128C1
Bechtel to repair 3 Mile I 2-12, 128G1
Kennedy attacks Carter policies 2-20, 130C2
Fla plant accident 2-26, modificatns planned 3-5, 169G1
Tenn plant gets start-up license 2-28, 169F2
NRC orders Babcock safety review 3-4, 169E2
Connally 'basic speech' excerpts 3-7, 184F2, B3
Ala plant FBI probe disclosed 3-7, 249F1-A2
Kennedy 'basic speech' excerpts 3-10, 183G2
3 Mile I gas venting proposed 3-12, Middletown (Pa) residents vs 3-20, 248B3
GPU sues Babcock & Wilcox 3-25, 249B1
Commonwealth Ed, 2 offcls indicted 3-26, 249D1
3 Mile I anniv marked by demonstratns 3-28—3-31, 248G3
3 Mile I health studies rptd 4-2, 4-15, 4-17, 332G1-B3
Ill A-plant '79 dischrg data rptd 4-7, revised 4-27, 441A2
NRC asks Babcock fine re '77 Ohio plant accident 4-10, 332B1
Va, NJ plants get start-up licenses 4-10, 4-16, 332E1
Citizens' Party seeks ban 4-13, 288C3
Calif lab cancer cases rptd 4-22, 356E3
Calif A-plant laws overturned 4-23, 331G3-332B1
DC protests held 4-26—4-28, 441G1
Ark A-plant accident 5-10, gas venting delay order defied 5-13, 441B1
3 Mile I containmt bldg entry fails 5-20, NRC OKs gas venting 6-10, 440F3, 441B1
NH A-protesters repulsed 5-24—5-26, 441E1
NRC '80 funds authrzn clears Cong, reforms set 6-10, 6-16, 497E1; Carter signs 7-1, 494F1
3 Mile I gas venting danger seen 6-18; radioactive water spilled 6-27, krypton vented 6-28—7-11; containmt bldg entered 7-23, 550C2-E3
Dem platform drafted 6-24, 479G2, A3
A-waste storage, fusion dvpt appropriatn clears Cong 6-25, 9-10; Carter signs 10-1, 803E2
Ala A-plant shutdown fails 6-28; NRC orders GE reactors probed 7-7, 551G1-C2
NRC membership scored 7-1; Carnesale named chrmn 7-7, 551A3
'79 A-plant data rptd 7-8, 509A3

1976

France OKs fast-breeder reactor 4-15, 372B3
ERDA focuses on conservatn 4-19, 184E3
Cong OKs '77 NRC funds 5-5, 5-10, 358G2; signed 5-22, 982E1
Bethe wins Niels Bohr award 5-6, 504D3
Carter urges A-plant curbs 5-13, 374F3
Canada bars India A-sales 5-18, India scores 5-20, 363A2
French-W Ger reactor pact OKd 5-18, 372F2
Giscard on export controls, S Korea plant sale cancellatn 5-20, 372D2
IEA OKs cooperatn pact 5-20—5-21, 372F3★
NATO cites Sovt-W Ger plan halt 5-21, 353G1
Plutonium use curbed 5-26, 398G1
Paris group in S Africa plant deal 5-28, US role rptd 6-1, 387F1, 388D1
Australia OKs A-ship visits 6-4, 455D3
US Dem platform text 6-15, 475E1, 476G2
Oldia expands A-plants 6-19, 538C2
US OKs reactor sale to Spain 6-21, fuel sale to India 7-21, 739B2
US econ aid curbs enacted 6-30, 533F1
W Ger, France conf 7-6, 521F1
Ford OKs '77 ERDA funds 7-12, 517G1, F2
W Ger reaffirms Brazil A-sale bar 7-15, 530A3
Sovt-French pact signed 7-16, 540E2
Ikle scores US A-aid 7-23, 739G2
US admits India A-blast aid 8-2, 581D3
GAO cites missing A-fuel 8-5, 739A3
French, S Africa plant deal signed 8-6, 630G3
US-Iran pact signed 8-7, 581B2
US-Pak discuss French A-plant 8-8—8-9; France protests 8-9, 581G2
Carter vs breeder reactor 8-9, 585C1
Carter vs moratorium on power 8-17, 617B2
US GOP platform text 8-18, 607B3, 610E2, E3, 611B1
Taiwan A-fuel reprocessing rptd 8-29, 732D1, 760G3
Mondale urges US restraint 8-30, 645C3
UK signs IAEA, Euratom pacts 9-6, 936A2
Taiwan rpts reprocessing halt 9-14, 858D2
Sweden A-policy cited 9-20, 714A2
Exporters warned on safeguards 9-21, 760D3
US House OKs export guidelines 9-22, 746D2, F2
Ford, Carter debate 9-23, 702D2
Carter urges curbs 9-25, 724A1
Export guidelines bill not cleared 10-2, 883B1, B3
US uranium enrichmt bill not cleared 10-2, 883A3
Ford, Carter debate 10-6, 742E1
French-Iran pact signed 10-6, 773E2
Carter scores Ford 10-8, 762A2
Sweden alters A-plans 10-8, 794G1
Benedict gets Science Medal 10-18, 858C3
Canada-Japan accord 10-26, 836B3
France issues guidelines 10-11, 772B3
Ford proposes fuel-processing curbs, Carter reacts 10-28, 848C3
UN vs West, Israel aid to S Africa 11-5, 842C3
Israel bars US sen inspection 11-8, 878F1
France to end S Africe sales 11-9, 928A1
Australia lifts uranium export ban 11-11, 888C1
Bonn program, poll rptd 11-11, 931B1
French drop Strasbourg plant 11-20, 1002F3
Canada A-sales irregularities rptd 11-22, 904A1, C1; Parlt probe opens 11-30, 923B3
Argentina probe of Canada sales rptd 11-27, 997A2
Canada probe continues 12-2—12-15, 962G2
House Dems back joint com legis powers end 12-6—12-9, 981A2, D2
Australia unions back uranium contracts 12-8, 923B1
USSR-India heavy water sale rptd 12-8, 955A2
France bans sale of reprocessing plants, to keep forgn pacts 12-16, 1002A3
Canada to audit A-sale agent 12-21; Argentina pact delay rptd 12-22, 998C1, G1
Canada tightens export rules, cuts Pak ties 12-22, 998A1

1977

Brazil-Venez ties deteriorate 4-1, 547G2★-B3
Babcock sues vs United Tech purchase 4-4, 274C3
Carter urges plutonium ban, breeder progrm curbs, intl safeguards 4-7; US, forgn reactn mixed 4-7—4-8, 267A3, 268D1
W Ger issues A-policy statemt 4-7, 268E2
US A-fuel export delays rptd 4-13, 4-14, 268C2
A-energy conf, US plutonium, breeder curbs scored by IAEA, others 4-13—5-2, 334E2-335B1
Carter energy plan 4-18, 4-20, 290E2, 295A1, F1; fact sheet 291F1, 293B2-E2
Carter energy plan reactn 4-20, 320A2, C3
W Ger vs US curbs 4-21, affirms A-export policy 4-26, 334A1
Japan moves vs US plutonium ban 4-21, 335D1
Japan breeder operational 4-24, 335B1
W Ger breeder, other A-research spending proposed 4-27, 333F2
Carter asks A-export bill 4-27, 334B1
'68 high seas uranium loss rptd 4-28—5-2, Israel denies role 4-29, 335D1-B2
Supplier natns meet in London 4-28—4-29, 403F1-A2
A-opponents conf in Salzburg 4-29—5-1, 335E1, 403E1
Salzburg intl conf; safeguards, safety issues debated 5-2—5-13, 402D2-403D1
NH A-plant foes tried, freed 5-4—5-13; LEAA bars funds 5-19, 409D3
Carter OKs uranium shipmts 5-6, 403A2
7-natn summit debates A-sales, sets study 5-7—5-8, 357D2, E2, 358E1
Trudeau, Giscard meet 5-13, 389B2
US concedes Brazil-W Ger deal 5-13, 414A2
US OKs Spain reactor sale 5-17, 398C2
US OKs Yugo parts sale 5-20, 398F2
Kosygin opens Finn A-plant 5-23, 391A2
Australia uranium comm rpt issued 5-25; reactn 5-31, 465A2-A3
Swiss urge A-power ban 5-28—5-29, Basel votes plant ban 6-12, 490A1
'68 uranium loss rptd Israeli plot 5-30, 416F2
French scientists vs A-breeder 5-30, 450A1
Australia threatens EC uranium export ban 6-1, 7-4, 595D3
Mrs Carter sees Brazil pres 6-7, 455G1
Carter energy plan scored 6-8, 443G2
Austria plant protested 6-12, 763A2
EPA OKs NH A-plant 6-17, 498D2
W Ger halts data exports 6-17, 566C3
Fire threatens Los Alamos lab 6-18, 660F3
COMECON seeks capacity rise 6-21—6-23, 513F1
Carter lauds Australia policy 6-21—6-23, 560C3
USSR, France back safeguards 6-22, 495E1
NH A-power backers rally 6-26, 498D3
EC ldrs defer JET site decisn 6-29—6-30, Callaghan concerned 7-1, 624G2-A3
French plant leaks radioactive gas 7-1, 543E2
Australia dockers protest uranium shipmts 7-2—7-3, 523D1
French 'Super Phoenix' OKd 7-5, environmentalists protest 7-31, 597B2-C3
Trudeau sees Schmidt 7-6—7-12, eases A-fuel export ban 7-12, 566F2, A3
Australia Labor backs uranium ban 7-7, 540E3
Canada A-agency head fired 7-7, 541E3
Schlesinger backs A-power 7-10, 538E2
Carter on US-USSR talks 7-21, 550B3
Carter backs Italy plants 7-25—7-27, 581A2
ERDA funds clear Cong, Clinch R projct deleted 7-25, 592F2-C3, ★ E3; Carter signs 8-5, 609D2
NRC OKs NH A-plant constructn 7-26, 702B2
Giscard reasserts A-policy 7-30, 597G2
A-growth standstill rptd 8-1, 717C2
US rpts fissionable material missing 8-4, 8-8, 717D1
Calif plant reopening opposed re quake faults 8-5, 838C2
A-plant protests in 4 states 8-6—8-8, 702D2
S Africa plutonium capacity chrgd 8-14, 657A1
Australia lifts uranium ban 8-25, USSR scores 8-25, 8-26, 693G1-E3
Australia uranium vote rejctd 9-7, 705C1
France confrms Pak deal 9-8, 1013A1
Japan-US reprocessing pact, safeguards provisn signed 9-12, 812B3
Reprocessed-fuel bomb use rptd 9-14, 812D2-B3
Australia union conf asks uranium referendum 9-15, 740B2
S Africa rpts open sector cyclotron constructn plans 9-15, 825A3
French, US talks 9-15—9-16, 1012E3
House backs Clinch R breeder, other research 9-20, 758C2
Supplier natns OK safeguard pact 9-21, 717A1
US spent-fuel storage problems rptd 9-23, 794C2
US plant-licensing halt urged, waste problem cited 9-29; Admin oppositn rptd 10-3, 794A3
Va quake fault cover-up rptd 9-30, 838D1
Carter at UN, stresses safeguards 10-4, 751G2, 752A1
Australia A-envoy named 10-6, 779E1

1978

FTC aide backs oil, gas firms' uranium reserves lid 4-5; Justice Dept proposal rptd 4-6, 282D2
US OKs EC uranium exports 4-9, 278F3
W Ger scores US-EC A-export renegotiatn 4-12, 255B1
Calif Sundesert plant voted down 4-13, 281B2
Plant constructn, union accord reached; Carter hails 4-18, 281A3
US comm bars uranium to India 4-20, 288A3; India scores 4-23, 4-24; Carter OKs sale 4-27, 313G1
Gen Atomic rpts new evidnc in United Nuclear case 4-20, 346F2-A3
Asbestos workers get health warning 4-26, 326A3
NH A-plant site review ordrd by NRC 4-28, constructn workers protest 5-10, 347A1
SC, Colo, NH A-plant protests 4-29—5-1, 347C1
Carter on waste disposal, plant sites 5-4, 321E1
Japan-US fusn research fund rptd discussed 5-4, 341B3
Energy Dept study sees growth 5-8, 366E2
Gulf chrgd re uranium cartel 5-9, 346D1-D2
Gulf sues Westinghouse 5-9, 346D2
Plutonium-fueled breeder dvpt backed by Rockefeller study 5-10, 346B3
Gen Atomic documts rule review declined by Sup Ct 5-15, 387E3
UK OKs Windscale funds 5-15, Japan reprocessing contracts rptd signed 5-25, 437F2-A3
Justice Dept backs 10% lid on oil, gas firms' uranium reserves 5-15, 471E2
Gen Atomic damages awarded United Nuclear, Ind & Mich 5-16, 366G2
New TVA chrmn takes over 5-19, 390G1, C2
US defers A-fuel export licenses 5-20, 408B2
Carter visits Oak Ridge, backs A-power 5-22, 386B3
US offers new long-term enriched uranium contracts 5-26, 408C1
Gen Atomic trial judge interference ruled by Sup Ct 5-30, 430A3
Australia OKs uranium mining, export rules 5-31, 434B3
Schmidt reviews Carter talks 6-1, 519C2
A-plant size, efficiency study rptd 6-2, 408D3
W Ger environmtlists gain in state electns 6-4, 456D2
IEA sees larger energy supply role 6-5, 449E3★, 450G1
Canada prov backs uranium dvpt 6-8, 647C2
US-India talks, A-cooperatn pledged 6-13—6-15, 466C3
EC seeks Australia uranium talks 6-13, 495A1
Swedish panel backs A-power 6-14, govt split rptd 6-15, 691F1-A2
W Ger A-plant accidents 6-20, 6-23, concern rptd 6-26, 500A2
Nicaragua pres studies US plants 6-22, 593B2
Japan breeder research pact with France, W Ger rptd 6-23, 548E3
NH A-plant protest 6-24—6-26, 494A1
Washn A-plant protests 6-25, 494G1
Accident liability law backed by Sup Ct 6-26, 567A1
US hints S Africa fuel supply 6-29, 536G3
UN sesn backs peaceful A-technology 6-30, 522C3
NH A-plant halt ordrd 6-30, 529F2
Dutch parlt backs Brazil uranium sale 6-30, 575A1
India uranium sale allowed by US House 7-12, 551D1
Australia, Finland sign uranium accord 7-20, 590C1
EC halts UK-Australia uranium pact 7-27, 666E1
Canada AECL reorganized 7-28, 590E3-591A1
GAO urges new US agency 7-31, 610E1
NH A-plant cooling plan OKd 8-4, constructn to resume 8-10, foes vow actn 8-7, 8-10, 609G1-A3
Ore, Calif A-foes protest 8-6—8-7, 609B3
Pl-Australia safeguards pact signed 8-7, 666G1
US-Australia safeguards pact signed 8-8, 666B2
France asks Pak contract revisn, US pressure cited 8-9; Pak scores, denies China agrmt 8-23, 668A2
France cancelatn of Pak deal cited 840A1
US fusn research advance rptd 8-12, 653F2
NH plant constructn resumes 8-14; protests continue 8-14—12-7, ct appeal fails 8-22, 914A1-E1
Wis bars new A-plants 8-17, 665F2
Ireland A-plant protest rptd 8-20, 671E3
Canada, Japan sign uranium pact 8-22, 667B1
Carter breeder research vow linked to gas plan vote 8-23—8-26, 677G3-678E1
UK plutonium facility closed over contaminatn 8-24, 667D2
Australia Aborigine uranium royalties set 8-25, 666A1
Calif protesters convicted 8-30, 941D2
Japan uranium import fund set 9-3, 694D1
US, Japan plan joint research 9-6, 695B3★
Australia uranium compromise OKd 9-8, 9-15, new dispute delays projct 9-19, 721A1

1979

NRC orders Babcock plants closed, 3 Mile I reaches shutdown 4-27, 321D3-322B2
Colo A-protesters arrested; other demonstratns in Vt, Ark, NY, NM 4-28—4-29, 322E3
NRC, 3 Mile I operators testify 4-30, 5-7; blast danger, radiatn levels rptd 5-1, 5-5, 344E1-E2
A-power radiatn risks reviewed 5-2, 609A3
3 Mile I radiatn estimate hiked 5-3, 344C1
Carter urges safety measures, scores Clinch R projct 5-4, 346F3
DC A-protest draws 65,000 5-6, Carter rejcts plant closings 5-7, 343A3-344C1
3 Mile I safety benefit seen 5-7, 373G3
Va plant sabotage probed 5-8, 5-10, 386D2
2 Cong coms seek plant limits 5-9, 5-10, 382A1
3 Mile I comm halts probe 5-17, gets subpoena power 5-17, 5-21, 417F2-F3
Silkwood Okla estate wins damages, plutonium find cited 5-18, 381D1
3 Mile I cattle deaths rptd 5-20, 382E1
NRC delays reactor licensing 5-21, 381D3
NJ A-plant reopening set 5-30, 610A1
NY, Okla, other protests 6-2—6-3, 416G1-D2
Met Ed blamed for 3 Mile I accident 6-5, 518A3
Connally on energy crisis 6-11, 439F3
Waste cleanup bill excludes 6-13, 441D2
A-waste transport rules set 6-15, 610B1
Va plant sabotage chrgs rptd 6-18, 466E1
GPU gains credit line 6-19, 519A1
A-protests held 6-22-10-1; NYC demonstratn draws 200,000 9-23, 742F1-743D1
Colo protesters convicted 6-22, 743D1
NRC orders 33 reactors inspected 6-25, 518D3
Calif A-protest draws 20,000 6-30, 519G1
Nev A-dump ordered closed 7-2, 519A2
NRC shuts undamaged 3 Mile I reactor No 1 7-2, extends order 8-9, 629D3-G3
NH '77 A-protest chrgs dropped 7-3, 519C1
Carter backs in new energy plan 7-16, 532G2
A-plant constructn halts linked to 3 Mile I, NRC regulatn 7-16—8-7, 609D3
NM waste spill 7-16, cleanup continues 9-5, 744A1
3 Mile I clean-up proposed 7-17, NRC urges water purificatn method 8-14, 629E2-D3
Va protesters convicted 7-17, 743B1
NRC asks A-plant changes 7-19, 609B3
Nev A-dump reopened 7-24, 561G2
WCC urges A-plant moratorium 7-24, 640F1
Citizens Party platform backs ban 8-1, 594G3
NRC: 3 Mile I preventable 8-2, 609E1
Silkwood damages award upheld 8-20, 629G3
3 Mile I property values rptd unaffected 8-20; evacuation size, costs rptd 9-23, 743G2-D3
S Pacific waste site disputed 8-21, 743D3
Carter defends A-power 8-22, 622D3
NRC reactor licensing freeze lifted 8-22, reversed 8-23, 664G3
NRC site rules chng seen 9-17, 743E1
NY plant shutdown urged 9-17, 743B2
'50s fallout, SAT decline linked 9-17, 747A2
Tenn fuel plant shut re uranium loss 9-18, FBI probes 10-10, 809A3
Va plant leak 9-25, probe rptd 10-2, 786G3-787B1
Ariz radioactive tritium plant seized 9-26, decontaminatn begun 9-29; Amer Atomics seeks reorganizatn 10-6, 806B2
NRC license policy case declined by Sup Ct 10-1, 768D2
Minn plant leak 10-2, cold shutdown reached 10-3; probe 10-7—10-9, 786C3
Washn, Nev close A-dumps 10-4, 10-22, cancer research threatened 10-23, 806G2-C3, 885G3*
NH plant site occupatn prevented 10-6—10-8, 806F3
NY rejects 2 reactors 10-12, 807B1
Calif pro-nuclear rally 10-13, 806D3
Va coal shift studied 10-15, 807A2
Va plant saboteurs convicted 10-16, 807D1
Indian Pt plant security said lax 10-16, 10-20, 807E1
Indian Pt FALN bomb threat rptd 10-18, 786E2
Met Ed fined $155,000 10-26, 826F1-E2
NYC protesters arrested 10-29, 827D2
3 Mile I comm final rpt: NRC abolitn urged, no A-constructn bar sought; reactn 10-30, 825C2-826F1
SC orders 50% A-dump cut 10-31, 851B2
Met Ed license challenged, rate hike asked 11-1, 826E2
A-plant cooling system hazard rptd 11-1, discounted 11-2, 849F1-C2
NRC reactor licensing freeze extended 11-5, 848G3
3 Mile I coal shift studied 11-5, 849C2
Brown for phaseout 11-8, 847G2
NRC fines Mich utility 11-9, 867A1

1980

GOP platform plank backs 7-10, 506C3
'79 A-plant mishaps rptd 7-14, 551D2
GOP platform adopted; text 7-15, 537B1, F1
Reagan pres nominatn acceptance speech 7-17, 532C2
NRC accident rules rptd tightened 7-24, 551D1
NRC clears Va plant of negligne 8-5, 648G3
Commonwealth Ed, 2 offcls acquitted 8-8, 649D1
GPU asks 3 Mile I cleanup aid, revises estimates 8-9, 649A3
Kennedy Dem conv speech 8-12, 610E2, 614F1
Dem platform planks adopted 8-13, 615G1
NRC staff backs 3 Mile I cleanup 8-14, 649D2
3 Mile I containmt bldg entered again 8-15, 649F1
Va plant conducts drill 8-16, NRC grants operating license 8-20, 648D3
Plutonium removing chem dvpt rptd 9-12, 9-13, 716A3
Tenn A-plant gets operating license 9-16, 723A2
Maine votes to keep A-plant 9-23, 723C2
Fusion dvpt bill clears Cong 9-24, signed 10-7, 981E2
Shoreham (NY) A-plant protest 9-29, 961C3
NYS A-waste storage clean-up enacted 10-1, 739D1
RR A-fuel tariffs case declined by Sup Ct 10-6, 782D2
Westinghouse to acquire Teleprompter 10-15, 836E1
Con Ed Indian Pt 2 leak controversy 10-17—10-23; NY judge backs rate surchrg 12-1, NRC staff seeks fine 12-11, 961C2
Carter, Reagan TV debate 10-28, 815F1
Anderson answers TV debate questns 10-28, 816D1
2d leak at Con Ed Indian Pt 2 11-3, 961B3
Mo, SD, Mont voters rejct A-power curbs; Washn, Ore OK 11-4, 847C2, G2
Vepco cancels N Anna 4 unit 11-25, 961F1
GPU seeks $4 bln from NRC 12-8, 960E3-961A1

1976

Obituaries
Warner, Roger S 8-3, 716F3
Safeguards Issue—*See 'Industrial Use' above*
Tests & Detection—*For U.S.-Soviet test ban developments, see under DISARMAMENT & Arms Control*
India bars A-tests end 1-14, 73G2

1977

NY Indian Pt plant found safe 10-12, 838F2
NRC nominee rejectd 10-17, 800E1
Australia anti-uranium drive mounts 10-17—11-3, 901F1-A2
Spent-fuel storage by govt backed by Carter 10-18, intl aid offered 10-19, 794F1
Intl fuel bank urged by Carter 10-19, 794C1
Resrch authorizatn, Clinch R dvpt OKd by Cong 10-20, 833A1, D1
Australia dockers back uranium boycott, demand vote 10-20, 901B2
Medit natns reach pollutn pact 10-21, 876D2
S Africa denies A-bomb vow to US 10-23, US issues Vorster letter 10-25, 825D2
Canada-Rumania pact set 10-24, 982D3
EC choses UK for JET site 10-25, 852G3
Clinch R, energy research authorizatn vetoed 11-5, 854E2-D3
US scientists ask A-plant closings, repairs, cite NRC rpt; NRC refuses 11-5, 917D1
US plant delays study discounts licensing 11-5, 917D2
Australia issues export rules 11-9, 901C1
Iran-W Ger A-plant deal set 11-10, 926C2
Australia uranium mining challenge planned 11-14, 901E1
ERDA authorizatn signed 11-15, 878A1, D1
Carter, Iran shah discuss A-plant sales 11-15, 11-16, 897G1
US, Canada OK uranium export pact 11-15, 913D1
US OKs Brazil uranium sale 11-16, 895G3; Vance-Geisel talks rptd 11-22, 912C3
4 Nobel, 10 other scientists back A-power 11-16, 936F3
Mich plant closed by NRC, studies set 11-18; Hart scores NRC 11-19, 917G1
Terrorists attack French power plants 11-19, 1011G3
Argentina to get US, Canada tech aid 11-21, 912A3
USSR-Japan pact rptd 11-21, 988G1
'78 NRC authorizatn, Clinch R provisn clears Cong 11-29, 938D1; signed 12-13, 1001G2
Solar energy backed for 3d World; A-dvpt seen 'trap' 12-11, 975A3, C3
Laser uranium enrichmt advances rptd 12-14, 12-17, arms spread risk seen 975F1-G2
Canada-Italy pact rptd 12-15, 982G2
Canada, EC OK uranium pact 12-20, 1010G1
US sale to Iran planned 12-31, 1001A1
Safeguards Issue—*See 'Industrial Use' above*
Tests & Detection—*See ARMAMENTS—Atomic Weapons; for U.S.-Soviet test ban developments, see under DISARMAMENT & Arms Control*

1978

NE A-plant delays threaten elec supply 9-11, 702B1
Canada uranium find rptd 9-13, 722B1
Carter simplifies forgn impact policy 9-26, 804F2
USSR-Libya power deal rptd 10-4, 821A1
Swedish govt falls on A-power issue 10-5, 764F2
US pub works veto upheld by House 10-5, 765E1
Bhutto on Pak A-capability, cites US oppositn to French deal 10-5, 798E1
Okla, Ind protesters arrested 10-7, 11-1, 941E2-F2
NH plant shutdown costs rptd 10-10, 914F1
Norway study com backs A-power 10-12, 884E1
Brazil program, W Ger purchases rptd lagging 10-15, 836A3
Australia bars Aborigine uranium dvpt veto 10-16, 812C3, D3 ★
Argentina plans plutonium processing plant 10-17, 840B3
France-China science, tech pact signed 10-20, 814B1
Waste disposal seen possible 10-20, 961B2
Iran plans cutback 10-22, 816A3
GAO links A-plants, arms productn 10-23, 900F1
Australia Aborigines OK uranium projct 11-3, 865E3
US cancels S Africa uranium contracts 11-4, 904C2
Austrians vote vs A-plant 11-5, 878E3
US-China atom smasher deal rptd 11-6, 871C2
Mont votes A-plant curbs 11-7, 847G1, 856E1
Australia centralizes waste monitoring 11-9, 900C2
US fuel rules unveiled 11-15, 919F3-920B1
France-China deal OKd by US 11-24; sale set 12-4, 986G1
NRC plant ratings released, safety progrm scored 11-25, 940B3, E3
Colo protesters convicted 11-29, 941A2
Solar cell competitive breakthrough rptd 11-30, 983F1
NH '77 protesters ruled illegal 12-6, 1009B3
NH A-plant bond guarantee rejctd 12-8, 1009G2
Reactor safety test called success 12-9, scientists score 12-10, 961E1-B2
EPA toxic-waste plan excludes A-wastes 12-14, 982G3
US to continue Taiwan pacts 12-15, 12-17, 973C2, 975B1, G1, C2
Canada, Rumania set reactor sales 12-15, 1013F2
NJ offshore A-plant contract canceled 12-19, 1009D3
Environmentalists criticize Carter 12-20, 1009E1
Ill utility orders 2 A-plants 12-20, 1009G3
Radiation—*See 'Industrial Use' above; for medical use, see MEDICINE—Cancer*
Safeguards Issue—*See 'Industrial Use' above*
Satellites—*See under ASTRONAUTICS*
Tests & Detection—*For testing and radiation issues, see ARMAMENTS—Atomic Weapons; for test ban developments, see DISARMAMENT*

1979

Midwest quake threat to 9 plants rptd 11-15, 954G1
Washn A-dump reopened 11-19, 885E3-886A1
Va plant saboteurs sentenced 11-27, 925B2
Carter on 3 Mile I comm rpt; replaces NRC head, creates advisory com, bars reactor licensing freeze 12-7, 940F1-E2
Kennedy scores Carter 12-13, 962B2
Industrial Use & Safeguards Issue (foreign)
US forgn projects impact rpts ordrd 1-5, 16F3
Australia uranium accord signed 1-9, 36C2
Canada-India quarrel end asked 57A3
US-China pact signed 1-31, 65C1
France A-plant constructn speedup ordrd 2-7, 82D3
Urenco plans W Ger A-enrichmt plant 2-7, 101D1
Westinghouse settles Swedish uranium supply suits 2-9, 131C3
Mex, US sign cooperatn pact 2-16, 124D3
Swiss vote backs A-progrm 2-18, 136F3
Spanish A-plant protests rptd 3-12, 192A2
Swedish energy bill rptd 3-13, A-waste plans faulted 3-14, 213D3-214D1
Brazil pres, Mondale confer on W Ger A-deal 3-22–3-23, 247F3, G3
US OKs India uranium sale 3-23, 416F2
Sweden OKs 2 reactors 3-29, 238E2
Foreign protests sparked by 3 Mile I A-accident, govt reactns vary 3-31–4-5, 246C1-B3
Oil producers see A-accident advantage 4-1, Australia fears uranium export drop 4-5, 246B3
France, Mex sign agrmt; US delay cited 4-1–4-4, 372B2
UK Labor seeks A-reactor hearings 4-6, 267G3
French factory, Iraq A-reactor sabotaged; forgn agents suspected 4-6, 276D1
US chrgs Pak A-arms plans, cuts econ aid 4-6; Pak denies 4-8; US jet offer rptd 4-16, 277B2, G2
Asia presses A-power progrms 4-6, Japan shuts plants after US safety warnings 4-14, 323B2
Belgian mayor closes A-plant 4-7, Cabt reverses 4-8, 276B2
Denmark defers plants 4-9, 276B2
W Ger protests rptd 4-9, sabotage attempt 4-13, 276C2
Spain oversight plans, protests rptd 4-9, 276D2
E Eur 3 Mile I media treatmt rptd 4-11, 323B1
USSR A-accidents disclosed 4-22, 323F1
Canada A-plant safety scored 4-27, 352A3
W Ger electn issue 4-29, 333A3
Japan OKs safety efforts 5-2, 320F2
USSR A-plant bid to India rejctd 5-2, 323F2
Swiss to probe Pak A-sales 5-2, 342F1
Eur A-Conf opens; Schmidt, Carter back A-power 5-7, 373F3-374C1
French loan to China signed 5-9, 370A2
France vows Iraq A-reactor replacemt 5-9, 371F2
France, W Ger resolve plutonium custody dispute 5-16, 380B1
W Ger reprocessing plant blocked 5-16, 410E3
Spain plans A-safety cncl 5-16, parlt debate rptd 5-17, 428C1
Spanish, French dockworkers boycott A-cargo 5-17, 390G2
Swiss OK tighter curbs 5-20, 390B3
IEA backs more use 5-22, 380F1
Eur, Canada A-protests 6-2–6-3, 416G1, E2
Spain A-protests 6-3, 6-5, 428G1-A2
USSR to build Turkey plant 6-5, 488F2
USSR urban A-plants rptd set 6-6, 476B3
EC comm backs dvpt, urges safety measures 6-13, 437G1
Pl suspends project 6-15, 487G3
W Ger FDP party backs A-power 6-16, 489F2
Canada A-plant accidents revealed 6-16, 6-19, 502B1
Sweden OKs plant fueling 6-25, 505G1-C2
Luxembourg plant plans dropped 6-27, 506A3
UK plant financing OKd 6-27, 524B3
Tokyo summit backs more use 6-29, 493E2
Comecon sets dvpt program 6-29, 497E1
Canada seeks dvpt 6-29, 501G3
W Ger sees long-term need 7-4, 506D1
US, Australia OK uranium pact 7-5, 501D1
French-Iraq reactor agrmt rptd 7-11, 564E1
Australia, UK sign pact 7-24, 562F2
France seeks Euratom revisn 7-24, 633B2
WCC urges A-plant moratorium 7-24, 640F1
BP to join Australia uranium mining project 7-27, 580G2, G3
Spain A-cncl, plant constructn OKd 7-30, 585D2
W Ger ends Iran plant deal 7-31, 586F2

1980

Industrial Use & Safeguards Issue (foreign)
Spain sets $1.4 bln for dvpt 1-8, 22B2
Canada PCs cite '74 India aid cutoff 1-8, 38F1
Italy panel backs A-dvpt 1-9, 20D3
USSR buys Italian equipmt 1-10, 28A1
Australia, Japan discuss pact 1-16, 78B2
Australia projcts rptd 1-19, 56E1
USSR constructn lag rptd 1-25, 79E3
Denmark defers A-plant decisn 1-26, 96D3
French protests staged 1-31, 2-9, 149A3
EC OKs A-fusion funds 2-5, 125B2
USSR '57 mishap confrmd by US probe 2-13, 153B1
France OKs 2 plants 2-20, 2 breeder reactors 2-26, 149D2, G2
W Ger reprocessing plant permit sought 2-27, 154A1
France OKs Iraq enriched uranium fuel, reactor; US scores 2-27, 192D3
Vienna conf backs plutonium fuel 2-27, 220D3
French A-protesters arrested 2-29, freed 3-17, 231C3
Australia plant rptd backed by France 3-3, 171A1
Argentine-Swiss heavy water deal opposed by US 3-10—3-11, contract signed 3-14, 229A2
US delays India uranium fuel shipmts 3-13, 181G3
Italy aid to Iraq seen; US concern noted 3-17, disputed 3-18, 220G2
Argentina opens Brazil talks 3-18, bilateral agrmts with 7 other Latin natns cited 229C2
Sweden referendum backs A-power 3-23, 2 A-reactors to start up 3-28, 219C3-220E1
US-Mex talks 4-2—4-3, 315A2
USSR 2d breeder reactor started 4-8, 316C1
US-Canada pact rptd 4-23, Swiss delay Canada pact 5-29, 429E1
Italy cuts Eurodif share 5-2, 409D1
US OKs Pl A-reactor 5-6, 440E3
Argentina-Brazil accord set 5-15—5-17, 405C2
US agency bars India uranium sale 5-16, 440C3
Australia questions US Pacific A-waste plan 5-21, 405G2, C3
Canada radioactive vegetables rptd 5-22, 406G2
French uranium find rptd 5-29, 407E2
W Ger protest village dispersed 6-4, 446C3
French power workers strike 6-12, 463A1
Carter OKs India uranium sale 6-19, 495F2
Venice summit endorses 6-23, 473F2
W Ger A-power moratorium urged 6-26, 581G1
W Ger, USSR sign pact 7-1, 489D2
OECD warns vs A-plant delays, '79 data rptd 7-8, 509F2
Dutch rpt backs A-plants 7-17, 565A2
UK tokamak fusion advance rptd 7-17, 715B3
Israel vs France-Iraq deal, US 'resigned' 7-28; France defends 7-29, 573A3, C3
France A-plant security rptd heightened 8-6, 670A2
Japan dvpt urged 8-18, 635A3
France uranium enrichmt process rptd 9-10, 707C3
Swiss reject US A-export protest 9-22, 754C2
US Cong fails to block India uranium sale 9-24, 723C1
Westinghouse Pl plant bldg resumes 9-25, 752C3
S Africa uranium plant capacity disclosed 9-30, 753G2
France sets A-tech dvpt 10-1, 749E3, F3
US uranium arrives in India 10-7, 830C2
France sets China A-reactor sale 10-17, 829A3
Taiwan-S Africa uranium deal cited 10-17, 831E2
Dutch protesters blockade A-plant 10-19-10-20, 830G2
Israel for Mideast A-ban 11-3, 864A2
Austria A-backers seek new referendum 11-3—11-10, 870C3
Iraq bars UN A-reactor inspectn 11-7, 864B2
Australia sets reprocessing terms 11-27, 919F3
Spain issues plant permit, A-power role downscaled 12-3, 923E2, A3
W Ger research office bombed 12-4, 969C2
USSR '79 shale oil detonatn cited 12-5, 951E3
Safeguards Issue—*See 'Industrial Use' above*

1976

'74 US info on India scored 1-20, 93B3
China test 1-23, Japan fallout rptd 2-1, 83D3
2 US tests 2-4, 84B1
US ups undergrnd pace, yield 2-13—3-17, 242D3
French undergrnd test 4-2, 243C1
France bars Pacific atmospheric tests 4-16, 372E3
US, UK joint A-test 8-26, 663D3
China tests 9-26, 10-17; US rpts fallout 10-5, 790E3
US confrms China computer sale 10-28, 832A3
China blast 11-7, called success 11-18, 871F3
Weapons—*For banning or control, see DISARMAMENT*
NATO A-group meets 1-21—1-22, 297G2
US-Spain pact signed 1-24, 77B1
Reagan scores US policy, Ford rebuts 2-10, 109A2, E2
US-Sovt supplies, research compared 2-10—2-27, 182F2-C3
Ford defends policy 3-5, 179C3
US estimates Israeli A-bombs 3-11, 216F2
Rpt stresses Sovt surprise attack capability, Europn independnc from US A-umbrella 3-15; NATO disavows rpt 3-16, 3-19, 297B2
Moynihan lands Israel A-bomb rpt 3-25, 234B2
Time rpts Israel '73 bomb strength; Israel denies 4-5, 243D1
Italy CP backs NATO A-policy 4-18, 297C1
UK A-fuel productn set 4-27, 4-28, 351E2-B3
French Cabt OKs '77-82 defense budget 5-5, 417E2-C3
US hearings on S Africa A-plant deal 5-26—5-29, 388F1
US Dem platform text 6-15, 476G2
US-Spain defns pact ratified 6-21, 7-23, 534F2, 541D3
Ford OKs '77 ERDA funds 7-12, 517G2
France, S Africa A-plant deal signed 8-6, 631A2
US rpts Taiwan A-bomb capacity, Taiwan denies 8-29, 760G3
Rumsfeld on Sovt readiness 9-27, 961F1
Sovt civil defns plans rptd 10-11, 934B1
France studies nonproliferatn 10-11, 1002B3
NATO warned re USSR 12-10, 933G2

1977

Weapons—*See ARMAMENTS, DISARMAMENT*

1978

Weapons—*See ARMAMENTS, DISARMAMENT; for safeguards issue, see ATOMIC Energy—Industrial Use*

1979

S Korea-Westinghouse reactor deal set 8-3, 742A2
US delays uranium to India 8-4, 646D2
Australian govt to sell uranium projct share 8-7, 600D1
Iran demands W Ger A-plant compensatn 8-10, 634E3
Canada uranium reserves estimate hiked 8-15, 613B2
Denmark referendum planned 8-22, 668D1
Spain issues 2 A-plant permits 8-25, protests staged 8-28–9-1, 670A3, D3
Argentine deals with W Ger, Swiss rptd; Canada installatn cited 10-1, 749D1
Canada scores Argentina sale loss 10-2–10-3, 788B3
W Ger A-power compromise rptd 10-2, 796C2
Ontario plants judged safe 10-3, 772B1
French protesters delay plant fueling 10-4, 772B3
USSR, E Ger sign pact 10-5, 761C2
Eur protests continue 10-9–10-15, 781F3
Sweden program halt study rptd 10-10, 795A2
USSR article on safety rptd 10-14, 815B2
France freezes Iran's stake in Eurodif 10-24, 976E2
Swiss plant attack rptd 11-4, 876A1
Cuban plant constructn plans rptd 11-8, 872B2
Spain factory bombed 11-13, 875A3
Connally campaign themes cited 11-15, 983B1
Sweden safety study issued 11-19, 910G2
Canada NDP conv debates 11-22–11-25, 927E1
W Ger Soc Dems back 12-6, 938G2
Australia sells uranium projct share 12-18, 992C2
UK OKs Westinghouse pressurized water reactor, A-needs detailed 12-18, 994B2
Radiation—*See 'Industrial Use' above*
Safeguards Issue—*See 'Industrial Use' above*
Tests & Detection—*For testing and radiation issues, see ARMAMENTS–Atomic Weapons; for test ban developments, see DISARMAMENT*
Weapons—*See ARMAMENTS, DISARMAMENT; for safeguards issue, see ATOMIC Energy–Industrial Use*

1976

ATOMS—*See PHYSICS*
ATRASH, Linda
Assassinated 5-27, 385D2
ATTENBOROUGH, Richard
Knighted 1-1, 80F2
ATTICA (N.Y.) Correctional Facility—*See 'Prisons' under CRIME*
ATWOOD, Angela
Cited in Hearst trial 2-9, 114A2, C3
AUBERT, Guy
Injured 8-30, 643D3
AUCHINCLOSS Sr., Hugh D.
Dies 11-20, 970B1
AuCOIN, Rep. Les (D, Ore.)
Reelected 11-2, 830C3
AUDI Nsu Auto Union A.G.—*See VOLKSWAGENWERK*
AUDUBON Society, National
Fla wetlands dvpt barred 4-16, 284D3
Stahr visits Carter 12-16, 937C2
AUGUST, Jan
Dies 1-17, 56A3
AUGUSTA, Ga.—*See GEORGIA*
AUGUSTA Chronicle (newspaper)
Ford endorsement rptd 10-30, 827G3
AULETTA, Egidio
Dies 10-20, 876B2
AUNE, Leif J.
Norway works, munic min 1-12, 30A2
AURORA, Ill.—*See ILLINOIS*
AUSTIN, Tex.—*See TEXAS*

1977

ATOMIC Energy Agency, International—*See 'International Atomic Energy Agency' under UNITED Nations—International Atomic Energy*
ATOMIC Industrial Forum Inc.
Carter A-proposals scored 4-7, 268D1
Backs spent-fuel storage by govt 10-18, 794D2
ATOMIC Safety & Licensing Appeal Board—*See U.S. GOVERNMENT—NUCLEAR Regulatory Commission*
ATO Tewodros Legesse
Killed 2-25, 238D3
AT&T—*See AMERICAN Telephone & Telegraph Co.*
ATTORNEY General, U.S.—*See BELL, Griffin*
AUBERT, Pierre
Elected Swiss forgn min 12-7, 1018E1
AUBREY, Crispin
Charged under Secrets Act 5-24, 526D3
AUBURN Dam (Calif.)
Carter proposes fund cut 2-22, 126E1
Carter for reconsideratn 4-18, 299C3
AUCTIONEER, The (book)
On best-seller list 3-6, 184G3
AUDITORS—*See ACCOUNTING*
AUDREY Rose (book)
On best-seller list 2-6, 120G3
AUDUBON Society
NY Times libel case review declined 12-12, 960E2
AUGUST, Steve
In NFL draft 5-3, 353B2
AUGUSTA, Ga.—*See GEORGIA*
AUGUSTINE, Norman R.
Replaced as Army undersecy 7-21, 626A3
AUKEN, Svend
Named Denmark labor min 10-1, 882F3
AUSCHWITZ (concentration camp)—*See NAZIS*
AUSTAD, Mark E.
Replaced as amb to Finland 5-25, 500B1
AUSTIN (U.S. tanker)
San Fran Bay oil spill 1-5, 214F2
AUSTIN, Tex.—*See TEXAS*

1978

ATOMIC Energy Agency, International—*See UNITED Nations—International Atomic Energy Agency*
ATOMIC Energy Commission—*See under U.S. GOVERNMENT*
AT&T—*See AMERICAN Telephone & Telegraph Co.*
ATTACHMENTS (book)
On best-seller list 9-4, 708D1
ATTALAH, Ibrahim Abdel-Rahman
Egypt industry min 10-5, 774B3
ATTENBOROUGH, Richard
Chess Players released 5-17, 619A1
Magic released 11-18, 970A2
ATTICA (N.Y.) Correctional Facility
Ex-inmate arrested in NYC police slayings, '76 Carey pardon scored 4-5, 388C3
ATTORNEY General, U.S.—*See BELL, Griffin*
ATTOUMANI, Said
Ousts Soilih in Comoro coup 5-13, 371A2
AT&T v. MCI Telecommunications Corp.
Case declined by Sup Ct 11-27, 937B2
ATWOOD, J. Brian
Says Saudis press jet sale 3-14, 177A1
AUBERJONOIS, Rene
Eyes of Laura Mars released 8-4, 970C1
AUBREY, Crispin
Maj secrets chrgs dropped 10-23, 838A3; sentncd re other chrgs 11-17, 924F1
AUBURN (Ala.) University
2d in NCAA indoor track championships 3-11, 692D3
Spann at US-USSR swimming meet 4-15—4-16, 780B3
McCall in NFL draft 5-2, 336G3
Mitchell in NBA draft 6-9, 457G3
AuCOIN, Rep. Les (D, Ore.)
Reelected 11-7, 852B1
AUDIARD, Michael
Dear Detective released 4-24, 619D1
AUDRAN, Stephane
Silver Bears released 4-20, 619G3
Violette released 10-9, 1030F3
AUDUBON Society, National
NH A-plant site review ordrd 4-28, 347B1
Carter gets high rating 12-20, 1009F1
AUERBACH, Arnold (Red)
Heinsohn fired as Celtic coach 1-3, 40G3
Rejcts Knicks offer, OKs Celtics contract 7-14, 656E1
AUGUSTIN, Monique
Arrested 5-5, jailed 8-21, 725D1
AUGUSTIN, Ronald
Sister jailed 8-21, 725D1
AUKEN, Svend
Named Danish labor min 8-30, 688A1
AURORA, Colo.—*See COLORADO*
AUSTIN, Tex.—*See TEXAS*

1979

ATOMIC Energy Agency, International—*See UNITED Nations–International Atomic Energy Agency*
ATOMIC Energy Commission—*See under U.S. GOVERNMENT*
ATOMIC Industrial Forum
Walske on NRC A-safety rule 1-20, 54B3
Perkins on Silkwood suit impact 5-18, 381C3
Walske on 3 Mile I comm final rpt 10-30, 826D1
ATOMIC Scientists, The Bulletin of the
Nuclear 'doomsday clock' unchngd 1-1, 13D1
AT&T—*See AMERICAN Telephone & Telegraph Co.*
ATTICA (N.Y.) Correctional Facility
'71 riot convict paroled 2-21, 156E1
Inmate slain in racial brawl 6-3, 548F2
ATTORNEY General, U.S.—*See BELL, Griffin; CIVILETTI, Benjamin R.*
AT&T v. MCI Communications
Case declined by Sup Ct 3-26, 231B1
ATWELL, Rick
Sarava opens 2-11, 292F2
AUBERJONOIS, Rene
Break a Leg opens 4-29, 711G1
Every Good Boy opens 7-30, 711F2
AUDUBON Society, National
Scores US wilderness proposal 1-4, 16C2
Peterson installed pres 4-1, 272D1
AUGUR v. Collins
Case declined by Sup Ct 1-22, 54A2
AUNT Erma's Cope Book (book)
On best-seller list 11-4, 892C3
AUREL, Jean
Love On The Run released 4-5, 528A3
AUSCHWITZ Death Camp
US CIA releases photos 2-22, 193D1
Mengele loses Paraguay citizenship 8-8, bounty offered 8-10, 616A3
AUSIELLO, Msgr. Renato
Flemish art stolen from Rome convent 6-3, 656F1
AUSTIN, Tex.—*See TEXAS*

1980

ATOMIC Energy Agency, International—*See UNITED Nations--International Atomic Energy Agency*
ATOMIC Industrial Forum
NRC reactor licensing resumptn urged 1-9, 17C1
ATOMIC Scientists, The Bulletin of
Nuclear 'doomsday clock' moved up 1-1, 12C3
ATROMID-S—*See MEDICINE--Drugs & Health-Care Products*
ATSELLIS, Stelios
Named Cyprus min to pres 9-9, 749F2
AT&T—*See AMERICAN Telephone & Telegraph Co.*
ATTAR, Issam al-
Claims backing for Moslem Brotherhood 213B1
ATTAWAY, Rowland
Denies attacking blacks 4-8, 333A1
ATTICA (N.Y.) Correctional Facility
Renewed violence, overcrowding rptd 1-31, 2-1, 112D3
'Son of Sam' Soc Sec benefits rptd 6-5, insanity plea rptd faked 8-4, 639E2
ATTORNEY General, U.S.—*See CIVILETTI, Benjamin R.*
ATUEGBU, Fidelis
USF wins NCAA soccer title 12-14, 1001E3
ATWATER Jr., H. Brewster
Named Gen Mills chief exec 12-16, 959E1
ATZORN, Robert
Marionettes released 11-7, 972F3
AUBURN (Ala.) University
Ralph Jordan dies 7-28, 608C2
AUCOIN, Rep. Les (D, Ore.)
Reelected 11-4, 844B1, 852F2
AUDIARD, Michael
Incorrigible released 3-3, 416A3
AUERBACH, Arnold (Red)
Named NBA top exec 5-29, 656D3
AUERBACH, Nobert T.
Named UA pres, chief officer 12-12, 986A3
AUERSWALD, Ingrid
Wins Olympic medal 7-26, 624G1
AUGUSTA—*See GEORGIA*
AUKEN, Sven
Overtime curbs planned 3-13, 256A1
AUNLI, Ove
Wins Olympic medal 2-17, 155B3
AUNT Erma's Cope Book (book)
On best-seller list 1-13, 40B3; 2-10, 120C3; 3-9, 200C3
AUSTIN—*See TEXAS*

1976

AUSTIN (U.S. warship)
In Intl Naval Review 7-4, 488D3
AUSTIN, J. Paul
Cosponsors Carter business mtg 7-22, 550G3
'70 Carter campaign donor 10-17, 805B1
AUSTIN, Richard A.
Loses Mich Sen primary 8-3, 565G1

1977

AUSTIN, Debbie
Wins LI Charity Classic 8-14, 951D1
LPGA top money winner 11-27, 951F1
AUSTIN, H. Gregory
On Maine Indian land claims 1-21, 59G1
AUSTIN, Tracy
Loses US Open match 9-7, 787E2
AUSTRAL Airlines
Argentine jet crash 11-20, 992D2
AUSTRALIA (sailboat)
Loses America's Cup 9-18, 828E2

1978

AUSTIN, Debbie
Wins Amer Cancer Society tourn 2-13, 355B3
2d in Sunstar tourn 3-12, 355E3
2d in Amer Defender Classic 4-23, 356A1
AUSTIN, J. Paul
China signs Coke deal 12-13, 1015B2
AUSTIN, John
Wins NCAA tennis title 5-29, 419E2
AUSTIN, Tracy
Loses Brinker tourn 3-12, 419A2
US wins Weisman Cup 4-23, 419C1
US Open results 9-10, 707E1
US wins Federatn Cup 12-3, 1027A1

1979

AUSTIN, Vice Adm Bernard L. (ret.)
Dies 8-21, 671F1
AUSTIN, Beth
Whoopee opens 2-14, 292F3
AUSTIN, Michael
Shout released 11-9, 1008E1
AUSTIN, Tracy
Avon tourn results 1-7, 2-4, loses title 3-25; wins Family Circle 4-15, 391A2, C2, C3
US wins Federatn Cup 5-6, 391E2
Wins Women's Italian Open 5-14, loses World Invitatn 5-20; Wimbledon results 7-6, 7-7, 570A1, B2, C2
Loses Volvo Cup 8-26, wins US Open 9-9, 734A1, D2

1980

AUSTIN Jr., J. Paul
Presses Guatemala Coca-Cola franchise sale 5-27, 464B1
Goizueta to replace 8-6, 600D2
AUSTIN, John
Wins Wimbledon mixed doubles 7-5, 606A3
AUSTIN, Tracy
Loses Colgate championship 1-7, Sunbird Cup 5-4; wins Clairol Championship 3-30, Family Circle 4-13, BMW Championship 6-21, 607E2, A3-C3, E3
Avon tourn results 1-13—3-16, wins title 3-23, 607A2
US wins Federatn Cup 5-25, 607B1
Wins Wimbledon mixed doubles; semifinal singles loss cited 7-5, 606D2, A3
Loses US Open semifinals 9-5, 691E2
Wins US Women's Indoor 10-5; loses Fla Fed 11-16, Lions Cup 11-23, 947G1-G2
AUSTIN (Tex.) American-Statesman (newspaper)
Ex-atheist apologizes in schl prayer dispute 5-9, 471F2
Anderson pres endorsemt rptd 11-1, 844F1

AUSTRALIA

1976

AUSTRALIA—*See also ADB, COMMONWEALTH of Nations, OECD*
Museums rptd neglected 1-16, 26D3
Divorce actns rptd 1-29, 97G2
Sept '75 populatn rptd 3-15, 204D1
NSW backs daylight-savings time 5-1, 349C3
'75 populatn rptd 5-18, 400D1
Immigrant quotas raised 5-20, 400E1
Intl Eucharist Cong 8-1—8-8, 596G2
Priests hold banned masses 8-31, 691E3
Population rpt notes decline 10-1, 749B3
Drought end causes flooding 10-5, 770D3; towns evacuated 10-16—10-18, 808E1
Eclipse seen 10-23, 808B2
Captain Bligh's log bought 11-25, 902A3
Gas spill in Tasmania 12-18, 997B3
Fly, locust plagues rptd 12-30, 997D3

1977

AUSTRALIA—*See also COMMONWEALTH of Nations, OECD, SEATO*
Sydney commuter train crash 1-18, 104C3
'75 divorce rate rptd up 1-27, 158A2
RAAF Mirage jet crashes 2-2, 113F2
Brushfires kill 5 2-12—2-13, 204G2
Gunman kidnaps students, others 2-14, 163C1
'76 census revised 3-15, 280G2
Immigratn study rptd 3-18, 218F1
Darwin mem'l unveiled 3-26, 280E2
Solar energy research set 4-6, 280G3
Morosi wins libel suit 4-22, 326A2
Indonesian quake recorded 8-19, 747A3
Natl park planned in North 8-25, 693A2
New pesticides developed 11-7, 945F1-A2
Queensland protesters arrested 11-11, 881B3
Atomic Energy & Safeguards—*See 'Uranium' below*
Cocos Islands—*See COCOS Islands*

1978

AUSTRALIA—*See also COMMONWEALTH of Nations, GATT, OECD, SOUTH Pacific Forum*
Rptr rescues Laotian girlfriend 5-27, 420D2
Qantas curbs on Jews probed 10-18, 836D1; 10-20, 900E3

Aborigine Affairs
Racism study issued 1-4, 6C2
Canberra to take over Queensland Aborigine affairs 3-22; Bjelke-Petersen scores 3-22, Aborigines back 3-25, 225E1
Queensland land control compromise rptd 4-11, 286F1, D2 ★
Uranium mining rules adopted 5-31, 434C3
Natl Front for apartheid 6-3, 495B1
Mineral revenue tax proposed 7-20, 570C2
Uranium royalties set 8-25, 666A1
Uranium compromise OKd 9-8, 9-15, new dispute delays projct 9-19, 721A1
Uranium dvpt veto barred 10-16, 812C3
Uranium mining OKd 11-3, 865E3

Atomic Energy & Safeguards
Foreign uranium export delayed for unions 1-6, 16E1
N Terr uranium deposit found, dvpt curbs rptd 2-3, 88A1
Unions vote to honor uranium contracts 2-10, 110B1
Nuclear Suppliers' Group joined 2-24, 129C2
A-test monitoring statn declassified 3-1, 145A2
Japan uranium treaty sought 3-20, 208B3
Uranium mining exports protested 4-1, 243E3
French neutron bomb test protested 4-21, 311B1
Uranium mining, export rules adopted 5-31, 434B3
Fraser urges A-arms curb 6-5, 450D3
EC seeks uranium trade talks 6-13, 495A1
Aborigine uranium revenue tax proposed 7-20, 570C2
Finland signs uranium accord 7-20, US A-policy cited 7-21, 590C1
EC halts Australia-UK uranium accord 7-27, 666E1
PI signs safeguards pact 8-7, 666G1
US interim safeguards pact signed 8-8, 666B2
Aborigine uranium royalties set 8-25, 666A1
Aborigine uranium compromise OKd 9-8, 9-15, new dispute delays projct 9-19, 721A1
Canada uranium deposit rptd 9-13, 722C1
Maralinga waste plutonium causes concern; UK denies negligence, offers aid 10-5—10-10, 771G2
Anthony bars Aborigine uranium dvpt veto 10-16, 812C3, D3 ★
Aborigines OK uranium project 11-3, 865E3
Waste monitoring centralized, safety concerns cited 11-9, 11-10, 900C2

Crime & Civil Disorders
New S Wales prisoners protest 1-5, McGeechan talks role ended 1-10, 34B3
Hilton Hotel bombed 2-12, 110E1 ★
Queensland demonstratn ban protested 3-4, 165B2
Bomb found at home of India amb 3-25, 225D2
8 MDs, 73 others chrgd in medical fraud 4-3, 243G3-244C1
Ananda Marga hq raided 6-17, 495D1
53 gays arrested in Sydney march 6-25, protesters battle police 6-26, 495C1
Drug smuggling patrols increased 7-9, 530B2
30 injured in prison riot 8-22, 646C2
Police, gay rights backers clash 8-27, 686C1
19 Croats rptd arrested 9-5, 796E3
NSW transport agency probe set 12-5, 963D2
Queensland march curbs protested 12-7, 963E2

1979

AUSTRALIA—*See also COMMONWEALTH of Nations, DISARMAMENT-Geneva Committee, GATT, OECD*
Queensland hit by cyclone 1-1—1-2, 18C2
Fire destroys SE woodland, heat wave hits Sydney 1-10, 18E2
Prawn arsenic levels rptd high 2-20, 188G2
Barrier reef park rptd urged 6-6, 423F2
Skylab crashes down 7-11, 509A1
Kangaroo kill quota hiked 7-25, 581C1
Communicatns satellite planned 10-18, 852B2

Aborigine Affairs
Setlmts flooded by cyclone 1-1, 18D2
Mining rights probe rptd 1-24, 94F2
Oil drilling on land OKd 6-18, 467G1
Health study ordered 11-28, 906D3

Atomic Energy & Safeguards
Ranger uranium accord signed 1-9, 36C2
Uranium mining projct OKd 3-1, 153D1
US A-accident impact on uranium sales seen 4-5, 246C3
US uranium accord signed 7-5, 501D1
UK uranium pact OKd by EC Comm 7-5, 522E1; signed 7-24, 562F2
BP to join uranium mining project 7-27, 580G2, G3
Govt to sell Ranger share 8-7, 600D1
Roxby Downs dvpt seen 9-16—9-17, 749C2; mining OKd 10-9, 810G3
Peko to buy govt Ranger share 12-18, 992C2

Crime & Civil Disorders
Melbourne paintings rptd stolen 1-3, 18F2
Surveillance bill proposed 3-8, 209F2
Perth bombings 4-4, 4-5, 266E2
Pan Am hijack bid foiled 4-4, 266F2
NSW police corruptn chrgd, comr quits; probe launched 6-5, 467B2
Drug bur inquiry rptd 6-20, 467F2
Drug traffic rpt issued, new narcotics force announced 11-6, 870D2

1980

AUSTRALIA—*See also ADB, ANZUS, COMMONWEALTH of Nations, GATT, GENEVA Committee, IEA, OECD*
Cyclone hits Goldsworthy 1-10, 56A1
Oldest life evidence rptd 4-2, 415A3
Barrier reef preservatn backed 6-10, 460F2
Oldest fossil life forms found 6-19, 715F2

Aborigine Affairs
Ethnic broadcast unit planned 1-24, 116A1
Mining efforts protested 5-8, 371A1
Anti-abortn bill defeated, pol impact seen 5-30, 428D3
Diamond mining projct OKd 7-27, 602C2
Sacred site drilling protested 8-11, 617G2
Sacred site drilling starts 8-29, govt scored 9-2, UN appeal made 9-3, mining negotiatns ban rptd 9-5, 686G1
Local worker recruitmt stressed 12-1, 940G3
NSW police brawl, 11 chrgd 12-2; racial tensns seen rising 12-3, 964D1-A2

Atomic Energy & Safeguards
Japan pact discussed 1-16, 78B2
Uranium mine plans rptd 1-19, 56E1
French enrichmt plant aid offered 3-3, 171A1
US Pacific A-waste plan questioned 5-21, 405G2, C3
Reprocessing terms set 11-27, 919F3

Crime & Civil Disorders
Prison unrest hits New South Wales 10-23, 828A1
NSW police brawl, 11 chrgd 12-2; racial tensns seen 12-3, 964D1-A2
Woolworth bomb blast 12-24; extortn demanded 991D2

1976

Economy & Labor (domestic)
Devaluation rpts denied 1-5, 7B3
Bank reserve deposit ratio raised 1-7, 26A3
Dec '75 budget deficit, reserve assets rptd 1-7, 26B3
Econ advisory group formed 1-20, 46G1
Iron workers strike 1-20, layoffs rptd 1-26, 97D2
Bank loan interest cut 1-22, 46B2
Business investmt, tax moves detailed 1-26, 97D1
New uranium yields rptd 1-28, govt ends role 2-1, 97A1
Victoria fuel projct rptd 1-28, 97D2
Fraser asks voluntary pay curbs, rpts govt spending cuts 2-2, 2-3, 97F1
Railway rate hike rptd 2-3, 97G2
State income tax proposed 2-4, 97B2
Govt defers bldg projcts 2-4, state premrs ask aid 2-5, 116G1
Jan jobless totals rptd 2-9, 137E2
Govt job cuts OKd 2-10, 137E2
4th ¼ '75 budget deficit up 2-10, 137F2
Wage hike OKd 2-13, 137G2
Air traffic controllers strike 2-20, 154F3
Steel plant deferred 2-24, 154D3
Copper mine closing set 2-24, 154E3
Manganese, other mineral ocean finds rptd 2-26, 154F3
Unions seek wage hike 3-2, 172B3
Steel price hike rptd sought 3-2, 172B3
Rice growers seek govt aid 3-2, 172C3
Wool, airport workers strike 3-5, 3-31, 249C3; wool strike ends 4-20, 287A3
Feb jobless total falls 3-8, 187F2
Steel price hike OKd 3-9, 187F2
New uranium find rptd 3-9, 187G2
Govt uranium mine for sale 3-10, 187A3
Jobless total rptd up 3-13, 297E3
Govt employe pensn plan offered 3-18, 203F3
Sept-Nov '75 consumer spending down 3-18, 204C1
NW coast opened for oil dvpt 3-22, 237E2
Natl energy cncl OKd 3-23, 237E1
Jobless benefits revised 3-23, 237E1
Cigaret, tobacco TV ads banned 3-23, 237G1
'75 crude oil output up 3-23, 237F2
Min wage increased 3-25, 237C2
Wage policy review set 4-1, 249E3
New uranium find rptd 4-5, 249B3
Jan-Mar budget deficit 4-8, 249F3
Reserve deposit ratio cut 4-8, 249F3
Tax-sharing plan agreed 4-9, 264D3
Mar jobless rate rptd up 4-12, 264F3
Govt spending curbs announced 4-19, 309A3
1st ¼ CPI rptd up 4-21, 287C3
Wage policy hearings 4-22—5-13, new policy set 5-28, 415A1
Govt meets cutback goals 4-28, 332C1
Parlt gets business tax plan 5-6, 362D3
Apr jobless total rptd 5-7, 362C3
NSW cost cuts announced 5-13, 362E3
New tax plan, Medibank subsidy, spending cuts set 5-20, 380C1
Immigrant quotas raised 5-20, 400F1
'76-80 defns budget set 5-25, 399E3
Unions ask mgt pay Medibank levy 5-26, 415C2
Aboriginal land bill terms set 5-27, 415B2
1st ¼ GDP rptd up 6-3, 415G1
Oil price hike asked 6-14, 455F3
Uranium enrichmt plant set 6-30, 496G1
Gen strike vs Medibank chngs 7-12, 520B2
States to get suplmtl funds 7-14, 554C2
2d ¼ CPI rptd up 7-16, 554D2
Secret papers rptd leaked 7-17, 537G1
July jobless rptd up 8-6, 587B2
Dock strike ends 8-10, 623C2
Wage hikes announced 8-12, 637C1
'76-77 budget introduced 8-17, 636D3
Budget cuts protested 8-23, 650B1
Whitlam scores budget proposals 8-24, 672B3
Fraser scores pol strikes 9-2, dockers protest 9-7, 691C3
Drought study issued, relief set 9-8, 709E2-E3
Drought relief set 9-8, 709E2-E3
2d ¼ wages rptd up 9-10, 730D1
Jobless relocatn plan set 9-12, 730A1
Aug jobless data rptd 9-13, 730D1
Econ advisory bd named 9-14, 730E1
Aug food prices rptd up 9-16, 709E3
Jobs plan set 9-21, 770A3
Qantas rpts '75 losses 9-23, 749D3
Drought ends, wheat crop cited 10-5, 770D3
Sept jobless rptd down 10-11, 789D2
3d ¼ CPI rptd up 10-21, 808A2
Stock prices drop 10-26, 870A1
Uranium mining backed 10-28, 835B2
GM-H sets major expansn 10-31, 870B1
Chrysler plans expansion 11-2, 835A3
Oil-shale find rptd 11-3, 835G2
Darwin '74 cyclone relief scored 11-4, probe ordrd 11-18, 902D2
Monetary curbs set, oppositn scores 11-7, 850C1
Productivity dept formed 11-7, 870A1
Mining to end on Fraser I 11-11, 888A2
Unions vs uranium ban end 11-12, 888F1
Inflatn rate rptd 11-15, 869D3
Copper find rptd 11-18, 902G2
Wkly wage, strike data rptd 11-29, 896D2
Unions back uranium contracts 12-8, 923C1
Tasmanian electn factor 12-11, 944B3
Pub spending cut set, budget deficit rptd 12-16, 961E2, F3 ★
Reserve bank cuts liquidity 12-21, 997F2 ★

1977

Economy & Labor (domestic)—*See also 'Uranium' below*
'76-77 wheat forecast hiked 1-3, 17E1
Air controllers slowdown 1-7, jobs threatened 1-11, 42F2
Dock union S Africa boycott fails 1-21, 67B3
Coal productn cuts seen 1-25, 81C3
Ct backs S Australia gas tax 2-1, 96E1
3d ¼ '76 strike data rptd 2-1, 96C2
Diamonds found in W Australia 2-1, 96A3
'77 inflatn rate forecast rptd 2-3, 96E2
Jan jobless rate rptd 2-5, 96B2
Dec '75-76 inflatn rate rptd 2-7, 87B2
Dieback fungus hits forests 2-14, 132C2
ACTU shipbldg plea 2-16, ANL contract job actn urged 2-17, 253F1, C2
Parkes Dvpts bankrupt 3-8, 237A1
Newcastle shipyd study rptd 3-10, 253D2
Wool floor-price drop barred 3-15, 236E3
Immigrant workers rptd needed 3-18, 218F1
Govt raises wages 3-31, 253E3
Public svc job cuts set 4-4, 303A1
Pensn benefits hiked 4-6, 302F3
Voluntary wage-price curbs asked 4-13, 302D3
US CIA union infiltratn chrgd; Fraser sets probe 4-27, 326D1-A2, 344F2
Victoria fuel strike ends 4-28, 346B1
US CIA probe calls mount 4-29, infiltratn chrgs continue 5-4, 372A1
Air controllers strike 4-29, 5-7—5-13, 388G3
Fraser halts CIA probe 5-3; allegatns continue 5-17—5-24, 410F1-B2
Ford plans NSW plant 5-5, 389D1
Feb-Apr jobless rate rptd 5-6, 389C1
Govt raises wages 5-24, 424C2
1st ¼ CPI rptd 5-24, 424C2
Uranium comm rpt issued 5-25, reactn 5-31, 465A2-A3
May jobless rate rptd 6-6, 484C3
1st ¼ retail sales down 6-9, 484B3
1st ¼ GDP, other output data drops; profits, wages up 6-10, 484B3
Peabody interests sold 6-30, 520A2
Wool prices up 7-4, '77-78 output at 20-yr low 8-12, 652E3-653A1
Alumina refinery canceled 7-7, 523F1-A2
Auto industry layoffs rptd 7-13, 560G3
$ devalued 1.5% 8-3, 615G2
US rptdly bars CIA union role 8-4, 633A1
Strikes blamed on UK immigrants 8-5, disputed 8-8, 632B3
Lynch presents '77-78 budget 8-16, Whitlam scores 8-23, 670E3, 671E1
Pub employe strikes banned 8-19, 652A3
Workers get 2% raise 8-22, 725F1-A2
NW Shelf gas search OKd 8-24, 704C3-705B1
ACTU cong 9-12—9-15, 740B2
Strike chrgs vs UK immigrants clarified 9-12, 762A3
Forced labor camps exposed 9-20, 779A2
Melbourne transit, power workers strike 9-27, 9-28; Sydney blackout 9-28, 762F2
Power worker, govt talks fail 10-7, 800C3; pay request rejected, strike continues 10-18, 822B1; ends 10-25, 839C2
UK immigrants chrgd again 10-9, 800B3
Anti-union bill signed 10-23, 839E2
Oil reserves seen depletn forecast 11-3, 862F1
Mt Lyell copper mine gets fed aid 11-10, 945A1
Sheep disease hits North 11-14, state of emergency asked 11-15, 881D3
Lynch land-deal scandal chrgd 11-15—11-21, resigns 11-18, 901C2
New animal disease lab OKd 11-15, 922G3
'77-78 wheat output forecast 11-28, 945C1
Plan to kill diseased cattle dropped 11-28, 945E1

1978

Economy & Labor (domestic)—*See also 'Atomic Energy' above*
Wool stock rise rptd 1-4, 6E2
Dec '77 jobless rptd; Dec '76, '75 rates cited 1-6, 53D2
Drought financial losses rptd 1-11, Bjelke-Petersen asks prayers 1-15, 16B1
Drought causes massive brushfires 1-13—1-18, livestock shot 1-16, 145G1
Workers get 1.5% wage hike 2-1, 88D1
Poseidon nickel mine to close 2-4, 88F1
Jan jobless rptd record 2-11, 145F1
Immigratn curbs asked 2-19, 129B2
Qantas '77 profit rptd 3-6, 225F2
'77 gold output at 5-yr high 3-15, 208D3
Feb jobless rate falls 3-20, 208F2
Whaling indus probe set 3-20, 208C3
Queensland bauxite mine planned 3-22, 225F1
Ports hit by job actns 4-9—5-2, 349F3-350B1
McNeill urges coal conversn, other energy measures 4-10, 265E3
Queensland mineral rights compromise rptd 4-11, 286A2
'77, 1st ¼ CPI rise rptd 4-27, 327D3
'78 inflatn drop, output forecast 4-27, 328A1
Chrysler layoffs, productn chngs set; '77 losses rptd 5-3, 349D3
Norfolk I offered home rule 5-8, 369D3
BP finds sulfides deposit 5-16, 411C2
Port congestn continues 5-22, 411A2
Fraser defends govt, cites inflatn curbs 5-29, 434B3
Port setlmt rptd; Sydney, Melbourne job actns end 6-5, 450F3
New immigratn policy set 6-7, 451B1, D1
Sheep, cattle herds rptd down 6-14, 472F1
1st ¼ GDP rptd up 2.4% 6-16, 472C2
'77 oil productn rptd up 3% 7-5, 514D2
Budget deficit 50% above forecast 7-7, 530E1
Coking coal mine strike rptd 7-13, 555C1
Domestic airlines hike fares 7-13, 555B2
2d ¼ inflatn rate rptd down 7-28, 590A2
'77 jobless rise rptd 7-28, 677D1
Port strikes 8-11—9-7; Sydney, Melbourne shipping disrupted 9-1, Port Kembla closed 9-6, 686F1
'78-79 budget presented, natl health insurnc dropped; oppositn, unions score 8-15, 628F1-E3
Budget protests; Sydney, Brisbane violence 8-17, 8-21, 646B1
Telecom strikers warned 8-22, setlmt reached 8-26, 721F1
Budget protests continue; soc svcs, tax cuts scored 8-23, 686E1
Indl tech impact study set 8-29, job training urged 9-3, 721B2
New South Wales coal find rptd 9-1, 686A1
Dockers close all major ports, other strikes hamper cargo shipmts; govt bars role 9-12—9-16, 738E2
Lynch, Holding land-deal scandal reopened; denials issued, judicial probe barred 9-14, 771D1
Bass Strait oil find rptd 9-21, 738D3
Fraser sees '79 jobless peak 9-28, 812G3-813A1
Brisbane right-to-march protest, 288 held 10-30, 866A1
State borrowing for indl projcts OKd 11-6, 878F2
Fraser budget scored by Melbourne inst 11-7, 878B2
Govt mfg subsidy fall rptd 11-13, 944D1
Fuel delivery strike ends 11-15, 921A1
Ruby field discovered 11-23, 920F3
Econ ministry split 11-30, 943F3
3d ¼ GDP rptd 12-7, 944A1
Slow econ growth rptd 12-7, 944A1
Real jobless rptd at 9% 12-12, 1013B1
Wage-monitoring com set by govt 12-13, 985E2
Whaling ban urged 12-18, 1012F3
Melbourne Inst urges econ stimulus 12-19, 1012D3

1979

Economy & Labor
Banking inquiry ordrd 1-23, 74A1
Aborigine mining rights probed 1-24, 94G2
Sales tax rejected 1-25, 73F2
'78 4th 1/4 inflatn rptd 1-31, 94E2
'78 retail sales rptd up 1-31, 113C1
'78 housing approvals, factory productn rptd up 2-1, 2-6, 113D1
Airline maintenance workers strike rptd 2-21, 188G3-189A1
Finance min resigns 2-22, 133C2; reinstated 2-25, 168C1
Fraser sees recovery signs 2-27, 168A1
Inflatn drop doubted 3-13, 189A1
Econ growth predicted 3-15, 209D3
Mineral processing backed 3-26, 233F1-A2
Fscl '78 GDP rise posted 3-28, 253D1
Farm income seen rising 3-29, 253F1
Truckers protest 4-6—4-11, 266C2
Alumax plans smelter 4-20, 311D1
Fraser vs union militants 4-22, 328F1-B2
Savings bond, other interest rates hiked 4-23, 311A1
Job-training study missn set 4-28, skilled worker shortage rptd 4-30; employers score 5-1, 351G2-D3
Victoria Liberals seek job funds 5-8, 387C1
Adelaide bank rescue set 5-14, 387C1
Indl task force formed 5-16, 423G2-C3
Austerity measures proposed 5-24, 404E2
Budget deficit underestimated 5-30, 443G1-C2
Barrier reef oil drilling banned 6-4, 423F1
1st 1/4 GDP, inflatn rptd up 6-11, 443C2
Union ldrs arrests spur mine strikes 6-12, 443E2; 6-21, 483A1
Inflatn pay raise granted, indexatn scored 6-27, 483E1
Energy measures announced 7-3, 522C1
Pub employe curbs enforced 7-13, Telecom workers end maintenance ban 7-17, 542A1
Labor troubles rptd 7-14, 542D1
Fraser scores strikers 7-22, some unions continue work bans 7-23, 562B2
Fscl yr inflatn, jobless rate rptd 7-25, 581A1
GDP '79 rise, other OECD forecasts rptd 8-3, 599E3-600A1
Pilbara mine strike ends 8-3, 666E3
Dock strike ends 8-8, 612A1
June '78-79 inflatn outpaces wages, consumer confidence rptd down 8-20, 650C2
Fscl '79-80 budget presented 8-21, 631E2
Defns budget detailed 8-23, 683G2
Farmers hurt by drought; Westn Australia, New South Wales cited 8-28, 650F2
Labor Party budget plans detailed 8-28, 684A1
Alcohol fuel projct rptd 8-30, 666D3
Queensland anti-strike bill proposed 9-4, 705E3-706A1
ACTU attacks wage restraints, Fraser scores 9-11, 728G1
Energy reserves seen abundant 9-13, 705C3
Econ policies linked to S Australia electn 9-15, 749B2
Roxby Downs dvpt seen 9-16—9-17, 749C2
Roxby Downs mining OKd 10-9, ACTU oppositn rptd 10-12, 810G3
Fraser scored re unemploymt, state aid 10-11, 832A2
Sept jobless rise rptd 10-11, 832D2
Arbitratn panel chngs OKd 10-18, 852D2
Diamond area found 10-20—10-21, 852B3
Queensland oil find 11-10—11-11, 888G1
Queensland backs rail electrificatn 11-12, 888C1
Murdoch ends Herald & Weekly Times takeover bid 11-22, 906G2
Fairfax acquires Herald interest 11-26, 966A3
Coal dvpt, rail electrificatn projcts backed 12-4, 947G3
Murdoch gains Ansett Transport control 12-18, 966E3
Environment & Pollution
NSW auto pollutn curbs disputed 10-31, 888A1
Queensland backs rail electrificatn 11-12, Sydney studies bus plan 11-13, 888C1
Coal dvpt, rail electrificatn projcts backed 12-4, 947G3

1980

Economy & Labor
Natl inflatn wage hike OKd; govt, Labor party score 1-8, 37B2
Cyclone hits mining town 1-10, 56B1
Diamond find rptd 1-11, 18E2
Stocks post strong advances 1-18, 56C1
Resource projct dvpt rptd 1-19, 56E1
Defns spending hike set 2-19, 132C1
Bond rate hike announced 3-2, 210G3
Budget moves, tax cuts announced 3-6, 210E2
Fuel tanker drivers strike 3-8—3-9, other New South Wales labor unrest rptd 3-11, 190F2
Tanker strike accord scored 3-14, 229B3
Wool strike accord rptd 3-21, 229F2-A3
'79 lost strike days up 3-21, 229A3
Labor job plan unveiled 3-23, 271G2
Fraser attacks unions 3-27, 271D3
Drought threat rptd 4-7, 272A1; aid planned 4-14, 309F2; threat ended 4-24, 334E1
Coal job dispute begins 5-2, 350A2
Aborigines vs mining efforts 5-8, 371A1
Harbor pilots strike rptd 5-16, 371F1
Journalists strike rptd 5-16, 371G1
Harbor pilots end strike 5-20, 405C3
Metalworkers seek 35-hr wk 5-22, 388B1
Journalists vote strike end 6-11, 443E1
Queensland hydrogen car plans set 6-22, 496E2
Power workers strike 6-24, layoffs estimated 6-25, 496C2
1st, 2d 1/4 growth rptd down 6-24, 519F3
GM unit to shut Sydney plant; unions, govt weigh retaliatn 7-1, 543A1
4.2% gen wage hike OKd 7-14, 542F2, G2
35-hour wk sanctns set 7-16, 602F1
Fscl inflatn rate at 10.7% 7-24, 576G3
Econ forecast rptd 7-29, 617C2
Sydney dockers strike 8-18—8-26, 650F2
New South Wales power statn builders strike 8-18, 650A3
'80-81 budget presented 8-19, 632D2
Labor budget offered 8-26, 667B2
Queensland coal strike compromise set 9-2, miners OK 9-4, 705A2
Electn issues cited 9-11, 727C3
Labor Party sets indl relatns policy 9-15, 727E3
Govt sets labor policy, Labor Party scores 9-18, 766C2
Murdoch TV takeover, Ansett deal rptd vetoed 9-29, 747G3
Wheat crop seen reduced 10-13, 827E3
Stock mkt jumps on Fraser win 10-21, 857E3
Fed job freeze, probe set 11-18, 900D1
3d 1/4 rise in forgn skilled workers rptd 11-18, 900A2
Coal strike, Panama Canal congestn linked 11-24, 895E3
Strikers pay setlmts scored 11-26; Victoria accord attacked 12-2, 940C2-D3
Local worker recruitmt stressed 12-1, 940D3
Interest rates hiked 12-2, 964A1
Energy—*See also 'Atomic Energy' above*
Queensland shale oil project rptd 2-12, 116F1
Oil levy plans rptd 3-6, 210F2
Fuel tanker drivers strike 3-8—3-9, 190G2; accord scored 3-14, 229B3
Fuel stockpiling backed 3-18, 229E3
Fraser scores tanker driver setlmt 3-27, 271F3
Saudi film oppositn linked 4-15, 310B1
Japan coal projct bid barred 4-15, 334F1
Aborigines protest Amax oil drilling 5-8, 371B1
Barrier reef protectn backed 6-10, 460F3
Queensland hydrogen car plans set 6-22, 496F2
Exxon shale-oil accord set 7-7, 520B1
Aborigine sacred site drilling protested 8-11, 617G2
Aborigine sacred site drilling starts 8-29, UN appeal made 9-3, mining negotiatns ban rptd 9-5, 686G1
Labor Party gas price freeze policy cited 9-11, 727D3
NW Shelf gas, Queensland coal conversn projects rptd 10-1, 10-2, 748E1

1976

Foreign Economic Developments
'75 UK missile deal rptd 1-6, 7E3
Dec '75 export-import data 1-12, 46B2
SDR rate rptd 1-15, 14A3
French Mirage purchase cited 1-16, 36C2
Japan coal deal OKd 1-20, 46G1
Getty unit rpts uranium find 1-28, 97C1
Wheat sales to China, India rptd 1-29, 97F2
US Westinghouse Corp uranium pact set 2-3, 115E3
'76 forgn aid cuts announced 2-4, 97B2
French trade drive, A-info exchng planned 2-4, 116A2
Japan trade talks 2-4—2-15, 137C3
Pakistan wheat deal OKd 2-11, 137F3
At intl econ conf 2-11—2-20, 148B1
Nissan buys VW plant 2-12, 137E3
2 US missile frigates bought 2-18, 154C3
Eur, Japan cos defer steel projct 2-24, 154D3
Japan sugar pact 2-26, 155A1
China sugar deal rptd 3-1, 190F1
In Jordan talks 3-2—3-9, 204C1
W Ger loan rptd 3-4, 172A3
PNG aid agrmt rptd 3-4, 172C3
SE Asia wheat deals rptd 3-11, 187D3
ILO rpts jobless rate 3-13, 297E3
US investors assured 3-17, 204A1
Papua New Guinea copper deal 3-22, 237D2
S Korean trade talks rptd 3-23, 237A2
Swiss loan OKd 3-23, 237F2
Investmt policy outlined 4-1, 249G2
Wool deals with Japan in peril 4-1, 249D3
Rumanian coal deal rptd 4-6, 250A1
Uranium safeguards rptd 4-8, 249B3
March export surplus rptd 4-8, 249G3
Eximbank loan OKd 4-13, 264E3
Indonesia aid set 4-14, 309F2
Sovt wheat purchase rptd 4-28, 321D3
OKs UN tin pact 4-28, 380F1
Lockheed payoff chrgd 4-29, 322F1-A2
Oil dvpt project set 4-29, 332B1
Forgn ownershp of mines rptd 5-2, 350A1
1st ¼ paymts deficit down 5-4, 349F3
Apr trade surplus rptd 5-7, 380B2
'77 forgn aid rise set 5-20, 380F1
US loan OKd 5-20, 400A1
Mine financing policy revised 6-2, 415E1
China sugar pact confrmd 6-2, 415A2
Japan auto projects OKd 6-10, 438B3
Japan trade reaffirmed 6-16, 481B1
Lockheed C130-H deal rptd 7-1, 481F1
IMF loan approved 7-2, 496B2
UK-Japan coal-mining project set 7-7, 496A2
Export racket uncovered 7-8, 537C1
Fraser in US investmt talks 7-27, 554F1
US mining deal rptd 7-28, 571G3-572B1
S Africa trade ban ends 7-31, 572B1
2d ¼ paymts, June trade surplus rptd 8-2, 587F1
Boneless beef sale to USSR set 8-3, 587C2
US firm to buy shelf gas 8-8, 650G1
Anthony sees UK trade secy; scores EC, Japan curbs 8-12, 623A2
Nissan car plant deal set 8-15, 650F1
US, French arms purchases budgeted 8-17, 636F3
Aug trade surplus rptd down 9-7, 692A1
US sugar duties tripled 9-21, 721D3
Qantas admits price cutting 9-23, 749D3
Japan iron ore pact rptd 9-23, 770E3
Vs World Bank funds rise 10-5, 778D1
Fraser arrives Indonesia, in ASEAN pact 10-10, 789A2
Sept trade surplus rptd 10-11, 789D2
3d ¼ paymts deficit rptd 10-13, 789E2
Canada sets meat import quota 10-19, 837B1
Uranium policy rpt issued 10-28, 835B2
US bond issue rptd set 11-4, 850E1
Productivity dept formed 11-7, 870A1
Oct trade surplus rptd 11-8, 869E3
PNG trade pact signed 11-8, 997A3
Oct payments deficit rptd 11-9, 869B3
Uranium export ban lifted 11-11, 888C1
Fraser I mineral sands export banned 11-11, 888A2
US antitrust actn blocked 11-18, Westinghouse pact cancelatn cited 11-19, 997C2
Murdoch to buy US paper 11-19, 887D2
Forgn reserves down 11-26; currency devalued, new exchng system set 11-28, 896C1
NZ, PNG devalue currencies 11-29, 896D1, G2
Currency revalued up 12-6, 922G3; 12-13, 944F2
Tariffs cut on 900 items 12-7, 944D2
Nov trade surplus rptd 12-9, 944D3
Aluminum refinery set 12-9, 961G3
Devaluatn a Tasmanian electn factor 12-11, 944C3
Peabody Coal to be sold 12-14, 985D1
'77 US beef export pact OKd 12-15, 976B2
NZ $ revalued up 12-20, 1013G1
Air fares to rise 12-21, 997B3

Foreign Relations (misc.)—*See also 'UN Policy' below*
Ports A-ship use OKd 1-15, 26E2; approval clarified 1-22, 46D1
Allied A-ships offered port use 1-15, 26E2; terms set 1-22, 46D1
Fraser at Razak funeral 1-16, in Asean talks 1-16—1-18, 46B1
Safety for A-ships demanded 1-22, 46D1
Leb secret army seized 1-27, 71G3
Consulate cutbacks announced 2-4, 97A2
UK joint rocket range to close 2-18, 154C3
Amb to Algeria named 2-18, 155B1
NZ, US joint manuevers set 2-19, 137D2

1977

Foreign Relations (misc.)—*See also 'Monetary, Trade & Aid', 'UN Policy' and 'Uranium' below*
Sovt ship asked to leave 1-4, 17G1; USSR complies 1-5, 42C3
Sovt chrgs on US bases denied 1-25, 81A2
PNG sets seabed border, Fraser suspends talks 2-7, 132C1
Queen Eliz arrives 3-7; monarchy ties protested 3-7—3-13, 199C1
Queen ends tour 3-30, 280D2
Sovt student defectn rptd 4-27, 314D3
'72 Allende coup role rptd 5-4, 372F1
NZ defense pact rptd 5-4, 410F2
Diplomatic corps cuts urged 6-2, 484D3

1978

Foreign Relations (misc.)—*See also 'Atomic Energy' above, 'Immigration', 'Monetary, Trade, Aid & Investment' and 'UN' below*
Indonesia '76 Timor takeover recognized 1-20, 72F1
Maltese envoy recalled 1-24, 228B3
Asian, Pacific Commonwealth ldrs hotel bombed 2-12, 110E1 ★; mtgs held 2-13—2-16, security rptd tightened 2-14, 121C2-D3
Bomb found at home of India amb 3-25, 225D2
UK defns resrch pact signed 4-18, 391E2
3 arrested in Thai emb bomb plot 4-21, 311A1

1979

Foreign Relations (misc.)—*See also 'Atomic' above, 'Monetary' and 'UN' below*
Viet refugees get asylum 2-12, 109A1
China Viet invasn concern voiced 2-18, 123G1
USSR culture, sci ties to be renewed 4-3, 253E1
Job-training study missn set 4-28, 351G2
Indochina refugee admissns set 5-7, 379E2
Thais hold Cambodia refugees for resetlmt 6-12, 436B1
NZ couple linked to drug bur probe 6-20, 467G2

1980

Foreign Relations (misc.)—*See also 'Atomic Energy' above, 'Monetary', 'UN Policy' below*
Japan premr visits, sees Fraser; Sovt Afghan invasn scored 1-16, Pacific orgn studied 1-20, 78E1-D2
Moscow Olympics shift backed 1-22, 45A3
Japan joins 4-natn Pacific naval games 2-26, 151C3
Iran asks neutrality on US hostages 4-11, 282G1
Fraser lauds USOC boycott vote 4-14, 283G2
UK film on Saudi princess barred 4-15, 309E3

1976

SEATO formally disbanded 2-20, 148C1
Iraq-Whitlam electn fund alleged 2-25—3-2, 172B2; **for subsequent developments, see 'Government & Politics' below**
CP delegatn in China 2-25, 189F1
Hussein visits 3-2—3-9, 204B1
Fraser in NZ; at S Pacific Forum, backs Anzus 3-8—3-11, 179B2, 187B3
Japan amb arrives 3-9, 187E3 *
China scores Sovt Indian O role 3-13, 265C3
Indochina refugees arrive 3-19, 237B2
Feakes named Malaysia High Comr 3-29, 237B2
Tennis team to visit China 4-6, 249G3
Peacock in Indonesia 4-14, 309F2
Angolan MPLA recognized 4-28, 332D1
Japan pact set 5-6, 349D3
'77 Concorde svc to UK, Bahrain, Singapore OKd 5-28, 400C1
Fraser policy speech scores Sovt mil expansion 6-1, 438C2
A-ship visits OKd 6-4, 455D3
Fraser in Japan, signs pact 6-16; arrives China; Cuba, Sovt, E Eur ambs snub 6-20, 481A1
Rpt Nigeria arrests natl in gun plot 6-19, 498F2
Secret papers rptd leaked 7-17, 537G1
'77 Concorde svc suit filed 7-20, 537A2
Whitlam in China quake 7-28—7-29, 545C2
Dependents quit China quake area 8-1, 561E2
'70 Viet massacre denied 8-3, 571E3
Anthony visits UK 8-12, 623C2
Viet refugees entry OKd 8-31, 672E3
Fraser tours Torres Strait I re PNG seabed pact 11-22—11-24, 961C3
Viet refugees admitted 12-18, 997C3

Government & Politics—*See also other appropriate subheads in this section*
'75 House electn results 1-2, 7G3
'75 divorce law in effect, judges sworn 1-5, 7D3
6 cabt coms formed 1-14, 26F2
Final '75 Sen electn results 1-15, 46E1
Listed as 'free' nation 1-19, 20B3
New S Wales premr named 1-20, 46F1
Old natl anthem restored 1-21, 46B2
Illegal immigrant amnesty set 1-25, 71E3
Labor caucus reelects Whitlam, sets electn rule 1-27, 71D3
Labor shadow cabt named 1-29, 116D1
Govt advisory bodies cut 2-2, 97G1
Garland quits in bribery probe 2-6, chrgd 2-17, 154A3
Whitlam chrgs 'deceit' in '75 ouster 2-9, 116E1
Labor Parlt boycott rptd planned 2-10, 116F1
Parlt opens, Labor boycotts 2-17, 137A3
Illegal immigrant amnesty rptd 2-18, 154G3
Garland denied Whitlam contempt order 2-24, 172F2
Whitlam-Iraq electn fund alleged, libel suits filed 2-25—3-2, 172B2
Labor '75 electn debt rptd 3-2, 172F2
Whitlam, Ellicott exchng chrgs 3-4, 187D2
Labor meets on Iraq fund; censures Whitlam, 2 others 3-5—3-7; Whitlam bars resignatn 3-7, 3-9, 187F1
Garland bribe case dropped 3-8, 187E2
Whitlam beats party ouster moves 3-17, 203C3
Govt info access bill planned 3-17, 203E3
New advisory parlt coms set 3-18, 203E3
Liberals win Victoria electn 3-20, 236G3
Labor shadow cabt changed 3-25, 237A1
Iraq fund probe rpt 3-25, 237C1
Labor wins in NSW electns 5-1, 349A3
S Australia party, Liberals merge 5-1; splinter forms new party 5-7, 349C3
Natl anthem for Olympics set 5-4, 349G3
NSW govt installed 5-12, plans set 5-13, 362E3
Air force to get new radar 5-12, 380B2
Aboriginal named S Australia gov 5-25, 424A2
Aboriginal land bill terms set 5-27, 415A2
State premrs meet Fraser, fed aid plans rptd 6-10, 456A1
Lord Casey dies 6-17, 524D2
Bland named ABC chrmn 7-4, 520E2
Environmt, repatriatn mins replaced 7-4, 520F2
Secret papers rptd leaked 7-17, 537F1
Kerr flees demonstratn vs Whitlam ouster 8-23, 650D1
Defns spending plan detailed 11-4, 850G1
Productivity dept formed 11-7, Macphee named min 11-8, 870A1
7 Navy planes destroyed in fire 12-5, 922E3
Liberals lose in Tasmania 12-11, 944B3

Medicine & Health
Govt spending cutbacks rptd 2-3, 97F1
Cigaret, tobacco TV ads banned 3-2, 237G1
Medibank tax levy set 5-20, 380E1; unions seek relief 5-26, 415C2
Medibank expansion rptd 6-8, 456B1
Medibank chngs protested 7-12, 520B2
Medibank rates undercut 8-10, 623E2
Medibank cuts protested 8-23, 650D1
Whitlam scores Medibank cuts 8-24, 672D3
Aborigine alcholism rptd 10-7, 869F3
Airline food probe set 12-6, 962A1

1977

Viet refugees rptd accepted 6-16, 497D1
Japan friendship treaty ratified 7-21, 596A1
Indochina refugee quotas eased 8-31, 685E2
Egypt drops anti-Copt plan 9-12, 863F2
Indian envoy assaulted 9-15, suspect arrested 9-18; guards assigned 9-20, 779F1
Qantas halts S Africa flights 9-20, 762C3
Rhodesia info center to close 9-20, 762D3
Viet refugee total rptd 11-23, 1018E2
Viet refugees arrive 11-29; Hanoi denied return 11-30, 1018D2
Pro-apartheid min fired 12-21, 982D2
USSR Jewish emigratn rptd up 12-21, 1017E2

Government & Politics—*See also other appropriate subheads in this section*
Nov '76 troop strength rptd 1-10, 96A2
Ct to cut Parlt size 2-1, 113F1
Liberals win WA electns 2-19, 158D1
Queens opens Parlt 3-8, 199D1
Whitlam ldrship challenged 3-9, 218G1
Final WA electn results 3-15, 253D3
Menzies honored 3-17, 280E2
1st ombudsman named 3-17, 280D3
Chipp quits Liberal Party 3-24, 280F3
Defns chief retires; MacDonald succeeds 4-20, 302F3
South Australia gov resigns 5-4, 346D1
Intelligence reorganizatn set 5-5, 371F3
Charter changes OKd 5-21, 447A1
Natl song chosen 5-21, 447G1
Whitlam reelected Labor Party head 5-31, 465D3
Labor Party conv 7-4—7-11, 503E3
Kerr quits as gov gen 7-14, 541C1
Cairns plans retiremt 8-10, Ellicott resigns over Whitlam probe 9-6, 693D1
N Territory electns 8-14, 725D1
S Australia electns 9-17, Dunstan triumph rptd 9-24, 740F1
Richardson to retire 9-20, 762E3
Early electns set 10-27, 839C3
Labor wins Greensborough by-electn 11-5, Chipp comments 11-18, 922B3
Queensland govt wins electn 11-12, campaign errors noted 11-15, 881F2
Intellignc agency advertises for spies 11-12, 923B1
Lynch resigns 11-18, 901C2
Marijuana Party enters Sen races 11-18, 945A1
Cowen sworn gov-gen 12-8, 963F3
Electn polls rptd 12-9, 963F2
Liberal, Natl Party coalitn wins reelectn; Chipp assured Sen seat 12-10; vote results analyzed 12-11—12-12, 963C2
Whitlam quits Labor Party ldrship, Hayden seeks post 12-10, 963D3
Cabt named; Lynch reapptd, Liberal Party ldrshp bid backed 12-19, 982D1-B2
Shiel fired re pro-apartheid stance 12-21, 982B2
Hayden elected Labor Party ldr, Bowen dep ldr 12-22, 1009C2 *

Medicine & Health—*See also 'Narcotics' below*
Cholera strain identified 3-9, 199G1
Cholera danger rptd past 3-16, 280C3
Intelligence agency to widen role 10-27, 862G1
Aborginal health team dismissed 11-8, 881C3

Monetary, Trade & Aid Issues (including all foreign business and economic developments)
Uranium export ban sought 1-3, 7A1
Record wool exports seen 1-4, stockpile cuts 1-15, 42B2
EEC beef import levy set 1-5, 60C2
Dec '76 capital inflow sets record 1-17, 42G2

1978

Fraser starts 18-day tour; UK, W Ger, France on agenda 6-1, 450E3
Natl Front for closer UK ties 6-3, 495B1
Indian sect hq raided 6-17, 495D1
Solomons gain independnc 7-7, 549E1
Mideast peace force rptd backed 8-31, 673G1
19 Croats rptd arrested 9-5, 796E3
China warns vs Sovt Asia role 9-6, 696D1
Antarctic activities increase urged 9-17, 900G2
Syria-imposed Qantas curb on Jews probed 10-18, 836E1; demands dropped 10-20, 900E3
USSR bugging of Moscow emb chrgd 11-14, 878C3

Government & Politics—*See also other appropriate subheads in this section*
Electn final results rptd 1-6, 53C2
S Australian police chief fired 1-17, successor named 1-19, 53F1
Fraser defends Kerr apptmt 2-10, Kerr resigns 3-2, 165E1-A2
Wartime hangings probe asked 5-8, 350C1
Norfolk I offered home rule 5-8, 369D3
Menzies dies 5-14, 440B3
Fraser defeats censure motn 5-29, 434G2
Natl Front opens branch 6-3, 495A1
N Terr granted partial self rule 7-1, 570G2-B3
Cocos I purchase announced 7-2, 514D1
Whitlam quits politics 7-14, 555A2
Fraser fires Withers in electoral boundary scandal 8-7, defends actn 8-8, 612F1
Fraser denies link to Withers scandal 8-21, no-confidence motn defeated 8-24, 703B2
Chaney replaces Withers as admin svcs min 8-25, 703G2
Lynch, Holding pol corruptn chrgd; denials issued, judicial probe barred 9-14, 771D1
Fraser shuffles Cabt, econ min split 11-30, 943E3
NSW transport agency probe set 12-5, 963D2

Immigration
Labor Party asks curb 2-19, 129A2
Indochina refugee entry OKd 3-15, policy rptd unchngd 3-17, 187E2
Vietnamese refugee asylum asked 4-9, 265B3
9,000 Indochinese to be admitted 5-17, 369A3
Natl Front for 'white Australia' 6-3, 495B1
New policy set; quotas raised, point system instituted 6-7, 451A1
Northn coast patrols increased 7-9, 530B2
Tax levy proposed 8-15, 628B2

Monetary, Trade, Aid & Investment—*See also 'Atomic Energy' above*
Malaysia sugar talks ended 1-11, 34C3; pact setld 1-13, 110A2
Dillingham to close mine operatns 1-17, 34F2
EC import curbs scored 1-24, boycotts threatened 1-25, 1-26, 69D2-D3

1979

Indochina refugee total rptd 6-28, 473F2
UK prime min visits, hints Zimbabwe sanctns end 7-1, 546C3
ANZUS meets on Indochina refugees, scores Viet 7-4—7-5, 495A2, F2
Zimbabwe recognitn terms agreed, Viet refugee quota hike sought 7-4, 501A1
NZ pol union explored 8-19, 8-21, 631G3, 632B1
In Zimbabwe peacekeeping force 12-23, 976E3

Government & Politics—*See also other appropriate subheads in this section*
Cabt operatns streamlined 2-4, 113F1
S Australia premr resigns 2-15, 153A1
Finance min resigns 2-22, 133C2; reinstated 2-25, 168C1
Surveillance bill proposed 3-8, 209F2
Liberals win Victoria electns 5-5, 387A1
NSW police comr quits 6-5, 467B2
Labor Party conf 7-19, 542F1
Labor wins Tasmania electn 7-28—7-29, 612D1
Labor loses S Australia electns 9-15, Tonkin takes office 9-18, 749E1
Hawke to run for Parlt 9-23, 771A2; wins ALP preselectn 10-14, 832D2
Liberal-NCP coalitn threatened by Queensland rift 9-24, 771C2
Sinclair quits as indus min, Fraser censure motn fails 9-27, 787G2
Fraser shuffles Cabt 12-8, 948D1

Monetary, Trade, Aid & Investment—*See also 'Atomic' above*
Asian oppositn to new air policy rptd 1-5, 6C1
US trade concessns obtained 1-8, 36F2
Bauxite Assn floor price rejected 1-9, to continue membership 1-10, 18D3
Taiwan trade rise cited 1-15, 27C3

1980

Zimbabwe gains indepndnc 4-18, 301E1
E Ger dancer's asylum rptd 4-22, 327A1
USSR May Day parade shunned 5-1, 354G2
China dep premr visits, pacts OKd 5-7—5-11, 387F3
China ICBM test rptd 5-18, 389B1
Queen Eliz visits 5-23—5-28, 405D3
Olympic com rejects boycott, Fraser scores 5-23, sports feds, athletes bar participatn 5-28, 421A1
Cambodia aid need stressed 5-27, 397B2
New Hebrides unrest linked 6-8, 436D2
Wilderness Conf meets 6-10, 460F2
Immigratn rules set 6-19, 485D2
20 Rumanian defectors seek refuge 7-3, 548E3
Egypt amb at shah's funeral 7-29, 571G1
Iran hostage appeal rptd 8-16, 634G3
Gandhi criticisms raise concern 11-6, 870G1
Forgn policy articles, book banned 11-8, 11-9, 885B1; upheld by High Ct 12-1, 919E2
Immigratn rptd up 11-18, 900G1
Forgn skilled workers 3d 1/4 rise rptd 11-18, 900A2
Banned forgn policy articles publshd 12-2, 991F2
Armenians kill 2 Turkish aides 12-17, 991A2

Government & Politics—*See also other appropriate subheads in this section*
Queensland police law disputed 4-9, 292D2
Sinclair chrgd 4-29, 334B2
Queensland rift threatns fed coalitn 6-16, 6-18, 485E3
Sinclair acquitted 8-14; rejoins Cabt 8-18, 650C2
Defense dvpt plans set 9-9, 705F1
Fraser sets electn date 9-11, 727B3
Labor advances in polls 10-15, 787A1
Fraser wins reelectn 10-18, 807E2
Fraser shuffles Cabt 11-2, 857E2
Queensland Liberal rift scored 11-11, govt coalitn loses Sen control 11-12, 885F1
Queensland electns held 11-29, 919G2

Medicine & Health
Agent Orange blamed in birth defects 1-3, 6A1; study ordrd 1-8, 37E2
Agent Orange rpt ordered 3-26, 252F2
Computer error re pharmacist overpaymts rptd 4-4, 292G2
Brain chem productn rptd 5-10, 715F1
Queensland anti-abortn bill defeated, pol impact seen 5-30, 428D2
'79 Malaria cases rptd 5-31, 478A2
Exercise study questns heart disease preventn 7-5, 715D3

Monetary, Trade, Aid & Investment
See also 'Atomic Energy' above
US backed on Sovt grain ban 1-7, USSR penalized for Afghan invasn 1-9, 9C2
USSR grain sale increase barred 1-12, 27E3
Japan talks note resources, air fare cuts 1-16, Pacific orgn 1-20, 78E1-D2
Stocks attract forgners 1-18, 56C1

1976

Portuguese Timor Relations—*See TIMOR*
Sports
Australian Open results 1-4, 31E3
Tennis team to visit China 4-6, 249G3
Summer Olympic results 7-18—7-31, 573E3, 574D2, 575F2, 576G3

1977

Japan trade mtg; beef, fishing pacts set 1-17—1-18, 60A2
Japan shipping dispute 1-17—2-21, ANL pact set 2-16, 253E1-D2
ASEAN review panel set 1-20, 60E2
ICFTU S Africa boycott fails 1-21, 67B3
'76 3d ¼ trade surplus rptd 1-24, 60F1
Wider ASEAN trade ties seen 1-24, 60E2
'76 coal exports set record 1-25, 81A3
'75-76 forgn investmt profits rptd 1-28, 158E1
UK radar equipmt deal planned 2-1, 96A2
SRD rate raised to 10% 2-2, 113C2
IMF SDR defined 87G2
4th ¼ '76 paymts deficit rptd 2-5, 280A3
Jan imports set record 2-9, 158G1
Czechs free Bonn newsman 2-14, 114D3
Textile quotas retained 2-16, 158B2
Canada beef sales limited 2-17, 179C1
US-Canada wheat pact agreed 2-25, 158G2
US-Canada wheat-price pact backed 3-1, 179C1
Japan to build Newcastle dock 3-15, 253D2
China wheat pact signed, '76 sales cited 3-16, 178F3
Feb trade deficit rptd 3-16, 199F1
Dollar hits US $1.10 mark 3-22, 236D3
China sugar deal set 3-30, 236G3
NZ textile import quota set 4-17, 346A1
Textile, clothing import quotas extended 5-2, 345F3
Ford plans NSW plant 5-5, 389D1
Israel gets US arms preference 5-12, 361E1
NZ textile plea rebuffed 5-18, 410C2
US sets arms-sales policy 5-19, 380G2
Fraser scores EC protectionism 6-1, 7-4, 595D3
3 trade offices urged closed 6-2, 484E3
Backs N-S $1 bln aid plan 6-3, 437F2
IAC warns vs high tariffs 6-15, 504A3
Asia econ grouping seen, trade data rptd 6-22, 504E2
IWC cuts whaling quotas 6-24, 496F3
ASEAN backs ties 6-27—6-29, 537E1
Japan sugar pact dispute 6-30—7-27, 578B3
China record wheat sale, '76-77 exports rptd 7-4, 578E2
Forgn loan curbs lifted 7-7, 523A1
Intl group cancels alumina plant 7-7, 523F1-A2
Fraser rejcts ASEAN criticism 7-9, 561A1
Car import quotas imposed 7-12, 560D3
Paymts deficit rptd 7-29, 615B3
Sovt wheat deal rptd 8-2, 596B1
Japan sugar talks fail again 8-4, 615C2
Sinclair: UK immigrants cause econ problems 8-5; UK refutes, compares export data 8-8, 632B3
PNG revalues currency 8-5, 639C2
Fraser sees ASEAN ldrs 8-6—8-7, 607A2
Japan coal contract signed 8-8, 615E2
US scores trust probe-blocking laws 8-8, 630A1
Fiji dock strike ends 8-8, 636C3
Gold reserves revalued 8-11, 725C2
NW Shelf gas search OKd 8-24, 704C3-705B1
Exported meat disease link denied 8-29, 725B2
Fraser rejcts uranium export vote 9-7, 705C1
Sinclair UK immigrant strike chrgs clarified 9-12, 762A3
Qantas halts S Africa flights 9-20, 762C3
Dillingham rejcts compensatn offer 9-22, Anthony comments 10-3, 762B2
Fraser warns Japan on trade disputes 9-23; more beef imports agreed 10-28, Anthony welcomes 10-30, 862A1
Japan bars beef import plan 9-26, 800C3
Japan sugar refiners sued by Queensland 9-28, 800E2
Car import curbs extended 10-6, 779C1
Intl sugar pact OKd, world mkt share cited 10-7, 855D1
UK immigrants scored again 10-9, 800A3
Exxon admits paymts 10-25, 818A2
Japan sugar pact set 10-26, 839G2-A3
EC rejcts beef import demand 10-30, 862D1
S Africa confrms livestock disease 923A1
US, 5 other govts ban livestock imports 11-23, 922F3
'77-78 wheat exports forecast, Egypt accord rptd 11-28, 945C1
Bauxite base price OKd 12-7, 975E1
Narcotics & Drugs
New S Wales eases pot penalties 4-20, 346E1
Wran chrgs abuses widespread, urges pot decriminalizatn 7-22, 944F3
New S Wales pot opponent missing 7-25, govt opens drug trade probe 7-27, 578G2
Narcotics Bur ex-chief accused of smuggling 8-8, 944F3
Smuggling, arrest data rptd 9-29, 944G3
Fraser sets drug trade probe 10-5, 779B2
Sen panel backs pot decriminalizatn 11-18, 944E3
Marijuana Party enters Sen races 11-18, 945A1
Norfolk Island—*See under 'N'*
Obituaries
Connor, Reginald F X 8-22, 696E2
Embry, Basil Edward 12-8, 1024F1
Ritchard, Cyril 12-18, 1024G2
Sports
Australian Open results 1-9, 103D3
US wins World Cup 3-11—3-13, 431F1
Courageous keeps America's Cup 9-18, 828E2
Wins Davis Cup 12-4, 970F1

1978

Malta aid bar rptd 1-24, 228B3
US exempts from arms sales ceiling 2-1, 106E2
Fraser scores EC policies 2-15, 121E2
Singapore scores trade barriers 2-15, 121F2
EC imposes steel duty 2-16, 129C2
Japan coal export pacts rptd 2-20, 145E1
PNG budgets '78 aid 2-22, 192B3
Brazilian coal pact signed 3-1, 165C2
Japan coal pact price cut rptd 3-1, 165D2
EC, Japan trade curbs scored 3-1, 3-7, 265E2
Jan paymts deficit rptd; Feb surplus, forgn reserves total 3-10, 187C3
'77 gold exports rptd 3-15, 208F3
Japan bars iron, coal curbs 3-20, 208A3
$ in new SDR basket 4-3, 300F3
S Africa ship blocked by unions 4-4, 243E3
Fraser threatens EC curbs 4-6, EC delays trade talks 4-14; Hayden scores 4-16, 310D3
Port strike setld 4-9—4-10, 350B1
McNeill warns vs oil imports, cites '85 cost 4-10, 265D3
200-mi fishing zone sought 4-13, 286D2
Wool exports rptd down 4-14, 411G1
Japan trade talks rptd, commodity fund planned 4-23, 391C2
Trade curbs, exchng rate adjustmts scored 4-27, 327F3
Land sale in US halted 5-1, 327F2-D3
Chrysler job cuts, productn chngs set; '77 losses rptd 5-3, 349D3
Mar paymts surplus rptd, Apr deficit 5-11, 530C1
New S Wales imposes coal export duties 5-19, 369F3
US '78 arms sales forecast 5-19, 387B1
Japan to import iron 5-25, 411D1
Fraser defends govt, cites investmt progrm 5-29, 434B3
US '77 thoroughbred import ban cited 539E2
Fraser in US for trade talks 6-1—6-5, 430E3
US hikes meat import quotas 6-8, 428E2
Garland in Brussels, EC bars coal import cuts 6-13, 494F3-495A1
Japan asks eased import curbs 6-27, iron contract revisns 7-4, 514G1
'77 oil imports rptd 7-5, 514E2
Drug smuggling patrols increased 7-9, 530B2
Steel import limits set 7-10, 530G1
Car import curb proposed 7-13, 530A2
Coking coal mine strike halts exports, '77 sales drop rptd 7-13, 555C1
'77-78 wool exports rptd down 7-18, 555F1
Mitsubishi investmt in Chrysler unit cited 8-10, 623D3
Trade levies proposed in '78-79 budget 8-15, 628B2, D3
Importers score proposed trade levies 8-17, 646A2
UK co takeover of Bushells blocked 9-7, 9-29, 754F2
China exports up 9-11; iron ore order rptd, Japan import lag cited 9-29, 754E2
US sets '79 arms sales lid 9-26, 734A2, E2
Joint W Ger coal conversn effort set 10-10, 793D3
UK air fare cut set 10-11, 793A3
China favored trade status set 10-11, 836G1
Chrysler import violatn fine set 10-19, 813B1
Mineral export policy set 10-24, 836A1
Mitsubishi to buy Chrysler share 10-25, 836B2
Treas Dept scores import curbs 10-31, 866C1
Import tariff curb seen 11-13, 944E1
Cut-rate US air fare proposed 11-14, 920E2
Reserves at high mark 11-21, 944E1
Japanese bonds issued 11-24, 944F1
3d ¼ export income rptd down 12-7, 944B1
US coal deal rptd signed 12-11, 963A2
Japan investmt rise seen 12-12, 985B2
Cut-rate US air fare pact set 12-13, 985G1-B2
Alcoa plant expansn planned 12-14, 963G2
Obituaries
Menzies, Robert Gordon 5-14, 440B3
Sports
Australian Open results 12-31-77—1-1, 22F3
Wickam sets 800-m freestyle mark 2-23, 780F2
US wins World Cup 3-9—3-12, 252C1

1979

Bank reserve requiremt raised 1-16, 57B1
Wheat deals with China, 4 other natns rptd 1-22, 56G2-F3
Forgn investmt record rptd 1-24, 56G3
US oil co opposed to aborigine demands 1-24, 94C3
Currency futures market set 2-1, 74B1
GM unit rpts '78 loss, expansn plans 2-6, 94E3
ICI petrochem plans rptd, Dow Chem dvpt seen unlikely 2-8, 94C3
Auto content rule eased, GM unit plant constructn plans cited 2-22, 133E2
IEA joined 3-2, 162C1
Japan iron ore price rise set 3-6, 188E2
$ supply growth cited 3-13, 189B1
Japan gets coal price cut 3-13, 233B2
Pre-export mineral processing backed 3-26, forgn dvpt needs noted 3-27, 233F1-A2
Exxon-Broken Hill Exmouth Plateau oil drilling rptd 3-28, 233D1
Beef, wheat sales, farm income hike linked 3-29, 253G1
Canada wheat accord set 4-3, 253A1
Whaling ban set 4-4, impact on Japan, USSR seen minimal 4-8, 284B2
Japan trade accord signed, beef industry impact cited 4-6, 266A2
China credit aid rptd 4-6, 284D2
Mineral export compromise set 4-23, 328A1
Oil co profits rptd down 5-8, 351E3
Mitsubishi acquires Chrysler unit share 5-14, 368F2
Exxon unit sees contd oil imports 5-18, 368D2
Coal export tax hike proposed 5-24, 404G2
EC trade accord set 5-29, 404F3-405C1
US oil co talks rptd 6-4, 423F2
Conzinc to buy Kaiser Steel Hamersley shares 6-4, 562B3
Amax unit oil drilling OKd 6-18, 467G1
UK hints Zimbabwe sanctns end 7-1, 546C3
Iron ore exports halted 7-14, 542E1
Fscl yr paymts deficit down; exports, imports up 7-19, 562A3
BP to join Olympic Dam mining project 7-27, 580G2
Alcan aluminum project rptd 8-3, 600A1
High tariffs end urged by OECD 8-3, 600A1
Iron mine strike ends 8-3, 666E3
Coal export duty cut set 8-21, 631F3
NZ trade union explored 8-21, 631G3-632B1
Tariff cut deferred 8-24, 650B2
Chrysler plans sale to Mitsubishi 9-15, 699A2
S Korea trade accord rptd 10-16, 788C1
200-mi fishing zone takes effect, Japan fee rptd set 11-1, 832G1-A2
Drug traffic rpt issued 11-6, 860G2
Oil exploratn permits granted, Fortescue field reclassified 11-27, future exploratn expenditures rptd 11-28, 925F2
Wheat sales to USSR detailed 11-28, 948B1
Sports
Australian Open tennis results 1-3, 103C2
Australian Hard Ct results 1-7, 391F2
US wins Federatn Cup 5-6, 391D2
Nations Cup won 5-14, 570C2

1980

Sovt trade curbs broadened, '79 trade data cited 1-28, 1-29, 116C1
EC steel accord rptd set 2-5, 132A1
Reynolds Metal unit in alumina plant consortium 2-8, 95E1
Sovt trade curbs lifted 2-12, 148A1
US mil purchase talks seen 2-19, 132E1
Defns spending compared 2-19, 132G1
US Eximbank loan offer to Murdoch co sparks probe 2-19, 989D1
PNG OKs gold, copper dvpt by Broken Hill 3-10, 195A1
Japan wool needs cited 3-11, 191B1
Amoco tanker strike accord scored 3-14, 229B3
Wool strike pact rptd 3-27, 229G2
US beef demand down 4-7, 272A1
US asks Iran export ban 4-13, 281D2
Saudi trade linked to film oppositn 4-15, 309G3
Japan coal projct bid barred 4-15, 334F1
UK tariff breaks to end 4-16, 309D3
Mitsubishi buys Chrysler unit 4-30, 350E1
Coal export problems seen 5-7, 350C2
China vows contd wheat purchases 5-7—5-11, 387F3
Amax oil drilling spurs Aborigine protests 5-8, 371B1; 8-11, 617G2
Pacific cable planned 5-19, 387E3
Antarctic fishing pact set 5-20, 398D1
Hunts bailout loan collateral listed 5-28, 426E1
USSR wheat sale hike rptd 6-17, 460E2
Sovt grain sale limit set 6-24, 496A2
GM unit to shut plant 7-1, 543A1
Exxon shale-oil accord set 7-7, 520B1
EC sheepmeat talks founder 7-15, 561C3
US OKs jet fighter sale 7-24, 561G3
S Pacific island trade pact rptd signed 7-24, 576F2
Shoe, textile, garment import tariffs kept 8-15, 632F2-D3
US '79 gold productn rptd 8-27, 685B3
Coal strike effect seen 9-4, 705C2
Antarctic fishing pact signed 9-11, 721B1
Airbus deal OKd, EC sheepmeat agreemt cited 9-29, 748B1
China wheat contract cited 10-13, 827F3
Forgn investmt rise seen 10-21, 857G3
Sovt grain embargo affirmed 11-18; Canada ends support, US-China pact cited 11-20, 900D2, F2
Obituaries
McEwen, John 11-20, 928A3
Press & Censorship
Murdoch TV takeover, Ansett deal rptd vetoed 9-29, 747G3
Forgn policy articles, book banned 11-8, 11-9, 885B1
Articles, book ban upheld by High Ct 12-1, 919E2
Banned articles publshd 12-2, 991F2
Sports
Australian Open tennis results 1-1, 1-2, 213E1
Australian Hard Ct results 1-6, 607D2
Moscow Olympics shift backed 1-22, 45A3

1976

UN Policy & Developments
Aborigines to ask trade sanctns 3-11, 187B2
Peacock at sea law conf 3-16, 203G3
Tin pact OKd 4-28, 380F1
Vs WHO anti-Israel stand 5-19, 355D2
Vs UNESCO Israel 11-22, 879A1
ILO rpts strike data 11-29, 896D2

U.S. Relations—*See also 'Foreign Economic Developments' above*
Fraser backs Indian O role 1-12, 26E2
New amb to US named 2-1, 97A3
Los Angeles consulate closed 2-4, 97A2
US amb to Australia confrmd 2-4, 110B2
Navigation base OKd 2-17, 137C2
US amb arrives 2-18, 155B1
Joint maneuvers set 2-19, 137D2
S Pacific Forum backs US role 3-8—3-9, 179C2
Peacock visits US 3-11—3-17, 203G3
Navigation base go-ahead 3-23, 237D1
Rockefeller visits 3-30—3-31, 249F2
Mine ownership data rptd 5-2, 350A1
Fraser reaffirms support 6-1, 438E2
Australia OKs A-ship visits 6-4, 455E3
Fraser on Indian O role 6-20, 481D1
Carter urges greater unity 6-23, 451F2
Ship in US Bicentennial event 7-4, 488D3
Fraser visits US 7-26—7-30, 554E1
US GOP platform text cites 8-18, 609A3
US A-ship docks, workers strike 9-7, 691C3

1977

UN Policy & Developments
UN Assemb member 3F3
Norfolk Decolonizatn Com plea 2-9, 132A2
Rhodesia office closure OKd 5-27, 457F1

Uranium
Protest blocks W Ger shipmt 1-2, 17B2
Scientists urge mining, export ban 1-3, 7B1; dvpt defended 1-11, 17B2
Westinghouse suit rptd 1-25, '76-82 sales contracts cited 1-26, 81F2
Mine losses rptd, stocks fall 1-26, 81D2
In US, Canada collaboratn exchng 2-4—3-11; US denies cartel agrmt 6-29, 624C3
Westinghouse rpts low-grade find 2-16, 158C2
US, PI, EC press Australia for deals 2-24—3-16, 218B1
Mine aid set 3-5, 179D1
Fox comm ends hearings 3-22, 253C3
Fraser sees major export role, strict controls; cites Carter exchng 3-23, 217G3
Japan contracts canceled 3-24, 218D1
Whitlam asks safeguards 3-29, 253G2
Cartel role rptd 4-25, 479F2
Export guidelines set 5-24, 465B3
Fox comm rpt issued 5-25, reactn 5-31, 465A2-A3
EC export ban threatened 6-1, 7-4, 595D3
Carter lauds safeguards policy 6-21—6-23, 560D3
Dockers protest shipmts 7-2—7-3, chrg police brutality 7-4; US shipmt leaves 7-5, 523D1
Labor backs mining ban 7-7, 540E3
Ban lifted 8-25; protests held, Labor, USSR score 8-25—8-26, 693G1, D3
Output, sales forecast; reserves estimated 8-25, 8-26, 693A3
Protesters surveillnc rpts unconfrmd 9-1, 923A1
Fraser rejects referendum 9-7, 705C1
ACTU conf asks referendum 9-15, 740B2
Fox named A-envoy 10-6, 779E1
Uren sees govt boycott measures 10-17, leaks Fox rpt on US A-policy 11-2; reactn 10-18, 11-3, 901F1-A2
Dock workers back boycott, demand referendum 10-20, 901B2
Prelim export rules issued 11-9, 901C1
North Terr plans mining challenge 11-14, 901E1
Backs UK vs US cartel probe jurisdictn 12-1, 1003F3

U.S. Relations—*See also 'Monetary, Trade & Aid' and 'Uranium' above*
Sovt chrgs on US bases denied 1-25, 81A2
CIA union infiltratn chrgd; Fraser sets probe 4-27, 326D1-A2; 344F2
CIA probe calls mount 4-29, pol party funding chrgd 5-4, 372A1
Alston confrmd amb 4-29, 418B1
Fraser halts CIA probe 5-3, allegatns continue 5-17—5-24, 410F1-B2
Diplomatic corps cuts urged 6-2, 484D3
Fraser in US, sees Carter 6-21—6-23, 560C3
US Labor conv observer accused as CIA agent 7-5, 541B1
US rptdly bars CIA role 8-4, 632G3
Courageous keeps America's Cup 9-18, 828E2
Navigatn statn OKd 9-23, 762B3
Pine Gap base pact renewed 10-19, 800E3
Carter cites ANZUS 11-9—11-10, 925E3

1978

US battles equine VD 3-15—7-13, 539E2
Golf tourn results 10-22—12-3, 990B2-E2
Australian Indoor results 10-22, 1027B2
US wins Federatn Cup 12-3, 1026G3
US wins Davis Cup 12-10, 1026E3

UN Policy & Developments
Kerr quits UNESCO post 3-2, 165E1-A2
Refugees comr visits, Indochinese to be admitted 3-15, 187F2
UNDOF mandate renewed 5-31, 400B2
Fraser addresses disarmamt sessn 6-5, 450D3
IAEA to monitor Finnish uranium accord 7-20, 590F1
ILO rpts '77 jobless rise 7-28, 677D1
Racism conf boycotted 8-26, 676B2
Assemb member 713B3

Uranium Issues—*See 'Atomic Energy' above*

U.S. Relations—*See also 'Monetary, Trade, Aid & Investment' above*
US troop presence rptd 1-2, 5D2
US alerts to Sovt A-satellite fall 57E1
A-test monitoring statn declassified 3-1, 145A2
US wins World Cup 3-9—3-12, 252C1
US natl arrested in Thai emb bomb plot 4-21, 311A1
Mondale visits 5-8, 360B3
Australia adopts uranium rules 5-31, 434E3
Fraser in US 6-1—6-5, 450D3
US A-policy cited re Finland, Australia uranium accord 7-21, 590G1
Interim safeguards pact signed 8-8, 666B2
Mideast peace force rptd backed 8-31, 673G1
McDonnell Douglas paymts rptd 12-15, 982G2

1979

Australian Indoor tennis results 10-21, 1003E3
US wins Davis Cup 12-16, 1003B3

UN Policy & Developments
Membership listed 695D2

Uranium Issues—*See 'Atomic' above*

U.S. Relations—*See also 'Atomic' and 'Monetary' above*
Ford head announces retiremt 3-14, 202G2
Pan Am hijack bid foiled 4-4, 266F2
Job-training study missn set 4-28, 351G2
US agrees on Zimbabwe recognitn terms, seeks Viet refugee quota hike 7-4, 501A1
Carter rues Skylab landing, Fraser replies 7-11, 509B1
US monitoring base backed by Labor Party, SALT cited 7-19, 542F1
Ex-amb scores Fraser ties 8-24, 650G2
Chrysler plans operatns sale 9-15, 699A2

1980

Olympic alternate games backed 3-18, 206C1
Fraser lauds USOC boycott vote 4-14, 283G2
Olympic com rejects boycott; Fraser, US score 5-23, athletes, sports feds bar participatn 5-28, 421A1
US wins Federatn Cup 5-25, 607B1
Moscow Olympics results 7-20—8-3; Campbell triple jump disallowed 7-25, IAAF backs Sovts 7-31, 588B3, 589D3, 623F2-D3, 624C1
Australia wins America's Cup trials 9-5, Freedom retains Cup 9-25, 834E1-D2
Czechs win Davis Cup 12-7, 946F3

UN Policy & Developments
Assemb res backing Palestinian state opposed 7-29, 572F1
Women's conf 5-yr plan opposed 7-30, 587A3
Aborigines appeal sacred site drilling, discriminatn 9-3, 686G1

U.S. Relations—*See also 'Monetary' above*
Mil cooperatn talks seen 2-19, 132E1
Pacific naval games start 2-26, 151C3
Pan Am revives discount coupons 3-10, 346E3
US asks Iran crisis support 4-8, 257D2
Iran asks neutrality on hostages 4-11, 282G1
US asks Iran pol sanctns 4-13, 281D2
Fraser lauds USOC boycott vote 4-14, 283G2
Pacific A-waste plan questioned 5-21, 405G2
Olympic com boycott rejectn scored 5-23, 421B1
Qantas flights increased 7-30, 617F2
Iran hostage appeal rptd 8-16, 634G3
B-52 base talks set 9-9, 705D1
Press articles, book on US ties banned 11-8, 11-9, 885B1; High Ct upholds 12-1, 919E2
Banned press articles publshd 12-2, 991F2

1976

AUSTRALIA, New Zealand, U.S. Treaty Organization (Anzus)
Australia, NZ score Sovt threat 3-8—3-11, 187C3
Australia OKs A-ship visits 6-4, 455D3

AUSTRIA—*See also ADB, IEA, OECD*
'75 women's rights bill in effect 1-1, 97B3
Wiesenthal rptd ending Nazi hunt 1-9, 97C3
SDR rate rptd 1-15, 14A3
Listed as 'free' nation 1-19, 20B3
Rptd in W Ger-Iran-USSR gas pipe pact 1-19, 97E3
Polaroid camera pact rptd 1-30, 97F3
Wick chrgd as ex-Nazi, Rotary nominatn protested 3-10, 3-11, 380E2
Soclst cong 3-11—3-13, 380C2
Rossi named cardinal 4-27, 336B2
Quake tremors rptd 5-6, 352B3
Consumer buying rptd up, indl output down 6-24, 572E1
Minority rights bill OKd 7-7, 554F2
Vienna bridge collapse 8-1, 796D2
Language census, Slovenes shun 11-14; govt-Slovenes talks set 11-28, 923D1
Ranks 1st in W Eur suicides 11-17, 944F3

Foreign Relations (misc.)—*See also 'UN Policy' below*
Chile presses on refugees 1-9, 47E2
Plyushch in Vienna 1-11, 30F2
Europn soclsts meet 1-18—1-19, 48A3
USSR to make more dailies available 1-21, 76G2
Chile emb refugees to get safe-conducts 1-25, 100C1

1977

AUSTRALIA, New Zealand, U.S. Treaty Organization (ANZUS)
NZ, US talks 11-9—11-10, 925E3

AUSTRIA—*See also IDB, IEA, OECD*
Defense min resigns 5-30, Cabt chng OKd 5-31, 424D3, 425C1
Soclsts win Burgenland electn 10-2, 763E1
Heroin use rptd up 10-17—10-21, 971E3

Economy & Labor (domestic)
Dec '75-76 inflatn rate rptd 2-7, 87A2
'76 GNP rptd 3-18, 763B1
A-plant protested 6-12, 763A2
Tax protest halts Vienna traffic 9-13, 763G1
Shilling devaluatn denied 9-28, 10-3, speculatn rptd 9-30, 763D1
Kreisky presents austerity plan; 1st ½ econ data rptd 10-3, 762F3

Foreign Relations (misc.)—*See also 'Monetary, Trade & Aid' and 'UN Policy' below*
IDB joined 1-10, 438E3
'76 Eur Cncl pact vs terrorism cited 9G2
In 14-natn sulphur-dioxide pact 1-19, 109B3
Czech dissidents offered asylum 1-25—1-31, rejcted 1-28, 82B3, D3
Kreisky sees PLO moderatn 2-13, 107G1
Czechs free Bonn newsman 2-14, 114D3
'76 Polish hijacker jailed 2-15, 425A2
Sovt Israeli emigrants seek resetlmt 4-24, 436E3
A-opponents meet in Salzburg 4-29—5-1, 335E1, 403E1

1978

AUSTRALIAN Land Title Ltd.—*See under MORLAN International Inc.*

AUSTRIA—*See also COUNCIL of Europe, EFTA, GATT, IDB, OECD*
Grain poisoning scandal rptd 2-8, 110G2
Quake felt 9-3, 759A1
June '77-78 world inflatn rates ranked 10-18, 914F1
A-plant opening rejctd by voters 11-5, 878E3

Foreign Relations (misc.)—*See also 'Monetary, Trade, Aid & Investment' and 'UN' below*
Kreisky visits USSR 2-6—2-8, 110C2
Sadat visits; seeks Mideast peace backing, sees Israeli oppositn ldr 2-11, 98F2
W Ger secret svc surveillnc protested 2-14, 110B3
Swiss host 4-natn terrorism mtg, 'hot line' set 4-8—4-9, 438B2
Eur conservative groups formed 4-24, 424C3
Turkish premr visits 5-16, 398G2
Nazi extraditn from Brazil rptd sought 6-8, 477C2
Kreisky, Brandt arrange Sadat-Peres talks, give peace plan 7-9; plan made pub 7-10, 521B2
Sadat meets Weizman 7-13, ends Austria visit 7-14, 546A2
Moscow expels rptr 9-30, 821E1 ★
Czech dissident begins 1-yr stay 10-28, 885E2

1979

AUSTRALIA, New Zealand, U.S. Treaty Organization (ANZUS)
Meets on Indochina refugees, backs Viet Cambodia exit 7-4—7-5, 495A2, F2

AUSTRIA—*See also COUNCIL of Europe, GATT, IDB, IEA, OECD*
Soclsts gain in electns, Kreisky wins 4th term 5-6, 352B1
Mid '78-79 inflatn rptd lowest in OECD 8-9, 627C1
Violin contest held 9-19, 892F2
Vienna fire kills 25 9-28, 918C1
Anti-inflatn methods cited 11-1, 827A1

Foreign Relations (misc.)—*See also 'Monetary' & 'UN' below*
Vienna hosts SALT II summit 6-15—6-18, 449A1, F1, 457E2
Nazi's extraditn denied by Brazil 6-20, 483A3
Arafat visits Kreisky 7-6—7-8, Israel recalls amb 7-8, 511A3, E3
E Eur defectns rptd rising 9-12, 697F2
Tourists killed in fire 9-28, 918C1
Czech revokes dissident's citizenship 10-8, 838A2

Helsinki Agreement—*See EUROPE—Security and Cooperation*

Monetary, Trade, Aid & Investment
Portugal sets farm seizure compensatn 1-11, 212E3
'78 trade deficit rptd 2-7, 181G3
GM expansn plans detailed 6-11, 555F1
Iran drops gas pipe plans 7-28, 583A1

Sports
World figure-skating results 3-14—3-17, 391D3-392A1

1980

AUSTRALIA, New Zealand, U.S. Treaty Organization (ANZUS)
Australia bans critical book 11-9, 885E1

AUSTRALIA, The (yacht)
Wins America's Cup trials 9-5; Freedom 3d race finals victory upheld 9-22, Freedom retains Cup 9-25, 834E1-D2

AUSTRIA—*See also ADB, COUNCIL of Europe, CSCE, GATT, IDB, IEA, OECD*

Atomic Energy & Safeguards
Vienna A-fuel conf ends 2-27, 220D3
A-backers seek new referendum 11-3—11-10, 870C3

Crime & Civil Disorders
Hosp scandal rptd spreading 8-27, 667G2
Hosp scandal spurs govt reform plan 9-3, reforms OKd 9-9, 705D2
Hosp scandal spurs Androsch confidence vote 10-8, 870F3
Androsch sets resignatn 12-11, 964A2

Economy & Labor
Labor costs rptd 8-12, 698E1

Foreign Relations (misc.)—*See also 'Monetary' below*
Moscow Olympics stand rptd 1-21, 45B3
Turkey envoy deaths cited 2-6, 197C2
Columbia amb seized in DR Emb raid 2-27, 141B1; freed 3-6, 180F2
Vienna A-fuel conf ends 2-27, 220D3
PLO aide gets special status 3-13; Israel protests 3-14, Arafat lauds 3-15, 205G3-206B1
Czech couple defects 3-17, 262E2
Iran asks neutrality on US hostages 4-12, 282F1
Colombia leftists delay flight to Vienna 4-27, 335C2
Gromyko sees Muskie 5-16, 378A1

1976

USSR chrgs emigre internmt 2-4, 122C2
Kreisky in Czech, pacts OKd 2-17—2-19, 289D2
Angola MPLA recognized 2-19, 163D1
Soclst cong; liberatn movts, detente backed 3-11—3-13, 380D2
Europn socialists meet 3-13—3-14, 222F3
Total IMF oil loan rptd 4-1, 340F2
Sadat visits 4-10—4-12, 275E2
Schmidt on Eur CPs 4-15, 503C1
Kreisky at intl soc dems mtg 5-23—5-25, 449B3
Ferreira gets Argentina emb asylum 5-24, 399D2
Israeli airport blast 5-25, 370F2
Ferreira quits Argentina emb 5-31, 441C2
IDB entry planned 6-3, 465D3
1st ¼ trade deficit rptd 6-28, 572E1
Schilling freed to float; gains vs US $, W Ger mark 7-13—8-4, 572C1
Argentina violence scored 8-26, 672D2
Cambodia ties restored 8-30, 679C1
Czech bars playwright visit 10-9; chrgs traded 10-12, 10-14, 852A1
Polish plane hijacked 11-4, 907G1
French amb to Yugo killed 11-6, 910A2
Yugo backs Slovenes 11-14, govt talks set 11-28, 923F1, A2
Jan-Sept trade deficit, GNP up 11-17, 923B2
Iran-Czech pipeline to supply gas 11-22, 946B2

Obituaries
Gabl, Gertrud 1-18, 56C3

Sports
Winter Olympics in Innsbruck 2-4—2-15, 158F2-159B3
Summer Olympic results 7-18—7-31, 573F3, 575A2

UN Policy & Developments
Abstains on UN rights comm resolutn vs Israel 2-13, 125E2
Vs WHO anti-Israel stand 5-19, 355D2
Waldheim wins 2d term 12-7, 12-8, 914C2

AUTH, Tony
Wins Pulitzer Prize 5-3, 352E3

AUTOMOBILE Racing
Carter at SC stock-car races 6-6, 663F3, 666C1

Winners
Daytona 500, Pearson 2-15, 424A3
Indy 500, Rutherford 5-30, 424F2
Western 500, Pearson 1-18, 56F2

1977

Venez pres visits 5-3—5-4, 362A1
Spain exiles Basque prisoners 6-9, 454B1
'75 Turk amb death cited 6-9, 565A2
Viet refugees rptd accepted 6-16, 497E1
Observer at USSR mil exercises 7-11, 551C1
USSR emigre details dissident detentns 8-31, 684B1
Eur Cncl to study Turkey rights abuses in Cyprus 9-8, 764G1-A2; rpt shelved, Greece protests 11-3, 946E3
W Eur heroin conf 10-17—10-21, 971E3
Swiss hold 2 students re Palmers kidnap 11-9, intl terrorist link seen 11-24, 991F1; capture 2 W Ger terrorists 12-20, 1017D3
Czech cooperatn pact signed 11-22, 936F2

Helsinki Agreement—*See EUROPE—Security and Cooperation*

Monetary, Trade & Aid Issues (including all foreign economic developments)
IMF SDR defined 87G2
1st ½ trade, paymts deficits up, tourism, reserves down 10-3, 763C1
Czech trade talks open 11-22, 936G2

Obituaries
Schoeffler, Paul 11-21, 952C3
Schuschnigg, Kurt von 11-18, 952C3

UN Policy & Developments
UN Assemb member 3F3
Abstains on Israel occupatn rule vote 2-15, 107E2
Waldheim in Vienna 2-16, 107D1
IAEA sponsors A-conf in Salzburg 5-2—5-13, 402D2-403D1

U.S. Relations
Czechs free US newsman 2-13, 114B3
Kreisky sees Clifford 2-16, 122A2
Kreisky visits US 3-14, 425E1
Wolf confrmd US amb 6-22, 626F3
'75 US double agent kidnap by Sovts cited 7-14, 564C2

AUSTRIAN, Dr. Robert
Pneumonia vaccine gets FDA OK 11-21, 907B1

AUTOMOBILE Racing
Citicorp to drop USAC sponsorship 6-24, 531F2
New USAC-Citicorp pact set 9-21, 871A1
Grand Prix final standings 10-23, 870C3, E3
USAC final standings, earnings 10-31, 870F3
NASCAR final standings, earnings rptd 11-20, 1020D3
Yarborough named top driver 12-8, 1020C3

Obituaries
Hulman, Tony 10-17, 872C2
Isaac, Bobby 8-14, 696G2

Winners
Calif 500, Unser 9-4, 870F3
Calif Grand Prix, Andretti 4-3, 870D3
Daytona 500, Yarborough 2-20, 531B2
Daytona endurance, Haywood, Graves, Helmick 2-6, 531D2
Drag racing, Bach 4-24, 531E2
Formula 1, Lauda 10-1, 870C3
Indy 500, Foyt 5-29, 531F1-A2
Japan Grand Prix, Hunt 10-23, 870E3
Le Mans, Ickx, Barth 6-12, 531A2
NASCAR, Yarborough 11-20, 1020C3
Schaefer 500, Sneva 6-26, 871C1
US Grand Prix, Hunt 10-1, 870D3
USAC, Sneva 9-4, 870F3

1978

Helsinki Agreement—*See EUROPE—Security and Cooperation*

Monetary, Trade, Aid & Investment
EC steel dumping probe begun 1-23, 80C2
USSR trade deficit talks, '77 data cited 2-6—2-8, 110C2
'77 trade deficit sets record 2-7, 110F2
Schilling in new SDR basket 4-3, 300G3
Hungary devalues forint 11-11, 906G2

Sports
3 win world skiing titles 1-29—2-5, 316D2, G2
Habeler climbs Everest without oxygen 5-8, 420C2
2d in Nations Cup 5-15, 419D1
World Cup soccer finals, sidelights 6-1—6-25, 519F3, 520F1, E3

UN Policy & Developments
Chile rights abuse res backed 3-6, 210F1
Unifil troops opposed 3-29, 214B1
UNDOF mandate renewed 5-31, 400B2
Assemb member 713B3

U.S. Relations
Pan Am to end Vienna svc 9-7, 701G1

AUTOBIOGRAPHY of Federico Sanchez (book)
Spain CP chief refutes 1-21, party ldrs rptd shaken 2-24, 136B2

AUTOGIRO Co. of America
Patent case review barred 1-23, 65E1

AUTOMATION Industries Inc.
Gen Cable plans purchase 3-15, 404F1

AUTOMOBILE Association, American—*See AMERICAN Automobile Association*

AUTOMOBILE Dealers Association Election-Action Committee, National
7th-leading PAC fund-raiser 9-7, 753B2

AUTOMOBILE Racing
USAC offcls die in charter plane crash 4-23, 460E2
Unser takes USAC 'Triple Crown' 9-3, 968F3
Andretti wins world title 9-10, 968C3
Italian Grand Prix site switched 10-27, 968E3
Unser sets USAC earnings record 12-24, 1028C2
USAC sets new rules, CART formatn cited 12-28, 1028A2

Obituaries
Peterson, Ronnie 9-11, 778A2

Winners
Calif 500, A Unser 9-3, 968F3
Daytona 500, Allison 2-19, 538A3
Daytona endurance, Hezemans, Stommelen, Gregg 2-5, 538C3
Indy 500, A Unser 5-29, 538B2
Ital Gr Prix, Andretti 9-10, 968C3
LeMans, Jaussaud, Pironi 6-11, 538F2
Schaefer 500, A Unser 6-25, 538E3
US Gr Prix West, Reutemann 4-2, 968F3
US Gr Prix, Reutemann 10-1, 968F3
USAC, Sneva 12-24, 1028C2

1979

Vienna Open tennis results 5-20, 570D2
Austrian Grand Prix tennis results 7-29, 734B2
Vienna Grand Prix tennis results 10-29, 1003E3

UN Policy & Developments
Membership listed 695D2

U.S. Relations
GM expansn plans detailed 6-11, 555F1
SALT II Summit in Vienna 6-15—6-18, 449A1, F1, 457E2
US amb met PLO rep 8-15, 605E1; Kreisky details 8-22, 625B1

AUTOMOBILE Association, American—*See AMERICAN Automobile Association*

AUTOMOBILE Club of New York Inc.—*See AMERICAN Automobile Association*

AUTOMOBILE Racing
CART-USAC rift detailed; Foyt quits CART, Woodward sues USAC 1-31, 5-27, 491F1
Allison, Yarborough collide 2-20, 3-4, NASCAR fines 2-20, 490F3, 491A1
Foyt takes 2 USAC natl titles; earnings record cited 7-29, 11-11, 1005F1
Brazil alcohol fuel race held 9-7, 871E2
Scheckter wins world title 9-9, 1005D1
Petty wins 7th NASCAR Gr Natl title; top $ winner 11-18, 1005A2

Winners
Belgian Gr Prix, Scheckter 5-13, 1005E1
Carolina 500, B Allison 3-4, 491B1
Daytona endurance, Field, Ongais, Haywood 2-4, 491C1
Daytona 500, Petty 2-20, 490F3
Indy 500, Mears 5-27, 490G2
Italian Gr Prix, Scheckter 9-9, 1005D1
LeMans, D Whittington, B Whittington, Ludwig 6-10, 490D3
LubriLon Gr Prix, Foyt 7-29, 1005F1
Monoco Gr Prix, Scheckter 5-27, 1005E1
Pocono 500, Foyt 6-24, 491D1
S African Gr Prix, Villenueve 3-4, 1005E1
Texas 250, Foyt 11-11, 1005G1
Times 500, Petty 11-18, 1005A2
US Gr Prix West, Villenueve 4-8, 1005E1
US Gr Prix, Villenueve 10-7, 1005F1

1980

Occupatn end anniv marked 5-16, 378D1
Olympic com rejects Moscow boycott 5-20, 379A3
Kreisky in Iran hostage mission 5-25—5-26; warns vs sanctns 5-27, 394C1
20 Rumanians defect 7-3, 548C3
Sovt dissident feminist arrives 7-20; expelled unionist chrgs KGB murdered wife 7-25, 680C2-B3
Jewish youth killed in Belgium blast 7-27, Palestinian seized 7-28, 573D2
Iraqi bomb plot fails 7-30, diplomats expelled 7-30, 7-31, 604G2
Westn labor costs compared 8-12, 698E1
Iran hostage appeal rptd 8-16, 634G3
Sovt violinist seeks W Ger asylum 8-19, 980E1
OPEC ministerial mtg 9-15—9-18, 694B3
Nazi kills self in Brazil 10-3, 810E1

Government & Politics—*See also other appropriate subheads in this section*
Occupatn end anniv marked 5-16, 378D1
Kirchschlager reelected pres 5-18, 388F1
Vorarlberg referendum backs autonomy 6-15, 520E1
Hosp scandal chrgs rptd denied 8-27, 667C3
Hosp scandal spurs Kreisky reform plan 9-3, reforms OKd, Androsch to comply 9-9, 705D2
Androsch wins confidence vote 10-8, 870F3
Androsch sets resignatn 12-11, 964A2

Monetary, Trade, Aid & Investment
GM plant set 2-20, 125A3
Yugo loan rptd 9-20, 833C2

Obituaries
Kokoschka, Oskar 2-22, 176A2

Sports
Moscow Olympics stand rptd 1-21, 45B3
Lake Placid Olympic results 2-12—2-24, 154F2, 155F2-156D1
Moser retires from skiing 3-16, 470A1
Austrian Indoor tennis results 3-23, 607G2
Olympic com rejects Moscow boycott 5-20, 379A3
Moscow Olympics results 7-20—8-3, 588B3, 622B2, A3, 623D2, 624G3
Austrian Grand Prix tennis results 7-27, 691A3

U.S. Relations
Italian banker convicted in NY 3-27, 237A2
Iran asks neutrality on hostages 4-12, 282F1
Muskie sees Gromyko 5-16, 378A1
Occupatn end anniv marked 5-16, 378D1
Kreisky in Iran re US hostages 5-25—5-26, warns vs new sanctns 5-27, 394C1
Iran hostage appeal rptd 8-16, 634G3

AUTOMOBILE Dealers Association, American Imported (AIADA)
McElwaine testifies on imports 10-11, 823G2

AUTOMOBILE Racing
USAC-CART reach compromise 4-3; USAC dissolves Champ Racing League, rift widens 6-30, 1002F1
Jones wins world title 9-28, 1001F3
Rival Gr Prix circuit set 10-31, 1002C1
Earnhardt wins NASCAR Gr Natl title; top $ winner 11-15, 1002D1
Rutherford named top driver; earnings cited 12-5, 1002E1

Obituaries
Galindez, Victor 10-26, 876E1
Gregg, Peter 12-15, 1004A2

Winners
Argentine Gr Prix, Jones 1-13, 1002B1
British Gr Prix, Jones 7-13, 1002B1
Canadian Gr Prix, Jones 9-28, 1001G3
Daytona 500, Baker 2-17, 637C3
Daytona endurance, Stommelen, Jost, Merl 2-3, 637E3
French Gr Prix, Jones 6-29, 1002B1
Indy 500, Rutherford 5-25, 637E2
LA Times 500, Parsons 11-15, 1002D1
LeMans, Rondeau, Jaussard 6-15, 637A3
Pocono 500, B Unser 6-22, 637G3
Spanish Gr Prix 6-1, 1002B1
US Gr Prix, Jones 10-5, 1002A1
US Gr Prix West, Piquet 3-30, 1002B1

AUTOMOBILES

1976

AUTOMOBILES—*See also 'Motor Vehicle' under ACCIDENTS; also BUSES, TRUCKS; company names*
Used-car trade rule proposed 1-2, 7B2
GM wins warranty-fraud case, other suits pending 4-1, 287D1
Ford urges regulatory reform 5-13, 346G3
Reagan: energy bill will cut car size, jobs 5-14, 356F3
Dem platform text 6-15, 471E2, 475A1
Sup Ct OKs traffic violatn search 7-6, 535C1
GOP platform text 8-18, 607G1
Steel price hike cancelled 8-30, 646G3
Elec car bill vetoed 9-13, overridden 9-17, 707D3
EPA ratings, table 9-22, 766G1-770C2
Research bill veto sustained 9-29, 745G3
Ford campaign donatns cited 10-22, 938F3
3 convctd in GM warranty-fraud case 12-23, 988E1

1977

AUTOMOBILES—*See also ACCIDENTS—Motor Vehicle; ROADS; company names*
DOT issues future trends rpt 1-15, 58G2
Ford productn halt ordrd 2-8, 113B1
Carter budgets elec car resrch 2-22, 125D2
Roy Abernathy dies 2-28, 164B2
FTC vs Tenneco bid for Monroe 3-15, 274G3
GM to end Vega, Astre productn 3-15, 463D3
Tire-grading case review denied 3-21, 230D2
License-plate slogans curbed 4-20, 342D2
GM offers engine switch controversy setlmt, NY suit resolved 4-25, 325F3
Metric road signs proposed; speedomtr, odomtr plans rptd 4-28, 369D1
Urban business confidence rptd 5-16, 384C3
Ill driver license law upheld 5-16, 419F1
Ford complaint vs FTC declined 5-16, 419D2
Small car mfr speedup urged 5-19, 408F2
Metric signs plan dropped 6-24, 522G1-A2
Norton Simon buys Avis 6-27, 519A2
Aluminum demand increase cited 6-27, 577C2
Mo House ex-speaker sentncd 8-16, 712B2

1978

AUTOMOBILES—*See also company names*
Midwest blizzard causes heavy losses 1-26—2-11, 105D3
Adams issues policy statemt 2-8, 109D1
FTC suit vs STP setld 2-9, 348C1
Coal strike threatens productn 2-11, 104E1
Boston Cadillac agency closes 3-1, 142F3
Spinks arrested 3-19, pays fine 5-18, 379C1
GM vows '78 exec pay curb 5-19, 427C3
Zinc demand drop rptd 6-1, 443C3
UAW pres quits Admin panel 7-19, 611G1
Natl Auto Dealers, UAW on top PAC fund-raisers list 9-7, 753C2
GM-UAW southn plant pact set 9-11, 699B3
GM, AMC, Chrysler sue vs FTC probe 9-11, 768C1
AMC, UAW sign 2-yr pact 9-25, 737G2-C3
Bank leasing case declined by Sup Ct 10-2, 751B2
VW Pa plant struck 10-9—10-15, 809C3
Ford settles FTC repossessed cars complaint 10-14, 942C1
Rental car parking ticket case refused by Sup Ct 10-30, 832F2
Police search power broadened by Sup Ct 12-5, 959C2
Calif franchise law upheld by US Sup Ct 12-5, 959C3

1979

AUTOMOBILES—*See also company names*
'73-77 crime survey rptd 1-18, 119A1
Detroit projct investmts cited 1-23, 70D3
King fined for drunk driving 2-16, 291D1
Chrysler, GM mkt share compared 2-23, 188E1
Ford heir rejcts dissident stockholders role, seeks bd spot 2-26, 202D3
Ford stockholders suit barred in NY 3-8, 202D3
Ford sets retiremt 3-14, 202G2
Faulty repairs rptd common 5-7, 595B3
PAC top '78 spenders rptd 5-10, 363F1
Corp execs '78 pay rptd high 5-14, 348A1
GM radio trust suit settled 5-14, 441F3-442A1
State-local '78 tax revenues up 5-16, 386C2
'Car of the future' plan set 5-18, 441C3
Ford heir barred from contesting will 7-16, 631C1
Auto-Train withdraws fed loan applicatn 8-21, Seabd extends pact 8-24, 726A2
AMC declares dividend, '79 revenues cited 9-21, 784E3
Auto-Train financing plan OKd 12-7, 989A3

1980

AUTOMOBILES
Ford kickback suit settled 1-11, 225C2
State ct jurisdictn narrowed by Sup Ct 1-21, 93A2, C2
Carter budget proposals 1-28, 73C1
Ford heir retains DC atty 3-12, 225D3
Ford resigns 3-13, 224C3
Box search case refused by Sup Ct 3-24, 265C2
Ford $1 bln credit line rptd added 3-24, 287G3
State-local '79 tax collectns rptd 4-17, 307D2
Ford, Chrysler families art auctned 5-12, 5-13, 472A1
Carter sees auto execs, vows actn 5-14, 384E1
Reagan hits regulation 5-15, 383A1
Mt St Helens damage assessed 5-24—7-4, 503E3
Borg-Warner, Bosch trust violatn rptd 7-11, 917F2
Reagan issues aid plan 7-12, 535D1
GOP platform adopted 7-15, 537C1
NCAA probe of UCLA basketball team 'rewards' rptd 7-27, 875D3
Auto-Train financial, svc difficulties detailed 7-31—9-26, DC investors rescue attempt rptd 11-26, 958C2-D3
Dem platform plank adopted 8-13, 614C3
Tenna liquidatn ordered 9-12, 985G3
Ford heir drops family suit 10-10, 985F2

1976

Foreign Developments (including U.S. international news)—*See also 'Labor' below*
UK Chrysler bailout plan signed 1-5; layoffs, terms rptd 1-14, 1-23, 72F2
Columbia '75 price hikes rptd 1-9, 31B1
Chile lifts import ban 1-9, 48A1
Datsun led '75 US imports 1-11, 280G1
Brazil '75 growth down 1-20, 98F2
'75 Italy productn rptd down 1-29, 74C3
UK '75 exports rptd up 1-29, 174G1
Argentina '75 productn down 2-11, 212C3
Nissan buys Australia VW plant 2-12, 137E3
Japan-EC Jan-Sept '75 exports rptd 2-24, 191F2
Jan US imports up 2-27, 168D3
Argentina-Paraguay smuggling cited 3-5, 206A1
Feb US imports down 3-26, 230A2
Arson at Fiat plant rptd 4-19—4-23, 297F1
VW OKs US plant 4-23, 321E2
US ends mktg probe 5-4; VW dumping rptd 5-6, 320E3
Brit Leyland rpts profit 5-17, 365C1
VW plans US plant 5-28—10-5, 987C3
Australia-Japan deals set 6-10, 438B3
Nissan in Australia deal 8-15, 650F1
Eur, Canada price hikes set 8-16, 10-12, 988B1
Aug, Sept US imports rptd up 9-7, 10-6, 747F3
Spain Ford plant opens 10-25, 929A2
Australia Chrysler unit to expand 11-2, 835A3
Chrysler sets S Africa merger 11-3, 856D1
Oct US imports rptd 11-3, 885F2
S Africa sales rptd down 11-4, 856F1
France, UK set cooperatn 11-12, 880C2
France rpts Oct export fall 11-18, 964E2
Libya buys into Fiat 12-1, 964G3-965E1
Nov US imports 12-3, 987F2
Ghana Mil Cncl retiremts linked to import fraud 12-3, 1003C2
Australia ends import limits 12-7, 944F2
Volvo US plant delayed 12-9, 987A3
Forgn paymts study rptd 12-20, 985D2
Turk Oyak-Renault to close 12-24, 1012A1

1977

Chrysler unveils 2 small, front-drive models 12-5—12-9, 962B1
Ga GM franchise case review refused 12-12, 960D2
Oregon 'guest passenger' law review refused 12-12, 960F2
GM $40 mln engine switch paymt, warranty extensn rptd 12-17, 1007E3
Foreign Developments (including U.S. international news)—*See also other appropriate subheads in this section*
Brazil industry at zero growth 3-25, 524A3
Japan mfrs study US investmt rise 3-28, 318F3
Honda overtakes VW in US mkt 4-11, VW seeks 2d US plant 6-15, 463E3
Ford plans new Australia plant 5-5, 389D1
Volvo, Saab agree to merge 5-6, 469B3
Egypt OKs Ford plant agrmt 5-10, 390A2
Greece sets big car tax 5-18, 487D3
UK lifts Leyland investmt freeze 6-29, OKs loan 7-25, 695A1
NZ to import Sovt Lada 7-4, 638F2
Australia import quotas imposed 7-12, 560D3
Volvo-SAAB merger called off 8-28, 709E1
Canada sets metric road signs 9-6, 705D2
Turkey bans 'luxury' imports 9-8, 709D2
Taiwan to hike output 9-22, 783F2
Australia extends import curbs 10-6, 779C1
'76 world top exporters, productn rptd 10-11, 853G2
'76 US dumping probe cited 10-19, 933G2
Ford, Egypt sign truck pact 10-29; AMC pact cited 863G1, B2
Japan assures GATT on tariff cuts 11-29, 933D2
E Ger in VW deal 11-30, 984E1
VW links $ drop, export harm in US mkt 12-7, 932D3
Israel-Rumania trade rptd 12-10, 987C3
Peugeot exec slain in Argentina 12-16, 981F3
Japan Sept-Nov productn rptd 12-20, 1015F1
Rootes Group founder dies 12-20, 1024A3

1978

Accidents—*See ACCIDENTS—Motor Vehicle*
Foreign Developments (including U.S. international news)—*See also other subheads in this section*
Dutch rescue Volvo car unit 1-5, 93G1
Budd reveals Thyssen bid 1-12, talks OKd 1-17, 66A2
Argentina '77 exports drop, worker layoffs rptd 1-13; hint GM to quit mfg 2-24, 310B2
Volkswagen ends 'beetle' line 1-19, 74D3
Japan '77 top export item 1-20, 44B3
Australia threatens EC boycott 1-25, 69C3
UK Leyland sets reorganizatn, job cuts 2-1, 112D1-D2
Japan bars UK export curbs 2-8, 112E2
UK Leyland to close plant, cut 3,000 more jobs 2-15, 132B1
US bans S Africa police sales 2-17, 135E1
UK Ford unit ends strike 2-20, 132C1
Sachs takeover halted by W Ger ct 2-23, 211B1
Japan to curb UK car exports 3-3, 168A1
Spain unsold inventory rptd 3-10, 394F3
UK Leyland '77 losses rptd 3-20; loan granted 3-23, cost cuts pledged 3-28, efficiency study rptd 3-30, 267C3-G3
AMC, Renault plan joint productn, distributn 3-31, 283F3-284B1
Italy showrooms bombed 4-6, 4-22, 4-30, 330D1, E1, G1; 5-22, 393F3
Brazil factory strikes 4-28—5-23, 411G3
Japan vows US export cut 5-3, 341F2
Chrysler Australia job cuts, productn chngs set; '77 losses rptd 5-3, 349D3
Fiat autos bombed in Milan 5-4, 393G1
Renault plants struck 5-25—6-27, 532G3
Alfa Romeo pres, 3 execs sentenced 5-29, 454E2
Renault Rumania expansn rptd 6-14, 651A1
Alfa Romeo exec shot in Naples 6-22, 517A2
Renault Basque office bombed 6-30, 649B2
Fiat showroom in Turin bombed 7-10, 574F1
Australia proposes import curb 7-13, 530A2
US rpts Japan export curbs affirmed 7-17, 544A2
US-Canada '77 trade rptd 8-2, 613F2
Argentina GM to shut down 8-4; Ford may hike investmts 8-17, 793B2, E2
Peugeot to buy Chrysler Eur units 8-10, 623C2-624A1
UK Leyland ex-exec jailed 8-11, 667G2
Australia sales tax cut proposed 8-15, 628B2
Australia sales tax cut, tariff proposals scored 8-17, 646B2
GM sets S Africa plant integratn 8-29, 742G2
UK Leyland labor troubles persist 9-11, 9-14; 1st ½ profits rptd 9-14, 739G2
UK Ford workers strike 9-21, 10-9, 763F1, D3
UK OKs Chrysler sale to Peugot 9-28, 764D1
Ford to regain Chile operatns 10-5, 796D1
Mitsubishi to buy Chrysler Australia share 10-25, 836B2
USSR Ladas rptd sold in Canada 11-13, 1020F3-1021A1

1979

Accidents—*See ACCIDENTS-Motor Vehicle*
Chrysler Issues—*See CHRYSLER*
Foreign Developments (including U.S. international news)—*See also 'Fuel Issues' and 'Mergers' below*
UK Rolls-Royce plant strike continues 1-8, 20C3
AMC, Renault sign sales pact 1-10, 131E2
Spain workers strike 1-15, 61G1
Japan '78 exports rptd 1-24, 98D2
Spain Chrysler 14% pay hike OKd 1-24, 100D3
Canada mfrs ruled liable for defects 1-25, 95C3
Volvo stockholders block Norway deal 1-26, 77G1
Volvo '78 earnings rptd up 1-26, 77D2
Spain '78 export hike rptd 1-31, 101A1
GM Australia unit rpts '78 loss, expansn plans 2-6, 94E3
BL Longbridge workers strike 2-7–2-14, co-wide strike rejected 2-9, 115B3-F3
Austria '78 imports down 2-7, 181G3
Australia eases local content rule, GM plant plans cited 2-22, 133E2
Brazil metalworkers strike 3-13–3-27, 210D1, 328A1
BL hit by wildcat strike 4-9, 285F3-286A1
Ford bars Europn plant 4-24; Renault, Peugot French plans rptd 4-25, 299G2
BL-Honda productn planned 5-17, 388B2
Renault Portugal expansn rptd 5-24, 409A3
Mex 1st 1/4 productn rptd 6-1, 487C2
Argentina 1st 1/4 sales rptd 6-2, 466F3
Spain GM plant agrmt rptd 6-6, 428A2
GM Eur expansn plans detailed 6-11, 555F1, A3
Fiat-Poland deal signed 6-18, 487F1-A2
USSR hikes prices 7-2, 504E2
Iran industries natlzd 7-5, 503F2, A3
Ford to invest $76 mln in Argentina; sales, Chrysler-VW plans cited 7-20, 562F1
VW plans 2d US car plant, Mercedes truck plant plan rptd 7-26, 663D3
Brazil tax set 8-1, 871C2
BL plans job cuts, 1st 1/2 profits rptd 9-10, 686D2
Fiat announces investmt plan 9-12, 709C2
Alfa Romeo plans joint ventures 9-13, 709E1
Dutch plan tax hike 9-18, 730C3
Ford sets Canada layoffs 9-27, 806F1
Brazil metalworkers strike again 10-29, 833B2
BL employes endorse cutbacks 11-1, 855F2-B3
USSR mil seen aided by US 11-8, 856F3
BL union militant fired, strikes ensue 11-19, interim pact OKd 11-27, 994G1
UK NEB members quit re Rolls-Royce transfer 11-20, 949C3
Ford fires 700 S African blacks 11-21, 899C3
S Africa ends job bias 12-1, 969B1
Fiat Turin workers, plants attacked by terrorists 12-11, 12-14, 12-21, 995C2, D2, A3
Japan productn rptd up 12-12, 963D3
US denies USSR plant mil use 12-17, 997F2
Renault to buy Volvo share 12-19, 993G3-994C1
UK vows BL aid 12-27, 994D1
BL-Honda accord signed 12-27, 994E1

1980

Bush vows investmt aid 10-16, 817B3
AMC credit agrmt reached 12-11, 938G2
Meese vows 'close look' 12-28, 980A3
Accidents—*See ACCIDENTS--Motor Vehicle*
Chrysler Issues—*See CHRYSLER Corp.*
Foreign Developments (including U.S. international news)—*See also 'Fuel Issues' below*
Ford rehires S Africa strikers 1-9, 60C3
Honda to open US plant 1-11, 35F2
UAW pres asks Japanese assemb plants in US 1-13, 35B2
Peugot, Chrysler productn talks, finance deal rptd 2-6; Mitsubishi to finance Chrysler imports 2-12, 127D2-G2
BL bars rehiring of fired steward 2-7, 117B3; strike rejected 2-20, 150D1
UAW pres in Japan, asks US plants 2-11—2-14; Japan urges action 2-12, Nissan, Toyota respond 2-18, response lauded 2-19, 127B1
VW sets 2d US plant site 2-12, 127B3
GM sets Eur plants 2-20, 125A3
Spain rpts '79 SEAT losses 2-21, 196F2, G2
Canada '79 steel demand drop cited 2-22, 211E2
Ford S Africa unit race policies evaluated 2-27, 195A2
EC warns US vs trade war 2-28, 204F2
Greece sets 20% import cut 3-4, 173D1
Connally 'basic speech' excerpts notes Japan imports 3-7, 184B2
Australia tanker drivers strike 3-8—3-9, 190G2; accord scored 3-14, 229B3
Ford Indonesia paymts probe rptd dropped 3-13, 224D3
Mitsubishi to continue Chrysler import financing 4-1, 287C1
BL workers bar strike 4-2, 274E2
Carter vs import bars 4-17, 287E2
Nissan seeks US truck plant, UAW pres asks car plants 4-17, 288D1
Ford, VW hit by Brazil metalworkers strike 4-19, 310C1
BL strike ends 4-21, 313E1
W Europn cos plan research 4-22, 303A3
Mitsubishi buys Chrysler Australia unit 4-30, 350E1
Brazil strike losses rptd 5-11, 388C2
Canada jobless rise linked 5-13, 388G2
US concerned re Japan imports 5-14, 384G1
Japan to end US auto parts tariff 5-15, 482B1
US raises truck import duty, Japan rues 5-20, 384A2
Fiat layoff plans rptd 5-20, 408D3
Fiat balks at SEAT acquisitn; Japan, W Ger talks rptd; '79, 1st 1/4 data cited 6-4, 467A3
Canada plant closing set 6-9; UAW workers stage sit-in 8-8—8-21, resume work 8-25, 650B3
UAW asks import curbs; '75-79 Japan Eur trade data cited 6-12, 457E2, A3
Ford plans Mex engine plant 6-12, 465B2
USSR strike rptd 6-13, 467E1-C2
Sovts seize license plates re Olympic traffic 6-14, 467C2
Australia plans hydrogen cars 6-22, 496E2
Rolls-Royce, Vickers to merge 6-25, 498G1
S Africa strike ends 6-25, 499B2
Kuwait buys 10% of Brazil VW unit, Daimler-Benz interest rptd 6-25, 542E3, 562C1
Vauxhill rpts '79 loss 7-1, 498F1
Australia GM unit to shut plant 7-1, 543A1
AMC gains Renault loan 7-1, 556B3
Japan import curbs asked by unions, Ford 7-1, 8-4, 599C1
Nissan fears US productn, tariff rise 7-1, 7-29, 599G1
Taiwan '79 sales rptd up 7-4, 567A3
Canada May, June sales down; US trade deficit up 7-5, 520G2, B3
Japan rptd top auto maker 7-7, 541E3
Carter seeks import curb ruling 7-8, 505B1
Toyota-Ford productn talks revealed 7-9; Ford rejectn rptd 7-14, 556G2-A3
Reagan vs import quotas 7-12, 535F1
US, Canada purchases compared 7-16, 562E3
Peugeot, Chrysler engine deal confrmd 7-17, 541E2
ITC blocks import probe speedup 7-18, 556G1-B2, 599F1
Canada, Japan talks held; US role cited 8-2—8-11, 618G1
Canada chrgs Sovt dumping 8-7; record sales rptd 8-8, 618C1-F1
Canada July sales rptd down 8-7, 618B2
Reagan vows Japan import curbs 9-2, 664F2
Fiat, Peugeot project set 9-15, 751F3
Alfa Romeo, Nissan project OKd 9-20, 751B3
Renault increases AMC share, rescue plan set 9-24, 724C3
Fiat cancels layoffs 9-27, 751E2
SEAT-Toyota talks rptd 10-8, 793A3*
US hearings on Japan imports 10-8—10-11, 823E1
BL seeks more UK aid 10-27; strike threatened 11-3, workers accept 7% pay deal 11-18, 886D2
GM, Ford units in UK rpt losses 10-31, 11-6, 886G2
ITC bars Japan imports curbs 11-10, 866D3
Polish govt retains productn control 11-19, 878F2

1976

1977

Fuel Conservation
Carter budgets elec car research 2-22, 125D2
GM drops rotary engine projct 4-12, 409D1
Carter energy plan 4-18, 4-20, 289D2, 290C1, 294E3, 295A1, A3; fact sheet 291C2-E2
Cong reactn to Carter plan 4-20, 294A1
Mfrs, poll reactns to Carter plan 4-21—4-24, 320C1, B3
Carter plan scored 4-30—6-8, GOP TV rebuttal 6-2, 443E1-G2
UAW pres vs Carter plan 5-19, 408F2
Carter, Cong tussle over plan 6-9—6-13, 460F1-A2
Carter warns vs energy lobby 6-10, 460A3
Adams sets '81-84 standards 6-26, 522E1
Gas rationing studied 7-10, 538C2
Energy-efficient motor oil rptd 7-11, 558D3
House OKs Carter energy pkg 8-5, 609F3
Sen votes gas-guzzler ban 9-13, 703C1
GM unveils diesel Olds, smaller mid-sized cars 9-13, 722G3-723B1
EPA ratings issued 9-19, 723B3
Sen com vs gas-guzzler tax, backs 4¢-gal extensn 9-20, 757E2, F2 ★
Elec car tax credit, 4¢-gal extensn OKd by Sen 10-31, 832F1, A3, D3

1978

Fuel Issues
New fuel standards for light trucks issued 3-15, 284F1-B2
Tax deductn end backed by House com 4-17—4-19, 305G3
Gas-guzzler standby tax status rptd 4-21, 305C1
Swiss rejct monthly ban 5-28, 558D2
NZ plans gas duty 6-1, 497C3
US, Canada tax policy scored 6-5, 449E3 ★, 450F1
Gas price hike urged by Sawhill 6-13, 450D2
Md refiner-run gas statn ban upheld by US Sup Ct 6-14, 491F3
Energy Dept offers standby gas ration plan 6-22, 511G1
Tax deductns cut by House com 7-27, 587A1
Mo rejects tax hike 8-8, 626C1
EPA ratings issued 9-15, 719F2
Aug price rise rptd 9-26, 752D1
Energy bill clears Cong 10-15, 787B2, E2
Carter toughens 55 mph enforcemt 11-8, 875A3
Premium unleaded gas shortage, price hikes rptd 11-20—11-21, 939E1
EPA tests questnd 11-21, 939C2
Shell trust probe rptd 11-28, suit filed 11-30, 939C3, D3
Shell, Amoco begin rationing 12-1; 3 others seek OK 12-3; artificial shortage discounted 12-4, 938F3-939E1
Shortage probe rptd, rationing studied 12-6, 962E3
'78 price rise rptd 12-19, 1010F1

1979

Fuel Issues
Adams backs '85 mileage standard 1-19, 87C3
Carter budget proposals 1-22, 45A2
Carter orders fed agency fuel-saving 2-6, 82C3
Kerr-McGee OKs price refund 2-8, 113B1
Carter backs 55-mph limit 2-12, 109D3
Adams outlines urban-aid policy 2-13, 129A3
Carter seeks conservatn powers 2-26, 145B3
Gasoline price controls eased 3-2, 162F1
Calif price law challenge declined by Sup Ct 3-5, 185E1
OTA sees auto use threatened 3-10, 187D3
Feb gas prices up 2% 3-25, 252F1
US conservatn lag rptd 3-28, 228A1
Mar-May car sales drop, gas fears linked 4-4, 5-3, 6-5, 441D2
Carter asks parking curbs, 55-mph speed limit 4-5, 250F3, 251A1
Gas anti-price gouging drive starts 4-16, 301C2
1st 1/4 gas demand hike rptd 4-22, 343E1
Texaco fined re Calif gas-switching 4-26, 301D2
150 gas price violatns rptd 4-27, 324C3
W Ger sets conservatn steps 4-30, 5-16, 373F2-C3, D3
Poll faults oil cos 5-4, 343A2
Calif gas shortage probe ordrd, rationing backed 5-5, 347D1
May gas supplies seen tightening, shortfall explained 5-7, 342G3
Jan-Apr wholesale price rise rptd 5-7, 343E1
Calif odd-even gas rationing begins 5-9, 342B3
Standby gas rationing defeated 5-10, 342A2
Carter scores House on gas ration defeat, calls for Cong plan 5-11; criticizes pub on shortage 5-15, 361A1
Carter sees Brown, hikes Calif gas allocatn 5-16; Ore gov scores, summer shortfall warned 5-17, 361F1-E2
State-local '78 tax revenues up 5-16, 386C2
Amerada Hess price violatns chrgd, other refiners warned; Jan-May hikes noted 5-17, 385A2; 396C1
'Car of the future' plan set 5-18, 441C3
Gas prices in W Eur, other natns rptd 5-19, 5-20, 396G3
Japan asks Sunday gas statn closings 5-21, 389B2
Bulgaria, Yugo curb auto use 5-21, 5-23, 397C1
Diesel fuel allocatn rules adopted 5-25, 395D2
Retail gas price rise rptd 5-26, 395D3
'78 state gas use rptd; chart 5-27, 395D2-A3
June gas supplies cut 5-29—5-30, 395B3
States get gas sales regulatn power 5-29, 395G3
Carter sees oil execs 5-31, Ind Dems 6-1, 418C1, G2
Calif energy plan proposed 5-31, 418G3
No-lead gas output incentives set 6-4, 418A3
Brazil alcohol use rptd 6-4, 430G1
UK to hike gas tax 6-12, 445E2
EC comm backs conservatn 6-13, 437B2
Auto role seen undiminished 6-18, 514A3
Odd-even gas rationing spreads to E Coast, Tex 6-19—6-21; Mobil asks standby plan 6-21, 462C2-C3
Gasohol tax exemptn proposed 6-20, 498F1
Diesel fuel allocatn rule canceled 6-22, 479C3
Gas shortage spreads, cos rpt July allocatns 6-23—6-27, 479B1
Md sues US re gas allocatn 6-26, 479G1
OPEC ups price, US hikes seen 6-28, 473F1
Carter vacatn cancelatn linked 7-1, 497A3
Carter calls NE govs 7-2, 497C3
Greece sets conservatn steps 7-3, 543G3, 544A1
Spain price hike rptd 7-3, 546C1
W Ger seeks more fuel efficiency, bars speed limit 7-4, 506C1, B2
Mondale on Admin plans 7-8, 517E3
China-Pl pact signed 7-8, 567C1
Intercity summer bus svc expansn OKd 7-12, 579C2
Carter 6-pt energy plan calls for gas rationing, conservatn 7-15, 532E2, 534D1-A2
Israel hikes gas prices 7-19, 566C1
Schlesinger fired, gas shortage linked 7-20, 530E1
Adams fired, cites fuel efficiency goal 7-20, 531B2
Gas rationing veto amendmt OKd in House, Carter scores 7-25, 557A2
Rumania hikes gas price 7-27, demands Westn money paymts 8-1, 645D3, G3

1980

AMC rpts Renault aid crucial 11-19, 883C2
W Ger lay-offs rptd planned 11 27, 924C3
Nissan-VW project planned 12-3, 924D3
Auto import curb res dies in Cong 12-4, 982B2
BL strike end urged by Thatcher 12-31, 994F1

Fuel Issues
Anderson backs 50 cents per gallon gas tax 1-5, 4D3
State of State messages 1-7—1-15, 403D2, A3, E3, 404E1; 1-15, 484F1
Carter sets alcohol productn goal 1-11, 33B2
Canada's Trudeau vs excise tax 1-12, 38C1
Carter asks gas rationing 1-21, 1-23, 41E2, 43A2, E3
Carter budget proposals 1-28, 73D1
Kennedy urges gas rationing, GOP scores 1-28, 74E2, E3, 75G1
Brookings economists back gas rationing 2-6, 2-7, 126G2
Ireland plans gas levy hike 2-27, 150G3
Australia tanker drivers strike 3-8—3-9, 190G2; accord scored 3-14, 229B3
Feb unleaded gas use rptd 3-12, 250C3
Worldwatch scores gasohol, asks automatic transmissn ban 3-15, 251A1
2d 1/4 gas use targets set, '80 consumptn drop 3-20, 250C3
UK plans tax hike 3-26, 232E1
Ashland unveils refining advance 3-31, 251E1
Carter scores small car productn lag 4-17, 287D2
State-local '79 tax collectns rptd 4-17, 307D2
Brazil alcohol fuel promotn outlined 4-20, progrm delays rptd 6-3; US sales surge 6-10, 460G3-461A2
US drivers rptd buying Canada gas 4-21, 334E3
W Europn cos plan research 4-22, 303B3
Chrysler plans K-cars 5-10, 383F2
US oil import fee blocked by Dist Ct 5-13, 366A1
Reagan hits regulatn 5-15, 383E1
Elec car dvpt claimed 6-5, reactn 6-9, 541F2
Standby gas rationing plan submitted by Carter 6-12, 551G3
Australia plans hydrogen cars 6-22, 496F2
Venice summit stresses conservatn 6-23, 473F2
Dem platform drafted 6-24, 479G2
Italy OKs gas price hike 7-2, 523E3
World glut cuts Eur prices 7-4—8-12, 628F1-B2
US econ rules reviewed 7-8, 505E1
5 cos cut gas prices 7-9, 553F1
GM pledges '85 fuel-efficient cars 7-9, 556C3
Reagan seeks gas allocatn rule repeal 7-12, 535E1
US 1st 1/2 gas consumptn rptd down 7-24, 553C1
Carter pres renominatn acceptance speech 8-14, 612G1, 613F1
Reagan scores fed regulatns 9-2, Admin disputes 9-3, 664F2
Anderson, Reagan TV debate 9-21, 721E3, 722A1
Rules revisns clear Cong 9-30, signed 10-10, 981C1
Carter lauds new cars 10-1, 739B2
Carter sees US productn 10-12, 779D1
Iran to triple prices 11-9, 879D3
ITC bars Japan auto curbs 11-10, 866D3
PPG accused of fuel-switching 11-25, 899C3

1976

Insurance Issues
US Sup Ct bars review of Conn no-fault insurnc law 1-12, 24C1
Sen rejects no-fault bill 3-31, 234C2
Carter vs no-fault law 8-9, 585E1
No-fault bill not cleared 10-2, 883A2

Labor
Spain Chrysler strike continues 1-19, 54D3
UK Chrysler strike ends 2-3, 174A2
Leyland Innocenti layoffs completed 2-4, 141C1
Argentina workers strike 3-8—3-9, 212G2
Trade Act aid to workers set 4-14, 4-26, 348E2-A3
Brit Leyland strikes rptd 4-22, 4-23, 365D1
Some Ford workers get Trade Act aid, total aid rptd 6-7, 431A2
Chrysler plant strike ends 7-11, 570C2
UAW contract talks 7-19, 7-20, 570E1
Brit Leyland strikes, layoffs rptd 8-10, 8-11, 638F1
UAW targets Ford 8-24, rejcts 1st offer 8-31, 669B2
UK Ford strikes end 8-26, 651B3
URW ends Goodyear, Firestone strikes 8-28, 8-29, 647A3
Argentina slowdown rptd 8-30, 650A1
Brit Leyland strikes end 9-10, 712B3
UAW strikes Ford 9-14, 689D2
Italy strke 10-8, 10-12, 10-13, 838D2
UAW ratifies Ford contract 10-12, 789B1
Strikes linked to Sept. Oct indl output, econ indicators 10-15, 10-29, 806G1, 833D1; 11-15, 866D3
Strikes linked to Oct sales 11-3, 885F2
UAW, Chrysler pacts 11-5, 11-7, 847A3
UAW sets GM strike deadline 11-8, 847C3
AMC workers get Trade Act aid 11-17, 855D2
Chrysler pact ratified 11-17, 887G1
GM pact set after 'mini-strike' 11-19, 887C1
UAW ratifies GM pact 12-8, 991E1
UAW wins GM vote in South 12-22, 991D1

Pollution—*See 'Automobile Pollution' under ENVIRONMENT*

Price Issues
Ford price hike in effect 1-5, rescinded 1-15, 280A3
Columbia '75 hikes rptd 1-9, 31B1
GM crash parts monopoly chrgd 3-22, 989E3
Car rental trust suit setld 7-12, 989G2
Eur, Canada hikes set 8-16, 10-12, 988B1
GM hikes '77 prices 8-25, 647A1
Ford urges '77 hikes reassessed 9-8, 665A2
Price boosts rptd 9-21—10-6, 747F2
AMC cuts '77 prices 11-4, offers rebates 11-9, 11-16, 885C1
GM offers rebates 11-10, 885B2
Steel prices hiked 11-24—11-29, 897C2

Safety Issues
Firestone settles on tire ads 2-16, 186A3
Nader analysis rptd, fed laxity re air bags chrgd 2-23, 186E2
Sup Ct backs recall fines 4-19, 331D2
US Dem platform text 6-15, 471F2

1977

Insurance Issues
Adams backs fed no-fault standards 7-15, 7-21, 594E3
Renault Argentina workers strike 10-11—10-14, 981B1

Labor
UK Rubery Owen job actn end agreed 1-4, 44F3
US gas shortage forces plant closings 1-17, 37C2
UK Leyland strike idles 21,000 2-18—2-28, 201C1
UK Leyland strikers return to work 3-21, 256B1
Ford, Chrysler layoffs 4-11—4-15, AMC 6-2, 463C3
Brazil GM unit lays off 400 5-6, 524G2
Mex Feb-Apr layoffs rptd 5-13, 527G3
AMC sued on age bias 5-20, 422A2
GM back-pay award case refused 6-29, 557C3
UK Lucas strike threatens Leyland productn 7-4, 695B1
Ford UK asks 15% pay hike 7-20, 581D1
UK Leyland workers rejct strike 8-29, 694F3
Chrysler plant closing, layoffs set 12-6, 962A1

Payments Issues
SEC sues Uniroyal 1-27, 93C3
GM rpts payoffs 3-31; Chrysler 6-13, Ford 6-15, 503F1-B2
Leyland bribery chrgs stir controversy 5-19—5-25, Ryder retires 7-1, 526C1, D1 ★

Pollution—*See ENVIRONMENT—Automobile Pollution*

Price Issues—*See also 'Statistics' below*
GM, Ford hike prices 1-3, 2-7, 155D3
AMC, GM extend rebates 1-9, 1-11, 39B1
VW hikes US prices 7-29, 585C2
GM hikes '78 models 8-23, cuts Chevette 9-15, 722B3
'78 hikes announced 9-30—10-18, 859G1
Toyota, Honda hike US prices 11-24, 932F3
VW hikes US prices, cites $ drop 12-14, 962D1

Recalls—*See 'Safety Issues' below*

Safety Issues
Adams backs mandatory air bags 3-21, 213B2
Air bags ordered on '82 cars 6-30, 521F3
Ford sets recalls for fan, fuel tank hazards 8-16, 651A3

1978

Insurance Issues
Cong scored re no-fault stand 3-4, 183C1
US diplomatic immunity law revisn signed 9-30, 750D3

Obituaries
Breech, Ernest Robert 7-3, 620E2
Davis, Francis W 4-16, 356E2
Harrah, William 6-30, 540G2
Lear, William Powell 5-14, 440B3

Pollution—*See ENVIRONMENT—Air & Water*

Price Issues—*See also 'Statistics' below*
USSR hikes spare part prices 3-1, 151A3
GM, Ford match import car price hikes 3-24, 4-17, 283B3
VW, Toyota boost US prices 3-31, 4-14, 283F2
GM, Ford hike prices; Strauss backs 4-28, 5-9, Meany scores 5-10, 361C3, E3, 362B2
US small-car prices hiked 5-26—6-6, 428A2
Japan, W Ger, US '78 import hikes rptd 7-17, 8-18, 665C1
GM cuts sporty car prices 9-13, 936A2
Ford, Chrysler hike prices 9-19, 10-2; GM 11-6, 936F1
Toyota, Datsun US prices hiked 10-8, 10-29, 935F3
GM vows price compliance 12-1, 934B3
Ford, Chrysler, GM hike prices, AMC cuts 12-12—12-22, 1004D1

Recalls—*See 'Safety Issues' below*

Safety Issues
'77 recall record rptd 1-1, 67D3
FTC cites Ford re engine defect 1-13, 67F2
Ford assessed $128.5 mln in Pinto crash case 2-6, 185B3

1979

US retail slowdown, gas shortage linked 7-27, 648G3
DR riots re prices 8-1, 575F3
Brazil, car cos set alcohol dvpt plan 8-18, 871C2
Gasohol supported by Carter 8-22, 622A3
9 states, DC lift odd-even rules 9-3–9-10; Calif retains 9-7, 683E1
Rumania eases paymt rule 9-3, 741G3-742A1
BL job cuts linked 9-10, 686F2
W Ger conservatn steps rptd 9-12, 733E2
Brazil tree rptd fuel source 9-15, 1000B2
Dutch plan tax hike 9-18, 730C3
Calif counties drop odd-even gas rationing 9-20–10-2, 850D1
Dutch Shell refinery struck 9-24, 731A2
Belgium to hike gas prices 10-2, 832B3
Norway plans gas tax hike 10-6–10-7, 774C1
House ends gas price controls 10-12, reverses decisn 10-24, 848E3
Calif odd-even gas rules reimposed 10-13, 870C1
Standby gas rationing OKd 10-17, 10-23, Carter signs 11-5, 848A3
Chevron cuts gas price 3¢ 10-26, 804G3
Canada gas price hike sought 11-12, 888E3
Kennedy vs gas tax 12-13, 962A2

Insurance Issues
Carter seeks fed no-fault standards 1-25, 70D2
Wage rate ruling voided by Sup Ct 3-5, 184F3
Nev repeals no-fault 5-29, 466E2-A3
Mich no-fault case refused by Sup Ct 6-11, 478G3

Labor Issues—*See also 'Foreign' above*
Workers idled by Teamsters strike 4-5, 251D2
Trucking stoppage over 4-10, 262C2
UAW conv; Fraser bars US talks role 4-17, 280A1
UAW warns Admin 6-30; Big 3 contract talks begin 7-16, Chrysler gets no-strike pledge 7-18, 598A1
UAW wins Okla City GM organizing vote 7-19, 598G1
UAW stages 'ministrikes' vs GM 8-23–8-27, 698E2
UAW targets GM in contract talks 8-30, 9-10; accord reached 9-14, signed 9-19, 698A1
GM-UAW pact provisn disclosed 9-18; contract rptd ratified, Kahn vs 9-30, 744F1
Ford sets layoffs 9-27, 10-22, 806F1
Ford ratifies UAW contract 10-22, 805G3
Chrysler, UAW reach accord 10-25, 805E2
Layoffs mount 12-4, 963B3

Mergers & Acquisitions
GM sells Frigidaire to White 1-31, 131A3
Renault buys Mack Trucks share 3-19, 3-20, 236E2, 283B1
Uniroyal to sell Eur operatns 4-17, 560F3
Borg-Warner, Firestone drop merger 4-24, 349D3
Mitsubishi acquires Chrysler Australia share 5-14, 368F2
VW-Chrysler merger denied 6-22, 576E2
Swiss firm acquires US parts maker 7-30, 770G2
Ford buys Mazda maker share; GM, Chrysler Japan interests cited 9-7, 745D3
Renault to buy interest in AMC, VW US plant cited 10-12, 784F2, G3
VW-Chrysler Argentina deal rptd set 11-19, 887F2

Obituaries
Bennett, Harry H 1-4, 104F2

Pollution—*See ENVIRONMENT-Air & Water*

Price Issues—*See also 'Statistics' below*
Chrysler, Ford hike prices 1-2, 1-3, 5C1
AMC wipes out price cut 1-2, 5D1
Wage-price compliance vowed 2-6, 128B1
OTA sees auto use cutbacks 3-10, 187D3, F3
GM hikes prices 3-31; Ford, Chrysler, AMC follow suit 305E2
UAW discounts wage-price guides 4-17, 280B1
GM radio trust suit settled 5-14, 441F3-442A1
USSR hikes prices 7-2, 504E2
GM hikes prices 10-1; Ford, Chrysler 10-10, 10-12, 963F3
Rebates reinstituted 11-5–11-16, 963A3

Safety Issues
Tire grading order upheld 2-8, 111D2
OTA sees auto use cutbacks 3-10, 187E3, G3
Radial tire grading ordrd 3-13, 208C3
Chrysler seeks fed aid, links rules cost 7-31, 576B1

1980

Labor & Plant Issues—*See also 'Foreign' above*
Ford sets layoffs, plant closings 1-3, 1-10; GM shuts Cadillac plant 1-10, bars more layoffs 1-14, 35F1-B2
GM to close 2 plants, replacemt sites set 1-31, 287B2
Jan jobless rate rptd up 2-1, 92C2
UAW OKs Chrysler concessns 2-1, 127C2
Productn cuts spur plant closings, layoffs 3-27—4-16, 287D1
'80, '81 jobless aid miscalculated 4-9, 330F1
UAW cancer probe rptd 4-22, 356G3
Plant, personnel retrenchmts continue 4-22—5-16, 383F3
April jobless rate rptd 5-2, 344B3
Fraser elected to Chrysler bd 5-13, 383C3
UAW conv held 6-1—6-6, 457G1
May jobless rate rptd 6-6, 437F2
Ford sees 800 new jobs 6-12, 465D2
Worker layoffs rptd 6-21, 481E3
Cong OKs jobless aid bill 7-2, Carter signs 7-8, 515G1
Carter unveils aid plan; GOP scores 7-8, 505A1-B2
Reagan issues aid plan 7-12, 535G1
Worker US jobless aid OKd 8-14, 647E3
Reagan sees Detroit execs, workers; scores imports, fed regulatns 9-2; Admin disputes 9-3, 664E2
Detroit tax revenue drop rptd 9-8, 743F2
Worker layoffs rptd 9-11, 701G2
AMC strike 9-16, UAW pact reached 9-17, 725B1
Carter cites fed aid 9-18, 698D3
Carter vows jobs aid 10-1, 739G1-C2
UAW gets US jobless aid 10-14, 823G2
Reagan visits Ohio plants 10-15, 780C1
Copper demand rptd down 10-24, 805B3
Special aid re imports rejected 11-5, 870B2
Ford settles job-bias case 11-25, 899B2
Chrysler K-car output rptd cut 12-9, 938F2
UAW urges Reagan to act 12-20, 980E2
UAW OKs Chrysler renegotiatn 12-22, 984D2

Obituaries
Dietrich, Raymond H 3-19, 279B2
Thompson, Joe 4-21, 360F3

Plant Issues—*See 'Labor & Plant Issues' above*

Pollution—*See ENVIRONMENT--Air & Water*

Price Issues—*See also 'Statistics' below*
Domestic prices hiked 1-2—1-11, 14D2
Platinum hits record high 1-17, 30F3
Copper futures trading limited 1-24, 69C1
Toyota, Chrysler, GM, Ford, VW hike prices 2-20—4-7, 288A1
'80 sales rise credited to rebates 4-4, 287B3
Ford hikes prices 5-5, offers rebates 5-9; Chrysler, AMC follow suit 5-13, 5-15, 384C2
Toyota raises prices 2.8% 5-27, 482A1
Ford asks suppliers to cut prices 6-21, 481G3
GM, Honda, AMC, Chrysler hike prices 7-1—7-9, 556D2
Sept producer prices reflect rebates 10-3, 783F1
Chrysler hikes K-car prices 10-15, 883A2
Chrysler rebates, Ford subsidies offered 12-5, 938C2

Safety Issues
Nader libel case declined by Sup Ct 2-19, 131F1
Crash test results rptd 2-28, 225A2
Uniroyal tire recall set 3-7, 348C2
Ford acquitted in Ind Pinto trial, evidence rptd restricted 3-13, 185B3-186D1

1976

Mondale legis record cited 512B3
Nader at air bag hearing 8-3; US bars mandatory requiremt, seeks demonstratn projct; reactn 12-6, 920G3, 921D1
Chrysler recall ordrd 12-10, 942D3

Statistics—*See also other appropriate subheads in this section*
'75, Dec-Mar '76 sales 1-8—4-6, 280E1-E2
Dec, '75 CPI 1-21, 90D1
'75, 4th ¼ profits 2-3—2-24, 215B3
Dec auto debt up 2-6, 169A1
Jan CPI 2-20, 168E2
Mar productn, layoffs 3-7—4-15, 280F2
Jan auto debt up 3-8, 199C3
Feb assemblies 3-16, 199A3
Mar assemblies 4-15, 279F2
1st ¼ profits 4-29, 376B3
'75 top 500 indls ranked 437A1, D1, F2
Apr-Sept new-car sales 5-5—10-6, 747B3
Mar credit 5-6, 375G3
April CPI 5-21, 375E1, F1
April debt up 6-7, 436F2
May CPI 6-22, 453C3
May debt 7-9, 519G1
2d ¼ profits 7-28, 708F3
July CPI 8-20, 635A2
Indl output index revised 9-16, 709E1
3d ¼ profits up 10-28, 866G2
Oct US-made car sales rptd 11-3, 885F2
Oct WPI rptd 11-4, 846C2
AMC rpts 4th ¼, '76 losses 11-10, 885F1
Oct CPI 11-19, 885A1
Nov new-car sales, productn 12-2, 12-3, 987F2
Nov indl output rise, post-strike dvpts linked 12-15, 958G2
Tires—*See RUBBER*

AVEBURY, Lord
Probes Argentine rights abuse 11-5—11-15, 996E2
AVERIN, Igor
Shipping talks fail 12-8, 947G3
AVERINA, Tatyana
Wins Olympic medals 2-5—2-8, 158G3-159A1
AVEROFF-Tossizza, Evangelos
Panagoulis mourners score 5-5, 352B1
AVIAN, Bob
Wins Tony 4-18, 460E2

AVIATION—*See also airline, aircraft company names; country names*
Portugal suspends Mozambique links 1-14, 52D1
China-Cambodia air route set 1-23, 100G3
Algeria bars Morocco flights 2-15, 178C3
S Pacific Forum meets 3-8—3-9, 179C2
Pak makes India overtures 3-27, 278F2
Canada to extend transport tax 5-25, 400E3
UK govt wins natlztn ruling 5-27, 401E3; defers plans 6-7, 407B3
Pak-India flights resume 7-21, 538G1 ★
Uganda suspends forgn flights 7-25, 548F2
Qantas admits price cutting 9-23, 749D3
Canada-Japan accord 10-26, 836B3
UK govt wins natlztn debate limit motion 11-8, 852G3

1977

Air bag, seat belt order operative 10-14, 796G3-797A1
Nader scores NHTSA admin 11-30, 1008D1

Statistics—*See also 'Labor' above*
'76, Dec productn rise 1-3, 38G3
'76, Dec new-car sales 1-6, 38D3
UK '76 imports up 1-8, 45B1
Dec '76 assemblies up 1-17, 93A1
Dec '76 new, used car prices 1-19, 78B1
W Ger '76 output, exports up 1-31, 139C2
Jan production, new-car sales, imports 2-1, 2-3, 155G3-156B1
Dec '76 loans record 2-7, 93F1
UN cites '76 output rise 2-14, 146B1
Jan assemblies drop 2-15, 129G3
EC '76 output up 12% 2-22, 146C2
Jan loans up 3-4, 176A3
Feb productn down 3-15, 194B1
Feb CPI rise 3-18, 215C1
Feb debt rptd up 4-5, 274E1
1st ¼ US imports rank 4-11, 463E3
1st ¼ purchases up 4-20, 300E1
AMC sales down 4-24, 320E1
Fortune ranks '76 top indls 340D1, A2
'76 state-local revenues 5-4, 388F1
Mar debt rise 5-5, 406C3
'60-61, '72-73 family spending compared 5-10, 423F2
Apr assemblies down 5-16, 384B1
'76 top 100 black-owned firms 6-1, 519G3
Feb-May new-car sales, imports up 6-3, 6-6, 463F2
Consumer spending, sales upturn linked 6-7, 518B3
Mex 1st ¼ productn down 6-7, 528A1
May CPI rise 6-22, 482B1
June, July new-car, import sales 7-6, 8-3, 629A2
'76 local tax revenue 7-7, 540A2
June CPI 7-21, 554C2
July productn up 8-15, 628F3
GM, Ford 2d ¼ profits up 8-15, 668F3
July CPI 8-19, 651E1
GM cites 5-yr inflatn, new car prices rise 8-23, 722D3
Aug new-car, import sales 9-6, 722F2, A3
LA June sales 9-6, 722A3
Sept-Nov, '77 new-car, import sales 10-4—12-7, 961E3-962C1
Japan Nov exports 12-16, 985E1
Nov CPI up 12-21, 977E1
AUTRY, Gene
Angel mgt realignmt rptd 12-17, 990B2
AVALANCHES & Landslides
S Africa mine avalanche 9-3, 768G3
AVEROFF-Tossizza, Evangelos
Named Greek defense min 11-28, 925B2
AVERY, Leonard
CIA damages recommended 5-12, 423C1

AVIATION—*See also airline, aircraft company names*
CAB fare actns 1-10—3-29, 324B3-325E1
US deregulatn bill proposed 1-13, 36F2
DOT issues future trends rpt 1-15, 58D3
US '78 budget proposals 1-17, 32F2, 33C1, B2
CAB acts re NY, O, Pa weather-related shortages 1-19, 54F1
'75-76 CAB commuter data rptd 2-2, 324E3
3 airlines indicted for rate-fixing 2-3, 93F2
CAB raises airline baggage liability 2-3, 4-15, 324F3, 325F1
'76 4th ¼ profits rptd 2-8, 301E1
Carter flies in wartime cmnd post 2-11, 110E3
Carter budget revision 2-22, 125B3

1978

GM assessed $2.5 mln in Chevelle crash case 2-9, 185E3
Ford engine flaw notificatn rptd 2-14, 348D1
Ford Pinto crash award cut 3-31, 264F3
Chrysler pollutn-control remedy, recall ordrd 4-20, 349D1
Chevette, Pinto fail tests 5-4, 5-8, 365F3
AMC '76 cars recalled 5-10, 349A1; recall expanded 5-19, 409F2
Ford recalls Pintos, Bobcats 6-9, more deaths rptd 7-6, 7-8, 569B3
Omnis, Horizons rptd unsafe 6-18; Canada, US deny 6-28, 7-7, 569D3
Firestone tire recall sought 7-8, 8-31, suits rptd 9-22, recall set 10-20, 834D3
Ford, NHTSA reach Pinto recall pact 8-21; Nader, Ford trade chrgs 8-22—8-30; sales rptd up 9-14, 719B1
Ford transmissn hazard warned by NHTSA 8-29, 719A2
Nader scores Vega safety 8-30, 722F1
Ford indicted in Ind Pinto deaths 9-13, 718F3-719A1
Carter toughens 55 mph enforcemt 11-8, 875A3

Statistics
'77, Dec US, import sales 1-5, 4C3
Argentina '77 exports down 45% 1-13, 310B2
W Ger '77 sales 1-20, 94A1
Volvo '77 profits, exports 1-27, 93E1
GM, Chrysler '77 4th ¼ profits 2-6, 2-23, 282F2
Jan-Mar US, import sales 2-6, 3-6, 4-5, 283D3
'77 4th ¼ profits 2-7, 282E3
Japan '77, Jan UK sales 2-8, 112F2, G2
Jan productn; US, import sales 2-15, 106F1, B2
'64-78 spending pattern chngs reflected in new CPIs 222D2
Renault '77 US sales cited 3-31, 284B1
Feb indicator index, sales drop linked 4-6, 262E2
Record 1st ¼ loss rptd 4-26, 623G3
1st ¼ '77, '78 profits rptd down 4-27, 403E2
Chrysler 1st ¼ losses rptd 5-3, 349F3
Apr-July US, import sales 5-4—8-4, 664F3
Big 3 on '77 Fortune 500 list 5-8, 325D1-E1
'77 top-paid execs ranked 5-15, 364F3, 365B1
'77 productivity rptd down 6-14, 470B1
Chrysler July sales rptd down 8-3, 623C3
2d ¼ employmt costs 8-30, 680B2
Aug-Nov US, import sales 9-7—12-6, 935D3
Japan Apr-June, Aug exports down 9-8, 9-13, 694C2, D2
Ford rpts Pinto sales up 9-14, 719B1
UK Leyland rpts 1st ½ profits 9-14, 739G2
Chrysler record 3d ¼ loss, divd cut 11-2, 936C1
Output near record in '78 12-21, 1004G1

AUTO Safety, Center for (Washington, D.C.)
On Firestone tire recall agrmt 10-20, 835B1, D1
AUTUMN of the Patriarch, The (Book)
Royalties to fund intl rights group 12-21, 1015C3
AUTUMN Sonata (film)
Released 10-8, 969B3
AVALANCHE (film)
Released 8-28, 969B3
AVCO Cup—*See HOCKEY—Winners*
AVEBURY, Lord
Scores Bolivia vote fraud 7-12, 571F1
AVEDON, Richard
Imposter sentenced 5-5, 380B2
AVERIN, Igor
Defends shipping policy 9-11, 820D3
AVERY, B. Leonard
CIA mail-opening damages upheld 11-9, 940D1
AVERY Federal Savings and Loan Association (Louisville, Ky.)
US bonds tax case refused by Sup Ct 10-30, 832B3
AVERY Federal Savings and Loan Assn. v. Meyers
Case refused by Sup Ct 10-30, 832B3

AVIATION—*See also airline, aircraft company names*
Lockheed strike ends 1-2, 4B2
Nader '73 'bumping' case award cut 1-10, 67F3-68A1
McDonnell Douglas strike 1-13—4-16, 284E2
Carter State of Union Message 1-19, 32B1
Carter budgets airports, traffic facilities 1-23, 47E3
Autogiro patent case review barred 1-23, 65D1
CAB Natl Airlines rule review barred 1-23, 65C2
Blizzards close Chicago, Boston airports 1-26—1-27, 2-5—2-10, 105C2, B3
Nader group scores CAB 1-31, 68A1
Delta damage suit vs US refused review 2-21, 126A2

1979

Nader, Garn clash in Sen hearing 11-20, 1005F3

Statistics (U.S.)
'78, Dec import sales 1-5, 4G3
Chrysler '78 loss, 4th 1/4 profit gain 2-26, 188F1
Mar-May domestic sales down, import sales up 4-4, 5-3, 6-5, 441D2
Apr indl output down truck strike linked 5-16, 362F3
Apr imports up 5-30, 402G3
Chrysler sales drop, inventory buildup 7-5, 7-31, 576A3
2d 1/4 GNP down 7-20, 556C3
Sales slump, June credit data linked 8-6, 622E1
2d 1/4 profits down 8-17, 628G2
June-Aug domestic sales, imports 9-5, 663B3
Aug indl output drop, car productn linked 9-14, 701C1
2d 1/4 paymts gap, forgn car sales linked 9-20, 701G2
Sept domestic sales, imports 10-4, 806G1-B2
2d 1/4 crime rise 10-9, 819B3
Sept indl output 10-16, 784B2
GM, Ford 3d 1/4 profits, sales 10-25, 806B1
3d 1/4 indus loss rptd 10-31, 923B1
Nov, Oct domestic sales, imports 11-6, 12-5, 963E2-A3
Nov indl output 12-14, 964B1
Nov CPI rise 12-21, 984E2
Supreme Court Rulings
Wage rate ruling voided 3-5, 184F3
Calif price law challenge declined 3-5, 185E1
Random checks by police barred 3-27, 263D1
NY gun-in-car law upheld 6-4, 438B3
Mich no-fault case refused 6-11, 478G3
Luggage search warrants backed 6-20, 516C2
Mass license suspensn rule upheld 6-25, 540A2
Motorist 'Miranda rights' case declined 10-9, 784D1
Makers' FTC challenge declined 11-5, 884E2
NJ Methodist munic powers case declined 11-13, 902G1
AUTO-Train Corp.
Fed loan applicatn withdrawn 8-21, Seaboard extends pact 8-24, 726A2
ICC OKs financing plan 12-7, 989A3
AVCO Cup—*See HOCKEY—Winners*
AVERY, Sewell L.
Barr dies 1-16, 104E2

AVIATION—*See also airline, aircraft company names*
SEC suit vs Hughes settled 1-19, 88A2
Carter budget proposals 1-22, 41G2, 45F1, B2
LA sues Krishna re airport solicitatns 1-25, 102F1
Fairchild acquitted on tax chrgs 2-7, 88A1
'78 4th 1/4 profit drop rptd 2-7, 201B3
NY flights cutback, fuel shortage blamed 2-13, 126C2
AF pilot drain, morale loss cited 2-15, 130E2
Airport luggage search case declined by Sup Ct 2-26, 164F3
CAB adopts new charter rules 3-1, 166C3
4 fuel-short airlines cut flights 3-6, 3-7, 162A2

1980

Seatbelt use decline rptd 3-26, 309A3
Chrysler to replace rusted fenders 4-11, 288F1
W Europn cos plan research 4-22, 303B3
Firestone fined 5-13, tire recall set 7-3, 702B2
Reagan hits regulatn 5-15, 383B1
FTC OKs used-car rule 5-16, 702F2
Ford transmissn hazard determined 6-11; denial issued, info suit filed 8-20, 702D1
Carter seeks eased curbs 7-8, 505B1-E1
FTC chrgs GM defect notificatn failure 8-8, 702A3
Reagan scores fed regulatn 9-2, Admin disputes 9-3, 664F2
Carter lauds new cars 10-1, 739C2
Air bag delay defeated by House 10-1, 982E1
EPA Chrysler recall order challenge refused by Sup Ct 12-1, 918E2

Statistics (U.S.)
'79, Dec domestic, import sales 1-4, 14A2
Jan domestic, import sales up 2-5, 127G2
'79, 4th 1/4 profits down 2-7, 222A2
Jan productn drop 2-15, 126B3
Ford '79 profit, 4th 1/4 loss 2-21, 287D3
Feb productn 3-14, 247G3
Mar domestic, import sales drop 4-3, 287F2-A3
1st 1/4 GM profits plunge 4-22; Ford, Chrysler post losses 4-28, 5-7, 384C1
Apr indl output down 5-16, 384C3
May sales plunge 6-5, 481C3
May indl output rptd 6-13, 455F1
June domestic, import sales drop 7-6, 556B2
June indl output up 7-16, 542A1
2d 1/4 GM, Ford, AMC losses 7-24, 7-29, 574A1
Chrysler 2d 1/4 record loss 7-31, 573F2
July domestic, import sales 8-5, 599A1
July indl output up 8-15, 631G1
Aug domestic, import sales drop 9-4, 701E2
'79 crime data 9-24, 971E1-A2
Sept domestic sales drop, imports rise 10-6, 784E2
Jan-June import sales up 10-11, 823F2
Sept indl output up 10-16, 783E1
GM, Chrysler 3d 1/4 losses 10-27, 10-29, 823C1
Ford 3d 1/4 loss 10-28, 823A1
Oct domestic, import sales 11-4, 856G3
AMC 3d 1/4 loss 11-7, 883B2
AUTO-Train Corp.
Financial, svc difficulties detailed 7-31—9-26; DC investors rescue attempt rptd 11-26, 958C2-D3
AVALOS Navarrete, Jose Ramon
Joins Salvadoran junta 1-9, 19G3
AVERBURY, Lord
Observes Guyana electns 12-15, chrgs fraud 12-19, 994A3
AVEROF-Tossizza, Evanghelos
Greek dep premr 5-8, 352D2
AVERY, Fred
Death rptd 9-1, 755B2

AVIATION—*See also airline, aircraft company names*
Washn State of State message 1-15, 484F1
'79 aerospace sales rptd, '80 sales forecast 1-25, 66B1
Carter budget proposals 1-28, 73C1
Smoking risk to nonsmokers rptd 3-26, 318B2
Nader '78 'bumping' award overturned 5-16, 703B2
Hughes flying boat to be dismantled 5-22, 560G2
DEA detainmt procedure backed by Sup Ct 5-27, 453G3-454A1
Eastern sets coast-to-coast svc 6-1, 516B2
Delta jet lands at wrong field 6-21, pilot suspended 6-22, 519C2
Ford electn to Tiger Intl bd rptd 6-25, 600A3

1976

Air France rpts deficit 11-18, 905B3
Greek pilots bar night flights 11-30, 1004C3
Australia probes food standards 12-6, 962A1
Australia fare rise set 12-21, 997B3

Accidents—*See 'Aviation' under ACCIDENTS*

1977

CAB orders bumping signs posted 3-1, rpts '76 data 4-7, 325A1, G1
Domestic local svc down in '75 3-3, 325B1
TWA tour case review barred 3-7, 211C2
CAB conduct rules issued 3-30, 325E1
Babcock sues vs United Tech purchase 4-4, 274B3
FAA sets rules on disabled 4-7, 325G2
CAB suspends license-fee rules 4-8, 325F1
Carter energy plan 4-20, 291D3
1st, 2d ¼ profits rptd 4-28, 7-28, 668C3, D3
Aerospace '76 sales, investor data rptd 340B1, B3
Ozone threat countered 5-6, 369G1
Urban business confidence rptd 5-16, 385C1
CAB 'no-frills' rule review denied 5-16, 419C2
United seniority rule upheld 5-31, 461G2
FCC revokes '76 Telpak order 6-1, OKs pvt rates 6-1, 6-8, 465D1
TWA 'on-time' ads curbed 6-13, 463D2
Eastn to add no-smoking seats 6-14, 593G1
NYC airports shut in blackout 7-13—7-14, 537F2
House OKs Carter energy pkg 8-5, 610C1
Braniff, Tex Intl indicted 8-16, 629C3
FAA rejects crew smoking ban 9-1, 778E3
CAB acts on NY-London budget fares 9-9, 9-15, Carter overrules 9-26, 860D2
Traffic controllers not covered in House mandatory retiremt curb 9-23, 737E2
CAB procedures case review refused 10-3, 760B3
Amer Air stewardesses win pregnancy suit 10-3, 819B1
Aerospace firms struck 10-4—12-31, 1005G1
3d ¼ aerospace profits rptd up 10-27, 11-14, 918C2
Cargo deregulatn bill signed 11-9, 899A3
CAB votes cigar, pipe smoking ban 11-22, 900G1
Test pilot age bias case refused 11-28, 919D2
Port Auth sets noise rule 12-14, Byrne vetoes 12-27, 1006E3
CAB eases charter curbs 12-21, 1006C3

Accidents—*See ACCIDENTS—Aviation*
Concorde—*See 'SST/Concorde Issues' below*
Foreign Developments (including U.S. international news)—*See also other appropriate subheads in this section*
Australia air controllers slowdown 1-7—1-11, 42F2
Air Canada cuts forgn svcs 1-12, 43C2
E Africa Airways folds 2-1, Kenya plans svcs 2-3, 88D1
US-Aeroperu rebate case settlmt rptd 2-18, 324G3
Canada raises domestic fares 2-24, 200E1
US-UK air treaty talks 3-10—3-11, 213A1
PI pilot kills 7 in theft plot 3-31, 312F3
US-Mex pot smuggling rptd 4-8, 332D3
Kenya cuts EAC svcs 4-19, 392G3
Air Canada '76 loss rptd 4-20, 372F3
US-UK treaty talks cited 4-22, 368B2
Australia controllers strike 4-29, 5-7—5-13, 388G3
UK natlizes aircraft industry 4-29, 526G2-B3
SAS strike settled 5-9—5-20, 469G3
Sweden domestic air strike starts 5-13, 469G3
Greek air controllers strike 5-13—5-23, 487E3
Eastn to lease Eur Airbus 5-24, 441B2
Miami airline drops Cuba svc plan 5-25, 456E2
Dassault natlizatn planned, '76 sales cited 6-8, 597D3
US OKs Laker 'Skytrain' svc 6-13, 500F2
US-UK air svc pact set 6-22, 500E1
Air France rpts '76 losses 6-27, 543G2
Albania-Greece air link set, other Albania links cited 7-18, 595F1
US-UK air svc pact signed 7-23, 593C1
Pan Am, TWA, Brit Airways seek lower US-UK fares 7-24, 7-29, 8-1, 593D1
Canada controllers strike 8-7—8-10, 616D1

1978

United Tech to buy Ambac 3-2, 185C1
CAB OKs more 'Super Saver' fares 3-3, 206A3
Kennecott blocks Curtiss-Wright takeover bid 3-13—5-24, 402B1-403D1
UAL maternity rule review refused by Sup Ct 3-20, 205G3
EPA revises emission rules 3-27, 263C2
Pan Am buys Lockheed L-1011 jets 4-4, 264D2
CAB OKs 3% fare hike 4-6, 264E3
Carter asks regulatory reform bill passage 4-11, 259F3
CAB proposes air-fare deregulatn 4-14, 284E1
Black woman qualifies as pilot 4-19, 420C1
1st ¼ '77, '78 profits rptd unchngd 4-27, 403D2
Northwest pilots strike 4-29—8-15, 680E3
Clemente family case vs FAA declined by Sup Ct 5-1, 364C1
LA to get 'Skytrain' 5-5, 2-carrier London svc 6-9, 570D1
McDonnell Douglas plans Data 100 purchase 5-18, 404F1
CAB OKs 1st-class air fare cut 5-19, 366F1
CAB revises 'bumping' penalty 6-1, 570B1
Bede Aircraft OKs FTC trustee plan 6-13, 702B2
Pan Am offers Boston-Amsterdam trial fare 6-15—7-31, 640C3
N Central, Southn airlines merger set 7-13, 684D1
UAL orders Boeing jets 7-14, 569F3
Eastern quits mutual-aid pact 7-14, 681A1
'77-78 2d ¼ profit rise rptd 7-28, 642C3
CAB ends most charter curbs 8-17, 640D2
TXI, Pan Am purchase of Natl stock OKd 8-17, 8-28; Pan Am, Natl set merger 9-7, TXI scores 9-12, 700G3
CAB OKs new air fare rules 8-25, 684E1
Western, Continental merger set 8-31, 684B1
Eastern orders Boeing 757s 8-31, 684F1
CAB OKs Pan Am Houston svc 9-1, 701E1
Fairchild, chrmn indicted 9-8, 808A3
Noise abatemt bill clears House 9-14, stalled in Sen 10-3, 765C3
United Tech seeks Carrier merger 9-18, bid rejctd 9-25, US sues vs takeover 11-13, 896D1
Kennecott victory over Curtiss-Wright voided 9-28, 752D2; cos settle 12-20, 1004G3
Deregulatn compromise clears conf com 10-6, 765D2-C3
Deregulatn clears Cong 10-14, Carter signs 10-24, 873F1
Deregulatn OK by Cong cited 10-15, 784F3
Amer, TWA begin 3-class svc 10-15, 812D2
3d ¼ aerospace profits rptd down 10-30, 919F2
UAL NYS maternity leave case refused by US Sup Ct 11-27, 937A2
TWA, Amer drop 3-class svc 12-6, 12-26, 1007E3
Eastn seeks Natl merger 12-11; Pan Am, TXI bids rptd probed 12-22, 1007B3
Navy, AF pilot drain to commercial jobs rptd 12-13, 984B2
Jet fuel shortage feared 12-14, 983G3-984B1
FAA proposes air-safety rules 12-27, 1006C3-1007B1

Accidents—*See ACCIDENTS—Aviation*
Foreign Developments (including U.S. international news)—*See also other appropriate subheads in this section*
Ethiopia airport rptd closed 1-3, 3E3
Australia to review EC pact 1-26, 69B3
France, W Ger OK B10 constructn 2-6—2-7, 122C1
Viet, Laos reopen aerial shortcut 2-11, 140B1
US-UK fare dispute 2-28, 3-7, agrmt reached 3-17; Braniff London svc starts 3-18, 206E1
Olympic Airways in 1-day strike 3-1, 149G3
Qantas '77 profit rptd 3-6, 225F2
USSR OKs French Airbus landings 3-8, 238D2
France acquires Dassault stock 3-8, 313E1
US, Dutch air svc accord 3-10, 206F2
Greece-Turkey airspace talks 3-10—3-11, 216G2
Japan airport riots 3-26—3-27; opening delayed 3-28, 227E3
Greek-Albania flights set 3-28—3-30, 374C2
NZ state-owned airways merge 4-1, 498D2
USSR, Turkey sign trade pact 4-5, 477C1
Eastern buys Eur Airbuses 4-6, 264B3
Hong Kong-Canton flights to resume 4-9, 259B3
ICAO picks US bad-weather landing system 4-19, 319A2-C3
S Korean jet downed over USSR, 2 die 4-20; USSR frees passengers, detains 2 crewmen 4-23, 301G3
USSR frees S Korean crewmen 4-29, 318D1
Japan to buy US DC-9s 5-3, 341G2
Aer Lingus strike ends 5-5, 393B1
Laker gets LA 'Skytrain' svc OK 5-5, 570F1

1979

NBC expense acct scandal grows 3-28, 334A3
1st 1/4 profits rptd down 4-27, 385D1
Corp execs '78 pay rptd high 5-14, 348A1
United strike ends 5-24, 402A2
Punitive damages vs unions barred by Sup Ct 5-29, 421D3
Allegheny Airlines name chng OKd 6-5, 465G2
Air travel increase seen 6-18, 514B3
1st transcontinental hang-glider flight 7-9–8-16, 656C3
FAA to upgrade small airports 8-7, 726D3
United strike, DC-10 groundings cited 9-8, 726B3
Carter copter technicians transferred, pot use alleged 9-12, 809A2
3d 1/4 profit drop rptd 10-31, 923B1
Midway Airlines begins svc 11-1, 989E1
Me airport bond issue OKd 11-6, 847B1

Accidents—*See ACCIDENTS–Aviation*
Fare Issues—*See also 'Foreign' below*
CAB intrastate fare order case refused by Sup Ct 1-8, 14D3
Pan Am ad deceptn chrgd 1-10, 35F2
$99 cross-country fares, new routes OKd 1-12, 35D2
CAB adopts new charter rules 3-1, 166C3
Domestic air fares rise 5-15, 465E3
United offers NY-LA, other discount plans 5-24, 402C2
Half-fare plan takes effect 7-1, 579G1
CAB grants 9.5% fare hike 8-31, clarifies rule 9-4, 725E3
CAB OKs 3.7% fare hike 10-26, 830A3
CAB ends IATA probe 12-5, 989C1
CAB OKs 3.3% fare hike 12-20, 989B1
Foreign Developments (including U.S. international news)—*See also other appropriate subheads in this section*
Iran controllers strike 1-1, 2D3
Asian oppositn to Australia fare policy rptd 1-5, 6C1
Canada tests back bilingualism 1-5, 18G3
UK airline '72 crash case refused by Sup Ct 1-15, 32D1
Pan Am, TWA warned on London fares 1-23, 87F3
Pan Am ends IATA membership 1-31, 112A1
Canada safety abuses rptd 2-8–2-14, 134B1
Rhodesia air svc cuts rptd 2-18, 2-22, 170F2, D3
Air Canada bilingual svcs scored 2-20, 168D3
Iberia workers stage slowdown 2-20, 192G1
Australia maintenance workers strike rptd 2-21, 188G3-189A1
Iran Air cuts back US, Eur svc; cancels Airbus, Boeing, Concorde contracts 2-25, 144E3
US OKs Libya 747 sales 3-2, 250G1
Aer Lingus struck 3-20, 211F3
UAL orders French-US engines 3-29, 309B1
Egypt, Israel set link 4-2–4-3, 248F3
IATA sets air fare hike 4-3, 324D1
GATT pact signed, tariff cuts seen 4-12, 273B2
US, Canada meet re bargain fares 4-18–4-20, 329E2
Aeroperu struck 5-7, 411F2
Saudi-Air Canada pact Arab boycott clause rptd 5-7, 467F3
US-French air svc pact rptd 5-12, 465A3
'78 world's busiest airports listed 421C1

1980

DEA detainmt procedure curbed by Sup Ct 6-30, 511G1
Crandall named Amer Airlines pres 7-16, 600F2
Deregulatn cited in Dem conv keynote address 8-11, Kennedy speech 8-12, 612A2*, D2, 614B1
Chevron cuts fuel prices 9-18, 786C1
Transport system expansn bill suspended by Cong 10-1, 982D2
LA airport nuisance award case refused by Sup Ct 10-6, 782A3
Itel rpts huge '79 loss 10-16, 784F1
Alaska bond issue OKd 11-4, 847A2
Continental strike ends 12-20, 988E1

Accidents—*See ACCIDENTS--Aviation*
Fare Issues
CAB OKs fare hikes 1-1, 2-26, 4-28, 346G3-347A1
Carter backs global hikes 2-18, CAB OKs 3-12, 3-24, 346D2
Pan Am revives discount coupons 3-10, 346D3
World Air cuts coast-to-coast fares 4-9, 346B3
CAB OKs fare hikes 5-13, Nader group sues 6-18, 515G3-516D1
CAB OKs some global fare hikes 5-15, 516E1
Coast-to-coast fare 'war' 6-6—7-1, 516A2
Air Canada cuts fares 6-12, 461E3
Foreign Developments (including U.S. international news)
El Al rep killed in Turkey 1-2, suspects arrested 2-13, 135G3, 136A1
US cuts Aeroflot flights 1-8, Australia bars flights 1-9, 9D1, E2
Zimbabwe air links restored 1-9, UK jet lands 1-11, 31D3
Brit Airways workers strike 1-10, 59F1
Aeroflot flights boycotted in NY, DC 1-11, 55C2; 1-18, 1-22, 45E1
Australia, Japan favor air fare cuts 1-16, 78A2
Minneapolis-St Paul-London svc set 1-24, 347A2
Aeroflot radar tampering probed 1-31, USSR to end NY flights 2-4, 114F3
Intl deregulatn clears Cong 1-31, 2-4, Carter signs 2-15, 346F1
US-UK air svc pact rptd revised 2-1, 346A2
Spain arrests Aeroflot exec 2-14, 141A3
Eximbank loan offer to Australia's Ansett sparks probe 2-19, 989D1
Turkey, Greece end Aegean dispute 2-22, 2-23, 150F2
US-UK svc expansn agreed 3-5, 172A3
Sydney airport labor unrest rptd 3-11, 191A1
Italy controllers stage job actn 3-12, 194A2
Pan Am Miami-London svc retentn OKd 4-7, 346G2
World Air Boston-London svc OKd 4-10, 346C2
Sweden workers strike 4-25, 355D2
Laker Miami-London svc OKd 5-15, 516D2
Portugal pilots strike 6-23—7-14, 580E1
Australia-US svc increase set 7-30, 617F2
Brit Airways '80 profits rptd 7-31, 578G2

1976

Hijackings & Bombings—*For Palestinian developments, see AVIATION Incidents under MIDDLE EAST*
Canada-US extradition treaty 3-22, 238D3
PI rebels hijack jet 4-7, surrender in Libya 4-14, 260B2
Libya denies hijackers asylum 4-15, hostages return to PI 4-16, 313B3
Gunman killed in Denver 4-19, 383E3
PI jet seized 5-21, gunmen routed 5-23, 383B3
US refuses '70 Sovt hijackers asylum 6-24; Turkey frees 7-10, Italy harbors 7-11, 543G3
Jet bombed at Boston Airport 7-2, 796C3
Libyan hijacker surrenders 7-6, 539G1, A2 ★
'72 Eastn jet hijackers sentncd 7-16, 544C1
GOP platform text 8-18, 604G1, D2
Egypt jet seized, recovered 8-23; Libya denies role 8-24, Egypt accuses 8-25, 629B2-B3
Israel lauds Egypt action 8-24, 629C3
Mondale scores Ford Admin 9-1, 665B3
Qaddafi denies Egypt hijack 9-2, 683A1 ★
Croats seize TWA jet in US 9-10—9-12; questnd on '75 LaGuardia blast 9-12, 685A1
Pak seizes Indian Airlines hijackers 9-11 685C3 ★
Sovt pilot defects to Iran 9-23; extradited 10-25, 854B2
Cuba jet bombed in Carib 10-6, 779A3; **for subsequent developments see 'Exiles' under CUBA**
Cuba renounces US pact 10-15, 779B3, 780A1
W Ger to try Czech hijacker 10-29, 946F1
Pole hijacks plane to Vienna 11-4, 907G1

1977

Canada controllers slowdown 8-18, 634A3
USSR bars French Airbus 9-1, 736D1
UK OKs Laker svc requests 9-14, 9-29; 'Skytrain' begins 9-26, profit rptd 10-24, 860B2
ESA-N Amer satellite plan shelved 9-19, 736B1
Qantas halts S Africa flights 9-20, 762C3
Iceland strike ends 10-25, 984A2
UK bans some SAS flights 10-30, 882G3
Kenya cuts Tanzania air links 11-1, 913E1
UK controllers end strike 11-1, 1013C2
Canada safety enforcemt scored 11-28, 965B3
Canada domestic charters rptd OKd 12-7, 965F3
US, Mex air svc accord 12-19, 1006A3
US svc to Eur expanded, new US 'gateway' cities opened 12-21, 1006B2
US eases charter rules 12-21, 1006C3

Hijackings & Bombings—*See also 'Middle East Incidents' below*
Pak frees Indians 1-5, India protests 1-6, 45F3
US asks Cuba pact talks 2-3, 180C2; 3-5 171B2
Austria jails '76 Polish hijacker 2-15, 425A2
Italian seizes Spain jet 3-14—3-16, 224A3
W Ger sentnc '76 Czech hijacker 3-31, 380B2
Cuba on US pact renewal 4-9, 283E1
Ethiopia attempt foiled 4-26, 328D1
US links 4 natns to terrorists 5-8, 380E1-B2
4 Croats convctd for '76 TWA hijack 5-5, 1 sentncd 5-12, 451G2
Miami airline offices bombed 5-25, 456E2
Sovt hijacks plane to Sweden 5-26, 429B1
US links Cuba pact renewal, full ties 6-3, 455G3
Amin Entebbe raid role rptd 6-8, 487A1
Chilean jet forced to Argentina 6-21, 537C2
Chilean hijacks jet to Peru 7-5, 537B2
Sovt jet hijacked to Finland 7-10—7-12, 537F1-A2
Croat hijackers sentncd 7-20, 7-21, 642A2
Japan jet forced to Bangladesh 9-28; surrendered in Algeria 10-3, 756G2, A3 ★
French jet seized, returned 9-30, 807C3
Japan hijackers boast 10-4; govt acts re future seizures 10-4—10-12, 801E3
Czechs hijack jet to W Ger 10-11, 848F3
Lufthansa jet hijacked 10-13, W Ger rescue raid in Somalia frees 86 10-18, 789A1-790D2, 791C2
Frontier Air jet hijacked 10-20, 807F3
IFALPA strike postponed 10-21, 868C3
W Ger tightens security 10-23—10-24, Algeria flight canceled 11-8, 868C3-E3
Lufthansa hijackers identified 10-25, 10-27, 868E2
Viets hijack jet to Singapore 10-29, 848C2
UN condemns; IFALPA cancels strike 11-3, 852B3
Lufthansa jets threatened 11-5, W Ger airports searched 11-6, 868G2
USSR hijackers sentncd 11-10, 988E2
Canada RCMP plot rptd 11-16, 945C3
Lufthansa bookings fall 11-29, 969D2
Malaysian hijacked jet crashes 12-4, 992B2
Viets jailed 12-15, 991F3
Middle East Incidents
Turk hijacks jet to Leb 3-19, 224F3
US scores Libya, Iraq 4-2, 381E1

1978

Singapore Airlines to buy Boeing jets 5-9, 365E2
UK, Rumania jet deal signed 6-15, 515G2
USSR downs 2 Iran army copters 6-21, 573F3
Greece, Turkey in Aegean talks 7-4—7-6, 624A1
Poland sale to USSR rptd 7-5, 650D2
US blacks urge S African Airways ban 7-6, 632E3
Australia domestic air fares rise 7-13, 555C2
French controllers delay Eur flights 7-14—8-21, 640F2-A3
US, Israel reach pact 7-15, 640B2
N Amers stranded in Amsterdam, London get aid 7-16, CAB waives charter rules 8-4, 640B3
US ends most charter curbs 8-17, 640D2
Cuba rptdly seeks US commercial air svc 8-17, 687G1
US intl policy outlined 8-21, 640E1-B2
Air Canada settles with pilots 8-24, suspends svc in IAM dispute 8-25—9-5, 686B2
Brit Airways orders Boeing 757s, Airbus Industrie scores 8-31, 684G1
Japan purchase, leasing funds set 9-3, 684D1
Pan Am to end svc to Moscow, 9 other Eur cities 9-7, 701F1
Mex controllers strike 9-17—9-18, 10-5, 818G1
Australia policy to cut UK, intl fares 10-11, 793A3
Qantas curbs on Jews probed by Australia 10-18, 836DD1; Syria drops demand 10-20, 900E3
UK Airbus role OKd by France 10-24, 10-25, 902A3
US, W Ger svc accord 10-25, 831E1
Mex air controllers end strike 10-28; ground workers strike 11-2, gain wage hikes 11-4, 904C1
Iran Air strike 11-1, 827E2
Lang on Air Canada-Nordair merger 11-7, 879E3
Delta to end IATA membership 11-11, 894C3
IATA revises structure 11-13, 894A3
Australia proposes cut-rate US fare, eases 2d US carrier oppositn 11-14, 920E2
Canada proposes airport flight tax hike 11-16, 901C1
France-China trade pact signed 12-4, 986A2
United fined re Rhodesia pilot training 12-8, 955G3-956A1
Australia, US set cut-rate fares, 2d US carrier OKd 12-13, 985G1-B2
US to continue Taiwan pacts 12-15, 12-17, 973C2, 975B1, G1, C2
World Ct bars Aegean dispute actn 12-19, 1000E3
UK-Scandinavian pact OKd 12-22, 1017F1

Hijackings & Bombings
Ecuador plane hijacked to Cuba 1-18, 212A3
2 Pak attempts foiled 1-21, 3-2, 212E2
Piedmont attempt foiled 1-28, 212C2
Czech hijacks jet to W Ger 2-6, 212D2
Palestinians seize jet in Cyprus 2-18, 117A1; **for subsequent developments, see MIDDLE EAST—PALESTINIAN Developments—Cyprus Terrorist Attack**
United attempt foiled 3-13, 212A2
Lufthansa '77 hijacker sentenced in Somalia 4-25, 353F3
Terrorist threats cut Lufthansa '77 profits 5-18, 417C2
3 Leb guerrillas slain at Paris airport 5-20, 383E3
Moscow Finnair office shootout 5-24, 416E2
Algeria ousts Japan Red Army hijackers 7-3, 524D3
US OKs USSR detectn equipmt sale 7-6, 10-13, 905C2
Hijacking agrmt signed by 7-natn Bonn summit 7-17, 544F2-C3
'77 papal role in W Ger hijack cited 8-6, 601E2
E Ger hijacks Polish plane to W Berlin 8-30, 894F3
Malaysian '77 crash rpt issued 9-7, 888F1
Finnair jet ransomed, hijacker arrested 9-30—10-1, 927B1
Czech hijacker sentncd in W Ger 10-4, 776E3
Sovt hijacker rptd killed 11-15, 927A1
France sentences Delta '72 hijackers 11-23, 926F3
TWA jet hijacked in Ill, teen-ager surrenders 12-21, 1029F1

1979

US grounds DC-10s indefinitely, bans forgn flights 6-6, 420E2, 421A1
Amer pedals across Eng Channel 6-12, 527F3
Airbus models rptd OKd by France 6-18, 485C2
Spain hikes air fares 7-3, 546D1
Iran industries natlzd 7-5, 503F2
PI flights to China, Taiwan OKd 7-8, 567D1
US lifts DC-10 flight ban 7-13, 538E2
Brit Airways share sales set 7-20, 564F3
IATA natns agree on fare hikes 7-30, 721F3
US to challenge coastal sea claims 8-10, 646F1
Canada '80 bilingual air control set 8-21, Allegheny warns flight cutoffs 8-24, 650D3
Sovt dancer detained in NY airport 8-24, released 8-27, 644G3
Nicaragua cancels commercial flights 8-25–8-26, 689A2
US halts Canada discount fares 8-30, 667D2
IATA gets limited trust immunity 9-10, 725G3-726A1
US-China charter svc pact OKd 9-17, 726D1
Pak Intl Air sues McDonnell Douglas re overchrg 9-25, 886B2
Canada to sell crown cos 9-28, 749G2
S Africa airport toilets integrated 9-30, 774E2
France air traffic disrupted by job disputes 10-2, 11-8, 11-12, 791D2, 872D3
UK-China pact OKd 11-1, 854A2
Mex ground workers strike 11-1, 874E3; setlmt agreed 11-27, 909F2
Spain, France in air traffic talks 11-26–11-27, 952G1

Hijackings & Bombings
Canada '69 suspect arrested 1-14, 37A2
Trapnell sentncd in escape try 2-9, 119C2
Air Rhodesia flight downed by guerrillas 2-12, 136A3
Australia hijack bid foiled 4-4, 266F2
Brussels El Al jet raid thwarted 4-16, 278A3
USSR swaps '70 hijack plotters 4-27, 317C2
Entebbe hijack case declined by US Sup Ct 4-30, 364F3
E Ger '78 hijacker freed in W Berlin 5-28, 430E2
Entebbe victim's body found 5-30, 429E1
Delta jet hijacked to Cuba 6-11, 442A1
Serbian seizes jet in Chicago 6-20, surrenders 6-21, 491E2
Spanish plane hijacked to Switz 8-4, 603F3
Leb Moslems seize Alitalia jet 9-7, surrender in Iran 9-8, 9-7, 677B3
Israel sentncs 2 W Gers for '76 plot 9-11, 677D2
Amer Airlines jet detained in El Paso, Iran flight demanded 11-24, 898E2
Baker urges '1st Brigade' 12-19, 983C1
Mergers & Acquisitions
Gulfstream '78 sale to Amer Jet cited 1-3, 16E1
United Tech-Carrier merger set 3-30, 349E3-350A1
N Central, Southn Airways merger OKd 6-5, 465D3
SEC faults United Tech-Carrier merger 6-25, shareholders back 7-5, 541A3
TXI, Pan Am bids for Natl OKd by CAB 7-10; TXI quits race 7-28, Pan Am buys TXI shares in Natl 8-2, 578D3
Seaboard, Tiger set merger 7-18, 579D1
Continental-Westn merger blocked by CAB 7-21, 579C1
Continental ends Westn bid 8-7, 830E1
Alaska Airlines stock ploy blocked by CAB 8-28, judge backs 10-4, 830F1
TXI eyes TWA merger 9-13; Trans World dirs vs 9-19, TXI undaunted 9-26, 830C1
Eastern-Natl link rejected by CAB 9-27; Pan Am-Natl merger OKd 10-25, Carter approval sought 10-29, 830A1
Beech Aircraft, Raytheon merger set 10-2, 785A1
Justice Dept asks Seaboard-Tiger merger ban 10-2, Seaboard shareholders OK rptd 10-19, 830B2
Wien Air stock sale to HFC rptd, Alaska Air sues 11-20; CAB rejcts Alaska NW sale 12-20, 989F1

1980

US bars Iraq commercial jet sale 8-29, 662C3
Canada air controllers stage job actns 9-5, 9-28, disciplined 9-26, 9-30, 808B2
US-China pact signed 9-17, 707A1, B1
Australia OKs Airbus deal 9-29, 748B[illegible]

Hijackings & Bombings
PR bomb plot foiled 1-7, 3 arrested 1-25, 94B1
NYC Aeroflot office bombed 1-13, 55A2
Delta jets hijacked to Cuba 1-25, 7-22, Amer flight in LA 4-9, 617A3
'71 hijack money believed found 2-10—2-13, 136E2
Paris Aeroflot office bombed 2-24, 149F3; French arrest 11 7-1, 522A2
Aeroflot Frankfurt office bomb found 3-7, 236B1
Rome Turkish Airlines office bombed 3-10, 316B2
Iranair office in Leb bombed 4-16, 300B2
Orly blast wounds 7 6-12, 463F1
Venice summit condemns 6-22, 473D1
'70 Delta hijacker jailed in US 6-30, 514D2
Argentina jet seized, finance min extortn fails 6-30—7-1, 519F2
PR navigatn statns bombed, air traffic rerouted 7-14, 559F3
Cuban refugees hijack Air Fla jets to Havana, '80 total rptd 8-10, 8-13, 617A2
Cuban refugees hijack more jets to Havana, 2 attempts foiled 8-14—8-17; FAA tightens security 8-15, 631B3
Eastn hijack attempt foiled 8-18, 667F1-A3
Cuban refugees continue US hijack attempts 8-26—9-17; Havana issues strong warning 9-16, returns 2 9-18, 704B1-B2
Cuban refugees storm Braniff jet in Lima 8-29, surrender 8-30, 672B2
Air France jet blown up in Guadeloupe 9-17, 769G1
Venez acquits '76 Cuba jet bombing suspects 9-26, 794G2
London Turkish Airlines office bombed 10-12, 794G1*
Cuba to free US prisoners 10-13, 789A1
Moslem extremists hijack Turkish jet 10-13, commandos overcome 10-14, 794A2
4 US hijackers freed by Cuba, arrested in Miami 10-27, 828D3
Uruguayan forces plane to Argentina 11-12, surrenders 11-13, 888C3
Venez jet hijacked 12-5, 30 arrested 12-6, 968D3
Mergers & Acquisitions
Pan Am-Natl merger completed 1-7, Pan Am Miami-London svc retentn OKd 4-7, 346F2
Seaboard-Tiger merger OKd by CAB 5-8, 516F1-A2
Fairchild, VSI to merge 8-26, 746C1
Pneumo, LTV to merge 8-28, 746B1

1976

Military Issues—*See 'Aircraft' under ARMAMENTS*

Obituaries
Hughes, Howard 4-5, 335B3
Laddon, I M 1-14, 80E3
Lippisch, Alexander 2-11, 160E3
Loening, Grover 2-29, 192E3
Reynolds, Milton 1-23, 80F3

Political Payments Issues—*See also BOEING, LOCKHEED, NORTHROP*
Dutch Dassault bribe case opens 2-10, 141D2; acquittal 2-25, 158E2
United Technologies, Rockwell rpt forgn paymts 4-9, 362C2, E2
Dutch Dassault bribe probe widens 4-13, 322B2
SEC lists corp paymts 5-12, 725G3, 726A1
Butler settles SEC suit 6-7, 986D2
Nixon bid for Grumman donatn chrgd 9-13; denied 9-15, 9-16, 979G1-E3
Forgn paymts studies issued 12-18, 12-20, 985G1, D2
CAB accuses Flying Tiger 12-29, 986D1

SST Issues
US holds Concorde hearing, EPA vs landing 1-5, 5C2
Rpt WMO urges limited fleet 1-17, 104A3
UK-Bahrain, Paris-Rio flights begin; London airport protest 1-21, 86A2
US OKs 16-mo test 2-4, oppositn continues 2-4—2-5, 94C2-E3
Brit Aircraft rpts layoffs 2-10, 174F1
Kennedy service barred 3-11, 378A3
CAB OKs Concorde fare hike 4-30, 378F3
French pres in 1st US landing 5-17, 372F1
US test decisn upheld 5-19, 5-22, 378G2
Concorde runs to US begin 5-24, 378C2, A3
Australia OKs '77 flights 5-28, 400C1
Australia environmtlists sue 7-20, 537A2
UK Concorde 1st ¼ losses rptd 8-26, 675B3
US Sup Ct bars landing rule 11-15, 882B2

U.S. Developments (domestic)—*See also 'Political Payments' and 'SST' above*
Natl Airlines strike ends 1-4, 5E1
Ford State of Union message 1-19, 37D3, 39C2
US budget proposals 1-21, 66C1
'75 4th ¼ airlines aerospace profits rptd 2-3, 215A3, B3
Ford urges regulatory reform 2-5, 110A1
Natl Airlines 'no strike' pact 2-19, 153A3
Sup Ct bars review of Westn Air San Diego-Denver request 3-8, 219B2
Sup Ct bars Westn Air ruling review 3-8, 219B2
CAB drops chrg vs Callaway 3-31, 745A2
Cockpit smoking ban sought 4-20, 308G1
1st ¼ profit loss rptd 4-29, 376B3
CAB OKs 2% fare hike 4-30, 378D3
'75 top 500 indls ranked 437D2
Pan Am sets flight marks 5-2, 5-3, 912F3
Palmer sets flight mark 5-19, 368F3
Sup Ct backs Nader on airline bumping 6-7, 435A2
Dem platform text 6-15, 474B2
Ct voids '75 route swap 6-30, CAB overrules 11-19, 992E2
'76-80 authorizatn signed 7-12, 567A1
2d ¼ profits rptd 7-28, 708F3
Cong clears airport funds 8-4, 646C2; signed 8-14, 982F1

1977

Leb hijacker overpowered in Kuwait 6-6, 497C3; freed 8-29, 736B2
Leb hijacks UK jet to Qatar 6-29, 535B2
PFLP hijacks Kuwait plane 7-8, frees hostages 7-9; surrenders in Syria, PLO denies role 7-10, 535B1
PLO denies W Ger hijack role 10-13; Arab rescue aid efforts rptd 10-20, 789E1, G2, 790G1, C2

Military Issues—*See ARMAMENTS—Aircraft*

Obituaries
Elder, Ruth 10-9, 872F1
Hobbs, Leonard 11-1, 952E2
Ilyushin, Sergei 2-9, 164B3
Magruder, William 9-10, 788F1
Pawley, William 1-7, 84D3
Solomon, Samuel 12-8, 1024C3

Payments Issues
Boeing tops '70-76 paymts list 1-21, 79F1
Japan Lockheed probe ends, 2 indicted 1-21; trials open 1-27, 1-31, 83B2
2 Italy ex-mins indicted 1-29, 116B3
Dynalectron rpts paymts 2-4, 94F1
TWA rpts paymts, rebates 2-8, 94A2
Amer Airlines settles SEC chrgs 2-9, 111F2
Japan Boeing kickback chrgd 2-14, probed 2-15, 136D1
Saudi US sales comms cited 2-22, 124A3
Italy trial set 3-10, 284B1
Aero Systems paymts rptd 3-11, 233E3
Lockheed rpts grand jury, IRS probes 4-8, 502F3
Lockheed overseas sales rptd unharmed 4-28, 502E3
Amer Airlines, Braniff paymts rptd 5-17, 503A1, B1
Lockheed rpts '70-75 total to SEC 5-26, 502E2-D3
W Ger clears Lockheed 6-22, 602E1

SST/Concorde Issues
BAC layoffs set, sales lag cited 2-1, 99D1
Braniff Dallas-DC-Eur pact rptd 2-11, 213B1
Carter backs Concorde, suit vs Port Authority delayed 2-16, 131D2
France warns US 3-4—3-8; Port Auth delays decisn 3-7; reactn 3-7, 3-9, 212D2
Carter call-in topic 3-5, 171D1, B3
Carter sees Carey 3-7, backs tests 3-9, 212C3, E3
UK prime min sees Carter 3-10—3-11, 213A1
US mfrs back Concorde 3-10, 3-11, 213E1
US House OKs research authorizatn, NY reps lead oppositn 3-17, 213G1, B2
Concorde noise data rptd 4-9—4-25, 368E2
NY protests 4-11, 4-17, 368D2
Giscard on NY landing rights 5-9, 358E2
Judge lifts NY ban; reactn 5-11, 368B1-D2
US House anti-Concorde move fails 6-8, 463B2
Appeals ct backs JFK Concorde ban 6-14, 463D1
Air France rpts '76 losses 6-27, 543G2
NY Concorde ban overturned; reactn 8-17, 627D1-B2
USSR bars Siberia refueling 9-2, 736F1
US, UK rpts score Concorde 9-16, 9-21, 738F3, 739A1
US expanded landing rights proposed; reactn 9-23, 738A2-C3
NY Concorde ruling upheld 9-29, 738D3
NY landing delay rejected 10-6, Marshall issues stay 10-7, Sup Ct denies 10-17, 797A3
NY Port Auth offers noise optns 10-8, draws protests 10-9, 10-17, 819E3
NY operatns begin, noise data cited 10-19, 10-20, 819A3
London-Bahrain-Singapore pact rptd 10-24, 905D3
USSR TU-144 starts passenger svc 11-1; 831F3
NY anti-Concorde protests 11-20, 11-22, 900E1
NY passenger svc begins 11-22, 900D1
Port Auth sets noise rule 12-14, Byrne vetoes 12-27, 1006E3

1978

Military Issues—*See ARMAMENTS—Aircraft*

Obituaries
Blair Jr, Charles F 9-2, 777F3
Breech, Ernest Robert 7-3, 620E2
Lear, William Powell 5-14, 440B3
Messerschmitt, Willy 9-15, 778E1
Nobile, Umberto 7-29, 620C3
Prescott, Robert 3-3, 252C3
Schwendler, William 1-14, 96E2

Payments Issues
Lockheed linked to W Ger scandal 1-13—1-17, 74C2
6 more Japanese tied to Lockheed bribe 1-30, 72C3
SEC sues Page Airways 4-13, 449G1-C2
Malaysian sentencd for Northrop kickback 6-6, 439E3
Italy pres resigns re Lockheed 6-15, 516F2
SEC chrgs Boeing, case setld 7-28, 642F3-643C1
Boeing, Lockheed, McDonnell settle FTC chrgs 8-18, 643C1
Lockheed ex-offcl cites Nakasone in Japan ct depositn; Nakasone denies 10-26, 838E3-839A1
McDonnell Douglas chrgd 12-14, case setld 12-15, 982D2

SST/Concorde Issue
E Coast booms linked to Concorde 3-15, 187G1
Sovt TU-144s rptd grounded after crash 10-27, 1032B1

1979

Murdoch gains Ansett Transport control 12-18, 966E3
Carter OKs Pan Am-Natl merger 12-22, 989C1

Military Issues—*See ARMAMENTS—Aircraft*

Obituaries
Conrad, Max 4-3, 356C3
Draper, Christopher 1-16, 104G2
Focke, Heinrich 2-25, 176G2
Frantz, Joseph 9-12, 756E2
Reitsch, Hanna 8-30, 671E3
Wallis, Barnes Neville 11-12, 932G3

Payments Issues
SEC sues Grumman, Gulfstream; case settled 1-4, 16D1-A2
Grumman Japan scandal probed 1-9, Nissho exec kills self 2-1, 98E2
Grumman discloses forgn paymts, denies Japan bribes 2-8, 305G2-D3
US drops Japan probe of 2 Lockheed ex-aides 2-15, 306C1
Lockheed discloses overseas paymts 2-16, 306F1-A2
6 Italians convicted re Lockheed 3-1, 155B2
4 indicted in Japan Nissho scandal 4-5, 5-15, 389D2
Textron pleads guilty to currency violatns 7-10, overseas payoffs admitted 7-26; Proxmire asks study 10-31, 923B2-B3
Italian ct statemt re Lockheed rptd 8-6, 603B1
Turkey chrgs Lockheed cover-up 9-20, 775F1
US indicts McDonnell Douglas, execs; Pak Intl Air suit cited 11-9, 886F1

Safety Issues
NYC near-collisn 2-11, FAA updates radar improvemt 3-12 206G1, C2; rpt issued 4-9, 412C2
FAA air-safety crackdown planned 3-16, 206C1
US grounds DC-10s for inspectn 5-29, engine mounting flaws rptd 5-30–5-31, 411E3-412E1
US grounds DC-10s indefinitely, travel chaos rptd 6-6, 420E2, F3
DC-10 legal barriers, engineering flaws discounted 7-10; flight ban lifted 7-13, 528E2
Chicago DC-10 crash rpt issued by FAA 7-10, findings disputed 7-12, 538E3-539E1
Munson death blamed on pilot error 9-16, 1002F3
DC-9 inspectns ordered 9-19, order expanded 10-9, 830C2
FAA grounds Prinair 10-25, 830F2
FAA seeks Braniff fine 11-6, 868B2
Amer, Continental pay fines on DC-10 11-16, 988D3
Controllers score computers 11-20, 988F3-989A1
Air safety panel formed 12-19, 988E3
Chicago DC-10 crash rpt issued by Safety Bd 12-21, 988F2

SST and Concorde Issue
Concorde Dallas-DC svc begins 1-12, 35A3
UK cancels British Airways Concorde debt 2-22, 154B2
Iran Air cancels Concorde deal 2-25, 144E3
Concorde program ended, unsold jets allocated 9-21, 721E2

1980

Continental-Westn bid renewed 9-22, 746E2
W Ger aerospace merger set 11-29—11-30, 925E2
Westn sought by UNC Resources 12-24, 985C1

Military Issues—*See ARMAMENTS--Aircraft*

Obituaries
Cochran, Jacqueline 8-8, 676B1
McDonnell Jr, James S 8-22, 676C2
O'Neill, Ralph A 10-23, 876A3
Patterson, William A 6-13, 528C3
Petrov, Boris N (rptd) 8-26, 676E2
Vodopyanov, Mikhail V (rptd) 8-14, 676E3

Payments Issues
3 get suspended sentnc in Japan Nissho case 7-24, 605C2

Safety Issues
DC-10 safety system chngs sought 1-12; no pylon defects found 1-23, 53B2-G2
McDonnell Douglas settles FAA fine 1-23, 53E2
Commuter pilot rules stiffened 2-6, 347E1
Airline ozone measures rptd 2-12, 159A1
'79 accident rate rise rptd 2-20, 347D1
San Diego air control zone set 3-22, 347A1
DC-10 probe ends, pylon chng ordered 5-16, 518C3
Amer Airlines ruled immune from DC-10 crash damages 5-23, 518F3
FAA claims computer data reliable 6-30, 666F3
Jet engine inspectns ordered by FAA 7-16, 667B1

SST/Concorde Issue
Braniff drops Dallas-DC Concorde svc 4-14, 346F3

1976

CAB OKs domestic fare hike 8-10, 992A3
GOP platform text 8-18, 607E1, F1
Dole legis record cited 614F2
Canada settles Northrop suit 9-7, 710G1-B2
Corp '74, '75 zero tax paymt rptd; effective tax rate cited 10-2, 10-14, 847F1, G1, D2
Deregulatn legis not cleared 10-2, 884F1
Pregnancy bias rulings rptd 10-14, 943A3
Noise rule extended to old planes 10-21, 849C1
3d ¼ profits rptd up 10-28, 866G2
US sets antinoise timetable 11-18, 868B3
Braniff job bias settlemt OKd 11-23, 943G2

U.S. Developments (foreign)—*See also 'Plane Hijackings', 'Political Payments' and 'SST' above*
Swiss, Delta pact rptd ended 1-9, 31G1
Canada Lockheed buy delayed 4-1, 250D2
Eximbank Australia loan rptd 4-13, 264E3
CAB OKs N Atlantic fare hikes 4-30, 378E3
US indicts Aeroflot 7-27, 908B1
French, US cos in jet accord 8-12, 588D3
Br Airways orders 12 Lockheed jets 8-18, 675D3
US extends noise rule to old planes 10-21, 849C1
Forgn airlines exempted from US noise rules 11-18, 868G3
Ford rejcts CAB transatlantic plan 12-28, 992A2

AVIATION Consumer Action Project
Testifies vs Concorde 1-5, 5C3
Seeks cockpit smoking ban 4-20, 308A2
AVILOV, Nikolai
Wins Olympic medal 7-30, 576C1
AVIONS Marcel Dassault-Breguet Aviation
Botterman acquittal urged 2-12, 141D2; acquitted 2-25, 158E2
Dutch bribe probe widens 4-13, 322B2
AVIS Inc.
FTC trust suit setld 7-12, 989A3
AVIS Rent-a-Car System Inc.—*See AVIS Inc.*
AVNERI, Shlomo
In Israel forgn min post 2-15, 125G2
Gets lie-detector test 759C3
AWACS (Airborne Warning & Control System)—*See 'Aircraft' under ARMAMENTS*
AWALEH, Aden Robleh
Arrest rptd 1-14, 85G3
AWARDS—*See subjects; also AWARDS & Honors under Ford*
AWOONOR, Kofi
Ghana confirms arrest 2-24, 208G2
Rptd freed 10-24, 858G1
AXEN, Hermann
E Ger Politburo enlarged 5-22, 381E2
AYLWIN, Patricio
Home bombed 2-26; scores rightists 3-3, 310C3
AYOROA Ayoroa, Gen. Juan
Bolivia expels 2-23; denies chrgs 2-25, 238D1
AYOROA Montano, Col. Miguel (ret.)
Deported to Paraguay 2-4, 237D3
AYOUBI, Mahmoud al-
Egypt talks called off 5-19, 370A2
AYUBI, Mahmoud al-
In Egyptian talks 6-23—6-24, 449D1
Quits as Syrian premier 8-1, 594F2
AZBEL, Mark
Exit visa denied 2-16, 421E2
AZORES (Portuguese Islands)
Cuba defies refueling ban 1-10—1-15; Portugal, US protest 1-13, 1-19, 53C2
Poll rejects autonomy 1-26, 143E2
FLA disruptive activities rptd 1-28, 2-10, 143G2-A3
PPD wins local electns 6-27; Eanes warns secessionists 6-28, 482F3
Venez air transport crash 9-4, 696F3
Assemb opens 9-4; US talks on Lajes base planned 9-5, 812F1
Portugal blocks US trip 10-23, 812B2
AZZAWI, Ahmed al-
Killed 7-10, 679A3

1977

AVIATION Consumer Action Project
Eastn to add no-smoking seats 6-14, 593A2
FAA rejcts crew smoking ban 9-1, 778F3
AVIATION Week & Space Technology (magazine)
Rpts Israel arms sale to Chile 1-8, 28D3
AVIONS Marcel Dassault-Breguet Aviation
Dassault cleared 4-21; natlizatn planned, '76 sales cited 6-8, 597D3-598B1
AVIS Inc.
Norton Simon buys 47% 6-27, 519A2
AVNERI, Uri
In Israel peace group 10E2
Asks contd Ofer probe 1-9, 21F1
AVON Books—*See HEARST Corp.*
AVONDALE Shipyards Inc.—*See OGDEN Corp.*
AWACS (Airborne Warning & Control System)—*See ARMAMENTS—Aircraft*
AWARDS—*See subjects; also AWARDS & Honors under CARTER*
AXELROD, Ernst
Arrested 9-21, 753B1
AXELSON, Kenneth S.
Named Treas dep secy 1-18, 52D3
Withdraws nomination 3-9, 191A2
AYER, Mary
Sets 400-mtr hurdles mark 6-9—6-11, 602C3
AYRES, William
Cited in Park indictmt 9-6, 688D1
AZAR, Shmuel (executed 1955)
Body returned to Israel 4-19, 297A2
AZBEL, Mark
Arrives Vienna 7-6, 512E3
AZEREDO da Silveira, Antonio
US A-talks fail 3-2, 190A1
Cancels Venez visit 4-1, 547B3
Sees Todman 5-12—5-14, 414G1
Greets Mrs Carter 6-6; scores US, press on rights issue 6-12, 455E1, B2
Scores OAS rights emphasis 6-15, 494B2
AZEREDO da Silveira, Antonio
Sees Vance, A-talks rptd fruitless 11-22, 912C3
AZIMI, Gen. Riza
Iran war min 8-7, 618F1
AZIZ, Abdul
Indicted 4-7, 396D1
AZORE Islands (Portuguese territory)
Portuguese min's home bombed 9-11, 887C1
AZPURUA Marturet, Lorenzo
Venez planning chief 1-7, 23F2

1978

AVIATION Consumer Action Project
CAB scored 1-31, 68A1
AVIATION Week and Space Technology (magazine)
Rpts Sovt success vs cruise missile 10-23, 877C2
AVICE, Edwige
Wins French legis seat 10-1, 815B2
AVILDSEN, John G.
Slow Dancing released 11-8, 970B3
AVINO, Antonio
Turin trial halted 3-10, 191F1
AVIS Inc.—*See under NORTON Simon*
AVIS Rent A Car System Inc. v. Chicago
Case refused by Sup Ct 10-30, 832F2
AVNI, Ran
Halloween Bandit opens 12-18, 1031A2
AVON Products, Inc.
Mitchell to leave bank bd 3-7, 163C1; Stevens 3-21, 205D1
'79 women's tennis sponsorship rptd 5-17, 419D2
AWACS (Airborne Warning & Control System)—*See ARMAMENTS—Aircraft*
AWAR, Salem
Executed 6-26, 499B1
AWARDS & Honors—*See under CARTER; specific subjects*
AWE, James
FBI rptd destroying old files 3-15, 186D3
AXEN, Hermann
Sees W Ger rep re ties 1-28—1-30, 61E3
AYALEW, Mandefro
Scores US re Ogaden 1-20, 43G2
Resigns, asks US residence 1-29, 137B2
AYLER, Ethel
Nevis Mt Dew opens 12-7, 1031E2
AZCUE Lopez, Eusebio
On Oswald Cuba emb visit 8-2, 831D1
AZERBAIJAN Soviet Socialist Republic—*See USSR—Republics*
AZHARI, Gen. Gholam Riza (Iranian premier)
Heads Iran mil govt 11-6, 857E2
Names 8 civilns to Cabt 11-16, 893G2
Vows to restore order 11-18, 893A3
Blames Tudeh for unrest 12-3, 929E1
Ties 'atheists, saboteurs' not Moslems to strife 12-5, 929G1
Warns strikers of pay loss 12-6, 929C1
Lifts march ban 12-8, 953E2
AZIZ, Tarek
In Arab summit delegatn to Cairo 11-4, 859D2
AZMOUN, Manuchehr
Named Iran exec affairs min 8-27, 668B1
Loses Iran Cabt post 10-30, 827F3
AZZOLINI, Lauro
Arrested 10-1, 817D1

1979

AVIATION Club, National (Washington, D.C.)
Pan Am, TWA warned on London fares 1-23, 87F3*
FAA air-safety crackdown planned 3-16, 206D1
AVON Products Inc.
Tiffany OKs takeover bid 1-18, 89E1
Navratilova wins tennis title 3-25, 391B2
AWACS (Airborne Warning & Control System)—*See ARMAMENTS-Aircraft*
AWOLOWO, Chief Obafemi
Loses Nigeria pres electn 8-11, 636F2
Shagari electn challenge defeated 9-26, 753E3
AWTREY, Dennis
Traded to Sonics 1-17, 526D2
AYALA, Benny
In World Series 10-10—10-17, 816D2
AYALA, Jose
Visits Nicaragua for Andean Group 6-11, 446E3
AYALA, Mike (El Cyclone)
Lopez KOs 6-17, 839A1
AYCKBOURN, Alan
Bedroom Farce opens 3-29, 711D1
AYDAN, Aynur
Gunes resigns 10-5, 795D3
AYDINOGLU, Ismail Hakki
Rpts hard currency use 7-31, 637D1
AYESH, Mohammed
Sentenced 8-7, executed 8-8, 602F2
AYKROYD, Dan
1941 released 12-14, 1008B1
AYLER, Ethel
Plays From Africa opens 1-14, 292D2
AYOROA, Col. Miguel
Retains Bolivia Cabt post 11-19, 907A2
AYRES, Richard
Vs EPA coal-use rule 5-25, 404A1
AZADI, Ali
Named Iran agri min 2-19, 125D1
AZENBERG, Emanuel
They're Playing Our Song opens 2-11, 292E3
Whose Life opens 4-17, 712E3
AZERBAIJAN Soviet Socialist Republic—*See USSR-Republics*
AZEVEDO, Mario
Heads Portugal Pub Works Min 7-30, 603E3
AZHARI, Gen. Gholam Riza
Replaced as Iran mil staff chief 1-4, 2B3; premier 1-6, 11E2
Iran urges assassinatn 5-13, 357G1
AZIZ, Ibrahim Abdul
Slain 12-15, 980F1
AZMOUN, Manuchehr
Executed 4-9, 276B3
AZZAM, Mohammed
Replaces Mohsen in PLO posts 8-3, 625E2

1980

AVIATION Consumer Action Project
Sues CAB on domestic fare hike OK 6-18, 516C1
AVILDSEN, John G.
Formula released 12-19, 1003A2
AVINS, Alfred
Del Law Schl libel case decined by Sup Ct 11-10, 868B3
AVINS v. White
Case declined by Sup Ct 11-10, 868B3
AVIONS Marcel Dassault-Breguet Aviation
W Europn fighter planned 4-14, 303F1
AVNET, Jon
Coast to Coast released 10-3, 836E2
AWACS (Airborne Warning & Control System)—*See ARMAMENTS--Aircraft*
AWAKENING, The (film)
Released 10-31, 972C3
AWFI, Maj. Fawzi al-
Security forces resignatn cited 1-1, 22E1
AXWORTHY, Lloyd
Canada employmt, immigratn min 3-3, 171C2
Hosts Liberal conv 7-4—7-6, asks equality for West 7-4, 543D2
On '81 immigratn data 10-31, 871E2
AYAT, Hassan
Tied to plot vs Bani-Sadr 6-19, 464F2
AYDELOTT, William
Return of the Secaucus 7 released 9-14, 836E3
AYERS, William
Dohrn surrenders 12-3, 928B1
AYKROYD, Dan
Blues Brothers released 6-20, 675A2
AYLING, Denys
Wins Oscar 4-14, 296A2
AZAR, Abraham el-
Killed 1-2, suspects arrested 2-13, 136A1
AZCUY, Isaac
Wins Olympic medal 7-28, 623D1
AZENBERG, Emanuel
Children of a Lesser God opens 3-30, 392E2
I Ought to be in Pictures opens 4-3, 392D3
Division St opens 10-8, 892B3
AZIZ, Tareq
Escapes assassinatn 4-1, 261C1
Sets Iraq-Iran peace terms 9-25, 718A3
Seeks Sovt arms 11-11—11-12, 879G2
AZIZ al-Turki, Abdul
Named to Aramco bd 7-8, 662F1
AZOFF, Irving
Urban Cowboy released 6-11, 675F3
AZORE Islands (Portuguese territory)
Quake kills 52 1-1, 24E2
AZZOLINI, Lauro
Accused re Moro affair 1-2, 20G2

B

1976

B-Plane Series—*See 'Aircraft' under ARMAMENTS*
BA, Andibrahima
Guinea internal trade min 12-11, 1005A2
BA, Mamadou
Guinea communicatns min 12-11, 1005G1
BAADER, Andreas
Trial testimony 1-13, 1-27, 77G2
Meinhof found hanged 5-9, trial adjourned 5-13, 383G1
Cohorts escape 7-7, 593C3

1977

B-Plane Series—*See ARMAMENTS—Aircraft*
BAADER, Andreas
Trial delayed 1-20, adjourned re bugging 3-17, 260B1
Sweden arrests terrorists 4-1, deports 2 4-3, 428E3
Buback killed 4-7, Baader-Meinhof linked 4-9, 4-13, 286B2, F2
Sentenced 4-28, 352F1
Hunger strike ends 9-2, Schleyer kidnapers ask release 9-6, 9-8, 695B2
Atty arrested 9-30, extradited 11-16, 968F2
Hijacked jet freed 10-18, 789B1
Kills self 10-18, reactn 10-18—10-20, 789C1, 790D2-791E1
Schleyer slain 10-18, 791F1
State issues suicide rpt 10-26, buried 10-27, 868D1

1978

B-15 (Calcium Pangamate)—*See FOOD*
B-Plane Series—*See ARMAMENTS—Aircraft, AVIATION*
BAADER, Andreas
Atty smuggled guns into prison 1-12, 21G3
Experts confirm suicide 1-23, 115A1
Parlt com rpt affirms suicide 2-23, 152A2
Stuttgart prosecutor's office affirms suicide 5-8, 354D1
Eur rights ct rejcts jail abuse chrgs 7-19, 651A3
Proll arrested in UK 9-15, 725A2
Memorial rally 10-18, 885G1

1979

B-PLANE Series—*See ARMAMENTS-Aircraft*
BA, Le Quang
Arrested 8-2, 604E1

1980

B-Plane Series—*See ARMAMENTS--Aircraft*

1976

BABASHOFF, Jack
Wins Olympic medal 7-25, 575E2
BABASHOFF, Shirley
Wins Olympic medals 7-18—7-25, 563A1, 575B3, C3
BABCOCK, Tim M.
Sentence upheld 2-10, 144G3
Hammer pleads guilty again 3-4, 180F3
Jail term set aside 6-4, 442B2
BABCOCK & Wilcox Co.
Ct curbs plutonium use 5-26, 398B2
BABITT, Judge Roy
OKs Abercrombie bankruptcy petitn 8-9, 984D3
BABIUCH, Edward
On Polish State Cncl 3-25, 268C2
BACAILLE, Dr. Maurice
Defends Ramses restoratn 11-8, 912B3
BACCHANTE (British warship)
In Intl Naval Review 7-4, 488C3
BACH, Gavriel
On Jerusalem prayer ruling 6-30, 528D2
BACHAUER, Gina
Dies 8-22, 892F2
BACH Cano, Ricardo
Believed arrested 12-30, 996F3
BACHFELD, Jochen
Wins Olympic medal 7-31, 574C1
BACHMAN, Dr. Leonard
On Pa mystery disease 8-5, 573A3
New Legion disease probe set 9-30, 815D1
BACHMAN, Maria Elena
Chile asks Vatican emb release 1-9, 47F2
Gets safe-conduct, Sweden offers asylum 1-28, 100B1
Arrives Sweden 2-22, 288C3
BACH: Sonatas & Partitas for Violin (record album)
Wins Grammy 2-28, 460D3
BACKE, John D.
Named CBS Inc pres 10-13, 892F1
BACKUS, John W.
Awarded Science Medal 10-18, 858C3
BACOS, Michel
Denies Uganda tie to hijackers 7-5, 485E2
BACTERIA
Gene research curbed 6-23, 735F3, 736A1
Synthetic gene implantatn rptd 8-28, 735F2
BADDELEY, Angela
Dies 2-22, 192C3
BADHAM, Robert E.
Elected 11-2, 829E1
BADI, Aquiles
Dies 5-8, 368D2
BADILLO, Rep. Herman (D, N.Y.)
Reelected 11-2, 830B2
BADRAN, Mudar
Named Jordan premr 7-13, quits 11-27, 949A3
BAER, Byron M.
Behind in primary tally 6-8, 410A1
Loses primary revote 9-21, 725C2
BAEZ, Federico
Kin found slain 3-7; identified as Reyes assassin 3-10, 212F1
BAEZA, Jose
Asks new cabt 2-20, 2-23, 154C2
BAFALIS, Rep. L.A. (R, Fla.)
Reelected 11-2, 829C2
BAFIA, Jerzy
Polish justice min 3-27, 268G2
BAFILE, Corrado Cardinal
Appointed cardinal 4-27, 336B2
BAGAZA, Lt. Col. Jean-Baptiste
Leads coup 11-1, assumes pres 11-3, 857G3 *
BAGLEY, William T.
On potato futures default 5-25, 5-26, 397D1
Warns NY commodity exchngs 9-15, 990E2
BAHADUR, Raj
Quits Cabt 12-22, becomes Gujarat gov 12-24, 1006D1
BAHAMA Islands—*See also COMMONWEALTH of Nations*
Gulf slush fund rpt detailed 133E1
Whitfield elected oppositn ldr 1-12, 104A2
Vesco, 6 others indicted 1-14, 78D2
Listed as 'free' nation 1-19, 20B3
Forgn cos rptd leaving 1-22, 104A2
Rpt Chile bought Sovt arms 2-25, 288F3
US censures Currie Bimini trip 3-16, 200A3
US rpts on Projct Haven probe 4-12, 283D3
Amer hanged for '74 murders 10-19, 1012D2
US probes S Korea gifts 11-7, 899E1
BAHR, Egon
Named Soc Dems secy-gen 12-15, 968A2

1977

Lufthansa jets threatened 11-5, 868A3
More explosives found 11-11, Schubert kills self 11-12, 888B2, C2
BAADER-Meinhof Gang—*See GERMANY, Federal Republic of—Terrorism*
BABALAU, Constantin
At miners strike 8-2, 947F3
Dismissed 12-15, 987A3
BABBITT, Bruce E.
Ariz murder plot, liquor probe cited 1-15, 1-27, 162B1, E1; 11-6, 871C2
Ariz murder plot cited 11-6, 871C2
BABCOCK, Barbara A.
Named asst atty gen 2-16, confrmd 3-4, 211D1
BABCOCK & Wilcox Co. Inc.
United Tech proposes purchase 3-29, 274B3
US blocks United Tech takeover 7-5, 520D1
McDermott wins bidding war, United withdraws 8-25, 666E3
McDermott takeover cited in table 880F1
McDermott to buy remaining shares 12-8; takeover cited 12-11, 1004C2, E2
BABIA Zingbi Malobia, Gen.
Named Army staff chief 4-5, 265E2
BACA County, Colo.—*See COLORADO*
BACALL, Lauren
Howard Hawks dies 12-26, 1024B2
BACH, Fred
Wins drag racing title 4-24, 531E2
BACH, Gavriel
On Nablus jail terror group 7-29, 589E1
BACH, Richard
Illusions on best-seller list 8-14, 643F1; 9-4, 712C3; 10-2, 808D3
BACH Cano, Ricardo
Novillo found dead 1-18, 197G3
BACKE, John D.
Paley sets retiremt 4-20, 356B1
CBS chief exec 5-11, 532F1
CBS realigns managemt, forms sports, entertainmt units 10-17, 846E1
BACKFIRE Bomber—*See ARMAMENTS—Aircraft*
BACTERIA—*See also MEDICINE, subheads 'Diseases' and 'Drugs'*
New life form identified 11-2, 907G3
Hormone made by DNA techniques 12-1, 1022G2
BADAL, Prakash Singh
India agri min 3-26, 240B1
Corruptn probe asked 4-1, 283D3
BADEN-Powell, Lady Olave
Dies 6-25, 532E2 *
BADILLO, Rep. Herman (D, N.Y.)
Koch wins mayoral primary 9-8, 723B2
BAD News Bears in Breaking Training, The (film)
Top-grossing film 8-3, 643B2; 8-31, 712G3
BADRAN, Mudar
Jordan-PLO tie OKd 2-22—2-23, 122E1
Dayan mtg rptd 9-20, 713G2
Vs Syria-Egypt rift 11-22, 894E1
BAER, Justice Harold
Jets-Mets dispute settled 5-26, 491B2
BAGAZA, Lt. Col. Jean-Baptiste
Sees Young 2-5, 105D1
BAGGE, Carl E.
On Carter energy plan 4-24, 319G3
BAGOADA, Hector
Arrested 4-26, 371B2
BAIBAKOV, Nikolai
Sets '78 econ plan 12-14, 987E3
BAINES, Harold
In baseball free-agent draft 6-7, 644A3

BAHAMA Islands—*See also COMMONWEALTH of Nations*
UN Assemb member 3F3
US sues Filipinos, co re payoffs 1-12, 79G2
UNCTAD shipping study rptd 4-17, 337E2
US ct bars IRS tax evidence; Castle Bank closes 4-28, 395C3
Pindling, PLP win electns; econ, corruptn issues cited 7-19, 578F3
Population growth rptd; Haiti, Jamaica immigratn 579E1
Pindling names new Cabt 7-29, 675C1
BDP secy gen resigns 8-19, 710E1
Govt seeks forgn investmt 8-19, 710F1
Pindling at Panama Canal pacts signing 9-7, 678C1
Queen opens Parlt 10-20, 844G2
Cabt salaries increased 10-29, 844A3
Gulf fined re laundered money 11-13, 881E2

1978

BAADER-Meinhof Gang—*See GERMANY—Terrorism*
BABA, James
Loses Danish libel suit 6-18, 688B1
BABASHOFF, Jack
Sets 400-m freestyle relay mark 8-22, 780C2
BABBAH, Mohammeden Ould
Named Mauritania defns min 1-26, 95D1
BABBITT, Acting Gov. Bruce E. (D, Ariz.)
Becomes Ariz gov 3-4, 186F3
Vs Carter water plan 6-7, 427C1
Wins primary 9-12, 736A2
Elected gov 11-7, 853D2, 855D1
BABCOCK & Wilcox Co.
McDermott takeover cited 9-25, 896G1
BABE, Thomas
Prayer For My Daughter opens 1-17, 760B3
Fathers & Sons opens 11-16, 1031E1
BABU, Abdulrahman
Freed 4-26, 479D2
BABY Come Back (recording)
On best-seller list 2-4, 116F3
BAC—*See BRITISH Aircraft Corp.*
BACCHUS, Haroon
Jim Jones ruled murder victim 12-22, 999F3
BACH, Johann Sebastian (1685-1750)
Arias wins Grammy 2-24, 316D1
BACH, Richard
Illusions on best-seller list 1-8, 24D3; 2-5, 116B3
BACHE Halsey Stuart Shields Inc.
Jacobs on $, stock mkt recovery 11-2, 827A1
BACIOGLU, Basir
Slain 6-2, 476D3
BACKFIRE Bomber—*See ARMAMENTS—Aircraft*
BACKUS, Richard
Gimme Shelter opens 12-10, 1031G1
BACON—*See MEAT*
BACTERIA
Anti-bacterial ocean organism rptd 5-3, 335B1
Legionnaires' disease isolated 8-11, 635C3
BADAWI, Maj. Gen. Ahmed
Egypt chief of staff 10-5, 774C3
BADEN, Dr. Michael
Testifies on King assassinatn 8-15, 641E1
Testifies on JFK assassinatn 9-7, 698C1
BADGER, Ed
Quits Bulls to coach Cincinnati U 4-9, 272G2
Costello named Bulls coach 6-5, 656D1
BADHAM, Rep. Robert Edward (R, Calif.)
Reelected 11-7, 850B2
BADILLO, Herman
Garcia wins US House seat 2-14, 108C2
On Carter urban-aid plan 3-27, 218B1
BAD News Bears Go To Japan, The (film)
Released 7-14, 969B3
BADRAN, Mudar (Jordanian premier)
Gives conditns for entering Israel-Egypt talks 2-27, 157A1
Meets US aide 3-5, 156G3
BAEZ, Joan
Renaldo & Clara released 1-25, 619D3
BAEZA, Rev. Alfonso
Union rights backed 10-23, 1014A3
BAFALIS, Rep. Louis A. (Skip) (R, Fla.)
Reelected 11-7, 850G2
BAGHAJATI, Adnan
Syria fires from newspaper post 6-19, 559A2
BAGLEY, Bill
Wins Cong primary in Wyo 9-12, 736D2
BAGNOLD, Enid
Intl Velvet released 7-19, 970G1

BAHAMA Islands—*See also COMMONWEALTH of Nations*
Nassau expenses rated 1-14, 28B3
Lloyd Carr fugitive '75 arrest cited 1-14, 83F2
Cabt com on investmt created 3-6, 194F1-A2
Vesco leaves CR 4-30, 354E2; visits on business 5-11, 478C3
Illegal aliens ordered out 6-29, 538B1
CR bars Vesco return 7-7, 558D3; rejcts citizenship 7-19, 617D2; denies appeal 8-23, 671E2
Haiti refugees arrive US 7-18, 7-22, 671C3
Citibank sued re forgn tax evasn 7-24, 717C3
Marathon swimmer departs for Fla 8-13, 653A2
UN Assemb member 713C3
Press freedom rptd by IAPA 10-13, 829A2
BAHERI, Mohammed
Out as Iran justice min 10-30, 827F3
BAHR, Chris
NFL '77 kicking ldr 1-1, 56B2
BAHR, Egon
USSR force cut talks cited 417B1
Spy scandal disclosed, smear campaign chrgd 8-31—9-6, 725C2
Spy probe dropped 9-26, 868A3

1979

BAADER-Meinhof Gang—*See GERMANY, Federal Republic of—Terrorism*
BABBITT, Gov. Bruce E. (D, Ariz.)
Named to 3 Mile I probe 4-11, 275C1
Scores NRC licensing decision 8-23, 665C1
Orders tritium seizure 9-25, 806B2
BABBITT v. United Farm Workers
Case decided by Sup Ct 6-5, 464A3
BABCOCK and Wilcox Co.—*See under McDERMOTT & Co.*
BABE (recording)
On best-seller list 11-7, 892E3
BABE, Thomas
Taken in Marriage opens 2-26, 292D3
Kid Champion opens 8-27, 712A1
BABILONIA, Tai
Wins world figure-skating title 3-14, 391G3
BACALL, Lauren
By Myself on best-seller list 2-4, 120B3; 3-4, 173D3; 4-8, 271A2; 5-6, 356D2
BACH, Steven
Butch & Sundance released 6-15, 819G3
BACHARDY, Don
Mtg By the River opens 3-28, 712D1
BACHE Halsey Stuart Shields Inc.
Wyser-Pratte drops McGraw-Hill proxy battle 2-23, 151D3
BACKFIRE Bomber—*See ARMAMENTS—Aircraft*
BACTERIA
Antibiotics in animal feed rptd risky 6-25, 734F3
Army sued on '50 serratia test 9-16, 727B1
BADEN, Dr. Michael
Roman autopsy rptd 6-17, 521C3
BAD Girls (recording)
On best-seller list 5-30, 448F3; 7-4, 548E3, F3; 8-1, 620E3, F3
BADHAM, John
Dracula released 7-13, 820A1
BADRI, Lt. Gen. Abdul Ali
Slain 2-11, 105G1
BAETZ, Reuben
On Loto Canada sale 9-4, 685G1-A2
BAEZ, Joan
Fonda pol stance scored 7-20, 593E2
BAFFI, Paolo
Chrgd re bank dealings 3-26, 237G1-D2
Resigns, named honorary gov 10-5, 793E1
Sarcinelli backed by ct 11-14, 909E2
BAGGE, Carl E.
Lauds EPA coal-use rules 5-25, 403G3
Scores rail decontrol bill 6-6, 579F2
BAGLEY, Smith W.
Indicted 3-14, SEC chrgs 3-15, 291G3
Acquitted 8-1, 578D2
BAGLEY, William T.
CFTC '78 resignation cited 9-5, 681C2

BAHAMA Islands—*See also COMMONWEALTH of Nations*
'60s Resorts Intl, organized crime links cited 2-26, 152A1
Shah arrives for extended stay 3-30, 247B3
Shah's presence opposed 5-30, 408E1
US law firm chrgd in visa fraud 6-1, 491F3
Shah leaves for Mexico 6-10, 445E3
Somoza expelled 8-2, 600E1
Nyad completes Fla swim 8-20, 656E3
UN membership listed 695E2
Shah's US entry cited 11-18, 879A2
Shah rules out asylum 12-5, 914D1
Land sales to forgners curbed, Colombian drug smuggling cited 12-7, 948F1
1st 1/4 real estate boom rptd 12-7, 948B2
BAHNA, Dr. Sami L.
Transplants fetal liver 8-20, 736B3
BAHONAR, Ayatollah
Named Iran educ dep min 7-19, 565F2
BAHR, Egon
Strauss loses electn dispute 10-5, 796B2

1980

BABATUNDE, Obba
Reggae opens 3-27, 392F3
BABBITT, Gov. Bruce E. (D, Ariz.)
State of State message 1-14, 268G3-269B1
BABE (recording)
On best-seller list 1-2, 40E3
BABE, Thomas
Salt Lake City opens 1-23, 136E3
BABILONIA, Tai
Retains US figure skating title 1-17, withdraws from world competitn 3-12, 470D2, E2
Withdraws from Winter Olympics 2-15, 154C3
BABIUCH, Edward (Polish premier; resigned Sept. 24)
Named Poland premier 2-18, 152D2
Appeals to strikers in TV talk 8-15, 625D1
Ousted, replaced 8-24, 641A1, F1, 658D2
Sovts rpt pol shuffle 8-24, 642G1
Purged by CP Central Com 10-6, 760C2
BACALL, Lauren
By Myself on best-seller list 2-10, 120D3
By Myself wins Amer Book Award 5-1, 692C2
BACH, Gavriel
Asked to explain W Bank ousters 5-20, 381E1
BACHE Group Inc.
Hunt group asked to cover silver futures trading 3-25; contracts sold 3-26, SEC halts trading 3-27, 223F1, B2
Hunt silver trading, preferential treatmt probed 3-31—4-2; additional debts rptd, shakeup seen 3-31, 245A2
Hunt silver debt repaid 4-8, 345E1
Hunt bank loans probed, deceptn chrgd 5-30, 425A2
Jacobs on Carter econ renewal plan 8-28, 633D3
Hunts liquidate stock holdings; '80 earnings rptd 10-21, 8673
BACHELET, Vittorio
Killed 2-12, 151A2
BACKE, John D.
Quits CBS post, Paley dispute hinted 5-8, 376D1
Wyman assumes CBS posts 6-2, 501G1
BACKFIRE Bomber—*See ARMAMENTS--Aircraft*
BACK in Black (recording)
On best-seller list 12-3, 948C3
BACK in the Race (play)
Opens 4-17, 392C2
BACTERIA
Animal gene differences rptd 1-23, 160B1
GE microbe patent upheld by Sup Ct; reactn 6-16, 452E2-453A2
BACZAKO, Peter
Wins Olympic medal 7-27, 624F2
BAD Girls (recording)
Summer said born-again 1-25, 199G2
BADHAM, Rep. Robert E. (R, Calif.)
Reelected 11-4, 842C2
BADRAN, Mudar (Jordanian prime minister)
Named Jordan prime min 8-28, 698G1
BAD Timing/A Sensual Obsession (film)
Released 9-21, 836D2
BADYLAK, Walenty
Kills self re Katyn protest 3-20, 262F3
BAEZ, Joan
At Cambodia border aid vigil 2-6, 108D2
BAEZA, Ernesto
Resigns 8-11, subordinates arrested 8-12, 618D3
BAFALIS, Rep. L. A. (R, Fla.)
Reelected 11-4, 842G2
BAFFREY, Doris
Admits PI bombing role 10-31, 874A2
BAGBY, Monica
Layton acquitted of attempted murder 5-22, 407F3-408B1
BAGHERI, Gen. Amir Bahaman
Replaced as AF cmdr 6-19, 464E2
BAHAMA Islands—*See also COMMONWEALTH of Nations*
3 killers hanged 1-29, 132A2
Bank looting case rptd 3-3, 228G3
Symonette death rptd 3-17, 280C2
Foreign Relations (misc.)
Cuban MiGs sink patrol boat, buzz island 5-10; talks open 5-12; UN protest filed 5-13, 371A2-B3
Pindling in UK 5-10, 371F2
US rescue copter buzzed by Cuba MiGs 5-12, 371C3
Cuba regrets US copter buzzing 5-15, 380B2
8 Cuban fishermen convicted of poaching 7-9, 563E2
Cuba patrol boat compensatn rptd 7-9, 563F2
Haitian refugees rptd stranded 10-9, evicted 11-13, 869F2
64 Haitians reach Harbour I 11-21; refugee rptd on Cayos Lobos 11-22, 920C1-E1
U.S. Relations
US rescue copter buzzed by Cuba MiGs 5-12, 371C3; Cuba regrets 5-15, 380B2
US cts power to suppress evidence curbed 6-23, 554C3
Vesco interviewed 7-27, B Carter role discounted 7-30, 570D1
US rpts stranded Haitian refugees 10-9; US news copter missing 11-13, 869F2, C3
BAHR, Matt
NFL '79 kicking ldr 1-5, 8B2
Steelers win Super Bowl 1-20, 61B3-62C1

1976

BAHRAIN—*See also ARAB League, NONALIGNED Nations Movement.*
Iran recalls amb 1-17, 12G3
Listed as 'partly free' 1-19, 20C3
Concorde service begins 1-21, 86A2
Sadat visits, gets aid vow 2-27, 162C1
Emir visits France 3-2, 204F3
Australia OKs '77 Concorde flights 5-28, 400D1
UK Concorde 1st ¼ losses rptd 8-26, 675B3
Cluverius confrmd US amb 9-30, 807F3
BAHRU, Brig. Gen. Tufa
Named Dergue cmdr 8-17, 674D2
BAILAR, Benjamin F.
Warns on high costs 3-8, 186D3
Reports 3d ¼ surplus 11-15, 869D2
BAILAR 3d, Dr. John
On breast X-ray dangers 8-23, 679G3
BAILEY, F. Lee
On Hearst trial strategy 1-26, 70C1
Hearst trial opens 2-4, 113G3
Hearst trial dvpts 2-12—3-10, sums up defns 3-18, 201G1, G2, 202D2, C3
Hearst freed on bail 11-19, 891D2
BAILEY, John M. (d. 1975)
Cleared in jai alai scandal 1-12, 271D1
BAILEY, Dr. Pearce
Dies 6-23, 524C2
BAJPAI, K. S.
Assumes amb post in Pak 7-21, 538G1
BAKER, Deane
Loses Mich Sen primary 8-3, 565A3
BAKER, Donald I.
Named asst atty gen 7-27; confrmd 8-6, 807D3
Asks stiff penalties in paperbd case 10-5, 885F3, 886B3
Asks jail terms for price-fixing 11-20, 885B3
BAKER Jr., Sen. Howard H. (R, Tenn.)
Ford lists as potential VP 1-22, 41A2
Detente resolutn blocked 3-22, 246A1
Campaigns with Ford 5-14, 374F1
Hosts Reagan 5-20, 374E1
Named to intelligence com 5-20, 377E1
In Iowa for Ford 6-18, 451D1
VP prospect cited 8-10, 584C1
GOP vp poll rptd 8-11, 583F3
Keynotes GOP conv 8-16, 601G3, 614E3
Wife's drinking problem rptd 8-17, 598A3
Ford selects Dole as vp 8-19, 598F1, G2
GOP conv vp vote table 8-19, 599E3
Gets Sadat peace bid 11-13, 878A1
BAKER 3rd, James A.
Promises delegate list 7-20, 531F3
Claims majority for Ford 7-23, 549D3
On Reagan delegate claim 8-2, 564B2
Rpts Ford delegate count 8-13, 583C2
Named Ford campaign chief 8-25, 631B1
Ford com wires blacks re Carter church bias 10-31, Weber deplores 11-2, 827A1
BAKER, Janet
Wins Grammy 2-28, 460E3
BAKER, Joy D(irksen) (Mrs. Howard H.)
Drinking problem rptd 8-17, 598A3
BAKER, Milton G.
Dies 8-7, 892F2
BAKER Irons & Dockstader Inc.
Boycott rpts released 10-18, 10-20, 785G3, 786A2
BAKERSFIELD, Calif.—*See CALIFORNIA*
BAKERY Goods
FDA bans Red #2 dye 1-19, 44D2
Dec, '75 CPI 1-21, 90A2

1977

BAHRAIN—*See also ARAB League, NONALIGNED Nations Movement*
UN Assemb member 3F3
Arab monetary fund created 4-18, 318C1
US Navy base pact ends 7-1, 511G3
Amnesty Intl lists lawmakers held 9-5, 753B2
Hijackers refuel 10-13, 789D1
London-Singapore Concorde pact rptd 10-24, 905D3
Assad visits re Cairo conf 12-10, 954F2
BAHRO, Rudolf
E Ger arrests 8-23, 684E1
BAHUGUNA, Hemvati N.
Quits party 2-2, 71E1
Named chemicals min, balks 3-26; relents, sworn 3-27, 239G3, 240C1
BA Ibrahima
Mauritania finance min 8-4, 772E1
BAINS, Hardial Singh
Accused 2-24, 159B1
BAJWA, Rafiq Ahmed
Illegal Bhutto mtg chrgd 3-14, 201E1
BAKER, Buddy
3d in Daytona 500 2-20, 531C2
NASCAR final standing, earnings rptd 11-20, 1020E3
BAKER, Dusty
In World Series 10-11—10-18, 806A2
BAKER Jr., Sen. Howard H. (R, Tenn.)
Elected minority ldr 1-4, 6E1
Ethics panel formed 1-18, 77F2
Votes vs Marshall 1-26, 52B3
On Sen reorganizatn 2-4, 91D1
American Airlines gift rptd 2-9, 112B1
Backs Carter arms stand 3-31, 247G1
On Carter energy plan 4-20, 293G3; 4-25, 320G3
Sees Carter on SALT 5-18, 401B1
Scores US-Cuba thaw 6-5, 455G3
Asks Korea probe prosecutor 6-9, 442E2
Amends '70 Clean-Air Act 6-9, 460G3
Sen backs compromise Korea amendmt 6-16, 477E3
Attacks Dems on cargo preference 8-1, 719B3
Sen campaign financing killed 8-2, 592C2
Delays Panama Canal pact judgmt 8-11, 622G1; 9-11, 698G2
Sen Canal hearings open, treaty clarificatn urged 9-26, 754G2, D3
Warns GOP vs Canal pact divisn; Javits vs oppositn role 11-13, 912D1
BAKER, Lenny
Wins Tony 6-5, 452D1
BAKER Industries, Inc.
Wells Fargo Armored Service Corp.
Ex-FBI official indicted 4-7, 275C2
Bid rigging chrgd 6-21, 520D3
BAKER & McKenzie
On 5 largest law firms list 5-16, 383A2
BAKERY Goods
Arbitratn under expired contracts affirmed 3-7, 211B3
BAKHT, Sikander
Indian works min 3-26, 240B1

1978

BAHRAIN—*See also ARAB League, NONALIGNED Nations Movement*
Bahrain city expenses rated 1-14, 28B3
Islamic, Arab poor-natn aid rise rptd 4-9, 257F2
Arab fund loan to Sudan rptd 8-17, 925F3
UN Assemb member 713C3
BAHRO, Rudolf
Sentenced 6-30, 585E3
BAIBAKOV, Nikolai Konstantinovich
Rpts '78 econ plan prelim results, '79 forecast 11-29, 1020A2
BAILEY, Bill
Death rptd 12-17, 1032C2
BAILEY, Don
Wins US House seat 11-7, 849F2, 852E1
BAILEY, F. Lee
On Lloyd Carr '77 revenues 1-24, 83G2
BAILEY, Pearl
Brother's death rptd 12-17, 1032C2
BAILEY, R. E.
Conoco chrmn, chief exec 9-20, 809B1
BAIRD, Joseph
On Mead oppositn to Occidental bid 12-20, 1004F3
BAKALIS, Michael J.
Wins Dem primary for Ill gov 3-21, 207A2
Loses electn 11-7, 853A2
BAKAYOGO, Lt. Col. Tiecore
Arrested 2-28, 250F3
BAKER, Dusty
Dodgers win NL pennant 10-7, 779D1
In World Series 10-10—10-17, 799A3
BAKER Jr., Sen. Howard H. (R, Tenn.)
In Panama, sees Torrijos 1-3—1-7; plans treaty amendmts 1-25, sees ratificatn 1-30, 58E1
Scores Carter energy plan 1-26, 63F1
Introduces Canal pact amendmts 2-7, 120D1
Canal neutrality pact amended 3-10, 3-13, ratified 3-16, 177E1, F2, G3-178A2
Vs neutron bomb cancellatn 4-4, 254B1
Votes for 2d Canal pact, ratificatn role cited 4-18, 273B1, F2
Scores Carter forgn policy 5-3, 342F2
Backs Mideast plane sales 5-15, 357G1
Sees CIA evidence on Cuba role in Zaire 6-2, 442F1
Gulf illegal paymt rptd 6-2, 449E1
On Cong security leaks 7-11, 524F2, E3
Endangered Species Act revised by Sen 7-19, 551D2
Wins primary 8-3, 606B2
Upset over Carter A-breeder deal 8-24, 678A1
On tour for Kemp-Roth bill 9-20—9-22, 734F3
Reelected 11-7, 848D3, 853D1
On new China policy 12-16, 12-19, 975D3
BAKER, Janet
Wins Grammy 2-24, 316D1
BAKER, John L.
Scores FAA air-safety proposals 12-27, 1007A1
BAKER, Len
Traded to Indians 10-3, 779A3
BAKER, Mark Linn
All's Well Ends Well opens 7-5, 760B1
BAKER Jr., Russell T.
Civiletti confirmed 5-9, 342E3
BAKER, Tommy
Indiana basketball coach dismisses 12-12, 1028A1
BAKERIES & Bakery Goods
DPF on '77 Fortune 500 list 5-8, 325B2
Pillsbury to acquire Green Giant 9-18, 752C3
OSHA drops 'nuisance' equipmt rules 10-24, 833D3
UK bakers strike 11-7, 882C3
UK strike ends 12-13, 987G3
BAKER Industries Inc.
Wells Fargo Armored Service Corp.
Fined on trust chrgs 4-22, 511D1
NYC armored truck heist 12-19, 1028E2
BAKER Street (recording)
On best-seller list 6-7, 460F3; 7-8, 579G3
BAKERY, Confectionery & Tobacco Workers International Union (AFL-CIO)
Formed 8-16, 700G1-B2
BAKERY and Confectionery Workers' International Union of America (AFL-CIO)
Local ldrs '76 earnings rptd 2-20, 365A2, C2
Merges with Tobacco Workers union 8-16, 700G1-B2
BAKHTIAR, Shahpur
Named to form Iran govt, shah foes vs 12-29; Natl Front ousts 12-30, 993A1
On Cabt plans, shah status 12-30, 993D1

1979

BAHRAIN—*See also ARAB League, NONALIGNED Nations Movement*
Egypt recalls envoy 4-7, 278D1
Egypt ships barred 4-17, 278A2
Libya fete attended by Arab ldrs 9-1, 688C3
UN membership listed 695E2
Khomeini envoy ouster cited 9-26, 752B3
Egypt offers Iran annexatn threat aid 9-28, offer rejected 10-2, 752C3
At Persian Gulf security conf 10-14—10-16, 804A2
US sets evacuations, travel curbs 11-26, 894G1
BAHRO, Rudolph
Freed 10-11, 761E2
Arrives in W Ger 10-17, 882G3
BAHUGUNA, Hemwati Nandan
Scores OPEC price hike 3-27, 227G3
Named Indian finance min 7-28, 573D1
BAIBAKOV, Nikolai Konstantinovich
Reveals '80 econ plan 11-28, 928C3
BAILEY, Douglas
Cited as top Baker strategist 11-14, 983A2
BAILEY, James
In NBA draft 6-25, 507A2
BAIM, Gary L.
Ice Castles released 2-22, 174F2
BAIR, Doug
Reds lose NL pennant 10-5, 797D2
BAIRD, John
Loudspeaker opens 4-30, 712C1
BAIRD, Roy
Quadrophenia released 11-2, 1008C1
BAIRD v. Sharp
Case refused by Sup Ct 5-14, 383E1
BAIRES, Jaime
Arrested 2-23, dies of burns 3-4, 235B1
BAKER, Blanche
French Postcards released 10-19, 1007D3
BAKER Jr., Sen. Howard H. (R, Tenn.)
Reelected Sen minority ldr 1-15, 30B2
Scores State of Union Message, budget 1-24, 48F1
At GOP conf, backs wide-ranging SALT debate 2-3, 86B1
Gallup GOP poll ratings 3-4, 185E3
Talks to Midwest GOP, urges SALT criticism; offcls rate 3-10, 185G3, 186B1
Asks Carter peanut loan probe 3-13, 184A2
Scores Carter peanut probe limits 3-20, 203D1
Scores SALT treaty 4-11, 295A2; backs chngs 5-10, 460A1; 6-27, 496C3
Sees oil-profits tax OK 4-23, 300E2
Addresses Mayors Conf 6-13, 439C3, 440A1
Scores Carter re energy 7-5, 497F3
Scores SALT at Sen com hearing 7-9, 510F1
Pres campaign funds rptd 7-12, 594A1
Asks Carter energy plan support 7-17, 534A3
Urban League pres on electn backing 7-22, 560E1
Carter boats down Mississippi 8-17—8-24, 622A2
On Carter speech re Sovt troops in Cuba 10-2, 737E2
Scores Connally Mideast peace plan 10-12, 783E2
Ford bars '80 pres bid 10-19, 808F1
SALT amendmt defeated 10-23, 822C2
Enters '80 pres race 11-1, 828D3
Concerned re natl security 11-2, 983D1
2d in Me straw poll 11-3, 866B3
Addresses GOP govs, vs Iran threats 11-18, backs Carter handling 11-18, 983F1
GOP poll results 11-25, 982E1
Pol dir quits, other staff chngs cited 12-3, 983G1
Urges anti-terrorist brigade 12-19, 983C1
BAKER, Leonard
Wins Pulitzer 4-16, 336G2
BAKER, Richard H.
Exxon unveils elec motor inventn 5-18, 404A2
BAKER, Russell
Wins Pulitzer 4-16, 336B3
BAKER, Samm Sinclair
Scarsdale Diet on best-seller list 3-4, 173E3; 4-8, 271A2; 5-6, 356C2; 6-3, 432A2; 7-1, 548B3; 8-5, 620C3, 9-2, 672B3; 10-14, 800B3; 11-4, 892B3
BAKER, Walter
Canada natl revenue min 6-4, 423F3
BAKER Hotel (Dallas, Tex.)
Closes 8-31, 887B2
BAKERIES & Bakery Goods
ITT bread fiber chrg setld 3-25, 308C3
Yellow No 5 labeling ordrd 6-26, 571B2
PCB contaminated products destroyed 9-17, 704E3
BAKER International Corp.
Fortune rpts '68-78 stock gain 5-7, 305B2
BAKER v. McCollan
Case decided by Sup Ct 6-26, 541A1
BAKHTIAR, Abbas Qoli
Named Iran industry min 1-6, 11G2
BAKHTIAR, Guy
On father's news conf 7-31, 582C3
BAKHTIAR, Shahpur
Civilian govt gets parlt OK, issues policy statemt 1-3; named premr 1-4, 2D2
Natl Front scores govt 1-4, 2G2
US for cooperatn 1-4; 3B1
Vows close US ties 1-5, 3D1
Govt installed 1-6; presents Cabt to lower house, outlines policy 1-11, 11D2, B3

1980

BAHRAIN—*See also ARAB League, NONALIGNED Nations*
French pres tours Arab states 3-1—3-10, 180B1
Iran hostage rescue try sparks protest 4-26, 324E2
Palestinian curbs rptd tightened 10-22, 821C2
BAHUGUNA, H. N.
Resigns govt posts 5-19, 487D2
BAIBAKOV, Nikolai
Rpts econ, agri problems 10-21, 798E1
BAILEY, Rep. Don (D, Pa.)
Reelected 11-4, 844E1
BAILEY, Jack
Dies 2-1, 175E3
BAILEY, Melvin Lee
Cuba to free 10-13, 789A1
BAILEY, Wendell
Elected to US House 11-4, 843D2, 851F1
BAITTINER, Jou
Slain 9-17, 697G2
BAKER, Buddy
Wins Daytona 500 2-17, 637C3
BAKER, Carroll
Watcher in the Woods released 4-16, 416G3
BAKER, Dusty
NL batting ldr 10-6, 926E2
BAKER, Herbert
Jazz Singer released 12-19, 1003B2
BAKER Jr., Sen. Howard H. (R, Tenn.)
FEC OKs Bush, Kennedy funds 1-2, 1-4, 5C2
In Ia GOP debate, scores Admin forgn policy 1-5, 4F2, D3
2d in Ia poll 1-11, 33E1, F1, G1
3d in Ia caucus vote 1-21, 50F1
Wins 4 Ark delegates 2-2, 92A1
Urges cong action on Abscam scandal 2-10, 110E3
Fails to gain more Ark delegates 2-16, 130G1
2d in PR primary, expenditures cited 2-17, 130A1, D1
NH gun control forum 2-18, GOP pres debate 2-20, 129B3, G3
Trails GOP in Times/CBS poll 2-20, 130F2
NH debate exclusn spurs controversy 2-23, 143D1
3d in NH primary vote 2-26, 142D3, G3, 143F1
Loses Mass, Vt primaries 3-4, quits pres race 3-5, 166E2-E3, 167A2
Loses matching funds 3-13, 209D1
Dole quits GOP race 3-15, 208E1
Backs Reagan 4-20, campaigns in Pa 4-20—4-21, 304E2
Addresses GOP conv 7-17, 531E3
Sees Reagan 11-18, 880G2
Backs toxic waste clean-up fund 11-24, 898B1
Named Sen majority ldr 12-2, 915C2
Sees Haig apptmt confrmd 12-9, 935A2
Vows fair-housing debate 12-9, 954C2
BAKER 3rd, James A.
On La primary results 4-5, 265B1
Vows Bush campaign to continue 5-6, 342A1
Named to Reagan com 7-22, 549A3
Named chief of staff 11-14, 881E1
Emergency econ action studied 12-17, 956C1
BAKER, Robert G. (Bobby)
Hill dies 6-15, 528A2
BAKER, Samm Sinclair
Scarsdale Diet on best-seller list 2-10, 120D3; 3-9, 200C3; 4-6, 280D3; 5-4, 359E3; 6-8, 448D3
BAKERIES & Bakery Goods
US dietary guidelines issued 2-4, 157B3
Reagan vs 'cheap food' 4-18, 328A1
BAKHMIN, Vyacheslav
Sentenced 9-24, 863D2
BAKHTIAR, Abbas-Qoli
Arrested in antigovt plot 7-17, 545G1
BAKHTIAR, Samsam
Arrested in antigovt plot 7-17, 545G1
BAKHTIAR, Shahpur
Linked to anti-Iranians in Iraq 4-9, 300C1
US gen tied to post-shah plot 6-2, 418G2
Anti-Khomeini plot rptd 6-15, 465A1
US anti-Khomeini broadcasts rptd 6-29, 490A3
Linked to Iran coup plot, lauds plotters 7-11, 539D2
Iran arrests 2 cousins in antigovt plot 7-17, 545G1
Escapes death try; 5 seized, PLO linked 7-18; Iran warned, denies role 7-18—7-19, 545A1
On shah's death 7-27, 571D2
Plans coup, denounces Khomeini rule 8-8, 644E2
UK missionary arrested 8-8, 671D3
Iran executes Jewish 'spy' 8-17, 644B3
US ex-amb scores Brzezinski '79 Iran policy 9-6, 694C1, E1
Plans exile govt 9-26, 769D1

1976

BAKKE, Allan P.
Sup Ct stays reverse bias ruling 11-15, 882D1
BAKKE, Hailvarad
Norway trade min 1-12, 30B2
BAKKE, Karl E.
Replaced as Commerce counsel 2-26, 186C2
Sovt conf-entry talks withdrawl urged 11-26, 948G1
BAKR, Ahmed Hassan al-
Scores Leb-Syria talks 2-8, 107C2
Meets Syrian defector 6-15, 430F1
BAKR, el-Rasheed el-Tahir
Named Sudan prime min 8-9, 857E2
BALAGUER, Joaquin
Spain king, queen visit 5-31—6-1, 459B2
Oppositn groups coalesce 11-12, 1001A3
'73 Philip Morris payoffs rptd 12-28, 1001C2
BALAKHONOV, Vladimir
UN staff ask release 3-30, 421B3

BALANCE of Payments, International
Jamaica IMF accord on currency reform 1-8, 13E1
S Africa '74, '75 deficits rptd 1-21, 76F2
W Ger '75 deficit rptd 2-3, 158D2
Australia '75 4th ¼ deficit rptd 2-10, 137F2
Japan Jan deficit rptd 2-10, 141C2; revised 2-27, 191E2
Israel '76-77 budget submitted 2-24, 157E1

1977

BAKKE, Allan P.
Justice Dept files brief 9-19; Sup Ct hears arguments 10-12, orders more briefs 10-17, 834F2-835G1
BAKKE, Karl E.
On Sea-Land rebate setlmt 1-5, 6G3
BAKR, Ahmed Hassan al- (Iraq president)
Vows aid to Palestinian rejectionists 7-16, 571D2
Expands Cmnd Council 9-4, 695E2
BAKR, el-Rasheed el-Tahir
Named Sudan forgn min 9-10, 844A1
BALAGUER, Joaquin (Dominican Republic president)
Sees Young 8-14, 647F1
Frees leftist guerrillas 9-2, 710D2
At Panama Canal pact signing 9-7, 678C1
Vs Wessin return for pres bid 10-2, 786F1
CP legalized 10-26, 844D3
Promotes army hardliner 11-4, gets reelectn support 11-5, 969D3

BALANCE of Payments, International—*For deficit aid, see also lending agencies (e.g., IMF, WORLD Bank Group)*
Viet '75, '76 deficits rptd 1-11, 23A3
Australia Dec '76 surplus rptd 1-17, 42A3
UK Dec '76 surplus rptd 1-18, 44A3
Ireland '76 deficit up 1-20, 64A2
EC '77 rate forecast 1-28, 74F1
Norway '76 deficit rptd 2-1, '77 forecast 2-2, 99F2

1978

BAKIR, Orhan
Death sentnc sustained 4-28, 378F2
BAKKE, Allan P.
Med schl admissn ordrd, race-based affirmative actn principle upheld by Sup Ct; opinion excerpts 6-28, 481A1, 483E1-487C2
Photo 482A1
Reactn to Sup Ct ruling 6-28, 482G1-483A1
Biographical data 483B2
Sup Ct cites ruling in Univ of NC case 7-3, 552C1
Weber reverse job-bias case accepted by Sup Ct 12-11, 980F2
BAKR, Ahmed Hassan al- (Iraq premier)
Sovt emb in Baghdad ordrd moved 5-25, 416E1
Naif shot 7-9, dies 7-10, 522E2
In PLO talks 8-9—8-11, feud ended 8-23, 674B1
Meets Assad; Syria, Iraq to join forces 10-24—10-26, 803F1
BAKSHI, Ralph
Lord of Rings released 11-15, 970A2
BAKUNAS, A. J.
Killed 9-22, 777E3
BALABIN, Pini
Convicted of '77 dealer's murder 10-6, 824D2
BALAGUER, Joaquin (Dominican president)
Gen Perez lauds, electoral bd bars pol statemts 1-20, 94C2
Warns Carib conf of 'soc catastrophe' 1-22, 100D3
PRD-PR shootout 1-26, 94D2
9th pres candidate sets bid 2-10, 136C3
2 die in campaign unrest 2-19, 152D2
Signs 'non-agressn pact' with PRD ldrs 3-10, 230D3
Trades vote fraud chrgs with PRD 4-26, 354A3
Vice pres nominee replaced 5-5, 354G2
Oppositn coalitn talks fail 5-6, 354A3
PRD harrassmt rptd 5-12—5-13, polls rptd divided 5-14, 372A2
Electns held 5-16, army suspends vote count, US scores 5-17; pledges fair electn, vote count resumes 5-18, 371A3, C3 ★ -372D1
PR, PRD trade vote fraud chrgs 5-21, 414E2
PRD wins electns 5-26; congratulates Guzman 5-27, 414G1
Final vote count rptd 6-2, 456G3-457A1
Electn defeat confrmd, party wins Sen majority 7-8, 558F3
On Sen seats ruling 7-20, 617G2
Govt scored by Guzman at inaugural 8-16, 648D1
Nivar loses army command 8-16, 648F2
Guzman kin get govt posts 8-23, 671G2
Guzman replaces admin offcls 8-25, 774C2
Sen rejects Guzman amb apptmts 11-9, 881A1
Guzman retires Perez y Perez 11-17, 989A3

BALANCE of Payments, International—*For deficit aid, see also lending agencies (e.g., WORLD Bank Group)*
Defined 50B1
W Ger '77 surplus rptd 1-4, 21E3
Sweden '77 deficit rptd 1-11, 21G1
US-Japan trade pact set, Japan paymts surplus cut vowed 1-13, 26F2, B3
Italy '77 surplus rptd 1-13, 38A1
China '77 surplus rptd 1-16, 89D2

1979

Ends censorship, eases martial law 1-6, 11A3
Rallies oppose govt 1-6–1-11, tribal group backs Khomeini 1-10, 11D3-12A1
Warning vs mil coup publshd 1-10, 12A2
US backs govt 1-11, 12F1
Regency council formed 1-13, 25F1
Khomeini forms Islamic Revolutn Cncl to replace govt 1-13, 25A2
Parlt OKs govt 1-15, 1-16, Justice min resigns 1-17, 25C2
Shah leaves Iran, permanent exile seen 1-16, 25C1, E1 •
Carter: give govt 'chance' 1-17, 26G1
Defies Khomeini on succession 1-18, 26B1
Tehrani in France to meet Khomeini 1-18, 49B3
Vows to keep office 1-19; rally ban reimposed 1-25, arms issued 1-27, 49B2
Army backs 1-22, Teheran pro-govt rally held 1-25, 49D2
Meets Khomeini aide 1-23, Army closes airports 1-24, 49E1
Shah vs US coalitn backing 1-23, 49D3
Khomeini rejects eiectn plan 1-24, 49C1
Offers Khomeini mtg in France 1-27; Khomeini rejects 1-28; return set 1-30, 67C1
Khomeini returns; arrest threatened, counter actn vowed 2-1, 66C3, 67B1
Khomeini bars backers in govt 2-2, outlines power transfer 2-4, 81F1
Warns Khomeini forces 2-4, 81B2
On Bazargan contacts 2-4, 82G1
Accepts Khomeni 'shadow govt', bars resignation 2-5, 2-6, 81C1, C2
US renews backing, Bazargan contacts cited 2-6, 82D2
Aide says govt functns blocked 2-7, 81E2
For vote on new govt, const chngs 2-8, 81G2
Scorns rebel attacks 2-10; **overthrown** 2-11, 105A1-F1, D2
Rptd in hiding 2-18, 125G12; 2-25, 144G3
Scores Khomeini govt 3-24, 229C1
French refuge rptd 3-30, 247C3
Iran urges assassinatn 5-13, 357F1
Khomeini rptdly backs executn 5-22, 389C1
Electn role seen 7-30, 582D3
In Paris, scores Khomeini 7-31, 582F2
UK Emb in Teheran seized 11-5, 841A2
BAKKE, Allan P.
Weber reverse job-bias case argued in Sup Ct 3-28, 262C3
DiLeo case declined by Sup Ct 4-23, 346D2
Govt minority constructn grants case argued in Sup Ct 11-27, 945C1
BAKR, Ahmed Hassan al- (Iraqi president; resigned July 16)
Meets Assad 6-17–6-18, joint pol cmnd set 6-19, 462D1
Quits, names Hussein 7-16, 544D3
Plotters arrested 7-28, 583D1
BALAGUER, Joaquin
Mil backers get forgn posts 1-12, 62D2
Gulf Western-DR sugar probe rptd 8-16, 632E3
Mil backers plot foiled 9-25–9-26, 751E3

BALANCE of Payments, International
Defined 33B1
Yugo '78 deficit rptd 1-5, 334A2
Italy '78 surplus rptd 1-18, 38F3
W Ger '78 surplus rptd 2-7, 137F1
OECD, OPEC, dvpg natns '78 data rptd 2-8, 161B1-D1
Canada '78 deficit up 3-7, 210E2
W Eur '78 surplus rptd 3-13, 180B2
US '78 gap rptd, '77 revised 3-21, 252C2

1980

BAKKE, Allan P.
Govt minority constructn grants upheld by Sup Ct 7-2, 510B1
BAKKE, Capt. Richard
Killed in Iran rescue mission 4-24, 321E2
BAKKER, Jim
TV revenues rptd 2-25, 413A2
BALABAN, Bob
Marie & Bruce opens 2-3, 136C3

BALANCE of Payments, International
Defined 34D1
Swiss deficit hike seen 1-11, 102B1
S Korea '80 deficit estimated 1-12, 101F1
UK '79 deficit rptd 1-16, 59E1
OECD sees Luxembourg-Belgium deficit 1-17, 56C2
Japan '79 record deficit rptd 1-25, 100A1
W Ger sees '79 current acct deficit, '80 deficit hike 1-30, 197E3

1976

Uruguay '75 deficit rptd 3-12, 383B1
US '75 3d, 4th ¼ basic balance; other data revised 3-24, 229G3
Turkey '75 deficit rptd 4-1, 315F1
Nigeria '75 deficit rptd 4-1, 366B2
UK rpts March surplus 4-14, 313B1
Japan '75 deficit rptd 4-16, 291C1
France 5-yr plan draft OKd 4-21, 312F1
Australia 1st ¼ deficit down 5-4, 349F3
Latin '75 deficit rptd up 5-10, 465G3
Data format revised 5-16; 1st ¼ capital flow rptd 5-17, 396B2
US 1st ¼ current acct deficit; '75 4th ¼ revised, 1st ¼ capital flow 6-18, 479E2-A3
France 5-mo deficit rptd 7-16, 555E3
S Africa deficit rptd 7-21, 540C1
Chad '75 deficit cited 7-29, 1012A3
Australia 2d ¼ surplus rptd 8-2, 587F1
Uruguay surplus rptd 8-4, 755E1
US GOP platform text cites 8-18, 610F2
Italy July surplus rptd 8-23, 676C3
Mex devalues peso 8-31—9-12, 694B2
IMF group drops debt moratorium demand 10-2, 778F1
Issue at IMF-World Bank mtgs 10-4—10-5, 777C1, G1, 778E1
'77 oil-importers deficit forecast 10-5, 778E1
W Ger Aug surplus rptd 10-7, 857B3
Portugal sets import curbs 10-8, 811B3
Australia 3d ¼ deficit rptd 10-13, 789E2
World Bank issues Venez study 10-16, 875C2
Australia to offer US bond issue 11-4, 850F1
Australia Oct deficit rptd 11-9, 869B3
Spain deficit forecast 12-1, 929F1
US 3d ¼ deficit rptd; 1st, 2d ¼ surpluses revised 12-22, 958C1
Deficit Aid—*See also lending agencies (e.g., IMF, WORLD Bank Group)*
Jamaica IMF accord on poor natns' aid 1-8, 14E1
EC OKs Ireland loan 2-16, 157B1 ★
US offers poor natns' aid plan 5-6, 317A2, 318D1
7-natn econ summit vows aid to Italy, others 6-27—6-28, 462A2
BALBIN, Ricardo
At intl soc dems mtg 5-23—5-25, 449B3
BALDI, Ubaldesc
Wins Olympic medal 7-20, 575A2
BALDUS, Rep. Alvin J. (D, Wis.)
Reelected 11-2, 831A3
BALDOVINOS, Carlos M.
Killed 9-12, 996D1
BALFOUR MacLaine International Ltd.
Chrgd re Arab boycott 11-17, 986C3
BAL Harbour, Fla.—*See FLORIDA*
BALL, George W.
Platform com testimony 5-18, 357C3
Carter campaign donatn rptd 10-22, 939B1
BALLA, Josef
Wins Olympic medal 7-31, 576E3
BALLANTINE Brewing Co.—*See FALSTAFF Brewing*
BALLARD, Florence
Dies 2-22, 192C3
BALLESTEROS Pulido, Jaime
Detained 11-28, 909C1
BALLOONS (& Balloonists)
Thomas Atlantic flight fails 7-1, 640E3
Yost breaks world records 10-10, 892E2
BALLOSTEROS, Severiano
Runner-up in Brit Open 7-10, 716E2
BALLUKU, Beqir
Hoxha on '73 coup plot, purge 11-1, 850A1
BALOUT, Lionel
Defends Ramses restoratn 11-8, 912B3
BALTIC Sea
'75 Sovt ship mutiny rptd foiled 1-22, 122A3
BALTIMORE, Md.—*See MARYLAND*

1977

Finland '76 deficit posted 2-2, 182G1
W Ger '76 surplus rptd 2-10, 118F1
Greek '76 deficit rptd 2-10, 134G3
US Jan paymts deficit rptd 2-14, 134F2
Asia '76 deficit rptd 2-16, 147D2
Canada '76 deficit rptd 2-21, 133E3
Spain $4 bln deficit rptd 2-22, 307B3
NZ '76 deficit narrowed 2-28, 222E2
World '76 deficits rptd 3-8, 188F2-A3
Latin '75-76 data; table 3-11, 189A1, A2 ★
W Ger '74-76, Jan-Feb '77 deficit data rptd 3-15, 3-28, 260E2
Canada '76 deficit down 3-16, 218C2
US '76, 4th ¼ paymts deficit rptd 3-23, 234C1
Eur pressure re US trade policy rptd 3-23, 249B1
Portugal Jan-Feb deficit rptd 4-2, 330E3
Venez '76 deficit rptd 4-4, 547E1
Arab monetary fund created 4-18, 318A1
7-natn summit meets 5-7—5-8, 357B1
Bonn, Japan OK deficit move 5-7—5-8, 357G2
'76 Swiss surplus rptd 5-12, 489E3
Peru '76 deficit rptd 5-17, 427C3
Intl bankers conf in Tokyo 5-22—5-25, 437D3
Turkish forgn reserves crisis 5-24—7-4, 565D2
US asks Japan, W Ger, Swiss, Dutch deficit move; notes US shift 5-25, 437D3
BIS warns US re deficit 6-12, 502D1
US 1st ¼ deficit record; '76, 4th ¼ revised 6-22, 501G3
Japan plans deficit 6-29, 544D3
OECD issues econ rpt 7-20, '77 deficits forecast 7-31, 586B2, D2
US backs $ depreciation vs mark, yen 7-21, 552D1
Andreotti, Carter talks 7-25—7-27, 581C2
Canada deficit $ drop linked 7-27, 597E1
Australia deficit rptd 7-29, 615B3
'76, '77 trade protectionism rise seen 7-31, 586B3
Japan, Bonn surplus, US trade gap rptd linked 8-8, 585A2
Portugal deficit rise cited 8-25, 886E1
Danish deficit rptd rising 8-31, 672F2, A3
IMF rpts '76 deficits, '77 forecast 9-11, 700F2
US 2d ¼ deficit rptd 9-21, 722E2
US '77 paymts gap forecast 9-27, 753G3
Jamaica Jan-June gap narrowed 9-27, 884B3
Austria 1st ½ deficit rptd 10-3, 763C1
Nobel won by Meade 10-14, 951F3
Norway '77 deficit forecast 10-14, Jan-July data rptd 10-27, 967D2
US Japan talks end 12-15, 974E1-A2
Japan vows surplus cut 12-19, 984E3
US 3d ¼ deficit rptd 12-21, 977B1
OECD backs US deficit 12-27, 999B1
US oil imports, paymts gap linked 12-30, 997A3
BALBIN, Ricardo
Cleared 7-2; army seeks new 'civic orgn' ldrs 7-3, 615E1
BALBO, Giuseppe
Arrest rptd 8-27, 783C1
BALDWIN, Alfred
Claims vs Nixon funds rptd 5-6, 482G2
BALDWIN, Howard
Named WHA pres 8-22, 1021D1
BALDWIN, Roger
FBI ACLU surveillance rptd 6-19, 481G1
BALDWIN Co., D. H.
FRB bars S&L ownership 2-22, 155E1
BALFOUR Declaration
Sadat, Begin cite in Knesset addresses 11-20, 892F2, 894B1
BAL Harbor, Fla.—*See FLORIDA*
BALIDAWA, Charles
Defects to UK 3-13, 308D2
BALKOS, Anastasios
Named Greek pub order min 11-28, 925B2
BALL, George
Vs science research curbs 2-22, 184F1
BALL Jr., John (deceased)
Inducted into golf HOF 8-23, 675F3
BALLANTINE Books
Presley book sets order record 8-20, 696D1
BALLARD, Greg
In NBA draft 6-10, 584A2
BALLI, Veli
2d in Boston Marathon 4-18, 603A1
BALLOT-Lena, Claude
3d in Le Mans 6-12, 531B2
BALMERINO (race horse)
2d in Arc de Triomphe 10-2, 971A2
BALSIGER, David
Lincoln Conspiracy on best-seller list 11-6, 872F3
BALTIMORE, Md.—*See MARYLAND*

1978

UK '77 surplus rptd 1-17, 132D1
Spain '77 deficit rptd 1-21, 395A1
US $ strategy re Bonn, Japan rptd 1-23, 27F2
Venez '77 deficit posted 1-27, 332C1
Finland '77 deficit rptd 1-30, 90B1
Barbados '77 deficit down 2-3, 152A2
Greece '77 deficit rptd 2-6, 149D3
Turkey '77 deficit rptd 2-6, 3-1, 170C3
Norway '77, '75-77 deficit rptd 2-10, 134C1
Denmark '77 deficit rptd 2-14, 2-22, 130G3
Dutch '77 surplus estimated 2-15, 169B3
Malta '77 surplus rptd 2-17, 228B3
France '77 deficit rptd 2-24, 149F1
N, S Korea paymts compared 2-27, 340E3
New Zealand '77 deficit rptd 3-7, 497D3
Australia Jan deficit, Feb surplus rptd 3-10, 187C3
Canada '77 deficit rptd 3-10, 187G3
Unctad poor-natn debt relief talks; '77 debt estimates cited 3-11, 301A1
US record '77, 4th ¼ deficits rptd 3-22, 221B3
Nigeria '77 deficit rptd 4-3, 248B1
Portugal deficit rptd set 4-3, 331C2
US deficit, $ drop linked 4-7—4-8, 257A3
Japan Mar surplus record rptd 4-15, 314C1
Zambia '80 deficit end agreed 4-26, 333F2
Australia deficit drop forecast 4-27, 328A1
Australia Mar surplus rptd, Apr deficit 5-11, 530C1
US 1st ¼ deficit, '77 revised; acctg tech chngs cited 6-21, 469C3
7-natn Bonn summit meets 7-16—7-17, 543D3
Rhodesia '77 deficit up 7-26, 616E1
Canada record 2d ¼ deficit rptd 9-8, C$ weakness linked 9-11, 703F3, 704C1
US 2d ¼ deficit rptd; 1st ¼ '77 data revised 9-19, 717B1
US '79 deficit drop seen 9-26, 731D3
OECD sees '79 gap narrowing 11-17, 918C1
US 3d ¼ deficit rptd, 2d ¼ revised 12-19, 982C1
BALANCHINE, George
Nabokov dies 4-6, 356C3
Baryshnikov joins NYC Ballet 4-26, 335F3
BALBIN, Ricardo
Detained re banned Radical mtg 5-1, 611E3
Sees Spain king 11-28, 968A1
BALBO, Giuseppe
Jailed in quake relief scandal 1-23, 103G3
BALCAZAR Monzon, Gustavo
Elected vice pres 10-11, 814G3
BALDERIS, Helmut
USSR wins world hockey title 5-14, 458D3
BALDUS, Rep. Alvin J. (D, Wis.)
Reelected 11-7, 852C4
BALDWIN, Faith
Dies 3-19, 252C2
BALDWIN, Howard
OKs NHL entry bids 2-22, 296B3
BALDWIN, James
Amen Corner opens 4-22, 760B1
BALDWIN v. Montana Fish and Game Commission
Hunting fee disparity backed by Sup Ct 5-23, 405F3
BAL Harbour, Fla.—*See FLORIDA*
BALL, Alex
Named Fury coach 6-16, 707D3
BALL, George
To review Iran crisis 12-4, 929E2
BALLARD, Greg
Bullets win NBA title 6-7, 457A2
BALLESTEROS, Severiano
Wins Greater Greensboro Open 4-2, 355G3
2d in French Open 5-15, 580E3
Ties for 2d in Irish Open 8-27, 672G3
BALLEW, Claude D.
Obscenity convictn overturned by Sup Ct 3-21, 220E3
BALLEW v. Georgia
Juries of less than 6 ruled illegal by Sup Ct 3-21, 220E3
BALL Four. My Life and Hard Times Throwing the Knuckleball in the Big Leagues (book)
Bouton returns to major leagues 9-10, 779E3
BALLOONS (& Balloonists)
2 Britons fail in Atlantic flight 7-30, 653B1
3 Amers cross Atlantic 8-11—8-17, 652D3
BALLROOM in St Patrick's Cathedral, The (play)
Opens 12-1, 1031A1
BALOPOULOS, Michael
Dies 3-3, 252C2
BALTAZAR, Rui
Named Mozambique finance min 4-22, 331D1
BALTIC Sea
Sweden fishing zones set 1-1, 21A2
Sweden protests Sovt sub patrols 3-1, spy trawlers rptd moored 3-11, 291A3
Danish fishermen protest quotas 5-5, 371D2; 5-10, 436A3
BALTIMORE, Md.—*See MARYLAND*
BALTIMORE Canyon—*See GAS, Natural; PETROLEUM—Offshore Development*

1979

OECD sees French surplus 3-25, 236A2
Netherlands '78 deficit rptd 3-28, 288D2
France plans maintenance 4-5, 267D2
Japan, US state goals 5-2; Ohira notes Apr 3-wk deficit 5-3, 320F1, B3
Portugal '79 deficit forecast 5-25, 409E2
Venez '78 deficit rptd 5-28, 429D3
Mex 1st 1/4 deficit rptd 6-1, 487F2
US 1st 1/4 surplus rptd; '78, 4th 1/4 revised 6-21, 463B2
Tokyo summit ends 6-29, 493D1
OECD sees more deficits 7-19, 554D3
Australia fscl yr deficit down 7-19, 562A3
Guyana '78 deficit rptd 8-28, 687F2
IMF sees gap widening 9-16, 720D1
Dutch see '80 surplus 9-18, 730F3
US 2d 1/4 deficit rptd, 1st 1/4 revised 9-20, 701F2
Norway sees '80 deficit reductn 10-6—10-7, 774C1
Japan 1st 1/2 deficit rptd 10-30, 836G2
Denmark record deficit seen 11-4, 855D1
Peru '80 surplus seen 11-26, 951G2
Brazil '79 deficit forecast 12-7, 948A3
US 3d 1/4 surplus rptd, 2d 1/4 revised 12-20, 984A3
BALANCHINE TV Great Performance (TV program)
Wins Emmy 9-9, 858F2
BALDERIS, Helmut
Sovts win Challenge Cup 2-11, 118D3, E3
BALDERSTON, John L.
Dracula released 7-13, 820A1
BALDWIN, James
Malcolm X neutralizatn plan by FBI rptd 11-5, 886C3; 12-4, 993D3
BALDWIN, Michael
Phantasm released 6-1, 820G2
BALDWIN, Nigel
Just a Little Less opens 5-20, 712A1
BALL, Alan
Whitecaps win NASL title, named playoff MVP 9-8, 775B3, D3
BALLANCHINE, George
Baryshnikov named Amer Ballet dir 6-20, 527E3
BALLARD, David (d. 1977)
Murderer executed 10-22, 817D2
BALLEN Cordovez, Sixto Duran
Loses Ecuador pres bid 4-29, 329F3
Roldos sworn Ecuador pres 8-10, 613D2
BALLESTEROS, Severiano
Wins British Open 7-21, 586G3
US wins Ryder Cup Matches 9-16, 969E3
BALLESTRERO, Cardinal Anastasio Alberto
Installed cardinal 6-30, 640D2
BALLET—*See DANCE*
BALLOONS (& Balloonists)
DaVinci Trans-America flight falls short 10-2, 992A3
BALLY Manufacturing Corp.
NJ casino license rptd pending 2-26, 152C1
Mays to cut baseball ties 10-29, 1002G3
BALTIMORE, Md.—*See MARYLAND*
BALTIMORE Canyon—*See PETROLEUM—Offshore Developments*

1980

Norway surplus seen 2-5, 100F2
Ireland plans deficit cut 2-27, 151B1
Canada '79, 4th 1/4 deficit down 3-8, 211B2
US '79 4th 1/4 deficit rptd, 3d 1/4 surplus revised 3-20, 263A3
W Ger deficit seen 3-24, 236F2, A3
Sovt bloc '79 deficit up 4-1, 285A3
Dutch '79 deficit doubles 4-2, 277C1
IMF $ support plan shelved 4-24, 302F1
Denmark deficit spurs plan 5-5, 351C2
Jamaica rpts Dutch loan 6-4, 465D1
'79 Yugoslav deficit cited 6-5, 468D3
Yugoslav deficit reductn seen 6-6, 468E3
US 1st 1/4 deficit rptd; '79, 4th 1/4 revised 6-19, 455C1
S Korea '80 deficit revised up 7-1, 499C3
Canada current acct deficit widens 9-9, 687E1
IMF role in oil debt studied 9-15, 695E2
Westn natns '80 deficit forecast 9-16, 695G3
US 2d 1/4 deficit rptd, 1st 1/4 revised 9-18, 725G1-A2
Yugo seeks deficit reductn 9-18, 833D2
Canada current acct gap narrows 12-9, 941G1
US 3d 1/4 deficit rptd, 2d 1/4 revised 12-18, 984B2
BALDASAR v. Illinois
Case decided by Sup Ct 4-22, 344B1
BALDING, Rebecca
Silent Scream released 2-2, 216E3
BALDRIGE, Malcolm
Named Commerce secy 12-11, 935B1
BALDUS, Rep. Alvin (D, Wis.)
Loses reelectn 11-4, 851G2
BALDWIN, Adam
My Bodyguard released 8-1, 675B3
BALDWIN, Doug
Front Page opens 12-22, 1003B3
BALDWIN, Judge Ernest F.
Sentences polygamist ldr 6-2, 502B3
BAL Harbour—*See FLORIDA*
BALLA, Jozsef
Wins Olympic medal 7-31, 624E3
BALLANTRAE, Baron (Bernard Edward Ferguson)
Dies 11-28, 928B2
BALLERINO, John T.
Charged in GSA scandal 1-15, 112F1
BALLESTEROS, Severiano
Wins Masters 4-13, 412G1
BALLOONS (& Balloonists)
2 Amers cross N Amer 5-12—5-15, 470E3
BALLY Manufacturing Corp.
NJ gambling license issued 12-29, 988B3
BALTIC Sea
W Ger lifts navy curbs 7-18, 540F1
BALTIMORE—*See MARYLAND*

1976

BALTIMORE News American (newspaper)
Ford endorsement rptd 10-30, 827G3
BALTIMORE Sun, The (newspaper)
India newsman loses certificatn 2-14, 139C3
Carter interview 9-4, 664C1, F1
Trewhitt on pres debate panel 10-6, 740F2
Audit of Pallottine Fathers rptd 10-24, 950F3
Ford endorsement rptd 10-30, 827G3
BANANA, Rev. Canaan
Freed 1-15, 53G3
To join Geneva conf 10-19, 797G1
BANANAS—*See FRUITS & Vegetables*
BANCAL Tri-State Corp.
Rptd on FRB 'problem' list 1-22, 111A3
Bank of California (San Francisco)
Rptd on comptroller's 'problem' list 1-26, 113E1
BANCROFT, David
Hearst pretrial move 1-23, 70A1
BANCSHARES of North Carolina
Rptd on FRB 'problem' list 1-22, 111A3
Bank of North Carolina (Jacksonville)
Rptd on comptroller's 'problem' list 1-26, 113E1
BANDA, Hastings Kamuzu
UK scores re Goans 5-16, 382D2
Chrgs Goans seek deportatn 5-29, 497D3
Cuts new Cabt, takes justice post 5-31, 497D3
BANDARNAIKE, Sirimavo
Vs student boycott 11-22, 890B2
BANDO, Sal
AL batting ldr 10-4, 796C1
Contract rptd signed 12-5, 951D3
BANDUSHA, Maj. Jean
Burundi pub health min 11-13, 1012G2
BANG, Nguyen Luong
Vice pres of united Viet 7-3, 502E3

BANGLADESH (formerly East Pakistan)—*See also ADB, COMMONWEALTH of Nations, NONALIGNED Nations Movement*
Listed as 'not free' nation 1-19, 20D3
Rebels take border post 1-23—1-24; India denies aid 1-26, 156B2
Rebel leader identified 156C2
Total IMF oil loan rptd 4-1, 340B2
Indian clashes 4-19—4-20, 290F1
Exiled army men visit 4-20—4-30, 332A2
Air chief Tawab quits, replaced 5-1, 332F1
Army split claimed 5-2, 332F1
Ganges dam protested 5-16—5-17, 365F1
Chrgs India border raid 5-18, 382A2
44 pol prisoners freed 7-16, 543C2
17 socialist plotters sentenced 7-17, 543B2
Intl Eucharist Cong rice progrm lauded 8-2, 596D2
Qazi Nazrul Islam dies 8-29, 1015F1
4 sentncd as plotters 9-20, Dutchman deported 9-23, 734B3
Chrgs India aids rebels 9-25, India denies 9-26, 755B1
Masters confrmd US amb 9-30, 808C1
'71-75 starvatn deaths rptd 10-28, 863A2
Abud Hamid Bhashani dies 11-17, 970B1
Electns postponed 11-21, 923F2-A3
Rahman takes full powers, pol foes seized 11-29, 11-30, 12-7, 923D2
BANGOR, Wash.—*See WASHINGTON*
BANGOR Punta Corp.
Smith & Wesson
Libya defrauded in French binocular deal 12-25—12-30, 1006D3
BANGOURA, Mamadou
Guinea dvpt min 12-11, 1005G1

1977

BALTIMORE Sun (newspaper)
Trust suit setld 5-26, 504A2
On most reliable govt news source list 12-10, 1009B1
BALTIMORE & Ohio/Chesapeake & Ohio Railroad Co.—*See CHESSIE System*
BALZANO, Michael P.
Brown succeeds 2-25, 148C3
BANANA, Rev. Canaan
Arrested 1-25, 50B1
BANASZAK, Pete
Raiders win Super Bowl 1-9, 24E3, F3
BANCAL Tri-State Corp.
Bars British takeover 3-1, 155A2
Bank of California
Sells 27 branches 7-6, 578D1
Japan unit purchases challenged 8-9, 669A3
BANCO do Brasil
Named world's 8th largest bank 6-21, 578A2
BANDA, Hastings Kamuzu (Malawian president)
2 sentenced in plot 2-14, 309E2
Cabt dismissed 7-7, replaced 7-8, 772C1
BANDA, Zongani
Dismissed as Zambia power min 4-24, 490B2
BANDARANAIKE, Anura
Mother ousted in elections 7-21, 571E3
BANDARANAIKE, Sirimavo (Sri Lanka prime minister; replaced July 23)
Warns emergency rule 1-25, 68B3
Ends parlt 2-12, foes score 2-15, 137E3
Subasinghe quits Cabt, Freedom Party 3-1, 183G1
Defectors form new party 4-10, 309D3
Loses electn 7-21, replaced 7-23, 571B3
Boycotts Assemb vote 10-5, 843E3
BANDARANAIKE, Solomon (West Ridgway Diaz) (d. 1959)
Wife loses election 7-21, 571F3
BANDERA, Girolamo
Arrest rptd 8-27, 783D1
BANDO, Chris
Ariz State wins coll baseball title 6-18, 568A1
BANDO, Sal
Ariz State wins coll baseball title 6-18, 568A1

BANGLADESH (formerly East Pakistan)—*See also COMMONWEALTH of Nations, NONALIGNED Nations Movement*
Mushtaque sentenced 2-26, 183C1
Mushtaque acquitted of 2d chrg 3-10, 309G1
Tornado kills 900 4-1, 312E2
Pres Sayem quits, Rahman sworn 4-21, 309F1
Martial law policies approved 5-29, 451D2
Malaria upsurge rptd 9-4, 747F3
Cholera outbreak rptd 9-21, 748D1
Rebel raid rptd 9-30, 763D2
Army coup crushed 10-2; death toll 230 10-3, 763B2
3 parties banned 10-14, 805E2
Coup ldrs executed, sentncd 10-19, 805G2
Army coup plotters sentncd 10-27, 969F2
Foreign Relations (misc.)
UN Assemb member 3F3
OPEC allocates loan funds 1-10, 12A3
Sweden budgets aid 1-10, 23B1
India Ganges talks collapse 1-23, 64D1
Nixon reminisces 5-12, 386B2
Japan jet hijacked 9-28—10-3, 756G2, C2
India Ganges R pact 11-5; map 896D3
Sweden cancels debts 11-8, 904A1
BANGOR Punta Corp.
Chris-Craft damages voided 2-23, 150A2
Smith & Wesson
'66-75 Latin arms sales rptd 4-8, 415G2

1978

BALTIMORE Sun, The (newspaper)
USSR seizes Piper's notes 3-2, US protests 3-8, 180E1
USSR accuses Piper 6-28, 518C1, D2; convicts 7-18, 575D2
Piper fine paid 8-4, 634B1
USSR closes Piper case 8-18, 651F1; issues warning 8-24, 670C2
BAMBERGER, George
Signs as Brewers mgr 1-20, 195A1
BANANAS—*See FRUITS & Vegetables*
BANCA Nazionale Del Lavoro (Rome bank)
Not on '77 top 10 bank list 11-8, 914D1
BANCO de Brasil (Brazilia bank)
Ranked '77 9th biggest in world 11-8, 914B1, D1
BANCO Latinoamericano de Exportaciones, S.A.
Opens 9-8, 828C3
BANDA, Hastings Kamuzu (Malawian president)
Meets forgn press; defends ousters, S Africa ties 6-30, 534E3
Bars forgn rptrs 8-14, 677G1
BANDERA, Girolamo
Jailed in quake relief scandal 1-23, 103F3

BANGLADESH (formerly East Pakistan)—*See also COMMONWEALTH of Nations, GATT, NONALIGNED Nations Movement*
UK prime min visits 1-4—1-5, 37B1, A2
Islamic bank poor-natn aid rise rptd 4-9, 257F2
Burma Moslems seek refuge 4-30; Dacca rally scores Burma 5-6; exodus toll at 100,000 5-10, 412E2
Burma blames Bengalis 5-7, Islamic League concerned 5-8, 412A3
US A-fuel export license deferral rptd 5-20, 408B2
Rahman reelected pres, foes chrg fraud 6-3; Rahman denies 6-5, 435A1
New Cabt sworn 6-29, 538D1
Burma refugee pact reached 7-9, 538G1
Dutch cancel debts 7-10, 575E1
UK cancels debts 7-31, 592D1
UN Assemb member 713C3
BANGOR Punta Corp.
'77 sales rise rptd 5-8, 325C2

1979

BALTIMORE Sun, The (newspaper)
Franklin wins Pulitzer 4-16, 336C3
Groden JFK autopsy photo forgery claim denied 7-9, 520A3
BALTIMORE-Washington Airport (Friendship, Md.)
8 armed Iranians seized 11-15, 879F1
BANANAS—*See FRUITS & Vegetables*
BANCO Caley-Dagnall, S.A.
Nicaraguan operatns curbed 7-25, 574B1
BANGEMANN, Martin
To inform UK Liberals re EC Parlt exclusn 7-18, 537C3

BANGLADESH (formerly East Pakistan)—*See also COMMONWEALTH of Nations, GATT, NONALIGNED Nations Movement*
Freedom House lists as partly free 13A1
Nationalist Party wins parlt electns 2-18, martial law end set 2-19, 172F3
Martial law lifted 4-7, 328F2
Foreign Relations (misc.)—*See also 'UN' below*
UK ends fiancee immigrant virginity tests 2-2, 96D3
India accords reached 4-18, 328C2
Iran detains natl in US Emb 11-5, 841E1; frees 11-22, 895A3
Anti-US protests 11-22—11-23, 894D1
US sets evacuatns, travel curbs 11-26, 894G1
UN Policy & Developments
Membership listed 695E2
Iran sanctns res abstentn 12-31, 974G2
BANGUI, Sylvestre
Asks French asylum 5-22, 387B2
BANI-Assadi, Hossein
Iran deputy premier 4-24, 297B2
BANI-Sadr, Abolhassan
Installed Iran forgn min, backs US Emb takeover 11-10, 862F1
Asks UN Cncl mtg on US hostages, sets new terms 11-13, 862C1
Defends US asset withdrawal 11-14, 861C2
US women, black hostages ordrd freed 11-17, 878B1
Repudiates forgn debts 11-23, 896B2
OKs UN Cncl debate on Iran 11-25, asks delay 11-27, 896C1
Khomeini vs UN Cncl debate 11-27, fires 11-28, 896E1
Heads Azerbaijan peace missn 12-10, 936D1
Defies US sanctns threat 12-22, 974D3

1980

BALTIMORE News American (newspaper)
Agnew interview publshd 4-20, 333C3
BALTIMORE Sun (newspaper)
Corddry in pres TV debate 9-21, 721C3
BALZAC, Honore de (1799-1850)
Heartaches of a Pussycat opens 3-19, 392A3
BALZAMO, Vincenzo
Italy science min 4-4, 275G3
BAMBERGER, George
Suffers heart attack 3-6, returns to manage Brewers 6-4, 636G3
BANANA, Rev. Canaan (Zimbabwean president)
Zimbabwe indepndnc proclaimed; sworn 4-18, 301D1
BANANAS—*See FRUITS & Vegetables*
BANCROFT, Anne
Fatso released 2-1, 216E2
BANDARANAIKE, Felix Dias
Sri Lanka parlt ousts 10-16, 810B1
BANDARANAIKE, Sirimavo
State of emergency set 10-14, ousted from parlt 10-16, 810A1

BANGLADESH—*See also ADB, COMMONWEALTH of Nations, GATT, NONALIGNED Nations*
Freedom House lists as partly free 87E3
Foreign Relations (misc.)—*See also 'UN Policy' below*
Islamic conf summit proposed 1-7, 67E2
India hit by Assamese-Bengali unrest 3-24—4-7, 275B1
Assam unrest continues 4-12—4-29, 352G2
W Ger pol asylum rules rptd tightened 7-31, 581E2, F2
Burma citizenship law rptd proposed 8-13, 617F3
World Bank '80 loans rptd 9-22, 720E1
India unrest renewed 10-19—11-2, 729C2
Assam protests renewed 10-19—11-2, 873A1
UN Policy & Developments
Iran sanctns vote absentn 1-13, 29A1
Choudhury vs apptmt to shah probe comm 2-17, 122C1
Cncl scores Israel Jerusalem move 8-20, 627C2
Cncl seat replacemt set 11-13, 896E1
BANI-Sadr, Abolhassan
Vs Sovt Afghan invasn 1-16, 27D2
Elected pres 1-25; final results 1-28, 66C3
On US hostage resolutn, scores militants 1-26—1-28, 67B1
US sees hostage hope in electn 1-28, 67E1
Militants cancel rally; newspr closes 2-3, 88C2, D2
Inaugurated pres 2-4, 88G1
Consolidates Rev Cncl power 2-5, 2-7; denounces US Emb militants, curbs media access 2-6, 105G1
US delays sanctns 2-7, 88F2
Sets hostage release terms 2-11—2-13, rpts secret plan OKd 2-13, 105D1
OKs UN comm to probe shah 2-18, 2-19, 122D1
Heads armed forces 2-19, 122D2
Meets UN comm 2-24, 137F2
Denies US moderate claim; at anti-US rally, urges people's army 2-25, 137D2
Hostage visit with UN comm rptd planned 2-28, 138C1
Overruled by Khomeini on hostages 3-10, vs militant-govt stand 3-11, 177B1, D1
Vows vote fraud probe 3-16, gets complaint 3-18, 218F1
Arabs vs stand on gulf states, islands 261B1
Rally protests hostage policy 3-25, Islamic ldr asks trials 3-26, 217F2
US denies 'apology' notes 3-29, 3-30, 241D2, 242A1, B1
EC sends US hostage release plea 3-31, 242D1
Sets US hostage transfer terms 4-1, 241B1-F1
Khomeini bars hostage shift to govt 4-7, 258B1
EC votes hostage plea 4-10, 281G2
Warns Iraq vs attack 4-11, 300D1
EC, Japan ask hostage release 4-12, 282E1
Says US blocked shah's query in Panama 4-16, US denies 4-17, 283C1
Warns US vs more sanctns 4-18, 298C2
Vs Moslem attacks on leftists 4-20, 4-22, 299D3
Confirms hostage transfer 4-26, 322D3
Lauds UK Emb rescue 5-5, 337D1

1976

BANKAMERICA Corp.
Clausen in Mex talks 1-26, 75F1
FRB acquisition bar cited 8-19, 667C2
Boycott rpts released 10-18, 10-20, 786B1, A2
Bank of America National Trust & Savings Association
Not on 'problem' bank list 1-11, 110F2
Argentina grain export credits set 1-28, 96B3
Gas pact with Japan, USSR reached 3-31, 655C3
Raises prime rate 5-28, 436C3
Heads E Ger Euro$ loan group 6-4, 417B2
Syndicate OKs Bolivia loan 6-18, 456A3
Rpt Spain seeks intl loan 6-23, 501A3
Spain Eurocurrency loan rptd 7-13, 541B3
Spain signs intl loan 8-9, 929G1
Arab boycott noncompliance rptd 10-24, 11-10, 986F2
Lowers prime rate 10-29, 846E2
Calif boycott law compliance set 11-3, 12-1, 987C1
Lowers prime rate 12-10, 939B3
BANKERS Association, American—*See AMERICAN Bankers Association*
BANKERS Club of America (N.Y.)
Mondale addresses 8-25, 645A3
BANKERS Trust Co. (Miss.)
Sued 5-7, declared insolvent 6-8, 438E1
Miss closes S&Ls 6-20; run halted 7-8, 494G3-495B1
BANKERS Trust New York Corp.
FRB bars acquisition, cites money troubles, stock drops 8-19, 667F1
Bankers Trust Co. (N.Y.)
Rptd on FDIC 'problem' list 1-23, 112C2
Del Farmers Bank default rptd 2-4, 437C3
AJC scores re boycott 3-18, 747A2
Drops Zaire loan suit; new paymt plan OKd 10-13, 890G2-C3
Bankers Trust Savings and Loan Association (Jackson)
Receiver named 5-20, 438E1
Bankers Trust International
Hungary loan rptd 7-2, 925D2
Syndicate lends USSR $250 mln 7-16, 540D2
Boycott rpt released 10-19, 786C1
BANK for International Settlements (BIS)
Gold purchases rptd planned 1-8, 14D1
IMF gold purchase rptd 6-3, 430E2
Loan to prop UK £ OKd 6-7, 407A2
Buys IMF gold 10-29, 832F2
BANK for Reconstruction and Development, International—*See under WORLD Bank Group*
BANKHEAD, Dan
Dies 5-2, 368D2
BANK Leu Ltd. (Zurich)
IMF gold buyer 9-15, 739D3
BANK Leumi Trust Co.
Buys Amer Bank & Trust 9-16, 940D1
BANK of California—*See under BANCAL Tri-State Corp.*
BANK of New Orleans & Trust Co.—*See NEW Orleans Bancshares Inc.*
BANK of North Carolina—*See under BANCSHARES of North Carolina*
BANK of Oman Ltd.
Buys IMF gold 10-29, 832E2
BANK of the Commonwealth (Detroit)
1st Arabian acquisitn OKd 12-19, 983F3

1977

BANKAG Bank (Zurich)
Liquidation set, '76 arrests cited 8-19, 658E1
BANKAMERICA Corp.
Bank of America National Trust & Savings Association
IBEC loan cancelled 1-26, 123E2
Venez Eurocurrency loan set 3-28, 547D1
Listed as world's biggest 6-21, 578G1
Rpts '76 China trade surplus 8-11, 635E3
Argentina loan co-financed 11-10, 981G2
Mex $1.2 bln loan rptd 11-18, 967C1
BANKER, The (magazine)
World's top 10 banks rptd 6-21, 578G1
BANKERS Association, American
Blumenthal addresses conv 10-19, 792G2, 798G1
BANKERS Trust New York Corp.
Bankers Trust Co. (N.Y.)
On Sovt-bloc Western debt 2-13, 335F3
Pension managemt cited 6-28, 578C2
SEC rpt chrgs NYC '74-75 financial deceptn 8-26; reactn 8-26—8-27, 665A3, 666A1
Bankers Trust International
Venez Eurocurrency loan set 3-28, 547D1
BANK for International Settlements (BIS)
UK sterling balances accord 1-10, 20C2; Callaghan to supervise 1-21, 44E2
Sovt-bloc Westn debt rptd 2-23, 335D3, F3
Warns US re paymts, trade gaps 6-12, 502D1
BANK for Reconstruction and Development, International—*See under WORLD Bank Group*
BANK Leumi Trust Co.
Graiver scandal breaks in Argentina 4-11, 345C2; 'proof' rptd 5-4, 371A2
BANK of America National Trust & Savings Association—*See under BANKAMERICA Corp.*
BANK of California—*See BANCAL Tri-State Corp.*
BANK of the Commonwealth (Detroit)
Pharaon sale cited 12-27, 1003A3

1978

BANKAMERICA Corp.
Bank of America National Trust & Savings Association
Brazil loan syndicatn rptd 3-10, 311G1
S Africa loans backed 3-22, 237E2
Panama refinance pkg planned 6-22, 632D2
Giraldi named Latin export bank vice pres 9-8, 828D3
Ranked world's biggest bank 11-8, 913G3-914A1
BANKER, The (British magazine)
Ranks '77 world's top 10 banks 11-8, 913G3, 914A1
BANKER International
Graiver indicted in US 4-12, 326B2
BANKERS Life & Casualty Corp.
John MacArthur dies 1-6, 96G2
BANKERS Trust New York Corp.
Bankers Trust Co. (N.Y.)
Stock sale case refused by Sup Ct 3-28, 241E3
Chile loans rptd undercutting US rights policy 4-11, 312F1
BANK for International Settlements (BIS)
US moves to halt $ slide 1-4, 27A2
BANK Leumi Trust Co.
Graiver indicted for Amer Bank & Trust embezzlemt 4-12, 326G1
BANK of America National Trust & Savings Association—*See under BANKAMERICA Corp.*
BANK of Credit & Commerce International S.A. (London)
Financial Gen sues vs takeover 2-17, 204A3
SEC files chrgs 3-18, complaint setld 3-19, 204A2
BANK of London and South America
Nicaragua mgr attacked by guardsmen 11-6, 883B2
BANKOV, Stefan
Rpts '74 attack 9-14, 749B1
BANK Robberies—*See BANKS—Crime Issues*

1979

BANI-Sadr, Ahmed
Named Iran econ dep min 7-19, 565F2
BANKAMERICA Corp.
Bank of America National Trust & Savings Association
Poland econ monitor plan set 1-11, 59G3
Ecuador loan set 1-30, 101G1
Iran banks natlzd 6-7, compensatn vowed 6-10, 469G1
Ranked '78 world's biggest bank 6-19, 476A2
Nicaragua operatns curbed 7-25, 574B1
Mex oil loan agrmt rptd 7-28, 584E1
Nicaragua debt paymts in doubt 9-28, 753F2
El Salvador office bombed 10-28, 834F2
Pak branch sacked 11-21, 893F1
Iran sues UK branch for assets freeze 11-30, 915A2
BANKER, The (British magazine)
Top '78 300 banks rptd 6-19, 476A2
BANKERS Association, American
Wire-transfer thefts discounted 3-25, 239D2
Automatic funds shift voided 4-20, 303A3
Reuss abandons FRB aid bill 4-24, 303C2
Carter bank law reform proposal backed 5-22, 403A2
Volcker addresses 10-9, 764C3
BANKERS Association, Independent
Automatic funds shift voided 4-20, 303B3
BANKERS Life & Casualty Corp.
Colo land sale refunds set 5-8, 596A1
BANKERS Trust New York Corp.
Bankers Trust Co. (N.Y.)
Poland econ monitor plan set 1-11, 59G3
Branch robbed of $2 mln 8-3, 2 suspects arrested 8-8, 8-9, 656C1
Prime rate lowered 11-15, 941C1
Iran assets seized for loan repaymts 11-16, 879F3
Iran sues UK branch for assets freeze 11-30, 915A2
BANK Leumi Trust Co.
Graiver ruled dead, chrgs vs Amer Bank & Trust dismissed 1-8, 161C1
BANK Markazi (Iran)
US banks sued for UK, French assets freeze 11-30, 12-5, 915A2
UK upholds US assets freeze 12-5, 915G1
France upholds US assets freeze 12-12, 12-21, 976B2
BANK of America National Trust & Savings Association—*See under BANKAMERICA*
BANK of Credit & Commerce International S.A. (London)
Lance '78 aid cited 4-9, 306B1
BANK of Tokyo
Iran banks natlzd 6-7, compensatn vowed 6-10, 469A2
BANK Omran (Iran) (defunct)
Shah chrgd with embezzlemt 12-11, 935D2
BANK Robberies—*See BANKS-Crime Issues*

1980

Khomeini OKs premr apptmt 5-9, Rev Cncl bars 5-12, 373F1
Strips Khalkhali of power 5-13, 373C2
On renewal of UN comm missn 5-17; West warning to Waldheim cited 5-23, 393G2, 394B1
Khalkhali orders executns 5-21, 419D3
Addresses new parlt 5-28, 394G1, C2
Clark OKs panel to probe US 6-4, 418C3
Vs trial for hostages 6-9, 433G1
2 close aides quit 6-17, 6-19; shifts army cmnd 6-19, 464B2
Plot to overthrow rptd 6-19, 464E2
Khomeini scores rule 6-27; responds 6-29, 490D1-D2
Calls hostage crisis 'insoluble' 6-28, 490D2
Names Bojnourdi Rev Guard cmdr, Sharif dep 6-29, 490C2
Meets MD protesters 7-2, 507B1
Women protest clothing rule 7-5, 507B1, D1
Mil coup plot fails 7-10, 539D2
Formally sworn 7-22, 571A3
US, UK rptrs flee Iran 7-25, 572C1
Nominates premier 7-26, 571E2
Hostage status unaffected by shah's death 7-27, 571C2
Sends message to jailed Iranians in US 8-5, 587D1
Premr nominee rejctd, Rajai named 8-9; parlt agrees 8-11, 620A1
Vs new Cabt 8-31, parlt delays OK 9-2, 671B2
Khomeini asks to OK partial Cabt 9-5; OKs 14 mins 9-7, parlt OKs 9-10, 688G3*-689C1
US favors probe, backs Khomeini terms 9-17, 693B2
On Iraq ending border pact, sees all-out war 9-17, 694C2
Calls up reservists in Iraqi war 9-20, 717C1
Vs UN truce bid 10-1, 734A1
Seeks world arms purchase 10-7, 757G2
Waldheim asks truce 10-10; replies 10-13, 774F1
Khomeini cedes war powers 10-12, 773D2
Scores Ghotbzadeh arrest 11-7, 862E1
Backs quick hostage setlmt 11-10, 861G1
Meets UN Iran-Iraq peace delegate 11-20, 894B3
Announces 'new war phase' vs Iraq 12-3, 913D1
Khalkhali quits as drug prosecutor 12-7, 943F1
BANKAMERICA Corp.
Intl Group OKs Polish loan 8-22, 642C2
Clausen named World Bank pres 10-30, 826G1
Armacost named pres, chief exec 12-1, 959C1
Bank of America National Trust & Savings Association
El Salvador natlzatn set 2-11, 117F2
Brazil oil loan rptd 3-5, 191F1
Credit restrictions rptd 3-27, 222G2
Prime rate hiked to 19.5% 3-28, 20% 4-2, 247D2
Prime rate cut to 17.5% 5-7, 367D3
Prime cut to 14.5% 5-23, 401G1
Prime cut to 14% 5-30; 12.75% 6-12, 438B1, D1
Prime cut to 11.5% 7-7, 514A1
Bolivian debt paymts postponed 9-3, 686F2-B3
Nicaragua debt rescheduled 9-5, 689G2
BANKERS Association, American
Kaufman addresses 2-21, 144F3
BANKERS Trust New York Corp.
Fla 'parochial' banking practices curbed by Sup Ct 6-9, 512F2
Bankers Trust Co. (N.Y.)
Prime rate dropped to 18.5% 4-28, 329A2
Prime rate cut to 17.5% 5-6, 367C3
Prime cut to 15.5% 5-22, 14% 5-27, 401F1, C2
Prime cut to 13% 6-5, 438C1
Prime cut to 11% 7-21, 574E3
Nicaragua debt rescheduled 9-5, 689A3
Major banks hike prime to 14% 9-12—10-2, 764E2
FRB OKs commercial paper sales 9-29, 986B2
BANK for International Settlements (BIS)
W Ger bond redemptn questnd 6-3, 446G3*
BANK of America National Trust & Savings Association—*See under BANKAMERICA Corp.*
BANK of New York Co. Inc., The
Bank of New York, The
Prime rate cut to 14% 5-28, 13% 6-5, 438B1, C1

1976

BANKRUPTCY—*See also company, country names*
Hamilton Bancshares, 3 units file 2-20, 166E3
Cong clears city reform bill 3-25, 246D2; Ford signs 4-8, 982E1
Grant adjudged bankrupt 4-13, 984F3
Abercrombie petitn granted 8-9, 984D3
Ford, Carter debate 9-23, 702D2; 10-22, 802B1
Fiscl '76 petitns down 10-20, 984C3
Carter scores Ford record 10-31, 827A2
Carter bars NYC bankruptcy 12-28, 978D2

1977

BANKRUPTCIES—*See also company, country names*
UM&M files 7-12, 612F1-F2
Grant '75 bankruptcy cited 7-12, 612E2
Abercrombie closes 12-14, 980E3
Milwaukee Rd files 12-19, 1006G3

1978

BANKRUPTCIES
Church bond losses rptd 2-27, 295F3
Penn Central reorganizatn plan OKd 3-9, 185F3-186F1
REA case review refused by Sup Ct 3-20, 206A1
Japan Mar record rptd 4-10, 314A2
Tax liability backed by Sup Ct 5-22, 388B1
Bede Aircraft OKs FTC trustee plan 6-13, 702C2
HFC lending violatns chrgd 7-7, 589F1
Revisn bill delay sought by Burger 9-28; Cong clears 10-6, 788D2-789B1
Food Fair files for protectn 10-1, 752G3
Milwaukee Rd wins merger appeal 10-5, 812C2
Penn Central reorganizatn ends 10-24, 875F3
Revisn bill signed 11-6, 1003B1

1979

BANKRUPTCIES
Food Fair closes 123 supermkts 1-27, 131G2
State rent collectn laws backed by Sup Ct 2-21, 128G3
Chase REIT files 2-22, 131G1-E2
Allied Artists files for reorganizatn 4-4, 430G3
Milwaukee Rd svc cut denied 6-1, 465A2
Antioch averts 6-4, 482G1-B2
Personal data collectn backed by Sup Ct 6-4, 439B2
Milwaukee Rd trustee quits 6-15, 867G2
City Stores files 7-27, 648F3
Rock Island RR 'cashless' findings rptd 9-21, 9-26, 722B2-F2
Penn Central reorganizatn challenges declined by Sup Ct 10-1, 768E1
Worldwide Church receivership challenge refused by Sup Ct 10-1, 768A2
Reform act takes effect 10-1, 991C1
Amer Atomics seeks reorganizatn 10-6, 806F2
Rock Island RR reorganizatn plan ordered 10-10, 830E3
Milwaukee Rd embargoes track 11-1, Carter signs aid bill 11-4, 867E2
Fscl '79 petitns rptd up 11-15, 991B1
Milwaukee Rd bailout ruled legal 11-25, 989A2
Methodist legal immunity cases declined by Sup Ct 11-26, 919F2
Rock I reorganizatn plan filed 12-28, 989C2

1980

BANKRUPTCIES
Lafayette Radio files 1-4, 131E3
Milwaukee Rd westn track purchase rejected in '79 1-7, 53C1
Rock I RR liquidatn ordrd 1-25, 131G1
Pa scandal indictmts 2-12, 502D2
Personal filings rptd up 3-25, 263C3
Penn-Dixie files 4-7, 985F3
Small business failure rise rptd 5-15, 455G2
Lake Placid Olympics com threat rptd 6-1, 421A2
Rock I RR abandonmt OKd, worker aid law upset 6-2; Sup Ct bars actn 7-2, 11-10, 868E2
Chrysler stops supplier paymts 6-11, 457B1
AMA threat cited 7-22, 583A3
White Motor files 9-4, 985E3
Auto-Train files 9-8, ct blocks creditors svc cut 9-26; DC investors rescue attempt rptd 11-26, 958C2, B3
Natl Student Mktg liquidates 9-10, 985F3
Tenna liquidatn ordered 9-12, 985G3
Mansfield Tire liquidates 9-19, 985F3
Barber Oil liquidates 10-2, 986A1
Kress liquidatn set 11-6, 986B1
NY Mafia boss convicted of fraud 11-21, 971G2
NRC lists GPU aid optns 11-28, 961B1
Methodists settle Pacific Homes suit 12-10, 963D3
Natl Shoes files 12-11, 985F3
New Haven RR reorgn challenge refused by Sup Ct 12-15, 957D2
Reading emerges 12-31, 985G3

BANKS (& BANKING)

1976

BANKS (& Banking)—*See also CREDIT, Consumer; MONETARY Developments; EXPORT-Import Bank and FEDERAL Reserve System under U.S. GOVERNMENT; WORLD Bank Group; also bank, country names*
Bloomfield (NJ) bank fails 1-10, sold 1-11, 167B2
Major banks rptd on 'problem' list, Cong asks regulatory reform 1-11—2-9, 110D2-113D2
Colo bank fails, sold 1-12, 167B2
Ford State of Union message 1-19, 37D3, 39C2
'77 budget seeks rules revisn 1-21, 65E3
Del Farmers Bank rpts loss 1-29; state, FDIC bailout dvpts 2-4—6-10, 437F2
'75 4th ¼ profits rptd 2-3, 215A3
Hamilton Natl fails, sold 2-16; reopens 2-17; parent co files bankruptcy 2-20, 166E3-167A2
'Problem' savings & loans rptd 2-17, 185C1
Mercantile (Mo) pol costs rptd 2-27, 181A1
Houston bank failure, sale rptd 3-3, 167C2
Volcker vs regulatory merger 3-9, 185F3
Detroit notes purchased 3-24, 994D2
Govt access to records upheld 4-21, 331C1
House com acts on 2 Reuss reform bills 4-30, 5-3; House OKs FRB bill 5-10, 345D1
Miss S&Ls crisis 5-7—6-8, 438E1
San Leandro (Calif) bank fails 5-22, Lloyds reopens 5-23, 438B1
NY business loans rptd up 6-2, 436E3
Houston bank closed 6-3, 438D1
Sup Ct rules on venue of suits 6-7, 435G1
NJ, Colo, Ky banks closed 6-14, 6-25; NJ bank reopens 6-15, 495F1
Dem platform text 6-15, 469E3
Miss S&Ls closed 6-20, run halted 7-8, 494F3-495E1
Treas anti-bias actn scored 7-1, 943D3
Nader rpt scores diversificatn 7-5, 495B2-A3
Texas bank fails 7-7, 940B2
2d ¼ profits rptd 7-28, 708F3
Business loans rptd down 7-29, 568E2
Sen curbs IRS record access 8-6, 586G1
Fed bds make-up scored 8-15; Burns disputes 8-30, 666G3
GOP platform text 8-18, 604F2
FRB bars Bankers Trust acquisitn, cites finances 8-19, 667F1
Open govt bill protects privacy 9-13, 688F3
Amer Bank & Trust fails 9-15, sold 9-16, 940A1
Boston bank fails, sold 9-15, 984A1
Cong clears IRS records access curbs 9-16, 706F1
Carter vs redlining 9-25, 724F1
'75 zero, under 10% tax paymts rptd 10-2, 10-14, 847F1-D2
Sup Ct bars review of electronic banking rule 10-4, 807B2
Franklin bank failure handling scored 10-6, 940B2
Rural agri loan problems cited 10-12, 787F3
Firms effective tax rate cited 10-14, 847D2
Phila bank fails 10-20, sold 10-21, 940G1
Problem bank list grows 11-2, 866D1, E1 ★
Mayors ask urban dvpt bank 11-8, 845D3
RI bank fails 11-16, 940F1
New Orleans banks fails 12-3, sold 12-5, 939E3-940A1
Detroit bank acquisitn OKd 12-19, 983F3

1977

BANKS (& Banking)—*See also CREDIT, MONETARY Developments; also bank, country names*
GAO scores fed regulators 1-31, 154E3
Record '76 savings inflow rptd 2-1, 155G1
NYC debt repaymt dvpts 2-8—3-11, 193C1-G3
FRB bars bank S&L ownership 2-22, 155D1
NYC banks chrgd re job bias 2-23, 279G1
Bancal rejcts takeover bid 3-1, 155A2
Okla, Conn, Ga banks fail 3-10, 3-28, 5-20, 578C1
Problem bank list rptd up 3-11, 194C2
'73-76, bank failures cited 3-11, 194F2
Ill bank withdraws farmland fund plan 3-11, 195A1
Carter drops tax rebate plan 4-14, 271F1
NBA aids ailing teams 6-15, 584E1
Foreclosure delays upheld 6-17, 518F2
Pension mgt concentratn chrgd 6-28, 578B2
Lance's Ga bank rpts 1st ½ loss 7-5, 7-13, 514D2
Bancal to sell 27 Calif branches 7-6, 578D1
2 women's banks chartered 7-6, 578F1
Privacy comm submits rpt, scores FRB computer plan 7-12, 632B1, D1
Kan wheat farmers' debts rptd 8-8, 612B1
1st Penna takes over NFL Eagles 8-8, 659A1
Ga bank omits dividend 8-9, 626F1
Carter sees rules reform need 8-23, 649F1
Carter to reimburse Ga bank for plane use 8-24, 649E3
Labor Dept warns Harris Trust re bias 8-25, 669G2
SEC rpt chrgs NYC '74-75 deceptn 8-26; reactn 8-26—8-27, 665C2, 661A1
Regulators see no major chngs needed; FDIC to study loan, overdraft policy 9-26, 761B2
Interest-bearing fed tax, loan accts clear Cong 10-14, 815A3; signed 10-28, 1001D2
Bancal sale of 19 Calif branches cleared 10-19, 979D2
La judicial conduct code review refused 11-7, 857E2
Right to sue natl banks widened 11-8, 857C1
S&L redlining curbed 11-9, 898D2
Carter denies FRB rift 11-10, 877C1
Lehman Bros, Kuhn Loeb plan merger 11-28, 1004F2-A3
Cleveland schl debt repaymt OKd 12-7, 939F2

1978

BANKS (& Banking)—*See also CREDIT, MONETARY Developments; also bank names*
Key figures in NYC fscl crisis listed 86E3
Econ indicator index described 128B1
Lance loans rptd repaid 1-17, 2-13, 3-22, 204C3
NYC fscl recovery plan issued 1-20, 87A2, B2
'53, '78 cong membership compared 1-30, 107G2
Sen Banking Com rpt vs future NYC aid 2-9, 87A1
Lance sued by Financial Gen, SEC 2-17, 3-18; SEC chrgs setld 3-19, 204F1, A3
Holding cos insurance sales denied review 2-27, 143B2
Blumenthal proposes NYC long-term loan guarantees 3-2, Carter signs bill 8-8, 608C1, F2
Cleveland schls denied loans 3-23, 279E2
Carter unveils urban-aid plan 3-27, 217A3
Stock sale checking-acct case refused by Sup Ct 3-27, 241D2
Bankers Trust stock sale case refused by Sup Ct 3-28, 241E3
Pan Am buys Lockheed jets 4-4, 264F2
Lance scores press coverage 4-12, 324F3-325A1
Pulitzer awarded for Lance disclosures 4-17, 315B2
SEC, comptroller chrg Lance, 2 banks; case setld 4-26, 324G2-E3
Corp pol free speech backed by Sup Ct 4-26, 343G2
Check-bouncing protectn OKd, NOW acct use cited 5-1, 5-5, 345D3
Mgt gains for women rptd 5-22, 554F3
NYC control bd-MAC bill signed 6-2, 608F3
Admin asks exec pay curbs 6-6, 428B1
Columbia U sets stock sale 6-6, 633C1
Carter campaign com, Ga bank fined for '76 plane use 6-26, 509A3
Gartner Minn loans rptd 6-27, 513E3
Solar, other renewable energy business loan aid signed 7-4, 512F1
NYC $2.55 bln loan agreed 7-27, 609B1
Consumer co-op bank clears Cong 8-9, signed 8-20, 663E1
Auto-leasing case declined by Sup Ct 10-2, 751B2
Mellon Bank SC-immunity case refused by Sup Ct 10-10, 789F2
FDIC paymt case refused by Sup Ct 10-16, 789B1
FRB hikes reserve requiremts 11-1, 825E1
Morgan Stanley sued re Olinkraft merger 11-8, 896D3
3 US banks on world's '77 top 10 list 11-8, 913F3
Reform bill signed 11-10, 1002E3
Carter reaffirms natl dvpt bank support 11-27, mayors oppose 11-29, 914B3, G3
Reuss Open Market Com case declined by Sup Ct 11-27, 937F2
FRB holding co power backed by Sup Ct 12-11, 980D3
Cleveland defaults 12-16, ct actn delayed 12-28, 1008A2, C2, D3
Nov indicators drop, NOW accts use linked 12-28, 1003C3

1979

BANKS (& Banking)—*See also CREDIT, MONETARY Developments; also bank names*
FRB discourages 'long float' check delays 1-10, 15E2
Carter budget proposals 1-22, 44C2, D3
'78 problem banks listed by FDIC 1-30, 113A2
Buckley, Sitco partners settle SEC chrg 2-7, 132E1
Dvpt finance progrm proposed 3-1, 164G1
NYC occupancy tax collectn curbed by Sup Ct 3-5, 185E1
FRB clears Cleveland bank 3-14, 204D2
Indicators index revised, NOW accounts cited 4-1, 252A2
3 Mile I A-accident impact rptd 4-2, 245B3
Treas calls in tax receipts 4-2, 251C3
Carter urges privacy bill 4-2, 264F3
FEC clears Carter primary spending, rpts minor violatn 4-2, 265B1, D1
FRB membership cost cited 4-9, Reuss abandons bill 4-24, 303D1
BayBanks '77 FRB withdrawal cited 4-9, 303A2
Automatic funds shift voided 4-20, 303C2
Carter proposes bank law reforms 5-22, regulators set chngs 5-30, 403B1
Antioch averts bankruptcy 6-4, 482G1
Cleveland repaymt plan agreed 6-9, 579F3
Citicorp unit applicatn case declined by Sup Ct 6-11, 478G3
KKK law use curbed by Sup Ct 6-11, 479B1
US banks slip in world's '78 top 300 list 6-19, 476G1
GPU gains credit line 6-19, 519A1
Carter proposes solar energy bank 6-20, 498A1
GOP credit card plan blocked 6-21, 595G1
Cleveland default tied to anti-mayor moves 7-17, 579A3
FBI charter expands record access 7-31, 599A3
Boston bank A-protesters arrested 8-31, 742F3
Cleveland defaults again 8-31, repays over $3.7 mln 9-26, 920B3
Legislators' incomes studied 9-1, 701D3
Fla '78 FRB deposit growth, drug traffic linked 9-6, 840E3
Comptroller warns vs credit overextensn 9-13, 681D1
FRB sets new reserve rule, monetary policy 10-6; Volcker addresses bankers assn 10-9, 764F1, C3
Banking svcs case declined by Sup Ct 10-15, 847A3
Mfrs Hanover admits money supply error 10-26, 828C2
Mfrs Hanover cautious re Chrysler loans 10-30, Carter rescue plan proposed 11-1, 845C3
Martin vs bank 'greed' 11-1, 827C1
Cleveland plight cited 11-6, 846G2
Chicago mayor seeks schl note repaymt guarantee 12-7, 944A1
Rockefeller sets Chase retiremt, Butcher to succeed 12-18, 986B2
Chrysler credit set 12-21, 981E3-982A1
Chicago schl rescue barred 12-21, 991A2
Stopgap checking acct interest bill signed 12-28, 987B3

1980

BANKS (& Banking)
Money market, mutual funds defined 223A3
Cleveland debt cited 1-4, 187E1
Saco (Me) '79 default rptd 1-7, 54E1
'79 money supply growth rptd 1-10, 52A2
Merrill Trust Saco (Me) loan cited 1-10, 187F1
FRB fears membership exodus 1-23, 2-4; map, defectn chart 113B1-C3
Ia grain elevator owner's debt rptd 1-31, 238B1
FRB sets new monetary supply terms 2-7, 113C3
Carter unveils anti-inflatn plan 3-14, 201F1, G1
Employee uniform case declined by Sup Ct 3-17, 226F1
Class actn 'moot' standard redefined by Sup Ct 3-19, 250D1
Money mkt funds bank drain controversy rptd 3-20—3-21, 223C3
Ford Motor $1 bln credit line rptd 3-24, 287G3
Credit rptd tightened on FRB moves 3-27, 222D2
Deregulatn bill clears Cong 3-27, 3-29, Carter signs 3-31, 245C3
Top 10 money mkt funds chart 3-31, 223F3
Credit controls modified by FRB 4-2, 263F2
Chrysler aid deal planned 4-2, 287A1; loan guarantees OKd 5-10, 383A3
Money supply, business loans rptd down 4-4, 263F1-B2
Speculative investmt loan curbs urged 4-15, 290B1
FRB increases farm, small business loans 4-17, 286A2
First Penn bailout set 4-28, 329D3
First Chicago officers ousted 4-28, 456A2
Hunt silver bailout set 5-2, 344G3
DIDC proposes bank gift ban 5-6, oppositn rptd 7-18, 560E3
FRB eases credit controls 5-22, credit issuers rptd cautious 5-27, 399F3, 400G1
Hunts bailout loan paid 5-27, collateral listed 5-28, 425E2, B3-426F1
Hunt silver deals, Bache deceptn probed; FRB regulatn studied 5-29—5-30, 425D1-B3
Fla bank rules tightened 6-3, drug money linked 6-5, 502A1-A2
Fla 'parochial' practices curbed by Sup Ct 6-9, 512F2-A3
Chrysler stops supplier paymts 6-11, 457B1
Mello named First Women's pres 6-12, 600G2
US Chrysler aid plan backed by 2 holdout banks 6-20, 481D2
First Chicago chrmn named 6-24, 600C2
Chase names pres, chrmn 6-25, 600C2
FRB ends credit controls 7-3, 513E1
Carter seeks car dealer loan guarantees 7-8, 505F1
Financial futures trading expands 7-24, 8-7, 617D1
Cleveland default setlmt, bond purchase agreed 7-29, 743B3
Money supply rptd up 8-15, 630D3
DIDC tightens new acct gift rules, bans finder's fees 9-9, 986D1
Chicago OKs emergency borrowing 9-10, 743E3
Citicorp Choice Card introduced 9-16, FRB orders end 10-10, 985D3
AMC rescue plan proposed 9-24, 724D3
FRB OKs commercial paper sales 9-29, 986A2
Housing, community dvpt authrzn clears Cong 9-30, signed 10-8, 804B2

1976

Arab Boycott—*See under BUSINESS*
Crime Issues—*See also 'International Developments' below*
Ticor indicted 1-14, unit chrgd 2-2, 160A1
2 ex-Franklin offcls plead guilty 1-20, 78F2
US Financial ex-chrmn sentncd 2-3, 124D1
6 ex-Franklin aides sentncd 3-9, 271B2
Lefferdink sentncd in Miami 4-26, 384G2
W Va gov, aide acquitted 5-5, 342E3
Cunningham indicted 5-26, 442F2
Ex-SBA offcl sentenced 6-25, 596G1
Amer Bank & Trust fraud rptd 9-25, 940E1
Saxe mistrial declared 10-13, 816B2
'75 embezzlmt sentncs cited 11-20, 885D3

International Developments—*See also 'Interest Rates' above*
Colombia natlztn law rptd 1-2, 31A1
Consortium loan to Mex set 1-2, 75D1
US agrmt on forgn deposit disclosures rptd 1-18, 44A3
Panama Chase exec exiled 1-20, 121A3
Italy seeks US, Bonn loans 1-22, 74A2, E2
US-Dutch deal rptd 1-23, 102C2
US, Mex ldrs vow cooperatn 1-26, 75E1
US grain credit to Argentina set 1-28, 96B3
Deutsche mark bond issue set 1-28, 158E1
N Sea oil Euroloans rptd 2-4, 2-5, 173E3
Italy ups reserve requiremts, curbs speculatn 2-11, 140G2
Italy to get consortium-backed EC loan 2-16, 141A1
Japan-UK-US syndicate aids Hamilton Natl 2-20, 167D1
Canada sets curbs 2-20, 188A2
Bolivia gets UK, Canada loans 3-12, 4-14, 416E1
Swiss loan to Australia OKd 3-23, 237F2
US-USSR-Japan gas pact reached 3-31, 655C3
Canada-Lockheed contract deferred 4-1, 250D2; signed 4-30, 332F2; deal fails 5-18, 362G3
EC credits to Portugal set 4-6, 276E2
Iran, Pak, Turkey pact signed 4-22, 298B2
UK bank staff probed 4-28, 458B1
US proposes intl resources bank 5-6, 317C1, B2
Algeria gets Euro$ loan 5-6, 455D1
1st ¼ US loans to foreigners up 5-17, 397A1
US-Australia loan OKd 5-20, 400A1
UNCTAD vs US plan 5-30, US scores 6-1, 388E2, B3
IMF gold purchases rptd 6-3, 6-9, 430D2
Loan to prop UK £ OKd 6-7, 407A2
US-led syndicate OKs Bolivia loan 6-18, 456A3
Rpt Spain seeks intl loan 6-23, 501G2
Nigeria sets partial takeover 6-29, 1007D3
Quebec Olympic loans planned 6-30, 529F1
Hungary Euro loan rptd 7-2, 925D2
Spain intl loan rptd 7-13, 541B3
USSR gets $250 mln intl loan 7-16, 540D2
Riviera bank theft 7-16, 560E2
Argentina intl loan rptd 7-23, 554B1
Algeria $ securities issue rptd 7-27, 902B2
Citibank, others sue Eximbank re Zaire loan 8-9, 621B2
Paris bank robbery 8-13, 574F3-575A1
Canada proposes forgn unit operatns 8-23, 637C2
Herstatt, 7 others arrested 8-26, 678G3
Venez loan set 9-15, 875C1
Bank Leumi buys Amer Bank & Trust 9-16, 940D1
Venez, UK, Kuwait banks form finance co 9-17, 875E1
3d IMF gold auction 9-25, 739D3
Rpt Greece OKs Iran bank 9-29, 854G1
US forgn bank bill dies in Cong 10-2, 940F2
Libra Bank sets Chile loan 10-20, 871D1
4th IMF gold auction 10-27, 832E2
7 seized re Riviera heist 10-27, 876F3
Poland, W Ger credit deal rptd 11-4, 907F1
Bank of Eng defers special deposit paymts 11-5, 853C3
Australia ups reserve floor 11-7, 850D1
Zaire paymt plan rptd OKd 11-8, 890B2

1977

Crime Issues—*See also 'International Developments' below*
Saxe pleads guilty 1-17, sentncd 2-11, 140E1
Franklin, Hamilton auditors sued 2-9, 2-11, 155A3, C3
Chemical Bank indicted 2-24, 155C2
Chemical, 2 ex-offcls plead guilty 3-3, 4-14, 540A3
Security Natl double jeopardy bar upheld 3-28, 276F3
Mafia infiltratn rptd 5-16, 568E1
Franklin ex-v chrmn pleads guilty 6-21, 540G2
Mercantile bank of Chicago ex-chrmn pleads guilty 6-21, 540B3
'76 embezzlemt costs rptd 11-17, 919C1

International Developments—*See also 'Interest Rates' above*
'76 Swiss credits rptd 1-4, 48F2
UK gets $1.5 bln consortium loan 1-24, 99G1
Quebec bars forgn control 1-25, 81G3
Bank of Amer group cancels IBEC loan 1-26, 123D2
Australia SRD rate raised 2-2, 113C2
Sovt-bloc Western debt rptd 2-13—4-13, 335C3
'76 US bank lending record 2-17, 145E2
S Africa small bank aid set 2-22, 160E3
Bancal rejects UK unit takeover bid 3-1, 155A2
'76 US bank interventn rptd 3-2, 188E3
Swiss bank closed 3-2, 489D3
Riviera bank robber escapes 3-10, 288E2
FRB asks OPEC lending role 3-10; IMF debt managing role rptd 3-28, 362E3-363D1
Iran, Pak, Turkey sign pact 3-12, 190C2
'76, 4th ¼ bank lending rptd 3-23, 234G1
Jamaica to natlize Barclays 3-23, 257A2, D2
Venez gets Eurocurrency loan 3-28, 547C1
'66-75 Latin arms purchases rptd 4-8, 415E2
Argentina Graiver guerrilla fund scandal 4-11—4-23, 345A2; 4-23—5-4, 371G1
US loans to Indonesia rptd risky 4-18, 392G2
Chase curbs S Africa loans 4-19, 350C2
3 Swiss officers arrested 4-24, 350F2-B3
Swiss scandal spreads 4-26—6-20, new bank rules signed 6-2, 564A3, E3
Geneva pvt bank fails 5-9, 489B3
Tokyo monetary conf 5-22—5-25, 437B3
Forgn lending rptd up, US '76 loans 6-5, 438B1
Brazil gets intl consortium loan 6-20, 524D2
World's top 10 rptd 6-21, 578G1
Liechtenstein signs new rules 6-27, 564D3
Bancal to sell 27 Calif branches 7-6, 578E1; Japan unit purchase disputed 8-9, 669A3
Australia lifts loan curbs 7-7, 523A1
ASEAN reserve fund set 8-5, 607D1
Geneva Union Bank dir chrgd 8-12, 658D1
Swiss close Hervel, officers sought 8-15, 658B1
Zurich Bankag Bank liquidatn set, '76 arrests cited 8-19, 658E1
Panama Canal treaty backing seen 8-22, 679C1; opponents plan campaign 9-9, 698B3
Swiss banks adopt new rules 8-23, 658F1
Lloyds Lugano branch to close 8-24, 658E1
Nigeria Euroloan rptd 9-1, 746C3
Dresdner Bank gets new hd 9-9, 969B2
Quebec gets US loan 9-13, 742D1
Reps at IMF-World Bank mtgs 9-26—9-30, 753D2
Japan unit Bancall purchase cleared in Calif 10-19, 979D2
3 Chiasso offcls fired 10-31, Swiss Credit fined $28 mln 11-10, 904F1-D2
Lloyds, Bank of Amer co-finance Argentina loan 11-10, 981G2
Japan sets 'free yen' reserve deposits 11-17, 932G2
OPEC plans developing natn investmts 12-7, 997E3
Saudi buys Lance Ga bank shares 12-27, 1003E2

1978

Crime Issues—*See also 'Foreign Developments' below*
Hearst rehearing appeal rejctd 1-4, 24F2
US crime code revisn clears Sen 1-30, 64D2
Chase branch in PR bombed 2-8, 116B1
PR bank branches bombed 2-16, 129F1
Ala treasurer indicted 3-21, 380A1
Graiver, 4 others indicted 4-12, 326C1
Hearst convictn review denied by Sup Ct 4-24, 322F1
Chicago 1st Natl offers reward in '77 theft 5-1, 380C1
Ala treasurer convicted 5-25, 6-25, sentncd 6-8, 886F3
2 convicted in Wash, Ore robberies 7-11, 824A3
Franklin ex-offcls indicted 7-13, Bordoni pleads guilty to '75 chrgs 9-5, 681B1
Ray III '67 robbery role cited 8-17, 641A3; 11-15, 898A3; Ray's brother denies role 11-30, 938D1
5 Teamsters indicted 10-5, 770G3
Flood indicted 10-12, 792C1
Pornographer arrested in Conn 10-25, 971B2
LA bank robbed by phone 10-25, computer consultant arrested 11-5, chrgd 11-20, 991G3-992D1
Unificatn Church abuses chrgd by House subcom 11-1, 862C3
Cleveland mayor's brother arrested 12-18, 1008G3

Foreign Developments (including U.S. international news)—*See also 'Interest Rates' below; also country names*
Mozambique natlizatn rptd 1-4, 22D2
Italian suit vs Swiss Credit probed 1-10, secrecy breach denied 1-11, 151C1
Italy bank offcl held in Sindona case 1-11, 19G2
Westdeutsche bank chief fired, W Ger state finance min resigns 1-17, 55D1
Lance loans rptd repaid 1-17; Saudi deal, Abedi role cited 2-13, 3-22, 204C3
LeClerc arrested in Switz 1-19, 95A2
Belgian bank fails 1-24, 94E1
US, Canada banks curb Jamaica operatns 2-3, 95A1
Swiss Credit to sell Chiasso Texon holdings 2-10, 151A2
Lance, Arabs sued by Financial Gen, SEC 2-17, 3-8; SEC chrgs setld 2-19, 204F1, A3
Swiss Credit rpts '77 Chiasso losses 3-1, 151F1
Turkey '77 loan defaults rptd 3-1, 170B3
UAW acts vs S Africa loans 3-6, 193B3
Brazil loans, debts rptd 3-10—4-8, 311E1-C2
Peru loan refinancing barred 3-10, 353F1, B2
Barone resigns over Sindona link 3-10, 454C2
S Africa loans barred by Citibank, '74-76 joint loans cited 3-11, 193F2
Unctad poor-natn debt relief talks; '77 debt estimates cited 3-11, 301A1
Denmark '77 forgn loans rptd 3-14, 189D3
Japan doubles reserve requiremt on free yen deposits 3-15, 235F1
Nicaragua rebel robberies 3-17, 4-7, 376F1
Chem Bank rpts S Africa loan bar 3-21, BankAmer backs loans 3-22, 237D2
Nigeria withdraws Barclays funds in S Africa dispute 3-22; '76, '77 data cited 237A2
UK bank S Africa loan policy rptd 3-25, 237C2
Canada standby credit fund increased 4-3, 244D1
Forgn activity in US rptd up 4-3, 4-12, 263A2
Italy rejcts Sindona appeal 4-3, US orders extraditn 5-19, 454F1
Hongkong Bank to buy Marine Midland 4-5, 263E1-A2
Chile gets $210 mln loan 4-7, 312E1
US loans to Chile rptd undercutting rights policy 4-11, 312F1
Graiver, 4 others indicted in US 4-12, 326C1
Canada gets W Ger loan 4-28, confrms US talks 5-1, 328C1
OPEC investmt shift rptd 4-28, 344A3
Chile Citibank branch bombed 5-1, 351E3
Singapore Airlines to buy Boeing jets 5-9, 365F2
NatWest to buy Natl Bank of NA 5-12, 364F1
Peru offcls meet intl bankers 5-23—5-24, 394C2
'Hungarian Circle' forgers sentncd 5-31, 824B3
Westdeutsche bank chief's dismissal upheld 6-1, 456F3
Bordoni extradited to US 6-2, arraigned 6-5, 454C2
UK bank to buy Union Bancorp 6-8, 553B1
Zaire loan deal cited 6-14, 478F1
Spain admits forgn banks 6-16, 822E1
Bank of Amer plans Panama refinancing pkg 6-22, 632D2

1979

Carter Personal Issues—*See CARTER–PERSONAL; LANCE, Thomas Bertram*
Crime Issues—*See also 'Foreign Developments' below*
Graiver ruled dead, chrgs dismissed 1-8, 166B1
3 Franklin ex-offcls convicted 1-23, 205G2-D3
Hearst released from prison 2-1, 79F1
Chicago embezzler convicted 2-7, 119A3
Bagley indicted in NC 3-14, 291G3
Sindona, Bordoni indicted 3-19, 205C2
2d LA bank wire-transfer theft 3-25, 239C2
LA computer consultant sentncd 3-26, 239G1
Franklin ex-offcls sentncd 3-26, 3-27, 291E3
Moon church fraud chrgd, '77 complaint cited 5-1, 376D2; chrg setld 6-6, 547E2
Bagley acquitted 8-1, 578E2
NYC record robbery 8-3, 2 suspects arrested 8-8, 8-9, 656C1
Sindona rptd kidnaped 8-6, 635A3
Robberies rise sharply 8-12, 619G2
13 NYC banks robbed, 2 suspects arrested 8-21—8-22; police protectn ordrd 8-22, 656A1
Canadian sentncd in Calif wire theft 9-24, 840C3
Sindona reappears, enters NY hosp 10-16, 793E2
Smith damage judgemt rptd 12-24, 991G3

Foreign Developments (including U.S. international news)—*See also 'Interest Rates' and 'Mergers' below*
Poland econ to be monitored by Westn banks 1-11, 59E3-60C1
Australia banking probe rptd 1-23, 74A1
Spain OKs forgn bank activities 1-26, 100E3
US loans to Ecuador set 1-30, 101G1
Credit Lyonnais employes chrgd 2-5, 96F2
Canada sets Japan loan 2-14, seeks Swiss loan 2-28, 153E1-A2
Swiss Credit Chiasso scandal chrgs filed 2-15, 23C1
Montreal bank heist 2-23, 220G2
Iran forgn assets, debts rptd 2-25, 144F3
China branch to open in US 3-1, 146E2
4 Swiss bank offcls convicted 3-1, 155F2
Japan bias vs US branches chrgd 3-4—3-5, 160C1
S Africa stock divestitures by Columbia U, other colls rptd 3-10—3-24, 270G3
Petroperu debts rptd 3-16, 256D1
DR gets intl loan 3-20, 256B3
Belgian banker killed 3-22, 228B3
Italy central bank offcls chrgd 3-24, 3-26, 237G1-D2
Poland signs US, UK, Canada bank loan 3-30, 279G2
Hungary to seek US loan 3-30, 279B3
S Africa '72-78 loans rptd 4-2, 270D2
Egypt blocks Arab League asset shift 4-7, 278F1
Lance '78 Arab aid, influence attempt chrg linked 4-9, 306A1
Canada Imperial named in Woolworth suit 4-12, 304A1
S Korea scandal, 4 chiefs ousted 4-13, 287A2
Italy central bank offcl suspended 4-17, 313D2
S Korea replaces 10 dirs 4-29, 324E1
Paris Rothschild branch bombed 5-1, 330D2
French loan to China signed 5-9, 370A2
Australia Adelaide bank rescue set 5-14, 387C1
W Ger reforms proposed 5-22, 411C1
Portugal gets $300 mln intl loan 5-25, 409D2
China loan agrmt with Chase canceled 5-29, 445B1
Turkey aid package set 5-30, 397B2
Argentina 1st 1/4, May reserves rptd 6-2, 466G2
Iran nationalizes banks 6-7, 469E1-C2
Japan $500 mln Mex loan rptd 6-8, 487F3
Arabs halt Canada deposits 6-19, 467B3
Japan banks dominate world's '78 top 300 list 6-19, 476G1
Lloyds Bank execs ransomed in El Salvador 7-2, 547G1
Swiss Credit Chiasso sentnces given 7-3, 505C2
Nicaragua nationalizes pvt banks, curbs forgn 7-25, 574A1
Mex oil co to get US bank loan; '78 Brazil-US loan cited 7-28, 584E1, D2
Turkey OKs debt restructuring pact 8-29, 711A1
UK seeks Irish crackdown on IRA robberies 9-5, 669C3
Greek intl bank loan set 9-7, 708C2
Nigeria ends Barclays boycott 9-26, 796D3
Nicaragua debt paymts in doubt 9-28, 753F2

1980

Reagan backs deregulatn 10-2, 738E2
Anderson campaign loan plan fails 10-2, abandoned 10-15, 818E1
Bush addresses conv, vows fewer regulatns 10-15, 817E2
Small bank weekly rpts reduced by FRB 10-22, 857F1
Money supply rptd up 11-18, 882D3
Money growth targets lowered 11-24, 897C3
AMC credit agrmt set 12-11, 938G2
Crime Issues—*See also 'Foreign' above*
Prosecution disparities rptd 1-6, 24B3, C3
NY businesswoman, 2 partners indicted 1-10, 216C1
Lance trial opens 1-14, chrgs reduced 4-9, 291E3
Smith jury award upheld 1-18, 55D2
Franklin Bank fraud appeals refused by Sup Ct 2-19, 131A1
Sindona convicted 3-27, 237D1
Sindona fraud suit ruling refused by Sup Ct 4-21, 344A2
Sindona aide sentenced 4-23, 415B1
Lance cleared on fund misuse 4-30, 332D3
Lance case dropped 6-9, 459F2-A3
Cts power to suppress evidence curbed 6-23, 554C3
'50 Brinks robber dies 9-27, 756B2
Offshore fraud indictmts 10-20, 860G2-E3
W Sutton dies 11-2, 928E3
NY businesswoman, partner convicted 12-21, 997F2
Foreign Developments (including U.S. international news)—*See also 'Interest', 'Mergers' below*
Iran assets in Eur rptd moved 1-2, 29D2
Venezuela loan talks rptd 1-14, 103C1
France freezes Citibank funds on Iran request 1-16; Citibank appeals 1-17, freeze upheld 1-21, 48B1
Greek workers strike 1-17, 98E1; strike ends 2-23, 150A3
Eur deposits in US banks rptd down 1-18, 48A2
Australia '79 stock gains cited 1-18, 56D1
W Ger sets curbs on gold, other metal holdings 1-23, 103C2
Turkey ends forgn bank curbs 1-25, 80C1
Panama Peoples Temple funds located 2-6, returned to US 2-28, 170C3, E3
El Salvador natlzatn set 2-11, 117E2
Hungary loan rptd 2-18, 142B3
Japan hikes reserve rate 2-18, 151E3
W Ger ex-terrorist sentncd, freed 2-22, 154E1
Japan sets yen rescue plan 3-2, 173F2
Bahamas bank looting suit rptd 3-3, 228G3
Italy loan fraud chrgd, 38 held 3-4, 173F1
Brazil oil credit rptd 3-5, 191F1
Brazil banks natlized, forgn units exempt 3-7, 192G1-B2
Italcasse 'black funds' scandal implicates 44 3-7, 212G2
US churches cut Citibank ties re S Africa loans 3-24, 277G3
Sindona extraditn sought by Italy 3-27, 237A2
Argentina closes major pvt bank 3-28, 252B2
10 Italcasse suspects freed 4-1, new Italy fraud chrgs rptd 4-2, 254G3
Portugal to seek $350 mln in loans 4-2, 277G2
Jamaica loan request rejctd 4-7, 287A1
'79 forgn investmt in US rptd 4-8, 329C1
Jamaica debt accord reached 4-15, 314C2
Swiss arrest French natls 4-15; Swiss Bank Paris office searched 5-7, 407C2
US widens Iran sanctns, asks assets use 4-17, 281B1, D1
Zaire debt rescheduled 4-23, 356G1
Sindona aide sentenced, Italy return seen 4-24, 415D1
Argentina pvt banks shaken by bankruptcies; govt assumes control, raises deposit guarantees 4-25, 349D3
W Ger suspect arrested 5-5, 411B3
Canada, US OK Chrysler loan guarantees 5-10, 383A3
DR central bank dir quits 5-28, 462A2
Chrysler stops supplier paymts 6-11, 457B1
Iran withdraws gold in Eur 6-17, 464A3
Swiss convict French natls 6-18, 522F2
Turkey '79 debt rptd 6-19, 468E1
Venice summit backs 3d World aid 6-23, 474B1
Mex gets record World Bank agri loan 7-10, 605D2
W Ger fraud cases rptd 7-24—7-28, 581E1
Saudis, Kuwait freeze loans to World Bank over PLO issue 8-2, 592A2
Polish loans granted 8-12, 8-22, 642C2
Swiss end forgn deposit curbs 8-27, 673B3
Bolivia debt paymts postponed 9-3, 686F2-B3
Canada profits rptd down 9-5, 686F3-687B1
Nicaragua forgn debt rescheduled 9-5, 689C2-A3
IMF revises SDR valuatn method 9-17, 695A2
Abu Dhabi bank gets US branch OK 10-1, 806F3
Japan eases forgn currency lending limit 10-16, lifts account ceiling 12-1, 966G3, 967A1
US offers Iran assets, hostage deal 10-20; Iran rejcts 10-22, 800A1
FRB backs free-trade zones 11-19, 958D1

1976

'75-76 US forgn lending rptd up; Citibank sees no threat, cites Jan-July total 11-10, 915E1
Vt rpts Canada deposits up 11-21, 903F3

Interest Rates—*For mortgage developments, see HOUSING*

Rates, stock prices linked 1-2—3-11, 184F2
Prime cut, raised 1-7—2-27, 167E2
FRB 'problem' list rptd 1-22, 112E3
Swedish discount rate cut 1-29, 104B1
Dutch discount rate cut 2-2, 102A3
Italy raises discount 2-2, 140F2
Finland ups import credit fees 2-4, 155E2
FRB cuts discount rates, acts on fed funds rate 2-27, 167C3
Canada ups bank, prime rates 3-8, 204G1
Stock mkt retreat, rates linked 3-11—5-28, 413G1, C2
Belgian ups discount rate 3-17, 7-23, 572F1
Prime lowered, raised 4-30—6-4, 436A3
Lower rates, tighter credit cited 5-3, 347C3
'74 rates, tax avoidance linked 5-5, 480D1
Fed funds rate hike rptd 6-5, 436E3
Dem platform text 6-15, 470C1, A2
Mondale cites high rates 7-15, 507G2, 511C2
S Africa ups bank rate 7-21, 540A1
France raises discount rate 7-22, 555E3
Prime lowered 7-26, 568C2
Carter stresses stability 7-28, 551B1
Dutch ups prime, Belgium ups short-term rates 7-30, 594C1
Stock mkt gain, prime cut linked 9-1, 9-21, 846A3, G3
UK raises lending rate 9-10, 694B1
French bank rate hiked 9-23, 731A3
Prime lowered 9-24, 10-28—10-29, 846E2
Denmark discount rate raised 10-5, lowered 12-6, 1001A2
UK hikes rate 10-11, 773C1
Australia ups rates 11-7, 850D1
Dow rise, prime cut linked 11-18—12-31, 984D1
Fed Reserve cuts discount, fed funds rates 11-19, 939E2
Prime lowered re 11-19, 12-10, 939A3
Canada cuts rates 11-22—11-23, 888C3; $ falls 11-24, 904B2
More Canada rates cut 11-24—12-1, 945D2
Canada cuts rates again 12-22—12-24, 998G2

1977

Interest Rates

Belgium discount rates cut 1-5, 24F1; 2-16, 199F3
Dutch discount rate cut 1-6, 24C2
Canada cuts bank, prime rates 2-1, 97G2
'76 US bank loans abroad rptd up 2-17, 145F2
Lower rate, mergers linked 2-18, 274C2
Japan discount rate cut 3-12, 3-16, 201C2
Ceiling powers cleared 4-5, 273A2; Carter signs 4-19, 380E3
Tax rebate plan dropped, rate dips 4-14, 271B2
Japan discount rate cut 4-18, 329G3
Belgium discount rate cut 5-5, 466E1
Dutch discount rate lowered 5-6, 412G1
Canada bank, prime rates cut 5-9, 5-10, 372E2
Low US rates, forgn investmt rise linked 5-11, 5-25, 385C3
Oct '74-May '77 prime rate graph 407A1
Prime raised, 5-13, FRB fed funds rate cited 5-30, 407D1
Citibank raises prime 5-27, Lance scores 6-1, 6-7; Morgan, others lower 6-13, 577D3
Morgan ups prime 8-1, Citibank 8-21, Chase 9-13, 703G3-704B1
US discount rate raised, money growth targets cited 8-29, 703D3
France asks discount rate cut 9-7, 744G1
Turkey raises bank rate 9-8, 709D2
US rate rise, housing inflatn linked 9-12, 722A1
Wells Fargo hikes prime 10-4, 798E2
Canada $ drop, higher US rates linked 10-17, 792E3
Admin warns FRB re rate rise 10-20, 798B3; Burns responds 10-26, 817G2-A3
Citibank hikes prime 10-21, 817C3
FRB hikes discount, heavy bank borrowing cited 10-25, 817B3
High UK yield on govt securities cited 10-31, 829B2
S&L rate differential extended 11-16, 878G1

1978

Citibank pullout from Nigeria cited 6-26, 799B1
Peking OKs Hong Kong 'capitalist' method; China, Hong Kong operatns cited 7-6, 532E1
S Africa sanctns urged by US blacks 7-6, 632E3
Sindona, Bordoni named Franklin co-conspirators 7-13; Bordoni pleads guilty on '75 chrgs 9-5, 681D1
Portugal gets French loans 7-19—7-21, 667C2
Peru debt repaymt pact signed 7-19, 669A2
Citibank sued re Eur tax evasn 7-24, 717B3
Comecon loan shunned by US 8-17, 660D3
US forgn bank regulatn clears Cong 8-17, 663A1
Brazil rated top Jan-June intl borrower 8-25, 828C3
Iceland halts currency transactns 8-28, 689B1
S Africa loans rptd rising 8-29, 669F3
Japan Ex-Im Bank loan unit set 9-3, 694D1
Japan proposes China loans 9-6, 695E2
Latin export bank founded 9-8, 828C3
FDIC paymt case refused by Sup Ct 10-16, 789C1, F1
Turkey plans debt restructuring 10-24, 840A2
Japan banks set Brazil loan 10-25, 837A1
World's '77 10 biggest banks ranked 11-8, 913F3
US backs interest paymt on frozen forgn assets 11-14, 977E1
US ct upholds Sindona extradtn 11-15, 906A3
Swiss Credit Bank robbed 12-27, 1028B3

Interest Rates—*For mortgage rates, see under HOUSING*

Discount, fed fund rates described 679B1
US hikes discount rate 1-6, Partee issues dissent 1-9; reactn 1-23, 28A1
Citibank ups prime rate 1-6, 28D2
US hikes fed fund rate 1-9, 28B2
Carter backs lower rates 1-12, 12B1
'77 futures trading, rate rise linked 1-12, 84B1
Carter links lower rates, forgn investmt 3-2, 140F3
Canada hikes bank rate 3-8, prime 3-9, 187G3
Japan Bank cuts discount rate 3-16, 235F1
Canada lending rate up 4-4, 244D1
UK proposes rate hike 4-11, 267F2
High rates boost sagging $, weakness persists 4-19—7-14, 523B2
Chase hikes prime rate 4-28, 326B2
Admin vs short-term rates 5-9, FRB hikes discount 5-11, 361C2
ALF-CIO links rates, wage hikes 5-10, 362B1
FRB cut linked to Carter tax plan 5-12, 361G1
US prime rate hiked to 8.5% 5-25, 403F2
US prime rate hiked 6-16, 6-30, 8-30, 679B2
May rate rise, housing slowdown linked 6-18, 470E1
Greece hikes deposit, loan rates 6-18, 631F1
US hikes discount rate; Miller vs, Admin scores 6-30, 679G1
Canada bank, prime rates raised 7-26, 8-1, 591B1
Harris cancels cong testimony, criticism of Fed cited 8-7, 605B2
Meany links to inflatn 8-8, 624A3; 9-18, 715D2
Fed funds rate hiked to aid $ 8-16, 622A2
Comecon loan shunned by US 8-17, 660F3
US hikes discount, fed funds rate 8-18, 679A1, A2
Canada bank, prime rates hiked 9-11, 9-12, 703G3, 704B1
Prime rate raised 9-15, 9-25, 752A1
Business cash holdings, high rates linked 9-18, 716F3

1979

Chile loan disclosures sought by US 10-1, 750C2
Italy central bank gov resigns, execs strike 10-5, 793E1
Venez rptdly seeks forgn loans 10-6, 837D3
Swiss secrecy laws challenged 10-8, 795E2
US consortium barred Jamaica loan 10-9, 996B1
US to weigh S Korea intl loans 10-17–10-19, 803A3
Bank of Amer El Salvador office bombed 10-28, 834F2
Hungary opens E-W bank 11-9, 882A3
US freezes Iran assets; reactn 11-14, 861B1, F1, G2
Cuba debts rptd 11-14, 876E2
US confrms Iran assets freeze 11-15, 11-16, ups assets estimate 11-19; risks detailed 11-15–11-18, 879C3-880G1
Minneapolis bank branch opened in Hungary 11-15, 882B3
UK extends curbs 11-15, 889E2
Swiss arrest W Ger robber 11-20, 998D3
Bank of Amer Pak branch sacked 11-21, 893F1
Chase declares Iran default 11-21, 896D2
Iran repudiates forgn debts 11-23, 896B2
Iran bars US $ paymts 11-23, orders hostile natns boycott 11-25, 896D3
Saudi assured on US assets freeze 11-25, 896C3
Pahlevi family assests rptd in Switz, France, US 11-26, 897D2, F3
Iran interest in Wis bank rptd 11-26, 898A1
Brazil gets $1.2 bln loan 11-26, 907F2
Peru debt prepaymt agreed 11-26, 951C2
Japan forgn exchng controls adopted 11-27, 12-3, 12-5, 996C2
Nicaragua $155 mln credit line rptd 11-27, 909G3
Morgan Guaranty attaches Iran W Ger assets 11-28, 896E2
Japan bank rpts Iran loan paymt 11-28, 896G2
Iran sues US banks for UK, French assets freeze 11-30, 915A2
Bolivia bankers strike 12-3, 926E1
Telefunken rescue plan rptd 12-4, 998G2
Iran assets freeze upheld by UK 12-5, 915F1
W Ger curbs Iran credit guarantees 12-7, 934A1
Japan dominated syndicate retain 2 Iran loans 12-7, 976G1
US scores Japan on Iran assets freeze 12-10, 933D2
Shah chrgd with embezzlemt 12-11, 935G1
Saudi theft rumor rptd 12-12, 968D3
France upholds Iran assets freeze 12-12, 12-21, 976B2
US Eximbank declares Iran in default 12-21, 976E1
Chrysler credit set 12-21, 981E3
El Salvador Citibank branch bombed 12-27, 993G2

Interest Rates—*For mortgage rates, see under HOUSING*

Discount, prime rates explained; '79 movemt cited 621E1
Canada prime, bank, savings acct rates hiked 1-3–1-4, 6F1
US savings bond sales linked 1-10, 133A2
Chase, Citibank cut prime to 11.5% 1-30, 2-9, 131E1
S Africa cuts bank rate 2-6, 171E3
UK lending rate linked 2-8, 116B1; cut to 13% 3-1, 154G2
Chase REIT bankruptcy linked 2-22, 131C2 205A2
US anti-inflatn guides set 3-16, 264C2
Japan to hike discount rate to 4.25% 4-16, 615D3
Australia hikes savings bond, other rates 4-23, 311A1
W Ger probes banks 5-17, 374E1
Carter proposes fed ceiling phase-out 5-22; FRB, FHLBB hike savings rates 5-30, 403B1-G2
UK hikes lending rate to 14% 6-12, 445G2
Carter proposes solar energy bank 6-20, 498C1
W Ger discount, Lombard rates hiked 7-13, 586B1
FRB hikes discount rate to 10%, $ rebounds 7-20, 531E3
Canada bank, prime rates hiked 7-23–7-24, 562D3
Tex disaster relief authorized 7-28, 638E3
FRB raises discount rate to 10.5%, prime hiked to 12% 8-16, 621A1
Rate rise, gold price hike linked 8-30, 645A3
Canada hikes bank rate 9-7; prime hits 13% 9-10, 9-11, 684F2
FRB hikes discount rate to 11%, prime rate cited 9-18, 701C2
Prime hiked to 13.25% 9-19, 13.5% 9-28; Bentsen asks halt 9-20, Proxmire backs hikes 9-26, 745F1
FRB sets monetary policies 10-6; ends fed funds rate interventn, financial mkts in chaos 10-8–10-12, 764C1-765B2
Prime hiked to 14.5% on FRB credit move 10-9, 764E1, B3

1980

Canada OKs new Bank Act 11-26, 920A2
W Ger bank earnings rptd 12-5, 12-10; Kaufhof holdings sold to Swiss bank 12-12, 696E1

Interest Rates—*See also HOUSING (U.S.)--Mortgage Rate Issues*

Discount, prime rates explained 247E2
S Korea rates hiked 1-12, 101G1
Chile '79 usury rate rptd 1-14, 19A3
Kennedy cites tripling 1-20, 50E2
Turkey sets hike 1-25, 80C1
Kennedy urges controls, scores Carter 1-28, 74F3, G3
Kennedy urges freeze 2-6, 90G3
FRB hikes discount rate to 13% 2-15, prime hits 15.75% 2-19, 126A1-E1
Hungary loan terms rptd 2-18, 142C3
AFL-CIO scores hikes 2-18, 146F3
Japan hikes discount rate to 7.25% 2-18, 151E3
Swiss end forgn acct ban 2-20, 153F2
Prime rises to 16.5% 2-22, 2-25, 16.75% 2-29, 144D2
Belgium hikes rptd 2-27, W Ger, Swiss 2-28, Denmark 2-29, 153A3, C3
'77-80 prime rate chart 2-29, 144A1
Reagan 'basic speech' excerpts 2-29, 207B2
Kennedy links rates, Mass primary win 3-4, 167A1
Prime at 17.25% 3-4, 17.75% 3-7, 167F2
Money mkt rates near 15% 3-6, 222C3
Canada sets bank rate float 3-10, 191D2
Prime hits 18.25%, spurs FRB discount rate hike speculatn 3-13, 182F2
FRB sets discount rate surchrg 3-14, 201A2
Prime rises to 18.5% 3-14, 19% 3-18, 209B2
Canada bank, prime rates climb 3-14—3-28, 252D3
US $ soars on forgn exchngs; Swiss, W Ger, Japan intervene 3-17, 202G2
Japan hikes discount rate 3-18, 276B2
Belgium hikes discount rate 3-19, 237C1
Kennedy stresses in NY 3-25, 221C2
SDR rate hiked to 10.25% 3-27, 302A2
Prime rises above 19% 3-28, 4-1, hits 20% 4-2, 247C2-A3
Banking deregulatn bill signed 3-31, 245G3
Brown scores Carter policies 4-1, 246C3
Canada bank, prime rates peak 4-2, fall 5-1, 334D2
Bush attacks Admin 4-7, 264D2
Chase cuts prime to 19.75% 4-16, 286D2
Kaufman sees '80 prime drop 4-16, 286E2

1976

Venez pledges Italy, UK deposits 11-21, 11-23, 929D3, E3
Montreal gets Olympic loan 12-31, 998D3

1977

Lance Finances—*See LANCE, Thomas B.*
Obituaries
Eccles, Marriner 12-18, 1024D1

1978

US hikes discount rate to aid $ 9-22, efforts fail 9-27, 731D2, 732D2
Carter scores FRB rate hikes 9-27, 9-28, 751C3
Chase hikes prime 10-12, 791C1
'74-78 prime, discount, fed funds rates chart 791D1
Canada bank, prime rates hiked 10-13, 10-16, 794D2
FRB Open Mkt Com debate on high rates vs slow growth rptd 10-16, 791C2
Mortgage-credit crunch avoided, 6-mo certificate use cited 10-18, 790E3
Prime rate boosted 10-23—11-3, 827C1
Discount, fed funds rate hiked by FRB 11-1, 826B1, D1, 827B1
Meany scores discount rate hike 11-1, 863E2
Prime rate hiked 11-13, 11-24, 918C1
Small business rates set by Pitts, Boston banks 11-14, 918E1
Oct indl output rise, rising rates linked 11-15, 919A2
State credit card rates backed by US Sup Ct 12-18, 981C2
Prime rate hiked 12-20, 1003D3

Obituaries
Bierwirth, John E 4-3, 356B2
Harriman, E Roland 2-16, 196A3
MacArthur, John 1-6, 96G2
Pierson, Warren Lee 1-12, 96C3
Sproul, Allan 4-9, 356D3
Redlining—*See under HOUSING*
Savings and Savings Banks
S&L redlining curbed 5-18, 410D2
Variable rate mortgages OKd 7-24, HUD secy vs 605D2
Ky franchise tax case refused by Sup Ct 10-30, 832A3
Ill redlining case refused by Sup Ct 10-30, 832C3
3 new mortgages OKd, '75 Cong actn cited 12-14, 962A1

1979

Canada bank rate, prime hiked to 13%; US discount rate hike linked 10-9, 771F2
Carter calls too high 10-11, 807F2
Canada bank rate, prime hiked to 14% 10-25, 811E3-812B1
Greenspan warns re competitive intl rate hikes 10-29, 826E3
FRB money supply data error, investmt losses linked 10-30, 828F2-A3
W Ger again hikes discount, Lombard rates 10-31, 838C1
Dutch key lending fee hiked 10-31, 838G1
Japan hikes discount rate 11-1, 836D2, 838G1
Swiss hike lending fees, Lombard rate, cut negative interest rate 11-2, 875E3
UK hikes lending rate 11-15, 889C2
Prime rises to 15.75% 11-16, falls to 15% 12-4, 940E3
Bolivia usury rates hiked 12-3, 926E1
W Ger drops cartel probe 12-13, 998A3
Stopgap checking acct bill signed 12-28, 987B3

Lance Issues—*See LANCE, Thomas Bertram*
Mergers & Acquisitions
United Financial purchase by Natl Steel planned 3-6, 205A2
FRB to bar hostile forgn takeovers, OKs 3 forgn bank acquisitns 3-13, 3-16, 205B1-A2
NY bank heads Houdaille takeover 4-2, 283A1
Australia Adelaide merger urged 5-14, 387D1
Barclays purchase of Amer Credit OKd 5-29, 440B3
2 Canadian banks to merge 6-29, 601A2
Midland Bank to buy Walter Heller Corp 7-6, 682B3
Obituaries
Dillon, Clarence 4-14, 356D3
Karpis, Alvin 8-26, 671E2
Meyer, Andre 9-9, 756B3
Savings & Savings Banks
Natl Steel plans United Financial purchase 3-6, McKinney concerned 3-7,
Indicators index revised, NOW accounts cited 4-1, 252A2
US savings bond sales suspended 4-2, 251C3
Carter proposes interest rate, other reforms 5-22; FRB, FHLBB set chngs 5-30, 403B1-G2
Banking svcs case declined by Sup Ct 10-15, 847B3

1980

FRB increases farm, small business loans 4-17, 286B2
Prime drops to 19.5% 4-18, 19% 4-23, 305D3
Prime drops to 18.5% 4-28—5-2, 329A2
W Ger hikes discount, Lombard rates 4-30, 356A1
Prime drops to 16.5% 5-5—5-12, 367B3
FRB ends discount rate surchrg 5-6, 344C2
Canada bank, prime rates fall 5-15, 388C3
Prime drops to 14% 5-19—5-27, 401E1-C2
FRB eases credit controls 5-22, short-term rates fall 5-23, 399F3-400F1
FRB drops discount rate to 12% 5-28, 400B2
Prime drops to 12% 5-28—6-12, 438A1
DIDC sets interest rate rules 5-28, S&Ls file suit 6-16, 516A3
UAW head scores Carter 6-1, 457D2
UK rate cuts seen 6-6, 444F3
Turkey regulatn eased 6-6, 446B1
FRB cuts discount to 11% 6-12, 438E1
Prime drops to 11.5% 6-23, 7-7, 514A1
IMF sees rate hikes 6-24, 477B3
UK cuts lending rate 7-3, 523F1
Prime drops to 10.75% 7-11—7-24, 574D3
Reagan vs pres credit controls 7-12, 535E1
Ford, Vander Jagt score Carter 7-14, 7-16, 534B2, E2
Carter links rate drops, housing starts 7-17, 542D1
Financial futures trading expands 7-24, 8-7, 617B1
FRB cuts discount to 10% 7-25, 574F3
Kennedy Dem conv speech, wins platform planks 8-12, 610G1, F2, 613F1, 614D2, F2, D3
Prime rises to 11.25% 8-19, 630F3
Japan cuts discount rate 8-19, 672C1
Prime rises to 11.5% 8-26, 666C2
Prime hiked to 14% 9-12—10-2, 763A1, 764D2
W Ger cuts Lombard rate 9-18, 925B2
FRB ups discount to 11% 9-25, 764A3
Italy hikes discount rate 9-28, 751D2
Housing, community dvpt authrzn clears Cong 9-30, signed 10-8, 804B2
Canada prime, bank rates rise 10-1—10-2, 767B1
Reagan vows lower rates 10-2, 738E2
Carter scores FRB policies, banks 10-2, 10-8; criticism deplored 10-2—10-3, 762F3-763A2
Student loan rate rise set 10-3, 803B3
Prime hiked to 14% 10-17, 14.5% 10-29, 15.5% 11-5, 11-6, 845D1, 867F1
UK min lending cut backed 10-28, 859B2
Reagan scores Carter record 10-29, 817G1
Canada prime, bank rates raised 10-30, 11-3, 871E1
S Korea rates cut 11-12, 944G3, 945C1
FRB hikes discount to 12%, sets surchrg 11-14, 882B3
Prime soars to 20% 11-17—12-10, 937D3
Fed funds rate range hiked 11-24, 897F3
Fed funds rate nears 19% 11-26, 937G3
Canada prime, bank rates hiked 11-28, 920B3
Fed deficit estimate rises 12-2, 916E2
Boston bond rating lowered 12-2, 939F3
Australia hikes rates 12-2, 964A1
FRB ups discount to 13%, surchrg to 3% 12-4, 937G3, 938A1
Chrysler rebates, Ford subsidies offered 12-5, 938C2
Chrysler K-car output cut rptd linked 12-9, 938G2
US $ rises on forgn exchngs, commodity prices fall 12-10, 932E1
Canada bank, prime rates raised 12-11, 12-12, 964C3
Prime hits 21% 12-16, 21.5% 12-19; some drop to 20.5% 12-23—12-29, 983A3
Brazil frees '81 rates 12-17, 991B1
Canada prime, bank rates hiked 12-18, 12-19; bank rate dropped 12-23, 992C2
Mergers & Acquisitions
Mfrs Hanover to buy First Penn units 6-3, 557B2
Ahmanson to acquire Fidelity 7-1, 557C2
Forgn bank takeover moratorium ends 7-1, 806A3
Midland sets Crocker takeover 7-15, 557G1
Great Western acquires Financial Federation 7-15, 557D2
Arabs to buy Financial Gen 7-25, 600D3
GAO asks forgn takeover ban 8-28; FRB tightens rules 9-17, 806F2
FRB OKs forgn branch rules 11-13, 867G2
Obituaries
Saxon, James J 1-28, 104F3
Wallenberg, Jacob 8-2, 676F3
Savings & Savings Banks
Mortgages defined 266F3
FRB sets new monetary supply terms 2-7, 113D3
Carter unveils anti-inflatn plan 3-14, 201F1
Calif redlining law curbed 3-17, 226C1
Money mkt funds drain controversy rptd 3-20—3-21, 223C3
Banking deregulatn bill signed 3-31, 245D3
Renegotiated-rate mortgages, funds infusn OKd by FHLBB 4-3, 266E2, F3
Mortgage rates decline 5-6—5-19, 384G3
DIDC proposes bank gift ban 5-6, oppositn rptd 7-18, 560E3

1976 1977 1978 1979 1980

1980

DIDC sets interest rate rules 5-28, S&Ls file suit 6-16, 516A3
S&Ls wider credit powers OKd 7-3, 516E2
Calif mortgage rates rise 7-23, 575A1
Financial futures trading expands 7-24, 8-7, 617D1
FHLBB proposes S&L loan plan 7-31, 600A1
Calif mortgage rate hikes continue 7-31—8-19, 631A1
DIDC tightens new acct gift rules, bans finder's fees 9-9, 986D1
Rates continue to rise 9-25, 10-1, 10-7, 867B2
Reagan backs interest-tax break 10-2, 738E2
Calif mortgage rates rise 11-7—12-16, 983F3

1976

BANKS, Dennis J.
Nov '75 indictment cited 7G1
Ariz BIA bomb threat 1-1, 7G1
BANKS, John
UK mercenaries leave for Angola 2-3, 81G2
Halts Angola mercenary operatn 2-8, 106E1
Named in Angola trial 6-11, 480E2
BANQUE Nationale d'Algerie
$ securities issue rptd set 7-27, 902B2
BANQUE pour L'Amerique du Sud (Brussels)
Graiver fraud rptd 9-25, 940C1, E1
BANTAM Books Inc.—*See under AMERICAN Financial Corp.*

1977

BANKS, Ernie
Inducted into baseball HOF 8-8, 643E3
BANQUE de Paris et des Pays Bas
Brazil steel loan granted 6-20, 524E2
BANQUE pour L'Amerique du Sud (Brussels)
Argentina Graiver scandal breaks 4-11, 345C2
BANTAM Books Inc.—*See under AMERICAN Financial Corp.*

1978

BANKS, Dennis
Calif bars extraditn to SD 4-19, 327E1
BANKS, Ernie
Mathews inducted into baseball HOF 8-8, 617E3
BANKS, Eugene
Kentucky wins NCAA basketball title 3-27, 272F1
BANKS, Peter
Faces Ga primary runoff 8-8, 625C3
Loses primary runoff 8-29, 683E1
BANNA, Sabry—*See NIDAL, Abou*
BANNI-Ahmad, Ahmad
Calls martial law illegal 9-17, 740D1
BANNISTER, Floyd
Traded to Mariners 12-8, 1026D1
BANQUE pour L'Amerique du Sud
Graiver indicted in US 4-12, 326A2
BANTAM Books Inc.—*See under AMERICAN Financial Corp.*

1979

BANQUE National de Paris
Iran banks natlzd 6-7, compensatn vowed 6-10, 469A2
BANTAM Books—*See under AMERICAN Financial Corp.*

1980

BANNISTER, Floyd
AL pitching ldr 10-6, 926G3
BANNON, Kenneth
Replaced as UAW vp 6-4, 457A2
BANQUE Keyser Ullmann en Suisse SA
Auto-Train loan set 8-22, dropped 9-8, 958E2, G2
BANTA, Dr. David
On MD oversupply 4-17, 318D1, F1

1976

BANZER Suarez, Gen. Hugo (Bolivian president)
Torres asks ouster 1-5, 27G1
Shifts mil 1-6, cabt 1-12, 26F3-27A1
Names Natl Maritime Cncl 1-7, 27B1
Student, labor unrest; plots chrgd 1-22—3-6, 237A3
Reque scores 5-17; threatens press curbs, press protests 5-20—5-23, 415E3
Torres found dead 6-2, 415F2, A3
Offers pol exiles amnesty 6-3; opponents arrested 6-6, 415A3
Chrgs leftist plot 6-7; offers miners pay hike 6-11, 456A2, C2
Aide scores Peru seaport plan 11-23, 975B2
Bars Chile, Peru arms race 12-7, 975E2
BAPTIST Ministers Union (Oakland, Calif.)
Funds returned to Carter 8-10, 585C3
BAPTISTS
Carter reassures Jews 6-6, 410F3
Carter teaches Bible class 7-18, 532C3
Calif black mins funds returned to Carter 8-10, 585B3
Women rptrs cover Carter class 8-15, 617C1
Carter Playboy interview disclosed 9-20, 704B2
Carter in Cleveland church 10-9, 762C2
Tex ldr backs Ford 10-10, 763C2
Carter church bars blacks 10-31, 826D3
Carter church ends black bar 11-14, 864C2
Blacks attend Carter church 11-21, 881F3
Southern Baptist Convention
Ford addresses 6-15, 433A2
Meets in Va 6-15—6-18, 951E2, G2 ★
BARAHENI, Reza
Chrgs police torture 5-28, 418E2
BARBADOS—*See also CARIBCOM, COMMONWEALTH of Nations, IDB, OAS*
Listed as 'free' nation 1-19, 20B3
Barrow chrgs US 'destabilizatn' campaign vs Jamaica 5-25, 522G1
Winston Scott dies 8-9, 892E3
At nonaligned conf 8-16—8-20, 622C1
BLP wins electns 9-2; Adams sworn prime min 9-3, 672F3
Smith named DLP ldr 9-24, 962F1
Cuba jet crashes 10-6, trial rejected 10-15, Venez offers info 10-16, 779A3, G3
Castro chrgs CIA re July bombing 10-15, 780B2
Cuba exile terrorist plan rptd 10-19, 780C2
2 Amers ousted in plot 10-25, Barrow denies DLP link 11-12, 962C1
Venez indicts 4 Cubans in jet crash 11-2, 843G2
BARBER, Samuel
Gets Arts & Letters award 5-19, 504C3
BARBERO, Carmelo
Signs peace pact 12-23, 1008G3
BARBERTON, O.—*See OHIO*
BARBIE, Klaus (alias Klaus Altman)
Bolivian envoy slain 5-11, 350F3
BARBITURATES—*See NARCOTICS & Dangerous Drugs*
BARCLAYS Bank
Arab boycott noncompliance rptd 11-9, 986B3
BARCO, Victor Renan
Colombia justice min 10-19, quits 11-17, 925B1
BARE, Frank
Confrms US gym team S Africa tour 7-20, 528E3

1977

BANZER Suarez, Gen. Hugo (Bolivian president)
Sees Todman 5-16, 414F2
At Panama Canal pact signing 9-7, 678C1
2 mins quit in oil tax dispute 10-11; 2 others ousted in road scandal, Cabt revised 10-13, 902A1
Sets '78 electns, lifts pol party ban 11-9; interim resignatn plan rptd 11-10; oppositn, exiles score 11-11, 901F2
Names Pereda AF chief 11-30, 1009A3
Bars '78 pres bid 12-1, parties score electn plan 12-26, 1009F2
Plot rptd foiled 12-9, 1009C3
BAPTISTS
Carter Ga church bars black member 1-9, 53C2
Carter joins DC church 1-23, 53C2
Sovt dissident rptd jailed 4-4, 314E2
Coll prof chrgs divorce bias 5-2, 472C1
Graham fund disclosed 6-26, 731E3-732A1
Charismatics meet 7-20—7-24, 620D3
Graham tours Hungary 9-3—9-14, 732A1
USSR dissidents, police clash 9-7, 753F1
Graham assn rpts finances 10-21, 845C1
BARAK, Aharon
Ofer probe dropped 1-9, 21D1
BARAKAT, Daud
On Israel electn 5-19, 401B3
BARAZZUTTI, Corrado
Loses Monte Carlo WCT 4-10, wins Charlotte 4-24, 430G2, A3
US Open results 9-11, 787E1
Australia wins Davis Cup 12-4, 970G1, F2
BARBADOS—*See also COMMONWEALTH of Nations, IDB, OAS*
UN Assemb member 3F3
Cuba details Angola war role, US interventn 1-9, 19G1
'75-76 trade, paymts table 3-11, 189A2 ★, C2
'61-75 GDP variatn table 5-30, 439A1
Belize independnc backed 6-16, 494G2
Seizes Israel arms for Guatemala; Belize claim cited 6-25, 553E2
Commonwealth finance mins meet 9-21—9-24, 936C2
Venez tries 4 Cubans in '76 crash 10-10, 867G3
U.S. Relations
Ortiz confrmd US amb 7-13, 626C3
Young visits 8-16—8-17, 646E1, 647E2
BARBER, Miller
2d in Texas Open 10-16, 950E3
PGA top money winner 10-30, 950G3
BARBITURATES—*See NARCOTICS & Dangerous Drugs*
BARBOUR, George
Dies 7-11, 604E2
BARCAK, Andrej
Norway cancels visit 1-20, 99C3
BARCIKOWSKI, Kazimierz
Dismissed 12-17, 987F1
BARCLAYS Bank Ltd.
Jamaica to natlize unit 2-23, 257D2
Arab boycott list drops 6-19, Israel operatns end denied 6-24, 511E3
World's 12th largest bank 6-21, 578B2
BARD, Brig. Gen. John C.
W Point apptmt cited 1-5, 41E1
Lectures in USSR 9-26, 9-28, 866F1
BARDELLA, Claudio
Asks return to democracy 2-18, 281C2
BARDIN, David
Winter fuel shortage plan set 12-1, 942D3
BARENTS Sea
USSR ousts EC trawlers 9-24, curbs fishing 9-27, 771F2

1978

BANZER Suarez, Gen. Hugo (Bolivian president)
Grants full amnesty 1-18; labor, student groups regain rights 1-25, 411B3
Electns annulled 7-19; Pereda ousts 7-21, 570D3, 571B1
Named Argentina amb 10-6, 823E2
BAPTISTS
Carter on mission program 1-30, 62E3
Carter: stabilizing factor 2-18, 123C3
Tenn clergy pub office ban upset by Sup Ct 4-19, 309D1
Gray wins Pa cong primary 5-16, 389D3
Howard elected NCC pres 11-4, 907F1
Southern Baptist Convention
Female clergy survey rptd 3-23, 295A2
'76 membershp growth rptd 6-12, 907B3
Carter addresses Baptist group 6-16, 510B1
BARAHONA, Lt. Juan Angel
Chrgs mil role in drug trade arrested 4-24, 614E3
BARAKAT, Col. Antoine
Blamed for Leb, Syria clashes 2-8, 79G1
BARAZZUTTI, Corrado
Loses King Classic 4-30, 419D1
French Open results 6-11, 540E1
BARBADOS—*See also CARIBBEAN Community, COMMONWEALTH of Nations, GATT, IDB, OAS*
'77 paymts deficit down 2-3, 152A2
GNP up 3% in '77, inflatn at 8% 3-10, 211B2
Belize defense aid agreed 3-10, 211C2
UN Assemb member 713C3
Press freedom rptd by IAPA 10-13, 829A2
BARBARO, Gary
NFL '77 interceptn ldr 1-1, 56D2
BARBARO, Guido
Names Turin trial defns atty 3-13, 191C2
BARBER, Anthony
UK bank to buy Union Bancorp 6-8, 553B1
BARBER, Bill
Wales Conf wins NHL All-Star game 1-24, 76D3
BARBER, Miller
Wins Phoenix Open 1-16, 76D1
BARBER, Red
Wins Frick broadcast award 8-8, 618A1
BARBOUR, Dick
2d in Daytona endurance 2-5, 538D3
BARCLAY, Dr. William R.
Asks smallpox lab virus destructn 10-27, 927C2
BARCLAY Hotel (N.Y., N.Y.)
Loews buys 5-31, 404A2
BARCLAYS Bank Ltd. (London)
Nigeria withdraws funds in S Africa dispute 3-22; '76, '77 data cited 237A2
Not on top '77 10 bank list 11-8, 914C1
BARDIN, David
Lobbyist's links to Energy Dept scored 5-15, 408B3
Defends Energy Dept on oil price fraud 12-10, 983E3
BARENTS Sea
USSR-Norway tensn rptd 10-12, 820F2

1979

BANZER Suarez, Gen. Hugo (ret.)
Returns to Bolivia, sees electn role 3-16, 233D2
3d in Bolivia electn 7-1, 501G1
Guevara electd interim pres 8-6, 600C2, A3
BAPTISM—*See RELIGION*
BAPTISTS
USSR emigratn rptd backed in US 2-26, 172F2
Baptism rites agrmt reached 3-31, 375A3
USSR dissident freed 4-27, at Carter church svc 4-29, 318A1; family leaves USSR 6-13, 476A3
Va religious schl expulsn upheld 8-23, 650A2
Progressive National Baptist Convention (N.Y.)
Jordan criticism of blacks scored 10-14, 780A3
Southern Baptist Convention
China property access rptdly asked 3-16, 218B1
Ga pastor joins Carter staff 4-15, 300E3
BARAKULLAH Khan
Bares Sovt mil role 8-21, 666E2
BARASCH, David
On 3 Mile I A-accident 4-4, 260B2
BARAZZUTTI, Corrado
Loses Paris Open 11-4, 1003F3
US wins Davis Cup 12-16, 1003A3
BARBADOS—*See also CARIBBEAN Community, COMMONWEALTH of Nations, GATT, IDB, OAS*
St Lucia defense pact seen 2-19, 181B3
Grenada rebel regime recognized 3-21, 236A3
St Vincent volcano erupts 4-13, 399C1
Crippled Greek tanker sinks off coast 8-2, 592A3
McComie elected OAS asst secy gen 10-24, 824E2
UN membership listed 695E2
BARBER, Miller
2d in Memorial Tourn 5-27, 587G2
BARBOUR, Clifford E.
Dies 1-10, 104E2
BARBOUR, Dick
2d in LeMans 6-10, 490D3
BARBRASH, Bob
Black Hole released 12-31, 1007A3
BARCHI, John
Harness-racing suspensn voided by Sup Ct 6-25, 540E1
BARCIA, Jose Rubia
Wins Natl Book Award 4-23, 356B2
BARCLAYS Bank Ltd.
Amer Credit purchase OKd 5-29, 440B3
Nigeria boycott rptd ended 9-26, 796D3
BARDIN, David J.
On diesel fuel allocatn rules 5-25, 395C2
BARDOT, Brigitte
Marks 45th birthday 9-28, 860A1
BARDSTOWN, Ky.—*See KENTUCKY*

1980

BANZER Suarez, Hugo
Rightists riot in Santa Cruz 6-18, 496B3
Electns held 6-29; Siles leads, lacks majority 7-3; Paz coalitn weighed 7-4, 508F3, 509A1
Paz quits pres race, Siles victory assured 7-9, 543C1
Peru firm files campaign plagiarism suit 7-12, 543E1
BAPTISTA, Jose Abraham
Bolivia junta tied to drug trafficking 8-15, 668B1
BAPTISTA, Jose Viana
Portuguese pilots strike 6-23—7-14, 580F1
BAPTISTS
Adams dies 2-27, 175C3
Carter seeks black support 10-20, 803B1
Southern Baptist Convention
Smith disparages Jewish prayers 8-22, religious ldrs denounce 9-18, 9-19, 811A1
BARABASS, Ingrid
Arrested 5-5, 411A3
BARABBA, Vincent P.
Lauds '80 census, scores revisns 12-31, 983B1
BARAMKI, Gabi
Arrested 12-1, 912A2
BARAZZUTTI, Corrado
Wins Naples Grand Prix 10-19, 947B2
Czechs win Davis Cup 12-7, 946E3
BARBADOS—*See also COMMONWEALTH of Nations, GATT, IDB, OAS*
Hurricane Allen hits 8-4, 621B2
Canada fines S Africa arms seller 8-14, 618A1
BARBARO, Gary
NFL '79 interceptn ldr 1-5, 8C2
BARBEAU, Adrienne
Fog released 2-29, 216E2
BARBERO, Carmelo
Subversn crackdown set 7-20, 566C1
BARBER Oil Corp.
Liquidates, Petro-Lewis buys unit 10-2, 986A1
BARBOUR, Dick
Daytona endurance results 2-3, 637F3
BARBUTO, Judge James V.
Acquitted of sex-bartering, convicted of other chrgs 6-13, 503B2
BARDON Munoz, Alvaro
Chile econ recovery detailed 1-14, 19C3
BARENTS Sea
NATO exercise held, USSR increased presence noted 3-14—3-19, 285F3
Norway, USSR OK talks 12-22—12-23, 979D2

1976

BARISHNIKOV, Alexander
Wins Olympic medal 7-24, 575F3
BARKAN, Alexander E.
AFL-CIO pol action planned 2-18, 149B1
BARKER, Bernard L.
Conviction reversed 5-17, 379D1
BARKER, John D.
Sentenced to die 6-28, 480G1
Executed 7-10, 519A3
BAR-Lev, Lt. Col. Baruch
Amin lauded Israeli raid 7-9, 515G1
BAR-Lev, Chaim
Cancels flight to US 10-19, 810G3
BARLEY
New support-rate set 10-13, 787G3
BARNARD, Doug
Elected 11-2, 822E1, 829D2
BARNET, Richard
Chrgs Chile in Letelier murder 9-21, 710F2
BARNETT, Joel
Ups '76 inflatn target 10-14, 810A2
BARNETT, Robert E.
FDIC chrmn 3-3; confrmd 3-17, 232C1
Rpts FDIC problem-bank data 11-2, 866D1, E1 *
BARNHARDT, Ray
Reagan sweeps Tex vote 5-1, 322G3
Heads Alaska pipeline probe 7-6; rpt issued 9-10, 690A3, E3, 691A1, A2
GOP conv vp vote table 8-19, 599F3
BARNUM, John W.
Greets Concorde arrival 5-24, 378E2
BAR of the City of New York, Association of the
Ct disbars Nixon 7-8, 493C3
BARON, Alvin
Indicted 11-30, 991C1
BARONA, Cmdr.
Captured 638A3
BARQANI, Mohammed
In Damascus raid 9-26, executed 9-27, 720C3, 721A1
BARR, Glen
Rpts extremist pressure 1-6, 19A3
BARRE, Maj. Gen. Mohamed Siad
At Sovt CP Cong 2-24—3-5, 195B3
BARRE, Raymond (French premier)
French trade min 1-12, 49C2
Named French premier 8-25, 637C3
Biographical sketch 638C1
Names Cabt, takes finance post 8-27, Cabt meets 8-28, 650A3
Details inflatn curbs 9-22, 712B2
Curbs spark 1-day strike 10-7, 772A3
Trade deficit rise rptd 11-18, 964E2
BARREIROS, Acacio
Anti-Spinola motn fails 8-10, 732G3
BARRETO, Humberto
Corruptn expose cites 8-3—8-5, 851B1
BARRETT, 1st Lt. Mark T.
Killed in Korea 8-18, 618C3
BARRETT, Nicole
Takes drug overdose 11-16, committed 11-19, 890F3, 891A2
Gilmore ends hunger strike 12-14, 952A3 *
BARRETT, Rep. William A. (D, Pa.)
Dies 4-12; nominated in primary 4-27, 305B1, 315F3
BARRIENTOS Ortuno, Gen. Rene (1920-69)
Gulf paymts rptd 134C1
Gulf rpts '66 bribe, Bolivia denies 1-14, 147G1
Rptdly ordered Guevara executn 5-9, 5-13, 415D3
BARROSO Hurtado, Rear Adm. Gutemberg
Bolivia navy chief 1-6, 26G3
BARROW, Judge Allen E.
Home-Stake fines rptd 12-22, 1016D2
BARROW, Earl
Chrgs US 'destabilizatn' campaign vs Jamaica 5-25, 522G1
Replaced as DLP ldr 9-24, 962F1
Denies DLP link to plot 11-12, 962E1
BARROW, Errol
DLP loses electns 9-2; replaced 9-3, 672G3
BARRY Lyndon (film)
Top-grossing film 2-25, 208G3

1977

BARGHOORN, Elso S.
Oldest fossils of life found 10-15, 908G1
BARK, L. Dean
On drought effects 2-21, 183C2
BARKER, Bernard L.
Nixon com to pay $50,000 2-22, 157G2
BARKER, Sue
Loses Bloomington Va Slims 1-30, 104A1
Va Slims tourn results 2-27, 3-6, 3-27, 431C1, F1
Wade wins Wimbledon 7-1, 548A2
BARLEY
Carter cuts '78 acreage 11-15, 916C2
BARLOW, Perry
Dies 12-26, 1023G3
BARNARD, Dr. Christiaan N.
Baboon heart implant fails 6-20, 619B3
Sees forced retiremt 7-11, 619G3
Chimpanzee implant fails 10-17, 847C3
BARNES, George
Dies 9-4, 787F3
BARNES, Leroy (Nicky)
Convicted 12-2, 972D1
BARNES, Marvin
Released from jail 10-14, 870F2
Traded to Braves 11-23, suspended 12-12, reinstated 12-21, 991C1
BARNES, Robert Gaylord
Dies 10-24, 872A1
BARNES, Wiley
Hiring defended 3-23, 3-25, 236D1
BARNETT, Robert
Rpts problem bank list up 3-11, 194D2
BARNUM, John W.
Replaced in Transport post 2-10, 148D3
BARNWELL, S.C.—*See SOUTH Carolina*
BAR-On, Hanan
Assured on Carter Mideast views 3-9, 165G2
BAROOAH, Dev Kant
Quits as Cong Party pres 4-13, 392B2
BARRANTES Lingan, Alfonso
Arrest rptd 3-11, 241F2
BARRE, Maj. Gen. Mohamed Siad (Somalian president)
Sees Young 2-5, 105D1
Sees Castro 3-12—3-14, 249C2
At Red Sea summit 3-22—3-23, 208F2
Sees Podgorny 4-2, 248C1
Rejcts Africa Horn federatn 5-18, 428E2
Visits USSR 8-29—8-31, Egypt 8-31, 684A3
In Saudi Arabia 9-14, 715A3
US arms aid assurances rptd 9-19, 715E3
W Ger raid frees hijacked jet 10-18, 789C2
USSR arms cut scored 10-21, 830A1
Cuba denies troop chrg 11-5, 875F1
BARRE, Raymond (French premier)
Defends Daoud release 1-13, 27B2
Inflatn curbs effective 1-26, unions protest 1-26—2-1, 159D2
On S Africa A-bomb capacity 2-17, 160C2
Urges Chirac-Giscard unity 3-20, 221B2
Names new Cabinet 3-30, 239C1
Econ plan protested 4-18, 4-26, Assemb OKs 4-28, 328B3, F3
On steel industry aid 4-19, 391D2
Viet premr visits 4-25—4-28, 329A1
OKs A-plant 5-12, scored 5-30, 450B1
Mitterrand TV debate 5-12, 542G3
Unions strike vs wage curbs 5-24, 486D2
Textile import curbs imposed 6-19, 1012D2, D3
Bars A-weapons abroad 6-23, 1012F3
Freezes imported food prices 6-28, 1012D2
Sees Andreotti 7-19, 581E2
In US, asks 'organized free trade' 9-15—9-16, 1012B3
Sets food price curbs 11-3; strikes called, shopkeepers rptd angry 11-8—11-15, 1012B2
Defends defense budget cuts 11-18, 924A2
Raises min wage, pensns 11-30, 1012G1
Giscard backs econ program 12-8, 1012F2, A3
BARRETO, Humberto
Backs Figueiredo pres bid 7-12, 615G3
BARRETT, Edith
Dies 2-22, 164C2
BARRETT, Edward J.
Dies 4-4, 356F2
BARRETT, Rev. Elizabeth
Ordained 1-10, 845C2
Episcs vs homosexuality 10-3, 845C2
BARRON, Brian
Rhodesia ousts 8-2, 599F2
BARROW, Judge Allen E.
Fines Phillips 11-22, 944C1

1978

BARGER, James
Testifies at JFK assassinatn hearing 9-11, 698A2
Backs acoustics experts on JFK death 12-29, 1002G1
BARKAT Gourad Hamadou (Djibouti premier)
Named premr 9-21, 840E3
BARKER, Stonie
Coal setlmt reached 3-14, 182A1
BARLEY—*For feed grain, see GRAIN*
BARNA, Minhaj
Released 10-10, 818A3
BARNARD Jr., Rep. D. Douglas (D, Ga.)
Reelected 11-7, 850B3
BARNES, Judge Ernest G.
Voids AMA ad ban 11-29, 947E2
BARNES, Joe
Montreal loses Grey Cup 11-26, 1025F1
BARNES, Leroy (Nicky)
Sentenced to life 1-19, 95E3
BARNES, Marvin
Traded to Celtics 7-7, 655A3
BARNES, Michael D.
Wins US House seat 11-7, 848A3, 851B1
BARNETT, Don
Wins Sen primary in SD 6-6, 448G1
Loses electn 11-7, 855B1
BARNETT, Joel
Hikes offshore oil tax 8-2, 591D3
Scores Ford strike 9-25, 764B1
BARNWELL, S.C.—*See SOUTH Carolina*
BAROCCO (film)
Released 4-7, 618B3
BARON, Alvin
Sued by US on Teamster pensn funds 2-1, 83C1
BARONE, Mario
Arrested in Sindona case 1-11, 19G2
Resigns as Banco di Roma dir 3-10, 454C2
BARR, Jim
Signs with Angels 12-3, 1025F3
BARRA Garcia, Felix
'77 arrest for corruptn cited 3-21, 289A3
BARRE, Maj. Gen. Mohamed Siad (Somalian president)
Asks Westn arms aid 1-16, 43A3
OAU presses Ethiopia mediatn 2-9, 100F1
Sees Italy CP rep 2-20—2-22, 138A1
Scores Ethiopia border, US exit call 2-21, 138A1
Plot rptd 2-28, 269G1
Sees US envoy 3-20—3-22, 215D2
Revolt crushed 4-9, 269E1
Rpts 20 killed in revolt 4-11, 353F2
In China 4-13—4-15, 353E2
BARRE, Raymond (French premier)
Presents govt electn progrm 1-7, campaign plans 1-9; Gaullists rptd angered 1-11, 54B2
Small govt parties form electn accord 1-10; Gaullists break pact 1-11; plays down split 1-13, 54B3
Visits China 1-19—1-24, 71D1
Giscard backs govt program 1-27, 70E3
Disputes Chirac electn claims 3-20, rift seen 3-21, 201E1
Announces tanker rules 3-23, 238G1
Reappointed premr 3-31, names Cabt 4-5, 245C2, F2
Presents econ program, retains austerity measures 4-19; Cabt wins confidence vote 4-20, 312B3
Defends pub svc price hikes 4-27, 352B2
Begins price control phase-out 6-1, 473G2
Asks Iraq try emb guards 8-2, 582C2
Socialist censure motion fails 10-4, 815D2
French-Chinese missile deal confrmd 10-20, 814A1
Delays EMS start 12-29, 999B1
BARREIROS, Maj. Adalto
Arrested 10-12, corroboratn of govt corruptn, tap chrgs cited 10-17, 836F2
BARRELS—*See CONTAINERS & Packaging*
BARRERA, Rev. Ernesto
Killed 11-29, archbp denies guerrilla chrg 12-19, 987A1
BARRERA, Laz
Affirmed wins Triple Crown 6-10, 539A2
Named top trainer 12-13, 1028G1
BARRETO, Bruno
Dona Flor released 2-26, 619F1
BARRETO, Humberto Esmeraldo
Paymts from US billionaire rptd 1-13, 165G3
BARRETO, Luiz Carlos
Dona Flor released 2-26, 619F1
BARRIE, George
Fingers released 3-2, 619G1
BARRIE, Gerald
Info Dept audit cited 6-15, 498B3
BARRIE, Sir James M(atthew) (1860-1937)
Fay Compton dies 12-12, 1032D2
BARRIE, Wendy
Dies 2-2, 196B2
BARRON, Gayle
In Boston Marathon 4-17, 692A3
BARROT, Jacques
Named French commerce min 4-5, 245G2
BARROW, Thomas D.
Kennecott chrmn; Curtiss-Wright dispute settled 12-15, 1005A1
BARRY, Marion
Elected DC mayor 11-7, 848A2

1979

BARGER, James
Defends JFK acoustics evidence 1-5, 4B2
BARGER, Ralph (Sonny)
Arrested 6-14, 492D1
BARHYDT, Frank
Quintet released 2-8, 174D3
BARKER, Sue
Loses Boston Avon tourn 3-18, 391D2
Loses Chichester tourn 6-17, 570D2
Wins Greater Pittsburgh Open 9-16, 734E2
US wins Wightman Cup 11-4, 1003C3
BARLETTA, Vicente
Arrested in Panama coup plot 10-24, 836E3
BARLOW, Judge George H.
Newark ex-mayor paroled 10-2, 891A2
BARLOW, Sir William
On Post Office reform 9-12, 687B1
BARNEGAT, N.J.—*See NEW Jersey*
BARNES, Benny
Steelers win Super Bowl 1-21, 63D1
Rozelle admits Super Bowl officiating error 2-22, 175C3
BARNES, Brian
Wins Italian Open 5-6, 587F2
BARNES, Ernest G.
Scores Horizon land sales 10-3, 903E1
BARNES, Maurice
Rubstic wins Grand Natl 3-31, 448A3
BARNETT, Joel
Spending plans unveiled 1-17, 59F2
BARNS, Christopher
Wild Oates opens 1-8, 292G3
BAROODY, Jamil M.
Dies 3-4, 272A2
BARR, John A.
Dies 1-16, 104E2
BARR, Richard
Sweeney Todd opens 3-1, 292C3
BARRANTES, Alfonso
Arrest rptd 1-8, 39F1
BARRE, Gabriel
What the Devil opens 4-16, 712E3
BARRE, Maj. Gen. Mohamed Siad (Somalian president)
Hints better USSR ties 1-21, 85F3
US scored re arms delay 2-7, 193A2
BARRE, Raymond (French premier)
Lists econ goals 1-4, 20A2
Announces job measures 1-16, 37A3
'78 trade balance surplus rptd 1-17, 37E3
Defends econ plans 2-2, 96B2
In Canada, hedges separatism issue 2-8—2-13, 133C3
At 'Lulu' debut 2-25, 174A1
Leftist censure votes fail 3-16, 235C2
On econ stimulus measures 4-4, 267A2
Sees Mauritania premr 5-3, 324A1
OPEC price hike impact seen 5-28, 473B2
US oil import subsidy scored 6-1, 417B2
New Airbus models rptd backed 6-18, 485C2
In Iraq, oil agrmt rptd 7-11, 564D1
Soclsts chrgd on broadcasts 8-24, 653D1
Seeks union 'dialogue' 8-29, 652C3
Rpt backs A-arms priority 9-11, 686G1
CGT, CFDT adopt jt progrm 9-19, 729C3
Talks with unions 10-2, 791F2
Meets Hua 10-15, 789F2
Chirac scores on econ 10-19, 834E3
On Boulin suicide 10-30, 835B1
Sees Spanish premr in Paris 11-26—11-27, 952D1
BARRERA, Laz
Pulls Affirmed from Marlboro Cup 9-4; sets earning record 10-6, 876F2, A3
Named top trainer 12-11, 1005C1
BARRETT, Judge James E.
Named to wiretap ct 5-18, 442C3
BARRETT, Stan
Sets land speed record 12-18, 1006D1
BARRIE, George
Class of Miss MacMichael released 1-26, 528A2
BARRIE, James M. (1860-1937)
Peter Pan opens 9-6, 956F3
BARRIENTOS Ortuno, Rene
Guevera elected Bolivia interim pres 8-6, 600G2
BARRON, Fred
Short of Paradise released 10-5, 1008F1
BARRON, Judge John
Quits Davis divorce trial 3-25, 271G3
BARROS, Jose Miguel
Recalled 6-21, 506F2
BARROW, Gen. Robert H.
Named Marine Corps head 4-18, 307G2
On Marine manpower reductn 9-10, 724D3
BARRY, Justin (Sam) (d. 1950)
In basketball HOF 4-30, 526F3
BARRY, Leo
Warns vs oil 'hysteria' 9-21, 728A3
BARRY Jr., Mayor Marion (Washington, D.C.)
Teachers end strike 3-29, 262A3
Rpts minorities business law ignored 6-13, 442E3

1980

BARGER, Ralph (Sonny)
Acquitted 7-2, 568B2
BARINOV, Juri
Wins Olympic medal 7-28, 622F2
BARKER, Len
AL pitching ldr 10-6, 926G3
BARKER, Sue
US wins Wightman Cup 11-1, 946G3, 947A1
BAR-Lev, Chaim
Visits Egypt 11-7—11-9, 863F2
BARLEY
Canada sale to USSR rptd 2-29, 171E2
EC to resume Sovt sales 10-23, 832B1
BARNARD, Dr. Christiaan
El Salvador kidnap offer cited 10-9, 789D3
BARNARD, Rep. D. Douglas (D, Ga.)
Reelected 11-4, 842B3
BARNARD College (N.Y., N.Y.)
Mattfeld resigns 5-28, 471B1
BARNES, Bill
Goodbye Fidel opens 4-23, 392G2
BARNES, Leroy (Nicky)
Convictn review refused by Sup Ct 4-21, 344G1
BARNES, Rep. Michael (D, Md.)
Reelected 11-4, 843B1
BARNES v. U.S.
Case refused by Sup Ct 4-21, 344G1
BARNETT, David H.
Indicted on espionage 10-24, pleads guilty 10-29, 855G2
BARNUM (play)
Opens 4-30, 392D2
Dale, Mitchell win Tonys 6-8, 692C3
BARNUM, Phines Tayler (1810-91)
Barnum opens 4-30, 392D2
BARNWELL—*See SOUTH Carolina*
BARON, Bengt
Wins Olympic medal 7-21, 623E2
BARONE, George
Sentenced 1-11, 64G1
BAROODY Sr., William J.
Dies 7-29, 608B1
BARQUERO, William
Released 4-4, 293B3
BARR, Richard
Lady From Dubuque opens 1-31, 136C3
BARRAGAN, Polly Baca
Loses US House electn 11-4, 851E3
BARRANTES, Alfonso
Left wins Arequipa electns 11-23, 923B1
BARRAULT, Marie-Christine
Stardust Memories released 9-26, 836F3
BARRE, Maj. Gen. Mohamed Siad (Somali president)
People's Assemb opens, '79 electn cited 1-24, 103A3
Asks more UN refugee aid 9-21, 736C1
Chrgs Ethiopia, Kenya invasn plan, calls Assemb sessn 12-7, 933A2
BARRE, Raymond (French premier)
Price hikes rptd OKd 1-2, 6C3
On autonomy trends 1-10, 58E2
On Sovt relations 2-7, 106G2
Chirac scores re econ 2-25, 193A1
At Tito funeral 5-8, 339B1
On forgn student rules 5-16, 407F1
Purchasing power decline rptd 6-14, 463D1
In Spain, sees Suarez 7-2—7-3, 567G1
Anderson visits 7-15, 550B1
Announces export, econ stimulus plan 9-3, 669G3
Jewish protectn measures set 10-8, 767F3
BARRERA, Enrique
Kidnaped, slain 11-27, 921F1
BARRETT, Bill
Sets 200-m individual medley mark 8-1, 834B3
BARRON, Brian
Amin interview aired 6-3, 446D2
BARRON, Holly
Mecca opens 2-2, 136D3
BARRON, John
Article questns Chappaquiddick 1-15, 32G3
BARROW, Barbara
Wins Birmingham Classic 4-27, 412E3
BARRY, Donald (Red)
Dies 7-17, 608C1
BARRY, Gene
Guyana released 1-25, 216F2
BARRY, Mayor Marion (Washington, D.C.)
Senghor visits US 4-4—4-6, 336D2
Proposes fiscal recovery plan 7-19, 742A3
At Reagan DC fete 11-18, 880E3
BARRY, Philip
Happy New Year opens 4-27, 392A3

1976

BARTELS Jr., John R.
Replaced As DEA head 2-5, 110A2
BARTLETT, Sen. Dewey (R, Okla.)
Scores NATO defns 11-14, 879D3
BARTON, Charles C.
'70 Carter campaign donor 10-17, 805B1
BARTU, Jan
Wins Olympic medal 7-22, 575B1
BARUA Castaneda, Luis
Sets austerity measures 1-12, 142D1
On Group of 24 debt moratorium issue 10-2, 778F1
BARWICK, Sir Garfield
Whitlam chrgs '75 ouster collusn 2-9, 116F1
BARYL, Jan
On Czech Presidium, Secretariat 4-16, 289B2
BARZEGAR, Mansour
Wins Olympic medal 7-31, 576D3
BAS, Pierre
Parlt gets 'franglais' ban bill 1-4, 50A2

BASEBALL
US bars US-Cuba series 1-7, 23E1
Martin's daughter sentncd 1-21, 160A3
Season opens 4-8, 272B2
Mid-yr standings 7-13, 544D2
Candelaria pitches no-hitter 8-9, 596G3
Montefusco pitches no-hitter 9-29, 756G2
Final standings 10-4, 795C3-796E1
Attendance record set 816D1
Honors & Awards
Lynn gets AP award 1-13, 31F3
6 named to HOF 8-9, 816B1
Palmer, Jones get Cy Young awards 11-2, 11-10, 952C1
Fidrych, Zachry, Metzger named top rookies 11-12, 11-30, 952E1
Munson, Morgan voted MVPs 11-16, 11-24, 952D1
Obituaries
Bankhead, Dan 5-2, 368D2
Carey, Max 5-30, 484D3
Combs, Earle 7-21, 656E3
Earnshaw, George 12-1, 1015C1
Murtaugh, Danny 12-2, 932F3
Warneke, Lon 6-23, 524G3
Player & Executive Developments
'75 free agent ruling upheld 2-4, 3-9, 951G3
3 A's stars sold for $3.5 mln 6-15, Kuhn voids sales 6-18, 444B3-F3
LaSorda succeeds Alston as Dodgers mgr 10-3, 816A1
Williams named Expos mgr 10-4, 815G3
McNamara rehired by Padres 10-4, 816A1
Schoendienst ousted as Cardinals mgr 10-5, 816B1
Free agent draft held 11-4, contracts rptd signed 12-5, 951C3-952C1
Jackson signs with Yankees 11-29, 951B3
Winners
NL wins All-Star game 7-13, 544F1
Reds, Yankees win pennants 10-12, 10-14, 796E1
Reds win World Series 10-21, 815F1-F3

1977

BARRYMORE, Ethel (1879-1959)
Daughter dies 5-22, 452F2
BARSHAI, Rudolf
Emigrates to Israel 1-30, 117G1
BARTELS, Judge John R.
Sentences '76 Croat hijackers 7-20, 642A2
Upholds LI ocean dumping 9-19, 723G3
BARTH, Dale
EPA backs DNA controls 3-8, 184B3
BARTH, Jurgen
Wins Le Mans 6-12, 531A2
BARTHOLOMEW, Peter
Subpoena rptd 6-18, 556C3
BARTLETT, Sen. Dewey (R, Okla.)
Warsaw Pact rpt released 1-24, 70A2
BARTON, Graham & Fatima
Chrg Leyland payoffs 5-19, arrested for forgery 5-21, 526D1
BARUA Castaneda, Luis
Quits as econ min 5-13, 427C2

BASEBALL
Carter call-in on US Cuba games 3-5, 171F1
US OKs Cuba games, Kuhn balks 3-8, 181C1
FCC pay-TV rules voided 3-25, appeal set 4-14, 376F2
Cuba-US all-star plans cited 4-11, 283B2
Mid-yr standings 7-19, 567A3
Orioles forfeit vital game 9-14, 748A3
Mets blamed for NYC '84 Olympics bid loss 9-25, Grant scores Carey 9-26, 828D3
Season ends, attendance rptd up 10-2, 767C3
Final standings 10-2, 767E3
Final batting, pitching, stolen base ldrs listed 10-2, 926B3-927A1
House subcom probes TV coverage 11-2, 949E3
Awards & Honors
Hall of Fame selectn review set 8-7, 644C1
Hall of Fame inducts 6 8-8, 643E3
Brock award for base-stealing created 8-17, 768C1
Oh wins Japan Medal of Honor 9-5, 748G2
Hall of Fame entrance rule eased, selectn com expanded 10-3, 768G1-A2
Jackson World Series MVP 10-18, 806D1
Lyle, Carlton win Cy Young awards 10-25, 11-2, 927D1
Weaver, Lasorda named top mgrs 10-25, 10-26, 927A2
Foster, Carew named MVPs 11-8, 11-16, 927B1
McCovey wins Hutch Award 11-14, 990E2
Murray, Dawson named top rookies 11-22, 11-23, 927F1
Obituaries
Hubbard, Cal 10-17, 872C2
Harris, Bucky 11-8, 952D2
Lollar, Sherman 9-24, 788D1
Lombardi, Ernie 9-26, 788D1
Meusel, Bob 11-28, 952B3
Smith, (Edward) Mayo 11-24, 952D3
Wrigley, Philip 4-12, 356G3
Player & Executive Developments
Jets to remain at Shea 2-18, 163D3
Finley, Kuhn clash over player sales 2-18—4-8; Finley loses suit 3-17 310A3
Randle slugs Ranger mgr 3-28, suspended 4-5, 310E3 *
Turner loses interim mgr dispute 5-11—5-13, Kuhn's suspensn power upheld 5-19, 567C3
Mets-Jets dispute settled 5-26, 491A2
Baines in free-agent draft 6-7, 644A3
Seaver traded to Reds, other last day trading rptd 6-15, 644B2
Jackson-Martin dispute 6-18, 6-21, 644B3
Robinson fired as Indian mgr 6-19, joins Angels 7-11, 644G1
Lucchesi fired as Ranger mgr 6-22, 644B3
Stankey hired as Ranger mgr 6-22, quits 6-23; Hunter replaces 6-27, 644B3
Randle fined 7-28, 644G2
Major league owners meet on trading, designated hitter, other measures; attendance, DC team pledge unresolved 8-17, 768A1
B Robinson retires 8-21, honored 9-18, 768E2
'No-litigatn' clause upheld 8-30, 768D1
Finley heart surgery 9-15, 768C2
Bavasi quits Padres, Kroc shifts front office 9-20, 768E2
Lucchesi sues Randle 9-21, 768D2
O'Connell fired as Red Sox gen mgr 10-24, AL owners veto team sale 12-8, 989E2

1978

BARRY, Rick
NBA free-throw ldr 4-9, 271F1, F2
Signs with Rockets 6-17, 656D1
Warriors OK compensatn award 9-5, 1027D3
BARRYMORE, John (Blythe) (1882-1942)
Fay Compton dies 12-12, 1032D2
BARSKI, Odile
Violette released 10-9, 1030E3
BARTELS, Anna
Rptd sentenced 1-14, 36B2
BARTELS, Karl
Rptd sentenced 1-14, 36B2
BARTER v. U.S.
Marrieds tax law review barred 1-9, 13B2
BARTHELME, Donald
Elected to Arts Institute 2-7, 316D1
BARTKOWSKI, Steve
Falcons win in playoffs 12-24, 1024D1
BARTLETT, Sen. Dewey F. (R, Okla.)
Votes vs Panama Canal neutrality pact 3-16, 177G2
Votes vs 2d Canal pact 4-18, 273B1
Coal conversn bill clears Sen 7-18, 550B1
Not running for reelectn 8-22, 683C1
Boren wins seat 11-7, 855G2
BARTOK, Bela (1881-1945)
Serly dies 10-8, 888E3
BARTON, Fatima
Acquitted 8-11, 667A3
BARTON, Graham
Sentenced 8-11, 667G2
BARULLI, Umberto
Reaches accord with Soclsts 6-23, 575A2
BARWOOD, Hal
Corvette Summer released 8-4, 970A1
BARYSHNIKOV, Mikhail
Joins NYC Ballet 4-26, 335E3
BASCHNAGEL, Brian
NFL '77 kick return ldr 1-1, 56G3
BASEBALL
Clemente family case vs FAA declined by Sup Ct 5-1, 364C1
Yankee surge, Red Sox decline detailed 5-24—9-17, 778G2
Mid-yr standings 7-11, 560A1
Season ends; Yankees win AL East playoff, Dodgers set attendance mark 10-2, 778D2
Final standings 10-2, 778B3
Final batting, pitching, stolen base ldrs listed 10-2, 928D2-G3
Awards & Honors
Garvey named All-Star Game MVP 7-11, 559C3
Hall of Fame inducts 3; Allen, Barber honored 8-8, 617D3-618A3
Dodgers dedicate playoff, Series to Gilliam 10-7, 10-8, 779E1
Dent named Series MVP 10-17, 799F2
Perry, Guidry win Cy Young Awards 10-24, 11-1, 928F1
Lemon, Altobelli named top mgrs 10-24, 928B2
Rice, Parker named MVPs 11-7, 11-15, 928D1
Horner, Whitaker named top rookies 11-20, 11-21, 928A2
Golden Glove winners named 11-21, 928C2-B3
Obituaries
Bostock, Lyman 9-23, 777G3
Cox, Billy 3-31, 252F2
Frick, Ford C 4-8, 356F2
Gilliam, Jim (Junior) 10-8, 779F1
Gordon, Joe (Flash) 4-15, 356G2
Haines, Jesse (Pop) 8-5, 708G2
Harris, Vic 2-23, 196B3
McCarthy, Joseph V 1-14, 96G2
Player & Executive Developments
Carew gets $100,000 bonus 1-6, 195D1
Bench ethnic jokes upset audience 1-7, 195B1
Bamberger signs as Brewers mgr 1-20, 195B1
Kuhn cancels Blue sale to Reds 1-30, 20 owners back 3-3, 194G2
F Robinson named Orioles coach 2-11, 195D1
Blue traded to Giants, other deals 3-15; Kuhn bars role 3-16, 194F3
Messersmith hurts shoulder 3-16, 195C1
Dark fired as Padres mgr, Craig named 3-21, 355B2
Bonds, others traded 3-23—10-3, 779G2-C3
A's sale fails, Davis scores Finley 3-27, 354F3
Kuhn upheld again on player sales 4-7, 355F1
Reggie candy bar debuts 4-13, 779F3
Rapp fired as Cardinals mgr 4-25, Boyer named 4-28, 355C2
Robinson to manage Rochester Triple-A club 5-8, 355D2
Winkles quits as A's mgr, McKeon replaces 5-23, 560D1
Garcia fired as Angels mgr, Fregosi replaces 6-1, 560E1
Amateur draft held, Horner 1st pick 6-6, 779G3
Cepeda sentncd on pot chrgs 6-14, 1026F2
Lemon quits as White Sox mgr, Doby replaces 6-30, 560E1
Jackson suspended 7-17; Martin assails Jackson, Steinbrenner 7-23; quits Yankees, Lemon named 7-24; Martin rehired for '80 7-29, 618A1
Umpires strike 8-25—8-26, 779F1
Bouton returns to major leagues 9-10, beats Giants 9-14, 779D3
Houk sets retiremt as Tigers mgr, Moss to replace 9-21, 1026G1
Women rptrs gain locker room access 9-25, 1026A3

1979

BARRY, Rick
NBA free-throw ldr 4-8, 290F2, A3
BARRYMORE, John (1882-1942)
Dolores Costello dies 3-1, 272C2
BARRY v. Barchi
Case decided by Sup Ct 6-25, 540F1
BARTH, Alan
Dies 11-20, 932B2
BARTLETT, Dewey F.
Dies 3-1, 272A2
BARTNOFF, Judith
On Sterns '57 spy chrg dismissal 3-22, 232F1
BARYSHNIKOV, Mikhail
Named Amer Ballet dir 6-20, 527E3
BARZANI, Gen. Mustafa al-
Dies 3-1, 272B2
BASCHNAGEL, Brian
NFL '78 kick return ldr 1-6, 80G2

BASEBALL
Easter killed in holdup 3-29, 1002E3
Padres ex-owner convicted 5-7, sentncd 5-31, 442F2
Umpires' 3-mo walkout setld, terms rptd 5-18, 569B2
Mid-yr standings 7-17, 569E1
Munson plane crashes 8-2, 671A3; death blamed on pilot error 9-16, 1002F3
Season ends 9-30, 797C1
Final standings 9-30, 797E1
Final batting, pitching, stolen base ldrs listed 9-30, 955D2-G3
'Lone Ranger' hired by Rangers 11-15, 1002E3
Awards & Honors
Hall of Fame rule chngs rptd 3-4, 618F3
Parker named All-Star Game MVP 7-17, 569A2
Hall of Fame inducts Mays, 2 others 8-5, 618C3
Stargell named Series MVP 10-17, 815F3
Weaver named top mgr 10-17, top AL mgr 10-19, 956A1
Williams named top NL mgr 10-23, 956A1
Flanagan, Sutter win Cy Young Awards 10-30, 11-7, 955C2, A3
Stargell, Hernandez named NL MVPs 11-13, 955F1
Golden Glove winners named 11-20, 956B1
Baylor named AL MVP 11-21, 955B2
Castino, Griffin named top AL rookies 11-26, 955B3
Sutcliffe named top NL rookie 11-28, 955C3
Rose named Player of Decade 12-29, 1003E1
Obituaries
Easter, Luke 3-29, 1002E3
Fitzsimmons, Freddie 11-18, 1008F2
Giles, Warren 2-7, 176B3
Munson, Thurman 8-2, 671A3
O'Malley, Walter F 8-9, 671C3
Player & Executive Developments
Carew traded to Angels 2-3, Kuhn discloses $ deal ban 2-4, 619D1
Marshall named A's mgr 2-12, 619B2
Player trades 3-27–11-13, 1002G2
Astros sale set 5-11, NL owners OK 5-16, 619D1
Martin setls battery chrg 5-24, returns as Yankees mgr 6-19, 619G1-B2
Horner contract dispute settled 6-4, 1003B1
Moss fired as Tigers mgr, Anderson replaces 6-12, 619C2
Orioles sold 8-2, 619A1
Kessinger quits as White Sox mgr, LaRussa replaces 8-2, 619C2
Aaron assails baseball racism 8-15, 1003D1
Kroc rpts record fine, to give up Padres operatn 8-24, 1003A1
Ozark fired as Phillies mgr 8-31, Green replaces 10-18, 1002F1
Altobelli fired as Giants mgr 9-6, Bristol replaces 9-14, 1002F2
Craig fired as Padres mgr 9-30, Coleman replaces 10-1, 1002F1
Hartsfield fired as Blue Jays mgr 9-30, replaced by Mattick 10-18, 1002F1
Herzog fired as Royals mgr 10-2, replaced by Frey 10-24, 1002F1
Martin in brawl 10-23, Yankees fire 10-28; Kuhn, MacPhail warn 11-29, 12-13, 1002B1
Mays to cut baseball ties 10-29, 1002G3

1980

BARRY, Rick
NBA free-throw ldr 3-30, 278D3, F3
BARRY, Tom
Dies 7-2, 608C1
BARRY v. American Financial Enterprises Inc.
Case refused by Sup Ct 12-15, 957E2
BARSZCZ, Edward
Ousted from Polish Cabt 11-21, 909D2
BARTHES, Roland
Dies 3-25, 279D1
BARTLEY, Robert L.
Wins Pulitzer 4-14, 296G2
BARTZ, Manfred
Arrest rptd 1-4, 57C2
BARYSHNIKOV, Aleksandr
Wins Olympic medal 7-30, 624D1
BARYSHNIKOV on Broadway (TV special)
Wins Emmy 9-7, 692E1
BARZANI, Gen. Mustafa
'65-75 Israel aid rptd 9-29, 735B3

BASEBALL
Topps card trust violatn rptd 7-2, 917F3
AL, NL midseason standings 7-8, 636E2
Season ends; final standings 10-6, 795C2, C3
Final batting, pitching, stolen base ldrs listed 10-6, 926D2-G3
Awards & Honors
Rose gets Player of Decade award; Aaron boycotts ceremony, chrgs racism 1-28, 637F1
Francona named NCAA MVP 6-6, 796F2
Griffey named All-Star MVP 7-8, 636D2
Hall of Fame inducts Snider, Kaline, 2 others 8-3, 796B2
Schmidt named Series MVP 10-21, 811C2
Virdon named top mgr 11-1, top NL mgr 11-17; Martin named top AL mgr 11-20, 926B1
Carlton, Stone win Cy Young Awards 11-4, 11-12, 925E3, G3
Brett named AL MVP 11-18, 925D3
Schmidt named NL MVP 11-26, 925B3
Howe, Charboneau named top rookies 12-1, 12-2, 926A1
Golden Glove winners 12-6, 926C1
Obituaries
Ashford, Emmett 3-1, 279D1
Howard, Elston 12-14, 1004B2
Marquard, Richard 6-1, 528E2
Page, Joe 4-21, 360F2
Player & Executive Developments
Mets sold 1-24, 795G2
Marshall fired as A's mgr 2-13, Martin replaces 2-21, 637A2
Sutter awarded $700,000 salary by arbitrator 2-25, 637A1
Munson family files wrongful-death suit 2-27, 637E1
Welch reveals alcoholism treatmt 3-4, 637F1
Bamberger suffers heart attack 3-6, returns to manage Brewers 6-4, 636G3
Porter leaves Royals for alcohol, drug treatmt 3-14; returns 4-26, 637E1
Players threaten strike 4-1, talks held 5-15—5-26; strike averted; free agent dispute deferred, other issues setld 5-23, 401G3-402C2
Terrell votes vs strike 4-1, 637C2
Mets fined for ad campaign 5-1, 637C1
Mets draft Strawberry 6-3, 636G3
Tigers sign Cuban refugee 6-3, 637C1
Marshall released by Twins 6-6, 637C1
Boyer fired as Cardinals mgr, Herzog replaces 6-8, 637B2
McCovey sets retiremt 6-22, 637B1
Kingman quits as sportswriter 7-2, 637B2
Gomez fired as Cubs mgr; Amalfitano replaces 7-25, 926A2
Richard suffers stroke 7-30, recovery seen 8-4, 636E3
Johnson fired as Mariners mgr; Wills replaces 8-4, 926A2
Herzog quits as Cardinals mgr, becomes gen mgr 8-29, field mgr 10-24, 926B2
Garvey article reprint OKd 8-14, 637D2
NL owners reject designated-hitter rule 8-14, 795G2
White Sox sale OKd by bd 8-23, 795A3
A's sold 8-23, 795B3
Mauch quits as Twins mgr; Goryl replaces 8-24, 926B2
Zimmer fired as Red Sox mgr 10-1, Houk replaces 10-28, 926A3
Corrales fired as Rangers mgr 10-5, Zimmer replaces 11-12, 926A3
DeBartolo White Sox purchase rejctd 10-24, 12-11, 1000E1
Free-agent draft held 11-13: Sutton, Roberts sign with Astros 12-3, 12-10; Winfield signs record pact with Yankees 12-15, 999F1-1000D1

1976

BASEBALL Players Association, Major League
Miller at hearing on A's sale 6-17, 444E3
BASFORD, Stanley Ronald
Morgentaler convictn set aside 1-22, freed 1-26, 72G1
Judge chrgs mins interfere 2-20, 187G3
Retains posts 9-14, 692B2
Sets Peltier extraditn 12-17, 999B1
BASF-Wyandotte Corp.
US files consent decree 11-16, 989C1
BASHA, Maj. Gen. Hassan Abu
Libyan saboteurs seized 3-9, 3-11, 205G1
BASHAR, Air Commodore Mohammed Khademul
Bangladesh air chief 5-1, 332F1
BASKETBALL
Nets win ABA finals 5-13, 424E2
Celtics win NBA finals 6-6, 424C2
Final ABA, NBA standings 424D2
Olympic results 7-27, 573G3

1977

Bristol fired as Braves mgr 10-25, Cox replaces 11-22, 927B2
North arrested on drug chrgs 10-28, 927B2
Jackson assault case dismissed 11-1, 927C2
Free agent draft held 11-4, contract signings 11-8—12-9, 989C3
Sudol retiremt announced 11-14, 990C2
Brewers name Dalton gen mgr, confirm Grammas firing 11-20, 990B2
NL pres robbed, beaten 11-30, 990F2
Paul resigns as Yankee pres 12-1, 990D2
Major league owners meet on Cleveland refinancing, World Series share proposals 12-4—12-8, 989F3
Kuhn lifts Turner suspensn 12-8, 990D2
Blue traded, Kuhn weighs challenge 12-9; other trades rptd 12-5—12-9, 990A1
Denver oilman buys A's 12-14, Oakland sues Finley to block deal 12-15, 989A2
Angels mgt realignmt rptd 12-17, 990G1
Records & Achievements
Colborn, Eckersley pitch no-hitters 5-14, 5-30, 644E1
Brock sets stolen base mark; table 8-29, 748D3
Oh breaks Aaron HR mark 9-3, 748E2
Jackson sets Series records 10-11—10-18, 807C1
McCovey grandslam homer mark cited 11-14, 990F2
Winners
Ariz State wins coll title 6-18, 568A1
NL wins All-Star Game 7-19, 567A2
Taiwan wins Little League title 8-27, 768B2
Yankees, Dodgers win pennants 10-8, 10-9, 807D1
Yankees win World Series 10-18, 806C1-807C1
Braves win Japanese title 10-27, 927D2

BASEBALL Writers Association of America (BBWAA)—*See BASEBALL*
BASES, Military—*See U.S. GOVERNMENT—DEFENSE; also country names*
BASFORD, (Stanley) Ronald
US-Canada trust com rptd set 6-18, 525G2
Pledges RCMP documts to royal comm 12-7, 965D1
BASHIR, Mohammed el-
Killed in air crash 2-9, 87D1
BASKETBALL
Awards & Honors
Sanders named NIT MVP 3-20, 262F2
5 named to Hall of Fame 5-2, 490E3
Dantley named rookie of yr, all-rookie team chosen 5-16, 584E3
Nissalke named NBA coach of yr 5-19, 584F3
Abdul-Jabbar named NBA MVP 5-23, 584F3
Walton named NBA playoff MVP 6-5, 490E3
NBA all-star team named 6-13, 584G3
Collegiate—*See also 'Awards' above*
NCAA conv 1-10—1-12, 104A2
SD team Cuba games OKd 3-5, 181C1
Tex Southn wins NAIA tourn 3-12, 262F2
NCAA Div II, III titles 3-19, 262D2
St Bonaventure wins NIT title 3-20, 262E2
Marquette wins NCAA title 3-28, 262E1
SD team in Cuba 4-4—4-8, 282B3
NBA draft held; table 6-10, 584A2, C3
Las Vegas placed on NCAA probatn 8-25; coach fired 9-9, reinstated 9-30, 870D2
Ind team dies in jet crash 12-13, 1023C2
Obituaries
Kennedy, Walter 6-26, 532B3
Rupp, Adolph 12-10, 1024B3
Professional—*See also 'Awards' above*
NBA final standings, table 4-10, 331B3
NBA referees strike 4-10—4-25, 331G3
NBA playoffs 5-22—6-5; Portland wins title 6-5, 490G2
NBA draft held; table 6-10, 584A2, C3
NBA aids ailing teams 6-15, 583D3
NBA owners set 11-man rosters 6-15, arbitrator upholds 11-4, 870C1
Nets move to NJ set 7-26, 584F1
Bing retires 9-26, signs with Celtics 9-28, 870A3
Storen fired as Hawks pres 9-27, 870B3
Knicks trade Frazier 10-8, 870G2
NJ Sports Auth OKs Meadowlands arena 10-13, 870C2
Barnes released from jail 10-14, 870F2
Archibald injures ankle 10-15, 870G2
Abdul-Jabbar punches player 10-18, fined $5000 10-20, 870E1

1978

Twins owner causes furor with remarks on blacks, players 9-28—10-2, 779B2
Hunter fired as Rangers mgr, Corrales replaces 10-1, 1026G1
Kuhn authority challenge refused by Sup Ct 10-2, 751A2
Devine quits as Cardinals gen mgr, Claiborne replaces 10-18, 1026A3
Doby fired as White Sox mgr, Kessinger replaces 10-19, 1026G1
Gamble, Lyle sent to Rangers 10-25, 11-10, other trades 12-5—12-15, 1026B1-E1
Free-agent draft held 11-3, contracts signed 11-13—12-3; Rose, Phillies agree 12-5, 1025C3
Grant quits as Mets chrmn 11-8, 1026E2
Martin in barroom brawl 11-11, chrgd with assault 11-12, 1026D2
Anderson fired as Reds mgr, McNamara replaces 11-28, 1026E1
Owners meet 12-1—12-8; Kuhn scores free-agent system 12-5, 3-div proposal to be pursued 12-7, 1026A2
Bouton return to sportscasting rptd 12-6, 1026G2
Carew rejcts Giants trade 12-7, 1025G3-1026A1
Lucchesi settles Randle suit 12-8, 1026F2
Simon bid to buy Orioles rptd 12-21, 1026F2
Records & Achievements
Forsch pitches no-hitter 4-16, 355A2
Rose gets 3000th hit 5-5, 559F3
Mendon pitches NAIA championship no-hitter 6-1, 560A2
Rose hits in 44 straight games 6-14—7-31, 618E2-A3
Seaver pitches no-hitter 6-16, 559G3
McCovey hits 500th homer 6-30, 560A1
Stargell becomes all-time strikeout ldr 8-6, 779D3
Oh hits 800th homer 8-30, 780A1
World Series attendance mark set 10-10—10-17, 799F2
Jackson sets Series HR mark 10-10, 799C3
Yankees win 107 Series games 10-17, 799F2
Winners
Emporia State wins NAIA title 6-1, 560A2
USC wins NCAA title 6-8, 560F1
NL wins All-Star Game, Garvy named MVP 7-11, 559F2
Taiwan wins Little League title 8-26, 779F2
Yankees win AL East playoff 10-2, 778D2
Dodgers, Yankees win pennants 10-7, 778E3
Yankees win World Series 10-17, 799D2-800G2

BASEBALL Writers Association of america (BBWAA)—*See BASEBALL*
BASES, Military—*See U.S. GOVERNMENT—DEFENSE; country, territory names*
BASFORD, (Stanley) Ronald
Sets retiremt 1-13, 89C1
Clears MP re RCMP spy rpt 3-17, 209B1
Scores MP C$ speculatn chrg 5-23, 413C1
Lang replaces 8-9, 647C1
BASHIR, Faisal
On Saudi dvpt plans 2-20, 122F1
BASIE, Count
Band wins Grammy 2-24, 315F3
BASKETBALL
Awards & Honors
Smith named NBA All-Star game MVP 2-5, 271C3
Lee named coll player of yr 3-13, 272D2
5 named to Hall of Fame 5-1, 457D3
Davis named NBA top rookie 5-9, 457A3
H Brown named NBA top coach 5-15, 457B3
Walton named NBA MVP 5-24, 457A3
NBA all-star team named 6-13, 457C3
Collegiate—*See also 'Awards' above*
AIAW chngs scholarship rules 1-7—1-11, 40A3
NCAA conv 1-11—1-13, 40D1-B2
NCAA Div II, III titles 3-18, 272B2
Grand Canyon wins NAIA title 3-18, 272B2
Texas wins NIT 3-21, 272G1
Kentucky wins NCAA title 3-27, 272A1
Mullaney to coach Brown U 4-3, 272F2
Badger to coach Cincinnati U 4-9, 272G2
NBA draft held; table 6-9, 457B2, F2
Ind team '77 air crash blame fixed 8-18, 758C3
Indiana players disciplined re pot 12-12, 1028A1
Professional—*See also 'Awards' above*
AABA debuts 1-6, folds 2-4, 271E3
Johnson fired as Kings coach, Staverman named 1-8, 272F2
NCAA modifies NBA 'hardship' draft rule 1-11—1-13, 40G1
Taylor leaves Nuggets in contract dispute 1-17, 272G2
Havlicek sets retiremt 1-29, plays last game 4-9, 271B3
Washington reinstated 2-1, 271A2
East wins NBA All-Star game, Smith named game MVP 2-5, 271C3
NBPA quits violence com 2-10, 271B2
Porter sets NBA assist record 2-24, 271A2
Powers suspended in zone defns dispute 3-2, 271A3
Drollinger rejcts Nets offer 3-15, 272E2
NBA season ends; final standings, statistical ldrs 4-9, 271B1, C2-G2
Badger quits as Bulls coach 4-9, 272G2
Thompson signs Nuggets deal, becomes top-paid NBA player 4-18, 656F1

1979

Free-agent draft held 11-2; Ryan signs with Astros, becomes top-paid player 11-19; other contracts signed 11-8—12-19, 1001D3
Cepeda hired by White Sox 11-20, 1002F3
Owners meet: labor talks, free agents discussed; players traded 12-3—12-7, 1002A2
Records & Achievements
K Forsch pitches no-hitter 4-7, 619E2
Oh hits 814th home run 5-20, 1003C1
Yastrzemski hits 400th homer 7-24, 619E2
Rose sets NL singles mark 8-5, 619F2
Brock gets 3000th hit 8-13, 619C2
Chen Chao-an sets Little League strikeout mark 8-23, 797B3
Yastrzemski gets 3000th hit 9-12, 1002D3
Brock breaks all-time stolen base mark 9-23, 1003D1
Winners
Cal State-Fullerton wins NCAA title 6-8, 569A3
NL wins All-Star game, Parker named MVP 7-17, 568C3
Taiwan wins Little League semifinal 8-23, title 8-25 797G2
Pirates, Orioles clinch pennants 10-5, 10-6, 797A2
Pirates win World Series 10-17, 815D3-817C1
Hiroshima wins Japanese title 11-4, 1002G1

BASEHART, Richard
Great Bank Hoax released 3-22, 528C2
BASES, Military—*See U.S. GOVERNMENT—DEFENSE*
BASILE (Italian fashion house)
'79 fashion roundup rptd 1006A2
BASKETBALL
Italy-Israel game protested 3-7, 212E1
American Game released 4-28, 528B1
US coach at Pan Am Games arrested 7-8, sentncd 9-10; team wins gold medal 7-13, 798B3-799A1
Awards & Honors
Meyers named '78 top female athlete 1-10, 103C2
Thompson named All-Star MVP 2-4, 175A1
Top coll players named 3-12, 3-29, 290E3
Easterling named WBL All-Star game MVP 3-14, 507G1
Hodges named top coll coach 3-24, 290F3
Chamberlain, 6 others in HOF 4-30, 526B3
Fitzsimmons named NBA top coach 5-11, 526A2
Ford named NBA top rookie 5-16, 526A2
Malone named NBA MVP 5-23, 526F1
Johnson named NBA playoff MVP 6-1, 507B1
NBA all-league teams announced 6-6, 526B2
Collegiate—*See also 'Awards' above*
West Pt recruiting abuses probed 1-4, 175B3
NCAA vows Title IX fight, rejcts reforms 1-8—1-10, 102C3
LSU suspends Scales 3-5, 291B1
Drury wins NAIA title 3-17, 239B1
NCAA Div II, III titles 3-17, 239B1
Indiana wins NIT 3-21, 238E3
Old Dominion wins AIAW title 3-25, 239A1
Mich State wins NCAA title 3-26, 238F2
Brown named UCLA coach 3-27, 291E1
NCAA panel rejcts shot clock, amends rules 3-31, 290G3
Big East conf formed 5-29, 6-26, 526F3
WBL holds draft 6-12, 526F2, A3
NBA draft held; table 6-25, 507G1-B3
U of New Mex scandal detailed 12-13—12-21, 1003E1
Obituaries
Gottlieb, Eddie 12-7, 1008G2
Rudolph, Marvin (Mendy) 7-4, 588C3

1980

Howser quits as Yankee mgr; Michael replaces 11-21, 926E1
Records & Achievements
Jenkins gets 100th AL win 5-3, 636C3
Japanese player gets 3000th hit 5-31, 637D1
Reuss pitches no-hitter 6-28, 636B3
Carlton breaks southpaw strikeout mark 7-6, 636D3
Jackson hits 400th homer 8-11, 636A3
Aikens sets Series homer mark 10-18, 812G1
Wilson sets Series strikeout mark 10-21, 812G3
Winners
All-Star Game, NL 7-8, 636B1
Little League final, Taiwan 8-30, 796G2
NCAA title, Ariz 6-6, 796E2
NL West playoff, Astros 10-6, 795D2
Pennants; Royals, Phillies 10-10, 10-12, 795F3
World Series, Phillies 10-21, 811A2-812G3

BASES, Military—*See under U.S. GOVERNMENT--DEFENSE*
BASKETBALL
Afghan players defect to Pak 6-20, 475D2
Moscow Olympic results 7-26—7-30, 588G2-D3, 622D1
Awards & Honors
Gervin named All-Star MVP 2-3, 279A1
Jackson named NAIA tourn MVP 3-15, 240D3
Sampson named NIT MVP 3-20, 240A3
Top coll players, coach named 3-21, 3-26, 240F3
Nissen named AIAW tourn MVP 3-23, 240B3
Griffith named NCAA tourn MVP 3-24, 240D2
Johnson named NBA playoff MVP 5-16, 432A2
Abdul-Jabbar named NBA MVP 5-29, 656A3
Fitch named NBA top coach 5-29, 656C3
Bird named NBA top rookie 5-29, 656C3
Auerbach named NBA top exec 5-29, 656D3
NBA all-league teams announced 6-2, 656D3
Collegiate
NCAA OKs women's title tourns 1-8, 103C3
Lieberman named top '79 female athlete 1-8, 104D1
NCAA Div II, III titles 3-15, 240C3
Cameron wins NAIA title, Jackson named tourn MVP 3-15, 240D3
Virginia wins NIT, Sampson named tourn MVP 3-20, 240E2
Aguirre, Lieberman named top players; Meyer top coach 3-21, 3-26, 240F3
Old Dominion wins AIAW title, Nissen named tourn MVP 3-23, 240A3
Louisville wins NCAA title, Griffith named tourn MVP 3-24, 240D1-D2
NBA draft held; table 6-10, 447A1, E1
UNM coach acquitted of US chrgs 6-20, 875E3
NCAA probe of UCLA team 'rewards' rptd 7-27, 875C3
Ore U indictmts cited 10-15, 875C3
Ariz U to seek athletic dept fraud probe 10-16, 875A3
Obituaries
Furlow, Terry 5-23, 656A2

1976

BASS, Dennis
'Dirty dozen' list issued 3-25, 220A1
BASSHAM, Lanny
Wins Olympic medal 7-21, 575A2
BASSO, Lelio
Russell ct meets 1-10—1-17, 61D2, F2
BATES, Ruby—*See SCHUTS, Ruby*
BATH Iron Works Corp.
Asks contract relief 5-4, 454D1
BATLLE, Jorge
Loses pol rights 9-1, 678F1
BATMAN (comic books)
Peru bans 2-3, 142F3
BATON Rouge, La.—*See LOUISIANA*
BATON Rouge State Times (newspaper)
Ford endorsement rptd 10-30, 827G3
BATTEN, William M.
Named NYSE chrmn 4-27, 347F3-348F1
BATTISTI, Judge Frank
Denies school constructn bar in Cleveland 1-6, 6C2
BAUCUS, Rep. Max S. (D, Mont.)
Reelected 11-2, 824B2, 830B1
BAUDRIN, Germain
Sentenced 2-23, 220A3
BAUKHAGE, Hilmar R.
Dies 2-1, 124C3
BAUM, Most Rev. William Wakefield
Appointed cardinal 4-27, 336G1

1977

Shue fired as 76er coach 11-4, 991B1
Knicks sue Nets over paymts 11-7, 870A2
Bradley sets US Sen bid 11-14, 991A1
Havlicek becomes 3d all-time NBA scorer 11-14, 991D1
Barnes traded to Braves 11-23; suspended 12-12, reinstated 12-21, 991C1
Players' agent sentenced 11-28, 1021A2
Hopkins fired as Sonic coach 11-30, 991C1
Issel scores 15,000th point 12-3, 991B1
LA player injures rival 12-9, fined $10,000 12-12, 990G2-G3
LA acquires Dantley 12-13, 990G3
Brown fired as Pistons coach 12-15, 991E1
Celtics trade Scott, suspend Washington 12-27, 1021A1
BASKETBALL Referees, National Association of (NABR)
NBA strike 4-10—4-25, 332A1
BASOV, Nikolai
Endorses A-power 11-16, 936F3
BASQUES—*See SPAIN*
BASS River State Forest (N.J.)
Fire kills 4 7-23, 660E3
BASU, Jyoti
West Bengal chief min 6-21, 488A1
BATCHELOR, Clarence Daniel (C. D.)
Dies 9-5, 787F3
BATEMAN, Raymond H.
Wins primary for gov 6-7, 446D3
Loses election 11-8, 855A2
BATLLE, Jorge
Seeks Blancos aid vs repressn 7-16, 601A1
Newsman seized 7-20—7-21, 601B2
BATTASH, Awni
Hijackers release 7-10, 535B2
BATTERY—*See ASSAULT & Battery*
BATTISTI, Judge Frank
Orders Cleveland schls kept open 10-19, 939F2
BAUDOUIN, King (Belgium)
Asks Tindemans to form govt 4-22, 326A3
Bars Tindemans resignatn 6-2, swears Cabt 6-3, 465E3
BAUGHMAN, J. Ross
Rpts Rhodesia atrocities 12-2, 1015G3-1016C1

1978

Vitale named Pistons coach 5-1, Kauffman quits as gen mgr 7-14, 656B1
Nets owner sued 5-2, 656B2
Fitzsimmons named Kings coach 5-10, 656C1
NBA playoffs 5-21—6-7; attendance record set 5-30, Bullets win title 6-7, 457B1-A2
Costello named Bulls coach 6-5, 656D1
Davis traded to Pacers 6-8, 437C2
Knicks, Nets settle financial dispute; Jackson traded 6-8, 457D2
NBA draft held; table 6-9, 457B2, F2
NBA owners OK 3-pt experimt, add 3d referee 6-15, 6-16, 655E3
Barry signs with Rockets 6-17, 656D1
Nuggets, Lakers, Kings in 4-player trade 6-26, 656A1
Celtics, Braves swap owners; Braves move to San Diego, renamed Clippers 7-7, 655E2, B3
Celtics, Clippers in 7-player deal 7-7, 8-15; Shue named Clippers coach 8-1, 655G2
NBA realignmt OKd 7-7, 655C3
Wilkens signs Sonics contract 7-11, 656A2
Auerbach rejcts Knicks offer, OKs Celtics multiyr contract 7-14, 656E1
Tatum traded to Celtics 7-19, 655G3
Caldwell pensn upheld by NC ct 7-19, 656F1
Webster declared free agent 7-31, 656F1
Trail Blazers OK Walton trade 8-4, 1027F3
McGinnis traded to Nuggets for Jones, Simpson 8-16, 655F3
Webster signed by Knicks 8-28; Shelton, other compensatn awarded Seattle 10-29, 1027B3
Nets sale agreed 8-28, 1027E3
Warriors OK Lucas as Barry compensatn 9-5, 1027D3
Free traded to Clippers 10-12, 1028A1
Celtics name Cowens coach 11-14, Knicks name Holzman 12-11, 1027E2
Women's league begins play 12-9, 1027F2
BASNETT, David
Backs Labor Party 10-4, 763F2
BASQUES—*See SPAIN*
BASSI, Pietro
Given 15-yr term in Turin trial 6-23, 516E3
BAST, William
Betsy released 2-9, 618C3
BATE, Walter Jackson
Wins Natl Book Award 4-10, 315D2
Wins Pulitzer Prize 4-17, 315C1
BATEMAN, Marv
NFL '77 punting ldr 1-1, 56B3
BATES, Alan
Unmarried Woman released 3-4, 620B1
BATESON, Joseph
Gets life sentence 5-26, 474A3
BATHROOMS
OSHA drops toilet seat 'nuisance' rule 10-24, 833E3
B.A.T. Industries Ltd.
British-American Cosmetics Ltd.
Yardley, Germaine Monteil ownership cited 5-5, 345D3
British-American Tobacco Co. Ltd.
Brown & Williamson ownership cited 5-5, 345C3
British-American Tobacco Investments Ltd.
NRC OKs Appleton Papers divisn sale 5-5, 345B3
International Stores Holdings Ltd.
Gimbels, Saks ownership cited 5-5, 345D3
BATTERY—*See CRIME—Assault & Battery*
BATTISTI, Judge Frank J.
Defers Cleveland busing program 8-25, 699D1
Fines Seatrain, Ocean Equipmt 10-23, 876B3
BATTLE of Chile, The (film)
Released 1-12, 618C3
BAUCUS, Rep. Max (D, Mont.)
Wins Sen primary 6-6, 448A2
Wins Sen seat 11-7, 846G1, 848D2, 856D1, E1
BAUDOUIN, King (Belgium)
Greets Carters 1-6, 1E1
Gets Tindemans resignatn 6-15, rejcts 6-19, 612E2, D3
Tindemans resigns 10-10, 764A2
BAUER, Fred
Buddy Holly Story released 7-21, 969E3
BAUGHAM Jr., U(rbanus) E.
Dies 11-6, 972E2
BAUGHER, Scott
Hopkins wins NCAA lacrosse title 5-27, 540B2
BAUGHMAN, J. Ross
Wins Pulitzer 4-17, photo authenticity questnd 4-21, 4-22, 315B2, F2
Rhodesia mil atrocities probe rptd ended 4-22, 455C2
BAUM, Gerhart
Named W Ger interior min 6-6, 456C3
Lauds Bulgaria on terrorist transfer 6-22 500B1
Orders border police probe 7-5, 651F2
Sees neo-Nazis terror 7-25, 652D1
Sees UK home secy 9-4—9-5, 688B2
BAUM, Marlyn
My Cup Runneth Over 6-22, 760F2
BAUM, Werner A.
Protests secrecy order 5-11, 514A1

1979

Professional—*See also 'Awards' above*
Robinson traded to Suns, other NBA deals 1-5–5-30, 526C2
Harlem Globe Trotters meet Teng 1-29, 66C2
NBA coaching chngs 2-1–4-12, 290C3
NBA owners meet; ponder declining status, vote to expand 2-3–2-4, 175C1
West win NBA All-Star game, Thompson named MVP 2-4, 175A1
NBA players meet, urge game chngs 2-5, 175G1
McAdoo traded to Celtics 2-12, 507D2
King fined for drunk driving 2-16, 291D1
Taylor joins Clippers 2-20, 291E1
LSU suspends Scales 3-5, 291B1
East wins WBL All-Star game, Easterling named MVP 3-14, 507F1
Chamberlain scores Abdul-Jabbar 3-21, 291C1
WBL season ends 4-7, 507E1
NBA season ends; final standings, statistical ldrs 4-8, 290A2-C3
WBL playoffs 4-17–5-2, Angels win title 5-2, 507C1
NBA OKs Celtics sale 5-7, 527C1
NBA playoffs 5-20–6-1, Sonics win title 6-1, 506B3
Lakers, Forum arena rptd sold 5-30, 527D1
Bird signs with Celtics 6-8, 507E2
NBA OKs Jazz move to Utah 6-8, 527B1
WBL expands, holds draft 6-12, 526F2
NBA OKs 3-pt goal test, 10 sec rule; drops 3d referee 6-21, 526D1
NBA draft held; table 6-25, 507G1-B3
Pacers drop woman player 9-9, Meyers signs with Gems 11-14, 1003E2
Walton compensatn set 9-18, voided 9-19, 1003B2
BASNETT, David
Scores top salaries hike 6-5, 425E2
Scores proposed union curbs 7-9, 524A3
BASQUES—*See SPAIN*
BASSETT Hall (estate)
Willed to Williamsburg Foundatn 4-13, 672E2
BASTURK, Abdullah
Arrest re May Day rally cited 5-1, 333D1
Rptd freed 5-22, 398F1
BATASUNA, Herri
Slain 9-28, 754E2
BATES, Alan
Shout released 11-9, 1008E1
Rose released 11-17, 1008D1
BATES, Harvey
Drug bur inquiry rptd 6-20, 467G2
BATES, Tom
CIA-disputed article publshd 4-19, 309B3
BATES & Co., Ted
Bristol-Myers ads assailed by FTC 10-12, 903A1
BATH, Mathias
Prisoner exchange rptd 7-20, 586E2
BATHGATE, Andy
NHL scoring mark cited 4-8, 356A1
B.A.T. Industries Ltd.
British-American Tobacco Co. Ltd.
Brown & Williamson ordrd to obey FTC subpoena 1-25, 91D3
BATON Rouge, La.—*See LOUISIANA*
BATT, Neil
On Labor win in Tasmania 7-29, 612G1
On S Australia electn loss 9-15, 749B2
BATTISTA, Lloyd
King of Schnorrers opens 11-28, 956C3
BATTLE Creek, Mich.—*See MICHIGAN*
BATTLESTAR Galactica (film)
Released 5-17, 528C1
Top-grossing film 5-23, 448G3
BATTLESTAR Galatica (TV series)
Mattel recalls toys 1-11, scored 2-27, 308B3
BAUCUS, Sen. Max (D, Mont.)
Sen income limit stayed 3-8, 185F2
Tours Cambodia refugee camps in Thailand 10-21–10-23; in Cambodia, proposes food convoy 10-24; rpts to Carter 10-26; Cambodia vs plan 10-27, 823C3-824E1
BAUDIN, Robert
Buzzes NYC bldgs 10-11, 860F1
BAUDOUIN, King (Belgium)
Announces new govt coalitn 4-2, 253B2
BAUGH, Laura
Ties for 2d in Mayflower Classic 7-8, 587E3
BAUM, Gerhart
Backs Gorleben A-reprocessing plant 5-16, 411A1

1980

Professional
King arrested for sex abuse, drug possessn 1-2; sentncd 6-4, 656G1
NBA OKs Dallas expansn 2-2, 119C2
East wins NBA All-Star Game; Gervin named game MVP 2-3, 279A1
NBA labor pact OKd; details 2-4, 119G1
NBA coaching chngs 3-1—7-18, 656D3
WBL season ends 3-15, 432C2
NBA season ends; final standings, statistical ldrs 3-30, 278F2-279A1
WBL playoffs 4-3—4-10, Stars win title 4-10, 432A2
Dallas NBA team OKd 5-1; expansn draft held 5-28, 447D1
NBA playoffs 5-4—5-16, Lakers win title 5-16, 431F3
Furlow dies in car crash, drugs found 5-23, 656A2
Hunts Chicago Bull bailout loan collateral listed 5-28, 425E3
Parrish traded to Celtics 6-9, 447B1
NBA draft held; table 6-10, 447A1, E1
Ransey, Lester traded 6-10, 447C1
Johnson chrgd with cocaine possessn 7-13, 656B2
NBA cocaine use rptd widespread 8-19; league warns players, assn vows fight 8-20, 656E1, G2
BASNETT, David
Scores new budget 3-26, 232F2
BASU, Tarun
Claims Bengalis massacred 6-22, 578E3
BATEMAN, Jaime
Sees rptr 4-17; govt mtg asked 4-19, rejctd 4-21, 311F2, C3
BATEMAN, Robert
Sentenced 1-11, 64A2
BATES, Alan
Nijinsky released 3-20, 216D3
BATES, Lucius Christopher
Dies 8-22, 676A1
BATESON, Gregory
Dies 7-4, 608D1
BATHGATE, Andy
'61-62 NHL scoring title tie cited 4-6, 295F3
B.A.T. Industries Ltd.
Bruce Gimbel dies 10-17, 876F1
BATTEN, William M.
NYSE contract extended 7-2, 600C3
BAUCH, Herbert
Wins Olympic medal 8-2, 622A2
BAUCUS, Sen. Max (D, Mont.)
Chastises B Carter re Libya 8-22, 647F1
On B Carter probe 9-17, 701A2
BAUDOUIN, King (Belgium)
Govt resigns 4-3, 4-9, 272D1
Swears in new govt 5-18, 388A2
Asks Martens delay resignatn 10-5, accepts resignatn 10-7, 766F2
New govt sworn 10-22, 860C2
BAUM, Gerhart
On neo-Nazi group ban 1-30, 103G1
Strauss scores re Munich bombing 9-27, 755A1
Sworn W Ger interior min 11-5, 925E1
BAUM, Thomas
Carny released 6-13, 675B2
BAUM, Cardinal William
Named to Vatican educ post 1-15, 199B2

1976

BAUMAN, Rep. Robert E. (R, Md.)
Nominates Helms as GOP vp 8-19, 598E2
GOP conv vp vote table 8-19, 599F3
Reelected 11-2, 829A4
BAUMGARTL, Frank
Wins Olympic medal 7-28, 576B1
BAUTISTA, Daniel
Wins Olympic medal 7-23, 575E3
BAUXITE—*See ALUMINUM & Bauxite*
BAXLEY, William J. (Bill)
Reopens '63 church bomb probe 2-18, 159D3
3 freed in '57 slaying 4-14, 316F2
BAXTER Laboratories Inc.
Rpts foreign payoffs 2-23, 361B3
SEC lists paymts 5-12, 726D2
BAXTRUM Jr., George P.
Rpts FBI SWP burglaries 7-29, 569G3
BAY City (Mich.) Times, The (newspaper)
Newhouse buys Booth chain 11-8, 901B3
BAYERISCHE Motoren Werke A.G.
US ends car dumping probe 5-4, 321D2
BAYH, Sen. Birch E(vans) (D, Ind.)
Gets US campaign aid 1-2, more funds OKd 1-8, 22E3, F3
Common Cause rpts code backing 1-9, 23A1
2d in Iowa precinct vote 1-19, 41A1
3d in NH primary 2-24, 148F1, B3
7th in Mass primary 3-2, 165B1
Quits campaign 3-4, 165C2
Fed fund total listed 3-4, 180C3
Endorses Carter 5-3, 323G3
Named to intelligence com 5-20, 377D1
Oregon primary results 5-25, 374E3
RI primary results 6-1, 390C2
Calif primary results 6-8, 409B1
FEC ends fed funds 6-23, total rptd 7-1, 490F3★, 491A1
FEC certificatn total rptd 12-31, 979F2
BAY Hill Country Club (Orlando, Fla.)
Ford golf outings rptd 9-23, 722B3
BAYLOR, Don
AL batting ldr 10-4, 796D1
Contract rptd signed 12-5, 951D3
BAYLY Sr., George V.
Indicted 2-18, stiffer penalties asked 10-5, 886E1; sentncd 11-30, 921F2
BAY of Pigs—*See 'U.S.' under CUBA*
BAY State (U.S. warship)
In Intl Naval Review 7-4, 488E3
BAZELON, Judge David L.
Orders A-plant hearings 7-21, 570B3
OKs release of Nixon tapes 10-26, 849B3
BAZYNSKI, Leszek
Wins Olympic medal 7-31, 574A1
BBC—*See BRITISH Broadcasting Co.*
BEACHES—*See PARKS*
BEALL Jr., Sen. J. Glenn (R, Md.)
Unopposed in primary 5-18, 357A2
Seconds Ford nominatn 8-18, 597G2
AMA donatn rptd 10-22, 938E3
Loses reelection 11-2, 819E3, 821D1
BEAM Distilling Co., James B.
Boycott rpt released 10-18, 786A1
Arab boycott noncompliance rptd 10-28, 986A3
BEAME, Mayor Abraham D. (N.Y.)
Plans '78 Soc Sec withdrawal 3-22, 994F1
Endorses Carter 5-26, 390B3
James Farley dies 6-9, 444B1
Carter meets NY delegates 6-14, 432C1
Dem conv speaker 7-12, 508C1, 509B1
Mondale visits 8-26, 645G2
Carter thanks New York 11-3, 845E3
Police win '75 increase 12-22, 991D2
Carter sees, renews aid vow 12-28, 978D2
BEARD, Rep. Edward P. (D, R.I.)
Wins primary 9-14, 704F3
Reelected 11-2, 821C3, 830G2
BEARD Jr., Rep. Robin L. (R, Tenn.)
Reelected 11-2, 830B4
BEARS—*See WILDLIFE*
BEASLEY Jr., Gerald
Defeated 11-2, 822G2

1977

BAUMAN, Rep. Robert E. (R, Md.)
Cargo preference defeated 10-19, 815G1
BAUMER, Jim
Brewers confirm resignatn 11-20, 990C2
BAUTISTA, Brig. Gen. Teodulfo
Slain 10-10, 803F2
BAUXITE—*See ALUMINUM & Bauxite*
BAUXITE Association, International
Base price set by 10 natns 12-7, 975D1
BAVASI, E. J. (Buzzie)
Quits Padres 9-20, 768E2
Joins Angels 10-24, mgt realignmt rptd 12-17, 990A2
BAXLEY, William J.
'63 church bomber convictd 11-18, 907C3
BAXTER State Park (Me.)
Fire destroys 3,500 acres 7-17—8-2, 660C3
BAYARDO Bengoa, Fernando
Uruguay justice min 1-27, 351G2
BAYER AG
Miles purchase OKd 10-17, 880E1
BAYI, Filbert
Wins mile run 2-25, 602D3
BAYLOR, Elgin
In basketball HOF 5-2, 490F3
BAYLOR University (Waco, Tex.)
Green in NFL draft 5-3, 353B3
BAY of Pigs—*See CUBA—U.S. Relations*
BAYONA Jimenez, Rafael
Assassinated 2-13, 255B1
BAYONNE, N.J.—*See NEW Jersey*
BAZ, Osama el-
At Cairo conf 12-14—12-15, 953G1
BAZ, Sama el-
Quits re Sadat Israel trip 11-18, 890C2
BAZELON, Judge David L.
Vs FCC obscenity order 3-16, 216A1
BBC—*See BRITISH Broadcasting Corp.*
BEACHES—*See PARKS & Recreation Areas*
BEAGLE Channel
Chile-Argentina dispute cited 11-4, 944C3
BEALE, Edith Bouvier
Dies 2-5, 164C2
BEAL v. Doe
Pa abortn funding denial upheld 6-20, 516E2
BEAM Distilling Co., James B.—*See AMERICAN Brands Inc.*
BEAME, Mayor Abraham D. (N.Y., N.Y.)
Debt repaymt talks 2-8—3-9, plan OKd 3-10; US loan released 3-11, 193B1-D3
Jets to remain at Shea 2-18, 163D3
Carter visits 3-17, 191B1
Revokes NY Airways landing rights 5-16, 412C3
Scores Con Ed, orders blackout probe 7-13—7-14, 537B3
Vs NY Concorde ban end 8-17, 627G1
SEC rpt chrgs '74-75 financial deceptn 8-26; reactn 8-26, 8-27, 665C2, D3
Defeated in primary 9-8, 723A2
Carter visits NYC, tours S Bronx 10-4—10-5, 761A1, B1
NYC clean-air case review declined 10-17, 797D3
Koch elected mayor 11-8, 855E2
Scores Moody's note rating 11-10, 881E1
BEAME v. Friends of the Earth
Review declined 10-17, 797C3
BEAMS, Jesse W.
Dies 7-23, 604E2
BEAN, Andy
Wins Doral Open 3-13, 311A2
BEASLEY, Robert P.
Indicted, Firestone paymts cited 10-25, 818C2
BEATRICE Foods
Discounts, overbilling rptd 3-14, 233C2
BEAUDOIN, Cheryl
Murdered 7-22, suspect indictd 9-7, 712E1

1978

BAUMAN, Charlie
Punched by Hayes in Gator Bowl 12-29, Hayes fired 12-30, 1025A3
BAUMAN, Rep. Robert E. (R, Md.)
Reelected 11-7, 851B1
May join China policy suit 12-20, 975C3
BAUMANN, Juergen
Free Dems lose 2 state electns 6-4, 456G2
Resigns 7-3, 651B2
BAUXITE—*See ALUMINUM & Bauxite*
BAXLEY, Ga.—*See GEORGIA*
BAXLEY, Bill
Faces Ala primary runoff 9-5, 699B2
Loses runoff 9-26, 769E1
BAXTER Jr., James H.
Wins Sen primary in Del 9-9, 736G1
Loses electn 11-7, 848A1
BAXTER, Paul
Nordiques win WHA All-Star game 1-17, 76G3
BAXTER, Ron
Texas wins NIT, named co-MVP 3-21, 272A2
BAYER, Gary
History of Amer Film opens 3-30, 760D2
Porch opens 11-14, 1031G2
BAYER A.G.
Allegheny drops unit sale plan 10-24, 897G1
El Salvador plant bombed 11-24, 986G3
BAYH, Sen. Birch E(vans) (D, Ind.)
Backs Carter intell reorganizatn 1-24, 49B2
Backs Sen intell bill 2-9, 107E1
Reads Torrijos drug link rpt to Sen 2-21, 120C2
Votes for Panama Canal neutrality pact 3-16, 177D2
Votes for 2d Canal pact 4-18, 273B1
Sen ethics com rpts Park gift disputed 6-19, 527E2
Perjury probe sought in Korean scandal 10-16, 832D1
BAYI, Filbert
Buerkle sets indoor mi run record 1-13, wins Wanamaker 1-27, 76D2, B3
BAYKAL, Deniz
Named Turkey energy min 1-5, 21F2
BAYLOR, Don
AL batting ldr 10-2, 928E3-F3
BAYNE, Trudy
Pins & Needles opens 7-6, 760B3
BBC—*See BRITISH Broadcasting Corp.*
BBWAA (Baseball Writers Association of America)—*See BASEBALL*
BCOA—*See BITUMINOUS Coal Operators Association*
BEAGLE, Peter S.
Lord of Rings released 11-15, 970A2
BEAGLE Channel
Argentina-Chile dispute dvpts 1-6—2-10, 100F3; map 101E1
Chile, Argentina chiefs meet 2-20; formal talks begin 3-1, arbitratn disputed 3-10, 216D1
Argentina-Chile talks fail 5-22—11-2; forgn mediatn set 11-7, 860B2
Argentine forgn min quits 10-27, 840A3
Pope, US ask more talks, Argentina-Chile talks fail 12-12; armies on alert 12-15; Argentina urges peaceful setlmt 12-16, 979D2-B3
Argentina scores Chile, rejects papal mediatn 12-21, 999C3
Pope to mediate dispute 12-22; envoy named 12-23, visits Argentina 12-26, 999A3
BEALL Jr., J. Glenn
Wins primary for Md gov 9-12, 716G1
Loses electn 11-7, 848B2
BEAME, Abraham D.
Goldin role in NYC fscl crisis 86A3
NYC fscl '79 budget OKd, 'windfall' funds found 6-28, 609D1
BEAN, Andy
2d in San Diego Open 1-29, 76E1
2d in Houston Open 4-23, 355G2
Wins Kemper Open 6-4, Memphis 6-11, 580E3, F3
Wins Western Open 7-3, 672C3
PGA top money winner 10-31, 990B3
Wins Dunlop Phoenix tourn 11-26, 990D2
BEARD, Rep. Edward P. (D, R.I.)
Wins renomination 9-12, 716A3
Reelected 11-7, 852A2
BEARD Jr., Rep. Robin L. (R, Tenn.)
Reelected 11-7, 852D2

1979

BAUXITE—*See ALUMINUM & Bauxite*
BAUXITE Association, International
Australia rejects floor price 1-9, to continue membership 1-10, 18D3
BAXTER, Keith
Mtg By the River opens 3-28, 712D1
BAYBANKS Inc.
'77 FRB withdrawal, reserve requiremt cost cited 4-9, 303A2
BAY City, Tex.—*See TEXAS*
BAYH, Sen. Birch Evans (D, Ind.)
Justice closes Korean probe 1-5, 4A3
Intelligence Com chrmn 1-23, 71E2
Urges Paisley death probe 1-24, 55A1
Disputes balanced budget amendmt status 2-6, 86D2
Wife dies 4-24, 356B3
Sen rejcts direct pres vote 7-10, 515A1
BAYH, Marvella (Mrs. Birch Evans)
Dies 4-24, 356B3
BAYI, Filbert
Coe breaks 1500-m run mark 8-15, 911F1
BAYLOR, Don
NL wins All-Star Game 7-17, 568F3-569B1
AL batting ldr 9-30, named MVP 11-21, 955B2, E3, F3
BAYLOR, Elgin
Fired as Jazz coach 4-12, 290D3
BAYLOR University (Waco, Tex.)
Breast-feeding survey rptd 1-5, 64C2
Hawthorne in NFL draft 5-3, 335G2
Johnson in NBA draft 6-25, 507A3
Wins Peach Bowl 12-31, 1001B3
BAY Village, O.—*See OHIO*
BAZARGAN, Mehdi (Iranian premier; resigned Nov. 6)
Bars Iran regency cncl apptmt 1-13, 25G1
Meets Bakhtiar 1-23, 49E1
Bakhtiar cites contacts 2-4, 82G1
Named to head provisional govt 2-5, 81A1
US cites contacts 2-6, 82E2
Bakhtiar OKs '80%' of views 2-8, 81G2
Revolt overthrows Bakhtiar 2-9—2-11, office attacked 2-13; names Cabt 2-12—2-13, 105A1, E2
US recognizes govt 2-16, 125B3
Names more new Cabt mins 2-19, 125D1
Seeks oil export resumptn, names state co chrmn 2-19, 125D2
Gens rptd executed by Khomeini cncl 2-20, 125F1
Israel, S Africa oil ban cited 2-20, 126A3
Scores Khomeini cncl, threatens resignatn 2-28, 144G2
Khomeini rivalry cited 161E2
Khomeini calls govt 'weak' 3-7; Khomeini bars resignatn 3-8, asks backing for govt 3-9, 179B3
Women protest dress curb 3-8, 179E2
Pahlevi ex-offcls executed 3-13, 179B3
Scores trials, executns 3-14; Khomeini suspends 3-16, 199D1
Komitehs rptdly opposed 4-12, 297E2
Backed Sanjabi resignatn 4-16, 277A1
Murder try at Qaraneh funeral denied 4-24, 297E1
Names Yazdi forgn min 4-24, 297B2
Komiteh purge launched 4-25, 321C3
Motahari slain 5-1, 321D1
Protesters ask press freedom 5-19, 389E1
Scores Khomeini policies 5-28, 407B3
On bank seizures 6-8, 469F1
Denied militia curbs, scores guerrillas 7-1, 503B3
Key industries nationalized 7-5, 503F2
Khomeini declares gen amnesty 7-9, 524E3
Mil police cmdr defies dismissal order 7-9, 525G1
Khomeini to share power 7-19, 565D2
Khomeini foes march to office 8-12, 614C3
Khomeini says govt lacks zeal 8-17, 635B1
Iraq gets complaint on Kurdish rebels 8-25, 653F2
Offers resignatn 8-31, 670E1
Fires oil chief, shifts Cabt 9-28, 752B2
Warns US re shah's entry 10-21, 879B2
Meets US aide in Algiers 11-1, clergy vs 11-4, 842B2
Resigns 11-6, 841C1, 842G1
Entezam arrested 12-19, 976A1
BBDO International Inc.
Chrysler drops account 3-1, 188D1
BEAGLE Channel
Chile asks Argentina free prisoners 1-5, 51E3
Papal mediatn agreed 1-8, envoy returns to Vatican 1-9, 51B3
Argentina '78 arms purchases cited 1-10, 40B3
BEAN, Andy
Ties for 2d in Crosby Pro-Am 2-4, 220D3
Wins Atlanta Classic 6-10, 587B3
PGA top money winner 11-30, 969F2
BEAR, Robert L.
Acquitted in abductn case 12-4, 932C1-A2
BEARD, Rep. Edward P. (D, R.I.)
Joins draft-Kennedy move 5-23, 384C2
BEARD Jr., Rep. Robin L. (R, Tenn.)
Chrgs Pentagon cover-up re volunteer mil failure 9-12, 724B3
Vs Rev King holiday bill 12-5, 945D2
BEAR Stearns & Co.
Brooke joins 5-23, 392C2
BEASLEY, Larry
Pleads no contest re '77 loan chrg 5-14, 380E3

1980

BAUMAN, Rep. Robert E. (R, Md.)
Sees unbalanced '81 budget 6-12, 452E1
Calls synfuel bill fascism 6-26, 479E2
Vs Nicaragua aid bill 7-2, 515F1
Loses reelectn 11-4, 846B2, 848C2
BAUME, Peter
Australia aborigine min 11-2, 857F2
BAUXITE—*See ALUMINUM & Bauxite*
BAXTER, Richard Reeves
Dies 9-26, 755B2
BAXTER, Teri
Ties for US 200-m breaststroke title 7-31, 834E3
BAYARD, Henri
Renamed to Haitian Cabt 4-26, 335G3
BAYER A.G.
Iran takeover rptd 7-9, 546E2
BAYH, Sen. Birch Evans (D, Ind.)
Paisley cleared by Sen com 4-24, 459D1
Sen passes oversight bill 6-3, 458D3
Named B Carter probe chrmn 7-24, 548G3
Plans B Carter panel probe 7-25—7-31, 569E1-G1
Backs Civiletti re B Carter probe 8-6, 595C2
Watergate counsel declines B Carter probe role 8-7, 595E3
Exempts Carter from personal testimony 9-24, 764D1
Loses reelectn 11-4, 837D1, 845A2, 850F3
Carter aide cleared in spy leak 12-5, 940A3
BAYI, Filbert
Wins Olympic medal 7-31, 624D1
BAYLOR College of Medicine (Houston, Tex.)
Exercise, reduced heart attack risk linked 2-14, 158F1
BAYON, Ignacio
Named Spain indus min 5-2, 355D1
BAYULKEN, Umit Haluk
Named Turkey defense min 9-21, 720C3
BAZARGAN, Mehdi
Bani-Sadr cited Cabt mins 6-29, 490A2
Scores Ghotbzadeh arrest 11-7, 862E1
BBC—*See BRITISH Broadcasting Corp.*
BEACHAM, Robert M.
Charged in GSA scandal 1-15, 112E1
BEAGLE Channel
Pope offers solutn to Chile-Argentina dispute 12-12, 978C3-979A1
BEAMON, Bob
Dombrowski sets sea level long jump mark 7-28, 589C1
BEAN, Andy
Wins Hawaiian Open 2-10, 412D2
2d in Atlanta Classic 6-8, PGA 8-10, 714C2, 715B1
PGA top money winner 10-12, 971E3
BEARD, Rep. Edward P. (D, R.I.)
Wins primary 9-9, 700G2
Loses reelectn 11-4, 849B1
BEARD Jr., Rep. Robin L. (R, Tenn.)
Chrgs Sovt SALT violatns, US denies 9-18, 730C2
Reelected 11-4, 844D2
BEARDSLEY, Craig
Sets 200-m butterfly mark, beats Fesenko Olympic time 7-30, 834A3

1976

BEATON, Roderick
Vs developing natns press pool 7-19, 619B3
BEATRICE Foods Co.
Vows no boycott compliance 3-18, 747B2
BEATTY, Warren
Carter at Hollywood affair 8-22, 631G2
BEAUDRY, Pierre
Vs new air rules 7-27, 572D2
BEAUSIRE, Marie Anne
'75 CR asylum cited 47F2
In CR, Chile asks extraditn 2-2, 100A1
BEAUSOLEIL, Maj. Gen. Charles
Retiremt rptd 11-17, car import fraud linked 12-3, 1003D2
BEAZLEY, Kim
Quits shadow cabt post, replaced 3-15, 237B1
BEBER, Sam
Dies 8-25, 656E3
BECERRA, Franklin
Uruguay emb incident, ties cut 6-28—7-6; returns Venez 7-7, 542D2-A3
BECHTEL Corp.
US sues on Arab boycott issue 1-16, 44D2
To buy Peabody Coal shares 12-14, 985C1
BECKER, Henning
Viet orphans to stay 3-16, relocated 3-19, 3-21, 252E1
BECKER, Marion
Wins Olympic medal 7-24, 576F1
BECKER, Ralph E.
Named Honduras amb 8-21; confrmd 9-8, 807E3
BECKETT, Samuel
Pleas for Sovt dissident 3-24, 421A3
BECVAR, Rudolf
Hijacks plane 10-28, faces W Ger chrgs 10-29, 946F1
BECVAR, Stepan
Brother named in shooting 10-29, 946G1
BEDARD, Marc-Andre
Named justice min 11-26, 903G2
Orders Morgentaler chrgs dropped 12-10, 946C1
BEDELL, Rep. Berkley W. (D, Ia.)
Chrgs grain scandal cover-up 1-29, 136D1 ★
Reelected 11-2, 829D3
BEDFORD-Stuyvesant Restoration Corp.
Thomas rptdly rejctd HUD post 12-16, 937A2
BEEBE, Rev. Peter
Convictn reversed 4-9, denied new trial 6-11, 755A3
BEECHER, Henry K.
Dies 7-25, 680F3
BEEF—*See MEAT*
BEER—*See ALCOHOLIC Beverages*
BEESLEY, Allan
On sea law conf impasse 5-7, 342A2
BEETHOVEN: Symphonies (record album)
Wins Grammy 2-28, 460D3
BEETZ, Jean
Vs inflatn plan ruling 7-12, 554F3

1977

BEAUDOIN, Frederick
Wife, 7 children slain 7-22; suspect indictd 9-7, 712E1
BEAUDRY, Paul
On '72 RCMP news agency raid 10-26, 841G1
BEAUFORT Sea
Canada OKs oil search 6-1, 425E3
Eskimos concerned re drilling 6-13—6-17, 619F2
BEAUJON, Aristides
Drops Copei pres nod bid 8-18, 674F1
BEAULIEU, Andre
Named North Stars coach 11-24, 1021F1
BEAULIEU, Priscilla
Ex-husband dies 8-16, 696A1
BEAUTIFUL Swimmers: Watermen, Crabs, and the Chesapeake Bay (book)
Wins Pulitzer Prize 4-18, 355E2
BEAUTY Contests
Miss Univ crowned 7-16, 808G2
Miss America crowned 9-10, 808A3
BEAVERBROOK Newspapers Ltd.
Sold 6-30, 526F3
BECERRIL, Carlos
Escalera KOs 5-16, 395D1
BECHTEL Corp.
Settles Arab boycott suit 1-10, 78B2-A3
Peabody Holding Co.—*See separate listing*
BECKENBAUER, Franz
Signs with Cosmos 5-25, named NASL MVP 8-18, 676F3
Cosmos win NASL title 8-28, 676F2
BECKER, Jurek
Visits West 12-19, 984A2
BECKER, Dr. Leonard
Oxygen, anesthesia mixup rptd fatal 9-10, 748G1
BECKS, Michael Steven
Flees to Brazil 2-9, 144E3
BECVAR, Rudolph
Sentenced 3-31, 380B2
BEDARD, Marc-Andre
On Levesque auto mishap 2-25, 159C1
RCMP '73 PQ raid revealed 10-28, 840G3
Extends Quebec RCMP probe 11-3, 902A3
Confrms police raids on prov pol parties 11-31, 945G3; details distilleries paymts probe 12-6, 965E2
BEDOYA, Maria
Disappears 6-25, 595F2
BEEL, Louis J. M.
Dies 2-11, 164C2
BEELAERTS van Blokland, Pieter
Named Dutch housing min 12-19, 986B1
BEER—*See ALCOHOLIC Beverages*
BEETHOVEN, Ludwig van (1770-1827)
China lifts ban 3-26, 449D3
BEG, Mirza Hameedullah
Opposed as chief justice 1-25; named 1-28, sworn 1-29; ct boycotted 1-31, 71A3
BEGAM, Robert G.
Vs fed no-fault auto insurnc standards 7-18, 595A1
BEGGARMAN, Thief (book)
On best-seller list 12-4, 1021G2

BEGIN, Menahem (Israeli premier)
Facts on 377D2
Likud wins electns 5-17, Peres rejcts unity bid 5-19, 377A1
Assures US, Arabs on peace; affirms occupatn policy 5-17, 377B2
PLO, Arab reactn to Likud victory 5-18—5-24, 401B3

1978

BEASLEY, Robert P.
Pleads guilty to embezzlemt 2-28, 142C3
Sentenced 5-31, 404D2
BEASTS, The (play)
Opens 2-8, 760C1
BEATHERD, Bob
Named Redskins gen mgr 2-24, 171A3
BEATLES, The (singing group)
Presley offer to aid FBI rptd 7-14, 554A1
BEATRICE Foods Co.
To buy Tropicana 3-5, 184F3
Tropicana trust challenge rejcted 8-2, cos merge 8-7, 767C2, D3
BEATRIX, Crown Princess (Netherlands)
Bomb defused at Hague 5-11, 454E3
BEATTIE, Jim
Yankees win AL pennant 10-7, 778F3
In World Series 10-10—10-17, 800B2
BEATTY, Ethel
Eubie opens 9-20, 1031E1
BEATTY, Warren
Heaven Can Wait released 6-27, 619D2
BEAUCHAMPS Javier, Gen. Juan
Denies coup rumors, urges fair vote count 5-17—5-18, 371B3 ★, C3 ★
Sen rejects amb post apptmt 11-9, 881B1
BEAUDINE Jr., William
Magic of Lassie released 8-3, 970B2
BEAUFILS, Georges
Jailed as Sovt spy 7-12, 649G3
BEAUFORT Sea
Yukon dvpt halted 7-6, 531A3
BEAUMONT, Tex.—*See TEXAS*
BECHTEL Corp.
Bechtel Power in A-plant constructn accord 4-18, 281B3
BECHTLE, Judge Louis C.
Sentences paper cos, offcls 9-21, 768F2
BECK, Robert A.
Prudential chrmn, chief exec 9-1, 809A1
BECK, Stanley
Straight Time released 3-18, 620A1
BECKENBAUER, Franz
On NASL All-Star team 8-20, 707B3
BECKER, Elizabeth
In Cambodia 12-9, escapes gunman 12-23, 997A2
BECKER, Ernest A.
On builders profit margin 5-16, 362F1
BECKER, Friedhelm
Sentenced for terrorist publicatn sale 5-17, 439B2
BECKER, Verena
Sentence rptd 4-26, 354A1
BECKETT, John R.
On United Artists policy 1-17, 75B3
BECKETT, Sir Terence
Calls Ford strike 'political' 9-25, 764A1
Vs Ford sanctns 11-27, 11-28, 923B3
BECKWITH, Horace
Dismissal for FBI break-ins seen 12-5, 939A3
BECTON Dickinson & Co.
Sun Oil buys controlling interest 1-17; Wms Act violatn chrgd, Cong com chrmn ask probe 1-27, 65F3
SEC sues to rescind Sun Oil takeover 3-9, 223F1
BEDARD, Marc-Andre
FLQ exiles ask amnesty 1-3, 7E1
Vows Quebec language law ruling appeal 1-24, 70F2
6th Cross kidnaper alleged 11-2, withholds name 11-8, 880B1
Quebec language law appeal denied 11-28, 964C1
BEDDING Industry
Cotton dust rules issued 6-19, 472B1
BEDE Aircraft Inc.
FTC trustee plan agreed 6-13, 702B2
BEDELL, Rep. Berkley (D, Iowa)
Reelected 11-7, 850C4
BEDSON, Henry
Kills self 9-6, 927A2
BEECHER, Henry Ward (1813-87)
Thread of Scarlet opens 12-8, 1031B3
BEEF—*See MEAT*
BEE Gees (singing group)
Stayin' Alive on best-seller list 2-4, 116F3; 3-8, 196A; 4-5, 272F3; 5-3, 356D1
Win Grammy 2-24, 315F3
Night Fever on best-seller list 3-8, 196B1; 4-5, 272F3; 5-3, 356D1
Sgt Pepper released 7-21, 970B3
BEER—*See ALCOHOLIC Beverages*
BEETHOVEN, Ludwig van (1770-1827)
Sonata for Piano wins Grammy 2-24, 316D1
BEGELMAN, David
Film industry probes rptd 2-4, 2-11, 2-13, Valenti denies 3-2, 251D2
Quits Columbia Pictures in embezzlemt scandal 2-9, indicted 3-31; film contract rptd 3-13, 251C1
3 stockholder suits rptd filed 4-1, 251C2
Fined in theft case 6-28, 599A2
New film indus probe set 7-14, 599F2
Columbia fires Hirschfield 7-20, 599D2
BEGGARMAN, Thief (book)
On best-seller list 9-4, 708D1
BEGHIN, Ferdinand
Corsican castle destroyed 8-11, 649D3
BEGIN, Menahem (Israeli premier)
Vs Sadat, Hussein re US pressure call, W Bank plan 1-3, 2B3
Lauds Sadat-Carter talks 1-4, 3A1
Sadat sees 'no hope' for talks 1-12, 26B2
Scores Egypt forgn min on talks 1-17, meets 1-18, 25C1, G1

1979

BEASLEY, Robert P.
Firestone sued re gold trading 3-15, 202C2
Firestone indicted on tax chrgs 7-11; pleads guilty, fined 7-26, 648D3
BEATLEMANIA (play)
'78-79 success rptd 11-4, 956E2
BEATLES, The (singing group)
Ex-mgr convicted on tax fraud 4-26, 392F3
Ex-mgr sentenced 7-10, 656E2
BEATTIE, Ann
Head Over Heels released 10-19, 1007D3
BEATTIE, Jim
Yastrzemski gets 3000th hit 9-12, 1002D3
Traded to Mariners 11-1, 1002C3
BEATTS, Anne
Gilda Radner Live opens 8-2, 711C3
BEATTY, Nevada—*See NEVADA*
BEATTY, Ned
Great Bank Hoax released 3-22, 528C2
Promises in the Dark released 11-2, 1008B1
1941 released 12-14, 1008B1
BEATTY, Perrin
In Canadian Cabt 6-4, 423G3
BEAUCHAMP, Gen. Rene
Textron pleads guilty to currency violatns 7-10, 923G2
BEAUDOIN, Cheryl (d. 1977)
Acquin convicted in mass murder 10-19, 819C2
Acquin sentenced 11-30, 954A1
BEAUDOIN, Louise
Loses by-electn 4-30, 329E1
BEAUFORT Sea
Canada oil find discounted 9-13, 728C3
BEAU'S Eagle (race horse)
2d in Santa Anita Derby 4-1, 448D3
BEAUTY Contests
NYS to be reimbursed 3-27, 308E3
BEAVER Valley Power Station—*See PENNSYLVANIA-Atomic Energy*
BECHTEL Group of Companies, The
Bechtel Power Corp.
3 Mile I clean-up study rptd 7-17, 629F2
Trust suit re boycott cited 8-27, 648G2
BECK, Barry
Soviets win Challenge Cup 2-11, 118B3
BECK, Michael
Warriors released 2-9, 174F3
BECKENBAUER, Franz
Named to NASL All-Star team 8-27, 776E1
BECKER, Harold
Onion Field released 9-19, 820E2
BECKER, Leon
Once A Catholic opens 10-10, 956F3
BECKERMAN, Sidney
Bloodline released 6-28, 819F3
BECKETT, Samuel
Mercier & Camier opens 10-25, 956C3
BECKLER, Robert W.
Lockheed ex-aides' probe dropped 2-15, 306C1
BECKMAN Instruments Inc.
2 execs kidnaped in El Salvador 9-21, 729D2
Ads run to free execs 10-10, 790D3
Execs freed, ransom rptd 11-7, 872E2
BECKWITH, Horace
Webster rescinds dismissal, orders demotn 1-26, 92F2
BECTON, Dickinson & Co.
Sun stock sale ruled illegal 7-9, 541E2
Sun sets divestiture 12-19, 985G1
BEDERT, Ulrich G.
Vows Nicaragua refugee aid 7-19, 536A1
Guatemala relief convoy for Nicaragua set 7-21, 574B2
On Nicaragua food shipmts 8-4, 603C3
BEDNAROVA, Otta
Arrested 5-29, sentncd 10-23, 802B2
BEDREGAL Gutierrez, Guillermo
Role in mil coup rptd 11-1, 833D1
BEDROOM Farce (play)
Opens 3-29, 711C1
BEECH Aircraft Corp.
Raytheon acquisitn set 10-2, 785A1
BEEF—*See MEAT*
BEE Gees (singing group)
Too Much Heaven on best-seller list 1-10, 80E3; 2-14, 120E3; 3-7, 174E1
Spirits Having Flown on best-seller list 2-14, 120F3; 4-4, 271E2
Win 4 Grammys 2-16, 336C3
Tragedy on best-seller list 3-7, 174D1; 4-4, 271D2
BEER—*See ALCOHOL*
BEGELMAN, David
Named MGM movie pres 12-18, 1007D1
BEGGARS Soap Opera, The (play)
Opens 7-23, 711D1

BEGIN, Menahem (Israeli premier)
Israelis rally vs new setlmts 1-13, 28G2, A3
Canada oppositn ldr in Israel 1-14—1-17, 57B3
Blames Egypt for US mediatn failure 1-28, 69D1
Denies Arab torture chrg 2-11, 108C2

1980

BEATLES, The (singing group)
McCartney deported from Japan 1-26, 200E2
Lennon slain in NYC, ex-mental patient chrgd 12-8; reactn 12-9; background, photos 933D2-943F3
BEATON, Sir Cecil
Dies 1-18, 104F1
BEATRICE Foods Co.
Kidnap liability barred 1-6, 18B1-B2
Tropicana merger found illegal 11-28, 917G3
Bob Evans merger cancelled 12-29, 985D1
BEATRIX, Queen (Beatrix Wilhelmina Armgard) (Netherlands)
Mother to abdicate 1-31, 100D1
Invested as queen 4-30, 353C3
BEATTIE, Richard
Gets Educ Dept transitn post 1-9, 18B2
BEATTS, Anne
Gilda Live released 3-28, 416G2
BEATTY, John Lee
Wins Tony 6-8, 692C3
BEAUTY Contests
Miss America emcee dropped 1-4, replacemt named 3-5, 198G3
BECHTEL Group of Companies, The
Shultz named pres 12-2, 959D3
Bechtel Power Corp.
3 Mile I repairs contract rptd 2-12, 128G1
BECK, Gilbert
Ala death penalty struck down by Sup Ct 6-20, 555C1
BECK, Volker
Wins Olympic medal 7-26, 624A1
BECKENBAUER, Franz
Cosmos win NASL title 9-21, 770A2
BECKER Inc., A.G.
FRB OKs commercial paper bank sales 9-29, 986B2
BECKER, Alan S.
Wins US House primary 9-9, 700B2
Loses US House electn 11-4, 849E2
BECKER, Richard S.
Kate Smith estate feud setld 9-4, 908D2
BECKER, Sabine
Wins Olympic medals 2-14, 2-20, 156A1, B1
BECKERMAN, Sidney
Serial released 3-28, 416E3
BECKETT, Dr. Arnold H.
On Olympic drug use 8-3, 590B3
BECKETT, Terence
Econ outlook grim, backs lending rate cut 10-28, 859A2
BECKMAN, Aldo
Dies 9-10, 755C2
BECKMAN Instruments Inc.
El Salvador police storm occupied plant 3-17, 212A1
BECK v. Alabama T
Case decided by Sup Ct 6-20, 555C1, 869B1
BECKWITH, Col. Charles A.
On aborted Iran rescue mission 5-1, 322D2
Testifies on Iran rescue missn 5-7, 338A1
BECTON, Dickinson & Co.
Dickinson ct damages action dropped 2-14, 558A2
BEDELL, Rep. Berkley (D, Iowa)
Reelected 11-4, 842D4
BEDJAOUI, Mohammed
On UN comm to probe shah 2-17, hints comm hostage role 2-20, 122C1, F1
Vows probe of shah's rule 2-28, 138D1
BEDOYA Reyes, Luis
3d in Peru pres electn 5-18, 390B2
BEEF—*See MEAT (& Meat Products)*
BEEN in the Storm So Long: The Aftermath of Slavery (book)
Wins Pulitzer 4-14, 296E2
BEER—*See ALCOHOL*
BEER, Wolfgang
Dies in crash 7-25, 581C1
BEGGS, Richard
Wins Oscar 4-14, 296A2

BEGIN, Menachem (Israeli prime minister)
In Sadat autonomy talks 1-7—1-10, 12E1
Meets US mediator 1-30, 89B2
Vows Christn protectn re vandals 2-4, 133D3
Vows aid to Christn Leb forces 2-7, 107D3

1976

1977

Asks more W Bank setlmts 5-19; scores US peace plan, PLO role 5-22, 401F2
Hospitalized 5-23, 401D2
Seeks DMC coalitn 5-24, 401B2
Carter sees moderation 5-26, 417A2
Delays Dayan appointment 5-29, 450A2
Aide in US 6-2, 440C2
Named to form govt 6-7, 450C2
Gives Agudat Israel concessns 6-9, 474A3
Likud adopts forgn policy plank 6-17, 474F2
NRP, Agudat Israel join Likud 6-19; presents Cabt to pres 6-20; wins parlt confidence vote, becomes premr 6-21, 474G1
OKs Viet refugee asylum 6-21, 497A2
Denies 'ultimatum' 6-23, 495B3
Thanks Carter for arms sale plan 6-26, 511A2
US worried re views 6-27, 495G2
Carter sets 'moratorium' on Mideast remarks 6-30, 510B1
Vs EC on Palestine state 6-30, 510E1
Sen Javits visits 509E1
Asks Oct Geneva conf, Sadat OKs 7-4; replies 7-5, 509D1
Bomb blast in Israel 7-6, 511B3
Meets Carter 7-19—7-20; airs peace plan 7-20; cites US-Israel differences 7-21, 549A1-B2
Arab, Israeli reactn to plan 7-19—7-21, 549C2-550A1
Labor Party gets peace plan 7-19, 549G2
US OKs mil aid package 7-22, 570C3
Asks Waldheim aid on Syrian Jews 7-22, 570G3
3 W Bank towns legalized 7-26; scores US criticism, wins confidence vote on US visit 7-27, 570C1, D2
Carter: W Bank plan, PLO Geneva stance block peace 7-28, 570D1
Lauds Sadat pre-Geneva conf plan 8-3, 588D3
Admits aid to Leb Christns 8-8, 605A2
Sees Vance; bars PLO role, W Bank, Gaza exit 8-9, 605F1
Says Sadat no moderate 8-11, 623C3
Defends rights move for W Bank, Gaza Arabs 8-15, 623F1, G1
US vs new W Bank setlmts 8-18, 623A1
Visits Rumania 8-25—8-29, 663C2
Gets new setlmt plan 9-2, 685G1
Katz vs US policy 9-13, 697G1
Dayan briefs on Jordan mtg 9-17, 714A1
Bars 2 W Bank setlmts 9-25, 9-28, 734F2
Torrijos visits 9-27—9-30, 755E3
Hospitalized 9-30, heart ailmt rptd 10-3, 749F1
Weighs US-Israel Geneva agrmt 10-5, 749F1
Katz on W Bank descriptn 10-10, 793D2
DMC votes to join govt 10-20, 801A3; 4 join Cabt 10-24, 827B2
Vs US W Bank plan 11-6, 850B2
On air raid vs PLO bases 11-10, 849D1
USSR Jews immigratn rptd up 12-21, 1017F2

Sadat Peace Exchanges (& aftermath)

In Sadat exchng on Israel visit 11-11, 11-12, 11-14; extends formal invitatn 11-15; Sadat accepts 11-17, 873A1
To ask Jordan, Syria, Leb ldrs to Israel 11-15, 873G1
US, Arab, Sovt reactn 11-15—11-16, 873F2
Ceausescu go-between role rptd 11-16, 873C2
Arab reactn to Sadat visit 11-17—11-22, 890D2-D3, 894E1
US, Sovt reactn to Sadat visit 11-17—11-22, 894E2
Thanks Ceausescu 11-18, 895B1
Sadat arrives Israel 11-19; tours Jerusalem, addresses Knesset 11-20, 889A1
Addresses Knesset, asks Arab ldrs visit 11-20, 889B2
Knesset speech text 11-20, 893D1-894D3
Holds news conf with Sadat, final communique released 11-21, 889D2-890F1
Names Cairo conf envoys 11-28, 909E2
Carter hails breakthrough 11-30, 913A2-C3
Visits UK 12-2—12-7, 930C3
Meets Vance, hopeful on peace 12-10—12-11, 954A1
Arrives US 12-14; Carter on missn 12-15, 955A1
Gives Carter peace plan 12-16, says US backs 12-17, Carter lauds plan 12-28, Begin pleased 12-29, 994A3
Ismailia summit, impasse, new talks set 12-25—12-26; airs peace plan, text 12-28, 993A1-994A3

1978

Meets Vance on talks breakdown 1-19, 25D2
Rpts progress in Egypt talks 1-19, 25D2
On Egypt talks breakdown, chrgs press anti-Semitism 1-21—1-23; Egypt press denies 1-24, 41E1, A2-42D1
On Egypt press attacks 1-29, 60C1
Gets Carter note on setlmts 1-29, clarifies policy to US amb 2-1, 60A2, E2
Labor Party, press vs Shiloh stand 2-2, 2-3, 2-5, 78C2
Carter plea on peace try 2-3, 77E1
In US feud over setlmts 2-3, 2-7, 78F1; text of US statemt 79B1-B2
Sadat chrgs intransigence 2-6, 77D2
Vs US arms to Egypt 2-8, 78C1
UK prime min on Sadat mtg 2-9, 98D2
Peres: cleared Sadat mtg 2-11, 98G2
Protests US Sinai setlmt oppositn 2-12, 2-13, 98B1, F1
Vs US jets to Egypt, Saudis; plans US visit 2-15, 97F1
Clarifies statemts on Carter setlmt stand 2-15, 97B2
US aide resumes mediatn 2-21—3-6; gets Sadat note 3-2, replies 3-6, 156D3, F3
US: jet sale pkg deal 2-24, 139C1
Setlmt policy retained 2-26, 139A1
Carter for Begin-Sadat talks 3-2, 140E3
Vs US stand on Res 242 3-4, 156G1
Weizman bars new setlmts 3-6, 3-7, 157D1
Opposed in Israel on Res 242 stand 3-7—3-9, 156B3
Efforts to bar Carter confrontatn cited 3-9, 176B3
Postpones US visit 3-11, 175E3, 176B2
Details PLO raid 3-12, 175D1
Warns reprisal vs PLO 3-12, 3-13, 175E3
On Israel invasn of Leb 3-15, 173C2
Meets Carter 3-20—3-21; queried by US Cong coms 3-21, 199B1
Carter says talks failed 3-23, 214F2
Asks US public support 3-23, 214B3
Weizman asks coalitn govt; comments 3-24, 214C2, D3
Weizman backs on Carter talks 3-24, 214D2
Returns Israel, says Carter talks 'difficult' 3-24, 214C3
Cabt, Knesset back policies 3-26, 3-29, 214D1, G1
Israel, US deny US plan to oust 3-26, 214F1
Seeks new Egypt talks 3-28, 3-29, 235B3
Israel rally urges concessns 4-1, 235E3
Ceausescu gets note 4-3—4-4, 235E3
Sadat urges flexibility 4-5, 235C3
Israel denies arms pact breach in Leb invasn 4-6, 236F2
Briefs Cabt on Leb invasn 4-11, 256A3
Carter lauds Ceasescu '77 go-between role 4-11, 291D1
Israel rallies; statemts back, oppose policies 4-15, 4-25, 4-26, 300D1
Israel reaffirms Res 242 stand 4-16, 275B1
Meets Waldheim, assures on Israeli Leb exit 4-18, 274B2, G2
Arrives US 4-30; meets Carter, US aid reaffirmed 5-1; tours US, asks Arab talks 5-2—5-8; returns Israel 5-9, 339G1
Carter backs W Bank self-rule plan 4-30, 339E2
Scores US Sen jet pkg OK 5-16, 358G1
US asks peace talk renewal 5-19, 424D2
Navon sworn Israel pres 5-29, 418C2
Scores Sadat war threat 6-8, 462A1
UK lauds Rumania peace role 6-14, 515C3
Cabt, parlt back stand on W Bank, Gaza 6-18—6-19, 461A1
Weizman denies plan to quit 6-23, 489E1
Vs Carter statemt on Israel rejectn of Egypt plan 6-27, 489A1
Sees Mondale; OKs Egypt-Israel conf, renewal of talks 7-2, 7-3, 502A1, B1
US OKs jet sale to Taiwan 7-2, 524B3
Egypt details peace plan 7-5, 501A1, E1
Syrians warned on Leb Christn attacks 7-6, 503B1
Scores Shcharansky trial 7-10, 543A1
Cabt scores Weizman, Peres mtgs with Sadat 7-16, 546D2
Sadat preference for Weizman, Peres seen 7-16, 546G2
Clash with Peres on Sadat mtg 7-19, 546B3
Labor Party questns health 7-20, MD calls fit 7-21; Begin, Cabt score Labor 7-23, 563C2
Sadat calls 'obstacle' to peace 7-22, 563B1
Bars El Arish, Mt Sinai return to Egypt 7-23, 563E1
Sees hardened Egypt stand 7-26, 562B3
Wins confidence vote 7-26, 563A1
Sadat scores Sinai plan rejectn 7-30, 582A1
Lauds US rebuke of Egypt 7-31, 582C1
Jets raid PLO base in Leb 8-3, 583C1
Meets Vance 8-6—8-7; OKs summit talks with Carter, Sadat; reactn 8-8, 601G2, E3
Gets plea to let Leb army move south 8-8, 638C3
Yadin barred com actn on W Bank setlmts 8-14, 639A1
6 in DMC quit coalitn, keeps Knesset control 8-23, 668F1
Parlt members warn Syria on Leb 8-28, 674F1
Tells US aide of Leb crisis 8-30, 674D2
Vs US troops in W Bank, Gaza 8-31, 673C2
Sees Carter in pre-summit 9-5; **Camp David talks start 9-6—9-7, 673A1**

1979

Denies Dayan PLO policy shift 2-13, 144E1
Hints Carter mtg 2-26, high-level talks minus Sadat barred 2-27, 142F2, C3
Says Israel, Egypt far apart 2-28, 143B1
In US; vs 'sham' peace, meets Carter 3-1, 143D1
Carter in Israel 3-10—3-13, Cabt OKs proposals 3-12; Sadat OKs, Knesset to vote 3-13, 177A1, F1, A2
Vs US govt briefing press on talks 3-13, 177C2
Carter lauds on Egypt pact 3-14, 177F2
USSR: offered US use of Haifa port 3-15, 178D2
NRP to quit re Egypt pact 3-18, 197B1
Vows no Palestine state 3-20, 197D1
Meets Vance, settles Sinai oil issue 3-24; meets Sadat, oil turnover OKd 3-25, 221F2
Signs Egypt peace treaty 3-26, 221A1
Arafat scores for Egypt pact 3-26, 222C2
Returns from DC 3-29, 250A1
Meets Sadat in Cairo, OKs agrmts 4-2—4-3; briefs parlt 4-4, 248E3
Denies Christian-Leb troop role 4-19, 278B1
Sadat deplores PLO raid 4-22, 296B3
US vs 2 new W Bank setlmts 4-23, 296B2
Asks death penalty for terrorists 4-24, Cabt OKs 4-29, 319C3
Pact documts exchngd 4-25, 295E2
Greets Sovt dissidents 4-29, 317C2
Vows contd strikes vs PLO, Leb vs peace bid 5-7, 341D1, E1
Scores executn of Iranian Jew 5-9, 353D2
Arab group vows to 'bring down' 5-10, 341E2
Weizman, Dayan vs Palestinian autonomy plan 5-17; drop oppositn 5-21, 394F2
Jordan rejcts peace talks bid 5-19, 379B1
Meets Vance, says Sadat vowed open border 5-24, 394D2
Iran protesters assail 5-24, 407A3
Announces Egypt border opening 5-27, 394B3
Says Sadat vs Israel settlers in El Arish 5-28, 395C1
Nablus setlmt voted, lauds 6-3, 415F1, A2
Dayan reaffirms W Bank, Gaza hold 6-4, 415G2
Bars Palestinian state, reelected Herut chrmn 6-6, 436F2
Defends setlmts policy; scores Brzezinski, NY Times 6-10, 436G1-D2
US Jews vs setlmt policy 6-20, 462A1
Sets preemptive strikes vs PLO 6-25, 475D2
US deplores Leb raid, Syria jet clash 6-27; vows contd raids 6-28, Cabt backs 7-1, 496A2
Strauss sees, scores West Bank setlmts 7-2, 511A2
Meets Sadat on Palestinian autonomy 7-10—7-11, hails mtg 7-12, 511F2
In hosp 7-19; brain artery rptd blocked 7-23, recovery seen 7-30, 583G2
Govt wins confidence vote 7-30, 583D2
Carter assures of contd support 8-4, 591C2
Leaves hospital 8-4, 591D2
Vs US UN res plan on Palestinians 8-19, 8-20, 623F2
Vows contd strikes in Leb 8-27, 643A2
Vs US criticism of Israel Leb raids 8-30, 658B3
Rumania bid to mediate PLO, Syria feud 8-31; rejects 9-2, 659B2
Meets Sadat; Sinai patrols, oil sale OKd 9-4—9-6, 658D1
Briefs Strauss on autonomy talks; reassured on PLO policy, other issues 9-11—9-12, 676E2, B3, E3
Carter phones on Camp David anniv 9-17, 695F1
Favors Jesse Jackson mtg, Dayan vs 9-20, 694F2
Senegal ldr chrgs racism 9-20, 721G1
Shuns Jesse Jackson 9-25, 762G3
Dayan offers resignatn 10-2, quits over Palestinian issue 10-21, leaves office 10-23, 801A1
Meets pro-Israel US black group 10-17, 780E3
Defeats no-confidence motions 10-23, 801G1
Shifts Cabinet 10-29, 856B2
Mt Sinai returned to Egypt 11-15, 881E3
Sees Linowitz 12-10, 938C1

1980

Hebron setlmt vote delayed 2-17, 218D3
Gets Carter explanatn on UN vote 3-4, 163D3
Scores UN setlmts res, US vote reversal 3-6, 179B1-B2
Shamir named forgn min 3-9, 179B3
Defends Jerusalem land seizure 3-13, 178C3
Carter invites to talks 3-19, 260B3
Sadat demands deadline for autonomy talks 3-21, 219E1
Sees Linowitz; vs setlmt freeze, security talks 3-25, 219G1-A2
Scores US on Sovt Jewish emigres 4-2, 262C3
Cabt limits talks with Carter 4-9; meets Carter on Palestinian autonomy 4-15—4-16; Sadat OKs talks speedup 4-16, 284F1
On US hostage rescue try 4-25, 324E1
Vs PLO talks 4-28, 418C2
Weizman quits 5-25; scores Begin rule, Begin assails 5-27, 429A3
Invites Saudi's Faud to Israel 5-27, 395G1
Cabt apptmt proposals opposed 5-27; to keep defns post in interim 6-1, 429E3
Scores W Bank bombings 6-2, 417D1
Plans 10 new W Bank setlmts, confirms Hussein-W Bank talks 6-4, 434F1
Vs Egypt briefing PLO on autonomy talks 6-8, 434A2
Vs Muskie remark on setlmts 6-10, 434F1
Scores EC stand on PLO 6-15, 449F1
To move office to E Jerusalem 6-22; US queries 6-25, objects 6-26, 476F1-A2
Suffers heart attack 6-30, 498G2-B3
Anderson visits 7-11, 549G3
French-Iraqi A-deal protested 7-28, 573A3
Meets EC rep, vs PLO talks 7-31, 585F2
Sadat asks delay in autonomy talks re Jerusalem 8-3; replies, chrgs Egypt aide breaches peace pact 8-8, 585A1, G1
Sadat autonomy talks exchngs rptd 8-11, 8-12, 627C1
Sadat asks new 3-way summit 8-15, response cool 8-19, 627F1
Defends Jerusalem move; scores US stand, Saudi threat 8-28, 660G2
Meets US aide on autonomy talks 9-1—9-2; OKs talks renewal 9-3, 660C2
Arens vs defense min post 9-1, 712D2
Says Syria unrest prompts Libya merger 9-9, 697D2
'65-75 Israel aid to Iraqi Kurds rptd 9-29, 735A3
OKs 2 W Bank mayors' return to appeal ouster 10-6; rejects plea 10-21, 822G2-A3
On Jordan war aid to Iraq 10-7, 757F1
Scores France anti-Semitism 10-13, 790A1
Discounts US warning on Leb raid 10-17, 800A3
Iraq sees US, Israel, Iran plot 10-18, 799B2
Vs Weizman electn tour with Carter 10-28, 830D2
Noncommital on Reagan electn, sends message 11-5, 841D2
Oppositn ldrs visit Egypt 11-7—11-9, 863G2
Arrives US 11-9; meets Carter 11-13; cuts visit for confidence vote 11-19, 880D2
Survives no-confidence vote 11-19, 880D1
Vows contd W Bank security control 11-20, 895G1
Warns interventn in Jordan-Syria feud 11-26, 911E3
Bans pro-PLO conf 12-1, 912F1
Orders 2 W Bank mayors redeported 12-5, 931D2
Linowitz suggests Reagan summit mtg 12-7, 930D3
Peres scores Sinai 'giveaway' 12-17, 966G1
Reaffirms Camp David process 12-18; US list obstacles 12-19, 952C3
Peres to run vs in '81 12-18, 966E1

1976

BEGIN, Monique
Sworn natl revenue min 9-15, 692D1
BEHRING International Inc.
Boycott rpts released 10-19, 7-20, 786C1, A2
BEIDA, Mahfoud Ali
SADR cabt min 3-5, 178A3
BEILENSON, Anthony Charles
Elected 11-2, 829C1
BEISHEIM, Justice George
Bronfman trial verdict 12-10, 952B3
BEITH, Alan
Grimond succeeds Thorpe 5-12, 364F3
BEITZ, Berthold
Signs Iran-Krupp pact 10-19, 782C2
BEJM, Tadeusz
Polish transport min 3-27, 268G2
BELAUNDE Terry, Fernando
Begins Peru visit 1-4, lauds Morales 1-5, 55A3
Returns to Peru 5-15; rpt civilian govt sought 6-11, 499B3
BELENKO, Viktor Ivanovich
Defects 9-6; US grants asylum 9-7, arrives 9-9, 695E1-696D1
USSR, Japan trade chrgs re defectn 9-9, 9-20, 10-5; bars return 9-28, 839F2

BELGIUM—*See also ADB, EUROPEAN Community, IEA, NATO, OECD*
Cafe fire 1-1, 80D1
Listed as 'free' nation 1-19, 20B3
Govt acts re potato shortage 1-21, 84C1
Walloons fail re FDF govt entry, reaffirm coalitn support 2-21, 220B3
Bank discount raised 3-17, 7-23, 572F1
Quake tremors rptd 5-6, 352B3
Express train derails 6-27, 560F3
Short-term interest rates hiked 7-30, 594C1
Drought measures announced 8-24, 630E1
Natnwide local electn results 10-10, 857D3
Mid Oct-Nov jobless rate up 11-29, 935C2
Tindemans reshuffles Cabt 12-8, 1012E2
European Force Reduction Issues—*See under EUROPE*
Foreign Relations (misc.)—*See also 'UN Policy' above*
SDR rate rptd 1-15, 14A3
French Mirage purchase cited 1-16, 36C2
Southn socialists meet 1-24—1-25, 120B1
Sovt Jewry conf held 2-17—2-19, 206F2-C3
Angola MPLA recognized 2-20, 163B1
Phone head sentncd re ITT bribe 2-23, 220A3

1977

BEGIN, Monique
Named Canada health min 9-16, 725F2
Yields women's post 9-23, 763C3
BEGUN, Iosif
Detained 2-28, 3-10, US protests 3-1, 226D2, D3
Sentenced 6-1, 436E2
BEJARES, Gen. Hernan
Chrgs Christian Dem 'plot' 3-11, 219C3
BEJM, Tadeusz
Dismissed 12-17, 987F1
BEKER Industries Inc.
Rpts payments 1-4, 94D2
BELAUNDE Terry, Fernando
Vs constituent assembly plan 8-25, 673B2
Party demands immediate electns 10-5, 784A2

BELGIUM—*See also EC, ESA, IDB, IEA, NATO, OECD*
Brussels hotel fire kills 15 5-22, 429B3
Prigogine wins Nobel 10-11, 951B3
Economy & Labor (domestic)
Bank discount rate cut 1-5, 24F1
'76 factory wage study rptd 1-28, 158B3
Franc devaluatn rejctd 2-3, 199D3
Dec '75-76 inflatn rate rptd 2-7, 87A2
Austerity program set 2-13, unions strike 2-24—3-9, 199F2
'76 econ growth rate rptd 2-22, 146C2
Jan jobless rate rptd 2-28, 199A3
Unemploymt at 9% 4-18, 326C3
Bank discount rate cut 5-5, 466E1
Econ reform measure OKd 6-9, 561C1
Aug jobless rate rptd 9-26, 771A2
'75 world pay rank rptd 11-6, 853E3
Foreign Relations (misc.)—*See also 'Monetary, Trade & Aid' and 'UN Policy' below*
'76 Eur Cncl pact vs terrorism cited 9G2
Mobutu visits 1-17—1-24, 199G3
In 14-natn sulphur-dioxide pact 1-19, 109B3
Benin coup attempt detailed 2-1, 96F1
ESA flight set 2-16, 170C3
USSR sentences natl 3-25, 314B3
Sahara captured arms displayed 3-28, 337B2
Rumania blocks dissident contact 4-2, 315F1
Zaire mil advisors rptd 4-12, 265F2

1978

USSR says NATO ties sought 9-6, 673G2
Transport min resigns 9-13, 798F3
DMC splinter party formed, to oppose policies 9-14, 798F3
Camp David summit ends; signs pacts with Carter, Sadat; photo 9-17, 709C1, B2
Text of agrmts 9-17, 711A1-712C3
Carter details pacts to US Cong, lauds role 9-18, 709E2
Carter: summit faced collapse 9-18, 710D1
Peres backs pacts, 2 aides doubt 9-18, 712E3
Gush Emunim seize W Bank hill in pact protest 9-19, 712C3
Disputes US on setlmts; says Carter, Sadat yielded on Golan, E Jerusalem 9-20, 710F1
Assad chrgs mil plans vs Syria 9-20, 712D2
Camp David summit letters released 9-22, 729F1; text 730C2-G3
Hussein on summit stand 9-22, 730G1
Bars separate summit pacts vote 9-24, 729C1
Backs Sadat on Sinai setlmt demand 9-25, 729F1
Threatens to quit unless summit pact OKd 9-27, 729D1
Carter disputes on W Bank setlmts 9-27, 729D2
Carter: backed Sarkis Leb govt 9-28, 745D1
Carter asks Leb truce role 10-5, 761C1
Vows aid to Leb Christns 10-8, 762D1
Carter links West Bank issue, peace talks 10-10, 766E3
Says Israel to expand setlmts 10-25, 10-26, 802F1
Wins Nobel Peace Prize 10-27, 886D1
Reaffrms setlmt expansn plan to Carter 10-29, 858G3
Meets Carter, Vance 11-2, 858A3
Carter: vs separate Egypt pact 11-9, 858G3
Says Israel ready to discuss W Bank-Gaza autonomy, Carter satisfied 11-21, 892F2
Jerusalem stand cited 11-21, 893A1
Gets new Egypt pact stand 11-30, 930F2
Accepts Nobel award 12-10, 950B3-951A1
Meets Vance on new Egypt pact draft 12-11, 950A3
Cabt, parlt back stand vs Egypt pact revisn 12-15, 12-19, 978G2
Egypt denies pact change 12-15, 978E3
Vs US criticism of Israel Leb raid 12-21, 997C3
Sadat says Arab oppositn aids pact impasse 12-25, 997F3
Says ready for new Egypt talks 12-26, 997G3
BEGLE, Edward G.
Dies 3-2, 252D2
BEGUN, Iosif
Arrested 5-17, sentenced 7-28, 543C1
BEIKMAN, Charles
Seized in Amos murders 11-25; Guyana cultists held as witnesses 11-28, 910E2
Amos murder hearing 12-4, 955A2
Stephan Jones confesses 12-18, Guyana indicts 12-19, 1000A1
BEILENSON, Rep. Anthony Charles (D, Calif.)
Sees Castro, Zaire role denied 6-13, 442F2-A3
Reelected 11-7, 850G1
BEILIN, Dina
Visa OK rptd 3-7, 180G1
BEIS, Dimitrios
Elected Athens mayor 10-22, 816D2
BELANGER, Mark
Wins Golden Glove Award 11-21, 928A3
BELAUNDE Terry, Fernando
Party registered for June electns 2-3, 134D2
Accepts AP pres bid 10-3, 776C1
BELGER, Mark
Sets indoor 880-yd run record 1-13, 76E2
BELGIUM—*See also COUNCIL of Europe, EC, GATT, IDB, IEA, NATO, OECD*
Industrialist kidnaped 3-8, 232A2; found slain 4-10, 379C3
Brussels statue stolen 4-25, 4-27, 335C2
Campers killed in Spanish blast 7-11, 636E1
Deligne wins Field Medal 8-15, 1023F2
African Relations
Zaire executes 13 in plot 3-17, 230A3
Zaire rescue operatn, French tensn rptd 5-18—5-23; troops exit 5-22, 381A1-382A1
USSR scores Zaire rescue 5-22, 382D1
Tindemans sees Zaire pres, African security force backed 5-24, 417D3
USSR chrgs troops massacred Zaire whites 5-25, 417C3
Zaire death toll rptd 5-30, 417G2, B3
Western natns meet on pan-Africa force 6-5, 441E2
Zaire pullout set 6-7, 441D1
Zaire rebel ldr ousted 6-7, 441E1
Zaire defns force training rptd 6-10, 441F1
Zaire emergency aid OKd 6-13—6-14, 478A1
Zaire role cited in govt crisis 6-15—6-19, 612F2
Mozambique chrgs natls killed in Rhodesia raid 6-23, 594B3
Comoro mercenary role chrgd 7-8, 561F2; mercenary ouster rptd 7-23, 596D1

1979

BEGIN, Monique
Warns provs re health insurance 3-12, 211D1
BEGLARI, Gen. Mohammed Amin
Found slain 2-12, 105A2
BEHBAHANI, Seyyed Mohsen
Slain 7-21, 565D3
BEHBEHANIAN, Mohammed
Shah chrgd with embezzlemt 12-11, 935D2
BEHESHTI, Ayatollah Mohammed
Chrgs Hassan with treason 425G3
On US hostage trial 12-5, 934B2
BEHRMAN, S. N.
Grand Tour opens 1-11, 292E1
BEHZADNIA, Ali
Defends ouster of LA Times rptr 7-1, 525D2
Ousts NYT rptr 7-22, curbs press 7-23, 565F3
BEIKMAN, Charles
Jonestown radio message transcripts rptd 1-29, 118F1
BELANGER, Mark
In World Series 10-10–10-17, 816A1
BELCO Petroleum Corp.
Peru orders contract renegotiated 12-7, 951A2
BELEW Jr., Judge David O.
Racial slur rptd 7-14, 901B3
BELGIUM—*See also COUNCIL of Europe, DISARMAMENT–Geneva Committee, EC, GATT, IDB, IEA, NATO, OECD*
Explosn injures 15 8-28, 641E2
Flemish militants riot 10-21, 832F2
African Relations
Zaire to get troops 2-6, 137F2; troops leave 3-15, 215D2
Belgian-trained Zaire troops replace Shaba intl force 8-14, 733G3
Atomic Energy & Safeguards
Huy mayor closes A-plant 4-7, Cabt reverses 4-8, 276B2
Economy & Labor
'78 living standards ranked 2-2, 109A2
Banker slain 3-22, suspect arrested 3-24, 228B3
'78 per capita GNP ranked 6th 7-24, 575E3
Westn wage rates compared 9-19, 697D3
'80 deficit measures rptd 10-2, Francophone Soclsts back 10-13–10-14, 832A3
Energy—*See also 'Atomic' above*
Oil consumption curbs set 4-12, 396E3
European Force Reduction Talks—*See under EUROPE*
Foreign Relations (misc.)—*See also 'Monetary' and 'UN' below*
UK amb's life threatened 3-23, 228A3
Bhutto executn scored 4-4, 247A2

1980

BEGIN, Monique
Canada health min 3-3, 171B2
BEHARA, Hassan
Wins Olympic medal 7-24, 624C3
BEHESHTI, Ayatollah Mohammed
Hints delay in US hostage release 2-27, 137E1
Asks hostage trials 3-26, 217F2
Aide tied to plot vs Bani-Sadr 6-19, 464F2
On US hostage response 11-12, 861C2
BEIDERBECKE, Bix (Leon Bismarck) (1903-31)
Elected to Recording Arts HOF 2-27, 296C3
BEIKMAN, Charles Edward
Sentenced 4-8, 313B3
Appeals sentence 5-22, 408B1
Guyana rptdly drops chrgs 9-20, 751B1
BEILENSON, Rep. Anthony Charles (D, Calif.)
Reelected 11-4, 842G1
BEINECKE, Frances
Scores offshore leasing speedup 6-17, 552G2
BEING There (film)
Douglas wins Oscar 4-14, 296G1
Top-grossing film 4-23, 360B1
BELAUNDE Moreyra, Antonio
Eludes Colombia emb raiders 2-27, 141C1
BELAUNDE Terry, Fernando (Peruvian president)
Elected Peru pres 5-18, 390A2
Banzer sued for campaign plagiarism 7-12, 543E1
Inaugurated, outlines goals 7-28, 579E3
Snubs Argentina pres 7-28, 580C1
Condemns Bolivia coup 7-29, 577D1
Bars Cuban refugee exit demands 8-29, 672E2
Munic electns held 11-23, 923A1
Attends Santa Marta conf 12-17, 992A3
BELCHER, Page
Dies 8-2, 676A1
BELCO Petroleum Corp.
Peru tax positn said unaffected 1-9, 21A3
Peru contract signed 4-30, 354F1
BELENKO, Lt. Viktor
US asylum cited 9-15, 705A1
BELFER, Arthur
On Peru tax effect 1-9, 21A3
BELFIELD, David (Daoud Salahuddin)
Sought in Tabatabai slaying 7-23, 545C2
Flees US 8-6, 671D3
BEL Geddes, Barbara
Wins Emmy 9-7, 692C1
BELGIUM—*See also ADB, COUNCIL of Europe, CSCE, EC, GATT, GENEVA Committee, IDB, IEA, MBFR, NATO, OECD*
Fourons riots staged 3-8—3-9, demonstratns barred 3-11, 182F1
Bus hijackers foiled 11-14, 920E1-A2
Economy & Labor
OECD sees slowdown 1-17, 56C2
Discount rate hiked 2-27, 153D3; 3-19, 237C1
Govt spending cuts rptd 3-24, 237B1
Labor costs rptd 8-12, 698C1, F1
Hormones in cattle feed barred 10-1, 737C3
Austerity plan set 10-16, 787E1
Energy
Econ slowdown forecast linked 1-17, 56D2
Conservatn steps rptd 3-24, 237C1
Italy cuts Eurodif share 5-2, 409D1
Gasoline prices cut 8-12, 628A2
Foreign Relations (misc.)—*See also 'Monetary', 'UN Policy' below*
Olympic com to decide on Moscow role 1-21, 45B3; rejects boycott 3-22, 259C3
Mex emb occupied 2-18, 152A1
IRA claims credit for past bombings 2-19, 194C1
150 Cuban refugees offered asylum 4-16, 285C1
Europn CPs meet 4-28—4-29, 327C2

1976

US Lockheed bribe probe set 3-9, 220B3
To join A-safeguards group 3-13, 243F2
France quits currency 'snake' 3-15, 229A2
Franc snake role bolstered 3-17, 7-23, 572F1
Eur liberals meet 3-26—3-27, 260C3
Total IMF oil loan rptd 4-1, 340F2
US ends car dumping probe 5-4, 321C2
N Chaval kidnaped in Mex 5-25, ransomed 5-29, 419A2
IDB entry planned 6-3, 465D3
Loan to prop UK £ OKd 6-7, 407C2
Paris Club defers Zaire debt 6-17, 488A2
France vs joint Eurpn steel firm 7-6, 521G1
Spy arrested in W Ger 8-16, 640B2
Plane pact signed 8-24, 734D3
2 US banks drop Zaire loan suits 10-13, 890A3
W Ger mark revalued 10-17, 782B1
DISC program ruled illegal 11-5, 976E3
France bars jt Eur defns 11-30, 905A3
In IMF UK loan 12-21, 1004B1
Sports
Summer Olympic results 7-18—7-31, 573E3, 574B2-E2, 575G3, 576D1, E1
UN Policy & Developments
Vs WHO anti-Israel stand 5-19, 355D2
Vs anti-S Africa aid stand 11-5, 842C3
Vs black Namibia support 12-20, 955C1

1977

Mex '76 kidnapers seized 4-13—4-14, 528G3
Spain exiles Basque prisoners 5-22, 454A1
France expels Agee 8-18, 654E2
Indochina refugee quotas eased 8-31, 685E2
Eur Cncl to study Turkey rights abuses in Cyprus 9-8, 764G1-A2; rpt shelved, Greece protests 11-3, 946B3
Government & Politics—*See also other appropriate subheads in this section*
Budget vote splits coalitn 3-3, RW mins ousted 3-4; gen electn called 3-9, 199B2
Electn results 4-17; Tindemans named caretaker premr 4-22, asks 'grand coalitn' 4-27, 326D2
Federatn plan OKd 5-24; FDF stalls govt formatn 6-2, Cabt sworn 6-3, 465E3
Tindemans wins confidence vote, devolutn plan OKd 6-9, 561B1
Spaak elected FDF chrmn 6-15, 561D1
Helsinki Agreement—*See EUROPE—Security and Cooperation*
Monetary, Trade & Aid Issues (including all foreign economic developments)
'76 Eur snake loan, forgn reserves cited 1-5, 24G1
In UK sterling balance pact 1-10, 20C2
US F-16 sale review set 1-17, 70D3
Exporters seek franc devaluatn 1-20, rejctd 2-3, 199D3
ICFTU S Africa boycott fails 1-21, 67B3
Air Canada to end svc 1-28, 43D2
IMF SDR defined 87G2
Brazil mil aid request seen 3-7, 168B1
Zaire gets arms 3-17, 207D3
A-supplier natns meet, Carter plan scored 4-28—4-29, 403F1-A2
US F-16 pact signed 5-5, 441A2
Carter OKs uranium shipmt 5-6, 403C2
'68 Israeli uranium purchase rptd 5-30, 416B3, D3
Group of 10 membership cited 438F1
Zaire debt rescheduled 7-7, 583E1
Sweden quits 'snake' 8-29, 709A1
A-supplier natns OK export safeguards 9-21, 717D1
US co chrgs steel dumping 10-20, 836E3
Exxon admits paymts 10-25, 818A2
UN Policy & Developments
UN Assemb member 3F3
UN Assemb Israel occupatn res opposed 11-25, 910D2
S Africa oil ban abstentn 12-16, 1016A2
U.S. Relations—*See also 'Monetary, Trade & Aid' above*
Mondale visits 1-23—1-24, 69B1, 70C1
US-ESA space flight set 2-16, 170C3
Chambers confrmd amb 4-29, 418D1
Agee visit OKd 8-18, 645D2
ESA satellite launching aborted 9-13, 735G3
Carter visit scheduled 9-23, 738F1
Carter visit deferred 11-7, 854A1; rescheduled 11-29, 914B2
Carter begins world tour 12-29, 1000G3

1978

Comoro mercenary quits army 9-27, 798C3
Cholera emergency aid program rptd 10-12, 927E2
Atomic Energy & Safeguards
'77 A-export safeguard pact detailed 1-11, 11B2
US alerts to Sovt A-satellite fall 57E1
Nuclear plant leak disputed 1-25, 69F3
Australia joins A-suppliers' group 2-24, 129C2
US study backs breeder dvpt 5-10, 346G3
Economy & Labor (domestic)
'77 inflatn rate drop rptd 1-3, 35B1
Brussels expenses rated 1-14, 28G2, A3
Oil workers' dispute setld 1-17, 70A1
Bank van Loo et Cie fails 1-24, 94E1
'77, Jan jobless rates rptd 2-7, 115C2
Armed forces protest pay, job conditns 3-4, 170F3
Workers protest unemploymt 4-5, 258F2
Econ policy crisis resolved 6-15—6-19, 612F2-B3
Steel strike 6-22—6-27, 612F3
June '77-78 world inflatn rates ranked 10-18, 914F1
Steel rescue plan announced 11-24, 921C1
European Force Reduction Talks—*See under EUROPE*
Foreign Relations (misc.)—*See also 'Atomic Energy' above, 'Monetary, Trade, Aid & Investment' & 'UN' below*
Ulster arms shipmt rptd seized 1-6, 7F3
Greek premr in Brussels 1-26, 149B2
At USSR mil maneuvers 2-6—2-10, 103B2
France, W Ger OK ESA rocket launcher 2-6—2-7, 122B1
Eur fascists meet 3-4—3-5, 238D3
Chile pol exile arrives 4-15, 287F2
Eur conservative party union shunned 4-24, 424D3
Corsica army bldgs bombed 5-6, 352E2
ESA communicatns satellite launched 5-12, 384D3
Turkish premr visits 5-17, 398B3
USSR scores Zaire rescue 5-22, 382D1; chrgs massacres 5-25, 417C3
Westn natns meet on pan-Africa force 6-5, 441E2
'60 Cuba ship blast tied to CIA 8-1, 831C1
Czech ousts rptr 8-10, Boel cancels visit 8-11, 691B3
Government & Politics—*See also other appropriate subheads in this section*
Devolutn dispute rptd 1-6, 34F3
Devolutn plan accepted 1-17, 69D3
Coalitn splits on econ policy, devolutn 6-15; crisis resolved, Tindemans resignatn rejctd 6-19, 612E2-F3
Coalitn disputes devolutn, Tindemans resignatn accepted 10-10, 764A2
Caretaker govt formed, Boeynants premr 10-20, 813D1
Soclsts split on linguistic lines 10-28, 968F1
Electns held, results indecisive 12-17, 1013D1
Helsinki Agreement—*See EUROPE—Security and Cooperation*
Monetary, Trade, Aid & Investment—*See also 'Atomic Energy' above*
Ulster arms shipmt rptd seized 1-6, 7F3
Franc in new SDR basket 4-3, 300F3
Graiver indicted in US 4-12, 326C1, A2
US F-16 review urged 4-24, 407D2
Zaire aid OKd 6-13—6-14, 478A1
French workers block traffic 6-23, 6-27, 532C3
Zaire cholera aid rptd 10-12, 927E2
W Ger mark revalued up 10-16, 798C2
Hungary devalues forint 11-11, 906G2
At Brussels monetary summit, EMS entry backed 12-4—12-5, 952C2
Ireland to join EMS 12-15, 979F1
US probes steel dumping chrgs 12-28, 1006B1
Sports
Merckx retires from cycling 5-18, 692C2
Pollentier suspended from Tour de France 7-16, Hinault wins race 7-23, 692B2
UN Policy & Developments
Sea Law Conf talks continue 5-23—7-15, 8-21—9-16, 732E3
Racism conf boycotted 8-26, 676B2
Assemb member 713C3
U.S. Relations—*See also 'Monetary, Trade Aid & Investment' above*
US troop presence rptd 1-2, 5C2
Carter visits 1-6, 1C1
US alerts to Sovt A-satellite fall 57E1
Teller at A-plant hearings 1-25, 69G3
US study backs breeder dvpt 5-10, 346G3
US launches ESA satellite 5-12, 384D3
US seabed mining bill debated at UN conf 8-21—9-16, 732E3
ITT unit linked to forgn paymts 11-2, 876E1, E2
$2.1 mln in stolen bank funds rptd unrecoverable 11-5, 992D1

1979

PLO raid on El Al jet thwarted 4-16, 278A3
Spain bomb blast hurts 2 6-30, 504G3
IRA, explosn link disputed 8-28, 641E2
USSR prisoner total estimate rptd 9-14, 697E2
Dutch Shell strikers vowed union support 9-24, 731C2
Iran: US aide held false passport 12-6, 914G2
UK letter bombs, IRA linked 12-17, 994F3
Government & Politics—*See also other appropriate subheads in this section*
New coalitn announced 4-2, Martens sworn premr 4-3, 253B2
Eur Parlt electns 6-7, 433A1, 434C1
Francophone Soclsts meet 10-13—10-14, 832C3
Helsinki Agreement—*See EUROPE—Security and Cooperation*
Monetary, Trade, Aid & Investment
Ireland ends UK £ parity 3-30, 268F3
Uniroyal operatns sale set 4-17, 560G3
W Ger ranks exporter labor costs 5-1, 374B2
EC green currencies revised 6-21, 513G1
EMS currencies realigned 9-24, 719A1
Sports
Scheckter wins Grand Prix 5-13, 1005E1
UN Policy & Developments
Membership listed 695E2
Pol Pot govt seat upheld 9-19, 695C2
U.S. Relations
US A-accident linked to plant dispute 4-7, 276A2
ITT unit to aid paymts probe 8-8, 648F1
False passport rptd held by US aide in Iran 12-6, 914G2

1980

USSR May Day parade shunned 5-1, 354G2
Surinam coup fails, mercenaries seized 5-1—5-2, 410A3
Tito funeral held 5-8, 339B1
Olympic com OKs Moscow participatn 5-20, 379A3
ESA rocket test fails 5-23, 397G2
W Ger backs NATO A-missiles 7-15, 540C1
ESA plans comet probe 7-15, 548A1
Jewish youth killed in Antwerp blast 7-27, Palestinian seized 7-28, 573D2
Westn labor costs compared 8-12, 698C1, F1
Iran parlt ldr rebuffs hostage appeal 8-17, 634D3
Turkey coup, NATO maneuvers withdrawal linked 9-15, 696B2, F3
Sovts scored at CSCE conf 11-12, 863C1
Government & Politics—*See also other appropriate subheads in this section*
Martens reunites coalitn in Brussels linguistic dispute 1-10, 37G2
FDF leaves coalitn 1-16, Martens shuffles Cabt 56F1
Govt resigns re autonomy plan rejectn 4-3, 4-9, 272B1
New 6-party govt sworn 5-18, 388A2
Regional autonomy plan OKd 8-5, 602F2
Martens submits resignatn 10-4, delay asked 10-5; resignatn OKd 10-7, 766F2
Martens sets new coalitn 10-16, 787C1
Martens coalitn sworn 10-22, 860C2
Monetary, Trade, Aid & Investment
Luxembourg joint current acct deficit seen 1-17, 56C2
US Steel files dumping complaint 3-21, 225D1
Paymts deficit reductn steps rptd 3-24, 237C1
US sets steel import probe 4-10, 367E3
US finds steel import damage 5-1, 456C1
Italy cuts Eurodif share 5-2, 409D1
US arrests businessman as Sovt trade spy 5-18, sentenced 8-1, 598B2
Dutch to probe S Africa sanctns 6-27, 499A2
Sports
Moscow Olympics stand rptd 1-21, 45B3
Olympic com rejcts Moscow boycott 3-22, 259C3
Olympic com OKs Moscow participatn 5-20, 379A3
Eur Soccer Championship lost 6-22, 771C2
Moscow Olympics results 7-20—8-3, 588C3, 623D1
UN Policy & Developments
Assemb Palestinian state res abstentn 7-29, 572F1
U.S. Relations
US Steel files dumping complaint 3-21, 225D1
US sets steel import probe 4-10, 367F3
US finds steel import damage 5-1, 456C1
US arrests businessman as Sovt trade spy 5-18, sentenced 8-1, 598B2
Iran parlt ldr rebuffs hostage appeal 8-17, 634D3
A-missile deploymt OKd 9-19, 737A2

1976

BELHUMEUR, David
Accused 10-12, 999A1
BELIAEV, Evgeny
Wins Olympic medal 2-8, 159C1

1977

BELGRADE Conference (Helsinki Agreement)—*See EUROPE—Security and Cooperation*
BELINFANTI, A. U.
Jamaica agri min 1-4, 46C1

1978

BELGRAVE, Cynthia
Amen Corner opens 4-22, 760B1
BELIEVE It (race horse)
3d in Ky Derby, Preakness 5-6, 5-20, 539C1-E1
BELISLE, Danny
Hired as Caps coach 10-9, 991C1

1979

BELHUMEUR, David
Cleared re Giguere case 12-7, 949C1
BELIN, David W.
Scores House JFK death probe final rpt 7-17, 538B2
BELISLE, Danny
Fired as Caps coach 11-13, 1004F1

1980

BELHUMEUR, David
Acquittal appeal set 1-4, 6A2

1976

BELIZE (formerly British Honduras) (British colony)—*See also CARIBCOM*
Price in UK re independnc 1-5, 55B2
Guatemala rejcts UK quake aid 2-11, 120C3
Guatemala accepts pvt UK quake aid 2-12, 155D3
Guatemala, UK continue independnc talks 9-21—9-22, 10-26—10-28, 977E3
Offshore oil deposits rptd 10-4, 978A1
BELKIN, Samuel
Dies 4-18, 315G3
BELKNAP (U.S. missile cruiser)
'75 collisn ct martial verdicts 5-12, 6-22, 941G2
Repair authorizatn signed 7-14, 517D1
BELL, Rep. Alphonzo (R, Calif.)
Loses Senate primary 6-8, 409D2
BELL, Carolyn Shaw
Cited as Carter adviser 4-23, 305E2
BELL, Earl
Sets pole-vault record 5-29, 424D3
BELL, Griffin Boyette
Named atty gen 12-20; desegregatn rulings, pvt club membership scored 12-20—12-22, 956F1, G2
Photo 956A1
Biog sketch 957D1
BELL, Ricky
2d in Heisman balloting 11-30, 969E2
BELL, Terrel H.
Quits as Educatn comr 5-2, 412A2
BELLAH, James Warner
Dies 9-22, 1015B1
BELLER, Gary
Testifies at privacy hearings 2-11, 151D2
BELLEVUE Stratford Hotel (Philadelphia, Pa.)
Mystery disease kills 23 8-5, 573A3
Disease probe continues 8-6—8-31, 656E2, F2
Closes 11-18, 911F2
BELL & Howell Corp.
Polaroid Austrian deal rptd 1-30, 97F3
BELLMON, Sen. Henry L. (R, Okla.)
Milk price veto upheld 2-4, 88G1
Retains Senate seat 3-4, 180C2
BELLO, Alfred P.
Carter, Artis judge disqualified 10-19, 860B1
Carter, Artis convicted 12-21, 1015D3
BELLOW, Saul
Wins Pulitzer Prize 5-3, 352C3
Wins Nobel Prize 10-21, 840D1
Rptd fired, runs for House seat 12-7, 925B2

1977

BELIZE (formerly British Honduras) (British colony)
Guatemala illegal immigratn rptd 1-30, 415E1
Defense force set 2-13, 10-yr UK pact sought 5-20, 415C1
OAS backs Guatemala claim 3-1, 190G2
Guatemala backs contd UK talks, warns vs independence 5-17, 415D1
Guatemala severs Panama ties 5-19; chrgs exchngd 5-20, 5-24, Latin mediatn asked 5-27, 414G2
Price starts Panama visit 5-20, 414C3
Commonwealth conf gets Guatemala plea 6-8—6-15, 487E1
Panama, Carib natns back independnc 6-16; Guatemala threatens war 6-18, 494G2
Barbados seizes Israel arms for Guatemala 6-25, 553E2
Guatemala chrgs Cuba arms transit 7-4, 673F1
UK-Guatemala talks 7-6—7-7, Guatemala demands rptd 7-6—7-9, 553F1
Israel arms sale to Guatemala rptd 7-6, 553E2
UK sends troops, jets 7-7—7-8, Guatemala protests 7-8, 553E1, G1
Anti-independnc rally held 7-11, 553D2
UK-Guatemala talks 7-26—7-28; UK bars troop exit 7-28, Laugerud scores 8-5, 706C2
US independnc backing rptd 8-12, 706G2
UK dep secy on Latin tour, affirms independnc 9-8; Guatemala scores, cites troop presence 9-23, 767B1
Spain king backs Guatemala 'aspiratns' 9-13; Mex comments 9-17, 805C1
CR backs independence 9-30, 786D1
Price fears Guatemala invasn, Guatemala scores 11-18, 969A3
UN Assemb backs independnc 11-28, 969G2
UK troops sent to Bermuda 12-4—12-6, 935F2, G3
UK rpts Guatemala talks 12-9, 969A3
BELKHOJA, Tahar
Dismissed 12-23, 1019D2
BELL, Eric
Jamaica educatn min 1-4, 46C1
BELL, Griffin Boyette
NAACP opposes 1-10, 59B3
Confrmatn hearings 1-11—1-18; confrmatn recommended 1-19, delayed 1-20, 34C1
Confrmd 1-25, sworn 1-26, 52D2, G2
King probe rpt cited 2-2, 77C2
Modifies dual prosecutn rule 2-11, 821B1
On King assassinatn rpt 2-13, 2-24, 149D2
Rpts personal finances 2-25, 147D3
FBI health care probe agreed 3-20, 236A1
ERA rescissions memo rptd 3-26, 3-27, 279G3
Proposes illegal alien plan 4-27, 370C2
Handicapped anti-bias rules signed 4-28, 338C3
Natl crime data plan opposed 6-8, 480C3
Puts FBI on Ray case 6-10, 459A2
US-Canada trust com rptd set 6-18, 525G2
Study urges LEAA reorganizatn 6-30, 630A2
Sees Korean probe prosecutns 7-18, 556E2
Extends Hyde Amendmt scope 7-27, 786C2
Turner testifies on CIA mind-control tests 8-3, 611B2
Korean lobbying info sharing agreed 8-3, 688D2
Carter offers illegal alien plan 8-4, 592C1
Vows multinatl trust probes 8-8, 629E3
Opposes grand jury changes 8-9, 630E1
OKs 15,000 Viet refugees 8-11, 739F3
Johnson named FBI dir 8-17, 626A2
Announces Park indictmt, seeks extraditn 9-6, 687D2, F3
Panama Canal tap hearings postponed 9-30, 756E1
Torrijos drug rpts denied 10-13, 792E1
Carter: no decisn re Helms indictmt 10-27, 814C1
Clashes with FBI probe attys 12-7, 940A1
Names new FBI probe team, drops indictmt oppositn 12-13, 979B3
BELL, Richard E.
Replaced as Agri asst secy 4-6, 272A3
BELL, Ricky
USC wins Sugar Bowl 1-1, 8F3
In NFL draft 5-3, 353G1, A2, D2
BELLAMY, Carol
Wins city cncl pres runoff 9-19, 723C2
Elected city cncl pres 11-8, 855F2
BELLANGER, Claude
Parisien Libere strike ends 8-16, 654D3
BELLEVUE Hospital Center (N.Y.)
NYC blackout 7-13—7-14, 537F2
BELL & Howell Co.
Powell apologizes to Percy 9-14, 701B3
BELLOW, Saul
Backs Czech dissidents 1-21, 82G2
BELL Savings Bank (Philadelphia, Pa.)
Saxe sentenced 2-11, 140G1
BELL Telephone Laboratories Inc.—*See AMERICAN Telephone & Telegraph*

1978

BELIZE (formerly British Honduras) (British colony)—*See also CARIBBEAN Community*
UK cancels El Salvador armored car sales, Guatemala backing cited 1-19, 75A1
Price in UK, sees forgn secy 1-24—1-25, 94F1
Guatemala hints land compromise 2-24, 230C3
Barbados, Guyana, Jamaica in defns accord 3-10, 211C2
Mex '76 oil find rptd 4-21, 354B2
Guyana backs independnc, affirms defns pledge 5-6, 354C2
Guatemala reaffirms independnc demands 5-18, 478E2
Price, Lindo vow non-pol independnc talks 6-2, 478D2
Carter hopeful for Guatemala setlmt 6-21, 489C3
Guatemala pres asks 'peaceful' solutn 7-1; new UK contacts rptd 7-6, 538E1
Panama, Guatemala resume ties 8-29, 798A3
New independnc talks begin 9-25, 798G2
BELKHODJA, Tahar
Gen strike provokes violence 1-26—1-28, 74D1
BELKIN, Alan
Different Story released 6-13, 619E1
BELKNAP, Allen R.
Beasts opens 2-8, Modigliani 5-17, 760C1, E2
Approaching Zero opens 11-30, 1031A1
BELL, Buddy
Traded to Rangers 12-8, 1026D1
BELL, Griffin Boyette
Marston dismissal controversy 1-10, 1-12, 12D2, G2; ousts 1-20, 32F1
On past FBI corruptn 1-10, 15F1
Webster named FBI dir 1-19, 32D1
Justice clears on Marston ouster 1-24, 62C2
Carter defends Marston ouster 1-30, 62F1-B2
Bars shipping rebate probe delay 2-3, 184D3
Disputes Burger on trial lawyers 2-12, 108C1
Explains US suit vs ex-CIA agent 2-14, 129E1
Taft-Hartley invoked in coal strike 3-6; gets ct order 3-9, 159C2, 160C2; order takes effect 3-13, 181G2
Picks Marston successor 3-23, 243B3
Rpts Gray, 2 other FBI ex-aides indicted; asks disciplinary actn vs LaPrade, 68 agents 4-10, 262A1
LaPrade seeks debate 4-13, 285D1
House OKs tuitn tax credits 6-1, 431D3
FBI informant case declined by Sup Ct 6-12, 468E1
Legislative vetoes deplored 6-21, 466E1
Backs LTV-Lykes merger 6-21, 492C3
Lauds Sup Ct Bakke ruling 6-28, 482B2
Cited for contempt in FBI informants case 7-6, 507A2
Fires LaPrade 7-6, 507G2
Contempt order stayed 7-7, 524G3
Cuba offers pol offenders to US 8-31, 687D1
Kirbo rpts GSA probe talks 9-7, 715E1
Backs warrantless tap curbs 9-8, 697D1
Names Lynch to head GSA probe 9-20, 753F3
Cong clears bankruptcy law revisn 10-6, 788G2
Kennedy asks FTC probe Lykes-LTV merger 11-9, FTC rejcts 11-21; shareholders OK merger 12-5, 935E2
To admit more Indochina refugees 11-28, 932G3-933D1, 934F1
BELL, Jeffrey
Wins Sen primary in NJ 6-6, 425B1, 447F3
Loses electn 11-7, 849A1
BELL Canada
Bias end ordrd 9-11, guidelines issued 9-21, 772F3
BELLECOURT, Vernon
Asks Carter mtg 7-18, Indian commitmt 7-23, 569B1, E1
BELLE of Amherst (recording)
Wins Grammy 2-24, 316B1
BELL Helicopter Textron—*See TEXTRON*
BELL & Howell Co.
Berkey wins trust suit vs Kodak 1-21, 67G1
BELLITTO, N. D.
Contessa of Mulberry St opens 1-4, 887E1
BELLMON, Sen. Henry (R, Okla.)
Votes for Panama Canal neutrality pact 3-16, 177F1, F2
Votes for 2d Canal pact 4-18, 273B1
Visits USSR 11-11—11-18, 905C1
BELLOLI, Giovanni
Magistrate resigns in kidnap controversy 1-22, 133B3
BELLOW, Saul
Alimony, child-support ordrd by ct 9-10, 844F3
Letter to Carter chrgs pro-Egypt stand 12-19, 979A1
BELLOW, Susan
Wins alimony, child-support 9-10, 844F3
BELL Telephone Laboratories, Inc.—*See AMERICAN Telephone & Telegraph*
BELL v. Ohio
Ohio death penalty law voided by Sup Ct 7-3, 552D1-A2
BELL v. Socialist Workers Party
FBI informant case declined by Sup Ct 6-12, 468E1

1979

BELIZE (formerly British Honduras) (British colony)—*See also CARIBBEAN Comumunity*
UDP Dec '78 munic electn win rptd 1-19, 78B1
Commonwealth conf backs indepndnc 8-7, 590E2
PUP wins parlt electns; US, UK territorial guarantees on indepndnc sought 11-21, 906F3-907D1
BELKNAP, Allen R.
Nature & Purpose opens 2-23, 292C2
BELKNAP, U.S.S. (cruiser)
Recommission announced 1-23, 89B3
BELL, Buddy
AL batting ldr 9-30, wins Golden Glove Award 955F3, 956C1
BELL, Griffin Boyette
JFK, King murder plot reviews delayed 1-2, 4C1
Warns anti-shah rioters in US 1-4, 3G1
FBI ex-agent's statemt in SWP trial sought 1-16, 92C2
Paisley death probe urged 1-24, 55B1
For 6-yr pres term 1-25, 110G1-A2
Webster rescinds FBI agent's dismissal, orders demotn 1-26, 92F2
Foreign students surveyed, visa probe planned 1-29, 93F2
Reassures ABA on minority apptmts 2-12, 130F1
Announces student visa crackdown 3-8, 167F2
Refugee bill proposed 3-8; extends Sovt, Indochinese paroles 3-26, 307G3-308D1
Contempt citatn overturned 3-19, 207E1
Names Carter peanut probe spec counsel, GOP scores limits 3-20, 203A1
Carter probe spec counsel gains new power 3-23, 301G2-B3
Orders fed judge's murder probed 5-29, 431E2
7 shipping cos indicted 6-1, 423C2
Resignatn accepted, replacemt named 7-19, 529C1, E1
Signs Phila police brutality complaint 8-10, 610D2
Scores Carter 8-14, leaves office 8-16, 608C3
Errors in '77 Sup Ct tax case cited 10-8, 848A2
Contempt case declined by Sup Ct 10-9, 783D3
Testifies in Vesco case 12-4, 943F2, G2
BELL, Jesse E.
Loses Gary mayoral primary 5-8, 363G2
BELL, Mike
In NFL draft 5-3, 335E1
BELL, Peter
Solid hydrogen rptd formed 3-2, 290C1
BELL Canada
Ontario, Quebec strike starts 8-12, 613F1; ends 9-6, 685E1
Saudi deal delayed 10-18, 833A3
BELLER, Kathleen
Promises in the Dark released 11-2, 1008B1
BELLEVUE Hospital (N.Y., N.Y.)
Morales escapes prison ward 5-21, 431E1
BELL Helicopter Textron—*See TEXTRON*
BELL & Howell Co.
Home-study student reimbursement agreed 3-26, 308D3
BELL & Howell Co. v. NLRB
Case declined by Sup Ct 6-18, 499E2
BELLIN, Dr. Howard
Loses malpractice suit 5-3, 392A3
Malpractice suit award cut 6-4, 527F2
BELL Jar, The (film)
Released 3-20, 528C1
BELLMON, Sen. Henry (R, Okla.)
Vs SALT treaty 4-5, 258G1
BELLON, Yannick
Rape of Love released 9-23, 820A3
BELLONI, Judge Robert C.
Bars CIA Ore Magazine censorship stay 4-19, 309D3
BELLOTTI v. Baird
Case decided by Sup Ct 7-2, 559G1
BELLOW, Saul
Vs Israel setlmt policy 6-20, 462B1
Book awards protest rptd 8-9, 755F3
BELL v. Wolfish
Case decided by Sup Ct 5-14, 383G1
Marshall decries ruling 5-27, 422C1

1980

BELK, W. E.
Hostages' letters publshd 1-18—1-20, 47C3
BELKNAP, Allen R.
Interview opens 4-24, 392C3
BELL, Buddy
AL batting ldr 10-6, 926D3
Wins Golden Glove Award 12-6, 926D1
BELL, Eric
Resigns 3-26, 276B1
Forgn bank debt accord reached 4-15, 314F2
BELL, Griffin Boyette
Vesco grand jury ends 4-1, 251D3
Scores Sovts at CSCE conf 11-13, 863C1
BELL, Ricky
NFL '79 rushing ldr 1-5, 8E3
BELLAND, Bruce
Quick Change opens 10-30, 892D3
BELL Canada
Interconnect monopoly curbed 8-5; rate hike OKd 8-12, consumer group protests 8-15, 632D3, 633A1
Monopoly charged 9-23, denied 9-24, 748G2
BELLI, Melvin
Flynn biographer suit 8-1, 639F1
BELL Laboratories—*See AMERICAN Telephone & Telegraph Co. (AT&T)*
BELLMON, Sen. Henry (R, Okla.)
Okla primary results 8-26, 682G3
Primary runoff results 9-16, 724A3
Nickles wins Sen seat 11-4, 845C3, 850B1
Estimates '81 budget deficit 11-20, 896D2
Budget reconciliatn signed 12-5, 936G1
BELLUOMINI, George
Drug links rptd under investigatn 8-21, 647B2

1976

BELMAR, Innocent
Rptd fired, runs for House seat 12-7, 925B2
BELOVA, Elena
Wins Olympic medal 7-24, 574G2
BELYAK, Konstantin N.
Named to Central Com 10-26, 839E2
BEMANANJARA, Jean
Named transport min 8-20, 926B1
BEMAYEL, Bachir
Admits camp atrocities 8-13, 618A1
BENCH, Johnny
NL wins All-Star game 7-13, 544G1
In World Series, named MVP 10-16—10-21, 815B2
BENCHLEY, Peter
Deep on best-seller list 12-5, 972E2
BENDER, Albert E.
Dies 2-16, 160C3
BENDIX Corp.
Argentina execs assassinated 1-29, 96A2
Blumenthal named Treas secy 12-14, 936C1, F2
BENEDICT, Manson
Awarded Science Medal 10-18, 858C3
BENENSON, Peter
Harrises indicted 9-29, 735E2
BENET, Jacques
Rousseaux arrested 1-8, denies link 1-15, 45B3, C3
BENHELEL, Hamdane
Named as hijacker 9-4, 662F2
BENIN, People's Republic of (formerly Dahomey)—*See also AFRICAN Development Bank, NONALIGNED Nations Movement, OAU*
Listed as 'not free' nation 1-19, 20D3
Oct '75 plotters sentncd 2-1—2-2, 404C1
Nigeria ousts UK newsman 2-16, 192A1
Togo border reopened 3-27, 372C1
At France-Africa summit 5-10—5-11, 355A3
ECOWAS rptd ratified 11-6, 974E2
UN Policy & Developments
Council member 62F2; 720C1
OKs pro-Palestine resolutn 1-26, 59G2
Waldheim warns Cncl on Leb 3-30, 226B2
Not in Timor Cncl vote 4-22, 334F3
Shuns UNFICYP extensn vote 6-16, 457C1
OKs Israel Arab land exit 6-29, 464C1
Anti-Israel resolutn withdrawn 7-14, 515F3
S Africa arms ban vetoed 10-19, 781D3
Shuns UNDOF vote 11-30, 895B2
BENITEZ, Antonio
Pol rights revoked, arrest ordrd 6-23, 520C1
Indicted 10-25, 997E1
BENITO, Maria Inmaculada
Acquitted of adultery 10-9, 909A3
BENJAMIN Jr., Adam
Defeats Madden 5-4, 323A2
Elected 11-2, 823B2, 829B3
BENJAMIN, Fred I.
Loses MD malpractice suit 6-1, 1016C3
BENKERT, Adm. William M.
On tanker grounding 12-22, 969B1
BENN, Anthony Wedgwood
Bids for prime min 3-17, withdraws 3-25, 239A2 ★
Retains Cabt post 4-8, 266D3
BP, govt to share North Sea fields 7-1, 522A1
Retains Cabt post 9-10, 693F3, 694A1
Signs Norway N Sea oil pact 9-10, 832E3
Assailed by moderate Laborites 11-16, 906C1
BENNATON Ramos, Abraham
United Brands details '74 bribe 12-10, 985E3
BENNEKOM, Pieter
Ecuador ousts 1-13, 28F2
BENNETT, Rep. Charles E. (D, Fla.)
Reelected 11-2, 829B2
BENNETT, David
Malagasy ousts 9-23, 926A1
BENNETT, Michael
Wins Tony award 4-18, 460E2
Chorus Line wins Pulitzer 5-3, 352C3
BENNETT, Gov. Robert F. (R, Kan.)
Links Butz, Carter remarks 10-3, 744D2
BENNINGTON (Vt.) College
Pres, vice pres resign 1-29, 271F3
BENOIT, Gary
Nominated for vp at Dem conv 7-15, 506B3
BENSINGER, Peter B.
DEA head 12-9-75; confrmd 2-5, 110A2
Denies US-Mex strife 6-8, 420A1
BENSON, Dr., Herbert
Relaxatn Response on best seller list 1-25, 80C3; 2-29, 208F3; 12-5, 972C2
BENSON, Lucy W.
Named Carter advisor 11-19, 881D3
BENSON, Raymond
Harrassed at US Sovt emb 4-6, 260C1
BENTSEN Jr., Sen. Lloyd M. (D, Tex.)
Gets US campaign aid 1-2, 22D3
Common Cause rpts code backing 1-9, 23A1
Miss caucus vote results 1-24, 94F3, 95A1
3d in Okla caucuses 2-7, 129E1
Ends pres bid 2-10, 129G1
Fed fund total listed 3-4, 180C3
Renominated; Carter sweeps pres delegate vote 5-1, 323A1
Lauds Carter 6-10, 432E1
Fed funds total rptd 7-1, 491A1
AMA donatn rptd 10-22, 938E3
Reelected 11-2, 820D1, 822E3, 828C3
FEC certificatns total rptd 12-31, 979F2

1977

BELORUS Machinery of U.S.A. Inc.
Sovt ownership cited 10-31, 949G1
BEN-Ami, Jacob
Dies 7-22, 604E2
BENCHLEY, Peter
Deep on best-seller list 6-4, 452B2; 7-3, 548F3
BENDER, Traugott
Baader trial adjourned 3-17, 260C1
BENDIX Corp.
Blumenthal sets up trust 2-25, 147E3
BENEDETTI, Mario
Uruguay bans books 10-17, 905A2
BENEFICIAL Corp.
Rebate rpt cited 1-5, 6E3
FTC ad dispute review refused 4-25, 342B3
BEN-Elissar, Eliahu
Named Israel Cairo conf envoy 11-28, 909E2
At Cairo conf 12-14—12-15, 953C1
BENELLI, Msgr. Giovanni
Inducted Florence archbp 6-27, 768G2
BENET, Steven Vincent (1898-1943)
FBI surveillance rptd 6-19, 481E1
BENHABYLES, Abdelmalek
Algeria justice min 4-27, 470C2
BENHAM, Dorothy
Succeeded as Miss Amer 9-10, 808A3
BENIN, People's Republic of (formerly Dahomey)—*See also NONALIGNED Nations Movement, OAU*
UN Assemb, Cncl member; Ignacio-Pinto on World Ct 3F3, 4E1, F1
Coup foiled 1-16, borders closed 1-17, 48B1
Coup attempt detailed 2-1, 2-4, UN probe set 2-8, 96C3
Morocco protests coup chrgs 2-25, 160D1
Waldheim gets UN probe rpt 3-8, 243A3
UN Cncl condemns coup try 4-14, 309A2
At France-Africa summit 4-19—4-20, 316F3
OAU mtgs boycotted 6-23—7-5, Amin cites coup plot 7-4, 512B1, A2
Bantin inducted as cardinal 6-27, 768B3
UN Cncl electns held 10-24, 852F3
UN S Africa econ, permanent arms sanctns vetoed; apartheid res OKd 10-31, 851G2
Cuba security aides rptd 11-17, 896F1
BENJAMIN, Guy
Stanford wins Sun Bowl 12-31, 1020D2
BENJAMIN, Robert S.
Replaced as Pub Broadcast chrmn 3-9, 396D3
BENJAMIN Harrison Bridge (Hopewell, Va.)
Ship hits 2-24, 204F3
BENN, Anthony Wedgwood
Shell, Exxon sign UK N Sea pact 1-5, 20F3
BENNETER, Klaus-Uwe
Ousted as SPD youth-wing head 4-27, 353E1
BENNETT Jr., Douglas J.
Named State asst secy 1-21, 53C1
Cuba prisoner rpt released 5-13, 390C1
BENNETT, John J.
Replaced as Navy asst secy 4-25, 418E1
BENNETT, Leslie J.
CIA interrogatn chrgd 11-23, 923G1
BENNETT Jr., W. Tapley
Named NATO amb 4-7, confrmd 4-25, 418C1
BENNINGTON (Vt.) College
'77-78 costs rptd 3-27, 483G1
BENNY, Jack (1894-1974)
'Rochester' Anderson dies 2-28, 164B2
BENOIST, Emil Pierre
Kills 6, self 8-26, 807A3
BEN Salah, Ahmed
Sentenced in absentia 8-20, 867E2
BENSON, Kent
In NBA draft 6-10, 584A2, D3
Punched by Abdul-Jabbar 10-18, 870F1
BENSON, Lucy Wilson
Named State undersecy 1-7, 14G1
Guatemala rejcts mil aid 3-16, 187A2
BENTES Monteiro, Gen. Euler
Leads exec pres poll 11-7, gains mil backing 12-2, 964A2
BENTON & Bowles Inc.
Sued on cereal ads 6-30, 613B2
BENTROVATO, Anthony
Kickback chrg dropped 11-11, 928D1
Reindicted 12-19, 991C3
BENTSEN Jr., Sen. Lloyd M. (D, Tex.)
'76 specl interest gifts rptd 2-15, 128D2; 3-7, 232G2
On Carter energy plan 4-20, 293F3, 294B1
Vs bank pension mgt concentratn 6-28, 578C2

1978

BELMAR, Innocent
Shot 1-4; dies, 3 suspects held 1-5, 94F2
BELSON, Jerry
'End' released 5-10, 619G1
BELUSHI, John
Animal House released 7-27, 970D2
BENAVIDES, Magda
Rpts home bombed 9-3, 775G3
BENAVIDES, Gen. Raul
Quits as Chile interior min, named defns min 4-12, 350E3
Ben BELLA, Ahmed
Boumedienne dies 12-27, 1012D2
BENCH, Johnny
Ethnic jokes upset audience 1-7, explains 1-11, 195B1
BENCHLEY, Peter
Jaws 2 released 6-16, 619E2
'Island' record film price rptd 9-1, 759E2
BENDELL, Vivian
Wins Ilford North by-electn 3-2, 167E2
BENDIX Corp.
ICAO picks US bad-weather landing system 4-19, 319C3
Ben ELIEZER, Col. Benjamin
Heads W Bank mil govt, promotn set 5-2, 340C2
Ben-ELISSAR, Eliahu
Warns Syria on Leb Christn attacks 7-6, 503B1, E1
BENES, Bernardo
Sees Castro, flies ex-prisoners to Miami 10-21, 880F2
BENESTAD, Torleaf
Indicted 4-12, 326A2
Ben-GAL, Maj. Gen. Avigdan
On Israel exit from south Leb 6-13, 462D1
BENIN, People's Republic of (formerly Dahomey)—*See also GATT, NONALIGNED Nations Movement, OAU*
6 W African natns back ECOWAS 3-18, USSR scores 3-20, 237E1
Gabon ousts workers 7-23, 596A2
UN Assemb member 713C3
Polisario recognitn cited 11-10, 999G2
BENIQUEZ, Juan
Traded to Yankees 11-10, 1026B1
BENJAMIN Jr., Rep. Adam (D, Ind.)
Reelected 11-7, 850A4
BENJAMIN, Robert S.
Resigns from United Artists 1-13, 75A3
BENNATON Ramos, Abraham
Named co-conspirator re United Brands bribe 7-19, 643G1; B2
BENNETT, Rep. Charles E. (D, Fla.)
On Flood-Eilberg probe 3-15, 240A3
Reelected 11-7, 850F2
BENNETT, James V.
Dies 11-19, 972E2
BENNETT, Gov. Robert F. (R, Kan.)
Wins renomination 8-1, 606D1
Loses reelectn 11-7, 847A1, 854E2
BENNY, Jack (1894-1974)
Noble dies 4-3, 356C3
Niece sues deprogrammer 4-7, 295D3
BENSON, Charles
Arrested in parole payoff 12-15, 1011F1
BENSON, Lucy W.
On '77 arms request rejctns 5-19, 386G3
BENTES Monteiro, Gen. Euler (ret.)
Leads Figueredo oppositn, seeks MDB support 5-29—7-9, 555F2-556A1
Magalhaes drops pres bid 8-8, 646E2
Joins MDB 8-17, pres nominatn seen 8-18, 646F2
Gets MDB pres nominatn 8-23, 671B2
Scores Abreu arrest 10-2; disillusn with MDB rptd 10-6, 771F3
Loses pres electn 10-15, 794B1
BENTON, Robert
Superman released 12-14, 1030E3
BENTRO, Anthony (Anthony Bentrovato)
Convicted in kickback case 3-25, 232C2
Sentenced 7-11, 560E2
BENTROVATO, Anthony—*See BENTRO, Anthony*
BENTSEN Jr., Sen Lloyd M. (D, Tex.)
Votes for Panama Canal neutrality pact 3-16, 177D2
Votes for 2d Canal pact 4-18, 273B1
Backs Mideast plane sales 5-15, 357D2
Personal finances rptd 5-19, 385D3
Carter backs judges merit selectn 11-8, 873B3

1979

BELMONT, Eleanor Robson
Dies 10-24, 860A2
BELOUSOVA, Ludmila
Defects to Switzerland 9-18, 721B3
Gets asylum 10-30, 939G3
BELRIDGE Oil Co.
Mobil suit fails 12-7; Shell acquires 12-10; Mobil, Texaco sue 12-11, 942D1
BELTRAN Espantoso, Pedro Gerardo
Dies 2-16, 176E2
BELUSHI, John
Old Boyfriends released 3-21, 528C3
Shame of Jungle released 9-14, 820C3
1941 released 12-14, 1008B1
BEN Bella, Ahmed
House arrest lifted 7-4, 521E3
BENCHLEY, Peter
Island on best-seller list 7-1, 548B3; 8-5, 620B3
BENDA, Vaclav
Named Charter 77 ldr 2-8, 126F3
Arrested 5-29, sentncd 10-23, 802A2
BENDER, Friedrich
Signs China pact 6-19, 637G3
BENDIX Corp.
Wage-price compliance vow unwritten 2-6, 128B1
Wins Warner & Swasey bid 12-17, 986F2
BENEATH the Valley of the Ultravixens (film)
Released 5-11, 528D1
BENEDICT, Keith
Shelley opens 4-14, 712D2
BENEDICT, Paul
Billy released 1-31, 174C2
BENEFICIAL Corp.
Credit bias suit filed 5-8, 596F1
Ben-ELIEZER, Brig. Gen. Benyamin
Nablus mayor freed 12-5, 916B3
Ben-ELISSAR, Eliahu
Egypt-Israel pact in effect 4-25, 295E2
BENENSON, Bill
Boulevard Nights released 3-22, 528E1
BENGSCH, Alfred Cardinal
Dies 12-13, 1008A2
Ben-GURION, David (1886-1973)
Rabin book rpts '48 Arab expulsn order 10-22, Allon denies 10-24, 823G1
BENIN, People's Republic of (formerly Dahomey)—*See also GATT, NONALIGNED Nations Movement, OAU*
Absent from UN rights comm votes 2-21, 148E1
UN membership listed 695E2
BENIQUEZ, Juan
Traded to Mariners 11-1, 1002C3
BENISCH, Robert G.
Argues govt minority constructn grants case in Sup Ct 11-27, 945A1
BENITEZ, Manuel (El Cordobes)
Gives command performance 7-22, 656F3
BENITEZ, Wilfredo
Decisns Palomino for WBC welterwgt title 1-14, 79A3
Decisns Weston 3-25, 412F3
Leonard TKOs for WBC welterwgt title 11-30, 1004B3
BENJAMIN, P. J.
Savara opens 2-11, 292F2
BENJAMIN, Richard
Love At First Bite released 4-12, 528G2
Scavenger Hunt released 12-25, 1008E1
BENJEDID, Col. Chadli (Algerian president)
Elected pres 2-7, 94B2
Names Cabt 3-8, 215E2
Liberalizatn moves rptd 5-11, 522A3
Lifts Ben Bella house arrest 7-4, 521E3
BENMAR Transport & Leasing Corp.
ICC order upheld by Sup Ct 10-15, 847G3
BENN, Anthony Wedgwood
Left gains at Labor Party conf 10-1—10-5, 773D1
Left to dominate Labor Party probe 10-24, 873F2-B3
BENNETT, Rep. Charles E. (D, Fla.)
Ethics Com chrmn vote delayed 1-23, 71G1
Elected Ethics Com chrmn 1-31, 87A1
Bars S Africa bribe probe 3-21, 213C2
BENNETT, Harry H.
Dies 1-4, 104F2
BENNETT, John B.
Man, Woman & Bank released 9-28, 820G1
BENNETT, W(illiam) A. C.
Dies 2-23, 176F2
BENNETT, William Richards
On resource co stock giveaway 1-11, 37F2
BENNINGTON (Vt.) College
Forgn student recruitmt abuses rptd 3-2, 167B3
BENOIT, Joan
In Boston Marathon, sets US record 4-16, 911D3
BENSON, Andrew A.
Rpts benzaldehyde cancer research 1-28, 139D1
BENSON Jr., Charles
Indicted 3-15, 309D2
BENSON, George
Wins Grammy 2-16, 336E3
BENSON, Robby
Ice Castles released 2-22, 174F2
Walk Proud released 6-15, 820F3
BENT (play)
Opens 12-2, 1007B2
BENTON, Robert
Kramer vs Kramer released 12-19, 1007F3
BENTSEN Jr., Sen. Lloyd M. (D, Tex.)
Shuns Teng 2-2, 83C3, F3
Scores Japan trade policy 5-3, 320G2
Finances disclosed 5-18, 383D2

1980

BELMONDO, Jean-Paul
Incorrigible released 3-3, 416B3
BELOGLAZOV, Anatoly
Wins Olympic medal 7-30, 624C3
BELOGLAZOV, Sergei
Wins Olympic medal 7-31, 624C3
BELRIDGE Oil Co.—*See SHELL Oil Co.*
BELSON, Jerry
Roast opens 5-8, 392G3
Smokey & the Bandit II released 8-15, 675E3
BELUSHI, John
Blues Brothers released 6-20, 675A2
BELZBERG, Hyman
Hunts' Bache shares acquired 10-21, 867B3
BELZBERG, Samuel
Hunts' Bache stock acquired 10-21, 867B3
BELZBERG, William
Hunts' Bache shares acquired 10-21, 867B3
BENACERRAF, Dr. Baruj
Wins Nobel 10-10, 889F3
BENATAR, Pat
Crimes of Passion on best-seller list 10-8, 796C3
BEN Bella, Ahmed
Freed from prison 10-30, 870E1
BENCHLEY, Peter
Island on best-seller list 4-6, 280D3
BENDES, M. Albert
Indicted 1-10, 216C1
BENDIGO Shafter (book)
Wins Amer Book Award 5-1, 692G2
BENDIX Corp.
Cunningham controversy, resignatn rptd 958D3
Warner & Swasey trust chrgs rptd setld 7-14, 917E2
Asarco shares sold back 10-29, 985F2
BENEDICT, Clive
Elected to US House 11-4, 844B4, 850G2
BENEDICTOS I (Vassilios Papadopoulos)
Dies 12-10, 1004A1
BENEFICIAL Corp.
FTC credit pact complaint setld 5-12, 703F1
BENEFICIAL National Life Insurance Co.
Fafian named pres 9-28, 959B3
BEN-ELIEZER, Brig. Gen. Binyamin
On Hebron PLO attack 5-3, 340G1
BEN-GAL, Maj. Gen. Avigdor
Meets Christn militia, UNIFIL cmdrs 4-14, 284B1
BENHAMOUDA, Boualem
Named Algeria interior min 1-13, 55G3
BENIN, People's Republic of—*See also GATT, NONALIGNED Nations, OAU*
Chad peacekeeping force arrives 1-18, 119A1
Libyan role in Chad splits OAU 12-23—12-24, 979C1
BENJAMIN Jr., Rep. Adam (D, Ind.)
Reelected 11-4, 842A4
BENJAMIN, P. J.
Charlie & Algernon opens 9-14, 892B3
BENJEDID, Col. Chadli (Algerian president)
Bouteflika ousted 1-13, 56A1
Syria says Israel plans attack 2-23, 140C3
At hard-line Arab summit 4-14—4-15, 284G2
Ben Bella freed from prison 10-30, 870F1
BENN, Anthony Wedgwood
Labor bars Trotskyist probe rpt publicatn 1-23, 79D2
Left advances at Labor Party conf 9-29—10-3, urges House of Lords abolitn 9-29, 768D2, F3
Speaks at disarmamt rally 10-26, 886G3
Foot elected Labor ldr 11-10, 872F2
Not in Labor shadow Cabt 12-4, 942E2
BENNENT, David
Tin Drum released 4-11, 416F3
BENNER, Richard
Happy Birthday Gemini released 5-2, 416A3
BENNETT, Rep. Charles E. (D, Fla.)
Seeks to broaden Abscam probe 2-3, 82A2
Abscam spec counsel hired 2-13, 143D2
House backs ethics com Abscam probe 3-27, 267B1
Ethics com asks Myers expulsn 9-24, House expels 10-2, 740B1
Reelected 11-4, 842F2
BENNETT, John C.
Dies 5-4, 448C1
BENNETT, Michelle
Marries Duvalier 5-27, 471F1
BENNETT, Robert W.
Abortn funding cases argued in Sup Ct 4-21, 306D3
BENNETT, Wallace C.
Silent Scream released 2-2, 216E3
BENNETT, William Richards
Sets uranium mining ban 2-27, 148E2
Vs Canada bill of rights 9-18, 728B2
BEN Nevis (race horse)
Wins Grand Natl Steeplechase 3-29, 448A1
BEN-Shalom, Miriam
Army reinstatmt ordered 5-20, 428A3
BENSON, John
Loses NCAA doubles tennis title 5-26, 607D1
BENSON, Robby
Die Laughing released 5-23, 675C2
Tribute released 12-13, 1003F2
BENTON, Robert
Wins Oscar 4-14, 296G1
BENTON & Bowles Inc.
FTC bike ad chrg setld 7-31, 703D1
BENTON Harbor—*See MICHIGAN*
BENTSEN Jr., Sen. Lloyd M. (D, Tex.)
Heads Dem econ task-force 6-26, 480B3
On '81 tax cut 7-1, 492C3

1976

BENZAHRA, Moussa
Spared from guillotine 8-4, 589A1
BERAS Rojas, Msgr. Octavio
Appointed cardinal 4-27, 336A2
BERBERICH, Monika
Escapes from jail 7-7, recaptured 7-21, 593D3
BERBEROGLOU, Ahmet Midhat
Loses Turk Cypriot pres electn 6-20, 457A1
BERCEANU, Gheorge
Wins Olympic medal 7-24, 576F2
BERDICHEVSKY, Gen. Jose
'75 plot vs Pinochet rptd 1-9, 47F1
BERENGER, Paul
Party wins electns 12-20, 1013F1
BERG, Harold E.
Getty Oil Co pres 7-9, 680G2
BERG, John
Paris paper links to CIA 1-13, 49F3
BERGE Istra (Norwegian freighter)
Lost at sea 1-19, 79D3
BERGEN, Michael
Paris paper links to CIA 1-13, 49F3
BERGER, Helga
Seized as E Ger spy 5-14, 383D1
BERGER, Marilyn
On pres debate panel 10-15, 782B3
BERGER, Moise
Resigns as prosecutor 7-6, 859A3
BERGER, Thomas
NW gas pipe hearings end 11-17, 998D2
BERGLAND, Rep. Bob (D, Minn.)
Reelected 11-2, 829G4
Named Agri secy 12-20, 956F1
Photo 956C2
Biog sketch 957E1
BERGMAN, Bernard
Blumenthal case dismissed 4-13, 271C1
BERGMAN, Ingmar
Hospitalized 2-3, chrgs dropped 3-24, 271C3 ★
Quits Sweden 4-22, 368C3
BERGONETTI, Carlos Antonio
Assassinated 8-19, 672B1
BERGSTEIN, Frank D.
Indicted 2-18, stiffer penalties asked 10-5, 886E1; sentncd 11-30, 921G2
BERHANU, Maj. Bayeh
Dergue com chrmn 7-16, 674D2
BERHANU, Col. Haile
Rptd executed 7-25, 674B2
BERKELEY, Busby
Dies 3-14, 240D3
BERLE, Peter A. A.
GE signs PCB pact 9-8, 691A3
BERLIN, Dr. Leonard
Wins malpractice suit 6-1, 1016A3
BERLINGUER, Enrico
Addresses Sovt CP Cong 2-27, sees Brezhnev 3-1, 195E3
Backs entente with Christian Dems 4-10, 296E3
Urges post-electn coalitn 5-13, 352D1
Opens CP electn campaign 5-16, bars premr bid 5-28, 402F2, B3
Repeats NATO assurance, discounts Sovt threat 6-15, 446C1
Hails electn 6-21, 6-23, 445F1
At E, W Eur CP conf 6-29—6-30, 461E1
At Spain CP mtg in Rome 7-28, 753G1
On confidence vote abstentn 8-10, 624E1
Backs austerity plan 10-18, 838B2
Hails US electn results 11-3—11-4, 826E1
BERMUDA (British colony)
Davis elected Rotary pres 6-14, 484D2
Summer Olympic results 7-18—7-31, 573F3, 574E1
BERMUDA Triangle
Ship disappears 10-15, 912D1
BERNARDIN, Archbishop Joseph L.
Scores Ecuador re bishops expulsn 8-20, 692G3
Scores Carter re abortion issue 8-31, 645D2
On Ford abortn stand 9-10, 686E1
Bishops neutral in pres race 9-16, 686G1-A2
On mass absolutn 12-8, 951A2
BERNARDINO, Bishop Angelico
Scores prisoner 'suicide' 1-26, 98D1
BERNER, Arne
Sworn Finnish trade min 9-29, 750D3

1977

BEN Yahia, Mohamed
Algeria finance min 4-23, 470C2
BENZA Chacon, Capt. Manuel (ret.)
Expelled 1-8, 46A3
BENZENE
Worker exposure curbed 4-29, 345D1
BENZIDINE—*See CHEMICALS*
BERECZ, Janos
Scores Eurocommunism 7-24, 590D3
BERG 3rd, Vernon E.
Discharge upgraded 4-27, 344F1
BERGER, Helge
Sentenced in W Ger for spying 11-2, 968D2
BERGER, Raoul
Scores Sup Ct rulings 10-31, 878E3
Says House must OK Canal pacts 11-3, 912A2
BERGER, Thomas
Rpt asks gas pipeline delay 5-9, 372G1
NWT scores rpt 5-16, 389B3
BERGERAC, Michel C.
Top '76 salary rptd 5-23, 408D3
BERGERON, Andre
Force Ouvriere vs gen strike 12-1, 1012D1
BERGEROV, Pierre
Left-wing talks fail 11-9, 924C3
BERGLAND, Robert (Bob) Selmer
Sen com OKs nominatn 1-11, confrmd 1-20, 34B1, C3
GOP wins Minn seat 2-22, 128A1 ★
Rpts personal finances 2-25, 147D3
Canada wheat-price pact agreed 2-25, 158F2
Farmland fund plan withdrawn 3-11, 195C1
Hikes milk price supports 3-22, 213E3
Outlines farm proposals 3-23, 214C1
Presents food-stamp plan 4-5, 250A2
Vows USDA reform 4-14, 365D1
Tours Calif 4-14—4-18, rpts on drought conditns 4-18, 365D1, 376E3
Fla drought aid asked 6-27, 659G3
Carter cuts wheat acreage 8-29, 666C2
Proposes Minn wilderness area 9-13, 724D1
Meyer's personal lobbying halted 9-30, 773C1
Meyer resigns 10-20, 814C2
Vs disaster aid ceiling for '77 crops 10-25, 833D3
On USSR grain purchases 11-2, 948B3
BERGMAN, Ingrid
Roberto Rossellini dies 6-3, 532F3
BERGSTEN, C. Fred
Named Treas asst secy 1-18, 52E3
USSR sets 200-mi limit 3-1, 147E1
BERGSTROM, Dr. K. Sune D.
Wins Lasker Award 11-16, 927A3
BERGUS, Donald C.
Named amb to Sudan 5-13, confrmd 5-25, 499D3
BERKOWITZ, David Richard (Son of Sam)
Son of Sam sought 6-26, 532C1
Kills Moskowitz, blinds Violante 7-31, 641D3
Arrested 8-10; arraigned 8-11, indicted 8-15, pleads not guilty 8-16, 641B3
Tapes impounded 8-16, 642A1
Heller becomes atty of record 8-16, 642A1
Court-apptd MDs call insane 8-30, 848D3
Found fit for trial 10-21, 848B3
BERLINGUER, Enrico
Sees Marchais, Carrillo in Spain 3-2—3-3, 242F3
On Christian Dem-CP pact 6-29, 544E2
Addresses Sovt Central Com, parlts 11-3, 865G3
BERLIN Issue—*See GERMAN Democratic Republic—West German Relations*
BERMAN, Pandro S.
Wins Oscar 3-28, 264D1
BERMUDA (British colony)
No-confidence move fails 2-11, 4 Cabt mins resign 2-15, 374C2
UNCTAD shipping study rptd 4-17, 337E2
'73 death sentncs confrmd 5-2, 374D2
US-UK air svc pact signed 7-23, 593C1
Sharpe resigns 8-26, 675E1
Gibbons elected prime min 8-29, names Cabt 8-31, 969B3
Executns spark riots, arson 12-1—12-3; emergency declared 12-2, UK troops dispatched 12-4, 935D2
Princess Hotel fire kills 2 Amers 12-2, 935C3
UK troops exit, curfew eased 12-6, 935G3
Oppositn ldr to seek no-confidence vote 12-6, 936A1
BERNARDIN, Archbishop Joseph L.
On female ordinatn study 1-27, 119F2
Urges evangelism 11-14, succeeded as Bishops' Conf pres 11-15, 906A3, C3

1978

BENYLIN (diphenhydramamine hydrochloride)—*See MEDICINE—Drugs*
BENZ, Josef
Wins 2-man bobsled champ 2-5, 316F3
BENZENE—*See CHEMICALS*
BERAN, Josef Cardinal (1889-1969)
Tomasek named church ldr 1-10, 17D3
BERARDI, Rosario
Slain 3-10, 191G1
Turin cop killed, Brigades gunman captured 4-11, 329D3
BERARDINO, Tito
Shot 5-12, 393F2
BERBERICH, Monika
Sentenced 4-27, 354A1
BERE, James F.
Borg-Warner, Firestone to merge 11-28, 935F1
BEREMENYI, Geza
Rain & Shine released 12-21, 1030D3
BERENSON, Stephan
Dead End opens 5-4, 760A2
BEREUTER, Douglas K.
Wins US House seat 11-7, 851E2, 854G3
BERG 3rd, Vernon E.
Navy dischrg held unfair, review ordrd 12-6, 960B2
BERGEN, Candice
Oliver's Story released 12-14, 1030C3
BERGEN, Edgar
Noble dies 4-3, 356C3
Dies 9-30, 777E3
BERGER, Thomas
Rpt asks pipeline monitoring agency 1-12, 130E1
BERGLAND, Robert (Bob) Selmer
Tours Westn states 1-9—1-13, 34E1
Farmers meet in DC 1-20, Sen testimony 1-24, 163C2-F2
Sadat asks for US food 2-6, 77G2
Pelted on farm tour 2-21, 163E2
Seeks food-stamp cut-off to striking miners 3-10, 182D2
Farmers occupy USDA 3-16, 219F1
Vs Sen farm aid bill 3-21, 218F3
Presents Carter farm aid plan; denies Sen bill 'derailmt' bid, links food price rise 3-29, 218D1-D2, E2
Opposes farm bill 4-6, 261D2
Carter denies rift 4-11, 260G3
On Carter strategy session 4-26, 306B3
Haskell scores 5-2, 342B2
Farm bill clears Cong 5-4, 343C1
Begins USSR grain tour 5-9, 499D2
On meat import quota hike 6-8, 428F2
Ends 10-day China visit 11-14, 902A1
BERGMAN, Bernard
Sentenced for bribery 2-2, 232F3
BERGMAN, Ingmar
Serpent's Egg released 1-27, Little Night Music 3-7, Summer Paradise 3-11, 619A3, F3, 620A1
Autumn Sonata released 10-8, 969B3
BERGMAN, Ingrid
Autumn Sonata released 10-8, 969B3
BERING Strait
USSR icebreaker reaches 6-12, 506B2
BERKELEY, Edward
Taxi Tales opens 12-29, 1031A3
BERKEY Photo Inc.
Kodak trust suit won 1-21, 67C1
Kodak trust damages awarded 3-22, 205A1
Kodak award reduced 7-3, 808E2
Kodak lawyer pleads guilty 9-21, sentncd 10-17, 808C2
BERKOWITZ, David Richard (Son of Sam)
Pleads guilty 5-8, sentenced 6-13, 500F2
BERLIN, Irving
Wins Tony 6-4, 579A3
BERLINGUER, Enrico
Backs anti-terrorism bills 3-20, 200D2
Lauds Moro; urges CP, Christian Dem rift healed 5-9, 338D1
Asks tougher party line vs Christian Dems, affirms coalitn 5-27, 454A1
BERLIN Issue—*See GERMAN Democratic Republic—West German Relations*
BERLOUIS, Ogilvy
Chrgs Kenya coup plot role 4-29, 378D3
BERMAN, David
Pins & Needles opens 7-6, 760B3
BERMAN, Jason
Perjury probe sought in Korean scandal 10-16, 832E1
BERMAN, Jerry
Lauds House curbs on natl security taps 9-7, 697B1
BERMAN, Ronald
Sees USSR air threat to NATO 1-29, 81B3
BERMUDA (British colony)
US troop presence rptd 1-2, 5E2
UK comm urges independnc, econ measures 8-2, 603E3
BERNAL Escalante, Gen. Rene (ret.)
Bolivia pres nominatn rptd 5-26, 478G2
Rptd 3d in pres vote count 7-11, 530G2
Rptd underground 7-24, 571D1
BERNARDI, Roy A.
Loses US House electn 11-7, 849B2
BERNER, T. Roland
Sees Milliken on Kennecott takeover 3-15; denunciatns exchngd 4-6—5-2, bid blocked 5-24, 402E1, D2, D3, 403A1
Curtiss-Wright, Kennecott settle 12-20, 1005A1

1979

Hackler nominatn rptd blocked 8-3, 647D1
Vs interest rate hikes 9-20, 745B2
Ben YAHIA, Mohamed Seddik
Named Algeria forgn min 3-8, 215E2
BENZ, Josef
Swiss win world 2-man bobsled title 2-18, 392E1
BENZALDEHYDE—*See MEDICINE-Drugs*
BENZECRI, Alfonso
Venez health min 3-10, 192C3
BENZOCAINE—*See MEDICINE-Drugs*
BERE, James F.
Calls off Firestone merger 4-24, 349C3
Rpts Borg-Warner elec motor-control device 10-2, 770F2
BERENBAUM, Barry
Sentncd in bank wire theft 9-24, 840C3
BERENGER, Tom
In Praise of Older Women released 2-8, 174A3
Butch & Sundance released 6-15, 819G3
BERENJIAN, Gen. Hasehm
Executed 4-13, 276D3
BERENSON, Red
Hired as Blues coach 12-10, 1004F1
BERETTA, David
Sees Kahn, wage-guide compliance urged 4-20, 344G3
BERG, Alban (1885-1935)
Complete 'Lulu' debuts in Paris 2-25, 173G3-174C1
BERG, Helene (d. 1976)
Complete 'Lulu' debuts in Paris 2-25, 174B1
BERGER, Senta
Nest of Vipers released 9-7, 820C2
BERGERON, Andre
Assails govt 8-7, 633C3
BERGLAND, Robert (Bob) Selmer
Sees no farm price support hike 2-6, 109E2
On USSR grain purchases 7-13, 568B1
Hikes USSR grain sale ceiling, US wheat acreage 8-1, 636C3
Intl sugar agrmt OKd by US Sen 11-30, 987A3
BERGMAN, Lowell
Loses libel case 4-18, 334C2
BERGMAN, Martin
Joe Tynan released 8-17, 820C3*
BERGMOSER, J. Paul
Named Chrysler pres 9-20, 700A1
BERK Co., F. W.
NJ Meadowlands cleanup ordrd 8-26, 704B2
BERKER, Feyyaz
On currency measures 8-1, 637F1
BERKEY Photo Inc.
Kodak award reversed 6-25, 517C2-A3
BERKLEY, Richard L.
Elected KC mayor 3-27, 231A3
BERKOWITZ, David Richard (Son of Sam)
Prison interview 2-22, pre-arrest evidence rptd 2-26, 156F2
BERKOWITZ, Martin
Found slain in Iran 1-15, 26D1
BERKS, Robert
Einstein sculpture unveiled 4-22, 392E2
BERLANGA Robles, Francisco
Killed by bomb 1-2, 40F1
BERLIND, Roger
Festival opens 5-7, 711A3
1940's Radio Hour opens 10-7, 956F3
BERLINGUER, Enrico
Withdraws govt support 1-26, 76F1-B2
Affirms PCI parlt oppositn role 7-3, 525A3
Gains power in CP shakeup 7-10, 525F3
Seeks talks with Soclsts 8-11, 615G1
China premr in Italy 11-3—11-6, 854E2
BERLIN Issue—*See GERMAN Democratic Republic-West German Relations*
BERMAN, Jason
Perjury probe closed 1-5, 4A3
BERMAN, Jerry J.
On FBI charter 7-31, 599B3
BERMAN, Lester
Short of Paradise released 10-5, 1008F1
BERMAN, Paul
Madman and Nun opens 1-18, 292A2
BERMUDES, Wilfredo Francisco
Arrested in Panama coup plot 10-24, 836C3
BERNAC, Pierre
Dies 10-17, 860A2
BERNAL Escalante, Gen. Rene (ret.)
Bolivia pres bid rptd 3-16, 233G2
BERNARD, Judd
Class of Miss MacMichael released 1-26, 528A2
BERNARD, Kathy
Miracle Worker opens 1-6, 292C2
BERNARD, Thelonious
Little Romance released 4-27, 820F1
BERNARDI, Herschel
Goodbye People opens 4-30, 711D3
BERNARDIN, Archbishop Joseph L.
Named to '80 Rome synod 5-3, 376A1
BERNER, Gary
Minnesota Moon opens 1-31, 292B2
BERNERO, Robert
On 3 Mile I radioactive iodine 4-8, 261E1

1980

BEN-YOSEF, Baruch
Seized as anti-Arab plotter 5-13, 362B3
BENZENE—*See CHEMICALS*
BERENDT, Lee
Denies Comex silver regulatn conflict 5-30, 425A3
BERESFORD, Bruce
Getting of Wisdom released 8-5, 675F2
BERETTA, David
On Uniroyal tire losses 1-22, 52A3
Flannery elected Uniroyal chief exec 2-22, 225A1
BEREUTER, Rep. Douglas K. (R, Neb.)
Reelected 11-4, 843E2
BERG, A. Scott
Max Perkins wins Amer Book Award 5-1, 692C2
BERG, Paul
Wins Nobel Prize 10-14, 889F2
BERGEN, Candice
Marries 9-27, 908F1
BERGEN, Edgar (1903-78)
Daughter weds 9-27, 908G1
BERGER, Helen
Denies Olympic women's gymnastics score fixing 7-24, 589E2
BERGER, Mark
Wins Oscar 4-14, 296A2
BERGER, Samuel David
Dies 2-12, 175E3
BERGESCH, Bill
Becomes Yankee gen mgr 11-21, 926G1
BERGHOF, Herbert
Charlotte opens 2-27, 392D2
BERGLAND, Robert (Bob) Selmer
Admin to buy Sovt grain contracts 1-7, 9G2
Tours la, on grain embargo 1-8, 1-9, 10E1
Grain 'diversn' paymts studied 1-18, 44G3
On dietary guidelines 2-4, 157D3
Grain 'diversn' paymt plan dropped 2-29, 168F3
Grain price support increase ordered 7-28, 575F1
US-China grain pact signed 10-22, 801A2, B3
Block criticizes 12-23, 980G1
BERGMAN, Ingmar
Marionettes released 11-7, 972F3
BERGREN, Eric
Elephant Man released 10-3, 836E2
BERKELEY (Calif.) Barb, The (newspaper)
Folds 7-3, 582E3
BERKEY Photo Inc.
Antitrust appeal refused by Sup Ct 2-19, 130F3
BERKEY Photo Inc. v. Eastman Kodak Co.
Case refused by Sup Ct 2-19, 130G3
BERKLEY, Mayor Richard L. (Kansas City, Mo.)
Fire fighters end strike 3-22, 227E3
BERKOWITZ, David Richard (Son of Sam)
Soc Sec benefits rptd 6-5; insanity plea faked 8-4, 639E2
BERLIN, Irving
Kate Smith estate feud setld 9-4, 908C2
BERLIN, Spencer H.
Watch on the Rhine opens 1-3, 136F3
Lady From Dubuque opens 1-31, 136C3
BERLIND, Roger
Lady From Dubuque opens 1-31, 136C3
BERLINGUER, Enrico
Sees French CP ldr, Sovt Afghan invasn scored 1-5, 57B3
Scores Sovt Afghan invasn, US 2-17, 134E1
PCI rejects Paris CP parley 4-2, 254F3
Visits China 4-14—4-22; renews PCI ties 4-15, vs Sovt front 4-22, 314F1, B2
At Tito funeral 5-8, 339C1
Carter sees 6-20, 474A2
Lauds govt defeat 9-27, 751C2
BERMAN, Dan
Wins US Sen primary 9-9, 700A3
Loses US Sen electn 11-4, 852D1
BERMUDA (British colony)
Olympic boycott OK rptd 2-2, 85C1
BERNAL Pereira, Gen. Waldo
Leads mil coup in Bolivia 7-17, 546A3
BERNAYS, Doris F(leishman)
Dies 7-11, 608D1

1976

BERNHARD, Prince (Bernhard Leopold Frederick Everhard Julius Coert Karel Gotfried Pieter) (Netherlands)
Lockheed payoff cited 2-6, 130F3
Cabt confrms Lockheed bribe 2-8, sets probe 2-9, 131D2
Parlt backs probe 2-10, 3-man comm opens inquiry 2-11, 131G2
Swiss lawyer denies payoff role 2-10, 131A3
Swiss OK Dutch probe 2-25, comm rpts interviews 3-5, 254G2
US data documts payoff 2-27, 254B3
Latin trip canceled 3-4, US conf 3-5, 254C3
US Sen subcom confirms payoff 3-10, 200D2
'51 Argentina bribe rptd 3-12, 254E3
Dutch press rpts Lockheed link 4-21, 322A3
Sees Den Uyl on probe rpt 8-23, 626A3
Probe rpt detailed to Parlt, resigns posts 8-26, 626F1; text excerpts 627A1, D2
Parlt votes vs prosecutn 8-30, 642C2
Pressured Schmidt on '71 jet buy 9-2, 684F2
Payoff chrgs traded in W Ger campaign 9-29, 10-1, 754C3
BERNHARDT, Sarah (1844-1923)
Adolph Zukor dies 6-10, 444A3
BERNSHTAM, Mikhail
In CSCE monitor group 5-13, 408B2
BERNSTEIN, Carl
Final Days on best-seller list 12-5, 972A2
BERNSTEIN, Carol
'72 campaign gift listed 4-25, 688D1
BERRA, Yogi
Reds win World Series 10-16—10-21, 815F3
BERRIGAN, Daniel
Begins jail term 1-19, 160F2
BERRIGAN, Philip
Begins jail term 1-19, 160F2
BERRY, Lt. Gen. Sidney B.
On West Pt cheating 5-24, 394G3, 395A1
At Sen honor code hearing 6-21, 670C3
Scores cadet defns lawyers 8-27, 670A3
BERRY & McCarthy Shipping Co.
Boycott rpt released 10-18, 786C1
BERSON, Dr. Solomon A. (deceased)
Yalow wins Lasker award 11-17, 910E3
BERT Breen's Barn (book)
Wins Natl Book Award 4-19, 292D3
BERTOLUCCI, Bernardo
Rpt Brazil offcls see banned film 8-3—8-5, 851C1
BERTRAM, Arnold
Wins Jamaica House seat 12-15, 965A2
BERTSCH, Dale
Wins Rockefeller award 11-16, 911E3
BERUBE, Yves
Named resources min 11-26, 903A3
BERUTOWICZ, Wlodzimierz
Replaced as justice min 3-27, 268G2
BESSELL, Peter
Rpt admits Thorpe coverup 5-11, 351B1; on coverup role 5-12, 364F3
BEST, Judge Hollis
Newsmen jailed 9-3—9-17, 700A3
BEST Friend (play)
Opens 10-19, 1014E3
BETACHEW Nadew, Brig. Gen.
Rptd killed 7-13, 523D3
BETANCOURT, Romulo
Opens intl soc dems mtg 5-23, 449G2
BETETA, Mario Ramon
In US talks 1-26, 75F1
On peso float 8-31, 694B2
BETHE, Hans A.
A-materials export ban urged 1-19, 115D3
Wins Neils Bohr award 5-6, 504D3
Awarded Science Medal 10-18, 858C3
BETHEA, Thomas Edward
Sentenced 7-21, 544D1
BETHLEHEM Steel Corp.
Fined 4-10, 988E3
Withdraws price hike plan 8-30, 646C3
Ford admits golf trip 9-28, 722D3
'75 zero tax paymt rptd 10-2, 847F1
Hikes prices 6% 11-29; Admin, Carter reactn 12-29—12-2, 897F2, C3

1977

BERNHARD, Prince (Bernhard Leopold Frederick Everhard Julius Coert Karel Gotfried Pieter) (Netherlands)
Boeing denies consultant 1-5, 215C3
25th Bilderberg conf 4-21—4-24, 359B3 ★
Return to pub life rptd 8-28, 986B2
BERNIER, Serge
Quebec wins WHA title, named playoff MVP 5-27, 430C1
BERNSTEIN, Carl
Final Days on best-seller list 2-6, 120G3; 3-6, 184G3
Nixon scores 5-25, 420F1, E2
Chrgs CIA press links 9-12, 720F2-721C1
BERRY, Mary F.
Named HEW asst secy 1-19, 53A1
BERRY, Lt. Gen. Sidney B.
Replacemt set, reforms planned 1-5, 41D1, G1
Replaced as West Pt dir 4-4, 354B2
BERSON, Dr. Solomon A. (1918-72)
Yalow wins Nobel Prize 10-13, 951C3
BERTOLACCINI, Silvia
Wins Colgate Far East tourn 11-13, 951E1
BERTOLUCCI, Paolo
Wins German Intl 5-15, 431B1
Australia wins Davis Cup 12-4, 970E2
BERTRAM, Byron
Borg wins Wimbledon 7-2, 548E1
BETA-Blockers—*See MEDICINE—Drugs*
BETANCOURT, Argenis
Arrest rptd 10-13, 867E3
BETANCOURT, Carlos
Brother rptd arrested 10-13; leads rural attack 10-26, 867E3
BETANCOURT, Romulo
Protests Videla visit 5-20, 547D2
Urges big AD primary turnout 7-17, 566F1
Ottolina pres bid backing rptd 8-26, 674D2
BETANCUR, Belisario
Conservative pres nod seen 7-25, 727D2
BETHE, Hans A.
Says A-energy 'necessity' 5-9, 403D1
Endorses A-power 11-16, 936G3
BETHEL, Phillip M.
Bahamas transport min 7-29, 675D1
BETHEL Baptist Church (Birmingham, Ala.)
'58 bombing suspect surrenders 9-28, 907E3
BETHLEHEM Steel Corp.
Pa coal mine fire 2-7—4-5, 396C2
Contract OKd 4-9, 273G2
Water pollutn control deadline upheld 4-18, 342A1
Prices hiked 5-12, 385C2
Johnstown flood damage rptd 7-20, 604A1
Prices hiked 7-22, 577A1
Dividend cut planned, Dow drops 7-27, 593D3
1st ½ earnings drop rptd 7-27, 612E1
Lackawanna layoffs, plant closing rptd 8-18, 9-30, 775D3
Md files water pollutn suit 9-20, settles 9-22, 762E1
Chrgs Japan, India dumping 10-17; Canada 11-3, 836C3, F3
Posts record 3d ¼ loss 10-26, 836E2
3d ¼ loss depresses business profits 10-27, 918A2
LTV, Lykes to merge 11-4, 943G2
US probes Japan, India dumping 11-22, 933B3
Supertankers collide 12-16, 999F3
Prices hiked 12-19, 1003B2
BETHLEM, Gen. Fernando Belfort
Brazil army min 10-12, 840B1

1978

BERNHARD, Prince (Bernhard Leopold Frederick Everhard Julius Coert Karel Gotfried Pieter) (Netherlands)
26th Bilderberg Conf held 4-21—4-23, 302D3
BERNHARD, Harvey
Damien released 6-8, 619D1
BERNHARD, Horst
Wins 4-man bobsled Championship 2-12, 316G3
BERNHARDT, Melvin
Da opens 3-13, 887E1
Wins Tony 6-4, 579F2
BERNSTEIN, Barry Armyan
Thank God It's Fri released 5-19, 620B1
BERNSTEIN, Robert
Scores Snepp ruling 7-7, 527B3
BERNSTEIN, Walter
Betsy released 2-9, 618C3, 620B1
BERNSTEIN, William
Resigns from United Artists 1-16, 75A3
BERRELLEZ, Robert
Accused of perjury 3-20, 206C3
US drops 3 chrgs vs Gerrity 8-18, 643C3
BERRI, Claude
First Time released 3-28, 619A2
BERRY, Bob
Hired as Kings coach 4-21, 458B3
BERRY, John
Major secrets chrgs dropped 10-23, 838A3; sentncd re other chrgs 11-17, 924E1
BERRY, John (producer)
Bad News Bears released 7-14, 969C3
BERRY, Ken
Cat From Outer Space released 6-30, 618F3
BERSTER, Kristina Katherina
Seized in US 7-16, W Ger issues arrest warrant 7-24, 577A1
3 US citizens chrgd 8-12, US asylum rptd sought 8-15, 651D3
2 US citizens plead guilty 8-28, 8-31, 725D1
BERTO, Juliet
Celine & Julie released 2-24, 618G3, 619A1
BERTOIA, Harry
Dies 11-6, 972F2
BERTOLACCINI, Silvia
2d in Far East Open 11-12, 990D2
BERTONI, Daniel
Argentina wins World Cup 6-25, 520G2
BERTRAM, Byron
Loses N Amer Zone Davis Cup matches 3-17, 3-19, 252B1
BERTUCELLI, Jean-Louis
No Time For Breakfast released 9-15, 970D2
BESNARD, Jean Marie
Bonjour Amour released 6-11, 618D3
BESSELL, Peter
Testifies at Thorpe hearing 11-20—11-21, 945A1
BESSY, Maurice
King of Hearts opens 11-22, 1031C2
BEST, Dr. Charles H.
Dies 3-31, 252D2
BEST, George
FIFA to ban 10-10, 969D2
BEST Little Whorehouse in Texas, The (play)
Opens 4-17, 760D1
BESTONSO, Ippolito
Wounded 9-29, 816G3
BETA Blockers—*See MEDICINE—Drugs*
BETANCOURT, Rev. Ivan (d. 1975)
Murderers sentenced 2-2, 194C2
BETANCOURT, Romulo
AD to control Senate 12-3, 952C3
BETANCUR, Belisario
Turbay wins Liberal pres nominatn 2-26; campaign name-calling rptd 2-28, 147D1
Scores Turbay, ends pres campaign 5-28, 413A2
Loses pres electn 6-4; disputes count, Conservatives protest 6-5—6-9; recount begins 6-11, 443E1-E2
Loses pres vote recount 6-15, concedes 6-20, Turbay scores 6-23, 629G3
BETHEA, Larry
In NFL draft 5-2, 336G2
BETHGE, Raimund
2d in 2-man bobsled champ 2-5, 316F3
BETH Israel Hospital (Boston, Mass.)
Union organizing backed by Sup Ct 6-22, 508E3
BETH Israel Hospital v. NLRB
Hosp union organizing backed by Sup Ct 6-22, 508E3
BETHLEHEM Steel Corp.
In Dow Jones indl avg 66E2
Hartford arena roof collapses 1-18, 95D3
'76 tax nonpaymt rptd 1-27, 65G2
Scores US trigger plan 2-12, 158C1
Carter sees Foy on coal strike 2-24, 122F3
Price hike undercuts US Steel, sees increases 3-31, 262F3, 263C1
Foy sees Carter, backs inflatn plan 4-20, 361G3
'77 loss cited in Fortune list 5-8, 325B3
Price hike held to 3%, Admin hails 6-12, 470B2
To expand China mine 12-4, 986F2
BETHLEM, Gen. Fernando Belfort
Discounts prison torture chrgs 2-19, 166C1
BETHUNE Jr., Edwin R.
Wins US House seat 11-7, 850C1, 855A2
BETSY, The (film)
Released 2-9, 618C3
Top-grossing film 3-1, 196A1

1979

BERNHARD, Prince (Bernhard Leopold Frederick Everhard Julius Coert Karel Gotfried) (Netherlands)
Lockheed rpts Dutch bribes 2-16, 306G1
BERNING, Susie
2d in LPGA Team tourn 9-16, 970E1
BERNISCHKE, Rolf
NFL '78 kicking ldr 1-6, 80B1
BERNSTEIN, Carl
'Brethren' publicatn stirs controversy 12-2, 988B2
BERNSTEIN, Ira
1940's Radio Hour opens 10-7, 956F3
BERNSTEIN, Robert
USSR bars re book fair 8-23, 689F3
BERNSTEIN, Theodore M.
Dies 6-27, 508D2
BERNSTEIN, Walter
Almost Perfect Affair released 4-26, 528B1
Yanks released 9-19, 820G3
BERRELLEZ, Robert
US drops perjury chrgs 2-8, 88C1
US drops chrgs vs Gerrity 3-7, 188A2
BERRY, Chuck
Pleads guilty to '73 tax evasn 6-12, 527A3; sentncd 7-10, 656D2
BERRY, Clayton
Table Settings opens 3-23, 712G2
BERRY, David
GR Point opens 4-16, 711E3
BERSTER, Kristina Katherina
Sentenced 2-7, release set 2-23, 119F2
Returns to W Ger 11-1, 998F3
BERTELL, Rosalie
Scores 3 Mile I A-accident 4-7, 261C1
BERTI, Humberto Calderon
Elected OPEC pres 12-20, 977A2
BERTOLACCINI, Silvia
2d in Rail Charity Classic 9-3, Mixed Team tourn 12-9, 969D3, 970C1
BERTOLUCCI, Giovanni
Innocent released 1-11, 174G2
Stay As You Are released 12-21, 1008G1
BERTOLUCCI, Paolo
US wins Davis Cup 12-16, 1003A3
BERYLLIUM
H-bomb letter, diagram cites 9-16, 9-18, 715E3-716F2, 717G1
BESSELL, Peter
Thorpe acquitted 6-22, 486B1
BEST, George
Suspensn lifted 3-28, 655C2
BEST of Earth, Wind and Fire Vol. 1 (recording)
On best-seller list 1-10, 80F3
BETELGEUSE (French tanker)
Sinks, 50 killed 1-8, 201C1
Oil loss rptd 8-15, 608F1
BETHE, Hans
Cited in H-bomb letter 9-16, 9-18, 715G2-A3, 717E1
BETHESDA (Md.) Naval Hospital
Sen Talmadge admitted 1-22, 176E1
Powell surgery 3-15, tumor rptd benign 3-22, 231A2
Rep Bolling admitted 6-25, 527A3
Brennan confined 9-10—9-13, 744F3
Marshall admitted 10-17, 848G2
BETH Israel Hospital (Boston, Mass.)
Cancer linked to genetic defect 9-13, 735B2
BETHLEHEM Steel Corp.
In Dow Jones indl avg 72E1
US Steel cites undercutting 7-2, 942C1
Wheeling-Pittsburgh fed aid scored 8-28, 682A1
'77 3d 1/4 loss cited 10-30, 845G3
BETSY, The (film)
Allied Artists files bankruptcy 4-4, 431A1

1980

BERNHARDT, Melvin
Hide & Seek opens 5-4, 392B3
BERNSTEIN, Ira
Roast opens 5-8, 392G3
BERNSTEIN, Leonard
West Side Story opens 2-14, 136G3
BERNSTEIN, Walter
Little Miss Marker released 3-21, 216C3
BERRIOS Martinez, Ruben
Loses PR gov electn 11-4, 852E3
Romero declared winner in recount 12-18, 988A2
BERRY, William W.
On N Anna 4 A-plant cancellatn 11-25, 961B2
BERTELLI, Carlo
On 'Last Supper' fresco crack 6-16, 472G3
BERTOLINI, Pierre
Separatists take captive 1-6, release rptd 1-14, 58C1, A2
BERTOLUCCI, Paolo
Loses Italian Indoor 11-23, 947F2
Czechs win Davis Cup 12-7, 946E3
BERTRAND, Robert
Chrgs Bell Canada monopoly 9-23, 748G2
BERUBE, Yves
On asbestos co purchase 5-8, 371E3-G3
BEST, David
Wins Fla US House primary 9-9, 700B2
Loses US House electn 11-4, 849E2
BEST Boy (film)
Wins Oscar 4-14, 296A2
BEST Sellers—*See LITERATURE--Best Sellers*
BETANCOURT, Armando
USF wins NCAA soccer title 12-14, 1001D3
BETANCOURT de Liski, Regina
Sees Colombia by-electn win; elected 3-9, 181A1, 231G2
BETANCUR, Belisario
Leftists ask Panama mtg 4-19, 311G2
BETHEL Baptist Church (Birmingham, Ala.)
Stoner convicted, sentncd 5-14, 405B1
BETHLEHEM Steel Corp.
In Dow Jones indl avg 76E1
Trautlein named chairman 1-31, 224F3
W Va miners strike 2-21—3-3, 170A1
Foy warns vs dumping 2-28, 204G2
USW contract settled 4-15, 289A2
Cort dies 5-25, 448D1
Prices cut 7-1, 575F2
Bribe case guilty pleas 7-24, 8-7, 600E1, A2
Bribe case fines set 8-25, 957E3
Trautlein on Carter econ renewal plan 8-28, 663B3
Ex-offcl sentenced 10-27, says bribes 'condoned', civil suit ruling rptd 12-8, 957F3, 958B2
BETHLEMI, Idilefonso
Limon KOs for WBC super featherwgt title 12-11, 1001B1
BETHUNE Jr., Rep. Edwin R. (R, Ark.)
Reelected 11-4, 842C1

1976

BETTENDORF, Ia.—*See IOWA*
BETTMAN, Gilbert
Sentences 2 Ohio police 7-6, 524D1
BEULLAC, Christian
Named labor min 8-27, 650E3, G3
Defends Parisien Libere raid 12-6, 964C1
BEVERAGES—*See also ALCOHOLIC Beverages*
FDA bans Red #2 dye 1-19, 44D2
Plastic bottles challenged 4-21, 308A2
4 states vote on container deposits 11-2, 821D1, 823F2, 824F1, 825B3
BEVILL, Rep. Tom (D, Ala.)
Reelected 11-2, 828G2
BEYEN, Johan Willem
Dies 4-29, 368E2
BEYENE, Lt. Seleshi
Rptd executed 8-12, 674C2
BEYER, Richard K.
Sentenced 7-6, 524D1
BEYER, Udo
Wins Olympic medal 7-24, 575F3
BHAGAT, Bali Ram
Gandhi backs rights curbs 1-5, 28F3
BHARGAVA, G. S.
Loses press certificatn 2-14, 139C3
BHASHANI, Abud Hamid
Dies 11-17, 970B1
BHASHANI, Maulana Abdu Hamid Kha
Leads dam protest 5-16—5-17, 365G1
BHUTAN—*See also NONALIGNED Nations Movement*
Listed as 'partly free' 1-19, 20C3

BHUTTO, Zulfikar Alli
In Canada A-talks 2-23—2-25, 175A1
Says IAEA OKs French A-plant sale 2-25, 175C1
Seeks India ties 3-27, Gandhi OKs talks 4-11, 278E2
Signs Iran, Turk econ pact 4-22, 298A2
Sees Mao in China 5-27, 439D2
In US talks on French A-plant 8-8—8-9, 581A3
Frees Khan from jail 8-28, 679B2
Regrets Mao death 9-9, 657E2

1977

BETTANIN, Leonardo
Killed 1-1, 16D3
BETTELHEIM, Bruno
Scores Califano on quotas 3-31, 235E2
Wins Natl Book Award 4-11, 355A2
BETTIS, Tom
Named interim Chiefs coach 10-31, fired 12-19, 1020A2
BEUCLER, Jean-Jacques
Named war vets min 9-26, 744G2
BEULLAC, Christian
Named labor min 3-30, 239G1
BEVAN, David C.
Acquitted 3-11, 491E3
BEVERAGES—*See also ALCOHOLIC Beverages*
Pepsico's Pizza Hut takeover cited in table 880G1
US, Canada set saccharin ban 3-9; reactn 3-9—3-11, 176D3-177B2
Coca-Cola rpts forgn paymts 4-1, 503F2
US denies Zaire aid request 4-21, 317C3
Environmentalists urge bottle deposits 4-21, 320B2
Coca-Cola Bottling of LA OKs NW takeover 10-17, 880A2
BEVERLY, Trazana
Wins Tony 6-5, 452D1
BEVERLY Hills Supper Club (Southgate, Ky.)
Fire kills 161 5-28, 429D2
Fire laid to wiring 6-10, 740A1
Death toll rises 6-12—7-29, damage suits rptd 7-29, 740B1
BEVILACQUA, Joaquim
Scores forgn publicatn censorship 5-28, 524D3
BHAKTIVENDANTA, A. C. (Swami Prabhupada)
Dies 11-14, 952C2
BHUSHAN, Shanti
India law min 3-26, 240B1
BHUTAN—*See also NONALIGNED Nations Movement*
UN Assemb member 3G3
BHUTTO, Benazir
Vs father's jailing 9-28, arrested 9-29, 765E2
BHUTTO, Nusrat
Heads People's Party 765F2
Husband's petitn overturned 9-25, 765B3
Govt seizes trust 10-17, 885G2
Ct upholds husband's detentn 11-10, 885E2
Govt returns newspaper 12-6, 968A1
BHUTTO, Zulfikar Ali (Pakistan prime minister; ousted July 5, 1977)
Proposes agrarian reforms 1-7, 24D2
Sets electns 1-7; 2 mins resign 1-13, 66E2
Party wins electns 3-7, 3-10; foes chrg fraud 3-8, ask resignatn 3-12, 201F1
Asks foes end boycott 3-12, 3-14, 202D1
Post-electn riots 3-16—3-22, 222G3
Foes vs peace bid 3-24, ouster rejctd 3-27, 259B1
Reelected 3-28; forms Cabt, cedes forgn post 3-30, 258A3
4 quit party 4-8; 2 ambs quit 4-13, 4-14, 305D2, F2
Followers asked to fight back 4-14, 305D2
Holds Cabt mtgs 4-15—4-16, 305C2
Ousts Hayat from Parlt 4-16, 395G1
Announces reforms 4-17, foes rejct 4-18, 305D1
Assumes emergency powers 4-21, 313A1
Meets party on crisis 4-22, 313F1
Foes plan march 4-24, govt seeks ban 313C2
Mil chiefs vow support 4-27, 313E2
Stand rptd eased 4-27, 313G2
Renews bid to PNA 4-28, 4-29, protest march blocked 4-29, 4-30, 349A1
Tribesmen join ouster drive 4-28—5-4, 349C1
Chrgs US plot 4-28, US denies 4-28, 5-3, 349E1
Sees Libya forgn min 5-4, 348E3
PNA ldrship demand resignatn 5-5, 348G3
Foes demonstrate, violence erupts 5-6—5-15, 378D2
Asks PNA ldr drop demands 5-11, 378A2
Proposes referendum 5-13, 378D1
Pir of Pagaro chrgs terrorism 5-23, 450B3
PNA talks falter 6-14—7-4, 509B2
Army overthrows, detains 7-5, 509A1
Army coup plan detailed, Zia vs trial 7-8, 544E3
Fed security force probe rptd 7-13, 545C1
Release planned 7-14, 545D1
Freed 7-28, vs martial law 7-29, 599E1
Bar group asks arrest 8-28, 707A3
Arrested for 2 murders 9-5, 3d murder hinted 9-6, 707B2, G2
Freed on bail 9-13, rearrested 9-17; followers rally, PPP plans electn strategy 9-18, 730F2
Ct to hear arrest petitn 9-20, petitn overturned 9-25, 765A3
Daughter arrested, wife warned 9-29, 765E2
Electns postponed 10-1, 765C2
Denounces emergency rule extensn 10-3, 765G2
Formally chrgd 10-11, 803C1
Vote after trial vowed 10-13, 803A1, B1
Govt seizes trust 10-17, 885G2
Ct upholds detention 11-10, 885E2
Loses court appeal 11-20, 987A1
Barred as parlt candidate 11-25, 986F3
Security force disbanded 11-30, 968A1
Newsmen strike re new Musawat mgt 12-3; govt returns Musawat to wife 12-6, 967E3

1978

BETZ, Carl
Dies 1-18, 96C1
BEULLAC, Christian
Named French educ min 4-5, 245G2
BEVACQUA, Kurt
Traded to Padres 10-25, 1026B1
BEVERAGES—*See also ALCOHOLIC Beverages*
Jan, Feb CPIs rptd 2-27, 222F1
Coca-Cola chosen for '80 USSR Olympics 3-14, Fanta deal rptd 3-16, 230C1
Coke, Pepsi bottler curbs barred 4-25, 346C1
Mar CPI rise rptd 4-28, 344G3
7-Up OKs Philip Morris takeover bid 5-15, 364F2-C3
May CPI rise rptd 6-30, 506G3
Chelsea soft drink ads halted 7-22, 941F3-942A1
Neb, Alaska voters rejct container deposits 11-7, 847B3, 854G3
Liggett to buy SC Pepsi bottler 11-16, 1005C2
BEVERLY Hills Supper Club (Southgate, Ky.)
Pulitzer awarded for '77 fire coverage 4-17, 315A2
'77 fire indictmts ruled out 8-2, 972C1
BEVILL, Rep. Tom (D, Ala.)
Reelected 11-7, 850B1
BEYCHOK, Shelly
November People opens 1-14, 760A3
BEYE, Blondin
Named Mali youth min 1-7, 75F1
BEYER, Udo
Sets shot-put mark 7-6, 692G3
BHATTACHARYA, Saroj K.
'Test-tube baby' delivered 10-3, 824E3
BHUTAN—*See also NONALIGNED Nations Movement*
UN Assemb member 713C3
BHUTTO, Benazir
Freed from detentn 1-13, 55A3
Arrested, detained, backers riot 10-4, 775C2
BHUTTO, Nusrat
Freed from detentn 1-15, 55A3
Daughter detained at home 10-4, 775D2
Ct orders freed 11-18, 925C3

BHUTTO, Zulfikar Ali
Wali Khan cleared 1-1, 8B1
Backers riot, seized 1-4, 55G2
Pak agrmt on UK compensatn rptd 1-12, 37A2
Daughter, wife freed from detentn 1-13, 1-15, 55A3
Gets death sentnc 3-18, files plea 3-25; followers riot 3-18—3-20; intl pleas vs sentnc 3-22, 228D3-229C1
Rashid arrested 4-7, 268C2
Shah warns Pak vs executn 5-19, 391G1
Moslem League men in Cabt 7-17, 559C1
Chaudhry quits as Pak pres 9-14, 740E2
Backers riot 10-2, 775A2
Denies '77 electn fraud, says Pak was near A-capability 10-5, 798E1
Pol parties curbed 10-16, newspapers 10-17, 818F2, C3
Wife ordered freed 11-18, 925C3

1979

BEVERAGES—*See also ALCOHOL*
Amer Brands acquires FDS 2-14, 132B2
Additive-safety law revisns urged 3-2, 195F1
Feb CPI costs up 3-25, 252E1
Mar CPI rise rptd 4-26, 324F3
Labor pact bargaining backed by Sup Ct 5-14, 383B2
Apr CPI rise rptd 5-25, 402E3
Yellow No 5 labeling ordrd 6-26, 571B2
Coca-Cola '84 Olympic sponsorship rptd 8-20, 798C1
Washn, O, Me deposit-bottle initiative results 11-6, 846B2, E3
Intl sugar agrmt OKd by US Sen 11-30, 987A3
BEVERLY Hills, Calif.—*See CALIFORNIA*
BEYOND the Poseidon Adventure (film)
Released 5-24, 528D1
BHUTAN—*See also NONALIGNED Nations Movement*
UN membership listed 695E2
BHUTTO, Benazir
Freed 5-28, vows pol struggle 5-29, 430D2
Chrgd 9-1, detained 10-17, 794F1
BHUTTO, Shah Mawaz
Warns vs father's executn 2-13, executn stayed 2-14, 116C2
BHUTTO, Nusrat
Heads People's Party 5-4, freed 5-28, 430E2
Detained 10-17, 794F1

BHUTTO, Zulfikar Ali
Supporters arrested 2-2, univs closed 2-5, 2-2, 116D2
Prisoner clemencies exclude 2-10, 116A3
Sons warn vs executn 2-13; Zia scorns intl pleas, executn stayed 2-14, 116G1
Clemency pleas ignored 3-29, 4-1; **executed 4-4**; protests ensue, Zia defends actn 4-4—4-5, 247A1-A2
Nepal students protest executn 4-5, 389C3
Widow heads People's Party 5-4; followers freed 5-21; daughter vows contd pol struggle 5-29, 430C2
Daughter chrgd 9-1; widow, daughter detained 10-17, 794F1

1980

BETTENHAUSEN, Gary
3d in Indy 500 5-25, 637G2
BETTS, James E.
Loses US Sen electn 11-4, 851C2
BEVERAGES—*See also ALCOHOL*
USDA 'junk food' rules rptd 1-27, 157F3
Charles Hires Jr dies 3-19, 279D3
Coca-Cola ends USSR shipmts 3-21, 259E1
Guatemala Coca-Cola plant unrest, intl protests 4-16—5-27, 463B3
Mar CPI rptd 4-22, 305C2
Coca-Cola reorganizatn rptd 5-30, 8-6, 600D2
May CPI rptd 6-24, 481B1
FDA issues caffeine warning 9-4, 726A2
Coca-Cola sets NY bottling deal 11-24, 985B2
Beatrice, Tropicana merger found illegal 11-28, 917F3
Nov CPI rptd 12-23, 983D3
US '80 orange juice futures price down 12-31, 984G3
BEVERLY, David
NFL '79 punting ldr 1-5, 8F3
BEVILL, Rep. Tom (D, Ala.)
Reelected 11-4, 842B1
BEWERSDORF, Uwe
Wins Olympic medal 2-17, 155F3
BEYER, Udo
Wins Olympic medal 7-30, 624D1
BHUTAN—*See NONALIGNED Nations*
BHUTTO, Benazir
Detentn order lifted 4-8, 336C2
BHUTTO, Nusrat
Detentn order lifted 4-8, 336C2

BHUTTO, Zulfikar Ali (1928-79)
US issues rights rpt 2-5, 87D1
Widow, daughter freed 4-8, 336C2

1976

BIAGGI, Rep. Mario (D, N.Y.)
Reelected 11-2, 830A2
BIAMBY, Pierre
Haiti interior, defense min 4-1, 267D2, G2
BIATHLON
Winter Olympic results 2-6, 2-13, 159F1
BIBBY, Jim
AL pitching ldr 10-4, 796D1
BIBEAU, Gilles
Billingualism rpt released 8-17, 637D1
BICA, Antonio
To be replaced 1-6, 11B2
BICENTENNIAL, American Revolution
French offer US gifts 1-12, 80A3
Leek wins NJ lottery 1-27, 160G2
Cong OKs Magna Carta trip 3-17, 4-5, 283G2
Rockefeller in Australia 3-30—3-31, 249F2
French pres visits US 5-17—5-22, 372E1
Spain king, queen open exhibits 6-3, 6-5, 459G2, C3
Trudeau visits Ford 6-16, 481A3
Venez: give back Panama Canal 6-22, 793C1
Operatn Sail, Intl Naval Review, other festivities, protests mark 6-26—7-5; NY harbor photo 7-4, 488C1-489D2
Queen Eliz arrives US 7-6, 489E2
Rpt Rumanian seeks US asylum 8-7, 907B3
GOP platform text cites 8-18, 608A2
Ford urges Land Heritage Act 8-31, 644E2
Mondale at NJ parade 9-11, 687F1
US team climbs Mt Everest 10-8, 876B3
Ford, Carter debate 10-22, 799G2, 800G3, 802G2
Moscow shows opens 11-11, bomb scare closes 11-17, 907F3
Moscow exhibit closes 12-13, 948A2
BICUDO, Helio
Book links death squads, army chiefs 12-26, 997G3
BIDDEFORD, Me.—*See MAINE*
BIDEGAIN, Oscar
Pol rights revoked, arrest ordrd 6-23, 520C1
BIDEN Jr., Sen. Joseph R. (D, Del.)
Questns Kissinger on Sovt policy 1-29, 88E3
Named to intelligence com 5-20, 377E1
BIDGOOD, Don
Named in grain fraud 3-11, 247D3
BIDWELL, Sidney
Seeks riot probe 8-31, 651E2
BIENKOWSKI, Wladyslaw
Police brutality chrg rptd 10-14, 966G1
BIENVENUE, Jean
Asks eased student language rules 11-2, 851C2
BIERBAUM, Karl
Pleads guilty 8-12, 988G1
BIERMANN, Wolf
Exiled 11-16; protests 11-17—11-19, 905A2
Protesters arrested, expeled 12-10—12-12, 12-26, 1001E3
BIERWIRTH, John C.
Denies Nixon bid for Grumman donatn 9-15, 979C3, E3
BIFFEN, John
Shadow cabt energy spokesman 1-15, 101B2
BIGEARD, Marcel
Resigns defense post 8-4, 588B3
BIGELOW, Gloria
Named in Getty will 6-8, 444C2
'BIG Government' Issue—*See REGULATORY Agencies (& Issues) under U.S. GOVERNMENT*
BIG Thompson River (Colo.)
Floods canyon 7-31, 595E2, G2 ★
Flood rpt issued 8-10, death toll at 138 8-22, 756A2
BILAK, Vasil
On Czech Presidium, Secretariat 4-16, 289F1, A2
BILANDIC, Michael A.
Named Chicago acting mayor 12-28, 994A1
BILGE, Col. Sinan
Pleads innocent 4-7, 298G1; acquitted 4-30, 322B3
BILLINGHAM, Jack
In World Series 10-16—10-21, 815F2
BILOXI-Gulfport South Mississippi Sun (newspaper)
Ford endorsement rptd 10-30, 827G3
BILSKI, Jean
Kills Chaine, self 5-14, 381C3
BIMINI—*See BAHAMA Islands*
BINGHAM, Rep. Jonathan Brewster (D, N.Y.)
House OKs boycott provisns 9-23, 746B2
Scores Ford re boycott legis 10-7, 786E3
Reelected 11-2, 830B2
BINGHAM, Stephen M.
San Quentin 6 verdict 8-12, 656C1
BINGHAMTON, N.Y.—*See NEW York State*
BINH, Nguyen Thi
Vows forgn oil cooperatn 5-7, 367A3
United Viet educ min 7-3, 502F3
BINOCULARS
Libya defrauded in French deal 12-25—12-30, 1006D3
BIOCHEMISTRY
Henrik Dam dies 4-17, 368E2

1977

BIA—*See U.S. GOVERNMENT—INTERIOR—Indian Affairs, Bureau of*
BIAGGI, Rep. Mario (D, N.Y.)
In South Korea 4-12, 305F3
BIAYENDA, Emile Cardinal
Killed 3-23, 220C2
Killers executed 3-26, 282A3
BIBRING, Dr. Grete L.
Dies 8-10, 696C2
BICENTENNIAL, American Revolution
Ford State of Union message 1-12, 13F1
Carter drops land funds 2-22, 125F2
BICYCLING & Bicycles
House OKs Carter energy pkg 8-5, 610C1
BIDDLE, Francis (1886-1968)
Widow dies 12-30, 1023G3
BIDDLE, Katherine C. (Katherine Garrison Chapin)
Dies 12-30, 1023G3
BIDDLE Jr., Livingston R.
Named arts endowmt chrmn 10-31, confrmd 11-4, sworn 11-30, 927F3
BID Rigging—*See ANTITRUST*
BIEGLER, John C.
Backs stronger SEC regulatn 5-10, 519B3
BIEMILLER, Andrew J.
Scores energy tax plans 5-19, 443C2
BIERMAN, Bernard W. (Bernie)
Dies 3-7, 264C2
BIERMANN, Wolf
Kirsch quits E Ger 8-29, 684D1
BIERWIRTH, John
Iran comm settlemt rptd 12-15, 978C1
'BIG Government' Issue—*See REGULATORY Agencies (& Issues) under U.S. GOVERNMENT—REGULATORY Agencies (& Issues)*
BIGGS, E. Power
Dies 3-10, 264D2
BIG Sandy River (Ky., Va.)
Floods Ky-W Va towns 4-3—4-6, 311G2
BIJEDIC, Dzemal
Dies 1-18, 48G2
Tito Egypt visit canceled 1-20, 43F3
Replaced as premr 3-15, 224A1
BIKO, Khaya
Arrested, freed 12-2, 934E1
BIKO, Solomon
Arrested, freed 12-2, 934E1
BIKO, Steven
Arrested 8-18, fast rptd 9-5, 707D3
Dies in jail 9-12; domestic, US reactn 9-13—9-15, 707C3-708D1
Death rpts vary 9-15—9-17; protests 9-18—9-19, 735B2
Vorster on death 9-16, 747C1
Buried, envoys attend 9-25, 735C3
Govt, press clash on death coverage 10-7—10-12, 804D2
Black groups banned 10-19, 803E3
Kruger on prelim autopsy rpt 10-21, 825F1
Autopsy rpt leaked 10-25, judicial inquest ordrd 10-26, 887E1
Inquest opens 10-27, testimony rptd 11-14—11-15, 887D1, C2
US House expresses concern 10-31, 852D1
Kruger confrms autopsy rpt 11-9, 887B2
Inquest clears police 12-2; US, S Africa score 12-2—12-3, 933F3
Kin arrested, freed 12-2, 934E1
BILANDIC, Mayor Michael A. (Chicago, Ill.)
Cracks down on child porno 5-20, 432D3
Sees Puerto Rican ldrs 6-6, 464D3
Elected mayor 6-7, 446B3
Greets Venez pres 7-1, 546C2
Fires accuser 11-21, 944C2
BILDERBERG Conference
25th meeting held 4-21—4-24, 359A3
BILETNIKOFF, Fred
Wins Super Bowl, named MVP 1-9, 24G3
BILLY Graham Evangelistic Association
Special fund disclosed 6-26, 731E3-732A1
Rpt filed 10-21, gift annuities OKd 10-26, 845C1
BINDER, Robert H.
Replaced in Transport post 2-10, 148E3
BING, Dave
Retires 9-26, signs with Celtics 9-28, 870A3
BINGHAM, Eula
Named Labor asst secy 3-11; confrmd 3-18, 272F2
1,100 OSHA rules to be dropped 12-5, 937D3
BINGHAM, Rep. Jonathan Brewster (D, N.Y.)
Visits Cuba 2-10, rpts 2-15, 110E1; 2-16, 180E2
BIOLOGICAL Warfare—*See CHEMICAL & Biological Warfare*
BIOLOGICS, Bureau of—*See under U.S. GOVERNMENT—FOOD & Drug Administration*

1978

BIA—*See U.S. GOVERNMENT—INTERIOR—Indian Affairs, Bureau of*
BIAGGI, Rep. Mario (D, N.Y.)
IRA link rptd scored 2-22, 289C1
Vs Turkish arms embargo end 4-5, 276F3
Reelected 11-7, 851D3
Visits Ireland re 'peace forum' 11-14, 923E1
BICYCLING & Bicycles
Merckx retires 5-18, 692C2
Smog regulatn eased 6-16, 512G2
Belgian suspended from Tour de France 7-16, Hinault wins race 7-23, 692A2
BIDEN Jr., Sen Joseph R. (D, Del.)
Carter attends fund-raiser 2-20, 123C3
Votes for Panama Canal neutrality pact 3-16, 177D2
Votes for 2d Canal pact 4-18, 273B1
On Carter secrecy rules 6-29, 508A2
Unopposed in primary 9-9, 736G1
Reelected 11-7, 848D1
BIDNE, Jim
Hopkins wins NCAA lacrosse title 5-27, 540B2
BID Rigging—*See ANTITRUST*
BIDWILL, Bill
Fires Coryell as Cardinals coach 2-10, hires Wilkinson 3-2, 171B3
BIEBER, Margarete
Dies 2-25, 196C2
BIERMANN, John
Cyprus presses chrgs 2-22, drops case 2-24, 138E2
BIERMANN, Wolf
Supporters barred from writers cong 4-26, 360C2
BIERWIRTH, John E.
Dies 4-3, 356B2
BIGELOW-Sanford, Inc.—*See SPERRY & Hutchinson*
BIG Fix, The (film)
Released 10-6, 969C3
BIGGS, Ronald Arthur
'65 prison escape cited 12-18, 1028C3
BIGGS-Davison, John
Vs Ulster troop pullout 9-19, 723B2
BIG Rock Point, Mich.—*See MICHIGAN*
BIG Wednesday (film)
Released 7-27, 969C3
BIKEL, Theodore
Inspector Gen revived 9-21, 1031A2
BIKINI Island (U.S. trust)
'54 A-test radiatn imperils residents, relocatn planned 4-12, 278C2-A3
Residents relocated to Kili 8-31, 685A3
BIKO, Steven (d. 1977)
Family sues offcls 1-3, 20A3
Amnesty Intl chrgs 20 detainee deaths 1-18, 39E1
Kruger vows detainee protectn 1-31, 92G1
Govt actn vs police barred 2-2, 92F1
Australia union blocks S African ship 4-4, 243F3
'Biko Inquest' opens in US 5-17, 760D1
Friends, family rptd arrested 9-12, 742D2
BIKO Inquest, The (play)
Opens 5-17, 760D1
BILANDIC, Mayor Michael (Chicago)
Carter host 11-2, 862B2
Chicago offcls pay hike compromise set 12-13, 957D3
BILANDZIC, Ivan
2 Croatians free Chicago emb hostages 8-17, 706C3
BILANDZIC, Stefan
2 NYC bombs defused 8-14, 706D3
2 Croatians seize W Ger emb in Chicago, ask release 8-17, 706F2
W Ger extraditn ruling protested 8-18, 706D3
W Ger rules out extraditn 9-13, 706F3
Yugo scores W Ger on extraditn 9-13, 725F1, G1 ★
US convicts 2 for W Ger emb seizure 12-1, 933B3
BILDERBERG Conference
26th meeting held 4-21—4-23, 302B3
BILINGUALISM—*See also country names*
Carter urges educ aid 3-2, 141D3
Educ progrm scored 5-9, 348F3-349A1
BILLBOARD (magazine)
Best-selling recordings listed 2-4, 116E3
BILL of Rights—*See HUMAN & Civil Rights, PRIVACY Issues; U.S. GOVERNMENT—SUPREME Court—Defendants Rights*
BILOXI, Miss.—*See MISSISSIPPI*
BILTMORE Hotel (N.Y, N.Y.)
Loews buys 5-31, 404A2
BINGHAM, Eula
Issues benzene exposure rule 2-2, 85A3
Blames grain dust for '77 blasts 3-30, eases elevator checks 7-18, 636C2, D2
On W Va scaffold collapse 6-8, 459B3, G3
928 'nuisance' rules cut 10-24, 833E3
BINGHAM, Rep. Jonathan Brewster (D, N.Y.)
India uranium sale OKd 7-12, 551E1
Reelected 11-7, 851F3
BINGHAM, Thomas
Rhodesia oil-sanctns violatn study released 9-19, 755G3
Callaghan urges Rhodesia sanctn violatns inquiry 12-15, 987A3
BIOCHEMISTRY
Electron beam specimen studies rptd 5-5, 334F3
DuVigneaud dies 12-11, 1032F2
BIOLOGICAL Warfare—*See CHEMICAL & Biological Warfare*

1979

BIA—*See U.S. GOVERNMENT-INTERIOR-Indian Affairs Bureau of*
BIAGGI, Rep. Mario (D, N.Y.)
Arms sales to Ulster police suspended 8-2, 601G3
BIANCHI, Dan
Loudspeaker opens 4-30, 712C1
BIANCHI, Kenneth A.
Gets life for Washn, Calif slayings 10-19, 10-22, 818D2
BIANCO, Gerardo
Elected Christian Dem whip 7-3, 525B3
BIBBY, Jim
In World Series 10-10—10-17, 817D1
BIBLE, The (book)
USSR smuggling rptd 3-13, 238E1
Spoof causes furor, legal moves 8-27—10-30, 859E1-E2
BICAT, Nick
Teeth 'n' Smiles opens 8-13, 712A3
BICAT, Tony
Teeth 'n' Smiles opens 8-13, 712A3
BICKHAM, Jack M.
Apple Dumpling sequel released 8-31, 819E3
BICYCLING & Bicycles
AMF to produce safety ads 7-8, 595G2
Hinault wins Tour de France 7-22, 655D2
BIDDLE, James
Announces retirement 9-12, 892C2
BIDEN Jr., Sen. Joseph R. (D, Del.)
China offers to monitor SALT 4-19, 312D1
Labor '78 campaign gifts rptd 6-13, 595E1
Co-sponsors FBI charter 7-31, 599B3
In USSR re SALT 8-28—8-30, 657F2
Sees SALT delay re Cuba troop issue 9-6, 674B1
Chrysler aid compromise set 12-19, 981G2
BIDWELL, William
Fires Wilkinson 11-28, 1001D1
BIEDENKOPF, Kurt
Secy's E Ger defectn rptd 3-13, 180A3
BIERMAN, Robert
Loses libel suit 1-17, 57A2
BIFFEN, John
UK chief Treas secy 5-5, 338G1
Defends govt spending plan 11-1, 855D2
BIG Bad Burlesque (play)
Opens 8-14, 711E1
BIKO, Steven (d. 1977)
Kruger loses justice post 6-14, 469G2
Family wins setlmt 7-27, 585E1
Atty leaves S Africa 8-10, 617F2
BILANDIC, Mayor Michael (Chicago, Ill.)
Upset in primary 2-27, 149E3-150A1
BILECKI, Zeljko
NASL goalkeeping ldr 8-12, 654G3
Whitecaps win NASL title 9-8, 775A3, B3
BILINGUALISM
Educatn progrm oppositn rptd 1-29; '68, '79 costs compared 1-30, 127G1
HEW proposes new rules 6-29, 596F3
Ann Arbor standard English teaching plan ordrd 7-12, 597B1
NY Hispanic programs ordrd 7-18, 7-20, 597C1, D1
Ann Arbor OKs 'Black English' teacher progrm 8-15, 650A3
BILL, Tony
Going in Style released 12-25, 1007D3
BILLUPS, Ouida
Homeland opens 4-16, 711F3
BILLY Graham Evangelistic Association
'77 financial rpt cited 1-17, 102E1
Funds deficit rptd 9-21, 755A3
BILLY in the Lowlands (film)
Released 1-31, 174C2
BILSON, Bruce
N Amer Irregulars released 4-12, 528B3
BINAISA, Godfrey Lukwangwa (Ugandan president)
Named Uganda pres 6-20, 488D3
Lule freed in Tanzania 7-8, 637A3
Stages OAU walkout 7-18, 552D2
Sets reward for Amin capture 8-5, 637B3
Sees Young, scores aid lack 9-19, 721D1
Shuffles Cabt 11-19, defends actn 11-22, 998G1
BINDRIM, Paul
Novelist libel case refused by Sup Ct 12-3, 964G1
BINGHAM, George Caleb (1811-79)
Church painting sold for record sum 10-25, 891G3
BINGHAM-Willamette Co.
3 Mile I A-plant pump design defended 3-28, 241D2
BINGO—*See GAMBLING*
BIOCHEMISTRY
Vitamin C anti-infectn role studied 5-5, 691D2
Obituaries
Chain, Ernst B 8-12, 671G1
Lynen, Feodor 8-8, 671G2
Rolf, Ida P 3-19, 272E3
BIOGRAPHY: A Game (play)
Opens 4-5, 711E1
BIOLOGICAL Warfare—*See CHEMICAL & Biological Warfare*

1980

BIA (Indian Affairs, Bureau of)—*See under U.S. GOVERNMENT--INTERIOR*
BIAGGI, Rep. Mario (D, N.Y.)
Reelected 11-4, 843D3
BIAGGINI, Benjamin F.
On Santa Fe, Southn Pacific merger proposal 5-15, 427D3
BIANCA, Enrico
French arrest 3-28, 255E1
BIASINI, Oddo
Italy culture min 4-4, 275G3
Plans monument preservatn 5-20, 409A1
BIATHLON
Winter Olympic results 2-16—2-22, 155D3
BIAYENDA, Emile Cardinal (d. 1977)
Pope lauds 5-5, 363F2
BIBBY, Jim
NL wins All-Star Game 7-8, 636C2
NL pitching ldr 10-6, 926G2
BIBLE, Dana
Dies 1-19, 104F1
BIBLE, The (book)
US teen reading survey rptd 1-18, 157F1
Ex-atheist apologizes in schl dispute 5-9, 471G2
Ky 10 Commandmts schl law upset by Sup Ct 11-17, 881B3, E3
BICYCLING & Bicycles
Moscow Olympic results 7-20—7-28, flag controversy 7-24, 588E1, 622E2
Zoetemelk wins Tour de France 7-20, 835D1
Benton & Bowles settles FTC ad chrg 7-31, 703E1
BIDEN Jr., Sen. Joseph R. (D, Del.)
Schmidt assures re NATO vows 451B1
BIDNE, Jim
Hopkins wins NCAA lacrosse title 5-31, 638B1
BIEBER, Owen
Named UAW vp 6-4, 457B2
BIERIA, Roman
Wins Olympic medal 7-23, 624B3
BIERMAN, Robert
Wins libel appeal 2-15, 148D3
BIERRENBACH, Flavio
Rightists' bomb threat rptd 8-27, 705B3
BIG Brothers-Big Sisters of America Inc.
Westheimer dies 12-30, 1004F3
BIGNARD, Leon Albany (Barney)
Dies 6-27, 528B1
BIG Sandy/Leather Britches (recording)
Watsons win Grammy 2-27, 296D3
BIKO, Steven
MD's probe squashed 6-29, 525C1
BILAK, Vasily
Warns Poland, hints mil interventn 10-8, 10-19, 831E1
BILANDIC, Michael A.
Byrne scores 'past admins' 1-30, 186G2
Ill non-labor picketing rights affirmed by Sup Ct 6-20, 555D2
BILBY, Judge Richard M.
Declares mistrial in Ariz alien case 7-29, 713F2
BILGIC, Sadettin
Pres impasse continues 4-10, 278B2
BILINGUALISM
Hispanic immigrants in US surveyed 5-11—5-14, 396D2
Fla voters end govt use 11-4, 847B3
BILL, Tony
My Bodyguard released 8-1, 675B3
BILLY Bishop Goes to War (play)
Opens 5-29, 756B3
BILLY Graham Evangelistic Association
TV revenues rptd 2-25, 413A2
BINAISA, Godfrey Lukwangwa (Ugandan president)
Ousts Muwanga 2-10, 125F3
Bans pol parties 5-5, ousts army chief 5-10; mil seizes power 5-11—5-14, 375B1
Olympic boycott stand reversed 5-24, 421G1
Obote scores 5-27, 446F1-A2
Obote party ousts Cabt rivals 9-17, 731C1
Obote frees 12-15, 968C3
BINDER, David
Rpts US anti-Khomeini broadcast 6-29, 490G2
BINGHAM, Eula
OSHA cancer rules set 1-16, 36C1, F1
BINGHAM, Rep. Jonathan Brewster (D, N.Y.)
Reelected 11-4, 843F3
BIOCHEMISTRY
Obituaries
Roberts, Richard 4-4, 360B3
Sisler, Frederick D 3-2, 280B2
Stein, William H 2-2, 176D3
BIOGEN, S. A.
Interferon rptd produced in lab 1-16, 62A3
BIOLOGICAL Warfare—*See CHEMICAL & Biological Warfare*

1976

BIOLOGY
Jacques Monod dies 5-31, 404D2 ★
Gorini dies 8-13, 892A3
BIOMEDICAL Research—*See 'Research' under MEDICINE*
BIRCH Society, John—*See JOHN Birch Society*
BIRD, Doug
Yankees win pennant 10-14, 796A2
BIRD, Vere
Antiguan prime min 2-18, 270D1
BIRDS—*See WILDLIFE*
BIRENBAUM, William M.
Elected Antioch Coll pres 4-12, 504F2
BIRLA, K. K.
Heads Indian Express 1-3, 73F3
BIRMINGHAM, Ala.—*See ALABAMA*
BIRMINGHAM Post-Herald (newspaper)
Ford endorsement rptd 10-30, 827F3
BIRMINGHAM Southern Railroad
Black employes win suit 1-9, 25D3
BIRNS, Justice Harold
Nixon disbarred in NY 7-8, 493F3
BIRNS, Laurence R.
On Argentine rights abuse rpt 12-19, 996A3
BIRO, Joszef
Rpts Sovt barter pact 4-1, 543A3
BIRON, Bob
Protests Norton defeat decisn 9-29, 756E2

BIRTH Control & Family Planning—*See also ABORTION*
Kistner changes view on pill 1-10, 32A2
'77 US budget proposal 1-21, 65F1
Sequentials withdrawn 2-25, 224B3
Sup Ct bars pvt hosp sterilizatn rule review 3-1, 170C1
Cath decline linked to '68 ban 3-23, 443F3
India birth-control plan set 4-16, 290B1
US Sup Ct backs Utah contraceptive rule 5-24, 393D2
US Dem platform text 6-15, 476E3
US forgn aid funds signed 6-30, 533E2
Carter urges strong family planning progrm 8-3, 564B3
India orders civil servant plan 9-6, 676E1
Laos bans birth control 9-9, 735F1
India riot deaths rptd 10-17, 10-27, 810C2
Detroit Cath mtg backs 10-21—10-23; Natl Conf vs 11-8—11-11, 859D1, G1
Moslems score India riot deaths 10-28, 837A3
World populatn growth down 10-28, 863F1
'72-74 IUD abortn deaths rptd 11-18, 931E2
Tenn bishop grants absolutn 12-5, 12-12, 951F1
BIRTHS (including pregnancy)
US infant mortality rate down 1-12, 32B1 ★
'75 US fertility rate rptd 3-5, 224F3
Sup Ct bars review of rule on husband in delivery room 4-5, 262B2
India rpts birth rate 4-16, 290E1
'20-73 data rptd 4-27, 379F3
E Ger maternity benefits extended 5-29, 417G1
Airline pregnancy bias rulings rptd 10-14, 943A3
Carter on prenatal care 10-19, 785C2
Sup Ct vs mandatory pregnancy benefits 12-7, 919G3
SC sterilizatn suit cited 12-13, 960D3
BISAGLIA, Antonio
Sworn Italy state min 7-30, 573G1
BISALLA, Maj. Gen. Iliyasu D.
Executed 3-11, 222C2, E2
Cabt shuffled 3-11, 222A3
BISCAYNE Bay, Fla.—*See FLORIDA*
BISCAYNE Bay Yacht Club (Miami, Fla.)
Exclusn of blacks, Jews upheld 4-15, 307G3
Sup Ct bars review of bias case 10-4, 766B1
BISHOP, Capt. Burk E.
Scores honor-code proceedings 8-4, 670B2
BISHOP, Carl
Firing upheld 6-10, 552D2
BISHOP, Kelly
Wins Tony award 4-18, 460E2
BISHOP, Capt. Wayman R.
At Bronson trial 6-18, 493E2
BISMARK (N.D.) Tribune (newspaper)
Ford endorsement rptd 10-30, 831F2
BITSIOS, Demetrios
Initials US pact, letters exchng on Cyprus released 4-15, 259D1, A2
Warns Sovt amb vs pol mtgs 5-16, 402G1
Debates Aegean at UN 8-12—8-13, sees Kissinger 8-14, 622D2
Plans new Turk talks 8-25, 643F2

1977

BIOLOGY
Textbook barred in Indiana 4-14, 471D3
DNA research defended 6-17, 847B1
Vladimir Timakov dies 6-21, 532F3
NSF '78 authorizatn signed 8-15, 689E1
Jean Rostand dies 9-3, 788D2
Methanogens identified as 3d life form, evolutn theory detailed 11-2, 907G3
Antarctic ice shelf penetrated 12-9, 971A3
BIOLOGY: A Search for Order in Complexity (book)
Ind ct bars PS use 4-14, 471E3
BIRCH, Charles
Urges uranium ban 1-3, 7B1
BIRD, Rose Elizabeth
Named Calif chief justice 2-12, 140C3
Confirmed 3-11, 396B3
BIRDS—*See WILDLIFE*
BIRDSALL, Judge Ben C.
Bolles suspect pleads guilty 1-15, 161B3
BIRDSONG, Otis
Houston loses NIT tourn 3-20, 262F2
In NBA draft 6-10, 584A2
BIRMINGHAM, Ala.—*See ALABAMA*
BIRNBAUM, Norman
CIA damages recommended 5-12, 423C1
BIRQADAR, Usama
Bomb blast near home 4-8, 266E3

BIRTH Control & Family Planning—*See also ABORTION*
HEW reorganizatn effected 3-9, 175B3
Birth pill-smoking risk rptd 3-29, 287E3
India eases birth curb program 4-2, 283G3
Pill warning to MDs, druggists ordrd 4-8, 355D1
RC bishops uphold ban 5-3—5-6, 375D1
DES cancer risk rptd cut 5-3, 432C1
Ireland reform legis defeated 5-5, 567B1
FDA orders IUD labeling 5-6, 431E2
Hysterectomy excesses chrgd 5-9, 732G2
Vaginal foam exempted from fluorocarbon ban 5-11, 387A2
NY contraceptive curbs voided 6-9, 501G1
6 groups score Carter abortn stand, submit plan 7-19, 786C3
'78 family planning authorizatn OKd 8-1, 689A3
US House populatn com set 9-24, 834A1
India drops forced measures 10-3, 842G2-B3
Spain contraceptive ban to end 10-25, 867B1
BIRTHS (including pregnancy)—*See also ABORTION*
Ford '78 budget proposal 1-17, 32D3
Italy dioxin deformities rptd 2-18, 135G3
Chicago DES suit filed 4-25, 431C3
Pregnant job bias rule review denied 5-16, 419B2
Mich '74 DES suit dismissed 5-16, 431F4-432B1
Pregnant women warned vs alcohol 6-1, 472E1
Teenage rates rptd high 7-19, 786E3
Luxembourg decline 7-21, tax benefits weighed 8-31, 745A3
Pregnancy provision in AT&T pact agreed 8-6, 613A3
Canada Anglicans gets euthanasia rpt 8-17, 732G1
Tris sterility danger warned 8-30, 820D2
Sterility-linked pesticide curbed 9-8, 723D2
Pregnancy benefits voted by Sen 9-16, 737G3
'76 US data rptd 9-19, 962A3
Stewardesses win pregnancy suit 10-3, 819B3
Princess Anne has son 11-14, 1021E2
Lasker Award presented 11-16, 927B3
Maternity leave seniority rights upheld 12-6, 938C2
Maternity sick-leave pay case ordrd reexamined 12-6, 938A3
BIS—*See BANK for International Settlements*
BISHOP, Cameron David
'75 bombing convictn reversed 4-5, 484E1
BISHOP, Maurice
Scores Chile-Grenada ties 10-26, 869B1
BISSELL, Richard
Dies 5-4, 452D2
BISSON, G. E.
Chrgs Pl rights violatns 7-31, 618G3
BITSIOS, Demetrios
Meets Turk forgn min 1-29, 122D2

1978

BIOLOGY
Neurotransmitter measurability rptd 334B2
Salamander magnetic orientatn rptd 1-19, 334C1
Brain protein study rptd 2-18, 334D1
Vegetable immunization rptd 3-2, 334G1
Protein spatial structure predictn rptd 3-16, 334F2
Key vision dvpt chemical rptd 4-15, 334C3
Anti-viral protein advance rptd 4-16, 334A3
Female hormone rptd in male boars 4-20, 334F3
Early mammals held nocturnal, cool-blooded 4-24, 334D3
Anti-bacterial ocean organism rptd 5-3, 335B1
Electron beam specimen studies rptd 5-5, 334F3
'Test-tube' baby born in UK 7-25, 596D3; India 10-3, 824D3
BIRCH Society, John—*See JOHN Birch Society*
BIRD, Doug
Royals lose AL pennant 10-7, 779B1
BIRD, Larry
3d in coll basketball 3-13, 272E2
In NBA draft 6-9, 457C2, F2
BIRD, Judge Rose Elizabeth
Wins voter confirmatn 11-7, 856D2
BIRDS—*See WILDLIFE*
BIRHANU Baye, Maj.
Denies USSR, Cuba troop role 1-18, 43E3
BIRKENHEAD, Susan
Working opens 5-14, 887E3
BIRMINGHAM, Ala.—*See ALABAMA*
BIRMINGHAM Medical School, University of (Great Britain)
Embryo transplant research rptd 7-25, 597B1
BIRNBAUM, Norman
CIA mail-opening damages upheld 11-9, 940D1
BIRO, Andre
Sentncd for fraud 5-31, 824C3
BIROBIDZHAN Jewish Autonomous Region—*See USSR—Republics*
BIRON, Bob
Norton named WBC champion 3-18, 211G3
BIRTH Control & Family Planning—*See also ABORTION*
Pill warning label revised for smokers 1-11, 23E2
Searle dies 1-21, 96E3
Cath views polled 3-2, 295A1
Clinic firebombings, vandalism rptd up 3-7, 5-17, 744A2
Contraceptive foams exempted from fluorocarbon ban 3-15, 186B2
Judicial immunity in sterilizatn case backed by Sup Ct 3-28, 241F2
Irish bishops ease stand vs contraceptive sales 4-5, 289A2
Cath contraceptive use rptd up 4-15, 295E1
Surgical sterilizatn rise, pill decline rptd 4-15, 598C2
Spain contraceptn bill OKd 4-26; 70% use despite ban rptd 6-23, 576F2
Mich MDs liable for vasectomy failures 5-23, 597B2
Nonprofit lawyer soliciting backed by Sup Ct 5-30, 430D2
Teen contraceptn rptd effective 6-7, 598A2
Papal policy cited 8-6, 601D1; 8-26, 658B1
Spain enacts contraceptive law 10-12, 822B2
Rubella vaccinatn costs cited 11-10, 927B3
US aid to Mex proposed 12-20, 1010E2
BIRTH Defects—*See CHILDBIRTH*
BIRTHS (including pregnancy)—*See ABORTION, CHILDBIRTH*
BISACCIA, Bob
Bistro Car opens 3-23, 887B1
BIS—*See BANK for International Settlements*
BISAGLIA, Antonio
Named Italy indus min 3-11, 191C1 ★
BISHOP, Kelly
Piano Bar opens 6-8, 887E2
BISSET, Jacqueline
Greek Tycoon released 5-12, 619D2
Great Chefs of Eur released 10-6, 970E3
BISTRO Car on the CNR, A (play)
Opens 3-23, 887A1
BISZKU, Bela
Replaced Hungary SWP admin secy 4-20, 534G1, B2
BITAT, Rabah
Algeria interim pres 12-27, 1012C3

1979

BIOLOGY
Ultraviolet impact on aging rptd 3-20, 290G1
GE, Upjohn microbe patents reaffirmed 3-29, 265F2
Big worm seen as new phylum 3-31, 290E1
Magnet-synthesizing bacteria rptd 4-8, 691C2
Dinosaur extinctn, extraterrestial event linked 5-28, 691B3
Surviving ape hybrid rptd 7-21, 692B2
GE, Upjohn microbe patents case accepted by Sup Ct 10-29, 884D1
Central nerve regeneratn studied 12-14, 1000C2
BIRCH, Patricia
Gilda Radner Live opens 8-2, 711C3
BIRD, Larry
Named top coll basketball player 3-12, 290E3
Mich State wins NCAA basketball title 3-26, 238G2, C3
Signs with Celtics 6-8, 507E2
BIRD, Judge Rose Elizabeth
Sup Ct inquiry ends 11-5, 869A2
BIRDS—*See WILDLIFE*
BIRENBAUM, William M.
Sees Antioch chngs 6-18, 482A2
BIRINYI, Michael (d. 1975)
Viet defoliant suit filed 2-1, 90C1
BIRMINGHAM, Ala.—*See ALABAMA*

BIRTH Control & Family Planning—*See also ABORTION*
Cyanamid sterilizatn suit threatnd 1-4, 56A3
Frozen sperm study rptd 1-7, 64G2
Carter budget proposals 1-22, 44A3
US retains Afghan program 2-22, 147D1
Minn Planned Parenthood funds ban upset 2-23, 310D2
Pope presents 1st encyclical 3-15, 216G3
China measures rptd 4-24, 5-1, 370D2
Ulcer drug-sperm study rptd 5-3, 354E3
Pill-hypertensn study rptd 5-7, 355F1
Ulcer drug OKd by FDA panel 6-1, 471C2
DES 'morning-after' contraceptn cited 6-28, 571B3
Prescription drug leaflets urged 6-29, 571G1
Vatican criticism of sexual ethics book rptd 8-11, 640G2
India problems rptd 8-13, 687G2
Pope in US, affirms oppositn 10-3—10-7, 758B3, 759B2, C2, G3, 760C1
Chinese efforts rptd 10-10, 789G3
BIRTHS—*See CHILDBIRTH*
BISAGLIA, Antonio
State co nominees rptd dropped 1-8, 21B1
BISHARA, Abdalla Yaccoub
US UN Amb Young met PLO rep 7-26, 605F1
On UN Palestinian res vote delay 8-24, 642E1
BISHOP, Elizabeth
Dies 10-6, 860B2
BISHOP, Jesse Walter
Executn stay denied 10-21, dies in Nev gas chamber 10-22, 817G1-F2
BISHOP, John
Winter Signs opens 3-11, 712F3
BISHOP, Maurice (Grenadan prime minister)
Leads Grenada coup; scores Gairy, vows reform 3-13, 190A3
Diplomatic overtures, recognitn rptd 3-15—3-24, 236C3, E3
Chief aides rptd 3-23, 237A1
Suspends Const, affirms Commonwealth ties 3-25, 236F3
Closes oppositin paper 10-15, 792B3
Coup plot fails 11-3, 855G3-856A1
US sets Carib policy 11-29, 960E3
BISHOP, Stephen
Wins Grammy 2-16, 336G3

1980

BIOLOGY
Upjohn microbe patents case remanded by Sup Ct 1-14, 37D1
GE microbe patents case cited 3-5, 318B1
Chicken teeth rptd grown 3-8, 415D2
Oldest life evidence rptd 4-2, 415A3
Sovt Soyuz 35 launched 4-9, 365A2
GE microbe patent upheld by Sup Ct; reactn 6-16, 452E3-453A2
Oldest fossil life forms found 6-19, 715F2
Mammoth-elephant link rptd 7-11, 715F3
Photosynthesis step rptd replicated 7-17, 715G3
Enzyme-lifespan link rptd 8-21, 716E1
Obituaries
Keeton, William 8-17, 676G1
Kendrick, Pearl 10-8, 876B2
BIONIC Woman, The (TV series)
'Bionic' trademark case declined by Sup Ct 3-31, 291D3
BIRCH, Patricia
Really Rosie opens 10-12, 892E3
BIRCH, Reg
On Aborigine exploitation 9-5, 686E2
BIRD, Larry
In NBA All-Star Game 2-3, 279B1
Named NBA top rookie 5-29, 656C3
On NBA all-league team 6-2, 656D3
BIRD, Vere (Antiguan prime minister)
Reelected 4-24, 411D3
BIRDSAIL, Judge Ben C.
Sentences Bolles killer 11-14, 926C3
BIRDSONG, Otis
NBA scoring ldr 3-30, 278C3
BIRDY (book)
Wins Amer Book Awards 5-1, 692G1, E2
BIRENDRA Bir Bikram Shah Deva, King (Nepal)
Voters back partyless govt 5-2; vows reforms 5-14, 409G3
BIRK, Roger E.
Named Merrill Lynch chrmn, chief exec 12-17, 959E1
BIRKENMEIER, Hubert
NASL goalkeeping ldr 8-24, 770D3
Cosmos win NASL title 9-21, 770E2
BIRLADEANU, Ion
Wins Olympic medal 8-2, 622C2
BIRMINGHAM—*See ALABAMA*
BIRON, Rodrigue
Quits UN, backs referendum 3-3, 230D1

BIRTH Control & Family Planning—*See also ABORTION*
Va sterilization program rptd 2-23, 158D3
Des Moines Register privacy case refused by Sup Ct 2-25, 188A1
FTC chrgs misleading suppository ads, complaint setld; '77-78 sales cited 2-28, 358F2
Pills rptd most effective 7-13, 584A2
Dem platform planks adopted 8-13, 615D1, E1
Mich contraceptive distributn case declined by Sup Ct 10-6, 782G2
Foreign Developments (including U.S. international news)
Dutch bishops affirm traditionalism 1-31, 156F3
Pope in Africa, affirms oppositn 5-2—5-10, 363F1, A3
Pope affirms traditionalism 6-1, 476F3
World Bank rpt urges human dvpt program 8-17, 628B3
RC bishops family life conf opens 9-26, ban challenged 9-29—9-30, 810D2, E2, C3
Pope in W Ger, affirms traditionalism 11-15—11-19; youth ldrs denounce 11-19, 905D1, F2
BIRTHDAY of the Infanta, The (book)
Wins Amer Book Award 5-1, 692B2
BIRTHS—*See CHILDBIRTH*
BISAGLIA, Antonio
A-dvpt go-ahead seen 1-9, 20E3
Italy industry min 4-4, 275F3
Denies oil tax evasn chrgs 10-28, 873A3
BISHARA, Abdalla Yaccoub
UN oil focus warning rptd 8-27, 643B1
BISHOP, Maurice (Grenadan prime minister)
Escapes assassinatn 6-19, calls war alert 6-20, 498B2
In Nicaragua, marks Somoza downfall 7-19, 565F2
BISHOP, Randy
Reggae opens 3-27, 392F3

1976

BITTNER, Rev. Merrill
Quits Episc Church 4-9, 755E3
BIZRI, Amin
Leb transport min 12-9, 913E2
BJELKE-Petersen, Johannes
Rptd vs PNG seabed pact 11-25, 961E3
BJOERNEBOE, Jens
Dies 5-9, 404F1
BJORK, Kaj
On bombed Cambodian town 3-6, 238B2
BLACK, Charles
Denies delegate bribe chrgs 8-16, 616E1
BLACK, Eli M.
'74 Honduras bribe detailed 12-10, 985E3
BLACK, Dr. James W.
Wins Lasker award 11-17, 910E3
BLACK Americans—*See also organization names*
Mormons void ordinatn 4-3, 951C2
Fla club exclusn upheld 4-15, 307G3
Report on women issued 4-27, 379G3
Ford Bicentennial address cites 7-5, 489A1
Justice Marshall has heart attack 7-5, 519D2
'60s natl strategy vs chrgd 8-12, 671F2
Sup Ct refuses Fla club bias case 10-4, 766A1
Farm populatn drop rptd 10-5, 833G1
Bell pvt club membership disputed 12-20—12-22, 956G2

Crime & Civil Disorders
Williams freed 1-16, 79A1
'72 Wilmington 10 convictn review denied 1-19, 43E1
Carson, 5 others acquitted 2-6, 124E1
Cleaver Defns Fund formed 2-17, 272E1
'63 Ala church bomb probe reopened 2-18, 159D3
Sup Ct curbs jury bias questioning 3-3, 219E1
4 sentncd in 'Zebra' killings 3-29, 292F3
FBI Cointelpro papers freed 4-5, 248B2
Sen intellignc com rpts student protest probes 4-28, 330F1
Rights rally in Phila 7-4, 489C1
San Quentin 6 verdict 8-12, 656B1
Cleaver freed on bail 8-13, 640C3
Detroit youth gangs disrupt concert 8-15; Hart named police chief 9-28, 776F1, C2
House sets King death probe 9-17, 728G3-729G2
H Rap Brown paroled, '68 La arms chrgs dropped 10-21, 912C3
'Scottsboro Boy' pardoned 10-25, 859G3-860B1
Sup Ct bars review of jury bias questioning rule 11-1, 867D3

1977

BITUMINOUS Coal Operators' Association (BCOA)
UMW strike begins 12-6, 937B1-E2
UMW talks break off 12-30, 1005F2
BJELKE-Petersen, Johannes
PNG border disputed 2-2, 2-7, 132F1, G1
Queensland govt wins electn 11-12, 881F2
BLACK, Douglas M.
Dies 5-15, 452D2
BLACK 4th, E. Neubold
Elected USOC 2d vp 4-29, 491A3
BLACK, Hugo (1886-1971)
LBJ '48 Sen primary plea cited 7-30, 631D2
BLACK, William Joseph
Czech rpts permit request 1-14, 83A1
BLACK & African Festival of Arts & Culture, World (Festac)
Held 1-15—2-12, 106B1
BLACK Americans
Roots makes TV history 1-23—1-30, 118D3
Ga adoptn curb review refused 6-20, 517C1
Miss Univ crowned 7-16, 808G2
'76 real family income, inflatn compared 10-3, 822A1
DAR rpts 1st black member 12-3, 1021D2
Life expectancy rptd 12-13, 962C3
Business
'76 top 100 firms rptd 6-1, 519F3
SBA aid program scored 7-6, halted 7-8, 577G2
SBA ends moratorium 11-4, 859F3
Minority contract goes to white firms 12-13, 979C1

Crime & Civil Disorders
Death penalty survey rptd 2-7, 594B3
Carter speaks to Ohio kidnaper 3-9, 178B3
Chesimard convicted, sentenced 3-25, 288B3
New Haven surveillnc abuses chrgd 5-12, 422E3
Wilmington 10 denied retrial 5-20, 531C3
'77 death row populatn rptd 6-7, 594B1
SC death penalty bill signed 6-8, 594D2
Chicago cops win Panther suit 6-21, 540E2
Newton to face murder chrgs in Calif 6-24, 531G3
Ohio KKK rally disrupted 7-4, 540E1
Bus hijacked in NY 2 slain 7-4, 568F3
NC sniper hits picnickers 9-5, 848G2
'58 Ala church bomber surrenders 9-26, '63 bomber convicted 11-18, 907G2, D3
Canada RCMP barn burning probed 10-20, 841E2; 11-1, 902C3
'73 Hanafi massacre figure acquitted 11-5, 871G2
Amnesty Intl probes US prisoners 11-5, 943A1
FBI Cointelpro papers released 11-21, 940B3
Wilmington 10 pardon sought 12-4, 943B1
Amnesty Intl chrgs US rights abuses 12-8, 956D2
Low life expectancy linked 12-13, 962C3
Dawson 5 murder chrgs dropped 12-19, 991B2

1978

BITUMINOUS Coal Operators Association (BCOA)
Coal talks resume 1-12, 62B2; **for subsequent developments, see COAL—Strike**
BITUMINOUS Contractors, Association of
Tentative pact reached 3-28, 217E1
BJELKE-Petersen, Johannes
On Queensland drought 1-15, 16B1
Queensland demonstratn ban protested 3-4, 165C2
Affirms Queensland Aborigine policy 3-22, 225B2
Reaches Aborigine land control compromise 4-11, 286F1
Brisbane protest march 10-30, 866A1, C1
BJOERK, Kjell
Kidnaped in El Salvador 8-14, ransomed 8-25, 722A2, 723F2 ★
BLACK, Eli M.
Named co-conspirator re United Brands bribe 7-19, 643A2, B2
BLACK, Karen
Capricorn One released 6-2, 618E3
BLACK Americans
Bench jokes upset audience 1-7, 195B1
Carter State of Union Message 1-19, 29C2, 30A3
Webster queried re clubs 1-30, 83A1
Black, white female consumers compared 4-12, 811G3-812D1
Rap Brown rpts conversn, name chng 6-15, 844D2
Carter sees Houston ldrs 6-24, 509F3
Black-owned farms vanishing 7-20, 811G2
Urban League conf opens 8-6, 810E3, 811B1, F1
Urban League dir scores pols, Admin 8-6, 8-8, Mondale defends Admin 8-7, 811A1, B1
'75 illegitimate births rptd 8-10, 744D1
Gallup Poll: black bias down 8-27, 811E3
CORE conv; Innis elected chrmn, dir 9-8—9-10, ex-ldrs vs 9-18, 810C1
Sickle cell trait study 9-28; test rptd 11-4, 948D1
Fire victim data rptd 10-8, 972C2
Marian Anderson honored 10-17, 844F1
Urban population growth at standstill 11-30, 943E1
Ldrs meet Carter, score budget plans 12-4, 936A3
Carter cites repression 12-6, 934C1
Kennedy, blacks score Carter budget plans 12-9, 956G1, G2
Carter commemorates King 12-9, 956C3
Carter soothes NAACP ldrs on budget plans 12-11, 980A2

Crime & Civil Disorders—*See also KING Jr., Martin Luther; for political corruption, see 'Politics & Government' in this section below*
Wilmington 10 denied convictn review 1-5, 24D2
Wilmington 10 sentences cut 1-23, Wright paroled 6-1, 560B2
Death sentencing bias rptd 3-6, 389A1
Phila radicals blockaded 3-8, surrender 5-7, 410D1-C2
CIA spying rptd 3-17, 243E2, A3 ★
Newton arrested 5-11, assault chrg dropped 7-13; convicted on gun chrg 9-28, sentncd 11-3, 971F2
5 youths sentncd in '76 NYC racial assault 5-12, 380D3
Little extradited to NC 6-9; indicted 6-18, sentenced 7-12, 560E3
KKK informant for FBI rptd agent-provocateur 7-9, 7-11; violence, cover-up probed 7-12, 527E3-528B2
KKK informant indicted in '65 Liuzzo slaying 7-20, 720D2
Ga prison racial violence 7-23, 8-16, 627G2
Phila radicals routed; cop killed, 12 chrgd 8-8, 645D1
Soledad Brother chrgd in Calif murder 8-25, 886G3
France sentncs '72 Delta hijackers 11-23, 926F3
Carter warned on urban unrest 12-4, 936A3, C3

1979

BITUMINOUS Coal Operators Association (BCOA)
UMW plans strike fund 12-13, 987B1
BIVENS v. Federal Narcotics Agents
Case cited by Sup Ct 6-5, 464D1
BJELKE-Petersen, Johannes
Offers Queensland anti-strike bill 9-4, 705E3-706A1
Warns Liberals re coalitn 9-24, 771D2
On Queensland rail electrificatn 11-12, 888C1
BJORNSTAD, Eric
Wine Untouched opens 6-22, 712F3
BLACK, Karen
In Praise of Older Women released 2-8, 174A3
Killer Fish released 12-7, 1007F3
BLACK, Noel
Man, Woman & Bank released 9-28, 820G1
BLACK Americans
Carter seeks natl holiday for King 1-14, 31G2
Urban League rpt details econ plight 1-17, 35D1-C2
Thomas named Ford Foundatn pres 1-30, 78E3
Racial attitudes surveyed 2-20, 306C3
SCLC ousts Williams 4-10, 283F1
NC PCB disposal disputed 6-5, 597D3
Carter sees ldrs at Camp David 7-6—7-11, 513F2; thanks 7-30, 608F2-609A1
Jackson ends S Africa visit, controversy spurred 8-1, 617D1-C2
Nobel awarded to economist 10-17, 858A2
Connally vs affirmative actn 11-15, NAACP scores 11-26, 982G3-983A1
'78 median family income rptd 11-24, 965F2
King holiday bill withdrawn 12-5, 945B2

Crime & Civil Disorders—*See also KING, Jr., Martin Luther; for political corruption, see 'Politics & Government' in this section below*
KKK informant's extraditn OKd 2-7, 120D1
Baltimore looting 2-18; curfew imposed 2-19—2-20, arrests rptd 2-22, 176C2
Little convictn reversed 2-27, 156B1
KKK growth, renewed activity rptd 3-15, 7-22, 11-11, 865A1
Newton murder case ends in mistrial 3-24, 239C1
Fla death penalty appeal refused by Sup Ct 3-26, 231A1
Ga wildlife refuge protesters jailed 5-4—5-10, 368E1
KKK, blacks parade, clash in Ala 5-26, 6-9; Ga 8-18; 5 slain in NC 11-3, 864C2-F3, 865E3-866G1
Attica inmate slain in racial brawl 6-3, 548G2
Fed power to void state convictns backed by Sup Ct 7-2, 558E3
Ala police slaying protested 7-20, 869C3
Phila police brutality chrgd, Rizzo calls suit political 8-13, 610G1, C2
FBI sets '70 Black Panther murder convictn probe 9-24, 886E2
Newton murder case ends in 2d mistrial, chrgs dropped 9-27, 818B3
Phoenix (Ill) mayor shot 10-16, dies 10-18, 840C2
Phila police brutality suit dismissed 10-30, 831E3
Chesimard escapes NJ prison 11-2, 953C2
Malcolm X neutralizatn plan by FBI rptd 11-5, 886A3
Black Muslims rpt harrassmt 11-24, 898B2
Death row populatn rptd 11-25, 989F3
Cleaver murder chrgs rptd dropped 12-3, 1006E1

1980

BITTON, Charlie
Meets Arafat, 3 W Bank mayors 9-25, 736E3
BIVENS v. Federal Narcotics Agents
Case cited by Sup Ct 4-22, 343G3
BJELKE-Petersen, Johannes
Defends Queensland police law 4-9, 292D2, E2
Anti-abortn bill defeated, pol impact seen 5-30, 428E2
Threatns Liberal coalitn end 6-16, 485E3
Rpts hydrogen car plans 6-22, 496E2
Queensland electns held, lauds win 11-29, 919G2
BLACK, Charles
Reagan fires as pol dir 2-26; scores 2-28, 143G1-C2
BLACK, Conrad
Thomson wins FP bid 1-11, 38A2
BLACK, Don
Endorses Reagan 9-2, 664F1
BLACK, Joe
Walk pitches Series opener 10-14, 811E2
BLACK, Robert
On malaria outbreak 5-31, 478B2, A3
BLACK, Shirley Temple
Father dies 9-30, 756F2
BLACK, Judge Susan
Orders ILA end Sovt boycott 2-1, 169F1
BLACK Agenda for the 80's, Conference on a
Held 2-29—3-2, Jackson addresses 2-29, 190C2
BLACK Americans
Urban League rpt doubts '70s progress 1-22, 94B2
King Peace Prize award rptd 1-28, 200B1
Natl conf held 2-29—3-2, 190C2
Latin immigratn attitudes polled 5-20, 396C3
NAACP conv held 6-30—7-4, 515D2
Angela Davis marries 7-5, 639A1
US proposes, withdraws racism motion at UN women's conf 7-28, 587E2

Crime & Civil Disorders
Cleaver gets 5 yrs probatn 1-3, 64E3
'58 Ala church bombing suspect extradited 1-11, 55B3
Okla shooting spurs violence 1-20, murder chrg filed 1-21, 94E1
Ex-Black Panther denied parole 2-5, 215A2
'63 Ala church bombing prosecutn rptd blocked, FBI informant '65 murder probed 2-18, 227C2
Calif killers sentenced 2-27, 238C3
KKK rallies, violence in Tenn, Calif, Ind, NC 3-15—4-26, 333E1-G1
Hines '78 rape convictn overturned 3-18, 215E2-A3
Wrightsville (Ga) rallies spur violence 4-8—4-19, FBI probe rptd 4-14, 332G3
Wichita rampage 4-22, 333F1
Phila radicals convicted in '78 murder 5-8, 414A1
2 climb Statue of Liberty in protest 5-11, 667D1
'58 Ala church bomber sentncd 5-14, 405A1
4 Miami cops acquitted in exec's '79 death 5-17, rioting erupts 5-17—5-19, 382E2
Wrightsville unrest continues 5-19, 5-22, mtg held 5-23; 18 chrgd 5-29, 460B2
Miami exec's case probed by grand jury 5-21, 401E3
Miami declared disaster area 5-22, riot death toll 5-26, 401D3
Jordan shot in Ft Wayne (Ind) 5-29, 401D2
Hooks warns re despair 5-29, 460F1-A2
Jordan visited by Carter; transferred to NY hosp 6-12, 442G1
Panther shootout retrial order declined, legal fees award voided by Sup Ct 6-2, 513A1
Carter booed in Miami 6-9, 439D1
US comm cautns re police 7-9, 519G1
Sailor convicted of sex harassmt 7-11, 598G1
Miami violence erupts again 7-15—7-17, 560A1
KKK members acquitted in Chattanooga shooting 7-22, racial disorders erupt 7-22—7-26, 575F3
Dade Cnty ex-cop indicted 7-28, 576B1
KKK assaulter convicted 10-2, 884F3
Miss police shooting protested 10-4, 884E3
Buffalo area slayings, other racial incidents prompt probe 10-13, 997C1
Mass death penalty law struck down 10-28, 868E3
Anti-KKK suit filed 11-4, 884G3

1976

Education—*For school integration and busing issues, see EDUCATION*
NAACP loses Cleveland schl constructn plea 1-6, 6C2
Sen intelligence com rpts FBI student probes 4-28, 330F1
'71-75 reading study released 9-21, 993C2

Employment—*For bias and quota issues in general, see MINORITIES*
Quotas set for Chicago police 1-5, 6A2
RR workers win suit 1-9, 25D3
Race quotas for NY principals voided 1-19, 42G1-C2
EEOC suit vs GE affirmed 1-23, 70C3
Jan jobless rate rptd 2-5, 153A1
Boston schl admins quota set 2-24, 202E3
Sup Ct bars Colo bias rule review 3-1, 170C1
Feb jobless rate rptd 3-5, 198G3
Sup Ct backs retroactive seniority 3-24, 218A2
Mar jobless rate down 4-2, 263D1
'64-75 black-white data rptd 4-27, 380B1
Black Dem caucus for full employmt bill 5-1, 5-2, 343C3
Apr jobless rate rptd 5-7, 347D2
AFSCME sues ACTION 6-2, 414C1
May jobless rate rptd 6-4, 412A3
Merrill Lynch OKs job quotas 6-4, 414F1
DC police job test upheld 6-7, 435A1
Dem platform text 6-15, 469C2
Sup Ct extends rights laws 6-25, 479C2
J P Stevens bias end ordrd 6-25, 944C1
June jobless rate rptd 7-2, 494E1
Reagan scores reverse bias bias 7-6, 490F2
Kissinger jeered 8-2, State Dept issues job data 8-3, 922G1
July jobless rate rptd 8-6, 586C3
NYC constructn union quotas ordrd 9-1, 943G3
Aug jobless rate rptd 9-3, 667A3
Fed advisory bds bias chrgd 9-17, 944F1
Ford, Carter debate 9-23, 701C1
Mondale on jobs 9-26, 725C1
Sept jobless rate rptd 10-8, 769A3
Westn Elec bias damages, quotas ordrd 10-22, 943D2
Jobless rate rptd high 11-2, study urged 11-3, 922C2
Oct jobless rate rptd 11-5, 846A2
NYC teacher-job bias chrgd 11-9, 922A1
New exam-bias rules set 11-17, 884E2
Braniff bias setlmt OKd 11-23, 943G2
Boston sued re bias 11-26, 944E1
'74 average earnings rptd 11-28, 943G1
Sup Ct refuses La HS reverse bias case 11-29, 900F3
NJ quotas barred 11-30, 943C2
Nov jobless rate rptd 12-5, 918B1

Housing
Home loan bias suits filed 4-16, 285C2
Cross-dist housing upheld 4-20, 308C2

1977

Education—*For school integration and busing issues, see EDUCATION*
Jensen AAAS honors scored 2-23, 183C3
Carter rebuts Jordan criticism 7-25, 573F1
SAT '63-77 scores drop 8-23, test critics respond 8-24, 739F1, C2
U of Ark football players suspended 12-21, bias suit dropped 12-29, 1020E2

Employment
Detroit police chrg reverse bias 1-4, 278A3
Dec '76 jobless rate rptd 1-12, 37E3
Jan jobless rate drops 2-4, 111F1
Chicago police hiring goals accepted 2-6, 279B3
Sup Ct bars NYC compensatn case review 2-28, 175C2
Cities Svc bias setlmt rptd 3-2, 279D1 *
Frontier Air bias suit rptd 3-15, 279B2
Califano backs quotas 3-17, 217B3; retracts 3-31, 235B2
Avondale accord rptd 3-21, 279C2
March jobless rate up 4-1, 252F1
Apr jobless rate rptd 5-6, 383G3
Coors OKs antibias pact, EEOC drops suit 5-9, 819D1
UAW pres for more black ldrs 5-18, 408F1
Pre-'64 seniority bias upheld 5-31, 461C2
Police, firefighters job bias chrgd in LA 6-2, NYS 9-8, NJ 10-4, 819B2, D2
May jobless rate rptd 6-3, 445C1
Hazelwood (Mo) teacher bias suit vacated 6-27, 538G3
NAACP scores Carter 6-27—6-28; Bond scores 8-15, SCLC 8-18, Meany 8-30, 702A2
GM back-pay award case refused 6-29, 557C3
La cities OK police, firefighter job quotas 6-29, 819F1-A2
Jordan scores Carter 7-24, Carter rebuts 7-25, 7-28, 573E1, A3
July jobless rate rptd 8-5, 611C3
CSA worker ordrd to pay bias suit costs 8-23, 669G3
15 ldrs meet, score Carter 8-29, 702D1
July record youth jobless rate rptd 8-31, 692C2
Aug jobless rate rptd 9-2, 692A2
Carter vows jobs actn 9-7, 702A1
House minimum wage bill scored 9-17, 758F3
Chicago police quota case review refused 10-3, 760A3
Sept jobless rate rptd 10-7, 776C3
46 Lee Way truckers win record back pay 10-11, 818G3
Detroit topic for Carter 10-21, 817A1
Oct jobless rate rptd 11-4, 858E2
Black Caucus for full employmt compromise bill 11-14, 877B1
Nov jobless rate rptd 12-3, 961C3
TVA bias suit case review refused 12-5, 939D1
Jobs stressed at Carter mtg 12-14, 960E1
Carter-Burns policy dispute cited 12-28, 1000D2

Housing
Sup Ct backs Ill restrictive suburban zoning 1-11, 15A1
Sup Ct bars review of New Castle (NY) fed land dvpt grants 1-17, 58C1
Sup Ct voids Indianapolis busing plan 1-25, 80A1
'For sale' sign ban lifted 5-2, 406G1
Jordan scores Carter 7-24, Carter rebuts 7-25, 7-28, 573E1, A3
Low life expectancy linked 12-13, 962C3

1978

Education—*For school integration and busing issues, see EDUCATION*
SC teacher tests backed by Sup Ct 1-16, 33D2
Davis joins SF State U faculty 1-26, 172B2
Ala State Univ white job bias ruled 5-1, 348B1
Bakke med schl admissn ordrd, race-based affirmative actn principle upheld by Sup Ct; reactn, opinion excerpts 6-28, 481A1-483A1, E1-487C2
Harvard admissns progrm described 483B2
'77 med, law schl enrolmt down 10-8, 811C2
Ga schl bd pol rule struck down by Sup Ct 11-28, 937F3

Employment & Business
Dec '77 jobless rate rptd 1-11, 50G3
NAACP hits Carter energy plan 1-11, 68D1
3 named for astronaut spots 1-16, 157E3
Davis joins SF State U faculty 1-26, 172B2
Jan jobless rate 2-3, 127E3
Feb jobless rate 3-10, 222A1
Jordan: youth jobless at 60% 3-15, 811B2
Mar jobless rate rptd 4-7, 262C2
Media racism scored 4-7—4-8, 419E3
Full employmt seen vote issue by black ldrs 4-10, 7-21, 568C2, F2
Low-level jobs, earnings rptd by Carnegie Corp 4-10, 811F1
Black, white women compared 4-12, 812B1
Woman qualifies as airline pilot 4-19, 420C1
Apr jobless rate rptd 5-5, 345F1
Black-white wage gap rptd narrowed 5-8, Urban League disputes, rpts black jobless hike 8-8, 810B3, F3-811A1
May jobless rate rptd 6-2, 429E2
Sup Ct '77 retroactive seniority case cited in Bakke decisn 6-28, 482F1
June jobless rate rptd 7-7, 552F2
US Steel guilty of bias 8-3, 811B3
July jobless rate rptd 8-4, 607C3
Mondale cites Admin plans 8-7, 811C1
LA mayor on jobless 8-8, 811G1
Gannett TV statn purchase set 8-20, 759G3
Aug jobless rate rptd 9-1, 679E3
Pub works minority business quota provisn upheld 9-23, 811F2
Dan River settles bias suit 9-28, 811C3
Sept jobless rate rptd 10-6, 790B3
Viet vets jobless rtpd high 10-10, 878C1
Humphrey-Hawkins bill cleared 10-15, 808A1; Carter signs 10-27, 873A2
'67-78 minority-white earnings gap rptd 10-19, 812G2
Oct jobless rate rptd 11-3, 864D3
Ldrs score Carter budget plans 12-4, 936A3
Nov jobless rate rptd 12-8, 958E1, F1
Weber reverse job-bias case accepted by Sup Ct 12-11, 980A3

Housing
Carter State of Union Message 1-19, 30G2
Widespread bias rptd 4-17, 285C2
LA mayor cites improvemt 8-8, 811G1
Gallup poll: black bias down 8-27, 811F3
CORE Arab-financed NY plan cited 9-18, 810G1
NYS redlining study finds race bias 12-7, 942G2-A3

1979

Education—*For school integration and busing issues, see EDUCATION*
'Italian Bakke case' declined by Sup Ct 4-23, 346F2
Coll enrollmt rptd up 5-12, 367C2
Carter links vote, bias 5-20, 384G2
Ann Arbor standard English teaching plan ordrd 7-12, 597B1
Fla HS literacy test voided 7-12, 785E3
Ann Arbor OKs 'Black English' teacher progrm 8-15, 650A3
Va religious schl expulsn upheld 8-23, 650A2
Woman wins Rhodes scholarship 9-9, 1005F2

Employment & Business
Dec '78 jobless rate rptd 1-14, 34C1
Urban League rpts jobless 1-17, 35E1
AT&T cleared on '73 decree 1-17, 92A2
Jan jobless rate rptd 2-2, 110D3
Racial attitudes surveyed 2-20, 307D1
Safeway firing case declined by Sup Ct 2-21, 128D3
Feb jobless rate rptd 3-8, 182C3
NYC Transit Auth ex-addict ban backed by Sup Ct 3-21, 231C2
Weber reverse bias case argued in Sup Ct 3-28, 262D3
Retroactive seniority case declined by Sup Ct 4-2, 281C2
Mar jobless rate rptd 4-6, 280B3
Apr jobless rate rptd 5-4, 362D3
Carter links jobs, vote 5-20, 384G2
May jobless rate rptd 6-1, 422D2
Sup Ct workforce data rptd 6-11, 464A2
Weber affirmative actn challenge rejctd by Sup Ct, reactn; majority opinion excerpts 6-27, 477C1-478E1
June jobless rate rptd 7-6, 516E3
Jackson scored re youth jobless 7-28, 617F1
July jobless rate rptd 8-3, 621G2
Aug jobless rate rptd 9-7, 680F3
Sept jobless rate rptd 10-5, 766C2
Carter sees affirmative action success 10-9, 767F1
Sears sued by US re bias 10-22, 885C3
Westn Elec bias case refused by Sup Ct 10-29, 884C2
Oct jobless rate rptd 11-2, 866D3
Govt constructn grants case argued in Sup Ct 11-27, 945A1
Nov jobless rate rptd 12-7, 941G1

Housing
Racial attitudes surveyed 2-20, 307E1
Racial 'steering' suits allowed by Sup Ct 4-17, 325A3
Carter links vote, bias 5-20, 384G2
Soul City support withdrawn 6-28, 665F1

Jewish Relations
Carter compares Palestinian issue, US civil rights drive 7-31; scored 8-1, 575C1
Jews, blacks seek to heal rift 8-15, 8-16, 606E1-B2; 8-19, 8-22, 624F1
SCLC meets PLO, Israeli, Jewish ldrs; backs PLO 8-21, 623F3
Jewish groups reject criticism 8-23, 661B3
Harris seeks black-Jewish reconciliatn 8-29, 661G2
Carter urges black-Jewish amity, denies Young tap 8-30, 661B2
McHenry named UN amb 8-31, 661A1
NAACP dirs meet, affirm intl role 9-8–9-9; back US-PLO talks, Israel existence 9-11, 677D1
Ga SCLC chapter honors Qaddafi 9-16, 694B3
SCLC ldrs in Leb 9-18–9-20; Israel rebuffs visit 9-20, 694F1, E2
SCLC ends Leb visit 9-21, 763C2
Young: black PLO support 'natural' 9-22, 721B2
Carter denies US Jewish pressure to oust Young 9-23, 763E2
Young: Dayan aired Terzi mtg 9-24; Young meets Dayan, absolves 9-26, 763G2
Jesse Jackson in Mideast, Israeli offcls snub; meets Arafat 9-25–10-5; PFLP scores 10-6; briefs Strauss, Saunders 10-8, 762F3
2 Jewish ldrs quit Jackson trip 9-26, 763B2

1980

Atlanta child slayings probe continues 11-6, 927C3
6 Klansmen acquitted in '79 NC slayings 11-17; US vows review, other reactn 11-17—11-18, 898D2-C3
Hines declared unfit for retrial 11-21, 927F1
Wilmington 10 convictn reversed 12-4, 940C1
Miami riots, racism linked 12-6, 963D1
Black sentncd for Miami riot role 12-11, 990A1
FBI informant cleared '65 murder 12-15, 990B1
Dade Cnty ex-cop acquitted 12-17, 989F3

Education—*See also EDUCATION--School Integration*
Young Mich State U post rptd 1-18, 199A1
Coll freshmen survey rptd 1-20, 320B1
College enrollmt rptd up 1-22, 94E2
Newton awarded PhD 6-15, 638F3
ABA backs law schl 'opportunities' 8-6, 744D1

Employment & Business
Carter asks youth training progrm 1-10, 16F2
Lee Way settles job bias suit 1-10, 17D2
Dec '79 jobless rate rptd 1-11, 33F2
US rights comm rpts jobless rate 1-15, 36D3
Urban League rpts '70s jobless hike 1-22, 94E2
Jan jobless rate rptd 2-1, 92D2
Calif dual seniority system backed by Sup Ct 2-20, 146F2-B3
Jobless rate for youths said higher 2-28, 228A3
Feb jobless rate rptd 3-7, 182D3
Mar jobless rate rptd 4-4, 263E1
Amoco settles credit bias suit 4-29, 370B3
Apr jobless rate rptd 5-2, 344A3
Sears Ala bias suit dropped 5-22, 485D1
Hooks warns re despair 5-29, 460A2
IBM sued re Md bias 6-3, 485G1
May jobless rate rptd 6-6, 437E2
Carter stresses jobs progrm 6-9, 439F1
Anderson addresses NAACP 7-1, 515A3
Govt constructn grants upheld by Sup Ct 7-2, 510C1
June jobless rate rptd 7-3, 513A3
Reagan vows jobs, business expansn 7-15, 534B1
July jobless rate rptd 8-1, 599F2
Urban League issues jobless study 8-2; conv hears pres candidates 8-3—8-6, 597B1, E2
Aug jobless rate rptd 9-5, 684A1
NY Times settles '74 bias suit 9-17, 746B3
Bush for jobs 'with dignity' 9-18, 781B1
Motorola bias suit rptd setld 9-23, 746E3
Sept jobless rate rptd 10-3, 783E2
'79 median family income rptd 10-23, 824B1
Oct jobless rate rptd 11-7, 867D1
LA settles job bias suit 11-21, 962A3
Nov jobless rate rptd 12-5, 938C1
Boston settles US job bias suit 12-5, 962B3
NAACP held liable in Miss boycott 12-10, 963C2
Bobbie Brooks '77 case setld 12-21, 988C1

Housing
'70s home owners rptd up 1-22, 92F2
Vanderbilt drops River House suit 6-12, 639G1
Integratn rptd linked to busing 11-16, 989B3

1976

Military
Angola Unita aid plea 2-3, 82C1
CORE Angola policy scored 2-10, 2-14, Farmer to quit 2-19, 163A3
Marine bias chrgd 6-4, 435A3
Manpower study scored 6-7, 454A2
Ford, Carter debate 10-22, 801G3
NAACP—*See NATIONAL Association for the Advancement of Colored People*

Obituaries
Bankhead, Dan 5-2, 368D2
Harris, Walter 8-8, 816E3
Henderson, Vivian 1-28, 124E3
Hubbard, DeHart 6-23, 524G2
Johnson, Mordecai 9-11, 716C3
Long, Herman 8-8, 816F3
McDonald, Henry 6-12, 524B3
Newman, Cecil 2-7, 160G3
Robeson, Paul 1-24, 80F3

Politics & Government
Wallace denies 'racism' chrg 1-9, 22E2
Diggs at OAU summit 1-10—1-13, 16G1
Reagan concedes budget plan flaw 1-16, 41F1
Shriver wins black support in Miss 1-24, 95A1
Black conv plans pres candidacy; 2 decline ticket 3-15—3-20, 214E2
Metcalfe wins Ill Cong primary 3-16, 196F2
Carter 'ethnic purity' remark stirs controversy 4-4—4-13, 260D2-261F2
FBI Cointelpro papers freed 4-5, 248B2
Jackson wins NY primary 4-6, 245A1
Black Caucus, Natl Urban League score Carter 4-8, 261D1
Carter backs Black Caucus-supported jobs bill 4-8, 261G1
Metcalfe tax probe dropped 4-15, 286F3
Carter addresses DC med students 4-16, 281D3
Carter wins in Pa 4-27, 305F1
Dem caucus drafts platform, hears pres candidates 4-30—5-2, 343A3, 358A1
Ala primary results 5-4, 323D2
Carter urges compensatory rights 5-4, 324E1
Noel quits Dem Platform Com 5-14, 357F3
Detroit mayor on Carter-Udall choice, cites Udall Mormon background 5-15, 357C1
Dem Platform Com hears Rev Jackson 5-20, 357E3
Dem delegate selectn bias chrgd 5-27, 413G3
Kirksey runs in Miss Sen primary 6-1, 411A2
Carter stresses commitmt 6-14, 433D1
US Dem platform text 6-15, 478C3
Black Assemb picks pres nominee 6-18, 490D3
Dems plan '80 conv rules 6-20, 451A2
Carter sees NY Dems 6-23, 452E1
Pa Dem delegate tiff setld 6-29, 490A1
Gibson heads Mayors Conf 7-1, 493B1
Jordan Dem conv keynoter 7-12, 508D1
Carter resolves conv issues 7-12, 513E1-C2
Dem Conv rpt on role 7-13, 509G1
Young gets Carter conv role 7-14, 506A1
Carter seeks bias end 7-15, 507E1, 510A3
Carter record cited 512C1-B2
Austin loses Mich Sen primary 8-3, 565F2
Delegate representatn at GOP conv rptd 8-7, 8-8, 616C2
Mins' funds returned to Carter 8-10, 585B3
Reagan, Ford seek conv delegates 8-16, 8-17, 601G2, B3
GOP conv delegates' views on house sales to blacks rptd 8-17, 616G2
Carter visits Watts 8-23, 631E2
Dems seek voter registratn 8-23, 631F2
Carter visits Ga vote-drive group 8-30, 645A2
Black Caucus vs Vorster-Kissinger mtg 9-2, 660C3
Mondale visits Chicago area 9-16, 687B2
Henry greets Carter in Miss 9-17, 704A3
Black Caucus backs King murder probe 9-17, 729G1
Carter, Ford debate 9-23, 701C1
Carter vs redlining 9-25, 724F1
Mondale sees Md group 9-26, 725B1
Carter scores Butz remark 10-2, 743B1

1977

Military
Volunteer army rptd success 9-25, 777F2
Enlistees rptd rising 11-15, 920A2
NAACP—*See NATIONAL Association for the Advancement of Colored People*

Obituaries
DuBois, Shirley Graham 3-27, 356A3
Hamer, Fannie Lou 3-14, 264F2
Henderson, Edwin 2-3, 164A3
Hobson, Julius 3-23, 264A3
Powell, Clilan 9-22, 788C2
Schuyler, George 8-31, 788E2
Waters, Ethel 9-1, 788A3

Politics & Government
Carter church rejects member 1-9, 53C2
Bell confrmatn hearings, Black Caucus oppositn cited 1-11—1-18, 34E1
Mitchell named Carter asst 1-14, 35C3
Harris confrmd HUD dir 1-20, 34B1, E2
Bell confrmd 1-25, 52G2
Young confrmd UN amb 1-26, 52C3
Sup Ct backs racial redistricting 3-1, 174E3-175D1
Marsh elected Richmond (Va) mayor 3-8, 252C3
Young seat runoff set 3-15, 191G3; held 4-5, 252B1
Bradley reelected LA mayor 4-6, 252C3
NAACP conv scores Carter 6-27—6-28; Bond scores 8-15, SCLC 8-18, Meany 8-30, 702A2
Minority-aid use re Nixon votes chrgd 7-6—7-8, 577D3
Jordan scores Carter 7-24, Carter rebuts 7-25, 7-28, 573C1, F2
Black Caucus backs Carter criticism 7-29, 592G3
15 ldrs meet on crucial issues, score Carter 8-29, 702D1
Carter sees Black Caucus 9-7, 702A1
Pa gov defends Tucker ouster 9-28, 800C2
Jackson reelected in Atlanta 10-4, 879E1
Black Caucus stand in Bakke case cited 10-12, 834D3
Black Caucus scores minority contract bidders S Africa partnership 10-15, 979G1
Black Caucus asks actn vs S Africa 10-21, 825B1
Electn results 11-8, 855F1, G2, C3, D3
Morial elected New Orleans mayor 11-12, 879C1
Black Caucus for full employmt compromise bill 11-14, 877B1
Natl Women's Conf OKs minority res 11-19—11-21, 917C3
Hinds Cnty (Miss) voter apportnmt case refused 11-28, 919F2
Black caucus chrmn seeks Wilmington 10 pardon 12-4, 943C1
Jordan bars 4th House term 12-10, 1005B3
Carter meets ldrs, urban policies stressed 12-14, 960B1
Carter cites campaign vow 12-28, 1002A1

Religion
Carter church rejcts member 1-9, 53C2
Ex-Mormon loses church suit 3-10, 310A2
Howze installed Miss bishop 6-6, 471B2
Walker installed DC Episc bishop 9-24, 845F2

1978

Military
Army notes disciplinary problems 8-15, 683F1
Army study on equal opportunity rptd 8-16, 683A2
Army 2-yr enlistmt plan rptd 11-10, 895G2-A3
'70-78 enlistmt rise rptd 12-6, 960A1

Obituaries
Bailey, Bill (rptd) 12-17, 1032C2
Bradford, Alex 2-15, 196D2
Brown, Zara Cully 2-28, 196D2
Emmerich Sr, John 8-17, 708F2
James Jr., Daniel 2-25, 196C3
Jones, Blanche Calloway 12-16, 1032A3
Metcalfe, Ralph H 10-10, 853B2, 888C3
Pittman, Portia 2-26, 196E3
Still, William 12-3, 1032F3
Turner, Thomas Wyatt 4-21, 356E3
Waddy, Joseph C 8-1, 708G3

Politics & Government
Jackson addresses GOP com 1-20, 568D2-B3
'53, '78 cong membership compared 1-30, 107E2
Black Caucus vs Rhodesia pact 3-9, 193A2
Diggs indicted 3-23, 220C2
Jackson, Jordan, Brooke interviewed re black vote, Carter 4-10, 568F2-B3
'76 pres vote turnout rptd 4-13, 285C2
Gibson reelected in Newark 5-9, 363G1
Nix loses Pa primary to Gray 5-16, 389D3
Brooke admits false loan disclosure 5-23, 406B1
Leland wins Tex primary runoff 6-3, 426F2
Hatcher refuses White House job 6-6, 568B3
Carter job apptmt data rptd 6-15, 811E1
Mitchell scores Bakke ruling 6-28, 482F2
Hooks addresses GOP com 7-21, 568A2
LA mayor: more blacks elected 8-8, 811G1
Martin named Carter aide 8-11, 663G3-664A1
DC voting amendmt clears Cong 8-22, 661C1, G1-C2
Gallup poll: black-pres bias down 8-27, 811E3
DC voting amendmt OKd in NJ 9-11, rejctd in Pa 11-14, 878A3
Urban League dir sees HEW employes 9-21, 811C1
Carter assures Black Caucus on Humphrey-Hawkins bill 9-29, 808C1
Diggs convicted 10-7, 791D3; sentncd 11-20, 900A2
Cong action vs Roybal scored 10-12, 831G3
Cleveland city cncl pres indicted 10-27, 1008F3
Election results 11-7, 845E1, D2, 846E1, G2, 847G2, 848B1, A2, 849E2, 852F2, 853B2, 854B1, 855D3, 856F2-A3
Diggs reelected 11-7, 846E2, 851F1, 854B1
Carter backs judges merit selectn 11-8, 873C3
Payton quits Peace Corps 11-24, 915G1
GOP govs note black vote 11-27, 916B1
State post electn losses rptd 11-28, 915C3
Ga schl bd elective office rule struck down by Sup Ct 11-28, 937F3

Religion—*See also PEOPLES Temple*
Mormons end priesthood ban 6-9, ordain 1st black 6-11, 480G2
Muhammad quits as Muslim ldr 9-10, 810A2
Mormon missionary work cited 10-13, 907B2
7th-day Adventists refused separate role 10-20, 907F2
Howard elected NCC pres 11-4, 907F1

1979

Jordan, Hooks vs PLO support 10-11, 10-14; Baptist Conv scores criticism 10-14, 780C2-A3
SCLC drops invitatn to Arafat 10-11, 780F3
US Arab group gives PUSH $10,000 10-13, 780G3
NAACP, Urban League, others in Israel; back govt, Palestinians; oppose PLO support 10-14—10-17, 780C3
Hooks, 3 other black ldrs ask halt to debate; Jordan, Jackson 'reaffirm unity' 10-17, 780B3
US rep rebuts Young on Terzi mtg 10-28, 823D2

Medicine & Health
Cancer rate rptd up 2-16, 139E2
Strokes rptd down 2-23, 2-28, 195B2, F2, A3
Cancer death rates detailed 3-5, 195B3
Edelin gets Boston U post, '75 convictn reversal cited 3-15, 272B1
Birth pill-hypertensn link discounted 5-7, 355F1
City hosp closings rptd 9-2, 970G3-971A1

Military
Marine Corps names 1st brig gen 2-23, 272C1
Navy recruiting bias chrgd 6-14, 519C3
Racism seen 7-23, 561B3
West Pt names 1st brigade cmdr 8-11, 609D1
Navy orders anti-racist policy, remedial educatn program 8-29, 664E2
West Pt hazing scandal surfaces 11-9, 868D3

Obituaries
Burrell, Berkeley G 8-31, 671G1
Douglas, Aaron 2-2, 176G2
Easter, Luke 3-29, 1002E3
Mingus, Charles 1-5, 104D3
Muse, Clarence 10-13, 860G2
Parks Jr, Gordon 4-3, 356F3
Randolph, A Philip 5-16, 432E3
Smith, Charlie 10-5, 860E3
White, Charles W 10-3, 860G3

Politics & Government—*See also 'Jewish Relations' above*
Detroit chosen GOP conv site 1-23, 70C3
Racial attitudes surveyed 2-20, 307E1
Brooke cleared of wrongdoing 3-20, 208F2
KC mayoral candidate loses 3-27, 231B3
San Antonio city cncl shifts to whites 4-7, 265B2
Southn regulatory bds found segregated 4-9, 307F1-A2
Hatcher renominated in Gary 5-8, 363F2-A3
Bowser loses Phila mayoral primary 5-15, 363D2
Carter chides on voting 5-20, 384F2-A3
Southn offcls hold conv 5-25—5-27, 423D1
Sup Ct workforce data rptd 6-11, 464A2
Hooks sees Kennedy win, grudging Dem support 6-24, 559E3
NAACP maps pol activism, other reforms; gives Mondale cool receptn 6-25—6-30, 559B3, E3
Sen rejcts direct pres vote 7-10, 515C1
All-white judicial memberships assailed 7-14, 9-19, 9-25, 901E2
Cleveland cncl pres acquitted 7-18, 580G1
Urban League conf 7-22—7-25; Jordan scores Carter, vs 'dumping,' urges voter strength 7-22, 560D1
Hatchett joins fed appeals ct in Fla, sets precedent 8-4, 656G3
1st black woman US magistrate sworn 8-7, 901F3
Mich HS voter turnout law signed 8-14, 724E2
'70-76 Ga registered voter increase cited 8-14, 724G2
Young quits as UN amb re PLO contact 8-15, US black reactn 8-15, 8-16, 606E1-B2
Carter praises Young, denies tap 8-30, 661F2
Castro sees 2 Black Caucus reps 10-13, 779E1
Voter registratn drive launched 10-25, 808G1
Arrington elected Birmingham mayor 10-30, 829B1
Wayne Cnty (Mich) govt reorgnztn accord reached 11-1, 921D1
17 blacks elected to Miss legis 11-6, 846E2
3 voted to Houston cncl 11-6, 904E3
Diggs conviction upheld 11-14, 900A3
Higgs loses Memphis mayoral vote 11-15, 904E3

Religion—*See also 'Jewish Relations' above; also PEOPLES Temple*
Bradford elected 7th-day Adventists vp 1-11, 78D3
Mormon Church integratn rptd 6-8, 6-15, 508A1
Black Muslims rpt harrassmt 11-24, 898B2

1980

Obituaries
Ashford, Emmett 3-1, 279D1
Bates, Lucias C 8-22, 676A1
Buchanan, Bessie A 9-7, 755D2
Davis, John W 7-12, 608E1
Garret, Leroy 7-21, 608G1
Griffin, L Francis 1-18, 104F2
Hayden, Robert 2-25, 176E1
Hurley, Ruby 8-10, 676F1
Owens, Jesse 3-31, 280E1
Patterson, William L 3-5, 280F1
Randolph, Lillian 9-12, 756A2
Thomas, Billy 10-11, 876E3

Politics & Government—*See also other appropriate subheads in this section*
2 Ala dist judges named 1-10; controversy ensues 5-19—9-17; Clemon confrmd 6-26, Gray withdraws 9-17, 744B2
Black Caucus scores Carter budget 2-5, 94F2
SC reapportionmt suggestd 2-14, 185B2
Natl conf sets '80 goals 2-29, 190C2
All-white club judicial memberships censured by US Conf 3-6, 250D2
Sumter Cnty (Ga) ruled biased 4-7, 309A2
Sheffield named Va dist judge 4-9; tax probe halts Sen hearings 8-27, fight vowed 9-9, 744D3
SC reapportionmt suit filed 4-18, 349A2
At-large local electns upheld by Sup Ct 4-22, 343A2
Black Caucus presses Carter on Haitian refugee plight 5-7, 340C1
Diggs convictn review refused by Sup Ct 6-2, Diggs resigns 6-3, 428A1
Rodino wins NJ primary 6-3, 439A3
Carter sees Black Caucus 6-9, 439F1
San Fran OKs at-large vote 8-19, 632B3
NYC media gets NSC Africa memo 9-16, Admin calls forgery 9-17, 726E3-727B1
Census revisn ordrd 9-25, 741E2
5th judicial circuit split 10-14, 918D3
Electn results 11-4: cong 846B2, D3; state 850E3
Troup (Tex) to end svcs bias 12-11, 963A2

Presidential Election (& Transition)
Mrs Reagan makes racial gaffe in Ill 2-17, 128D2
Candidates scored at natl conf 2-29, 190E2
Kennedy fails to win Fla, Ala, Ga primary voters 3-11, 189D3
Candidates address NAACP 6-30—7-4, 515D2
Hooks sees black vote for Dem 7-6, 515B3
GOP delegates see Reagan; Hooks addresses conv 7-15, 533A3, F3, 535A1
News conf topic 8-4, 593B2
Urban League hears candidates 8-4—8-6, 597A1
Reagan sees Chicago ldrs 8-5, 597B3
Dem platform plank adopted 8-13, 610A3, 614F2
Hooks addresses Dem conv 8-13, 611E3
Mrs King seconds Carter renominatn, Dellums makes token challenge 8-13, 811C3
Carter sees conv delegates 8-15, 629E3
Mondale in Cleveland 9-1, St Louis 9-18, 780E1, D2
Carter addresses Phila Baptists 9-3, 699A1
Reagan tours Cleveland 9-10, 699C3
Carter deplores Reagan racism 9-16, clarifies 9-18, 698A2
Bush stresses jobs issue 9-18, 781B1
Journalists hear Anderson 9-29, 739E2
Bradley campaigns with Mondale 10-3, 817B1
Carter warns vs Reagan win 10-6, 762E3
Reagan deplores Carter 'hysteria' 10-7, 763D2
Carter softens Reagan attack 10-9, 778C2

1976

Butz quits re racist remarks 10-4, 743F3-744E3
Carter in Salt Lake City 10-7, Cleveland 10-9, 762C1, C2
Dole sees GOP slump re Butz 10-8, 763G3
Ford, Carter debate 10-22, 799G3, 801F3
Carter church incident mars final tour 10-31—11-2, 826D3
Key support in Carter win 11-2, 818G2
Election results 11-2, 820C2, 822D1, D3, 825A2, 830E4
Carter support cited 11-11, 845D2
Carter church ends ban 11-14, 864C2
3 attend Carter church 11-21, 881F3
Carter transitn team named 11-23, 881C3
GOP urged to seek vote 11-29, 917B3
Young named UN amb 12-16, 936C2
Carter rpts 4 barred Cabt posts 12-16, 937B1
Carter sees Black Caucus 12-16, 937B2
Civil rights groups score Bell apptmt 12-20—12-22, 956G2
Cabt selectn process disputed 12-20, 957B1
Harris named HUD secy 12-21, 956G1
Presidential Election—*See 'Politics & Government' above*
Sports
Charleston named to HOF 8-9, 816C1
Robinson rehired by Indians 10-4, 815G3

BLACK Caucus—*See 'Politics & Government' under BLACK Americans*
BLACK Community Organizations, United Federation of
Scores CORE Angola recruitmt 2-14, 163B3
BLACK & Geddes Inc.
Boycott rpt released 10-18, 786A1
BLACK Lawyers, National Conference of
Vs Calif reverse bias appeal 11-11, 882F1
BLACK Lung Disease—*See 'Heart & Lungs' under MEDICINE*
BLACKMAN, Herbert N.
Questns ILO job rpt 6-18, 449F3
BLACK Mountain, N.C.—*See NORTH Carolina*
BLACKMUN, Justice Harry A(ndrew)—*For Supreme Court developments not listed here, see SUPREME Court under U.S. GOVERNMENT*
Bars stay on beef standards 1-9, 24B2
Backs IRS emergency procedure 1-13, 23F3
Vs Pa police misconduct rule 1-21, 42F3
Rules on campaign law 1-30, 87A1, A2
Backs retroactive seniority 3-24, 218E2
Backs drug convictn ruling 4-27, 349C2
Voids drug price ad ban 5-24, 393F1
Vs alien civil svc rule 6-1, 414B2
Vs NC police firing 6-10, 552F2
Vs silence-on-arrest ruling 6-17, 552C3
Backs some church-coll aid 6-21, 452F3
Rules on US wage laws 6-24, 468D2
Vs sex-show zoning 6-24, 479A1
Backs patronage ouster bar 6-28, 468E3
For business records seizure 6-29, 535B2
Vs press gag order 6-30, 491F3
Backs abortion consent rulings 7-1, 518D3, F3
Ct upholds death penalty; voids NC, La laws 7-2, 491G2, C3
Backs sympathy strikes 7-6, 535E1
Cited in Ford biog sketch 614D1
For review of NM strikers pay rule 10-4, 807F2
For review of Border Patrol car search 10-18, 867F2
Vs carry-back tax ruling 11-2, 867C2
Vs jury death sentnc ruling 12-6, 920C3
Vs pregnancy benefits 12-7, 920E1
Vs vacating Gilmore stay 12-13, 952F2

1977

Sports
Willis named to HOF 1-17, 164C1
Cooper in basketball HOF 5-2, 490F3
Baseball HOF inducts 2, selectn comm end cited 8-8, 644B1, D1
US Open racial dispute 9-8, 787F2
Baseball HOF entrance rule eased, selection com expanded 10-3, 768G1-A2
U of Ark football players suspended 12-21, bias suit dropped 12-29, 1020E2
Welfare & Poverty
CBO issues poverty rpt 1-13, 80G3
Welfare study group scored 2-11, 176A1
Welfare study issued 4-15, 302D1
NAACP scores Carter 6-27—6-28, Bond scores 8-15, SCLC 8-18, Meany 8-30, 702A2
Jordan scores Carter 7-24, Carter says 'no apologies' 7-25, 7-28, 573C1, F2
15 ldrs score Carter 8-29, 702D1
Low life expectancy linked 12-13, 962C3
BLACK Caucus—*See BLACK Americans—Politics & Government*
BLACK Elected Officials, National Council of Local
Rattley at black ldrs mtg 8-29, 702F1
BLACK Lawyers, National Conference of
Vs Bell confrmatn 1-11—1-18, 34A2
BLACKLEDGE v. Allison
Fed ct review of guilty pleas ordrd 5-2, 406E2
BLACK Liberation Army
Chesimard convicted, sentncd 3-25, 288B3
BLACKMUN, Justice Harry A(ndrew)—*For Supreme Court developments not listed here, see U.S. GOVERNMENT—SUPREME Court*
Bars Gilmore executn stay 1-16, 40B2
Backs racial voter redistricting 3-1, 175C1
Rules on Mich electn law 3-21, 230D3
Rules on death sentencing 3-22, 231A1
For Miranda rule review 3-23, 276D1
Watergate appeals decisn leaked 4-21, 382C2
Backs Iowa obscenity convictn 5-23, 444E2
Backs Ohio job benefits law 5-31, 461E3
Backs 1-man police lineups 6-16, 518D1
Vs Medicaid abortn curbs 6-20, 516B3
Backs HEW jobless-benefits standards law 6-20, 516F3
Vs Justice Dept warrantless searches 6-21, 539D1
Backs legal fee ads 6-27, 538D3

1978

Sports
Spinks-Ali rematch plan protested 3-8, site shifted 3-9, 212E1
US-S Africa Davis Cup protests 3-17—3-19, 251A1
Spinks-Ali rematch contract signed 4-11, 378F3
Williams in NFL draft 5-2, 336B2
Doby named White Sox mgr 6-30, 560E1
Mitchell claims bias, traded 8-23, 1024B3
Twins owner causes furor 9-28—10-2, 779B2
Welfare & Poverty
Adult, child poverty data rptd 4-11, 811F1
Guaranteed income study rptd 5-19, 720F3
'77 poverty level data rptd 8-12, 684E2
Urban League dir sees HEW employes 9-21, 811D1

BLACK Body Blues (play)
Opens 1-24, 887B1
BLACK Caucus—*See BLACK Americans—Politics & Government*
BLACK Hawk (helicopter)—*See ARMAMENTS—Aircraft*
BLACK Lung Disease (pneumoconiosis)—*See MEDICINE—Heart & Lungs*
BLACK Marble, The (book)
On best-seller list 2-5, 116B3; 3-5, 195D3
BLACKMUN, Justice Harry A(ndrew)—*For Supreme Court developments not listed here, see U.S. GOVERNMENT—SUPREME Court*
Cancer operatn rptd 1-9, 13E3
Vs EPA asbestos rule curb 1-10, 13A3
Not in forgn natn trust suit rule 1-11, 33D3
Not in SC teacher tests rule 1-16, 33D2
Backs 'prehire' union picketing 1-17, 34B1
Vs prosecutors' plea-bargaining power 1-18, 65A1
Not in job bias case legal fees rule 1-23, 65C2
For Mo univ Gay Lib status review 2-21, 125E3
Vs Multistate Tax Compact rule 2-21, 126A2
Not in age bias job suit ruling 2-22, 126F2
Not in holding co tax ruling 2-22, 126G2
Not in sub-subcontractor paymt bond ruling 2-22, 126A3
Vs med student ouster rule 3-1, 143B3
Not in Maritime Comm labor contract ruling 3-1, 144C1
Not in suspended students damage case 3-21, 220D3
Vs cities' liability under trust law 3-29, 280D2
Not in A-plant rulings case 4-3, 280B3
Not in Minn pensn law case 4-3, 309A1
Vs Ark defendants rights rule 4-3, 309B1
Backs tax breaks in lease-back deals 4-18, 309A2
Not in clergy pub office case 4-19, 309F1
Backs bar on sex-based pensn plans 4-25, 322E3
Vs engineers' fee code 4-25, 323C1
Backs state stevedoring tax 4-26, 344C1
Curbs SEC trading suspensns 5-15, 387G1
Not in Indian tribal authority case 5-15, 387D3
Backs corp takeover tax liability 5-22, 388G1
Backs OSHA warrantless searches 5-23, 405F2
Backs Mont hunting fee disparity 5-23, 405G3
Vs NH rape law ruling 6-5, 431D2
Not in emergency welfare standards case 6-6, 447E2
Backs Skokie Nazi rally delay 6-12, 447B3
Not in double jeopardy evidence cases 6-14, 468F3
Vs Md refiner-run gas statn ban 6-14, 492E1
Backs Tellico Dam vs rare fish 6-15, 468C2
Vs Iowa business tax formula 6-15, 468E2
Not in press prison data access case 6-26, 566D3
Backs evidence hearing rules 6-26, 566E3
Vs Bakke med schl admissn, backs race-based affirmative actn principle; opinion excerpt 6-28, 481C1-F2, 486E2
Not in Minn pensn funds case 6-28, 567E1
Not in gypsum price fixing case 6-29, 567C3

1979

Sports
Knoetze boxing match protested 1-13, 79C2
NBA owners ponder declining league status 2-3—2-4, 175E1
Easter killed in holdup 3-29, 1002E3
Aaron assails baseball racism 8-15, 1003D1
Tate decisns Coetzee for WBA heavywgt title 10-20, 838E2
Welfare & Poverty
Black-white gap rptd 1-17, 35F1, C2
'78 poverty data rptd 11-24, 965F2

BLACK Caucus—*See BLACK Americans–Politics & Government*
BLACK Fox Nuclear Station—*See OKLAHOMA–Atomic Energy*
BLACK Hawk (helicopter)—*See ARMAMENTS– Aircraft*
BLACK Hills (S.D., Wyo.)
SD Sioux awarded $100 mln 6-13, 464D3-465A1
BLACK Hole, The (film)
Released 12-21, 1007G2
BLACKLEDGE, Barbara
Wild Oates opens 1-8, 292G3
BLACK Liberation Army
Chesimard escapes NJ prison 11-2, 953D2
BLACKMUN, Justice Harry Andrew—*For Supreme Court developments not listed here, see U.S. GOVERNMENT—SUPREME Court*
Backs Boston referendum spending case review 1-8, 14C3
Vs Pa abortn control law 1-9, 14D1
Backs IRS tax acctg limits 1-16, 32A3
Vs rail pensn in divorce pact 1-24, 54C1
Vs corp name curbs 2-21, 128G2
Vs Ill right-to-counsel rule 3-5, 185D2
Vs muffler assn tax break 3-20, 203F3
Vs broader grant of immunity 3-20, 204D1
Backs jobless pay for strikers 3-21, 231G1
Backs church schl labor interventn 3-21, 231G2
Vs NYS alien teacher ban 4-17, 325E3
Vs unwed father damage suit bar 4-24, 364G1
Vs Calif cargo container taxes 4-30, 364B3
Vs pvt Title IX suit 5-14, 382F3
Vs mutual fund dirs' power 5-14, 383D1
Vs Scientology documts seizure 5-14, 383A3
Discloses finances 5-15, 382E2
Backs some punitive damages vs unions 5-29, 421D3
Vs co-defendant confessns 5-29, 422B1
Backs personal bankruptcy data collectn 6-4, 439B2
Backs broader Cong legal immunity 6-18, 498G3
Backs warrantless phone surveillnc 6-20, 516D1
Vs luggage search warrants 6-20, 516C2
Vs gender-based welfare plan 6-25, 539E3
Backs Wolston libel suit right 6-26, 540D3
Vs Weber affirmative actn challenge 6-27, 477G1
Backs unwed mothers survivors' aid 6-27, 558B2
Vs dockworker negligence suits 6-27, 558C2
Vs ctroom pub access curbs 7-2, 515A3
'78-79 Sup Ct term ends, voting alignmt rptd 7-2, 558A1, C1
Backs power to void state convictns 7-2, 558G3
Vs Mass abortn-consent law 7-2, 559D2
Comments on trial closures cited 9-8, 745E1
Backs 'exclusionary rule' case review 10-1, 768B3
Not in Minn pensn funds case 10-15, 847F3
Backs NYC schl aid denial 11-28, 944D2
Backs extended searches 11-28, 944B3
Backs pub access to waterways 12-4, 988C1
Backs Taiwan treaty case review 12-13, 940D1

1980

Young campaigns for Carter 10-10, racial remark repudiated 10-15, 803D1
Abernathy, Williams back Reagan 10-16, Evers 10-22, 802B2
Bush vows hiring support 10-16, 817G2, A3
Carter seeks support, Lowery endorses 10-20, 10-23, 803B1
Carter, Reagan TV debate 10-28, 814B2
Carter hits Reagan debate statemt 10-29, 816D2
Reagan pledges cities aid 12-1, 914G2
Reagan meets ldrs in NYC 12-9, DC, vows rights defense 12-11, 956A2-F2
Reagan aide, Sowell address conservative conf 12-14, 956G2
Reagan rpts Cabt-level apptmt 12-22, 979E2
Sports
Aaron boycotts awards ceremony, chrgs racism 1-28, 637F1
Davenport, Gadley on US Olympic bobsled team 2-24, 154C3
Ashe retires from tennis competitn 4-16, 607A2
Wills hired as Mariners mgr 8-4, 926A2
Hagler wins world middlewgt title 9-27, 772B2
NFL hiring practices scored 10-27, 998C3
USC coach defends athletic admissns policy 10-29, 875F2

BLACK Caucus—*See BLACK Americans–Politics*
BLACK Hawk (helicopter)—*See ARMAMENTS–Aircraft*
BLACK Hills (S.D., Wyo.)
Sioux compensatn upheld by Sup Ct 6-30, 511B1
Oglala Sioux seek compensatn award 7-18, 560F1-B2
Oglala Sioux compensatn suit dismissed 9-11, 704B2
BLACK Hole, The (film)
Top-grossing film 1-9, 40G3
BLACK Journalists, National Association of
Anderson addresses 9-29, 739E2
BLACK Like Me (book)
John H Griffin dies 9-9, 755C3
BLACKMUN, Justice Harry Andrew—*For Supreme Court developments not listed here, see U.S. GOVERNMENT–SUPREME Court*
Backs inmate escape justificatn 1-21, 92G3
Vs narrowed state ct jurisdictn 1-21, 93B2
Vs Customs Svc goods liability 1-21, 93B3
Ex-clerk named Abscam leaks prosecutor 2-11, 111G1
Vs tax liability in RR worker compensatn 2-19, 131D1
Backs pvt coll faculty unions 2-20, 146A2
Vs NYS pvt schl reimbursemt 2-20, 146E2
Vs Calif dual seniority system 2-20, 146A3
Vs fed gun law prior convictn limit 2-27, 188A3
Not in Kissinger records case 3-3, 210B1
Backs 'insider' stock trading convictn 3-18, 226F2
Backs Indian land 'inverse condemnatn' 3-18, 226G3
Backs Vt tax on forgn dividends 3-19, 249A3
Backs mutual fund insurance case review 3-24, 265G1
Backs inmate mental health case dismissal 3-25, 265F2
Backs at-large local electns 4-22, 343F2
Vs Atlanta schl integratn ruling 5-12, 386C3
Backs narrow Ga death law applicatn 5-19, 440A1
Vs land-grant exchng ban 5-19, 440B2
Vs lower PR welfare aid 5-27, 453E3
Vs SEC fraud intent proof 6-2, 512E3
Vs Fla 'parochial' banking practices 6-9, 512G2
Backs use of jail informants 6-16, 511C3
Backs state sales preference 6-19, 554E2
Rules on utilities' free speech 6-20, 555C2
Vs Ill non-labor picketing rights 6-20, 555E2
Vs donated porno warrants 6-20, 555B3
Backs cts power to suppress evidence 6-23, 554E3
Rules on lawyer legal fee penalty 6-23, 555B1
Backs unpatented key ingredient monopolies 6-27, 511C2
Vs Medicaid abortn funding limits 6-30, 492E1
Backs Sioux $122.5 mln award 6-30, 511C1
Backs govt minority constructn grants 7-2, 510D1
Backs open criminal trials 7-2, 510A3
Backs OSHA benzene standard 7-2, 511A1
'79-80 Sup Ct term ends, voting alignmts rptd 7-2, 540B2
Backs unwed couples child custody case review 10-20, 807C1
Backs Ky 10 Commandmts schl law 11-17, 881G3
Backs lenient sentence appeal 12-9, 936C3
Backs defendants fed ct civil rights suits 12-9, 937C1
Not in judicial pay hikes case 12-15, 957D1

1976

BLACK Muslims
4 sentncd in 'Zebra' killings 3-29, 292F3
BLACK Panther Party
Cleaver Defense Fund formed 2-17, 272E1
Sen com rpts FBI tactics 4-28, 330E2
Sen com staff study details FBI harrassmt 5-6, 344A2
Cleaver freed on bail 8-13, 640C3
BLACK Political Assembly, National
Plans pres bid; Bond, Dellums decline 3-15—3-20, 214E2
Kirkpatrick named pres candidate 6-18, 490D3
BLACKWELL, Robert J.
On US-Sovt shipping talks 10-7, 856B3
Talks end 12-8, USSR scored 12-10, 947F3
BLAGOEV, Blagoi
Wins Olympic medal 7-24, 576E2
BLAGOYEVA, Yordanka
Wins Olympic medal 7-28, 576G1
BLAIR, David
Dies 4-1, 484C3
BLAIR, Robert
Hijacker killed 4-19, 383F3
BLAIS, Jean-Jacques
Sworn postmaster gen 9-15, 692F1
Bans strikes 10-5, 10-7, 808G3, 809A1
Bars postal mediatn 10-22, 836F3
BLAKELEY, William
Dies 1-5, 56A3
BLAKENEY, Allan
Scores US potash suit 9-21, 750B2 ★
On fed-prov tax plan 12-15, 962E2
BLANCHARD, Gen. George S.
Fair resignatn rptd 1-16, 43F2
BLANCHARD, Rep. James J. (D, Mich.)
Reelected 11-2, 829E4
BLANCHET, Paul
Loses Haiti Cabt post 4-1, 267D2, F2
BLANCO, Hugo
Expelled from Peru 7-10, arrives Sweden 7-11, 590F3
BLAND, Sir Harry
Named ABC chrmn 7-4, 520E2
BLANKENHORN, Dr. David H.
Rpts new artery x-ray system 1-21, 159D2
BLANKENSHIP, G. T.
Edwards elected 11-2, 822A3
BLAZIC, Viktor
Arrested 5-17, sentncd 9-16, 910D1
BLAZING Saddles (film)
Top-grossing film 3-31, 240B3
BLEICHER, Michael
Conv platform proposal rejctd 7-13, 509A2
BLIGH, Adm. William (1754-1817)
Australia purchases log 11-25, 902A3

1977

BLACK Muslims—*See ISLAM in the West, World Community of*
BLACKOUTS—*See ELECTRIC Light & Power*
BLACK Panther Party
New Haven surveillnc abuses chrgd 5-12, 422E3
Chicago police win civil suit 6-21, 540E2
Newton to face US murder chrgs 6-24, in Canada custody 6-25—6-29, 531G3
Canada RCMP barn burning probed 10-20, 841E2; 11-1, 902C3
BLACK Sea
Rumania oil find 4-20, 468E3
BLACK Sunday (film)
Top-grossing film 4-27, 356E2
BLACKWELL, Robert
On Sovt shipping pact 2-7, 161B1
On Alaska oil transport 6-24, 498C2
BLACK and White in Color (film)
Wins Oscar 3-28, 264D1
BLAIN, Col. Kesner
Rptd still held in Haiti 9-30, 805E3
BLAIR, Eric—*See ORWELL, George*
BLAIR, Paul
In World Series 10-11—10-18, 806A2
BLAIR, Robert
Lauds NEB pipeline rpt 7-4, 525E2
BLAIS, Jean-Jacques
On RCMP mail opening 11-9, 882E1
Admits RCMP cooperatn 11-17, 923F2
Sets postal rate hike 11-21, 983C1
BLAKE, Jack
Carlucci named CIA dept dir 12-22, 1001F3
BLAKE, Vivian
Jamaica industry min 1-4, 46C1
BLAKENEY, Allan
NDP wins by-electn 6-8, 466E3
On oil royalty tax setlmt 11-24, 923F3
BLALOCK, Jane
Wins Colgate Triple Crown 1-15, 104C1
2d in Women's Intl 4-17, 951B1
3d in Muscular Dystrophy Open 9-5, 951D1
LPGA top money winner 11-27, 951F1
BLANCHARD, Francis
ILO drops Israel inquiry 3-21, 227D2
BLANCO, David
Named Bolivia finance min 10-13, 902C1
BLANCO, Jaime
Police assault 8-27, Cortes furor ensues 9-12—9-15, 826E3
BLANTON, Gov. Ray (D, Tenn.)
Death penalty veto overridden 4-11, 594E1
Urges cautn in Ray chase 6-11, asks US custody 6-13, 459B2, E2
BLAUVELT, Howard W.
Replies to Carter attack 10-13, 773A1
BLEJER, Hector
Scores arsenic rpt 6-6, 448D1
BLIND Ambition (book)
On best-seller list 2-6, 120F3
BLINDNESS—*See MEDICINE—Handicapped*
BLINN, William
Wins Emmy 9-11, 1021G3
BLISS, George
Rpts on child porno 5-15—5-18, 432G2
BLIVEN, Bruce
Dies 5-27, 452E2
BLIZZARDS—*See STORMS*

1978

Vs Ohio death penalty law 7-3, 552G1, A2
Voting alignmt shift noted 7-3, 565E3-566C1
Backs employer retaliatn case review 10-2, 751D1
Backs Mellon Bank immunity case review 10-10, 789A3
Urges new fed ct 12-4, 958E3
Backs extraditn probe bar 12-18, 981B2
BLACK Muslims—*See ISLAM in the West*
BLACKOUTS—*See ELECTRIC Light & Power*
BLACK Panther Party
CIA spying rptd 3-17, 243E2, A3 ★
Newton arrested 5-11, assault chrg dropped 7-13; convicted on gun chrg 9-28, sentncd 11-3, 971F2
France sentncs '72 Delta hijackers 11-23, 926F3
BLACKS, The (play)
Opens 5-24, 887B1
BLACK Sea
Turkey, USSR sign fishing, oil pacts 6-21—6-23, 595E2
BLACK v. U.S.
Postal competitn convictn refused by Sup Ct 3-27, 241E2
BLACKWELDER, Brent
On Carter natl water policy plan 6-6, 427A1
BLACKWOOD, Lyle
NFL '77 interceptn ldr 1-1, 56C2
BLAHEMORE, Michael
Players opens 9-6, 887E2
BLAIR Jr., Charles F.
Killed 9-2, 777F3
BLAIR, John W.
Wins Pulitzer 4-17, photo mix-up setld 4-21, 314F3, 315B2
BLAIR, Jon
'Biko Inquest' opens 5-17, 760D1
BLAIR, Pamela
King of Hearts opens 11-22, 1031C2
BLAIR, Paul
In World Series 10-10—10-17, 799F3
BLAIS, Jean-Jacques
Named Canada solicitor-gen 2-2, 70F1
On '75 Allmand, MP wiretaps, US informer 2-27, 166A2
Admits RCMP Ontario health file access 3-1, 209F1
Chrgs MP re RCMP spy rpt 3-2, 209C1
Bars actn vs RCMP officers 4-24, 311B3
On RCMP candidate monitoring 4-26, 328B2
Rpts RCMP documts destroyed 4-26, 328E2
Denies RCMP officers shielded 10-25, 837F2
BLAISDELL, George G.
Dies 10-3, 888D2
BLAKE, Eubie
Eubie opens 9-20, 1031D1
BLAKENEY, Allan Emrys
NDP wins prov electn 10-18, 813C2
BLAKEY, Deborah Layton
Guyana cult abuses detailed in affidavit 6-15, 891D3 ★
BLAKEY, G. Robert
JFK death hearings end 9-28, 749F3, 750A1
Denies Ray payoffs, FBI link in King murder 11-15, 11-17, 898A3, C3
On JFK murder film 11-26, 916D2
Details Ray family plot 11-27, links Raoul 11-30, 938A1, C1
BLALOCK, Jane
Wins Orange Blossom Classic 2-20, 355C3
2d in Birmingham Classic 4-16, 355G3
Greater Baltimore Classic results 5-14; Lady Keystone 6-15, Bankers Trust 6-18, 580F2-G3
Wins Mayflower Classic 7-3, Wheeling Classic 7-9, 672B3, C3
2d in Sarah Coventry Open 9-17, 990A2
LPGA top money winner 11-20, 990C3
BLANCHARD, Rep. James J. (D, Mich.)
Reelected 11-7, 851A2
BLANCHARD, Tom
NFL '77 punting ldr 1-1, 56F3
BLANCO, Hugo
Newsman kidnaped 9-3—9-10, rpts gang assault 9-15, 776B1
BLANKS, Larvell
Traded to Rangers 10-3, 779A3
BLANTON, Gov. Ray (D, Tenn.)
Retiring; primary results 8-3, 606A2
Alexander elected gov 11-7, 853C1
Aides arrested in parole payoff 12-15; pardons voided 12-20, defended 12-22, 12-24, 1011E1-E2
BLAUVELT, Howard W.
Sees Carter on coal strike 2-24, 122G3
To retire as Conoco chrmn 9-20, 809B1
BLAZEJOWSKI, Carol
Unsigned by WBL 12-9, 1027A3
BLAZEY, Thomas W.
Indicted 9-13, 737A2
BLEACHER Bums (play)
Opens 4-24, 760E1
BLIER, Bertrand
Get Out Handkerchiefs released 12-17, 1030A3
BLINDNESS—*See HANDICAPPED*
BLISS, George
Kills self 9-11, 777F3
BLIX, Hans
Swedish forgn min 10-18, 822F2
BLIZZARDS—*See STORMS*

1979

BLACK Muslims—*See ISLAM of the West*
BLACK Panther Party
Newton murder case ends in mistrial 3-24, 239C1
FBI admits '70 Seberg slander 9-14, 705A1
FBI sets '70 Pratt murder convictn probe 9-24, 886E2
Newton murder case ends in 2d mistrial, chrgs dropped 9-27, 818B3
Cleaver murder chrgs rptd dropped 12-3, 1006E1
BLACK Sea
Rumania oil find rptd 11-19, 910A2
BLACKTON, Jay
I Remember Mama opens 5-31, 711G3
Oklahoma opens 12-13, 1007D2
BLACKWELDER, Brent
Scores Carter re Tellico Dam bill signing 9-26, 766D3
BLACKWELL, Doretha R.
Sentncd in GSA kickback scandal 3-28, 367A3
BLACKWELL, Lucien E.
3d in vote for Phila mayor 11-6, 846A3
BLAHUT, Regis T.
CIA ouster rptd re rifled JFK death probe files 6-17, 6-18, 466B3
BLAIR, Eric—*See ORWELL, George*
BLAIR, Linda
Pleads guilty to drug chrgs 9-6, 859C3
Roller Boogie released 12-19, 1008C1
BLAKE, Judith
Abortn study cited 11-11, 930D2
BLAKE, William (1757-1827)
Book sold for record sum 6-13, 672E1
BLAKELY, Susan
Concorde Airport '79 released 8-3, 820A1
BLAKEMORE, Richard
Magnet-synthesizing bacteria rptd 4-8, 691C2
BLAKER, Peter
Rpts Hong Kong gov reapptmt 9-25, 730C2
BLAKEY, G. Robert
Defends JFK acoustics evidence 1-5, 4E2
Reaffirms JFK acoustics evidence 3-16, 205A1
CIA agent rptd ousted re rifled JFK death probe files 6-17, 6-18, 466D3
Denies JFK autopsy photo forgery claim 7-9, 520G2*, B3
House com final rpt released 7-17, 538F2
BLALOCK, Jane
Wins Orange Blossom Classic 2-26, 220F3
Wins Lady Citrus Classic 4-22, Otey Crisman 4-29, Sarah Coventry 6-17, 587D2, E2, B3
LPGA top money winner 11-30, 969G2
BLANCHARD, Rep. James J. (D, Mich.)
Vs neighborhoods panel rpt 3-15, 208B3
BLANCHARD, Tom
NFL '78 punting ldr 1-6, 80F2
BLANCORNELAS, Jesus
Newspaper stormed 11-1, 875B1
BLANEY, Neil
Wins Eur Parlt seat 6-7, 434C2
BLANKS, Larvell
Traded to Braves 12-7, 1002F2
BLANTON, Ray
Pardons felons 1-16; replaced as gov, releases blocked 1-17, 36F1-B3
Ray parole deal rptd too costly 1-18, 156D2
Seeks prisoner release, Sen censures 1-19; pardons still in dispute 1-31, 152F2
Hyden sentncd 1-26, 156E2
6 indicted in pardon sales 3-15, appeals ct upholds pardons 4-10, 309C2
BLANTON, Thomas (1872-1957)
Diggs censure seen 6-29, 515F1
Diggs censured 7-31, 578E1
BLAZER, Philip
Quits J Jackson Mideast tour 9-26, 763B2
BLECKNER, Jeff
Goodbye People opens 4-30, 711D3
BLEDSOE, Aleck Lee
Wins religious schl expulsn suit 8-23, 650A2
BLEIER, Rocky
Steelers win Super Bowl 1-21, 63B1
BLEMING, Thomas J.
Arrested in Panama coup plot 10-24, 836C3
BLINDNESS—*See HANDICAPPED*
BLISS & Laughlin Industries Inc.
AEA Investors purchase bid rptd 8-10, 942B2
BLIZZARDS—*See STORMS*

1980

BLACK Muslims—*See ISLAM of the West*
BLACK Panther Party
Cleaver gets 5 yrs probatn 1-3, 64E3
FBI Seberg probe rptd extensive 1-9, 55C1
Pratt denied parole 2-5, 215A2
2 protest Pratt appeal denial 5-11, 667D1
Stender dies 5-21, 448G2
Chicago shootout retrial order declined, legal fees award voided by Sup Ct 6-2, 513A1
Newton awarded PhD 6-15, 638F3
French newspr rpt on Cleaver asylum cited 11-7, 872F1
BLACK Sea
US, Turkey sign bases pact 3-29, 255C3
BLACK Stallion, The (film)
Top-grossing film 4-23, 360B1
BLACKTHORN (U.S. Coast Guard cutter)
Collides with oil tanker 1-28, suit rptd filed 2-3, hearing begins 2-6, 256D2
BLACKWOOD Brothers (singing group)
Win Grammy 2-27, 296E3
BLAGIDZE, Vakhtang
Wins Olympic medal 7-23, 624A3
BLAGOEV, Blagoi
Wins Olympic medal 7-26, 624F2
BLAHOVA, Dagmar
Apple Game released 1-16, 216B2
BLAIS, Jean-Jacques
Canada supply min 3-3, 171B2
BLAIS, Madeleine
Wins Pulitzer 4-14, 296G2
BLAKE, Jay Don
Wins NCAA golf title 5-31, 714F3
BLAKE, Robert
Coast to Coast released 10-3, 836E2
BLAKENEY, Allan
Vs Canada bill of rights 9-18, 728B2
Scores budget, energy plan 10-29, 858C3
BLALOCK, Jane
Wins Arden Classic 2-10, 2d in Lady Citrus 4-20, 412D2, D3
2d in LPGA Championship 6-8, 714C3
LPGA top money winner 10-12, 971F3
BLANCHARD, Francis
Praises Polish workers 9-1, 659G3
BLANCHARD, Rep. James J. (D, Mich.)
Reelected 11-4, 843A2
BLANCO, Alberto
Wins Olympic medal 7-28, 624F2
BLANCO, Rolando
Freed 4-19, 311C3
BLANTON, Ray
Ex-aides bid-rigging indictmts rptd 7-5, 655A2
BLANTON, Thomas (1872-1957)
Wilson censured 6-10, 438D2
BLASS, Bill
'80 fashion roundup rptd 998F1
BLATT, Jerry
Divine Madness released 9-25, 836E2
BLATTY, William Peter
Twinkle, Twinkle Killer Kane released 8-8, 675E3
BLAUBERG, Maija S.
Dinnan resumes teaching 10-6, 890D3
BLECHMAN, Burt
My Mother, My Father opens 1-9, 136D3
BLEICH, William
Hearse released 6-7, 675G2
BLILEY Jr., Thomas J.
Elected to US House 11-4, 844D3, 850D2
BLINOV, Aleksandr
Wins Olympic medal 7-27, 622G2

1976

BLOCH, Mrs. Dora
Left behind after Uganda raid 7-3, 485C1
UK-Uganda controversy on disappearance 7-7—7-12; body rptd seen 7-13, 515D2
Uganda tells UN of disappearance 7-9, 516A1
UK cuts Uganda ties 7-28, 547G3
Uganda photographer rptd dead 10-21, 874B2
Uganda issues raid rpt 11-16, 861C2
BLOOD—*See under MEDICINE & Health*
BLOOM, Robert
Bars bank rpts release 1-20, 111F3
Sees bank industry recovery 11-2, 866F1
BLOOMFIELD, N.J.—*See NEW Jersey*
BLOOMFIELD, Richard J.
Amb to Ecuador 3-22; confrmd 4-1, 262C3
BLOOMGARDEN, Kermit
Dies 9-20, 970C1
BLOOMINGTON, Ill.—*See ILLINOIS*
BLOUIN, Rep. Michael T. (D, Ia.)
Reelected 11-2, 829C3
BLOUNT, Frank
Suspended, DEA probe rptd 8-20, 776D2
BLUBBERS, Willi
Shot by E Ger guard 7-28, freed 8-11, 630D3
BLUE, Vida
Sold to Yankees 6-15, Kuhn voids 6-18, 444B3-F3
BLUE Coal Corp.
Indicted 11-19, 989D2
BLUE Cross Association
Studies alcohol coverage 6-9, 443F1
BLUE Diamond Coal Co.
Scotia mine blasts 3-9—3-11, 256A3
Scotia bodies recovered 11-19, 892B1
BLUE Eyes Crying in the Rain (recording)
Wins Grammy 2-28, 460A3
BLUE Ribbon Frozen Food Corp.
Named in Army meat fraud probe 5-10, 395B2
BLUM, Arlene
US team climbs Mt Everest 10-8, 876B3
BLUMBERG, Dr. Baruch Samuel
Wins Nobel Prize 10-14, 840C1
BLUMENTHAL, Albert H.
Case dismissed 4-13, 271B1
BLUMENTHAL, W. Michael
At Carter econ briefing 12-1, 898F2
Named Treas secy 12-14, 936C1
Biog sketch 936D2

1977

BL Ltd. (formerly British Leyland)
Longbridge workers strike 2-7–2-14, co-wide strike rejected 2-9, 115B3-F3
Wildcat strike hits 4-9, 285F3-286A1
Honda joint productn planned 5-17, 388B2
!ran interests natlzd 7-5, 503A3
Job cuts planned, 1st 1/4 profits rptd 9-10, 686D2
Workers back cutbacks 11-1, 855F2-B3
Union militant fired, strikes ensue 11-19, interim accord reached 11-27, 994G1
NEB members resign over Rolls-Royce transfer 11-20, 949F3
UK aid promised 12-20, 994C1
Honda accord signed 12-27, 994E1
BLOCH, Dora (d. 1976)
UK recognizes new Uganda govt 4-15, 288C2
Body found 5-30, 429D1
BLOCK, Herbert L.
Wins Pulitzer 4-16, 336B3
BLOCH, Dora (d. 1976)
Amin ex-min rpts death ordrd 6-8, 487A1
BLOCH, Ernst
Dies 8-3, 696D2
BLOCK, Dennis H.
Loses mayoral vote 6-7, 446B3
BLOCK, Howard
'74 murder rptd 10-4, 871E3
BLOOD—*See under MEDICINE*
BLOOM, Robert
Rpts problem bank list up 3-11, 194E2
BLOTTA, Oscar
Kidnaped 3-1, freed 3-7, 198C1
BLOUIN, Rep. Michael T. (D, Ia.)
'76 specl interest gifts rptd 2-15, 128F2
BLOUNT, Mel
Named Pro Bowl MVP 1-17, 104E1
Slander suit vs Noll cited 7-22, 659E1
BLUCHER, William
On Norfolk I pol status 2-9, 132B2
BLUE, Vida
Finley feud, sale halted 4-5—4-8, 310D3
Traded to Reds, Kuhn doubts 12-9, 990A1
BLUEBONNET Bowl—*See FOOTBALL—Collegiate*
BLUE Coal Corp.
Fined 3-21, ex-pres indicted 6-2, 520A3, C3
BLUE Cross Association
Carter asks hosp cost controls 4-25, 322D1
CAT scanner study rptd 5-2, 869D3
HMOs hailed for cost control 8-5, 643E2
BLUE Diamond Coal Co.
'76 Scotia mine blasts laid to spark 6-13, 8-10, widows' suit dismissed 9-12, 900F3, 901A1
Stearns mine violence 10-17, 937F2
BLUE-Gray Game—*See FOOTBALL—Collegiate*
BLUE Laws—*See BUSINESS*
BLUE-Ray Inc.
Chrgd re Arab boycott 1-7, 167A2
BLUM, Arlene
Tris sterility peril warned 8-30, 820D2
BLUM, Barbara
Named EPA dep admin 2-16, confrmd 3-4, 211D1
US agencies told to end pollutn 10-20, 800A2
BLUMENTHAL, W(erner) Michael
Sen com OKs nominatn 1-18, confrmd 1-20, 34A1, E3
Testifies on econ aid plan 1-27, 52A1, 89C2
Sees US, Bonn, Japan GNP hike as aid to world trade 1-28, 92D2
Acts to ease gas transport 2-2, 2-3, 76E1
Rpts personal finances 2-25, 147E3
Warns NYC on loans 2-27, 3-3, 3-10, releases funds 3-11, 193D1, G2, E3
Rpts fscl '77 spending lag 3-2, 174A3
Vs investmt tax credit bar 3-8, 174F2
Carter drops tax rebate, credit plans 4-14, 270D3, G3, 271A1, E1
London summit lodging shifted 5-5, 359G2
Sees Speer on imports, price hikes 5-5, 385D2
On steel price hike, prenotificatn 5-11, 385C2
Addresses Japan intl bankers conf 5-25, 437D3, 438A1
Forecasts '77 trade deficit 5-25, 445D1
Urges IDB rights stand 5-30—5-31, 438E3
Sees USSR '77 import cut 6-10, 530E1
Paymts, trade deficits views cited 6-22, 502B1
Backs $ depreciatn vs mark, yen 7-21, 552F1
Backs strong $ 7-28; US trade deficit-reducing strategy rptd challenged 8-8, 585B2-F2
Cargo preference debated 8-1, 719C3
Turner given new powers 8-4, 610B3
Sees Peru pres re econ crisis 9-8, 785G1
On '77 trade gap, capital inflow 9-27, 753F3
On May-July indicators index lag 9-29, 761F3
Carter asks intl loan policy review 10-6, 815C2
On $ drop, lack of business confidence in Admin 10-19, 792G2, 798F1
Rptd vs Burns 12-28, 1000D2

1978

BL Ltd. (formerly British Leyland)
Callaghan warns workers 1-26; Edwardes sets reorg, job cuts 2-1, 112D1-D2
Japan bars auto export curbs; '77, Jan sales rptd 2-8, 112G2
Liverpool assemb operatn to end, 3000 more jobs cut 2-15, 132B1
Japan to curb UK car imports 3-3, 168C1
Massive '77 losses rptd 3-20; govt loan granted 3-23, cost cuts pledged 3-28, efficiency study rptd 3-30, 267C3-G3
NEB '77 losses rptd 4-5, 268A1
Ex-exec jailed for forgery 8-11, 667G2
Labor troubles persist 9-11, 9-14; rpts 1st ½ profits 9-14, 739G2-740A1
Chrysler sale to Puegeot OKd 9-28, 764G1
BLM—*See U.S. GOVERNMENT—INTERIOR—Land Management, Bureau of*
BLOCK, Otto
Guatemala communicatns, works min 7-21, 722C3 ★
BLOCK Drug Co.
Polident ad complaint rptd setled 8-31, 702E2
BLOOD and Blood Pressure—*See under MEDICINE & Health*
BLOODBROTHERS (film)
Released 9-27, 969D3
BLOODLINE (book)
On best-seller list 3-5, 195D3; 4-2, 272A3; 4-30, 356F1; 6-4, 460B3; 7-2, 579B3; 8-6, 620A2; 9-4, 708B1
BLOOD Tie (book)
Wins Natl Book Award 4-10, 315D2
BLOOM, Jeremiah
3d in NY primary for gov 9-12, 716A2
BLOOM, Paul
On Gulf price suit setlmt 7-27, 610A3
BLOOMFIELD, Conn.—*See CONNECTICUT*
BLOOMINGTON, Ind.—*See INDIANA*
BLOOMINGTON, Minn.—*See MINNESOTA*
BLOUIN, Rep, Michael T. (D, Iowa)
Loses reelectn 11-7, 854D2
BLUE, Vida
Kuhn cancels sale to Reds 1-30, traded to Giants 3-15, 194G2, F3
A's sale fails 3-27, 355D1
NL wins All-Star Game 7-11, 559A3
NL pitching ldr 10-2, 928G2
BLUEBONNET Bowl—*See FOOTBALL—Collegiate*
BLUE Collar (film)
Released 2-9, 618D3
BLUE Cross & Blue Shield Associations
Hosps asked to reduce beds 6-20, 577E2
Carter health plan backed 7-29, 586F2
BLUE-Gray All-Star Game—*See FOOTBALL—Collegiate*
BLUE Sea Line
FMC rebate chrgs setld 9-18, 752F3
BLUM, Barbara
Asbestos rule amended 6-15, 512E3
BLUM, Yehuda Z.
Scores Palestinian Solidarity Day at UN 11-29, 951A3
BLUMENTHAL, Judge M. Joseph
Sets stiff trust penalties 2-3, 142G1
BLUMENTHAL, W(erner) Michael
Role in NYC fiscal crisis 86D2
NYC fscl recovery plan issued 1-20, 87E1
Sees Schmidt, growth rate hike barred 2-13, 119C1
Presents aid plan for NYC 3-2, 141B1
Proposes NYC long-term loan guarantees 3-2, Carter signs bill 8-8, 608C1, E2
Crude oil tax threat urged 3-24, 220B2
Vs soc sec revisn, oil tax use 4-5, 241D1
Asks oil price freeze; vows $ defns energy policy enactmt 4-21, 523G1
Tax-cut plan scaled back 5-12, 361E1
Soc Sec rptd sound, hosp insurnc reform urged 5-16, 368C3
Asks exec pay curbs 6-6, 428B1
Natl health plan delay urged 6-26, 491F2
Rpts EC monetary zone reservatns 7-18, 545G3
Carter asks aid re $ drop 8-16, 622G1
Backs growth rate convergence; sees '79 paymts deficit, inflatn drop 9-26, 731D3
Tax cut bill cleared 10-15, 785E1
In US-USSR trade talks 12-4—12-7, 966B1
In Rumania 12-8—12-9, 965C3-966A1
Testifies to Joint Econ Com 12-14, 980D1
At Boumedienne funeral 12-29, 1012B3

1979

BLODGETT, Katharine Barr
Dies 10-12, 860B2
BLONDELL, Joan
Dies 12-26, 1008B2
BLONDES Have More Fun (recording)
On best-seller list 2-14, 120F3; 4-4, 271E2
BLONDIE (singing group)
Heart of Glass on best-seller list 5-2, 356G2; 5-30, 448E3
BLOOD & Blood Pressure—*See under MEDICINE*
BLOODLINE (book)
On best-seller list 3-4, 173F3; 3-7, 174E1; 4-8, 271B2; 5-6, 356E2; 7-1, 548D3
BLOODLINE (film)
Released 6-28, 819E3
BLOOM, Murray Teigh
Last Embrace released 5-3, 528G2
BLOOM, Paul
On oil firm overchrgs 5-2, 343E2
BLOOMINGTON, Ind.—*See INDIANA*
BLOSSOM, Roberts
Escape from Alcatraz released 6-21, 820B1
BLOUNT, Mel
Steelers win Super Bowl 1-21, 63B1
BLUE Cross & Blue Shield Associations
2d opinion surgery plans evaluated 1-29, 140A1, C1
Hosp test paymts curbed 2-6, 138F1-C2
Tex drug plan trust rule upheld by Sup Ct 2-27, 165B1
Unneeded surgery debated 3-19, 218D3
3 Mile I A-accident evacuatn rptd 4-2, 245A3
Presurgery tests discouraged 5-1, 404C3
BLUE Diamond Coal Co.
Scotia mine widows suit challenge declined by Sup Ct 10-1, 768F1
BLUE Diamond Coal Co. v. Boggs
Case declined by Sup Ct 10-1, 768F1
BLUE Laws—*See RETAIL Trade*
BLUE Poles (painting)
Matisse work sold for record sum 7-3, 672B1
BLUES Brothers (singing group)
Briefcase Full of Blues on best-seller list 1-10, 80F3; 2-14, 120F3; 3-7, 174E1
BLUESTONE, Irving
UAW reaches accord with GM 9-14, 698D2
BLUHDORN, Charles G.
DR sugar probe rptd 8-16, 632E3-633A1
Sued for fraud, scores chrgs 11-26, 923D1, G1
BLUM, Barbara
2 weed killers banned 3-1, 167A2
BLUM, Jack
On Calif gas shortage 5-7, 343C1
BLUM, Len
Meatballs released 7-3, 820A2
BLUM, Yehuda
Vs UN W Bank setlmt probe 3-22, 198F2
Backs Unifil extensn 6-14, 436C3
Vs UN panel rpt on setlmts 7-18, 551E2
Vs UNTSO in Sinai 7-24, 551C1
US rpts Amb Young-PLO mtg 8-13, comments 8-14, 605B2, G2
SCLC pres meets on Young resignatn 8-21, 624B1
Scores Young's remarks, UN res on Palestinians 8-23, 642B2, C2
Defends Israel Leb policy 8-29, 658G2
BLUME, Judy
Wifey on best-seller list 8-5, 620D3; 9-2, 672D3
BLUME, Robert R.
Manny opens 4-18, 712C1
BLUMENTHAL, Eileen
Separatn rptd 4-14, 392F3
BLUMENTHAL, W(erner) Michael
On Taiwan, China, US trade ties 1-15, 27B3
Defends 'wage insurnc' tax credit plan 1-18, 55C3
Bendix wage-price compliance vow unwritten 2-6, 128C1
On Schlesinger oil warning, vows $ defense 2-8, 82A3, 83F1-B2
Affirms China econ ties 2-23; arrives for talks 2-24, asks Viet exit 2-27, signs assets accord 3-1, 141C2, 146B2-A3
Visits Japan, warns re trade imbalance 3-4–3-5, 159F3-160D1
Urges debt ceiling bill OK, fears default 4-2, 251D3
Separatn rptd 4-14, 392F3
US-China financial claims pact signed 5-8, 370C1
40 congressmen protest IMF-Nicaragua loan 5-10, 373A1
Carter names top econ spokesman 6-4, 463C1
At OECD mins mtg, sees oil price impact 6-14, 437B3
Dismissal rumored 7-17; fired, replacemt named; reactn 7-19, 529C1-531B2
Backs Volcker nominatn 7-25, 555D2
Addresses Urban League 7-25, 560C1
Named Burroughs chrmn 9-1, 859F3

1980

BL Ltd. (formerly British Leyland)
'79 union militant barred reinstatemt 2-7, 117B3; strike rejctd 2-20, 150D1
Layoffs announced 2-11, pay pact rejected 2-12, 117G2
Unions bar strike, back pact 4-2, 274E2
Union back wildcat strike 4-11, agrmt reached 4-21, 313E1
Research collaboratn set 4-22, 303B3
More govt aid sought 10-27; strike threatened 11-3, workers accept 7% pay deal 11-18, 886D2
Thatcher urges wildcat strike end 12-31, 994F1
BLOCH, Scotty
Act of Kindness opens 9-11, 756B3
BLOCK, Irwin J.
Miami riots, racism linked 12-6, 963F1
BLOCK, John R.
Named Agri secy 12-23, 980E1
Criticizes Bergland 12-23, 980G1
BLOCK, Larry
Coming Attractions opens 12-3, 1003A3
BLONDIE (singing group)
Call Me on best-seller list 3-5, 200E3; 4-2, 280E3; 4-30, 359G3; 6-4, 448E3
BLOOD & Blood Pressure—*See under MEDICINE*
BLOOD Feud (film)
Released 2-22, 216B2
BLOOD Wedding (play)
Opens 6-2, 756B3
BLOOM, Paul
Standard Oil price setlmt OKd 12-3, 960D1
BLOOMFIELD, George
Nothing Personal released 4-18, 416D3
BLOS, Joan W.
Gathering of Days wins Amer Book Award 5-1, 692D2
BLOT, Jacques
Scores UK on EC budget 4-28, 327F1
On Franco-Sovt summit 5-19, 378A3
BLUCKER, Robert
Hostages' letters published 1-18—1-20, 47C3
BLUE, Vida
NL pitching ldr 10-6, 926F2
BLUE Bell Inc.
Levi win in Wrangler trademark suit rptd 11-19, 917B3
BLUE Fire (freighter)
Intercepted off Cuba 7-4, 515A1, B1*
BLUE Kentucky Girl (recording)
Harris wins Grammy 2-27, 296D3
BLUE Lagoon (film)
Released 6-20, 675G1
BLUES Brothers, The (film)
Released 6-20, 675G1
Top-grossing film 7-2, 568G3
Heaven's Gate withdrawn from theaters 11-19, 906E1
BLUESTONE, Irving
Replaced as UAW vp 6-4, 457A2
BLUM, Barbara
On Love Canal 5-17, 387A1
BLUM, Harold H.
Hijack attempt foiled 8-18, 667F1-A3
BLUM, Richard
Marries San Fran mayor 1-20, 199E1
BLUM, Yehuda
UN res vs Israel setlmts voted 3-1, 163C1
Defends W Bank deportatns 5-8, 340D3
Scores UN censure of Israel 5-20, 381D1
Scores UN Cncl vote on W Bank bombings 6-5, 417C2
Calls UN mtg on Palestinians illegal 7-23, Assemb vote unsuccessful 7-29, 572A2, C2
Scored by Jordan 12-8, chrgs anti-Semitism 12-10, 952A3
Scores UN res on 2 W Bank mayors 12-19, 952D2
BLUMENFELD, Judge M. Joseph
Voids Conn oil tax pass along ban 7-9, 553D3
BLUMENFELD, Michael
Confrmd Panama Canal comr 4-2, 308E3
BLUMENTHAL, Richard
Named Abscam leaks prosecutor 2-11; may subpoena rptrs 2-12, 111E1
BLUMENTHAL, W(erner) Michael
Reagan 'basic speech' cites 2-29, 207C2
Named Burroughs chief exec, chrmn 9-25, 958G3

1976

BLYLEVEN, Bert
AL pitching ldr 10-4, 796D1
BLYTH Eastman Dillon & Co. Inc.
Rptd disciplined re boycott 8-11, 747C2
B'NAI B'rith
Cancels Brazil vacation tours 1-15, 27G2
Vs Austrian as Rotary pres 3-10, 380F2
Sam Beber dies 8-25, 656E3
Carter, Ford address DC conv 9-8, 9-9, 664G2, 665B2
Anti-Defamation League (ADL)
Meets 11-16—11-24, ldrs see Pope 11-24, 912C1
BNAI Zion
Cancels Brazil vacation tours 1-15, 27G2
BO, Hideo
Japan finance min 12-24, 1006B3
BOATS & Boating
Brazil bars S Africa race 1-2, 11C3
Olympic results 7-25, 7-30, 7-31; 2 Rumanians defect 7-28, 7-29, 562E2, 574E1, A2, 575C1, E1
BOAVIDA, Diogenes de Assis
Angola justice min 11-27, 995C3
BOAZ, Dennis
Conflict-of-interest rptd 11-12, 891F1
BOBBIO Centurion, Gen. Carlos
Mil revolt fails 7-9, 591A1
BOBSLEDDING
Winter Olympic results 2-7, 2-14, 159F1
BOCA Raton, Fla.—*See FLORIDA*
BOCHER, Main Rousseau—*See MAINBOCHER*
BODNARAS, M. Emil
Dies 1-24, 160C3
BODNER, Guillermo
Flies to Mexico 3-16, 382C3
BODYUL, Ivan
Visits Rumania 12-3—12-7, 1010E1
BOE, Archie R.
On air bag ruling 12-6, 921F1
BOEING Co., The
'75 arms sales listed 2-6, 147D2
SEC sues 2-12, ct OKs privacy 2-22, 362B2
Egypt probes payoff chrg 2-19, 138F2
US OKs Angola plane delivery 2-21, 163F1
Rpts foreign paymts 3-5, 362G1-B2
Confirms Iran jet-oil barter talks 5-11, 340B1
SEC notes paymts probe 5-12, 726D2
Ford campaigns 10-25, 802E3
B-1 contract awarded 12-2, 942E1
Top fscl '76 defns contractor 12-21, 961B3
BOEX, Heinrich
Suspended 5-17, 383E1
BOGGS, Rep. Corinne C. (D, La.)
Conv nominates Carter 7-14, 505F1
Reelected 11-2, 822B2, 829F3
BOGGS, Capt. Philip
Wins Olympic medal 7-22, 563B1, 575D3
BOGLIOLI, Wendy
Wins Olympic medal 7-22, 575A3
BOHARI, Lt. Col. M.
Nigeria oil min 3-15, 222A3
BOHLEN (tanker)
Sinks off France 10-14, 912E2
BOHMAN, Gosta
Named to Swedish Cabt 10-8, 794C2
BOHMER, Peter
FBI-terrorist ties chrgd 1-11, 42D1, F1
BOILERMAKERS, International Brotherhood of (AFL-CIO)
La oil refinery blast 8-15, 816B2
BOKASSA I, Emperor (Jean-Bedel Bokassa)
Assassinatn try fails 2-3, 204B2
Assumes 7 Cabt posts, army power 4-7, 288D2
Rptdly expels French plotter 4-30, 503F2
China ties restored 8-20, 949B2
Appoints council 9-5, 924D2
Names Dacko adviser 9-17, 858B1
Converts to Islam 10-19, 924C2
Visits China 11-15, 871C3
Declares CAR empire 12-4, 924B2
BOLAND, Rep. Edward P. (D, Mass.)
Reelected 11-2, 829B4
BOLBOSHIN, Nikolai
Wins Olympic medal 7-24, 576B3
BOLD Forbes (race horse)
Wins Ky Derby 5-1, 336F2
3d in Preakness 5-15, 368G3
BOLDT, Harry
Wins Olympic medal 7-30, 574D2

1977

BLUNDELL, Sir Denis
Successor named 3-7, 222B2
BLYLEVEN, Bert
AL pitching ldr 10-2, 927A1
Traded to Pirates 12-8, 990C1
BLYTH Eastman Dillon & Co. Inc.
Simon named adviser 4-4, 396F3
B'NAI B'rith
Hanafis seize intl hq 3-9—3-11, 192G2, B3
Hanafis indicted 5-3, 396A1
Hanafis sentncd 9-6, 711D1
Anti-Defamation League (ADL)
Scores Dixon anti-Nader slur 1-17, 96B1
House OKs antiboycott bill 4-20, 323A3
Boycott exemptns agreed 5-3, 460B1
Vs US-Sovt Geneva plan 10-3, 750G1
Sakharov, Shcharansky honored; Mondale reaffirms rights commitmt 11-20, 955F1
BOARD of Trade of Kansas City, Mo. v. U.S.
Sup Ct bars rate order review 10-3, 760D2
BOATS & Boating
Carter energy plan 4-20, 291D3
House OKs Carter energy pkg 8-5, 610C1
Courageous retains America's Cup 9-18, 828E2
BOBICK, Duane
Norton KOs 5-11, 395E1
BOBO, Donny
Suspended 12-21, drops bias suit 12-29, 1020E2
BOCCIA, Ubaldo
On Italy crime 1-5, 65D1
BOCK, Lothar P.
NBC gets Moscow Olympics 2-1, Satra suit rptd 2-14, 131D1, F1
BODINE, Albert
Wins United Tech suit 9-28, 860C1
BOE, Roy
NY Nets move to NJ set 7-26, 584F1, F2
BOECKER, Wallace S.
Questns coal impact on climate 5-31, 499C1
BOEHM, Franz
Dies 9-26, 872A1
BOEING Co., The
Forgn consultants rptd 1-5, ct backs secrecy 2-25, 215C3
Questionable paymts total cited 1-21, 79F1
Japan kickback chrgd 2-14, probed 2-15, 136D1
Concorde landings backed 3-11, 213F1
US-Canada sign probe pact 3-15, 200F1
Canary I crash suits filed 3-31—4-6, 311G3-312B1
Urban business confidence rptd 5-16, 385C1
IAM strikes 10-4—11-17, 1005A2
Nigeria copter purchase set 10-17, 986B3
Peabody Holding Co.—*See separate listing*
BOGART, Humphrey (1899-1957)
Howard Hawks dies 12-26, 1024B2
BOGGS, Tommy
Traded to Braves 12-8, 990B1
BOHAN, Marc
'77 fall fashions rptd 7-29, 1022C1
BOHANON, Judge Luther
Grants laetrile access 4-8, 4-17, 376C1
BOHLMANN, Hans-Joachim
Charged 10-8, 848E2
BOISE, Ida.—*See IDAHO*
BOKASSA I, Emperor (Jean-Bedel Bokassa) (Central African Empire)
US, UK rptrs held 7-14—8-15, US protest rptd 8-16, 634E3, 635B1
Coronation 12-4, 946D2-A3
BOKASSA, Empress Catherine
Crowned 12-4, 946E2
BOKASSA, Prince Jean-Bedel Georges
At coronation 12-4, 946F2
BOLAN, Marc
Killed 9-16, 787G3
BOLAND, Rep. Edward P. (D, Mass.)
To head intell com 7-14, 577B2
BOLD Reasoning (race horse)
Seattle Slew wins Triple Crown 6-11, 491A1

1978

BLUM v. Toomey
NYS welfare eligibility case refused by Sup Ct 6-12, 468C1
BLYLEVEN, Bert
NL pitching ldr 10-2, 928G2
BLYTH, Eastman Dillon & Co.—*See INA Corp.*
BLYTH, Eastman Dillon & Co. Inc. v. Rolf
Case refused by Sup Ct 12-4, 959B1
BMI—*See BROADCAST Music Inc.*
B'NAI B'rith
Vs UN pro-Palestinian drive 10-7, 762C3
Anti-Defamation League (ADL)
Sadat peace plea reply denied 2-1, 60D3
Forster lauds Bakke ruling 6-28, 482C3
B'NAI Torah Institute (Brooklyn, N.Y.)
Flood '74-76 influence selling rptd 1-27, 240C2
Pinter pleads guilty to bribery, tax chrgs 5-11, 363D2; sentenced 6-22, 500F3
BOADELLA, Albert
Escapes to France 2-27, play actors sentncd 3-7, 250A2
BOAM, Jeffrey
Straight Time released 3-18, 619G3
BOARD of Curators v. Horowitz
Horowitz ouster upheld 3-1, 143B3
BOARD of Education v. U.S.
Case declined by Sup Ct 12-4, 959A2
BOARD of Governors v. First Lincolnwood Corp.
FRB bank-holding co power backed by Sup Ct 12-11, 980E3
BOARD of Trustees v. Sweeney
Sex-bias ruling voided by Sup Ct 11-13, 874F1-C2
BOATS & Boating
Heyerdahl burns boat 4-4, 420G1
1st woman sails world solo 6-8, 653C2
BOBO, Donny
Arkansas wins Orange Bowl 1-2, 8C3
Suspended 12-14, 1025C3
BOBOKOV, Angel
Named Bulgaria agri dir 4-29, 531A1
BOBSLEDDING
Swiss win 2-man champion 2-5, 316F3
E Gers win 4-man champion 2-12, 316F3
BOBST, Elmer Holmes
Dies 8-2, 708A2
BOC International Ltd.
Airco OKs takeover bid, FTC trust fight cited 4-7, 403D3
BODOH, Allan F.
Go Tell Spartans released 9-23, 970E1
BODY Snatchers, The (book)
Movie remake released 12-21, 1030A3
BOE, Jason
On DC voting amendmt ratificatn 8-22, 661D2
BOE, Roy L.
Sued 5-2; Islanders fscl mgr named 6-6, refinancing plan OKd 8-10, 656B2
Nets sale agreed 8-28, 1027E3
BOEING Co., The
4th in '77 defns contracts 3-28, 224F2
Pan Am buys Lockheed jets 4-4, 264E2
McDonnell Douglas strike ends 4-16, 284G2
Singapore Airlines to buy jets 5-9, 365E2
UAL orders jets 7-14, 569F3
SEC chrgs, case settled 7-28, 642F3-643C1
FTC paymts chrgs settled 8-18, 643C1
Eastern, Brit Airways order 757s 8-31, 684G1
10th-ranked cash-rich US co 9-18, 716E3 *
AWACS purchase set by NATO 12-5, 954C2
China deal signed 12-19, 1015B2
BOEKER, Paul
Bolivia aid suspensn rptd 7-23, 571A2
BOEL, Henri
Cancels Czech visit 8-11, 691B3
BOEYNANTS, Paul Vanden
Belgium caretaker premr 10-20, 813D1
Electns held 12-17, submits resignatn, caretaker role asked 12-18, 1013E1
BOGAZIANOS, Vasili
PS Your Cat is Dead opens 3-22, 887F2
BOGGS, Rep. Corinne C. (Lindy) (D, La.)
Reelected 11-7, 850F4
BOGICEVIC, Vladislav
Signs with Cosmos 1-4, 23A2
BOISE Cascade Corp.
Indicted for price fixing 1-25, 67D2
Price fixing plea, fine rptd 10-16, 1005B3
BOIVIN, Leo
Fired as Blues coach 2-16, 458B3
BOK, Derek
Harvard revises curriculum 5-2, 348C2
Harvard-CIA secret ties revealed 12-1, 962A3
BOKASSA I, Emperor (Jean-Bedel Bokassa) (Central African emperor)
Maidou named premier 7-14, 596C1
BOLAN, Thomas
Ford sued 4-25, suit amended 5-16, 390B3
BOLAND, Bill
'50 Ky Derby victory cited 5-6, 539D1
BOLAND, Rep. Edward P. (D, Mass.)
Reelected 11-7, 851C1

1979

BLUNT, Anthony
Identified as 4th spy 11-15; controversy ensues 11-15–11-21, issues statemt 11-20, 908C2-909F1
BLYLEVEN, Bert
Rose sets NL singles mark 8-5, 619G2
NL pitching ldr 9-30, 955G2
Pirates win NL pennant 10-5, 797D2
In World Series 10-10–10-17, 816F1
B'NAI B'rith
Anti-Defamation League (ADL)
Henry Schultz dies 5-5, 432F3
Timerman wins Freedom Prize 6-17, 467E1
Weber case Sup Ct ruling scored 6-27, 477E2
Carter Palestinian-US civil rights analogy scored 8-1, 575E1
Young mtg with PLO rep opposed 8-15, 606A2
Young resignatn pressure denied 8-19, 624A2
Black criticism rejctd 8-23, 661E3
Timerman expelled from Argentina 9-25, 728B1
KKK membership study rptd 11-11, 865D1
BOARD of Education v. Harris
Case decided by Sup Ct 11-28, 944A2
BOARD of Governors of the Federal Reserve System v. United States League of Savings Associations
Case declined by Sup Ct 10-15, 847D3
BOARDWALK (film)
Released 11-14, 1007A3
BOATS & Boating
Sales unaffected by oil prices 3-28, 228A1
10-ft craft crosses N Atlantic 7-24, 656C3
Fastnet yachting disaster 8-14, 799F3; rpt issued 12-10, 955C1
USSR rptd kidnaped defector 10-15, 856C3
BOBRICK, Sam
Murder at Howard Johnson's opens 5-17, 712E1
BOBSLEDDING
Swiss win world 2-man title 2-18, 392D1
W Gers win world 4-man title 2-25, 392D1, E1*
BOBU, Emil
Named Rumania labor min 1-31, 171B1
BOCHTE, Bruce
NL wins All-Star Game 7-17, 569B1
AL batting ldr 9-30, 955E3
BODCAW Co.
Intl Paper purchase set; Weyerhaeuser, Mobil out bid 3-8, 350A1
1st 1/4 merger rise rptd 4-10, 349B3
Intl Paper buys 8-9, 664F1
BOEING Co., The
Teng visits Seattle plant 2-4, 83G3
Iran Air cancels 747 deal 2-25, 144E3
Missile info leak alleged 3-1, 207D2
US OKs Libya jet sale 3-2, 250G1
4 indicted in Japan bribe scandal 4-5, 5-15, 389F2
Wilson, Stamper on '78 top-paid execs list 5-14, 347F3
DC-10s grounded 6-6, 421A1
W Ger AWACS deal threatened 8-1, 586G1
7th in '78 defns contracts 8-1, 609C1
3 employes killed in Turkey 12-14, 998C1
BOETTCHER, Hermine
Acquitted re war crimes 4-19, 333E3
BOEYNANTS, Paul Vanden
Replaced as Belgian premr 4-3, 253C2
BOGARDE, Dirk
Despair released 2-15, 174D2
BOGDANOVICH, Peter
Saint Jack released 4-26, 528E3
BOGICEVIC, Vladislav
NASL assist ldr 8-12, 655A1
BOHAN, Alan
Cleared in youth's slaying 7-4, 565B1
BOHAN, Marc
'79 fashion roundup rptd 1006D2
BOHEMIAN Grove (race horse)
3d in Irish Derby 7-1, 876E3
BOHMAN, Gosta
Falldin named premier 10-9, 795A2
BOHNE, Gerhard Johannes
Argentina '66 extraditn cited 8-8, 617B1
BOIARDO, Ruggiero (Richie the Boot)
Indicted 5-23, 508A2
BOISE Cascade Corp.
Stone Container offer rptd 1-22, 89E1
Paper workers strikes end 1-30, 2-13, 345E2, F2
Stone Container rejcts merger 1-30, Lone Star purchase agreed 4-11, 440E3
BOKASSA I, Emperor (Jean-Bedel Bokassa) (Central African emperor; ousted Sept. 20)
Scores rioting 1-23, 62B2
On student death 5-17, 5-22, 387A2
Linked to student massacre by African probe 8-6, 601G2
Massacre order rptd 8-16, 697F3
Dacko deposes 9-20; France bars asylum 9-21—9-24, Ivory Coast accepts 9-24, 720E1-E2
Gifts to Giscard alleged 10-10, 791D1; 12-4, 993D3
BOLD Agent (race horse)
2d in Queen's Plate 6-30, 876D3
BOLD Bidder (race horse)
Kentucky Derby legacy rptd 5-5, 448F2
BOLD Ruler (race horse)
Kentucky Derby legacy rptd 5-5, 448E2
BOLDT, Judge George H.
Washn Indian fishing treaties upheld by Sup Ct 7-2, 559D1

1980

BLUNT, Anthony
Quits academy 8-18, controversy rptd 8-24, 652D1
BLYLEVEN, Bert
NL pitching ldr 10-6, 926G2
BLYTH Eastman Paine Webber Inc.
Money mkt fund unit listed 3-31, 223G3
Hunt silver debt repaid 4-16, 345F1
Genentech stock offer success rptd 10-14, 806A1
B'NAI B'rith
Pres candidates address conv, vow Israel support 9-3—9-4, 681A3
Anti-Defamation League (ADL)
Redgrave TV role protested 1-13, 120D2
BOARD and Care (film)
Wins Oscar 4-14, 296A2
BOARD of Regents v. Tomanio
Case decided by Sup Ct 5-19, 440G2
BOARD of Trade v. CFTC
Case declined by Sup Ct 4-28, 369E1
BOATS & Boating
UK indep Olympic boycott spreads 5-17, 379E2
Brit Rail plans sales 7-15, 544E1
Moscow Olympic results 7-20—8-3, 588F2, 622B2-D2, 623F1-B2, 624F3
Atlantic sailing record set 8-1, 907G3
Courageous eliminated from America's Cup trials 8-25; Turner sells 9-25, 834F1
Freedom, Australia win America's Cup trials 8-29, 9-5, Freedom retains Cup 9-5, 834E1-D2
Tayor killed in record run 11-13, 1002A2
BOB Evans Farms Inc.
Beatrice merger cancelled 12-29, 985D1
BOBSLEDDING
Lake Placid Olympic results 2-16, 2-24, 156C1
2 blacks on US Olympic team 2-24, 154C3
BOCHINA, Natalya
Wins Olympic medal 7-30, 624B2
BODY Human: the Magic Sense, The (TV special)
Wins Emmy 9-7, 692D1
BODYUL, Ivan I.
Named Sovt dep premr 12-19, 996C2
BOEING Co., The
Cruise missile problems rptd 1-7, 16G2
Jet productn cited 1-25, 66B1
Turkey '79 murder suspects arrested 2-13, 135G3
Eximbank loan offer to Australian co sparks probe 2-19, 989D1
Named cruise missile contractor 3-25, 228D1
Gen Dynamics wins short-range cruise missile contract 4-2, 267B3
Iran copter deliveries canceled 4-8, 282D1
7th in '79 defns contracts 5-28, 403F1
FAA orders jet engine inspectns 7-16, 667B1
3 get suspended sentnc in Japan bribe case 7-24, 605D2
US bars jet sale to Iraq 8-29, 662C3
BOEING v. Van Gemert
Case decided by Sup Ct 2-19, 131B1
BOELLING, Klaus
On Franco-Sovt summit 5-19, 378D3
BOGART, Humphrey (1899-1957)
Sam Marlow released 10-3, 836E3
BOGDANICH, Walt
Wins Polk award 2-25, 692E3
BOGDANOVA, Yulia
Wins Olympic medal 7-23, 623C3
BOGGS, Rep. Corinne C. (D, La.)
Wins primary 9-13, 724G2
Reelected 11-4, 842F4
BOGLEY Inc. v. U.S.
Case declined by Sup Ct 1-21, 93B3
BOGOMOLOV, Oleg
Sovts pledge COMECON energy export rise 10-1, 753B3
BOHMAN, Gosta
'81 budget rptd 1-11, 102A1
BOHRINGER Mannheim G.m.b.H.
Iran takeover rptd 7-9, 546E2
BOISE—*See IDAHO*
BOISE Cascade Corp.
Fine paper trust suit acquittal rptd 12-3, 917A2
BOISE State University
Wins NCAA Div I-AA football title game 12-20, 999B3
BOISI, James O.
Defends Hunt bailout loan 5-30, 425D2
BOJNOURDI, Kazem
Named Iran Rev Guard comr 6-29, 490C2
BOKASSA, Jean-Bedel
Confirms Giscard gifts 9-17, 728G3
French newspaper cites Giscard gifts 11-7, 872G1
French free Giscard gift figure 11-29, 921A3
Giscard cousins paid damages re gifts story 12-23, 996D3
BOLAND, Rep. Edward P. (D, Mass.)
Reelected 11-4, 843C1
BOLDEN, Jeanette
Sets indoor 640-yd relay mark 2-29, 892F1
BOLD Forbes (race horse)
Hunts bailout loan collateral listed 5-28, 426C1

1976

BOLIVIA—*See also ANDEAN Group, IDB, OAS, SELA*
'74 mil forces rptd 1-2, 60F2
Torres asks Banzer ouster 1-5, 27G1
Mil cmdrs, 2 mins replaced 1-6, 1-12, 26F3-27A1
Listed as 'not free' nation 1-19, 20D3
Police, guerrillas clash 4-2; guerrillas arrested 4-4, 4-8, 415G3-416C1
Controversy over Guevara, Zenteno slayings 4-14—5-23, 415B3
Torres found dead 6-2, protests staged 6-3, state funeral barred 6-6, 415D2-A3
Pol exiles offered amnesty 6-3; Banzer opponents arrested 6-6, 415A3
Torres death protests spread, leftist plot chrgd 6-7—6-19; siege imposed 6-9, 456D1
Santa Cruz jet crash 10-13, 876G2
'75-76 repressn rptd up 10-31, 975D1

Economy & Labor (domestic)
'74 defns budget rptd 1-2, 60F2
'75 GNP up, inflatn down 1-9, 27G1
Labor, student unrest grows; govt chrgs plots, deports ldrs 1-22—3-6, 237G2
Teachers wages hiked 3-5, 238G1
Miners strike, rejct pay hike 6-3—6-19; siege imposed 6-9, 415F2, 456D1

Foreign Relations (misc.)
Chile sea outlet plan scored 1-1—1-3, 1-9; terms rptd 1-2, study panel named 1-7, 26F3, 27A1
Gulf rpts bribes, Bolivia denies 1-14, 134C1, 147G1
Russell ct scores rights abuse 1-17, 61D2
Canada co labor dispute spurs unrest 1-22—3-6, 237A3
'75 OAS embargo end cited 138C2
YPFB gets UK, Canada bank loans 3-12, 4-14, 416E1
Pereda: Chile, Argentina, Peru leftists aid ELN 4-8, 416C1
World Bank dvpt loan rptd 4-13, 416C1
Forces tin price hike, signs intl pact 4-30, 416F1
Paris envoy slain 5-11, 350D3
Torres kidnaped in Argentina 6-1, found dead 6-2, body flown to Mex 6-7, 415D2-A3
Latin pol exiles greet Torres' widow in Mex 6-7, Torres buried 6-9, 456F2
Kissinger visits 6-7, 465E2
Forgn banks OK dvpt loan 6-18, 456A3
At nonaligned conf 8-16—8-20, 622C1
Chile rejcts seaport plan 11-26, 975G1
Vows neutrality in Chile-Peru war 12-7, 975D2

1977

BOLEN, David B.
Replaced as amb to Botswana, Lesotho, Swaziland 6-23, 626B3
Named amb to E Ger 7-8, confrmd 7-28, 626D2

BOLIN, Wesley
Sworn Ariz gov 10-20, 817B2

BOLIVIA—*See also ANDEAN Group, IDB, OAS*
'76 amnesty for 70 rptd 1-1, 3D1
US envoy visits, rights abuses detailed 5-14—5-17, 414D1, C2
'61-75 GDP variatns table 5-30, 439A1
Patino's niece kidnaped 10-3, freed 10-13, 871F1
2 mins quit in oil tax dispute 10-11, 2 others ousted in road scandal; Cabt revised 10-13, 902A1
Banzer sets '78 electns, lifts pol party ban 11-9; interim resignatn plan rptd 11-10; oppositn, exiles score 11-11, 901F2
Pol exiles rptd at 5000 11-11, 901F3
Pereda named AF chief 11-30, navy rptdly backs for pres 12-22, 1009A3
Banzer bars '78 pres bid 12-1, parties score electn plan 12-26, 1009F2
Anti-Banzer plot rptd foiled 12-9, 1009C3
Amnesty for 284 exiles set 12-21; union secret reentries rptd 12-22, 1009F3

Foreign Relations (misc.)—*See also 'Monetary, Trade & Aid' below*
UN Assemb member 3G3
Peru-Chile border buildup rptd 1-10, 2G2
Israel rptd prime arms seller 1-15, 28E3
Uruguay release of Mex newsman urged 7-15, 601F1
Banzer at Panama Canal Pact signing 9-7, 678C1
UN Cncl elects member 10-24, 852F3

Monetary, Trade & Aid (including all foreign economic developments)
Tin pact ratificatn barred 1-10, 169F1
Higher tin price backed 1-19, 169C2
'75-76 trade, paymts table 3-11, 189A2★, C2
Tin pact ratificatn agreed 3-29, 298C1
'66-75 arms transfers table 4-8, 415A2
UK cancels loan re miner abuse 8-9, 902B2
Forgn bankers confident in econ; '76, '77 loan data rptd 10-7, 902D1

U.S. Relations
Govt scores rights abuse chrgs, churches form panel 5-14, 414E2
Cocaine traffic rptd 8-29, 972F1
Banzer at Panama Canal Pact signing 9-7, 678C1
Govt econ data doubted; smuggling effect cited 10-7, 902E1-A2
US electn pressure noted, Banzer denies 11-11, 901G3
US drug prisoner pact set 12-20, 1010C3
Gulf ex-chrmn convicted 12-23, 1010A1

1978

BOLGER, William F.
New labor pact reached 7-21, 564E2
Postal pact revised 9-15, 765G3-766A2

BOLIN, Gov. Wesley H. (D, Ariz.)
Dies 3-4, 186F3
Babbitt elected gov 11-7, 855D1

BOLIO Bremen, Marina
To be CR human promotn min 3-4, 171A1

BOLIVIA—*See also ANDEAN Group, IDB, OAS*
Hunger strike wins full amnesty 1-18; labor, student groups regain rights 1-25, 411B3
Students seize La Paz univ 4-27; 40 ordered arrested, 3 seized 5-2, 411D3
35 seized in labor march 5-1, 411F3
Labor ldrs chrg govt harassmt 5-5, 411F3
Univ reopened, offcls replaced 5-30, 478A3
Patino art collectn auctnd 6-29, 579E1
Tin miners strike vs Pereda 7-21; arrests rptd 7-25, 571B1
Peasants, soldiers clash in Coritapa 7-25, violence rpts vary 7-26, 7-27, 671A2
News media strike prevented 8-18, 691D2
Guerrilla ldr rptd arrested 9-1, 691F2
Press freedom rptd by IAPA 10-13, 829A2
Miners reject govt wage offer 10-20, 840D3

Foreign Relations (misc.)
Chile ties broken 3-17, sea outlet impasse cited 3-19, 216A1
Amazon 8-natn pact signed 7-3, 829C2
Electn fraud chrgd by intl observers 7-12, 7-19, 571E1
UN Assemb member, named to Cncl 9-19, 713A3, C3
Banzer named Argentina amb 10-6, 823E2
World Bank oil loan set 10-8, 840D3
Argentine pres sees Pereda, backs sea outlet 10-25, 860C3
Chile sea access dispute cited re Cabt shuffle 11-1, 11-6, 868E3
Chile war fears cited 11-2, 860B3
Drug smuggling drive begun 11-15, 913G1

Government & Politics—*See also other appropriate subheads in this section*
3 oppositn candidates set pres bids 4-10—5-12; Lechin rejcts 5-5, leftist coalitn fails 5-11, 411E2, A3
Pereda rptdly leads pres race 4-21, 411F2
Paz Estenssoro pres bid set 5-24; Bernal, Amurrio bids rptd 5-26, 5-30, 478F2
Electns held, fraud chrgd 7-9; Pereda leads vote count, oppositn scores electns 7-11, 530D2
Campaign harassmt rptd 7-9, 530C3
Intl observers chrg electn fraud 7-12, 7-19, 571E1
Electns annulled 7-19, 570C3-571G1
Pereda seizes power 7-21, swears Cabt, on democracy 7-24, 570C3-571B1
Oppositn ldrs rptd underground 7-24, 571B1
Post-coup detainees ordrd freed 7-26, 617C2
Siles asks new electns, warns strikes 7-29, oppositn ldrs rptdly shun 7-30, 617B2
'80 electns set, Pereda bars pres bid 8-6, 617A2
State of siege lifted; natl security law, govt svc law revoked 8-11, 671G1
Press freedoms guaranteed 8-18, 691D2
Leftist coup rptdly foiled, Siles followers arrested 10-29, 840C3
Cabt quits 11-1; mil controls new Cabt 11-6, 868D3
Army officers seized in 'plot' 11-2, 868D3
Pereda presses anti-curruptn drive 11-15, 11-21; offcl oppositn cited 11-24, 913F1
Siles kin homes bombed 11-23, 913B2
Pereda ousted in bloodless coup; Padilla vows July '79 electns, swears Cabt; Siles backs plan 11-24, 913B1, C2

U.S. Relations
Gulf Oil compensatn paymt rptd 4-14, 478A3
US A-fuel export license deferral rptd 5-20, 408B2
Carter hopeful for sea outlet solutn 6-21, 489C3
US rues coup 7-22; aid suspensn cited 7-23, cutoff seen 7-26, 571G1
US mil aid resumed 8-15, 671A2

1979

BOLESLAUS II, King (d. 1081)
St Stanislaus murder cited 6-2, 414A2

BOLGER, William F.
Rpts Postal Svc surplus 11-27, 921B2

BOLIN, Molly
Angels win WBL title 5-2, 507D1

BOLIVIA—*See also ANDEAN Group, IDB, LAFTA, NONALIGNED Nations Movement, OAS*

Economy & Labor
Gen strike, bank closings halt business 11-14, 888C2
Econ reforms set; bankers strike, peasants demonstrate 12-3, unions ask natl protest 12-5, 926C1

Foreign Relations (misc.)—*See also 'Monetary' and 'UN' below*
Chile sea access dispute cited 1-20, 52B1
El Salvador migratn pact rptd 2-12, 235A2
Padilla at Brazil pres inaugural 3-15, 210D1
Banzer ends Argentina exile 3-16, 233D2
Nonaligned movemt joined 9-3, 675E1
OAS Assemb hosted, Pacific access asked 10-22–10-31, 824E1
Tourists evacuated 11-7, 853C1

Government & Politics—*See also other appropriate subheads in this section*
Freedom House lists as partly free 13B1
Lechin rejcts pres bid; asks police, mil cuts 3-12, 233G2
Banzer returns, sees electn role; pres candidates listed 3-16, 233D2
Coup attempt averted, defns min resigns 6-29, 501G2
Electns held, Siles leads vote count 7-1, 501F1
Voting deadlocked 8-3–8-4; Guevara elected provisional pres, civiln govt restored 8-6, 600G1
Army units rebel, govt reaffirms control 10-11, 811D1
Mil coup ends democracy, Natusch named pres 11-1, 832E3
Cong dissolved 11-2, martial law declared, mil split rptd 11-3; crisis continues 11-4–11-6, martial law lifted, death toll rptd 11-7, 852D3
Mil officers ask Natusch resignatn 11-14, Natusch resigns, Gueiler replaces 11-16, 888A2
Cabt sworn 11-19, 907G1
Army cmdr rebels 11-23; Gueiler meets demands, names successor 11-25, 907D1

Monetary, Trade, Aid & Investment
US scored on tin sales 10-22, 824F1
US cuts aid 11-2, 833F1; sets terms 11-16, 888B3
'79 trade deficit, forgn debt estimated 11-16, 888G2
Peso devalued; IMF, Venez loans, US aid set 12-3, 926D1, G1

UN Policy & Developments
Israel setlmt policy opposed in comm rpt 7-14, 551B2
Membership listed 695E2

U.S. Relations
US issues rights rpt 2-10, 107E3
US cocaine trade growth rptd 9-5, 972A3
US scored on tin sales 10-22, Vance lauds dem rule 10-23, 824F1
Vance warns vs coup 10-23, US cuts aid 11-2, 833D1
US tourists evacuated 11-7, 853C1
US sets aid terms 11-16, 888B3; 12-3, 926G1

1980

BOLGER, William F.
Postal rate hike proposed for '81 4-21, 347B2

BOLIN, Molly
Stars win WBL title 4-10, 432B2

BOLIVAR, Simon (1783-1830)
Santa Marta conf marks death 12-17, 992A3

BOLIVIA—*See also ANDEAN Group, IDB, NONALIGNED Nations, OAS*

Economy & Labor
Lechin arrested 7-17, feared dead 8-1, 602C3

Foreign Relations (misc.)
Mex gets UN Cncl seat 1-7, 12B2
Colombia envoy seized in DR emb raid 2-27, 141B1; siege ends, envoy freed 4-27, 335G1
Argentina A-pact cited 3-18, 229E2
Olympic role ruled out, econ blamed 5-2, 379D2
Peru firm sues Banzer 7-12, 543E1
UN women's conf held 7-14—7-31, coup protested 7-18, 587C3
Peru vows border dispute setlmt 7-28, 580B1
Andean Group members condemn coup 7-29; Taiwan, 3 Latin natns recognize mil govt 7-31, 577D1
Garcia scores Andean Group 8-6, 602F3
Brazil offers Siles family asylum 8-12, 668G1
Gueiler gets exit OK 9-15, 728A1
Siles surfaces in Peru 9-15, Paz joins 9-16, 728B1
Gueiler leaves for France 10-4; in W Ger, scores Garcia govt 10-5, 787C2
Amazon pact signed 10-28, 865D2
OAS scores coup, asks rights probe 11-27, 913E3
Santa Marta conf boycott set 12-10; conf condemns coup 12-17, Andean Group participatn end threatnd 12-18, 992A3

Government & Politics—*See also other appropriate subheads in this section*
Freedom House lists as partly free 87E3
Cabt resigns amid coup rumors 3-26; new mins sworn, mil gets 2 posts 4-7, 272E1
Coup rumors intensify 5-30—6-10, mil asks electn delay 6-9, denied 6-10, 443A2
Mil again asks electn delay, Gueiler bars 6-19, 496D3
Electns held, mil silent 6-29; Siles leads, lacks majority 7-3; coalitn movemt mounts 7-4, 508D3-509A1
Paz quits pres race, Siles victory assured 7-9, 543C1
Banzer sued for campaign plagiarism 7-12, 543E1
Mil coup ousts Gueiler, disbands Cong; Soclst ldr slain 7-17; miners resist, Siles supports 7-20, 546E2
Mil junta moves to consolidate power 7-17—7-31; Siles forms clandestine govt, urges 'passive resistence' 7-30, 577A1
2 high ranking officers replaced 7-30, mil rival pledges support 8-5, 602D3
Compulsory govt svc decreed 8-1, 602B3
Garcia delivers independnc day speech, Siles issues counter statemt 8-6, 602E3

Sports
Olympic role ruled out, econ blamed 5-2, 379D2

Unrest
Leftist priest slain 3-22, mil coup plot fails 3-23; Cabt shuffled 4-7, 272E1
La Paz bomb blasts 5-30, 443B2
Siles aides die in plane crash, sabotage blamed 6-2, 728D1
Gueiler assault attempt fails 6-7, 443A3
Rightists riot in Santa Cruz, US facilities ransacked 6-18; Gueiler scores 6-19, 496G2
Mil coup ousts Gueiler, Soclst ldr slain 7-17; miners resist 7-20, 546E2
Miners attack army barracks, mining camps raided 7-23, 577B1
Pol suspects, rptrs detained; churches raided, 11 priests missing 7-23, 577C1
Siles forms clandestine govt, urges 'passive resistance' 7-30, 577A2
1,000 still missing; Gueiler gets church protectn, Lechin feared dead 8-1, 602C3
US journalist detained 8-6—8-12, arrest total rptd 8-14, 668D1
Siles family offered Brazil asylum 8-12, 668G1
La Paz archbp denounced 9-3, church chrgs rights abuses 9-10, 686C3
Gueiler gets exit OK 9-15, 728A1
Siles surfaces in Peru, vows resistance 9-15, 728B1
Gueiler leaves for France 10-4, scores Garcia regime 10-5, 787C2
OAS asks rights probe 11-27, 913E3

U.S. Relations
Amb presents credentials; warns mil vs coup, links aid 3-26, 272B2
US moves vs coup rptd 5-31—6-4; mil scores, asks amb's ouster 6-5—6-9, 443C2
Rptr detained 6-9, 443F2
Anti-US riots in Santa Cruz 6-18, 496A3
US protests coup; recalls amb, suspends mil aid 7-17, 546D3
US cuts off aid 7-25, 577E1
Garcia scores US 8-6, 602F3
US journalist detained 8-6—8-12, arrest total rptd 8-14, 668D1
US cuts emb staff, halts drug progrms 8-13; junta trafficking rptd 8-15, 667E3

1976

BOLL, Heinrich
Pleads for Sovt dissident 3-24, 421A3
BOLLE, Elvind
Norway fisheries min 1-12, 30A2
BOLLES, Don
Bomb injures, land fraud probe cited 6-2; dies 6-13; Adamson chrgd 6-21, 483F2
Murder case dvpts 7-2—10-26, mistrial declared 10-21, 859E2
18 indicted re land fraud 9-14, 859D3
Press probes Ariz crime 10-2, 849B2
New judge OKd 11-19, trial site shifted 12-7, 971D3
Wins Ariz U posthumous award 12-9, 971G3
BOLLING, Klaus
On abandoned Sovt A-plant 3-31, 243D2
On French troop reductn 10-9, 852A3
BOLLING, Rep. Richard (D, Mo.)
Reelected 11-2, 830A1
Loses majority ldr bid 12-6, 919B1
BOMBINGS—*See under CRIME; also country names*
BOMMARITO, Peter
Rubber strike starts 4-21, 309A1, B1
BOND, Gov. Christopher S. (R, Mo.)
Fords lists as potential VP 1-22, 41A2
Reagan sweeps Mo delegates 6-12, 432E2
VP prospect cited 8-10, 584C1
Addresses GOP conv 8-16, 615B1, D1
Loses reelection 11-2, 820G2, 823B3
BOND, Julian
Cleaver Defense Fund formed 2-17, 272E1
Declines pres bid 3-15, 3-20, 214F2, A3
Bell apptmt scored 12-20, 956G3
BONDA, Alva Ted
'72 campaign gift listed 4-25, 688D1
BONDARCHUK, Anatoli
Wins Olympic medal 7-28, 576B1
BONDS—*See STOCKS, Bonds & Securities*
BONGO, Omar (formerly Albert-Bernard Bongo) (Gabonese president)
At France-Africa summit 5-10—5-11, 355G2
Names new mins 10-19, 1003A2
Freezes forgn debts 12-6, 1003C2
Ashland '72 paymts rptd 12-20, 985B3
BONIFACIO, Franco
Italian justice min 2-11, 140B2
BONIFACIO, Paolo
Sworn Italy justice min 7-30, 573F1
BONIFAS, Capt. Arthur G.
Killed in Korea 8-18, 618C3
BONIOR, David E.
Elected 11-2, 823E2, 829E4
BONK, Gerd
Wins Olympic medal 7-27, 576F2
BONKER, Rep. Don (D, Wash.)
Reelected 11-2, 831A2
BONNET, Christian
Meets wine growers 1-7, 138B3
Seeks EEC drought aid 7-19, 548E3
Announces drought aid 8-25, 675C1
Named agriculture min 8-27, 650G3
BOOKER McConnell Ltd.
Guyana unit natlizatn set 2-23, 252C3
BOOK of Common Prayer
Revisn approved 9-20, 755G1, E2
BOOKS—*See LITERATURE*
BOOMS, Rev. Albert
Deported from Pl 11-20, 890D1
BOONCHAI Bamroonphong, Gen.
Named dep premier 10-22, 813F2
BOONE, Pat
Butz resigns 10-4, 743G3
BOONSANONG Punyodyana
Assassinated 2-28, 176E3
BOOTH, Albert
Named employment secy 4-8, 266F3
Retains Cabt post 9-10, 694A1
Rpts job measures 9-23, 773A2
BOOTH Newspapers Inc.
Acquired by Newhouse 11-8, 901F2

1977

BOLLES, Don (d. 1976)
Adamson pleads guilty, 2 others arrested 1-15, 161D3
Ariz Mafia ties probed 3-13—3-20, 568G1
Trial judge's daughter found dead 9-20, 871G2
2 convicted of murder 11-6, 871B2
BOLLINGER, Elizabeth (Mrs. Jacques)
Dies 2-22, 164C2
BOLTON, Frances Payne
Dies 3-9, 264D2
BOLWELL, Edwin
Named NY Post editor 1-8, 48G3
BOMBECK, Erma
Grass is Always Greener on best-seller list 3-6, 184F3; 10-2, 808F3
BOMBINGS—*See under CRIME; also country names*
BO Moya
Asks US to aid separatists 779A3
BOMPENSIERO, Frank
Slain 2-10, linked to porno 7-3, 568D2
BONAIRE—*See NETHERLANDS Antilles*
BOND, Julian
Vs Bell confrmatn 1-11—1-18, 34A2
Scores Carter 8-15, 702A2
BONDA, Ted
Fires Robinson as Indian mgr 6-19, 644G1
BONDS, Bobby
AL batting ldr 10-2, 926F3, 927A1
Traded to White Sox 12-5, 990C1
BONDS & Bond Issues—*See STOCKS, Bonds & Securities; also city, state names*
BONESTEEL 3rd, Gen. Charles H.
Dies 10-13, 872B1

BONGO, Omar (formerly Albert-Bernard Bongo) (Gabonese president)
Sends Morocco OAU plea 512C1
Opens OAU summit 7-2, 512C1
Seeks Goldsmith release 8-11, 635B1
BONIFACIO, Jose
Asks Cong draft reform aid 4-2, 281D1
BONKER, Rep. Don (D, Wash.)
Sees Ethiopia ldr 12-13, rpts terror 12-16, 998C2
BONNER, Neville
At Commonwealth finance mins conf 9-21—9-24, 936E2
BONNET, Christian
Named interior min 3-30, 239A2
On Creys-Malville A-protest 8-2, 597A3
BONNEVILLE Power Administration—*See under U.S. GOVERNMENT—INTERIOR*
BONSAL, Judge Dudley B.
Drops Teamster kickback chrg 11-11, 928C1
BOOK of Common Prayer
Dissident Episcs rejct revisn 9-14—9-16, 731D2
BOOK of Lists, The (book)
On best-seller list 7-3, 548E3; 8-14, 643G1; 9-4, 712D3; 10-2, 808E3; 11-6, 872E3; 12-4, 1021G2
BOOK-of-the-Month Club Inc.
Time Inc to buy 7-5, 519D2
BOOKS—*See LITERATURE*
BOONLERT Kaewprasart, Maj.
Gets life sentence 4-21, 331E2
BOONVILLE, Calif.—*See CALIFORNIA*
BOOT and Shoe Workers Union (AFL-CIO)
Scores Carter re shoe imports 4-2, 248B2
BOOZ, Allen & Hamilton Inc.
Simon named adviser 3-7, 396E3
BOPHUTHATSWANA
Independence declared 12-5, 935A2

1978

BOLL, Heinrich
Loses libel suit 5-30, 439E2
BOLLAND, Robert
Scores NRC A-reactor safety test 12-10, 961A2
BOLLES, Don (d. 1976)
Killers sentenced to death 1-10, 24B2
Dolan gives family Pulitzer money 4-17, 315A2
State witness jailed 12-9, 992D2
BOLLING, Rep. Richard (D, Mo.)
House votes $16 bln tax cut 8-10, 604C1
Reelected 11-7, 851D2
BOMBECK, Erma
If Life Is a Bowl of Cherries on best-seller list 4-30, 356G1; 6-4, 460B3; 9-4, 708B1; 7-2, 579C3; 8-6, 620A2; 10-9, 800B3; 11-6, 888A1; 12-3, 971B1
BOMBINGS—*See under CRIME; country names*
BOND, Edward
Spring Awakening opens 7-13, 887B3
BOND, Langhorne M.
Proposes FAA air-safety rules 12-27, 1006D3, 1007B1
BOND Buyer, The (magazine)
Rpts on electn results 11-7, 915B2
BONDESTAM, Anitha
Swedish communicatns min 10-18, 822A3
BONDS, Bobby
Traded to Rangers 5-17, Indians 10-3, 779G2
BONDS & Bond Issues—*See STOCKS, Bonds & Securities; city, state names*
BONER, Bill
Wins US House seat 11-7, 852D2, 853E1
BONGO, Omar (formerly Albert-Bernard Bongo) (Gabonese president)
Student riots shut univ 2-4, 94E2
Page Airways paymt chrgd 4-13, 449B2
Asks African defns force 5-22, 382B3
Ousts Benin workers 7-23, 596A2
BONIFACIO, Francesco Paolo
Named Italy justice min 3-11, 191B1
BONIN, Justice Robert M.
Suspended as Mass Sup Ct justice 4-13, censured 7-8, resigns 8-6, 844A1
BONIOR, Rep. David E. (D, Mich.)
Reelected 11-7, 851F1
BONJOUR Amour (film)
Released 6-11, 618D3
BONKER, Rep. Don (D, Wash.)
Rpts Egypt, Sudan vow Somali aid 1-26, 99F3
Doubts CIA evidence on Cuba role in Zaire 6-8, 442D2
Reelected 11-7, 852A4
BONN Economic Summit
UK prime min urges plan 3-14, sees Carter 3-23, 226G2
Carter money plan reservatns rptd 6-18, 546A1
7-natn econ summit; ldrs vow inflatn fight, output hike, sign hijacking agrmt 7-16—7-17, 543B3-544C1
W Ger econ stimulus plan rptd 7-28, 583E3
US demands farm produce agrmt 9-7, 695D1
Carter affirms inflatn, trade vows at IMF-World Bank mtg 9-25, 731G2
BONNET, Christian
Renamed French interior min 4-5, 245F2
On Orly airport shootout 5-20, 383F3
BONNET, Henri
Dies 10-25, 888D2
BONNEVILLE Power Administration—*See under U.S. GOVERNMENT—INTERIOR*
BOOCK, Peter
Arrested in Yugo 5-11, extraditn unresolved 5-11—5-31, 439B1
Yugo bars extraditn 11-17, release rptd 11-18, 906A2
BOOCK, Waltraud
Husband arrested in Yugo 5-11, 439B1
BOOGIE Oogie Oogie (recording)
On best-seller list 9-6, 708E1; 10-11, 800E3
BOOKBINDER, Hyman
Mondale reassures on Mideast jet sale 5-15, 358C1
BOOK of Lists, The (book)
On best-seller list 1-8, 24E3; 3-5, 195F3; 4-2, 272C3
BOOK-of-the-Month Club Inc. (of Time Inc.)
FTC complaint rptd setld 9-7, 702G1
BOOKS—*See LITERATURE*
BOONE, Bob
NL wins All-Star Game 7-11, 559E3
Wins Golden Glove Award 11-21, 928B3
BOONE, Debby
Wins Grammy 2-24, 315F3
BOONE, Pat
Daughter wins Grammy 2-24, 315F3
Held liable for acne ads 5-11, 702F2-A3
BOONE, Ron
Traded to Nuggets, Lakers 6-26, 656A1
BOOTH, Col. Ferris (deceased)
Nephew convicted in widow's murder plot 4-26, 380G2
BOOTH, Lillian
Nephew convicted in murder plot 4-26, 380G2
BOPHUTHATSWANA
Spinks-Ali rematch plan protested 3-8, site chngd 3-9, 212B1, E1
Blacks denied S Africa passports 6-9, 536C3
Malawi bars passport holder 6-10, 536E3

1979

BOLLERS, Harold
Dismisses Layton chrgs 3-7, 220E1
BOLLING, Gary
Glorious Monster opens 7-10, 711D3
BOLLING, Rep. Richard (D, Mo.)
Rules Com chrmn 1-24, 71E1
Hospitalized for alcoholism 6-25, 527A3
BOLSHOI Theatre
Godunov defects to US 8-23; US detains wife 8-24, releases 8-27, 644D3-645F1
Kozlovs defect to US 9-16, 697C2
Godunov ABT resigntn rptd 11-21, 1005E3
BOLT, Tommy
2d in Legends of Golf tourn 4-29, 587E2
BOLTON, Bruce
Alabama wins Sugar Bowl 1-1, 8F2
BOLTON, Guy Reginald
Tip Toes opens 3-26, 712A3
Dies 9-5, 756A2
BOMBECK, Erma
If Life is a Bowl of Cherries on best-seller list 4-8, 271B2; 5-6, 356E2; 6-3, 432C2
Aunt Erma's Cope Book on best-seller list 11-4, 892C3
BOMMARITO, Peter
In 'Big 4' contract talks, wage guides in dispute 2-2—5-9; ct ruling sought 5-2, 344C3-345A2
Ct bars wage-guide contract denial, sees Uniroyal setlmt 5-31, 399D3
Pacts set with Goodrich 6-15, Uniroyal 6-18, 480E1
BOND, Christopher
Flying Blind opens 11-15, 956B3
BOND, Langhorne M.
Details FAA air-safety crackdown 3-16, 206C1
Rpts DC-10 safety flaws 5-29, 411F3
Grounds DC-10s indefinitely 6-6, 420C3
Lifts DC-10 flight ban 7-13, 538G2
BONDS, Bobby
Traded to Cardinals 12-7, 1002F2
BONDS & Bond Issues—*See STOCKS, Bonds & Securities*
BONE, Raleigh
Deadly Delilah opens 7-6, 711D2
BONIFAZ, Oscar
Retains Bolivia Cabt post 11-19, 907A2
BONILLA, Ruben
Elected LULAC pres 6-17, 810E1
Scores judge in Torres case 10-30, 839F3
BONIOR, Rep. David E. (D, Mich)
Asks US-USSR airlift aid to Cambodia 11-1, 863B3
BONNANO, Joseph
Galante slain 7-12, 548C1
BONNANO Jr., Joseph C.
Indicted on conspiracy chrgs 4-27, 368F1
BONN Economic Summit
W Ger parlt OKs budget 1-26, 77F2
BONNELL, Barry
Traded to Blue Jays 12-5, 1002E2
BONNIER Newspaper Group
Esquire purchase rptd 5-1, 334D2
BOOKS—*See LITERATURE*
BOONCHU Rojanasathien
Thai finance post rejctd 5-25, 429A1
BOONE, Bob
NL wins All-Star Game 7-17, 568G3
Wins Golden Glove Award 11-20, 956D1
BOORSTEIN, William
Held by strikers 8-17—8-18, 652G2
Escapes 8-24, flees to US 8-28 668B2
BOPHUTHATSWANA
Venda declared independent 9-13, 732G1

1980

BOLL, Heinrich
Papal petitn rptd 11-15, 905B1
BOLLER, Thomas
Ia schools buy White House uniforms 5-16, 460A3
BOLLES, Don (d. 1976)
Killers convictns overturned 2-25, 214G2
Killer convicted 10-17, 860E3
Killer sentenced 11-14, 926B3
BOLLING, Rep. Richard (D, Mo.)
Reelected 11-4, 843D2
BOLSHOI Theater
Vlasova seeks US return 8-1, 638B2
BOLT, Tommy
Wins Legends of Golf 4-27, 412E3
BOMBECK, Erma
Aunt Erma's Cope Book on best-seller list 1-13, 40B3; 2-10, 120C3; 3-9, 200C3
BOMBINGS—*See under CRIME*
BOMMARITO, Peter C.
Votes vs natl accord 5-6, 385B2
BONANNO, Joseph C. (Joe Bananas)
Mafia, pizza indus ties probed 8-24, 714G1
Convicted 9-2, 712E3
BOND, Alan
Protests Freedom America's Cup 3d race victory 9-21, victory upheld 9-22, 834C2
BOND, Christopher S. (Kit)
Wins Mo primary for gov 8-5, 682F3
Elected Mo gov 11-4, 845G2, 847B1, 851G1
BOND, Langhorne M.
San Diego air control zone set 3-22, 347A1
Claims FAA computer data reliable 6-30, 666F3
BONDS & Bond Issues—*See STOCKS*
BONDUE, Alain
Wins Olympic medal 7-24, 622F2
BONELLI, Richard
Dies 6-7, 528C1
BONER, Rep. Bill (D, Tenn.)
Reelected 11-4, 844C2
BONFILS Foundation, Helen & Frederick G.
Times Mirror Co to buy Denver Post 10-22, 857D1
BONHAM, John
Dies 9-25, 755C2
BONIN, William George
Chrgd in Calif 'freeway murders' 7-29, 654B2
4th chrgd in 'freeway murders' 8-22, 727G1
BONIOR, Rep. David E. (D, Mich.)
Reelected 11-4, 843F1
BONISOLI, Franco
Accused re Moro affair 1-2, 20G2
BONKER, Rep. Don (D, Wash.)
Reelected 11-4, 844B3
BONNER, Ruth
Sakharov exiled 1-22, 46D3
Police block Sakharov apartmt 3-4, 3-5, 181B3
BONNER, Yelena
Sakharov expelled 1-22, 46F2
Delivers Sakharov statemts 1-28, 2-4, 86D1, A2-D2
BONNET, Christian
Bars negotiatns with Corsica militants 1-10, 58E2
Vows more protectn for Jews 9-28, 750E1
On US journalist's ouster 10-3, 790B2
Meets Jewish ldrs re synagogue blast 10-4, 767D2
BONNET, Neil
3d in Daytona 500 2-17, 637D3
2d in LA Times 500 11-15, 1002D1
BOOGIE Wonderland (recording)
Earth, Wind & Fire wins Grammy 2-27, 296D3
BOOK of the Dun Cow, The (book)
Wins Amer Book Award 5-1, 692G2
BOOKS—*See LITERATURE*
BOONCHU Rojarsthien
Thai deputy premier 3-12, 196F3
BOONE, Bob
In World Series 10-14—10-21, 811G2-812G3
BOONE, Ron
NBA free-throw ldr 3-30, 278D3
BOOTHE, Powers
Wins Emmy 9-7, 692D1
BOPHUTHATSWANA
Econ aid need rptd 2-8, 134F2
S Africa rptd planning consolidatn 2-9, 134G2-A3
Mafeking transfer set 3-27, 278D1
Mafeking transferred 9-19, 753A2
Boxing title bout held, riots erupt 10-25, 887E3, 1000E3

1976

BORANES—*See CHEMICALS*
BORBELY, Sandor
Named to Secretariat 10-27, 947B1
BORBON y Battenberg, Don Juan de (Count of Barcelona) (Spain)
Urges Spain back king 6-14, 459E1
BORBON y Borbon, Prince Juan Carlos de (Spain)—*See JUAN Carlos I, King*
BORBON y Parma, Prince Carlos Hugo de (Spain)
2 followers slain 5-9, brother expelled 5-14, 422F2
BORBON y Parma, Prince Sixto Enrique de (Spain)
2 Carlists slain 5-9, expelled 5-14, 422G2
BORD, Andre
Quits as UDR chief 4-9, 312A3
BORDABERRY, Juan Maria
Human rights abuse chrgd 3-5, 207D3
Nov vote rptd canceled 3-12, 4-11, 382F2
Sees Stroessner 3-24—3-27, Pinochet 4-21—4-24, 382D3
Talks with mil reps end 5-7, sees ldrs 5-21, 6-1, ousted 6-12, 440D3
Sovt dissidents score rights abuse 5-10, 441A2
US House panel vs Uruguay mil aid 6-5, 441G1
New pres named 7-14, 542A1
Pol rights restored 10-7, 814B3
BORDERS, Archbishop William Donald
On Pallotine Fathers audit 6-18, 950G3
BORDER Steel Rolling Mills Inc.
Fined 4-10, 988E3
BORDONI, Carlo
Indicted 1-20, 78A3
BOREN, Gov. David L. (D, Okla.)
Okla Dem caucuses results 2-7, 129E1
Carter gives energy role 7-6, 492G3
New death penalty law enacted 7-24, 568C3
BORG, Bjorn
Loses US pro indoor 2-1, 123A3
Wins WCT 5-9, Wimbledon 7-3, 504E1, G1
Wins US pro tennis 8-31, 716G1
Runner-up in US Open 9-12, 716A1
BORG Olivier, George
Labor electn win rptd 9-20, 713E1, A2
BORK, Robert H.
Backs death sentence 3-30, 3-31, 262A1
Backs Levi on busing review 5-29, 392B1
BORMAN, Frank
To head honor code study 8-23, 670E2
BORT Jr., James H.
Jailed 9-3—9-17, 700B3
BORTNICK, Alan
Kidnaped, ransomed 1-12—1-17, 159F3
Kidnapers sentencd 7-21, 544D1
BORZOV, Valery
Wins Olympic medal 7-24, 575F3
Death threat rptd 7-31, 562A3
BOSCH, Juan
Russell ct meets 1-10—1-17, 61E2
BOSCH, Orlando
Exile coalitn, Letelier murder links rptd 10-11, 10-12, 10-19, 779D3, 780F2, C3; rpts denied 10-21, 844E2
'68 US convictn cited 779F3, 844G1
Exile killed in PR 10-25, 844C3
Morales cited re US rptrs expulsn 11-1, 844G1
Cuba airline office bombed in Spain 11-7; CORU claims credit 11-9, 844B3
BOSCO, Henri
Dies 5-4, 368E2
BOSE, Wilfred
Killed 7-3, named as hijacker 7-5, 485C1, G2
Say planned Uganda landing 7-13, 516G1
BOSHOFF, Linky
Wins US Open doubles 9-12, 716D1
BOSTER, Davis Eugene
Named Guatemala amb 8-24; confrmd 8-26, 807E3; replaced as Bangladesh amb 9-30, 808C1
BOSTOCK, Lynn
AL batting ldr 10-4, 796B1-D1
BOSTON, Mass.—*See MASSACHUSETTS*

1977

BORAG (Kuwait tanker)
Breakup off Taiwan rptd 3-3, 214C3
BORBON y Borbon, King Juan Carlos de (Spain)—*See JUAN Carlos I, King*
BORD, Andre
Named Parlt relatns min 9-26, 744G2
BORDELEAU, Christian
Quebec wins WHA title 5-27, 430C1
BORDELEAU, Paulin
Quebec wins WHA title 5-27, 430C1
BORDENTOWN, (N.J.) Reformatory—*See 'Crime' under NEW Jersey*
BORDER Patrol, U.S.—*See U.S. GOVERNMENT—JUSTICE—Immigration & Naturalization Service*
BOREN, Gov. David L. (D, Okla.)
OKs executn by drugs 5-10, 594F1
BORG, Bjorn
Wins Pepsi Grand Slam 1-23, 103G3
Wins US Indoor 3-6; WCT, Grand Prix tourns 4-10, 4-24, 430G2, C3, 431B1
Wins Wimbledon 7-2, 548D1
Quits US Open 9-6, 787E2
BORG, C. Arthur
Promoted 1-21, 53E1
WCT settles suit 12-6, 1020B3
BORGHESE, Prince Valerio
Miceli treason trial opens 5-30, 1014G3
BORGONOVO Pohl, Mauricio
Kidnaped 4-19, slain 5-10, 373A2
FPL members sought 9-17, 747F1
BORK, Robert H.
Sup Ct voids homosexual dismissal ruling 1-10, 57C1
Replaced as solicitor gen 3-4, 211F1
BORMAN, Frank
Hoffman rules on honor code 1-5, 41A1, B1
Eastern to lease Airbus 5-24, 441B2
BOROS, Julius
Wins PGA Seniors title 1-30, 104D1
BORTHWICK, Brian
Tried in absentia 2-10, 100B1
BOSA, Peter
Named to Canada Senate 4-5, 281B3
BOSCH, Orlando
Venez pres sues 7-4; mil ct '76 jet bombing trial rptd 10-10, 868B1
Letelier murder probe continues 9-10, 743A3
BOSLEY, Thad
Traded tO White Sox 12-5, 990C1
BOSMAN, Jackie
Sentncd re Mandela trial 9-7, 825G3
BOSTOCK, Lyman
AL batting ldr 10-2, 926F3-927A1
Signs with Angels 11-21, 989D3
BOSTON, Mass.—*See under MASSACHUSETTS*
BOSTON College
Schindler in NFL draft 5-3, 353B3

1978

Tswanas denied S African citizenship 6-12, 536F3
S Africa poll examines racial attitudes 6-15, 6-22, 536A3
UN racism conf vs indep recognitn 8-26, 676A2
2 guerrillas killed in police shootout 10-27, 904E3
BORACK, Carl
Big Fix released 10-6, 969C3
BORAN, Behide
Scores party members slaying 10-9, 822E3
BORDENKIRCHER v. Hayes
Prosecutor plea-bargaining power expanded 1-18, 64D3
BORDER Patrol, U.S.—*See U.S. GOVERNMENT—JUSTICE—Immigration & Naturalization Service*
BORDLEY, Bill
USC wins NCAA baseball title 6-8, 560G1
BORDONI, Carlo
Extradited to US 6-2, arraigned 6-5, 454C2, D2 ★
Named Franklin co-conspirator 7-13, pleads guilty on '75 chrgs 9-5, 681D1
BOREN, Gov. David L. (D, Okla.)
Faces US Sen primary runoff 8-22, 683A1
Denies homosexual charge 8-23, 683B1
Wins runoff 9-19, 736G3
Wins seat 11-7, 846G1, 848G2, 855G2
BORETZ, Alvin
Brass Target released 12-21, 1030E2
BORG, Bjorn
USTA ranks 2d 1-5, 22E3
Loses Grand Prix Masters 1-8, 22A3
Wins Birmingham WCT 1-15, Pepsi Grand Slam 1-22, Scandinavian Cup 3-8, WCT Tourn of Champs 3-26, Milan WCT 4-2, Italian Open 5-28, 418D2-419B1
Quits Grand Prix bonus chase 6-2, 540G1
Wins French Open 6-11, 3d consecutive Wimbledon title 7-8, 539E3, 540D1
Loses US Open 9-10, 707A1, D1
Wins Smash '78 10-29, Tokyo Intl 11-5, 1027C2
BORGE, Tomas
Hunger strikers protest jail treatmt 4-4—4-27, leaves solitary 4-19, 375A3, F3
BORGES, Jorge Luis
Scores World Cup 6-12, 520D3
BORGHESE, Prince Junio Valerio (Italy) (deceased)
Andreotti testifies at Miceli trial 1-9, 19A2
BORG-Warner Corp.
Firestone merger planned 11-28, 935D1
BORJA, Rodrigo
Dem Left nominates for pres 2-21, 148D2
Rptd 4th in pres electn 7-16, 557A1
BORK, Robert
Says Bakke ruling not 'landmark' 6-28, 482D3
BORLAND, Hal
Dies 2-22, 196C2
BORMAN, Frank
Gets space medal of honor 10-1, 861C2
Eastern seeks Natl merger 12-11, 1007D3
BORN Again (film)
Premieres in DC 9-24, 844D1
BORN Innocent (TV film)
Sex abuse suit vs NBC OKd by Sup Ct 4-24, 322B2; dismissed 8-8, 635C2-A3
BORODINA, Natasha
US wins Weisman Cup 4-23, 419C1
BOROS, Julius
Sues PGA over exemptn rule 1-23, 76F1
BOROWSKI, Irwin M.
GSA special counsel, inspector gen candidate 11-13, 899B2
BORQUEZ, Israel
Letelier extraditn hearings to be secret 9-22; US protests 9-28, 755A3
Contreras rptdly sees US evidence 10-13, 795G2
Queries Letelier murder suspects 10-17—10-24, 1014C3
Orders probe of lime kiln bodies rpt 12-6; 27 bodies rptd unearthed 12-12, 1013G3-1014A1
BORST, Stephen
Cops opens 3-28, 760F1
BORTKEVICH, Leonid
Marries Olga Korbut 1-7, 95G3
BOSCH, Hieronymus (1450-1516)
Conjurer stolen 12-13, 1029A1
BOSCH, Orlando
2 Cuban exiles seized in Letelier probe 4-14, 287D2
BOSCHWITZ, Rudy
Wins Sen primary in Minn 9-12, 716D1
Elected 11-7, 846C1, F1, 854A3, 858D2
BOSMAN, Jackie
Appeal rptd lost 1-23, 114F1
BOSSIER City, La.—*See LOUISIANA*
BOSSY, Mike
NHL scoring ldr 4-9, 296E1, E2
Named NHL top rookie 6-12, 458E2
BOSTOCK, Lyman
Killed 9-23, 777G3
BOSTON (singing group)
Don't Look Back on best-seller list 9-6, 708F1; 10-11, 800F3
BOSTON, Mass.—*See MASSACHUSETTS*
BOSTON Co. Institutional Investors
SEC censures re Equity Funding 9-4, 681A2
BOSTON College
Loses NCAA hockey title 3-25, 296B3

1979

BORBON, Pedro
Traded to Giants 6-28, 1002A3
BORDABERRY, Juan Maria
Colombian pol situatn compared 11-14, 993G1
BORDEN Inc.
Price compensatn case declined by Sup Ct 1-22, 54B2
A&P milk price actn backed by Sup Ct 2-22, 150A3
BORDEN Inc. v. Bergland
Case declined by Sup Ct 1-22, 54B2
BORDER Gas Inc.
Mex natural gas purchased 10-18, 814E3
Mex natural gas purchase finalized 12-29, 996A3
BORDER Patrol, U.S.—*See U.S. GOVERNMENT-JUSTICE-Immigration & Naturalization Service*
BORDONI, Carlo
Indicted 3-19, 205C2
BORELLI, Carla
Seduced opens 2-1, 292A3
BOREN, Sen. David L. (D, Okla.)
In USSR re SALT 8-28—8-30, 658D1
BORG, Bjorn
Boycotts Grand Prix Masters 1-14, 103A3
Named '78 top player by ITF 1-18, 103F2
Wins Richmond Classic 2-4, Pepsi Grand Slam 2-11, Rotterdam WCT 4-8, 391D1, F2-C3
Grand Prix dispute setld 2-10, 391F1
Wins French Open 6-10; Wimbledon, sets win mark 7-7, 569C3, 570E1
Wins Swedish Open 7-22, Canadian Open 8-20, 734B2
Wins Tokyo World Singles 11-4, WCT Challenge Cup 12-9, 1003C3, F3
BORGE, Tomas
Rpts Nicaragua rebel offensive 5-29, 409B2*
Named Nicaragua interior min 7-23; army cmnd member 7-29, 573C2
Meets US amb, asks for arms 7-28, 573E2
Frees Natl Guard prisoners 8-11—8-12, 616G1
Scores murder of Somoza's nephew 10-5, 793G3
Accuses Somoza, son in Chamorro death 10-9, 794A1
Alleged abuses admitted 12-3, 951E1
BORG-Warner Corp.
Elec motor-control device developed 10-2, 770E2
BORICUA Popular Army (Macheteros)
Claims credit for Navy ambush 12-3, 924C3
BOROS, Julius
Wins Legends of Golf title 4-29, 587D2
BOROWSKI, Irwin
Muellenberg named GSA inspector gen 1-30, 92E3
BORG-Warner Corp.
Firestone merger called off 4-24, 349C3
BORQUEZ, Israel
US submits more data in Letelier case 1-8, 19C3
Letelier extraditns seen unlikely 2-7, 114B3
Rejcts US extraditn request 5-14, 369C2
Bars US extraditn request, frees 3 army offcrs 10-1, 750G1
US reduces Chile aid 11-30, 927G2
BORROMEO Mata, Carlos
Killed by guerrillas 3-3, 234E3
BOSCHWITZ, Sen. Rudy (R, Minn.)
Finances disclosed 5-18, 383E2
BOSMAN, Jacqueline
Jailed 12-13, 969F1
BOSOMS and Neglect (play)
Opens 5-3, 711F1
BOSSY, Mike
Sovts win Challenge Cup 2-11, 118D2-G2
NHL scoring ldr 4-8, 355D2, G3
BOSTON, Mass.—*See MASSACHUSETTS*
BOSTON College
In Big East basketball conf 5-29, 526G3

1980

BOPP, James
Scores Families Conf 6-21, 601B2
BORCKINK, Anne
Wins Olympic medal 2-14, 156A1
BORDEN Inc.
Amax buys unit 5-16, 746E1
BORDER Gas Inc.
Mex-US gas sales begin 1-15, 60E1
BORDERLINE (film)
Released 10-31, 972C3
BORDONI, Carlo
Sentenced 4-23, 415B1
BORG, Bjorn
Wins Grand Prix Masters 1-13, 213G1
Named top '79 player by ITF 1-21, 213D2
Wins Pepsi Grand Slam 2-10, WCT Tourn of Champs 2-24, Nice Open 3-30, Monte Carlo WCT 4-6, Grand Prix of Tennis 4-27, 607F2-B3
Wins French Open, sets win marks 6-8, 606A3
Wins Wimbledon 7-6, 606G1
USTA, pros settle rules dispute 7-16, 691G3
Defaults in Canadian Open 8-17, 691B3
Loses US Open 9-7, 691F1, B2
Declines S Africa match 10-16, 947E1
Loses Swiss Indoor 10-19, wins Stockholm Open 11-10, 947B2, D2
BORGE, Tomas
Ousts radio commentator 2-1, 118C1
Announces Larios arrest 9-11, 709C3
BORG-Warner Corp.
FTC trust violatn rptd 7-11, 917F2
BORISOV, Vladimir
Arrested, placed in mental hosp 3-29, 262G1
Sovts expel 6-22; in Austria, chrgs KGB murdered wife 7-25, 680A3
BORK, Robert
At GOP platform hearings, sees weakened presidency 1-14, 32E1
BORMANN, Martin (1900-45?)
Farago dies 10-15, 876D1
BORN Free (Book)
Adamson found dead 1-3, 104D1
Adamson slaying suspect chrgd 2-2, 238B3
BORRELLI, Jim
Bull Pen opens 6-12, 756C3
BOSCH, Orlando
Acquitted in '76 Cuba jet bombing 9-26, 794G2
BOSCH G.m.b.H., Robert
FTC trust violatn rptd 7-11, 917F2
BOSHOFF, Carel
Chosen Broederbond head 9-26, 753E2
BOSQUE, George M.
Sought in San Fran Brinks theft 7-15, 654A3
BOSSA Lopez, Simon
Kidnaped 8-13, freed 8-14, 707E2
BOSTON—*See MASSACHUSETTS*
BOSTON Children's Hospital
New blood disease treatmt rptd 1-23, 159D3
BOSTON College
MacArthur WWII 'gift' dispute rptd 1-30, 1-31, 115F1

1976

BOSTON Globe (newspaper)
Schl integratn study rptd 1-24, 95F2
Ariz crime probed 10-2, 849B2
Carter endorsement rptd 10-30, 831G2
Vs death penalty 11-13, 891C2
BOSTON Herald-American (newspaper)
Forman wins Pulitzer 5-3, 352E3
Ford endorsement rptd 10-30, 827G3
BOSTON Tea Party Museum
Fire breaks out 5-29, 392D1
BOSTON University
Gets hypertension grant 1-30, 123G3
BOSTWICK, Don P.
Sued re stock sale 8-9, 709C3
BOSWELL, Connee
Dies 10-11, 816D3
BOTERO, Rodrigo
Minimizes econ problems re unrest 8-13, 731D2
BOTHA, George
Detained 12-10, rptd killed 12-15, 1010F2
BOTHA, Michael C.
Meets Soweto ldrs 6-19, 447A2
Forced Afrikaans use dropped 7-6, 500A2 *
Eases housing curbs 8-14, reaffirms racial separatn 8-20, 639B3, D3
BOTHA, Pieter K.
Confrms Angola troop exit, defends role 1-26, 57A2
Rpts Angola buffer force 2-3, oppositn scores 2-5, 106G1
Sets Angola troop exit 3-25, 228A1
Denies Angola attack 11-11, 862E2
BOTHA, Roelof F.
Chrgs Sovt, Cuba Angola threat 1-31, 103F2
Defends Angola role 3-30, 228A3
Kissinger confirms Vorster mtg 6-17, 427F1
At Kissinger-Vorster mtg 6-23—6-24, 446C3
At mtg re Rhodesia fund 10-5—10-7, 781B3
Windhoek conf adjourned 10-22, 832G1
Scorns UN resolutn 12-22, 954D3
BOTHA, Stephanus
S Africa cabt shifted 1-22, 76G1
BOTHMAN, Russell
Arrest presumed 8-17, 624E3
BOTOMBELE, Bokonga Ekanga
Named French amb 10-18, 949G3

BOTSWANA—*See also AFRICAN Development Bank, COMMONWEALTH of Nations, NONALIGNED Nations Movement, OAU*
Listed as 'free' nation 1-19, 20B3
US statemt, reactn 4-27, 293C2, 294D2
Kissinger sees forgn min 5-5, 318C3
Replaces rand with pula 8-23, 857E3
Khama in Tanzania re ANC rift 9-6—9-7, 661D3
UK African conf plan hailed 9-29, 718F1
US '77 aid funds signed 10-1, 806D3
S Africa student refugees rptd 11-19, 927E1
Rebel asylum barred 12-7, 1009D3
Rhodesian Relations—*See 'African Relations' under RHODESIA*
BOTTERMAN, Johannes
Dutch Dassault bribe case opens 2-10, acquittal asked 2-12, 141E2
Acquitted 2-25, 158E2
BOTTLES—*See CONTAINERS*
BOTTOM, Joe
Wins Olympic medal 7-21, 575D2
BOUDIN, Leonard
On SWP suit 8-8, 635B1
BOUEY, Gerald
Rpts bank rate rise 3-8, 204A2
On interest rate cut 11-19, 888D3, E3
On 2d interest rate cut 12-22, 998G2

1977

BOSTON Edison Co.
Retroactive rate rise let stand 11-14, 878C3
BOSTON Globe, The (newspaper)
Wins Pulitzer Prize 4-18, 355G2
Polaroid-S Africa sales revealed 11-16, 934F2
BOSTON Herald-American, The (newspaper)
Wins Pulitzer Prize 4-18, 355G2
BOSTON Psychopathic Hospital—*See MASSACHUSETTS Mental Health Center*
BOSTON Stock Exchange
'68 NYS stock transfer tax amendmts ruled illegal 1-12, 57F2
Shut 7-14, 537B3
SEC scores natl mkt move delay, ITS cited 12-1, 1004F1
BOSTON Stock Exchange et al v. New York State TAX Commission
'68 NYS stock transfer tax amendmts ruled illegal 1-12, 57F2
BOSTON University
Drug death study rptd 2-28, 224D2
Smoking-menopause link rptd 6-25, 620D1
BOSTROM, Pat
Loses Port Washn Cup 4-17, 430F3
BOSTWICK, Barry
Wins Tony 6-5, 452C1
BOSWORTH, Barry P.
Named wage price cncl dir 7-8, confrmd 7-22, 626D2
On steel price hikes 12-18, 12-22, 1003C2
BOTELER Jr., E. L.
Convicted 1-8, 60D1
BOTHA, Michiel
Businessmen ask black mgr ban end 7-26, 600C2
Quits educ office 10-3, 826A1
BOTHA, Pieter
Sets draft extensn, air base 4-21, 350B2
Rpts arms self-sufficiency 4-28, 350C2
Asks nonwhite govt role 5-26, 428B3
BOTHA, Roelof F.
S Africa forgn min 2-11, 160D3
Denies Zaire aid offer 4-9, 265F2
Wins Parlt seat 5-11, 428C3
Vance speech reactn rptd 7-4, 535F3
Asks sex laws repeal 7-7, 564A1
Scores UK 7-28, backs Smith 8-4, 599B2
Denies A-capacity 8-21, 657C1
Asserts A-bomb ban 8-30, 663G3
Rpts arms self sufficiency 10-26, scores UN ban 11-4, 851D2
BOTHA, Stephanus P.
Black job restrictns eased 12-14, 1016G2

BOTSWANA—*See also COMMONWEALTH of Nations, NONALIGNED Nations Movement, OAU*
UN Assemb member 3G3
Journalist escapes from S Africa 1-5, 3D3
Southn Africa bps score apartheid 1-10, 100A3
US modifies duty-free list 2-28, 189E3
Lesotho trade rptd 4-9, 490E1
Norland confrmd US amb 6-23, 626B3
US aid authorizatn OKd 8-4, 668D1
Sweden cancels debts 11-8, 904A1
Rhodesian Relations—*See RHODESIA*
BOTTLES—*See CONTAINERS*
BOTULISM—*See FOOD—Contamination*
BOUABID, Abderrahim
Resigns 6-6, 467D2
BOUCETTA, Muhammad
Named Morocco forgn min 10-10, 772F1
BOUCHARD, Charles
Bank fails 5-9, found dead 5-11, 489D3
BOUCHER, Paul
Joins FBI probe 12-13, 979C3
BOUEY, Gerald
On bank rate cut 1-31, 97A3

1978

BOSTON Edison Co.
Power failures 2-7—2-9, 105D2
Mass rate-limit case refused by Sup Ct 10-30, 832G2
BOSTON Edison Co. v. Massachusetts
Case refused by Sup Ct 10-30, 832G2
BOSTON Globe, The (newspaper)
Brooke admits false disclosure 5-26, 406C1
Turner interview rptd 12-1, 962G2
BOSTON Marathon—*See TRACK & Field*
BOSTON University
Bldg purchase rptd planned 3-1, 142G3
Wins NCAA hockey title 3-25, 296B3
Study rpts women smokers risk heart attacks 6-8, 727A1
BOSTWICK, Barry
Movie, Movie released 11-22, 970C2
BOSWORTH, Barry
Backs Meany wage stand 5-11, 362C1
On Apr CPI, Admin inflatn plan 5-22, 428C3
Links govt regulatn cost, inflation 6-12, 427A3
Hails steel price hike restraint 6-12, 470C2
On steel trade-aid price curb tradeoff 6-19, 428G1
Links productivity, inflatn 7-27, 606D3
Meany scores re wage pacts, Carter names panel 8-7, Meany lauds 624B2
Sees US role in Teamster talks 8-22, 680F2, B3
Kahn named wage-price cncl chrmn 10-25, 806E2
Paper union sues Admin re wage-price plan 12-1, 934D2
BOSWORTH, Patricia
Choices opens 12-10, 1031C1
BOTELHO Gonsalvez, Raul
Bolivia forgn min 11-24, 913D1
BOTHA, Michiel
Replaced in S Africa black post 1-25, 55C1
BOTHA, Pieter Willem (South African prime minister)
On Angola raid 5-4, 338B3
Named S African prime min 9-28, 742D1
Cabt denies Namibia plan rejectn 10-3, 819F2
Sees Namibia contact group 10-16—10-18; gets Carter note 10-16; vows UN Namibia vote OK 10-19, 819G2
Ahtisaari talks to reopen 10-19, 819E3-F3
Sets Info Dept probe 11-6; closes Mostert probe 11-7, 868F1
Sets parlt Info Dept probe, oppositn boycotts 11-7, 904G3
Shuffles Cabt 11-14, 904A3
Rhodesia ldrs see 11-15; warning vs vote delay rptd 11-23, 912A2
Treurnicht electn seen as setback 11-25, 946E2
Extends Info Dept probe mandate 12-1, rpt clears 12-5, 946G1, A2
Sets secret projects limit, warns re press curbs 12-7, 989A1
Advises UN Namibia plan OK 12-22, 1020G1
BOTHA, Roelof Frederik ('Pik')
UK, UN reps see re Rhodesia talks 1-9, 59G1
Quits Namibia mtg 2-12, 113E3
Denounces Kapuuo killing 3-28, 229E2
Sees Owen, Vance on Rhodesia 4-16, 290C3
Scores US re Angola raid warning 5-12, 475E3
In US A-talks 6-25—6-29, 537A1
Warns UN re Walvis Bay 7-27, 562C1
Fails in bid for prime min 9-28, 742E1
Prime Min bid linked to Info Dept scandal 10-29, 868C1
Closes Forgn Affairs Assn 11-21, 946B2
Sees Waldheim, Vance 11-27; Carter 11-30, 988G3-989A1
BOTHA, Stephanus P.
Sets enriched uranium expansn 2-13, 135A1
Loses Transvaal ldrshp bid 11-25, 946D2
BOTSWANA—*See also COMMONWEALTH of Nations, NONALIGNED Nations Movement, OAU*
S Africa editor arrives 1-3, 8E1
Westn indep plan for Namibia backed 3-26, 248G2
UK student, 2 S Africa natls killed 3-27; student cleared of chrgs 5-17, 596A1
US bars Peace Corps from S Africa hosps 5-15, 633A1
Namibia rebels OK talks 6-11, 475D3
S Africa holds cleric re refugee rebel infiltratn 6-26—8-7, 633A3
Westn indep plan for Namibia OKd 7-12, 547F2
UK cancels debts 7-31, 592D1
UN Assemb member 713C3
Zambia fertilizer stranded 10-10, 783A3
Soldier cleared in UK, S Africa deaths 11-13, 906D2
Rhodesian Relations—*See RHODESIA*
BOTTLES—*See CONTAINERS*
BOTTOMS, Timothy
Other Side of Mt released 3-24, 619C3
BOTULISM—*See FOOD—Contamination Issues*
BOUEY, Gerald
Bank rate raised 7-26, 591B1
BOULANGER, Daniel
King of Hearts opens 11-22, 1031C2

1979

BOSTON Globe, The (newspaper)
Sunday circulatn listed 6-6, 431D1
Kennedy interviewed re Chappaquiddick 7-17, 539F1
BOSTON Herald-American, The (newspaper)
Staff wins Pulitzer 4-16, 336B3
Conrail employee fund depletn rptd 5-27, 465D2
BOSTON Museum of Fine Arts
Stuart portraits sale to DC museum halted 4-14, 374E3
BOSTON Pops Orchestra
Fiedler opens 50th season 5-1, 392A2
Fiedler dies 7-10, 588F2
BOSTON Symphony Orchestra
Fiedler conducts 3-25, 272F1
BOSTON University
Uterine cancer study rptd 1-31, 139E1
Edelin gets med schl post, '75 convictn reversal cited 3-15, 272B1
Faculty, other strikes 4-5—4-22, 326D3
Stock sold re S Africa 4-26, 333A1
Test scores of future teachers rptd down 10-4, 810B2
BOSTON v. Anderson
Boston referendum spending case refused by Sup Ct 1-8, 14B3
BOSWORTH, Barry
On Feb producer price rise, guidelines compliance 3-8, 182E3
Tightens price rules 3-29, 264D1
Defends wage hike limit 5-10, 362D2
On UAL contract terms 5-28, 402E2
Ct bars wage-guide contract denial 5-31, 399B2
Carter, Eizenstat rptd vs controls remark 6-4, resignatn plan rptd 6-16, 463E1
On May CPI rise 6-26, 480B3
BOTHA, Pieter Willem (South African prime minister)
Mulder quits Parlt 1-24, 99B2
Rhoodie hints scandal disclosures 3-7, denounced 3-10, 191A1, E1
Asks Rhoodie arrest 3-16, bars resignatn 3-22, 213B1, B2
Scores US envoy spying 4-12, 286F3
Fewer black curbs urged 5-8, 373B2
Erasmus comm rpt clears 6-4, 427F3
Shuffles Cabt 6-14, 469F2
Muzorewa visit rptd 6-20, 490D2
Names Viljoen Namibia head 8-1, 585G1
Namibia assemb gets powers 8-13, 617B3
In Soweto, vows improvemts 8-31, 732B3
Offers marriage, sex law chngs 9-25, 774B2
Party loses by-electn, vows eased apartheid 11-8, 889F3
Bars majority rule, coloreds denounce 11-9, 889G3
Admits Zimbabwe mil role 11-30, 937B2
BOTHA, Roelof Frederik ('Pik')
Rejcts UN Namibia plan, scores contact group 3-5, 171F1, A2
Meets UN contact group 3-19—3-22, on Namibia assemb power increase 5-8, 354C2
Denies Namibia talks failure sought 4-14, 287G1
Muzorewa visit rptd 6-20, 409D2
Scores US black rights ldr 7-28, 617F1
Vs Commonwealth Zimbabwe plan 8-7, 589F2
Denies S Africa A-blast 10-26, 824C3
BOTHA, Stephanus P.
Miners end strike 3-14, 191A2
Sets black labor rights 5-2, 332F2
Gives migrant blacks union rights 9-25, 732C2
Sets job reservatn end 11-26, 969A1
BOTHA, Thozamile
Ford fires 700 blacks 11-21, 899D3
BOTLEY, Betty
Portrait of the Artist released 4-21, 528D3
BOTSWANA—*See also COMMONWEALTH of Nations, NONALIGNED Nations Movement, OAU*
S Africa border clash 1-14, 171C3
Uganda govt recognized 4-12, 288C2
S Africa atty's entry rptd 8-12, 617E2
UN membership listed 695E2
S Africa unions bar natls 9-25, 732E2
Khama reelected, Parlt majority increased 10-20, 815A3
Zimbabwe Rhodesian Relations—*See ZIMBABWE*
BOTTING, Ronald
City Suite opens 4-2, 711B2
BOTTLES—*See CONTAINERS*
BOTTOMS, John
Holeville opens 12-4, 956B3
BOUABID, Maati (Moroccan premier)
Named Moroccan premr 3-23, 271E1
BOUCEIF, Col. Ahmed Ould (Mauritanian premier; replaced May 31)
In France; seeks aid, sets Polisario talks 5-3, 324A1
Dies in plane crash 5-27, 412E1
Salek resigns 6-4, 417E1
BOUCHARD, Dan
NHL goaltending ldr 4-8, 355E2
BOUDIN, Leonard
Scores Bell contempt citatn rule 3-19, 207B2
BOUEY, Gerald K.
Explanatn asked re C$ drop 1-31, 95C2
On bank rate hike 7-22, 562E3; 9-7 684F2; 10-9, 771A3; 10-25, 811F3, 812A1
BOULANGER, Nadia
Dies 10-22, 860C2

1980

BOSTON Edison Co.
NRC reactor licensing resumptn urged 1-9, 17D1
BOSTON Globe, The (newspaper)
Wins 3 Pulitzers 4-14, 296C2, F2, G2
Muskie interviewed 9-7, 680A1
BOSTON Pops Orchestra
Williams named conductor 1-10, 199F2
BOSTON University
Craig on Olympic hockey team 2-24, 155B2
BOSWELL, Tom
NBA field-goal ldr 3-30, 278D3
BOSWORTH, Barry
Urges wage-price controls, gas rationing 2-6, 126G2
BOTHA, Pieter Willem (South African prime minister)
Reorganizes Natl Security Dept 1-15, 60E3
Plans black ldr conf 2-15, 174C2
On Zimbabwe vote 3-4, 162C1
Scores Treurnicht 3-7, Cabt ouster bid fails 3-11, 3-12; poll backs 3-16, 255B2
Vows legis powers for Namibia assemb 5-1, 374E2
Vows educ spending review 5-5, 374B3
Party wins by-electn 5-7, 374E1
Backs nonwhite cncl, const change 5-8, 373G3, 374C1
Vows crackdown on unrest 5-30, 466A2, E2
Discloses raid on SWAPO bases 6-13, 466F2
Namibia defense force set 8-1, 711A1
Abandons black cncl 8-8, 652E3
Shuffles Cabt 8-26; scores hardliners 9-2, supporter wins by-electn 9-3, 689E3
On Mafeking transfer to Bophuthatswana 9-19, 753B2
Broederbond address rptd 9-26, 753F2
Names multiracial cncl 10-2, 793A1
Visits Taiwan 10-13—10-17, 831D2
BOTHA, Roelof Frederik ('Pik')
On Namibia plan 5-12, 374C2
Admits SWAPO operatn, denies Angola raid chrgs 6-27, 524F3
Chrgs UN, Waldheim SWAPO support 8-29; McHenry denies 9-9, 710D3
UN Namibia talks agreed 11-25, 967C2
BOTHA, Thozamile
Held re demonstratn 1-10, 60G3
Banned re Port Eliz protest 2-27, 195A3
Rptd in Lesotho 5-6, 374A3
BOTHMAN v. Warren B.
Case refused by Sup Ct 3-31, 291B3
BOTSWANA—*See also COMMONWEALTH of Nations, NONALIGNED Nations, OAU*
At regional econ unity mtg 4-1, 243D1
Khama dies 7-13, Masire elected pres 7-18, 562A1
UN Namibia talks schedule agreed 11-24, 967B2
BOUCHER, Gaetan
Wins Olympic medal 2-19, 155G3
BOUCHER, Phillippe
Govt chrgs re ct system articles 11-7, 872D1
BOUDIN, Eugene Louis (1825-98)
Painting sold for record sum 5-13, 472G1
BOUDIN, Kathy
Weathermen fugitive surrenders 7-8, 576E3
BOUEY, Gerald K.
Announces bank rate float 3-10, 191G2

1976

BOULEZ, Pierre
Wins Grammy 2-28, 460D3
BOULIN, Robert
Named parlt min 8-27, 650E3, G3
BOUMEDIENNE, Houari (Mohammed Ben Brahim Boukharouba) (Algerian president)
Arab natns seek Sahara setlmt 1-27—1-29, 58C2
Sees Castro 3-12—3-14, 251C3
Algeria, Niger, Libya set closer ties 4-8, 372A1
Voters OK natl charter 6-27, 543G1
Arafat tells of Leb crisis 7-11, 514G2
Gets Arafat plea vs Syria 10-13, 758D2
Voters OK new const 11-19, 902F1
Reelected 12-10, 1012C2
BOURASSA, Robert
Trudeau scores 3-5, 238B3
Scores teachers strike 4-13, 288F1
Quebec eases school language rules 11-2, 851A2
Loses election 11-15, 870E1
To quit Liberal ldrship 11-19, 903E3
Levesque sworn 11-25, 903E2
BOURGES, Yvon
Army union probe documts bared 1-15, 119F3
Ousts Sanguinetti 1-22, 139E1
At sub H-bomb ceremony 1-24, 139C2
On arms to Egypt 3-26, 275F1
Named defense min 8-27, 650F3
Rpts '77 defns budget hike 11-9, 905F2
BOURGUIBA, Habib
Sahara plea rptd 1-29, 58D2
Libya assassinatn plot foiled 3-22, 239C2
Wife dies 11-14, 932C3
BOURGUIBA, Moufida
Dies 11-14, 932C3
BOUVIER, Antonio Degas
Tied to Uganda hijackers 7-5, 486B1
BOUVIER, Maurice
Rpts French crime rate up 12-7, 1003C1
BOWDLER, William G.
At Kissinger-Vorster mtg 6-23—6-24, 446C3
BOWEN, Rep. David R. (D, Miss.)
Reelected 11-2, 829G4
BOWEN, Lionel
Loses Labor Party ldrship bid 1-27, 71D3
BOWEN, Gov. Otis R. (R, Ind.)
Reelected 11-2, 820E3, 823C2, 831E1
BOWEN, William G.
Announces Rockefeller awards 11-16, 911C3
BOWERS, David W.
Testifies in Schorr probe 7-19, 748D3
BOWIDOWICZ, Thomas C.
ELF frees 1-9, 31E1
BOWLING, Lt. Cmdr. Roy Howard
Vietnam rpts killed 9-6, 678B3
BOWLING Green Park (Ky.) City News (newspaper)
Ford endorsement rptd 10-30, 827G3
BOWMAN Transportation Co.
Loses retroactive seniority suit 3-24, 218E2
BOWO, Sawito Kartowi
Arrested as plotter 9-14, 735B1

BOXING
Ali beats Young, Dunn 4-30, 5-25, 424B3
Olympic results 7-31, 574A1
Ali decisns Norton 9-28, 756C2
Pal Carbo dies 11-9, 970D1

1977

BOULDER, Colo.—*See COLORADO*
BOULIN, Robert
Named dep finance min 3-30, 239G1
BOUMEDIENNE, Houari (Mohammed Ben Brahim Boukharouba) (Algerian president)
Sees Castro 3-1, 249G1
Shuffles Cabt 4-23, 4-27, 470A2
6 French natls freed 6-19, 566G3
At OAU summit 7-2—7-5, 512D1
Mediates Egypt-Libya clashes 7-24—7-25, 569F2
Indl investmt cuts seen 9-5, econ priorities shifted 12-4, 963E1, B2
Gets Giscard Sahara warning 10-30, sees Libya premr 11-2, 852B2
At Tripoli anti-Sadat mtg 12-2—12-5, 929B2
BOURGES, Yvon
In Egypt on jet deal 1-5—1-9, 10B3
Named defense min 3-30, 239G1
Sahara kidnap prompts Cabt mtg 10-27, 831A3
In US, bars arms sales curb 11-22, 1012E3
BOURGUIBA Jr., Habib
Named pres adviser 12-26, 1019E2
BOURNE, Dr. Peter
Named Carter special asst 1-14, 35C3
On pot decriminalizatn 3-14, 332G3
Urges narcotics study for pain relief 11-16, 992E3
BOURNE, Col. Robin
Rpts security suspects list 8-9, 633C3
BOUTEFLIKA, Abdelaziz
6 French natls freed 6-19, 566G3
BOUTTOS, Ioannis
Named Greek finance min 11-28, 925B2
BOWDLER, William G.
At Biko funeral 9-25, 735D3
US recalls for talks 10-21, 825A1
Returns to Pretoria 11-5, 852C1
BOWEN, Rep. David R. (D, Miss.)
S Africa sugar lobby gift alleged 7-20, 614F1
BOWEN, Lionel
Labor Party ldrship bid seen 12-10, 963F3
Elected Labor Party dep ldr 12-22, 1009C2 ★
BOWEN, Gov. Otis R. (R, Ind)
Laetrile legalized 5-1, 375F3
BOWLES, Heloise
Dies 12-28, 1023G3
BOWLING
Sup Ct voids ruling vs Brunswick 1-25, 80E2
BOWMAN, Ralph S.
Sentenced 5-16, 508E2
BOWMAN, Scotty
Named NHL coach of yr 5-13, 429G3

BOXING
US-USSR tourn results 1-29, 2-3, 2-5, 263F1
Duran KOs Fernandez 1-29, 263C2
Young decisns Foreman 3-17, 263B1
Escalera KOs Garvey 3-17, 263F1
ABC suspends US Championships 4-16, issues report 9-3, 828B1
Norton KOs Bobick 5-11, 395E1
Ali decisns Evangelista 5-16, 395A1
Escalera KOs Becerril 5-16, 395D1
Duran decisns Muniz 5-16, 395D1
Gazo TKOs Wajima 6-7, 828B1
DeJesus KOs Saldivar 6-27, 828A1
Cervantes TKOs Jiminez 6-27, 828A1
Monzon decisns Valdes, sets retiremt 7-30, 827G3
Duran decisns Viruet 9-17, 827G3
Ali decisns Shavers, fight sets TV viewing record 9-29, 827C3
House subcom probes TV coverage 11-2, 949F3, 950A1
Norton decisns Young 11-5, 970C2
Valdes decisns Briscoe for middleweight title 11-5, 970B3
Spinks decisns Righetti, '78 Ali fight set 11-18, 970C2, C3 ★
Galindez decisns Gregory 11-20, 970D3
WBC softens threat vs Ali 12-1, 970A2
Zarate TKOs Rodriguez 12-2, 970D3
'77 champions listed 12-17, 970A2 ★
Lastra decisns Ortega for featherweight title 12-17, 970D3 ★

1978

BOULIN, Robert
Named French labor min 4-5, 245F2
BOUMEDIENNE, Houari (Mohammed Ben Brahim Boukharouba) (Algerian president)
Visits Malta 1-2, 39C2
Orders French import cuts 1-11, 11C3
Says radicals back PLO 2-2, 78A3
Ahmed Kaid dies 3-5, 252A3
Irate over hardline conf feuds 9-24, 730C1
Dies; facts on 12-27; buried 12-29, 1012B2
BOURASSA, Robert
Ryan replaces as party ldr 4-15, 328G2
BOURGES, Yvon
Renamed French defense min 4-5, 245F2
BOURGUIBA, Habib (Tunisian president)
Workers protest rule 1-26—1-28, 74B1
Labor army draft plan rptd 3-3, 170A2
BOURNE, Dr. Peter G.
Armed forces drug abuse rise rptd, tests backed 4-27, 368D2-A3
Resigns in drug prescriptn scandal 7-20, 549F2
Cocaine use rptd, denies; on drug use by White House aides 7-20, 568C1
BOUTEFLIKA, Abdelaziz
On anti-Sadat summit 2-5, 78F2
Sees Giscard on Sahara 8-1, 676F2
BOUTON, Jim
Returns to major leagues 9-10, beats Giants 9-14, 779D3
Return to sportscasting rptd 12-6, 1026G2
BOUTTOS, Ioannis
Presents '78 budget 2-16, 149F2
Named Greek agri min 5-10, 373E3
BOWA, Larry
NL wins All-Star Game 7-11, 559B3
NL batting ldr 10-2, wins Golden Glove Award 11-21, 928F2, A3
BOWDLER, William G.
Presses Somoza re plebiscite, oppositn demands 12-7—12-27, 1018E2-A3
BOWEN, Rep. David R. (D, Miss.)
Reelected 11-7, 851B2
BOWEN, Gov. Otis R. (R, Ind.)
Rpts coal shortage, sees power cuts 2-10, 104D1
Estimates blizzard losses 2-11, 105D3
Uses guardsmen on coal convoys 2-14, 160D2
BOWERS, Dr. William J.
Death sentencing study finds bias 3-6, 389A1
BOWES, Dr. James E.
On armed forces measles infestatn 11-10, 927A3
BOWLES, Robert
Slaying rptd, Cluchette chrgd 8-25, 887A1
BOWLING Green (O.) State University
Wins NCAA hockey match 3-25, 296C3
BOW Valley Industries Ltd.
Canada uranium find rptd 9-13, 722B1
BOXING
Lyle chrgd in shooting death 1-6, 56C1
Spinks title bout defns in dispute, Ali rematch set 2-17—3-16; Nev comm suspends 3-9, WBC withdraws title, names Norton champ 3-18, 211B3-212D1
Spinks-Ali rematch plans protested 3-8, site shifted to Mauritius 3-9, 212E1
Spinks arrested on auto, drug chrgs 3-19, 4-21; avoids indictmt, pays fine 5-18, 379A1
Holmes decisns Shavers 3-25, 600B1
Spinks-Ali rematch contract signed 4-11, TV rights rptd 5-2, 378E3
FCC faults ABC tourn 4-25, 379D1
World Amateur tourn results 5-6—5-20, 600C2
Ali wins 3d heavywgt title 9-15, TV viewing record rptd 9-20, 726B1, E2
Lyle acquitted 12-16, 1028D2
Obituaries
Jacopucci, Angelo 7-21, 600B2
Tunney, Gene 11-7, 972F3
Title Bouts
Canto decisns Oguma 1-4, 56B1
Parlov KOs Cuello 1-8, 56C1
Duran TKOs DeJesus for lightwgt title 1-21, 55E3
Arguello TKOs Escalera 1-28, 379A2
Gushiken KOs Vargas 1-29, 379A2
Palomino KOs Sorimachi 2-11, 379A2
Spinks decisns Ali for heavywgt title 2-15, 171B1-C2
Lopez TKOs Kotei 2-15, 379B2
Serrano decisns Martinez 2-18, 379B2
Zarate KOs Davila 2-25, 379B2
Cuevas TKOs Weston 3-4, 379B2
Mattioli KOs Obed 3-11, 379C2
Palomino KOs Mohatar 3-18, 379C2
Lujan TKOs Ruvaldino 3-18, 379C2
Pedroza TKOs Lastra 4-16, 379D2
Corro decisns Valdes for middleweight title 4-22, 379F1
Arguello TKOs Tam 4-29, 379D2
Cervantes KOs Tongta 4-29, 379D2
Galindez decisns Lopez 5-6, 379E2
Netrnoi decisns Castillo 5-6, 379E2
Mattioli KOs Duran 5-14, 379E2
Arguello KOs Alcala 6-3, 600F1
Holmes decisns Norton for heavywgt title 6-9, 600A1

1979

BOULEVARD Nights (film)
Released 3-22, 528E1
BOULEZ, Pierre
Complete 'Lulu' debuts in Paris 2-25, 174C1
BOULIN, Robert
On steel worker unrest 2-6, 96F1
Suicide discovered; Peyrefitte, others blamed in note 10-30, 834F3-835A2
Matteoli named successor 11-8, 872F3
BOUMEDIENNE, Houari (d. 1978)
Benjedid elected pres 2-7, 94B2
Ben Bella freed 7-4, 521F3
BOURGES, Yvon
Rpt backs A-arms priority 9-11, 686G1
BOURNE, Jeff
NASL scoring ldr 8-12, 654G3
BOURNE, Dr. Peter G.
Hired by UN 4-25, 392G1
BOUTEFLIKA, Abdelaziz
Benjedid elected pres 2-7, 94C2
Named Algeria pres adviser 3-8, 215E2
BOVIN, Alexander
Scores Iranian rule 9-8, 688D1
BOWA, Larry
NL batting ldr 9-30, 955F2
BOWDLER, William G.
Meets Nicaraguan rebels 6-27, 475G2
In Nicaragua rebel talks 7-12, 512F1
BOWDOIN College (Brunswick, Me.)
Benoit in Boston Marathon, sets US record 4-16, 911D3
BOWERS, Kenneth L.
On 3 Mile I A-accident 4-9, 261F2
BOWIE, Robert R.
Rpts CIA Iran statn closure 1-18, 26E2
BOWLES, J. C.
Disputes JFK acoustics evidence 1-5, 4A2
BOWMAN, Margaret (1956-78)
Bundy gets death penalty for '78 slaying 7-31, 604D2
BOWMAN, Scotty
Soviets win Challenge Cup 2-11, 118C2
Resigns as Canadiens coach 6-10, signs as Sabres gen mgr 6-11, hires Neilson to coach 6-20, 470G2
BOWSER, Charles W.
Loses Phila mayoral primary 5-15, 363D2

BOXING
US revokes Knoetze visa 1-9, judge enjoins 1-11; Knoetze KOs Sharkey, fight protested 1-13, 79C2
Duran abandons world lightwgt title 2-1, 412G3
Ali retires 6-26, 838G2
Pan Am Game results 7-1—7-15, 798G2
Claussen KOd 11-23, dies 11-28; NYS comm suspends boxing, probes death 11-28—12-27, 1004E3
Obituaries
Claussen, Willie 11-28, 1004E3
Galento, Tony (Two-Ton) 7-22, 588G2
Title Bouts
Pedroza TKOs Kobayashi 1-9, 79C3
Benitez decisns Palomino for WBC welterwgt title 1-14, 79A3
Cervantes decisns Montilla 1-18, 79D3
Gonzalez, Oguma draw 1-29, 412C3
Arguello TKOs Escalera 1-29, 412D3
Serrano decisns Valdez 2-18, 412D3
Gomez KOs Jiminez 3-9, 412D3
Lopez KOs Castanon 3-10, 412E3
Kudo decisns Gonzalez 3-14, 412E3
Park decisns Canto for WBC flywgt title 3-18, 412E3
Holmes TKOs Ocasio 3-23, 412A3
Shavers KOs Norton 3-23, 412C3
Benitez decisns Weston 3-25, 412F3
Gushiken KOs Lopez 4-8, 412F3
Lujan KOs Garcia 4-8, 412F3
Galindez KOs Rossman for WBA light heavywgt title 4-14, 412F2
Watt KOs Pitalua for WBC lightwgt title 4-17, 412F3
Zanon decisns Evangelista for Eur heavywgt title 4-18, 412G3
Franklin KOs Johnson for WBC light heavywgt title 4-22, 412G3
Park decisns Igarashi 5-20, 838G3
Kim decisns Giussipi 6-3, 838G3
Pintor decisns Zarate for WBC bantamwgt title 6-3, 838G3
Lopez KOs Ayala 6-17, 839A1
Kudo KOs Gonzalez 6-20, 839A1
Holmes KOs Weaver 6-22, 838B3
Antuofermo decisns Corro for world middlewgt title 6-30, 838E3
Gonzalez KOs Oguma 7-6, 839A1
Arguello TKOs Limon 7-8, 839B1

1980

BOUMEDIENNE, Houari (d. 1978)
Ben Bella freed from prison 10-30, 870E1
BOUQUARD, Rep. Marilyn Lloyd (D, Tenn.)
Reelected 11-4, 844C2
BOURGUIBA, Habib (Tunisian president)
Sees Carter 2-29, 197C1
Carter sees son, vows support 2-29, 197D1
Names Mzali interim premr 3-1, 197A1
BOURNE Identity, The (book)
On best-seller list 3-9, 200A3; 4-2, 280A3; 5-4, 359C3; 6-8, 448B3; 7-13, 568B3; 8-17, 640E3
BOURQUE, Ray
Named NHL top rookie 6-6, 488C1
BOUSQUET, Charles
Jewish militants attack 10-8, 767G3
BOUSSAC, Marcel
Dies 3-21, 279E1
BOUTEFLIKA, Abdelaziz
Ousted as Benjedid aide 1-13, 55G3
BOUTERSE, Daisy
Ousts Surinamese pres, names premr to post 8-13, 653F2
BOUTS, Dierick (1420-75)
Painting sold for record sum 4-16, 472G2
BOUTWELL, Dr. Joseph
On faulty lab tests 3-23, 358G3-359A1
BOWA, Larry
In World Series 10-14—10-21, 811G2-812G3
BOWDLER, William D.
At Nicaragua anniv fete 7-19, 565F2
BOWEN, Rep. David R. (D, Miss.)
Reelected 11-4, 843C2
BOWEN, Gov. Otis R., (R, Ind.)
Orr elected Ind gov 11-4, 847E1
BOWERS, Alexander S.
Really Rosie opens 10-12, 892E3
BOWERS, George
Hearse released 6-7, 675G2
BOWES, Bill
Jamaica moves to quell violence 7-18, 579G1
BOWLING Green—*See KENTUCKY*
BOWMAN, Margaret (1956-78)
Bundy gets 3d death sentence 2-12, 136E2
BOWRING & Co., C. T.
Marsh & McLennan to buy 4-14, 386B1
BOXER, Nat
Wins Oscar 4-14, 296A2

BOXING
5 die from matches 1-1—11-3; Canada launches safety probe 7-7, 907A3
Ali named Athlete of Decade 1-13, announces comeback 3-3, 320G3
Scott convictn appeal refused 1-14, 320F3
Jones arrested for rape 1-31, complaint dropped 2-1, 320D3
Gomez sets consecutive title KO mark 2-3, 320B3
US AAU team killed in Polish jet crash 3-14, 213E3; engine failure seen 3-31, 256C3
Kid Gavilan rptd broke 4-1, 320E3
Moscow Olympic results 8-2, 589E1, 622E1
Ali-Holmes fight sets live gate record; Holmes sets heavywgt KO mark 10-2, 772E1
Weaver win spurs S Africa riots 10-25, 887E3
Duran fined 11-26, rejcts retiremt 11-28, 1000A3
Obituaries
Denny, Cleveland 7-7, 907B3
Donovan, Arthur 9-1, 755G2
Galindez, Victor 10-26, 876E1
Hoosier, Harlan 1-18, 907E3
Newell, Charles 1-17, 907E3
Owens, Johnny 11-3, 907A3
Thomas, Tony 1-1, 907E3
Title Bouts
Arguello KOs Castillo 1-20, 320A3
Pedroza decisns Nemeto 1-22, 320A3
Sanchez TKOs Lopez for WBC featherwgt title 2-2, 320F2
Holmes TKOs Zanon 2-3, 320F1
Gomez KOs Valdez, sets consecutive KO mark 2-3, 320A3
Kim KOs Ibarra for WBA flywgt title 2-17, 320B3
Mamby KOs Kim for WBC super lightwgt title 2-23, 320B3
Watt TKOs Nash 3-15, 320B3
Minter decisns Antuofermo for world middlewgt title, victory disputed 3-16, 320B2
Zapata decisns Nakajima for WBC junior flywgt title 3-24, 320C3
Saad Muhammad TKOs Conteh 3-29, 320C3

1976

BOYA, Thomas S.
Waldheim warns on Leb 3-30, 226A2
BOYD, Aquilino
Panama forgn min, canal negotiator 4-1; scores Reagan 4-16, 291B2, F2
Chrgs CIA 'destabilizatn' plan 9-17; asks new US talks 9-22, 792F1, B2-B3
Sees Kissinger, canal talks set 10-7, 792E3
Sees US advisers 12-1—12-3, 1008C2
BOY Meets Girl (play)
Opens 4-13, 1014C3
BOY Scouts of America, Inc.
Ford suspends HEW ruling 7-7, 535F2
BOYSE, Dr. Edward A.
Gets Adler Prize 2-11, 272C1
BOYS From Brazil, The (book)
On best-seller list 12-5, 972F2
BOYSON, Rhodes
In new UK shadow Cabt 11-19, 1004A2
BRABEC, Vratislav
Sentenced 9-23, 851E3
BRADEMAS, Rep. John (D, Ind.)
Scores State of Union speech 1-19, 40B1
Scores Greek, Turkish arms pacts 4-15, 259B2
Admits Park gifts; anti-aid votes cited 10-26, 900E1; 981F1
Reelected 11-2, 829B3
Named majority whip 12-8, 981D1
BRADLEY, Arthur D.
Carter, Artis convicted 12-21, 1015D3
BRADLEY, Bruce
Loses electn 11-2, 821D1
BRADLEY, Mayor Thomas (Los Angeles, Calif.)
Carter settles black issues 7-12, 513C2
Carter rpts Cabt post declined 12-16, 937A2
BRADLEY University (Peoria, Ill.)
Ford speech 3-5, 179D3
BRADSHAW, Terry
In Super Bowl 1-18, 56B1
BRADSHAW, William
On Canada A-sales 11-30, 923B3
BRADWELL, Baron (Tom Driberg)
Dies 8-12, 892G2
BRAHIM, Hakim
'75 defns budget, mil forces rptd 1-2, 60F2
SADR cabt min 3-5, 178A3

1977

BOYCE, Christopher John
Arrested on spy chrgs 1-16, 41D2-A3
Chrgs CIA Australia union infiltratn 4-27, 326D1-A2, 344E2
Convicted 4-28, 344A2
Lee convicted 5-15, 409C3
Lee gets life sentence 7-18, 576F3
Cited re Australia-US talks 8-4, 633A1
Sentenced to 40 yrs 9-12, 732E3
BOYD, Alan
Signs UK air svc pact 7-23, 593C1
BOYD, Aquilino
Quits as forgn min, canal negotiator 2-9, 379A1
BOYD, Stephen
Dies 6-2, 532E2
BOYENGE Singa, Brig. Gen.
Named Shaba cmdr 3-31, 260D3
BOYER, Ernest L.
Named US educ comr 1-19, 52G3
Educ Office reorganized 4-11, 301D3
BOYLAN, Jim
Marquette wins NCAA title 3-28, 262A2
BOYLE, W. A. (Tony)
Convictn upset, retrial ordrd 1-28, 95D3
BOY Scouts of America, Inc.
N Orleans unit sex crimes chrgd 4-11, 432G2
BOYS Farm Inc.
Child porno scheme rptd 5-15, 432E2
BOYS From Brazil, The (book)
On best-seller list 4-3, 264A2
BP—*See BRITISH Petroleum*
BPA—*See U.S. GOVERNMENT—IN-TERIOR—Bonneville Power Administration*
BP Pipelines Inc. v. U.S.
Sup Ct upholds Alaska pipe rate order 11-14, 878E2
BRACY, Terrence L.
Confrmd Transport asst secy 2-10, 148C3
BRADA-Miller Freight System
ICC sues 11-3, 861D1
BRADEMAS, Rep. John (D, Ind.)
On-site picketing defeated 3-23, 229F1
Visits China 4-9—4-17, 298C2
Carter agrees to sign HEW-Labor funds 6-15, 459D3
Cited in Park indictmt 9-6, 688C1
BRADFORD, Ned
Kissinger sells memoirs 2-7, 131A2
BRADFORD, Robert W.
Sentenced 5-16, 508E2
BRADLEE, Benjamin C.
Carter mtg rptd 2-25, 151G2
Sees Castro 2-26—2-27, 180C3
BRADLEY, Bill
Seeks US Sen nominatn 11-14, 991A1
BRADLEY, Pat
2d in LPGA Championship 6-12, 951C1
2d in Colgate Far East tourn 11-13, 951E1
LPGA top money winner 11-27, 951F1
BRADLEY, Mayor Thomas (Los Angeles, Calif.)
Reelected 4-6, 252B3
LA picked for '84 Olympics 9-25, 828B3
BRADSHAW, Robert (St. Kitts-Nevis prime minister)
Scores Nevis colonial vote 8-19, 675C2
BRADY, James
Named NY mag editor 1-8, 48G3
BRAE Corp.
Seeks Green Bay line purchase 11-22, 1007C1
BRAFF, Ruby
George Barnes dies 9-4, 787F3

1978

Zarate KOs Hernandez 6-9, 600G1
Lopez decisns Burnett 7-3, 600G1
Serrano KOs O Young Ho 7-9, 600A2
Minter KOs Jacopucci 7-19, Jacopucci dies 7-21, 600B2
Netrnoi TKOs Estaba 7-29, 600A2
Corro decisns Harris 8-5, 969D1
Kudo decisns Gazo 8-9, 969D1
Cervantes TKOs Sekgapane 8-26, 969E1
Ali decisns Spinks for 3d heavywgt title 9-15, 726B1
Rossman TKOs Galindez for light heavywgt title 9-15, 726C2
Lopez KOs Malverez 9-15, 726C2
Lujan decisns Davila 9-15, 726D2
Gushiken KOs Chung 10-15, 969E1
Lopez TKOs Clemente 10-21, 969E1
Gomez KOs Zarate 10-28, 969F1
Holmes KOs Evangelista 11-10, 969A1
Arguello decisns Leon 11-10, 969D1
Corro decisns Valdes 11-11, 969F1
Canto decisns Tacomron 11-20, 969F1
Pedroza decisns Solis 11-27, 969G1
BOYD, Alan S.
Named Amtrak pres 4-25, facts on 349A2
BOYD, Julianne
Eubie opens 9-20, 1031E1
BOYER, Charles
Kills self 8-26, 708B2
BOYER, Ken
Hired as Cardinals mgr 4-28, 355C2
BOYLE, John
Killed 7-11, 630B3
BOYLE, W. A. (Tony)
Gag-order case remanded 1-9, 13G1
Convicted again 2-18, 129A1
UMW pensn attachmt case review refused by Sup Ct 4-3, 309B1
BOYNES, Winford
In NBA draft 6-9, 457G2 ★
BOY Scouts of America
Handicapped Eagle Scout honored at White House 7-21, 844G1
BOYS From Brazil (film)
Released 10-5, 969D3
BOYS In Company C, The (film)
Released 1-31, 618D3
BOZZO, Ferdinando
Swiss Credit secrecy breach probed 1-10, chrg denied 1-11, 151D1
BPA—*See U.S. GOVERNMENT—IN-TERIOR—Bonneville Power Administration*
BP Minerals—*See BRITISH Petroleum Co. Ltd.*
BP Pipelines Inc. v. U.S.
ICC Alaska pipe rates backed by Sup Ct 6-6, 447B2
BRABOURNE, John
Death On Nile released 9-29, 970B1
BRACEWELL, Ken
Named Stompers coach 5-24, 707C3
BRACHT, Baron Charles Victor
Kidnaped 3-8, 232A2
Found slain 4-10, 379C3
BRACKEN, Eddie
Hello Dolly opens 3-5, 887A2
BRACKMAN, Jacob
King of Hearts opens 11-22, 1031C2
BRADBURY, Norris
A-arms test oppositn rptd 11-3, 877A2
BRADEMAS, Rep. John (D, Ind.)
Vs Turkish arms embargo end 4-5, 276E3; 5-3, 378G1
Ethics com notes Park gift 7-13, 527C2
Reelected 11-7, 850B4
BRADEN, Spruille
Dies 1-10, 96D1
BRADFORD, Alex
Dies 2-15, 196D2
BRADFORD, Robert
Protests Westminster mass 7-6, 557F3
BRADLEE, Benjamin C.
Stands by SALT 'freeze' rpt 6-2, 422A3
BRADLEY, Bill
Wins Sen primary in NJ 6-6, 447G3
Elected 11-7, 845E1, 846E1, 848E2, 849A1
BRADLEY, Luther
In NFL draft 5-2, 336F2
BRADLEY, Pat
Kent Golden Lights results 5-29; wins Lady Keystone 6-15, 580G2, G3
Borden Classic results 7-16, wins Hoosier Classic 7-30, 672D3, E3
Wins Rail Charity Classic 9-4, Mixed Team tourn 12-3, 990D1, G1
LPGA top money winner 11-20, 990C3
BRADLEY, Mayor Thomas (Los Angeles, Calif.)
Plans drastic layoffs 6-7, 425B3
Addresses Urban League 8-8, 811F1
LA OKs '84 Olympic pact 10-12, 842F3
BRADLEY University (Peoria, Ill.)
Phegley in NBA draft 6-9, 457G3
BRADSHAW, Robert
Dies 5-24, 440D2
BRADSHAW, Terry
NFL '77 passing ldr 1-1, 56A2
BRADY, Gen. Herman
Quits as defns min; named Pinochet aide 4-12, gens' cncl liaison 4-28, 350E3, 351D1
BRAGA, Sonia
Dona Flor released 2-26, 619F1

1979

Pedroza KOs Olivares 7-22, 839B1
Kim decisns Carupo 7-28, 839B1
Espana TKOs Lira 8-4, 839B1
Saad Muhammad decisns Conteh 8-18, 839C1
Park, Canto draw 9-9, 839C1
Lopez OKs Caba 9-26, 839C1
Holmes TKOs Shavers 9-28, 838C3
Gomez TKOs Mendoza 9-28, 838E3
Kim KOs Yokai 10-4, 839C1
Sanchez decisns Jurietti 10-7, 839D1
Tate decisns Coetzee for WBA heavywgt title 10-20, 838F2
Scypion KOs Claussen 11-23, 1004E3
Leonard TKOs Benitez for WBC welterwgt title 11-30, 1004B3
Antuofermo, Hagler draw 11-30, 1004D3
Johnson KOs Galindez for WBA light heavywgt title 11-30, 1004D3
BOYCE, Christopher John
US spy satellite data rptd compromised 4-28, 318A3
BOYD, Alan S.
Rpts Amtrak staff shake-up 9-26, 868E1
BOYD, Jamie
Blames drug dealers in Tex judge's death 5-29, 431E2
BOYD, John
Scores truckers' strike 1-11, 20G2
BOYLE, Lord
Top salaries hike OKd 6-5, 425D2
BOYLE, Andrew
Philby spy ring explored 10-28, 10-29, 873F3
Blunt named 4th spy 11-15, 908D2
BOYLE, Judge James A.
Kennedy on Chappaquiddick 7-17, 539D2
BOYLE, John (d. 1978)
2 soldiers face murder chrgs 2-1, 97C1
Soldiers cleared in killing 7-4, 565B1
BOYLE, Peter
Hardcore released 2-8, 174F2
BOYLE, W. A. (Tony)
Sentenced again 10-11, 840B1, C1*
BOYNTON, Homer
Declines comment on Sullivan memoirs 6-24, 521B1
Denies destruction of FBI files 6-26, 520F3
Named FBI exec asst 8-8, 611C1
BOYS, Barry
Candida opens 3-6, 711A2
BRABOURNE, Lady
Injured, father killed by IRA 8-27, 641B1
BRABOURNE, Lady (dowager)
Injured by IRA 8-27, dies 8-28, 641B1
BRABOURNE, Lord
Injured by IRA 8-27, 641B1
BRACY, Terrence L.
Jordan vs 7-19, resigns 7-20, 530G1, A3
BRADEMAS, Rep. John (D, Ind.)
House majority whip 71A1
On Camp David mtg 6-2, 418D2
BRADFORD, Charles E.
Elected 7th-day Adventists vp 1-11, 78D3
BRADFORD, Peter A.
Vs uranium sale to India 3-23, 416G2
Votes to revoke Met Ed license 10-26, 826A2
BRADFORD-White Corp.
Acquitted of price-fixing 10-22, 986E1
BRADLEY, Sen. Bill (D, N.J.)
Finances disclosed 5-18, 383D2
In USSR re SALT 8-28—8-30, 658D1
BRADLEY, Dudley
In NBA draft 6-25, 507B2
BRADLEY, Gen. Omar
Allen dies 9-27, 756A2
BRADLEY, Pat
Loses LPGA match-play title 2-4, 220D3
2d in Honda Civic Classic 3-18, Otey Crisman 4-29, Lady Michelob 5-13, Golden Lights 6-3, 587A2-B3
2d in Barth Classic 8-20, 970B1
LPGA top money winner 11-30, 969G2
BRADLEY, Mayor Tom (Los Angeles, Calif.)
Urges fed aid for '84 Olympics 5-28, 798D1
Attends Carter dinner 10-24, 961F2
BRADSHAW, Terry
NFL '78 passing ldr 1-6, 80A1
Steelers win NFL conf title 1-7, 8E3
Steelers win Super Bowl; named MVP 1-21, 62E3-63A2
BRAFF, Dr. Erwin
Rpts refugees strain SF health svcs 7-18, 550D2
BRAHMS, Johannes (1833-97)
Concerto for Violin wins Grammy 2-16, 336G3

1980

Weaver KOs Tate for WBA heavywgt title 3-31, 320C1
Gregory TKOs Johnson for WBA light-heavywgt title 3-31, 320E1
Holmes TKOs Jones 3-31, 320F1
Camel decisns Parlov for WBC cruiserwgt title 3-31, 320B2
Leonard KOs Green 3-31, 320E2
Lujan TKOs Isogami 4-2, 320C3
Serrano TKOs Kazama 4-3, 320C3
Randolph TKOs Cardona for WBA junior featherwgt title 4-4, 1000F3
Cuevas KOs Volbrecht 4-6, 320D3
Oguma KOs Park for WBC flywgt title 5-18, 1000F3
Watt decisns Davis, retains WBC lightwgt title 6-8, 1000F3
Duran decisns Leonard for WBC welterwgt title 6-20, 772D2
Sanchez TKOs Lopez, retains WBC featherwgt title 6-21, 1000G3
Kim decisns Arrozal, retains WBA flywgt title 6-29, 1000G3
Zapata TKOs Nakajima, retains WBC jr flywgt title 6-29, 1000G3
Holmes TKOs LeDoux, retains WBC title 7-7, 1000D3
Hearns TKOs Cuevas for WBA welterwgt title 8-2, 907E2
Pintor KOs Owen 9-19, Owen dies 11-3, 907A3
Hagler TKOs Minter for world middlewgt title 9-27, 772A2
Holmes KOs Ali 10-2, Ali blames drug misuse 10-7, 771F3
Pedroza decisns Lockeridge, retains WBA featherwgt title; post-fight drug test negative 10-4, 1001A1
Weaver KOs Coetzee, retains WBA title 10-25, 1000E3
Leonard TKOs Duran for WBC welterwgt title 11-25, 907B2
DeLeon decisns Camel for WBC cruiserwgt title 11-25, 1001A1
Saad Muhammad KOs Mwale, retains WBC light-heavywgt title 11-29, 1001B1
Mustafa Muhammad TKOs Koopmans, retains WBA light-heavywgt title 11-30, 1001B1
Limon KOs Bethlemi for WBC super featherwgt title 12-11, 1001B1
Mathebula decisns Kim for WBA flywgt title 12-13, 1001B1
BOYCE, Christopher John
Prison escape rptd 1-22, 55E1
BOYD, Julian Parks
Dies 5-28, 448C1
BOYD, Julianne
Onward Victoria opens 12-14, 1003E3
BOYER, Herbert W.
Genentech stock offer success rptd 10-14, 805G3
BOYER, Ken
Fired as Cardinals mgr 6-8, 637B2
Replaced as Cardinals mgr 6-28, 926C2
BO Yibo (Po Yi-po)
Signs US trade pact 9-17, 707A1
BOYLE, Peter
In God We Trust released 9-26, 836C3
True West opens 12-23, 1003F3
BOYLE, Raelene
Bars Olympic participatn 5-28, 421D1
BOYLE, William
Sentenced 1-11, 64G1
BOYNTON, Homer
On Soviet double agent 3-3, 189G1
BOZERMAN, Mary
Sim opens 6-2, 756G3
BOZZUTO, Richard C.
Loses Sen primary 9-9, 700C2
BRABOURNE, John
Mirror Crack'd released 12-18, 1003C2
BRACH, Gerard
Tess released 12-12, 1003E2
BRACKETT, Leigh
Empire Strikes Back released 5-21, 675D2
BRADEMAS, Rep. John (D, Ind.)
Loses reelectn 11-4, 837E2, 846D1, 850G3
Foley succeeds as whip 12-8, 936D2
BRADFORD, Barbara Taylor
Woman of Substance on best-seller list 7-13, 568D3; 8-17, 640G3; 9-14, 716C3; 10-12, 796F3
BRADFORD, Naomi
Loses US House electn 11-4, 851D3
BRADLEY, Sen. Bill (D, N.J.)
FCC backs WOR-TV move to NJ 11-6, 906G1
BRADLEY, Ed
Wins Polk award 2-25, 692F3
BRADLEY, Pat
2d in Sarah Coventry 6-29, wins Greater Baltimore 7-20, 715B1, D1
Wins Peter Jackson Classic 8-10, 2d in Japan Classic 11-9, 972F1, F2
LPGA top money winner 10-12, 971F3
BRADLEY, Mayor Tom (Los Angeles, Calif.)
LA adults-only housing barred 1-31, 115C2
Campaigns with Mondale 10-3, 817B1
BRADLEY Beach—*See NEW Jersey*
BRADSHAW, Terry
Steelers win NFL conf title 1-6, 8E1
Steelers win Super Bowl; named MVP 1-20, 61B3-62C1
BRADY, James
8 Cabinet posts filled 12-11, 934G3
On Presser's transitn role 12-18, 956A1
BRAELOW, Bonnie
We Won't Pay! opens 12-17, 1003G3
BRAHMS, Johannes (1833-97)
Symphonies Complete, A German Requiem win Grammys 2-27, 296F3

1976

BRAILOWSKY, Alexander
Dies 4-25, 524C2
BRANCH, Taylor
Arrives Venez 10-21, ousted 10-22, 844F1
BRANDAO, Evil
Torture death rptd 7-9, 836B2
BRANDLER, Judge Mark
Hearst stands 'mute' on trial 5-12, 367E3
Enters Hearst pleas 5-28, 423G1
Harrises convicted 8-9, denies mistrial 8-10, 596C1
Sentences Harrises 8-31, 679C3
BRANDON, Dr. Milan L.
Rpts new asthma drug 2-17, 159F2
BRANDT, Willy
At Europn socialist confs 1-18—1-19, 48G2; 3-13—3-24, 222F3
Spanish socialist aid set 1-24, 120A2
E Ger seeks Guillaume visit 1-25, 158B2
Reply to Kissinger letter on CP ties 2-5, 120C2
CDU wins Lower Saxony revote 2-6, 157G2
Announces Eur Parlt bid 2-6, 158B2
At intl soc dems mtg 5-23—5-25, 449A3
Addresses SPD conv 6-19, 503B1
Elected Soc Intl pres 11-26, 935F2
Spain OKs Socialist conf 11-27, 908E3
BRANDY—*See ALCOHOLIC Beverages*
BRANIFF International Corp.
SEC lists paymts 5-12, 726B1, D2
Braniff Airways, Inc.
Job-bias setlmt OKd 11-23, 943G2
CAB reporting penalty cited 12-29, 986G1
BRANSON, George Howard
Chrgd in bribery probe 2-17, 154B3
Whitlam contempt order denied 2-24, 172G2
Bribe case dropped 3-8, 187D2
BRATTELI, Trygve
Resigns 1-9, replaced 1-12, 30F1
BRAUN, Franziska
Dies 1-13, 56A3
BRAUN, Gregor
Wins Olympic medal 7-22, 574B2
BRAWER, Paul
Sentenced in USSR 8-27, 655F1-A2
Loses appeal 10-26, 857F1

BRAZIL—*See also DISARMAMENT—Geneva Committee, IDB, LAFTA, OAS, SELA*
Oppositn legislators fired 1-6, 27A2
'75 meningitis deaths total 1-8, 27A3
Geisel mil support rptd, plot aborted 1-9, 98A2
Sao Paulo prisoner 'suicide' 1-17, army chief fired 1-19; prisoner deaths scored 1-26, 1-29, 97G3
Listed as 'partly free' 1-19, 20C3
Legislators' ouster scored 1-23, 98G1
'Death squad' victims found 1-29, 98B2
Prestes chrgs MDB-PCB ties 2-8, MDB denies 2-10, 287G3
MDB arrests rptd 2-21—3-26, protested 3-31, 287G3
3 MDB deputies score govt 3-20; fired 3-29, 4-1 287D3
Widespread ABA, police violence rptd 7-9—10-14, 835B3
Govt corruptn detailed; 5 lose pol rights 8-3—8-5, 850E3
Kubitschek dies 8-23; mourning set 8-27, 836F2
Rpt communists chrg pretrial torture 9-10, 850C3
Police rptd held in death squads, murders 10-11, 850C2
Burnier co offices bombed 10-22, 850F2
'75-76 repressn rptd up 10-31, 975D1
Govt wins munic vote 11-15; Geisel, MDB ldrs comment 11-19—11-20, 902C3
Book links death squads, army chiefs 12-26, 997F3
Church Developments
Priests score prisoner 'suicide' 1-26, 98D1
Lorscheider named cardinal 4-27, 336C2
Bishop attacked 9-23; Jesuit priest killed, reactn 10-12—10-16, 835E3, 836B1
Priest murder protested 10-29, 850E2
Priest arrested in Para 10-31, 903D2
Bishops mtg re violence, Geisel-archbp mtg rptd 11-5, 850G2, A3
Bishops score violence 11-16, 903D1
IAPA asks 'terrorism' end 11-17, 916A2
Economy & Labor (domestic)
New oilfield found 1-6, 27D2
'75 cruzeiro devaluatns total 21.9% 1-9, 98E2
'75 COL up, Jan price hikes rptd 1-16, 98C2
Bahia drought, food airlift rptd 1-16, 98E2
'75 auto industry growth down 1-20, 98F2
50% inflatn in '76 seen 6-28, 836E2
Govt corruptn detailed 8-3—8-5, 850G3
Bishops score govt policy 11-16, 903E1, A2
'76 inflatn rate 46% 12-31, 997F3
Foreign Economic Developments
'75 trade, debt servicing data 1-6; coffee export income 1-9, 27E2

1977

BRAINWASHING—*See MIND Control*
BRAMLET, Al
Found slain 3-17, 261C3
BRANCH, C. B.
'76 salary rptd 5-23, 408C3
BRANCO, Castello
Lacerda dies 5-21, 452E3
BRANDT, William
Yoshimura convicted 1-20, 60B1
BRANDT, Willy
Backs Czech dissidents 1-22, 82G2
Warns on W Berlin 1-24, 102F1
CIA payments rptd 2-19, 124G1; Carter rpts error 2-24, 151A2
Warns of Nazi revival 8-19, 658G1
'70 Warsaw visit cited 11-21, 926G1
Rich-poor comm meets 12-9—12-11, 997F3
BRANIFF International Corp.
Concorde pact rptd 2-11, 213B1
VOA promotion rptd 5-17, 503B1
Indicted 8-16, 629C3
Carter OKs Dallas-London route 12-21, 1006D2
BRAUER, Richard D.
Dies 4-17, 356G2
BRAUNSCHWEIG, Andre
Scores Croissant extraditn 11-27, 969D1
BRAVO, Alfredo
Disappears 9-8, arrest admitted 9-20, 922G1-A2
BRAY 3rd, Charles W.
On El Salvador rights abuses, aid cutoff 3-9, 207A1
US withholds Nicaragua aid 4-7, 475B3
BRAZIER, Eugenie
Dies 3-3, 264E2

BRAZIL—*See also DISARMAMENT—Geneva Committee, IDB, OAS*
Atomic Energy & Safeguards
Mondale urges Bonn curb A-sales 1-25, 69B2
Canada asks A-safeguards treaty OK 1-28, 190F1
US rptd vs Bonn A-deal 2-7, curbs hinted 2-8, 118A1
Argentina backs Bonn A-deal 2-7, 190G1
US links aid, A-safeguards 3-1; talks on Bonn deal fail 3-2, intl pressure rptd 3-11, 189F3
Argentina A-race admitted 3-11, 190C1
Ueki: A-progrm to continue 3-26, 268F3
US presses Bonn on A-deal 3-31; W Ger honors pact 4-5, 268F2
Venez ties deteriorate 4-1, 547G2-B3
US A-fuel export delay rptd 4-14, 268C2
W Ger reaffirms A-deal 4-21, 334B1
US concedes W Ger A-deal 5-13, 414G1, A2
Mrs Carter, Geisel discuss safeguards 6-7, 455G1
W Ger halts data export 6-17, 566C3, E3
Schmidt sees Carter 7-13—7-14, 566F2
Alerts Carter on S Africa A-test 8-6; Carter confrms, vows actn 8-15, 663C3
US OKs uranium sale 11-16, 895G3, 912D3
Vance-Geisel safeguards talks rptd fruitless 11-22, 912C3, F3
Venez backs A-policy 11-25, 912D3
Economy & Labor (domestic)
'75 coffee crop damage, '76 harvest cited 74A3, C3
Coffee reserves total rptd 1-4, 74G3
Gomes asks democracy 1-21, 2-2; quits Cabt 2-8, replaced 2-9, 281B2
'76 factory wage study rptd 1-28, 158B3
Business ldrs ask democracy 2-2, 2-18; govt econ plans rptd 3-25, 281B2
Interest rates to be cut 2-9, 281E2
Auto industry at zero growth 3-25; GM lays off 400 5-6, 524G2
Salvador mayor fired 4-11, 303F2
Vacatns extended, rent law repealed 4-13, 303D1
Wages raised 44.1% 5-1, 524F2
Geisel sets price freeze, curbs 5-18, 524E2

1978

BRAIN—*See under MEDICINE & Health*
BRAINWASHING—*See MIND Control*
BRANCH, C. B.
To retire as Dow chrmn 5-3, 809F1
BRANCH, Cliff
NFC wins Pro Bowl 1-23, 56E1
BRAND, Jack
Cosmos win NASL title 8-27, 707D2
BRAND, Norman
Fined in Rhodesia arms scandal 7-23, 616A2
BRANDO, Marlon
Superman released 12-14, 1030E3
BRANDON, Johnny
Eubie opens 9-20, 1031E1
BRANDON, Michael
FM released 4-28, 619A2
BRANDON, Robert
Tax cut bill criticism rptd 10-16, 785E2
BRANDT, Willy
Schmidt reshuffles Cabt 2-3, 93C2
Vogel asks local curbs on Nazis 2-4, 114C2
Arranges Sadat-Peres talks, gives peace plan 7-9; plan made pub 7-10, 521B2
Filbinger quits over Nazi chrgs 8-7, 616G3
Denounces SPD spy scandal 9-2, 725G2
SPD to ease pub employe hiring rules 10-16, 823E1
BRANDY—*See ALCOHOL*
BRANIFF International Corp.
'71 Panama-US heroin transfer rptd 2-21, 120G2
UK air-fare dispute flares 2-28, 3-7, setlmt reached 3-17; Dallas/Fort Worth-London svc starts 3-18, 206G1, E2
BRASS—*See COPPER & Brass*
BRASSEUR, Claude
We Meet Paradise released 5-22, 620C1
BRASS Target (film)
Released 12-21, 1030E2
BRAUNSCHWEIG, Andre
Croissant '77 extraditn upheld 7-7, 649B3
BRAUNWALD, Dr. Eugene
On artery spasm research 12-7, 992C3
BRAVO, Alfredo
Moved to house arrest 6-18, 793A1
BRAY, John R.
Dies 10-10, 888E2

BRAZIL—*See also DISARMAMENT—Geneva Committee, GATT, IDB, OAS*
Rio Modern Art Museum burns 7-8, 579A2
Atomic Energy & Safeguards
'77 safeguard pact detailed 1-11, 11G1
US sees no A-bomb before '84 1-26, 61C2
Dutch OK uranium sales 2-1, protest held 3-4, 162C2, F2
Geisel in W Ger talks, US A-deal oppositn cited 3-6—3-10, 332D3
Carter stresses safeguards 3-29, W Ger A-deal oppositn scored 3-30, 233A2, C2
A-power program, W Ger purchases lagging 10-15, 836A3
Economy & Labor (domestic)
Rio de Janeiro expenses rated 1-14, 28B3
'77 inflatn rptd 38.8% 3-1, 1st ¼ COL 4-21, 311A2
Jobless rate rptd 8%-9% 3-17, 311B2
'77 growth rate rptd 5% 4-8, 311F1
Minimum wage hiked 4-28; indl workers strike 4-28—5-23, 411G3
Real wages decline, indl job instability cited 5-24, 412B2
Union curbs rptd retained 6-30, 555C3
Strikes continue 7-11—9-4, 772F1
Anti-strike decree set 8-4, unions score 8-15; govt warns unions 9-10, 772C2
May strike reprisals rptd 8-15, 772B2
Anti-inflatn petitn submitted; govt rejects, church backs 10-13, 836F3

1979

BRAIN—*See under MEDICINE*
BRALY, Malcolm
On The Yard released 1-18, 174C3
BRAMBLE, Mark
Grand Tour opens 1-11, 292E1
BRAMLETT, Leon
Loses Miss GOP gov primary 8-7, 680F2
BRANCHART, Georges
Arrested re fraud 2-5, 96F2
BRANDEIS University (Waltham, Mass.)
Ford bond sold re S Africa 4-27, 333A1
BRANDLING-Bennett, Dr. David
On flu progrm underutilizatn 5-18, 471D1
BRANDO, Marlon
Apocalypse Now released 8-15, 819D3
Wins Emmy 9-9, 858E2
BRANDT Jr., Jerrold
Bell Jar released 3-20, 528D1
BRANDT, Rut Hansen (Mrs. Willy)
Files for divorce 3-8, 271F3
BRANDT, Willy
Files for divorce 3-8, death plot foiled 3-20, 271E3
Greets Arafat 7-6—7-8, 511B3
W Ger assures Israel on Arafat mtg 9-10, 677C1
Mex visit scored 10-30, 874G3
BRANDY, Tamara
Big Bad Burlesque opens 8-14, 711E1
BRANIFF International Corp.
Dallas-DC Concorde svc begins 1-12, 35A3
Trust fine paid 2-23, 206D2
US-French air svc pact rptd 5-12, 465C3
FAA seeks airlines fine 11-6, 868B2
BRANNAN, Mike
2d in Houston Open 5-6, 587E2
BRASCAN Ltd.
Seeks Woolworth, takeover sought by Edper 4-9; Woolworth spurns 4-11; suits, other dvpts 4-12—4-23, 303B3-304C2
Edper buys stock 4-30—5-1; Woolworth bid set back 5-25; offer dropped, suits setld 5-29; Edper renews takeover effort 5-30, 440C2
Edper completes takeover 6-14, 6-29, 542D3
McDougall scored as Petro-Canada breakup study head 9-5, 685B1
BRASCO, Frank J.
Disbarmt challenge declined by Sup Ct 4-16, 303C1
BRASCO v. The Joint Bar Association
Case declined by Sup Ct 4-16, 303C1
BRASS—*See COPPER & Brass*
BRASS Ring, The (play)
Opens 7-2, 711F1
BRATKOWSKI, Stefan
Asks free discussn re econ 5-4, 374A3
BRAUN, George
Umbatha opens 4-9, 712B3
BRAZIL—*See also DISARMAMENT-Geneva Committee, GATT, IDB, OAS*
E central states hit by floods 2-7, 120B2
Atomic Energy & Safeguards
Mondale, Figueiredo confer on W Ger A-deal 3-22—3-23, 247F3
Economy & Labor
Sao Paulo indl workers, Rio bus drivers, teachers strike 3-13, 210C1
Metalworkers strike 3-13—3-27, 328A3
Figueiredo vows agri, econ reforms; '78 inflatn cited 3-15, 210B1
'68-74 GDP, other data rptd 3-29, 328E3
Metalworkers reach wage agrmt 5-11; govt interventn ended, union ldr reinstated 5-15, 399G1
Alcohol fuel use rptd 6-4, 430G1
Frost damages coffee crops 6-4, 430F1
Indian lands protected 6-22, 483A2
Belo Horizonte constructn workers strike, violence erupts 7-29—8-3; govt, unions back demands 8-3, 8-10, 612C2-A3

1980

BRAILOVSKY, Irina
Husband arrested 11-13, 863G1
BRAILOVSKY, Viktor
Arrested, freed 4-10, 326G2
Hosts Jewish scientist conf 4-13—4-15, 326E2
Sovts arrest 11-13, 863G1
BRAITHWAITE, Hilton L.
Marries Angela Davis 7-5, 639A1
BRALY, Malcom
Dies 4-7, 360C1
BRAMBLE, Mark
Barnum opens 4-30, 392D2
BRAND, Jack
Sets NASL shutout mark 7-3, NASL goalkeeping ldr 8-24, 769G3, 770D3
Named NASL top N Amer player 9-15, 1001A3
BRAND, Millen
Dies 3-19, 279F1
BRANDLING-Bennett, Dr. A. David
On US influenza deaths 2-15, 158A3
BRANDO, Marlon
Formula released 12-19, 1003A2
BRANDSTETTER, Wanda
Indicted in ERA bribe probe 6-5, chrgs denied 6-6, 441D3
Fined in ERA bribe case 11-7, 997A3
BRANDT, Willy
N-S study urges aid plan 2-12, 124A3
Berlinguer mtg cited 4-2, 254G3
SPD wins North Rhine-Westphalia vote 5-11, 390E3
BRANIFF International Corp.
Dallas-DC Concorde svc dropped 4-1, 346F3
Cuban refugees storm jet in Peru 8-29, surrender 8-30, 672C2
Lawrence resigns as chrmn, chief exec 12-31, 986A3
BRANTI v. Finkel
Case decided by Sup Ct 3-31, 291G1
BRAQUES, Georges (1882-1963)
Loren art collectn claim rptd denied 2-9, 200B2
BRASS—*See COPPER & Brass*
BRAUN, Zev
Fiendish Plot of Dr Fu Manchu released 8-8, 675E2
BRAUNSTEIN, George
Fade to Black released 10-17, 836F2
BRAVE New World (book)
GE microbe patent upheld by Sup Ct; reactn 6-16, 453G1

BRAZIL—*See also GATT, GENEVA Committee, IDB, OAS*
Jet crash kills 54 4-12, 527G3
Polio drive stalled, data questnd 4-16, 310G1-C2
Atomic Energy & Safeguards
Argentina talks open 3-18, bilateral agrmt with 7 other Latin natns cited 229C2
Argentina accord set 5-15—5-17, 405C2
Figueiredo scores arms race 7-28, 605G2
Economy & Labor
Agrarian reform initiated, 9 large estates expropriated 2-5, 95G1
'79 inflatn rate 77.2%, GDP rptd up 7% 2-14, 191C2
Gasohol seen as food productn threat 3-15, 251C1
Dockers strike 3-17—3-21; metalworkers walk out 4-1, rejct ct-ordrd setlmt 4-7, 272D2-B3
Metalworkers clash with police, vow to continue walkout 4-18; strike ldr arrested 4-19, 310B1
Alcohol fuel promotn outlined 4-20, progrm delays rptd 6-3, 460G3
Metalworkers clash with police, 22 arrested 5-5; strike ends, auto mfg losses rptd 5-11, 388C2

1976

Argentina tourism, wheat smuggling up 1-9, 96A3
Multinatls panel issues rival rpts 1-9, 98G2
French Mirage purchase cited 1-16, 36C2
Amazon bauxite operatn begun 1-16, 98F2
Paraguay steel mill planned 1-16, 205F3
Mex joint iron venture set 1-23, 75C1
At intl econ conf 2-11—2-20, 148B1
Kissinger rptdly sees no US trade ties chng 2-19—2-22, 177F1
Northrop bribes rptd admitted 2-23, 147F1
Latin press scores US pact 2-23, 177D1
'75 imports from US down 3-19, 466B1
US bars shoe import curb 4-16, 322C1
'75 Sovt trade rptd 5-5, 341A1
Intl banks OK Bolivia loan 6-18, 456A3
'75 Uruguay trade rptd 7-9, 542A2
W Ger reaffirms A-sale bar 7-15, 530A3
'75-76 US bank loans cited 11-10, 915F1
Iran buys into 2 Krupp units 11-23, 949E1
'76 intl borrowing rptd 12-22, 976G1

Foreign Relations (misc.)
S Africa recalls amb 1-2, 11C3
Russell ct scores rights abuse 1-17, 61D2
Concorde flights begin 1-21, 86A2
Venez fears Cuba troops in Guyana 1-24, 138B2
Spinola in Switzerland 2-7, 315B1
Prestes addresses French CP Cong 2-8, 288A1
Guyana denies Cuba, China mil presence 2-23—3-10, 253B1
Portugal to seek closer ties 7-19, 558F1
At nonaligned conf 8-16—8-20, 622C1
IAEA dir cites 9-21, 760F3

1977

Coffee prices frozen 5-20, 458A2
'61-75 GDP variatns table 5-30, 439A1
58 censor positns opened 6-1, 524E3
Business failures up 6-3, 524A3
Jan-May oil consumptn cut 6-24, 524B2
MDB ldr scores econ structure 6-27, 523F2

Foreign Relations (misc.)—*See also 'Atomic Energy' above, 'Human Rights' and 'Monetary, Trade & Aid' below*
UN Assemb member 3G3
Venez ties deteriorate 4-1, 547G2 ★ -B3
Forgn publicatns to be censored 5-28, 524B3
Australia emb abolitn urged 6-2, 484D3
Haiti amb slain 7-3, aide held 7-12, 583C2
Uruguay arrests rptr 7-14, 601F1
Pereira at Panama Canal pact signing 9-7, 678A1
Venez pres visits 11-16—11-20, 912E3

Government & Politics—*See also other appropriate subheads in this section*
Independt govt branches urged 2-25, 281E2
'78 MDB gov electns predicted 3-4, 281F1
MDB blocks judicial reform bill 3-30; Geisel suspends Cong 4-1, 281A1
Salvador mayor fired 4-11, 303E2
Geisel decrees judicial reforms 4-13, tightens mil rule 4-14, 303B1
Bar Assn scores judicial reforms 4-19, 523A3
ARENA ldrs score pol measures 4-29, 5-4, 523A3
Cols ask return to democracy 5-26, 523B3
Geisel fires MDB deputy 6-14, 523E3
Divorce legalized 6-23, 524F3
MDB ldrs urge democracy 6-27, poll backs 6-29, 523B2
MDB oppositn ldr banned; Frota, Figueiredo pres bids cited 7-1, 541E1, B2
Barreto backs Figueiredo 7-12; Geisel support for Gomes Monteiro rptd 7-22, 615G3
Attys, scientists, mil ask democracy 7-16—8-13, 633B1, A2
Sen ldr sets '78 pres bid 7-26, 615D3
Politicians, soldiers ask pol reforms; Magalhaes gains support, mil back Figueiredo 8-22—9-24, 740D3, G3 ★
Students rally for democracy 8-23—9-23, 740A3
Magalhaes Pinto on pres bid 9-30, 840F1
Frota fired as army min 10-12, pol activities rptd 10-14, 839E3
Cabt mins back Figueiredo 10-21, 840D1
Geisel: pol system 'relative democracy' 11-4, 964E1
Bentes leads exec pres poll 11-7, gains mil support 12-2; Figueiredo rptd Geisel choice 11-17, 964F1
MDB ldr acquitted of electn law violatn 11-30, 964B2
Geisel backs pol reforms 12-1, MDB ldrs score plan 12-9, 12-13, 964A1
Divorce bill cleared 12-4, 964D3; signed 12-26, 1018F3

Human Rights (including political prisoner issues)—*See also 'Press & Censorship' below*
800 pol prisoners rptd 1-1, 3B1
Democracy return urged by Gomes 1-21, business ldrs 2-2, 2-18, 281B2
Cnclman chrgs torture schls 2-1, loses pol rights 2-2, 168E1
French lawyers chrg minors tortured 2-13, 168C1
2d cnclman loses pol rights 2-16, MDB warned vs criticism 2-26, 186F2
Prisoner torture exam barred 2-16, 186B3
Gen asks freedoms restored 2-25, 281E2
Bishops conf scores repressn 2-26, 186A3
US mil aid rejctd, rights rpt scored 3-5, 3-7; MDB backs 3-6, 167E3
US mil aid pact canceled 3-11, 186C2
US issues rights rpt 3-12, 187D1

1978

Govt OKs collective bargaining, Sao Paulo, Rio raises cited 10-27, 879A2

Foreign Relations (misc.)—*See also 'Atomic Energy' above, 'Monetary, Trade, Aid & Investment' below*
Uruguay frees newsman 1-5, 136F3
UN res on Chile rights abuse opposed 3-6, 210F1
Alleged Nazi arrested 5-30; W Ger, 3 others ask extraditn 5-31, 6-8, 477G1
Cuba pressure re Africa rptd asked 6-11, 443C1
Amazon 8-natn pact signed 7-3, 829C2
Amer Human Rights Conv enacted 7-18, 829A1
Portugal ex-pres ends exile 7-23, 594F1
UN Assemb member 713C3
French pres visits 10-4—10-8, 772F2
Argentina fears role in possible Chile war 11-2, 860B3

Government & Politics—*See also other appropriate subheads in this section*
Geisel confrms Figueiredo pres choice; MDB, others score 1-4—1-5, 6G2
Figueiredo scored by Abreu rpt 1-13, 165F3
Ex-trade min backs Magalhaes for pres, scores Geisel 1-20, 165C3
Magalhaes scores Figueiredo, asks direct electns 2-15, 165B3
Figueiredo favors 'gradual' democracy 2-23, 165E2
Figueiredo gets Arena pres nod 4-8, 555E3
Bentes, Magalhaes set anti-Figueiredo front, ask MDB support 5-29; Gomes backs Bentes 7-6, MDB wary 7-9, 555F3-556A1
Figueiredo candidate loses Sao Paulo gov race 6-5, 556B1
Army capt runs on MDB ticket; scores Figueiredo, jailed 6-16, 556C1
Const reforms submitted; MDB reps score, ask direct electns 6-23, 555E2
Industrialists ask full democracy 6-27, 556E3
Figueiredo warns vs MDB cong win 7-9, 556B1
Figueiredo scores oppositn demands 7-27, vows restore democracy 7-28, 646C3
Civilians found pro-democracy center 8-1, 646E3
Magalhaes drops pres bid, Bentes rivalry cited 8-8, 646E2
Bentes joins MDB 8-17, pres nominatn seen 8-18, 646F2
Brasilia voting bar cited 8-22, 661E1
Bentes, Brossard get MDB pres, VP nominatns 8-23, 671B2
MDB scores pol reforms 9-19; Cong OKs, 'bionic' sens remain 9-21, 772B1
Abreu jailed, Bentes protests 10-2, 771E3
Bentes rptdly may end candidacy 10-6, 772A1
Figueiredo elected pres 10-15, 794A1
Figueiredo reaffirms dem goal 10-16, 836D2
Govt corruptn chrgs rptd, Figueiredo admits taps 10-17; son implicated 10-20, 836E2
MDB Cong candidates rptd harrassed 10-31, 11-13, govt chrgs CP infiltratn 11-14, 921D2
Govt retains control in Cong electns, MDB makes gains 11-15, 921G1
New party system planned 11-15, 921F2

Human Rights (including political prisoner issues)
Uruguay frees newsman 1-5, 136F3
Prisoners: torture continues 2-19, 166A1
Allege 'death squad' ldr seized 2-22, 166E1
Figueiredo bars amnesty; on rights law chngs 2-23, 165F2
Alleged 'death squad' chief freed on bail 3-3, 412C2
UN res on Chile rights abuse opposed 3-6, 210F1
Carter cites concern 3-29; sees Mesquita Neto, Arns 3-31, 233E2
Indl strike news blackout 4-28—5-23, 412F1
Press censorship ends, broadcast curbs retained 6-9, 555D2
Civilians found pro-democracy center 8-1, 646E3

1979

Oil prices hiked, auto tax set 8-1, 871C2
July inflatn, '79 forecast rptd 8-13, 612B3
Delfim outlines new anti-inflatn plan 8-15, 612B3
Alcohol fuel dvpt plan set 8-18, 871C2
Copa-ba tree rptd fuel source 9-15, 1000B2
Metalworkers strike in Sao Paulo, 250 arrests rptd. 10-29, 833G1-A2
State co supervisn set, deficits rptd 10-29, 871B1
Minimum wage raised 10-31, 871F1
Sao Paulo metalworkers strike continues, violence erupts 11-6–11-8, 871G1
Gas prices raised 58% 11-23, taxi drivers strike 11-26–11-27, 907B2
Inflatn to top 70% 11-26, 907E2
Figueiredo redirects econ policy; inflatn, energy costs targeted 12-7, 948C2

Foreign Relations (misc.)—*See also 'Atomic' above, 'Monetary' & 'UN' below*
Beagle Channel papal mediatn agreed 1-8, 51D3
Uruguayans '78 kidnap admitted 1-17, Brossard scores police probe 1-23, 95F1
CELAM mtg opens in Mex 1-27, 68B2; Pope backed 2-3, Nicaragua, El Salvador prelates 2-12, 108F3
Forgn ldrs at Figueiredo inaugural 3-15, 210D1
Mideast, SALT briefing 3-22, 248A1
Nazi's extradtn denied 4 natns 6-20, 483A3; confinemt rptd 8-8, 617C1
Latin pol refugees occupy Swedish consulate, protest Argentina repressn 8-6; UN responds 8-8, 627D1, F1
Figueiredo in Venez 11-6–11-7, 953E1

Government & Politics—*See also other appropriate subheads in this section*
Figueiredo names Cabt, vows democracy 1-19, 94G3, 95B1*
Sarney sees democracy in 2 yrs 3-13, 210A1
Figueiredo sworn, reaffirms democracy pledge 3-15, 209F3
Silveira named amb to US 3-23, 248C1
Indian lands protected 6-22, 483G1-G2
Simonsen quits planning post, Delfim named 8-10, 612A3
Party reform law implemented, Arena, MDB disolved 11-30, 926D2

Human Rights
Freedom House lists as partly free 13A1
New yr legal chngs; repressive laws expire; death penalty, life jail terms abolished; pol rights restored 22B2
'Death squad' victims cited 1-18, 97D2
Figueiredo vows freedom of expressn 3-15, 209G3
Mondale, Figueiredo confer 3-22–3-23, 247F3
PEN Club meets 7-21, 554A1
Latin pol refugees occupy Swedish consulate, protest Argentina repressn 8-6; UN responds 8-8, 627D1, F1
Pol amnesty law signed 8-28, 926B2

1980

Metalworkers strike ldrs released 5-19, 405E3
Unemploymt seen rising 5-23, 405G3
Pope urges reforms, sees Indian ldrs 6-30—7-11, 537A2-538F2
Oil rig accident cuts productn 20% 9-7, 731A3
'80-81 coffee productn forecast 10-1, price, revenue drop seen 10-7, 777A3
Gas prices hiked, rationing studied 10-3, 759F1
'81 budget OKd, inflatn forecast; '80 inflatn rptd 12-17, 991A3

Foreign Relations (misc.)—*See also 'Atomic Energy' above, 'Monetary', 'UN Policy' below*
Argentina escapees '79 sanctuary rptd 2-4, 95B1
Colombia amb seized in DR Emb raid 2-27, 141B1; injury rptd 3-10, 180B3
Cuban refugees offered asylum 4-16, 285C1
Colombia DR Emb siege ends, amb freed 4-27, 335G1
Figueiredo in Argentina, ties strengthened 5-15—5-17, 405B2
Pope visits, urges reforms 6-30—7-11; mass marred by violence 7-9, 537A2-538F2
Mex pres visits 7-27—7-31, 605F2-A3
Bolivia mil govt recognized 7-31, 577F1; Siles family offered asylum 8-12, 668G1
Nazi kills self 10-3, 810E1
Italy priest expelled, immigratn law controversy rptd 10-30, 870G3

Government & Politics—*See also other appropriate subheads in this section*
Finance min quits 1-15, 95C2

Human Rights
Freedom House lists as partly free 87E3
Cath clergy attacks rptd, violence debated 1-11, 95A3
Pope asks 'just society' 6-30—7-11, 537A2-538F2
Rightists continue terror campaign vs reforms 8-27—8-29, 705G2
RC priest vs mass request 9-7, expelled 10-30, 870G3

1976

Obituaries
Goulart, Joao 12-6, 970G1
Maluf, Chafic 12-27, 1015A2
Pontes, Paulo 12-28, 1015D2
Press & Censorship
Newsmen score Herzog 'suicide' rpt 1-13, legislators' ouster 1-23, 98F1
Konder, lawyers group denounce Herzog death 1-26, 1-29, 98E1
Santana Machado arrest confrmd 3-9, 288B1
MDB protest rpts cut 3-31, 288C1

1977

MDB sen scores rights abuse 3-22, 281A2
MDB youths arrested 3-27—3-29, 281A2
US pressure scored 3-28, 268E3
MDB blocks judicial reform bill 3-30; Geisel suspends Cong 4-1, 281A1
Geisel decrees judicial reforms 4-13, tightens mil rule; MDB, press score 4-14, 303B1
Students, workers seized 5-1; widespread protests, church backs 5-3—6-4, 447B2
US envoy conciliatory 5-13, 414G1, B2
US missionaries held 5-15—5-18, 455A2
Arns honored in US 5-22, 447A3
Cols ask pol amnesty 5-26, 523C3
Mrs Carter visits 6-6—6-9, sees US missionaries 6-8; Brazil scores US stand 6-12, 455E1
Student protests continue 6-6—6-22; Mrs Carter gets plea 6-6, 523F3-524E1
Geisel fires MDB deputy 6-14, 523E3
Cath educator acquitted 6-24, 525C1
MDB ldrs score govt abuses 6-27, 523B2; Furtado banned 7-7, 541E1
Rio 'death squad' kills 55 7-1—8-10, police role rptd 8-9, 633A3
Maoists sentenced 7-8, 633D2
Lawyers, scientists, mil ask rights observance 7-16—8-13, 633B1, A2
Brazilia students expelled 7-21; strike continues, 100 seized 7-25—8-3, 633E1
US missionary expelled 7-27, police beating denied 8-6, 633F2
Army col jailed 8-18—9-2, 741C1
Rio prison hunger strike rptd 8-18; Rio, Sao Paulo torture rpts continue 8-31, 9-11, 741G1
Student protest rallies smashed 8-23—9-23, 740A3
Cop seized in 'death squad' murders 8-31; 2-mo toll passes 70 9-4, 805A3
US missionary rpts jail abuses, 'reign of terror' in slums 9-1, 741B2
Amnesty Intl lists lawmakers held 9-5, 753B2
Archbps score police raids on univ 9-25, 9-27; security chief justifies raids 9-27, 840G1
Student 'extremists' seized 9-28, 840C2
Fleury acquitted in 3 'death squad' murders 10-14, 840E2
'Death squad' kills 12 10-18, 840D2
Pol prisoners detail torture 10-26, 11-10, pub outcry rptd 11-10, 964C2
Alleged Communists acquitted 10-28, 840C2
'Death squad' probe asked 11-7, more murders rptd 11-14; '77 Rio toll at 95 11-17, 964B3
Female prison conditns protested 11-10, 964A3
Monetary, Trade & Aid (including all foreign economic developments)—*See also 'Atomic Energy' above*
'77 coffee exports rptd 74C3, D3
Coffee export tax raised 1-4, 1-17, 74F3
Boeing rpts consultants 1-5, ct backs secrecy 2-25, 215C3
US coffee price hike rptd 1-19, 74D3, 78A1
Coffee export tax raised 2-16, 3-7, producers warned vs withholding 3-1, 168G3
Japan raw material orders rptd 2-21, 253B2
US chrgs coffee price manipulatn 2-22, 169C1
US modifies duty-free list 2-28, 189E3
US mil aid rejctd 3-5, 3-7, 167E3; pact canceled 3-11, 186C2
Cruzeiro devalued 3-8, 209F1
Coffee export tax raised 3-9, 209F1
'75-76 trade, paymts data; table 3-11, 189C1, A2 *
'76 trade data rptd 3-11, 524B2
US bars Rhodesia chrome 3-18, 191E1
Carter bars shoe import curbs 4-1, 248E2, B3
'66-75 arms transfers table 4-8, 415A2, F2, C3
US coffee prices raised 4-18, 319C1
Cruzeiro devalued 2.2% 5-1, 524G2
Coffee exports limited 5-20, 458A2
IMF, US '76 bank loans rptd 6-5, 438E1, F1
Steel co gets forgn loan 6-20, 524C2
Iran trade pact signed 6-23, 524F1
IWC cuts whaling quotas 6-24, 496F3
Hydroelec talks with Paraguay, Argentina 9-22—9-23, 794D3; Paraguay arrest of critics rptd 9-23, 803G1
Intl sugar pact OKd, world mkt share cited 10-7, 855D1
US Cong bars mil credit sales 10-19, 815A3; bill signed 11-1, 834D1
10 coffee exporters ratify boycott strategy 10-21; Brazil alters policy, sets Colombia pact 11-4, 3 others join actn 11-9, 876G2-D3
Exxon admits paymts 10-25, 818A2
Coffee exports, trade deficit concern linked 11-7, 876D3
Paraguay vs elec grid frequency chng 11-11, 976B1
Cruzeiro devalued 11-14, 12-6; total '77 devaluatns 27.9% 12-6, 964E3
Obituaries
Lacerda, Carlos 5-21, 452D3
Pignatari, Francisco 10-27, 872F2
Press & Censorship
Jornal do Brasil scores Geisel reforms 4-14, 303C2
Forgn publicatns to be censored 5-28, 524B3
58 censor positns opened 6-1, 524E3
2500 rptrs score censorship 6-8, 524D3
Uruguay arrests rptr 7-14, 601F1

1978

MDB asks 'arbitrary' rule, torture end 9-19; govt pol reforms passed 9-21, 772C1
Journalist's '75 death marked 10-25; govt blamed, probe asked 10-28, 879D1
Newspr dir indicted 10-27, 879G1
MDB campaign press curbs rptd 11-14, 921C2
Monetary, Trade, Aid & Investment—*See also 'Atomic Energy' above*
US bars chrome duty hike 1-29, 80F3
Canada agri equipmt firm cancels dividends, sales drop cited 2-15, 146E1
Australian coal pact signed 3-1, 165C2
'77 trade surplus rptd; coffee, mfg exports up 3-1, 311D1
EC seeks steel export agrmt 3-2, 158C2
Geisel visits W Ger 3-6—3-10, 332D3
3 forgn loans for $610 mln rptd 3-10, 311G1
Hydro project gets forgn bank loan 3-30, 311C2
'77 forgn debt rptd $31.2 bln 4-8, 311E1
Arab aid rise rptd 4-9, 257C2
Venez oil deal signed 4-28, 332B1
Swedish, W Ger, US auto plants struck 4-28—5-23, 412A1
UK conglomerate retail operatns cited 5-5, 345D3
Paraguay steel loan rptd 5-5, 395E3
E Ger trade pact rptd 7-13, 649C1
Jan-June intl bank top borrower 8-25, 828C3
World Bank top borrower 9-15, 828B3
Argentina disrupts Chile auto delivery 9-15, 860A3
French trade, tech pacts signed 10-4—10-8, 772F2
Parana waters diverted for itaipu dam, Argentine fears cited; Eur cos sign turbine pact 10-20, 829F2
Cruzeiro devalued 2%, '78 total 22% 10-25, 837A1
Japan banks set steel loan 10-25, 837A1
Coffee export tax raised, US price hikes seen 10-25, 837B1
China to buy steel 11-1, 879E2
Bank ranked '77 9th biggest in world 11-8, 914B1, D1
Cruzeiro devalued 12-6, 12-21, 1021F2
Mex '79 oil price hike set 12-20, 978F2
Press & Censorship—*See 'Human Rights' above*

1979

Monetary, Trade, Aid & Investment—*See also 'Atomic' above*
Trade levies altered, cruzeiro devalued 2-2, 210F1-A2
Metalworkers strike halts productn at forgn affiliates 3-13—3-27, 328A3
El Salvador coffee price squeeze chrgd 3-13, 348B2
Figueiredo vows trade reforms; '78 forgn debt, oil imports cited 3-15, 210B1
Canada co utility share cited 4-9, 303F3
China trade missn arrives 5-21, maritime pact signed 5-22, 443B3
Cruzeiro devalued 5-30, 430E1
Coffee exports suspended 6-4, 430F1
Jari projct probe set 6-8, 443G2
Oil import ceiling set 7-11, 871B2
Jari projct to be Brazil-run 7-12, 542B2
'78 US oil loan cited 7-28, 584C2
Spain RR, mining deals rptd 8-3; seeks trade parity, '78 gap noted 8-6, 654B2
'84 export goal set, trade cncl revived 8-17, 871E1
Forgn cos set alcohol fuel dvpt plan 8-18, 871D2
Multinatl code set 10-1; forgn investmt, debt rptd 10-2, 870G3
Argentina, Paraguay dam accords signed 10-19, 845A1
Ford, Caterpillar, Olivetti units hit by metalworkers strike 10-29, 833B2
Cruzeiro devalued 10-31, 871D1
Jan-Sept trade gap up 11-1, 871F2
Figueiredo in Venez trade talks 11-6—11-7, 953F1
Oil import costs to exceed $7 bln 11-26, 907E2
$1.2 bln alcohol fuel loan rptd 11-26, 907F2
Forgn exchng operatns suspended 12-6, 948D2
Figueiredo devalues cruzeiro 30%, revises trade rules; forgn debt, oil costs targeted 12-7, 948E2
Obituaries
Novaes, Guiomar 3-7, 272D3
Press & Censorship—*See 'Human Rights' above*

1980

Monetary, Trade, Aid & Investment
Cruzeiro devalued 3.2%, '79 devaluatns cited 1-8, 191B2
Iraq oil accord signed 1-9, 95F2
USSR grain embargo rejected 1-14, 28D1
Mex '80 oil imports seen 1-15, 60B2
'79 trade deficit rptd, '80 forecast 1-15, 95D2
Forgn reserves used to offset debt 3-5, 191C1
'80 oil loan rptd; imports, debt svc costs cited 3-5, 191F1
Feb trade deficit rptd; Mar, Apr forecast 3-5, 191C2
IDB meets, Jamaica debt accord set 4-15, 314C2
Ford, VW hit by metalworkers strike 4-19, 310C1
Metalworkers strike ends, auto mfg losses rptd 5-11, 388D2
Argentina trade accords signed 5-15—5-17, 405E2
Apr 1st 1/4 trade deficit grows; forgn debt repaymt revised 5-24, 406B1
Cruzeiro devalued, '80 total at 19.56% 5-28, 406C1
US alcohol fuel sales surge; 1st 1/4, Apr data 6-10, 461E1
Kuwait buys 10% of VW unit 6-25, 542E3, 562C1
Mex oil, trade talks 7-27—7-31, 605F2-A3
Bolivia gas deal sought 7-31, 577G1
Jari project halt threatnd 8-5, govt reactn rptd 10-16, 787D2-C3
World Bank '80 loans rptd 9-22, 720E1
Sovt oil purchase, deals with 6 other natns rptd 10-2, 759G1-A2
Coffee glut weakens ICO cartel, liquidatn set 10-7, 777F2
Amazon pact signed 10-28, 865D2
Iraq oil shipmts set 11-20, 894C2
'80 exports, trade deficit rptd; '81 oil costs, trade forecast 12-17, 991D3, F3
Obituaries
De Moraes, Vinicius 7-9, 608F1
Portella Nunes, Petronio 1-6, 104E3

1976

Gomes da Silva torture rptd 4-15, 288D1
Cong bans radio, TV campaigns 6-28, 836D2
Govt corruptn detailed 8-3—8-5, 850E3
AAB bombs press assn hqs 8-19, Marinho home 9-23; threatns newsmen 10-8, 835D3
O Expresso accuses CP 8-27, 836B2
Opiniao offices bombed 11-15, IAPA asks 'terrorism' end 11-17, 916A2
Bishops score suppressn 11-16, 903A2
MDB links campaign curbs, electn loss 11-20, 903A1
Sports
Summer Olympic results 7-18—7-31, 573F3, 576C1, F3
U.S. Relations
US Jews cancel hotel reservatns 1-15, 27G2
Amazon bauxite operatn begun 1-16, 98G2
Kissinger visits, signs consultative pact 2-19—2-22; pact denounced 2-23, 2-26, 177A1, D1
Northrop bribes rptd admitted 2-23, 147F1
'75 imports from US down 3-19, 466B1
US bars shoe import curb 4-16, 322C1
Ship in US Bicentennial event 7-4, 488D3
Sugar duties tripled 9-21, 721D3
'75-76 US bank loans cited 11-10, 915F1
US '64 coup aid rptd set 12-29, 998A1

1977

Scientists score censorship 7-22, 633C1
Geisel bans party broadcasts 7-26, 616B1
Novelist arrested 7-27, 633C2
Folha writer arrested, Sao Paulo exec editor replaced 9-21, 741D1
Movimento seized, MDB news coverage barred 9-23, 741F1
Leftist infiltratn chrgd 10-12, 840A1
O Estado scores 'relative democracy' 11-4, 964E1
U.S. Relations—*See also 'Atomic Energy', 'Human Rights' and 'Monetary, Trade & Aid' above*
US natl seeks refuge 3-2, 144E3
US rift rptd 3-28, 268E3
Todman scores 5-11; visits, 'consultant status' pledged 5-12—5-14, 414D1
Mrs Carter visits 6-6—6-9, 454E1, 455E1
Panama Canal pact backing rptd 9-3, 678D1
Santos sees Carter 9-6, at Canal pact signing 9-7, 678A1
Carter visit scheduled 9-23, 738F1
Carter visit deferred 11-7, 854A1; rescheduled 12-1, 914C2
Vance visits, sees Geisel 11-22—11-23, 912D2, C3

1978

Sports
World Cup soccer finals 6-1—6-25, coach scored 6-7, 519D3—520A2, C3
U.S. Relations—*See also 'Atomic Energy' and 'Monetary, Trade, Aid & Investment' above*
Paymts to govt offcls from US billionaire rptd 1-13, 165G3
Carter visits 3-29—3-31, 233B1, A2
Cuba pressure re Africa rptd asked 6-11, 443C1

1979

Sports
Alcohol fuel auto race held 9-7, 871E2
UN Policy & Developments
Refuge comr responds to Latin pol protesters 8-8, 627F1
Spain premr visits 8-6—8-8, 654F1-C2
Membership listed 695E2
U.S. Relations
2 CIA alleged agents named 1-4, 17C3
Metalworkers strike halts productn at US affiliates 3-13—3-27, 328A3
El Salvador coffee price squeeze chrgd 3-13, 348B2
Marshall, Mrs Mondale at Figueiredo inaugural 3-15, 210E1
Mondale visits 3-21-3-23; Silveira named amb to US 3-23, 247D3, 248A2
Jari projct probe set 6-8, 443G2
US basketball coach arrested in Pan Am Games assault 7-8, 798E3
Jari projct to be Brazil-run 7-12, 542B2
'78 US oil loan cited 7-28, 584C2
Ford, Caterpillar units hit by metalworkers strike 10-29, 833B2

1980

Sports
Moscow Olympic results 7-20—8-3, 623A3, 624A1, F3, G3
Brazil Open golf results 11-24, 972G2
UN Policy & Developments
Refugee comm '79 sanctuary for Argentines rptd 2-4, 95B1
WHO polio data questned 4-16, 310B2
U.S. Relations
Sabin polio drive stalled 4-16, 310G1-C2
US alcohol fuel sales surge 6-10, Admin oppositn rptd 6-18, 461E1
Jari project halt threatnd 8-5, govt reactn rptd 10-16, 787D2-C3

1976

BRAZINSKAS, Algirdas & Pranas
Refused US asylum 6-24; freed 7-10, fly to Rome 7-11, 544A1
BRAZ Teixeira, Antonio
On Macao autonomy statute 1-10, 53A3
BRAZZAVILLE—*See CONGO Republic*
BREAUX, Rep. John B. (D, La.)
Reelected 11-2, 829G3
BRECKENRIDGE, Rep. John B. (D, Ky.)
Reelected 11-2, 822F1, 829F3
BREHMER, Christina
Wins Olympic medal 7-29, 576A2
BREITEL, Chief Judge Charles D.
Rules NYC debt moratorium unconstnl 11-19, 887G3
BREKKE, Gerald W.
Wins Minn Sen primary 9-14, 705B1
Loses electn 11-2, 823G2
BREMENT, Marshal
Sovt reentry bar rptd 11-17, 907B3
BREMER, Arthur Herman
Wallace taunted in Wis 3-30, 245E3
BRENNAN, Col. Jack
Calls Nixon 'love letters' 'hoax' 6-4, 438B2
BRENNAN, Thomas
Loses Mich Sen primary 8-3, 565A3

1977

BRAZZAVILLE—*See CONGO Republic*
BREEDER Reactors—*See ATOMIC Energy—Industrial Use*
BREKALO, Jozo
Invades UN missn 6-14, held 6-16, 497D2
BREN, Donald
Group wins Irvine Co 5-20, 519E1, F1
BRENNAN, Joseph E.
Disputes Indian land claims 1-21, 59F1
BRENNAN, Joseph P.
UMW wildcat strikes 6-18—9-6, 690G2, A3
UMW strike begins 12-6, 937E1

1978

BRAZZAVILLE—*See CONGO Republic*
BREAD—*See BAKERIES & Bakery Goods*
BREAD and Chocolate (film)
Released 7-14, 969E3
BREA Garo, Gen. Robinson
Loses police command 10-2, 881C1
BREAUX, Rep. John B. (D, La.)
Cited in Passman indictmt re Korea 3-31; gift disputed 4-3—4-5, 239F1, C3
Ethics com cites Park gift testimony conflict 7-13, 527E1
Reelected 11-7, 851A1
BRECKINRIDGE, Rep. John B. (D, Ky.)
Defeated in primary 5-23, 406D2
Hopkins wins seat 11-7, 853B3
BREECH, Ernest Robert
Dies 7-3, 620E2
BREEDER Reactors—*See ATOMIC Energy—Industrial Use*
BREEST, Gunther
Record wins Grammy 2-24, 316C1
BREL, Jacques
Dies 10-9, 888E2
BRENNAN, Joseph E.
Wins Me gov primary 6-13, 466G3
Elected 11-7, 847E2, 853F2

1979

BRAZZAVILLE—*See CONGO Republic*
BREAD—*See BAKERIES & Bakery Goods*
BREAK a Leg (play)
Opens 4-29, 711G1
BREAKFAST In America (recording)
On best-seller list 5-2, 356A3; 5-30, 448F3; 7-4, 548F3; 8-1, 620F3; 9-5, 672F3; 10-3, 800F3
BREAKING Away (film)
Released 7-17, 819F3
Top-grossing film 9-26, 800G3
BREAST-Feeding—*See CHILDREN–Health*
BREAUX, Merlin
Oil worker pact setld 1-11, 87F1
BRECHT, Bertolt (1898-1956)
FBI '43-56 surveillnc rptd 3-29, 367C3
BRECKINRIDGE, John Bayne
Dies 7-29, 588D2
BREEDER Reactors—*See ATOMIC Energy–Industrial Use*
BREER, Murle
Wins Mixed Team tourn 12-9, 969C3
BRENES, Cpl. Lorenzo
Questnd in death of US rptr 6-21, 461A3
Named in ABC rptr's death 6-30, 512C3
BRENNAN, Gov. Joseph E. (D, Me.)
Vetoes pub mtg smoking ban 3-13, 218F2
Asks potato futures trading halt 5-9, 348G1
Abstains in gov vote on Carter '80 support 7-8, 518D1
Gets reassurance on heating fuel supply 8-28, 703C2
Endorses Kennedy 10-19, 847C2
BRENNAN, Marjorie
Husband's '80 retiremt seen 10-23, 848F2

1980

BREAKING Away (film)
Tesich wins Oscar 4-14, 296G1
BREAUX, Rep. John B. (D, La.)
Wins primary 9-13, 724A3
Reelected 11-4, 843A1
BRECHT, Bertolt (1898-1956)
Lusitania Songspeil opens 1-10, 136B3
Mother Courage opens 5-13, 392E3
BREEDER Reactors—*See ATOMIC Energy--Industrial Use*
BREGMAN, Martin
Simon released 2-29, 216E3
BREMER, Rev. Jack
Visits US hostages in Iran 4-6, 258D2
BRENNAN, Edwin A.
Named Sears president 3-12, 225B1
BRENNAN, Gov. Joseph E. (D, Me.)
State of State message 1-2, 269C2
Fills Muskie Sen seat 5-8, 367B2

1976

BRENNAN Jr., Justice William J(oseph)—*For Supreme Court developments not listed here, see SUPREME Court under U.S. GOVERNMENT*
Upholds non-fed tax on imports 1-14, 23B3
Vs Pa police misconduct rule 1-21, 42F3
Vs warrantless arrests 1-26, 87F2
Rules on campaign law 1-30, 87A2
Upholds state alien job curbs 2-25, 169G1
Vs Firestone libel ruling 3-2, 169B3
Backs limited prosecutor immunity 3-2, 169E3
Vs shopping cntr pickets rule 3-3, 218G3
Vs jury bias questioning curb 3-3, 219F1
Backs retroactive seniority 3-24, 218D2
Vs mil pol activity curb 3-24, 218A3
Va homosexual ban upheld 3-30, 261C3
Vs redistricting review rule 3-30, 262D1
Backs city-suburb housing plan 4-20, 308B3
For convicts 5th Amendmt rights 4-20, 331F2
Vs govt access to bank records 4-21, 331E1
Vs drug convictn rule 4-27, 349D2
Vs prisoner garb ruling 5-3, 359A2
Vs limiting grand jury bias challenge 5-3, 359B2
Swears in FEC members 5-21, 391B3
Rules on alien jury duty bar 6-1, 414D2
Vs fed employe job bias suit rule 6-1, 414G2
Dissents on police job test rule 6-7, 435E1
Vs NC police firing 6-10, 552F2
Vs trial transcript ruling 6-10, 552A3
Vs teacher dismissal ruling 6-17, 552D3
Vs some church-coll aid 6-21, 452F3
Vs local zoning referendum 6-21, 453D1
Vs police bargaining summary rule 6-21, 553A1
Rules on US wage laws 6-24, 468E2
Vs sex-show zoning 6-24, 479A1
Vs 'doorway' arrests rule 6-24, 553D1
Vs defns info-access rule 6-24, 553E1
Vs prison transfer ruling 6-25, 552B2
Vs schl rezoning bar 6-28, 478F3
4-state strip mining stay voided 6-28, 569B1

1977

BRENNAN Jr., Justice William J(oseph)—*For Supreme Court developments not listed here, see U.S. GOVERNMENT—SUPREME Court*
Vs Ill restrictive suburban zoning 1-11, 15D1
Vs govt wiretap use expansn 1-18, 58D2
Swears Califano 1-25, 52F2
On Miranda rights curb 1-25, 80B2
Vs secondary strike curb 2-22, 149G3
Vs police informant ruling 2-22, 150C1
Backs racial voter redistricting 3-1, 175C1
Vs Soc Sec widower benefits rule 3-2, 192F1
Vs death sentencing rule 3-22, 230G3
Vs 'comity' extensn to civil actns 3-22, 231G2
Sidesteps Miranda rule review 3-23, 276B1
Affirms intra-group grand jury bias 3-23, 276E2
Vs death penalty 6-6, 478E2
Voids NY contraceptive curbs 6-9, 501B2
Vs price-fixing suit curbs 6-9, 501A3
Vs Medicaid abortn curbs 6-20, 516B3
Vs Justice Dept warrantless searches 6-21, 539D1
Vs aid for church schls 6-23, 539B3
Backs US custody of Nixon papers 6-28, 539D3
Bans Kent State gym 9-6, ban withdrawn 9-8, 820A3
Reinstates Las Vegas basketball coach 9-30, 870F2
Hears Bakke case arguments 10-12, 835F1
Vs Alaska pipe rate order 11-14, 878G2
Backs taxes on state police meal stipends 11-20, 919G1

1978

BRENNAN Jr., Justice William J(oseph)—*For Supreme Court developments not listed here, see U.S. GOVERNMENT—SUPREME Court*
Cancer treatment rptd 1-9, 13D3
Vs EPA asbestos rule curb 1-10, 13A3
For SC teacher tests review 1-16, 33D2
Vs prosecutors' plea bargaining power 1-18, 65A1
Vs sub-subcontractor paymt bond rule 2-22, 126A3
Vs PR welfare benefits exclusn 2-27, 143D1
Vs med student ouster rule 3-1, 143B3
Vs Maritime Comm labor contract jurisdictn 3-1, 144B1
Vs curbs on oil tanker regulatn 3-6, 162B1
Not in Indian ct trial rule 3-6, 162E1
Vs testimony thru illegal search 3-21, 221A1
Vs state police alien ban 3-22, 221D1
Not in judicial immunity sterilizatn case 3-28, 241E3
Backs cities' liablity under trust law 3-29, 280A2
Not in Minn pensn law case 4-3, 309A1
Denies broadcasters Nixon tapes 4-18, 308B2
Vs clergy pub office ban 4-19, 309E1
Backs Hearst convictn review 4-24, 322A2
Backs NBC sex abuse suit review 4-24, 322E2
Not in sex-based pensn plans case 4-25, 322G3
Not in engineers' fee code case 4-25, 323D1
Vs corp pol free speech 4-26, 343D3
Not in state stevedoring tax case 4-26, 344D1
Not in Va judicial inquiry case 5-1, 363E3
Curbs SEC trading suspensns 5-15, 387F1
Vs trespass laws union rule 5-15, 387D2
Vs fed tap power 5-15, 387G2
Backs Calif jurisdictn in child-support case 5-15, 387G3
Vs tax liability in bankruptcy 5-22, 388E1
Vs corp takeover tax liability 5-22, 388F1
Not in OSHA searches case 5-23, 405F2

1979

BRENNAN Jr., Justice William Joseph—*For Supreme Court developments not listed here, see U.S. GOVERNMENT—SUPREME Court*
Backs Boston referendum spending case review 1-8, 14C3
Vs limited lawyers' interstate rights 1-15, 31F3
Tex abortn record access case declined 1-22, 54A2
Vs Blue Shield drug plan trust rule 2-27, 165G1
Vs single-sex alimony 3-5, 184D2
Backs job-testing data disclosure 3-5, 184D3
Backs SC abortn prosecutn ban 3-5, 185B1
Vs Ill right-to-counsel rule 3-5, 185C2
Backs jobless pay for strikers 3-21, 231A2
Vs NYC Transit Auth ex-addict ban 3-21, 231C2
Backs church schl labor interventn 3-21, 231F2
Backs Fla death penalty appeal review 3-26, 231A1
Backs cable TV pub-access rule 4-2, 281B2
Vs IRS tap evidence 4-2, 281E2
Vs NYS alien teacher ban 4-17, 325E3
Vs 'state of mind' libel queries 4-18, 302F1
Vs covert US entries for 'bugging' 4-18, 346A2
Vs unwed father damage suit bar 4-24, 364G1
Vs verbal rights waiver 4-24, 364C2
Backs mutual fund dirs' power 5-14, 383C1
Vs pretrial detentn curbs 5-14, 383A2
Backs fed ct welfare suits 5-14, 384A1
Discloses finances 5-15, 382E2
Backs state age bias filings 5-21, 400E2
Vs innocence instructn refusal 5-21, 400E3
Vs state parole discretn 5-29, 421A3
Vs co-defendant confessns 5-29, 422B1
Vs NY gun-in-car law 6-4, 438E3
Not in NJ ex-offcls rejailing case 6-4, 438G3
Vs vets' job-preferne law 6-5, 421A2

1980

BRENNAN Jr., Justice William Joseph—*For Supreme Court developments not listed here, see U.S. GOVERNMENT--SUPREME Court*
Vs citizenship revocatn law 1-15, 51E2
Backs inmate escape justificatn 1-21, 92G3
Vs mil petitn limits 1-21, 93E1
Vs narrowed state ct jurisdictn 1-21, 93B2, D2
Vs CIA disclosure limits 2-19, 130F3
Backs pvt coll faculty unions 2-20, 146G1-A2
Vs NYS pvt schl reimbursemt 2-20, 146E2
Vs Calif dual seniority system 2-20, 146A3
Vs IRS handwriting orders 2-20, 170G1
Vs govt damage suits geographic relevance 2-20, 170C3
Backs fed gun law prior convictn limit 2-27, 188A3
Backs Kissinger records access 3-3, 210A1
Backs fed funded group info access 3-3, 210D1
Not in Calif wine pricing case 3-3, 210G1
Vs Tex habitual-offender law 3-18, 226C3
Backs ctroom ID in illegal arrest 3-25, 265B3
Backs Indian land managemt fed liability 4-15, 306G1
Vs 'good faith' municipal immunity 4-16, 328F2
Vs at-large local electns 4-22, 343A3
Backs prisoners right to sue 4-22, 343E3
Vs police interrogatn rule 5-12, 386B3
Vs Atlanta schl integratn ruling 5-12, 386C3
Vs Ga death penalty 5-19, 440B1
Vs narrowed 'exclusionary rule' 5-27, 453E2
Vs lower PR welfare aid 5-27, 453E3
Vs DEA detainmt procedure 5-27, 454A1
Vs SEC fraud intent proof 6-2, 512E3
Vs pre-1920 oil shale mining claims 6-2, 513D1
Vs defendant pre-arrest silence testimony 6-10, 512E1
Vs GE microbe patent 6-16, 453D1

1976

Backs patronage ouster bar 6-29, 468C3
Vs business records seizure 6-29, 535C2
Vs illegitimates benefits rule 6-29, 568E3
Vs press gag orders 6-30, 492A1
'72 vote vs death penalty cited, dissents in '76 decision 7-2, 491A2, G2
Vs fed cts criminal appeals curb 7-6, 534E3
Vs warrantless questioning of aliens 7-6, 535A1
Vs inadmissible criminal evidence use 7-6, 535B1
Vs warrantless car search rule 7-6, 535C1
Vs sympathy strike rule 7-6, 535G1
For review of Fla club bias case 10-4, 766A1
For housing bias ruling review 10-4, 766B1
For review of NM strikers pay rule 10-4, 807F2
For arguments on double jeopardy protectn case 10-12, 848E2
Vs carry-back tax ruling 11-2, 867C2
Backs review of Ind auto suit curbs, scores summary decisns 11-8, 883E3
Vs parole revocatn hearing rule 11-15, 882D2
For review of Pa youth curfew 11-15, 882E2
Okla gag order stayed 11-24, 901E2
Vs Austin busing rule 12-6, 920F2
Backs pregnancy benefits 12-7, 920F1
Vs pub employe contract debate right 12-8, 960B2
Vs vacating Gilmore stay 12-13, 952F2
For Mo tuitn aid case review 12-13, 960A3
For Ky maiden name case review 12-13, 960B3
Vs EEOC grievance-delay ruling 12-20, 960C1
Voids Okla beer-buying law 12-20, 960D1

BRESLIN, Jimmy
Carter, Artis get new trial 3-17, 256G3
BRETT, George
AL batting ldr 10-4, 796B1, C1
BREWER, Dr. George E.
Rpts sickle cell zinc treatmt 2-24, 159G2
BREWSTER, Robert C.
Quits amb post 3-17, 232G1
Replaced as amb to Ecuador 4-1, 262C3
BREYTENBACH, Breyten
Rhodesia sanctn violatns chrgd 6-21, 621F1 *
BREZHNEV, Leonid Ilich (Soviet president)
Meets Berlinguer 3-1, 195F3
New Politburo, Secretariat listed 3-5, 195F1, B2, E2
Not at Bulgaria CP Cong, Zhivko lauds 3-29—4-2, 250E1
Zagladin on independent CPs 4-20, 341A2
Promoted to field marshal, bust dedicated 5-8, 421G1
Mozambique ldr visits 5-17—5-23, 403D1
Signs India amity vow 6-11, 440B1
Meets Tito 6-28, 461D2
Opens E, W, Eur CP conf 6-29, 461G1
Rpt vs Syria Leb policy 7-19, 528F1
Mil rank cited 7-30, 908A2
Asks Syria quit Leb 9-11, Assad rejects 10-1, 10-5, 737G1
W Ger visit rptd set 10-4, 754G2
Scores Westn pressure re arms buildup 10-5, 739F1
Sees Neto 10-7, signs treaty 10-8, 856C3
Gets Arafat plea vs Syria 10-13, 758E2
Signs Mongolia pact 10-19, 949B3
Addresses Central Com on econ, forgn affairs 10-25, 839F1
Seeks closer Albania ties 10-25; Hoxha scores USSR 11-2, 849G3
Sees Gierek, signs aid pact 11-9—11-15, 907C1
Sees Tito, denies threat 11-14—11-17, 909D3, 955A2
Sees Ceausescu, 11-22—11-24, 907A2
At Warsaw Pact summit 11-25—11-26, 896E3
Qaddafi visits 12-6—12-9, 949B1
W Ger visit confrmd 12-16, 968C2
United States
In Kissinger SALT talks 1-21—1-23, 61A3, F3
'74 A-test pact implementatn delayed 4-9, 242E2
Signs A-pact after US delay 5-28, 371C2; treaty text 387A1
Meets Harriman 9-20; regrets Nixon resignatn 9-29, 752B1
Ford, Carter debate 10-6, 740G3
Sees Hammer 10-20, 947E3

1977

BRETHREN Church (Dunkers)
Gilbert Dodds dies 2-3, 164F2
BRETT, George
AL batting ldr 10-2, 926F3
In AL playoff 10-5—10-9, 807A2
BRETT, Ken
Traded to Angels 6-15, 644F2
BREWER, James W.
Indicted 3-3, 204D1
BREWER, William D.
Replaced as amb to Sudan 5-25, 499D3
BREWER v. Williams
Miranda rule review declined 3-23, 275A3
BREWSTER Jr., Kingman
Named amb to UK 4-7, confrmd 4-29, 418C1
Successor at Yale named 12-20, 1021C2
BREYTENBACH, Breyten
Acquitted 7-15, 564D1
BREZHNEV, Leonid Ilich (Soviet president)
Yugo bars mil pact 1-9, 24B1
In Italy trade talks 1-10—1-13, 64C3
Soyuz 24 lands 2-25, 170F2
Sees Castro 4-4—4-6, 249F3
Japan affirms Kurile claim 4-13, 319E2
Podgorny ousted 5-24, 412B2
Vows 'Stalinism' end 5-24, 433F2
Constitutn draft issued 6-4, 433C1
Elected pres 6-16, 469C2
In Paris, sees Giscard 6-20—6-22, 494D3-495A2, B2
Giscard denies US-USSR mediator role 6-22, 495C2
Giscard evaluates talks 7-25, 551A1
Tito visits 8-16—8-18, 640C2, 709E3
Ex-prisoners emigratn plea rptd 9-23, 753C1
Scores West re rights 10-4, 785A3
Kuznetsov named 1st vp 10-7, 785C3
Sees Owen; backs Rhodesia plan, signs A-war pact 10-10—10-11, 812F3
Meets India prime min 10-21—10-26, 842F2
Marks 60th anniv of revolutn, warns vs Eurocommunism 11-2; photo 11-7, 865F2, C3
Grain harvest shortfall rptd 11-2, 948D2
Africa
Warns vs Zaire meddling 4-18, 317C2
Sees Mengistu 5-6, 391A1
Somalia scored re Ogaden 9-28, 830C1
Angola pres visits 9-28, 830D1
Sees UK forgn secy, backs Rhodesia plan 10-10—10-11, 812F3
Middle East
Meets Arafat 4-7, Assad 4-18—4-22, 297C2
Sees Fahmy in Moscow 6-10, 457A3
Meets Fahmy in Belgrade 6-15, rpt better Egypt ties set 6-22, 496B2
Rpt asked new Egypt pact 7-16, 550C1
United States
Asks SALT II pact, scores mil aims rpt 1-18, 70F1
US defends Sakharov letter 2-18, 137F2
US sens protest Zavurov jailing 2-19, 226A2
Scores Carter rights stance 3-21, 226A1

1978

Backs exclusn of children from porno rule 5-23, 405E1
Vs Mont hunting fee disparity 5-23, 406A1
Not in lawyer soliciting cases 5-30, 430G2
Not in newsroom searches case 5-31, 430B2
Not in arson search warrants case 5-31, 431E1
Vs municipal legal immunity 6-6, 447E1
Not in FCC cross media case 6-12, 468A1
Backs '75 double jeopardy doctrine 6-14, 468D3
Vs Iowa business tax formula 6-15, 468F2
Backs Freedom of info in NLRB cases 6-15, 468G2
Backs union supervisor discipline 6-21, 509D2
Backs hosp union organizing 6-22, 508E3
Vs Alaska oil job preference law 6-22, 508G3
Backs press prison data access 6-26, 566D3
Backs Grand Central office complex 6-26, 567A1
Vs Bakke med schl admissn, backs race-based affirmative actn principle; opinion excerpt 6-28, 481C1-F2, 485C1
Backs Minn pensn funds law 6-28, 567E1
Vs juvenile case reviews 6-28, 567A2
Vs FCC 'Filthy Words' ban 7-3, 551E3
Not in death penalty cases 7-3, 552B2
Vs Calif, NM water rights 7-3, 552C2
Voting alignmt shift noted 7-3, 565G3-566C1
Denies Chicago Nazi rally delay 7-7, 529B2
Backs employer retaliatn case review 10-2, 751D1
Backs coll sex-bias ruling 11-13, 874C2
Vs cities' power over suburbs 11-28, 937D3
Vs new fed ct 12-4, 959A1
Vs broader police auto search power 12-5, 959C3
Backs Calif auto franchise law 12-5, 959E3
Backs extraditn probe bar 12-18, 981B2

BRETON Revolutionary Army—See *FRANCE—Terrorism*
BRETT, George
NL wins All-Star Game 7-11, 559A3
AL batting ldr 10-2, 928E3
Royals lose AL pennant 10-7, 779B1
BREWER, Albert
Loses primary for Ala gov 9-5, 699B2
BREWER, Brig. Gen. Margaret A.
Promoted by Marine Corps 5-11, 420E1
BREWER, Ron
In NBA draft 6-9, 457F2
BREWSTER Jr., Kingman
Sees Rhodesia rebel ldrs 3-13—3-14, 193B1
BREZHNEV, Leonid Ilich (Soviet president)
Gets Order of Victory 2-20, 151C3
Addresses CP Central Com re agri 7-3, targets OKd 7-4, 518G2-B3
Kulakov dies 7-16, 620G2
Mikoyan dies 10-22, 888D3
Chernenko elected to Politburo 11-27, 924C3
Announces '78 record harvest 11-27, 966E2
Foreign Developments
Warns NATO vs neutron bomb 1-23, 103C2
Sees Austria chancellor 2-8, 110E2
Grigorenko citizenship revoked 2-13, 179G2
UK scores campaign vs neutron bomb 2-21, 140D1
Japan vs peace bid 2-22; draft publshd 2-23, 121D3
Scores US ties; SALT, trade pact delays 2-24; US blames Africa role 2-25, 137A1
On China border tour 3-28—4-9, bars pullback 4-1, 237F3, G3
W Ger weighs uranium deal 4-2, 258C2
Scores US SALT 'indecisn' 4-7, 297C2
Sees Vance on SALT 4-22; rpts progress, backs neutron bomb restraint 4-25, 297B1, G1
Offers mutual force cuts, warns vs neutron bomb deploymt 5-2, 417C1
Visits Bonn 5-4—5-7, trade pact signed 5-7, 417A1-B2
Czech dissidents arrested 5-30, 504F1
Scores NATO defns plan, Zaire interventn 5-31, 423G1
Schmidt reviews Carter talks 6-1, 519A2
Carter issues detente warning 6-7, 423B3
Scheel plea for Hess release rptd rejctd 6-11, 477E3
E-W Ger ties rptd improved 6-24, 622G2
Scores US China ties 6-25, 488A3; Carter reassures 6-26, 491B1
Carter protests Shcharansky trial 7-12, 543F2
Sees Ceausescu on Hua trip 8-7, 678A1
Sees Hammer 8-25, 670A2

1979

Backs sex-bias suits vs congressmen 6-5, 464C1
Backs 'probable cause' in detentns 6-5, 464D2
Differs on Ariz farm labor law finding 6-5, 464B3
Not in consumers' right to sue case 6-11, 478E2
Backs broader Cong legal immunity 6-18, 498G3
Vs Helstoski indictmt rule 6-18, 499B1
Vs Mont 'deliberate homicide' convictn 6-18, 499G1
Vs child mental commitmt rules 6-20, 516B1
Vs warrantless phone surveillnc 6-20, 516F1
Backs youth probatn officer consultatn right 6-20, 516C2
Vs 'good faith' arrest 6-25, 540E1
Vs broader libel suit rights 6-26, 540B3, D3
Backs Idaho takeover law challenge 6-26, 540F3
Vs rights violatn proof in false arrest suits 6-26, 541A1
Vs Weber affirmative actn challenge; majority opinion excerpts 6-27, 477C1-478E1
Backs unwed mothers survivors' aid 6-27, 558A2
Vs dockworker negligence suits 6-27, 558C2
Backs wage-price case review 7-2, 498D2
Vs ctroom pub access curbs 7-2, 515A3
'78-79 Sup Ct term ends, voting alignmts rptd 7-2, 558A1
Vs Mass abortn-consent law 7-2, 559C2
Suffers stroke 9-4, 744E3
Backs Bell contempt case review 10-9, 783E3
Criticizes press 10-17, 848C1
Backs Bishop executn stay 10-21, 817D2
'80 retiremt seen 10-23, 848D2
Stays Georges Bank offshore lease sale 11-6, stay lifted 11-9, 867E1
Vs advisor investor suit curbs 11-13, 902D1
Backs VA malpractice ruling 11-28, 944F3
Backs pub access to waterways 12-4, 988C1
Vs union wildcat strike liability 12-10, 988E1
Vs Taiwan treaty case review 12-13, 940D1
Again stays, lifts Georges Bank lease sale 12-18, 990A2

BRENNAN v. U.S. Postal Service
Case declined by Sup Ct 1-15, 32A1
BRENT, George
Dies 5-26, 432D2
BRENTWOOD, N.Y.—See *NEW York State*
BREST, Martin
Going in Style released 12-25, 1007D3
BRETHREN, The (book)
Publicatn stirs controversy 12-2, 988A2
BRETT, George
NL wins All-Star Game 7-17, 568F3
AL batting ldr 9-30, 955D3-F3
BREWER, Jim
Traded to Pistons 2-15, 526F2
BREWER Carias, Charles
Venez youth min 3-10, 192C3
BREZHNEV, Leonid Ilich (Soviet president)
Warning vs Westn links to China cited 1-5, 12C3
Congratulates Cambodia rebels 1-9, 11G1
Carter cites China ties concern 1-17, 29E3
Pak pres scorns Bhutto clemency plea 2-14, 116B2
Scores China, backs SALT 3-2, 172A1
Podgorny pol career ends 3-4, 237F2
Reelected, ill health cited 4-18, 314B1
Sees Giscard: pacts signed; space flight, arms talks unsetld 4-26—4-28, 323A3
SALT II pact drafted, Carter summit planned 5-9, 338C3, 339B1, D1
Tito visits 5-16—5-18, 379D3
In Hungary: backs Carter summit, improved China ties; health rptd good 5-30—6-1, 416F3
Desai vs plea on Afghan aid 6-14, 443E1
At Vienna summit 6-15—6-18; **SALT II pact signed 6-18**, 449A1-C2; texts 450A1-458E2
Carter asks SALT II ratificatn 6-18, 449E2
U-2 SALT verificatn talks rptd 6-21, 497D1
Carter: denied Viet bases 6-23, 474F2
Byrd sees re SALT 7-4, 510B3
Kosygin repeats Backfire pledge 8-30, 657E2
Gets Carter message on Cuba troops 9-25, responds 9-27, 737D1
In E Ger 10-4—10-8; offers troop cut, missile freeze 10-6; reactn 10-7, 10-9, 761C1-F3
Vs NATO A-missiles 10-13—11-6, 880G2
Signs S Yemen pact 10-25, 802B1
NATO group backs A-missiles 11-14, 880A2
Scores US A-war alert 11-16, 882D2
Scores econ chiefs; rpts low grain harvest, urges oil conservatn 11-27, 928A3
Tikhonov named full Politburo member 11-27, 929C1

1980

Vs state sales preference 6-19, 554G2
Backs cts power to suppress evidence 6-23, 554E3
Vs nursing home summary aid cutoff 6-23, 554G3
Vs magistrates pretrial role 6-23, 555A1
Backs broader right to sue states 6-25, 540E3
Vs narrowed illegal search protectn 6-25, 541A2
Vs unpatented key ingredient monopolies 6-27, 511D2
Vs Medicaid abortn funding limits 6-30, 492E1
Not in Potts executn stay vote 6-30, 511F1
Backs govt minority constructn grants 7-2, 510D1
Backs OSHA benzene standard 7-2, 511A1
'79-80 Sup Ct term ends, voting alignmts rptd 7-2, 540C2
Permits draft registratn 7-19, 597F3*, 598A1
Backs unwed couples child custody case review 10-20, 807C1
Stays PR refugee camp transfers 10-24, 825A3
'Mr Justice' title dropped 11-14, 882A3
Male-only draft case accepted 12-1, 918F1
Vs lenient sentence appeal 12-9, 936E3
Vs rail pensn revisn 12-9, 937B1
Backs defendants fed ct civil right suits 12-9, 937C1
Vs job bias suit filing time limit 12-15, 957C2

BRESLIN, Catherine
Unholy Child on best-seller list 12-7, 948F3
BRESSLER, Richard
Named BN pres 5-19, 456F2
BRETHREN, The (book)
On best-seller list 1-13, 40B3; 2-10, 120C3; 3-9, 200B3; 4-6, 280C3
Powell refutes Sup Ct media image 5-1, 368G2
BRETT, George
AL batting ldr 10-6, 926D3, E3
Royals win AL pennant 10-10, 796A1
In World Series 10-14—10-21, 811C2-812B3
Named AL MVP 11-18, 925D3
BREWER, Graeme
Wins Olympic medal 7-21, 623G2
BREWERS Association, California
Dual seniority system backed by Sup Ct 2-20, 146F2-B3
BREWSTER, Daniel
Williams indicted in Abscam probe 10-30, 824C3
BREZHNEV, Leonid Ilich (Soviet president)
Carter scored for Afghan criticism 1-3, 1F2
Afghan exiles protest Sovt interventn 1-4, 3B1
Marchais leaves for USSR 1-7, 57E3
Scores US Afghan reactn 1-12, 26C2
CP Olympic handbook rptd 1-19, 68C1
Backs detente 2-4, 84E3
Gets Tito detente plea 2-21, 139B3
Offers Afghan pullout for neutrality vow 2-22, Carter responds 2-25, 139E2, G2
Sees US oil exec, Afghan pullout hint rptd 2-27, 165G1
China vs Afghan neutrality plan 3-2, 165D1
Killanin asks Carter mtg 4-23, 325F2
Meets with Killanin on Olympics 5-7, 379E1
At Tito funeral 5-8, 339A1
Sees Giscard on Afghan 5-19, 378G2-379D1
Carter backs Eur-Sovt ties 6-23, 473G1
Lauds Afghan interventn 6-23, 475F1
Schmidt in USSR; discusses A-missiles, urges Afghan exit 6-30—7-1, 489A1, G1
US, French independnc day broadcasts barred 7-4, 7-14, 566D3
Opens Moscow Olympics 7-19, 588B1
Asks US arms talks 8-22, US denies delay 8-26; Muskie indicates US ready 9-7, 679D3
Lauds Polish CP promotn 9-6, 678A3
Sees Polish ldrs, aid hike pledged 9-10—9-11, 679D1
Asks Iraq-Iran war setlmt, blames US 9-30, 758G2
Signs Sovt-Syria friendship pact 10-8, 759D2
E Ger Poland warning rptd 10-8, 761D1
Urges US arms talks resume 10-14, 776C3
Meets Afghan pres, vows contd aid 10-16; communique 10-19, 827C1
Rpts econ, agri problems 10-21, 797E2
Carter questns Reagan ability 10-21, 802G3

1976

Urges US arms, trade pacts 11-30, 947A3
Not to 'test' Carter; Carter to push SALT 12-3, 916E2
Carter sees summit 12-27, prospect welcomed 12-29, 978G2

BRICENO, Gen. Gonzalo
Officers rptd seized 8-13, 652D2
BRIDENBAUGH, Dale G.
Quits GE A-post 2-3, 115C1
BRIDGE (card game)
Crawford dies 2-14, 160C3
Fishbein dies 2-19, 192D3
US wins world title 5-8, 352G3
BRIDGES & Tunnels
NYC bridge toll hikes upheld 4-26, 308C1
Dem platform text 6-15, 474A2
Vienna bridge collapses 8-1, 796D2
Swiss complete longest tunnel 12-16, 1011D3
BRIGITHA, Enith
Wins Olympic medals 7-19, 7-22, 575B3
BRIGGS, Ellis O.
Dies 2-21, 484C3
BRIGUGLIO, Salvatore
Indicted 6-23, 460A1
BRIMMER, Andrew F.
At Carter econ briefing 12-1, 898F2
BRING on the Empty Horses (book)
On best seller list 1-25, 80C3; 2-29, 208E3; 12-5, 972B2
BRINKLEY, Rep. Jack Thomas (D, Ga.)
Reelected 11-2, 829D2
BRINK'S, Inc.
Record Canada theft 3-30, 250F3
BRISTOL-Myers Co.
SEC lists paymts 5-12, 726E2
'69 trust suit ends in mistrial 8-17, 988B3
Sup Ct bars review of trust case 10-4, 807B3
BRITISH Aircraft Corp. Ltd.
Australian SAM deal rptd 1-6, 7E3
Layoffs announced 2-10, 174E1
Govt wins natlzn ruling 5-27, 402D1
Signs Iran oil-arms deal 11-18, 906F1
BRITISH Airways
Concorde svc to NY barred 3-11, 1st flight to US lands in DC 5-24, 378D2-C3
Lockheed jet purchase set 8-18, 675D3
Rpts 1st ¼ Concorde losses 8-26, 675B3
Collisn over Yugo 9-10, 696B3
Australia probes food standards 12-6, 962B1
BRITISH Broadcasting Corp. (BBC)
Airs Solzhenitsyn warning vs communism 3-24, 424F1
Spain oppositn ldrs arrested 4-3, 269D1
Amin threatens rptr 6-14, 502E2
Closes India office 8-5, 621D1
Sudan scores, bars film crew 8-6, 8-7, 592G2, 857D2
BRITISH Honduras—*See BELIZE*
BRITISH Leyland Ltd.
Italy Innocenti layoffs completed 2-4, 141C1
Arab boycott lifted 3-24—4-3, 242C1
Plant strikes rptd 4-22, 4-23, 365D1
US ends car dumping probe 5-4, 321D2
6-mo profit rptd 5-17, 365C1
Govt loan set 7-21, 556F2
Plant strikes, layoffs rptd 8-10, 8-11, 638F1

1977

SALT talks open 3-28; US bids rejctd, Geneva talks agreed 3-30, 225A1, C2
Sees SALT compromise 4-5, reassures Carter 4-8, 400D3
Nixon reminisces 5-12, 385E3, 386D1, F1
Carter defends rights stand 6-13, 473G1
Giscard denies US-USSR mediator role 6-22, 495C2
Vance briefed on Giscard talks 6-24, 495B2
Carter proposes preliminary talks 6-30, 515D1
Sees US amb; rejcts Carter rights stand, preliminary talks 7-5, 529E3
Ford '76 letter re agent rptd 7-15, 564F2
Giscard scores Carter on detente 7-25, 551A1
Replies to Carter Charleston speech 8-16, 640B2
Gromyko sees Carter summit 9-23, 10-1, Carter vague 9-29, 750F3
Backs A-test ban 11-2, 996G3-997A1
Carter gets letter 11-18, 894E3
Scientists aks Shcharansky trial observers 12-15, 1017F1
Carter sees vist after SALT accord 12-28, 1002C1

BRIBERY—*See under CRIME*
BRIDGES, Harry
Sovt offcls denied visas 4-16, 306G2
Retires 4-18, 324G2
Herman elected ILWU pres 6-23, 481E3
BRIDGE, Structural and Ornamental Iron Workers, International Association of (AFL-CIO)
Lawyer fees case refused 11-14, 878E3
BRIDGES & Tunnels
Thousand Islands Bridge pact signed 2-5, 133B1
Ship hits Va bridge 2-24, 204F3
Richmond-San Rafael pipe laid 6-7, 492B3
NYC clean-air case review declined 10-17, 797D3
BRIDGE Too Far, A (film)
Top-grossing film 7-6, 548G3
BRIDGMAN, Mich.—*See MICHIGAN*
BRIEDENBACH, Andrew W.
Replaced as EPA asst admin 6-21, 626F2
BRIGADE 2506 (Bay of Pigs veteran group)
More attacks pledged 8-31, 686D1
BRIGGS & Stratton Corp.
'76 Fortune 500 list drops 341D1
BRIMMER, Andrew A.
US shoe, auto industry comparison rptd 8-8, 587G2
BRINKMEYER, Glenn
Cited re Houston police indictmt 10-20, 821A1
BRINK'S Inc.—*See PITTSTON Corp.*
BRISCOE, Bennie
Valdes decisns for middleweight title 11-5, 970B3
BRISCOE, Gov. Dolph (D, Tex.)
Scores Carter energy plan 4-20, 320D2
OKs executn by drugs 5-11, 594G1
Signs Seadock funding bill 7-27, 725A1
Carter awards Braniff London route 12-21, 1006E2
BRISCOE, Frank
Loses mayoral election 11-22, 900B3
BRISCOE v. Bell
Atty gen voting rights power ulheld 6-20, 516A1
BRISTOL, Dave
Turner loses interim mgr dispute 5-11—5-13, 567F3
Fired as Braves mgr 10-25, 927B2
BRISTOL-Meyers Co.
Clairol Inc.
Hair dye linked to cancer 10-17, benzidine use denied 12-14, 962G3, 963D1
BRITANNIA Hotel (London)
Carter entourage lodged 5-5, 359G2
BRITISH Aerospace Ltd.
Formed 4-29, 526B3
BRITISH Aircraft Corp. Ltd. (BAC)
Australia to buy radar equipmt 2-1, 96A2
Nationalized 4-29, 526B3
Concorde Developments—*See AVIATION—SST/Concorde*
BRITISH Airways
Strike ends 4-27, 392B1
Yugo air controller sentncd re '76 crash 5-16, 497A3
US air svc pact set 6-22, 500A2, D2
US-UK fare cut sought 7-24, 593G1
CAB acts on NY-London budget fare 9-9, 9-15, Carter overrules 9-26, 860E2
Concorde Developments—*See AVIATION—SST/Concorde*
BRITISH American Commodity Options Corp. v. Bagley
'74 commodity law challenge declined 11-7, 857F1
BRITISH Broadcasting Corp. (BBC)
India lifts ban 1-6, 45G3
Uganda atrocity rpt aired 3-13, 308E2
Andrew Young interview 4-5, 272E1
Pak protests role 4-28, 349A2
Rhodesia ousts rptr 8-2, 599F2
BRITISH Caledonian Airways
Scores US-UK air svc pact 6-22, 500E2
BRITISH Commonwealth—*See COMMONWEALTH of Nations*
BRITISH Gulf Air
Jet hijacked to Qatar 6-29, 535B2
BRITISH Honduras—*See BELIZE*
BRITISH-Irish Association
O'Brien addresses 9-18, 782A3
BRITISH Leyland Ltd.
Strikes idle 21,000 2-18—2-28, 201C1
Strikers return to work 3-21, 256B1
Payoff chrgs stir controversy 5-19—5-25; NEB chrmn retires 7-1, 526C1
Govt lifts investmt freeze 6-29, OKs loan 7-25, 695A1

1978

Sees Kennedy 9-9, 742F3
Vs Camp David summit 9-22, 731E1
Carter asks Leb truce role 10-5, 761C1
Meets Syrian pres, more arms vowed 10-5—10-6, 762C3
Vance sees on SALT 10-23, 803D3
Signs Viet pact 11-3, 859E2
W Ger hwy to Berlin OKd 11-16, 905G3
Sees US sens; rpts Sovt neutron bomb test, backs SALT 11-17, 905C1, D1
Warns US vs Iran interventn, US rebuts 11-19, 893D3
Signs Ethiopia pact 11-20, 922C3
Kennedy emigratn interventn cited 11-30, 946G2
Meets Afghan premr 12-4, signs friendship pact 12-5, 943D2
Vs Warsaw Pact defns spending curbs 12-5, 930E1
US offcls see re trade 12-6, 966C2
US-China tie reactn termed positive 12-19, 973C1, 976E1; denies positive reactn 12-21, 995E1; SALT pact delay linked 12-26, 12-26, 996C1

BRIBERY—*See BUSINESS—Payments Issues, CRIME—Bribery*
BRICKMAN, Marshall
Wins Oscar 4-3, 315B3
BRICUSSE, Leslie
Stop the World opens 8-3, 887C3
BRIDGES, James
'Sept 30 1955' released 3-31, 619E3
BRIDGES, Jeff
Somebody Killed Her Husband released 9-29, 970C3
BRIDGESTONE Tire Co. of America
FTC complaint rptd setld 9-14, 942A1
BRIDGE, Structural and Ornamental Iron Workers, International Association of—*See IRON Workers, etc.*
BRIDGES & Tunnels
Carter budgets constructn, repairs 1-23, 47A3
Italy plans Messina bridge 7-13, 689E3
BRIDGMAN, Mich.—*See MICHIGAN*
BRIGGS, Warren
Loses US House electn 11-7, 849D3
BRIGHAM Young University (Provo, Utah)
Wrestling rank rptd 3-13, 379A3
Interracial marriage discouraged 7-15, 907C2
BRIGHT, Richard S.
History of Amer Film opens 3-30, 760D2
BRIGHT and Golden Land, The (play)
Opens 4-3, 760E1
BRIGUGLIO, Salvatore
Slain 3-21, 232F2
BRILEY, John
Medusa Touch released 4-14, 619B3
BRILL, Debbie
Sets indoor high jump mark 2-24, 600E3
BRINK, Robert
Gay Divorce opens 3-9, 760C2
BRINKLEY, Rep. Jack Thomas (D, Ga.)
Reelected 11-7, 850A3
BRINKS Inc.—*See under PITTSTON*
BRINNIN, John Malcolm
Elected to Arts Institute 2-7, 316E1
BRISCOE, Gov. Dolph (D, Tex.)
Loses primary 5-6, 362D3
BRISTOL & Co., John W.
SEC censures re Equity Funding 9-4, 681A2
BRISTOL-Myers Co.
Forgn natn tetracycline trust suit OKd 1-11, 33E3
FDA OKs butorphanol tartrate 8-30, 727E3
BRITISH Aerospace Corp.
Brit Airways orders Boeing 757s, Airbus Industrie scores 8-31, 684A2
BRITISH Aircraft Corp. Ltd. (BAC)
Rumania jet deal signed 6-15, 515A3
BRITISH Airways
LA gets 2-carrier London svc 6-9, 570F1
Boeing 757s ordrd, Airbus Industrie scores 8-31, 684F1
Australia fare cut announced 10-11, 793C3
UK role in Airbus OKd 10-24, 10-25, 902E3
BRITISH American Commodity Corp.
Mail case refused by Sup Ct 6-26, 566F3
BRITISH-American Cosmetics Ltd.—*See under B.A.T. Industries*
BRITISH-American Tobacco Co. Ltd.—*See under B.A.T. Industries*
BRITISH-American Tobacco Investments Ltd.—*See under B.A.T. Industries*
BRITISH Broadcasting Corp. (BBC)
Parlt sessns broadcast 4-5, 268A1
Bulgaria employes slain 9-11, 10-2, 748D3, 749B1
BRITISH Caledonian Airways
US air-fare dispute flares 2-28, 3-7, setlmt reached 3-17, 206B2
UK-Scandinavia pact OKd 12-22, 1017B2
BRITISH Columbia (Canadian province)—*See CANADA*
BRITISH Commonwealth—*See COMMONWEALTH of Nations*
BRITISH Honduras—*See BELIZE*
BRITISH Leyland—*See BL Ltd.*

1979

Schmidt plans '80 mtg 12-4, 938F2
Lauds new Afghan pres 12-28, 973C2
Carter warns on Afghan invasn 12-28, gets Mrs Thatcher protest 12-29, 973G2, 974C2

BRIBERY—*See under CRIME*
BRIBIESCA, Dr. Sergio
Mex immigratn study rptd 2-12, 127A3
BRICENO, Mercedes Pulido de
Venez women's min 3-10, 192D3
BRICKMAN, Marshall
Manhattan released 4-24, 528A3
BRIDGE (card game)
Howard Schenken dies 2-20, 176E3
BRIDGEFORTH, Ruffin
On black progress in Morman Church 6-15, 508A1
BRIDGEPORT, Conn.—*See CONNECTICUT*
BRIDGES, Beau
Norma Rae released 3-1, 174C3
5th Musketeer released 9-7, 820B1
BRIDGES, James
China Syndrome released 3-16, 528G1*
BRIDGES, Jeff
Winter Kills released 5-17, 528G3
BRIDGES, Lloyd
5th Musketeer released 9-7, 820B1
BRIDGES & Tunnels
Mo, Me bond referenda OKd 11-6, 847B1
BRIEFCASE Full of Blues (recording)
On best-seller list 1-10, 80F3; 2-14, 120F3; 3-7, 174E1
BRIGHAM Young University (Provo, Utah)
Loses Holiday Bowl 12-21, 1001A3
BRIGUGLIO, Gabriel
Indicted 2-22, 155G3
Sentenced 7-10, 548E1
BRILL, Lt. Col. Arthur
On pot linked transfers 9-12, 809A2
BRISTOL, Dave
Hired as Giants mgr 9-14, 1002F1
BRISTOL Foods Inc.
Settles '78 beef-price suit 10-22, 985E3
BRISTOL-Myers Co.
FTC offcl assails ads 10-12, 902F3
BRITISH Aerospace Corp.
Govt proposes shares sale 7-23, 564B3
BRITISH Airways
Asian oppositn to Australia fare policy rptd 1-5, 6D1
Dallas-DC Concorde svc begins 1-12, 35A3
'72 crash case refused by US Sup Ct 1-15, 32D1
UK cancels Concorde debt 2-22, 154B2
Govt proposes shares sale 7-20, 564B3
Concorde program ended, unsold jets allocated 9-21, 721F2
BRITISH-American Tobacco Co. Ltd.—*See under B.A.T. Industries*
BRITISH Broadcasting Corp. (BBC)
Rhoodie interview aired 3-21, 213A1, C1
Iran ousts 2 newsmen 8-21, 635A2
Tories plan '81 subsidy cut 11-1, 855C2
BRITISH Commonwealth—*See COMMONWEALTH of Nations*
BRITISH European Airways v. Benjamins
Case refused by US Sup Ct 1-15, 32E1
BRITISH Honduras—*See BELIZE*
BRITISH Independent Steel Producers' Association
'78 steel output rptd 1-11, 38D1
BRITISH Leyland—*See BL Ltd.*
BRITISH National Oil Corp.
N Sea oil assets sale barred 9-14, 707F1
Price hike set 11-6, 864B2
BRITISH Petroleum Co. Ltd. (BP)
Iran oil crisis forces sales curbs 1-6, 83B1
Westn consortium barred from Iranian oil exports 2-27, 146A1
Deutsche BP-Veba deal OKd 3-5, 214F3
Cited in Exxon sales curb 3-13, 183A3
Australia profits rptd down 5-8, 351F3

1980

Announces Kosygin resignatn, Tikhonov successn 10-23, 797B1, F1
Lauds Kosygin 10-24, 831E3
Meets Polish ldrs, affirms ties 10-30, 860A1
Sees US Sen Percy 11-26, 915C1
In India 12-8—12-11; meets Gandhi 12-8—12-9, joint declaratn 12-11; offers Persian Gulf peace plan in parlt speech 12-10; US rejects 12-11, 930D1-A3
Percy rpts on talks 12-12, 950B3
Kosygin death rptd 12-19, 951C1; confrmd 12-20, 996A2
Meets Polish forgn min, reaffirms 'confidence' 12-26, 976A3

BRIBERY—*See CRIME--Bribery, Fraud & Extortion*
BRICKMAN, Marshall
Simon released 2-29, 216E3
BRIDGE (card game)
Michael Gottlieb dies 4-8, 360G1
BRIDGEPORT—*See CONNECTICUT*
BRIDGES, James
Urban Cowboy released 6-11, 675F3
BRIDGES, Lloyd
Airplane released 7-2, 675G1
BRIDGESTONE Museum of Fine Art (Tokyo)
Picasso painting bought for record sum 5-12, 472C1
BRIDGES & Tunnels
Mt St Helens damage assessed 5-24—7-4, 503E3, 504A3
Swiss open longest road tunnel 9-5, 754B3
BRIGADOON (play)
Opens 10-16, 892A3
BRIGHAM Young University (Provo, Utah)
Wilson in Senior Bowl 1-12, 62B2
Wilson in NFL draft 4-29, 336F3
2d in NCAA team golf championship 5-31, 714F3
Marsh sets 3000-m steeplechase mark 6-28, 891B2
Wins Holiday Bowl 12-19, 999B3
BRIGHT, Rev. Bill
Addresses DC Christian rally 4-29, 348E3
BRIGHT, Cyril
Executed 4-22, 353G1
BRIGHT Flows the River (book)
On best-seller list 1-13, 40D3
BRIGHTMAN, Carol
Drawings & Digressns wins Amer Book Award 5-1, 692B2
BRILAB Probe—*See under U.S. GOVERNMENT--FEDERAL Bureau of Investigation*
BRINK, Gary
Wins Oscar 4-14, 296A2
BRINKLEY, Rep. Jack Thomas (D, Ga.)
Reelected 11-4, 842B3
BRINKLEY, Joel
Wins Pulitzer 4-14, 296G2
BRINK'S Inc.—*See PITTSTON Corp.*
BRISBIN, David
Dead End Kids opens 11-18, 1003A3
BRISTOL—*See TENNESSEE*
BRISTOL-Myers Co.
'79 top TV advertiser 4-4, 376B2
BRITISH Aerospace Corp.
W Europn fighter planned 4-14, 303F1
BRITISH Airways
Workers strike 1-10, 59F1
Pan Am Miami-London svc retentn OKd 4-7, 346A3
World Airways Boston-London svc OKd 4-10, 346D2
Braniff drops Dallas-DC Concorde svc 4-14, 346F3
Fiscal '80 profits rptd 7-31, 578G2
BRITISH Bancorp.
Auto-Train loan set 8-22, dropped 9-8, 958E2, G2
BRITISH Broadcasting Corp. (BBC)
Cutbacks announced 2-28, 172F3
Amin interview aired 6-3, 445F3
Assad death try rptd 6-28, 525F3
Cutbacks rptd modified 7-31, 670D3
USSR jams broadcasts 8-20, 626E2
Rockefeller cable network wins US program rights 12-11, 1002B3
BRITISH Colombia (Canadian province)—*See CANADA*
BRITISH Commonwealth—*See COMMONWEALTH of Nations*
BRITISH Honduras—*See BELIZE*
BRITISH Leyland—*See BL Ltd.*

1976

BRITISH National Oil Corp.
North Sea find rptd 5-28, 521D3
To share BP North Sea fields 7-1, 521F3
BRITISH Petroleum Co. Ltd. (BP)
Norway to buy subsidiary 1-7, 30D2
French coastal oil traces rptd 1-31, 139G2
Admits Italy bribes 4-13, 267F1
Rhodesia sanctin violatns chrgd 6-21, 621A2
Govt to share North Sea fields 7-1, 521F3
Joint probe with Norway set 8-6, 590C2
In Australia gas deal 8-8, 650B2
Irish Sea well rptd dry 8-13, 638A2
S Africa investmt plans rptd 8-26, 714B1
UK announces stock sale 12-15, 1003G2
Del R oil spill 12-27, 1014E1
BRITISH Solomon Islands—*See ADB*
BRITISH Steel Corp.
EC aid set 3-25, 529A3
Fiscal '75 losses rptd 7-28, 589G1
BRITISH West Indian Airways (BWIA)
Castro chrgs CIA re Barbados blast 10-15, 780B2
BRITT Jr., Raymond C.
Testifies re '57 Ala murder 2-26, 316G2
BRITTEN, Benjamin
Dies 12-4, 970C1
BRKIC, Dusan
Sentenced for emigre plot 3-12, 223B3
BROADBENT, Edward
Scores judicial interfernc, handling 3-12, 221E1
BROADCASTING—*See also PRESS; also network, country names*
CIA manipulatn rptd 1-16, 1-17; House com rpt leaked 1-23, 92C2
House OKs educ funds 1-20, 94A2
Sen OKs copyright revisns 2-10, 152C2
Firestone settles on safety ads 2-16, 186A3
FCC equal-time rules upheld 4-12, 282D1
'75 Fortune 500 rptd 437D2
Boston Community Broadcasting cited in SEC chrgs vs Gen Tire 5-10, 360A2
Cong clears educ funds 5-25, 434B3; Ford signs 6-5, 982F1
Cong clears copyright revisns 9-30, 764E3; Ford signs 10-19, 982G1
Sup Ct bars equal-time review 10-12, 765D3
Nixon tapes release OKd 10-26, 849A3
Awards
Emmys presented 5-17, 460A2
Obituaries
Baddeley, Angela 2-22, 192C3
Baukhage, Hilmar 2-1, 124C3
Cowan, Louis 11-8, 970D1
Davis, Rupert 11-22, 970E1
Erskine, Laurie York 11-30, 1015D1
Ford, Paul 4-12, 316A1
Friis, Harold T 6-15, 524E2
Halop, Billy 11-9, 970A2
Hughes, Richard 4-28, 368F2
Lowry, Judith 11-29, 932E3
McBride, Mary Margaret 4-7, 272F3
McCoy, George Braidwood 12-22, 1015A2
Neuman, Herman 5-4, 524C3
Roy, Mike 6-26, 524E3
Smith, Frederick 8-14, 656G3
Young, John 1-12, 56G3
Presidential Broadcasts—*See PRESS & Broadcasting under FORD*
Presidential Election (& transition)—*See also 'Presidential Campaign TV Debates' under POLITICS*
Muskie rebuts Ford message 1-21, 40E1
FCC rules on 2 pol ads 3-4, 180E2-A3
Reagan address 3-31, 232B2
Goldwater ad vs Reagan 5-8—5-9, 342B3
Carter scores Udall ads 5-28, 390G2
Ford ads vs Reagan aired 6-5, 410G1, B2 ★
Carter natl spot broadcast 6-6, 411E1
Dem platform text 6-15, 473E1
Brown address 6-25, 468G1
Reagan address 7-6, 490F2
GOP platform text 8-18, 604C2, 608A2, 610B3
Carter scores coverage 11-5, 845F1
Carter TV spending rptd 11-17, 938B2
Carter news confs 12-14, 12-16, 936D1, B3

1977

Lucas strike threatens productn 7-4, 695B1
Birmingham workers rejct strike 8-29, 694F3
Dobson address 9-27, bias chrgd 10-20; quits post 10-21, Edwardes named 10-25, 863G3

BRITISH Petroleum Co. Ltd. (BP)
Kuwait purchase cutbacks rptd sought 1-20, 107F3
Extra Saudi purchases rptd 2-16, 108B1
Lonrho sues vs sanctn abuses 5-31, 413C2
Overseas paymts admitted 6-3, 526A2
Alaska pipeline opens 6-20, 476B3; ICC proposes rates 6-28, 498F1
Zambia sues re Rhodesia sanctns 8-22, 662D1
Australia OKs NW Shelf gas search 8-24, 704E3
Sup Ct OKs Alaska pipe interim rate rise 10-20, upholds order 11-14, 878E2
BRITISH Shipbuilding Corp.
Formed 7-1, 526D2
BRITISH Steel Corp. (BSC)
TUC scores Port Talbot strikers 5-18, 392E1
Apr-Sept record losses rptd 10-20; TUC, Parlt comment 11-11, 883D2
Armco chrgs dumping 12-5, 933A3
BRITTON Jr., Theodore
Replaced as amb to Barbados, Grenada 7-13, 626C3
BROACKES, Nigel
Beaverbrook chain purchased 6-30, 527A1
BROADBENT, Edward
Scores budget proposal 3-31, 254A2
Backs pipeline rpt 5-9, 372D2
Scores police dischrg 6-16; chrgs Goyer, RCMP cover-up 6-17, 485C1, E1
Requests security file 8-12, 633F3
Fox vague on RCMP file 8-29, 705E1
BROADCASTERS, National Association of
FCC obscenity order voided 3-16, 216B1
BROADCASTING—*See also PRESS; also network, country names*
GOP for House coverage 1-4, 36G3
Ford budgets educ cuts 1-17, 32D2
Joint media ownership barred 3-1, 216B1
Paley sets CBS retiremt 4-20, 355G3
'76 stockholder equity rptd 340A3
FCC reverses pol air time rule 5-6, 376G1
'69-76 Sup Ct rulings rptd 5-17, 419A3
White House distributes Panama Canal 'fact sheet' 8-4, 590B1
Carter seeks more pub broadcasting funds 10-6, 846A1
Awards
NBC cancels Emmy broadcast 4-15, 355B3
Emmys presented 9-11, 11-6, 1021F3
Obituaries
Anderson, Eddie (Rochester) 2-28, 164B2
Cabot, Sebastian 8-23, 696E2
Carlson, Richard 11-25, 952C2
Carr, John Dickson 2-27, 164D2
Devine, Andy 2-18, 164F2
Finklehoffe, Fred 10-5, 872F1
Grauer, Ben 5-31, 452A3
Howe, Quincy 2-17, 164A3
Jaffe, Saul 11-1, 952E2
Kamen, Milt 2-24, 164B3
Markel, Lester 10-23, 872E2
Marx, Groucho 8-20, 696C3
Payne, Virginia 2-10, 164D3
Prinze, Freddie 1-29, 84E3
Tetzel, Joan 10-31, 872A3
Tourtellot, Arthur 10-18, 872B3
Waters, Ethel 9-1, 788A3
Presidential Broadcasts—*See CARTER—PRESS & Broadcasting*

1978

BRITISH Petroleum Co. Ltd. (BP)
BP Minerals finds Australia sulfides deposit 5-16, 411C2
ICC Alaska pipe rates backed by Sup Ct 6-6, 447B2
UK hikes offshore oil tax 8-2, 591G3
Rhodesia sanctns-breaking study released 9-19, 756B1-E3
Rhodesia sanctions violatn denial changed 10-22, 838E2
Japan faces Iran oil cutback 11-7, 858D2
BRITISH Shipbuilders Ltd.
Massive losses rptd 6-27, limit set 7-10, 573A3
BRITISH Steel Corp. (BSC)
'77 losses rptd 1-10, rptg scored 1-11, defended 1-16; govt cuts investmt 1-17, 36G2
Shipbldg losses rptd 7-10, 573D3
BRITTAN, Robert
Gay Divorce opens 3-9, 760C2
BRITTANY—*See FRANCE*
BRITTON, Jeff
Bistro Car opens 3-23, 887B1
BRIZ Lopez, Antonio (d. 1977)
Murder suspects arrested 1-20, 112C1
BRK Electronics—*See PITTWAY Corp.*
BROAD, Thomas
Indicted 3-23, 243F1
BROADBENT, Edward
Disputes Trudeau on econ recovery 3-21, 225E3
BROADCAST Enterprises Network Inc.
Gannett TV statn purchase set 8-20, 759F3
BROADCASTERS, National Association of
Wasilewski vs children's TV ad curbs 4-10, 347D2
BROADCASTING—*See also PRESS; also network, country names*
HEW anti-smoking campaign set 1-11, 23F2
Fla tape curb challenge refused by US Sup Ct 3-20, 206B1
Media racism scored 4-7—4-8, 419E3
Burger warns media giants 4-26, 343G3
'77 Fortune 500 data rptd 5-8, 325B2, C3, 326A1
'77 top-paid execs ranked 5-15, 364F3, 365B1
FCC 'fairness doctrine' case refused by Sup Ct 5-30, 430C3
Class actn certificatn appeals curbed by Sup Ct 6-21, 509G2
FCC 'Filthy Words' ban upheld by Sup Ct 7-3, 551F2
Leonard to head CBS News 7-14, 599A3
FCC rejcts censorship role 7-21, 599E1
FCC's Brown scores agency 10-11, 908D1
NY newspaper strike ends 11-6, 865G1
Awards
Allen, Barber win Frick 8-8, 618A1
Emmys presented 9-17, 1030E1
Obituaries
Ahn, Philip 2-28, 196B2
Barrie, Wendy 2-2, 196B2
Bergen, Edgar 9-30, 777E3
Betz, Carl 1-18, 96C3
Brown, Zara Cully 2-28, 196D2
Crane, Bob 6-29, 540E2
Daly, James 7-3, 620F2
Damerel, Myrtle Vail 9-18, 778A1
Etting, Ruth 9-24, 778B1
Evans, Bergen 2-4, 196G2
Fields, Totie 8-2, 708F2
Fontaine, Frank 8-4, 708G2
Frick, Ford C 4-8, 356F2
Geer, Will 4-22, 356F2
Goff, Norris 6-7, 540G2
Highet, Gilbert 1-20, 96C2
Homolka, Oscar 1-27, 96E2
Jones, Blanche Calloway 12-16, 1032A3
Kiernan, Walter 1-8, 96D2
McGrath, Paul 4-13, 356B3
Morris (the cat) 7-7, 620B3
Morrison, Bret 9-25, 778F1
Nebel, Long John 4-10, 356C3
Noble, Ray 4-3, 356C3
Rockwell, George L 3-3, 252D3
Sylvester, Victor 8-14, 708E3
Whitehead, Edward 4-16, 356F3
Wood, Peggy 3-18, 252F3
Presidential Broadcasts—*See CARTER—PRESS & Broadcasting*

1979

UK to sell shares 6-12, 445G2
Nigeria cuts sales, S Africa shipments cited 7-12, 545A2
UK plans shares sale 7-24, 564F3
Australia joint mining venture set 7-27, 580G2
Nigeria nationalizes assets, S Africa sales cited; UK scores 7-31, 584D2-D3
2d 1/4, 1st 1/2 profits soar 9-6, 686F3
Australia OKs Roxby Downs mining 10-9, 811A1
UK plans stock sale 10-16, 792D2
'53 Iran coup book rptd recalled 11-10, 886G3
BRITISH Shipbuilders Ltd.
Denatlztn deferred 7-23, 564F3
BRITISH Steel Corp. (BSC)
'78 output rptd down 1-11, 38D1
Plant closings planned, losses cited; scored 7-12, 549F1
'80 strike called, 1st 1/2 losses cited 12-7, 949G2
BRITT, Harry
On White convictn 5-22, 386C1
BRITZ, Jerilyn
2d in LPGA Champ 6-10, wins US Women's Open 7-15, 587D1, F1
BRIZENDINE, John
Defends DC-10 design 7-12, 539E1
Indicted on paymts chrg 11-9, 886A2
BRIZOLA, Leonel
Brazil amnesty law signed 8-28; returns 9-7, form PTB 11-30 926C2, C3
BROAD, Thomas
Convicted 8-16, 704F1
Fined, put on probatn 12-10, 947B1
BROADBENT, Edward
Scores corp profit rpt 2-7, 114E1
Starts electn campaign 3-27, 3-29, 266G2, F3
In TV debate, asks econ dvpt plan 5-13, 368C3, F3
Backs PC govt, warns vs Petro-Canada divestiture 5-30, 424D1
Scores Petro-Canada breakup 9-5, 385A1
Scores PQ white paper 11-1, 853D2
NDP conv backs ldrship 11-22–11-25, 927D1
BROADCASTERS, National Association of (NAB)
Carter addresses conv 3-25, 230E1
Justice Dept sues over TV ad limit 6-14, 618G2-A3
FCC children's TV staff rpt scored 11-1, 858D3
BROADCASTING—*See also PRESS; network, country names*
Carnegie Comm rpt urges pub broadcast chngs 1-30, 78B2
ABC, NBC wage-price compliance rptd, CBS vow conditnal 2-6, 128C1
Buckley, Sitco partners settle SEC chrg 2-7, 132B1
Carter addresses broadcast conv 3-25, 230E1
Starr ex-execs settle SEC chrgs 3-27, 4-9; Shamrock transfer OKd 6-8, 588F1
1st 1/4 profits rptd down 4-27, 385D1
'78 Fortune 500 data rptd 5-7, 305D1, G1
Press freedom insurnc plan set 9-27, 859F2
UPI press partnership sale rptd 10-4, 859G2
Macmillan accepts ABC merger offer 10-16, ABC ends talks 11-22, 942A3
Library link-up urged 11-16, 901D1
Carter pol broadcast aired 12-4, 918A3, 919C1
Awards & Honors
Emmys presented 9-9, 858D2
Obituaries
Blondell, Joan 12-26, 1008B2
Buchanan, Edgar 4-4, 356C3
Coughlin, Charles E 10-27, 860A2
Crockett, James 7-11, 588E2
Gargan, William 2-16, 176A3
Hall, Jon 12-13, 1008A3
Hodge, Al 3-19, 272F2
Leonetti, Tommy 9-15, 756F2
Manion, Clarence E 7-28, 588A3
Newhouse, Samuel I 8-29, 671B3
Pious, Minerva 3-16, 272D3
Sheen, Fulton J 12-9, 1008E3
Vance, Vivian 8-17, 671F3
Presidential Broadcasts—*See CARTER–PRESS*

1980

BRITISH Petroleum Co. Ltd. (BP)
Canada unit hq slates Montreal move 1-26, 116C3
Selectn Trust takeover set 7-7, 523A2
Rhone-Poulenc sells share 7-9, 522C2
Nigeria '79 assets natlzn cited 10-3, 792E2
BRITISH Shipbuilders Ltd.
Fiscal '80 losses rptd 7-31, 578E2
'81 govt aid hike seen 11-6, 886C3
BRITISH Steel Corp.
Steelworkers strike 1-2, 6D3
Pvt steelworkers join strike 2-1—2-3, 97E3
Union immunities curb asked 2-19, 150C2
Annual 1 bln pound loss seen 3-6, 193B3
Strikers OK vote on pay offer 3-9, 193D2
Strike settled, loss estimated 4-1, 254B2
MacGregor chosen as chrmn 5-1, 352E1
Record loss rptd 7-30, 578B2
Lords rule on Granada case 7-30, 634G1-E2
Aid hike set 9-26, 750D2
Granada case dropped 9-30, 750F3
'81 govt aid hike seen 11-6, 886C3
Recovery plan outlines 12-10; wage curbs sought 12-11, layoffs set 12-12, 965E2
BRITTEN, Benjamin (1913-76)
Peter Grimes wins Grammy 2-27, 296F3
BRITTON, Barbara
Dies 1-17, 104G1
BRITZ, Jerilyn
Ties for 2d in Arden Classic 2-10, 412D2
Alcott breaks US Women's Open scoring mark 7-13, 714B3
Wins Dallas Classic 9-29, 972C2
BRIZ Armengol, Gen. Enrigue
Assassinated 9-2, 673G2
BRIZOLA, Leonel
Metalworkers strike ldr arrested 4-19, 310F1
BROADBENT, Edward
Vs separatism 5-11, 372C2
Backs auto plant sit-in 8-11, 650F3
BROADCASTERS, National Association of (NAB)
Wasilewski assails FCC cable-TV deregulatn moves 7-22, 583F1
Copyright royalty fee divisn assailed 7-29, 640A3
VHF TV statn expansn proposal scored 9-18, 732C1
Comsat TV plan oppositn cited 10-2, 907B1
BROADCASTING
Valente becomes RCA pres 1-1, fired 6-18, 582G1
FTC funding blocked 3-15—4-30; agency shuts down 5-1, reopens 5-2, 348C1
'79 Fortune 500 data rptd 5-5, 291E1
Backe quits CBS post 5-8, 376D1
Jankowski CBS resignatn hoax 5-23, 501A2
Wyman assumes CBS posts 6-2, 501G1
NBC realigns managemt, Segelstein promoted 6-3, 501D2
Pfeiffer sees Silverman 7-7, relieved of duties 7-8; resigns as NBC chrmn, RCA dir 7-10, 582B1
S Korea orders media regrouping 11-14, 888B1
Awards & Honors
Polk Memorial presented 2-25, 692D3
Emmys presented 9-7, 692B1
Mergers & Acquisitions
Times Mirror Conn divestiture ordered 1-24, 120B1
RCA OKs Random House sale 2-6, 386D1
Cox to drop GE merger plans 4-25; FCC OKs merger 4-28, 386E1
Times Mirror to buy Denver Post 10-22, 857C1
Obituaries
Bailey, Jack 2-1, 175E3
Banghart, Charles K (rptd) 5-31, 528B1
Britton, Barbara 1-17, 104G1
Dragonette, Jessica 3-18, 279C2
Durante, Jimmy 1-29, 104C2
Enlow, Grayson Maynard 5-18, 448E1
Fielding, Jerry 2-17, 176A1
Garret, Leroy 7-21, 608G1
Hitchcock, Alfred 4-29, 360A2
Hurleigh, Robert F 8-10, 676F1
Jackson, Eddie 7-16, 608B2
Janney, Leon 10-28, 876B2
Janssen, David 2-13, 176F1
Kintner, Robert E 12-20, 1004C2
Lauck, Chester 2-21, 176B2
Levenson, Sam 8-27, 676G1
McCarty, Mary 4-5, 360D2
Medford, Kay 4-10, 360E2
Mueller, Merrill 12-1, 1004B3
Nielsen, Arthur C 6-1, 528A3
Patrick, Gail 7-6, 608F2
Randolph, Lillian 9-12, 756A2
Renaldo, Duncan 9-3, 756B2
Shelley, Norman 8-22, 676A3
Silverheels, Jay 3-5, 280A2
Stone, Milburn 6-12, 528E3
Tobias, George 2-27, 176G3
Tovorov, Orin 8-16, 676D3
Tuckner, Howard 8-2, 676E3
Presidential Broadcasts—*See under CARTER*
Presidential Election (& Transition)
GOP Ia pres debate aired 1-5, 4C2
Kennedy broadcasts aired 1-14, 32B3; 1-28, 75A1
Connally sponsors natl telethon 2-14, 129E1
Kennedy assails Carter media use 2-14, 130B2
GOP candidates debate in NH 2-20, 129A3

1976

Radio—*See also 'Presidential Campaign TV Debates' under POLITICS*
RFE Olympics coverage barred 2-4, 158B3
Brunswick execs sentncd 4-12, 316E3
Latin conf 7-12—7-21, 619F3
Canada OKs US FM on cables 9-23, 771E3
'60-75 consumer spending rptd 11-23, 959G2
Sovt interfernc rptd eased 12-28, 1011B1

Television—*See also 'Presidential Campaign Developments' above; also 'Presidential Campaign TV Debates' under POLITICS*
1st S Africa broadcast 1-5, 11A3
FCC cable TV curbs scored 1-26, 2-5, 135B3, D3
FCC eases cable TV rules 4-2, 249B2
Sup Ct bars review of CPB bias-control case 4-19, 331B2
Walters signs ABC contract 4-22, 504A2
Latin conf 7-12—7-21, 619F3
Canada ends ad tax deductn for US TV 9-22, 771C3
NBC, US set programming pact 11-17, 869D1
FCC networks probe asked 11-23, 901D1
'60-75 consumer spending rptd 11-23, 959G2

1977

Radio
Vatican boosts Sovt bloc broadcasts 2-16, 471E2
'75 WBAI obscenity rule voided 3-16, 215D3-216B1
Carter asks more intl funds 3-22, 229F3; USSR scores 3-24, 226G2
Pa statn loses license 4-4, 395A3
FCC raises CB penalty 4-26, 345B1
'76 corp gifts rptd 5-12, 409C2
ABA issues ad rules 8-10, 630G1

Television
NBC trust accord OKd 1-2, 918B3
FCC OKs network probe 1-14, 119C1
Canada ends ad deletns from US programs 1-21, 60G3
Roots sets viewing record 1-23—1-30, 118B3
NBC signs Ford 1-29, 236C3
NBC to air Moscow Olympics 2-1, Satra sues 2-14, 130G3, 131E1
Vitamin ads to children barred 2-7, 217C1
Top 10 audiences listed 2-9, 119A1
House subcom hearings on violence, family hr set 2-9, 157G3
Anti-violence outcry grows 2-14—2-18; FCC chrmn, NBC address programmers 2-14, 157D3
FCC pay-TV rules voided 3-25, Sup Ct appeal OKd 4-14, 376C2
McCarthy pres debate suit review declined 4-4, 341D3
NBC cancels Emmy broadcast 4-15, 355B3
Nixon-Frost interview 5-4, 365G3-567B1; 5-12, 385D3; 5-19, 405C3; 5-25, 419B3
Tennis tourn fee disclosures 5-7—5-20, FCC rpts probe 7-8, 548C2
'76 corp gifts rptd 5-12, 409C2
GOP energy plan rebuttal 6-2, 443E1
Castro interview 6-9, 456E1-B2
Canada scores US influence 6-14, 485G2
NBA aids teams 6-15, Pacers hold telethon 7-4, 584B1, E1
Performers' suits affirmed 6-28, 557F3
FCC suspends probe 6-30, 583E2-A3
Gen Foods sued on cereal ads 6-30, 613C2
Fla OKs TV trials 7-5; TV violence cited in Zamora plea 10-7, 807F2; Zamora sentncd 11-7, 907F3
Emmy dispute ends 7-12, 583A3
Libel suit vs NBC dismissed 7-12, 643B1
ABA issues ad rules 8-10, 630G1
US study chrgs bias 8-15, 642G2
NBC-TV pres fired 8-22, 658A3

1978

Radio
Minority ownership aid proposed 1-31, 195A2
Natl Pub Radio airs Sen Canal pact debate 2-8—2-22, 120E1
UK Parlt sessns broadcast 4-5, 268A1
Nixon tape access denied by Sup Ct 4-18, 308C1
Gannett plans Combined purchase 5-8, 345F2
FCC OKs WTOP sale 5-11, 599G3
NM info order review refused by Sup Ct 5-15, 388B1
FCC cross-media ban backed by Sup Ct 6-12, 467B3
FCC 'Filthy Words' ban upheld by Sup Ct 7-3, 551G2
SD statn rptd purchased by TV host 11-16, 919D3
FCC proposes more AM channels 12-19, 1030G1

Television
Cowles Communicatns to liquidate 1-6, 75G3
Football contract tax value backed 1-9, 13B2
FCC OKs WJLA, KOCO-TV exchng 1-12, scores Allbritton 2-13, 109A3
Super Bowl viewing record rptd 1-17, 39F3
Silverman to head NBC 1-20, ABC replaces with Thomopoulos 2-1, 75D2
Minority ownership aid proposed 1-31, 195A2
Justice trust probe rptd 2-4, 251E2
Minow named PBS chrmn 2-5, 335F2
Reagan Canal pact address 2-8, 121A1
Columbia Pictures pres quits in embezzlemt scandal 2-9, indicted 3-31, 251C1
CBS pact with Spinks, Top Rank rptd 2-17, 211E3
FCC cable-TV access rules voided 2-24, 195D2-C3
FTC proposes children's ad curbs 2-28, 4-28, Cong wary 4-26—5-2, 347G1, D2
Wilkinson named Cardinals coach 3-2, 171D3
WJLA-TV swap OKd again 3-9, Allbritton halts deal 3-24, 270G2
Canada bars pay TV 3-13, 226C1
Wussler quits CBS Sports 3-15, FCC censures 'Heavyweight Championship' tennis tourn 3-16, 252D1
NFL OKs instant replay 'dry run' 3-17, 336D3
'Holocaust' aired 4-16—4-19, NBC rpts 120 mln viewers 4-20, 316F1
Nixon tape access denied by Sup Ct 4-18, 308C1
ABC news show chngs set 4-19, Reasoner move to CBS set 5-12, 419A3, C3
Sex abuse suit vs NBC OKd by Sup Ct 4-24, 322A2
FCC faults ABC boxing tourn 4-25, 379D1

1979

Radio
Carnegie Comm rpt urges pub broadcast chngs 1-30, 78E2
Paramount resumes 'Warriors' ads 2-22, 174F1-A2
Fairbanks Colo U football deal leaked 4-2, 335D2
FCC doubts RKO Gen license fitness 7-18, 618B2
Jaffe linked to KGB 8-11, 611A2
USSR denies VOA rptr visa 9-5, 690C1
Deregulatn proposed 9-6; Nader opposes 9-11, ACLU asks pub review 11-5, 858E3
World Admin Conf held 9-27-12-6, 1006A3
'John Hour' debuts in NYC 10-23, 887E1
FCC OKs more AM statns 12-12, 1006E3

Television
HEW to step up anti-smoking drive 1-11, 23D1
Knoetze boxing match protested 1-13, 79D2
ABC to cut children's ads 1-18, 78A3
Super Bowl viewed by 95 mln 1-21, 62D3
Sony video recorder copyright trial opens 1-22, 120E2
W Ger airs 'Holocaust' 1-22–1-26, 137B2
Haldeman discloses '75 CBS interview fee 1-27, 176C1
Carnegie Comm rpt urges pub broadcast chngs 1-30, 80E2
NBA owners ponder rating decline 2-3–2-4, 175D1
Soviets win Challenge Cup 2-11, 118G1
Wichita rptr contempt convictn review refused by Sup Ct 2-21, 128C3
GE, Cox merger agreed 2-21, 188C2-A3
Paramount resumes 'Warriors' ads 2-22, 174F1-A2
Nixon Admin pub TV moves disclosed 2-24, 194A1
Washn Post viewing survey rptd 2-28, 3-1, 173B1
US House coverage begins 3-19, 208D1
Bell & Howell to reimburse home-study students 3-26, 308D3
NBC ex-official pleads guilty 3-28, expense acct scandal grows 4-19, 334E2
Cable TV pub-access rule upset by Sup Ct 4-2, 281F1
Fairbanks Colo U football deal leaked 4-2, 335D2
Sup Ct rulings disclosed 4-16, 4-17, ct worker fired re leaks 4-20, 302G2
FCC cable TV rate case declined by Sup Ct 4-16, 302G3
Music license fee case remanded by Sup Ct 4-17, 326A1
'State of mind' libel queries backed by Sup Ct, reactn 4-18, 302A1, B2

1980

Carter '79 ad bid upheld by ct 3-14, 221F3
Bush Pa town mtgs cited 4-22, 304D2
Carter interview aired 6-1, 422F3
Kennedy on Meet the Press 6-1, 422G3
Carter bars Kennedy debate 6-5, 423F1
Evangelical Christian pol role profiled 7-11—9-15; voters surveyed, Falwell ministry detailed 9-15, 818C3-819F3
Carter, Reagan campaign ad budget rptd 9-4, 665B3
Reagan scores 'stealth' plane disclosure; Brown, Perry testify on leaks 9-4, 665E3
Reagan asks equal time 9-18, 698A3; bid rejctd 9-19, 723B1
Reagan, Anderson debate; Carter absence noted 9-21, 721C2-722E2
2d pres debate plans falter 9-25, vp debate canceled 9-29, 739F3
Anderson addresses Religious Broadcasters 9-29, 739D2
Carter interviewed by Walters 10-8, 778B2
Carter interviewed in St Petersburg 10-10, 778C3
Carter gives paid radio speech 10-12, 779A1
Commoner uses vulgar ad 10-15, 818A3
Bush on Detroit area TV show 10-16, 817A23
Reagan peace pledge aired 10-19, 801C2-802B1
Carter radio address 10-19, 802F2
Carter, Reagan debate set 10-21, 801F3
Reagan paid TV address 10-24, 817B2
Carter, Reagan debate 10-28, 813A1-815E3
Anderson answers debate questns on cable TV 10-28, 815F3
Reagan final TV appeal 11-3, 840A3
TV debate impact polled 11-4, 838G2
NBC defends electn projectns 11-5, Carter on early concessn 11-12, 865E3, 866D1

Radio
FCC sets RKO Gen license hearings 1-24, 119C3
Ohio DJ fired, '79-80 'captivity' cited 2-6, 199D3
Airwave evangelism symposium held 2-6—2-7; broadcast growth rptd 2-25, 413C1-D2
FCC seeks more FM channels 3-5, 239F3-240A1
Spanish statns in US rptd 5-11—5-14, 396F2
ESA satellite venture fails 5-23, 397A3
Protected AM signals limited 5-29, 519A2
Pope scores mass-media 7-5, 538C1
Frederick rptd honored 7-7, 638E2
Evangelists assume pol role 7-11—9-15, Falwell profiled 9-15, 818E3, 819B3
Copyright royalty fees divided 7-29, 640F2-A3
USSR jams Westn broadcasts 8-20, reactn 8-21, 626D2, C3
Kate Smith estate feud setld 9-4, 908C2
NYC black statns get NSC Africa memo 9-16, Admin calls forgery 9-17, 726E3-727B1
Poland RC Sunday mass broadcast 9-21, 720G2
Westinghouse to acquire Teleprompter 10-15, 836F1
T Leary rptd fired 11-1, 890D2
San Fran statn acquired by Charter Co 11-6, 907A2
Iran hostage interview broadcast 11-11, 862B1
Lennon slaying reactn 12-9, 934A1

Television—*See also 'Presidential Election (& Transition)' above*
Miss America emcee dropped 1-4, replacemt named 3-5, 198G3
CBS 'dovish' complaint case refused by Sup Ct 1-7, 16A1
Rozelle defends Oilers call 1-7, 23A2
Iran bars CBS-TV 29A3
CBS, RCA sign video disk pact 1-10, 120F1
Redgrave role protested 1-13, 120B2
Iran ousts US newsmen 1-14, defends move 1-15, 29D2-A3
NBC $ loss re Moscow Olympic boycott rptd 1-20, 45E3
FCC lifts 3 RKO Gen licenses 1-24, 119F2
ABC wins '84 Winter Olympic rights 1-24, 206F1
GOP rebuttal to State of Union aired 1-28, 75D1
FCC OKs Westinghouse unit license 1-30, 119C3
Comsat direct satellite svc OKd 1-30, 240A1
Mobil ad rejectn rptd 1-31, 120D1
CBS forms video divisn 1-31, 239E3
NBA Dallas expansn OKd 2-2, 119E2
NBA labor pact OKd, cable TV suit dropped 2-4, 119C2
Airwave evangelism symposium held 2-6—2-7; broadcast growth, revenues rptd 2-25, 413C1-D2
Rather named Cronkite successor 2-15, 198E3
Dick Cavett sued 2-15, 199E2
Okla State of State message 2-19, 404A1
RCA to rent AT&T satellite, missing Satcom cited 2-20, 160B3
CBS rpts Israel A-test 2-21; Israel cancels rptr's credentials 2-24, 141E3
'60 Minutes' airs Iran segmt 3-2, govt pressure rptd 3-6, 239B1
Zenith, RCA in video disk pact 3-3, 239C3

1976

1977

SAT '63-77 scores drop 8-23, 739E1
NBC sex-bias suit settled 8-31, 979C2
FCC cable TV obscenity rule ordrd suspended 9-1, 846B2
Nixon-Frost interview 9-3, 692C3
Canada actors' union bars forgners 9-7, 742E2
ESA satellite missn aborted 9-12, 736A1
Ali fight sets viewing record 9-29, 827D3
FCC pay-TV rule review declined 10-3, 760A3
House subcom probes TV sports 10-4, 11-2—11-3, 949C3
House subcom violence rpt scored 10-24, 921F1-C2
Viacom-RCA satellite pact rptd 10-25, 921D1
NFL record pact rptd 10-26, 950D1-A2
Journalists thoughts protected 11-7, 920A3
Canada ad deletn upheld 11-30, 946F1
Sevareid retires 11-30, 1021E2
Viewing decline rptd 12-6, 1021D3
Heisman trophy presented 12-8, 950D2
Satra drops NBC suit 12-9, 971D2
Most reliable govt news sources listed 12-10, 1008G3
Time plans cable-TV purchase 12-22, 1004C3

1978

Spinks-Ali rematch rights rptd sold 5-2, 378G3
Gannett plans Combined purchase 5-8, 345F2
Sears withdraws TV ads, aids PTA 5-12, 599B3
FCC OKs WTOP-TV swap 5-18, 599F3
Solzhenitsyn scores West 6-8, 444B3
FCC cross-media ban backed by Sup Ct 6-12, 467B3
WPIX-TV license renewed 6-16, 672C1
Unions curbed on supervisor discipline by Sup Ct 6-21, 509E1
AAU suspends 4 track stars 6-23, 692F2
Press prison data access curbed by Sup Ct 6-26, 566A3
Begelman fined in theft case 6-28, 599A2
Moving indus defamatn chrg rebutted 6-30, 589F2
Tex executn filming case declined by Sup Ct 7-3, 552D2
FCC to renew children's TV probe 7-28, 672A2
Courtrm cameras backed by state judges 8-3; ABA vs, OKs lawyer ads 8-9, 626A3, C3
Sex abuse suit vs NBC dismissed 8-8, 635C2-A3
Gannett to sell WHEC-TV 8-20, 759F3
US statns protest Canadian tax law 8-29, 686A3
Indep news producers sue networks 9-11, 759F1
Pfeiffer named NBC chrmn, RCA dir 9-13, 759B3
Fleming named CPB pres 9-14, 759E3
Ali-Spinks bout 9-15, viewing record rptd 9-20, 726D2
WESH-TV license renewal voided, ct sets guidelines 9-25, 907D3
Jarvis tax-cut message 9-26, 735D3
Zamora loses violence suit 9-26, 759F2
FCC drops cable-TV svc rule 9-27, OKs 'distant' signal importatn 11-2, 1030B2, C2
USSR color TV deals rptd 10-5, 820F3
FTC child ad probe curbed 11-3; stay denied, probe affirmed 11-17, 941G2-C3
FCC orders NYC, Phila statn studios in NJ 11-9, 1030D2
SBA loan guarantee to Today's Brokaw rptd 11-16, 919D3
Music licenses challenged 11-27, 1030A1
Nixon on Paris progrm 11-28, 942B2
NBC drops fall lineup 11-29, 1030C1
Bouton return to sportscasting rptd 12-6, 1026G2

1979

Cable WTCG to expand programming 4-23, 334D3
Carson won't quit Tonight Show 5-2, 334B3
Another Sup Ct ruling disclosed 5-18, 382A3
Panax granted Mich licenses 5-31, FCC revokes 7-12, 618E2
NAB sued over ad limit 6-14, 618G2-A3
ABC rptr slain in Nicaragua 6-20, 461F2
PBS reorganizatn approved 6-25, 588C1
ABC rptr's slayer confesses 6-30, 512B3
AMF to produce bike safety ads 7-8, 595G2
FCC doubts RKO Gen license fitness 7-18, 618G1
ABC affiliates rptd on par with rivals 7-31, 588A2
Bundy televised trial ends 7-31, 604D2
Iran ousts NBC 4-man crew 8-6, 602D2
Kerkorian trust suit dismissed 8-14, 756D1
LA '84 Olympic costs projected 8-15, 798B1
Amer Express travelers check ad chngd 8-29, 903C1
Actor defies ct order in Lone Ranger case 8-30, 859D3
Sears TV repair recall set 8-31, 903E1
MCA, IBM in video disk venture 9-5, 756F1
Cocaine use cited 9-5, 972G2
ABC wins rights to '84 LA Olympics 9-25, 797C3
World radio conf held 9-27–12-6, 1006C3
Pope's US visit gets record coverage 10-1–10-7, 760E3
NBC '77 trust setlmt challenge refused by Sup Ct 10-1, 768C2
Video recorder use upheld 10-2, 858F2
'John Hour' debuts in NYC 10-23, 887E1
Children's programming scored 10-30, NAB responds 11-1, 858A3-E3
'Jaws' viewed by 80 mln 11-4, 1006F3
Reagan pres bid aired 11-13, 866G2
FCC 'family hour' power backed 11-20, 1007B1
Mecca mosque militants ask ban 11-20, 899B1
FCC upholds Carter ad bid 11-20, 918G3
Walters interviews shah 11-22, 897C3
AAU reinstates Stones 11-28, 956E1
NBC '77 trust setlmt challenge refused again by Sup Ct 12-10, 988A2
RCA loses satellite 12-10, 991E1
Connally switches strategy 12-15, 982A3, B3
FCC modifies children's TV plan 12-19, 1006G3

1980

Iran readmits newsmen 3-7, 178C2
Olympic alternate summer games financing studied 3-18, 206D1
Freedom of Info ct order bar backed by Sup Ct 3-19, 250B1
Pioneer to enter US video disk mkt 3-26, 376E3
NBC barred from Moscow Olympic coverage, $61 mln rptd lost 3-28, 259D1
'Bionic' trademark case declined by Sup Ct 3-31, 291D3
Stapleton to quit series 4-2, 471B3
Ad rates rptd soaring, '79 top 10 advertisers listed 4-4, 376F1, A2
Editors vs US Olympic policy 4-9, 264F1
Iran hostage film purchase offer rejected 4-10, 282C3
UK film on Saudi princess strains ties 4-10, 294B1; 4-22—4-25, 313C2-B3
NBC hints revised Olympic coverage 4-14, 283F2
Australia bars Saudi film showing 4-15, 309E3
US asks Iran Intelsat bar 4-17, 281E1
Ctroom cameras case accepted by Sup Ct 4-21, 344E1
Methodists set TV venture 4-21, 413D3
'79-80 Nielsen ratings rptd, CBS regains lead 4-22, 376A1
Getty Oil in pay-TV film venture 4-22, Justice Dept to probe 4-24, 376D2
Iran shows film of US hostage rescue site 4-26, 323C1
French-W Ger satellite pact signed 4-30, 356D1
'Charlie's Angels' fraud probe rptd 5-1, 376F2
NBC drops Olympic telecast, estimates loss at $22 mln 5-6, 379D3
Carson NBC contract signing rptd 5-6, 470G3
Saudi film protested in US 5-8, PBS airs 5-12; cts rule on telecast 5-9, 5-12, 375E2-376A1
CBS, US settle trust dispute 5-8, 501C3
Spanish statns in US rptd 5-11—5-14, 396F2
CBS barred from Cuba telecast, previous transmissns cited 5-22; policy review rptd 5-23, 397C1
UK regrets Saudi film 5-22, 407A3
Donahue, Thomas marry 5-22, 471A2
Baseball contract dispute setld 5-23, 402A2
CBS Cuba broadcasts cleared 6-1, 420G2
Cable news network debuts 6-1, 422F3, 501A3
FTC child ad probe case refused by Sup Ct 6-16, 511D3
Charlie's Angels role filled 6-17, 638C2
Prime-time rule failure seen 6-18, 501C1
Kalb, Mudd join NBC 6-18, 7-1, 638F2
Duran-Leonard fight revenue rptd 6-20, 772E2
FCC seeks cable-broadcast ownership ban 6-24, 583B2
USSR bars US, French independnc day speeches 7-4, 7-14, 566B3
Pope scores mass-media 7-5, 538C1
Evangelists assume pol role 7-11—9-15, Falwell profiled 9-15, 818E3, 819B3
Sovts bar W Ger program 7-13, 590D1
US networks Sovt Olympic contract rejectn rptd 7-13, 590A2
Pay-TV lobbying group formed 7-15, 639G3
Afghan Olympic team denies defectn plan 7-21, 590B2
Actors strike; home video mkt, minimum wage at issue 7-21, 684A3
Cable-TV distant signal, syndicatn limits lifted by FCC 7-22, 583B1
3 UK rptrs flee Iran 7-25, 572B1
Idaho statn raided by police 7-26, 582A2
UK-Saudi ties restored 7-28, 578A3
Copyright royalty fees divided 7-29, 640E2-A3
UK press confidentiality ruling 7-30, 634G1-E2
Idaho prosecutor sued over statn raid 8-1, 732A3
Getty Oil pay-TV film plan draws trust suit 8-4, 639D3
ABC ties to Spelling-Goldberg rptd probed by SEC 8-7—8-8, 640B1
Moscow Olympics anti-US film rptd aired 8-9, 590A1
ABC settles US trust suit 8-22, 732E1
Hoffman fugitive yrs recapped 9-4, 713A2, B2
FCC proposes UHF, VHF statn expansn 9-9, 9-18, 731C3
'Shogun' aired by NBC 9-15—9-19; top ratings rptd 9-24, 835E2-B3
Pa announcer chrgd in lottery fraud 9-19, 786B3
RKO General to buy Cablecom 9-24, 746G1
UK press confidentiality case dropped 9-30, 750F3
Redgrave film aired by CBS, Jews protest 9-30, 835B3
Appeals ct backs Abscam tapes broadcast 10-1; Sup Ct refuses stay, tapes aired 10-14, 781C2
Comsat satellite plan advances 10-2, 906D3
GTE sells Philco, Sylvania to N Amer Philips 10-2, 985E2
FCC revokes Faith Center license 10-10, 907B1
Evangelist reverses Jewish prayer stance 10-11, 811F1
Westinghouse to acquire Teleprompter 10-15, 836E1

1976

BROADCASTING, Corporation for Public
Sup Ct bars review of FCC bias-control case 4-19, 331B2
T Macdonald dies 5-21, 404B2
BROCK, Lou
NL batting ldr 10-4, 796A1
BROCK 3rd, Sen. William (Bill) Emerson (R, Tenn.)
Ford lists as potential vp 1-22, 41A2
Unopposed in primary 8-5, 633G1
Withdraws as vp prospect 8-9, 584E1
GOP conv vp vote table 8-19, 599F3
Loses reelection 11-2, 819F3, 822C3
BROCKETT, E. D.
McCloy rpt scores 133D2, C3
Barred from Gulf bd mtg 1-15, 133A1, C3
BRODERICK, Henry
San Quentin 6 verdict 8-12, 656D1
BRODHEAD, Rep. William M. (D, Mich.)
Reelected 11-2, 829E4
BROKEN Hill Proprietary
In Australia gas deal 8-8, 650B2
BRONER, Julio
Quits CGE 3-8, 212A3
BRONFMAN, Edgar Miles
Cosponsors Carter business mtg 7-22, 550G3
Trial verdict 12-10, 952B3
BRONFMAN 2d, Samuel
Trial verdict 12-10, 952A3
BRONSON, S. Sgt Harold L.
Court-martial starts 6-14, 435D3
Acquitted 6-28, 493B2
Wallraff convicted 7-19, 586E3
McClure prosecutns end 9-1, 942D2
BRONX, N.Y.—See NEW York City
BROOKE, Sen. Edward William (R, Mass.)
Ford lists as potential vp 1-22, 41A2
Admin seeks busing rule review 5-20, 377C3
Releases desegregatn data 6-19, 992C3
Withdraws as vp prospect 8-9, 584E1
Seconds Ford nominatn 8-18, 597G2
Sen com ends Scott probe 9-15, 980B1
Asks Butz dismissal, Butz apologizes 10-1, 744E1
BROOKHAVEN National Laboratory (Upton, N.Y.)
Ting wins Nobel 10-18, 840G1
BROOKINGS Institution (Wash., D.C.)
Urges new role for Marines 2-2, 95B3
Publishes study vs B-1 productn 2-8, 183F1
Gordon dies 6-21, 484D3
BROOKLYN, N.Y.—See NEW York City
BROOKLYN College—See NEW York, City University of
BROOK Park, O.—See OHIO
BROOKS, Gwendolyn
Admitted to Natl Inst of Arts & Letters 5-19, 504C3
BROOKS, Rep. Jack (D, Tex.)
On revenue sharing 2-23, 149D3
Reelected 11-2, 830D4
BROOMBERG, Elly
Shifted to info post 1-13, 53E3
OKs Rhodesia conf 10-11, 781G1
BROOMFIELD, Rep. William S. (R, Mich.)
S Korea probe rptd 10-30, 11-13, 900G1
Reelected 11-2, 829F4

1977

BROADCASTING, Board for National—See under U.S. GOVERNMENT
BROADCASTING, Corporation for Public
Carter seeks more funds 10-6, 846B1
BROCK, Lou
Sets stolen base mark; table 8-29, 748D3
BROCK 3rd, William (Bill) Emerson (R, Tenn.)
Elected GOP natl chrmn 1-14, 40E3
Scores Viet pardon action 1-21, 51D2
'76 spec interest gifts rptd 2-15, 128E2; 3-7, 236C2
Confers with Ford 3-25, 236C2
Scores Carter energy taxes 4-25, 320G3
Rebuts Carter energy plan 6-2, 443E1
Demands Young ouster 6-6, 443D3
Asks Korea probe prosecutor 7-16, 556C2
Attacks Dems on cargo preference bill 8-1, 8-27, 719B3, E3
Base-stealing award created 8-17, 768C1
8 Sens score Canal pact opponents 912E1
BROCK Award, Lou—See BASEBALL—Awards
BROCKWAY Glass Co.
Strike ends 10-14, 818F3
BRODEUR, Claude
Testifies on '72 barn burning, dynamite theft 11-1, 902C3
BRODOCK, Susan
Sets mile walk mark 2-25, 602E3
BROKEN Hill Proprietary Co. Ltd.
NW Shelf gas search OKd 8-24, 704E3
BRONFMAN, Edgar Miles
2 sentncd for extortn 1-6, 103D1
BRONFMAN 2d, Samuel
2 sentncd for extortn 1-6, 103D1
BRONSTEIN, Lev Davidovich—See TROTSKY, Leon
BRONX, N.Y.—See NEW York City
BROOK, Peter
Wins by-electn 2-24, 201A1
BROOKE, Sen. Edward W. (R, Mass.)
Bell confrmd atty gen 1-25, 52G2
Backs Javits on Mideast 6-27, 496A1
Backs urban aid bill 10-8, 796E2
BROOKE Army Medical Center (San Antonio, Tex.)
Canary I crash victims arrive 3-30, 244E1
2 Canary I crash victims die 4-19, 312B1
BROOK Farm (Boston, Mass.)
Fire destroys 3-27, 396B2
BROOKHAVEN National Laboratory (Upton, N.Y.)
Coal use seen pub health threat 7-17, 559F1-A2
Goudsmit gets Sci Medal 11-22, 952A1
BROOKINGS Institution (Washington, D.C.)
Bergsten named to US post 1-18, 52E3
Schultze rpts '76 income 2-25, 148D1
Yost in Viet missn 3-16—3-20, 206C1
Bosworth confrmd wage price cncl dir 7-22, 626D2
Israeli aide vs Carter Mideast stand 9-13, 697G1
Issues US defense needs study 9-26, 858A1
BROOKLYN College—See NEW York, City University of
BROOKS, Geraldine
Dies 6-19, 532F2
BROOKS, Rep. Jack (D, Tex.)
'76 special interest gifts rptd 2-4, 128G3, 129C2-F2
Reorganizatn powers cleared 3-31, 228E1, G1
BROOKS, Van Wyck (1886-1963)
FBI surveillance rptd 6-19, 481E1
BROOMBERG, Elly
Scores cleric killings 2-8, 85D1
Replaced as info min 9-18, 824E3
BROOMFIELD, Rep. William (R, Mich.)
Cited in Park indictmt 9-6, 688D1
BROOTEN, Kenneth
Assassinatn com compromise offered 2-25, 149D1

1978

BROADCASTING, National Citizens Committee for
FCC cross-media ban backed by Sup Ct 6-12, 467E3
BROADCAST Music Inc. (BMI)
TV music licenses challenged 11-27, 1030A1
BROADWAY Musical, A (play)
Opens 12-21, 1031A1
BROCK 3rd, William (Bill) Emerson
Marston dismissed 1-20, 32B2
Black GOP support sought 7-21, 568D2
Decries Griffin reassignmt 8-5, 605D3
Backs DC voting amendmt 8-22, 661B2
Leads Kemp-Roth tax-cut bill tour 9-20—9-22, 734F3
Vs Carter anti-inflatn plan 10-24, 807A1
Sees GOP 'momentum' 11-8, 845B1
Urges appeal to minorities 11-28, 916C1
Scores Admin China policy 12-15, 974B3
BRODERICK, Ken
Nordiques win WHA All-Star game 1-17, 76F3
BRODHEAD, Rep. William M. (D, Mich.)
Reelected 11-7, 851F1
BRODKIN, Herbert
'Holocaust' aired 4-16—4-19, NBC rpts 120 mln viewers 4-20, 316A2
BRODOCK, Susan
Sets indoor mile walk mark 2-24, 600D3
BROKAW, Tom
SBA loan guarantee rptd 11-16, 919D3
BROMBERG, Michael
Scores US cost guideline 12-28, 1012G1
BROMBERGER, Herve
Violette released 10-9, 1030E3
BRONFMAN, Edgar
Stages opens 3-19, 760D3
BRONFMAN, Edward
Sells NHL Canadiens 8-3, 656A3
BRONFMAN, Peter
Sells NHL Canadiens 8-3, 656A3
BRONSON, Charles L.
JFK murder film assessed 11-26, 916F1
House com asks JFK murder film review 12-30, 1002D1
BRONSON, William E.
Unopposed in Mass cong primary 9-19, 736C3
BRONX, N.Y.—See NEW York City
BROOKE, Sen. Edward W. (R, Mass.)
Role in NYC fiscal crisis 86A3
Vs NYC fed aid renewal 1-4, 87A1
Votes for Panama Canal neutrality pact 3-16, 177F1, F2
On Carter urban-aid plan 3-27, 217G3
Interviewed re black vote, Carter 4-10, 568G2-A3
Votes for 2d Canal pact 4-18, 273B1
Admits false loan disclosure 5-26, 406B1
Wins primary 9-19, 736F2
Loses reelectn 11-7, 845E1, D2, 846E1, 847F2
Ethics com probe to end 12-19, 982A1
BROOKHAVEN National Laboratory (Upton, N.Y.)
Hydrogen storage study rptd 4-18, 293G3 *
BROOKINGS Institution (Washington, D.C.)
USSR air threat to NATO seen 1-29, 81B3
US land missile risks seen 5-24, 407E1
US arms sales policy assessed 7-16, 564F1
Mil manpower cost cuts urged 9-5, 683A3
Carter backs Okun pay insurance plan 10-24, 805G2
BROOKLYN, N.Y.—See NEW York City
BROOKS, Lt. Gen. Edward H. (ret.)
Dies 10-10, 888F2
BROOKS, Rep. Jack (D, Tex.)
With Carter in Tex 6-24, 509F3
Reelected 11-7, 852A3
PAC contributns rptd 12-24, 1008D1
BROOKS, Joel
Halloween Bandit opens 12-18, 1031A2
BROOKS, Joseph
Wins Grammy 2-24, 315E3
Wins Oscar 4-3, 315C3
If I See You released 5-24, 619D2
BROOMFIELD, Rep. William S. (R, Mich.)
Reelected 11-7, 851A2
BROSSARD, Paulo
Gets MDB vp pres nominatn 8-23, 671C2
BROSTEN, Harve
Wins Emmy 9-17, 1030F1

1979

BROADCASTING, Board for International—See under U.S. GOVERNMENT
BROADCAST Music Inc. v. Columbia Broadcasting System
Case remanded by Sup Ct 4-17, 326A1
BROCA'S Brain (book)
On best-seller list 9-2, 672C3
BROCCOLI, Albert R.
Moonraker released 6-29, 820B2
BROCK, Lou
NL wins All-Star Game 7-17, 568G3
Gets 3000th hit 8-13, 619C2
Breaks all-time stolen base mark 9-23, 1003D1
BROCK 3rd, William (Bill) Emerson
Scores B Carter remarks 1-11, 31E2
Detroit named '80 conv site 1-23, 70B3
Scores State of Union Message, budget 1-24, 48A3
GOP ldrs meet, reject balanced budget amendmt 2-4, 86G1
Scores Carter defns policy 3-1, 165B3
Scores Carter energy speech 7-16, 534G2
Scores US Intell policy 8-6, 610D3
BROCKETT, Don
Big Bad Burlesque opens 8-14, 711E1
BROCKMEYER, John D.
Enchanted Pig opens 4-23, 711F2
BRODERICK, Judge Raymond J.
Eilberg pleads guilty in plea-bargain 2-24, 152E2
BRODERICK, Judge Vincent L.
Sentences Beatle ex-mgr 7-10, 656E2
BRODEUR, Richard
WHA goaltending ldr 4-18, 355G2
BRODIE, Israel
Dies 2-13, 176F2
BRODOCK, Sue
Sets 5000-m walk mark 6-16, 10000-m walk mark 6-17, 911C2
BRODY, Burton
NCAA rejcts reform proposal 1-9, 102G3
BROKEN Hill Proprietary Co. Ltd.
Offshore oil drilling rptd 3-28, 233E1
Australia oil shortages seen 5-18, 368E2
BROKENLEG v. Butts
Case refused by Sup Ct 6-18, 499A2
BROLIN, James
Amityville Horror released 7-27, 819D3
BROMBERG, Michael
Vs hosp cost-control bill 3-9, 194A3
BRONFMAN, Edward
Brascan control sought 4-30—5-1, 5-30, 440B3
Brascan takeover completed 6-14, 6-29, 542E3
BRONFMAN, Peter
Brascan control sought 4-30—5-1, 5-30, 440B3
Brascan takeover completed 6-14, 6-29, 542E3
BRONX Zoo, The (book)
On best-seller list 5-6, 356D2; 6-3, 432B2; 7-1, 548C3; 8-5, 620C3
BROOKE, Edward W.
Sen ethics com clears 3-20, 208F2
Remarries 5-12, joins investmt firm 5-23, 392C2
BROOKE, Remigia
Ex-husband remarries 5-12, 392C2
BROOKINGS Institution (Washington, D.C.)
Older soldiers rptd more productive 6-17, 519E2
BROOKLYN, N.Y.—See NEW York City
BROOKS, Albert
Real Life released 3-1, 174E3
BROOKS, Avery
Spell #7 opens 7-15, 712E2
BROOKS, Foster
Villain released 7-20, 820E3
BROOKS, Rep. Jack (D, Tex.)
Gov Operations Com chrmn 1-24, 71D1
Sees Teng, lauds 1-30, 66C1
BROOKS, Jacqueline
On Mount Chimborazo opens 5-21, 712A2
BROOKS, Jeff
Nature & Purpose opens 2-23, 292C2
BROOKS, Cadet Vincent K.
Named West Pt brigade cmdr 8-11, 609D1
BROOTEN, Kenneth
On Oswald 'look-alike' death 1-18, 93C2, E2
BROPHY, John
Named WHA top coach 5-16, 470G2
BROSSARD, Paulo
Scores police re Uruguayans '78 kidnap 1-23, 95G1

1980

Moore's son kills self 10-15, 890A2
Actors end strike 10-23, 805B3
Pol airtime case accepted by Sup Ct 11-3, 856D2
Ferrigno wins suit 11-3, 890F2
FCC backs WOR-TV move to NJ 11-6, 906E1
Ctroom cameras case argued in Sup Ct 11-12, 882A2
'Dallas' episode aired 11-21, viewing record rptd 11-25, 905A3
McCarthy film libel case refused by Sup Ct 12-1, 918D2
LA DA ends 'Charlie's Angels' probe 12-2, 1002E2
ABC-Warner Amex cultural cable deal set 12-2; CBS seeks FCC ownership rule revocatn 12-8, details cable plans 12-10, 1002G3-1003C1
NASL retrenches 12-8, 1001B2
Lennon slaying reactn 12-9, 934A1
RCTV wins BBC rights 12-11, 1002B3
BROADCASTING Advertisers Reports Inc.
'79 top 10 TV advertisers listed 4-4, 376B2
BROCK, Carol
Navy drops lesbian chrgs 8-21, 898G3
BROCK, Stan
In NFL draft 4-29, 336F2
BROCK 3rd, William (Bill) Emerson
Attacks Carter forgn policy 1-1, White rebuts 1-2, 5A1
GOP platform hearings open 1-14, 32A1
Calls Reagan 'nominee' 5-26, 399A1
Reagan keeps as GOP head 6-13, 452G2-B3
Scores Carter Detroit visit 7-8, 505B2
Addresses GOP conv 7-16, 531E3
Renamed GOP chrmn 7-18, 549F2
Sees 'new coalition' 11-4, 838A3
GOP gains in state legislature 11-4, 847A2
Meets with Reagan 12-10, 956C2
BROCKUNIER, Charles
Afghans arrest 2-21—2-22, free 3-27, 272E2
BRODERICK, Judge Vincent L.
Orders Evans probatn 10-7, 890F1
BRODHEAD, Rep. William M. (D, Mich.)
Reelected 11-4, 843A2
BROKEN Hill Proprietary Co. Ltd.
Australia alumina plant planned 2-8, 95F1
Papua New Guinea gold, copper dvpt conditionally OKd 3-10, 195A1
Australia gas project rptd set 10-1, 748F1
BRONCO Billy (film)
Released 6-11, 675A2
BRONSON, Charles
Borderline released 10-31, 972D3
BROOKING, Terry
West Ham United wins English FA Cup 5-10, 771D3
BROOKINGS Institution (Washington, D.C.)
Economists urge controls, gas rationing 2-6, 2-7, 126F2
Arthur Okun dies 3-23, 280D1
BROOKS Inc., Bobbie
Cleared of '77 job bias chrgs 12-21, 988B1
BROOKS, Edwin
Scores interest rate rules 6-12, 516C3
BROOKS, Herb
US hockey team beats Sovts 2-22, wins Olympic gold medal 2-24, 155F1
BROOKS, Rep. Jack (D, Tex.)
Reelected 11-4, 844A3
BROOKS, Mel
Nude Bomb released 5-9, 675B3
BROOKS, Michael
In NBA draft 6-10, 447F1
BROOKS, Rich
U of Oregon transcript scandal rptd 2-14, 469F2
BROOKS, Tim
Complete TV Director wins Amer Book Award 5-1, 692E2
BROOMFIELD, Rep. William S. (R, Mich.)
Urges US, allies protect raw material natn sea routes 1-14, 32D1
Protests Saudi film telecast 5-8, 375B3
Reelected 11-4, 843A2
BROSIO, Manlio Giovanni
Dies 3-14, 279F1

1976

BROUMAND, Garsivaz
Slain 5-4, linked to Cuba 5-10, 365D2
BROUSSE, Pierre
Named commerce min 8-27, 650G3
BROUSSE, Robert
Sees major Guadeloupe volcano eruptn 8-16, 643G3
Guadeloupe warning scored 9-2, 674D3
BROWN, Rep. Clarence J. (R, Ohio)
Vs gas regulatn extensn 2-5, 108F2
Backs Admin econ recovery plan 3-10, 230C3
Releected 11-2, 830G2
BROWN, Lt. Col. Daniel W.
On Pendelton transfers 11-28, 983A2
BROWN, Donald S.
Wins Rockefeller award 11-16, 911F3
BROWN Jr., Gov. Edmund G. (Jerry) (D, Calif.)
Farm labor dispute continues 1-22—2-11, 153D2
MDs end slowdown 2-5, 144D3
Enters Calif pres primary 3-12, 197F2
Md campaign dvpts 4-28—5-11, 343A2
At black Dem caucus 5-2, 343B3
In DC 5-6, 343E2
Wins Md primary 5-18, 356E2, 357E1, F1
Talks to NJ delegates 5-18, 390D3
Campaigns in Ore 5-20, 373D3
Wins Nev, 3d in Ore 5-25, 373E1, F2-B3, 374C3, D3
NJ slate backs 5-27, 390C3
Wins RI primary 6-1, 389G2, 390C2
Signs A-plant safety bill 6-3, 409F2
Wins Calif primary, NJ slate beats Carter 6-8, 409B1, A2, E3
Primary delegates totaled 6-8, 409A3
Visits La 6-10, NY 6-14, 432F1
Campaign debt rptd 6-16; fed funds total 7-1, 490G3, 491A1, E1
In Tex for Strauss dinner 6-18, 452F1
Paid TV speech 6-25, 468G1
29 Dem govs back Carter 7-6, 492C3
Nominated at conv, 3d in vote 7-14, 505G1, 506E1, 507A2
Dem conv pres vote, table 7-14, 507A2
Conv rules debated 7-15, 513F2
In Plains 8-12—8-13, 616G3
Campaigns with Carter 9-25—9-26, 724D1
Signs 'right-to-die' bill 9-30, 770E2
Lauds Carter 10-7, 762D1
Carter, Ford debate 10-22, 800E3
Stumps with Carter 11-1, 827D1
Carter primary spending rptd 11-17, 938A3
Rpts Christopher State apptmt 12-31, 978E3
FEC certificatn total rptd 12-31, 979F2
BROWN, Frederick Z.
Scores Guyana premier 10-20, 844E2
BROWN, Rep. Garry (R, Mich.)
Reelected 11-2, 829D4
BROWN, George
Carter meets black leaders 7-12, 513D2
BROWN Jr., Rep. George E. (D, Calif.)
Reelected 11-2, 829E1
BROWN, George M.
Wins sen primary 9-21, 804D3
Loses election 11-2, 825E1
BROWN, Gen. George S.
'74 remark vs Jews cited 787D1
Statemts re Israel, Iran, GB rptd 10-17—10-18; explains 10-18; Rumsfeld, Ford, back 10-18, 10-20; Carter, others score 10-20, 787C1
Ford, Carter debate remarks 10-22, 799F3, 801D1, C2
BROWN, Gordon
Arraigned 4-22, 309D3
BROWN, H(ubert) Rap (Gerold)
Paroled '68 La arms chrg dropped 10-21, 912C3

BROWN, Harold
Carter briefing session 7-26, 551D1
Named Defense secy 12-21, 956G1
Photo 956D2
Biog sketch 957G1
On $5-7 bln spending cut 12-28, 978D1

1977

BROTMAN, Judge Stanley S.
Declares Dufala case mistrial 3-10, 261F2
BROTZMAN, Donald G.
Replaced as Army asst secy 5-27, 500A1
BROUN, Heywood (1888-1939)
FBI surveillance rptd 6-19, 481E1
BROWN, Arnold
Named Salvation Army pres 5-5, 532G1
BROWN, Ben
Named Dem dep chrmn 1-21, 53B2
BROWN, Rep. Clarence J. (R, Ohio)
Rebuts Carter energy plan 6-2, 443G1
Sees Alcan finance problem 11-2, 856D3
BROWN, Edmund G. (Pat)
Champion named to HEW post 1-19, 53A1
BROWN Jr., Gov. Edmund G. (Jerry) (D, Calif.)
Names Bird chief justice 2-12, 140C3
Bird confirmed 3-11, 396B3
Carter calls 'good friend' 5-12, 381D1
With Carter in Calif 5-17, 381C3
Vetoes death penalty 5-27, 594A2
Death penalty veto overridden 8-11, 652D2
LA picked for '84 Olympics 9-25, 828B3
BROWN, Frederick Z.
On Cuba troops in Angola 2-2, 105F1
BROWN, George
Shapp defends black's ouster 9-28, 800E2
BROWN Jr., Rep. George E. (D, Calif.)
Scores Dodd Clinch R amendmt 9-20, 758D3
BROWN, George F.
Bribery chrgd 2-16, 215E2
BROWN, Gen. George S.
On US retaliatory power 1-30, 70A3
Scores Cong, backs mail surveillnc 3-27, 231F3
Singlaub loses Korea comnd 5-21, 403G2
Sees Korea ldrs on US troop exit 5-24—5-26, 440G3
Sees Ford on Canal pact 8-16, 622D1
Sees ret officers on Canal pact 8-29, 679A1
Defends Canal treaty support 9-27, Thurmond doubts sincerity 10-4, 755A2

BROWN, Harold
Sen com OKs nominatn 1-13, confrmd 1-20, 34A1, D3
Proposes '78 defns budget cuts 1-25, 1-26, limits cruise missile dvpt 2-2, 94E2
On Carter budget changes 2-22, 125C1
Rpts personal finances 2-25, 147F3
Vs mil unionizatn ban 3-18, 343C1
Panel scores breeder reactor, plutonium use 3-21, 234F3
Rpts upgrading of Viet dischrgs authorized 3-28, 231B3
Doubts early arms pact, sees spending rise 4-1, 247D1
Meets Sadat 4-5, 245B1
Consolidates arms dvpt, procuremt 4-25; orders more Minuteman IIIs 5-3, 343A3
AF computer projct scored 4-27, 421F2, C3

1978

BROTHERHOOD of Railway, Airline and Steamship Clerks, Freight Handlers, Express and Station Employes—*See RAILWAY, Airline and Steamship Clerks, etc.*
BROTHERHOOD of Sleeping Car Porters—*See PORTERS, Brotherhood of Sleeping Car*
BROTHERS Johnson (instrumental group)
Win Grammy 2-24, 315G3
BROUDRE-Groeger, Joachim
Accused of spying, smear campaign chrgd 8-31—9-6, 725C2
Spy probe dropped 9-26, 868A3
BROWN, Barry M.
Platinum opens 11-12, 1031F2
BROWN, Bobby
Traded to Yankees 6-14, 779B3
BROWN, Charles L.
Named AT&T chrmn, chief exec 10-18, 808D3
BROWN, Rep. Clarence J. (R, Ohio)
Vs pvt energy com mtgs 4-13, 304E2
Scores energy bill 10-15, 786C3
Reelected 11-7, 851E3
BROWN, David
Jaws 2 released 6-16, 619E2
Benchley book sets record film 9-1, 759E2
BROWN, Eddie
NFL '77 kick return ldr 1-1, 56G3
BROWN, Edmund G. (Pat)
Kalmbach joins law firm 7-11, 844C1
BROWN Jr., Gov. Edmund G. (Jerry) (D, Calif.)
At Mondale-Westn govs mtg 1-13, 34E1, A2
A-plant rejected by Kern Cnty 3-8, 184F1
On Sundesert A-plant defeat 4-14, 281D2
Bars Banks extraditn to SD 4-19, 327E1
Property-tax cut amendmt voted 6-6; freezes hiring 6-7, vows aid, spending cuts 6-8, 425A3, D3
Wins primary 6-6, 425E3, 447E3
Allocates surplus budget to aid local govts hit by Propositn 13 6-24, 525C3
Urges state-local govt spending curb 6-24, 525E3
Signs budget 7-6, 525F3
White discounts Carter challenge 7-26, 682B3
3d in Dem pres poll 8-13, 682E2
Urges state reimbursemt for fed programs 8-28, govs back 8-29, 681D3, 682E1
Signs $1 bln income tax cut 8-30, 735E2
Carter in Sacramento 11-3, 862B2
Reelected 11-7, 845B2, 847B1, 853D2, 856C2
BROWN, Freddie (Downtown)
NBA free-throw ldr 4-9, 271F2
Bullets win NBA title 6-7, 457E1
BROWN, Rep. Garry (R, Mich.)
Loses reelectn 11-7, 854B1
BROWN, George
Sentncd in '72 hijacking 11-23, 926F3
BROWN Jr., Rep. George E. (D, Calif.)
Reelected 11-7, 850B2
BROWN, Gen. George S.
Backs pension overhaul 1-18, 53D1
Sees USSR mil gains 2-2, 81A3
Successor named to head Joint Chiefs 4-5, 281F1
Dies 12-5, 1032C2
BROWN, Graham
Nevis Mt Dew opens 12-7, 1031E2
BROWN, H. Rap—*See AMIN, Jamil Abdullah-al*

BROWN, Harold
Urges arms buildup in defns posture statemt 2-2, 81A1
Sadat asks for US arms 2-6, 77G2
US to bolster S Korea air power 2-18, 135G2
Affirms Asia, Pacific commitmt 2-20, 126B3
Warns vs mil aid bar to Korea 2-22, 204D1, E1
Successor at Caltech named 3-6, 172E3
Weizman in US re arms request 3-8, 176E3
In Carter, Tito talks 3-8, 194C1
Links neutron bomb cancellatn, Sovt arms restraint 3-10; USSR rejects 3-11, 254F1
Backs shipbldg cuts 3-24, 223A3
Vs A-weapons material ban 3-31, 4-3, 277D2

1979

BROSZEY, Christel
Defectn to E Ger rptd 3-13, 180A3
BROTEN, Neal
Minn U wins NCAA hockey title 3-24, 356E1
BROTON Benelto, Francisco
Escapes Spain jail 12-17, 997E3
BROWN, Judge Bailey
Confrmd to Appeals Ct, all-white club membership disputed 9-25, 901C3
BROWN, Curtis
NFL '78 kick return ldr 1-6, 80D2
BROWN, Dale
Suspends Scales from basketball 3-5, 291B1
BROWN Jr., Gov. Edmund G. (Jerry) (D, Calif.)
To seek US budget amendmnt 1-8, 13B2
Carter vs budget amendmt 1-17, 29D2
US budget amendmt thrives 2-6, 86C2
At Mex worker's funeral 2-14, 327G1
AFL-CIO offcls assess 2-19, 2-21, 149F1
Govs vs budget amendmt 2-26, 150A2
Scored re Tex pipeline cancelatn 3-13, 183E1
Asks Rancho Seco A-plant shutdown 4-1, 245D1
Rancho Seco operatn OKd 4-6, 260C3, 261E3
In Africa, marks birthday 4-7, 271E3
Urges end to US A-power use 4-24, 322G3
Welcomes Carter to Calif 5-4, 347A1
Carter backs gas rationing plan 5-5, 347E1
Scores A-energy at DC protest 5-6, 343C3
Orders gas rationing 5-8, rationing starts 5-9, 342C3
Sees Carter, gets gas vow 5-16, 361F1
Proposes energy, transit plan 5-31, 418F3
Backs SALT II, scores MX 6-29, 496G3
At Diablo Canyon A-protest 6-30, 519G1
Absent in govs' vote on Carter '80 support 7-8, 518D1
Fonda, ex-POW appts cause furor; legis rebuffs detailed 7-13—8-8, 593A2-B3
Scores Carter on A-power stance 7-16, 532A3, 534B3
N Amer energy mkt backed 7-20, 581B2
Pres com formed, Mex trip begins 7-30, 593E1
Asks odd-even gas rules retentn 9-7, 683G1
Vetoes anti-UFW bill 9-7, 698E3
Addresses NH Dem picnic 9-8, 680E1
Gay sworn judge 9-17, appeals judge arrested 9-20, 748F1-A3
Signs order ending some odd-even gas rules 9-20, 850D1
Reimposes odd-even gas rules 10-13, 870C1
State Sup Ct inquiry ends 11-5, 869A2
Enters pres race 11-8, 847E2
Representative at Dem Natl Com mtg 11-9, 961D2
Offers 'new econ order' 11-9, 962D2
Seeks flexible credit system, stresses inflatn, energy 11-20, 962G2
Invited into Iowa debate 12-4, 962A3
Kopp loses San Fran mayoral vote 12-11, 946F3
Gubernatorial powers for Curb upheld re state absence 12-27, 983D3
Vs Carter la debate bar 12-28, 12-29, 983F2
BROWN, Freddie (Downtown)
NBA free-throw ldr 4-8, 290F2
Sonics win NBA title 6-1, 507B1
BROWN, Georgia
Carmelina opens 4-8, 711A2
BROWN, Gordon
Chrg dismissed 10-15, 812D2
BROWN, Graham
Season To Unravel opens 1-25, 292G2
BROWN, Harold
A-target chng urged 1-13, 52A3
Calls '80 defns budget 'austere' 1-22, 42G3
Warns of Sovt threat in defns posture statemt, cong testimony 1-25, 52A2
Urges US response to Sovt surrogates 2-8, 89B2
Visits Saudi 2-10—2-11, Jordan 2-12, Israel 2-13—2-15, Egypt 2-16—2-18, 143B2-D3
Sees US defns of Mideast interests 2-25; Admin clarifies remarks 2-26, 2-27, 143D3-144B1
Meets Israel defns min 3-17; Israel, Egypt mins 3-19, 198G1, C2
Backs SALT II ratificatn 4-5, 257F2
On SALT II missile verificatn 4-17, 279E2
OKs XM-1 tank productn 5-8, 386A1

1980

BROWN, Alice
Sets indoor 640-yd relay mark 2-29, 892F1
BROWN, Arvin
Watch on the Rhine opens 1-3, 136F3
BROWN, Blair
One-Trick Pony released 10-3, 836D3
BROWN, Charles
Home opens 5-7, 392C3
BROWN, Charles L.
On AT&T reorgn 8-20, 648E2
BROWN, Rep. Clarence J. (R, Ohio)
On Carter econ renewal plan 8-28, 663A3
Reelected 11-4, 843D4
BROWN, Clay
BYU wins Holiday Bowl 12-19, 999B3
BROWN, Cooper
Wins Hawaii US Sen primary 9-20, 745E1
Loses US Sen electn 11-4, 852C2
BROWN, Drew (Bundini)
Holmes KOs Ali 10-2, 772E1
BROWN Jr., Gov. Edmund G. (Jerry) (D, Calif.)
Scores Carter forgn policy 1-5, 1-8; in Iowa 1-9, 13A2
State of State message 1-10, 482G3-483D1
Ia poll standing: 4% 1-11, 33A2
Debates Mondale, Kennedy in Ia, vs forgn policy, grain embargo 1-12, 32D2
3d in Me caucus vote 2-10, 109C1
Trails Dems in Times/CBS poll 2-20, 130E2
Wins 10% of NH vote 2-26, 142E2, F2, 143A1
Last in Mass primary 3-4, 166D2, D3
Wins token vote in Fla, Ga, Ala primaries 3-11, 183A3
Loses matching funds 3-13, 209D1
Gets 3% vote in Ill 3-18, 206C2
Conn primary vote 3% 3-25, 221D3
Offshore oil leasing opposed 3-28, 330G3
Wis, Kan primary results 4-1, 246G1-E2
Ends pres bid 4-1, 246C2, B3
Tex primary results 5-3, 342F2
Mich, Ore primary votes 5-20, 383D1-G1
Miller loses supervisor vote 6-3, 439E2
Greets Carter 7-3, 505D2
Signs water bill 7-18, 632A2
Addresses Dem conv 8-13, 611E3
At Mondale rally 9-5, 780G1
Jackson death sentnc upheld 10-23, 868G3
Campaigns with Mondale 10-26, 816F3
BROWN Jr., Rep. George E. (D, Calif.)
Reelected 11-4, 842B2
BROWN, Gordon
Convicted re Sky Shops bribe conspiracy 2-8, 148A3
Fined, jailed 3-7, 230G2
BROWN, Hank
Elected to US House 11-4, 842D2, 851D3

BROWN, Harold
In China mil talks 1-6—1-9; Sovts score 1-7, 11F2
Scores Sovt criticism 1-11, tours mil hq 1-12, ends China visit 1-13; in Japan, urges defns spending hike 1-14, 31F1
China briefs Pak on Peking visit 1-18—1-21, 44A3
China to buy US mil gear 1-24, 46B2
Asks mil mobility in defns posture statemt, cong testimony 1-29, 65E1
Details Iran rescue mission 4-25, 321C1, F1
On MX deploymt chng 5-6, 369E2
China mil gear sale OKd 5-29, 397D3, G3
Computer errors trigger A-alerts 6-3, 6-6; discounts war 6-9, 457E3
Tells mil recruiters to stress unemploymt 6-11, 458C2
Adm Hayward backs draft 6-19, 478G3

1976

BROWN, Jonathan
Bank diversificatn scored 7-5, 495B2
BROWN, L. Dean
Arrives in Leb 3-31, 226E1
Mediates in Leb 4-1—4-5, 241E2
In Leb talks 4-8, 4-10, 4-12, 258E1
Rpts to Ford, Kissinger; returns to Leb 4-30; leftists score 5-2; meets Karami 5-4, 319D1
Ends Lebanon mission 5-11, 337C2
BROWN, Lester R.
Rpts world populatn growth 10-28, 863A2
BROWN, Paul
Quits as Bengals coach 1-1, 31C2
BROWN, R. Harper
Indicted 2-18, stiffer penalties asked 10-5, 886E1; sentncd 11-30, 921E2
BROWN Jr., Samuel W.
Dem com OKs platform 6-15, 432G3
BROWN, Judge Thomas L.
Orders Mich police unit disbanded 1-18, 45F1
BROWN, Virgil E.
Seconds Ford nominatn 8-18, 597G2
BROWN Co.
Trust suit dvpts 2-18—10-5, 886C1, E2; Dilno sentncd 11-30, 921A3
BROWNING Jr., James L.
Hearst trial opens 2-4, 113D3-114C3
Hearst trial dvpts 2-12—2-23, sums up 3-18, 201A2-F3, 202A3
BROWNING-Ferris Industries Inc.
SEC lists paymts 5-12, 726D2
BROWNS Ferry, Ala.—*See ALABAMA*
BROWN & Sites Co.
Boycott rpt released 10-18, 786B1
BROWN University (Providence, R.I.)
Brown quits as pres 6-30, Swearer succeeds 8-14, 640G3
BROYHILL, Rep. James Thomas (R, N.C.)
Reelected 11-2, 830F2
BRUCE, David K. E.
Quits as NATO amb 1-30, replaced 3-3, 186D2
Gets Medal of Freedom 2-10, 272C1
BRUCHERT, Hans-Bieter
Wins Olympic medal 7-31, 576C3
BRUERA, Ricardo
Argentina educ min 3-29, 236B1
BRUESEWITZ, Rev. Oskar
Dies in anti-govt protest 8-22, 772C2
BRUNDTLAND, Gro Harlem
Norway environmt min 1-12, 30A2
BRUNEI (British protectorate)
Listed as 'not free' nation 1-19, 20D3
BRUNER, Mike
Wins Olympic medal 7-18, 575D2

1977

Sees limited SALT agrmt 5-6, 401C1
Backs cutbacks 5-10—6-1, 420C3
OKs US-UK mil info exchng 5-16, 379G3
NATO defns mins OK spending hike 5-18, 379D3
On Singlaub incident 5-21, 5-22, 404B1
Assures Saudis on arms 5-24, 402D1
CIA control of NSA, NRO rptd opposed 6-10, 6-12, 576G2
On Carter B-1 decision 7-1, 514D3
In S Korea troop talks 7-25—7-26; briefs Japan 7-27, 572D1, A2
Turner given new powers 8-4, 610A3
Campaigns for Canal pact ratificatn 8-15, 622C1
Cruise missile debate delays Gromyko-Vance mtg 9-11, 751D2
Defends Canal pact at Sen hearings 9-27, 755D2
Rpts USSR satellite destructn capability 10-4, 777A2
Backs M-X dvpt 10-6, 10-8, 777A1
Bars mil strikes, organizing 10-6, 777E3
NATO debates neutron bomb, cruise missile 10-11—10-12, 956A3
Yugo mil cooperatn set 10-13, 785F3
Orders budget process revamped 10-26, 857F2
On '78, '79 defns budgets 11-6, 857B3
Meets Bourges, arms sales curb refused 11-22, 1012E3

BROWN, Herb
Fired as Pistons coach 12-15, 991E1
BROWN, Hubie
Storen fired as Hawks pres 9-27, 870B3
BROWN, Ian Ramsey
Accused of smuggling 8-8, 944F3
BROWN, Larry
Retires from football 7-26, 659B2
Brother fired as Pistons coach 12-15, 991E1
BROWN, Bishop Leslie
On Luwum death 2-21, 139D1
BROWN, R. Harper
Sentence cut 2-17, 504E1
BROWN, Ralph
Jamaica local govt min 1-4, 46C1
Jamaica ruling party secy 9-18, 884D2
BROWN Jr., Samuel W.
Confrmd ACTION dir 2-25, 148C3
BROWN, William
Chrgs El Salvador vote fraud 3-9, 206C3
BROWN, Willie
Raiders win Super Bowl 1-9, 24F3
BROWNE, Alice
Sets swim record 8-21, 828E3
BROWNE Jr., Ernest C.
Loses mayoral electn 11-8, 855G2
BROWNER, Ross
Wins Downtown AC Trophy 12-8, 950E2
BROWN-Evans, Lois
Urges riots end, blames racism 12-1—12-3, to seek no-confidence vote 12-6, 935E3, 936A1
BROWNING Jr., James A.
Hearst convictn upheld 10-2, 839A1
Antarctic shelf penetrated 12-9, 971G2
BROWNMAN, Harold L.
Replaced as Army asst secy 4-25, 418D1
BROWN University (Providence, R.I.)
'77-78 costs rptd 3-27, 483G1
S Africa detains Harper 6-10, 469A2
Hartwick wins NCAA soccer title 12-4, 1020E3
BROWN v. Board of Education
Cited re Bakke case 10-12, 834C3
BROZ, Jovanka (Mrs. Josip Broz Tito)
In seclusn 6-15, illness denied 10-11, 786A1
House arrest, probe re Serb backing rptd 10-25, 844G1
BRUCE, David K. E.
Dies 12-4, 1024A1
BRUDZINSKI, Bob
In NFL draft 5-3, 353C2
BRUMA, Eddy Johan
Party leaves govt coalitn 9-23, 767B3

1978

Urges Turkish arms embargo end 4-6, 276F2
GAO sees Trident cost overruns 4-13, 407C2
Haig resignatn threat rptd 4-25, 298G2-A3
Armed forces drug abuse rise rptd 4-27, 368D2, A3
Assures Sen com on Saudi jet use 5-10, 357A2
Clarifies CIA evidence on Cuba role in Zaire 6-4, 442G1
Civil defns reorganizatn concern rptd 6-20, 466G2
Lauds cruise missile test 6-21, 493C2
Affirms US mil superiority; concedes Sovt troop threat in Eur, NATO weakness 6-23, 493D2
At Carter mtg on security leaks 7-11, 524G2
Gets study on Joint Chiefs 7-12, 528C2
In S Korea mil talks, North threat seen 7-26—7-27, 594G3
Laser weapon use confrmd 8-23, 684A1
Vs USSR oil equipmt sale 9-6, 743D1
In Camp David summit talks 9-7, 673E1
Yugo defns min visits 9-24—9-29, 758E1
Pentagon studies gen purpose missile 9-26, 738C1
US vows Israel air base aid 9-28, 9-29, 746F1
In S Korea 11-6—11-8, joint cmnd set 11-7; in Japan 11-8, Japan to pay more for US forces 11-9, 872B3-E3
Rpts USSR Pacific buildup 11-9, 914F1
Gets Army 2-yr enlistmt plan 11-10, 895F2
Vance rebuts Sovt chrg on Iran 11-19, 893G3
Gets JCS draft proposal 11-21, 895A1
Urges mil pensn reform 12-14, 1009C2
Arms sales talks dispute rptd 12-19, 996D3

BROWN, Harry
Wilson dies 4-9, 356G3
BROWN, Hubie
Named top NBA coach 5-15, 457B3
BROWN, J(ohn) Carter
Rpts Natl Gallery commissns 6-1, 578C3
BROWN, Jill E.
Qualifies as airline pilot 4-19, 420C1
BROWN, John
'Test-tube' daughter born 7-25, 596E3
BROWN, John Y.
NBA OKs Celtics-Braves ownership swap 7-7, 655F2
BROWN, Ken
Wins Irish Open 8-27, 672G3
BROWN, Lennox
Twilight Dinner opens 4-18, 760F3
BROWN, Lesley
'Test-tube' daughter born 7-25, 596E3
BROWN, Louise
1st 'test-tube' baby 7-25, 596E3
BROWN Jr., R. Manning
Quits Stevens' bd 9-12, 699C2
BROWN, Robert
Arrives Guyana 11-15, visits cult commune 11-17, killed 11-18, body flown home 11-21, 889F2, A1-891C1
BROWN, Sam
Payton quits Peace Corps 11-24, 915F1
BROWN, Ted
NC State wins Tangerine Bowl 12-23, 1025D2
BROWN, Tyrone
Vs WPIX-TV license renewal 6-16, 672E1
Scores FCC performance 10-11, 908D1
BROWN, William F.
Wiz released 10-25, 970E3
Broadway Musical opens 12-21, 1031A1
BROWN, Zara Cully
Dies 2-28, 196D2
BROWN Brothers Harriman & Co.
E Roland Harriman dies 2-16, 196B3
BROWNE, Jackson
Running On Empty on best-seller list 3-8, 196C1; 4-5, 272G3; 5-3, 356E1
BROWNER, Ross
In NFL draft 5-2, 336F2
BROWNLEE, Vivian
2d in Mixed Team tourn 12-3, 990D1
BROWN Lung Disease (byssinosis)—*See MEDICINE—Heart & Lungs*
BROWN Transport Co.
Freight-rate case refused by Sup Ct 12-4, 959B2
BROWN Transport Co. v. Atcon Inc.
Case refused by Sup Ct 12-4, 959B2
BROWN University (Providence, R.I.)
Mullaney to coach basketball 4-3, 272G2
BROWN & Williamson Tobacco Corp.—*See B.A.T. Industries—British-American Tobacco Co. Ltd.*
BROYHILL, Rep. James Thomas (R, N.C.)
Hosp cost lid rejected by com 7-18, 550F3
Reelected 11-7, 851C3
BRUCE, Ailsa Mellon (1901-69)
Natl Gallery additn opens 6-1, 578E2
BRUCE, Terry L.
Loses US House electn 11-7, 853B2
BRUCETON, Pa.—*See PENNSYLVANIA*
BRUGNON, Jacques (Toto)
Dies 3-20, 252D2
BRUNEI (British protectorate)
Independence set; Malaysia, Indonesia back 6-30; facts on 533D3
Oil output, revenue cited 534A1
Viet refugee boat barred 12-23, 997F2
BRUNELIN, Andre G.
No Time For Breakfast released 9-15, 970D2

1979

Backs SALT II draft treaty 5-9, 338D3
NATO defense mins back SALT 5-16, 359A3
Sees USSR 1st-strike ability 5-30, 410G1
At SALT II summit 6-15–6-18, 449G1; cited in communique text, Carter address 6-18, 457B1, 458E3
Confirms N Korea mil buildup 6-21, 495A2
Backs SALT in Sen hearings 7-9, 510D1; 7-18, 536A2
Mil retiremt plan proposed 7-19, 628A2
Mil volunteer shortage rptd 8-20, 649B2
On MX 'racetrack' deployment 9-7, 677G3
Israel defense min seeks more arms, jet co-productn 9-13–9-14, 693C2
Concern re W Ger defense spending rptd 9-21, 733B2
Bars USSR computer sale 9-27, 775C1
Staff rpt on US arms to China publshd 10-3, 789F1
USSR vs Japan visit 10-16, 803E3
In S Korea for mil talks 10-17–10-19, visits Japan 10-20, 803E2, C3
Morocco arms sale rptd backed 10-22, 804B1
US carrier, AWACS sent to S Korea 10-28, 822D1
False A-war alert placed 11-9, 869G2
JCS backs increased mil pay 11-13, 903E3
Halts flight training for Iranians 11-23, 898G1
Bars Marine manpower reductn 12-5, 923G3
Urges NATO reinforcemt plans 12-11, thanks re Iran support 12-12, 959C2
On Carter defense spending plan 12-13, 963B2

BROWN, Herbert C.
Wins Nobel Prize 10-16, 858B1
BROWN Jr., Judge Ira
To place Peoples Temple in receivership 1-23, 117C2
BROWN, John
Test-tube daughter marks 1st birthday 7-25, 656B2
BROWN, John (deceased)
Secret marriage to Queen Victoria alleged 5-22, 388F2
BROWN, John N.
Dies 10-9, 860D2
BROWN Jr., John Y.
NBA OKs Celtics sale 5-7, 527C1
Wins primary for Ky gov 5-29, 420C1
Elected 11-6, 846C2
BROWN, Joseph
Paintings rptd stolen 1-3, 18F2
BROWN, Ka-Ron
Sancocho opens 3-28, 712C2
BROWN, Larry
Quits as Nuggets coach 2-1, named UCLA coach 3-27, 290C3, 291E1
BROWN, Lesley
Test-tube daughter marks 1st birthday 7-25, 656B2
BROWN, Louise
Marks 1st birthday 7-25, 656A2
BROWN, Miles J.
Dismisses du Pont monoply case 9-17, 810C1
BROWN, Dr. Norman K.
Terminally ill treatmt study rptd 5-31, 471E2
BROWN, Rebecca
Sentenced 3-6, 316A2
BROWN, Robert K.
Chrysler resignatn rptd 2-23, 188E1
BROWN, Sam
Peace Corps dir picked 3-29, 310G2
BROWN, Steve
Strider opens 5-31, 712F2
BROWN, Ted
In NFL draft 5-3, 335F1
BROWN, Tyrone
Sup Ct workforce data rptd 6-11, 464A2
BROWNE, Jackson
At Diablo Canyon A-protest 4-7, 262A1
Performs at NYC A-protest 9-23, 742G2
BROWN University (Providence, R.I.)
Baker addresses 11-2, 983E1
BROWN v. Board of Education
Case cited by Sup Ct 7-2, 539A3
BROWN v. Felson
Case decided by Sup Ct 6-4, 439B2
BROWN v. Texas
Case decided by Sup Ct 6-25, 540D2
BROWN v. Traub
Case refused by Sup Ct 12-3, 964A2
BROWN & Williamson Tobacco Corp.—*See B.A.T. Industries–British-American Tobacco*
BROZ, Jovanka
Tito '78 divorce rptd 2-4, 176C1
BRUCE, Earle
Hired as Ohio State football coach 1-12, 175D3
BRUCE, George
5th Musketeer released 9-7, 820B1
BRUCE, J. Campbell
Escape from Alcatraz released 6-21, 820B1
BRUEGHEL, Pieter (d. 1569)
Painting stolen in Italy 2-1, 119G1
BRUNDAGE, Percival F.
Dies 7-16, 588D2
BRUNEI
UK independence pact signed 1-7, 40D3

1980

Meets Saudi defense min on F-15 gear 6-26, 538D3
Sees Canada defns min, F-18 deal agreed 7-8, 544A1
A-war strategy revised 8-5, 595A1; reassures allies, Muskie not consulted 8-8, 615E2, E3
Lobbies for MX plank 8-13, 611D2
Outlines A-strategy, sees ICBM vulnerability 8-20, 630D1
To form counterterrorist unit 8-23, 644F1
Testifies on 'stealth' plane disclosure 9-4, 665G3
Scores Dutch, Danish mil spending 10-3, 737D1
US sends Saudis more air defns gear 10-5, 758A1
Admits Pentagon MX distortn 10-5, 897B1
US undecided on Saudi F-15 gear 10-27, 821C1
Sen OKs research, readiness appropriatn 11-21, 896E3
Europns defend mil spending 12-9—12-10, 949D2
Warns Sovts on Poland invasn 12-10, 949B2
In Japan; asks arms outlay hike, cites Sovt threat 12-11—12-12; in S Korea, pleas for Kim Dae Jung 12-13, 952G3-953E1
Scores W Ger mil spending target 12-18, 950B1
Calls Iran hostage demand ransom 12-21, 973G1

BROWN, Harold O. J.
On evangelical Christian pol movemt 8-19, 819D1
BROWN, Judge Ira
Gets rpt on Peoples Temple assets 2-6, 170F3
BROWN, J. Carter
At Reagan DC fete 11-18, 880E3
BROWN, Jesse
On Mass welfare fraud case 5-13, 414G3
BROWN, Julie
Of the Fields opens 5-27, 756F3
BROWN, Larry
Louisville wins NCAA basketball title 3-24, 240G1
BROWN, Lester R.
Sees gasohol as world food threat 3-15, 251B1
BROWN, Paul
Fined for autobiography chrgs 1-22, 175B3
BROWN, Paul L.
On G&W elec car dvpt 6-9, 541E3
BROWN, Ricky
In NBA draft 6-10, 447F1
BROWN, Robert (d. 1978)
Layton faces murder chrgs 5-22, 407G3
BROWN, Sandra
Indicted 1-10, 216C1
Convicted 12-21, 997F2
BROWN, Steve
Hijinks! opens 12-18, 1003B3
BROWN, Wendell
Up the Academy released 6-6, 675F3
BROWN Co.
James R Corp purchase agreed 2-1, 3-27, 385E3
BROWNE, Jackson
Hold Out on best-seller list 8-13, 640C3; 9-10, 716F3
BROWNE, Leslie
Nijinsky released 3-20, 216D3
BROWNE, Robert M.
Onward Victoria opens 12-14, 1003E3
BROWNE, Virgil
Dies 1-7, 104G1
BROWNJOHN, John
Tess released 12-12, 1003E2
BROWN'S Ferry Nuclear Power Plant—*See Atomic Energy*
BROWN University (Providence, R.I.)
Mattfeld resigns as Barnard pres 5-28, 471B1
Keeney dies 6-18, 528C2
BROWN v. Glines
Case decided by Sup Ct 1-21, 93B1
BROYHILL, Rep. James Thomas (R, N.C.)
Reelected 11-4, 843C4
BROZ, Jovanka
Mourns Tito 5-5, 338A3
BRUBAKER (film)
Top-grossing film 7-2, 568G3
BRUCKHEIMER, Jerry
American Gigolo released 2-1, 216A2
BRUCKNER, Roland
Wins Olympic medals 7-25, 622E3, F3
BRUMA, Edy
Gets Surinam civiln post 2-28, 174F3
BRUNE, Mayor Eugene C. (Somerville, Mass.)
On tank car accident 4-3, 392A2

1976

BRUNNER, Guido B.
European Comm meets 12-22—12-23, 977F1
BRUNO, Hal
On pres debate panel 10-15, 782B3
BRUNS, Gunter
Killed in Portugal 1-1, 11A1
BRUNSWICK Record Corp.
Execs sentenced 4-12, 316B3
BRUNSWICK (Me.) Times-Record (newspaper)
Carter endorsement rptd 10-30, 831G2
BRUST, Joseph A.
Indictmt dismissed 12-1, 1016B2
BRUTUS, Dennis
Supports Olympic boycott 7-17, 528C3
BRUYNTJES, Hans
US team climbs Mt Everest 10-8, 876C3
BRYAN, Judge Albert V.
Ordrs Westn Elec bias end 10-22, 943D2
BRYANT, Foy
Baron indicted 11-30, 991C1
BRYANT, Judge William B.
'75 legal costs ruling rptd 1-1, 6F3
Rules football player draft illegal 9-8, 736B3
BRYN Mawr (Pa.) College
McBride dies 6-3, 484F3

BRZEZINSKI, Zbigniew
Platform com testimony 5-19, 357D3
Sees Australia prime min 7-26, 554G1
Carter briefing session 7-29, 551E1
Named natl security aide 12-16, 936A3, C3
Bio sketch 937F1
Linowitz mtg rptd 12-19, 975C1
BUBACH, Siegfried
On spy arrests 6-2, 6-5, 441G3
BUBAR, Benjamin C.
Final pres vote tally 12-18, 979C2
BUBBLING Brown Sugar (play)
Opens 3-2, 1014B3
BUCARAM, Asaad
Immediate electns asked 2-3—3-16, 363F2
To help draft const 10-11, 872G2

1977

BRUNNER, Guido
Gets Eur Comm post 1-7, 74A2
BRUNSWICK Corp.
Sup Ct voids trust ruling 1-25, 80E2
BRUSHY Mountain State Prison, Tenn.—*See TENNESSEE*
BRYAN Jr., Lt. Gen. Blackshear M. (ret.)
Dies 3-2, 264D2
BRYANT, Anita
Vs White House gay rights hearing 3-27, 278E2
Miami homosexual rights law repealed 6-7, 446F2
Gays launch educatn campaign 6-13, 560A3
Fla citrus comm renews contract 11-16, 927G2
BRYANT, Rosalyn
Sets dash, run marks 1-28—2-25, 602G3, 603A1
BRYANT, Warren
In NFL draft 5-3, 353A2
BRYANT, Judge William B.
Rules FBI raids on Scientology offices illegal 7-27, 628B2
Jails Scientologist for contempt 7-29, frees 9-14, 940D2

BRZEZINSKI, Zbigniew
Sworn natl security adviser 1-23, 52E2
Young rpts on Africa trip 2-13, 106A1
Sees Carter on Amin exit bar 2-25, 141C1
Rpts net worth 2-25, 147G3
Assures Israel on Carter views 3-9, 166F2
Kreisky in US talks 3-14, 425E1
Optimistic re early arms pact 4-1, 247E1
Sees Dobrynin on SALT 4-13, 400C3
On Carter-Assad talks 5-9, 360D2, G2
Sees Frei 5-25, 493D1
Czechs charge Dubcek support 6-13, 512G3
Greets Venez pres 6-28, 546E1
In Carter conf with US Jews 7-6, 510A1
USSR wiretap com rptd 7-10, 551B2
Turner given new powers 8-4, 610G2, B3
Sees Church re Cuba visit 8-8, 653F3
Panama Canal pact ratificatn campaign underway 9-7, 678G3
Announces Carter 8-natn trip 9-23, 738G1
Assures Israel on Geneva plan 10-2, 750D2
Sees improved USSR ties 10-18, 866D1
Sees Young on S Africa sanctns 10-24, 851D3
Offers W Bank plan 11-5, Israel vs 11-6, 850B2
Meets with Wyszynski 12-30, 1001B2
BUBACK, Siegfried
Killed 4-7, Baader-Meinhof linked 4-9, 4-13; funeral 4-13, 286A2
Baader, others sentenced 4-28, 352A3
Murder suspect seized 5-3, 601E3
Bank chief slain 7-30, 601A3
Schleyer kidnaped 9-6, 695A2
2 suspects captured 9-22, 11-10, 888A1, E1
Slayers linked to Schleyer murder 10-20, 791B2
Baader atty linked to suspects 11-18, 969A1
BUCARAM, Asaad
Velasco scores pres bid 3-3, challenged 3-4, 348A1
Civilian rule delayed 4-22, 347D3
Launches pres bid 7-18, 842F1

1978

BRUNHART, Hans (Liechtenstein premier)
Elected Liechtenstein premier 2-3, 95B1
BRUNNER, Guido
Sees Garland on coal, uranium imports 6-13, 495A1
Halts UK-Australia uranium pact 7-27, 666E1
On OPEC oil-refining role 10-9, 871F1
OPEC price hike bad for EC 12-18, 978F1
BRUNSWICK, O.—*See OHIO*
BRUSATI, Franco
Bread & Chocolate released 7-14, 969E3
BRYAN Jr., Judge Albert V.
Asked to bar Thi ouster 2-8, issues stay 2-10, 103B3
Litton indictmt dismissal reversed 4-5, 368G1 *
Sentences 2 for Viet spying 7-7, 555B1
BRYAN, Frederick van Pelt
Dies 4-17, 356C2
BRYANT, Chris
Joseph Andrews released 4-13, 619F2
BRYANT, Cullen
Rams win in playoffs 12-31, 1024A2
BRYANT, Hazel
Blacks opens 5-24, 887C1
BRYANT, Paul (Bear)
Alabama wins Sugar Bowl 1-2, 8D3
BRYANT, Rosalyn
Forde breaks 500-mtr run record 1-15, 76A3
BRYANT, Judge William B.
Hanna pleads guilty 3-17, 202F3
Sentences Hanna 4-24, 323F3
Denies 3 FBI ex-offcls' dismissal motn 11-30, 939E3
BRZEZINSKI, Zbigniew
Arafat vs PLO stand 1-2, 3D1
Scored re PLO aide's murder 1-5, 3G1
Sees Sovt, China 'proxy war' in Viet-Cambodia clashes 1-8; Sovts score 1-9, 9C2
Sees Dobrynin on Sovt satellite reentry 1-12, 1-17, 57B1, F2
Viets assail 'proxy war' chrg 1-16, 43E1
To head counterintell oversight com 1-24, 49D2
Rpts Sovt, Cuban role in Ethiopia expanding 2-24, 137E1
Links SALT delay, Horn of Africa interventn 3-1, 178F3
Vs Jewish critics on Mideast 3-8; Jewish ldrs vs policy 3-9, 176B3
In Carter, Tito talks 3-8, 194C1
Brown vs A-weapons material ban 3-31, 277E2
At 26th Bilderberg Conf 4-21—4-23, 302C3
Reassures Mideast jet sale opponents 5-15—5-16, 358C1
In China; backs ties, scores USSR 5-20—5-22; briefs Japan 5-23—5-24, 384D2
In S Korea, US support assured 5-24—5-25; ldrs skeptical 5-29, 399C2
SALT, US global views rptd discussed in China 5-27, 5-29, 399G1
Scores USSR, Cuba; cites Africa role 5-28; Pravda denounces 5-30, 399B1
Evaluates US SALT offer 5-28, 422C3
Carter stresses unified Admin forgn policy 6-8—6-26, 490E2, A3, G3
China airborne device sale rptd 6-9, 436G1
Castro scores Zaire chrgs 6-13, 442B3; calls 'liar' 6-18, 687B2
Brezhnev warns vs China ties 6-25, 488B3
At Carter mtg on security leaks 7-11, 524G2
Vs USSR oil equipmt sale 9-6, 743D1
In Camp David summit talks 9-7, 673E1
Giscard gives Leb peace plan 10-2, 745F1
US OKs West arms sales to China 11-9, 901D3
US rebuts Sovt chrg on Iran 11-19, 893F3
Carter rptd critical of pol intellignc 11-25, 917C1
On human rights issue 12-6, 934D1
Teng invited to US 12-11, 974D1
US-China ties agreed 12-14, 973G2
Reassures Dobrynin re US-China tie 12-15, Pravda scores 12-19, 976G1
Giscard talks re US-China tie rptd 12-16, 977C1
Arms sales talks dispute rptd 12-19, 996D3
Defends China negotiatns 12-20, 975E3, 996F1
Criticized in US Iran intelligence feud 12-20, 994E2
BRZOZOWSKI, Andrzej
Landscape After Battle released 2-9, 619F2
BUARQUE de Holanda, Sergio
Founds pro-democracy center 8-1, 646E3
BUBACK, Siegfried (d. 1977)
Dutch protest for Baader-Meinhof 3-14, 192G1
Goettingen U editors fined 4-5, 353D3
Yugo arrests 4 W Ger terrorists 5-11, 438G3
Slaying suspect killed 9-6, 724F3
Speitel captured 9-24, 885A1
Folkerts extradited 10-17, 885D1
BUBLIK, Viktor
Walk to Sweden rptd 11-1, 947A1
BUCARAM, Asaad
Rightist, center-left parties vs pres bid 1-6, 1-13, 111G3
Backs new const 1-14, 111G3
Arrested 1-15, freed 2-4, 112A1

1979

BRUNNER, Guido
On Iran oil cutoff impact 2-13, 126E2
Scores OPEC price hike 3-28, 227F3
Scores US oil import subsidy 5-30, 417G1
Energy plan proposed 6-13, 437F1
Carter energy plan praised 7-16, 534G3
BRUNO, Vincent
Strike collapses 3-4, 165G3
BRUNSWICK Steam Electric Plant—*See NORTH Carolina—Atomic Energy*
BRUSHY Mountain State Prison, Tenn.—*See TENNESSEE*
BRUTON v. U.S.
Case cited by Sup Ct 5-29, 422A1
BRYAN Jr., Judge Albert V.
Named to wiretap ct 5-18, 442D3
Sentences Madsen for espionage 10-26, 831F3
BRYAN, Wayne
Festival opens 5-7, 711A3
BRYANT, Bobby
NFL '78 interceptn ldr 1-6, 80G1
BRYANT, Gunnery Sgt. Charles L.
Marines suspend 6-27, beating incident probed 7-7, 520B1
BRYANT, Hazel J.
Second Thoughts opens 5-4, 712C2
BRYANT, Robert M.
Sentenced in GSA scandal 5-30, 964B3
BRYANT, Judge William B.
Vesco jury foreman resigns, claims cover-up 8-29, 647G2
Vesco case perjury comments denied by Heymann 8-30; rejects jury foreman resignatn 9-7, 725G2, C3
Cuts '71 protesters' award 12-13, 991G2
BRYN Mawr (Pa.) College
McPherson removed as Wilson Coll trustee 5-26, 482E1
BRZEZINSKI, Zbigniew
Addresses businessmen on China ties impact 1-15, Admin controversy denied 1-16, 27A2
Host to Teng 1-28, 66B2
Seeks Saudi, Jordan support for Israel-Egypt pact 3-17—3-18; rpts on missn 3-19; Hussein scores 3-20, 197B2, 198D1
Backs SALT II ratificatn 4-4, 257G2, 258B1
USSR dissident-spy swap talks rptd 4-27, 317D1
Defends 'new diplomacy' 5-1, 347F1, C2
Sees OAS ambs, explains US 'globalism' 5-10, 416D3
Lauds Israeli protest vs setlmt 6-10; Begin criticizes 6-11, 436C2
Cited in SALT II communique 6-18, 457B1
S Korea troop exit halted 7-20, 567F2
Access to Carter cited 7-25, 556F1
Warns Sovts vs Afghan role 8-2, 580C2
Strauss rpts on Mideast missn 8-21, 623G2
Carter denies Strauss feud on Mideast mediator role 8-22, 623D3
USSR bars book entry 9-4, 690E1
On Sovt troops in Cuba 9-8, 673D1
Sees Nicaragua junta ldrs 9-24, 731D3
Rebuts Ford re SALT criticism 9-27, 739A3
Morocco arms sale rptd backed 10-22, 804B1
Meets Bazargan in Algiers 11-1, Iran clergy vs mtg 11-4, 842B2
Sees intl pressure vs Iran 12-9, 933F2
Assures Pak on Afghan coup 12-30, 974A2
BUA, Judge Nicholas J.
Rules Chicago patronage illegal 9-24, 770D3
BUCARAM, Assad
Roldos wins pres bid 4-29, 329G3
Roldos Cabt resigns 11-29; meets Roldos 12-4, new Cabt named 12-9, 967A3-968A1

1980

BRUNO, Angelo
Slain 3-21, 237B2
BRUNSON, Larry
NFL '79 kick return ldr 1-5, 8C3
BRUSATI, Franco
To Forget Venice released 1-28, 216F3
BRUSSTAR, Warren
Phillies win NL pennant 10-12, 796G1
In World Series 10-14—10-21, 812C2
BRUZELIUS, Nils J.
Wins Pulitzer 4-14, 296F2
BRYAN, William Jennings (1860-1925)
Vance resignatn compared 4-28, 323D2
Hicks dies 6-27, 528A2
Mondale compares Reagan 9-19, 780E2
BRYANT, Anita
Files for divorce 5-22, 471D3
Divorce rptd 8-21, 639C1
BRYANT, Chris
Awakening released 10-31, 972C3
BRYANT, Cullen
Steelers win Super Bowl 1-20, 61C3-62C1
BRYANT, Paul (Bear)
Alabama wins natl title 1-2, 23A1
BRYANT, Rosalyn
Sets indoor 440-yd dash mark 2-29, 892D1
BRYANT, Judge William B.
Vesco grand jury ends 4-1, 251E3
2 FBI ex-offcls convicted 11-6, 884F2
Drops chrgs against Gray 12-11, 940G1
Sentences 2 FBI ex-offcls 12-15, 963A3
BRYANT v. Yellin
Case decided by Sup Ct 6-16, 511E2
BRYN Mawr (Pa.) College
Carpenter dies 1-2, 104B2

BRZEZINSKI, Zbigniew
Arrives Pak, reassures India 2-1; in defense talks 2-2—2-3; briefs Saudis 2-4—2-5, 83A1-G1
Pakistan dismisses aid offer 3-6, 165C2
Says Sovts vs Afghan settlemt 3-12, 205D1
On shah's move to Egypt 3-23, 218A1
Muskie named secy of state 4-29, 323F2
Muskie denies possible rivalry 5-7, 343E1
Signed oath re leaks 7-16—7-17, 549A2
B Carter Libyan mtg rptd 7-22, 549B1
Carter rpts on brother's Libyan role 8-4, 593G2, C3, E3, 594E2
A-war strategy revised 8-5, 595A1; Muskie not consulted 8-8, 615E2, D3
Sullivan scores Iran '79 policy 9-6, 694B1
Testifies in B Carter probe 9-17, 701F1-A2
NSC Africa memo called forgery 9-17, 726G3
Sen subcom issues critical rpt in B Carter case 10-2, 763F3-764A1, E1
Scores W Ger mil spending target 12-18, 950B1
BUBACK, Siegfried (d. 1977)
Folkerts sentenced 7-31, 581B1
BUCARAM, Assad
Roldos calls plebiscite on const reform, breaks with CFP 4-11, 312A1
Roldos cancels plebiscite 5-19, 462B3

1976

BUCHAN, Alistair
Dies 2-4, 123D3
Kissinger mem'l address 6-25, 466D1
BUCHANAN, J. Judd
Sworn pub works min 9-15, 692E1
BUCHANAN Jr., Rep. John Hall (R, Ala.)
Reelected 11-2, 828G2
BUCHEN, Philip W.
Sees Curtis on Morton role 1-19, 41E2
OKs Ford tax info release 9-30, 761E1
On Ford '73 IRS audit, funds issue 10-8, 764B1-A2
BUCKLEY, Sen. James L. (Conservative-R, N.Y.)
Testifies vs Concorde 1-5, 5B3
Sup Ct rules on campaign law 1-30, 86F1
Kissinger letter released 3-29, 232B3
Rptd Ford vp prospect 8-10, 584E1
GOP vp poll rptd 8-11, 583F3
GOP pres bid promoted 8-11, 8-12, 584A3
Withdraws GOP pres bid 8-16, 615E3
Wins NY Sen primary 9-14, 687F2
Rptdly seeks Brown dismissal 10-20, 787C3
AMA donatn rptd 10-22, 938E3
Loses reelection 11-2, 819C3, E3, 821F2
Medicaid abortn stay barred 11-8, 848A2
BUCKLEY, Sheila
Trial begins 4-27, 313E1
Convicted 8-6, 589B1
BUCKLEY Jr., William F.
Saving the Queen on best seller list 2-29, 208E3; 12-5, 972F2
GOP conv vp vote table 8-19, 599E3
Carter, Ford debate 10-22, 800E3
BUCKNER, Bill
NL batting ldr 10-4, 795F3
BUCYRUS-Erie Co.
Vows no boycott compliance 3-18, 747B2
BUDDHISM
South Vietnam Developments—*See VIETNAM, South*
BUDEIRY, Brig. Gen. Misbah
Released 6-23, 448F2
BUENA Vista, Calif.—*See CALIFORNIA*
BUFFALO, N.Y.—*See NEW York State*
BUFFALO Courier-Express (newspaper)
Ford endorsement rptd 10-30, 831F2
BUFFALO Forge Co.
Sup Ct rules vs sympathy strike injunctns 7-6, 535G1
BUFFALO News (newspaper)
Ford endorsement rptd 10-30, 831F2
BUFKIN, David
Named in Angola trial 6-11, 480F2
BUGLIOSI, Vincent
Helter Skelter on best seller list 1-25, 80C3; 2-29, 208F3
BUJUKOV, Nikolai
Wins Olympic medal 2-8, 159C1
BUKHARI, Ijaz
On WHO anti-Israel stand 5-19, 355D2
BUKOVSKY, Vladimir
Eur Parlt scores mistreatmt 7-9, 540B3
Exchngd for Corvalan 12-18; press conf 12-19, 955D2-F3
BULGARIA—*See also COMECON, DISARMAMENT—Geneva Committee, WARSAW Pact*
Census results rptd 1-3, 104C2
Listed as 'not free' nation 1-19, 20D3
Balkan natns meet 1-26—2-5, 213E3
Castro visits, sees Zhivkov 3-8—3-12, 251C3
11th CP Cong held 3-29—4-2, 250B1
Zhivkov in Greece 4-9—4-11, 333A2
Yugo sentences Cominformists 4-14, 542G3
Shuns China fete for Egypt vp 4-19, 275A3
Vs Chile at UNCTAD conf 5-5, 320C2
'75 Sovt trade rptd 5-5, 340F3
Addresses E Ger SED cong 5-19, 381A2
Canada amb named 7-7, 910E2
China quake casualty data rptd 8-1, 562C1
UK corp truck pact rptd 9-8, 910E2
Role in Sovt space program set 9-14, 684D1
Rpt US seizes fishing boat 9-30; 3 ask asylum 10-15, 910D2
Sovt-Egypt talks in Sofia 11-3—11-4, 841F2
European Force Reduction Issues—*See under EUROPE*
Sports
Olympic results 7-18—7-31, 573C3, 574A1, C1, 576G1-E3
BULLFIGHTING
Sidney Franklin dies 4-26, 368F2
BULLOCK, Judge J. Robert
Sets Gilmore executn date 12-15, 952F1
BULTMANN, Rudolf
Dies 7-30, 816E3
BUMPERS, Sen. Dale (D, Ark.)
Scores Sen subcoms 4-4, 247A2
BUNDY, William P.
Answers Allon on map use 9-17, 699A3
BUNGE Corp.
Mulloy sentncd in grain probe 1-9, 43E3
6 ex-employes sentncd 2-4, 135E3
Grain abuse plan cited 3-16, 248C1
Ex-inspector rptd indicted 9-13, 990D3
BUNKER, Ellsworth
Testifies on Panama Canal talks 4-8; testimony released 4-13; on Panama control of zone 4-15, 291G2
Canal talks continue 10-19—10-26, 12-13—12-18, 1008F1
Canal talks suit thrown out 12-18, 1008E2

1977

BUCHANAN, J. Judd
Named Canada science min 9-16, 725B3
BUCHANAN, Patrick J.
On Nixon-Frost interview 5-16, 367G3
BUCHANAN Jr., Wiley T.
Replaced as amb to Austria 6-22, 626F3
BUCKLEY, James L.
'76 specl interest gifts rptd 2-15, 128E2
BUCKLEY, William F.
Sup Ct bars libel case review 1-17, 58B1
BUCKNER, Milt
Dies 7-27, 604F2
BUDGET, U.S.—*See under U.S. GOVERNMENT*
BUDKER, Gersh
Dies 7-6, 604F2
BUFALINO, Russell A.
Sentenced 10-21, 991D3
BUFFALO, N.Y.—*See NEW York State*
BUFFER Stocks—*See COMMODITIES*
BUFKIN, David
On Cuba-Rhodesia spy plan 1-10, 17A3
Rpt CIA denies hiring 1-16, 61D1
CIA denies Zaire mercenary recruitmt 4-17, 317D3
BUGGING—*See WIRETAPPING & Electronic Surveillance*
BUHLER, Frederic
Chrgd with fraud 8-15, 658D1
BUJNOWSKI, Arthur J.
'76 St Thomas crash probe rptd 3-6, 312A2
BUKOVSKY, Vladimir
French CP scores USSR 1-6, 63D2
In US, urges rights stand 2-23—3-1; USSR scores 2-24, 142G2
USSR scores Carter rights stance 3-2, 3-21, 226D1, E1
US scores Shcharansky chrg 6-2, 436F1
Addresses AFL-CIO 12-12, 961D1
BULGARIA—*See also COMECON, DISARMAMENT—Geneva Committee, WARSAW Pact*
2 die in Sovt hotel blaze 2-25, 204D2
Earthquake kills 50 3-4, 204F1
Velchev ousted 5-12, 451E2
Single party-state ldr cited 6-16, 469F2
Charter jet crashes in Libya 12-2, 992E2
Foreign Relations (misc.)
UN Assemb member 3G3
UK 200-mile limit in effect 1-1, 21A1
'76 OECD trade gap rptd 1-26, 123D2
Spain ties rptd renewed 1-27, 242C2
UN chrgs Rhodesia sanctn violatns 2-10, 123A1
Westn debt rptd mounting 2-13—4-13, 335C3
Exiles ask W Eur CP support 2-23, 314C2
Colombia studts ban emb car 3-25, 347C2
Newsman gets French asylum 7-7, 606G2
Eurocommunism rptd scored 7-8, 590B3
Argentina seizes 2 fishing boats 10-1, 944F2
Malta premr provokes walkout in Peking 11-3, 925G2
Helsinki Agreement—*See EUROPE—Security and Cooperation*
U.S. Relations
US adopts fishing agrmt 2-21, 173D3
Garthoff named US amb 7-28, 626E2
Travel limits eased 11-9, 989E1
BUMBA Moasso Djogo, Gen.
Replaced as Army staff chief 4-5, 265E2
BUMBRY, Al
AL batting ldr 10-2, 926F3
BUMPERS, Sen. Dale (D, Ark.)
On DNA research regulatn 2-4, 184C3
BUNCONJIC, Marijan
Invades UN missn 6-14, held 6-16, 497D2
BUNDY, McGeorge
On Ford quitting foundatn 1-12, 56D1
BUNGE Corp.
Rail grain-car deals curbed 8-1, 613D1
BUNKER, Ellsworth
Rpts Canal accord 8-10, begins ratificatn campaign 8-16; House com scores 8-17, 621D1, 622C1-A2
Sees Reagan, Canal pact fight vowed 8-25, 678G2
Canal pact ratificatn campaign underway 9-7, 678G3
On Panama rights record 9-8, 699E1
Testifies on Canal talks tap rpt 9-16, 9-19, 716D2
Testifies on Canal pact discrepancies 9-26, 754F2, D3

1978

Pres bid barred, protests 2-20, 148G1
Pres vote won by son-in-law 7-16, runoff set 7-18, 557B1
BUCARO, Col. Hugo Tulio
Guatemala finance min 7-21, 722D3 ★
BUCHANAN, J. Judd
Canada Treas Bd pres 11-24, 921C3
BUCHANAN, John
Wins Nova Scotia electn 9-19, 739B2
BUCHANAN Jr., Rep. John Hall (R, Ala.)
Reelected 11-7, 850B1
BUCHER, Gaetan
Heads DR sugar cncl 8-25, 774D2
BUCHHOLZ, Earl (Butch)
WTT clubs fold 10-27—11-11; plans new franchises 12-1, 1027B1
BUCK, Harold
Spinks decisns Ali 2-15, 171C1
BUCKEYE Pipeline Co.—*See PENN Central*
BUCKLER, Annerose Lottmann
Error in Schleyer hunt rptd 3-7, 332D2
BUCKLEY, Robert A.
Hello Dolly opens 3-5, 887A2
BUCKLEY Jr., William F.
Stained Glass on best-seller list 7-2, 579C3
BUCKNER, Bill
NL batting ldr 10-2, 928D2
BUCY, J. Fred
Vs USSR oil equipmt sale 9-6, 743D1
BUDD Co.
Takeover bid revealed 1-6, Thyssen named suitor 1-12, talks OKd 1-17, 66A2
BUDDHISM
China curbs rptd eased 3-10, 294E1
Thien Minh death rptd 10-26, 888F3
BUDDY Holly Story, The (film)
Released 7-21, 969E3
BUDGET, U.S.—*See under U.S. GOVERNMENT*
BUERKLE, Dick
Sets indoor mile run record 1-13, wins Wanamaker 1-27, 76D2, B3
BUFFALO, N.Y.—*See NEW York State*
BUFORD, Terri
Switzerland trip re cult money rptd 12-15, denied by lawyer 12-16; testifies 12-21, 1000E1
Grand jury questions 12-21, 1000D1
BUGGING—*See WIRETAPPING*
BUILDING & Builders—*See CONSTRUCTION Industry, HOUSING*
BUJOLD, Genevieve
Coma released 2-1, 619B1
BUKICH, Steve
UCLA ties in Fiesta Bowl 12-25, 1025E2
BUKREYEV, Vladimir
Tied to KGB, quits ILO post 676D1
BULA Hoyos, German
Colombia agri min 8-7, 629D3
BULGAKOV, Mikhail
Moliere opens 3-12, 887B2
Master & Margarita opens 11-11, 1031D2
BULGARIA—*See also COMECON, DISARMAMENT—Geneva Committee, WARSAW Pact*
'77 agri output down, other econ results rptd 2-9, 531A1
Sofia air crash kills 73 3-16, 271A1
Dissident manifesto rptd 4-3, 276F1
Agri officials ousted 4-29, 530F3
Intl CP conf 12-15, 1020C1
European Force Reduction Talks—*See under EUROPE*
Foreign Relations (misc.)
EC imposes steel dumping levies 1-23, 80B2
Yugo disputes Macedonians, chrgs UN Charter violatns 6-15—6-25, 531B1
4 W Ger terrorists arrested, extradited 6-22, 500A1
Danes give envoy asylum 7-26, 688D1
UK defector dies 9-11, ruled murder 9-29; 2d defector found dead 10-2; French, US incidents rptd 9-14, 748C3
UN Assemb member 713C3
Rumania troop entry refusal cited 11-25, 913B3
Helsinki Agreement—*See EUROPE—Security and Cooperation*
BULGARI of Rome
Stolen diamond recovered in autopsy 5-4, 380F1
BULL, John S.
On Kennecott bd rival slate 3-27, 402G3
BULLY, John
Loses Dominica pres electn 12-21, 1021G2
BULUTOGLU, Kenan
Named Turkey econ managemt min 1-5, 21F2
BUMPERS, Sen. Dale (D, Ark.)
Votes for Panama Canal neutrality pact 3-16, 177D2
Votes for 2d Canal pact 4-18, 273B1
Carter A-breeder deal threatens gas compromise support 8-26, 678C1
BUNDY, McGeorge
Warns vs excessive CIA curbs 4-19, 306F2
BUNKER, Edward
Straight Time released 3-18, 619G3

1979

BUCCI, Frank
Gold wins ASL title 9-16, 776C2
BUCHANAN, Beau
Peoples Temple tape copy rptd 3-15, 219G2
BUCHANAN, Edgar
Dies 4-4, 356C3
BUCHANON, Willie
NFL '78 interceptn ldr 1-6, 80G1
BUCHELI, Fausto
Kidnaped 9-21, 729D2
Freed 11-7, 872F2
BUCHNER, Georg
Woyzeck released 8-24, 820F3
BUCKLEY, John
On heating fuel supply 10-11, 786B3
BUCKLEY Jr., William F.
Admits misled in '57 Smith case 1-22, 78G3
Settles SEC charge 2-7, 132A1
BUCK Rogers (film)
Released 3-29, 528E1
BUDDHISM
Carter discloses Park conversn effort 8-5, 639C2
BUDDY Holly Story, The (film)
Renzetti wins Oscar 4-9, 336B2
BUDGE, Don
Borg named '78 top player 1-18, 103G2
BUDGET, U.S.—*See under U.S. GOVERNMENT*
BUERKLE, Dick
Coghlan wins Wanamaker Mile 2-9, 911C2
BUETTNER-Janusch, John
Indicted 10-4, 839G3
BUFALINI, Paolo
Dropped from Italy CP secretariat 7-10, 525F3
BUFFALO, N.Y.—*See NEW York State*
BUFMAN, Zev
Peter Pan opens 9-6, 956G3
Oklahoma opens 12-13, 1007D2
BUFORD, Terri
Says most cult money in Panama 1-17, 117G2
BUGGING—*See WIRETAPPING*
BUGNINI, Msgr. Annibale
In Iran plea re US hostages 11-8—11-10, 862C2
BUIAN, Nicholas
Damage case declined by Sup Ct 4-23, 346G2
BUIAN v. Baughard
Case declined by Sup Ct 4-23, 346A3
BUILDING & Builders—*See CONSTRUCTION Industry, HOUSING*
BUJOLD, Genevieve
Murder By Decree released 2-8, 174B3
BUKOVSKY, Vladimir
'76 exchange cited 4-27, 317C1
BULGARIA—*See also COMECON, DISARMAMENT—Geneva Committee, WARSAW Pact*
Bible availability cited 3-13, 238F1
Hosp personnel cigaret ban rptd 3-19, 218F2
1st cosmonaut in flight 4-10—4-12, 279B2
Energy conservatn measures implemented 5-21, 397C1
Agri decentralizatn rptd 7-16, 741B3
2 women banned from track 10-26, 912A1
European Force Reduction Talks—*See under EUROPE*
Foreign Relations (misc.)
Cambodia downfall rptd lauded 1-10, 11A2
China invasn of Viet scored 2-19, 122F2
Israel-PLO prisoner swap aided 3-14, 178G2
Cosmonaut aboard Sovt Soyuz 33 4-10—4-12, 279B2
Westn investmt rptd OKd 9-8, 741D3
UN membership listed 695E2
USSR troop absence rptd 761G2
Taiwan trade bar affirmed 11-28, 952B3
Helsinki Agreement—*See EUROPE—Security and Cooperation*
U.S. Relations
US A-accident media coverage rptd 4-11, 323C1
BULLE, Ernest
Zimbabwe commerce min 5-30, 393E1
BULLFIGHTING
El Cordobes gives command performance 7-22, 656F3
BULLOCK, H. Ridgely
Utter Glory opens 5-13, 712C3
BULLOCK, Ridgely
Comin' Uptown opens 12-20, 1007C2
BULOFF, Joseph
The Price opens 4-19, 712B2
BUMBRY, Al
AL stolen base ldr 9-30, 955F3
Orioles win AL pennant 10-6, 797F2
In World Series 10-10—10-17, 816A1
BUNDY, McGeorge
Elliott dies 1-9, 104A3
Ford Foundatn retiremt set 1-30, 78D3
BUNDY, Theodore R.
Gets death penalty for '78 Fla slayings 7-31, 604C2

1980

BUCH, Henri
On rightist police infiltratn 10-4, 767F2
BUCHAN, John
39 Steps released 5-2, 416F3
BUCHANAN, Bessie A.
Dies 9-7, 755D2
BUCHANAN Jr., Rep. John Hall (R, Ala.)
Not in subcom Somali mil pact protest 8-28, 661B3
Loses Ala primary 9-2, 682E2
Smith wins seat 11-4, 849F1
BUCHANAN, Mary Estill
Wins Sen primary 9-9, 700D2
Loses US Sen electn 11-4, 846B3, 851C3
BUCHEGGER, Christine
Marionettes released 11-7, 972F3
BUCKLEY, James L.
At GOP platform hearings, urges fed responsibility shift; Sen bid cited 1-14, 32G1
Wins Sen primary 9-9, 700C2
Loses US Sen electn 11-4, 848B1
BUCKLEY Jr., William F.
Stained Glass wins Amer Book Award 5-1, 692F2
Cancels Vassar appearance 5-19, 471B2
BUCKNER, Bill
NL batting ldr 10-6, 926D2-F2
BUCYRUS-Erie Co. v. Department of Industry
Case declined by Sup Ct 1-14, 37C1
BUDDE, Brad
In NFL draft 4-29, 336F2
BUDGET, U.S.—*See under U.S. GOVERNMENT*
BUDLONG, Morrison
Sentenced 12-19, 997C3
BUEHNING, Fritz
Loses S African Open 12-2, 947A3
BUETTNER-Janusch, John
Convicted 7-16, 607F3-608A1
Sentenced 11-13, 997D3
BUFFALO—*See NY*
BUFMAN, Zev
West Side Story opens 2-14, 136G3
Brigadoon opens 10-16, 892A3
BUFORD, Gordon
Herbie Goes Bananas released 9-12, 836B3
BUGAR, Imrich
Wins Olympic medal 7-28, 624C1
BUGGING—*See WIRETAPPING*
BUGNINI, Msgr. Annibale
In Iran crisis media group 4-5, 258D1
Visits US hostages 12-25, 974G1
BUILDING (& Builders)—*See CONSTRUCTION Industry, HOUSING*
BUJOLD, Genevieve
Incorrigible released 3-3, 416B3
BULGARIA—*See also COMECON, CSCE, GENEVA Committee, MBFR, WARSAW Pact*
'79 econ rpt issued 1-23, 166E1
Foreign Relations (misc.)
USSR Afghan invasn backed 1-10, 11A1
Yugo scores re territorial claims 1-18, 49F2
Communists meet on USSR Afghan invasn 2-6—2-7, 109A2
UN anti-Sovt Afghan res opposed 2-14, 123E3
Joint venture law enacted 3-25, 365D2
Israeli parlt members meet Arafat 9-25, 736D3
Libya-Iran airlift rptdly uses airspace 10-10, 774D2
Iraq seeks arms 11-11—11-12, 879A3
Government & Politics—*See also other appropriate subheads in this section*
Chervenkov dies 10-21, 876B1
Sports
Lake Placid Olympic results 2-12—2-24, 154F2, 155F2-156D1
Moscow Olympic results 7-20—8-3, 588A3
BULL, Gerald
Admits S Africa arms sales 3-25, 278F1
BULLARD, Edward
Dies 4-3, 360C1
BULLFIGHTING
Colombia bullring collapse kills 222 1-21, 80C3
BULL Pen (play)
Opens 6-12, 756C3
BUMBRY, Al
AL batting, stolen base ldr 10-6, 926E3, F3
BUMPERS, Sen. Dale (D, Ark.)
Scores oil import fee 6-6, 437A2
Reelected 11-4, 840C1, 845A3, 849G1
BUNDY, Theodore R.
Gets 3d death sentence 2-12, 136C2
BUNGE, Bettina
Loses Women's Stockholm Open 11-2, 947C2
BUNIN, Charlotte
Act of Kindness opens 9-11, 756B3

1976

BURCH, Francis B.
Announces Pallotine pact 8-24, 951C1
BURCH, Rosabella
Named in Getty will 6-8, 444D2
BURDEN, Don W.
FCC ruling stands 5-24, 393E2
BURD & Fletcher Co.
Trust suit dvpts 2-18—10-5, 886C1, E2
BURDICK, Sen. Quentin N. (D, N.D.)
Reelected 11-2, 820D1, 823D3, 828A3
BURFEINDT, Betty
Wins LPGA title 5-30, 424C3
BURG, Yosef
Vs no-confidence motion 12-14, 964E3
Removed from Cabt 12-19, 964C3
BURGENER, Rep. Clair W. (R, Calif.)
Reelected 11-2, 829F1
BURGER, Heinrich & Kathryn
Seized on spy chrgs 6-14, 441E3
BURGER, Stanley C.
Wins Senate primary 6-1, 411F1
Loses election 11-2, 824A2
BURGER, Chief Justice Warren E(arl)—*For Supreme Court developments not listed here, see SUPREME Court under U.S. GOVERNMENT*
Scores Cong re fed judgeships 1-3, 24C2
Backs IRS emergency procedure 1-13, 23F3
Rules on campaign law 1-30, 86A3, 87A1-A2
Bars Red #2 dye ban delay 2-13, 137F1
Lauds fed judges, urges new judgeships 2-15, 136A3
Vs retroactive seniority 3-24, 218D2
Backs drug convictn ruling 4-27, 349B2
Backs FPC job bias powers 5-19, 393B3
Rejects Concorde case 5-22, 378G2
Rules on drug price ads 5-24, 393G1
Vs alien civil svc rule 6-1, 414B2
Vs guilty plea ruling 6-17, 552C3
Backs some church-coll aid 6-21, 452F3
For local zoning referendum 6-21, 453C1
Rules on US wage laws 6-24, 468D2
Vs patronage ousters bar 6-28, 468E3
Backs nonlawyer judge rule 6-28, 492E1
Vs press gag order 6-30, 491F3
Vs abortn rights extensn 7-1, 518E3
Marks Bicentennial 7-2, 489A2
Ct upholds death penalty; voids NC, La laws 7-2, 491G2, C3
For fed cts criminal appeals curb 7-6, 534E3
Backs sympathy strikes 7-6, 535E1
For review of Border Patrol car search 10-18, 867E2
Vs carry-back tax ruling 11-2, 867C2
Urges shorter briefs 11-9, 882B3
Vs MD office abortn rule 11-29, 900D3
Vs Gilmore executn stay 12-3, 952D2
Vs Austin busing plan 12-6, 920E2
Vs jury death sentnc rule 12-6, 920C3
Vs pregnancy benefits 12-7, 920E1
For pub employe contract debate right 12-8, 960A2
Vs Okla beer-buying rule 12-20, 960E1
BURGSTALLER, Eugen F.
Paris paper links to CIA 1-13, 49D3
BURKE, Rep. J. Herbert (R, Fla.)
Reelected 11-2, 829C2
BURKE Jr., Jack
Named to PGA Hall of Fame 1-27, 123G2
BURKE, Rep. James A. (D, Mass.)
Reelected 11-2, 829C4

1977

BUNKER, Laurence
Dies 10-10, 872B1
BURBANK, Calif.—*See CALIFORNIA*
BURCH, Francis B.
Baltimore press suit setld 5-26, 504B2
Rules on Mandel governorshp 8-25, 652C1
BURDICK, Sen. Quentin N. (D, N.D.)
Scores IJC rpt on Garrison 9-16, 726C1
BURFIENDT, Betty
2d in Muscular Dystrophy Open 9-5, 951D1
BURG, Yosef
Israel interior min 6-20, 474E2
BURGER, Chief Justice Warren E(arl)—*For Supreme Court developments not listed here, see U.S. GOVERNMENT—SUPREME Court*
Issues annual rpt 1-1, 15F1-C2
Swears in Carter, photo 1-20, 25A1, F1
Swears in Cabt members 1-23—1-27, 52E2, A3, C3
Vs racial voter redistricting 3-1, 175B1
Rules on old-age benefits bias 3-21, 230C2
Rules on deaths sentencing 3-22, 231B1
For Miranda rule review 3-23, 276D1
Vs double jeopardy protectn rule 4-4, 341C3
Curbs license-plate slogans 4-20, 342E2
Watergate appeals decisn leaked 4-21, 382C2
Vs inmate legal aid 4-27, 383E1
Disputes high ct critics 5-17, 419E2-B3
Addresses ABA conf 5-27, 444C3
Backs Fla retroactive death sentnc 6-17, 518C2
Vs Justice Dept warrantless searches 6-21, 539D1
Backs Detroit remedial educ bias progrms 6-27, 538B3
Vs US custody of Nixon papers 6-28, 539F3
Backs executn for rape 6-29, 557E2
Hears Bakke case arguments 10-12, 835F1
Backs bowhead whaling ban 10-24, 835G1
Legal scholar scores Sup Ct rulings 10-31, 879A1
Blocks FBI use of Scientology documts 12-8, 940F2
Backs mandatory pensn-plan retiremts 12-12, 960B2
BURGHOFF, Gary
Wins Emmy 9-11, 1022A1
BURGLARY—*See CRIME—Robberies*
BURKE, Glenn
In World Series 10-11—10-18, 806G1

1978

BUNKER, George M.
On Kennecott bd rival slate 3-27, 402G3
BUNZ, Dan
In NFL draft 5-2, 336G2
BURCH, Preston M.
Dies 4-4, 356C2
BURDEN, Carter
Wins US House nominatn 1-15, overturned 1-18, 108G1-A2
BURDEN, William Douglas
Dies 11-14, 972F2
BURDICK, Sen. Quentin N. (D, N.D.)
Votes vs Panama Canal neutrality pact 3-16, 177F2
Votes vs 2d Canal pact 4-18, 273B1
Visits USSR 11-11—11-18, 905A2
BURGENER, Rep. Clair W. (R, Calif.)
Reelected 11-7, 850C2
BURGER, Chief Justice Warren E(arl)—*For Supreme Court developments not listed here, see U.S. GOVERNMENT—SUPREME Court*
Issues annual rpt, urges jury selectn chngs 1-1, 12D3
Vs trust suits by forgn natns 1-11, 33B3
Trial lawyer competency disputed 2-10—2-13, defends criticism 2-12, 107F3
For Mo univ Gay Lib status review 2-21, 125E3
Vs limited immunity for prison offcls 2-22, 126E2
Backs Indian ct trials of non-Indians 3-6, 162E1
Backs state police alien ban 3-22, 221B1
Vs NH gov flag-lowering curb 3-24, 221E2
Backs cities' liability under trust law 3-29, 280C2
Vs Minn pensn funds law 4-3, 309A1
Vs clergy pub office ban 4-19, 309D1
Vs bar on sex-based pensn plans 4-25, 322E3
Backs corp free speech, warns media giants 4-26, 343F3
Vs Va judicial inquiry law 5-1, 363B3
Vs utility customer hearings 5-1, 364B1
Urges improved law student skills, discounts Carter criticism 5-16, 388C2
Backs corp takeover tax liability 5-22, 388G1
Backs exclusn of children from porno rule 5-23, 405B3
Backs natural gas diversn 5-31, 431C1
Vs NH rape law ruling 6-5, 431D2
Backs munic legal immunity 6-6, 447A2
Backs FBI informant case review 6-12, 468E1
Vs lengthening double jeopardy protectn 6-14, 468G3
Backs rare fish vs Tellico Dam 6-15, 468B2
Vs IRS summons power 6-19, 492G2
Vs union pol organizing 6-22, 508D3
Vs computer program patent curbs 6-22, 509D1
Vs Ark prison attys added fees 6-23, 566A2
Backs NJ waste dumping law 6-23, 566C2
Vs press prison data access 6-26, 566B3
Vs evidence hearing rules 6-26, 566F3
Backs Grand Central office complex 6-26, 567A1
Backs Bakke med schl admissn, vs race-based affirmative actn principle 6-28, 481F1, C2
Backs juvenile case reviews 6-28, 567G1
Backs US offcls' legal immunity 6-29, 567E2
Backs gypsum price fixing ruling 6-29, 567A3
Vs Ohio death penalty law 7-3, 552E1
Voting alignmts shift noted 7-3, 565E3-566C1
Urges judgeshp bill passage 7-23, 626D3
Addresses ABA, renews trial lawyer criticism 8-9, 626A2, G2-A3
Urges study of US govt 9-21, 751F2
Rejects RR strike appeal 9-26, 809A3
Intervenes re bankruptcy bill 9-28, Cong clears 10-6, 788E2, D3
Receives Fordham Stein Award, defends judicial lobbying 10-25, 832D3
Urges new fed ct 12-4, 958E3, G3
Backs extraditn probe bar 12-18, 981G1
BURGER Chef Systems Inc.—*See under GENERAL Foods*
BURGESS, Joyce Tillerson
Sentncd in '72 hijacking 11-23, 926F3
BURGESS, W. Randolph
Dies 9-16, 778A1
BURGHARDT, Arthur
Amen Corner opens 4-22, 760B1
BURGLARY—*See CRIME—Robbery*
BURGUET, Frantz-Andre
Servant & Mistress released 6-6, 619F3
BURGUND, Reynolds
On deal to build China hotels 11-9, 880B2
BURIED Child (play)
Opens 11-6, 1031B1
BURKE, Rep. J. Herbert (R, Fla.)
Wins renominatn 9-12, 734C3
Pleads guilty on 2 bar chrgs, no contest on 3d 9-26, 734G2
Loses reelectn 11-7, 846D2, 849E3
BURKE, Jack
Sues PGA over exemptn rule 1-23, 76G1
BURKE, Rep. James A. (D, Mass.)
Donnelly wins seat 11-7, 847D3
BURKE, John R.
On Guyana cult suicide victims 11-21, 891B1

1979

BUONO, Angelo
Chrgd in 'Hillside Stranglings' 10-19, 818F2
BURCH v. La.
Case upheld by Sup Ct 4-17, 325F3
BURCKNER, Clara
All-Round Reduced Personality released 4-23, 528A1
BUREAU, The: My 30 Years in Hoover's FBI (book)
Posthumous publicatn rptd set 6-24, 521B1
BURG, Yosef
Palestinian autonomy talks open 5-25, 394G1-A2
Palestinian autonomy talks held 7-29—7-31, warns vs state 8-2, 574D3
Vs Res 242 change 8-6, 591D3
Backs Dayan on US policy shift chrg 8-7, 591F2
Autonomy talks held, sees Palestinian entry 9-26—9-27, 740A3
BURGER, Heinrich
Prisoner exchange rptd 7-20, 586D2
BURGER, Chief Justice Warren Earl—*For Supreme Court developments not listed here, see U.S. GOVERNMENT—SUPREME Court*
Backs Pa abortn control law 1-9, 14A2
Names special prosecutor panel 1-12, 56F1
At Rockefeller funeral 2-2, 104D2
Notes bail crime rise, scores trial judges 2-11, 130D1
Vs Blue Shield drug plan trust rule 2-27, 165A2
Backs nonpatent royalties 2-28, 165D2
Backs single-sex alimony 3-5, 184E2
Vs broader grant of immunity 3-20, 204D1
Vs church schl labor interventn 3-21, 231F2
Vs LA fire dept bias case finding 3-27, 263A2
Hears Weber case argumt 3-28, 263B1
Fires Sup Ct worker re news leaks 4-20, 302F2; transferred to Govt Printing Office 4-27, 382B3
Vs unwed father adoptn consent role 4-24, 364E1
Backs Okla minnow sale ban 4-24, 364D2
Backs tighter mental hosp commitmt standard 4-30, 364F2
Replaced as Natl Gallery bd chrmn 5-3, 375E1
Discloses finances 5-16, 382C2
Names 10 to wiretap ct 5-18, 442A3
Backs state age bias filing time limit 5-21, 400G2
Backs state parole discretn 5-29, 421G2
Backs some punitive damages vs unions 5-29, 421E3
Vs sex-bias suits vs congressmen 6-5, 464D1
Vs 'probable cause' in detentns 6-5, 464F2
Backs consumers' right to sue 6-11, 478F2
Vs use of 'open-ended' warrants 6-11, 478B3
Backs broader Cong legal immunity 6-18, 498E3
Backs child mental commitmt rules 6-20, 515F3
Backs end to AFDC-UF welfare plan 6-25, 540A1
Backs 'good faith' arrest 6-25, 540D1
Backs Mass driver license suspensn rule 6-25, 540G1
Assails 2 admitted to Sup Ct bar 6-25, 541B1
Backs broader libel suit rights 6-26, 540A3
Backs Weber affirmative actn challenge 6-27, 477A2
Vs eased criminal evidence standard 6-28, 558B3
Backs ctroom pub access curbs 7-2, 515F2
'78-79 Sup Ct term ends, voting alignmt rptd 7-2, 558A1
Vs Dayton (O) busing order 7-2, 539B3
Vs power to void state convictns 7-2, 559A1
Vs Ga laws in church land dispute 7-2, 559C1
Vs Mass abortn-consent law 7-2, 559B2
Comments on trial closures 8-8, 630G2
Backs Amtrak KC train cut 9-30, 868D1
Backs 'exclusionary rule' case review 10-1, 768B3
Hears govt minority constructn grants case argumts 11-27, 945B1
Backs extended searches 11-28, 944B3
'Brethren' publicatn stirs controversy 12-2, 988A2
Swears in Hufstedler 12-6, 946F2
Vs Taiwan treaty case review 12-13, 940C1
BURGER King—*See PILLSBURY Co.*
BURGESS, Guy
Spy ring scandal reopened 10-28, 10-29, 873G3
Blunt named 4th spy 11-15, issues statemt 11-20, 908D2-B1, 909D1
BURGLARY—*See CRIME—Robbery*
BURHENNE, Dr. H. Joachim
Removes gallstone from shah 11-26, 897F1
BURIED Child (play)
Shepard wins Pulitzer 4-16, 336E2, G2
BURKE, John R.
State Dept rpt finds Guyana cult probe neglect 5-3, 335F3

1980

BUPRENORPHINE—*See MEDICINE—Drugs & Health-Care Products*
BURDICK, Sen. Quentin N. (D, N.D.)
Scores farm amendmt 12-4, 954F3
BURG, Yosef
Egypt vs autonomy plan 1-17; sees Egypt hard line 1-20, 48C2
Autonomy talks progress 1-31—2-1, 89G1
Autonomy talks speedup OKd 3-17, 219F1
Misses Hebron setlmt vote 3-24, 218C3
On Egypt autonomy talks delay 5-15, 362C2
Autonomy talks renewal OKd 7-2—7-3, 539D1
Denies major concessn in autonomy talks 10-14, 775C3
Orders Israeli police chief ousted 12-31, 994D3
BURGENER, Rep. Clair W. (R, Calif.)
Reelected 11-4, 842C2, 852C2
BURGER, Norbert
Loses Austria pres electn 5-18, 388G1
BURGER, Chief Justice Warren Earl—*For Supreme Court developments not listed here, see U.S. GOVERNMENT—SUPREME Court*
'79 judiciary study rptd 1-3, 51F2
Backs trust suits vs real estate brokers 1-8, 16E1
Gives 'State of Judiciary' address 2-3, 114E2
Backs contd abortn aid order stay 2-19, 130A3
Backs testimony by spouse 2-27, 188C2
Backs Cleveland busing challenge review 3-17, 225G3
Backs 'insider' stock trading convictn 3-18, 226F2
Backs Tex porno film restraints 3-18, 226F3
Vs state legislators' immunity 3-19, 249D3
Vs class actn 'moot' standard redefinitn 3-19, 250E1
Backs inmate mental health case dismissal 3-25, 265F2
Backs warrantless home arrests 4-15, 306E1
Not in Indian land managemt liability rule 4-15, 306G1
Backs 'good faith' municipal immunity 4-16, 328A3
Vs multiple sentencing curbs 4-16, 328C3
Hears abortn funding cases 4-21, 306C3
Backs at-large local electns 4-22, 343D2
Vs prisoners right to sue 4-22, 343G3
Declines Wilmington (Del) busing case review 4-28, 368F3
Backs police interrogatn rule 5-12, 386G2
Vs EEOC class actn process avoidance 5-12, 426B2
Finances rptd 5-15, 555C3
Backs Ga death penalty applicatn 5-19, 440B1
Vs land-grant exchng ban 5-19, 440B2
Warns vs ct system 'merger' 6-10, 632D1
Backs GE microbe patent 6-16, 453A1
Vs use of jail informants 6-16, 511B3
Pretrial data secrecy rule rptd OKd by Judicial Conf 6-19, takes effect 8-1, 632A1
Vs Ill non-labor picketing rights 6-20, 555E2
Vs container pact ban refusal 6-20, 555G2
Vs donated porno warrants 6-20, 555B3
Vs cts power to suppress evidence 6-23, 554E3
Vs lawyer legal fee penalty 6-23, 555B1
Vs broader right to sue states 6-25, 540F3
Backs Medicaid abortn funding limits 6-30, 491G3
Backs govt minority constructn grants 7-2, 510D1-F1
Backs open criminal trials 7-2, 510G2-A3
'79-80 Sup Ct term ends, voting alignmts rptd 7-2, 540B2
5th judicial circuit split, backing cited 10-14, 918D3
Stays GOP campaign aid ruling 10-17, 856F1
Backs inmate legal fees case hearing 11-10, 868F1
Ctroom cameras case argued 11-12, 882C2
'Mr Justice' title dropped 11-14, 882A3
Backs Ky 10 Commandmts schl law 11-17, 881G3
Hears Nixon taps case 12-8, 937F2
Backs judicial pay hikes 12-15, 956F3-957D1
BURGESS, Guy
USSR honors Philby 7-15, 566A3
BURGLARY—*See CRIME—Robbery*
BURGMEIER, Tom
AL pitching ldr 10-6, 926G3
BURHOE, Ralph Wendell
Wins Templeton prize 5-13, 471D2
BURING, Julie E.
On saccharin cancer risk 3-6, 317A2

1976

BURKE, Richard
European Comm meets 12-22—12-23, 977G1
BURKE, Rep. Yvonne Brathwaite (D, Calif.)
Carter meets black leaders 7-12, 513C2
Seconds Brown at Dem conv 7-14, 506F1
Seconds Mondale at conv 7-15, 506B3
Reelected 11-2, 829D1
BURLESON, Rep. Omar (D, Tex.)
Reelected 11-2, 830E4
BURLINGTON, Vt.—*See VERMONT*
BURLINGTON Northern Inc.
'75 tax paymt rptd 10-2, 847A2
BURLISON, Rep. Bill D. (D, Mo.)
Travel expense probe ends 10-27, 981G3
Reelected 11-2, 830B1
BURMA—*See also ADB, DISARMAMENT—Geneva Committee, NONALIGNED Nations Movement*
Listed as 'not free' nation 1-19, 20D3
Rebels rptd repelled, flee to Laos 2-11, 144G2
Govt-rebel clashes 3-22—3-28, 264G3
Rpt Reds get Viet war arms 3-31, 265B1
Govt-Karen clashes rptd 265B1
45 die in rebel raid 4-26, 422C3
Govt-rebel clashes 5-1, 422D3
Mil plotters arrested 7-2, 543D2
Rangoon martial law lifted 9-1, 679D1
Cuba ties set 10-11, 832G3
BURMAH Oil Co., Ltd. of the UK
UK loan rptd 1-13, 173F3
UK buys interest in Ninian Field 3-10, 521D3
Rpts North Sea find 7-9, 521C3
BURN, Dennis
Sentenced in USSR 8-27, 655F1-A2
Loses appeal 10-26, 857F1
BURNAP, Willard H.
Indicted 6-1, 412E3
Fired 12-15, denies chrgs 12-16, 986B1
BURNETT, Chester (Howlin' Wolf)
Dies 1-13, 56B3
BURNHAM, Forbes
PPP backs govt 2-21, 252G3
Sets Booker natlizatn 2-23, 252C3
Denies Cuba, China, E Ger mil presence 3-3, 3-6, 253A2
Hails govt schl takeover 10-1, 1005D2
Chrgs US re Cuba jet crash 10-17; US scores 10-20, 844D2
BURNIER, Brig. Gen. Joao Paulo
Co bombed 10-22, 850F2
BURNS, Arthur F.
On bank regulatory reform, data disclosures 1-21, 2-6; FBI probe asked 1-25, 111G3-112F1
Testifies on money growth targets 2-3, 168A1
On money growth targets 5-3, 347E2
House OKs FRB bill 5-10, 345A2-D2
Sees Australia prime min 7-27, 554F1
Defends dist bd make-up 8-30, 667D1
Predicts IMF loan to UK 11-11, 853F2
Warns vs stimulative policies, rpts lower MI target 11-11; denies Carter rift 11-12, 865E1
Carter sees compatibility 11-15, 863F3
Monetary curbs eased 11-19, 12-17, 939G2
Briefs Carter 11-22, 881D1, D2
BURNS, Brian
Loses Vt primary for gov 9-14, 705B2
BURNS, Emmett
Scores Miss boycott ruling 8-12, 671E2
BURNS, George
Wins Oscar 3-29, 240A3
BURNS, Robert
Named Canada house ldr 11-26, 903A3
BURROUGHS Corp.
SEC lists paymts 5-12, 726E2
BURST, Elizabeth
Killed in Ethiopia 8-4, 581C1
BURT, Leo
Fine arrested 1-7, 32F2
BURT Co., F. N.
Trust suit dvpts 2-18—10-5, 886C1, E2
BURTICA, Cornel
Scores US policies 4-13, 277D1
BURTON, Rep. John L. (D, Calif.)
Reelected 11-2, 829A1
BURTON, Rep. Philip (D, Calif.)
Reelected 11-2, 829A1
Loses majority ldr bid 12-6, 919B1

BURUNDI—*See also AFRICAN Development Bank, NONALIGNED Nations Movement, OAU*
Listed as 'not free' nation 1-19, 20D3
Recognizes Sahara republic 3-5, 178G2
Total IMF oil loan rptd 4-1, 340B2
At France-Africa summit 5-10—5-11, 355A3
Kenya chrgs Uganda seized oil shipmt 7-16, 548A2
Micombero ousted in coup 11-1; Bagaza replaces 11-3, 857G3 *
Bagaza apptd pres 11-10; Cabt named 11-13, 1012F2

1977

BURKE, Mike
NY Mets move to NJ set 7-26, 584B3
BURKE, Randy
In NFL draft 5-3, 353C2
BURKE, Richard
Gets Eur Comm post 1-7, 74B2
BURKE, Rep. Yvonne Brathwaite (D, Calif.)
Backs pot decriminalizatn 3-14, 332B2
BURKHARDT, Francis X.
Named Labor asst secy 3-11; confrmd 3-18, 272F2
BURLESON, Rep. Omar (D, Tex.)
Spec interest gifts rptd 3-7, 232B3
BURLESON, Rick
AL batting ldr 10-2, 926G3
BURLINGTON Northern Inc. (BN)
Milwaukee Rd merger rejctd 2-16, 213F2
SEC complaint setld 4-28, 368F3
Green Bay rail purchase OKd 7-15, 613D1
ICC OKs Green Bay line purchase 11-30, offer dropped 12-1, 1007B1
Frisco merger OKd 12-5, 1007D1
BURLINGTON, Vt.—*See VERMONT*
BURMA—*See also DISARMAMENT—Geneva Committee, NONALIGNED Nations Movement*
UN Assemb member 3G3
Rebel-govt clashes 2-18, 183E1
Ruling party vs Premr Sein econ policy 2-22; Maung named 3-29, 243B3
Karen rebel base taken 3-27, 243C3
Poppy crop cited 4-1, 393E3
US asked to aid separatists 779A3
Govt-rebel clashes rptd 7-11, 567A1
Ne Win seeks China CP rebel aid end; China, N Korea visits cited 779F2
5 separatists held in plot 9-3, 779D2
CP rebels expand operatns 10-6, 779E2
Political shakeup rptd 10-8, 779B3
W Eur heroin conf 10-17—10-21, 972A1
Rebel losses listed 10-21, 844B3
US heroin flow rptd down 11-7, 972B1
BURMAH Oil Co. Ltd. of the UK
Reynolds takeover of oil unit cited in table 880F1
Gen Dynamics wins US loan guarantee, Park fee cited 1-19, 55E1-F2
Australia OKs NW Shelf gas search 8-24, 704E3
BURNETT, Archbishop William B.
S Africa schl desegregatn set 1-22, 67F1
BURNHAM, Forbes (Guyana prime minister)
CIA payments rptd 2-19, 124F1
Young vows more econ aid 8-10, 646A3
Rejects Jagan coalitn plan 9-9, 767C2
BURNHAM, Joseph
Dies 10-10, 872B1
BURNS, Arthur F.
Scores Carter econ plan 2-3, 89A3
Asks OPEC banker role 3-10, 363C1
On Carter trade policy dilemma 3-22, 249C1
Carter rpts monthly mtgs set 4-15, 299B1
At White House mtg on spending 5-2, 364C2
Reuss scores FRB actns 5-24, 406E3
Vs $ drop 7-26, 585F2
Asks 'bold' Admin econ moves 10-26, 813C3, 817D2-A3
Carter on policy criticism, reappointmt 10-27, 813C3
Carter sees no discord 11-10, 877C1
Links merger activity, capital spending decisns 11-14, 879D3
Sen confirmatn bill signed 11-16, 878B2
Carter unsure re reapptmt 11-30, 914F1
Miller named successor 12-28, reactn 12-28, 12-29, 997B3, 1000D1
BURNS, George
Ties 2d in Greensboro Open 4-3, 311F1
2d in Kemper Open 6-5, 676E1
BURNS, Raymond
Dies 7-7, 604G2
BURNS International Security Services Inc.
Raymond Burns dies 7-7, 604G2
BURRELL, Berkeley
Blacks meet re govt 'neglect' 8-29, 702F1
BURROUGHS, Jeff
NL batting ldr 10-2, 926C3
BURROUGHS Corp.
To promote S Africa equality 3-1, 160B3
BURROWS, Erskine
Death sentence confirmed 5-2, 374D2
Executn stay fails, riots erupt 12-1—12-3, hanged 12-2, 935G2
BURROWS, Stephen
'77 fall fashions rptd 6-6, 1022C1
BURTICA, Corneliu
Named Rumania dep min 1-25, 100F1
BURTON, Rep. Phillip (D, Calif.)
Backs cong electn funds bill 3-16, 232G3
Chairs Redwood Pk hearings 4-13, 4-14, 323D1

BURUNDI—*See NONALIGNED Nations Movement, OAU*
UN Assemb member 3G3
IMF loan set 2-4, 87E2
Young sees Bagaza 2-5, 105D1
IDA OKs educ credit, '75-76 enrolmt cited 2-10, 161E2
Uganda mercenary aid rptd 3-28, 308G1
At France-Africa summit 4-20—4-21, 316F3

1978

BURKE, Mike
Scores Webster compensatn award 10-29, 1027C3
BURKE, Richard
Warns vs USSR shipping takeover 9-11, scored 9-19, 820A3, E3
BURKE, Rep. Yvonne Brathwaite (D, Calif.)
Loses electn for Calif atty gen, US House seat filled 11-7, 856G2, E3
BURKHARDT, Francis X.
On Teamster pensn fund suit 2-1, 83D1
BURKS v. U.S.
Double jeopardy evidence rule backed by Sup Ct 6-14, 468F3
BURLESON, Rep. Omar (D, Tex.)
Not standing for reelectn 5-6, 363A1
Stenholm wins seat 11-7, 855D3
BURLESON, Rick
Misses All-Star Game 7-11, 559G2
BURLINGTON, Vt.—*See VERMONT*
BURLINGTON Northern Inc. (BN)
Milwaukee Rd wins merger appeal 10-5, 812B2
Chessie, Seaboard to merge 11-16, 897B1
BURLISON, Rep. Bill D. (D, Mo.)
Reelected 11-7, 851D2
BURMA—*See also DISARMAMENT—Geneva Committee, GATT, NONALIGNED Nations Movement*
Ne Win reelected 1-15, 145D2
China dep premr visits 1-26—1-31, 111F2
Rebel-govt clashes rptd 2-17, '77 rebel toll 136B3
Govt foes sentenced 2-23, 145B2
Rangoon plane explosn kills 48 3-25, 271B1
Moslems flee to Bangladesh 4-30; Dacca rally scores Burma 5-6; exodus toll at 100,000, exterminatn campaign denied 5-10, 412E2
Burma blames Bengalis 5-7; Islamic League concerned 5-8, 412A3
Bangladesh refugee return pact reached 7-9, 538G1
UN Assemb member 713C3
China dep premr visits 11-14, 894G1
BURMAN, Harold
Sovt blocks US emb entry 7-27, 634D1
BURNAP, Willard H.
Pleads no contest to paymts chrg 8-9, 610E3
BURNETT, Carol
Wedding released 9-29, 970D3
BURNETT, Jesse
Lopez decisions 7-3, 600A2
BURNHAM, Forbes (Guyanan prime minister)
On const reform bill 4-10, 378B3
Ends Moscow visit, communique 4-22, 301G3
In UK, backs Belize independnc 5-6, 354C2
Sees '78 electns stay 5-15, lauds PNC const draft 6-9, 478F3
Wins const referendum 7-10, Assemb term extended 7-21, 688D2
Says IMF econ targets possible 8-8, 688B3
Jonestown cult ties cited 11-21, 891G1
BURNS, Arthur F.
Carter on interest rates 1-12, 12C1
Cites inflatn danger, asks energy plan OK 1-30, 161D3
Resigns from FRB 1-31, 161C3
Miller confirmed 3-3, 161E1
Urges gold sale, other $ defense measures 3-31, 235B2
Admin oppositn re tight credit cited 8-18, 679E1
Teeters named to fill FRB term 8-28, 664C1
BURNS, George
Noble dies 4-3, 356C3
BURNS, Helen
Catsplay opens 4-16, 887C1
Inspector Gen revived 9-21, 1031A2
BURNS, W. Sherman
Dies 1-5, 96D1
BURNS International Security Services Inc.
W Sherman Burns dies 1-5, 96D1
BURROUGH, Ken
NFL '77 touchdown ldr 1-1, 56B2
BURSEY, Brett
On SC A-plant protest 5-1, 347E1
BURSTON, Samuel
Threatens EC boycott 1-25, 69B3
BURSTYN, Ellen
Same Time Next Yr released 11-22, 970A3
BURTICA, Cornel
Loses CP post, named trade min 3-7, 193B2
BURTIS, Thomas A.
Named Sun chief exec 9-9, 809D1
BURTON, Rep. John L. (D, Calif.)
Reelected 11-7, 850D1
BURTON, Rep. Phillip (D, Calif.)
Redwood Park expansn bill OKd 2-9, 85G2
Parks bill OKd by House 7-12, 526B3
Reelected 11-7, 850E1
BURTON, Richard
Medusa Touch released 4-14, 619B3
Wild Geese released 11-11, 970E3
BURUNDI—*See also GATT, NONALIGNED Nations Movement, OAU*
Tribal warfare rptd 3-1, 395C3
Ndabemeye freed 5-6, 596B1
UN Assemb member 713C3
Cholera outbreak, Belgian aid rptd 10-12, 927E2
Polisario recognitn cited 11-10, 999G2

1979

BURKS v. Lasker
Case decided by Sup Ct 5-14, 383A1
BURLESON, Rick
NL wins All-Star Game 7-17, 569C1
Wins Golden Glove Award 11-20, 956C1
BURLESQUE—*See THEATER*
BURLINGTON, Ia.—*See IOWA*
BURLINGTON Northern Inc. (BN)
EEOC data curb upheld by Sup Ct 2-21, 128F3
Rock Island takeover ordered 9-26, 722C3
BURMA—*See also DISARMAMENT–Geneva Committee, GATT, NONALIGNED Nations Movement*
Aides in Cambodia escape to Thailand 1-8, 10A1
US to challenge coastal sea claims 8-10, 646A3
UN membership listed 695E2
Nonaligned movemt quit 9-28, 742C2
BURMAH Agate (Liberian tanker)
Collides, explodes off Texas 11-1, 954F3
BURNETT, Archbishop Bill
To defy S Africa apartheid 12-7, 969D1
BURNETT, Howard J.
Class Enemy opens 6-18, 711C2
BURNHAM, Forbes (Guyanan prime minister)
Strikes prompt pol crisis 7-23–8-28, 687A2
Postpones electns amid pol crisis 10-22, 814B1
BURNS, Allan
Little Romance released 4-27, 820F1
Butch & Sundance released 6-15, 819F3
BURNS, Arthur F.
'72 tight money easing cited 7-25, 555E2
BURNS, Duane T.
Union dues case refused by Sup Ct 1-8, 14E3
BURNS, George
Just You & Me Kid released 7-27, 820E1
Going in Style released 12-25, 1007D3
BURNS, George (golfer)
Ties for 2d in Greater Greensboro Open 4-8, 587C2
Wins Natl Team Championship 10-28, 970A2
BURNS, Jack
Muppet Movie released 6-22, 820C2
BURNS, John
Shares 6000-m relay mark 4-28, 911A3
BURNS, Randall
Pleads guilty to PCB dumping 6-4, 597G2
BURNS, Robert
Quits 5-17, 378B1
BURNS Jr., Robert J.
Improper PCB storage chrgd 3-9, 206F3
Pleads guilty to PCB dumping 6-4, 597G2
BURNS, Timothy
Pleads guilty to PCB dumping 6-4, 597G2
BURRELL, Berkeley G.
Dies 8-31, 671G1
BURRELL, Pamela
Biography: A Game opens 4-5, 711E1
BURRIS, Ray
Traded to Yankees 5-23, 1002G2
BURROUGHS, Edgar Rice
Shame of Jungle released 9-14, 820C3*
BURROUGHS Corp.
Blumenthal named chrmn 9-1, 859F3
BURRUS, Glenn E.
Settles SEC chrg 2-7, 132D1
BURTON, Shelly
Electric Horseman released 12-21, 1007C3

BURUNDI—*See also GATT, NONALIGNED Nations Movement, OAU*
Forgn missnaries expelled 6-12, 470D1
UN membership listed 695F2

1980

BURKE, Mike
NBA cocaine use rptd 8-19, 656G2
BURLINGTON—*See VERMONT*
BURLINGTON Free Press, The
Anderson pres endorsemt rptd 11-1, 844F1
BURLINGTON Northern Inc. (BN)
ICC orders coal shipping refund 1-4, Sup Ct refuses stay 1-14, 37A3
Milwaukee Rd track deal set 3-19, 346E1
Frisco merger OKd by ICC 4-17, 345D2
Bressler named pres 5-19, 456F2
Frisco merger stayed by Powell 11-21; appeals ct OKs link 11-24, Sup Ct lifts stay 11-25, 937G2-A3
BURLINGTON Northern Inc. v. U.S.
Case refused by Sup Ct 1-14, 37A3
BURLISON, Rep. Bill D. (D, Mo.)
Loses reelectn 11-4, 851F1
BURMA—*See also ADB, GATT, GENEVA Committee, NONALIGNED Nations*
Olympic role ruled out, athletic skill blamed 5-19, 379F2
U Nu returns from exile 7-29, 617C3
NE rebel fighting rptd 8-10, 8-15, 668A2
Two-tier citizenship rptd proposed 8-13, 617E3
BURMEISTER, Dr. Leon
On Iowa cancer rpt 4-15, 357B3
BURNETTE, Mila
Mecca opens 2-2, 136D3
BURNHAM, Forbes (Guyanan president)
Opponent killed in bomb blast 6-13, 469F1
Assumes presidency, names Reid prime min 10-6, 791E1
Reelected 12-15, intl observers chrg fraud 12-19, 994F2
BURNS, Arthur F.
Anti-inflatn com sets policy 6-21, 481D1
Regrets Carter FRB criticism 10-3, 763F1
Vs emergency act now; issues Amer Institute Enterprise study 12-24, 980B3
BURNS, Britt
Jackson hits 400th homer 8-11, 636A3
AL pitching ldr 10-6, 926F3
BURNS, George
Wins Crosby Pro-Am 2-3, 412C2
Oh, God! II released 10-3, 836D3
PGA top money winner 10-12, 971E3
BURNS, Ralph
Wins Oscar 4-14, 296G1
BURPEE, David
Dies 6-24, 528C1
BURRETT, William Arthur
Convicted 4-23, 372B1
Sentenced 6-16, 486F1
BURRILL, Frederick T.
Retires as Calif Fed pres 12-18, 959A2
BURROUGHS Corp.
Mirabito retires, Blumenthal named chief exec, chrmn 9-25, 958G3
BURROWS, James
Wins Emmy 9-7, 692C1
BURROWS, Millar
Dies 4-29, 360D1
BURTON, Eric
Retains Antigua parlt seat 4-24, 411E3
BURTON, Gary
Wins Grammy 2-27, 296E3
BURTON, Rep. John L. (D, Calif.)
FAA computer reliability probed 6-30, 666F3
Reelected 11-4, 842D1
BURTON, Rep. Phillip (D, Calif.)
Reelected 11-4, 842E1
BURTSEV, Mikhail
Wins Olympic medal 7-25, 622B3

BURUNDI—*See also GATT, NONALIGNED Nations, OAU*
UN Afghan res abstentn 2-14, 123E3

1976

BURWOOD-Taylor, V. H.
Eritrea rebels free 5-3, 335G1
BUSBEE, Gov. George (D, Ga.)
Ford, Carter debate 9-23, 702E1
BUSCAYANO, Bernabe
Captured 8-26, 638F2
Rivera leads NPA 11-24, 1009E1
BUSES—*See also 'Motor Vehicle' under ACCIDENTS; for school busing issue, see 'School Integration' under EDUCATION*
NJ line struck 3-9—3-22, 220G1
Dem platform text 6-15, 474B2
BUSH, Dorothy V.
Renamed to Dem post 7-16, 532B3
BUSH, George Herbert Walker
Confrmd CIA dir 1-27, 68B1
Limits CIA-media contacts 2-11, 150A3
Vs CIA contacts disclosure 2-15, 150G2
Ford revises intelligence command 2-17, 127D1
Sen com drops request for media contacts 2-17, 150E2
Scores House rpt leak 2-22, 151F1
Scores rpt of AIAA briefing 3-16, 216A3
Rebuts Pike chrgs 3-16, 217B1
Sees Nixon rpt on China 3-22, 215B1
Replaced as amb to China 4-1, 262C3
US newsmen in USSR linked to CIA 5-25, 371B3
At emergency mtg on Leb 6-16, 425C2
Briefs Carter 7-28, 551C1
In Plains 8-12; Carter praises, disavows dumping memo 8-13, 616D3
GOP conv vp vote table 8-19, 599F3
On Sov defns outlays 10-5, 960G3
Briefs Carter 11-19, 881F1
Resigns CIA post 11-24, 917C2
BUSIA, Kofi
Ghana confiscates assets 3-16, 503G2
BUSIC, Zvonko and Julienne
Hijack TWA jet 9-10, arraigned 9-13, 685C2

1977

BUSCAYANO, Bernabe
Gets death sentence 11-25, 947B1
BUSE, Don
NBA final standings 4-10, 331C3
BUSES—*See also TRANSPORTATION—Mass Transit*
Carter energy plan 4-18, 4-20, 291D3, 295A1
Intercity fare increases 5-15, 423A2
NYC hijacking, 2 slain 7-4, 568D3
O'Neal rpt scores ICC 8-3, 651A3
House OKs Carter energy pkg 8-5, 610C1
Riders' 'bill of rights' set 8-8, 627B2
EPA sets exhaust rules 9-5, 739D3
BUSH, Dorothy Vredenburgh
Renamed Dem party secy 1-21, 53B2
BUSH, George Herbert Walker
CIA rpt on Sovt aims stirs controversy 12-22-76—1-18, 39G2, E3
Defends CIA security 1-2, 41A2
1st Intl Bancshares dir 2-23, 140G2
NATO replacemt named 2-25, 148G3
CIA-press links charged 9-12, 720A3
Turner curbs CIA news media contacts 11-30, 941C1
BUSHELL, John C. W.
Gets Pak protest on BBC 4-28, 349A2
BUSIA, Kofi
Cedi devaluatn cited re ouster 7-1, 598E2
BUSIC, Julienne
Convicted 5-5, 451A3
Sentenced 7-20, 642A2
BUSIC, Zvonco
Convicted 5-5, 451A3
Sentenced 7-20, 642A2
BUSINESS Council (Washington, D.C.)
Carter addresses 12-14, 976E3

1978

BUSBEE, Gov. George (D, Ga.)
Wins renomination 8-8, 625D3
Rpts prison probe indictmts 9-14, 771B1
Reelected 11-7, 852F1, 853E2
BUSCH, August
Devine retires as Cardinals gen mgr 10-18, 1026A3
BUSES—*See also TRANSPORTATION—Mass Transit*
Carter budget proposals 1-23, 47B3
AMC to end productn 5-31, 665B2
Mt Hood trust award vs Greyhound curbed by Sup Ct 6-19, 492A3
New Orleans schl drivers strike 9-1, 698G2
Accidents—*See ACCIDENTS—Motor Vehicle*
BUSEY, Gary
Buddy Holly Story released 7-21, Big Wednesday 7-27, 969D3, E3
BUSH, Blair
In NFL draft 5-2, 336F2
BUSH, George Herbert Walker
Vs excessive intellignc agency curbs 4-5, 306A2
BUSH, George W.
Wins Tex Cong primary runoff 6-3, 426F2
BUSHNELL, John A.
Denies Guyana cult probe neglect, cites Rep Ryan briefing by State Dept 11-20, 891F2-A3
BUSHUYEV, Konstantin Davidovich
Dies 10-26, 888F2
BUSIA, Kofi
Dies 8-28, 708C2
BUSIC, Bruno
Assassinated 10-16, 805A2

1979

BUSBEE, Gov. George (D, Ga.)
At Teng luncheon in Atlanta 2-1, 83F2
OKs FBI ex-informant's extraditn 2-7, 120C1
BUSCHE, Heinz
W Gers win world 4-man bobsled title 2-25, 392F1
BUSES—*See also TRANSPORTATION—Mass Transit*
Carter State of Union Message asks deregulatn 1-23, 46G3
Adams outlines urban-aid policy 2-13, 129A3
EPA tightens exhaust rule 2-15, 187C1
Intercity summer svc expansn OKd 7-12, Greyhound sues ICC 7-13, 579B2
Trailways sale completed 8-21, 682E3
NJ line fires Iranian drivers 11-22, 898C2
BUSH, George Herbert Walker
Talks to Midwest GOP, vs Admin forgn policy; offcls rate 3-10, 185G3, 186B1
Enters '80 pres race 5-1, 326B1
Pres campaign funds rptd 7-12, 593G3
Ford bars '80 pres bid 10-19, 808F1
Wins Me straw poll 11-3, 866A3
Keene campaign post cited 11-14, 982E2
3d in Fla straw vote 11-17, 887D1
BUSH, Prescott
Son enters pres race 5-1, 326C1
BUSHNELL, David I.
Peabody to sell Inman portraits 2-9, 173G2
BUSIA, Kofi (d. 1978)
Owusu pol agreemt cited 6-22, 485C3
BUSINESS Council (Washington, D.C.)
Carter addresses 12-12, 962G3

1980

BUSBEE, Gov. George (D, Ga.)
State of State message 1-15, 483A2
Sends troopers to Wrightsville 4-8, 333B1
BUSES—*See also TRANSPORTATION--Mass Transit*
EPA sets exhaust rule 1-2, 5F2
Lake Placid problems mar Olympics 2-13—2-18, 155D2
Fla regulatn ends 7-1, 558D2
Greyhound-Mt Hood trust case declined by Sup Ct 10-6, 782C2
Diesel emissns rule set 12-24, 987E2
BUSEY, Gary
Carny released 6-13, 675B2
Foolin' Around released 10-17, 836G2
BUSH, George Herbert Walker
Voices urgency re Iran 1-2, 5E1
FEC OKs matching funds 1-2, 5B2
In Ia GOP debate; Des Moines Register poll cited 1-5, 4E2, G3
3d in Ia poll 1-11, 33E1-G1
Attacks Carter 1-20, 50E2
Beats Reagan in Iowa caucus 1-21, 50D1
Reagan steps up pace 1-22—2-5, 91F2
Wins 1 Ark delegate 2-2, 92A1
Reagan assails stances 2-5, 2-6; answers on abortn 2-7, 128F2, A3
Denies '70 campaign gift coverup 2-7, 128E3
Connally campaigns in SC 2-14, 129A2
Anderson publicity problem rptd 2-15, 129E2
Gains another Ark delegate 2-16, 130G1
Wins PR primary, expenditures cited 2-17, 130A1, D1
NH gun control forum 2-18, GOP pres debate 2-20, 129B3, C3, G3
Gains in Times/CBS poll 2-20, 130F2
NH limited GOP debate dispute sparked 2-23, 143C1
2d in NH primary 2-26, 142G2-143B1, F1
'Basic speech' excerpts 3-3, 208C2-G3
Wins Mass primary, 3d in Vt 3-4, 166D2-E3
Trails in SC primary 3-8, 183F3
Fares poorly in Fla, Ga, Ala primaries 3-11, 183B3, E3
In Ill GOP forum 3-13, 206E2
FALN raids NY hq 3-15, 208C3-209A1
3d in Ill primary, delegate count cited 3-18, vows continued race 3-19, 206D2, 207A1, C1
Wins Conn primary, 2d in NY 3-25, 221A2, E2, B3
Gallup Poll results 3-31, 247B1
Wis, Kan primary results 4-1, 246G1, A2, A3
Loses La primary 4-5, 264G3, 265B1
Addresses newspr eds, attacks Admin 4-7, 264C2
Poll rating negative 4-18, 304G3
Anderson calls 'evasive' 4-20, 328C1
Scores Carter on Iran 4-20, 328B2
Scores Reagan, Admin 4-21, 304F2
Wins Pa primary 4-22, 304A1, C2
Loses Tex primary 5-3, 342A2
Reagan delegate gains rptd 5-3, 342D3
Loses Tenn, Ind, NC primaries; wins DC 5-6, 341G2-342A2
Md, Neb primary results 5-13, 366F2-D3
Wins Mich primary, loses Ore 5-20, to reassess candidacy 5-21, 382E3-383E1
Ends pres run 5-26, 398E2-399B1
Ida, Ky, Nev primary votes 5-27, 399B2-F2
8 primary results 6-3, 423B2-G2
Delegate count table 6-28, 506B2
Reagan names as vp choice; wins nominatn, makes acceptance speech 7-17, 529D1-530A1, A2
Reagan pres nominatn acceptance speech 7-17, 531B1
Photo with Reagan, Ford 7-17, 529A1
Biog sketch 530C3
Campaigns in Detroit, Houston 7-19, 549E2
Laxalt lauds as nominee 7-22, 549G1
Baker named to Reagan com 7-22, 549A3
In Japan, China; denies Reagan '2-China' policy 8-19—8-22; clarificatn issued 8-25, 645E2, 646A1-F1
Stresses econ, forgn issues; coins 'Carterism'; other campaign highlights 8-30—10-7, 780G2-781C2
With Reagan in DC 9-15, 699F3
Anderson, Reagan TV debate 9-21, 722F1
TV debate canceled 9-29, 740A1
Hits Carter econ policies, vows fewer govt regulatns 10-15, 10-16, 817E2
With Reagan in Detroit 10-16, 802B2
Scores Carter forgn policy, backs Israel 10-16, 10-19, 817C3
NRA endorses 11-1, 844F2
Joins Reagan campaign windup 11-3, 840A3
Elected vice pres 11-4, 837F1
At Reagan news conf 11-6, 839C2
Baker gets key Admin post 11-14, 881G1
At GOP govs mtg 11-17, joins Reagan in DC 11-18, 880F2
Electoral College votes 12-15, 956F1
BUSHEHRI, Behruz
Iraq captures 10-31, 854E3
BUSHNEL, John Alden
Confrmd Panama Canal comr 4-2, 308E3

1976 1977 1978 1979 1980

BUSINESS & INDUSTRY

1976

BUSINESS & Industry—*See also ANTITRUST Actions, BANKRUPTCY, BANKS, CONSUMER Protection, ECONOMY, LABOR, TAXES and other related headings; also company, industry, country names*
House OKs pub works bill 1-29, 93F1; Ford vetoes 2-13, 127E3
Ford seeks curbs on CIA spying 2-18, 127C3
Sen OKs expanded pub works bill 4-13, 283C1
CIA ownership rptd 4-26, 299C2, 302A2
FEC revisn bill signed 5-11, 346F2
Ford urges regulatory reform 5-13, 346G3
Cong clears ACE, SCORE funds 5-13, 393D1
1st ¼ US capital flow rptd 5-17, 396C2, 397A1
Bank loans rptd up 6-2, 436E3
New Orleans vendor curb upheld 6-25, 552F1
Bank loans rptd down 7-29, 568E2
House com scores Fed Reserve dist bd make-up 8-15, 666G3
Inventories cited re pause in econ recovery 8-30, 647G1
Open govt bill signed 9-13, 688G3
AT&T rpts $1 bln Aug ¼ profit 9-15, 984F1
US execs visit to Cuba rptd 9-27, 791B2
US business role in new Rhodesia govt rptd sought 10-18, 781B3
Mayors ask urban dvpt bank 11-8, 845D3

Arab Boycott
US sues Bechtel 1-16, 44D2
Israeli shipping blacklisted 2-21, 145A2
Rumania joins boycott vs Israel 3-11, 242D1
22 cos vow no compliance 3-18, 747G1
16 firms blacklisted, 43 removed 3-24—4-3, 242B1
6 cos fined 4-19, 4-20, 747F1
Gen Tire suit settled 5-10, 359G3, 360F1
SEC chrmn on rptg rules 6-4, 747E2
Firms warned vs Sinai drilling 7-24, 561B2
US Sen curbs tax benefits 8-6, 586F1
2 NASD members disciplined 8-11, 747C2
Carter vs co compliance 8-18, 617B2
Sen OKs boycott curb 8-27, 746D2
House panel chrgs Commerce Dept aid 9-7, 746E3, G3, ★ 747B1
Carter, Ford assail 9-8, 9-9, 664C3, 665E2
Oil cos warn vs House bill 9-12, 9-19, 746C3
US Cong OKs tax benefits curb 9-16, 705E2, 706E1
House bill bars co compliance 9-22, 746A2

1977

BUSINESS & Industry—*See also ANTITRUST Actions, CONSUMERS, ECONOMY, LABOR, MERGERS, TAXES and other related headings; also company, industry, country names*
Carter issues conflict-of-interest code 1-4, 4C2
Carter econ plan scored 1-10, 14C1
'76 cong contributns rptd 1-15, 2-4, 2-15, 128C1-129F2
Sen subcom rpt scores independent audits 1-17, 79B1
CEA rpt to Cong 1-18, 35E3, 36F1
Reps at White House reception 1-21, 53A2
Sen rpt scores regulatory agency apptmts 2-9, 131E3
Corp merger activity rptd up 2-18, 274G1
Giaimo proposes '78 budget 3-23, 229A1
SBA loan ceiling hike signed 3-24, 250D3
Double jeopardy bar upheld 3-28, 276F3
Carter drops rebate, tax credit plans 4-14, 271B1-C2
Carter outlines anti-inflatn plan 4-15, 298G3
Admin backs pollutn fines 4-18, 342D3
Carter energy plan 4-20, 290G1; fact sheet 292F1; reactn 4-21—4-24, 319B3, 320C1
Mass blue laws upheld 4-21, 388F1
Pentagon retiree hiring amendmt OKd 4-25, 324E1
'76 pres, cong donatns rptd 4-28, 482D1
'76 money for arts rptd 5-12, 409C2
Cong sets '78 budget target 5-17, 405A1
EPA cites water cleanup deadline 6-21, 483B3
USSR tap on US phones chrgd 7-10, 551E1-A2
Small business bill signed 8-4, 689B3
Lance for business role in govt 9-15, 701A3
Gold-paymt for contracts OKd by Cong 10-14, 815D3
Blumenthal on business lack of confidence in Admin 10-19, 798F1
Burns asks 'bold' Admin econ moves 10-26, 813C3, 817D2
Bethlehem posts record 3d ¼ loss 10-26, 836E2
Carter on lack of confidence 10-27, 813C3
SEC disclosure policy backed 11-3, 859D3
SBA ends moratorium 11-4, 859F3
NY business loan bond issue rejected 11-8, 879G1
'76 crime cost rptd 11-17, 919B1
'76 forgn investmts analyzed 12-5, 997C3
Ldrs see recessn, score Admin 12-14, 962E1
Carter seeks confidence 12-14, 976E3
Miller to replace Burns 12-28, reactn 12-28, 12-29, 1000F2
Carter fears spending lag threatens balanced '81 budget 12-28, 1000G2
Carter cites campaign vow 12-28, 1002A1

Arab Boycott
7 cos chrgd re rptg violatns 1-7, 167G1
Bechtel, US settle suit 1-10, 78B2-A3
Canadian group seeks ban 1-13, 60F2
Canada orders compliance rpts, bars aid 2-16, 158E3
SEC policy rptd reversed 2-18, 167E1
Arabs ease boycott vs Israel 2-18, 167D2
Vance backs curb, vs Sen bills 2-28, 166A3
Israel agency combats 3-7, 167A2
US House OKs bill 4-20, 323C2
Egypt OKs Ford plant agrmt 5-10, other US deals rptd 5-16, 390A2
Arabs revise list 6-8—6-20, 511C3
US Cong clears bill 6-12, 459G3-460E1
Ford, Egypt sign truck pact 10-29; contd boycott vs Ford vowed 10-30, 11-3, 863G1
Saudis extend Israel boycott 12-10, 955C1
Canada bars cos disclosure 12-15, 12-16, 1010A2

1978

BUSINESS & Industry—*See also ANTITRUST Actions, ECONOMY, FOREIGN Trade, LABOR, MERGERS, STOCKS, TAXES & other related headings; also company, industry, country names*
OPIC loses new policy-writing power 1-1, trade protectionism cited 1-3, 67A1
EEOC to monitor corporatns 1-4, 5B1
Westn execs assured by Mondale 1-9—1-13, 34C2
'78 capital spending rise seen; '77, '76 data 1-12, 65B3
Carter State of Union Message 1-19, 29G1, 30E2
Carter Econ Message 1-20, 48C3
Carter budget proposals 1-23, 44G2, 46G2; tables 45E2, 46B2
'77 forgn investmts in US rptd, '75 revised 1-24, 65C3
'53, '78 cong membership compared 1-30, 107F2
GOP attacks Carter budget 1-31, 63C1
NE, Midwest blizzard losses 2-5—2-11, 105B2, D3
'77 med costs, HMO plans rptd 3-10, 5-10, 578D1
Carter unveils urban-aid plan 3-27, reactn 3-27—3-30, 217C2-218D1
Corp execs exempted from mandatory retiremt curb 4-6, 238G3
Carter unveils anti-inflatn plan, reactn 4-11, 259D2, 260E2
Carter cites July '76-77 profits rise 4-11, 260B2
S Bronx offered fed aid 4-12, 285G1
OPIC extensn signed 4-24, 323C2
Lobbying bill OKd by House 4-26, 323A2
Corp pol free speech backed by Sup Ct 4-26, 343D2
Talcott to sell 2 divisns to Gulf + Western 5-7, 404E1
Fortune ranks 500 top indls 5-8, 325B1
Corp hq shift data rptd 5-8, 326B1
Corp execs '77 pay rise rptd, top 10 listed 5-15, 364C3-365C1
Cong '79 budget target res cleared 5-17, 385F2
Admin jawboning produces exec pay curbs 5-19—6-1, campaign stepped up 6-6, 427B3-428B1
Dental insurnc coverage rptd up 5-21, 578C2
Tax liability in bankruptcy backed by Sup Ct 5-22, 388B1
Corp takeover tax liability curbed by Sup Ct 5-22, 388F1
Mgt, professional gains for women rptd 5-22, 554E3
Carter plans budget cuts 5-25, 404G2
Dymo OKs Esselte takeover 5-26, 404B1
Corp forgn earnings case refused by Sup Ct 6-5, 431F2
'76, '77 exec pay hikes in top 100 indls rptd 6-6, 428C1
Promotn quotas barred by House 6-13, 445G3
Freedom of Info in NLRB cases barred by Sup Ct 6-15, 468F2
Carter sees Houston ldrs 6-24, 509F3
US-based corps S Africa guidelines expanded 7-5, 632F3
Regulatory overhaul asked by ABA 8-8, 626D2
Corp PACs multiply, 'PAC democracy' feared 9-7, 753C2, G2
Record cash holdings rptd, top 10 listed; econ uncertainty blamed 9-18, 716B3
Gas bill OKd by Sen 9-27, 733D3
College aid grows 10-4, 754B2
Bankruptcy law revisn clears Cong 10-6, 788D2-789B1; signed 11-6, 1003B1
Black opportunities seen rising in '77 10-8, 811E2
Carter 'export consequences' order scored 10-10, 804G2
Labor-business coalitn vs energy bill rptd 10-16, 787F3
Cater anti-inflatn plan sets voluntary wage-price guidelines 10-24, 805B2-807B1; **for subsequent developments, see ECONOMY—Carter Anti-Inflation Plan**
Small business aid vetoed 10-25, 897F2
FTC data cases refused by Sup Ct 11-6, 873D3
SBA minority-aid abuse detailed 11-21, 919A3

Arab Boycott
Canada issues compliance rpt, disclosures pledged 5-30; Westinghouse unit named 6-1, 435C2
Canadian subsidiaries ordrd to comply with US law 6-2, 435B3
Camp David summit pact abolishes 9-17, 711G3, 712B3
Qantas bar of Jews re Syria demand probed by Australia 10-18, 836D1; demand dropped 10-20, 900E3

1979

BUSINESS & Industry—*See also ANTITRUST Actions, ECONOMY, FOREIGN Trade, MERGERS, STOCKS, TAXES and other related headings; also company, industry, country names*
SEC corp suit findings retrial barred by Sup Ct 1-9, 14A2
Businessmen at State Dept mtg on US-China trade 1-15, 27B2, G2
Carter budget proposal tables 1-22, 42E2, 43A2, B2
Carter State of Union Message 1-23, 46E2, D3, G3, 47B1, G1
Investmt drop cited in productivity decline 2-9, 111C1
ABA rejcts white-collar crime proposal, OKs cong testimony 2-13, 130A2
US, Mex sign cooperatn pact 2-16, 124D3
Professnl use of corp names curbed by Sup Ct 2-21, 128D2
Carter proposes dvpt financing progrm 3-1, 164F1
Kennedy introduces merger-limit bill 3-8, 202D2
Corp crime study rptd 3-8, 240A1
'78 profit rise cited 3-13, 182D1
US rule compliance costs rptd 3-14, 3-29, 230E2-C3
Carter on '78 profits, inflatn 3-29, 264C1
B Carter denies Libya plans 4-15, 310D1
Reverse Freedom of Info suits curbed by Sup Ct 4-18, 345D3
Fortune ranks 500 top indls 5-7, 304D2
PAC '78 gifts rptd up 5-10, 363G1
US-China pact set 5-13, 370F1
Corp execs '78 pay rise rptd, top 10 listed 5-14, 347C3-348C1
DC rpts minorities contract law ignored 6-13, 442E3
'77, '78 forgn investmt rptd 6-13, 463F3
Arts cncl sets business skills program 7-4, 672F2
Carter sees ldrs at Camp David 7-6-7-11, Admin briefing planned 7-12, 513E2, F2
Time, Control Data to sponsor art shows 7-19, 672C2
Carter thanks Camp David participants 7-30, 608F3-609A1
Citizens Party platform backs controls 8-1, 595A1
Legislators' incomes studied 9-1, 701D3
Kennedy lauds free enterprise 9-27, 962A1
Pay Advisory Com set 9-28, members named 10-16, 829D2-B3
SBA minority-aid abuse rptd 9-28, 947B2-B3
Mail order finance chrg case refused by Sup Ct 10-1, 768B2
Franchise terminatn case refused by Sup Ct 10-29, 884B1
Carter proposes indl innovatn 10-31, 829D3
NY indl dvpt bond issue rejected 11-6, 846C2, 847A1
Terrorism rptd up 11-15, 882E1

Arab Boycott
Canada oppositn ldr vows actn 57G2
Arabs urge boycott vs Egypt 3-14, 178D1
Canada scores prov law 3-20, 267A1
Arab League imposes Egypt boycott 3-31; US, Egypt score 4-1, 4-2, 248B2, B3
Air Canada-Saudi contract boycott clause rptd 5-7, 467E3
Arab People's Cong presses curbs 5-10, 341E2
Canada warned vs Israel Emb move 6-19, 467B3
Continental Grain unit fined 8-27, 648G2
Canada deal losses, Israel Emb move linked 10-18—10-29, 833D2, G2
Cameron fine rptd 11-1, 923B3

1980

BUSINESS & Industry—*See also related subjects (e.g., ECONOMY, LABOR, TAXES); also company, industry, country names*
Small business defined 455D3
Paper work costs rptd 1-3, 17C3
$2 bln youth training progrm asked 1-10, 16C2
Small business hardships blamed on Carter 1-13, 5-15, 5-29, 455E2
Carter cites corp profit rise 1-20, 50D2
State ct jurisdictn narrowed by Sup Ct 1-21, 93F1
Customs Svc goods liability backed by Sup Ct 1-21, 93A3
'79 forgn mfg investmt rptd up 2-6, 92B3
'79 Chrysler loss sets record 2-7, 127E1-A1
Ford acquitted in Pinto trial 3-13, 185B3
Carter anti-inflatn plan unveiled to ldrs 3-14; reactn rptd 3-15, 3-17, 201A1, 202E1
FTC funding blocked 3-15—4-30; agency shuts down 5-1, reopens 5-2, 348C1
USOC boycott pressure rptd 3-21, 258C3
'79 forgn investmt rptd 4-8, 329A1
NY transit strike impact rptd 4-10, 268D2
FRB small business loans increased 4-17, 286A2
'Big Business Day' held 4-17, 308G1
Exxon 1st 1/4 profit sets record 4-23, 331B1, D1
Fortune ranks 500 top indls 5-5, 290C2
Fed unincorporated trust suits backed by Sup Ct 5-19, 440E2
Credit fixing curbed by Sup Ct 5-27, 453F2
CPSC seeks asbestos use data 5-30, 703F2
Wis out-of-state corp earnings tax backed by Sup Ct 6-10, 511E3
Standby gas rationing plan submitted by Carter 6-12, 552A1
State sales preference backed by Sup Ct 6-19, 554E2
Venice summit urges pvt sector shift 6-23, 473C3
Dem platform backs minorities' aid 6-24, 480A1
Financial futures trading expands 7-24, 8-7, 617D1
Forgn investmt said dangerous 8-7, 601D3
ABC ties to Spelling-Goldberg rptd probed by SEC 8-7—8-8, 640B1
AT&T begins reorgn 8-20, 648E1-A3
Reindustrializn bd backd by AFL-CIO cncl 8-21, 647D3
Contract awards amendmt OKd by House 9-16, 741E1
Small business aid bill signed 9-19, 784C2
FRB OKs commercial paper bank sales 9-29, 986A2
Clean water amendmts clear Cong 10-1, signed 10-21, 981E1
Calif 'pub figures' libel case refused by Sup Ct 10-6, 782E2
Itel rpts $443.3 mln '79 loss 10-16, 784D1
Islamic econ conf 11-4—11-6, 865B1
Patent law revisn clears Cong 11-21, 915F3; signed 12-12, 982A1
NAACP held liable in Miss boycott 12-10, 963C2

Arab Boycott
Egypt ends boycott of Israel 2-5, 107G2
Arab hardliners urge reinforcemt 4-15—4-16, 284G2
Dutch threats force Israel Emb move 8-26, 643F2
US data rptd 10-20, 800F3
3M fined 10-30, 985G2

1976

2 US reps, State Dept warn vs House bill 9-22, 9-27; Saudi threat rptd 9-26, denied 9-27, 746F2
Calif bill signed 9-27, 5 other state laws cited 12-1, 987D1
Israel orders probe of Amoco-Egypt agrmt 9-29, 759B3
US panel rpts bank compliance 9-29, 986G3
94% compliance rate rptd 9-30, 747C1
Cong bills die; Ford extends '69 Export Admin Act 9-30, 786C3, 883B1, 884B2
Ford, Carter debate 10-6, 740D2, 741F3, 742A1
Ford modifies disclosure stand, discrepancy explained 10-7, 785F2-786G3
Commerce Dept on disclosures 10-7; sets new rptg rules, chrgs 7 cos 10-8, 785A3
Ford, Admin rptd vs tax bill penalties 10-7, 787A1
Carter scores Ford 'discrepancy' 10-8, 762B2
Commerce Dept releases compliance rpts, chrgs 8 more cos 10-18—10-20, 785E3
US banks role cited 785F3, 786A3
Carter vows to end 10-19, 785E2
Ford news conf remarks, scores Carter 10-20, 784F2
Richardson testifies before House sub com, 2 members seek compliance halt 10-20, 786E2-B3
Boycott ban in 5 states cited 10-20, 786G2
More cos rpt boycott requests, noncompliance 10-24—11-10, 986E2-B3
UK bank, co on blacklist 10-29, 889D3
5 cos chrgd with rpt violatns 11-3, 986B3
Bank of Amer vows noncompliance 11-3, modifies policy 12-1, 987C1
Treas issues guidelines 11-7, Ribicoff scores 12-8, 987C2
Commerce Dept modifies rpt rules 11-18, 986C3
Eximbank confrms loan bar 12-7, 986G3

Multinationals—*See also 'Political Payments' below; also country, organization names*

Brazil panel issues rival rpts 1-9, 98G2
SELA backs Latin regulatn 1-15, 60A3
UN Transnatl Comm meets 3-2—3-12, 297G3
OECD OKs code 5-21, 430C3
ILO conf 6-2—6-18, 449F3
US Dem platform text 6-15, 476D2
OECD adopts code, US backs 6-21, 450D1
Carter vows tax reform cautn 7-22, 550D3, E3
Ford, Carter debate 9-23, 701G2

Political Payments Issues—*See also BOEING, GULF Oil, LOCKHEED, NORTHROP*

13 drug cos rpt forgn paymts 1-9—4-27, 361G1-362G1
Jones pleads guilty 1-29, 134D1
Pentagon gets Rockwell guest lists 2-3, 3-17; censures officials 3-16, 200G2
Ford orders probe 2-10, 134A2
IRS ordrd to expand probe 2-10, 134D2
Dutch Dassault bribe case opens 2-10, 141D2; acquitted 2-25, 158E2
Babcock sentence upheld 2-10, 144G3
Occidental Venez bribes rptd 2-14—2-19, 147F1, F3
W Ger, French cos' Colombia bribes rptd 2-16, 2-23, 147G2
'64-70 Mo bank costs rpts 2-27, 181A1
Rollins admits Mex payoffs 3-3, 419D3
Hammer pleads guilty again 3-4, 180F3
US proposes bilateral data disclosure, UN agrmt 3-5; OECD, Chamber of Commerce plans rptd 3-8, 199F3
Argentina '51 Dutch paymts rptd 3-12, 254D3
ITT forgn paymts rptd 3-12, 4-16, 5-12, 360F3-361G1
Ford names probe panel 3-21, 262C2
Hammer, Babcock spared jail terms 3-23, 6-4, 442B2
United Technologies, Rockwell rpt forgn paymts 4-9, 362C2, E2
BP, Shell admit Italy bribes 4-13, 267F1
UK bank staff probed 4-28, 458B1
Army meat scandal chrgd 5-7—5-12, 395A2
SEC settles with Gen Tire 5-10, Emersons 5-11, 359B3-360D3, 419D3
SEC lists cos chrgd 5-12, 725E3-729F2
OECD OKs multinatl code 5-21, 430D3
R J Reynolds, Sea-Land paymts rptd 5-28, 8-23, 9-13, 689G2
Kaiser, Reynolds Metals admit forgn paymts 6-2, 6-10, 690D2
Butler settles SEC suit 6-7, 986D2
Venez Occidental rpt issued 6-8, arrests ordrd 7-14, 593B1
Richardson-Hills quarrel re SEC actns 6-11—6-17, 668E3
US Dem platform text 6-15, 476E2
OECD adopts multinatl code, US backs 6-21, 450D1
Sen com OKs anti-bribe bill 6-22, 668B3
US Cong to get pres rpts 6-30, 533G1
Foremost admits paymts 7-3; SEC sues, settles 7-7, 669D1

1977

Multinationals—*See also 'Payments' below; also country, organization names*

3d World cooperatn seen 3-31, 257G3
UN rpt scores Namibia bias 4-19, 349G2
North-South talks end 6-3, 437A3, B3
Venez pres seeks regulatn 6-28, 546B2
US denies uranium cartel rpts 6-29, 624E3
FALN bombs NYC bldgs 8-3, 613F3
Bell vows trust probes 8-8, 629E3
Panama Canal treaty backing seen 8-22, 679C1
Canal pact opponents plan campaign 9-9, 698B3
Meany scores 12-8, 960F3

Obituaries

Eccles, Marriner 12-18, 1024D1

Payments Issues—*See also KOREA (South)—U.S.-Korea Political Payments; also LOCKHEED*

Sterling Drug rpts '70-76 paymts 1-3, 94B1
Carter-Wallace rpts paymts 1-3, 94C1
Beker rpts '72-75 paymts 1-4, 94D2
Sea-Land case setld, rebate probe continues 1-5, 6B2
Canada A-sale agent linked to '72 paymt 1-7, 42G3; AECL warned vs disclosure 1-25, 114C1
CIA, US multinatls Allende bribes chrgd 1-9, 1-11, 18C2, F2
GTE bribery suits filed, settled 1-12, 1-27, 79G1, F2-D3
Sen subcom rpt scores independent auditors 1-17, 78B3
Hasbro rpts '71-75 rebates 1-19, 94E2
Hughes Aircraft payoffs to Indonesia chrgd 1-25, govt probes 2-4, 2-14, 182G2
SEC sues Uniroyal 1-27, 93C3
Olin rpts '71-76 paymts 1-27, 94E1
ARA Svcs rpts rebates 1-28, 94D1
Natl Distillers kickbacks, pol paymts rptd 1-28, 215G1
2 Italy ex-mins indicted 1-29, 116B3
Deere rpts '72-76 paymts 2-1, 94G1
Canada rejcts UDI books in Korea A-sale probe 2-1, 114G1
Dynalectron rpts '72-76 paymts 2-4, 94F1
Olympia disclosures rptd 2-4, 215D2
AMF rpts '71-76 paymts 2-8, 93G3
TWA rpts rebates, paymts 2-8, 94A2
Canada Polysar admits illegal rebates 2-8, 114B2
Amer Airlines settles SEC chrgs, CAB setlmt cited 2-9, 111F2, E3
Japan Boeing kickback chrgd 2-14, probed 2-15, 136D1
Loew's disclosure rptd 2-14; Shell 2-16; Dresser 2-17; Wean 3-8; Singer, E-Systems 3-10; Medtronic, Aero-Systems 3-11; Beatrice Foods 3-14; Cargill 3-18; Motorola 3-23; Dow 3-28; Ogilvy & Mather 3-30, 233B2
Jones guilty plea cited 2-16, 111G3
Aeroperu rebate case rptd setld 2-18, 324G3
Ct backs Boeing on secrecy 2-25, 215G2, A3 ★
Castro scores US rights pressure 2-26—2-27, 180E3
Sales seen unhurt by crackdown 2-28, 233C1

1978

Multinationals—*See also 'Payments' below; also country, organization names*

IBM quits Nigeria; Colgate, Citibank pullouts cited 6-26, 798G3-799B1
OAS sets Latin guidelines 7-1, 505D2

Obituaries

Dassler, Adolf (rptd) 9-18, 778B1
Bierwirth, John E 4-3, 356B2
Blaisdell, George G 10-3, 888D2
Bobst, Elmer Holmes 8-2, 708A2
Cushman, Austin T 6-12, 540E2
Farrell Jr, James A 9-15, 888A3
Harrah, William 6-30, 540G2
Hasselblad, Victor 8-6, 708A3
Hood, Clifford F (rptd) 11-27, 972C3
Meadows, Algur Hurtle 6-10, 540C3
Messerschmitt, Willy 9-15, 778E1
Mortimer, Chas G 12-25, 1032C3
Prouvost, Jean 10-17, 888D3
Rockwell, Willard F 10-16, 888D3
Weicker Sr, Lowell P 11-25, 972G3
Welch, Leo D 10-22, 888G3

Payments Issues—*See also KOREA (South)—U.S.-Korean Political Payments*

Shipping line chrgs vs Garmatz dropped 1-9, 15G3
Westinghouse A-contract fee to Herdis rptd 1-13, PI ordrs probe 1-16, 38C2
Lockheed linked to W Ger scandal 1-13—1-17, 74C2
Miller queried re Textron Iran, Nigeria paymts 1-24—2-28, CIA, Defense info re Khatemi rptd 1-25, 2-17, 161F1-G2
Flood, Eilberg probed 1-27—3-15, 239G3-240A3; win renominatn 5-16, 389E3
US crime code revisn clears Sen 1-30, 64D3
6 more Japanese tied to Lockheed bribe 1-30, 72C3
Shippers denied immunity from Justice rebate probe 2-3, 184E3
Shipping rebate fine total cited 184F3
Southn Bell pleads guilty 2-13, fined 2-16, 116G2
McDermott pleads guilty, fined 2-22, 142E2-B3
Firestone ex-offcl pleads guilty 2-28, 142C3
SEC seeks Textron subpoena 3-2, 161A2
Seatrain, others indicted re shipping rebates 3-8, plead guilty 3-16, 184B3
Schlitz sued re kickbacks 3-15, 223C2
Williams, Control Data plead guilty, fined 3-26, 4-26, 448B3
Anheuser-Busch fined re rebates 3-31, 449F2
Sea-Land pleads guilty re rebates, fined 4-11, 449E2
SEC sues Page Airways 4-13, 449G1-C2
Gurney trial press-curbs review declined by Sup Ct 4-17, 308D2
Mendelsohn suit setld 4-18, named US aide 6-10, 446F3-447B1
OPIC extensn curbs paymts 4-24, 323A3
Ford Indonesia bribe probe rptd, stockholder suit filed 4-25, 5-16, 390G2
Wild gives SEC depositn 4-26, settles Gulf paymt chrgs 5-11; gift recipients rptd 6-2, 449B1
Textron bribe evidence rptd destroyed 5-8, 448G3
Firestone ex-offcl sentncd 5-31, 404D2
Malaysian sentncd for Northrop kickback 6-6, 439E3
Reynolds settles SEC chrgs 6-6, 449C2

1979

Multinationals—*See also 'Payments' below; also country, organization names*

Canada indus control by US cited 3-24, 234F1

Obituaries

Burrell, Berkeley G 8-31, 671G1
Clore, Charles 7-26, 588E2
David, Donald K 4-13, 356C3
Eaton, Cyrus S 5-9, 432E2
Garbisch, Edgar William 12-14, 1008G2
Kleberg Jr, Richard 5-8, 432B3
Murchison, John D 6-14, 508C3
Power, Donald C 3-11, 272E3

Payments Issues—*See also KOREA (South)–U.S.-Korean Political Payments*

Gruman Japan scandal probed 1-9, Nissho exec kills self 2-1, 98E2
Jamaica offcl fired re US kickbacks 1-29, 101B2
Fairchild acquitted on tax chrgs 2-7, 88A1
Grumman discloses forgn payoffs, denies Japan bribes 2-8, 305G2-D3
US drops Japan probe of 2 Lockheed ex-aides 2-15, 306C1
Lockheed discloses overseas paymts 2-16, 306F1-A2
Eilberg pleads guilty in plea-bargain 2-24, 152C2
Italians convicted re Lockheed 3-1, 155B2
Ford stockholders suit barred in NY 3-8, 202A3
REA vp indicted 3-8, 239F3
Tenneco fined in La bribe case 3-17, 239B3
Mays chrmn convctd of IRS bribe 3-26, 239E3
Alexander's sentncd re TV rebates 3-29, 298C3
4 indicted in Japan Nissho scandal 4-5, 5-15, 389D2
Stevedoring exec indicted 4-9, 292B1
2 US oil execs chrgd re '76 Qatar bribe, Lance '78 influence role alleged 4-9, 305E3-306C1
Allied Chem indicted on kickbacks 4-17, 985B3
Lockheed guilty in Japan payoffs, fined 6-1, 422F2
ISC accused of forgn paymts 7-9, 541E3
Textron pleads guilty to currency violatns 7-10, admits overseas payoffs 7-26; Proxmire asks study 10-31, 923B2-B3
FCC doubts RKO Gen license fitness 7-18, 618A2
Miller rptd cleared in Textron case 8-2, 627C2
Kenny fined for Cook I '78 electn fraud role 8-2, 648G1
Italian statemt re Lockheed rptd 8-6, 603B1
ITT settles SEC chrgs 8-8, 648D1
Turkey chrgs Lockheed cover-up 9-20, 775F1
Southn Bell NC paymts scored by FCC 9-20, 870F1

1980

Obituaries

Browne, Virgil 1-7, 104G1
Cort, Stewart 5-25, 448D1
Evers, John W 12-5, 1004E1
Hires Jr, Charles E 3-19, 279D3
Leftwich, James T 7-6, 608C2
Reynolds, Richard S 10-5, 876D3
Sanders, Harland 12-16, 1004C3
Semenenko, Serge 4-24, 360E3

Payments Issues

Control Data case refused by Sup Ct 1-7, 16A1
FCC lifts 3 RKO Gen licenses 1-24, 119A3
FCC backs Westinghouse unit TV license 1-30, 119D3
Textron settles SEC chrgs, Miller payoffs knowledge alleged 1-31, Miller denies 2-1, 92C1-A2
Miller testifies re Textron 2-8, spec prosecutor sought 2-8—2-11, 145E1-B2
Seatrain settles disclosure suit 2-8, 558B1
Sears indicted on Japan TV rebates 2-26, 251G3
Miller-Textron spec prosecutor rejected 3-11, 185C2
US Ford-Indonesia probe rptd dropped 3-13, 224E3
Justice Dept offers forgn paymts advice, SEC vs 3-24, 227G1-C2
Canada exchng offcl chrgd 5-5, 406C3
NY Deliverers Union head convicted 5-15, 370E3; sentncd 6-26, 656D1
Venice summit vows curbs 6-23, 474D1
Bethlehem Steel, ex-offcl plead guilty 7-24, 8-7, 600E1, A2
3 get suspended sentnc in Japan Nissho case 7-24, 605C2
Bethlehem Steel fines set 8-25, 957E3
SEC cooperatn pledged 8-28, 958B1
Bethlehem Steel ex-offcl sentenced 10-27, says bribes 'condoned', civil suit ruling rptd 12-8, 957F3, 958B1
Harrah's gets temp NJ gambling license, Webb Corp ties rptd severed 11-1, 988D3
Marubeni, Hitachi units convicted 11-5, 957B3
NYC TV statn move to NJ backed 11-6, 906F1
SEC parallel probe case refused by Sup Ct 11-17, 882E1
Tesoro Petro case setld 11-21, 957D3

1976

Alcoa admits '70-72 forgn paymts, Jamaica rptd recipient 7-9—7-19, 690C1-D2
3M tax case dismissed 7-27, 566B2
Ford submits legis 8-3, 668A2
UN, OECD actn cited 8-3, 668A3
Sen curbs tax benefits 8-6, 586F1, 669C1
Carter mocks Ford legis proposal 8-9, 8-11, 584F3, 585D2
US GOP platform text cites 8-18, 611A1
Carter backs pub prosecutn 8-18, 617B2
Sen OKs anti-bribe bill 9-15, 708B1
US Cong clears tax bill 9-16, 706E1
Carter queried on Ga favors, hits Ford 10-2, 743C1
Anti-bribe bill not cleared 10-2, 884B2
Ford on golf trips 10-14, 761D3
US criminal probe task force named 10-14, 985B3
Southn Bell accepts blame, chrgs vs 11 dropped 10-25, 939C1
Cannon reelected 11-2, 824C2
Canada A-sales irregularities rptd 11-22, 904A1, C1; Parlt probe opens 11-30, 923B3
United Brands rpts more paymts 12-10, 985C3
Continental Oil fires 2 12-15, rpts paymts 12-16, 986A1
Canada sets guidelines 12-16, UDI audit 12-22, 998C1
Forgn paymts studies issued 12-18, 12-20, 985E1-B3
Philip Morris DR payoffs rptd 12-28, 1001B2
CAB chrgs Flying Tigers, 4 others cited 12-29, 986D1
SEC sues Amer Hosp 12-29, 986G1

Pollution Issues—*See appropriate subheads under ENVIRONMENT & Pollution*

Presidential Election (& transition)

Carter sees support 6-14, 433E1
Dem platform text 6-15, 469E3, 470C1-B2, 471B2, 473F3, 477B2
Carter on multinatl reforms 7-22, 550D3, E3
GOP conv delegates compared 8-7, 8-8, 616D2
Carter mocks Ford pol paymts legis 8-9, 8-11, 584F3, 585D2
Carter vs fed chartering 8-9, 585E1
GOP platform text 8-18, 603A2, 606E3
Carter on pol paymts, Arab boycott 8-18, 617B2
Dole acceptance speech 8-19, 613C1
FEC rules on pres debate financing 8-30, 644D1
Carter, Ford score Arab boycott 9-8, 9-9, 664C3, 665E2
Ford, Carter debate 9-23, 701G2
Carter queried on corp favors in Ga, hits Ford 10-2, 743C1
Ford, Carter debate Arab boycott 10-6, 740D2, 741F3, 742A1
Carter scores Ford 'discrepancy' re boycott rptg 10-8, 762B2
Ford visits LA group 10-8, 763B1
Carter sees Cleveland group 10-9, 762D2
Dole, Mondale debate 10-15, 783F2, A3
Carter vows Arab boycott end 10-19, 785E2
Ford scores Carter re Arab boycott 10-20, 784G2-B3
Ford, Carter debate 10-22, 802A1
Ford scores Carter re tax loopholes 10-28, 803A2
Carter notes bankruptcies 10-31, 827A2
Carter to tighten post-govt job rules 11-29, 898C3

Statistics

Nov inventories, sales; Oct revised 1-15, 91G2
Dec, '75 indl output; Nov revised 1-16, 91E3
'75 4th ¼ data 1-20, 89D2, A3
Econ Rpt forecasts outlays 1-26, 67F1
Dec '75 indicators, Nov revised 1-28, 90E3
Jan indl output; Nov, Dec revised 2-13, 168E2
Dec inventories, sales 2-13, 169C1
Jan indicators, Dec revised 2-27, 168A3
Jan inventories, sales; Dec revised 3-16, 199G1
Feb indl output; Dec '75, Jan revised 3-16, 199G2
'75, 4th ¼ profits rptd; 3d ¼ revised 3-19, 215B2
Nov '75-Feb indl output revised 3-26, 279G2
Feb indicators, Jan revised 3-29, 229F2
Feb inventories, sales up; Jan revised 4-14, 279G3
March indl output 4-15, 279E2
Mar indicators, Feb revised 4-28, 306E2, A3 ★
Wall St Journal rpts 1st ¼ profits 4-29, 376G2
'75 top 500 indls ranked 436F3
Mar, 1st ¼ inventories, sales; Feb revised 5-13, 376C1
Apr indl output, Feb, Mar revised, '70-Apr '76 graph 5-14, 375A2
1st ¼ profits, 4th ¼ '75 revised 5-20, 376E2
Apr indicators, Mar revised 5-28, 395B3
Apr inventories, sales 6-14, 479D3
May indl output, Apr revised 6-16, 479B3
May indicators, Apr revised 6-29, 494A3
May inventories, sales rptd; Apr revised 7-14, 536F2-A3
2d ¼ productivity, labor costs; 1st ¼ revised 7-27, 567D2
June indicators, May revised 7-28, 567E3

1977

Foremost pleads no contest 3-7, 215E1
Voluntary rptg plan end seen 3-7, 233A2
Rorer-Amchem rpts paymts 3-9, sued 3-16; GM rpts 3-31; Coca-Cola 4-1; White Consolidated 4-3; Emhart 4-6; Petrolane 4-7; Cincinnati Milacron 4-11; McDermott 4-12; United Tech 4-28; Studebaker 5-4; Cook Industries 5-5; Jones Constructn 5-16; Kraft 5-22; Global Marine 6-2; Central Soya 6-9; Chrysler 6-13; Ford 6-15; CRS Design 6-23, 503C1
Amer Brands rpts Beam gifts 3-10, 215C2
US, Canada sign Boeing probe pact 3-15, 200F1
Interstate United rebates, pol paymts rptd 3-16, 215F2
Corp double jeopardy bar upheld 3-28, 276G3
Agnew friend sentncd 4-4, 312C3
SEC sues Schlitz 4-7, Occidental 5-3, Anheuser-Busch 5-19, 503B3-504A1
Gerber reveals Anderson Clayton paymts 4-25, suit set 9-15, 799G1
7-natn summit scores bribery, Carter comments 5-8, 357D2
Sup Ct declines Wild waiver case 5-16, 419A2
SEC opens some files; Amer Airlines, Ashland, Braniff, Butler paymts rptd 5-17, 502F3-503B1
UK Leyland payoff chrgs stir controversy 5-19—5-25, NEB chrmn retires 7-1, 526C1
US Lines settles SEC chrgs 6-6, 651B1
Gulf indicted re IRS gifts 6-15, 504A1
Venez pres seeks regulatn 6-28, 546B2
Canada AECL pres fired 7-7, 541E3
Canada Polysar scored by Parlt 7-7, 541G3
Korea Assemb asks US act vs unfair chrgs 7-7, 551F3
S Africa sugar lobby sued 7-20, 614A1
Sony settles FMC chrgs 8-19, 650G3-651A1
SW Bell loses slander suit 9-12, 724B2
NYS chrgs Schenley rebates 10-6, 860E1
Seagram admits paymts 10-14, 818B2
Jacquin settles SEC rebates chrgs 10-17, 860E1
Defns contractor gifts scored by Proxmire 10-24, 920C2
Exxon settles SEC chrgs 10-25, 818D1-A2
Beasley indicted, Firestone paymts cited 10-25, 818C2
Gen Tire offcls to repay gifts 10-27, 860A2
Gulf fined re laundered money 11-13, 881D2
Anti-bribery bill clears Cong 12-7, 937G3; signed 12-19, 1001G2
Goodyear settles SEC chrgs 12-21, 1005A1
Massey Ferguson admits overbilling 12-29, 1010G2

Statistics

Dec '76 retail sales 1-10, 38C2
'77 capital spending rise forecast; '76 data rptd 1-11, 56G3-57A1
Nov '76 inventories, sales; Oct revised 1-14, 56E2
Dec '76 indl output 1-17, 92G3
Canada firms expansn in US up in '76 1-25, 132F3
Indicators index described 1-28, 92C3
Dec '76 indicators up, Jan-Nov revised 1-28; graph 92F2
AT&T rpts record '76 earnings 2-1, 93B3
'76 4th ¼ profits 2-8, 3-21, 301A1
Jan indl output 2-15, 129D3
'76, Dec inventories, sales; Nov revised 2-16, 130F2
Jan indicators, Dec '76 revised 2-28, 154E1
Feb indl output, Jan revised 3-15, 194A1
Jan inventories, sales 3-17, 194F1
Workweek data 3-18, 194G2-A3
Feb indicators 3-30, 234A2
Jan-Mar retail sales cited 4-14, 271F1
Mar indl output; graph 4-14, 300A1, A3
Feb inventories, sales; Jan revised 4-15, 300F3
1st, 2d ¼ profits rptd 4-28, 7-28, 8-19, 668F2, C3
Mar indicators; Jan, Feb revised 4-29, 399E2
Fortune ranks '76 top 500 indls 340A1
'76, '77 forgn investmt in US 5-11, 5-25, 385F2
Apr indl output, Feb revised 5-16, 384A1
Mar inventories, sales; Feb revised 5-16, 384F1-A2
Urban confidence rptd, econ data table 5-16, 384A2, D2
'76 salaries up, top 10 execs listed 5-23, 408B3
'76 top 100 black-owned firms rptd 6-1, 519F3
'77 capital spending upturn seen 6-7, 6-24, 6-27, 518G2
Apr, May indicators 6-29, 502C2
'74-77 indl output graph 7-15, 553E3

1978

SEC upheld on disclosure power 6-8, Schiltz settles 7-9, 642C3
United Brands-Honduras paymts rptd 6-9, 614C3, 615A1
Italy pres resigns over Lockheed chrgs 6-15, 516F2
United Brands pleads guilty re Honduran bribe, fined 7-19, 643F1
Boeing chrgd, settles 7-28, 642F3-643C1
SEC sues Parsons, case settled 8-4, 643C2 ★
Conoco ex-offcl pleads no contest 8-9, 610D3
UK Leyland ex-exec jailed for forgery 8-11, 667G2
3 aircraft makers settle FTC chrgs 8-18, 643C1
Katy, 2 offcls chrgd; suit setld 8-30, 737A1
Flood indicted 9-5, 685B1
Fairchild, chrmn indicted 9-8, 808B3
SEC sues Seagram, case setld 9-8, 961E3
Eilberg chrgd by ethics com 9-13, 697F1
Goodrich chrgd with tax fraud 9-13, 737F1
Seatrain fined for rebates, other shipping setlmts rptd 9-18, 10-1, 752E3
ICC ex-offcl indicted 9-22, pleads not guilty 9-29, 770E2
Seatrain, Ocean Equipmt fined 10-23, 876B3
Westinghouse plea rejected 10-23, Egypt payoff figure named 10-26, co fined 11-20, 961F2
Eilberg indicted 10-24, pleads not guilty 11-1, 835C2
Lockheed ex-offcl cites Nakasone in Japan ct depositn; Nakasone denies 10-26, 838E3-839A1
Hosp Corp Saudi paymts chrgd, settles 10-26, 876E3-877C1
Schlitz pleads no contest, fined 11-1, 877C1
ITT sued re forgn paymts 11-2, 876B1-B3
Shipping malpractice bill vetoed 11-4, 897G2
Eilberg loses reelectn, Flood wins 11-7, 846D2, E2
Japan shippers settle US rebate chrgs 11-8, 961F3
SEC sues McDonnell Douglas 12-14, suit setld 12-15, 982D2
PAC gifts to cong com chrmn rptd 12-24, 1008B1

Price Issues—*See appropriate subheads under ECONOMY; also commodity names*

Statistics

Indl output index described 52F1
Indicator index described 127F3-128D1
'77, Dec indl output; Sept-Nov revised 1-17, 52D1
'77 4th ¼ spending 1-19, 50G1
Dec '77 indicators; July-Nov revised 1-30, 127E3
'77 4th ¼ profits 2-7, 3-20, 282B3
Jan indl output 2-15, 106E1
Jan, Dec '77 retail sales 2-15, 106A2
Jan indicators 2-28, 223A1
Feb indl output 3-16, 223D1
Feb indicators; Nov-Dec '77, Jan revised 4-6, 262D2
Mar indl output; Jan, Feb revised 4-14, 304A1
1st ¼ '77, '78 profits compared 4-27, 403G1
Mar indicators 5-1, 344B3
Apr indl output, Mar revised 5-16, 389A2
1st ¼ profits, 4th ¼ '77 revised 5-18, 403D1
Apr leading indicators; Jan, Feb revised 6-1, 429C1
'77 indl productivity 6-14, 469G3-470B1
May indl output; Mar, Apr revised 6-15, 470B1
May indicators, Apr revised 7-3, 507G1
June indl output; Apr, May revised 7-14, 552G3
'77-78 2d ¼ profits 7-28, 642A3
June indicators; Mar, Apr, May revised 7-31, 607E2
July indl output, Apr-June revised 8-15, 643C3
2d ¼ profits; '77, 1st ¼ revised 8-18, 642E2-A3
July indicators, Apr-June revised 8-31, 680E1
Aug indl output; June, July revised 9-15, 717E1
Aug indicators, July revised 10-1, 752B2
'50-78 productivity decline analyzed by Admin 10-4, 790C1
Sept indl output up; chart 10-17, 790C2

1979

Seagram unit admits Pa bribery 9-27, 809E3
Atlantica consortium fine for rebates rptd 10-31, 985G2
US indicts McDonnell Douglas, execs; Pak Intl Air suit cited 11-9, 886F1
Southn Railway fined 11-12, 868F1-A2
Italy ENI scandal spurs Saudi oil cutoff 12-5, 995A3

Price Issues—*See appropriate subheads under ECONOMY; also commodity names*

Statistics

Indl output index described 33G3
'78, Dec indl output; Nov revised 1-17, 33F3
Dec '78 indicators, Nov revised 1-31, 111A2
Feb indl output, Jan revised 3-16, 252E3
Feb indicators, Dec '78 revised 4-1, 252G1
'78, 4th 1/4 profits up 2-7, 3-20; reactn 3-20–3-21, 201A2-B3
Jan indl output 2-15, 151E2
Jan indicators; Dec, Nov '78 revised 3-1, 151E1
Mar indl output, Feb revised 4-13, 280F3
1st 1/4 profits, 4th 1/4 '78 revised 4-27, 5-19, 385A1
Mar indicators; Jan, Feb revised 4-30, 325E1
Apr indl output; Feb, Mar revised 5-16, 362E3
Apr indicators, Jan-Mar revised 5-31, 463E2
May indl output, Apr revised 6-15, 463B3
2d 1/4 profits 6-26, 8-17; 1st 1/4, '78 4th 1/4 revised 8-19, 628D2
May indicators; Mar, Apr revised 6-29, 517C1
June indl output; Apr, May revised 7-13, 557B1
June indicators; Apr, May revised 7-30, 577E2
July indl output, June revised 8-16, 622D1
July indicators, Apr-June revised 8-29, 646D3
July inventories 9-11, 701D1
Aug indl output; June, July revised 9-14, 701A1
Aug indicators, July revised 9-28, 745F2
Sept indl output; July, Aug revised 10-16, 784G1-B2
Sept indicators 10-30, 866E3

1980

Presidential Election (& Transition)

Kennedy urges profit controls 1-28, 74F3
Kennedy urges energy conservatn incentives 2-2, 91E1
Kennedy urges profits freeze 2-6, 90G3
Reagan 'basic speech' urges deregulatn 2-29, 207E3
Connally 'basic speech' excerpts 3-7, 184C3
Kennedy 'basic speech' excerpts 3-10, 183E1
Citizens' Party target 4-11—4-13, 288B3-D3
Reagan vows minority business expansn 7-15, 534B1
Dem conv keynote speech 8-12, 612D2
Dem platform planks adopted 8-13, 614D2, C3, 615F1
Carter offers econ renewal plan; reactn 8-28, 663A1-D3
Bush hits regulatn issue 9-18, 781A1
PAC donatns case accepted by Sup Ct 10-6, 782B2
Reagan proposes ombudsman 11-3, 840B3
Trade assn PAC funds soliciting ban challenge refused by Sup Ct 11-3, 856E2
Reagan aide, Sowell address black conf 12-14, 956G2

Statistics

Small business data 455D3
Indl output index described 34A3-35A1
'79, Dec indl output; Oct, Nov revised 1-16, 34A2
Dec '79 indicators, Nov revised 1-30, 92D2
'79, 4th 1/4 profits up 2-7, 3-19, 222C1-A2
Jan indl output, Dec '79 revised 2-15, 126A3
Jan indicators, Oct-Dec '79 revised 2-29, 167G3
Feb indl output 3-14, 247F3
Feb indicators; Dec '79, Jan revised 3-31, 247E3
Loans decline 4-4, 263F1
Mar indl output, Feb revised 4-15, 286A3
1st 1/4 inventories, '79 4th 1/4 revised 4-18, 305C3
Mar indicators; Jan, Feb revised 4-30, 329D2
Apr indl output, Mar revised 5-16, 384A3
Apr indicators, Mar revised 5-30, 424C3
May indl output, Apr revised 6-13, 455E1
May indicators, Apr revised 6-30, 492B2
June indl output, May revised 7-16, 541G3
2d 1/4 inventories, 1st 1/4 revised 7-18, 556B1
June indicators; May, Apr revised 7-30, 574E1
July indl output, June revised 8-15, 631F1
July indicators, June revised 8-29, 666B1
Aug indl output, July revised 9-16, 701A3
Aug indicators; July, June revised 9-30, 740G3
Sept indl output, Aug revised 10-16, 783D1
Sept indicators; Aug, July revised 10-30, 824B1
Oct indl output; Sept, Aug revised 11-14, 957F2
Oct indicators; Sept, Aug revised 12-1, 916B2

1976

2d ¼ profits, 1st ¼ revised 8-19, 708C3
Dow reactn to 2d ¼ profits 8-19—8-20, Aug indicator 9-28, 846F3, 847A1
July indicators; '75, '76 revisns 8-27, 708F2
June-Aug indl output; Jan '73-May '76 revised 9-16, 708G3; table 709A1
Aug indicators rptd, Sept '75 revised 9-28, 768A1
Sept indl output, Aug revised 10-15, 806F1
Aug inventories, sales; July revised; June data cited 10-15, 806F2
3d ¼ productivity, labor costs; 2d ¼ revised 10-27, 918D1
Sept indicators, Aug revised 10-29, 833A1
Oct indl output, Sept revised 11-15, 866C3
Oct indicators, July-Sept revised 12-1, 918G2
'70-76 indicators graph 918A2
Oct inventory, sales; Sept revised 12-14, 958B3
Nov indl output; Sept, Oct revised 12-15, 958F2-A3
1st ¼ '75—3d ¼ '76 mfg utilizatn rate rptd 12-17, 958E3
Nov indicators up, July-Oct revised 12-29, 983C2
Wage-Price Developments—*See under ECONOMY*

1977

May, June, 1st, 2d ¼ indl output; Mar, Apr revised 7-15, 554G3
Apr, May inventories, sales; Mar revised 7-15, 555A2
June indicators, May revised 7-29, 593E3
July indl output, May revised 8-15, 628D3
'76 US investmts abroad 8-29, 669D1
July indicators, June revised 8-30, 668G3
Aug indl output, July revised 9-16, 722C1
Aug indicators, May-July revised 9-29, 761E3
Sept indl output, Aug revised 10-14, 798G1
'76 forgn investmt in US, '75 revised 10-26, 836F3
3d ¼ profits, 2d ¼ revised 10-27, 11-14, 11-17, 918F1
Sept indicators, May-Aug revised 10-28, 836A1
Oct indl output 11-15, 898D3
Oct indicators; Aug, Sept revised 11-30, 941C2
Nov indl output 12-14, 961C3
Nov indicators, Oct revised 12-30, 1003A2
Transfer Payments—*See INCOMES*
Wage-Price Developments—*See under ECONOMY*

1978

Sept indicators, June-Aug revised 10-30, 864F2-A3
3d ¼ profits, 2d ¼ revised 10-30, 11-21, 919A2, D2
Oct indl output; July, Aug revised 11-15, 919F1-A2
Oct indicators, Aug revised 11-29, 918E3
Nov indl output 12-15, 982B1
Factory capacity record in Nov 12-15, 982C1
Nov indicators, Aug-Oct revised 12-28, 1003A3
Transfer Payments—*See INCOMES*
Wage-Price Developments—*See under ECONOMY*

1979

3d 1/4 profits, 2d 1/4 revised 10-31, 11-20, 922E3-923C1
Oct indl output 11-15, 922F1
Oct indicators, July-Sept revised 11-30, 922D1
Nov indl output; Sept, Oct revised 12-14, 964A1
Nov indicators, Oct revised 12-31, 985E1
Wage-Price Developments—*See under ECONOMY*

1980

Nov indl output; Oct, Sept revised 12-16, 984D1
Nov indicators; Oct, Sept revised 12-31, 984C1
Wage-Price Developments—*See under ECONOMY*

1976

BUSINESS International (N.Y. research group)
Forgn payoffs study rptd 12-20, 985B2
BUSING Issue—*See under EDUCATION*
BUSSI, Gen. Antonio
Says ERP wiped out in Tucuman 11-24, 996C1
BUSTAMANTE, Jose Luis
Chile-Bolivia sea outlet study 1-7, 27C1
BUTCHER, Willard C.
Bars testimony on Chase 1-16, 111E3
BUTHELEZI, Chief Gatsha
Zulu pol struggle setld 1-15—1-19, 76A2
Zulus shift capital 1-19, 76E2
Demands majority rule 3-14, 428C3
On black violence 8-15, 8-17, 639D1
In Johannesburg 8-27, scores police 8-28, Vorster 8-29, 653A1, D1
Forms anti-govt front 10-8, 793C3
In US, asks black aid 11-9; lauds Carter 11-18, 928F1
Scores students 11-18, forms party 11-29, 928C1
BUTLER, Darelle
Acquitted 7-16, 640E2
BUTLER, Rep. M. Caldwell (R, Va.)
Reelected 11-2, 830G3
BUTLER, R. Gordon
Edgerly guilty, GM suits cited 4-1, 287F1
Convicted 12-23, 988F1
BUTLER, Dr. Robert N.
Wins Pulitzer Prize 5-3, 352D3
BUTLER, William J.
Charges Iranian torture 5-28, 418C2
BUTLER Chevrolet Inc.
Edgerly guilty in warranty case; pending suits cited 4-1, 287D1
BUTLER National Corp.
SEC lists paymts 5-12, 726E2
Settles SEC suit 6-7, 986D2
BUTROS, Fuad
Leb defense min 12-9, 913D2
Gemayel vs arms surrender 973D2
BUTTS, James
Wins Olympic medal 7-30, 576C1
BUTZ, Earl L.
Some Ford support 'erosion' 1-4, 3A3
On US grain shipmts inspectn 2-3, 136C1
Milk price bill veto upheld 2-4, 88E1, F1
Ford names new policy com 3-5, 180A1
On '76 food prices 5-3, 396B1
Testifies in Callaway probe 5-13, 745E1
Ford advocate in Calif 5-24, 374A1
Strauss deplores GOP Admin 7-12, 508G3
Mondale scores 7-31, 565E1
Dems score at Farm Fest 9-15, 686D3
Racist remarks scored by Ford, others 10-1—10-3; regrets 10-1; resigns 10-4, 743F3-744E3
Carter scores remarks 10-2, 743B1
Sen rpt on Callaway cites memo 10-5, 745D1
Dole admits GOP slump 10-8, 763G3
Israel agri deal delayed 10-18, 811A1
BYELORUSSIAN Soviet Socialist Republic—*See 'Republics' under USSR*
BYINGTON, John S.
Consumer comm chrmn 5-4; confrmd 5-26, 412D1
BYKOV, Anatolyi
Wins Olympic medal 7-24, 576A3
BYKOVSKY, Col. Valery
Soyuz 22 launched 9-15, 684C1
BYONG Uk Li
Wins Olympic medal 7-31, 574A1
BYRD Jr., Sen. Harry F. (Ind, Va.)
Sen OKs anti-bribe tax curbs 8-6, 669C1
Reelected 11-2, 820E1, 823B1, C3

1977

BUSINESS League, National
Burrell at black ldrs mtg 8-29, 702F1
BUSINESS Roundtable, The
US House OKs antiboycott bill 4-20, 323A3
Boycott exemptns agreed 5-3, 460B1
BUSING—*See EDUCATION—School Integration*
BUSNELL, Bennie
Gilmore executed 1-17, 40F1
BUSTAMANTE, Alexander
Dies 8-6, 696D2
BUSTAMANTE, Jorge
Scores Carter alien plan 8-28, 746A2
BUTCHMAN, Alan A.
Confrmd Transport dep secy 2-10, 148D3
BUTHELEZI, Chief Gatsha
Lauds Young 5-22, 399C3
Scores govt crackdown 10-19, 804E1
Scores pass law revisn plan 11-3, 852G1
BUTLER, Lois
Albert record subpoena rptd 12-1, 915F1
BUTLER, Mike
In NFL draft 5-3, 353B2
Mex payoff recipient named 5-17, 503B1
BUTLER, Thomas
Dies 10-30, 872C1
BUTLER, William J.
Chrgs Pl rights violatns 7-31, 618G3
BUTROS, Fuad
Sees Gemayel on hq blast 1-4, 2F1
Meets US aide on Syrian troop moves 1-29, 2-1, 72B1
Sees Sovt amb 3-1, 143D2
League force extended 6 mos 3-9, 188B2
Sees US aide on fighting 9-14—9-16, 714B3
Scores Israeli raid 11-9, 849A2
Briefs Arab League on Leb 11-14, 874A2
Rejcts Cairo conf invitatn 12-1, 930G2
BUTTE, Mont.—*See MONTANA*
BUTTER—*See DAIRY Products*
BWANALI, Edward
Named Malawi trade min 7-8, 772C1
BYELORUSSIAN Soviet Socialist Republic—*See USSR—Republics*
BYINGTON, Rev. Edward
Cath editor fired 6-16, 471A2
BYKOVSKY, Col. Valery
Soyuz 22 landing rptd 109G3
BYRD Jr., Sen. Harry F. (Ind, Va.)
Votes vs Marshall 1-26, 52B3
US to seek Rhodesia amendmt repeal 1-31, 72F3
Rhodesia chrome imports banned 3-18, 191C1
Cited in Park indictmt 9-6, 688E1

1978

BUSINESS Council (Washington, D.C.)
Miller addresses Va mtg 5-13, 361B2
BUSINESS Roundtable, The
Backs Carter inflatn plan 4-11, 260E2
BUSINESS Week (magazine)
'77 top-paid corp execs, labor ldrs ranked 5-15, 364G3, 365D1
BUSING—*See EDUCATION—School Integration*
BUTANE—*See GAS, Natural*
BUTCHER, Jake
Wins primary for Tenn gov 8-3, 606G1
Loses electn 11-7, 853D1
BUTERA, Robert J.
Loses primary for Pa gov 5-16, 389C3
BUTHELEZI, Chief Gatsha
At nonwhite united front mtg 1-11, 20C3
Scores bantustans; urges electn boycott, schl return 1-29, 92B2
Youths attack at Sobukwe funeral 3-11, 193C3
Heads nonwhite party, Zulu electn win rptd 3-14, 229A3
S Africa poll rpts blacks back 6-15, 536G2
Inkatha to pressure forgn cos 7-13, 633E1
BUTLER, John M.
Dies 3-16, 252E2
BUTLER, Landon
On labor-pact panel 8-7, 624D2
BUTLER, Rep. M. Caldwell (R, Va.)
Reelected 11-7, 852D3
BUTORPHANOL Tartrate (Stadol)—*See MEDICINE—Drugs*
BUTROS, Fuad
Meets Syrians on truce 2-8, 79G1
On plan to shift army to south 7-28, 581E1, F1
Meets Assad on Leb clashes 8-29, 674A2
Ambush thwarted 11-2, 828A2
BUTROS, Ghali
Vs Parlt move to bar Israel talks 4-13, 299C3
BUTTE, Mont.—*See MONTANA*
BUTTER—*See DAIRY Products*
BUTTERFIELD, Fox
Pl electn coverage protested 4-11, 269C1
BUTTY, Julius
Sentncd for assault 8-18, Munro interventn prompts resignatn 9-8, 721E2
BUTZ, Earl L.
Bench jokes upset audience 1-7, 195C1
Legal immunity defined by Sup Ct 6-29, 567B2
BUTZ v. Economou
US offcls' legal immunity defined by Sup Ct 6-29, 567B2
BUWONO, Sultan Hamengku
Replaced as Indonesia vp 3-22, 246E1
BUZHARDT Jr., J. Fred
Dies 12-16, 1032D2
BYELORUSSIAN Soviet Socialist Republic—*See USSR—Republics*
BYERS, Russell George
Alleges King murder plot 7-26, 589G2
Discloses King murder bounty 11-29, 938G1
BYERS, Walter
NCAA meets, House subcom probe cited 1-11—1-13, 40B2
BYINGTON, S. John
Scored in Civl Svc rpt 1-12, resigns as CPSC chrmn 2-8, 185E2-A3
King named CPSC chairwoman 6-29, 589A2
BYKOVSKY, Col. Valery
Docks with Salyut 8-27, returns 9-3, 714A1
BYRD Jr., Sen. Harry F. (Ind, Va.)
Votes vs Panama Canal neutrality pact 3-16, 177F2
Votes vs 2d Canal pact 4-18, 273B1
Personal finances rptd 5-19, 385D3
BYRD, Adm. Richard Evelyn (1889-1957)
Frederick Crockett dies 1-17, 96E1
Poulter dies 6-14, 540E3

1979

BUSINESS Roundtable, The
Regulatory costs rptd 3-14, 230E2
BUSINESS Week (magazine)
Amer Express seeks McGraw-Hill 1-9, 16A1
Muir dies 1-30, 104E3
'78 top-paid corp execs ranked 5-14, 347D3-348C1
BUSING—*See EDUCATION—School Integration*
BUSS, Jerry
Buys Lakers, Kings, Forum arena 5-30, 527E1
BUSTELO, Carlos
Parlt energy debate rptd 5-17, 428B1
In GM talks 6-5, plant agrmt reached 6-6, 428A2
BUTCHER, Willard C.
Named Rockefeller successor 12-18, 986B2
BUTCHMAN, Alan A.
Dismissal sought 7-19, resigns 7-20, 530G1, A3
BUTCH and Sundance: The Early Days (film)
Released 6-15, 819F3
BUTHELEZI, Chief Gatsha
Meets with US' Jackson, domestic black ldrs 7-30, 617B2
BUTKUS, Dick
Enters HOF 7-28, 1001C1
BUTLER, Adam
Brit Shipbldrs denatlzn deferred 7-23, 564G3
BUTLER, Jerry
In NFL draft 5-3, 335F1
BUTLER, Jim
'78 extortn convictn cited 1-26, 156F2
BUTLER, Michael
Hair released 3-13, 528D2
BUTMAN, Hillel
Release cited 4-29, 317D2
BUTNER v. U.S.
State rent collectn bankruptcy laws backed by Sup Ct 2-21, 128G3
BUT Never Jam Today (play)
Opens 7-31, 711G1
BUTROS, Fuad
Scores Israel air raid on Leb 4-11, 278E2
Asks US pressure Israel re raids 8-26, 643A2
BUTTERFIELD, Alexander P.
Dismissed by Calif Life 8-16, 656F2
BUTTERWORTH v. Walker
Case refused by Sup Ct 10-29, 844B2
BUTTREY Food Stores Inc.
PCB contaminated eggs destroyed 9-17, 704D3
BUTZNER Jr., Judge John D.
Mandel conviction upset 1-11, 18B1
BUTZ v. Economou
Case cited by Sup Ct 6-5, 464D1
BUZZANCA, Thomas
Indicted 3-6, 220C2
BUZZI, Ruth
Villain released 7-20, 820E3
BUZZI, Stephen R.
Convicted 2-22, sentncd 3-19, 220G2
BYAM, Suzanne
Homeland opens 4-16, 711F3
BYELORUSSIAN Soviet Socialist Republic—*See USSR-Republics*
BYERS, Walter
Scores House subcom probe 1-10, 103F1
Vs Title IX sports guidelines 12-4, 1000C3
BYMAN, Bob
Wins Citrus Classic 3-4, 220F3
BYRD Jr., Sen. Harry F. (Ind, Va.)
Finances disclosed 5-18, 383D2
Res' scores Carter Taiwan treaty move 6-6, 440B2
Zimbabwe trade amendmt OKd by Sen 6-12, 435A1
Vs SALT ratificatn 7-30, 644B1
BYRD, Adm. Richard Evelyn (1889-1957)
Antarctic DC-10 crash kills 257 11-28, 912E1

1980

BUSINESS Week (magazine)
US arms productn rptd 1-25, 65F2, 70D3
Wage-price controls backed 2-22, 144G3
Top 10 money market funds listed 3-31, 223F3
BUSING—*See EDUCATION--School Integration*
BUSSERT, Meg
Brigadoon opens 10-16, 892A3
BUSSIERES, Pierre
Canada finance min 3-3, 171C2
BUSTAMENTE y Rivero, Jose
Honduras, El Salvador sign peace pact 10-30, 872C3
BUSTELO, Carlos
Spain sets energy conservatn 1-8, 22B2
Ousted as indus min 5-2, 355D1
BUTCHER, Willard C.
Named Chase chrmn 6-25, 600D2
BUTHELEZI, Chief Gatsha
Backs black community cncls 5-10, 374C1
Botha abandons black cncl 8-8, 652G3
BUTLER, George A.
On First Penn bailout 4-28, 329F3, 330A3
BUTLER, Horace
Arrested in Tabatabai slaying 7-23, 545C2
BUTLER, Rep. M. Caldwell (R, Va.)
Reelected 11-4, 844D3
BUTLER, Merrill
Scores US housing actions 4-17, 286A2
BUTLER, Michael
Reggae opens 3-27, 392F3
BUTLER, Owen B.
Named Procter & Gamble chrmn 12-9, 959B1
BUTLER, Sidney
US to buy Sovt-bound chickens 1-21, 44E3
BUTLIN, Billy
Dies 6-12, 528D1
BUTROS, Fuad
Sees US amb, reassured on peace efforts 8-28, 643G3
Retained as Leb forgn min 10-25, 874A1
BUTTE—*See MONTANA*
BUTTER—*See DAIRY Products*
BUTTRICK, Rev. Dr. George A.
Dies 1-23, 104A2
BUTTS, Vernon Robert
Chrgd in Calif 'freeway murders' 7-29, 654C2
4th chrgd in 'freeway murders' 8-22, 727G1
BUTUZOVA, Natalya
Wins Olympic medal 8-2, 622D1
BUZZANCA, Thomas
Sentenced 5-20, 927F2
BYELORRUSSIAN Soviet Socialist Republic—*See UNION of Soviet Socialist Republics--Republics*
BYERLY, Terry Lee (alias Davis Earl Keene)
Remains in Cuba 10-27, 828D3
BYFIELD, Alfredo
Released 4-6, 293B3
BYKOV, Anatoly
Wins Olympic medal 7-23, 624B3
BY Myself (book)
Wins Amer Book Award 5-1, 692C2
BYONG Uk Li
Wins Olympic medal 8-2, 622E1
BYRCH, Dr. Milan
Bjelke-Petersen scored 6-22, 496F2
BYRD Jr., Sen. Harry F. (Ind, Va.)
Va dist judges named 4-9; scores Sheffield nominatn, vows fight 4-9, 9-9, 744E3, 745C1
BYRD, Henry (Professor Longhair)
Dies 1-30, 104A2
BYRD, Adm. Richard Evelyn (1889-1957)
Finn Ronne dies 1-12, 104F3

1976

BYRD, Sen. Robert C(arlyle) (D, W. Va.)
Declares pres bid 1-9, 21D3
Seeks Sen majority post 3-5, 181F1
Kissinger vs chrome amendmt 4-27, 293E1
Wins pres. Sen primaries 5-11, 342C3
Ford urges regulatory reform 5-13, 347A1
Releases pres delegates 6-10, 432E1
Dem platform text cites amendmt 6-15, 478E3
Dem conv pres vote, table 7-14, 507E2
Reelected 11-2, 820D1, 823E1, 828D3
Carter meets cong ldrs 11-17, 864A2
BYRNE, Gov. Brendan (D, N.J.)
Endorses Carter 4-29, 324A1
Signs income tax bill 7-8, 995A2
NE govs seek aid 11-13—11-14, 864B3
BYRNE, Dominic P.
Bronfman case verdict 12-10, 952A3
BYRNE, Donald
Dies 3-4, 484C3
BYRNE, Patricia M.
Named Mali amb 9-3; confrmd 9-15, 807E3
BYRNE, Robert
US wins chess crown 11-10, 969B3
BYRNE, Thomas R.
Amb to Czech 3-31; confrmd 4-28, 412E1
Replaced as amb to Norway 4-1, 262B3
BYRNES, George V.
Guild strikes Time 6-2, 398C1
BYRON, Rep. Goodloe E. (D, Md.)
Scored by environmt group 3-25, 220B1
Reelected 11-2, 829A4
BYRON, Katharine E.
Dies 12-28, 1015B1

1977

BYRD, Sen. Robert C(arlyle) (D, W. Va.)
Wins Sen majority post 1-4, 5E3-6C1
Carter econ plan disclosed 1-7, 5B2
Ethics panel formed 1-18, 77F2
On Sen reorganizatn 2-4, 91D1
Backs Warnke nominatn 3-5, 3-9, 172B2
On water projct cuts 3-11, 209G3
Backs cong pub electn funds 3-19, 232E3
Backs ethics code 4-1, 251C2
Lauds tax rebate plan withdrawal 4-14, 270E3
On Carter water projct cuts 4-18, 299E3
'76 campaign surplus rptd 5-4, 482G1, A2
Urges energy tax change 5-19, 443B2
Scores Japan export curb agrmt 5-20, 416F1
On Carter-Cong energy tussle 6-11, 460A2
Backs water projcts compromise 6-15, 459F3
Sen backs compromise Korea, Cuba amendmts 6-16, 477F3-478B1
House votes busing curbs 6-16, 478D1
Vs B-1 bomber 6-24, 514D2
Backs Carter Mideast moves 6-29, 496C1
Delays Panama Canal vote 9-10, 698E2
Sees Lance resignatn 9-10, 701E3
Rpts mail vs Canal pacts; says Sen lacks ratificatn votes 9-24, 755A3
Gas bill filibuster ends 10-3, 757G2, 758A1
Says Torrijos cleared re drug rpts 10-13, 792E1
Lauds Carter-Torrijos Canal pact statemt 10-15, 791G3
Energy tax bill OKd 10-31, 832G1
Sees shift toward Canal pact 11-8, 911F3
In Panama, sees Torrijos 11-9—11-12, 911B2, E3
BYRNE, Gov. Brendan T. (D, N.J.)
Com issues terrorism rpt 3-2, 483G3
Concorde stand rptd 3-9, 212D3
Signs casino gambling act 6-2, 423G3
Wins renomination 6-7, 446C3
Carter stumps in NJ 9-10, 761C1
Reelected 11-8, 855E1, A2
Signs permanent income tax bill 12-15, 1008D3
Vetoes Port Auth aircraft noise rule 12-27, 1006E3
BYRNE, Dominic P.
Sentenced for extortn 1-6, 103C1
BYRNE, Jane M.
Fired 11-21, 944D2
BYROADE, Henry A.
Replaced as amb to Pak 6-7, 499F3

1978

BYRD, Sen. Robert C(arlyle) (D, W. Va.)
Backs Panama Canal pacts 1-13; plans amendmts 1-25, sees ratificatn 1-30, 58E1
Introduces Canal pact amendmts 2-7; in Sen debate 2-9, 120D1, G1
Sees no Torrijos drug link 2-22, 120C3
Canal pact procedural ploy defeated 2-22, 120E3
Canal neutrality pact amended 3-10, 3-13, ratified 3-16, 177E1, D2, G3-178A1
Vs neutron bomb cancellatn 4-6, accepts deferral 4-7, 254A1
Discounts Torrijos moves on DeConcini reservatn 4-8, 255B3
DeConcini OKs noninterventn 'understanding' 4-13, 255F3
Votes for 2d Canal pact, ratificatn role cited 4-18, 273B1, F2
For Mideast jet-sale legis delay 4-25, 307B1
Vs Soc Sec rollback 5-19, 386D1
Disputes Carter on Africa aid curbs 5-20, 383D1
Sees CIA evidence on Cuba role in Zaire 6-2, 442F1
Gulf illegal paymt rptd 6-2, 449E1
On labor law revisn setback 6-22, 508D2
Gas bill filibuster avoided 9-14, 733C2
Praises 95th Cong 10-15, 784F2
BYRNE, Gov. Brendan T. (D, N.J.)
Legalizes laetrile 1-10, 23B3
Urges offshore leasing legis 2-21, 125B3
Pocket vetoes death penalty bill 3-3, 388E3
Scores Ulster violence 3-16, 373C3
BYRNE, Seamus
Wounded in Belfast 6-27, 630A3
BYRNES, Marty
In NBA draft 6-9, 457G2
BYRON, Beverly
Wins US House seat 11-7, 846F2, 848A3, 851B1
BYRON, Rep. Goodloe E. (D, Md.)
Dies 10-11, 888G2
Wife wins US House Seat 11-7, 848A3
BYSSINOSIS (brown lung disease)—See *MEDICINE—Heart & Lungs*

1979

BYRD, Sen. Robert Carlyle (D, W.Va.)
Proposes Sen delay tactics curb 1-15, 30A2
Sen majority ldr 71A2
Sen OKs filibuster curb 2-22, 150D2
Sen income limit stayed 3-8, 185G2
Schl prayer amendmt shifted 4-9, 326D2
Sees oil-profits tax OK 4-23, 300E2
Resources Dept plan dropped 5-15, 365A2, D2
Lauds EPA coal-use rule 5-25, 403F3
Links MX OK, SALT pact 6-10, 438C1
In USSR re SALT 7-1–7-5; sees Brezhnev 7-4; warns vs amendmts on US TV 7-8, 510B3
Defends Carter '80 bid 7-28, 593E3
Defends Young UN resignatn 8-16, 606B2
Bars SALT, Cuba troop issue linkage 9-8, 674G1
On Carter speech re Sovt troops in Cuba 10-1, 737C2
Backs SALT ratificatn 10-25, 822C3
Delays SALT debate till '80 12-6, 938E3
BYRNE, Gov. Brendan (D, N.J.)
Gets reassurance on winter heating fuel supply 8-28, 703C2
Attends Carter dinner 10-24, 961F2
BYRNE, Mayor Jane M. (Chicago, Ill.)
Wins Chicago mayoral primary 2-27, 149E3-150A1
Elected Chicago mayor 4-3, 251G3
Attacks Carter policies 6-9, 439C3
Princess Margaret in Chicago 10-13, 860B1
Gets Kennedy telegram, support sought; lauds Carter record 10-15, 807A3
FALN bombs office 10-18, 786B2
Endorses Kennedy 10-30, 847C2
Backs Kennedy at Dem Natl Com mtg 11-9, 961D2
On city job reductn 11-16, 921A1
Goldschmidt threatens US fund loss 11-20; scores 11-20, 11-21, 983F3
Scores offcls re schl fscl crisis 12-5, on note repaymt 12-7, 943F3, 944A1
Skips Carter fete 12-6, 961D3
Transit strike 12-17–12-20, 987C2
Schls miss payday 12-21, 991A2
BYRNE, Judge Richard
OKs respirator removal 2-15, 291B2
BYRNES, Marty
Traded to Jazz 1-12, 526C2
BYRNE v. Public Funds for Public Schools
Case affirmed by Sup Ct 5-29, 421G3
BZ (3-quinuclidinyl benzilate)—See *NARCOTICS & Dangerous Drugs*

1980

BYRD, Sen. Robert Carlyle (D, W. Va.)
Vs Clark warning to Sovts 2-2, 83D2
Backs '81 budget cuts 3-5, 168E3
Carter coal-fired utilities plan presented 3-6, 169F3
Urges Carter to campaign 4-26, 328A2
Muskie named secy of state 4-29, 323B3
Urges Carter to debate 5-10, 367A1
Scores Carter budget stand 5-28, 424B2
Meets Carter on Cuban refugees 6-4, 435C1
On oil import fee 6-6, 437A2
Sen OKs Iran hostage resolutn 6-18, 460B1
Pledges tax-cut plan 6-26, 480G2
Joins open-conv move 8-2, 596F2
Sees Reagan, vows cooperatn 11-18, 880G2, C3
Backs toxic waste clean-up fund 11-24, 898B1
Retains Sen Dem posts 12-4, 936G2
Warns on Haig apptmt 12-6, 935G1
Urges fair-housing bill 12-6, 954C2
Haig appointed 12-16, 955B2
BYRD International Airport (Richmond, Va.)
Taxiway bid-rigging scandal rptd 7-5, 655B2
BYRNE, Gov. Brendan (D, N.J.)
Proposes casino comm reform 2-11, 111D1
BYRNE, Mayor Jane M. (Chicago, Ill.)
State of State message 1-8, 403E3
Appoints spouse press secy 1-9, 199F1
Chicago budget deficit rptd 1-12, names Yeo chief fscl adviser 1-22, 186E2
Assails 'past admin' fscl actns 1-30, tax error levy backed 2-14, 186F2, B3
Kennedy campaign said troubled 3-4, 167B1
Firemen end strike 3-8, 187F2
Ill primary results 3-18, 206G2
ERA rejected by Ill house 6-18, 482D3
Helps Mondale campaign 9-9, 780A2
Sets water rationing 9-12, 9-22, 947C3
At Carter rally 10-6, 762B3
Daley elected Cook Cnty state attorney 11-4, 850E3
BYRNE, Kevin
2d in 6,000-m Penn Relays 4-25, 892D2
BYRON, Rep. Beverly (D, Md.)
Reelected 11-4, 843B1
BYRUM, John
Heart Beat released 4-25, 416A3
BYSTROM, Marty
In World Series 10-14, 812F2

C

1976

C-Plane Series—See *'Aircraft' under ARMAMENTS*
CABALLERO, Luis
Goods frozen 7-1, 520A2
CABINDA—See *under ANGOLA*
CABRAL, Amilcar (d. 1973)
Rousseaux claims death role 1-9, 45D3
CABRAL, Luis
Sees Castro, Neto, Sekou Toure 3-15—3-16, 251E3
CABRERA, Manuel
Church excommunicates 8-17, 711A2
CACM—See *CENTRAL American Common Market*
CADDELL, Patrick H.
Analyzes electn 11-5, 11-11, 845G1
CADEMARTORI, Jose
Exiled 12-11, 963D1
CADILLAC Gage Co.—See *EX-Cell-O Corp.*
CADMIUM
UN Medit pollutn pact signed 2-16, 126D3
CAFFERATA Marazzi, Adm. Geronimo
Peru housing min 7-17, 590D3
CAFIERO, Antonio
Says Peron to retire 1-13, 71B3
Signs Venez econ pact 1-14, 96D3
Negotiates wage hike 1-22, 96D2
Loses cabt post 2-3, 154G2
CAGIANESE, Dominick
Arrested 5-17, 401B2, D2
CAGIELSKI, Longin
Named Polish dep premr 3-27, 268E2
CAGLAYANGIL, Ihsan Sabri
Cyprus peace talks resumptn set 1-18, 48E2
Signs US base pact 3-26, 244G1
Turkey OKs PLO office 5-12, 373B2
On Aegean oil feud 8-11—8-14, 622C2-B3
Plans new Greek talks 8-25, 643F2
CAGNOTTO, Franco
Wins Olympic medal 7-22, 575D3
CAHILL, Thomas J.
Vesco, 6 others indicted 1-14, 78E2
CAHILL, William T.
Norcross wins Sen primary 6-8, 410A1
Sup Ct bars review of Gross conviction 10-4, 766E1
CAIRNS, Dr. James
'70 Australia Viet massacre denied 8-3, 571F3
CALABRO, Victorio
Mil ldrs block provincial takeover 1-8, 26E1
Scores Peron pol isolatn 1-27, 71G2

1977

CAAMANO, Claudio
Freed in amnesty 9-2, 710D2
CAB—See *U.S. GOVERNMENT—CIVIL Aeronautics Board*
CABANAS, Lucio (d. 1974)
Brother rptd jailed 5 yrs 3-30, 528E3
CABANAS, Pablo
Rptd jailed 5 yrs 3-30, 528E3
CABANILLAS, Pio
Cabt backs center-right coalitn 1-21, 68B2
Spain culture, welfare min 7-5, 545A2
CABINET, U.S.—See *under U.S. GOVERNMENT*
CABLE TV—See *BROADCASTING—Television*
CABO, Dardo
Killed 1-6, 42C1
CABOT, Sebastian
Dies 8-23, 696E2
CABRERA, Edilberto
Arrest rptd 8-26, chrgs jail beatings 9-7, 726G3
CABRERA, Francisco
Uganda visit cited 3-3, 308C2
CABRINI, Saint Frances Xavier (1850—1917)
Neumann canonized 6-19, 731C3
CACCIAFESTA, Remo
Shot 6-21, 1014A3
CACERES Monie, Gen. Jose Rafael (ret.)
Arrested 5-4, 371B1
Freed 6-13, 522D3
CADDELL, Patrick
Carter ciarifies memo 5-12, 381B1
Carter on mtg re polls drop 10-27, 814A1
CADMAN, Radclyffe
Names S Africa party head 10-5, 826C1
CAFIK, Norman A.
Canada multiculturalism min 9-16, 725F2
CAGLAYANGIL, Ihsan Sabri
Meets Greek forgn min 1-29, 122D2
Signs Treaty of Izmir 3-12, 190D2
CAGLE, Vice Adm. Malcolm W. (ret.)
Acquitted in Iran contract fraud 11-24, 942F2
CAIN, James Mallahan
Dies 10-27, 872C1
CAIRNS, James F.
Morosi wins libel suit 4-22, 326B2
Plans retiremt 8-10, 693D1
CAISSE Nationale de Credit Agricole
World's 3d largest bank 6-21, 578A2
CALABRO, Victorio
Graiver probe protectn rptd 4-22, 371E2
CALAMAI, Peter
Czechs seize belongings 4-24, 314A3

1978

CAAN, James
Comes A Horseman released 11-1, 969G3
CAB—See *U.S. GOVERNMENT—CIVIL Aeronautics Board*
CABAL OF Hypocrites, A (play)
Moliere opens 3-12, 887B2
CABELL, Enos
NL batting ldr 10-2, 928F2
CABINET, U.S.—See *under CARTER and U.S. GOVERNMENT*
CABLE TV—See *BROADCASTING—Television*
CABRAL, Manuel Jose
Named DR finance min 8-16, 648D2
CADBURY Schweppes Ltd.
Cmdr Whitehead dies 4-16, 356F3
CADDELL, Patrick
Hired by Venez pres candidate 5-5, 395G1
CADILLAC Mountain (Me.)
Sun Day observed 5-3, 321G3
CAESAR'S Palace Hotel (Las Vegas, Nev.)
FCC censures CBS 'Heavyweight Championship' tennis tourn 3-16, 252F1, B2
CAFIERO, Eugene A.
Iacocca replaces, named Chrysler vice chrmn 11-2, 936B1
CAILLOL, Alain
Captured 3-24, 232F1
CAIN, Darryl L.
US drops dual prosecutn 7-14, 991D3
CAINE, Michael
Silver Bears released 4-20, 619G3
California Suite released 12-21, 1030E2
CAISSE Nationale de Credit Agricole (Paris bank)
Ranked '77 3d biggest in world 11-8, 914A1, D1
CAKMUR, Yuksel
Named Turkey youth min 1-5, 21F2

1979

C-Plane Series—See *ARMAMENTS—Aircraft*
CAAN, James
Chapter Two released 12-14, 1007B3
CAB—See *U.S. GOVERNMENT-CIVIL Aeronautics Board*
CABA, Jose
Lopez KOs 9-26, 839C1
CABAN v. Mohammed
Case decided by Sup Ct 4-24, 364B1
CABINET, U.S.—See *under U.S. GOVERNMENT*
CABLE TV—See *BROADCASTING—Television*
CAESARS World Inc.
Boardwalk Regency casino opens 6-26, 520D1
NJ hikes gambling tax 9-18, 851G1
CAETANO, Marcello
Sa Carneiro oppositn cited 12-2, 917D1
CAFFEY, Richard
Buck Rogers released 3-29, 528E1
CAFFREY, Judge Andrew
Swears 1st black woman US magistrate 8-7, 901F3
CAFIERO, Eugene A.
Chrysler resignatn rptd 3-1, 188D1
CAGE aux Folles (film)
Released 5-12, 528F1
CAHILL, Kevin
N Ireland remarks rptd 4-20, 312C3
CAHILL, Mike
Loses Stowe Grand Prix 8-19, 734C2
CAIN, Harry Pulliam
Dies 3-3, 272B2
CAINE, Michael
Beyond the Poseidon Adventure released 5-24, 528E1
CAISSE Nationale de Credit Agricole (Paris bank)
Ranked '78 world's 2d biggest bank 6-19, 476B2
CALAVERAS Fault, Calif.—See *CALIFORNIA*

1980

CAAN, James
Hide in Plain Sight released 3-21, 216G2
CAB (Civil Aeronautics Board)—See *under U.S. GOVERNMENT*
CABANAS, Roberto
Cosmos win NASL title 9-21, 770E2
CABINET, U.S.—See *under U.S. GOVERNMENT*
CABLECOM General Inc.
RKO General buys 9-24, 746G1
CABLE News Network (CNN)
Debuts, Carter interview aired 6-1, 422F3, 501A3
CABLE TV—See *BROADCASTING--Television*
CABRAL de Almeida, Luis (Guinea-Bissau president; ousted Nov. 14)
Ousted in coup 11-14; safety assured 11-18, 887B1
CACERAS Lehnhoff, Eduardo
Dies in fire at Spanish emb 1-31, 98C2
CACTUS (Panamanian freighter)
Collides with US aircraft carrier 7-29, 674E1
CADDELL, Patrick H.
On vote results 11-4, 838E2
CADDYSHACK (film)
Top-grossing film 8-6, 640D3
CADMIUM
Medit pollutn pact signed 5-17, 381C3
CAERHAT, Ludwig
Revson heir, financier indicted 8-19, 713G3
CAESARS World Inc.
NJ gambling license issued 10-25; '79 '80 revenues rptd 12-12, 988F2-B3, E3
CAETANO, Marcello
Dies 10-26, 876A1
CAFFEINE
FDA issues warning 9-4, 726A2
CAGLAYANGIL, Ihsan (Turkish president)
Pres electn deferred 3-22, 236G1
Takes over as acting pres 4-6, 278B2
Anti-terrorist bills set 7-24, 580B3
CAGNOTTO, Franco
Wins Olympic medal 7-23, 623E3
CAHN, Judge Edward
Blocks draft registratn 7-18, 597G3
CAIN, Melanie
Jacobson sentenced for murder 6-3, 502A2
CAIN, William
Of the Fields opens 5-27, 756F3
CAJAL y Lopez, Maximo
Flees Guatemala emb fire 1-31, takes refuge with US amb 2-1, 98B2, A3
CAJUSO, Eduardo
Signs with Tigers 6-3, 637C1
CALANDRA Sr., John P.
Acquitted in FBI bribery case 7-3, 655E2

1976

CALDER, Alexander
Dies 11-11, 970C1

CALDERON, Gen. Jose Ramon
Lockheed paymts rptd 2-8, 147F2
Rpt Lockheed papers confirm bribe 8-24, 740A2

CALGON Corp.
Nalco boycott noncompliance rptd 11-7, 986B3

CALHOUN, Jesse A.
On Ford fund probe 9-21, 722F2
Carter campaign donatn rptd 10-22, 939B1

CALIFANO Jr., Joseph A.
Carter names spec adviser 8-3, 564C3
Argues vs Schorr subpoena 9-13, 749D1
Named HEW secy 12-23, 956E2
Photo 956D3
Biog sketch 957D2
Sees welfare reform delay 12-28, 978G1

CALIFORNIA
Drought ends 2-5, 271C3
Lone Pine A-test tremor rptd 2-13, 243A1
28 die in Yuba HS bus crash 5-21, 383G3
San Leandro bank fails 5-22; Lloyds reopens 5-23, 438B1
NASA Jupiter symposium 5-24, 443C3
Moon property assessed 6-2, 971E1
Getty funds Mailbu mausoleum 6-8, 444G1-A2
US Sup Ct rules on Pasadena schl rezoning 6-28, 478G3
US Sup Ct declines zoning rule review 6-28, 569D1
Yuba HS bus crash rpt 7-22, 595A3
Fscl '75 per capita income, tax burden rptd 9-15, 10-12, 959E1, E2

1977

CALDERA, Rafael
Scores AD pres primary 7-17, 566D1
Copei platform lauds admin 8-18, 674G1
MEP pres candidate named 9-25, 867B3

CALDERO, Michael A.
Secret news source case review refused 10-31, 835F2

CALDERON Munoz, Abdon
Pres candidacy rptd 8-26, 842F1

CALDWELL, Dr. Glyn G.
A-test linked to cancer 12-13, 1022E3

CALDWELL, John L.
On US business in S Africa 11-23, 934B3

CALDWELL, Philip
On Ford chief exec panel 4-14, 409C1

CALHOUN (Ga.) First National Bank
Lance cleared 8-18, 625F1, B3
Carter defends Lance, concedes reforms needed 8-23, 649F1
Lance irregularities chrgd 9-5—9-7, 690A1-A2
Lance defends practices 9-15, 700G3-701F2
Sen com hearings on Lance 9-16—9-19, govt affidavit released 9-20, 718D2-G3
Carter cites Lance controversy 9-21, 718F1

CALDWELL, Taylor
Ceremony on best-seller list 11-6, 872E3

CALIFANO Jr., Joseph A.
Confrmatn hearings 1-13; confrmatn recommended 1-18, delayed 1-20, 34C1, E3
Confrmd 1-24, sworn 1-25, 52D2, F2
Forms welfare study group 1-26, meets 2-11, 175F3-176B1
Fredrickson retained at NIH 2-3, 211B1
Asks Sencer resignatn 2-4, 103D3
On DNA patent order 2-7, 184C2
Orders flu shots resumed 2-8, 103F2
Tells Carter budget too low 2-14, 110C3
On schl aid cutoffs; Ark, Tex review ordrd 2-17, 156C3
On Carter budget revision 2-22, 125E3
Rpts personal finances 2-25, 147G3
Walsh resigns 3-6; Calif health probe curb chrgs denied 3-19; Walsh, Sen com statemts 3-23, 235F2
HEW reorganization set 3-8, 175E2
Backs schl admissn, job quotas; vs busing curbs 3-17, 217B3
FBI to aid health fraud probe 3-20, 236A1
Hirings questioned 3-23—3-26, 236B1
Retracts quota statemt 3-31, 235B2
Guidelines for colls in 6 states reordrd 4-1, 446C1
Names Foege CDC dir 4-5, 287D3
Handicapped protest 4-5—4-16, vows rules review 4-5, 301D2
Sets immunizatn drive 4-6, 287E2
On fed DNA curbs 4-6, 452A1
Educ Office reorganized 4-11, 301D3
Hosp cost controls urged 4-25, 322F1
Proposes illegal alien plan 4-27, 370C2
Signs handicapped rules 4-28, 338E2
Testifies on hosp waste 5-24, MD fees 6-7, 479F1
Outlines Carter welfare plan 5-25, scores spending lid 5-27, 445D2-E3
Backs coll admissn 6-5, 445F3
On Medicaid cuts 6-8, 460C3
Carter agrees to sign HEW-Labor funds 6-15, 459C3
Rpts Medicaid fraud cases 6-18, 643G2
Addresses AMA 6-19, 479B1
NYC spec schl aid withheld 7-5, 631G1
On Admin adoptn proposal 7-12, 628G2-A3
Bars phenformin sales 7-25, 603A2
Turner on CIA mind-control tests 8-3, 611A2
Bans fed subsidies for abortn 8-4, 786G1
Urges Cong action on hosp costs 8-17, 643A3
Addresses govs conf 9-8, 719G1
Vs GOP Soc Security plan 9-9, 720C2
Hosp cost cutbacks proposed 9-26, 869D2
Urges abortn issue setld 10-11, 786C2
Chicago teachers assigned by race 10-12, 837F2
Hails Kaiser-Permanente HMO 10-26, 869G3

CALIFANO v. Abbott
Old-age benefits test voided 3-21, 320F1

CALIFANO v. Goldfarb
Statute vs widowers' benefit voided 3-2, 192D1

CALIFANO v. Jablon
Old-age benefits test voided 3-21, 230F1

CALIFANO v. Jobst
Disability benefits loss upheld 11-8, 857A1

CALIFANO v. Silbowitz
Old-age benefits voided 3-21, 230E1

CALIFANO v. Webster
Old-age benefits sex bias upheld 3-21, 230B2

CALIFORNIA
'68 NYS stock-transfer tax amendmts ruled illegal 1-12, 57F2
Forest Svc employes taxatn upheld 1-25, 80G2
Edwards AF Base space shuttle test 2-18, 170B3; **for subsequent developments, see 'Space Shuttle' under ASTRONAUTICS**
Carter vs Auburn Dam $s 2-22, 126E1
Bank of Calif takeover rejected 3-1, 155A2
Irvine Co takeover battle rptd 3-3, 274E3
Palmdale land swell chng rptd 3-3, 288G1
UFW-Teamsters sign pact 3-10, 177D3
Moon disciples in parental custody 3-24, Boonville seminars halted 3-28, 286F3

1978

CALCIUM Pangamate (B-15)—*See FOOD*

CALDER, Alexander
Natl Gallery commissn rptd 6-1, 578B3

CALDERA, Rafael
Copei candidate elected pres; AD to control Sen 12-3, 952C3

CALDERON Fornier, Rafael Angel
To be CR foreign min 3-4, 171A1

CALDERON Munoz, Abdon
5th in Ecuador pres race 7-16, 557A1
Shot 11-29, dies 12-9; suspect rptd seized 12-13, 989D3
Ecuador interior min, police chief fired; murderer rptdly identified 12-20, 1021C3

CALDERON Velarde, Alfonso
OKs probe of rptr's death 2-16, 289G3

CALDER Trophy—*See HOCKEY—Awards*

CALDWELL, Joe
ABA pensn upheld by NC ct 7-19, 656G1

CALDWELL, Malcolm
In Cambodia 12-9, slain 12-23, 997A2

CALDWELL, Mike
AL pitching ldr 10-2, 928F3-G3

CALDWELL, Philip
Promoted 6-8, Iacocca fired 7-13, 642E1
Named Ford pres 10-16, 808E3

CALERO Portocarrero, Adolfo
Arrest rptd 9-4, 690C3

CALHOUN (Ga.) First National Bank
SEC, comptroller chrgd ; case setld 4-26, 324G2-E3

CALIFANO Jr., Joseph A.
Sets HEW anti-smoking crusade; Nader, other lobbyists score 1-11, 23B2, G2
Issues HEW abortn rules 1-26, 116D1
Rpts Va, Ga, NC coll integratn plans rejctd; Ark, Okla, Fla OKd 2-2, 85E1
Coll student aid plan unveiled 2-8, 84A2
NC, Ga, Va coll integratn plans OKd 3-8—5-12, 369B1
Soc Sec rptd sound, hosp insurnc reform urged 5-16, 368C3
Delays USSR trip 5-30, 401A2
Welfare reform compromise prepared 6-7, 446B2
Natl health plan readied 6-26, 491E2
Lauds Sup Ct Bakke ruling 6-28, 482C2
Scores hosp cost lid rejectn by House com 7-18, 550G3 ★
Defends Carter health plan 7-28, outline released 7-29, 585F2, 586D2
Announces measles campaign 10-4, 927D3
Vs new med schools 10-24, 948C3
Guyana releases letter lauding Rev Jones 11-20, 891D1
On natl health plan at Dem midterm conf 12-9, 956D2
OKs recombinant DNA rules 12-16, advisory panel expanded 12-27, 1022F3-1023E1
Sets hosp cost guide 12-28, 1012F1

CALIFANO v. Aznavorian
SSI forgn travel rule backed by Sup Ct 12-11, 981A1

CALIFANO v. Mandley
State emergency welfare standards backed by Sup Ct 6-6, 447E2

CALIFANO v. Torres
PR welfare benefits exclusn upheld 2-27, 143D1

CALIFANO v. White
Expedited disability benefits rule review declined 2-27, 143F1

CALIFORNIA
Indians begin 'Longest Walk' from Alcatraz 2-11, 568D3
Child-support case jurisdictn denied by US Sup Ct 5-15, 387F3
Presbyterian Assemb opens in San Diego 5-16, 409F3-410B1
Space shuttle launching base authorizatn clears US House 5-22, 407B1
Nixon hosts ex-POWs at San Clemente 5-27, 513D2
UK bank to buy Union Bancorp 6-8, 553B1
May mortgage rates rptd up 6-18, 470F1
Petaluma developers fee set 7-21, 611D2
Ky leads refugee welfare protest 8-2, 844E2

1979

CALCAGNO, Judge Walter F.
Sentences White in Moscone-Milk slaying 7-3, 547F3

CALDERON Berti, Humberto
Venez mines, energy min 3-10, 192C3

CALDERON Munoz, Abdon (d. 1978)
Ecuador ex-min linked to death 1-12, 62E2
Police catch alleged killer, Jarrin to be tried in mil ct 3-12, 256E3

CALDER Trophy—*See HOCKEY-Awards*

CALDWELL, Gisela
Hitting Town opens 1-6, 292F1

CALDWELL, L. Scott
Old Phantoms opens 2-8, 292D2

CALDWELL, Philip
Elected Ford chief exec 5-10, 366C2
'78 pay rptd 5-14, 348B1

CALEXICO, Calif.—*See CALIFORNIA*

CALHOUN (Ga.) First National Bank
Lance, 3 others indicted 5-23, plead not guilty 5-24, 380B2

CALIFANO Jr., Joseph A.
Orders A-test cancer rpts probed 1-8, 17E2
HEW smoking rpt issued 1-11, 23B1
Separates from wife 1-19, 79A2
2 unions ask HEW radiatn safety studies 1-30, 90E3
Carter hosp cost plan faces Cong hurdles 2-13, 110C1
Backs natl health insurnc 2-13, 110E1
Soc Sec chng re women urged 2-15, 132E3
Rejcts Darvon ban; orders FDA hearings, MD warning 2-15, 138F2
Sees low-level radiatn risks 2-27, 208A1
Medicaid '78 abortn decline rptd 3-8, 315A1
Backs hosp cost-control bill 3-9, 194D3
Testifies on 3 Mile I radiatn, sets study 4-4, 260E1
Lauds FDA's Kennedy 4-17, 310A3
Soc Sec COL hike rptd 4-26, 310F1
On teenaged smoking 4-27, 970D3
Hikes 3 Mile I radiatn estimate 5-3, 344C1
Warns WHO vs Mideast politics 5-8, 398G2
Defends Carter natl health plan 5-14, 362G1
Mental health bill proposed 5-15, 365C1
Welfare plan presented 5-23, 384F1
Sends PHS team to Asia 6-5, 550E2
Backs pot controls 6-6, 492D2
Sets methapyrilene drug recall 6-8, 471F1
Guillain-Barre flu shot claims rptd stalled 6-10, 470E3
In China 6-28, Hawaii 7-4, 495A3
Dismissal rumored 7-17, fired 7-18; replaced, reactn 7-19, 529C1-531B2, A3
Carter denies firing rpt 7-20, bars details 7-25, 556C1
Harris confrmd HEW secy 7-27, 577C1
Immunizatn progrm rptd effective 9-11, 736D3

CALIFANO Jr., Trudy (Mrs. Joseph A.)
Separates from husband 1-19, 79A2

CALIFANO v. Boles
Case decided by Sup Ct 6-27, 558F1

CALIFANO v. Wescott
Case decided by Sup Ct 6-25, 539E3

CALIFANO v. Yamasaki
Case decided by Sup Ct 6-20, 516D2

CALIFORNIA
ITT LA long-distance phone svc OKd 1-4, 15E2
Paramount resumes 'Warriors' ads 2-22, 174G1-A2
LA art museum willed Renoir painting 3-7, 375B2
Pt Reyes Light wins Pulitzer 4-16, 336D2, A3
Examiner loses libel judgmt 4-18, 334B2
Grand jury transcript examinatn barred by US Sup Ct 4-18, 346C2
La-Pacific '78 sales gain rptd 5-7, 305G1
FTC opens film industry probe 5-23, 430C3
Sacramento paper tied to S Africa scandal 6-4, 427E3

1980

CALDERON, Jose
Arrested in Anderson assault 8-5, 596G3-597A1

CALDERON Berti, Humberto
Sets 6% oil productn cut, curbs multinatl sales 1-16, 102E3, 103A1
Seeks OPEC mtg 10-22, Venez lifts fuel-oil prices 10-27, 822B2
Stresses OPEC unity 12-15, 951D2

CALDWELL, L. Scott
Home opens 5-7, 392C3

CALDWELL, Philip
On '79 forgn earnings 2-21, 287F3
Praises Ford Pinto trial acquittal 3-13, 185F3
Named Ford chairman 3-13, 224C3
Testifies on auto imports 10-9, 823C2

CALDWELL, Taylor
Bright Flows the River on best-seller list 1-13, 40D3

CALIFANO Jr., Joseph A.
Hired as Haig atty 12-22, 980B1

CALIFORNIA
'79 forgn mfg investmt rptd 2-6, 92C3
Coors trust case declined by US Sup Ct 2-19, 131D1
USSR scientists barred from 2 confs 2-22, 135D1
Wine pricing law held illegal by Sup Ct 3-3, 210E1
Hunts bailout loan collateral listed 5-18, 425F3, 426E1
Credit fixing curbed by Sup Ct 5-27, 453G2
Shopping cntr petitn access backed by Sup Ct 6-9, 512A2
Mex seizes tuna boats 7-8, 7-10, 565D1
Major gold deposit found, '79 productn rptd 8-27, 685F2
Itel rpts huge '79 loss 10-16, 784D1

1976

Anti-boycott law signed 9-27; Bank of Amer vows compliance 11-3, modifies policy 12-1, 987D1
'Right-to-die' bill signed 9-30, 770E2
Richardson vows boycott info 10-20, 786G2
Fscl '76 bankruptcy petitns rptd 10-20, 984C3
US Sup Ct stays U of Calif med schl reverse bias ruling 11-15, 882C1
Calif U to appeal reverse bias ruling 11-19, 995F2

Brown Presidential Campaign—*See BROWN Jr., Gov. Edmund G.*
Crime & Civil Disorders—*See also 'Politics' and city subheads; also HEARST, Patricia; SYMBIONESE Liberation Army*
Fine arrested in San Rafael 1-7, 32E2
San Simeon, Wyntoon Hearst homes bombed 2-12, 3-11, 201A3-B3
US Sup Ct rules on convict silence right 4-20, 331F2
7 killed on State U campus 7-12, 860G1
Chowchilla schlchildren kidnaped 7-15, suspects arrested 7-23, 7-29, 560A1
Harrises convicted 8-9, 595B3
San Quentin 6 verdict 8-12, 656B1
Sen com chrgs Medicaid fraud, 8-30, 715B1
Harrises sentenced 8-31, 679B3
Fresno Bee newsmen jailed 9-3—9-17, 700C2
Cornfeld sentncd 9-27, 860A3
Harrises indicted for Hearst kidnap 9-29, 735E2
Chowchilla kidnap trial moved 11-10, 876E3
Camp Pendleton racial assault, KKK link probed 11-13—12-6, 983C1
Legis for Tokyo Rose pardon 11-17, 892C2
Weapons cache found 12-4—12-11, Wiggins, 2 others chrgd 12-15, 952D3

1977

Sup Ct curbs weight-labeling rules 3-29, 277A1
Weight-labeling rules curbed by Sup Ct 3-29, 277A1
US sues vs union loans 3-30, 261G3
US water rights upheld 4-4, 253B1
Mail-order operatns tax upheld 4-4, 341E3
Parents lose Moon disciple custody 4-11, 310B1
'74 Turk jet crash setlmt 4-14, 312C1
Hughes property assessmt rptd 4-14, 354A3
San Diego on '75 10 largest cities list 4-14, 388B1, D1
Biology text barred in Ind 4-14, 471E3
Auburn Dam reconsidered 4-18, 299C3
'76 per-capita income table 5-10, 387G2
Long Beach, Oakland, San Diego business confidence rptd, econ data table 5-16, 384G2, 385C1
Irvine Co bought by Taubman group 5-20, 519B1
Porpoise kills curbed 6-11, 443A1
Schl financing rule review rejctd 6-20, 517D1
Sylvania retail sales rules upheld 6-23, 539G1
Bank of Calif sells 27 branches 7-6, 578D1; Sumitomo purchase challenged 8-9, 669A3
Fires destroy Santa Barbara homes, forests 7-26—8-23, 660B2-G2
US clean-air bill enacted 8-8, 610C2
DBCP productn suspended 8-12, 723F2
Rains flood south 8-15—8-17, 747F2
Farm holding breakup asked by US 8-18, 8-22, 703A2, G2
New youth job corps cntr opens 8-31, 692E2
June new-car sales rptd 9-6, 722B3
Rare meteorite awarded to state 9-7, 712G2
'76 per capita income, tax burden table 9-13, 10-18, 821F2, G3
Phone co refunds ordrd 9-13, 839G1
GM cuts '78 Chevette price 9-15, 722F3
Lockheed Burbank, Palmdale, Sunnyvale machinists strike 10-10—12-31, 1005A2, C2
San Diego liquor license revocatn case review refused 10-17, 797F3
Sumitomo bank acquisitns OKd 10-19, 979D2
Landowners satellite constructn dispute declined 11-7, 857E2
Mitsubishi TV plant cited 12-14, 974B2
Oakland A's sold to Denver oilman 12-15, city sues Finley 12-15, 989A2
Farm strike support seen small 12-22, 1003D1
Bakke Case—*See BAKKE, Allan*

Crime—*See also HEARST, Patricia*
Riverside student arrested as spy 1-16, 41D2-A3
Great Westn land case setld 1-26, 156D1
San Diego Mafia ldr slain 2-10, Mafia operatns rptd widespread 5-16—7-3, 568E1, A2, D2
Mardian bar reinstatemt cited 2-28, 175C2
Pot decriminalizatn impact rptd 3-14, 3-31, 332E2, A3
Polanski indicted 3-24, 262D1
Woolbright convicted 4-22, 396G1
Edgar Smith sentenced 4-25, 396E1
Riverside student convicted as spy 4-28, 344A2; accomplice convicted 5-15, 409B3
Alioto wins libel award 5-3, 532B2
'76 death row populatn rptd 5-5, 594A1
Child porno prostitution rptd 5-15, 5-27, 432A2-E2
Laetrile smugglers sentncd 5-16, 508E2
ICC to curb movers 5-23, 423F3
Death penalty bill vetoed 5-27, 594A2
Porno trial ad role upheld 6-6, 478B3
San Fran LEAA office to close 6-20, 630E2
Haldeman in Lompoc jail 6-21, 483G2
Homosexual slain 6-22, 560D2
Newton to face '74 murder chrgs 6-24, 531G3
Mafia porno operatns rptd 7-3, 568D2
Trashbag murder suspect indicted 7-13, 603F2
Riverside student gets life 7-18, 576E3
'76 Chowchilla kidnapers plead guilty 7-25, 642D1
Van Houten mistrial declared 8-6, 711C2
Polanski pleads guilty 8-8, mental exam ordered 9-19, 732C3
Death penalty veto overridden 8-11, 652D2
San Fran Chinatown gang killings 9-4, 9-11, 711G2
Mendelsohn campaign funds suit cited 11-11, 877B2
Pot law detailed 12-11, 972D3
Glendale Hillside Strangler sought 12-14, 992B1
Chowchilla kidnapers convicted 12-15, 992D1
Trashbag killer sentncd 12-21, 991A3
Drought (& developments)
23 cnties get drought relief 1-20, 77A1
Marin Cnty water rationing starts 2-1, 76C3

1978

Emmys presented in Pasedena 9-17, 1030E1
United Methodist immunity case declined by US Sup Ct 10-16, 789E2
San Diego-Mex border fence planned 10-24, 818D1
Mortgage rate hiked to 11% 11-17, 919C1
Auto franchise law upheld by US Sup Ct 12-5, 959D3
San Diego, San Jose populatn ranked 12-6, 942E3, G3
S&L variable rate mortgages OKd, '75 Cong actn cited 12-14, 962A1

Accidents & Disasters
Rain rptd, drought near end 1-8, 24C1
Ford liability in '72 car crash rptd 2-6, 185B3; award cut 3-31, 264F3
Rain floods drought areas 2-10, disaster declared in 8 counties 2-16; cloud-seeding link probed 2-14, 105F3, 106B1
Drought end declared, reservoirs rptd 90% normal 3-5, 207B2
Rainstorm, floods kill 8 3-6, 207D2
Squaw Valley tram car falls 4-15, 460A2
Earthquakes recorded 4-25, 6-3, 480F1
Crop damage, US food inflatn linked 5-30, 428C2
San Andreas Fault shift rptd 6-18, 480C1
Santa Barbara quake 8-13, 759B1
Firestone suits rptd 9-22, 835F1
San Diego air crash kills 150 9-25, 758D2
'57 AF jet wreckage identified 10-12, 843E3
FAA proposes air-safety rules 12-27, 1006C3, E3

Crime & Civil Disorders—*See also HEARST, Patricia*
Lloyd Carr fugitive '76 arrest cited 1-14, 83F2
Segretti law practice suspensn ends 1-27, 172G2
Polanski flees US 2-1, 116A2
2 Hughes ex-aides indicted on drug chrgs 2-16, 459G1
'76 Chowchilla kidnapers sentncd 2-17, 232C3
Trash bag killer pleads guilty 2-21, 232B3
Swindler sentenced 4-10, 380C2
Banks extraditn barred 4-19, 327E1
Sex abuse suit vs NBC OKd by US Sup Ct 4-24, 322D2
MD mistrial in abortn death 5-5, 369C2
Newton arrested 5-11, assault chrg dropped 7-13; convicted on gun chrg 9-28, sentncd 11-3, 971F2
Children excluded from porno rule by US Sup Ct 5-23, 405G2, F3
AIM activists acquitted 5-24, 396B2
Admitted murderer sentenced 5-24, 396F2
'77 prison populatn rptd down 6-3, 440D1
Press prison data access curbed by US Sup Ct 6-26, 566A3
Kalmbach reinstated by bar, joins ex-gov's law firm 7-11, 844B1
Compton woman chrgd in welfare fraud 7-25, 684F3; convicted 11-31, sentncd 12-28, 1029C1
Sex abuse suit vs NBC dismissed 8-8, 635B2-A3
Cluchette chrgd in Oakland murder 8-25, 887A1
Synanon loses damage suit 9-19; atty attacked by rattler 10-10, 2 members chrgd 10-17, 841F2, D3
Angels outfielder slain 9-23, 777G3
Hypnosis-related murder case refused by US Sup Ct 10-2, 751C2
Harrises sentncd 10-3, 823F3
Van Houten sentncd 10-11, 824F2
Synanon incidents probed 10-15, task force formed 10-17, 841G3-842B1
LA bank robbed by phone 10-25, computer consultant arrested 11-5, 991G3-992D1
Death penalty list extended 11-7, 847A2, 856A3; 920C2
Synanon ranch searched 11-21, 971A2
Croatian killed 11-22, 933E3

1979

Welfare cuts set 6-19, 561G1
LA condominium growth rptd 6-23, 482B3
Actor defies ct order in Lone Ranger case 8-30, 859D3
Nixon San Clemente estate expenses disputed 9-5—9-6, 683B2
2 Bolshoi dancers defect in LA 9-16, 697D2
'78 per capita income rptd 9-16, 746E1, G2
Nixon San Clemente repaymt asked by Cong 9-26, 883F2
Imperial Group-Howard Johnson merger bar seen 10-12, 942E3
LA-area '78 beef-price suit setld 10-22, 985C3
Pahlevi family real estate holdings rptd 11-26, 898B1
Lugosi heirs publicity right denied 12-3, 1005E2
Iran consulate staff in San Fran ordrd cut 12-12, 933C1
San Fran '79 living costs ranked 12-28, 991A1

Accidents & Disasters
Calaveras fault quakes, San Fran jolted 5-7, 8-6, 619D3
Range fires 6-8—6-11, 572E3
Forest fires rptd 8-12, 620D1
Brush fires destroy 130,000 acres 9-11—9-23, 799E2
Imperial Valley quake; Caltexico, El Centro damaged, LA jolted 10-15, 799A2
Midwest quake threat rptd, San Andreas fault compared 11-15, 954E1
Atomic Energy
Rancho Seco (Clay Statn) A-plant called unsafe 1-26, 90D3
Rancho Seco A-plant shutdown asked 4-1, 245D1
Rancho Seco reactor cleared, operatn OKd 4-6, 260C3, 261E3
Diablo Canyon A-plant protested 4-7, 261G3, 262A1
Pacific Gas shareholders defeat A-power delay 4-18, 322F3
Brown urges end to A-power use 4-24, 322G3
Rancho Seco A-plant shut by NRC 4-27, 321G3
San Onofre A-plant pipe leaks rptd 5-2, 322B3
Diablo Canyon reactor licensing delayed 5-21, 381G3
San Onofre A-plant pipe cracks rptd 6-25, 518G3
Brown backs SALT II, scores MX 6-29, 496G3
Diablo Canyon A-protest draws 20,000 6-30, 519G1
Ariz cancels A-plant, blames regulators 7-16, 609F3
Diablo Canyon '77 protest chrgs dropped 8-10, 742G3-743A1
'50s fallout, SAT decline linked 9-17, 747C2
San Luis Obispo pro-nuclear rally 10-13, 806D3
Diablo Canyon reactor licensing delay extended 11-5, 849C1
Brown Presidential Campaign—*See BROWN Jr., Gov. Edmund G.*
Crime & Civil Disorders—*See also HEARST, Patricia*
Beverly Hills anti-shah riot 1-2, 3F1
San Fran '78 Nazi activity cited 1-19, 102B1
UFW strike violence 2-10, 2-21, 327F1; 6-11, 698B3
LA investmt fraud plea bargains rptd 2-13, 119B3
SLA '75 Oakland murder convictn reversed 2-27, 156C1
1st 'house arrest' sentnc 3-6, 316A2
Newton murder case ends in mistrial 3-24, 239D1
2d LA bank wire-transfer theft 3-25, 239C2
LA bank computer consultant sentncd 3-26, 239G1
IRS tap evidence backed by US Sup Ct 4-2, 281D2
Pt Reyes Light wins Pulitzer re Synanon rpts 4-16, 336D2, A3
Mafia alleged chieftain indicted 4-27, 368G1
Smith convicted 5-4, 5-7, sentncd 5-31, 442C2
San Fran ex-supervisor convicted in Moscone-Milk slaying, gays protests 5-22, 385G3
Hell's Angels arrested 6-14, 492B1
Lakeside KKK member sentncd for '78 murder 6-19, 492G1
'78 inmate totals rptd 6-21, 548C2
Juvenile 'Miranda rights' case remanded by Sup Ct 6-25, 540B2
Truckers protest 6-28, 479C2
San Fran ex-supervisor sentenced in Moscone-Milk slaying 7-3, 547E3
Camp Pendleton beating incident probed 7-7, 520B1
2 FBI agents slain in El Centro 8-9, 727E3
KKK Castro Valley clash 8-19, 865B1, 866A2
Cocaine trade growth, profit investmt in real estate rptd 9-5, 972F2, G2
Jordan LA cocaine use alleged 9-13—9-21, 767C2, G2
Judge arrested on drug chrgs 9-20, 748F1
Canadian sentncd in bank wire theft 9-24, 840C3
Newton murder case ends in 2d mistrial, chrgs dropped 9-27, 818B3
San Diego schl sniper pleads guilty 10-1, 819E2

1980

Accidents & Disasters
Cruise missile crashes rptd 1-7, 16A3
Greenville fault quakes; San Fran, Sacramento jolted; Livermore lab evacuated 1-24—1-27, 80E2
Rainstorms, flooding hit 2-13—2-22, disaster declared 2-21, 213F2
Yosemite area quakes, LA jolted 5-25, 5-27, 527D3
Brush fires destroy 86,000 acres 11-15—11-30, disaster declared 11-29, 948A1
Arts & Culture
SF museum buys Cassatt print for record sum 2-14, 472B2
Moore's son kills self 10-15, 890A2
Artist royalties case declined by Sup Ct 11-10, 868C2
Heaven's Gate withdrawn by UA 11-19, 906A1
Atomic Energy & Safeguards
State of State message 1-10, 483B1
Quakes force Livermore lab evacuatn 1-24—1-27, 80G2
Babcock plant review ordrd 3-4, 169F2
Demonstratns mark 3 Mile I anniv 3-28—3-31, 249B1
A-plant laws overturned 4-23, 331G3-332B1

Brown Presidential Campaign—*See BROWN Jr., Gov. Edmund G. (Jerry) (D, Calif.)*
Crime & Civil Disorders
Cleaver gets 5 yrs probatn 1-3, 64E3
Parole offcls immunity upheld by US Sup Ct 1-15, 51F1
James Garner assaulted 1-16, 200E1
Smith jury award upheld 1-18, 55D2
Ehrlichman bar resignatn accepted 1-19, 199D1
Boyce Lompoc escape rptd 1-22, 55E1
Indian activist sentenced 1-23, 349E1
Ex-Black Panther denied parole 2-5, 215A2
FBI Brilab probe, LA judge bribe plot rptd 2-8—2-9, 111E2, C3, 112A1
'Church' founder, aide convicted of fraud 2-9, 157B2
FBI 'Miporn' probe rptd 2-14, 136F1
2 sentenced for random black murder 2-27, 238C3
2 kidnaped boys found 3-1, 3 chrgd 3-2, 238C2
San Fran Chinatown gang ldr convicted of murder 3-10, 238A2
Oceanside Klan rally spurs melee 3-15, 333E1
Car box search case refused by Sup Ct 3-24, 265C2
San Diego schl sniper's father marries cellmate 3-26, 638G3
Determinate sentnc impact rptd 3-29, 359B2
LA Amer Airlines flight hijacked to Cuba 4-9, 617A3
'Charlie's Angels' LA fraud probe rptd 5-1, 376F2
Judge resigns in pot case, sentenced 5-5, 414F1
Hearst probation rptd ended 5-9, 471E3
2 protest Pratt appeal denial 5-11, 667F1
'Pyramid' schemes rptd growing 5-17, collapses rptd 6-18, 655G2-E3
Teamster offcl sentenced 5-23, 482F2
Jordan cleared re LA cocaine chrgs 5-28, 402E3
Female Secret Svc agent slain 6-5, 503E2
Col sentenced for sex harassment 6-28, 598G1
Hell's Angels mistrial declared 7-2, 568G1
NY-fugitive horse trainer recaptured 7-9, 997D2
Synanon founder convicted in murder attempt 7-15, 655E3
Garner assailant convicted 7-19, 639B3

1977

Snowfall rptd below normal 2-1, 76G3
Alameda, Contra Costa counties ration water 2-8, Monterey 2-19, 153A1
Conservatn urged 2-15, 152E3
Science group focuses on weather 2-21, 183A3
LA groundwater pumping cut 3-1, 492E3
Agri, other losses estimated 3-7, 3-8, 244E2
Voltage cut test set 3-18, 278B1
San Fran sets water rations 3-22, 244C3
Econ losses scaled down, new wells set 4-9, 376D3
Bergland tours 4-14—4-18, rpts on conditns 4-18, 365D1, 376E3
Record conditns rptd 5-4, 376B3
LA votes water rationing 5-12, 492D3
Carter visits San Joaquin Valley 5-17, 381B3
Santa Catalina cuts water use 5-25, 492F3
Marin pipeline laid, Calif Aqueduct cited 6-7, 492A3
Dry spell continues 6-16, 492A3
Drought impact rptd 7-28; agri losses projected, water rationing cited 8-9, 659E3, 660C1
Forest fires 7-28—8-23, 660B2-G2
Unchngd by southn rains 8-15—8-17, 747G2

1978

San Fran mayor, supervisor slain 11-27; ex-supervisor chrgd 11-29, 920G1-D3
Haldeman leaves Lompoc prison 12-20, 1011A3
San Fran museum art theft 12-25, 1028G3-1029A1

1979

Hell's Angels trial opens 10-4, 840E1
'Hillside Strangler' gets life, accomplice chrgd 10-19, 10-22, 818D2
Scientologists convctd as spies 10-26, 839F2; sentncd 12-6–12-7, 1000B1
Pot farm growth rptd 10-29, 972F1
Bird ruling oppositn cited 11-5, 869B2
Sirhan parole hearing denied 11-7, 953B3
Iranians protest in Beverly Hills 11-9, 863C1
Manson denied parole 11-27, 953D3
San Diego schl sniper sentenced 11-30, 953F3
Cleaver chrgs rptd dropped 12-3, 1006E1
Smith damage judgemt rptd 12-24, 991G3
Carter nephew paroled 12-24, 1006B1

1980

RFK's son arrested in drunken driving case 7-27, 639C2
Atkins denied parole 7-29, 639D2
'Freeway murder' suspects chrgd 7-29, 654B2
ABC ties to Spelling-Goldberg rptd probed by SEC 8-7—8-8, 640B1
San Fran Brink's truck robbed 8-15, 654G2
'Playmate of Yr' found slain 8-15, 713D3
Hell's Angels sentenced 8-18, 714B1
Drug investigatn of 2 B Carter associates rptd 8-21, 647A2
4th charged in 'freeway murders' 8-22, 727E1
Religious deprogrammer convicted 8-29, 727B1; sentncd 9-26, 857B3
Bonanno, nephew convicted 9-2, 712E3
Synanon founder gets probatn 9-3, 860D2
Redgrave TV film protested 9-30, 835C3
Hollywood travel agency bombed 10-12, 794F1
LA 'alphabet bomber' convicted 10-16, sentncd 11-24, 927A2
Jackson death sentnc upheld 10-23, 868F3-869A1
LA DA ends 'Charlie's Angels' probe 12-2, 1002E2
Ark prison probe curbed by Sup Ct 12-8, 937C1
Methodists settle retiremt home fraud suit 12-10, 963C3
La Scola insulin-slaying chrgs reduced 12-29, 997G1

1976

Energy Developments
GE A-engineers quit re safety 2-3, 115A1
Ford seeks Alaska gas pipe plan 2-26, 149B2
Cong opens Elk Hills, Buena Vista reserves 3-31, 246A3
Utah power project dropped 4-14, 284E2
A-plant safety bill signed 6-3, 409E2
Voters rejct A-plant curbs 6-8, 409D2
'75 offshore lease sale cited 8-25, 648E3
Alaska oil surplus export opposed 11-30, 991F3

1977

Energy Developments
Natural gas use curbed 2-1, 76D1
Peak-load elec pricing urged 3-11, 277D3
Utilities to test volt cuts 3-18, 278A1
Offshore oil sales delayed 5-17, 498F3
Humboldt Bay A-plant reopening opposed 8-5, 838C2
Diablo Canyon A-plant protest 8-7, 702F2
Washington sues 10 oil cos 8-16, 691E3
Oil cos settle fed suit 8-31, 691C3
State oil trust suits merged 9-12, 691G3
Tex oil pipe OKd 12-2, 942E3
Carter to hike Elk Hills oil output 12-20, 997A3

1978

Energy Developments
A-plant rejected by Kern Cnty, water problems cited 3-7, 184B1
Sundesert A-plant rejctd 4-13, Brown statemt 4-14, coal plant studied 4-18, 281B2
Solar power tower constructn rptd 5-3, 321F3
Elk Hills oil cut opposed, residual fuel exports backed 5-26, 408F1
New oil rules set, residual fuel exports OKd 6-15, 470B3-471B1
June housing starts, indicators rise linked to energy saving rules 7-19, 7-31, 607F2, F3
Diablo Canyon A-plant protested 8-6—8-7, 609B3, D3
July housing starts, indicators; June revised 8-16, 8-31, 680F1, E2
A-plant moratorium cited 8-17, 665F2
Diablo Canyon A-plant protesters convicted 8-30, 941D2
Southn Cal Edison refund case refused by US Sup Ct 10-16, 789A2
Eureka Humboldt Bay A-plant rating rptd 11-25, 940D3
Pub utilities refund cases refused by US Sup Ct 12-11, 981D1

1979

Energy—*See also 'Atomic' above*
Fuel price law challenge declined by US Sup Ct 3-5, 185E1
Tex pipe canceled, state regulatns scored 3-13, 183D1
Carter asks Tex pipe resumptn 4-5, 250E3
Gas price-fixing rule overturned 4-18, 346C2
Texaco, distributor fined re gas-switching 4-26, 301D2
LA gas price violatns rptd 4-27, 324C3
Carter orders gas shortage probe, backs rationing 5-5, 347D1
Gas shortage explained 5-7, 343C1
Odd-even gas rationing begins 5-9, 342B3
Standby gas rationing rejcted by US House 5-10, 342G2
Carter sees Brown, hikes gas allocatn 5-16; Ore gov scores 5-17, 361F1-E2
Tex pipe cancellatn reaffirmed 5-24, 396F1
'78 per capita gas use rptd 5-27, 395G2
Brown proposes plan 5-31, 418F3
Odd-even rationing spreads to E Coast, Tex 6-19–6-21, 462C2
Brown backs research fund shift 6-29, 497A1
Offshore oil, gas lease bids placed 6-29, 518B2
Oil spot mkt purchases rptd 7-16, 494E2
Offshore lease bids accepted 8-7, 649E1
Alaska, Indonesia LNG imports OKd 8-14; Pt Conceptn terminal chosen 9-26, projct approved 9-27, 769C2
Odd-even gas rules retained 9-7, 683G1
Odd-even gas rules dropped by some counties 9-20–10-2, 850D1; reimposed 10-13, 870C1
Shell acquires Belridge Oil 12-10; Mobil, Texaco sue 12-11, 942F1

1980

Energy—*See also 'Atomic Energy' above*
State of State message 1-10, 483B1
Carter seeks more coal-fired utilities 3-6, 169D3
2d 1/4 gas use target set 3-20, 250G3
Offshore leasing pressed, '81-85 reoffering sale planned 3-28, 330C3
Gulf natl park drilling rights affirmed 3-31, 291A3
Oil profits tax rejected by voters 6-3, 439D2
Elk Hills oil stockpiling site studied 6-16, 552D2
Offshore oil, gas leasing speedup OKd 6-17, 552F2
$5 bln water projct OKd 7-18, 632G1

1976

Environment & Pollution—*See also 'Energy' above*
AMC fined, 3 models banned 1-5, 5D3
Sen votes Death Valley mining halt 2-4, 135A2, C2
US cncl rpt cites car pollutn 2-27, 171D2
Asbestos found in San Fran water 4-30, 349F1
Ford vs tuna-porpoise ruling 5-24, 374A1
Death Valley mining curbed 9-28, 834B2
Desert land-use study 10-21, 834E1
Air quality progress rptd 12-8, 943C1

1978

Environment & Pollution—*See also 'Accidents & Disasters' and 'Energy' above*
'77 open-space effort rptd 85C2
Redwood Park expansn clears Cong 2-9, 85D2; 3-21, Carter signs 3-27, 218D1
Wilderness area clears Cong 2-9, 109D2; signed 2-24, 218A2
LA-Long Beach area, San Diego clean-air ratings rptd 2-23, 144D3, E3
AMC auto recall excludes 5-10, 349C1; expanded 5-19, 409F2
Water rights backed by US Sup Ct 7-3, 552B2
LA, San Fran, Sacramento make bad-air list 7-5, 513C1, D1
Parks bill clears House 7-12, 526E3
Bad-air list corrected 7-19, 644B2
King Range authorzn signed 8-20, 697D2
US parks bill cleared 10-13, 834A3, C3
Long Beach voters OK Sohio lease 11-7, 857B1
IWC La Jolla mtg rptd 12-8, 1001B3

1979

Environment & Pollution
LA bad air quality cited 1-25, 90C2
Oil Spill Conf held in LA 3-20, 200F3
Hooker Lathrop chem dumping, well pollutn rptd 6-18; US, state probe 6-19, 6-21, 597F1
Interior Dept seeks to protect primitive areas 9-7, 703C3
San Fran '50 germ warfare test suit rptd 9-16, 727B1

Family Issues
Hearst legal separatn rptd 1-25, 79G1
Unwed couple suits rptd 2-22, 3-16, 289G2-B3
Marvin breach of contract suit setld 4-18, 289B1
Steiger pre-nuptial agrmt upheld 7-5, 527D3

Hearst Case—*See HEARST, Patricia*

Immigration Issues
San Diego illegal alien welfare study rptd 1-29, 127F1
San Diego border fence repairs set 4-26, 327G2
Viet refugee influx rptd, svcs rptd strained 8-5, 659F3-660A3
INS curb on gays lifted 8-14, 631A3
INS neighborhood raids curbed 11-26, 924B1

1980

Environment & Pollution
State of State message 1-10, 483B1
LA air problem noted 2-19, 145E2
Mex tomatoes found toxic 2-20, border checks tightened 3-12, 233A3
LA sewage permit extensn backed by Sup Ct 3-18, 226E3
Offshore drilling pressed, oppositn rptd 3-28, 330C3
Gulf natl park drilling rights affirmed by Sup Ct 3-31, 291A3
Water law compliance rptd 4-10, 308E1, F1
Zoning ordinances backed by Sup Ct 6-10, 512F1
Imperial Valley water rights upheld by Sup Ct 6-16, 511E2
$5 bln water projct OKd 7-18, 632G1
Reagan smog stance controversial 10-7—10-13, 779A3-D3
Reagan cites record in TV debate 10-28, 815G1
Parklands bond issue OKd, Lake Tahoe propositn defeated 11-4, 847F3
EPA halts aid funds 12-11, 963B1
Desert protectn plan issued 12-22, 986G3-987C1

Family Issues
Pension divorce setlmt case declined by Sup Ct 1-14, 37B1
LA adults-only housing barred 1-31, 115C2
S Ford paternity suit settled 2-28, 199A2
Retarded youth surgery case refused by Sup Ct 3-31, 291B3
San Jose, Santa Clara voters reject gay rights referenda 6-3, 439F2
White House Conf meets in LA 7-10—7-12, 601G1

Housing
State of State message 1-10, 483A1
La adults-only housing barred 1-31, 115C2
Mortgage rate at 14% 2-22, 145C1
Redlining law curbed by Sup Ct 3-17, 226C1
Mortgage rate hits 17.5% 3-19, 222D3
LA home prices rptd 3-29, 248A1

1976

Hearst Case—*See HEARST, Patricia*
Labor
US Sup Ct declines review of women's overtime rule 1-12, 24D1
Farm labor dispute continues, boycott renewal planned 1-22—2-11, 153G1
Alien job curbs upheld 2-25, 169F1
LA hosp interns denied unionizatn 3-22, 220F1
Soc Sec withdrawals rptd 3-23, 994G1
San Fran strike 3-31—5-8, 348C3
Van Nuys Anheuser-Busch strike ends 6-6, 436B2
Min wage ruled not binding on states 6-24, 468A3
Chavez speaks at Dem conv 7-14, 506E1
Cannery strike ends 7-31, 570C1
Passman denies rice sale chrg 8-16, 633C1
Carter backs farm workers referendum, Chavez endorses Carter 9-25, 724D1
Sup Ct bars review of farm worker organizing rule 10-4, 766E1
Dole scores organizing propositn 10-30, 827G2
Voters reject proposition 11-2, 825B1, E3
Los Angeles
CIA bars data on Hughes burglary 1-5, 24E2
Ticor indicted 1-14, unit chrgd 2-2, 160A1
Watson warrantless arrest upheld 1-26, 87B2
MDs end insurance slowdown 2-5, 144B3
Japan Socialists, Kotchian meet 2-13, 132E1
Hosp interns denied unionizatn 3-22, 220F1
Ford at GOP fund-raiser 3-26, 232A1
VA overpaymts rptd 3-26, 262A3
Reagan press conf 4-2, 245C2
Chamber of Commerce tap rptd 5-9, 344F2
Ehrlichman break-in verdict upheld 5-17, 379C1
Teachers sue vs desegregatn plan 5-22, 453E2
Ford at Press Club 5-25, 374C1
Reagan meets reporters 5-28, 391B2
Reagan campaigns 6-7, 410E3
Nixon disbarred in NY 7-8, 493E3
Carter visits 8-22—8-23, 631D2
Mondale campaigns 9-1, 9-7, 665G2, B3
'74-75 SAT average rptd 9-13, 993G1
Carter campaigns 9-25, 724E1
Carter campaigns 10-7, 762D1
Ford visits 10-7, 762G3, 763B1, A2
Mondale campaigns 10-18, 803D3
Ford campaigns 10-24, 802E3
Carter rally 11-1, 827C1
US Sup Ct bars review of theater, bookstore obscenity rule 11-1, 868A1
Air quality progress rptd 12-8, 943C1
Heroin use rptd 12-12, 972C3
Carter rpts Bradley rejctd US post 12-16, 937A2
Tanker explodes in harbor 12-17, 969F1
Farr wins 5-yr ct test 12-21, 995C1
Politics—*See also city subheads; also BROWN Jr., Gov. Edmund G.*
Primary date set 22C2
GOP del selectn rule upheld 1-19, 42G3
Hinshaw convicted 1-26, 95E3
Brown enters pres primary 3-12, 197F2
Ford sees GOP ldrs in Fresno 3-27, 232A1
Reagan cites record as gov 3-31, 232B2, E3

1977

Hearst Case—*See HEARST, Patricia*
Los Angeles
Rpt on Hughes '38 will ordrd 1-17, 120B2
US rights comm backs city-suburb busing 2-15, 112E1
Students boycott re busing 2-18, 216E3
Groundwater pumping cut 3-1, 492E3
Busing plan OKd by bd 3-3, 216D3
Saccharin worker layoffs set 3-10, 177B1
Amer Air NYC 'Super-Saver' fare OKd 3-15, 325D1
Bradley reelected mayor 4-6, 252B3
On '75 10 largest cities list 4-14, 388A1, C1
Ford address 4-16, 321G3
Woolbright convicted of '74 Summa theft 4-22, 396G1
Water rationing voted 5-12, 492D3
Child porno, prostitutn rptd 5-15, 5-27, 432A2-E2
Housing sales rptd, econ data table 5-16, 384G2, 385C1
Carter addresses UAW conf 5-17, 381F2, B3
Police job bias chrgd 6-2, 819D2
Aqueduct water allotmt denied 6-7, 492C3
UK air svc pact set 6-22, 500G1, F2
Gays march for equal rights 6-26, 560E2
Mafia porno operatns rptd 7-3, 568D2
Schl integratn plan rejected 7-6, 8-8, 630G3-631C1
4 Episc priests deposed, parishes sued 8-5; new diocese formed 9-14—9-16, 731E2, G2
USC med cntr burn patient death choice rptd 8-11, 712D2
EPA sues on sewage 8-12, 724C1
Flash floods 8-15—8-17, 747G2
June new-car sales rptd 9-6, 722B3
Named '84 Olympics site 9-25, 828G2
PI plotters escape 10-1, 10-2, 803B3
Carter at Dem dinner 10-22, 817D1
Minority constructn quota ruled unconst 10-31, 978F3-970C1
USSR exhibit opens 11-12, 988C2
Medicine & Health
Laetrile OKd by San Diego ct 1-21, 376E1
DNA patent order lifted 2-7, 184C2
Germ warfare tests rptd 3-8, 195E2, G2
San Jose health care probe dispute 3-8—3-23, 235G2
Right to die law cited 3-31, 355D1
Psychotherapist rule review declined 4-4, 341E3
Handicapped protest at HEW 4-5—4-16, 301D2
Handicapped rules signed 4-28, 338F2
Laetrile smugglers sentenced 5-16, 508E2
AMA mtg in San Fran 6-19, 479C1
HMOs hailed for cost control 8-5, 643E2
Burn patient death choice rptd 8-11, 712D2
DBCP production suspended 8-12, 723F2
Free abortions continued 10-12, 787A1
May Romm dies 10-15, 872G2
HMO unit certified 10-26, 870A1
Maternity sick-leave pay case ordrd reexamined 12-6, 938A3
Politics & Government—*See also other appropriate subheads in this section*
Legislature schedule rptd 6C2
Bird named chief justice 2-12, 140C3; confrmd 3-11, 396B3
Justice McComb forced to retire 5-2, 388B2
1-family housing boom, speculatn rptd 5-2—6-2, 554B3

1978

Hearst Case—*See HEARST, Patricia*
Labor
Lockheed strike ends 1-2, 4B2
McDonnell Douglas Long Beach strike 1-13—4-16, 284A3
UFW ends boycotts 1-31, 83F1
1st in US defns contracts 2-21, 127D2
Anaconda LA strike ends 4-3, 284E3
Unions held subject to trespass laws by US Sup Ct 5-15, 387A2
State hiring frozen, counties plan layoffs 6-7, 425A3
Carter sees jobless rate rise 6-14, 446D3
Contractors reverse bias case sent back by US Sup Ct 7-3, 552B1
Extended jobless aid rptd 7-10, 552A3; ends 8-4, 607D3
Postal pact oppositn rptd 7-21—7-23; Richmond workers strike 7-22, 29 fired 7-23, 564G3, 564A1
Watts jobless rate rptd high 8-8, 811G1
Gay teacher ban rejctd 11-7, 847A3, 857A1
Oakland fire dept minority plan overturned 12-26, 1006F2
Los Angeles
Busing plan set for Sept 1-3, 5E1-A2
Vance visits re Canal pacts 1-13, 58B2
Natl Airlines Miami-LA rule review denied 1-23, 65C2
Pacific Exchng vs consolidatn 2-1, 66C3
Rain floods area 2-10, damage rptd at $23 mln 2-27; cloud-seeding link probed 2-14, 105G3, 106B1
Laity conf backs broader role 2-19, 294B3
Clean-air rules violated 2-23, 144D3
Rainstorms, floods kill 8 3-6, 207D2
Dutch air svc accord reached 3-10, 206A3
UK air-fare dispute setld 3-17, 206D2
Anaconda strike ends 4-3, 284E3
Schl system 2d largest in US 4-12, 264A1
Mandatory busing plan set 4-14, 309E2
Sex-based pensn plans barred by US Sup Ct 4-25, 322B3
Earthquakes recorded 4-25, 6-3, 480F1
Begin visits 5-2, 339E2
Carter addresses ABA unit 5-4, 320A3
'Skytrain' svc set 5-5, 2-carrier London svc 6-9, 570D1
AIM activists acquitted 5-24, 396C2
Ex-POWs hold conv 5-27, 513D2
Layoffs, schl cutbacks planned 6-7, 425B3
MD malpractice claims studied 6-8, 577F3
Air rated worst in US 7-5, 513C1
FBI '77 Scientology raids upheld 7-6, 554E1
New film indus probe set 7-14, 599F2-A3
Air quality rpt corrected 7-19, 644B2
Postal pact oppositn rptd 7-21—7-23, 565A1
Rams plan '80 Anaheim move, Coliseum suit vs NFL cited 7-25, 1023F3
Schl busing appeals rejctd 8-3—9-9; busing starts peacefully, 10,000 boycott 9-12, 698A3-699A1
Urban League conf opens, Bradley addresses 8-8, 810E3, 811F1
Scientology ldrs indicted 8-15, 644E3, 645C1
Pan Am Houston svc OKd 9-1, 701E1
GOP tax-cutters on tour 9-22, 734F3
IOC OKs '84 Olympics pact 10-9, City Cncl approves 10-12, 842F3
Van Houten sentncd 10-11, 824F2
Sec Pacific bank robbed by phone 10-25, computer consultant arrested 11-5, 991G3-992D1
WTT Strings fold 11-7, new franchise planned 12-1, 1027B1, C1
Populatn ranked 12-6, 942D3
Medicine & Health
Right-to-die law use rptd 3-18, 597D3
Heart attack risk rptd cut by strenuous work 3-24, 597F3
Mrs Ford hospitalized in Long Beach 4-10—5-5, 420A1
LA MD malpractice claims studied 6-8, 577F3
Sperm bank suit rptd 8-1, 597A2
SF MD surplus by '90s seen 8-3, 597D2
Infant botulism traced to honey 11-1, 948A2
Smoking-ban propositn fails 11-7, 847A3, 856G3
Obituaries
Ketchum, William M 6-24, 540B3
Poulter, Thomas 6-14, 540E3
Peoples Temple—*See separate listing*
Politics & Government—*See also other appropriate subheads in this section*
Legislature schedule rptd 14D3
Mendelsohn suit setld 4-18, named US aide 6-10, 446F3-447B1
Primary electns, property tax initiative 6-6, 425A1, E1-426F1, 447C3
Brown urges local-state spending curb 6-24, 525E3

1979

Labor & Employment
Chavez union strikes lettuce farms 1-19, violence erupts 2-10, 2-21; natl boycott set 4-26, 327A1
Rail pensn excluded from divorce pact by US Sup Ct 1-24, 54A1
Paper mill strike ends 2-20, 345A3
LA Fire Dept bias case found moot by Sup Ct 3-27, 263A2
Truck mechanics end strike 4-16, 384F3
Prop 13 effects rptd 6-3–7-2, 499G2-500D1
UFW lettuce strike violence 6-11, strike settled 8-31, 698B3
Truckers protest 6-28, 479C2
LA Cnty deputies end 'sickout' 7-12, 599E1
BART svc curtailed 8-31–11-21, 922B3
Brown vetoes anti-UFW bill 9-7, 698E3
LA teachers threaten sickout 9-10, San Fran teachers strike 9-11, 679B1, C1, E1
Lawyer survey rptd 9-17, 787D1
San Fran teachers strike ends 10-23, 850F1
Medicine & Health
Breast-feeding survey rptd 1-5, 64C2
Malpractice arbitratn rptd 1-28, 139D3
Laetrile shipmt recalled 3-8, 196A1
Hearing-aid ad case refused by US Sup Ct 3-19, 203B3
MD-managed insurnc plan cuts hosp costs 6-14, 570E3
Medicaid cuts set 6-19, 561G1
Rabies cases rptd up 7-14, 620A3
San Fran health svcs strained by Indochina refugees 7-18, 550C2
Tuberculosis, parasites rptd in Viet refugees 8-25, 659D3
San Fran '50 germ warfare test suit rptd 9-16, 727B1
Laetrile ban challenge declined by Sup Ct 11-13, 902E1
Peoples Temple—*See PEOPLES Temple*
Politics & Government—*See also other appropriate subheads in this section*
Legislature schedule rptd 5C3
Brown to seek US budget amendment 1-8, 13B2
Nev joint planning agency immunity curbed by US Sup Ct 3-5, 185C1
State ct immunity curbed by US Sup Ct 3-5, 185D1

1980

Mortgage rates drop 5-6—5-19, 384G3
Mortgage rate fall continues 5-22—6-30, 514B1
Rent-control repeal, San Jose, Santa Clara gay rights referenda rejected by voters 6-3, 439E2, F2
Mortgage rates rise 7-23, 575A1
Mortgage rate rise continues 7-31—8-19, 631A1
Mortgage rates continue to rise 9-25, 10-1, 867B2
LA airport nuisance award case refused by Sup Ct 10-6, 782A3
San Bernardino, Riverside integratn, busing study rptd 11-16, 989E3
Methodists settle retiremt home suit 12-10, 963C3
Labor & Employment
Ford shuts Pico Rivera plant 1-10, 35A2
State of State message 1-10, 483A1
Pension divorce case declined by Sup Ct 1-14, 37B1
FBI Brilab probe rptd 2-8—2-9, 111E2, C3
LA, San Fran purchasing power rptd high 2-12, 125D3
Brewers dual seniority system backed by Sup Ct 2-20, 146F2-B3
LA parade backs OCAW strike 3-1, 187D2
LA police female job bias case declined by Sup Ct 4-28, 369B2
UAW conv in Anaheim 6-1—6-6, 457G1
San Jose, Santa Clara voters reject gay rights referenda 6-3, 439F2
San Fran layoffs planned 6-4, 744A1
AFSCME conv in Anaheim 6-10, 438D3
NEA conv in LA 7-3—7-4, 505C2
San Fran 27-day hotel strike ends 8-12, 647G3-648B1
Winery strike ends 9-22, 747A3*
LA settles bias suit 11-21, 962A3
LA pact ratified 12-12, 988A1
Medicine & Health
State of State message 1-10, 483D1
Retarded youth surgery case refused by Sup Ct 3-31, 291B3
Gonorrhea epidemic cited 4-9, 584F3
Livermore lab cancer cases rptd 4-22, 356E3
DES in cattle rptd 4-24, 358F1
DES liability case declined by Sup Ct 10-14, 781D3
Shockley rpts Escondido sperm bank donatns 10-28, 990D2
Smoking-ban propositn fails 11-4, 847A3
Peoples Temple—*See PEOPLES Temple*
Politics & Government—*See also other appropriate subheads in this section*
Legislature schedule rptd 18C1
State of State message 1-10, 482G3-483D1
GOP platform hearing set in Los Angeles 1-14, 32A1
San Fran mayor marries 1-20, 199E1

1976

Morton sees GOP in San Jose 4-4, 245D2
'72 Nixon spending rptd 4-25, 688A2
Kissinger cancels speeches 5-18, 359D1
Carter, Ford campaign 5-20—5-25, 373C3, G3
Reagan campaigns 5-26—6-1, 391A2-C2
Reagan, Ford campaign dvpts 6-2—6-7, 410B1-G2, E3
Primary results 6-8, 408F2, 409A1, A2
2 Compton offcls sentncd 6-21, 860C2
Cella convicted 6-24; sentnc rptd 7-20, 860D2
Dem conv women delegates, table 508B2
Chavez speaks at Dem conv 7-14, 506E1
Dem conv pres vote, table 7-14, 507B2
GOP pre-conv delegate count 8-14, 583B3
GOP conv pres, vp vote tables 8-18—8-19, 8-19, 599B1, B3
GOP conv delegates vs Dole as vp 8-19, 598C2
John Costello dies 8-28, 892F2
Mondale in Santa Monica 9-1, 665B3
Fresno Bee newsmen jailed 9-3—9-17, 700D2
Carter tours with Brown 9-25—9-26, 724D1
Dole visits Reagan 9-25, 724E3
Hinshaw expulsn blocked; primary loss noted 10-1, 807E1
Mondale campaigns 10-18—10-19, 803D3
Dole campaigns 10-29—10-30, 827G2
Carter stumps 11-1, 826G3, 827B1, D1
Election results 11-2: pres 818A1, G1, 819B1; cong 817E1, 819D3, 820D2, 828C1, G3-829F1; state 824F3, 825B1, E3
Ford starts Palm Springs vacatn 11-7, 845E2
Carter primary spending, gifts rptd 11-17, 938E2-A3

San Diego

Newspaper chrgs FBI backed terrorists 1-11, 42A1
Rival Viet refugees split 2-20, 176C3
Westn Air ruling review denied 3-8, 219C2
McClure dies 3-13, Marine cts-martial ordered 4-28, 378A1
FBI efforts vs Panthers rptd 5-6, 344C2
Ford visits 5-24, 374A1
Ford TV interview 6-4, 410F2
Marine ct-martial starts 6-14, 435D3
Marine acquitted 6-28, 493B2
US Sup Ct declines zoning rule review 6-28, 569D1
'76 Marine ct-martials rptd 7-18, 7-21; Wallraff convicted 7-19, 586G3
Mondale tours naval facilities 9-7, 665G2
Carter campaigns 9-25, 724B1
Mondale campaigns 10-19, 803E3
Ford campaigns 10-24, 802E3

San Francisco

Ford plotter gets life term 1-15, 23F1-D2
Kissinger policy speech 2-3, 88A2
Ford at GOP fund-raiser 3-26, 231D3
4 sentncd in 'Zebra' killings 3-29, 292F3
Craft strike 3-31—5-8, 348C3
Asbestos found in water 4-30, 349F1
USSR scores labor delegatn visa denials 5-25—5-28, 408A1
Moon properties assessed 6-2, 971E1
Reagan press conf 6-3, 410E1
Sailboats mark Bicentennial 7-4, 489E2
Carter queried on nephew's sentence 7-26, 551G1
Black mins return funds to Carter 8-10, 585B3
Carter at fund-raiser 8-23, 631E2
Mondale visits 8-30, 845C3
2d Ford-Carter debate set 703A2
Dole visits 687B1
2d Ford, Carter debate 10-6, 740F2
Carter campaigns 10-7, 762B1
Carter visits 10-31, 827F1
Heroin use rptd 12-12, 972C3

1977

Meyer personal lobbying halted 9-30, 773F1
Meyer quits US post 10-20, 814B2
Mendelsohn Interior nominatn withdrawn 11-11, 877A2

San Francisco

San Fran Bay oil spills 1-5, 2-10, 214F2, A3
Germ warfare tests rptd 3-8, 195E2, G2
Amer Air NYC 'Super-Saver' fare OKd 3-15, 325D1
Water rationing set 3-22, 244C3
NFL OKs 49er sale 3-29—4-1, 263F2
Redwood Pk hearings 4-13, 4-14, expansn asked 4-19, 322F3, 323C1
Archbishop installed 4-26, 375A3
Handicapped rules signed 4-28, 338F2
Alioto wins libel award 5-3, 532B2
Largest US law firms rptd 5-16, 383B2
Econ data table 5-16, 384G2
AMA mtg 6-19, 479C1
LEAA office to close 6-20, 630E2
Bank of Amer ranked world's largest bank 6-21, 578G1
UK air svc pact set 6-22, 500A2
Homosexual slain 6-22, gays march for equal rights 6-26, 560D2
CIA mind-control tests rptd 8-1—8-9, 611C1
Baseball owners fail to solve attendance problem 8-17, 768A1
Chinatown gang killings 9-4, 9-11, 711G2
Episc diocese formed 9-14—9-16, 731E2
CIA mind-control tests probed 9-20, 9-21, 721A2, E2
New Viet refugees arrive 9-20, 739E3
Concorde landing rights proposed, scored 9-23, 738B2, B3
Milk elected supervisor 11-8, 855D3
Natl League of Cities conf 12-7, 959C3

1978

Budget signed, drop cited 7-6, 525F3
DC voting rep amendmt ratificatn delayed 878A3
Brown addresses govs conf 8-28, resolutn adopted 8-29, 681D3, 682E1
Carter in Sacramento 11-3, 862B2
Election results 11-7: cong 846D2, A3, 848D1, 850D1, 856B3; state 845B2, 847C1, A2, A3, 853D2, 856C2, 915D2, 920C2
Black lt gov noted 11-28, 915E3

San Francisco

Angela Davis joins State U faculty 1-26, 172B2
Pacific Exchng vs shift to LA 2-1, 66C3
UAL hijack attempt foiled 3-13, 212A2
UK air-fare dispute setld 3-17, 206D2
Oakland A's sale fails 3-27, 355A1
Mendelsohn suit setld 4-18, 446G3-447B1
Sex abuse suit vs NBC OKd by US Sup Ct 4-24, 322D2
Gay rights repeal petitns rptd 4-25, 327B2
'77 living costs rptd 4-26, 349F1
Singapore Airlines '79 svc set 5-9, 365G2
KQED-TV prison data access curbed by US Sup Ct 6-26, 566A3
Air quality rated poor 7-5, 513D1; corrected 7-19, 644B2
Museum gets Rockefeller art 7-20, 628E1
Sperm bank suit rptd 8-1, 597A2
MD surplus by '90s seen 8-3, 597D2
Sex abuse suit vs NBC dismissed 8-8, 635C2-A3
Pan Am Houston svc OKd 9-1, 701E1
Rev Jones-Moscone pol ties cited 11-21, 891B2
Moscone, supervisor slain 11-27; ex-supervisor chrgd 11-29, 920G1-D3
Populatn ranked 12-6, 942F3
De Young museum art theft 12-25, 1028G3-1029A1
Oakland fire dept minority plan overturned 12-26, 1006F2

Sports

NASL '77 club moves to San Diego, Oakland, Anaheim cited 1-5, 23B1
Oakland A's sale fails 3-27, 355A1
NBA OKs Braves move to San Diego 7-7, 655E2
Rams plan '80 Anaheim move, LA Colliseum suit vs NFL cited 7-25, 1023F3
Angels outfielder slain 9-23, 777G3
IOC OKs '84 Olympics pact 10-9, LA Cncl OKs 10-12, 842F3
1st woman claims El Capitan alone 10-26, 843A3
LA, San Diego, Anaheim WTT teams fold 11-7—11-10; new franchises planned 12-1, 1027B1, C1

Tax Issues

'67, '77 sales-tax rates rptd 1-5, 15D3
State tax revenue data 1-9, 84C2, F3
Hughes legal residence dispute in US Sup Ct 3-29, 459D1
Moody's Standard & Poors suspend bond ratings 4-13, 6-7, 426D1
Propositn 13 property tax-cut amendmt OKd by voters 6-6; text 425A1, E1, F2
Property tax revenue data rptd 6-6, 425D2
Brown freezes state hiring 6-7; pledges aid, spending cuts 6-8, 425A3, D3
LA plans layoffs, schl cutbacks 6-7, 425B3
Budget surplus rptd, local autonomy threat seen 6-7, 425C3
Propositn 13, HEW fund cuts linked 6-13, 445G2
Carter evaluates Propositn 13 impact 6-14, 446D3
Propositn 13 topic at natl convs 6-17—7-6, 525F3
Hughes estate dispute interventn refused by US Sup Ct 6-22, 509A1
Budget surplus aid to local govts signed 6-24, 525C3
US Sen ratifies UK pact 6-27, 588B3
Cong Budget Office rpts on Propositn 13 impact 7-6, 525E2
Propositn 13 defns spending impact rptd 7-11, 526C2
NAACP vs 'Propositn 13 mentality' 7-21, 568C2
July US income rise, Propositn 13 linked 8-17, 643E3
Jarvis spearheads natl tax-cut movemt 8-17—9-26, 735A3
Brown, Kennedy urge budget restraints, cite Propositn 13 8-28, 681D3
$1 bln income tax cut enacted 8-30, 735E2-A3
June bldg surge, Propositn 13 linked 8-31, 680G1
GOP tax-cut tour in LA 9-22, 734F3
Propositn 13 upheld by ct 9-22, 735B2
Propositn 13, US public works veto linked 10-5, 765C1
Tax-cut referenda OKd by 13 states, Propositn 13 cited 11-7, 847E1, 856D1, 857G1
Pub utilities refund cases refused by US Sup Ct 12-11, 981D1

1979

Viet War era CIA surveillnc rptd 3-9, 207C2
Long Beach, Fresno fiscal status rptd 3-20, 204G1
Ft MacArthur to close 3-29, 265F3
GOP wins Ryan House seat 4-3, 265E1
Brown in Africa 4-7, 271E3
Carter in San Fran, LA 5-4–5-5, 346C3, 347A1
Carter alleged death plot probed 5-5–5-29, 404C1
Fonda, ex-POW apptmts cause furor; Brown legis rebuffs detailed 7-13–8-8, 593A2-B3
Brown pres com formed, Mex trip begins 7-30, 593E1
Cranston vs Carter '80 nominatn support 8-20, 627B3
FBI admits '70 Seberg slander 9-14, 705B1
GOP retains primary rules 9-16, 724B1
Gay sworn as judge 9-17, 748B2-A3
LA all-white club judicial membership surveyed 9-19, 901F2
Brown judicial apptmt scored 9-20, 748F1
LA, San Diego bond ratings listed 9-20, 920E3, F3
Carter in San Diego 10-11, 807E2
State Sup Ct inquiry ends 11-5, [illegible]
State, San Fran electn results 11-6, 846A2, D3, F3
Brown enters pres race 11-8, 847E2; **see BROWN, Gov. Edmund**
Reagan enters pres race 11-13, 866C2; **see REAGAN, Ronald**
Renfrew named US dep atty gen 11-20, 946A3
Kennedy in LA 11-30, San Fran 12-2, 12-14, 918C3, 962F1, A2
Feinstein elected San Fran mayor 12-11, 946E3
US Rep Wilson chrgd re House rules violatns 12-13, 945E2
Gubernatorial powers for Curb upheld re Brown state absence 12-27, 983D3

Religious Issues—*See also PEOPLES Temple*

Worldwide Church sued, put in receivership 1-3, 23G2
Krishna sued re airport solicitatns 1-25, 102F1
Worldwide Church audit set 3-16, receivership lifted 3-17, 376B2
Archbp Quinn named to '80 Rome synod 5-3, 376A1
Scientology documts '76 seizure upheld by Sup Ct 5-14, 383A3
Worldwide Church receivership challenge refused by Sup Ct 10-1, 768A2
Scientologists convicted as spies 10-26, 839F2; sentncd 12-6–12-7, 1000B1
Methodist legal immunity cases declined by Sup Ct 11-26, 919E2

School Issues

Coll enrollmt rptd down 1-29, 367E2
Schl aid rptd 3-5, 282D3, F3
Pvt coll openings rptd 3-19, 282C3
LA busing plan challenged 8-27, referendum rptd set 9-2, 679C3 679C3
San Diego busing rptd set 9-2, 679E3
LA teachers threaten sickout 9-10, San Fran teachers strike 9-11, 679B1, C1, E1
Lawyer survey rptd 9-17, 787D1
San Fran strike ends 10-23, 850F1
NAACP sues vs anti-busing measure 11-14, 991A2
Religious teacher firing case dismissed by Sup Ct 12-10, 988F1

Sports

NCAA, AIAW conventns 1-18–1-10, 102B3-103C2
Burger King donates $2 mln to Olympics 5-15, 798F1
Bradley urges fed aid for '84 Olympics 5-28, 798D1
NBA Lakers, NHL Kings rptd sold 5-30, 527D1
San Fran, LA get WBL teams 6-12, 526G2
Allen pedals aircraft across Eng Channel 6-12, 527F3
Hang-glider leaves Long Beach on transcontinental flight 7-9, 656C3
Rafferty completes Death Valley run 7-15, 656D3
LA '84 Olympic costs projected 8-15, Coca-Cola sponsorship rptd 8-20, 798A1
ABC wins TV rights to '84 LA Olympics 9-25, 797C3
Land speed record rptd 12-18, 1006D1
Davis Cup finals in San Fran 12-14–12-16, 1003G2

Tax Issues

Brown proposes income tax cut 1-8, 13D2
Prop 13 impact on Dec '78 CPI rptd 1-24, 73F1
Coll enrollmt decline, Prop 13 linked 1-29, 367E2
Fscl '78 tax revenue rptd 2-13, 152B2
Schl aid by state up, Prop 13 linked 3-5, 282D3, F3
1st 'house arrest' sentnc, Prop 13 linked 3-6, 316B2
LA cargo container taxes voided by US Sup Ct 4-30, 364A3
State-local revenues, Prop 13 linked 5-16, 386A2
Energy, transit plan proposed 5-31, 418F3

1980

Lobbyist ban case refused by Sup Ct 1-21, 93G2
Rep Wilson found guilty of financial misconduct 4-16, censure asked 4-24, 333F3
Primary, referendum results 6-3, 439G1-F2
San Fran fscl referendum held 6-3, 744A1
Rep Wilson censured 6-10, 438F1-E2
Ex-Rep Douglas dies 6-28, 528E1
Reagan record noted 7-16, 534D1
Reagan rpts '79 tax data 7-31, 570D3-571A2
San Fran OKs at-large vote 8-19, 632A3
PAC donatns case accepted by Sup Ct 10-6, 782A2
Election results 11-4: cong 837E1, E2, 840C1, 842D1, 845A3, 846E1, F1, B2, C2, E3, F3, 852G1; state 845D2, 847A3, F3
'80 census rptd, reapportmt seen 12-31, 983D1

Presidential Election (& Transition)

Mondale, Kennedy visit 5-15, 383A2
Kennedy counting on win 5-28, 399E1
Kennedy in San Fran 5-30, 422G3
Primary results 6-3, 422E2, 423B2, 424C1
Poll rpts voter discontent 6-3, 423B1
Kennedy in Anaheim 6-10, 438C3
Carter in LA 7-3, at Merced town mtg 7-4, 505C2-G2
Reagan-Ford ticket problems noted 7-16, 530C1
Carter trails Reagan, Anderson in poll 7-30, 570C2
Brown addresses Dem conv 8-13, 611E3
Mondale in LA, San Fran; Brown lends support 9-5, 780G1-A2
Bush campaigns in San Fran 9-11, 10-1, 780F3, 781A2
Anderson debates Reagan record 9-21, 722F1
Carter in LA, San Jose 9-22—9-23, 722A3, E3, G3
Mondale in LA; stumps with Brown, Bradley 10-3, 10-26, 816E3, 817B1
Reagan stirs pollutn controversy 10-7—10-13, 779A3-D3
Reagan cites pollutn control record 10-28, 815G1
Press endorsemts rptd 11-1, 841F3
Reagan in San Diego 11-3, 840A3
Election results 11-4, 838A1, 839A1, D3
Reagan returns to LA 11-21, 897G2
Reagan home for holidays 12-13, 956C2

Press & Broadcasting

LA TV statn license lifted 1-24, 119F2
San Fran TV statn license OKd 1-30, 119C3
'Charlie's Angels' LA fraud probe rptd 5-1, 376F2
SF telecast of Saudi film cleared 5-12, Nielsen rating rptd 5-13, 375F3, G3
Berkeley Barb folds 7-3, 582F3
ABC ties to Spelling-Goldberg rptd probed by SEC 8-7—8-8, 640B1
'Playmate of Yr' found slain 8-15, 713D3
Redgrave TV film protested in LA 9-30, 835C3
Corp 'pub figures' libel case refused by Sup Ct 10-6, 782E2
Faith Center San Bernadino TV license revoked 10-10, 907B1
T Leary radio statn firing rptd 11-1, 890D2
LA DA ends 'Charlie's Angels' probe 12-2, 1002E2

Religious Issues—*See also PEOPLES Temple*

'Church' founder, aide convicted of fraud 2-9, 157B2
Worldwide Church probe case declined by Sup Ct 6-2, 513C1
Religious deprogrammer convicted 8-29, 727B1; sentncd 9-26, 857B3
Faith Cntr TV license revoked 10-10, 907B1

School Issues

2 profs suspended re sex harassmt 1-9, 77D3, F3
State of State message 1-10, 483A1
LA busing plan ordered 5-19, 426E3
Reagan record noted 7-16, 534E1
San Jose teachers strike 9-3, 723E3
LA busing begins peacefully 9-16, 724C1
San Bernardino, Riverside busing, housing integratn study rptd 11-16, 989E3

Sports

Raiders need NFL OK for LA move 1-18, 62C1
ASL LA Skyhawks fold 1-29, 771D1
Raiders LA move attempt sparks controversy 2-22—3-5, 175E1-C2
NL wins All-Star Game 7-8, 636B1
Moscow Olympic flag controversy 7-16—8-3, 588F1
Oakland A's sold 8-23, 795B3
LA hosts WBC bantamwgt bout 9-19, 907A3

Tax Issues

State of State message 1-10, 483A1
Fscl '79 revenue rptd 2-20, 307B3
San Fran faces budget crisis; Prop 13, 9 cited 3-8, 186F3
Income, oil tax proposals rejected by voters 6-3, 439C2

Transportation

Union Pacific, MoPac set merger 1-8, 52C3
Westn Pacific RR sale set 1-21, 131C2

1976

CALIFORNIA, Gulf of—*See GULF of California*

CALIFORNIA, University of
UCLA wins Rose Bowl 1-1, '75 rank rptd 1-2, 31B3
Viet refugee group barred 176D3
Chern gets Science Medal 10-18, 858D3
Berkeley's Chern wins Sci Medal 10-18, 858D3
Sup Ct stays Davis med schl reverse bias ruling 11-15, 882C1
Davis med schl ruling appeal voted 11-19, 995E2

CALIFORNIA Institute of Technology (Caltech) (Pasadena, Calif.)
New artery x-ray system rptd 1-21, 159E2
Rpts on Nev A-test 3-14, 243B1
Pickering gets Science Medal 10-18, 858F3
Brown named Defense secy 12-21, 956G1
Jet Propulsion Laboratory—*See under 'J'*

CALIFORNIA Rock and Gravel Co.
Owner's son arrested 7-22, 560A2

CALIFORNIA State University
Fullerton Campus
Gunman kills 7 7-12, 860G1

CALIFORNIA Suite (play)
Opens 6-10, 1014D3

CALKINS, John T.
Loses Cong election 3-2, 166E2

1977

CALIFORNIA, University of
Student attitudes survey released 1-14, 157F1-F2
Riverside studnt seized as spy 1-16, 41D2-A3
Davis reverse bias case cited 3-17, 217C3
Williams confrmd to SEC 4-7, 272D3
Albrecht in NFL draft 5-3, 353B3
SF rpts insulin gene reproductn 5-23, 451D3
Johnson in NBA draft 6-10, 584A3
Tris sterility warning 8-30, 820D2
Bakke brief filed 9-19; Sup Ct hears arguments 10-12, orders more briefs 10-17, 834F2-835G1
Pneumonia vaccine success rptd 10-26, 907D1
San Fran DNA research-produced hormone rptd 12-1; research violatns probed 12-16, 1022F2
Robinson wins Downtown AC Trophy 12-8, 950E2

CALIFORNIA American Water Co.
Water rationing begins 2-19, 153B1

CALIFORNIA Asiatic Oil Co.—*See under STANDARD Oil Co. of California*

CALIFORNIA Baptist College (Riverside, Calif.)
Fulmer chrgs divorce dismissal 5-2, 472C1

CALIFORNIA Institute of Technology (Caltech) (Pasadena, Calif.)
Kanamori revises Richter scale 2-14, 161B3
Brown rpts net worth 2-25, 147F3

CALIFORNIA Society of Dentistry for Children
Sues Gen Foods on cereal ads 6-30, 613F2

CALIFORNIA State University
Kennedy-Minott confrmd amb 8-3, 626G2

CALIGUIRI, Richard S.
Elected mayor 11-8, 855G1, A3

1978

CALIFORNIA, University of
Hughes Mormon will ruled fake 6-8, trial costs rptd 6-12, 458G3, 459A1
Berkeley Campus
San Andreas Fault rptd challenged 6-20, 480D1
Davis Campus
Laetrile danger rptd 3-6, 598B3
Bakke med schl admissn upheld, minority admissns plan voided by Sup Ct; reactn, opinion excerpts 6-28, 481A1-487C2
Bakke photo, biog data 482C1, 483B2
Los Angeles Campus (UCLA)
Tully sets indoor pole vault record 1-7, 76G2
Angela Davis joins SF State 1-26, 172B2
Tully sets pole vault marks 3-11, 5-19, 692D3, F3
AIAW basketball title 3-25, 272C2
Electrode implant paralysis treatmt rptd 5-6, 1023F1
Lund damage rptd in chronic marijuana users 5-15, 728G2
Austin, Nichols win NCAA tennis 5-29, 419E2
2d in NCAA outdoor track champ 6-1—6-4, 600F3
Quasar found near Earth galaxy 6-8, 654F1
Townsend in NBA draft 6-9, 457G3
Ties in Fiesta Bowl 12-25, 1025E2
San Diego Campus
Spectral line, ferromagnetism studies rptd 2-25, 3-16, 293G2, D3
San Francisco Campus
Heart research rptd 3-24, 597G3
2 new cholesterol drugs rptd 5-27, 1023G1
Sickle cell anemia test rptd 11-4, 948D1
Santa Barbara Campus
Quake damage rptd 8-13, 759B1

CALIFORNIA & Hawaiian Sugar Co.
Trust chrgs settled 6-12, 511C1

CALIFORNIA Institute of Technology (Caltech) (Pasadena)
Goldberg named pres 3-6, 172E3
Black hole at center of galaxy rptd 3-9, 293E3
Vision dvpt study rptd 4-15, 334C3
Uranus rings studied 5-27, 654E1

CALIFORNIA State University
Long Beach Campus
Bunz in NFL draft 5-2, 336G2
San Francisco Campus
Davis joins faculty 1-26, 172B2
Fractional chrg experimts rptd 2-16, 293B3

CALIFORNIA Suite (film)
Released 12-21, 1030E2

CALIFORNIA Superior Court v. General Council on Finance and Administration of the United Methodist Church
Case declined by Sup Ct 10-16, 789F2

CALIFORNIA v. Southland Realty
Natural gas diversn curbed by Sup Ct 5-31, 430F3-431D1

CALIFORNIA v. U.S.
Calif water rights backed by Sup Ct 7-3, 552B2

CALLAGHAN, Sir Bede
Japan investmt rise seen 12-13, 985D2

1979

Prop 13 effects; Jarvis, Gann new pursuits reviewed 6-1–7-2, 499F2-500B2
Utilities refund stay refused by Sup Ct 10-1, 768C1; appeal denied 10-15, 848B1
Prop 13 cited re San Fran teacher layoffs 10-23, 850F1
Mil spending return ranked 1st 11-18, 904A2
Transportation
CAB fare order case refused by US Sup Ct 1-8, 14D3
$99 cross-country air fares, new routes OKd 1-12, 35E2
San Diego '78 air crash rpt issued 4-19, 412D2*
United offers new NY fare 5-24, 402C2
Brown offers mass transit plan 5-31, 418F3
LA, San Fran on '78 world's busiest airport list 6-1, 421C1
DC-10s grounded, Laker LA svc halted 6-6, 421B1
Amtrak funding offered 8-31, 868B1, C1
BART svc curtailed 8-31–11-21, 922B3
San Fran-Shanghai air charter svc set 9-17, 726E1
San Fran cable cars shut down 9-26, Goldschmidt backs fund request 10-13, 831C1
San Fran cable cars resume svc 11-5, 989E3

CALIFORNIA, University of
Prop 13 effects reviewed 6-3, 499E3
Berkeley Campus
Forgn student enrollmt listed 167E3
White claims new hominid species 1-18, 137F3
Milgrom on Dead Sea Scroll 3-2, 217G2
Newell in basketball HOF 4-30, 526E3
San Fran quake epicenter rptd 8-6, 619D3
Colombia quake rptd 11-23, 912G2
Loses Garden State Bowl 12-15, 1001G2
Los Angeles Campus (UCLA)
Meyers named '78 top female athlete 1-10, 103C2
Forgn student enrollmt listed 167E3
Brown named basketball coach 3-27, 291E1
Tuiasosopo, Robinson in NFL draft 5-3, 335F2
Wins NCAA tennis title 5-24, 570A2
3 in NBA draft 6-25, 507A3, B3
Meyers waived by NBA team 9-9, signs with WBL Gems 11-14, 1003F2
Pot use concern rptd 10-14, 971G3
Abortn study cited 11-11, 930D2
San Diego Campus
Lyon rpts Brecht '43-56 FBI surveillnc 3-29, 367C3
Gov Brown addresses 6-29, 496G3
Santa Barbara Campus
'75 A-safety rpt called unreliable 1-19, 54C2
Peale's Jupiter theory rptd 3-17, 216G2

CALIFORNIA Institute of Technology (Caltech) (Pasadena)
Goldreich Uranus ring theory rptd 1-11, 289G3
Ingersoll on Jupiter findings 3-8, 216D1
14th Jovian moon rptd discovered 10-17, 1000D2
Hufstedler named Educ secy 10-30, 829A2

CALIFORNIA Life Corp.
Butterfield dismissed 8-16, 656F2

CALIFORNIA State University
Prop 13 effects rptd 6-3, 499E3
Fullerton Campus
Wins NCAA baseball title 6-8, 569A3

CALIFORNIA Suite (film)
Top-grossing film 1-10, 80G3; 2-7, 120G3
Smith wins Oscar 4-9, 336A2

CALIFORNIA v. Civil Aeronautics Board
Case refused by Sup Ct 1-8, 14E3

CALIFORNIA v. Patrick Steven W.
Case remanded by Sup Ct 6-25, 540B2

CALIFORNIA Young Lawyers Association
Lawyers survey rptd 9-17, 787D1

CALIG and Waterman v. Supreme Court of Ohio
Case refused by Sup Ct 11-5, 884B3

1980

San Fran fare hike proposal cited 3-8, 187B1
Pan Am revives discount coupons 3-10, 346E3
San Diego air control zone set 3-22, 347A1
World Air cuts fares 4-9, 346B3
LA Amer Airlines flight hijacked to Cuba 4-9, 617A3
Qantas Australia svc increase set 7-30, 617F2
NY-Peking air svc sets San Fran, LA stopovers 9-17, 707C1
LA airport nuisance award case refused by Sup Ct 10-6, 782A3
EPA halts highway funds 12-11, 963B1
Welfare & Social Services
Moffet sailors rptd seeking food stamps 4-24, 428G1

CALIFORNIA, University of
'79 endowmt earnings rptd 3-24, 319B2
Berkeley Campus
Rose in E-W Shrine Game 1-5, 62A2
Hermassi suspended re sex harassmt 1-9, 77F3
Rosen on mortgage rates 3-7, 222B3
Arvidsson sets swim marks 3-28—3-29, 4-11; team wins NCAA title 3-29, 834F3, 835B1
Breast cancer, enzyme link rptd 3-29, 415B3
Oldest life evidence rptd 4-2, 415A3
Ariz wins NCAA baseball title 6-6, 796E2
Sup Ct '79-80 term analyzed by Choper 7-2, 540G2
Mammoth-elephant link rptd 7-11, 715F3
Pac-10 transcript scandal penalties avoided 8-11, 875B2
George Stewart dies 8-22, 676C3
Plutonium removing chem dvpt rptd 9-12, 9-13, 716F2
Milosz wins Nobel 10-9, 889D2
Irvine Campus
Neutrino mass proposed 4-30, 416G1
Los Angeles Campus (UCLA)
FDA OKs Laetrile testing 1-3, 23F2
Freshmen student survey rptd 1-20, 319C3-320B1
Transcript scandal rptd 2-22, 469C2, F2
Loses NCAA basketball title 3-24, 240D1-D2
DNA transfer between living mice rptd 4-3, 415F3
Loses NCAA tennis team title 5-22, 607C1
2d in NCAA outdoor track champ 6-5—6-7, 892B1
Vandeweghe in NBA draft 6-10, 447F2
NCAA probe of basketball team 'rewards' rptd 7-27, 875D3
Barrett sets swimming mark 8-1, 834B3
Pac-10 punishes in transcript scandal 8-11, 875D1, G1
San Diego Campus
DES, problem pregnancy study rptd 1-25, 63D2
Smoking risk to nonsmokers rptd 3-26, 318A2
Bernd Matthias dies 10-27, 876F2
San Francisco Campus
Fetal skin disease test rptd 1-10, 64D1
Brain chem productn rptd 5-10, 715F1
Santa Cruz Campus
Newton gets PhD 6-15, 638F3

CALIFORNIA Bar Association
Ehrlichman resignatn accepted 1-19, 199D1

CALIFORNIA Brewers Association v. Bryant
Case decided by Sup Ct 2-20, 146B3

CALIFORNIA Fair Political Practices Commission v. Institute of Government Advocates
Case refused by Sup Ct 1-21, 93G2

CALIFORNIA Federal Savings & Loan Association
Morgage rate cut 5-22, 6-23, 514B1
Mortgage rate raised to 14% 10-1, 867C2
Mortgage rate hiked to 15% 11-7, 16% 12-3, 983F3
Burrill retires, Janis named pres 12-18, 959G1

CALIFORNIA Institute of Technology (Caltech) (Pasedena)
'Big Bang' remnants rptd 1-20, 415C2
'79 endowmt earnings rptd 3-24, 319C2

CALIFORNIA Liquor Dealers v. Midcal Aluminum
Case decided by Sup Ct 3-3, 210E1

CALIFORNIA Medical Assocation v. Federal Election Commission
Case accepted by Sup Ct 10-6, 782C2

CALIFORNIA State Polytechnic University
San Luis Obispo Campus
Wins NCAA Div II football title game 12-13, 999G2

CALIFORNIA State University
Northridge Campus
Nava named Mex amb 4-3, 315F1
San Jose Campus
Jacklin fired re sex harassmt 1-9, 77E3
Thomas in Senior Bowl 1-12, 62B2
Inskster wins US Women's Amateur golf title 8-17, 714E3

CALIFORNIA v. Yellin
Case decided by Sup Ct 6-16, 511E2

CALIGUIRI, Mayor Richard (Pittsburgh, Pa.)
Carter loses primary 4-22, 304D1

CALIGULA (film)
Released 2-2, 216C2
Boston judge rules not obscene 8-1, 640B2

1976

CALLAGHAN, James
Argentina ousts amb re Falklands dispute 1-13, 26F1
Iceland fishing talks set 1-19, 50D3
Rpts on Rhodesia const talks 3-2, 176B2
Sees Sovt amb on Africa interventn 3-15—3-19, Gromyko denies roles 3-25, 228G3, 229A1
In prime min race 3-17, balloting results 3-25, 3-29, 239G1
Rpts Rhodesia charter plan 3-22, 240C1
Elected prime min 4-5, 252G1
Names Cabinet 4-8, 266D3
'74 Cyprus policy scored 5-19, 457E1
Govt wins ship natlzn ruling 5-27; meets Thatcher 5-28, 402B1; defers plan 6-7, 407B3
Deplores racism 6-15, 482B1
French ldr ends visit 6-24, 481C3, E3
At 7-nation econ summit 6-27—6-28, 461G2, 462E1, G1
Visits Belfast 7-5, 498B3
Angola appeal rptd 7-5, 519D3
Uganda lauds Kenya crisis aid 7-20, 548D2
Scores UK amb's slaying 7-21, 538G2
UK cuts Uganda ties 7-28, 548B1, D1
Kissinger backs Rhodesia plan 8-2, meets 8-5, 580D3
Names Howell re drought 8-24, 630D1
Sees Kissinger on S Africa 9-6, 660E2
Reshuffles Cabt 9-10, 693C3
In Canada 9-11—9-18, 730G1
Seamen's strike averted 9-22, 750E3
Smith accepts proposal 9-24, 717B1, A2
Addresses Labor conf 10-1, 791C3
Thatcher ties to econ collapse 10-8, 791E3
Lending rate hiked 10-11, 773E1
Foot elected dep ldr 10-21, 853A2
On £ fall, IMF loan terms 10-25; oppositn scores 10-26, 810A1
Rhodesia conf opens, statemt read 10-28, 797B1
On by-election losses 11-4, 853G1
£ edges up 11-7, 853C2
Govt wins 3 votes 11-8, loses 2 11-10, 852F3
Richard sees 843D1
Meets Giscard, backed on IMF loan, sterling balances 11-11—11-12, 880B2 ★

CALLAHAN, Nicholas P.
FBI probe rptd 3-21, 248G1
Fired 7-16, 634C1

CALLAN, Col. Tony—*See GEORGIOU, Costas*

CALLAWAY Jr., Howard H. (Bo)
Says White House too apolitical 1-8, 21A3
Scores Reagan budget plan 1-8, 22A1
Fla primary comments 3-9, 179E1, F1
Chrgd 3-12, steps aside during probe 3-13, 197G1
Quits Ford campaign post 3-30, 233B1
CAB dismisses chrg 3-31, 745A2
Army recruitmt bias coverup chrgd 6-7, 454G1
Sen subcom rpt accuses; scores rpt 10-5, 744F3, 745G1

CALLEY Jr., William L.
Sup Ct bars case review 4-5, 262F1
Favors uncondtinal amnesty 9-8, 680A3

CALLIAN, Georges
Rpt CAR expels 4-30, 503G2

CALTEX Oil Co.
Rhodesia sanctn violatns chrgd 6-21, 621A2

CALVO, Carlos
Bolivia finance min 1-12, 27A1

CALVO Serer, Rafael
Arrested 6-3, freed on bail 6-18, 459F1

CAMACHO, Marcelino
Sees political changes 1-6, 12C2
Seized 3-29, chrgd 4-1, 269A1
Freed 5-25, 422F2
Gracia Trevijano freed on bail 6-12, 459G1
Scores Suarez 7-3, 500G3

CAMARATA, Peter
Proposes Teamsters reform 6-15, 436B1

CAMARA, Favo
Named Guinea amb to Algieria 12-11, 1005A2

CAMARA, Moussa Sandiana
Named Guinea gov 12-11, 1005A2

CAMBODIA (Khmer Republic)—*See also ADB, NONALIGNED Nations Movement*
Sihanouk ends forgn tour; presides at cabt mtg 1-3, 8B1
Natls quit S Vietnam 1-3, 11G3
New charter in effect 1-5, 8A1
Paris embassy closed 1-7, 139D2
Listed as 'not free' nation 1-19, 20D3
Mass population shift rptd 1-19, 46D2
China air route set 1-23, 100G3
Troops slay fleeing refugees 1-26, 98E3
Thais list total escapees 98G3
Natl elections set 2-4, 98B3
Laos, N Viet bolster ties 2-11, 121E1
Forgn aides visit Siem Reap 3-2—3-4, 238B2
Refugees land in Australia 3-19, 237B2
People's Assembly elected 3-20, 238A2
Rpt Burma CPs get war arms 3-31, 265B1
Sihanouk, cabt resign 4-5, 4-7, 250F1-A2
Assemb OKs new govt 4-11—4-13; Cabt announced 4-14, 265C1
Mass executns rptd 4-21, 5-7, 350B1
Opposition group formed 4-21, 350G1
Pilot defects to Thailand 4-30, asks asylum 5-2, 335E1

1977

CALLAGHAN, James (British prime minister)
On sterling balances accord 1-11, 20B3
To supervise indl, sterling policies 1-12, 1-13, 44B2
Carter backs Concorde trial 1-16, 131F2
Mondale visits 1-27, 69C1
Names Owen forgn secy 2-21, 200F3
Sees Carter re Concorde, air treaty 3-10—3-11, 213A1
Lauds unions re Leyland threat 3-16, 256D1
Rpts Liberal pact 3-22, wins no-confidence vote 3-23, 239A2
Vance arms talks rptd 3-31, 247A1
Sees Muldoon 3-31, 258B2
Carter asks Portugal aid 4-1, 330C3
Tours UK with Carter 5-6, hails visit 5-8, 359C2
At 7-natn econ summit, Jenkins role disputed 5-7—5-8, 357B1, F1, 358G1
At 4-power NATO talks 5-9, min mtg 5-10, 358C2
Jay appointmt opposed 5-11, 391F3
Sees Mondale 5-22, 398E1
Scores Leyland payoff chrgs 5-24, 526E1
Bars Amin from Commonwealth conf 6-8—6-15, 486E3
On EC JET delay 7-1, 624A3
Lynch asks mtg on united Ireland 7-6, 599B1
Grunwick strike violence 7-11, 543G3
Unions end wage restraint 7-13, 544A1
Says Rhodesia electns 'irrelevant' 7-19, 563E3
On anti-inflatn pkg OK 7-20, 580E3
Denies Wilson bugged 8-23, 745D2
TUC backs once-a-yr raises 9-7, 745B2
SDLP urges Irish link 9-21, 783A3
Dobson chrgs weak on unions 9-27, 864C1
Liberals back Labor pact 9-28, 745D1
Meets Lynch on Ulster power-sharing 9-28, 782A2
Opens Labor Party conf 10-4, 863C3
West rpts Unionst devolutn stand 10-8—10-9, 783E3
Lynch asks UK back reunificatn 10-12, 782F2
Schmidt thanks re hijack rescue aid 10-18, 790F1
Sees Schmidt, JET site vote agreed 10-18; Culham chosen 10-25, 853A1
OKs W Ger mil 'offset paymt' terms 10-18, 926F2
Scot, Wales home rule motn passes Commons 11-16, 903D2
Meets Israel premier 12-4, 931D1
In French summit 12-12—12-13, 1013G1

CALLAS, Maria
Dies 9-16, 787G3

CALLAWAY Jr., Howard H. (Bo)
Probe dropped 1-11, 59D2

CALLEA, Harry Desmond
Sentence commuted 1-25, 139E3

CALLIMAHOS, Lambros D.
Dies 10-28, 872C1

CALLISTER, Judge E. Talbot
Hearst pleads no contest 4-18, 302D2
Sentences Hearst 5-9, 370E3

CALMON de Sa, Angelo
Brazil industry min 2-9, 281D2

CALORIE Control Council
Saccharin ban scored 3-9, 176G3

CALTEX Oil Co.
To promote S Africa equality 3-1, 160B3
Sued re Rhodesia sanctns 5-31, 413C2
Zambia sues re Rhodesia sanctns 8-22, 662D1

CALVO, Carlos
Quits Cabt in oil dispute 10-11, 902A1

CALVO Sotelo, Leopoldo
UCD launched 5-3, 453G1

CAMARA, Archbishop Helder
Scores police raids on univ 9-27, 840A2

CAMARGO, Col. Jose Maria de Toledo
On prisoner torture chrgs 11-10, 964A3

CAMARGO-Seixas, Angela
France expels Agee 8-18, 654F2

CAMBODIA (Khmer Republic)—*See also NONALIGNED Nations Movement*
Postwar conditns rptd 5-2, 337A1
Pol Pot identified as premr, CP head 8-19, 9-25, 741C2
2½ mln rptd killed since '75 9-12, 710G1
Pol Pot on evacuatn move 10-2, 779E3
Party, govt ldrs named 780A1
Pol Pot denies widespread killings 840C3
Rpt armed forces purged 10-19, 840A3
Foreign Relations (misc.)—*See also 'UN Policy' below*
UN Assembly member 4B1
Raids Thai villages 1-28—1-29; Thailand closes border 1-30, alerts army 1-31, 87D3
Chrgs Thai border raids 2-4, 2-12, 138G1
OPEC loan offer rejctd 3-3, 183F1
Thai border clashes 5-6, 5-8, 5-12, 393G2
Viet border clashes rptd 5-8—8-8, 607C2-B3
ASEAN backs ties 7-5—7-8, 537C1
Thai border clashes 7-20—7-22; Thai protest 7-25, 571G3
Thai clashes continue 7-23—8-8, Thanin confrms 8-6, 607A3, B3
ASEAN asks ties, press scores 8-5, 607E1

1978

CALLAGHAN, James (British prime minister)
Lynch cites '77 talks 1-8, 18D3
Mondale on Westn tour 1-9—1-13, 34G1
Sees Caramanlis on EC entry 1-25, 149B2
Warns Leyland workers 1-26, 112C2
Scores Thatcher immigratn stand, rpts '77 total 1-31, 90G1
Meets Sadat, hints peace role 2-9, 98D2
Sees Mason on Belfast bombing 2-19, 132D2
Defends neutron bomb, scores SS-20 2-21, 140D1
Scores Tory immigratn policy 3-3, 167D3
Urges Bonn econ summit plan 3-14, sees Carter in US 3-23, 226B3
For govt oil revenue plans 3-21, 227D1
On '78-79 stimulus budget 4-11, 267D2
Labor wins Scot by-electn 4-14, 288C1
Disclaims UK defns chief's remarks on USSR 5-1, 329A3
Bars confidence vote, scores tax cuts 5-11, 415C2
Sees Kaunda, OKs extra aid 5-15, 395D2
Botswana clears dead student 5-17, 596A1
On Liberal-Labor pact end 5-25, 453A1
NATO summit ends, scores US emphasis on Africa 5-31, 397G1
Labor wins Hamilton by-electn 6-1, 437C2
Sees Ceausescu, lauds Mideast peace role 6-13—6-16, 515F2, C3
Govt narrowly wins confidence vote on Healey's salary 6-14, 496F2
On EC monetary zone proposal 7-7, 545D1, B3
Scores Shcharansky, Ginzburg trials 7-10, 542B3
Asks Israel-Egypt conf shift re security 7-15, 546G1
At 7-natn Bonn econ summit 7-16—7-17, 543C3, 544C2
Regrets Kenyatta death 8-22, 639B3
Delays gen electn; Thatcher, Steel score 9-7; Healey defends decisn 9-8, 704D3
Sees Kaunda re Rhodesia sanctns-breaking 9-22, 756A3
Defends 5% pay-hike policy 10-1, 10-3, 763B1, G1
Sees China forgn min 10-10—10-13, 796G1
TUC rebuffs govt on pay, price statemt 10-14, 903G1
2 Vauxhall plants bar strike 10-23, 10-24, 816D1
Poll rpts policy backing 10-28, 867E1, F1
Legis plans outlined 11-1, 838D1, F1
Wins confidence vote 11-9, 866F3
Names new Rhodesia envoy 11-23, 911F3
Defends sanctns vs Ford Motor 11-28, 923F3
Vs EMS entry 12-5, 951G3, 952A1
Tories score pay sanctns 12-13; renounces, wins confidnc vote 12-14, 964E2
Urges Rhodesia sanctns probe 12-15, 987A3

CALLAHAN, Nicholas
Past FBI corruptn rptd 1-10, 15A2, C2

CALLOWAY, Cab (deceased)
Sister dies 12-16, 1032A3

CALM Prevails Over the Country (film)
Released 4-6, 618E3

CALORIES—*See FOOD—Diets*

CALTEX Petroleum Corp.
S Korea '71 campaign gifts rptd 11-1, 862E3

CALUMET Farm
Alydar loses Triple Crown 6-10, 539A1

CALVERT, Judge David
Fines Wichita strikers 9-17, 9-27, 753E1

CALVET, Maria Dolores
Rpts illegal abortns 4-26, 576B3

CALVO Ortega, Rafael
Named Spain labor min 2-24, 394G2

CALVOSO, Fedele
Killed 11-8, 1018F1

CALVO Sotelo, Leopoldo
Named Spain EC negotiator 2-10, 395C1

CAMACHO Leyva, Gen. Luis Carlos
Named Colombia defns min 8-7, 629C3, D3

CAMARGO, Pedro P.
Rpts W Ger terrorists in Colombia 2-18, 147C3

CAMBODIA (Democratic Kampuchea)—*See also NONALIGNED Nations Movement*
Massacres denied 7-17, 548B3
Govt denies rights breach 7-21, 660B1
'75 urban ousters defended 7-28, 583B3
New purges rptd, refugees flee 8-8, Lon Nol aides rptd targets 8-10, 659F3-660B1
Lon Nol: 3 mln killed since '75 9-21, 748A2
Refugee exit data rptd 10-11, 776C2
Revolt rptd 10-23, 803G2
Refugee flow rptd high 11-10, 870A3
Revolt rptd spreading 11-25, 933D2
Anti-govt front rptd 12-3; front scores govt 12-4, 933E1-D2
Foreign Relations (misc.)—*See also 'UN' and 'Vietnam Conflict' below*
China lauds army 1-16, 42C3
Scandinavian ambs end visit 1-21, call Pnompenh 'ghost city' 1-22, 43A2; Thai min disputes 2-2, 61E1
China aide ends missn 1-22, 80G1
Thai border clash, 7 die 1-23; '77 casualties cited 61C1
Thai talks, ties renewal set 1-30—2-2, 61B1
Thai refugee policy rptd 2-16, 139F3

1979

CALLAGHAN, James (British prime minister; replaced May 4)
At 4-natn Guadeloupe summit, endorses SALT 1-5–1-6, 12E2, B3, 40C2
China jet deal revealed 1-5, 12B3
Truckers' strike sanctned by union despite appeal 1-11, 20E2
Revises wage policy, scores truckers 1-16, 37G3
Abandons Rhodesia conf plan 1-17, 39D3
City, rail workers strike 1-22, 1-23, 59C2
Truckers' strike ends 1-29, 75E3
Meets TUC ldrs, warns on pol impact of strikes 1-29, 76C1
Rejects wage-price freeze 1-30, 75E3
Scores public worker strikes 2-1, 75F3
Poll rpts approval drop 2-6, 116B1
Backs Scottish, Welsh devolutn 2-12, 2-21, 135G1
TUC-govt accord announced 2-14, 115D2, A3
Backs fall electn 2-26, 154F1
Scottish, Welsh devolutn set back in vote 3-1, 168F3
Manual workers OK pact 3-6, 211D2
Amb to Holland killed 3-22, 228F2
Loses confidence vote 3-28, sets May electns 3-29, 228C1
Lauds Neave 3-30, 254B2
Says UK A-plants safe 4-3, 246G2
Labor manifesto issued 4-6, 267E3
On mil pay comparability goal 4-17, 331E1
Vs Natl Front rally violence 4-24, 313D1
Tories win electn 5-3, resigns as prime min 5-4, 537A1, F1, D2
Reelected Labor head 5-9, 359F1
Scores Tory programs 5-15, 359D1
Scores budget 6-12, 445G1
'77 N Ireland visit cited 8-29, 669E2
N Sea oil assets sale barred 9-14, 707A2
Left advances at Labor Party conf 10-1–10-5, 773D1, D2, E2
Left to dominate Labor Party probe 10-24, scores 10-31, 11-2, 873F2-C3

CALLAHAN, Rev. William J.
Silenced, ordrd relocated; female ordinatn issue cited 12-1, 999F3

CALLERI Oil Co.
Fined re gas-switching 4-26, 301D2

CALLUM, B.
Beneath the Valley of Ultravixens released 5-11, 528D1

CALOGERO, Pietro
Rpts Moro probe progress 4-16, 313G2

CALS, Cesar
Brazil mines min designate 1-19, 95D1

CALVIN, Melvin
Tree rptd fuel source 9-15, 1000B2

CAMACHO, Marcelino
Scores govt econ policy, calls for soclst-CP front 10-15, 795D1

CAMACHO, Umberto
Cited in Carter death plot probe 5-5–5-29, 404F1

CAMACHO Leyva, Gen. Luis Carlos
Pol power rptd 11-14, 993F1

CAMARA, Archbishop Helder
Backs Pope 2-3, Nicaragua, El Salvador prelates 2-12, 108F3

CAMBELL, Edward J.
Vs NLRB USW decisn 7-3, 561B1

CAMBODIA—*See also NONALIGNED Nations Movement*
Natlst front revealed 10-12, 779B2
Pnompenh populatn rptd 11-12, 863A3
Famine
Rice shortages seen, famine feared, UN aid limits rptd 4-22, 4-28, 318B2
Rice growing halted, famine confrmd 8-3, 600B3
US issues food aid plea 8-8–8-9, 600E3
Christian Conf, Thais see famine 8-23, 8-30; Red Cross air lifts food, medicine 8-29, 9-8, 684F1
Forgn relief seen blocked 9-22; UNICEF, Red Cross aid set 9-26; Viets score 9-30, 740G3-741E1
US warns of starvatn threat 9-27, 741D1
Viets deny famine 10-4, score forgn aid 10-14, 779D2
Carter sees food aid 10-9, 767A2
Sihanouk asks US aid bar, fears Viet soldier theft 10-11, 811E2
Natlst group starts aid program 10-12, 779B2
Govt denies emergency 10-12, 811A2
UNICEF, Red Cross aid starts 10-13, 10-14, 10-16, 779G1

1980

CALLAGHAN, James
Labor bars Trotskyist probe rpt publicatn 1-23, 79C2
US amb's pol gaffes rptd 1-30, 200D2
Labor censure vote defeated 2-28, 172G1
Scores new budget 3-26, 232F2
Urges Sovt Afghan exit, mil cutbacks 5-31, 429F2
Scores econ policies; Thatcher wins no confidence vote 7-29, 578D1
Addresses TUC, urges 'new partnership' 9-2, 688D2
Pol future undecided, leftists advance at Labor Party conf 9-29—10-3, 768D2, G3
Quits as Labor ldr 10-15, 790F3
Foot elected Labor ldr 11-10, 872B2

CALLAWAY, Howard H. (Bo)
Loses Sen primary 9-9, 700E2

CALL Me (recording)
On best-seller list 3-5, 200E3; 4-2, 280E3; 4-30, 359G3; 6-4, 448E3

CALMETTE, Dr. Albert (1863-1933)
TB vaccine cited 1-20, 63B2

CALTAGIRONE, Camillo
Fled Italy, evades arrest 2-11, 151E2
Tax debt estimated 3-12, 255G1

CALTAGIRONE, Francesco
Fled Italy, evades arrest 2-11, 151E2
Tax debt estimated 3-12, 255G1

CALTAGIRONE, Gaetano
Fled Italy, evades arrest 2-11, 151E2
Evangelisti quits Cabt post 3-4, 173A2
Tax debt estimated 3-12, 255G1

CALVALIGI, Enrico
Slain 12-31, 995D1

CALVO Sotelo, Leopoldo
Named Spanish dep premr 9-8, 690E2

CAMACHO Leyva, Gen. Luis Carlos
On DR Emb siege end 4-28, 335B3
Directs search for escaped guerrillas 6-25, 521C2

CAMBODIA (Democratic Kampuchea)—*See also ADB, NONALIGNED Nations*
Khieu, Ieng refute Pol Pot excesses 2-28, 181F1
'70-79 populatn drop rptd 5-24, 397D2
Ieng on Pol Pot ouster, exile govt reform proposals 11-29, 913E2-A3
Famine
UN World Food Program halts Jan aid; UNICEF, Red Cross rpt backlogs 1-2, 12C2
US chrgs aid blocked 1-8, 49F1
Thais suspend refugee aid 1-10; resume 1-20, 49F1
Intl relief move averts 'disaster' 1-23, 2-10; Thai border statn suspends operatns 2-7, 108D1-B2
Thai intl aid convoy blocked; US, French protest 2-6, 108B2
Reagan 'basic speech' scores US-USSR detente 2-29, 207A3, F3
Red Cross, World Food Program dispute shipmts 3-10, 261G3
UNICEF fears renewal 3-21, UN conf seeks aid 3-26; Red Cross, UNICEF begin airlift 4-4, 261C3, 262A1
UN sponsors conf on aid 5-26—5-27, 397A2

1976

Missn in France asked to leave 7-30, request scored 7-31, 572G2-B3
Teng Sary visits Peking 8-7, 588D2
UK ties restored 8-9, 589B2
Thai border reopened 8-30, 677F3
Austria ties restored 8-30, 679C1
Thai rebel aid rptd 9-3, 677D3
Thais asked to extradite 4 ex-offcls 9-4, 734E3
China delegatn views Mao body 9-13, 711F3
Thais return 26 refugees 11-23, 929B2
Thais chrg Viet invasn plan 12-8, 949D3

U.S. Relations

Rpt US jets raid Siem Reap 2-25; US, Thais deny 2-27; troops protest 2-29, 172D3
Forgn aides visit Siem Reap 3-2—3-4, 238B2
Reagan scores Ford policy 3-4, 165G3
Nixon cites bombing policy 3-10, 184A2
US Sen com cites US projcts 4-26, 304D2
NY Times writer wins Pulitzer 5-3, 352D3
US Dem platform text 6-15, 475G3
'75 refugee funds use extended 6-30, 533C2
Carter cites war 7-15, 507D1, 510E2
US GOP platform text 8-18, 609F2, A3, 610A2
Ford acceptance speech cites 8-19, 612A1
Dole legis record cited 614G2
US limits forgn aid use 10-1, 806E3
GAO study faults '75 US Mayaguez actn 10-5, 749B2
Ford, Carter debate 10-6, 741D1, 742A2
Ford, Carter debate 10-22, 800D3

1977

Malaysia eases refugee ban 8-31, 685D2
Lon Nol discounts Viet border clash rpts 9-12, 710G1
Pol Pot in China 9-28, 741G2
Pol Pot on Viet, Thai clashes 9-28, 741C3, E3
Pol Pot ends China trip, '75 visit disclosed 9-28—10-2, 779E3, 780A1
Thais repel border incursns 10-15—10-16, 10-31, 841D3
Refugees get Viet asylum 10-19, 841G2
New Thai rulers for ties 10-21, 827D1
UK bars ties 10-24, 864F1
Thai border clashes 12-21—12-22, 999C3
Viet border clashes 12-22, 12-24, 12-27; Cambodia cuts ties 12-31, 999D2

UN Policy & Developments

Dues disputed, vote right suspended 9-20, 713B1
Dues payment rptd 10-4, 770B2

U.S. Relations

US sees no cooperatn re MIAs 2-25, 206F2
US travel ban end set 3-9, 172F3, 173D1
Postwar conditns rptd 5-2, 337A1
Nixon reminisces 5-12, 386B1
Nixon backs US '70 invasn 5-19, 406A1
US Sen vs loans 6-14, 477C3
US offcls rpt high death toll 7-26, 590C2
US aid bar signed 8-4, 668B2
MIAs listed by US 9-30, 795E1
Pol Pot cites war deaths 841C3
US intl agency loan policy set 10-19, 815A2-C2

1978

Thai civlns abducted 3-5, 237C3
Canada Parlt scores killings 301B2
Thai rebels get aid in clash 4-9, 301A3
Thai CP rebels rptdly extend frontier control 4-10, 301F2
Ex-info min urges intl aid vs killings 4-19, 301D2
Cambodia rptd clearing out civlns near Viet, Thai border areas 4-19, 301A3
Oslo mtg gets atrocity rpts 4-21—4-23, 301C2
Thais put refugees in camps 4-30, 341C2
Australia to admit 9,000 refugees 5-17, 369A3
Chinese ethnics plight cited 5-29, 399G3
Ieng in Thailand, China role cited; border pact agreed 7-14—7-17, 548F2, B3
UK interventn re rights chrgd 7-21, 660C1
'75 border closure defended 7-28, 583B3
Refugees flee to Thailand 8-8, 659F3
Ieng in Pl 10-19, 803E2
China backs vs Vietnam 11-5, 894G1
UK prof arrives 12-9, slain 12-23; rebel plot seen 12-24, 997G1
Pl signs US mil base pact, Pnompenh pressure cited 12-31, 1000A3

UN Policy & Developments

Ieng addresses disarmamt sessn 6-9, 490E1
US, UK chrg cruelty; rpt to UN cited 8-31, 9-20, 748E1
UN Assemb member 713D3
Lon Nol asks 'free Khmers' in UN seat 9-21, 748A2
US sens urge death probe 10-12, 794F1
Waldheim gets invite 10-13, 794D1
Waldheim OKs visit 11-1, 859G3

U.S. Relations

US chrgs 'proxy war' re Viet-Cambodia clashes 1-8; scored 1-9, 1-16, 9C2, 43E1
US chrgs rights breach 1-18, 43F1
US distressed by Thai refugee policy 2-16, 140B1
Viet buldup re Cambodia rptd 4-7, 277D3
Mayaguez '75 seizure cited 4-7, 278B1
'Holocaust' chrgd at DC news conf 4-19, 301D2
Carter assails on rights 4-21, 301G1
Solzhenitsyn scores US capitulatn 6-8, 444C3
Viet, US plots chrgd 6-13, 6-24, 6-25, 548C2
Viet scores China backing 6-20, 464G2
CIA-Viet coup plot chrgd 6-25, Hanoi denies 6-27, 490C2
Sen McGovern for intl force to oust govt 8-21, US bars 8-22, 659B3
US chrgs cruelty 8-31, 748E1
US sens urge UN probe deaths 10-12, 794F1
McGovern: Cambodia vs intl force 10-12, 794A2
US vows neutral stance 10-25, 830D1
US seeks to avert major Viet clash 11-5, 859D3
US backs interest paymts on frozen forgn assets 11-14, 977G1
US to admit more refugees 11-28, 932G3-933D1, 934E1
2 US rptrs arrive 12-9, escape gunman 12-23, 997A2

Vietnam Conflict

USSR, China hint backing for Viets, Cambodians 1-1, 4F1
Border clashes rptd, Viets take Parrot's Beak 1-2—1-5; Pnompenh claims counterdrive 1-3, 1-4, 3G3
USSR group urges talks 1-2, 4A2
Cambodia vs negotiatns 1-3, 4D1
Amb to Vietnam leaves 1-3, 4E1
Cambodia seeks N Korea aid 1-3, 4E1
Viet asks peace talks 1-5, 1-12, 42D3
Border clashes ebb, Viets control Parrot's Beak 1-6, 9A1
Cambodia claims victories, high losses inflicted 1-6—1-9, 9B1
Viets chrg massacre 1-6, 9F1
Battle zone map 9F1
Viets chrg Cambodian raid 1-7, 9B2
US sees Sovt-China 'proxy war' 1-8; USSR scores 1-9, Viet 1-16, 9C2, 43E1
USSR concerned re clashes 1-8, 10A1
Viet protests China press rpts 1-9, China rpts rival battle versns 1-10, 42G2
Both sides chrg raids 1-18, 1-24, 1-25; Viets warn retaliatn 1-20, 42C2
China delegatn in Cambodia 1-18, 42C3
Viet denies 'federatn' plan 1-18, 43C1
China chrgs Hanoi agressn 1-22, bars mediatn 2-1, 80F1
Clashes 1-24—2-9, 80A1
Viet troop advance through Laos rptd 2-1, 80D1
Viet peace bid 2-5; Cambodia vs, UN gets copy 2-8, 79G3
3 border prov clashes 2-11, 2-16, 2-18, 121E1
Viet says China arms Cambodia 2-21, 121C1
Viets: 300 Cambodians slain 201G2
Viets deny federatn plan 201B3
Viets chrg incursn 3-16, 3-17, 201F2
Cambodia asks negotiatns 3-16, 201A3
Pol Pot vs Viet federatn plan 3-19, 201B3
Cambodia: Viet invasn repulsed 4-7; Viets deny 4-13, 4-14, 277C3
US rpts Viet buildup 4-7, 277D3
Viets cite offshore dispute 4-7, 278A1
Viet agressn chrgd 4-13, 4-16, 277E3
Cambodia rptd clearing out civlns in border area 4-19, 301B3
Lull broken by heavy clashes 5-14, 6-16—6-23, 490F1
Hanoi offers truce 6-6, 490C1
Cambodia chrgs agressn at UN 6-8, 6-9, 490E1

1979

Aid rptdly reaches Pol Pot forces 10-17, 779E2
Viet chrgs Thai war role 10-18, 811D3
US sens tour Thai camps 10-21—10-23, meet Cambodia offcls 10-24; Carter gets rpt, names Clark to head aid effort 10-26; Pnompenh rejcts food convoy proposal 10-27, 823C3-824E1
Carter vows $70 mln food aid 10-24, 811F1
UN vows relief aid 11-5, 863B3
UNICEF, Red Cross call relief inadequate 11-25, 917D2
Forgn relief rptd blocked, Pnompenh denies 12-2—12-3, 917G1
Sovt bloc aid listed 12-3, 917A2
Thais block border relief, blame Free Khmer 12-3, 917F2
US, intl relief groups rpt aid shipmts stalled; Sovt, Viet, Cambodia role disputed 12-5—12-24, 977G2-978G3

Foreign Relations (misc.)—*See also 'Famine' above, 'UN' and 'Vietnam Conflict' below*

Sihanouk in China 1-6—1-8, NY 1-9, 10F2
Sihanouk sees China dep prime min in DC 1-31, 66D2
Red Cross missn confrms famine, torture 8-3, 600B3
UK ends Pol Pot ties 12-6, 978G3

Government & Politics—*See also other appropriate subheads in this section*

Sihanouk freed from house detentn 1-5, 10G2-A3
Rebel govt policies outlined 1-6, 10D1
Pol Pot govt ousted, rebel United Front in power 1-8, 9E1
Heng heads Cncl, other members listed 1-8; '78 pol activities cited 10A1
Sihanouk on Pol Pot govt 1-8, 10F2
Pol Pot still in Cambodia 1-10, 9F2
Sihanouk to remain in West 1-18, 68G3
Heng chrgs Pol Pot govt massacres 1-25, 68E3
Sihanouk sees return 2-11, 2-13, 142D2
Heng govt admits shortcomings 3-24, 229C2
Pol Pot, Ieng Sary get death sentnc 8-19, 666F3
Khieu replaces Pol Pot as premr 12-27, 977E2

Refugees—*See 'Vietnam Conflict' below; also INDOCHINA-Refugees*

UN Policy & Developments—*See also 'Famine' above*

Cncl aid vs Viet urged 1-2, 1E1
Sihanouk asks aid 1-9, Cncl meets 1-11—1-12, 10G1, A3
Waldheim urges war end 2-18, 123B1
Cncl meets, US asks Viet exit 2-23; actn stalled 2-28, 142A1
USSR vetoes Cncl resolutn 3-16, 200E1
UNICEF missn confrms famine, torture 8-3, 600B3
Pol Pot govt recognitn, forgn support linked 8-30, 674D3
Pol Pot govt seat challenged by Viet 9-18; seat upheld 9-19, 695B2
Membership listed 695F2
Pol Pot govt retains seat 9-21, 741F1
Assemb votes Viet exit 11-14, 863E3

U.S. Relations—*See also 'Famine' above, 'Vietnam Conflict' below*

Sihanouk in NY 1-9, 10F2
Sihanouk meets Vance, US stay OKd 1-18, 69A1
Debt to US rptd past due 2-5, 84C3
US rights rpt omits 2-10, 107A2
Pol Pot govt UN seat upheld 9-19, 695C2
Pol Pot govt UN seat backed 9-21, Sovts score 9-22, 741G1, B2
Congresswomen in Pnompenh 11-12, 863F2

Vietnam Conflict—*See also 'Famine' above*

Rebel successes rptd 1-1, 1-3, 1-4, 1F2
Cambodia ties USSR to invasn 1-2, 1E1
UN interventn asked 1-2; US backs bid 1-3, qualifies 1-4; Viet scores bid, chrgs China link 1-4, 1E1
Viet, rebel troops rptd closer to Pnompenh 1-4, 1-5, 1B1, C2
Viets seize 1/4 of country 1-4, 1D2
Neak Luong bombed 1-4, 2A1
USSR rpts rebel advance in Cambodia 1-4, 2A1
China vs troops to Cambodia 1-5, 1D1
Pol Pot: 'life-or-death struggle' 1-5, 1D2
US tells Sovts of concern 1-5, 11B1
Guadeloupe summit topic 1-5—1-6, 12G2
Battle map 9A1
Pnompenh, Kompong Som captured 1-7, 9D1, D2
US, China score Viet 1-7, 1-8; USSR hails Pnompenh capture 1-7, 11A1
Rebels: all provinces 'liberated' 1-8, 9G1
Forgn offcls escape to Thailand 1-8, 9G2
Sihanouk asks UN, US aid 1-9, 10A3
USSR, allies laud Pol Pot overthrow 1-9; Rumania scores 1-10, 11E1
Dep premr flown to Thailand 1-11, China 1-12, 9F2
UN hears plea 1-11—1-12, 10G1
Nonaligned natns reactn rptd uncertain 1-11, 11B2
Strong govt resistance rptd 1-12, 9E2
Fighting near Thai border, Angkor temples 1-13—1-17, 28A1-C1
Govt loses Siem Reap, Battambang 1-13, Nimit 1-14, 28B1, D1
ASEAN demands Viet pullout 1-13, 28B2

1980

Intl aid halted 6-17, Viets blamed 7-9; Thais, Red Cross, UN OK renewal 7-27, 591C2
UNICEF, Red Cross aid resumes 8-4, 644F3
Red Cross ends food aid, UNICEF plans '81 halt 12-16, 951E3

Foreign Relations (misc.)—*See also CAMBODIA (Democratic Kampuchea)--Famine, CAMBODIA (Democratic Kampuchea)--Vietnam Conflict*

India prime min backs Heng 1-6, 11G3
USSR backs detente 2-4, 84E3
Morocco king vs Sihanouk plan 2-22, 141D2
China joins IMF 4-17, 302E2
India sets ties; ASEAN, US, China score; USSR lauds 7-7, 547F2
Pol Pot delegate shunned at UN women's conf 7-17, 587C2
Pol Pot govt keeps UN Assemb seat 10-13, 775B2

Refugees—*See under INDOCHINA*

UN Policy & Developments—*See CAMBODIA (Democratic Kampuchea)--Famine*

U.S. Relations—*See also CAMBODIA (Democratic Kampuchea)--Famine, CAMBODIA (Democratic Kampuchea)--Vietnam Conflict*

US issues rights rpt 2-5, 87G1
Sihanouk in US, backing for armed group denied 2-22, 141B2
Connally cites Sovt threat 3-7, 184F3
US mil computer failure rptd re Mayaguez seizure 3-10, 210D2
US scores India ties 7-7, 547G2

Vietnam Conflict

Refugees fight near Thai, 1000s cross border 1-4—1-6, 12B3
Thai-Cambodia border battles 1-25—1-31, 68C2
US sees major Viet drive near Thai border 1-26, 68F2
US pres candidates' 'basic speeches' cite Viet takeover 2-29, 3-3, 207B3, 208C3
China vows guerrilla aid 3-9; Khieu asks intl backing 3-11, 181E1
Pol Pot forces ambush train 6-10, 475G3
China vs Viet Thai raids 6-25, 7-2, 508A2, D2
US asks Viet Thai raid halt 6-25, Moscow aid 6-25, 6-26, 508B2
Viets capture 4 Westn civilians 6-25, release 6-29, 508F2
Viet thrust drove 100,000 Cambodians to Thailand 6-26, 508D1
ASEAN conf scores Viet Thai incursn; Viet deny frontier breach 6-26, 508E1-A2
Thai-Viet clashes near border; Pol Pot backers pursued into Thai 6-28, kill 20 Viets 7-1, 508C1
US arms lift to Thai starts, USSR scores 7-5, 508B1
Carter, Hua meet 7-10, 506C1
Thais vs Viet Cambodia-Thai DMZ plan at forgn min talks 7-18, 591F1
Thai mil raids chrgd, DMZ plan rejectn scored 7-26, 591G1-C2
ASEAN vs Cambodia-Thai DMZ plan, offers alternative plan 8-1, 591E1
Waldheim seeks Thai, Viet peace pact 8-2—8-5, 591A1
Commonwealth scores Viet role 9-8, 680C1
China sees war danger 9-11, 706F3
UN asks Viet exit 10-22, Viet rejects 10-23, 801C1
China, Thai peace talks 10-30, 952B1
Refugees return from Laos, Thai, Viet 11-13, 951G3

1976

1977

1978

Viets, US CIA tied to coup trys 6-13, 6-24, 6-25, 548C2
Viet scores China Cambodia backing 6-20, 464G2
Cambodia chrgs Viet-US CIA overthrow plot 6-25, Hanoi denies 6-27, 490C2
Viet claims mil gains 6-27, 6-29, 548G1-B2
Major Viet invasn rptd 6-28; Hanoi denies 6-29, 548E1
Cambodia war summary claims high Viet death toll 7-3, 548B2
Ieng Sary chrgs threat 7-17, 548G2
Cambodia asks nonaligned oust Viet 7-25—7-30, 583B3
Vietnam: Cambodian units destroyed 7-30, 660E2
Parrot's Beak clashes rptd fierce 7-31, 660E2
Cambodia: 1,200 Viets killed in July 7-31, 660E2
Rpt Viet air strikes aid troops 8-1, 660C2
China chrgs Viet aggressn 9-19, 748A1
Plea for Viet treaty 10-12, 794F1
Viet seizure plan chrgd 10-13, 794E1
Viets say China force aids 10-18, 803D2
Cambodia chrgs raids 10-18, Sovt aid 10-19, 803E2
Viet rpts revolt 10-23, 803G2
Viets chrg China aids 11-2, 859C3
US seeks to avert major clash 11-5, 859D3
China delegatn in Cambodia 11-5—11-6, 894G1
Cambodia chrgs gas bombs fired 11-7, 859F3
Both sides use jets 11-24, 11-28, 933G2
Viet: Cambodia revolt spreading 11-25, 933D2
Cambodians battle Viets, rebels; Viets thrust 70 mi 11-28—12-29, 996G3
Viets drive inside Cambodia 12-2, 12-6, 933E2
Viet rpts rebel front in Cambodia 12-3, 933E1
Cambodia rebel front scores China 12-4, 933C2

1979

Govt tries to set up mt defense 1-14, 28D1
Viets set up mil depots 1-15, 28D1
Sovts, Czechs veto UN action 1-15, 28E1
Govt retakes Kompong Som 1-16; Viets mount air strikes, rush reinforcemts 1-17, 27E3
Khmer Rouge troops flee to Thailand 1-18, 68F2
Viets retake Kompong Som 1-18, 68F2
Viets attack temple ruins, Khmer Rouge retake Takeo prov capital 1-19, 68G2
Rebels claim total control 1-20, 68E2
US hikes Thai mil aid 1-21, 84E2
Heng lauds Viets for aid 1-25, 68G3
Loyal troop advances rptd 1-28, 68D2
China hints at mil move vs Viet 1-30, 1-31, 65F2
Khmer Rouge raid near Pnompenh 1-30, 68A3
Heng concedes resistance 2-6, 142D1
Teng: Viets must be 'punished' 2-7, 84C1
US vows aid to Thais 2-7, 84B2
USSR warns China on Viet attack 2-8, 106D3
US warns China on Viet attack, scores Viet invasn 2-9, 106A3
Sihanouk return rebuffed, China welcomes 2-13, 142D2
Viet peace missn 2-16–2-20, friendship pact signed 2-18, 123B2
China retaliates vs Viet, troops launch invasn 2-17, 121E1
US scores Viet, links China invasn 2-17, 2-20, 122B3
Waldheim asks hostilities end 2-18, 123B1
China, Pol Pot aides score Viet pact 2-18, 142A2
Rumania scores Viet troop presence 2-19, 122E2
Carter bars interventn, seeks fighting end 2-20, 123E2, C3
Pol Pot forces press drive, advances rptd 2-21, 2-22, 142C1
Carter defends stand 2-22, 124D1
UN Cncl meets, US asks Viet exit 2-23; actn stalled 2-28, 142A1
China vs Viet role 2-27, 141F2
Carter bars US role 2-27, 149B2
Cambodian spillover into Thailand 3-4, 229B2
Pol Pot forces control admitted 3-14, 229C2
USSR vetoes UN res 3-16, 200E1
Sihanouk asks peace talks 3-19, 229E2
Laos troops aid Viets, Pol Pot group asks support 3-24, 229E1
Pol Pot group scores Viet-Cambodia pact 3-25, 229A2
US intell praised 3-25, 231F3-232B1
Pol Pot forces claim victories 3-27, 278G3
New Viet drive rptd 3-31; Pol Pot hq taken, escape to Thailand rptd 4-5; Cambodian civilns flee 4-12, 278E3
Cambodia civilns, Pol Pot troops flee to Thailand; forced back, shelling chrgd 4-16–4-29, 318B1-B2
Refugee setlmt data rptd 4-25, 379F2
China asks Viet exit 4-26, 298F1
More soldrs, civilns flee 5-9–5-11, 360C2
Pol Pot rptd alive, in Cambodia mtg with Khieu Samphan 5-14, 360E2
Yugo-USSR dispute cited 5-18, 380B1
Pol Pot seeks alliance with ex-foes 5-31, 6-2, 443D3
Viets: China seeks Pol Pot comeback 6-1, 474F2
Cambodia refugees rptd killed 6-4, 436A1
Thais return refugees 6-11; permit 1,430 temporary stay, ask Pol Pot stop flow 6-12, 435E3, 436B1
Pol Pot forces claim victories 6-15, 6-18, 550B3
Cambodia chrgs Thais kill refugees 6-22, 474G1
Sovts deny bases 6-23, 474F2
ASEAN, ANZUS back Viet exit 6-30, 7-5, 495C2, A3
Thais rptdly halt refugee expulsns 6-30, 1,000 granted temporary stay 7-10, 550F1
Viet links troop exit, China 'aggressn' end 7-5, 537B1
China anti-Thai radio statn closing linked 7-11, 537E3
Pol Pot forces attacked 7-18; total victory claimed 7-22, mass acres chrgd 7-26, 550F2, C3
Viet bars discussn in China talks, scores China re refugees 7-20, 575B3
US, China vs Heng, Pol Pot role 8-28, 644F2
Pol Pot, Heng recognitn splits nonaligned natns 8-28–9-9, 674B3-675A1, D1
China asks Viets quit 8-29, 660A2
Thais score Hanoi 8-30; fighting intensifies, refugees mass near border 9-9, 684C2
New Viet offensive rptd 9-25, US warns 9-27, 740D3, 741E1
Thais to accept refugees 9-26, 764A2
Viets score forgn relief aid to Cambodia 10-4, 10-14, 779E2
Sihanouk rpts guerrilla group formatn 10-4, to seek US, Westn aid 10-4, 10-12, 811B2
Fighting escalates near Thai border 10-10–10-20, 811B3
Defns offcl in USSR; scores West, China 10-12, 811A2

1980

1976

CAMBRIDGE, Mass.—*See MASSACHUSETTS*
CAMBRIDGE, Godfrey
Dies 11-29, 932D3
CAMEJO, Peter
Chrgs police re FBI thefts 3-28, 234F3
FCC rejcts pres debate bid 9-20, 703F2
Sup Ct bars equal-time review 10-12, 765E3
Final pres vote tally 12-18, 979B2
CAMERON, Mark
Disqualified at Olympics 7-30, 563B2
CAMERON Financial Corp.
Rptd on FRB 'problem' list 1-22, 111A3
CAMEROON—*See also AFRICAN Development Bank, NONALIGNED Nations Movement, OAU*
Listed as 'partly free' 1-19, 20C3
Equatorial Guinea exiles rptd 1-24, 62A2
Recognizes Angola MPLA 2-2, 82G2
At intl econ conf 2-11—2-20, 148B1
Total IMF oil loan rptd 4-1, 340B2
IMF loan rptd 6-30, 910F2
EC aid set 7-8, 529A3
Olympic withdrawal rptd 7-21, 528B3
Gabon clash rptd 11-16, border closed 11-17, 1003B2
Listed as not free 12-22, 977B3
CAMI, Tefta
Albania educ min 4-30, 331F3
CAMIEL, Peter J.
Jackson loses primary 4-27, 305D1
CAMPA, Valentin
Named CP pres candidate 1-9, 75D2
Loses pres electn 7-4, 498D1
CAMPAGNOLO, Iona
Sworn fitness, state min 9-15, 692G1
CAMPANERIS, Bert
AL batting ldr 10-4, 796D1
Contract rptd signed 12-5, 951E3
CAMPANO Lopez, Lt. Gen. Angel
Replaced as Civil Guard chief 12-23, 1011G2
CAMPBELL, Bill
Contract rptd signed 12-5, 951E3
CAMPBELL, Clarence S.
Flyers beat Sovt team 1-11, 56G1
Arraigned 4-22, 309C3
CAMPBELL, J. Phil
Cited in rpt on Callaway 10-5, 745C1, E1
CAMPBELL, James F.
Replaced as El Salvador amb 8-4, 808B1
CAMPBELL, Robert D.
Named Newsweek chrmn 10-5, 892A2
CAMPBELL, Ross
Testifies re A-sales 11-24, 904F1
A-sale probe continues 11-30, 923D3
Vs A-sale disclosures 12-9, 962C3
CAMPBELL, Steven
Eritrea rebels free 5-3, 335G1
CAMPBELL, William
AL pitching ldr 10-4, 796D1
CAMPBELL Soup Co.
Boycott rpt released 10-20, 786A2
CAMPILLO Sainz, Jose
In US talks 1-26, 75F1
CAMPINOS, Jorge
In Yugoslavia 1-13, 143B1
CAMPORA, Hector Jose
Arrest rptd 3-26, 236D3
Junta freezes bank acct 3-30, 236C3
Rptd in Mexico emb 5-20, 399E3
Rights revoked, arrest ordrd 6-23, 520C1
Magazines rptd closed 7-23, 620D3
Cited re Spinola-Eanes link 8-11, 733B1
CAMPOS, Gen. Cesar
Replaced as interior min 1-31, 142A3
CAMUS, Bishop Carlos
Scores govt repressn, fear 8-22, 711F1
CANACHE Mata, Carlos
Hails Carter electn 11-3—11-4, 826D2

1977

CAMBRIDGE, Mass.—*See MASSACHUSETTS*
CAMDEN, N.J.—*See NEW Jersey*
CAMERA Never Blinks, The (book)
On best-seller list 9-4, 712E3
CAMERAS—*See PHOTOGRAPHY*
CAMERON, Clyde
Chrgs CIA govt meddling 5-4, 372D1
CAMERON, Dr. D. Ewen (d. 1967)
CIA mind-control tests revealed 8-1—8-9, 611C1
CAMERON, Ron
On Australia SRD rate hike 2-3, 113E2
CAMEROON—*See also NONALIGNED Nations Movement, OAU*
UN Assemb member 3G3
Nigeria frees US natl 3-7, 393F2
CAMILION, Oscar
Argentina backs Brazil A-deal 2-7, 190A2
CAMPAIGN Financing—*See under POLITICS*
CAMPANA Lopez, Ramon
FRAP hijackers seek release 8-21, 746A1
CAMPANO Lopez, Lt. Gen. Angel
Named 7th mil region chief 1-15, 68D2
CAMPBELL, Alexander
Scores Levesque language offer 7-27, 596E3
CAMPBELL, Anne
Wins Dem state chrmn post 3-31, 251B1
CAMPBELL, Billy Lee
Lance controversy 9-5, 690A1
CAMPBELL, Clarence S.
Replaced as NHL pres 6-22, 548B3
CAMPBELL, Duncan
Charged under Secrets Act 5-24, 526D3
CAMPBELL, Earl
Wins Heisman, Downtown AC trophies 12-8, 950A2
CAMPBELL, Rev. Ernest T.
Rev Coffin succeeds 8-14, 808C2
CAMPBELL, Joe
In NFL draft 5-3, 353A2
CAMPBELL, Ross
Named AECL temporary pres 7-7, 541G3
CAMPBELL College (Bules Creek, N.C.)
Loses NAIA basketball title 3-12, 262F2
CAMPORA, Hector Jose
Mex asks Argentina safe-conduct 1-18, 66B2, D2 ★
Montoneros ldr killed 9-7, 922A1
CAMPS, Alberto Miguel
Killed by soldiers 9-7, 921G3
CAMPS & Camping—*See PARKS & Recreation Areas*
CAMUNAS Solis, Ignacio
Spain min for Cortes relatns 7-5, 545C2

1978

CAMBRIDGE University (England)
Anti-tick virus rptd 2-23, 334F1
Test-tube baby born 7-25, 596F3, 597B1
CAMERAS—*See PHOTOGRAPHY*
CAMERON, Donald (balloonist)
Atlantic balloon flight fails 7-30, 653B1
CAMERON, Donald N.
Fraser fires Cabt min 8-7, 612A2
CAMERON, Neil
In China, remarks on USSR cause uproar 5-1, 329F2
CAMEROON—*See also GATT, NONALIGNED Nations Movement, OAU*
Islamic bank poor-natn aid rise rptd 4-9, 257F2
Mboumoua replaced at OAU 7-22, 561D2
UN Assemb member 713D3
CAMICIA, Nicholas
Sees Carter on coal strike 2-24, 122G3
Coal settlemt reached 3-14, 182A1
CAMPAIGN Financing—*See under POLITICS*
CAMPBELL, Alan K.
On Civil Svc chngs 8-11, 625D2
Civil Svc reform enacted 10-13, 787C3
CAMPBELL, Alexander B.
Wins reelectn 4-25, 312C1
Reelected PEI premr 4-25, 312C1
Resigns 9-11, 739D2
B Campbell confrmd premr 12-9, 964A2
CAMPBELL, Bennett
Elected PEI premr 9-18, 739E2
Confirmed premier 12-9, 964F1-A2
CAMPBELL Jr., Carroll A.
Wins US House seat 11-7, 852B2, 853C1
CAMPBELL, Duncan
Maj secrets chrgs dropped 10-23, 838A3; sentncd re other chrgs 11-17, 924F1
CAMPBELL, Earl
Notre Dame wins Cotton Bowl 1-2, 8B3
Houston obtains draft rights 4-24, signs multiyr contract 5-2, 335G3, 336E2
Rushes for 199 yds, 4 TDs 11-20, 1024B1
Oilers win in playoffs 12-31, 1024F1
CAMPBELL, Judge Levin H.
Delays offshore lease sale 1-30, 108D2
CAMPBELL, Robert
Sentenced to life 9-6, 722F3
CAMPBELL, Ross
Sets AECL reorganizatn 7-28, 590E3
CAMP David Summit—*See under MIDDLE EAST—EGYPT-Israel Peace Moves*
CAMPISANO, Joseph
Indicted 10-5, 770F3
CAMPONE, Merv
Bistro Car opens 3-23, 887B1
CAMPORA, Hector Jose
Remains in Mexico emb 1-19, 208C2
CAMPS, Hugo
Czechs arrest 8-8, expel 8-10, 691B3
CAMPUS Crusade for Christ International
Laity ldrshp role cited 2-19, 294C3
Drollinger rejects Nets offer 3-15, 272E2
CAN, Mehmet
Named Turkey justice min 1-5, 21E2

1979

Viet rpts intl relief aid reaches Pol Pot forces 10-17, 779E2
China, USSR differ on talks agenda 10-17, 803A2
Huang warns vs Viet success 10-18, 789A3
Viets chrg Thai, US, China role 10-18; Thais, Viets confer 10-19—10-20, 811C3
UN asks Viet exit 11-14, 863F3
CAMBRIA, Paul
Lawyers' interstate rights limited by Sup Ct 1-15, 31D3
CAMBRIDGE, Mass.—*See MASSACHUSETTS*
CAMBRIDGE, O.—*See OHIO*
CAMBRIDGE University (England)
Tremaine Uranus ring theory rptd 1-11, 289G3
Solar neutrino theory rptd 4-12, 691E3
Blunt named 4th spy 11-15, 908A3
CAMDEN, Ark.—*See ARKANSAS*
CAMERON, Dr. D. Ewen (deceased)
'71 LSD tests cited 1-29, 96A1
CAMERON Iron Works Inc.
US fine rptd 11-1, 923B3
CAMEROON—*See also GATT, NONALIGNED Nations Movement, OAU*
Young, US trade delegatn visit 9-15, 720A3, 721A1
UN membership listed 695F2
CAMPAIGN Financing—*See under POLITICS*
CAMPAIGN for Economic Democracy
Hayden, Fonda set tour 9-23, 742B3
CAMPANERIS, Bert
Traded to Angels 5-4, 1002G2
CAMPBELL, Alan K.
Civil Svc Comm replaced 1-1, 6A1
CAMPBELL, Alexander B.
MacLean elected PEI premr 4-23, 311F1
CAMPBELL, Bennett
Replaced as PEI premr 4-23, 311F1
CAMPBELL, Clarence
Trial ordrd re Sky Shops 4-26, 329F1
Chrg dismissed 10-15, 812D2
CAMPBELL, Earl
NFL '78 touchdown, rushing ldr 1-6, 80B1, B2
Steelers win NFL conf title 1-7, 8E3
Named NFL MVP, top rookie 1-19, 175B2
Oilers win in playoffs 12-23, 12-29, 1001A1
CAMPBELL, J. K.
Banking inquiry rptd 1-23, 74B1
CAMPBELL, Ross
Scores Argentina A-sale loss 10-2, 788C3
CAMPBELL, Scott
WHA penalty minutes ldr 4-18, 355G2
CAMPECHE, Bay of
Mex oil well blows out 6-3, 462B2
CAMPORA, Hector Jose
Given safe passage 11-20, 906A2
CAMP Pendleton, Calif.—*See CALIFORNIA*

1980

CAMBRIDGE Hospital (Mass.)
D Kennedy MD found guilty on drug chrgs 1-18, 199G3
CAMBRIDGE University (England)
Schizophrenia, dopamine link rptd 1-10, 415E1
Blunt resignatn cited 8-24, 652F1
Sanger wins 2d Nobel 10-14, 889G2
CAMDEN—*See NEW Jersey*
CAMEL, Marvin
Decisns Parlov for WBC cruiserwgt title 3-31, 320B2
DeLeon decisns for WBC cruiserwgt title 11-25, 1001A1
CAMERAS—*See PHOTOGRAPHY*
CAMERON College (Lawton, Okla.)
Wins NAIA basketball title, Jackson named tourn MVP 3-15, 240D3
CAMEROON—*See also GATT, NONALIGNED Nations, OAU*
Chad refugee total rptd 4-23, 311B2
Chad premr flees, signs cease-fire 12-16, 965D1
Libyan role in Chad opposed 12-23—12-24, 979E1
CAMP, Kay
At anti-US conf in Iran 6-2—6-5, 418D2, 419D1
CAMP, Rick
NL pitching ldr 10-6, 926G2
CAMPAIGN Financing—*See POLITICS--Campaign Finances & Practices*
CAMPBELL, Bill
2d in US Senior Open 6-29, 715C1
CAMPBELL, Rep. Carroll (R, S.C.)
Reelected 11-4, 844B2
CAMPBELL, Clarence
Convicted re Sky Shops bribe conspiracy 2-8, 148A3
Sentenced 3-7, NHL compensatn rptd 3-13, 230G2
CAMPBELL, Earl
NFL '79 touchdown, rushing 1-5; Steelers win NFL conf title 1-6, 8E1, B2, B3
Named NFL MVP 1-9, 175A1
NFC wins Pro Bowl 1-27, 175D1
Raiders win playoffs 12-28, 999E1
CAMPBELL, Edward J.
Praises USW contract 3-28, 251F2
CAMPBELL, Ian
Moscow Olympics triple jump disallowed 7-25; IAAF backs Sovt officiating 7-31, 589D3
CAMPBELL, Jimmy Lee (d. 1979)
Slayers sentenced 2-27, 238D3
CAMPBELL, Marion D.
Atlantic Monthly sale rptd 3-1, 239F1
CAMPBELL, Tisha
Really Rosie opens 10-12, 892E3
CAMPEAU, Robert
Trustco takeover bid fails, urges probe 10-2, 766F3, 767A1
CAMPEAU Corp.
Trustco takeover bid set 8-27; bid fails 10-2, 766E3-767A1
CAMPORA, Hector J.
Dies 12-19, 1004B1
CAMPOS, Judge Santiago
Rescinds Gannett purchase of NM paper 6-30, 582F2-A3
CAMPUS Crusade for Christ International
DC rally held 4-29, 348E3

CANADA

1976

CANADA—*See also ADB, COMMONWEALTH of Nations, DISARMAMENT—Geneva Committee, IDB, IEA, NATO, OECD*
Brink's van hijacked 3-30, 250F3
Toronto police brutality rptd 7-28, 587G3
Pope, Coggan dispute female ordinatn 8-20, 756D1
Immigratn curb urged 8-22; Jan-June data rptd 11-3, 851D1
Croats divert TWA jet to Montreal, Newfoundland 9-10, 685D1
Indians file land claim, Eskimo claim noted 10-25, 851G2
Orthodox Jews meet 11-25—11-28, 912A1 ★
Anglicans ordain 6 women 11-29, 932C1
Indians lose land claim moratorium 12-22, 998E2

1977

CANADA—*See also COMMONWEALTH of Nations, DISARMAMENT—Geneva Committee, IDB, IEA, NATO, OECD*
Tanker rptd sunk off Cape Cod 1-11, 104E3
Ottawa Caths granted absolutn 3-15, 375B2
'76 population data rptd 3-25, 237D2
Cobalt (Ontario) fire 5-23, 604D2
Anglican synod meets 8-17, 732G1
Metric highway signs go up 9-6, 705D2
Air-traffic safety enforcemt scored 11-28, 965B3

1978

CANADA—*See also COMMONWEALTH of Nations, DISARMAMENT—Geneva Committee, GATT, IDB, IEA, NATO, OECD*
Cults probe asked 11-30, 911A3
Accidents
BC Pacific Westn jet crashes 2-11, 271A1
13 canoers drown in Lake Temiscamingue 6-11, 460D2
Toronto jet crash kills 3 6-26, 636D3
Bus plunges into Lac D'Argent, 41 die 8-4, 636A3
7 natls die in US hotel fire 11-26, 971B3

African Relations
Namibia conf held 2-11—2-12, progress rptd 2-13, 113A3
UN abstentn on Rhodesia pact vote 3-14, 192F3
Front-line natns back Namibia plan 3-26, 248G2
Algerian immigrant rptd kidnaped 4-24, Canada protests 7-1, 7-4, 531D3
Namibia plan OKd by Vorster 4-25, 299C1
S Africa business code issued 4-28, 377F1
Namibia rebel ldr cancels talks 5-7, 339D1
Namibia rebels OK talks 6-11, 475C3
Zaire aid OKd 6-13—6-14, 478A1
Saudi offcl visits 6-29, 635B1
Namibia plan OKd by SWAPO 7-12, 547C2

1979

CANADA—*See also COMMONWEALTH of Nations, DISARMAMENT–Geneva Committee, GATT, IDB, IEA, NATO, OECD*
Mrs Trudeau rpts intimacies 3-8, 3-20; women's group honors 3-23, 271C3
Toronto archbp installed cardinal 6-30, 640B2
Accidents & Disasters
Air safety abuses rptd, Lang replies 2-8—2-14, 134B1
Quebecair crash kills 17 3-29, 240D3
Manitoba floods 4-26—4-30, 472A2
Acid rain perils noted 7-12, 7-17, 581G2
Rideau Club burns 10-23, 834A1
Train derailed 11-10—11-11, Mississauga evacuated 11-11—11-14, 871D3
Mississauga evacuees return 11-15, compensatn paymts begun 11-19, 927C2
African Relations
UN rights comm res vs white-minority regimes opposed 2-21, 148G1
S Africa rejcts Namibia plan 3-5, 171B2
Namibia compromise proposed 3-19—3-22, Pretoria bars 5-7, extends assemb powers 5-8, 354F2
S Africa scored by UN vote 5-31, 428B1
Namibia UN talks reopen 11-12—11-16, 889D3

1980

CANADA—*See also COMMONWEALTH of Nations, CSCE, GATT, GENEVA Committee, IDB, IEA, MBFR, NATO, OECD*
Divorced woman awarded 1/2 ex-spouse's stock 3-26, 273A2
Accidents & Disasters
Quebec fire kills 42 1-1, 24C2
Mt St Helens erupts 5-18, 378E1
Val d'Or mine caves in 5-20, 603G1
Forest fires rptd 5-24, 5-26, 406C2
Mt St Helens damage assessed 5-24—7-4, 503F3
Drought eased by rain, haylift 6-27, 7-3, 520B2
Forest fire losses rptd 8-2, 633G1-C2

1976

Economy (domestic)—*See also 'Labor' below*
Trudeau econ remarks scored, liberal split seen 1-5—1-11, 27A3, B3 ★
'75 monetary reserves down 1-5, 28D1
Ontario OKs inflatn progrm 1-13, 46E3
Javelin ex-chrmn, 4 others rptd sought 1-14, 28B1
Dec '75 CPI, '75 monthly inflatn rptd 1-15, 46G3, 47A1
Alcan Brazil operatn begun 1-16, 98F2
Trudeau defends policies 1-19, 46A3
$ strengthens 1-26, 99D1
Rail reorgnzatn plan presented, '74 losses cited 1-29, 98G3
Jan CPI up 2-12, 188F1
Commons gets '76-77 spending estimates 2-18, '75 supplemental request 3-12, 188C1
Chartered banks curbed 2-20, 188A2
Commons OKs ad tax amendmt 2-25, 188A3
Wage, price controls extended 3-8, 204F1
Bank, prime rates raised 3-8, 204G1
Feb-Apr CPI, inflatn data rptd 3-11, 4-8, 5-12, 351A2
Fed-prov finance talks open 4-1, 265F1
Ontario sets restraint budget 4-6, 265F2
New energy plan set 4-27, 332B2
Trudeau, premrs in oil price talks 5-6, 380D3
Oil price rise set 5-18, 380B3
'76 record budget presented 5-25, 400F1
Quebec dairy farmers riot 6-3, 416F2
Sarnia-Montreal pipeline opens 6-6, 6-15, 438D3

1977

Atomic Energy & Safeguards—*See also 'Uranium' below*
Pak to buy French A-plant 1-3, 12C3
AECL Argentina A-sale agent linked to '72 Ont pol paymt 1-7, 42G3
AECL warned vs Argentina agent disclosure 1-25, contract cancellatn barred 2-3, 114C1
Brazil, Argentina A-safeguard treaty OK asked 1-28, 190F1
UDI books in Korea A-sale probe rejctd 2-1, 114G1
Australia rpts US A-safeguards exchng 3-23, 218A1
US A-fuel export delay rptd 4-14, 268C2
Supplier natns score Carter plans 4-28—4-29, 403F1-A2
7-natn summit debates A-sales, sets study 5-7—5-8, 357D2, E2
Trudeau, Giscard meet 5-13, 389B2
Trudeau sees Schmidt 7-6—7-12, eases A-fuel export ban 7-12, 566F2, A3
AECL pres fired; '75-77 losses, sales cited 7-7, 541E3
CP asks US neutron bomb ban 8-8, 640A3
Supplier natns OK safeguards 9-21, 717D1
Rumania cooperatn pact set 10-24, 982D3
Argentina to sign weapon-ban pact, tech aid seen 11-21, 912A3
Italy cooperatn pact rptd signed 12-15, 982G2

Crime—*See also 'RCMP' below*
Vancouver bank heist foiled 1-10, 5 chrgd 1-11, 162G3
Montreal crime rate surges 1-31—2-3, 97C2
Montreal bomb threat, prison reforms vowed 2-10, 159G1
Leftists held in Waterloo raid 2-24, 159B1
US-Canada prisoner exchng treaty 3-2, 200B1
Sup Ct backs lie detector ban 3-22, 237C3
Laetrile smuggling into US rptd 5-6, 375C3
Prison system scored in Commons rpt 6-7; Fox, Caouette comment 6-8, 466F1
New Brunswick jail blaze 6-21, 604C2
Newton detained 6-25—6-29, 531G3
Ottawa-sniper attack kills policeman 7-11, 596C2
Gun controls, wiretap curbs in criminal code amendmts 7-18, 596A2
US ratifies prisoner exchng treaty 7-19, Carter signs enabling legis 10-28, 834E1
Fox pledges prison reform 8-5, 634B1
New Brunswick jail arsonist sentncd 9-30, 848D2
Bilingual cts proposed in Throne Speech 10-18, 822F2
Drug probe raids 11-17—12-8, arrests rptd 12-15, 1010A3

Defense & Armed Forces
Defns conf asks forces hiked 1-13—1-15, 82F1-B2
'76-77 budget rptd 1-14, 82A2
Mil equipment modernizatn set 7-13, 579D3
Mil forces increase set, budget rise estimated 7-15, 579C3
Army mail opening, union surveillnc bared 11-11—11-12, 882C2
Navy modernizatn program set 12-22, 1010F1

Economy (domestic)—*See also 'Energy' and 'Labor' below*
Nov 12-mo consumer price rise rptd 1-7, 29C3
Ct bars Quebec cable TV control 1-12; min vows appeal 1-14, 43B2
Air Canada cuts svcs 1-12, 43C2
Dec '76, '73-76 yrly CPI rise rptd 1-14, 43E2
BC offers '77-78 budget 1-24, 346G3
Levesque outlines asbestos natlizatn, other plans 1-25; reactn 1-26—1-28, 81F3
Bank, prime rates cut 2-1, 97G2
Govt, provinces in offshore mineral pact 2-1, 133B3
Dec '75-76 inflatn rate rptd 2-7, 87A2
Jan CPI record rise rptd 2-11, 133F3
Domestic air fares raised 2-24, 200E1
Quebec bond issue sold 3-1, 158F3
'76 GNP rptd 3-1, 218A2
$ at 7-yr low 3-9, 179E2
Quebec, Saskatchewan end price controls 3-10, 3-17, 218F2
Saskatchewan offers '77-78 budget 3-10, 372C3
Feb CPI up 3-11, Jan WPI 3-15, 200C2
Alberta offers '77-78 budget 3-11, 346F3
Seal hunt revenue estimated 3-15, 237G3
New Brunswick offers '77-78 budget 3-15, 346E3
Nova Scotia offers '77-78 budget 3-29, 372C3
Fed '77-78 budget presented 3-31, 253F3-254B2
Dairy subsidies raised; surplus butter, milk rptd 4-4, 304D1

1978

S Africa Zulus back labor code 7-13, 633F1
Beirut emb staff cut 7-27, 581E2
Namibia electn delay barred 10-14; contact group sees Botha, Steyn 10-16—10-18, 820A1
S Africa arms sales suspected 11-6—11-7, 904E2
UN abstentn on Namibia electn warning 11-13, 904B2

Atomic Energy & Safeguards—*See also 'Soviet Satellite Issue' below*
A-export safeguard pact detailed 1-11, 11B2
EC uranium ban lifted; UK, W Ger shipmts, inspectn set 1-16, 102D3
Japan uranium pact initialed 1-26, 88E3
Australia joins A-suppliers' group 2-24, 129C2
AECL probe ends, asks agent paymts withheld 2-27, 166G2
AECL regulatns cited 2-27, 166C3
United Nuclear wins uranium cartel suit, impact on other Gulf suits seen 3-2, 144A2, C2
US chrgs Gulf re uranium cartel 5-9, 346B2
A-arms role in Eur to end 5-26, 422A1
Australia sets uranium rules 5-31, 434D3
Saskatchewan rpt backs uranium dvpt, safeguards 6-8, 647C2
AECL reorganized, '76-77 loss cited 7-28, 590E3-591A1
Quebec heavy-water plant canceled 8-16, 666E2
Japan uranium pact signed 8-22, 667B1
Saskatchewan uranium find rptd 9-13, 722A1
Rumania reactor deal signed 12-15, 1013F2

Crime—*See also 'RCMP' below*
'70 Cross kidnapers seek amnesty 1-3, 7C1
Prison file access OKd 3-1, 188F1
Quebec prison siege ends 3-22, 244E3
Cuban exile seized by US re bomb plot 4-14, 287D2
Algerian immigrant rptd kidnaped 4-24, Canada protests 7-1, 7-4, 531D3
NHL player fined on '77 drug chrg 4-24, 656F3
Giguere cleared re Sky Shops 6-29, 514E3
Laporte '71 kidnapers paroled 7-16, 7-17, 556D3
Hijacking pact signed 7-17, 544G2
US prisoner exchng treaty OKd 7-19, 572B1
Ontario solicitor-gen phones atty 8-14, resigns 9-9, 721D3
US smuggling operatn rptd 8-16—8-18, 641A2
Hamilton landlord sentncd for assault 8-18, Munro interventn prompts resignatn 9-8, 721E2
Singer wins '70 arrest suit 9-12, 755D2
BC ex-min fined for fraud 9-18, 739E2
MP sentncd in arson case 10-6, 794G2
Sugar refineries fined record sums 10-6, 794F3
US, Canada exchng prisoners 10-12—10-13, 794D3
Rolling Stone's heroin sentnc suspended 10-24, band OKs benefit 10-26, 842E1
FLQ 6th Cross kidnaper alleged 11-2, 11-8, 880B1
BC addict treatmt law set, drug-related crime cited 12-18, 1013B3

Economy (domestic)—*See also 'Labor' below*
Sun Life to quit Quebec 1-6, 16F1; stockholder vote delayed 1-14, 35D3
Inflatn plan protested 9-17—10-14, 771A1
AIB tightens indl price controls 9-27, 750F1
Trudeau sets inflatn plan end 10-7, 771F2
Sept CPI rptd 10-7, 808A3
Trudeau parlt address vows econ recovery 10-12, 771D2
Yr-end, Oct CPI rptd 10-25, 11-10, 888A3
Stats Canada chrgd re GNP estimates 11-8, Chretian defends 11-15, 888A3
Quebec separatists win electn 11-15, 870F1, A2
Stock decline, $ transfer from Quebec rptd 11-16, 870D2
Banks cut interest, mortgage rates 11-22—11-23, 888C3
6 more banks cut rates 11-24—12-1, 945D2
Strike data rptd 11-29, 896D2
Macdonald, prov finance mins meet on taxes, revenue sharing 12-6—12-7, 945A1
Oct '75-76 inflatn rate rptd 12-6, 976B1
Macdonald sees continuing inflatn 12-7, 945B2
Nov CPI rptd 12-8, 945A2
Trudeau, prov premrs OK 5-yr plan 12-13—12-14; press protests closed mtg 12-13, 962F1
Banks cut rates again 12-22—12-24, 998G2

1979

Atomic Energy & Safeguards
Lake Huron A-plant safety doubted 4-27, 352A3
Darlington A-protest staged 6-2, 416G1, E2
Ontario A-plant accidents revealed 6-16, 6-19, 502B1
Clark seeks dvpt 6-29, 501G3
Uranium reserves estimate hiked 8-15, 613B2
Argentine plant deal cited 10-1, 749E1; loss scored 10-2—10-3, 788B3
Ontario plants judged safe 10-3, 772B1
PC asks parliamentary com review 10-9, 788E2
NDP conv debates 11-22—11-25, 927E1

Crime & Civil Disorders—*See also 'RCMP' below*
Marion kidnap suspect acquitted 1-2, 6A2
Lanctot arrested 1-6, 19F1; bail set 1-11, 37B2
3 arrested in stock fraud 1-10, 37C2
FLQ '69 bombing suspect arrested 1-14, 37G1-A2; sentncd 3-26, 254C1
BC cartoonist loses libel suit 1-17, 57G1
Montreal bank robbed by 2 in copter 2-23, 220G2
Goyer wins libel suit appeal 3-30, 253F3
Marion kidnaper sentncd 4-6, 267D1
Campbell trial ordrd re Sky Shops 4-26, 329F1
Dredging scandal trial ends, 5 convicted 5-5, 352F1
Union ldr jailed re '78 strike 5-7, 352D1
Dredging cos fined, 5 sentncd 6-11, 468A2
Giguere cleared of Liberal Party funds misuse 7-20, 563D1
Cossette-Trudels sentncd 8-7, 632B3
Rondeau gets hiked sentnc 9-11, 685C1
Bank wire thief sentncd 9-24, 840C3
BC addict law overturned 10-11, 853D2
Campbell, Brown Sky Shops chrg dismissed 10-15; Giguere chrg dropped 10-19, 812D2
Lanctot sentncd 11-8, 872D1
Union ldr jailing scored by NDP 11-22—11-25, 927A2
Giguere cleared in ad agency influence peddling 12-7, 949A1
FLQ bomb suspect returns 12-23; arraigned 12-24, 992F3

Defense & Armed Forces
Women to get more duties 1-29, 95F2
Treu cleared 2-20, 189A2
Security clearance review asked 2-23, 189C2
In US naval maneuvers off PR 5-9—5-19, 385D3

Economy—*See also 'Labor' below*
Bank prime rates raised 1-3—1-4, 6E1
BC resource co stock giveaway set 1-11, 37F2
Unity Cncl rpts top concern 1-16, 57C1
Dec '78 CPI, '78 inflatn rate rptd 1-18; '78 food prices, inflatn linked 1-29, 95D2
Unity Task Force asks more prov powers 1-25, 74D2, B3
Auto makers ruled liable for defects 1-25, 95C3
Const reforms debated 2-5—2-6, 113B3, G3
'78 corp profits up 2-6, Trudeau defends 2-7, 114B1
Jan CPI rise rptd 2-19, 168G2
'78, 4th 1/4 GNP rptd 2-27, 168E2
Inflatn comm created 3-2, 168B2
Feb CPI climbs 3-16, 210E3
'78 real income decline rptd; $ drop, inflatn cited 3-23, 234A2
Science Cncl sees tech lag 3-24, 234D1
Clark backs budget deficit 3-27, 266F3
Broadbent for 3-, 5-yr plans 3-29, 266G3
Hudson's Bay bought by Thomsons 4-8, 284E3
Edper seeks Brascan 4-9, reneges 4-11, new offer barred 4-11, 303C3, G3, 304B2
Mar CPI jump rptd 4-12, 284B3
Corp mergers rise rptd 4-16, 285D1
Tech funds set, Telesat gets satellite dvpt grant 4-17, 311A3
Govt to buy more domestic goods 4-17, 311E3

1980

Atomic Energy & Safeguards
PCs cite '74 India A-aid cutoff 1-8, 38F1
BC sets 7-yr uranium mining ban 2-27, 148D2
US nonproliferatn pact rptd 4-23, Swiss delay deal 5-29, 429F1
Radioactive vegetables near A-plant rptd 5-22, 406G2
7-natn Venice summit backs 6-23, 473F2
Trudeau, Cossiga agree on reactor sale 6-24, 486F1
USSR to pay for '78 satellite crash 11-21, 920C3

Crime & Civil Disorders—*See also 'RCMP' below*
Giguere acquittal appeal set 1-4, 6G1; appeal rejctd 1-7, 57A1
Campbell, Brown convicted in Sky Shops bribe conspiracy 2-8, 148A3
BC cartoon libel ruling upset 2-15, 148C3
Bahamas bank looting suit rptd 3-3, 229C1
Campbell, Brown get 1-day sentence, fine 3-7, NHL compensatn rptd 3-13, 230G2
Statistics Canada cleared 4-1, 272F3
Rooney cleared re influence chrgs 4-3, 273F1
'68 FLQ bomber sentenced 4-8, '69 bomber paroled 4-11, 310F3
Ontario butchers fraud chrgs dropped 4-11, 372E1
6 convicted in Ontario, Quebec meat fraud 4-23, 372A1
Quebec referendum campaign unrest scored 5-2, 350A3
Vancouver exchng ex-vp chrgd 5-5, 406C3
Olympics contractor chrgd 5-9, 406E2
6 sentncd in meat fraud 6-16, 486E1
KKK opens Toronto hq 6-26, 497D1
Rape case questioning broadened 6-27, 520C3
US crime rates compared 7-16, 562C3
Montreal prison escape foiled, hostages taken 8-25; convicts surrender 8-28, 668F3
'76 Olympic fraud indictmts rptd 10-2, 788D1

Defense & Armed Forces
Pacific naval games start 2-26, 151C3
F-18As chosen for AF 4-16, 293C2
Lamontagne sees Brown, OKs F-18 deal 7-8; US discount offered; NORAD, NATO benefits seen 7-11, 543E3
Navy to upgrade destroyers 8-8, 618D2

Economy—*See also 'Labor' below*
Clark, Trudeau seek spending cuts 1-2, 1-12, 37G3, 38B1, C1
Hiram Walker, Consumer gas merger set 1-9, 19D1
Quebec Liberals propose const reform 1-10, 18F3
PCs reaffirm mortgage tax relief plan 1-15, 38A1
Dec '79 CPI up, '79 inflatn total rptd 1-23, 79A1
Stock exchngs cut hrs; Jan records cited 2-4, 96B2
'79 corp profits rptd up 2-7, 116A2
Toronto, Montreal exchngs resume normal hrs 2-11, 116F3
Jan CPI hits 200, 12-mo inflatn up 2-14, 148A2
'79, 4th 1/4 corp profits up 2-22, 211D2
'79, 4th 1/4 factory use rptd 2-26, 211F2
Toronto stocks hit record high 2-27, 148D1
Toronto stocks peak 2-29, plummet 3-3—3-10, 191B3
Whales damage Newfoundland fishing 461F2
Bank rate float set 3-10, 191D2
Interest rate rumors spur C$ drop 3-10, 191F3
Feb CPI hike rptd; '76-80 CPI chart 3-13, 230C2, E2
Bank, prime, mortgage rates climb 3-14—3-28, 252D3
Toronto stocks plummet 3-17—3-27, recover 3-28, 253B1
Metric conversn resumed by Liberals, rptd 50% complete 3-31, 335C1
Statistics Canada cleared 4-1, 272F3

1976

May CPI rptd 6-10, 416F3
Plumptre quits inflatn bd 6-10, 439A1
Premrs vs fed finance stand 6-14—6-15, 456E3
New wage-price controls set 6-16, 456D3
Econ growth cited 6-27—6-28, 462E1
BC wins seabed case 6-30, 520C3
Inflatn plan upheld, Ontario entry voided 7-12, 554C3
BC-Alberta oil pipe planned 7-16, 587E3
Pepin, business ldrs meet on inflatn plan 8-9; CLC sets protest 8-12, reactn 8-12—8-15, 623A3 ★
Menzies named AIB v chrmn 8-9, 750B2
Energy agency vs bilingualism 8-11, 637A2
July CPI rptd 8-13, 623D3
Oil subsidy law rptd chngd 8-25, 650F2
1st ¼ GNP rptd 8-30, 650C2
Postal rate hiked 9-1, 692A3
Potash prices cited 9-1, 750D2
Natural-gas surplus rptd 9-3, 710A1
Corp profit limit eased, investmt credit set 9-7, 730G2
Aug CPI rptd, July revised 9-10, 709F3
Quebec plans US Olympic loan 6-30, 529F1
EEC pact signed 7-6, 496D3
7-natn A-waste conf opens 7-12, 739G1
BC-Alberta oil pipe planned, export to US cited 7-16, 587E3
Law vs ad tax deductn for US TV passed 7-16; in effect 9-22, 771C3
Algeria constructn pact rptd 7-16, 902C2
North-South conf deadlocked 7-17, 530F1
Italy loan ban disclosed 7-17, 531A1
Lockheed deal resigned 7-21, 554G3
Argentina bank loans, debt renegotiatn rptd 7-23, 7-25, 553G3, 554B1
US ties rptd strained 7-26, 587C3
US admits India A-blast aid 8-2, 581E3
Saskatchewan potash natlzn cited 8-12, US trust suit scored 9-21, 750B2 ★
Ivory Coast loans rptd 8-12, 1012G3
US OKs car price adjustmt 8-16, 988D1
Forgn bank operatns proposed 8-23, 637C2
US chrgs potash price fixing 8-30, 673E2
Oil export levies cut 9-1, 710F1
US, Canada oil exchngs set 9-2, 650D2
Settles Northrop suit 9-7, 710G1-B2
US oil exports prices raised 9-10, quota cut 9-14, 710C1
Royal Bank in Venez intl bank loan 9-15, 875C1
Callaghan, Trudeau talks 9-16, 9-18, 730B2
UK seizes Rhodesian tobacco 9-18, 713F2
US FM signals allowed 9-23, 771E3
US copyright bill clears Cong 9-30, 765D1; 10-19, 982G1
Backs World Bank funds rise 10-5, 778D1
US beef quota scored 10-11, 837A1
US oil exports 10-13, 11-23, levies adjusted 11-1, 11-10, 945F2
Meat import quota set 10-19, 837B1
'69-73 meat import data cited 837C1
Trudeau in Japan 10-20—10-26, pact signed 10-21; Japan trade cited 836G2
Sets 200-mi fishing limit 11-2, 889A1
Cuban fishing boats seized 11-8, 11-9, 888F3
Power co natlzd by Venez 11-12, 875F2
US road pact rptd 11-12, 945E3
$ down after Quebec electns 11-16, 870E2
Ford to close plants 1 wk 11-16, 885C2
Canada Vt deposits rptd up 11-21, 903F3
Argentina, S Korea A-sales probed 11-22, 11-24, 904A1, C1; 11-29—12-2, 923B3; 11-27, 997A2
Spain tax pact signed, '73-76 trade data rptd 11-23, 962G3
Grain sale to Poland set 11-24, 889B1
Polysar rebates rptd 11-26, 904G1; Trudeau defends, probe OKd 11-30, 924A1
$ falls 11-26, forgn borrowing noted 11-29, 904B2
Telemedia buys TV Guide units 11-27, 945F3
Marubeni rptd Japan A-sale agent 11-29, 923G3
'77 clothing imports curbed 11-29, 924F1
US $ reserves rptd down 12-2, 945E2
A-sale probes continue 12-2—12-15, 962G2
US rpt backs gas pipeline 12-7, 998A2
China wheat sale rptd 12-8, 946B1
USSR-India heavy water sale rptd 12-8, 955C2
US rejects Laval bonds 12-9, 945B3
North-South conf delayed 12-9, 976F3
'77 US beef import pact disputed 12-15, 976B2
New guidelines set 12-16, UDI audit OKd 12-21, 998D1
US paymts study rptd 12-20, 985B2
In IMF UK loan 12-21, 1004B1
'76 intl borrowing rptd 12-22, 976A2
A-export rules tightened, Pak rejcts 12-22, 998A1
Argentina A-plant pact delay rptd 12-22, 998G1
Quebec, US banks sign Olympic loan 12-31, 998D3

1977

March CPI up 4-7, 282B1
Quebec, Ontario set '77-78 budgets 4-13, 4-19, 303G2
$ up slightly 4-14, 303G3
Prov fed aid losses rptd 4-16, 327C1
Prov inequalities scored 4-20, 326D3
Air Canada rpts '76 loss 4-20, 372F3
Fed budget OKd by Commons 4-21, 327F1
Manitoba sets '77-78 budget 4-22, 327G1
Wage-price control mtg 4-22, 327C2
Prov inequalities rpt erred 4-22, 346C3
Natl RR shows '76 profit 4-26, 372D3
Govt rpts Quebec cos exodus 4-28, reactn 4-28—4-30, 346C2
New AIB head named 4-28, 346B3
Newfoundland offers '77-78 budget 4-28, 372A3
Maple Leaf Mills '76 purchase cited 340C1
Inflatn measures pledged 5-7—5-8, 357D1
Indepndnt Quebec econ ties opposed, industry favoritism noted 5-8, 425C3, D3
Bank, prime rates cut 5-9, 5-10, 372E2
Alcan unit sets Quebec expansn 5-31, 425B3
Phone rate hikes OKd, conditns imposed 6-1, 448F1
Apr, May CPI up 6-11, 505D2
1st ¼ GNP rptd up 6-22, 525C3
Home insulatn tax credit set 6-27, 505B1
Xerox wins IBM patent suit 7-5, 525B3
June CPI rptd up 7-13, 561F3
$ drop, inflatn talk cited 7-27, 597E1
Quebec rejcts home insulatn funds 7-28, 597B1
Record '77 wheat crop seen 7-29, 612A1
Wage-price controls end proposed 7-29, 616A3
July CPI rptd up 8-12, 634B3
Stock mkt down 8-12, 634D3
Wage-price curbs plan rejctd 8-17, 634E2
Alberta rejcts home-insulatn plan 8-17, 653A3
IBM appeals Xerox ruling, copiers ordrd removed 8-17, 705A3
Provs ask controls end, stimulus program 8-19, 653F1
2d ¼ GNP dips 8-30, 694C2
Aug CPI rptd 9-14, 725E3 ★
Ontario lumber co expansn bid cited 764A1
Govt decentralztn plan set 10-3, 801C1
Inter-prov trade asked 10-5—10-6, 780E2
$ at 10-yr low 10-6, 780E3
Sept CPI rise rptd 10-12; AIB claims progress vs inflatn 10-21, 822F3, G3 ★
$ falls; slow growth, inflatn cited 10-17, 792E3
Controls end, stimulus progrm outlined in Throne Speech 10-18, schedule set 10-20, 822F2-F3
'76 income rise rptd 10-18, 823B1
$ hits 40-yr low 10-18—10-24; govt bars money curbs 10-20, sets credit deal 10-27, 841A3
Jan-Sept nickel surplus rptd; 3d ¼ prices, profits down 10-20, 923G3
Trudeau sees Alberta, BC ldrs 10-31—11-1, 882A3
Oct CPI up 11-15, 903B2
Postal rate hike set 11-21, 983C1
3d ¼ GNP up, 2d ¼ revised 11-28, 1010C2
$ rptd down 11-30, recovers 12-8, 932E3, 933C1
Cable TV fed control upheld 11-30, 946E1
Airlines domestic charters rptd OKd 12-7, 965F3
Nov CPI up 12-13, 1010F2

1978

Newfoundland defends seal hunt 1-9; '76 earnings, '78 quotas rptd 1-12, 35F2
Metric chng set in constructn, food, textile industries 1-16, 89B1
Dec '77 CPI, '77 inflatn rptd 1-17, 70G2
US ties seen welcome 1-23, 53E3
Govt, business, labor reps confer 2-1, 111G1
Trudeau, prov premrs hold summit mtg; Quebec airs dissatisfactn 2-13—2-15, 111D1
Jan CPI rise rptd 2-15, 145G3
Massey-Ferguson cancels Mar dividends 2-15, 146D1
'78-79 spending plan unveiled 2-22, 145B3
Liberals stress econ; back guaranteed income, spending cuts 2-24—2-26, 145E2, A3
'77, 4th ¼ GNP rptd 2-28, 187E3, F3 ★
ECC named new wage-price monitor 3-11, 209D2
Pay TV barred by CRTC 3-13, 226C1
Feb CPI rise rptd 3-15, 209B2
Trudeau rpts recovery in NY speech; NDP ldr disputes 3-21, 225F2
Saskatchewan potash purchases rptd 3-27, pro-rationing policy ruled illegal 10-3, 773D1-A2
US TV statn ordered dropped; ad deletn policy cited 3-28, 226A2 ★
CLC drops business-labor-govt confs 4-3, backs natlizatn 4-7, 266A2, E2
'78-79 budget set; tax cut plans offered, deficit forecast 4-10; Levesque scores 4-11, prov reactn rptd 4-12, 265F3
Quebec cuts sales taxes 4-11, selectivity scored 286G2
Mar CPI rptd up 4-12, 286E3
Sun Life shareholders OK move 4-25, Quebec Assemb scores 4-26, 311D2-A3
Liberal popularity rptd down 5-2, 350G1
'78 per capita income ranked 5-12, 384F3
Quebec '77 tax rebate proposed 5-15, 369G3, 370A1 ★
Apr CPI rise slows, inflatn rate rptd 5-16, 370B2
Quebec tax rebate stirs dispute, MP ejected from Parlt 5-16—5-18, 391G2
Corp merger study released 5-16, 392B1
Quebec tax dispute setld 6-8, 451A2
Husky Oil stock soars 6-8, probe launched 6-19, 629G1
May CPI surge rptd 6-14, 473E1
Quebec rejcts sales tax plan 6-14, Chretien bars chng 6-16, 495E1
1st ¼ GNP rise rptd 6-23, 495F2
Chretien, prov finance mins meet; tax rebates, Loto Canada debated 7-6, 531B2
Yukon land dvpt halted 7-6, 531A3
BC Loto Canada curb rptd 7-7, 531F2
June CPI rise rptd 7-12, 556F2
NW Terr Inuit land pact set 7-14, 556B2
Trudeau pledges 5% output hike 7-17, 544B2
Trudeau offers stimulatn plan 8-1, 613D1
Quebec tax rebate rptd sent, Chretien letter scored 8-1, 613C3
Prov premrs ask regulatory powers 8-10, 647F1
July CPI rise rptd 8-15, 666D3
Stimulatn plan spending cuts detailed 8-16, 8-24, 666C2-C3
2d ¼ GNP rise rptd 8-29, 666F3-667A1
Andras, Chretien set more stimulatn plan cuts 9-8; provs score 9-11, 739B1
Bank, prime rates hiked 9-11, 9-12, 704B1
Aug CPI rise rptd 9-13, 704C1, G1
Trudeau sets '79 electn, stimulatn plan implementatn linked 9-15, 739A1
Econ issues linked to PCs Nova Scota win 9-19, 739C3
PCs offer mortgage tax relief 9-21; Chretien, Andras score 9-28, 755A2
Abitibi plans Price Paper takeover 9-29, 772C3
Sugar refineries fined record sums 10-6, 794F3
Sept CPI rptd down 10-11, 794E2
Bank, prime rates hiked 10-13, 10-16, 794D2
PC tax relief plan, electn wins linked 10-16, 813C2
Saskatchewan resource policy backed in prov electn 10-18, 813D2
June '77-78 world inflatn rates ranked 10-18, 914F1
Const talks: power-sharing agreed, regional conflicts exposed 10-30—11-1, 866F1, B3
Bank, prime rates hiked 11-6, 879F2
Air Canada takeover of Nordair rescinded 11-7, 879E3
'78-79 revised budget set: tax cuts, business incentives offered; deficit rise seen 11-16, 900F3-901F1
Saskatchewan potash tax upheld by ct 11-17, 922D1
Cabt Econ Dvpt Mins Bd set 11-24, 921G2
Oct CPI rptd up 11-24, 922B1
Trudeau, prov premrs hold 2d summit 11-27—11-29; govt regulatn rpt presented 11-28, 944G1-B3
3d ¼ GNP lags 11-27, 944C3
Simpsons drops Sears merger plan, Hudson's Bay takeover seen 12-18, 986B1
Nov CPI rise rptd 12-19, 1013B2
Trudeau admits prices out pace wages 12-19, 1013D2
Family allowance cuts rptd OKd 12-22, 1013A2

1979

Edper renews Brascan bid 4-30—5-1, 5-30, 440C2
Quebec plans asbestos co takeover 5-2, 352D2
Dredging scandal trial ends, 5 convicted 5-5, 352F1
Broadbent for dvpt plan 5-13, 368F3
Apr CPI, 12-mo inflatn rptd 5-18, 377A2, 378E1
PC win linked, policies rptd 5-22, 377E1, E2
Wage-price controls failure rptd 5-24, 405D1
Quebec rpt cites cos exit 5-26, 405A3
Inco strike effects assessed 6-4, 444F1
Metric conversn scored in PC study 6-6, 444A2
Dredging cos fined, 5 sentncd 6-11, 468A2
7-natn indicators index rptd 6-11, 513A3
May CPI hike rptd 6-15, 468F1
1st 1/4 GNP rptd up 6-19, 468B1
Quebec expropriatn bill enacted, asbestos co sues 6-21; takeover halted 6-27, 484F1
Oil price rise, inflatn linked 6-29, 502A1
2 Montreal banks to merge 6-29, 601A2
June CPI increase slows 7-13, 543A1
Acid rain perils noted 7-17, 581B3
Bank rate hits new high 7-23, prime hiked 7-24, 562D3
Quebec asbestos co loses expropriatn injunctn suit 7-25, 563A1
Inflation comm disbanded 7-25, 581D1
Crosbie sees slowdown 7-26, 612E3
Fiscal restraint urged, '79 OECD forecasts rptd 8-2, 601D1
US recessn threat seen 8-7, 8-9, 601B1
Corp profits rptd up in 2d ¼ 8-9, 600G3-601A1
July CPI up, 12-mo inflatn down 8-17, 632F1
Prov premrs ask budget role, vow spending cuts 8-17, 632B2
Loto Canada sale to provs agreed 8-21, 651D2; price set 9-4, 685F1-A2
2d ¼ GNP drop rptd, 1st ¼ revised 8-31, 667B1
Quebec cos exit rptd 9-5, 750D1
Nova Scotia, Newfoundland to get resource control 9-5, 9-14, 706G2
PQ econ policy paper issued 9-6, 750C1
Bank rate hiked 9-7; prime hits 13% 9-10, 9-11, more hikes rptd 684F2
Mortgage tax credit plans announced by Saskatchewan 9-14, PCs 9-17, 706A1, F1
CPI rise slows in Aug 9-14, 706A2
Crown corps sales set 9-28, govt ownership rptd 9-29, 749E2
Bank rate hits 13%; prime raised, stocks fall 10-9, 771F2
PC backs pvt enterprise 10-9, 788G1
Cable TV accord set 10-17, 853B3
Sept CPI jumps 10-18, 833A3
Bank rate probe by Parlt com opens 10-23, 812A1
Bank rate at 14%, prime raised 10-25, 811E3-812B1
PQ white paper presented 11-1, 853E1
Interest rates spur no-confidence vote 11-6, 871B3
PQ electn defeat linked 11-14, 889B2
CDC divestiture planned 11-19, 908B1
NDP backs more govt control, central econ planning 11-22—11-25, 927G1, B2
3d 1/4 GNP up, recessn seen 11-29, 926E3
Statistics Canada probes launched 12-10, 967D2
Budget introduced 12-12, defeated 12-13; govt falls 12-14, 936F2-D3
Nov CPI, 12-mo inflatn rate up 12-15, 967E1
PQ referendum bill presented 12-17, 997C3

1980

Bank, prime rates peak 4-2; fall 5-1, 334D2
Hiram Walker, Consumers Gas merger OKd 4-8, 310D3
Throne speech vows more govt control, budget deficit cut, mortgage tax relief plan cutback 4-14, 292E3, 293C1
Mortgage rates rptd, home purchases unaffected 4-14, 4-29, 334A3
Mar CPI rise rptd 4-18, 311C1
Tax changes set; '80 budget deficit, inflatn estimated 4-21, 310D2-A3
Bank, prime rates fall 5-15, record govt bond redemptn noted 5-16, 388C3
Apr CPI, 12-mo inflatn rptd; auto prices cited 5-16, 388G2
Toronto stocks up 5-21, 377A2
Georges Bank fishing quota hiked 6-12, 461B2
Air Canada cuts fares 6-12, 461E3
1st 1/4 corp profits rptd up 6-12, 461F3
1st 1/4 GNP rptd down 6-17, 461C3
Drought hurts retail sales 6-27, 7-3, 520G2
Liberals back rail freight rate freeze, guaranteed annual income 7-4—7-6, 543E2
May, June car sales down 7-5, 520G2
Prelim const talks held 7-8—7-24, 603B1
US consumptn compared 7-16, 562D3
Alcan pipe impact seen 7-17, 562F2
Bell interconnect monopoly curbed 8-5; rate hike OKd 8-12, consumer group protests 8-15, 632D3, 633A1
July car sales rptd down 8-7, 618B2
July CPI rptd 8-15, 633F1
'79 gold productn rptd 8-27, 685C3
Campeau sets Trustco takeover bid 8-27; bid fails 10-2, 766E3-767A1
2d 1/4 GNP rptd down, CPI rptd up 8-29, 668D2
Ottawa, Ontario reject Massey-Ferguson aid 9-4; 3d 1/4 loss rptd 9-8, 728D2
Bank profits decline, Royal Bank gets new chrmn 9-5, 686F3-687C1
Const talks held 9-8—9-13, 706D1
August CPI rise rptd 9-15, 706A2
Bell monopoly chrgd 9-23, denied 9-24, 748G2
Prime, bank rates raised 10-1—10-2, 767B1
'81 budget, tax plan set; deficit, inflatn, productn forecast 10-28; oppositn heated 10-29—10-30, 857G3-858D3
Prime, bank rates hiked 10-30, 11-3, 871E1
Ontario offers 2 tax moves to offset fed econ plan 11-14, 885C2
New Bank Act OKd 11-26, 920A2
Prime, bank rates raised 11-28, 920B3
GNP, inflatn rptd up 12-6, 964G3
Bank, prime rates raised 12-11, 12-12, 964C3
Massey-Ferguson equity plan proposed 12-13, '80 loss rptd 12-17, 12-17, 992D1-B2
Bank, prime rates hiked 12-18, 12-19; Parlt debates 12-19; bank rate dropped 12-23, 992C2

1976

1977

Energy—*See also 'Atomic Energy' above*
Saskatchewan, Alberta oil output drop cited 1-6, 18C1
US OKs natural gas purchase 1-19, 53G3
Saskatchewan, Alberta cut oil royalties 1-19, 3-22, 237E1
More US gas purchases OKd 1-27, 1-28, 75C3, 76E1
US '75 gas reserves rptd down 1-28, 76B3
US pipeline pact signed 1-28, 82B2
US OKs gas-elec exchng 2-5, 91C3
US gas exports continue 2-13—2-19, 152D2
US gas pipe talks 2-21—2-23, 132C3
Fed, prov energy mins in oil-price impasse 4-6—4-7, 281F3-282A1
Carter energy plan 4-20, 291D2
US splits on Alaska gas route 5-2, 369C2
Berger rpt asks US gas pipe delay 5-9, 372G1; NWT scores 5-16, 389B3
Oil, gas land-use rules rptd 5-10, 8-10, 634A2
Prov oil, gas price hikes OKd 5-12, 410F3
Beaufort Sea oil search OKd 6-1, 425E3
Gulf, Mobil units halt Mackenzie drilling 6-4, 466A3
Eskimos vs Beaufort drilling 6-13—6-17, 619F2
Oil, gas price hikes set 6-23, 504E3
Home insulatn tax credit set 6-27, 505B1
US gas pipe route OKd 7-4, 525E1, A2 ★
Alcan pipe rpts issued 7-28, 8-2, 596E2-C3
Quebec rejcts home insulatn funds 7-28, 597B1
US cos back Alcan route 7-29, 596C3
Parlt OKs US gas pipe 8-8, 616B2
Alberta rejcts home-insulatn plan 8-17, 653A3
Provs scores resource policy 8-19, 653A2
Cabt OKs Alcan gas pipe 9-6; Trudeau, Carter announce agrmt 9-8, 687B1
US cos OK Hydro-Quebec loan 9-13, 742D1
Alcan gas pipe pact signed 9-20, 725C3
Quebec blackout 9-20, 742A3
Alcan rte clears US Cong 11-2, Carter signs 11-8, 856C3
Postal rate hike set, fuel costs cited 11-21, 983D1
Saskatchewan oil royalty tax ruled illegal 11-23, 923D3
Home insulatn rebate rules dropped 12-1, 966A1

Environment & Pollution
Water radiatn treatmt set 1-5, 43G2
IJC bd scores US Garrison projct 1-7, 60C3
Yellowknife arsenic pollutn chrgd 1-16, probe set 1-18, 61E1
Parlt com chrgs govt rules misuse 2-3, 133C2
US halts Garrison projct 2-18, 133A1
US gas pipeline talks 2-21—2-23, 132C3

1978

Energy—*See also 'Atomic Energy' above*
US '75 oil, gas investmts rptd 1-10, 70C3
Berger rpt urges gas pipe monitoring agency 1-12, 130E1
Metric chng set in oil industry 1-16, 89B1
US natural gas import rise, joint oil reserve storage study OKd 1-17, 53G2
Alcan gas pipe legis introduced 2-3, NEB sets pipe specificatns 2-20, 130A1
Kitimat oil depot barred 2-23, 130E1
Trudeau lauds Alcan project in NY speech 3-21, 225A3, D3
NW Terr Indians seek Metis pipe support 3-29, 244C3
Alcan gas pipe legis cleared 4-4, signed 4-13; US delay seen 8-16, 647F2
Oil exploratn tax credits budgeted 4-10, 266F1
Fuel prices, Mar CPI rise linked 4-12, 286F3
Conservatn effort rated 6-5, 449E3 ★, 450F1
Petro-Canada, Occidental in Husky Oil bidding war; collusn chrgd, Husky bd member quits 6-10—7-27; Alberta Gas wins control 6-27, 628E3-629E2
BC-Alberta gas find bared 6-27, 571F3
Yukon exploratn permits halted 7-6, 531B3
NW Terr Inuit oil, gas claims settled 7-14, 556G1
Gasoline tax lowered, natural gas deregulatn hinted 8-24, 666F2, A3
Natural gas indus reassured on deregulatn 8-30, 739F1
US gas export hike urged; graph 9-1—9-8, 704A2, C2
Viet oil exploratn pact rptd 9-7, 686G3
Saskatchewan interest on illegal oil tax ordrd 10-3, 773B2
Const talks: power-sharing agreed, regional conflicts exposed 10-30—11-1, 866G1, C3
Petro-Canada buys US-owned unit 11-10, 11-20, 901A2
1st ½ '78 oil productn rptd down 11-14, 871B2
Revised budget extends incentives 11-16, 901A1
Oil price rise OKd by Alberta, Ottawa 11-27; provs score 11-29, 944A2, E2
Oil, gas prices set by Alberta, Ottawa 12-8, 985E3
Algerian natural gas pipe rejctd by US 12-18, 983E3

Environment & Pollution—*See also 'Atomic Energy' and 'Energy' above, 'Soviet Satellite Issue' below*
Newfoundland defends seal hunt 1-9; '76 earnings, '78 quotas rptd 1-12, 35F2
Yukon land dvpt halted, caribou study set 7-6, 531A3
NW Terr Inuit land claims setld 7-14, 556F1
Prov premrs ask regulatory powers 8-10, 647F1

1979

Energy—*See also 'Atomic' above*
BC sets resource co stock giveaway 1-11, 37A3
Const reforms debated 2-5–2-6, 114A1
Alberta oil output rise OKd 2-12, 153A3
Exxon cuts oil shipmts, Gillespie scores 2-15–2-19, 153B2
Alberta gas reserve estimate hiked 2-16, 153C3
Oil price hike rptd sought 2-27, 145B3
US gas export hike urged 2-28, 210B3
US affirms Alcan pipe plan 3-3, 168F1
Petro-Canada oil import hike ordrd 3-13, 210G2
Alberta PCs win electn 3-14, 210D2
Oil spill off Nova Scotia 3-15, 201D1
Clark vows actn vs oil cos, Exxon cited 3-27, 266E3
Trudeau scores oil producing provs 3-28, 266C3
Broadbent for forgn oil sales curb 3-29, 267A1
Trudeau offers US oil pipe routes 4-10, 284E2
Oil prices, mergers rise linked 4-16, 285D1
Alberta Gas to take over Husky 5-13, 405F2
Major gas find announced 5-15, 405B2
Petro-Canada divestiture vow by PC cited 5-30, 424D1
US oil-sands study pact signed 6-4, 444D2-A3
Iraq threatns oil cutoff 6-27, 502B2
Tokyo summit 6-28–6-29, 493B1-F2
Clark seeks oil price rise, other sources 6-29, 501B3-502A1
US GAO doubts Alcan viability 7-4, 7-5, 522A2
Sable I gas find rptd 7-10, 542G2
World's top gas user 7-11, 542B3
Oil, gas export prices raised 7-13, 7-19, 542D2
US environmt commitmt sought 7-20, 581D3
Tenneco seeks UV assets 7-23, 770B3
US energy plan model cited 7-25, 557D3
N Amer common mkt opposed 7-26, 581A2
Alberta OKs 3d oil-sands plant 8-3, 651D1
Prov premrs conf topic 8-16–8-17, 632C2
Oil price hike spurs CPI rise 8-17, 632A2
Great Canadian, US' Sun Oil merge 8-22, 651A2
US gas purchase price cited 8-31, 689A1
Petro-Canada breakup study rptd 9-5, 684E3
Labrador, Baffin offshore potential rptd at intl petro cong 9-11, 728B3
PC MPs urge price hike 9-11, 728D3
Beaufort Sea oil find discounted 9-13, 728C3
Alberta offers fed loan for oil price hike, OKs Quebec loan 9-13, 728F3
Oil exports to US cut 9-19, 706E2
Newfoundland oil find, Dow rise linked 9-21, 745C3
Newfoundland strike rptd 9-21, 728F2
Crown co sale set 9-28, 749G2
US gas export price hiked 10-5, 788G3
PC speech asks '90 self-sufficiency 10-9, 788B2
Petro-Canada stock giveaway urged in govt rpt 10-14, 812B1
Sept CPI jumps 10-18, 833A3
Alberta oil price hike accord rptd near 10-22; Lougheed threatns cutoff 10-29, Clark assures Parlt re flow 10-30, 853E2
James Bay generator started, NY elec sales cited 10-27, 833D3
US oil prices hiked 10-31, 864F1
Prices spur no-confidence vote 11-6, 871A3

Environment & Pollution
Seal-hunt protests canceled 3-17, 3-24, 250E3
7-natn A-waste conf opens 7-12, 739G1
Arctic drilling banned 7-27, 587F3
US Lonetree Reservoir constructn protested 10-12, 945G3
Prelim pipeline rpt urges delay 11-1, comm hearings end 11-17; Sup Ct bars moratorium 12-22, 998C2

1980

Energy—*See also 'Atomic Energy' above*
Domestic, export oil prices hiked 1-1, 6F1
Clark seeks new policy, higher prices 1-2, 37G3
Newfoundland oil find confrmd 1-3, 6D1
BC, Indians sign gas revenue sharing pact 1-7, 57C1
Consumers Gas, Hiram Walker merger set 1-9, 19D1
US OKs Alcan pipe sectn 1-10, westn sectn constructn to begin 1-22, 56F3, G3
Trudeau vows self-sufficiency, vs gas excise tax 1-12, 38C1
Carter OKs all-US oil pipe route; Trudeau, Clark comment 1-17, 1-18, 56B3
US oil, gas export prices raised 1-21, 2-1, 79C1
Gasoline prices linked to CPI rise 1-23, 79C1
BP Canada slates Montreal hq move 1-26, 116C3
Gas tax hike plan, PC defeat linked 2-18, 121D1
Trudeau reelected, policies cited 2-18; vows oil indus ownershp increase 2-19, 121C2, E2
US blocks gas purchase re price hike 2-19, delays ban 2-20, 191F3-192A1
Mobil rpts Newfoundland finds 2-20, 2-21; C$ rise linked 2-21, 148F1
'79 4th 1/4 corp profits rptd up 2-22, 211E2
Oil cos lead stock mkt boost 2-27, 148F1
Stock mkt fall linked to Mobil offshore doubts 3-10, 191D3
Mex hikes gas prices 3-18, 234F1
US gas export price pact set 3-24, 229G3-230C1
Tar-sand oil price cut set 3-28, 272C3
Engelhard acquires Hunts' Beaufort Sea holdings 3-31, 244F3
Consumers Gas, Hiram Walker merger OKd 4-8, 310D3
Throne speech vows Canada oil ownership rise, price chngs 4-14, 293A1, B1
Oil price hike tied to deficit reductn 4-21, 310E2
US drivers rptd buying gas 4-21, 334E3
Alcan pipe eastn leg OKd by US 4-24, 331A1
Hunts Beaufort Sea property transfer cleared 4-28, 345D1
Alberta seeks oil price hike 5-6, offers productn bill 5-7, 428G3
Gas pipe extensn to Quebec OKd, 5 oil projects planned 5-16, 406D1
Newfoundland oil productn delay rptd 5-20, 429C1
Const talks vowed 5-21, 377F1
Mex oil-trade agrmt signed 5-27, 409A3
Alberta vs Ottawa oil price proposals 5-30, 428E3
Alberta, Ottawa oil price talks 6-18—6-19, extend deadline 6-19, 486C1
7-natn Venice summit 6-22—6-23, 473A1-474E1
US energy policy scored 6-23, 486A3
Ottawa gets US assurances on Alcan pipe completn 6-27—7-17, OKs southn leg pre-bldg 7-17, 562F1-F2
Trudeau affirms policy, backs moderate price rise 7-6, 543C2
Mobil wells off Newfoundland rptd productive 7-10, 7-11, 544B1-D1
Oil levy raised 75% 7-11, 543C3
Atco bid for Calgary Power stalled 7-16, 543F2
NEB OKs Foothills pipe financing, Olson gives construction go-ahead 7-22, 577D3
NDP filibuster vs Alcan pipe defeated 7-23, 577A3
Alberta, Ottawa oil talks fail 7-25, Alberta hikes price 7-31, 577A2, F2
Petro-Canada to buy Newfoundland refinery 8-1, 633B1
'79 oil profits rptd up 8-12, 618A1
Mobil halts Newfoundland Ben Nevis drilling 8-22, 668D3
Dome gets Japanese loan 8-23, 651C1
Alberta, Ottawa gas pricing pact rptd extended 8-28, Alberta hikes price 8-31, 669F1
Alberta delays oil, gas price hikes 9-30, 788B1
Lalonde urges Ottawa oil revenue hike 10-1, 788A1
Ottawa, Alberta talks fail again 10-2, 787C3
Exxon Beaufort Sea oil find rptd 10-3, 785E2-A3
Natl plan presented 10-28; oppositn strong, Alberta threatns oil productn cut 10-29—10-30, Ottawa offers price negotiatns 10-31, 857G3-858E3
Oil chiefs reject Ottawa plan 11-5, 11-7, 871A3
Alberta sets Mar '81 oil cutback 11-7, 885G2
Alberta oil sands projects stalled 11-19, 920E3
Alberta oil cutback, separatism polls linked 11-24, 11-25, 941B1, D1
BC bars fed gas tax paymt 12-20, 991G3

Environment & Pollution
Acid rain perils rptd 2-2, 2-19, 145F2, B3
Newfoundland fishermen shoot whales 461F2
Acid rain damage stressed 6-23, 486F2
Acid rain pact signed with US 8-5, 603E1

1976

Foreign Relations (misc.)—*See also 'UN Policy' below*
Mackenzie King '45 diary cites Sovt spy case 1-1, 8F1
Trudeau in Mex, Cuba, Venez 1-24—2-2; defends trip 2-3, 116C2
Bars Cuba Angola airlift refueling 1-30, 106D2
Angola MPLA recognized 2-18, 163D1
Leb emb siege 2-23, 145G2
Norway seal-hunt protests canceled 3-17, 3-24, 250E3
Sovt occupatn of Arctic island chrgd 6-17, 456C3
Bulgaria names amb 7-7, 910E2
12 Chile refugees leave Argentina emb 7-15, 1000 to get asylum 7-19, 571F2
Rumania, Sovt athletes defect 7-28—8-4, 562C2
Uganda expels 2 priests 8-13, 874D2
Callaghan visits 9-11—9-18, 730G1
Cuba to honor hijack pact 10-15, 780D1
Rhodesia fund backed 10-15, 843D2
Sovt envoy ousted 12-9, 963B1
Spain forgn min visits 12-22—12-23, 963A1

1977

Seal hunt scored 3-15, 237E3
Detroit sued on Lake Erie 5-6, 422F2
Berger com asks gas pipe delay 5-9, 372G1; NWT scores 5-16, 389B3
Oil, gas land-use rules rptd 5-10, 8-10, 634A2
Beaufort sea oil search OKd 6-1, 425F3
Gulf, Mobile units halt Mackenzie drilling 6-4, 466C3
Yellowknife arsenic probe rptd 6-6, 447E3
Eskimos vs Beaufort drilling 6-13—6-17, 619F2
IWC cuts whaling quotas 6-24, 496G3
US gas pipe route backed 7-4, 525F1, C2
Indians sue Ontario lumber co 7-7, expansn bid probed 764A1
Alcan gas pipe rpts issued 7-28, 8-2, 596E2-C3
Parlt backs US gas pipe 8-8, 616D2
Trudeau, Carter OK Alcan gas pipe 9-8, 687G1
IJC scores Garrison projct 9-19, 725G3
Alcan gas pipe pact signed 9-20, 725C3
Japan indl ldrs score rules 9-27, 780F2
Ontario tightens cleanup enforcemt 9-28, 763F3
Ontario lumber co fined 9-29, 763E3

Foreign Relations (misc.)—*See also 'Atomic Energy' and 'Energy' above, 'Monetary, Trade & Aid' and 'UN Policy' below*
Alleged Cuban spies ordrd ousted 1-10, 17E2
Cuba admits spy operatns; 4 expelled 1-12, 42D3
Seaborn '64-65 Viet missn cover-up rptd 1-14, 97B3
'76 Cuba spy surveillnc rptd 1-16, 61C1
Angola war rpt published 1-31, 86A1
Sovt sailor defects in US 2-8, 117G1
UK 'subject' status ends 2-15, 133A3
Sovt scientist deported as spy 2-24, 159E1
Chile withdraws amb nominee 2-26, 219G2
S Africa rejcts Namibia plan 4-7, 285C1
Scientists at Sovt seminar 4-18—4-20, 315D2
Czechs seize rptr's belongings 4-24, 314A3
S Africa sees Namibia compromise 4-29, 349C2
S Africa OKs Namibia const concessns 5-9, 400D1
Trudeau in France, sees Giscard, warns re Quebec 5-11—5-14, 389G1
Quebec modifies NATO stand 5-29, 425F2
S Korea amb rptd KCIA agent 6-5, 442A1
S Africa OKs Namibia plan 6-10, 457B2
Uganda arrests rptr 6-22, rptr interviews Amin 7-10, 600A3
Schmidt visits 7-6—7-12, detente pledged 7-7, 566G1, F2
USSR envoy chrgd as indl spy 7-20, 579F3
Tanzania pres visits 8-2—8-3, 624C1
SWAPO ldr joins Namibia talks 8-8, 639D3
Namibia compromise plan OKd 8-19, 699D3
Indochina refugee quotas eased 8-31, 685E2
Trudeau at Panama Canal pact signing 9-7, 678C1
Egypt drops anti-Copt plan 9-12, 863F2
ESA satellite projct shelved 9-19, 736B1
Namibia conf stalled 9-22—9-26, 770D2
Torrijos begins Canal treaty tour 9-24, 755F3
China forgn min visits 10-4—10-7, 801D1
Cuba '60, '70 aid to US radicals rptd 10-9, 896A3
Queen Eliz visits, promotes unity 10-14—10-19, 822A2
Levesque in France, gets Legion of Honor 10-23—11-4; Ottawa scores 11-4, 862B2, B3
Namibia tour fails to win SWAPO concessns 11-21—12-7, 1016E3
China ousts Toronto rptr 11-27, 946B2
France clarifies Quebec ties 12-9, 965G2
Togo assassinatn plot rpt cites Canadian mercenary 12-15, 988A3

1978

Const talks: power-sharing agreed 10-30—11-1, 866G1
Inuit land pact initialed 10-31, 866C3
Revised budget extends tax write-offs 11-16, 901B1

European Force Reduction Talks—*See under EUROPE*

Foreign Relations (misc.)—*See also 'Atomic Energy' above, 'Monetary, Trade, Aid & Investment', 'Soviet Satellite Issue' and 'UN' below*
US prisoner arrives from Cuba 1-2, 22D1
Jamieson in China 2-1, 80G1
USSR natls expelled for spying 2-9, 110D3
USSR spy rpt leaked 3-7, 208F3-209E1
USSR chrgs natl framed as spy 3-15, 209E1
Parlt res vs Cambodia killings 301B2
Cuban exile seized by US re Canada bomb plot 4-14, 287B2
Viet refugees ferried to Malaysia 4-14—4-17, 341B2
Hijacking pact signed 7-17, 544G2
Queen Eliz visits 7-26—8-6, 647B2
Monarchical role curbs debated 8-10, 8-16, 647E1, G1
Air Canada shutdown strands travelers in UK 8-25—9-5, 686F2
Viet refugees accepted 11-26, 11-29, 932E3

1979

European Force Reduction Issues—*See under EUROPE*

Foreign Economic Developments
Gulf payments detailed 133G3
SDR rate rptd 1-15, 14A3
Alcan Brazil operatn begun 1-16, 98F2
US pipeline delay rptd 1-20, treaty initialed 1-28, 116C3
Bata Bolivia unit unrest 1-22, 237A3
Trudeau in Latin trade talks 1-24—2-2, 116C2
$ trades above US parity 1-26, 99D1
S Korea A-reactor agrmt 1-26, 103C3
7-natn A-safeguards agrmt 1-27, 84A1
'75 trade deficit rptd 1-30, 116F2, A3
Guyana to buy Alcan unit 1-30, 252F3
Reader's Digest rpts ad tax agrmt 2-3, 116E3
At intl econ conf 2-11—2-20, 148B1
Pakistan A-talks 2-23—2-25; suspended 3-2, 174G3
Ad tax amendmt OKd, Time halts editn 2-25, 188G2
Ford seeks Alaska gas pipe plan 2-26, 149A2
China wheat deal set 2-27, 190G1
EC talks open 3-11, 204E1
US-run Newfoundland refinery bankrupt 3-12, 221C2
Bolivia oil co gets bank loan 3-12, 416F1
US threatens steel quotas 3-16, 212G3
Lockheed contract deadline extended 4-1, 250D2
Total IMF oil loan rptd 4-1, 340F2
Rockwell rpts paymts 4-9, 362A3
Sovt wheat purchases rptd 4-27, 321D3
New oil import plan set 4-27, 332C2
$1 bln Lockheed contract signed 4-30, 332F2
US ends car dumping probe 5-4, 321D2
'75 Sovt trade rptd 5-5, 340B3
1st ¼ US bond sales peak 5-17, 397A1
Lockheed deal collapses 5-18, 362G3
Bars India A-sales 5-18, India scores 5-20, 363A2
Sovt fishing zone pact 5-19, 200-mi limit set 6-4, 417D1
Tariff extensn proposed; UK, Ireland tax raised 5-25, 400D3
7-natn summit set 6-1, 6-3, 388G3
Lockheed Cabt repercussns 6-1—6-8, 416A2
Reynolds admits paymts 6-2, 690E2
Loan to prop UK £ OKd 6-7, 407C2
Petro-Canada buys Arco unit 6-7, 417C1
US sets steel quotas 6-7, 430G3, 431D1
Gas export price rise set, US role noted 6-10, 416G3
NATO OKs W Ger tank purchase 6-11, 449B2
US oil exports cut 6-11, 481B3
US Dem platform text cites ties 6-15, 478F2
Export credit terms tightened 6-15, 529F3
Oil exports to US cut 6-16, 481B3
Paris Club defers Zaire debt 6-17, 488A2
Intl banks OK Bolivia loan 6-18, 456A3
At 7-natn econ summit 6-27—6-28, 461G2
US potash producers indicted 6-29, 748A1
Clark meets premrs: seeks oil price rise, energy bank, other steps; US cited 11-12, 888C3
Heavy oil deposits estimated 11-26, 953E1
Clark Prairie prov support rptd high 12-3, 927C1
9-mo oil export data error rptd 12-10, 967F2
Price, excise tax hikes budgeted 12-12; defeated 12-13, 936C3, D3

European Force Reduction Talks—*See under EUROPE*

Foreign Relations (misc.)—*See also 'Atomic' above, 'Monetary' and 'UN' below*
UK envoy kidnap suspect arrested 1-6, 19G1; bail set 1-11, 37B2
Clark in Japan 1-7-1-11, India 1-11-1-14, 57E2
USSR gets satellite search bill 1-23, 96D1
Levesque: indep Quebec would keep Westn defns ties 1-25, 74F3
Monarchy role chng barred, const amendmt process debated 2-5–2-6, 113G2, E3
French premr in Ottawa, Quebec 2-8–2-13, 133C3
Indochina refugees get asylum 2-12, 109A1

1980

Foreign Relations (misc.)—*See also 'Atomic Energy' above, 'Monetary', 'Soviet-Afghan Issue', 'UN Policy' below*
NATO engineer accused of passing secrets to China 1-11, 78B3
Pacific orgn studied 1-20, 78C2
Japan joins 4-natn Pacific naval games 2-26, 151C3
RCMP '71 suspect list rptd sent abroad 2-28, 192A1
Activist role planned 4-14, 293E1
Mex pres visits 5-25—5-28, 409G1, A3
7-natn Venice summit 6-22—6-23, 473A1-474E1
Westn labor costs compared 8-12, 698E1
MacGuigan scores S Africa, USSR 9-22, 748G3-749B1
Guyana electn observed 12-15, declared 'fraudulent' 12-19, 994A3

148 CANADA— FACTS—ON—FILE

1976

Government & Politics—*See also other appropriate subheads in this section*
Mackenzie King diaries publshd 1-1, 8C1
Listed as 'free' nation 1-19, 20B3
Ouellet ruled in contempt 1-23, 72E1
Turner quits Commons 2-13, 188F2
Judicial interference chrgd 2-20; probe barred 3-3; chrgs denied 3-3, 3-4, 187E3, F3 ★
PC conv ends; Clark elected ldr 2-23, 188B2
Penal reforms proposed 2-24, 250A3
Trudeau seeks BNAA return 3-5, 238A3
Judicial probe rpt presented, Drury resignatn rejctd 3-12, Ouellet's OKd 3-16; PC, NDP start slowdown 3-15, no confidence move defeated 3-16, 220D3, E3 ★ -221B2
Morality law review urged 3-25, 250C3
Fed cleaning contracts probed 3-29, 265G2
Trudeau on charter proposals 4-1, 4-9, 265C2
Sky Shops probe jurisdictn disputed 4-21—4-23; 5 arraigned 4-22, 309B3-310A1
Ontario Liberals form 2 wings 4-25, 350C2
Giguere accused 5-5, 380G3
Const issue deferred 5-6, 380F3 ★
MPs vote bribery chrg probe 5-7, 350B2
Keenan quits airport safety probe comm 6-7, 416E3 ★
Plumptre quits AIB 6-10, denies rift 6-11, 439A1
Marchand quits 6-28, 496E2; acting min named 7-12, 555E1
Newfoundland by-electns 6-30, 520B3
Commons votes civiln death penalty end 7-14, 520G2
Liberals popularity down 9-4, 692A2
Cabt reorgnzd 9-14, sworn 9-15, 692B1
Const talks 10-1—10-2, 749F3
Diefenbaker accuses JFK 10-4, 837C1
PC, Clark favored in polls 10-9, 10-16, 808F2
2d Parlt sessn opens, Trudeau policy speech read 10-12, 771D2
Giguere chrgd 10-12, trial set 11-26, 988G3
Defense min quits, replaced 10-13, 790D1
Liberals lose 2 by-electns 10-18, 808B2
Ct rules on Ouellet appeal 10-20, 851F2
Urban, defns mins named 11-3, 851E2
Statistics Canada employes chrgd 11-3, check ordrd 11-4; conflict-of-interest guidelines legis rptd 11-10, 870G2-F3
PC wins 3 PEI by-electns 11-8, 888C2
Rpt Statistics Canada OKd '73 fund solicitatn 11-12; irregularity denied, Parlt hearing set 11-15, 888D2
Separatists win Quebec electn 11-15, Trudeau, Levesque statemts 11-15, 11-16, 870C1
Bourassa to quit party ldrshp 11-19, 903E3
Poll: fewer back Quebec separatn 11-22, 903D3
Acctg method scored, study comm named 11-22, 903G3; Caron quits comm 11-25, 924A2
Levesque sworn 11-25; names cabt 11-26, 903E2
Trudeau in unity appeal 11-25; Levesque scores 11-26, 903B3
PQ wins seat in recount 12-1; 2d recount stalled 12-3, 924D1
PQ wins 2d recount 12-22, 998B3

1977

Government & Politics—*See also other appropriate subheads in this section*
Dec poll: 47% back PC 1-5, 7B2
'71 blacklist revealed 1-25, 1-26, 97A1; **for subsequent developments, see 'Crime' above**
Parlt OKs TV coverage 1-25, 114E2
Trudeau ends by-electn tour 1-28, 113A3
Parlt com chrgs rights violatns 2-3, 133A2
Levesque in car mishap 2-6, 113D2; cleared in death 2-21, 2-25, 159C1
Trudeau leads Clark in poll 3-5, 218D3
Levesque opens Quebec Assemb 3-8, 179F1
4 named to Senate 4-5, 281A3
Trudeau, wife separatn rpts 4-8, 4-11, 281C3
Trudeau campaigns 4-18—4-20, 346F1
Horner quits PC 4-20, 304A1
Yukon Cncl asks expansn 5-4; NWT asks more self-rule, on native land claims 5-16, 389E2
Liberal popularity poll 5-11, 410D3
By-electns, Liberals gain 5-24, 410G2-E3
Trudeau, wife separate 5-27, 426F1
Saskatchewan NDP wins by-electn 6-8, 466D3
Ontario PC wins legis electns 6-9, 466F2
Lavoie quits PC 6-14, 505C2
Unity task force formed 7-5, 542D1
Liberals lead in poll 7-13, 580A1
Parlt OKs bills, recesses 7-25, 596D1
Premiers conf 8-18—8-19, 653A1
Nadon quits, Simmonds replaces 9-1, 742B2
Macdonald resigns 9-6, 694B2
Cabt shuffled 9-16, 725E2, G2 ★
Begin yields women's post 9-23, 763C3
Decentralizatn plan set 10-3, 801B1
Manitoba PCs win electn upset 10-11, 823C1
TV Parlt coverage starts 10-17, 863F1
Queen Eliz opens Parlt 10-18, 822A2, D2
Trudeau in Alberta, BC 10-31—11-1, 882A3
Quebec Liberal, Union Nationale party records seized 11-30, 945G3; returned 12-11, 965D2
Fed audit rpt sees less waste 12-1, 946A1
Queen ends govt duties 12-30, 1010D1
Helsinki Agreement—*See EUROPE—Security and Cooperation*
Immigration
US immigratn rptd up 1-13, 43A2
Quebec orders French schl transfers 1-24, English progrm end 1-25, 113F3-114A1
Parlt com chrgs govt rules misuse 2-3, 133C2
Sovt sailor seeks asylum 2-8, 117G1
Requirements eased 2-15, 133E2
'76 immigratn down 4-13, 389C2
Poll: racial tension up 4-21, 327F1
Ottawa-Quebec pact reached 5-27, 425B2
Immigratn Act revisn passed 7-25, 596D1

1978

Government & Politics—*See also other appropriate subheads in this section*
Basford sets retiremt 1-13, 89C1
Metric chngs set 1-16, 89B1
Lamontagne named min without portfolio 1-19, postmaster gen 2-2, 70F1
Fox quits as solicitor-gen re abortn illegality 1-30; statemt text; Blais replaces 2-2, 70B1
MP chrgd with influence peddling 1-31, 88A2
1st comptroller-gen named 2-20, 145E3
'78-79 spending plan unveiled 2-22, 145B3
Fox avoids chrgs, Trudeau backs 2-23, 166C2
Liberal Party rally 2-24—2-26, 145E2
Human Rights Act enacted 3-1, 188E1
Goyer to resign 4-6, 287E1
NDP gets labor support 4-7, 266C2
'78-79 budget set 4-10; prov, other reactn 4-10, 4-12, 265F3
Civil servant wins libel suit vs Goyer 4-13, 286G3
Ryan wins Quebec Liberal post 4-15, 328G2
Prince Edward I electn 4-25, 312B1
Reznowski elected Soc Credit ldr 5-7, 392A1
Gen electn delayed, Apr poll cited 5-11, 350E1
Levesque scores electn delay 5-14, 370D1
MP ejected in Quebec tax debate 5-16, 391G2
Statistics Canada sets conflict-of-interest rules 6-10, 495A3
Const plan, rights charter proposed 6-12, 451E1
Const legislatn presented, detailed 6-20, 472F2
Giguere cleared re Sky Shops 6-29, 514E3
Quebec by-electn won by Liberal 7-5, 514F2
Col scores defns min 7-10, transferred 7-12, 556G2
Trudeau on spending plan, gen electn stay, PO status 8-1, 613D1
Post Office crown corp shift set 8-1, 613G1
Lang sworn justice min 8-9, 647C1
Prov premrs summit ends, Const plan scored 8-10; Trudeau, Lalonde defend 8-16, 646F3-647B2
Ontario solicitor-gen phones atty 8-14, Munro scandal spurs resignatn 9-9; replaced 9-12, 721E3
Munro phones judge 8-18, probe rpt prompts resignatn 9-8, 721C2
Const chngs scored by Indians 8-29, 8-30, 755D1
More spending cuts announced 9-8, provs score 9-11, 739B1
Levesque divorced 9-8, 844G3
PEI premr quits 9-11, new premr named 9-18, 739D2
Const plan sent to Sup Ct 9-13, Trudeau scores prov premrs 9-15, premrs reaffirm plan oppositn 9-25, 754E3
Trudeau sets '79 electn 9-15, 738F3
Davis resigns BC legis seat 9-17, 739F2
Nova Scotia PCs win electn 9-19, 739B2
By-electns held, Liberals suffer setbacks 10-16, 813E1
Saskatchewan NDP wins electn 10-18, 813C2
New Brunswick PCs reelected 10-23, 837C3
Const talks: power-sharing agreed, regional conflicts exposed 10-30—11-1; '79 chngs seen 11-2, 866E1-C3
Yukon PCs win assemb control 11-20, 944E3
Auditor-gen rpts contd fiscal mismanagemt 11-23, 921F3
Cabt shuffled, Munro replaced by O'Connell; Econ Dvpt Mins Bd set, Urban Affairs Min end seen 11-24, 921G2
PC leads Liberals in poll 12-6, Turner favored as Liberal ldr 12-9, Trudeau bars resignatn 12-14, 985G2, C3
Schreyer named gov gen 12-7, 963B3
PEI Liberals confirm Campbell 12-9, 964F1-A2
Parlt ends '78 sessn, spending cuts set 12-22, 1013A2
Helsinki Agreement—*See EUROPE—Security and Cooperation*
Immigration
Ottawa, Quebec sign pact 2-20, 146A1
US RCMP informer's illegal entry cited 2-27, 166B2
New regulatns set 3-8, 188G1

1979

Viet diplomat expelled 3-29, 267E1
216 Viet refugees arrive 4-5, 299F1
Newspaper avoids trial re USSR spy rpt 4-23, 311B2
Australia sets job study missn 4-28, 351G2
Nicaragua fighting rptd 5-29, 409A2
Indochina refugee admissns hiked 6-21, 474B2
Indian chiefs in UK 7-2–7-3, 522E3
RCMP plans Emb taps 7-4, 522F2
Indochina refugee admissns to hit 50,000 by '80 7-18, 549D2
Gov Gen sees Indians 7-19, 632G2
UK envoy's kidnapers sentncd 8-7, 632B3
Citizen slain in Afghanistan 9-8, 696C1
PC asks parliamentary com review 10-9, 788E2
UK envoy's 3d kidnaper sentncd 11-8, 872D1
FLQ exile leaves Cuba 12-23, 992F3
Government & Politics—*See also other appropriate subheads in this section*
'48 Mackenzie King diaries released 1-1, 19A2
Clark 4-natn pol tour 1-7–1-18, 57E2
Liberal gain rptd in Dec '78 poll 1-10, 36E3
Manitoba NDP ldr named 1-13, 57C3
Unity Cncl rpts pub indifference 1-16, 57C1
BC pol cartoonist fined 1-17, 57G1
Unity Task Force rpt asks more prov powers, const, Parlt, Sup Ct chngs 1-25; reactn 1-25, 1-26, 74D1-F3
Const talks continue, minor reforms OKd 2-5–2-6, 113F2-114B1
Natl Party of Canada conv 2-11, 189F1
Social Credit ldr quits 2-22, 189E1
Natl Inflatn Comm created 3-2, 168B2
Liberal MP joins PCs; Parlt party standings rptd 3-7, 189C1
Liberals lead in Feb poll 3-7, 189G1
Alberta electns, PCs win 3-14, 210B2
Newfoundland gets new premr 3-17, 233F3
Electns set, Parlt increase noted 3-26, 233B3
Gen electn campaign opens 3-27–3-29, 266G2
Goyer wins libel suit appeal 3-30, 253F3
Roy named Soc Credit head 3-30, 254A1
Levesque remarries 4-12, 392D2
PEI Liberals lose electn 4-23, 311F1
Prov govt ruling parties cited 311A2
Quebec by-electns go to Liberals, Natl Assemb standing cited 4-30, 329A1
Trudeau backs const patriatn 5-9, 368D3
BC Socreds win, majority reduced 5-10, 369B1
Davis reelected to BC legis 5-10, 369D1
Poll shows slim Liberal lead 5-12, 368G3
Pol ldrs in TV debate 5-13, 368C3
Quebec Cabt min quits 5-17, 378B1
PCs win electn; Clark heads minority govt, policies rptd; vote breakdown 5-22, 377A1-F2
Clark photo 5-23; facts on 377E1, F2-378B1
Employmt min secret papers found in garbage 5-26, 444A3
Jamieson quits Parlt for Newfoundland premr bid 5-27, 424C1
PC wins Nova Scotia seat in recount 5-29, 424D1
NDP ldr backs PCs, warns vs Petro-Canada divestiture 5-30, 424D1
Clark sworn, Cabt named 6-4, 423C3
PC hiring freeze set 6-8, 444A1
PC majority hiked in Newfoundland electn, Jamieson wins seat 6-18, 467G3
Const patriatn scored by Indians 7-3, 522E3
Trudeau unveils shadow cabt, vows to remain Liberal ldr, scores PC Parlt delay 7-19, 563B2
Giguere cleared of Liberal funds misuse 7-20, 563D1
Inflatn comm dispanded 7-25, 581E1
Decentralizatn plans cut back 7-27, 581E3
'79-80 pub svc cuts ordrd, hiring freeze ends 8-15, 632C1
Prov premrs meet 8-16–8-17, 632B2
Socred MP joins PCs 9-19, 729B1
Quebec Cabt shuffled, min quits 9-21, 750B1
NWT cncl elected 10-1, 772E1
Grafftey gets new Cabt post 10-8, 789A3
Parlt opens; PC speech asks decentralizatn, Parlt reform; Jerome named House speaker 10-9, 788E1-A3
Yukon cncl gets more power, comr resigns 10-10, 833F3
No-confidence votes defeated 10-12, 10-15, 11-6, 871A3
Liberals meet, score Trudeau 10-12–10-14, 812F1
Giguere influence peddling chrgs dropped 10-19, 812C2; 12-7, 949A1
Clark meets prov premrs 11-12, 888C3
PQ loses by-electns 11-14, 889G1-B2; 11-26, 907G3-908B1
PC edge cut in by-electns 11-19, 907E3
Trudeau quits Liberal ldrship 11-21, 907G2
NDP conv held, Broadbent reconfrmd ldr 11-22–11-25, 927D1
Poll finds PC support down 12-3, 927A1

1980

Government & Politics—*See also other appropriate subheads in this section*
Campaigning begins 1-2, 1-12, 37E3
Liberals lead PCs in poll 1-2—2-4, 96B1
Jerome named Fed Ct justice 1-4, 38C2
Giguere Sky Shops acquittal appeal set 1-4, 6G1; rejctd 1-7, 57A1
Quebec Liberals propose const reform 1-10, 18E3
Trudeau reelected, Liberals win Commons majority; vote breakdown chart 2-18, 121A1
Sauve named Commons speaker 2-29, 171C2
Trudeau sworn, names Cabt 3-3, 171D1
Biron quits UN party, Le Moignan succeeds as ldr 3-3, 230D1
NWT prov status rejected 3-6, 273C1
NS Liberal paymts to Regan, corp paymts to NS parties rptd 3-17, 253E1
NB premr admits PC paymts 3-22, repaymt rptd 3-25, 253B2
Liberal wins Quebec by-electn 3-24, 230E3
Lamer named Sup Ct judge 3-28, 273C2
Kirkham quits Statistics Canada 3-31, 273B1
Parlt opens, Throne Speech read 4-14, 292E3
Fscl '79 spending rpt issued 4-26, 334B3
NDP meets, seeks const chng 5-9—5-11, 372A2
Const talks vowed 5-21, 377E1
Const negotiatns set 6-9, 443C3
Const talks jeopardized 6-19, 486E1; 7-25, 577F2
'O Canada' proclamed natl anthem 7-1, 496E3-497C1
Liberal conv in Winnipeg 7-4—7-6, Trudeau affirms const vow 7-6, 543A2
Prelim const talks held 7-8—7-24, 602G3-603D1
Freedom of info legis introduced 7-16, 562E3
NDP filibuster defeated, Parlt recesses 7-23, 577A3
Const talks fail 9-8—9-13, 705E3
Trudeau meets Liberal caucus, Cabt 9-17, 9-18; recalls Parlt for const 'patriatn' 9-18, 728E1
Roy quits as Socreds pres, Hattersley named 11-3, 885E3
NWT assemb OKs split 11-6, ministry set 11-7, 885B3
Toronto mayor loses reelectn 11-11, 900D3
Liberals win Quebec by-electns 11-17, Conservative wins in Ontario prov 11-20, 900A3
Westn separatism polls rptd 11-24, 11-25, 941A1, D1
Patriatn plan opposed in poll 12-10, 964D2
Immigration
US draft dodgers warned 2-7, 95G3
300 Cuban refugees offered asylum 4-16, 285C1
Sovt Armenian entries estimated 5-24, 467F2
KKK opens Toronto hq 6-26, 497D1
US data compared 7-16, 562A1
E Eur records rptd found 8-20, 651F1-C2
'81 refugee total rptd cut 10-31, 871E2

1976

Labor & Employment
Dec '75 jobless rate rptd 1-13, 28C1
Toronto teachers end 9-wk strike 1-19, 72A1
Quebec paper mill strikes end 1-21, 47B1
Olympics facilities completn delay cited 1-28, 99G1
Jan jobless down 2-10, 188G1
Wage, price controls extended 3-8, 204F1
Jobless rate rptd up 3-13, 297E3
UAW special conv 3-18—3-20, 220C1
CLC denounces controls 3-22; quits CLRC, Econ Cncl 3-23, 238D2
Quebec teachers anti-strike law passed 4-8, teachers strike 4-13, 288E1
Feb-Apr jobless rptd 5-11, 350G1
CLC Cong, decisn-making role demanded 5-16—5-21, 400F3
'76 budget presented 5-25, 400D2, G2
Air controller strike averted 5-31, 416C3 ★; **for subsequent developments, see 'Language Issue' below**
May jobless rptd 6-8, 416F3
New wage-price controls set 6-16, 456D3
Olympics bldg fraud chrgd 6-30, 529B2
Inflatn plan upheld, Ontario entry voided 7-12, 554C3
CLC sets inflatn plan protest 8-12, reactn 8-12—8-15, 623A3 ★
Quebec teachers OK contract 8-31; 9 schl bds protest 9-1, 673F1-B2
'76 wage rise avg: 12.11% 9-7, 730D3
Experts hit bargaining tactics 9-10, 771C2
June-Sept jobless rptd 9-14—10-12, 808B3
Quebec Cath teachers end strike 9-15, Protestant teachers walkout 10-1, 750E1
CLC vp warns on inflatn plan 9-17, 771E1
Labor bd vs wage cuts 9-17, 771A2
Postal workers strike 10-3—10-7; govt mediatn plan scored 10-11, 808D3
Oct jobless rptd up 10-9, 888C3
Trudeau parlt speech vows fight vs unemploymt 10-12, 771D2
Strike vs inflatn plan 10-14, 771A1
Strikers penalized 10-19, 10-21, 836D3
Quebec Protestant teachers end walkout 10-19, 836G3
Postal mediatn ends 10-21; Blais bars 10-22, 836F3
Immigratn linked to job needs 11-2, 851F1
Quebec Sept jobless rptd 11-12, 870F1
'77 clothes imports curbed 11-29, 924G1
Nov jobless rptd down 12-8, 945C2

Language Issue
Bilingualism program scored 3-31, 250B2
Air controller strike averted 5-31, Keenan quits 6-7, 416C3 ★

1977

Indians & Inuit (Eskimos)
Yellowknife arsenic pollutn chrgd 1-16, probe set 1-18, 61E1
Yukon Cncl asks expansn 5-4; NWT asks more self-rule, on native land claims 5-16, 389E2
Berger com asks gas pipe delay 5-9, 372A2
Land-use rules rptd 5-10, 634C2
Inuit file new land claim 5-13, 411D1
Yellowknife probe rptd 6-6, 447E3
Inuit at intl conf 6-13—6-17, 619D2
Inuit vs Beaufort drilling 6-13—6-17, 619F2
Ontario lumber co sued 7-7, expansn bid probed 764A1
NWT prov plan offered 7-14, rejctd 8-3, 616D2
Yukon settlemt aid asked re gas pipe project 8-2, 596B3
Prison reform pledged 8-5, 634F1
Quebec Inuit protest language bill, police dispatched 8-22—8-26; Crees dissociate 8-26, 671F2
Language bill dispute continues 8-30—9-2; Inuit ask James Bay land pact delay, Crees vs 9-1, 693E3
Allmand's ouster scored 9-16, 725A3
US dam projct danger cited 9-19, 726B1
Inuit protest abates 9-22, 742C1
James Bay land pact becomes law 11-1, 862D3, E3 ★

Labor & Employment—*See also 'Language Issue' below*
'76 strike illegality rejected 1-6, 18D1
Dec '76 jobless rate rptd 1-11, 17D3
Quebec ends govt wage curbs 1-15, 43G1
Dock union S Africa boycott fails 1-21, 67B3
'76 factory wages rptd 1-28, 158A3
Montreal police slowdown 1-31—2-3, 97C2
Alcan strike pact reached 1-31, 114A2
Jan jobless rate sets record 2-8, 114A1
Mins meet, fail to end wage curbs 2-22, 158C3
Levesque opens Quebec Assemb 3-8, 179D2
Quebec, Saskatchewan end wage controls 3-10, 3-17, 218F2
Feb jobless rate rises 3-15, 200A2
BC farm workers unionize 3-21, 237E2
March jobless rate up 4-13, 282C1
Quebec, Ontario set '77-78 budgets 4-13, 4-19, 303A3, E3
Prov unemploymt actn urged 4-20, 327A1
Racial tension rise rptd 4-21, 327F1
Budget OKd by Commons 4-21, 327F1
Manitoba jobless data rptd 4-22, 327B2
Wage-price control mtg 4-22, 327D2
Prov inequalities rpt erred 4-22, 346D3
New AIB head named 4-28, 346B3
Newfoundland factory closing set 4-28, 372B3
Quebec cos exodus rpt questnd 4-30, 354D2
Apr jobless rate up 5-10, 372G2
Union rptd liable re '76 strike 5-18, 411A1
Govt OKs educ funds 5-20, 411C1
May jobless rate down 6-14, 505E2
June jobless rate rptd 7-12, 561G3
Wage-price controls end proposed 7-29, 616A3
Air controllers strike 8-7—8-10, CATCA vs Parlt order 8-10, 616D1
July jobless rate rptd 8-9, 634A3
CLC rejcts wage-price curbs plan 8-17, 634E2
Air traffic controllers slowdown rptd 8-18, 634A3
Provs asks controls end 8-19, 653F1
ACTRA, film producers feud 8-31—9-12, 742E2
Aug jobless rate rptd 9-13, 725F3
BC pensioners win union fight 9-24, 764B1
Govt decentrlztn plan set 10-3, 801C1
Sept jobless rise rptd 10-11, 823B1
Controls end, stimulus progrm outlined in Throne Speech 10-18, 822F2, A3
3,000 nickel worker layoffs set 10-20, 923F3
Oct jobless steady 11-8, 903C2
Army spying on unions rptd 11-11—11-12, 882C2
Postal rate hike set 11-21, 983D1
Fed audit rpt scores jobless benefit waste 12-1, 946E1
Footwear indus jobless rptd 12-2, 983A1
Nov jobless up 12-6, 1010E2

Language Issue
French ban at intl airports upheld 1-12, 17B3
Air Canada to cut svcs 1-12, 43D2
Airport hearings open 1-17, 43F1

1978

'77 total rptd 3-9, 188C2
Algerian rptd kidnaped 4-24, protested 7-1, 7-4, 531D3

Indians & Inuit (Eskimos)
USSR satellite radiatn danger discounted 1-25, 57C2
Treaty Indian status defined 244C3
NW Terr group OKs Metis members 3-29, 244B3
USSR satellite hazard feared 7-5, 514D3
Yukon land dvpt halted 7-6, Inuit laud 7-7, 531C3
NW Terr Inuit land pact set, other native groups score 7-14, 556F1
'Longest Walk' protesters see amb to US 7-18, 569C1
Const reform plan scored 8-30, 755D1
US gas export hike opposed 9-1, 704A3
Mackenzie R Indian, Metis legal funds halted 9-27, 866E3
Inuit land pact initialed 10-31, 866C3
Indians win Yukon seats 11-20, 944F3

Labor & Employment—*See also 'Language Issue' below*
Dec '77 jobless rise rptd 1-10, 16D2
Govt, business, labor reps confer 2-1, 111G1
Jan jobless drop rptd 2-7, 145F3
Trudeau cites 8% jobless rate 2-13, 111E1
Quebec to control temporary worker entry 2-20, 146C1
'78-79 spending plan unveiled 2-22, 145C3
Air traffic controllers pact rptd 2-23, 166G3
Liberals stress jobs, res adopted 2-24—2-26, 145E2, A3
Sex bias in govt jobs outlawed 3-1, 188F1
Feb jobless rptd 3-14, 209A2
Trudeau addresses NY investors 3-21, 225G2
'76 illegal strike rule upheld 3-21, 244B2
CLC conv ends: natlizatn, other chngs voted; postal union rift healed 4-7, 266A2
Labor ldrs score '78-79 budget 4-10, 266G1
Mar jobless rise rptd 4-11, 286D3
Jobless overpaymts rptd 5-5, 350G2
Apr jobless unchngd; % employed at record high 5-9, 370F1
Statistics Canada employe rules issued 6-10, 495A3
May jobless rate unchngd 6-14, 473C1
Quebec curbs constructn workers, Ontario scores 7-1; labor mins meet 7-12, 7-20; CLC backs Quebec 7-21, 571G2-F3
June jobless rate unchngd 7-11, 556E2
Trudeau pledges job growth 7-17, 554B2
'77 jobless rise rptd 7-28, 677D1
Post Office reorgnizatn set 8-1, 613A2
July jobless drop rptd 8-8, 666C3
Civil Svc job cuts planned 8-16, 666E2
Jobless benefits cut set 8-24, 666A3
Air Canada settles with pilots 8-24, suspends svc in IAM dispute 8-25—9-5, 686B2
25,000 jobs seen in US gas export hike 9-1—9-8, 704G2
Munro quits as labor min 9-8, 721C2
More Civil Svc hiring, jobless benefit cuts set 9-8, 739C1
Toronto transit workers strike 9-11, arbitratn ordrd 9-13, strike ends 9-15, 721G3
Bell Canada bias end ordrd 9-11, guidelines issued 9-21, 772F3
Aug jobless rise rptd 9-12, 739G1
Stat Canada ends job rpts 9-13, 739A2
Jobs program support linked to PCs Nova Scota win 9-19, 739C2
AMC, UAW in 2-yr pact 9-25, 737C3
Sept jobless rate unchngd 10-10, 813E3
Jobless benefit curbs to be eased 10-10—10-11, 813E3
Postal strike 10-16—10-25, 813B3
Noranda, Inco copper strike cited 10-20, 805C1
Jobless, interest rates linked 11-6, 879B3
Oct jobless drop rptd 11-7, 901F1
Revised budget sets tax incentives 11-16, 900G3, 901A1, F1
O'Connell named labor min 11-24, 921E3
Nov jobless up 12-6, 964C1
March hidden jobless rptd 12-8, 964D1
Trudeau admits wages lag 12-19, 1013D2
Jobless benefit cuts passed 12-21, 1013A2

Language Issue
Insurance co to leave Quebec 1-6, 16F1; delays vote on move 1-14, 35D3
Quebec language requiremt ruled invalid, appeal set 1-24, 70B2

1979

Statistics Canada probes launched 12-10, 967D2
Govt defeated on budget 12-13; House dissolved, electns set 12-14, 936F2-E3
Trudeau to remain Liberal ldr 12-18, 966G3

Helsinki Agreement—*See EUROPE–Security and Cooperation*

Indians & Inuit (Eskimos)
BC cartoonist loses libel case 1-8, 57A2
Unity Task Force urges larger role 1-25, 74B3
Indian chiefs in UK, protest Const patriatn 7-2–7-3, 522E3
Schreyer meets Indian reps 7-19, 632G2
Women meet Clark, protest bias 7-20, 601D2
Alberta tribes to administer fed funds 8-13, 632D2
NWT cncl elected 10-1, 772F1
PC pledges jobs 10-9, 788B2

Labor & Employment—*See also 'Language Issue' below*
Dec '78 jobless drop rptd 1-9, 19E1
Job rise seen 2-6, 2-7, 114C1, E1
Jan jobless rise rptd, Chretien defends govt record 2-6, 134G1-C2
Inflation comm created 3-2, 168B2
Feb jobless down 3-13, 210D3
'78 wage lag rptd 3-23, 234A2
Mar jobless rate rptd unchngd 4-10, 284G2
Parrot jailed re '78 postal strike 5-7, 352D1
Inco strikers rejct contract 5-12, 369E1
Apr jobless unchngd 5-15, 378D1
Wage-price controls failure rptd 5-24, 405D1
Inco strike ends 6-4, 444E1
PC govt hiring freeze set 6-8, 444A1
May jobless drop rptd 6-12, 468E1
June jobless rate drops 7-10, 542F3
Inflatn comm disbanded 7-25, 581G1
Jobless hike seen 7-26, 612E3, G3
Ontario, Quebec Bell workers strike 8-12, 613F1
'79-80 pub svc cuts ordrd, hiring freeze ends 8-15, 632C1, F1
July jobless drop rptd 8-16, 612C3
Quebec job loss rptd 9-5, 750D1
Ontario, Quebec Bell strike ends 9-6, 685E1
Aug unemploymt rate rptd 9-11, 706C2
Montreal Star folds, strike linked 9-25, 729D1
Ford sets auto layoff 9-27, 806F1
Union reactn to crown co sales 9-28, 749C3
PC pledges more jobs 10-9, 788B2
Sept jobless drops 10-9, 833C3
Quebec bars pub employe strikes 11-13, 889A2
PQ electn defeat linked 11-14, 889B2
CDC divestiture impact seen 11-19, 908E1
Parrot jailing scored by NDP 11-22–11-25, 927A2
Statistics Canada probes launched 12-10, 967G2
Jobless insurnc cost rise budgeted 12-12, defeated 12-13, 936E3
Nov unemploymt down, total labor force drop rptd 12-12, 967G1-A2
Nova Scotia OKs labor law 12-28, 992D3

Language Issue
Bilingual air control backed in tests 1-5, 18G3
Unity Cncl rpt criticizes 1-16, 57F1

1980

Indians & Inuit (Eskimos)
BC, Fort Nelson Indians sign gas revenue sharing pact 1-7, 57C1
BC cartoon libel ruling upset 2-15, 148E3
NWT prov status rejected 3-6, 273E1
Ottawa plan scored 9-30, Alberta agrees 10-4, 828E1, A2
NWT divisn OKd by assemb 11-6, 885B3

Labor & Employment—*See also 'Language Issue' below*
UAW bars Chrysler concessns 1-3, 14F1
Trudeau vows more jobs 1-12, 38C1
Dec '79 jobless down, '79 average rptd 1-16, 78F3
Jan jobless rate up, part-time workers cited 2-12, 148C2
Nurses win equal-pay suit 2-25, 171F2
Quebec teachers end strike 2-25, 211E1
Feb jobless rate steady, total labor force up 3-12, 211G1
Mar jobless rate rptd unchngd 4-10, 311A1
Female jobs legis planned 4-14, 293C1
Ford Ontario plant shut 4-15, 287F1
Civil Svc cuts recommended 4-16, 334A3
'80 jobless rate estimated 4-21, 310G2-A3
Apr jobless hike rptd 5-13, 388E2
Const talks vowed 5-21, 377F1
Union wage hikes avg rptd 5-27, 406A2
Postal contract ratified 6-2, 443G3
Oshawa auto plant closing set 6-9; UAW workers stage sit-in 8-8—8-21, resume work 8-25, 650B3
Abitibi contract talks fail 6-20, paperworkers strike 6-27; CNTU follows suit 7-1, 497G1-F2
Liberals back guaranteed annual income 7-4—7-6, 543E2
Jan-June auto worker layoffs rptd 7-5, 520A3
US median income compared 7-16, 562G2
Abitibi strike ends 7-31, 603B2
July auto layoffs cited 8-7, 618E1
Minumum wage hike rptd 8-11, study scores 8-18; Regan backs 8-20, 650G3-651D1
Labor costs rptd 8-12, 698E1
Air controllers stage job actns 9-5, 9-28, disciplined 9-26, 9-30, 808B2
Const talks held 9-8—9-13, 706E1
August jobless rise rptd 9-10, 687G1
'79 average income rptd, Alberta tops list 9-10, 728A3
Govt workers threaten strike 9-22—9-26, walk out 9-29; strike spreads, setlmt reached 10-1—10-14, 807G3
Sept jobless rate rptd down 10-14, 828C1
'81 budget set, unemployment forecast 10-28, oppositn heated 10-29—10-30, 858A1, C2
Oct jobless rise rptd 11-8, 941C1
Nov jobless drop rptd 12-10, 941D1

Language Issue
Quebec Liberals propose rights bill 1-10, 19B1
More French mgt hiring urged 1-23, 116F3

1976

Air pilots, controllers strike 6-20—6-28; Trudeau backs bilingualism 6-23, 481G1-A3
Marchand quits re airport pact 6-28, 496E2
French air controller slowdown 7-1, 496C3
Bilingual comm limits airport pact 7-6, 537F2
Air controller transfer benefits rptd 7-6, 537A3
Trudeau pushes bilingualism 7-9, 537B2
Rpt fed govt to ignore Quebec bill 7-10, 537F2
Air rules curb French 7-23, 7-27; CATCA bars strikes 7-26, Quebec union protests 7-27, 572A2
2 Liberal MPs to represent Quebec union 8-3, 587G2
Air Canada seeks fare hike 8-10, 587E2
Civil svc bilingualism debated 8-11—8-17, Bibeau rpt issued 8-17, 637C1
Air pilots ask French manuals 8-12, workers sue for bilingualism 8-20, 637B2
Bilingual govt workers get pay hike 8-31, 673B2
Ct OKs bilingual pilots, orders French manuals 9-7, 692C2
Quebec to aid air controllers 9-7, 692F2
Air Canada appeal rejected 9-22, 730D2
Air group rejects govt aid 9-22, 730F2
Air Canada OKs French 9-29, 790G1
Trudeau parlt speech cites policy 10-12, 771B3
Defense min quits, replaced 10-13, 790D1
Quebec eases rules re immigrant students 11-2, 851A2

1977

Quebec orders immigrants French schl shift 1-24, 113F3
Quebec to end English immigrant progrm 1-25, 114A1
Pilots OK St Hubert bilingualism, controllers score 2-15, 133F1
Pilots fined for '76 strike 2-16, 133C1
Levesque affirms Eng-French coexistence 3-8, 179A2
Quebec white paper vs bilingualism 4-1, 254B2; Trudeau scores 4-5, 281F2
Quebec language bill introduced 4-27, Trudeau scores 4-28, 346F2
Quebec hiring stand rptd eased 5-17, 425A3
PQ rejcts English-schl ban 5-29, 425G2
Ottawa backs language choice 6-21, Trudeau comments 6-23, 505F1-A2
Quebec bill withdrawn 7-8, revised bill introduced 7-12; Trudeau, business ldrs score 7-13, 7-14, 561E1
Comm backs bilingual air traffic 7-8, 561A3
Quebec offer to provs 7-22; reactn 7-27—7-29, 596D3
English parents back rebel school bds 7-25, 597C1
French controllers reject strike 8-7—8-10, 616G1
Provs rejct Quebec deal, OK educ study 8-19, 653A1
Inuit protest Quebec bill 8-22—8-26, Crees dissociate 8-26, 671F2
Quebec passes bill, chngs noted 8-26, 671G1
Montreal Prot schl bds defy bill 8-29, educ min warns 9-2, 694D1, F1
Quebec schl admin detailed 694E1
'71-76 French populatn rptd 8-29, 742F1
Inuit protest continues; Cree rift widens, Levesque scores govt 8-30—9-2, 693E3
Quebec special-status offer rejected 9-9, 741F3
Inuit protest abates 9-22, 742C1
Civil svc bilingual rules revised 9-30, 763E2
Trudeau bars Quebec bill battle 10-6, 780C1
Ct voids Quebec bill documt proviso 10-6, 780A2
Bilingual cts, rights amendmt proposed in Throne Speech 10-18, 822G2
James Bay land pact becomes law 11-1, 862E3 ★

1978

Eng version of Bill 101 signed 2-1, 88C3
Free choice for teaching use OKd by premiers 2-22—2-23, 166D3
Liberals back bilingualism, fed funding 2-26, 145A3
Ottawa sets fund for ct challenges 3-10, 188C2
Fed bilingual svc held inadequate, Bill 101 scored 3-21, 225F3
Insurance co shareholders OK move 4-25, 311D2-A3
Rights guarantees proposed in new constitutn 6-12, 451G1
Const legis presented, guarantees cited 6-20, 472E3, 473A1
Appeals ct upholds airport French ban 6-29, Trudeau backs 6-30, 515B1
Quebec OKs English in corp offices 7-19, 571C2
Montreal Prot schls end bill defiance, RCs to continue 7-31, 613G2
Fed bilingual bonus end planned 8-16, 666E2
New Francophone ldr named 9-7, 721F3
Const talks: guarantees opposed by provs 10-30—11-1, 866A2, C2
Quebec loses language requiremt appeal 11-28, 964A1

1979

Unity Task Force backs Quebec, urges minority rights protectn by provs 1-25; Trudeau reacts 1-26, 74F2, C3
Const reforms debated 2-5–2-6, 114A1
French premr assured re rights 2-8, 133E3
Bilingual budget cut set 2-19, 168E3
Yalden rpt chrgs bilingual lag, scores budget cut 2-20, 168B3
Social Credit ldr quits 2-22, 189F1
Liberal MP joins PCs 3-7, 189D1
Civil svc bilingual bonus extended 3-21, Yalden scores 3-22, 234A1
Clark backs const guarantees re schooling 3-27, 266F3
Quebec rpt cites cos exit, job losses 5-26, 405B3
Quebec offcl language decisn reserved by Sup Ct, Manitoba case cited 6-11, 484A1
US asbestos unit challenges Quebec expropriatn law 6-21, 484D2
'80 bilingual air control set 8-21, reactn 8-22, 8-24, 650D3
Quebec job losses rptd 9-5, 750F1
Montreal Star closes 9-25, 729D1
US asbestos unit takeover prepared 10-4, 772A1
Sup Ct voids Bill 101 parts, Manitoba law 12-13, 948C3
US asbestos unit wins stay 12-13, 949A1
Quebec restores English 12-14, 967B2

1980

BP hq to move from Montreal 1-26, 116F3
Yalden rpt: bilingualism effort failing 4-22, 351A1
'O Canada' proclaimed natl anthem 7-1, 497C1
Const talks held 9-8—9-13, 706D1

Medicine & Health

1976

Morgentaler freed from jail 1-26, 72G1
Morgentaler acquittal upheld 3-15, 537B3
Flu immunizatn shots set 3-30, 238E3
3d Morgentaler acquittal 9-18, chrgs dropped 12-10, 946C1
Flu vaccine limit set 9-28, 795F2
Prov insurnc subsidy OKd 12-7, 945F1; 12-14, 962A2

1977

Yellowknife arsenic pollutn chrgd 1-16, probe set 1-18, 61E1
Hospital drug deaths rptd 2-28, 224E2
Ottawa backs abortn clinics 3-4, 237A3
Saccharin ban set 3-9, 177E1
Saccharin ban delayed 4-19, 304B1
Laetrile smuggling into US rptd 5-6, 375C3
Yellowknife probe rptd 6-6, 447E3
Saccharin linked to human cancer 6-17, 530D3
Anglican church gets euthanasia rpt 8-17, drops abortn debate 8-18, 732G1
Ulcer drug Tagamet OKd in US 8-23, 748E2
RCMP data access bared 11-14, 882F1
RCMP file access probe set 12-1, 945A2

1978

Brain neurotransmitter measurability rptd by McMaster Univ 334B2
Quebec to control medical treatmt entry 2-20, 146C1
'78-79 spending plan unveiled 2-22, 145C3
RCMP Ontario file access admitted 3-1, 209F1
Dialysis data rptd 4-27, 578A2
Saskatchewan A-safeguards backed 6-8, 647D2
Polio cases confrmd in 3 provs 8-10, 635B3
Provs score fed aid cuts 9-11, 739D1
BC addict treatmt law set 12-18, 1013B3

1979

Provs warned re health-care funds 3-12, OHIP MDs rptd leaving plan 3-13, 211B1
Broadbent backs govt paymt system 3-29, 266F3
Radiatn study urged 10-3, 772E1
Mississauga chlorine spill evacuatn 11-11–11-14, 871D3; evacuees compensated 11-19, 927C2

1980

Nurses win equal-pay suit 2-25, 171F2
Valium mfr convicted 2-26, 116E2-C3
US health costs, infant mortality rates compared 7-16, 562C3
MDs scored in rpt 9-23, 687A2

Middle East Relations

1978

UN rights comm res on Israel, PLO 2-14, 99A2, B2
Leb peace force (Unifil) formed 3-19, 197D2; **for peacekeeping developments, see MIDDLE EAST—LEBANON**
Mideast oil undersells Venez 4-16, 332A1
Arab boycott compliance rpt issued, disclosures pledged 5-30; Westinghouse unit named 6-1, 435C2
UNDOF mandate renewed 5-31, 400B2
US peace force proposal rptd backed 8-31, 673G1
Bell Canada bias in Saudi ordrd ended 9-11, guidelines issues 9-21, 772F3

1979

'70 Israel envoy kidnap chrg cited 1-6, 19A2
Clark in Israel 1-14–1-17, Jordan 1-17–1-18, 57E2
UN rights comm res for Palestinian state opposed 2-21, 148F1
Ontario anti-Arab boycott law scored 3-20, 267A1
Saudi-Air Canada pact rptd 5-7, 467F3
Israel emb in Jerusalem promised 6-5, 424B1
Israel Emb move plans protested by Arabs 6-7, 6-19, Mideast mission studied 6-14, 467B3
Israel Emb move delayed, Mideast study set 6-23, 502F1
Iraq threatens oil cutoff 6-27, Arab League halts econ ties 6-29, 502B2
Israel Emb move, refugee admissns plan scored by Trudeau 7-19, 563D2
Stanfield tours Mideast 9-9–10-20, warns vs Israel Emb chng 10-20; move dropped 10-29, 833B2
Arab deal losses, Israel Emb move linked 10-18–10-29, 833D2, G2

1980

Canada aids 6 US diplomats flee Iran, closes Teheran emb 1-28; Clark denies pol aim 1-29; Iran warning dismissed 1-30, 66C1-B3
Iran emb escapee airs more details 2-12, 106E1
Israel emb controversy, PC defeat linked 2-18, 121G1
Stanfield rpt backs more PLO ties 2-29, 230C3
Iran sanctns asked by US 4-13, 281D2
Iran sanctns imposed 4-23, 298B3
Iran protests cultural exhibitn bar, Egypt pavillion rental 7-3, 520F3-521B1
8 honored for Iran escape role 7-25, 578A1
UN res on Palestinian state opposed 7-29, 572F1

1977

Monetary, Trade & Aid Issues (including all foreign economic developments)—*See also 'Atomic Energy' and 'Energy' above, 'Payments Issues' and 'Uranium' below*
Quebec W Ger bond sale 159A1
Cuban boats fined, patrol costs noted 1-4, 7F1
$ nears US parity 1-5, 17E3
Intl investors score Saskatchewan, Manitoba; rebuttal 1-6, 17G3
French trade min in Canada 1-9—1-12, Quebec 1-11, 43D1
In UK sterling balances pact 1-10, 20C2
Ghana loan rptd 1-13, 48G1
Arab boycott ban urged 1-13, 60F2
US TV ad deletn policy halted 1-21, 60G3
ICFTU S Africa boycott fails 1-21, 67B3
'76 trade surplus, paymts deficit rptd 1-21, 2-21, 133D3
Levesque asks US business investmt, sees asbestos industry natlzatn 1-25; reactn 1-26—1-28, 81D3
Canada cos '76 US expansn rptd 1-25, 132F3
Bank of Amer group cancels IBEC loan 1-26, 123D2
Johns-Manville delays expansn 1-28, 82D1
'76 factory wage study rptd 1-28, 158A3
IMF SDR defined 87G2
Arab boycott compliance rpts ordrd, aid barred 2-16, 158E3
Australia limits beef sales 2-17, 179C1
Norwegian fishing ship fined 2-22, 147A2
US fishing zone agrmt rptd 2-23, 132B3
NHL team gets loan 2-23, 164E1
US wheat-price pact agreed 2-25, 158F2

1978

Monetary, Trade, Aid & Investment—*See also 'Atomic Energy' and 'Energy' above*
'75 US, other forgn investmt total rptd 1-10, 70B3
US tariff cuts, corp disclosure agrmt, other econ cooperatn set 1-17; US ties seen welcome 1-23, 53G2, E3
US estimated annual trade rptd 1-19, 53F3
EC imposes steel dumping levies 1-23, 80B2
'77 merchandise trade surplus, exports, imports rptd up 1-28, 88G3
C$ falls below 90¢ 2-1—2-20; forgn borrowing set to boost C$ 2-21, 129D3
Montreal bank curbs Jamaica operatn 2-3, 95A1
USSR trade min canceled visit 2-14, 111A1
Brazil, N Amer farm equipmt sales drop rptd 2-15, 146E1
Steel dumping measures rptd 2-21, 244G2-B3
US bond sales, other credits rptd 2-27—3-13; C$ sinks 3-8, recovers 3-11, 188B1
Bank rate hiked 3-8, prime rates 3-9, 187G3
'77 paymts deficit rptd 3-10, 187G3
Bank of Nova Scotia bars Peru loan refinancing 3-10, 353F1, B2

1979

Monetary, Trade, Aid & Investment—*See also 'Atomic' and 'Energy' above*
Peru bank debt renegotiated 1-2, 22C3
C$ rises vs US$ 1-3, 6A2
US fishing talks progress seen 1-10, 37A1
Poland econ to be monitored by bank 1-11, 59F3, G3
Taiwan trade rise cited 1-15, 27C3
US Atlantic fish pact drafted 1-23, 95D3
Levesque: indep Quebec would seek US investmt 1-25, 74F3
C$ below 84¢ 1-31; '78 forgn reserve expenditure rptd 2-2, 95A2
French premr in trade talks 2-8–2-9, 133E3
Carter Westn econ summit warning to Japan rptd 2-10, rpt disputed 2-15, 160F1
Japan loan to boost C$ set 2-14, Swiss loan sought 2-28, 153E1-A2
'78 export value rptd up; C$ value vs US $, 10 other currencies rptd down 2-27, 168F2
US labor ldrs urge shoe import cap 3-6, 207C1
'78 forgn deficit rise rptd 3-7, 210E2
C$ above 85¢ 3-12–3-16, 210F2
Food duties cut 3-12, 210F3
Mack Trucks to mkt Renaults 3-19, 283B1
DR Royal Bank loan OKd 3-20, 256B3

1980

Monetary, Trade, Aid & Investment
See also 'Atomic Energy', 'Energy' above, 'Soviet-Afghan' below
Clark seeks more trade 1-2, 37G3
Thomson buys FP Publicatns 1-11, 38G1
Pacific orgn studied 1-20, 78C2
Mex silver, gold sales tax scored 1-25, 68G3
'79 merchandise trade surplus up 2-2, 96G1-B2
'79 US mfg investmt rptd 2-6, 92C3
Valium mfr convicted re price-cutting 2-6, 116E2-C3
Trudeau vows forgn investmt scrutiny; US investmts cited 2-19, 121E2
Turkey aid sought 2-19, 135D3
C$ over 87 cents 2-21, 148G1
Natlst trend seen in Cabt 3-3, 171E1
Bahamas bank looting suit rptd 3-3, 229C1
Brazil oil loan rptd 3-5, 191F1
'79, 4th 1/4 current acct deficit down 3-8, 211B2
C$ below 86 cents 3-10, 191F3
C$ at 84 cents 3-24, 253D1
S Africa arms sales admitted by US-Canada co 3-25, 278F1
US farmers ask potato imports ban 3-27, 368D2
C$ nears record low 4-2, US loan limits urged 4-14, 334D2
'79 US investmt rptd 4-8, 329C1
'79 debt rptd up 4-11, 310A3

1976

Obituaries
Caouette, Real 12-16, 970D1
MacMillan, H R 2-9, 160E3
Penfield, Wilder 4-5, 316C1
Walsh, Eric 2-14, 524G3

Prisons & Prisoners
'74-76 BC incidents cited 789F3-790B1
BC guards ban overtime, curtail duties 9-9, reach accord 9-20, 789C3
Wilkins quits 9-17, probe set 9-20, 809C1
BC convicts riot 9-24, seize hostages 9-27; hostages freed, demands met 9-28—10-1, 789F2
Montreal unrest 9-24—10-5, 790B1
Therrien resignatn asked 10-1, ct actn warned 10-5, 789D3
Therrien to honor pact 836C3
BC convict transfer set 10-11, 789E3
Ontario unrest 10-16—10-17, 790D1
BC guards drop suit plan 10-19, 836B3
Ontario bars prisoner deals 10-20, 836D3

1977

Quebec asbestos natlzatn eased 2-28; Johns-Manville to resume expansn 3-7, 254F2
US sets 200-mi fishing limit 3-1, 147G1
Australia backs US wheat-price pact 3-1, 179C1
'76 forgn exchng mkt tensns rptd 3-2, 188D3
US food import costs up 3-11, 3-15, 200E2
US execs sentncd for Sovt sales 3-14, 203F2
Norway in seal hunt 3-15, 237F3
'76 paymts, capital flow rptd 3-16, 218C2
Forgn investmt rules eased, '76 new projects rptd 3-23, 218G2
Kenya holds rep re Canada rail contract 5-4, 393C1
At 7-natn econ summit 5-7—5-8, 357A1-358B2
Intl consortium OKs Egypt aid 5-11—5-12, 390C3
GATT to study US ruling on Japan elec duties 5-23, 416C2
$ drops 6-1, US bond issue cited 6-6, 448D1
N-S $1 bln aid plan backed 6-3, 437E2
Group of 10 membership cited 438F1
US-Canada trust com rptd set 6-18, 525G2
IWC cuts whaling quotas 6-24, 496G3
US interim fish pact OKd 6-25, 525F2
ASEAN backs ties 6-27—6-29, 537E1
Zaire debt rescheduled 7-7, 583E1
W Ger Leopard, Lockheed Orion deals set 7-13, 579E3
Temporary fishing rights pact signed 7-26, 688D3
$ down, paymts deficit cited 7-27, 597D1
US scores trust probe-blocking laws 8-8, 630A1
$ at 8-yr low 8-12, 634D3
Provs ask greater US trade role 8-19, 653A2
Spain-Venez RR pact signed 9-10, 805A1
US textile duties cut 9-12, 705F2-A3
Asia investmt sought 9-22—10-4; Japanese, Hong Kong business ldrs score 9-27, 10-4, 780F2
Xerox OKs IBM patent use 9-23, 764D1
USSR grain sales rptd 9-30, 948C3
China min asks trade hike 10-4—10-7, 801E1
Finance mins back free trade 10-5—10-6, 780C2
Quebec ct upholds US chem co suit 10-6, 780B2
$ falls; paymts deficit, US interest rates cited 10-17, 792D3
$ hits 40-yr low 10-18—10-24; govt bars money curbs 10-20, sets credit deal 10-27, 841A3
Japan, W Ger, S Africa steel dumping chrgd 10-18, 862G3
Intl nickel cartel asked 10-21, US dumping seen 10-24, 924B1
Forgn aid progrm scored, Haiti scandal cited 10-27; Dupuy defends 11-3, 863B1
8 US cos chrg steel dumping 11-3, 836E3
4th in China forgn trade 11-7, 882D3
Poland wheat sale rptd 11-9, 987B2
US OKs Inco acquisitn of ESB 11-11, 918E3
Australia livestock banned 11-23, 922G3
$ rptd down 11-30, recovers 12-8, 932E3, 933C1
US TV ad deletn upheld 11-30, 946F1
Footwear imports curbed 12-1; US EC protests rptd 12-14, 982G3
France, Quebec OK 5-yr copper deal 12-6, 965B3
US vs Revere sale to Alcan 12-9, 1004F3
Arab boycott list disclosure barred 12-15, 12-16, 1010A2
St Lawrence Seaway toll hike set 12-16, 982D3
S Africa econ ties cut 12-19; '76 trade rptd 1016C2
Massey Ferguson admits overbilling 12-29, 1010F2

Obituaries
Fortin, Andre 6-24, 532A3
Johnson, Harry G 5-8, 452C3

Payments Issues
Polysar admits illegal rebates 2-8, 114B2
US Boeing probe pact signed 3-15, 200F1
Polysar scored in Parlt rpt 7-7, 541G3
Seagram admits paymts 10-14, 818B2
Quebec police raid prov pol parties 11-30, 945G3; liquor co kickbacks alleged 12-6, 965E2
US carnival co '75 Alberta police payoffs rptd 12-6, 12-8, 965B2

Prison Issues—*See 'Crime' above*

Press & Broadcasting
Ad deletns from US progrms ended 1-21, 60G3
Parlt OKs TV coverage 1-25, 115E2
CBC bias probe asked 3-4, 179A3
3 guilty in '72 APLQ break-in 5-26, 426D1; freed, Quebec sets probe 6-16, 484F3
US TV influence scored 6-14, 485G2
LaMarsh rpt scores media violence, asks curbs 6-15; reactn 6-15—6-16, 485G1
'72 Quebec APLQ break-in dvpts 6-20—6-23, 541F2, B3
CBC bias chrgd, reorganizatn asked 7-20, 579F1
ACTRA, film producers feud re forgn stars 8-31—9-12, 742D2
Quebec APLQ break-in probe opens 10-3, 800F3
RCMP break-in authorizatn disputed 10-25—10-26, 841F1

1978

UK prime min urges Bonn summit plan 3-14, sees Carter 3-23, 226D3
Trudeau woos NY investors, backs free trade 3-21, 225F2
US TV statn ordered dropped re ads 3-28, 226A2 *
AMC, Renault plan joint distributn 3-31, 283G3
C$ falls below 88¢; bank rate hiked, US $ fund increased 4-3, 244D1
C$ in new SDR basket 4-3, 300F3
US thoroughbred imports banned 4-3, 539G2
C$ hits 45-yr low 4-4, 235D1
Lockheed deal collapse cited 4-13, 287B1
C$ falls below 87¢ 4-13; boosted by W Ger loan 4-28, US talks 5-1, 328B1
Mideast oil undersells Venez 4-16, 332A1
S Africa business code issued 4-28, 377F1
US loan set 5-3, C$ rises above 90¢ 5-15, 370E2
US blocks fishing boats 5-5, treaty problems cited 5-9, 350B2
Forgn-investmt ban enforcemt urged 5-16, 392E1
Quebec hints new currency 5-16, C$ falls below 90¢ 5-17—5-23, 412C3
MP chrgs C$ speculatn 5-20, retracts 5-24, 412F3
US fish talks adjourn 5-26, 413D1
Arab boycott compliance rpt issued, disclosures pledged 5-30; Westinghouse unit named 6-1, 435C2
US fishing boats banned, US retaliates 6-2, 6-4, 435D1
Subsidiaries ordrd to comply with US law 6-2, 435B3
Zaire aid OKd 6-13—6-14, 478A1
1st ¼ trade balance rptd 6-23, 495G2
Forgn competitn concern voiced 7-6, 531D2, G2
C$ rises vs US$ 7-14, 523C3
At 7-natn Bonn econ summit 7-16—7-17, 543C3, 544B2, G2
C$ down 7-25; bank, prime rates raised 7-26, 8-1, US rate rise cited 7-26, 591B1
US sees Ottawa 'interventn practices' as trade pacts danger 8-1, 613E2
IBM, Xerox settle patent dispute 8-1, 665F2
'77 auto trade deficit with US rptd 8-2, 613F2
Ford plans Ontario plant, US scores Ottawa grant 8-3, US-Canada offcls meet 8-4, 613B2
C$ rises vs US$ 8-15, 622F1
Royal Bank in Mex agri loan 8-15, 690G1
Forgn aid freeze planned 8-16, 666E2
1st ½ trade surplus, 2d ¼ shrinkage, July deficit rptd 8-25; C$ weakness linked 9-11, 703F3, 704E1
July merchandise trade deficit rptd 8-29, 667A1
US TV statns protest tax law 8-29, 686A3
C$ Aug defense costs rptd 9-5, 703D3
Spain joint Venez RR deal rptd 9-7, 821G3
2d ¼ record paymts deficit rptd 9-8, 704C1
C$ hits 45-yr low 9-11; bank, prime rates hiked 9-11, 9-12, money growth targets narrowed 9-11, C$ rises 9-12, 703D3, F3 *
Bell Canada bias in Saudi ordrd ended 9-11, guidelines issued 9-21, 772F3
C$ dips 9-26, 10-2; standby credit deals renegotiated 10-12, govt bonds offered 10-18, 813E2
Saskatchewan potash export curbs ruled illegal 10-3, 773D1
June '77-78 US$ rise rptd 10-4, 790F1
US$ declines 10-30; rescue plan set, $ recovers 11-1, 825E2, 826A1
Oreck trust case refused by US Sup Ct 10-30, 832A3
US union asks United Tech-Carrier merger bid reviewed 10-30, 896F2
Alberta, Saskatchewan vs export controls 10-31, 866C3
Bank, prime rates hiked; US discount rate rise cited 11-6, 879G2
S Africa arms sales suspected 11-6—11-7, 904E2
USSR Ladas rptd sold 11-13, 1020F3-1021A1
Ottawa budget, US growth estimates linked 11-16, 901E1
US exports rptd down, 3d ¼ GNP lags 11-27, 944E3
Chile trade boycott impact rptd 12-15, 1014A2
Simpsons-Sears merger blocked 12-18, 986B1

Obituaries
Atkinson, Walter 1-6, 96C1
Robson, Mark 6-20, 540F3

Press & Censorship
Prov film censorship upheld, '73 Nova Scotia case cited 1-19, 111A2
Press freedom rptd by IAPA 10-13, 829A2
Newspr letters to ed curbed 11-21, 964C2

1979

Ontario anti-Arab boycott law scored 3-20, 267A1
'78 $ drop effects cited 3-23, 234B2
US multinatls cited re tech lag 3-24, 234F1
Trudeau ties $ fall to PQ 3-29, 266C3
Broadbent for forgn investmt curb 3-29, 267A1
Poland loan signed 3-30, 279G2
Hungary loans cited 3-30, 279C3
Australia wheat accord set 4-3, 253A1
'78 debt rptd C$118 bln 4-7, 311E3
C$ tops 87¢ 4-9, 284D3
Brascan seeks Woolworth 4-9, spurned 4-11; other dvpts 4-12—4-23, 303B3-304C2
US scores Air Canada bargain fares 4-18—4-20, 329E2
GATT pact signed, aircraft tariff cuts seen 4-19, 273B2
Brascan control sought by Edper 4-30—5-1; Woolworth bid delayed 5-25; offer dropped, suits setld 5-29; Edper renews takeover effort 5-30, 440C2
Quebec plans US asbestos co expropriatn, C$ drops 5-2, 352D2
Saudi-Air Canada pact signed, Arab boycott clause rptd 5-7, 467F3
Broadbent scores forgn investmt 5-13, 368F3
$ fall, jobless rate linked 5-15, 378D1
Imports cited in econ controls rpt 5-24, 405F1
C$ below 85¢, recovers 6-4, 444B1
US trade rptd hurt by metric conversn 6-6, 444C2
Edper completes Brascan takeover 6-14, 6-29, 542D3
Arabs halt bank deposits, Bell Canada rptd warned by Saudis 6-19, 467B3
Quebec asbestos takeover scored in US 6-19; expropriatn bill enacted, Asbestos Corp sues 6-21; takeover halted 6-27, 484F1
Iraq threatns oil cutoff 6-27, Arab League halts econ ties 6-29, 502B2
Import tariffs cut 7-12, 543C1
US discount rate hike spurs bank rate rise 7-23, 562E3
'79 record trade deficit seen 7-24, 613D1
US asbestos co loses suit 7-25, 563A1
US recessn seen, 2d ¼ trade impact forecast 8-7, 601C1
Denison Mines bid accepted by Reserve Oil 8-14, agrmt ended 10-31, 986B3
US airline warns flight cutoffs re bilingualism 8-24, 651C1
US tuna boats seized 8-26, Canada tuna exports embargoed 9-4, 667D1
US halts Air Canada discount fares 8-30, 667D2
US econ, GNP drop linked 8-31, 667C1
Gold Maple Leaf coin on sale 9-6, 684C3
PQ econ policy paper issued 9-6, 750C1
US discount rate hike, bank rate increase linked 9-7, 684A3
C$ above 86¢ 9-11, 684B3; 9-13, 676D2
Crown co US unit sale set 9-28, 749G2
US asbestos co takeover prepared 10-4, 771D3
US discount rate, paymts deficit linked to bank rate hike 10-9, 771G2
C$ below 86¢ 10-9, 771C3
AMC to sell Renault cars in Canada 10-12, 784B3
Arab deal losses, Israel Emb move linked 10-18—10-29, 833D2, G2
C$ up 10-25, 811G3
Mex vegetable prices probed by US 10-30, 831A2
PQ white paper presented 11-1, 853F1
3d 1/4 exports rptd up; US econ downturn impact seen 11-29, 926G3, 927A1
Gold Maple Leaf rptd preferred to USSR coin 11-29, 929G1
9-mo trade surplus error rptd 12-10, 967F2
US asbestos co wins stay 12-13, 948G3
Dominion Bridge loses Warner & Swasey bid 12-17, 986F2
PQ referendum bill presented 12-17, 997C3
'Michelin Bill' OKd by Nova Scotia 12-28, 992F3
US $ closes down 12-31, 978F3

Obituaries
Bennett, Wm 2-23, 176F2
Diefenbaker, John G 8-16, 671A2
Dionne, Oliva 11-15, 932E2

Press & Censorship
Montreal-Matin closure rptd 1-6, 6D2
Toronto Sun secrecy trial barred 4-23, 311B2
Montreal Star closes 9-25, 729D1

1980

US asks Iran export ban 4-13, 281D2
Throne speech vows forgn takeover, meat import curbs 4-14, 293A1, C1
US F-18As purchase set 4-16, 293C2
Iran sanctns imposed 4-23, 298B3
US A-pact rptd 4-23, 429E1
Turner & Newall asbestos units sold to Quebec, US co sought 5-8, 371D3
Chrysler loan guarantees OKd 5-10, 383D2
Pacific cable planned 5-19, 387E3
C$ over 86 cents 5-21, 377A2
Mex credits set, joint projcts studied 5-27, 409A3
N&W, Southn RR merger sought 6-2, 427E2
Apr trade deficit rptd, US exports cited 6-3, 444A2
US co sets Oshawa plant closing 6-9; UAW workers stage sit-in 8-8—8-21, resume work 8-25, 650B3
US auto trade pact cited 6-12, 457A3
Atlantic fishing quota raised re US pacts ratificatn failure 6-12, 461B2
Labatt to brew Anheuser-Busch beer 6-17, 486D2
7-natn Venice summit 6-22—6-23, 473A1-474E1
US hit by paperworkers strike 6-27, 7-1, 497E2
Drought forces rise in US barley, corn imports 6-27, 520C2
US auto trade deficit up, sales down 7-5, 520G2, B3
Canada OKs F-18 deal 7-8, US discount offered 7-11, 543E3
Japan auto, trade talks held; US role cited 8-2—8-11, 618G1
June trade surplus rptd 8-2, 618F2
Sovt auto dumping chrgd 8-7; record sales rptd 8-8, 618C1-F1
'79 forgn-based oil co revenues rptd down 8-12, 618A1
S Africa arms seller fined 8-14, 618F2
MacGuigan on 3d World aid 8-26, rpt sees survival threatened 8-27, 669B1, E1
US trade drop, 2d 1/4 GNP decline linked 8-29, 668F2
July trade surplus rptd down 9-5, 687C1
Nicaragua debt rescheduled 9-5, 689G2
Current acct deficit widens 9-9, 687E1
US tax treaty signed 9-26, 748B2
Gold reserves rptd 9-30, Sept sales 10-3, 767E1
MacEachen scores forgn aid record 10-1, 766A3
C$ above 85 cents 10-3, 767E1
Aug trade surplus rptd up; US, Japan, Eur trade cited 10-4, 788G1
Algeria quake aid rptd 10-11, 776E1
Belzbergs buy Hunts' Bache stock 10-21, 867B3
Sovt 13-yr debt dispute rptd settled 10-22, 828B2
C$ below 85 cents 11-3, 871C2
Sept trade surplus drop rptd 11-19, 941E1
New Bank Act OKd 11-26, 920A2
Haiti aid talks shunned 12-8, 942C3
Current acct deficit narrows 12-9, 941G1
C$ at 47-yr low 12-11, 964F3
C$ below 83 cents 12-16, near 84 cents 12-31, 992F2
MacEachen scores US tight money policy 12-19, 992E2

Obituaries
Harsh, George 1-25, 104G2
Leger, Jules 11-22, 928F2
Lessage, Jean 12-11, 1004D2
McLuhan, Herbert Marshall 12-31, 1004F2
Smythe, Conn 11-18, 928E3

Press & Censorship
Freedom of info legis asked 1-11, 78G2
N Amer Newspaper Alliance replaced 3-3, 239E2
Freedom of info legis introduced 7-16, 562E3
Ottawa Journal, Winnipeg Tribune closings spur deals 8-27, 668G2-D3
Uruguay detains CBC rptr 11-7—11-10, 888B3

1976

Quebec—*See other appropriate subheads in this section; for separatist issue, see 'Government & Politics'; for Olympics, see under SPORTS*

1977

Quebec Separatist Issue—*See also 'Language Issue' above; for other Quebec news, see appropriate subheads in this section*
US immigratn rptd up 1-13, 43A2
Levesque: independnc 'inevitable' 1-25, Trudeau scores 1-26, 81D3, 82E1
Levesque seeks early vote 1-27, Trudeau stakes career 1-28, 113A3
Trudeau reassures US 2-22, Levesque discounts 2-23, 132G2, D3
Carter on issue 2-23, 126A3
Network bias probe asked 3-4, 179A3
Levesque opens Natl Assemb 3-8, 179G1
$ at 7-yr low 3-9, 179G2
Trudeau in unity plea 4-18—4-20, 346F1
Fed govt rpts cos exodus 4-28, reactn 4-28—4-30, 354C2
Chirac backs separatism 4-29, 346A3
Provs vs indepndnt Quebec econ ties 5-8, 425C3
France warned vs support 5-13, 389G1
Unity support seen in by-electns 5-24, 410A3
PQ modifies stand 5-29, 425E2
CBC bias chrgd 7-20, 579F1
Separatists behind in poll 8-17, 672B1
Independnc vote rules issued 8-24, 671E3
Bar assn backs unity 9-1, 694G1
Trudeau to rejct independnc vote 9-9, 742E1
Queen Eliz visit promotes unity 10-14—10-19, 822A2
Chretien links separatism, econ crisis 10-20, 822F3
Levesque in France, gets Legion of Honor 10-23—11-4; Ottawa scores 11-4, 862B2, B3
Trudeau sees Alberta, BC premrs 10-31—11-1, 882A3
France clarifies Quebec ties 12-9, 965G2

RCMP & Other Intelligence Issues
'71 blacklist revealed 1-25, 1-26, access disputed 1-26—2-3, 97A1
Blacklisted cleared 5-24, 426C1
RCMP denies '70 document theft 5-25, cleared 5-27, 426A1
3 police guilty in '72 break-in 5-26, 426D1
Fox, Goyer sued 6-13; deny blacklist 6-29, 541G2-B3
3 police freed in '72 break-in 6-16; MPs score, Quebec sets probe; govt claims cover-up 6-16—6-17, 484F3
RCMP '72 Quebec break-in dvpts 6-20—6-23, 541F2, B3
RCMP probe set, prov probes cited 7-6, 541E2
Police tap curbs in criminal code amendmts 7-18, 596C2
USSR envoy chrgd as indl spy 7-20, 579F3
Security-risk suspect list rptd 8-9—8-13, Broadbent protests 8-10, 633C3
RCMP admits files on MPs, Clark scores 8-17; RCMP clarifies 8-18, 653B2
RCMP probe of NDP members rptd 8-25, 705B2
Fox vague on Broadbent RCMP file 8-29, 705E1
RCMP admits MP tapped 9-20, 742A2
Quebec RCMP probe opens 10-3, RCMP denies documts 10-4, 800F3
Alberta RCMP probe rptd 10-20, 841B2
More RCMP chrgs hinted; '72 barn burning, dynamite theft rptd 10-20, 841D2
RCMP '72 raid authorizatn disputed 10-25—10-26, 841F1
RCMP probe overseer named 10-25, 841B2
'73 PQ break-in bared 10-28; Trudeau, Levesque, Keable comment 10-28, 11-2, 840E3
Tap device found by PC MP 10-31, 841E2
2d tap device found by PC ldr 10-31; Parlt informed, RCMP role disputed 11-1, 11-3, 11-4, 902C2
Fox admits '72 raid info 10-31, defends PQ surveillnc 11-3, 902G3
Quebec probe hears '72 barn burning, dynamite theft testimony 11-1; scope widened 11-3, 902B3
NDP '71-73 surveillnc bared 11-1, 11-3, 903B1
Trudeau backs 11-2, 882F2
Quebec probe asks '73 PQ break-in documents 11-2, Fox limits 11-11, 903A1
'72 raid authorizatn, prior knowledge chrgd 11-2—11-11, 903D1
Fox defends watchdog role 11-6, 11-13, 882A2
Mail opening, break-ins, med file abuses confrmd 11-9—11-14, 882A1
Army mail opening, union spying bared 11-11—11-12, 882C2
Defns min admits spying 11-14, 945D3
'Featherbed' files on Trudeau, Cabt mins chrgd 11-15; Fox confrms 11-16, 923A2
Trudeau discounts 'Featherbed' impact 11-16; defends RCMP mail opening, bars Cabt resignatns 11-18, 923C2
Offenses vs Arab residents, other improprieties rptd 11-16—11-23, 945C3
Postmaster gen admits RCMP cooperatn 11-17, 923F2
Drug probe raids 11-17—12-8, arrests rptd 12-15, 1010A3
CIA link alleged; mail surveillnc, interrogatn rptd 11-23, 11-24, 923C1
Ottawa fails to halt Quebec probe 11-23, 11-25, 923G1
Fox sets security svc curbs 11-24, 945A3
Ottawa Univ tap role denied 11-29, 945F3

1978

Quebec Separatist Issue—*See also 'Language Issue' above; for other Quebec news, see appropriate subheads in this section*
Trudeau threatens force vs separatn 1-1; reactn 1-2, 1-3, 6F3-7C1
FLQ amnesty sought by '70 Cross kidnapers 1-3, 7C1
US-Ottawa ties seen improved 1-23, 53E3
PQ denies forgn funding 2-3, 129A3
Liberals play down separatn issue 2-24—2-26, 145E2
Trudeau cites re econ problems 3-21, 225A3
CLC backs Quebec right to choose 4-3, 266D2
Emigratn to other provs up 4-25, 311A3
Liberal poll standing rptd down 5-2, 350G1
Levesque ties fed electn, referendum dates 5-14, 370E1
Cultural policy presented 6-6, 473F1
Independnc referendum law passed 6-23, 495B2
PQ loss seen re by-electn 7-5, 514B3
FLQ convicts paroled 7-16, 7-17, 556D3
Landry named Francophone ldr 9-7, 721E3
Singer wins '70 arrest suit 9-12, 755D2
Levesque asks sovereignty-fed assn agrmt 10-10; Ryan rebuts 10-11, 837C1
Levesque joins Const power-sharing talks 10-31—11-1, 866F2
FLQ 6th Cross kidnaper alleged 11-2, 11-8; RCMP informer denied 11-6, 880B1
PQ backs Levesque plan 12-3, 963E3-964A1
Cossette-Trudels return, arrested 12-13, 964A2

RCMP & Other Intelligence Issues
Fox bares fake FLQ communique, informant recruiting tactics; stresses document control 1-9, 35C1
FLQ '72 infiltratn rptd 1-10, 35A2
RCMP '74 break-in outside Quebec bared 1-11, 1-12, 35C2
APLQ '72 raid aim disputed 1-13, 35E2
'73 PQ break-in explained 1-19—1-26, 88E2-C3
PQ forgn funding, spy infiltratn alleged 2-2; PQ denies 2-3, 129B3
13 Sovts expelled for spying 2-9, 110D3, 111C1
Quebec probe halted by ct 2-21, 129E2
'78-79 hiring increase planned 2-22, 145C3
'75 wiretap of ex-solicitor gen, MP chrgd 2-22, called accident; US informer cited 2-27, 166F1
Govt file access OKd 3-1, 188E1
Ontario health file access admitted 3-1, 209F1
USSR spy rpt leaked 3-7, newspr chrgd 3-17; MP cleared 3-7, 208F3, 209B1
USSR chrgs natl framed re spy 3-15, 209E1
2 chrgd in '77 PC MP taps 4-3, 244G1
Goyer to resign 4-6, 287F1
Tap cover-up bared 4-11; warrantless break-ins revealed 4-18, 311F3-312B1
Blais bars actn vs officers 4-24, 311B3
Candidate monitoring rptd 4-26, Trudeau admits 4-27, 328E1
Documents rptd destroyed 4-26, 328E2
Treu sentncd for documt possessn 5-5; secret trial scored 6-13—6-14, 451B3
Quebec probe rule delayed 5-26, inquiry closed 5-31, 451F2
Alberta probe rptd 7-25, 590D2
Poll finds mail-opening backed 8-30, 686C3
'72 dynamite theft, barn burning admitted 9-13, 837B3
Alberta bars criminal chrgs 9-27, 837A3
McDonald probe asks Cabt papers 10-13, granted 10-27; mins knowledge of illegalities chrgd 10-24, 837F1
RCMP agent protectn chrgd, denied 10-25, 837F2
Quebec probe limited by ct 10-31, 879B3
'70 Cross kidnap informer denied 11-6, 880E1

Soviet Satellite Issue
US alerts to Sovt satellite fall 57E1
USSR satellite falls in NW Terr 1-24; radiatn detected, debris found 1-25—2-1, 57A1
USSR gets satellite protest 1-25; US, USSR defend cooperatn 1-27, 1-28, 57D2
Satellite search cost rptd 2-3, paymt claim planned 2-13, 103E1
Satellite debris retrieved, Sovt scientist admits error 2-4, 103A1
USSR offers satellite damages 2-14, 238A2
Satellite search rptd ended 4-2, 238C2
Satellite search pressed, hazard feared; total cost cited 7-5, 514C3
Satellite search ends 10-18, 1013G2

1979

Quebec Separatism Issue—*See also other appropriate subheads in this section*
Lanctot returns, arrested 1-6, 19F1
Lanctot chrgd, bail set 1-11, 37B2
FLQ '69 bombing suspect returns, arrested 1-14, 37G1-A2; sentncd 3-26, 254C1
Unity Cncl rpts indifference 1-16, 57C1
Unity Task Force rpt backs free choice, more powers; Levesque shuns 1-25, 74A3-E3
French premr hedges issue 2-13, 133F3
Trudeau says ignoring 'treason' issue, ties $ fall to PQ 3-29, 266A3
PQ Cabt min quits, sees separatn defeat 5-17, 378B1
Business exodus rptd 5-26, 405A3
PQ conf opens, Levesque details limited autonomy plan 6-1; plan backed 6-3, 424E1-F2
Levesque sets '80 referendum, Ryan scores delay 6-21, 483D3
Trudeau backs unity 7-19, 563C2
Giguere cleared re '70 funds 7-20, 563F1
Cossette-Trudels sentncd 8-7, 632B3
Prov premrs rejct autonomy plan 8-17, 632C2
Job loss rptd 9-5, 750D1
PQ econ policy paper issued 9-6, 750C1
Alberta offers prov loan 9-13, 729A1
PQ poll: federalism backed 9-28, 749F3-750A1
Liberals score Trudeau policies 10-14, 812B2
PQ white paper presented, reactn 11-1-11-2, 853D1-D2
Lanctot sentncd 11-8, 872D1
PQ loses by-electns 11-14, 889G1-B2; 11-26, 907G3-908B1
NDP backs self-determinatn 11-22-11-25, 927G1
PQ referendum bill presented 12-20, 992E2

RCMP & Other Intelligence Issues
Keable inquiry reopens 2-13, 189D2
Treu cleared 2-20, 189A2
Security clearance review asked 2-23, 189C2
Ontario health plan probe continues 3-9, 189A3
Documts, ex-offcrs hold Cabt aware of RCMP lawbreaking 3-28-3-30, 253D2-E3
Allmand admits break-in knowledge 4-3-4-5, 311D2
Toronto Sun secrecy trial barred 4-23, 311C2
McIlraith: Cabt discussed lawbreaking 4-26, 329A2
Clark backs more RCMP power 5-13, 368F3
Emb wiretaps planned 7-4, 522F2
APLQ '72 break-in described by Dare 7-4, 522B3

1980

Quebec Separatism Issue
Clark asks improved ties 1-2, 37G3
Quebec Liberals set confederatn plan 1-10, 18E3
Trudeau victory speech stresses central govt 2-19, 121G2
Biron quits UN party, backs referendum 3-3, 230D1
Poll: majority vs separatn 3-7, 230A2
Drummond backs referendum 3-19, 230G1
Assemb OKs referendum bill 3-20, 230C1
Trudeau backs unity 4-14, 293E1
Referendum date set, Trudeau bars negotiatn 4-15, 293F1
Trudeau campaigns vs referendum in Montreal, Levesque scores 5-2, 350D2
NDP seeks const chng 5-11, 372A2
Referendum defeated 5-20, 377A1
Const talks held 9-8—9-13, 705G3

RCMP & Other Intelligence Issues
McDonald comm probe rpt issued: Secrets Act revisn, freedom of info legis asked; Treu accused of passing secrets 1-11, 78E2-E3
Sovt spy ring uncovered, 3 envoys expelled 1-21, 56F2; USSR expels diplomat 1-31, Canada chrgs retaliatn 2-7, 95E3
'71 suspect list rptd sent abroad 2-28, 192A1
Treu denied legal costs compensatn 3-17, 211D1
RCMP '70s sabotage unit rptd 4-20, 350A3
RCMP Cabt informers rptd 4-24, 350E3
2 guilty in '77 MP bugging fraud 4-28, 335A1

Soviet-Afghan Issue
Afghan aid cut off 1-5, 10B3
US backed on Sovt grain embargo 1-7, 9C2
Trudeau asks consultatn 1-7, PCs bar 1-8, 38D1
USSR credit, tech cuts set 1-11, 28A2
USSR Olympics move backed by Clark 1-11, 28C3; 1-21, 45A3
Sovt airline diverted to Montreal 1-11, 55C2
USSR grain sale increase barred 1-12, 27E3
3 Sovts expelled re spying 1-21, USSR links to Afghan invasn 1-22, 56F2
USSR, Canada, expel envoys 1-31, 2-7, 95E3
Trudeau eases Olympics boycott conditions 2-19, 121F2
USSR grain purchase rptd 2-29, 171E2
Olympic com rejcts Moscow boycott 3-30, 259G2
Olympic com sees boycott 4-14, 283A3
Moscow boycott backed, Olympic com scores 4-22, 325A3
Olympic com OKs Moscow boycott 4-26, 379B2
Canada Cup hockey tourn cancelled 4-30, 488B3
USSR May Day parade shunned 5-1, 354G2
Afghan frees UN offcl 6-22, 486B2
Grain embargo lifted 7-24, 577F3
Sovts scored at UN 9-22, 748G3-749B1
Sovts scored at CSCE conf 11-12, 863C1
Sovt grain embargo support ended, US-China pact cited 11-20, 900B2

Soviet Satellite Issue
USSR to pay for '78 crash 11-21, 920C3

1976

Sports—*See also 'Olympics' under SPORTS*
Sovt hockey tour ends 1-12, 56F1
NHL pres arraigned 4-22, 309B3
Canadiens win Stanley Cup 5-16, 404E3
Canada wins Canada Cup 9-15, 736F3

UN Policy & Developments
Abstains on rights comm resolutn vs Israel 2-13, 125E2
ILO rpts jobless rate 3-13, 297E3
Vs 2 WHO anit-Israel resolutns 5-17, 5-19, 355F1, D2
Vs UNESCO anti-Israel res 11-22, 879A1
ILO rpts strike data 11-29, 896D2

U.S. Relations—*See also 'Foreign Economic Developments' above*
Mackenzie King diaries publshd 1-1, 8F1
Protests Cuba airlift refueling 1-23, 106D2
New extraditn treaty 3-22, 238D3
Enders warns vs cut in ties 6-13, 438F3
Trudeau visits Ford, Clark visit cited 6-16, 481A3
O'Donnell on Canada strike 6-24, 481E2
Ship in US Bicentennial event 7-4, 488B3
Rpt finds ties strained 7-26, 587A3
Chowchilla kidnap suspects arrested 7-29, 560B1
US GOP platform text cites 8-18, 609D3
Diefenbaker accuses JFK 10-4, 837C1
US Lonetree Reservoir constructn protested 10-12, 945G3
Peltier extraditn set 12-17, 999B1

1977

Ontario med file access probe set 12-1, 945A2
Quebec '69 PQ break-in tap bared 12-1, 945E2
Tax data use confrmd 12-2, 945F2
McDonald royal comm hearings open 12-6; '72 news agency break-in, PQ info-gathering network detailed 12-7—12-8, 965C1
Alberta probe bares corruptn 12-6, 12-8, 965B2
Royal comm gets RCMP cooperatn pledge 12-7, 965D1
Parizeau, Levesque confrm PQ info-gathering network 12-9, 965A2
3d bid to halt Quebec probe foiled 12-11, 964F3
Quebec probe halt barred, suspensn cited 12-16, 982E2

Sports
'76 Olympic TV costs cited 2-3, 131A1
US NHL team gets loan 2-23, 164E1
Czechs keep hockey title 5-8, 430B2
WHA championship game 5-27, 430B1
US hockey player arrested 8-18, 1012F1
Montreal wins Grey Cup 11-27, 950E2
Lafleur named top male athlete 12-19, 1021E1

Trans-Alaska Pipeline—*See 'Energy' above*

UN Policy & Developments
Assemb, Cncl member 3F3, 4E1
Vs resolutn on Israel occupatn abuses 2-15, 107E2
Maputo conf rep bars S Africa, Rhodesia embargo 5-21, 399F2
Namibia vote abstentns 11-4, 851E1
Assemb condemns Israel occupatn 11-25, 910D2
S Africa oil, investmt ban abstentns 12-16, 1016A2

Uranium
Saskatchewan defends policy 1-6, 18C1
In US, Australia uranium collaboratn exchng 2-4—3-11; cartel agrmt denied 6-29, 624D3
Uranium cartel, Gulf role rptd 4-25; US probes 6-9—6-17; Macdonald blames US uranium embargo 6-16, 6-17, 479A2-480F2
Carter OKs uranium shipmt 5-6, 403C2
US-Canada trust com rptd set 6-18, 525A3
Australia lifts uranium ban 8-25, 693C3
Cartel trust probe opens 10-3, Denison scores 10-19, 895F2
Cartel info disclosure ban relaxed 10-14; ban lifted for MPs 11-10, 895C3
US pact OKd 11-15, 913D1
TVA sues producers 11-18, 895F1
Backs UK vs US cartel probe jurisdictn 12-1, 1003F3
Italy suit vs pricing policy rptd 12-13, 982B3
Italy supply pact rptd 12-15, 982A3
EC pact signed 12-20, 1010G1

U.S. Relations—*See also 'Energy', 'Monetary, Trade & Aid', 'Payments Issues' and 'Uranium' above*
IJC bd scores US Garrison projct 1-7, 60C3
Quebec emigratn bids rptd up 1-13, 43A2
'64-65 Seaborn Viet missn cover-up rptd 1-14, 97B3
Levesque in NY 1-21—1-25, 81D3
St Lawrence bridge pact signed 2-5, 133B1
Canada amb quits 2-14, policy dispute denied 2-17, 132D3
Trudeau Cong address scheduled 2-17, 127E3; in US 2-21—2-23, 132F2
US halts Garrison project 2-18, 133A1
Carter on Quebec issue 2-23, 126G2
Trudeau assassinatn plot rptd 2-23, 261A3
US prisoner exchng treaty 3-2, 200B1
Carter on water projects 3-16, 210C1
'70 US antiwar bomber arrested 4-9, 492C1
Canada '76 immigratn rptd 4-13, 389D2
Laetrile smuggling rptd 5-6, 375C3
Detroit sued on Lake Erie pollutn 5-6, 422F2
Towe named amb 6-3, 525A3
US TV influence scored 6-14, 485G2
Rpt asks TV shows cutback 6-15, 485A2
Canada detains Newton 6-25—6-29, 531G3
Trudeau sees Schmidt 7-6—7-12, scores Carter rights policy 7-14, 566F2
US ratifies prisoner exchng treaty 7-19, Carter signs enabling legis 10-28, 834E1
CBC reliance on US shows scored 7-20, 579D2
Controllers strike jams US airports 8-7—8-10, 616E1
Canada CP asks neutron bomb ban 8-8, 640A3
US hockey player arrested on drug chrgs 8-18, 1021F1
Provs ask greater role 8-19, 653G1
Trudeau at Panama Canal pact signing 9-7, 678C1
Actors' union bars US star 9-7, 742F2
IJC scores Garrison projct 9-19, 725G3
Cuba aid to US radicals rptd 10-9, 896A3
CIA link to RCMP alleged 11-23, 11-24, 923C1

1978

Sports
Queen's Plate metric conversn set 1-16, 89C1
US thoroughbred imports banned 4-3, 539G2
NHL player fined on '77 drug chrg 4-24, suspended 7-24, 656F3
Loto Canada extensn planned, provs score 7-6; BC curbs 7-7, 531E2
2 balloonists depart from Newfoundland 7-26, 653C1
NHL Canadiens sold 8-3, 656A3
Canadian Women's Amateur golf results 8-12, 990E1
Canadian Open tennis results 8-19, 1027B2
Kissinger named NASL bd chrmn 10-4, 969C2
'76 Olympic debt noted 10-12, 842G3
Edmonton wins Grey Cup 11-26, 1025E1

UN Policy & Developments
IAEA uranium shipmt inspectn set 1-16, 102F3
Rights comm resolutns on Israel, PLO 2-14, 99A2, B2
USSR vetoes satellite safety 2-14, 238A2
Abstains on Rhodesia pact vote 3-14, 192F3
Leb peace force (Unifil) formed 3-19, 197D2; **for peacekeeping developments, see MIDDLE EAST—LEBANON**
Assemb disarmamt sessn opens 5-23, Trudeau ends Eur A-arms role 5-26, 421G1, 422A1
Sea Law conf talks continue 5-23—7-15, 8-21—9-16, 732E3
UNDOF mandate renewed 5-31, 400B2
USSR satellite search pressed 7-5, 514C3
ILO rpts '77 jobless rise 7-27, 677D1
Racism conf boycotted 8-26, 676B2
Cncl, Assemb member 713A3, D3
S Africa arms sales suspected 11-6—11-7, 904E2
Cncl abstentn on Namibia electn warning 11-13, 904B2

Uranium—*See 'Atomic Energy' in this section above*

U.S. Relations—*See also 'Atomic Energy', 'Energy' and 'Monetary, Trade, Aid & Investment' above*
US troop presence rptd 1-2, 5E2
US prisoner arrives from Cuba 1-2, 22D1
Newfoundland premr in US, defends seal hunt 1-9, 35F2
Quebecor Phila Journal '77 debut cited 1-9, 75F3
US alerts to Sovt satellite fall 57E1
Lloyd Carr fugitive '75 arrest, extraditn fight cited 1-14, 83E2
Mondale visits 1-17—1-18, 53F2
Canada ties seen improved 1-23, 53E3
USSR satellite falls in NW Terr 1-24; radiatn detected, debris found 1-25—2-1, 57A1
US, USSR defend satellite reentry cooperatn 1-27, 1-28, 57D2
RCMP informer, illegal entry cited 2-27, 166B2
CAB OKs 'Super Saver' fares 3-3, 206B3
Trudeau addresses NY investors, lauds US ties 3-21, 225F2, D3
Cuban exile seized re Canada bomb plot 4-14, 287D2
US bans recreatn fishing 6-4, 435G1
US compact cars declared safe 6-28, 569E3
Caribou protectn talks set 7-6, 531C3
W Ger terrorist seized 7-16, 577A1
Indians see amb to US 7-18, 569C1
Prisoner exchng treaty OKd 7-19, 572B1
Ray admits smuggling operatn 8-16—8-18, 641A2
Seabed mining bill debated at UN conf 8-21—9-16, 732E3
Mideast peace force rptd backed 8-31, 673G1
US sues Seagram re paymts, case settled 9-8, 961E3
AMC, UAW in 2-year pact 9-25, 737C3
Prisoners exchanged 10-12—10-13, 794D3

1979

Sports
US wins Can-Am Bowl 1-6, 8C3
Sovts win Challenge Cup 2-11, 118B2, F3
NHL-WHA merger set 3-22, details OKd 3-30, 355G1, A3
Soccer players strike 4-13—4-18, 431D3
Sovts retain world ice hockey title 4-25, 448D1
Winnipeg takes WHA title 5-20, 447F3
Montreal wins Stanley Cup 5-21, 447E2
Canadian Open golf results 6-24, 587B3
Pan Am Games results 7-1—7-15, 798F2
Canadian Open tennis results 8-20, 734D2
Loto Canada sale agreed 8-21, 651D2; price set 9-4, 685A2
Edmonton wins Grey Cup 11-25, 1001F1
WCT Challenge Cup results 12-9, 1003D3

UN Policy & Developments
Rights comm resolutns on Israel, south Africa, pro-Palestinian state opposed 2-21, 148E1
S Africa rejcts Namibia plan 3-5, 171B2
Namibia compromise proposed 3-19—3-22; Pretoria bars 5-7, extends assemb powers 5-8, 354F2
Namibia vote abstentn 5-31, 428B1
Indochina refugee conf asked 6-28, 473E2
Membership listed 695F2
MacDonald rights speech scored 10-2, 788D3
PQ white paper presented 11-1, 853G1
Namibia talks reopen 11-12—11-16, 889D3
Eur pollutn pact OKd 11-13, 864A3

U.S. Relations—*See also 'Energy' and 'Monetary' above*
Levesque visits, assures re indep Quebec defense ties 1-25, 74F3
GM ruled liable for car defects 1-25, 95D3
'71 CIA drug tests on MP's wife rptd 1-29, 95F3-96B1
Student enrollmt in US rptd 167D2
Trudeau in US, sees Carter 3-3, 168E1
Joint naval maneuvers off PR 5-9—5-19, fishermen protest 5-16, 5-19, 385D3
PC policy continuity seen 5-22, 377F2
RCMP plans emb taps 7-4, 522A3
US environmt commitmt sought 7-12, 7-20, air agrmt set 7-26, 581D2, C3
Seagram unit admits bribery 9-27, 809G3
Clark pledges freedom of info act 10-9, 788E2
Reagan urges closer ties 11-13, 866D2

CANADIAN Imperial Bank of Commerce (Toronto)
Named in Woolworth suit 4-12, 304A1

CAN-Am Bowl—*See FOOTBALL—Collegiate*

CANARD Enchainé, Le (Paris newspaper)
Bokassa gift to Giscard alleged 10-10, 791D1
Giscard tax rpt arrest made 10-12, 791B2
Boulin suicide linked 10-30, 834G3, 835C1, A2
Bokassa gift to Giscard chrgd again 12-4, 993D3

1980

Sports
Moscow Olympics move backed by Clark 1-11, 28C3; 1-21, 45A3
Lake Placid Olympics results 2-12—2-24, 154F2, 155F2-156D1
Trudeau eases Olympic boycott conditions 2-19, 121F2
Olympic com rejcts Moscow boycott 3-30, 259G2
Olympic com sees boycott 4-14, 283A3
Moscow boycott backed, Olympic com scores 4-22, 325A3
Olympic com OKs Moscow boycott 4-26, 379B2
Sims hints CFL move, Cousineau '79 signing cited 4-29, 336C3
Canada Cup hockey tourn cancelled 4-30, 488B3
'76 Olympics contractor chrgd 5-9, 406E2
Hart KOs Racine 5-17, Denny 6-20; Denny dies, govt launches probe 7-7, 907B3
NASL Challenge Cup results 5-21—5-26, 770F3
Drapeau blamed for '76 Olympic debt 6-5, 444C1
Quebec Liberals keep '76 Olympic contributns 6-6, 444G1
Drapeau scores '76 Olympic debt rpt 6-14, 461A3
Montreal hosts WBC welterwgt bout 6-20, 772D2
Canadian Open golf results 6-22, 715B1
NHL club sale, transfer to Calgary OKd 6-24, 488A2
Players Challenge tennis results 7-20, Canadian Open 8-17, 691G2, B3
Jackson Classic, World Cup golf results 8-10, 12-14, 972F1, G2
Jones wins Gr Prix, world title 9-28, 1001F3
'76 Olympic fraud indictmts rptd 10-2, 788D1
NASL NLRB order refused by US Sup Ct 10-14, labor pact set 12-5; owners, player reps ratify 12-12, 12-18, 1001F2
Edmonton wins Grey Cup; Moon named game MVP 11-23, 999B2
Montreal, Calgary to get NASL clubs 12-8, 1001F1
WCT Challenge Cup results 12-14, 1002D2

UN Policy & Developments
Afghan frees official 6-22, 486B2
Assemb res backing Palestinian state opposed 7-29, 572F1
Women's conf 5-yr plan opposed 7-30, 587A3
S Africa arms seller fined 8-14, 618F2
MacGuigan addresses 11th special sessn 8-26, 669B1
MacGuigan addresses Assemb 9-22, 748E3-749B1
Namibia talks schedule agreed 11-24, 967C2
Cuba ex-offcl asks prison hunger strike probed 12-4, 963D2

U.S. Relations—*See also 'Energy', 'Monetary' above*
UAW bars Chrysler concessns 1-3, 14F1
USSR Olympics move backed 1-11, 28C3; 1-21, 45A3
3 Sovts ousted re spying 1-21, 56F2
Canada aids 6 US diplomats escape Iran 1-28, 66C1-B3
US thanks for Iran rescue 1-30, 1-31, 88A3
Draft dodgers warned 2-7, 95G3
US emb escapee airs more details 2-12, 106E1
US ties seen hurt by Trudeau electn 2-19, 121E2
Pacific naval games start 2-26, 151C3
Iran crisis support asked 4-8, 257D2
US asks Iran pol sanctns 4-13, 281D2
Ford Ontario plant shut 4-15, 287F1
MacGuigan scores US policies 6-1, 429A2
Fisheries issue imperils ties 6-12, 461E2
US acid rain policy scored 6-23, 486F2
KKK opens Toronto hq 6-26, 497C1
Demographic data compared 7-16, 562G2-D2
8 honored for Iran escape role 7-25, 578A1
Acid rain pact signed 8-5, 603E1
E Eur immigratn records rptd found 8-20, 651F1-C2

1976

CANARY Islands (Spanish territory)
Univ concert cancelatn protested 3-3, 207D2
CANCER—*See under MEDICINE & Health*
CANCER Society, American—*See AMERICAN Cancer Society*
CANDELARIA, John
Pitches no-hitter 8-9, 596G3
NL pitching ldr 10-4, 796A1
CANNES (France) Film Festival
Prizes awarded 5-28, 460F1
CANNING Industry—*See CONTAINERS & Packaging*
CANNON, Sen. Howard W. (D, Nev.)
Wins renomination 9-14, 705C1
Com ends Scott probe 9-15, 980A1
Reelected 11-2, 820D1, 824C2, 828C2
CANOEING—*See BOATING*
CANTON, O.—*See OHIO*
CAOUETTE, Real
Quebec dairy farmers riot 6-3, 416A3
Dies 12-16, 970D1
CAPE Canaveral, Fla.—*See FLORIDA*
CAPE Cod Commercial Fishermen's Coalition
Nantucket oil spill suit delayed 12-30, 1014A1
CAPELLINI, Brig. Jesus Orlando
Named Cordoba AF chief 4-10, 264C1
CAPE Verde Islands—*See also NON-ALIGNED Nations Movement, OAU*
Listed as 'partly free' 1-19, 20C3
Sovt shipping pact rptd 3-6, 404D1
China ties set 4-25, 404D1
At France-Africa summit 5-10—5-11, 355A3
Wells confrmd US amb 9-15, 808D1
Listed as not free 12-22, 977B3
CAPITAL Bank & Trust Co. (Boston, Mass.)
Assumes New Boston assets 9-15, 984A1
CAPITAL City Club (Atlanta, Ga.)
Bell membership scored 12-20—12-22, 956F3
CAPITAL Growth Co.
Receiver sues Figueres 9-22, 1000G2
CAPITAL National Bank of Miami—*See PEOPLE'S Downtown National Bank of Miami*
CAPITAL Punishment—*See under CRIME; also country names*
CAPITAL Times (Madison, Wis. newspaper)
NLRB rules on ethics code 4-8, 272D2
CAPLING, Maj. Elwyn Rex
Rptd killed in Viet 9-6, 678B3 ★
CAPPADORO, Gerry
Barbados deports 10-25, 962D1
CAPPEART, F. L.
'72 campaign gift listed 4-25, 688C1
CAPPELLONI, Guido
Italy CP bares '75 finances 1-16, 74E3
CAPTAIN and Tenille, The (music group)
Wins Grammy 2-28, 460A3
CAPTIVE Nations Committee, National
Viksnins scores Ford E Eur remark 10-7, 762C3
CAPUCCI, Archbishop Hilarion
Hijackers demand release 6-29, 463D1
Hijackers seek release 9-4, Israel bars 9-6, 662A3
CAPUTO, Bruce F.
Elected 11-2, 821G2, 830B2

1977

CANADA Development Corp.
Polysar admits illegal rebates 2-8, 114B2
Polysar scored in Parlt rpt 7-7, 542G3-543C1
CANADIAN Arctic Gas Pipeline Ltd.
FPC splits on Alaska pipe route 5-2, 369B3
Canada com asks pipe delay 5-9, 372A2
Canada bd backs Alcan route 7-4, 525F1
CANADIAN Pacific Air (CP Air)
Pilots fined for '76 strike 2-16, 133E1
Domestic fares raised 2-24, 200E1
Domestic charters rptd OKd 12-7, 966A1
CANADIAN Pacific Ltd.
Soo bid for Green Bay line rejctd 7-15, 613E1
CANALS—*See specific names*
CANARY Islands (Spanish territory)
S Africa Airways offices bombed 1-3, 22C3
747s crash on Tenerife 3-27, 244C1
Crash suits filed in US 3-31—4-6; probe begun 4-4, 311B3-312C1
Prison riot quelled 7-21, 582G2
CANCER—*See under MEDICINE*
CANCER Institute, National—*See U.S. GOVERNMENT—PUBLIC Health Service—National Institutes of Health*
CANCER Therapy Inc., Committee for Freedom of Choice in
At FDA laetrile hearings 5-2, 376C1
Laetrile smugglers sentncd 5-16, 508E2
CANDELARIA, John
NL pitching ldr 10-2, 926E3
CANDILLO, Ringo
Americans win ASL title 9-4, 827B3
CANNING Industry—*See CONTAINERS & Packaging*
CANNON, Sen. Howard W. (D, Nev.)
'76 special interest gifts rptd 1-15, 128F3, 129B1
CANNON, Isabella
Elected mayor 11-8, 855D3
CANNON, Bishop William
Gives inaugural prayer 1-20, 25F1
CANO, Juan
Americans win ASL title 9-4, 827B3
CANO, Ricardo
Wins Davis Cup matches 4-29—5-1, 353C3
CANODE, Hal
2d in drag racing champ 4-24, 531F2
CANTEEN Corp.—*See under TRANS World Airlines*
CANTLEY, Sir Joseph
Threatened 1-24, sentences IRA gunmen 2-10, 222G2
CANTO, Miguel
'77 boxing champion 12-17, 970A3
CAOUETTE, Gilles
Wins electn 5-24, 410B3
CAOUETTE, Paul
Scores prison rpt 6-8, 466D2
Lauds Fox reform pledge 8-5, 634G1
CAOUETTE, Real
Son wins Parlt seat 5-24, 410B3
CAPE Cod, Mass.—*See MASSACHUSETTS*
CAPE Verde Islands—*See also NONALIGNED Nations Movement, OAU*
UN Assemb member 3F3
At France-Africa summit 4-20—4-21, 316F3
Sahel dvpt plan OKd 6-1, 458F3
New Sahel famine seen 9-19, 770A2
Cuba medical aides rptd 11-17, 896F1
CAPILLA, Doug
Traded to Reds 6-15, 644E2
CAPITAL Cities Communications, Inc.
Buys Kansas City Star Co 2-15, 216F1
CAPITAL Flow—*See BALANCE of Payments*
CAPITAL Punishment—*See under CRIME*
CAPITAL Spending—*See BUSINESS*
CAPOZELLA, Capt. Norberto
Arrested for Kappler escape 9-8, 729E1
CAPPALLI, Patti
'77 fall fashions rptd 6-6, 1022D1
CAPRIO, Msgr. Giuseppe
Vatican state dep secy 6-14, 768A3
CAPUANO, Thomas M.
Detained 5-15—5-18, sees Mrs Carter 6-8, 455A2
Brazil expels 7-27, police beating denied 8-6, 633F2
On Recife jail, slums 9-1, 741B2
CAPUCCI, Archbishop Hilarion
Vatican asks release 10-30; Israel frees 11-6, 850G2-D3
CAPUTO, Rep. Bruce F. (R, N.Y.)
Chrgs Nixon Admin Korea scandal cover-up 7-7, 557A1
CARABALLO, Gustavo
Arrested 4-14, 345B3
CARABELLI, Gabriela
US science acad seeks info 4-27, 315A2

1978

CANADIAN Football League—*See FOOTBALL*
CANAGARATNAM, M.
Shot 1-27, 293A1
CANALITO, Lee
Paradise Alley released 10-10, 970F2
CANALS—*See specific names*
CANARY Islands (Spanish territory)
Tenerife 747 crash cited 1-6, 24B1
Spain king in Libya re independnc 1-21; OAU panel urges separatist support 2-21, 136E1
Separatist bombings 1-21, 1-31, 136E1, A2
Separatist ldr wounded in Algiers 4-5; Spain blamed 4-20; 2 tried, sentncd 5-6—5-7, 576C3
Spanish premr visits, sets navy base constructn 4-26, 576F3
Spain sets Tenerife, other pub works projcts 6-7, 576F3
Separatists bomb Spanish installatns, S Africa Airways office 6-15—7-8, 576F3
Spain dismisses 2 cops for defns of ousted police chief 8-31, 706C2
Tenerife '77 crash rpt issued 10-18, Dutch score 10-23, 888A2
CANAVAN, Dennis
Scores El Salvador repressn 12-10, 987D1
CANCER—*See under MEDICINE; for radiation issues, see ATOMIC Energy—Industrial Use*
CANDIA, Col. Mario
Bolivia energy min 11-24, 913E1
CANDLESHOE (film)
Released 8-4, 969F3
CANDY
Reggie bar debuts 4-13, 779F3
Hershey price rise opposed by Carter 11-9, 875C1
Hershey bar price hike OKd 11-20, 917G3
Hershey to buy Friendly Ice Cream 12-26, 1005G1-A2
CANDY Eclair (race horse)
Named top 2-yr old filly 12-12, 1028C1
CANE, Paulos Ngolosi
Dies 7-13, 3 policemen suspended 7-20, 633D2
3 policemen sentncd in death 11-3, 904D3
CANELLOPOULOS, Athanasios
DCU resignatn rptd 4-11, 374A1
Named Greek finance min 5-10, 373E3
Presents '79 budget 11-24, 924B2
CANNELLA, Judge John
Sentences NY rabbi in Flood case 6-22, 500E3
CANNING Industry—*See CONTAINERS & Packing*
CANNOLD, Michael
Go Tell Spartans released 9-23, 970E1
CANNON, Dyan
Revenge of Pink Panther released 7-19, 970A3
CANNON, Sen. Howard W. (D, Nev.)
Votes for Panama Canal neutrality pact 3-16, 177F1, D2
Sen OKs 2d Canal pact amendmt, votes for pact 4-18, 273B1, B2, E2
Airline deregulatn compromise clears conf com 10-6, 765C3
CANTEEN Corp.—*See under TRANS World Airlines*
CANTO, Miguel
Decisions Oguma 1-4, 56B1
Decisns Tacomron 11-20, 969F1
CANTOR, Arthur
My Astonishing Self opens 1-18; Biko Inquest 5-17, 760D1, F2
Playboy of Weekend World opens 11-16, 1031G2
CANTRELL, Judge Ben
Orders Nashville prison bldg closed 1-30, 440E1
CAN'T Smile Without You (recording)
On best-seller list 4-5, 272F3; 5-3, 356D1
CANTU Pena, Fausto
Arrested 4-25, chrgd re coffee smuggling, tax fraud 4-29, 517E3
CAOUETTE, Real (d. 1976)
Reznowski replaces as party ldr 5-7, 392A1
CAPE Canaveral, Fla.—*See FLORIDA*
CAPE Horn
Argentina-Chile Beagle Channel talks 5-22—11-2, 860E2
New Beagle Channel talks fail 12-12, 979E2
CAPELLA, Jacques
Killed in Iraq emb raid 7-31, French police protest 8-3, 649D3
CAPE Verde Islands—*See also NON-ALIGNED Nations Movement, OAU*
UN Assemb member 713D3
CAPITAL Gains Tax—*See TAXES*
CAPITAL Punishment—*See under CRIME*
CAPONE, Al (Alfonso) (1899-1947)
Ex-chauffeur dies 4-25, 356G2
CAPONE, Roberto
Killed 11-8, 1018F1
CAPPELLETTI, John
Rams win in playoffs 12-31, 1024G1
CAPUTO, Rep. Bruce F. (R, N.Y.)
On Park testimony 1-13, 63E3
Doubts Park testimony 4-3, 239D2
Rpts of reps linked to Kim 5-25, 432C3
Loses electn for NY lt gov, Peyser wins US House seat 11-7, 849A2

1979

CANARY Islands (Spanish territory)
Separatists win Cong seats 3-1, 191F2
Regionalists score in munic vote 4-3, 256F2
Dutch probe '77 Tenerife crash 5-29, 412C2
Spain air fare hikes exclude 7-3, 546D1
Iberian jet hijacked 8-4, 603F3
Spain defends nonaligned conf plans 8-10, 8-13, 654G2
CANAVAN, Linda
King of Schnorrers opens 11-28, 956C3
CANCEL-Miranda, Rafael
Sentence commuted 9-6, 666E1
Freed 9-10, returns to PR 9-12, 682G3
CANCER—*See under MEDICINE*
CANDELARIA, John
In World Series 10-10—10-17, 816C2
CANDIDA (play)
Opens 3-6, 711A2
CANDY
Hershey fears 3 Mile I impact 4-9, 261E2
Benzocaine OKd as diet aid 5-12, 572A1
CANDY-O (recording)
On best seller list 7-4, 548F3; 8-1, 620F3; 9-5, 672F3; 10-3, 800F3
CANETE, Ricardo
Cites Letelier murder boast by Ross 1-30, 75D1
CANISTRACCI, Paul
Slain in Attica racial brawl 6-3, 548G2
CANIZARO, Joseph C.
New Orleans real estate investmt rptd 11-26, 897G3-898A1
CANNELLA, Judge John
Fines shipping consortium 10-31, 985G2
CANNING Industry—*See CONTAINERS & Packing*
CANNON, Edward
Going in Style released 12-25, 1007D3
CANNON, Geraldine
Pvt Title IX suit allowed by Sup Ct 5-14, 382D3
CANNON, Sen. Howard W. (D, Nev.)
Commerce Com chrmn 1-23, 71C2
Clashes with Kennedy over trucking deregulatn 2-7, 111G2
Ends Kennedy trucking dispute 3-21, 308G3
CANNON, Mark
Sup Ct workforce data rptd 6-11, 464G1
CANNON v. University of Chicago
Case decided by Sup Ct 5-14, 382D3
CANOEING—*See BOATING*
CANONERO II (race horse)
Preakness track record retained 5-19, 448G2
CANSINO, Gen. Jose
Assassinated 6-10, 445B3
CANTEEN Corp.—*See under TRANS World Corp.*
CANTELEY, Joseph
Thorpe acquitted 6-22, 486A1
CANTO, Miguel
Park decisns for WBC flywgt title 3-18
Draws with Park 9-9, 839C1
CANTOR, Arthur
On Golden Pond opens 2-28, 712G1
CANTRELL, Ed
Faces murder trial 2-7, 156A1
CAPE Canaveral, Fla.—*See FLORIDA*
CAPEHART, Homer E.
Dies 9-3, 756B2
CAPE Verde Islands—*See also NONALIGNED Nations Movement, OAU*
Young visits, urges Israel 'dialogue' 9-5, 720B3
UN membership listed 695F2
CAPITAL Punishment—*See under CRIME*
CAPITOL International Airways Inc.
$99 cross-country fares, new routes OKd 1-12, 35E2
CAPP, Al (Alfred Gerald Caplin)
Dies 11-5, 932C2
CAPRIO, Cardinal Giuseppe
Named Vatican finance dir 4-30, 376G1
Installed cardinal 6-30, 640C2
CAPUCCI, Archbishop Hilarion
Named Melkite inspector, Israel reassured 5-7, 376B3 •

1980

CANALETTO (1697-1768)
Loren art collectn claim rptd denied 2-9, 200B2
CANARD Enchaine, Le (Paris newspaper)
De Broglie scandal deepens 4-14, 312F2, B3
Bokassa confirms Giscard gifts 9-17, 728G3
Giscard cousins paid damages re Bokassa story 12-23, 996D3
CANARY Islands(Spanish territory)
Tenerife jet crash 4-25, 392B1
Spain escorts stricken Cuban tankers to Las Palmas 7-14, 562E2
Basques threaten bombings 7-23, 580G2
CANBY, Vincent
Scores Heaven's Gate 11-19, 906C1
CANCER—*See under MEDICINE*
CANCER Research, American Association for
Interferon success rptd 5-28, 526D2
CANDY
USDA 'junk food' rules rptd 1-27, 157F3
Guatemala Nestle exec kidnaped 6-17, 487F2
CANE, Melville H.
Dies 3-10, 279G1
CANNON, Dyan
Coast to Coast released 10-3, 836E2
CANNON, Sen. Howard W. (D, Nev.)
On RR deregulatn bills 10-14, 783F3
CANNONE, Steven
Indicted 3-3, 215D1
CANOEING—*See BOATS & Boating*
CANONERO II (race horse)
Hunts bailout loan collateral listed 5-28, 426C1
CANTERBURY Tales (play)
Opens 2-12, 136A3
CANTEY, Joe
Temperence Hill wins Belmont 6-7, 447A3
CANTON, Mark
Die Laughing released 5-23, 675C2
CAPE Verde Islands—*See also NONALIGNED Nations, OAU*
Mondale in African tour 7-17—7-23, 620D2
Guinea-Bissau pres ousted in coup 11-14, 887B1
CAPITAL Cities Communications Inc.
RKO General buys Cablecom 9-24, 746G1
CAPITAL Holding Corp.
Natl Liberty merger set 6-13, 746E1
CAPITAL Punishment—*See under CRIME*
CAPONE, Al (Alphonso) (1899-1947)
Froelich dies 2-5, 176B1
CAPOTE, Truman
Music for Chameleons on best-seller list 9-14, 716C3; 10-12, 796E3
CAPRIA, Nicola
Italy south region min 4-4, 275F3
CAPTAIN J. H. (U.S. shrimp boat)
Ferries Cuban refugees, faces fine 4-26, 326D1
CAPTAIN & Tennille (singing group)
Do That To Me on best-seller list 2-6, 120F3
CAPUCCI, Archbishop Hilarion
Visits US hostages in Teheran 2-8, 106D1
In Iran crisis mediatn group 4-5, 258D1
Arranges repatriatn of dead US raiders 4-29—5-6, 337A2

1976

CARAMANLIS, Constantine
Shifts 2 cabt mins 1-5, 73D2
Clerides drops peace talks resignatn 1-18, 48E2
Balkan natns meet 1-26—2-5, 213E3
On EC applicatn delay 1-29, 84E2 ★
Educ reforms enacted 1-31, 221G3
Welcomes EC entry vote 2-10, 164E2
US-Turkish pact protested 3-31, 4-12, 259E1, D2
Ceausescu visit rptd 4-8, 333B2
Zhivkov visits 4-9—4-11, 333A2
Makes peace bid on Turkey 4-17, 278D2
Tito visits 5-10—5-13, 543C3
Vs Demirel on Aegean feud 8-20, 643B3
Asks Aegean talks 9-4, 845B2
Vs NATO Cyprus mediatn 11-12, 897A3
CARAZO, Fidel
Scores govt reform plans 1-28, 144E1
CARBO, Paul John (Frankie)
Dies 11-9, 970D1
CARCICH, Rev. Guido John
Pallotine fund probe set, reassignmt rptd 8-24, 951D1
CARDOSO, Capt. Jose Luis
Beja apptmt rptd 9-27, 811B3
CARDOSO Amaral, Maj. Fernando
On Angola refugee problems 1-22, 53F2
CARDOZO, Gen. Cesareo
Assassinated 6-18, 495E3
CARDWELL, James B.
Reports SSI overpaymts 1-20, 128C2
CARDWELL, William C.
Scores shipyd cost overruns 6-7, 454B1
CARE (Cooperative for American Relief Everywhere)
Guatemala quake aid rptd 2-10, 120E3
CAREW, Rod
AL batting ldr 10-4, 796B1, C1
CAREY, Alford R.
Pleads guilty, sentncd 1-9, 32F2
CAREY, Gov. Hugh L. (D, N.Y.)
Signs anti-boycott law 1-1, 987B2
Names Sandler to Murtagh post 1-16, 79A1
Concerned about Concorde 2-4, 94D3
Endorses Carter 6-12, 432D1
Declares LI shore disaster area 6-23, 454F2
Dismisses Nadjari 6-25, 1016D1
Dem conv speaker 7-12, 508C1, 509B1
NYC hosp strike ends 7-17, 553G2
Welcomes Mondale 8-25, 645G2
GE signs PCB pact 9-8, 691B3
NE govs seek aid 11-13—11-14, 864A3
Accepts NYC debt ruling 11-19, 888B1
Visits Carter 12-28, 978C2
Pardons Attica ex-inmates 12-30, 995C2
CAREY, Max
Dies 5-30, 484D3
CARGILL, Inc.
3 La grain inspectors indicted 1-19, 44E1
In grain abuse agrmt 3-16, 248A1
Sovt grain sales rptd 4-28, 321C3
India sues 5-3, 333E2
USSR buys soybeans 7-2, 540A2
CARGO, William I.
Succeeded as amb to Nepal 3-3, 186B2
CARIBBEAN—*See LATIN America*
CARIBBEAN Common Market and Community (Caribcom) (Barbados, Belize, Dominica, Grenada, Guyana, Jamaica, Montserrat, St. Kitts-Nevis-Anguilla, St. Lucia, St. Vincent, Trinidad & Tobago)
Kissinger pledges US support 2-17, 177C2
CARIBCOM—*See CARIBBEAN Common Market and Community*
CARILLO, Santiago
At E, W Eur CP conf 6-29—6-30, 461C2
CARLES, Ruben Dario
Arrested 1-15, exiled 1-20, 121A3
CARLOS—*See SANCHEZ, Ilich Ramirez*
CARLOUGH, Edward J.
Quits Ford panel 1-8, 4C1
CARLSON, Everett
Indicted 7-14, sentncd 10-8, 796B3
CARLSON, Frank
Cited in Dole biog sketch 614D2
CARLSON, Jack
Replaced in Interior post 3-23, 232D1
CARLTON, Steve
NL pitching ldr 10-4, 796A1
Reds win pennant 10-12, 796F1
CARLTON College (Northfield, Minn.)
Swearer named Brown U pres 8-14, 640G3

1977

CARAMANLIS, Constantine
Meets US envoy 2-17—2-19, 122B2
Plans early Greek electns 9-19, 728D2
Replaces 3 mins 10-21, 925C2
Party wins electns 11-20, 11-23, 924E3
Names Cabt 11-28, 925F1
CARANSA, Maurits
Kidnaped 10-28, freed 11-2, 871D1
2 W Ger terrorists captured 11-10, 888B1
CARAZO, Rodrigo
Named Oppositn Union '78 pres candidate 3-13, 506C2
Asks Vesco, Oduber prosecutn 5-19, 506D1
'78 pres race underway 9-2, 710B2
CARBON Industries
ITT takeover cited in table 880G1
CARBON Monoxide—*See TOBACCO—Smoking-Health Link*
CARBON Tetrachloride—*See CHEMICALS*
CARBORUNDUM Co.
Kennecott purchase backed by bd 11-16; merger table cited 880A1, F1
Kennecott takeover cited 12-11, 1004E2
CARDOZA, Norman F.
Wins Pulitzer Prize 4-18, 355F2
CARDOZO, Gen. Cesareo (d. 1976)
Murder suspect killed 1-19, 197E3
CARDOZO, Brig. Jose
Rejects US aid 3-1, 142C2
CAREW, Rod
NL wins All-Star Game 7-19, 567D2
Named AL batting ldr 10-2; MVP 11-16, 926F3-927B1
CAREY, Gov. Hugh L. (D, N.Y.)
NYC debt repaymt plan scored 3-4, 193A2
Carter Concorde talk rptd 3-7, 212C3
Carter meets 3-17, 191B1
Asks halt to US IRA aid 3-17, 222E3
In Ireland 4-22—4-25, scores IRA 4-22, 329G1
Scores NY Concorde ruling 5-11, 368C2
Orders NYC blackout probe 5-14, 537C3
Farley quits Athletic Comm 6-3, 828B2
Vetoes death penalty bill 7-12, 594F2
NYC loses '84 Olympics bid, blames Grant 9-25, 828B3, D3
Koch elected NY mayor 11-8, 855E2
Byrne vetoes Port Auth aircraft noise rule 12-27, 1006F3
CAREY v. Population Services International
Contraceptive restraints voided 6-9, 501A2
CARGILL Inc.
Forgn paymts rptd 3-18, 233C2
ICC curbs rail grain-car deals 8-1, 613D1
CARGO Preference—*See SHIPS*
CARIBBEAN Region—*See LATIN America*
CARIBBEAN Sea
US transit cited re Latin A-ban pact 4-14, 295G2
CARILLO Marcor, Alejandro
Rpts drought crisis 8-8, 660D1
CARIM, Tara
Assassinated 6-9, 565G1-A2
CARITY, Chester
Sentenced 3-10, 203B3
CARLIN, George
FCC obscenity order voided 3-16, 215E3
CARLOS—*See RAMIREZ Sanchez, Illich*
CARLSON, Richard
Dies 11-25, 952C2
CARLTON, Steve
NL pitching ldr 10-2, 926E3
Wins Cy Young Award 11-2, 927E1

1978

CARAMANLIS, Constantine (Greek premier)
OKs Ecevit talks 1-23, 2-9, 170C2
Visits 4 EC natns for entry talks 1-25—2-1, sees NATO head in Brussels 1-26, 149G1
In Ecevit summit talks 3-10—3-11, oppositn scores 3-12, 216D2
Ecevit chrgs US summit pressure 3-10, stand rptd hardened 3-12, 216E3
Scores US on proposed Turkey arms embargo end 4-7, 277C1
Turkish talks delayed 4-11, 277E1
Shuffles Cabt 5-10, woos DCU 5-11, 373C3
Links Cyprus setlmt, NATO role 5-27, 398C3
Sees Ecevit in US, more talks set 5-29; confers with Carter 5-31, 398B2
Aegean talks resume 7-4—7-6, 624B1
CARAVANS (film)
Released 11-1, 969F3 ★
CARAZO Odio, Rodrigo (Costa Rican president)
Elected pres 2-5, vows Vesco ouster 2-7, 89E2
Plans Somoza land expropriatn 2-22, 151A1
Pledges Vesco expulsn 2-22, 152C2
Names Cabt 3-4, 170G3
Vesco indicted 3-16, 269D3
Vesco vs ouster 5-6, plans return to CR 5-11, 478D3
Sworn as pres; Vesco expulsn hinted, reentry bar rptd 5-8, 354D2
At Panama Canal pact instrumts exchng 6-16, 463F2, 464A1
Bars Vesco return 7-7, 558D3
Ct rejcts Vesco citizenshp plea 8-23, 671E2
CARBONNEAU, Jean-Marc
6th Cross kidnaper hinted 11-2, 880C1
CARBORUNDUM Corp.—*See under KENNECOTT Corp.*
CARCICH, Rev. Guido John
Indicted 1-6, 24G2
Pleads guilty, sentenced 5-9, 380F1-A2
CARDOZO, Hilarion
Accused of '72 vote-buying 5-5, 395A2
CARDWELL, James B.
Ross named Soc Sec comr 8-24, 664B1
CARENA-Bancorp. Inc.
NHL Canadiens sold 8-3, 656A3
Grundman assumes Canadiens post 9-6, 991B1
CAREW, Rod
Given $100,000 bonus 1-6, 195D1
NL wins All-Star Game 7-11, 559A3
Griffith remarks cause furor 9-28—10-2, 779E2
AL batting ldr 10-2, 928D3-F3
Rejcts Giants trade 12-7, 1025G3-1026A1
CAREY, Gov. Hugh L. (D, N.Y.)
Role in NYC fiscal crisis 86B2
For more NYC fed aid 1-9, 87F2
Laetrile bill veto cited 1-10, 23C3
Proposes state budget 1-17, agrees on NYC aid funds 2-6, 87C2
Scores Sen Banking Com rpt on NYC 2-9, 87C1
Orders Little extradited 2-23, 431A2
Scores Ulster violence 3-16, 373C3
On Carter urban-aid plan 3-27, 218B1
NYC policemen slain; '76 Attica pardon scored, death penalty pressed 4-5, 388C3
Vetoes death penalty bill 4-11, veto override fails 5-2, 388G2-B3, D3
Signs NYC control bd-MAC bill 6-2, 608D3
Vows Niagara disaster area cleanup aid 8-7, 703E1
Carter signs NYC aid bill 8-8, 608E1, F2
Wins primary 9-12, 716G1
Reelected 11-7, 845B2, 847C1, 849D1, 853D3
Signs mortgage rate lid hike, anti-redlining bill 12-8, 962F1
CAREY, Richard J.
3d in primary for Me gov 6-13, 467A1
CAREY v. Piphus
Suspended student damages curbed by Sup Ct 3-21, 220G2
CARIBBEAN Common Market—*See CARIBBEAN Community*
CARIBBEAN Community (Antigua, Barbados, Belize, Dominica, Grenada, Guyana, Jamaica, Montserrat, St. Christopher-Nevis-Anguilla, St. Lucia, St. Vincent, Trinidad & Tobago)
Caricom dvpt plans collapse 1-13, 100E2
CARIBBEAN Region—*See LATIN America*
CARIBOU—*See WILDLIFE*
CARICOM—*See CARIBBEAN Community*
CARIELLO, Vito
Indicted 10-5, 770F3
CARITA, Maria
Dies 9-6, 778A1
CARLIN, George
FCC 'Filthy Words' ban upheld by Sup Ct 7-3, 551G2
CARLIN, John W.
Wins Kan primary for gov 8-1, 606E1
Elected 11-7, 847A1, 853F2, 854E2
CARLSBAD, N.M.—*See NEW Mexico*
CARLSON, David E.
Questns solar cell advance 11-30, 983C2
CARLSON, Jack
Links govt regulatn cost, inflatn 6-19, 427A3
Vs price guideline tightening 12-13, 957A2
CARLTON, Steve
Phillies lose NL pennant 10-7, 779C1

1979

CARAMANLIS, Constantine (Greek premier)
Signs EC entry treaty 5-28, 407B2
EC entry treaty ratified 6-28, 543C3
On inflatn, energy problems 9-8, 707E3
CARAZO Odio, Rodrigo (Costa Rican president)
In Mex 5-20, 409A1
Ousts 3 Sovt envoys 8-19, 667B3
CARBAUGH, John
Zimbabwe conf role rptd 9-19; UK denies protest 9-20, 718G1
CARBONDALE, Ill.—*See ILLINOIS*
CARBON Fuel Co.
Wildcat strike liability limited by Sup Ct 12-10, 988D1
CARBON Fuel Co. v. United Mine Workers
Case decided by Sup Ct 12-10, 988C1
CARBORUNDUM Corp.—*See KENNECOTT Corp.*
CARDENAL Martinez, Rev. Ernesto
Nicaragua culture min 7-23, 573C2
Visits Cuba 7-26, 574C2
CAREW, Rod
Traded to Angels 2-3, 619D1
CAREY, Dr. Freeman H.
Rpts Powell tumor benign 3-22, 231A2
CAREY, Gov. Hugh L. (D, N.Y.)
Inaugural 1-1, 13E2
Asks $225 mln tax cut 1-3, 13G2
'76 Attica commutatn cited 2-21, 156E1
Scores UK on N Ireland 4-22, 312B3
Invited UK-Ireland offcls to Ulster peace conf 8-6, 602E1
Gets support re Northeast Energy Corp proposal, reassurance on winter heating fuel 8-28, 703B2
Kennedy discussn re '80 pres bid rptd 9-8, 680B1
New Haven A-reactors rejected 10-12, 807B1
Scotto indicted 11-15, 890B2
Boxing suspended in NYS 11-28–12-27, 1004F3
CAREY, John
Quits Chicago schl post 11-30, 943G3
CAREY, John M.
Lauds vets' job-preferne ruling 6-5, 421C2
CARIBBEAN Community (Caribcom) (Antigua, Barbados, Belize, Dominica, Grenada, Guyana, Jamaica, Montserrat, St. Kitts-Nevis-Anguilla, St. Lucia, St. Vincent, Trinidad & Tobago)
New Grenada regime makes diplomatic overtures 3-15, wins recogntin 3-24, 236A3
CARIBBEAN Group for Cooperation & Economic Development
Formatn, forgn aid pledges rptd 7-6, 960F3
CARIBBEAN Region—*See LATIN America*
CARIBBEAN Sea
2 tankers collide off Tobago 7-19, record oil spill rptd 7-21, 553G2
Crippled tanker sinks off Barbados 8-2, 592A3
US to up mil activity 10-1, 737A1, G1, 739A1
CARIOU, Len
Sweeney Todd opens 3-1, 292C3
One Man released 7-27, 820E2
CARLIN, Gov. John W. (D, Kan.)
Scores rail decontrol bill 6-6, 579G2
CARLISLE, Mark
UK educatn secy 5-5, 338G1
CARLTON, Steve
NL wins All-Star Game 7-17, 568E3
NL pitching ldr 9-30, 955G2

1980

CARAMANLIS, Constantine (Greek president)
To seek permanent Olympic site 1-18, 45C3
Sets Acropolis rescue plan 4-15, 285D2
Elected pres 5-5, Rallis selected premr 5-8, 352B2, D2
Sworn 5-15, 407E3
Kouris sentncd re embezzlemt story 12-30, 996F3
CARAZO Odio, Rodrigo (Costa Rican president)
IMF '79 austerity pkg rptd 2-1, 117F1
Protests Cuba refugee policy, shuns Nicaragua anniv fete 7-15, 565G2
Attends Santa Marta conf 12-17, 992A3
CARDEN, William
Back in the Race opens 4-17, 392C2
CARDENAL, Jose
In World Series 10-14—10-21, 812C3
CARDINALE, Claudia
Immortal Bachelor released 2-22, 216A3
CARDONA Jr., Rene
Guyana released 1-25, 216F2
CARDONA, Ricardo
Randolph TKOs for WBA junior featherwgt title 4-4, 1000F3
CAREW, Rod
NL wins All-Star Game 7-8, 636E1
AL batting ldr 10-6, 926D3
CAREY, Bernard
Loses Cook Cnty state atty electn, chrgs vote fraud 11-4, 850D3
CAREY, Gov. Hugh L. (D, N.Y.)
State of State message 1-9, 270A1
Orders Lake Placid Olympics transit takeover 2-16, 155E2
NY primary results 3-25, 221B3
NYC transit strike ends 4-11, 289D2
Asks open Dem pres conventn 5-5, 342E3
Urges US aid re Love Canal 5-21, 387C1
Signs gun control bill 6-13, 470G2
At NYFE opening 8-7, 616E3
Backs open conv in rules fight 8-11, 610A1
Praises Carter econ renewal plan; vows reelectn support 8-28, 663E2
A Hoffman commendatn cited 9-4, 713C2
Accompanies Mondale in NYC 9-15, 780B2
Greets Carter 9-29, 739C1
CAREY, Ron
Fatso released 2-1, 216E2
CAREY v. Brown
Case decided by Sup Ct 6-20, 555D2
CARGILL Inc.
Paint-resin price trust setlmt reached 7-22, 917E1
CARHUFF, Jack
Munic bond mkt comments rptd 2-28, 186G1
CARIBBEAN Sea
Cuba gets 3d Sovt sub 1-17, 192F1
Hurricane Allen hits 8-4—8-7, 621G1
US news copter missing 11-13, 869D3
CARIONE, Tony
Protests Minter middlewgt victory 3-16, 320D2
CARLIN, Gov. John (D, Kansas)
State of State message 1-7, 403F2
CARLSBAD—*See NEW Mexico*
CARLSON, Gerald R.
Wins Mich US House primary 8-5, 682D3
Loses US House electn 11-4, 851D1
CARLSON v. Green
Case decided by Sup Ct 4-22, 343C3
CARLSSON, Lars-Goran
Wins Olympic medal 7-26, 623D2
CARLTON, Steve
Breaks southpaw strikeout mark 7-6, 636D3
NL pitching ldr 10-6, 926F2, G2
Phillies win NL pennant 10-12, 796B1
In World Series 10-14—10-21, 811C3, 812D3
Wins Cy Young Award 11-4, 925E3
CARLTON Fields Ward Emmanuel Smith & Cutler
Smith installed ABA pres 8-6, 744B2

1976

CARNATION Co.
SEC lists forgn paymts 5-12, 726E2
CARNEGIE Endowment for International Peace (N.Y.)
Herzog speaks at cntr 1-12, 18E1
CARNEY, Rep. Charles J. (D, O.)
Reelected 11-2, 830B3
CARON, Marcel
Quits spending probe 11-25, 924A2
CARPENTIER, Alejo
Elected to Natl Assemb 11-2, 1001A1
CARPENTER, Liz
ERAmerica DC office opens 2-25, 172F1
CARPENTER Jr., Walter S.
Dies 2-2, 124D3
CARPENTERS and Joiners of America, United Brotherhood of (AFL-CIO)
Sidell quits Ford panel 1-8, 4C1
CARPETS
Dacron price raised 11-30, 898G1
CARR, Rep. Bob (D, Mich.)
Reelected 11-2, 829D4
CARR, Shirley
Warns on anti-govt action 9-17, 771E1
CARRADINE, Keith
Wins Oscar 3-29, 240A3
CARREIRA, Cmdr. Henrique Teles
Angola defns min 11-27, 995C3
CARRERO Blanco, Luis (1903-73)
Spain royal adviser killed 10-4, 774A3
Oriol kidnapped 12-11, 967F2
Memorial service held 12-20, 967D2
CARRIER Corp.
SEC lists forgn paymts 5-12, 726F2
CARRILES Galarraga, Eduardo
Finance min 7-8, 523E2
CARRILLO, Santiago
Raimon audience cheers 2-5, 144E2
At CP exec mtg in Rome 7-28—7-31, 753F1
Secret Spain visits rptd 8-15, passport rejctd 8-26, 753A3
Arrested 11-22, 967A3
Freed on bail 12-30, 1011E2
CARRIO, Genaro
Scores OAS re Chile rights abuse 3-5, 310F1
CARRIZO Springs, Tex.—*See TEXAS*
CARROLL, Francis
Scores banned Masses 8-30, 692A1

1977

CARLUCCI, Frank C.
Named CIA dep dir 12-22, 1001E3
CARMEL River, Calif.—*See CALIFORNIA*
CARNE, Marcel
Jacques Prevert dies 4-11, 356E3
CARNEGIE Council on Policy Studies in Higher Education—*See CARNEGIE Foundation for the Advancement of Teaching*
CARNEGIE Endowment for International Peace (N.Y.)
Maynes named to US post 1-21, 53D1
CARNEGIE Foundation for the Advancement of Teaching
Urges coll curriculum reform 12-15, 1009C1
CARNER, JoAnne
2d in Colgate Winners Circle 4-3, 951B1
3d in US Womens Open 7-24, 951A1
LPGA top money winner 11-27, 951E1
CAROL II, King (Rumania) (1893-1953)
Widow dies 6-29, 532C3
CAROLINA Environmental Study Group
A-plant accident liability limit voided 3-31, 277D2
CAROLINE, Princess (Monaco)
Engagement announced 8-25, 808B3
CARPENTER, Edward
Scores NH A-plant OK 6-17, 498D3
CARR, Rep. Bob (D, Mich.)
Backs Carter on B-1, FB-111H 10-8, 796D1
CARR, Canon Burgess
Scores Luwum killing 2-17, 2-19, 139A1
CARR, John Dickson (Carr Dickson, Carter Dickson)
Dies 2-27, 164D2
CARR, Kenny
In NBA draft 6-10, 584A2
CARR, Sam
Son of Sam arrested 8-10, 641F3
CARREIRA, Henrique Teles (Iko)
Angola war role rptd 1-31, 86C1
CARRERO Blanco, Adm. Luis (d. 1973)
Spain exiles assassins 5-22—6-9, 454B1
CARRICK, John
Named Australia educ min 12-19, 982A2
CARRIE (book)
On best-seller list 2-6, 120G3
CARRIEN, Jerome
Guillotined 6-23, 543G1
CARRIER Corp.
Inmont purchased 8-11, 629A3
CARRILES Galarraga, Eduardo
Spain sets econ package 2-22, 307A3
CARRILLO, Santiago
Meets oppositn ldrs 1-4; negotiatn team excludes 1-7, 22A3
Heads PCE candidates list 2-21, 285C3
Hosts Marchais, Berlinguer; scores Sovt rights abuse 3-2—3-3, 242F3
On PCE legalizatn 4-9, 4-14, 285E2, B3
Elected to parlt 6-15, 453F1, C2
USSR scores Eurocommunism 6-23, response 6-25, 6-27, 507F1
Sovt bloc reactn to Moscow stance 7-3—7-24, 590A3
USSR renews attack 7-6, 545C3
Pol, econ pacts OKd by govt, oppositn 10-8—10-9, 867C1
USSR bars speech 11-3, 865G2
CARROLL, Archbishop Coleman F.
Dies 7-26, 604G2

1978

CARLUCCI, Frank C.
Confrmd CIA dep dir 2-9, 83A1
CARMET, Jean
Violette released 10-9, 1030F3
CARMICHAEL, Harold
NFL '77 pass receiving ldr 1-1, 56F2
CARMO, Isabel do
Arrested in violence probe 6-22, 594E1
CARNEGIE Corp. of N.Y.
Rpts on black jobs, wages, poverty 4-10, 811E1
CARNEGIE-Mellon University (Pittsburgh, Pa.)
Simon wins Nobel Prize 10-16, 886G2
CARNELIA, Craig
Working opens 5-14, 887E3
CARNER, JoAnne
Wins Colgate Triple Crown 1-29, 76E1
2d in LPGA Classic 5-21, Kent Golden Lights 5-29; wins Peter Jackson Classic 6-4, 580F2, G2, G3
Wins Borden Classic 7-16; 2d in US Women's Open 7-23, Hoosier Classic 7-30, Eur LPGA 8-6, 672G2, C3, E3
LPGA top money winner 11-20, 990C3
CARNEY, Rep. Charles J. (D, Ohio)
Wins primary 6-6, 448D1
Loses reelectn 11-7, 854E1
CARNEY, Daniel
Wild Geese released 11-11, 970E3
CARNEY, Mary
Othello opens 1-30, 887D2
CARNEY, William
Wins US House primary in NY 9-12, 716C2
Elected 11-7, 849A2, 851C3
CARNIE, Mark
Killed 7-19, 630E3
CARO, Anthony
Natl Gallery commissn rptd 6-1, 578C3
CAROLINA Power and Light Co.
Harris elected Chamber of Commerce chrmn 4-29, 420G1
CAROLINE, Princess (Monaco)
Wedding plans announced 4-24, 420G2
Married 6-28, 6-29, 580D1
CARPENTER, John
Eyes of Laura Mars released 8-4, 970C1
Halloween released 10-15, 970E1
CARR, Allen
Grease released 6-16, 619C2
CARR, James A.—*See ABRAHAMS, Alan*
CARR, Rep. M. Robert (D, Mich.)
Israel frees US Arab 10-18, 783E2
Reelected 11-7, 851E1
CARRADINE, David
Serpent's Egg released 1-27, 619F3
CARRADINE, Keith
Duellists released 1-14, Pretty Baby 4-5, 619F1, D3
CARRERO Blanco, Adm. Luis (d. 1973)
Killers get amnesty 1-20, 135F3
Gen, aide assassinated 7-21, 576B1
Murderer killed in France 12-21, 1022F1
CARRIER Corp.
United Tech seeks merger 9-18, bid rejected 9-25, US sues vs takeover 11-13, 896D1
Plans Jenn-Air acquisitn 10-4, 896F2
UAW rptd vs United bid 10-30, NY stay lifted 11-10, 896D2
CARRILLO, Heliodoro
Kidnaped 6-1, 414C1
CARRILLO, Santiago
Refutes critical book, party ldrs rptd shaken 2-24, 136A2
Reelected CP chief, 'Leninist' label dropped 4-19—4-23, 821C3
Sees Giscard in Madrid 6-30, 649A2
Scores gen's assassinatn 7-21, 576A1
CARROLL, George
Indicted 7-19, 598F3

1979

CARLYLE Hotel (N.Y., N.Y.)
H Ford expenses rptd repaid 4-12, 366A3
CARMELINA (play)
Opens 4-8, 711A2
CARMICHAEL, Gil
Wins Miss GOP gov primary 8-7, 680F2
Loses electn 11-6, 846E2
CARMICHAEL, Laurie
Arrest touches off strike 6-12, 443E2
CARMONA v. Ward
Case declined by Sup Ct 1-8, 14D3
CARNEGIE, Pa.—*See PENNSYLVANIA*
CARNEGIE Corp.
Comm rpt urges pub broadcast chngs 1-30, 78C2
PBS reorganizatn approved 6-25, 588C1
CARNEGIE Council on Policy Studies in Higher Education—*See CARNEGIE Foundation for the Advancement of Teaching*
CARNEGIE Foundation for the Advancement of Teaching
Cncl rpts on coll ethics 4-18, 282A2
Cncl rpts on high schls 11-27, 925D1-A2
CARNEGIE Institute Museum of Art (Pittsburgh, Pa.)
Arkus retiremt set 5-11, 375C2
CARNER, JoAnne
Wins LPGA match-play title 2-4, 220D3
Wins Honda Civic Classic 3-18, Women's Kemper 4-1; 2d in Lady Citrus 4-22, 587A2-D2
LPGA top money winner 11-30, 969G2
CARNES, Rev. Paul N.
Dies 3-17, 272C2
Succeeded by Pickett 4-29, 376A2
CARNEY, Art
Going in Style released 12-25, 1007D3
CARNEY, Dennis
Backs Wheeling-Pittsburgh fed aid 8-28, 682B1
CAROLINA Power & Light Co.
A-plant plans canceled 1-4, 186D2
CARON, Leslie
Goldengirl released 6-15, 820C1
CARPENTER, M. Kathleen
On military racism 7-23, 561B3
CARPENTER, Paul
Scores Fonda pol stance 7-20, 593E2
CARPENTER, Rob
Oilers win in playoffs 12-29, 1001A1
CARR, Judge George
Voids Fla HS literacy test 7-12, 785D3
CARR, James A.—*See ABRAHAMS, Alan*
CARR, M. L.
NBA stolen-ball ldr 4-8, 290A3
CARR, Richard T.
Beasley pleads no contest re '77 loan 5-14, 380F3
Indicted 5-23, pleads not guilty 5-24, 380D2
CARR, Terry
Almost Perfect Affair released 4-26, 528B1
CARRADINE, Keith
Old Boyfriends released 3-21, 528C3
Almost Perfect Affair released 4-26, 528C1
CARRASCO, Santiago C.
Admits killing ABC rptr 6-30, 512B3
CARRERA, Vinicio
Venez transport min 3-10, 192C3
CARRERO Blanco, Adm. Luis (d. 1973)
Gen, 2 cols assassinated 5-25, 428E2
CARRICK, John
Cabt operatns streamlined 2-4, 113D2
CARRIER Corp.
United Tech merger OKd by ct 1-31, terms set 3-30, 349E3-350A1
SEC scores United merger 6-25, shareholders back 7-5, 541A3
CARRILLO, Santiago
Asks unity with Soclsts 4-4, 256A3
CARRINGTON, Lord
UK foreign secy 5-5, 338D1, F1
Sees Vance re Zimbabwe Rhodesia 5-21–5-23, 393E2
Zimbabwe Rhodesia envoy set 5-22, 393C2
Backs common NATO policy re SALT III 5-30, 415E3
Iraq ties rptd restored 7-5, 583B2
On Zimbabwe recogntn proposal 7-10, 546C3
Australia A-pact signed 7-24, 562G2
Opens Zimbabwe conf 9-10; const chng, agenda debated 9-11, 9-12, 675E2-676A1
Protest re US aides' Zimbabwe conf role rptd 9-20, 718A2
Zimbabwe const proposal OKd 9-21, 9-24, 718C1
Offers Zimbabwe const 10-3, delivers Patriotic Front ultimatum 10-11, opens unilateral talks 10-16 777B2
Tories endorse Zimbabwe policy 10-10, 791G2, B3
Patriotic Front OKs const 10-18, 844F1
Offers Zimbabwe transitn plan 11-2, 844D1, B2
On Zimbabwe sanctns lapse 11-7, 881A2
Zimbabwe transitn talks continue 11-9–11-14, Patriotic Front OKs plan 11-15, 880G3, 881C1
Offers Zimbabwe cease-fire plan 11-16, Muzorewa OKs 11-26, Patriotic Front OKs gen terms 12-5, 936G3-937F1
Zimbabwe cease-fire signed 12-21, 976B3
CARROLL, Gordon
Alien released 5-24, 528A1
CARROLL, James
Mortal Friends on best-seller list 7-1, 548D3

1980

CARMAN, Greg
Elected to US House 11-4, 843C3
CARMET, Jean
Soupcon released 3-26, 416E3
CARMICHAEL, Harold
NFL '79 touchdown ldr 1-5, 8E2
CARMICHAEL, Stokely
At DC draft protest 3-22, 228A1
CARNEGIE Foundation for the Advancement of Teaching
Cncl rpts on declining coll enrollmt 1-22, 319D2
CARNEGIE Institution of Washington (Washington, D.C.)
Animal, bacteria gene differences rptd 1-23, 160D1
Planetary core study rptd 6-19, 715B2
CARNER, JoAnne
Wins Whirlpool Championship 2-3, Bent Tree Classic 2-24, Sunstar Classic 3-9, Honda Civic 3-16, 412D2, G2, A3
Wins Lady Keystone Open 6-22, 2d in Mayflower 7-6, 715B1, C1
2d in Peter Jackson Classic 8-10, 972F1
LPGA top money winner 10-12, 971F3
CARNESALE, Albert
Named NRC chrmn 7-9, 551A3
CARNEY, Rep. William (R, N.Y.)
Reelected 11-4, 843C3
CARNY (film)
Released 6-13, 675B2
CAROLINE, Princess (Monaco)
Divorced 10-9, 890D3
CAROTHERS, A. J.
Hero at Large released 2-8, 216F2
CARPENTER, Elizabeth S.
Educ Dept transitn aide 1-9, 18C2
CARPENTER, John
Fog released 2-29, 216E2
CARPENTER, Rhys
Dies 1-2, 104B2
CARPENTER, Thelma
Turns opens 6-16, 756G3
CARPENTERS & Joiners of America, United Brotherhood of (AFL-CIO)
Sidel confrmd Panama Canal comr 4-2, 308E3
CARR, Austin
In NBA expansn draft 5-28, 447D1
CARR, Rep. Bob (D, Mich.)
Loses reelection 11-4, 851C1
CARR, John
Families Conf opens in Md 6-5, 442E3
Families Conf meets in Minn 6-19—6-21, LA 7-10—7-12, 601B2
CARR, Richard T.
Fraud chrgs reduced 4-9, 292A1
Cleared on 3 counts, mistrial declared on 3 4-30, 332F3
US case dropped 6-9, 459A3
CARRIER Corp.
United Tech suit settled 3-6, 558E1
CARRIERE, Jean-Claude
Tin Drum released 4-11, 416F3
CARRILLO, Santiago
Sees police ldrs, vows support 10-22, 832B2
CARRINGTON, Lord
In Pak, India on Afghan crisis 1-16, 27E1, A2
UK retaliates vs Sovts re Afghan 1-26, 67C3
Chrgs Mugabe voter intimidatn 2-6, 118E2
On Afghan neutrality plan 2-19, 123G3
Vance asks backing vs Sovt Afghan invasn 2-21, 139C2
On Zimbabwe vote 3-4, 161G2
In Rumania 3-13, Sovt Afghan move scored 3-14, 205G1
Gibraltar links to Spain set 4-10, 274G2
Saudi ties strained 4-10, 4-11, 294E1
Says EC bars Iran oil purchase 4-22, 298F1
Regrets Saudi TV film 5-22, 407A3
Asked UN Cncl Res 242 chng to aid Palestinians 5-31, 418B1
Wage curbs rptd rejected 6-7, 444E3
On New Hebrides unrest 6-11, 436B2
Hopeful on Reagan electn 11-5, 841B3

1976

CARROLL, Dr. Robert G.
Pittsburgh radiatn subjects recalled 5-12, 384C2
CARSON, Robert C. (Sonny)
Acquitted, '74 convictn cited 2-6, 124E1
CARSTENS, Karl
Scores W Ger detente policy 1-29, 157G3
W Ger Parlt pres 12-14, 968B3
CARSWELL, G. Harrold
Cited in Ford biog sketch 614C1
CARTER, Amy
To attend DC public schl 11-28, 917D2
CARTER, Billy
Gas station blast 8-7, 585A2
Family holdings rptd 8-19, 646B1
'70 Carter campaign donor 10-17, 805B1
CARTER, Don
'70 Carter campaign donor 10-17, 805B1
CARTER, Harlan
Scores gun control 3-2, 170B2
CARTER, Hugh
'70 Carter campaign donor 10-17, 805A1
CARTER, Judge James
Porpoise killing curbed 10-15, 902C1
CARTER, Jeff
Dole cites remark on Graham 10-6, 763F3

1977

CARROLL, John
Rejects govt pay proposal 6-29, 599C3
CARRUTHERS, Ian K.
Sues govt, Rudnicki suit cited 6-13, 541A3
CARS—*See AUTOMOBILES*
CARSON, Jack W.
Scores Carter econ plan 1-10, 14C1
CARSWELL, Andrew
Rpt scores air safety enforcemt 11-28, 965C3
CARSWELL, G. Harrold
Byrd support cited 1-4, 6B1
CARTELS—*See ANTITRUST*
CARTER, Amy
Nursemaid granted reprieve 2-3, 254D2
CARTER, Billy
Brother sets up trust 1-4, 5A1
Pres tax data issued 6-24, 499E2
CARTER 3rd, Chip (James Earl)
At Indian rite, meets Gandhi 2-13, 116B1
Pres call-in topic 3-5, 171F1
Visits China 4-9—4-17, 298B2
China goodwill message rptd 4-22, 321A3
CARTER 3rd, Hodding
Named State Dept spokesman 1-17, 53F1
Scores Dole Canal cable release 10-5, 755C1

1978

CARROLL, Gov. Julian (D, Ky.)
Sees Carter on coal strike 2-23, 122E3
On coal pact chances 2-27, 160D1
Backs Carter on budget 12-20, 980E2
CARROLL, Wallace E.
Sued re Katy bribe 8-30, 737B1
CARROLL County, Ill.—*See ILLINOIS*
CARROLL v. Department of HEW
Fed fund bar for ct-ordrd desegregatn refused review 2-27, 143F1
CARS—*See AUTOMOBILES*
CARS, Hadar
Swedish trade min 10-18, 822A3
CARSTENS, Karl
Confirms past Nazi membership 11-10, 872G1
CART (Championship Auto Racing Teams)—*See AUTOMOBILE Racing*
CARTELS—*See ANTITRUST*
CARTER, Amy
In S Amer, Africa 3-28—4-3, 233B1
CARTER, Dixie
Fathers & Sons opens 11-16, 1031E1
CARTER 3rd, Hodding
Defends US Jonestown pre-suicide probes 11-24, 910B1
On US proposal re Cyprus dispute 11-29, 922B2
CARTER, J. Michael
Indicted 7-13, 681B1

1979

CARROLL, Joe Barry
Indiana wins NIT 3-21, 238F3
CARROLL, John (Julian La Faye)
Dies 4-24, 356C3
CARROLL, Lewis (1832-98)
But Never Jam Today opens 7-31, 711G1
CARROLL, Vinnette
But Never Jam Today opens 7-31, 711G1
CARS (singing group)
Candy-O on best-seller list 7-4, 548F3; 8-1, 620F3; 10-3, 800F3
CARSON, Johnny
Won't quit Tonight Show 5-2, 334B3
Linked to Nev casino purchase 12-21, 992B2
CARSON, Willie
Troy wins Irish Derby 7-1, 876E3
CARSTENS, Karl (West German president)
Elected W Ger pres, Nazi past protested 5-23, 410F2
Poehl named Bundesbank chief 9-19, 733A3
CARSWELL, G. Harold
Assaulted in Atlanta 9-11, 859D3
CARSWELL, Robert G.
On Iran assets freeze 11-16, 879E3
Japan vows pressure vs Iran 12-17–12-18, 959B1
CART (Championship Auto Racing Teams)—*See AUTOMOBILE Racing*
CARTAGENA, Desiderio
Testimony on soclsts '78 deaths rptd 5-3, 350E2
CARTELS—*See ANTITRUST*
CARTER, Amy
Visits Japan 6-24–6-29, 494B1
Boats down Mississippi 8-17–8-24, 622G1, F2
CARTER, Billy
Hosts Libyans 1-9, rptd anti-Semitic remarks spur controversy 1-11–1-13, 31C2; Carter defends 2-27, 149E2
Lance banking favors rptd 1-17, 31A1
Hospitalizatn rptd 2-27, 149F2
Brother's trustee buys land 3-1, 'hush money' hinted 3-22, 203G1
Hospitalized for alcohol abuse 3-7, 271A3
Peanut loan scheme alleged 3-11–3-13, spec prosecutor sought 3-13, 183F3-184B2
Peanut probe spec counsel named 3-20, 203B1
Peanut probe spec counsel gains more power 3-23, 301G2-B3
Denies peanut loan -'76 campaign link, false bank rpts 4-11, 301C3
Confrms Libya financed '78 trip, denies business dealings 4-15, 310C1
Testifies on family business loans 5-18, 380G3
Brother releases financial data 5-31, 420G1
Brother's optn on business rptd 6-19, 500E2
At Qaddafi coup celebratn 9-1, 688D3
Cleared in family business probe 10-16, 782G2-783A1
CARTER, Bonita
Slain by police 6-22, 2,000 protest 7-20, 869D3
CARTER, Butch
Indiana wins NIT, named co-MVP 3-21, 238G3
CARTER, Chip
In missn to Saudi, Jordan 3-17–3-18, 198B1
Fla delegate rule lobby failure rptd 8-2, 593D1
At Park funeral 11-3, 843F3
CARTER, Dixie
Taken in Marriage opens 2-26, 292D3
CARTER, Donald C.
Oklahoma! opens 12-13, 1007D2
CARTER, Gary
NL wins All-Star Game 7-17, 569B1
CARTER, Cardinal Gerald Emmett
Installed cardinal 6-30, 640B2
CARTER 3rd, Hodding
Kennedy anti-shah remark deplored 12-3, 918D3
CARTER, J. Michael
Convicted 1-23, 205A3; sentncd 3-27, 291E3

1980

CARROLL, Joe Barry
NCAA basketball tourn results 3-24, 240E1
In NBA draft 6-10, 447A1, E1
CARS (recording)
On best-seller list 6-4, 448E3
CARSON, Johnny
NBC contract rptd signed 5-6, 470G3
CARSON, Willie
Henbit wins English Derby 6-4, 448B1
CARSTENS, Karl (West German president)
Greets Pope 11-15, 905C1
CARTER, Amy
DC draft protest held 3-22, 227G3
Father cites in TV debate 10-28, 815C1
CARTER, Billy
Registers as Libyan agent 7-14, 542A2
Libyan role rptd, Sen probe set 7-22—7-24, 548F2
Libyan role controversy grows; veracity questioned, cables released 7-22—7-31; Vesco connectn discounted 7-30, 569A1-570D1
Dem open conv move forms 7-25—7-31, 570E1
Byrd scores Pres Carter's judgemt 7-26, 8-2, 596A3
Releases secret cable on Libya 8-1, 595D1
Pres Carter denies impropriety; rpts to Sen panel, natn 8-4, 592F1; news conf text excerpt 593A2
Sen probe opens 8-4, 8-6, 595F2
Civiletti withheld info 8-6, Justice probe begun 8-7, 595G1, D2
Watergate counsel declines Sen probe role 8-7, 595E3
Sen probe counsel named 8-11, 647E2
Sen probe continues, 2 associates rptd under investigatn 8-19—8-21, 647A2
Testifies before Sen probe 8-21—8-22, 647A1-A2
Sen probe hearings 9-4—9-17, 700D3
Sen probe concluded 9-22—9-24, critical rpt issued 10-2, 763B3-764F1
Charter Media dissolved 9-30, 836C2
Govt informant indicted in bank fraud 10-20, 860C3
Pres Carter faulted on Sen probe 10-29—11-1, 841E1
Bob Hope stumps for Reagan 11-3, 840A3
CARTER, Caron
Divorced 2-29, 199G1
Remarries 6-21, 639B1
CARTER, Chip
Divorced 2-29, 199G1
Ex-wife remarries 6-21, 639B1
CARTER, Gary
NL batting ldr 10-6, 926E2
2d in NL MVP vote 11-26, wins Golden Glove 12-6, 925C3, 926E1
CARTER 3rd, Hodding
US regrets Abscam term 2-12, 111A2
Vs Kennedy Iran remarks 2-13, 109G2
Assails Sovt Olympic moves 4-4, 259F1, C2
Refused oath re leaks; resignatn cited 7-16—7-17, 549B2
CARTER, J. Michael
Bank fraud appeal declined by Sup Ct 3-17, 226G1
CARTER 4th, James Earl
Parents divorced 2-29, 199A2

CARTER, JIMMY (JAMES EARL JR.)

1976

Abortion—*See 'Medicine & Health' below*

1977

ABORTION—*See MEDICINE in this section below*
AGE and Aged Persons
Seeks Soc Security chngs 5-9, 363F2
Scores liberals' criticism 5-12, 380F3
Signs job funds 5-13, 380D3
Soc Security Miss town mtg topic 7-21, 575F1
GOP offers Soc Sec plan 9-9, 720A2, D2
House votes mandatory retiremt curb 9-23, 737B3
Delays tax pkg, asks Soc Sec actn 10-27, 813A1, A3, C3
Hopeful on Soc Sec legis 11-30, 914A1
Lauds Soc Sec bill passage 12-15, 957E3, 958C1; signs 12-20, 1001C2
Medicare—*See under MEDICINE in this section below*

1978

ABORTION—*See MEDICINE in this section below*
AGE and Aged Persons
State of Union Message 1-19, 30E2
Budget proposals 1-23, 44E2, 46F3, 47B1, 48B2; table 45C2, E2
Seeks job-bias unit reorgn 2-23, 124A1
Links Soc Sec hike, tax cuts 3-2, 141D1
Soc Sec rollback opposed 4-5, 240D3
Signs mandatory retiremt curb 4-6, 238E2
Soc Sec rollback veto warned 5-17, 386C1
Cites US commitmt 11-27, 914C3
Medicare—*See under MEDICINE in this section below*

1979

ABORTION—*See MEDICINE in this section below*
AGE and Aged Persons
Budget proposals 1-22, 41C2, F2, 43G2; tables 42A1, C2, D2
Soc Sec cuts opposed in Cong 1-23, 55A3
Defends Soc Sec budget 1-26, 70B1
Medicare—*See under MEDICINE in this section below*

1980

ABORTION—*See MEDICINE & Health in this section*
AGE and Aged Persons
Asks Soc Sec fund boost 1-21, 43F3
Budget proposals 1-28, 70A2, 72G1; tables 69G3, 70C1, D1
Pensn chngs urged 5-23, 404A2
Scored by GOP plank 7-10, 506A3; rebuts chrgs 7-17, 532E1
Renominatn acceptance speech cites 8-14, 612G3, 613F1, B2
Attacks Reagan Soc Sec stand 9-3, 699B1
Signs multi-employer pensn plan reform 9-26, 856C3
Backs expanded Soc Sec, natl health insurnc 10-10, 778B3, C3, 779A2
Ridicules Reagan 'secret plan' 10-22, 802E3
Chrgs Reagan 'flipflop' on Soc Sec 10-27, 816B3
Debates Soc Sec with Reagan 10-28, 813B2, 815A2

1976

Amnesty Issue—*See 'Foreign Policy & Defense' below*

1977

AGRICULTURE
Keeps Ford budget total 2-22, 125B2
Call-in topic 3-5, 171D1
Milk price supports hiked 3-22, 214A1
Requests drought aid 3-23, 210B2
Bergland on farm plan 3-23, 214C1
Giaimo proposes budget 3-23, 229A1
Favors reserves build-up 4-15, 299A1
Bars sugar import quotas 5-4, 457D3
McGovern scores farm policy 5-13, 381D2
Cong sets '78 budget target 5-17, 405A1
Would veto Sen farm bill 5-26, 417C1; O'Neill cautns 6-1, 459A3
Signs '78 funds bill 8-12, 688G2
Sugar subsidies ruled illegal 8-19, 854G3
Cuts wheat acreage, asks reserves; ups corn price supports 8-29, 666B2
Signs farm bill 9-29, 736D2, G2
Halts aide's personal lobbying 9-30, 773C1
Meets farm editors 10-2, 761E2
Visits Iowa, Diehl farm 10-21, 817B1
Sets sugar price-support loan guarantee, import duty hike 11-8, 854D3
Signs '77 crop disaster-aid ceiling removal 11-8, 1001E2
Cuts feed grain acreage 11-15, 916C2
Farmers protest in Plains 11-25, 916E1
Meets striking farmers 12-24, 1002F3
Stresses campaign vow 12-28, 1002A1
AID—*See FOREIGN Aid in this section below*
AMNESTY Issue—*See DEFENSE in this section below*
APPOINTMENTS
Issues conflict-of-interest code 1-4, 4C2
Signs formal nominatns 1-20, 25D2
Proposes ethics law 5-3, 338B1
Cabinet & Subcabinet
Aaron, HEW asst secy 1-19, 53B1
Adams confrmd Transport secy 1-20, 34B1, B3
Alexander, Army secy 1-19, 52F3; nominated 2-2, confrmd 2-11, 148C3
Anderson, Treas undersecy 3-4; confrmd 3-29, 272E2
Andrus confrmd Interior secy 1-20, 34B1, G3
Axelson, Treas dep secy 1-18, 52D3; withdraws 3-9, 191A2
Babcock, asst atty gen 2-16; confrmd 3-4, 211D1
Bell atty gen confrmatn hearings 1-11—1-18; delayed 1-20, 34C1; confrmd 1-25, sworn 1-26, 52G2
Bennett, State asst secy 1-21, 53C1
Benson, State undersecy 1-7, 14G1
Bergland confrmd Agri secy 1-20, 34B1, C3
Bergsten, Treas asst secy 1-18, 52E3
Berry, HEW asst secy 1-19, 53A1
Bingham, Labor asst secy 3-11; confrmd 3-18, 272F2
Blumenthal confrmd Treas secy 1-20, 34A1, E3
Bracy, Transport asst secy 2-7, confrmd 2-10, 148C3
Brown confrmd Defense secy 1-20, 34A1
Burkhardt, Labor asst secy 3-11; confrmd 3-18, 272F2
Butchman, Transport dep secy 2-7, confrmd 2-10, 148D3
Califano HEW secy confrmatn hearings 1-13; delayed 1-20, 34C1, E3; confrmd 1-24, sworn 1-25, 52D2, F2
Carter, State asst secy 1-17, 53F1
Champion, HEW undersecy 1-19, 53A1; Sen com OKs 3-23, 235E3
Christopher, State dep secy 2-7, confrmd 2-24, 148D3
Civiletti, asst atty gen 2-16; confrmd 3-4, 211D1
Civiletti, dep atty gen 12-6, 1001D3
Claytor, Navy secy 1-19, 52G3; nominated 2-7, confrmd 2-11, 148D3
Cooper, State undersecy 1-7, 14B2
Davenport, Transport asst secy 2-7, confrmd 2-10, 148E3
Days, asst atty gen 2-16; confrmd 3-4, 211E1
Duffey, State asst secy 1-21, 53C1
Duncan, Defns dep secy 1-28, confrmd 1-31, 148E3 ★
Flaherty, dep atty gen 3-9; confrmd 4-5, 272G2
Foreman, Agri asst secy 3-7; confrmd 3-24, 272A3
Gibbs, Army asst secy 4-7; confrmd 4-25, 418D1
Habib retained at State 1-7, 14A2
Harman, Commerce undersecy 1-6, 14F1
Harris confrmd HUD secy 1-20, 34B1, E2
Hathaway, Agri asst secy 3-24; confrmd 4-6, 272A3
Herbst, Interior asst secy 3-3; confrmd 4-1, 272A3
Hidalgo, Navy asst secy 4-1; confrmd 4-25, 418E1
Janis, HUD undersecy 3-4; confrmd 3-23, 272B3
Katz, State asst secy 1-21, 53E1
Kreps confrmd Commerce secy 1-20, 34B1, A3
LaBerge, Army undersecy 6-27; confrmd 7-21, 626A3
Lance confrmd OMB dir 1-20, 34B1, 35A1
Mark, AF undersecy 5-23; confrmd 7-21, 626A3
Marshall Labor secy confrmatn delayed 1-20, 34C1, G3; confrmd 1-26, sworn 1-27, 52B3
Martin, Interior asst secy 3-3; confrmd 4-11, 272B3
Martinez, HEW asst secy 1-19, 53B1
Maynes, State asst secy 1-21, 53D1
Meador, asst atty gen 2-14; confrmd 3-18, 211F1

1978

AGRICULTURE
State of Union Message 1-19, 30F3
Budget proposals 1-23, 44F2, 48D1; table 45E2
Vs parity demand, on migrant workers 1-30, 62C3, D3, 163D2
Signs drought aid extensn 2-7, 218A2
Meets protesting farmers 2-14, 163D2
Backs emergency farm bill 3-13, 177A3
Farm bill clears Sen 3-21, wage-price cncl scores 3-22, 218G3, 219C1
OKs set-aside paymts, grain reserve ceiling drop; sees income hike; Cong bill veto warned 3-29, 219C1-D2
Vows farm bill veto 4-6, 4-11; House defeats 4-12, 259G3, 261C1, D2, F2
Signs compromise farm bill, orders wheat support level hike 5-15, 465D3
Plans severe budget cuts 5-25, 404A3
Hikes meat import quotas, cites beef price rise 6-8, 428D2
Addresses farm assn in Mo 8-14, 626C1
Vows beef import limit, vs price controls 8-14, 626F1
Signs land purchase registratn 10-14, 897B2
Environmtlists score pesticide policy 12-20, 1009E1
APPOINTMENTS
Defends apptmt of US attys 2-17, 123E2
Minority data disclosed 6-15, 811D1
Backs judges merit selectn 11-8, 873F2-C3
Environmentalists laud 12-20, 1009D1

Allen, AF chief of staff 4-5, 281A2
Ball, NSC member 12-4, 929E2
Brewer, Marine Corps gen 5-11, 420F1
Carlucci confrmd CIA dep dir 2-9, 83A1
Civiletti confirmed dep atty gen 5-9, 342D3
Cohen, CAB chrmn 10-25, 806E2
Costle, Regulatory Cncl dir 10-31, 863C3
DeLuca, acting US Phila atty 1-24, 62D2
Earle, SALT negotiator 10-20, 804A2
Fettig, purchasing cncl chrmn 5-18, 405A2
Freeman, TVA bd chrmn 5-16, 390G1-G2
Gartner confrmd to CFTC 5-17; resignatn asked 6-26, refused 6-28, 513G2
Geller, telecommunicatns agency dir 3-28, 270C2
Hatcher rejcts White House liaison post 6-6, 568B3
Hayward, Navy operatns chief 4-5, 281A2
Jones, Joint Chiefs chrmn 4-5, 281F1
Kahn, anti-inflatn chief, Wage-Price Cncl chrmn 10-25, 806C1
King, CPSC chairwoman 6-29, 589A2
Kneip to Singapore (rptd) 6-6, 448G1
Kraft, pol group liaison 4-27, 306G3
Martin, pres asst 8-11, 663G3-664A1
McGarry, interim FEC member 10-25; Common Cause sues 10-26, 831F2-B3
Miller confirmed FRB chrmn 3-3, 161E1
Mondale, Arts cncl honorary dir 2-28, 335E2
Rafshoon, pub relatns aide 5-18, 386C3
Rockefeller, coal indus study comm chrmn 5-26, 405A1
Ross, Soc Sec comr 8-24, 664B1
Seignious, ACDA head 10-20, 804A2
Strauss, inflatn spec counsel 4-11, 259E2
Teeters to FRB 8-28, 664C1
Webster, FBI dir 1-19, 32C1; confrmd 2-9, 82G3
Weddington, pres asst 8-31, 681C3
Wexler, pres asst 4-19, 306F3
Zagoria, FEC nominatn withdrawn 8-12; to CPSC 9-29, confrmd 10-10, 831C3

1979

AGRICULTURE
Backs tobacco subsidies 1-17, 30C1
Budget proposals 1-22, 45G3-46D1; table 42F2
State of Union Message 1-23, 46F1, 47B1
Bergland bars price support hike 2-6, 109E2
On farmers' protest 2-27, 149A3
Proposes meat, poultry inspectn reform 3-25, 230A2
Vows farm energy supplies 5-4, 346C3
Seeks solar heat tax credit 6-20, 498E1
Cancels diesel fuel allocatn rule, farmers score 6-22, 479D3
Kennedy scores 11-12, 11-29, 962D1, E1
APPOINTMENTS
Askew, Immigratn Policy comr 2-16, 127A1; spec trade rep 8-8, 647B1*
Atherton, amb to Egypt 5-8, 347B3
Barrow, Marine Corps head 4-18, 307G2
Blumenthal, chief econ spokesman 6-4, 463C1
Brown confrmd to Appeals Ct 9-25, 901C3
Celeste, Peace Corps dir 3-29, 310F2
Chambers, Women's Natl Advisory Com acting head 1-16, 30B3
Civiletti, atty gen 7-19, 529E1; confrmd 8-1, sworn 8-16, 700A3
Claytor, Transportatn temp secy 7-20, 529D1; confrmd Defense dep secy 7-27, 577D1
Cutler, White House counsel 8-17, 623E1
Donovan, senior adviser 7-25, 556E1
Duncan, Energy secy 7-20, 529D1; confrmd 7-31, 627B2; sworn 8-24, 623E1
Freeman, GSA head 3-23, 232B2; confirmed 6-27, 965A3
Friedersdorf confrmd to FEC 2-21, 130B3
Gaskins, ICC chrmn 10-12, 831A1
Goldschmidt, Transportatn secy 7-27, 577B1
Harris, HEW secy 7-19, 529D1; confrmd 7-27, 577C1
Hidalgo, Navy secy 9-13, 700B3; confirmed 10-19, 965B1
Hufstedler, Educ secy 10-30, 829F1; confrmd 11-30, sworn 12-6, 946F2
Jordan, chief of staff 7-17, 529A1, G1
Klutznick, Commerce secy 11-16, 883C3
Kraft, campaign dir 8-10, 608F2
Krueger, Mex amb-at-large 6-22, 793D3
Landrieu, HUD secy 7-27, 577B1; confrmd 9-12, 700F2
Maddox, speechwriter 4-15, 300E3
McDonald, pres asst 8-10, 608G2
McGarry confrmd to FEC 2-21, 130B3
McHenry, UN Amb 8-31, 660F2; sworn 9-23, 763F2
Meyer, Army staff chief 5-2, 347F2
Miller, Treas secy 7-19, 529D1; confrmd 8-2, sworn 8-6, 627B2, D2
Muellenberg confirmed 4-10, 965A3
Laingen, amb to Iran 10-2, 752F2
Linowitz, Mideast envoy 938A1
McGill, Natl Agenda Comm chrmn 10-24, 810A3
Muellenberg, GSA inspector gen 1-30, 92D3
Pay Advisory Com 10-16, 829E2
Peterson, Consumer Affairs Cncl 9-26, 902C3
Renfrew, dep atty gen 11-20, 946A3
Robb, Women's Natl Advisory Com head 5-9, 351G1-A3
Seignious confrmd ACDA dir 3-1, 271C1
Stone confrmd CFTC chrmn 4-11, 681D2
Strauss, campaign chrmn 11-6, 961A2
3 Mile Island probe comm 4-11, 275C1
Torres, Mex-Amer affairs asst 8-10, 608F2
Valdez, chief of protocol 9-13, 700B3; confirmed 11-5, 965B1
Volcker, FRB chrmn 7-25, 555B2; confrmd 8-2, sworn 8-6, 627B2, E2
Watson, amb to USSR 7-20; confrmd 8-1, 794D3-795A1
Weddington, senior aide 8-10, 608E2
Woodcock confrmd China amb 2-26, 146D1

1980

AGRICULTURE
To ease farmer burden 1-4, 1B1, F1; Amer Agri Movemt seeks grain loans 1-6, 10C1, D1
Mondale defends grain embargo, Kennedy, Brown score 1-12, 32F2
Budget proposals 1-28, 73A2; table 70F1
Orders grain support loan rate hiked 7-28, 575E1
Renominatn acceptance speech cites grain embargo, farm subsidies 8-14, 613B1, B2
Reagan assails policy 9-30, 738A3
Says USSR hurt by grain embargo 11-12, 865E3
Canada ends grain embargo support 11-20, 900B2
Signs '80 Agri Act 12-3, 981G1
Signs '81 Agri appropriatn 12-15, 982B1
Signs plant protectn amendmt 12-22, 981A1
Soviet Grain Embargo—*See under GRAIN under 'G'*
APPOINTMENTS
Aiello, ethnic affairs aide 1-3, 5G3
A-waste disposal panel 2-12, 128C1
Carnesale, NRC chrmn 7-9, 551A3
Clausen, World Bank pres 10-30, 826A2
Clemon, US dist judge 1-10; confrmd 6-26, 744C2, C3
Dickenson, Park Svc dir 5-1, 333D2
Eidenberg, pres asst 6-11, 439B1
Gray, US dist judge 1-10, withdraws 9-17, 744C2, D3
Jordan, campaign dep chrmn 6-11, 438G3
Lubbers confrmd NLRB cncl 4-23, 333E2
Muskie, secy of state 4-29, 323A2-C3; confrmd 5-7, sworn 5-8, 343A1
Nava confrmd Mex amb 4-3, 315E1
Panama Canal Comm confrmd 4-2, 308C3
Sawhill, Synfuels Corp chrmn 9-10, Sen panel OKs 9-25, 699C1, 725E2
Sheffield, US dist judge 4-9; Sen confirmatn hearings halted 8-27, 744E3
Synfuels Corp interim bd 10-5, 786E2-A3
Thompson, US dist judge 9-17, 744D3
Watson, chief of staff 6-11, 438G3
Winberry US dist judgeship nominatn rejctd 3-4, 250E2

1976 1977 1978 1979 1980

Medina, HUD asst secy 4-25; confrmd 5-25, 500A1
Mendelsohn, Interior asst secy nominatn withdrawn 11-11, 877A2
Moose, State dep undersecy 1-7, 14A2
Murray, Defense asst secy 4-1; confrmd 4-25, 418F1
Nelson, Army asst secy 5-19; confrmd 5-27, 500A1
Nye, State undersecy 1-21, 53D1
Packer, Labor asst secy 3-11; confrmd 3-18, 211F1 *
Pierre, Army asst secy 4-25; confrmd 5-9, 418G1
Read, State undersecy 7-25; confrmd 8-3, 626D3
Richmond, HEW asst secy 6-9; confrmd 6-28, 626D3
Ross, Defense asst secy 1-19, 52G3; confrmd 3-4, 211F1
Schlesinger, Energy secy; confrmd 8-4, 591C2
Shanahan, HEW asst secy 1-19, 53B1
Simons, HUD asst secy 3-11, confrmd 3-23, 272C3
Solomon, Treas undersecy 1-18, 52D3
Thomas, State asst secy 1-21, 53E1
Vance confrmd State secy 1-20, 34A1, C3
Vest, State asst secy 5-5; confrmd 5-25, 500C1
Wald, asst atty gen 2-16; confrmd 3-4, 211G1
Warden, HEW asst secy 3-11; confrmd 3-29, 272D3
Weddington, Agri gen counsel 7-15; confrmd 8-4, 626F3
White, Agric dep secy 3-10; confrmd 3-15, 211G1
White, Defense asst secy 4-21; confrmd 5-9, 418A2
Woodworth, Treas asst secy 1-7, 14C2; nominated 2-18, confrmd 2-21, 148G3
Woolsey, Navy undersecy 2-21; confrmd 3-4, 211A2

Diplomatic

Alston to Australia 4-7; confrmd 4-29, 418B1
Bennett to NATO 4-7; confrmd 4-25, 418C1
Bergus to Sudan 5-13; confrmd 5-25, 499D3
Bolen to E Ger 7-8; confrmd 7-28, 626D2
Brewster to UK 4-7; confrmd 4-29, 418C1
Castro to Argentina 8-19; sworn 10-20, 817B2
Chambers to Belgium 4-7; confrmd 4-29, 418C1
Cohen to Senegal, Gambia 6-10; confrmd 6-23, 626D2
Eagleburger to Yugo 5-13; confrmd 6-7, 499E3
Fox to Trinidad 5-17; confrmd 6-7, 499E3
Gardner to Italy 1-7, 14D2
Garthoff to Bulgaria 7-8; confrmd 7-28, 626E2
Goheen to India 4-7; confrmd 4-25, 418D1
Hartman to France 5-13; confrmd 6-7, 499E3
Haynes to Algeria 4-27; confrmd 4-27, 418E1
Heck to Nepal 5-3; confrmd 5-25, 499F3
Hummel to Pak 5-23; confrmd 6-7, 499F3
Irving to Jamaica 5-19; confrmd 5-25, 499F3
Jones to Haiti 7-26; confrmd 8-3, 626E2
Kaiser to Hungary 6-22; confrmd 6-30, 626F2
Kennedy-Minott to Sweden 7-26; confrmd 8-3, 626G2
Killgore to Qatar 7-26; confrmd 8-3, 626G2
LeMelle to Kenya, Seychelles 4-7; confrmd 5-9, 418F1
Lerner to Norway 7-1; confrmd 7-13, 626A3
Lewis to Israel 4-7; confrmd 4-25, 418F1
Linehan to Sierra Leone 5-23; confrmd 6-23, 626A3
Lowenstein to Luxembourg 5-13; confrmd 5-25, 499G3
Lucey to Mex 5-19; confrmd 5-25, 499G3
Mansfield to Japan 4-7; confrmd 4-21, 418G1
Miller to Malaysia 5-13; confrmd 5-25, 500A1
Norland to Botswana, Lesotho, Swaziland 4-25; confrmd 6-23, 626B3
Ortiz to Barbados, Grenada 6-29; confrmd 7-13, 626C3
Parker to Leb 2-4, confrmd 2-10, 148F3
Pezzullo to Uruguay 7-1; confrmd 7-13, 626C3
Richardson, amb at large 1-17, 53F1; nominated 2-22, confrmd 2-24, 148F3
Ridgway to Finland 5-3; confrmd 5-25, 500B1
Schaufele to Greece 6-23; confrmd 7-13, 626E3
Shannon to Ireland 6-20; confrmd 6-21, 626E3
Shlaudeman to Peru 5-13; confrmd 5-25, 500B1
Smythe to Cameroon 4-25; confrmd 5-9, 418A2
Solaun to Nicaragua 7-8; confrmd 7-28, 626E3
Spiers to Turkey 4-15; confrmd 5-25, 500B1
Strauss, trade rep 3-11; confrmd 3-29, 272C3; sworn 3-30, 249D1 *
Sullivan to Iran 4-7; confrmd 5-25, 500C1
Toon to USSR 4-25; confrmd 6-7, 500C1

1976

1977

Warner to Switz 5-26; confrmd 6-7, 500D1
Warnke, SALT negotiator 2-2; controversy ensues 2-3—2-8, 88F3; 2-9—3-9, confrmd 3-9, 171G3-172D2
Weissman to CR 5-19; confrmd 5-25, 500D1
West to Saudi Arabia 5-24; confrmd 6-7, 500D1
Wolf to Austria 6-16; confrmd 6-22, 626F3
Woodcock, Peking liaison 5-12, 381A2
Young confrmd UN amb 1-26, 52C3

Miscellaneous

Abzug declines post 2-19, 140B3
Biddle, arts endowment chrmn 10-31; confrmd 11-4; sworn 11-30, 927G3
Blum, EPA dep admin 2-16; confrmd 3-4, 211D1
Borg, State exec secy 1-21, 53E1
Bosworth, wage-price cncl dir 7-8; confrmd 7-22, 626D2
Boyer, Educ comr 1-19, 52G3
Brown, ACTION dir 2-18, confrmd 2-25, 148C3
Carlucci, CIA dep dir 12-22, 1001E3
Claybrook, Natl Highway Traffic Safety admin 3-18; confrmd 4-6, 272G2
Cleland, VA admin 2-18, confrmd 2-25, 148E3
Costle, EPA admin 2-16; confrmd 3-4, 211E1
Edey rejctd for environmt cncl 10-17, 800G1
Falco, State drug advisor 1-21, 53D1
Frank, NOAA dir 6-30; confrmd 7-13, 626E2
Fredrickson retained at NIH 2-3, 211B1
Goldman, FEA asst admin 4-7; confrmd 5-12, 418E1
Gramley to CEA 1-18, 52E3
Griffin, Gen Svcs acting admin 2-15, 148F3
Hansen rejctd for NRC 10-17, 800E1
Johnson, FBI dir 8-17, 626A2; withdraws nominatn 11-29, 914C2
Jorling, EPA asst admin 6-1; confrmd 6-21, 626F2
King, ACTION dep dir 2-24; confrmd 3-4, 211E1
Laise, Forgn Svc dir gen 1-21, 53E1
Lake, Policy Planning dir 1-7, 14B2
Lewis, ACTION assoc dir 7-13; confrmd 8-4, 626A3
McCree, solicitor gen 2-16; confrmd 3-4, 211F1
McIntyre, OMB dir 12-27, 1001B3
Military Compensatn Comm 6-27, 499A3
Miller, FRB chrmn 12-28, 1000D1
Morton, US treasurer 6-7; confirmd 8-2, 626B3
Mundheim, Treasury gen counsel 6-15; confrmd 8-2, 626B3
Nimetz, State counselor 1-7, 14C2
Nordhaus to CEA 1-18, 52E3
Norton, EEOC chrmn 5-16; confrmd 5-27, 500A1
Page, Urban Mass Transport admin 6-13; confrmd 7-1, 626C3
Pertschuk to FTC 3-25; confrmd 4-6, 272B3
Peterson, consumer affairs adviser 4-4, 354D2
Reinhardt, USIA dir 1-7, 14G1
Rollins, FEA asst admin 7-14; confrmd 8-4, 626D3
Saunders, State intellignc bur dir 1-21, 53E1
Schultze confrmd CEA chrmn 1-20, 34B1, 35A1
Siemer, Defense gen counsel 4-1; confrmd 4-25, 418G1
Sorensen withdraws CIA nominatn 1-17, 35B1, B2
Speth to environmt cncl 3-7; confrmd 4-4, 272C3
Sullivan, Fed RR admin 4-29; confrmd 6-23, 626F3
Turner, CIA dir 2-7, confrmd 2-24, 148G3
Warnke, arms control agency dir 2-2, controversy ensues 2-3—2-8, 88F3; 2-9—3-9, confrmd 3-9, 171G3-172D3
Williams to SEC 3-30; confrmd 4-7, 272D3
Zwick, Mil Compensatn Comm chrmn 6-27, 499D3

White House

Aragon, spec asst, ombudsman 1-14, 35D3
Bourne, mental health asst 1-14, 35C3
Costanza, pres asst 1-14, 35F2
Eizenstat, domestic affairs asst 1-14, 35A3
Jordan, pres asst 1-14, 35F2
King, asst for personnel 1-14, 35B3
Kraft, apptmts asst 1-14, 35A3
Lipshutz, pres counsel 1-14, 35E2
Mitchell, spec projects asst 1-14, 35C3
Moore, cong liaison asst 1-14, 35A3
Watson, intergovt asst, Cabt secy 1-14, 35G2

ARMAMENTS—*See ATOMIC Energy, DEFENSE, DISARMAMENT and FOREIGN Policy in this section below*

ARMS Control—*See ATOMIC Energy, DISARMAMENT and FOREIGN Policy in this section below*

ARTS & Culture
Asks State Dept bur reorganizatn 10-11, 797C2

ASTRONAUTICS
Keeps Ford budget figure 2-22, 125B2
Call-in topic 3-5, 171C1
Signs NASA '78 authorizatn 7-30, 688G3

1978

ARMAMENTS—*See also DISARMAMENT and FOREIGN Policy in this section below*
Gets '77 mil strategy rpt 1-6, 5G2
State of Union Message 1-19, 29B1, A3, 31B2
Budget proposals 1-23, 45B1-46B1
Signs B-1 fund rescissn 3-7, 160F2
Shipbldg goals reduced 3-24, 223F2
Defers neutron bomb productn 4-7, 253A1
Haig resignatn threat re neutron bomb rptd, denied 4-25, 298E2-B3
Sen budget target res sets higher ceiling 4-26, 305B3
Singlaub scores on neutron bomb, B-1 4-27, 321F2; 6-2, 433B2
Affirms A-parity with USSR 6-7, 424A1
Threatens carrier authrzn veto 6-8, 432A1
Neutron bomb indecisn scored by 2 sens 6-11, 469B3
New Sovt A-bomber rptd 6-19, 518E3
Sales policy assessed 7-16, 564F1
Vetoes '79 authrzn, scores A-carrier funds 8-17, 621A1
51 reps protest MAP missile plan 9-22, 737D3
Signs '79 aid authorzn, sets arms sales lid 9-26, 734C1, A2
Pentagon studies gen purpose missile 9-26, 738C1
Signs '79 defns funds 10-13, 833D1
Orders neutron parts productn 10-18, signs authorzn 10-25; USSR scores 8-26, 833B2, E2
Signs '79 aid funds 10-18, 862C2
Signs '79 revised authorzn 10-20, 833F1-A2
Cong com rpts A-arms reliability debate 11-3, 877G1
Cites '79 authorzn veto 11-6, 862D1
Plans '80 defns budget hike 11-9, 874E3, 875F1
Pentagon asks M-X, Trident 2 funds 11-15, 916C3
Discusses A-strategy, M-X, Trident 2 use 11-30, 916F2, B3

ARTS & Culture
Opens Natl Gallery additn 6-1, 578D2
Honors Marian Anderson 10-17, 844F1

ASTRONAUTICS
Budget proposals 1-23, 46C1; table 45D2
Defends Sovt satellite cooperatn 1-27, 57D2
Urges satellite safety rules, A-ban; discounts Sovt mil threat 1-30, 57E2, 62E1, G2-A3

1979

ARMAMENTS—*See also DISARMAMENT and FOREIGN Policy in this section below*
US A-target chng urged 1-13, 52B3
Budget proposals 1-22, 42A2-43G2
State of Union Message 1-23, 47F2, D3, 48E1
On MX deploymt 5-29, 402D1
OKs MX dvpt 6-8, reactn 6-9—6-11, 437E2-438D1
Sen OKs '80 authrzn 6-13, 438E1
Signs MX dvpt funds bill 7-25, 700A2
Vs budget, SALT linkage 7-27; US sens react 8-2, 8-3, 590G2
Chooses 'racetrack' MX deployment plan, diagram 9-7, 677F2, 678A2
Asks budget hike 9-11, 687D1
MX dvpt rptd assured 10-25, 822C3
Cites cruise, MX, Trident dvpt 12-12, 963E1

ARTS & Culture
Budget proposals 1-22, 46A3

ASTRONAUTICS
Budget proposals 1-22, 46E1; table 42F2
Addresses Cong on SALT II 6-18, 459E1
Offers Australia Skylab aid 7-11, 509B1
Signs '80 NASA funds bill 11-5, 883A3
Space shuttle support affirmed 11-14, 883E3

1980

ARMAMENTS
OKs FX jet for export 1-4, 16B3
A-blast mystery off S Africa unsolved 1-23, 49A3
Kennedy A-arms policy 2-20, 130D2
Reagan 'basic speech' excerpts 2-29, 207F2
MX deploymt rptd chngd 5-6, 369C2
Dem platform backs MX 6-24, 479A3, C3
Neutron bomb deferral cited 6-26, 486D3
Brown reassures allies on A-strategy shift, Muskie not consulted 8-8; Sovts score 8-11, 615D2-616B1
Wins MX plank 8-13, 611C2, 615B2
Muskie regrets A-strategy ommissn, sees enhanced role 8-13, 630E2
Renominatn acceptance speech; text 8-14, 612D1, F3, 613B1
Brown outlines A-strategy, ICBM vulnerability seen 8-20, 630D1
Defends A-strategy shift 8-21, 629F2
Blasts Reagan on A-race 9-2, 664A3
Signs '81 arms authrzn 9-8, 764F3
Signs '81 arms appropriatn 10-1, 803F2
Assails Reagan on A-superiority 10-16, 10-19, 802E2, A3
Debates with Reagan 10-28, 814F2
Anderson answers debate questns 10-28, 815G3
Hits Reagan on A-arms 10-29, 816C2
Plans spokesman role, on Reagan policy support 11-12, 865F2, A3
Signs A-arms authrzn 12-17, 981C1

ARMED Forces—*See DEFENSE & Armed Forces in this section*

ARTS & Culture
Signs Arts and Humanities Act 12-4, 982A1
Lauds John Lennon 12-9, 934B2

ASTRONAUTICS
Budget outlays, table 1-28, 70F1
Revised budget proposals 3-31, 244E1

1976 1977 1978 1979 1980

1977

ATOMIC Energy & Safeguards—*See also DEFENSE and DISARMAMENT in this section below*
In Australia safeguards, uranium collaboratn exchng 2-4, 3-11, 624G3
'78 budget revisns 2-22, 124E3, 125B2, C2
Outlines energy plans 3-17, 186C1, 191A1
Sees Japan premr re reprocessing plant 3-22, 209G2
Australia safeguards exchng rptd 3-23, 217F3
Asks plutonium ban, forgn A-fuel reprocessing curbs 4-7, 267A3
Plutonium ban assailed 4-13—5-2, 334E2
Presents energy plan 4-18, 4-20, 290E2, 295A1, F1; fact sheet 291F1, 293B2-E2
Asks A-export curbs 4-27, 334B1
Supplier natns score proposals 4-28—4-29, 403F1-A2
Salzburg intl conf 5-2—5-13, 402E2, F2, 403A1
OKs uranium shipmts 5-6, 403A2
7-natn summit debates A-sales, sets study 5-7—5-8, 357E2
Sees Schmidt 5-7, 358E1
Backs Italy A-plants 7-25—7-27, 581B2
Brezhnev rpts S Africa A-test plan 8-6, Carter confirms, vows actn vs 8-15, 663C3
Says S Africa denies A-plans 8-23, 649E2
Japan reprocessing pact 9-12, 812B3
Clinch R breeder OKd by House, veto confrontatn seen 9-20, 758C2
Addresses UN, stresses safeguards 10-4, 751G2, 752E1
Backs govt storage of spent fuel 10-18, offers intl aid 10-19, 794G1
Backs intl fuel bank 10-19, 794C1
Clinch R breeder funds clears Cong 10-20, 833A1
Vorster denies A-bomb vow 10-23, US releases letter 10-2, 825D2
On weapon spread policy 10-27, 813A3
Vetoes Clinch R breeder, other authorizatns 11-5, 854E2-D3
A-plant delays not linked to licensing 11-5, 917E2
Shah of Iran visits 11-15—11-16, 897F1
Signs NRC funds bill 12-13, 1001G2
Sets Iran sale details 12-31, 1001A1

AWARDS & Honors
Presents ecology award 4-15, 354F1
Plaque presented to Pele 10-1, 827D2
Awards Medals of Sci 11-22, 951G3-952C1

BANKS & Banking
Signs interest rate ceiling 4-19, 380E3
Gets privacy panel rpt 7-12, 632B1
Lance cleared of financial irregularities 8-18, 625E1-626F1
Sees bank reform need 8-23, 649G1
Admits overdrafts 8-23, 649C2
Lauds Burns, undecided on reapptmt 10-27, 813F3
Signs fed funds interest deposit bill 10-28, 1001D2
Denies FRB rift 11-10, 877C1
Signs S&L interest-rate extensn, FRB revisns 11-16, 878G1
Unsure re Burns reapptmt 11-30, 914F1

BLACK Americans
Plains church rejcts black 1-9, 53C2
Backs civil rights acts 2-16, 110D2
Speaks to Ohio kidnaper 3-9, 178B3
NAACP scores 6-27—6-28, Julian Bond 8-15, SCLC 8-18, Meany 8-30, 702A2
'No apologies' to blacks, poor; rebuts Jordan criticism 7-25, 7-28, 573C1, F2
Black Caucus backs Jordan 7-29, 592G3
15 ldrs form coalitn vs 8-29, 702G1
Vows jobs action 9-7, 702A1
Jobs a Detroit round-table topic 10-21, 817A1
Sees ldrs at White House 12-14, 960B1
Stresses campaign vow 12-28, 1002A1

BROADCASTING—*See PRESS below*

BUDGET—*See also other appropriate headings in this section*
Studies econ stimulus plan 1-7, 5G1-A2; labor, mgt score 1-10, 14D1
Outlines econ plan 1-27, 51G3; submits 1-31, 75A2
Cong, Admin debate econ plan 1-27—2-4, 89A2
Plans tough review of Cabt requests 2-14, 110B3
Fscl '78 revisns, table 2-22, 124B3-126E1
Vows balanced, zero-based budget 3-16, 190E3
On needless spending 3-16, 210B1
Giaimo proposes budget 3-23, 228D3
Vs tax rebate funds diversion 4-14, 270B3
Outlines anti-inflatn plan 4-15, 299A1, C1
Estimates energy plan impact 4-22, 321F2
GOPs score energy taxes 4-25, 320F3
Stresses balanced budget 5-2, 364B2
Scores liberals' criticism 5-12, 381A1
Signs $20 bln funds bill 5-13, 380D3
Reaffirms goal 5-17, 381G2
Cong sets '78 targets, table; '77 levels revised 5-17, 404D3, 405A1, E1
Would veto 3 spending bills 5-26, 417B1
Sees balanced budget by '81 7-21, 575E1
Cong sets binding '78 budget levels 9-15, 719G2
Defers naming new dir 10-2, 761D2

1978

GAO rpt on satellite radiatn hazards issued 2-6, 103F1
Marks NASA anniv: outlines US goals, confrms spy satellites, honors astronauts 10-1, 861A2

ATOMIC Energy & Safeguards—*For weapons issues, see ARMAMENTS above, DISARMAMENT below*
OKs uranium sale to India, safeguards discord revealed 1-2, 1F2
State of Union Message 1-19, 29B1, A3, 31D2
Budget proposals, omits Clinch R breeder 1-23, 46G1, D2
Defends Sovt satellite cooperatn 1-27, 57D2
Urges satellite A-curbs 1-30, 57E2, 62A3
GAO rpt on satellite radiatn hazards issued 2-6, 103F1
Backs state option right 2-17, 123E2
Rpts waste-disposal plan 2-27, 145A1
Signs Clinch R funds, plans terminatn use 3-7, 160C3; GAO says halt illegal 3-10, 183D2
Signs A-export controls 3-10, 183E1, B2
Waste storage rpt issued, task force study set 3-15, 183A3
A-plant licensing chngs proposed, scored 3-17, 205B2
Clinch R compromise proposal rptd 3-17, 3-23, 242C1
Stresses Brazil safeguards 3-29, 233A2
Hails union-contractor accord 4-18, 281A3, D3
Uranium sale to India barred 4-20, 288B3; OKs sale 4-27, 313G1
On waste disposal plan, A-plant sites 5-4, 321E1
Visits Oak Ridge, backs A-power 5-22, 386G2-B3
New uranium enrichmt contracts set 5-26, 408E1
Pledges India A-cooperatn 6-13—6-15, 466C3
Uranium sale to India allowed by House 7-12, 551E1
Breeder research backing linked to gas price compromise 8-23—8-26, 677F3-678E1
Eases forgn environmt impact policy 9-26, 804F2
Environmentalists score 12-20, 1009E1

AWARDS & Honors
Honors handicapped Scout 7-21, 844G1
Presents Space Medal of Honor to 6 10-1, 861A2
Honors Marian Anderson 10-17, 844F1
Cited by Nobel Peace Prize Com 10-27, 886E1
Gets family award from Mormons 11-27, 914G3

BANKS & Banking
On interest rates 1-12, 12B1
Links interest, forgn investmt 3-2, 140F3
Presents urban-aid plan, would create natl dvpt bank 3-27; reactn 3-27—3-30, 217A3, F3
OKs consumer co-op bank 8-20, 663E1
Scores FRB rate hike 9-27, 9-28, 751C3
Meany scores wage-price plan, asks interest rate curbs 10-31, 863B2
Signs banking reform bill 11-10, 1002E3
Reaffirms natl dvpt bank plan 11-27, mayors oppose 11-29, 914B3, G3

BLACK Americans
State of Union Message 1-19, 29C2, 30A3
Jordan urges job pressure 3-15, HEW aid 9-21, 811D1, B2
Black ldrs critical 4-10, 568A3
Hatcher rejcts liaison post 6-6, 568B3
Job apptmt data disclosed 6-15, 811E1
Sees Houston ldrs 6-24, 509F3
Mondale details proposals, scores Cong 8-7, 811C1
Names Martin spec liaison 8-11, 663G3
Meets Cong Black Caucus on Humphrey-Hawkins bill 9-29, 808C1
Rpts on Viet vets 10-4, 878C1
Signs Humphrey-Hawkins bill 10-27, 873A2
Meets ldrs, budget plans scored 12-4, 936A3
Cites US repressn 12-6, 934C1
Budget scored at govs conf 12-9, 956G2
Commemorates King 12-9, 956C3
Soothes NAACP ldrs on budget plans 12-11, 980A2

BROADCASTING—*See PRESS in this section below*

BUDGET—*See also LANCE, Thomas Bertram; other appropriate headings in this section*
State of Union Message 1-19, 29D2, 30C3
Econ Message 1-20, 48G2
Submits to Cong, summary 1-23, 44C2-48E2
Federal budget dollar table 63A1
GOP rebuttal 1-31, 62F3
Affirms '81 balanced budget pledge 2-17, 123E2
Signs debt ceiling extensn 3-27, 261A3
Vows to meet fscl '79 deficit target 4-11, 259D3
Asks Cong inflatn impact rpts 4-11, 259E3
Sen votes budget target res 4-26, 305C2
Zero-based budgeting assessed 5-2, 344E1-A2
Fscl '79 deficit target cut 5-12, 361D1
Plans sharp fscl '80 cuts 5-25, 404F2
Threatens vetoes to hold spending 6-8, 431G3

1979

ATOMIC Energy & Safeguards—*For weapons issues, see ARMAMENTS above, DISARMAMENT below*
GE worker chrgd in uranium theft 2-1, 119G3
NRC OKs India uranium sale 3-23, 416F2
Proposes regulatory reform 3-25, 230A2
Visits 3 Mile I A-accident site 4-1, 241D1, 244F2, B3, 245B1
Forms 3 Mile I probe panel, gets Nader proposals 4-5; issues food safety assurnc 4-6, 260C2, A3, G3
Vows 'full account' re 3 Mile I 4-5, 251A1
Reaffirms commitmt; vows 3 Mile I apptmts, A-plant licensing reform 4-10, 263A3
Names 3 Mile I probers 4-11, 275C1
Cited in 3 Mile I NRC transcripts 4-12, 276C1
Gov Brown urges end to A-power use 4-24, 323A1
Shuns A-hecklers 4-25, 300C1
Urges safety measures, scores Clinch R projct 5-4, 346F3
Scored at DC A-protest 5-6, rejcts A-plant closings 5-7, 343E3, G3
Eur A-Conf message affirms US supplier role 5-7, 374B1
Waste cleanup bill excludes 6-13, 441D2
Backs A-power in new energy plan 7-16, 532G2
Defends A-power 8-22, 622D3
3 Mile I comm scores NRC reactor licensing decision 8-23, 665B1
Gets 3 Mile I comm final rpt: NRC abolitn urged, no A-constructn bar sought; reactn 10-30, 825C2-826F1
Responds to 3 Mile I comm rpt; replaces NRC head, vs reactor licensing freeze, backs A-power 12-7, 940F1-E2
Kennedy scores 12-13, 962B2

BANKS & Banking
Budget proposals 1-22, 44C2, D3
Proposes interest rate, other reforms 5-22; regulators set chngs 5-30, 403B1-G2
Proposes solar energy bank 6-20, 498A1
Calls interest rates too high 10-11, 807F2
Signs stopgap banking bill 12-28, 987B3

BLACK Americans
Seeks natl holiday for King, marks death anniv 1-14, 31G2
Jordan seeks aid, scores budget plans 1-17, 35A2, C2
At Cheyney coll, urges vote exercised 5-20, 384F2-A3
Pol conv splits on support 5-25—5-27, 423A2
Hooks sees Kennedy edge, grudging black support 6-24, 559E3
Sees ldrs at Camp David 7-6—7-11, 513F2; thanks 7-30, 608F3-609A1
Urban League pres scores 7-22, 560D1
Compares Palestinian issue, US civil rights drive 7-31; scored 8-1, 575E1
SCLC asks Jewish mtg following Young resignatn 8-16, 606A2
Times clarifies Palestinian-rights remark 8-18, 607C1
Urges black-Jewish amity, denies Young tap 8-30, 661B2

BROADCASTING—*See PRESS in this section below*

BUDGET—*See also other appropriate headings in this section*
Restores some '80 budget cuts 1-2—1-5, 3C3
Kennedy, O'Neill, ADA score plans 1-13—1-26, 70C2
Vs proposed balanced budget amendmt, on '80 deficit 1-17, 29C2
Urban League dir vs plans 1-17, 35C2
Submits to Cong, summary 1-22, 41A1-46B3
State of Union Message 1-23, 46D2, E3, 47G1-A2, E2, 48A1
GOP attacks State of Union Message, proposals 1-24, 48F1-B2
House com opens hearings; Miller, Rivlin testify 1-25, 48E3
Defends plans 1-26, 70A1
Balanced budget amendmt status disputed 2-6, 86F2
Urges Cong 'hold line' 2-12, 109F3
'80 resolutns clear Cong 5-25, 11-28, 900A1
Stresses deficit cut 5-29, 402B1

1980

ATOMIC Energy & Safeguards—*See also ARMAMENTS, DISARMAMENT & Arms Control in this section*
State of Union asks NRC reorganizatn, A-waste progrm 1-21, 43E3
A-waste storage plan outlined, advisory panel named 2-12, 127D3, 128C1
Kennedy scores indl policy 2-20, 130C2
Uranium sale to India backed 5-7, NRC blocks 5-16, 440C3
NRC '80 funds authrzn clears Cong, reforms set 6-10, 6-16, 479E1
OKs uranium sale to India 6-19, 495F2
Dem platform drafted 6-24, 479G2, A3
Signs '80 NRC funds authrzn 7-1, 494F1
Names Carnesale NRC chrmn 7-9, 551A3
Cong fails to block uranium sale to India 9-24, 723C1
Signs NYS A-waste storage clean-up 10-1, 739C1
Signs A-waste storage, fusion dvpt appropriatn 10-1, 803E2
Signs fusion dvpt bill 10-7, 981E2
Anderson answers debate questns 10-28, 816D1
Signs low-level A-waste bill 12-22, 981D1

BANKS & Banking
Reagan 'basic speech' cites interest rates 2-29, 209B2
Unveils anti-inflatn plan 3-14, 201F1, G1
Signs deregulatn bill 3-31, 245C3
Brown scores interest rates 4-1, 246C3; UAW pres 6-1, 457D2
FRB ends credit controls 7-3, 513F1
Ford, Vander Jagt score interest rates 7-14, 7-16, 534B2, E2
Links interest rate drop, housing starts 7-17, 542D1
Scores FRB, banks re interest rates 10-2, 10-8; criticism deplored 10-2—10-3, 762F3-763A2
Signs housing, community dvpt authrzn 10-8, 804B2
Prime rate rise continues 10-17—11-6, 867B2
Reagan hits interest rates 10-29, 817G1

BLACK Americans
Names 2 Ala dist judges 1-10, controversy ensues 5-19—9-17, 744C2
Black Caucus scores budget 2-5, 94F2
Home cnty ruled biased 4-7, 309A2
Names Va dist judge, Byrd scores 4-9, 744E3
Black Caucus pleas for Haitian refugees 5-7, 340D1
Acts to stem Miami rioting 5-19, 382A3
On V Jordan shooting 5-29, 401B3
Hooks warns re despair 5-29, 460A2
Visits Jordan in hosp 6-1, 442D2
In Miami, draws protests 6-9, 439C1
Sees Black Caucus 6-9, 439F1
Addresses NAACP 7-4, 515E2, A3
News conf topic 8-4, 593B2
Addresses Urban League, visits Jordan 8-6, 597B2, D2
Sees Dem conv delegates 8-15, 629E3
Scores Reagan Klan remark 9-2, 664B1
Addresses Phila Baptists 9-3, 699B1
Deplores Reagan racism 9-16, clarifies 9-18, 698A2
NSC Africa memo called forgery 9-17, 726E3-727B1
Anderson criticizes 9-29, 739E2
Warns vs Reagan win 10-6, 762E3
Reagan deplores campaign 'hysteria' 10-7, 763D2
Softens Reagan attack 10-9, 778C2
Young campaigns 10-10, racial remark repudiated 10-15, 803D1
Seeks support, Lowery endorses 10-20, 10-23, 803B1
Debates with Reagan 10-28, 814B2
Hits Reagan debate statemt 10-29, 816D2
Meets ldrs, antibusing veto vow backed 12-4, 954C1

BROADCASTING—*See PRESS & Broadcasting in this section*

BUDGET—*See also other appropriate headings in this section*
State of Union proposals 1-21, 1-23, 41F2, 43C2, C3, E3
Submits to Cong, summary 1-28, 69B2-74B1
Black Caucus scores 2-5, 94F2
Cong asks budget cuts 2-27, 2-28, O'Neill scores 3-5, 168E2-F3
'80, '81 deficits seen higher 3-5, 168A2
Anti-inflatn plan sets fscl '81 spending cut 3-14, 201A1
Submits revised '81 budget; Kirkland, Gunther score 3-31, 243D2-244E1
GOP budget proposed 4-1, 244G1
Warns vs Sen cutbacks 4-1, 247E1
Scores Cong fscl '81 res 5-27, Dem ldrs back res 5-28, House rejects 5-29, 424C1-C3
UAW head scores 6-1, 457D2
Offers econ renewal plan, revenue-sharing rise 8-28, 663B2
Scores Reagan plans 10-14, 779A2

1976

Busing Issue—*See 'Civil Rights' below*
Cities & States
In NY debate 4-1, 233D2
'Ethnic purity' incident 4-4—4-13, 260D2-261F2
Vs 'instant' plans 6-3, 411D1
Addresses US Mayors Conf 6-29, 468A1
Vows state-fed cooperatn 7-6, 492D3
On revenue sharing 7-6, 492F3
Stresses local actn 9-6, 664B2
On urban issues 10-27, 803D2
Thanks NYC re electn 11-3, 845E3
US Mayors urge commitmt, Samuels at conf 11-7—11-8, 845G2-B3
Mayors urge econ aid 12-9, 12-14, 937A3
Renews pledges to NYC 12-28, 978C2

1977

Signs HEW-Labor funds 12-9, 1001F2
Stresses business spending rise to balance budget 12-28, 1000G2
Admits balancing difficult 12-28, 1002B1
BUSINESS—*See also other appropriate headings in this section*
Sets conflict-of-interest code 1-4, 4C2
Plans 'econ stimulus' tax cuts 1-7, 5E1
White House reception 1-21, 53A2
Cong gets tax cut plan 1-27, 52D1
On investmt tax credit option 1-31, 89G3
Ullman, Burns on tax proposals 2-1, 2-3, 89D2, A3
GOP offers alternate tax plan 2-2, 89G2
Arab boycott guidelines rptd 2-28, 167A1
House drops tax option 3-8, 174D2, F2
Signs SBA loan ceiling hike 3-24, 250D3
Drops tax credit plan, reactn 4-14, 270F2, 271B1
Urges anti-inflatn effort 4-15, 298G3
Presents energy plan 4-20, 290G1; fact sheet 292F1
Energy plan reactn 4-21—4-24, 319B3, 320C1
Hints tax credits veto 4-22, 321G2
Scores steel price rise hikes 5-6, 385G1, D2
Denounces bribery at 7-natn summit 5-8, 357D2
Clarifies tax credits plan 5-12, 381B2
Cong sets '78 budget target 5-17, 405A1
Energy plan criticism continues 5-18, 443C2
Vs steel price hikes 7-21, 577B1
Signs small business bill 8-4, 689B3
Orders steel industry study 8-5, 612C1
Signs debt collection rules 9-20, 761D1
Gets wage-price panel steel industry analysis 10-7, 776G1
Links US, intl steel woes 10-13, 775F1
On lack of confidence in Admin 10-27, 813C3
Addresses Business Cncl 12-14, 976E3
Signs ban vs forgn bribes 12-19, 1001G2
To ask $6-7 bln tax cut 12-20, 976B2
Fears spending lag threatens balanced budget 12-28, 1000G2
CABINET & White House Staff—*See also APPOINTMENTS above, RESIGNATIONS below, also specific department under U.S. GOVERNMENT*
Sets conflict-of-interest code 1-4, 4C2
Urges limo svc, legal staff cuts 1-24, 53D2
Asks inflatn monitoring 1-31, 89G3
Stresses cutbacks 1-31, 2-14, 110A3
Cuts limo svc, White House staff; revises rule procedures 2-2, 75B1, F1
Pay raise takes effect 2-20, 127E2
Financial statemts issued 2-25, 147A3-148F1
Cuts paperwork 2-28, 148B3
Sen OKs reorganizatn powers 3-3, 191F2
Califano hirings disputed 3-23, 3-25, 236B1, A2
Reorganizatn powers cleared 3-31, 228A1
Signs reorganizatn powers, issues plans 4-6, 250B3
Cabt-level educ dept vow cited 4-11, 302B1
Signs pay raise procedure chngs 4-12, 272E3, 273B1
On cutting staff size 4-15, 299C2
Proposes ethics law 5-3, 338B1
Backs spec prosecutor bill 5-3, 338F1
On promiscuity 6-30, 515B2
Sen com clears Lance 7-12—7-25, 573C3-574D2; **for subsequent developments, see LANCE, Thomas B.**
Submits staff reorganizatn plan 7-15, 555D3
Women aides vs abortn curbs 7-15, 786E2
Halts farm aide's personal lobbying 9-30, 773D1
CAMPAIGN Finance—*See POLITICS in this section below*
CITIES, Suburbs & Towns
'78 budget changes 2-22, 125A2, E2
Reaffirms NYC aid pledge 3-1, 3-11, 193B3
Sees NYC mayor 3-17, 191B1
Backs graffiti cleanup 5-17, 381C3
Cong sets '78 budget target table 5-17, 405A1
Environment message 5-23, 404B2
Orders NYC blackout probe 7-14, 537B3
'No apologies' to blacks, poor; rebuts Jordan criticism 7-25, 7-28, 573C1, A3
Black Caucus backs Jordan 7-29, 592G3
Tours South Bronx 10-5, 760G3
Signs urban, housing aid 10-12, 796G1
Sees black ldrs 12-14, 960B1

1978

Stresses Cong restraint 6-14, 446B3
Backs restraint 6-23—6-24, 509G3
'79 deficit forecast revised 7-6, 506D3
Cites sharp '80 cuts at Bonn summit 7-16—7-17, 544E1
Signs debt ceiling rise 8-3, 625F2
Cites '80 deficit cut goal 8-14, 626F1
'Budget-busting' veto threat rptd 8-29, 682B1
Signs fscl '78 added funding 9-8, 681F2
Cong res sets '79 levels 9-23, 734C1
Links spending restraints, interest rate cuts 9-27, 751D3, E3
Scores Labor, HEW bills 9-28, 751G3
Balancing still a goal 10-10, 766G2
Anti-inflatn plan sets deficit, spending cuts by fscl '80 10-24; reactn 10-25, 805G2-D3, 806C3
Meany scores spending cut plan 10-31, 863B2
Plans 'tight' '80 budget 11-6, 862F1; 11-9—11-14, 874D3-875A2
Stresses tight '80 budget 11-27, 914F2
'80 budget mtgs cited 12-4, 936E3
Dem midterm conf debates; anti-Carter res rejctd 12-8—12-10, 956D1-C3
Defends '80 budget plans amid protests 12-11, 12-14, 12-20, 979F2-980E2
Downplays Dem dissent 12-12, 956D3
Restores $2 bln to '80 budget, totals estimated 12-22, 1002C3
BUSINESS
Econ Message 1-20, 48C3
Budget proposals 1-23, 44F2, 46G2; tables 45E2, 46B2
Vows coal indus study 3-25, 217G1
Presents urban-aid plan 3-27, reactn 3-27—3-30, 217C2-218D1
Scores steel price hike 3-30; hike undercut, rolled back 3-30—4-3, 262G3
Sets anti-inflatn plan, asks voluntary restraint, reactn 4-11, 259D2, 260E2
Cites July '76-77 profits rise 4-11, 260B2
Sees execs, gets inflatn plan support 4-20, 5-11; critics scored 5-8, 361A3, G3
Signs OPIC extension 4-24, 323C2
Scales down tax-cut plan 5-12, 361A1
'Citizen rate' proposal rejctd 5-12, 389F1
Jawboning holds exec pay hikes 5-19—6-1, 427B3-428A1
Plans severe '80 budget cuts 5-25, 404G2
Sets up coal industry panel 5-26, 405A1
Sees Houston ldrs 6-24, 509G3
Signs solar, other renewable energy loan aid 7-4, 512E1
Dow drops on inflatn fears 10-16—10-31, rebounds on $ aid steps 11-1—11-3, 825B1, 826D1-827A1
Vetoes aquaculture bill 10-19, 807E3
Vetoes small business aid 10-25, 897F2
Signs bankruptcy revisn bill 11-6, 1003B1
Pocket vetoes Tris compensatn bill, asks SBA aid 11-8, 941C3
Scores Hershey price hike 11-9, 875C1
SBA minority aid abuse briefing rptd 11-21, 919C3
Anti-Inflation Plan—*See under ECONOMY under 'E'*
CABINET & White House Staff—*See also APPOINTMENTS above, RESIGNATIONS below; also specific departments under U.S. GOVERNMENT*
Jordan legal separatn rptd 1-9, 96B1
State of Union Message 1-19, 29E2, 31E1, 32A1
Educ dept not in budget 1-23, 47A2
Jordan rptd in barroom tiff 2-19; defns issued 2-20, comment 3-2, 141G1-B2
Freezes salaries 4-11, 259D2
Lauds Cabt, staff; bars chngs 4-11, 260F3
Proposes Educatn Dept 4-14, 279A1-B2
Strategy sessns 4-15—4-16, Cabt image chngs rptd planned 4-17—4-29, 306G2
Regrets Bourne prescriptn scandal 7-20, 549F2
Warns staff vs drug use 7-24, 568B1
Harris cancels cong testimony, White House disagrmt cited 8-7, 605F1
Jordan linked to Vesco 'pol fix', denials issued 9-1—9-15; Anderson revises article 9-11, 719D3
Signs ethics bill 10-26, 832F1-B2
CITIES, Suburbs & Towns
Gets Proxmire-Brooke letter vs NYC aid renewal 1-4, 87A1
State of Union Message 1-19, 29G3, 30G1, 31B1, 32A1, C1
Budget proposals 1-23, 44F2, C3, 47F3, table 45E2
Federal budget dollar table 63A1
Meets with NYC mayor 2-2, 87B1
Defends NYC aid plan 3-2, 141A1
Presents urban-aid plan 3-27, reactn 3-27—3-30, 217C2-218D1
S Bronx aid vowed 4-12, 285F1
Cautions NYC re aid 4-25, 307F3
Backs NYC long-term loan guarantees 4-25, signs aid bill 8-8, 608C1, A3

1979

ADA scores priorities 6-24, 982E2
Signs '80 contd funds resolutns 10-12, 11-20, 900F1, A2
BUSINESS & Industry
Natl trust comm rpt issued 1-16, 88C2
State of Union Message 1-23, 46E2, D3, G3, 47B1, G1
Seeks price-fixing consumer suit bill, fed no-fault auto insurnc standards 1-25, 70C2, D2
Kennedy introduces merger-limit bill 3-8, 202F2
On '78 profits 3-29, 264C1
Sees business ldrs 5-15, 361D1
Asks waste cleanup fund 6-13, 441G1
Seeks solar heat tax credit 6-20, 498E1
Sees ldrs at Camp David 7-6—7-11, 513F2
Thanks Camp David participants 7-30, 608F3-609A1
Bars Chrysler cash advance, backs loan guarantee 8-9, 8-22, 662E1, D2
Proposes indl innovatn 10-31, 829D3
Proposes Chrysler rescue plan 11-1, 845B2
Chrysler aid bill OKd 12-21, 981E1
Anti-Inflation Plan—*See under ECONOMY under 'E'*
CABINET & White House Staff—*See also APPOINTMENTS above, RESIGNATIONS below; also specific departments under U.S. GOVERNMENT*
Proposes Educ Dept 1-22, 44D2; 2-8, 110F2
Cautions re press leaks 2-12, 109G3-110B1
Ex-aide Bourne gets UN post 4-25, 392G1
Sen OKs Educ Dept 4-30, 326B2
Drops Resources Dept plan 5-15, 365A2
Ex-aide scores staff 5-18, 627F2
Energy reorgn optns cited 7-8, 514A1
Asks mass resignatn, names Jordan staff chief 7-17, 529A1, E1
Staff evaluatn forms issued 7-17, 529G1, 530C2, 531C1
Fires 4 Cabt offcrs, names replacemts; reactn 7-19—7-20; defends moves 7-20, 529A1-531G3
Defends shake-up, Jordan apptmt 7-25, 555D3-556D1
Staff shuffled 8-10, 608C2
Jordan denies cocaine use 8-24, aides back 8-25, Landau disputes 8-28, 647D1-E2
Vesco jury foreman resigns, claims cover-up 8-29, 647E2
Vesco perjury, cover-up chrgs denied 8-31, juror resignatn rejected 9-7, 725F2-E3
Jordan cocaine probe continues 8-31—9-28, FBI expands inquiry 9-13; news conf 'comment' 10-9, 767B2, C2
Expects campaign activity 11-5, 961F2
Jordan cocaine probe spec prosecutor named 11-29, 900C3
Bell testifies in Vesco case 12-4; Carter to videotape testimony 12-5; Civiletti quits probe 12-7, 943C2-C3
CITIES, Suburbs & Towns
To resubmit countercyclical aid plan 1-2, 3E3
Budget proposals 1-22, 44B3; table S1-22, 42F2
Resubmits countercyclical aid plan 3-6, 164A2
Mayors Conf backs policies 6-13, 439F2-440A1
Sees mayors at Camp David 7-6—7-11, 513F2
Thanks Camp David participants 7-30, 608F3-609A1

1980

Debates with Reagan 10-28, 813A2, E2, 814D1
'80 budget deficit doubles 10-29, 824F3
Reagan says data withheld 10-30, 840A1
Meets cong Dems on fscl '81 11-13, 866G1
Signs 'reconciliatn' bill 12-5, 936D1
Signs '81 revenue sharing appropriatn 12-15, 982B1
Signs debt limit hike 12-19, 981E1
Signs '81-83 revenue sharing extensn 12-28, 982C1
BUSINESS & Industry
Signs Chrysler aid bill 1-7, 14A1
Policies blamed for small business hardships 1-13, 5-15, 5-29, 455E2
Scores small car productn lag, vs import bars 4-17, 287D2
Optimistic on steel indus 5-14, 367G3
Sees auto execs, vows actn 5-14, 384E1
In Detroit, unveils auto industry aid plan 7-8, 505A1-A2
Signs Chrysler loan guarantee bill 7-8, 515G1
Auto import probe speedup denied 7-18, 556G1-B2
Offers econ renewal plan; reactn 8-28, 663A1-D3
Cites car-industry aid 9-18, 698D3
Unveils steel indus aid plan 9-30, 740G2-D3
Scores Reagan on Chrysler aid 10-1, 739A2
Backs tax depreciatn write-offs 10-14, 779F1
Funds UAW jobless aid program 10-14, 823G2
Reagan scores auto indus policies 10-15, 780C1
Signs patent law revisn 12-12, 982A1
Signs fishing indus aid 12-22, 982C1, 995B3
Wage-Price Developments—*See under ECONOMY (U.S.) under 'E'*
CABINET & White House Staff—*See also APPOINTMENTS, RESIGNATIONS in this section*
Vs Miller resignatn 2-2, 92A2
Miller probe sparks controversy 2-8—2-11, 145A2
Griffin gets Chrysler post 3-13, 199B3
Vesco grand jury ends 4-1, 251B3
Jordan cleared re cocaine chrgs 5-28, 402C3
Mil aide rptd reassigned in tax dispute 6-10, 638E3
Jordan joins campaign com, Watson named chief of staff 6-11, 438G3
Campaign role planned 7-15, 549C3
Aides took oaths re leaks 7-16—7-17, 549G1
FEC issues campaign rules 9-5, Admin sets guidelines 9-8, 681D2
Kraft cocaine probe rptd, steps down as campaign mgr 9-14, 700B1
Holds final session 12-3, 935F2
Kraft probe suspended 12-12, 989F2
CITIES, Suburbs & Towns
State of Union topic 1-23, 43A2, F2
Budget proposals 1-28, 73E1; table 70F1
Revised budget proposals, Gunther scores 3-31, 244A1, C1, F1
Sees mayors on Haitian refugee plight 5-7, 340C1
Addresses Mayors Conf 6-10; Kennedy speech canceled 6-11, 438E2-E3
Offers econ renewal plan 8-28, 663B2
Reaffirms NYC aid pledge 9-29, 739B1
Signs NYC funds rider 10-1, 826C2
Warns vs Reagan win 10-6, 762E3
Reagan deplores campaign 'hysteria' 10-7, 763D2

1976

Civil Rights
Disputes Jackson re busing 3-3, 166E1
Says Southn bias absent 3-19, 214A2
'Ethnic purity' incident 4-4—4-13, 260D2-261F2
In Ohio, urges blacks' rights 5-4, 324E1
Backs ERA, names women's advisory com 6-13, 432B2
Stresses 6-14, 433C1, F1
Pres nominatn acceptance speech 7-15, 510G1, D2
On busing 8-3, 564B3
Women rptrs cover church class 8-15, 617C1
Playboy interview lauds LBJ 9-20, 704C2
Sees black mins 9-25, 724E1
Scores Butz remark on blacks 10-2, hits Ford handling 10-4, 743B1, 744F1, C3
Sees feminists, backs ERA 10-2, 10-7, 762D1
Seeks rights for blacks, sees Mormon ldr 10-7, 762C1
Debates Ford 10-22, 801F3, 802C2
Plains church incident; comments 10-31, 11-1, 826D3
Church ends ban vs blacks 11-14, 864C2
Blacks attend Plains church 11-21, 881F3
Rpts blacks, others minorities rejctd posts 12-16, 937A1
Sees Black Caucus delegatn 12-16, 937B2
Bell apptmt scored 12-20—12-22, 956G2

Courts
Vs Sup Ct actn rules 8-9, 585B1
Scores judicial system 8-11, 585A3
Backs Sup Ct 9-13, Mondale comments 9-14, 686G2, 687G1
On judicial apptmts 10-15, 785A2
Debates Ford 10-22, 802A2

Defense Issue—*See 'Foreign Policy & Defense' below*

Delegates & Endorsements—*See also 'Democratic National Convention', 'Labor' and 'Primaries' below*
Wins Iowa precinct vote 1-19, 40G3
2d in Miss caucuses 1-24, 94F3
Leads in Okla caucuses 2-7, 129D1
Leads Ford in Gallup poll 3-15, 197D1
Wins 35 NY delegates 4-6, 244G3
Leads in delegate count 4-9, 261A1
King, other prominent blacks endorse 4-13, 261G1
In NJ 4-27, Byrne backs 4-29, 324A1
Would like Humphrey backing 4-28, 324D1
Bayh, Wallace back 5-3, 5-5, 323G3-324A1
Delegate count rptd 5-4, predicted 5-5, 322G2-D3
H Ford lauds 5-7, 343D2
Delegate backing in non-primary states slipping 5-22—5-25, 373E3
Endorsed by Beame 5-26, 390B3
Ribicoff endorses 6-7, 411B1
Primary delegates totaled 6-8, 409A3
Daley, Wallace endorse, Stevenson frees delegates; Jackson, Humphrey, Kennedy vow unity 6-9, 408G3
Leadings Dems endorse; Church, Udall end bids 6-10—6-16, 431F2-432F1
Sees NY delegates 6-14, 432C1
Sen Dems endorse 6-24, 490D2
Brown would support 6-25, 468G1
Sees NJ state sens, delegates 6-30, 468F1
Dem govs endorse 7-6, 492A3
Pacifies black leaders 7-12, 513E1
Press endorsemts rptd 10-30, 11-8, 827D3

Democratic National Convention
Fla delegates seated 6-28, 490B1
Women's equal-representation issue resolved 7-11—7-15, 509F3
Platform debate rejected 7-13, 509B2
McGovern hails leadership 7-13, 509G2
Wins pres nomination 7-14, 505D1
State roll-call of votes, table 7-14, 507A2
Acceptance speech 7-15, 506D3; text 510A1-511A1
Debate on rules 7-15, 513D2
Names Mondale vp choice, ratified 7-15, 506G1, A3
Mondale acceptance speech 7-15, 507F2-508B1; text 511B2
Photo with Mondale 7-15, 505A1

1977

CIVIL Rights—*See HUMAN & Civil Rights in this section below*
CONGRESSIONAL Relations—*See also other appropriate subheads in this section; also personal names*
Moore named cong liaison 1-14, 35A3
White House reception 1-21, 53G1
Concedes mistakes 2-8, 88E3
Pay raise takes effect 2-20, 127E2
Sees growing cooperation 2-23, 126B3
Call-in on pay raise 3-5, 171D1
Lauds cooperatn 3-16, 190F3
Sen adopts ethics code 4-1, 251D2
Signs pay raise procedure chngs 4-12, 272E3, 273B1
Breakfast mtg with Dem ldrs 4-19, 321E3
Veto cautn urged 6-1, tensn eased 6-15, 459G2-F3
Cites progress 7-12, 534D1
Cites growing admiration 7-28, 574D3
Signs '78 Cong funds 8-5, 689B1
Plans easier agenda 12-15, 976F3-977B1; admits expectatns unrealistic 12-28, 1002A1
CONSUMER Affairs
Backs class-action suits 3-5, 171G2
Backs US agency 4-6, 250F2-B3
Energy plan scored 5-18, 443D2
Urges consumer agency bill 6-1, 417E3
Signs debt collectn rules 9-20, 761D1
Signs saccharin ban delay 11-23, 1001F2

COURTS
Burger lauds re merit selectn 1-1, 15C2
Pay raise takes effect 2-20, 127E2
Signs extended legal aid for poor 12-28, 1002G2
CRIME
On Cuba hijack pact 3-5, 171C2
Speaks to Ohio kidnaper 3-9, 178B3
Backs spec prosecutor bill 5-3, 338F1
Cong sets '78 budget target 5-17, 405B1
On law enforcemt reorganizatn 6-29, 499G2
Pardons jailed PR natlst 10-6, 808A2
DEFENSE & Armed Forces—*See also FOREIGN Policy and INTELLIGENCE Issues in this section*
Inaugural 1-20, 27E1
Pardons draft evaders, reactn 1-21, 51A2, D2
Brown on defense cuts 1-25, 94G2
Wants strong, lean force 2-2, 75B2
Flies in wartime command plane 2-11, 110E3
Plans Ford budget cut 2-12, 110D3
'78 budget revisions 2-22, 124B3, 125A1, B2
Plans mil pensn, draft reviews 3-1, 148F2
War powers, amnesty, draft among call-in radio topics 3-5, 171D1, E2
A-carrier funds rescinded 3-15, 195E3
Repeats fund-cut pledge 3-16, 190E3
Giaimo proposes budget 3-23, 228G3
OKs upgrading of Viet dischrgs 3-28, 231B3
Not to reprimand Brown 3-28, 232C1
Poll standing on pardon low 4-4, 251C1
NE-Midwest base-closing ban asked 4-6, 423G2
House OKs '78 arms bill 4-25, 323F3
AF computer project scored 4-27, 421F2
Confrms antimissile beam research 5-3, 343F3
Dischrg upgrade response weak 5-10, 421B1
Cong sets '78 budget targets 5-17, 404D3; table 405A1, B1
B-1 cost estimate hiked 5-18, 420G3
Removes Singlaub from S Korea cmnd 5-21, 403G2
On Singlaub's removal 5-26, 417A2
Takes ride on A-sub 5-27, 417C3
Names manpower costs panel 6-27, 499A3
Vs B-1, backs cruise missile 6-30, 514C1
Defers neutron bomb decisn 7-12, 533A1, E1; facts on bomb 534A2
Weapons, civil defns authorizatn cleared 7-14, 575F3
Neutron bomb topic at Miss town mtg 7-21, 575B1
Seeks arms sales curbs 7-28, 574G2
Signs mil constructn authorizatn 8-1, funds 8-15, 668B2
Slovik widow seeks case review 8-16, 808G1
B-1 cut from '78 funds 9-9, 704F2-A3
Signs '78 weapons, civil defns funds bill 9-21, 834D1
Vets-dischrg benefits review bill clears Cong 9-23, 759C2; signs 10-8, 773A2
Vet benefits no-veto vow 9-28, 796B3, C3
Signs vet-disability pensn hike 10-3, 877F3
Discharge-review phone svc ends 10-4, 759G2
B-1, FB-111H policy clarificatn cited 10-8, 796C1
Neutron-bomb protesters disrupt church svcs 10-16, 797G2
B-1 revival fails in House 10-20, 795E3

1978

Hatcher rejcts liaison post 6-6, 568C3
Addresses mayors on budget 11-27; anti-inflatn plan backed, natl dvpt bank opposed 11-29, 914F2-G3
Black ldrs warn on unrest 12-4, 936A3, C3
Budget plans scored by ldrs 12-9, 956G3
Sees mayors on budget 12-20, 980C2
Inner-city health progrm urged 12-20, 1009F1
Restores '80 budget funding 12-22, 1002D3
CIVIL Defense—*See DEFENSE in this section below*
COAL—*See ENERGY, LABOR in this section below*
CONGRESSIONAL Relations—*See also FOREIGN Policy, LEGISLATION, MESSAGES to Congress and other appropriate headings in this section; also U.S. GOVERNMENT—CONGRESS; personal names*
'77 support rptd 1-7, 12A3
Griffin firing strains O'Neill-White House ties 7-28—8-7, 605E2
Scores spec interests 8-14, 626D1
Meets Black Caucus on Humphrey-Hawkins bill 9-29, 808C1
Praise of 95th Cong rptd 10-16, 784F2
Signs ethics bill 10-26, 832F1-B2
Gives midterm assessmt 11-6, 862C1
CONSUMER Affairs
State of Union Message 1-19, 31B1, 32B1
Consumer agency bill defeated 2-8, 82G1
Bolsters White House office 4-27, 347D3
Backs CPSC reauthorizatn 4-27, 347F3
Chastises lawyers 5-4, 320F2; 5-5, 342B1
'Citizen rate' mail proposal rejctd 5-12, 389F1
Names King CPSC chairwoman 6-29, 589A2
OKs consumer co-op bank 8-20, 663E1
Pocket vetoes Tris compensatn bill, asks SBA to aid firms 11-8, 941C3
Vs boycotts of wage-price violators 12-12, 957B1
COURTS & Legal System
Scores attys; proposes criminal code reform, other judicial chngs 5-4, 320F2; 5-5, 342B1
Burger comments on censure 5-16, 388F2
Legal aid plan rejctn scored 8-7, 626D2
Signs judgeships bill 10-20, backs merit selectn 11-8, 873C2-C3
Signs ethics bill 10-26, 832F1-B2
Signs bankruptcy revisn bill 11-6, 1003B1
CRIME
Signs child porno, prostitutn bill 2-6, 218A2
Testimony presented at Ga trial 4-19, 309E3
Signs child abuse extensn, black mkt adoptn study 4-24, 323E3
Proposes criminal code, prison, other reforms 5-4, 320A3
Proposes LEAA revisn, pub housing anti-crime plans 7-10, 525C1, G1
Backs GSA paymts probe 9-4, 685E2
Hearst pardon petitioned 9-26, 824C1
Signs diplomatic immunity revisn 9-30, 750D3
Black ldrs warn on urban unrest 12-4, 936A3, C3
Launches HEW anti-fraud drive 12-13, 984A3
DEBT, Public—*See BUDGET in this section above*
DEFENSE & Armed Forces—*See also ARMAMENTS above, FOREIGN Policy below*
Gets '77 mil strategy rpt 1-6, 5G2
State of Union Message 1-19, 29A3, 31B2, C2
Budget proposals 1-23, 44E2, D3, G3-46B1; table 45D2, E2
Federal budget dollar table 63A1
Names Jones Joint Chiefs chrmn; Allen, Hayward to AF, Navy posts 4-5, 281F1
Double-dipping barred in pension revisn plan 4-10, 281C1
Sen budget target res sets higher ceiling 4-26, 305B3
Singlaub scores 4-27, resigns 4-28; Goldwater comments 5-1, 321D2-B3
Scored by GOP sens 5-3, 342G2
Names 1st female Marine Corp gen 5-11, 420F1
Exempts natl defens contracts from purchasing controls 5-18, 405G1
Singlaub continues criticism 6-2, 433A2
Proposes new civil defns agency 6-19, 466D2-B3
Visits Ft Hood (Tex) 6-24, 509G3
Revises secrecy classificatn rules 6-29, 508F1
Signs Coast Guard '79 authrzn 6-30, 525C2
Vetoes '79 civil defns authrzn 8-17, 621D2
Vets job preference retained by House 9-11, other reforms OKd 9-13, 696C2-D3
Rpts on Viet vets; ACLU, vets cncl score 10-10, 878A1-G1
Signs '79 funds bill 10-13, 833B1
Signs '79 revised authorzn, Navy contract setlmt funds 10-20, 833A2
Cites '79 authorzn veto 11-6, 862D1
Plans '80 budget rise 11-9, 874E3, 875F1
Gets Army 2-yr enlistmt plan 11-10, 895F2
Plans civil defns spending hike 11-12, 895E1

1979

CIVIL Defense—*See DEFENSE in this section below*
COAL—*See ENERGY in this section below*
CONGRESSIONAL Relations—*See also FOREIGN Policy, LEGISLATION, MESSAGES to Congress and other appropriate headings in this section; also U.S. GOVERNMENT–CONGRESS; personal names*
Deplores special interests 5-25, 401D1
Hosts House Dems 6-1–6-2, 418B2
CONSUMER Affairs
Seeks price-fixing suit bill, fed no-fault auto insurnc standards 1-25, 70C2, D2
Proposes bank loan reforms 5-22, 403B1
Oil decontrol protested 6-1, 418A1, F1
Creates Consumer Affairs Cncl 9-26, 902B3
COURTS & Legal System
Sued over judicial pay limit 11-9, 901C2
CRIME & Civil Disorders
Grants Hearst clemency 2-1, 79F1
Pardoned PR natlst dies 3-7, 272D2
Orders fed judge's murder probed 5-29, 431E2
Warns vs truck strike violence 6-21, 479C3
Harden mtg re Vesco rptd 8-30, denies cover-up chrgs 8-31, 725B3-C3
Commutes sentncs of 4 PR natlsts 9-6, 666C1
PR natlsts freed 9-10, return to San Juan 9-12, 683A1
Orders KKK probe 11-6, 865D3
Kennedy scores 11-9, 962C1
NH kidnapers demand audience 11-23–11-24, 898D2
DEBT, Public—*See BUDGET in this section above*
DEFENSE & Armed Forces—*See also ARMAMENTS above, VETERANS below*
Mil ex-ldrs warn of Sovt challenge 1-12, 15A1
Women's unit attacks budget 1-12, 30E2
Vs proposed balanced budget amendmt 1-17, 29D2
Budget proposals 1-22, 41B2, 42C1-43F2; tables 42A1, D2
State of Union Message 1-23, 47B1, D2, 48E1
GOP chrmn backs budget proposal 1-24, 48A2
Defends budget plans 1-26, 70A1
GOP denounces policies 3-1, 165A3
Vs draft revival 4-10, 263E3
Sen OKs '80 arms authrzn 6-13, 438E1
'Quick-strike' force planned 6-21, 482D3
Signs supplemental funds bill 7-25, 700A2
Mil volunteer shortage rptd 8-20, 649C2
Seeks budget hike 9-11, 678D1
False A-war alert placed 11-9, 869G2
Signs '80 mil constructn funds 11-30, 845F1
Marines to join 'quick-strike' force 12-5, 923E3
Pledges 5-yr spending hike 12-12, turnaround noted, Sen reactn cool 12-13, 962F3-963E2

1980

Softens Reagan attack 10-9, 778C2
Signs '81-85 coastal zone mgt authrzn 10-17, 981A2
Vows Medicaid, welfare relief 10-20, 803F1
Chrgs Reagan 'flipflop' on NYC aid 10-27, 816B3
Debates with Reagan 10-28, 814G1-C2
Anderson answers debate questns 10-28, 816B1
Migratn to Sun Belt, suburbs urged by advisory panel 12-29, 990G1
CONGRESSIONAL Relations—*See also LEGISLATION, MESSAGES to Congress in this section*
Sen com asks consultatn on Iran 4-24, 297C2, 298B1
Meets with jr members 7-30, 570B3
Reagan hits 'legis chaos' 9-15, 699F3
Cites work with Cong 9-18, 698D3
Meets Dems, lame-duck agenda set 11-13, 866G1
CONSUMER Affairs
Addresses Consumer Federatn of Amer, upholds FTC role 2-7, 91F1
Signs FTC emergency funding bills 3-28, 5-1, 348B1, D1, B2
Signs FTC authrzn 5-28, appropriatn 6-4, 702C3
Rpts '79 exec order implemented 6-9, 703B1
Plans to speak out 11-12, 865F2
COURTS & Legal System
Names Ala dist judges 1-10, controversy ensues 5-19—9-17, 744C2
ABA finds judicial appointee 'unqualified' 3-2, Sen panel rejects 3-4, 250E2
Judges granted 12.9% pay hike 3-24, 250F1
Names Va dist judges 4-9, 744E3
Warns vs GOP Sup Ct apptmts 7-4, 515A3
OKs 5th judicial circuit split 10-14, 918A3
Scores Reagan Sup Ct apptmt vow 10-15, 779A1
Signs judicial discipline bill 10-15, 918F3
Judicial pay hikes backed by Sup Ct 12-15, 956E3-957D1
CRIME & Civil Disorders
FALN raids Chicago campaign hq 3-15, 208B3-209A1; supporters rptd threatened 4-7, 309B1
Vesco grand jury ends 4-1, 251B3
Hearst probatn rptd ended 5-9, 471F3
Acts to stem Miami rioting 5-19, 382A3
On V Jordan shooting 5-29, 401B3
NAACP warns re blacks' despair 5-29, 460A2
In Miami, draws protests 6-9, 439C1
Anderson answers debate questn 10-28, 816B1
DEFENSE & Armed Forces—*See also ARMAMENTS, VETERANS in this section*
State of Union sets Persian Gulf defns, budget hike 1-21, 1-23, 41A1, 42F2, A3, 43B1, F3
Budget proposals 1-28, 69C3, 70B2-71E2; tables 69G3, 70D1
Kennedy scores Persian Gulf doctrine 1-28, 74E2-E3
GOP vs Persian Gulf doctrine, backs spending hike 1-28, 75C1
Admits US Persian Gulf weakness 1-29, 65A1
Black Caucus scores budget 2-5, 94F2
Reagan assails policies 2-15, 128B3
GOP candidates score weakness 2-20, 129G2, D3
Revised budget proposals 3-31, 244B1
Weighs Persian Gulf force 4-1, 247C1
'80 spending cut rptd 4-17, 330E1
Declares offcl mourning for dead Iran raiders 5-6, 337D2
Greets Nimitz crew 5-26, 403G1-A2
Backs mil compensatn bill 5-26, 403A2
Scores Cong fscl '81 budget 5-27, backs own proposal 5-28, Joint Chiefs assail 5-29, 424C1-G2
Points to spending rise 5-29, 423E3
Computer error triggers A-alert 6-3, 457E3
Dem platform drafted 6-24, 479G3
Ford scores 7-14, 534F2
Moynihan cites spending hikes 8-11, 612D3
Anderson attacks policy 8-19, 629G3
US 'stealth' fighter said to evade radar 8-20, 630D2
Pledges spending growth, defends policies 8-21, 629D2-A3
Backs gradual spending hike 9-2, 664C3
Reagan scores 'stealth' plane disclosure 9-4, 665D3
Signs '81 mil pay, benefit authrzns 9-8, 764F3, 765C1
Hits 'war-and-peace' issue 10-2, 10-6, 762B2
Attacks Reagan stand 10-9—10-14, 778D2, G2, D3, 779A2
Continues to hit 'war-and-peace' issue 10-16—10-19, 802D2
Reagan: mil strength 'eroding' 10-19, 801F2

1976

Economy—*See also other appropriate subheads*
Issues policy paper 4-23, 305A2
Stresses commitmt to poor, sees farmer support 6-14, 433E1
Vows state cooperatn 7-6, 492D3
Pres nominatn acceptance speech 7-15, 507F1; text 510D2, F2

1977

Visits SAC hq in Neb 10-22, 817D1
Budget reform ordrd by Brown 10-26; '78, '79 budgets compared to Ford's 11-6, 857F2-C3
Eases POW info-disclosure code 11-3, 858E1
Signs ERDA authorizatn, neutron bomb provisn 11-15, 878A1
Signs supplemental authorizatn 11-15, 1001E2
Signs GI Bill revision 11-23, 1001F2
Signs vets pension bill 12-2, 1001F2
B-1 decisn scored by Jane's 12-7, 942B1

DEPRESSED & Disaster Areas
OKs Colo drought relief 1-29, 76G3
State disaster aid, emergency status granted 2-5, 91A2; Ohio asks status 2-8, 92B1
Call-in on Westn drought 3-5, 171C1
Requests drought aid 3-23, 210A2
Signs drought aid 4-7, 273E1
Declares Ky, W Va, Va, Ala disaster areas 4-7, 4-9, 311F2, A3
Gets Bergland drought rpt 4-18, 376E3
Signs drought relief funds 5-13, 380D3
Signs drought aid authorizatn 5-23, 405A3
Names 7 Pa counties disaster areas 7-21, 604A1
Broadens small business loans 8-4, 689D3
Declares Kansas City disaster area 9-14, 768C3
Sets dam-inspectn progrm 11-30, 914E1

DISARMAMENT & Arms Control—*See also DISARMAMENT under 'D'*
Inaugural 1-20, 26C1, 27F1
Statemt to world 1-20, 26F1, C2
To seek A-test ban, arsenal limit 1-24, 51G2
'Fireside chat' stresses 2-2, 75C2
Backs Warnke 2-4, 2-8, 88F3, 89D1
'78 budget revisns 2-22, 125C1
Urges strong Warnke vote 3-9, 172G1
Addresses UN 3-17, 185B1, F2
IISS scores policy 4-28, 401D1
Sees cong arms experts 5-18, 401A1
Sets arms-sales policy 5-19, 380D2
Signs Latin A-ban pact 5-26, 415D3
Wife on Latin tour 5-30—6-12, 454D3, 455A1, E1
Joint Perez communique issued 7-1, 546E2
Rpts A-test talks set 7-28, 574E2
Signs '78 arms control funds 8-2, authorizatn 8-17, 689G1, C2
Addresses UN, urges intl code 10-4, 751G2, 752A1

Soviet Issues (including SALT)
To seek early Salt II pact 1-27, 70D1
Urges quick arms accord, other proposals 2-8, 88A2
Sees Sovt stance unchngd 3-9, 172D3
USSR rejects SALT bids 3-30, 225D1
Vows arms limitatn fight 3-30, 225E2
Gromyko scores arms proposals 3-31; stands firm 3-31, 4-2, 246G2, B3
Cong reactn to arms stand 3-31, 247F1
Gets Brezhnev SALT reassurance 4-8, 400E3
Sees Dobrynin 4-12, 400B3
Optimistic re Sovt talks 4-15, 299A2
Rebuffs Pravada re SALT proposals 4-15, 400G3
Assesses SALT talks 5-26, 417F1
Denies rights issue link 6-30, 515A1
Asks Brezhnev prelim talks 6-30, 515D1; Brezhnev bars 7-5, 529F3
Defends policy, defers neutron bomb 7-12, 533D1, F1
Sees Schmidt 7-13—7-14, 566B2
Backs missile cuts 7-21, 550D3
Rpts A-test talks set 7-28, 574E2
Brezhnev sees arms race, backs SALT solutn 8-16, 640E2
Cruise missile debate delays mtg 9-11, 751E2
Meets Gromyko on SALT 9-23, 9-27; rpts progress 9-29, 750E3
Gromyko sees Brezhnev summit 9-23, 10-1, 750F3, 751B1
Significant agrmt in sight 10-4, 752A1
Sees accord in 'few weeks' 10-21, 817C1
Sees SALT progress 10-27, 813A3, G3
NATO backs SALT stand 12-9, 957A1
Sees Brezhnev visit after accord 12-28, 1002C1
Warsaw news conf remarks 12-30, 1001D1

DROUGHTS—*See DEPRESSED & DISASTER Areas above*

ECONOMY—*See also other appropriate headings in this section*
Sees Cong ldrs on 2-yr, $30 bln plan 1-7, 5C1
Labor, mgt groups score plan 1-10, 14C1
Ford's CEA econ rpt stresses differences 1-18, 35F3-36F1
$31 bln stimulus plan outlined 1-27, 51G3

1978

'80 budget hike seen 11-15, oppositn rptd 11-18, 895A2
Pentagon asks '79 suplmtl budget 11-15, 916C3
To scrutinize budget 11-27, 914E3
Powell: inflatn threatens budget plans 11-28, 980F1
Discusses civil defns, spending plans 11-30, 916F2-A3
Defends budget plans 12-9, 12-12, 956F2-G3
Defends budget plans, 2 cong ldrs score 12-14, 979F2-980B1
Brown urges pensn reform 12-14, 1009C2

DEPRESSED & Disaster Areas
Declares Ohio disaster area 1-26, 105A3
Signs drought aid extensn 2-7, 218A2
Declares Mass disaster area; RI, Mass, Conn emergency aid 2-10, 105C2
Declares 8 Calif counties disaster areas 2-16, 106A1
Signs added disaster funds 4-4, 261C3
Proposes new emergency agency 6-19, 466D2-B3
Declares Niagara (NY) disaster area 8-7, 703A1, D1

DISARMAMENT & Arms Control—*See also DISARMAMENT under 'D'*
US-India declaratn vows A-weapons reductn 1-3, 1D2
Sets arms sales ceiling for non-allies 2-1, 106D2
Vance rptdly backs A-weapon material ban 4-3, 277B2
To seek 5-yr test ban 5-20, 996E2
UN Assemb sessn opens, absence scored 5-23, 421F1
Lauds Latin A-ban pact adherence 6-21, 489C3
Optimistic on Europn troop-cut talks 6-26, 491F1
Admits spy satellite use 10-1, 861B2
3-yr A-test ban order rptd 10-5, 996E2
Warnke resigns post 10-10, 766F3, 804F1; replaced 10-20, 804A2
Cong com rpts A-test ban doubts 11-3, 877G1

Nuclear Safeguards Issue—*See ATOMIC Energy in this section above*

Soviet Issues (including SALT)
Pledges to consult NATO 1-6, 1D1
State of Union Message 1-19, 29B1, A3, 31B2
Warns USSR vs Horn of Africa role 3-2, 140E2, 179A1
Warns USSR vs mil buildup, interventn; Tass scores 3-17, 202G1-A3
Defers neutron bomb, asks comparable Sovt restraint 4-7, 253B1
Vs Sovt offer re neutron bomb 4-25, 307A2
Lauds Sovt effort on SALT 5-5, 342F1
Warns USSR on Africa role 5-25, 418C1
Sees Gromyko, Africa role disputed 5-27, 422C1-A2
Denies SALT 'freeze' rpt 6-2, 422F2
Issues detente warning, sees SALT progress; Tass replies 6-7, 423E2, 424E1
Vance stresses priority, denies Africa policy link 6-19, 490B3, D3
Sees SALT success, Sen treaty OK 9-27, 751E3
Sees Gromyko on SALT 9-30—10-1, 747F2
3-yr A-test ban rptd 10-5, 996E2
Prefers SALT pact as treaty 10-10, 766G3
Names new SALT negotiator 10-20, 804A2
Plans priority effort 11-6, 862E1
SALT mtg with sens 12-7, 996E1
On SALT pact delay, links to Sovt summit 12-12, 957C1, D1
China tie linked to SALT pact delay 12-26, 996C1

ECONOMY—*See also other appropriate headings in this section*
London Times scores policy, links $ weakness 1-4, 27B3
Warns steel industry on quotas 1-18, 80D3
State of Union Message 1-19, 29F1, B2, A3, 30G1-F2, D3, 31A1, F2, G3
Economic Message 1-20, 48E2

1979

DEPRESSED & Disaster Areas
NOAA flood statistics rptd 2-11, 120A2
Declares Mo disaster area 4-21, 472D2
Declares Tex disaster area 7-28, 638E3

DISARMAMENT & Arms Control
State of Union Message 1-23, 47C3
Lauds Mex support 2-14–2-16, 124F2
'77 total A-reductn call cited 8-30, 658C1
Sees Pope, issues joint statemt 10-6, 759C3; photo 758C1

Nuclear Safeguards—*See ATOMIC Energy in this section above*

Soviet Issues (including SALT)
UK, W Ger back SALT accord at Guadeloupe summit 1-6, 12F2
US mil ex-ldrs warn of Sovt challenge 1-12, 15D1
Denies SALT security threat 1-17, 29G3
State of Union Message notes SALT 1-23, 46C2, D2, 47G2-E3, 48C1
Sets SALT pact ratificatn as top forgn goal 1-25, 70B2
Arms dvpt restraint confrmd, exec agrmt rpt denied 2-23, 258B2
Brezhnev sees SALT agrmt 3-2, 172C1
On SALT linkage, emerging pact 2-20, 123F2, F3-124B1
Sens score SALT treaty 3-4, 258D1
SALT ratificatn pressed 4-4, 4-5, 257F2
Baker urges SALT chngs 4-11, 295A2
Urges scientists back SALT 4-23, 300F2
Urges SALT pact ratificatn 4-25, 294A2
US spy satellite data rptd compromised 4-28, 318G2, 319A1
Would uphold SALT terms without ratification 4-30, 319A1
SALT draft announced, Brezhnev summit planned 5-9, 338C3, 339B1
SALT debate priority stressed 5-15, 365D2
On MX deploymt 5-29, 402D1
Brezhnev backs SALT summit 6-1, 417B1
OKs MX dvpt 6-8; Sovts score, SALT pact cited 6-10, 438B1-D1
At Vienna summit 6-15–6-18; **SALT II pact signed 6-18,** 449A1-C2; texts 450A1-458E2
Addresses Cong on SALT II 6-18, 449C2; text 458F1-459E3
U-2 verificatn talks rptd 6-21, 497D1
Vs arms budget tie to SALT 7-27; US sens react 8-2, 8-3, 590E3
Chooses 'racetrack' MX deployment plan; diagram 9-7, 677G2, 678A2
Rejects SALT-Cuba troop link 9-8, 673C1
Ford scores SALT 9-26; Brzezinski rebuts 9-27, 739F2, A3
Urges SALT ratificatn despite Cuba troops 10-1; speech text; Sen, Sovt, Eur reactn 10-1–10-3, 737A1-739D2
Scores Eur missile freeze offer 10-9, 761A3
Byrd rpts assurance on MX dvpt 10-25, 822C3
SALT, defense budget hike linked 12-13, 963A2-D2
Rejects SALT treaty vote delay 12-16, 979A2

ECONOMY—*See also other appropriate headings in this section*
Budget proposals 1-22, 41A1, A2, 44B3
State of Union Message 1-23, 46C2, E2-G3, 47C1-B2

1980

Claims mil prepared 10-24, 816A3
Debates with Reagan 10-28, 813B1, A2, C2-814A1, B3, 815G2, B3, D3
Anderson answers debate questns 10-28, 815G3
Presses 'war-and-peace' issue 10-29, 816B2
Sen OKs '81 defns appropriatn 11-21, 896B3; clears Cong 12-5, 935A3
Signs '81 appropriatn 12-15, 982B1
Signs Army LSD setlmt 12-18, 982A1
Signs mil pay benefits 12-23, 982C1

Draft Registration
Asks draft registratn 1-23, 41A1, 43B1
Kennedy vs, GOP backs 1-28, 74B3, 75E1; 2-12, 110C2
Issues registratn plan 2-8, 110F2
Says youth 'overreacting' 2-13, 110D1
AFL-CIO backs draft registratn 2-25, 147A1
Female registration rejected by House subcom 3-6, 188B3
DC protest held 3-22, 227G3-228A1
House OKs funding amendmt, bars female funds 4-22, 349A2
Adm Hayward backs draft 6-19, 478F3
Anti-draft group scores 6-24, 478D3
Dem platform drafted 6-24, 479E3
Signs bill 6-27, 478C1, F1
Issues registratn proclamatn 7-2, 493B3
Brennan OKs registratn 7-19, 598A1
Renominatn acceptance speech cites 8-14, 613C1

DEPRESSED & Disaster Areas
Declares Ariz disaster area 2-20, Calif 2-21, 213D3
Mo seeks disaster aid 5-13, 391F2
Declares Washn disaster area 5-21, 382B2
Orders Love Canal aid 5-21, 386D3
Declares Grand I (Neb) disaster area 6-4, 527C3
Visits stricken Neb area 6-10, 439D1
Signs Mt St Helens victim aid bill 7-8, 515F1
Declares drought disaster in 7 states 7-16, 616F1
Offers econ renewal plan 8-28, 663B2
Declares NJ emergency 10-19, 947D3
Declares Calif disaster area 11-29, 948E1

DISARMAMENT & Arms Control
Renominatn acceptance speech; text 8-14, 612D1, F3, 613B1, A3
Blasts Reagan on A-arms race 9-2, 664B3
Debates with Reagan 10-28, 813A1, E1, A2, 814F2, B3,815G2
Hits Reagan nonproliferatn stance 10-29, 816C2
Plans spokesman role; on Reagan policy support 11-12, 865F2, A3
Urges Latin A-arms treaty 11-19, 881A3

Soviet Issues (including SALT)
To delay SALT for Afghan invasn 1-2, 1B2
State of Union topic 1-23, 41C2, 42A2
Kennedy scores arms race 2-20, 130D2
Reagan 'basic speech' scores SALT 2-29, 207G2
Hints SALT renunciatn, doubts Sen ratificatn 3-14, 209D1
Discusses W Ger-USSR A-missile talks 7-2, 489C1
Weighs Sovt A-weapon talks proposal 7-5, 506A1
Brezhnev asks talks 8-22, US denies delay 8-26; Muskie indicates US ready, hints SALT ratificatn 9-7, 679D3-680B1
Cites arms talks 9-18, 698B3
Muskie praises SALT 9-18, 10-16, 776A2
Reagan would redo SALT 9-30, 738E3
Scores Reagan SALT stand 10-1, 739B2; 10-2, 10-6, 762B2
Attacks Reagan stand 10-8—10-10, 778B2, F2, D3
Assails Reagan, sees 'nuclear precipice' 10-16, 10-19, 802D2
Reagan pledges SALT III talks 10-19, 801C2, 802A1
Debates issue with Reagan 10-28, 813A1, E1, 814F2, B3, 815G2
Anderson answers debate questns, backs SALT II 10-28, 816C1
Hits Reagan SALT stance 10-29, 816D2
Hits arms-control issue 10-30, 841B1
Meets Schmidt 11-20, 903G3-904A2
Percy 'confident' of new talks 12-12, 950D3

ECONOMY
State of Union proposals 1-21, 1-23, 41D1, F2, 43C2, D2, B3
On '79 inflatn rise 1-25, 75C3
Budget forecasts, proposals 1-28, 69B2-E3; table 1-28, 71A2
Econ Message, CEA rpt 1-30, 74B1
Kennedy scores record 2-6, stages mock debate 2-7, 91C1, G1

1976

Record cited 512C2
Dow trend after nominatn 7-15—11-10, 846D3, 847A1-D1
Sees business ldrs 7-22, 550B3
Briefed 7-27, sets forth goals 7-28, 550G3
Sees Nader 8-7—8-8, 585F1
Addresses Nader forum on consumer issues, corp bribery, govt controls, trust legis 8-9, 584D3-585F1
Backs 2 trust bills 8-9, 585A1, D1
Vows 'clean' govt 8-11, 585D2, A3
Sees film, TV execs 8-22, 631E2, G2
Sees Ia farmers, scores GOP farm policy 8-24, 8-25, 631G2, G3-632E1; Dole rebuts 8-26, 632E2
Scores Ford park plan 8-29, 644D3
Stresses inflatn curbs, balanced budget 9-3, 664D1
Scores Arab boycott 9-8, 664C3
On SBA mismanagemt 9-13, 686D2
On fed funds 9-14, 686A3
Sees SD, Minn farmers, scores GOP econ policies 9-15, 9-16, 686B3
Outlines econ policy 9-24, 724A3
Vows redlining end 9-25, 724E1
Scores GOP econ mismanagemt 9-26, spec interests 9-27, 724F1
On Aug econ indicators 9-27, Sept WPI 10-7, 768D1, 769G3
Stresses inflatn 9-30, 742E3
Sees NE govs 10-1, 743A1
Chrgs Ford, GOP indifferent to poverty 10-4, 743D1
Ford scores on budget, econ 10-7—10-13, 763G1, B2
Ford: Carter would spend more 10-14, 761F3
Backs grain-loan rate hike 10-14, 787E3
Ford scores on soc prgrms 10-19, 784B2, D2
Vows Arab boycott end 10-19, 785E2
On 3d ¼ GNP, inflatn rpt 10-19, 805F1
Ford vs Arab boycott stand 10-20, 784G2
Ford scores re spending 10-28, 803G1
Stresses econ 10-29—10-31, 827F1-B2
On Sept indicator drop 10-29, 833B1
Caddell: econ a secondary issue 11-5, 845D2
Burns warns vs stimulating 11-11, denies rift 11-12, 865G1
Reuss on monetary policy, sees Burns cooperatn 11-12, 865B2
NE govs seek aid 11-13—11-14, 864A3
Top news conf topic 11-15, 863D2
Fed Reserve eases curbs 11-19, 12-17, 939G2
Plans early program 11-23, 881B2
Concerned re steel price hike 11-29—12-2, 897D3
See top advisers 12-1, 898B2
Renounces controls vs steel price rise 12-3, 917E1
Plans aid program 12-9—12-14, 937C2-938A1
Sees advisers, rpts positive trend 12-27, 978C2
Cabinet unit set up 12-29, 978E2

Energy
Urges A-plant curbs 5-13, 374F3
Sees Houston oil execs 7-1, 490E2
Urges natural gas deregulatn 7-6, 493A1
Vows tax reform caution 7-22, 550D3
Stresses conservatn, not A-power; vs oil industry breakup 8-9, 585B1, D1
Experts brief; repeats oil industry stance 8-17, 617G1-B2
Connally scores energy policy 8-27, 645C1
Proposes Cabt-level energy dept 9-21, 704F1, E2
Urges A-fuel curbs 9-25, 724A1
Urges natl policy 9-30, 742F3
Sees NE govs 10-1, 743A1
Debates Ford 10-6, 740E2, 741D3
Scores Ford on A-safeguards 10-8, 762A2
Debates Ford 10-22, 800D1, 801E2, A3
On Ford A-fuel policy 10-28, 848C3
Backs Atlantic offshore oil exploratn 10-30, 827G1
Egypt reactn to Carter win 11-4, 826C2
Rep addresses mayors 11-7, 845B3
Urges restraint on oil prices 11-15, 864A1
Urges oil price restraint 12-14, 12-16, 935C1, 937E2
Cabinet unit set up 12-29, 978E2

1977

Submits stimulus plan to Cong 1-31, 75A2
On wage, price monitoring 1-31, 89E3
Defends stimulus plan 2-2, 75A2
News conf remarks on plan 2-8, 88C3
CBO questns Carter goals 2-15, 126E1
Submits '78 budget revisns 2-22, 124D3
Seeks voluntary wage, price control 2-23, 126C3
'77 budget levels cleared 3-3, 174B1
Giaimo proposes budget 3-23, 228D3
Poll standings 4-4, 251D1, F1
Urges stimulus plan passage 4-7; drops rebate, credit plans 4-14, 270F2
Outlines anti-inflatn plan 4-15, 298G2
Admits energy plan inflationary 4-15, 299E1
Presents energy plan 4-18, 289B2, 290B2, 295A1, A2; fact sheet 291A1
Defends energy plan 4-22, 321E2
Stresses fscl restraint 5-2, 364B2
Stimulus funds cleared 5-5, 365D2; signed 5-13, 380D3
Vs steel price hikes 5-6; prenotificatn cited 5-11, 385G1, D2
At 7-natn London summit 5-7—5-8, 357A1-358A1; diplomacy hailed 5-8—5-16, 359D1
Scores liberals' criticism 5-12, McGovern responds 5-13, 380F3, 381D2
Hails London summit 5-12, 381G1
Signs stimulus pub works bill 5-13, 380D3
Cong OKs stimulus tax bill 5-16, 381D3-382E1
Environment message 5-23, 404C2
Would veto spending bills 5-26, 417D1
On local dvpt reorganizatn 6-29, 499G2
Cites stimulus legis 7-12, 534E1
Miss town mtg topic 7-21, 575D1
Vows to meet '77, '78 growth goals 9-26, 753E2
News conf remarks on policy criticism, inflatn, 10-27, 813B3
Top priority in '78 12-14, 976E3; 12-28, 1002B1

EDUCATION
'78 budget revisns 2-22, 124C3, 125A2, 126A1, C1
Bars student draft defermts 3-1, 148A3
Giaimo urges 'impact aid' end 3-23, 229A1
Educators vs quotas 3-31, 235D2
Cabt-level dept vow cited 4-11, 302B1
Presents energy plan 4-20, 290G1; fact sheet 292C1
Cong sets '78 budget target 5-17, 405A1
Would veto impacted aid 5-26, 417C1
Agrees to sign HEW-Labor funds 6-15, 459B3
Sen OKs HEW-Labor funds 6-29, 515F2
Gets privacy panel rpt 7-12, 632B1
Rebuts Jordan criticism 7-25, 573F1
Signs vets dischrg-benefits review 10-8, 773A2
Asks State Dept bur reorganizatn 10-11, 797C2
Signs career guidance aid 12-13, 1001G2

ELDERLY—*See AGE and Aged Persons in this section above*

ENERGY—*See also ATOMIC Energy in this section*
Asks thermostats lowered 1-21, proposes emergency gas reallocatn legis 1-26, 53D3
Rescinds gas price decontrol order 1-24, 55C1
Warns of permanent shortage 1-30, 75C3
'Fireside chat' outlines plans 2-2, 75D1
Fuel-cost threatens recovery plan 2-2, 76A1
Signs emergency gas legis 2-2, 76B2
Names Dunham gas act admin 2-2, 91G2
Sees sacrifices, vs undue profits 2-8, 88B3
Kissinger to head nongovt panel 2-12, 110E3
'78 budget revisns 2-22, 125G1, A2
On gas deregulatn, supply 2-23, 126D3
Submits energy debt bill 3-1, 148F1
Call-in topic 3-5, 171E1
Vows comprehensive policy 3-16, 190E3
Asks intl cooperatn 3-17, 185E2
At Charleston (W Va) seminar 3-17, 190G3
On CIA oil forecast 4-15, 294D1
Concedes plan inflationary 4-15, 299E1
Presents natl policy plan to natn 4-18, addresses Cong 4-20, 289A1-290B1

1978

Urges proposals kept intact 1-30, 62B3
Affirms '78 top priority 2-17, 123A2
Calls steel price hike inflationary 3-30, 262G3
Sets anti-inflatn plan: asks fed pay hike limit; freezes White House, exec pay; names Strauss coordinator 4-11, 259C2
Cites accomplishmts 4-11, 260A2
Anti-inflatn plan reactn 4-11, 4-12, 260E2
Consumer price table 427F2
Inflatn fight aimed at sagging $, weakness persists 4-19—7-14, 523F1, C2
Sees business ldrs, gets inflatn plan support 4-20, 5-11; critics scored 5-8, 361A3, G3
Poll drop tied to inflatn 4-24, 308B1
Vows contd inflatn fight 4-25, 307C3
Bids attys restrain fees 5-4, 320C3
Bars wage-price controls 5-4, 321C2
Sees Meany, labor ldrs; wage-restraint plea rejctd 5-10; Bosworth backs 5-11, 361F2, D3
Orders govt-purchasing controls 5-18, 405E1
Jawboning inflatn strategy rptd successful 5-19—6-1, 427B3-428A1
Plans severe budget cuts 5-25, 404F2
Blamed for inflatn surge 6-19, 427D2
Revises secrecy classificatn rules 6-29, 508F1
Vows anti-inflatn measures at Bonn summit 7-16—7-17, 544A1, E1
Cautions Cong re inflatn 7-20, 549E3
Poll finds pessimism growing 8-13, 679E2
Stresses inflatn in farm assn address 8-14, 626C1
GM hikes '79 model prices, deceleratn vow cited 8-18, 665G1
Asks 5.5% fed pay hike 8-31, 681E2
Vows new anti-inflatn plan 9-20, 715E1
At IMF-World Bank mtg, vows inflatn fight 9-25, 731G2
Scores FRB rate hike, asks tougher fscl anti-inflatn role 9-27, 9-28, 751C3
Vetoes pub works bill as inflationary 10-5, 765D1, D2
Readies anti-inflatn program 10-10, 766F2
Unveils anti-inflatn plan 10-24, 805B2-807B1; **for subsequent developments, see ECONOMY—Carter Anti-Inflation Plan**
$ rescue plan, inflatn fears linked 11-1, 825B2-827A1
Vows inflatn curbs 11-2, 862A2
Gives inflatn curb top priority, bars mandatory wage-price controls 11-6, 862D1, E1
Says '79 recessn, depressn unlikely 11-16, 11-30, 917D3
Links inflatn fight, oil prices 11-17, 899E3
Inflatn, econ growth linked to budget problems 11-28, 12-14, 980C1
Blacks score budget plans 12-4, 936A3

EDUCATION
State of Union Message 1-19, 29F2, 30G1, G2, 31B1, E1, G3
Budget proposals 1-23, 44E2, 46F1, F3, 47D1, 48C2; table 45E2
Unveils coll student aid plan 2-8, 84A2
Scores student-loan defaults 2-17, 123F2
Submits aid plan to Cong 2-28, 141A3; House rebuffs 3-20, 202B3
Vs tuitn tax credit 4-11, 260G3
Proposes new Cabt dept 4-14, 279A1-B2
Plans severe budget cuts 5-25, 404A3
Addresses Naval Acad commencemt 6-7, 423D2
Threatens tuitn tax credit, coll student aid bill vetoes 6-8, 431D3, F3
Admin lauds Bakke ruling 6-28, 482B2
Vs tuitn tax credit, HEW budget bills 9-28, 751G3
Rpts on Viet vets; ACLU, vets cncl score 10-10, 878D1, G1
Coll student aid plan cleared, tuitn tax credit rejected 10-15, 807G1
Signs '79 HEW funds 10-18, 873F1
Signs coll student aid bill 11-2, 873E1
Gets Army GI benefits plan 11-10, 895F2
Higher-educ groups protest '80 budget plans 12-14, 980G1
Restores '80 budget funds 12-22, 1002E3

ENERGY—*See also ATOMIC Energy in this section above*
London Times scores policy, links $ weakness 1-4, 27B3
NAACP scores plan 1-11, 68C1
News conf remarks on legis, world tour 1-12, 11F3, 12A1
State of Union Message 1-19, 29C1, D1, 30G1, A2, 31A1, F2
Econ Message 1-20, 48B3, D3
Budget proposals 1-23, 44E2, D3, 46E1; table 45D2
Acts to avert energy crisis in 9-state area 2-11, 2-16, 104C1-D2
Legis logjam, $ weakness linked 2-24—3-6, 119A1
Signs research authrzn 2-25, 218B2
Sees govs on natl plan 2-27, 144G3
Signs black lung eligibility 3-1, 218B2
Links oil import cuts, $ defns 3-2, 140G3
Links energy crisis, poll drop 3-2, 141E1
On Midwest coal shortage 3-6, 160A2
Cong legis deadlock persists 3-7—3-22, 219F2-220B2
Crude oil tax passage doubted 3-7, 3-8; Blumenthal import fee backing rptd 3-24, 220E1, B2
On coal output, reserves 3-9, 160B2
Says gas deregulatn acceptable 3-9, 160D3

1979

Wage insurnc tax credit opposed in Cong 1-23, 55C3
Greenspan sees inflatn worsening 1-24, 48B2
Econ Message, CEA rpt 1-25, 48C2-49A2
Miller, Rivlin vs '79 econ forecasts 1-25, 48E3
Outlines legis program 1-25, 70B2
Poll rating drops 3-29, 231D3, F3
Calls inflatn control 'urgent' 4-10, 263C3, 264D1
Sees contd inflatn 4-25, 300C1
Warns Dems vs inactn 5-25, 401D1
Calls inflatn top priority 5-29, 402A1
Sees consumerists 5-31, Dems 6-1–6-2, 418A1, G1, F2
Revamps econ team 6-4, 463C1
Vs Bosworth controls remark 6-4, Bosworth resignatn plan leaked 6-16, 463E1
Rep Anderson scores 6-8, 439E2
ADA scores 6-24, 982D2
On OPEC price hike impact 7-1, 494C2
Low poll rating linked 7-1, 497G1
Conducts policy review; sees US ldrs, resets natl speech 513C2
Miller named chief econ aide, vows steady policy 8-6, 627D2
Defends record 9-25, 723F2
Sets Pay Advisory Com 9-28, 829C2-B3
On FRB credit-tightening moves 10-6, 10-9, 765G3-766A1
Kennedy scores on inflatn 11-7, 847F1
Cites inflatn as issue 12-4, 918C2
Anti-Inflation Plan—*See under ECONOMY under 'E'*

EDUCATION
Some '80 budget cuts restored 1-5, 3D3
Budget proposals 1-22, 41C2, 44G1-D2, F2, 46C1; table 42E2
State of Union Message 1-23, 46G3
Proposes Cabt-level dept 2-8, 110F2
Vs pro-schl prayer legis 4-10, 263F3
Hails Sen re Educ Dept OK 4-30, 326C2
Links black vote, bias 5-20, 384G2
Sees ldrs at Camp David 7-6–7-11, 513F2
Thanks Camp David participants 7-30, 608F3-609A1
NEA endorses 9-28, 782F2
Signs IRS tax power curbs 9-29, 883E2
Backs Head Start expansn 10-15, 807A3
Backs 'minimized' busing 10-16, 807C3
Signs Educ Dept bill 10-17, 782A2
Proposes expanded indl research grants 10-31, 829G3
Forgn-language study urged 11-7, 944F1
Emphasizes libraries 11-16, 901B1

ENERGY—*See also ATOMIC Energy in this section above*
Confident despite Iran unrest 1-17, '26D2
Sees eventual oil-price rise, on Mex prospects 1-17, 30B1
Budget proposals 1-22, 45B2; table 42F2
Drafting dvpt legis 1-25, 70D2
Oil-profits remark scored 1-26, 70F1-A2
Orders fed agency fuel-saving 2-6, 82C3
Urges voluntary conservatn, cites oil worker setlmt 2-12, 109C3, E3
In Mex oil, gas talks 2-14–2-16, 124F1
Seeks oil conservatn powers 2-26, plans cautn 2-27, 145B3
Backs Canada pipeline 3-3, 168F1
Schlesinger sees no voluntary cuts 3-12, 183C2
Calif-Tex pipe canceled, Alaska oil swap seen 3-13, 183A2
Ends domestic oil price controls; asks profit tax, conservatn, other measures 4-5, 250B2-251A1
Canada offers oil pipe routes 4-10, 284F2
Sees climbing oil prices, gas shortage; home-oil reserve ordrd 4-25, 300D1

1980

Connally scores inflatn 2-14, 129F1
Anti-inflatn policy cited 2-15, 126F2
GOP candidates score weakness 2-20, 129G2
Says inflatn at crisis stage 2-25, 144G2
Reagan 'basic speech' excerpts 2-29, 207B2
Kennedy calls policy intolerable 3-9, 206E3
Ford calls program 'disaster' 3-12, 207G1
Unveils 5-pt inflatn plan 3-14; Cong, other reactn 3-14—3-17, 201A1-202F2
Revised budget forecasts, proposals 3-31, 243D2-244E1
Kirkland scores policies 3-31, 247A2
Brown scores policies 4-1, 246C3
Bush, Reagan, Kennedy score 4-7—4-10, 264C2, F2, B3
Sees short recessn 4-17, 285F2
Pa campaign intensifies 4-18—4-23, 304F1, A2
Reagan scores policy 5-2, 344C3
On inflatn prospects 5-9, 367G1, F2
Vows lower inflatn rate 5-29, 423F3
Says recessn steeper 6-1, 424E3
UAW head scores 6-1, 457E2
Reagan scores inflatn 6-3, 423C3
Kennedy on public anguish 6-5, 423F1
Says inflatn corner turned; Reagan, Anderson score 6-6, 437F2, A3
Vows cooperatn to mayors 6-10, 438E2
Reagan scores 6-25, 480B2
FRB ends credit controls 7-3, 513F1
GOP plank scores 7-10, 506G2-A3
Ford, Vander Jagt score 7-14, 7-16, 534A2-F2
Plans 'econ renewal' program 8-6, 597C2
Kennedy wins platform planks 8-12, issues statemt 8-13, 609D1, 610F2, 611F1, 614C2
Renominatn acceptance speech; text 8-14, 612F1, F3, 613A2
Sees Kennedy on econ program 8-25, 646G2
Reagan sees 'Carter depressn' 8-27, defends remark 9-1, 664A2, C2
Offers renewal plan; reactn 8-28, 663A1-D3
Reagan assails 'mess' 9-9, 699D2
Sees 'encouraging' signs, vs 'quick-fix' approach 9-18, 698C3, G3
Bush attacks 'sorry' performance 9-26, 781F1
Reagan attacks policies 10-1, 738B1
Calls Reagan proposals inflationary 10-6, 762G2-B3
Reagan says data doctored 10-6, 763A3
Promises 'renaissance' 10-12, 10-14, 779A1, E1
Bush scores fscl policy 10-15, 10-16, 817E2, G2
Reagan: strength 'eroding' 10-19, 801F2
Foresees 'full recovery' 10-20, 803A1
Reagan hits record, gives 8-pt plan 10-24, 10-29, 817G1-E2
Debates with Reagan 10-28, 813B1, 814B1, 815G2, E3
Anderson answers debate questns 10-28, 816A1
Inflatn influenced electn, exit-poll rptd 11-4, 837F1, 838F1, E3
Vs emergency act now 12-24, 980B3
Wage-Price Developments—*See under ECONOMY (U.S.) under 'E'*

EDUCATION
State of Union proposals 1-21, 1-23, 43A2, F2, D3
Budget proposals 1-28, 69E3, 73E2; table 70E1
Black Caucus scores budget 2-5, 94G2
Addresses NEA 7-3, endorsemt renewed 7-4, 505C2
Renominatn acceptance speech cites 8-14, 613A1, B2
Gets AFT endorsemt 8-21; addresses conv, sees clear choice 8-22, 646E2
Signs higher educ authrzn 10-3, 803A3
Calls Reagan proposals inflationary 10-6, 762B3
Signs vet aid 10-17, 856F2
Scientific literacy study issued 10-22, 990G1
Vows antibusing rider veto 12-4, vetoes 12-16, 954B1, E1

ENERGY
Sets alcohol productn goal 1-11, 33B2
OKs Alaska oil pipe route 1-17, 56B3
State of Union proposals 1-21, 1-23, 41A1, D2, 42C1, 43F1, D3, F3
Budget proposals 1-28, 70A1-B1, 71E3-72C1, 74A1; table 70F1, G1
Kennedy, GOP score re Persian Gulf defense 1-28, 74E2, F2, E3, 75C1
'77 forgn oil use pledge cited 1-29, 77D2
Kennedy attacks policy 2-2, 91C1
Links Cong inactn, inflatn 2-25, 144G2
Oil stockpiling stalled 3-5, 165B3
Seeks more coal-fired utilities 3-6, 169A3
Ford attacks policies 3-12, 207G1
Gasohol seen as world food threat 3-15, 251B1
Voluntary state gas use targets set, '80 consumption drop 3-20, 250D3
Scores Mobil pricing policies 3-28, 4-1, 248F1
Revised budget proposals 3-31, 243G2, 244D1
Scores controls 4-1, 247C1
Signs windfall oil profits tax 4-2, 244B2
Assures Japan re Iran oil imports loss 5-1, 341F1
Oil import fee blocked by Dist Ct 5-13, 366A1

1976

Finances
Gets US campaign subsidy 1-2, more funds OKd 1-8, 22E3, F3
Fed fund total listed 3-4, 180C3
Loses Sup Ct funds plea 4-23, 306C1
Fed funding resumed 5-21, 391D3
At Dallas fund-raiser 6-14, 433B1
Campaign debt rptd 6-16; fed funds total 7-1, 491A1, C1
At Houston, Boston, NYC Dem fund-raisers 6-18—6-23, 452E1
Still eligible for fed funds 6-23, 490G3
At Chicago, Houston fund-raisers 7-1, 490D2

1977

Text of address to natn 4-18, 294D2-295C1
Cong reactn to natl policy plan 4-20, 290B3, 293G1
Natl policy plan fact sheet 4-20, 291A1-293F3
Domestic, forgn reactn to plan 4-20—4-24, 319A3-320F3, 324B2
Castro lauds policy address 4-20, 4-21, 390E1
House forms energy panel 4-21, 321B1
Defends plan 4-22, 321D1
GOPs score proposed taxes 4-25, 320F3
UN resource rpt backs conclusns 4-26, 362G2
Cong, labor, business, consumers score plan 4-30—6-8; GOP TV rebuttal 6-2, 443E1-G2
Gets FPC Alaska gas pipe rpt 5-2, 369C2
AFL-CIO scores plan 5-4, 364D3
Cites finite resources at 7-natn summit 5-8, 358D1
McGovern scores policy 5-13, 381D2
On fuel crisis, clean air 5-17, 381B3
Cong sets '78 budget target 5-17, 405A1
Sen OKs Cabt-level dept 5-18, 405E1
UAW pres vs car proposals 5-19, 408F2
Environment message 5-23, 404B2
US oil imports poll rptd 6-2, 464A3
Cong tussle continues 6-9—6-14, 460E1-C2
Warns vs oil, auto lobbies 6-10, 460A3
Welcomes OPEC price freeze 6-30, 515A2, 535A3
Alcan gas pipe route backed 7-4, 525F1
US tanker cargo preference backed 7-11, 538B2
Oil tanker cargo preference controversy 7-11—9-9, 719B3-G3
Cites Cong action 7-12, 534E1
Orders NYC blackout probe 7-14, 537C3
Coal progrm health hazard seen 7-17, 559F1
Miss town mtg topic 7-21, 575E1
Strip-mine rules cleared 7-21, 575D2
For Atlantic oil exploratn 7-22, 575G1
Backs gas-tax proposal 7-22, 575B2
Scores oil imports use 7-28, 574C3
Signs Energy Dept bill, names Schlesinger secy 8-4, 591C2
Warns of 'impending crisis' 8-4, 591E3
House OKs legis package 8-5, 609E2-610C1
Signs ERDA funds 8-8, 609D2
OKs Alcan gas pipe 9-8, 687B1
Coal-conversn, gas guzzler bills clear Sen 9-8, 702A3-703F1
Govs assured of conf 9-8, 719A2
Sen sets back progrm, OKs deregulatn 9-14—10-4; veto threatened 9-24, press conf 9-29, 757A1
IEA seeks oil use lid 10-5—10-6, 794B1
Urges Nigeria curb oil price hikes 10-12, 797G1
Scores oil industry; reactn 10-13, 772E2, F3
'78 research authorizatn clears Cong 10-20, 832G3
Topic on Iowa visit 10-21, 817C1
Offshore leasing bill blocked by House com 10-25, 833A3
Delays tax pkg, asks energy progrm enactmt 10-27, 813A1-F3
Cites poll rating drop 10-27, 814B1
Sen passes tax bill 10-31, 832C1-F3
Alcan gas rte clears Cong 11-2, signed 11-8, 856C3, F3
Defers world trip 11-7, 854A1
Address to nation 11-8, 854A1
Signs ERDA mil authorizatn 11-15, 878A1
Iran backs oil price freeze 11-16, 897B1, B2
Schlesinger comments re legis compromise draw fire from House 11-21—11-23, 916B3-917C1
Reschedules world tour 11-29, 12-1, 914B2
News conf remarks on legis 11-30, 914A1, B1
LNG import policy faulted by GAO 12-12, 962G1
Sees as failure of yr 12-15, 975G3
Cong com adjourns without compromise 12-22, 1002F1
Legis priority in '78 12-28, 1002B1, D1

ENVIRONMENT & Pollution
Statement to world 1-20, 26G1, A3
Vows strip-mining, oil-spill bill 2-2, 75E1
'78 budget revisns 2-22, 125A2, 126D1
Call-in on Concorde 3-5, 171D1, B3
Sen vs water projct cuts 3-10, 174C2
On water project cuts 3-16, 3-23, 210C1, D1
Asks oil-spill legislatn, intl conf 3-18, 214G1-D2
Presents energy plan 4-18, 4-20, 289G1, 295A1, C1-E1, A2; fact sheet 291B1, F1, 293A2-B2
Backs some water projects 4-18, 299E2
Energy plan reactn 4-20—4-24, 319G3-320A1, A2, B3
Water projct funds impoundmt barred 5-3, 365C2
Signs water projct provisn 5-13, 380D3
On fuel crisis 5-17, 381B3
Message to Cong, reactn 5-23, 404G1-G2
Urges end to whaling 6-20, 496F3
Signs strip mine bill 8-3, 592F1
For eased steel industry curbs 10-13, 775G2
Signs drinking water bill 11-16, 1001F2
Signs endangered species bill 12-19, 1001A3
Signs clean-water revisn 12-20, 1001A3

1978

Oil import curbs backed by FRB chrmn 3-15, 181C1
Plans coal industry study 3-25, 217G1
Meets key Cong conferees in pvt sessns 4-11, 4-12, House protests 4-13, 304F1-A3
Meets GOP conferees 4-12, 304C2
Abourezk demands gas deregulatn veto 4-17, assured 'open' debate 4-18, 273C2
Mock Cong fetes mark anniv of plan; appeals to Cong 4-20, 304A3
Cong breakthrough; backs gas price compromise 4-21, 304E1-305A2
Cites Cong progress 4-25, 307A3
Marks Sun Day; vows solar energy strategy, renewable fuel projct funds 5-3, 321C3
Names new TVA chrmn 5-16; visits facility, urges broader energy role 5-22, 386G2-B3, 390G1-G2
Lauds cong gas price compromise 5-24, 446C1
Warns Cong on oil import fee 6-22, 511F2
Stresses need for legis 6-23—6-24, 509G3
Scores Sen oil import fee bar 6-27, 511B3, 523A3
CBO crude oil tax study rptd 6-29, 512D1
Signs solar, other renewable energy business loan aid 7-4, 512E1
Vows '78 plan, oil import cuts at Bonn summit 7-16—7-17, 544A1
Coal conversn bill clears Sen; program status rptd 7-18, 549G3-550F1
Coal slurry pipe bill defeated 7-19, 550G1
Urges crude oil tax legis 7-20, 549D3
Gas price compromise in trouble, lobbying effort rptd 8-17—9-1, 677A3-678B2
Solar panel draft study issued 8-25, 718A2; final study rptd, spending hike backed 12-12, 982G3
Govs conf OKs legis delegatn 8-28, 682G1
Plans gas bill lobbying effort 8-30, 664G1
On cong conf com vote 8-31, lauds Sen vote on compromise natural gas bill 9-27, 733A1, D1
Japan joint research planned 9-6, 695C3
Stresses legis package 10-10, 766G2
Hails Cong OK of plan 10-15, 786A2
Signs natl security progrm authorzn 10-25, 833C2
Natural gas supplies rptd plentiful 10-29, 899G3
Signs 5-part bill, backs oil import curbs 11-9, 873A1
Vs OPEC oil price hike 11-17, 899E3
Natural gas controls suit filed 11-20, 900D1
Urges OPEC price restraint 12-12, 957E1
Vows actn vs oil indus abuses 12-12, 983D2

Coal Strike—*See under LABOR in this section below*

ENVIRONMENT & Pollution—*See also RESOURCES, Natural in this section below*
Budget proposals 1-23, 44E2, 47B2, E3, 48G1; table 45D2
Suspends Ohio, Ind pollutn curbs 2-11, 2-16, 104G1
Signs sewage treatmt funds 3-7, 160F2
Urges Liberia tanker safety rules 4-3, 234E1
Signs ocean pollutn study 5-8, 343B2
Signs Coast Guard '79 authrzn 6-30, 525C2
Vetoes wildlife program 7-10, 567G3
Declares Niagara dump-site disaster area 8-7, 703A1, D1
Halts forgn impact statemts 9-26, 804F2
Signs natl parks authorzn 11-10, 897A2
Signs endangered species revisn 11-10, 1003B1
Gets 'outstanding' rating 12-20, 1009D1

EUROPEAN Community—*See under FOREIGN Policy in this section below*

1979

Urges Cong OK standby controls 4-30, 324F2-A3
Vows supplies for farmers 5-4, 346C3
Orders Calif gas shortage probe, backs rationing; scores Cong 5-5, 347D1
Standby gas rationing defeated, temp controls clear Cong 5-10, 342A2
Scores House on gas ration defeat, calls for Cong plan 5-11; criticizes pub on shortage 5-15, 361A1
Sees Brown, hikes Calif gas allocatn 5-16; Ore gov scores, summer shortfall warned 5-17, 361F1-E2
Warns Dems re inactn 5-25, 401D1, G1
Gives states gas sales regulatn power 5-29, 395G3
Sees oil execs 5-31, consumerists, Dems 6-1—6-2, 417G3-418G2
Cleveland Elec air rule eased 6-6, 422E3, 423B1
Meets Schmidt for talks 6-6, 430A1
Connally at Mayors Conf 6-11, 439E3-440A1
Proposes oil spill cleanup 6-13, 441F1
Presents solar energy plan 6-20, 498A1
Cancels diesel fuel allocatn rule 6-22, 479D3
Scores OPEC price hike, urges energy dvpt funds 6-28, 473A2
At Tokyo summit, defends oil policy 6-28—6-29; Giscard criticism rptd 7-2, 493B1-494C1
Scores OPEC price hike 7-1, 494C2
Poll rating low 7-1, 497G1, G2
Plans new progrm, address 7-2, 7-3, cancels speech 7-4; reactn 7-5, 497F1
Conducts policy review; sees US ldrs at Camp David, resets natl speech 7-6—7-12, 513C2, G3
Eizenstat memo leaked 7-7, 513C3
Mondale addresses govs 7-8, 517B3, D3
Assured on Saudi oil output hike 7-9, 536D3
Orders temp controls 7-10, 514G1
TV address on new 6-pt program 7-15, text; KC, Detroit speeches detail plan 7-16; reactn 7-15—7-17, 532A1-535C1
Brown backs N Amer common mkt 7-20, 581B2
Canada seeks environmt commitmt 7-20, 581D3
Accepts Cong energy plan delay 7-24, scores House re gas rationing veto amendmt 7-25, 557A2-D2
Kennedy-Durkin plan unveiled 7-25, 557C3
Thanks Camp David participants 7-30, 608F3-609A1
Standby gas rationing passes House 8-1, Sen rejcts 8-2, 595B1
Energy, Justice clear oil cos on hoarding; probe to go on 8-6, 628B3
AFL-CIO cncl backs plan 8-6, 629D2
Defends plan in Miss R boat trip 8-17—8-24, 622F1-623D1
UAW job action 8-22, 831A3
Calls for program passage 9-3, 661F1
Asks heating oil price freeze 9-8, 9-12, oil cos respond 9-16—9-19; Dem House caucus asks controls 9-19, 703A1-G1
Agrees to plan modificatns 9-11, 702D2
Oil exec scores policies 9-12, 702F3
New Eng energy mailing planned 9-17, 703E2
Predicts plan passage 9-25, 723B3
Sees Mex pres 9-28—9-29, 753B2
Energy mobilizatn bd bill clears Cong 10-4, 11-1, 961E1
Backs Westn states water control 10-10, 807E2
Links windfall tax, oil co profits 10-25, 804E2
Kennedy scores 11-2—12-13, 962B1, E1, A2
Signs standby gas rationing bill 11-5, 848A3
Sees environmentalists 11-7, 961A3
Synfuel authorizatn clears Sen 11-8, 961C1
Energy Dept funds; synfuel dvpt, heating aid clears Cong 11-9, 883E1; signed 11-27, 920B1
Urges govs aid oil conservatn 11-16, 879A3
Sees dependnc as security threat 11-28, 894D3
Cites as campaign issue 12-4, 918C2
Kennedy 'anti-coal' chrg rebutted 12-13, 987D1
Kennedy scores oil pricing 12-20—12-21, 983G2

Decontrol & Tax Plans—*See PETROLEUM—Carter Decontrol*

ENVIRONMENT & Pollution
Orders rpts on forgn impact 1-5, 16F3
Budget proposals 1-22, 45A3; table 42F2
Vows rule enforcemt 2-27, 149G2-A3
Hints rules delay 4-5, 250G3
Plans Viet war herbicide study 5-30, 419B2
Sees reps re oil policy 5-31, 417G3
Cleveland utility air rule eased 6-6, 422D3, 423B1
Proposes waste cleanup 6-13, 441F1
Canada seeks commitmt 7-20, 581D3
Interior Dept seeks to protect primitive areas 9-7, 703D3
Signs '80 water funds, Tellico Dam legis 9-26, 766F2
Mex oil blowout talks agreed 9-28—9-29, 753A2
Signs '80 EPA funds bill 11-5, 883A3
Sees environmentalists 11-7, 961F2

1980

Sees 'energy security' 5-29, 423E3
Vetoes oil import fee bar res 6-5, Cong overrides 6-5, 6-6, 436G2-437B2
Standby gas rationing plan submitted to Cong 6-12, 551E3
Synfuel bill clears Cong 6-19, 6-26, 479B2; signs 6-30, 494G1-A2
Oil import fee proposal dropped 6-19, 551D3
Dem platform drafted 6-24, 479G2
Energy Mobilizatn Bd defeated by House 6-27, 515A2
Attacks GOP inactn 7-17, 532E1
Assures Canada on Alcan pipe completn 7-17, 562G1-A2
Signs W Ger, Japan synfuel pact 7-31, 666D2
Oil planks voted 8-13, 611F2
Renominatn acceptance speech; text 8-14, 612E1, F3, 613F1, B3
Anderson scores Arab oil dependnc 9-4, 682A1
Rebuts Reagan attack 9-10, 699C1
Synfuels Corp bd named 9-10, 9-13, 699C1, 725E2
Bush attacks policy 9-10, 780F3
Hails fed progrm results 9-18, 698D3
Saudi secret talks 9-18, US stockpiling rptd resumed 10-27, 826B1
Attacks Reagan policy 9-22, 722G2
Signs energy appropriatn 10-1, 803A2
Names interim Synfuels Corp bd 10-5, 786E2-A3
Signs auto fuel standards revisn bill 10-10, 981C1
Cites Admin effort 10-12, 10-14, 779B1, F1
Debates with Reagan 10-28, 813D1, 814B1, 815D1
Anderson answers debate questns 10-28, 816A1
Signs Alaska lands bill 12-2, 916C1
Signs Gasohol Competitn Act 12-2, 982A1
Signs Pacific NW power bill 12-5, 981A2
Signs wood reuse bill 12-19, 982C1

ENVIRONMENT & Pollution
Budget proposals 1-28, 70A2, 73E2; table 70F1
Orders Love Canal aid 5-21, 386D3
Seeks eased auto emissn curbs 7-8, 505B1-E1
Global forecast gloomy 7-23, 573F1
Renominatn acceptance speech cites 8-14, 613F1
House passes clean-up funds 9-19, 9-23; Sen OKs 'superfund' 11-24, 897G1
Signs non-game wildlife law 9-29, 915B3
Asks steel indus deadlines delayed 9-30, 740B3
Signs Love Canal relocatn aid 10-1, 739E1
Dam support scored 10-1, 803A3
Foresees clean America 10-12, 779D1
Signs '81-85 coastal zone mgt authrzn 10-17, 981A2
Signs clean water amendmts 10-21, 981E1
Signs toxic dumping controls 10-21, 981F1
Ridicules Reagan on 'tree' pollutn 10-22, 802F3
Debates with Reagan 10-28, 815F1-A2
Anderson answers debate questns 10-28, 816D1
Plans to speak out 11-12, 865F2
Signs Alaska lands bill 12-2, 916C1
Signs toxic waste clean-up 12-11, 936C1
Signs '81 Interior funds 12-13, 982B1
Signs '81 EPA appropriatn 12-15, 982B1
Signs pesticide progrm extensn 12-17, 982C1

1976

At NY fund-raisers 7-16, 532G2
Ticket gets fed funds 7-20, 565A3
At NH fund-raiser 8-3, 564C3
Undocumented spending rptd 8-8, 585E3
Black mins funds returned 8-10, 585B3
Backs cong pub financing 8-11, 585A3
At San Fran fund-raiser 8-23, 631F2
Nomination costs rptd 8-28, 688F3
At NY fund-raiser 8-31, 645D2
Addresses AFL-CIO groups 9-10, 9-15, 686B2, 686D3
On Ford fund probe 9-29, 9-30, 723D1, A2
Admits UK, Israel underwrote trips 9-29, 723D2
Queried re corp favors in Ga 10-2, 743B1
At LA fund-raiser 10-7, 762D1
Scores Ford on finances 10-8, 762E1, B2
Lists '70 campaign donors 10-17, 804E3
FEC lists major backers 10-22, 939A1
Pres campaign cost rptd 11-17, 12-7, 938F1-A3
FEC certificatns rptd 12-31, 979E1, F2

Foreign Policy & Defense—*See also 'TV Debates' below*
Joins Kissinger critics 3-15, 198D1
Visits Meany 5-14, Meany reaction rptd 5-19, 391A1
Seeks 'men of faith' 6-19, 452B1
Urges intl cooperatn 6-23, 451D2
Airs forgn policy views 6-24, 490C1
Pres nominatn acceptance speech 7-15, 507C1
Briefed on defns, forgn policy 7-26—7-29, 551C1
Adviser sees Australia prime min 7-26, 554G1
Ford submits paymts disclosure bill 8-3, 668B3
Briefed on intl econ; gives views 8-18, 617E1, B2
Addresses Amer Legion on amnesty 8-24, 631F2, E3; Dole rebuts 8-25, 632B2
On US mil posture 8-24, 631F3
Scores GOP farm export policy 8-25, Dole rebuts 8-26, 632C1, E2
Ford, Connally hit inexperience 8-27, 644G3
Mondale stresses arms control 8-30, 645C3
Forgn policy speech stresses human rights, scores Arab boycott, arms sales 9-8, 664G2
Sees defense waste, Ford mounts attack 9-9, 664F3, 665B2
Dole scores inexperience 9-9, 666A1
Stresses defense issue 9-13, 686E2
Harriman Yugo visit canceled 9-16, 734A3
Harriman sees Brezhnev 9-20, 752B1
B-1 delay in '77 funds bill 9-22, 707D1
Dole scores grain embargoes 9-22, 9-23, 724D3
Panama asks immediate canal talks 9-22, 792A3
Urges A-fuel curbs 9-25, 724A1
Backs US initiative in southn Africa 9-27, 724B2
Scores arms sales to Saudi, backs commitmt to Israel 9-30, 742F3
Confers with Schlesinger 10-3, 743E1
Dole attacks 10-4, 10-5, 743F1-B2
Ford scores on defense 10-7, 763A2
Scores Ford on A-safeguards, other 'discrepancies' 10-8, 762E1-A2
Vs Ford chrgs re defns cuts 10-15; Ford reply 10-16, 785B1
Ford scores on defns 10-16, 10-19, 784C2, D2
Ford disputes re world prestige loss 10-18; scientists score 10-26, 840B2, D2 ★
Vows Arab boycott end 10-19, 785E2
US-Panama canal talks continue 10-19—10-26, 12-13—12-18, 1008F1, D2
Ford scores re Arab oil embargo, boycott 10-20, 784G2
Gen Brown reprimand request rptd 10-20, 787C3
Debates Ford 10-22, 800F3
Brezhnev scores statemts 10-25, 839B2
Cables Sovt Jew 10-25, 857B1
Ford scores; Carter rebuts re Yugo 10-26, 802G3-803D1
Plans bipartisan conf 10-26, 803C2
Sees continuity 11-4, 819G2
Egypt cites bias to Israel 11-4, 826C2, 841G2
Sadat asks Mideast move 11-13, 11-17, 878B1, C1
Urges restraint on oil prices, hopeful re SALT 11-15, 864A1
Buthelezi lauds 11-18, 928F1
Sees Kissinger, Cabt 11-19—11-22, 881C1
Kissinger denies Rhodesia mil guarantee 11-20, 879D2
SALT talks adjourn 11-20, 916C1
Weighs intl econ conf 11-22, 881A1
Chile denies seeking favor 11-22, 963E1
To upgrade econ aspect 11-23, 881A2
Plans Viet pardon action 11-27, 898C3
Wife in Mex 11-30—12-2, 906A3
Brezhnev asks SALT talks renewal 11-30, 947A3
Sen com remarks on Cyprus, bipartisanship rptd 12-1, 916B3
Limited B-1 contracts awarded 12-2, 942C1
Brezhnev forswears any 'test'; to push SALT 12-3, 916A3
NATO hears pledge 12-9, 933B2
North-South conf delayed 12-9, 976G3
Urges oil price restraint 12-14, 12-16, 935C1, 937E2
Panel advises on Latin Amer 12-14, 974D3

1977

FOOD Stamps—*See under WELFARE in this section below*
FOREIGN Aid—*See also country subheads under FOREIGN Policy in this section below*
Call-in topic 3-5, 171E1
Fscl '78 proposals 3-17, 210C3
Vs human rights amendmt 4-15, 299B2
Sen backs rights, aid link 6-14, 477F2
Signs '78 mil authorizatn 8-4, 667G3
Signs '78 econ authorizatn 8-4, 668F1
Intl lending agency authorizatn, rights amendmt cleared 9-21, 737C3; signs 10-3, 834D1
Backs World Bank capitalizatn hike 9-26, 754B2
Signs Food for Peace extensn 9-29, 737B2
Seeks intl lending agency funding, rights link compromise 9-30; asks goals review 10-6, 815B2
Intl lending agency, other '78 funds clear Cong 10-19, 815A2; signs 11-1, 834D1
FOREIGN Policy—*See also other appropriate headings in this section; for Administration policy and actions, see country or subject headings in Index*
Backs world-wide ties 3-17, 186B2
Defends speaking out 3-24, 230B1
Poll standings 4-4, 241E1
Cong sets '78 budget target 5-17, 405A1
Outlines new approach 5-22, 397A1
Goldwater: 'cool it' 7-29, 593A1
Announces 8-nation trip 9-23, 738F1
World trip deferred 11-7, 854A1; rescheduled 11-29, 12-1, 914B2
Energy to be world tour issue 12-28, 1002D1
Begins world tour 12-29, 1000E3
Africa—*See also specific countries in this section*
Young rpts on trip 2-13, 106A1
Call-in on Cuba role 3-5, 171B2
Backs majority rule 3-17, 186D1 ★
Seeks more VOA funds 3-22, 230A1
OKs Sudan jet sale 4-7, 327G3
Backs Young views 4-12, 272D1
Outlines policy 5-22, 397D1
Backs Young 5-23, 444B1; 5-26, 6-6, 417B3
Sees Young 6-7, 444A1
Says Young to shift focus 6-10, 460E2
Seeks arms sales curbs 7-28, 574B3
OKs southn regional aid fund 8-4, 668D1
OKs Sahel region aid 8-4, 668G1
On US leadership role 10-27, 813B3
Algeria
Favors Sovt challenge 6-10, 460D2
Angola
Scores Cuba role 2-16, 110A1, 180G2
Vs Cuba interventn 5-22, 397F1
Signs arms aid bar 8-4, 668B1
Argentina
Aid cut 2-24, 142E1
Signs arms aid bar 8-4, 668B1
Encouragemt of Radical ldr rptd 9-2, 922E1
Videla vow to end rightist terror rptd 9-12, 922E1
Asia—*See also specific countries in this section*
Seeks more VOA funds 3-22, 230A1
Vows closer cooperatn 5-22, 397F1
Australia
In uranium collaboratn exchng 2-4—3-11, 624G3
Fraser rpts A-safeguards exchng 3-23, 217F3
Sees Fraser 6-21—6-23, 560C3
CIA role rptdly barred 8-4, 633A1
Austria
Kreisky in US talks 3-14, 425E1
Belgium
Plans to visit 9-23, 738F1
Visit deferred 11-7, 854A1; rescheduled 11-29, 914B2
Botswana
OKs regional aid fund 8-4, 668D1
Brazil
Mil aid rejctd 3-5, 167E3; pact canceled 3-11, 186D2
Lauds Cardinal Arns 5-22, 447A3
Wife gets student rights plea 6-6, 524D1
Assured on Canal pact backing 9-3, 678D1
Sees vice pres 9-6, 678A1
Plans to visit 9-23, 738F1
Visit deferred 11-7, 854A1; rescheduled 12-1, 914C2
Uranium export OKd 11-16, Venez backing cited 11-25, 912D3
Burma
Asked to aid separatists 779A3
Cambodia
To lift US travel ban 3-9, 172F3
House panel asks to end repressn 7-26, 590E2
Signs aid bar 8-4, 668B2
Refugee quotas eased 8-31, 685D2
Canada
Trudeau in US 2-21—2-23, 132B3
Vs Quebec separatism 2-23, 126G2
At 7-natn econ summit 5-7—5-8, 357B1
Alcan gas pipe route backed 7-4, 525F1
Trudeau scores rights stand 7-14, 566G2
Signs temp fishing rights pact 7-26, 688D3
OKs Alcan gas pipe 9-8, 687B1
Signs Alcan gas rte res 11-8, 856F3
Chile
Frei rpts paymts apology 3-4, 219A2
Disavows Tyson apology on coup, campaign statemts noted 3-8, 3-9, 219A1, C1
Spain Soclst sees Chile rights role 8-31, 743D2
Sees Pinochet 9-6, 678A1

1978

EXECUTIVE Orders
Reorganizes intell unit 1-24, 49A2
'Plain English' rulemaking 3-23, 218D2
Forms telecommunicatns agency 3-28, 270C2
Broadens consumer office powers 4-27, 347D3
Revises secrecy classificatn rules 6-29, 508B1
Broadens Contract Compliance Office powers 10-6, 811G2
Backs judges merit selectn 11-8, 873F2-C3
FOOD Stamps—*See under WELFARE in this section below*
FOREIGN Aid—*See also country, region subheads under FOREIGN Policy in this section below*
Signs '79 funds, IMF contributn 10-18, 862C2, F2
FOREIGN Investment—*See BUSINESS above, FOREIGN Policy below*
FOREIGN Policy—*See also other appropriate headings in this section; for Administration policy and statements, see country or subject headings in Index*
Ends world tour 1-6, 1B1; news conf remarks 1-12, 12A1
State of Union Message 1-19, 29F2, 31F1
Budget proposals 1-23, 44F2; table 45D2
Attacked by GOP sens 5-3, 342G2
Revises secrecy classificatn rules 6-29, 508F1
Signs mil, security aid authrzn 9-26, 734C1-G2
Signs diplomatic immunity revisn 9-30, 750D3
Afghanistan
Discusses new govt with India 6-13—6-15, 466G3
Africa—*See also country names in this section*
Scores Sovt role 1-12, 12F1
State of Union Message 1-19, 31G2
Warns USSR re Horn role 1-25, 43D3; 3-2, 140E2, 179A1
Warns USSR, Tass scores 3-17, 202E1, G2
Scores Cuba mil role 3-28, 4-1, 233D1, G2
Scores Soviet role 5-5, 342E1
Orders aid curb review 5-16, scores Cong restraints 5-19, 5-23, 382D3
Warns Cuba, USSR; scores Cong aid curbs 5-25; Cuba denies chrgs 5-30, 418D1, F1
Addresses NATO summit on USSR, Cuba threat 5-30, 397E1
Outlines goals, asks USSR cooperatn 6-7, 424B1
House com seeks policy clarificatn 6-8; Vance briefs, denies SALT 'link' 6-19, 490A3, C3
Brazil, Venez pressure on Cuba rptd asked 6-11, 443C1
Vance policy statemt, rights stressed 6-20, 487E1
Silent on Cuba role at OAS 6-21, 489A3
Optimistic in policy appraisal 6-26, 490D2, 491A1
Lauds Young 7-20, 549E2
Signs southn Africa aid authorzn 9-26, 734G1
Algeria
Lauds Boumedienne 12-27, 1012C3
Angola
Scores Cong curbs on rebel aid 5-23, 383B1
Denies knowledge of Clark mtg 5-24, 443D1
Chrgs Zaire role 5-25, 5-30, 418A1, B1, G1
Denies knowledge of rebel aid 6-26, 491G1-A2
Signs econ aid authorzn bar 9-26, 734G1
Signs econ aid funds bar 10-18, 862E2
ASEAN
At econ talks 8-3—8-4, 603C3
Asia—*See also country names in this section*
State of Union Message 1-19, 31G2
Warns USSR vs mil buildup, interventn 3-17, 202F1
At ASEAN econ talks 8-3—8-4, 603C3
Australia
Exempts from arms sales ceiling 2-1, 106F2
Signs mil, security aid authorzn 9-26, 734A2, E2
Belgium
Visits 1-6, 1C1
Belize
Cites Guatemala land dispute 6-21, 489C3
Bolivia
Cites sea outlet dispute 6-21, 489C3
Brazil
Visits; stresses rights, A-safeguards 3-29—3-31, 233B1, A2, 262G3
Cuba pressure re Africa rptd asked 6-11, 443C1
Cambodia
Scores rights breach 4-21, 301G1
Vows refugee aid 12-6, 934E1
Canada
Ties seen improved 1-23, 53E3
China
Seeks cooperatn, reassures USSR 6-26, 491B1
Meets amb on ties 9-19, sets target date 11-4, 974A1
Bars arms sales, seeks full ties 11-30, 936F2
Posters urge rights stand 12-10, 949F2

1979

EXECUTIVE Orders
State gas sales regulatn powers 5-29, 395G3
Consumer Affairs Cncl 9-26, 902B3
Cuba policy directive rptd 10-16, 781D2
Trade reorganizatn 10-25, 803B1
FOOD Stamps—*See under WELFARE in this section below*
FOREIGN Aid—*See also country, region subheads under FOREIGN Policy in this section below*
Budget proposals 1-22, 41C2; table 42E2
FOREIGN Investment—*See BUSINESS above, FOREIGN Policy below*
FOREIGN Policy—*See also other appropriate headings in this section; for Administration policy and statements, see country or subject headings in Index*
Orders environmental impact rpts 1-5, 16F3
Budget proposals 1-22, 41C2; table 42E2
State of Union Message 1-23, 46E2, D2, E1
Warns staff re press leaks 2-12, 109G3
Dole, Reagan score 2-16, 2-18, 124D1
Policy speech stresses ally ties 2-20, 123D2-124B1
Vs simplistic criticism 2-22, 124C1
Defends policy stance 2-27, 149G1
Addresses govs 2-27, 150C2
'New diplomacy' defended 5-1, 347F1-F2
Secret tapes denied 10-29, 869F1
Forgn-language study urged 11-7, 944F1
Afghanistan
SALT II summit topic 6-15—6-18, 449D1
Warns USSR on invasn 12-28, contacts Pak pres 12-30, 973G2, 974A2
Africa—*See also country names in this section*
Guadeloupe summit discusses aid 1-5—1-6, 12G2
SALT II summit topic 6-15—6-18, 449D1
Addresses Cong on SALT II 6-18, 449E2, 459A3
Young rpts on trip 9-22, 721C2
Asia—*See also country names in this section*
SALT II summit topic 6-15—6-18, 449D1
Australia
Rues Skylab debris 7-11, 509B1
Fraser scored by ex-amb 8-24, 650G1
Austria
At SALT II summit in Vienna 6-15—6-18, 449A1, F1, 457E2
Brazil
Intl role, close ties seen 3-22, 248A1
Cambodia
Guadeloupe summit discusses Viet dispute 1-5—1-6, 12G2
Links Viet, China invasns 2-20, 122C3
Bars Viet dispute role, seeks fighting end 2-20, 123E2, C3; 2-22, 124D1; 2-27, 149B2
Backs food aid 10-9, 767A2
Sihanouk sends plea on food aid, Thai refugees 10-11, 811E2
Vows $70 mln in food aid 10-24, 811F1
3 sens rpt on famine, Clark heads aid effort 10-26, 823E3
Reps urge US-USSR airlift 11-1, 863A3
Canada
'78 fish war truce proposal cited 1-10, 37E1
Westn econ summit warning to Japan rptd 2-10, rpt disputed 2-15, 160E1
Sees Trudeau, backs Alcan pipeline 3-3, 168F1
Trudeau offers oil pipe routes 4-10, 284F2
Canada seeks environmt commitmt 7-20, 581D3
OKs discount flight halt 8-30, 667D2
Cancels trip 11-8, 842E2
China
Guadeloupe summit topic 1-5—1-6, 12E2, G2, C3
US mil ex-ldrs warn of Sovt threat 1-12, 15C1
US OKd Taiwan arms ban in tie talks 1-12, 27D1
Vance-Brzezinski rift denied 1-16, 27G2
Sees peaceful Taiwan setlmt, invites Nixon to Teng dinner, reassures Sovts on ties 1-17, 29D3, E3
Proposes Taiwan ties legis, to veto anti-Peking bills 1-26, 66E2
Teng visits DC 1-28—2-1, in talks 1-29—1-30, signs pacts 1-31; communique issued 2-1, 65A1-D2, 66D1
Accepts China invite, asks Hua to visit US 1-29, 65A2
Sovts assured on Teng talks 2-1, 65D2
Tass: Teng trip undermines SALT 2-1, 84F1
Links Viet, Cambodia invasns 2-20, 122C3
Seeks Viet dispute end, defends ties normalizatn 2-20, 123E2, C3;
Asks Viet exit, bars role; defends trade talks 2-27, 141C2, 149C2
US, China open embs 3-1, 146B3
Teng vs rights complaints 3-16, 259B1
Signs Taiwan relatns bill 4-10, 259C2
Addresses Cong on SALT II 6-18, 459E2

1980

EXECUTIVE Orders
Trade reorganizatn 1-2, 94G2
Rpts '79 consumer order implemented 6-9, 703B1
Uranium sale to India 6-19, 495F2
Draft registratn 7-2, 493B3
FAMILIES & Family Life
Opens Families Conf 6-5, 442E2
White House Conf meets in Minn 6-19—6-21, LA 7-10—7-12, 601G1
FOOD Stamps—*See under WELFARE and Poverty in this section below*
FOREIGN Aid—*See also FOREIGN Policy in this section*
Budget proposals, table 1-28, 70E1
Signs '81 authrzn 12-16, 981C3
FOREIGN Policy—*See also other appropriate headings in this section; for Administration policy and statements, see country or subject headings in Index*
GOP chrmn scores 1-1, 5A1
Kennedy, Brown score 1-12, 32E2
Stresses policy re renominatn 1-20, 50G1
Budget proposals, table 1-28, 70E1
Kennedy blasts 2-12, 110F1
Reagan assails 2-15, 128B3
Ford attacks 3-12, 208A1
Bush scores 4-7, 264C2
Sees 'stronger' Muskie role 5-9, 367D1
Ford, Kissinger score 7-14, 7-15, 534G2, C3
Anderson scores 7-14, 550A1
Aides took oaths re leaks 7-16—7-17, 549G1
Bush scores weak policies 9-24, 781D1
Reagan asserts peace priority 10-19—10-20, 801C2-802D1
Debates with Reagan 10-28, 814E2, G2
Forgn reactn to Reagan electn 11-5, 11-6, 841B2-D3
Afghanistan
USSR invasn reactn 1-1—1-6, 2D2; for subsequent developments, see 'USSR' in this section below
Africa
State of Union address 1-23, 42C3
A-blast mystery off S Africa unsolved 1-23, 49A3
NSC memo called forgery 9-17, 726E3-727B1
Argentina
Rights policy scored 11-20, 913C3
Asia—*See also specific countries in this section*
Cites Indian Ocean policy 1-23, 42F2, C3
State of Union address 1-23, 42C3
Australia
Eximbank loan to Ansett, mtg with Murdoch sparks probe 2-10, 989E1
Cambodia
Signs refugee aid bill 7-8, 515F1
Scores USSR re Viet invasn support 7-10, 506D1
Canada
OKs all-US oil pipe route 1-17, 56B3
Thanks Clark for envoy rescue 1-31, 88A3
Assures on Alcan pipe completn 7-17, 562G1-A2
Sovt grain embargo support ended 11-20, 900B2
China
Cites diplomatic role 1-20, 50G1
State of Union address 1-23, 42C3
Meets Hua in Tokyo; USSR scores 7-10, 506B1, F1
Signs trade pact 9-17, 707A1
Cites normalized ties 9-18, 698B3
China (Taiwan)
Arms sale OKd 1-3, 11G2
Eases TV import curbs 6-30, 515C3
Reagan scores policy 8-25, 646G1
Colombia
Hails DR Emb siege end 4-28, 335A3
Cuba
State of Union address 1-23, 42G1
Reagan 'basic speech' scores ties 2-29, 207B3
Refugees granted conditional stay 4-24, 301B1
Offers refugees 'open arms' 5-5, declares Fla emergency 5-6, 339D2, C3
Curbs 'open arms' policy, orders flotilla end; 5-pt progrm detailed 5-14, 361A1
Gives refugees pol asylum 5-21, 380B1
Cuban flotilla boat seizures protested 5-28, 700 face fines 5-29, 396G1
Consults Cong ldrs 6-4; orders criminal refugees expelled 6-7, 435A1, E1, G1
Sees Miami Hispanic ldrs re refugees 6-9, 439E1
Signs refugee resetlmt aid bill 7-8, 515F1
Castro lauds Latin policy 7-18, 565B3
Sets 3-pt refugee resetlmt plan 9-18, 742G1
Quotes Reagan blockade proposal 9-23, 722D3
Cuba to release US prisoners 10-13, 789E1
Scores Reagan blockade proposal 10-16, 802F2
30 US prisoners freed 10-27, 828D3
Matos asks UN probe prison hunger strike 12-4, 965D2
Developing Nations—*See also specific countries, regions*
Notes improved ties 1-23, 42C3, 43D1
Addresses World Bank-IMF mtg, vows aid 9-30, 761G3

1976

Sees Sovt summit 12-27, Brezhnev rptd favorable 12-29, 978G2, B3
Seeks SALT agrmt, A-curbs 12-27, 978A3
Defns cut stance explained 12-28, 12-29, 978D1
Plans mtgs with Mideast ldrs 12-29, 978C3

1977

Pinochet OKs UN rights probe 9-7, 743B1
Backs Helms setlmt 11-10, 877G1

China

Backs closer ties 3-17, 186B2
Son Chip visits 4-9—4-17, 298B2
Rpts goodwill message 4-22, 321A3
Rpts claims talks under way 5-12, 381A2
Says key to world peace 5-22, 397D2
Favors Sovt challenge 6-10, 460D2
Backs full ties 6-30, 515F1
Stresses Taiwan ties 8-19, 645C2
Gets Taiwan protests 8-20, Peking regrets stand 8-29, 664F2, A3
On Vance mission 8-25, 645B1
Hua lauds '72 communique stance 8-25, 645C1
Vance briefs on trip 8-28, 664C2

China (Taiwan)

On China ties 6-30, 515F1
Stresses ties 8-19, 645C2
Gets letters vs Peking ties 8-20, Peking regrets stand 8-29, 664F2, A3

Colombia

To aid drug effort 6-10, 455D2
Sees Lopez Michelsen 9-6, 678A1

Cuba

Castro lauds, sees ties 2-9, scores rights pressure 2-26—2-27; reactn 2-19, 180B2, C3
On key to normal ties 2-12, 2-16, 110A1, 180G2
Mex offers aid re Cuba ties 2-15, 110D1
On pol prisoners, US ties 2-23, 126E2, G2
Call-in topic 3-5, 171F1, A2
To lift US travel ban 3-9, 172F3, 180B2
Currency curbs eased 3-25, 283E2
Assures Castro on ties, lauds fishing talks; reactn 4-9, 283C1, F1
Castro lauds energy plan 4-20—4-21, 390E1
Doubts Zaire troop role 4-22, 321C3
Trade curb ease, shipmt halt authority voted by Sen com 5-10, 5-11, 389D3, F3
Deplores Angola role 5-22, 397F1
Dellums briefs on Castro talk 6-3, 456C2
Castro lauds 6-9, 456A2
Favors Sovt challenge 6-10, 460D2
Sen backs compromise policy 6-16, 477D3, G3
OKs aid bar 8-4, 668B2
Church missn, sees Castro 8-8—8-11, 653C3, F3, 654A1, D1
Hails release of natls, kin 9-22, 781D2
Castro reaffirms Africa role 12-5, 1011F2

Cyprus

Clifford missn 2-17—2-26, 122F1, 146G3
Sets Turkey arms aid terms 4-19, 351F1
Sees Caramanlis, Demirel 5-10, 359C1
OKs security aid 8-4, 668D1
Urges new talks 8-25, 764E1

Czechoslovakia

Gets pleas for dissidents 1-19, 82A3

Developing Nations—*See also specific countries, regions in this section*

Inaugural 1-20, 26B1, 27E1
Statemt to world 1-20, 26A3
Cites N-S talks at 7-natn summit 5-8, 358D1
Reaffirms faith in Young 5-23, 444B1

Ecuador

Bars Israel jet sale 2-7, 87A3
Israel jet sale bar scored, wife clarifies 6-2, 454C3
Seeks trade curbs end 6-2, hails democratizatn plan 6-3, 454D3

Egypt—*See also 'Middle East Conflict' in this section below*

On Libya conflict restraint 7-28, 574B3
OKs security aid 8-4, 668D1

El Salvador

Mil aid rejected 3-16, 206A3

Ethiopia

Aid cut 2-24, 142E1
Meets Shah on Somalia conflict 12-31, 1001A1

Europe—*See also 'NATO' and specific countries in this section*

Briefs Mondale 1-23, lauds missn 2-1; Mondale rpts 2-2, 69E1
Explains human rights stand 2-23, 126C2
Asks more RFE transmitters 3-22, 229F3
Stresses human rights 5-2, 338A2
Sees Schmidt; OKs MBFR initiatives, eases CSCS rights stand 7-13—7-14, 566B2, E2
Cites troop cut talks 7-21, 550B3

France

Vs Daoud release 1-12, 10B1
Talks to Giscard 1-13, cooperatn vowed 1-14, 27G2
Backs Concorde trial 2-16, 131D2
Giscard warns vs Concorde ban 3-4, Le Monde scores 3-7, 212B3
Asks Portugal aid 4-1, 330C3
Stresses rights in TV interview 5-2, 338B2
At 7-natn econ summit 5-7—5-8; sees Giscard 5-9, diplomacy hailed 5-11, 357B1, 358F1, E2, 359E1, G1
Giscard denies USSR mediator role 6-22, 495C2
Giscard scores on detente 7-25, 550D3
Seeks arms sales curbs 7-28, 574A3, B3
Sees Barre, 'organized free trade' asked 9-15—9-16, 1012B3
Barred Mitterand mtg 9-16, 883D3
Plans to visit 9-23, 738F1
Visit deferred 11-7, 854A1; rescheduled 11-29, 914B2
Sees Bourges, arms sales curb refused 11-22, 1012E3

1978

Announces ties, assures Taiwan 12-15, 973A1; text 975A1
Brzezinski visit cited 973G2
US reactn to ties mixed 12-15—12-20, 974A3, 975A3-976E1, 995C2
Eur, Asia back ties; call to Japan rptd 12-16, 977B1
Calls Brezhnev reactn to ties 'positive' 12-19, 976E1; Brezhnev denies 12-21, 995E1
Ties, SALT pact delay linked 12-26, 996C1

China (Taiwan)

Sees China amb on ties, sets terms 9-19, 974B1
Announces Peking ties; to end defns pact, assures Taiwan 12-15, 973A1; text 975A1
US reactn to China ties mixed 12-15—12-20, Goldwater threatens suit 12-15, 974A3, 975A3-976E1
Goldwater, 14 other congressmen sue vs defns pact end 12-22, 995C2

Colombia

Consults Lopez on DR electn 5-19, 414C2

Costa Rica

Wife at Oduber inaugural 5-8, 354D2
Oduber on DR electn 5-19, 414C2

Cuba

Urges Ethiopia exit 3-7—3-9, 194A1
Scores Africa mil role 3-28, 4-1, 233D1, G2
Scores US curbs on Africa aid 5-19, 383A1
Gets CIA evidence on Zaire role 5-19, 442A1
Chrgs Zaire role 5-25, 5-30; Cuba denies 5-30, 418A1, E1
Addresses NATO summit on Africa threat 5-30, 397E1
Briefs Cong ldrs on Zaire role 6-2, 442E1
Brazil, Venez pressure re Africa rptd asked 6-11, 443C1
Rebuts Castro denial on Zaire 6-14, 443A1
Castro lauds, scores Brzezinski 6-18, 687B2
Vance briefs House com, notes Africa role concern 6-19, 490D3
Silent on Africa role at OAS 6-21, 489A3
Castro would like mtg 6-27, 687A2
Castro rptdly asked concessns re dual citizens release 8-17, 687G1
USSR assures re MiGs 11-20, 1016G1
Scored by '80 pres hopeful 11-29, 938E3
Vows help for pol refugees 12-6, 934E1

Cyprus

Lauds Sadat on Cyprus raid 2-23, US denies taking sides 2-26, 138G2
Vows renewed peace effort 8-1, 587B3
Signs refugee aid authorzn, end to Turkey arms embargo 9-26, 734G1, B2

Developing Nations—*See also specific countries, regions in this section*

Urges US, Eur aid 1-4, 2E1
Links aid price stabilizatn 3-29, 233F1
Sees 'new era' 4-18, 274B1

Dominican Republic

Vote count suspensn scored, Balaguer pledge cited 5-17, 371D3
Consults latin ldrs warns Balaguer vs vote fraud 5-19; Guzman victory accepted 5-27, 414B2

Egypt—*See also 'Middle East Conflict' in this section below*

Visits 1-4, 1C1, 2A2
Sadat asks arms 1-20, 1-21, 41G1
Briefed on Somalia aid 1-26, 99G3
Defends jet sale 2-17, 123C2
Lauds Sadat on Cyprus raid 2-23, US denies taking sides 2-26, 138G2
Vs jet sale legis delay 4-25, 307A1, B1
Hopeful on jet sale legis 5-4, 321D2
Seeks Sen support for jet sale, lauds passage 5-15, 357D1, 358A1
Reassures jet sale opponents 5-15—5-16, 358B1
Signs econ aid authorzn 9-26, 734E1

El Salvador

Cites Honduras border dispute 6-21, 489C3

Ethiopia

Scores Sovt Ogaden role 1-12, 12E1
Warns USSR 1-25, 43D3
Briefed on Somalia aid pledges 1-26, 99G3
Warns vs Somalia invasn 2-17, Mengistu vow rptd 2-21, 137G1
Warns USSR vs mil role 3-2, 140E2, 179A1
Urges USSR, Cuba exit 3-7—3-9, 194A1
Lauds Somali withdrawal 3-9, 179F2
Denies knowledge of Clark mtg 5-24, 443D1

Europe—*See also 'European Community', 'NATO' and country names in this section*

Vows US commitmt 1-4, 2E1
State of Union Message 1-19, 31B2
Warns USSR vs mil buildup 3-17, 202E1
Optimistic on troop-cut talks 6-26, 491F1
Vetoes shipping malpractice 11-4, 897G2

European Community (EC)

Visits hq, reassures 1-6, 1C1, D1
Monetary plan reservatns rptd 7-18, 545G3

France

Visits 1-4—1-6; sees Mitterrand, Fabre; declines Chirac mtg 1-6, 1B1, 2C1

1979

Mondale briefs on visit 9-4, 660E2
OKs trade benefits 10-23, 834E1

China (Taiwan)

US OKs arms ban in Peking tie talks 1-12, 27D1
Sees peaceful Peking setlmt 1-17, 29E3
Proposes legis on relatns, to veto anti-Peking bills 1-26, 66E2
Signs US relations bill 4-10, 259C2
US cong defns treaty suit dismissed, Sen rebukes policy 6-6, 440F1, B2
Loses defns treaty suit 10-17, 777A1
Defns treaty abrogatn upheld 11-30, 919D1
Defns treaty case refused by Sup Ct 12-13, 940A1

Cuba

Addresses Cong on SALT II 6-18, 449E2, 459A3
Warns USSR re troops; statemt text 9-7, 673A1
On USSR troops 9-25, 723E2
Castro scores re troop rpt 9-28, 737G2
Orders increased surveillnc; speech text 10-1; Sen, Sovt, Eur reactn 10-1—10-3, 737A1-739D2
Marines begin Guantanamo maneuvers 10-17, 781C2

Cyprus

State of Union Message 1-23, 48F1

Developing Nations—*See also specific countries, regions in this section*

Budget proposals 1-22, 41C2
Urges science aid 4-23, 300B3
Addresses Cong on SALT II 6-18, 459A3

Egypt—*See also 'Middle East Conflict' in this section below*

Trade group visits 4-17, 296C1
Asked Saudis end Egypt feud 5-21, 378D3
Addresses Cong on SALT II 6-18, 459A3

Europe—*See also 'NATO' and country subheads in this section*

US mil ex-ldrs warn of Sovt threat 1-12, 15C1
A-Conf message affirms US supplier role 5-7, 374B1
Addresses Cong on SALT II 6-18, 459E2

France

At Guadeloupe summit 1-5-1-6, 12D2-D3, 40C2
Westn econ summit warning to Japan rptd 2-10, rpt disputed 2-15, 160E1
Francois-Poncet visits US 6-4-6-5, 485C1
Giscard critizes policy, rebuts 6-28; Giscard comments publshd 7-2, 493F2

GATT

State of Union Message 1-23, 46G3
Hails pact 4-12, 274B1
Submits trade bill to Cong 6-19, sets tariff cuts 6-21; House OKs bill 7-11, 541F1-A2

Germany (East)

Scores USSR troop cut plan 10-9, 761A3

Germany (West)

At Guadeloupe summit 1-5-1-6, 12D2-D3, 40C2
Westn econ summit warning to Japan rptd 2-10, rpt disputed 2-15, 160E1
Meets Schmidt 6-6, 430A1
Israeli setlmt pressure rptd sought 7-9, 511B2

Great Britain

At Guadeloupe summit 1-5-1-6, 12D2-D3, 40C2
Westn econ summit warning to Japan rptd 2-10, rpt disputed 2-15, 160E1
Congratulates Thatcher 5-4, 338A2
Backs Thatcher on Zimbabwe plan 8-6, 590C2
Lynch visits, seeks cooperatn on Ulster 11-8, 874A2
Iran assets freeze upheld 12-5, 915F1
Thatcher visits, backs on Iran 12-17, 968G1

Grenada

Recognizes new govt 3-22, 236G2

Guinea

Sees Toure, gives aid pledge 8-8, 796C3

India

Addresses Cong on SALT II 6-18, 459E2
Students burn effigy 11-30, 915D1

Indochina—*See country names in this section*

Iran

Cancels US naval move 1-2, 3E1
Orders probe of US anti-shah riot 1-4, 3G1
Guadeloupe summit topic 1-5-1-6, 12G2
US jets to visit Saudi 1-10, 12C2
Policy protested in Ga 1-14, 31A3
Backs Bakhtiar, existing arms pacts; on intellignc posts 1-17, 26G1
Khomeini vs cooperatn plea 1-18, 26A1
State of Union Message 1-23, 48F1
Shah vs coalition backing 1-23, 49C3
Seeks Khomeini ties 2-12, 106A1
Bars interventn, warns USSR 2-20, 123E2, A3
Vs simplistic criticism 2-22, 124D1
Protesters assail 5-24, 407A3
SALT II summit topic 6-15-6-18, 449D1
Pres campaign muted 10-24-12-13, 961G1
US Emb takeover forces Canada trip cancellatn 11-8, 842E2
Denounces terrorism 11-8, 874B2
Asks US calm, meets hostage kin 11-9, 863A1

1980

Ecuador

Quotes Reagan on '75 fishing war 9-23, 722D3

Egypt

Sadat defends shah's asylum 3-25, 217C2
Sadat regrets electn defeat 11-5, 841C2
Signs '81 aid authrzn 12-16, 981C3

Ethiopia

Mengistu scores re Somali pact 9-12, 736A1

Europe—*See also specific countries in this section*

Iran support withheld 4-10, 281G2
Visits 6-19—6-26, backs Eur-Sovt ties 6-23, 473C1-475C1

European Community (EC)

US Steel suit oppositn rptd 3-27, 243C1
Backs Spain entry 6-25, 474D3

France

Citibank assets froze 1-16, 48B1
Sees allied unity re Sovt Afghan invasn 2-13, 110C1
Backs Eur-Sovt ties 6-23, 473F1
Neutron bomb test rptd 6-26, 486D3
Urges Poland aid 8-29, 659C1
Debates with Reagan 10-28, 814E2

Germany (West)

State of Union address 1-23, 42G1
Meets Schmidt, discusses Afghan 3-5, 205B2
Sends letter vs E-W missile freeze 6-16, Schmidt seeks mtg 6-18, 450B3-451D1
Sees Schmidt, USSR visit criticism disputed 6-21, 473E1
Sees Genscher re W Ger-USSR A-missile talks, lauds Schmidt trip 7-2, 489C1, E1
Signs synfuel pact 7-31, 666D2
Urges Poland aid 8-29, Schmidt responds 9-3, 659C1, C2
Meets Schmidt 11-20, 903G3-904A2

Great Britain

Fiber import curbs sought 2-5, 125G1
OKs Trident purchases 7-14, 544D2
Urges Poland aid 8-29, 659C1

Greece

Hails NATO mil wing re-entry 10-20, 800F1

Haiti

Refugee pol asylum pressed 5-7, 340C1
Refugees granted 6-mo reprieve, get pub assistance 6-20, 484B3-485D1
Signs refugee resetlmt aid bill 7-8, 515F1
Sets 3-pt refugee resetlmt plan 9-18, 742G1

India

Assures on aid to Pak 1-16, 27G1
Clifford in talks 1-30—1-31, 83C2
Uranium sale backed 5-7, NRC blocks 5-16, 440C3
OKs uranium sale 6-19, 495F2
Cong fails to block uranium sale 9-24, 723C1

Iran—*See also 'Iran-Iraq War' in this section below*

GOP chrmn chrgs Carter deceptn 1-1, 5A1, E1
Brown scores 1-5, 1-8, 13B2
Waldheim rpts on missn 1-6, 3B3
Sees no break in crisis 1-8, 1-9, 29B3
Poll status slips 1-10, 32G2
Mondale boosts policy 1-12, 32E2
France freezes Citibank funds 1-16, 48B1
Hostage letter cited 1-17, 47F3
State of Union topic 1-21, 1-23, 41E1, 42B1, D1, 43G3
Reagan scores 1-24, 91A3
Kennedy blames Carter, asks intl probe comm 1-28, 74C3
Thanks Clark for envoy rescue 1-31, 88B3
Wife campaigns 1-31, 91E2
Me pol ads cited 2-10, 109E1
Kennedy, Admin exchng chrgs re intl probe comm, other issues 2-12—2-13, 109B2-110D2
Backs intl comm plan, sees 'positive signs' for hostage release 2-13, 105A1, 109C2, C3
Warns vs 'pessimism' on hostage release 2-24, 137C2
Vs apology to Iran govt 3-8, 177F2
Defends immigration policy 3-14, 209G1
Sadat defends shah's asylum 3-25, 217C2
'Apology' note denied 3-29, 4-1, 241G1, C2
Student deportatn ban denied by Sup Ct 3-31, 291G2
Delays added sanctns 4-1, 241A1-F1
Sees breakthrough, campaign impact noted 4-1, 246F2
Bars apology 4-1, 247B1
Cuts ties, ousts Iran aides, imposes sanctions; state text 4-7, 257A1-C2
Bush: 'manipulated' media 4-7, 264E2
Khomeini hails end of US ties 4-8, 258F1
Sanctns threaten Japan econ 4-8, 276B2, F2
Defends policy 4-10, 264G1
US allies withhold support 4-10, 281G2
Presses allies to back sanctns 4-13, 281D2
Threatens mil actn, widens sanctns 4-17, 281A1
Anderson, Bush score 4-20, 328D1, B2
Vs hostage kin visits 4-21, 299B2
Mil action decision denied 4-23, 298F2
Methodists urge restraint 4-23, 324F3
Rpts aborted hostage rescue 4-25, 297C1
Khomeini, Ghotbzadeh, Bani-Sadr score rescue try 4-25, 4-26, 322A3, B3, 323A1
Details US rescue mission 4-27, 321C1
Scores display of dead US raiders 4-28, 323D1

1976 | 1977 | 1978 | 1979 | 1980

1977

Germany (East)
E Ger ousts Nitsche 8-29, 684E1
Germany (West)
Brandt paymt chrg regretted 2-24, 151A2
Rpts Uganda mediatn role 2-27, 141F1
Asks Portugal aid 4-1, 330C3
Stresses rights in TV talk 5-2, 338B2
At 7-natn econ summit 5-7—5-8; sees Schmidt 5-7, diplomacy hailed 5-11, 357B1, 358E1, 359E1, B2
Sees Schmidt 7-13—7-14, lauds econ plans 7-15, 566G1
Schmidt mark revaluatn backing rptd 7-21, 552G1
Schmidt rptdly vs reflationary proposals 8-8, 585B2
Scores econ expansn policy 9-26, 753F2
Aids hijacked jet rescue 10-17, Schmidt thanks 10-18, 789E2, 790F1
Great Britain
Backs Concorde trial 2-16, 131D2
Concorde, air treaty talks with Callaghan 3-10—3-11, 213A1
Asks Portugal aid 4-1, 330C3
Backs Young 'racism' apology 4-7, 272B2
Stresses rights in TV talk 5-2, 338B2
In London for econ summit; tours NE, sees Thatcher 5-5—5-8; visit hailed 5-8, 357B1, 358F1, 359E1, C2
OKs Laker 'Skytrain' svc 6-13, 500F2
Hails air svc pact 6-22, 500C2
Sees Owen re Rhodesia 7-23, 581B3
On A-test talks, arms sales curbs 7-28, 574E2, A3
Sees Thatcher 9-13, 883C3
Greece
Clifford missn 2-17—2-26, 122F1, 146G3
Sees Caramanlis 5-10, 359C1
OKs arms aid 8-4, 668C1
Guatemala
Mil aid rejected 3-16, 187A2
Arms sales resumed 9-7, 706A3
Hungary
B Graham bears message 9-8, 732D1
India
Mother, son at Ahmed rite 2-13, 116B1
OKs nutrition aid 8-4, 668A2
Plans to visit 9-23, 738F1
Visit deferred 11-7, 854A1; rescheduled 11-29, 914B2
Indonesia
OKs arms aid 8-4, 668C1
Iran
Hoveida denies rights policy prompted pub trial 4-11, 527A2
Plans AWACS sale 7-7, drops deal 7-28, 8-2, 611D2
Plans to visit 9-23, 738F1
Visit deferred 11-7, 854A1; rescheduled 11-29, 914B2
7 US AWACS purchased 11-8, 905A3
Shah visits 11-15—11-16, strong Iran backed 11-16, 897A1
Visits 12-31, 1000E3
Iraq
Favors Sovt challenge 6-10, 460D2
Ireland
Fitzgerald visits US 3-16—3-19, 329E1
Israel—*See also 'Middle East Conflict' in this section below*
Bars Ecuador jet sale 2-7, 87A3; Ecuador scores 6-2, 454C3
Reviews concussn bomb sale 2-8, 88A3
Drops concussn bomb sale 2-17, 121E1
Affirms F-16 sale 3-7—3-8, 165A2
Blamed for Likud electn win 5-17, reactn 5-18, 377B2, 378C1; 5-25, 402B1
OKs security aid 8-4, 668D1
Italy
At 7-natn econ summit 5-7—5-8; diplomacy hailed 5-11, 357B1, 359A2
Sees Andreotti, rights stand backed 7-25—7-27, 581A2
Seeks arms sales curbs 7-28, 574B3
Jamaica
Manley visits 12-16, 1019G1
Japan
Briefs Mondale 1-23, lauds missn 2-1; Mondale rpts 2-2, 69E1
Plans S Korea pullout 3-9, 202E3
Meets Fukuda 3-21—3-22, 209E2
Asks Portugal aid 4-1, 330C3
At 7-natn econ summit 5-7—5-8; sees Fukuda 5-7, 357B1, 358F1
Fukuda rptdly vs reflationary proposals 8-8, 585B2
Scores econ expansn policies 9-26, 753F2
Jordan—*See also 'Middle East Conflict' in this section below*
Lauds Hussein 2-18, defends CIA 2-23, 123D3; 2-24, 151E1
Post mtg on paymts story rptd 2-25, 2-28, 151G2
OKs arms, security aid 8-4, 668C1, D1
Kenya
Kaunda lauds 5-23, 400A1
Korea (North)
To lift US travel ban 3-9, 172F3, 173D1
Rpts US copter downed 7-14, welcomes release of men 7-16, 552G2, B3, F3
Korea (South)
Rptdly barred Mondale visit 1-28, 70A1
Cites pol prisoners 2-23, 126E2
Plans troop exit, stresses rights 3-9, 202D3
Reassures Japan on troop exit 3-22, 209F2
Gets clerics protest on rights 4-19, 305C3
Removes Singlaub as forces staff chief 5-21, 403G2
On Singlaub's removal 5-26, 417A2
GOP ldrs ask spec prosecutor 6-9, 442E2
Sen OKs troop exit amendmt 6-16, 477D3, G3
Bars spec prosecutor, backs Justice probe 7-18, 556D2

1978

Mitterrand mtg scored in France 1-6—1-10, 54D1
Neutron bomb test rptd 4-17, 313D1
Pak A-contract pressure cited 8-9, 668B2
China ties reactn 12-16, 977C1
Germany (East)
On rights abuse, Ger reunificatn 7-15, 544F3
Germany (West)
Schmidt eases $ crisis tensns, joint approach proposed 3-9, 234E2
Schmidt clarifies neutron bomb stand, warns vs policy shift 4-12, 254B3
Sees Schmidt 5-30—5-31, 519F1
Schmidt cites mtg 7-7, 545G2
Visits, reaffirms US commitmt 7-14—7-15, 544D3-545D1
At Bonn econ summit 7-16—7-17, 553C3, 546A1
Parlt OKs $7.8 bil econ stimulus 11-24, 925E2
China ties backed 12-16, 977C1
Great Britain
State of Union Message 1-19, 31D2
On air-fare dispute 3-7, hails setlmt 3-17, 206E1, B2
Backs joint Rhodesia plan 3-9, 161D1
Windscale A-reprocessing plant OKd 3-22, 227A2
Sees Callaghan on world econ 3-23, 226G2
Seeks new Rhodesia peace conf 4-2, 234B1
Cites Belize-Guatemala land dispute 6-21, 489C3
China ties backed 12-16, 977B1
Greece
Meets Caramanlis 5-31, 398D2
Guatemala
Cites Belize land dispute 6-21, 489C3
Guyana
On Rep Ryan murder 11-19, 891B3
Honduras
Cites El Salvador border dispute 6-21, 489C3
India
Visits, OKs uranium sale; A-safeguards discord revealed 1-1—1-3, 1E1
State of Union Message 1-19, 31B3
US comm bars uranium sale 4-20, 288B3
OKs uranium sale 4-27, 313G1
Sees Desai; pledges A-cooperatn, trade measures 6-13—6-15, 466C3
Cong allows uranium sale 7-12, 551E1
Indochina
Vows refugee aid 12-6, 934E1
Iran
Reaffirms support for shah 9-10, 693E2
Moslem ldr scores 9-13, 740F2
Supports shah again 10-10, 797A3
Sees shah's son, gives support 10-31, 827G3-828A1
Sees Cabt on crisis 11-6, 858B2
Brezhnev warns vs interventn, US rebuts 11-19, 893F3
Rptd critical of US intellignc 11-25, 917C1
Backs shah, shuns interventn 11-30, 936E2
Doubts shah survival, US denies confidence loss 12-7, 953E3
Blames Khomeini for unrest, backs shah 12-12, 953C3
Israel—*See also 'Middle East Conflict' in this section below*
Sees Dayan 2-16, 139F1
Defends jet sale 2-17, 123C2
Vs jet sale legis delay 4-25, 307A1, B1
Hopeful on jet sale legis 5-4, 321D2
Seeks Sen support for jet sale, lauds passage 5-15, 357D1, 358A1
Reassures jet sale opponents 5-15—5-16, 358B1
Signs econ aid authorzn 9-26, 734E1
Italy
Warns vs CP govt role 1-12, 19E1
Japan
Exempts from arms sales ceiling 2-1, 106F2
Hikes CB radio tariffs 3-28, 443E3
Overrules steel import minimum price order 4-24, 444B1
Sees Fukuda re trade surplus 5-3, 341E2
Joint energy research planned 9-6, 695C3
Signs mil, security aid authorzn 9-26, 734A2, E2
Vetoes shipping malpractice 11-4, 897G2
Ohira call re China ties rptd 12-16, 977C1
Jordan—*See also 'Middle East Conflict' below*
Sees Hussein 1-1—1-2, 2A2, E2
Signs econ aid authorzn 9-26, 734F1
Kenya
Assures Moi on arms aid 3-2, 289F2
Regrets Kenyatta death 8-22, 639B3
Korea (North)
Tito rptdly asked US, N-S Korea talks 4-5, 4-19, 277A3
Korea (South)
Dissidents score rights rpt 2-17, 135C2
Tito rptdly asked US, N-S Korea talks 4-5, 4-19, 277A3
Slows US troop exit 4-21, 301C3
Signs defns equipmt transfer authorzn 9-26, 734F2
China ties reactn 12-16, 977D1
Laos
Vows refugee aid 12-6, 934E1
Latin America—*See also country names in this section*
State of Union Message 1-19, 31G2
Addresses OAS, reaffirms rights commitmt 6-21, 489D2-D3
Amer rights conv enacted 7-18, 829B1

1979

Khomeini scores 11-11, 862C2
Bans oil purchase 11-12; freezes assets, reactn 11-14, 861A1, G2
Pres candidates' reactns to policy 11-14-12-26, 982A2, B3, 983F1, B2
Scores hostage detentn 11-15, 877F2, 885E1
Assets freeze order confrmd, clarified 11-15, 11-16; risks detailed 11-15-11-18, 879D3, 880C1
Warns vs domestic retaliatn 11-16, 898D1
Wife rpts on crisis 11-17, 887C1
Threatens US mil move, Khomeini scores 11-20, 877A1, F1
Chase declares loan default 11-21, 896D2
Sees advisers 11-22, threatens mil retaliatn 11-23, 894C2
Stresses firmness in hostage release; defends shah's entry, denies Kissinger role 11-28, 894G2
Sends shah to US AF base 12-2, 914A1
Silent on Kennedy anti-shah remarks 12-3, 918E3
Plans econ pressure vs Iran 12-4, 913B2
Mutes reelectn bid announcemt 12-4, 918F2, 919C1
UK upholds assets freeze 12-5, 915F1
Poll gain linked 12-5, 918E2
Briefs hostage kin 12-7, 934D1
Poll leads, crisis linked 12-11, 962E3
NBC hostage interview scored 12-11, 934D3
Drafts plan to free hostages 12-8, 934C1
Rptd encouraged by dvpts 12-14, 958E2
Thanks Panama for taking shah 12-15, 957B1
Khomeini scores re shah exit 12-17, 958B1
Japan vows pressure vs Iran 12-17–12-18, 959A1
Thatcher backs re crisis 12-17, 968G1
Seeks UN sanctns 12-21, 974C3
To skip Ia debate 12-28, 983E2
Ireland
Lynch visits, seeks cooperatn on Ulster 11-8, 874A2
Islamic Nations—*See also country names in this section*
Affirms ties 11-28, 895E1
Israel—*See also 'Middle East Conflict' in this section below*
US mil ex-ldrs urge support 1-12, 15C1
Trade group visits 4-18, 296C1
Begin thanks re Sovt dissidents swap 4-29, 317C2
Addresses Cong on SALT II 6-18, 459E2
Vows support 9-25, 723F2
Italy
Westn econ summit warning to Japan rptd 2-10, rpt disputed 2-15, 160E1
Japan
Warning re trade surplus rptd 2-10, rpt disputed 2-15; Ohira seeks mtg 2-22, 160E1-160A2
Meets Ohira on trade goals 5-2, 320F1
Addresses Cong on SALT II 6-18, 459E2
Visits 6-24–6-27; at Tokyo energy summit 6-28–6-29, 493A1-494B2, 495E2
Japan vows pressure vs Iran 12-17–12-18, 959B1
Jordan—*See 'Middle East Conflict' in this section below*
Korea (North)
Communique on reunificatn 7-1, S Korea visit scored 7-4, 494D3-495B1, D1
North vs 3-way talks 7-10, 537E1
DMZ tunnel discovered 9-1, 709G3
Korea (South)
Stratton vs troop exit 1-3, 39C1
Dissidents assured on rights 3-7, 390A1
Japan talks noted 5-2, 320D2
Dissident releases tied to visit 5-12, oppositn ldr vs visit 5-15, 389E3
Dissidents detained re visit 6-28, 495C1
Visits, meets Park, dissidents; joint communique 6-29–7-1, 493B3-494C1
North vs 3-way talks 7-10, 537E1
86 dissidents freed 7-17, 567B3
Halts troop pullout 7-20, 567F2-A3
Discloses Park conversn effort 8-5, 639B2
ROK to up defns outlay 8-8, 654D1
NDP ldr. scores visit 9-16, 710B3
Park gets note on dissent 10-18, 803F2
Lauds Park 10-27, 822G1
Latin America—*See also country names in this section*
Addresses Cong on SALT II 6-18, 449E2, 459A3
Mexico
On oil, gas prospects, upcoming trip 1-17, 30B1
Mexicans protest visit 2-7, 2-15, 124A3
Visits; oil, gas, alien issues discussed; cooperatn pact signed 2-14–2-16, 124F1, 127A1
Rpts gas talks 4-5, 250E3
Mex border fence dropped 4-26, 327A3
Vows aliens protectn 5-5, 347B1
Names amb-at-large 6-22, Lucey resigns 10-8, 793D3
Sees Lopez, oil spill talks agreed 9-28–9-29, 753G1-C2
Lopez lauds Latin policy 10-1, 754C1
Middle East Conflict
Guadeloupe summit topic 1-5–1-6, 12G2
Urges talks flexibility 2-20, 123G2

1980

Vance resigns re rescue oppositn 4-28, 323A2, E2
Defends rescue missn 4-29, 323D3
Ends campaign travel ban 4-30, 328F1, A2
Beckwith rpts on rescue mission 5-1, 322F2
Ohira urges moderatn 5-1, 341E1
Declares offcl mourning for dead US raiders 5-6, 337D2
Leads in ABC poll 5-6, 342G1
Rescue missn defended in Sen probes 5-8, 338D1
Tito funeral absence linked 5-8, 338D3
Student immigratn case refused by Sup Ct 5-19, 440B2
Cites 'terrorism' 5-29, 423F3
Iran ties Huyser to post-shah plot 6-2, 418F2
Khomeini scores on hostages 6-4, 418D3
Iran calls Clark secret agent 6-6, 433B1
UPI admits error in Clark story 6-6, 507D2
Backs Clark prosecutn re travel ban 6-10, 6-16; reacts 6-11, 459A3, F3
Bars force to free hostages 6-12, 506F3
Yugo joint communique backs hostage release 6-25, 474C3
Scores hostage policy 7-4, 505E2
Thanks Japan for sanctns support 7-8, 506E1
Calls hostage release 'humanitarian' 7-10, 539A2
Iran assets seizure damages backed by US ct 7-10, 546A2
Sees Queen 7-19, 546A1
Mourns shah's death 7-27, 571E2
Protesters burn in effigy 8-2, 586D3
Invasn plan rptd, denied 8-16, 635A1
Sullivan scores Brzezinski '79 policy 9-6, 694D1
Khomeini asks shah wealth returned, frozen assets unblocked 9-12, 693C1
Scores Reagan hostage stance 9-15, admits release prospects bleak 9-15—9-18, 699E1
Cites efforts to free hostages 9-18, 698C3
Signs hostage relief act 10-14, 981B2
Seeks Rajai mtg in NYC 10-16, 799G3
Offers to unfreeze assets for hostages 10-20, Iran rejcts 10-22, 799G3
Reagan hits hostage issue 10-20—10-22, 802D1, F1
Ridicules Reagan hostage stance 10-21, 10-22, 802C3
Debates hostage issue with Reagan 10-28, 813D1, 814D2-B3, 820B3
Hostage issue interrupts campaign windup 11-2, 841A1
Iran parlt OKs hostage release terms; sees hope 11-2; Iran vs message 11-3, 853B1, F2, E3
Electn influence seen, exit poll rptd 11-4, 837E1, 838G1, E2, E3
Iran reactn to Reagan win 11-5, 11-6, 853G3
Reagan offers hostage 'help' 11-6, 839C2
Iran gets US hostage response, comments 11-12, 861F1, 865D3
Assets freeze backed by US ct 11-13, 861D2-862A1
Iran urges accept demands for hostages 12-19, 973E1
On Algerian rpt on hostages 12-26, 974D2
Iran-Iraq War
Vows neutrality 9-23, 718F3
Seeks continued oil flow 9-24, 718B2
US urges free oil passage, hints at intl force 9-26, 735C2
Iraq sees US, Israel, Iran plot 10-18, 799B2
Iraq warns vs arms to Iran 10-25, 10-26; King Hussein warns 10-29, 820G2-B3
Debates with Reagan, affirms neutrality 10-28, 814D2
Khomeini blames for invasn 10-29, 820C1
Iraq—*See also 'Iran-Iraq War' in this section above*
Persian Gulf vow scored 1-25, 65D1
Commercial jet sale barred 8-29, 662C3
Islamic Nations—*See also specific countries in this section*
State of Union address 1-23, 42C2, D3
Israel
Weizman on campaign jet 10-27, 816C3
Israel vs Weizman electn trip 10-28, 830D2
Signs '81 aid authrzn 12-16, 981C3
Italy
Visits Rome, sees ldrs 6-19—6-21, 474A2
Japan
Yen continues dollar slide 4-8, 276B2
Rice pact set 4-12, 314B3
Meets Ohira, sci pact signed 5-1, 341B1
Lifts TV import curbs 6-30, 515C3
Thanks for Iran sanctns support 7-8, 506E1
Seeks auto import ruling 7-8, probe speedup denied 7-18, 556G1-B2, 599F1
At Ohira rites 7-9; meets Hua, USSR scores 7-10, 506B1-G1
Signs synfuel pact 7-31, 666D2
Unveils steel indus aid plan 9-30, 740C3
ITC bars auto import curbs 11-10, 866E3
Jordan
King Hussein warns vs arms to Iran 10-29, 820B3
Kenya
Moi visits, aid hike OKd, bases rptd discussed 2-20—2-22, 142A2
Korea (South)
State of Union address 1-23, 42G1
Eases TV import curbs 6-30, 515C3
Govt reforms asked 8-28, 673A2
Kim leniency asked 12-13, 953C1

1976 1977 1978 1979 1980

1977

Assures Park on troop exit 7-25, 572A2
OKs Cong policy role 8-17, 667A3
Park Tong Sun extraditn sought 9-6, 9-8, 687F3, 688A1
Park Tong Sun immunity offer rptd 9-17, 774G1
Rpts to Cong on Park immunity offer, scores Korea 11-5, 915F2

Laos
Gets rpt on US MIA missn 3-23, 206A1
OKs aid bar 8-4, 668B2
Refugee quotas eased 8-31, 685D2
Food aid sought, barred 12-16, 989C1

Latin America—*See also OAS and specific countries in this section*
Cites human rights issue 2-23, 126E2
Vows closer cooperatn 5-22, 397F1
Signs A-ban pact 5-26, 415D3
Wife on Latin tour 5-30—6-12, 454D1
Says Young to shift focus 6-10, 460F2
Vance visits Argentina, Brazil, Venez 11-20—11-23, 912E2-913C1

Lebanon—*See also 'Middle East Conflict' in this section below*
OKs security aid 8-4, 668D1

Lesotho
OKs regional aid fund 8-4, 668D1

Libya—*See also 'Middle East Conflict' in this section below*
Qaddafi lauds, asks closer ties 6-12, 488B1
On Egypt conflict restraint 7-28, 574B3

Mexico
Lopez Portillo visits 2-14—2-17, 110D1, 136B3
Pol prisoners freed 4-11, 528C3
Mex expert vs alien plan 8-28, 746A2
Assured on canal pact 9-3, 678D1

Middle East Conflict
Vs Daoud release 1-12, 10B1
Rpts Vance tour planned 1-24, 51G3
Plans to meet leaders 2-23, 126F2
Boycott guidelines rptd 2-28, 167A1
Sees Rabin, offers peace plan 3-7—3-8, 165A1-A2
Plans mtgs with Arab ldrs 3-8, 165A2
Outlines setlmt views 3-9, 165B1, B2
Egypt, Israel react to peace plans 3-12—3-15, 187C2
Backs Palestine 'homeland' 3-16; Israel, PLO reactn 3-17, 187D3
Addresses UN; greets PLO rep, bars follow-up 3-17, 185G1, 186D1
Defends speaking out 3-24, 230D1
Meets Sadat 4-4—4-5, Sadat rpts differences 4-6, 245A1
Allon sees US-Israel tensns 4-24, 316G1
Sees Hussein, for Geneva conf delay 4-25—4-26, 315G3-316B1
PLO questns 'homeland' stand 5-1, 360F3
Sees Assad, backs Palestine 'homeland' 5-9, 358D2, 360G1-A3
Egypt, Israel increase war games 5-9, 361B2
Israel briefed on Assad talks 5-11, 361A1
Assures Israel on arms 5-12, 361D1
Stresses peace chance 5-22, 397B1
Begin vs proposals 5-22, 401G2
Fahd in DC talks 5-24—5-25, 401F3
Sees moderatn by Begin 5-26, 417G1
For Palestine homeland, compensatn; statemt clarified 5-26; Israel protests 5-28—5-31, 440B1
King Hussein backs moves 5-31, 496E1
Arabs warn vs boycott laws 6-8, 511F3
Rpt urged Israel keep Golan, holy shrines 6-11, 6-13, 474B1
Assures Israel chief rabbi 6-15, 474A1
Denies vs Palestine state 6-16, 496G1
Mondale on policy 6-17; Israel sees no change 6-19, 473C2,
Seeks arms sale to Israel 6-25, Begin thanks 6-26, 511F1
Begin mtg scheduled 6-27, 495A3
Javits vs peace plan 6-27, 495E3
Rabin scores Arab homeland support 6-28, 495D3
9 sens back efforts 6-29, 496B1
Sets moratorium on US statemts; stresses Israel support 6-30, 510A1, C1
Sadat: Israel ties impossible 7-2, 509G1
Assures US Jewish ldrs on Israel support, Arab recogntn 7-6, 509E2
Lauds Sadat peace moves, Hussein mtg 7-12, 533E2
Meets Begin 7-19—7-21; Begin airs peace plan 7-20, cites differences 7-21, 549A1-B2
Reaffirms Vance missn 7-20, 549A2
Rpt Fahd transmitted Arafat note 7-20, 550B2
Israel mil aid package OKd 7-22, 570B3
Says Israel W Bank plan blocks peace 7-28, 570D1
Sadat for Israel-Arab pre-Geneva mtg 8-2, 588D2
Signs '78 arms, security aid 8-4, 668A1
Backs PLO shift on UN Res 242 8-8, 605E1
Vance Geneva plan link to Carter's seen 8-10, 605E2
Briefed on Vance missn, renews Israel peace plea 8-14, 623C2
Vs new W Bank setlmts 8-18, 623A1
Scores Israeli W Bank setlmts 8-23, 649D3
Sovts score W Bank setlmt stand 9-2, 685C2
Sees Dayan, urges Leb restraint 9-19, 713G1, 714B3
Sees Egypt forgn min 9-21, 714D1
Meets Syria, Jordan reps 9-28; for PLO peace role 9-29, 734A1, F1
Cong ldrs score US-Sovt Geneva plan 10-2, 750F1
Meets Dayan, Geneva conf approach OKd 10-4—10-5, 749C1-A2

1978

Scored by '80 pres hopeful 11-29, 938F3

Lebanon—*See also 'Middle East' in this section below*
Vows help for refugees 12-6, 934E1

Liberia
Visits 4-3, 233B1, 234C1

Mexico
Bars migrant workers 1-30, 62D3

Middle East Conflict
In talks with Hussein 1-1—1-2, King Khalid 1-3, Sadat 1-4; Begin lauds Sadat talks 1-4, 1C1, 2G1-B3, 3A1
PLO vs Palestine stand 1-1, 1-2, 1-4, 3B1
For Palestinian vote, vs separate state 1-6, 10E2
Says Sadat views 'almost identical' 1-12, 12G1-A2
Asks Sadat to renew Israel talks 1-18, 25F2
State of Union Message 1-19, 29B1, B3, 31E2
Syria chrgs Sadat compliance 1-19, 42A2
Sadat requests arms 1-20, 1-21, 41G1
Queries Begin on setlmts 1-29, 60A2
Defines real peace 1-30, 62E2
Dayan denies '77 setlmt vow 2-1, 60F2
Sets arms sales ceiling 2-1, 106F2
Meets Sadat 2-3—2-5, 77B1-B2
In Israel feud over setlmts 2-3, 2-7, 78F1 text of US statemt 79B1-B2
Mtgs with cong, US Jewish ldrs rptd 2-9, 98A1
Israel peace plan support denied 2-12, 98D1
Begin to visit US 2-15, 97A2
Begin clarifies statemts on setlmt stand 2-15, 97B2
Sees Dayan on Saudi jet sale 2-16, 139G1
Defends Saudi, Israel, Egypt jet sale 2-17, 123C2
Lauds Sadat on Cyprus raid 2-23, US denies taking sides 2-26, 138G2
Backs UN Res 242, Begin-Sadat talks resumptn; links poll standings 3-2, 140G2-E3, 141F1
Vs Israel stand on Res 242 3-7, 3-9, 156E2
Begin freezes setlmts pending talks 3-7, 157F1
Jewish aide quits staff 3-8; Carter, aide statemts 3-9, 176C2
Meets Israel defense min 3-8, 176E3
US Jewish ldr vs policy 3-9, 176G2
Efforts to bar Begin confrontatn cited 3-9, 176B3
Begin postpones visit re terrorist attack 3-11, 175E3, 176B2
US asks Israel quit Leb 3-16, 173G2
Warns USSR vs mil buildup, interventn 3-17, 202F1
Begin in US talks, impasse remains 3-20—3-21, 199B1
Says Begin talks failed 3-23, 214F2
Weizman backs Begin on talks 3-24, 214D2
Israel Cabt, Knesset back Begin 3-26, 3-29, 214E1
Sadat lauds peace role 4-5, 235D3
Lauds Ceausescu '77 go-between role 4-11, ends talks 4-13, 291D1
Sees jet sale as pkg deal, vs legis delay 4-25, 307A1, B1
Sees peace progress 'steady' 4-25, 307G1
Vs indep Palestinian state 4-30, Egypt reassured 5-1, 339E2
Meets Begin, reaffirms support 5-1, 339G1
Arafat scores Palestine statemt 5-1, 339E3
Hopeful on jet sale legis 5-4, 321D2
Khalid stresses F-15 need 5-13, 358E2
Seeks Sen support for jet sale, lauds passage 5-15, 357D1, 358A1
Reassures jet sale opponents 5-15—5-16, 358B1
Asks Begin, Sadat, Khalid for peace talks renewal 5-19, 424C2
Vows peace commitmt, scores Israel rejectn of Egypt plan 6-26, 491F1
Begin vs statemt on Israel rejectn of Egypt peace plan 6-27, 489A1
Mondale in Israel 6-30—7-3, Egypt 7-3, 501B2
Hints at Geneva conf 6-30, 502C1
Urges end to Beirut fighting 7-6, 503G2
Israel: Sadat plan tougher than Aswan formula 7-11, 521E1
Sadat lauds mediatn 7-22, 563C1
Sadat rebuked for refusing new Israel talks 7-31, 582A1
Decides on Sadat, Begin summit 7-31, mtg set 8-8, 601G2
On US troops to Mideast 8-30, 673F1
In pre-summit talks with Begin 9-5; **Camp David talks start,** meets Begin, Sadat 9-6—9-7, 673A1
House backs peace moves, upholds defns veto 9-7, 677E2
Camp David summit ends; signs pacts with Sadat, Begin; photo 9-17, 709C1
Text of pacts 9-17, 711A1-712C3
Details pacts in Cong address 9-18, 709E1, E2-710B1
Says Camp David summit faced collapse, Sadat confrms 9-18, 710D1
Arafat: will 'pay' for agrmts 9-19, 712F1
Begin notes setlmts dispute, Golan, E Jerusalem compromise 9-20, 710E2-F2
Stresses US peace role 9-20, 715B3
Camp David summit letters released 9-22, 729F1; text 730C2-G3
Stresses Camp David on stump; poll status jumps 9-22—9-24, 736B1
Leb fighting mounts, conf plan cited 9-24—10-4, 745G2
Vance briefs on missn 9-25, 731B1

1979

Asks high-level Egypt, Israel talks; Sadat balks 2-25; Israel bars Begin talks minus Sadat 2-27, 142F2, A3
Brown, Schlesinger see US defns of oil interests 2-25; remarks clarified 2-26, 2-27, 143D3-144B1
Says Israel-Egypt differences minor 2-27, Begin disagrees 2-28, 143C1
Meets Begin 3-1, 143E1
Begin OKs pact plan 3-2—3-4, Israel Cabt OKs 3-5, 157B1
Egypt, Israel trip set 3-5; in Cairo, meets Sadat, gets counterproposals 3-8, 157A1
Gets Israel, Egypt OK on pact 3-8—3-13; in US, briefs Congress 3-14, 177A1, F2, 178A1
Begin vs Powell press briefing 3-13, 177C2
PFLP cites Israel-PLO prisoner swap 3-14, 178A3
Sets missn to Saudi, Jordan 3-15, 197C2
Hails Knesset OK of peace pact 3-22, 197A2
On US-Palestinian ties 3-23, 222G2
Signs Egypt-Israel treaty 3-26, 221B1
Arafat scores for Israel-Egypt pact 3-26, 222C2
Says Israel eases W Bank, Gaza rule 3-27, 222C3
Egypt-Israel pact spurs poll gain 3-29, 231D3
Names Strauss 'superamb' 4-24, 295G3-296C1
Arab group vows to 'bring down' 5-10, 341E2, F2
Asked Saudis end Egypt feud 5-21, 378D3
Backs Palestinian rights 6-6, 430C1
Begin denies setlmt suspensn vow 6-10, 436B2
SALT II summit topic 6-15—6-18, 449D1, 458A2
Palestinian autonomy espousal denied 6-15, 475A1
Addresses Cong on SALT II 6-18, 459A3
W Ger pressure vs Israeli setlmts rptd sought 7-9, 511B2
Israel: reneges on Sinai force 7-24, 551D1
Signs treaty funds bill 7-25, 700A2
Likens Palestinian claims to US civil rights drive 7-31; US Jews, blacks, Israel protest 8-1, 8-2, 575C1
Assures Begin of support 8-4, meets Israel amb re growing rift 8-8, 591F1-C2
Bars chng on Res 242 8-8, 591A2
Vs Palestinian state 8-10, 606G2
Young quits as amb to UN re PLO contact 8-15, SCLC asks mtg with Jews 8-16, 605B1, 606A2
Times clarifies Palestinian-rights remark 8-17, 607C1
Arafat warns vs oil takeover 8-20, 659A2
Strauss rpts on missn to Israel, Egypt 8-21, 623G2
Denies Strauss feud on mission 8-22, 623D3
Says Arabs vs independent Palestinian state, urges PLO recognize Israel; denies Arab oil threat 8-30, 659C1
Urges black-Jewish amity, denies Young tap 8-30, 661B2
At Camp David anniv rites; phones Sadat, Begin 9-17, 695D1
Denies US Jewish pressure to oust Young 9-23, 763E2
Sees Pope, issues joint statemt 10-6, 759D1
Connally scores policy 10-11, 783B2

Namibia (South-West Africa)—*See 'South Africa' below*

NATO
Haig sets resignatn 1-3, 3B2
State of Union Message 1-23, 47D2
Mins back contd budget hike 5-15, 359C3
Backs modernization 6-6, 430A1
Addresses Cong on SALT II 6-18, 459D1
Urges A-arms deploymt 10-9, 761A3
Seeks Dutch, Norway A-missile support 12-7, 938D1

Netherlands
Sees van Agt, seeks A-missile support 12-7, 938E1

Nicaragua
State of Union Message 1-23, 48F1
40 congressmen protest IMF loan 5-10, 373A1
Long-term ties detailed 535F3
Sees 3 junta ldrs 9-24, 731C3

Northern Ireland
Sees Pope, issues joint statemt 10-6, 759D3
Lynch visits, seeks cooperatn on Ulster 11-8, 874A2

Norway
Sees Nordli, seeks A-missile support 12-7, 938D1

OPEC
On price hikes 2-27, 145E3
Scores price rise 6-28, 473A2; 7-1 494C2
Gets Eizenstat memo 7-7, 513E3
Kennedy vs re price hikes 12-20—12-21, 983A3

Pakistan
Zia scorns Bhutto clemency plea 2-14, 116B2
Zia asks aid renewal 9-22, 794E2
Contacts Zia on Afghan crisis 12-30, 974A2

1980

Kuwait
Persian Gulf vow scored 1-25, 65C1

Latin America—*See also specific countries in this section*
Addresses OAS, cites accomplishmts 11-19, 881E2, 913C3
Argentina scores rights policy 11-20, 913C3

Lebanon
Quotes Reagan on '76 civil war 9-23, 722D3

Libya
Brother registers as Libyan agent 7-14, 542A2; for subsequent developments, see CARTER, Billy
Hits Reagan on A-arms spread 10-29, 816C2

Middle East—*See also specific countries in this section*
Cites Egypt-Israel peace-treaty role 1-20, 50G1
State of Union address 1-23, 42G1, B3
PLO scores Persian Gulf vow 1-25, Saudis hopeful re Palestinian recognitn 1-26, 65D1
Assures Israel on arms to Egypt 2-25, 140F2
Disavows US UN vote vs Israel 3-3, Begin gets statemt 3-4; Vance takes blame 3-4; Sen com probe set 3-5, 162F2, 163D1, D2, D3, 164A1
Reassures US Jews re Israel 3-4, 164D1
Begin scores UN setlmts reversal 3-6; takes blame, vs W Bank outposts 3-8, 179A2
Terms UN vote gaffe 'honest breakdown', says US policy unchngd 3-14, 209F1
Kennedy scores UN gaffe 206F3
Invites Begin, Sadat 3-19; meets Sadat on autonomy impasse 4-8—4-9, 260F2, B3
Vance defends UN vote, disavowal 3-20, 3-21, 218B2, F2
Lauds Camp David pact on 1st anniv 3-23, 260C3
Meets Begin on Palestinian autonomy 4-15—4-16, 284F1
Israel Labor Party ldr gives W Bank plan 4-24, 324G3
Asks Sadat to renew autonomy talks 5-13; Sadat OKs 5-14, again suspends 5-15, 362D1
Cautns W Eur vs UN Cncl Res 242 chng 5-31, 417F2
Asks Sadat to renew Palestinian autonomy talks 6-8, 434D1
Hussein visits, opposes peace talks role 6-17—6-18; Jordan tank sale vowed 6-19, 450A1, E1
PLO: reneged on recognitn pledge 7-22, 572C2
Sadat asks delay in autonomy talks re Jerusalem 8-3, 585B1
Renominatn acceptance speech cites accord 8-14, 613D1
Sadat asks new summit 8-15, Begin cool 8-19, 627F1
Vows Israel support, bars PLO ties; Reagan, Anderson score policies 9-3—9-4, 681E3
Cites peace efforts 9-18, 698B3
Scores UN move to oust Israel 9-29, 739A1
Bush scores 'flipflop' 10-16, 10-19, 817C3
Vs some Saudi F-15 gear 10-24, 821A1
Mondale: 'delivered' for Israel 10-26, 816F3
Debates with Reagan 10-28, 813G2, 814E2
Hits Reagan on A-arms spread 10-29, 816C2
Meets Begin, autonomy talks stressed 11-13, 880E2

Morocco
Aides took oaths re leaks 7-16—7-17, 549A2

NATO
State of Union address 1-23, 42G1, A3
Urges Spain membership 6-25, 474D3
Discusses W Ger-USSR A-missile talks 7-2, 489C2
OKs UK Trident purchases 7-14, 544D2
Meets Schmidt 11-20, 903G3-904A2

Nicaragua
Signs aid bill 7-8, 515D1
Castro lauds policy 7-18, 565B3
Releases $75 mln in aid 9-12, 709E2-B3
Blamed for Somoza downfall 9-17, 721F1

Nigeria
Meets Shagari 10-7, 792G2

OAS
Addresses Assemb, affirms rights stance 11-19, 881E2, 913C3

OPEC
Links oil prices, inflatn 1-23, 43B2
Saudi secret talks 9-18, US stockpiling rptd resumed 10-27, 826C1

Pakistan
Gets US Cong backing on arms 1-3, 27B1
Weighs mil aid to counter Sovt threat 1-4, 1F1
Assures India on aid to Pak 1-16, 27G1
Asks mil, econ aid pkg 1-21; warns USSR 1-23, 41C2, 42D3, 43D3

Panama
Reagan 'basic speech' scores re Canal 2-29, 207G2
Cites treaty adoptn 11-19, 881A3

1976

1977

Reaffirms Israeli commitmt, Palestinian rights at UN; sees Fahmy 10-4, 749A2, 751D3
Snubs Koch after protest 10-4, 761B1
Israel Cabt OKs Geneva working paper 10-11, Dayan airs text 10-13, 769B1
Sadat asks PLO at Geneva 10-19, 793A1
Assad vs US-Israel Geneva plan 10-21, 831B2
On peace overture moves 10-27, 813G2
Survey sees political harm 10-31, 831F1
Assures US Jews on policies 11-2, 830A3
Urges Geneva talks, lauds Sadat stand 11-10, 850C2
Sadat for US Palestine rep to Geneva 11-12, 873D2
Lauds Sadat Israel visit 11-15, 873F2
Calls Begin 11-17, Sadat 11-18, lauds Sadat trip 11-20, 11-22, 894F2
Sees Dobrynin 11-18, 894E3
Backs Sadat moves, names Cairo conf envoy 11-30, 910C1, 913A2-E3
Sadat lauds peace stand 12-6, 930A1
Asks Israel response to Sadat visit 12-9, 954B1
Vance rpts on trip 12-15, 954D2
Says PLO blocks peace; on Sovt role, Begin missn to US 12-15, 954B3
Chrgs PLO inflexible 12-15, PLO rebukes 12-16, 995C1
Begin gives peace plan 12-16, lauds 12-28; reactn 12-29, 12-31, 994A3-995C1
On US stance 12-30, 1001E1
In Iran, sets mtg with Sadat 12-31, 1000F3
Mozambique
Signs arms aid bar 8-4, 668B1
NATO
To study defns needs 1-23—1-24, 69E2
At 4-power London talks 5-9, addresses mtg 5-10, 358C2, G2-359C1
Mtg ends, arms proposals backed 5-11, 359E3
Defers neutron bomb decisn 7-12, 533C2
New Zealand
Sees Muldoon 11-9—11-10, 925E3
Nicaragua
Aid vs govt terror sought 3-2, 168E2
Latins ask Somoza aid halt 3-25, 476B1
Koch chrgs US aid stance misrepresented 7-1, 656C3
Guerrilla asks aid cutoff 10-26, 864G3
Visit deferred 11-7, 854A1; rescheduled 12-1, 914C2
Nigeria
Apartheid effort lauded 8-25, 662B1
Plans to visit 9-23, 738F1
Sees Obasanjo 10-11—10-12, 797D1
Northern Ireland
Vows US peace aid 8-30, 729E3
OAS
Addresses 4-14, 295C2-296C1
Seeks budget share cut 5-13, 415F1
Joint Venez communique backs rights comm 7-1, 546D2
OPEC
Cites at 7-natn summit 5-8, 358C1
Welcomes price freeze 6-30, 515A2, 535A3
Panama
Latin ldrs back Panamanian canal demands 1-18, 46F1
Linowitz joins treaty talks 2-8, 379B1
Call-in on Canal 3-5, 171E1, D2
Rpts treaty talks progress 6-30, 515G1
On Canal treaty talks 7-21, 575C1
On 2d Canal 7-21, experts react 7-25, 589E3
Venez advice on Canal talks rptd 7-27, 590D1
Sees negotiators, writes Torrijos 7-29, 589D2-D3
Latin ldrs laud talks 8-6, 606C3
Canal treaty compensatn rptd resolved 8-8, 607B1
Details Canal treaty 8-12, 621D1
Vows Canal treaty ratificatn campaign 8-15, 622C1
ACU campaigns vs canal pacts 8-21, 678E2
On proposed treaty 8-23, 649F2
Brazil, Mex reassure on Canal pact backing 9-3, 678D1
Sees Torrijos, Latin ldrs 9-6; signs Canal treaties 9-7, 677A1, G2
Canal pact ratificatn campaign underway 9-7, 678F3
Torrijos lauds 9-9, 698B2
US mil chiefs reaffirm treaty support 9-27, 755F1
Briefed on Torrijos drug rpts 10-13, 792E1
Clarifies Canal pacts with Torrijos 10-14, 791A3
Treaties a topic in Denver 10-22, 817D1
Treaty a '78 priority 12-28, 1002B1
Paraguay
Prisoners released 1-27, 2-23, 167G2
Sees Stroessner 9-6, 678A1
Stroessner impressn rptd favorable 9-23, 803A2
Peru
Morales vows '80 electns 7-28, 618D2
Sees Morales Bermudez 9-6, 785G1
Philippines
OKs arms aid 8-4, 668C1
US base talks resume 9-22—9-23, 824B3
Poland
Plans to visit 9-23, 738F1
Visit deferred 11-7, 854A1; rescheduled 11-29, 914B2
Visits 12-29—12-30, 1000E3, 1001B1
Portugal
Urges Westn aid 4-1, sees Soares 4-20—4-22, 330B3
Signs mil aid bill 4-30, 339G1

1978

Signs regional aid authorzn 9-26, 734F1
Disputes Begin on W Bank setlmts 9-27, 729D2
On Camp David accords re Israeli setlmts 9-27, 859B1
Urges Leb peace conf 9-28, 9-30; Chamoun backs 9-20, Syria vs 9-30, 745A1, B2
Urges world ldrs back Leb truce effort, contact with Giscard cited 10-5, 761B1
On upcoming Egypt-Israel talks, seeks future Jordan, Palestinian role 10-10, 766D3
Opens Israel-Egypt pact talks 10-12, intervenes 10-17, 782C2, F2; 10-21, 802A3
Vs Israel setlmt expansn 10-26, 802F2
Sadat heeds plea not to recall pact talks delegatn 10-27, 858G2
Camp David role cited by Nobel Com 10-27, 886E1
Stresses talks on stump 10-28, 831C2
Begin reaffrms stand on setlmt expansn 10-29, 858G3
Meets Begin 11-2, 858A3
Cites Camp David in midterm assessmt 11-6, 862B1
Asks end to Israel-Egypt linkage feud 11-9, 858E3
Hassan: gave Sadat pledge on E Jerusalem, W Bank 11-10; US denies 11-12, 892E3-893B1
Begin says satisfied with Israel Cabt action 11-21, 892F2
Deplores Israel-Egypt pact impasse 11-30, 12-7, 930A2, 936C2
Gets new Sadat pact stand 12-1, 930F2
Lauds Sadat on new pact draft, cites W Bank-Gaza vote deadline 12-13, says treaty now up to Israel 12-14, 951A1
Recalls Vance from Egypt, Israel shuttle 12-15, 950D2
Egypt denies Israel pact chng 12-15, 978E3
US Jewish ldrs chrg pro-Egypt stand 12-19, 979A1
Mozambique
Signs econ aid authorzn bar 9-26, 734G1
Signs econ aid funds bar 10-18, 862E2
Namibia—*See 'South Africa' below*
NATO
Visits hq; vows consultatn, more troops 1-6, 1D1
W Ger gun picked for XM-1 1-31, 82B1
Exempts from arms sales ceiling 2-1, 106F2
Defers neutron bomb 4-7, deploymt issue cited 4-9, 253D1, F2
Haig agrees to remain cmdr 5-19, 398D3
Addresses summit; lauds defense plan, scores USSR 5-30—5-31, 397C1
Affirms sustained mil spending, USSR scores 6-7, 424B1, F1
Optimistic re Eur troop-cut talks 6-26, 491F1
Turkey assures on role 6-30, 595D2
Signs mil, security aid authorzn 9-26, 734A2, B2, E2
'80 defns budget hike seen 11-15, 895B2
On defns budget goal 11-30, 916A3
NATO warns vs arms spending drop 12-6, 954F2
New Zealand
Exempts from arms sales ceiling 2-1, 106E2
Signs mil, security aid authorzn 9-26, 734A2, E2
Nicaragua
Food, educ aid released 5-16, 593D2
Somoza scores rights stance 5-30, 593A2
Lauds Somoza rights vow 8-1, 593C2
Somoza fires Natl Guard ldrs 8-18, 659A3
Signs econ aid funds bar 10-18, 862E2
Nigeria
Visits; asks Cuba exit, majority rule 3-31—4-3, 233B1, F2-234C1
OAS
Opens assemb, stresses rights 6-21, 489E2
OPEC
Urges poor natn aid 3-29, 233G1
Vs oil price hike 11-17, 899E3
Urges price restraint 12-12, 957E1
Pakistan
French A-contract pressure cited 8-9, 668B2
Panama
Vance backs Canal pacts in 'Jan blitz' 1-11—1-13, 58A2
State of Union Message 1-19, 29B1, B3, 31A3
Sen com OKs pacts, asks addenda 1-30, 58B1
In TV appeal for treaty 2-1, 58E2
Reagan rebuts treaty TV appeal 2-8, 121A1
Lauds treaties at NH town mtg, gets ovatn 2-18, 123B3
Sen amends Canal neutrality pact 3-10, 3-13, OKs reservatns 3-16, 177G1, G3-178A1
Canal pact vote deals rptd, denied 3-13; Packwood scores 3-14, 177G1, A3
Enlists wife in pact campgn 3-14, 177D3
Placates Torrijos on DeConcini treaty reservatn 3-15, 255A2
Lauds Sen neutrality pact vote 3-16, 178G1
Venez backs Canal pacts 3-28, 233D1
Warns Torrijos on treaty ratificatn 4-7, 255B3
DeConcini OKs noninterventn 'understanding'; Moynihan, Haskell threaten vote vs pact 4-13, 255F3
Sees Abourezk, Hayakawa on Canal pact vote 4-17, 273C2

1979

Panama
Sees GOP ldrs re Canal pact legis 6-7, 419D3
Royo lauds re Canal pacts 9-5, 675A2
Signs Canal treaty implementatn 9-27, 723A2
Philippines
Macapagal vs Marcos support 9-15, 815F1
Rhodesia—*See 'Zimbabwe Rhodesia' in this section below*
Saudi Arabia—*See also 'Middle East Conflict' above*
US jets to visit 1-10, 12C2
Offers security talks 2-11, 143D2
Fahd cancels visit 2-22—2-24, 143F1
Rules out mil bases 2-27, 144B1
Asked end to Egypt feud 5-21, 378D3
Assured on oil output hike 7-9, 536D3
Arms aid OK seen 7-13, 536B3
Lands '79 oil productn rise 9-26, 781E1
Kennedy scores re Saudi oil price hike reactn 12-21, 983B3
South Africa
State of Union Message cites Namibia 1-23, 48F1
Mahlangu clemency plea rptd 4-6, 270C3
Thailand
USSR, Viet warned re threat 1-17, 30A1
Meets Kriangsak, vows arms speedup 2-6—2-7, 84A2
Sihanouk sends Cambodia refugee plea 10-11, 811F2
Wife visits Thai refugee camps 11-8—11-10, orders food airlift 11-13, 863G1, E2
Turkey
Guadeloupe summit topic 1-5—1-6, aid offer rptd 1-12, 12G2, 40C2
House bars new mil aid 6-21, 488C2
United Nations
Denies Jewish pressure to oust Young 9-23, 763E2
Young quits re PLO contact 8-15, 605B1
McHenry named amb 8-31, 660F2
Backs Cambodia food aid 10-9, 767A2
UK vows support re Iran 12-17, 968A2
Seeks Cncl sanctns vs Iran 12-21, 974C3
USSR—*See also DISARMAMENT above*
Guadeloupe summit topic 1-5—1-6; backs detente 1-6, 12E2, G2, C3
US mil ex-ldrs warn of Sovt challenge 1-12, 15A1
Vance-Brzezinski rift denied 1-16, 27G2
Reassures on China ties, warns on Thailand, sees no Sovt mil edge 1-17, 29F3-30A1
State of Union Message 1-23, 47D3, 48E1
Teng sees war threat 1-29, 65F1
Tass: Teng trip undermines SALT 2-1, 84F1
Sci group in Moscow 2-5—2-7, 100C1
Warns vs Iran interventn 2-20, 123B3
GOP scores defns policy 3-1, 165B3
Brezhnev optimistic re mtg 3-2, 172D1
Sovt dissidents, spies exchngd 4-27, 317C2
Brezhnev in Hungary, backs mtg 5-30—6-1, 416G3, 417B1
At Vienna summit 6-15—6-18, 449A1; communique text 457A1-458E2
Sovts deny Viet bases 6-23, 474F2
Warns re Cuba troops 9-7; rejects SALT linkage 9-8; statemt text 673A1-A2
On Cuba troops 9-25, 723E2
Orders increased Cuba surveillnc, urges SALT ratificatn; speech text 10-1; Sen, Sovt, Eur reactn 10-1—10-3, 737A1-739D2
Scores troop cut plans 10-9, 761A3
OKs China trade benefits 10-23, 834E1
Brezhnev scores A-war alert 11-16, 882D2
Bars ammonia import curbs 12-11, 939D2
Warns Brezhnev on Afghan invasn 12-28, 973G2
Vatican
Sees Pope, issues joint statemt 10-6, 757E1, 759B3; photo 758C1
Vietnam
Guadeloupe summit discusses Cambodia dispute 1-5—1-6, 12G2
Warns re Thailand threat 1-17, 30A1
Links Cambodia, Viet invasns 2-20, 122C3
Bars dispute interventn, seeks fighting end 2-20, 123E2, C3; defends stand 2-22, 124D1
Asks China exit, bars role; defends trade talks 2-27, 141C2, 149B2, D2
Sovts deny Viet bases 6-23, 474F2
In Japan refugee talks 6-26, 494A2
Doubles refugee quota 6-28, 473D2
Refugees strain US health svcs 7-18, 550D2
Ordrd Navy refugee rescue 7-21, 549E1
Exodus spurred by rescue missn 7-28, 575C2
Yemen (North)
Ordrs US arms speedup 3-7, 178B3, 179B1
Zimbabwe Rhodesia
State of Union Message 1-23, 48F1
Helms asks sanctns end 4-24, 293F2
Muzorewa scores 4-29, 332C2
Sen votes sanctns end 5-15, 359A2
To keep trade ban 6-7; Sen votes to end 6-12, 434D2, 435A3, 438F1
Blamed for guerrilla activity 6-13, 547A1

1980

Persian Gulf
State of Union declares area vital to US 1-23, 41A1, 42F2; reactn 1-25, 1-26, 65B1; 1-28, 74E2, F2, E3, 75C1
Admits defense weakness 1-29, 65A1
Clark warns Sovts on move 1-31; Vance, Byrd rebut remark 2-1, 2-2, 83C2
Pentagon rpt on defns ability issued 2-1, 84A1
Issues draft registratn plan 2-8, 110G2
Amphibious assault force dispatched 2-12, 106A2
Weighs force 4-1, 247C1
Bush attacks policy 9-25, 781D1
Debates with Reagan 10-28, 813G2
Peru
Lauds Belaunde electn 5-18, 390A3
Poland
Urges Westn aid 8-29, 659C1
Praises striking workers 9-1, 664D2
Labor unrest statemts scored by Sovts 9-2, 659E2
Cautns US union on aid 9-4, 659E3
$670 mln grain credit OKd, praise strike dignity 9-12, 710F2, C3
Sovts warned vs mil interventn 12-2, 12-3, 910G2, B3
Portugal
Visits, backs govt 6-26, 474C3, 475B1
Saudi Arabia
Persian Gulf vow lauded 1-26, 65D1
Sens vs F-15 gear sale 7-8, 538G2
Vs some F-15 gear 10-24, US says undecided 10-27; Saudi scores 10-30, 821A1-F1
Reelectn rptd favored 10-27, 826G1
Senegal
Senghor in US 4-4—4-6, 336A3
Somalia
Ethiopia scores re mil pact 9-12, 736A1
House subcom backs arms sales 9-30, 735B3
South Africa
Backs Namibia majority rule 10-7, 792G2
Spain
Visits; backs EC, NATO membership 6-25, 474D3
Thailand
Orders arms airlift 7-1, 491A3
Tunisia
Sees Bourguiba's son, vows support 2-29, 197C1
Turkey
Bases, aid pact signed 3-29, 255B3
United Nations
Waldheim rpts on Iran missn 1-6, 3B3
Iran probe comm controversy 2-12—2-13, backs probe comm at news conf 2-13, 105B1, 109B2-E3
Calls Israel setlmt vote mistake 3-14, 309F1
Kennedy scores vote gaffe 3-18, 206F3
UN Charter backed 6-25, 474B3
Matos asks Cuba prison hunger strike probed 12-4, 965D2
USSR—*See also DISARMAMENT & Arms Control in this section*
Intl reactn to Afghan invasn retaliatn 1-1—1-6, 2D2
GOP comments re Afghan 1-1—1-3, 5B1, E1, B2
Sovts score Afghan 'invasn' remarks 1-3, punitive steps 1-5, 1-6, 1F2
Alcoa suspends smelter talks 1-3, 9B2
Announces econ, pol measures vs Afghan invasn 1-4; more moves planned 1-5, 1B1
Brown scores re Afghan 1-5, 13B2
Olympic boycott weighed 1-7—1-18, 28E2
Brezhnev scores 'lies' re Afghan 1-12, 26C2
Mondale defends grain embargo; Kennedy, Brown score 1-12, 32E2
Connally vs 'appeasemt' 1-17, 91E3
Limits '80 ammonia imports 1-18, 45A2
Urges shift of Moscow Olympics 1-20, 45B2
State of Union topic 1-21, 1-23, 41A1, E1-C2, 42B1, 43D3
Sakharov exiled 1-22, 46D3
Tass scores State of Union address 1-24, 43A3
Cong, USOC back Olympic stand 1-24—1-29, 67E3
Reagan: weak re Afghan 1-24, 1-27, 91A3, B3
Kennedy scores Carter re Afghan 1-28, 74F2-A3, B3
GOP vs Persian Gulf doctrine 1-28, 75D1
Admits Persian Gulf mil weakness 1-29, 65A1
Wife campaigns 1-31, 91E2
Defends Olympic stand 2-1, 85B1
UK support re Afghan cited 2-5, 125A2
Sovt aide warns W Eur on new Cold War 2-7, 107B1
Issues draft registratn plan 2-8, 110F2
Me pol ads cited Afghan 2-10, 109E1
Persian Gulf assault force dispatched 2-12, 106A2
Urges USOC boycott decisn 2-12, 107E1
Kennedy attacks re Afghan 2-12, 110G1-A2
Firm re Afghan, Olympics boycott, Yugo aid, draft registratn 2-13, 110B1-D1
Connally scores appeasemt 2-14, 129F1
Afghan rebel arms rpt denied 2-16, 123A1
Brezhnev seeks Afghan neutrality vow 2-22; responds 2-25, 139F2, G2
Orders phosphate export halt 2-25, 139D3
Reagan 'basic speech' scores detente 2-29, 207A3
Sees Schmidt re Afghan 3-5, 205B2
Asks Olympics product ban 3-12, 206G1

1976

1977

OKs arms aid 8-4, 668C1
Signs loan authorizatn 8-4, 668C1
Rhodesia
Clarifies Young remark re Kissinger 2-13, 105G2
Backs UN econ sanctns 3-17, 186E1
Sees UK forgn secy 7-23, 581B3
Sees Nyerere on majority rule 8-4—8-5, 623F3
Backs majority rule at UN 10-4, 751F3
Sees Nigeria ldr 10-11, 797E1
Saudi Arabia—*See also 'Middle East Conflict' above*
Rpt confrmd secret pact 6-27, 474F1
Seeks arms sales curbs 7-28, 574B3
Visit scheduled 11-29, 914B2
Somalia
Favors Sovt challenge 6-10, 460D2
Contacts on hijacked jet 10-17, 789E2
Meets Shah on Ethiopia conflict 12-31, 1001A1
South Africa
Clarifies US policy 6-10, 460G2
Vorster hits policy 8-5, 639G2
Brezhnev rpts A-test plan 8-6; rpt confrmd, actn pledged 8-15, 663C3
Says no A-bomb test planned 8-23, 649E2
Apartheid effort lauded 8-25, 662B1
Backs Namibia indepndnc at UN 10-4, 751F3
Vorster scores crackdown criticism 10-19, 804C2
US amb recalled for talks 10-21, 825A1; returns to Pretoria 11-5, 852C1
Vorster denies A-bomb vow 10-23, US releases letter 10-25, 825D2
Sees Young on UN sanctns 10-24, 851D3
Backs UN arms sanctns, bars spare parts 10-27, 851G3-852C1
Spain
OKs arms aid 8-4, 668C1
Gonzalez sees Chile rights role 8-31, 743D2
Swaziland
OKs regional aid fund 8-4, 668D1
Sweden
Vs Young remark on racism 6-10, 460F2
Syria—*See also 'Middle East Conflict' in this section above*
OKs security aid 8-4, 668D1
Taiwan—*See 'China (Taiwan)' above*
Tanzania
Sees Nyerere 8-4—8-5, 623F3
Signs arms aid bar 8-4, 668B1
Thailand
OKs arms aid 8-4, 668C1
Turkey
Clifford missn 2-17—2-27, 122F1, 146G3
Backs arms aid agrmt 4-19, 351E1
Sees Demirel, vows more mil aid 5-10, 359C1
OKs arms aid 8-4, 668C1
Uganda
Backs Young on deaths 2-20, 139C1
Scores re human rights 2-23, 126E2
Amin bars US natls exit, relents 2-25—3-1, 141A1
United Nations
Rejcts Uganda mediatn role 2-27, 141F1
Addresses Gen Assemb 3-17, 185A1-186B2
Backs Japan permanent Cncl seat 3-21, 209C3
Links Viet ties, entry 3-24, 229B3
Viet entry Miss town mtg topic 7-21, 575B1
Chile rptdly OKs rights probe 9-7, 743B1
Addresses Gen Assemb 10-4, 749A2, 751G2-752G1
Signs rights pacts 10-5, 769D2
US withdraws from ILO 11-1, 829E1
USSR—*See also DISARMAMENT above*
Gets Sakharov plea 1-28, backs 1-30; sees Dobrynin 2-1, 84C1
Reaffirms rights commitmt 2-8, 88F2
Sakharov gets reply 2-17, 137B2
Explains human rights stand 2-23, 126B2
Sees Bukovsky 3-1, 142G2
Rights stand defended 3-17, 185B1
Asks more Radio Liberty funds 3-22, 229F3; USSR scores 3-24, 226G2
Poll standings 4-4, 251D1, F1
On fishing violatns 4-10, 270G1
USSR union reps barred 4-16, 306B3
Discounts antimissile beam rpt 5-3, 343F3
Outlines policy 5-22, 397E1-D2
Congressmen vs computer sale 6-5, 469F2; US bars 6-23, 501E3
Helsinki violatns scored 6-6; rebuttals 6-8, 6-13, 473C1, F1
Tass scores rights stand 6-7, 436E2
Plans challenge in key areas 6-10, 460D2
Scores Toth detentn 6-16, 475C1
France denies mediator role 6-22, 495C2
Reaffirms rights stand, welcomes Brezhnev mtg 6-30, 515A1
Pravda scores cruise missile deploymt 7-3, 514G3
US amb rights speech barred 7-4, 530A1
Brezhnev scores rights stand, bars mtg 7-5, 529F3
Defends US policy, rights stance; downplays Sovt eavesdropping 7-12, 533B1, C2
Sees Schmidt, eases rights stand 7-13—7-14, 566D2
Double agent's release sought 7-14, 564B2
Bars cold war, arms race; affirms rights commitmt 7-21, 550E2
Seeks arms sales curbs, lauds restraint 7-28, 574A3
Arbatov chrgs ties 'worse' 8-3, 590D1
Brezhnev rpts S Africa A-test plan 8-6; rpt confrmd, actn pledged 8-15, 663C3

1978

Sen ratifies 2d Canal pact; hails vote, sees 'new era' 4-18, 273A1, G2
Singlaub scores pacts 4-27, 321G2
Consults Torrijos on DR electn 5-19, 414C2
Visit protested, 2 students die 6-14; govt ups security 6-15, 463E3
Exchngs treaty instrumts with Torrijos 6-16, addresses Zonians 6-17, 463F2, 464B1
Says pacts good Latin omen 6-21, 489B3
Philippines
China ties backed 12-16, 977D1
Poland
State of Union Message 1-19, 31B3
Rhodesia
Calls internal pact inadequate 3-9, 161C1
Asks majority rule 4-1, says US, UK seek new peace conf 4-2; Rhodesian blacks reject 4-3, 233G2, 234B1
Asks USSR support for majority rule 6-7, 424B1
Trade sanctns conditnl end backed by Cong 8-2, 588C1
Signs sanctions end 9-26, 734D1, C2
On US peace role 10-10, 767A1
Shuns Smith during US tour 10-10, 819A1
Rumania
Sees Ceausescu on Mideast, trade, rights 4-12—4-13, 291C1
Saudi Arabia—*See also 'Middle East Conflict' above*
Visits 1-3, 1C1, 2A2
Sees Dayan on jet sale 2-16, 139G1
Defends jet sale 2-17, 123C2
Vs jet sale legis delay 4-25, 307A1, B1
Hopeful on jet sale legis 5-4, 321D2
Khalid stresses F-15 need 5-13, 358E2
Seeks Sen support for jet sale, lauds passage 5-15, 357D1, 358A1
Reassures jet sale opponents 5-15—5-16, 358B1
Somalia
Scores Sovt Ogaden role 1-12, 12E1
Briefed on Egypt, Sudan aid 1-26, 99G3
Warns USSR vs Ethiopia aid 3-2, 140E2
South Africa
Clark scores chrome import move 1-29, 80G3
Vorster: 2-faced on rights 3-31, 234A1
Asks majority rule 4-1, 233G2
Asks USSR support for Namibia solutn 6-7, 424B1
Botha gets note on Namibia 10-16, 819B3
Sees Botha on Namibia 11-30, 989A1
Cites repression 12-6, 934C1
Spain
Lauds const referendum result 12-7, 967B1
Sudan
Briefed on Somalia aid 1-26, 99G3
Syria—*See also 'Middle East Conflict' in this section above*
Signs econ aid authorzn 9-26, 734F1
Tanzania
Nyerere lauds Angola contact plan 6-25, 487E3
Signs econ aid authorzn bar 9-26, 734G1
Thailand
China ties backed 12-16, 977D1
Turkey
Dispatches diplomatic missn 3-29; briefed, asks arms embargo end 4-1, 276B2
Congressmen oppose embargo end 4-5, US Greeks protest 4-16, 276D3, 277E1
Move to lift arms embargo set back 5-3, 5-11, 378B1
Meets Ecevit 5-31, 398D2
Ecevit reassures on NATO role 6-30, 595D2
Urges end to arms ban 7-20, 549F3
Arms embargo end gets Cong OK 8-1, reactn 8-2, 587D2-588B1
Signs arms embargo end 9-26, 734D1, G1, B2
Uganda
Amin threatens trade ban retaliatn 10-12, 823A1
United Nations
Reaffirms Res 242 support 3-2, 140D3
Disarmamt sessn opens, absence scored 5-23, 421F1
Rebukes Young 7-12—7-15, 7-20, 542C2, 549E2
Marks Human Rights Declaratn anniv, urges Genocide Conv ratificatn 12-6, 934A1
USSR—*See also DISARMAMENT above*
A-parity seen in '77 rpt 1-6, 5G2
Scores African role 1-12, 12E1
Warns re Ethiopia role 1-25, 43D3
Defends satellite cooperatn 1-27, 57D2
Urges satellite safety rules, A-ban; discounts mil threat 1-30, 57E2, 62G2-A3
Warns vs Ethiopia mil role 3-2, 140E2, 179A1
Urges Ethiopia exit 3-7—3-9, 194A1
Warns vs mil buildup, interventn; Tass scores 3-17, 202C1-A3
GOP sens attack policy 5-3, 342E2
Vs Africa role, chrgs 'racism' 5-5; Tass rebuts 5-6, 342E1
Scores US curbs on Africa aid 5-19, 383A1
Chrgs Zaire role 5-25, 418B1
Issues detente warning; denounces domestic, forgn policy in Annapolis speech 6-7, 423D2
Tass calls Annapolis speech 'strange' 6-7, 424C1; Kremlin rebuts 6-17, 464C3-465C1

1979

Muzorewa in US talks 7-11, 546C2
House rejects sanctns end 7-11, 546B3
Backs Commonwealth plan 8-6, 590C2
Retains sanctns 11-14, 881B2

1980

Adamant on Olympic boycott 3-21, 3-22, threatens emergency powers use 4-10, 258E2
Orders Olympic products ban 3-28, 259B1
Reagan on Olympic boycott 4-8, 264A3
Newspr eds vs Olympic curb 4-9, 264F1
Defends Afghan, Olympic policy 4-10, 263G3
Reagan backs Olympic boycott 4-10, 288D2
USOC backs Olympic boycott; reactn 4-12, Sovts denounce move 4-13, 283E1, C2, B3
Sees Iran threatened 4-17, 281A2
Anderson scores re Afghan 4-20, 328D1
Killanin asks Brezhnev mtg 4-23, 325F2
Afghan linked to India uranium sale support 5-7, 440D3
Scores policies, threatns detente end 5-9, 367G1
Meets with Killanin on Olympics 5-15, 379E1
Cites 'aggressn' in Afghan 5-29, 423F3
Schmidt gets letter vs E-W missile freeze 6-16, seeks mtg 6-18, 450B3-451D1
OKs uranium sale to India 6-19, 495A3
On detente 6-20, scores Afghan invasn 6-20, 6-23, 473C1, 474B2
Schmidt vs USSR trip criticism 6-21; Eur-Sovt ties backed 6-23, 473E1
Backs Afghan transitnal plan 6-24, USSR scores 6-25, 474F2-B3
Portugal joint communique urges anti-Sovt steps re Afghan 6-26, 475C1
Lauds Schmidt Moscow visit 7-2, 489E1
Signs draft registratn proclamatn, scores Afghan invasn 7-2, 494A1
Sovts reject Afghan peace plan 7-2, 507C3
Reaffirms grain embargo 7-4, 505F2
Brezhnev shuns Independnc Day greeting 7-4, 566D3
Thanks Japan for Olympic boycott support 7-8, 506E1
Meets Hua in Tokyo, scores USSR; Sovts vs mtg 7-10, 506C1, F1
Kissinger seeks Sovt curbs 7-15, 534D3
Killanin rips boycott 7-18, 590E3
Defends Olympic boycott 7-30, 590C3
Adopts new A-war strategy 8-5, 591D3
Muskie unaware of A-strategy shift 8-8; Sovts score 8-11, 615C2, G3
Moynihan cites US defense spending hikes 8-11, 612D3
Muskie regrets A-strategy ommissn, sees enhanced role 8-13, 630E2
Renominatn acceptance speech cites 8-14, 613C1
Brown outlines A-strategy, ICBM vulnerability seen 8-20, 630D1
Poland labor unrest remarks scored 9-2, 659E2
Quotes Reagan on Afghan crisis 9-23, 722D3
Brezhnev: no pres preference 10-14, 776D3
Scores Reagan Afghan response 10-16, 802F2
Mondale hails grain embargo 10-26, 816E3
Chrgs Reagan 'flipflop' on grain embargo 10-27, 816B3
Says USSR hurt by grain embargo 11-12, 865E3
Canada ends grain embargo support 11-20, 900B2
Warns vs Poland mil interventn 12-2, 12-3, 910G2, B3
Vatican
Sees Pope 6-21, 474A2, D2
Venice Summit
Attends 6-22—6-23, 473C1-474E1
Dem platform vs A-power stand 6-24, 479B3
Vietnam
Reagan 'basic speech' cites war 2-29, 207D2
Scores USSR re Cambodia invasn support 7-10, 506D1
Debates with Reagan 10-28, 814A1
Warsaw Pact
State of Union address 1-23, 42G1
Yugoslavia
Would aid vs Sovt threat 2-13, 110D1
Sends Tito letter re Afghanistan 2-25, 139A3
On Tito death, vows Yugo support 5-4; funeral absence scored 5-8, 338E2, B3
Visits, backs indepndnc 6-24; joint communique issued 6-25, 474D2-C3
Zimbabwe
Cites diplomatic role 1-20, 50G1
Renominatn acceptance speech cites 8-14, 613D1
Meets Mugabe, praised 8-27, 674D2, E2

1976

Government Reorganization & Regulation
On goals 6-14, 433F1
Pres nominatn acceptance speech cites 7-15, 507F1, 510F2, C3
Record cited 512A2
Vs industry links 8-9, 584E3
On apptmts 8-9, 8-11, 585G1, C2
Urges restructuring 8-16, 617F1
Scores Ford priorities 8-30, 645B2
Urges Cabt-level energy dept 9-21, 704F1, E2
Debates Ford 9-23, 702C1
Debates Ford 10-22, 800F3
Reaffirms plans 11-15, 864A1
Seeks legis 11-17, 864A2
Urges Cong act 11-17, 864A2
Sees Glenn 12-16, 937B2

1977

Brezhnev replies to Charleston speech 8-16, 640B2
W Bank setlmt stand scored 9-2, 685C2
Urges Indian O restraint at UN 10-4, 751G3
Sees Dobrynin, gets Brezhnev note 11-18, 894E3
On Sovt Mideast role 11-30, 913G2-C3
Uruguay
Aid cut 2-24, 142E1
Pol ldrs back rights stance 4-1, 351E3
Venezuela
Perez paymt chrg regretted 2-22—2-24, 124A2, 151A2
Perez lauds rights stand 2-27, 142F2
Sees Perez 6-28—6-29; joint communiques issued 7-1, 546D1
Perez advice on Panama Canal rptd 7-27, 590D1
Plans to visit 9-23, 738F1
Visit deferred 11-7, 854A1; rescheduled 12-1, 914C2
Brazil A-policy backing by Perez rptd 11-25, 912E3
Vietnam
Plans missn to Hanoi 2-11, 110A2
Call-in topic 3-5, 171E1, E2
To lift US travel ban 3-9, 172F3
Cites mission in UN talk 3-17, 186C2
Gets rpt on US MIA missn, OKs talks on ties 3-23, 206A1
Links ties, econ aid; lauds MIA missn 3-24, 229G2-E3
Asked to bar US aid 5-4, 333E1
Favors Sovt challenge 6-10, 460D2
OKs aid bar 8-4, 668B2
Refugee quotas eased 8-31, 685D2
Food aid sought, barred 12-16, 989C1
Yugoslavia
Kardelj visits 9-28—10-4, 785E3
Lauds Mihajlov release 11-25, 956A2
Zaire
Vs tank sale, doubts Cuba troop role 4-22, 317A3, 321B3
Signs arms aid curb 8-4, 668E1
Zambia
Signs arms aid bar 8-4, 668B1

FOREIGN Trade—*See also country subheads under FOREIGN Policy above*
TV import duty hike asked 2-14, 208A3
Modifies duty-free list 2-28, 189E2
Sugar quota cut asked 3-14, 189D1
Tin reserve release sought 3-16, 298G1
Addresses UN 3-17, 185D2
Trade policy dilemma seen, Strauss role outlined 3-22—3-31, 248E3-249D1 ★, E1
Bars shoe-import curbs 4-1, scored 4-1—4-5, 248C1
UNCTAD commodity talks deadlocked 4-3, 297F3
Sees labor ldrs on import curbs 4-6, 4-13, comments 4-18, 271D2
Presents energy plan 4-18, 4-20, 289B2, 290A3, 295C1, G1; fact sheet 291B1, A2, D2, A3, 293D3
Bars sugar import quotas 5-4, 457D3
At 7-natn econ summit 5-7—5-8, 357G1
US tanker cargo prefernc backed 7-11, 538B2
Cargo preference controversy 7-11—9-9, 719B3-G3
Sees arms sales curbs 7-28, 574G2
US deficit-reducing strategy rptd challenged 8-8, 585A2, F2
Addresses IMF-World Bank mtg on econ growth, trade; cites US deficit 9-26, 753E2
Signs sugar tariff bill 9-29, 736D3
Stresses arms sales curbs at UN 10-4, 751G2, 752F1
Vs voluntary steel curbs 10-13, 775F1
Vows actn vs steel dumping, bars trade curbs 10-13, 775D2
Hikes sugar levies 11-8, 854E3
Plans export tax break phaseout 12-20, 976B3
Backs agri loans, vs forgn oil reliance 12-20, 997A3

GOVERNMENT Reorganization
Fireside chat outlines plans 2-2, 75D1, F1
Submits energy dept bill 3-1, 148F1
Sen OKs pres powers 3-3, 191F2
Vows 'sunset laws' 3-16, 190E3
Pres powers cleared by Cong 3-31, 228A1
Signs reorganizatn power bill 4-6, 250B3
Cabt-level educ dept vow cited 4-11, 302B1
USDA bureaucracy scored 4-12, 364F3
Urges energy dept 4-18, 4-20, 293D3, 295E1
Disbands Forgn Intell Bd, names 3 to Oversight Bd 5-5, 462C2

1978

House com asks Brzezinski 'hardline' clarified 6-8, Vance outlines policy 6-19, 490A3
Warns on ship insurance bias 6-9, 499D3
New A-bomber rptd 6-19, 518E3
Stresses unified Admin policy 6-20, 6-23, 490F3-491A1, 510A1
Sees stable ties; explains China policy, trade, rights 'linkage' 6-26, 490D2, 491A1
2 Sovt spy suspects, US businessman freed 6-26, 506F1
Cruise missile strategy seen 6-27, 563F3
Shcharansky trial seen as challenge 7-10, 541G1
Protests Shcharansky trial 7-12, 7-14, 541G2 ★ -542A1, 543E3
Rebukes Young for US 'pol prisoners' remark 7-12—7-15, 7-20, 542C2, 549E2
Computer sale barred, oil sale review set 7-18, 542E1
Denies 'vendetta'; deplores Shcharansky, Ginzburg convictns, US Olympics boycott 7-20, 549B2, C3
Brezhnev rptdly wants mtg 8-25, 670A2
OKs oil equipmt sale 9-6, 743D1
On Shevchenko-CIA affair 10-10, 844B3
On Sovt forgn motivatn 11-13, 914D2
Assured on Cuba MiGs 11-20, 1016F1
Bars arms sales 11-30, 936F2
US-USSR trade reps in Moscow talks 12-4—12-7, 966B1
Cites repression 12-6, 934C1
Brezhnev gets letter backing trade rise 12-6, 966D2
Terms Brezhnev reactn to China ties positive 12-19, 976E1; Brezhnev denies 12-21, 995E1
Venezuela
Visits; signs maritime, drug pacts 3-28—3-29, 233B1, C1
Consults Perez on DR electns 5-19, 414C2
Cuba pressure re Africa rptd asked 6-11, 443C1
Vietnam
Vows refugee aid 12-6, 934E1
Warsaw Pact
Optimistic re Eur troop-cut talks 6-26, 491F1
Yugoslavia
Sees Tito, joint statemt issued 3-7—3-9, 194A1
Tito rptdly asked US, N-S Korea talks 4-5, 4-19, 277A3
Zaire
Gets CIA evidence on Cuba role 5-19, 443A1
Chrgs Cuba, USSR role 5-25, 5-30; Cuba denies 5-30, 418A1, E1
Briefs Cong ldrs on Cuba role 6-2, 442E1
Rebuts Cuba denial 6-14, 443A1
Zambia
Sees Kaunda 5-17—5-18, 395E2
Signs econ aid authorzn bar 9-26, 734G1

FOREIGN Trade—*See also country, organization subheads under FOREIGN Policy above*
Reaffirms free-trade policy 1-6, 1D1
Urges energy legis 1-12, 12A1
Backs specialty steel quotas 1-18, 80C3
State of Union Message 1-19, 29F1, 30D2, 31A1, D2
Bars chrome alloy duty hike 1-29, 80E3
Bars nut, bolt import curbs 2-10, 181A2
Vows arms sales curbs 2-17, 123D2
Links oil import cuts, $ defns 3-2, 140G3
OKs copper stockpile purchase 3-13, 177B3
Blumenthal oil import fee backing rptd 3-24, 220B2
Hikes CB radio tariffs 3-28, 443C3
Anti-inflatn plan cites trade deficit, export study plan 4-11, 260G1
Hikes meat import quotas 6-8, 428D2
Warns Cong on oil import fee 6-22, 511F2
Scores Sen oil import fee bar 6-27, 511B3, 523A3
Bars import curbs on stainless steel utensils 7-2, clothespins 10-2, 805E1
Vows oil import cuts 7-16—7-17, 544A1
Vows beef import limit 8-14, 626F1
To seek intl steel pact, dumping end 9-20, 715A3
At IMF-World Bank mtg, vows export hike 9-25, 731G2
Export promotn plan set, 'export consequences' 9-26; business scores order 10-10, 804B2, G2
Sees deficit cut as goal 10-10, 766G2
Bars copper import curbs 10-20, 804E3-805B1
Nut, bolt duty rise backed by ITC 10-31; OKs hike 12-26, 998D3
Meany scores $ rescue plan 11-1, 863F2
OKs ferrochrome tariff hike 11-2, 999B1
Vetoes textile amendmt, vows waiver extensn 11-11, 998E1

GAS, Natural—*See ENERGY above*
GOVERNMENT Employment—*See LABOR in this section below*
GOVERNMENT Reorganization
State of Union Message 1-19, 29B1, E2, 31C1, E1
Reorganizes intell agencies 1-24, 49A2; legis introduced 2-9, 106D3
Seeks job-bias unit reorgn 2-23, 123D3-124B1
Proposes Civil Svc revisn 3-2, 141B2
Presents urban-aid plan 3-27, 217A3
Forms telecommunicatns agency 3-28, 270C2
Sets anti-inflatn plan 4-11, 259E3
Proposes Educ Dept 4-14, 279A1-B2
Signs adoptn revisns 4-24, 323E3
Urges Civil Svc revisn 4-25, rptd top goal 4-26, 306D3, 307D3

1979

FOREIGN Trade—*See also country, organization subheads under FOREIGN Policy above*
State of Union Message 1-23, 47B1
Urges world pact 2-25, 150C2
Hails GATT pact 4-12, 274B1
Sets specialty steel curbs phaseout 6-12, 466A2
Submits trade bill to Cong 6-19, sets tariff cuts 6-21; House OKs bill 7-11, 541F1-A2
Asks trade functn reorganizatn 7-19, Sen OKs trade bill 7-23, signs 7-26, 646E3-647C1
Submits trade reorganizatn plan 10-25, 803B1

GAS, Natural—*See ENERGY above*
GOVERNMENT Employment—*See LABOR in this section below*
GOVERNMENT Reorganization
Civil Svc Comm replaced 1-1, 6A1
Backs Educ Dept, Natl Dvpt Bank; ends Travel Svc, Youth Corp 1-22, 44D2, D3, 45A2, 46D1
State of Union Message 1-23, 46F3, G3
Proposes Educ Dept 2-8, 110F2
Proposes Natural Resources Dept 3-1, 164B1
Proposes dvpt finance progrm 3-1, 164G1
Plans pipeline regulatory agency 3-3, 168A2
Asks Energy Security Fund 4-5, 250C3
Hails Sen re Educ Dept OK 4-30, 326B2

1980

FOREIGN Trade—*See also FOREIGN Policy in this section above*
Signs trade reorganizatn plan 1-2, 94G2
OKs FX jet for export 1-4, 16B3
'77 oil use pledge cited 1-29, 77D2
Vs auto import bars 4-17, 287E2
Oil import fee blocked by Dist Ct 5-13, 366C1
TV import curbs asked 5-13, 368C2
Truck import duty raised 5-20, 384B2
Seeks auto import curb ruling 7-8, 505B1
Proposes steel trigger price mechanism 9-30, 740G2-D3
ITC bars auto import curbs 11-10, 866E3

GOVERNMENT Reorganization
Signs trade plan 1-2, 94G2
Asks NRC reorganizatn 1-21, 43E3
Island territories get econ plan 2-14, 495A1
Rpts 35 agencies implement consumer progrms 6-9, 703B1
Creates Econ Revitalizatn Bd 8-28, 663C2
Signs Forgn Svc bill 10-17, 981D2
EDA powers expansion dropped by Cong 11-20, 982B2
Regulatory reform bill dies 12-16, 982G2

1976

1977

Backs consumer agency bill 6-1, 417E3
Names mil manpower costs panel 6-27, 499A3
Stresses 4 initial areas 6-29, 499G2
Lauds Cong action 7-12, 534E1
Submits exec office plan 7-15, 555D3
Miss town mtg topic 7-21, 575E1
Authorizes Young Adult Conservatn Corps 8-5, 609C2
Proposes AFDC, SSI, food stamp progrms end 8-6, 608C3
Submits USIA-educ, cultural bur reorgn plan 10-11, 797C2
Signs mine agency reorganizatn 11-9, 855G3
Signs FRB procedures revisn 11-16, 878B2

HEALTH—*See MEDICINE & Health below*
HEALTH Insurance—*See MEDICINE in this section below*
HOUSING
'78 budget revisions 2-22, 125E2
Carter on Harris policy 3-9, 178F1
Presents energy plan 4-18, 4-20, 289E2, 290E1, 295A2; fact sheet 291F3-292F1
'77 rent subsidy rise cleared 4-28, 339A1; signed 4-30, 380E3
Rebuts Jordan criticism 7-25, 7-28, 573E1, A3
Signs urban aid bill 10-12, 796G1
Signs S&L interest-rate extensn 11-16, 878G1

HUMAN & Civil Rights
Backs civil rights acts 2-16, 110D2
Disputes Young on Nixon, Ford racism 6-6, 443E3
Sees Young, backs speaking out 6-7, 440A1
Gets privacy panel rpt 7-12, 632B1
ACLU calls record 'poor' 7-20, 575C2
Miss town mtg topic 7-21, 575F1
Foreign Issues—*See also country subheads under FOREIGN Policy above*
Inaugural 1-20, 25G2, 27E1
Statemt to world 1-20, 26F1, A3
Fireside chat 2-2, 75C2
Reaffirms commitmt 2-8, 88F2
Explains stand 2-23, 126B2
Aid to 3 natns cut 2-24, 142D1
For world ldrship role 3-9, 173B1
Town meeting 3-16, 190F3
Addresses UN 3-17, 185A1, 186E1-A2
Links to aid program 3-17, 210C3
Reaffirms commitmt 3-22, 3-30, 225G2, 226E2
58 sens support stand 3-25, 226E3
Rhodes scores policy 3-31, 247G1
Defends OAS stand, backs Amer Conv ratificatn 4-14, 295C2
Vs House aid bill amendmt 4-15, 299B2
IISS scores stance 4-28, 401D1
Stresses in Eur TV talk 5-2, 338A2
7-natn summit debates stand 5-7—5-8, 357F2, 358E1
Explains policy to NATO 5-10, 359A1
Outlines new policy 5-22, 397B2, E2
Affirms faith in Young 5-23, 444B1; 5-26, 6-6, 417B3
Wife on Latin tour 5-30—6-12, 454G1
USSR scores re Helsinki rpt 6-8, Carter rebuts 6-13, 473F1
Sen backs vs lending agency-rights amendmt 6-14, 477F2
Issues joint Venez communique 7-1, 546D2
Latin mtgs protested 9-6—9-7, 678B1
Cong clears lending agency bill, rights amendmt 9-21, 737C3
USSR ex-prisoners emigratn plea rptd 9-23, 753C1
Ukrainian writer rptd jailed re open letter 9-26, 753B1
Seeks lending agency, rights link compromise 9-30, 815B2; signs authorizatn 10-3, funds 11-1, 834D1
Signs UN pacts 10-5, 769D2
Shah of Iran visits; demonstratns 11-15—11-16, 897D1
Warsaw remarks 12-29, 1001G1

IMMIGRATION
Gets illegal alien plan 4-27, 370E1
On illegal alien plan, reactn 8-4, 591F3
Young in Mex talks 8-8, 646D2
Mex expert vs alien plan 8-28, 746A2

INAUGURATION
Celebrations 1-19, 1-20, 26D2
Sworn 1-20, 25C1, 26D2; photo 25A1
Address 1-20, 25E2; text 26G2
Statemt to world 1-20; text 26D1, A2

INDIANS—*See MINORITIES in this section below*

1978

Proposes law enforcemt revisn 5-4, 320A3
Stresses reform theme 5-25, 404F3
Proposes emergency agency 6-19, 466D2-B3
Says exempt from legis vetoes 6-21, 466E1
Forms new intell classificatn unit 6-29, 508D1
Proposes LEAA revision 7-10, 525C1
Vs cong com Civil Svc chngs 7-20, 549F3
Defends Civil Svc reform 8-3, 605E3
Sets collective bargaining panel 8-7, 624C2
Civil Svc Comm chngs take effect 8-11, overall reform pending 8-12, 625A2-F2
OKs consumer co-op bank 8-20, 663E1
Civil Svc reforms clear Sen 8-24, 661C3, 662A1; House 9-13, 696C2-D3
Broadens Contract Compliance Office powers 10-6, 811G2
Signs Inspector Gen Act 10-12, 899C2
Signs judgeships bill 10-20, backs merit selectn 11-8, 873C2-C3
Anti-inflatn plan backs regulatory cncl creatn 10-24, 805D3
Meany scores regulatn plan 10-31, 863B2

HEALTH—*See MEDICINE in this section below*
HISPANIC Americans—*See MINORITIES in this section below*
HOUSING
State of Union Message 1-19, 30G2, 31G3
Budget proposals 1-23, 46F1, 47F3, 48A1; table 45E2
Presents urban-aid plan 3-27, reactn 3-27—3-30, 217D3-218A1, C1
Anti-inflatn plan cites higher costs 4-11, 260A1
Unveils anti-crime plan 7-10, 525A2
Harris cancels cong testimony, White House disagreemt cited 8-7, 605F1
HUD sets Fannie Mae authority 8-14, 628B1
Urges relaxed urban bldg codes 11-27, 914D3

HUMAN & Civil Rights—*See also FOREIGN Policy subheads above, MINORITIES and group names in this section*
World tour theme 1-1—1-4, 1F1, 2D1
Cited re world freedom gains 44B2
State of Union Message 1-19, 29F2, 31G1, C3
Orders intell agency curbs 1-24, 49A2; legis introduced 2-9, 106D3, 107F1
Sees intl impact 4-11, 260E3
Rebukes Young for US 'pol prisoners' remark 7-12—7-15, 7-20, 542C2, 549E2
Signs mil, security aid authorzn 9-26, 734D2
Stresses as goal 11-13, 914C2
Defends policy 11-30, 936A3
Reaffirms policy 12-6, 933G3-934F1

IMMIGRATION
Illegal alien plan deferred 10-15, US House com scores 12-20, 1010A3

INDIANS—*See MINORITIES in this section below*

1979

Drops Resources Dept plan 5-15, 365A2
Proposes trade functn shift 7-19, 647A1
Consumer Affairs Cncl created 9-26, 902B3
Sets Pay Advisory Com 9-28, 829C2-B2
Submits trade plan 10-25, 803C1

HEALTH—*See MEDICINE in this section below*
HISPANIC Americans—*See MINORITIES in this section below*
HOUSING
Budget proposals 1-22, 42C1, A2, 44E3, 45D2
Seeks property bias curbs 1-25, 70C2
Asks fuel-saving measures 4-5, 250F3
Links black vote, bias 5-20, 384G2
Orders more timber sales 6-11, 441A1
Proposes solar energy plan 6-20, 498A1
Signs '80 HUD funds bill 11-5, 883A3

HUMAN & Civil Rights—*See also FOREIGN Policy subheads above; also MINORITIES and group names in this section*
State of Union Message 1-23, 47E2, E3
Seeks privacy protectn, property bias bills 1-25, 70C2
Proposes privacy legis 4-2, 264C3
SALT II summit topic 6-15—6-18, 449D1
Addresses Cong on SALT II 6-18, 459A3
Sends FBI charter to Cong 7-31, 599B2
Sees Pope, issues joint statemt 10-6, 759D3; photo 758C1

IMMIGRATION
In Mex illegal alien talks; vows cooperatn, names policy comr 2-14—2-16, 124G1, 127A1
Mex border fence dropped 4-26, 327A3
Vows Mex aliens protectn 5-5, 347B1
Sees Ohira on Indochina refugees 6-26, 494A2
Doubles Indochina refugee quota 6-28, 473D2
Indochina refugees strain US health svcs 7-18, 550D2
Indochina refugee rescue ordrd 7-21, 549E1
Scores 'melting pot' concept 8-7, 592F3
Defends Indochina refugee policy 8-22, 622A3

INCOMES
State of Union message 1-23, 46E2, 47B1

1980

HEALTH—*See MEDICINE & Health in this section*
HISPANIC Americans—*See MINORITIES in this section*
HOUSING
Budget proposals 1-28, 69D3, 70A2, 73E1; table 70F1
Backs subsidized mortgages 4-17, 286D1
On June starts 7-17, 542D1
Renominatn acceptance speech cites 8-14, 612G1
Offers econ renewal plan 8-28, 663B2
Signs housing, community dvpt authrzn 10-8, 763A2, 804B2
Names task force, advisory com; issues white paper 10-8, 763B2
Signs Natl Historic Preservatn Act Amendmts 12-12, 981C2
Signs '81 HUD appropriatns 12-15, 982B1

HUMAN & Civil Rights
State of Union topic 1-23, 41C2, 43D1
Stresses 6-21, 474D2
Cites basic campaign issues 8-15, 629D3
Debates with Reagan 10-28, 814A2, 815D3
Plans to speak out 11-12, 865F2
Vows rights cause to endure 11-19, 881D2, 913C3

IMMIGRATION
Seeks more refugee aid 1-28, 72D2
Defends Iranian entries 3-14, 209G1
Signs refugee reform bill 3-17, 249A2
Offers Cuban refugees 'open arms' 5-5, declares Fla emergency 5-6, 339D2, C3
Haitian pol asylum pressed 5-7, 339G3
Curbs Cuban 'open arms' policy, orders flotilla end; 5-pt program detailed 5-14, 361A1
Gives Cuban refugees pol asylum 5-21, 380B1
Sees Cong ldrs on Cuban refugees 6-4, orders criminals ousted 6-7, 435A1, E1, G1
Sees Hispanic ldrs re Cuban refugees 6-9, 439F1
Signs Cuban, Haitian, Cambodian refugee aid bill 7-8, 515F1
Sets 3-pt resetlmt plan 9-18, 742G1
Signs refugee aid to states 10-10, 785B1
El Salvador alien deportatn proceedings begin 10-18, 826A1
Panel backs higher quotas, amnesty for illegal aliens 12-7, 939B1
PR refugee camp blocked again 12-18, 988C2
Lauds House deportatn res bar 12-24, 989B2

1976

Labor
Backs jobs bill 4-8, 261F1
Offers jobs plan 4-23, 405A2, D2
Wins in Pa 4-27, 305C1, F1
Endorsed by Woodcock 5-7, 343D2
Dem com OKs platform 6-15, 432A3
Visits Meany 6-30, 468E1
Endorsed by AFL-CIO bd 7-19, 532D2
Endorsed by AFL-CIO union ldrs 7-22, 551E1
Says jobs top econ goal 7-28, 550G3
Sees AFL-CIO bd, Meany vows support 8-31, 645B2, C2
Sees jobs as inflatn cure 9-3, 664F1
Prefers work to welfare 9-6, 664C2; 9-13, 686D2
Addresses AFL-CIO groups 9-10, 9-15, 686B2, 686D3
Debates Ford 9-23, 700F3, 701A1-B2; 702C1, 702A2, C2, A3
Endorsed by Chavez 9-25, 724D1
Sees Westn AFL-CIO ldrs 9-27, 724C2
Stresses jobs in Buffalo 9-30, 742E3
Sees San Fran, Cleveland groups 10-7, 10-9, 762B1, C2
Vows no tax rise for workers 10-14, 785C2
Mondale, Dole debate 10-15, 782F2, 783D2
Debates Ford 10-22, 800D1-F2, F3, 801A3, 802B1
Meets NJ ldrs 10-27, at Bklyn,rally 10-28, 803E2, G2
Mayors urgs jobs aid 11-8, 845C3
News conf statemts on jobs 11-15, 863E2-E3
Plans early program 11-23, 881C2
Lance sees jobless rate problem 12-5, 917A1
Plans jobs progrms 12-9—12-14, 937D2-938A3

1977

INTELLIGENCE Issues
CIA review rptd, forgn paymts ordrd ended 2-18, 123C3
Inouye rpts Sen com watch 2-22, 150F3
News conf on CIA activities 2-23, 123E3
Defends CIA activities, urges secrecy 2-24, 151E1
Post mtg on paymts story rptd 2-25, 2-28, 151G2
Vs criminal penalties for leaks 3-9, 212C1
Micronesia watch rptd 5-3, 387C1
Alleged Nazi sympathizer vindicated 5-3, 532C2
Disbands Forgn Intell Bd, names 3 to Oversight Bd 5-5, 462C2
Proposes wiretap curbs 5-18, 386E2
Downplays Sovt eavesdropping 7-12, 533C2
Gets privacy panel rpt 7-12, 632B1
House creates intelligence panel 7-14, 557G1
Double agent's Sovt release sought 7-14, 564B2
Gives Turner new powers 8-4, 610F2
No decisn on Helms indictmt 10-27, 814C1
Backs Helms case handling 10-31, 838F3
Backs Helms setlmt 11-10, 877F1

LABOR
Major jobs effort planned 1-7, 5F1; labor scores 1-10, 14C1
Inaugural 1-20, 27A2
White House reception 1-21, 53A2
Econ recovery plan revised 1-27, 52B1-A2
Cong hearings on econ plan 1-27—2-4, 89A2
On wage, price monitoring 1-31, 89E3
Defends econ recovery plan 2-2, 75A2
On public works spending 2-8, 88D3
'78 budget revisions 2-22, 124F3, 126D1
Sets hiring ceiling 3-2, 148E2
Call-in topic 3-5, 171C1-E1, G2
Asks youth programs 3-9, 173D1-A2
Giaimo proposes budget 3-23, 228E3, 229A1
Constructn-site picket bill fails 3-23, 229E1
Oppositn to 'double dipping' cited 3-23—3-26, 236B2
$2.50 minimum wage asked 3-24, 229D2
Rejcts shoe-import curbs 4-1, reactn 4-1—4-5, 248F1
Sees ldrs on import curbs 4-6, 4-13, comments 4-18, 271D2
Extends jobless benefits 4-12, 272E3
Urges anti-inflatn effort 4-15, 298G3
Presents energy plan 4-18, 4-20, 289B2, 290G1, 295C1; fact sheet 291B1, 292B1, C1
Defends energy plan 4-22, 321F2
Outlines welfare reform goals 5-2, 337C3-338A1
Pub works jobs bill cleared 5-3, 365E1
AFL-CIO ldrs score 5-4, 364B3
At 7-natn London summit 5-7—5-8, 357A1
Scores liberals' criticism 5-12, McGovern replies 5-13, 380F3, 381D2
Signs pub works jobs bill 5-13, 380D3
Addresses UAW conv 5-17, 381E2
Energy plan criticism continues 5-19, 443C2
Environment message 5-23, 404B2
Agrees to sign HEW-Labor funds 6-15, 459B3
Signs CETA extensn 6-15, 500F3
Sen OKs HEW-Labor funds 6-29, 515F2
Backs $2.65 min wage 7-12, 533B1, 534A1
Proposes labor law reform; reactn 7-18, 555C2-C3
Law reform, jobless topics at Miss town mtg 7-21, 575B1, D1
Rebuts Jordan criticism 7-25, 7-28, 573E1, A3
On illegal alien plan, Meany scores 8-4, 592B1-E1
Signs youth jobs bill 8-5, 609A2
Proposes welfare job plan 8-6, 608C2-609E1
Vows jobs actn to blacks, full employmt bill problems rptd 9-7, 702A1
House votes mandatory retiremt curb 9-23, 737B3
Jobs a Detroit roundtable topic 10-21, 817A1
News conf cites jobless rate drop 10-27, 813F3
US withdraws from ILO 11-1, 829E1
Signs minimum wage bill 11-1, 834B1
Signs mine safety rules 11-9, 855E3
On jobless problem, stimulus program 11-10, 877E1
Backs 'full employmt' bill compromise 11-14, 876E3
Urges US jobs for women 11-17, 914E2
Meany lauds, gets White House invitatn 12-12, 960G3, 961B1
Sees black ldrs on jobs issue 12-14, 960E1
Stresses campaign vow 12-28, 1002A1
Sees jobless goal difficult 12-28, 1002B1

1978

INTELLIGENCE Issues
Reorganizes agencies, details curbs 1-24, 49A2
Legis on reorganizatn, curbs introduced 2-9, 106D3, 107F1
Natl security warrantless taps curbed by Sen 4-20, 306G1
Revises secrecy classificatn rules 6-29, 508B1
Complains of security leaks to Cong ldrs 7-11, 524E2-F3
Natl security warrantless taps curbed by House 9-7, 696E3
Signs intell agencies authorzn 9-17, 715C3
On Shevchenko-CIA affair 10-10, 844B3
Signs natl security warrantless tap curbs 10-25, 863A1
Note critical of pol analysis rptd 11-25, confrmd 11-30, 917B1, E1

JEWS
Deplores Ill Nazi march, bars interventn 1-30, 62E1, D3
Mtgs with ldrs on Mideast rptd 2-9, 98A1
Reassures ldrs on Mideast jet sale 5-15—5-16, 358B1

JUDICIARY—*See COURTS & Legal System*

LABOR—*See also PENSIONS & Retirement in this section below*
State of Union Message 1-19, 29B1-D2, F3-30C2, A3-E3, 31B1, G3
Econ Message 1-20, 48A3, C3
Budget proposals 1-23, 44E2, D3, 46E2, 47G3; tables 45E2, F2, 46B2
On jobs program, migrant workers 1-30, 62A3, C3
Signs black lung benefits fund 2-10, 125E2
Meany scores ldrship, jobs policy 2-20—2-24, 142B1
Seeks job-bias unit reorgn 2-23, 123D3-124B1
Proposes Civil Svc reform 3-2, 141B2
Vows coal indus study 3-25, 217G1
Presents urban-aid plan 3-27, reactn 3-27—3-30, 217F2-218D1
Concerned re Redwood Park law job protectn provisn 3-27, 218G1
Anti-inflatn plan asks voluntary restraint, reactn 4-11, 259D2, 260F2
Cites jobless rate drop 4-11, 260A2
Hails A-plant constructn accord 4-18, 281A3, D3
Renews jobless pledge, urges Civil Svc revisn 4-25, 307C3, D3; 4-26, 306D3
Bars wage-price controls 5-4, 321C2
Sees Meany, labor ldrs; wage-restraint plea rejctd 5-10; Bosworth backs 5-11, 361F2, D3
Scales down tax-cut plan 5-12, 361B1
Orders purchasing control exemptn 5-18, 405G1
Plans severe budget cuts 5-25, 404A3
Sees Calif jobless rise 6-14, 446D3
Vetoes fire fighters workweek cut 6-19, 465B3
Cotton dust rules issued 6-19, 471G3
UAW pres quits advisory panel 7-19, 611B2
Vs cong com Civil Svc chngs 7-20, 549F3
Meany, Fraser score health plan 7-29, 586G1
Defends Civil Svc reform 8-3, 605E3
Meany scores Bosworth, panel compromise agreed 8-7; dispute flares over reform legis, postal pact 8-8—8-11, 624A2-G3
Civil Svc Comm chngs take effect 8-11, overall reform pending 8-12, 625A2-F2
Poll finds pessimism growing 8-13, 679F2
Backs Humphrey-Hawkins bill 8-18, 9-29, 808C1
Civil Svc reforms clear Sen 8-24, 661C3, 662A1; House 9-13, 696C2-D3
Proposes 5.5% fed pay hike 8-31, 681D2
Meany tempers remarks 9-18, 715E2
Addresses USW conv, vows labor law legis 9-20, 715E1-B3
Jordan urges black job pressure 9-21, 811B2
Scores Labor Dept budget bill, threatens pub works veto 9-28, 751G3
Orders rail strike end 9-28, 809B2
Vetoes pub works bill 10-5, 765C2
Broadens Contract Compliance Office powers 10-6, 811G2
Rpts on Viet vets; ACLU, vets cncl score 10-10, 878B1-D1, G1
Signs '79 Labor funds 10-18, 873F1
Signs Humphrey-Hawkins bill 10-27, 873A2
Signs CETA extension 10-27, 873B2
Cites pub works veto in midterm assessmt 11-6, 862C1
Plans contd fed job freeze 11-9, 874G3
Meany evaluates electn results 11-9, 875C2
Black ldrs score budget plans 12-4, 936A3
Job safety chngs urged 12-8, 984D3
Budget plans scored by ldrs 12-9, 956G2
CWA pres scores Meany criticism 12-11, 960F3
Restores CETA '80 budget funds 12-22, 1002D3

Anti-Inflation Plan—*See ECONOMY under 'E'*

Coal Strike
Bars interventn 1-30, 62B3
Brings talks to White House as energy crisis looms 2-3—2-16, 104A1, D3-105E1
Sees talks progress, jobs as '78 priority 2-17, 123F1, B2
Threatens 'drastic action' 2-18; briefs cong ldrs, coal-state govs, indus execs 2-23—2-24, 122E2
Meany scores inactn 2-23, 142D1

1979

INTELLIGENCE Issues
CIA dissatisfactn rptd 2-22, 133B1
CIA tap of US citizen in Iran rptd barred 3-11, 180D1
Assures SALT verificatn 4-25, 294D2
Sends FBI charter to Cong 7-31, 599B2
Secret tapes denied 10-29, 869F1

JEWS & Judaism
On brother's remarks 2-27, 149E2
Scored on Palestinian-US civil rights analogy 8-1, 575F1
SCLC asks black-Jewish mtg following Young UN resignatn 8-16, 606A2
Urges black-Jewish amity, denies Young tap 8-30, 661B2
Denies pressure to oust Young 9-23, 763E2

LABOR
To resubmit countercyclical aid plan 1-2, 3E3
Bars min wage, constructn wage chngs 1-4, 3F3
Rail clerks, N&W sign pact 1-8, 87C2
Mtg with Meany 'clears air' 1-12, 13B3
On '80 budget funds 1-17, 29F2
Warns vs Teamsters strike 1-17, 251D2
Fitzsimmons asks ICC chrmn firing 1-18, 111G3
Budget proposals 1-22, 41G1, D2, 44A1, B1; tables 42C2, E2, 43B2
State of Union Message 1-23, 46F2, D3, 47D1, E1, G1, C2
Fed pensn cuts, wage insurnc tax credit opposed in Cong 1-23, 55B3, C3
Seeks less union recruitmt curbs 1-25, 70D2
AFL-CIO offcls assess 2-19—2-21, 149D1
Resubmits countercyclical aid plan 3-6, 164A2
Proposes privacy bill 4-2, 264G3
Teamsters' pact lauded 4-11, 262A2
Averts rail dispatchers strike 5-8, 598G2
Links black vote, bias 5-20, 384G2
Offers pub-svc jobs plan 5-23, 384C1
Asks fed pay revisn 6-6, 419C2
Addresses Food Workers 6-7, 419E3
Waste cleanup bill provisn scored 6-13, 441B2
Acts on truckers' demands, forms task force 6-21—6-22, 479B3
Sees ldrs at Camp David 7-6—7-11, 513F2
Signs fed pay hike funds bill 7-25, 700G1
6 ldrs back reelectn 7-30, 593B3
Thanks Camp David participants 7-30, 608F3-609A1
AFL-CIO cncl backs energy plan 8-6, 629D2
OKs '80 pol Census hiring 8-9, 631E1
UAW energy job action 8-22, 831A3
Proposes 7% '80 fed pay hike 8-31, 700D2
Praises at picnic 9-3, 661C1
Orders Rock I RR strike end 9-20, unions agree 9-26, 722B2-A3
Defends employment record 9-25, 723F2
Announces natl labor accord, sets Pay Advisory Com 9-28, names members 10-16, 829C2-B3
Sees affirmative action success 10-9, 767F1
Vows no constructn job losses 10-11, 807F2
At AFL-CIO conv, lauds Meany; reelectn support sought 11-15, 877F2, 885A1, C1
Notes jobs issue 12-4, 918B3

Anti-Inflation Plan—*See ECONOMY under 'E'*

1980

INTELLIGENCE Issues
Urges charter passage, restraints lifted 1-23, 41D1, 43C1
Backs newsmen as CIA agents 4-12, 459B1
Signs oversight bill 10-14, 804D1
Aide cleared in spy leak 12-5, 940B2

JEWS & Judaism
Honors Simon Wiesenthal 8-5, 638G1
Addresses B'nai B'rith conv 9-4, 681E3
Warns vs Reagan win 10-6, 762E3
Reagan deplores campaign 'hysteria' 10-7, 763D2
Drops Reagan attack 10-9, 778D2
Heckled in NYC 10-13, 778E3

LABOR
LIRR pres strike bd rpts 1-14, 53F1
ILGWU endorses 1-15, 32A3
Cites jobs, jobless gains 1-20, 50D2
State of Union proposals 1-21, 1-23, 41G2, 43A1, C2, D3
Budget proposals 1-28, 69C2, E2, D3, E3, 72D1; tables 70D1, E1, 71B
AFL-CIO backs draft registratn 2-25, 147A1
Revised budget proposals, Kirkland scores 3-31, 244B1, E1, 247A2
Addresses AFL-CIO 4-1, 241G1, 247B1
AFSCME backs Kennedy 4-2, 247G1
Acts to delay PATH strike 4-12, 704B3
Sees AFL-CIO ldrs on Haitian refugees 5-7, 340C1
Pensn chngs urged 5-23, 404A2
UAW head scores 6-1, 457D2
Reagan on jobless 6-3, 423C3
Stresses jobs progrm 6-9, 439F1
Vows cooperatn to mayors 6-10, 438F2
Reagan scores 6-25, 480B2
In Detroit, unveils auto worker aid plan; GOP scores 7-8, 505A1-B2
Signs jobless aid bill 7-8, 515G1
Ford, Vander Jagt score 7-14, 7-16, 534A2, E2
Kennedy wins platform plank 8-12, issues statemt 8-13, 609D1, 610F2, 611F1, 614F2, F3
Renominatn acceptance speech cites 8-14, 613A1, A2, C2
Pledges massive jobs program 8-15, 629E3
Endorsed by AFL-CIO exec cncl 8-20, 647F2-B3
Gets AFT endorsemt 8-21; addresses conv, sees clear choice 8-22, 646E2
Sees Kennedy on jobs plan 8-25, 646G2
OKs fed pay raise 8-29, 685C2
Jobless benefits extended 9-8, 684B1
Cites steel worker recalls, scores 'quick-fix' approach 9-18, 698D3-G3
Addresses Calif AFL-CIO unit 9-22, 722A3
Signs multi-employer pensn plan reform 9-26, 856C3
Addresses ILGWU 9-29, 738G3
Sees NYS civil svc workers, scores Reagan 10-1, 739F1
Vows aid to auto workers 10-1, 739G1-C2
Signs public works appropriatn 10-1, 803D2
Reagan says steel plan borrowed 10-2, 738D2
Warns vs Reagan win 10-6, 762D3
Scores Reagan on min wage, jobless benefits 10-10, 778D2
Sees 'full employmt' 10-12, 10-14, 779D1, E1
Sees expanding jobs 10-20, 803A1
Ridicules Reagan 'secret plan' 10-22, 802F3
Reagan hits record, cites 'misery index' 10-24, 10-29, 817G1-B2
Chrgs Reagan 'flipflop' on min wage 10-27, 816B3
Debates with Reagan 10-28, 813C1-814B2, 815G2, D3
Plans to speak out 11-12, 865F2
Judicial pay hikes backed by Sup Ct 12-15, 956E1-957D1

Wage-Price Developments—*See under ECONOMY (U.S.) under 'E'*

176 CARTER (LABOR)—
FACTS—ON—FILE

1976

1977

LEGISLATION
Proposals & Requests—*For Congressional action, see U.S. GOVERNMENT—CONGRESS, subheads 'Legislation'*
Emergency gas reallocatn 1-26, 53D3
$31 bln econ plan 1-27, 51G3; 1-31, 75A2
'78 budget revisns 2-22, 124B3-126E1
Energy dept 3-1, 148F1
Youth job programs 3-9, 173D1-A2
Marijuana decriminalizatn 3-14, 332G1
Foreign aid program 3-17, 210C3
Oil spill 3-18, 214G1-D2
Election law changes 3-22, 210C2
Intl broadcasting funds 3-22, 229F3
Drought aid 3-23, 210B2
$2.50 minimum wage 3-24, 229D2
Consumer agency 4-6, 250F2-B3
Tax rebate, business credit plan withdrawn 4-14, 270F2
Energy 4-20, 289A1, G2-290B3
Hospital cost controls 4-25, 322A1
Child health program 4-25, 322G1
A-export curbs 4-27, 334B1
Ethics in Govt Act 5-3, 338A1
Soc Security reform 5-9, 363F3
Wiretap curbs 5-18, 386E2
Environment message 5-23, 404G1-G2
Child adoption subsidies 7-12, 628E2-B3
Exec office reorganizatn 7-15, 555D3
Labor law reform 7-18, 555C2
Drug abuse curbs, pot decriminalizatn 8-2, 609E1-A2
New welfare system 8-6, 608C2-609E1
Grain reserves 8-29, 666D2
Pub broadcasting funds 10-6, 846A1
USIA educ, cultural bur reorgn 10-11, 797C2
Plans no new bills for '78 10-27, 813D2
Plans more realistic agenda 12-15, 976F3-977A1
Signed
Emergency natural gas 2-2, 76B2
Fishing rights 2-21, 3-3, 173C3
Rhodesian chrome ban 3-18, 191B1
SBA loan ceiling 3-24, 250D3
Govt reorganizatn powers 4-6, 250B3
Drought aid 4-7, 273E1
Jobless benefits, Cong pay-raise procedures 4-12, 272F3
Interest rate ceiling powers 4-19, 380E3
Portugal mil aid 4-30, 339G1
More '77 rent subsidies 4-30, 380E3
Supplemental funds 5-4, 339D1
Drought relief funds 5-13, 380D3
Pub works jobs, water projct provisn 5-13, 380D3
Econ stimulus, other funds 5-13, 380D3
Drought aid authorizatn 5-23, 405A3
Tax cut, simplificatn act 5-23, 417F3
CETA extensn 6-15, 500F3
Coast Guard authorizatn 7-1, 592G1
Cong COL hike bar 7-11, 592G1
State income tax rule for Cong 7-19, 592A2
Interior Dept funds 7-26, 592D3
Canada temp fishing rights pact 7-26, 688D3
Weapons, civil defns authorizatn 7-30, 592A2
NASA '78 authorizatn 7-30, 688G3
Mil constructn authorizatn 8-1, funds 8-15, 668B2
Health programs extensn 8-1, 689G2-B3
State, Justice, Commerce, other '78 funds, '77 suplmt 8-2, 667B3
Arms control funds 8-2, authorizatn 8-17, 689G1, D2
Water research, saline conversn 8-2, 689E2
Strip mine bill 8-3, 592F1
Energy Dept creatn 8-4, 591C2
Mil aid authorizatn 8-4, 667G3
Foreign econ aid 8-4, 668F1
Small business aid 8-4, 689B3
Youth job programs 8-5, 609A2
'78 Cong funds 8-5, 689B1
Pub works, ERDA funds 8-8, 609D2
Clean-air amendmts 8-8, 610D1-F2
Agri funds 8-12, 688G2
NSF '78 authorizatn 8-15, 689D1
State authorizatn, visa provisn 8-17, 667D2-B3
Debt collection rules 9-20, 761D1
Defense Appropriation Act 9-21, 834D1
Farm, food stamp bill 9-29, 736D2
Juvenile Justice Amendmts 10-3, 797B1
Intl lending agency authorizatn 10-3, 834D1
Vets disability-pensn hike 10-3, 877F3
Debt ceiling increase 10-4, 773E2
HUD, VA, NASA, other funds 10-4, 796G2-F3
Vets dischrg-benefits review 10-8, 773A2
Urban, housing aid authorizatn 10-12, 796G1
HEW hq renaming 10-23, 817E1
Medicare, Medicaid abuse curbs 10-25, 814D1
Mex, Canada prisoner exchng 10-28, 834E1

1978

Announces tentative setlmt, urges ratificatn 2-24, 122D2
Hopeful on setlmt 2-26, 160A1
Defends role, links poll drop 3-2, 141C1, F1
Invokes Taft-Hartley, names facts bd 3-6, sees compliance 3-9, 159A2-B3
On strike-related jobless, supplies 3-6, 3-9, 160A2
Meany vs food-stamp cutoff to strikers 3-11, 182D2
Hails tentative pact 3-14, 182B2
Hails pact ratificatn, vows industry study panel 3-25, 217F1
Sets up coal indus panel 5-26, 405A1
LANGUAGE
Urges bilingual educ aid 3-2, 141D3
Signs 'plain English' order 3-23, 218D2
LEGISLATION
Urges actn on sunset, other bills in anti-inflatn plan 4-11, 259F3, 260D1
Compares Admin, Cong 4-11, 260F3
Backs lobbying limits 4-25, 307A3
To focus on attainable goals 4-26, 306C3
Protests legislative vetoes 6-21; reactn 6-21, 6-22, 466E1-C2
Scores pork barrel allocatns 9-28, 751G3
Gives midterm assessmt 11-6, 862C1
Proposals & Requests—*For congressional action, see U.S. GOVERNMENT—CONGRESS—Legislation*
State of Union 1-19, 29A1-32C1; text 30A1-31F2
Tax reductn, reform 1-21, 48F3
Budget 1-23, 44C2-48E2
College student aid plan 2-8, 84A2
CETA extensn, revisn 2-22, 124B1
Job-bias unit reorgn 2-23, 123D3-124B1
Education aid 2-28, 141A3
NYC aid 3-2, 141B1
Civil Service revision 3-2, 141B2
A-plant licensing changes 3-17, 205B2
Urban-aid plan 3-27, 217G2-E3
Education Dept 4-14, 279A1-B2
Water policy 6-6, 426A3
Water projects 6-9, 446F2
New emergency agency 6-19, 466D2
Health plan 7-29, 585G2, 586A1
Fed pay hike 8-31, 681D2
Viet vets 10-10, 878B1
Signed
Child porno, prostitutn bill 2-6, 218A2
Drought aid extensn 2-7, 218A2
Black lung benefits fund 2-10, 125E2
Timber sales bidding 2-20, 218A2
New wilderness areas 2-24, 218A2
Energy research authrzn 2-25, 218B2
Black lung benefits eligibility 3-1, 218B2
'78 supplemental funds; Clinch R provisn, B-1 rescissn 3-7, 160F2
A-export controls 3-10, 183E1
Redwood Park expansion 3-27, 218E1
Debt ceiling extension 3-27, 261A3
Disaster added funds 4-4, 261C3
Mandatory retiremt curb 4-6, 238E2
OPIC extension 4-24, 323C2
Child abuse extensn, adoptn provisns 4-24, 323B3
Ocean pollutn study 5-8, 343B2
Farm price supports 5-15, 465D3
Investor protectn 5-21, 386D2, E2
DC '78 funds 6-5, 432B1
State soc svc claims setlmt 6-12, 465F3
Medicare kidney progrm revisns 6-13, 466A1
Coast Guard '79 authrzn 6-30, 525B2
Solar, other renewable energy business loans 7-4, 512E1
Debt ceiling increase 8-3, 625F2
NYC long-term aid 8-8, 608C1
Consumer co-op bank 8-20, 663E1
Land Managemt Bur '79-82 authrzn 8-20, 697C2
Customs law revision 9-3, 750A1
Fscl '78 supplemental funding 9-8, 681F2
Intell agencies authrzn 9-17, 715C3
Forgn arms, security aid authorzn, end to Turkey arms embargo, Rhodesia sanctns 9-26, 734C1-G2
'79 HUD, VA, NASA, EPA, other funds 9-30, 750C2
'79 NASA authorzn 9-30, 750A3 ★
Diplomatic immunity revisn 9-30, 750D3
Inspector General Act 10-12, 899C2
Civil Svc reform 10-13, 787G2-788A1
'79 defns funds, abortn curb 10-13, 833B1
Land purchase registratn 10-14, 897B2
Tanker safety rules 10-17, 807B3
'79 forgn aid funds, IMF contributn 10-18, 862C2, F2
Labor, HEW '79 funds 10-18, 873F1
'79 revised arms authorizn 10-20, 833F1-A2
Judgeships increase 10-20, 873C2
Inland Waterways authorzn 10-21, 897C2
Airline deregulation 10-24, 873F1
Energy Dept security progrm authorzn, neutron parts productn 10-25, 833B2
Natl security warrantless tap curbs 10-25, 863A1
Govt ethics 10-26, 832F1-B2
Humphrey-Hawkins full employmt 10-27, 873A2
CETA extension 10-27, 873B2
Nazi deportatn 10-30, 872D2
Pregnancy benefits 10-31, 873G1
Amer Samoa House del 10-31, 1003A1
Conrail aid 11-1, 875C3
College student aid 11-2, 873E1
Presidential papers 11-4, 897D2
Tax cut 11-6, 873E1
Bankruptcy revisn 11-6, 1003B1
Surface transit funds 11-8, 875D2
Amateur sports 11-8, 1003B1
Energy bill, gas deregulatn provisn 11-9, 873A1

1979

LEGISLATION
Vows fight for program 5-29, 401F3
Meets with GOP ldrs 6-7, 419D3
Proposals & Requests—*For congressional action, See U.S. GOVERNMENT-CONGRESS-Legislation*
State of Union Message 1-23, 46F3, 47A2, 48A1; detailed 1-25, 70A2
Educ Dept 2-8, 110F2
Oil conservatn powers 2-26, 145B3
Natural Resources Dept 3-1, 164B1
Dvpt financing progrm 3-1, 164F1
Hospital cost control 3-5, 163A2
Urban aid 3-6, 164A2
Regulatory reform 3-25, 230E1
Privacy protectn 4-2, 264C3
Roadless forest lands 4-16, 282E1
Drug regulatn reform 4-20, 315A2
Oil-profits tax plan 4-26, 300G3
Mental health 5-15, 365B1
Water projct cost-sharing 5-16, 365E2-A3
Bank law reforms 5-22, 403B1
Welfare reform 5-23, 384B1
Fed pay revisn 6-6, 419C2
Natl health plan 6-12, 438G1
Hazardous waste cleanup 6-13, 441E1
Trade liberalizatn 6-19, 541E1
Solar energy 6-20, 498A1
FBI charter 7-31, 599B2
China trade benefits 10-23, 834E1
Industrial innovatn 10-31, 829D3
Chrysler rescue plan 11-1, 845B2
Signed
Debt ceiling, balanced budget optn 4-2, 251F2, F3
Duty waiver 4-3, 298E3
US-Taiwan relations 4-10, 259C2
'79 supplemental funds; fed pay hike, Mideast peace treaty 7-25, 700F1
Trade liberalizatn 7-26, 646E3
'79 emergency food stamp funds 8-2, 700B2
'80 State, Justice, other funds 9-24, 766E3
'80 water funds, Tellico Dam 9-26, 766F2
Panama Canal treaty implementatn 9-27, 723A2
Amtrak fund authorizatn 9-29, 867C3
'80 Treas, Postal, other funds 9-29, 883C2
'80 continuing appropriatn resolutns 10-12, 900F1; 11-20, 900A2
Educ Dept 10-17, 782A2
DC '80 funds 10-30, 870A1
Milwaukee Rd aid 11-4, 867E2
'80 HUD, VA, NASA, other funds 11-5, 883A3
Standby gas rationing 11-5, 848A3
'80 Agri funds 11-9, 920A1
'80 Interior, Energy funds 11-27, 920B1
'80 Transport funds 11-30, 920C1
'80 mil constructn funds 11-30, 945F1
Stopgap banking bill 12-28, 987B3

1980

LEGISLATION
Proposals & Requests—*See also under CONGRESS*
Youth training progrm 1-10, 16G1-F2
State of Union 1-21, 1-23, 41A1-43G2, B3
Budget 1-28, 69B2-74B1
Draft registratn 2-8, 110F2
A-waste storage 2-12, 127D3
Coal-fired utilities plan 3-6, 169A3
Revised budget 3-31, 243D2-244E1
Standby gas rationing plan 6-12, 551E3
Econ renewal plan 8-28, 663A1-D3
Signed
Chrysler bailout 1-7, 14A1
Intl airline deregulatn 2-15, 346F1
Refugee reform 3-17, 249A2
FTC emergency funding 3-28, 5-1, 348D1, B2
Banking deregulatn 3-31, 245C3
Windfall oil profits tax 4-2, 244B2
Emergency food stamp funds 5-27, 402F3
FTC authrzn 5-28, appropriatn 6-4, 702C3
Amtrak, Rock I RR aid 5-30, 427E1
Draft registratn funding 6-27, 478C1
Synfuel dvpt 6-30, 494G1-A2
Trucking deregulatn 7-1, 494B1
'80 NRC funds authorizatn 7-1, 494F1
Viet War mem'l 7-1, 496B1
'80 supplemental funds, Nicaragua aid 7-8, 515D1
Eximbank funding 8-29, 989B1
'81 arms, mil pay authrzn 9-8, 764F3
Mil benefits authrzn 9-8, 765C1
Small business aid 9-19, 784C2
Multi-employer pensn plan reform 9-26, 856C3
Wildlife Conservation Act 9-29, 915B3
NYS A-waste storage clean-up 10-1, 739D1
Love Canal relocation aid 10-1, 739E1
Stopgap funds, NYC rider 10-1, 785B1, 826C2
Energy, water appropriatn 10-1, 803A2
Higher educ authrzn 10-3, 803A3
Mental health authrzn 10-7, 803E3
Fusion dvpt 10-7, 981E2
IMF fund quota hike authrzn 10-7, 981E3
Housing, community dvpt authrzn 10-8, 763A2, 804B2
'81 Transport funds 10-9, 980F3
Refugee aid to states 10-10, 785B1
Auto fuel standards revisn 10-10, 981C1
RR deregulatn 10-14, 783D3
Intelligence oversight 10-14, 804D1
Newsroom searches curb 10-14, 835F1-C2
5th judicial circuit split 10-14, 918A3
Iran hostage relief act 10-14, 981B2
Household moving 10-15, 915G2
Judicial discipline 10-15, 918F3
Vet educ aid 10-17, 856F2
'81-85 coastal zone mgt authrzn 10-17, 981B2
Forgn Svc reorgn 10-17, 981D2
Toxic dump controls 10-21, 981F1
Clean water amendmts 10-21, 981F1
Alaska lands 12-2, 915G3-916D1
Gasohol Competitn Act 12-2, 982A1
Agri Act 12-3, 981G1
Arts and Humanities Act 12-4, 982A1
Budget reconciliatn 12-5, 936D1
Medicare, Medicaid changes 12-5, 981A1
Child nutritn authrzn 12-5, 981B1
Pacific NW power 12-5, 981A2
Paperwork Reductn Act 12-11, 935C3
Toxic waste clean-up 12-11, 936C1
Natl Historic Preservatn Act Amendmts 12-12, 981C2
Patent law revisn 12-12, 982A1
NSF authrzn 12-12, 982B1
'81 Interior funds 12-12, 982B1
'81 Defense appropriatn 12-15, 982B1
'81 HUD, VA appropriatn 12-15, 982B1
'81 Agri appropriatn 12-15, 982B1
'81 forgn aid authrzn 12-16, 981C3
Stopgap funds; IMF funding rider 12-16, 981E3, 982C1
A-arms authrzn 12-17, 981C1
Pesticide program extensn 12-17, 982C1
Army LSD setlmt 12-18, 982A1
Debt limit hike 12-19, 981E1
Wood energy use 12-19, 982C1
Plant Variety Protectn Act amendmt 12-22, 981A1
Low-level A-waste 12-22, 981D1
Fishing indus aid 12-22, 982C1, 995B3
Mil pay benefits 12-23, 982C1
Revenue sharing renewal 12-28, 982C1
Vetoed—*See also CONGRESS--Veto Action*
Dioxins study 1-2, 17G2
Debt limit; oil import fee bar res 6-5, 436G3-437A1
VA MD pay hike 8-22, 649C3
'81 State, Justice, Commerce funds; busing amendmts 12-16, 954E1
Forgn tourism bill 12-25, 982D1

1976

Medicine & Health
Biographical sketch 511G2-512E2 ♦
Proposes natl health plan 4-16, 281D3
Vs 'instant' approach 6-3, 411D1
Lauds Europe 6-23, 451A3
Pres nominatn acceptance speech cites 7-15, 507E1, 510G2, A3
Spending record cited 512B3
Teaches Bible class 7-18, 532B3
On jailed nephew 7-26, 551F1
Cites abortn 8-3, 564B3
Family holdings rptd 8-19, 646A1
See RC bishops 8-31, 645C2, 686F1
Cites Medicaid waste 9-6, 664D2
Phila church mtg shifted, Scranton anti-abortn protests 9-7, 664A1
Defends abortn stand 9-9, 664D3
Hits Medicaid mismanagemt 9-13, stresses health care 9-14, 686D2, A3
Bishops vs abortn stand 9-16, 686G1
Debates Ford 9-23, 702F1
On health care 10-19, 785A2
Debates Ford 10-22, 801C3, D3, 802C1
AMA backs natl health insurance 12-7, 931D2

1977

Indochinese refugee aid 10-28, 834B2
Minimum wage 11-1, 834B1
Intl lending agency, other forgn aid funds 11-1, 834D1
Alcan gas pipe rte res 11-8, 856F3
Farm disaster aid ceiling removal 11-8, 1001E2
Mine safety rules, agency reorganizatn 11-9, 855E3
Air cargo deregulatn 11-9, 899A3
Child nutritn, schl lunch 11-10, 897D2
Maritime aid authorizatn 11-12, 1001E2
ERDA authorizatn, neutron bomb provisn 11-15, 878A1
Defns supplemental authorizatn 11-15, 1001E2
S&L interest-rate extensn, FRB revisns 11-16, 878G1
Rail mass transit aid 11-16, 900A1
Drinking water authorizatn 11-16, 1001F2
Vets educ benefits 11-23, 1001F2
Saccharin ban delay 11-23, 1001F2
Vets pension revision 12-2, 1001F2
HEW-Labor funds 12-9, 1001F2
NRC fund authorizatn 12-13, 1001G2
Career guidance aid 12-13, 1001G2
Rural health services 12-13, 1001G2
Corp forgn bribe bar 12-19, 1001G2
Endangered species bill 12-19, 1001A3
Soc Sec tax rise 12-20, 1001C2
Med schl transfer revisn 12-20, 1001A3
Clean Water Act amendmts 12-20, 1001A3
Interest deposits for US $ 12-28, 1001D2
Legal aid for poor (LSC) extensn 12-28, 1002G2

Vetoed
Clinch R A-breeder other energy authorizatns 11-5, 854E2-D3
Rabbit meat inspection 11-10, 897B3

MEDICAID—*See under MEDICINE in this section below*
MEDICARE—*See under MEDICINE in this section below*
MEDICINE & Health—*See also NARCOTICS in this section below*
Ford '78 budget proposal 1-17, 32F1
Statement to world 1-20, 26G1, A3
Carter budget revision 2-22, 125A2
Call-in topic 3-5, 171D1
Consumer agency 4-6, 250F2-B3
Plans hosp cost-cutting 4-15, 299C1
Presents energy plan 4-20, 290G1; fact sheet 292C1
Urges hosp cost controls 4-25, 322A1
Asks child health progrm 4-25, 322G1
Scores liberals' criticism 5-12, 380F3
Vows natl health insurnc plan 5-17, 381F2
Affirms anti-abortn stand 5-17, 381C3
Cong sets '78 budget target 5-17, 405A1
Backs Sup Ct abortn rulings 7-12, 533B1, F2-534A1
Asks child adoptn subsidies 7-12, 628E2-B3
Gets privacy panel rpt 7-12, 632B1
Abortn stand scored by family planning groups 7-19, 786C3
Natl insurance topic at Miss town mtg 7-21, 575B1
Rebuts Jordan criticism 7-25, 573G1
Signs health program extensn 8-1, 689G2-B3
Signs '78 food funds bill 8-12, 688A3
Signs vets disability pensn hike 10-3, 877F3
Signs vets dischrg benefits review 10-8, 773A2
Vetoes rabbit meat inspectn 11-10, 897B3
Signs rural services bill 12-13, 1001G2
Signs med schl transfer revisn 12-20, 1001A3
To offer natl insurnc plan in '78 12-28, 1002B1

Medicaid
Budget revisions 2-22, 125G3
Asks hosp cost controls 4-25, 322D1, G1
Backs Sup Ct abortn rulings 7-12, 533B1, F2-533A1
Women aides vs abortn curbs 7-15, 786E2
Signs abuse curbs 10-25, 814D1

Medicare
Budget revisions 2-22, 125F3
Asks hosp cost controls 4-25, 322D1
Child health plan scored 6-22, 643C3
Signs abuse curbs 10-25, 814D1

MESSAGES to Congress—*See also LEGISLATION—Proposals above*
Econ plan 1-31, 51G3, 75A2, 89F3
Fscl '78 budget revisns 2-22, 124B3-126E1
Foreign aid 3-17, 210C3
Oil-spill legislatn 3-18, 214G1-D2
Election law changes 3-22, 210C2
Intl broadcasts 3-22, 229F3
Drought aid 3-23, 210B2
Consumer agency 4-6, 250F2-B3
Energy 4-20, 289A1, G2-290B3
Hospital cost controls 4-25, 322A1
A-export curbs 4-27, 334C1
Ethics law 5-3, 338A1
Environment 5-23, 404G1-G2
Drug abuse curbs, pot decriminalizatn 8-2, 609E1-A2
New welfare system 8-6, 608C2-609E1
USIA-educ, cultural bur reorgnzatn 10-11, 797C2
Clinch R A-plant veto 11-5, 854F2

MINORITIES—*See also BLACK Americans in this section above*
Indian claims backed 2-28, 197C1
Call-in on jobs 3-5, 171F1
On housing program 3-9, 178F1
Educators vs quotas 3-31, 235D2
Poll standing 4-4, 251G1
On quotas issue 7-28, 574G3
Signs youth jobs bill 8-5, 609B2

1978

Natl parks authorzn 11-10, 897A2
Banking reform 11-10, 1002E3
Endangered species revisn 11-10, 1003B1

Vetoed
Fire fighters workweek cut 6-19, 465B3
Wildlife program authrzn 7-10, 567F3-568B1
'79 arms authrzn 8-17, 621A1
Public works 10-5, 765A1-D2
Aquaculture authorzn 10-19, 807E3
Small business aid 10-25, 897F2
DC pension reform 11-4, 897E2
Shipping malpractice 11-4, 897G2
Tris compensatn 11-8, 941C3
Hollings textile trade amendmt 11-11, 998E1

MEDICAID—*See under MEDICINE in this section below*
MEDICARE—*See under MEDICINE in this section below*
MEDICINE & Health—*See also NARCOTICS in this section below*
State of Union Message 1-19, 31B1, 32A1, B1
Budget proposals 1-23, 44F2, 46G1, 47B1, E1, 48G1; table 45E2
Signs black lung benefits fund 2-10, 125E2
Vs fed funds for abortns 2-17, 123G2-A3
Anti-inflatn plan asks hosp costs bill OK 4-11, 259F3
Signs child abuse extensn 4-24, 323B3
Attacks AMA 5-5, 342A1
Cotton dust rules issued 6-19, 471G3
Natl health plan readied, inflatn stalls implementatn 6-26, 491E2
On hospital-costs bill 7-20, 549E3
Vs House com on hosp costs 7-20, 549E3
Sees Kennedy on health plan; Kennedy, labor ldrs score 7-28; health plan outlined 7-29, 585F2; text 586A1
Scores HEW budget bill 9-28, 751G3
Rpts on Viet vets; ACLU, vets cncl score 10-10, 878D1, E1, G1
Signs mil abortn fund curb 10-13, 833F1
Signs '79 HEW funds 10-18, 873F1
Anti-inflatn plan to monitor costs, urges hosp cost-control bill OK 10-24, 806D1
Signs pregnancy benefits bill 10-31, 873G1
Job safety chngs urged 12-8, 984D3
Inner-city progrm urged 12-20, 1009F1
Restores '80 budget funds 12-22, 1002E3

Medicaid
Budget proposals 1-23, 48A2-C2

Medicare
Budget proposals 1-23, 48B2

MESSAGES to Congress—*See also LEGISLATION—Proposals above*
State of Union 1-19, 29A1-32C1; text 30A1-31F2
Economic 1-20, 48E2
Budget 1-23, 44C2-48E2
Water policy 6-6, 426A3
Legislative veto protest 6-21, 466E1
Fed pay hike 8-31, 681D2
Camp David summit pacts 9-18, 709E2
Viet vets 10-10, 878A1

METALS (& Metal Products)
Backs specialty steel quotas 1-18, 80C3
Bars chrome alloy duty hike 1-29, 20E3
Bars nut, bolt import curbs 2-10, 181A2
OKs copper stockpile purchase 3-13, 177B3
Scores steel price hike 3-30; hike undercut, rolled back 3-20—4-3, 262G3
Overrules Japan steel import minimum price order 4-24, 444B1
Bars import curbs on stainless steel utensils 7-2, 805E1
To seek intl steel pact, dumping end 9-20, 715A3
Bars copper import curbs 10-20, 804E3-805B1

MINORITIES—*See also BLACK Americans and JEWS in this section above*
State of Union Message 1-19, 29C2, 30A3
To recruit judges 5-4, 320B3
On Indian land claims 5-4, 321C1
Apptmt data disclosed 6-15, 811E1
Admin lauds Bakke ruling 6-28, 482B2
Indians ask mtg 7-18, AIM ldr scores 7-23, 569B1, E1
Broadens Contract Compliance Office powers 10-6, 811F2
SBA aid abuse briefing rptd 11-21, 919C3
Cites US repression 12-6, 934C1

1979

MEDICAID—*See under MEDICINE in this section below*
MEDICARE—*See under MEDICINE in this section below*
MEDICINE & Health—*See also NARCOTICS in this section below*
Some '80 budget cuts restored 1-4, 3D3
Warns on smoking perils 1-17, 30C1
Budget proposals 1-22, 41D2, 44D2-B3; table 42D2
State of Union Message 1-23, 46F3, 47A2, 48A1
Drafting mental health progrm 1-25, 70D2
Wife asks more mental health funds 2-7, 112B1
Urges hosp cost curb legis 2-12, 109F3
Hosp cost plan faces Cong hurdles 2-13, 110C1
Califano backs natl health insurnc 2-13, 110E1
Sends hosp cost-control bill to Cong 3-5, opens lobbying campaign 3-6, 163A2-C3
Hosp cost-control hearings open 3-9, 194E2
Proposes privacy bill 4-2, 264D3
Califano defends natl health plan 5-14, 362F1
Proposes mental health plan 5-15, 365B1
Cites hosp cost-control bill defeat by House panel 5-25, 401B2
Unveils natl health plan 6-12, 438G1
Waste cleanup bill provisn scored 6-13, 441B2
Indochina refugees strain US health svcs 7-18, 550D2
On Kennedy health plan record 9-25, 723E3
Hosp cost-control bill defeated by House 11-15, 883A1
Abortn stand linked to NOW reelectn oppositn 12-9, 961B3

Medicaid
Budget proposals 1-22, 41D2, 44E2
Sends hosp cost bill to Cong 3-5, 163B3
Unveils natl health plan 6-12, 438A2, D2

Medicare
Budget proposals 1-22, 41E2, 44E2; table 42E2
Sends hosp cost bill to Cong 3-5, 163B3
Unveils natl health plan 6-12, 438A2, D2

MESSAGES to Congress—*See also LEGISLATION—Proposals above*
Regulatory reform 3-26, 230E1
State of Union 1-23; text S1-23, 46C2-48F1
GOP reactn to State of Union 1-24, 48F1-C2
Economic 1-25, 48C2
State of Union detailed 1-25, 70B2
Urban aid 3-6, 164A2
Privacy protectn 4-2, 264C3
Oil-profits tax plan 4-26, 300G3
Welfare reform 5-23, 384G1
SALT II treaty 6-18, 449C2; text 458F2-459E3
Solar energy 6-20, 498A1
FBI charter 7-31, 599B2

MINORITIES—*See also BLACK Americans and JEWS in this section above*
Seeks property bias curbs 1-25, 70C2
At Mex-Amer fete in LA 5-5, 346C1, 347B1
Sees affirmative action success 10-9, 767G1

1980

MEDICINE & Health
State of Union proposals 1-21, 1-23, 43A1, F2, F3
Budget proposals 1-28, 69D3, E3; table 70E1
Black Caucus scores budget 2-5, 94F2
Dem platform backs abortn 6-24, 479G2, B3
Issues platform statemt, disavows abortn plank 8-13, 611E1
Vetoes VA MD pay hike bill 8-22, Cong overrides 8-26, 649C3
Signs mental health authrzn 10-7, 803E3
Backs natl health insurnc 10-10, 778B3
Debates natl insurnc with Reagan 10-28, 814C2
Signs Army LSD setlmt 12-18, 982A1

Medicaid
Scores Reagan stand 10-1, 739B2
Vows fed aid to cities 10-20, 803F1
Signs paymt revisns 12-5, 981A1

Medicare
Budget proposal, table 1-28, 70E1
Renominatn acceptance speech cites 8-14, 613A1
Scores Reagan oppositn 10-1, 739B2; 10-10, 778C3, D3
Ridicules Reagan 'secret plan' 10-22, 802F3
Debates with Reagan 10-28, 813B2, 815D2
Signs paymt revisns 12-5, 981A1

MESSAGES to Congress
State of Union rpt 1-21, 43B3
State of Union address; text 1-23, 41A1-43G2
Reagan State of Union reactn 1-24, 91A3
Budget 1-28, 69B2-74B1
Economic 1-30, 74B1
A-waste storage plan 2-12, 127D3
Coal-fired utilities plan 3-6, 169A3
Revised budget 3-31, 243D2-244E1
Uranium sale to India 6-19, 495G2

MINORITIES—*See also BLACK Americans, JEWS & Judaism in this section above*
Sees Fla Hispanic ldrs re Cuba refugees 6-9, 439F1
Mondale seeks Hispanic vote 10-3, 10-26, 816G3-817B1
Kennedy stumps in Tex 10-22, 817E1
Debates with Reagan 10-28, 814G1, A2
Hits Reagan debate statemt 10-29, 816D2
Plans to speak out 11-12, 865F2

1976

PERSONAL
Vacations 11-6—11-11, 845F2
Amy to attend public schl 11-28, 917E2
Lance on bank loan 12-5, 917C1
At Daley funeral svc 12-22, 969D3

Polls
Leads Ford 3-15, 197D1
Leads Ford, Reagan 4-12—8-1, 564F3
Lead drops, Southn base firm 8-25, 8-28, 9-1, 644G1
Trails in 1st debate poll 9-30, 725E1
Lead drops to 8% 9-30, 725A2
Lead rises after 2d debate 10-15, 1st debate results cited 764B2
Lead up 6 points 10-21, 804B3
On poll lead loss 10-22, 799F3, 800G2
3 give edge over Ford, 1 to Ford 10-27, 10-31, 11-1; Gallup statemt 11-3, 825F3
Ford on decline 10-28, 803G1
NBC polls electn issues 11-2, 818B3
Caddell analyzes electn 11-5, 11-11, 845G1

Presidential Campaign & Election—*See also 'Transition' below; for specific issues, see other appropriate subheads*
Common Cause rpts campaign code backing 1-9, 23A1
Campaigns in Fla 2-26—3-4, 166E1
Campaigns in Raleigh 3-19, 214A2
In Wis; rebuts Humphrey, Jackson 3-24—3-31, 233F1, 245B3, D3
Humphrey rules out campaign 4-29, 305A3
In Tex, scores Ford ldrshp 4-30, 324D1
Jackson suspends candidacy 5-1, 324A3
Seeks Dem unity 5-2, 323F3
At black Dem caucus 5-2, 343A3
On Neb vote 5-6, 5-12, 343G1
On Brown 5-6—5-11; Brown on Carter 5-11, 343A2, G2
Says Reagan sways Ford 5-14, 390E3
Kennedy denies pres bid rpt 5-20, 357F2
For 'aggressive' presidency 5-20, 373C3
In NJ, warns of reactn in south 5-26, 390A3
Scores critics 5-27—5-31, 390E1-A3
Reagan ready to take on 6-1, 391C2
Vs 'wish-box' platform 6-3, 411C1
Reassures Jews 6-6, 410F3
Natl TV spot broadcast 6-6, 411E1
In NJ, Ohio 6-7, 411C1
Sees Wallace 6-12, 432A2
Dem com adopts platform 6-15, 432F2
Ford addresses Baptists 6-15, 433D2
Sees black ldrs in NY 6-23, 452E1
Sees Daley 7-1, 490D2
Sees Houston execs, Hispanic ldrs 7-1, 490E2
Ford or Reagan 'tough' opponent 7-6, 489D3
Target of Reagan TV talk 7-6, 490F2
Sees Boren, Walker 7-6, 492G3
Arrives NYC 7-10, on Meet the Press 7-11, 509E1
Pres nominatn acceptnc speech 7-15, 507A1; text 510D2, G2

1977

MONETARY Developments—*See also country subheads under FOREIGN Policy above*
At 7-natn London summit 5-7—5-8, 357A2
Schmidt backed mark revaluatn 7-21, 552G1
Blames $ drop on oil imports, backs more US output, agri loans 12-20; $ rallies 12-21, 997G2-B3
$ drops on Miller apptmt 12-28, 997B3

NARCOTICS & Dangerous Drugs
Call-in topic 3-5, 171E1
Backs pot decriminalizatn 3-14, 332G1
To aid Colombia drug effort 6-10, 455D2
Urges pot decriminalizatn, drug abuse studies 8-2, 609E1-A2
Rpts heroin abuse down 11-7, 972A1
Pot stand backed by AMA, ABA 11-13, 972B3
NIDA rpts barbiturates study 11-27, 972E3

NATURAL Resources—*See RESOURCES, Natural in this section below*

PERSONAL
Sets up trust 1-4, 4C2, G3
In Plains 1-7, 5B2; 2-11—2-13, 106A1, 110C1, C3, E3
Joins DC Baptist Church 1-23, 53C2
Call-in on son's White House residence 3-5, 171F1
Cuts summit entourage, chngs hotel 5-5, 359F2-A3
Book proceeds for library 5-26, 417D2
In Ga for holidays 5-27, 417D3
Issues '76 tax return data 6-24, 499C2
To leave papers to nation 6-30, 515B2
On staff promiscuity 6-30, 515C2
Sister at charismatic conf 7-20—7-24, 620F3
Vacations in Plains 8-6, 608D2
Admits bank overdrafts 8-23, 649C2
Mother wins Synagogue Cncl prize 9-25, 808A3
Protestors seized at church 10-16, 797G2
With family at Camp David 10-25, 961E1

POLITICS—*See also POLLS, WATERGATE in this section below*
Sends PR gov message 1-2, 16G2
Names Curtis Dem chrmn 1-6, 14D2
Cong declares pres winner 1-6, 14F2
Ford State of Union message 1-12, 13G1, D2
White House receptions 1-21, 53G1
Natl com fills posts 1-21, 53A2

1978

MONETARY Developments—*See also BANKS above; also country subheads under FOREIGN Policy above*
Pledges strong $ 1-6, 1D1
Urges energy bill 1-12, 12A1
State of Union Message 1-19, 29C3, 31A1, G2
$ weakness, energy legis logjam linked 2-24—3-6, 119A1
Vs more vigorous $ defns 3-2, 140F3
Sees strong $ 3-9, 160G3-161A1
FRB chrm backs oil import curbs 3-15, 181C1
Anti-inflatn plan cites $ drop impact 4-11, 260E1
Moves to boost sagging $, weakness persists 4-19—7-14, 523F1, C2, A3
Scales down tax-cut plan 5-12, 361B1
At 7-natn Bonn summit; vows import cuts, inflatn measures 7-16—7-17, 543C3, G3, 544A1, D2, 546A1
Worried re $ drop; cites inflatn, trade gap links 8-16, 622C1-D2
At IMF-World Bank mtg, vows strong $ 9-25, 731E2
On boosting $ 10-10, 766G2
Signs suffragette coin bill 10-10, 788B2
Signs '79 forgn aid funds, IMF contributn 10-18, 862F2
$ rescue plan set; $, stock mkt recover from record losses 11-1; reaction 11-2—11-3, 825A1-827A1
Meany scores $ rescue plan 11-1, 863E2
Vows responsible policy 11-2, 862A2
Links $ rescue, oil prices 11-17, 899E3

NARCOTICS & Dangerous Drugs
Signs Venez cooperatn pact 3-28, 233E1
Signs state soc svc claims setlmt 6-12, 465F3
Regrets Bourne prescriptn scandal 7-20, 549F2
Staff use rptd 7-20, 7-22, warns aides 7-24, 568B1
White House pot use rptd 11-19, 943B3

NATO—*See under FOREIGN Policy above*

NATURAL Resources—*See RESOURCES, Natural in this section below*

NEUTRON Bomb—*See ARMAMENTS in this section above; for foreign reaction, see appropriate subheads under FOREIGN Policy above*

OPEC—*See under FOREIGN Policy above*

PARKS & Recreation Areas—*See RESOURCES, Natural in this section below*

PENSIONS & Retirement
Signs mandatory retiremt curb 4-6, 238E2
Double-dipping barred in mil pensn revisn plan 4-10, 281C1
Vetoes DC pension reform 11-4, 897E2

PERSONAL—*See also LANCE, Thomas Bertram*
Ends Plains visit 5-22, 386G2
Vacations in Ida, Wyo 8-19—8-30, death threat rptd hoax 8-30, 664D1
Gets family award from Mormons 11-27, 914G3
In Plains for Christmas, hemorrhoid attack rptd 12-21, 1003E1

PETROLEUM—*See ENERGY above*

POLITICS—*See also POLLS in this section below*
Mondale tours 7 Westn states 1-9—1-13, 34D1
Defends Marston ouster 1-12, 12C2, 32G1; 1-30, 62D1
Humphrey eulogy 1-15, 32A3
Justice Dept clears on Marston ouster 1-24, 62A2, C2

1979

MONETARY Developments—*See also BANKS above; also country subheads under FOREIGN Policy above*
$ rescue plan, paymts surplus linked 6-21, 463C2

NARCOTICS & Dangerous Drugs
Panel rpts pot use up 5-21, 492G2
5 White House copter technicians transferred 9-12, 809A2

NATO—*See under FOREIGN Policy above*

NATURAL Resources—*See RESOURCES, Natural in this section below*

OPEC—*See under FOREIGN Policy above*

PARKS & Recreation Areas—*See RESOURCES, Natural in this section below*

PERSONAL
Brother hosts Libyans 1-9, rptd anti-Semitic remarks spur controversy 1-11–1-13, 31C2; defends brother 2-27, 149E2
Ga bank details favors 1-17, 30E3-31B2
Sister arrested 2-24, 271B3
Brother hospitalized 2-27, 149G2
Trustee buys land from brother 3-1, 'hush money' hinted 3-22, 203G1
Peanut loan scheme alleged 3-11–3-13, spec prosecutor sought 3-13, 183F3-184B2
Brother hospitalized for alcohol abuse 3-7, 271A3
Bagley chrgd re stock fraud 3-14–3-15, 291G3
Peanut probe spec counsel named, GOP scores limits 3-20, 203A1
Peanut probe spec counsel gains new power, GOP reacts 3-23, 301G2-C3
Nephew's marriage rptd 4-4, 271B3
Denies knowledge of peanut loan illegalities 4-10, 263F3
Brother, NBG pres deny peanut loan, '76 campaign link 4-11, 301C3
Ends 10-day vacatn 4-22, 300G3
USSR dissident at church svc 4-29, 318A1
Purported death plot probed 5-5–5-29, 404C1
Brother testifies on family business loans 5-18, 380G3
Peanut business documts rptd subpoenaed 5-27, 5-28, 401A2
Releases financial data 5-30, 5-31, 420F1-D2
Curran blocks Lance witness plea bargain 6-6, 500A3
Option to buy brother's business share rptd 6-19, 500E2
Hawaii vacatn canceled 7-1, 497G2
Stevens sees 'mental problem' 7-20, 531B3
Travels down Mississippi 8-17–8-24, 622F1-623D1
Rabbit attack rptd 8-29, 661G1
Brother at Libya fete 9-1, 688D3
Drops out of foot race 9-15, said healthy 9-16, 700D3-701A1
Signs entertainmt funds bill 9-29, 883F2
Cleared in peanut business probe 10-16, 782G2-783A1
At World Series 10-17, 817D1
Nephew paroled 12-24, 1006B1

Lance Finances—*See LANCE, Thomas Bertram*

PETROLEUM—*See ENERGY above*

POLITICS—*See also POLLS in this section below; for specific issues and reactions to policies, see other headings in this section*
Aide warns Dems face 'new realities' 1-4, 3C2
State of Union Message 1-23, 46F3
Connally announces pres bid 1-24, 70F2
At Rockefeller funeral 2-2, 104D2

1980

MONETARY Developments—*See also BANKS & Banking, FOREIGN Policy in this section above*
Econ Message backs restraint 1-30, 74D1
Reagan 'basic speech' excerpts 2-29, 207B2
Addresses World Bank-IMF mtg, warns vs 'politics' 9-30, 761G3
Signs IMF fund quota hike 10-7, appropriatn rider 12-16, 981E3, 982C1

PERSONAL
Nephew reimprisoned 2-13, 200D2
Son divorced 2-29, 199G1
Releases financial data 4-15, 305B1
Son's ex-wife remarries 6-21, 639B1
In Plains 7-4-7-8, 505G2
Brother registers as Libyan agent 7-14, 542A2
Brother's Libyan role rptd, Sen probe set 7-22—7-24 548F2
Brother's Libyan role controversy grows 7-22—7-31, 569A1-570D1
Brother releases secret cable 8-1, 595D1
Rpts to Sen, natn on brother's case; denies impropriety 8-4, 592F1-593A3; news conf text excerpt 593A2
Brother probed by Justice, Sen 8-4—8-7, 595G1-E3
Brother's Sen probe continues, 2 associates rptd under investigatn 8-19—8-22, 647A1-E2
Brother's Sen probe continues 9-4—9-17, 700D3
Brother's Sen probe concluded 9-22—9-24, critical rpt issued 10-2, 763B3-764F1
Issues rules re family dealings 10-1, 764G1
Mother has hip surgery 10-2, 908E2
Faulted on brother's Sen probe 10-28—11-1, 841E1
Discusses future plans 11-12, 865E1-A3
At Camp David 12-13, 956C2
Breaks collar bone 12-27, 989A3

PETROLEUM—*See ENERGY in this section above*

POLITICS—*See also POLLS in this section below*
FEC OKs Bush, Kennedy funds 1-2, 1-4, 5C2
Mondale, wife in Iowa 1-4—1-10, 12F2-13B1
Brown scores Ia debate withdrawal 1-9, 13A2
Mondale debates Kennedy, Brown 1-12, 32D2

1976

Record cited 512A2
Sees natl com; outlines campaign strategy, lauds Strauss 7-16, 532F2
Ford scores ticket 7-17, 531F2
Scores Nixon pardon 7-20, 532G1
Names Jordan, Lipshutz top campaign aides 7-20, 565F3
Sees Time, Hearst editors 7-22, 551E1
Sees Talmadge 7-24, 551F1
Scores lack of ldrshp, family structure 8-3, 564D2
Names Califano spec adviser 8-3, 564C3
Meets DC press editors 8-4, 564E3
Sees natl com; plans 'aggressive' campaign 8-4, 565D3
Vows 'clean' govt 8-11, 585A2-A3
Meets Ital-Amer group 8-12, 616G3
Disavows 'dumping' memo 8-13, 616B3
Briefed on issues 8-16—8-18, 617E1
On GOP conv attacks vs 8-17, 617D2
Scores GOP policy of 'drift', 'continuity' of Nixon 8-20, 632E1
Visits W Coast, Ia 8-22—8-25, 631D2-632E1
Scores Ford list of issues 8-30, 645A2
Sees Jews in Ga 8-30; in DC mtgs with bishops, NY mtgs with Jews, Ital-Amers 8-31, 645A2, D2
Dole scores veto criticism 9-3, 665G3
Kicks off campaign 9-6—9-9, 663F2-664F3
Scores Ford ldrshp 9-6, 663F2, 664G1
Seeks Southern, Midwest votes 9-10—9-16, 686B2
Vows voter registratn at 18 9-10, 686C2
Dole attacks 9-10, 9-11, 686G3, 687A1
Ford hits 'trust me' 9-15, 685F2
RC bishops assert neutrality 9-16, 686G1
In Miss with Eastland, Stennis 9-17, 704E1, G2
Playboy interview disclosed 9-20, regrets LBJ remark 9-22, 704F1
'Whistlestop' tour 9-20, 704F1, A3
Explains Playboy interview, regrets LBJ remark 9-24, 9-27, 724C2
Addresses Polish-Amer conv 9-24, 725A1
Sharpens attack vs Ford in NE 9-30—10-2, 742C3, 743A1
Dole attacks in NE swing 10-1—10-5, 743E1-E2
Voter mail registratn bill not cleared 10-2, 883E1
Butz, Playboy remarks compared 10-3, 744D2
Dole scores 10-6, 10-8, 763E3-764A1
Links Ford to Nixon 10-9, 10-10, 762C2, F2
Sees Polish-, Greek-Amers 10-10, 762F2
Baptist ldr scores on Playboy 10-10, 763D2
Lauds Daley 10-11, 762G2
Campaign tactics scored 10-11, 763E2
In NY, NC 10-14, 10-19, 827E1
Dole, Mondale debate Playboy 10-15, 783F3
Ford continues criticism, on Playboy 10-15—10-20, 784E1-D3
Wires Ford on chrgs 10-15; Ford replies 10-16, 785B1
Scores Nixon, Ford programs 10-15, 10-19, 785E1
Dole attacks 10-16—10-26, 804C1-E2
At Al Smith fete in NYC 10-21, 785E1
Urges big vote turnout 10-23, 10-26, 803B2, E2
Final tour 10-29—11-1, 826D3-827B2
Final TV plea 11-1, 826G2
Dole attacks 11-1, 827B3
Elected 11-2, Ford concedes 11-3, 817D1-819D2
Popular, electoral vote table 818C1, map 819A1
Gold price reactn to electn 11-2—11-15, 915G3
Stock mkt reactn 11-3—11-4, 826B1
Forgn pol, econ reactn 11-3—11-4, 826C1-F2
Photo with wife 11-3, 826D1
Thanks NYC 11-3, 845E3
Holds news conf 11-4, 819D2
Upset at TV coverage 11-5, 845F1
Caddell electn analysis 11-5, 11-11, 845G1
Sees unifying effect 11-22, 880G3
Electoral College votes 12-13, 979A1
Final tally rptd 12-18; table 979C1, A2
Primary Results
Wins NH primary 2-24, reacts 2-25, 148E1, F2, B3
4th in Mass primary 3-2, 165A1
Wins Vt primary 3-2, 165G1
Wins Fla primary 3-9, 179D1
Wins Ill primary 3-16, 196D2-D3, 197C1
Wins NC primary 3-23, 213G3, 214C1
Wins Wis primary 4-6, 245B1
Wins Pa primary 4-27, 304E3, 305C1
Wins Tex primary 5-1; Ind, Ga, Ala 5-4, 322G2, G3, 323D1-F2
Church wins in Neb 5-11, 342D1
Edges Udall in Conn vote 5-11, 342E3
Wins in Mich, loses in Md 5-18, 356D2, F2, 357E1, G1
Wins in Ark, Tenn, Ky 5-25, 373D1, F2, 374B2
Wins in SD, loses Mont, RI 6-1, 389F2-390B1, B2, A3
Wins in Ohio, loses in NJ, Calif 6-8, 408F2-409D1, B2

1977

Mass town mtg 3-16, 187D3, 190A3
Sees Carey, Beame in NYC 3-17, 191B1
Asks election law changes 3-22, 210C2
Confers with Ford 3-24, 236C2
Urged to consult with state party units 4-1, 250G3
Early poll ratings high 4-4, 251C1
Nixon offers assistance 4-19, 321E3
On Ford criticism 4-22, 321D3
Backs spec prosecutor bill 5-3, 338F1
Meany, McGovern on image-making 5-4, 5-7, O'Neill defends 5-8, 364F2, B3
Scores liberals' criticism 5-12, McGovern replies 5-13, 380F3, 381D2
On Caddell memo, liberal threat 5-12, 381B1
Thinks Nixon violated law 5-12, 381C2
Visits Calif, sees Brown 5-17, 381E2
Sen com clears Lance 7-12—7-25, 573C3-574D2; **for subsequent developments, see LANCE, Thomas B.**
Tours South 7-21—7-22, 574G3
Miss town mtg 7-21, 575A1; 589E3
Backs public financing of Sen campaigns 7-28, 574F3
Cargo preference backing held 'payoff' 8-1, 8-27, 719B3-G3
To reimburse bank for plane use 8-24, 649E3
Stumps in NJ 9-10, Va 9-24, 761C1
Powell apologizes to Percy 9-14, 701D3
Halts farm aide's personal lobbying 9-30, 773C1
Snubs Koch after protest 10-4, 761B1
Cross country tour 10-21—10-23, 817A1
On 'style/substance' criticism 10-27, 813F2
Registratn issues lose in Ohio, Washn 11-8, 879F2
Curtis to resign Dem post 12-7, 960B3
Jordan bars 4th term 12-10, 1005C3
Ford visits 12-20, 976E3
TV interview on 1st yr 12-28, 1001G3
Names White as Dem chrmn 12-28, 1005D3

1978

At Dem natl chrmn installatn, vows closer party ties 1-27, 87A3
On post-presidential plans 1-30, 62E3
Visits RI, Me, NH, Del; holds news conf, town mtgs; backs Dem sens reelectn bids 2-17—2-20, 123D1-C3
Defends apptmt of US attys 2-17, 123E2
On Marston replacemt delay 3-9, 161A1
Marston successor picked 3-23, 243C3
Black ldrs critical 4-10, 568A3
On Admin image, reelectn plans 4-11, 260D3, E3
Cabt, staff strategy sessns 4-15—4-16; image chngs rptd planned 4-17—4-29, 306G2
Testimony presented at Ga corruptn trial 4-19, 309E3
Sen com finds no Marston cover-up, Mathias disputes 4-24, 309A3
Tours 4 Westn states 5-3—5-5, new style rptd 5-6, 320A3, G3, 321D3, 342A1, G1-D2
Denies liability to Dems 5-4, 321A2
Visits Tenn 5-22, 386G2-B3
Visits Ill, W Va 5-25—5-26, 404B3-405A1
Gulf '70 illegal paymt rptd 6-2, 449D1
Dems chng pres nominatn rules 6-9, 448D2
Affirms religious role 6-16, 510B1
Visits Texas 6-23—6-24, 490F3, 509F3
Campaign com fined $1200 for '76 plane use 6-26, 509A3
Riley wins SC gov runoff 6-27, 510D1
To back PR status vote 7-25, 627G1-A2
White on '80 prospects 7-26, 682A3
Crane scores ldrship, sets pres bid 8-2, 606C1
Visits Va, NC 8-3, 8-5, 605D3
Expects Kennedy reelectn support 8-11, 682E2-A3
Visits farm belt 8-14, 626C1
DC voting amendmt clears Cong 8-22, 661D2
Dem govs' back performance 8-28, 682G1
Jordan, Kirbo linked to Vesco 'pol fix,' denials issued 9-1—9-15; Anderson revises article 9-11, 719D3
Backs GSA paymts probe 9-4, 685E2
Kirbo to monitor GSA probe 9-7, 715D1
Stumps 4 states 9-22—9-23, 736A1
Visits W Va 10-7, 769A2
Visits Tenn, Fla 10-26; 4 states in NE 10-28, 831A2, B2
Signs Amer Samoa House del bill 10-31, 1003A1
Takes 6-state tour 11-2—11-3, 862G1
Signs Presidential Records Act 11-4, 897D2
Gives midterm assessment 11-6, 862A1
Electn results 11-7, 852F3, 853A1, E1
Evaluates electn results, Meany differs 11-9, 875A2-D2
On presidency, goals 11-13, 914B2
Prefers one-term to inflatn plan failure 11-30, 917F3
Dems hold midterm conf 12-8—12-10, addresses 12-8, 956D1-C3
Downplays Dem, Kennedy dissent; assesses '78, noncommital re '80 12-12, 956D3-957B2

1979

AFL-CIO offcls assess 2-19, 2-21, 149E1
Addresses govs 2-25, 2-27, 150C2
Revisits Elk City (Okla) 3-24, 230C2
FEC OKs primary spending 4-2, 265A1
Ex-aide calls 'arrogant' 4-22, 300B3
Visits NH 4-25, 300A1
Dobelle cited as campaign com head 4-25, 300B1
Favors 6-yr pres term 4-27, 326E1
Lauds Ribicoff 5-3, 326A2
Visits Iowa, Calif 5-4—5-5, 346C3-347E1
Ex-aide scores staff 5-18, 627F2
Urges blacks to vote 5-20, 384F2-A3
Draft-Kennedy move launched 5-23, 384C2
Addresses Dem Natl Com 5-25, 401D1
'76 campaign ad financing probed 5-25, 401A3
Black pol conv splits on backing 5-25—5-27, 423A2
Hosts House Dems 6-1—6-2, 418B2
Campaign com billed $50,203 6-4, 419G2
Scores spec interest groups 6-7, 420B1
Anderson enters pres race 6-8, 439E2
Confident vs Kennedy '80 bid 6-12, 440D1
'76 campaign ad financing improprieties denied 6-22, 500B2
ADA opts for Kennedy 6-24, 482C2
Hooks sees Kennedy edge, grudging black support 6-24, 559E3
NYC chosen '80 Dem conv site 6-28, 518E1
Reviews policy at Camp David, sets key natl speech 7-6—7-12, 513C2
Dem govs back reelectn 7-8, 518B1
Sen rejects direct pres vote 7-10, 515C1
Campaign funds rptd 7-12, 594B1
Asks mass Cabt resignatn, names Jordan staff chief 7-17; fires 4 offcrs, reactn 7-19—7-20; defends moves 7-20, 529A1-531G3
Staff evaluatn forms issued 7-17, 529G1, 530C2, 531C1
Urban League vs 'dumping' 7-22, 560E1
Jackson sees Kennedy '80 bid 7-24, responds 7-25, 556B2-D2
McGovern backs Kennedy '80 bid 7-26, 556A2
Byrd defends '80 bid 7-28, 593E3
Brown forms pres com 7-30, 593F1
6 union ldrs back reelectn 7-30, 593B3
Thanks Camp David participants 7-30, 608F3-609A1
Visits Ky, Ind 7-31, Md 8-7, 592E2
Kennedy primary tension rptd 8-2, Mass legis bars date chng 8-6, 592G3-593E1
OKs pol '80 Census hiring 8-9, 631E1
Staff shuffled 8-10, 608C2
Bell scores performance 8-14, 608C3
Travels down Mississippi 8-17—8-24, 622F1-623D1
Tex gov discounts Kennedy '80 run 8-19, 627D3
Cranston vs '80 nominatn support 8-20, 627B3
'76 general campaign financing cleared 8-21, 661G3
Visits Iowa 8-22, 662D2
Vesco jury foreman quits, claims cover-up 8-29, 647E2; chrgs denied 8-31, juror resignatn rejected 9-7, 725F2-E3
Mondale '80 pres race suggested 9-5, 662B1
Kennedy considers '80 race 9-6—9-11, 679E3-680A2
Orders Kennedy Secret Svc protectn 9-20, 723G3
Holds NYC town mtg, comments on Kennedy 9-25, sends Kennedy letter 9-26, 723C2-F3
Gets NEA endorsemt 9-28, 782E2
Kennedy pres funding challenged 10-4, 783A3
Comments on '80 race 10-9, 766F3-767D1
In Southwest 10-10—10-11, Midwest 10-15—10-16, NJ 10-25; with Kennedy at JFK library dedicatn 10-20, rivalry intensifies 10-22, 807C2-808F1, 905D1
Fla pres caucuses 10-13, win rptd 10-19, 783B1
Clark joins Kennedy campaign 10-19, 847C2
Fundraiser joins Kennedy camp 10-24, 847G1
Pres campaign muted 10-24—12-13, 961G1-B3
At DC Dem rally 10-24, 961E2
Secret tapes denied 10-29, 869F1
Mayor Byrne endorses Kennedy 10-30, 847B2
Kennedy attacks 11-2—12-13, 961F3, 962B1-B2
Wins Ia straw vote 11-3, Kennedy '80 debate set 11-6, 866G2-A3
Expects Cabt campaign role 11-5, 961F2
Strauss named campaign com head 11-6, at Dem Natl Com mtg 11-9, 961A2, E2
Kennedy enters pres race 11-7, 847C1
Brown enters pres race 11-8, 847F2
White endorses 11-8, 961C2
Attacks Kennedy positns 11-15, 885E1
Wins Fla straw vote 11-18, 887C1
Goldschmidt threatens Chicago aid loss 11-20, 983G3
FCC backs on TV ad bid 11-20, 918G3
Mondale, kin campaign 11-28—12-8, 961B3-E3
Brown invited into Ia debate 12-4, 962A3

1980

ILGWU backs ticket 1-15, 32A3
Mondale ends Iowa tour 1-19, 50F2-A3
Stresses forgn policy role 1-20, 50G1
Bush attacks econ, forgn policies 1-20, 50E2
Beats Kennedy in Iowa caucus 1-21, 50D1
Kennedy makes major speech; rebutted 1-28, 74E2, 75B1
Wife campaigns in Buffalo 1-31, Mondale in Maine 2-5, 91D2
Kennedy stages mock debate, vs lack of dialogue 2-7, 91F1, A2
Wins Maine caucus vote 2-10, 109C1, D1
Kennedy scores debate bar 2-12; defends 2-13, 109G3, 110C2
Kennedy assails policies in NH, Mass 2-14—2-20, 130G1
Wins NH primary 2-26, 142E2, F2, E3
Bush 'basic speech' excerpts 3-3, 208E2, F3
Wins Vt primary, loses Mass 3-4, 166C2-G3
Connally 'basic speech' excerpts 3-7, 184C2
Connally calls popularity 'fantasy' 3-9, 184B1
Wins Fla, Ga, Ala primaries 3-11, 182G3
Wins 4 state caucus votes 3-11—3-12, 209B1
Ford attacks Admin 3-12, 207G1
Ford visits 3-13, 207F1
FALN raids Chicago hq 3-15, 208B3-209A1
Wins PR primary 3-16, 208B2
Wins Ill primary, delegate count cited 3-18, 206B2-207A1
Loses NY, Conn primaries; delegate strength tops 50% 3-25, 221A2, A3, C3
Wins Wis, Kan primaries 4-1, 246E1-G2
Brown ends pres bid 4-1, 246C3
AFSCME backs Kennedy 4-2, 247G1
Wins La primary 4-5, 264F3, G3
Bush, Reagan, Kennedy score 4-7—4-10, 264C2-D3
Supporters threatened by FALN 4-7, 309B1
Terkel: same as Reagan 4-11, 288D3
Kennedy financial data scored 4-15, 305E1
Anderson comments 4-20, 328D1
Kennedy: 'no more Carter' 4-21, 304F1
Loses Pa primary 4-22, 303G3, 304A2
GOP target in Pa 4-22, 304D2
Strauss on Kennedy effort 4-23, 304B2
Anderson announces independent bid 4-24, 303F3
Edged by Kennedy in Mich 4-26, 327E2
Kennedy supporters' petitn rejected by Sup Ct 4-28, 369A2
Sears: Anderson could win 4-29, 328E1
Ends campaign travel ban 4-30, 328F1
White readies fall campaign 5-2, Kennedy assails 5-5, 366E3-367A1
Wins Tex primary 5-3, 342A2, E2
Ill gov scores 5-4, 342E3
Carey asks open conventn 5-5, 342E3-343A1
Wins Tenn, Ind, NC primaries; loses DC 5-6, 341E2-342A2
At Phila town mtg 5-9, 367D1, F2
Byrd urges debate 5-10, 367A1
Wins Md, Neb primaries 5-13, 366D2-D3
Kennedy debate rejected 5-15, 383A2
On incumbency at campaign hq 5-19, 399B3
Wins Ore primary 5-20, 383D1
Bush ends pres bid 5-26, 398G2
Wins Ark, Ky, Nev, Ida primaries 5-27, 399B1-E2
Bars debate with Anderson, Reagan favors 5-27, 399A3
Reagan would debate 5-27, 399B3
Campaigns in Ohio 5-29, 423C3
Kennedy calls Reagan 'clone' 5-30, bars platform offer 6-1, 422G3
Makes overtures to Kennedy 5-31—6-4, mtg set 6-4, 422G2
Final primaries held; gains delegate majority 6-3, 422D2, 423B2-G2, 424C1
Pres delegate count, primary vote total 6-4, 596A2
Meets Kennedy 6-5, 423D1
Meets with state Dem chrmn 6-6, 439B1
Jordan joins campaign com 6-11, 439A1
ADA head sees disaffectn 6-15, 480G1
Voter discontent rptd 6-18, 493B3
Anderson: on the wane 6-20, 493A2
Dem platform drafted 6-24, Kennedy vows floor fight 6-25, 479F2-480D1
NEA renews endorsemt 7-3, 505D2
At Merced (Calif) town mtg 7-4, 505E2
GOP scores Detroit visit 7-8, 505B2
GOP plank: must go 7-10, 506G2
GOP conv attacks 7-14—7-17, 529G2-535E1
GOP platform adopted; text 7-15, 536E1-G3
Anti-Reagan strategy set 7-15, 549C3
Reagan nominatn acceptance speech 7-17, 531B2, 532A2, 533C1
Congratulates Reagan on nominatn; seeks debate, Reagan accepts 7-17, 532D1
Tours Fla 7-17, 532D1
Reagan campaign themes set 7-19, 549B3
Meets with conv delegates, scores Ford vp 'debacle' 7-19, 549D3
Visits Ky, Dallas 7-21, 549E3
Kennedy quits B Carter Libyan probe 7-23, 549E1
Open conv move forms, popularity dips 7-25—7-31; Kennedy-Anderson news conf 7-31, 570E1-D3
Scores 'open conv' 8-1, 8-4, 596A3
Byrd joins open conv move 8-2, 596F2
Dem govs neutral on open conv 8-3—8-5, 596A1

1976

1977

POLLS
Standings drop 10-10, 10-18, 817F1
On Caddell-Rafshoon mtg, rating drop 10-27, 814A1
Commentary survey sees Mideast policy harm 10-31, 831F1

1978

POLLS
On poll-standings drop 3-2, 141E1
Ratings plummet 3-30, 4-24, 307G3
Econ issues rating rptd down 4-12, 260A3
Strategy sessns held 4-15—4-16, 306A3
Trails in popularity vs Kennedy, Ford, Reagan 5-7—5-24; says not concerned 5-25, 404B3, C3
Dem chrmn explains low ratings 7-26, 682C3
Ratings still bleak 8-10—8-27, 682A2
Camp David summit boosts ratings 9-22, 9-24, 736B1
Rating steady at 50% 12-28, 1003C1

1979

Announces reelectn bid, urges Mondale renominatn 12-4, 918A2, F2, A3
Bell testifies in Vesco case 12-4; Carter to videotape testimony 12-5; Civiletti quits probe 12-7, 943C2-C3
Wife, Mondale in NY 12-5, 918A3
NOW vs reelectn 12-9, 961A3
Feinstein voted San Fran mayor 12-11, 946F3
Declines Ia debate 12-28; reactn 12-28–12-31, 983E2

POLLS
Mideast role spurs gain 3-29, 231D3
Trails Kennedy 4-26, 384F2
Says not 'afraid' of polls 5-25, 401D2
Labor ldr compares Truman 6-7, 419G3
Gallup approval rating 29% 7-1, 497G1
Ratings still bleak 7-1, 7-9, 514D1
AP-NBC rating drops 9-13, 680A2
Kennedy endorsemt by Mayor Byrne linked 10-30, 847B2
Kennedy ahead 11-4, 847D2
Iran crisis spurs gain 12-5, 918E2
Takes poll leads 12-11, 962C3, E3

1980

Denies impropriety re brother; rpts to Sen, natn 8-4, 593A1-A3, G3
Kennedy post-conv unity pledged; platform, rules debate agreed 8-5, 596E1
Kennedy ends bid after open conv move fails 8-11, 609C1, E1
Kennedy wins econ, other platform planks 8-12, 609D1, 610F2-611C1
Kennedy speech stirs conv 8-12, 609D1, 610D1, 613D2-614B3
Wins renominatn on 1st ballot, blacks make token challenge 8-13—8-14, 609C1, 611G2-E3
Brown pledges support 8-13, 611G3
Issues platform statemt; Kennedy endorses, conv adopts 8-13, 609D1, 611C1; text excerpts 614C2-615C3
Photo with Kennedy 8-14, 609A1
Renominatn acceptance speech 8-14, 609E1, 611G2, 612D1-A2; text excerpts 612E2-613C3
Addresses Dem Natl Com, states basic issues 8-15, 629C3
Reagan to ignore 'distorted' chrgs 8-16, 629C2
Endorsed by AFL-CIO cncl 8-20, 647F2-B3
Kennedy greets warmly, urges reelectn 8-21, 629A3, B3
Endorsed by AFT 8-21, 646G2
Kennedy: to 'campaign actively' 8-25, 646G2
Lucey scores record 8-25, 646C3, D3
Econ renewal plan offered; Reagan scores; Carey vows support; other reactn 8-28, 663A1-D3
Anderson platform scores 8-30, 664G3
Launches campaign in Tuscumbia, Reagan notes Klan 'birthplace' 9-1; remark stirs furor 9-2, 663D3, 664D2
Bush scores Admin record, coins 'Carterism' 9-2—10-7, 780C3, 781A1, B2
FEC issues campaign rules 9-5, Admin sets Cabt guidelines 9-8, 681D2
NY Liberal Party endorses Anderson 9-6, 681E1
Rejcts 3-way debate 9-9, controversy ensues 9-9—9-10, 680D2
Kraft cocaine probe rptd, steps down as campaign mgr 9-14, 700B1; for subsequent developments, see KRAFT, Tim
Attacks Reagan in Tex visit 9-15, 699C1
Reagan asks equal TV time 9-18, 698A3
Seeks debate with Reagan 9-18, 698E3
Reagan, Anderson debate on TV; absence noted 9-21, 721C2, D3
Raises warmonger issue 9-22—9-23; Reagan, Anderson protest 9-23, 722F2
Reagan declines debate 9-25, 739F3
Dems for Reagan formed 9-29, 738F2
In NYC 9-29, Niagara Falls 10-1, 738G3
Warns vs Reagan win 10-6, 762B3
Reagan deplores campaign 'hysteria' 10-7, 763C2
Admits attacks on Reagan 'ill-advised' 10-8, shifts tone 10-9, 778A2, C2
Says Reagan 'bad' for US 10-10, 778D3
Stumps in NE, Ill; Kennedy, Jackson pitch in 10-13, 10-15, 778E3
Commoner uses vulgar radio ad 10-15, 818A3
Shares dais with Reagan in NY 10-16, 803G1-A2
TV debate with Reagan set 10-21, 801F3
Questns Reagan ability 10-21, 802G3
Reagan calls 'incompetent' 10-22, 10-23, 802A2
Kennedy stumps Tex 10-22, 817C1
Mondale sees close Carter win 10-26, 816C3
Chrgs Reagan 'flipflop' on issues 10-27, 816A3
Debates Reagan on TV 10-28, 813A1-815E3
Anderson answers debate questns on cable TV 10-28, declares 'draw' 10-29, 815F3
Israel vs Weizman electn trip 10-28, 830D2
Says Reagan age not issue 10-29, 816E2
Reagan chrgs ineptitude 10-29—11-3, 840A1, A2, A3
Winds up campaign 10-29—11-3, 841A1
Press endorsemts rptd 11-1, 841E3-G3
NRA endorses Reagan 11-1, 844F1
Reagan favored by London gamblers 11-3, 844F3
Reagan wins electn; breaks Dem coalitn, wins Sen control 11-4, 837C1-838B3
Concedes electn 11-4, vows 'fine transitn' 11-4—11-5, 837E2, 838B3
Popular vote table 838A1; electoral vote table, map 839A1, D3
On future role 11-12, 865G1-A3
On early concessn 11-12, 866D1
FEC paymt $29.4 mln 11-13, 866G1
Still DC 'outsider' 11-18, 880F3
Electoral College votes 12-15, 956F1
Gets '80 census rpt 12-31, 982D3

POLLS
Leads Kennedy, GOP 1-8, 1-9, 13F1, F3
Iran crisis support ebbs 1-10, 32G2
Leads in Ia poll 1-11, 33G1
Increases lead over Kennedy 2-20, 130D2
Trails Ford, leads Reagan 3-9, 208B1
NY pre-primary polls cited 3-25, 221B2
Leads Kennedy 3-31, Reagan 4-1, 246E3-247A1
Leads in Wis primary 4-1, 246G2
50% dissatisfied with Carter, Reagan choice 4-18, 304E3, 305B1
Leads in ABC poll 5-6, 342G1
Tied with Reagan 5-19—6-23, 452G1
Leads Kennedy 2 to 1 6-1, 452E2

1976

1977

POVERTY—*See WELFARE and Poverty in this section below*
PRESS
AP, UPI interview 1-24, 51B3
'Fireside chat' 2-2, 75A1
News conf 2-8, 88A2, 89D1
News conf in Plains 2-12, 110C1, D3
News conf 2-23, 123E3, 126B2
Post mtg on paymts story rptd 2-25, 2-28, 151G2
Call-in radio broadcast 3-5, 171A1-G3
News conf 3-9, 165B1, B2, 172G1, D3, 173A2, 178C3, 202E3
News conf 3-24, 210E1, 230B1
News conf 4-15, 294D1, 298F2
TV addresses on energy 4-18, 4-20, 289A1-290B3, 294D2-295C3
News conf 4-22, 321D1-D3
Interview aired in Eur 5-2, 338A2
News conf 5-12, 380F3-381C2
Live TV program in Calif 5-17, 381B3
News conf 5-26, 417B1
Magazine publishers interview 6-10, 460C2
News conf, summary 6-30, 510A1, 514C1, 515A1, 535A3
News conf, summary 7-12, 533A1-534E1
News conf, summary 7-28, 570D1, 573F2, 574E2, G2
Interviewed, sees energy crisis 7-29, 591E3
News conf 8-6, 609D2
News conf 8-23, 649F1
Phone talks to San Fran news dir mtg 9-15, 701G3
News conf on Lance 9-21, 718A1
News conf, energy plea 9-29, 757C1
Addresses farm editors 9-30, 773G1
Meets farm editors 10-2, 761E2
Seeks more public broadcasting funds 10-6, 846A1
Asks USIA reorgnizatn 10-11, 797C2
News conf 10-13, 772E2, 773B1, 775F1
News conf 10-27, 813A1; 852A1
Energy address on TV 11-8, 854A1
News conf 11-10, 877C1-A2
News conf 11-30, 913A2-914A2
News conf 12-15, 954C3
TV interview 12-28, 1001G3
News conf in Warsaw 12-30, 1001B1
PUBLIC Works—*See LABOR above*
RACISM—*See HUMAN & Civil Rights and MINORITIES above*
RELIGION
Plains church rejcts black 1-9, 53C2
Inaugural 1-20, 25E2
Joins DC Baptist church 1-23, 53C2
Gets clerics protest on Korea 4-19, 305C3
Meets with Coptic Pope 4-20, 471G2
On Plains church donatns 6-24, 499F2
Miss town mtg topic 7-21, 575F1
Sister: charismatic Christian 7-21, 620G3
Graham bears message to Hungary 9-8, 732D1
RESIGNATIONS
Cabinet & Subcabinet
Flaherty, dep atty gen 11-26, 914D2
Lance, Budget dir 9-21, 718A1
Meyer, Agri asst secy 10-20, 814B2
Miscellaneous
Hills, SEC chrmn 3-2, 211B2
Pepitone, Selective Svc dir 3-9, 211A2
Robson, CAB chrmn 211A2
Schultze, Econ Policy Group co-chrmn 3-15, 211A2
Sirica, fed judge 10-4, 927E3
Walsh, HEW inspector 3-6, 235F3
RESOURCES, Natural
Inaugural 1-20, 25G2, 27C1
Statemt to world 1-20, 26G1
OKs Colo drought aid 1-29, 76G3
Plans strip-mining bill 2-2, 75E1
Cuts water project funds 2-22, 126D1
More water project cuts studied 2-23—3-24, 209D3
Addresses UN 3-17, 185E2
Requests drought aid 3-23, 210B2
Backs some water projects 4-18, 299E2
Water project funds impoundmt barred 5-3, 365C2
Cong sets '78 budget target 5-17, 405A1
Environmt message 5-23, 404B2, F2
Would veto water projects 5-26, 417C1, D1; O'Neill cautns 6-1, 459A3
Cong water projct differences eased 6-15, 459E3
Water project funds OKd by Cong 7-25, 592G2-B3
Signs water research, saline conversn bill 8-2, 689E2
Signs strip mine bill 8-3, 592F1
Signs water projct bill 8-8, 609D2

1978

POSTAL Service
'Citizen rate' mail proposal rejctd 5-12, 389F1
POVERTY—*See WELFARE and Poverty in this section below*
PRESS
News conf 1-12, 11F3-12D3
News conf 1-30, 57E2, 62C1, E2; 163D2
2d fireside chat 2-1, 58E2
News conf in RI 2-17, 123F1
News conf 3-2, 140D2-141B2
News conf 3-9, 159F2, 160F1, B2, D3-161D1; 178F2
Addresses editors, broadcast execs 4-7, 255B3
Addresses newspaper editors 4-11, 259E2, 260C3-261C1
TV address on Canal 4-18, 274A1
News conf 4-25, 306G3-307F3
News conf in Ore 5-4, 320G3-321D2
News conf in Chicago 5-25, 404B3, 418B1
News conf 6-14, 446B3-E3
News conf 6-26, 490D2, 491A1-F2
News conf 7-20, 549B2
Addresses mag editors 8-11, 682F2-A3
Anderson revises Vesco 'pol fix' chrg 9-11, 719D3
TV news conf 9-28, 751E3
News conf 10-10, 766F2
Unveils anti-inflatn plan 10-24, 805B2
News conf in KC 11-9, 873C1, 874E3, 875A2
Moyers TV interview 11-13, 914B2
News confs 11-16, 11-30, 916F2-B3, 917E1, D3
Broadcast eds interview 11-17, 899E3
News confs 11-30, 936B2-A3; 12-12, 956D3, 983D2
Walters TV interview 12-14, 979G2, F3
PUBLIC Works—*See LABOR above*
REGULATORY Agencies
Vows regulatn cost cutting 10-24, cites Kahn success 10-25, 805D3, 806F2
RELIGION
Backs Baptist missn progrm 1-30, 62E3
Sees as 'stabilizing factor' 2-18, 123B3
Mormons give family award 11-27, 914G3
On rights abuses 12-6, 934D1
RESIGNATIONS
Bourne, drug abuse aide 7-20, 549F2
Burns, FRB 1-31, 161C3
Costanza, pres asst 8-1, 605G3
Fraser, labor-mgt panel 7-19, 611G1
Jenkins, TVA bd 5-5, 390A2
Payton, Peace Corps dir 11-24, 915F1
Singlaub, Ft McPherson head 4-28, 321E2
Wagner, TVA bd 5-18, 390G1
Warnke, arms control dir 10-10, 766F3
RESOURCES, Natural—*See also METALS above*
Budget proposals 1-23, 44F2, 47D2, 48G1; table 45D2
Signs timber sales sealed-bid repeal 2-20, 218A2
Signs wilderness area bill 2-24, 218A2
Signs Redwood Park bill 3-27, 218E1
Asks timber harvest rise 4-11, 260A1
On water, forest policy, Indian land claims 5-4, 320G3-321E1
Unveils natl water plan 6-6; reactn 6-6—6-7, 426A3
Asks 26 water projcts 6-9, House bill veto threatened 6-9, 6-14, 446E2, C3
Signs land bur authrzn 8-20, 697C2
Vetoes public works bill, House upholds 10-5, 765A1-D2, 769B2
Signs timber land purchase registratn 10-14, 897B2
Signs natl parks authorzn 11-10, 897A2
Protects Alaska lands 12-1, 936F3
Environmtlists laud Alaska conservatn, water projcts veto 12-20, 1009D1

1979

POVERTY—*See WELFARE and Poverty in this section below*
PRESS
News conf 1-17, 26G1, 29C2-30D1, C3, 251D2
News conf 1-26, 66D2, 70A1
News conf; warns staff re leaks 2-12, 106A1, 109C3-110B1
Addresses editors' conf 2-22, 124C1
News conf 2-27, 144B1, 145D3, 149G1-D3
Addresses broadcast assn 3-25, 230E1
Urges restricted newsroom searches 4-2, 264D3
Energy message on TV 4-5, 250B2-251A1
News conf 4-10, 263C2-G3, 264B1, B2
Addresses Newspr Publishers 4-25, 294A2
Sees newspaper editors 4-27, 326E1
News conf 4-30, 319A1, 324C2
News conf in Iowa 5-4, 346C3, E3
News conf 5-29, 396B1, 401F3-402D1
News conf 6-12, 438F2
News conf 7-1, 494C2
Energy mtgs covered; TV address announced 7-2, canceled 7-4, 497A3
TV address on new energy plan 7-15, 532A1
Press conf, plans regional mtgs 7-25, 555F2, E3, 556A1
TV address on Sovt-Cuba troop issue 10-1, 737A1
News conf 10-9, 766A1, F3-767B2
FCC backs on TV ad bid 11-20, 918G3
News conf 11-28, 894G2
Pol broadcast aired 12-4, 918A3, 919C1
PUBLIC Works—*See LABOR above*
REGULATORY Agencies
Regulatory calendar issued 2-28, 164E2
Outlines reform proposals 3-25, 230E1
RELIGION
Vs pro-schl prayer legis 4-10, 263F3
Sees ldrs at Camp David 7-6—7-11, 513F2
Thanks Camp David participants 7-30, 608F3-609A1
Discloses Park conversn effort 8-5, 639B2
Sees Pope at White House 10-6, 757E1, 759B3; photo 758C1
Lauds papal visit 10-9, 767F1
Quotes Pope in KC speech 10-15, 807G2
RESIGNATIONS
Adams, Transportatn secy 7-20, 529D1
Bagley CFTC resignatn cited 9-5, 681C2
Bell, atty gen 7-19, 529C1
Blumenthal, Treas secy 7-19, 529C1
Cabt, staff 7-17, 529F1, B2
Califano, HEW secy 7-19, 529C1
Castillo, INS head 8-10, 630D3
Clark, refugee aide 10-30, 847C2
Horgan, pres asst 8-9, 747B3
Kennedy, FDA comr 4-17, 310G2
Kreps, Commerce secy 10-4, 829B2
Lipshutz, pres counsel 8-10, 608C2
Lucey, Mex amb 10-8, 793A3
O'Leary, Energy dep secy 7-9, 514A1
O'Neal, ICC chrmn 10-4, 831B1
Schlesinger, Energy secy 7-20, 529D1
Seevers CFTC resignatn cited 9-5, 681C2
Solomon, GSA head 3-21, 232C2
Straus, VOA dir 10-1, 771D1
Strauss, Mideast amb 11-6, 961B2
Young, UN amb 8-15, 605B1
RESOURCES, Natural
Budget proposals 1-22, 45D3; table 42F2
State of Union Message 1-23, 46G2, 47C2, 48A1
Proposes Cabt-level dept 3-1, 164B1
Proposes forest lands bill 4-16, 282E1
Drops Cabt-level dept plan 5-15, 365A2
Proposes water projct cost-sharing 5-16, 365E2-A3
House OKs Alaska land bill 5-16, 367A1
Orders more timber sales 6-11, 441A1
Backs westn states water control 10-10, 807E2

1980

Voter discontent rptd 6-3, 423B1
Job rating declines 6-16, 452C2
Job rating at new low; trails Reagan, Anderson in Calif 7-30, 570E1, B2, C2
Doubts veracity 8-4, 593E1
Ratings revive 8-17, 8-19, 630B1
Anderson vote shift in NY seen 9-5, 681F1
Discounts ratings 9-18, 698F3
Post-debate poll findings 9-23—9-28, 739A3
Standings tighten, indicate toss-up 10-23—10-27, 816G1
Exit polls find 'dissatisfactn' 11-4, 838F1
POVERTY—*See WELFARE and Poverty in this section*
PRESS & Broadcasting
TV address on Sovt Afghan invasn 1-4, 1B1
Meet the Press remarks 1-20, 45C2, 50G1-D2
News conf 2-13, 105A1, 109C2, C3-110E1
Kennedy chrgs media misuse 2-14, 130B2
News conf 3-14, 201B1, C2, 209D1-A2
'79 TV ad bid upheld by ct 3-14, 221F3
News conf 4-1, 241B1
Bush scores media use 4-7, 264E2
Newspr eds vs Moscow Olympic curbs 4-9; addresses 4-10, 4-9, 264E1, F1
TV interview 4-13, 281C2
News conf 4-17, 285F2, 286D1, 287D2
News conf 4-29, 323E2, D3
Cable News interview 5-31, 422E3
On Face the Nation 6-1, 424E3
Aides took oaths re leaks 7-16—7-17, 549G1
News conf 8-4, 592F1; text excerpt 593A2
Campaign ad budget rptd 9-4, 665B3
News conf 9-18, 698C2, A3, E3
Reagan asks equal TV time 9-18, 698A3
Reagan equal-time bid rejected 9-19, 723B1
LA TV interview 9-23, 722E3
Walters ABC-TV interview 10-8, 778B2
St Petersburg TV interview 10-10, 778C3
Signs newsroom searches curb 10-14, 835F1-C2
Radio address 10-19, 802F2
Debates Reagan on TV 10-28, 813A1-815E3
Newspaper endorsemts rptd 11-1, 841E3-G3
Pol airtime case accepted by Sup Ct 11-3, 856D2
News conf 11-12, 861F1, 865E1-E3
On early concessn 11-12, 866D1
REGULATORY Agencies
Reform bill dies in Cong 12-16, 982G2
RELIGION
Sees Methodist delegatn 4-23, 324F3
Evangelical Christian votes profiled 9-15, 819A2
Warns vs Reagan win 10-6, 762E3
Reagan deplores campaign 'hysteria' 10-7, 763D2
Drops Reagan attack 10-9, 778D2
RESIGNATIONS
Carter, State spokesman (rptd) 7-17, 549B2
Dougherty, FTC trust bur dir 5-27, 703A1
Friedersdorf, FEC chrmn 12-16, 955D3
Vance, secy of state 4-28, 323G1
RESOURCES, Natural
Alaska gov cites '78 lands issue 1-15, 268D3
Asks Alaska lands protectn 1-21, 43F3
Budget proposals 1-28, 73D3; table 70F1
Alaska lands protectn extended 2-12, 131A3
Global forecast gloomy 7-23, 573F1
Hails Alaska lands bill 8-19, 631E2, A3
Signs water appropriatn bill 10-1, 803A2
Alaska lands bill clears House 11-12, 866E2-C3
Signs Alaska lands bill 12-2, 915G3-916D1

1976

Republican National Convention
Opens, speakers attack 8-16, 601G3, 614E3, 615B1
Connally attacks 8-17, 601A2
On attacks vs 8-17, 617D2
Ford, Reagan nominated 8-18, Ford wins 8-19, 597G2, 598B1
Platform text cites 8-18, 602B1

Security
Briefed 7-26, 7-28, 551C1; 8-12, 616D3
Scores Kelley 8-13, 617B1
Scores abuses 9-6, 664B2
Fences with Ford on firing Kelley 9-7—9-9, 664D2, E3, 665D1
Cabinet unit set up 12-29, 978E2

Taxes
Presents health plan 4-16, 281E3
States goals 4-23, 305B2, D2
Vows reform 7-15, 507E1, 510G2
Pres nominatn acceptance speech 7-15, 510D2
Defends Mondale special interest bill 7-20, 532C2
Vows reform caution 7-22, 550B3
Outlines goals 7-28, 551A1
Vows to end inequities 8-11, 585A3
Notes issue 8-30, 645B2
Disputes Ford on tax-relief proposals 9-17—9-20, 703G2-704C1
Debates Ford 9-23, 701D1, F1, A2-E3, 702G1, C3
Campaigns 9-24, 9-26, 724F1, A3
Church taxation disputed 10-2, 743C2
Baptist ldr scores 10-10, 763D2
Ford: big taxer 10-13, 763G2
Says no hike for workers 10-14, 785C2
Vs Ford chrgs 10-15; Ford replies 10-16, 785C1
Mondale on Cong compromise 10-17, 803C3
Debates Ford 10-22, 800C1, F3, 801F1
On conditns to cut 10-27—10-28, 803F2; 11-4, 819F2
Scores Ford proposal 10-30, 827F1
Sees tax cuts 11-4, 819F2
Burns warns vs stimulating econ 11-11; denies Carter rift 11-12, 865A2
On cuts, revisn 11-15, 863E3, G3, 864A1
On tax-cut possibility 12-6, 917B1
Plans tax cuts 12-9—12-14, 937E2-938A1

Transition Developments—*Note: All appointments and Carter-Ford Administration developments are listed here. For all other post-election developments, see 'Presidential' and other subheads in this section*
Watson, Ford reps meet 11-5, 845C1
Powell on transitn study 11-11, 845F2
On personnel selectn; names Powell press secy 11-15, 863G3, 864B1
To see Ford, Kissinger 11-16, 864B2
Meets Dem cong leaders 11-17, 864E1
Sees Ford Cabt members 11-19—11-22, 881C1
Advisory panel named 11-19, 881C3
Visits Ford 11-22, 880F2
On Capitol Hill 11-23, 881G1
Transition team named 11-23, 881D2
Lance slated for Cabt 11-23, 898D2 ★
Harriman a visitor 11-29, 898B3
To tighten rules re post-govt posts 11-29, 898C3
Confers with Vance 11-30—12-1, 898B3
Names Vance secy of state, Lance OMB dir 12-3, 916C1
'Rigid' re Cabt member business holdings 12-3, 917E1
Names Treas, Transport secys 12-14, 936C1
Fills UN, CEA, natl security posts 12-16, 936G1-937A1
Rpts blacks, other minorities rejctd posts 12-16, 937A1
Sees Glenn 12-16, 937B2
Sees environmt groups 12-16, 937B2
Completes Cabt with Bell, Brown, others; names CIA, energy chiefs 12-18—12-23, 956E1
Cabinet photo 956A1
Bell apptmt scored 12-20—12-22, 956G2
Names Defense, State dep secys 12-21, 12-21, 978D3, G3
Meets Cabt nominees, Mondale 12-27—12-29, 978B1-G2
Concerned about isolation 12-30, 978C3

TV Debates
Ford asks debate 8-19, 599E2
League of Women Voters sets dates 8-19, 632E3
Ford asks earlier dates, Carter rep rejcts 8-24, 632G3-633A1
Negotiators meet 8-26, 632C3
FEC OKs debates 8-30, 644D1
Debate ground rules, topics set 9-1, 644A1
McCarthy, Maddox threaten suits 9-2, 644F1
Sees 'tie' as victory 9-4, 664F1

1977

Water policy a Denver round table topic 10-22, 817D1
Signs mine safety rules 11-9, 855E3
Dam-inspectn program set 11-30, 914E1

RURAL Affairs
On gas-tax plan 7-22, 575C2
Signs '78 dvpt funds 8-12, 688B3, C3

SCIENCE
For Latin training programs 4-14, 296A1
Cong sets '78 budget target 5-17, 405A1
Signs NSF '78 authorizatn 8-15, 689D1
Awards Medals of Sci 11-22, 951G3-952C1

SOCIAL Security—*See AGE and Aged Persons in this section above*

SOCIAL Services—*See also WELFARE in this section below*
Stresses fscl restraint 5-2, 364C2

SPORTS
Call-in on Cuba games 3-5, 171F1
Honors Pele 10-1, 827D2

STATE-Federal Relations—*See also other appropriate headings in this section*
Call-in topic 3-5, 171E1

TAXES
Sees Cong ldrs on econ plan 1-7, 5D1
Econ aid plan revised 1-27, 51G3-A2
Cong hearings on plan 1-27—2-4, 89A2
On payroll credit plan 1-31, 89G3
Plans reforms for '77 2-2, 75E1
Plans new standard credit 2-10, 110D2
'78 budget revisns 2-22, 124D3, E3
Call-in topic 3-5, 171D1, A3
House OKs cuts, investmt credit killed 3-8, 174D2
Vows revisions 3-16, 190D3
Giaimo proposes budget 3-23, 228D3
Urges rebate plan passage 4-7, drops rebate, business credit plans; business reactn 4-14, 270F2-271C2, 300D3
Would veto GOP tax-cut plan 4-15, 299G1
Presents energy plan 4-20, 289D1, 290D1-G1, B2-A3; fact sheet 291C2-293D3
Energy plan reactn 4-21—4-24, GOPs score 4-25, 320C1, C2, B3, F3
Defends energy plan, hints business credits veto 4-22, 321D1, G2
Rebate withdrawal linked to debt cut 4-27, 407E3
Asks credits for working poor 5-2, 337G3
Labor scores energy plan 5-4, 364E1
Seeks Soc Security chngs 5-9, 363F2
Scores liberals' criticism 5-12, McGovern replies 5-13, 380F2, 381D2
Clarifies business credits plan 5-12, 381B2
Stimulus cuts OKd by Cong 5-16, 381D3-382E1
Signs tax-cut bill 5-23, 417F3
Cong tussle over energy plan 6-9—6-14, 460F1-C2
Issues '76 personal data 6-24, 499C2
Miss town mtg topic 7-21, 575E1, F1
Backs gas-tax proposal 7-22, 575B2
Rebuts Jordan criticism 7-25, 573G1
Proposes new welfare system 8-6, 608D2-609E1
Expects cut in '78 10-13, 773B1
Delays reform proposals, asks Soc Sec actn 10-27, 813A1, B3-E3
Sen passes tax bill 10-31, 832C1-F3
Plans '78 cut, reforms 11-30, 913E3
Laurence Woodworth dies 12-4, 1024G3
Lauds Soc Sec bill passage 12-15, 957E3
To ask $25-bln cut in '78 12-20, 976A2

TRADE—*See FOREIGN Trade above*

TRANSPORTATION
Ford urges airline deregulatn bill 1-13, 36G2

1978

SCIENCE
Budget proposals 1-23, 44F2; table 45D2
Revises secrecy classificatn rules 6-29, 508F1

SOCIAL Security—*See AGE and Aged Persons in this section above*

SOCIAL Services—*See also other appropriate headings in this section*
Signs state-fed claims setlmt 6-12, 465F3

SOLAR Energy—*See ENERGY above*

SPORTS
Vs US Olympics boycott in '80 7-20, 549C3
Signs amateur sports bill 11-8, 1003B1

STATE of the Union Message
Delivers 1-19, 29A1-32C1; text 30A1-31F2
GOP rebuttal 1-26, 63D1

TAXES
Reaffirms plans to cut 1-12, 12B2
State of Union Message 1-19, 29B1, G1, B2, D2, F3, 30E2, F2
Econ Message 1-20, 48A3
Submits tax-cut, reform plan to Cong 1-21, 48F3
Budget proposals 1-23, 44G2, F3, 46E3, 47A2; table 45C2
Federal budget dollar table 63A1
Urges proposals kept intact 1-30, 62B3
Vs educ credit 2-8, 85B1
Vs martini-lunch deduction 2-17, 123G1
Links cuts, Soc Sec hike 3-2, 141D1
Crude oil tax passage doubted 3-7, 3-8; Blumenthal oil import fee backing rptd 3-24, 220E1, B2
On tax-cut plan equity 3-9, 160G3-161A1
Presents urban-aid plan 3-27, reactn 3-27—3-30, 217F2-218D1
Soc Sec rollback opposed 4-5, 240D3
Vs schl tuitn credit 4-11, 260G3
Stock mkt gains linked to plan 4-14, 303C1
House com pares reform plan 4-17—4-19; sees 3 reps 4-20, reactn rptd 4-23, 305C3
Sen backs plan, disputes starting date 4-25, 4-26, 305E2
Defends tax-cut, reform plan 4-25, 305F2, 306C1, G3, 307B2-A3
Scales down, delays tax-cut plan 5-12, 361A1
Threatens schl tuitn credit veto 6-8, 431G3
On Calif tax initiative 6-14, 446D3
Warns Cong re crude oil tax passage 6-22, 511F2
Scores capital gains plans 6-26, 491A2
CBO crude oil study rptd 6-29, 512D1
Cites oil tax, reform plan at Bonn summit 7-16—7-17, 544B1, E1
Vs capital gains proposals 7-20, 549E3
House com OKs $16 bln cut, discards 'reforms' 7-27; rptd dissatisfied 7-31, 586G2-F3
House votes $16 bln tax cut bill 8-10, 604A1
Vs tax cut, tuitn credit bills 9-28, 751G3
Scores Sen tax-cut bill 10-10, 766A3
Cong clears $18.7 bln cut, Admin reactn 10-15, 785D1-786C1
Signs Inland Waterways authorzn 10-21, 897C2
To sign tax-cut bill 10-26, 831B2
Meany scores wage-price rebate plan 10-31, 863B2
Signs tax-cut bill 11-6, 873E1
Plans no Soc Sec chng 11-9, 874G3

TRADE—*See FOREIGN Trade above*

TRANSPORTATION
State of Union Message 1-19, 32A1-B1
Budget proposals 1-23, 44F2, 47G2; table 45E2

1979

SCIENCE & Technology
Budget proposals 1-22, 46A2; table 42F2
Urges innovatn, dvpg natn aid 4-23, 300A3

SOCIAL Security—*See AGE and Aged Persons in this section above*

SOCIAL Services—*See also other appropriate headings in this section*
Vs proposed balanced budget amendmt 1-17, 29E2
Proposes privacy bill 4-2, 264F3

SOLAR Energy—*See ENERGY above*

STATE of the Union Message
Delivers 1-23; text 46C2-48F1
GOP reactn 1-24, 48F1-C2
Cong gets detailed text 1-25, 70A2
On 'new foundatn' theme 1-26, 70E1

TAXES
Budget proposals 1-22, 41D2, E2 44F1; tables 42A1, C2, 43B2
Soc Sec, wage insurnc credit plans opposed in Cong 1-23, 55A3
Urges wage insurnc credit plan 2-12, 109F3
Asks oil profits tax 4-5, 250B2, B3
Cites wage insurnc credit plan defeat by House panel 5-25, 401B2
Doubts '80 tax cut 5-29, 402A1
Asks waste cleanup fund 6-13, 441G1
Seeks solar heat credit, gashol exemptn 6-20, 498E1
Sees possible tax cut 9-25, 723A3
Signs IRS tax power curbs 9-29, 883E2
Proposes indl innovatn 10-31, 829E3

Oil Profits Tax Plan—*See PETROLEUM–Carter Decontrol*

TRADE—*See FOREIGN Trade above*

TRANSPORTATION
Rail clerks, N&W sign pact 1-8, 87C2
Adams' rail deregulatn plan rptd 1-15, 35C3

1980

RURAL Affairs
State of Union topic 1-23, 43A2, F2
Warns vs Reagan win 10-6, 762E3
Reagan deplores campaign 'hysteria' 10-7, 763D2
Softens Reagan attack 10-9, 778C2

SCIENCE & Technology
Suspends USSR tech equipmt sale 1-4, 1D1; affirms ban 1-23, 41B2, 42D2
Budgets research funds; table 1-28, 69D3, 70F1
Japan research pact signed 5-1, 341C1
Renominatn acceptance speech cites computers 8-14, 612F1
Offers econ renewal plan 8-28, 663C2
Scientific literacy study issued 10-22, 990G1
Signs NSF authrzn 12-12, 982B1
Signs '81 NASA, NSF appropriatns 12-15, 982B1

SPORTS
Threatens Moscow Olympics boycott 1-4, 1E1; 1-23, 41B2, 42D2
Urges shift of Moscow Olympics 1-20, 45B2
House com backs Olympic stand 1-23, 45G3; Cong, USOC 1-24—1-29, 67E3
Ali to promote Olympic stand in Africa 1-31, 68F1
Defends Moscow Olympic stand 2-1, 85B1
Urges USOC boycott decisn 2-12, 107E1
W Ger joint communique backs Moscow Olympics boycott 3-5, 205B2
Asks Moscow Olympics product ban 3-12, 206G1
Adamant on Moscow Olympic boycott 3-21, 3-22, threatens emergency power use 4-10, 258E2
Orders Moscow Olympic products ban 3-28, 259B1
Reagan on Moscow Olympic boycott 4-8, 264A3
Newspr eds score Moscow Olympic curbs 4-9; reasserts stance 4-10, 264E1, F1
Reagan backs Olympic boycott 4-10, 288D2
USOC backs Olympic boycott; reactn 4-12, Sovts denounce move 4-13, 283E1, C2, B3
Killanin asks Brezhnev mtg 4-23, 325F2
Meets with Killanin on Olympics 5-15, 379E1
Thanks Japan for Olympic boycott 7-8, 506E1
Killanin rips boycott 7-18, 590E3
Defends Olympic boycott 7-30, 590C3

STATE of the Union Message
Released 1-21, 43B3
Address to Cong; text 1-23, 41A1-43G2
Tass calls 'demagogical' 1-24, 43A3
Reagan reactn 1-24, 91A3; Kennedy 1-28, 74F3; 2-12, 110D2
GOP rebuts 1-28, 75C1

TAXES
State of Union defers '80 cut 1-21, 43C3
Budget proposals 1-28, 69F2, 70A1, 72A2; tables 69G3, 70D1
Revised budget proposals 3-31, 243F2, G3
Signs windfall oil profits tax 4-2, 244B2
Says tax cut possible 5-9, 367G1
Oil import fee blocked by Dist Ct 5-13, 366A1
Vetoes oil import fee bar 6-5, Cong overrides 6-5, 6-6, 436G2-437B2
Scores 'easy' talk of cuts 6-10, 438G2
Reagan scores 6-25, 480B2
'81 tax cut backed 6-29—7-1, 492B3-493A1
Scores GOP plan 7-3, 505C2; 7-17, 532D1; 8-6, 597B2
To aid car makers 7-8, 505B1
Renominatn acceptance speech; text 8-14, 612E1, F3, 613G1
Offers econ renewal plan, rejcts pre-electn cut; reactn 8-28, 663A1-D3
Scores 'quick-fix' cut 9-18, 698C3, 699A1
Unveils steel indus aid plan 9-30, 740A3
Scores Reagan plan, backs business write-offs 10-14, 779F1
Hits Reagan massive cuts 10-24, 816G2
Debates with Reagan 10-28, 813D1, E1, E2, 814D1, 815A3
Anderson answers debate questns 10-28, 816A1, B1
Would veto tax-cut bill 11-12, 866B2

TECHNOLOGY—*See SCIENCE & Technology in this section above*

TRANSITION Developments
Pledges 'fine transition' 11-4, 11-5, 837E2, 838B3
Reagan in DC 11-17—11-19, 880G1; visits White House 11-20, 897E2

TRANSPORTATION
LIRR pres strike bd rpts 1-14, 53F1
Asks trucking, rail deregulatn 1-21, 43F3
Budget proposals 1-28, 72G3; table 70E1

1976

More rules rptd 9-8, 700F3
2d, 3d debates set 703A2
3d-party challenges rejctd 9-17, 9-20, 703D2
Networks OK rules 9-18, 9-20, 703B2
1st Ford debate 9-23, 700E2-703A2
Experts rate 1st debate 9-23, 9-30; sound loss explained 9-24, 725D1
Ga gov protests Ford Medicaid remark 9-25, 725G1
Trails in 1st debate poll 9-30, 725E1
2d Ford debate 10-6, 740B2-742G2
On Ford E Eur 'blunder'; other reactn 10-7—10-10, 762A1, F1, B3, D3
Ford refers to 'quiz show' 10-7, 763G1
Torrijos scores Panama Canal stand 10-7, 792F3
Scores Ford Arab boycott remark 10-8, 762A2
Dole disputes re Iran, Saudi arms sales 10-8, 764A1
Ford lists debate 'errors' 10-9, 763C2
Sup Ct bars equal-time review 10-12, 765D3
Ford scores forgn policy chrg 10-14, 761F3
Poll lead up after 2d 10-15, 1st cited 764B2
Dole, Mondale debate 10-15, 782E1-784E1
3d Ford debate 10-22, 799E2-802C3
Ford, Dole score Yugo remark 10-26, 803C1, 804F2
Yugo scores 10-27, 910B1
Says key to victory 11-5, 845D1
Caldell minimizes Ford E Eur gaffe 11-11, 845E2
Sees unifying result 11-22, 880G3

Vice Presidential Nomination Issue
Vs speculatn 6-9, 431G3
Vs FBI checks on list 6-17, 452D1
Panel to aid in search set 6-17, 489A3
Sees Meany 6-30, 468E1
Invites Muskie to Ga 7-4, 489B3
Plans 'strong role' 7-5, 489C3
Sees Mondale, Glenn 7-8, 489E3
Sees Jackson 7-10; Church, Stevenson 7-12, 506A2
Cuts candidate list to 7 7-11, 506G1
Rodino bows out 7-12, 506A2
Names Mondale 7-15, conv ratifies 506D2, A3
Mondale biog sketch 512E2

Welfare
Vs 'instant' reform 6-3, 411D1
Favors natl progrm 7-6, 492E3
Pres nominatn acceptance speech 7-15, 510D2, G2; record cited 512C2
Briefed 8-16, 617F1
Scores Ford priorities 8-30, 645B2
Debates Ford 9-23, 701F1, 702E3
Theme in NYS 9-30, 742E3
Debates Ford 10-22, 801D3
NE govs urge reform 11-14, 864A3, F3
Reform delays seen 12-28, 12-29, 978G1-B2

1977

Backs Concorde trial 2-16, 131D2; 3-9, 212E3
'78 budget revisns 2-22, 125A2, G2
Giscard warns re Concorde 3-4, Le Monde scores 3-7, sees Callaghan 3-10—3-11, 212B3-213A1
Call-in on Concorde 3-5, 171D1, B3
Concorde talk with Carey rptd 3-7, 212D3
Backs Concorde trial 3-9, 212E3
For surface-mode deregulatn 3-16, 190E3
Asks oil-tanker safety rules 3-18, 214G1-D2
Presents energy plan 4-18, 4-20, 289F1, 290C1, 295A1; fact sheet 291C2-F3, 293F3
Defends energy plan 4-22, 321B2
Signs rail rehabilitatn loan progrm 5-13, 380D3
Energy plans scored by UAW pres 5-19, 408F2
Warns vs auto lobby 6-10, 460A3
OKs Laker 'Skytrain' svc 6-13, 500F2
Hails UK air svc pact 6-22, 500C2
US tanker cargo preferenc backed 7-11, 538B2
Cargo preference controversy 7-11—9-9, 719B3-G3
O'Neal report scores ICC 8-3, 651E2
OKs NY-London budget air fares 9-26, 860D2
Signs air cargo deregulatn 11-9, 899A3
Signs maritime aid bill 11-12, 1001E2
Signs rail mass transit aid 11-16, 900A1
OKs new air routes to Eur 12-21, 1006B2
CAB eases air charter rules 12-21, 1006C3

TRAVEL
For eased curbs on US visits 2-23, 126C2; 3-17, 186G1
To lift travel bans on US natls 3-9, 172F3
Review of US curbs rptd 4-16, 306A3
Eases curbs on visas to US 8-17, 667D2-B3

VETERANS—*See DEFENSE & Armed Forces above*

WATER—*See RESOURCES, Natural above*

WATERGATE
Commutes Liddy's term 4-12, 325C3
Lauds Sirica 10-7, 927F3
Says no Liddy contact 10-27, 814D1

WELFARE and Poverty
Inaugural 1-20, 26B1, 27E1
Statemt to world 1-20, 26A3
Reform rpt in works 2-2, 75E1
Study group meets 2-11, 176B1
'78 budget revisions 2-22, 124C3, 125A2
Call-in topic 3-5, 171D1
Giaimo proposes budget 3-23, 229A1
Outlines reform goals 5-2, 337C3-338A1
Labor scores spending curb 5-4, 364D3
McGovern scores reforms 5-13, 381D2
Cong sets '78 income security target 5-17, 405A1
Reforms outlined 5-25, spending lid affirmed 5-26, 445D2-E3
Agrees to sign HEW-Labor funds 6-15, 459B3
Sen OKs HEW-Labor funds 6-29, 515F2
Miss town mtg topic 7-21, 575F1
'No apologies' to blacks, poor; rebuts Jordan criticism 7-25, 7-28, 573C1, F2
Black Caucus backs Jordan 7-29, 592G3
Proposes new system, summary 8-6, 608C2-609E1
Govs back reform plan 9-9, 719F1
Cites problem 10-27, 813A3-E3
Extends legal aid for poor 12-28, 1002G2

Food Stamps
Food-stamp plan proposed 4-5, 250A2
Signs '78 food stamp funds 8-12, 688A3
Signs revisions 9-29, 736D2, 737B1

Medicaid—*See under MEDICINE above*

WHITE House Staff—*See CABINET & White House Staff above*

WIRETAPPING & Electronic Surveillance—*See INTELLIGENCE Issues above*

WOMEN
ERA rejected in NC 3-1, 197C2
Call-in on ERA, draft 3-5, 171E1, F2
Educators vs quotas 3-31, 235D2
Poll standing 4-4, 251G1
White House aides vs abortn curbs 7-15, 786E2
Backs ERA, proclaims Equality Day 8-16, 669B2
Urges US job opportunities 11-17, 914E2
Natl Women's Conf adopts platform 11-19—11-21, 917A3
Stresses campaign vow 12-28, 1002A1

YOUTH
Proposes job programs 3-9, 173D1-A2
Job funds cleared 5-3, 365E1; signed 5-13, 380D3
Signs jobs bill 8-5, 609A2
Jobs for blacks a Detroit topic 10-21, 817A1

1978

On UK air-fare dispute 3-7, hails setlmt 3-17, 206E1, B2
Asks trucking regulatn probe, airline reform bill 4-11, 259F3
Plans severe budget cuts 5-25, 404A3
Warns USSR on ship insurnc bias 6-9, 499D3
Gives LA 2-carrier London svc 6-9, 570D1
Signs Coast Guard '79 authorzn 6-30, 525C2
Intl aviatn policy outlined 8-21, 640F1
Scores highway bill 9-28, 751G3
Signs Inland Waterways authorzn 10-21, 897C2
Signs airline deregulatn 10-24, 873F1
Signs Conrail aid bill 11-1, 875C3
Vetoes shipping malpractice 11-4, 897G2
Signs mass transit, road fund bill 11-8, 875D2
Environmtlists urge natl policy 12-20, 1009F1

VETERANS—*See DEFENSE & Armed Forces above*

WATER—*See RESOURCES, Natural above*

WELFARE and Poverty
State of Union Message 1-19, 30G1, E2, B3, 31B1, 32A1, B1
Budget proposals, defers reform 1-23, 44C3, 46F1, F2, C3, 47A1, D1, 48C1, D2
Scores lawyers 5-4, 320F2, D3
Reform compromise prepared 6-7, 446E1
Signs state soc svc claims setlmt 6-12, 465F3
Scores HEW budget bill 9-25, 751G3
Signs '79 HEW funds 10-18, 873F1
Cites US commitmt 11-27, 914C3
Launches anti-fraud drive 12-13, 984A3

Food Stamps
Cutoff to striking miners opposed by Meany 3-11, 182D2

WHITE House Staff—*See CABINET & White House Staff above*

WILDLIFE—*See ENVIRONMENT in this section above*

WIRETAPPING & Electronic Surveillance—*See INTELLIGENCE Issues above*

WOMEN
State of Union Message 1-19, 29C2, 30A3
Would sign ERA extension 2-17, 123G2
Meets natl conf members, vows more effort 3-22, 218B2
To recruit judges 5-4, 320B3
Names 1st Marine Corp gen 5-11, 420F1
Backs ERA in Ill 5-26, 494C2
Apptmt data disclosed 6-15, 811E1
Urges ERA extensn 7-12, 529F2
Weddington named pres asst 8-31, 681C3
ERA extensn cleared by Sen 10-6, 788B1, D1
Signs suffragette coin bill 10-10, 788B2
Signs pregnancy benefits bill 10-31, 873G1
Natl Advisory Com cancels mtg 11-22, 915D1
Mormon award opposed 11-27, 915B1
Cites US repression 12-6, 934C1
Cites ERA support 12-8, 956E2

YOUTH
State of Union Message 1-19, 29B1, C2, 30B3
Budget proposal 1-23, 46F2
Black ldr scores on jobless 12-4, 936B3

1979

Fitzsimmons asks ICC chrmn firing 1-18, 111G3
Budget proposals 1-22, 41G2, 45B1; table 42E2
Drafting maritime legis 1-25, 70D2
Seeks fed no-fault auto insurnc standards 1-25, 70D2
Amtrak route cutback plan revised 1-31, 129B1
Backs 55-mph limit 2-12, 109D3
Proposes regulatory reform 3-25, 230G1
Averts rail dispatchers strike 5-8, 598G2
Sets 'car of the future' plan 5-18, 441C3
OKs N Central, Southn Airways merger 6-5, 465D3
Acts on truckers, demands, forms task force 6-21-6-22, 479B3
Backs Amtrak 8-7, 592E3
Signs Amtrak funding authrzn 9-29, 867C3
Names Gaskins ICC chrmn 10-12, 831A1
Signs Milwaukee Rd aid bill 11-4, 867E2
Goldschmidt threatens Chicago aid loss 11-20, 983G3
Milwaukee Rd bailout ruled legal 11-25, 989B2
OKs Pan Am-Natl merger 12-22, 989C1

Oil Profits Tax Plan—*See PETROLEUM—Carter Decontrol*

VETERANS
Budget proposals 1-22, 41C2, 43F3, 44F1; table 42E2
Vows aid for Viet vets 5-30, 419A2
Signs '80 VA funds bill 11-5, 883A3

WATER—*See RESOURCES, Natural above*

WELFARE and Poverty
Vs proposed balanced budget amendmt, on '80 budget plans 1-17, 29E2, F2
Budget proposals 1-22, 43G3-44A1, B1, F1, 45D2; table 42E2
Defends budget 1-26, 70A1
Proposes privacy bill 4-2, 264F3
Offers welfare reform plan 5-23, 384B1
Scores welfare system 10-15, 807A3

Food Stamps
Seeks budget rise 1-22, 46B1; table 42E2
Seeks cash substitute re SSI progrm 5-23, 384D1
Signs '79 emergency funds bill 8-2, 700B2

Oil Profits Tax Plan—*See PETROLEUM-Carter Decontrol*

WHITE House Staff—*See CABINET & White House Staff above*

WIRETAPPING & Electronic Surveillance—*See INTELLIGENCE Issues above*

WOMEN
Ousts Abzug from women's panel 1-12, resignatns, protests ensue 1-12-1-17; Chambers named acting head 1-16, 30C2
Names Robb women's panel head 5-9, 351G1-A3
NOW vs reelectn 12-9, barred from White House mtg 12-13, 961G2, A3

YOUTH
Budget proposals 1-22, 44B1, A3, 46D1
Soc Sec cuts opposed in Cong 1-23, 55B3

1980

Signs intl airline deregulatn 2-15, 346F1
OKs global airfare hike 2-18, 346D2
Revised budget proposals 3-31, 244D1
CAB OKs Seaboard-Tiger merger 5-8, 516G1
Signs Amtrak, Rock I RR aid bill 5-30, 427E1
Rock I RR aid law upset 6-2; Sup Ct bars actn 7-2, 11-10, 868F2
Trucking deregulatn clears Cong 6-19, 6-20, 479A1; signed 7-1, 494B1
Fla deregulates trucking 7-1, 558F2
Plans mass transit boost 8-6, 597C2
Renominatn acceptance speech; text 8-14, 612F1, G1, 613F1
Offers econ renewal plan 8-28, 663B2
Lauds new US cars 10-1, 739B2
Signs '81 Transport Dept funds 10-9, 980F3
Signs RR deregulatn 10-14, 783D3

VETERANS
Vetoes dioxins study 1-2, 17G2
Budget proposal, table 1-28, 70E1
Signs Viet War mem'l bill; speech scored 7-1, 496B1-F1
Awards WWII vet Medal of Honor 7-19, 638E1
'Antiveteran' says Reagan 8-18, 629D1
Vetoes VA MD pay hike 8-22, Cong overrides 8-26, 649C3
Signs educ aid 10-17, 856F2
Signs '81 VA appropriatn 12-15, 982B1

WELFARE and Poverty
State of Union asks revisns 1-21, 43F3
Budget proposals 1-28, 69D3, 72B2; table 70E1
Revised budget proposals 3-31, 244B1
Attacks GOP stands 7-17, 532E1
Renominatn acceptance speech; text 8-14, 612F1, F3, 613A2
Attacks Reagan 8-22, 646F2
Calls Reagan proposals inflationary 10-6, 762B3
Vows fed aid to cities 10-20, 803F1
Debates with Reagan 10-28, 814C2

Food Stamps
Budget outlays up; table 1-28, 70E1, 73D2
Signs emergency funds legislatn 5-27, 402F3
Signs '81 appropriatn 12-15, 982B1

WHITE House Staff—*See CABINET & White House Staff in this section above*

WOMEN
Backs equal rights, ERA 1-23, 43A1, F2
Seeks draft registratn 2-8, 110E2, G2
AFL-CIO backs draft registratn 2-25, 147A1
ERA rejected by Ill House 6-18, 482D3
Issues platform statemt, backs ERA planks 8-13, 611D1
Renominatn acceptance speech cites 8-14, 612G3
Scores GOP stand 9-29, 739A1
Scores Reagan Sup Ct apptmt vow 10-15, 779A1
Debates with Reagan 10-28, 813B2, 814B2, 815C2, A3
Plans to speak out 11-12, 865F2

YOUTH
Asks training program 1-10, 16G1-F2
State of Union proposals 1-21, 1-23, 41G2, 43D2, D3
Budget proposals 1-28, 69D3, 72D1
Revised budget proposals 3-31, 244B1
GOP plank scores 7-10, 506A3
Debates with Reagan 10-28, 814G1
Signs child nutritn authrzn 12-5, 981B1

Draft Registration—*See under DEFENSE & Armed Forces in this section above*

CARTER, Lillian Gordy
Carter biog sketch 511G2
Family holdings rptd 8-9, 646B1
Campaign donatn rptd 10-22, 939B1

CARTER, Mark Bonham
Meets Southall ldrs on racism 6-8, 482D1

CARTER, Judge Oliver J.
Hearst mental exams disputed 1-7—1-23, 69E3
Denies Hearst pretrial motns 1-26, 70B1
Hearst jury selectn starts 1-27, 69C3
Hearst jury selectn ends 2-3, trial opens 2-4, 113E2
Hearst trial dvpts 2-11—3-18, 201C1-202E3

CARTER, Jeff (Donnel Jeffrey)
In London summit entourage 5-5—5-8, 359F2
At Pele tribute 10-1, 827D2

CARTER, Lillian Gordy
Son sets up trust 1-4, 5A1
At Indian rite, meets Gandhi 2-13, 116B1
Pres tax data issued 6-24, 499E2
Wins Synagogue Cncl prize 9-25, 808A3

CARTER, Judge Robert L.
Rules on Knicks-Nets dispute 7-18, Nets NJ move agreed 7-26, 584G2

CARTER, (Mother) Maybelle
Dies 10-23, 888G2

CARTER, Michael
Held in Guyana murder probe; rpts Jonestown-Sovt tie 11-28, 910F2, B3, 911A1

CARTER, Mike
Sets jr shot-put mark 6-25, 692G3

CARTER, Nell
Ain't Misbehavin' opens 5-9, 760B1 *
Wins Tony 6-4, 579A3

CARTER, Pancho
2d in Calif 500 9-3, 968G3

CARTER, Judge Robert L.
Orders 'strip-frisk' prison searches ended 4-22, 440G1

CARTER, Judy
Campaigns in NH 11-29, 961E3

CARTER, Lillian
Lance banking favors rptd 1-17, 31A1
Peanut probe spec counsel named 3-20, 203B1
On Kennedy '80 pres bid 9-8, 680C1
Campaigns in NH 11-29, 961E3

CARTER, Judge Robert L.
Rules Sun, Becton stock purchase illegal 7-9, 541F2
Voids Webster '78 compensatn 9-19, 1003C2

CARTER, Joseph
Raging Bull released 11-14, 972G3

CARTER, Lillian
At Tito funeral 5-8, 338B3
Undergoes hip surgery 10-2, 908E2

1976

Hearst convctd, sets sentencing 3-22, 220C2
Sentences Hearst 4-12, 367C3
Dies 6-14, 524D2
Hearst sentenced 9-24, 735A2
CARTER, Rosalynn Smith (Mrs. Jimmy)
Carter biog sketch 511G3
'Whistlestop' tour 9-20—9-21, 704C3
Visits Lady Bird Johnson 9-23, 724B3
Campaign donatn rptd 10-22, 939B1
Campaigns with husband 10-23, 803C2
Photo with husband 11-2, 817A1
Visits White House 11-22, 880F2
Amy to attend public schl 11-28, 917F2
In Mexico 11-30—12-2, 906A3
CARTER, Rubin (Hurricane)
Gets new trial 3-17, bail 3-19, 256D3
Retrial opens 10-12, 11-11, 860B1
Found guilty 12-21, sentencing set 12-23, 1015C3
CARTER, Rep. Tim Lee (R, Ky.)
Travel expense probe ends 10-27, 981G3
Reelected 11-2, 829E3
CARTER Jr., W. Beverly
Amb to Liberia 3-22; confrmd 4-1, 262C3
CARTER Farms Inc.
Carter biog sketch 512B1
CARTONS—*See CONTAINERS & Packaging*
CARTOONS & Cartooning
Auth wins Pulitzer 5-3, 352E3
Sup Ct bars LA Times libel suit review 10-4, 807D2
CARTWRIGHT, Rev. Lucius S.
Pleads guilty 8-6, sentncd 9-17, 776F2
CARTY, Rico
AL batting ldr 10-4, 796B1, C1
CARVAJAL, Vice Adm. Patricio
On Bolivia seaport plan 11-26, 975B2
CARVALHO, Maj. Otelo Saraiva de
Seized in '75 plot, denies chrgs 1-19, 53C1
Republica ordrd returned to owners 1-28, 143D2
Freed 3-3, 383G2
Sets pres bid 5-27, Eanes wins 6-27; backers warned 6-28, 482C3-483C2
Rpt Eanes scores '75 revolt 6-4, 483B2
Backers vow fight 7-5; govt reasserts revolt role 7-13, 558G2
Spinola, Eanes link cited 8-11, 733B1
Scores govt 10-3; arrested 10-23, 811G3
Released from prison 11-12, 966E2
Electn results 12-12, 966E2
CARVER, Roy
'72 campaign gift listed 9-25, 688B1
CASALDALIGA, Bishop Pedro
Jesuit priest killed 10-12, 836C1
CASALS, Rosemary
Wins Federatn Cup tennis 8-29, 716A2
CASANAS, Alejandro
Wins Olympic medal 7-28, 576A1
CASE, Sen. Clifford P. (R, N.J.)
Named to intelligence com 5-20, 377E1
CASEY, Lord (Richard Gardiner Casey)
Dies 6-17, 524D2
CASEY, Rep. Robert (Bob) (D, Tex.)
Confrmd to Fed Maritime Comm 1-21, 68C1
Resigns House seat 1-22, 68D3
Gammage wins House seat 11-2, 822G3
CASH, Dave F.
NL wins All-Star game 7-13, 544B2
NL batting ldr 10-4, 795G3
Contract rptd signed 12-5, 951D3
CASPIAN Sea
Iran-Czech pipeline pact rptd 11-22, 946B2
CASS, John P.
On Australia wheat crop 10-5, 770E3
CASSERLY, Jack
Shifted from White House 1-21, 40D3
CASSIDY, Jack
Dies 12-12, 1015C1
CASSIDY, Dr. Sheila
Torture chrg backed 1-1; Chile denies 1-5, 8C2
UN testimony on Chile torture 1-19, 47G1
Gutierrez linked to arrest 1-24, 100B1
Chile prisoners' rights decreed 1-28, 100F1
CASSIN, Rene
Dies 2-20, 192C3
CASSON, Sir Lewis (d. 1969)
Widow dies 6-9, 444A3
CASTANEDA, Jorge
On offshore econ zone 6-6, 420C2
CASTELLITO, Anthony (d. 1961)
Slayers indicted 6-23, 460C1
Fed chrgs vs slayers dismissed 10-29, 972C1
CASTELLS, Miguel
Spanish torture alleged 5-13, 422D2
CASTELLO Branco, Carlos
Scores Herzog 'suicide' rpt 1-13, legislators' ouster 1-23, 98G1
CASTELO Soto, Eduardo
Killed 4-3, 264F1
CASTIELLA y Maiz, Fernando Maria
Dies 11-25, 970D1

1977

CARTER, Rosalynn Smith (Mrs. Jimmy)
Urges Ind ERA OK 1-18, 59B2
Holds Bible at inaugural, photo 1-20, 25A1, F1
ERA fails in NC 3-1, 197D2
Plans conf on aging 4-18, 322B2
Undergoes minor surgery 4-28, 322D2
Takes A-sub ride 5-27, 417D3
On Latin tour 5-30—6-12, 454D1
Gets Brazil student rights plea 6-6, 524D1
Tax return data issued 6-24, 499C2
Ecuador visit cited 7-5, US affirms jet sale ban 7-6, 511C1
Brazil expels US missionary 7-27, 633G2
Carter-Caddell-Rafshoon mtg cited 10-27, 814A1
At Natl Women's Conf 11-19, 917E3
With Pres on world tour 12-29—12-31, 1000F3, 1001C2
CARTER, Rubin (Hurricane)
Sentenced 2-9, 140C1
CARTER Farms Inc.
'76 tax data issued 6-24, 499F2
CARTER Hawley Hale Stores Inc.
Edward Marcus dies 4-4, 356D3
CARTER-Wallace Inc.
Rpts forgn paymts 1-3, 94C1
CARTER-Waters Corp.
Price-fixing chrgd 6-6, 504B1
CARTIER Inc.
Jules Glaenzer dies 8-16, 696G2
CARTOGRAPHY
Andrew Hagstrom dies 10-8, 872B2
CARTOONS & Cartoonists
Szep wins Pulitzer 4-18, 355G2
Ross Lewis dies 8-6, 696A3
Obituaries
Barlow, Perry 12-26, 1023G3
Batchelor, C D 9-5, 787F3
Crane, Roy 7-7, 604G2
Goscinny, Rene 11-5, 952D2
Gropper, William 1-6, 84B3
Hubley, John 2-21, 164B3
Musial, Joe 6-6, 532D3
Patterson, Russell 3-17, 264C3
CARVAJAL, Vice Adm. Patricio
Scores OAS rights emphasis 6-14, 494A2
Sees US amb 11-17, 983E2
CARVER, Lord (Richard Michael Power Carver)
Rptd named Rhodesia comr 9-2, 810A1
Smith invites 9-28, 810B1
Tours southn Africa 10-30—11-9; briefs Owen 11-10—11-1, 875G2, 876B1
CARVALHO, Maj. Otelo Saraiva de
Cuba role in Angola detailed 1-9, 19C1
CASALEGNO, Carlo
Shot 11-16, dies 11-29, 1014F2
CASALS, Rosemary
Wade wins Wimbledon 7-1, 548A2
To join new WTT team 12-10, 1020G2
CASANOVA Sandoval, Col. Eduardo
Kidnaped 5-29, freed 6-1, 438D2
CASCADE Mountains
Cloud-seeding program starts 2-28, 153E1
Snowpack below normal 4-26, 376C3
CASE, Sen. Clifford P. (R, N.J.)
On Sovt mil aims estimate 1-18, 40A1
Backs Panama Canal talks 2-2, 379A2
Bradley seeks Sen seat 11-14, 991A1
CASE, Ross
Apples win WTT title 8-27, 787E3
CASEY, Lane & Mittendorf
Sued re sugar lobby gifts 7-20, 614B1, E1
CASH, Dave
NL batting ldr 10-2, 926D3
CASPER, Wyo.—*See WYOMING*
CASPER, Billy
Watson breaks record 1-23, 104B1
CASPER, Dave
Raiders win Super Bowl 1-9, 24E3
Oakland wins in playoffs 12-24, 1019F3
CASS, John P.
On China wheat sale 3-8, 178G3
CASTILLO, Eduardo
Freed 8-24, 784E2

1978

CARTER, Rosalynn Smith (Mrs. Jimmy)
Husband ends world tour 1-6, 1E1, C2
Jordan legal separatn rptd 1-9, 96B1
Joins Canal pact vote drive 3-14, 177D3
In S Amer, Africa 3-28—4-3, 233B1
At CR pres inaugural 5-8, 354D2
At Pope Paul's funeral 8-12, 658B3
Guyana releases '77 letter to Rev Jones 11-20; denies remembering Jones 11-21, 891D1
Mormons give family award 11-27, 915A1
In Plains for holiday 12-21, 1003E1
CARTER, Steve
Nevis Mountain Dew opens 12-7, 1031E2
CARTER, Rep. Tim Lee (R, Ky.)
Reelected 11-7, 850E4
CARTER, Timothy
Held in Guyana murder probe; rpts Jonestown-Sovt tie 11-28, 910F2, B3, 911A1
Returns to US 12-29, 1000D2
CARTER Hawley Hale Stores Inc.
Drops Marshall Field bid 2-22, to buy Wanamaker 3-8, 185E1
CARTMELL, Mike
On Rev Jones sexual tyranny 11-24, 911A2
CARTOONS & Cartoonists
MacNelly wins Pulitzer 4-17, 315B2
Obituaries
Rockwell, George L 3-3, 252D3
Bray, John R 10-10, 888E2
Mullin, Willard 12-21, 1032C3
CARTWRIGHT, Veronica
Invasn of Body Snatchers released 12-21, 1030A3
CARTY, Rico
Traded to Blue Jays 3-15, 195A1
AL batting ldr 10-2, 928E3
Blue Jays reacquire on waivers 10-3, 799B3
CARUCCI, Frank
Coolest Cat opens 6-23, 760F1
CARVER, Lord (Richard Michael Power Carver)
Tours Africa re Rhodesia Malta mtg 1-6—1-9, at mtg 1-30, 59F1
In UK, US mtg with Patriotic Front 4-15, 290E2, G2-A3
Quits Rhodesia post, scores lack of progress 11-30, 946A1
CARY, Frank T.
On IBM 4-for-1 stock split 12-19, 1004C1
CASALS, Rosemary
Loses LA Va Slims 1-29, 419F1
CASE, Sen. Clifford P. (R, N.J.)
Votes for Panama Canal neutrality pact 3-16, 177F2
Votes for 2d Canal pact 4-18, 273B1
Vs Mideast jet package 5-15, 357F1
Defeated in primary 6-6, 425C1, 447F3
Sen votes conditnl end to Rhodesia sanctns 7-26, 588F1
Ex-aide's FEC nominatn withdrawn 8-12, gets consumer post 10-10, 831C3
Bradley wins seat 11-7, 849B1
CASEY, Robert P.
Loses primary for Pa gov 5-16, 389B3
CASEY, Warren
Grease released 6-16, 619C2
CASEY'S Shadow (film)
Released 3-17, 618F3
CASH, James (d. 1972)
GM liable in car crash 2-9, 185E3
CASS, Moss
Asks immigration curb 2-19, 129A2
CASSAVETES, John
Brass Target released 12-21, 1030E2
CASSEL, Jacqueline
Ballroom at St Patrick's opens 12-1, 1031A1
CASSIMO, Alberto
Named Mozambique labor min 4-22, 331E1
CASTANEDA, Carlos
Ring of Power on best-seller list 2-5, 116C3; 3-5, 195E3
CASTANO Espaillat, Julio Cesar
Named DR educ min 8-16, 648D2
CASTELLANO, Aracelli
Rapists convicted 5-3, 396C1
CASTELLITO, Anthony (Three Fingers) (d. 1961)
Briguglio shot to death 3-21, 232A3
Provenzano, Konigsberg convicted of murder 6-14, sentenced 6-21, 480B2
CASTELLO Branco, Carlos
Says MDB backed by majority 11-15, 921C2
CASTER, Richard
Traded to Oilers 8-17, 1024E3
CASTILLO, Col. Clementino
Guatemala educ min 7-21, 722D3 *
CASTILLO, Freddie
Netrnoi decisns 5-6, 379E2

1979

CARTER, Rosalynn Smith (Mrs. Jimmy)
Gacy '78 photo confrmd 1-21, 79A1
Asks more mental health funds 2-7, 112B1
Mental health bill proposed 5-15, 365B1, F1
Financial data released 5-30, 5-31, 420F1-D2
Visits Japan 6-24–6-29, 494D1
With husband in Pa; addresses Women's Natl Dem Club 7-12, 513F2, 514E1
Addresses Urban League 7-24, 560B1
At Ecuador pres inaugural 8-10, 613D2
Boats down Mississippi 8-17–8-24, 622G1-623D1
Defends Jordan on cocaine chrgs 9-21, 767C3
Greets Pope in Boston 10-1, 757F1
Husband defends campaign role 10-9, 767B1
Visits Thai refugee camps 11-8–11-10, food aid ordrd 11-13, 863G1, E2
Addresses Fla Dem conv 11-17, 887C1
Campaigns in NH 11-29, Ga, Ark 12-8, 961A2, D3
Subs for husband in NY 12-5, 918G2
CARTER, W. Beverly
Votes Israel UN condemnatn 9-5; US dissociates 9-6, 659E2
CARTER-Mondale Presidential Committee
Dobelle cited as head 4-25, 300B1
Strauss named head 11-6, 961B2
CARTER'S Farms Inc.
Carter releases financial data 5-31, 420G1-A2
B Carter optioning of business share rptd 6-19, 199G2
CARTONS—*See CONTAINERS & Packaging*
CARTOONS & Cartoonists
BC cartoonist loses libel case 1-17, 57G1
Obituaries
Capp, Al 11-5, 932C2
Fleischer, Dave 6-25, 508E2
CARTWRIGHT, Bill
In NBA draft 6-25, 507A2
CARTWRIGHT, Veronica
Alien released 5-24, 528A1
CARUPO, Siony
Kim decisns 7-28, 839B1
CARUSO, Barbara
Ride A Cock Horse opens 3-18, 292E2
CARUSO, Fred
Winter Kills released 5-17, 528G3
CARVAJAL, Jose Federico de
Assumes PSOE interim ldrship 5-20, 390F2
CARVER, Mayor Richard E. (Peoria, Ill.)
Heads US Conf of Mayors 6-13, 440C1
CARVER, Roy J.
Agrees to consent order 4-9, 305E3-306C1
CARY, Frank T.
US regulatory costs rptd 3-14, 230B3
CARY, Dr. Freeman H.
On Brennan stroke 9-17, 744E3
CASABLANCA Record & Filmworks Inc.
Records unit firings cited 8-10, 618E1
CASALS, Rosemary
US wins Federatn Cup 5-6, 391E2
US wins Wightman Cup 11-4, 1003C3
CASANAS, Alejandro
Pan Am Game results 7-1–7-15, 798C3
CASAROLI, Cardinal Agostino
Named Vatican state secy 4-30, 376F1
Installed cardinal 6-30, 640C2
Curia reforms urged 11-9, 931C2
CASE, Edson
On 3 Mile A-accident 3-28, 242G1
CASE Western Reserve University (Cleveland)
Breast cancer drug study rptd 9-11, 736C1
CASH, Rosalind
Class of Miss MacMichael released 1-26, 528A2
CASH, William
Backed Flood acquittal 2-5, 102C2
CASPER, Dave
NFL '78 receiving ldr 1-6, 80C1
CASS, Peggy
Once A Catholic opens 10-10, 956F3
CASSELL, Barry
On US beef concessns 1-8, 36G2
CASSEN, Patrick
Jupiter moon theory rptd 3-17, 216G2
CASSIDY, Mark
Acquitted re price-fixing 4-29, 327C3
CASTANEDA, Jorge
Named Mex forgn secy 5-17, 408C3
Rebuffs Iran threat on shah 6-11, 445F3
Vs Nicaragua interventn 6-21, 461A1
Bars shah's reentry 11-29, 897C1
CASTANG, Veronica
Ride A Cock Horse opens 3-18, 292E2
CASTANON, Roberto
Lopez KOs 3-10, 412E3
CASTELLANO, Lucio
Seized in Moro probe 6-6, 487C1
CASTELLITO, Anthony (Three Fingers) (d. 1961)
Provenzano, Konigsberg '78 murder convictns upset 6-7, 491G3
CASTELO, Joseph
Indicted 3-6, 220D2
CASTELO Jr., Manuel
Indicted 3-6, 220D2
CASTILLO, Bernardino
Scores union curbs 7-9, 523A2
CASTILLO, Jose Antonio
Slain 10-28, 834F2

1980

CARTER, Rosalynn Smith (Mrs. Jimmy)
Campaigns in Iowa, backs embargo 1-7, 13A1
Speaks in Buffalo 1-31, 91E2
B Carter Libyan role rptd 7-24, 549C1
Sen com seek B Carter testimony 7-25, 569E1
In Peru for Belaunde inauguratn 7-28, 579E3
Husband denies impropriety re brother 8-4, 592D3, 594E2
Mental health authrzn clears Cong 9-24, 9-30, signed 10-7, 804C1
Pinch hits for Mondale 11-2, 841C1
Reagans visit 11-20, 897E2
CARTER, Rep. Tim Lee (R, Ky.)
Rogers wins US House seat 11-4, 849B3
CARTER-Mondale Presidential Committee
Kennedy speech rebutted 1-28, 75A1
CARTER Moore & Co.
Italy ct rules vs fibers 4-4, 294B3
CARTER v. U.S.
Case declined by Sup Ct 3-17, 226G1
CARTOONS & Cartoonists
BC cartoon libel ruling upset 2-15, 148C3
Avery rptd dead 9-1, 755B2
CARVAJAL Moreno, Gustavo
Meets El Salvador leftist ldr 5-26, 444A3
CARVER, Mayor Richard (Peoria, Ill.)
Loses US Sen primary 3-18, 206D3
CARY, Frank T.
Carter names to Synfuels Corp bd 9-13, withdraws 9-24, 725F2
Opel named chief exec 12-21, 986F2
CASALS, Pablo (1876-1973)
Marta Istomin gets Kennedy Cntr post 2-26, 199D2
CASALS, Rosemary
US wins Federatn Cup 5-25, 607C1
Wimbledon results 7-5, 606A3
CASANAS, Alejandro
Wins Olympic medal 7-27, 624A1
CASAS, Roxanne (d. 1977)
Stone acquitted of murder 2-1, 238E1
CASCO Bank (Portland, Me.)
Saco (Me) '79 default rptd 1-7, 54E1
CASERO, Paco
Backs Andalusia hunger strike 8-19, 653A2
CASEY, Douglas R.
Crisis Investing on best-seller list 9-14, 716B3; 10-12, 796D3
CASEY, Joseph E.
Dies 9-2, 755D2
CASEY, William J.
Named Reagan campaign chief 2-26, 143C1
Reagan camp organizes 7-22, 549B3
Equal TV time asked 9-18, 698A3
Heads Reagan transitn team 11-6, 839A3
Named CIA dir 12-11, 935E1
CASPER, Dave
Raiders win playoffs 12-28, 999E1
CASPIAN Sea
USSR rpts drainoff plugged 3-2, 235F3
USSR caviar scandal rptd 4-15, 354E3
CASSADY, Carolyn
Heart Beat released 4-25, 416A3
CASSADY, Neal (deceased)
Heart Beat released 4-25, 416A3
CASSATT, Mary (1845-1926)
Print sold for record sum 2-14, 472B2
CASSAVETES, John
Gloria released 10-1, 836A3
CASSIDY, Sheila
UK to restore Chile relatns 1-16, 57A2
CASSON, John
On Carter econ forecasts 1-28, 69B3
CASTANEDA de la Rosa, Jorge
Rpts US gas price hike 3-18, 234F1
Bars US hurricane spotter 7-1, 524D2
Hints El Salvador leftist ties 8-18, 633B3
CASTEL, Michael
Don't Answer the Phone released 8-9, 675C2
CASTILLO, Jaime
Arrest rptd 11-18, 887C2

1976

CASTILLO, Gen. Victor
Leaves cabt, named army staff chief 1-12, 27A1
CASTILLO Velasco, Jaime
DINA rights abuse chrgs rptd 6-12, 465E1
Exiled 8-6; bishops score govt 8-18, 711C2
CASTLE, Barbara
Quits Cabt 4-8, 266G3
CASTLE & Cooke Inc.
SEC lists paymts 5-12, 726F2
Forgn paymts policy cited 12-18, 985A2 ★
CASTRO Madero, Capt. Carlos
Rpts Canada A-sale probe 11-27, 997A2
CASTRO Ruz, Gen. Fidel (Cuban president)
Sees Torrijos, signs pacts 1-10—1-15, 52C2
Vows contd MPLA aid 1-15, 16F3
Uruguay bans youth group 1-20, 208B1
Venez scores Angola role 1-24, 138G1
Sees Canada prime min 1-26—1-29, 116D2
Constitutn OKd in referendum 2-15, 138B1
Addresses Sovt CP Cong 2-25, 196E1
Ford calls an 'outlaw' 2-28, 165F2
US comm rptdly told of CIA attempts on life 3-1, 217E2
Tours E Eur, Africa 3-6—3-16; dismisses US warnings 3-14, 251G2-E3
CIA memo on JFK threat rptd 3-20, 3-21, 217D2
Sweden, US informed of Angola troop exit rate 5-21, 5-24, 370B3
NATO doubts Angola exit 6-13, 467E1
Vows Angola aid 7-26, 649E2
Exile murder plot rptd 8-17—8-18, 791F1
Cubans blamed for US-based terrorism 8-18, 8-22, 791B1
CIA assassinatn plot cited 791E1
On econ problems, Sovt aid 9-27, 771G3-772E1
Uruguay pres scores Kennedy 10-8, 814G1
On munic assemb electns 10-11, 858E1
Ties CIA to jet crash, new death plot, terrorism; voids US hijack pact 10-15, 779A3, 780B1-C2
Ex-aide killed in PR 10-25, 844C3
Elected to Natl Assemb 11-2, 1001A1
CORU claims credit for Spain bombing 11-9, 844B3
Nicaragua denies exile aid 11-16, 926F1
Addresses Natl Assemb 12-2, elected pres 12-3, 1000C3
Jamaica electn issue 12-15, 965A2, D2
CASTRO Ruz, Gen. Raul
New constitutn enacted 2-24, 251F3
CATHAY Pacific Airways
Smith quits 2-11, 132G2
CATHOLIC Bishops, U.S. National Conference of—*See 'U.S.' under ROMAN Catholic Church*
CATHOLIC Relief Services
Guatemala quake aid rptd 2-10, 120E3
CATIN, Carlo Donat
Sworn Italy industry min 7-30, 573G1
CATLETT, Claudia
Weinstein chrgs vs Hiss rptd 3-18, 218C1, F1
CATLETT, Perry
Hiss denies Weinstein chrgs 3-18, 218F1
CATTLE—*See LIVESTOCK*
CATYB, Albert
On La oil refinery blast 8-15, 816A2
CAVAILLE, Marcel
Announces US jet accord 8-12, 588D3

1977

CASTLE, Robert O.
On Calif land swell chng 3-3, 288G1
CASTLE, William
Dies 5-31, 452E2
CASTLE Bank and Trust (Bahamas) Ltd.
US ct bars tax info; closes 4-28, 395C3, F3
CASTRO, Julio
Missing 9-28; rptd in Argentina, kin fear dead 10-3, 905A2
CASTRO, Gov. Raul H. (D, Ariz.)
Named in Bolles murder testimony 1-26—1-27, 162A1, D1
Backs Central Ariz Project 3-21, 210F1
Sworn amb to Argentina 10-20, 817B2
CASTRO, Col. Ruy (ret.)
Jailed re civiln rule plea 8-18—9-2, 741C1
CASTRO Olivera, Raul
Killed by guerrillas 10-26, 921C3
CASTRO Ruz, Gen. Fidel (Cuban president)
On COMECON A-plant 1-6, 19E3
Cuba role in Angola detailed 1-9, 19A1
CIA linked to '71 swine fever 1-9, 19E2
US makes overtures 1-27—3-9; interviews back trade ties, score rights pressure 2-9, 2-6—2-27, 180B2
Carter on key to normal ties 2-12, 2-16, 110B1
US Rep Bingham rpts on talks 2-15, 110E1; 2-16, 180F2
Tours Africa 3-1—4-2; in E Ger 4-2—4-4, USSR 4-4—4-6, 249F1
US probes CIA plot 3-16, 228F2
Denies Zaire role 3-21, 261D1
Sees US legislators 4-9; McGovern rpts on mtg 4-11, 282E3, 283B1
Carter on US-Cuba ties 4-14, 295F3
Minn execs in Cuba 4-20—4-22, 390D1
Scores US trade curb amendmt 5-11, 389F3
Somalia rejects Horn of Africa union 5-18, 428E2
Guatemala pres cites 5-20, 414B3
Denies Ethiopia advisers 5-24, 427F1
Sees US rep 5-28; Ethiopia reassurances rptd 6-1, Carter briefed 6-3, 456C2
Jamaica seeks closer US ties 5-30—5-31, 454E2
Interviewed on US TV 6-9, 456D1-B2
Exile chrgs betrayal by Venez pres 7-4, 868C1
Torrijos ties noted re US-Panama Canal talks 7-27, 590C1
Frees exiled commandos 8-2, 654C2
Sees Sen Church 8-8—8-11; OKs US natls, families exit 8-11, 653B3-654D1
Young lauds Panama Canal pact backing 8-11, 646D3
On US emb renovatn costs 9-1, 686B1
Reagan warns vs Panama role 9-8, 699B1
US natls, kin fly to US 9-22, 781B2
Sees US thaw 'long, slow' 9-29, 781F2 ★
US adm chrgs 'Torrijos-Castro-Moscow axis' 10-10, 792A2
In Jamaica, pledges aid 10-16—10-21, 883E3-884E1
Sees US execs; trade ties, prisoners, CIA discussed 10-26, 896E2
CIA plots vs Jamaica ldr rptd 11-2, 884G1
Torrijos ties discounted by US sens 11-12, 911D3
Artime dies 11-13, 952B2
US warns on Africa mil buildup 11-17, 896D1
FBI Cointelpro papers released 11-21, 940E3
Vs Africa pullout 12-5, scored by Young 12-6, reaffirms stand 12-24, 1011F2
US prisoner to be freed 12-13, 1011D3
CASTRO Ruz, Juanita
Protests cruise to Cuba 5-15, 390A2
CASTRO Ruz, Gen. Raul
Sees US legislators 4-7—4-8, 282D3
CASTROVILLE, Tex.—*See TEXAS*
CAT (computerized axial tomographic) Scanner—*See X-RAYS*
CATECHETICAL Directory, National (book)
US bishops OK 11-17, 906E1
CATHOLIC Bishops, U.S. National Conference of—*See ROMAN Catholic Church—U.S.*
CATHOLIC Conference, U.S. (USCC)
New Viet refugees arrive US 9-20, 739G3
CATHOLIC-Jewish Liaison Committee, International
Proselytism scored at mtg 3-28—3-30, 492C2
CATHOLIC Jurists, International Commission of
Brazil torture of minors chrgd 2-13, 168D1
CATHOLIC Press Association
Gallup addresses conv 4-26—4-29, 470B3
CATHOLICS—*See ROMAN Catholic Church*
CATHOLIC Theological Society of America
US bishops score sex study 11-16, 906C2
CATHOLIC Women, The National Council of
Rally vs women's conf 11-19, 918A1
CATTLE—*See LIVESTOCK*
CAULKINS, Tracy
Sets 3 swim records 8-18—8-21, 828E3
CAUTHEN, Steve
Sets earnings marks 10-24, 12-10; named top jockey 12-10, sportsman of yr 12-14, 970F2
CAVAILLE, Marcel
In Japan on shipbldg 1-21, 73C3
Backs NY Concorde ruling 5-11, 368A2
Scores Sovt Airbus bar 9-1, 736D1
Scores US Concorde proposal 9-23, 738F2

1978

CASTILLO Valdez, Rafael
Guatemala forgn min 7-21, 722C3 ★
New Belize independnc talks begin 9-25, 798A3
CASTILLO Velasco, Jaime
Chile allows return 4-4, 267F1
CASTLE, Jerome
Indicted for fraud 10-10, 808F2
CASTLE & Cooke Inc.
Standard Fruit & Steamship Co.
Honduras payoffs admitted 6-9, 615A1
CASTRO, Raul H.
Successor as gov dies 3-4, 186F3
CASTRO Ruz, Gen. Fidel (Cuban president)
Sees US reps on embargo, Africa role 1-2, 22E1
Raul Castro rptd in Ethiopia 1-12, 43F3
Mengistu visits Cuba 4-21—4-27, 372B3 ★
Eritrea talks rptd favored 4-27, 372G2
US seeks Cuban exiles in Letelier murder case 5-4, 370E3
Sees US envoy, denies Zaire role 5-17, 382A1
Guatemala pres scores 6-1, 497C1
Denies Zaire role 6-13; US disputes 6-12—6-14, 442F2, 443A1
Chrgs CIA aids UNITA 6-18, 645E3
Lauds Carter, scores Brzezinski 6-18, 687B2
Wants Carter mtg 6-27, 687A2
Somoza blames for Nicaragua unrest 7-22, 593F1
CIA death plots chrgd 8-2—8-4, 831D1
OKs dual US citizens release, asks Carter concessns 8-17, 687G1
Exiles bomb Cuba UN mission 9-9, 777B1
Hosts Spain premier 9-9—9-10, 821G3
In Ethiopia 9-12—9-19; Libya, Algeria 9-19, 776E3
Cited at JFK death hearings 9-19, 9-27, 749G2, F3, 750A2
Sees Miami exile ldrs, ex-prisoners fly to US 10-21, 880C2-B3
Overtures divide US exiles 10-24; US cites improved ties, remaining problems 11-13, 880D3
US exiles invited for pol talks 11-4, 880B3
Meets exile ldrs, sets prisoner release prisoner terms 11-21—11-22, 12-8—12-9; ex-prisoners fly to US 12-12, Venez 12-24, 1016A1
US pres hopeful scores 11-29, 938E3
CASTRO Ruz, Gen. Raul
Ethiopia visit rptd 1-12, 43F3
CASTROVILLE, Tex.—*See TEXAS*
CATERING Industry
Canteen kickbacks to Ford alleged 4-25, 390A3
CATERPILLAR Tractor Co.
USSR equipmt deal rptd 9-29, 821B1
CAT From Outer Space, The (film)
Released 6-30, 618F3
CATHOLIC Institute for International Relations
Bolivia vote fraud scored by Lord Avebury 7-12, 571F1
CATHOLICS—*See ROMAN Catholic Church*
CATHOLICS, Federation of Colored
Turner dies 4-21, 356E3
CATHOLIC University of America (Washington, D.C.)
Ellis gets Laetare Medal 3-6, 172F3
Pellegrino becomes pres 9-1, 844E1
CAT and Mouse (film)
Released 5-6, 618F3
CATARACTS—*See EYES & Eyesight*
CATSPLAY (play)
Opens 4-16, 887C1
CATTLE—*See LIVESTOCK*
CATTON, Bruce
Dies 8-28, 708C2
CAUCUS, Rep. Max (D, Mont.)
Parks bill OKd by House 7-12, 526G3
CAULKINS, Tracy
Leads US women's swimming resurgence, sets records 1-7—8-28, 780A1-D2, B3
CAUTHEN, Steve
Affirmed wins Triple Crown 6-10, 539C1-A2
McHargue breaks earnings mark 12-31, 1028E1
CAVAILLE, Marcel
Rpts USSR OKs Airbus landings 3-8, 238D2

1979

CASTILLO, Leonel J.
Resigns as INS head 8-10, 630D3
CASTILLO, Gen. Victor
Quells Bolivia army rebelln 10-11, 811D1
CASTINO, John
Named AL co-top rookie 11-26, 955B3
CASTLE, Jerome
Convicted for fraud 8-29, 655F3
CASTRE Madero, Rear Adm. Carlos
Rpts W Ger, Swiss A-plant deals 10-1, 749C1
On Canada A-sale loss 10-3, 788E3
CASTRO, Juanita
Demonstrates at anti-Fidel rally 10-12, 779C1
CASTRO, Capt. Lautaro
Held in '74 lime kiln murders 7-5, 523B1
CASTRO Hurtado, Gen. Arnaldo
Resigns as Venez army chief 5-22, 429B3
CASTRO Ruz, Gen. Fidel (Cuban president)
Scores US, Egypt, China 1-1; US cites obstacles to full ties 1-2, 20A1
Hosts US reps, asks trade embargo eased 1-7, 40E3
Exiles' murder trial opens in US 1-9—1-12, 19D2
CIA '63 death plot rptd confrmd 5-2, 367E3-368A1
Visits Mex 5-17—5-18, 372D2
US jet hijacked to Cuba 6-11, 442D1
Scores worker productivity 7-4, 685E3
US-Nicaragua ties detailed 535D3
'66 plotter pardoned 8-27, 686A1
Opens nonaligned summit, backs USSR 9-3, vows restraint as chrmn 9-9, 674C2, 675F1, B2
US-PR prisoner trade denied 9-6, 666F1
Frees 4 US prisoners 9-17, 706C3
Denies Sovt combat brigade presence, scores Carter 9-28, 737G2
Carter cites 'special' Sovt ties 10-1, 738A3
In US amid tight security 10-11—10-14; addresses UN, asks 3d World aid 10-12, sees 2 black congressmen 10-13, 778B2-779F1
Matos freed after 20 yrs 10-21, 812E2
Cuban NY mission bombed 10-27, 852E1
CASTRO Valley, Calif.—*See CALIFORNIA*
CATCHINGS, Harvey
Traded to Nets 2-7, Bucks 5-30, 526E2, F2
CATERPILLAR Tractor Co.
Fortune rpts '78 rank, sales gain 5-7, 305A1
UAW strikes 10-1—12-19, 987E1
Brazil metalworkers strike 10-29, 833B2
CATES, Gilbert
Promise released 3-7, 528D3
CATHOLIC Bishops, U.S. National Conference of—*See ROMAN Catholic Church—U.S.*
CATHOLIC Charities, National Conference of
KC conv; Jordan, Carter address 10-14—10-15, 780D2, 807G2
CATHOLIC Relief Services
East Timor famine aid rptd 10-30, 838C2
CATHOLICS—*See ROMAN Catholic Church*
CATHOLIC Theological Society
Vatican criticism of sexual ethics book rptd 8-11, 640G2
CATHOLIC University of America (Washington, D.C.)
Pope sees Cath scholars, backs acad freedom 10-7, 760B1
CATHOLIC Workers of Baltimore
White House A-protest 3-31, 261F3
CATLETTSBURG, Ky.—*See KENTUCKY*
CATO, Milton (St. Vincent prime minister)
Independence gained 10-27, 825E1
Party wins electns 12-5, 951A3
Union, Palm Island rebelln crushed 12-7—12-8, 951D3
CATONSVILLE 9—*See MARYLAND—Crime*
CATTLE—*See LIVESTOCK*
CAUCE, Caesar
Slain in NC 11-3, 864D3
CAULFIELD, Maxwell
Class Enemy opens 6-18, 711C2

1980

CASTILLO, Ruben
Arguello KOs 1-20, 320A3
CASTLE, Jerome
Penn-Dixie files for bankruptcy, '79 convictn cited 4-7, 985F3
CASTLE & Cooke Inc.
Nader coalitn attacks 4-17, 308B2
Standard Fruit & Steamship Co.
CR banana workers' strike ends 1-17, 117D1
CASTRILLO, Roberto
Wins Olympic medal 7-26, 623D2
CASTRO, Orlando
Hijacks Uruguayan plane 11-12, surrenders in Argentina 11-13, 888C3
CASTRO Caicedo, German
Sees M-19 ldr 4-17, Turbay 4-19, 311F2
CASTRO Ruz, Gen. Fidel (Cuban president)
Tightens rule, assumes key ministries 1-11, 38E2, C3
Reagan, Connally 'basic speeches' cite 2-29, 207C3; 3-7, 184G3
Allows Padilla to emigrate to US 3-16, 231A3
Offers asylum to DR Emb captors in Colombia 3-18, 211C3
Seeks to mediate Afghan-Pak feud 3-25—3-27, 271C2
French trade accord reached, Antilles non-interventn pledge linked 4-1, 253F2
Vows Peru Emb refugees safe passage 4-7, 261C2
Peru scores refugee policy shift 4-16, 285F1
Bay of Pigs marked 4-19, 300F2-B3
Goodbye Fidel opens 4-23, 392G2
US seeks airlift of refugees 5-1, 326A2
Skips Tito funeral 5-8, 339A1
Carter curbs 'open arms' policy, orders flotilla end; 5-pt progrm detailed 5-14, 361D1, B2
Blocks criminal refugees return 6-24, 514F2
In Nicaragua; marks Somoza downfall, evaluates US policy 7-18—7-19, 565G2
Greets Mex pres 7-31, 605B3
Cuban refugees seize jet in Lima, demand flight to US 8-29, 672D2
Venez acquits '76 jet bombing suspects 9-26; chrgs traded 9-29, 794G2, B3
Manley link spurs Jamaica electn issue 10-5, 791G3
Reagan criticism cited 10-13, 789F1
Frees 30 US prisoners 10-27, 828C3
Manley defeated in Jamaica 10-30, 854E1
Addresses 2d Cuban CP Cong, outlines 5-yr plan 12-17, 12-20, 992C3
CASTRO Ruz, Raul
'79 econ performance scored 1-1, 38B3
Bahamas patrol boat talks open 5-12, 371F2
CASTRO Spikula, Sergio de
On Chile econ recovery 1-14, 19F2, C3
CATALANO, Patti
2d in NYC Marathon 10-26, 891A1
CATALANO Inc. v. Target Sales Inc.
Case decided by Sup Ct 5-27, 453G2
CATES, Gilbert
Last Married Couple released 2-8, 216B3
Oh, God! II released 10-3, 836C3
Tricks of the Trade opens 11-16, 892G3
CATHER, Willa (1873-1947)
Harper's to cease publicatn 6-17, 501A1
CATHOLIC Charities, National Conference of
Mondale addresses NY mtg 9-23, 780F2
CATHOLIC Relief Service
Indonesia bars E Timor relief 12-9, 943D1
CATHOLICS—*See ROMAN Catholic Church*
CATHOLIC University (Washington, D.C.)
Busing, housing integratn rptd linked 11-16, 989B3
CATS
Tenn house rptd purchased 2-9, 200G1
CATTLE—*See LIVESTOCK*
CAUCUSES—*See POLITICS—Elections*
CAULKINS, Tracy
Sets 200-m breaststroke mark 4-9, 834G3
Sets 100-m breaststroke, 400-m individual medley marks 7-29, 7-30; ties for US 200-m breaststroke title 7-31, 834C3, D3
CAULTON, Christopher
Chrgd re business paymts 5-5, 406C3
CAVACO e Silva, Anibal
Named Portuguese finance min 1-3, 21F3
Submits '80 austerity budget 4-2, 277F2

1976

CAVANAUGH, John J.
Elected 11-2, 823D3, 830C1
CAVERT, Samuel McCrea
Dies 12-21, 1015C1
CAVETT, Dick (Richard)
Sup Ct bars review of Polish joke case 2-23, 170A1
CAWLEY, Evonne Goolagong—*See GOOLAGONG, Evonne*
CAYMAN Islands (British colony)
Forgn cos leave Bahamas 1-22, 104B2
CBS Inc.
Muskie rebuts Ford message 1-21, 40E1
Cronkite interviews Ford 2-3, 88A1
Schorr admits leaking House com rpt 2-12, suspended 2-23, 150D3, 151G1
Schorr dismissal urged 2-17, 216F3
House leak probe underway 3-2, 216E3
Wallace on Face the Nation 3-7, 179A3
Wood quits, Wussler named 4-9, 504C2
Boyd on Morning News 4-16, 291F2
Gives Church pol time 4-19, 282B1
Brown on Face the Nation 5-9, 343G2
Sovt editor on US spy chrg 5-26, 371D3
Ford on Face the Nation 6-6, 410B3
Rabin on Face the Nation 7-11, 515B2
Schorr probe hearings 7-19, 7-20, 8-25, refuses testimony 9-15; probe dropped 9-22, 748A3
US files consent decree 7-27, 989G1
On Ford delegate count 8-16, 601D3
Dole on Face the Nation 8-22, 631C2
'F-14' documentary televised 8-27, 979E3
OKs pres debate rules 9-20, 703C2
Schorr resigns, Salant comments 9-28, 749E1, A2
Signs USSR pact 10-6, 907G3
Hoover on Everest climb 10-8, 876D3
Taylor ousted, Paley to resign as chief exec 10-13, 892E1
Mondale on Face the Nation 10-17, 803C3
NYT Poll: Carter ahead 10-27, 826C1
Louis Cowan dies 11-8, 970D1
NBC, US in programing pact 11-17, 869B2
US asks FCC probe 11-23, 901D1
Cronkite interviews Carter 11-29, 897E3
Lance on Face the Nation 12-5, 917A1

1977

CAVANAUGH, Matt
Pitt wins Gator Bowl 12-30, 1020C2
CAVANZO, Josue
Assassinatn rptd 1-12, 255B1
CAVCAT (Yugoslav ship)
Poison cargo recovery begun 4-4, 284B3
CAVERO, Inigo
Spain educ, sci min 7-5, 545B2
CAVIN, Robert B.
Convicted 8-30, 691B3
Fined 9-16, 918F2
CAZAARES v. Indiana
Sup Ct refuses appeal 1-10, 57A2
CAZZANIGA, Vincenzo
Exxon settles forgn paymts chrgs 10-25, 818E1
CBOE—*See CHICAGO Board Options Exchange*
CB Radio—*See BROADCASTING—Radio*
CBS Inc.
Bush on Face the Nation 1-2, 39F3, 41A2
Korry on 60 Minutes 1-9, 18D2
FCC sets probe 1-14, 119E1
NBC gets Moscow Olympics 2-1, 131D1
Castro on Evening News 2-9, 180D2
Vance on Face the Nation 2-27, 151C2
John Dickson Carr dies 2-27, 164D2
Carter call-in sessn 3-5, 171A1-G3
Turner on Face the Nation 3-20, 211C3
Sadat interview 4-9, 267A3
Paley sets retiremt 4-20, 355G3
Schlesinger on Face the Nation 4-24, 319C3
Tennis tourn fee disclosures 5-7—5-20, FCC rpts probe 7-8, 548D2
Schultze on Face the Nation 5-8, 385A2
Backe named chief exec 5-11, 532F1
Child abuse police on 60 Minutes 5-15, 432A2
Brown on Face the Nation 5-22, 404C1
USSR claims Jews influence 7-22, 589B2
Study chrgs TV bias 8-15, 643B1
CIA-press link chargd 9-12, 721C1
Rpts US bugging of Panama Canal talks 9-16, 716A2
Managemt reorgnzd; sports, entertainmt units set 10-17, 846E1
Tourtellot dies 10-18, 872B3
NFL record TV pact rptd 10-26, 950E1-A2
House subcom probes TV sports 11-3, 949E3, 950B1
Wins Emmy 11-6, 1022B1
Journalists' thoughts for 60 Minutes protected 11-7, 920G2
Cronkite interviews Sadat, Begin 11-14, 873D1
Ex-CIA analyst on 60 Minutes 11-20, 898F1
Sadat interview 11-27, 909G1
Sevareid retires 11-30, 1021E2
NBC trust accord OKd 12-1, 918C3
On most reliable govt news source list 12-10, 1009B1
Begin on Face the Nation 12-18, 994B3
CEA—*See U.S. GOVERNMENT—ECONOMIC Advisers, President's Council of*
CEAUSESCU, Elena (Mrs. Nicolae)
Promoted 1-25, 100D1

1978

CAVANAUGH, Rep. John J. (D, Neb.)
Reelected 11-7, 851E2, 854F3
CAVARRETTA, Phil
Dark fired as Padres mgr 3-21, 355B2
CAVCAT (Yugoslav ship)
Italy completes poison cargo recovery 4-25, 330E3
CAVENHAM Ltd.—*See GENERALE Occidentale S.A.*
CAWLEY, Evonne Goolagong—*See GOOLAGONG, Evonne*
CAWLEY, Helen
Loses Australian Open 1-1, 22F3
CAYMAN Islands (British colony)
Vesco leaves CR 4-30, 354E2
CAZACU, Virgil
Named to Rumania CP central com, dep prime min 3-7, 193C2
CAZALE, John
Dies 3-12, 252E2
CB (citizens band) Radio—*See ELECTRIC & Electronics*
CBS Inc.
Football TV contract tax value backed 1-9, 13C2
Super Bowl viewing record rptd 1-17, 39F3
Panama Canal poll cited 1-19, 58D2
Silverman to head NBC 1-20, 75E2
Reagan scores Canal pacts in TV address 2-8, 121B1
IMS purchase sought 2-15, rejctd 2-22, 185B1
TV pact with Spinks, Top Rank rptd 2-17, 211E3
Leonard vs children's TV ad curbs 2-28, 347C2
Ali on Sports Spectacular 3-4, 212A1
Tito interview 3-8, 194B1
Wussler quits CBS Sports 3-15, FCC censures 'Heavyweight Championship' tennis tourn 3-16, 252E1
Carter poll standing down on econ issues 4-12, 260A3
Reasoner move from ABC set 5-12, 419C3
Colby on 60 Minutes 5-14, 367D3
US trust suit seeks Fawcett divestiture 6-1, 510E3
Popular Library, Fawcett '76 sales rptd 6-1, 510F3
Moving indus defamatn chrg rebutted 6-30, 589F2
Leonard to head news divisn 7-14, 599A3
Gannett to sell TV statn 8-20, 759G3
Independent news producers sue 9-11, 759G1
Fla slayer loses TV violence suit 9-26, 759G2
NBC drops fall TV lineup 11-29, 1030D1
China policy poll 12-19, 976E1
Face the Nation
Begin 7-23, 563F1
Brzezinski 1-8, 9D2
Dayan 10-8, 762C1
Eizenstat 10-15, 785E1
Hussein 10-1, 762A2
Jones 11-21, 895A1
Marshall 2-26, 160A1
Meany 11-5, 863F2
O'Neil 1-22, 64C1
Preyer 9-24, 898E1
Schlesinger 6-25, 511F3
Turner 10-22, 940F2
Ullman 4-2, 241C1
CBS Reports—*See CBS Inc.*
CCD—*See DISARMAMENT—Geneva Committee*
CDC (Center for Disease Control)—*See U.S. GOVERNMENT—PUBLIC Health Service—Disease Control, Center for*

1979

CAVANAGH, Jerome Patrick
Dies 11-27, 932C2
CAVANAUGH, Daniel
Convicted in '77 Papa slaying 10-23, 840A2
CAVANAUGH, Rev. John Joseph
Dies 12-28, 1008B2
CAVANAUGH, Lt. Col. Michael
Beaten in Afghan 9-8, leaves 9-9, 696E1
CAVARA, Paolo
Stay As You Are released 12-21, 1008G1
CAZACU, Virgil
Ousted as Rumania dep premr 1-31, 171C1
CBOE—*See CHICAGO Board Options Exchange*
CBS Inc.
Knoetze boxing match protested 1-13, 79D2
Haldeman discloses 60 Minutes interview fee 1-27, 176C1
Wage-price compliance, postal rate rollback linked 2-6, 128C1
Salant NBC apptmt rptd 3-29, 335A1
'State of mind' libel queries backed by Sup Ct, '73 60 Minutes suit cited; Leonard scores 4-18, 302A1, B2
O'Leary on news program 5-7, 343B1
Sevareid, St Pierre wed 6-30, 527E2
Kennedy interviewed re Chappaquiddick 7-17, 539F1
ABC-TV affiliates rptd on par 7-31, 588B2
1st $\frac{1}{2}$ profits down, records unit fires staff 8-10, 618D1
Ex-newsman linked to KGB 8-11, 611A2
Small named NBC News pres 8-28, 756A2
NBC '77 trust setlmt challenge refused by Sup Ct 10-1, 768C2
FCC scores children's TV 10-30, NAB responds 11-1, 858B3, D3
NBC '77 trust setlmt challenge refused again by Sup Ct 12-10, 988A2
NBC Iran hostage interview scored 12-11, 934D3
Face the Nation
Brown 2-25, 143D3
Brzezinski 12-9, 933F2
Byrd 7-8, 511A1
Church 9-9, 674C1
Schlesinger 8-5, 629A2
Webster 7-2, 561F3
Young 8-19, 624D3
Polls
Midwest GOP offcls 3-10, 185F3
Carter rating up 3-29, 231D3
A-power 4-10, 259G2
Kennedy leads 11-4, 847D2
Abortn, women's ordinatn 11-11, 930A2
CBS Inc. v. U.S.
Case refused by Sup Ct 10-1, 768D2; 12-10, 988A2
CCD—*See DISARMAMENT–Geneva Committee*
CDC (Center for Disease Control)—*See U.S. GOVERNMENT–PUBLIC Health Service–Disease Control, Center for*
CE, Cardinal Marco
Installed cardinal 6-30, 640C2
CEA—*See U.S. GOVERNMENT–ECONOMIC Advisers, Council of*
CEASAR'S World
NJ casino license rptd pending 2-26, 152C1
CEAUSESCU, Elena (Mrs. Nicolae)
Ordrs CP purge 9-18—9-19, 910D2

1980

CAVANAUGH, Rep. John J.(D, Neb.)
Daub elected to US House 11-4, 851A2
CAVETT, Dick
Hellman sues 2-15, 199E2
CAVIAR—*See FISHING Industry*
CAWLEY, Roger
Wife wins Wimbledon 7-4, 606G2
CAWTHORN, Robert
Interferon patent applicatn rptd 1-16, 62E3
CAYETANO Carpio, Salvador
Salvadoran leftists launch offensive 12-26, 993D2
CAYMAN Islands
Mystery freighter intercepted off Cuba 7-4, 515B1
CBS, et al v. FCC
Case accepted by Sup Ct 11-3, 856D2
CBS Inc.
'Dovish' complaint case refused by Sup Ct 1-7, 16A1
Kalb rpts Ghotbzadeh slur vs Khomeini, Iran bars CBS-TV 29A3
RCA video disk pact signed 1-10, 120F1
Redgrave TV role protested 1-13, 120D2
Boston affiliate loses license 1-24, 119F2
Mobil TV ad rejectn rptd 1-31, 120E1
Video divisn formed 1-31, 239E3
Rather named news anchorman 2-15, 198E3
Raviv rpts Israel '79 A-test 2-21, loses credentials 2-24, 141E3
Bradley wins Polk award 2-25, 692F3
'60 Minutes' airs Iran segmt 3-2, govt pressure rptd 3-6, 239B1
Iran hostage film purchase rejected 4-10, 282C3
'79-80 Nielsen ratings rptd, TV lead regained; 'Guyana Tragedy' cited 4-22, 376A1
Backe quits, Paley dispute hinted 5-8, 376D1
US trust dispute setld 5-8, 501C3
Cuba broadcasts barred, previous transmissns cited 5-22; policy review rptd 5-23. 397C1
Wyman named pres, chief exec 5-22; assumes posts 6-2, 501G1
Jankowski resignatn hoax 5-23, 501A2
Cuba broadcasts cleared 6-1, 420G2
Kalb, Mudd join NBC 6-18, 7-1, 638F2
Times/CBS protectionism poll rptd 6-26, 515F3
Reasoner files divorce suit 6-30, 639A1
Rather denies Afghan gang slaying role 8-4, 602E1
ABC settles US trust suit 8-22, 732F1
Kraft cocaine-use probe rptd 9-14, 700D1
'Shogun' aired by NBC 9-15—9-19, top ratings rptd 9-24, 835B3
Redgrave TV film aired, Jews protest 9-30, 835C3
Appeals ct backs Abscam tapes broadcast 10-1; Sup Ct refuses stay, tapes aired 10-14, 781F2
'Dallas' TV episode aired 11-21, viewing record rptd 11-25, 905A3
FCC cable ownership rule revocatn sought 12-8; cultural cable move detailed 12-10, 1003A1
RCTV wins BBC rights 12-11, 1002C3
CBS Toys
Toy gym recall set 6-2, 703G2
Face the Nation
Bush 1-20, 50E2
Carter 6-1, 424E3
Fraser 8-31, 659A3
Hooks 7-6, 515B3
Kennedy 3-9, 206E3
Meese 12-28, 980G2
Muskie 9-7, 679D3
Proxmire 2-10, 145A2
Holt, Rhinehart & Winston
Photocopy co sued 2-5, 119G3
Photocopy suit rptd setld 3-21, 376D3
Presidential Campaign & Election
See also 'Face the Nation' above
Reagan on 60 Minutes 1-27, 91B3
Times/CBS pres poll rptd 2-20, 130D2
Carter ad bid upheld by ct 3-14, 222B1
Times/CBS Ill primary poll cited 3-18, 206F2
Reagan scores press 4-10, 288B2
Times/CBS pres poll rptd 4-18, 304E3
Reagan delegate majority rptd 5-20, 382F3
Times/CBS pres poll rptd 6-3, 423B1
Cronkite interviews Ford 7-16, 530C1, E1
Reagan equal-time bid rejctd 9-19, 723B1
Post-debate pres poll rptd 9-28, 739C3
Pres poll standings tighten, toss-up seen 10-23, 816A2
Pol airtime case accepted by Sup Ct 11-3, 856D2
Electn-exit poll results 11-4, 838G2
Electn projectns lag explained 11-5, 865F3
CD (Committee on Disarmament)—*See GENEVA Committee*
CDC (Disease Control, Center for)—*See under U.S. GOVERNMENT--PUBLIC Health Service*
CE, Cardinal Marco
Warning re banned mass rptd 4-26, 364E1
CEA (Economic Advisors, Council of)—*See under U.S. GOVERNMENT*
CEAUSESCU, Elena
Named Rumania dep premr 3-29, 412B1

1976

CEAUSESCU, Nicolae (Rumanian president)
At Sovt CP Cong 2-24—3-5, 195B3, 196C1
Visit to Greece rptd 4-8, 333B2
Addresses culture cong 6-2, 420C2
Shuffles Cabt 6-15, 440A2
At E, W Eur CP conf 6-29—6-30, 461D2
In Yugoslavia 9-8—9-10, 734F2
Brezhnev visits 11-22—11-24, 907A2
Sees Elliot Richardson 11-22, 907E2
Moldavian ldr visits 12-3—12-7, 1010E1
CEBALLOS, Col. Jorge (ret.)
Scores mil junta 1-12, 28F1
CECCALDI, Etienne
Transfer disputed 5-16, 537F3
CECO Corp.
Fined 4-10, 988E3
CEDAR Coal Co.
Wildcat strike spreads 7-19—7-27, 553G1
CEDAR Rapids, Ia.—*See IOWA*
CEDAR Rapids-Marion Gazette (newspaper)
Ford endorsement rptd 10-30, 827G3
CEDARS-Sinai Medical Center (Los Angeles, Calif.)
Intern unionizatn barred 3-22, 220F1
CEDENO, Cesar
NL wins All-Star game 7-13, 544C2
NL batting ldr 10-4, 796A1
CEDERBERG, Rep. Elford A. (R, Mich.)
Reelected 11-2, 829D4
CEJAS, Jesus
Vanishes in Argentina 8-9, 'desertn' rptd 8-16, 672F1
CELANESE Corp.
SEC rpts no corp paymts 5-12, 726F2
CELEBES Sea
Quake hits Pl 8-17, 619A2
CELIS, Miguel D.
Seized in US 5-15, 401D2
CELLA Jr., Dr. Louis
Convicted 6-24, sentnc rptd 7-20, 860D2
CELLINI, William
Seconds Ford nominatn 8-18, 597G2
CELLULOSE
UK, Japan cos set Paraguay investmts 4-30, 403B3
CEMENT (& Cement Industry)
Trinidad plant expansn set 1-2, 55D3
Angola natlizes Portugal co 5-6, 371A2
CENSORSHIP—*See PORNOGRAPHY; specific media (e.g., MOTION Pictures); also country names*
CENTENNIAL (book)
On best seller list 1-25, 80D3; 2-29, 208F3
CENTENNIAL Bank (Philadelphia, Pa.)
Fails 10-20, sold 10-21, 940G1
CENTER for Community Change (Washington, D.C.)
Study scores revenue sharing 3-2, 187B1
CENTER for Improved Education (Columbus, O.)
Prisoner job training rpt issued 3-9, 271D2
CENTER for National Policy Review (Washington, D.C.)
Study scores revenue sharing 3-2, 187B1
CENTER for the Study of Democratic Institutions (Santa Barbara, Calif)
John Cogley dies 3-28, 272E3

1977

CEAUSESCU, Nicolae (Rumanian president)
Rpts '76 indl output, '77 forecast 1-1, 100G1-A2
Party shuffled, wife promoted; son rptd CP youth ldr 1-27, 100D1
Scores human rights plea 2-17, 137A2
Asks quake relief halt 3-8, discounts warning 3-10, 204A2
Declares general amnesty 5-9, 437A1
US coal deal signed 5-30, 468E3
Sets press self-censorship 6-30, 567F1
Miners strike 8-1, reforms vowed 8-3; reprisals rptd 9-1, 947E3, G3
Meets with Begin 8-25—8-29, 663C2
Rptd Begin-Sadat go-between 11-16, 873C2
Begin thanks 11-18, 895B1
On '81-85 econ plan 12-7, 987E2
CEAUSESCU, Nicu
Rptd Rumania CP youth ldr 1-27, 100E1
CECO Corp.
Price-fixing chrgd 6-6, 504B1
CEDENO, Cesar
NL batting ldr 10-2, 926D3
CEKADA, Anthony
Ordained by Lefebvre 6-29, 620G2
CELOTEX Corp.—*See WALTER Corp., Jim*
CEMENT Industry
Sup Ct rejects US Steel case 2-22, 149B3
2d ¼ profits rptd up 7-28, 668C3
Record trust fine levied on Medusa unit 10-5, 918D2
CENSORSHIP—*See PORNOGRAPHY; specific media (e.g., MOTION Pictures); also country names*
CENSUS, Bureau of the—*See under U.S. GOVERNMENT—COMMERCE*
CENTENO, Norberto
Kidnaped 7-6, found dead 7-12, 595E2
CENTER for Defense Information
US-Sovt strategic weapons compared 751C3
CENTER for Disease Control—*See U.S. GOVERNMENT—PUBLIC Health Service—Disease Control*
CENTER for Law and Social Policy
Frank confrmd NOAA dir 7-13, 626E2
CENTER for National Security Studies
Backs FBI curbs 2-15, 157C3
CENTO—*See CENTRAL Treaty Organization*

1978

CEAUSESCU, Nicolae (Rumanian president)
Meets Sadat 2-12, 98A3
Shuffles CP, govt posts 3-7, 193B2
Meets Dayan, gets Begin note 4-3—4-4, 235D3
In US 4-11—4-18, sees Carter 4-12—4-13, 291C1
Visits UK 6-13—6-16, jet deal signed 6-15, 515F2
Reassures Brezhnev on Hua visit 8-7, 678A1
Pacepa defectn rptd 8-8, 651A1
Hua visits Rumania 8-16—8-21; communique issued 8-18, agrmts signed 8-21, 674A3-675A2
USSR scores Hua joint statemt 8-21, 675D3
Pacepa defectn triggers purges 9-1, 9-6, 741B3
Bars Warsaw Pact defns hike 11-25, 913F2
Hua visit cited 11-25, 913B3
Affirms Warsaw Pact defns spending curbs 11-29—12-1, Brezhnev scores 12-5, 929F2
Sees US Treas Secy Blumenthal 12-9, 965D3
CECIL, Dick
NASL OKs Caribous sale, Atlanta move 10-3, 969A3
CEDDO (film)
Released 2-16, 618G3
CEDERBERG, Rep. Elford A. (R, Mich.)
Loses reelectn 11-7, 854B1
CELANESE Corp.
Mitsubishi unit indicted 5-9, 404B2
Olin takeover set 10-3, 767G3
Olin merger ended 11-10, 897C1
CELAYA, Gen. Amilcar
In Honduras mil junta 8-7, 614A3
CELESTE, Lt. Gov. Richard F. (D, Ohio)
Wins primary for Ohio gov 6-6, 448C1
Loses electn for Ohio gov 11-7, 854D1
CELINE and Julie Go Boating (film)
Released 2-24, 618G3
CELOTEX Corp.—*See WALTER Corp., Jim*
CEMENT Industry
Kaiser, Medusa to merge 3-16, 283D1
1st ¼ '77, '78 profits rptd up 4-27, 403E2
Southn workers sign pact 5-22, 429E3
'77-78 2d ¼ corp profit rise rptd 7-28, 642C3
Kaiser-Medusa deal canceled 8-22, Crane-Medusa deal set 9-1, 700C3
Penn Dixie ex-offcl indicted 10-10, 808F2
Nigeria '75 scandal, French suit cited 11-30, 934A3
CENSORSHIP—*See PORNOGRAPHY; specific media (e.g., MOTION Pictures); country names*
CENSUS, Bureau of the—*See under U.S. GOVERNMENT—COMMERCE*
CENTENNIAL (book)
On best-seller list 11-6, 888B1; 12-3, 971C1
CENTER for Disease Control—*See under U.S. GOVERNMENT—PUBLIC Health Service*
CENTER for National Security Studies
Carter intell reorgn, curbs scored 1-24, 49B3
CIA informant in DC schls rptd 3-30, 243A3 ★
Black ldr cited in FBI anti-King effort 5-29, 410G2

1979

CEAUSESCU, Nicolae (Rumanian president)
Shuffles Cabt 1-31, 171B1
Agri reform rptd 2-6, 170F3
Govt posts shuffled 3-30, 279D3
Seeks Israel-PLO-Syria feud mediatn 8-31; Israel rejects 9-2; Arafat mtg cited 659B2*
Wife ordrs CP purge 9-18–9-19, 910C2
Skips E Ger fete 10-7, 761E2
12th CP cong held 11-19–11-23, Pirvulescu scores 11-23, 910C1
CEDANO Suero, Gen. Demetrio
Arrested 9-25, plot exposed 9-26, 751F3
CEDENO, Leonel
Quits Ecuador Cabt 11-29, 967E3
CEFOXITIN—*See MEDICINE–Drugs*
CELAM—*See LATIN American Episcopal Conference*
CELEBREZZE Jr., Anthony J.
HEW post cited 7-27, 577E1
CELESTE, Richard F.
Named Peace Corps dir 3-29, 310F2
CEMENT Industry
Price guidelines tightened 3-29, 264A2
Boise Cascade to buy Lone Star unit 4-11, 440E3
India, Bangladesh accord set 4-18, 328E2
1st ¼ profits rptd down 4-27, 385D1
Ideal Basic price violatn chrgd 5-9, 385A2
CEMENTON, N.Y.—*See NEW York State*
CENSUS, Bureau of—*See under U.S. GOVERNMENT–COMMERCE*
CENTENNIAL (book)
On best-seller list 1-7, 80D3
CENTER for Defense Information
US, USSR strategic weapons compared 338G3
CENTER for Policy Research
Viet vet study released 9-25, 725E1
CENTER for Science in the Public Interest
Urges beer warning label 9-19, 736B1
CENTER for Strategic and International Studies of Georgetown University (Washington, D.C.)
Schlesinger apptmt rptd 9-1, 859F3*

1980

CEAUSESCU, Nicolae (Rumanian president)
Scores USSR re Afghanistan 1-1, 11A1
Sees Gromyko, bars Afghan support 1-31—2-2, 109A1
Wife named dep premr 3-29, 412B1
Calls for trade balance 6-4, 465D3
Scores Polish CP, unionists 10-21, 831B1
At Moscow summit on Poland 12-5, 929D1
CEBRIAN, Juan Luis
Sentenced for 'insults' 5-9, 410B2
CECCALDI, Daniel
Charles & Lucie released 5-9, 675B2
CECIL, Al
Files Okla murder chrg 1-21, 94A2
CECIL, Donald
Clothes for a Summer Hotel opens 3-26, 392E2
CEDARS Sinai Hospital (Los Angeles, Calif.)
James Garner assaulted 1-16, 200E1
CEDENO, Cesar
NL batting ldr 10-6, 926D2
CEFALO, Dan
Missing in Carib copter crash 11-13, 869E3
CEFALO, Jim
Brother missing in Carib copter crash 11-13, 869E3
CELASUN, Gen. Sedat
In Turkey mil junta 9-21, 720C3
CELOVSKY, Boris
Statistics Canada cleared 4-1, 273A1
CEMENT Industry
Spain sets energy conservatn 1-8, 22C2
Turkey sets price hike 1-25, 80B1
Penn-Dixie files for bankruptcy 4-7, 985F3
State sales preference upheld by Sup Ct 6-19, 554F2
Taiwan '79 sales rptd down 7-4, 567B3
Polish shortage rptd 11-12, 878B3, C3
CENDANA, Gregoria
Named Pl info min 1-17, 100B3
CENTENARY College (Shreveport, La.)
Sutton 2d in NCAA golf championship 5-31; wins US Amateur 8-31, 714D3, F3
Reagan addresses 10-22, 802A2
CENTER for Science in the Public Interest
Alcohol ingredient labeling order scored 6-10, 485C3
FDA caffeine warning scored 9-4, 726E2

1976

CENTRAL African Empire (formerly Central African Republic)—*See also AFRICAN Development Bank, NONALIGNED Nations Movement, OAU*
Listed as 'not free' natn 1-19, 20D3
IMF OKs SDR purchase, rpts '75 export drop 2-2, 204C2
Bokassa assassinatn try fails 2-3, 8 sentncd 2-14, 204B2
Quainton confrmd US amb 2-4, 110C2
Plotters' executn rptd 3-23, 288E2
Total IMF oil loan rptd 4-1, 340C2
Bokassa takes mil control, 7 Cabt posts; Domitien dismissed 4-7, 288D2
Bokassa expels jailed French natl 4-30, 503F2
At France-Africa summit 5-10—5-11, 355A3
Olympic withdrawal rptd 7-21, 528B3
China ties restored 8-20, 949A2
Bokassa names council 9-5, 924D2
Bokassa names Dacko adviser 9-17, 858B1
Bokassa in China 11-15, 871C3
Bokassa declares empire 12-4, 924B2
OPEC grants loan 12-23, 975F3
CENTRAL African Republic—*See CENTRAL African Empire*
CENTRAL America—*See LATIN America; specific countries, organizations*
CENTRAL American Common Market (CACM) (Costa Rica, El Salvador, Guatemala, Nicaragua)
Kissinger pledges US support 2-17, 177C2
CENTRAL Banking System
Rptd on FRB 'problem' list 1-22, 111B2
Central Bank (Oakland, Calif.)
Rptd on comptroller's 'problem' list 1-26, 113E1
CENTRAL National Chicago Corp.
Rptd on FRB 'problem' list 1-22, 111A3
Central National Bank (Chicago)
Rptd on comptroller's 'problem' list 1-26, 113E1
CENTRAL Railroad Company of New Jersey
Conrail begins operation 4-1, 235E1

1977

CENTRAL African Empire (CAE) (formerly Central African Republic)—*See also NONALIGNED Nations Movement, OAU*
UN Assemb member 3F3
Uganda claims invasn threat 2-22, 141D2
At France-Africa summit 4-20—4-21, 316F3
Zaire rpts forces sent 5-13, 394D1
US, UK rptrs arrested 7-14, freed 7-21, 8-15; US protest rptd 8-16, 634E3
Bokassa crowned emperor 12-4, 946D2-A3
Per capita income, other econ data cited 946A3
CENTRAL America—*See LATIN America; specific countries, organizations*
CENTRAL Arizona Project—*See ARIZONA*
CENTRAL Hotel (Galveston, Tex.)
Burns 4-19, 508G3
CENTRAL Intelligence Agency—*See under U.S. GOVERNMENT*
CENTRAL Soya Co.
Rpts payoffs 6-9, 503D1
ICC curbs rail grain-car deals 8-1, 613D1

1978

CENTRAL African Empire (CAE)—*See also GATT, NONALIGNED Nations Movement, OAU*
Maidou named premier 7-14, 596C1
UN Assemb member 713D3
CENTRAL Florida Enterprises Inc.
WESH-TV license renewal voided, ct sets guidelines 9-25, 907E3
CENTRAL Illinois Public Service Co. v. U.S.
Retroactive withholding tax on lunch allowances barred 2-27, 143A2
CENTRAL Intelligence Agency—*See under U.S. GOVERNMENT*
CENTRAL Selling Organization (London)
De Beers sets diamond surchrg 3-28, 4-27, 319B1
Diamond prices hiked 8-8, 622F2

1979

CENTRAL African Republic (CAR) (formerly Central African Empire)—*See also GATT, NONALIGNED Nations Movement, OAU*
Student riots 1-20–1-21, Zaire troop role denied 1-23, 62A2
Students rptd slain 5-14; Bokassa admits, amb to France resigns 5-22, 387E1
US amb resumes post 6-21; abuses protested, aid halt planned 8-9, 601B3
Bokassa linked to student massacre by African probe 8-6, 601G2
Massacre confrmd 8-16, France cuts aid 8-17, 697F3
UN membership listed 695F2
Dacko deposes Bokassa, restores natn's ex-name 9-20, rpts on French aid 9-22, troop presence 9-24, 720E1-C2
Bokassa denied French asylum 9-21–9-24, Ivory Coast accepts 9-24, 720D2
37 Libyans arrested 9-22, 720C2
Bokassa gifts to Giscard alleged 10-10, 791D1; 12-4, 993D3
CENTRAL American Common Market (CACM) (Costa Rica, El Salvador, Guatemala, Honduras, Nicaragua)
Central American Bank for Economic Integration (BCIE)
Nicaragua $50 mln credit rptd 11-27, 909G3
CENTRAL European Bank Ltd.
Opens 11-9, 882A3
CENTRAL Hudson Gas and Electric Corp. v. Public Service Commission
Case accepted by Sup Ct 11-26, 919A3
CENTRAL Hudson Gas & Electric Corp.
Shareholders defeat A-power delay 4-3, 322F3
CENTRAL Intelligence Agency—*See under U.S. GOVERNMENT*
CENTRAL Louisiana Energy Corp.
Gulf States purchase agreed 2-12, 132G1
CENTRAL State University (Edmond, Okla.)
Loses NAIA Div I football title game 12-15, 1001G2

1980

CENTRAL African Republic—*See also GATT, NONALIGNED Nations, OAU*
USSR, Libya ties broken 1-22, 336B2
US issues rights rpt 2-5, 87E2
S Africa trade cited 4-1, 243B2
Bokassa confirms Giscard gifts 9-17, 728G3
French newspr rpt on Giscard gifts cited 11-7, 872G1
French free Bokassa-Giscard gift figure 11-29, 921A3
Libyan Chad role opposed 12-23—12-24, 979E1
CENTRAL Hudson Gas & Electric Corp. v. Public Service Commission
Case decided by Sup Ct 6-20, 555F1
CENTRAL Intelligence Agency—*See under U.S. GOVERNMENT*
CENTRAL Maine Power Co.
Maine votes to keep A-plant 9-23, 723D2

1976

CENTURY National Bank (N.Y.)
Amer Bank & Trust fails 9-15, 940B1
CEPERNIC, Jorge
Rights revoked, arrest ordrd 6-23, 520C1
CERAMICS
US eases import curbs 4-30, 322D1
CEREALS
FDA bans Red #2 dye 1-19, 44D2
Dec, '75 CPI 1-21, 90A2
CEREBROVASCULAR Disease—*See 'Diseases & Epidemics' under MEDICINE*
CERMAK Nursing Home (Cicero, Ill.)
Fire kills 7 2-4, 271B3
CERONI, Franco
Named in grain fraud 3-11, 247D3
CERRO Corp.
SEC rpts paymts probe 5-12, 726F2
CERTIFIED Color Manufacturers Association
Red #2 dye ban in effect 2-12, ct challenge continues 2-13, 137D1
CERUTTI, Paul
Disqualified at Olympics 7-19, 563B2
CERVETTI, Giovanni
Backs Italy NATO, EEC role 4-18, 297A1
CESNER Jr., Robert
Angola mercenary trial 6-11—6-28, 480B2, F2
CEYLON—*See SRI Lanka*
CHABOT, John
Hiss book review publshd 3-18, 218E1
CHAD—*See also AFRICAN Development Bank, NONALIGNED Nations Movement, OAU*
Listed as 'not free' nation 1-19, 20D3
French premier visits 3-5—3-6, 204F3
Total IMF oil loan rptd 4-1, 340C2
Malloum assassinatn try fails 4-13, 270E3
Mercenary role in Sudan coup chrgd 7-6, 501E3
287 rebels surrender 7-8, 559E3
Rpt Libya gives rebels arms 7-15, 531F1
Olympic withdrawal rptd 7-21, 528B3
IMF loan rptd 7-29, 1012A3
Libyan invasn plan chrgd 8-13, 629G3
Rpt Libya annexes border areas 9-9, 696F2
CHAFEE, John H.
Nominated for RI Sen seat 9-14, 704G3
Elected 11-2, 820B1, 821C3, 828B3
CHAFETZ, Dr. Morris E.
On Rand alcohol study 6-9, 443B1
CHAGGAR, Gurdip Singh
Murdered 6-4, 482D1
CHAIKIN, Sol C.
Endorses Jackson 1-6, 22B3
Endorses Carter 7-22, 551E1
CHAINE, Jacques
Slain, wife hurt 5-14, 381B3
CHAINE, Mrs. Jacques
Injured, husband slain 5-14, 381C3
CHAKRAVARTY, Nikhil
Closes newspaper 12-28, 1006B1
CHALANDON, Albin
Rptd for Eur defns group 1-15, 126D2
CHALARD Hiranyasiri, Gen.
Purged 10-11, 775C3
Retires; becomes monk 10-19, 813D3
CHALMERS, Dr. Thomas C.
Panel scores FDA rpt 5-23, 392G1
CHAMBER of Commerce, International
Rptd drafting ethics code 3-8, 200A2
Cited re Venez-US co talks 11-1, 874F3

1977

CENTRAL Treaty Organization (CENTO) (Great Britain, Iran, Pakistan, Turkey, U.S.)
Meets in Iran, acts vs subversn 5-14—5-15, 380B1
CENTURY National Bank (N.Y.)
Argentina Graiver scandal breaks 4-11, 345C2; 'proof' rptd 5-4, 371A2
CEREALS—*See also GRAIN*
Gen Foods sued on ads 6-30, 613A2
Gambia projcts drought losses 8-22, 660E1
CEREMONY of the Innocent (book)
On best-seller list 11-6, 872F3
CEREZO Arevalo, Vinicio
Says 'civil war' exists 8-12, 673B1
CERRO Marmon Corp.
On '76 Fortune 500 list 341B1
CERTIFIED Public Accountants, American Institute of
Sen subcom staff rpt issued 1-17, 78F3
CERVANTES, Antonio (Kid Pambele)
TKOs Jiminez 6-27, 828A1
CESARSKY, Jorge
Held in Spanish killing 1-30, 101G3
CEY, Ron
NL batting ldr 10-2, 926C3
In World Series 10-11—10-18, 806F1
CEYLON—*See SRI Lanka*
CEZARSKY, Jorge
Arrested in Spain 3-2, 307F2
CF&I STEEL Corp.—*See CRANE Co.*
CFS Continental Inc.
Continental ups coffee prices 3-14, 209G1
CFTC—*See U.S. GOVERNMENT—COMMODITY Futures Trading Commission*
CHABLAN-Delmas, Jacques
Meets with Giscard 12-8, 1012A3
CHAD—*See also NONALIGNED Nations Movement, OAU*
UN Assemb member 3F3
Sets S Africa boycott 1-16, 29G2
Claustres released 1-30, 84C2
Afro-Arab policy statemt scored 3-3—3-5, 170B2
'76 plotters sentncd 3-26; 4 executed 4-4, 309B2
Coup attempt rptd crushed 4-1, 309B2
9 plotters executed 4-6, 490D2
At France-Africa summit 4-20—4-21, 316F3
Sahel dvpt plan OKd 6-1, 458E3
Libya frontier seizure chrgd 7-2—7-5, 512E1
Libya agressn chrgd 7-14, denied 7-15, 597A2
France rptd mil aid 7-18, 597F1
Egypt asks Libya halt 'agitatn' 7-25, 569G2
UK consul seeks Goldsmith release 635C1
CHAFFEE, Sen. John (R, R.I.)
Votes vs Bell confrmatn 1-19, 34D1
CHAIKIN, Sol
Sees Carter on textile curbs 4-13, 271A3
CHAKAIPA, Archbishop Patrick
Scores clerics massacre 2-7, 85B1
CHAKOVSKY, Alexander
US bars entry visa 1-12, 22D1
CHALARD Hiranyasiri, Gen.
Coup try fails, seized 3-26, 243E1 ★
Executed 4-21, 331E2
CHALERM Khamropvong, Lt. Gen.
Sentenced in absentia 5-10, 393C3
CHAMBERLAIN, Wilt
All-time NBA score cited 11-14, 991D1
CHAMBER of Commerce, U.S.-Arab
Rpts Israel boycott eased 2-18, 167D2

1978

CENTREX—*See AMERICAN Telephone & Telegraph*
CENTURION, Faustino
Arrested in Paraguay 11-17, 989F3
CERAMICS
Shoji Hamada dies 1-5, 96C2
CEREALS
Australia vs EC import curbs 1-24, 69G2
FTC proposes children's TV ad curbs 2-28, 4-28, Cong wary 4-26—5-2, 347B2, D2
FTC children's ad probe curbed 11-3; stay denied, probe affirmed 11-17, 941G2-C3
CERO, Comandante—*See PASTORA, Eden*
CERRITOS (Calif.) College
McTear sets indoor 60-yd dash records 1-7, 1-27, 76G2, B3
CERVANTES, Antonio
KOs Tongta 4-29, 379D2
TKOs Sekgapane 8-26, 969E1
CESPEDES, Gen. Hugo
Bolivia defense min 11-24, 913D1
CESSNA Planes—*See ARMAMENTS—Aircraft*
CETA (Comprehensive Employment and Training Act)—*See LABOR—Employment*
CETIN, Hikmet
Named Turkey state min 1-5, 21E2
CEY, Ron
Dodgers win NL pennant 10-7, 779D1
In World Series 10-10—10-17, 799B3
CEYLON—*See SRI Lanka*
CEZANNE, Paul (1839-1906)
3 paintings stolen in Chicago 12-27, 1028E3
CFTC—*See U.S. GOVERNMENT—COMMODITY Futures Trading Commission*
CHABAN-Delmas, Jacques
Elected Natl Assemb pres 4-3, 245G2
CHABROL, Claude
Violette released 10-9, 1030E3
CHACON, Col. Francisco Rene
Murdered 2-6, 136D3
CHAD—*See also GATT, NONALIGNED Nations Movement, OAU*
Rebels rpt forgn natls captured 2-2, town taken 2-15, 130C2
Rebel advances, airport capture rptd 2-3, 2-7; Habre cease-fire pact 2-5, 89F1
Libya ties cut; rebel aid, land seizure chrgd 2-6, 89E1
Cease-fire set 2-20, 4 natns OK peace plan 2-24, 130A2
French presence increased 4-6, 4-19, renewed fighting rptd 4-15, 287G1
Rebels free forgn natls 4-14, 287B2
Anti-French riots 4-24, 572A2
France confrms troop role 4-26, 572G1
French Chadians halt rebels 5-18—6-2, 572E1
French mil aid rptd 5-24, 382C3
Libyan invasn chrgd 6-22, troops estimated 7-5, 572B2
Govt-rebel talks fail 7-3—7-6, 572B2
OAU asks Libya border solutn 7-22, 561F1
Habre named premier 8-29, 732G3
UN Assemb member 713D3
CHAFEE, Sen. John H. (R, R.I.)
Votes for Panama Canal neutrality pact 3-16, 177F2
Votes for 2d Canal pact 4-18, 273B1
CHAFFEY, Don
Magic of Lassie released 8-3, 970B2
CHAIKIN, Sol C.
Sees Pinochet, says labor repressn continues 5-23, 452C3
CHAIN Saw Manufacturers Association
To set safety rules 3-31, 348E1
CHAIN Saws—*See MACHINES*
CHAIN Stores—*See DEPARTMENT & Variety Stores; SUPERMARKETS & Chain Stores*
CHAI Tse-min
Named China envoy to US 5-19, 384C3
Meets Carter on ties 9-19, 974A1
Teng invited to US 12-11, 974D1
CHAMBERLIN, Janice Darlene
Marries Mickey Rooney 7-28, 844D3
CHAMBERLAIN, Richard
Fathers & Sons opens 11-16, 1031E1
Last Wave released 12-18, 1030B3
CHAMBERLAIN, Wilt
Havlicek plays last game 4-9, 271B3

1979

CENTRAL Treaty Organization (CENTO) (Great Britain, Iran, Pakistan, Turkey, U.S.)
Iran plans withdrawal 2-6, 81C2
Pakistan quits 3-12, 181B3
CENTURY 21 Real Estate Corp. v. Nevada
Nev real estate ad rule affirmed by Sup Ct 3-5, 185A1
CEPEDA, Orlando
Hired as White Sox instructor, scout 11-20, 1002F3
CERDAN Calixto, Enrique
Escapes Spain jail 12-17, 997E3
CEREALS
Yellow No 5 labeling ordrd 6-26, 571B2
Army '50 rust spore tests rptd 10-7, 770G3
Battle Creek seeks trust suit environmt impact statemt 10-9, 809G3
CERHA, Friedrich
Complete 'Lulu' debuts in Paris 2-25, 174B1
CERONE, Rick
Traded to Yankees 11-1, 1002C3
CERRO Corp.
Chile expropriatn cited 5-10, 369C3
CERVANTES, Antonio (Kid Pambele)
Decisns Montilla 1-18, 79D3
CERVI, Tonino
Nest of Vipers released 9-7, 820C2
CERVONE, Vittorio
Contact with Red Brigades confrmd 2-7, 97D3
CESAR, Alfredo
Forgn debt paymt talks rptd 11-27, 909D3-910A1
CESIUNAS, Vladislavas
Rptd kidnaped 10-15, 856C3
CESPEDES, Gen. Hugo
Resigns 6-29, 501G2
CETA (Comprehensive Employment and Training Act)—*See LABOR–Employment*
CEY, Ron
NL wins All-Star Game 7-17, 569C1
CEYLON—*See SRI Lanka*
CFTC—*See U.S. GOVERNMENT–COMMODITY Futures Trading Commission*
CH-Helicopter Series—*See ARMAMENTS-Aircraft*
CHABAN-Delmas, Jacques
On Boulin suicide 10-30, 835A1, E1
CHA Chi Chol
Slain 10-26, Kim plot chrgd 10-28, 821G1-G2
Assassinatn rpt confrms Kim plot 11-6, 843G2-A3
CHACON, Francisco Saa
Ecuador pub works min 12-9, 967F3
CHACON, Juan
Vows continued struggle 11-6, 872C3
CHAD—*See also GATT, NONALIGNED Nations Movement, OAU*
Freedom House lists as not free 13A1
Rebel clashes 2-12–2-15, truce rptd 2-19, Nigeria mediatn OKd 3-1, 153G3
Habre rebelln thwarted 2-14, 114G1-A2
Moslems rptd massacred 3-6, 3-9, 211B2
Govt, Frolinat sign peace accord 3-16; France to withdraw troops 3-20, 211F1
Oueddei heads provisnal govt, Malloum leaves 3-23, 329C3
Moslem strife rptd renewed 4-6, deaths estimated 4-9, 329C3
Libya invasn of Aouzou fails 4-20, 329A3
France debt relief vow rptd 5-4, 371C3
Oueddei to head 3d provisnal govt 8-21, 638D2
UN membership listed 695F2
French troops aid CAE coup 9-20, 720G1
CHADMEN, Christopher
Dancing in Dark opens 1-21, 292D1
CHAFFE, Sen. John (R.I.)
US Quebec asbestos takeover 6-19, 484A2
CHAFIK, Shariar Mustapha
Assassinated 12-7, Iran role seen 12-8, 935B1
CHAGRA, Jimmy
Tex judge slain 5-29, 431G2
Convicted of drug smuggling 8-15, 818F3
CHAIKIN, Joseph
Re-Arrangements opens 3-9, 292E2
CHAIKIN, Sol C.
Urges Meany emeritus role, less Carter criticism 2-20, 149C1
ILGWU gets NE pact 5-30, 402F1
Backs Carter reelectn 7-30, 593C3
CHAIN, Ernst B.
Dies 8-12, 671G1
CHAIN Stores—*See DEPARTMENT & Variety Stores; SUPERMARKETS & Chain Stores*
CHAISSON, Eric
Black hole at galaxy cntr seen 3-31, 290E1
CHAI Tse-min
Lauds US-China ties 1-1, 2E1
China opens US Emb 3-1, 146B3
CHALFEN, Morris
Dies 11-4, 932D2
CHALK, Dave
Traded to Rangers 5-4, 1002G2
CHALLE, Gen. Maurice
Dies 1-18, 104F2
CHALLIF, Jamie
Till Marriage Do Us Part released 7-20, 820E3
CHAMBERLAIN, Neville (1869-1940)
GOP compares Carter defns policy 3-1, 165B3
CHAMBERLAIN, Wilt
Interview scores Abdul-Jabbar 3-21, 291C1
In basketball HOF 4-30, 526B3

1980

CEPEDA, Orlando
Schmidt named NL MVP 11-26, 925C3
CESSNA Aircraft Co.
Munson family sues 2-27, 637E1
CEZANNE, Paul (1839-1906)
Painting sold for record sum 5-13, 472G1
Painting stolen in Argentina 12-25, 991E1
CFTC (Commodity Futures Trading Commission)—*See under U.S. GOVERNMENT*
CHABAN-Delmas, Jacques
Cuts USSR visit re Sakharov 1-23, 86C1
CHABOT, Michel
Scores chrg vs Treu 1-12, 78E3
CHACON, Juan
Denies death rumor, scores US 3-28, 253G3
Kidnaped, slain 11-27, 921F1
CHAD—*See also GATT, NONALIGNED Nations, OAU*
Congo troops arrive, peacekeeping force listed 1-18, 119A1
CAR breaks USSR, Libya ties 1-22, 336C2
Fighting resumes; US, Europns evacuated; death toll at 700 3-22—3-25, 221E1
Truce efforts fail; Congo troops, foreigners leave; refugee, death tolls up 3-25—4-23, 311E1
French forces withdraw 5-16, 390F3
USSR envoy dies 6-7, body misplaced 6-17, 491C3
OAU truce failure scored 7-4, 509B2
Peace conf in Togo fails 10-18—10-19, 810F1
Islamic League meets 11-10, 895B2
Cease-fire agrmt reached 11-28; Libyan troops occupy capital, Habre flees to Cameroon, signs agrmt 12-16, 965D1
OAU split on Libyan role in war 12-23—12-24, 979B1
CHADHA, Jagdish Rai
Ct bars US House deportatn res 12-24, 989G1
CHAEV, Alexander
Wins Olympic medal 7-22, 623A3
CHAIKIN, Sol
Seconds Carter renominatn 8-13, 611C3
CHAIN Stores—*See DEPARTMENT & Variety Stores, SUPERMARKETS*
CHAKRABARTY, Ananda M.
GE microbe patent upheld by Sup Ct 6-16, 452F3
CHAKULYA, Wilson
In Zambia Cabt shift 12-4, 969F2
CHALK, Dave
In World Series 10-14—10-21, 811E3
CHAMBERLAIN, Richard
'Shogun' aired by NBC 9-15—9-19, top ratings rptd 9-24, 835F2
CHAMBERLAIN, William
Dies 3-24, 279G1

1976

CHAMBER of Commerce of the U.S.
Ford at NH dinner 2-7, 109E1
Ford speaks on econ 4-26, 307G2
CHAMBER of Commerce of the U.S., Junior—*See JAYCEES*
CHAMBERS, Anne Cox (Mrs. Robert W.)
'70 Carter campaign donor 10-17, 804F3
CHAMBERS, Robert W.
'70 Carter campaign donor 10-17, 804G3
CHAMBERS, Whittaker
Weinstein chrgs vs Hiss rptd 3-18, 217E3
CHAMBLISS, Chris
Yankees win pennant 1-14, 796G1
AL batting ldr 10-4, 796C1
In World Series 10-16—10-21, 815D2
CHAMOUN, Camille
Says Palestinians main combatant 1-8, 17G1
Druze attack Damur 1-12—1-15, 17E3
Fighting spreads to Chuf area 1-13, 17G3
Air strike order rptd 1-16, 33D2
Assails alleged Damur massacre 1-20, 34D1
Chrgs Syria army in Leb 1-21, 34B2
Backs Syria peace move 1-24, 59F1
Assured on Leb sovereignty 1-25, 59G1
OKs mil pullback 1-25, 59A2
Vs cabinet enlargement 162F2
Vs new peace plan 4-19, 273F1
Asks electn delay 4-28, 296C1
Denies arms bought in Egypt 5-24, 369E2
Backs Syrian invasion 6-6, 406B2
Vs Arab peace force 6-11, 429D2
Egypt scores re Leb clashes 6-29, 464A1
Israel arms rptd 7-3, 487B1
Bars Leb truce 7-12, 514E2
Vs Arab troop replacmnt 7-25, 546A2
League presses truce accord 7-26, 546B2
Christians disavow Tel Zaatar truce 7-26, 546E2
Jt Christian force planned, deplores rival clash 7-27, 546B3
On Syria, PLO pact 7-29, 547C1
Tel Zaatar wounded removed 8-4, 561E1
Chrgs Iraq troop role 8-5, 577B2
Chrgs Libya jet shipmt 8-9, 577D2
Named acting premr, defns min 9-15, 682F2
Christian rivals clash 9-20, 720A3
Vs Saudi interventn 10-15, 779B1
Sees Sarkis on Riyadh pact 10-20, 779C1
Meets Jordan aide 11-1, 841G1
Sees Sarkis, OKs Arab force 11-9, 841E1
Car ambushed 12-12, 953D1
CHAMOUN, Dany
On Tel Zaatar losses 8-13, 617G3
CHAMPAIGN, Ill.—*See ILLINOIS*
CHAMPION, Charles
On Alaska pipeline rupture 7-15, 690G3
CHAMPION International Corp.
Antitrust suit dvpts 2-18—10-5, 886C1, E2
CHAND, Lt. Gen. Prem
Resigns 11-19, 963C3
CHANDLER, Dr. Chris
Climbs Mt Everest 10-8, 876B3
CHANDLER, Jennifer
Wins Olympic medal 7-20, 563B1, 575E3
CHANDLEY, Peter
Visited hijacked hostage 7-7; Uganda ousts 7-13, 515F2, Ae, 548D1
CHANG Chun-chiao
Chou En-lai dies 1-8, 8E3, 9A1
Hua rptd acting premr 2-7, 117C2
Meets W Ger delegatn 2-14, 189F1
Radical strength rptd 4-27, 333E1
Cited as possible Mao successor 9-9—9-10, 658D1
Listed in China ldrship 9-10, 712A1
Rptd arrested 10-12, 10-13, 757A2
Plot, purge confirmed 10-22, 790C2, C3
Scored at Hua rally 10-24, more accusatns rptd 10-25, 10-26, 809A2
Porters detail plot role 10-30, 11-8, 871C2
Loses Shanghai post 10-30, 871A3
Tied to indl disruptn 11-2, 871G2
Blamed for Fukien unrest 11-23, 904F3
Drive vs backers asked; restraint urged 11-28, 904A3
Fighting rages in central provs 12-6—12-31, 1000C1-D2
Accused 12-18, faces possible executn 12-23, 999E3
Hua sees '77 natl purge 12-24, 999A3
CHANG Dae Hi
Finland expels 10-20, 799C3, E3
CHANG Key Young
Asks N-S pol talks resumptn 7-4, 557A3
CHANG Kung Soon
In S Korea Cabt 12-4, 928A3
CHANG Kuo-tao
Cited in Mao death announcemt 659C2
CHANG Tsai-chien
Signs Egypt jet pact 4-21, 275F2
CHANG Wen-chin
On Taiwan Olympics ouster 7-16, 529E1

1977

CHAMBER of Commerce of the U.S.
Carson vs Carter econ plan 1-10, 14C1
On anti-inflation plans 4-15, 299E2
Kissinger addresses 5-4, 333A2
On Carter Social Sec plan 5-9, 364A2
Carter energy plan scored 5-18, 443C2
Welcomes OSHA refocusing 5-19, 422A2
Carter labor law reforms scored 7-18, 555B3
Alaska parks plan challenge filed 9-14, 739C3
Pollutn violatns by fed facilities rptd 9-19, 800B2
US withdraws from ILO 11-1, 829A1
Revised jobs bill scored 11-14, 877B1
S Africa unit opens 11-23, 934B3
Poll: business fears recessn 12-14, 962F1
CHAMBERS, Bishop Albert A. (ret.)
Episc dioceses formed 9-14—9-16, 731F2
Episc bishops score 10-5, 845D2
CHAMBERS, Anne Cox
Named amb to Belgium 4-7; confrmd 4-29, 418C1
CHAMBERS, Julius L.
Blacks meet re govt 'neglect' 8-29, 702F1
CHAMBLISS, Chris
In World Series 10-11—10-18, 806F1
CHAMBLISS, Robert Edwards
Indicted 9-26, convicted 11-18, 907G2
CHAMBRIER, Eloi
Replaced as Gabon tourism min 7-13, 772B1
CHAMORRO, Pedro Joaquin
Asks Carter rights pressure 3-2, 168D2
CHAMOUN, Camille
Vs Palestinian arms 1-10, 28B2
Proposes UN troop use 2-27, 143C2
Heads Lebanon Front 3-18, 208C2
Asks Christns protectn 3-19, 208C2
Calls strike vs new army head 3-28, 227B2
Syria asks Israel ties end 4-9, 266C2
Seeks PLO curbs 4-19, 316A3
Rpt sought Israel mil aid 8-22, 648F1
Chrgs Palestinians arm 8-25, 647G3
CHAMPION, Hale
Named HEW undersecy 1-19, 53A1
Califano denies probe curb chrg 3-17, 235E3
Sen com OKs nominatn 3-23, 235F3
Backs 2d surgical opinion 11-1, 869E3
CHAMPION International Corp.
Hoerner Waldorf takeover cited in table 880G1
Trust convictn review declined 11-7, 857B2
CHAN, Julius
PNG dep prime min 7-12, 639G1
CHAND, Lt. Gen. Prem
Named UN Rhodesia rep 9-29, 809G2-810A1
Tours southn Africa 10-30—11-9, 875G2
CHANEY, Don
Traded to Celtics 12-27, 1021A1
CHANG Chun-chiao
Rpt province unrest quelled 1-4, 1D1
Blamed for Fukien unrest 1-4, 1G1
Blamed for econ lag 2-1, 98G1
Heightened drive vs urged 2-5, 2-7, 98C1
Chekiang offcls disgraced 3-2, 179D3
Kweichow progress lauded 3-5, 179F3
Radical accused of bugging 3-9, 180E1
Liaoning offcl arrested 3-14, 220D1
Blamed for Hangchow unrest 4-11, 282B2
New leap forward set 5-4, 449F2
Tied to Shanghai plot 5-17, 449C3
Arrest ended Nanchang riots 6-5, 449B3
Scored at Kiangsi rally 6-6, 505D3
Cited for Hupei unrest 6-8, 505E3
Scored in Liaoning Prov 6-24, 562D1
Tied to Yunnan agents 6-29, 562C1
Rpt ousted from party 7-22, 571G2
Anti-Mao stand cited 9-8, 694B3
Mao policy distortn chrgd 9-10, 706F1
Replaced as forces pol dir 9-25, 743D3
Arrest date confrmd 10-6, 780F3
'71-75 China trade rptd up 11-6, 882C3
Yu suicide rptd 11-8, 882E3
CHANGING (book)
On best-seller list 4-3, 264A2; 6-4, 452A2
CHANGNON, Stanley A.
St Louis environment study rptd 2-24, 184B1
CHANG Tieh-sheng
Arrested 3-14, 220E1
CHANG Ting-fa
In Politburo 8-21, 645G2
CHANG Yie-joon
Orders textile growth curb 10-5, 804D3
S Korea energy head 12-20, 1017D1

1978

CHAMBER of Commerce of the U.S.
Lesher hails consumer agency defeat 2-8, 82A2
Okla ERA boycott evaluated 3-20, 494G2
Harris elected chrmn 4-29, 420G1
Carlson links govt regulatn cost, inflatn 6-19, 427A3
Labor law revisn set back 6-22, 508G2
Carter health plan endorsed 7-29, 586E2
Carlson scores price rule tightening 12-13, 957A2
CHAMBERS, David
History of Amer Film opens 3-30, 760C2
CHAMBERS, M. M.
State aid to colls rptd up 10-10, 770C2
CHAMBERS, Wally
Traded to Buccaneers 4-12, 336F1
CHAMBLISS, Chris
Wins Golden Glove Award 11-21, 928A3
CHAMBLISS, Robert
FBI informant probed 7-12, 528B1
CHAMORRO, Javier
On drive to oust Somoza 2-1, 73F2
CHAMORRO, Pedro Joaquin
Murdered 1-10, 19C3
1000s mourn 1-10—1-11, riot 1-11—1-12; 4 held in murder 1-11, 72G3
Pol group bars Somoza dialogue 1-15, 73D3
Strikers ask full probe, Somoza resignatn; students demonstrate 1-23—1-30, 73A2
La Prensa backs strike vs 2-1, 73F2
Riots mark death 2-10, 115C3
Somoza vows murder probe panel 2-26, 150F3
Newsmen protest murder 3-1, 150C3
Somoza mil aide killed by rebels 3-8, 192C2
Vs Arab mil aid to PLO in Leb 3-24, 213C2
Anti-govt unrest continues 3-31—4-28, 375F2
Somoza names death probe panel, 4 shun 4-6, 376B2
Ramos extraditn from US sought 4-11, 376C2
Cousin murdered 5-8, 376E1
IAPA scores murder probe 10-13, 829F1
CHAMORRO, Pedro Jose
Murdered 5-8, 376E1
Bombings mark death anniv 7-10, 592G3, 593A2
CHAMOUN, Camille
Chrgs Tyre arms shipmts to PLO 1-25, 79E2
Hails PLO exit from Saida 2-3, 79D3
Vs Leb-Syria mil ct 2-14, 99C1
Warns re Leb troops to south 6-5, 463A1
Christn factns clash 6-15, 462A3
On Christn massacre 6-28, 502C2
In intl plea to end Syrian attacks 7-2, 502G2
Scores Arab League force 7-4, 502A3
Vs Sarkis resignatn move 7-12, 522D1
Urges Syrians leave Leb 7-12, 522E1
Says Syrians try to undermine summit 9-10, 713B2
Backs US Leb peace plan 9-29, 745D2
France blames for Leb clashes 10-16; denies, blame Syria 10-17, 783C1
PLO seeks accord 11-13, 870A1
CHAMOUN, Dany
Blames PLO for clashes 4-12, 256F1
CHAMOUN, Dory
Says Syria death toll high in Beirut, lauds Israel aid 8-31, 674E2
CHAMOUN, Pierre
Vs Sarkis talks with Assad 10-9, 761A2
CHAMPION, Gower
Broadway Musical opens 12-21, 1031B1
CHAMPION International Corp.
Settles '76 trust suits 10-2, 768C3
CHAMPIONSHIP Auto Racing Teams (CART)—*See AUTOMOBILE Racing*
CHANAB River (India)
Pak, India dam talks to resume 2-6—2-7, 113B1
CHAND, Lt. Gen. Prem
Tours Africa re Rhodesia Malta mtg 1-6—1-9; at mtg 1-30, 59F1
In UK, US mtg with Patriotic Front 4-15, 290E2
CHANDLER Jr., Alfred D.
Wins Pulitzer Prize 4-17, 315C1
CHANDLER, Bob
NFL '77 pass receiving ldr 1-1, 56C2
CHANDLER, Wes
In NFL draft 5-2, 336E2
CHANDLER, Mayor Wyeth (Memphis, Tenn.)
Police, firemen end strike 8-18, 644E2
CHANEY, Frederick
Named Australia admin svcs min 8-25, 703G2
Aboriginal Affairs min 11-30, 943F3
CHANG Chun-chiao
Saifudin replaced as Sinkiang CP ldr 1-29, 89C2
Teng cleared of '76 Peking riots 2-15, 111C2
Spared executn 2-21, 130A3
Tied to Tsao persecutn 6-28, 515B2
Cited for freedom lack 7-3, 532C2
China pragmatic approach seen 532A2
Wu ousted as Peking mayor 10-10, 773G3
Mao tied to 'Gang of 4' 11-19, 901E2
CHANG Nien-shang
Ousted in test scandal 2-20, 130F2
CHANH, Nguyen
Signs China trade pact 1-10, 21A3

1979

CHAMBER of Commerce of the U.S.
SEC role in pensn plans barred by Sup Ct 1-16, 32D2
Cong chrmn at natl mtg 4-30, 327B2
US pay-scale revisn backed 6-6, 419G2
Fraser scored re UAW job action 8-22, 831B3
CHAMBERS, Marjorie Bell
Named Natl Advisory Com acting head 1-16, 30B3
CHAMBLISS, Chris
Traded to Blue Jays 11-1, Braves 12-5, 1002E2, C3
CHAMORRO, Pedro Joaquin (d. 1978)
Protesters mark death anniv 1-10, 21A3
La Prensa offices burned 6-11, 446A3
Widow named to provisional junta 6-17, 461A2
Somoza, son accused in death plot 10-9, 794B1
CHAMORRO, Violeta Barrios de (Mrs. Pedro Joaquin)
Scores govt inaction on husband's murder 1-10, 21E3
Named to Nicargua provisional junta 6-17, 461G1
Meets US envoy in Panama, plans outlined 6-27, 475A3
Announces currency rate, other decrees 9-3, 689E2
CHAMORRO Cardenal, Jaime
Proposed for Nicaragua junta 7-6, 504D1
CHAMOUN, Camille
Backs Haddad mil role 4-21, 296F3
Leb Christn group co-ldr 5-16, 378E2
CHAMOUN, Pierre
Asks army end Beirut clashes 6-18, 462F1
CHAMP, The (film)
Released 4-3, 528F1
Top-grossing film 5-2, 356F2; 5-23, 448G3
CHAMPION International Corp.
Civil trust setlmt revealed 5-1, 327F3
CHAMPIONSHIP Auto Racing Teams (CART)—*See AUTOMOBILE Racing*
CHAMRAN, Mostafa
Named Iran defense min 9-28, 752C2
CHAMS, Princess (Iran)
Anti-shah riot at US home 1-2, 3F1
CHANDLER, Wes
NFL '78 kick return ldr 1-6, 80G2
CHANDLER, Mayor Wyeth (Memphis, Tenn.)
Reelected 11-15, 904E3
CHANG Ching-fu (Zhang Jingfu)
Rpts '79 budget 6-21, 484B3
On mil budget rise 6-29, 502C3
CHANG Kuo-tao
Dies 12-4, 1008C2
CHANG Ting-fa
Identified as Viet invasn cmdr 2-21, 122D1
CHANG Wen-jin
Blames Viet for refugees 7-20, 549A2
CHAN Ven
Cambodian educatn min 1-8, 10B1

1980

CHAMBER of Commerce of the U.S.
Anti-labor filibuster broken 4-22, 333F2
Mex investmt growth rptd 6-13, 465E2
Verity on Carter econ renewal plan 8-28, 663B3
PAC funds soliciting ban challenge refused by Sup Ct 11-3, 856E2
Donovan named Labor secy 12-16, 955B3
CHAMBERS, Dorothea Lambert (deceased)
Goolagong wins Wimbledon 7-4, 606F2
CHAMBLISS, Robert Edwards
'77 murder convictn cited 2-18, 227E2
CHAMI, Sheik Mohammed
Slain 2-2, 154C2
CHAMORRO, Violeta Barrios de (Mrs. Pedro Joaquin)
Quits junta 4-19, La Prensa struck 4-20, 315B2
Replaced on junta 5-18, 390C1
CHAMOUN, Camille
Phalangists defeat NLP 7-7—7-8; militia merger rptd 7-9, 524E1, G1
CHAMOUN, Dany
Quits militia cmnd, scores rival 7-9, 524F1
CHAMPION, Gower
Dies 8-25, 676A1
42d Street opens 8-25, 756D3
CHAMPION International Co.
Fine paper trust suit acquittal rptd 12-3, 917B2
CHAMPLIN, Bill
Wins Grammy 2-27, 296D3
CHAN, Julius (Papua New Guinea prime minister)
Sworn PNG prime min 3-11, 194F3
CHANDLER, Noel
Ctroom cameras case argued in Sup Ct 11-12, 882A2
CHANDLER, Raymond (1888-1959)
Sam Marlow released 10-3, 836E3
CHANDLER, Wes
NFL '79 receiving ldr 1-5, 8F2
CHANDLER v. Florida
Case accepted by Sup Ct 4-21, 344E1
Case argued in Sup Ct 11-12, 882A2
CHANG Chun-chiao—*See ZHANG Chunqiao*
CHANGELING, The (film)
Released 3-28, 416E2
CHANGE of Seasons, A (film)
Released 12-17, 1003F1
CHANGING Times (recording)
Mighty Clouds win Grammy 2-27, 296E3

1976

CHAPARRO, Sergio
Says inflatn under control 11-5, 871F1
CHAPMAN, William
Scores Ford park plan 8-31, 644B3
CHAPPELL Jr., Rep. William V. (D, Fla.)
Reelected 11-2, 829B2
CHARBONNEAU, Yvon
Teachers strike 4-13, 288G1
CHARLES, Pearnel
Interrogatn re JLP plot rptd 6-30, 522E1
CHARLES, Ray
Wins Grammy 2-28, 460A3
CHARLESTON, W. Va.—*See WEST Virginia*
CHARLESTON, Oscar (d. 1954)
Named to Hall of Fame 8-9, 816C1
CHARLOTTE, N.C.—*See NORTH Carolina*
CHARLOTTE Observer (newspaper)
Carter endorsement rptd 10-30, 831G2
CHARLOTTESVILLE, Va.—*See VIRGINIA*
CHAROENWONGSA, Pifit
New Bronze Age date set 5-13, 504F1
CHARRON, Claude
Named youth, sports min 11-26, 903A3
CHARTERED Bank of London (San Francisco)
Boycott rpts released 10-18, 10-20, 786B1, A2
CHARUMBIRA, Zefania
Named to Rhodesia Cabt 4-27, 295C2
CHASE Bag Co.
Co, execs indicted 10-29, 11-4, 886C3
CHASE Manhattan Corp.
Rptd on FRB 'problem' list 1-22, 111A3
'75 tax paymt rptd 10-2, 847A2
Chase Manhattan Bank (N.Y.)
Rptd on comptroller's 'problem' list 1-11; Rockefeller, Butcher reply 1-11, 1-16, 110D2-111C1, E3
Capital-assets ratio rptd 1-20, 112F2
Panama exec exiled 1-20, 121A3
Zaire copper projct halt rptd 1-27, 335D2
AJC chrgs boycott compliance 3-18, 747A2
Lowers prime rate 12-10, 939C3
CHASE Sardi, Miguel
Rpts arrested, tortured 4-5, 403F2
CHATICHAI Choonhaven, Maj. Gen.
Leaves Thailand with Praphas 8-22, 640A2
Leaves Thailand 10-16, 813D3
CHATTANOOGA, Tenn.—*See TENNESSEE*

1977

CHANNEL Industries Gas Co.—*See TENNECO Inc.*
CHANNEL Islands (British)
UK-French dispute cited 329C2
CHANNELS—*See RIVERS & Waterways*
CHAPIN, Katherine Garrison—*See BIDDLE, Katherine C.*
CHAPIN Jr., Roy D.
Quits as AMC chief 10-21, 962C1
CHAPLIN, Sir Charles (Charlie) Spencer
Dies 12-25, 1024B1
CHAPMAN, Judge Robert F.
Exempts SC mill from Tris ban 5-24, 483E2
Upsets Tris ban 6-23, enjoins recall 6-26, 560C1
CHAPPAQUIDDICK, Mass.—*See MASSACHUSETTS*
CHARIOT (Israeli tank)—*See ARMAMENTS—Tanks*
CHARISMATIC Movement
US data rptd 4-26—4-29, 470D3
Ecumenical conf 7-20—7-24, 620A3, D3
At RC bishops conf 11-14—11-17, 906B3
CHARITIES—*See PHILANTHROPY; specific organization names*
CHARLES, Pedro
JFK assassinatn files released 12-7, 943B2
CHARLESTON, S.C.—*See SOUTH Carolina*
CHARLESTON, W. Va.—*See WEST Virginia*
CHARLOTTE, N.C.—*See NORTH Carolina*
CHARLOTTE Observer (newspaper)
Rpts Graham fund 6-26, 731E3-732A1
CHARREN, Peggy
Scores FTC re ads for children 2-7, 217E1
CHARTER 77—*See CZECHOSLOVAKIA—Human Rights*
CHARTS—*See ILLUSTRATIONS—Tables, Charts & Graphs*
CHASE, Goodwin
Chrgs Lockheed overbilled Navy 6-13, 482G2
Admits Lockheed chrg error 8-22, 649G3
CHASE Bag Co.
Rue, co convicted 11-23, 918G2, A3
CHASE Manhattan Corp.
Chase Manhattan Bank, N.A. (N.Y.)
Kissinger named to intl com 3-21, 396D3
Venez Eurocurrency loan set 3-28, 547D1
S Africa loans curbed 4-19, 350C2
Rockefeller at Bilderberg conf 4-21—4-24, 359C3
Brazil steel loan granted 6-20, 524E2
World's 4th largest bank 6-21, 578A2
Pensn managemt control rptd 6-28, 578C2
SEC rpt chrgs NYC '74-75 financial deceptn 8-26; reactn 8-26—8-27, 665A3, 666A1
Poland gets copper dvpt loan 8-31, 886A1
UK unit in Nigeria loan 9-1, 746C3
Prime linked 9-13, 704A1
CHATTANOOGA, Tenn.—*See TENNESSEE*
CHATTANOOGA Glass Co.—*See under DORSEY Corp.*
CHATTANOOGA News-Free Press (newspaper)
Hood wins Pulitzer 4-18, 355A3

1978

CHANNING, Carol
Hello Dolly opens 3-4, 887G1
CHAO-Min Pan
Taiwan wins Little League title 8-26, 779G2
CHAOTE v. U.S.
Case refused by Sup Ct 11-6, 874C1
CHAPIN Jr., Roy D.
To retire as AMC chrmn 10-20, 809A2
CHAPLIN, Sir Charles (Charlie) Spencer (1889-1977)
Body stolen 3-2, 232D3
Woman of Paris released 4-13, Gentleman Tramp 4-26, 619B2, 620D1
Body recovered 5-17, 380D1
'78 high chic fashion rptd 8-4—8-11, 10-27—11-3, 1029B2
CHAPLIN, Geraldine
Wedding released 9-29, 970D3
CHAPMAN, Ann (d. 1971)
CIA implicated in death 7-24, Moundis convictn questnd 7-31, 631F2
CHAPMAN, Clarence
NFL '77 kick return ldr 1-1, 56G3
CHAPMAN, Oscar
Dies 2-8, 196D2
CHAPMAN, Richard D. (Dick)
Dies 11-15, 972G2
CHAPMAN, Robin
Force 10 released 12-21, 1030G2
CHAPPEL Jr., Rep. William V. (D, Fla.)
Reelected 11-7, 850F2
CHAPTER Two (play)
Wedgeworth wins Tony 6-4, 579A3
CHARITIES—*See PHILANTHROPY; organization names*
CHARLES, Eugenia
Scores Dominica independence 11-2, 861D3
CHARLESTON, S.C.—*See SOUTH Carolina*
CHARLESTON, W. Va.—*See WEST Virginia*
CHARLIE'S Angels (TV series)
Silverman to head NBC 1-20, 75F2
Sears withdraws ads 5-12, 599C3
CHARLOTTE'S Web (book)
White wins Pulitzer citatn 4-17, 315B1
CHARNIN, Martin
Record wins Grammy 2-24, 316B1
CHARTER Co., The
Oil pricing scheme indictmts 9-14, 718A3
CHARTER International Oil Co.—*See CHARTER Co., The*
CHARTER 77—*See CZECHOSLOVAKIA—Human Rights*
CHARTS—*See under ILLUSTRATIONS*
CHASE, Chevy
Foul Play released 7-19, 970D1
CHASE, Goodwin
GAO clears Lockheed on overbilling chrg 6-22, 493C3
CHASE, Ilka
Dies 2-15, 196E2
CHASE Bag Co.
Fined, Rue sentncd 9-21, 768G2-B3
CHASE Manhattan Bank, N.A.—*See under CHASE Manhattan Corp.*
CHASE Manhattan Corp.
'76 tax nonpaymt rptd 1-27, 65G2
Jamaica operatns cutback set 2-3, 95B1
Rockefeller sees Carter, backs inflatn plan 4-20, 361G3
Rockefeller scores Carter 'export consequences' order 10-10, 804B3
Chase Manhattan Bank, N.A. (N.Y.)
PR branches bombed 2-8, 116B1; 2-16, 129F1
Chile bank loan set 4-7, 312E1
Prime rate hiked 4-28, 326B2
Prime rate hiked 8-30, 679C2
Prime rate hiked 10-12, 791C1; 10-31, 827C1
Ranked '77 6th biggest in world 11-8, 914A1, B1
Nigeria loan set 11-30, 934G1
Chase World Information Corp.
On Algeria dvpt plans 2-20, 122A2
Rpts Arab forgn aid rise 4-9, 257B2
CHASTENET, Jacques
Dies 2-7, 196E2
CHATHAM County, Ga.—*See GEORGIA*
CHATICHAI Choonhavan
Says China set leng trip to Thailand 7-14, 548C3

1979

CHAO Tsi-yang
Promotn to Politburo rptd 9-28, 750D3
CHAPIN, Doug
When A Stranger Calls released 10-12, 1008A2
CHAPIN, Miles
French Postcards released 10-19, 1007D3
CHAPLIN, Sir Charles (Charlie) Spencer (1889-1977)
Mary Pickford dies 5-29, 432D3
CHAPMAN, Brenda
WBL scoring ldr 4-7, 507F1
CHAPMAN, Chuck
On Australia energy reserves 9-13, 705C3
CHAPMAN, Graham
Life of Brian released 8-17, 820A2
CHAPMAN, Lee
Boardwalk released 11-14, 1007A3
CHAPMAN v. Houston Welfare Rights Organization
Case decided by Sup Ct 5-14, 384A1
CHAPPAQUIDDICK Island, Mass.—*See MASSACHUSETTS*
CHAPTER Two (film)
Released 12-14, 1007A3
CHARETTE, Jean-Pierre
Returns to Canada, arrested 1-14, 37G1-A2
Sentncd 3-26, 254C1
CHARITIES—*See PHILANTROPY; organization names*
CHARITY Hospital (New Orleans)
Fetal liver transplanted 8-20, 736B3
CHARLAP, Mark
Peter Pan opens 9-6, 956F3
CHARLES, Prince (Charles Philip Arthur George) (Prince of Wales) (Great Britain)
Attends Mountbatten funeral 9-5, 669C1
CHARLES, Bob
2d in Australian PGA 11-11, 970B2
CHARLES, Mary Eugenia
Unions urge govt takeover 5-30, 424A3
CHARLESTON, S.C.—*See SOUTH Carolina*
CHARLESTON, W. Va.—*See WEST Virginia*
CHARLIE Daniels Band
Devil Went Down on best-seller list 9-5, 672E3
Mln Mile Reflectns on best-seller list 9-5, 672F3*
CHARLOTTESVILLE, Va.—*See VIRGINIA*
CHARNIN, Martin
I Remember Mama opens 5-31, 711G3
CHARO
Concorde Airport '79 released 8-3, 820A1
CHARTER Co., The
To seek ERC Corp 10-18, 986C3
CHARTER 77—*See CZECHOSLOVAKIA-Human Rights*
CHARTOFF, Robert
Rocky II released 6-15, 820B3
CHARTRAW, Rick
Montreal wins Stanley Cup 5-21, 447E3
CHARTS—*See under ILLUSTRATIONS*
CHASE Manhattan Bank N.A. v. New York City
NYC occupancy tax collectn curbed by Sup Ct 3-5, 185E1
CHASE Manhattan Corp.
Chase Manhattan Bank, N. A. (N.Y.)
Spain OKs local operatn 1-26, 100F3
Prime rate lowered 1-30, 131E1
NYC occupancy tax collectn curbed by Sup Ct 3-5, 185E1
China loan canceled 5-29, 445B1
Iran banks natlzd 6-7, compensatn vowed 6-10, 469G1-A2
'78 world's 10th biggest bank 6-19, 476B2
Prime hiked 8-16, 621E1
Armored truck holdup nets $2 mln 8-21 656B1
Nicaraguan debt paymts in doubt 9-28, 753F2
Prime rate hiked, Reuss scores 11-7; lowered 11-27, 940G3, 941B1, D1
D Rockefeller blamed for shah's US entry 11-14, 861C2
Iran assets attached for loan repaymts 11-16, 879F3
Iran loan default declared 11-21, 896D2
Iran '73-78 oil revenue deposits rptd 11-26, 897F3
Iran sues UK branch for assets freeze 11-30, 915A2
Iran assets freeze upheld in UK 12-5, 915F1
Iran syndicate loans retained 12-7, 976G1
Rockefeller sets retiremt, Butcher to succeed 12-18, 986B2
Chase Merchant Banking Group
DR loan OKd 3-20, 256B3
CHASE Manhattan Mortgage and Realty Trust
Voluntary bankruptcy filed 2-22, 131G1-E2

1980

CHAO Chi-yang—*See ZHAO Ziyang*
CHAO Hsing-chi
Vs Reagan '2-China' stand 6-15, 452D3
CHAPIN, Frederic L.
Expelled from Ethiopia 7-29, 661G2
CHAPMAN, Mark David
Chrgd in Lennon slaying 12-8, 933F2
CHAPMAN, William C.
Charged in GSA scandal 1-15, 112F1
CHAPOT, Jean
Charles & Lucie released 5-9, 675B2
CHAPPAQUIDDICK—*See MASSACHUSETTS*
CHAPPELL Jr., Rep. William V. (D, Fla.)
Reelected 11-4, 842F2
CHAPPIE, Eugene A.
Elected to US House 11-4, 842D1, 846E1, 852A2
CHAPTER Two (film)
Top-grossing film 2-27, 200G3
CHARBONEAU, Joe
Named top AL rookie 12-2, 926B1
CHARETTE, Jean-Pierre
Allard sentenced 4-8, 310F3
CHARITIES—*See PHILANTHROPY*
CHARLES, Prince (Charles Phillip Arthur George) (Prince of Wales) (Great Britain)
Marks Zimbabwe independence 4-17—4-18, 301C1
CHARLES, Mary Eugenia (Dominican prime minister)
Party wins landslide, named prime min 7-21, 635G3
CHARLES and Lucie (film)
Released 5-9, 675B2
CHARLESTON—*See SOUTH Carolina*
CHARLIE & Algernon (play)
Opens 9-14, 892A3
CHARLIE Daniels Band
Wins Grammy 2-27, 296D3
CHARLIE'S Angels (TV series)
Fraud probe rptd 5-1, 376F2
Roberts gets role 6-17, 638C2
ABC ties to Spelling-Goldberg rptd probed by SEC 8-7—8-8, 640B1
LA DA ends fraud probe 12-2, 1002E2
CHARLOTTE—*See NORTH Carolina*
CHARLOTTE (play)
Opens 2-27, 392D2
CHARTER 77—*See CZECHOSLOVAKIA--Human Rights*
CHARTER Co., The
Occidental drops Permian sale talks 3-17, 385G2
Media unit formed, buys Phila Bulletin 4-10, 376F3
On '79 Fortune 500 list 5-5, 291C1, F1
ERC OKs Getty offer 6-5, 557A3
Pres Carter quizzed re brother 8-4, 594G3
B Carter probe under way 8-20, 647B2
Media unit dissolved 9-30, 836A2
Phila Bulletin, San Fran radio statn acquired from Eller 11-6, 907G1-A2
CHARTOFF, Robert
Raging Bull released 11-14, 972G3
CHARTS—*See ILLUSTRATIONS—Charts, Graphs & Tables*
CHASE, Chevy
Seems Like Old Times released 12-19, 1003D2
CHASE, David
Wins Emmy 9-7, 692D1
CHASE Bag Co.
Price fixing appeal declined by Sup Ct 1-14, 37E1
CHASE Manhattan Corp.
Labreque named pres, Butcher chrmn 6-25, 600C2
Chase Manhattan Bank, N.A. (N.Y.)
MacArthur WWII 'gift' dispute rptd 1-30, 1-31, 115G1
Prime rate hiked to 17.25% 3-4, 167F2
Khomeini overrules on hostages 3-10, hopeful on UN comm return 3-11, 177B1, E1
Prime rate hiked to 18.25% 3-13, 182F2
Prime rate raised to 19% 3-18, 209C2
Credit restrictions rptd 3-27, 222G2
Prime rate hiked to 19.75% 4-1, 20% 4-2, 247D2, A3
Prime rate cut to 19.75% 4-16, 286D2
Prime rate cut to 19.5% 4-18, 19% 4-23, 305E3
Prime rate cut to 18.5% 5-1, 329A2
Prime cut to 18% 5-5, 17% 5-7, 367B3, C3
Prime cut to 15.5% 5-22, 14% 5-27, 401E1, C2
Mortgage rate cut to 13% 5-27, 514C1
Prime cut to 13% 6-4, 438C1
Sullivan named First Chicago chrmn 6-24, 600C2
Prime cut to 11.5% 7-7, 514A1
Mortgage rate cut to 12% 7-15, 575B1
Prime cut to 11.25% 7-17, 10.75% 7-24, 574D3, E3
Prime rises to 11% 8-7, 11.25% 8-19, 630F3
Prime hiked to 11.5% 8-26, 666C2
Prime hiked to 13.5% 9-12—10-1, 764D2
Prime rate hiked to 15.5% 11-6, 867A2
Prime rate hiked to 18.5% 12-2, 937F3
Prime rate hits 21.5% 12-19, dropped to 20.5% 12-23, 983B3
CHATAK, Elmer
Asks Japan auto import curb 7-1, 599E1
CHATEL, Gilles
On Iran cultural exhibitn bar 7-3, 521A1
CHATTANOOGA—*See TENNESSEE*
CHATTANOOGA News-Free Press, The (newspaper)
Partially joins with Chattanooga Times 5-12, Civiletti OKs 9-2, 732E2
Chatanooga Times pact gets final OK 11-6, 907E1

1976

CHATTANOOGA Times (newspaper)
Carter endorsement rptd 10-30, 831B3
CHATTI, Habib
Protests EC pact 'bias' 2-3, 164F2 *
CHAVAL, Andre
Daughter kidnaped 5-25, freed 5-29, 419A2
CHAVAL, Nadine
Kidnaped 5-25, ransomed 5-29, 419A2
CHAVAN, Yeshwantaro B.
India, China to trade ambs 4-15, 278D3
Pakistan ties set 5-18, 356C2
Scores Canada A-sales bar 5-20, 363C2
CHAVEZ, Cesar
Teamsters dispute continues, boycott renewal planned 1-22—2-11, 153F2
Nominates Brown at conv 7-14, 506E1
Dem conv pres vote, table 7-14, 507E3
Endorses Carter 9-25, 724D1
Ford scores Carter 10-15, 784F1
Calif voters reject proposal 11-2, 825B1, E3
CHAVUNDUKA, Gordon
Chrgs pro-Nkomo plot 11-28, 893C2
CHAZARO Lara, Ricardo
Mexico navy min 12-2, 907A1
CHEATHAM, Thomas B.
Chrgs Nixon bid for Grumman donatn 9-13, 979G1-D3
CHEBOKSAROV, Vladimir
Wins Olympic medal 7-24, 576A3
CHECKING Out (play)
Opens 9-14, 1014D3
CHEEK, Rev. Alison
Rejcts church compromise 4-4, forms separate unit 5-9, 755C3
CHEHABI, Maj. Gen. Hikmat
Mediates Leb pact 1-21—1-22, 33F1
Sahara missn rptd 1-29, 58C2
CHEMETRON Corp.
Votator chrgd re Arab boycott 10-19, 786E1
CHEMICAL & Biological Warfare (CBW)
Horses found dead near Utah cntr 7-4, Army denies leak 7-9, 7-24, 587C1
CHEMICAL and General Workers Unions, International Federation of
Backs rubber boycott 4-27, 308F3
CHEMICAL New York Corp.
'75 zero tax paymt rptd 10-2, 847F1
Chemical Bank (N.Y.)
Security Natl '75 classified assets rptd 1-11, 110D3
Argentina to get grain credits 1-28, 96B3
Rptd on FRB 'problem' list 1-29, 113A1
AJC chrgs boycott compliance 3-18, 747A2
In Venez intl bank loan 9-15, 875E1

CHEMICALS (& Chemistry)—*See also country, company names*
China-W Ger deal rptd 1-6, 78B1
Dec '75 output rptd up 1-16, 92A1, C1
NYS accuses GE re PCBs 2-9, 171E3
EPA urges toxic chem law 2-26, 171E2
US cncl rpt cites pollution threat 2-27, 171D2
FDA seeks chloroform ban 4-6, 249D2
ACN, vinyl chloride link cited 4-21, 308B2
Ford urges regulatory reform 5-13, 346G3
Dem platform text 6-15, 471F2
SEC sues Foremost 7-7, 669A2
Nickel carbonyl tested in Pa mystery probe 8-6—8-31, 656G2
GOP platform text 8-18, 608B1
Sulfuric acid spill off Va 8-18, 796F2-A3
NYS, GE sign PCB pact 9-8, 691F2-B3
Aerosol curb urged 9-13, 691E2
Indl output index revised 9-16, 709E1
Red #4, carbon black dyes curbed 9-22, 729A3
'75 tax paymt data rptd 10-2, 10-14, 847B2, C2
Toxic substances bill, PCB ban signed 10-12, 764E2
FDA to phase out aerosol fluorocarbons 10-15; aerosol warning labels proposed 10-19—11-23, 901E3
Lipscomb wins Nobel re boranes 10-18, 840E1
Science Medals awarded 10-18, 858E3-G3
Pa plant illness identified 11-5, 911G1

1977

CHATTI, Habib
Resigns 12-25, 1019D2
CHATTOPADHAYA, D. P.
Arrested 10-3, 765C1
CHAUVIN, Adolphe
Sees Amalrik 2-24, 143B1
CHAVAL, Nadine
Kidnapers seized 4-13—4-14, 528G3
CHAVAN, Yeshwantaro B.
Named Cong Party Parlt ldr 3-23, 205E2
Party exec com splits 12-27, 1013F3
CHAVEZ, Cesar
Signs Teamsters pact 3-10, 177E3
CHAVIS, Benjamin F.
Wilmington 10 denied retrial 5-20, 531D3
CHAYEFSKY, Paddy
Wins Oscar 3-28, 264C1
CHAYET, Claude
In Polisario talks 11-7, 852E2
CHEATHAM Jr., Thomas P.
Hughes Indonesia payoff rptd 1-25, 182D3
CHECKER Express Co.
ICC sues 11-3, 861C1
CHECKER Motors Corp.
Edward Cole dies 5-2, 452E2
CHEEMA, Hafizul
Loses Assemb seat 3-31, 258D3
CHEESE—*See DAIRY Products*
CHEEVER, John
Falconer on best-seller list 4-3, 264G1; 5-1, 356B2; 6-4, 452G1; 7-3, 548D3; 8-14, 643F1
CHEEVERS, Jerry
Montreal wins Stanley Cup 5-14, 429F3
CHEMETRON Corp.
Allegheny wins control 9-8, 880C2
CHEMICAL & Biological Warfare
'49-69 Army tests revealed 3-8, 195C2
CIA study rpts WWII use 3-9, 195B3
US effort rptd 3-21, 232E1-A2
Dow paymts rptd 3-28, 233D2
US, USSR OK working group 3-30, 225G1
Carter cites US-USSR talks 7-21, 550B3
US, USSR note arms ban progress 8-30, 686G2
CHEMICAL New York Corp.
Chemical Bank (N.Y.)
Indicted 2-24, 155C2
2 ex-offcls plead guilty 3-3; bank fined 4-14, 540A3
Security Natl double jeopardy bar upheld 3-28, 276F3
Venez Eurocurrency loan set 3-28, 547D1
Gilpatric '74 interest conflict chrgd 5-24, 407D1
Lance cleared in govt probe 8-18, 625A3
SEC rptd chrgs NYC '74-75 financial deceptn 8-26; reactn 8-26—8-27, 665B3, 666A1
CHEMICAL and Pollution Sciences Inc.
Quebec ct backs injunctn 10-6, 780B2

CHEMICALS & Chemistry
Benzidine pollutn curb set 1-3, 95A2
Nitrates cited re Peru-Chile border buildup 1-10, 2A3
EPA bars PCB dischrg 1-19, GE finds PCB replacemts 2-7, 95E1, G1 *
Olin Corp rpts paymts 1-27, 94E1
Canada co admits rebates 2-8, 114B2
'76 4th ¼ profits rptd 2-8, 301D1
Sovt bloc chrgd re Rhodesia sanctns 2-10, 123A1
Colo, Washn weather modificatn rptd 2-21, 2-28, 153C1
Aerosols, weather chngs linked 2-21, 183G2
EC '76 econ growth rptd 2-22, 146C2
EPA water pollutn curbs upheld 2-23, 150D2
Ore aerosol ban in effect 3-1, 323B2
Carbontetrachloride dischrg shuts FMC plant 3-9, EPA pact 3-15, 196B3
FDA orders fluorocarbon aerosol warning 4-26, 323E1
1st ¼ profits drop rptd 4-28, 668E3
US curbs worker benzene exposure 4-29, 345D1
Carter environmt message 5-23, 404C2
S Korea ends import curbs 6-14, 470G2
'71 Ga plant blast ruling 6-23, 604B1
Canada co scored 7-7, 541G3
Danes block PVC plants 7-7, 672E1
Hercules buys Warren-Teed 7-19, 650F3
Gulf buys Kewanee 8-9, 612E2
Cimetidene ulcer use OKd by FDA 8-23, 748C2
Tenneco buys Phila Life 8-25, 650G3

1978

CHATTERTON, Michael
Kidnaped in El Salvador 12-1, negotiatns for release rptd 12-21, 986C3
CHAUDHRY, Fazal Elahi
Quits as pres 9-14, 740C2
CHAVES, Aureliano
Geisel taps for vice pres 1-5, 6E3
CHAVET, Yitzhak
Quits Israel pres race 418C2
CHAVEZ, Carlos
Dies 8-2, 708C2
CHAVEZ, Cesar
Announces end to boycotts 1-31, 83G1
CHAVEZ, Federico
Dies 4-24, 356C2
CHAVEZ, Judith Taylor
Shevchenko denies CIA financed gifts 10-13, 844A3
CHEAP Detective (film)
Released 6-22, 619A1
Top-grossing film 7-6, 579F3
CHEATERS (play)
Opens 1-15, 760E1
CHEESE—*See DAIRY Products*
CHEIKHOL-Eslamanzadeh, Chojaeddin
Arrested 9-12, 693G1
CHEMICAL Bank—*See under CHEMICAL New York Corp.*
CHEMICAL & Biological Warfare
US reemphasis rptd, USSR advantage cited 6-5, 433E1
500 Viet vets claim Agent Orange disabilities 10-11, critic dies 12-4, 984D1-A2
US nerve gas productn order rptd 10-19, 833F2-A3
CHEMICAL New York Corp.
Milan branch mgr shot 5-11, 393D2
Chemical Bank (N.Y.)
S Africa loan bar rptd 3-21, 237D2
Chile loans rptd undercutting US rights policy 4-11, Reuss scores 4-12, 312G1
Prime rate hiked 10-23, 827C1
Not on '77 world top 10 list 11-8, 914C1
Prime rate hiked 12-20, 1003D3

CHEMICALS
Hair-dye warning proposed 1-4, 86A1
NJ cancer death rate link studied 1-12, 23E3
4MMPD, tetrachlorethylene curbs urged 1-13, 86A1
Acrylonitrile rule issued 1-16, 85F3
Grace plans King's purchase 1-23, 66C2
'77 forgn investmts rptd 1-24, 65D3
EPA asks trihalomethane water filtratn 1-25, 86B1
US curbs benzene exposure, API scores 2-2, 85G2, C3
Chlorine gas spilled in Fla derailmt 2-26, 196F1
Dow, USSR sign 10-yr pact 2-28, 151F3
EPA sets fines for spills 3-3, 163G3
Fluorocarbon aerosols banned 3-15, 186G1-E2
EPA sues vs PCB pollution 3-17, 243B1
Methoxychlor, malathion rptd non-carcinogenic 3-21, 3-24, 727D3
French industry hurt by oil spill 3-23—3-29, 238D1, F1
Du Pont titanium dioxide monopoly chrgd 4-10, 346A1
PCB contaminated animal feed recalled 4-12, 727C3
Norepinephrine role in vision dvpt rptd 4-15, 334B3
CPSC curbs benzene use 4-27, 348G1
Fortune ranks '77 top indls 5-8, 325F1
Mitsubishi unit indicted 5-9, 404C2
Nitrite-cured bacon curbed 5-15, 728F1
Polymer with elec conductivity rptd 5-18, 654D1

1979

CHATTERTON, Michael
Freed in El Salvador 7-2, 547G1
CHAVAN, Yeshwantrao B.
Asked to form new govt 7-18, 544E1
Gives up Cabt try 7-22, 573B1
Named dep prime min 7-28, 573D1
CHAVEZ, Cesar
Calif lettuce strike starts 1-19, natl boycott set 4-26, 327A1
Calif lettuce strike ends 8-31, 698G2
CHAYKIN, Maury
Leave It to Beaver opens 4-3, 712B1
CHEAN Vamm
Cambodia aid program rptd 10-12, 779C2
CHEAP Trick (singing group)
At Budokan on best-seller list 5-2, 356B3; 5-30, 448F3; 7-4, 548F3; 8-1, 620F3
CHEA Sim
Cambodian interior min 1-8, 10B1
CHEESEBOROUGH, Chandra
Sets indoor 220-yd dash mark 2-23, 911E2
CHEEVER, John
Stories on best-seller list 2-4, 120B3; 3-4 173D3
Wins Pulitzer 4-16, 336E2, G2
Natl Book Awards rptd 4-23, 356G1
CHEEVERS, Gerry
Sovts win Challenge Cup 2-11, 118C3, E3
CHEMICAL Bank—*See under CHEMICAL New York Corp.*
CHEMICAL & Biological Warfare
'63 Utah land mines destroyed 3-27, 307C3
US, USSR reject Geneva conf weapons ban proposal 4-26, 625A3
SALT II communique backs ban 6-18, 457F3
Army sued on San Fran '50 germ test 9-16, 727B1
BZ tested by Army in '64, stockpile rptd 9-24, 727F1
US Army '50 grain blight tests rptd 10-7, 770G3
Army seeks test subjects 11-2, 850E2
Laos rebel gas attacks rptd 11-3, 12-12, 979A1
'60s drug tests on Pa prisoners rptd 11-25, 947E1
'50s CIA NYC tests chrgd 12-3, 946A1
CHEMICAL Industry Institute of Toxicology (N.C.)
Formaldehyde-cancer link rptd 10-18, 971C1
CHEMICAL Manufacturers Association
Waste cleanup bill opposed 6-13, 441C2
Dump site list issued 11-1, 886B1
CHEMICAL New York Corp.
Chemical Bank (N.Y.)
Poland econ monitor plan set 1-11, 59G3
Prime rate hiked 9-19, 745F1
UK upholds Iran assets freeze 12-5, 915F1

CHEMICALS
Fluorocarbon suit setld by Allied 1-5, 56G1
EPA wants advance data 1-10, 16G3-17A1
Carter budgets toxic control funds 1-22, 45A3
Grace acquires Daylin 1-24, 88E3
Viet Agent Orange suit filed 2-1, 90A1
US sues NJ cos on hazardous wastes 2-7, 129G3-130B1
2 herbicides banned, dioxin link cited 3-1, 167E1
Food-safety law revisns urged 3-2, 195D1
Pa co sued re PCB storage 3-9, 206D3
NYS bird deaths laid to nitrate poisoning 3-18, 206G3
Fla, NY, Pa, Ohio tank car derailmts 4-8, 5-3, 5-6, 472D3
Jan-Sept '78 tank car derailmts rptd 4-9, 472C3
Niagara dump hearings, Hooker knew of seepage in '58 4-10, 4-11, 281B3
PCB rules issued 4-19, 281G3-282A1
Velsicol indicted for Mich PBB cover-up 4-26, pleads not guilty 5-7, 597E3
Methapyrilene product ban asked 5-1, 354C3
NC PCB dumping chrgd 6-4—6-13, disposal disputed 6-5, 597G2-E3
Carter proposes hazardous waste cleanup, cites Niagara dump 6-13, 441E1

1980

CHATTANOOGA Times, The (newspaper)
Partially joins with Chattanooga News-Free Press 5-12, Civiletti OKs 9-2, 732E2
News Free-Press pact gets final OK 11-6, 907E1
CHATTI, Habib
Iran rejects Islamic war mediatn 10-19, 10-20, 799B3
CHAUCER, Geoffrey (1340-1400)
Canterbury Tales opens 2-12, 136A3
CHAUSSOL, Maria Elena
Seized in DR Emb raid 2-27, 141B3
Freed 2-27, 311C3
CHAVES, Aureliano
Hikes gas prices, studies rationing 10-3, 759F1
CHAVES Belaunde, Fernando
Bars chrgs vs Cuban refugees 8-30, 672G2
CHAVEZ, Cesar
Brown quits pres race 4-1, 246D3
Campaigns with Mondale 10-26, 816F3
CHAVEZ, Leonor
Gives birth 4-26, 326E1
CHAVEZ Mena, Fidel
Signs Honduras, El Salvador peace pact 10-30, 872C3
CHAVIS, Rev. Ben
Wilmington 10 convictn reversed 12-4, 940E1
CHEAPOO, Chea
Sets businessmen's arrest 4-25, 353D2
CHEEKS, Maurice
Lakers win NBA title 5-16, 432B1
CHEESE—*See DAIRY Products*
CHEESEBOROUGH, Chandra
Ottey breaks indoor 220-yd dash mark 2-29, 892E1
CHEEVERS, Gerry
Escapes fine over NYC brawl 1-25, 198D3
CHEKHOV, Anton (1860-1904)
Sea Gull opens 11-11, 892E3
CHEKHOVA, Olga
Dies 3-29, 279A2
CHELSEA College (London)
Glucose fertilizatn role rptd 7-3, 715G2
CHEMCENTRAL-Detroit Corp.
EPA toxic waste suit filed 10-7, 825G1
CHEMICAL Bank—*See CHEMICAL New York Corp.--Chemical Bank (N.Y.)*
CHEMICAL & Biological Warfare
US rights rpt scores Sovt Afghan moves 2-5, 87B1
US Rift Valley Fever testing cited 3-2, 318D3
Geneva meets, reviews '72 treaty 3-3—3-21, 235G2*
Sovt Afghan poison gas use rptd 3-4—3-5, 205G2-B3
USSR anthrax stockpile suspected by US 3-18, 235C2
UK weighs chem weapons acquisitn, Sovt threat cited 4-2, 274F1
NATO plans better defenses 5-14, 377E2
US chrgs Sovt anthrax cover-up 6-29, 500A1
US chrgs Sovt, Viet, Laos use 8-7, 628C3
Sovt Afghan use disputed 8-21, 650F1-A2
House defeats productn funds challenge 9-16, 741C3
Sen excludes productn appropriatn 11-21, 896F3
Nerve gas funds omitted from '81 defns appropriatn 12-5, 935B3
CHEMICAL New York Corp.
Chemical Bank (N.Y.)
Credit restrictions rptd 3-27, 222G2
Prime rate hiked to 20% 4-2, 247D2
Prime rate cut to 17.5% 5-6, 367C3
Mortgage rate cut to 13.5% 5-19, 385B1
Prime cut to 15% 5-22, 401F1
Prime rate cut to 14% 5-28, 438B1
Prime cut to 10.75% 7-24, 574E3
Prime hiked to 11% 8-4, 630G3
Prime hiked to 13.5% 9-12—10-1, 764E2
Prime rate hits 21.5% 12-19, dropped to 20.5% 12-29, 983B3
CHEMICAL Recovery Systems Inc.
EPA Ohio toxic waste suit filed 10-7, 825F1
CHEMICALS
NJ State of State message 1-8, 403F3
Dopamine, schizophrenia link rptd 1-10, 415E1
Workplace cancer rules set 1-16, 35G3
Budget proposes pollutn fees 1-28, 73G2
NJ waste suit partially setld, Edison dump to be covered 1-30, 93D3
GAO scores cancer-nitrite study 1-31, 159F1
EPA sets toxic waste rules 2-26, 145D3
OSHA rpts Va shipyd abuses 2-27, 147E3
Ark dump suit filed 3-4, 190E3
McCormick vs Sandoz merger bid 3-18, 386B1
CPSC sued over Tris ban 3-24, 348F2
Memphis area illness probed 4-2, 331A3
Boston area phosphorous trichloride fumes spur evacuatn 4-3, 392E1
Office cancer risks linked to nitropyrene 4-11, 357B1-A3
Iowa farm cancer study rptd 4-15, 357D3
Mich PBB cleanup sought 4-17, 331D2, F2
NJ dump burns 4-22, 331B2
US sues Union Corp re PCBs 4-24, 331E3
NY sues Occidental, Hooker re Love Canal dumping 4-28, 331D3
EPA adopts toxic waste rules 5-5, 387E1
PCB rules published 5-9, 387G1
Love Canal dump health defects rptd 5-16, US sets evacuatn 386D3-387D1

1976

9 dye cos consent decree filed 11-16, 989B1
Legion disease probe scored 11-23—11-24, 911B2
Canada rebates rptd 11-26, 904G1; Trudeau defends co, probe set 11-30, 924A1
Moorhead scores price hikes 12-2, 898B2
Tex workers rpt nerve disorders 12-6, 950B2
Coleman to OK superport 12-17, 992E1
Forgn payments studies issued 12-18, 12-20, 985G1, D2
Chemical Warfare—*See CHEMICAL & Biological Warfare*
Cosmetics—*See COSMETICS*
Fertilizers—*See under 'F'*
Obituaries
Curme, George 7-28, 716A3
Frumkin, Alexander 5-27, 404G1
Onsager, Lars 10-5, 970G2
Polanyi, Michael, 2-22, 192F3
Ruzick, Leopold 9-26, 932F3
Pesticides—*See PESTICIDES*
Petrochemicals—*See PETROLEUM*

CHENEY, Richard B.
Transition work under way 11-5, 845D1
CHEN Hsi-lien
Chou En-lai dies 1-8, 8E3
Hua named 'acting' premr 2-7, 117C2
Listed in China ldrship 9-10, 712A1
At Hua rally 10-24, ldrship rank rptd 10-25, 809F1
CHENNAULT, Anna C.
CAB complaint filed 12-29, 986F1
CHEN Tu-hsiu (1879-1942)
Cited in Mao death announcemt 659B2
CHEN Yung-kuei
Listed in China ldrship 9-10, 712B1
CHERN, Shiing-Shen
Awarded Medal of Science 10-18, 858D3
CHERNOBYLSKY, Boris
Sees Shchelokov 10-21, arrested 10-25, 856G3
Freed 11-15, 966D3
CHERNE, Leo
Named to intelligence bd 2-17, 127E1
CHERNENKO, Konstantin U.
Named to CP Secretariat 3-5, 195F2
CHERRY Hill, N.J.—*See NEW Jersey*

1977

Govt acts on nitrates in meats 8-31, 10-18, 820A1
Allegheny wins Chemetron control 9-8, 880C2
Nitrous oxide-oxygen hosp mixup rptd fatal 9-10, 748G1
Fyrol FR-2 warnings rptd 9-29, 820B2
Canada ct backs US co 10-6, 780B2
Nobel won by Prigogine 10-11, 951A3
4MMPD in hair dye linked to cancer 10-17, 12-14, 962D3, 963A1
Medit natns reach pollutn accord 10-21, 876D2
Sweden sets aerosol can ban 11-10, 904E1
Sci Medals awarded 11-22, 952B1
E Ger-Pl trade pact set 12-7, 1000C2
NJ treatmt plant blast 12-8, 1023D3
Israel-Rumania trade rptd 12-10, 987C3
Unilever plans Natl Starch takeover 12-11, 1004D2
Coloring dyes banned by FDA 12-12, 980G3
Natl Distillers, Emery plan merger 12-19, 1004C3
EPA orders cos to rpt 12-22, 1007A2
Obituaries
Coolidge, Albert S 8-31, 696E2
Fieser, Louis 7-25, 604B3
Pesticides—*See under 'P'*
Tris
Tris sleepwear banned 4-7, 302E2 ★, F2 ★
Ban extensn, recall cost-sharing ordrd 4-28, 5-3, upheld 5-19, 483A2
Woolworth suit setld 5-18, 483D2
SC mill gets ban exemptn 5-24, 483E2
CPSC ban upset 6-23, recall enjoined 6-26, 560C1
Appeals ct curbs ban 8-12; CPSC sues 2 chain stores 8-19, 8-22, sale halted 8-20, 651F3
Sterility danger warned 8-30, 820D2
Federated settles CPSC complaint 8-31, 820D2
CPSC sues Montgomery Ward 10-16, 820A2

CHEMICAL Warfare—*See CHEMICAL & Biological warfare*
CHENARD, Laurent
Ethiopia ousts 4-25, 327C3
CHENG Chao-chang
Slain 8-30, 706G1
CHEN Hsi-lien, Gen.
Posters assail 1-9, 61C2
In Politburo 8-21, 645G2
Posters assail 10-20, 823F2
CH'EN Li-li
Wins Natl Book Award 4-11, 355B2 ★
CHEN Mu-hua
Gets econ post 1-14, 61F2
CHEN Pi-hsien
Named to Yunnan CP posts 2-12, 134B1
CHEN Yung-kuei
In Politburo 8-21, 645G2
CHEPKWURUI, Paul
Carter protests Amin exit bar 2-25, 141C1
CHERCOVER, Murray
Vs LaMarsh rpt proposals 6-16, 485F2
CHERNENKO, Konstantin Ustinovich
Named to Politburo 10-3, 785C3

1978

Tenneco offers Albright & Wilson purchase 5-23, 404F1
CPSC adopts cancer agent rules 6-1, 703C3
PCB ban formally proposed 6-7, 513A1
EPA sets indl water dischrg rule 6-20, 512F3
Ky chlorine leak sickens swimmers 6-28, 636E3
Saccharin, cyclamate studies rptd inconclusive 7-19, 7-28, 727B3
Italian panel condemns Seveso firm for '76 dioxin blast 7-27, 689E1 ★
Niagara dump site declared disaster area 8-7, 703A1
Justice Dept probes Occidental-Mead merger plan 8-18, 767G2-A3
Occidental opens USSR ammonia plant 8-22, 670F1
Nitrite additives linked to cancer 8-11, FDA proposes phase-out 8-31, 727G3
Italy plant accident kills 3, toxic cloud spreads 9-19, 724G2
Acrylonitrile final rule set 9-29, 753G3
Celanese plans Olin takeover 10-3, 767G3
Benzene exposure rule upset 10-5, 833G3-834C1
PBBs contaminate Mich populatn, breast-milk studies cited 10-9, 769C2
US sues vs Occidental-Mead merger 10-11, Occidental offers concessns 10-23, US expands chrgs 10-25, 895B3
500 Viet vets claim dioxin disabilities 10-11, critic dies 12-4, 984F1, A2
Allegheny drops planned sale to Bayer unit 10-24, 897E1
Italy indus rescue plan proposed 10-26, 817B2
Mich PBB suit dismissed 10-27, 834C1
Diamond Shamrock to buy Falcon Seaboard 11-2, 1005A2
Celanese-Olin merger ended 11-10, 897C1
EPA warns on hazardous dump sites 11-21, 899D2
Borg-Warner, Firestone to merge 11-28, 935E1
Amorphous silicon, fluorine rptd in new solar cell 11-30, 983G1
Toxic-waste rules proposed 12-14, 982C3
Pesticides—*See PESTICIDES*
Tris
CPSC votes garment export ban 5-5, 347A3
Compensatn bill pocket vetoed 11-8, 941C3

CHEMISTRY
Nobel won by Mitchell 10-17, 886C2
Obituaries
Conant, James B 2-11, 196F2
Norrish, Ronald George Wreyford 6-7, 540D3
DuVigneaud, Vincent 12-11, 1032F2
CHEMOTHERAPY—*See MEDICINE—Cancer*
CHENEY, Richard
Wins US House primary in Wyo 9-12, 736D2
Elected 11-7, 852D4, 856G1
CHEN Hsi-lien, Gen.
Posters rptdly score 4-9, 287F3
Loses Peking mil post 10-17, 814B2
Chin gets top Peking post 11-22, 950A2
CHENIVIERE, Lionel
Arrested for Versailles bombing 6-30, chrgd 7-4, 533F2
CHEN Mu-hua
Named dep premier 2-26—3-5, 153E1
CHEN Po-ta
Attack on Tao Chu chrgd 12-10, 950F1
CHEN Yun
In China Politburo 12-22, 1015E1
CHERNENKO, Konstantin Ustinovich
Elected to USSR Politburo 11-27, 924B3
CHERNYAYEV, Rudolf
Arrested as Sovt spy 5-20, 409B3
Dobrynin takes custody 6-26, 506G1
Crawford sentence suspended 9-7, 742E3
Convicted as spy 10-13, sentncd 10-30, 835A2
USSR demands return, denounces sentnc 11-4, 863E1
CHERRY, Evelyn
Defends SBA loan guarantee to TV host 11-16, 919E3

1979

Hooker Calif dumping, well pollutn rptd 6-18; US, state probe 6-19, 6-21, 597F1
Hooker sued for Mich clean-up 6-22, Fla abuses rptd 8-5, 597C2
Yellow No 5 (tartrazine) labeling ordrd 6-26, 571G3
Allied Chem to buy Eltra 6-28, 560G1
PCB limits in food cut 6-28, 571C2
DES banned in animal feed 6-28, 571F2
Olin convicted for Niagara dumping 8-16, 704E1
NJ Meadowlands cleanup ordrd 8-26, 704A2
Solar cell silicon productn method rptd 8-27, 649B1
Hooker chrgd in LI dumping 8-31, 665F3
Fluoride dental value doubted 9-1, 1000A2
Toxic chems, sterility linked 9-11, 736F1
Hydrocarbon sap rptd fuel source 9-15, 1000B2
PCBs contaminate food in West 9-17, 704A3
Du Pont titanium dioxide monopoly case dismissed 9-17, 810C1
Nitrosamines found in beer, warning urged 9-19, 9-22, 735E3-736B1
Mich PBB contaminatn rpt issued 10-9, Velsicol settles suits 10-23, 808G2-D3
Hooker settles Mich dump suit 10-24, 808E3
Dump sites listed 11-1, 886B1
US Steel, Texaco set venture 11-14, 941D3
Halocarbon aerosol risk estimate revised up 11-17, 1000E2
US troops Agent Orange exposure rptd 11-24, 5 mfrs sued 11-26, 904B2-A3
US sues Occidental, Olin re Niagara dumps 12-20, 990F1
Foreign Developments (including U.S. international news)
GATT pact signed, tariff cuts seen 4-12, 273G1
Turkey imports set 7-31, 637E1
E Ger output rptd down 8-1, 741F3
Hooker-USSR phosphorus deal rptd 8-5, 597F2
W Ger factory peril forces evacuatns 9-17, 796C2
Dutch Shell plant struck 9-24, 731A2
USSR, E Ger sign pact 10-5, 761C2
Sovt ammonia import curbs asked 10-5, 802B3
Formaldehyde-cancer link rptd 10-18, 971C1
'Laughing gas' hazard rptd 10-24, 971E2
Canada chlorine spill evacuatn 11-11—11-14, 871D3; evacuees compensated 11-19, 927C2
Sovt ammonia import curbs barred 12-11, 939D2
CHEMICAL Society, American
Sterility, toxic chem link rptd 9-11, 736F1
CHEMICAL Workers Union, International (AFL-CIO)
Wins Allied Chemical suit 1-5, 56C2
CHEMISTRY
US-China pact set 5-13, 370E1
Coll test score rise rptd 10-4, 810D2
Nobel won by 2 10-16, 858B1
Obituaries
Natta, Giulio 5-2, 432C3
Woodward, Robert Burns 7-8, 588G3
CHEM-Nuclear Services Inc.
15 protesters arrested 10-1, 742D3
Barnwell A-dump cut ordrd 10-31, 851C2
CHEN, L. K.
On Taiwan A-power progrm 4-6, 323C2
CHEN Chao-an
Sets Little League strikeout mark 8-23, team wins title 8-25, 797A3
CHEN Chieh
Vs US textile quotas 5-14, 370B1
CHEN-Chu
Backs Cambodia UN motion vs Viet 1-11, 10B2
Backs UN res on Viet, Cambodia conflicts 3-16, 200F1
Backs Pol Pot govt UN seat 9-21, 741G1
CHENG Heng
Sihanouk exile group formatn disclosed 10-4, 811C2
CHEN Mu-hua
Populatn limit planned 8-13, 652C1
Corruptn probe target 8-22, 652A1
CHEN Yun
China dep premier 7-1, 502E2
Heads anti-corruptn drive 8-22, 651F3
CHEREAU, Patrice
Complete 'Lulu' debuts in Paris 2-25, 174C1
CHERNE, Leo
Chrgs Cambodia food aid blocked 12-18, 977G3, 978G1
CHERNENKO, Konstantin Ustinovich
In Hungary with Brezhnev 5-30—6-1, 417A1
At SALT II summit 6-15—6-18, 449F1; cited in communique 6-18, 457C1
CHERNISHCH, Yuri
Ousted from CR 8-19, 667C3
CHERNYAYEV, Rudolf
Freed in dissident exchng 4-27, 317B1
CHEROKEE Indians—*See INDIANS, American*
CHERRY, Don
Released as Bruins coach 5-24, signs with Rockies 5-29, 470C3
Creighton succeeds as Bruins coach 7-5, 655B3

1980

OSHA chlorine rules partial stay granted by Sup Ct 5-19, 440A3
CPSC seeks asbestos use data 5-30, 703F2
Unpatented key ingredient monopolies backed by Sup Ct 6-27, 511C2
US com urges tighter controls 6-29, 494F2-A3
OSHA benzene standard rejected by Sup Ct 7-2, 510D3
La dump suit filed 7-15, 558F3
Tex chem workers cancer cases rptd 7-24, 584C2
Nitrate ban rejected by US 8-19, 726C1-A2
PCB cleanup methods rptd 8-21, 9-11, 747B2
House passes clean-up funds 9-19, 9-23; Sen OKs 'superfund' 11-24, 897G3-898G1
GE OKs Hudson R dump site cleanup 9-24, 825E2
Love Canal relocatn aid enacted 10-1, 739E1
Toxic dumping controls clear Cong 10-2, signed 10-21, 981F1
EPA toxic waste suits filed 10-7, 10-9, 825A1-A2
EPA policy scored 10-31, 869B2
FMC pleads guilty re tetrachloride pollutn 11-10, 869A2
Du Pont, New England Nuclear merger set 12-8, 985A2
Waste clean-up bill signed 12-11, 935E3-936C1
Foreign Developments (including U.S. international news)
Australia study blames Agent Orange in birth defects 1-3, 6A1; study ordrd 1-8, 37E2
Societa Italiana aid OKd 1-11, 20F3
US limits USSR ammonia imports 1-18, 45A2
OECD sees food shortages 1-23, 49E3
France-India pact signed 1-28, 97C3
Canada '79 profits rptd up 2-7, 116B2
Sierra Leone rejects US co waste dump plan 2-20, 154A2
Montedison ends losses 3-20, 233D2
'76 Seveso dioxin blast damages agrmt with Roche rptd 3-26, 233A1
Australia orders Agent Orange rpt 3-26, 252F2
African dependnc on S Africa cited 4-1, 243A2
Rhone-Poulenc sells units 7-9, 522C2
US banned item export curb set 8-2, 599G2
Poland gets USSR loan 9-3, 658A3
Polish productn drop rptd 11-12, 878C3
Pesticides—*See PESTICIDES*

CHEMISTRY
Nobel won by 3 10-14, 889F2
Obituaries
Libby, Willard F 9-8, 756A1
Watts, George W 3-29, 280E2
CHEN Boda
Gang of 4 trial set 9-27, delayed 11-1, 859B1
Indictmt aired 11-15—11-18, trial starts 11-20, 877C1
Admits Liu persecutn 11-28; admits all chrgs 12-18, 975G1
CHENEY, Rep. Richard (R, Wyo.)
Reelected 11-4, 844D4, 852E1
House GOP policy com chrmn 12-8, 936D2
CHEN Hsi-lien, Gen.
Ousted from Politburo, loses regional cmnd 2-29, 171F3
Resigns as dep premr 4-16, 351F1
CHERIF, Ezzedine
Hanged 4-17, 316A3
CHERNE, Leo
Cambodia blocks aid convoy 2-6, 108B2
CHERRY Hill—*See NEW Jersey*
CHERSEKOVA, Marina
Wins Olympic medal 2-17, 155F3
Wins world figure skating title 3-12, 470B2
CHERVENKOV, Vulko
Dies 10-21, 876B1

1976

CHESAPEAKE Bay
Kepone found in fish 2-26, 171C3
CHESAPEAKE & Ohio Railroad—*See under CHESSIE System*
CHESAPEAKE & Potomac Telephone Co.
Cleared re Halperin tap 12-16, 981B1
CHESS
Byrne dies 3-4, 484C3
Sovt's Korchnoi defects 7-27, 558F3
Korchnoi loses Sovt honors 9-4, 857C1
US wins crown 11-10, 969A3
CHESSIE System, Inc.
Conrail labor talks fail 3-23, 235D2
Pa-Baltimore rail link agreed 9-15, 988A1
'75 tax paymt rptd 10-2, 847A2
Chesapeake & Ohio Railroad
ICC fund powers upheld 6-17, 552F3
CHESTNUT, Jack L.
Sup Ct bars convictn review 10-4, 766D1
CHEVERLY, Md.—*see MARYLAND*
CHEVRON Oil Co.—*See STANDARD Oil Co. (California)*
CHEVY Chase, Md.—*See MARYLAND*
CHEYENNE, Wyo.—*See WYOMING*
CHEYENNE Indians—*INDIANS, American*
CHEYSSON, Claude
Rpts EC pacts with Tunisia, Morocco 1-13, 84E2
European Comm meets 12-22—12-23, 977F1

1977

CHESAPEAKE Bay
Md asks US aid for fishermen 1-20, 54D2
US disaster aid rptd granted 2-5, 91B2
Bethlehem Steel Sparrows Pt cleanup agreed 9-22, 762E1
CHESIMARD, Joanne D.
Convicted, sentncd 3-25, 288B3
CHESSIE System, Inc.
ICC curbs B&O, Chesapeake grain-car deals 8-1, 613C1
Chicago, South Shore & South Bend Railroad
Operatn ordrd contd 4-8, 325F2
CHETTLE, John R.
Sued re sugar lobby gifts 7-20, 614B1
CHEVALLAY, Georges-Andre
Presents austerity budget 10-21, 904E2
CHEYSSON, Claude
Gets Eur Comm post 1-7, 74B2
CHIA Chi-yun
Out as Yunnan CP chief 2-12, 133G3
CHIANG Chen-dung
Taiwan wins Little League title 8-27, 768B2
CHIANG Ching (Chiang Ch'ing)
Rpt province unrest quelled 1-4, 1D1
Blamed for Fukien unrest 1-4, 1F1
Blamed for Teng ouster 1-6, 1C2
2 backers assailed 1-9, 61C2
Blamed for econ lag 2-1, 98G1
Heightened drive vs urged 2-5, 2-7, 98C1
More consumer goods asked 2-24, 200E3
Chekiang offcls disgraced 3-2, 179D3
Kweichow progress lauded 3-5, 179F3
Radical accused of bugging 3-9, 180E1
Liaoning offcl arrested 3-14, 220D1
Blamed for Hangchow unrest 4-11, 282B2
Mao work sabotage chrgd 4-15, 347D1
New leap forward set 5-4, 449F2
Arrest ended Nanchang riots 6-5, 449B3
Scored at Kiangsi rally 6-6, 505D3
Cited for Hupei unrest 6-8, 505E3
Scored in Liaoning Prov 6-24, 562D1
Tied to Yunnan agents 6-29, 562C1
Rpt ousted from party 7-22, 571G2
Anti-Mao stand cited 9-8, 694G2-B3
Mao policy distortn chrgd 9-10, 706F1
Arrest date confrmed 10-6, 780F3
'71-75 China trade rptd up 11-6, 882C3
Yu suicide rptd 11-8, 882E3
Police charge abuses 12-8, 983F3

1978

CHERYAYEV, S.
Named as Sovt spy 3-30, 247F3
CHESAPEAKE (book)
On best-seller list 8-6, 620A2; 9-4, 708B1; 10-9, 800A3; 11-6, 887F3; 12-3, 971A1
CHESAPEAKE Bay, Md.—*See MARYLAND*
CHESHIRE, Maxine
Calls McCarthy drug addict, notes White House pot use 11-19, 943A3
CHESS
Karpov retains world title, final game table 7-18—10-17; Fischer to end retiremt 10-20, 843A1
CHESS Federation, International—*See CHESS*
CHESSIE System Inc.
Seaboard merger set 11-16, 897A1
CHESS Players, The (film)
Released 5-17, 619A1
CHESTER, Raymond
Traded to Raiders 7-21, 1024D3
CHESTNUT, Fien
Indicted 10-5, 770F3
CHESTNUT, Jack
Campaign finance sentnc cited 33E1
CHEVES, Joe
2d in PGA Senior tourn 2-5, 355A3
CHEVRON Oil Co.—*See under STANDARD Oil Co. of Calif.*
CHEWING Gum
Amer Chicle '76 blast chrgs dismissed 2-15, 212D3
CHEYNEY (Pa.) State College
Wins NCAA Div II basketball title 3-18, 272B2
CHEZ, Heinz (d. 1974)
Catalan actors sentncd 3-7, 250G1
CHHANG Song
Chrgs Cambodian killings 4-19, 301D2
CHIANG Ching
Saifudin replcd as Sinkiang CP ldr 1-29, 89C2
Teng cleared of '76 Peking riots 2-15, 111C2
Spared executn 2-21, 130A3
'76 riot role scored 4-7, 287E3
Posters vs Hua, Gen Chen rptd 4-9, 287F3, G3
Tied to Tsao persecutn 6-28, 515B2
Cited for freedom lack 7-3, 532C2
China pragmatic approach seen 532A2
Chinese get 1st cigaret warning 8-28, 727A2
Wu ousted as Peking mayor 10-10, 773G3
Mao tied to 'Gang of 4' 11-19, 901E2
Poster links to Mao 11-23, 949F1
Attack on Tao Chu chrgd 12-10, 950F1

1979

CHESAPEAKE (book)
On best-seller list 1-7, 80A3; 2-4, 120A3; 3-4, 173C3; 4-8, 271G1; 5-6, 356C2; 10-14, 800C3; 11-4, 892D3
CHESAPEAKE Bay
'78 collisn rpts 1-20, 140F3; 2-26, 3-2, 240E3; Cuyahoga cmdr convicted 11-3, 887B3
Va oil refinery OKd by army 10-4, 769G3-770F1
CHESIMARD, Joanne D.
Escapes NJ prison 11-2, 953C2
CHESS
Karpov marries 6-1, 527D2
Korchnoi gets Swiss asylum 9-24, 721E3
CHESSIE System Inc.
Shareholders back Seaboard merger 2-13, 205E3
Seaboard cleared of trust chrgs 2-22, 206B1
Cyrus Eaton dies 5-9, 432E2
CHESTER, William T.
Sentenced in GSA scandal 7-12, 964F3
CHETTY, Shun
Leaves S Africa 8-10, rptd in Botswana 8-12, 617D2
CHEVALLAZ, Georges-Andre
'80 austerity budget proposed 9-26, 754B3
CHEVASSUS, Alix
Marries Niarchos 6-5, 527E2
CHEVRON Standard Ltd.—*See under STANDARD Oil Co. of California*
CHEVRON U.S.A.—*See under STANDARD Oil Co. of California*
CHEWING Gum
Benzocaine OKd as diet aid 5-12, 572A1
CHEYNEY (Pa.) State College
Carter addresses 5-20, 384G2-A3
CHIANESE, Pasqualina
Gives birth to octuplets 8-16, 656C2*
CHIANG Ching
Rptd in secret prison 5-6, 353F1

1980

CHESAPEAKE (book)
On best-seller list 1-13, 40D3
CHESAPEAKE Bay
Environmental decay rptd 2-19, 145G2
CHESAPEAKE & Potomac Telephone Co.
See AMERICAN Telephone & Telegraph Co. (AT&T)
CHESS
Soviets dominate Olympiad 12-7, 972A3
CHESSIE System Inc.
Seaboard Coast Line merger set 9-24, 745A3
CHESSON, Joseph J. F.
Executed 4-22, 353G1
CHESTERTON, G(ilbert) K(eith) (1874-1936)
Harper's to cease publicatn 6-17, 501B1
CHEVENEMENT, Jean-Pierre
Withdraws pres bid, backs Mitterrand 11-8, 886B2
CHEVRON U.S.A.—*See under STANDARD Oil Co. of California*
CHEWNING, Emily Blair
Anatomy Illustrated wins Amer Book Award 5-1, 692C2
CHANG Ching—*See JIANG Qing*

1976

CHIANG Ching
Mao backs arts policies 1-1, 9E3
Role in anti-Teng drive rptd 2-26—3-9, 189D2
Radical strength rptd 4-27, 333E1
May Day CP unity rptd 5-2, 332E3
Cited as possible Mao successor 9-9—9-10, 658F1
Cited in Mao biog 659G1
Listed in China ldrshp 9-10, 712A1
Mourns Mao 9-12, 711D3
Rptd arrested 10-12, 10-13, 757F1-E2
Posters denounce 10-15—10-18, 790G2
Plot, purge confirmed 10-22, 790A2
Scored at Hua rally 10-24, more accusatns rptd 10-25, 10-26, 809A2
Posters detail plot role 10-30, 11-8, 871C2
Aides lose Shanghai posts 10-30, 871A3
Tied to indl disruptn 11-2, 871G2
Blamed for Fukien unrest 11-23, 904F3
Drive vs backers asked; restraint urged 11-28, 904A3
Fighting rages in central provs 12-6—12-31, 1000C1-D2
Chrg sought power, Yao backed 12-18; faces possible executn 12-23, 999E3
Hua sees '77 natl purge 12-24, 999G2
CHIANG Ching-Kuo
Rpts A-fuel reprocessing halt 9-14, 858D2
Heads Kuomintang Party, vows mainland recovery 11-18, 890D3
Ad chrgs execution plan 11-27, 1007A2
Says 254 dissidents jailed 12-25, 1007G1
CHIANG Kai-shek (d. 1975)
Cited in Mao biog 658B3-659B1
Son vows mainland recovery 11-16, 890E3
CHIAO Kuan-hua
Nixon visits 2-21—2-29, 189A3
Score USSR at UN 10-5, 759F3
Meets Kissinger 10-9, 858B1
Ousted as foreign min 12-2, 904D2
CHIAPPE, Francois
Convicted 12-9, 971F2-C3
CHICAGO, Ill.—*See ILLINOIS*
CHICAGO (play)
Long run listed 12-31, 1014G3
CHICAGO, University of
Friedman, Bellow win Nobels 10-14, 10-21, 839G3, 840D1
CHICAGO Milwaukee Corp.
SEC sues, settles 6-29, 984G1
Chicago, Milwaukee, St. Paul & Pacific Railroad—*See separate listing*
CHICAGO, Milwaukee, St. Paul & Pacific Railroad
SEC sues, settles 6-29, 984A2
CHICAGO News (newspaper)
Carter endorsement rptd 10-30, 831G2
Lisagor dies 12-10, 1015A2

1977

CHIANG Ching-kuo (Taiwanese president)
Peking asks US cut ties 8-22, 645G1
Briefed on Vance China trip 8-26, 664F2
CHIANG Kai-shek (d. 1975)
CIA payments rptd 2-19, 124E1
Yang Sen dies 5-15, 452G3
Ma Chao-chun dies 9-19, 788F1
CHIANG Nan-hsiang
Rehabilitatn rptd 3-9, 180G1
CHICAGO, Ill.—*See under ILLINOIS*
CHICAGO, University of
Divinity schl conf 4-18, 492E2
DES study suit filed 4-25, 431A3
DES cancer risk rptd cut 5-3, 432D1
Gray named pres 12-10, 1021B2
CHICAGO Board of Trade
Hunts sued on soybean futures 4-28, 341F1
Hunts countersue 5-4; ct lifts trading ban 5-6, backs comm curbs 6-7, 464B1
Hunt soybean trading ruled illegal 9-28, 858E3
CHICAGO Board Options Exchange (CBOE)
Amex options war rptd 2-17, 521F1
SEC limits trading, begins probe 10-18, 859C3
CHICAGO Daily News, The (newspaper)
Edgar Ansel Mowrer dies 3-2, 264C3
Bilandic fires accuser 11-21, 944E2
CHICAGO Milwaukee Corp.
Rail co-BN merger bid rejected 2-16, 213E2
Milwaukee Rd stock purchase OKd 7-15, 593C2
Green Bay rail purchase rejctd 7-15, 613E1
ICC curbs rail grain-car deals 8-1, 613C1
Milwaukee Rd bankrupt 12-19, 1007A1
CHICAGO, Milwaukee, St. Paul & Pacific Railroad Co.—*See CHICAGO Milwaukee Corp.*
CHICAGO & Northwestern Transportation Co.
Green Bay rail purchase rejected 7-15, 613E1
ICC curbs rail grain-car deals 8-1, 613C1
FRA to buy stock 9-9, 778B3
CHICAGO, Rock Island & Pacific Railroad Co.
ICC curbs grain-car deals 8-1, 613C1

1978

CHIANG Ching-kuo (Taiwanese president)
Peking plea to Taiwan Chinese 12-27-77, 1-4, 17A3
Li Huan post resignatn cited 1-6, 38C2
Elected Natlst China pres 3-21, 251A1
Japan LDP ldrs rptd vs China talks 4-7, 278C2
Sworn pres; names premr, Kuomintang head 5-20, 401G3
Scores US-Peking ties, bars reconciliatn 12-16, 12-18, 974G1-F2; statemt text publshd 12-17, 975F1, 976B2
US aide rpts on Taipei attack 12-28, 994C3
CHIANG Hua
Admits injustices, torture 10-26, 827E3
CHIANG Kai-shek (d. 1975)
Cited in Taiwan statemt on US-Peking ties 12-17, 976B3
CHIC (singing group)
Le Freak on best-seller list 12-6, 971D1
CHICAGO, Ill.—*See ILLINOIS*
CHICAGO, Art Institute of—*See ART Institute of Chicago*
CHICAGO, University of
Molecular sieve announced 2-9, 293C3
CHICAGO Board of Trade
'77 trading rise rptd 1-12, 84A1
Futures vol rptd down in '78 1004A3
CHICAGO Board Options Exchange (CBOE)
Optns trading record, seat price rptd 12-29, 1004B3
CHICAGO Daily News (newspaper)
Ceases publicatn 3-4, 195E1
CHICAGO Milwaukee Corp.
Milwaukee Rd wins BN merger appeal 10-5, 812B2
CHICAGO, Milwaukee, St. Paul & Pacific Railroad Co.—*See CHICAGO Milwaukee Corp.*

1979

CHIANG Ching-kuo (Taiwanese president)
Urges China reconquest 1-1, 2A2
Pvt institute to continue US ties 2-15, 146F1-A2
CHIANG I-chen
For US coordinatn on Indochina refugees 6-29, 495B3
CHIANG Nan-hsiang
Named China educ min 2-6, 134A3
CHIC (magazine)
Flynt convctd in retrial 3-28, 240D1
CHIC (singing group)
Le Freak on best-seller list 1-10, 80E3; 2-14, 120E3; 3-7, 174D1
Good Times on best-seller list 8-1, 620E3; 9-5, 672E3
CHICAGO, Ill.—*See ILLINOIS*
CHICAGO, University of
Pvt Title IX suit allowed by Sup Ct 5-14, 382D3
Primary care MD study rptd 6-14, 571A1
Hears Vernon Jordan 10-17, 780C3
Schultz wins Nobel Prize 10-17, 858G1
CHICAGO Board of Trade
CFTC orders Mar wheat trading halt 3-15, cts stay 3-18—3-19; trading ends, speculators named 3-21, 201C3
CFTC OKs T-notes futures trading 6-19, 681C3
CHICAGO Board Options Exchange (CBOE)
Stock options trading described 348D2
DEA raid nabs 10 cocaine traders 2-7, 119C3
SEC asks trading overhaul 2-15, freeze end seen 2-22, 348B3, 349C1
CHICAGO Mercantile Exchange
CFTC OKs T-notes futures trading 6-19, 681C3
CHICAGO Milwaukee Corp.
Milwaukee Rd borrowing OKd 5-4, svc cut denied 6-1, 465F1
Hillman quits Milwaukee Rd bankruptcy post 6-15, 867F2
Milwaukee Rd takeover of Rock Island ordered 9-26, 722C3
Milwaukee Rd embargoes westn track 11-1, Carter signs aid bill 11-4, embargo lifted 11-5, 867E2-C3
Milwaukee Rd bailout ruled legal 11-25, 989A2
CHICAGO, Milwaukee, St. Paul & Pacific Railroad (Milwaukee Road)—*See CHICAGO Milwaukee Corp.*
CHICAGO & North Western Transportation Co.
Rock Island takeover ordered 9-26, 722C3
CHICAGO, Rock Island and Pacific Railroad
Unions strike 8-28, 8-29, Carter orders cooling-off period, asks ICC actn 9-20; judge bars bankruptcy 9-21, ICC orders takeover 9-26, 722A1-C3
Svc resumes 10-5, judge orders reorganizatn plan 10-10, contract accord reached 10-22, 830C3

1980

CHIANG Ching-kuo (Taiwanese president)
Crackdown protested by US delegatn 1-19—1-24, 102A2, E2, G2
CHIARELLA, Anthony F.
'Insider' stock trading convictn voided by Sup Ct 3-18, 226B2
CHIARELLA v. U.S.
Case decided by Sup Ct 3-18, 226B2
CHICAGO—*See ILLINOIS*
CHICAGO, University of
Chile econ recovery detailed 1-14, 19G1
DES-linked problem pregnancy studies rptd 1-25, 63D2, F2, A3
'79 endowmt earnings rptd 3-24, 319B2
Hans Morgenthau dies 7-19, 608E2
Cronin wins Nobel 10-14, 889C3
CHICAGO Board of Trade (CBT)
Silver futures trading curbed 1-22, 68D3; restraints upheld 2-11, 114E1
T-bill futures trading OK sought 3-20, NY units announce merger 3-21, 224F1
CFTC emergency order case declined by Sup Ct 4-28, 369E1
Currency futures trading on NYSE unit OKd 5-28, 481B2
Hunts weigh legal actn 5-30, 425A3
Treasury futures trading exclusivity awarded to NYSE unit 7-15; CFTC order overturned 7-17—7-18, enforcemt chief quits 7-22, 558A3
Financial futures trading expanded, '79 vol rptd 7-24; NYFE opens 8-7, 616F3
Grain futures hit record highs 10-28, 855D1
Rosenthal nominated chrmn 11-24, 960A1
Chicago Board Options Exchange
SEC ends ban on trading 3-26, 224B2
New issues banned 10-10, 986D2
CHICAGO Mercantile Exchange
Amex, NYSE commodity units to merge 3-21, 224F1
Treasury futures trading exclusivity awarded to NYSE unit 7-15; CFTC order overturned 7-17—7-18, enforcemt chief quits 7-22, 558A3
Financial futures trading expanded, '79 vol rptd 7-24; NYFE opens 8-7, 616F3
CHICAGO Milwaukee Corp.
Milwaukee Rd gets fed loan; westn track purchase rejected in '79 1-7, 52G3
Milwaukee Rd svc cut set 2-25, ICC spurns reorganizatn plans 3-19, BN, Union Pacific track deals set 3-19, 4-1, 345E3-346F1
CHICAGO Rock Island and Pacific Railroad
Liquidatn ordrd 1-25, bids rptd 2-4; svc extensn asked 2-14, 131F1
Svc extensn granted 2-22, 147F3
Svc continues 3-31, judge warns ICC on paymt 4-1, 345C3
Aid bill clears Cong 5-22, Carter signs 5-30, 427E1

1976

CHICAGO Sun-Times (newspaper)
Hoge moderates pres debate 10-15, 782B3
Carter endorsement rptd 10-30, 831G2
CHICAGO Symphony Orchestra
Wins Grammy 2-28, 460D3
CHICAGO Tribune (newspaper)
Wins Pulitzer Prize 5-3, 352E3
Prints Croat hijacker demands 9-11, 685E1
Ariz crime probed 10-2, 849D2
Ford endorsement rptd 10-30, 827G3
CHICANOS—*See MEXICAN-Americans*
CHIGOWE, Tyupo Shumba
Sentenced to die 4-14, 428C2

CHILDBIRTH—*See BIRTHS*

1977

CHICAGO Daily News, The (newspaper)
Edgar Ansel Mowrer dies 3-2, 264C3
CHICAGO, South Shore & South Bend Railroad—*See under CHESSIE System*
CHICAGO Seven
Froines named to OSHA 9-30, 808B2
CHICAGO Sun-Times (newspaper)
Ross named Defns asst secy 1-19, 52G3; confrmd 3-4, 211G1
Gen Brown article rptd 3-27, 231G3
Powell apologizes to Percy 9-14, 701C3
CHICAGO Tribune (newspaper)
Child porno series 5-15—5-18, 432E2
On most reliable govt news source list 12-10, 1009B1
CHICANOS—*See MEXICAN Americans*
CHICKENS—*See POULTRY*
CHIEN Kuo-tung
China sports min 1-29, 98C2
CHIGINYA, Bishop Tobias
Named Rhodesia RC bishop 2-22, 375A3
CHIKEREMA, James
In Rhodesia 9-18; backs Smith re army 9-19, 735F1-B2
Kaunda backs Patriotic Front 10-21, 810F2
CHIKESI, Chakamyuka
Quits Muzorewa group 8-8, 662D2
CHIKWANDA, Alexander
Named Zambia agri min 4-24, 490G1
CHILDBIRTH—*See BIRTHS*

1978

CHICAGO Sun-Times (newspaper)
Chicago Daily News folds 3-4, 195E1
CHICAGO Symphony Orchestra & Chorus
Wins Grammys 2-24, 316C1
CHICAGO Tribune, The (newspaper)
Johnrae Earl dies 1-10, 96F1
Geo Bliss kills self 9-11, 777F3
CHICHESTER, Sir Francis
Woman tops world sail record 6-8, 653D2
CHICKENS—*See POULTRY*
CHIDAMBER, Pratap—*See CHITNIS, Lord*
CHIEF Justices, Conference of
Vt mtg; TV cameras in ctrooms backed 8-3, 626A3
CHIEU, Nguyen Thi
Humphrey convicted as Viet spy 5-19, 390A1
CHI Hoa-tien
In Zaire 6-24, 652G2
CHILDBIRTH (including pregnancy)—*See also ABORTION*
Breast cancer immunity, early pregnancy link rptd 1-19, 334A1
Carter budgets Medicaid 1-23, 48C2
Birth defect programs halted by March of Dimes 3-8, 744B2
UAL maternity rule review refused by Sup Ct 3-20, 205G3
Rural deaths rptd 4-6—4-7, 577E3
Cath fertility rate rptd down 4-15, 295D1
Firestone jobless benefits challenge declined by Sup Ct 4-17, 308B3
Childbirth-linked hormone rptd in male boars 4-20, 334F3
Municipal legal immunity ended by Sup Ct 6-6, 447D1-A2
Pregnancy x-ray risk seen 7-11, 598G2
NYC embryo implant trial opens 7-17, 597G1; damages awarded 8-18, 770G1
'Test-tube baby' (embryo implant) born in UK, reactn 7-25, 596D3-597F1
Calif sperm bank suit rptd 8-1, 597A2
Niagara retardatn, chem dump site linked 8-7, 703B1
Illegitimate births rptd 8-10, 744D1
Eisenhower baby born 8-15, 844G3
W Ger birth rate rptd down 8-16, 725A3
Sterility-linked pesticide curbs asked 9-19, 719C2
Rural health progrm planned 10-2, 770G1
'Test-tube baby' born in India 10-3, 824D3
Miscarriages in Mich, PBBs linked 10-9, 769F2
Progestin birth-defect risk warning ordrd 10-12, 948D2
Thalidomide victim bears child 10-13, 948F3
ACLU hails pregnancy benefits law 10-20, 981B3
Pregnancy benefits bill signed 10-31, 873G1
UAL NYS maternity leave case refused by US Sup Ct 11-27, 937G1
Microwave safety scored 12-11, 936C3

1979

ICC extends takeover order 11-28; reorganizatn plan filed 12-28, 989B2
CHICAGO Sun-Times (newspaper)
Pulitzer Prizes awarded 4-16, 336F2
Daily, Sunday circulatn listed 6-6, 431C1, D1
CHICAGO Tribune, The (newspaper)
Gapp wins Pulitzer 4-16, 336C3
Daily, Sunday circulatn listed 6-6, 431C1
H-bomb letter published 9-18, 713B2; text of letter, diagram 714D1-717E3
Municipal bond ratings listed 9-20, 920F3
2d Daley salary disclosed 12-4, 946G3
CHICKENS—*See POULTRY*
CHIKEREMA, James
UANC ousts 5-12, Muzorewa blocks 5-13, 359F2
Forms oppositn party 6-20, 490G1

CHILDBIRTH (including pregnancy)
Lead exposure sterilizatn controversy in W Va 1-4, 56A3
Fluorocarbon-birth defect study cited 1-5, 56G1
Frozen sperm study rptd 1-7, 64E2
'Test-tube baby' born in Scotland 1-14, 79C2
Smoking tied to birth perils 1-16, 63E3
Childbirth drug effects rptd 1-16, 64C1
Carter budgets prenatal program 1-22, 44B3
VD warning issued 2-19, 140E1
Ore miscarriages, herbicide ban linked 3-1, 167E1
Colo radium waste sites rptd 3-5, 187G1
Nixon grandchild born 3-14, 271F2
3 Mile I A-accident, evacuatn urged 3-28—4-3, 241C1-245F3
3 Mile I radiatn study set 4-4, advisory lifted 4-9, 260F1, 261A2
Ford grandchild born 4-22, 392G3
Prenatal hemophilia test rptd 4-26, 315D2
Nutritn-related deaths rptd down 4-30, 386A3
Swedish queen gives birth 5-13, 392G3
NZ woman gives birth after hysterectomy 5-16, 392B3
Carter unveils natl health plan 6-12, 438C2
PCB limits in food cut 6-28, 571D2
Peru annual birth rate 3.5% 7-19, 566F3
UK test-tube baby marks 1st birthday 7-25, 656A2
Octuplets born in Italy 8-16, 656C2*
Sterility, toxic chems linked 9-11, 736F1
FBI admits '70 Seberg slander 9-14, 705B1
USSR birth rate rise urged 10-10, 857D1
Pot use risks rptd 10-14, 972D1
'Laughing gas', miscarriages linked 10-24, 971E2, A3
Ind pregnancy jobless pay case refused by Sup Ct 11-13, 902A2
Abortn funding cases accepted by Sup Ct 11-26, 919A2
Sex seen as pregnancy risk 11-29, 971B3

1980

ICC urges svc cutback 5-27; OKs segment sale 6-10, 598B3-F3
ICC extends svc again 5-30, 427B2
Abandonmt OKd, worker aid law upset 6-2; Sup Ct bars ruling 7-2, rail law study 11-10, 868E2
CHICAGO Sun-Times (newspaper)
Carter pres endorsemt rptd 11-1, 841G3
John Fischetti dies 11-18, 928D2
CHICAGO Tribune (newspaper)
Kingman quits as sportswriter 7-2, 637B2
Aldo Beckman dies 9-10, 755C2
Reagan pres endorsemt rptd 11-1, 841F3
CHICKENS—*See POULTRY*
CHICOPEE Falls—*See MASSACHUSETTS*
CHILD, Julia
More Company wins Amer Book Award 5-1, 692D2

CHILDBIRTH (including pregnancy)
Australia blames Agent Orange in birth defects 1-3, 6A1; study ordrd 1-8, 37F2
Maternity smoking, drinking risks rptd 1-4, 23C3
US 'test-tube baby' clinic OKd 1-8, 24E1--B2
Fetal skin disease test rptd 1-10, 64C1
Tex woman gives birth to 21st child 1-12, 200F1
Conn ERISA maternity case declined by Sup Ct 1-14, 37B1
US rpts smoking-health risks 1-14, 40C2
DES, problem pregnancies rptd linked 1-25, 63C2
VD linked dangers rptd 2-5, 158B1
S Ford paternity suit settled 2-28, 199A2
Shockley rpts Calif sperm bank donatns 2-28, 990D2
Saccharin warning rptd 3-6, 317C2
Australia orders Agent Orange rpt 3-26, 252F2
Smoking risk to nonsmokers rptd 3-26, 318C2
3 Mile I study rptd 4-2, 332A2, G2
US median age linked 6-21, 519E1
Sovt '71-76 infant mortality rise rptd 6-25, 525D2
Glucose fertilizatn role rptd 7-3, 715G2
US, Canada infant mortality rates compared 7-16, 562C3
Mex birth rate at 2.9% 9-1, 730D1
FDA issues caffeine warning 9-4, 726A2
France seeks increase 10-1, 749D3

1976

CHILDREN—*See also EDUCATION*
Peru renews comics ban 2-3, 142E3
Edmonds wins Natl Book Award 4-19, 292D3
Benefit curbs re illegitimacy upheld 6-29, 568D3
US funds UN progrm 6-30, 533E2
Carter asks improved adoptn rules 8-3, 564B3
GOP platform text 8-18, 603E3, 605A2
Farm populatn drop rptd 10-5, 833A2
Sup Ct stays gag order in Okla murder case 11-24, 901C2
Benefits for divorced mothers barred 12-13, 940C3
Day Care Issues
Mondale record cited 512C3
'77 budget proposal 1-21, 65F1
ERA disputed 2-13, 172G1
Cong clears funds bill 3-24, 234D1
Funds bill veto sustained 5-5, 345G3
Sen OKs tax credit 8-6, 586B1
GOP platform text 8-18, 602E3, 604D3, 605A3
Ford signs revised bill 9-7, 665C1
Tax credit clears Cong 9-16, 705F3
Health & Safety
Ford State of Union message 1-19, 38G2, 39G2
'77 budget proposals 1-21, 62B3, 65B2
Ford rpts govs back budget plan 1-22, 41C2
Sen OKs paint poison bill 2-19, 170F3
Ford signs '77 food funds 7-12, 533C3
Ford signs day-care bill 9-7, 665C1
Polio vaccine shortage, danger rptd 9-21, 9-23, 776B1
Cong sets HMO aid rules 9-23, 765C2
Nutritn block-grant bill not cleared 10-2, 884A2
Health manpower aid signed 10-13, 788E2
Welfare Issues—*See under POVERTY*

1977

CHILDREN
Welfare cost rptd 2-19, 176C1
HEW reorganizatn effected 3-9, 175B3, D3
'75 FCC obscenity order voided 3-16, 215E3-216B1
Porno, prostitutn network rptd 4-11—5-27, 432G1-G3
Child-abuse law hearing 5-23, 432F3
Carter welfare reform plan 8-6, 608C3
House subcom TV violence rpt scored 10-24, 921G1-C2
Day-care, abuse cntrs urged by Natl Women's Conf 11-19—11-21, 917D3
Adoption & Foster Care—*See also 'Supreme Court Cases' below*
Adoption subsidy bill OKd by House 6-7, 628C3
Admin subsidies proposed; current US foster care spending cited 7-12, 628E2-C3
Carter abortn alternative scored 7-19, 786D3
Education—*See under 'E'*
Health & Safety
Ford '78 budget proposals 1-17, 32B3
FTC bars vitamin pitch 2-7, 217C1
Carter budget revision 2-22, 125F3
Reye's syndrome cases up 3-11, 224E1
Measles upsurge rptd 3-19, 224D1
HEW sets immunizatn drive 4-6, WHO launches global projct 4-7, 287E2, B3
Sleepwear flame-retardant banned 4-7, 302E2★, F2★; **see 'Tris' under CHEMICALS**
Carter asks medicaid care program 4-25, 322G1
Pa mental health rights case refused 5-16, 418G3
Edith Jackson dies 6-5, 532B3
Laetrile overdose death 6-11, 508E1
Medicaid care found lacking, Carter plan scored 6-22, 643B3
Gen Foods sued on cereal ads 6-30, 613B2
McDonald's halts glass promotn 7-8, 7-17, sues Mass 7-12, 560B1
'78 health progrm authorizatn OKd 8-1, 689A3
'78 nutritn funds OKd 8-12, 688A3

1978

CHILD Development, Office of—*See under U.S. GOVERNMENT—HEALTH, Education & Welfare*
CHILDREN—*See also YOUTH*
Porno, prostitutn curbs clear Cong 1-24, 82D3; signed 2-6, 218A2
Porno film distributor sentenced 5-19, 396G3
Morocco child labor rptd 5-29, 596F2
Intellgnc dvpt study rptd 7-8, 1023E2
Grandparent child-care tax credit clears Cong 10-15, 786D1
Adoption & Foster Care
Father's role limited 1-10, 13C3
Adoptn bill signed 4-24, 323E3
Day Care
Carter budget proposals 1-23, 47C1
Backed in Humphrey-Hawkins bill 3-16, 182D3
State soc svc claims setlmt signed 6-12, 465F3
Education—*See EDUCATION*
Health & Safety
Bias in govt progrms rptd 1-10, 14C1
HEW anti-smoking drive set 1-11, 23C2
Carter budget proposals 1-23, 47C1, 48F1, B2
Epilepsy drug OKd 2-28, 231C2
FTC proposes TV ad curbs 2-28, 4-28, Cong wary 4-26—5-2, 347G1, D2
Toys sharp-edge tests OKd 3-10, 264G3
Water toy recall set 4-13, 348F1
Educ Dept nutritn unit proposed 4-14, 279D1
'73 abuse act extensn signed 4-24, 323B3
Tris garment exports banned 5-5, 347A3
Spleen regeneratn rptd 6-22, 598F1
Chelsea soft drink ads halted 7-22, 941G3-942A1
FCC to renew TV probe 7-28, 672A2
Niagara retardantn, chem dump site linked 8-7, 703B1
Small toy ban proposed 10-5, 769D3
Fire victim data rptd 10-8, 972C1
FTC TV ad probe curbed 11-3; stay denied, probe affirmed 11-17, 941G2-C3
Tris compensatn bill pocket vetoed 11-8, 941C3
US Army rules tightened 11-29, 960F2
Supreme Court Cases
Wis remarriage law voided 1-18, 65B1

1979

CHILD Development, Office of—*See under U.S. GOVERNMENT–HEALTH, Education & Welfare*
CHILDREN—*See also YOUTH*
Cable TV 'superstatn' to expand programming 4-23, 334D3
TV network programs scored 10-30, NAB responds 11-1, 858A3-E3
Library outreach urged 11-15–11-19, 901G1
FCC modifies TV plan 12-19, 1006G3
Adoption & Foster Care
Fed welfare paymts backed by Sup Ct 2-22, 151B1
Unwed father consent role backed by Sup Ct 4-24, 364A1
Half-Indian custody case refused by Sup Ct 6-18, 499A2
Day Care
Steinem cites as '80 electn issue 7-13–7-15, 578C3
Education—*See EDUCATION*
Health & Safety Issues
Breast-feeding rptd up in pvt hosps 1-5, 64B2
Mattel recalls space toys 1-11, ACT: recall ineffective 2-27, 308A3
Lawyers' interstate rights limited by Sup Ct 1-15, 31C3
Crib death preventive device test rptd 1-15, 64G1
Crib death risk increased by smoking 1-16, 64B1
Childbirth drug effects rptd 1-16, 64C1
ABC to cut TV ads 1-18, 78A3
Mil family abuse data rptd 1-21, 93E3
Carter budget proposals 1-22, 44A3
Illegitimate child abuse data rptd 1-26, 93C3
Leukemia study sees less therapy 2-9, 139A2
Utah '50s leukemia study rptd 2-14, 112B2
Calif ct OKs respirator removal 2-15, 291B2
VD warning issued 2-19, 140E1
Vegetarian diet rptd risky 2-22, 140F1
Cancer diagnosis secrecy study rptd 2-26, 218F1
3 Mile Island A-accident, evacuatn urged 3-28–4-3, 241C1-245F3
3 Mile I advisory lifted 4-9, 261A2

1980

CHILDREN
LA adults-only housing barred 1-31, 115C2
State of State messages 1-14, 483D3; 2-6, 269G1
GOP platform adopted; text 7-15, 535E3, 536A1
Adoption & Foster Care
Families Conf opens 6-5, 442C3
Ark brothers rptd reunited 6-29, 638A3
Stepfather adoptn rights case accepted by Sup Ct 10-6, 782B3; vacated 11-17, 882F1
Day Care
Neb State of State message 1-10, 403C3
GOP platform adopted; text 7-15, 535G2
Dem platform plank adopted 8-13, 614F3
Anderson platform offered 8-30, 665C2
Health & Safety Issues
Stuttering, genetics link rptd 1-5, 63B3
Kan State of State message 1-15, 403G2
Carter budget proposals 1-28, 72B3
VD linked diseases rptd 2-5, 158B1
FBI 'Miporn' probe rptd 2-14, 136A2
Va sterilizatn progrm rptd 2-23, 158E3
Crib death heredity link rptd 2-28, 358C3
Saccharin warning rptd 3-6, 317C2
Ct limits harvest work, US pesticide study plan cited 3-20, 227C1
CBS unit toy gym recall set 6-2, 703G2
Benton & Bowles settles FTC bike ad chrg 7-31, 703E1
Immigratn econ impact rptd 9-22, 826F3
Mental health authrzn clears Cong 9-24, 9-30, signed 10-7, 803G3
Nutritn authrzn clears Cong 12-3, signed 12-5, 936F1, 981B1
Nutritn funds clear Cong 12-4, 954D3; signed 12-15, 982C1
Supreme Court Rulings
Fed worker illegitimate child aid backed 2-26, 188F1
Del 'unfit' parent case accepted 3-24, 265A2
Labor law fines upheld 4-28, 369A1
FTC TV ad probe case refused by Sup Ct 6-16, 511D3
Stepfather adoptn rights case accepted 10-6, 782B3; vacated 11-17, 882F1
Unwed couples custody case refused 10-20, 807A1

1976

CHILDREN'S Defense Fund
Edelman named Carter aide 11-23, 881E3
CHILDREN'S Hospital (Philadelphia, Pa.)
Virus linked to MS 2-28, 224F2
CHILE—*See also ANDEAN Group, IDB, LAFTA, OAS, SELA*
2 ex-presidents OK advisory roles 1-2, 1-4; Frei rejcts 1-2, 8D2
'74 mil forces rptd 1-2, 60F2
Mil staff chief quits 1-3, replaced 1-6; oppositn to Pinochet rptd 1-4—1-10, 47C1
Chile U purge rptd 1-8, 47C3
Listed as 'not free' nation 1-19, 20D3
Pinochet scores Frei 1-21; denies mil rift, junta backs 1-28, 99D3
Aylwin home bombed 2-26; rightists scored 3-3, 310C3
Cabt, mine mgrs quit 3-5; Cabt shuffled 3-8, 288F2
Guerrilla arsenal rptd seized 8-15, 711E1
Church Developments
Vatican pressed on refugees 1-9, 47F2
Pol prisoner, jobless aid set 1-16, 47A3
Pinochet, church ldrs meet 1-20; bishop lauds 1-21, 100D2
Bishops ask forgn priests stay, note '75 ousters 1-23, 100B2
Precht rpts torture continues 1-26, 100A2
Vatican emb refugees get safe-conducts 1-28, 100A1
Vatican emb refugees exiled to Sweden 2-21, 288B3
US reps chrg repressn 3-17; Zalaquett seized, exiled 4-5, 4-12, US scores 4-19, 310C2
Montealegre arrested 5-12, 465G1
DINA rights abuse chrgs rptd 6-3, 465F1
Santiago rejects chrgs vs Montealegre 7-16, 711D2
2 attys exiled 8-6; bishops score govt 8-18, 711C2
Bishops stoned 8-15; govt agents excommunicated 8-17, bishops see Pinochet 8-18, 711G1
Bishop scores repressn, fear 8-22, 711F1
UN panel chrgs abuses 10-14, 963F2
Rpts detainees missing up 11-5, 963G1
Copper Issues
$800 mln loss in '75 rptd 1-29, 99A3
World Bank loan, US OKs 2-3, 99F2
US, other forgn role in Codelco set 3-5, 288A3
Mine mgrs quit 3-5, 288A3
Intl price rise cited 6-30, 871G1
'70 Anaconda anti-Allende offer rptd 12-23, 999A2
Economy & Labor (domestic)—*See also 'Copper Issues' above*
'74 defns budget rptd 1-2, 60F2
'75 inflatn rate down 1-6, 8F2
Peso devalued 1-7, 48A1
Church jobless aid set 1-16, 47A3
Peso devalued 1-16, 1-28, 99A3
Peso revalued upward 6-30; new devaluatn set 11-4, 871G1
Santiago Jan-June jobless rate up 8-13, 871A2
Bishop scores unemploymt 8-22, 711F1
500 state cos sold since '73 coup 10-16, 871B2
Jan-Oct inflatn 151.3% 11-5, 871F1

1977

Meningitis A vaccine rptd 9-28, 907G1
Fyrol FR-2-treated sleepwear warning issued 9-29, 820C2
Schl lunch, nutritn bill signed 11-10, 897D2
Supreme Court Cases
Custody jurisdictn review denied 1-25, 80G2
Illegitimates' rights rulings 4-26, 382G2-C3
Pa mental health rights case refused 5-16, 418G3
Burger cites '69-76 cases 5-17, 419B3
NYS foster care rule upheld 6-13, 517D2
HEW jobless-benefits standards law upheld 6-20, 516D3-517A1
Ga racial adoptn curb review refused 6-20, 517C1
CHILDREN'S Defense Fund
Edelman in Viet missn 3-16—3-20, 206C1
Medicaid child care found lacking 6-22, 643B3
CHILDREN'S Television, Action for
FTC bars vitamin pitch to children 2-7, 217E1
CHILDREN'S Television, Committee on
Sues Gen Foods on cereal ads 6-30, 613E2
CHILE—*See also ANDEAN Group, IDB, OAS*
'60 quake measure revised 2-14, 161B3
Santiago bomb blasts 10-4—11-5, 983G2
Church Developments
Pol prisoners estimated 1-1, 3C1
Vatican scores Pinochet 1-9, 18D3
Lefebvre on Latin tour 7-13—7-26, 620F1
Repressn vs Vicariate rptd down 11-11, house raided 11-16, 983A2, C2
Economy & Labor (domestic)
'76 inflatn rptd 1-4, 18F1
Southern oil find rptd 1-6, 18A3
Pvt investmt cos ordrd to register 1-7, 18A2
Pvt investmt bankruptcies cited 219E3
'76 3d ¼ jobless rate down 2-11, govt work progrms cited 3-18, 6-5, 448D3
'76 pvt investmt cos scandal rptd 2-18, 449A2
Peso revalued upward 3-4, 449G1
Jan-Mar inflatn down 4-5, cost to poor noted 5-3, 448C3
New econ measures enacted 5-1, reactn 5-3—5-9, 448E2
'61-75 GDP variatns table 5-30, 439A1
Low agri, indl productn cited 6-5, 448E3
Pinochet lauds econ program, union curbs to continue 9-11, 742E3
Poll: 71% back govt policy 9-21, 743A2
Copper mine struck 11-2; labor ldr banishmt rptd 12-4, 1019B1

1978

Indian tribal authority backed 5-15, 387B3
Calif jurisdictn in support case denied 5-15, 387F3
Children excluded from porno rule 5-23, 405G2-F3
NH rape law case refused 6-5, 431C2
NYS illegitimate child inheritance law upheld 12-11, 981B1
Welfare & Poverty
Carter budget proposals 1-23, 46D3, 47A1, C1
Unificatn Church '77 solicitatn bar cited 2-22, 295B3
Black data rptd 4-10, 811F1
AFDC minimum in reform compromise 6-7, 446G1
Waste limits proposed 7-10, AFDC '77 paymt errors rptd 8-12, 685A3
HEW vows 'runaway' father crackdown, '77 data rptd 7-19, 685A1
CHILDREN'S Defense Fund
Head Start shift opposed 4-14, 279A2
CHILDREN'S Television, Action for
FTC proposes children's TV ad curbs 2-28, 4-28, 347C2
CHILDS, Henry
NFL '77 touchdown ldr 1-1, 56E2
CHILE—*See also GATT, IDB, OAS*
Quake hits northn areas 8-3, 759B1
Beagle Channel Dispute—*See BEAGLE Channel*
Church Developments
Bishops score plebiscite 1-2, 16E3, F3
Amnesty decreed 4-19, actn on missing asked 4-25, 351E2, A3
Rights year launched 4-25, 351B3
Hunger strikers occupy churches, ldrs mediate 5-22—6-9, 452D2
Govt statemt on missing unchngd 6-23; bps issue plea for info 7-15, 573B1
UN rights panel ends probe 7-27, 591D2
Bishops ask data on missing 10-12, 795F3
Union ban protested 10-23, 1014G2
Papal plea on Beagle Channel issued 12-12, 797A3
Papal mediatn of Beagle Channel dispute set 12-22, envoy in Argentina 12-26, 999A3
Economy & Labor (domestic)
GDP rptd 8.6% in '77 2-10, 312F2
Govt sets jobs cut 3-1; Santiago jobless 13.3% in Dec '77 3-3, 312F2
'77 inflatn 63.5%, 1st ¼ '78 inflatn 7.8% 4-14, 312E2
Trade union repressn rptd 5-23, 452C3
16 unions back hunger strikers 5-31, 452G2
Jan-June inflatn 14.7% 7-28, 795E1
70 seized in copper mine protest 7-31—9-16, miners benefits hiked 9-23, 795F1-E2
Santiago jobless 12.8% 9-1, 795F1
Steelworkers ask wage hike 9-7, 795E2
Agri productn down 9-15, 795D1
Land reform to end 10-6, 795A1
June '77-78 world inflatn rates ranked 10-18, 914E1
7 'Marxist' unions banned 10-20, church protests 10-23; pvt co union electns held 10-31, 1014E2

1979

Nutritn-related deaths rptd down 4-30, 386A3
Virus found to cause diabetes 5-23, 471F3
Siamese twins separated 5-30, 527F2; leave hosp 7-17, 656C2
Carter unveils natl health plan 6-12, 438C2
CPSC adopts small toy ban 6-17, 596B2
Mental commitmt rules backed by Sup Ct 6-20, 515E3
AMF to produce bike safety ads 7-8, 595A3
Hyperactivity treatmt cited 7-16, 571F3
FDA drive vs lead in canned food rptd 8-11, 736G3
Fluoride efficacy doubted 9-1, 1000B2
Immunizatn progrm rptd effective, childhood diseases down 9-11, 736D3
Supreme Court Rulings
Foster care benefits backed 2-22, 151B1
Alimony rule in NYS custody case backed 3-19, 203F2
Unwed fathers adoptn, damage suit rights defined 4-24, 364A1
Fed custody fights curbed 6-11, 478F3
Mental commitmt rules backed 6-20, 515E3
Gender-based welfare rules illegal 6-25, 339D3
Unwed mothers denied survivors' aid 6-27, 558A2
Welfare & Social Services
Foster care benefits backed by Sup Ct 2-22, 151B1
Gender-based plan ruled illegal by Sup Ct 6-25, 539D3
Unwed mothers denied survivors' aid by Sup Ct 6-27, 558A2
CHILDREN of Sanchez (recording)
Mangione wins Grammy 2-16, 336E3
CHILDREN'S Hospital Medical Center (Boston, Mass.)
Needleman lead study rptd 3-29, 266G1
CHILDREN'S Television, Action for
Stricter toy missile regulatns asked 2-27, 308A3
CHILDS, Dean
Shares 6000-m relay mark 4-28, 911A3
CHILDS v. Childs
Case decided by Sup Ct 3-19, 203G2
CHILE—*See also GATT, LAFTA, IDB, OAS*
Beagle Channel Dispute—*See BEAGLE Channel*
Economy & Labor
Union ldrs see labor min 1-2, offered more freedom 1-3, 6F2
'78 inflatn 30.3% 1-4, 19G3
Union reforms seen limited; labor min cancels Group of 10 mtg 1-12, 28G3-29B1
Econ upswing seen; growth rate, inflatn rptd 5-21, 369D3
Anchovy catch drops; '78, '79 fish-meal output data rptd 7-3, 555C1
Labor decrees curb unions 7-9, 523E1
Pinochet defends policies, sets poverty plan 9-11, 685C2

1980

CHILDREN of a Lesser God (play)
Opens 3-30, 392D2
Wins Tonys 6-8, 692B3
CHILDREN'S Emergency Fund, UN International—*See UNITED Nations–UNICEF*
CHILDS, Dean
Wins 6,000-m Penn Relays 4-25, 892C2
CHILE—*See also GATT, IDB, OAS*
Beagle Channel Dispute—*See BEAGLE Channel*
Economy & Labor
'75-79 econ recovery plan detailed; '79 unemploymt, inflatn, interest rates cited 1-14, 19F1
Teniente copper mine struck 1-19, 57E1

1976

Foreign Relations (misc.)—*See also 'Copper Issues' above; 'Human Rights' and 'Refugee Issues' below*

Bolivians vs sea outlet plan 1-1—1-3; Bolivia, Peru name study panels 1-7, 27B1
Italy aide asks democracy restored 1-3, 47D2
Bolivia mil chngs rptd 1-9, 26F3
Auto import ban lifted 1-9, 48A1
Argentina holds UK subjcts 1-12, 26A2
Bishops ask forgn priests stay, note '75 ousters 1-23, 100B2
'75 oil imports up $300 mln 1-29, 99A3
Bolivia deports 'plotters' 2-22, 238D1
CR students chrg US coup role 2-23, 178F1
Sovt arms rptdly bought 2-25, 288E3
Venez detains natls 3-2, 208D2
Orfila lauds Pinochet 3-18, rebuts Mex press criticism 3-19, 310G1
World Bank loan protested 3-19, 3-23; McNamara defends 4-12, 310E2
Total IMF oil loan rptd 4-1, 340C2
Argentina govt policies, pol image compared 4-2, 4-7, 264E1, B3
Bolivia: MIR aids guerrillas 4-8, 416C1
Enriquez rptd seized in Argentina 4-10, 399B1
Pinochet in Uruguay 4-21—4-24, 382D3
UNCTAD delegatn questioned 5-5, 320C2
Exiles greet Torres widow in Mex 6-7, 456F2
Argentina arrests seminarian 8-3, 672C1
Ecuador expels bishops 8-15, 711A2
Coup anniv scored in Panama 9-10, 792E1
Letelier buried in Venez 9-29, 780F3
Andean Group membership dropped 10-6, 999D1
Venez chrgs vs Cuba exiles rptd 10-12—10-20, 779B3, 780F2, B3
Exile link to Letelier denied 10-20—10-21, 844E2
Forgn group sets agri loan 10-20, 871D1
Bolivia seaport plan rejctd 11-26, 975A2
Bolivia bars Peru war role 12-7, 975D2
World Bank OKs 2 loans 12-21, 999F1

Human Rights (including political prisoner issues)—*See also 'Church Developments' above, 'Refugee Issues' below*

UK envoy backs MD torture chrg 1-1, Chile denies 1-5, 8C2
Russell ct scores rights abuse 1-17, 61D2
UN panel gets UK MD torture testimony 1-19, 47G1
Gutierrez linked to UK MD arrest 1-24, 100C1
Prisoners' rights decreed 1-28, ICJ scores 2-2, 100D1
UN, OAS, US, Venez units chrg abuses 2-10—4-24; Chile denies 2-18, 4-24, 310A1
US Sen protests abuses 2-18, 151F3
Velasco, Weibel seized 3-24, 3-29, 310A3
US rep: abuse extensive 4-21, 382G3
Prisoner release, arrest data 5-6—5-26, 6-7, 464D3
Amnesty Intl chrgs terrorism 5-24, 399D2 ★
Scored at intl soc dems mtg 5-25, 449F2, C3
DINA abuses chrgd 6-3, 6-9, 6-12, 465A1-F1
OAS mtg issue 6-4—6-18, 464B2
Kissinger on rights abuse 6-8, 465B2
OAS panel rpt, govt denial publshd 6-9, 464G3
Prisoner abuse rpt cited 6-21, 465C1
US ties econ aid, abuses 6-30, 533C1
2 leftists found dead 7-16, 9-12; UN presses Soria probe 12-14, 963A2
Rpt 250 unable to find exile homes 8-4, 711G2
Flores freed, exiled to US 8-5, 711F2
47 detainees rptdly vanish 8-7, 711C1
Rpt guerrilla arsenal seized 8-15, 711E1
Amnesty Intl: repressn continues 8-23, 711A1
ICJ: abuses continue 8-31, 711B1
US sen cites Uruguay torture 9-28, 814G2
UN panel rpts more abuses, urges econ pressure 10-14, 963E2
US aid rejected 10-19, 10-20, 870G3 ★
'75-76 repressn rptd up 10-31, 975D1
Cited re forgn agri loan 11-5, 871E1
Pol prisoner total rptd down, disappearncs up 11-5, 963F1
304 pol prisoners freed 11-17—11-18; denies Carter favor sought 11-22, 963D1
8 leftists rptd missing 12-15, 12-20, 12-22, 999E2
Corvalan, Bukovsky exchngd, US role rptd; Cuba rejcts Montes-Matos trade 12-18, 955D2-G3
Trucco: 1 pol prisoner left 12-18, 963B1
World Bank voices 'concern' 12-21, 999G1

Press & Censorship

'75 censorship decree scored 1-9, 47E3
Christian Dem radio closed 1-20, 99F3
Govt OKs Frei book 1-23, bars press debate 1-31, 99B3
Christian Dem radio statn reopens 2-6; closed 3-22, Velasco seized 3-24, 310A3
Ercilla closed 3-23, 310C3
OAS rights abuse rpt, govt denial publshd 6-9, 464G3
Amnesty Intl rpts newsmen seized 8-23, 711B1

Refugee Issues (including safe-conducts)

Forgn embs pressed on refugees 1-9, 47E2

1977

Foreign Relations (misc.)—*See also 'Human Rights' and 'Monetary, Trade & Aid' below*

UN Assemb member 3F3
Antarctic claim renewed 1-5, 18B3
Canada amb nominee withdrawn 2-26, 219G2
Spain infiltrates exile groups 3-5, 307F2
Sweden arrests terrorist 4-1, 429B1
'76 MD exodus rptd 5-3, 448B3
Australia '72 Allende coup role rptd 5-4, 372F1
Jets hijacked to Argentina 6-21, Peru 7-5, 537B2
Bolivia miners rptd exiled 8-9, 902C2
Peru border dispute buildup rptd 8-31, 785C1
Pinochet at Panama Canal pact signing 9-7, 678A1
Letelier murder probe implicates DINA, Cuban exiles 9-7—9-10, 743D2
USSR aggressn in Latin Amer blamed on US 9-11, 724F3
Grenada oppositn ldr scores ties 10-26, 869B1
Argentina Beagle Channel setlmt cited 11-4, 944C3

Government & Politics—*See also other appropriate subheads in this section*

Christn Dem 'plot' chrgd 3-11, denied 3-13; pol parties banned 3-12, 219A3
State of siege extended 3-11, 219G3
Limited electns by '85 vowed 7-9, 635F2
Pinochet defends rule, bars early pol chng 9-11, 742B3
'85 electn plan rptd scored by students, unions 9-16, 743F1
Poll: most Chileans back govt 9-21, 743G1

Human Rights (including political prisoner and refugee issues)

Prisoner estimates rptd 1-1, 3C1
Corvalan pension restored 1-5, 18B3
Lavin asked to end US visit 1-28, govt denies chrgs 2-2, 219D2
Radio Balmaceda closed 1-28, 219E3
Ercilla rptd under govt control 2-3, new publicatns curbed 3-11, 220A1
Canada amb nominee withdrawn re DINA link 2-26, 219G2
US aide regrets '73 coup role 3-8; US disavows apology, Carter stance contradictns noted 3-8, 3-9, 218E3
UN comm adopts resolutn 3-9, 219F1
UN comm chrgs cited 3-11, 207A2
Amnesty Intl rpts 1500 missing 3-16, 493A2
Forgn natns force quick debt repaymt 5-3, 449D1
US rights stand scored 6-1, 439D1
Hunger strikers protest disappearances 6-14—6-27, 493F1
Montes exchngd for E Ger prisoners 6-18; arrests rptdly continue 6-19, 476E1
US blocks 2 loans 6-28, 493A1
US aid rejected 6-28, 512G2
US lauds electn plan 7-11, reaffirms rights concern 8-1, 635F2
US aides visit, conditns rptd improved 8-8—8-12; 8 dissidents detained 8-11, 635B2
DINA blocks disappearnc probes 8-11, 635E2
DINA abolished, Natl Intell Cntr created 8-12, 635D1
Spain Soclst ldr visits, sees rights improvemt, Carter role 8-28—8-31, 743C2
Soclst Intl asks econ sanctns 8-31, 743B2
Disappearance probes rptd dropped 9-5, 743B1
Amnesty Intl lists lawmakers held 9-5, 753B2
Pinochet visit protested in US 9-6—9-7, 678B1
Pinochet rptdly OKs UN panel visit 9-7, 743B1
EEC to close Santiago office 9-7, 743B2
State of siege continues 9-11, 742C3
Pinochet: US attitude 'improving' 9-11, 743A1
Some pol repressn ease rptd 9-15—9-16, 743E1
Repressn rptd down; prisoner trials, DINA probe rptd 11-11, 983G1-C2
Vicariate house raided 11-16, 983D2
47 seized at protest rally 11-17, 983D2
3 rights activists expelled, enter US 11-23, reject govt return bid 11-28, 983E2
Amnesty Intl lists jailed medical workers 11-28, 956G2
UN rights comm rpt scored 12-2; Assemb res vs Chile 12-16, 983D1

1978

Foreign Relations (misc.)—*See also 'Human Rights', 'Letelier Murder Probe' and 'Monetary Trade, Aid & Investment' and 'UN' below*

Bolivia breaks ties 3-17, cites sea outlet impasse 3-19, 216A1
Nicaragua anti-govt protest barred 9-5, 796B1
Bolivia sea outlet impasse spurs Cabt shuffle 11-1, 11-6, 868E3

Government & Politics—*See also other appropriate subheads in this section*

Plebiscite scored by Frei 1-2; protests, arrests rptd 1-2—1-3, 16D3
Plebiscite opponents ignored by press 1-2—1-3, 17A1
Plebiscite backs Pinochet 1-4, junta dissent cited 1-5, Pinochet interview 1-8, 16F2, D3 ★
Poll on govt, Pinochet support 3-4—3-6, 209F3
State of siege lifted; emergency stays in effect 3-9, 209E3
Ex-DINA chief quits army, govt 3-21, 209G2
Leigh scores Pinochet, asks civiln rule 3-26; Pinochet plays down rift 3-29, 267A2
Night curfew lifted 3-31, 267E1
New const ordrd 4-5, 267D1
Cabt quits 4-12; reshuffled, civln majority cited 4-12, 4-21, 350E3
New const draft detailed 4-13, 351E1-A2
Pinochet: mil govt not 'transitory' 6-17, 478B3
Leigh offers dem rule plan 7-18, Pinochet backers score 7-20, 7-21; AF support rptd 7-25, 572G2
Christian Dems called 'No 1 enemy' 7-21, 572C3
Leigh dismissed from junta, AF post; Matthei replaces 7-24, 572D2, E3
AF gens replaced 7-25, Leigh drops appeal 7-26; Pinochet rptd in total control 7-29, 591E1-C2
'Protected democracy' const drafted 7-29, 591B2
Cabt shuffled 12-26, 1014D1

Human Rights (including political prisoner and refugee issues)

Plebiscite on UN rpt, 'intl aggressn' 1-4; Pinochet on UN probes 1-4, 1-5; US scores vote 1-5, 16G2, A3, 17E1, A2
ICJ: rights abuse continues on reduced scale 1-4, 17C2
12 Christian Dems seized 1-13, banished 1-14; ct ruling rptd 1-31, 210B1
UN comm cites contd abuses, asks fund for victims 3-6, 210D1
State of siege lifted, emergency still in effect 3-9, 209G3
Amnesty chrgs MDs with torture 3-11, 180C3
Lazo prison term commuted to exile 3-27, flies to France 4-1, 267F1
Castillo return allowed 4-4, 267F1
Amnesty for pol prisoners set, numbers disputed 4-5, 267A1
Repressn rptd eased, US probe linked 4-8, 267A2
US bank loans rptd undercutting rights policy 4-11, US rep scores 4-12, 312F1
Cabt reshuffled, intl image linked 4-14; Pinochet denies US role 4-21, 351B1
AF ex-officers exiled, depart for UK, Belgium 4-15, 287F2
Amnesty decreed 4-19; 69 pardoned, reactn 4-20—4-29, 351B2, G2
Mil rift rptd, Pinochet denies 4-21; Brady named liaison 4-28, 351C1
Church launches rights yr 4-25, 351B3
100s seized in May Day rallies, 5-1, jail abuses rptd 5-15, 351C3
Leighton, 102 exiles to return 5-13, 452B3
Hunger strikers ask data on missing 5-22—6-9; govt agrees 6-7, protesters arrested 6-8, 452C2
US labor ldrs visit, say repressn continues 5-23, 452C3
UN comm sets relief fund 6-2, 452D3 ★
UN comm probe OKd by govt 6-9, 452A2
OAS rpt chrgs abuse 6-21; Jamaica, US score govt 6-23, 489G2, E3, G3
US recalls amb, plans rights review 6-23, 495G3
Govt statemt on missing unchngd 6-23; church issues plea for info 7-15, 572G3
US comm chrgs abuse 6-24, 490C1
OAS asks eased repressn 7-1, 505B2
UN panel probe opens 7-12, 572F3; ends 7-27, 591C2
Leigh offers dem rule plan 7-18, Pinochet backers score 7-20, 7-21; Leigh dismissed 7-24, 572D2
Gen scores govt on dissent, Leigh dismissal 8-24; Leigh agrees 8-31, 796C1
Women protesters detained 8-30, 796B1
Law students demonstrate 9-5, 796A1
40 seized, 8 missing in Sept 9-22, 796A1
Church asks data on missing 10-12, 795F3
IAPA urges press freedom 10-13, 829D1, A2
Trade boycott set by forgn unions 11-24; Pinochet, US reactn 12-6—12-15, 1014E1
Corpses found in lime kiln 12-6, 12-12, '74 shooting recalled 12-18; US offcls ask intl probe 12-8, 1013F3-1014D1

Letelier Murder Probe (& developments)

US seeks 2 in Letelier, Moffitt deaths probe 2-21, Cuba exiles implicated 2-22; Chile claims no record of suspects 2-24, 146G1, E2

1979

Foreign Relations (misc.)—*See also 'Human Rights', 'Letelier' and 'Monetary' below*

Argentina release of prisoners asked 1-5, 51E3
Newsman disappears in Argentina 40C3; freed 1-11, 117C1
Colombia rebels rptdly planned amb kidnap 1-7, 115E1
Peru executes spy, expels Chile amb; land dispute cited 1-20, 51F3
Grenada coup ldr vs ties 3-13, 190D3
Europn Migratn Comm rpts refugee relocatns 5-7, 369G2
Nicaragua expels radicals 8-16, 636C2
UN membership listed 695F2
Bolivia demands access to Pacific 10-22, 824F1

Government & Politics—*See also other appropriate subheads in this section*

Pinochet state-of-the-natn address 9-11, 685B2

Human Rights

Freedom House lists as not free 13A1
Castro: US caused Chile repressn deaths 1-1, 20B1
US rights rpt omits 2-10, 107A2
'76 Corvalan-Bukovsky swap cited 4-27, 317C1
Pol prisoner relocatn rptd 5-7, 369G2
8 police held in '74 lime kiln murders 7-5, 523B1
PEN Club condemns 7-21, 554B1
Pol refugees occupy Swedish consulate in Rio, protest Argentina repressn 8-6; UN responds 8-8, 627D1, F1
Pinochet bars civil rule 9-11, 685B2
Mass grave discovered at Yumbel 10-4, 789B1
OAS scores abuses 10-30, 824F2

Letelier Case

US judge gets 2d death threat 1-3, 6B3
Contreras, aide get temp hosp leave 1-6, 1-11, 19B3
US submits more data vs Contreras, 2 aides 1-8, 19C3

1980

Foreign Relations (misc.)—*See also 'Human Rights', 'Monetary' below*

UK to restore relatns 1-16, 57G1
Olympic boycott OK rptd 2-2, 85C1
Argentine A-pact cited 3-18, 229E2
Pinchot cancels 11-day Asian tour 3-22, cuts PI ties 3-24; assassinatn plot alleged 3-25, 230F3-231E1
PI ties restored 4-2, 311D2
Grenada scores Allende overthrow 6-20, 498F2
Peru vows border dispute setlmt 7-28, 580B1
Israel Emb shift rptd 8-26, 643E2

Government & Politics—*See also other appropriate subheads in this section*

Forgn min dismissed 3-25, Rojas named 3-28, 255G3
Draft const submitted to junta 7-11, 563B1
Army officer assassinated, Allende's nephew blamed 7-15, 563A1
Security chief removed 7-24, 603E2
Pinochet sets draft const vote 8-8; rally held, Frei denounces plebiscite 8-27; other oppositn surfaces 9-2, 669B2
Internal security shakeup, dir quits 8-11, 618D3
Draft const approved by voters, Pinochet retains power; Christian Dems denounce plebiscite 9-11, 706B2

Human Rights

Freedom House lists as partly free 87D3
US issues rights rpt 2-5, 87A3
French CP cites Pinochet 2-20, 1493
UK natl detained 7-16—7-18, torture chrgs disputed 7-29, 8-6, 749E1
Student's death spurs rightist death squad chrgs 8-2, 603F2
Cardinal rpts death threats, students score terrorism 8-4, 603D3
Internal security shakeup, dir quits 8-11; 20 subordinates arrested for right-wing terror 8-12, 618A3
Pinochet oppositn surfaces, mil rule scored 8-27, 9-2, 669B2
Amnesty Intl issues rpt, protests abuses 9-8, 749C1
OAS cites poor record 11-27, 913D3
Amnesty Intl scores 12-10, 978A3

Letelier Case

Contreras linked to tax scandal 8-4, 603B3
US ct overturns convictn of 3 Cubans, new trial ordrd for 2 9-15, 703C3
US ct awards Letelier, Moffitt kin 11-5, 869F3

1976

CR '75 asylum to 2 cited 47F2
UN refugees start hunger strike 1-13, 47G2
Emb refugees to get safe-conducts 1-25, 1-28, 100A1
Exiles chrg Colombia harassmt 1-28, 2-1, 118A3
Pascal, Beausire in CR; Chile asks extraditn 2-2, 99G3
Gutierrez exiled 2-21, vows return 2-22, 288B3
Refugees leave Venez, Hungary embs 3-6, 2-4, 2-16, 288D3
Argentina seizes 35 4-3; rejects return 4-9, 264B2
CR denies Pascal extraditn 4-9, 288C3
Amnesty Intl chrgs terrorism 5-24, 399D2 ★
23 kidnaped in Argentina 6-11, freed 6-12, 495G3
Protests staged in Argentina 7-6—7-18; Canada, 4 W Eur natns OK visas 7-19, 571E2
12 in Argentina flee to Canada 7-15, 571G2
Flores exiled to US 8-5, 711F2
Venez emb rptdly harbors MIR, Red Sept members 8-27, 9-8, 711D1
Letelier citizenship revoked 9-10, 710C3
Letelier killed in US; DINA accused, US probe asked 9-21—9-23, 710C2
13 pol prisoners exiled 11-17—12-11, 963D1

U.S. Relations—*See also 'Copper Issues' and 'Human Rights' above*
US oppositn to Pinochet rptd 1-10, 47F1
'70 CIA media manipulatn rptd 1-16, 92B3
Russell ct scores '73 US coup aid 1-17, 61C2
US sens CIA contacts rptd 1-23, 1-26, 93G1, D2
'75 deportatn of nuns cited 1-23, 100C2
US aid rptdly continues 1-26, 99B2
US Sen bars arms aid authorizatn 2-18, 151F3
CR students score Kissinger re coup role 2-23, 178F1
Cocaine flow to US cut 3-1, 288F3-289A1
House vetoes arms sales ban 3-3, 181D2
Nixon testimony on Allende 3-11, 183G2
World Bank loan protested 3-19, 3-23; McNamara defends 4-12, 310E2
US Cong com OKs cash arms sales 3-31, 310A2
Zalaquett exile scored 4-19, 310D2
US Sen com cites US projcts 4-26, 304D2
Simon visits 5-7—5-8; for contd econ aid 5-16, 464D3
Gen Tire payoffs chrgd 5-10, 360B1-B2; ITT rpts '70 payoffs 5-12, 361E1
Drug dealer arrested in US 5-27, pleads guilty 11-5, 971A3

1977

Monetary, Trade & Aid Issues (including all foreign economic developments)
Drops Andean investmt, tariff rules dropped 1-3, 18G1
Israel arms sales rptd 1-8, 28D3
US, UK arms embargo cited 1-10, 2C3
'75-76 trade, paymts data; table 3-11, 189B1, A2 ★, B2
New forgn investmt law set 3-18, 448G3
'76 forgn credits total rptd 3-18, 449E1
Anaconda settles OPIC claim 3-31, 449F1
'66-75 arms transfers table 4-8, 415A2
Import taxes reduced 5-1, 448G2
Debt-svc paymts triple 5-3, 449D1
US blocks 2 loans 6-28, 493A1
US aid rejected 6-28, 512G2
More debt paymts planned 9-11, 742E3
Cheap copper exports, US woes linked 10-31, 859B1
Copper cutback barred 12-7, 975A1
Frei at Brandt intl dvpt comm mtg 12-9—12-11, 998A1
Exxon copper mine buy rptd 12-28, 1019B1

Obituaries
Allende, Beatriz 10-12, 871G3

Payments Issues
Exxon admits paymts 10-25, 818A2

U.S. Relations—*See also 'Human Rights', 'Monetary, Trade & Aid' and 'Payments Issues' above*
CIA, US cos '64 actn vs Allende chrgd 1-9, 1-11, 18B2
US sentncs drug dealer 1-21, 103B1

1978

Letelier probe pressed, suspects identified 3-2—3-9; Pinochet backs probe 3-6, panel visits US 3-9—3-10, 188F2-189B1
Letelier probe witness rptd dead 3-8, 189B1
Pinochet lifts state of siege 3-9, 209G3
US identifies murder suspects 3-20, 209B3
Ex-DINA chief quits army, govt 3-21, 209A3
Chile investigator quits 3-21, 209D3
Chile OKs questioning of murder suspects, disputes false identities 3-23, 266C3
Townley takes 5th in testimony, Fernandez rptd cleared 4-1, 266B3
Pinochet vows cooperatn 4-5; Townley denies murder, scores US 4-6, 266F3
Townley deported to US 4-8, arraigned 4-10, 266F2
US probe, rights moves linked 4-8, 267A2
Townley's wife chrgs junta betrayal 4-10, 266G3
2 Cuban exiles arrested in US 4-14; 3d rptd questnd 4-17, 287C2; jailed in NY 4-28, 370F3
Amnesty decree excludes 4-19, 351C2
US phone records link Townley, Cuban exiles 4-19, 370B3
Murder evidence rptdly removed by Contreras 4-20; magazine scores govt silence 8-10, 648A1
Townley friends say extraditn illegal 4-21, 371C1
Mrs Townley rptdly DINA agent 4-21, 371D1
Osorio autopsy details leaked by US 4-21, 371F1
US chrgs Townley 4-26; probe cooperatn, plea bargaining rptd 4-27, 370G2, 371A1
Townley implicated in Latin bombings 4-26, 371B1
Mrs Townley: DINA chose husband for Letelier murder, Pinochet urged probe cooperatn 5-2; US sources confirm 5-5, 370F3-371A1
Govt denies Townley DINA agent, wife cites paychecks 5-3, 371E1
US issues warrants for 3 more Cuban exiles 5-4; Novo arrested 5-4, bail set 5-8, 370G2, D3
US probe dir visits 5-22—5-25; interior min scores, Pinochet embarrassmt noted 5-26, 452D1
Indictmt of high offcls seen 5-23, 452D1
Pinochet 'disloyalty' seen by ex-DINA men 5-23, 452G1
US reveals death details, Cuban exiles role; Ross moved to DC 6-2, 451E3
Ex-DINA chief rptdly barred murder rap 6-5, 452F1
Washn Post asks Pinochet resign 6-10, 452A2
US recalls amb, chrgs probe noncooperatn; govt denies, scores US 6-23, 495D3
US indicts 3 Chileans, 4 Cuban exiles; Contreras, DINA aides seized 8-1; Pinochet asks 'proof' for extraditn, denies govt imperiled 8-2, 613E3-614G1
Townley plea-bargain pact to be studied 8-3, 614C1
Mrs Letelier sues Chile govt 8-8, 647G3
Townley admits placing bomb, judge OKs plea-bargain pact 8-11, 647A3
Cuba exiles plead not guilty 8-11, 647F3
US asks 3 extradited 9-20; judge sets secret hearings 9-22, US protests 9-28, 755F2
Pinochet rptdly denies Contreras tie 9-21, 755E3
US evidence rptdly seen by Contreras 10-13, 795F2-A3
3 Chilean suspects queried 10-17—10-24, Contreras claims innocence 10-24; US judge, prosecutor rptd threatnd 12-14, 1014C3
Townley, other witnesses rptd under US protectn 10-18, 795B3
US probe clears CIA 10-18, 795C3

Monetary, Trade, Aid & Investment
Exxon buys copper mine 1-24, 312C2
'77 trade deficit $120 mln, non-traditnl exports up 2-3, 312G2
Goodyear buys tire co 2-9, sets job cuts 3-29, 312C2
Peso to devalue 21.4% in '78 2-17, 312F2
US, other forgn banks OK $210 mln loan 4-7, 312E1
US bank loans rptd undercutting rights policy 4-11, US rep scores 4-12, 312F1
Food imports rptd up 9-15, 795D1
Ford to regain facilities 10-5, 796D1
Copper indus troubles cited 10-20, 805C1
Beagle Channel dispute halts Argentina trade 11-2, 860A3
Trade boycott set by forgn unions 11-24; Pinochet, US reactn 12-6—12-15, 1014E1

UN Policy & Developments—*See also 'Human Rights' above*
Decolonization com abstentn on PR colony status 9-13, 979E3
UN Assemb member 713D3

U.S. Relations—*See also 'Human Rights', 'Letelier Murder Probe' and 'Monetary, Trade, Aid & Investment' above*
CIA anti-Allende press briefing detailed 1-4, 14B3
Plebiscite scored 1-5, 17A2
Christian Dems banishmt scored 1-17, 210B1

1979

US trial opens 1-9, jury chosen 1-12, 19C2-A3
CIA '71, '73 'interest' in Townley svcs rptd 1-11, 19D3
US trial testimony begins 1-15; Townley cites Cuban exile tie, discounts Ross role 1-18–1-24, 57D3-58A3
Info curbed by '78 US-Chile pact 1-23, 74G3
Ross murder boast cited by FBI informer 1-30, 75D1
Extraditns seen unlikely 2-7, 114A3
Townley called CIA agent by Chile press 2-7, 114D3
Pinochet linked to assassins 2-9, 114E3-115B1
Townley credibility debated 2-12–2-13, 114F2
3 Cubans convicted; Silbert, Mrs Letelier laud verdict 2-14, 114B2-A3
3 Cubans sentenced 3-23, 234D2
Townley sentncd 5-11, 369E2
US extraditn request for Contreras, 2 aides rejctd 5-14, amb recalled 5-15, 369C2
US amb returns 6-7, Chile recalls amb 6-21, 506G2
US extraditn request rejctd, 3 army officers freed 10-1; US recalls amb 10-22, 750F1
US probes Contreras funds transfer, link to convicted Cubans alleged 10-9, 772A2
US cuts back ties 11-30, 927E2

Monetary, Trade, Aid & Investment
Union ldrs-labor min mtg averts trade boycott 1-3, 6F2
Trade boycott dropped by ORIT 1-15–1-16, 28D3
Anaconda sets copper exploratn 5-10, 369B3
'78 forgn debt rptd 5-21, 369F3
US trade boycott studied 10-1, 750D2
US reduces aid 11-30, 927E2

U.S. Relations—*See also 'Human Rights', 'Letelier' and 'Monetary' above*
US drops case vs ITT execs 2-8, 88C1; 3-7, 188G1
Refugee relocatn rptd 5-7, 369A3
Pinochet recalls amb to US 6-21, 506F2
ISC paymts alleged 7-9, 541F3
US denies spy aid 8-9, 664D2
Pinochet scores US ldrship 9-11, 685D2

1980

Monetary, Trade, Aid & Investment
US, forgn investmt rptd 1-14, 19C2
Oil import costs rptd 1-14, 19G2
UK lifts arms embargo 7-22, Amnesty Intl protests 9-8, 749E1
US export fraud indictmt rptd 8-4, 603B3
Soviet debt rescheduled 11-26, 965G1

Sports
Olympic boycott OK rptd 2-2, 85C1

U.S. Relations—*See also 'Human Rights', 'Monetary' above*
US amb to Bolivia in Santiago 7-20, 546D3
Tax fraud scandal rptd 8-4, 603C3
US 'regrets' const plebiscite 9-11, Pinochet rues interventn 9-12, 706A3
Letelier murder convictns overturned, new trial ordrd 9-15, 703C3

1976

US rep indicted 6-2, 414C3
US Dem platform text cites 6-15, 478F2
US bars arms aid, sales 6-30, 533C1
Ship in US Bicentennial event 7-4, 488A3
Flores exiled to US 8-5, 711F2
Exiles hold US rally; Letelier scores 'fascists' 9-10, 710G3
Letelier killed in US 9-21; DINA accused, US reps ask probe 9-21—9-23, 710C2
Letelier mass in DC 9-26, 781G3
Ford, Carter debate 10-6, 741D1, E2, F2
US widens Letelier probe 10-9; links Cuba exiles, doubts DINA role 10-12, 780C3-F3
Rpt FBI to probe Letelier case in Venez; exile-DINA link chrgd 10-18, 844F2
US aid rejected 10-19, 10-20, 870G3 ★
Hendrix chrgd re ITT probe 11-5, 869F2
US arms imports cited 12-7, 975E2
US OKs World Bank loan 12-21, 999G1

CHILE Human Rights Committee
Holds NY rally vs mil junta 9-10, 710G3

CHILES, Sen. Lawton (D, Fla.)
On mil meat-purchase fraud 5-8, 395E2
Unopposed in primary 9-7, 687C3
Reelected 11-2, 820C1, 822B1, 828D1

1977

Lavin asked to end US visit 1-28, 219D2
CIA paymts to Frei rptd 2-19, 124F1
Frei denies paymts 2-21, rpts Carter apology 3-4, 219A2
US aide regrets '73 coup role 3-8; US disavows apology, Carter stance contradictns noted 3-8, 3-9, 218E3
Nixon-Frost interview 5-25, 419D3
Frei sees Mondale 5-25, Almeyda sees Christopher 5-27; US denies backing oppositn 5-30, 493D1
US lauds '85 electns plan 7-11, 635F2
Pinochet sees Carter 9-6, at Panama Canal pact signing 9-7, 678A1
Letelier murder probe implicates DINA, Cuban exiles 9-7—9-10, 743D2
Alliance for Progress scored 9-11, 742F3
Ex-CIA head Helms pleads no contest on '73 testimony chrgs 10-31, 838B3
Helms sentncd 11-4, 861F1; Carter comments 11-10, 877G1
New US amb sees forgn min 11-17, 983E2

CHILES, Sen. Lawton (D, Fla.)
Scores SBA minority aid progrm 7-6—7-8, 577G2

CHIMPANZEES
Heart implant fails 10-17, 847C3

1978

UN rpt on rights abuse backed, abstains on fund for victims 3-6, 210F1, G1
2 ITT execs sued, 3-20; ex-amb, OPIC chrgs re CIA rptd 3-21, 206C3
Pinochet denies rights pressure 4-21, 351B1
Citibank branch bombed 5-1, 351E3
US recalls amb, plot vs Pinochet chrgd 6-23, 465D3, 496A1
US drops 3 chrgs vs ITT exec 8-18, 643C3
Book links CIA, Amer's death 9-12, 795D3
UN PR colony status vote abstentn 9-13, 979E3
ITT paymts chrgd 11-2, 876C1, E2
US asks more Beagle Channel talks 12-12, cites peace role 12-15, 979B3

CHILES, Sen. Lawton (D, Fla.)
Votes for Panama Canal neutrality pact 3-16, 177D2
Votes for 2d Canal pact 4-18, 273B1
Scores GSA probe bickering 9-8, 715C1

CHIMPANZEES
Goodall rpts violent behavior 4-19, 335A1

1979

CHILES, Sen. Lawton (D, Fla.)
Aging Com chrmn 1-23, 71C2

CHILES, Lois
Moonraker released 6-29, 820B2

CHILLECOTHE, O.—*See OHIO*

CHILLY Scenes Of Winter (book)
Head Over Heels released 10-19, 1007D3

1980

CHINA, PEOPLE'S REPUBLIC OF

1976

CHINA, People's Republic of
Rpt Chin Dynasty laws found 3-28, 265F3
Meteorite shower rptd 4-21, 443D3
Romanized script introduced 8-1, 588B2
Crimes, unrest rptd in Hunan, Shensi, other provinces 8-15—9-2, 673C3
Birth rate drop rptd 10-28, 863G1

Defense & Armed Forces
Manned space program gains rptd 1-7, 1-8, 78E1
18th A-test conducted 1-23, 83D3
Teng army policy attacked 2-16, 189E1
ICBM projct rptd dropped 2-24, 190C1
Inner Mongolia defns tunnels rptd 3-2, 190E1
Teng ousted 4-7, 243D3
US arms control rpt cites 7-29, 739E2
6th satellite launched 8-30, 674D1
19th, 20th A-tests 9-26, 10-17; US rpts fallout 10-5, 790E3
Equipmt modernizatn rptd 10-5, 961E1
Army backs Hua 10-17, 10-19, 790D3
A-test 11-17; called success 11-18, 871F3
Satellite launch rptd 12-18, 961C2

Earthquakes—*See also 'Economy' below*
2 major earthquakes hit Tangshan area 7-28; rescue efforts rptd, 100,000 feared dead 7-29—7-31, 545A1
Massive relief effort rptd, forgners leave; more quakes feared 7-30—8-3, 561D2
Quake disease preventn rptd 8-7, other effects rptd 8-8, 8-11; new tremors 8-8, 8-9, Peking warned 8-10, 588C1
Peking bldgs repaired 8-13, alert lifted 8-15, 619E2
Szechuan hit 8-16, 619C2
Szechuan hit by 2d quake 8-21, 674F1
Tangshan death toll rptd 100,000 8-23, 674G1
Peking rally honors relief workers, Hua scores looting 9-1, 673G2
US confrms computer sale 10-28, 832F2-B3

Economy & Labor (domestic)
Mao: 4th 5-yr plan met 1-1, 9E3
Youth movt to rural areas rtpd 1-6, 48G1
2 NE oil pipelines rptd 1-8, 78A1
'75 grain purchase goals exceeded 1-22, 100B3
1 mln rptd in Tachai movt 2-6, 117D3
Teng policies attacked 2-10, 2-17, 188E3, 189G1
'75 Tibetan wheat record rptd 2-14, 190G1
Oil need rise, Taching losses cited 4-6, 265E3
New oil terminal opened 6-9, 521B1
1st ½ oil growth rate slows 7-13, 521C1
1st ½ industrial output, other data rptd 8-30, 674A1
Tangshan indl area quake damage rptd, Tientsin port closed 8-30, 674C1
Record harvest rptd 9-1, 809A3
Tangshan coal mines resume operatn 9-28, 809C3
'75 indl, grain output rptd 10-5, 961E1
Agri conf backs mechanizatn 12-10—12-24, 999D3

Foreign Economic Developments
Sri Lanka aid, trade pacts rptd 1-2, 78D1
W Ger chem plant deal rptd 1-6, 78B1
US rpt disputes oil export role 1-8, 10A1
W Ger raises import quotas 1-22, 158C2
Japan to up oil imports 1-22, 208C3
Cambodia air route set 1-23, 100G3
Japan fertilizer deal rptd 1-26, 100F3
EC trade talks rptd set 1-27, 84B3
Rumania trade pact signed 1-29, 117D1, E3
'75 Indonesia oil output rptd 2-11, 144A3
3d ¼ '75 Taiwan trade rptd 2-12, 265G3
Canada wheat deal set 2-27, 190G1
Australia sugar deal rptd 3-1, 190F1
Laos aid pact signed 3-18, 222A2
Ethiopia pact signed 3-22, 311D3
India rpts arms aid to Pak 3-31, 278C3
Feb-Mar oil exports to Japan cut, steel deal canceled 4-5, 265D3
Egypt arms pact signed; USAF comment 4-21, 275E2, B3

1977

CHINA, People's Republic of
'76 Tangshan quake toll rptd 1-5, 120E2
'78 science parley rptd set 9-22, 781D1

Defense & Armed Forces
Defense mtgs held 2-6, 134E1
Army urged to stress skills 2-26, 180A1
Sinkiang gets new army chief 8-3, 616E3
Sub force ranked 3d 8-25, 686F2
A-tipped missile tested 9-12, 706B2
USSR backs A-test ban 11-2, 997B1

Economy & Labor (domestic)
'76 oil, gas output hike, new oilfield rptd 1-6, 1F2
Poster scores shortcomings 2-1, 98E1
Private productn urged 2-24, 200C3
Energy, food, indl shortages rptd 3-11, 200G2-C3
Drought spreads 3-18—3-24; food supply threat rptd 3-25, 238A1
Hua plan outlined, recovery seen 4-11, 282E1
Conf asks indl goals 4-20—5-13, new leap forward set 5-4, 449B2
Prolonged drought rptd 7-6, 578F2
Jan-June output up 7-15, 562D1
CIA rpts mixed econ outlook 8-15, 635B3
OECD rpts econ growth 8-16, 635G2
Tighter controls urged 9-12, 705E3
Pay hikes rptd; indl, agri forecast 10-23, 823A2
Poor grain harvest cited 11-15, 916F2
'77 indl, oil output up 12-26, 1010C3

1978

CHINA, People's Republic of
Sci conf held, drive launched 3-18—3-31; plan outlined 5-28, 436C1
1st cigaret warning issued, cancer deaths noted 8-28, 727F1

Cambodia-Vietnam Dispute—*See CAMBODIA—Vietnam Conflict*

Defense & Armed Forces
'76 arms spending rptd 7-23, 585C2
ICBM deploymt rptd possible 9-1, 676F3
'76 A-test linked to world fallout rise 11-5, 1000G3
A-test at Lop Nor rptd 12-14, radioactive debris breaks up 12-23, 1001A2

Economy & Labor (domestic)
10-yr plan OKd by People's Cong 2-26—3-5, 153C2, 154B1
Oil find rptd in S China Sea 5-6, 436E2
Dvpt plan outlined 5-28, 436F1
Hua urges econ growth, rpts Jan-June productn data 7-7, 532B1
'77 tobacco indus data rptd 8-28, 727C2
Hua on progress 10-1, 773B3
Speedup urged, '78 data rptd 10-3, 773F2
New oil find rptd 10-12, 871A3
CP conf sets '79 goals 12-22, chngs disclosed 12-24, 1015B1
'78 oil output rise rptd 12-26, 1000C3

Foreign Relations (misc.)—*See also 'Monetary, Trade, Aid & Investment' and 'UN' below, also CAMBODIA—Vietnam Conflict*
Forgn trip curbs eased 1-4, 17G2-A3
USSR fears Japan pact 1-9—1-10, 28E3
Cambodia army lauded 1-16, 42C3
French premr visits 1-19—1-24, 71D1
Teng ends Cambodia missn 1-22, 80G1
Teng visits Burma 1-26—1-31, Nepal 2-3—2-5, 111F2
Geneva conf chrmnshp debated 1-31, 61C3
Canada forgn min visits 2-1, 80G1
Japan vs Sovt protest on proposed treaty 121G3

1979

CHINA, People's Republic of—*See also DISARMAMENT—Geneva Committee*
Population estimate revisn rptd 12E3
Pinyin transliteratn system set 1-1, 75D2
Peking jet crash kills 44 3-14, 240G2
Birth control steps rptd 4-24, 5-1, '77 populatn data 5-14, 370D2
Teeth rptd replanted 5-1, 355B1
MDs build hand 5-2, 355A1
Quake kills 11 7-9, 619G3
Peking bishop elected 7-25, 639E2
Population limit planned 8-13, 652C1
Populatn control efforts rptd 10-10, 789G3

Atomic Energy & Safeguards
Nuclear 'doomsday clock' unchngd 1-1, 13F1
'78 underground tests rptd 3-6, 625D3
A-test fallout contaminatn in US cited 4-3, 245G3
Libyan '71 A-bomb bid rptd 4-14, 299C3
Mystery A-test ruled out 10-26, 824D3

Cambodia-Vietnam Conflict—*See CAMBODIA—Vietnam Conflict*

Defense & Armed Forces—*See also 'Atomic' above*
Viet invasn cmdrs identified 2-21, 122D1
'79 mil budget up 6-29, 502C3
'77 mil spending total rptd 10-13, 804F1

Economy & Labor
Business class rehabilitated 1-25, 75G1-C2
Shanghai econ protests 2-10, govt warns 2-12, 134D2
Birth control steps linked 4-24, 5-1, 370E2
Heavy industry cut back 5-2, 5-6, 352E3-353C1
Li speech details problems 6-14, 444C3
Hua admits econ errors, rpts '78 data 6-18, 484E2
'79 budget, econ plan rptd 6-21, 484A3
Poor stage Peking protests 8-8, 651F2-A3; 9-6, 985G2
Populatn limit planned 8-13, 652D1
Offshore oil find rptd 8-24, 664E3
Geology min created 9-13, 729B2
Oil reserve estimate raised 9-18, 2d offshore find rptd 10-10, 790D1
RR workers protest 9-20, 751C1
Farm dvpt plan OKd 9-28, 750E3
Food prices hiked, city workers given subsidies 11-1, 854D3
More oil finds rptd 11-26, 918F1

Foreign Relations (misc.)—*See also 'Atomic' above, 'Monetary' and 'UN' below*
Rhodesian dispute role cited 170D2
Cuba pres scores, rep quits rite 1-1, 20A1

1980

CHINA, People's Republic of—*See also GENEVA Committee*
Panda finding mission begins 5-12, 389E1
Peking blast kills 9 10-29, bomber rptd killed 11-3, 858E3
Peking bomb incident detailed 11-10, 878A1
Illiteracy study rptd 12-4, 953A3

Atomic Energy & Safeguards
'70-79 A-tests rptd 1-17, 31F3
A-test conducted 10-16, fallout hits US 10-20, 828A3
France A-reactor deal set 10-17, 829A3

Cambodia-Vietnam Conflict—*See CAMBODIA (Democratic Kampuchea)—Vietnam Conflict*

Defense & Armed Forces—*See also 'Atomic Energy' above, 'Foreign' below*
Mil ldrshp shuffle rptd 2-14, 2-19, 132C2
ICBM test rptd successful 5-18, 389A1

Economy & Labor
Sichuan decentralizatn experimt rptd 1-17, 132A3
Forgn currency black mkt rptd, coupon use set 3-1, 132E2
'79 econ rpt issued 5-1, 521C1
'79 oil rig collapse rptd 7-6, 621E3
Oil min scored re '79 accident 8-24; fired, vice premr censured 8-25, 651B3
Profits, local control stressed in new financial plan 8-30, 678C1
'79, '80 spending, farm productn rptd 9-1, 678G1
Hua announces new 5-yr plan 9-7, 677F2

1976

Albania metal combine opens 4-30, 331E3
Australia sugar pact confrmd 6-2, 415A2
Yields Tanzam RR control 7-14, 560A1
Japan shipping talks canceled 7-16, 555E2
IMF takes no actn on Taiwan ouster 10-8, 778D2
Hua at '74 Tibet agri conf cited 758B1
US-built fertilizer plants open 10-25, 832D3
US confrms computer sale 10-28, 832F2-B3
NATO sales scored 11-4, 880B1
'76 US loan default cited 11-11, 915G2
Canada wheat sale rptd 12-8, 946B1
Forgn paymts rptd unknown 12-20, 985A3

Foreign Relations (misc.)—*See also 'UN Policy' below*

Chou rites closed to foreigners 1-9, 48B1
UK Tory ldr attack on Sovt detente backed 1-24, 101A2
Morocco summons amb re Sahara 1-28, 58B2
Angola MPLA scores 2-2, 82F2
Hua sees Venez envoy 2-7, 117D1
Leftists meet W Ger, Australia CP delegatns 2-14, 2-25, 189E1
Guyana mil presence denied 2-23—3-10, 253B1
Forgn aides visit bombed Cambodia town 3-2—3-4, 238B2
Australia tennis team to visit 4-6, 249G3
India reports amb exchng 4-15, 278D3
Egypt vp visits, arms pact signed 4-18—4-21; Sovt bloc shuns fete 4-19, 275E2
Cape Verde ties set 4-25, 404D1
Albania reveals plot 4-30, 331C3
Mao sees NZ, Singapore, Pak ldrs 4-30—5-27; ends state visit role 6-15, 439D2
Australia lauds ties 6-1, 438G2
Fraser visits 6-20—6-23, 481A1
India amb takes post 7-7, 538C2
Portugal to seek full ties 7-19, 558E1
US asks 4-power conf on Korea 7-22, 557C2
Ex-Australia prime min in Tientsin 7-28—7-29, 545C2
Foreigners quit quake area 8-1, 561E2
Cambodia forgn min visits 8-7, 588D2
US again urges 4-power conf on Korea 8-19, 619A1
CAE restores ties 8-20, 949A2
Rhodesia ANC factn aid rptd 8-23, 661G3
Polish ouster of newsman regretted 8-24, 674E1
Thai rebel aid rptd 9-3, 677D3
Korea DMZ partitn OKd 9-6, 660G1
Intl reactn to Mao death 9-9—9-10, 657C2
Foreigners view Mao body 9-13, 711E3
Malta ties cited 9-20, 713F1
US asks 'phased' Korea talks 9-30, 719E2
Mao widow, others scored re ties 10-24, 809B2
Albania leftist support seen 11-1, 849F3
French journalists visit 11-2, 871D3
Bokassa feted 11-15, 871C3
Taiwan ldr vows mainland recovery 11-16, 890D3
Rumania defns min in Peking 11-22, 907C2

Government & Politics—*See also other appropriate subheads in this section*

Facts on Chou En-lai 9C1
'65 Mao poems, editorial publshd 1-1, 9D2
Mao backs Chiang Ching arts policies 1-1, 9E3
Press accuses 'Revisionists' 1-1, 2-6, 188E3
Chou En-lai dies 1-8, 8G2
Final Chou rites 1-15, 48B1
Listed as 'not free' nation 1-19, 10D3
New edition of Mao poems publshd 1-19, 100E3
Mao's educatn policies backed 1-21—1-27, 100G2
Coll grads rptd 'outstanding' 1-22, 100A3
Educ debate rptd under party control 1-23, 1-26, 100E2
'Deviationists' scored 2-6, moderate-radical rift rptd 2-8, 117G1
Chou 'pol will' disavowed 2-6, 118A1
Hua Kuo-feng named 'acting' premr 2-7, 117C1
Anti-Teng drive launched 2-10, Central com rptd split 2-17, Chiang Ching role rptd 2-26, 3-4, 188C3-189G2
Radical violence threatened 3-9, 244D1
Radical-moderate compromise urged 3-10—3-28, 243F3
Educators rptly repent 3-25, 266A1
5 banned journals to be reissued 3-25, 266B1
Pro-Chou rallies 4-1—4-4, riot 4-5, 243C3, 244A1
Teng ousted, Hua named premr 4-7, 243B3
Teng purge, Hua elevatn backed 4-8—4-28, 332F3 ★
Posters demand Teng's death 4-9, 332G3
2 die in prov unrest 4-10, 4-22, 333C1
Radical strength rptd 4-27, 333D1
May Day radical-moderate unity rptd 5-2, 332C3
Li Ta-chang dies 5-3, 368G2
Anti-rightist drive pressed 5-7, 5-16, 5-18, 439B1
Mao ends greeting forgn ldrs 6-15, 439B2
Chu Teh dies 7-6, buried 7-11, 520E3
Posters attack prov ldrs 7-19, 555C2

1977

Foreign Relations (misc.)—*See also 'Monetary Trade & Aid' and 'UN Policy' below*

Czech dissidents backed 1-26, 82A3
Greater Japan output noted 2-1, 98G1
Concorde purchases cited 2-1, 99E1
Ethiopia ldr receives amb 2-11, 238A3
Liberia ties set 2-22, 243D3
Zaire invasn chrg rpt 3-23, 261E1
Pak tribesmen hold workers hostage, seek interventn 4-28—5-4, 349C1
Albania scores, rift seen 7-8, 540D3
Albania air link cited 595F1
Thais protest Cambodia raid 7-25, 572C1
Albania dispute continues, rift denied 7-26—8-2; 3-worlds theory cited 595C1
Japan, S Korea briefed on Vance missn 8-26, 8-27, 664D2
Tito visits, ideological rift detailed 8-30—9-8; Albania scores Tito 9-2, 710B1, C1
Albania anti-China purge rptd 9-9, 731A1
Panama Canal pacts lauded 9-10, 699B2
Cambodia leader visits 9-28, 741G2
Cambodia premr ends visit, '75 trip disclosed 10-2, 779E3-780A1
Huang in Canada 10-4—10-7, 801D1
Brazil gen scores ties 10-12, 840A1
Malta premr provokes Sovt, E Eur walkout 11-3, 925E2
Canada rptr expelled 11-27, 946B2

Government & Politics—*See also other appropriate subheads in this section*

Troops sent to Honan rail junctn 1-3; provincial unrest rptd quelled 1-4, 1B1
Fukien unrest detailed 1-4, 1F1
Posters urge Teng rehabilitatn 1-6, 1-7, 1G1
Yao anti-Chou act chrgd 1-6, 1D2
Chou anniversary rites 1-8, 1E2
Mayor Wu Teh accused 1-8, 1F2
Posters back Teng 1-9—1-11, 61B2
Wu Teh, Chen Hsi-lien scored 1-9, 61C2
'76 Peking riot toll rptd, Liu Chuan-hsin linked 1-10, 61D2
Teng seen in Cncl post 1-13, 61E2
Chen Mu-hua gets econ post 1-14, 61F2
Teng reinstatemt seen 1-20, 1-23, denied 1-24, 97F3
Paoting unrest crushed 1-28, 98A1
3 apptmts announced 1-29, 98B2
Poster scores soc breakdown, crime 2-1, 98F1
Drive vs gang of 4, greater discipline urged 2-5, 2-7, 98B1
Yunnan CP shift 2-12, 133G3
Tuan named rail chief 2-20, 134D1
3 Chekiang offcls disgraced 3-2, 179C3
Govt foes, others sentncd, executed 3-2, 3-12, 3-17, 238G1
Heilungkiang, Chekiang, Kiangsu name CP chiefs 3-4, 179B3
Kweichow rally hails progress 3-5, 179E3
More Kiangsu apptmts, Kweichow shift 3-6, 179D3
Govt press editors chngd 3-7, 179G3
Radical accused of bugging 3-9, 180E1
2 educators rehabilitated 3-9, 180G1
Liaoning Prov unrest 3-17, 220C1
'76 Peking rioters freed 3-18, 220B1
Beethoven, Shakespeare ban lifted 3-26, 5-25, 449D3
Hanchow unrest detailed 4-11, 282A2
Mao's 5th volume publshd 4-15, 347B1
Chang tied to Shanghai plot 5-17, 449C3
Wang tied to post-Mao violence 6-3, 449G2
Gang of 4 arrests ended Nanchang riots 6-5, 449B3
Kiangsi chief urges purge 6-6, 505C3
Gang of 4 tied to Hupei unrest 6-8, 505E3
Kansu, Anhwei prov chiefs purged 6-22, 6-27, 505G2

1978

Pl Spratly isle takeover opposed 3-11, 290G1
Japan LDP ldrs rptd vs talks 4-7, 278B2
Hong Kong-Canton flights to resume 4-9, 259B3
Boats anchor off Senkakus 4-12; Japan protests 4-14, chrgs denied 4-15; boats rptd out 4-16, 278C1
Somali pres visits, pact signed 4-13—4-18, 353E2
India confrms '65 US A-device loss 4-17, 288D2
UK defns chief visits, remarks on USSR cause uproar 5-1, 329G2
Hua in N Korea; backs Korea merger, vs US mil presence 5-5—5-10; S Korea scores 5-11, 340D2
Ghana '66 emb raid rptd proposed by US CIA 5-8, 368C1
Japan briefed on US visit, renewed peace talks rptd backed 5-23—5-24, 384B3
Yugo dissident compares rights 6-6, 504B3
Huang ends Zaire visit; scores USSR, Cuba role 6-7, 441D2
Japan peace talks to resume 6-14, open 7-21; pact signed 8-12, 637A1
Spain king visits 6-16—6-19, 576A2
Zaire rpts naval advisers 6-18, 478C2
UK cites more China ties as warning to USSR 7-10, 542B3
Role in Cambodia aide visit to Thailand rptd 7-14, 548B3
Fatah chrgs Iraq seizes cargo 7-17, 546E3
Albania letter details split 7-30, 635C1
Libya premr visits 8-4—8-10, ties set 8-9, 691F2
Hua, party ldrs visit Rumania, Yugo, Iran 8-16—9-1, 674G2-675D3
Albania scores Hua trip, chrgs Balkan war plot 9-3, 676B1
Sovt SE Asia role scored 9-6, 696D1
Foreigner contacts ban lifted 9-9, 773D2
Huang visits UK 10-10—10-13, 796G1
Japan Diet OKs pact 10-16, 10-18, 802A1
Teng starts Japan visit 10-22, peace pact implemented 10-23; pact text 801A1-802A1
Mex pres visits, sees Hua 10-24—10-30, 903B3
Teng backs Korean reunificatn 10-25, 802D1
Rhodesia Patriotic Front backing cited 10-25, 906F3
Teng visits Thailand, Malaysia, Singapore, Burma 11-5—11-14, 894B1
Delegatn in Cambodia, backs vs Viet 11-5—11-6, 894G1
Teng scores Sovt-Viet pact 11-8, 894C1
Hong Kong emigratn up 11-11, 902C1
China linked to Australia tap chrg vs USSR 11-14, 878D3
Zambia MiGs cited 11-20, 912D1
Hua visit to Rumania cited 11-25, 913B3
Eur, Asia laud US-China ties 12-15, 12-16, 977B1
Rumania policy scored by USSR 12-15, 1020D1
Pl signs US mil base pact, SE Asia pressure cited 12-31, 1000A3

Government & Politics—*See also other appropriate subheads in this section; TIBET*

Teng aides get key posts 1-2, 53G3
Sinkiang ldr replaced 1-29, 89A2
Teng cleared of '76 Peking riots 2-15, 111B2
CP Central Com backs Natl People's Cong plans 2-18—2-23, 154D2
Hupeh offcls ousted 2-20, 130D2
'Gang of 4' spared executn 2-21, 130G2-A3
Consultative Conf meets 2-24—3-8, Teng named chrmn, new Const OKd 3-8, 154F2
People's Cong preparatory mtg OKs agenda 2-25, 154D2
People's Cong OKs new Const, Hua renamed premr, Teng allies get maj posts 2-26—3-5, 153A1-154C2
8 Hangchow executns rptd 2-27, 287C3
Rights abuses publicized 2-28, 146A3
Social sci courses revived 2-28, 146E3
New anthem approved 3-5, 154B2
Religious curbs rptd eased 3-10, 294C1
Shanghai purge victims rptd rehabilitated 3-13, 287G2
Peking mayor scored at rally 4-7, 287D3
Anti-Gen Chen posters rptd 4-9, 287F3
Posters vs Hua rptdly torn down 4-9, 287F3
Anhui injustice chrgd 4-11, 287A3
Inner Mongolia ldr arrested 4-11, 287B3
Reevaluatn of Mao ideas rptd urged 6-3, 532E2
110,000 rightist detainees freed, rehabilitatn program set 6-5, 435D3-436C1
Shanghai ex-mayor rehabilitated 6-23, ashes brought to Peking 6-28, 515G1
CP 75th anniv marked; Mao scored re democracy lack; Lin, Gang of 4 scored; Mao '62 speech cited 7-3, 532B2
Pragmatic approach seen since Mao, Gang of 4 era 7-6, 532A2
Sci Acad employes cleared 837F3
29th anniv marked 10-3, 773F2
Peking Mayor Wu ousted, Lin named 10-10, 773F3
Peking mil region head ousted 10-17, 814B2
Province purges rptd 10-23, 814F1
Injustices, torture admitted 10-26, 837E3

1979

Westn-natn Guadeloupe summit discusses, Brezhnev warning cited 1-5—1-6, 12E2, G2, C3
Sihanouk visits 1-6—1-8, 10F2-11A1
Li in Pak 1-20, vows aid vs 'aggressn' 1-22, 59C3
Jesuits return rptd discussed 1-23, 218C1
Albania CP ldr scores Mao, Teng 1-27, 69C3
Geneva Com sessn attendance barred 1-27, 625G2
Teng visits Japan 2-6—2-7, 84B1
Portuguese ties set 2-8, 134C3
Sihanouk returns to Peking 2-13, 142C2
Pak pres scorns Bhutto clemency plea 2-14, 116B2
Iran leftists reject alignmt 2-14, 125C1
India forgn min ends visit, Viet invasn scored 2-18; ties rptd unaffected 2-21, 123D1
Asian, Oceanic natns voice concern over Viet invasn 2-18—2-20, 123F1
Rumania splits with Sovt bloc, Albania over Viet invasn 2-19, 2-22, 122E2
Cuba role in Africa, Mideast scored 2-27, 141E2
Viet role in Cambodia, Laos scored 2-27, 141F2
USSR rpts Laos border troop mass 3-2; Laos asks end to road bldg 3-7, China regrets request 3-15, 200B1, D1
Laos chrgs incursns 3-7, 3-14, 3-15, 199G3-200B1
Libyan '71 A-bomb bid rptd 4-14, 299C3
Hong Kong immigratn rptd up 5-11, 379E2
Yugo-USSR dispute cited 5-18, 380B1
Afghan rebel role chrgd 6-11, 443C1
Forgn students in Shanghai attacked 7-3—7-10, 523F3
Hong Kong illegal emigratn penalties rptd 7-4, 524C1
Viet offcl defects 7-5; Hanoi, Peking confirm 8-6, 8-8, 604C1
Thai CP radio statn shut 7-11, 537C3
Indochina refugee resetlmt vowed at intl conf 7-20—7-21, 549D1
Afghans chrg rebel aid 8-9, 666F2
Israel blamed for Young resignatn 8-16, 606F2
Vatican rejcts Peking bishop 8-17; Pope seeks ties, church recognitn disputed 8-19—8-21, 639D2-C3
Thai anti-rebel pledge by Laos rptd 8-25, 659C3
Cuba scores US tie 9-3, 674C2
Spratly I annexed by Pl 9-7, 660C3
Hong Kong emigration cited 9-17, 730F2
Eur, Japan ties seen 9-22, 751C2
UK ties linked to Hong Kong gov reapptmt 9-25, 730C2
Hua visits 4 W Eur natns 10-15—11-6, 789E2, 853D3-854F2
Mongolia troop exit by USSR sought 11-30, 918A1
Japan premr visits; Indochina, Korea discussed 12-5—12-7, 939C3
Sovt Afghan invasn opposed 12-29, 974D2

Government & Politics—*See also other appropriate subheads in this section*

Teng photo 83D3
Freedom House lists as not free 12E3
Poster campaign supported 1-3, 7B1
Hu gets top party posts, Wang demoted 1-4, 6D3, G3
Peking rallies demand food, democracy, work 1-8, 1-14—1-15, 58A3
Business class rehabilitated 1-25, 75G1-C2
Liu death confrmd 1-28, 75E1
Chiang Nan-hsiang named educ min 2-6, 134A3
3 dissidents rehabilitated 2-6, 134B3
Teng warns protesters 3-16, 3-18; protests curbed, placards barred 3-29—4-1; activists score 4-1, 259A1-B2
Poster ban pressed 4-4, Shanghai posters appear 4-15, 312F1-C2
Pol prisoner torture rptd 5-6, 353D1
Teng replies to critics rptd 5-25, 406F1
Teng rptd scored on Hunan radio 5-29, 406B1
Natl People's Cong opens 6-18, 484F2
Natl People's Cong ends; 3 dep premrs named, govt changes, new legal code set 7-1, 502D2
Mao critics rehabilitated 8-3, 651A3
Anti-corruptn effort launched 8-22, 651D3
Writers meet 9-9, HS graduates protest 9-10, 685G2
Rights ldrs missing 9-12; Peking rally scores abuses, demands free electns 9-13, 685D2
3 new ministries created 9-13, 729A2
Protesters promised redress, comm rptd set up 9-15, 729F1
Mongolia pre-'69 borders restored 9-17, 729C2
Dissidents continue protests 9-20, 9-22, 751B1
Cultural Revolutn victims promoted 9-28, movemt deplored 9-29, 750E2, C3, E3*
Unoffcl art exhibit shut 9-29, protested 10-1, 750F3
Army use of Peking campus protested 10-10, withdrawal set 10-13, 789C3
Wei sentenced 10-16, 789C2
Dissident's trial halted 10-17, recess explained 10-29, 854F2

1980

Foreign Relations (misc.)—*See also 'Monetary', 'Soviet-Afghan Issue', 'UN Policy' below*

Canada engineer accused of passing secrets 1-11, 78B3
Huang in Pak, briefs Zia on US talks 1-18—1-21, 44F2
Japan arrests 3 as Sovt spies 1-18, 60D1
Pacific orgn studied 1-20, 78C2
Spratly, Paracel I claimed 1-30, 132C3
Geneva disarmamt conf opens 2-5, 108A1
French CP issues rights rpt 2-20, 149E3
Pakistan cites ties 3-5, 165E2
Italy CP ldr plans visit 4-2, 254G3
Japan defns support cited 4-7, 314E3
Italy CP ldr visits 4-14—4-22; renews PCI ties 4-15, vs Sovt front 4-22, 314F1, B2
Li visits Australia, pacts OKd 5-7—5-11, 387F3
Tito funeral held 5-8, 339B1
Hua visits Japan 5-27—6-1, 421G3
Viets scored re Thai raids 6-25, 7-2, 508A2, D2
India-Cambodia ties regretted 7-7, 547A3
Japan, US, China 'axis' chrgd by USSR 7-8, 7-10, 506F1
Hua at Ohira rites 7-9, 506B1
India launches satellite 7-18, 547E3
Burma citizenship law rptd proposed 8-13, 617F3
Forgn Ministry orders public portraits removed 8-16, 651F2
Chinese dual citizenship barred 9-10, 677C2
NZ, Kenya ldrs visit 9-11, 9-14, 706D3, G3
Viet rptd vs US MIA proposals 10-6, 855C2
Iran attacks ships 10-7, 758G2
N Korea uses airspace for Iran airlift 10-8, 774F2
French pres visits 10-15—10-22, 829A3
Hong Kong bans illegal immigrants 10-23, 855D2-C3
In Thai talks on Cambodia conflict 10-30, 952B1

Government & Politics—*See also other appropriate subheads in this section*

Freedom House lists as partly free 87E3
Teng yields army post to Yang Dechi 2-25, 172A1
Liu rehabilitated, Politburo shifted 2-29, 171C3
Wang named propaganda chief 3-7, 231A2
New party guidelines issued 3-15, 231E1
US exile named to sci post, 2 others cited 3-17, 231B2
Chao, Wan named dep premr 4-16; power shift seen 4-17, 351E1
Liu memorialized 5-17, 388F3-389A1
Tsinghai Prov reforms set 6-8, 462E1
Bureaucrats blamed in '79 oil rig collapse 7-6, 621G3
Mao policies scored 7-8, 8-10, public portraits ordrd removed 8-11, 8-16, 651C2
Oil min fired re '79 accident, vice premr censured 8-25, 651B3
Natl People's Cong 8-30—9-10: Hua submits resignatn as premr, local control plan set 8-30; Zhao named premr, other posts filled; reforms set 9-10, 677A1-678E2
Zhao photo 9-10, 677C1
Zhao vows govt reforms 9-11, 706C3
Hua on resignatn 9-27, 788B3
Gang of 4, others testify 11-23—12-29; trial delayed 11-1; Peking blast not linked 11-3, 858G3
Hua '76 promotn criticized 9-28, 788G2
Rights abuses admitted 10-2, 788C2
2 dead security aides purged 10-31, 859E1
28 Shanxi offcls ousted 11-8, 877F2
Gang of 4, other indictmts aired 11-15—11-18; trial starts 11-20, 877A1
Gang of 4, others testify 11-23—12-29; trial ends, death penalty asked for Jiang 12-29, 974F2-975E2
Hua scored in press 12-16, 12-30, 975C3
Mao scored by press for Cultural Revolutn role 12-22, 975F2

1976

Wu Teh to head People's Cong 7-24, 555F1
Hua scores 'class enemies' 9-1, 673G2
Mao dies 9-9, 6 seen as successors 9-9—9-10, 657A1; announcemt text excerpts 659A2-F3
Facts on Mao 658B2
Mao funeral com list publshd 9-10, 3 offcls rptd omitted 9-11, 711G3
Mao mourning period 9-11—9-18, 711A3
Editorial on party unity 9-16, 712C1
Hua succeeds Mao 10-7, 871E2
Mao body to be embalmed 10-8, 758D1
Hua appointmts announced 10-12; oppositn rptd 10-14, 757A1, D2
Facts on Hua 757B1-758D1
Press backs Hua, Mao directives 10-12, 10-14, 757D1, E2
Chiang, other radicals rptd purged, arrested, Mao will forgery cited 10-12—10-14, 757F1-E2
Purged ry min rptd reinstated 10-14, 809G2
Peking posters, demonstratns denounce plotters 10-15—10-23, 790A2, G2
Army backs Hua 10-17, 10-19, 790D3
Editorial denounces plotters 10-19, 790E2
Radical plot, purge confirmed 10-22, 790A2
Hua honored at rallies; Chiang, other radicals scored 10-23, 10-24; more accusatns rptd 10-25, 10-26, 809E1-G2
Fukien Prov clashes 10-27; army quells unrest, Chiang group blamed 11-23, 904D3
Chiang group plot detailed 10-30, 11-8, 871C2
Shanghai leadership shift 10-30, 871G2
Chiang group tied to indl unrest 11-2, 871G2
Obedience to govt asked 11-23, 905A1
Wang tied to Hangchow unrest 11-24, 904C3
Drive vs Chiang backers asked; restraint urged 11-28, 904A3
Forgn Min Chiao ousted, Huang named 12-2, 904D2-A3
Clashes in central provs, Paoting, Szechwan; Chiang 'gang of 4' linked 12-6—12-31, 1000B1-D2
More chrgs vs gang of 4 12-18, 12-23, 999E3
Hua sees '77 purge, blames gang of 4 12-24, 12-28, 999G2

Japanese Relations

Miki OKs peace treaty 1-13, 29F3
Japan to up oil imports 1-22, 208C3
Fertilizer deal rptd 1-26, 100F3
A-test fallout rptd 2-1, 83G3
Feb-Mar oil exports cut, steel deal canceled 4-5, 265D3
Japan warns US vs concessns 7-12; China cancels shipping talks 7-16, protests 7-19, 555E2
Reactn to Mao death 9-9, 657D2

Macao—*See MACAO*

Obituaries

Hsu Chin-chiang 7-21, 656F3
Lin Yutang 3-26, 316D1
Liu Wen-hui 6-24, 524G3
Mao Tse-tung 9-9, 657A1, 658A2

1977

Gang of 4, Mao nephew scored in Liaoning 6-24, 562C1
3 offcls scored at Kunming rally 6-29, 562A1
Teng rehabilitated 7-22, 511D2
Huang Ko-cheng rehabilitated 8-1, 8-2, 616C3
11th CP Cong: Central Com, Politburo elected; new charter adopted 8-12—8-18; results rptd 8-20—8-23, 645D2, F2★, G2★
CP membership at 35 mln 8-20, 646C1
Fukien army offcr slain 8-30, 706F1-A2
'71 anti-Mao plot detailed 9-8, 694D2
Mao creed modificatn urged 9-9, 694B3
Mao mausoleum opened 9-9, 706A1
Lo Jui-ching promoted 9-9, 706B1
Mao policy chng hinted 9-10, 706C1
Hupei unrest indicated 744D1
Army discipline urged 9-19, 743E3
Kwangsi dissent hinted 9-22, 744B1
Wei named forces pol dir 9-25, 743D3
Gang of 4 arrest date confrmd 10-6, 780E3
Wu, Chen scored in posters 10-20, 823F2
Educatn norms upgraded 10-21; concern re level drop rptd 10-24, 823B2
Pol executns rptd 10-21, 10-29, 11-1, 841E3-842A1
Natl People's Cong set for '78 10-23, 823E1
Yu suicide rptd 11-8, 882D3
Police abuses charged 11-28, 983A3
Ct sentences defended 12-4, 983D3
Police score radical abuses 12-8, 983E3

Monetary, Trade & Aid Issues (Including all foreign economic developments)

'76 oil exports cited 1-6, 2B1★
'75-76 Japan trade drop rptd 2-15, 180C1
Australia wheat pact signed, '76 sales cited 3-6, 178F3
Gold prices climb 3-18, 336C1
Tanzania aid total rptd 247D3
Australian sugar deal set 3-30, 236G3
Zaire arms aid set 4-7, 265E2
US sees normal trade ties 4-22, 321B3
US money-claim talks resume 5-1, 333B2
S Korea-Japan oil pact scored 6-8, 467B2
Pl rebel arms aid rptd 6-11, 468B3
Egypt arms deal rptd 6-25, 496C2
Australia record wheat buy, '76-77 imports rptd 7-4, 578E2
India aids Tibet rebels 8-6, 616E3
'76 trade data rptd 8-11, 635E3
USSR '77-78 trade pact rptd 8-15, 853F2
Somalia arms aid offer rptd 8-16, 649B1
Burma seeks rebel aid end 779F2
Guyana textile plant aid rptd 9-2, 710B3
Zenith plans TV operatns 9-27, 974D2
Canada trade hike asked 10-4—10-7, 801E1
US rpts '72-75 trade up 11-6, 882B3
Jan-June trade rptd down 11-7, 882C3
Malta aid announced 11-16, 925A3

1978

2 dep premrs promoted 10-26, 837G3-838A1
Mao '65 Cultural Revolutn backing scored 11-15, 901B3
'76 Peking riots termed revolutionary 11-16, 901C3
Rehabilitatn set for Cultural Revolutn victims 11-16, 901C3
Mao linked to 'Gang of 4' 11-19, 901E2
'76 Peking rioters cleared 11-19, 901A3
Poster drive widens, rallies held; Hua, Mao criticized, 11-20—12-10, 949A1
Peking region gets new pol ldr 11-22, 950G1
Teng: '76 purge 'wrong' 11-26, 950B1
Teng denies break with Hua 11-27, 949G2
Govt orders halt to anti-Hua posters, rallies 11-30, 949D1
Poster scores 'Gang of Four' 12-3, 949E2
Tao, Peng rptd cleared 12-10, 12-11, 950D1
CP Central Com mtg ends; 4 added to Politburo, 3 purged ldrs cleared 12-22, 1015C1
Peng Teh-hua, Tao Chu rites held 12-24, 1015G1

Monetary, Trade, Aid & Investment

Viet pact signed 1-10, 21G2
'77 forgn trade hits record 1-16, 89D2
French EC role lauded 1-20, accord signed 1-21; '76, '77 trade data cited 71D1
Equatorial Guinea aid rptd 1-25, 152A3
Rhodesia rebel aid cited 59C1
EC 5-yr trade pact initialed 2-3, USSR scores 2-6, 2-9, 102F2-D3
US OKs Japan computer sale 2-8, 111D2
Japan pact signed 2-16, 103C3
Malta '77 aid rptd 2-17, 228B3
Viet chrgs Cambodia arms aid 2-21, 121C1
US bars glove import curbs 3-15, 443G3
Albania-Greek trade pact signed 3-28—3-30, 374D2
EC 5-yr trade pact signed 4-3, USSR denounces 4-4, 302E3
Hongkong Bank to buy US bank 4-5, 263A2
Somali pact signed 4-13—4-18, 353E2
US oil drilling equipmt purchases cited 5-6, 436F2
US bars airborne device sale 5-8, lifts ban 6-9, 436G1
Viet aid cut set 5-12, Hanoi scores 5-30, 399A3
Cambodia mil aid cited 5-17, 490A2
US A-fuel export license deferral rptd 5-20, 408B2
Viet aid cut, talks rejctd 6-5, 6-7, 464G1
Argentina trade pact signed 6-9, 793G2
Spain air, trade pacts signed 6-16—6-19, 576A2, F2
Zaire receives mil delegatn, arms aid review seen 6-24, 652G2
Carter seeks more trade 6-26, 491C1
US bars Taiwan jet sale 6-30, 506C1
Viet econ aid ended 7-3, Hanoi discounts impact 7-4, 504B3
Hong Kong 'capitalist' bank methods OKd 7-6, 532E1
US scientists visit, trade rise seen 7-6—7-10, 564C2-C3
Hua urges intl trade growth 7-7, 532B1
Albania aid ended 7-13, technicians exit set 7-16, 549A1
Libya cooperatn pacts signed 8-9, 691F2
Japan peace pact signed, econ exchngs urged 8-12, 637B1
Rumania econ, tech cooperatn backed 8-18, agrmt signed 8-21, 675C1
Pak denies A-plant aid agrmt 8-23, 668F2
Japan seeks closer trade ties 9-6, 695C2
Jan-June forgn trade rise rptd 9-6, 773C3
Australia imports up 9-11, iron ore order rptd 9-29, 754E2
US demands contd Taiwan arms sales 9-19, 12-7, Peking acquiesces 12-16, 973E2, 974B1-E1
US bars clothespin import curbs, workgloves curb cited 10-2, 805E1
Australia sets favored trade status 10-11, 836G1
Taiwan oil claims cited 10-16, 871G2
French sci, tech pact signed; missile deal confrmd 10-20, 814A1
Japan pact implemented 10-23, 801B1, D2
Mex pres sets trade expansn 10-24—10-30, 903B3
USSR warns Eur vs arms sales 10-26, 814B1
France-USSR tensns re arms deal cited 10-29, 830G3
Brazil steel purchase set 11-1, 879E2
US OKs West arms sales 11-3, 11-9, 901D3
US firm to build hotels 11-6, 880A2
US OKs UK diesel engines sale 11-7, 901G3
US agri secy ends visit; sees more grain, cotton sales, agri exchngs 11-14, 902A1
US backs interest paymts on frozen forgn assets 11-14, 977F1
Japan business offices set 11-28—11-29, 986F2
Carter bars arms sales 11-30, 936F2
France trade pact signed, A-sale agreed 12-4, 986G1

1979

Wall posters scored by govt 11-3, 854C3
Ct rejects Wei appeal 11-6, 949F1
7 arrested at Democracy Wall 11-11, 11-18, 949E1
Democracy Wall closed 12-6, new wall used for posters 12-8, 949D1

Monetary, Trade, Aid & Investment—*See also 'U.S.' below*

UK jet, indl pkg revealed at Guadeloupe summit, W Ger warning cited 1-5, 12B3
Australia wheat deal rptd 1-22, 56G2-F3, 253G1
Japan plant equipmt deals canceled 2-26, 181D3
UNCTAD commodity fund set 3-20, 200E2
Australian credit aid rptd 4-6, 284D2
$7 bln French bank loan signed 5-9, 370G1
Gets Japan Eximbank credit 5-15, 484G3
Trade missn arrives Brazil 5-21, maritime pact signed 5-22, 443B3
Egypt arms deal set 6-5, 415A3
Japan contracts revived 6-12, 484E3
W Ger tech, raw materials pact signed 6-19, 637E3
'79 trade total, loans estimated 6-21, 484E3
Egypt jet exchng rptd 6-22, 475C1
Viet refugee aid weighed 6-28, 495A3
Forgn investmt rules issued 7-8, 523A3
Pl trade pact signed, '78 data cited 7-8, 567B1
EC textile pact initialed 7-18, 554E3
France pacts signed 10-17, 789B3
W Ger, Italy pacts signed 10-24, 11-6, UK jet sales seen 10-28, 854D1, G1, D2
Taiwan affirms trade ban 11-28, 952B3
Japan premr visits, pacts signed 12-5–12-7, 939C3

1980

Monetary, Trade, Aid & Investment
See also 'Soviet-Afghan Issue', 'U.S. Relations' below

Pacific orgn studied 1-20, 78C2
Forgn currency black mkt curbed 3-1, 132E2
Taiwan customs-free exports OKd 4-7, 295C2
World Bank dir in Peking 4-11—4-16, IMF admits 4-17, 302C2
'79 econ rpt issued, trade deficit up 5-1, 521D1, G1
Australia contd wheat purchases vowed 5-7—5-11, 387F3
World Bank admits 5-15, 389C1
USSR trade pact signed, trade drop cited 6-6, 451F3
Burma rebel aid rptd 8-10, 8-15, 668C2
Forgn debt rtpd 9-1, 678C2
Forgn firms, people to be taxed 9-2, 677C2-E2
Tanzam RR aid pledged 9-2, 731B2
Australia wheat crop seen reduced 10-13, 827F3
Canada ends Sovt grain embargo support, US deal cited 11-20, 900C2
'79 3d World arms sales rptd 12-10, 933C3
Parallel exchng rates set 12-15, 975F3

1976

Soviet Relations
Mao poems, editorial publshd 1-1, 9A3, D3
UN clash on Mideast 1-15, 60A1
US CIA media manipulatn rptd 1-17, 92D3
UK Tory ldr attack on Sovt detente backed 1-24, 101A2
USSR doubts improved ties 2-10, 117B3
Sinkiang border clashes rptd 2-12, 190A1
Hua scores detente 2-22, 189D3
Brezhnev scores 2-24, 194B2
Shuns Sovt CP Cong 2-24—3-5, 195B3
Sovt Indian O role scored 3-13, 265C3
Nixon rpts on China visit 3-22, 215D1
UN clash on Angola 3-26, 3-30, 228E2
Kirilenko scores CP 4-13, 289G1
Hua lauds end of Egypt-Sovt pact 4-19, 275A3
USSR asks renewed border talks 4-28, 341F2
Sovt Peking emb blast, 2 die 4-29; saboteur chrgd 4-30, 341B2
USSR scored re pro-Chou riot, Teng 5-18, 439G1
Suslov scores re detente 5-19, 381G1
Australia on Sovt containmt 6-1, 438G2
US Dem platform text cites 6-15, 477E3
Scores Sovt Angola role 6-23, 455G1
USSR accuses re drugs 7-24, 655A2
Mao death condolences sent 9-9, 658A1; rejected 9-14, 712E1
USSR makes UN overture 9-28, 719D3
USSR asks better ties 10-1, 752D1
China scores at UN 10-5, 759F3
Sovt mil strategy rptd 10-5, 961E1
Posters chrg Chiang link 10-18, 790C3
Brezhnev: ties possible 10-25, 839C2
Congratulatns to Hua rejctd 10-28, 871F3
Vs friendlier Sovt ties 11-2, 11-15, 871B3
Sovt revolutn anniv lauded 11-7, 871E3
China shuns UN vote on Angola entry 11-22, 879E1; 12-1, 895C3
Rumania defns offcl in China 11-22, 907C2
Border talks resume 11-30, 908C1
Sovt 'hunter-killer' spacecraft rptd 12-18, 961C2

Sports
Australia tennis team to visit 4-6, 249G3
Asks Taiwan Olympics ouster 7-16, 529E1

1977

Obituaries
Lin Li-ming 8-19, 696A3

Soviet Relations
Sovt threat stressed 1-26, 61G2
Scores USSR re Czech dissidents 1-26, 82A3
USSR urges A-test ban 2-15, 147D1
Sovt border talks end 2-28, 161D1
Sovt Zaire invasn role chrgd 3-23, 261E1
Pravda scores China 5-14, USSR protests 5-26, 458D2
US to challenge Sovt role 6-10, 460D2
US gen reprimanded for speech 6-17, 482E3
'77-78 trade pact rptd 8-15, 853F2
Sub forces ranked 8-25, 686F2
River rights accord set 10-7, 853D2
USSR backs A-test ban 11-2, 997B1
Malta premr provokes Sovt walkout 11-3, 925E2

Sports
Soccer team plays US Cosmos 9-17, 9-20; tours US 10-6—10-10, 827G2

Taiwan Relations
Peking stresses Sovt threat 1-26, 61G2
Peking exile money claims cited 5-1, 333D2
Peking vs more US scholar exchngs 6-28, 505G3
Taiwan vs US-China ties 7-2; Peking vows force vs Taiwan 7-4, 514A1
Peking pilot defects 7-7, seeks US aid 7-8, 536E3-537C1
US-Peking talks on Taiwan ties 8-22—8-25, 645A1
Taiwan briefed on Vance missn 8-27, 664E2
Li regrets US stand 8-29, 664A3
China sees setback to US ties 9-6, Ford denies pledge 9-7, 686D3-687B1
Anti-Taiwan stand reaffirmed 10-2, 10-4, 780G3

1978

2 US cos in iron-ore deals 12-4, 12-6, 986F2
Japan steel co to build mill 12-5, 986D2
US, USSR clash on arms sales, talks stalled 12-5—12-5, 996A3
Coke, Boeing deals signed 12-13, 12-19, 1015A2
US announces China ties, sees expanded trade 12-15, 973G1, 975B1, A2
Taiwan trade, mail svc asked 12-31, 995C1

Obituaries
Kuo Mo-jo 6-12, 540B3
Lo Jui-ching 8-3, 708A3
Pi Shu-shih, Ignatius 5-16, 440C3

Soviet Relations
US chrgs 'proxy war' in Viet-Cambodia clashes 1-8; scored 1-9, 1-16, 9C2, 43E1
USSR fears Japan pact 1-9—1-10, 28E3
USSR border areas closed to foreigners 1-19, 39B2
Geneva conf chrmnshp debated 1-31, 61C3
USSR scores EC trade pact 2-6, 2-9, 102B3; 4-4, 302G3
USSR rptly sought '69 joint US A-attack; US, USSR deny 2-16, 124B2
Japan rejcts Sovt protest on proposed treaty 121G3
US sees 'uncertainty', confirms Asia commitmt 2-20, 126D3
USSR makes overtures 2-24, China rebuffs 3-26; Brezhnev bars border pullback 4-1, 237D3
USSR stages border maneuvers 4-5, 238A1
USSR envoy arrives, border talks set 4-26, 360A3
UK defns chief's remarks on USSR cause uproar 5-1, 329G2
China rpts border raid 5-11, USSR claims mistake 5-12, 360C2
USSR 'hegemony', Africa links scored by US 5-20—5-22, 384F2, A3
SALT status briefing by US rptd 5-27, 399G1
USSR border buildup scored by US 5-28, 399D1
Huang chrgs USSR war threat 5-29, 422A1
Huang scores USSR role in Africa 6-7, 441D2
USSR role in Viet feud chrgd 6-7, 464A2
USSR warns US re China ties 6-17, 465A1
Japan-China pact opposed 6-19, 8-12, 637G1
Sovt border force concentratn noted 6-23, 493F2
Brezhnev warns US vs thaw 6-25, 488A3; Carter replies 6-26, 491B1
China ends Viet econ aid 7-3, 504D3
Viet-USSR plot to control SE Asia chrgd 7-12, 547G3
USSR scores Hua visit to Rumania, Yugo, Iran 8-5, 8-21, 8-27; Rumania pres reassures Brezhnev 8-7, 675D3-676A1
Hua visits Rumania, Yugo, Iran to counter Sovt influence 8-16—9-1, 674G2-675D3
USSR Viet backing, SE Asia role scored 9-6, 696C1
USSR assails Huang 10-10, 796C2
Huang chrgs USSR threat 10-13, 796B2
Toon calls USSR 'paranoid' 10-14, 821C1
Teng calls USSR threat 10-23, 10-25, 802A1, E1
USSR warns Eur vs arms sales 10-26, 814B1
Teng calls USSR world threat 11-6, scores Viet treaty 11-8, 894B1
USSR border buildup rptd 11-9, 914A2
China linked to Australia tap chrg vs USSR 11-14, 878D3
USSR fear of mil buildup cited 11-25, 913A3
USSR, US clash on arms sales, talks stalled 12-5—12-15, 996A3
US-China ties agreed 12-14, announced 12-15, 12-16, 973C1
US briefs USSR on China ties 12-15, reactn rptd 'positve' 12-16, 12-19, 976E1
Eur, Asia laud US-China ties 12-15, 12-16, 977B1
USSR scores Rumania stance on China 12-15, 1020D1
Brezhnev denies 'positive' reactn to US ties 12-21, 995E1
SALT pact delay linked to US-China ties 12-26, 996B1

Taiwan Relations
Plea to Taiwan Chinese 12-27-77, 1-4, 17A3
Taiwan mil offered money to defect 2-23, 146D3
US improved ties linked to Taiwan exit 5-20, 384F2
US bars Taiwan jet sale 6-30, 506C1
Libya retains Taiwan link, sets Peking ties 8-9, 691F2
Japan peace pact scored, reaffirms Senkaku claim 8-12, 637F1, D2
Background to US-Peking negotiatns 9-19—12-12, 974A1-E1
Peking oil claims cited 10-16, 871G2
Teng asks US cut ties 10-25, 802C1
US-Peking ties agreed 12-14, announced 12-15, 12-16; US to end Taiwan defns pact, retain other ties 973A1
Texts of US announcemt 12-15; US, Peking, Taiwan statemts publshd 12-17, 975A1-976C3; text of '72 Shanghai communique 976D2
US domestic reactn to Peking ties 12-15—12-20, 974A3, 975A3-976E1; congressmen file suit 12-22, Admin defends 12-27, 995B2

1979

Obituaries
Chang Kuo-tang 12-4, 1008C2

Soviet Relations
Westn-natn Guadeloupe summit reassures USSR on China ties, Brezhnev warning cited 1-6, 12E2, C3
Brezhnev links China to Cambodia 'hateful' govt 1-9, 11A2
Sovt Taiwan interference opposed 1-9, 26D3
Sovt mil buildup in Viet chrgd 1-11, 10C2
US mil ex-ldrs warn of Sovt threat 1-12, 15C1
Vance, Brzezinski on US ties 1-15, 27C2
US reassures USSR on ties 1-17, 29E3
USSR border mil outlay rptd 1-25, 99B3
Albania CP ldr chrgs US-USSR war favored 1-27, 69E3
Teng chrgs Sovt threat 1-29, 2-5, 65F1, G1
US-China communique criticizes USSR, US reassures 2-1, 65B2, D2
Teng vs Sovt 'hegemony' 2-1, 83E2
Teng visit to US scored 2-1, 2-4, 84D1
US sci group in Moscow 2-5—2-7, 100D1
Sovts deploy naval force off Viet 2-7, 107A1
China warned on Viet attack 2-8, 106D3
US seeks China-Sovt restraint 2-17, 122D3
USSR issues Viet invasn warning 2-18, accuses US 2-19—2-20, 122F1
China warns vs Viet arms aid 2-21, 122C1
USSR denounces Rumania stand on Viet invasn 2-21, 122F2
USSR scores Viet invasn 2-23, 2-26; Teng counterchrgs, doubts interventn 2-27, 141E2, F2
USSR, China trade chrgs at UN Cncl 2-23—2-28, 142A1
Brezhnev scores Peking 3-2, 172A1
USSR rpts Laos border troop mass 3-2, 200D1
China aid to Afghan rebels chrgd 3-18, 209D2
US intell on China-Viet war praised 3-25, 232B1
US rpts Sovts use Viet Cam Ranh base 3-27, 340F2
Peking OKs '50 pact lapse 4-2, USSR scores 4-4, 258C3
Sovt amb gets offer re improved ties 5-5, Brezhnev backs 6-1, 417B1
Viet-China conflict role backed by French CP 5-10—5-15, 371A2
Yugo-USSR dispute cited 5-18, 380B1
Teng policy rptd scored, improved ties hinted 5-29, 406D1
USSR chrgs Afghan rebel aid 6-11, 443C1
Border clash kills 1 7-16, 554F1
Talks resumptn OKd 7-25, 554A2
USSR, pol corruptn linked 8-24, 652B1
US aid vs hegemony asked 644B3
US-China ties backed 9-18, 9-22, 751B2, C2
China 'tricks' chrgd 9-22, 741B2
China envoys in Moscow 9-23, formal talks begin 10-17, 803F1
Sovt encroachmt in Sinkiang chrgd 9-29, 803A2
US Defns Dept backs arms to China 10-3, Vance reaffirms ban 10-4, 789E1
Hua Eur visit prompts chrgs 10-16, 10-18, 789G2
Hua warns vs Sovt threat 10-22, 10-28, 853G3, 854E1
Formal talks end 11-30, 917G3

Sports
Table tennis tourn results 4-30, 527E1
FIFA readmits 10-14, 1004F2
Taiwan sues over Olympic 2-China plan 11-15, IOC OKs plan 11-26, 1000C3

Taiwan Relations
Chiang vows reconquest 1-1, 2A2
Taiwan vs trade, other links 1-1; rejcts air landing offer 1-4, 2B2
Peking for peaceful merger 1-2, 2F1
Taiwan offered autonomy 1-9, rejects 1-11, 26A3
Reunificatn offer called 'trick' 1-11, 27B1
US OKd Taiwan arms ban in tie talks 1-12, 27D1
Carter sees peaceful Peking-Taiwan setlmt 1-17, 29D3
Carter urges Taiwan ties legis, to veto anti-Peking bills 1-26, 66E2
US reactn to Teng visit 1-28, 1-29, 66B1, F
Teng hints at mil actn 1-30, 65E2
Portugal backs Peking claim 2-8, 134D3
US role in Viet invasn chrgd 2-18, 123F1
US-Taiwan relatns bill protested 3-16, 259C3
US-Taiwan ties scored 4-19, 312A1
'77 populatn data rptd 5-14, 370A3
US cong defns treaty suit dismissed, Sen rebukes Carter 6-6, 440F1, B2

1980

Obituaries
Zhao Dan 10-10, 876G3

Soviet-Afghan Issue
Sovts chrg Afghan rebel training 1-1, 'aggressn' 1-5, 1E2, 2A1
Pak aid vowed 1-8—1-21, 44F2
Afghan rebel arms aid hike agreed 1-16, 31A2
Sovt talks cancelled 1-19, 45G3
Olympic stand rptd 1-21, 45C3; boycott hinted 1-25, 68E1
Afghan rebel arms aid chrgs continue 1-28, 67G2
Olympic boycott backed 2-1, 84G3
Geneva conf denunciatn 2-5, 108B1
Afghan subversn chrgd 2-22, 138F2
Brezhnev sees Peking threat 2-22, 139E2
EC, US neutrality plans scored 3-2, 165D1
US Afghan 'spy' chrgs sabotage 4-3, 271F2
Olympic boycott conditn set 4-24, 325G3
May Day parade shunned 5-1, 354G2
IOC issues Olympic acceptance list 5-27, 420E3
Afghans blame for Kabul riots 6-8, 442G2
Viet Thai raids linked 7-2, 508D2
Hua, Carter meet 7-10, 506D1
Moscow Olympics boycotted 7-19—8-3, 587F3
Arms rptd seized 9-1, 686C1
Zhao: Sovt moves pose war threat 9-11, 706F3
Sovt annexatn of border area rptd 11-4, 900B1
Canada ends grain embargo support, US deal cited 11-20, 900B2

Soviet Relations—*See also 'Soviet-Afghan Issue' above*
US-China mil talks opposed 1-7, 11F2; Brown rejcts Sovt criticism 1-11, 31G1
Japan arrests 3 as Sovt spies 1-18, 60D1
Improved ties sought 4-7, new China amb arrives in Moscow 4-20, 354F3
Teng scores USSR 4-17, 314G1
Italy CP vs anti-Sovt front 4-22, 314B2
China rpts ICBM test 5-18, 389B1
US OKs China tech sales 5-29, 398A1
USSR trade pact signed, trade cited 6-6, 451F3
US, China, Japan 'axis' chrgd 7-8; Carter-Hua mtg scored 7-10, 506C1, F1
3 Sovt spies sentenced 7-20, 563G1
USSR denounces anti-Mao directives 8-17, 651F2
Zhao chrgs 'aggressive' policies 9-11, 9-14, 706F3
Giscard warns of power monopoly 10-17, 829C3
USSR offers Persian Gulf peace plan 12-10, 930E1

Sports
Lake Placid Olympics controversy 1-15—2-12, Taiwan excused 2-13, 154D3
Moscow Olympics stand rptd 1-21, 45C3
Olympic boycott hinted 1-25, 68E1
Olympic boycott movemt joined 2-1, 84G3
Olympic boycott terms set 4-24, 325G3
IOC issues Olympic acceptance list 5-27, 420E3
Moscow Olympics boycotted 7-19—8-3, 587F3
Canton Grand Prix results 10-19, 947C1

Taiwan Relations
US OKs Taiwan arms sale, bars long-range planes 1-3, 11F2-A3
US arms to Taiwan opposed 1-9, 11E2
Taiwan Olympics controversy 1-15—2-12, Taiwan excused 2-13, 154D3
Customs-free exports to Taiwan OKd 4-7, US trade sought 4-9, 295C2
'79 Taiwan fishermen rescue rptd; smuggling activity cited 4-9, 295F2
Taiwan replaced in IMF 4-17, 302C2
Taiwan journalist sentenced 5-15, 375D2
Taiwan sentncs unificatn backer 5-15, 375E2
Taiwan replaced in World Bank 5-15, 389C1
Reagan backs US ties, triggers rift 8-16—8-26, 645E2
US amb scores Reagan remarks 8-26, 664D3
Hua vs Reagan stance 9-7, 678A1
Taiwan-US pact scored 10-4, 762E1
Peking cites Reagan stance, Taiwan welcomes electn 11-5, 841E2

1976

UN Policy & Developments
Cncl member 62F2; 720C1
Sovt Cncl clash on Mideast 1-15, 60A1
Shuns Cncl pro-Palestine vote 1-26, 59G2
Cncl clash on Angola 3-26—3-30, abstains on S Africa censure 3-31, 228B2
Shuns UNDOF extensn vote 5-28, 385G3
Shuns UNFICYP extensn vote 6-16, 457C1
Shuns Angola membership vote 6-23, 455F1
OKs Israel Arab land exit 6-29, 464C1
Shuns vote on anti-terror 7-14, 515G3
IAEA membership cited 8-29, 761A1
USSR makes UN overture 9-28, 719D3
Scores Sovt at Gen Assemb 10-5, 759F3
S Africa arms ban vetoed 10-19, 781D3
Bars vote on UNEF 10-22, 799B2
Shuns Angola membership vote 11-22, 879C1; 12-1, 895C3
Shuns UNDOF vote 11-30, 895B2
Waldheim wins 2d term 12-7, 914E2, F2
Shuns Assemb Geneva conf vote 12-9, 914D1

U.S. Relations
Chou En-lai dies; US lauds 1-8, 8A3, 9A2
Rpt disputes oil export role 1-8, 10A1
Kissinger pays Chou condolence visit 1-15, 48F1
CIA media manipulatn rptd 1-17, 92D3
Ford State of Union message 1-19, 38B3
US Dem policy rptd 1-21, 40F2
US rpts on 18th A-test 1-24, 83E3
US defns needs outlined 1-27, 68D2
US Marines reorganizatn urged 2-2, 95C3
Nixons to visit 2-6, Ford comments 2-10, 109F3, 117F2
Reagan scores Ford 2-10, 109D2
Ford on Nixon visit 2-17, 129G2
Nixons visit 2-21—2-29, Admin seeks rpt 3-2, 189A3
China ICBM projct rptd dropped 2-24, 190C1
Ford vs word 'detente' 3-1, 165E3
Forgn aides in bombed Cambodia town 3-2—3-4, 238B2
Reagan attacks Ford anew 3-6, 180E1
Chiang talks with US scholar scored 3-8, 189G2
US sets Taiwan force cut 3-11, 254E2
Nixon trip rpt 'useful' 3-22, 215A1
Cuba chrgs CIA collusn in Angola 3-29, 228G2
Gates confrmd amb 4-1, 262C3
US views on Egypt jet deal 4-21, 275B3
CIA book cited 4-26, 299E1
US Dem platform text cites 6-15, 477E3, 478E2
Carter for full ties 6-23, 451D3, 452A1
Veneris US visit OKd 6-29, 484F2
Japan warns US vs concessns 7-12, 555E2
Kissinger asks 4-power conf on Korea 7-22, 557C2
US offers quake aid, experts visit rptd 7-29, 545B2, D2
China cited in US arms control rpt 7-29, 739E2
US dependents quit quake area 8-1, 561E2
US GOP platform com plank 8-12, 582A2
US S Korea pullout asked 8-15, 619F1
US GOP platform text cites 8-18, 609B3
Ford acceptance speech cites 8-19, 612B1
Kissinger sees Huang Chen re Korea, urges 4-power conf 8-19, 619A1
USDA rpts China wheat crop up 9-1, 809A3
Reactn to Mao death 9-9, 657C2, 658C1
Schlesinger views Mao body 9-13, continues China tour 9-14, 711F3
Kissinger stresses mutual interests, asks 'phased' Korea talks 9-30, 719C2, E2
China cited in US Mayaguez rpt 10-5, 749D2
China vs for barring Viet UN seat 10-5, 760A1
US rpts A-test fallout 10-5, 790G3; 12-27, 992F1
Ford, Carter debate 10-6, 742B1
Chiao sees Kissinger 10-9, 858B1
US-built fertilizer plants open 10-25, 832D3
US confrms computer sale 10-28, 832F2-B3
China silent on Carter win 11-3—11-4, 826G1
Rpt hits NATO sales 11-4, 880B1
'76 US loan default cited 11-11, 915G2
US radioactive alert after A-test 11-17, 871G3
US China expert dies 12-4, 1015D1
US study rpts no forgn paymts 12-20, 985A3

1977

Tibet—*See under 'T'*

UN Policy & Developments
Assemb, Cncl member 3F3, 4D1
World Food Cncl OKs rice plan 6-23, 513E3
Shuns Rhodesia vote 9-29, 809G2
Shuns vote on UNEF extensn 10-21, 812A1
Shuns Israel occupatn vote 11-25, 910D2

U.S. Relations
CIA mail-opening prosecutns barred 1-14, 41E3
Sovt threat stressed 1-26, 61G2
More exchange visits set 3-13, 220F1
Carter backs closer ties 3-17, 186B2
US cong group visits 4-9—4-17, 298B2, C2 ★
Nixon vow of normal ties rptd 4-10, 298D2
Young scores US Africa policy 4-11, 271D3
Carter rpts goodwill message 4-22, 321A3
Money-claim talks resume 5-1, 333B2
Woodcock named liaison, claims talks rptd 5-12, 381A2
Nixon-Frost interview 5-12, 385E3, 386C1, C2
Carter: key to world peace 5-22, 397D2
US assured on S Korea exit 6-5, 440F3
US to challenge Sovt role 6-10, 460D2
US gen reprimanded for speech 6-17, 482E3
US scholar exchngs barred 6-28, 505E3
US backs full ties 6-29, Taiwan warns 7-2; Peking vows force 7-4, 513F3
Carter backs full ties 6-30, 515F1
Defector seeks US aid 7-8, 537B1
Albania scores improved ties 7-8, 540E3
US seeks Korea talks 7-27, 572C2
US Taiwan stand regretted 7-29, 664A3
China econ rpts issued 8-11, 8-15, 635B3
'76 US trade drops 8-11, 635F3
US stresses Taiwan ties 8-18—8-19, 645A2
Vance visits; normal ties sought, Taiwan discussed 8-22—8-25, 645A1-A2
Carter on Vance visit 8-25, 645B1
Sub forces ranked 8-25, 686F2
Vance briefs Japan on missn 8-26, returns to US 8-27; briefs Carter, no closer ties seen 8-28, 664C2
Taiwan, S Korea briefed on Vance missn 8-26, 8-27, 664E2
China sees setback to ties 9-6, Ford denies pledge 9-7, 686D3-687B1
Soccer team plays Cosmos 9-17, 9-20; tours US 10-6—10-10, 827G2
US arms shipmts to Taiwan scored 10-2, 10-4, 781A1

1978

US to continue arms sales 12-16, 973E2, 974E1
US-Peking accord denounced 12-16—12-18, 974F1; mobs attack US delegatn 12-27, talks on ties fail 12-28—12-29, 994A3
Peking conciliatn hinted 12-16, 12-17; Chiang vs talks 12-18, 974F2
US stresses Taiwan ties, sees no Peking invasn 12-17, 973B2, D2
Taiwan amb to US leaves post 12-29, ties formally ended 12-31, 995A1

Tibet—*See under TIBET*

UN Policy & Developments
Leb asks anti-Israel actn 3-15, 174D3
Leb force vote shunned 3-19, 197C1
Leb force expansn vote shunned 5-3, 340F1
Assemb disarmamt sessn opens 5-23; Huang hints Geneva role, scores USSR 5-29, 421C2, G2-422A1
UNDOF renewal vote shunned 5-31, 400A2
WHO notes cancer deaths 8-28, 727A2
PR called US colony 9-13, 979E3
Unifil extensn vote shunned 9-18, 713C1
Cncl, Assemb member 713A3, D3
Namibia vote shunned 9-29, 819E2
USSR assails Huang disarmamt speech 10-10, 796C2
Calls UNESCO press declaratn 'ambiguous' 11-22, 931E1

U.S. Relations
US sees better ties 1-7, 17E2
US chrgs 'proxy war' in Viet-Cambodia clashes 1-8; scored 1-9, 1-16, 9C2, 43E1
Geneva conf chrmnshp debated 1-31, 61C3
US info leaks in Viet spy chrgs 1-31, 68E3
US OKs Japan computer sale 2-8, 111D2
Rights rpt released 2-9, 102C1
Nixon ex-aide chrgs USSR sought '69 joint A-attack; US, USSR deny 2-16, 124B2
US bars glove import curbs 3-15, 443G3
Hongkong Bank to buy Marine Midland 4-5, 263A2
India confirms '65 A-device loss 4-17, 288D2
Hua backs N Korea on US mil exit 5-5—5-10; S Korea scores 5-11, 340E2
Oil drilling equipmt purchases cited 5-6, 436F2
Ghana '66 emb attack rptd proposed by CIA 5-8, 368C1
US bars airborne device sale, fears mil use 5-8; lifts ban 6-9, 436G1
Chai named envoy to US 5-19, 384C3
Brzezinski visits; backs ties, scores USSR 5-20—5-22; briefs Japan 5-23—5-24, 384D2
A-fuel export license deferral rptd 5-20, 408B2
SALT, US global views rptd discussed by Brzezinski 5-27, 399G1
Brzezinski scores USSR mil buildup 5-28, 399D1
Vance pledges A-weapons restraint 6-12, 445A2
USSR warns vs close ties 6-17, 465A1; 6-25, 488A3
US mil superiority affirmed, Sovt border forces noted 6-23, 493F2
Carter seeks cooperatn, scores USSR warning 6-26, 491B1
US bars Taiwan jet sale 6-30, 506C1
US scientists visit 7-6—7-10; US agri aide remains 7-17, 564C2-C3
Albania cites improved ties re split 7-30, 635D1
USSR scores US policy 8-5, 675G3
Japan-China pact lauded 8-12, 637F2
PR called colony by UN panel 9-13, 979E3
Background to negotiatns: Chai-Carter mtg 9-19; draft communique sent 11-4, 12-4; Teng US visit dvpts 11-25—12-12, 973G2-974E1
US bars clothespin import curbs, workglove curb cited 10-2, 805E1
Huang says US on defensive 10-13, 796B2
Toon calls USSR 'paranoid' 10-14, 821C1
US cites Taiwan oil claims 10-16, 871G2
China scholars end US visit 10-22, acad exchng set 10-23, 814D1
Teng repeats terms for ties 10-25, 802C1
US firm to build hotels 11-6, 880A2
US OKs Westn arms to Peking, sees no security threat 11-7, 11-9, 901E3, G3
USSR border buildup rptd 11-9, 914A2
US agri secy ends visit; sees more grain, cotton sales, agri exchngs 11-14, 902A1
US backs interest paymts on frozen forgn assets 11-14, 977F1
France-China A-sale OKd 11-24, 986C2
Poster lauds 11-25, 949B2
US lauds on rights recognitn 11-28, 950A2

1979

Pl flights to Taiwan OKd 7-8, 567D1
US, China discuss 8-28, 644E2
Carter loses Taiwan defns treaty suit 10-17, 777A1
Taiwan sues IOC over Olympic plan 11-15, plan OKd 11-26, 1000C3
Taiwan affirms trade ban 11-28, 952B3
Taiwan defns treaty abrogatn upheld 11-30, 919D1
Taiwan treaty case refused by US Sup Ct 12-13, 940E1

Tibet
'59 revolt prisoners freed 3-31, 312C2
Chineses offcls' transfers rptd 6-13; Dalai Lama rptdly backs Teng 6-14, 444F3
Dalai Lama invited to return 7-18, refuses 7-19, 563A3
Dalai Lama arrives in US 8-3, 685A3
People's Cong electns, Tian Bao chosen chrmn 8-6—8-14, 685D3

UN Policy & Developments
Viet aggressn in Cambodia chrgd 1-7, 11C1
Cambodia motion vs Viet backed 1-11, 10B2
Unifil extensn vote shunned 1-19, 51D1
Cncl meets on Viet invasn 2-23, actn stalled 2-28, 142A1
Viet, Cambodia res backed 3-16, 200F1
UNCTAD commodity fund set 3-20, 200E2
UNDOF renewal vote shunned 5-30, 395E1
Unifil renewal vote shunned 6-14, 436A3
Indochina refugee aid vowed 7-21, 549D1
Membership listed 695F2
Pol Pot govt seat upheld 9-19, 695C2
Pol Pot govt retains seat 9-21; USSR chrgs 'tricks' 9-22, Peking issues counter-chrgs 9-27, 741G1
Viet refugee resetlmt grant OKd 11-11, 863D3
Cncl debate on Iran, US hostage release urged 12-1—12-2, 913F1

U.S. Relations—*See also CAMBODIA–Vietnam Conflict, VIETNAM–China Conflict*
Ties formally established 1-1, 2B1
Teng meets US reps, invites Goldwater 1-2, 2F1
US Steel signs contract 1-5, 7D1
Sovts reassured re US-China ties by Westn natn Guadeloupe summit 1-6, 12E2
FBI warns of Chinese spies 1-7, 17G2
4 US sens meet Teng 1-9, 26B3
US expanded naval force backed 1-9, 26D3
US mil ex-ldrs warn of Sovt threat 1-12, 15C1
US OKd Taiwan arms ban in tie talks 1-12, 27D1
Vance, Brzezinski, others address US businessmen on US-USSR ties 1-15; Admin controversy denied 1-16, 27A2, G2
'78 US trade total rptd 1-15, 27A3
Carter sees peaceful Taiwan setlmt, invites Nixon to Teng dinner, reassures Sovts on ties 1-17, 29D3, E3
Carter urges Taiwan ties legis, to veto anti-Peking bills 1-26, 66E2
Albania ldr chrgs US-China plot 1-27, 69C3
Teng in US 1-28; meets Carter, US sens 1-29—1-30; pacts signed 1-31; communique issued 2-1, 65A1-66D2
Teng visits Atlanta, Houston, Seattle 2-1—2-5; leaves for home 2-5, 83D2-84B1
Debt to US rptd past due 2-5, 84C3
Science group '78 visit cited 2-5—2-7, 100D1
Teng vs Iran, Cuba stand 2-7, 84B1
Thai premr lauds ties 2-7, 84B2
US rights rpt omits 2-10, 107A2
US econ ties affirmed 2-23; Blumenthal arrives for talks 2-24, signs frozen assets accord 3-1, 141C2, 146B2
US open port pact rptd 2-23, 146G2
Woodcock confrmd US amb 2-26; US, China embs open 3-1, 146D1, A3
Carter defends trade talks 2-27, 149D2
US church reimbursemt set 3-16, 217G3
Teng vs rights complaints 3-16, 259B1
US-Taiwan relatns bill protested 3-16, Carter signs 4-10, 259C3
Taiwan ties protested 4-19, 312A1
US trade missn arrives 5-5, 352G3
Trade talks start 5-7, financial claims pact signed 5-11; sci, tech exchng announced 5-13; trade pact initialed 5-14, 369G3
'78 trade data cited 5-14, 370B1
US mil officers end visit 5-15, 370C2
Direct mail svc set 5-25, 406A1
Chase loan agrmt canceled 5-29, 445B1
Textile talks collapse 5-30, US sets quotas 5-31; Peking blames US 6-1, 405C3
4 papers to open offices 5-30, 406B2
Taiwan defns treaty suit dismissed, Sen rebukes Carter 6-6, 440F1, B2
US plea on Viet refugees rejected 6-16, 460G2
Carter addresses Cong on SALT II 6-18, 459E2
HEW secy visits, US coordinatn on Indochina refugees sought 6-28, 495A3
Trade pact signed 7-7, 523C2
Viet war role debated 7-20, 575E2

1980

Tibet
Yin Fa-tang rptd new CP ldr 5-29, 462D1
Reforms announced 5-31, 462A1
Exiles visit spurs demonstratns 7-29, visit curbed 7-31, 603E3-604A1

UN Policy & Developments
Iran sanctns vote shunned 1-13, 29A1
Indl dvpt aid fund disputed 2-9, 124D2
Palestinian state res backed 4-30, 325D1
UNESCO illiteracy study rptd 12-4, 953A3
UNIFIL mandate debate shunned 12-17, 977D3

U.S. Relations—*See also 'Soviet-Afghan Issue' above*
US OKs Taiwan arms sale, bars long-range planes 1-3, 11F2-A3
Defns Secy Brown in mil talks 1-6—1-9, 11B2
US' Meany opposed ties 1-10, 14E3
Brown rejcts Sovt criticism 1-11, tours mil hq 1-12, ends visit 1-13, 31F1
Alaska gov cites visit 1-15, 268C3
Huang briefs Pak on Brown visit 1-18—1-21, 44A3
Carter notes ties impact 1-20, 50G1; 1-23, 42C3
US to sell mil gear, no arms; earth statn, trade pacts OKd 1-24, 46B2
US issues rights rpt 2-5, 87B2
Reagan 'basic speech' excerpts 2-29, 207G3
Bush 'basic speech' excerpts 3-3, 208D3, E3
CIA alleged agents listed 3-7, 189G2
Power pact signed 3-15, 231A2
US exile gets govt post, 2 others cited 3-17, 231C2
US trade sought 4-9, 295D2
Teng on rapprochemt 4-17, 314A2
Shanghai consulate reopened 4-28, 351G1
China rpts ICBM test 5-18, 389B1
Reagan favors '2-China' policy 5-18, Peking scores 6-13—6-15, 452B3
US OKs mil gear sale 5-29, 397D3
Carter meets Hua in Tokyo; USSR scores 7-10, 506B1, F1
US GOP platform adopted 7-15, 537A1
Reagan backs Taiwan ties, triggers rift 8-16—8-26, 645E2
Woodcock: Reagan perils Peking ties 8-26, 664C3
Mondale scores Reagan gaffe 9-3, 9-19, 780F1, E2
Hua vs Reagan stance 9-7, 678A1
Trade pact signed 9-17; US clothing execs vs 9-18, 706G3-707G1
Carter cites normalized ties 9-18, 698B3
US weighs police gear request 9-20, 788D2
New US-Taiwan pact scored 10-4, 762E1
US ties, Viet MIA plan rejectn rptd linked 10-6, 855C2
France of power monopoly 10-17, 829C3
Reagan gives policy tenet 10-19, 801C3
A-test fallout hits US 10-20, 828B3
Grain pact signed 10-22, 801G1
Reagan electn reactn 11-5, 841E2
Canada ends Sovt grain embargo support, US deal cited 11-20, 900B2
Panama Canal clogged by trade shipmts 11-24, 895E3

1976

1977

1978

Press scores US re Guyana cult deaths 11-30, 911G2
Carter seeks more ties, notes changing attitude 11-30, 936F2
Bethlehem, US Steel in iron-ore deals 12-4, 12-6, 986F2
US, USSR clash on arms sales, talks stalled 12-5—12-15, 996A3
Ties agreed 12-14; Carter, Hua announce 12-15, 12-16; Teng US visit set 973A1
Texts of US announcemt 12-15; US, China, Taiwan statemts publshd 12-17, 975A1-976C3; text of '72 Shanghai communique 976D2
US domestic reactn to Peking ties 12-15—12-20, 974A3, 975A3-976E1; congressmen file suit 12-22, Admin defends 12-27,995B2
US briefs USSR on China ties 12-15, USSR reactn rptd 'positive' 12-16, 12-19, 976E1
Eur, Asia laud ties 12-15, 12-16, 977B1
US to continue Taiwan arms sales 12-16, 973E2, 974E1
Taiwan denounces US-Peking accord 12-16—12-18, 974F1
US stresses Taiwan ties, no Peking invasn 12-17, 973B2
Brezhnev denies 'positive' note on US-China ties 12-21, 995E1
CP Central Com mtg discusses ties 12-22, 1015F1
China A-test debris rptd over US 12-23, 1001A2
SALT pact delay linked to ties, Moscow denies 12-26, 996B1
Taiwan mobs attack US delegatn 12-27, talks on future ties fail 12-28—12-29, 994A3
Taiwan amb to US leaves post 12-29, ties formally ended 12-31, 995A1

Vietnam Dispute—*For Cambodia border dispute, see CAMBODIA—Vietnam Conflict*

Viet border clashes rptd 4-20, 5-1, 341F1
Chinese flee Viet 5-1—5-9, Peking concerned 5-1, 340G3-341D1
Viet aid cut set 5-12, Hanoi scores 5-20, 399A3
Viet expulsns chrgd 5-24; sea evacuatn, other measures rptd 5-27—5-30; Viet denies chrgs, seeks talks 5-28, 5-29, 399E2
Viet resetlmt directives issued 5-30, 400B1
Viet aid cut, talks rejctd 6-5, 6-7, 464G1
Viet OKs ethnic Chinese evacuatn 6-5; ships sail 6-15, evacuatn plan disputed 6-19, 6-22, 464C2
USSR role in Viet feud chrgd 6-7, 464A2
Amb to Hanoi recalled 6-15, 464B2
3 Viet consulates ordrd closed 6-17, 6-19; Hanoi protests 6-20, 464B2, G2
Viet OKs consulate in Ho Chi Minh City 6-17, 464C2
Jets rptd over Viet 7-9, China denies 7-12, 547F3
Ethnic Chinese evacuatn talks rptd at impasse 7-11, 548A1
Viet-USSR plot to control SE Asia chrgd 7-12, 547G3
Ethnic Chinese entry curbed 7-12, 7-13; Viets score move 7-14, 547G3, 548B1
Low-level refugee talks stalled 602D3
China asks dep forgn min talks on refugees 7-19, Hanoi accepts 7-23, talks start 8-8, 602B3
Chrgs traded on refugee exodus 7-20—8-4, 603B1
Laos backs Viet 7-22, 603F1-B2
Forced border repatriatns chrgd 8-8, 8-12, 660G1
Ethnic Chinese ousted from Hanoi hotel 8-12, 660B2
Ethnic Chinese talks resume 8-15, suspended 8-28, 660D1
USSR scores China, Rumania communique 8-21, 675E3
Border clash, Viets occupy China land 8-25, 'provocatns' rptd 8-26, 660D1
Refugees forced into China 9-2, 9-5, 747D1
Border violatns chrgd 9-4, 9-5, 695E3
USSR Viet backing scored 9-6, 696C1
Talks resume 9-7, 695E3
Aggressn chrgs traded 9-11, 9-19, 9-25, 9-27, 747G3-748E1
Viet talks ended 9-26, 747C3
Viet refugee flow linked 10-11, 776C2
China raids, troop mass chrgd 10-13, 10-18, 10-24, 803C2, G2
Border clash 11-1, chrgs exchngd 11-2, 11-7, 859B3
Viet-USSR friendship pact signed, China scored 11-3, 859G2
Teng scores Sovt-Viet pact 11-8, 894C1
Fishing boat clashes 12-9, chrgs traded 12-10, 12-11; China protests 12-13, 997D1
Viet blames re refugees 12-11, 956B1
Viet intrusns chrgd 12-14, 12-23, 997F1

1979

Dalai Lama arrives in US 8-3, 685A3
US Mideast peacemaker role scored 8-16, 606F2
VFW vs US recognitn 8-21, 628D1
US sees '85 oil imports 8-24, 664F3
Mondale arrives 8-25, meets Teng, Hua 8-27–8-28, pacts signed 8-28, 644B2
Mondale opens US consulate, ends visit 8-31; rpts to Carter 9-4, 660D2
Cuba scores China-US tie 9-3, 674C2
Nixon backs arms aid 9-15; visits Peking, evaluates ties 9-17–9-22, 751F1
Air charter svc pact OKd 9-17, 726D1
US shirt embargo rptd 9-27, 834D1
Defns Dept issues arms study 10-3, Vance reaffirms ban 10-4, 789E1
Carter loses Taiwan defns treaty suit 10-17, 777A1
Wei sentence deplored 10-17, 789E2
Carter OKs trade benefits 10-23, 834E1
US asks calm in S Korea crisis 10-27, 822F1
US sets new textile quotas 10-30, 834B1
Teng DC protesters freed 11-14, 904F3
Taiwan defns treaty abrogatn upheld 11-30, 919D1
US backed in UN debate on Iran 12-1–12-2, 913F1
Taiwan treaty case refused by US Sup Ct 12-13, 940E1

Vietnam Dispute—*See VIETNAM-China Conflict; for Cambodia dispute, see CAMBODIA-Vietnam Conflict*

1980

1976

CHINA, Republic of (Taiwan)—*See also ADB*
'75 electn fraud rptd chrgd 1-2, 123E1
Listed as 'not free' nation 1-19, 20E3
3d ¼ '75 China trade rptd 2-12, 265G3
US force cut announced 3-11, 254E2
US bars shoe import curbs 4-16, 322C1
Bus-train collisn 4-21, 404D3
US Dem platform text cites 6-15, 478F2
Carter urges more trade 6-23, 452A1

1977

CHINA, Republic of (Taiwan)
Rpts '76 mainland quake toll 1-5, 120E2
Tanker debris found 1-7, crew rptd lost 1-11, 104E3
Praphas returns to Thailand 1-8, 47C3
'76 trade surplus rptd 1-12, 139E3
Rpts Teng back in China Cncl 1-14, 61F2
'76 econ growth rptd 2-16, 147C2
Liberia ties cut 2-23, 243D3
Oil spill rptd off Keelung 3-3, 214C3

1978

CHINA, Republic of (Taiwan)
Freedom House lists as partly free 44A2
Kuomintang reshuffled 1-6, 38A2
'77 GNP, income, price data rptd 1-9, 38E1
6 sentncd on spy chrgs 1-17, 38C1
A-capability by '79 seen 1-26, 61B2
Chiang elected pres 3-21, 251A1
Chiang sworn pres; names premr, Kuomintang head 5-20, 401G3

1979

CHINA, Republic of (Taiwan)
Oppositn ldr arrested as spy 1-21, 116E1
'79-80 budget set, defns funds hiked 4-1, 286B2
Taipei blast kills 18 6-13, 572C3
Offshore territorial, econ zones extended 9-6, 733F3
Tanker, freighter collide off US 11-1; 15 rptd dead 11-9, 955A1

1980

CHINA, Republic of (Taiwan)—*See also ADB*
Freedom House lists as partly free 87E3
Dec '79 arrests protested 1-3—1-24, 102A2
'79 protesters tried 3-18—3-28, sentenced for seditn 4-18, 316E1
Journalist sentenced 5-15, 375D2
Rev Kao, 9 others sentncd 6-5, 468B1

1976

Liu Wen-hui dies 6-24, 524G3
Canada disputes Olympic role, US scores 7-11—7-17; Taiwan quits 7-16, 528F3
Japan warns US vs policy chng 7-12, China protests 7-16, 7-19, 555E2
Ex-min cleared of bribery 8-6, 679D2
US GOP platform com OKs plank 8-13, 582A3
Praphas quits for Thailand 8-15, returns 8-22, 640C1-A2
US GOP platform text cites 8-18, 609D3, 610A2
CAE restores China ties 8-20, Taiwan natls rptd ousted 8-27, 949B2
Opera barred from Denmark 8-21, 712G1
A-fuel reprocessing rptd 8-29, 732D1
A-bomb capacity rptd 8-29, 760G3
Barbados warns re ties 9-3, 673E1
Mao's death rptd celebrated 9-10, 657G2
To halt A-fuel reprocessing 9-14, 858D2
Ford, Carter debate 10-6, 741E2, 742C1
IMF takes no actn on ouster 10-8, 778D2
Kissinger sees Chiao 10-9, 858B1
Chiang heads Kuomintang 11-18, 890D3
8 pro-Peking agents sentncd 11-27, 949C3
Executn plan chrgd 11-27; Chiang: 254 dissidents jailed 12-25, 1007G1

CHINAMANO, Josiah
Rhodesia conf delegate 10-14, 781D2

CHING Ti
Attacked in Nanking posters 7-19, 555D2

CHINH, Truong
United Viet assemb com chrmn 7-3, 502F3
In Politburo 12-19, 967E3

CHIPENDA, Daniel
FNLA-Unita clashes rptd 1-10—1-27, 58A1

CHIRAC, Jacques
Govt programs outlined 1-14, 49F2
Wine growers vs Italy imports 1-14, 138B3
On arms sales policy 1-15, 1-25, 126E2, G2
Visits Brittany 1-16—1-17, 139B1
In India, signs pacts 1-22—1-26, 139E2
Bars regional autonomy 2-24, 205B1
Visits Chad 3-5—3-6, 204F3
Ends Libya visit 3-22, 239B3
To coordinate parlt coalitn 3-26; scores left 3-27, 4-1, 312B3
Meets Sadat 4-3—4-5, 275E1
Sees Giscard 6-6—6-7, 417E3
Spain premier visits 7-13, 541C3
Quits as premier 8-25, 637C3
Drought aid announced 8-25, 675D1
Barre names new Cabt 8-27, 651C1
Regains parlt seat 11-14, 872A3
Forms new party 12-5, 963D3

1977

Thai coup plotters barred 3-27, 243B2
Viet refugees barred 6-8, 497A2
Forgn investmts encouraged 6-20, 467B3
Typhoons hit 7-25, 7-31, 928D3
Jan-July trade surplus rptd 8-14, 641G2
Econ expansion planned 9-22, 783D2

Obituaries
Ma Chao-chun 9-19, 788F1
Yang Sen 5-15, 452G3

Peking Relations—*See CHINA, People's Republic of—Taiwan Relations*

Sports
Baseball team wins Little League title 8-27, 768B2

U.S. Relations
US shoe-import injury ruled 1-6; Carter bars curbs, talks underway 4-1, 248D1, D2-B3
CIA paymts to Chiang Kai-shek rptd 1-19, 124E1
US adopts fishing agrmt 2-21, 173D3
US modifies duty-free list 2-28, 189E3
US rules TV import injury 3-8, tariff hike asked 3-14, 208D3
Nixon '72 vow to Chou rptd 4-10, 298A3
US shoe export prelim pact OKd 5-14, 416C2
Shoe export pact signed 6-14, 587E2
Peking vs more US scholar exchngs 6-28, 505G3
US backs full Peking ties 6-29, Taiwan warns 7-2; Peking vows force 7-4, 513F3
Carter backs Peking ties 6-30, 515F1
Peking pilot defects 7-8, 537B1
US stresses ties 8-18—8-19, 645A2
Carter gets letters on ties 8-20, 664F2
US-Peking talks on Taiwan ties 8-22—8-25, 645A1
Peking asks end to US-Taiwan ties 8-22, 645F1
US briefs on Vance Peking trip 8-26, 664E2
Peking vs US stand 8-29, 664A3
Peking says Ford vowed break 9-6, Ford denies 9-7, 686E3-687B1
Witteveen scores shoe pact 9-26, 753F3
Peking vs US arms sales 10-2, 10-4, 781A1

CHINAGLIA, Giorgio
Cosmos win NASL title, sets scoring record 8-28, 676F2

CHINAMANO, Joseph
Rpts natlist arrests 6-30, 536D2

CHINA Sea
S Korea-Japan oil pact signed 6-8, 467A2

CHINCHILLA Carcamo, Gen. Mario
Named Honduras staff chief 1-3, 45E1

CHINKULI, Gen. Kingsley
Named Zambia mines min 4-24, 490G1

CHIORATO, Elena Lima de
Kidnaped 9-6, 710F2

CHIPIMO, Elias
Urges Zambia natlizatn end 6-16, 490C2

CHIPP, Donald
Resigns from Liberal Party 3-24, 280F3
On Greensborough by-electn 11-18, 922D3
Wins Sen seat 12-10, 963A3

CHIRAC, Jacques
Servan-Schreiber wins electn 1-6, 63A2
Backers score de Broglie case 1-9, 44F1
To run for mayor of Paris 1-19, 63C1
Munic electns 3-13, 3-20; in d'Ornano pact 3-15; elected Paris mayor 3-20, 221A1, D1
New Cabinet named 3-30, 239E1
On left '78 electn victory 4-3, 255F2
Assemb passes econ plan 4-28, 328C3
Backs Quebec separatism 4-29, 346A3
Faure loses Radical electn 5-15, 450A1
Soisson vows cooperatn 5-20, 449F3
Vs Eur Parlt direct electns 6-16, 598D1
Greets Brezhnev 6-21, 495E1
Parisien Libere strike ends 8-16, 654E3
4 govt parties set electn agrmt 10-21, 924B2
Sees Giscard on '78 electns 12-7; stresses unity 12-8, bars coalitn platform 12-13, 1012E2

1978

Quakes hit 9-1—9-6, '78 total: 43 9-6, 759C1
Parlt electns delayed, forgn min quits 12-16, 974C2
Arms spending hiked 12-18, 974E2

Foreign Relations (misc.)—*See also 'Monetary, Trade, Aid & Investment' below*
Laos, Viet bar from air lane 2-11, 140B1
PI occupies Spratly isle 3-11, 290G1
Japan LDP ldrs rptd vs China talks 4-7, 278C2
Senkakus claim cited 4-16, 278E1
Ethnic Chinese evacuatn from Viet set 6-20, 464A3
Libya retains links, sets Peking ties 8-9, 691F2
Rescues Viet refugees 12-4, 932C3
Thailand sees contd US links 12-16, 977D1
Viet refugee boat chngs course 12-19, 997F2

Monetary, Trade, Aid & Investment
'77 trade surplus rptd 1-10, 38F1
US textile agrmt rptd 2-27, 140B3
US A-fuel export license deferral rptd 5-20, 408B2
US bars jet sale 6-30, 506C1
US OKs Israeli jet sale 7-2, 7-4, Taiwan rejcts 7-6, 524D2
US bars stainless steel utensil tariff hike 7-2, 805G1
Currency revalued 7-10, 574B3
Trade surplus cuts set 7-17, 574D3
US demands contd arms sales 9-19, 12-7, Peking acquiesces 12-16, 973E2, 974B1-E1
Peking oil claims cited 10-16, 871G2
US again bars advanced jet sale, OKs more F-5s, Kfirs 11-6, 872E2
Peking asks trade, mail svc 12-31, 995C1

Peking Relations—*See CHINA, People's Republic of—Taiwan Relations*

Sports
Little League title won 8-26, 779F2

U.S. Relations
US troop presence rptd 1-2, 5D2
US '77 study warns vs Far East troop cuts 1-6, 5E3
CIA sees A-capability by '79 1-26, 61B2
Textile agrmt rptd 2-27, 140B3
Peking links US exit, ties 5-20, 384F2
A-fuel export license deferral rptd 5-20, 408B2
US bars jet sale 6-30, 506C1
US OKs Israel jet sale 7-2, 7-4, Taiwan rejcts 7-6, 524D2
US bars stainless steel utensil tariff hike 7-2, 805G1
Currency revalued up vs US$ 7-10, 544B3
US demands contd arms sales 9-19, 12-7, Peking acquiesces 12-16, 973E2, 974B1-E1
US cites Peking oil claims 10-16, 871G2
Peking asks US cut ties 10-25, 802C1
US again bars advanced jet sale, OKs more F-5s, Kfirs 11-6, 872E2
US reduces mil force 11-6, 872A3
US-Peking ties agreed 12-14, announced 12-15, 12-16; US to end Taiwan defns pact, retain other ties 973A1
Texts of US announcemt 12-15; US, Peking, Chiang statemts publshd 12-17, 975A1-976C3; text of '72 Shanghai communique 976D2
US domestic reactn to Peking ties 12-15—12-20, congressmen plan suit 12-15, 974A3, 975A3-976E1
Chiang denounces US on Peking ties 12-16, 12-18, thanks US 'friends' 12-16; anti-US demonstratns 12-16, 12-17, 974F1
Thailand sees contd US interest 12-16, 977D1
US sees contd ties, no Peking invasn 12-17, 973B2
US congressmen sue vs defns treaty end 12-22, Admin defends actn 12-27, 995B2
Mobs attack US delegatn 12-27, talks on future ties fail 12-28—12-29, 994A3
Amb to US leaves post 12-29, **ties formally ended 12-31, 994D3-995B1**

CHINAGLIA, Giorgio
NASL scoring ldr 8-6, 655E1, C2
On NASL All-Star team 8-20, wins scoring award 8-23, in NASL title game 8-27, 707D2, G2, B3

CHINCHILLA, Maj. Jose Enrique
Sentncd in '75 land reform murders 2-2, 194C2

CHIN Chi-wei
Named Peking pol head 11-22, 950G1

CHINESE Americans
Firecracker ban review refused by Sup Ct 3-27, 241D2
Oil of wintergreen warning issued 8-17, 727F3

CHINSAMY, Y. S.
At nonwhite united front mtg 1-11, 20C3

CHIPPEWA Indians—*See INDIANS, American*

CHIRAC, Jacques
Carter declines to visit 1-4—1-6, 2G1
Guena on Barre electn program 1-11, 54F2
Gaullists break govt electn pact 1-11, plays down split 1-13, 54D3
Backs Giscard on leftist bar 1-27, 70F3
Campaign speech rouses Gaullists 2-11, 149A1
Govt coalitn wins legis electns 3-12, 3-19, 200B3, F3
Claims electn victory, Barre disputes 3-20; rift seen 3-21, 201D1

1979

Coal conversn, other indl projcts rptd; Jan–Sept oil consumptn down 11-6, 952C3
'80-90 growth plan set; '79 growth, Jan–Sept inflatn rptd 12-3, 952F2, C3

Atomic Energy & Safeguards
A-policy affirmed despite US accident 4-3, 246G2
A-power program to continue 4-6, 323C2

Foreign Relations (misc.)—*See also 'Monetary' below*
Peking vs Sovt interference 1-9, 26D3
Portugal backs Peking claim 2-8, 134D3
Pilots to fly jets for N Yemen 5-29, 395F1
Indochina refugee entry barred, aid offered 6-21, 474C2
PI flights OKd by Peking 7-8, 567D1
Spratly I annexed by PI 9-7, 660C3

Monetary, Trade, Aid & Investment
US OKd arms shipmt ban in Peking tie talks 1-12, 27D1
US businessmen assured re trade 1-15, 27B2, G2
US '78 trade total rptd 1-15, 27A3
US color-TV export limit OKd, '78 data cited 1-17, 160B2
Dollar floated 2-1, 98C3
Debt to US rptd past due 2-5, 84C3
Sovt bloc, China trade bar affirmed 11-28, 952B3
Forgn mkt expansn set; Jan–Sept exports rptd, '80 2-way trade forecast 12-3, 952B3
Japan Jan–Oct trade rptd 12-4, 952F3

Obituaries
Chang Kuo-tao 12-4, 1008C2

Peking Relations—*See CHINA–Taiwan Relations*

Sports
Pitcher sets Little League strikeout mark 8-23, team wins title 8-25, 797G2
FIFA readmits mainland China 10-14, 1004F2
Olympic 2-China plan suit filed 11-15, IOC OKs plan 11-26, 1000C3

U.S. Relations—*See also 'Atomic' and 'Monetary' above*
US cuts ties, sets Peking ties 1-1, 2B1
Carter sees peaceful Peking setlmt 1-17, 29D3
Carter proposes legis on relatns, to veto anti-Peking bills 1-26, 66E2
US reactn to Teng visit 1-28, 1-29, 66B1, F1
Pvt institute to continue US ties 2-15, 146F1-A2
China Viet invasn collusn chrgd 2-18, 123F1
US Emb closes 3-1, 146B3
Student enrollmt in US rptd 167D2
Peking vs US ties 3-16, 4-19, 312A1
US-Taiwan relatns bill signed 4-10, 259C2
Cross named Amer inst head 4-21, 299E2
Pilots to fly US jets for N Yemen 5-29, 395F1
US cong defns treaty suit dismissed, Sen rebukes Carter 6-6, 440F1, B2
US denies spy aid 8-9, 664C2
US, Peking discuss 8-28, 644E2
Carter loses defns treaty suit 10-17, 777A1
US blamed for econ growth decline 11-6, new mkts sought 11-28, 952G2
Carter defns treaty abrogatn upheld 11-30, 919D1
Defns treaty case refused by US Sup Ct 12-13, 940A1

CHINAGLIA, Giorgio
NASL scoring ldr 8-12, 654F3, 655A1
Named to NASL All-Star team 8-27, 776E1

CHINA Grove, N.C.—*See NORTH Carolina*

CHINA Syndrome, The (film)
Released 3-16, 3 Mile A-accident impact rptd 3-29, 4-1, 243C1, 246D3, 528G1*
Top-grossing film 4-4, 271F2; 5-2, 356F2

CHINCHILLA (play)
Opens 6-4, 711B2

CHINESE Americans
Calif newspr loses libel case 4-18, 334C2

CHIPANGA, William
Freed 5-6, 374C3

CHIPPERFIELD, Ron
Sets WHA playoff scoring record 5-18, Winnipeg wins title 5-20, 448C1

CHIPPEWA Indians—*See INDIANS, American*

CHIRAC, Jacques
Gaullist support rptd 1-15, 135G1
Vs concessns to EC natns 2-10–2-11, 135E1
Scored at UDF parley 2-17–2-18, 135C1, F1
Reelected RPR head 3-31, scores Giscard 4-3, 267B3
Eur Parlt electns held 6-10, 433B2
'80 budget scored 10-19, 834E3

1980

Kuomintang wins parlt electns 12-6, 969D3

Economy & Labor
Defns-GNP ratio rptd 2-19, 132G1
'79 top 500 sales rptd up 7-4, 567G2-B3

Foreign Relations (misc.)—*See also 'Monetary' below*
China claims Spratly, Paracel I 1-30, 132D3
Bolivia mil govt recognized 7-31, 577F1
S Africa prime min visits 10-13—10-17, 831D2

Monetary, Trade, Aid & Investment
US OKs arms sale, bars long-range planes 1-3, 11F2-A3
China concerned re US arms sale plan 1-8, 11E2
'79 US trade growth, surplus rptd 1-10, 102G2
China OKs custom-free exports 4-7; US trade sought 4-9, 295C2
IMF removes, debt setlmt rptd 4-17, 302C2
US seeks TV import curbs extensn 5-13, 368A2
World Bank expels 5-15, 389C1
US eases TV import curbs 6-30, 515C3
1st 1/2 trade deficit rptd 7-11, 567E2
S Africa uranium deal, trade cited 10-17, 831E2, A3
Japan trade talks fail, '81 missn set 11-28, 967C1

Peking Relations—*See CHINA–Taiwan Relations*

Sports
Lake Placid Olympics controversy 1-15—2-12, team excused 2-13, 154D3
IOC bans from Moscow Olympics 5-27, 420D3
Little League title won 8-30, 796G2

U.S. Relations—*See also 'Monetary' above*
Dec '79 arrests protested by US delegatn, Chinese-Americans 1-19—1-24, 102A2
US policy scored by Reagan 2-20, 129D3
Reagan 'basic speech' excerpts 2-29, 207G3
Reagan backs '2-China' policy 5-18, Peking vs 6-13—6-15, 452B3
US GOP platform adopted 7-15, 537A1
Reagan backs ties, triggers China rift 8-16—8-26, 645E2
Reagan stance scored by Lucey 8-25, 646F3
Woodcock scores Reagan remarks 8-26, 664D3
Reagan policy scored by Peking 9-7, 678A1
'Nondiplomatic' pact signed 10-2, Peking scores 10-4, 762E1
Reagan electn win welcomed 11-5, 841E2

CHINAGLIA, Giorgio
Sets NASL career scoring mark 5-9, NASL scoring ldr 8-24, 769F3, 770D3
Cosmos win Challenge Cup 5-26, 771A1
Sets NASL playoff scoring mark 8-31; Cosmos win NASL title; named playoff, Soccer Bowl MVP 9-21, 770D2, E2

CHIN A Sen, Henk R. (Surinamese president)
Confrms mercenary coup attempt 5-6, 410A3
Named Surinam pres 8-13, 653F2

CHINESE Americans
Taiwan crackdown protested 1-19, 102E2
San Fran gang ldr convicted of murder 3-10, 238A2

CHINKULI, Gen. Kingsley
China pledges Tanzam RR aid 9-2, 731B2

CHIPP, Don
Labor coalitn wins Sen control 11-12, 885F1

CHIRAC, Jacques
Scores Giscard 2-25, 192G3
Scores UK re EC budget contributn 3-17, 242G2
Details econ plan 4-14, 312B2
Debre enters pres race 6-30, 522D1

1976

CHIRAU, Jeremiah
Named to Rhodesia Cabt 4-27, 295B2
Quits Cabt, forms party 12-29, 1009G3
CHISHOLM, Rep. Shirley (D, N.Y.)
Equal-time rules upheld 4-12, 282F1
Sup Ct bars equal-time review 10-12, 765E3
Reelected 11-2, 830A2
Foley voted Dem Caucus chrmn 12-6, 919G1
CHISSANO, Joachim
Nigeria aids Rhodesia guerrillas 7-6, 488A1
CHITACUMBI, Ruben
Denies MPLA mil claims 1-25, 57F1
CHI Teng-kuei
Hua named 'acting' premr 2-7, 117D2
Listed in China ldrship 9-10, 712A1
CHITEPO, Herbert (d. 1975)
Murder rpt released 4-9, guerrilla chrgd 4-21, 428G1-C2
CHITTENDEN Trust (Burlington, Vt.)
Rpts Canada deposits up 11-21, 903F3
CHIZOVA, Nadezhda
Wins Olympic medal 7-31, 576B2
CHLOROFORM—*See CHEMICALS*
CHOCHISHVILI, Shota
Wins Olympic medal 7-31, 575B1
CHOI Kyu Hah
Elected premier 3-12, 223A2
Warns more crackdowns 3-16, 223G1
CHOIRBOYS, The (book)
On best seller list 1-25, 80B3; 2-29, 208E3; 12-5, 972E2
CHOI Yong Kun
Dies 9-20, 970B2
CHONG Bo
Reports executions 4-21, 350F1
CHOQUETTE, Auguste
Accuses MPs 5-6, probe voted 5-7, 350B2
CHORUS Line, A (play)
Wins Pulitzer Prize 5-3, 352C3
Long run listed 12-31, 1014G3
CHOU En-lai
Facts on 9C1
Dies 1-8, 8G2
'Pol will' disavowed 2-6, 118A1
Hua named 'acting' premr 2-7, 117C1
Anti-Teng drive launched 2-10, 189A1-F1, A2
Hua sees Nixon 2-21—2-26, 189C3
US sets Taiwan force cut 3-11, 254E2
Backers rally 4-1—4-4, riot 4-5, 244A1
Teng ousted 4-7, 243C3
Prov unrest rptd 4-10, 4-22, 333C1
USSR scored re rally riot 5-18, 439G1
Chu Teh buried 7-11, 521B1
Mao dies 9-9, 6 seen as successors 9-9—9-10, 657D1, 658F1, G1
Cited in Mao biog 658F2
Mao mourning period ends 9-18, 711G3
Cited in Hua biog 758C1
Radical attacks rptd 10-24, 10-25, 809C2, G2
CHOUINARD, Julien
On air safety comm 6-28, 481G2
CHOU Jung-hsin
Rptdly repents errors 3-25, 266A1
Rptd purged from ldrshp 9-11, 712B1
CHOWCHILLA, Calif.—*See CALIFORNIA*
CHRETIEN, Jean
Rpts '76-77 spending plans 2-18, 188C1
Judicial interference chrgd 2-20; denied, libel suit weighed 3-3, 3-4, 187G3
Cleared in Deschaines rpt, '70 incident cited 3-12, 220F3
On Olympics lottery takeover 5-15, 529A2
Air pact talks cited 7-1, 496A3
Discounts bilingualism rpt 8-17, 637G1
Sworn industry min 9-15, 692D1
On Statistics Canada probe 10-20; rpts to parlt 11-3, 870A3
Parlt plans statistics hearings; defends GNP data 11-15, 888G2
On clothing import curb 11-29, 924G1
CHRIST, Disciples of—*See CHRISTIAN Church*
CHRISTIAN, Betty Jo
ICC member 12-8-75; confrmd 3-18, 232C1
CHRISTIAN, Desmond
Rptd deported from Grenada 12-7, 925A2
CHRISTIAN Church
Carter addresses conv 6-19, 452B1
Paraguay arrests 6 workers 4-10, 4-23, 403C2
CHRISTIAN Nationalist Crusade (Disciples of Christ)
Gerald L K Smith dies 4-15, 316C1
CHRISTIAN Radich (Norwegian sailing ship)
In Operation Sail 7-4, 488A3
CHRISTIAN Science Monitor (newspaper)
Rpts secret Israel-Jordan talks 1-12, 19D1
Angola ousts Wright 6-9, 480B3
CHRISTIANSEN, Ragnana
Norway transport min 1-12, 30A2
CHRISTIANSEN, Steven
FBI-terrorist ties chrgd 1-11, 42E1
CHRISTIANS and Jews, National Conference of—*See NATIONAL Conference, etc.*

1977

CHIRAU, Jeremiah S.
On Smith race reforms 2-23, 123E1
Lauds UK-US Rhodesia plan 9-2, 699A3
Rpt US bars entry 9-25, 811A3
OKs Smith majority-rule talks 11-25, 910B3
Sees Smith re majority rule 12-2—12-29, 1015F2
CHIRIBOGA, Jorge
Resignatn asked in striker deaths 10-25, 823B3
CHISSANO, Joaquim
At Frelimo cong 2-3—2-7, 137D1
CHISUPA, Remi
Named Zambia indus min 4-24, 490G1
CHI Teng-kuei
Vs more US scholar exchngs 6-28, 505F3 *
In Politburo 8-21, 645G2
CHLORDANE—*See PESTICIDES*
CHLOROFLUORCARBON—*See CHEMICALS*
CHOI Gak Kyu
S Korea commerce min 12-20, 1017D1
CHOLERA—*See MEDICINE—Diseases*
CHONA, Mainza (Zambia prime minister)
Named prime minister 7-20, 583F1
CHOU En-lai (1898-1976)—*See 1976, p. 9C1 for biog. data*
Yao chrgd re curbing praise 1-6, 1D2
Death anniversary noted 1-8, 1B2, E2
Wu Teh, Chen Hsi-lien scored 1-9, 61C2
'76 rioters freed 3-18, 220B1
Nixon '72 vow rptd 4-10, 298E2, A3
Gang of 4 chrgd 7-22, 571A3
'75 mtg with Cambodia ldr rptd 10-2, 780A1
Posters score Wu, Chen 10-20, 823F2
US rpts China '71-75 forgn trade up 11-6, 882C3
CHOU Jung-hsin (d. 1976)
Liu gets educatn post 1-29, 98B2
CHOWCHILLA, Calif.—*See CALIFORNIA*
CHRETIEN, Jean
Sees Rossi 1-9—1-12, 43E1
US-Canada trust com rptd set 6-18, 525G2
Named Canada finance min 9-16, 725G2 *
Vs Japan econ criticism 9-29, 780C3
On govt agency decentralizatn 10-3, 801C1
Sets controls end, stimulus progrm 10-20, 822A3
Bars govt actn re $ 10-20, 841C3
On footwear indus employmt 12-2, 983A1
CHRIS-Craft Industries Inc.
Sup Ct voids damage award 2-23, 150A2
CHRIST, Disciples of—*See CHRISTIAN Church*
CHRISTIANA Securities Co.
Du Pont merger OKd 6-16, 518A1
CHRISTIAN Church (Disciples of Christ)
United Church of Christ proposes merger 7-5, 642D2
CHRISTIAN Dior—*See DIOR, House of*
CHRISTIANITY Today (magazine)
B Graham fund disclosed 6-26, 731G3
CHRISTIAN Science Monitor (newspaper)
Rpts Israel arms sales to Greece, Turkey 1-6; Israel denies chrg 1-7, 28C3
On most reliable govt news source list 12-10, 1009B1

1978

Sees Giscard 3-26—3-31, 245F3
Barre renamed premr 3-31, 245D2
Faure loses Assemb pres bid 4-3, 245A3
Rpts truce with Barre govt 10-10, 815A3
Attacks Giscard 12-6, Gaullists quarrel 12-13—12-19, 987E1-E2
Peyrefitte suspended 12-20, 1016D3
CHIRAU, Chief Jeremiah
Facts on 59B2
Scores Muzorewa walkout 1-27, 59B3
OKs majority-rule pact 2-15, in transitn govt talks 2-16—2-20, 119B2-B3
Signs internal pact 3-3, 154A3
Sworn state cncl member 3-21, 210A2
Reveals pol detainees freed 4-6, 290F3
Council of mins sworn 4-14, 291B1
Sees Owen, Vance 4-17, 290E3
Black min ousted 4-28; govt split threatened, probe set 4-28—5-2, 317G1, C2
Govt split averted despite black ouster 5-14, 376G3
In US 10-15—10-20, 818D3
Armed backers cited 11-7, 867D3
Ndiweni quits ZUPO post 11-8, 884G2
Sees Botha 11-15; warning vs vote delay rptd 11-23, 912B2
Backs electn delay 11-16, 893B2
CHISHOLM, Rep. Shirley Anita (D, N.Y.)
Reelected 11-7, 851D3
CHI Teng-kuei
Replaced in Peking post 11-22, 950G1
CHITNIS, Lord (Pratap Chidamber)
El Salvador repressn scored 12-10, 987D1
CHLOE (French couture house)
'78 high chic fashion rptd 8-4—8-11, 10-27—11-3, 1029D2
CHLORDIMEFORM—*See PESTICIDES*
CHLORINE—*See CHEMICALS & Chemistry*
CHOATE, Judge Raymond
Awards Calif woman Synanon damages 9-19, 841D3
CHOCK Full O'Nuts Corp.
Uganda coffee ban backed 5-19, 416F3
CHOCOLATE—*See COCOA*
CHOICES (play)
Opens 12-10, 1031C1
CHOLERA—*See MEDICINE—Diseases*
CHOLESTEROL
2 new drugs rptd 5-27, 1023G1
FTC egg ad case declined by Sup Ct 10-2, 751D2
CHOMSKY, Marvin H.
Wins Emmy 9-17, 1030F1
CHONG, Tommy
Up In Smoke released 9-22, 970C3
CHONG Chun Gi
Vs S Korea trade bid 6-23, 497F2
CHOU En-lai (1898-1976)—*See 1976, p. 9C1 for biog. data*
Widow heads group to China 1-18, 42C3
Teng cleared of '76 riots 2-15, 111D2
Wu '76 riot role scored 4-7, 287E3
Chinese get 1st cigaret warning 8-28, 727B2
'76 Peking rioters cleared 11-19, 901A3
Posters ask '76 Peking riot probe 11-20, 949E1
US-China ties agreed 12-14, 973F1
Shanghai communique text excerpts 976D2
Widow named to Politburo 12-22, 1015F1
CHOWCHILLA, Calif.—*See CALIFORNIA*
CHRETIEN, Jean
Sees Sun Life offcls on relocatn 1-12, 35E3
Sets forgn loan to boost C$ 2-21, 129E3
Sets US standby fund increase 4-3, 244E1
Introduces '78-79 budget 4-10, 265F3
Cuts Quebec tax compensatn 4-13, 286C3
Confirms W Ger, US loans 5-1, 328D1
Rpts US loan set 5-3, 370E2
Sets Quebec tax rebate 5-15, 369G3
MP ejected in Quebec tax dispute 5-16, 391G2
Settles Quebec tax dispute 6-8, 451B2
Bars '78 Quebec tax credit 6-16, 495F1
Sees prov finance mins; sets tax rebate end, Loto Canada extensn 7-6, 531A2
Stevens scores re tax rebate letter 8-1, 613D3
Details budget cuts, gas deregulatn 8-24, 666C2, F2-C3
Sets further spending cuts 9-8, 739B1
Bars spec C$ support 9-27, 813F2
Scores PC mortgage tax relief 9-28, 755B2
Sets revised '78-79 budget 11-16, 900F3
CHRIST, Disciples of—*See CHRISTIAN Church*
CHRIST, United Church of—*See UNITED Church of Christ*
CHRISTIAN, Desmond
Queries Jones's son on Amos murder 12-18, indicted 12-19, 1000B1
CHRISTIAN, George
Son kills teacher 5-18, 396B2
CHRISTIAN, John Daniel
Kills teacher 5-18, 396A2
CHRISTIANBURG Garment Co. v. E.E.O.C.
Employers curbed on bias-case legal fees 1-23, 65A2
CHRISTIAN Church (Disciples of Christ)
Roy Ross dies 1-8, 96D3
Female clergy survey rptd 3-23, 295G1
CHRISTIAN Council, United—*See UNITED Christian Council*
CHRISTIAN Science Monitor (newspaper)
Strout wins Pulitzer citation 4-17, 315A1
CHRISTIANSEN, Arne
Named Danish trade min 8-30, 688A1

1979

CHIRAU, Chief Jeremiah
Rhodesian dispute role described 170C3
Whites OK draft const 1-30, 77B1
In Rhodesian electn 4-17—4-21, 293E1
On Commonwealth Zimbabwe plan 8-6, 589E2
CHIRIMBANI, John
Rhodesia parlt speaker 5-8, 354D1
CHIROPRACTORS
AMA chrgd in NY trust suit 7-5, 570E2
CHISHOLM, Rep. Shirley Anita (D, N.Y.)
On Camp David mtg 6-2, 418D2
Scores Educ Dept bill amendmts 7-11, 514E3
CHLOE (French couture house)
'79 fashion roundup rptd 1006C2
CHLORINE—*See CHEMICALS*
CHO, C. H.
Named in McDonnell Douglas paymts chrg 11-9, 886D2
CHO, C. K.
Named in McDonnell Douglas paymts chrg 11-9, 886D2
CHOI Kyu Hah (South Korean president)
Named acting ROK pres 10-26, urges unity 10-27, 821B1, 822A1
Meets Vance 11-3, 843F3
Announces electn plans 11-10, 875B2
Pres electn plan protested, dissidents seized 11-24, 928B2
Elected pres 12-6, lifts dissident decree 12-7, 951E3-952D2
Names pemr 12-10, Cabt 12-14; inaugurated 12-21, 997E1
CHOLERA—*See MEDICINE–Diseases*
CHO Lin
Visits US with Teng 1-28, 66B2
CHONG Mun Su
Arrested 4-13, 287C2
CHON Too Hwan, Maj. Gen.
Leads army rebels 12-12; shifts cmnd 12-13, 959B3, C3
CHOU En-lai (1898-1976)
Rally marks death anniv 1-8, 58B3
Rights drive curbed 3-31, 259B2
Widow rptd corruptn drive ldr 8-22, 651F3
CHOUFI, Mahoud el-
Denies Jewish rights abuse 2-22, 148A3
CHOU Yang
Promotion rptd 9-28, 750E3
CHRETIEN, Carmelina
Husband sentncd in rape case 9-24, 819A2
CHRETIEN, James K.
Sentncd for wife's rape 9-24, 819F1
CHRETIEN, Jean
Defends govt job policy 2-6, 134B2
Creates new inflatn comm 3-2, 168B2
In Trudeau shadow cabt 7-19, 563G2
Inflation comm disbanded 7-25, 581G1
Crosbie on '79-80 budget 7-26, 613A1
CHRIST, Disciples of—*See CHRISTIAN Church*
CHRISTENSEN, Ione
Quits as Yukon cncl comr 10-10, 833G3
CHRISTIAN, Henkell
Resigns 6-16, 468E2
CHRISTIAN Church (Disciples of Christ)
Baptism rites agrmt reached 3-31, 375A3
CHRISTIAN Conference of Asia
Rpts Pnompenh famine threat 8-23, 684B2
CHRISTIANITY—*See also religious denominations*
Khomeini views publshd 50C1
Pope cites re Poland history 6-4, 413D2
Carter discloses Park conversn effort 8-5, 639B2
S Korea teachers chrg torture 8-6—8-10, 654A1
Uganda ban rescinded 11-7, 998D2
CHRISTIANS and Jews, National Conference of—*See NATIONAL Conference, etc.*

1980

CHIRICO, Giorgio de (1888-1978)
Loren art collectn claim rptd denied 2-9, 200B2
CHIROPRACTORS
NYS civil rights suit filing limit upheld by Sup Ct 5-19, 440G2
AMA adopts ethics code 7-22, 583F2
CHISHOLM, Rep. Shirley Anita (D, N.Y.)
Scores Haitian refugee policy 6-17, lauds reprieve 6-20, 484E3, 485B1
Addresses Urban League 8-3, 597F2
Wins econ platform plank 8-12, 611A1
Reelected 11-4, 843E3
Ferraro gets House caucus post 12-8, 936E2
CHLOE (French couture house)
'80 fashion roundup rptd 12-31, 998C2
CHLORINE—*See CHEMICALS*
CHLORINE Institute Inc. v. OSHA
Chlorine rules partial stay granted by Sup Ct 5-19, 440B3
CHLOROQUIN—*See MEDICINE--Drugs & Health-Care Products*
CHOI Kyu Hah (South Korean president; resigned Sept. 16)
17 protesters sentnced 1-25, 2 spared 1-29, 101D1
Amnesties 687 dissidents 2-29, 195C3
Slanderous statemts barred 5-18, 380F2
Vows political reforms 5-18, 380G2
Visits Kwangju, urges peace 5-25, 394B3
Security com formed 5-31, 430E2
Chon sees mil ldrship 8-8, 620A3
Resigns 8-16, Chun replaces 8-27, 645G1, B2
CHOJECKI, Miroslaw
Rptd cleared 5-15, 381B2
CHOLESTEROL
US dietary guidelines issued 2-4, 157A3
Exercise, low blood levels linked 2-14, 158F1
Drug risks rptd, warning issued 2-17, 159G2
NAS rpt discounts health impact 5-27, stirs controversy 6-1, 432E2
CHOMBA, Frederick
Named Zambia home affairs min 12-4, 969G2
CHOMSKY, Marvin
Wins Emmy 9-7, 692D1
CHONES, Jim
Lakers win NBA title 5-16, 432F1
CHON Too Hwan—*See CHUN Doo Hwan*
CHOPER, Jesse H.
Sup Ct '79-80 term analyzed 7-2, 540G2
CHORNOVIL, Vyacheslav
Sovt sentence 6-9, 680C3
CHOUDHURY, Abu Sayeed
Rejcts Iran probe comm apptmt 2-17, 122C1
CHOU En-lai—*See ZHOU Enlai*
CHOUFI, Hammoud el-
Quits UN post 12-27-79, 22F2
CHRETIEN, Jean
Named Canada justice min 3-3, 171A2
Treu denied compensatn 3-17, 211D1
Prelim const talks held 7-8—7-24, 603A1
Backs Canada patriatn plan 12-10, 964B3
CHRISTENSON, Larry
In World Series 10-14—10-21, 812G1
CHRISTIAN Church (Disciples of Christ)
Protestant unity mtg ends, common ministry OKd 1-24, 156G2
Intercommunion poll rptd 4-4, 413A3
CHRISTIAN Freedom Foundation
Political actn profiled 7-11—9-15, 819G1
CHRISTIANITY
Conservatives hold DC rally 4-29, 348C3-349B1
Sioux Falls (SD) schls case refused by Sup Ct 11-10, 868A2
Domestic violence victims bill dropped 11-17, 982A2
CHRISTIAN Methodist Episcopal Church
See under METHODISTS
CHRISTIAN Science Monitor (newspaper)
'79 Afghan massacre rptd 2-4, 85A2
Ellis on pres TV debate panel 10-28, 813F1
CHRISTIANSEN, Robert
Hide in Plain Sight released 3-21, 216G2

1976

CHRISTIE, Agatha
Dies 1-12, 56B3
Curtain on best seller list 1-25, 80B3; 2-29, 208E3; 12-5, 972E2
Sleeping Murder on best-seller list 12-5, 972G2

CHRISTIE, John D.
FEA asst admin 2-12; confrmd 3-23, 232D1

CHRISTMAS, June
Carter transition aide 11-23, 881C3

CHRISTOPHER, Warren M.
Named State dep secy 12-31, 978D3

CHRISTOPHIDES, John
Chrgs Greek Cypriot expulsns continue 6-16, 457C1

CHRISTOVA, Ivanka
Wins Olympic medal 7-31, 576B2

CHROME & Chromite
Kissinger vs Byrd amendmt 4-27, 293E1, 294F1
Carter scores Ford Rhodesia stand 5-14, 390F3
US Dem platform text cites Byrd amendmt 6-15, 478E3

CHRYSLER Corp.
UK bailout plan signed 1-5; layoffs, terms rptd 1-14, 1-23, 72F3
Mich police file access chrgd 1-18, 45A2
Spain strike continues 1-19, 54D3
UK strike ends 2-3, 174A2
US may buy Ger tank 2-12, 183C2
'75, 4th ¼ profits rptd 2-24, 215C3
Workers denied Trade Act aid 4-14, 348G2
Argentina exec killed 4-14, 398G3
On '75 Fortune 500 list 437B1
US ends car dumping probe 5-4, 321D2
Total Trade Act aid rptd 6-7, 431B2
Mich plant strike ends 7-11, 570C2
UAW opens Big 3 talks 7-19, 570F1
VW buys Pa plant 9-15, 987D3
EPA fuel-econ ratings 9-22, 766B2-770C2
US files pollutn suit 9-27, 729E3
Car prices hiked 9-30, 747A3
Australia unit plans expansn 11-2, 835A3
Sets S Africa merger 11-3, 856D1
UAW pacts reached 11-5, 11-7, 847A3
1-wk plant closings rptd 11-9, 885C2
Wins Army tank contract 11-12, 941C3
UAW pact ratified 11-17, 887G1
GM pact set 11-19, 887D1
EPA orders large recall 12-10, 942D3

1977

CHRISTIE, Agatha
Sleeping Murder on best-seller list 2-6, 120E3; 3-6, 184E3

CHRISTIE, Perry G.
Bahamas health min 7-29, 675D1

CHRISTOPHER, Warren M.
Named State dep secy 2-7, confrmd 2-24, 148D3
Brazil A-talks fail 3-2, Bonn talks planned 3-11, 189F3, 190E1
Protests Sovt fishing violatns 4-5, 4-11, 270E1
Sees Almeyda 5-27, 493D1
Protests Sovt detentn of US rptr 6-14, 475F1
Chile loans blocked 6-28, 493B1
Whitlam mtg re CIA role rptd 8-4, 632G3
On Panama Canal treaty interpretatn 10-5, 755D1
Evaluates Sadat Israel trip 11-22, 894F2

CHROME (& Chromite)
US backs Rhodesia sanctns 1-31, 72F3
US bans Rhodesia imports 3-18, 191C1
OAU chrgs US, Japan re Rhodesia imports 6-28, 512C2
US '76 Rhodesia imports rptd 7-26, 581G3
US, Japan pact vs Rhodesia imports rptd 8-3, world output cited 662E1

CHRONICLE of Higher Education (magazine)
Student loan defaults rptd 9-6, 739F2

CHRYSLER Corp.
'76 productn, sales rptd up 1-3, 1-6, 38E3, 39A1
Layoffs 4-11—4-15, May new-car sales down 6-3, 463C3, D3
Carter energy plan reactn 4-24, 320D1
On '76 Fortune 500 list 340E1
Rpts '71-76 forgn payoffs 6-13, 503F1
Air bag order scored 6-30, 522C1
Australia layoffs rptd 7-13, 560G3
EPA suit dismissed 8-22, 723E3
GM hikes '78 prices, Chrysler to follow 8-23, 722D3
Aug new-car sales rptd up 9-6, 722G2
'78 model prices linked 10-6, 859B2
Argentine exec's home attacked 10-13, 921A3
Argentina exec's guards killed 12-2, 981F3
New front-drive cars unveiled 12-5—12-9, 962B1
Plant closing, layoffs planned 12-6; '77 mkt sales share rptd down 12-7, 962A1

1978

CHRISTIANSON, Larry
Phillies lose NL pennant 10-7, 779A1

CHRISTIE, Agatha (1891-1976)
Widower dies 8-19, 708B3
Death On Nile released 9-29, 970A1

CHRISTIE, Joe
Loses Sen primary in Tex 5-6, 362F3

CHRISTIE, Julie
Heaven Can Wait released 6-27, 619D2

CHRISTIE, Manson & Woods International Inc.
Gutenberg Bible auctioned 4-7, 295E2

CHRISTMAS at Candleshoe (book)
Candleshoe released 8-4, 969F3

CHRISTOPHER, Paula
Taxi Tales opens 12-29, 1031A3

CHRISTOPHER, Warren M.
Chrgs Cambodia rights breach 1-18, 43G1
Dispatched to Turkey 3-29; briefs Carter arms embargo end agreed 4-1, 276C2
W Ger neutron bomb pressure rptd 4-17, 253F1
Says terrorism no excuse for rights abuse 6-23, 489F3
Heads delegatn to Taiwan, attacked 12-27; talks on future ties fail 12-28—12-29, 994B3

CHRISTOPHERSEN, Henning
Named Danish forgn min 8-30, 688A1

CHRISTOPHIDES, John
Replaced as Cyprus forgn min 3-8, 189E1

CHRISTY, James W.
Discovers Pluto moon 7-7, 623G1

CHROMIUM (& Chromite)
Carter bars alloy duty rise 1-29; '77 forgn imports, Rhodesian ban cited 80E3
Mich sues Ford re pollutn 2-1, 163D3
Dutch impound Rhodesia cargo 12-13, 965D2

CHRONICLE of Higher Education (magazine)
'78-79 coll costs rise rptd 4-10, 264A2
State aid to colls rptd up 10-10, 770C2

CHRYSLER Corp.
In Dow Jones indl avg 66E2
'77 sales drop rptd 1-5, 4D3
'77 4th ¼ loss rptd 2-23, 282F3
EPA orders pollutn remedy, recall 4-20, 349C1
1st ¼ record loss rptd 4-26, 623G3
Australia job cuts, productn chngs set; '77, 1st ¼ losses rptd 5-3, 349D3, F3
On '77 Fortune 500 list 5-8, 325E1
Brazil factory strike rptd 5-22, 412D1
Small-car prices hiked 6-2, 428B2
Equity cash raised 6-20, 5-yr dvpt plan cited 8-10, 623E3-624A1
Canada, US declare Omnis, Horizons safe 6-28, 7-7, 569D3
July sales rptd down 8-3, 623C3
Peugeot to buy Eur units 8-10, 623B2-624A1
Brazil, S Africa, Turkey, Australia sell-off plans cited 8-10, 623C3
Sues to block FTC probe 9-11, 768C1
AMC, UAW sign 2-yr pact 9-25, 737B3
UK unit sale to Peugeot OKd 9-28, 764D1
Hikes '79 model prices 10-2, 936A2
Colombia store bombed 10-9, 814C3
Australia unit to be fined 10-19, 813B1
Mitsubishi to buy Australia share 10-25, 836B2
Iacocca named pres; record 3d ¼ loss, divd cut, stock price rise rptd 11-2, 936A1
Stock rises on Iacocca apptmt 11-2, 936D1
Nov sales drop rptd 12-6, 935E3
'79 model prices hiked 12-14, 1004D1

1979

CHRISTIE, Agatha (1891-1976)
Agatha released 2-8, 174C2

CHRISTIE, Judge Andrew
Sentences Pa robber 11-30, 953G2

CHRISTIE, Manson & Woods International Inc.
Blake book auctioned for record sum 6-13; Matisse, Picasso paintings 7-3, 672B1, F1

CHRISTMANN, Kurt
Arrest rptd 11-14, 876C2

CHRISTMAS Carol, A (book)
Comin' Uptown opens 12-20, 1007C2

CHRISTMAS Eve on Sesame Street (TV program)
Wins Emmy 9-9, 858E2

CHRISTOPHER, Dennis
Breaking Away released 7-17, 819F3

CHRISTOPHER, Warren M.
US-Turkey prisoner accord initialed 1-11, aid plans rptd 1-12, 40C2, A3
Protests Sovt role in Kabul shootout 2-14, 106F2
Gets Dobrynin regrets re Dubs 2-16, 147E2
In missn to Saudi, Jordan 3-17–3-18, 198B1
In Turkey for US base talks 5-7, 5-8, 397A3
China rptd vs plea on Viet refugees 6-16, 460B3
Backs Nicaragua aid 9-11, 731A3
Sees Nicaragua junta ldrs 9-24, 731D3
Urges calm re Iran emb takeover 11-8, 842D3

CHRISTOPHERSON, Stephanianne
Umbrellas Of Cherbourg opens 2-1, 292F3

CHRISTY, Arthur H.
Named Jordan cocaine probe spec prosecutor 11-29, 900C3-901A1

CHROMALLOY American Corp. v. Marshall
Case refused by Sup Ct 10-1, 768C1

CHRONICLE of Higher Education (magazine)
Pvt coll decrease rptd 3-19, 282A3
Birenbaum interviewed 6-18, 482B2

CHRYSLER Corp.
In Dow Jones indl avg 72E1
Prices hiked 1-2, 5C1
'78 sales drop rptd 1-5, 5B1
Diesel exhaust rule protested 1-10, 16E3
Spain workers strike 1-15, 61G1
Spain 14% wage hike OKd 1-24, 100D3
Wage-price compliance claimed 2-6, 128A1
Sales, mkt share drop cited; Brown resignatn rptd 2-23, 188E1
'78 loss, 4th 1/4 profit gain rptd 2-26, 188F1
New ad agency, Cafiero resignatn announced 3-1, 188B1
XM-1 tank engine problem rptd 3-2, 207A3
Price hike rptd 3-31, 305E2
Trucking stoppage over 4-10, 262D2
Reverse Freedom of Info suits curbed by Sup Ct 4-18, 345E3
On '78 Fortune 500 list 5-7, 304E1, 305F1
XM-1 tank productn OKd 5-8, 386E1
Ford firing of Iacocca scored 5-10, 366G2
Iacocca '78 recruitmt bonus rptd 5-14, 348B1
Australia unit share sold to Mitsubishi 5-14, 368F2
'Car of the future' plan set 5-18, 441D3
Mich plant to shut 5-29, 576G2
VW sale rumor denied 6-22, 576E2
Dow Jones index drops listing 6-28, 481E2
June sales drop rptd 7-5, 576B3
UAW opens contract talks; gives no-strike pledge, backs fed aid 7-18, 598A1, E1
VW joint venture in Argentina cited 7-20, 562A2
2d 1/4 loss rptd, fed aid sought 7-31, analysis; dividend omitted 8-2, 576A1-G3
GM chrmn vs fed aid 8-2, 576G3
UAW vs wage freeze plea, backs natlzn 8-3, Miller bars natlzn 8-9, 662A2, B3
Carter bars cash aid, backs loan guarantee 8-9, 8-22; Riccardo comment 8-9, 662E1-G2
Receivables, realty unit sold 8-10–8-22, 663F1
Rebate program starts 8-15, Aug sales rptd 9-5, 663F2, C3
UAW job action scored 8-22, 831A3
Exec salaries cut, savings estimated 8-30, 8-31, 662F3
Jan-Aug cost savings rptd 8-31, 662G2
Japan interests cited 9-7, 745E3
UAW reaches accord with GM 9-14, 698B1
Aid request submitted, rejctd; '79 record loss forecast, product dvpt plan outlined 9-15, 698G3-699G2
Riccardo sets resignatn 9-17, Iacocca, ex-Ford execs get top posts 9-20, 699B3
AMC chrmn backs fed aid 9-18, 699G2
Rebate end set, inventory rptd down 9-20, 700E1
Sept sales rptd up 10-4, 806B2
Financial woes cited in AMC-Renault deal 10-12, 784D3
'80 model prices hiked 10-12, 963G3
UAW accord reached, $203 mln saved 10-25, 805E2
Bank chrmn cautious re loans 10-30, 845C3

1980

CHRISTIE, Agatha (1891-1976)
Mirror Crack'd released 12-18, 1003B2

CHRISTIE, Renfrew
S Africa sentncs for espionage 6-3, 466D3

CHRISTIE Manson & Woods International Inc.
Hann icons sold for record sum 4-17, 472A3
Record art auctns held 5-12—5-16, 471G3-472A2
Da Vinci ms sold for $5.28 mln 12-12, 997E3

CHRISTOPHER, Dennis
Fade to Black released 10-17, 836F2

CHRISTOPHER, Warren M.
Arrives London 1-11; attends NATO Brussels mtg on Afghan crisis, sees Schmidt 1-15, 28E1
In Pak 2-1—2-3, 83G1; A-warning cited 2-27, 165G2
Says Sovts execute Afghans 3-28, 271G1
Defends Iran rescue missn 5-8, 338D1
Protests Saudi film telecast 5-8, 375A3
Scores Viet, USSR re Cambodia aid conf boycott 5-26, 397B2
Protests UN rejctn of Israeli constructn bid 6-19, 476C2
Urges uranium sale to India 6-19, 495B3
Backs extensn for Nicaragua refugees 6-30, 495C2
Briefs 3 Westn ldrs on hostages in Iran 9-19, 719C3
Warns Iraq vs Iran oil seizure 9-28, 735B2
Offers air defns gear to Gulf states 10-7, 758A1
In Algeria, delivers US response to Iran hostage demands 11-10—11-11; comments 11-12, 861A1, F1
In Algiers for US hostage talks 12-2—12-3; US rpts 12-4, 912F3-913A1
On new US hostage-asset plan 12-30, 973E2

CHRISTOPHER Cross (recording)
On best-seller list 8-13, 640C3; 9-10, 716F3

CHRISTOV, Valentin
Wins Olympic medal 7-29, 624G2

CHRISTY, Arthur H.
Studio 54 owners sentenced 1-18, 64D3
Grand jury clears Jordan 5-28, 402C3

CHROMIUM (& Chromite)
US defns posture, supply shortage linked 1-25, 65G2

CHRYSLER Corp.
Canadians bar UAW concessns 1-3, US contract revisns set 1-5; Carter signs aid bill 1-7, UAW council OKs pact 1-8, Mich aid set 1-9, 14A1-A2
'79 sales rptd down 1-4, 14A2
Prices hiked 1-11, 14G2
XM-1 tank full-scale productn rptd OKd 1-21, 54E3
UAW locals OK concessns 2-1, 127C2
Jan sales rptd down 2-5, 127A3
Puegot productn talks, finance deal rptd 2-6; Mitsubishi to finance imports 2-12, 127D2-G2
'79 loss sets record, viability questioned 2-7; Iacocca optimism disputed 2-13, 2-19, 127E1-C2
Horizon, Magnum-Cordoba pass crash test 2-28, 225B2
Mich loan rptd OKd 3-7, Mitsubishi to continue financing 4-1, $650 mln aid plan rptd 4-2, 287A1-D1
Prices hiked 3-7, 4-7, 288A1, C1
Ford Pinto trial evidence cited 3-13, 186C1
Griffin gets DC post 3-13, 199B3
Layoffs rptd 4-3, 287B2
Mar sales drop rptd 4-3; rebates cited for Jan, Feb sales rise 4-4, 287A3, C3
Losses seen greater 4-10, finance unit sale fails 4-11, 286E3
Aspen, Volare fender replacemt set 4-11, 288F1
White-collar staff cut 20% 4-22; Lynch R plant closing, full-size productn end set 5-16, 383F3, 384A1
Australia unit bought by Mitsubishi, '79 earnings rptd 4-30, 350E1
On '79 Fortune 500 list 5-5, 290F1, 291E1
1st 1/4 losses rptd 5-7, 384E1
Canada, US OK loan guarantees, K-cars planned 5-10; rescue law chngs rptd 5-12, 383C2
Fraser elected to bd of dirs 5-13, 383C3
Rebates offered 5-13, 384D2
US raises truck import duty 5-20, 384B2
Peugeot sales set 6-2; auto size policy chngd 6-3; VW mgrs hired 6-9; Sinatra offers aid 6-11, 457C1-G1
Steep keeps UAW post 6-4, 457C2
May sales plunge rptd 6-5, 481E3
Supplier paymts stopped 6-11, 457A1
Banks back govt plan 6-20; loan board OKs $500 mln note sale 6-24; Iacocca sees 4th 1/4 profit 6-25, 481D2
Worker layoffs rptd 6-21, 481F3
Loan guarantee bill clears Cong 515G1
Canada May, June sales down 7-5, 520A3
June sales rptd down 7-6, 556D2
Prices hiked 7-9, 556F2
GM pledges '85 fuel-efficient cars 7-9, 556F3
$250 mln loan OKd, 1st 1/2 loss rptd 7-15; cutbacks set 7-16; Peugeot engine deal confrmd, Iacocca asks tax credit 7-17, 541A2
Record 2d 1/4 loss rptd 7-31, 573F2
$300 mln loan guarantee OKd 7-31, 574A1

1976

CHTEREVA, Nikolina
Wins Olympic medal 7-26, 576F1
CHU Chiu-pai (1899-1935)
Cited in Mao death announcement 659B2
CHU Mu-chih
Rptd purged from ldrshp 9-11, 712B1
CHUNG Chung Bong
Sentenced 5-3, 334D2
CHURCH, Sen. Frank (Forrester) (D, Ida.)
Scores Lockheed payoffs 2-4, 130G1
Addresses Sovt Jews rights conf 2-17, 206A3
Ends Bonn payoff probe 3-10, 200A2
Scores Nixon testimony 3-11, 183F3
Sen com rpt transmittal letter 4-26, 300A1
Rules Com OKs temporary intellignc com 4-29, Sen creates permanent com 5-19, 376E3, 377D1
Italy pres cleared 6-15, 445D2
Listed as possible vp choice 489F3
Carter interviews 7-12, 506B2
Dem conv speech 7-13, 509D3
Nixon bid for Grumman donatn chrgd 9-13, 979C3
Sen vs forgn paymts amendmt 9-15, 708B1
Backs Uruguay mil aid ban 9-28, 814F2
FEC certificatn total rptd 12-31, 979F2
Presidential Campaign Developments
Fed fund total listed 3-4, 180C3
Enters pres race 3-18, 197D2
Scores Ford 4-19, 282A1
Loses Sup Ct funds plea 4-23, 306C1
At black Dem caucus 5-2, 343A3
Wins Neb primary 5-11, 342D1; comments 5-12, 343G1
Campaigns in Ore 5-20, 373D3
FEC funding resumed 5-21, 391E3
Wins in Ore, Ida 5-25, 373E1, F2-B3, 374D2-D3
Wins in Mont, 3d in RI 6-1, 389G2, G3-390C1, B2
Ohio, NJ primary results 6-8, 409B1, G2, F3
Primary delegates totaled 6-8, 409B3
Ends pres bid, backs Carter 6-14, 431F2, F3
Campaign debt rptd 6-16; fed funds total 7-1, 491A1, E1
FEC ends fed funds 6-23, 490F3
Dem conv pres vote, table 7-14, 507E2
CHURCH, Wade
Sup Ct bars review of libel suit 4-5, 262A2
Loses Ariz Sen primary 9-7, 687B3
CHURCHES—*See denominations, church names*
CHURCHES, All Africa Conference of—*See ALL Africa Conference of Churches*
CHURCHILL, John
On women Rhodes Scholars 12-19, 993E3
CHURCHILL, Winston
In new shadow Cabt 11-19, 1004A2
CHURCH of Christ, United—*See UNITED Church of Christ*
CHURCH of England—*See ANGLICANS*
CHU Teh
Dies 7-6, buried 7-11, 520E3
Successor named 7-24, 555G1
Cited in Mao biog 658D3
CHYUNG Yil Hyung
Sentenced 8-28, 655D1
CIA and the Cult of Intelligence, The (book)
Colby disputes CIA budget figure 3-17, 217F1
CIBA-Geigy Corp.
US files consent decree 11-16, 989C1
CICERO, Ill.—*See ILLINOIS*
CIERPINSKI, Waldemar
Wins Olympic medal 7-31, 576E1
CIGARETTES—*See TOBACCO*

1977

CHRYSOSTOMOS, Archbishop (Chrysostomos Aristodomou)
Facts on 924E1
Named to succeed Makarios 8-3, 617D1
Formally elected archbp 11-12, ordained 11-13; pol role seen 11-14, 924C1
CHUANG Tse-tung
Replaced in sports post 1-29, 98C2
CHUKCHI Sea
USSR sets 200-mi limit 3-1, 147E1
CHU Ko-chia
Scored at rally 6-29, 562A1
CHUNDER, Pratap Chandra
India educatn min 3-26, 240B1
CHUNG, Harry C. C.
Charges dismissed 12-27, 1008G1
CHURCH, Foster
Wins Pulitzer Prize 4-18, 355F2
CHURCH, Sen. Frank (Forrester) (D, Ida.)
Korry: '76 testimony 'bottled up' 1-9, 18E2
Scores Carter plutonium ban 5-2, 334D3
US denies uranium cartel agrmt 6-29, 624E3
Visits Cuba, sees Castro 8-8—8-11, 653C3-654D1
US natls, kin leave Cuba 9-22, 781B2
Demands Panama Canal treaty clarificatn 10-5, 755E1
Scores handling of Helms case 10-31, 838F3
CHURCHES—*See denominations, church names*
CHURCHES, All Africa Council of—*See ALL Africa Council of Churches*
CHURCHES, National Council of—*See NATIONAL Council of Churches*
CHURCHILL, Sir Winston Leonard Spencer (1874-1965)—*See 1965, p. 25B3 for biog. data*
Eden dies 1-14, 84G2
Widow bars financial aid 2-22, 140D3
Lord Moran dies 4-12, 356E3
Widow dies 12-12, 1024D3
CHURCHILL, Mrs. Winston—*See SPENCER-Churchill, Lady Clementine*
CHURCH of England—*See ANGLICANS*
CHURCH of the Lamb of God
Allred slain 5-10, 6 chrgd 9-27, 847F3
CHURSKY, Tony
Cosmos win NASL title 8-28, 676E2
CHU Teh (d. 1976)
Cong to elect successor 10-23, 823F1
CHYLAK, Nestor
In World Series 10-11—10-18, 806G1
CHYUNG Yil Hyung
At US reception in Seoul 5-26, 441C1
CIA—*See U.S. GOVERNMENT—CENTRAL Intelligence Agency*
CIACCIA, John
Vs bilingualism end 4-1, 254F2
CIA and the Cult of Intelligence, The (book)
RCMP-CIA link chrgd 11-24, 923D1
CIANFRANI, Henry J.
Rptr linked romantically 8-27, quits NY Times 9-12, 920E3
CIAPPI, Father Luigi
Inducted as cardinal 6-27, 768B3
CIBA-Geigy Corp.
Phenformin sales barred 7-25, 603B2
CIGARETTES—*See TOBACCO*
CIGARS—*See TOBACCO*

1978

CHU Mu-chih
Gets CP post 1-2, 54A1
CHUNG Fu-hsiang
Replaced as posts min 10-26, 838A1
CHUNG Hsi-tung
In Viet-China refugee talks 8-8, 602B3
Chrgs Viet aggressn 9-19, 747G3
Severs Viet talks 9-26, 747C3
CHUNG Mong Ku
Seized in housing scandal 7-14, 594E3
CHUNG Sung-il
Gushiken KOs 10-15, 969E1
CHUN-LI, Chen
Opium War released 8-14, 970E2
CHUQUIAGO (film)
Released 4-18, 619A1
CHURCH, Sen. Frank (D, Ida.)
Says Canal pacts protect Latins from communism 2-8, 120F1
Votes for Panama Canal neutrality pact 3-16, 177D2
Votes for 2d Canal pact, ratificatn role cited 4-18, 273B1, F2
Doubts CIA evidence on Cuba role in Zaire 6-9, 442E2
Reservatn added to UK tax pact 6-27, 588A3
CHURCHES—*See denominations, church names*
CHURCHILL, Mrs. Winston—*See SPENCER-Churchill, Lady Clementine*
CHURCHILL, Sir Winston Leonard Spencer (1874-1965)
'54 portrait rptd destroyed 1-11, 335D2
CHURCH of England—*See ANGLICANS*
CHU Teh, Marshal (d. 1976)
Yeh succeeds 2-26—3-5, 153C1
CIA—*See U.S. GOVERNMENT—CENTRAL Intelligence Agency*
CIANFRANI, Henry J.
Begins jail term 2-20, 172A3
CIBA-Geigy Corp.
FDA OKs metoprolol 8-7, 727E3
CICCHETTI, Charles
Wis A-plant moratorium ordrd 8-17, 665G2
CIGARETTES—*See TOBACCO*

1979

3d 1/4 record loss posted, sales down, other financial data rptd 10-30; dividend omitted 11-1, 845E3-846F1
3d 1/4 loss cited 10-31, 923B1
Carter rescue plan proposed, reactn 11-1, 845B2
FTC challenge declined by Sup Ct 11-5, 884G2
Rebates reinstituted 11-5, 963A3
Oct, Nov sales slump rptd 11-6, 12-5, 963F2
VW Argentina deal rptd set 11-19, 887F2
XM-1 tank defects said solved 11-20, 925C1
Industry layoff total cited 12-4, 963C3
Bernice Garbisch dies 12-14, 1008F2
Cong debates bailout bill 12-18–12-20, OKs 12-21, 981D1
CHRYSLER Corp. v. Brown
Case decided by Sup Ct 4-18, 345E3
CHUNG Seung Hwa, Gen.
Named ROK martial law head 10-27, 821C1
Link to Park death sought 11-6, 843E2-C3
Assails dissidents, oppositn ldr 11-28, 928F2
Arrested re Park murder 12-12, ousted as martial law head 12-13, 959A3
Formally detained 12-24, 997E1
CHURCH, Sen. Frank (D, Ida.)
Forgn Relatns Com chrmn 1-23, 71D2
Vs proposed Taiwan legis 1-26, 66A3
Meets Teng, Taiwan ties scored 4-19, 312B1
Backs SALT treaty chngs 5-15, 460B1
Conservative PAC plans drive 8-16, 627F3
Sees SALT vote delay re Sovt troops in Cuba 9-5, 657F1; 9-9, 674C1-E1
On Carter speech re Sovt troops in Cuba 10-1, 737D2
Offers SALT additn re Cuba 10-11, 822B3
Intl sugar agrmt OKd 11-30, 987G2, A3
Sees Waldheim on US hostages 12-1, 913E1
CHURCH, Frederic Edwin (1826-1900)
Painting sold for record sum 10-25, 891F3
CHURCH Jr., Samuel Morgan
Named UMW pres 11-16, 885D2, F2
UMW conv held 12-10–12-20, 986D3, 987A1
CHURCHILL, Dr. W. Hallowell
Cancer cocoon discovery rptd 8-20, 735G1
CHURCHILL, Winston
Admits liaison 12-15; Thatcher backs Churchill re security 12-17, 994G2
CHURCHILL, Sir Winston Leonard Spencer (1874-1965)
Maze dies 9-17, 756A3
China premr compares Thatcher 10-28, 854F1
CHURCH Mutual Insurance Co.
Iowa OKs malpractice insurnc 4-9, 376D1
CHURCH of England—*See ANGLICANS*
CHURCH of God International
'78 founding cited 1-3, 23E3
Membership rise rptd 5-4, 640A1
CHURCH of Scientology of Calif. v. Blumenthal
Case decided by Sup Ct 5-14, 383A3
CHURCH of the Lamb of God
4 acquitted in Allred '77 death, 2 sought 3-20, 240B2
CHURCH Rock, N.M.—*See NEW Mexico*
CHYNOWETH, Mark
Acquitted in polygamist's '77 death 3-20, 240B2
CHYNOWETH, Rena
Acquitted in polygamist's '77 death 3-20, 240B2
CHYNOWETH, Victor
Acquitted in polygamist's '77 death 3-20, 240B2
CIA—*See U.S. GOVERNMENT-CENTRAL Intelligence Agency*
CIAMPI, Carlo
Named central bank gov 10-5, 793F1
CIANFRANI, Henry J.
'80 parole granted 1-11, 102A3
CIGARETTES—*See TOBACCO*

1980

K-car sales rptd 8-5, prices listed 10-15, 883E1
Reagan sees auto execs 9-2, 664E2
Aug sales rptd down 9-4, 701G2
Detroit tax revenue drop rptd 9-8, 743G2
Worker layoffs rptd 9-11, 701A3
Carter scores Reagan on aid 10-1, 739B2
Sept sales rptd down 10-6, 784G2
3d 1/4 loss rptd 10-29, 823D1
McGagh resigns as vp, treas 10-29, 959C3
Oct sales rptd up 11-4, 857B1
GPU fed bailout considered 11-28, 961B1
EPA '76 recall order challenge refused by Sup Ct 12-1, 918E2
Rebates offered 12-5, 938C2
K-car output rptd cut 12-9, 938F2
New financial plan proposed 12-17, UAW OKs renegotiatn 12-22; $400 mln loan asked 12-23, 984D2
Mich asks worker insurnc 12-26, 984G2
Meese on fed aid 12-28, 980A3
CHRYSLER Corp. v. EPA
Case refused by Sup Ct 12-1, 918F2
CHUN Doo Hwan (Chon Too Hwan) (South Korean president)
Heads KCIA 4-14, 295A1
Students demand ouster 5-2, 5-10, 375B1
Students riot, 100 die 5-18—5-27, 394G2
Heads security com 5-31, quits KCIA post 6-2, 430F2
Extends mil power 6-4; govt denies mil power rules 6-16, 466G3-467C1
US retaliates vs power extensn 6-12, 467D1
KCIA purged 6-20, 499E2
New KCIA chief named 7-14, 566A2
Orders journalists fired 7-30, 620B3
Promoted to full gen 8-6; sees mil ldrship, US denies pres support 8-8, 620F2
US affirms support denial 8-11—8-16, 645B2
Choi resigns 8-16, nominated pres 8-18, 628B1
Quits mil 8-22; elected pres, fills key posts 8-27, 645G1
US qualifies support, asks govt reforms 8-28, 673F1
Sworn pres, vows martial law end 9-1; names Cabt 9-2, 673A1, C1
N Korea pres scores 9-25, 737B1
Unveils new business policy 9-29, 809C3
Korea Univ closed after riots 10-17, 810A1
811 politicans purged 11-12, 874G2
US pleas for Kim, discusses N Korea threat 12-13, 953D1
CHUNG Il Kwon
Pol activities curbed 11-12, 874B3
CHUNG Jai Suk
Purged 7-9, 525A2
CHUNG Seung Hwa, Gen.
Trial starts 3-5, sentncd 3-13, 195G3
CHURCH, Sen. Frank Forrester (D, Ida.)
US UN anti-Israel vote probe set 3-5, 164A1
On Admin forgn policy 3-27, 243C2
Sen com asks consultatn on Iran 4-24, 297D2
Vs extra gear for Saudi F-15s 6-17, 450C2
Backs India uranium sale 9-24, 723F1
Loses reelection 11-4, 837D1, 845A2, 851E3
CHURCH, Frederic Edwin
Homer oil sold for $1.7 mln 10-17, 998A1
CHURCH Jr., Samuel Morgan
W Va strike 2-21—3-3, 170B1
CHURCHILL, Winston
At Cambodia border aid vigil 2-6, 108D2
CHURCHILL, Sir Winston Leonard Spencer (1874-1965)
Sutherland dies 2-18, 176F3
Norman Shelley dies 8-22, 676A3
CHURCH of Christ Uniting
Protestant unity mtg ends, common ministry OKd 1-24, 156C2
CHURCH of Rasheed
Founder, aide convicted of fraud 2-9, 157B2*
CHURCH of the Brethren
Intercommunion poll rptd 4-4, 413A3
CHURCH of the Lamb of God
LeBaron convicted of murder 5-28, sentenced 6-2, 502B3
CHU Yong Bock
Retained as S Korea min 9-2, 673B1
CHU Yu-huai
Gets suspended death sentnc 7-20, 563B2
CHYTILOVA, Vera
Apple Game released 1-16, 216B2
CIA (Central Intelligence Agency)—*See under U.S. GOVERNMENT*
CIANCI Jr., Mayor Vincent (Providence, R.I.)
Addresses GOP conv 7-14, 531D3
Nominated for gov 9-9, 700A3
Loses gov electn 11-4, 849A1
CIANFRANI, Henry J.
Released from prison 5-16; marries ex-rptr 7-14, 890A2
CIBA-Geigy Corp.
Anturane aids heart attack survival 1-31, 159E2
FDA blocks Anturane sale 4-25, 527B1
CICHON, Aleksandr
Wins Olympic medal 7-29, 624E3
CID de la Paz, Horacio
Describes Argentina detentn 2-4, 95B1
CIENFUEGOS, Ferman
Proclaims major leftist offensive 12-26, 993C2
CIERPINSKI, Waldemar
Wins Olympic medal 8-1, 624E1
CIGARETTES—*See TOBACCO*
CILA, Renato
Arrows win MISL title 3-23, 771A2

1976

CILLIE, Piet
Reform plea rptd 11-9, 928D2
CINCINNATI, O.—*See OHIO*
CINCINNATI, University of
Finds thermography use limited 7-28, 680B1
CINCINNATI Enquirer (newspaper)
Ford endorsement rptd 10-30, 831F2
CINCINNATI Symphony Orchestra
Gets grant 1-12, 32E3
CINERAMA Inc.
Hotel unit indicted 11-17, 989F2
CIOARA, Gheorghe
Ousted as Rumania CP head 6-15, 440D2
CIRCLE in the Square, Inc. (N.Y.)
Wins Tony award 4-18, 460F2
CIRILLO Brothers Petroleum Corp.
In oil spill suit 12-22, 969E1
CISNEROS, Gen. Luis
Peru interior min 1-31, 142A3
CIS Oceanair Services
Boycott rpt released 10-18, 786B1
CITICORP (First National City Corp.)
FRB acquisitn bar cited 8-19, 667C2
'75 US tax paymt rptd 10-2, 847A2
Montreal Olympic loan rptd 12-31, 998D3
Citibank (First National City Bank) (N.Y.)
Rptd on comptroller's 'problem' list 1-11; Wriston, Spencer reply 1-11, 1-16, 110D2-111C1, E3
Cuts prime rate 1-16, chngs formula 1-23; cuts rate again 1-30, raises 2-27, 167G2
Capital-assets ratio rptd 1-20, 112F2
Del Farmers Bank default rptd 2-4, 437C3
AJC chrgs boycott compliance 3-18, 747A2
Rentschler plead guilty 4-20, 316E3
Lowers, raises prime 4-30—6-4, 436B3
Quebec loan planned 6-30, 529G1
Sues Eximbank re Zaire loan 8-9, 621B2
Drops suit re Zaire; new paymt plan OKd 10-13, 890G2-C3
Boycott rpt released 10-18, 786B1
Lowers prime 10-29, 846E2
Sees no threat re forgn loans outstanding, Jan-July data cited 915C2
Total Zaire debt cited 11-9, 890C2
Lowers prime rate 12-10, 939B3
Citicorp International Ltd.
In Venez intl bank loan 9-15, 875E1
CITIES, National League of
Fed min wage ruled not binding on states 6-24, 468G2
Delegation sees Carter 12-14, 937B3
CITIES Service Co.
In Viet oil talks 4-24, 352B2
SEC lists forgn paymts 5-12, 726F2
CITIES, Suburbs & Localities—*See also CRIME, EDUCATION, ENVIRONMENT & Pollution, HOUSING, MAYORS, TRANSPORTATION; city names*
Major banks on 'problem' list 1-11, 110F3
Bankruptcy bill clears Cong 3-25, 246D2; Ford signs 4-8, 982E1
Sup Ct rules on withholding union dues 6-7, 435A2
US min wage laws ruled not binding on localities 6-24, 468A2
Anti-porno zoning upheld 6-24, 479A1
Mayors on financial plight 6-26, 493A2
Federal Aid—*See also 'State-Local Aid' under U.S. GOVERNMENT—BUDGET; specific city, state names*
Federal aid program reviewed 1-8, 25E1
'77 budget proposals 1-21, 63F1, 65B3
Fiscal '77 US budget estimate talbes 231B1, 358C2
Carter gets aid plans 12-14, 937A3
Presidential Election (& transition)
Black Dems draft plank 5-1, 343D3
Dem platform priority item 5-20, 357A3
Beame endorses Carter 5-26, 390B3
Carter vs 'instant answers' 6-3, 411D1
Brown on urban decay 6-14, 432A2
Dem platform text 6-15, 469G1, D2, D3, E3, 470F2, 472F3, 473F1-474A3, 475G1
Carter lauds Eur planning 6-23, 451A3
Carter assures mayors on aid 6-29, 468C1
Daley cites natl problem 7-13, 509B3
Ford urges ldrship leeway 7-17, 531F2
GOP platform text 8-18, 602F1, 606A3
Ford acceptnc speech 8-19, 612C2
Carter stresses local actn 9-6, 664B2
Ford, Carter debate 9-23, 701C1, A2
Ford on aid plan 10-14, 761G3
Mondale addresses Calif conv 10-19, 803E3
Ford, Carter debate 10-22, 799G3, 801C3
Carter scores Ford 10-27, 803D2

1977

CIMETIDENE—*See CHEMICALS*
CINCINNATI, O.—*See OHIO*
CINCINNATI, University of
Bingham confrmd to Labor post 3-18, 272F2
CINCINNATI Milacron Inc.
Rpts forgn payoffs 4-11, 503E1
CINCINNATI Symphony Orchestra
Thomas Schippers dies 12-16, 1024B3
CINERAMA Hawaii Hotels Inc.—*See CINERAMA Inc.*
CINERAMA Inc.
Hawaii unit fined 5-11, 504D2
CINZANO (race horse)
Vet indicted in horse-switch scandal 12-2, 971B1
CIRCUS
Zacchini media suit affirmed 6-28, 557F3
CISNEROS Vizquerra, Gen. Luis
Scores Revolutionary Socialist Party 46B3
Sees '78 munic electns 2-12, 241D1
CITIBANK—*See under CITICORP*
CITICORP (First National City Corp.)
To promote S Africa equality 3-1, 160B3
Experts visit Zaire 3-17—3-26, 394D2
USAC sponsorship to end 6-24, 531F2
Lance cleared in govt probe 8-18, 625C2
New USAC pact set 9-21, 871A1
Citibank (First National City Bank) (N.Y.)
Zaire loan effort rptd 4-28, 394C2
Prime raised 5-13, 407D1
Prime raised 5-27, formula altered 6-10, 577D3, G3
World's 2d largest bank 6-21, 578A2
Pension managemt control rptd 6-28, 578C2
Venez pres sees dirs 6-30, 546B2
Prime hiked 8-21, 704A1
SEC rpt chrgs NYC '74-75 financial deceptn 8-26; reactn 8-26—8-27, 665A3, 666A1
Prime hiked 10-21, 817C3
NCC urges S Africa ties cut 11-10, 934D3
Citicorp International Bank Ltd.
Venez Eurocurrency loan set 3-28, 547D1
CITIES, National League of
Harris rpts new grant program 3-7, 178C1
Conf debates Admin plans 12-4, 12-7, 959B3
CITIES Service Co.
Oil co bias setlmt rptd 3-2, 279D1 *
Raises copper price 3-18, 209C2
Copper strike begins 7-1, 558G1
Seadock backing rptd 7-19, 559F2
CITIES, Suburbs & Towns—*See also CRIME, EDUCATION, ENVIRONMENT & Pollution, HOUSING, TRANSPORTATION; also city names*
Ford State of Union message 1-12, 13G2
Carter '78 budget revisns 2-22, 125A2
Rural migratn rptd 2-24, 183G3
Carter proposes youth corps 3-9, 173F1
Fed aid planned 3-10, 193F3
NE-Midwest House coalitn vs fed spending policy 4-6, 423D3
'75 top 10 cities rptd 4-14, 387B3; chart 388A1
Neighborhoods comm bill cleared 4-28, 339A1
Cong sets '78 budget target 5-17, 405A1
NAACP scores Carter 6-27—6-28, Bond scores 8-15, SCLC 8-18, Meany 8-30, 702A2
'76 tax revenue data 7-7, 540G1
Jordan scores Carter 7-24, Carter says 'no apologies' 7-25, 7-28, 573C1, A3
Black Caucus backs Jordan vs Carter 7-29, 592G3
Black ldrs score Carter 8-29, 702D1
Bond yields rptd down 9-6, 691E2
Carter vows actn to blacks 9-7, 702A1
'78 HUD funds signed 10-4, 796D3
Urban aid bill signed, NE-Midwest grants hiked 10-12, 796G1
Fscl '76 local per capita burden rptd 10-18, 821F3
Energy tax credit OKd by Sen 10-31, 832G2
'Full employmt' compromise bill backed 11-4, 877B1
ERA conv boycott rptd 11-14, 918B1
Admin urban policy debated 12-4, 12-7, 959B3
Black ldrs see Carter 12-14, 960B1
Federal Revenue Sharing & Grants-in-Aid—*See U.S. GOVERNMENT—BUDGET—Revenue Sharing; specific city, state names*

1978

CIMINO, Michael
Deer Hunter released 12-14, 1030F2
CINCINNATI, O.—*See OHIO*
CINCINNATI, University of
Badger to coach basketball 4-9, 272G2
CINCINNATI Enquirer (newspaper)
Gannett plans purchase, circulatn rise seen 5-8, 345G2
CINZANO (race horse)
Vet sentncd in '77 horse switch 11-3, 1028G1
CIRCUS
Wallenda dies in fall 3-22, 252F3
CISNEROS Vizquerra, Gen. Luis
Replaced as Peru interior min 5-15, 394E2
CISSOKO, Col. Charles Samba
Arrested 3-9, 250G3
C.I.T. Financial Corp.
National Bank of North America (N.Y.)
UK bank to buy 75.1% interest 5-12, 364F1
'67 Meadow Brook merger cited 364B2
CITIBANK—*See under CITICORP*
CITICORP (First National City Corp.)
Jamaica operatns cutback set 2-3, 95B1
Moore on Kennecott bd rival slate 3-27, 402E3
Chile loans rptd undercutting US rights policy 4-11, Reuss scores 4-12, 312G1
Canada loan set 5-3, 370E2
Zaire loan deal cited 6-14, 478F1
S Africa investmt total disputed 8-29, 669F3
Nigeria loan set 11-30, 934G1
Citibank (First National City Bank) (N.Y.)
Prime hiked 1-6, 28D2
PR branch bombed 2-16, 129G1
Peru loan refinancing barred 3-10; Sovt-Peru deal cited 3-14, 353F1, B2
S Africa loans halted 3-11, 193F2
Brazil-Paraguay hydro loan rptd 3-30, 311C2
Brazil $2.5 bln debt rptd 4-8, 311F1
Chile branch bombed 5-1, 351E3
Peru offcls meet intl bankers 5-23—5-24, 394C2
Nigeria exit cited 6-26, 799B1
Forgn tax evasn chrgd 7-24, 717B3
Prime rate hiked 11-3, 827C1
Ranked '77 world's 2d biggest bank 11-8, 913G3-914A1
Prime rate hiked 11-24, 918D1
CITIES (non-U.S.)—*See also country names*
Costliest cities rated, table 1-14, 28G2
CITIES, National League of
Carter addresses 11-27, support pledged 11-29, 914F2, F3
CITIES, Suburbs & Towns (U.S.)—*See also CRIME, EDUCATION, ENVIRONMENT & Pollution, HOUSING; also city names*
Segregatn growth linked to local govt housing policies 1-8, 13F3
Carter State of Union Message 1-19, 29G3, 30G1, 31B1, 32A1, C1
Carter budget proposals 1-23, 44F2, C3, 47F3; table 45E2
Federal budget dollar table 63A1
GOP attacks Carter budget 1-31, 63D1
'77 environmental decline rptd 85C2
FCC cable-TV access rules voided 2-24, 195F2
New CPIs described 222A2
Jan, Feb CPI rptd 2-27, 3-28, 222F1
Cities subject to US electn law 3-6, 162F1
Carter unveils urban-aid plan 3-27, reactn 3-27—3-30, 217C2-218D1
Cities trust law liability upheld by Sup Ct 3-29, 280F1-E2
Gambling legalizatn impact rptd 4-2, 434E2
Blacks stress urban needs as voting issue 4-10, 568F2, G2
'77 living costs, incomes ranked 4-26, 349E1
Cong '79 budget target res cleared 5-17, 385F1
Water-based land claims barred by Sup Ct 5-31, 431F1
Munic legal immunity ended by Sup Ct 6-6, 447C1-A2
Kreps warns re Propositn 13 6-21, 526E1
MD fee hikes forecast 7-23, 577D3
LNG safety measures urged 7-31, 609G3
July CPI rise rptd 8-29, 679G2
'79 community dvpt, state-local govt fed aid signed 9-30, 750E2-A3
Inner city crime survey rptd 10-16, 842A2
NYS property-tax-limit case refused by US Sup Ct 10-30, 832C3
Neb spending referendum loses 11-7, 854G3

1979

CIMETIDINE (Tagamet)—*See MEDICINE—Drugs*
CIMINO, Michael
Wins Oscar 4-9, 336G1
CINCINNATI, O.—*See OHIO*
CINCINNATI Bengals v. Hackbart
Case declined by Sup Ct 10-29, 884G1
CIOARA, Gheorghe
Named Rumania energy min 1-31, 171C1
CIRCULATIONS, Audit Bureau of
US top papers listed 6-6, 431D1
CIRCUS
Emmett Kelly dies 3-28, 272G2
CIRUOS Jr., William J.
On Morales escape 5-21, 431G1
CISNEROS, Gabriel
Ambushed by Basque terrorists 7-3, 505D1
C.I.T. Financial Corp.
RCA seeks merger 7-5, talks end 7-10, 517E1
RCA to buy 8-17, Integon talks end 8-24, 682A2-F2
National Bank of North America (N.Y.)
FRB OKs UK bank purchase 3-16, hitch seen 3-19, 205D1
CITIBANK—*See under CITICORP*
CITICORP
Ecuador loan set 1-30, 101G1
S Africa '72-78 loans rptd 4-2, 270D2
Amer Express travelers check TV ad chngd 8-29, 903D1
Greek intl bank loan set dup banks-intl 9-7, 708C2
Advance Mortgage Corp.
Applicatn case declined by Sup Ct 6-11, 479A1
Citibank (N.Y.)
Poland econ monitor plan set 1-11, 59G3
Spain OKs local operatn 1-26, 100F3
Prime rate lowered 2-9, 131F1
Zaire loan plan rptd dropped 3-26, 999F1
Turkey aid package set 5-30, 397B2
Iran banks natlzd 6-7, compensatn vowed 6-10, 469G1
'78 world's 3d biggest bank 6-19, 476A2
Nicaragua operatns curbed 7-25, 574B1
Prime rate hiked 9-28, 745G1
Nicaragua debt paymts in doubt 9-28, 753E2
Reuss vs prime rate hikes 10-31; prime rate hiked 11-16, lowered 12-14, 940G3
Iran assets freeze backed 11-14, 861G2
Iran assets attached for loan repaymts 11-15, 879F3
Pahlevi family fund transfer documented 11-26, 897E2
Iran sues UK, French branches for assets freeze 11-30, 12-5, 915A2
France upholds Iran assets freeze 12-12, 12-21, 976B2
El Salvador branch bombed 12-27, 993G2
Citicorp Real Estate Inc.
Condominium trend rptd 6-23, 482G2-A3
CITICORP v. Board of Governors, Federal Reserve
Case declined by Sup Ct 6-11, 479A1
CITIES Service Co. (Citgo)
US files overchrg suit 1-5, 17B1
Gasoline allocatns announced 2-28, 146C1
July gas supplies rptd 6-25, 479E1
Heating oil shortfall seen 6-28, 514G2
Overchrg penalties accepted 11-1, 850B1
CITIES, Suburbs & Towns (U.S.)—*See also city names*
Carter to resubmit countercyclical aid progrm 1-2, 3E3
Carter budget proposals 1-22, 44B3; table 42F2
Boston Navy Yd renovatn set 2-1, 93G3-94B1
Adams outlines urban-aid policy 2-13, 129A2
HUD rpts revitalizatn impact on poor 2-13, 132G2-C3
Carter submits countercyclical aid plan 3-6, 164A2
Neighborhoods panel issues rpt 3-15, 208G2
Fiscal status of cities rptd 3-20, 204E1
US ups poverty levels 4-9, 283D3
Racial 'steering' suits allowed by Sup Ct 4-17, 325G2
Urban malnutritn rptd down 4-30, 386G2
'78 tax revenues up 5-16, 386G1
US Mayors Conf held, Carter policies backed 6-9—6-13, 439C2-440D1
Md sues US re NE urban gas allocatn bias 6-26, 479A2
Carter sees mayors 7-6—7-11, 513F2
Landrieu, Goldschmidt records cited 7-27, 577E1-D2
City hosps decline rptd 9-2, 970E3-971C1
Municipal bond ratings listed 9-20, 920F3
'80 HUD funds clear Cong 10-24, Carter signs 11-5, 883G2
Urban fscl policy chngs predicted 10-24, 920G1
Reagan seeks fed progrm, tax shift 11-13, 866E2
Library fund shift urged 11-15—11-19, 901F1
'79 living costs ranked 12-28, 990E3

1980

CILLIE, Petrus M.
'76 riot rpt issued 2-29, 174D1-C2
CIMINO, Michael
Heaven's Gate withdrawn from theaters 11-19, 906B1
CINCINNATI—*See OHIO*
CIPERE, Dumitru
Wins Olympic medal 8-2, 622E1
CIRCUS
Fla Ringling Bros tax case refused by Sup Ct 3-24, 265A2
CITGO—*See CITIES Service Co.*
CITICORP
Nader coalitn attacks 4-17, 308B2
'Choice Card' introduced 9-16, FRB orders end 10-10, 985D3
Citibank (N.Y.)
France freezes funds on Iran request 1-16, decisn appealed 1-17, freeze upheld 1-21, 48B1
El Salvador natlzatn set 2-11, 117F2
USSR office to close 2-20, 134G3-135A1
Mortgage rate at 14% 2-26, 145C1
Prime rate hiked to 18.5% 3-14, 209B2
Churches cut ties re S Africa loans 3-24, 277G3
Credit restrictions rptd 3-27, 222G2
Prime rate hiked to 19.25% 3-28, 19.5% 4-1, 20% 4-2, 247D2, A3
Prime rate cut to 19.75% 4-18, 305E3
Home mortgage rates lowered 5-1, 329D2
Prime rate cut to 18.5% 5-2, 329A2
Hunt silver debts rptd 5-2, 345C1
Prime cut to 17.5% 5-7, 367D3
Mortgage rate cut to 15.5% 5-8, 14% 5-13, 385A1
Prime cut to 14.5% 5-23, 401G1
Prime cut to 14% 5-30; 12.75% 6-12, 438B1, D1
Mortgage rate cut to 12.25% 7-9, 514D1
Prime cut to 11.25% 7-11, 574D3
Nicaragua debt rescheduled 9-5, 689G2
Prime hiked to 14% 9-12—10-2, 763A1, 764D2
Mortgage rate at 14.25% 10-7, 867D2
Prime rate hiked to 16.75% 11-21, 19% 12-5, 937E3, F3
Canada OKs new Bank Act 11-26, 920C2
Prime rate at 21.5% 12-27, 983B3
CITIES, National League of
Conv hears Reagan pledges, sees New Deal era end; Hudnut elected pres 12-1, 914D2-F3
CITIES, Suburbs & Towns (U. S.)—*See also city names*
'67-77 elected offcls drop rptd 1-2, 5D3
State of State messages 1-8, 1-9, 1-15, 403B3, 404A1, F1
Sewer projects scored 1-9, 54F1-D2
'79 municipal bond sales rptd up 1-16, 92A3
Carter State of Union topic 1-23, 43A2, F2
Carter budget proposals 1-28, 73E1; table 70F1
Urban purchasing power rptd tops 2-12, 125D3
Canceled bond issues rptd 2-26, 2-28, 186D1
Miami Beach redvpt voted 3-11, 185B1
Carter anti-inflatn plan sets fed spending cuts 3-14, 201C1
NY vote called 'protest' 3-25, 221A3
Carter revised budget proposals, Gunther scores 3-31, 244A1, C1, F1
'Good faith' legal immunity ended by Sup Ct 4-16, 328D2
'79 tax collectns rptd 4-17, 307B2
Latin immigrants surveyed 5-11—5-20, 396B2
Mex-Canada projcts agreed 5-27, 409C3
Black ldr warns re despair 5-29, 460F1-A2
Mayors Conf 6-8—6-10, 438E2-G3
US summer jobs progrm rptd 6-30, 495G3
Census revisn ordrd 9-25, 741D2
Clean water amendmts clear Cong 10-1, signed 10-21, 981E1
'81-85 coastal zone mgt authrzn clears Cong 10-1, signed 10-17, 981A2
Busing, housing integratn rptd linked 11-16, 989B3
Natl League conv hears Reagan pledges, sees New Deal era end 12-1, 914D2-F3
Migratn to Sun Belt, suburbs urged by Pres advisory panel 12-29, 990G1

1976

Mayors seek Carter commitmt, Samuels at Mayors Conf 11-7—11-8, 845G2
Carter gets aid plans 12-14, 937A3

CITIZENS Bancshares Inc.
Rptd on FRB 'problem' list 1-22, 111B3
CITIZENS Research Foundation (Princeton, N.J.)
Alexander book excerpts publshd 4-25, 688E1
CITIZENS & Southern Holding Co.
Rptd on FRB 'problem' list 1-22, 111A3
Citizens & Southern National Bank (Atlanta)
Rptd on comptroller's 'problem' list 1-26, 113E1
CITIZENS Trust Bank—*See CITIZENS Bancshares Inc.*
CITIZENS State Bank (Carrizo Springs, Tex.)
Fails 7-7, 940B2
CITROEN S.A.
Peugeot merger rptd 10-1, 773B1
CITY National Corp.
Rptd on FRB 'problem' list 1-22, 111B3
City National Bank (Beverly Hills, Calif.)
Rptd on comptroller's 'problem' list 1-26, 113F1
CIVIL Rights—*See HUMAN & Civil Rights; specific areas, subjects of abuse*
CLABIR Corp.
'75 Flinchbaugh arms sales listed 2-6, 147C3
CLAGGET, Brice
Lauds Sup Ct campaign law ruling 2-1, 86G1

1977

CITIZENS Band Radio—*See 'Radio' under BROADCASTING*
CITIZENS For the Republic
Warns vs Panama Canal pact 9-1, 678G1, F2
CITIZENS & Southern National Bank (Ga.)
Anderson confrmd to Treas post 3-29, 272E2
Lance cleared of financial illegalities 8-18, 625B3
Ga right to sue affirmed 11-8, 857D1
CITIZENS & Southern National Bank v. Bougas
Right to sue natl banks widened 11-8, 857E1
CITRUS Fruits—*See FRUITS & Vegetables*
CITY of Hope Medical Center (Duarte, Calif.)
Hormone made from bacteria 12-1, 1022G2
CIVIL Aeronautics Board (CAB)—*See under U.S. GOVERNMENT*
CIVIL Defense—*See U.S. GOVERNMENT—DEFENSE; country names*
CIVILETTI, Benjamin R.
Asst atty gen 2-16; confrmd 3-4, 211D1
Agee prosecutn barred 3-18, 212A2
Named dep atty gen 12-6, 1001D3
Heads FBI break-in probe 12-7, 940G1
CIVIL Rights—*See HUMAN & Civil Rights; specific areas, subjects of abuse*
CIVIL Rights, Commission on—*See under U.S. GOVERNMENT*
CIVIL Service System—*See under U.S. GOVERNMENT*
C&K Petroleum Inc.
US cancels offshore lease 6-8, 499C1
CLAIROL Inc.—*See under BRISTOL-Meyers Co.*
CLAMSHELL Alliance
NH A-plant protest 4-30—5-3, 344B3
NH protesters tried, freed 5-4—5-13, 409E3

1978

Carter warns mayors, urban offcls on aid 11-27; anti-inflatn plan backed, natl dvpt bank opposed 11-29, 914F2-G3
GOP govs urge commitmt 11-27—11-28, 915G3
Conn legal immunity ruling vacated by US Sup Ct 11-27, 937B2
Cities' power over suburbs backed by Sup Ct 11-28, 937G2
Black populatn growth at standstill 11-30, 943F1
'75-77 migration of poor from South reverses 12-3, 943A1
Top 20 ranked, populatn losses rptd 12-6; table 942A3, D3
Kennedy, urban ldrs score Carter budget plans 12-9, 956G1, G2
Carter sees mayors on budget 12-20, 980C2
Inner-city health progrm urged 12-20, 1009F1
Carter restores budget cuts 12-22, 1002E3
CITIZENS Band (CB) Radio—*See ELECTRIC & Electronics*
CITIZENS Bank & Trust Co. (Ill.)
John MacArthur dies 1-6, 96G2
CITIZENS Committee for the Right to Keep and Bear Arms
False mailings admitted 1-16, 68E2
CITIZENS Engaged in Reuniting Families
'Moonie' deprogramming suit rptd 4-16, 295E3
CITROEN S.A.—*See PEUGEOT-Citroen*
CITRUS Fruits—*See FRUITS & Vegetables*
CITY Investing Co.
GDV bid for Servomation control accepted 8-31, 700A3
CITY of Hope National Medical Center (Duarte, Calif.)
Insulin from synthetic gene rptd 9-7, 947C3
CITY of West Haven v. Turpin
Legal immunity ruling vacated by Sup Ct 11-27, 937C2
CITY Sugar (play)
Opens 6-5, 887C1
CITY to City (recording)
On best-seller list 6-7, 460G3; 7-5, 580A1
CIULEI, Liviu
Inspector Gen revived 9-21, 1031A2
CIVIL Aeronautics Board—*See under U.S. GOVERNMENT*
CIVIL Aviation Organization, International—*See UNITED Nations—International Civil Aviation Organization*
CIVIL Defense—*See also U.S. GOVERNMENT—DEFENSE*
Carter proposes emergency agency 6-19, 466D2-B3
CIA issues USSR study 7-19, 563F3
US Cong pro-defns coalitn formed 8-8, 604C3
Carter vetoes '79 authrzn 8-17, 621D2
Carter plans spending hike 11-12, 895E1
CIVIL Disorders—*See CRIME—Riots & Civil Disorders*
CIVILETTI, Benjamin R.
On cong indictmts in Korean scandal 1-18, 1-26, 63C2
Sen com backs confirmatn 4-14, rpts no Marston cover-up 4-24, 309C3, D3
Sen rejcts com cover-up rpt, chrgs 'whitewash' 5-4, 342G3
Confirmed dep atty gen 5-9, 342D3
Sees Korea indictmts ended 6-1, 432G2
Sees Carter, Solomon on GSA probe 9-4, 685E2
Plans GSA probe coordinatn 9-18, 715B1
CIVIL Rights—*See HUMAN & Civil Rights; specific areas, subjects of abuse*
CIVIL Rights, Commission on—*See under U.S. GOVERNMENT*
CIVIL Rights, Office for—*See under U.S. GOVERNMENT—HEALTH, Education & Welfare*
CIVIL Service System—*See under U.S. GOVERNMENT*
CLACK, Jim
Traded to Giants 4-17, 336G1
CLAIBORNE, Jack
Named Cardinals gen mgr 10-18, 1026A3
CLAMSHELL Alliance
Seabrook A-plant protested 6-24—6-26, 494B1
Seabrook A-plant rulings scored, protests vowed 8-7, 8-10, 604C2, G2-A3
Seabrook constructn resumes 8-14; protests continue 8-14—12-7, ct appeal fails 8-22, 941A1-E1
Seabrook shutdown costs rptd 10-10, 941G1
Seabrook '77 protests ruled illegal 12-6, 1009B3

1979

CITIZEN Kane Soundtrack (recording)
Wins Grammy 2-16, 336F3
CITIZENS Against Nuclear Power
Zion A-protest rptd 9-29, 742E3
CITIZENS Committee on Indochinese Refugees
Cambodia food aid rptd blocked 12-18, 977G3, 978G1
CITIZENS For Law and Order Inc.
Calif judge scored for drug arrest 9-20, 748B2
CITIZENS Opposed to Rearranging Kids
Cleveland schl boycott urged 9-9, 679D2
CITIZENS Party
Formed, platform outlined 8-1, 594E3-595A1
CITRUS Fruits—*See FRUITS & Vegetables*
CITY Investing Co.
Rheem Mfg acquitted 10-22, 986E1
CITY Management Association, International
Fscl policy chngs seen 10-24, 920F1
CITY National Bank—*See under CITY National Corp.*
CITY National Corp.
City National Bank (Los Angeles)
Wire-transfer theft nets $1.1 mln 3-25, 239C2
CITY of Hope National Medical Center (Duarte, Calif.)
MS, depressn study rptd 1-4, 289E3
CITY on Fire (film)
Released 9-14, 819G3
CITY Stores Co.
Files voluntary bankruptcy; Sloan, Franklin Simon cited 7-27, 648F3
CITY Suite, The (play)
Opens 4-2, 711B2
CIVARDI, Cardinal Ernesto
Installed cardinal 6-30, 640D2
CIVIL Aeronautics Board—*See under U.S. GOVERNMENT*
CIVIL Defense
US spending hike favored 2-4, 89G1-B2
CIVILETTI, Benjamin R.
Rpts Bayh Korean probe closed 1-5, 4A3
Backs eased pot laws 6-9, 492A2
Named atty gen 7-19, 529E1
Confirmed 8-1, sworn 8-16, 700A3
Jordan cocaine use probe rptd 8-24, 647E1
4 PR natlsts' sentncs commuted 9-6, 666B2
Brown confrmd to Appeals Ct 9-25, 901D3
Rpts 2d 1/4 crime rise 10-9, 819A3
Carter peanut business cleared 10-16, 782B3
Renfrew named dep atty gen 11-20, 946A3
Orders probe of PR prisoner's death 11-23, 904B3
OKs Cincinnati papers joint pact 11-26, 1007G1
Curbs INS neighborhood raids 11-26, 924C1
Urges restraint re Iranians in US 11-27, 898C1
Asks Jordan cocaine probe spec prosecutor 11-29, 900C3
Quits Vesco probe 12-7, 943B3
Files World Ct plea on Iran hostages 12-10, 933D1
On World Ct decisn vs Iran 12-15, 957F2
CIVIL Rights, Commission on—*See under U.S. GOVERNMENT*
CIVIL Service System—*See under U.S. GOVERNMENT*
CIVIL War (U.S.) (1860-65)
US House expulsns cited 3-1, 165A3
CLAIBORNE, William
Iran informs of press curbs 7-23, 566A1
CLAMSHELL Alliance
Seabrook protesters arrested 3-9, 186E2
Boston A-power protest 4-1, 261F3
Plymouth (Mass) protest 6-3, 416D2
NH '77 A-protest chrgs dropped 7-3, 519E1
4,000 at Seabrook rally 7-21, 7-22, 743B1
Boston bank A-protesters arrested 8-31, 742G3

1980

Presidential Election (& Transition)
GOP platform planks urge fed responsibility shift 1-14, 32G1, A2
Kennedy urges urban renewal 1-28, 75A1
Kennedy 'basic speech' excerpts 3-10, 183B2
Mayors Conf visited by Reagan 6-8, Anderson 6-9, Carter 6-10, 438E2-G3
Kennedy urges jobs progrm 6-10, 438B3
Dem platform drafted 6-24, 480A1
Anderson urges uplift 7-1, 515A3
Reagan acceptance speech 7-17, 533A1
Urban League hears pres candidates 8-4, 8-5, 597E1, F1
Hooks addresses Dem conv 8-13, 611E3
Dem platform planks adopted 8-13, 614F2, 615A1
Carter offers econ renewal plan 8-28, 663B2
Reagan, Anderson debate aid 9-21, 721E2, 722C1
Reagan backs fed aid to NYC 9-27, 10-1, 738C1, E1
Carter warns vs Reagan win 10-6, 762E3
Reagan deplores Carter 'hysteria' 10-7, 763D2
Carter softens Reagan attack 10-9, 778C2
Mondale denounces Reagan tax cuts 10-16, 817B1
Carter vows welfare, Medicaid relief 10-20, 803F1
Carter chrgs Reagan 'flipflop' 10-27, 816B3
Carter, Reagan TV debate 10-28, 814G1-C2
Anderson answers TV debate questns 10-28, 816B1
Reagan sends Natl League message 12-1, 914D2
CITIES Service Co.(Citgo)
Phillips, Arco price pacts OKd 9-25, 9-26, 960G1
CITIZEN/LABOR Energy Coalition
Oil price setlmts suit filed 10-8, 960A2
CITIZENS' Party
Conv held 4-11—4-13, Commoner named pres candidate 4-13, 288A3
Commoner uses vulgar radio ad 10-15, 818A3
CITY of Anniston v. Scott
Case declined by Sup Ct 4-28, 369B2
CITY of Black Jack v. Bates
Case refused by Sup Ct 2-25, 188B1
CITY of Rome v. U.S.
Case decided by Sup Ct 4-22, 344D1
CIULLA, Anthony (Big Tony)
Errico convicted 5-19, 447B3
CIUZIO, Eugene
Indicted in Abscam probe 7-15, 554A2
CIVIL Aeronautics Board—*See under U.S. GOVERNMENT*
CIVIL Defense
Carter signs '81 authrzn 9-8, 765B1
CIVILETTI, Benjamin R.
Justice to probe JFK murder 1-4, 17G1
Urges cong coms delay Abscam probe 2-5, 2-6, 82B2
Backs Miller, vs spec prosecutor 2-5, 92A2
Proxmire scores on Miller-Textron issue 2-10, sens ask spec prosecutor 2-11, 145A2
Names Abscam leaks prosecutor 2-11, 111E1
Rejects Miller-Textron spec prosecutor 3-11, 185C2
Chicago strip search suit setld 3-26, 404E2
Warns vs FTC debt 4-25, 348E1
On Houston schl desegregatn suit 5-15, 559C1
Acts to stem Miami rioting 5-19—5-20, 382G2, D3
NAACP warns re blacks' despair 5-29, 460A2
Warns vs Iran travel ban violatn 5-30, 419B1
Carter orders criminal refugees expelled 6-7, 435E1
Clark probe requested 6-7, 459C3
Rpts Carter briefed on brother's case 7-25, 569A1, A2
Carter denies impropriety re brother; rpts to Sen, natn 8-4, 592C3, G3, 593B2, 594B3, 595B1
Withheld B Carter info 8-6, Justice probe begun 8-7, 595G1, D2
OKs Chattanooga papers' joint pact 9-2, 732E2
Lisker: ordrd B Carter case delay 9-4; denies order 9-5, 700G3, 701A1
'81 refugee quota cut 9-19, 883A3
Sen subcom issues critical rpt in B Carter case 10-2, 763F3-764A1
Interdept rpt faults in B Carter case 10-29—11-1, 841A2
Gives final OK to Chattanooga papers' pact 11-6, 907E1
Scores antibusing provisn 11-17, 881A1
Troup (Tex) to end black svcs bias 12-11, 963A2
Informer cleared re Ala '65 murder 12-15, 990B1
CIVIL Rights, Commission on—*See under U.S. GOVERNMENT*
CIVIL Service Employees Association
Carter addresses NYS conv 10-1, 739F1
CIVIL Service System—*See under U.S. GOVERNMENT*
C&K Petroleum Inc.
Alaska Interstate merger set 8-18, 745F3
CLAIRBORNE, Craig
Gourmet Diet on best-seller list 10-12, 796E3
CLAIRBORNE, Judge Harry A.
Rules on Columbia suit vs Kerkorian 10-20, 906B3

1976

CLANCY, Rep. Donald D. (R, Ohio)
Scored by environmt group 3-25, 220A1
CLARK, Sen. Dick (D, Iowa)
Feels tide vs Angola aid 1-29, 88D3
Vs US A-aid to S Africa 5-26—5-29, 388A2
CLARK, Joseph
Scores judicial interfernc handling 3-12, 221E1
Ford meeting cited 6-16, 481B3
Hits anti-inflatn plan 9-25, 9-26, 771G1
Poll backs as prime min 10-16, 808F2
Liberals lose by-electns 10-18, comments 10-19, 808E2
CLARK, Ramsey
Says 2 mln eligible for amnesty 1-6, 4B2
Loses NY Sen primary 9-14, 687D2
CLARK College (Atlanta, Ga.)
Vivian Henderson dies 1-28, 124E3
CLARKE, Horace
Scores oppositn 11-12, 965G2
CLARKSBURG (W. Va.) Exponent (newspaper)
Carter endorsement rptd 10-30, 831B3
CLASS Actions—*See COURTS*

1977

CLANCY, Rep. Donald D. (R, Ohio)
Spec interest gifts rptd 3-7, 232B3
CLAPP, Peter
Surrenders 6-21, 839F1
CLARAMOUNT, Col. Ernesto (ret.)
Loses electn 2-20; chrgs fraud 2-21, exiled 2-28, 181B2-A3, 182A1
CLARIDGES' (London hotel)
Lodging for Carter aides canceled 5-5, 359G2
CLARK, Sen. Dick (D, Iowa)
On US Rhodesia mission 1-10, 11C3
Sponsors cong electn fund bill 3-7, 232D3
CLARK, Jimmy
USSR tour results 1-29—2-5, 263A2
CLARK, Joseph
Trails Trudeau in poll 3-5, 218D3
Scores Horner defectn 4-20, 304B1
Backs pipeline rpt 5-9, 372D2
Electn law challenge rejctd 6-6, 478F3
Scores RCMP files on MPs 8-17, 653E2
Tap device found 10-31, dispute ensues 11-1, 11-3, 11-4, 902C2
CLARK, Mark (d. 1969)
Chicago cops win Panther suit 6-21, 540E2
CLARK, Monty
Fired as 49er coach 4-6, 1020A2
CLARK, Ramsey
Backs FBI legis curbs 2-15, 157B3
UK sets Agee ouster 2-16, 134B2
Agee prosecutn barred 3-18, 212B2
Father dies 6-13, 532F2
Vs Manila as Law Conf site 8-21, 665A1
CLARK, Dr. Roy S.
Calif awarded rare meteorite 9-7, 712B3
CLARK, Tom C.
Dies 6-13, 532G2
CLARK, Woody
USSR tour results 1-29—2-5, 263C2
CLARKE, Bobby
NHL season ldr 4-3, 262F3
CLARKE, Horace
Jamaica pub utilities min 1-4, 46C1
CLASS Actions—*See COURTS; company, industry names*

1978

CLAPPER, Aubrey (Dit)
Dies 1-20, 96E2
CLAPTON, Eric
Slowhand on best-seller list 3-8, 196B1; 4-5, 272G3; 5-3, 356E1
Lay Down Sally on best-seller list 4-5, 272F3
CLARK, Bruce
2d in Outland vote 11-25, 1025A2
CLARK, Bryan E.
Winning Isn't Everything opens 12-3, 1031C3
CLARK, Dennis Lynton
Comes A Horseman released 11-1, 969G3
CLARK, Sen. Dick (D, Iowa)
Scores Carter chrome import move 1-29, 80G3
Votes for Panama Canal neutrality pact 3-16, 177D2
Votes for 2d Canal pact 4-18, 273B1
Ex-agent says CIA misled re Angola 5-8, 367E2
S Africa reelectn oppositn rptd 5-13, 498D3
Carter scores Africa aid curbs 5-19, 5-23; Angola, Ethiopia plan rptd rejctd 5-24, 483A2
Carter denies knowledge of Angola, Ethiopia aid plan mtg 5-24, 443D1
Renominated 6-6, 448E1
Doubts CIA evidence on Cuba role in Zaire 6-9, 442E2
Loses reelectn 11-7, 846B1, 854C2
CLARK, Earl H. (Dutch)
Dies 8-5, 708D2
CLARK Ed
Loses electn for Calif gov 11-7, 856D2
CLARK, Frank
Indicted 9-5, 685D1
CLARK, Jack
NL batting ldr 10-2, 928E2-F2
CLARK, James G.
Arrested on marijuana chrgs 7-14, 844G2; sentncd 12-1, 992G1
Chrgd with fraud in NY 10-27, 992A2
CLARK, Joseph
Trudeau notes lack of support 2-24, 145F2
On Trudeau NY speech 3-21, 225E3
2 chrgd in '77 office tap 4-3, 244A2
Offers mortgage tax relief plan 9-21, 755A2
CLARK, Mario
NFL '77 interceptn ldr 1-1, 56D2
CLARK, Monty
49ers successor fired 1-10, 171D2
Named Lions coach 1-11, 171C2
CLARK, Ron
Revenge of Pink Panther released 7-19, 970A3
CLARK, Vernon (Rip) (d. 1977)
Lyle chrgd with slaying 1-6, 56C1
Lyle acquitted 12-16, 1028D2
CLARKE, Bobby
Wales Conf wins NHL All-Star game 1-24, 76D3
CLARKE, Maj. Gen. Mary
Promoted 7-1, 843C3
CLARKSDALE, Miss.—*See MISSISSIPPI*
CLARK University (Worcester, Mass.)
Power plant size, efficiency study rptd 6-2, 408D3
CLASS Actions—*See COURTS*

1979

CLANTON, David A.
AMA ad ban ordrd ended 10-24, 902G2
CLARK, Bob
Murder By Decree released 2-8, 174B3
CLARK, Brian
Whose Life opens 4-17, 712E3
CLARK, Bruce
Wins Lombardi Award 1-18, 175G2
CLARK, Candy
When You Comin' Back released 2-8, 174F3
More Amer Graffiti released 8-17, 820B2
CLARK, Carroll (deceased)
Death tied to '53 A-test 8-4, 630D1
CLARK, Charles (Booble)
NFL injury suit ruling declined by Sup Ct 10-29, 884F1
CLARK, Dick
S Africa '78 campaign gifts to Jepsen chrgd 3-21, 213C1
Labor '78 campaign gifts rptd 6-13, 595D1
To head Cambodia aid effort 10-26, 823G3
Quits refugee post, joins Kennedy campaign 10-30, 847C2
CLARK, Ed
Heads '80 Libertarian pres ticket 9-8, 680G2
CLARK, Frank
Sentncd 6-12, 442G2
CLARK, (Charles) Joseph (Canadian prime minister)
In Asia, Mideast tour 1-7—1-18, 57E2
Starts electn campaign 3-27, 266G2, E3
In TV debate, backs more RCMP powers 5-13, 368C3, E3
Wins electn 5-22; photo 5-23; facts on 377A1-378B1
Quebec negotiatns bar cited 6-3, 424E2
Sworn, names Cabt 6-4, 423C3
Vows Israel Emb in Jerusalem 6-5, 424B1
Weighs Mideast missn re Israel Emb 6-14, 467D3
Delays Israel Emb move, sets Mideast study 6-23, 502G1
At Tokyo energy summit 6-28—6-29, 493B1
Seeks Canada oil price rise, other energy sources 6-29, 501B3
Trudeau scores 7-19, 563C2
Indian women protest bias 7-20, 601D2
Prov premrs ask budget role 8-17, 632B2
Loto Canada sold to provs 8-21, 651D2; final price set, Baetz lauds 9-6, 685A2
Promises prov resource control 9-5, 9-14, 706G2
Janelle joins PCs 9-19, 729C1
Scores govt aid to business 9-27, 749D3
Parlt opens, Throne speech read 10-9, 788F1-788A3
Yukon cncl gets more power 10-10, 834A1
Rideau Club burns, office damaged 10-23, 834A1
Drops Israel Emb move plan 10-29, 833B2, E2
Assures Parlt re Alberta oil 10-30, 853G2
Scores PQ white paper 11-2, 853A2
Meets premrs; seeks oil price rise, other energy steps 11-12, 888B3
Poll ldrship rating low 12-3, 927C1
Defeated on budget vote 12-13, asks new electns 12-14, 936G2-D3
Trudeau to lead Liberals 12-18, 967B1
Scores PQ referendum bill 12-20, 992C3
CLARK, Josh
Just a Little Less opens 5-20, 712A1
CLARK, Kelvin
In NFL draft 5-3, 335G1
CLARK, Kenneth
Vs split in black ldrship 10-14, 780B3
CLARK, Ramsey
Spenkelink executed in Fla 5-25, 400C1
CIA surveillance rptd 7-16, 561B2
In Turkey, Iran bars US hostage release role 11-7; contacts PLO 11-8, 841D2, F2, 842F1
Recalled to US 11-14, 862G2
CLARK, Robert B.
Defends Valium 9-10, 734E3
CLARK, Ron
Murder at Howard Johnson's opens 5-17, 712E1
CLARK, Susan
Promises in the Dark released 11-2, 1108B1
CLARKE, Bobby
Soviets win Challenge Cup 2-11, 118C2
CLARK Oil & Refining Corp.
Mideast payment chrgs settled 7-19, 985F2
CLARKSBORO, N.J.—*See NEW Jersey*
CLASS Actions—*See COURTS*
CLASSEN, Willie
KOd 11-23, dies 11-28; death probed, boxing suspended in NYS 11-28—12-27, 1004E3

1980

CLANCY, Thomas J.
IRS prosecutn guidelines rptd 8-2, 601B3
CLAREMONT (Calif.) College
Reagan speech heckled 10-13, 779C3
CLARK, (Charles) Joseph (Canadian prime minister; replaced Feb. 18)
Begins electn campaign 1-2, 37E3
Names Jerome to Fed Ct 1-4, 38C2
Hints anti-USSR steps 1-5, 10B3
Sets USSR credit, tech cuts 1-11, 28A2
Backs USSR Olympics move 1-11, 28C3
Releases RCMP probe rpt 1-11, 78E2
Trudeau scores US pipe decisn 1-17; defends 1-18, 56E3
On US diplomats escape from Iran 1-29, 66G2
Carter thanks for Iran rescue 1-31, 88B3
Defeated by Trudeau 2-18, Trudeau sets policies 2-19, 121A1, F2
Vs Canada const 'patriatn' 9-18, 728D2
Backs PSAC strike 10-1, 808D1
Scores budget, energy plan 10-30, 858E2
Scored by Roy 11-3, 885EG3-886A1
Scores Trudeau patriatn plan 12-10, 964A3
CLARK, Allan
NFL '79 kick return ldr 1-5, 8D3
CLARK, Bill
Loses US Sen electn 11-4, 849A2
CLARK, Bob
Tribute released 12-13, 1003F2
CLARK, Bruce
In NFL draft 4-29, 336E2
CLARK, Ed
Urges Anderson quit pres race 8-20, 682B1
On 50 state ballots; ideology cited 10-28, 818E2
Press endorsemts rptd 11-1, 841E3
Popular vote table 11-4, 838A2
CLARK, Jack
Reuss pitches no-hitter 6-28, 636B3
CLARK, John W.
Confrmd Panama Canal comr 4-2, 308E3
CLARK, Judy
2d in LPGA Team tourn 10-5, 972D2
CLARK, Ken
NFL '79 punting ldr 1-5, 8F3
CLARK, Mark (d. 1969)
Panther Chicago shootout retrial order declined, legal fees award voided by Sup Ct 6-2, 513A1
CLARK, Ramsey
US warns vs trip to Iran; Gerassi Viet travel prosecutn cited 5-30, 419B1, E1
Heads US group at anti-US conf in Iran 6-2—6-5; asks Iran free hostages 6-3, OKs panel to probe US 6-4, 418D2, C3
Iran anti-US conf assailed, Ghotbzadeh defends 6-6, 433A1
Meets Iran militants 6-7; leaves Iran, defends visit 6-8, 433A2
US seeks Iran trip probe 6-7, Muskie seen lenient 6-8, Carter for prosecutn 6-10, 6-16; reacts 6-11, 6-15, 459A3
UPI admits error in Iran anti-US conf rpt 6-27, 507D2
CLARKE, Bobby
Canada Cup hockey tourn cancelled 4-30, 488C3
Islanders win Stanley Cup 5-24, 487E3
CLARKE, Jack G.
Saudi completes Aramco takeover, retains bd seat 9-4, 662A2
CLARKE, Maj. Gen. Mary E.
Testifies on sex harassment 2-11, 188F3
CLARKE, Maura
Found slain in El Salvador 12-4, 921B1
CLARKESVILLE—*See GEORGIA*

1976

CLAUSEN, Alden W.
In Mex talks 1-26, 75F1
At Carter econ briefing 12-1, 898F2
CLAUSEN, Rep. Don H. (R, Calif.)
Reelected 11-2, 829A1
CLAWSON, Carol
On Hays mental state 8-30, 646F1
CLAWSON, Rep. Delwin (Del) Morgan (R, Calif.)
Reelected 11-2, 829E1
Elected House GOP Policy Com chrmn 12-8, 981D3
CLAY, Richard
Indicted 1-14, 78C2
CLAY, Rep. William L. (D, Mo.)
Defends travel bills 3-23, 247E1
Travel expenses suit dropped 10-27, 981F3
Reelected 11-2, 820B2, 830A1
CLAYTON Brokerage Co.—*See GARNAC Grain*
CLEAN Air Coalition, National
Scores new EPA policy 11-10, 869C1
CLEAVER, Eldridge
Defense fund announced 2-17, 272E1
FBI role in split with Newton rptd 5-6, 344D2
Freed on bail 8-13, 640C3
CLEAVER, Kathleen
Cleaver Defense Fund formed 2-17, 272F1
CLEGG, Graham
Uganda detentn rptd 8-3, 581A1
Uganda frees 8-25, 874E1
CLEMENTON, N.J.—*See NEW Jersey*
CLEMENTS Jr., William P.
Pentagon offcls censured 3-16, 200D3
Decisn to pay shipyds rptd 4-8, 309A2
Maine shipyd asks contract relief 5-4, 454D1
Rpts shipyd paymt talks stalled 6-10, 453D3
At emergency mtg on Leb 6-16, 425C2
CLEMSON (S.C.) University
In NCAA soccer playoff 12-5, 969G2
CLERIDES, Glafkos
Quits peace talks 1-13, drops resignatn 1-18, 48D2
In new communal talks 2-17—2-21, 155C1
Quits communal talks 4-8, 311A2
Replaced 7-22, loses electn 9-5, 772G3-A2
CLEVELAND, O.—*See OHIO*
CLEVELAND, Rep. James (R, N.H.)
Scored by environmt group 3-25, 220A1
Reelected 11-2, 830C1
PLAIN Dealer, The (Cleveland newspaper)
Ford endorsement rptd 10-30, 831F2
CLEVELAND Press (newspaper)
Ford endorsement rptd 10-30, 831F2
CLEVETRUST Corp.
Cleveland Trust Co.
Lowers prime rate 1-7, 167F2
CLIBURN, Van
Lhevinne dies 11-9, 970C2
CLIFFORD, Belene
Named in Getty will 6-8, 444C2
CLIFFORD, Clark M.
Haldeman wiretap depositn 3-11, 184B2
Sees Carter 12-9, 937F3

1977

CLAUSEN, Ralph J.
On TV viewing decline 12-6, 1021E3
CLAUSTRE, Francoise
Released 1-30; thanks Qaddafi, scores French govt 2-1, 84C2
CLAUSTRE, Pierre
Released 1-30, 84C2
CLAVERO, Manuel
Spain regional min 7-5, 545A2
CLAY, Ken
In World Series 10-11—10-18, 806D3
CLAY, William L.
Loses St Louis mayoral race 4-5, 252F3
CLAYBORN, Raymond
In NFL draft 5-3, 353B2
CLAYBROOK, Joan Buckler
Named Natl Highway Traffic Safety admin 3-18, confrmd 4-6, 272G2
Nader scores, asks resignatn 11-30, 1008A1
CLAYTOR Jr., W. Graham
Named Navy secy 1-19, 52G3; nominated 2-7, confrmd 2-11, 148D3
Upgrades homosexual's dischrg 4-27, 344F1
Expanded sea duty for women backed 12-21, 978G2
CLEAMONS, Jim
Traded to Knicks 10-8, 870A3
CLEAN Air—*See ENVIRONMENT—Air & Water*
CLELAND, Joseph Maxwell
Named VA admin 2-18, confrmd 2-25, 148E3
On veterans' alcholism 6-7, 472A2
CLEMSON (S.C.) University
Rollins in NBA draft 6-10, 584B3
Loses Gator Bowl 12-30, 1020C2
CLERC, Loly
Czechoslovakia expels 3-2, 220E3
CLERGY & Laity Concerned
Luce scores PI rights abuses 8-25, 665A1
CLERIDES, Glafkos
Drops pres bid 12-16, 984B1
CLEVELAND, O.—*See OHIO*
CLEVELAND-Cliffs Iron Co.
USW settles, ends strike 11-21, 977C2
CLEVELAND National Forest (Calif.)
Fire destroys 3,000 acres 7-28—7-31, 660F2
CLIFFORD, Clark
Sees Waldheim, Kreisky 2-16; starts Aegean missn 2-17—2-22, 122F1
Ends missn in Cyprus 2-23—2-26; briefs UK 2-26—2-28, 146G3
At Makarios funeral 8-8, 617E1
CLIFFORD Warnke Glass McIlwain & Finney
Warnke named to US post 2-2, 88G3
CLIMATE—*See WEATHER*
CLINCH River (Va., Tenn.)
Floods rptd 4-3—4-6, 311A3
Tenn A-project curbed 4-7, 267E3
A-project funds dropped from bill 7-25, 592A3
House OKs A-projct, Carter veto seen 9-20, 758C2
A-projct authorizatn clears Cong 10-20, 832G3; vetoed 11-5, 854E2
'78 NRC authorizatn clears Cong 11-29, 938E1
CLINE, Ray
Backs CIA-press links 12-27, 1006G1
CLINTON, Mass.—*See MASSACHUSETTS*
CLINTON County, N.Y.—*See NEW York State*

1978

CLAUDON, Paul
Get Out Your Handkerchiefs released 12-17, 1030A3
CLAUSEN, Rep. Don H. (R, Calif.)
Reelected 11-7, 850D1
CLAWSON, Rep. Del (R, Calif.)
Grisham wins seat 11-7, 856F3
CLAY, Ken
Yankees win AL pennant 10-7, 778F3
In World Series 10-10—10-17, 799B3
CLAY, Gen. Lucius D. (ret.)
Dies 4-16, 356D2
CLAY, Rep. William L. (D, Mo.)
Scores A-worker firing, seeks GAO review 3-29, 242B2
Scores press, Korean scandal probe 10-13, 832B1
Reelected 11-7, 851C2
CLAYBORN, Raymond
NFL '77 kick return ldr 1-1, 56C3
CLAYBURGH, Jill
Unmarried Woman released 3-4, 620B1
CLAYTON, Stanley
Jonestown suicide resistance rptd 11-26, 911D1
CLAYTOR Jr., William Graham
Backs medium-sized carriers 2-21, 127G1
On carrier constructn, Admin shipbldg cuts 3-27, 223F3
Sees US anti-sub tech edge 5-24, 407B3
Hails Gen Dynamics, Litton contract dispute setlmts 6-9, 6-20, 469B1, A2, E2
Gay dischrg policy chng rptd 8-21, 683G2
CLEAN Air—*See ENVIRONMENT—Air & Water*
CLEARWATER, Fla.—*See FLORIDA*
CLEAVER, Eldridge
CIA spying on Black Panthers rptd 3-17, 243A3
CLELAND v. National College of Business
VA educ curbs backed by Sup Ct 3-20, 205E3
CLEMSON (S.C.) University
Wins Gator Bowl; Ohio coach punches player 12-29, coach suspended 12-30, 1025F2, G2
CLEMENT, Frank Goad (1920-69)
Son loses Tenn primary 8-3, 606B2
CLEMENT, Robert N.
Loses Tenn primary for gov 8-3, 606G1
CLEMENTE, Fel
Lopez TKOs 10-21, 969E1
CLEMENTE, Roberto (1934-72)
Family case vs FAA declined by Sup Ct 5-1, 364D1
CLEMENTE v. FAA
Clemente family suit vs FAA declined by Sup Ct 5-1, 364D1
CLEMENTS, Daniel
4 plead guilty to GSA corruptn 10-4, 753E3
CLEMENTS, Dave
Fired as Caribous coach 6-27, 707D3
CLEMENTS Jr., William P.
Wins primary for Tex gov 5-6, 362E3
Elected 11-7, 846B3, 853E3, 855A3
CLENCHED Hand, The (sculpture)
Stolen 2-20, 335D1
CLERC, Jose-Luis
Loses Canadian Open 8-20, 1027B2
CLEVELAND, O.—*See under OHIO*
CLEVELAND, James
Wins Grammy 2-24, 316A1
CLEVELAND, Rep. James C. (R, N.H.)
Reelected 11-7, 847F3, 851F2
CLEVELAND, Reggie
Traded to Brewers 12-15, 1026D1
CLEVELAND Electric Illuminating Co.
Cleveland defaults 12-16, Muny Light purchase studied 1008G2-A3
CLEVELAND National Air Races
'73 auto crash award 5-3, 460D1
CLEVETRUST Corp.
Cleveland Trust Co.
City debt collectn deferred 12-28, 1008D3
CLIFFORD, Clark M.
Vs specific intell curbs 4-4, 306C2
CLIFFORD Glass, McIlwain & Finney
Finney dies 1-30, 96G1
CLIFTON, John
Bistro Car opens 3-23, 887B1
CLIMATE—*See WEATHER*
CLINCH River (Va., Tenn.)
A-project not budgeted 1-23, 46C2
A-project authrzn dropped 2-8, 107A2, B2
A-projct funds signed, Carter plans halt 3-7, 160C3; GAO: halt illegal 3-10, 183E2
A-projct compromise proposal rptd 3-17, 3-23, 241F3
Carter visits Oak Ridge 5-22, 386B3
Carter A-breeder deal, gas compromise linked 8-23—8-26, 678A1
CLINE Maxon Inc.
Anacin ads ruled misleading 9-16, 770B1
CLINGER Jr., William F.
Wins US House seat 11-7, 849E2, 852E1
CLINKSCALES Jr., William
Testifies on GSA abuses 9-19, 714F2
CLINORIL (sulindac)—*See MEDICINE—Drugs*
CLINTON, Bill
Wins primary for Ark gov 5-30, 426C2
Elected 11-7, 853D2, 855F1
CLIOQUINOL (quinoform)—*See MEDICINE—Drugs*

1979

CLASS Enemy (play)
Opens 6-18, 711C2
CLASS of Miss MacMichael, The (film)
Released 1-26, 528A2
CLASS Reunion (book)
On best-seller list 9-2, 672B3
CLAY Station, Calif.—*See CALIFORNIA*
CLAYTON, Zack
Benitez decisns Palomino, denies fix 1-14, 79B3
CLAYTOR Jr., William Graham
Named Transportatn temp secy 7-20, 529D1
Confrmd Defense dep secy 7-27, 577D1
CLEAR, Mark
2d in AL top rookie vote 11-26, 955C3
CLEAVER, Eldridge
Murder chrgs rptd dropped 12-3, 1006E1
CLEESE, John
Life of Brian released 8-17, 820A2
CLEMENT, Dick
Prisoner of Zenda released 5-25, 820A3
CLEMENTE, Michael
Indicted 3-6, 220C2
CLEMENTS, B. Gill
On Sedco oil spill suits 10-19, 809G2
CLEMENTS, Daniel M.
Scores Gasch GSA sentences 5-29, 964B3
CLEMENTS Jr., Gov. William P. (R, Tex.)
Orders odd-even gas rationing 6-19, 462F2
Discounts Kennedy '80 run 8-19, 627D3
Sedco oil blowout liability unclear 8-23, 689C1
On Baker Hotel closing 8-31, 887D2
Lifts odd-even gas rules 9-3, 683F1
Sedco links rptd probed 9-22, 718B3
CLEMSON (S.C.) University
Football '78 rank rptd 1-2, 1-3, 8E2
Butler, Fuller in NFL draft 5-3, 335F2, G2
Loses NCAA soccer title game 12-9, 1004G1-A2
Loses Peach Bowl 12-31, 1001C3
CLERC, Jose Luis
Loses Argentine Open 11-25, 1003G3
CLEVELAND, O.—*See OHIO*
CLEVELAND Electric Illuminating Co.
City bond issue ban declined by Sup Ct 2-21, 128B3
Bank cleared re stock buy 3-14, 204D2
Ohio coal-use ruling issued 5-7, 351F1
EPA eases air rule 6-6, 422D3-423C1
City default tied to anti-mayor moves 7-17, 579B3
Muny Light rpts '78 profit 7-29, 580E1
CLEVELAND Trust Co.—*See under CLEVETRUST Corp.*
CLEVETRUST Corp.
Cleveland Trust Co.
FRB rpt clears 3-14, 204D2
Default tied to anti-mayor moves 7-17, 579B3
CLIFFORD, Clark M.
Sees Carter 7-7, 514C1
CLIMATE—*See WEATHER*
CLIMATE of Treason, The (book)
Philby spy ring explored 10-28, 10-29, 873G3
Blunt named 4th spy 11-15, 908D2
CLINARD, Marshall B.
Corp crime study rptd 3-8, 240B1
CLINCH River (Va., Tenn.)
A-project not budgeted 1-22, 45A3
Carter vs A-projct 5-4, 346G3

1980

CLASS Reunion (book)
On best-seller list 7-13, 568D3
CLAUDE, Sylvio
Arrested 10-13; family members arrested 11-29, 922B3
CLAUSEN, A. W.
Nominated World Bank pres 10-30, 826G1
CLAUSEN, Rep. Don H. (R, Calif.)
Reelected 11-4, 842D1
CLAVELL, James
Shogun aired by NBC 9-15—9-19, top ratings rptd 9-24, 835F2
Shogun on best-seller list 10-12, 796E3
CLAVERO Arevalo, Manuel
Resigns Cabt post 1-16, 101A3
Andalusia autonomy vote falls short 2-28, 174B3
Suarez shuffles Cabt 5-2, 355B1
CLAY, Rep. William L. (D., Mo.)
Wilson reprimand motn rejctd 6-10, 438B2
Reelected 11-4, 851C2
CLAYBROOK, Joan
On car crash tests 2-28, 225D2
On seatbelt use decline 3-26, 309A3
CLAYTON, Billy Wayne (William)
FBI Brilab probe target 2-9, 111F2
Indicted 6-12, 454E2, A3
Acquitted 10-23, 971B2
CLEAMONS, Jim
In NBA expansn draft 5-28, 447E1
CLEARE, Cedric (d. 1977)
Murderers hanged 1-29, 132B2
CLEARY, Catherine
Carter names to Synfuels Corp bd 9-13, Sen panel OKs 9-25, 725F2
Carter names to interim Synfuels Corp bd 10-5, 786F2
CLEAVER, Eldridge
Gets 5 yrs probatn 1-3, 64E3
French newspr rpt on asylum cited 11-7, 872F1
CLEMENS, Brian
Watcher in the Woods released 4-16, 416G3
CLEMENTE, Michael
Convicted 5-2, sentncd 5-20, 927E2, A3
CLEMENTS Jr., Gov. William P. (R, Tex.)
Paroles Hayes 2-6, 175G2
On Tex primary results 5-3, 342G2
Visits Reagan 11-16, 881A2
CLEMON, U. W.
Named US dist judge 1-10; ABA scores 5-19, Sen confrms 6-26, 744C2
CLEMSON (S.C.) University
NCAA basketball tourn results 3-24, 240A2
Stuckey in NFL draft 4-29, 336F3
CLERC, Jose-Luis
Argentina wins Nations Cup 5-12, 607A2
Loses Washn Star Intl 7-27, wins US Clay Cts 8-10, 691A3, B3
CLEVELAND—*See OHIO*
CLEVELAND Board of Education v. Reed
Case refused by Sup Ct 3-17, 226A1
CLEVELAND Electric Illuminating Co.
EPA tightens air rule 6-17, 494C3
CLEVELAND Press (newspaper)
Bogdanich, Johns win Polk award 2-25, 692E3
Sold 10-31, 1003D3
CLEVER, Edith
Left-Handed Woman released 4-2, 416C3
CLIFFORD, Clark M.
In India, assures on US arms to Pak 1-30; warns Sovts vs Persian Gulf move 1-31; Vance, Byrd rebut 2-1, 2-2, 83C2
Deplores W Europe failure to back US on Sovt sanctions 3-18, 205F1
Financial Gen deal set 7-25, 600F3
CLIFFORD, W. B. (Pete)
Wins Ala US House primary 9-2, 682F2
Loses US House electn 11-4, 849G1
CLIMATE—*See WEATHER*
CLINCH River (Va., Tenn.)
A-project not budgeted 1-28, 71G3
CLINGER Jr., William F.
Elected to US House 11-4, 844E1
CLINKSALES Jr., William A.
Testifies on GSA abuses 1-19, 112A2
CLINTON, Gov. Bill (D, Ark.)
A-plant defies gas venting order 5-13, 441D1
Activates Natl Guard at Chaffee 5-27, 396C1
Cubans riot at Chaffee 6-1; processing suspended, troops enforce calm 6-2, 420A1
Loses reelectn 11-4, 847B1, 849A2
CLINTON Correctional Facility (Dannemora, N.Y.)
Escapee chrgd in Halberstam slaying 12-6, 940A1
CLIPPER (yacht)
Freedom wins America's Cup trials 8-29, 834F1

1976

CLOSE, Brig. Gen. Robert
Defends Warsaw Pact attack theory 3-19, 297E2
CLOTHING
Dec '75 output rptd up 1-16, 92A1
Dec, '75 CPI 1-21, 90C1
Trade comm rules on shoe imports 2-21, 213D2
Ford bars shoe import curb 4-16, 321F3
Levi Strauss price-fixing chrgd 5-7, 989D3
Clothing, textile unions merge 6-3, 436E1
Dem platform text 6-15, 469C2
Warnaco admits rebates 9-13, 690B1
Aug CPI rptd 9-21, 708E2
Shoe import probe reopened 10-5; US industry ruled hurt by imports 12-28, 976C2
Mary Tolstoy dies 11-21, 970C3
'60-75 consumer spending rptd 11-23, 959G2
Canada curbs imports 11-29, 924F1
Dacron price raised 11-30, 898G1
Mainbocher dies 12-27, 1015A2
CLOTHING and Textile Workers Union, Amalgamated (AFL-CIO)
Established; to organize Stevens; boycott OKd 6-3, 436E1
CLOTHING Workers of America, Amalgamated (AFL-CIO)
Merges with Textile Workers 6-3, 436E1
CLOUD, Dr. Luther A.
Scores alcohol study 6-10, 443D1
CLUB des Amis du Sahel—*See SAHEL, Club des Amis du*
CLUB of Rome
UN world econ rpt challenges '72 study 10-13, 760E1
CLUVERIUS 4th, Wat T.
Named Bahrain amb 9-16; confrmd 9-30, 807F3
COADY, Msgr. Leo
Aids in Gearhart body return 7-13, 519E3
COAGE, Allen
Wins Olympic medal 7-26, 575A1

COAL—*See also country names*
Australia-Japan deal OKd 1-20, 46G1
Australia-Japan talks 2-4—2-15, 137D3
UNECE rpt issued 2-10, 164G1
US-Turkey venture failure rptd 2-21, 167B1
Australia-Rumania deal rptd 4-6, 250A1
Australia-UK-Japan mining project set 7-7, 496A2
E-W Ger lignite-mining pact rptd 7-15, 889C2
BP plans S Africa investmt rise 8-26, 714B1
W Ger backs Poland projct 12-8, 966E1
U.S. Developments (domestic)
Sup Ct to hear environmt case 1-12, 23G3
Ford State of Union message 1-19, 37F3, 39D2
'77 energy research budgeted 1-21, 64A3, C3
Dec, '75 CPI rptd 1-21, 90D1
Sup Ct upholds penalty procedure 1-26, 87B3
Jan CPI rptd 2-20, 168E2
House expands black-lung program 3-2, 181F3
Ky mine blasts 3-9—3-11, 256A3
Feb CPI rptd 3-19, 215A2
'75 energy use data rptd 4-4, 285C1
Utah power prjct dropped 4-14, 282B2
March CPI rptd 4-21, 306C2
Strip-mine rules adopted 5-11, 359D2-B3
Sup Ct backs Cheyenne rights 5-19, 394A1
Dem platform text 6-15, 470D3, 474E3, 475D1
Land leasing bill clears Cong 6-21, Ford vetoes 7-3, 518C1
Strip-mining stay reversed 6-28, 568G3
Black-lung law upheld 7-1, 568F3
Wildcat strike begins 7-19, 553F1
May, June CPI rptd 7-21, 536D2
Leasing veto overridden 8-3, 8-4, 566E2
Carter backs fuel use 8-9, 585C1
Wildcat strike ends 8-16, 669E3-670A1

1977

CLONING—*See GENETICS*
CLONTZ, Robert J.
Indicted 8-2, 631B3
CLOTHING
Dec '76 CPI rptd 1-19, 78B1
Australia import quotas retained 2-16, 158B2
Russell Patterson dies 3-17, 264D3
Labor ldrs ask garment-import curbs, workers protest Carter policies 4-6, 4-13, 271D2
Australia sets NZ import quotas 4-17, extends quotas 5-2, 345G3
March CPI rptd 4-21, 324C2
'60-61, '72-73 family spending compared 5-10, 423E2
Australia rebuffs NZ quota plea 5-18, 410C2
'77 fashion wrap-up 6-6, 7-29, 1022C1
Men's, boys' apparel workers get pact 6-9, 481B3
Robert Hall to close 6-16, 520B1
Australia rejects ASEAN trade criticism 7-9, 561A1
UM&M seeks bankruptcy 7-12, sells Robt Hall 8-8, 612F1-E2
June CPI rptd 7-21, 554C2
US hosts Sovt exhibit 11-12, 988D2
Shoes—*See under 'S'*
Sleepwear-Tris Issue—*See CHEMICALS—Tris*
CLOTHING Manufacturers Association
Men's, boys' apparel workers get pact 6-9, 481C3
CLOTHING and Textile Workers Union, Amalgamated (AFL-CIO)
Stevens mtg protest 3-1, 153E3
Findley sees Carter, workers protest imports 4-13, 271E2, A3
Men's, boys' apparel workers get pact 6-9, 481B3
Stevens fines set 10-27, trust suits filed 11-1, 11-10, 899B1
Stevens chrgd by NLRB law judge 12-21, 1005C1
CLOUGH, John W.
Antarctic shelf penetrated 12-9, 971G2
CLOUTIER, Real
Final WHA standings 4-7, 310E2
Quebec wins WHA title 5-27, 430C1
CLOUZOT, Henri-Georges
Dies 1-12, 84F2
CLUBS & Social Organizations—*See also specific names (e.g., FREEMASONS)*
3 chrgd in '76 NYC fire 1-2, 1-11, 140A2
Bell membershp dispute 1-11—1-18, 34G1
Kiwanis charter-withdrawal case review refused 10-3, 760D3
Carter plans business tax-break end 12-20, 976C3
CLUJO, Daniel
Kidnaped 9-11, 922D2
CLUJO, Monica
Kidnaped 9-11, 922E2
CLUNIES-Ross, John
In Australia talks 6-17—6-19, 504C3
CLUSKEY, Frank
Named party ldr 7-1, 530G2
CLYMER, Judge Lewis W.
Orders teachers strike halt 5-6, 481E2
C&NW—*See CHICAGO & North Western Transportation Co.*

COAL—*See also country names*
Ford energy message 1-7, 14C3
Mont Indian land leases revoked 1-13, 58F3
Ford budgets energy research 1-17, 31A3
Andrus backs strip mining curbs 1-18, 35A1
Pa mine fire 2-7—4-5, 396C2
Jan CPI rise rptd 2-18, 129C3
Carter submits budget revisns 2-22, 125D2
Carter asks energy dept 3-1, 148G1, D2
New burning process set 3-4, 278B1
'76 use rptd 3-13, 196B2
Carter for increased use 3-17, 191A1
Feb CPI rise rptd 3-18, 215C1
Ford-Mitre study issued 3-21, A-researchers dispute 3-26, 234B3, 235B1
6 cos fined 3-21, 2 execs indicted 6-2, 520G2
US '76, '71-76 elec power data rptd 3-23, 3-25, 277F1
Babcock sues vs United Tech purchase 4-4, 274C3
Carter asks plutonium ban 4-7, 268C1
Carter energy plan 4-18, 4-20, 289B1, E2, 290D2, 294A3, G3, 295A1-G1; fact sheet 291C1-G1, B3, 293C1-B2, A3
Admin backs 'scrubbers' 4-18, 322D3
Cong reactn to Carter energy plan 4-20, 293F2
Carter energy plan reactn 4-21—4-24, 319G3-320A1, B3
March CPI rptd 4-21, 324C2
Carter defends energy plan 4-22, 321D2
House OKs strip-mining curbs 4-29, 365G2
Climate impact studied 4-30, 5-31, 499C1
FEA proposes indl plant conversn 5-9, 369G3
Apr CPI rise rptd 5-22, 406B3
Carter environmt message 5-23, 404C2
Sen amends '70 Clean Air Act 6-10, 461E1

1978

CLOSE Encounters of the Third Kind (book)
On best-seller list 1-8, 24F3; 2-5, 116D3; 3-5, 195F3
CLOSE Encounters of the Third Kind (film)
Top-grossing film 1-4, 24G3; 2-1, 116E3; 3-1, 195G3; 3-29, 272E3
Wins Oscar 4-3, 315C3
CLOTHESPINS
US bars China import curbs 10-2, 805E1
CLOTHING & Fashion—*See also specific types*
US-Taiwan export agrmt rptd 2-27, 140B3
'64-78 spending pattern chngs reflected in new CPIs 222D2
USSR cuts synthetic prices 3-1, 151A3
Nigeria import ban rptd 4-4, 248C1
Quebec ends sales tax 4-11, 286G2
US Mar CPI rptd up 4-28, 345A1
US Tris exports banned 5-5, 347A3
US Apr CPI rise rptd 5-31, 428D3
Interco settles FTC chrgs 7-14, 768E3
'78 high chic fashion rptd 8-4—8-11, 10-27—11-3, 1029A2
US jeans co opens Hungary factory 8-8, 882D3
Australia import tax proposed 8-15, 628C2; scored 8-17, 646A2
US Aug CPI rise rptd 9-26, 752D1
US Sept CPI rise rptd 10-27, 864E1
US Oct CPI rise rptd 10-28, 918E2, A3
Carter pocket vetoes Tris compensatn bill, asks SBA to aid firms 11-8, 941C3
US jeans sold in E Ger 11-29, 1021A3
US Nov CPI rise rptd 12-22, 1003A2
Obituaries
James, Charles 9-23, 778D1
Paley, Babe 7-6, 620D3
Reid, Rose Marie 12-18, 1032D3
CLOTHING and Textile Workers Union, Amalgamated (AFL-CIO)
Stevens head forced off bank bd 3-7, 163A1
Avon chrmn quits Stevens bd, cites pressure 3-21, 205D1
Declared Stevens NC plant bargaining rep 3-26, 243B2
Stevens settles NLRB suit 4-28, 324F1-C2
Cotton dust rules challenged 6-19, 471E3
More Stevens bd chngs 9-11, 9-12, 699D2
CLOUD-Seeding—*See STORMS*
CLOUSE, Robert
Amsterdam Kill released 3-30, 618B3
CLOUTIER, Real
WHA scoring ldr 4-11, 296G2
CLUB Mediterranee
Paris hq bombed, '77 attacks cited 6-11, 473D3
CLUBS & Social Organizations—*See also club names*
Arsonist sentenced in '76 NYC fire 2-7, 380G3
Carter vs business tax breaks 2-17, 123A2
CLUCHETTE, John
Chrgd in Oakland murder 8-25, 886G3
CLUNIES-Ross, John
Australia announces Cocos I purchase 7-2, 514D1
CLUSKEY, Frank
Scores Lynch on reunificatn 1-9, 18E3
CLYNE, Judge John
Sentences Provenzano, Konigsberg 6-21, 480B2

COAL
Miners pensn jurisdictn case review barred 1-9, 13E2
Slurry study issued by OTA; reactn 1-18, 49A1-A2
Carter budgets research 1-23, 46G1
Black lung bills clear Cong 1-24, 2-15; finance measure signed 2-10, 125E1-E2; benefit eligibility bill signed 3-1, 218B2
Research authorizatn clears Cong 2-8, 107A3; 2-25, 218B2
Adams issues transportatn policy statemt 2-8, 109F1
Coal Policy Projct issues compromise rpt, EPC scores 2-9, 184G1-A3
EPA sulfur dioxide rules for Ohio upheld 2-13, 109A2
Mine constructn workers strike 3-27, reach tentative pact 3-28, 217E1
Mine constructn workers ratify pact 4-5, 265E1
Oil, gas firms' reserves lid backed by FTC aide 4-5; Justice Dept proposal rptd 4-6, 282D2, A3
Calif studies A-plant alternative 4-18, 281G2
House-Sen conferees OK conversn plan 4-21, 305C1, E1
W Va power plant scaffold collapses 4-27, 459G3
Anthracite pact ratified, '77 output rptd 4-30, 324E2
TVA pollutn setlmt scored 5-5, 5-18; new TVA chrmn backs alternatives 5-19, 390C2, D2
Energy rpt forecasts output rise 5-8, 366D2
Oil, gas firms' 15% reserves lid backed by Justice Dept 5-15, 471C2
US probes bias, orders affirmative actn progrms 5-30, 565A3
Power plant size, efficiency studied 6-2, 408D3
Gasificatn plant financing plan submitted 6-2, 471E2

1979

CLONING—*See GENETICS*
CLORE, Sir Charles
Dies 7-26, 588E2
CLOROX Co.
FTC '76 cleanser complaint setld 2-19, 308G2
CLOSE, Glenn
Wine Untouched opens 6-22, 712F3
CLOSE Encounters of the Third Kind (film)
Theme wins Grammy 2-16, 336G3
Columbia Pictures '78 equity return cited 5-7, 305A2*
CLOTHING & Fashion
US Dec '78 CPI rise rptd 1-24, 73A2
Daylin OKs Grace takeover 1-24, 88E3
Clothing, shoe unions merge 3-6, 207A1
Rumania sets price chngs 3-12, 279E3
GATT pact signed 4-12, 273G1, 274F1
'79 fashion roundup rptd 1006F1
Fortune rpts United Merchants sales drop 5-7, 305C1
ILGWU gets 25%, 3-yr pact 5-30, 402E1
USSR hikes coat, fur prices 7-2, 504D2
Canada tariff cuts rptd 7-12, 543E1
Franklin Simon parent co files bankruptcy 7-27, 648F3
Interco to buy Ethan Allen 8-13, 664B1
French knitwear import curbs protested in Italy 8-20, 668D3
Formaldehyde-cancer link rptd 10-18, 971E1
Sept CPI rise rptd 10-26, 828A1
Obituaries
Delaunay, Sonia 12-5, 1008D2
Hartnell, Norman 6-8, 508B3
Ratia, Armi 10-3, 860C3
Van Slyke, Helen 7-3, 588F3
CLOTHING and Textile Workers Union, Amalgamated (AFL-CIO)
Shoe workers union absorbed 3-6, 207A1
Stevens '77 suits dismissed 7-18, 8-6, 598C3
Stevens, others sued in Ga 7-18; Grumman, local offcls settle 8-1, 598E3
Finley backs Carter reelectn 7-30, 593D3
Potofsky dies 8-5, 671D3
CLOUSER, Ronald
Confesses in 'gentleman bandit' case 8-20, sentenced 11-30, 953G2
CLOUTIER, Real
WHA scoring ldr 4-18, 355F2, 356C1
CLUBS & Social Organizations
All-white judicial memberships assailed 7-14, 9-19, 9-25, 901E2
Canada's Rideau Club burns 10-23, 834A1
CLUTE, Howard Vander
VFW votes pol actn unit 8-21, installed cmdr 8-24, 628D1

COAL
Carter cuts research budget 1-22, 45F2
US cncl sees use cut 2-20, 132F2
Schlesinger backs as oil substitute 3-12, 183E2
W Va broker pleads guilty to fraud 3-13, 239G3
Ohio co sues vs clean-air rule 3-22, 206A3
Carter asks greater use 4-5, 250F3
NY power plant planned 4-5, 261B3
Carter stresses use, plans hearings 4-10, 263G2
Sick miner pay hike case declined by Sup Ct 4-30, 364C3
Low-level radiatn risk assessed 5-2, 609F2
EPA upheld re Ohio use 5-7, 351C1
Exxon unveils energy-saving device 5-18, 404B2
Utilities get clean-air rules; reactn 5-25, 403G2-404B1
EPA eases Cleveland utility air rule 6-6, 422D3-423C1
Rail decontrol bill scored 6-6, 579F2
Connally on energy crisis 6-11, 439F3
House OKs synthetic fuel bill 6-26, 498G1
Admin plans previewed 7-8, 517E3
Carter offers 6-pt energy plan 7-15, 7-16, 532C2, D2, 534A1, C1, B2
Sun Co purchase of Elk R Resources set 7-31, 986B3
NY energy plan outlined 8-7, 609G3
Interior Dept seeks to protect western lands 9-7, 703D3
Ky widows suit challenge declined by Sup Ct 10-1, 768F1
Pa mining accident, woman dies 10-2, 860G2
Va A-reactor shift studied 10-15, 807A2
RFK's son scores co profits 10-20, 807G3
House OKs Energy Dept authrzn 10-24, 848G3
Pa A-plant shift studied 11-5, 849C2

1980

CLITANDRE, Pierre
Arrested 11-28, 922G2
CLOHERTY, Jack
Wins Polk award 2-25, 692F3
CLOROX Co., The
'Playing for Time' sponsored 9-30, 835F3
CLOTHES for a Summer Hotel (play)
Opens 3-26, 392E2
CLOTHING & Fashion
CPSC sued over Tris ban 3-24, 348E2
NY transit strike impact cited 4-10, 268D2
Australia import tariffs kept 8-15, 632F2-D3
US-China textiles pact opposed 9-18, 707D1
Zimco special labor aid OKd 11-5, 870D2
Levi trademark suit vs Wrangler rptd won 11-19, 917B3
Levi retail price fixing suits rptd setld 12-2, 917G2
'80 fashion roundup rptd 998D1
Obituaries
Fogerty, Anne 1-15, 104E2
Jarman, Walton Maxey 9-9, 755D3
Rosenstein, Nettie 3-13, 280G1
Wilhemina 3-1, 280F2
CLOTHING & Textile Workers Union, Amalgamated (AFL-CIO)
Hollander dies 1-3, 104A3
Miller named to AFL-CIO exec cncl 8-21, 647C3
Stevens agrmt reached 10-19, 805B1-D2
Stevens plant access case refused by Sup Ct 10-20, 807A2
Deering Milliken '56 dispute setlmt OKd 12-14, 962E2
CLOUTIER, Real
In NHL All-Star game 2-5, 198A3
NHL scoring ldr 4-6, 296E1
CLUBS & Social Organizations
All-white judicial membership censured by US Conf 3-6, 250D2
CLURMAN, Harold E.
Dies 9-9, 755E2

COAL
ICC orders Burlington shipping refund 1-4, Sup Ct refuses stay 1-14, 37A3
Pa mine inspectn case declined by Sup Ct 1-7, 15F3
Union Pacific, MoPac set merger 1-8, 52D3
State of State messages 1-9, 270B1, 404E1; 1-9, 1-14, 483A3, 484B2
NAS backs more use 1-14, 53D3
Carter State of Union asks switch 1-21, 43D3
Carter budget proposals 1-28, 72B1, 74A1
Kennedy seeks oil-fired boiler shift 2-2, 91E1
W Va miners strike 2-21—3-3, 169G3-170D1
Carter plan seeks more use by utilities 3-6, 169A3
Connally, Kennedy back use in 'basic speech' 3-7, 184F2; 3-10, 183F2

1976

GOP platform text 8-18, 607D2, B3
July CPI rptd 8-20, 635A2
GAO vs synfuel project 8-24, 649G1
Ford, Carter debate 9-23, 702E2
UMW conv 9-23—10-2, 748F1
Syn fuel loan bill defeated 9-23, 883A3
Strip-mining bill not cleared 10-2, 883A1, F2
Sept indl output, strike linked 10-15, 806A2
Coke oven emissns curb set 10-20, 847E3-848A1
Sept CPI rptd 10-21, 805A3
Ky mines to hire women 10-21, 944A1
Ford, Carter debate 10-22, 801D2-E2, A3
Strikes linked to Conrail loss 11-11, 887D1
NE aid plan urged 11-14, 864F3
Bodies removed from Ky mine 11-19, 892B1
6 cos indicted 11-19, 989C2
Peabody Coal to be sold 12-14, largest US mine cited 12-15, 985B1, D1
Utah Intl, GE merge 12-16, 985A1

1977

'76 Ky mine blasts laid to spark 6-13, 8-10; widows suit dismissed 9-12, 900F3, 901A1
'76 strike productn losses estimated 462F3
UMW wildcat strikes 6-18—9-6, 690E2
May CPI rise rptd 6-22, 482B1
Raytheon to buy Falcon Seabd 6-22, 519C1
TVA sued on air pollution 6-22, 521B3
Slurry bill deferred 6-27, 515G3-516F1
Peabody sold 6-30, 520F1
Schlesinger backs A-energy 7-10, 538E2
Carter energy plan health threat seen 7-17, 559F1-A2
June CPI rptd 7-21, 554C2
Strip-mine bill clears Cong 7-21, 575D2-D3; Carter signs 8-3, 592F1
Energy Dept created 8-4, 591G2
Conrail 2d ¼ loss rptd 8-4, 612F3
House OKs Carter energy pkg 8-5, 609D3
Clean-air amendmts enacted 8-8, 610B2
July indl output down 8-15, 628E3
Sen OKs weakened coal-conversn bill, bars acquisitn curbs 9-8, 702B3, F3
Coal-leasing plan barred by ct 9-27, 1007C2
Sept indl output up 10-14, 798A2
Ky UMW strike violence 10-17, 937F2-B3
Sept income up 10-18, 798C2
Research authorizatn clears Cong 10-20, 833B1, E1
User-tax rebate for conversn clears Sen 10-31, 832E3
Columbus (O) voters OK elec plant 11-8, 879D2
Mine safety rules, agency reorganizatn signed 11-9, 855E3
Schlesinger comments draw fire from House 11-21—11-23, 916G3
Winter shortage plans set 12-1, 942A3
UMW strike begins 12-6, 937B1-E2; backed by AFL-CIO 12-13, 961E1
Cong energy conf com agrees on conversn 12-22, 1002B2
UMW talks break off 12-30, 1005F2

Foreign Developments (including U.S. international news)

20th Century Fund, OECD urge greater use 1-11, 1-27, 169E3, 170C1
Australia-Japan shipping dispute 1-17—2-21, 253B2
EC-Australia talks 3-14, 3-16, 218C1
Salzburg A-conf assesses risks 5-2—5-13, 402G3
US-Rumania sale set 5-30, 468C3
Australia-Japan pact signed 8-8, 615E2

1978

Mine safety inspectn case remanded by Sup Ct 6-5, 431E2
'77 mining productivity drop rptd 6-14, 470A1
EPA bars Ohio sulfur dioxide rule delay 7-6, 513E1
Carter vows dvpt measures at Bonn summit 7-16—7-17, 544D1
Conversn bill clears Sen 7-18, 549G3-550C1
Slurry pipeline bill defeated 7-19, 550F1
Miller recall barred by UMW bd 7-26, 624G3
Oil industry mining operatns rptd 9-8, 700D2
EPA proposes power plant scrubber installatn 9-11, 703F1
N&W Rwy strike ends 9-30, 809E2
US sues vs Occidental-Mead merger, cites coking coal reserves 10-11, Occidental offers concessns 10-23, 895B3
Conversn bill clears Cong 10-15, 786A2, 787G1; Carter signs 11-9, 873A1
Diamond Shamrock to buy Falcon Seabd 11-2, 1005B2
Energy Dept fuel rules unveiled 11-15, 919F3-920B1
Pa gas conversn plant closed 12-1, 962G3-963A1
Carter questns oil industry acquisitns 12-12, 983E2
TVA OKs pollutn pact 12-14, 982B3
'78 output rptd down 12-20, 1010A2
Miners sex bias suit setld 12-26, 1006F2

Foreign Developments (including U.S. international news)

China '77 trade hits record 1-16, 89E2
Japan, China sign pact 2-16, 103E3
Japan-Australia coal pacts rptd 2-20, 145E1
Australia-Brazil pact signed 3-1, 165C2
Japan wins Australia price cut 3-1, 165D2
Zambia coke delayed by port backlog 3-8, 170B1
Japan bars Australia import curbs 3-20, 208A3
New S Wales imposes export duties 5-19, 369F3
China dvpt plan outlined 5-28, 436F1
EC bars Australia import cuts 6-13, 494F3
Australia notes Japan import cuts 6-27, 514B2
China Jan-June output up 7-7, 532C1
Australia mine strike rptd, exports halted 7-13, 555C1
Dutch Shell drops Indonesia pact 7-24, 631G3
Australia export levy retained 8-15, 628A2
Australia find rptd 9-1, 686A1
Japan offers China dvpt loans 9-6, 695E2
US, Japan plan joint research 9-6, 695D3
Australia-W Ger conversn effort set 10-10, 793D3
Australia sets export plan 10-24, 836B1
US-China talks rptd set 11-6, 871D2
Australia-US deal rptd signed 12-11, 963A2

Strike & Effects

Talks resume 1-12, Carter bars interventn 1-30, 62B3
Dec '77 indl output index drop linked 1-17, personal income 1-18, 52E1, B2
Carter orders bargaining efforts intensified 2-3—2-13, announces White House talks 2-14, 104D3
Miller announces tentative contract 2-6, UMW bargaining cncl rejects 2-12; setlmt detailed 104D2-C3
Ohio declares energy emergency 2-9, 105C3
9-state area faces critical shortage; power cutbacks, worker layoffs imminent 2-10—2-11, 104C1
Carter grants Ohio, Ind emergency status 2-11, 2-16; sees 12 govs 2-16, 104E1, D2
Ind, W Va order power cutbacks 2-13, 104E3
Ind calls up natl guard 2-14, 160D2
UMW, operators resume talks at White House; deadlock continues 2-15—2-16, 104A1, 105B1
Ohio emergency task force meets 2-15, 104G1
Jan, Dec '77 econ effects rptd 2-15, 106C1, F1, A2, C2
Conrail aid sought 2-15, 224B3
Carter sees talks progress 2-17, 123F1
Carter threatens 'drastic action' 2-18; briefs cong ldrs, coal-state govs, indus execs 2-23—2-24, 122E2
UMW cncl reaches setlmt with P&M 2-20, BCOA rejcts as industry model 2-21, 122G3
$ drop rptd 2-23, 118E2
Meany scores Carter 2-23, 2-24, 142D1
Tentative setlmt reached, Carter urges ratificatn 2-24, 122D2
Carter, Marshall, Miller urge proposed pact ratificatn 2-26—3-1, 159G3-160D1
P&M setlmt rejectd by miners 2-26, 160A1
Jan indicators drop 2-28; Feb indl output 3-16, income 3-17, 223B1, D1
Carter defends role, links poll drop 3-2, 141C1, F1
Miners reject ratificatn 3-4—3-5, 159B2, G3
Jobless rptd 3-4, 160C2
Carter invokes Taft-Hartley, names inquiry bd, offers pay inducemts for return to work 3-6; sees compliance 3-9, 159A2, F2-B3
Carter on Midwest shortage, jobless 3-6, 160A2

1979

Connally campaign themes cited 11-15, 983B1
UMW plans organizing drive 12-10, strike fund 12-13, 986G3
Kennedy stresses use 12-13, 962B2
Kennedy: Carter 'anti-coal' 12-13, 987D1

Foreign Developments (including U.S. international news)

S Africa energy source 1-4, 22C1
USSR '78 plan shortfall rptd 1-19, 60G1, A2
Deutsche BP-Veba deal OKd 3-5, 215B1
S Africa miners protest 3-7, 171F3; end walkout 3-14, 191A2
Swedish energy bill rptd 3-13, 213E3
Japan gets Australia price cuts 3-13, 233B2
US-Japan research pact 5-2, 320E2
W Ger weighs research 5-16, 373D3
IEA backs more use 5-22, 380F1
Japan-US sales pact signed 6-2, 416E1
Luxembourg plans plant 6-6, 506B3
EC comm backs more use 6-13, 437G1
China rpts '78 output 6-18, 484A3
China, W Ger sign pact 6-19, 637G3
Tokyo summit backs more use 6-29, 493E2
W Ger plans more use 7-4, 506A1, E1
Canada seeks US environmt commitmt 7-20, 581E3
Australia sets export duty cut 8-21, 631F3
E-W Ger deal set 9-5, 796A3
W Ger seeks more use 9-12, 733E2
UK shortages seen 9-18, 752F1-A2
Swedish A-progrm alternative studied 10-10, 795C2
Taiwan conversn rptd 11-6, 952C3
Canada prime min backs use 11-12, 888F3
USSR rpts shortfall, '80 target 11-28, 928E3
Australia backs dvpt progrm 12-4, 947G3

1980

'79, 4th 1/4 profits rptd up 3-19, 222E1
Standard Oil (Ind) to buy LTV assets 3-25, 385C3
BN, Frisco RR merger OKd 4-17, 345F2
Hunt property transfers rptd 5-2, 345A1
Hunts bailout loan collateral listed 5-28, 426D1
EPA firms Cleveland utility air rule 6-17, 494C3, G3
GOP platform adopted; text 7-15, 536F3, 537B1, F1
Reagan pres nominatn acceptance speech 7-17, 532C2
ND synfuel plant loan OKd 7-18, 553B2
Dem platform planks adopted 8-13, 611F2, 615F1
Alaska lands bill clears Sen 8-19, 631C2
Multi-employer pensn plan reform signed 9-26, 856D3
Reagan in Ohio 10-7, clarifies pollutn stance 10-9, 779C2, A3
Carter sees future use 10-12, 779D1
Carter visits Ill mine 10-13, 778F3
Carter, Reagan TV debate 10-28, 815F1
ND synfuels plant gets $1.5 bln fed loan 11-19, ct blocks projct 12-8, 961E3
Vepco revises N Anna 4 plans 11-25, 961A2
Pittston unit fined $100,000 12-4, 962G3
Utah project OKd 12-16, 987B2

Foreign Developments (including U.S. international news)

Spain budgets power stations 1-8, 22C2
Australia mine plans rptd 1-19, 56E1
USSR '79 drop rptd 1-25, 79C3
Turkey sets price hike 1-25, 80B1
France-India pact set 1-28, 97B3
W Ger OKs plant project 1-30, 103E2
Australia strikes rptd 3-11, 190G3
France sets new energy measures 4-2, 254D1
Japan bid for Australia projct barred 4-15, 334F1
Australia job dispute begins 5-2, 350A2
Turkey mines rptd denatlzd 6-10, 445F3
Venice summit sets '90 output goal 6-22—6-23, 473A1, F2
UK miners seek 35% pay hike 7-8, 523C2
Dutch rpt vs coal 7-17, 565C2
UK fscl '80 productn rptd 7-30, 578E2
US, W Ger, Japan synfuel pact signed 7-31, 666F2
Japan dvpt urged 8-18, 635A3
Poland miners strike 8-29—9-1; accord reached 9-2, 15,000 stay out 9-3, 657B1, G1, 658B1, B2, E2
Australia strike ends 9-4, 705A2
World Bank '80 loans rptd 9-22, 720D1
Australia conversn project rptd set 10-2, 748A2
Polish productn drop rptd 11-12; govt retains control 11-19, 878F2-B3
Panama Canal congestn, trade increase linked 11-24, 895C3
UK miners OK 13% pay hike 12-1, 922B1

Mergers & Acquisitions

US Steel to sell assets to Sohio 12-2, 985B2
Mapco, Earth Resources merger set 12-5, 985E1
UNC Resources seeks Westn Air merger 12-24, 985C1

1976

COALITION of Northeastern Governors—*See GOVERNORS, U.S.*

COASTAL States Gas Corp.
- SEC lists forgn paymts 5-12, 726F2
- Holborn in oil spill suit 12-22, 969E1

COBALT
- Australia ocean find rptd 2-26, 154F3

COBB, Lee J.
- Dies 2-11, 160C3

COCA-Cola Co.
- Austin cosponsors Carter mtg 7-22, 550G3

COCAINE—*See NARCOTICS & Dangerous Drugs*

COCHISE College Park Co.
- 18 indicted in land fraud 9-14, 859D3

COCHRAN, Dwight M.
- Named to Lockheed probe 2-5, 131D2

COCHRAN, Rep. Thad (R, Miss.)
- Endorses Ford 7-30, 563F3
- Reelected 11-2, 830A1

COCKBURN, Dr. Charles
- Rpts no swine flu 6-3, 423F3

COCKS, Michael
- UK Labor Party whip 4-8, 267A1

COCO, Francesco
- Slain 6-8, 418A3

COCOA
- Nigeria evacuates Equatorial Guinea workers 1-26, 62E1
- 77 Group sets trade guidelines 2-10, 108C1
- Latin output rptd 5-7, 466C1
- UNCTAD OKs commodity fund 5-30, 388G2
- US warns NY commodity exchng 9-15, 990D2

CODD, Michael J.
- Police win '75 increase 12-22, 991D2

CODREANU, Roman
- Wins Olympic medal 7-24, 576B3

COELHO Ines, Jose
- Acquitted 10-11, 858F2

1977

COAL Association, National (NCA)
- Carter energy plan reactn 4-21, 4-24, 319G3-320A1
- Strip-mine bill scored 7-23, 575F2

COALITION for Responsible Genetic Research—*See GENETIC Research, etc.*

COAL Operators' Association, Bituminous—*See BITUMINOUS Coal Operators' Association*

COAL Operators' Association, National
- Wildcat strikes 6-18—9-6, 690G2

COASTAL States Gas Corp.
- Tex agency orders refunds, bars Lo-Vaca contract revisn 12-12, 980D1

COAST Guard—*See under U.S. GOVERNMENT*

COATS—*See CLOTHING*

COBALT
- UN Sea Law Conf adjourns 7-15, US scores rpt 7-20, 572B3

COBB, Donald
- Pleads guilty 5-26, 426D1
- Freed 6-16, 484G3
- Fox on RCMP raid probe 6-23, 541C3
- Testifies on '72 Quebec news agency break-in, PQ info-gathering network 12-7—12-8, 965E1

COBB, Michael
- In NFL draft 5-3, 353B2

COBB, Ty (1886-1961)
- Brock breaks stolen base mark 8-29, 748D3

COBBS, Elizabeth
- Testifies at Ala bomb trial 11-15, 907C3

COBHAM, Viscount (Charles John Lyttelton)
- Dies 3-20, 264E2

COBRA (Israeli helicopter)—*See 'Aircraft' under AVIATION*

COCA-Cola Bottling Co. of Los Angeles
- Northwest takeover OKd 10-17, 880A2

COCA-Cola Co.
- Duncan confrmatn recommended 1-13, 34D3; confrmd 1-31, 148E3
- Bell rpts stock holdings 2-25, 147D3
- Stock falls 3-9, saccharin substitute rptd 3-10, 177B1, A2
- Rpts forgn paymts 4-1, 503F2
- US denies Zaire request 4-21, 317C3
- Egypt contract rptd sought 5-16, 390E2
- India demands subsidy control 8-8, 637E2
- Egypt pact signed, contd Israel trade vowed 863B2

COCAINE—*See NARCOTICS*

COCHITI Lake, N.M.—*See NEW Mexico*

COCHRAN, Bob
- NFL officiating scored 12-18, 12-22, 1020G1

COCHRAN, Buddy D.
- Car rams KKK rally 7-2, chrgd 7-3, 540A1

COCHRANE, Sir Ralph
- Dies 12-17, 1024C1

COCKE Sr., Erle
- Dies 10-7, 872D1

COHUTTA Banking Co. (Chatsworth, Ga.)
- Lance role probed 9-7, 690B2

COCOA
- UN rpts '76 price rise 2-14, 145G3
- US inflatn forecast revised 5-25, 464B2
- France sets price freeze 6-28, 1012D2

COCOS Islands (Australia territory)
- Australia talks 6-17—6-19, 504C3

CODES—*See CRYPTOGRAPHY*

CODY, Thomas G.
- Replaced as HUD asst secy 5-25, 500A1

COE, Donald
- Cancer linked to A-test 12-13, 1022D3

1978

- Carter seeks violence preventn 3-6, govs vow cooperatn 3-7, 160C2
- Va declares emergency 3-7, 160D2
- Issues detailed 3-8, 159C3
- Return to work, talks resumptn ordrd; UMW, operator talks resumptn set 3-9, 159C2
- Carter vs confrontatn, mines seizure 3-9, 160E1
- Carter on output, reserves 3-9, 160B2
- UAW, USW aid strikers 3-9, 3-10, 182E2
- UMW, operator talks resumed, optimism rptd 3-10, 181E3
- Food-stamp cutoff to strikers sought by Admin 3-10, Meany scores 3-11, 182C2
- Inflatn impact cited 3-10, 221G3
- Taft-Hartley effected, defied 3-13, 181F2
- New tentative contract agreed, terms detailed; Carter lauds 3-14, 181D2, 182B1-C2
- Taft-Hartley extensn barred 3-17, 217C1
- New contract ratified 3-24, signed 3-25, Carter hails, vows industry study 3-25, 217A1, F1
- Layoff data cited 3-25, 217B1
- Construction worker strike delays return to work 3-27—3-28, 217D1
- US Steel hikes prices 3-29; price undercut, rolled back 3-30—4-3, 262D3
- Feb trade deficit linked 3-31, 262A2
- Feb indicators index linked 4-6, 262E2
- 1st ¼ real GNP drop rptd 4-19, 303A3
- 1st ¼ wage rise, pact linked 4-27, 389E2
- Utility chrgs to be probed 5-10, 366E3
- TVA rate hike moderatn asked 5-15, increase scaled down 5-17, 362A2
- Apr indl output rise, productn linked 5-16, 389B2
- 1st ¼ profits drop rptd 5-18, 403E1
- Carter names study panel 5-26, 405A1
- 1st ¼ record RR losses rptd 5-27, 433E3
- Rail lines fined in freight-car shortage 6-15, 7-3, 569C2
- Contract setlmt, inflatn linked 6-19, 427D2
- Energy Dept performance faulted 9-11, 701D2-A3
- '78 output rptd down 12-20, 1010A2

COAL Association, National
- '78 coal output rptd down 12-20, 1010A2

COALITION for a Democratic Majority
- Vs Vance-Gromyko SALT mtg 7-10, 543G2-A3

COALITION for Peace Through Strength
- Formed 8-8, 604A3

COALITION of American Public Employees
- Farmer scores Innis 9-18, 810F1

COAL Policy Project, National
- Compromise rpt issued, EPC scores 2-9, 184G1-A3

COAST Guard—*See under U.S. GOVERNMENT*

COATES, Anne V.
- Medusa Touch released 4-14, 619B3

COATES, John
- Remington air gun recall rptd, record setlmt cited 10-25, 942D1

COATES Hotel (Kansas City, Mo.)
- Fire destroys 1-28, 212C3

COBALT
- Zaire invasn pushes prices up 5-22; USSR, US buying rptd 5-23—5-24, 382A2
- Zaire mining resumptn rptd, shortage seen 7-14, 652B3
- US House OKs seabed mining bill 7-26, 588F3
- Zaire '78 productn drop rptd 11-21, 1021C2

COBB, Donald
- Fake FLQ communique bared 1-9, 35E1
- RCMP '74 break-in bared 1-11, 35D2

COBRA (helicopter)—*See ARMAMENTS—Aircraft*

COBURN, Donald L.
- Wins Pulitzer Prize 4-17, 315C1

COCA-Cola Co., The
- USSR '80 Olympics deal set 3-14; Fanta deal rptd 3-16, 230C1
- FTC orders bottler curbs lifted 4-25, 346C1
- Philip Morris to buy 7-Up 5-15, 364B3
- China deal signed 12-13, 1015A2

COCAINE—*See NARCOTICS*

COCHRAN, Rep. Thad (R, Miss.)
- Wins US Sen primary 6-6, 448B1
- Elected 11-7, 846D1, 848D2, 852F2, G2

COCKROFT, Don
- NFL '77 kicking ldr 1-1, 56B2

COCKTAIL Party, The (play)
- Nayatt School opens 5-12, 887B2

COCO, Francesco (d. 1976)
- Genoan police offcl killed 6-21, 517F1

COCOA & Chocolate
- Hungary hikes price 1-9, 55D2
- Ecuador '77 exchng reserves rptd 2-3, 148G2
- USSR hikes chocolate price 3-1, 151A3
- DR '77 trade deficit rptd 3-10, 230F3

COCOS Islands (Australian territory)
- Australia announces purchase 7-2, 514D1

CODEINE—*See NARCOTICS*

CODES—*See CRYPTOGRAPHY*

COE, Donald C.
- Wins A-test cancer claim 8-1, 702F3

COELHO, Tony
- Wins US House seat 11-7, 850F1, 856E3

1979

COAL Association, National
- EPA coal-use rules lauded 5-25, 403G3
- Bagge vs rail decontrol bill 6-6, 579F2

COALITION for a Democratic Majority
- Jackson addresses 6-12, 459F2

COALITION for a New Foreign and Military Policy
- MX 'racetrack' deployment plan scored 9-7, 678C1

COALITION for Direct Action at Seabrook
- Seabrook occupatn prevented 10-6–10-8, 806F3

COALITION for Peace Through Strength
- SALT treaty criticized 4-11, 294D3-295A2

COALITION to Ban Handguns
- Army guns NRA resale suit won 9-4, 747A2

COALPORT, Pa.—*See PENNSYLVANIA*

COARD, Bernard
- Grenada aide to prime min 3-23, 237A1

COASTAL (race horse)
- Wins Belmont Stakes 6-9, 448A2, C2
- 3d in Marlboro Cup 9-8, Jockey Gold Cup 10-6; 2d in Woodward Stakes 9-23, 876G2, A3, E3

COASTAL States Gas Corp.
- Hunt suit ruling declined by Sup Ct 12-10, 988G1

COAST Guard—*See under U.S. GOVERNMENT*

COBALT
- Zaire mining recovery rptd 1-25, 2-15, 137A3
- Canada strike continues 5-12, 369F1

COBLENZ, Walter
- Onion Field released 9-19, 820E2

COBRA (helicopter)—*See ARMAMENTS–Aircraft*

COBURN, James
- Goldengirl released 6-15, 820C1

COCA-Cola Co., The
- Natl Sports Festival held 7-21–8-1, 799C1
- '84 LA Olympic sponsorship rptd 8-20, 798C1
- Emory U to get $100 mln in stock 11-8, 902C2, E2

COCAINE—*See NARCOTICS*

COCHET, Henri
- Borg wins French Open 6-10, 570G1

COCKRELL, Mayor Lila (San Antonio, Tex.)
- Reelected 4-7, 265B2

COCKROFT, Don
- NFL '78 kicking ldr 1-6, 80B1

COCOA
- Brazil '78 exports to Spain rptd 8-6, 654B2

COCTEAU, Jean (1889-1963)
- Massine dies 3-16, 272B3

C&O Development Co.
- Liggett US cigaret business sought 3-28, 283E1
- Liggett merger talks end 6-14, 517G1

CODRON, Michael
- Night and Day opens 11-27, 956E3

COE, Sebastian
- Sets 800-m run mark 7-5, mile run mark 7-17, 1500-m run mark 8-15, 911A1, B1, E1
- Expense paymts probe rptd 11-12, named to UK Olympic team 11-13, 956A2

COETZEE, Gerrie
- Tate decisns for WBA heavywgt title 10-20, 838F2

COETZEE, Col. Gert J.
- US ousts 4-13, 287C1

1980

COALITION for Water Project Review
- Osann scores Carter dam support 10-1, 803A3

COALITION of Labor Union Women
- Miller named to AFL-CIO exec cncl 8-21, 647C3

COAL Miner's Daughter (film)
- Top-grossing film 3-26, 280G3

COAL Transportation Association, National
- Bush addresses 9-10, 780F3

COAST Guard—*See under U.S. GOVERNMENT*

COAST to Coast (film)
- Released 10-3, 836D2

COATS, Andy
- In Okla US Sen primary, runoff set 683B1
- Wins runoff 9-16, 724A3
- Loses US Sen electn 11-4, 850B1

COATS, Daniel R.
- Elected to US House 11-4, 842B3, 850G3

COBALT
- US defns posture, supply linked 1-25, 65G2
- USSR buying noted 2-5, 85E1

COBBS, Chris
- Rpts NBA cocaine use 8-19, 656F1

COCA, Col. Ariel
- Junta tied to drug trafficking 8-15, 668C1

COCA-Cola Bottling Co. of New York
- Coca-Cola sets purchase 11-24, 985B2

COCA-Cola Co., The
- USSR Coke shipmts ended 3-21, 259E1
- Guatemala plant labor unrest, intl protests; sale pressed 4-16—5-27, 463B3
- Goizueta named pres 5-30, chrmn 8-6, 600D2
- NY bottling deal set 11-24, 985B2

COCAINE—*See NARCOTICS*

COCHET, Henri
- Borg breaks French Open win mark 6-8, 606C3

COCHRAN, Jacqueline
- Dies 8-8, 676B1

COCOA
- US '80 futures price down 12-31, 984G3

CODD, Mary T.
- Loses NY US House primary 9-9, 682D2

CODEX (racehorse)
- Wins Santa Anita Derby 3-30; Preakness 5-17, victory upheld 6-4, 447C2, G3

COE, Frank
- Dies 6-2, 528D1

COE, Mark
- Killed 2-16, 194B1

COE, Peter
- A Life opens 11-3, 892G2

COE, Sebastian
- Sets 1000-m mark; Ovett breaks mile mark 7-1, 589C1
- Ovett ties 1500-m mark 7-15, 589A2
- Wins Olympic medals 7-26, 8-1, 589B2, 624A1, E1
- Ovett breaks 1500-m mark 8-27, 892G1

COELHO, Rep. Tony (D, Calif.)
- Reelected 11-4, 842F1

COETZEE, Gerrie
- Weaver KOs, loss spurs S Africa riots 10-25, 1000E3

1976

COFFEE
Brazil '75 exports down 1-9, 27F2
Colombia '75 price hikes rptd 1-9, 31B1
77 Group sets trade guidelines 2-10, 108C1
Uganda export drop cited 4-6, 502B3
Latin output rptd 5-7, 466C1
Gen Foods price cutting chrgd 7-16, 989B3
US warns NY commodity exchng 9-15, 990D2
COFFEY, Kenneth J.
Armed forces study scored 6-7, 454F1
COFFIN, Edmund
Wins Olympic medal 7-25, 574C2
COFFIN, Judge Frank M.
Upholds Boston busing plan 1-14, 42D2
COGGAN, Most Rev. Frederick Donald (Archbishop of Canterbury)
Pope disrupts female ordinatn 8-20, 756B1
Protests S Africa arrests, asks Mayson release 11-25, 927C2
COGLEY, John
Dies 3-28, 272E3
COHEN, Dr. Jonathan
At Marine Corps probe 6-9, 435C3
COHEN, Meyer Harris (Mickey)
Dies 7-29, 716G2
COHEN, Richard
US-Cuba baseball series vetoed 1-7, 23E1
COHEN, Rep. William S. (R, Me.)
Vs Connally vp selectn 8-5, 584F2
Reelected 11-2, 821D1, 829G3
COHERENT Radiation
SEC lists forgn paymts 5-12, 726F2
COINTELPRO—*See FEDERAL Bureau of Investigation under U.S. GOVERNMENT*
COJOT, Michel
Sees Uganda-hijacker ties 7-4, 485D2
COLBY, William E.
Cong briefing on CIA Italy aid rptd 1-7, 10A3
Denies Italy paymts chrg 1-9, 29B3
Scores House com rpt, denies leaked chrgs 1-26, 92F1, A3, 93E1
Replaced as CIA director 1-27, 68B1
CIA limits media contacts 2-11, 150B3
Vs CIA budget disclosure 3-17, 217D1
COLDS—*See 'Diseases' under MEDICINE*
COLE, Natalie
Wins Grammy 2-28, 460G2
COLE, The Rt. Rev. Ned
Schiess sues 7-8, 755E3
COLELLA, Rick
Wins Olympic medal 7-24, 575D2
COLEMAN, E. Thomas
Elected 11-2, 823B3, 830B1
COLEMAN, Jack
Pleads guilty 9-27, probatn rptd 11-4, 990G2

1977

COFFEE
World '76 crop, demand rptd; shortage causes cited 74G2, B3
Brazil '76 harvest, exports cited; taxes hiked, reserves total rptd 1-4, 1-17, 74C3-G3
Angola output rptd down 1-8, 86E1
US consumer boycott 1-11, 74G2
Colombia '76 smuggling losses rptd 1-11, 74G3
US '76 prices rptd up 1-19, 78A1
Gen Foods ups ground coffee price 1-20, 74F2
Dec '76 US imports rptd up 1-28, 92G1
FAO rpts no consumptn drop 2-3, 169B1
UN rpts '76 price rise 2-14, 145G3
Brazil ups export tax 2-16, 3-7, 168G3
3 US roasters up prices 2-19—3-3, 168D3
US House subcom hearings: price manipulatn chrgd 2-22, denied 2-22, 2-23, 169C1
Ethiopia forgn earnings rptd up 2-27, 328G1
US Jan trade deficit rptd 2-28, 154E1
Carter call-in topic 3-5, 171E1
NY thefts rptd 3-6, 169A1
Brazil raises export tax 3-9, 209F1
US Feb WPI rise rptd 3-10, 176E2
USDA, ICO supply, productn estimates rptd; '76 import, price data 3-10, 3-16, 209B1
Canada import costs up 3-11, 3-14, 200F2
Brazil '76 export earnings rptd 3-11, 524C2
US firms raise prices 3-14, 3-16, 209F1
Uganda smuggling rptd 3-16, 308D3
Colombia raises minimum price 3-23, 209A2
US Feb imports rptd 3-28, 234B1
Folger, Gen Foods up prices 3-30, 4-18, 319B1
General Foods blend rptd 4-4, 319F1
March CPI rise rptd 4-21, 324B2
Mar, Apr sales drop 4-22, 319D1
NYC consumptn rptd down 4-26, 319D1
Colombia halts exports 5-4, cuts price 6-16; Brazil limits exports 5-20, 458E1
US roasters cut prices 5-12, 6-2, 458C1
US 1st ¼ consumptn rptd down 5-19, 458B2
US inflatn forecast revised 5-25, 464B2
US Apr imports rise rptd 5-26, 445F1
US May import drop rptd 6-27, 502B2
France sets price freeze 6-28, 1012D2
NY commodity cntr opens 7-5, 521G2
Spain import costs raised 7-25, 582A2
Latin ldrs set intl fund 8-6, 608B2
July US imports drop 8-25, 651C2
2 US roasters cut prices 10-14, 10-17, 876F2
10 exporters back Brazil boycott strategy 10-21; Brazil, Colombia OK pact 11-4, 3 others join actn 11-9, 876C3
US consumptn rptd down 11-7, 876B3
Central African Empire exports cited 946B3
COFFEE Fund, International (Colombia, Costa Rica, Jamaica, Mexico, Panama, Venezuela)
Creatn set 8-6, 608A3
COFFEE Organization, International (ICO)
Forecasts tight supply 3-16, 209B1
COFFIN, Rev. William Sloane
Elected Riverside Church min 8-14, 808B2
COGGAN, Most Rev. Frederick Donald (Archbishop of Canterbury)
Scores Luwum death 2-17, Amin denounces 2-21, 139D1
Sees Pope, urges intercommunion 4-28—4-29, 374F2
Sees Eastn Orthodox ldr on female ordinatn 5-1, 374D3
Visits WCC in Geneva 5-3, 374F3
Sees Russian Orthodox Patriarch, debates female ordinatn 9-25, 845B3
COGGINS, Mayor Jyles (Raleigh, N.C.)
Loses reelectn 11-8, 855D3
COHEN, Herman J.
Named amb to Senegal, Gambia 6-10, confrmd 6-23, 626D2
COHEN, Manuel F.
Dies 6-16, 532F2
COHEN, Morris
Wins Medal of Sci 11-22, 951G3
COHEN, Stanley
Rpts on DNA recombinatn 10-8, 846E3
COHRS, Eberhard
Defection rptd 2-24, 315A1
COINTELPRO—*See U.S. GOVERNMENT—FBI*
COJUANGCO, Ramon
SEC sues 1-12, 79A3
COKER, Ehrlich Anthony
Executn for rape barred 6-29, 557C2
COKER v. Georgia
Death sentence vacated 6-29, 557C2
COL (cost of living)—*See country names*
COLBORN, Jim
Pitches no-hitter 5-14, 644E1
COLBY, William E.
Suits vs US spying rptd 5-22, 422C3
CIA-press links charged 9-12, 720A3
Disputes Viet evacuatn chrgs 11-22, 898B2
Defends CIA-press links, asks more agency 'covers' 12-27, 1005E3
COLE, Edward N.
Dies 5-2, 452E2
COLE, Robin
In NFL draft 5-3, 353B2
COLEMAN Sr., C. W.
Named in A&P overtime suit 9-27, 778E2
COLEMAN, John A.
Dies 2-23, 164D2

1978

COFFEE
Hungary hikes price 1-9, 55D2
Uganda smuggling rptd 1-10, 55C3
Guatemala '77 export-earnings rise, Central Amer prices cited 1-13, 168F3
Uganda pardons Kenya smugglers 1-31, 95C2
Ecuador '77 exchng reserves rptd 2-3, 148G2
USSR hikes price 3-1, 151G2, C3
Brazil '77 exports $2.6 bln 3-1, 311D1
Folger coffee price lowered 3-9, 181C3 *
8 Latin natns to withhold shipmts 3-10, 181A3
DR '77 trade deficit rptd 3-10, 230F3
Mex offcl chrgd with smuggling 4-29, 517E3
US importers to boycott Uganda 5-16—5-19, 416C3
Colombia '77 exports up 52% 5-19, 414E1
Uganda import ban voted by US Cong 6-12, 7-28; '77 productn rptd 6-24, 616D2, G2
Brazil hikes export tax, US price rise seen 10-25, 837B1
Kenya offcl quits 10-31, 885A3
COGGIOLA, Piero
Killed 9-28, 816F3
COHEN, Alain
First Time released 3-28, 619A2
COHEN, Alan N.
Replaced as Garden Corp pres 1-1, 95G3
Nets purchase agreed 8-28, 1027E3
COHEN, Jay J.
Eubie opens 9-20, 1031E1
COHEN, Ken
Patio/Porch opens 4-13, 887D2
COHEN, Marvin
Named CAB chrmn 10-25, 806E2
COHEN, Rob
Thank God It's Fri released 5-19, 620B1
Wiz released 10-25, 970F3
COHEN, Rep. William S. (R, Me.)
Unopposed in US Sen primary 6-13, 467B1
Elected 11-7, 846C1, F1, 847C2, 858C2
COHN, Roy M.
Sues Ford 4-25, queries on kickbacks 5-11, 390B3, 391C1
COL (cost of living)—*See ECONOMY—Inflation; country names*
COLBERT, Claudette
Kingfisher opens 12-6, 1031B2
COLBY, William E.
Backs intell curbs, secrecy provisn 4-5, 306D2
CIA ex-agent chrgs Cong misled on Angola 5-8, responds on 60 Minutes 5-14, 367D2, B3
COLD War—*See also USSR—U.S. Relations*
Brezhnev scores NATO, hints return 5-31, 423A2
COLE, Charles W.
Dies 2-6, 196E2
COLE, Homer
Named bakery, tobacco union vp 8-16, 700B2
COLE, Jerome F.
OSHA standard challenged 11-13, 899D3

1979

COFFEE
Kenya Jan-June '78 trade deficit rptd 1-5, 22A3
El Salvador price squeeze chrgd 3-13, 348G1
Brazil suspends exports 6-4, 430F1
Brazil '78 exports to Spain rptd 8-6, 654B2
Nicaragua export controls set, '78 trade cited 8-9, 616E1
Corning percolator recall set 9-4, 902E3
Nicaragua jobs progrm rptd 9-18, 732F1
Uganda vowed US aid 9-19, 721F1
Trading squeeze cited 12-31, 978A3
COFFIN Jr., Rev. William Sloane
Scores Iran sanctns 12-23; sees hostages 12-24–12-25, Iran forgn min 12-27, 975B1-B2
COGGAN, Most Rev. Frederick Donald (Archbishop of Canterbury)
Eulogizes Mountbatten 9-5, 669C1
Successor named 9-7, 755F2
COGHLAN, Eamonn
Wins Wanamaker Mile 2-9, 911C2
COHEN, Alexander H.
I Remember Mama opens 5-31, 711G3
Marshack publicity job rptd 11-13, 1005A3
COHEN, Andrew
Jordan cocaine probe immunity bid rptd 9-28, 767D3
COHEN, David
Scores Sen income limit stay 3-8, 185G2
COHEN, Dr. Ellis
On 'laughing gas' hazard 10-24, 971G2
COHEN, Joel
Rat's Nest opens 2-2, 292D2
COHEN, Marvin S.
Warns Pan Am, TWA on London fares 1-23, 87F3
Continental-Westn merger blocked 7-21, 579C1
COHEN, Neil
Rat's Nest opens 2-2, 292D2
COHEN, Dr. Sidney
Pot use concern rptd 10-14, 971G3
COHEN, Sen. William S. (R, Me.)
Meets Teng in China 1-9, 27B1
COHN, Roy M.
Backs Ford's nephew, suits cited 5-10, 366D2, G2
COL (cost of living)—*See ECONOMY–Inflation*
COLASURDO, Pat
In WBL draft 6-12, 526A3
COLAUTTI v. Franklin
Pa abortn control law voided by Sup Ct 1-9, 14A1
COLBERT, Jim
2d in Mixed Team tourn 12-9, 969D3
COLBY, William E.
CIA ex-agent cleared of Sovt spy charge 2-27, 152E3
Denies US newsman linked to KGB 8-11, 611B2
COLD War—*See also USSR–U.S. Relations*
Carter cites era re Cuba troop issue 10-1, 737C1, 738D2, 739D1
UK pro-Sovt spy scandal reopened 10-28, 10-29, 873F3
COLDWELL, Philip E.
Vs 'long float' check delays 1-10, 15G2
COLE, Albert L.
Nixon Admin pub TV moves disclosed 2-24, 194C2
COLE, Megan
Ride A Cock Horse opens 3-18, 292E2
COLEMAN, Cy
I Love My Wife opens 5-15, 711F3
COLEMAN, Delbert
Aladdin casino bid rejected 12-15, 965D1
COLEMAN, Jerry
Hired as Padres mgr 10-1, 1002F1

1980

COFFEE
El Salvador '79-80 crop hit by unrest 1-17, 39B1
Haiti crop destroyed by hurricane 8-5, 621C2
FDA issues caffeine warning 9-4, 726A2
ICO sets price limits, export quotas 10-3; glut weakens growers' cartel 10-7, 777D2
US prices rptd soft 10-6, 777B3
El Salvador optimistic on '81 ICO quota 10-15, 829G1
El Salvador leftists burn 4 mln lbs 11-22, 921B2
Price drops on higher US interest rates 12-10, 932B2
US '80 futures price down 12-31, 984G3
COFFEE Organization, International (ICO)
Price limits, export quotas set 10-3; coffee glut weakens growers' cartel 10-7, 777D2
El Salvador optimistic on '81 quota 10-15, 829G1
Price drops on US legislatn delay 12-10, 932B2
COGAN, David
Reggae opens 3-27, 392F3
COGGAN, Rev. Frederick Donald
Runcie enthroned Archbp of Canterbury 3-25, 364E2
COGHILL, Nevill
Canterbury Tales opens 2-12, 136A3
COGHLAN, Eamonn
Wins Wanamaker Mile 2-8, 892E2
COHEN, Alexander H.
Day in Hollywood opens 5-1, 392F2
COHEN, Chaim
Vs W Bank ldrs ouster 8-19, 627C3
COHEN, Geula
Parlt backs Jerusalem bill 7-23, 7-30, 572B3
COHEN, Jay J.
Horowitz & Mrs Washn opens 4-2, 392C3
COHEN, Rob
Small Circle of Friends released 3-9, 216F3
COHEN, Samuel E.
Caesars gets NJ gambling license 10-25, 988B3
COHN, Judge Avern
Fitzsimmons sentence rptd 2-19, 237G2
COHN, Roy M.
Ford kickback suit settled 1-11; replaced as Ford heir's counsel 3-12, 225D3-F3
McCarthy TV film libel case refused by Sup Ct 12-1, 918D2
COHN v. National Broadcasting Co.
Case refused by Sup Ct 12-1, 918E2
COINS—*See NUMISMATICS*
COLBERT, Jim
2d in Tourn of Champs 4-20, 412D3
COLBY, William E.
Damage suit geographic relevance backed by Sup Ct 2-20, 170A3
COLBY v. Driver
Case decided by Sup Ct 2-20, 170A3
COLD War
Kennedy warns Carter on reactn to Sovt Afghan move 1-28, 74A3
French premr, Sovt amb vs renewal 2-7, 106G2, 107A1
USSR chrgs US in UN Afghan invasn debate 11-20, 899G3
COLE, Joseph E.
Buy Cleveland Press 10-31, 1003D1
COLEAN, Miles Lanier
Dies 9-16, 755F2
COLEMAN, Cy
Barnum opens 4-30, 392D2
COLEMAN, Rep. E. Thomas (R, Mo.)
Reelected 11-4, 843D2
COLEMAN, Henry Randolph
Testifies at B Carter probe 8-19, 647E2
COLEMAN, Judge J. P.
5th judicial circuit split 10-14, 918C3
COLEMAN, Dr. John & Audrey
Arrested 8-9, 671D3

1976

COLEMAN, Ronald G.
Interior asst secy 4-27; confrmd 5-21, 412E1
COLEMAN Jr., William T.
Holds Concorde hearing 1-5, 5B2
OKs Concorde test 2-4, 94C2-B3
Conrail labor talks fail 3-23, 235F2
Justice Dept seeks busing rule review 5-14, 377C3
Concorde test decisn upheld 5-19, US svc set 5-24, 378E2
Noise rule extended to old planes 10-21, 849D1
Ford, Carter debate 10-22, 801G3
Sup Ct bars review of Concorde landing OK 11-15, 882B2
Sets aircraft noise rules 11-18, 868G3
Bars mandatory car air bags 12-6, 920G3
To OK 2 superports 12-17, 991G3
COLGATE-Palmolive Co.
SEC lists forgn paymts 5-12, 726F2
'75 tax paymt rptd 10-2, 847B2
COLLEGE Entrance Examination Board—*See under EDUCATIONAL Testing Service*
COLLEGES, Association of American
Sandler wins Rockefeller award 11-16, 911F3
COLLEGES & Universities—*See EDUCATION; college names*
COLLIER, Calvin Joseph
FTC comr 2-23; confrmd 3-18, 232D1
COLLIER, Peter
Rockefellers on best-seller list 12-5, 972C2
COLLINO, Maria Consolata
Wins Olympic medal 7-24, 574G2
COLLINS, Rep. Cardiss W. (D, Ill.)
Reelected 11-2, 829F2
COLLINS, Gerald
Scores Eire state of emergency 9-1, 676D2
COLLINS, Rep. James M. (R, Tex.)
Reelected 11-2, 830C4
COLMER, William
Endorses Ford 9-26, 723D3

COLOMBIA—*See also ANDEAN Group, IDB, LAFTA, OAS, SELA*
Vote age lowered, divorce legalized, other reforms rptd 1-2, 31A1
'74 defns budget, mil forces rptd 1-2, 60G2
Lopez reelectn move proposed 1-4, rejcted 1-7, 31B1
Low '75 inflatn rate rptd, prices hiked 1-9, 31B1
Lopez vows siege state end 1-16; unrest resumes, siege retained 1-19—2-5, 118B1
Listed as 'free' nation 1-19, 20B3
4 sentncd in Rincon death 1-30, 118A2
Student, labor unrest grows 2-12—4-7, 251A1
Students strike 4-7, riot 4-8; army rpts univ arsenal 4-15, 311B1
Ospina Perez dies 4-14, 316B1
UNO, MOIR chrg campaign arrests 4-15; priests urge anti-Marxist vote 4-16, 311A1
State, local electn results 4-18, 310D3
ELN scores Echavarria murder 4-18, 311G1
M-19 kills Mercado 4-19, union protests 4-21, 311C1
2 ransomed from ELN 6-14, 6-16, 731C2
Lifts state of siege 6-22, 731D2
Students riot 7-7—9-3, 731D1
FARC loots Sabanagrande 7-16; FARC, Army trade murder chrgs 7-25, 7-29, 731G1
Bombs blasts in Bogota, other cities 7-22—8-6, 731G1
Govt chrgs leftist plot 8-6, minimizes econ unrest 8-13, 731C2
MDs strike; hosp workers, students back 9-6—9-19, 730D3
Dike bursts 10-6, 816F1
State of seige reimposed 10-7; students riot, Natl Univ closed 10-8—11-17, 924G2
Labor min quits 10-10, Cabt 10-13; new govt named 10-19, justice min replaced 11-19, 924F3
Yopal air crash 10-25, 876F2
MD strike ends 10-26, 924A3
Foreign Economic Developments
'75 forgn bank natlzatn rptd 1-2, 31A1
French Mirage purchase cited 1-16, 36C2
Pledges Guatemala quake aid 2-4, 81F1
Lockheed bribes probed 2-8; French, W Ger paymts rptd 2-16, 2-23, 147E1, G2
Cuba trade pacts rptd 2-20, 251F3
US hands over Lockheed data 6-22; ct scores delays, takes over probe 9-1, 740F1
Import controls lifted 8-11, 731D2
At nonaligned conf 8-16—8-20, 622C1
US triples sugar duties 9-21, 721D3
Foreign Relations (misc.)—*See also 'UN Policy' below*
Russell ct scores rights abuse 1-17, 61D2, E2

1977

COLEMAN, Julia
Carter inaugural cites 1-20, 26G2
COLEMAN, Peter T.
Elected Amer Samoa gov 11-22, 943E3
COLEMAN Jr., William T.
On airline deregulatn bill 1-13, 36G2
Issues DOT forecast 1-15, 58E2
Air bag test pact OKd 1-18, 213D2
Rptd on IBM bd 2-22, 140A3
Adams backs mandatory air bags 3-21, 213C2
Rebuts Carter energy plan 6-2, 443G1
COLER, Jack (d. 1975)
Peltier sentncd 6-2, 492A1
COLLARES, Alceu
Scores Brazil econ structure 6-27, 523F2
COLLAZO, Abelardo
Arrested 2-11, 307E1
COLLECTED Poems 1930-1976 (book)
Wins Natl Book Award 4-11, 355A2
COLLECTION Agencies
Govt student loan collectn set 9-8, 739D2
COLLEGE Entrance Examination Board—*See under EDUCATIONAL Testing Service*
COLLEGES—*See under EDUCATION; college names*
COLLEY, George
Renamed Ireland finance min 7-5, 598F3
COLLINS, Addie Mae (d. 1963)
'63 Ala church bomber convictd 11-18, 907B3
COLLINS, Gerald
Named Ireland justice min 7-5, 599A1
COLLINS, Rep. James M. (R, Tex.)
'76 campaign surplus rptd 5-3, 482A2
COLLITT, Leslie
Czechs detain 2-4, US protests 2-8, 114B3 ★
Papers returned 3-1, 220F3

COLOMBIA—*See also ANDEAN Group, IDB, OAS*
Murder of unfaithful wives barred 3-23, 347A3
Lefebvre visits 7-12, 620G1
Economy & Labor (domestic)
Coffee crop damage cited, smuggling losses rptd 1-11, 74A3, G3
Drought effect on coffee crop rptd 4-18, 319C1
'61-75 GDP variatns table 5-30, 439A1
Jan-June COL up 26.2% 7-4, 636F1
Episc ldr scores govt 8-9, 727F2
Constructn halted by cement strike 8-12, 726B3
Gasoline shortage rptd 8-30, 726E3
Salaries Cncl representatn disputed 9-14—9-15, 9-19, 726D2
Jan-Aug inflatn at 30% 9-19, 726A3
Business ldr scores govt, cites agri output drop 9-30, 1011E1
Min wage raised 10-13, unions score govt 10-13, 11-18, 1011C1
'77 inflatn estimated by govt, IMF 11-9; Jan-June price rise rptd 11-14, 1011D1

Foreign Relations (misc.)—*See also 'Monetary, Trade & Aid' below*
UN Assemb member 3F3
Lopez Michelsen backs Panamanian canal demands 1-18, 46G1
Italian bank mgr kidnaped 3-13, 255G1
Bulgaria emb car stoned 3-25, 347C2
Panama seeks Guatemala mediatn 5-27, 415B1
Lopez sees Torrijos, regional ldrs 8-5—8-6; new Panama Canal pact backed 8-6, 606B3, 608A3
Lopez at Canal pact signing 9-7, 678A1

1978

COLEMAN, Cy
On Twentieth Century opens 2-19, 887C2
Wins Tony 6-4, 579A3
COLEMAN, Rep. E. Thomas (R, Mo.)
Reelected 11-7, 851D2, 854D3
COLEMAN, William T.
Adams issues transportation policy statemt 2-8, 109D1
COLES, Janet
Wins Lady Tara tourn 4-30, 356B1
COLESTIPOL—*See MEDICINE—Drugs*
COLGATE-Palmolive Co.
Stars defy 'Super Grand Prix' 4-23, 418D3
Nigeria exit cited 6-26, 799B1
COLGRASS, Michael
Wins Pulitzer Prize 4-17, 315C1
COLLECTED Poems (book)
Wins Natl Book Award 4-10, 315A3
Wins Pulitzer 4-17, 315C1
COLLEGE Entrance Examination Board—*See under EDUCATIONAL Testing Service*
COLLEGES—*See under EDUCATION*
COLLEGE Scholarship Service—*See EDUCATIONAL Testing Service—College Entrance Examination Board*
COLLETT, Wallace T.
Asks US oust Nicaragua pres 11-8, 883E3
COLLEY, George
Presents '78 budget 2-1, 72E2
COLLIN, Frank
Skokie Nazi march canceled, Chicago rally OKd 6-20—7-7; rally, counter-demonstratns held 7-9, 529G1
COLLINGS, Dale
Lobsters lose WTT title 9-21, 1027F1
COLLINS, Rep. Cardiss W. (D, Ill.)
Reelected 11-7, 850D3
COLLINS, Rep. James M. (R, Tex.)
Reelected 11-7, 852E2
COLLINS, Nancy
In Haldeman book scoop by-line 2-16, 124F2
COLLINS v. Young
Case refused by Sup Ct 11-13, 874C3
COLOMA Gallegos, Gen. Francisco
Catalan actors sentncd 3-7, 250A2

COLOMBIA—*See also ANDEAN Group, IDB, OAS*
Press freedom rptd by IAPA 10-13, 829A2
Economy & Labor (domestic)
Oil refinery workers strike 1-24; hospital MDs 2-1—2-3, 147A3
Lleras, Turbay support cited 2-27, 147C2
'77, 1st ¼ inflatn data rptd 4-28, 414D1
Urban transport fares hiked 5-8, drivers, pub employees strike 5-15, 5-18, 413D3
Marijuana cultivatn rptd; trade distorts econ, fuels inflatn 9-2, 815E1
Illegal strike penalties stiffened 9-6, 814E2
Bus fares, fuel prices hiked 10-11, 814F3
Jan-June inflatn 12.9% 10-11, 814G3
House, Sup Ct pay, min wage hikes set 11-10, 12-21, 1015E3

Foreign Relations (Misc.)—*See also 'Monetary, Trade, Aid & Investment' and 'UN' below*
Honduras sentncs 2 for '75 murder 2-2, 194C2
Lufthansa office bombed 2-17; W Ger terrorists take credit, 12 rptd in hiding 2-18, 147B3
Japanese terrorist plot rptd 2-18, 147C3
Nicaragua emb bombed 2-26, 151B1
Turbay postpones Venez trip 6-9, 443C2
Lopez Michelsen at Panama Canal pact instrumts exchng 6-16, 463F2, 464A1
8-natn Amazon pact signed 7-3, 829C2
Amer rights conv enacted, ct formed 7-18, 828E3-829C1
Peru rightists kidnap rptr 9-3—9-10, 776B1
Nicaragua oppositn weighs mediatn 9-14, 705C3

1979

COLEMAN Jr., William T.
Sup Ct workforce data rptd 6-11, 464A2
Backs IBM case judge's ouster 7-19, 610A3
COLLA, Richard A.
Battlestar Galactica released 5-17, 528C1
COLLAZO, Oscar
Sentence commuted 9-6, 666D1
Freed 9-10, returns to PR 9-12, 682G3
COLLAZO Araujo, Abelardo
Escapes Spain jail 12-17, 997E3
COLLEGE Entrance Examination Board—*See EDUCATIONAL Testing Service*
COLLEGES—*See under EDUCATION; specific names*
COLLEY, George
Presents '79 budget, notes '78 achievemts 2-7, 154E3, 155A1
On tax protest 3-20, 211G3
Defeated for prime min 12-7, 950E1
COLLINS, Bill
Shares indoor sprint medley mark 2-23, 911E2
COLLINS, Gerard
In UK-Eire security talks 10-5, 792E3
COLLINS, Dr. Harvey F.
Testifies on Hooker pollutn 6-19, 597A2
COLLINS, Robert
Walk Proud released 6-15, 820F3
COLLINS, Judge Robert
Blocks judicial financial disclosures 5-15, 382B2
COLLINS, Stephen
Promise released 3-7, 528D3
COLOM Argueta, Manuel
Called leftist 3-18, slain 3-22, 237B1
Army staff chief slain 6-10, 445D3

COLOMBIA—*See also ANDEAN Group, IDB, OAS*
Quake kills 60 11-23, 912F2-A3
Economy & Labor
'79 inflatn, min wage rptd 11-14, 993B2

Foreign Relations (misc.)
Nicaragua, Chile ambs rptd kidnap targets 1-7, 115E1
DR names Rosario mil attache 1-12, 62E2
CELAM '68 Medellin mtg cited 1-27, 1-28, 68A1, B2
Mex-CR missn on Nicaragua dispatched 5-21, 409B1
Venez offshore oil talks agreed 5-26—5-28, 398C2
Nicaragua expels radicals 8-16, 636C2
UN membership listed 695F2
Bahamas drug operatn cited 12-7, 948B2

1980

COLEMAN, Martha C.
V Jordan shot 5-29, 401G2, A3
Jordan case stymied 6-1—6-12; atty bars role in shooting 6-7, 442C2
COLEMAN Jr., William T.
Denies Ford transmissn hazard 8-20, 702E1
COLGATE-Palmolive Co.
FTC ends detergent indus probe 5-12, 703B2
COLINDRES, Eduardo
Taken hostage 2-5, 97C1
Freed 2-12, 117B2
COLINDRES, Julieta
Held by leftists 1-29, 97D1
Freed 2-12, 117B2
COLLARD, Claude
On French Olympic com vote 5-13, 379G2
COLLAZO Araujo, Abelardo
Killed 8-29, 673A3
COLLEARY, Bob
Wins Emmy 9-7, 692C1
COLLEGE and University Business Officers, National Association of (NACUBO)
'79 univ endowmt earnings rptd 3-24, 319F1
COLLEGE Entrance Examination Board—*See under EDUCATIONAL Testing Service*
COLLEGES—*See EDUCATION--Colleges*
COLLIER, John
Dies 4-6, 360D1
COLLIER, Robert Lewis
Death penalty appeal declined by Sup Ct 3-24, 265C2
COLLIER v. Georgia
Case declined by Sup Ct 3-24, 265C2
COLLIN, Frank
Arrested on sex chrgs 1-10, 55D3
COLLINS, Bill
Sets indoor sprint medley relay mark 2-29, 892F1
COLLINS, Dave
NL batting, stolen base ldr 10-6, 926E2, F2
COLLINS, Don
In NBA draft 6-10, 447G1
COLLINS, Rep. James M. (R, Tex.)
Reelected 11-4, 844D2
COLLINS, Larry
Fifth Horseman on best-seller list 10-12, 796D3; 12-7, 948D3
COLLINS, Pfc. Omester
Sentenced for sex harassment 3-6, 189B1
COLLINS, Richard Thomas
Convicted 4-23, 372B1
COLMER, William M.
Dies 9-9, 755F2
COLOMBIA—*See also ANDEAN Group, IDB, OAS*
Bullring collapse kills 222 1-21, 80C3

Foreign Relations (misc.)—*See also 'Monetary', 'Unrest' below*
Mex gets UN Cncl seat 1-7, 12A2
E Ger amb presents credentials 2-27, 141D1
Castro offers asylum to DR Emb captors 3-18, 211C3
Argentine A-pact cited 3-18, 229E2
Turbay in Peru for Belaunde inauguratn 7-28, 579E3
Bolivia coup condemned 7-29, 577D1
Jerusalem emb shift set 8-28, 660C3
Somoza adviser slain in Paraguay 9-17, 697G2
Cuba ex-offcl asks UN probe prison hunger strike 12-4, 965D2
Bolivia coup condemned by Santa Marta conf 12-17, 992A3

1976

Chile exiles chrg harassmt 1-28, 2-1, 118A3
Spain emb bombed 1-30, 118E1
Press scores US-Brazil pact 2-23, 177D1
Lopez on Panama Canal, Angola 2-23, 178D1
Uruguay pol refugees take asylum 3-3—3-12, 207G3
3 drug dealers arrested in Mex 3-5, 420D1
5 Uruguay refugees rptd in emb 5-18, 441D2
Dutch consul's ransom blocked 6-17, 731B2
Venez quits Uruguay emb 7-7, 542A3
Leftist plot chrgd 8-6, 731D2
Cuba to honor hijack pact 10-15, 780D1
Cuba exile terrorist plan rptd 10-19, 780D2
Venez gets illegal immigrants 12-5, 930F1

Narcotics & Drugs
Joint US drug drive agreed 1-20, 61A1
US baseball mgr's daughter sentncd 1-21, 160A3
Cocaine seized 1-24, 1-27, 118F2
US convicts drug pushers 1-26, 61A2
Airfields for US drug trade found 1-28, 118G2
Extensive marijuana cultivatn rptd 1-28, 118G2
3 dealers arrested in Mex 3-5, 420D1

UN Policy & Developments
Sovt vs on press plan 11-25, 896A1

U.S. Relations—*See also 'Foreign Economic Developments' and 'Narcotics' above*
Kissinger visits 2-22—2-23, 177A1; 178D1
US-Brazil pact scored 2-23, 177D1
Ship in US Bicentennial event 7-4, 488A3
US offices bombed 8-4—8-6, 731G1

COLOMBO, Emilio
Closes currency mkt to bolster lira 1-21, 74B2
On import controls 5-6, 365G3
New govt excludes 7-30, 573C1

COLOMBO, Vittorino
Sworn Italy post min 7-30, 573G1

1977

Government & Politics—*See also other appropriate subheads in this section*
Liberals OK '78 primary 3-21, 255A2
Bogota anti-corruptn drive rptd 7-8, 727G2
Cong corruptn rptd 7-8, 727A3
Pres race: leftist groups nominate Piedrahita 7-16, Pernia 8-7, Ramirez 8-10; Conservatives back Batancur 7-25, Patriotic Front launches Gen Valencia 9-16, 727G1-D2
Pres candidates chrg Lopez corruptn, repressn 7-16—9-16; Episc ldr chrgs 8-9, 727B2, F2
Liberal pres candidates affirm '78 primary plan 8-17, 727E2

Monetary, Trade & Aid (including all foreign economic developments)
'75-76 trade, paymts table 3-11, 189A2 ★
Export coffee price raised 3-23, 209A2
'66-75 arms transfers table 4-8, 415A2, F2
Coffee exports halted 5-4, price cut 6-16, 458E1
Intl Coffee Fund set 8-6, 608A3
Cement exports halted by strike 8-12, 726B3
Canal pact grants toll-free transit 9-7, 683D2
Exports rptd stagnating 9-30, 1011F1
In Brazil coffee-export pact 11-4, 876D3

Unrest
Pol prisoners estimated 1-1, 3G1
Strikes, pol violence continue 1-12—3-18, 254A3-255A2
US botanist kidnaped 2-14, 255F1
Italian bank mgr kidnaped 3-13, 255G1
Students riot, strike 3-24—4-24; Natl Univ closed 4-27, 347F1 ★
FARC, ELN guerrillas stage attacks, kidnapings 3-29—5-2, 347D2
May Day protests 5-1, Bogota bombings 5-2, 347G2
Pol violence, kidnapings, strikes continue 7-1—7-30; 500 rptd executed since '74 7-5, 635F3
Pres candidates score Lopez repressn, actn vs strikers 7-16—9-16, 727B2
Episc ldr scores govt 8-9, 727F2
Cement strike extended 8-12, 726B3
Ex-agri min kidnaped, co firings cited 8-19; freed 9-16, 727C1
Teachers strike 8-22, 726B3
Oil workers strike 8-25, police clash, arrests 8-26, 726C2, D3, G3
Measures vs strikers increased 8-26, 9-3, 9-8, 726F3, 727B1
Army seizes Cimitarra after FARC assassinatns 8-30, 727D1
FARC blamed for 3 Caqueta kidnaps 8-30, 727E1
Lopez labor talks fail 9-1, warns vs gen strike 9-12, 727A1
FARC blows up oil exec's home 9-3, pipelines 9-5—9-6, 727F1
Oil strike ldr chrgs jail beatings 9-7, 727A1
Gen strike, deaths rptd; Lopez scores, bars wage demands 9-14—9-15; Bogota curfew lifted 9-16; new strike threatnd 9-19, 726E1
Teachers strike ends 10-6, 1010F3
Guerrilla attacks rptd 10-19, 12-7, 1011B2
Govt: guerrillas moving to cities 11-1, 1011C2
Kidnap victims slain 11-3, 11-10, 12-22, 1011G1
Finance Min strike ends 11-4, 1010G3
Oil strike sabotage, arrests, dismissals rptd 11-11, 1010F3-1011A1
Labor unions demonstrate 11-18, 1011B1
Univs closed 12-13—12-14, 1011D2
95 seized re kidnaps, 15 chrgd 12-18—12-19; 3 kidnaps rptd 12-21, 1011F1

U.S. Relations
US botanist kidnaped 2-14, 255F1
'66-75 arms transfers table 4-8, 415A2, F2
Carter for rights conv ratificatn 4-14, 295E2
Coffee exports halted 5-4, price cut 6-16, 458E1
Todman visits 5-8—5-10, 414D1
Mrs Carter visits; drugs, prisoners discussed 6-9—6-10, 454E1, 455C2
Lopez lauds Panama Canal talks 8-6, 606C3
Lopez sees Carter 9-6, at Panama Canal pact signing 9-7, 678A1; text 683D2

COLOMBUS Australia (W. Ger. container-ship)
Australia dockers protest delays sailing 7-2—7-4, 523D1

1978

Nicaragua emb harbors refugees 10-13, 839F3
Nicaragua scores unrest, drug trade 10-14, 839C3

Government & Politics—*See also other appropriate subheads in this section*
Electoral ct collapses, Lopez electn favoritism chrgd 2-20, 147A2
Liberals win electns, Turbay gets pres nominatn 2-26, 147A1
Conservatives gain, leftists lose in cong electn results 3-2, 413B3
Pres campaign ends; Turbay, Betancur lead race 5-28, 413A2
Turbay elected pres 6-4; Betancur disputes count, Conservatives protest 6-5—6-9; recount begins 6-11, 443E1-E2
Turbay wins pres vote recount 6-15; Betancur concedes 6-20; Turbay scores 6-23, 629F3
Turbay, Cabt sworn 8-7; women score all-male Cabt 8-9, 629F2, F3
Uribe named forgn min 9-22, 815A1
Balcazar elected vice pres 10-11, 814G3

Monetary, Trade, Aid & Investment
'77 trade gap $33.5 mln 5-19, 414E1
Ecuador, Venez border projcts urged 8-7, 629A3
Chrysler operatns cited 8-10, 623F2
World Bank loans rptd up 9-15, 828B3

UN Policy & Developments
Leftist rights abuse chrgs rptd 2-20, 147E2
UN aide urges drug smuggling measures 9-2, 815F1
Assemb member 713D3
Lievano elected Assemb pres 9-19, 713F2

Unrest
FARC, M-19 guerrillas stage attacks 1-20—2-24, 147F2
Oil refinery workers strike 1-24, hosp MDs 2-1—2-3, 147A3
Troops patrol cities, arrest 100s 2-14—2-26; leftists chrg rights abuse 2-20, 147C2
Forgn guerrillas rptd active 2-17—2-18, 147B3
Guerrillas sack 3 towns 3-1—3-20, 414A1
Conservative ldr kidnaped 3-1, rptd freed 4-20, 414A1
Ex-amb kidnaped 3-25, abductors killed 4-14, 414B1
Rancher's son kidnaped 4-20, 414A1
Kidpnaped US jeweler found 4-30, 414C1
18 Bogota bombings 5-1, 2 killed 5-12, 413G3
Riots follow bus fare hike 5-8—5-31; drivers, pub employees strike 5-15, 5-18, 413C3
Troops deployed vs electn violence 5-28, 414C1
Liberal congressman kidnaped 6-1, 414C1
Bogota students riot 6-8—6-9, 443B2
FARC, ELN merger rptd 8-24, 814E3
'Security statute' enacted 9-6; bombings, murders continue 9-7—10-11, 814C2
US-owned stores bombed 10-9, 814C3
Bus fare hike protested 10-12—10-16, 814F3
Bus fare, security statute riots continue 10-25—11-4, 1015E2
30 guerrillas rptd seized 11-4, FARC attacks continue 11-10, 11-28, 1015C3
Mil jail torture rptd 11-8, 1015C2
Rights group formed by Garcia Marquez 12-21, 1015B3

U.S. Relations
Kidnaped US jeweler found 4-30, 414C1
Carter consults on DR electn 5-19, 414C2
Cepeda sentncd for pot smuggling 6-14, 1026F2
Lopez Michelsen at Canal pact instrumts exchng 6-16, 463F2, 464A1
Turbay: US ties 'cordial' 8-7, 629A3
Chrysler operatns cited 8-10, 623F2
Anti-drug pact signed 9-29, 815B1
US-owned stores bombed 10-9, 814C3

COLOMBO Sr., Joseph
Dies 5-22, 440D2

COLOMBO, Vittorio
Named Italy transport min 3-11, 191C1

COLONIAL Stores Inc.
Grand Union merger set 8-1, 718A1

1979

Unrest
Guerrillas raid mil arsenal 1-1, 100s arrested 1-1-2-9; const rights suspended 1-9, censorship lifted 2-9, 115C1
Texaco exec killed by guerrillas 1-4, 22D2
Soldiers, guerrillas in rural clashes 1-18-2-3, 115B2
Army rights abuses chrgd 3-12, power gain in '79 guerrilla drive rptd 11-14, 992G3
Buenaventura dock strike 5-29, 563E3

U.S. Relations
Texaco exec killed 1-4, 22D2
US amb rptd kidnap target 1-7, 115E1
US drug ring rptd broken 5-1, 492D3
US aide confers on Nicaragua 7-5, 504B1
US drug dealer convicted 8-15, 818F3
Calif pot output up 10-29, 972G1
Terrorist activity rptd up 11-15, 882A2

COLOMBO, Umberto
Nominated Italy A-energy group head 1-8, 21C1

COLON, Miriam
Simpson Street opens 3-5, 292A3

COLONEL Delmiro Gouveia (film)
Released 4-30, 528A2

COLONIAL Williamsburg (Va.) Foundation
Rockefeller estate willed 4-13, 672E2

1980

Government & Politics—*See also other appropriate subheads in this section*
Turbay's liberals win by-electns 3-9, 180F3
'Witch' wins local electn seat 3-9, 231G2

Monetary, Trade, Aid & Investment
Coffee glut weakens ICO cartel, liquidatn set 10-7, 777F2
Amazon pact signed 10-28, 865D2
US OKs Israeli jet sale 10-31, 865A2

Sports
World Cup golf tourn results 12-14, 972A3

Unrest
UK natls kidnaped 1-5, ransom demand rptd 1-7, 19D3
'78, '79 kidnapings rptd 1-5, 19F3
Guerrillas raid rural police statn 1-20, 96G2
Leftists seize DR emb; hold US, other forgn diplomats 2-27, 140F3
DR emb captors in govt talks 3-2—3-13; Austrian amb, 5 others freed 3-2, 3-6, Brazilian amb rptd injured 3-10, 180B2
Election security tight; liquor ban, sporadic violence rptd 3-8—3-11, 180G2, F3
Uruguay amb escapes DR Emb, Venez amb suffers 2d heart attack 3-17, 211G2-B3
DR Emb captors demands rejctd, more talks urged 3-18, 211C3
Castro offers asylum to DR Emb captors 3-18, 211C3
DR Emb talks resume 3-24, 3-26, 3 more hostages freed 3-25, 231D2-G2
DR Emb captors release 2 more hostages 3-30, resume talks 4-1, 253D2-F2
5 more DR Emb hostages released 4-4, 4-6, secy held as suspect 4-6, 298A3, C3
DR Emb raid topic in US pres race 4-7, 264D2
DR Emb talks continue, progress rptd 4-9, 4-11—4-13, 293D3
Uruguay Emb attack thwarted 4-14, 293G3-294A1
Amnesty Intl issues rpt, details torture 4-16; Turbey scores, asks OAS probe 4-20, 311F3, 335F2
Govt frees 9 leftists 4-18, 311D3
DR Emb captors ask Panama mtg, free CR envoy 4-19; govt bars 'dialogue' 4-21, 311F2-D3
OAS rights comm vists DR Emb hostages, DR envoy freed 4-22, 311E3
DR Emb takeover ends; captors fly to Cuba, free hostages 4-27; reactn 4-27—4-28, 335D1
2 M-19 guerrillas escape prison 6-25, 521A2
2 kidnaped UK natls freed 8-10, 707D2
M-19 guerrillas kidnap politician, 4 rptrs 8-13—8-14, 707E2
US agronomist kidnaped 8-16, 707B2
Troops move vs rebel camps in SE 8-26, 707G1
Caquetta peasants protest army presence 9-15, 788C3
Amnesty Intl issues 2d rpt, documts torture chrgs 9-22, 749A2
DR amb slain 11-16, 889C1

U. S. Relations
US co kidnap liability barred 1-6, 18A1-B2
8 convicted in US drug ring 2-4, 270F3
Peace Corps volunteer freed 2-11, 117A1
US amb seized in DR emb raid 2-27, 140F3, 141B1
DR Emb raid topic in pres race 4-7, 264D2
DR Emb siege ends, US amb freed in Cuba 4-27; Carter lauds 4-28, 335G1, B2, A3
Hispanic immigrants in US surveyed 5-11—5-14, 396G2
Fla banks linked to drug money 6-5, 502E1
US agronomist kidnaped 8-16, 707B2
US OKs Israeli jet sale 10-31, 865A2

COLOMBO, Emilio
Italy forgn affairs min 4-4, 275F3
On EC actn vs Iran 4-10, 282B1
Hails EC budget compromise 5-30, 421C3

COLOMBO, Felice
Soccer activity barred 5-18, 409C1

COLOMBO, Harry
Blood Feud released 2-22, 216C2

COLON, Maria
Wins Olympic medal 7-25, 624G1

COLONEL Moran (racehorse)
3d in Preakness 5-17, 447D2

COLON Osoric, Luis
Rptd missing 9-8, 786B2

1976

COLORADO
Woodmoor bank fails, sold 1-12, 167B2
Ford Vail condominium rptd 2-12, 129C2
Sup Ct bars job bias rule review 3-1, 170C1
Callaway chrgd re land dvpt 3-12, 197A2; **for subsequent developments, see CALLAWAY, Howard**
4 die in Vail gondola fall 3-26, 384F1
Reagan gets 3 delegates 6-19, 450G2
GOP delegate vote results 7-9, 7-10, 513B3
Dem conv women delegates, table 508B2
Dem conv pres vote, table 7-14, 507B2
Reagan loses delegate 7-27, 550A2
Big Thompson R flood 7-31, disaster declared 8-2, 595E2, G2 ★
Big Thompson R flood probe rptd 8-10, death toll at 138 8-22, 756G1
GOP pre-conv delegate count 8-14, 583B3
GOP conv pres, vp vote tables 8-18—8-19, 8-19, 599B1, B3
Ford in Vail 8-20, 631D1, B2, 632F3
Oil-shale leases suspended 8-23, 648G3
Ford in Vail 8-27, 8-29, 644F3, 645A1
Fscl '75 per capita income, tax burden rptd 9-15, 10-12, 959E2
Rpt on Ford '72 Vail ski expenses 10-8, 764F1
Election results 11-2: pres 818A1, 819B1; cong 824E1, 829F1; state 824F1, 825G2, A3-D3
Denver parish cuts Episc ties 11-28, 932F1
Flu shot paralysis rptd 12-17, 950E1
Fords in Vail 12-19—12-31, 980D2
Denver
US Sup Ct declines schl integratn rule review 1-12, 24E1
Violent crime rptd 3-2, 336D3
Westn Air ruling review denied 3-8, 219C2
Hijacker killed 4-19, 383E3
No asbestos found in water 4-30, 349G1
Coronado Natl Bank closed 6-25, 495G1
SWP office burglarized 7-7, 569G2-B3 ★; **for subsequent developments, see SOCIALIST Workers Party**
Mondale visits 9-2, 665B3
Carter campaigns 10-4, 743D1, 744C3
Mondale visits 10-18, 803D3
Transatlantic air route rejctd 12-28, 992E2
COLORADO River
Utah power prjct dropped 4-14, 282D2
COLOTKA, Peter
On Czech Presidium 4-16, 289A2
COLUMBIA, Md.—*See MARYLAND*
COLUMBIA, Mo.—*See MISSOURI*
COLUMBIA, S.C.—*See SOUTH Carolina*
COLUMBIA Broadcasting System—*See CBS Inc.*
COLUMBIA Record (newspaper)
Ford endorsement rptd 10-30, 831F2
COLUMBIA University (New York, N.Y.)
New atom particle observed 2-8, 124B1
Pulitzer Prizes awarded 5-3, 352B3
Brzezinski sees Australia prime min 7-26, 554G1
Lazarfeld dies 8-30, 680F3
Wu gets Science Medal 10-18, 858G3
Kupchan dies 10-19, 892B3
Brzezinski named Carter aide 12-16, 936A3, 937G1
COLUMBUS, O.—*See OHIO*
COMAN, Gen. Ion
Rumania defense min 6-15, 440B2
COMANECI, Nadia
Wins Olympic medals 7-19—7-22, 563B1, 574D3-F3
ComBANKS Corp.
SEC lists paymts 5-12, 727A1
COMBE, David
Censured re Iraq fund 3-7, 187A2
COMBS, Earle
Dies 7-21, 656E3
COMECON—*See COUNCIL for Mutual Economic Assistance*

1977

COLORADO
Legislature schedule rptd 6D2
Callaway probe dropped 1-11, 59E2
Great Westn land-fraud case setld 1-26, 156D1
13 cnties get drought relief 1-29, 76G3
Longet sentenced 1-31, 102E3
Cloud-seeding brings Aspen snow 2-21—2-22, 153C1
Baldwin S&L ownership barred 2-22, 155E1
Pueblo land developer pleads guilty 2-22, 156G1
Dust storm hits wheat 2-23, 153F1
Snowstorm kills 9 3-10—3-12, 204A3
Golden solar energy lab set 3-24, 278F1
Pot law impact rptd 3-31, 332A3
Alien schl voting law review declined 4-18, 342D1
EEOC drops antibias suit vs Coors 5-9, 819D1
'76 per-capita income table 5-10, 387G2
Boulder econ data table 5-16, 384F2
Drought continues 6-16, 492A3
Drought-related agri losses rptd 7-13, fed aid OKd 8-24, 660B1
Comanches, Utes end feud 7-24, 619A3
White River Natl Forest burns out 8-7, 660C3
'76 per capita income, tax burden table 9-13, 10-18, 821E2
Episc diocese formed 9-14—9-16, 731E2
USOC votes in Colo Springs 9-25, 828B3
Free abortions continued 10-12, 787A1
HMO unit certified 10-26, 870A1
Baca Cnty farmers movemt rptd 11-27, 916B2
Pot law detailed 12-11, 972D3
Denver
SWP break-in case closed 1-6, 15D3
Science group meets 2-21—2-25, 183C2-184C1
Water use drops 3-15, 244B3
Religious deprogrammer sentncd 3-28, 287F1
'75 bombing convictn reversed 4-5, 484E1
Econ data table 5-16, 384F2
NBA aids Nuggets 6-15, 583E3, G3
LEAA office to close 6-20, 630E2
Gays march for equal rights 6-26, 560E2
Water use drop rptd 7-13, 660B1
Carter visits 10-22, 817D1
Loses Dem '78 conv site bid 12-9, 960C3
Oilman buys Oakland A's, sets move 12-14, 989A2
'Gateway' air svc OKd 12-21, 1006C2
COLORADO, University of (Boulder)
Loses Orange Bowl 1-1, 8G3
Haas on drought measures 2-21, 183A3
Porter gets Medal of Sci 11-22, 952B1
COLORADO River
Spring runoff threatened 2-1, 76G3
S Calif water imports cited 3-1, 492F3
COLORADO Springs, Colo.—*See COLORADO*
COLOR Television, Committee to Preserve American
Vs Japan export level 5-18, 416C1
COLSON, Charles W.
Nixon-Frost interview 5-4, 366A2, F2
COLT, Ethel Barrymore
Dies 5-22, 452F2
COLUMBIA Broadcasting System—*See CBS Inc.*
COLUMBIA Gas System Inc.
FPC OKs emergency purchase 1-19, 53G3
US acts to ease transport 2-2, 76F1
Columbia Gas Transmission Corp.
FPC splits on Alaska pipe route 5-2, 369B3
COLUMBIA Gas Transmission Corp.—*See under COLUMBIA Gas System*
COLUMBIA River
Spring runoff threatened 2-1, 76G3
Flow decline rptd 3-8, 244A3
COLUMBIA University (New York, N.Y.)
Pulitzer Prizes awarded 4-18, 355C2
Venez pres visits 6-30, 546B2
Rudd surrenders 9-14, 839D1
Laser discoveries cited 10-11, 860A1
Turchin to accept post 10-14, 812C2
Said denies Geneva rep offer 11-15, 873E2
COLUMBUS, O.—*See OHIO*
COLVIN, Reynold H.
Argues Bakke case 10-12, Sup Ct orders more briefs 10-17, 834F3, 835A1, G1
COMANCHE Indians—*See INDIANS, American*
COMANECI, Nadia
TV producer gets US asylum 2-24, 315B1
COMECON—*See COUNCIL for Mutual Economic Assistance*

1978

COLORADO
Legislature schedule rptd 14D3
'67, '77 sales-tax rates rptd 1-5, 15D3
NASL '77 expansn cited 1-5, 23B1
Mondale tours Westn states 1-9—1-13, 34E1
State govt tax revenue table 1-9, 84C2
Wilderness area clears Cong 2-9, 109D2; signed 2-24, 218A2
Vail rpts record snow 3-14, 207C2
Aurora banker's wife ransomed 4-6, 396C3
Rocky Flats A-facility protested 5-1, 347F1
Sun Day marked in Golden, Colo Springs 5-3, 321D3, 322B1
Denver guaranteed income study rptd 5-19, 720F3
Tax relief measures rptd 5-25, spending curbs cited 6-6, 425D1
Grasshopper invasn rptd; spraying begun, EPA aid asked 7-12—7-31, 654A3
NHL OKs Rockies sale 8-9, 656B3
Primary results 9-12, 736D2
NASL OKs Caribous sale, Atlanta move 10-3, 969A3
Election results 11-7: cong 845D1, 846B1, 848D1, 850C2, 855F3; state 847C1, 853D2, 855F3, 897C3, 915D2
Black lt gov noted 11-28, 915E3
Rocky Flats protesters convicted 11-29, 941A2
Denver
Panama Canal 'truth squad' in Denver 1-19, 58C2
Clean-air rating rptd 2-23, 144E3
UAL hijack attempt foiled 3-13, 212A2
A's Denver sale fails 3-27, 354F3
Carter visits 5-3, 342B2
Utility settles FTC credit chrg 5-3, 434G1
EPA bars dam permit 5-25, 409A1
Makes bad-air list 7-5, 513C1
US state legislators meet 7-6, 526A1
Bad-air list corrected 7-19, 644B2
COLORADO, University of (Boulder)
Decker sets 1000-yd run mark 2-4, 692E3
Fairbanks suspended by Patriots, job offer cited 12-18; reinstated 12-20, 1024E2
COLORADO River
A-plant rejctd by Calif Assemb 4-13, 281C2
COLORADO Springs, Colo.—*See COLORADO*
COLSON, Charles W.
Haldeman book on Watergate rptd 2-16, 2-17; calls versn 'false' 2-16, 124A3, G3-125A1, E1
Nixon memoir excerpt cites Watergate role 4-30, 319F3, 320D1
Movie premieres in DC 9-24, 844D1
COLT Industries Inc.
Titanium unit indicted 9-28, 768D2
COLUMBIA Broadcasting System—*See CBS Inc.*
COLUMBIA Gas System Inc.
Coal gasificatn plant financing plan submitted 6-2, 471A3
COLUMBIA Pictures Industries Inc.
Begelman quits in embezzlemt scandal 2-9, indicted 3-31; film contract rptd 3-13, 251C1
3 stockholder suits rptd filed 4-1, 251C2
Melnick named TV chief 6-1; Hirschfield ousted as pres 7-20, Vincent replaces 7-21, 599C2
Begelman fined in theft case 6-28, 599A2
New film indus probe set, Screen Gems embezzlmt case cited 7-14, 599G2
COLUMBIA Presbyterian Medical Center (N.Y., N.Y.)
Embryo implant trial begins 7-17, 597G1; damages awarded 8-18, 770A2
COLUMBIA, S.C.—*See SOUTH Carolina*
COLUMBIA University (N.Y., N.Y.)
Gilbert Highet dies 1-20, 96C2
Pulitzer Prizes awarded 4-17, photo mix-up setld 4-21, 314D2-315B2
Haig addresses 4-25, 298A3
S Africa partial stock divestiture OKd 5-3, 377D1
Armstrong papers received 5-21, 844C2
S Africa bank stock sale set 6-6, 633C1
Embryo implant trial opens 7-17, 597G1; damages awarded 8-18, 770A2
'More' ceases publicatn, merges with Columbia Journalism Review 7-21, 672G1
COLUMBUS, Ga.—*See GEORGIA*
COLUMBUS, O.—*See OHIO*
COMA (book)
On best-seller list 1-8, 24F3; 2-5, 116C3; 3-5, 195F3; 4-2, 272C3; 4-30, 256B2
COMA (film)
Released 2-1, 619B1
Top-grossing film 3-1, 196A1
COMAN, Gen. Teodor
Dismissed 9-6, 741B3
COMBINED Communications Corp.
FCC OKs WJLA-KOCO TV exchng 1-12, 109B3
WJLA, KOCO-TV swap OKd again 3-9, Allbritton halts deal 3-24, 270A3
Gannett plans purchase; '77 profits, sales cited 5-8, 345E2, A3
Gannett to sell TV statn 8-20, 760A1
COMDEN, Betty
On Twentieth Century opens 2-19, 887C2
Wins Tony 6-4, 579A3
COMECON—*See COUNCIL for Mutual Economic Assistance*

1979

COLORADO
Legislature schedule rptd 5C3
Green River Basin oil find cited 1-5, 17G1
Denver breast-feeding survey rptd 1-5, 64C2
Oswald 'look-alike' dies 1-14, 93C2
Denver '78 Nazi activity cited 1-19, 102B1
Ft Carson child abuse rptd 1-21, 93E3
Denver bad air quality cited 1-25, 90C2
Denver fiscal status rptd 3-20, 204F1, C2
DiLeo case declined by Sup Ct 4-23, 346F2
Land sale refunds set 5-8, 595G3
Denver reelects McNichols 5-15, 363A3
Burger King donates $2 mln to Olympics 5-15, 798F1
Denver on '78 world's busiest airport list 6-1, 421C1
Haskell '78 labor gifts rptd 6-13, 595D1
Denver condominium growth rptd 6-23, 482B3
Bundy gets death penalty in Fla 7-31, 604E2, G2
Denver Chicano-Viet refugee violence 8-20—8-24, 660A1
Interior Dept seeks to protect primitive areas 9-7, 703C3
State worker Soc Sec non-participatn cited 9-10, 727B1
'78 per capita income rptd 9-16, 746F2
Iranian kills youth in Denver 11-11 12-10, 863E1
UMW conv in Denver 12-10—12-20, 986E3
Kennedy in Denver 12-13, 962A2
Atomic Energy
Rocky Flats A-protesters sentncd 1-8, 17D3
Denver radium waste sites rptd 3-5, 187F1
Ft St Vrain A-plant dispute rptd settled 4-3, 344E2
Rocky Flats A-protesters arrested 4-29, 322E3
Ft St Vrain protests staged 6-2, 416C2
Rocky Flats A-protesters convicted 6-22, 743D1
COLORADO, University of (Boulder)
Fairbanks to seek football post 4-2, Colo gov scores deal 4-3, 335E1
DiLeo case declined by Sup Ct 4-23, 346F2
COLORADO State University (Fort Collins)
Bell in NFL draft 5-3, 335E2
COLSON, Gary
Hired as U of New Mex basketball coach 12-21, 1003B2
COLT Industries Inc.
Crucible Alloy Division
EPA Pa cleanup pact set 5-7, 385G2-B3
COLUCCI, Vincent
Indicted 3-6, 220C2
COLUCCIO, Vincent
Sounders purchase OKd 10-15, 1004B2
COLUMBIA, S.C.—*See SOUTH Carolina*
COLUMBIA Artists Management
USSR cancels concert tour 9-27, 775A1
COLUMBIA Broadcasting System—*See CBS Inc.*
COLUMBIA Gas System Inc.
Columbia LNG Corp.
Iran to end shipmts 7-28, 583B1
COLUMBIA LNG Corp.—*See under COLUMBIA Gas System*
COLUMBIA Pictures Industries Inc.
Fortune rpts '78 equity return 5-7, 305A2*
Kerkorian trust case dismissed 8-14, 756C1
NBC '77 trust setlmt challenge refused by Sup Ct 12-10, 988A2
Begelman named MGM movie pres 12-18, 1007D1
COLUMBIA Pictures Industries v. U.S.
Case refused by Sup Ct 12-10, 988A2
COLUMBIA Union National Bank & Trust Co. (Kansas City, Mo.)
Burrus settles SEC chrg 2-7, 132E1
COLUMBIA University (N.Y., N.Y.)
McGill urges pub broadcast chngs 1-30, 78C2
S Africa bank stock sold 3-23, 270G3
Amer Assemb issues rpt 4-2, 282G2
A-reactor start-up halted 4-6, 261C3
Pulitzer Prizes awarded 4-16, 336C2
Cancer research threatened 10-23, 806C3
McGill named Natl Agenda Comm chrmn 10-24, 810A3
4th in NCAA soccer 12-9, 1004G1
COLUMBUS, Ga.—*See GEORGIA*
COLUMBUS, O.—*See OHIO*
COLUMBUS Board of Education v. Penick
Case decided by Sup Ct 7-2, 539E2
COLWELL, Lee
Named FBI exec asst 8-8, 611C1
COMANECI, Nadia
World Gym Championships results 10-5—10-9, 1005D2
COMBUSTION Engineering Inc.
A-reactor warning issued 4-12, 275B2*
NRC orders 8 A-reactors inspected 6-25, 518E3
COMECON—*See COUNCIL for Mutual Economic Assistance*
COMENCINI, Luigi
Till Marriage Do Us Part released 7-20, 820E3

1980

COLORADO
OCAW strike talks in Denver 2-28, 187D2
Oil leasing lottery suspended, scandal hinted 2-29; resumptn ordrd 4-7, 330E2
Denver-London air svc agreed 3-5, 172B3, E3
DES in cattle rptd 4-24, 358F1
Exxon buys Arco shale oil project 5-13, 553A3
Hunts bailout loan collateral listed 5-28, 426E1
Forest fire damage rptd 6-29, 616B2
Denver Post sale set 10-22, 857C1
Atomic Energy & Safeguards
Rocky Flats A-protesters arrested 1-1, 17G3
Rocky Flats A-protests held 4-19—4-20, 441F1
Crime & Civil Disorders
NY businesswoman, 2 partners indicted 1-10, 216C1, F1, A2
FBI 'Miporn' probe rptd 2-14, 136A2
'Pyramid' money schemes rptd 5-17, 655A3
Politics & Government—*See also other appropriate subheads in this section*
Legislature schedule rptd 18C1
State of State message 1-4, 269C1
Dem caucusing completed 6-4, 596A2
Govs Assn meets 8-3—8-5, 595F3
Anderson assaulted in Denver 8-5, 596E3-597A1
Sen primary results 9-9, 700D2
Bush speaks in Denver 9-10, 780E3
Newspaper pres endorsemts rptd 11-1, 841G3
Election results 11-4: pres 838A1, 839A1, D3; cong 840D1, 842C2, 845A3, 846B3, 851C3; state 845D2, 847C3
'80 census rptd, reapportmt seen 12-31, 983D1
COLORADO, University of (Boulder)
3d in NCAA skiing 3-8, 470B1
Haynes, Brock in NFL draft 4-29, 336F3
COLORADO River
Imperial Valley water rights upheld by Sup Ct 6-16, 511A3
COLUCCI, Vincent
Sentenced 5-20, 927F2
COLUMBIA Pictures Industries Inc.
In Getty Oil pay-TV film venture 4-22, Justice Dept to probe 4-24, 376E2
Pay-TV film plan draws trust suit 8-4, 639F3
Kerkorian, shareholders file suits 9-30, 10-7; dirs countersue 10-2, 10-20, 906D2
COLUMBIA River
Mt St Helens damage assessed 5-24—7-4, 504B3
COLUMBIA University (N.Y., N.Y.)
Sovern named pres 1-7, 200C1
'79 endowmt earnings rptd 3-24, 319B2
Pulitzer Prizes awarded 4-14, 296B2
Gene Weltfish dies 8-2, 676F3
Maurice Tauber dies 9-21, 756F2
John Randall dies 12-1, 1004B3
COLUMBUS—*See OHIO*
COMANECI, Nadia
Wins Olympic medals, disputes mar competition 7-23—7-25, 589D2-B3, 622G3, 623A1
COMBINED Communications Corp.
Ex-pres forms Charter Media, buys Phila Bulletin 4-10, 376G3
COMECON—*See COUNCIL for Mutual Economic Assistance*

1976

COMEDIANS (play)
Opens 11-28, 1014F3
COMIEZ, Maynard
On 1st ¼ GNP, inflatn data 4-19, 279B1
On Mar trade deficit 4-26, 307C1
On 1st ¼ corp profits 5-20, 376F2
On Apr trade deficit 5-26, 396G1
COMMERCE Clearing House, Inc. (CCH)
Rpts antipollutn spending 5-11, 414E3
Rpts '76 bankruptcies 10-20, 984C3
COMMERCIAL Metals Co.
Fined 4-10, 988E3
COMMISSION on United States-Latin American Relations—*See UNITED States-Latin American Relations, etc.*
COMMITTEE for a Constitutional Presidency—*See McCARTHY, Eugene J.*
COMMITTEE for Humane Legislation Inc.
Porpoise protectn voted 5-11, 398E2
COMMITTEE for Political Education (COPE)—*See under AMERICAN Federation of Labor*
COMMITTEE to Re-elect the President
Nixon disbarred in NY 7-8, 493E3
COMMODITIES & Commodity Trading—*See also commodity names*
Intl trade restructuring plan OKd at UNCTAD conf 2-10, 108A1
US offers poor natns buffer stock plan 5-6, 317E1, B2
Pacific exchng closes, US sues 5-10, 348C2
France proposes price stabilizatn plan 5-10—5-11, 355E3
Speculators default on potato futures 5-25; suit filed 5-27, 397C1-398B1
UNCTAD OKs price stabilizatn fund, vs US bank plan 5-30, US scores 6-1, 388E2, B3
Parsky on commodity pacts 6-1, 388E3
7-natn summit discusses UNCTAD fund plan 6-27—6-28, 462C2
Carter proposes stablizatn plan 7-28, 551A1
Mondale pledges agri loan rate revisn 7-31, 565G1
Potato futures default penalty set 8-31, ct delays setlmt 9-27, 990E1
US comm warns 5 exchngs 9-15, 990D2
Rosenthal & Co chrgd 10-21, ct blocks London optns rule 12-22, 990B2
New potato futures contract OKd 11-2, trading halted 11-3, 990A1

1977

COMMENTARY (magazine)
Carter Mideast policy survey 10-31, 831G1
COMMERCE—*See BUSINESS & Industry; FOREIGN Trade*
COMMERCE, Department of—*See under U.S. GOVERNMENT*
COMMERCE Clearing House (CCH)
State legislature mtgs table 6C2
Rpts fscl '76 state per capita tax burden, table 10-18, 821F2, F3
COMMISSIONER of Internal Revenue v. Kowalski
State police meal stipends ruled taxable 11-20, 919F1
COMMISSIONG, Janelle Penny
Crowned Miss Univ 7-16, 808G2
COMMODITIES & Commodity Trading—*See also commodity names*
Orange juice concentrate futures rise 1-28, 55B1; 1-31, 76C1
US to up Egypt import loan 2-1, 390E2
UN rpts '76 price rise 2-14, 145F3
IMF '76 lending rptd 3-7, 208G3
Buffer stock plan cited at Geneva 3-14—3-18, 209E2
Carter addresses UN 3-17, 185E2
UNCTAD talks deadlocked 4-3, 297C3
Carter UN address cited 4-3, 297F3
Carter 'open' to Latin price pacts, buffer stocks 4-14, 295G3
Carter outlines anti-inflatn plan 4-15, 299A1
Record Mar, 1st ¼ trading rptd 4-18, 301A2
7-natn summit backs common fund 5-7—5-8, 357C2
North-South talks end 6-3, 437A2-A3
NY trading cntr opens 7-5, 521F2
Hunt soybean trading ruled illegal 9-28, 858E3
'74 law challenge declined 11-7, 857F1
Unctad common fund talks fail 12-1; Perez cites re poor natn debt rise 12-20, 973D2, 974E2
US, Mex OK pact 12-2, 976G1

1978

COMEDIANS—*See BROADCASTING, MOTION Pictures, THEATER; personal names*
COMER, Steve
AL pitching ldr 10-2, 928F3
COMERT, Bedrettin
Slain 7-11, 595B3
COMES A Horseman (film)
Released 11-1, 969G3
COMING Home (film)
Released 2-15, 619B1
COMING Into the Country (book)
On best-seller list 2-5, 116C3
COMMERCE—*See BUSINESS & Industry, FOREIGN Trade*
COMMERCE, Department of—*See under U.S. GOVERNMENT*
COMMERCE Clearing House (CCH)
State legislature mtgs table 14G3
Rpts state sales-tax rates 1-5, 15A3
Ex-chrmn Thorne dies 2-15, 196F3
State tax relief measures rptd 5-25, 425D1
COMMIRE, Anne
Shay opens 3-7, 887B3
COMMITTEE for the Study of the American Electorate
Rpts voter turnout down 11-7, 915G2-A3
COMMITTEE for the Survival of a Free Congress
3d-leading PAC fund-raiser 9-7, 753B2
95th Cong rated 10-24, 865B3
COMMITTEE of Interns v. National Labor Relations Board
Hosp interns unionizatn bar denied review 2-27, 143B2
COMMITTEE on the Present Danger
Nitze scores SALT 12-14, 996B2
COMMITTEE to Re-elect the President
Nixon memoir excerpt cites Mitchell Watergate role 4-30, 319E3
COMMODITIES & Commodity Trading—*See also commodity names*
'77 trading rise, Chicago bd rank rptd 1-12, 83G3-84B1
Trader mail case refused by Sup Ct 6-26, 566F3
Common fund talks fail 11-30, 998F1
Options Trading
London trading explained 83E3
Lloyd Carr offcls arrested 1-10, Abrahams identity revealed 1-14, apprehended 1-24; co receiver named 1-19, 83B2-D3
London dealer probes cited 1-10, 83D3
London trading ban sought 1-31, 83E3
London sales suspended 4-5, 283A1
Abrahams sentncd on probatn violatn 4-20, 283C1
Abrahams, 11 others indicted 8-3, 665C2
Futures trading record, Chicago bd vol drop rptd 1004A3

1979

COMER, Steve
AL pitching ldr 9-30, 955G3
COMING Home (film)
Wins Oscars 4-9, 336F1, A2
COMINGS, David E.
Depressn, MS linked to heredity 1-4, 289E3
COMIN' Uptown (play)
Opens 12-20, 1007C2
COMMERCE—*See BUSINESS & Industry, FOREIGN Trade*
COMMERCE, Department of—*See under U.S. GOVERNMENT*
COMMERCE Clearing House (CCH)
State legislature mtgs table 5G3
State tax collectns rptd 2-13, 152G1
State-local tax revenues rptd 5-16, 386G1
Fiscl '79 bankruptcies rptd 11-15, 991B1
COMMITTEE for Economic Energy
Tex A-bond vote hailed 4-7, 261D3
COMMITTEE for Public Education and Religious Liberty v. Regan
NYC pvt schl reimbursemt bar voided by Sup Ct 4-2, 281A3
COMMITTEE of 75
Negrin slain 11-25, 906B1
COMMODITIES & Commodity Trading—*See also commodity names*
Treas bills, notes explained 681D2
Futures contract, arbitrage explained 72D2, F2
W Eur inflatn rise seen 3-13, 180B2
CFTC orders Chicago wheat trading halt 3-15, cts stay 3-18—3-19; trading ends, speculators named 3-21, 201C3
Holzer convicted of grand larceny 3-15, 239F2
UNCTAD fund set 3-20, 200D2
Stone confrmd CFTC chrmn 4-11, 681D2
UNCTAD aid pact rptd 6-3, 417D3
CFTC OKs T-bill, notes futures trading 6-19, NYSE asks trading OK 6-21, 681D2
Gulf Westn-DR sugar probe rptd 8-16, 632D3
FRB tightens credit, cites speculatn, Carter comments 10-6; Volcker warns bankers re loans 10-9, 764C1-E3, 765G3
Sugar futures soar 10-12, US bars supports 10-23, 808D2
Underregulatn said dangerous 11-1, 827A1
Eur, US, Canada pact vows raw material consumptn cut 11-13, 864B3
Gulf+Western sued by SEC 11-26, 923F1
Futures trade increase, squeezes cited 12-31, 978F2
Options Trading
Lloyd Carr offcls convicted 2-22, sentncd 3-19, 220E2
CFTC bars resumptn 9-5, 681F1

1980

COMENZO, Ron
Bull Pen opens 6-12, 756C3
COME Pour the Wine (book)
On best-seller list 12-7, 948D3
COMEX—*See COMMODITY Exchange Inc.*
COMING Attractions (play)
Opens 12-3, 1003A3
COMING Up (recording)
On best-seller list 6-4, 448E3; 7-9, 568E3
COMMERCE, Department of—*See under U.S. GOVERNMENT*
COMMERCE Clearing House (CCH)
State legislature mtgs table 18G1
State fscl '79 tax revenues rptd 2-20, 307E2-B3
State-local '79 tax collectns rptd 4-17, 307B2
346 referendum propositns in 42 states rptd 10-21, 847C2
COMMERCIAL Carriers Inc.—*See under TEXAS Gas Transmission Corp.*
COMMERZBANK A.G.
Earnings rptd down 12-5, Kaufhof shares sold 12-12, 969E1
COMMITTEE for an Open Convention
Formed 7-28, 570A2
Williams addresses Dem conv 8-11, 609F2
COMMITTEE for Public Education and Religious Freedom v. Regan
Case decided by Sup Ct 2-20, 146F2
COMMITTEE for the Defense of Elmer (Geronimo) Pratt
2 climb Statue of Liberty in protest 5-11, 667E1
COMMITTEE For the Survival of a Free Congress
Political actn profiled 7-11—9-15, 819G1
COMMITTEE on the Present Danger, The
US arms outlay increase urged 5-9, 369G2-C3
COMMODITIES & Commodity Trading—*See also commodity names*
Margin explained 899G1
Futures contract, arbitrage explained 76D2, G2
Gold, precious metal prices soar 1-2—1-18; Comex moves to curb silver specuatn 1-8, 1-10, 30F1-31E1
US suspends Sovt grain futures trade 1-6, 2B1
Round-the-clock gold trading detailed 1-7, 30D2
US rep urges raw material natn sea route protectn 1-14, 32D1
Grain prices stabilize 1-19, 44G3
Silver sales suspended by Comex, margin requiremt doubled 1-21; Chicago Bd sets curbs 1-22, 68A3
Gold hits record $875 1-21; plummets below $478 3-17, trading erratic 3-18—3-19, 203A1
Mex bans silver mine trading 1-24, imposes sales tax 1-25, 68E3
Copper futures trading curbed by Comex 1-24; prices drop 1-28, rebound 1-29, 69A1
Australia widens Sovt trade sanctns 1-29, 116D1; lifts curbs 2-12, 148A1
Silver futures trading curbs eased by Comex 1-30, 2-13, Chicago Bd restrictns upheld 2-11, 114B1, E1
Ia grain shortage scandal rptd, trading reforms sought 1-31, 238B1, C1
Kennedy on econ control exemptns 2-6, 91A1
Sugar futures soar, world stock fall seen 2-8, 182D1
Copper price hits record, falls 2-12—8-27, 805G2
Peru silver futures losses rptd 2-15, 152F1
London gold price chart 2-18—3-20, 202A3
Amex, NYSE futures trading units to merge 3-21, 224B1
Hunt group sets silver-backed bond issue 3-26, 222G3
Silver price plunges, Hunt empire totters 3-27, 223E1
Hunts use oil assets to settle Englehard debt, traders fear silver glut 3-31, 244F3
Occidental profits from futures trading hedge 3-31, 245D1
Hunt silver trading, Bache ties probed 3-31—4-2; additional debts rptd, shakeup seen 3-31, 245G1-B3
Sovt bloc '79 Westn exports cited 4-1, 285B3
Hunt silver trading debts repaid 4-8, 4-16, Canada OKs Engelhard setlmt 4-28, 345D1
Regulators debate speculatn curbs 4-14—4-15, 289F3
CFTC emergency order case declined by Sup Ct 4-28, 369E1
Hunts $1.1 bln silver bailout set 5-2, 344F3
Hunts testify at House, Sen probes; chrg SEC silver manipulatn 5-2, 345F1
IRS plans moves vs tax straddles 5-22, 481F1
Hunts bailout loans paid 5-27, collateral listed 5-28, 425E2, B3-426F1
Currency futures trading on NYSE unit OKd 5-28, 481B2
Hunt bank deals probed by Sen com; Comex scored, FRB regulatn studied 5-29—5-30, 425D1-B3
COMECON to keep fixed price system for Sovt purchases 5-29, 451F1
Engelhard sets NN Corp purchase 6-24, 557D3
USSR, W Ger sign pact 7-1, 489D2

1976

COMMODITY Exchange Inc.
US comm warns 9-15, 990D2
COMMON Cause
Rpts McCarthy, Reagan rejct campaign code 1-9, 22G3
Morton role questioned 1-22, 41G2
Wins FEC stay 2-27, 169F3
Scores Sikes, House Ethics Com 4-7, 286F2
Sikes hearing set 4-28, 309E2
Sikes reprimanded 7-29, 551F3
Lobbying bill not cleared 10-2, 883D1
COMMON Market—*See EUROPEAN Community*
COMMON Market Forwarders Inc.
Boycott rpts released 10-18—10-20, 786A1-G1
Sullivan on Israeli shipping rules 10-19, 786C2
COMMONWEAL (magazine)
John Cogley dies 3-28, 272E3
COMMONWEALTH Club Of California
Mondale addresses 8-30, 645C3
COMMONWEALTH of Nations (formerly British Commonwealth) (Australia, Bahamas, Bangladesh, Barbados, Botswana, Canada, Cyprus, Fiji, Gambia, Ghana, Great Britain, Grenada, Guyana, India, Jamaica, Kenya, Lesotho, Malawi, Malaysia, Malta, Mauritius, New Zealand, Nigeria, Papua New Guinea, Sierra Leone, Singapore, Sri Lanka, Swaziland, Tanzania, Tonga, Trinidad & Tobago, Uganda, Western Samoa, Zambia; special member: Nauru)
Seychelles independence OKd 1-22, 270G3
Plans Mozambique aid 3-4, 175F2
Seychelles joins 6-28, 799D2
Trinidad & Tobago becomes republic 8-1, 714B3
Gets UN observer role 10-18, 799C2
COMMONWEALTH Oil Refining Co. Inc.
Unit indicted 6-1, 412D3
COMMUNICATIONS—*See also ASTRONAUTICS; media (e.g., BROADCASTING)*
Ford State of Union message 1-19, 38G2
French-India pact signed 1-22—1-26, 139F2
Ford urges regulatory reform 5-13, 347A1
Latin natns hold conf 7-12—7-21, 619E3
Lord Thomson of Fleet dies 8-4, 816G3
Forgn paymts study rptd 12-20, 985D2
USSR interfernc rptd eased 12-28, 1011B1

1977

COMMODITIES Exchange Inc. (Comex)
NY trading cntr opens 7-5, 521F2
COMMODITY Credit Corp.—*See under U.S. GOVERNMENT—AGRICULTURE*
COMMODITY Futures Trading Commission—*See under U.S. GOVERNMENT*
COMMON Cause
Hails Carter conflict-of-interest code 1-4, 5C1
'76 spec interest Cong gifts rptd 1-15, 2-4, 2-15, 128C1-129F2
Sikes ousted as subcom head 1-26, 53G2
Gardner announces resignatn 2-5, 140D2
Rpts post-Watergate pol paymts prosecutn 2-16, 111G3
Waterman succeeds Gardner 4-23, 396C3
Flynt resignatn urged 7-16, 556C2
Gardner quits Rockefeller Fund 8-23, 927D3
Lists '76 maritime pol gifts 10-3, 815D1
COMMON Market—*See EUROPEAN Community*
COMMONWEALTH of Nations (formerly British Commonwealth) (Australia, Bahamas, Bangladesh, Barbados, Botswana, Canada, Cyprus, Fiji, Gambia, Ghana, Great Britain, Grenada, Guyana, India, Jamaica, Kenya, Lesotho, Malawi, Malaysia, Malta, Mauritius, New Zealand, Nigeria, Papua New Guinea, St. Lucia, Seychelles, Sierra Leone, Singapore, Sri Lanka, Swaziland, Tanzania, Tonga, Trinidad & Tobago, Uganda, Western Samoa, Zambia; special member: Nauru)
Canada drops 'subject' status 2-15, 133A3
NZ vs Uganda expulsn 3-31, 258C2
Amin threatens to 'crash' conf 6-7, curbs UK natls 6-8, 486F3
London conf backs Rhodesia, Namibia majority rule, condemns Amin 6-8—6-15, 486B3
Seychelles to remain member 6-8, 489B1
Uganda curbs UK natls 6-10, 508C1
Uganda lifts UK curbs 7-1, 600C3
Finance Mins meet; protectnism, poor natn aid discussed 9-21—9-24, 936C2
S Africa pressed on Rhodesia oil bar 10-19, 876B1
Canada cuts S Africa econ ties 12-19, 1016F2
COMMONWEALTH Oil Refining Co. Inc.
'75, '76 losses cited 340C2
Unit convicted 8-30, 691A3
Unit fined 9-16, 918F2
Ashland OKs stock purchase 9-22, 723B1
COMMUNICATIONS—*See also ASTRONAUTICS; media (e.g., BROADCASTING)*
'75 Ford Foundatn grants cited 1-11, 56E1
UK unions to boycott S Africa 1-13, 29A2; ICFTU boycott fails 1-21, 67A3
Sci Medal awarded 11-22, 952A1
Obituaries
Goldmark, Peter 12-7, 1024A2

1978

COMMODITY Credit Corp.—*See under U.S. GOVERNMENT—AGRICULTURE*
COMMODITY Futures Trading Commission—*See under U.S. GOVERNMENT*
COMMODORES (singing group)
3 Times a Lady on best-seller list 8-2, 620E1; 9-6, 708E1
Natural High on best-seller list 8-2, 620G1
COMMON Cause
Marston ouster scored 1-20, 32B2
House OKs lobbying bill 4-26, 323A2, C2
Cong electn funding bill rejctd 7-19, 550C3
'PAC democracy' feared 9-7, 753F2
FEC apptmt suit filed 10-26, 831A3
Wertheimer lauds ethics bill 10-26, 832G1
House ethics rule chng scored 12-6, 958E2
PAC cong com gifts rptd 12-24, 1008C1
COMMONER, Barry
Speaks at Sun Day rally in DC 5-3, 322A1
COMMON Market—*See EUROPEAN Community*
COMMONWEALTH Club of California
Brown addresses 6-23, 493D2
COMMONWEALTH Edison Co.
On Admin A-plant licensing revisn bill 3-17, 205B3
Coal strike billing to be probed 5-10, 367A1
2 A-plants ordered 12-20, 1009G3
COMMONWEALTH of Nations (formerly British Commonwealth) (Australia, Bahamas, Bangladesh, Barbados, Botswana, Canada, Cyprus, Fiji, Gambia, Ghana, Great Britain, Grenada, Guyana, India, Jamaica, Kenya, Lesotho, Malawi, Malaysia, Malta, Mauritius, New Zealand, Nigeria, Papua New Guinea, St. Lucia, Seychelles, Sierra Leone, Singapore, Sri Lanka, Swaziland, Tanzania, Tonga, Trinidad & Tobago, Uganda, Western Samoa, Zambia; special member: Nauru)
UK racial slurs disputed 1-6, 18G1
Australia hotel hosting Asian, Pacific ldrs bombed 2-12, 110E1 ★; security rptd tightened, Indian terrorists blamed 2-14, 121B3
Asian, Pacific conf meets 2-13—2-16; joint statemt on trade, energy, terrorism issued 2-16, 121C1
Australia Natl Front asks closer ties 6-3, 495B1
Australia raids Indian sect hq 6-17, 495D1
Canada plans Games financing extensn 7-6, 531F2
COMMUNICATIONS—*See also media (e.g., BROADCASTING)*
'53, '78 cong membership compared 1-30, 107G2
US telecommunicatn office reorganized 3-28, 270C2
Lobbying bill OKd by House 4-26, 323F1-C2
Zaire, W Ger deal rptd 7-19, 652A3
Viet, Thai cooperatn agreed 9-6—9-10, 696G1
Microwave safety scored 12-11, 936C3

1979

COMMODITY Exchange Inc. (Comex)
CFTC OKs T-bill futures trading 6-19, 681B3
Silver, copper prices rptd 10-2, 740D1, G1
Silver price soars 12-31, 978F2
COMMODITY Futures Trading Commission—*See under U.S. GOVERNMENT*
COMMODORES (singing group)
Midnight Magic on best-seller list 10-3, 800F3; 11-7, 892F3
COMMON Carrier Bureau—*See under U.S. GOVERNMENT—FEDERAL Communications Commission*
COMMON Cause
FEC apptmt upheld 1-8, 130D3
SWP wins funds rpt exemptn 1-9, 13F3
Sen income limit stay scored 3-8, 185G2
PAC spending rise scored 5-15, 363A2
Electn financing bill revival sought 5-24, 401D2
US pay-scale revisn backed 6-6, 419G2
Carter New England energy mailing scored 9-17, 703G2
COMMONER, Barry
Forms Citizens Party 8-1, 594F3
At NYC A-protest 9-23, 742G2
COMMON Market—*See EUROPEAN Community*
COMMONWEALTH of Nations (formerly British Commonwealth) (Australia, Bahamas, Bangladesh, Barbados, Botswana, Canada, Cyprus, Dominica, Fiji, Gambia, Ghana, Great Britain, Grenada, Guyana, India, Jamaica, Kenya, Lesotho, Malawi, Malaysia, Malta, Mauritius, New Zealand, Nigeria, Papua New Guinea, St. Lucia, St. Vincent, Seychelles, Sierra Leone, Singapore, Solomon Islands, Sri Lanka, Swaziland, Tanzania, Tonga, Trinidad & Tobago, Uganda, Western Samoa, Zambia; special member: Nauru, Tuvalu)
UK reopens Uganda office 4-21, 314D3
Zimbabwe Rhodesia recognitn barred 5-18, 393F2
UK plans Zimbabwe recognitn proposal 7-10, 546D3
UK delegatn vs Nigeria BP natlzn 7-31, 584B3, D3
Lusaka conf 8-1—8-7, Zimbabwe plan agreed 8-6, 589A1
Muzorewa, Patriotic Front to attend UK Zimbabwe conf 8-15, 8-20, 638B1
Australia-NZ trade union explored 8-21, 632A1
Australia defers tariff cut 8-24, 650C2
Zimbabwe transitn role offered 11-2, 844D2
UK OKs Zimbabwe peace force role 11-9, 881C1
Patriotic Front vs UK on Zimbabwe peace force size 11-19, 11-30, 937A1-E1
Zimbabwe peacekeeping force arrives 12-23, 976D3
COMMUNICATIONS—*See also media (e.g., BROADCASTING)*
Xerox plans WUI acquisitn 1-18, 89C1
NCR agrees to buy Comten 1-21, 89F1
Australia plans satellite system 10-18, 852B2

1980

Treasury futures trading exclusivity awarded to NYSE unit 7-15; Chicago ct overturns CFTC order 7-17—7-18, enforcemt chief quits 7-22, 558G2
CBT, Merc expand financial futures trading 7-24; NYFE opens, trading mixed 8-7, 616D3
ICO sets price limits, export quotas 10-3; coffee glut weakens growers' cartel 10-7, 777D2
Sugar futures hit 5 1/2-yr high 10-9, 777A2
Hunts liquidate Bache holdings 10-21, 867B3
Reagan electn welcomed by traders; gold prices gain, drop 11-5, 845A1, C1
CFTC sets tighter trading rules 11-25, 899B1
Prices drop on higher US interest rates 12-10, 932G1
US trading up 21% in '80 12-31, 984E3
Options Trading
Optns trader arrested in 'boiler room' swindle 1-2, 94B3
SEC ends ban, NYSE decision deferred; '79 trading vol rptd 3-26, 224A2
Lloyd Carr chief sentenced 6-20, 503C1
COMMODITY Exchange Inc. (Comex)
Silver speculatn curbs set 1-8, 1-10, 31C1
Silver futures trading suspended, margin requiremt doubled 1-21, 68A3
Gold hits record high 1-21, plummets on Carter anti-inflatn plan 3-17, 203B1
Copper futures trading curbed 1-24; prices drop 1-28, rebound 1-29, 69A1
Silver futures trading curbs eased 1-30, 2-13, 114B1
Copper price hits record, falls 2-12—8-27, 805G2
Peru silver futures trading losses rptd 2-15, 152F1
Amex, NYSE futures trading units to merge 3-21, 224E1
Hunt group sets silver-backed bond issue 3-26, 222G3
Silver price plunges, Hunt empire totters 3-27, 223E1
Hunts chrg SEC silver manipulatn 5-2, 345B2
Sen com probes Hunt bank deals; Proxmire scores bd, weighs FRB regulatn 5-29—5-30, 425D1, E2
Gold prices surge, drop on Reagan electn 11-5, 845C1
Copper price rises 11-12, 987G3
Prices drop on higher US interest rates 12-10, 932G1
COMMODITY Futures Trading Commission—*See under U.S. GOVERNMENT*
COMMON Cause
Cox elected chrmn 2-2, 115E2
Files campaign spending suit 7-1, 493B1
Reagan fund raising coms upheld by fed ct 8-28, 681G1
COMMONER, Barry H.
To accept teaching post 3-17, 471C3
Heads Citizens' Party pres ticket 4-13, 288B3, D3
Uses vulgar radio ad 10-15, 818A3
Popular vote table 11-4, 838A2
COMMON Market—*See EUROPEAN Community*
COMMONWEALTH Club (San Francisco, Calif.)
Mondale addresses 9-5, 780G1-A2
Bush addresses 9-11, 780F3
COMMONWEALTH Edison Co.
Co, 2 offcls indicted 3-26, 249D1
Ill A-plant '79 dischrg data rptd 4-7, revised 4-27, 441B2
Co, 2 offcls acquitted 8-8, 649D1
Evers dies 12-5, 1004E1
COMMONWEALTH of Nations (formerly British Commonwealth) (Australia, Bahamas, Bangladesh, Barbados, Botswana, Canada, Cyprus, Dominica, Fiji, Gambia, Ghana, Great Britain, Grenada, Guyana, India, Jamaica, Kenya, Lesotho, Malawi, Malaysia, Malta, Mauritius, New Zealand, Nigeria, Papua New Guinea, St. Lucia, St. Vincent, Seychelles, Sierra Leone, Singapore, Solomon Islands, Sri Lanka, Swaziland, Tanzania, Tonga, Trinidad & Tobago, Uganda, Western Samoa, Zambia, Zimbabwe; special members: Nauru, Tuvalu)
Zimbabwe joins 4-18, 301A2
Obote asks electn observers 5-27, 446B2
New Hebrides unrest, natls flee 5-28—6-3, 422B3
16 Asian, Pacific nations meet 9-4—9-8; Sovts, Viets scored for Afghan, Cambodia roles 9-8, 680B1
Uganda electn observed 12-10—12-11, 946B1, D1; Obote wins 12-13, 968A3
COMMUNICATIONS
Newhouse to buy Random House 2-6, 386D1
Carter seeks deregulatn legis 3-14, 201F1
US, Turkey sign bases pact 3-29, 255C3
Time names new mgt team 5-15, 456E2
Mex-Canada projcts agreed 5-27, 409C3
US OKs China sale 5-29, 397F3
Fairchild, VSI to merge 8-26, 746C1
Telecommunciatns bill tabled by Cong 9-30, 835D2
Japan-US trade talks resume 10-19, 864A3
Islamic econ conf 11-4—11-6, 865C1
Wage increases rptd 11-18, 883E1
Obituaries
McLuhan, Marshall 12-31, 1004F2

1976

COMMUNISM (U.S.)
Hall addresses Sovt CP Cong 3-1, 196E1
Rockefeller chrgs vs Jackson aides stir dispute 4-15—4-27, 305D3
Sen intelligence com rpt cites 4-28, 327D3, 330G1-A2, B3
Final pres vote tally 12-18, 979B2
COMMUNISM and Communist Countries (non-U.S.)—*See also country, organization names*
Czech 15th Cong, Sovt support stressed 4-12—4-16, 289B1
Kissinger warns on W Eur govts 4-13, 259A3
Schmidt on CPs in govt 4-15, 503E1
Sovt stand vs independent CPs seen eased 4-20, 341A2
Eur CPs meet, cong set 5-4—5-6, 341E1
Giscard on US misgivings 5-18, 372B2
E Ger SED Cong, Sovt intl leadershp stressed 5-18—5-22, 381B1
Rumania eases Eur CP mtg stand 6-2, 420A3
Spain PSP conv 6-5—6-6, 459B1
US Dem platform text 6-15, 478E1
E, W Eur CPs meet, rebuff USSR, back pluralism 6-29—6-30, 461A1
Reps at Albania cong 11-1—11-7, 849F3
Kissinger lobbying efforts rptd 2-5, 120B2
Sovt 25th CP cong 2-24—3-5; Brezhnev scores Westn parties 2-24, 193G1-196E1
El Salvador infiltratn chrgd 3-8, 289E3
Kissinger rebuts W Eur critics 3-11, 197G3
Solzhenitsyn warning aired 3-24, 424F1
Bulgaria 11th Cong 3-29—4-2, 250B1
Pravda, E Eur, Italy press score US critics 4-9—4-18, 276E3
Sen, House extend Export Admin Act in prelim votes 8-27, 9-22, 746C2
Castro sees trade rise 9-27, 772A1
'76 intl borrowing rptd 12-22, 976G1
COMMUNITY Broadcasting of Boston Inc.
SEC suit vs Gen Tire settled 5-10, 360A2
COMMUNITY National Bank—*See under PACIFIC Bancorp.*
COMORO Islands—*See also NONALIGNED Nations Movement, OAU*
Soilih elected pres, Mohammed vp 1-2; Cabt named 1-6, 1-10, 119A1
Listed as 'partly free' 1-19, 20C3
At France-Africa summit 5-10—5-11, 355A3
Joins Islamic Conf 5-12, 373B2
Comoro-Malagasy workers clash 12-20, forgn mins consult 12-23—12-26, 1013C1
Mayotte Separatist Issue
USSR scores French policy 2-5, 118G3
Mayotte votes to stay French 2-8, 118E3
France vetoes UN Cncl resolutn 2-8, 118G3
Stirn visits; bars mil base, sets vote on French ties 2-20—2-21, 205A1
Mayotte votes for French ties 4-11, France agrees 4-12, 538A3

1977

Kleinschmidt, Edward 8-9, 696A3
Kompfner, Rudolf 12-3, 1024C2
COMMUNICATIONS Satellite Corp. (Comsat)
McLucas elected Comsat unit pres 4-19, 396F3
FCC warns re escrow fund 9-11, ct upholds refund order 10-14, 944E1
COMMUNICATIONS Workers of America (CWA) (AFL-CIO)
AT&T pact reached 8-6, 613F2
COMMUNISM (U.S.)
Bertram Wolfe dies 2-22, 164G3
Will Herberg dies 3-27, 264G2
Sen subcom ends 3-31, 251F3
Carter stresses rights 5-2, 338A2
'20-42 FBI watch on ACLU rptd 6-19, 481B2
Sacco, Vanzetti vindicated 7-19, 652G2
FBI Cointelpro campaign detailed 11-21, 940B3, G3, 941B1
COMMUNISM and Communist Countries (non-U.S.)—*See also MARXISM; also country, organization names*
Spain-E Eur ties resumed 1-27, 2-9, 242C2
Reps at Frelimo cong 2-3—2-7, 137D1
Sovt bloc Westn debt rptd 2-13—4-13, 335B3
Vatican boosts Sovt bloc broadcasts 2-16, 471E2
Eurocommunists meet 3-2—3-3, 242E3
'76 E Eur trade data rptd 3-8, 188F2, B3
7-natn summit backs econ aid 5-7—5-8, 357E2
'76 E Eur export rptd up 6-14, 513B2
Yugo scores Sovt bloc dissidents at Helsinki preparatory conf 6-15, 473B1
USSR, Spain dispute Eurocommunism 6-23—6-27, 507F1
Hungary backs Eurocommunism, Spain 6-30; Rumania backs 7-5, 513E2
Hungary hardens re Spain, Eurocommunism 7-3, 7-24, 590D3
ASEAN backs Indochina ties 7-5—7-8, 537C1
USSR renews Spain dispute 7-6, 545C3
Albania scores China 7-7, 540D3
Sovt block reactn to Spain, Eurocommunism continues 7-8, 7-24, 590A3
Archbp Lefebvre attacks 7-12—7-26, 620F1
Albania-China dispute continues, rift denied 7-26—8-2, 595C1
28 CPs ask neutron bomb ban 8-9, 640G2
Sovt bloc vs UN desert fund 9-9, 770F1
Portugal CP backs USSR, scores Eurocommunism 10-28, 866F3
USSR revolutn 60th anniv feted 11-2—11-7; Carrillo speech barred 11-3, 865D2
Polish sexual permissiveness scored 12-4, 987E1
Amnesty Intl chrgs rights abuses 12-8, 956D2
U.S. Relations
US gets Sakharov plea on E Eur 1-23—1-29, 69A1
Carter on rights stand 2-23, 126C2
Carter asks more RFE funds 3-22, 229F3
W Eur CP policy affirmed 4-2, 4-6, 255E2
US House OKs export act 4-20, 323D3
US scores Sovt bloc re Helsinki pact 6-6, 473C1
Kissinger on W Eur CPs 6-9, 458B3
Eur CP travel ban end lauded 7-25—7-27, 581E2
US broadcasting scored by USSR 8-3, 590A2
US Cong comm scores re rights 8-5, 606B2
US eases visa curb 8-17, 667D2
B Graham on religion 9-15, 732E1
COMMUNITY of Peace People
Corrigan, Williams win Nobel 10-10, 951C2
COMMUNITY Relations Service—*See under U.S. GOVERNMENT—JUSTICE*
COMMUNITY Services Administration—*See under U.S. GOVERNMENT*
COMORO Islands—*See also NONALIGNED Nations Movement, OAU*
UN Assemb member 3F3
Citizen repatriatn from Madagascar sought 1-7, 24B2
At France-Africa summit 4-20—4-21, 316F3
Arab League seat denied 9-4, 685E1
UN asks French evacuatn of Mayotte 10-26, 869A1
Soilih backed in referendum 10-28, 868G3
COMPAGNIE Francaise des Petroles
To buy extra Saudi oil 2-16, 108B1, C1
Zambia sues re Rhodesia sanctns 8-22, 662D1
Gandhi arrested in bid-rigging scandal 10-3, 765B1
COMPAGNIE Luxembourgeoise de la Drensdner Bank AG
Brazil steel loan granted 6-20, 524E2
COMPANYS, Luis (d. 1940)
Barcelona riots mark death 10-15, 843G2
COMPLETE Auto Transit, Inc.
Miss interstate tax power backed 3-7, 192D2
COMPLETE Auto Transit Inc. v. Brady
States' tax power widened 3-7, 192D2
COMPLETE Book of Running, The (book)
On best-seller list 12-4, 1021A3

1978

COMMUNICATIONS Satellite Corp. (Comsat)
FCC dispute settled 5-9, 494C3
Welch dies 10-22, 888G3
COMMUNICATIONS Workers of America (CWA) (AFL-CIO)
AT&T bias case declined by Sup Ct 7-3, 552A1
Watts assails Meany 12-11, 960F3
COMMUNICATIONS Workers of America v. EEOC
AT&T bias case declined by Sup Ct 7-3, 551G3
COMMUNISM (U.S.)
Humphrey stand cited 32E3, F3
COMMUNISM and Communist Countries (non-U.S.)—*See also country, organization names (e.g., WARSAW Pact)*
W Ger '77 trade rptd 1-3, 21D3
Spain CP ldrs rptd shaken by book 1-21, 2-24, 136A2
UK ends propaganda unit 1-27, 71F2
Swiss rpt '77 asylum total 2-1, 151C2
Hungary '77 econ compared 2-9, 534F1
Unctad debt relief stand cited 3-11, 301D1
USSR '77 trade with bloc rpt 3-28, 230B1
Spain CP drops 'Leninist' label 4-19—4-23, PSOE drops 'Marxist' 5-22, 821C3
Sovt-bloc conv arms threat seen 5-25, 421F2
NATO rpt backs improved ties 5-30, 398A1
Brezhnev addresses Czech CP rally 5-31, 423A2
Africa role feared by Saudi 5-31, 441A2
Solzhenitsyn scores West 6-8, 444A3
Hungary backs Eurocommunism 6-10, 534B3
Rumania plans E Eur jet sale 6-15, 515B3
Tito backs Eurocommunism 6-20, 519G2
W Ger terrorists rptd in Sovt-bloc natns 6-22, 500F1
Italy CP scores USSR 7-11, 7-12, 543A1
Sovt gas export rise seen 8-13, 635A1
EC scores Sovt bloc shipping policy, USSR defends 9-11—9-19, 820B3-F3
Pole elected Pope 10-16, 781C2
Sovt-bloc debt rise rptd 11-21, 11-28, 999F1
Intl conf in Bulgaria, USSR scores Rumania 12-15, 1020C1
'78 oil output rise rptd 12-26, 1000B3
U.S. Relations
US oil shortage forecast disputed 1-18, 52E3
Sovt bloc protests US ouster of Viet UN amb 2-9, 103A3
Asia, Pacific mil commitmt affirmed 2-20, 126D3
Energy study forecasts oil imports 5-8, 366F2
'77 CIA oil study assessed 5-21, 384E1
Carter sees USSR model abandoned 6-7, 423G3
Vance pledges A-weapon restraint 6-12, 445A2
US favored-natn trade status cited 7-8, 534D2
Sovt bloc shipping growth rptd, West concerned 7-11—8-24, 670G2-E3
Latin subversn chrgs laid to CIA 8-1, 831C1
Cong pro-defns coalitn formed 8-8, 604C3
Control Data gets E Eur license 10-31, 841D1
Douglas FBI file detailed 11-14, 877E3
Interest paymts on frozen forgn assets 11-14, 977G1
King murder link rptd probed 11-22, 938F2
Carter scored on silence re Latin movemts 11-29, 938F3
COMORO Islands—*See also NONALIGNED Nations Movement, OAU*
Trial for alleged plotters demanded 1-22, 94B2
Malagasy sentences 54 for '76 riots 2-4, 115B3
Coup ousts Soilih, anti-religion stand cited 5-13, 371G1
Abdallah, Ahmed named ldrs 5-23, 445B3
Soilih killed in escape attempt 5-29, 445B2
Belgian mercenary ouster from govt rptd 7-23, 596D1
UN Assemb member 713D3
Belgian mercenary quits army 9-26, leaves 9-27, 798B3
Const draft OKd 10-1, Ahmed quits as pres 10-3, 885C2
COMPANY (play)
Revial opens 5-7, 887D1
COMPANY, The (book)
Ehrlichman freed from jail 4-27, 320E2
COMPLETE Book of Running, The (book)
On best-seller list 1-8, 24E3; 2-5, 116C3; 3-5, 195E3; 4-2, 272B3; 4-30, 356G1; 6-4, 460B3; 7-2, 579C3; 8-6, 620B2; 9-4, 708C1; 10-9, 800B3; 11-6, 888A1
COMPOSERS, Authors and Publishers, American Society of (ASCAP)
TV music licenses challenged 11-27, 1030A1

1979

COMMUNICATIONS Workers of America (CWA) (AFL-CIO)
Carter conv address set 7-12, 513D2; details energy progrm 7-16, 532F2
Watts backs Carter reelectn 7-30, 593D3
COMMUNISM (U.S.)
Anti-Teng protests in DC 1-29, 66E1
Brecht '43-56 FBI surveillnc rptd 3-29, 367C3
KKK clashes in NC 7-8, 11-3, 864E2, G3
COMMUNISM and Communist Countries (non-U.S.)—*See also country, organization names (e.g., WARSAW Pact)*
Sovt bloc lauds Viet re Cambodia invasn 1-9, 1-10; Rumania scores 1-10, 11E1
W Ger shipbldg competitn cited 1-21, 77F3
Westn banks to monitor Polish econ 1-26, 59E3-60C1
Bad weather cripples E Eur 1-31, 120C2
Amnesty Intl cites E Eur rights violatns 2-1, 85G2
Iran leftists rejct Sovt bloc 2-14, 125C1
Rumania splits with Sovt bloc, Albania over China Viet invasn 2-19, 2-22; USSR denounces 2-21, 122E2
W Eur CPs score China invasn of Viet 2-19, 122G2
UN rights comm res vs Israel backed 2-21, 148E1
NATO A-attack documts rptd held by defector 3-6, 180G3
Sovt-bloc spies in W Ger cited 3-13, 180D3
Bible availability rptd 3-13, 238E1
Sovt-bloc '78 Westn debt estimates rptd 3-20, 200C3
UNCTAD commodity fund set 3-20, 200E2
USSR hikes oil prices 3-21, 228B1
USSR '78 bloc trade surplus cited 3-28, 237C3
Forgn currency shops cited 285A2
RC dialogue seen 4-30, 376F1
French CP Eurocommunism shift seen 5-10–5-14, 371A2, E2
Sovt bloc faces fuel shortages, USSR warns 5-21–5-24; 1st 1/4 Comecon imports rptd 5-31, 397B1
Pope arrives Poland 6-2; on E Eur RC total, relig freedom 6-3, 413A2
Schmidt backs NATO modernizatn 6-6, 430A1
Sovt bloc econ difficulties rptd 7-16–9-8, 741F2
USSR oil export hike seen 7-18, 568G1
Rumania bars rubles for gas 7-27; Hungary, Czech order travel ban 8-1, 645D3, F3
Turkey sets trade hike 8-21, 637E2
E Eur defectns rptd rising 9-12, 697F2
USSR troop deploymt rptd 761F2
USSR sets E Ger troop cut 10-6, Westn reactn 10-7, 10-9, 761C1, A3-F3
USSR offers Eur troop, tank, missile cuts 10-13–11-6, 880G2
Cuban '77-78 trade rptd 11-14, 872C2
Rumania stresses indepndnc 11-19, 910B2
Taiwan seeks E Eur trade, affirms Sovt bloc bar 11-28, 952B3
Sovt bloc aid to Cambodia rptd 12-3, 917A2
U.S. Relations
Sovt bloc scored by Amnesty Intl 12-9, 980C2
US '78 trade surplus rptd 1-30, 71F3
E Eur 3 Mile I media treatmt rptd 4-11, 323B1
Carter backs NATO modernizatn 6-6, 430A1
Carter scores USSR E Ger troop cut plan 10-9, 761A3
COMMUNITY Broadcasting Inc.
FCC doubts RKO Gen license fitness 7-18, 618A2
COMMUNITY for Creative Nonviolence
White House A-protest 3-31, 261F3
COMMUNITY Energy Project
Rodberg sees jobs gain in solar energy use 4-21, 419A1
COMMUNITY and Junior Colleges, American Association of
Vance addresses 5-1, 347G1
COMMUNITY Relations Council of New York
Syrian abuse of Jews chrgd 2-22, 148A2
COMORO Islands—*See also NONALIGNED Nations Movement, OAU*
UN membership listed 695F2
COMPAGNIE Generale d'Electricite
Generale Occidentale share bought 3-16, 236B2
COMPLETE Posthumous Poetry, The (book)
Translatn wins Natl Book Award 4-23, 356B2
COMPLETE Scarsdale Medical Diet, The (book)
On best-seller list 4-8, 271A2; 5-6, 356C2; 7-1, 548B3; 8-5, 620C3; 10-14, 800B3; 11-4, 892B3
COMPOZ—*See MEDICINE–Drugs*

1980

COMMUNICATIONS Satellite Corp. (Comsat)
Direct TV service OKd 1-30, 240A1
CBS barred from Cuba broadcast 5-22, 397F1
CBS Cuba broadcasts cleared 6-1, 420G2
Broadcast satellite TV plan advances 10-2, 906D3
COMMUNICATIONS Workers of America (CWA) (AFL-CIO)
AT&T pact reached 8-9, 648B1
COMMUNISM (U.S.)
Wm Patterson dies 3-5, 280F1
Angela Davis marries 7-5, 639A1
Anderson assaulted in Denver 8-5, 596F3
Hall scores Polish strike setlmt 8-29, 659A
6 Klansmen acquitted in '79 NC slayings 11-17; reactn 11-17—11-18, 898D2-C3
COMMUNISM and Communist Countries (non-U.S.)—*See also country, organization names*
Sovt bloc reactn to Sovt Afghan invasn 1-1—1-10, 11A1
French CP-USSR rapprochemt, Eurocommunism decline seen 1-5—1-11, 57F2
W Eur CPs split on Afghan invasn 1-6, 2F2
Sakharov exile scored by W Eur CPs 1-22—1-24, 86A1
E-W Ger summit delayed, Sovt-bloc visits canceled 1-30, 103F1
Gromyko stresses Sovt bloc unity in Rumania visit 1-31—2-2, 109A1
Poor '79 econ growth rptd; slowdown seen, Westn debt estimated 2-4, 166D1-B3
Bulgaria mtg; N Korea, Rumania vs Sovt Afghan invasn 2-6—2-7, 109A2
French CP forms rights group, issues rpt 2-20, 149C3, E3
Italy CP funds from trade deals chrgd 3-7, 212C3
Nicaragua signs Sovt trade accord 3-19, delegatn in E Eur 3-22, 234F2
Sovt bloc '79 Westn debt rptd, rise in barter deals noted 4-1, 285A3
Italy CP rejects Paris parley; Spanish, Yugo boycott rptd 4-2, 254C3
EC-Yugo trade pact signed 4-2, 365B3
Italy CP renews China ties 4-15, 314F1
USSR trade sanctns opposed by W Ger 4-17, 303C2
Zimbabwe gains indepndnc 4-18, 301F1
Paris parley held 4-28—4-29, 327B2
Pope in Kenya scores 'atheistic ideology' 5-6, 363F2
W Eur trade ties cited 5-15, 378A1
E Ger gas cash sales barred 6-1, 431C3
Venice summit urges 3d World aid 6-23, 474B1
W Ger vows econ pact adherence 6-23, 474G1
SWAPO Sovt bloc arms displayed 7-2, 525B1
Moscow Olympics held 7-19—8-3, 587E3-588B1
Polish strikers demand pol reform 8-14—8-22; Gierek rejects 8-18; USSR, E Eur press rpts 8-19, 8-20, 625A1, G1, 626B2-B3
E Eur reactn to Polish unrest 8-25, 642G1
Poland affirms Sovt-bloc ties 9-4, 658C3
3d World arms sales rptd 12-10, 933A2
2d Cuban CP cong held 12-17—12-20, 992C3
U.S. Relations
Connally urges firm stand 1-17, 91E3
US issues rights rpt 2-5, 86B2, 87A3
US loan to Hungary confrmd 2-18, 142C3
5 Sovt bloc diplomats rptd ousted from US as spies 2-29, 189C2
Reagan 'basic speech' excerpts 2-29, 207D2
USSR trade sanctns opposed by W Ger 4-17, 303A3
Muskie asks 3d World aid 8-25, 642B3
COMMUNITY Broadcasting Inc.
FCC blocks WNAC-TV purchase 1-24, 119B3
COMMUNITY Nutrition Institute
US nitrite decision scored 8-19, 726G1
COMORO Islands—*See NONALIGNED Nations, OAU*
COMPACT (Committee to Preserve American Color Television)
Sears TV rebate indictmt hailed 2-26, 252B1
Japan TV dumping case setlmt scored 4-28, ct blocks setlmt 5-9, 368E1
TV import curbs continuatn asked 5-13, 368C2
Carter TV import curbs easing scored 6-30, 515E3
COMPAGNA, Francesco
Italy public works min 4-4, 275G3
COMPETITION, The (film)
Released 12-3, 972D3
COMPLETE Critical Prose and Letters, The (book)
Wins Amer Book Award 5-1, 692G2
COMPLETE Directory to Prime Time Network TV Shows: 1946-Present, The (book)
Wins Amer Book Award 5-1, 692E2
COMPLETE Scarsdale Medical Diet, The (book)
Tarnower slain 3-10, suspect chrgd 3-11, 214E3
On best-seller list 2-10, 120D3; 3-9, 200C3; 4-6, 280D3; 5-4, 359E3; 6-8, 448D3

1976

COMPTON, Calif.—*See CALIFORNIA*
COMPUTERS (& Computer Industry)—*See ELECTRIC & Electronics Industries*
CONABLE Jr., Rep. Barber B. (R, N.Y.)
Reelected 11-2, 830D2
Resigns GOP Policy Com post 12-8, 981E3
CONCEPCION, Dave
In World Series 10-16—10-21, 815D2
CONCORD, Mass.—*See MASSACHUSETTS*
CONCORDE (British-French SST)—*See 'SST' under AVIATION*
CONCORDIA Seminary (St. Louis, Mo.)
Preus ousts 4 re Seminex ordinatns 4-2, 776C3
CONDOR—*See 'Missiles' under ARMAMENTS*
CONDRA, Maj. Edward
Rpts marine abuse convictns 8-12, 586F3
CONFERENCE Board (N.Y.)
Rpts '60-75 consumer spending, income up 11-23, 959F1
CONFERENCE on Security and Cooperation in Europe—*See under EUROPE*
CONG, Vo Chi
United Viet Nam deputy premier 7-3, 502F3
CONGO Republic (formerly Brazzaville)—*See also AFRICAN Development Bank, NONALIGNED Nations Movement, OAU*
US chrgs Sovt warships near Angola 1-7, 2A2
Listed as 'partly free' 1-19, 20C3

1977

COMPTROLLER of the Currency, Office of the—*See under U.S. GOVERNMENT—TREASURY*
COMPUTERIZED Axial Tomographic (CAT) Scanner—*See X-RAYS*
COMPUTERS (& Computer Industry)
French oust Sovt spy 2-11, 159D3
US Cong probes AF projct 4-27—5-10, 421E2
Memorex, Teledyne '76 stock data rptd 340D2, B3. 341B1
US cong vs Sovt sale 6-5, 469F2
US crime info plan under review 6-16, 480B3
US bars Sovt sale 6-23, 501D3
ICC data-processing unit urged 8-3, 651F2
Nobel Prizes announced 10-11, 951A3
Potential crime loss rptd 11-17, 919C1
Japan assures GATT on tariff cuts 11-29, 933D2
COMSAT General Corp.—*See COMMUNICATIONS Satellite Corp.*
COMTOIS, Roland
Wins election 5-24, 410B3
CONABLE Jr., Rep. Barber B. (R, N.Y.)
Business tax credit stand cited 2-1, 89D2
Scores Soc Sec bill 12-15, 957D3
CONALCO Inc. (Consolidated Aluminum Corp.)
New USW pact reached 5-24, 422E1
Ormet—*See separate listing*
CONCENTRATION Camps—*See NAZIS*
CONCERNED Jewish Youth
Archbp Trifa suspended from NCC 2-4, 119G3
CONCORDE (British-French SST)—*See AVIATION—SST/Concorde*
CONCORDE, Emergency Coalition to Stop the
JFK protest held 10-9, 820A1
CONDOMINIUM (book)
On best-seller list 7-3, 548D3
CONDOR, Judge Dean E.
Rejects Gilmore stay 1-14, 40A2
CONE, Fairfax M.
Dies 6-20, 532G2
CON Ed—*See CONSOLIDATED Edison Co.*
CONEMAUGH River (Pa.)
Johnstown flooded 7-19—7-20, 603G3
CONESA, Roberto
Police rescue 2 officials 2-11, 307G1
CONFERENCE Board Inc.
Rpts Nov-Dec '76 consumer confidence up 1-9, 38F1
Rpts Canada cos '76 US expansn 1-25, 132F3
Rpts record '76, '77 forgn investmt in US 5-11, 5-25, 385G2
Ranks '75 world pay 11-6, 853C3
CONFERENCE of Presidents of Major American Jewish Organizations—*See JEWISH Organizations, etc.*
CONFERENCE on Charismatic Renewal in the Christian Churches—*See CHARISMATIC Renewal, etc.*
CONFERENCE on Security and Cooperation in Europe—*See under EUROPE*
CONGO, Democratic Republic of the—*See ZAIRE*
CONGO, People's Republic of the (formerly Brazzaville)—*See also NONALIGNED Nations Movement, OAU*
UN Assemb member 3F3
Angola rebel attacks, French natl kidnapings rptd 1-15, 1-17, 48D1

1978

COMPREHENSIVE Employment and Training Act (CETA)—*See LABOR—Employment*
COMPTON, Calif.—*See CALIFORNIA*
COMPTON, Fay
Dies 12-12, 1032D2
COMPTROLLER of the Currency, Office of the—*See under U.S. GOVERNMENT—TREASURY*
COMPUSTAT Services Inc.—*See STANDARD & Poor's Corp.*
COMPUTERS (& Computer Industry)
IRS project rptd dropped 1-9, 15C1
NJ cancer death rate studied 1-12, 23E3
IBM-Greyhound case review denied 1-16, 33E2
W Ger newspapers struck 1-19, 2-9, 115F1
US OKs Japan sale to China 2-8, 111D2
US bans S Africa police sales 2-17, 135E1
IMS rejects CBS bid 2-22, 185B1
IBM sues Xerox 2-23, 510B2
DEA ex-agents convicted in drug plot 3-10, 380B1
Dutch name 3 Sovts as spies 3-30, 247F3
US Wis U research secrecy order set 4-21, lifted 6-12, 513F3
Control Data fined for forgn paymts 4-26, 448F3
Honeywell Italy warehouse fire 5-12, 393G2
McDonnell Douglas plans Data 100 purchase 5-18, 404F1
US-China '76 deal cited 6-9, 436B2
Program patents curbed by Sup Ct 6-22, 509B1
IBM quits Nigeria 6-26, 798G3-799A1
NYC welfare fraud crackdown rptd 7-3, 684G3
IBM-Memorex case mistrial 7-5, 510F2
US cancels sale to USSR 7-18, 542E1; Carter denies vendetta 7-20, 549D2
Shroud of Turin studied 10-4, 11-7, 926B1
US-Sovt issue cited re Carter 'export consequences' order 10-10, 804A3
LA bank robbed by phone 10-25, consultant arrested 11-5, 991G3-992D1
Control Data deal with USSR set 10-31, 841C1
JFK murder film assessed 11-26, 916B1
IBM sets 4-for-1 stock split 12-19, 1003G3
COMSAT General Corp.—*See COMMUNICATIONS Satellite Corp.*
CONABLE Jr., Rep. Barber B. (R, N.Y.)
Rebuts Carter budget proposals 1-31, 63D1
Backs House com tax cut bill 7-27, 586D3
Reelected 11-7, 851A4
CONANT, James B.
Dies 2-11, 196F2
CONCEPCION, Dave
NL wins All-Star Game 7-11, 559D3, E3
CONCERNED Citizens of Montauk Inc.
NJ offshore oil drilling challenge refused 2-21, 125F2
CONCERT of the Century (recording)
Wins Grammy 2-24, 316B1
CONCKLIN, Eric
International Stud opens 5-22, 887A2
CONCORDE (British-French SST)—*See AVIATION—SST/Concorde*
CONCORDIA College (Moorhead, Minn.)
NAIA Div II football title won 12-9, 1025B2
CONCUTELLI, Pierluigi
Trial opens in Florence 1-30, 133B2
CON Ed—*See CONSOLIDATED Edison Co.*
CONFALONIERI, Cardinal Carlo
Eulogizes Pope John Paul I 10-4, 747B2
CONFERENCE Board Inc.
'77 forgn investmts in US rptd, '75 revised 1-24, 65C3
Consumer confidence down, inflatn chief worry 4-6, 260C3
Mgt, professional gains for women rptd 5-22, 554E3
CONFERENCE of Presidents of Major American Jewish Organizations—*See JEWISH Organizations etc.*
CONFERENCE of the Committee on Disarmament—*See DISARMAMENT—Geneva Committee*
CONFERENCE on Security and Cooperation in Europe—*See under EUROPE*
CONFESSIONS of Winfred Wagner, The (film)
Released 3-23, 619C1
CONGO, Democratic Republic of—*See ZAIRE*
CONGO, People's Republic of the (formerly Brazzaville)—*See also GATT, NONALIGNED Nations Movement, OAU*
Freedom House lists as not free 44F1
10 executed for '77 Ngouabi assassinatn 2-7, 115D2

1979

COMPREHENSIVE Employment and Training Act (CETA)—*See LABOR-Employment*
COMPTON, John (St. Lucian prime minister)
St Lucia gains independnc, oppositn boycotts fete 2-21, 181C2, G2
Party loses electns 7-2, 545B3
COMPUTERS (& Computer Industry)
IBM trust case marks 10th yr 1-17, 88D3
NRC agrees to buy Comten 1-21, 89F1
Sperry-USSR talks rptd 2-8 11-11,12-10, 237B3
5 US A-plants ordrd shut 3-13, 186G1-A2
2d LA bank wire-transfer theft 3-25, 239C2
LA bank consultant sentncd 3-26, 239G1
USSR to buy French Iris 80, '78 US ban cited 3-27, 237G2
'78 Sup Ct patent curb rule cited 3-29, 265F2
Sperry-USSR sale OKd 3-29, 287E2
Carter urges privacy legis 4-2, 264D3
NRC matches Comten bid, acquisitn agreed 4-23, 440G3
Data Gen '78 sales rise rptd 5-7, 305B2
IBM added to Dow Jones index 6-28, 481F2
IBM asks trust case judge ousted 7-19, 610G2
Control Data to sponsor art show 7-19, 672C2
FCC claims electronic mail project authority 8-1, Postal Svc sues 10-18, 921D2
Unified Industries-Liberia deal set 9-7, 720E3
US blocks USSR sale 9-27, 775C1
Sovt algorithm rptd programming breakthrough 10-6, 1000D2
IBM wins Transamerica trust suit 10-18, 851F2
Memorex rejects Amdahl, Storage Tech bids 10-28; ends Amdahl talks 11-20, 942D2
USSR mil aided by US sales 11-8, 857A1
Air controllers score radar system 11-20, 988F3-989A1
Western Union quits electronic mail project 12-4, 921G2, A3*
Saudis buy IBM notes 12-27, 986G1
COMTEN Inc.
NCR OKs purchase 1-21, 89F1
NRC matches Amdahl bid, acquisitn agreed 4-23, 440G3
CONABLE Jr., Rep. Barber B. (R, N.Y.)
GOP ldrs meet, reject balanced budget amendmt 2-4, 86G1
CONAGHAN, John (Johnny C)
Jordan cocaine use testimony rptd 8-31, 767D2
Indicted on drug chrgs 10-23, 891D3
Pleads guilty 12-18, 1000E1
CONCENTRATION Camps
US releases Auschwitz photos 2-22, 193D1
CONCEPCION (Spanish ship)
Treasure estimate rptd 1-1, 24F1
CONCEPCION, Dave
Wins Golden Glove Award 11-20, 956D1
CONCERTO for Violin in D Major (recording)
Wins Grammy 2-16, 336G3
CONCORD, Mass.—*See MASSACHUSETTS*
CONCORD (U.S. warship)
Personnel shortage rptd 11-22, 904C1
CONCORDE Airport '79, The (film)
Released 8-3, 819G2
CONCORD Fabrics Inc.
Textile union files Ga suit 7-18, 598F3
CONDOMINIUMS—*See HOUSING*
CONESA, Roberto
5 Grapo guerrillas escape jail 12-17, 998A1
CONFEDERATION of Iranian Students
US visa probes ruled illegal 12-11, 935G2
CONFERENCE Board Inc.
7-natn indicators index released 6-11, 513A2
Intl terrorism rptd up 11-15, 882E1
CONFERENCE Management Corp.
Intl arms exhibit spurs protests 2-18—2-19, 152F3
CONFERENCE of Presidents of Major American Jewish Organizations—*See JEWISH Organizations, etc.*
CONFERENCE of the Committee on Disarmament—*See DISARMAMENT-Geneva Committee*
CONFESSIONS of a Promiscuous Counterfeiter (book)
Author in aerial protest 10-11, 860G1
CONFORTI, Tony
Manny opens 4-18, 712C1
CONGO, People's Republic of the (formerly Brazzaville)—*See also GATT, OAU*
Yhomby Opango quits 1-6, Sassou-Nguesso replaces 1-8, 85E3
E Ger mil aid rptd 5-23, 406A3
UN membership listed 695F2

1980

COMPTROLLER of the Currency—*See under U.S. GOVERNMENT--TREASURY*
COMPUTERS (& Computer Industry)
Itel, Lloyd's settle 1-16, 131C3
NM State of State message 1-25, 269F3
Electronic mail plan OKd 2-22, 4-8, conflict of interest chrgd 2-27, 4-8, 347D2-E3
Reagan cites in 'basic speech' 2-29, 207A3
US defense warning system rptd unreliable 3-10, 210B2
Phone industry deregulatn set by FCC 4-7, 370F1
US errors trigger false A-alerts 6-3, 6-6, failed component blamed 6-17; valid warnings detailed 6-15, 457C3-458C2
FAA claims data reliable 6-30, 666F3
Carter cites job programs in pres renominatn speech 8-14, 612F1
AT&T begins reorgn 8-20, 648F1
Telecommunicatns bill tabled by Cong 9-30, 835E2
Itel rpts huge '79 loss 10-16, 784D1
US scientific literacy lag rptd 10-22, 990D1
US error A-alert rpt issued 10-29, 986B3
IBM win in Memorex trust suit rptd upheld 11-20, 917E3
Copyright protectn clears Cong 11-21, 915F3
Opel elected IBM chief exec 12-21, 986F2
Foreign Developments (including U.S. international news)
US suspends sale to USSR for Afghan invasn 1-4, 1D1; 1-9, 9F1
US rejects USSR export licenses 1-11, 28D2; 1-21, 45F1
US illegal sales to USSR probed 2-14, 135B1
USSR scientists barred from US conf 2-22, 135D1
Lloyd's leasing liability cited 3-31, 266F1
France facilities attacked 4-5, 4-15, 312F3
Sovt trade spy arrested 5-18, sentenced 8-1, 598B2
US OKs China sale 5-29, 397F3
W Ger, USSR sign pact 7-1, 489D2
Olympic gymnastics scoring malfunction 7-25, 589A3
France seeks dvpt 10-1, 749E3
Mergers & Acquisitions
Gould, Systems Engineering to merge 9-8, 746A1
Schlumberger, Data Systems to merge 9-18, 746B1
Source Telecomputing, Reader's Digest merge 9-24, 746F1
Obituaries
Haggerty, Patrick 10-1, 876G1
Mauchly, John 1-8, 104B3
COMSAT—*See COMMUNICATIONS Satellite Corp.*
COMSTOCK, George W.
Calls TB study results tragic 1-20, 63G1
CONABLE Jr., Rep. Barber B. (R, N.Y.)
Reelected 11-4, 843A4
Budget reconciliatn signed 12-5, 936E1
CONAGHAN, John (Johnny C)
Sentenced 6-12, 503F1-A2
CONCEPCION, Dave
NL wins All-Star Game 7-8, 636B2
CONCKLIN, Charles
Loses US House electn 11-4, 850B2
CONCORD—*See NEW Hampshire*
CONCORD Baptist Church (Brooklyn, N.Y.)
Carter addresses 2000 10-20, 803B1
CONFEDERATION of Iranian Students v. Civiletti
Stay denied by Sup Ct 3-31, 291G2
Case refused by Sup Ct 5-19, 440B2
CONFERENCE Board Inc.
'79 forgn mfg investmt rptd 2-6, 92B3
CONFERENCE of the Committee on Disarmament—*See GENEVA Committee*
CONFERENCE on Security and Cooperation in Europe (CSCE) (Helsinki Agreement) (Austria, Belgium, Bulgaria, Canada, Cyprus, Czechoslovakia, Denmark, East Germany, Finland, France, Great Britain, Greece, Hungary, Iceland, Ireland, Italy, Liechtenstein, Luxembourg, Norway, Poland, Portugal, Rumania, San Marino, Spain, Sweden, Switzerland, Turkey, U.S., USSR, Vatican, West Germany, Yugoslavia)
US, W Ger back talks 1-16, 28A2
Sci conf opens, scores USSR re Sakharov 2-18, 181A3
USSR-French talks held 4-24—4-25, 351F3
USSR sentences 2 monitors 6-9, 6-13, 680B3, C3
W Ger vows adherence 6-23, 474G1
NATO backs Sovt talks 6-26, 489G2
Spain readies forgn policy presentatn 9-8, 690C2
Madrid prep talks begin, Spain forgn min addresses 9-9, 679A3
Warsaw Pact mins set Madrid conf strategy 10-19—10-20, 800D2
Madrid review conf opens 11-11, Sovts scored 11-12, 11-13, 862C3
Madrid conf reaches compromise 11-14, 1st phase ends 12-19, 950E1
Pope affirms '75 rights provisns 11-16, 905G1
CONGER, Harry M.
Announces Calif gold find 8-27, 685A3
CONGO, People's Republic of the—*See also GATT, NONALIGNED Nations, OAU*
Chad peacekeeping force arrives 1-18, 119A1
Chad force begins exit 3-30, 311C2
Pope visits 5-5, 363E2

1976

Zaire recognizes Angola MPLA 2-28, 163A2
Zaire cites Sovt arms buildup 4-30, 318A3
Olympic withdrawal rptd 7-21, 528B3
Angola refugees rptd 10-2, 862D2
World Bank loan set 12-16, 1012A3
CONGRESSIONAL Quarterly (magazine)
Dem, GOP delegate box score 4-9, 261A1
Dem delegate totals cited 4-30, 324A3
'77 US budget estimates table 358B2
Corp paymts list 8-28, 729F2
Final pres vote rptd 12-18; table 979C1, A2
CONGRESS of Racial Equality (CORE)
Carson, 5 others acquitted 2-6, 124F1
Innis recruits for Angola 2-10; US blacks score 2-14, Farmer quits 2-19, 163A3
CONGRESS Watch (organization)
Lobbying bill not cleared 10-2, 883D1
CONLAN, Rep. John B. (R, Ariz)
Loses Ariz Sen primary 9-7, 687G2
Loses election 11-2, 824C1
CONNALLY Jr., John B(owden)
White House guest 4-1, Cabinet offer denied 4-19, 281A2
Reagan sweeps Tex vote 5-1, 322G3
Sup Ct bars Jacobsen plea-bargaining review 5-19, 393E3
Endorses Ford 7-27, 550B3
VP selectn disputed, campaign role seen 8-5—8-10, 584A2, C2-A3
GOP vp poll rptd 8-11, 583F3
On Watergate, Ford campaign 8-15, 8-18, 601C2
Addresses GOP conv 8-17, 601G1
Addresses VFW conv 8-18, 601E2
Ford sees Reagan re vp choice 8-19, 598F1
GOP conv vp vote table 8-19, 599E3
Nixon rptdly favors for vp 8-19, 616B1
Jacobsen get 2 yrs probatn 8-20, 1016A1
Rpt rejected GOP com post 8-22; sees Ford win 8-23, 631D1
Sees Ford, scores Carter 8-26—8-27, 645A1
With Ford in Dallas 10-9, 763B2
Campaigns with Ford 10-30, 826D3
Addresses GOP govs 11-29, 917G2-A3
Meets Ford on GOP unity 12-9, 938A1
CONNECTICUT
US Sup Ct bars review of no-fault insurnc law 1-12, 24C1
Bailey cleared in jai alai scandal 1-12, 271D1
Carter edges Udall in vote 5-11, 342E3
John McGuire dies 5-28, 524B3
Liability affirmed in reverse bias case 6-28, 569C1
Queen Eliz in New Haven 7-11, 489G2
Dem conv women delegates, table 508B2
Dem conv pres vote, table 7-14, 507B2
Ford wins 35 delegates 7-17, 531E2
New arthritis strain rptd 7-18, 911G2
Hurricane Belle damage rptd 8-11, 595D2
GOP pre-conv delegate count 8-14, 583B3
GOP conv pres, vp vote tables 8-18—8-19, 8-19, 599B1, B3
Carter in Groton 9-7, 663G3
US Sen primary results 9-7, 687D3
Fscl '75 per capita income, tax burden rptd 9-15, 10-12, 959G1, A2
Carter in Hartford 10-1, 742G3
Dole in New Haven 10-2, 743B2-E2
Hartford Times folds 10-20, 849F1
Election results 11-2: pres 818A1, 819A2; cong 820D1, F3, 825F2, 828C1, 829G1-A2
Greenwich teacher strike ends 11-24, 991G1
US Sup Ct backs closed primary 12-6, 920D3
Flu shot paralysis rptd 12-17, 950E1
Thames R oil leak 12-28, 1014G1

1977

French natls released 1-30, 84E2
IMF OKs loans 2-2, 203F1; 2-4, 87E2
Afro-Arab policy statemt scored 3-3—3-5, 170B2
Ngouabi slain 3-18, Massamba-Debat arrested 3-20, 220A2
Cardinal Biayenda slain 3-23, 220E2
Massamba-Debat, 6 others executed; Kikadidi sentncd in absentia 3-25, 3-26; plotter captured 4-11, 282G2
Opango named pres 4-3; suspends const, names Cabt 4-5; dissolves natl assemb, local govt 4-6, 282D2
US ties set 7-7, 583A2
Cuba mil presence detailed 11-17, 896G1

CONGRESS, U.S.—*See under U.S. GOVERNMENT*
CONGRESS of Racial Equality (CORE)
Backs Bell nominatn 1-11—1-18, 34B2
CONGRESS Watch
Consumer agency bill shelved 11-1, 856A3
Nader asks Claybrook quit NHTSA 11-30, 1008B1
CONLEY, Harold
Indictmt dropped 3-17, 287A2
CONNALLY, John B.
Nixon-Frost TV interview 5-12, 386A1
Houston bank ownershp cited 12-27, 1003G2
CONNECTICUT
Legislature schedule rptd 6D2
Indian land claims rptd 2-7, 197D1
Monroe Bank fails 3-28, 578C1
Fed spending inequities chrgd 4-6, 423D3
Schl funding held unconst 4-18, 302G2
'76 per-capita income table 5-10, 387C2
New Haven illegal surveillance chrgd 5-12, 422D3
US Sup Ct voids minor abortn rule 5-23, 444C3
Medicaid abortn fund curb upheld 6-20, 516D2
Danbury prison fire 7-7, 604F1
Family slain 7-22, suspect indictd 9-7, 712E1
State oil trust suits merged 9-12, 691G3
'76 per capita income, tax burden table 9-13, 10-18, 821A2
Welfare law re property sales upheld 10-17, 797F3
CONNELL Rice and Sugar Co.
Park Tong Sun paymts described 10-19—10-21, 816A3

1978

Angola, Zaire reconciliatn set 7-17, 562E1
Coup attempt chrgd 8-14, 660F3
UN Assemb member 713D3

CONGRESS, U.S.—*See under U.S. GOVERNMENT*
CONGRESSIONAL Quarterly (magazine)
Rpts Carter '77 cong support 1-7, 12A3
Poynter dies 6-15, 540F3
CONGRESS of Racial Equality (CORE)
Conv held, Innis reelected 9-8—9-10; Farmer, other ex-ldrs score 9-18, 810C1
CONGRESS of the Laity
LA conf stresses broader role 2-19, 294B3
CONGRESS Watch
Oil lobbyist role in Energy Dept policy questnd 5-15, 408E2-C3
95th sessn rated 10-28, 865B2-A3
Rpts big spenders win Sen races 11-15, 898B1
CONJURER, The (painting)
Stolen from Paris museum 12-13, 1029A1
CONKLING, Chris
Lord of Rings released 11-15, 970A2
CONNALLY, John B.
Testifies at JFK assassinatn hearings 9-6, 697F3
CONNALLY, Nellie (Mrs. John B.)
Testifies at JFK assassinatn hearings 9-6, 698B1
CONNECTICUT
Legislature schedule rptd 14E3
'67, '77 sales-tax rates rptd 1-5, 15D3
NASL '77 club move cited 1-5, 23A1
State govt tax revenue table 1-9, 84C2
Hartford suits vs suburbs review denied 1-16, 33G2
Hartford arena roof collapses 1-18, 95A3; rpt issued 6-15, 460C1
US emergency aid OKd 2-10, 105C2
7th in US defns contracts 2-21, 127D2
A-sub work stoppage feared 3-13, 224A2
GAO rpt scores Conrail safety efforts 3-15, 224F3-225A1
Waterbury, Ansonia Anaconda strike ends 4-3, 284E3
Pulitzer awarded for Stamford corruptn probe 4-17, 315A2
Ex-Sen Purtell dies 5-31, 440C3
'77 prison populatn rptd down 6-3, 440D1
Primary results 9-12, 716E2
New London A-sub theft foiled 10-4, 824F1; chrgs chngd 12-6, 2 convicted 12-14, 12-19, 992E1
Pornographer arrested in Bloomfield 10-25, 971B2
Carter at Hartford rally 10-28, 831C2
Election results 11-7: cong 846A3, 847C2, 848D1, 850D2; state 847C1, B2, 853E2
West Haven legal immunity ruling vacated by US Sup Ct 11-27, 937B2
Black treasurer noted 11-28, 915D3
CONNECTICUT Citizen Action Group
Nader '73 'bumping' case award cut 1-10, 68A1
CONNELL, Grover
Indicted re Korea sales, denies chrgs 5-26, 432E3
CONNELL Rice & Sugar Co. Inc.
Connell indicted 5-26, 432G3
CONNELLSVILLE, Pa.—*See PENNSYLVANIA*

1979

Pol Pot govt UN seat opposed 9-19, 695D2
Cuba rptd training children 12-4, 12-10, 981B2

CONGOLEUM Corp.
Fibic merger OKd 9-21, 942A2
CONGRESS—*See under U.S. GOVERNMENT*
CONGRESSIONAL Quarterly (magazine)
Legislators' incomes studied 9-1, 701C3-702B1
CONLEY, Raymond
Resigns as Dole aide 12-6, 983D2
CONNALLY, John Bowden
Announces pres bid 1-24, 70F2
Gains among GOP rivals 3-4, 3-10, addresses Midwest offcls 3-10, 185E3, 186A1
'Killer Bees' disrupt Tex Sen 5-18–5-22, 594C3
Addresses Mayors Conf 6-11, 439C3, E3
'Magic bullet' evidence cited 6-18, 466C3
Pres campaign funds rptd 7-12, 593G3
Scores Carter energy speech 7-15, 534F2
N Amer energy mkt backed 7-26, 581C2
Viguerie leaves Crane, joins campaign 8-8, 594C2
Outlines Mideast peace plan, Jewish groups vs 10-11; Baker, Dole score 10-12, 783G1-F2
Baker enters '80 race 11-1, 828F3, 829A1
3d in Me straw poll 11-3, 866B3
Scores affirmative actn 11-15, NAACP objects 11-26, 982G3-983A1
Campaign themes cited 983A1
2d in Fla straw vote 11-17, 887D1
GOP poll results 11-25, 982E1
Hits Kennedy Iran remarks 12-3, 918F3
Foregoes US matching funds, urges Reagan join la forum 12-12, 982B3
Campaign Strategy shifted 12-15, 982G2
Finance dir resigns, other staff chngs cited 12-19, 983C1
Thurmond, Edwards endorse 12-27, 982F2
CONNECTICUT
Breast-feeding survey rptd 1-5, 64C2
Hartford 2d opinion surgery plan evaluated 1-29, 140B1 479G1
Truckers stage protest 6-28, 479C2
Teachers' strikes rptd 9-12, 679B1
'78 per capita income rptd 9-16, 746G1, C2
Bridgeport Viet vet study released 9-25, 725A2
Iranians ordrd to leave 11-16, 879E1
Hartford '79 living costs ranked 12-28, 991A1
Atomic Energy
Haddam Neck A-plant called unsafe 1-26, 90C3
Millstone (Waterford) A-plant community studied 3-17, 207E3
Conn Yankee A-plant rptd top '78 performer 4-15, 322A3
Millstone, Conn Yankee A-plant pipe leaks rptd 5-2, 322B3
Millstone protesters arrested 8-30, 742G3
Crime & Civil Disorders
Hartford crime-control progrm rptd 2-25, 156C3
New London A-sub theft sentences 3-15, 3-20, 240E2
'57 spy chrgs vs Sterns dropped 3-22, 232E1
Waterbury armored car guards slain 4-16, 4 arrested 4-17, 316E1
Millstone A-protesters arrested 8-30, 742G3
Acquin convicted in mass murder 10-19, 819B2; sentenced 11-30, 954A1
Arson 'dual sovereignty' case refused by Sup Ct 11-13, 902A2
Energy—*See also 'Atomic' above*
Odd-even gas rationing begins 6-20, 462F2
July gas supply use rptd 6-23
Winter heating fuel supply promised 8-28, 703C2
Odd-even gas rules lifted 9-6, 683F1
Carter energy mailing planned 9-17, 703G2
Politics & Government—*See also other appropriate subheads in this section*
Legislature schedule rptd 5C3
Weicker announces pres bid 3-12, 185A3
Stamford, Hartford fiscal status rptd 3-20, 204F1
Legis OKs DC voting rep amendmt 3-28, 4-11, 367E1
Weicker ends pres bid 5-16, 363F3
CONNECTICUT, University of (Storrs)
In Big East basketball conf 5-29, 526G3
CONNECTICUT General Insurance Corp.
ERC Corp spurns offer 10-18, 986C3
CONNECTICUT Yankee Nuclear Power Station—*See CONNECTICUT–Atomic Energy*
CONNELL, Grover
Justice drops charges 4-16, 283D2
CONNELL, Mike
Named to NASL All-Star team 8-27, 776E1
CONNELLSVILLE, Pa.—*See PENNSYLVANIA*
CONNELL v. American Bankers Association
Case declined by Sup Ct 10-15, 847D3
CONNELLY, Brig. Gen. Donald W.
On Army recruiting abuses 11-19, 904A1

1980

Chad peace conf fails 10-18—10-19, 810G1
Libyan role in Chad spurs OAU rift 12-23—12-24, 979C1

CONGRESS—*See under U.S. GOVERNMENT*
CONGRESSIONAL Quarterly's Guide to the U.S. Supreme Court (book)
Wins Amer Book Award 5-1, 692D2
CONGRESS Watch
96th sessn rated 1-12, 53G2
CONLON, James
Convicted 7-28, fined 9-15, 927B3
CONNALLY, Dick
'Charlie's Angels' fraud probe rptd 5-1, 376C3
CONNALLY, John Bowden
Seeks US firmness on Iran, USSR re Afghan 1-3, 5F1
In Iowa GOP debate, scores Reagan absence 1-5, 4F2, F3
In Iowa, scores Reagan 1-8, 13D3
4th in Iowa poll 1-11, 33F1, G1
Sees Sovt role in Iran 1-11, 91F3
Speaks vs 'appeasemt' 1-17, 91E3
Marathon Iowa tour 1-19—1-20, 50C3
4th in Iowa caucus vote 1-21, 50F1
Blanked in Ark caucuses 2-2, 92A1
Saudi bank connectn, '78-79 fund transfers rptd 2-11, 129A2
Sponsors natl telethon 2-14, raises $1.5 mln 2-20, 129E1
Gains one Ark delegate 2-16, 130G1
Bush wins PR primary 2-17, 130B1, D1
NH gun control forum 2-18, GOP pres debate 2-20, 129B3, F3, G3
NH primary vote results 2-26, 142E3, G3
Mass, Vt primary results 3-4, 166F2, D3
'Basic speech' excerpts 3-7, 184B2, 185E1
2d in SC primary vote 3-8, 183E3
Ends pres bid, $12 mln rptd spent 3-9, 183F3
Endorses Reagan 3-25, 221F2
Addresses GOP conv 7-15, 531D3, E3
Visits Reagan 11-15, 881A2
CONNECTICUT
ERISA maternity case declined by Sup Ct 1-14, 37B1
Times Mirror media divestiture ordered 1-24, 120A1
Schl prayer law cited 2-6, 156A2
Influenza outbreak rptd 2-15, 158C3
Oil tax pass along ban voided 7-9, 553D3
KKK rally in Scotland 9-13, ldr arrested 9-14, 884C3
Bridgeport busing, housing integratn study rptd 11-16, 989E3
Phone harassmt law challenge declined by Sup Ct 12-1, 918G2
Levi trust case setlmt award rptd 12-2, 917A3
Atomic Energy & Safeguards
Demonstratns mark 3 Mile I anniv 3-28—3-31, 249B1
Politics & Government—*See also other appropriate subheads in this section*
Legislature schedule rptd 18D1
Buckley Sen bid cited 1-14, 32G1
State of State message 2-6, 269E1
US atty named Abscam leaks prosecutor 2-11, 111E1
Pres primary results 3-25, 221A2-D3
Grasso, Ribicoff vs open conv 8-11, 609G2, 610A1
Sen primary results 9-9, 700C2
Election results 11-4: pres 838A1, 839A2, D3; cong 840D1, 842D2, 845B2, B3, 848B1; state 845D2
'80 census rptd 12-31, 983D1
Gov Grasso ill, resigns 12-31, 990A3
CONNECTICUT College (New London)
Windmill christened 4-22, 307G3
CONNECTICUT General Insurance Corp.
ERC takeover bid dropped 6-8, 557G2
CONNECTICUT v. Pervel Industries
Case declined by Sup Ct 1-14, 37B1
CONNELLY, Marc
Dies 12-21, 1004B1

1976

CONNOR, James A.
Loses NH primary for gov 9-14, 705D1
CONNOR, Roger (d. 1931)
Named to Hall of Fame 8-9, 816D1
CONNORS, Jimmy
Tourn results 1-25, 2-1, 123G2
Tourn results 2-29, 3-14, 5-16, 7-27, 9-12, 716A1, B2-D2
Loses Wimbledon 6-29, 504F1
Wins Volvo intl 8-9, US clay ct 8-16, 656B2
CONRAD, Anthony L.
Quits RCA 9-16, 708G1
CONRAD, Larry A.
Loses electn 11-2, 820E3, 823C2
CONRAIL (Consolidated Rail Corp.)
Ford budget proposals 1-21, 66B1
Cong clears revised fund authorizatn 1-28, 68G3
Ford signs aid bill 2-5, 110B1
House votes funds 2-18, 152B1
Top offcls named 3-3, 235A3
Chessie, Southern drop out 3-23, 235E2
Ford signs funding bill 3-30, 233E2
Begins operatn, Amtrak to buy Boston-DC corridor 4-1, 235D1, B2
Rpts 1st ¼ loss 8-12, 648D1
Amtrak Boston-DC corridor buy set 8-29, 648G1
Fed loan hike signed 10-19, 834E2
Rpts 6-month loss 11-11, 887A2
Adams named Transport secy 12-14, 936F1, F3
CONRAN, J. V. (deceased)
Fed probe cited 2-27, 3-1, 181C1
CONSERVATION—*See RESOURCES, Natural*
CONSERVATION Voters, League of
Ford, Carter debate 10-22, 801E2
Edey sees Carter 12-16, 937C2
CONSERVATIVE American Christian Action Council
Sen intelligence com cites as target 4-28, 330F1
CONSOLIDATED Edison Co. (Con Ed)
On A-plant safety 2-9, 2-10, 115G1
CONSOLIDATED Packaging Corp.
Trust suit dvpts 2-18—10-5, 886C1, A2; 11-30, 921D3
CONSOLIDATED Rail Corp.—*See CONRAIL*
CONSTANTOPOULOS, Savas
Sentenced 1-21, 73E2

1977

CONNOLY v. Georgia
Ga search & seizure law voided 1-10, 57E1
CONNOR, Reginald F. X.
Dies 8-22, 696E2
CONNORS, Jimmy
Loses US Pro Indoor 1-3, Pepsi 1-23, 103F3
Loses WCT tourn 2-20, 4-10, wins WCT title 5-15, 430C2-F2
Wins 'heavyweight championship' 3-6; fee disclosures 5-7—5-20, FCC rpts probe 7-8, 548E2
US beaten in Davis Cup 4-29—5-1, 353E3
Wins King tourn 5-1, World Cup match 5-12, 430F3, 431F1
Loses Wimbledon 7-2, 548E1
Loses US Open 9-11, scores call 9-12, 787C1, F1, B3
CONRAD, Dr. Lyle
On measles increase 2-14, 224E1
CONRAIL (Consolidated Rail Corp.)
2 cleared, 1 convctd in '69 Penn Central case 3-11, 3-30, 491E3
'76-77 losses rptd 3-31, 325B2
2d ¼ loss rptd 8-4, 612D3
3d ¼ loss rptd 11-9, 899F3
Commuter line aid bill signed 11-16, 900B1
CONSALVI, Simon Alberto
Venez forgn min 7-15, 566A1
Sees Vance 11-23, 912F3
CONSCIENTIOUS Objectors, National Interreligious Service Board for
Scores Viet pardon actn 1-21, 51F2
CONSERVATION—*See ENERGY; RESOURCES, Natural*
CONSERVATION Foundation
Eastn forest expansn urged 4-28, 323D1
CONSERVATION Voters, League of
Edey environmnt nominatn deferred 10-17, 800G1
CONSERVATIVE Union, American
To fight Panama Canal treaty 8-15, 622A1
CONSOLIDATED Aluminum Corp.—*See CONALCO*
CONSOLIDATED Carriers Corp.
ICC probe rptd 6-3, 500D3
CONSOLIDATED Edison Co. (Con Ed)
NYC blackout 7-13—7-14, 537C2
Indian Pt plant found safe 10-12, reactn 10-25, 838F2
CONSOLIDATED Rail Corp.—*See CONRAIL*

CONSTITUTION, U.S.
Carter asks Electoral Coll end 3-22, 210G2
E Ger scores right-to-work omissn 9-28, 752B3
9 states seek anti-abortn amendmt 10-6, 786B3
Equal Rights Amendment—*See WOMEN—Politics & Government*

1978

CONNER, Judge William C.
Fines United Brands 7-19, 643F1
CONNOLLY, John S.
Loses Sen primary in Minn 9-12, 716C1
CONNOLLY, Maureen (1935-69)
US Open results 9-10, 707E1
CONNORS, Jimmy
USTA ranks 1st 1-5, 22E3
Wins Grand Prix Masters 1-8, 22G2
Loses Pepsi Grand Slam 1-22; wins US Pro Indoor 1-29, United Bank Classic 2-26, US Natl Indoor 3-5, Rotterdam WCT 4-9, 418G3-419B1
FCC censures CBS 'Heavyweight Championship' tennis tourn 3-16, 252E1
Defies 'Super Grand Prix,' loses Suntory Cup 4-23, 418B3
Wins Kent champ 6-10, Player Classic 6-16; loses Wimbledon 7-8, 539E3, 540C1
Wins Washn Star Intl 7-23, US Clay Ct 8-13, Australian Indoor 10-22, 1027A2, B2
Wins US Open 9-10, 707A1, C1
CONOCO—*See CONTINENTAL Oil Co.*
CONOMBO, Joseph (Upper Volta premier)
Upper Volta premier 7-7, 596C3
CONRAD Jr., Charles
Gets space medal honor 10-1, 861C2
CONRAD, Joseph
Duellists released 1-14, 619F1
CONRAIL (Consolidated Rail Corp.)
Jordan seeks more aid 2-15, Conrail '77 loss rptd 3-23, 224G2
Penn Central reorganizatn plan OKd 3-9, 185G3-186B1
GAO rpt scores safety efforts, Jordan disputes 3-15, 224E3-225A1
1st ¼ loss rptd 5-9, record rail industry losses 5-27, 433D3, F3
ICC fines in freight-car shortage 6-15, 569B2
2d ¼ Jan-June losses rptd 8-2, 684B2
ICC reduces fine 8-11, 643F2
Crew-size pact set 9-14, 700C1
Carter signs aid bill 11-1, 875C3
3d ¼ loss, 9-mo revenues rptd 11-1, 875E3
CONSERVATION—*See ENERGY; RESOURCES, Natural*
CONSERVATION Law Foundation of New England
Offshore lease sale delayed 1-28, 108E2
CONSERVATIVE Political Action Committee, National
2d-leading PAC fund-raiser 9-7, 753B2
CONSERVATIVE Union, American
Bell wins Sen primary 6-6, 447F3
CONSIDINE, John
Wedding released 9-29, 970D3
CONSOLIDATED-Bathurst Ltd.
Abitibi to buy Price interest 9-29, 772D3
CONSOLIDATED Carriers Corp.
ICC ex-offcl indicted 9-22, 770F2
CONSOLIDATED Edison Co. (Con Ed)
US blames for '77 NY blackout 7-6, 529F3
CONSOLIDATED Foods Corp.
'74 trust chrgs settled 6-12, 511C1
CONSOLIDATION Coal Co.—*See under CONTINENTAL Oil Co.*
CONSOLIDATION Coal Co. v. U.S.
Mine safety inspectn case remanded by Sup Ct 6-5, 431F2
CONSOLIDATED Foods Corp.
Hanes acquisitn set 9-14, 717G3
CONSOLIDATED Packaging Corp.
Indicted for price fixing 1-25, 67C2
Fined 10-13, 1005A3
CONSOLIDATED Rail Corp.—*See CONRAIL*
CONSTANCIO, Vitor
Portugal finance, planning min 1-30, 91C3

CONSTITUTION, U.S.
Proposed amendmt to bar deficit spending rptd endorsed by 23 legislatures 6-6, 425C1
Amendmt draft drive to curb US spending set 7-26, 735F3
DC voting rep amendmt clears Cong 8-22, 661A1-E2
DC voting rep amendmt OKd in NJ 9-11, Ohio 10-30; rejctd in Pa 11-14, 878G1, 1011F2
Burger urges study of US govt 9-21, 751G2
ACLU hails DC voting rep amendmt 10-20, 981B3

1979

CONNER, Judge William C.
Orders Curran repay NMU benefits 7-27, 744G2
CONNERY, Sean
Great Train Robbery released 2-1, 174F2
Meteor released 10-19, 1008A1
Cuba released 12-21, 1007B3
CONNOLLY v. Pension Benefit Guaranty Corp.
Case refused by Sup Ct 2-26, 164D3
CONNOR, Cam
In NHL expansion draft 6-13, 470A2
CONNOR, (Theophilus) Eugene (Bull) (d. 1973)
Ala police slaying protested 7-20, 869E3
CONNOR, John T.
On Pay Advisory Com 10-16, 829E2
CONNORS, Jimmy
Grand Prix Masters results 1-14, 103A3
Wins Birmingham WCT 1-21, US Pro Indoor 1-28, WCT Tourn of Champs 2-25, US Natl Indoor 3-4, Tulsa Grand Prix 4-15; loses Pepsi Grand Slam 2-11, King Classic 4-28, 391F2-C3
Grand Prix dispute setld 2-10, 391F1
French Open results 6-9, 6-10, Wimbledon 7-6, 7-7, 569D3, 570F1
Wins US Clay Cts 8-12, Stowe Grand Prix 8-19; US Open results 9-9, 734D1, C2
Loses Tokyo World Singles 11-4, WCT Challenge Cup 12-9; wins Hong Kong Grand Prix 11-11, 1003C3, F3
CONNOR v. Coleman
Miss legis redistricting ordrd by Sup Ct 3-26, 231C1
CONOCO Inc. (formerly Continental Oil Co.)
1st 1/4 profits rptd 4-27, 301B2
On '78 Fortune 500 list 5-7, 304F1
June gas supplies cut 5-30, 395C3
July gas supplies rptd 6-26, 479F1
US overchrgs alleged 10-18, 11-6, 849A3-D3; 11-8, 905F2; 11-18, 943F1
3d 1/4 profits rptd up 10-25, 804D2, D3
US overchrgs alleged 12-19, 990E2
Consolidation Coal Co.
Clean-air rule suit filed 3-22, 206A3
Ohio coal-use ruling issued 5-7, 351G1
UMW plans strike fund 12-13, 987B1
CONQUEROR, The (film)
Stars' deaths tied to '53 A-test 8-4, 630B1
CONRAD, Anthony L.
Pleads guilty 12-18, 1000F1
CONRAD, Max
Dies 4-3, 356C3
CONRAIL (Consolidated Rail Corp.)
Rail Labor Conf, clerks settle 1-13, 87F1
Carter budget proposals 1-22, 45B1
'78 4th 1/4 loss rptd 2-12, 167B1
New 5-yr plan submitted 3-15, 309F1
Rail clerks pact set 3-23, 262F2
1st ¼ loss rptd 4-24, '79 forecast lowered 6-1, 465E2
Tank car derails in Sunset Bay (NY) 5-4, 472F3
Employee fund rptd depleted 5-27, confirmed 5-30, 465G1
2d ¼ profit rptd 7-15; 3d ¼, 9-mo loss rptd 10-30, 989G2-A3
Joint study issued 9-11, optns narrowed 11-1, 989D2
Freight wreck kills 2 outside Phila 10-1, 912G3
3 Phila commuter trains collide 10-16, 912E3
CONSERVATION Law Foundation of New England
Mass offshore oil-lease ban lifted 2-20, 187A1
Mass offshore lease sale delayed 11-6, OKd 11-9, 867F1
Mass lease bids placed 12-18, 990A2
CONSERVATIVE Political Action Committee, National
Senate campaign planned 8-16, 627F3
CONSOLIDATED Edison Co. (Con Ed)
Indian Pt A-plant safety backed 9-17, 743D2
Indian Pt A-plant security rptd lax 10-16, 10-20, 807F1
Westchester rejects takeover 11-6, 846F3
CONSOLIDATED Edison v. Public Service Commission
Case accepted by Sup Ct 10-1, 919A3
CONSOLIDATED Packaging Corp.
Paperbd trust suit cited 6-28, 648B1
CONSOLIDATED Rail Corp.—*See CONRAIL*
CONSOLIDATED Truck Service Inc.
ICC order reinstated by Sup Ct 10-15, 847G3
CONSOLIDATION Coal Co.—*See under CONOCO*
CONSTANTIN, Nicolae
Rumania planning comm head 3-30, 279D3

CONSTITUTION, U.S.
Brown to seek budget amendmt 1-8, 13C2
Carter vs proposed balanced budget amendmt 1-17, 29E2
Bell for 6-yr pres term 1-25, 110G1-A2
Friedman group urges spending limit amendmt 1-30, 86G2
GOP vs balanced budget amendmt, backs spending limit amendmt 2-4, 86E1
Balanced budget amendmt status disputed 2-6, 86B2
Govs vs budget amendmt 2-26, 150B2
DC voting rep amendmt rejctd in NH, Ariz; OKd in Conn 3-7–4-26, 367D1

1980

CONNER, Dennis
Freedom wins America's Cup trials 8-29; 3d race finals victory upheld 9-22, Freedom retains Cup 9-25, 834E1-D2
CONNER, Judge William C.
Sentences NY drug dealer 6-12, 503G1-A2
Sentences Lloyd Carr chief 6-20, 503D1
CONNORS, Jimmy
Grand Prix Masters results 1-13, 213A2
Wins Birmingham WCT 1-20, US Pro Indoor 1-27, Tokyo Invitnl 4-13, Louisville Intl 5-18; loses US Natl Indoor 3-2, 607E2, G2, B3, D3
Wins WCT singles title 5-4; loses French Open semifinals 6-7, Wimbledon semifinals 7-5, 606B2, B3, 607A1
USTA, pros settle rules dispute 7-16, 691G3
Wins NH Grand Prix 8-3, loses US Open semifinals 9-6, 691A2, A3
Wins Canton Grand Prix 10-19, 947C1
Wins World Super tourn 11-2, 947C2
CONOCO Inc. (formerly Continental Oil Co.)
'79 profit rptd 1-29, 90F2, C3
1st 1/4 profit rptd 4-24, 331E1, G1
On '79 Fortune 500 list 5-5, 290F1
Gasoline prices cut 7-9, 553F1
Wholesale gas price cut rptd 8-1, 666D3
Consolidation Coal Co.
W Va wildcat strike 2-21—3-3, 170A1
CONRAC Corp.
Revlon heir, financier indicted 8-19, 713G3
CONRAD, Joseph (1857-1924)
Harper's to cease publicatn 6-17, 501A1
CONRAIL (Consolidated Rail Corp.)
Carter budget proposals 1-28, 73B1
'79 4th 1/4 loss rptd 2-12, 131D2
1st 1/4 loss rptd 5-1, 345G2
Jordan gets Cornell post 5-21, 456F2
2d 1/4, 1st 1/2 losses rptd 8-19; 3d 1/4 10-31, 857E1
Crane named chrmn, chief exec 9-29, 959C2
RR deregulatn bill signed 10-14, 784C1
Penn Central Transport takeover claim setld 11-17, 985B3
Reading emerges from bankruptcy 12-31, 986A1
CONROY, Edward T.
Loses US Sen electn 11-4, 848B2
CONSENTINO, Michael
On Ford acquittal in Pinto trial 3-13, 185E3
CONSERVATIVE Caucus
Political actn profiled 7-11—9-15, 819G1
CONSOLIDATED Aluminum Corp.
Alusuisse buys Phelps Dodge share 11-23, 985C2
CONSOLIDATED Edison Co. (Con Ed)
Indian Pt 2 A-plant leak controversy 10-17—10-23; NY judge backs rate surchrg 12-1, NRC staff seeks fine 12-11, 961C2
2d leak at Indian Pt 2 A-plant 11-3, 961B3
CONSOLIDATED Edison v. Public Service Commission
Case decided by Sup Ct 6-20, 555G1-C2
CONSOLIDATED Gold Fields Ltd.
Anglo-American buys 2-12, 398A3
CONSOLIDATED Rail Corp.—*See CONRAIL*
CONSTANTINE, King (Greece)
At shah's funeral 7-29, 571F1

CONSTITUTION, U.S.
GOP on budget amendmt deferral 1-28, 75F1
Bush vs abortn curb amendmt 2-7, 128B3
DC voting rep amendmt rejctd in Neb 2-11, 147B3
DC voting rep amendmt OKd in Md 3-17, Hawaii 4-17, 576F1
US intrastate gas sale power affirmed 6-6, 552C3
Human life amendmt debated at US Families Conf 6-19—6-21, 601A2, E2
GOP platform draft backs abortn ban amendmt 7-9, 506D2, F2

1976

CONSTRUCTION Industry—*See also HOUSING, PUBLIC Works*
Ford labor-mgt com formatn cited 3F3
On-site picket bill vetoed 1-2, union ldrs quit Ford com 1-8, 3C3, F3
Major banks on 'problem' list 1-11, 110F3
Dunlop quits Ford cabt 1-14, 23B1
Dec, '75 output rptd 1-16, 92B1
Ford State of Union message 1-19, 37C3
Boston GSA contracting violatns rptd 1-20, 71D1
Jan jobless rate rptd 2-5, 152F3
Jan output rptd 2-13, 168G2
House votes library aid 2-17, 170E3
Reagan vs on-site picket bill 2-28, 166D1
Feb jobless rate rptd 3-5, 199A1
Ford honored by contractors 3-9, 180C1
Feb output rptd 3-16, 199B3
Bldg supply profits rptd up 4-29, 376C3
Ford urges regulatory reform 5-13, 346G3
Apr output rptd 5-14, 375D2
Dem platform text 6-15, 469C2, 470C1, C3, 474B2
May indl output rise rptd 6-16, 479C3
Va builder sentenced 6-25, 860F2
Sup Ct declines Calif zoning rule review 6-28, 569D1
Ford signs housing aid bill 8-3, 566D3
Greenspan sees econ recovery pause 8-30, 647G1
NYC union bias barred 9-1, 943F3
Indl output index revised 9-16, 709E1
Carter, Ford debate 9-23, 701C1
Clean air amendmts not cleared 10-2, 883D2
Carter, Ford debate 10-22, 800E2
Oct jobless rate rptd down 11-5, 846G1
Green wins Rockefeller award 11-16, 911E3
Carter considers jobs plan 11-23, 881C2
Forgn paymts study rptd 12-20, 985D2, F2

CONSUMER Affairs—*See also NADER, Ralph; agency names under U.S. GOVERNMENT; industry and commodity names (e.g., AUTOMOBILES, FOOD, GAS); company names*
Carter legis record cited 512D2
Mondale record cited 512A3, C3
Muskie rebuts Ford 1-21, 40A2
House OKs trust bill 3-18, 246D3
Leasing protectn bill enacted 3-23, 234A1
Consumer confidnc rpt issued 3-26, 230A2
Product safety comm bill signed 5-11, 345G2
Dem platform text 6-15, 471C1, C2-F2, 473F3
Carter vows safeguards 7-15, 507F1, 510C3
Carter sees Nader 8-7—8-8; addresses Nader forum 8-9, 584D3, 585F1
GOP platform text 8-18, 603E2
Cong clears trust bill 9-16, 728E1
Protection agency bill not cleared 10-2, 883A1, A2
Ford, Carter debate 10-22, 800A2
CONSUMER Credit—*See CREDIT, Consumer*
CONSUMER Federation of America
Vs gas rate hike 7-28, ct modifies 8-9, 635G2
Praises Carter 8-9, 585F1
Foreman named Carter aide 11-23, 881E3
CONSUMER Price Index—*See 'Prices' under ECONOMY; also country names*
CONSUMER Reports (magazine)
Sup Ct bars Cong press gallery rule review 1-12, 24G1
CONSUMERS Union
Shuck on ABA advertising actn 2-18, 136G3
CONTAINER Corp. of America—*See MOBIL Oil*
CONTAINERS & Packaging
Paperbd trust suit dvpts 2-18—10-20, 885F3
FDA seeks chloroform ban 4-6, 249E2
Plastic beverage bottles challenged 4-21, 308A2
Anheuser-Busch strike ends 6-6, 436B2
Sen defeats nonreturnable ban 6-30, 833B3
Paper-bag makers chrgd 10-29, 886B3
4 states vote on mandatory deposits 11-2, 821D1, 823F2, 824F1, 825B3
Aluminum price hiked 11-29, 11-30, 898E1

1977

CONSTRUCTION Industry—*See also HOUSING, PUBLIC Works*
Bechtel setls Arab boycott suit 1-10, 78B2-A3
Deere rpts forgn paymts 2-1, 94G1
Secondary strikes curbed 2-22, 149D3
AFL-CIO backs on-site picket bill 2-22, 153C2
NYC union minority hiring rule overturned 3-21, 279D2
On-site picket bill fails 3-23, 229C1-D2
OSHA penalties upheld 3-23, 276F1
Boycott bill exceptn cited 4-20, 323E2
Apr indl output up 5-16, 384B1
Urban business confidence rptd, chart 5-16, 384C2, D3
Jones Constructn rpts payoffs 5-16, 503F1
Mafia infiltration rptd 5-16, 568E1
Concrete co price-fixing suit dismissed 6-9, 501F2
Female job quota proposed 8-16, 819E2
Anastasi acts on job bias 8-25, 669F2
Anatasi barred as fed contractor 8-25, 669F2; reinstated 11-23, 979F2
2d ¼ wage gains rptd 8-31, 704A2
AFL-CIO unit plan campaign vs common-site opponents 11-30, 961A2
White cos win minority-earmarked contract 12-13, 979C1
Cong com OKs conservatn measures 12-22, 1002B2
CONSULTATIVE Group for the Arab Republic of Egypt
Meets in Paris 5-11—5-12, 390F2
CONSUMER Credit—*See CREDIT, Consumer*
CONSUMER Federation of America
Elects O'Reilly dir 2-13, 217A2
Foreman confrmd Agri asst secy 3-24, 272A3
Carter energy plan scored 5-18, 443D2
CONSUMER Price Index—*See ECONOMY—Prices; country names*
CONSUMER Product Safety Commission—*See under U.S. GOVERNMENT*

CONSUMERS & Consumer Affairs—*See also NADER, Ralph; agency names under U.S. GOVERNMENT; industry and commodity names; company names*
Nov-Dec '76 confidence in business rptd up 1-9, 38F1
CEA rpt to Cong 1-18, 36B1, G1
FTC bars vitamin ads pitch to children 2-7, 217C1
Amer Consumer Fed names dir 2-13, 217A2
Carter for class-actn suits 3-5, 171G2
Carter backs US agency 4-6, 250F2-B3
Carter urges agency bill 6-1, 417E3
Spending, econ recovery linked 6-7, 6-24, 518B3
Price-fixing suits curbed 6-9, 501E2
Spending slowdown seen 7-15, 7-20, 555F1, B2
FTC corrective ad rule upheld 8-2, 613F1-A2
3d ¼ spending lag, GNP rate linked 10-19, 798C1
Fed agency bill shelved 11-1, 856F2
CONSUMER'S Union
Carter energy plan scored 5-18, 443E2
CONTAINER Corp. of America—*See MOBIL Oil*
CONTAINERS & Packaging
'76 paperbd execs sentncs cut 2-17, 504D1
Ore aerosol ban takes effect 3-1, 323B2
Teamsters, UFW sign pact 3-10, 177G3
State weight-labeling rules curbed 3-29, 277A1
Richmond OKs Continental bid 4-12, 274C3
E Coast dock protest 4-14—4-18, 324D2
Carter energy plan reactn 4-21, 320B2
FDA orders fluorocarbon aerosol warning 4-26, 323E1
Carter environmt message 5-23, 404E2
NC apple labeling rule voided 6-20, 517E1
Glass workers end strike 10-14, 818B3
Steelworkers OK can pacts 10-31, 837A1

1978

Goldwater plans treaty terminatn challenge 12-15, 974D3; suit filed 9-22, 995B2
Equal Rights Amendment—*See WOMEN—Politics & Government*

CONSTRUCTION Industry—*See also HOUSING, PUBLIC Works*
'Prehire' union picketing curbed 1-17, 33F3
US-Saudi contracts rptd 2-11, 113F2
Fed projct paymt bond coverage limited 2-22, 126A3
Engineers' fee code ruled illegal by Sup Ct 4-25, 323A1
W Va scaffold collapse kills 51 4-27, negligence chrgd 6-8, 459F2
Affirmative actn rules for women effected 5-7, 554G2
Southn jobs pact OKd 5-22, 429A3
Design deficiencies blamed in Hartford arena collapse 6-15, 460C1
Asbestos rule chngd by EPA 6-15, 512D3
Calif contractors reverse bias case sent back by Sup Ct 7-3, 552B1
SEC sues Parsons, case settled 8-4, 643C2 ★
2d ¼ employmt costs rptd 8-30, 680B2
16 cos, 10 execs chrgd re bid-rigging 9-27, 769A1
Aluminum wire dispute refused by Sup Ct 10-2, 751F1
Productivity decline rptd 10-4, 790D1
Public works veto upheld 10-5, 765C1
OSHA to consolidate rules 10-24, 833G3
Baltimore OKs bond issues 11-7, 915E2
Carter urges relaxed urban bldg codes 11-27, 914D3
Cities' power over suburbs backed by Sup Ct 11-28, 937A3, D3
CONSTRUCTORS Association, National
AFL-CIO unions sign pact 5-22, 429D3
CONSUMER Cooperative Bank, National
Created 8-20, 663E1
CONSUMER Credit—*See CREDIT, Consumer*
CONSUMER Federation of America (CFA)
Cong '77 ratings issued 3-4, 183B1
95th Cong ratings issued, consumer record hit 11-8, 981F2
CONSUMER Price Index (CPI)—*See ECONOMY—Price Indexes; also country names*
CONSUMER Product Safety Commission—*See under U.S. GOVERNMENT*
CONSUMERS & Consumer Affairs—*See also agency names under U.S. GOVERNMENT; industry and commodity names; company names*
Carter State of Union Message 1-19, 31B1, 32B1
'77 4th ¼ spending rise rptd 1-19, 50F1
Fed agency bill defeated 2-8, 82F1
Cong rated by Consumer Fed 3-4, 183B1; 11-8, 981F2
Black, white women compared 4-12, 811G3-812D1
Pupil competency testing rptd 5-9, 348A3
Co-op bank bill signed 8-20, 663E1
Aug spending rptd slowed 9-15, 717E1
3d ¼ spending rptd up, 2d ¼ revised 10-20, 863F3
Cong Watch rates 95th sessn 10-28, 865B2-A3
Carter vs boycotts of wage-price violators 12-12, 957B1
CONSUMERS Power Co.
Ct A-plant rulings curbed 4-3, 280F2
CONSUMERS Power Co. v. Aeschliman
Ct A-plant rulings curbed 4-3, 280F2
CONSUMERS Union
Omnis, Horizons rptd unsafe 6-18; Canada, US refute 6-28, 7-7, 569E3
CONTACT Lenses—*See EYES & Eyesight*
CONTAGIOUS Equine Metritis (CEM)—*See HORSE Racing*
CONTAINER Corp. of America—*See MOBIL Oil*
CONTAINERS & Packaging
Blood donor labeling ordrd 1-13, 231A3
Cardbd mfrs indicted 1-25, 67A2
Cosmetic ingredient label rule upheld 2-12, 231G3-232A1
Hypoallergenic label rule revoked 3-14, 231E3
Coke, Pepsi bottler curbs barred 4-25, 346B1
Time Inc to buy Inland Container 5-19, 403G2-C3
Appliance energy-cost labels OKd 6-28, 702A3
EPA to ease clean-water rules 8-10, 644A2
American Can to buy Fingerhut 8-14, 718D1
Oil of wintergreen warning issued 8-17, 727F3
Intl Paper settles '78 chrgs 8-25, 10-1; 3 other '76 defendants settle 9-25, 10-2, 768C3
Generic drug mislabeling probed 9-8, 727E2
Drug expiratn date labeling ordrd 9-13, 727F2
FDA sets calorie labeling rules 9-21, 770B1

1979

DC voting rep OKd in Minn, Mass 3-19, 204G2
Budget amendmt progress, Prop 13 linked 6-3, 500F1
Proposed amendmt to bar Electoral Coll rejected by Sen 7-10, 514G3-515D1
Anti-busing amendmt defeated in House 7-24, 559E2
Church-state issue challenged 9-13–10-3, 760A3
DC voting rep OKd in Wis 10-30, 11-1, 851C3
Equal Rights Amendment—*See WOMEN—Politics & Government*
CONSTITUTION Party
Thomson enters pres race 10-31, 829E1
CONSTRUCTION Industry—*See also HOUSING*
Carter bars wage rate chngs 1-4, 3F3
Chase REIT bankruptcy, costs linked 2-22, 131C2
Mont gross-receipts tax upheld by Sup Ct 2-22, 151C1
US no longer top DC area hirer 3-24, 232B2
Govt minority grant case accepted by Sup Ct 5-21, 400F3
NJ ex-offcls subject to rejailing by Sup Ct 6-4, 439A1
ISC accused of forgn paymts 7-9, 541E3
Carter pledges no job losses 10-11, 807F2
Lyons on Pay Advisory Com 10-16, 829A3
Peter Kiewit dies 11-2, 932B3
Govt minority grants case argued in Sup Ct 11-27, 944F3
CONSUMER Credit—*See CREDIT, Consumer*
CONSUMER Federation of America (CFA)
O'Reilly sees Carter 6-1, 418G1
CONSUMER Price Index (CPI)—*See ECONOMY—Price Indexes; also country names*
CONSUMER Product Safety Commission—*See under U.S. GOVERNMENT*

CONSUMERS & Consumer Affairs—*See also agency names under U.S. GOVERNMENT; industry and commodity names; company names*
'78, 4th 1/4 spending, savings rptd 1-18, 73C1
'79 spending forecast, '78 cited 1-25, 48D3
Carter seeks price-fixing suit bill, fed no-fault standards 1-25, 70C2
Kennedy offers trust suits bill 1-31, 308B2
Nader group suits curbed 3-14, 308G1
Carter urges actn vs price guide violators 3-25, 230B2
Carter urges privacy bill 4-2, 264F3
1st ¼ spending, savings rptd 4-19, 280D2
Automatic bank funds shift voided 4-20, 303F2
Right to sue protected by Sup Ct 6-11, 478D2
2d 1/4 spending, savings rptd; 1st 1/4 revised 7-20, 556A3
3d 1/4 spending, savings rptd; 2d 1/4 revised 10-19, 805A2
Warne honored 10-19, 903A2
CONSUMERS Power Co.
NRC fines for Palisades A-plant violatn 11-9, 867A1
CONSUMERS Union
Warne honored 10-19, 903A2
CONTACT Lenses—*See EYES & Eyesight*
CONTAINER Corp. of America—*See MOBIL Corp.*
CONTAINERS & Packaging
Boise Cascade offers to buy Stone Container 1-22, 89E1; bid rejected 1-30, 440E3
Food-safety law revisns urged 3-2, 195B1, D1
Radial tire grading label ordrd 3-13, 208D3
Food processing, storage rule chngs proposed 6-7, 572C2
Yellow No 5 labeling ordrd 6-26, 571G1
Paperbd trust suit setld 6-28, 647G3
Prescriptn drug leaflets urged by FDA 6-29, 571E1
FDA drive vs lead in canned food rptd 8-30, 736G3
Beer warning labels urged 9-19, 736B1
Washn, O, Me deposit-bottle initiative results 11-6, 846B2, E3

1980

Govs back power redistribution amendmt 8-5, 596D1
Reagan, Anderson debate abortn amendmt 9-21, 722C2
Ervin vs 'judicial verbicide' 10-22, 908A2
DC voters OK const conv; ERA, abortn rights threatened 11-4, 846E2, B3, 848F1,850C1
Reagan reaffirms abortn amendmt 11-6, 839C3
Equal Rights Amendment—*See WOMEN--Politics*
CONSTITUTIONAL Rights, Center for
Abortn funding cases argued in Sup Ct 4-21, 306G2
CONSTITUTION Party
Thomson ends pres run 4-14, 288G3
CONSTRUCTION Industry
Waterway injury case remanded by Sup Ct 1-14, 37F1
Copper futures trading limited 1-24, 69B1
Wyo State of State message 2-12, 484G2
US territories set projects 2-19—2-22, 495E1
Mar jobless rate, layoffs linked 4-4, 263F1
NYS resident jobs preference case declined by Sup Ct 4-21, 344C2
Apr jobless rate rptd 5-2, 344B3
Indian preference in contracts barred by Sup Ct 5-27, 454B1
May jobless rate rptd 6-6, 437E2
Govt minority grants upheld by Sup Ct 7-2, 510A1
SE road builders bid-rigging pleas, probe rptd 7-5, 655E1
USSR-US 1st 1/2 trade drop rptd 8-20, 711F2
Aug indl output rptd up 9-16, 701A3
Multi-employer pensn plan reform signed 9-26, 856D3
GM's Terex Div sold 9-28, 746A2
Sept indl output rptd up 10-16, 783E1
Copper demand rptd down 10-24, 805B3
CONSULTATION on Church Union—*See under PROTESTANTISM --See also specific denominations*
CONSUMER Alert
Keating scores 'Big Business Day' 4-17, 308D2
CONSUMER Credit—*See CREDIT, Consumer*
CONSUMER Federation of America (CFA)
Carter, Kennedy address 2-7, 91F1
CONSUMER Price Index (CPI)—*See ECONOMY--Price Indexes*
CONSUMER Product Safety Commission (CPSC)—*See under U.S. GOVERNMENT*

CONSUMERS & Consumer Affairs
Cong Watch rates 96th sessn 1-12, 53G2
'79, 4th 1/4 spending, savings rptd 1-18, 52C1
Carter, Kennedy address CFA 2-7, 91E1
'Big Business Day' scores corporatns 4-17, 308G1
1st 1/4 spending, savings rptd 4-18, 305C3
35 fed agencies implement programs 6-9, 703B1
Dem platform drafted 6-24, 480A1
US, Canada consumptn compared 7-16, 562D3
2d 1/4 spending, savings rptd 7-18, 556B1
Dem platform plank adopted 8-13, 614E3
Coalitn sues over oil price setlmts 10-8, 960G1
3rd 1/4 spending, savings rptd 10-17, 804D3
ITC bars Japan auto curbs 11-10, 866D3
Carter plans to speak out 11-12, 865F2
Block criticizes Bergland 12-23, 980G1
CONTA, Dennis
Loses Milwaukee mayoral bid 4-1, 247B2
CONTAINERS & Packaging
US dietary guidelines issued 2-4, 157C3
Paperbd trust setlmt case dismissed 10-20, 807A3

1976

CONTE, Rep. Silvio O. (R, Mass.)
Ousted as platform subcom chrmn 8-9, 583B1
Reelected 11-2, 829B4
CONTI, Haroldo
Kidnaped 5-5, 399A1
CONTI, Judge Samuel
Sentncs Moore to life 1-15, 23F1-D2
CONTINENTAL Airlines
CAB reporting penalty cited 12-29, 986G1
CONTINENTAL Can Co. Inc.—*See CONTINENTAL Group*
CONTINENTAL Grain Co.
Execs named in grain fraud 3-11, 247D3
Soviet grain sales rptd 4-28, 321C3
India sues 5-3, 333E2
Fined 5-4, 990C3
11-day Calif canners strike ends 7-31, 570C1
USW contracts extended 8-18, 670A1
CONTINENTAL Group Inc. (formerly Continental Can Co. Inc.)
Bars boycott compliance 3-18, 747B2
USW contracts extended 8-18, 670C1
Co, 4 offcls indicted 10-29, 11-4, 886C3
CONTINENTAL Illinois National Bank & Trust Co. (Chicago)
In Venez intl bank loan 9-15, 875E1
Boycott rpt released 10-20, 786A2
Lowers prime rate 10-28, 846E2
CONTINENTAL Oil Co. (Conoco)
N Sea oil find rptd 1-19, UK buys controlling interest 2-26, 173A3
North Sea find rptd 5-28, 521D3
Co, Kayo Oil indicted 6-1, 412D3, E3
Rptd vs boycott legis 9-19, 746C3
Sup Ct bars price hike review 10-4, 807A3
2 offcls fired 12-15, paymts detailed 12-16, 986A1
CONTRERAS Escobar, Eduardo
Rptd killed 11-7, 926D1
CONTROL Data Corp.
China, Sovt computer deals rptd 10-28, 11-1, 832G2-C3
CONVOY (song)
On best-selling list 1-28, 104G3
CONYERS Jr., Rep. John J. (D, Mich.)
Udall loses in Mich 5-18, 357C1
Ruff rejects Ford probe 10-15, 785A1
Reelected 11-2, 829D4
COOK, Donald C.
Announces retiremt 1-27, 160E2
COOK, Edward W.
Disputes Polish grain grading 3-12, 247E3
COOK, Marlow
Carter disavows dumping memo 8-13, 616F3
COOK County, Ill.—*See ILLINOIS*
COOKE, Judith
Killed 7-21, 538F2
COOK Industries, Inc.
Disputes Polish cargo grade, sues Agri Dept 2-26, 3-12, 247E3
Execs named in grain fraud 3-11, 247D3 *
Soviet grain sale rptd 4-28, 321C3
India sues 5-3, 333E2
Grain fraud indictmts 5-6—11-26, damages barred 12-15, 990F2
SEC lists paymts 5-12, 727A1

1977

CONTAMINATION Issues—*See under FOOD*
CONTI, Judge Samuel
Dismisses Atkinson slander suit 7-22, 659C1
CONTINENTAL Can Co.—*See CONTINENTAL Group*
CONTINENTAL Coffee Co.—*See CFS Continental*
CONTINENTAL Grain Co.
ICC curbs rail car deals 8-1, 613A1
Elevator blast kills 35 12-22, 1023E1
CONTINENTAL Group Inc., The (formerly Continental Can Co.)
Richmond takeover cited in table 880G1
Richmond OKs bid 4-12, 274D3
Steelworkers OK new pact 10-31, 837D1
Co, offcl convicted; 2 acquitted 11-1, 11-23, 918G2, A3
CONTINENTAL Illinois National Bank & Trust Co. (Chicago)
Farmland fund plan withdrawn 3-7, 3-11, 195A1
CONTINENTAL Oil Co. (Conoco)
Gulf of Mex gas probe set 2-17, 151F3
On '76 Fortune 500 list 340F1
Pipe Line Seadock backing rptd 7-19, 559F2
Trust chrg acquittal, unit convicted 8-30; another unit settles 8-31, 691B3, D3
Unit fined 9-16, 918F2
Blauvelt replies to Carter attack 10-13, 773A1
CONTINENTAL Pipe Line Co.—*See CONTINENTAL Oil Co.*
CONTINENTAL Trailways, Inc.—*See HOLIDAY Inns*
CONTINENTAL T.V. Inc.
Sylvania retail sales rules upheld 6-23, 539G1
CONTRACEPTION—*See BIRTH Control*
CONTRA Costa County, Calif.—*See CALIFORNIA*
CONTRERAS, Carmelo
Venez agri min 1-7, 23E2
Replaced as agri min 7-15, 566B1
CONTRERAS Sepulveda, Gen. Manuel
Letelier death ordr rptd, US denies 9-8, 743F2
CONTRERAS Tapia, Gen. Mario
DINA abolished 8-12, 635F1
CONTROL Data Corp.
Congressmen vs Sovt computer deal 6-5, 469A3
US bars Sovt computer deal 6-23, 501D3
CONWAY, James F.
Elected St Louis mayor 4-5, 252E3
CONWAY, William Cardinal
Dies 4-17, 356G2
Replaced as Irish Primate 8-22, 728F3
CONYERS Jr., Rep. John J (D, Mich.)
Black Caucus backs Carter criticism 7-29, 592G3
COOK, G. Bradford
Sup Ct disbars 5-31, 461G3
COOK, John William (Deceased)
Widow rptd kidnaped 2-25, 198B1
COOKE, Alistair
Six Men on best-seller list 11-6, 872E3
COOKE, Howard
Jamaica pub service min 1-4, 46C1
COOK Industries Inc.
Rpts payoffs, confrms grain fraud 5-4, 503B2
ICC curbs rail grain-car deals 8-1, 613D1
Sovt sale announced 8-9, 640B3

1978

Cosmetic label challenge refused by Sup Ct 10-10, 789D3
OSHA drops 'nuisance' barrel-making rules 10-24, 833D3
Neb, Alaska rejct mandatory deposits 11-7, 847B3
Liggett to buy SC Pepsi bottler 11-16, 1005C2
CONTAMINATION Issues—*See under FOOD*
CONTE, Rep. Silvio O. (R, Mass.)
Asks Argentina free Timerman 3-6, 208B1
Reelected 11-7, 851C1
CONTESSA of Mulberry Street, The (play)
Opens 1-4, 887D1
CONTINENTAL Air Lines Inc.
Western Airlines merger set 8-31, 684B1
Australia eases oppositn to 2d carrier 11-14, 920G2
US, Australia reach air accord 12-13, 985G1
CONTINENTAL Can Co.—*See CONTINENTAL Group Inc.*
CONTINENTAL Copper & Steel Industries Inc.
Price fixing suit rptd 9-21, 769C1
CONTINENTAL Grain Co.
La '77 grain elevator blast violatns rptd 5-16, 636F2
Pleads guilty 12-28, 1029D1
CONTINENTAL Group Inc., The (formerly Continental Can Co.)
Indicted for price fixing 1-25, 67C2
Clay dies 4-16, 356D2
Fined, Cooper sentncd 9-21, 768F2, A3
CONTINENTAL Illinois National Bank & Trust Co. (Chicago)
Prime rate hiked 5-25, 403F2
CONTINENTAL National Bank and Trust Co.
NCC withdraws funds re S Africa 9-21, 742F2
CONTINENTAL Oil Co. (Conoco)
US to drop trust suit vs Texaco 1-3, 67E2
Egypt pact signed 2-16, 139B3
Carter sees Blauvelt on coal strike 2-24, 122G3
Coal, uranium reserves lid backed by FTC aide 4-5, 282F2, G2
On '77 Fortune 500 list 5-8, 325F1
NJ offshore oil well rptd dry 6-2, 6-5, 449C3
Criminal pricing probe rptd 7-21, Burnap pleads no contest 8-9, 610D3
Chrmn Blauvelt to retire, Bailey named 9-20, 809B1
Gas rationing rptd sought 12-3, 939C1
NJ offshore wells rptd dry 12-6, 12-11, 12-27, 1010E1
Consolidation Coal Co.
Mine safety inspectn case remanded by Sup Ct 6-5, 431E2
Miners sex bias suit setld 12-26, 1006F2
CONTRACEPTION—*See BIRTH Control*
CONTRA Costa County, Calif.—*See CALIFORNIA*
CONTRACT Compliance Programs, Office of Federal—*See U.S. GOVERNMENT—LABOR—Employment Standards Administration*
CONTRERAS Sepulveda, Gen. Manuel
Osorio '77 death rptd 3-8, 189C1
Quits army, govt posts 3-21, 209G2
Letelier murder probe pressure rptd 4-9, 266E3
Letelier murder evidence removal rptd 4-20, magazine scores govt silence 8-10, 648A1
US indictmt in Letelier case seen 5-23, 452D1
Letelier death rap refusal rptd 6-5, 452F1
US indicts in Letelier murder, arrested 8-1; 'proof' for extraditn asked 8-2, 613F3-614F1
Townley admits link 8-11, 647D3
US asks extraditn 9-20, moved to mil hosp 9-22, 755G2, E3
Pinochet rptdly denies tie 9-21, 755E3
Rptdly sees US evidence 10-13, 795G2-A3
Queried by Sup Ct pres, claims innocence re Letelier 10-24, 1014C3
CONTROL Data Corp.
Pleads guilty, fined for forgn paymts 4-26, 448B3
USSR computer deal set 10-31, 841C1
Paymts suit cited 11-20, 961D3
CONVOY (film)
Released 6-28, 619C1
Top-grossing film 7-6, 579F3
CONYERS Jr., Rep. John J. (D, Mich.)
Reelected 11-7, 851D1
COOK, Crawford J.
US denies improper tie to West 3-30, 237A1
Saudis rptdly hired firm for F-15 sale 3-31, 236F3-237B1
COOK, John
Win US Amateur golf title 9-3, 990F1
COOK, Robin
Coma on best-seller list 1-8, 24F3; 2-5, 116C3; 3-5, 195F3; 4-2, 272C3; 4-30, 356B2
Coma released 2-1, 619B1
COOK, Rodney M.
Loses electn for Ga gov 11-7, 852F1
COOK, Vernon
Wins US Sen primary in Oregon 5-23, 406A3
Loses electn 11-7, 857A3
COOK Industries Inc.
'77 sales drop rptd 5-8, 325C2

1979

CONTEH, John
Saad Muhammad decisns 8-18, 839C1
CONTI, Judge Samuel
Hell's Angels trial opens 10-4, 840G1
CONTI, Tom
Whose Life opens 4-17, 712E3*
CONTIE Jr., Judge Leroy
Blocks Fuqua bid for Hoover 6-11, 560F2
CONTINENTAL Air Lines Inc.
DC-10 maintenance scored 7-10, 538F3
Westn Airlines merger blocked by CAB 7-21, 579C1
Westn merger talks end 8-7, 830E1
DC-10 safety fine paid 11-16, 988D3
CONTINENTAL Grain Co.
Jamaica fires Rose re paymts 1-29, probe rptd 2-4, 101C2
Swiss unit fined re boycott violatn 8-27, 648G2
CONTINENTAL Group Inc., The (formerly Continental Can Co.)
2 acquitted 4-29, civil trust setlmt revealed 5-1, 327C3, E3
Tyco drops Ludlow takeover bid 5-3, 560C3
Florida Gas purchased 8-28, 986C3
Continental Resources Inc. (formerly Florida Gas Co.)
Purchased 8-28, 986C3
Mex natural gas purchased 10-18, 814F3
CONTINENTAL Gummi Werke A.G.
Uniroyal Eur operatns sale set 4-17, 560F3
CONTINENTAL Illinois Corp.
Continental Illinois National Bank and Trust Co. (Chicago)
Iran banks natlzd 6-7, compensatn vowed 6-10, 469G1
Prime rate hiked 8-16, 621E1
CONTINENTAL Illinois National Bank and Trust Co.—*See under CONTINENTAL Illinois Corp.*
CONTINENTAL Oil Co.—*See CONOCO*
CONTINENTAL Telephone Corp.
Xerox plans WUI acquisition 1-18, 89D1
CONTRACEPTION—*See BIRTH Control*
CONTRACT Compliance Programs, Office of Federal—*See U.S. GOVERNMENT—LABOR—Employment Standards Administration*
CONTRERAS, Rufino
Killed 2-10, funeral 2-14, 327E1
CONTRERAS Sepulveda, Gen. Manuel
Freed to attend wedding 1-6; US submits more data in Letelier case 1-8, 19B3
Cited in Letelier trial testimony 1-16, 58B1, G2
Extraditn seen unlikely 2-7, 114C3
3 Cubans convictd re Letelier 2-14, 114E2
Avoids US extraditn 5-14, 369C2
Ct bars extraditn, frees 10-1, 750G1
US funds shift probed, link to convicted Cubans alleged 10-9, 772A2
CONTROL Data Corp.
Art show sponsorship rptd 7-19, 672C2
USSR sale blocked 9-27, 775C1
Signs USSR energy tech pact 12-14, 997E2
CONWAY, Kevin
Elephant Man opens 1-14, 292E1
CONWAY, Tim
Apple Dumpling sequel released 8-31, 819E3
CONYERS Jr., Rep. John J. (D, Mich.)
Joins dump-Carter move 5-23, 384C2
At black pol conv 5-25–5-27, 423D1
CONYERS, Judge Robert W.
Sentences Smith 5-31, 442D2
COOK, Charlie
Hired as Rogues coach 5-15, 1004D2
COOK, James
Peter Pan opens 9-6, 956G3
COOK, Maj. Jeff
On Army recruiting fraud probe 10-15, 850C2
COOK, John
Loses US Amateur golf tourn 9-2, 969D3
COOK, T. S.
China Syndrome released 3-16, 528G1
COOK County, Ill.—*See ILLINOIS*
COOK County Hospital (Chicago, Ill.)
City hosps decline rptd 9-2, 971A1
COOKE, Godwin
Resumes CEA post 6-21, 601B3
COOKE, Jack Kent
Sells Lakers, Kings, Forum arena 5-30, 527D1
COOK Industries Inc.
Grain export civil chrgs setld 9-26, 727G2-C3

1980

CONTE, Rep. Silvio O. (R, Mass.)
Reelected 11-4, 843C1
CONTEH, John
Saad Muhammad TKOs 3-29, 320C3
CONTI, Maria Teresa
Arrested 10-13, 791B3
CONTI, Judge Samuel
Sentences Hell's Angels 8-18, 714C1
CONTINENTAL Air Lines Inc.
Westn Airlines merger bid renewed, losses rptd 9-22, 746E2
Flight attendant strike ends 12-20, 988E1
CONTINENTAL Grain Co.
Jamaica sues US grain shippers 2-4, 99C3
CONTINENTAL Group Inc.
Price fixing appeal declined by Sup Ct 1-14, 37E1
CONTINENTAL Group Inc. v. U.S.
Case declined by Sup Ct 1-14, 37E1
CONTINENTAL Illinois Corp.
Continental Illinois National Bank and Trust Co. (Chicago)
Prime rate cut to 16.5% 5-7, 367E3
Prime rate hiked to 17% 11-20, 937E3
CONTINENTAL Oil Co.—*See CONOCO*
CONTINENTAL Telephone Co.
FCC OKs satellite launchings 12-4, 990E3
CONTRACEPTION—*See BIRTH Control*
CONTRERAS Sepulveda, Gen. Manuel
Linked to Chile tax scandal 8-4, 603A3
Letelier, Moffitt kin awarded $5 mln 11-5, 869F3
CONTROL Data Corp.
Payments case refused by Sup Ct 1-7, 16A1
CONVAIR—*See under GENERAL Dynamics*
CONVERGENCE of Interest (book)
Snepp manuscript rptd submitted for CIA OK 6-13, 517C1
CONWAY Jr., Henry N.
Chrgd in Bahamas bank looting suit 3-3, 229D1
CONWAY, Kevin
Mecca opens 2-2, 136D3
CONWAY, Justice Robert
Backs Con Ed rate surchrg 12-1, 961A3
CONWAY, Rose A.
Dies 3-17, 279A2
CONYERS Jr., Rep. John J. (D, Mich.)
Reelected 11-4, 843E1
COODY, Charles
Ties for 2d in Inverrary Classic 3-9, 412G2
COOK, Ellis
Named in Abscam indictment 5-22, 402B3
COOK, Tom H.
Testimony in Stoner case rptd 5-14, 405D1
COOK County—*See ILLINOIS*
COOKE, Brian
On World Air fare cuts 4-9, 346B3
COOKE, Michael-Eliot
Incomparable Max opens 6-15, 756D3
COOKE, Terence Cardinal
Lauds Medicaid abortn funding limit 6-30, 492A2
Reagan visits 12-9, 956A2

1976

COOKING—*See FOOD*
COOK Islands
S Pacific Forum meets 3-8—3-9, 179B2
COOKS, Jessie Lee
Convicted 3-13, sentncd 3-29, 292G3
COOK United Inc.
SEC lists paymts 5-12, 727B1
COOLEY'S Anemia—*See 'Blood' under MEDICINE*
COOLIDGE, Rita
Wins Grammy 2-28, 460C3
COOLIDGE Bank & Trust Co.—*See FIRST Coolidge Corp.*
COONEY, Patrick
In Rees security talks 1-8, 19F3
COOPER, Charles A.
Questns World Bank policies 12-26, 976C1
COOPER, Herman
NYC cops win '75 increase 12-22, 991C2
COOPER, James K.
Indicted 10-29, 886C3
COOPER, John Sherman
Quits as amb to E Ger 5-17, 412B2
COOPER, Owen
Named Carter adviser 11-19, 881E3
COOPER, Richard
Cited as Carter advisor 4-23, 305E2
At Carter econ briefing 12-1, 898F2
COOPER, Dr. Theodore
US health rpt issued 1-12, 32C1
Ford asks flu vaccine drive 3-24, 224C2
Flu vaccine tested 4-21, 316G1
Rpts flu vaccine error 6-2, 423C3
Halts flu vaccine progrm 12-16, 950D1
COOPERATIVE for American Relief Everywhere—*See CARE*
COOPER Industries Inc.
UK unit in Sovt deal 12-24, 1011A2
COPE—*See 'Committee for Political Education' under AMERICAN Federation of Labor*
COPELYN, John
Banned 11-18, 927C3
COPPER & Brass
Intl price fall cited 1-12, 142G1
Financing rptdly halts Zaire projct 1-27, 2-2, 335D2
Zambia transit problems rptd 1-30, 77G3
Canada '75 trade deficit rptd 1-30, 116B3
Zambia sees no earnings 1-30, 503C2
Zambia chrgs Angola seizure 2-20, 163E2
Australian mine closing set 2-24, 154E3
Australia ocean find rptd 2-26, 154F3
Mozambique actn spurs UK price rise 3-3, 175B3
Australia-PNG deal 3-22, 237D2
Zaire '75 export drop cited 3-23, 270F2
Kennecott signs Haiti pact 3-24, find rptd 3-25, 267A3
Uganda export drop cited 4-6, 502B3
Peru emergency set re miners strike 4-9, 499F2
1st ¼ US profits rptd 4-29, 376D3
UNCTAD OKs commodity fund 5-30, 388G2
Paris Club defers Zaire debt 6-17, 488B2
UN Sea Law Conf deadlocked 8-2—9-17, 700F1
Eximbank sued re Zaire loan 8-9, 621C2
Suit vs Eximbank re Zaire dropped 10-13, 890A3
W Ger-Poland pact 11-2; credit deal rptd 11-4, 907E1
Australia find rptd 11-18, 902G2
Kennecott to sell Peabody 12-14, 985B1
Chile Developments—*See under CHILE*
COPTIC Orthodox Church—*See under EASTERN Orthodox Churches*
COPYRIGHTS—*See also BROADCASTING, MUSIC, PUBLISHING; other subjects*
Sen OKs prelim revisns 2-10, 152B2
Sen OKs revisns 2-10, 152C2
Dem platform text 6-15, 473E1
Cong clears revisions 9-30, 764E3; Ford signs 10-19, 982G1
CORBETT, Raymond
Endorses Carter 7-22, 551F1
CORBETTA, Gen. Arturo
Replaced 7-6, 571C3
CORCORAN, Judge Howard F.
Stays food stamp revisns 5-28, 434D3
CORCORAN, Thomas G.
Wiretap rptd 5-10, 344G2
CORCORAN, Tom
Elected 11-2, 823G1, 829A3
CORDERO Jr., Angel
Wins Kentucky Derby 5-1, 336F2
Bold Forbes wins Belmont 6-5, 424E3
CORDOBA, Maj. Antonio
Arrested 3-13, 314B3
CORDOVA-Claure, Ted
On Guevara executn 5-13, 415D3, F3
COREA, Gamani
Submits UNCTAD report 5-4, 320D2
UNCTAD OKs commodity fund 5-30, 388F2
COREA, Chick, and Return to Forever (music group)
Wins Grammy 2-28, 460B3
CORE Laboratories Inc.
SEC lists paymts 5-12, 727B1
Arab boycott noncompliance rptd 11-9, 986B3
Forgn paymts policy cited 12-18, 985A2
CORGHI, Benito
Killed 8-5, 589B3
CORMACK, Bob
Climbs Mt Everest 10-8, 876B3
CORMAN, Rep. James C. (D, Calif.)
Carter offers health plan 4-16, 281G3
Reelected 11-2, 829C1
AMA vs health insurance bill 12-7, 931D2
CORN
Argentina drought 1-17, US credits set 1-28, 96B3

1977

COOK Islands (New Zealand territory)
NZ to set 200-mi fishing zone 9-7, 729B3
COOLIDGE, Albert S.
Dies 8-31, 696E2
COONEY, Patrick
Elected to Irish Sen 8-27, 728D3 *
COOPER, Charles (Tarzan)
In basketball HOF 5-2, 490F3
COOPER, Clifford
Resigns BDP post 8-19, 710E1
COOPER, Grant
Fasi trial folds 12-27, 1008G1
COOPER, James K.
Convicted 11-23, 918A3
COOPER, Jerome
Settles SEC chrgs 10-17, 860F1
COOPER, John Sherman
Replaced as amb to E Ger 7-28, 626D2
COOPER, Norman
Settles SEC chrgs 10-17, 860F1
COOPER, Paul
Cancer linked to A-test 12-13, 1022D3
COOPER, Richard N.
Named State undersecy 1-7, 14B2
Sen subcom staff rpt scores 1-17, 78C3
COOPER, Theodore
Replaced as HEW asst secy 6-28, 626D3
COOPERS & Lybrand
Big 8 acctg firms ranked 8-22, 650G2
Vesco auditing scored, ICC suit vs urged 11-29, 980B3
COORE, David
Jamaica finance min 1-4, 46C1
Cites IMF loan conditns 7-25, 884D3
COORS Co., Adolph
OKs antibias pact, EEOC drops suit 5-9, 819D1
COPAKEN, Richard
Seeks Shadrin release 7-14, 564D2
COPELAND, Barbara N.
Ordrd to pay govt bias suit costs 8-23, 669G3
COPERSUCAR
Hills Bros ups coffee price 3-3, 168G3
COPLEY News Service
CIA links chrgd, denied 9-12, 720B3, G3
COPPER & Brass
Arco buys Anaconda 1-12, 55F2
US modifies duty-free list 2-28, 189E3
Zaire's Shaba data cited 3-8, 207D3
No accord at Geneva talks 3-14—3-18, 209D2
US prices raised 3-18—3-22, 209A2
Anaconda settles OPIC Chile claim 3-31, 449F1
Zaire gets IMF loan 4-26, 394B2
US prices cut, worldwide surplus cited 6-1, 7-2, 7-20, 577C2
Kennecott sells Peabody 6-22, 520F1
US cos struck; Kennecott, Magma settle 7-1, 558B1
Zambia hit by low world prices 7-21, 583A2
Peru export prices cited 7-28, 618D2
Peru miners strike US co 8-2, 673D2
Zambia econ improvemt rptd 8-10, 675A1
July indl output down 8-15, 628E3
Peru export price rptd low 8-31, 784E3
Poland gets Chase loan 8-31, 886A1
Peru seeks forgn investmt 9-29, 785C2
Sept indl output up 10-14, 798B2
US financial woes rptd 10-31, 858G3
Australia mine gets fed aid 11-10, 945A1
Kennecott-Carborundum deal OKd 11-16, 880A1
France, Quebec in 5-yr deal 12-6, 965B3
Zaire, Zambia, Peru cut productn, Chile refuses 12-7, 975A1
London price rptd, world stockpile cited 12-7, 975C1
Lead-pollutn rule proposed 12-12, 1007C3
Exxon buys Chile copper mine 12-28, 1019B1
COPPER Exporting Countries, Intergovernment Council of (CIPEC) (Chile, Indonesia, Peru, Zaire, Zambia)
Zaire, Zambia, Peru to cut productn, Chile refuses 12-7, 975B1
COPPER Range Co.
Raises copper price 3-18, 209C2
COPTIC Orthodox Church—*See under EASTERN Orthodox Churches*
COPYRIGHTS—*See PUBLISHING*
CORDERO, Jose Angelo
Arrested 1-2, 140A2
CORDERO, Col. Luis
Bolivia energy min 10-13, 902C1
CORDERO, Rodrigo
CR pres candidate 9-2, 710B2
CORDLE, John
Quits Parlt over Poulson scandal 7-22, 581D1
CORI, Gerty T.
Yalow wins Nobel 10-13, 951E3
CORISH, Brendan
Replaced as party ldr 7-1, 530G2
CORMIER, Roger
Pleads guilty 5-26, 426D1
Freed 6-16, 484G3
On '72 RCMP raid authorizatn 10-25, 841A2
CORN
Carter farm plan outlined 3-23, 214D1
Refiners pollutn rules appeal refused 4-18, 342D1
Drought crop damage rptd 6-23—8-24, 659F3-660A1
Record US crop seen 7-29, 611G3
US sales to USSR rptd 8-9, 8-12, 640B3
Carter ups price supports 8-29, 666F2
Farm bill signed, target prices detailed 9-29, 736E2, B3
Garst dies 11-5, 952D2
Carter cuts '78 acreage 11-15, 916C2

1978

COOKING and Crafts Club—*See BOOK-of-the-Month Club*
COOK Islands (New Zealand territory)—*See also SOUTH Pacific Forum*
Henry, aides ousted over electn fraud; Davis sworn 7-25, 591F2
COOK, Reuf, Spann & Weiser
Saudis rptdly hired to lobby for F-15 sale 3-31, 236F3-237B1
COOLEST Cat In Town, The (play)
Opens 6-23, 760F1
COOPER, Brian
Saudis whip 5-15, return to UK 6-15, 515G3
COOPER, Cecil
AL batting ldr 10-2, 928D3
COOPER, James K
Sentenced 9-21, 768A3
COOPERS & Lybrand
Named in Ford suit 5-16, 391A1
COOPERS & Lybrand v. Livesay
Class actn certificatn appeals curbed by Sup Ct 6-21, 509G2
COPERSUCAR
Hills Bros to boycott Uganda coffee 5-17, 416F3
COPPER & Brass
Zambia revenue fall forces consumer subsidy end 1-1, 55E3
Exxon buys Chile mine 1-24, 312C2
Mich sues Ford re pollutn 2-1, 163D3
Zambia exports delayed 3-8, 170B1
US stockpile purchase OKd 3-13, 177B3
Kennecott blocks Curtiss-Wright takeover bid 3-13—5-24, 402B1-403D1
Zambia sets output cut, export backlog rptd eased 3-30, 333F2
Anaconda brass plants end strike 4-3, 284C3
Freeport Mineral '77 Indonesia bombings rptd 4-15, 319A1
OPIC extensn bill limits aid 4-24, 323G2
Anaconda '77 sales rptd up 5-8, 325A2
Zambia aid increased by US 5-18, 395G2
Zaire invasn pushes prices up, mine damage discounted 5-22, 382A2
Zaire security force backed 5-24, 417D3
W Ger to seek EC aid for Zambia, Zaire 6-30, 584D1
Zaire mining resumptn rptd 7-14, 652B3
US House OKs seabed mining bill 7-26, 588F3
Peru miners strike 8-4; US co halts shipmts 8-17, govt declares emergency 8-22, 669B1
Rhodesia mine strikers killed 8-15, 741A3
ITC urges US quota 8-23, Carter rejcts 10-20, 804E3-805B1
US oil industry diversificatn rptd 9-8, 700D2
Wire markers price fixing chrgd 9-21, 769B1
Kennecott victory over Curtiss-Wright voided, new electn ordrd 9-28, 752D2
Lead-pollutn rule issued 9-29, 754D1
Zambia reopens Rhodesia RR 10-10, 783A3
World price rise linked to forgn unrest, productn cuts 10-20, 805B1
Spain-Peru trade talks 11-22—11-26, 967A3
Chile trade boycott set by US, forgn unions 11-24; impact rptd 12-15, 1014G1
Kennecott, Curtiss-Wright settle 12-15, 1004G3
COPS (play)
Opens 3-28, 760F1
CORBETT, Brad
Vs Kuhn bar on Blue sale 3-3, 194F3
CORBITT v. New Jersey
NJ murder sentencing system upheld by US Sup Ct 12-11, 981C1
CORCORAN, Dan
Loses US House electn 11-7, 856F3
CORCORAN, Rep. Tom (R, Ill.)
Reelected 11-7, 850E3
CORDEN-Lloyd, Lt. Col. Ian
Killed in Ulster copter crash 2-17, IRA claims credit 2-18, facts on 132G2
CORDOBA, Alcira Rios de
Kidnaped 7-23, 792E3
CORDOBA, Luis
Kidnaped 7-23, 792E3
CORDOBA Rivas, Rafael
Bars 'dialogue' with Somoza 1-15, 73D3
On gen strike vs Somoza 2-7, 91B1
On Nicaragua oppositn comm 9-14, 705C3
CORE—*See CONGRESS of Racial Equality*
CORFU Island—*See GREECE*
CORLEY, Al
Taxi Tales opens 12-29, 1031A3
CORMAN, Gene
F.I.S.T. released 4-26, 619A2
CORMAN, Rep. James C. (D, Calif.)
Backs gas price compromise 8-17, 677B3, D3
Reelected 11-7, 850F1
CORN—*For feed grain, see GRAIN*
USSR orders rptd 2-28, 151G2
Farm aid, target price hike clears Sen 3-21, 218B3
Carter OKs set-aside paymt, sees income hike 3-29, 219C1, B2
Colombia '77 trade data rptd 5-19, 414F1
Argentina, China sign pact 6-9, 793A3
USSR purchases from US rptd 8-3, 634B3
Chile imports up 10-6, 796E1
US aid to Tanzania rptd 11-15, 870G2
USSR purchases from US rptd 12-26, 1020B3

1979

COOK Islands (New Zealand territory)
US co fined for '78 electn fraud role 8-2, 648A2
COOLIDGE, Calvin (1872-1933)
Phone monitoring claimed 10-21, 869C1
COOLIDGE, Rita
Performs in Cuba 3-1—3-4, 238D2
COOLIDGE 4th, Thomas Jefferson
Stuart portraits go to Natl Gallery 4-10, 375B1
COOLS-Lartigue, Sir Louis (Dominican president)
Resigns 6-16, 468E2
COONEY, Ray
Whose Life opens 4-17, 712E3
COOPER, Cecil
AL batting ldr 9-30, wins Golden Glove Award 11-20, 955F3, 956C1
COOPER, Jackie
Wins Emmy 9-9, 858D2
COOPER, Joseph W.
Martin punches 10-23, 1002C1
COOPER, Richard
Seeks Iran sanctns in W Ger 12-6, 934A1
COOPER, Robert
Running released 11-2, 1008D1
COOPER, Sydney
Guilty in dredging fraud 5-5, 352A2
Sentenced 6-11, 468C2
COOPERATIVE Apartments—*See HOUSING*
COOPER Industries Inc.
Gardner-Denver acquired 1-22, 89B1
1st ¼ merger rise rptd 4-10, 349B3
COOPER Laboratories Inc.
Long-wear contact lenses OKd 6-13, 572E1
COORDINATING Council In North America
Carter signs Taiwan relatns bill 4-10, 259B3
COPACABANA (recording)
Manilow wins Grammy 2-16, 336D3
COPE—*See MEDICINE–Drugs*
COPE, Newton
Radziwill postpones wedding 5-3, 392B2
COPELYN, John
'76 ban lifted 9-17, 732F2
COPLEY Plaza Hotel (Boston, Mass.)
Fire 3-29, busboy chrgd 3-30, 316C3
COPOLLA, Michael
Indicted 3-6, 220D2
COPPALINO, Dr. Carl A.
Paroled in Fla 10-16, 839G2
COPPER & Brass
Zaire mining recovery rptd 1-25, 2-15, 137A3
Peru miners strike 3-13—3-30, 255C2
Anaconda sets Chile exploratn 5-10, 369B3
Canada strike continues 5-12, 369F1
Iran industries natlzd 7-5, 503F2
China-PI pact signed 7-8, 567C1
BP to join Australia mining project 7-27, 580G2
S Australia mining dvpt seen 9-16—9-17, 749D2; projct OKd 10-9, 811A1
US penny minting cost, copper price linked 9-25, 727D2
Copper price soars 10-2, 740G1-A2
Zimbabwe warns Zambia 11-5, 844G2; cuts rail links 11-18, 899E2
Copper trading squeeze cited 12-31, 978A3
COPPOLA, Francis
Apocalypse Now released 8-15, 819D3
COPPOLLA, Leonardo
Slain 7-12, 548B1
COPYRIGHTS
Sony video recorder trial opens 1-22, 120E2
China-US pact signed 7-7, 523F2
Video recorder use upheld 10-2, 858G2
CORBELLINI, Francesco
Nominated Italy elec bd head 1-8, 21B1
CORCORAN, Des
Succeeds Dunstan as S Australia premr 2-15, 153B1
Loses S Australia electns 9-15, resigns 9-18, 749F1
CORCORAN, Judge Howard F.
NSA upheld on withholding data 10-29, 945E3
CORDERO, Angel
Instrument Landing wins Wood Meml 4-21, 448C3
COREA, Chick
Group wins Grammy 2-16, 336E3
CORENSWET Inc.—*See SELECT Brands*
CORENSWET Inc. v. Amana Refrigeration Inc.
Case refused by Sup Ct 10-29, 884B1
COREY, George
GOP wins US House seat 4-3, 265G1
CORIOLANUS (play)
Opens 3-14, 292C1; 6-28, 711C2
CORLL, Dean (d. 1973)
Henley convicted again 6-27, 819D1
CORMACK, Allan McLeod
Wins Nobel Prize 10-12, 858E1
CORMAN, Avery
Kramer vs Kramer released 12-19, 1007F3
CORMAN, Rep. James C. (D, Calif.)
Sponsors new welfare plan 5-23, 384A2
CORN
USSR '78-79 purchases rptd 3-15, 237D3
US price rises, Sovt crop blamed 7-2, orders confirmed 7-5, 567D3, G3
China-US pact signed 7-7, 523G2
US hikes USSR sale limit 8-1, 636D3
Brazil '78 exports to Spain rptd 8-6, 654B2
US '78 record harvest cited 9-21, 722E1
US harvest noted 10-1, 774D3
US OKs USSR '79-80 record sale limit, '78-79 sales totaled 10-3, 774B3

1980

COOK Islands—*See also ADB*
Island trade pact rptd 7-24, 576G2
COOMBS, W. P.
Swimming carnivorous dinosaurs rptd 3-14, 415G2
COONTZ (U.S. destroyer)
Trible says unfit, scores deploymt 6-30, 517F3
COOPER, Cecil
AL batting ldr 10-6, 926D3-F3
Wins Golden Glove Award 12-6, 926D1
COOPER, Christopher W.
Of the Fields opens 5-27, 756F3
COOPER, D. B.
'71 hijack money believed found 2-10—2-13, 136E2
COOPER, Earl
In NFL draft 4-29, 336F2
COOPER, John R.
USAC dissolves Champ Racing League 6-30, 1002F1
COOPERATIVE League of the U.S.A.
Anderson dies 6-25, 528A1
COORS Co., Adolph
Calif trust case declined by Sup Ct 2-19, 131D1
COPELAND, Rhonda
Abortn funding cases argued in Sup Ct 4-21, 7306G2
COPLAND, Aaron
Appalachian Spring wins Grammy 2-27, 296F3
COPOLLA, Michael
Sentenced 5-20, 927A3
COPOLYMER Rubber and Chemical Corp.
La chem-dump suit names 7-15, 558G3
COPPER & Brass
Chile '79 export earnings rptd 1-14, 19B3
Futures hit record high, Kennecott hikes prices 1-17, 30F3
Chile workers strike 1-19, 57E1
Comex limits futures trading, impact seen 1-24; prices drop 1-28, rebound 1-29, 69A1
USSR buying noted 2-5, 85E1
Comex prices hit record, fall 2-12—8-27, 805G2
Poland '79 exports rptd 2-26, 166A2
PNG OKs consortium dvpt 3-10, 194G3
Medit pollutn pact signed 5-17, 381C3
USW strike drags on 7-1—10-24; Kennecott, Phelps Dodge settle 8-27, 10-8, 805D2
Anaconda to close 2 Montana units 9-30, 825F2
USW settles with Asarco 11-10, strike ends 11-21, 987E3
Polish productn drop rptd 11-21; govt retains productn control 11-19, 878F2, C3
Comex prices rise 11-12, 987G3
Phelps Dodge sells Consolidated Alum share 11-23, 985C2
Zambia price drop cited 12-4, 969A3
Price drops on higher US interest rates 12-10, 932A2
'80 futures price down 12-31, 985A1
COPPOLA, Francis Ford
Brown quits pres race 4-1, 246D3
COPYRIGHTS
Photocopy co sued 2-5, 119F3
Photocopy suit rptd setld 3-21, 376C3
Cable-TV distant signal, syndicatn limits lifted 7-22, 583G1
Calif artist royalties case declined by Sup Ct 11-10, 868D2
Computer progrm protectn clears Cong 11-21, 915F3
CORBETT, William
Wounded 11-14, 994C1
CORCORAN, Judge Howard
Overturns Letelier murder convictns 9-15, 703F3
CORCORAN, Rep. Tom (R, Ill.)
Reelected 11-4, 842E3
CORDDRY, Charles
Panelist in pres TV debate 9-21, 721C3
CORDERO Jr., Angel
Codex wins Preakness, 5-17; victory upheld 6-4, 447C2
Errico convicted, Amy implicates 5-19, 447C3
CORDOVA—*See ILLINOIS*
CORDOVA Rivas, Rafael
Named to El Salvador junta 5-18, 390C1 *
Denies Somoza death role 9-17, 697E3
On Bluefields riot 10-1, 792G1
COREA, Chick
Wins Grammy 2-27, 296E3
COREY Jr., Ernest N.
Appeal refused by Sup Ct 4-14, 307B1
CORMAN, Rep. James C. (D, Calif.)
Loses reelection 11-4, 837E2, 846G1, 852A2
CORN
US rpts Sovt orders 1-3, suspends futures trading 1-6, 2C1-E1
US to buy Sovt contracts 1-7, 9F2
Iowa State of State message 1-15, 269A2
US studies crop 'diversn' paymts 1-18, 44F3
US Jan farm prices rptd down 1-31, 92F2
Ia grain elevator scandal rptd 2-25, 237F3
US crop 'diversn' paymt plan dropped, price rise cited 2-29, 169B1
US Mar farm price drop rptd 3-31, 263F3
USSR-Argentine 1st 1/4 trade rptd 4-15, 336G1
Iowa farm cancer study rptd 4-15, 357D3
USSR purchase of US soybeans in W Eur rptd 5-23, 431C1
US May farm price rptd up 5-30, 425D1
Mex crop threatened by drought 6-13, 524B2
US drought damage rptd 6-23—8-15, 616C2

1976

FDA bans Red #2 dye 1-19, 44D2
Hungary-Sovt barter pact rptd 4-1, 543A3
US sales to USSR rptd 4-28—5-4, 321G2
Latin maize output rptd 5-7, 466C1
US sales to USSR rptd 7-7—7-14, 540C2
US-USSR sale total rptd 8-31, 665E2
US-Sovt sale rptd 10-6, 752B2
US rpts record crop 10-12, 787E3
Ford hikes support rate 10-13, 787D3
US '76 record crop rptd 12-10, 983D3
Export Probe—*See under GRAIN*
CORNELL, Rep. Robert J. (D, Wis.)
Reelected 11-2, 831A4
CORNELL University (Ithaca, N.Y.)
Bethe gets Science Medal 10-18, 858C3
CORNFELD, Bernard
Convicted 8-15, sentncd 9-27, 860G2
CORNWELL, David L.
Elected 11-2, 823B2, 829C3
CORONADO National Bank (Denver, Colo.)
Closed 6-25, 495G1
CORONADO National Memorial (Ariz.)
Sen bars new mining claims 2-4, 135A2
Mining curbs signed 9-28, 834B2
CORPUZ, Victor
Captured 8-27, 695A1
CORRENT Jr., Domennic
Indicted 1-19, 44D1
CORRIGAN, Mairead
Car attacked 10-10, 773F3
Ulster peace rally in London 11-27, 1008E1
CORRIGAN, Richard
Lauds gun control bill vote 3-2, 170B2
CORSICA—*See under FRANCE*
CORTAZAR, Julio
Russell ct meets 1-10—1-17, 61E2
CORTEZ Pereira Araujo, Jose
Loses pol rights 8-4, 850F3
CORVALAN, Luis
Exchgd for Bukovsky 12-18, 955D2-E3
Chile arrests ex-secy 12-20, 999E2
CORVALAN Nanclares, Ernesto
Loses cabt post 1-15, 71B2
CORY Jr., Ernest N.
Mistrial in Mandel case 12-7, 922C3
COSGRAVE, Liam
Sends regrets re deaths 1-5, 19D2
Sees Wilson 3-5, 277G3
Scores UK amb slaying 7-21, 538G2
Asks state of emergency 8-31, 676F1, B2
O Dalaigh resigns 10-22, 837E3
Hillery named pres-elect 11-9, 873F1
Takes over defense post 12-2, 1006C2
COSMETICS & Toiletries
FDA bans Red #2 dye 1-19, 44A2
Red #2 ct challenge 1-27—2-13; FDA ban in effect 2-12, 137C1
FDA seeks chloroform ban 4-6, 249D2
Dem platform text 6-15, 471F2
Red #2 ban upheld 7-6, 571B1
Carbon black dye banned 9-22, 729A3
FDA bill not cleared 10-2, 883D2
Nigeria natlizatn rptd 10-29, 1007C3
COSMOPOLITAN (magazine)
Peru bans 1-10, 55C3
Peru renews ban 2-3, 142F3
COSMOSSHIPPING Co.
Boycott rpt released 10-18, 786B1
COSSIG, Francesco
Sworn Italy interior min 7-30, 573F1
COSSIGA, Francesco
Italian interior min 2-13, 140B2
COSTA Braz, Lt. Col. Manuel da
Portugal interior min 7-23, 558G1
Spinola ties cited 8-11, 733A1
COSTA Gomes, Gen. Francisco da
Oporto U head scores shooting 1-2, 11C1
Swears cabt members 1-6, 11C2
Names interim premier 6-24, 482D3
COSTANZA, Margaret
Seconds Carter nominatn 7-14, 505G2
COSTA Rica—*See also CACM, IDB, OAS, SELA*
San Jose riots 1-9, Oduber chrgs CP infiltratn 1-16, 123B1
Listed as 'free' nation 1-19, 20B3
Businessmen rptd vs tax hikes 1-20, 123C1
Foreign Relations (misc.)
'75 Chile refugees asylum cited 47F2
Joint US drug drive agreed 1-20, 61A1

1977

CORN, Morton
Replaced as Labor asst secy 3-18, 272F2
CORNELL University (Ithaca, N.Y.)
Rhodes named pres 2-16, 140F2
Rings around Uranus sighted 3-10, 908F2
Racker gets Sci Medal 11-22, 952B1
Nicholas Noyes dies 12-25, 1024E2
CORNING II, Mayor Erastus (Albany, N.Y.)
Reelected to 10th term 11-8, 855C3
CORNING Glass Works
Carter tours UK unit 5-6, 359E2
CORN Refiners Association Inc.
Sup Ct refuses pollutn rules appeal 4-18, 342D1
CORONADO National Forest (Ariz.)
9,000 acres burn 6-22, 660G3
CORPORATIONS—*See BUSINESS*
CORRIGAN, Mairead
NZ to let N Ireland detainees immigrate 2-21, 258D2
Wins Nobel Prize 10-10, 951C2
CORRUPTION, Political—*See under POLITICS*
CORSICA—*See under FRANCE*
CORSIGLIA, Robin
Wins 100-mtr breaststroke 8-18—8-21, 828F3
CORSON, Dale R.
Replaced as Cornell pres 2-16, 140F2
CORTEZ, Ricardo
Dies 4-28, 356A3
CORVALAN, Luis
Chile restores pension 1-5, 18B3
Marchais scores Sovt repressn 1-6, 63D2
CORY Jr., Ernest N.
Convicted 8-23, 652F1, A2 ★
Sentenced 10-7, 807E2
COSETTI, Joseph
3d in Pitts mayor electn 11-8, 855A3
COSGRAVE, Liam
NY gov visits 4-22, 329G1 ★
Govt loses election 6-16, 475G1-A3
Replaced as party ldr 7-1, 530F2
COSMAIR Inc.
Hair dye linked to cancer 10-17, 962G3
COSMETICS & Toiletries
Canada sets saccharin ban 3-9, 177F1
FDA orders fluorocarbon aerosol warning 4-26, 323E1
Fluorocarbon ban proposed 5-11, 387E1
John Powers dies 7-19, 604F3
Listerine ad order upheld 8-2, 613F1-A2
Hair dye linked to cancer 10-17, 12-14, 962D3, 963A1
Coloring dyes banned 12-12, 980G3
COSMETIC, Toiletry and Fragrance Association
Hair dye-cancer link scored 10-17, 962F3
COSSIGA, Francisco
On Italy police union 2-14, 135D3
Rpts terrorist attacks 12-2, 1014B1
COSSITT, Thomas
Accuses RCMP 11-15, 11-23, 923G1
Rpts RCMP files on Trudeau 11-15, chrgs 'Featherbed' info 11-18, 923A2, C2
Chrgs RCMP links with CIA 11-23, 923F1
COSTA, Jose Oliveira
Asks 'death squad' probe 11-7, 964C3
COSTAN, James
Chesimard convicted, sentncd 3-25, 288D3
COSTANZA, Margaret (Midge)
Named Carter asst 1-14, 35F2
Sees gay rights group 3-26, 278B2
Vs Carter abortn curbs 7-15, 786F2
Urges Lance resignation 9-10, 701E3
COSTA Rica—*See also IDB, OAS*
Facio abandons pres bid, reassumes min post 1-9, 48E1
Claramount exiled; Morales, 2 others get emb asylum 2-28, 181A3
PLN, Oppositn Union choose '78 pres candidates 3-13, 506C2
'61-75 GDP variatns table 5-30, 439A1
Villalobos chrgs dropped 7-11, 710C2

1978

CORN Belt—*See MIDWEST*
CORNELL, Rep. Robert J. (D, Wisc)
Loses reelectn 11-7, 854A2
CORNELL University (Ithaca, N.Y.)
DNA yeast transfer rptd 1-21, 333F3
Loses NCAA lacrosse title 5-27, 540A2
CORNICK, L. Carter
Reveals Letelier murder details 6-2, 451G3
CORNING Glass Works
Robert Murphy dies 1-9, 96B3
CORNWELL, Rep. David L. (D, Ind.)
Loses reelectn 11-7, 853A3
COROMINAS Petin, Rafael
Named DR pub works min 8-16, 648D2
CORPORATE Data Exchange (CDE)
S Africa investmt rpt cited 8-29, 669E3
CORPORATIONS—*See BUSINESS; also specific names*
CORPORATION Trust Co.
Kennecott Curtiss-Wright proxy votes counted, 1 mln misplaced 5-2, 403C1
CORRALES, Pat
Hired as Rangers mgr 10-1, 1026G1
CORRECTIONS Magazine
'77 state, natl prison populatn rptd 6-3, 440C1
CORRIGAN, Mairead
To quit peace movemt 4-15, disputes rptd 4-17, 373B1
CORRO, Hugo
Decisns Valdes for middlewgt title 4-22, 379F1
Decisns Harris 8-5, 969D1
Decisns Valdes 11-11, 969F1
CORRUPTION, Political—*See under POLITICS*
CORSI, Jim
Nordiques win WHA All-Star game 1-17, 76F3
CORSICA—*See under FRANCE*
CORTAZAR, Octavio
Teacher released 5-13, 620A1
CORTESI, Gaetano
Sentenced 5-29, 454E2
CORVETTE Summer (film)
Released 8-4, 969G3
CORYELL, Don
Fired as Cardinals coach 2-10, 171B3
Hired as Chargers coach 9-25, 1024A3
CORZINE, Dave
In NBA draft 6-9, 457G2
COSGROVE, James W.
Arrested in A-sub plot 10-4, 824F1
COSGRAVE, Liam
Garvey fired as police chief 1-19, 72D2
COSGROVE, James W.
Convicted 12-19, 992E1
COSKUN, Alev
Named Turkey tourism min 1-5, 21F2
COSMETICS & Toiletries—*See also HAIRDRESSING*
Ingredient label rule upheld 2-12, 231G3-232A1
Hypoallergenic label rule revoked 3-14, 231E3
Fluorocarbon aerosols banned 3-15, 186B2
Avon chrmn quits Stevens bd 3-21, 205D1
Listerine corrective ad review denied by Sup Ct 4-3, 280D3
'77 mail frauds cost $1 bln 4-3, 389G1
USSR, Turkey sign trade pact 4-5, 477D1
BAT industries Yardley, Monteil divisns cited 5-5, 345D3
Boone held liable for acne ads 5-11, 702F2-A3
Polident ad complaint rptd setld 8-31, 702E2
Label challenge refused by Sup Ct 10-10, 789D3
FTC injunctn halts acne cure ads 10-10, 942B1
COSMETIC Surgery—*See MEDICINE—Surgery*
COSMOS (Soviet satellite series)—*See ASTRONAUTICS—Satellites, Earth*
COSSETTE-Trudel, Jacques
Asks amnesty 1-3, 7D1
6th Cross kidnaper hinted 11-2, 880C1
Returns to Canada, arrested 12-13, 964A2
COSSETTE-Trudel, Louise (Louise Lanctot)
Asks amnesty 1-3, 7D1
6th Cross kidnaper hinted 11-2, 880C1
Returns to Canada, arrested 12-13, 964A2
COSSIGA, Francesco
Named Italy interior min 3-11, 191B1
Receives Moro letter 3-29, 246B3
Resigns as Italy interior min 5-10, 338F2
Andreotti takes over Interior post 5-11, 393F2
Replaced as Interior min 6-13, 558C2
COSSITT, Thomas
Cleared re RCMP spy rpt 3-17, 209B1
COSTA Gomes, Francisco da
At Dutch neutron bomb protest 3-18—3-19, 255D1
COSTANZA, Margaret (Midge)
To focus on women's issues 4-19, 306F3
Resigns as Carter aide 8-1, 605G3
COSTA Rica—*See also IDB, OAS*
'77 inflatn rptd under 5% 9-10, 828F2
Press freedom rptd by IAPA 10-13, 829A2
Foreign Relations (misc.)—*See also 'Monetary, Trade, Aid & Investment' below*
Nicaragua chrgs rebel bases 2-2, arms aid 2-3, 91F1
Latin rights abuse oppositn cited 91G2

1979

Zimbabwe bars Zambia shipmts 11-5, 844E2-A3
US rpts USSR purchases 11-28, 928C3
Sovt bloc relief to Cambodia rptd 12-3, 917A2
Mex productn down 18% 12-12, 950C2
Zimbabwe lifts Zambia embargo 12-17, 960G1
US sales to USSR rptd 12-20, 997F2
US record harvest rptd 12-31, 985B1
CORNELL University (Ithaca, N.Y.)
Gottfried cuts Soviet links 3-1, 172B2
NYC med cntr heart transplants rptd 5-6, 355E1
Med educ progrm funding scored 9-10, 734D3
Bethe cited in H-bomb letter 9-16, 9-18, 715G2-A3, 717E1
CORNERSTONE (recording)
On best-seller list 11-7, 892F3
CORNFELD, Bernard
Trial opens 9-24, acquitted 10-15, 817F3
CORNING Glass Works
Percolator recall set 9-4, 902D3
CORONADO, Capt. Robert
Gay rape chrg rejected 10-13, AF dismisses 10-15, 850C3
CORPORATION for Public Broadcasting—*See PUBLIC Broadcasting, Corporation for*
CORPORATIONS—*See BUSINESS; specific names*
CORRAL, Frank
NFL '78 kicking ldr 1-6, 80F1
NFC wins Pro Bowl 1-29, 79E3, G3
CORRETJER, Juan Antonio
Scores Rodriguez's death 11-15, 904C3
CORRO, Hugo
Antuofermo decisns for world middlewgt title 6-30, 838F3
CORRUPTION, Political—*See under POLITICS*
CORSARO, Frank
Whoopee opens 2-14, 292F3
Knockout opens 5-6, 712A1
CORSI, Jim
WHA goaltending ldr 4-18, 355G2
CORSICA—*See under FRANCE*
CORSINO Cardenas, Jose
Ecuador resources min 12-9, 967F3
CORTICOSTEROIDS—*See MEDICINE—Drugs*
CORVALAN, Luis
'76 exchange cited 4-27, 317C1
COSCARELLI, D. A.
Phantasm released 6-1, 820G2
COSCARELLI, Don
Phantasm released 6-1, 820G2
COSENTINO, Jerome
Chicago schls miss payday 12-21, 991G1
COSGROVE, James W.
Sentenced 3-20, 240E2
COSKUN, Alev
Greece tourism pact signed 6-5, 447B2
COSMETICS & Toiletries
Tiffany OKs Avon bid 1-18, 89E1
Schick sues Gillette over razors 6-14, 481D3
Acne ad refunds set 7-2, 596D2
Revlon to buy Technicon 9-6, 664A1
Formaldehyde-cancer link rptd 10-18, 971E1
COSMETIC Surgery—*See MEDICINE-Surgery*
COSMIC Rays
Low-level radiatn risk assessed 5-2, 609F2
COSMOPOLITAN National Bank (Chicago)
Embezzler sentncd 2-25, 156A2
COSMOS (Soviet satellite series)—*See ASTRONAUTICS-Satellites*
COSSETTE-Trudel, Jacques
Sentenced 8-7, 632B3
Lanctot sentncd 11-8, 872F1
COSSETTE-Trudel, Louise
Lanctot returns to Canada, arrested 1-6, 19G1
Sentenced 8-7, 632B3
Lanctot sentncd 11-8, 872D1
COSSIGA, Francesco (Italian premier)
Sworn Italy premier 8-5, 602D3
Wins confidence votes 8-11, 8-12, 615E1
Calls for energy sacrifices 9-14, 708B1
Greets China premr 11-3, 854C2
Suspends ENI head 12-7, 995E3
Sees Vance on Iran 12-11, 933G2
COSTA Lines Inc.
Charter ship burns, sinks off VI 3-30, 316B3
COSTANZO, Sarino R.
Law firm chrgd in visa fraud 6-1, 491E3
COSTA Rica—*See also IDB, OAS*
Cong emergency sessn, pub safety min censured 7-9, 512A3
Economy & Labor
Fuel prices hiked, oppositn scores 1-19, 238A2
Labor unrest hits Limon, pol subversn blamed 8-14—8-23, 667B3

1980

US drought damage final rpt 9-7, 857A3
US Sept farm prices rptd up 9-30, 741C2
US-China trade pact signed 10-22, 801G1
US futures hit 6-yr highs 10-28, 855D1
US '80 futures trading up 12-31, 984G3
Soviet Embargo—*See under GRAIN*
CORNELL, Robert J.
Priests barred from politics 5-4, drops electn bid 5-6, 341D2
CORNELL University (Ithaca, N.Y.)
'79 endowmt earnings rptd 3-24, 319B2
Jordan named business schl dean 5-21, 456F2
Hopkins wins NCAA lacrosse title 5-31, 638C1
Keeton dies 8-17, 676G1
Jordan named dean 9-29, 959D2
CORNERSTONE (recording)
On best-seller list 1-2, 40F3
CORNFELD, Stuart
Fatso released 2-1, 216E2
CORN Growers Association, National
Protests Sovt grain embargo 1-6, 10D1
CORPORATE Accountability Research Group
US releases Arab boycott data 10-20, 801B1
CORPORATIONS—*See BUSINESS*
CORPUS Christi—*See TEXAS*
CORRAL, Frank
Rams win NFL conf title 1-6, 8G1
Steelers win Super Bowl 1-20, 61C3-62C1
UCLA transcript scandal rptd 2-22, 469F2
CORRALES, Pat
Fired as Rangers mgr 10-5, 926A3
CORRIE, John
Bill sparks pro-abortn demonstratn 2-8, 132G3
CORRIVEAU, Leopold
Wins by-electn 3-24, 230F3
CORT, Stewart
Dies 5-25, 448D1
CORTESE, Joseph
Windows released 1-18, 216G3
CORYELL, Don
Named NFL top coach 1-9, 175C1
COSGROVE, Paul
Canada public works min 3-3, 171C2
COSME, Joao Batista
Ousted in Mozambique Cabt shuffle 3-21, 234E2
COSMETICS& Toiletries
TV ad rates rptd soaring 4-4, 376D2
Tighter chem controls urged 6-29, 494A3
Revlon heir indicted 8-19, 713F3
COSMOS (book)
On best-seller list 12-7, 948E3
COSMOS (Soviet satellite series)—*See ASTRONAUTICS--Satellites*
COSSIGA, Francesco (Italian premier)
Socialists end support 1-18, 59F2
Parlt OKs security rules 2-14, 98F3
Evangelisti quits Cabt 3-4, 173A2
On banking system 3-7, 212C3
Submits Cabt resignatn 3-19, 212D2
Postpones EC summit 3-24, 242G1
Heads new govt 4-4, 275A3, F3
On govt aims 4-14, 314C1
Chrgs vs Formica rptd 4-17, 314E1
Govt wins confidence vote 4-20, 314C1
At Tito funeral 5-8, 339B1
Cleared in terrorist tipoff scandal 5-29—5-31; CP vows full probe 6-2, coalitn scores 6-3, 430B1-D2
Local electns back 6-8—6-9, 445D2
Rpts EC mission to Mideast 6-13, 449E1
Carter visits Rome 6-19—6-21, 474A2
Sees Trudeau on A-reactors 6-24, 486F1
Parlt upholds terrorist tipoff innocence 7-27, 578G3
Wins confidence vote 7-31, 605A2
Visits Bologna after bombing 8-2, 605D1
OKs Alfa Romeo, Nissan project 9-20, 751B3
Loses econ vote, govt resigns 9-27; Forlani agrees to form govt 10-2, 751F1, A3
Fiat tentative labor pact set 10-15, 791F2
Forlani sworn premr 10-18, 808G3
COSTA Rica—*See also IDB, OAS*
Economy & Labor
Banana workers' strike ends 1-17, '79 data rptd 2-1, 117C1
Foreign Relations (misc.)—*See also 'Monetary' below*
Amb held hostage in El Salvador 1-11, freed 1-14, 38G3
Colombia amb seized in DR Emb raid, freed 2-27, 141B3, 311C3

1976

Exchng rates for imports rptd scored 1-20, 123C1
Takes Chile pol refugees, Chile asks extraditn 2-2, 99G3
Abstains on UN rights comm resolutn vs Israel 2-13, 125E2
Kissinger visits 2-23—2-24, 177A1, 178E1
Total IMF oil loan rptd 4-1, 340C2
Pascal extraditn to Chile denied 4-9, 288C3
Carter on Sovts 6-24, 490A2
IAPA, UNESCO press parleys 7-12—7-21, 619C3
US sugar duties tripled 9-21, 721D3
Figueres sued in US 9-22, 1000G2
Vs UN Gaza resetlmt resolutn 11-23, 878F2

Vesco Developments

Vesco, 6 others indicted 1-14, 78D2
'Vesco Law' repealed 11-2, 1000E2, F2 ★

COSTELLO, John A.
Dies 1-5, 56B3
COSTELLO, John M.
Dies 8-28, 892F2
COT, Jean-Pierre
Scores Tindemans rptd 1-29, 119C3
COTTER, Rep. William R. (D, Conn.)
Reelected 11-2, 829G1
COTTON
US budgets boll weevil drive 1-21, 66D2
Turkey export decline rptd 4-1, 315A2
France proposes price stabilizatn fund 5-10—5-11, 355E3
UNCTAD OKs commodity fund 5-30, 388G2
US warns NY commodity exchng 9-15, 990D2
EEC-Rumania pact rptd 11-12, 907F2
COTTON, Robert
Japan auto projects OKd 6-10, 438B3
COTTRELL, William C.
Slain 8-28, 652G1
COUGHLIN, Rep. Lawrence (R, Pa.)
Reelected 11-2, 830E3

1977

'78 pres campaign under way, 6 candidates rptd 9-2, 710A2

Foreign Relations (misc.)—*See also 'Monetary, Trade & Aid' below*

UN Assemb member 3F3
Oduber backs Panamanian Canal demands 1-18, 46G1
Vs UN resolutn on Israel occupatn rule 2-15, 107E2
El Salvador pol refugees accepted 4-19, 373C2
Panama seeks Guatemala mediatn 5-27, 415A1
Oduber sees Torrijos, regional ldrs 8-5—8-6; new Panama Canal pact backed, coffee fund set 8-6, 606B3, 608A3
US backs UN rights comr 8-8—8-9, 646G2
Oduber at Canal pact signing 9-7, 678C1
Canal pact grants transit right 9-7, 683E2
Spanish king visits 9-15—9-16, 804G3
Nicaragua plotters seized 9-25, 767A3
Oduber backs Belize independnc 9-30, 786D1
Nicaragua guerrillas begin offensive 10-12, 802D1, E2
Nicaragua border closed; boat strafed, chrgs exchngd 10-13—10-16, 802C3
Nicaragua rebels, deserter harbored 10-26—10-27, 865A1
Nicaragua border dispute probed by OAS 10-26, 865E1
Abstains on UN anti-Israel res 10-28, 830G2

Monetary, Trade & Aid Issues (including all foreign economic developments)

'75-76 trade, paymts table 3-11, 189A2 ★, B2
Intl Coffee Fund set 8-6, 608A3
Brazil coffee policy backed 10-21, 876C3

U.S. Relations

Carter for rights conv ratificatn 4-14, 295D2
Figueres links Monge, CIA 4-23, 506D2
Weissman confrmd amb 5-25, 500D1
Mrs Carter visits, beef exports discussed 5-31—6-1, 454E1, F2
Oduber backs rights stand 6-5, 454A3
Oduber lauds Panama Canal talks 8-6, 606C3
Young visits, backs UN rights comr 8-8—8-9, 646E1, F2
Oduber at Canal pact signing 9-7, 678C1
Canal pact grants transit right 9-7, 683E2

Vesco Developments

Pol financing scandal rptd 4-23—6-13, 506A1
Villalobos fires on Vesco home 6-2, 506A2
Cos rptdly chrgd re '75 gas distributors natlizatn 6-11, 506B2
Vesco wins libel suit, fraud trial ordrd 9-12, 767D1
ICC settles IOS Vesco claims 12-7, 980G2

COSTELLO, Declan
UK torture hearings 4-19—4-22, 315A3-F3
COSTELLO, Seamus
Killed 10-5, 782E3
COSTELLO v. Wainwright
1-judge prison ruling upheld 3-21, 230A3
COSTLE, Douglas M.
EPA admin 2-16, confrmd 3-4, 211E1
On air pollution stand 4-18, 322F2
OKs NH A-plant 6-17, 498D2
Proposes lead pollutn rule 12-12, 1007A3
Clean air 'long way' off 12-21, 1007F2
Plans chemicals inventory 12-22, 1007B2
COST-of-Living Index (COL)—*See ECONOMY, subheads 'Inflation' and 'Prices'; also country names*
COT, Jean-Pierre
Giscard scores US talks 4-2, 255D2
COTE, Corrine
In Levesque car mishap 2-6, 113D3
COTLER, Irwin
Urges Canada Arab boycott law 1-13, 60B3
COTTAGE Grove, Ore.—*See OREGON*
COTTEN, Robert
Named Australia counsul-gen in NY 12-19, 982F1
COTTON
US Feb WPI rise rptd 3-10, 176E2
Carter farm plan outlined 3-23, 214D1
Drought hits Tex High Plains 3-24, 244F3
Ga drought crop damage rptd 7-28, 659F3
Egypt curbs Sovt, Czech trade 8-14, 636A3
Farm bill signed, target prices detailed 9-29, 736D2, C3, F3
'77 disaster aid ceiling lifted by Cong 10-25, 833C3; signed 11-8, 1001E2
Egypt bans Sovt, Czech exports 10-26, 811F3
Central African Empire exports cited 946B3
COTTON, Robert
ASEAN trade criticism rejctd 7-9, 561A1
On car import quotas 7-12, 560E3
COTZIAS, Dr. George C.
Dies 6-13, 532G2
COULTER, Jessie L.
Kidnaps 8 2-11, chrgd 2-13, 163F1
Sentenced 9-12, 712G1

1978

Nicaragua pres land expropriatn planned 2-22, 151A1
El Salvador peasants, students seize emb 4-11—4-18, 723C3 ★
Nicaragua guerrilla seized 4-13, 376A2
Carazo at Panama Canal pact instrumts exchng 6-16, 463F2, 464A1
Nicaraguan dissidents return home 7-5, 593E1
Amer rights conv enacted, ct set 7-18, 828F3, 829A1
Nicaragua unrest role denied 7-28, 617F2
El Salvador guerrilla manifesto publshd 8-25, 722B2, 723F2 ★
Venez offers troops vs Nicaragua 9-13, Nicaragua oppositn weighs mediatn 9-14, 705C3, E3
UN Assemb member 713D3
Nicaragua pres estate ordrd seized 9-22, 823E2; Somoza scores 10-14, 839B3
Nicaragua guerrillas seized; deported to Venez, Panama 10-13, 839D3
Nicaragua censured by OAS for air raid 10-17, 839A3
Nicaragua troops drive guerrillas back 10-30, 839A2
Nicaragua refugees stream in 11-6, 883D2
Nicaragua border clashes, ties broken 11-21; Somoza closes border 12-26, 1018G3
Nicaragua border violatns scored by UN 12-15, 1019D1

Government & Politics—*See also other appropriate subheads in this section*

Figueres PLN control rptd lost 1-14, 89B3
Carazo elected pres 2-5, 89E2
Carazo names Cabt 3-4, 170G3
Carazo sworn pres 5-8, 354D2
Figueres reelected PLN chief 9-29, 823F2

Monetary, Trade, Aid & Investment'

Coffee exports to be withheld 3-10, 181B3
US urges Nicaragua rebel aid ended 12-11, 1018F3

U.S. Relations—*See also 'Vesco' below*

Mrs Carter at Carazo inaugural 5-8, 354D2
Carter consults on DR electn 5-19, 414C2
Carazo at Canal pact instrumts exchng 6-16, 463F2, 464A1
Nicaragua rebel aid end urged 12-11, 1018F3

Vesco Developments

Carazo vows Vesco ouster 2-7, 89C3; 2-22, 152C2
Asks CR citizenship, new govt to deny 2-23, 152B2
Indicted, posts bail 3-16, 269C3
Fraud chrgs dismissed, begins forgn trip 4-30, 354E2
Vesco appeals to Carazo 5-6, 478E3
Expulsn hinted by Carazo, reentry bar rptd 5-8, 354D2
Vesco in Bahamas, plans return to CR 5-11, 478C3
Fraud suit dismissal upheld 6-22, Carazo bars return 7-7, 558C3
Vesco denied citizenship 7-19, 617D2; appeal rejcted by ct 8-23, 671D2

COSTELLO, Larry
Named Bulls coach 6-5, 656D1
COSTLE, Douglas
Sets fines for chem spills 3-3, 163G3
Blocks Denver dam permit 5-25, 409D1
Denies Ohio clean-air delay 7-6, 513G1
OKs Seabrook cooling plan 8-4, 609B2
Proposes coal-fired utilities install scrubbers 9-11, 703G1
Fuel econ ratings issued 9-15, 719A3
Lead-pollutn rule issued 9-29, 754E1
Named Regulatory Cncl dir 10-31, 863C3
Toxic-waste rules proposed 12-14, 982E3
COST of Living (COL)—*See ECONOMY—Price Indexes; country names*
COTTER, Rep. William R. (D, Conn.)
Reelected 11-7, 850D2
COTTON
US pesticide sales curbed 2-15, 163B3
Paraguay '77 output up 2-17, 292E3
US-Taiwan textile agrmt rptd 2-27, 140C3
Farm aid clears Sen 3-21, 218F2-D3
Carter OKs planting cut paymts 3-29, 219C1, B2
US pesticide ban eased 3-30, 263D3
Farm aid defeated in House 4-12, 261C1
Farm bill compromise clears Cong 5-4, 343C1
Argentina, China sign pact 6-9, 793A3
Dust-exposure rules issued, suits filed 6-19, 471C3
E Ger-Brazil deal rptd 7-13, 649D1
DBCP pesticide curb asked 9-19, 719D2
Nicaragua '77 export drop cited re loan plea 11-1, 883B3
Bergland ends China visit, sees sales rise 11-14, 901G3-902A1
COTTON Bowl—*See FOOTBALL—Collegiate*
COUCH, Jerome B.
Loses US Sen electn 11-7, 849A3
COUGHLAN, Raymond
Loses Sen primary in NH 9-12, 736E1
COUGHLIN, Rep. Lawrence (R, Pa.)
Reelected 11-7, 852D1
COUGH Syrup—*See MEDICINE—Drugs*

1979

Foreign Relations (misc.)—*See also 'UN' below*

Nicaragua scores rebel aid 1-9, 21G3
Nicaragua border clashes continue 1-19, 76B3
Cuba pol prisoner entry OKd 2-2, 238F1
Venez rifle loan rptd 3-23, 238G1
UK reduces Nicaragua ties 3-29, 255B2
Nicaragua rebel arms-smuggling rptd 4-5, 254F3
Nicaragua patrols border 4-7—4-9, 269A3
El Salvador Emb seized 5-4, amb escapes 5-7, 370F3, 371A1
Carazo in Mex 5-20, Latin joint missn dispatched 5-21, 409A1
Nicaragua denounces rebel aid 5-27, 409D2
Nicaragua rebels launch offensive 5-29, 409G1, B2
Nicaragua warns 6-3; rebel aid curbs asked, border policing rejctd 6-4, 427D1
Andean Group warns Nicaragua 6-11, 446F3
Nicaragua pilot defects 6-13, 446E2
Nicaragua rebels launch southn offensive 6-16—6-17, 461C1
Tunisia intercepts Nicaragua rebel arms 7-11, 512E2
3 Sovt envoys ousted in labor unrest 8-19, 667B3
Matos, 26 other prisoners arrive 10-22, 812E2
Panama dissident coup plot fails 10-24, 836D3

UN Policy & Developments

Membership listed 695G2

U.S. Relations

US indicts 5 in Nicaragua arms plot 5-14, 386D3
US AF unit lands 7-8, ordered out 7-10, 512F2-A3
US embezzler's alleged murder rptd 8-20, 851E1

COSTELLO, Dolores
Dies 3-1, 272C2
COSTELLO, Larry
Fired as Bulls coach 2-16, 290D3
COSTELLO, Maurice (1877-1950)
Daughter dies 3-1, 272C2
COSTLE, Douglas M.
Presents diesel exhaust rule 1-10, 16B3
On anti-pollutn costs, gains 1-19, 129E3
Smog standard eased 1-26, 90E1
Regulatory calendar issued 2-28, 164F2
New fines proposed 3-21, 206F2
RR-yard noise rules proposed 4-16, 282C1
Hails US Steel agrmt 5-22, 385C2, F2
On coal-use rules 5-25, 403G3
No-lead gas output incentives set 6-4, 418B3, E3
Waste cleanup proposed 6-13, 441A2
To see Canada environmt min 7-26, 581F2
Lauds chem dump-site rpt 11-1, 886C1
On clean-air rule revisn 12-3, 924G3
COST of Living (COL)—*See ECONOMY-Price Indexes; country names*
COTE, Corinne
Weds Levesque 4-12, 392D2
COTTON
US-China textile talks collapse 5-30, US sets quotas 5-31, 405E3
US-China pact signed 7-7, 523G2
Nicaragua export controls set, '78 trade cited 8-9, 616E1
Cook sale to Mitsui cited 9-26, 727C3
COUGHLIN, Rev. Charles E.
Dies 10-27, 860D2

1980

300 Cuban refugees offered asylum, flights from Havana begin 4-16, 285B1
Cuba refugee flights suspended 4-18, 10,000 offered asylum 4-20; flights resume 4-24, 300C2, B3
Colombia envoy freed from DR Emb 4-19, 311C3
Cuba refugee conf opens 5-8, 361B1, A2
Cuba bars refugee talks 5-23, 396G1
Emb in El Salvador occupied by leftists 7-11, 563G2
Carazo protests Cuba refugee policy, shuns Nicaragua anniv fete 7-15, 565G2
El Salvador Emb refugees granted asylum 7-25, 203 flown to San Jose 7-26, 633D3
Carazo in Peru for Belaunde inauguratn 7-28, 579E3
Mex, Venez ldrs visit 8-3, 605C3
UN Cncl seat try ended 11-12, 896D1
Cuba ex-offcl asks UN probe prison hunger strike 12-4, 965D2
Bolivia coup condemned by Santa Marta conf 12-17, 992A3

Monetary, Trade, Aid & Investment

Mex '80 oil imports seen 1-15, 60B2
IMF '79 austerity pkg, standby credit rptd 2-1, 117F1
Mex, Venez sign oil supply guarantee 8-3, 605D3

COSTLE, Douglas M.
On diesel exhaust rules 2-21, 146B1
On toxic waste rules 2-26, 145E3
In Detroit re auto aid 7-7, 505A2
Disputes Reagan remark 10-8, 779F2
On scenic area air rules 11-25, 898C2
COSTLE v. Pacific Legal Foundation
Case decided by Sup Ct 3-18, 226D3
COTRONE, Joseph
Sentenced 1-11, 64A2
COTTEN, Joseph
Hearse released 6-7, 675G2
COTTER, Mick
Aborigines protest mining 5-8, 371D1
COTTER, Rep. William R. (D, Conn.)
Reelected 11-4, 842D2, 848C1
COTTON
Peru crop hit by drought 2-8, 234E3
Hunts bailout loan collateral listed 5-28, 425F3
Mex crop threatened by drought 6-13, 524B2
US drought damage rptd 6-23—8-15, 616C2
Tex hurricane losses rptd 8-13, 621B3
OSHA dust standard case accepted by Sup Ct 10-6, 782C1
US '80 futures trading up 12-31, 984G3
COTTONWOOD, Joe
Famous Potatoes wins Amer Book Award 5-1, 692D2
COUGHLIN, Rep. Lawrence (R, Pa.)
Reelected 11-4, 844D1

1976

COUNCIL Bluffs, Ia.—*See IOWA*
COUNCIL for Latin America—*See COUNCIL of the Americas*
COUNCIL for Mutual Economic Assistance (Comecon) (Bulgaria, Cuba, Czechoslovakia, East Germany, Hungary, Mongolia, Poland, Rumania, USSR, Yugoslavia)
EC trade talks open 2-16, 164E1
Brezhnev cites econ integratn progress 2-24, 194E2
'71-75 econ growth rptd up 3-18, 4-28, 341C3
USSR-Hungary barter pact rptd 4-1, 543A3
'75 Sovt trade rptd 5-5, 340G3
Summit sets goals 7-7—7-9, 722B2
EEC rejcts trade plan 11-15, 955E1
'75 trade deficit rptd 11-18, 977C1
Currency exchng rptd eased 12-17, 977A1
COUNCIL of the Americas
'70 anti-Allende aid offer rptd 12-23, 999B2
COUNCIL on Hemispheric Affairs—*See HEMISPHERIC Affairs, Council on*
COUNTER-Cyclical Aid—*See 'State-Local Aid' under U.S. GOVERNMENT—BUDGET*
COURSE of Time, The (film)
Wins Cannes award 5-28, 460G1
COURT, Sir Charles
Rpts steel project deferred 2-24, 154D3
Australia-Japan iron deal rptd 9-23, 770E3
Alumina refinery approved 12-9, 961F3

1977

COUNCIL for Mutual Economic Assistance (COMECON) (Bulgaria, Cuba, Czechoslovakia, East Germany, Hungary, Mongolia, Poland, Rumania, USSR; observers: North Korea, Vietnam, Yugoslavia)
To build Cuba A-plant 1-6, 19D3
Sovt oil price hike rptd 1-6, 67E3
Jamaica to seek pacts 1-19, talks rptd 1-28, 257E2
OECD '76 trade gap rptd 1-26, 123A2
W Ger '76 trade rptd 2-9, 102C2
Katushev named USSR rep 3-16, 306D3
Sovt '76 trade surplus up 3-21, 285B2
Sovt '76 oil exports rptd 6-11, 513F1
Premrs meet, stress energy needs 6-21—6-23, 513D1
EC formal talks OKd 9-21, 771C2
International Bank for Economic Cooperation (IBEC)
Bank of Amer group cancels loan 1-26, 123D2
COUNCIL of North Atlantic Shipping Associations—*See SHIPPING Associations, etc.*
COUNCIL on Hemispheric Affairs—*See HEMISPHERIC Affairs, Council on*
COUNTERCYCLICAL Aid—*See U.S. GOVERNMENT—BUDGET—Revenue Sharing*
COURAGEOUS (sailboat)
Retains America's Cup 9-18, 828E2
COURIER-Journal, The (Louisville, Ky.)
Presley insert record sales 8-22—8-24, 696F1
COURLANDER, Harold
Accuses Haley 4-22, 356E1
Sues Haley 5-24, 643D1
COURT, Sir Charles
Defends uranium developmt 1-11, 17C2
COURT, Sir John
Liberals win WA electns 2-19, 158D1
COURT, Margaret
Loses Hollywood Va Slims 1-6, 103G3
Loses Chicago Va Slims 2-13, 431E1

1978

COUNCIL for Financial Aid to Education—*See EDUCATION, etc.*
COUNCIL for Mutual Economic Assistance (Comecon) (Bulgaria, Cuba, Czechoslovakia, East Germany, Hungary, Mongolia, Poland, Rumania, USSR, Vietnam; associate member: Yugoslavia; observer: North Korea
Honecker complaint rptd 2-21, 505D1
EC seeks steel export agrmt 3-2, 158C2
Australia wool imports rptd down 4-14, 411A2
Poland default seen unlikely 6-1, 535G2
Summit mtg; Viet joins, Sovt bid for forced econ integratn fails 6-27—6-29, 504F3
OECD rpts '77 Westn debt rise 6-27, 505E1
China ends Viet econ aid 7-3, 504C3
US banks shun loan 8-17, 660D3
COUNCIL of Europe (Austria, Belgium, Cyprus, Denmark, France, Great Britain, Greece, Iceland, Ireland, Italy, Liechtenstein, Luxembourg, Malta, Netherlands, Norway, Portugal, Spain, Sweden, Switzerland, Turkey, West Germany)
Rights ct hears Isle of Man birching chrg 1-17, 36G3
Rights ct clears UK re Irish torture 1-18, 36E3
US Dems score UK re Ulster torture 3-16, 373A3
Rights ct model for Latin ct 7-18, 828F3
Rights ct rejcts Baader jail abuse chrgs vs W Ger 7-19, 651A3
Ulster prisoners plan rights ct plea vs UK 8-8, 630D2
Liechtenstein entry OKd 10-29, 777D2
COUNCIL of Vietnam Veterans—*See VIETNAM Veterans, Council of*
COUNCIL on Foreign Relations—*See FOREIGN Relations, Council on*
COUNCIL on Hemipsheric Affairs—*See HEMISPHERIC Affairs, Council on*
COUNTERSPY (magazine)
CIA attack re agent's death chrgd 1-4, 15A1
COUNTIES, National Association of
Carter urban-aid plan scored 3-27, 218B1
COUNTRY Instrumentalist of the Year (recording)
Robbins wins Grammy 2-24, 316A1
COUPEZ, Therese Ann
Convicted 7-11, 824G2
COURBET, Gustave (1819-77)
Paintings stolen in Marseilles 6-20, 579F1
COURLANDER, Harold
Alexander suit vs Haley dismissed 9-21, 759B3
Haley settles plagiarism suit 12-14, 1029E3
COURTER, James A.
Wins US House seat 11-7, 849C1, 851B3
COURTLAND, Jerome
Return From Witch Mt released 7-14, 970G2

1979

COUNCIL for Mutual Economic Assistance (Comecon) (Bulgaria, Cuba, Czechoslovakia, East Germany, Hungary, Mongolia, Poland, Rumania, USSR, Vietnam; associate member: Yugoslavia)
USSR 1st ¼ oil exports rptd 5-31, 397C1
Summit sets A-power expansn 6-26—6-29, 497E1
Rumania demands Westn money for gas, rejects transferable rubles 8-1, 645E3
International Bank for Economic Cooperation (IBEC)
Transferable ruble system cited 8-1, 645D3
COUNCIL of Europe (Austria, Belgium, Cyprus, Denmark, France, Great Britain, Greece, Iceland, Ireland, Italy, Liechenstein, Luxembourg, Malta, Netherlands, Norway, Portugal, Spain, Sweden, Switzerland, Turkey, West Germany)
Rights ct scores UK press censorship 4-26, 331A1
Lambertini installed cardinal 6-30, 640D2
UK Liberals to press electoral complaint 9-25—9-28, 792C2
COUNCIL on Foreign Relations—*See FOREIGN Relations, Council on*
COUNTERCOUP: The Struggle for Control of Iran (book)
Recalled for 'corrections' 11-10, 886F3
COUNTIES, National Association of
Carter speech planned 7-12, 513D2
Carter details new energy plan 7-16, 532B1, F2
COUNTY Court v. Allen
Case decided by Sup Ct 6-4, 438B3
COUP, The (book)
On best-seller list 2-4, 120B3
COURT, Charles
Export compromise set 4-23, 328C1
Scores Fraser on jobless, state aid 10-11, 832B2
COURTER, Rep. James A. (R, N.J.)
Gas price controls end passed 10-12, reversed 10-24, 848E3

1980

COUNCIL for Mutual Economic Assistance (Comecon) (Bulgaria, Cuba, Czechoslovakia, East Germany, Hungary, Mongolia, Poland, Rumania, USSR, Vietnam; associate member: Yugoslavia)
Kuwait OKs oil sales, 3-2; '79 imports, '80 estimate rptd 3-3 166C1
Fixed prices for Sovt purchases continue 5-29, 451F1
Sovts pledge energy export rise 10-1, 753B3
COUNCIL of Europe (Austria, Belgium, Cyprus, Denmark, France, Great Britain, Greece, Iceland, Ireland, Italy, Liechtenstein, Luxembourg, Malta, Netherlands, Norway, Portugal, Spain, Sweden, Switzerland, Turkey, West Germany)
EC positn on Iran endorsed 4-10, 282A1
COUNTERFEITING—*See under CRIME*
COUP De Tete (Hothead) (film)
Released 1-21, 216D2
COURAGEOUS (yacht)
Eliminated from America's Cup trials 8-25; Turner sells 9-25, 834F1
COURT, Charles
Aborigines protest mining 5-8, 371C1
COURT, Margaret
Evert Lloyd wins French Open 6-7, 606E3
COURTER, Rep. James A. (R, N.J.)
Reelected 11-4, 843B3

1976

COURTS & Legal Profession—*See also U.S. GOVERNMENT, subheads JUDICIARY and SUPREME Court*
ABA conv 2-15—2-17, 136B3-137C1
House OKs trust suits 3-18, 246D3-247B1
Sup Ct bars plea-bargaining case review 5-19, 393D3
Cunningham indicted 5-26, 442A3
Nadjari jurisdictn limited 6-3, indictmts dismissed 8-12—12-22, 1016E1
Sup Ct upholds alien jury duty bar 6-7, 414D2
Free trial transcripts for poor limited 6-10, 552G2
Dem platform text on legal aid 6-15, 471E2
Arrest silence rights affirmed 6-17, 552B3
Defns access to prosecutn info limited 6-24, 553E1
Nadjari dismissed 6-25, 1016D1
Use of nonlawyer judges upheld 6-28, 492E1
Sup Ct lets stand atty out-of-ct talk ruling 6-30, 492D1
State criminal trials without juries upheld 6-30, 552A3 ★
Fed ct illegal evidence challenge curbed 7-6, 534A3
Tax case use of inadmissible criminal evidence OKd 7-6, 535B1
NYS disbars Nixon 7-8, 493C3
Mondale actn on legal aid ruling cited 512A3
GOP conv delegates polled 8-7, 8-8, 616E2
Carter vs Sup Ct actn rules 8-9, 585B1
Carter scores judicial system 8-11, 585A3
GOP platform text 8-18, 604A2
Cong OKs state trust suits 9-16, 728F1
Sup Ct bars review of Ampex class-action ruling 10-4, 807B3
Double jeopardy protectn curbed 10-12, 848D2
Carter on judicial appmts 10-15, 785A2
Sup Ct eases retrial bids 10-18, 867F2
Civil-rights-suit fees bill signed 10-20, 788A2
Forgn natn immunity bill signed 10-21, 835A1
Ford, Carter debate 10-22, 802A2
Ford campaign donatns cited 10-22, 938F3
Sup Ct rules re plea-bargain confessns 11-1, 867D3
Sup Ct bars review of jury bias stand ruling 11-1, 867D3

1977

COURTS & Legal Profession—*See also U.S. GOVERNMENT, subheads JUDICIARY and SUPREME Court; also state names*
Sup Ct refuses Ind ct structure appeal 1-10, 57A2
Ford '78 budget proposals 1-17, 30A2, 32G2, 33D3
Carter inaugural 1-20, 27A2
Sup Ct bars child custody jurisdictn review 1-25, 80F2
Lawyers score regulatory agencies 2-9, 131E3
'59 dual prosecutn ban eased 2-11, 821B1
Carter budget revisions 2-22, 125B2
SC police informant curb voided 2-22, 150B1
Mardian reinstated to Sup Ct bar 2-28, 175B2
Sup Ct backs Ohio attys fee 2-28, 175D2
US issues terrorism rpt 3-2, 484C1
Carter for consumer class-actns 3-5, 171G2
DC reorganizatn upheld 3-22, 231D1-B2
Fed role in state civil actns curbed 3-22, 231B2
EC lawyer mobility OKd 3-23, 269D3
Intra-group grand jury bias affirmed 3-23, 276C2
ABA inmate rights rpt issued 4-26, 383C2
Jail inmate legal aid ordrd 4-27, 383D1
Plea bargaining review backed 5-2, 406D2
Law business boom rptd; largest firms table 5-16, 383F1-C2
Burger cites '69-76 right to counsel cases 5-17, 419A3
Guam Sup Ct jurisdictn curbed 5-23, 444A1
Grand jury witness rights clarified 5-23, 444F2, G2
Burger: too many lawyers 5-27, 444C3
Sup Ct disbars Cook 5-31, 461G3
Ala ct aid bill signed 6-13, 464F3-465A1
NYS political penalty voided 6-13, 517C2
Lawyers legal fee ads OKd 6-27, 538C3
Law groups vs fed no-fault auto insurnc standards 7-18, 595A1
ABA conv: grand jury chngs urged, ad rules set 8-4—8-11, 629F3, 630A1-A2
Sex-bias class actns settled by NBC 8-31, Reader's Digest 11-4, 979A2
Prisoner exchng bill signed 10-28, 834A2
Sup Ct disbars Mitchell, Ehrlichman 10-31, 835A3
Legal scholar scores Sup Ct rulings 10-31, 878E3, 879A1, B2
Dual fed-state prosecutns curbed 11-7, 857A2

1978

COURTS & Legal Profession—*See also U.S. GOVERNMENT, subheads JUDICIARY and SUPREME Court; also state names*
ABA links local govt housing policies, urban segregatn 1-8, 13F3
Segretti law practice suspensn ends 1-27, 172G2
'53, '78 cong membership compared 1-30, 107F2
Burger defends statemt backing trial lawyer 2-12, 107F3
Cong scored re class-actn stand 3-4, 183D1
Fla upholds gays' practice of law 3-20, 327C2
Mass Sup Ct justice suspended 4-13, censured 7-8; resigns 8-6, 844A1
Carter scores lawyers; backs class actns, low-cost optns, other reforms 5-4, 320F2; 5-5, 342B1
Burger urges improved law student skills, discounts Carter criticism 5-16, 388C2
Cong '79 budget target res cleared 5-17, 385F1
Women attys rptd up 5-31, 554E2
Solzhenitsyn scores Western legalism 6-8, 444D2
Garrison sworn La appeals ct judge 6-15, 843G3
Kalmbach reinstated by Calif bar, joins ex-gov's law firm 7-11, 844B1
Burger urges judgeship bill OK, notes caseload rise 7-23, 626D3
ABA conv: Burger renews trial atty attack; legal aid plan rejctd; TV ads, gag-order rules OKd 8-3—8-10, 626G1-C3
State judges meet, back ctroom cameras 8-3; ABA opposes 8-9, 626A3, C3
Class actns vs Firestone rptd 9-22, 835F1
'77 black law schl enrollmt rptd down 10-8, 811C2
Carter signs judgeships bill 10-20, backs merit selectn 11-8, 873C2-C3
Burger receives Stein Award, defends judicial lobbying 10-25, 832E3
DC pensn reform vetoed 11-4, 897F2
Carter econ plan sets fee hike ceiling 12-13, 957B2
Press search shield bill proposed 12-13, 1029D3
Marston Controversy—*See MARSTON, David*
Obituaries
Bryan, Frederick van Pelt 4-17, 356C2
Buzhardt Jr, J Fred 12-16, 1032D2
Chapman, Oscar 2-8, 196D2

1979

COURTS & Legal Profession—*See also U.S. GOVERNMENT, subheads JUDICIARY and SUPREME Court; also state names*
Tex kill-judge-for-hire trial ends 1-22, 64E3
Kennedy offers consumer class actn suits bill 1-31, 308B2
ABA mid-winter mtg: Burger, Bell address; new disciplinary rules OKd; other actns 2-7—2-14, 130C1
Criminal justice costs for drug abuse rptd 2-12, 140C2
Nader group suits curbed 3-14, 308G1
Judge quits Davis case, declares mistrial 3-25, 271G3
Eilberg Pa practice suspended 3-29, 272A1
Judges financial disclosure law blocked 5-15, 382A2; upheld 11-19, 901B2
Wiretap ct judges named 5-18, 442A3
Burger assails 2 admitted to Sup Ct bar 6-25, 541B1
All-white club judicial memberships assailed 7-14, 9-19, 9-25, 901E2
Trial closure efforts rptd on rise 8-4; Burger, Powell comment 8-8, 8-13, 630C2-C3
1st black joins fed appeals ct in south 8-4, 656G3
ABA conv rejcts 3d party search limits, death penalty, prisoner rights; other actns rptd 8-9—8-15, 768C3-769B1
Legislators' incomes studied 9-1, 701D3
Atty drug profiteering cited 9-5, 10-29, 972D2, E2
Stevens, Blackmun comment on trial closures 9-8, 745B1
Calif lawyer survey rptd 9-17, 787D1
Press freedom insurnc plan set 9-27, 859E2
Brennan criticizes press 10-17, 848E1
Minneapolis prostitutn expose 10-18, 887A2
Calif Sup Ct inquiry ends 11-5, 869G1
Carter sued over judical pay limit 11-9, 901C2
Judges financial disclosure law upheld 11-19, 901B2
FCC 'family hour' power backed 11-20, 1007B1
Kennedy scores 'legalisms' 11-30, 962F1
Obituaries
Duffy, F Ryan 8-16, 671B2
Fahy, Charles 9-17, 756C2
Gurfein, Murray I. 12-16, 1008A3
Hollister, John Baker 1-4, 104B3
Sorg, Herbert Peter 3-11, 272F3
Wood, John H 5-29, 431D2

1980

COURTS & Legal Profession—*See also subjects of rulings*
State of State messages 1-4, 1-9, 269D1, 270C1; 1-8, 403G3; 1-14, 483D2
Prosecutn disparities rptd 1-6, 24A3
2 Ala black dist judges named 1-10; controversy ensues 5-19—9-17; Clemon confrmd 6-26, Gray withdraws 9-17, 744B2
Ehrlichman Calif bar resignatn accepted 1-19, 199D1
ABA mid-winter mtg: Burger address; ethics code revisn unveiled; FBI charter backed; other actns 1-30—2-3, 114E2
ABA finds judicial appointee 'unqualified' 3-2, Sen panel rejects 3-4, 250E2
Affirmative actn jobs plan ordrd for fed cts 3-6, 250B2
Fla votes to ease backlog 3-11, 185A1
Ford heir chngs counsel in family suit 3-12, 225D3
Ill atty gen convicted of tax evasn 3-19, 215A3; sentenced 7-29, 654F2
Fed judges granted 12.9% pay hike 3-24, 250F1
Nixon impeachmt lawyer sentenced 6-10, 460B1
Burger warns vs ct systems 'merger' 6-10, 632D1
Vance resumes practice 6-11, 471G1
Ohio judge acquitted of sex-bartering, convicted of other chrgs 6-13, 503A2
Pretrial data secrecy rule rptd OKd 6-19, takes effect 8-1, 631G3
Canada broadens rape case questioning 6-27, 520C3
GOP platform adopted; text 7-15, 535A3, F3
ABA conv backs law schl minority 'opportunities', repudiates GOP plank; other actns rptd 7-31—8-6, 744C1-B2
Abscam judge quits cases 8-7, 599D3
Wayne Cnty (Mich) 'payless payday' 9-19, 743D2
Newsroom searches curb signed 10-14, 835A2-C2
5th judicial circuit split 10-14, 918A3
Ala death penalty dispute cited 10-15, 869D1
Judicial discipline bill signed 10-15, 918F3
Ervin vs 'judicial verbicide' 10-22, 908A2
Sup Ct drops 'Mr Justice' title 11-14, 882A3
Obituaries
Baxter, Richard Reeves 9-26, 755B2
Cane, Melville H 3-10, 279G1
Dixon, Robert G 5-5, 448E1
Donnell, Forrest C 3-3, 279B2
Douglas, William O 1-19, 50E3

1976

Burger urges short briefs 11-9, 882B3
De Ment gets Rockefeller award 11-16, 911C3
Sup Ct curbs anti-death juror exclusion 12-6, 920B3
Sup Ct declines SC ethics code case 12-13, 960D3
Obituaries
Armstrong, Barbar 1-18, 56G2
Ernst, Morris 5-21, 404F1
Hugh Auchincloss dies 11-20, 970B1
Kenny, Robert W 7-20, 716D3
Miller, William 4-12, 316B1
Morgan, Gerald 6-15, 484F3
COUTURE, Jacques
Named labor min 11-26, 903A3
COUTURE, John
Addresses Indep party conv 8-26, 666F1
COWAN, Louis G.
Dies 11-18, 970D1
COWDELL, Patrick
Wins Olympic medal 7-31, 574B1
COWPER, Reginald
Race reforms rejected 7-2, 522E3
Named Rhodesia defense min 9-9, 713E2
Extends mil duty 11-30, 1009F3
COWPERTHWAITE, Gordon
On Polysar rebates 11-29, 924C1
COX, Archibald
Udall 2d in Mass primary 3-2, 165F1
Nominates Udall at conv 7-14, 506B1
Mondale scores GOP ticket 10-5, 743D3, E3
COYOTES—*See WILDLIFE*
CPI (Consumer Price Index)—*See 'Prices' under ECONOMY; also country names*
CRAIG, Robert
Ct rules on immunity 1-5, 7B1
CRAIG, William G.
Loses Vt primary for gov 9-14, 705B2

1977

La judicial conduct code review refused 11-7, 857D2
ABA backs pot decriminalizatn 11-13, 972A3
Felony probatn-loss case review declined 11-14, 878B3
Lawyer fees case refused 11-14, 878D3
ICC lawyers scored re Vesco, suit vs urged 11-29, 980B3
McCarthy lawyer fee case declined 12-5, 939B1
Phone surveillnc orders backed 12-7, 939E1
Legal aid for poor (LSC) extended 12-28, 1002C2
Obituaries
Clark, Tom 6-13, 532G2
Dunn, Robert 1-21, 84G2
Jaffe, Saul 11-1, 952E2
Saypol, Irving 6-30, 532F3
Slesinger, Donald 10-13, 872G2
Szold, Robert 11-9, 952E3

1978

Finney, Thomas D 1-30, 96G1
Goodhart, Arthur Lehman 11-10, 972B3
Leibowitz, Samuel 1-11, 96F2
O'Neill, C William 8-20, 708C3
Pollak, Emile 1-6, 96C3
Ritter, Willis W 3-4, 252C3
Tobin, Austin 2-8, 196G3
Waddy, Joseph C 8-1, 708G3
Youngdahl, Luther W 6-21, 540G3
Supreme Court Rulings—*See also under U.S. GOVERNMENT*
Burger issues annual rpt, urges jury selectn chngs 1-1, 12D3
1-house veto case reviews barred 1-9, 13A1
Ohio, SC gag-order cases review denied, Pa case remanded 1-9, 13E1
Employers curbed on bias-case legal fees 1-23, 65A2
Trial lawyer competency disputed 2-10—2-13, Burger defends criticism 2-12, 107F3
Indian trials of non-Indians barred 3-6, 162D1
Juries of less than 6 ruled illegal 3-21, 220E3
Testimony thru illegal search backed 3-21, 220G3
Indian rape retrial backed 3-22, 221D1
Judge's jury instructn on silent defendant backed 3-22, 221F1
Judicial immunity in sterilizatn case backed 3-28, 241F2
A-plant rulings curbed 4-3, 280E2
Ark single-counsel convictns reversed 4-3, 309C1
Gurney trial press-curbs case declined 4-17, 308C2
Union legal fee liability case review denied 4-17, 308D3
Va inmate parole hearings case declined 4-24, 322E2
Va judicial inquiry law voided 5-1, 363G2-E3
Lawyer competency case declined 5-1, 363E3
Md U social-actn group case refused 5-1, 364C1
Speedy trial appeal procedure backed 5-1, 364D1
Indian tribal authority backed 5-15, 387A3
Calif jurisdictn in child-support case denied 5-15, 387G3
Lawyer soliciting rules set 5-30, 430B2
Gen Atomic trial judge interference ruled 5-30, 430G2
Presumptn of innocence jury chrg backed 5-30, 430A3
Newsroom searches by police backed 5-31, 430A1
Munic legal immunity ended 6-6, 447C1-A2
Double jeopardy ban redefined 6-14, 468G2
Class actn suits curbed 6-19, 492G1
US prosecutor legal immunity case declined 6-19, 492E2
Class actn certificatn appeals curbed 6-21, 509F2
Ark prison reform, attys fees backed 6-23, 566D1
Cong immunity case refused 6-26, 566D2
Evidence hearing rules drawn 6-26, 566D3
Juvenile case reviews upheld 6-28, 567F1
US offcls' legal immunity defined 6-29, 567A2
Hypnosis-related murder case refused 10-2, 751C2
Law firm dual-rep case refused 11-6, 873G3
Inmate suits judicial-aid case refused 11-13, 874B3
Conn legal immunity ruling vacated 11-27, 937B2
Cities' power over suburbs backed 11-28, 937A3
3 justices urge new fed ct 12-4, 958D3-959A1
Police auto search power broadened 12-5, 959C2
Mass drunk rights waiver ruling affirmed 12-11, 980G3
Extraditn probes barred 12-18, 981F1

1979

Supreme Court Rulings
SEC suit findings retrial barred 1-9, 14A2
Mo women jury exclusn law voided 1-9, 14G2
Lawyers' interstate rights limited 1-15, 31B3
UK airline '72 crash case refused 1-15, 32D1
La juvenile trial jury ban refused 2-21, 128B3
GM grand jury tax probe plea declined 2-26, 164G2
Lawyer phone waiver case declined 2-26, 164E3
Bi-state agency immunity curbed 3-5, 185C1
State ct immunity curbed 3-5, 185C1
Right-to-counsel doctrine clarified 3-5, 185F1-D2
Alimony rule in NYS child custody case backed 3-19, 203F2
Grant of immunity broadened 3-20, 203G3
IRS tap evidence backed 4-2, 281D2
Va inmate threat case refused 4-16, 302E3
Podell, Brasco disbarmt challenges declined 4-16, 303C1
Racial 'steering' suits allowed 4-17, 325A3
6-member jury convictn rule upheld 4-17, 325F3
'State of mind' libel queries backed 4-18, reactn 4-18, 4-23, 301F3, 302B2
Covert entries for 'bugging' upheld 4-18, 346E1
Calif grand jury transcript examinatn barred 4-18, 346C2
'Italian Bakke case' declined 4-23, 346D2
Unwed fathers damage suit bar upheld 4-24, 364A1, E1
Verbal rights waiver backed 4-24, 364A2
Mental hosp commitmt standard tightened 4-30, 364E2
Entebbe hijack case declined 4-30, 364F3
Pvt Title IX suit allowed 5-14, 382C3
Mutual fund dirs' power backed 5-14, 382G3
Fed ct welfare suits curbed 5-14, 384A1
A-test radiatn liability case refused 5-21, 400A3
Innocence instructn refusal backed 5-21, 400E3
Guilty plea incomplete info backed 5-21, 400G3
Punitive damages vs unions barred 5-29, 421B3
Co-defendant confessns allowed 5-29, 422A1
NJ ex-offcls subject to rejailing 6-4, 439A1
Lawyer's office statemts protected 6-4, 439E1
US maximum penalty prosecutn backed 6-4, 439E1
Personal bankruptcy data collectn backed 6-4, 439B2
Congressmen ruled liable to sex-bias suits 6-5, 463G3-464F1
Ariz farm labor law restored 6-5, 464A3
Consumers' right to sue protected 6-11, 478D2
'Open-ended' warrants use curbed 6-11, 478B3
ICC rail rate suspensn power backed 6-11, 478D3
Fed child custody fights curbed 6-11, 478F3
Cong immunity broadened 6-18, 498C3
Helstoski indictmt rule backed 6-18, 499A1
Customer suits vs accountants curbed 6-18, 499C1
Mont homicide convictn reversed 6-18, 499F1
Youth 'Miranda rights' limited 6-20, 516B2
Libel suit rights broadened 6-26, 540D2
Idaho takeover law challenge rejctd 6-26, 540E3
Rights violatn proof in false arrest suits backed 6-26, 540G3
Dockworker negligence suits backed 6-27, 558B2
Criminal evidence standard eased 6-28, 558D2
Ctroom pub access curbed; reactn 7-2, 515G1, C3
Power to void state convictns backed 7-2, 558E3
Mass abortn-consent law voided 7-2, 559G1-D2
Neb porno case jury challenge refused 10-1, 768F1
Ala legal counsel law challenge declined 10-1, 768A2
Bell contempt case declined 10-9, 783E3
Va trial closure case accepted 10-9, 783F3
Ill judge retiremt law challenge refused 10-9, 784F1
Neb rape bail case refused 10-15, 847E3
Mass jury selectn case refused 10-29, 884A2
Ohio atty billbd ad ban challenge refused 11-5, 884B3
NYS trial closure case declined 11-5, 884E3
Investor suits vs advisers curbed 11-13, 901G3
Arson 'dual sovereignty' case refused 11-13, 902B2

1980

Froelich, William J 2-5, 176B1
Glueck, Sheldon 3-10, 279B3
Hays, Paul 2-13, 176E1
Hicks, Sue Kerr 6-27, 528A2
Jenkins, Ray H 12-26, 1004B2
Lowenstein, Allard 3-14, 214C2
Reed, Stanly F 4-3, 360A3
Rodell, Fred 6-4, 528D3
Sebald, William J 8-10, 676G2
Stender, Fay 5-21, 448G2
Wolf, George 3-23, 280G2
Presidential Election (& Transition)
Dem platform reform planks adopted 8-13, 615C1
Reagan clarifies apptmt stand 9-30, 738C3
Mondale hails Hispanic apptmts 10-3, 817A1
Reagan vows female apptmts 10-14, 779A1, E3
Supreme Court Rulings
Environmental impact ct reviews limited 1-7, 15A3
'Petite' policy cited in Ky firearms case 1-14, 37G1
Parole offcls immunity upheld 1-15, 51E1
Inmate escape justificatn curbed 1-21, 92E3
State ct jurisdictn narrowed 1-21, 93F1
'Miranda rights' waiver proof backed 1-21, 93C3
Total plaintiff class lawyer fees backed 2-19, 131B1
Govt damage suits geographic relevance backed 2-20, 170A3
FTC trust procedure case accepted 2-25, 187E3
Coerced confessn search warrant case declined 2-26, 188A2
Spouse testimony upheld 2-27, 188A2
Fed gun law prior convictn rule upheld 2-27, 188E2
Kissinger records access blocked 3-3, 209G3
Immune grand jury testimony in perjury trials backed 3-3, 210D1
EPA dischrg permit ct reviews backed 3-17, 226F1
State legislators' immunity curbed 3-19, 249E3
Freedom of Info ct order bar backed 3-19, 250B1
Class actn 'moot' standard redefined 3-19, 250C1
Ctroom ID in illegal arrest backed 3-25, 265G2-C3
NYS political firings barred 3-31, 291A2
Retarded youth surgery case refused 3-31, 291B3
Warrantless home arrests curbed 4-15, 305F3
Cooperatn standard in sentencing backed 4-15, 306G1
'Good faith' municipal immunity ended 4-16, 328C2
Multiple sentencing curbed 4-16, 328B3
Ctroom cameras case accepted 4-21, 344E1
Prisoners right to sue broadened 4-22, 343B3
Misdemeanor 2d offense jailing limited 4-22, 344B1
CFTC emergency order case declined 4-28, 369E1
Mandatory civil jury cases refused 4-28, 369F1
Police interrogatn defined 5-12, 386B2
EEOC class actn process avoidance backed 5-12, 426G1
Atty conflict of interest probes backed 5-12, 426F2
Ga death law applicatn narrowed 5-19, 440C1
NYS rape shield law case dismissed 5-19, 440C2
Fed unincorporated business trust suits backed 5-19, 440E2
'Exclusionary rule' narrowed 5-27, 453A2
EPA guidelines appeals ct review backed 5-27, 453E3
DC professional tax case declined 5-27, 454A1
Pub offcl good faith defns defined 5-27, 454C1
State ct legal immunity defined 6-2, 512E3
Panther Chicago shootout trial lawyers' fees award voided 6-2, 513B1
Jail informant use curbed 6-16, 511C3
Ala death penalty struck down 6-20, 555C1
Donated porno warrants required 6-20, 555G2
Power to suppress evidence curbed 6-23, 554A3
Magistrates pretrial role upheld 6-23, 554G3
Lawyer legal fee penalty backed 6-23, 555A1
Right to sue states broadened 6-25, 540C3
Out-of-ct lawyers' fee awards backed 6-25, 540G3
Illegal search protectn narrowed 6-25, 541A1
Govt minority constructn grants upheld 7-2, 510E1
Open criminal trials backed 7-2, 510C2-C3
'79-80 term ends, decisns cited 7-2, 540E2
Mass rape trial press exclusn case remanded 10-14, 782B1
Unwed couples child custody case refused 10-20, 807A1
Trust damages liability sharing case accepted 11-3, 856C2
Inmate legal fees ruling upset 11-10, 868C1

1976

CRAMER, James A.
Wins VCU bias suit 5-28, 414A1
CRANE, Rep. Philip M. (R, Ill.)
Backs Buckley candidacy 8-11, 584D3
Buckley ends pres bid 8-16, 615E3
GOP conv OKs platform plank 8-18, 600C3
GOP conv vp vote table 8-19, 599E3
Reelected 11-2, 829G2
CRANE, Priscilla
On anti-bias revenue sharing efforts 3-2, 187E1
CRANES—*See WILDLIFE*
CRANMER, Thomas (1489-1556)
Episc Church OKs prayer bk revisn 9-20, 755F2
CRANSTON, Sen. Alan M(acGregor) (D, Calif.)
Rpts India A-plant leak 1-30, 156E2
Detente resolutn blocked 3-22, 246B1
Move to cut missile funds loses 5-26, 411C2
Credentials hearings end 7-1, 489G3
Dem conv panel rpts 7-13, 509F1
Carter meets cong ldrs 11-17, 864A2
Aide helps Carter 11-23, 881C3

1977

COUSY, Bob
Roche named ASL rookie of yr 9-8, 827C3
COUTELLIER, Jean
Pleads guilty 5-26, 426D1
Freed 6-16, 484G3
COUTURE, Jacques
On wage-price curbs end 2-22, 158C3
COVERDELL, Paul
Loses US House race 3-15, 192B1
COVINGTON, Harold A.
Nazi backer kills 2, self 9-5, 848A3
COWAN, Frederick W.
Kills 5, shoots self 2-14, 162E2
COWEN, Zelman
Replaces Kerr as gov gen 7-14, 541D1
Sworn gov-gen 12-8, 963F3
COWENS, Al
AL batting ldr 10-2, 926F3
Carew named AL MVP 11-16, 927D1
COWINS, Ben
Suspended 12-21, drops bias suit 12-29, 1020E2
COWLES Communications Inc.
Alioto wins libel award 5-3, 532B2
COWPER, Reginald E. D.
Extends mil call-ups 1-27, 73B2
Quits 2-11, 123F1
Mil call-ups increased 2-28, 144G2
Replaced as defns min 3-10, 223F2
COX, Archibald
Argues Bakke case 10-12, Sup Ct orders more briefs 10-17, 834F3, 835F1
COX, Bobby
Named Braves mgr 11-22, 927B2
COX, Robert J.
Detained 4-22—4-23, 345E3
COX, Wesley
In NBA draft 6-10, 584B2
COX, William
On abortn funding curb 12-7, 958C3
COX, William M.
Drops metric signs proposal 6-24, 522A2
COX Broadcasting Co.
Brzezinski rpts holdings 2-25, 147G3
COX Enterprises Inc.
Miami News scored re IRS rpts 1-6, 16B1
CP Air—*See CANADIAN Pacific Air*
CPC International Inc.
Indicted 3-30, fined 5-19, 504G1-A2
Sup Ct refuses pollutn rules appeal 4-18, 342D1
CPI (Consumer Price Index)—*See ECONOMY—Prices; also country names*
CPSC—*See U.S. GOVERNMENT—CONSUMER Product Safety Commission*
CRAMER, Haber & Becker
Nicaragua mil aid amendmt defeated 6-23, 656G2
CRANDALL, Del
Firing by Angels rptd 12-17, 990A2
CRANDALL, Robert W.
On aluminum price hikes 6-14, 577A2
CRANE, Rep. Philip M. (R, Ill.)
In TV campaign vs Canal pacts 10-29, 912C1
CRANE, Roy
Dies 7-7, 604G2
CRANE Co.
Anaconda takeover try cited 1-12, 55B3
Allegheny wins Chemetron control 9-8, 880C2
CF&I chrgs Japan, India steel dumping 10-17, 836C3; Canada 11-3, 836F3
US probes Japan, India dumping 11-22, 933B3
CRANSTON, Sen. Alan M(acGregor) (D, Calif.)
Elected majority whip 1-4, 6E1
Sponsors cong electn fund bill 3-7, 232D3
Lauds tax rebate plan withdrawal 4-14, 270E3
Doubts energy rebates 5-19, 443B2
Estimates Canal treaty votes 9-20, 755B3
On SALT extensn resolutn 9-26, 751B2

1978

COUSIN, Luis
Honduras health min 8-9, 691E3
COUTINHO, Claudio
Brazil soccer fans score 6-7, 520C3
COUTO e Silva, Gen. Golbery do
Embezzlemt, bribes chrgd 1-13, 166A1
COVINGTON, Ky.—*See KENTUCKY*
COVINGTON, Aubrey
Charged by SEC 10-5, 770C3
COVINGTON Knox Inc.
Charged by SEC 10-5, 770C3
COWAN, Patricia
Killed in audition 4-10, 380E2
COWARD, Sir Noel (Pierce) (1899-1973)
Fay Compton dies 12-12, 1032D2
COWDEN, Coy Dean
Retracts Ray alibi 8-18, 642B1
COWENS, Dave
NBA rebound ldr 4-9, 271F2
Named Celtics player-coach 11-14, 1027E2
COWINS, Ben
Arkansas wins Orange Bowl 1-2, 8C3
COWLES Communications Inc.
To liquidate 1-6, 75F3-76A1
WESH-TV license renewal voided, ct sets guidelines 9-25, 907E3
COX, Billy
Dies 3-31, 252F2
COX, Don
Dismissed from Indiana basketball team 12-12, 1028A1
COX, Mark
US wins Davis Cup 12-10, 1026F3
COX, Ted
Traded to Indians 3-30, 779C3
COZZENS, James Gould
Dies 8-9, 708D2
CPI (consumer price index)—*See ECONOMY—Price Indexes; also country names*
CPSC—*See U.S. GOVERNMENT—CONSUMER Product Safety Commission*
CRAGIN, Charles L.
Loses primary for Me gov 6-13, 467A1
CRAIG, Cleo F.
Dies 4-21, 356E2
CRAIG, Roger
Hired as Padres mgr 3-21, 355B2
CRANE, Bob
Killed 6-29, 540E2
CRANE, Daniel B.
Wins US House seat 11-7, 850F3, 853B2
CRANE, David
Loses US House electn 11-7, 853C2
CRANE, Dr. Norman
Indicted on drug chrg 3-16, 459G1
CRANE, Rep. Philip M. (R, Ill.)
Announces pres bid 8-2, 606C1
Vs Carter anti-infl plml 10-24, 807A1
Gets high rating from conservative group 10-24, 865B3
Reelected 11-7, 850E3, 853C2
Fernandez enters pres race 11-29, 938A3
CRANE, Stephen (1871-1900)
Crane's Way opens 7-12, 760G1
CRANE, Warren
Tribute opens 6-1, 887D3
CRANE Co.
Medusa OKs takeover 9-1, 700C3
CRANE'S Way (play)
Opens 7-12, 760G1
CRANSTON, Sen. Alan M (acGregor) (D, Calif.)
Redwood Park expansn bill OKd 1-31, 85G2
Votes for Panama Canal neutrality pact 3-16, 177D2
Votes for 2d Canal pact, ratificatn role cited 4-18, 273B1, F2
Greets Indian demonstrators 7-17, 569A1

1979

Methodist legal immunity case declined 11-26, 919E2
Extended searches curbed 11-28, 944E2-C3
Telex lawyer fee case declined 12-3, 964B2
Appointed lawyers legal immunity curbed 12-4, 987D3

COUSINEAU, Tom
In NFL draft 5-3, 335C1, E1
COUSINS, Robin
2d in world figure skating 3-15, 391F3
COUSINS Jr., Judge William
Declares Ill death penalty illegal 1-30, 400A2
COUSTEAU, Jacques-Yves
Son killed 6-28, 508D2
COUSTEAU, Philippe
Dies in plane crash 6-28, 508D2
COUSY, Bob
Firing forecast 11-19, quits as ASL comr 11-20, 1004A3
COUTO e Silva, Gen. Golbery do
Retains Brazil Cabt post 1-19, 95C1
Figueiredo sworn pres 3-15, 210F1
COUTURE, Donald
Arrested for theft, murder 4-17, 316G1
COUTURE, Donna
Arrested for theft, murder 4-17, 316G1
COVERT Action Information Bulletin
CIA alleged agents abroad listed 1-4, 17B3
COWANS Ford Dam, N.C.—*See NORTH Carolina*
COWART, Judge Edward D.
Sentences Bundy to death 7-31, 604E2
COWE, Roger
Backs Liberal res vs growth 9-28, 792B2
COWENS, Al
Traded to Angels 12-6, 1002F2
COWENS, Dave
To resign as Celtics coach 4-8, 290D3
Brown sale of Celtics OKd 5-7, 527D1
COX, Christopher Nixon
Born 3-14, 271F2
COX, Edward Finch
Son born 3-14, 271F2
COX, John
Pleads guilty 3-28, 334A3
COX, Patricia Nixon (Tricia) (Mrs. Edward Finch)
Son born 3-14, 271F2
COX, Ralph F.
Rpts Chile copper investmt 5-10, 369C3
COX, Robert
Tells of death threat 12-4, leaves Argentina 12-16, 966E2
COX, William
On '79 trade deficit 10-30, 828G1
COX Broadcasting Corp.
GE merger agreed 2-21, 188C2-A3
CPB—*See PUBLIC Broadcasting, Corporation for*
CPG Products Inc.—*See GENERAL Mills*
CPI (consumer price index)—*See ECONOMY-Price Indexes; also country names*
CPSC—*See U.S. GOVERNMENT-CONSUMER Product Safety Commission*
CRAIG, Roger
Fired as Padres mgr 9-30, 1002F1
CRAMER, Richard Ben
Wins Pulitzer 4-16, 336B3
CRANBERRIES—*See FRUITS & Vegetables*
CRANE, Rep. Philip M. (R, Ill.)
Talks to Midwest GOP, vs US monetary policy; offcls rate 3-10, 185G3, 186C1
Renews pres bid 5-16, 363E3
Scores Loeb sex allegatns 6-8, Viguerie quits campaign 8-8, 594G1-D2
Pres campaign funds rptd 7-12, 594A1
Me straw poll results 11-3, 866B3
4th in Fla straw vote 11-17, 887D1
CRANE, Warren
Faith Healer opens 4-4, 711G2
CRANE Co.
CF&I Steel Corp.
Wheeling-Pittsburgh fed aid scored, suit filed 8-28, 682A1, C1
CRANGLE, Joseph F.
Gets Kennedy campaign post 12-20, 983C3
CRANSTON, Sen. Alan MacGregor (D, Calif.)
Sen majority whip 71A2
Veterans' Affairs Com chrmn 1-23, 71E2
Carter warns re Taiwan legis 1-26, 66B3
Disputes balanced budget amendmt status 2-6, 86C2
Defends Carter Cabt, staff shake-up 7-19, 531B3

1980

Del Law Schl libel case declined 11-10, 868B3
Ctroom cameras case argued 11-12, 882A2
Extended judicial immunity barred 11-17, 882A1
SEC parallel probe case refused 11-17, 882D1
Pa pretrial press exclusn case refused 11-17, 882F1
Calif probe of Ark prisons curbed 12-8, 937D1
Nixon taps case argued 12-8, 937A2
Lenient sentence appeal backed 12-9, 936A3
Defendants fed ct civil rights suits curbed 12-9, 937B1
Judicial pay hikes backed 12-15, 956C3-957D1
FTC trust complaint challenge curbed 12-15, 957E1
COUSINEAU, Tom
CFL signing cited 4-29, 336C3
COUSINS, Norman
Anatomy of an Illness on best-seller list 2-10, 120C3; 3-9, 200C3; 5-4, 359E3
COUSINS, Robin
Wins Eur figure skating title 1-24, 470F2
Wins Olympic medal 2-19, 155E3
COUSINS, Tom
NHL OKs Flames sale 6-24, 488B2
COUSY, Bob
Machado named ASL com 12-17, 1001B3
COUTO e Silva, Gen. Golbery do
Ludwig threatns Jari project halt 10-16, 787E2
COVENANT, The (book)
On best-seller list 12-7, 948D3
COVERT Action Information Bulletin
CIA alleged agents abroad listed 3-7, 189F2
US Emb aide in Jamaica named as CIA operative 7-2, 564F3
COVINGTON, Harold A.
Draws NC votes for atty gen 5-6, 405G1
Hails NC KKK acquittals 11-17, 898B3
COWLEY, Malcolm
Writer's Trade wins Amer Book Award 5-1, 692C2
COX, Archibald
Elected Common Cause chrmn 2-2, 115E2
Campaign spending suit filed 7-1, 493B1
COX, Mark
Loses German indoor championship 3-16, 607G2
COX, Patricia Nixon (Tricia) (Mrs. Edward Finch)
Parents become NYC residents 2-14, 199C3
COX, William
On May indicators 6-30, 492C2
COX Broadcasting Corp.
GE merger plans dropped 4-25; FCC OKs merger 4-28, 386E1
COYLE, Ed
Quits Anderson campaign 8-28, 665C3
COYNE, James K.
Elected to US House 11-4, 844C1, 848G3
COYNE, William
Elected to US House 11-4, 844D1
CPI (consumer price index)—*See ECONOMY--Price Indexes*
C-Plane Series—*See ARMAMENTS--Aircraft*
CPSC (Consumer Product Safety Commission)—*See under U.S. GOVERNMENT*
CRAIG, James
Saudis order to leave 4-23, 313C2
CRAIG, Jim
US Olympic hockey team beats Sovts 2-22, wins gold medal 2-24, 155B2
CRAIG, Larry
Elected to US House 11-4, 842C3, 851F3
CRAIG Clairborne's Gourmet Diet (book)
On best-seller list 10-12, 796E3
CRANDALL, Robert L.
Named Amer Airlines pres 7-16, 600F2
CRANE, Arlene
Files suit vs W Ger magazine 7-16, 890C2
CRANE, Rep. Daniel B. (R, Ill.)
Reelected 11-4, 842A4
CRANE, L. Stanley
Resigns Southn Rail post; named Conrail chrmn, chief exec 9-29, 959C2
CRANE, Rep. Philip M. (R, Ill.)
In Ia GOP debate, scores Admin forgn policy 1-5, 4F2, E3
Ia poll results 1-11, 33F1, G1
5th in Ia caucus vote 1-21, 50F1
NH gun control forum 2-18, GOP pres debate 2-20, 129B3, D3, G3
NH debate exclusn spurs controversy 2-23, 143D1
NH primary vote results 2-26, 142E3, G3
Mass, Vt primary results 3-4, 166F2, D3
In Ill GOP forum 3-13, 206F2
Loses matching funds 3-13, 209D1
Wins 4 Ill delegates, cong primary 3-18, 206E2
Endorses Reagan 4-16, withdraws from pres race 4-17, 304B3
Evangelical Christian pol role rptd 7-11—9-15, 819C2
Wife sues W Ger magazine 7-16, 890C2
Gets votes as vp nominee 7-17, 529G1
Reelected 11-4, 842E3
CRANE, Stephen (1871-1900)
Harper's to cease publicatn 6-17, 501B1
CRANE Co.
CF&I Steel Corp.
Job bias suit setld 9-22, 746D3
CRANSTON, Sen. Alan MacGregor (D, Calif.)
On Carter anti-inflatn plan 3-14, 201E2
Wins renomination 6-3, 439A2
Homosexual entry bar repeal backed 6-20, 514D3

1976

CRANSTON, Toller
Wins Olympic medal 2-11, 159B1
CRASVAER, Peder
At boat collisn probe 10-25, 876B2
CRATER Lake National Park (Ore.)
Sen bars new mining claims 2-4, 135A2
Mining curb signed 9-28, 834C2
CRAVENS, Kenton R. (deceased)
Mercantile pol costs rptd 2-27, 181D1
CRAWFORD, H. R.
Succeeded in HUD post 3-11, 232F1
CRAWFORD, Hasely
Wins Olympic medal 7-24, 575E3
CRAWFORD, John R.
Dies 2-14, 160C3
CRAWFORD, Malcolm
£ in record 1-day drop 10-25, 809E3
CRAXI, Bettino
Named Soclst Party ldr 7-16, bars Cabt role 7-20, 539A1
CREAN, Frank
Loses Labor Party ldrship bid 1-27, 71D3
CREDIT, Consumer
Nov credit rptd, Oct revised 1-12, 91B3
Dec credit rptd; Oct, Nov revised 2-6, 168G3
Privacy comm hearings 2-11—2-13, 151A2
Jan credit rptd 3-8, 199B3
Discriminatn ban enacted 3-23, 233A3
Feb rise rptd 4-6, 279D3
Mar, 1st ¼ credit rptd 5-6, 375E3
Apr rise rptd 6-7, 436F2-A3
May credit up, Jan-Apr revised 7-9, 519F1, A2
GOP platform text 8-18, 602D3
June, July credit up 9-8, 709D2
Aug credit rise rptd 10-6, 806A3
Sept credit growth rptd 11-5, 866E3
Oct credit rptd up 12-6, 958A3
CREER, John P.
Loses Utah primary for gov 9-14, 705F1
CRENSHAW, Ben
Tourn results, top '76 money-winner 1-25, 2-1, 123E2
2d in Masters 4-11, 272G1
CRESTED Butte Development Corp.
Callaway chrgd 3-12, 197A2; **for subsequent developments, see CALLAWAY, Howard**
Sen rpt scores Calloway 10-5, 745D1
CRIA Cuervos (film)
Wins Cannes award 5-28, 460G1

1977

CRASH of '79, The (book)
On best-seller list 2-6, 120E3; 3-6, 184E3; 4-3, 264F1; 5-1, 356C2; 6-4, 452G1; 7-3, 548D3; 8-14, 643F1; 9-4, 712C3; 12-4, 1021A3
CRAWFORD, Cheryl
Wins Tony 6-5, 452F1
CRAWFORD, Jeff
On black festival violence 8-28—8-29, 672E3
CRAWFORD, Joan
Dies 5-10, 452F2
CRAWFORD, W. Donham
Vs Carter energy plan 4-24, 320A1
CRAWFORD, Willie
Traded to A's 6-15, 644G2
CREDIT, Consumer
Index described 56F3
Nov '76 data rptd 1-7, 56E3
Dec '76 credit rptd up 2-7, 93D1
Jan credit rptd 3-4, 176F2-A3
Feb rise rptd 4-5, 274E1
March credit rptd 5-5, 406B3
May '74-77 debt rise rptd, dangers debated 6-28, 555A1
Apr, May credit rptd up 7-8, 554G3 *
June credit up; May, Mar revised 8-8, 611D3
July credit rptd up 9-7, 704B2
Debt collectn rules signed 9-20, 761D1
Aug credit up 10-6, 798D2
Sept credit rptd, Aug revised 11-4, 858F2
Natl Women's Conf urges bias end 11-19—11-21, 917D3
Oct credit rise rptd 12-7, 961D3
CREDIT Unions
Loan, investmt rules clear Cong 4-5, 273C2; Carter signs 4-19, 380E3
CREIGHTON, The Right Rev. William F.
Succeeded by Walker 9-24, 845E2
CRENSHAW, Ben
2d in Byron Nelson Classic 5-8, 676C1
Wins Colonial Natl tourn 5-15, 676C1
2d in Irish Open 8-28, 676C2
CRESPIN, Jose Leonidas
Killed 2-20, 181A2
CRIALES de la Rosa, Humberto
Chrgs army murders 3-18, 255C1
Says 36 peasants killed 7-21—7-25, 636D1
CRICHTON, John H.
Dies 12-28, 1024D1
CRICHTON, Michael
Father dies 12-28, 1024D1

1978

CRASH of '79, The (book)
On best-seller list 1-8, 24F3
CRAWFORD, Cheryl
Somersaults opens 1-9, 760A2
CRAWFORD, Christina
Mommie on best-seller list 12-3, 971A1
CRAWFORD, Douglas
Tax vote rptd 5-11, 415A2
CRAWFORD, Francis Jay
USSR seizes 6-12, treatmt protested 6-13; chrgd 6-17, 476C2
Carter scores USSR treatmt 6-26, 491E1
Toon takes custody 6-26, 506G1
Harvester suspends Sovt deals 7-16, 575D3
Hammer rpts Brezhnev talk 8-25, 670B2
Trial opens 9-5, sentence suspended 9-7, leaves USSR 9-8, 742B3
Blumenthal scores Sovts 12-4, 966C1
CRAWFORD, Joan (d. 1977)
Estate auctioned 2-16, 172D2
CRAWFORD, Nancy Voyles
Caravans released 11-1, 969F3 *
CRAXI, Bettino
Soclsts gain in local electns 5-16, 375C2
Soclsts gain in Sicily electn 5-30, 453F3 *
Pertini elected pres 7-8, 558G1 *
CREDIT, Consumer
Data explained 128C3
Nov, Dec '77 credit rptd 2-10, 128A3
Jan credit rptd; Dec '77 revised 3-8, 222F3
Feb credit rptd 4-6, 262B3
Denver utility settles FTC chrg 5-3, 434G1
Mar credit rptd 5-5, 345C2
Apr credit, Jan-Mar revised 6-6, 429F2
May credit rptd 7-7, 552E3
HFC lending violatns chrgd 7-7, 589F1
Carter proposes LEAA revisn, pub housing plans 7-10, 525C1, G1
June debt rptd 8-4, 608A1
July credit rptd 9-8, 717C2
Aug-Oct credit rptd, May revised 12-6, 958B1
State interest rates on natl bank credit cards backed by US Sup Ct 12-18, 981C2
CREDIT Lyonnais (Paris bank)
7th in '77 world ranking 11-8, 914B1, D1
CREDIT Suisse (Swiss Credit Bank)
Chrmn probed 1-10, 151C1
To sell Texon holdings 2-10, rpts Chiasso scandal losses 3-1, 151F1-A2
Credit Suisse et de White Weld, Financiere du
Merrill Lynch to get 30% stake 4-14, 283D2
CREIGHTON, Douglas
Chrgd re USSR spy rpt leak 3-17, 208G3
CRENSHAW, Ben
2d in Crosby Pro-Am 1-23, 76C1
Ties for 2d in British Open 7-15, 580D2
2d in Australian Open 11-19, 990D2
CREOLE Gas Pipeline Co.
Interstate gas sale probed 6-22, 471A2
CRI, Un (book)
No Time For Breakfast released 9-15, 970D2
CRICHTON, Michael
Coma released 2-1, 619B1

1979

Vs arms hike link to SALT 8-3, 591D1
Conservative PAC plans drive 8-16, 627G3
Vs Carter '80 nominatn support 8-20, 627B3
CRAWFORD, Christina
Mommie Dearest on best-seller list 1-7, 80B3; 2-4, 120B3; 3-4, 173E3; 4-8, 271B2
CRAWFORD, Coral
Arrested in NYC bank robbery 8-9, 656D1
CRAWFORD, Fred
KKK analysis rptd 7-22, 865D1
CRAWFORD, Robert L.
Little Romance released 4-27, 820F1
CRAWFORD, William R.
US to send advisers to N Yemen 3-12, 178C3
CRAWLEY, Randall
Loses US amateur squash champs 1-21, 527B2
CRAXI, Bettino
Pertini asks to form govt 7-9, 525F2, D3
Abandons bid to form Cabt 7-24, 583A3
Red Brigades letter scores 8-10, 635F2
Berlinguer suggests talks 8-11, 615A2
ENI head suspended 12-7, 995F3
CRAYCRAFT, Charlene Baker
Rpts labor '78 cong campaign gifts 6-13, 595B1
CREDIT, Consumer
Data explained 34G3
Nov '78 credit rptd, Oct revised 1-5, 34E3
Dec '78 credit rptd 2-6, 111B2
Jan credit rptd 3-9, 182G3
Pvt debt collectn for US urged 3-10, 208E3
Carter urges privacy bill 4-2, 264F3
Feb credit rptd 4-6, 280D3
Mar credit rptd 5-3, 325F1-A2
Beneficial Corp bias chrgd 5-8, 596F1
Carter proposes bank loan reforms 5-22, 403B1
Montgomery Ward settles FTC chrg 5-29, 596A2
Apr credit rptd 6-6, 422E2
May credit rptd, Apr revised 7-6, 517B1
June credit rise rptd 8-6, 622D1
July credit rptd; May, June revised 9-10, 681B1
Heimann warns re credit overextensn 9-13, 681D1
Mail order finance chrg case refused by Sup Ct 10-1, 768B2
Aug credit rptd 10-5, 766C2
Economists fear rise 11-1, 827A1
Sept credit rptd 11-6, 866F3
Oct credit rptd 12-7, 941G1
CREDIT Commercial (France)
Pahlevi family fund transfers documented 11-26, 897E2
CREDIT Lyonnais (Paris bank)
Branchart arrested 2-5, 96F2
Iran banks natlzd 6-7, compensatn vowed 6-10, 469A2
CREDIT Suisse (Swiss Credit Bank)
5 chrgd in Chiasso scandal 2-15, 137D1
Chiasso sentncs given 7-3, 505C2
CREDIT Unions—*See FINANCIAL Services*
CREIGHTON, Douglas
Secrecy trial barred 4-23, 311C2
CREIGHTON, Fred
Fired as Flames coach 5-3, 470C3
Named Bruins coach 7-5, 655B3
CREIGHTON University (Omaha, Neb.)
Hickey in basketball HOF 4-30, 526E3
CREMER, Fritz
Arrested as E Ger spy 1-31, 77C3
CRENSHAW, Ben
Wins Phoenix Open 1-22, 220C3
2d in Canadian Open 6-24, Westn 7-8, British 7-21, 587A1, B3, D3
2d in PGA Championship 8-6, Pleasant Valley Classic 9-9; wins Natl Team Championship 10-28, 969E2, 970D1, A2
PGA top money winner 11-30, 969F2
CRESSON, James
Father's Day opens 6-21, 711A3
CRESTVIEW, Fla.—*See FLORIDA*
CREUSOT-Loire
US aid for Phoenix unit cited 8-28, 682G1
CREWS, Col. Alvin M.
S Africa ousts as spy 4-12, 286F3
CRIB Death (sudden infant death syndrome)—*See CHILDREN—Health & Safety Issues*
CRICHTON, Michael
Great Train Robbery released 2-1, 174E2
CRIGLER, Lynn
Whoopee opens 2-14, 292F3

1980

On Carter VA MD pay hike veto 8-26, 649E3
Reelected 11-4, 840C1, 845A3, 852G1
Reelected Sen Dem whip 12-4, 936G2
Scores Haig apptmt 12-16, 955A2
CRAWFORD, Christina
Mommie Dearest on best-seller list 1-13, 40C3
CRAXI, Bettino
Soclsts join new govt 4-4, 275C3
Local electns back coalitn 6-8—6-9, 445F2
Scores Pope abortn stand, coalitn strained 10-25, 873B2
Backs Red Brigade negotiatns 12-12, 966F2
CRAZY Little Thing Called Love (recording)
On best-seller list 2-6, 120F3; 3-5, 200E3; 4-2, 280E3
CREAN, Simon
Wool strike accord rptd 3-21, 229F2
CREDIT, Consumer
Data explained 15C2
Credit curbs modified by FRB 1-2, 263D2
Nov '79 credit, Oct revised 1-8, 15A2
'70-77 credit card use rise rptd 1-30, 92G2
Dec '79 credit rptd, Nov revised 2-7, 114A1
Default clause exclusn backed by Sup Ct 2-20, 170G2
Jan credit rptd, Dec '79 revised 3-10, 182E3
Carter anti-inflatn plan sets curbs 3-14; economists' reactn rptd 3-15, 201C1, 202E2
Credit rptd restricted on FRB moves 3-27, 3-28, 222D2-A3
Feb credit rptd, Jan revised 4-7, 263B2
Amoco settles bias suit 4-29, 370B3
Mar credit rptd, Feb revised 5-7, 344D3
Beneficial FTC complaint setld 5-12, 703F1
Auto sales impact rptd 5-14, 384F1
FRB eases controls 5-22, card issuers rptd cautious 5-27, 399F3, 400G1
Credit fixing curbed by Sup Ct 5-27, 453F3
Apr credit rptd 6-6, 437F3-438A1
FRB ends controls 7-3, 513E1
S&Ls wider powers OKd 7-3, 516E2
May credit rptd 7-9, 513E3
Reagan vs pres controls 7-12, 535E1
GOP platform text 7-15, 535G2, 536B2
Vander Jagt scores Carter 7-16, 534B2
June credit rptd 8-7, 684F1-B2
July, Aug credit rptd 9-10, 10-7, 783A3
Reagan assails Carter policies 10-2, 763C1
Sept credit rptd 11-7, 867E1
Oct credit rptd 12-3, 938D1
CREEL, Bob
Stoner convicted, sentncd 5-14, 405C1
CREGAR, William O.
Reveals ouster of 5 Sovt bloc diplomats 2-29, 189C2
CRENNA, Richard
Death Ship released 4-25, 416F2
CRENSHAW, Ben
2d in Tourn Players 3-23, Colonial Natl 5-18, 412A3, 413A1
3d in Brit Open 7-20, 714A3
Wins Busch Classic 9-28, 972C2
PGA top money winner 10-12, 971E3
CREUSOT-Loire
US protests Sovt steel deal 9-19, 728D3
US curbs imports 11-17, 886B1
CRIADO Amunategui, Gen. Arturo
Escapes death try 7-29, 605G3
CRIB Death (sudden infant death syndrome)—*See CHILDREN—Health & Safety Issues*
CRIDEN, Howard L.
Indicted in Abscam probe 5-22, 5-27, 5-28, 402E2, F2, B3; 6-18, 454G1
Convicted in Abscam trial 8-31, 684B2
Schwartz, Jannotti convicted 9-16, 740C2
Appeals ct backs Abscam tapes broadcast 10-1; Sup Ct refuses stay, tapes aired 10-14, 781D2
Thompson, Murphy convicted 12-3, 919E1

CRIME

1976

CRIME—*See also TERRORISM; country names*
Ford State of Union message 1-19, 38B2, 39E2, C3
Berrigans begin jail term 1-19, 160F2
ABA proposals on fed law enforcemt, pending case records 2-16, 137A1
Shooting incident at Sovt UN residence in NY 2-27, 229C2
Violent crime rptd up in 8 cities, LEAA vow cited 3-2, 336C3
US-Canada extraditn treaty 3-22, 238D3
Fiscal '77 US budget estimate tables 231B1, 358D2

1977

CRIME—*See also TERRORISM; country names*
Ford State of Union message 1-12, 13G2
FBI curbs proposed 2-15, 157B3
FBI rpts 324 'most wanted' captured 3-19, 288D2
DC ct reorganizatn upheld 3-22, 231D1-B2
Rudd, 3 other '60s Weathermen surrender 3-25, 6-21, 9-15, 839C1
Mil crimes rptd down 4-6, 343B2
Laetrile smugglers sentncd 5-16, 508E2
Cong sets '78 budget target 5-17, 405B1
Natl data svc under review 6-16, 480B3

1978

CRIME—*See also TERRORISM; country names*
Criminal code revisn OKd by Sen 1-30, 64F1
Criminal code revisn, other reforms backed by Carter 5-4, 320A3
Alaska plea bargaining rpt issued 5-15, 396E1
LEAA victimless crime study issued 9-11, 842B2
Diplomatic immunity law revisn signed 9-30, 750D3
Criminal code revisn dies 10-4, 785C1; ACLU hails 10-20, 981C3

1979

CRIME—*See also TERRORISM; country names*
LEAA '73-77 survey rptd 1-18, 118G3
ABA mid-winter mtg 2-7—2-14, 130E1
LEAA progrm in Conn rptd 2-25, 156C3
Corp crime study rptd 3-8, 240A1
Alcohol-related crimes rptd up 3-9, 218B3
Kennedy scores Carter 11-9, 962C1

1980

CRIME
State of State messages 1-4, 1-9, 269D1, 270C1; 1-8, 2-19, 403G3, 404C1; 1-14, 1-15, 483C2, D3, 484A2
Open trials backed by Sup Ct 7-2, 510C2-C3
Hispanic crime study rptd 7-28, 654C3
Dem platform criminal code plank adopted 8-13, 615D1
'79 US data rptd 9-24, 971D1
Libertarian pres candidate cites stance 10-28, 818G2
Criminal code revisn dies 12-16, 982E2

1976

'75 crime data rptd 3-25, 336G2
SD Indian leader shot 5-5, 384E2
Allied Chem indicted 5-7, other suits pending 349A1
Ex-Washn Post pressmen indicted 7-14, 7-21, 553B3
Ford urges Cong action 7-19, 532C1
Open govt bill signed 9-13, 688F3
Cong sets '77 budget levels, table 9-16, 706C2
Fed code revisn bill not cleared 10-2, 884F1
Allied Chem fined 10-5, 767D3
Sturz gets Rockefeller award 11-16, 911D3

Airplane Hijackings—*See under AVIATION*
Antitrust Actions—*See ANTITRUST*
Arson
'72 Wilmington 10 convictn review denied 1-19, 43E1
Ill nursing home 1-30, 1 chrgd 2-3, 271A3
Boston Museum fire 5-29, 392D1
NYC soc club 10-24, 876E2

Bombings
Ariz BIA office threatnd 1-1, 7F1
Fine arrested for '70 Wis bombing 1-7, 32C2
FBI-backed rt-wing blasts chrgd 1-11, 42C1
'75 data rptd 2-12, 159E3
Hearst Calif homes 2-12, 3-11, 201A3-B3
'63 Ala probe reopened 2-18, 159D3
Bomb defused at Sovt trading office in NY 3-25, 229A3
NE blasts 4-22—7-2; 4 suspects indicted 7-14, 1 sentncd 10-8, 796B3
Ariz reporter dies 6-13, 483G2; **see BOLLES, Don**
Letter bomb explodes in NY 6-14, FBI statemt 6-15, 504B1
Fine sentncd 8-6, 776G2
2 testify at '75 Miami bombers trial 8-17, 8-18, 791F1
Croat bomb kills NYC policeman 9-11, 685B1
Sovt ship in US port bombed 9-17, 908A1
Chile ex-min killed in US 9-21, 710C2; **for subsequent developments, see LETELIER, Orlando**
Explosives possessn crime rating up 10-4, 796G3
'74 Cuba exile convictn cited 10-20, 780A3

Bribery, Fraud & Extortion—*See also GRAIN—Export Probe, POLICE, POLITICS—Corruption Issues, STOCKS*
Ticor indicted 1-14, unit chrgd 2-2, 160A1
2 Franklin ex-offls plead guilty 1-20, 78F2
ABP, ex-offcl found guilty 1-21, 78B3
US Financial ex-chrmn sentncd 2-3, 124C1
Brunswick execs convctd 2-29, sentncd 4-12, 316B3
6 Franklin ex-offcls sentncd 3-9, 271B2
GM Mass auto dealer convicted, other suits cited 4-1, 287E1
Lefferdink sentncd in Miami 4-26, 384G2
Sea-Land rebates rptd 5-28—9-13, 689A3
Ariz reporter slain, land frauds linked 6-2—6-22, 483G2
Dem platform text 6-15, 473F3
Letter bomb explodes in NY, FBI statemt 6-15, 504B1
Pallotine Fathers fund fraud rptd 6-18—10-24, 950E3
Cella convicted 6-24, sentnc rptd 7-20, 860D2
Ex-SBA offcl sentncd 6-25, 596G1
Pomponio sentenced 6-25, 860F2
18 indicted in Ariz land fraud 9-14, mistrial declared in rptr's death 10-21, 859E2, D3
2 clerics sentncd in food-stamp swindle 9-17, 776F2
Cornfeld sentncd 9-27, 860G2
Cong OKs HEW inspector-gen bill 9-29, 765G2-B3; Ford signs 10-15, 982G1
Press probes Ariz crime 10-2, 849B2
Sup Ct bars review of suit vs Ampex 10-4, 807C3
3 seized in Phila extortn attempt 11-3, 972D1
'75 embezzlemt sentncs cited 11-20, 885D3
Sup Ct bars review of Ill legislator's case 12-6, 920C3
3 suspects rptd in Grenada 12-7, 925G1
2 convctd in Pittsburgh case 12-10, 952A3
Home-Stake fines rptd 12-22, 1016C2
3 convicted in Mass GM case 12-23, 988E1

1977

Croats in NY face US, NYS chrgs 6-16, 497D2
LEAA to close regional offices 6-20, study urges reorganizatn 6-30, 630A2, D2
Carter studies law enforcemt reorganizatn 6-29, 499G2
KKK rally assailant chrgd 7-3, 540A1
Raymond Burns dies 7-7, 604G2
SEC sues IDS, settles 7-19, 612A3
'76 FBI data rptd 9-27, 847D3
Chicago 7 figure gets OSHA post 9-30, 808B2
Carter cites 7% rate drop 11-7, 972C1
'76 cost to business rptd 11-17, 919B1
Airplane Hijackings—*See under AVIATION*
Antitrust Actions—*See under 'A'*
Arson—*See FIRES & Explosions*
Assassinations—*See under 'A'*
Assault & Battery—*See under 'A'*

Bombings
Bolles murder suspect pleads guilty 1-15, 161D3
Yoshimura convicted 1-20, 59G3; sentncd 3-17, 288A3
2 chrgd in Ariz fed bldg plot 2-14, 162F1
'75 Miami bomber sentncd 3-18, 288E3
FALN claims NYC blasts 3-21, 261A2
Bishop '75 convictn reversed 4-5, 484E1
Wis U '70 bomber sentncd 6-8, 6-10, 492C1
FALN hits 2 NYC bldgs 8-3, dud found 8-8, 613D3, G3
Ala '58 church bomb suspect surrenders 9-28, '63 bomber convicted 11-18, 907G2, D3

Bribery, Fraud & Extortion—*See also BUSINESS-Payments Issues; GRAIN-Export Probe; LABOR—Unions; POLITICS—Corruption*
2 in Bronfman case sentncd 1-6, 103C1
Amrep, 4 execs convicted 1-24, 156A2; sentenced 3-10, 203A3
Stirling Homex ex-offcls convicted 1-29, 103G1 ★; sentncd 3-11, 203F2
Teamster pres' son, others indicted 2-4, 102G3-103B1
Navajo ldr, ex-aide indicted 2-9, 162E3
Falstaff, Dixie cos chrgd 2-16, 215D2
McCulloch Properties pleads guilty 2-22, 156G1
Bond investmt scheme indictmts 3-3, 204C1
San Jose health care fraud chrgd 3-8, probe dispute 3-17—3-23, 235F2
2 NJ insurnc execs indicted 3-10, 203E3
2 '69 Penn Central plotters cleared 3-11, 1 convctd 3-30, 491E3
Elec execs sentncd for Sovt sales 3-14, 203D2
Hare Krishna indictmts dropped 3-17, 287F1
FBI to probe health care frauds 3-20, 236A1
IRS ex-offcl sentenced 3-31, 288G1
West convictn review declined 4-4, 341F3
Law firm settles Natl Studnt Mkting suit 5-2, 520A1
Mafia loan sharking role rptd 5-16, 568E1
Navajo fraud case dismissed 5-17, 492A1
537 Medicaid fraud cases rptd, pending legis cited 6-18, 643F2
Franklin bank ex-offcl pleads guilty 6-21, 540G2
Broadway producer chrgd 7-12, 10-13, 848F1
Boxing scandal rpt issued 9-3, 828D1
San Fran Chinatown slayings 9-4, 711B3
Vesco trial ordrd by CR 9-12, 767D1
State aid for food stamp cases set 9-29, 737F1, B2
Mafia's Bufalino sentncd 10-21, 991D3
Medicaid, Medicare curbs signed 10-25, 814D1

1978

Job tax credit for hiring felons clears Cong 10-15, 785D3
LEAA inner city survey rptd 10-16, 842A2
Press search shield bill proposed 12-13, 1029D3

Airplane Hijackings—*See under AVIATION*
Antitrust Actions—*See ANTITRUST*
Arson—*See FIRES & Explosions*
Assassinations—*See ASSASSINATIONS*
Assault & Battery
NBA player reinstated 2-1, 271A2
Calif bars Banks extraditn to SD 4-19, 327E1
Newton arrested 5-11, chrgs dropped 7-13, 971A3
5 youths sentncd in '76 NYC racial assault 5-12, 380D3
Calif woman wins Synanon suit 9-19; atty attacked by rattler 10-10, 2 members chrgd 10-17, 841G2, D3
Rep Burke pleads guilty 9-26, 734G2; loses reelectn 11-7, 846D2
Calif probes Synanon incidents 10-15, forms task force 10-17, 841G3-842B1
Atlantic City rate up 25% 11-10, 920F1
Martin chrgd 11-12, 1026D2
Ray's brother arrested in St Louis 11-27, 938F1
Synonon founder chrgd 12-3, 971A2
Lucchesi settles Randle suit 12-8, 1026F2

Bombings
Wilmington 10 denied convictn review 1-5, 24D2
Bolles killers get death 1-10, 24B2
Wilmington 10 sentences cut 1-23, Wright paroled 6-1, 560B2
Abortn clinic blasts rptd 3-7, 5-17, 744B2
Alaska '77 pipe saboteur convicted 5-11, 380A2
NY Sovt office bombed 7-10, 542A3
2 convicted for Washn, Ore bombings 7-11, 824A3
Cuba UN missn in NY bombed 9-9, 777B1
Chicago factory blast rptd 11-29, 933D3
Serbs held in Chicago plot 12-1, 933D3
Bolles state witness jailed 12-9, 992D2

Bribery, Fraud & Extortion—*See also BUSINESS—Payments Issues, POLITICS—Corruption*
Pallottine priest indicted 1-6, 24G2
SC gag-order case review barred 1-9, 13F1
Lloyd Carr fugitive arrested 1-24, 83B2-E3
Criminal code revisn OKd by Sen 1-30, 64C3, D3
Bergman sentenced 2-2, 232F3
Scientology founder sentncd 2-14, 232G3
Mattel offcls indicted 2-16, 116F2
McDermott pleads guity, fined 2-22, 142E2-C3
Grand jury probes new Estes chrgs 2-27, 172C3
Church-bond probes rptd 2-27, 295G3
Firestone ex-offcl pleads guilty 2-28, 142C3
Vesco indicted in CR 3-16, 269C3
Olin Corp indicted 3-23, 243E1
Bankers Trust stock sale case refused by Sup Ct 3-28, 241F3
REA ex-chief sentenced 3-31, 310C1
Mail frauds cost $1 bln 4-3, 389G1
Litton indictmt dismissal reversed 4-5, 368F1
Calif swindler sentenced 4-10, 380C2
Graiver, 4 others indicted for embezzlemt 4-12, 326C1
Lance, 2 banks chrgd, case settled 4-26, 324F2
Vesco chrgs dismissed by CR 4-30, 354F2
Avedon imposter sentenced 5-5, 380B2
2 chrgd in welfare frauds 5-8, 7-25; NY crackdown rptd successful 7-3, 684F3
Pallottine priest sentenced 5-9, 380F1-A2
NY rabbi pleads guilty 5-11, 363C2; sentenced 6-22, 500E3
Houston Univ ex-aide indicted 5-15, 380A3
Methodists settle pensn fund fraud suit 5-21, 480F3
Firestone ex-offcl sentenced 5-31, 404D2
22 indicted on port corruptn 6-7, 480D2
Union insurnc scheme chrgd 6-15, 560F2-D3

1979

Airplane Hijackings—*See under AVIATION*
Antitrust Actions—*See ANTITRUST*
Arson—*See FIRES & Explosions*
Assassinations—*See ASSASSINATIONS*
Assault & Battery
Utah man killed during arrest 1-18, 94B1
'73-77 survey rptd 1-18, 119A1
Cuban defector released from prison 2-21, 442G1
Martin setls chrg 5-24, returns as Yankees mgr 6-19, 619B2
Chippewas arrested in Minn violence 5-25, 465A1; sentncd 7-22, 630F3
Student violence rptd 7-5, 786F1
US basketball coach arrested at Pan Am Games 7-8, convctd 8-22, sentncd 9-10, 798D3
Carswell assaulted in Atlanta 9-11, 859D3
2d 1/4 rise rptd 10-9, 819B3
DC anti-Teng protesters freed 11-14, 904G3
Kennedy Secret Svc agents subdue woman with knife 11-28, 962D2
Cleaver guilty plea rptd 12-3, 1006E1
Mennonite farmer acquitted 12-4, 932C1-A2
Bombings
'78 data rptd 1-1, 102G2
Wis U '70 bomber paroled 1-11, 102F2
Wilmington 10 backed by Amnesty Intl 2-1, 85E2
Ill prison search nets bombs 3-3, 196G3
Morales convicted 3-9, sentncd 4-20; escapes 5-21, 431E1
Yoshimura '77 convictn upheld 4-5, 271A3
Serbian sentncd in '75 Chicago bombings 6-22, 491E2
NYC anti-Castro protests 10-12, 779C1
FALN bomb hoax in NYC 10-17; Chicago, PR blasts 10-18, 786A2
Cuban mission in NYC bombed 10-27, 852D1; 12-7, 947B3
Sovt UN missn in NYC bombed 12-12, 965C3

Bribery, Fraud & Extortion—*See also BUSINESS-Payment Issues, POLITICS—Corruption*
Graiver chrgs dismissed 1-8, 163B1
SEC role in pensn plans barred by Sup Ct 1-16, 32F1-D2
Scotto indicted 1-17, 87G2-C3
FBI ex-agent sentenced 1-17, 92B3
Fla ex-insurnc comr sentncd 1-18, 79C1
'Cross of Lourdes' mail fraud indictments set 1-19, 91B3
3 Franklin Bank ex-offcls convicted 1-23, 205G2-D3
Krishna cult sued re solicitatns 1-25, 102F1
Tenn ex-comr sentncd 1-26, 156E2
Houston ex-police chief sentncd 1-29, 79C1
GE worker chrgd in uranium theft 2-1, 119F3
Chicago bank embezzler convicted 2-7, 119A3; sentncd 2-25, 156A2
LA investmt fraud plea bargains rptd 2-13, 119B3
Estes indicted 2-22, 156G1
Lloyd Carr execs convicted, 2-22, sentncd 3-19, 220E2
Johns-Manville broker sentncd 3-13, 239C3
Coal broker pleads guilty 3-13, 239G3
Bagley chrgd 3-14, 3-15, 291G3
Holzer convicted of grand larceny 3-15, 239E2
Conn A-sub wire fraud sentences 3-15, 3-20, 240E2
Tenn pardon sale indictmts 3-15, 309E2
Sindona, Bordoni indicted 3-19, 205C2
Franklin Bank ex-offcls sentncd 3-26, 3-27, 291E3
NBC ex-offcl pleads guilty 3-28, expense acct scandal grows 4-19, 334E2
IRS tap evidence backed by Sup Ct 4-2, 281D2
Moon church bank fraud chrgd 5-1, 376D2
Holzer sentenced 5-3, 431A3
Securities law broker protectn backed by Sup Ct 5-21, 400C3
NJ indicts 8 in Genovese 'family' 5-23, 508G1

1980

Airplane Hijackings—*See AVIATION--Hijackings & Bombings*
Antitrust Actions—*See ANTITRUST Actions*
Arson—*See FIRES & Explosions*
Assassinations—*See ASSASSINATIONS*
Assault & Battery
Cleaver gets 5 yrs probatn 1-3, 64E3
James Garner assaulted 1-16, 200E1
FALN raids Carter, Bush campaign hqs 3-15, 208A3-209A1
Ctroom ID in illegal arrest backed by Sup Ct 3-25, 265A3
US, Sovt aides assaulted at UN mtg 4-30, 325G1
Koch egg assailant sentncd 6-6, 639G2
Garner assailant convicted 7-19, 639A3
Dade Cnty ex-cop indicted 7-28, 576B1
Ariz alien case mistrial declared 7-29, retrial sought 8-29, 713E2
Anderson assaulted in Denver 8-5, 596F3-597A1
'79 US data rptd 9-24, 971D1, F1
Domestic violence victims bill dropped 11-17, 982A2
'69 Weatherman fugitive surrenders 12-3, 928A1
Buffalo racial incidents prompt probe 12-13, 997E1
Bombings
Wis U '70 bomber rptd paroled 1-1, 24F3
Ala '58 church bomb suspect extradited 1-11, 55A3
NYC Aeroflot office bombed 1-13, 55A2
'63 KKK church bombing prosecutn rptd blocked 2-18, 227C2
Bolles killers convictns overturned 2-25, 214G2
11 FALN suspects arrested 4-4; houses raided, execs hit list seized 4-7, 4-8, 308F3-309E1
'58 Ala church bomber sentncd 5-14, 405A1
'70 Weatherman fugitive surrenders 7-8, 576A3
Chattanooga firebombings 7-22—7-24, 575G3
8 FALN suspects convicted 7-30, 1 suspect rptd extradited 8-4, 601C1
Nev casino bombed 8-27, 833F3
Phoenix CBS-TV statn firebombed 9-30, 835D3
Calif 'alphabet bomber' convicted 10-16, sentncd 11-24, 927A2
Bolles killer convicted 10-17, 860E3
'70 Weatherman sentncd 10-28; '69 fugitive surrenders 12-3, 928A1, D1
Bolles killer sentenced 11-14, 926B3-927A1
Wilmington 10 convictn reversed 12-4, 940C1
11 FALN members indicted in Chicago 12-10, 963F3
Bribery, Fraud & Extortion—*See also BUSINESS--Payments Issues, POLITICS--Corruption*
Commodity optns trader arrested 1-2, 94D3
Estes '83 parole rptd 1-3, 64F3
Prosecutn disparities rptd 1-6, 24B3
NY businesswoman, 2 partners indicted 1-10, 216B1
7 ILA ldrs, businessmen sentenced 1-11, 64E1-C2
NY-NJ Customs corruptn probed 1-11, offcl pleads guilty 2-13, 359C2-B3
Lance trial opens 1-14, chrgs reduced 4-9, 291E3
Smith jury award upheld 1-18, 55D2
Female white-collar crime rptd up 1-21, 215E3
Scotto, Anastasio sentenced 1-22, 1-23, 64D2
Fla drug trial bribe chrgd 2-4, 270G3
'Church' founder, aide convicted of fraud 2-9, 157B2
Pa bankruptcy scandal indictmts 2-12, 502D2
Franklin Bank fraud appeals refused by Sup Ct 2-19, 131A1
Charity solicitatn limit voided by Sup Ct 2-20, 170D2
la grain elevator scandal rptd 2-25, 237F3
NY record co, 2 execs indicted 2-28, 237B3
Oil leasing lottery suspended, scandal hinted 2-29; resumptn ordrd 4-7, 330B2
Bahamas bank looting suit rptd 3-3, 228G3
Franklin Natl ex-vp fraud appeal declined by Sup Ct 3-17, 226G1
Tex habitual-offender law upheld by Sup Ct 3-18, 226G2
Racketeer law cases declined by Sup Ct 3-24, 265D1
Mutual fund insurance case refused by Sup Ct 3-24, 265E1
Commonwealth Ed, 2 offcls indicted 3-26, 249D1
Sindona convicted 3-27, 237D1
Sindona fraud suit ruling refused by Sup Ct 4-21, 344A2
Sindona aide sentenced 4-23, 415B1

1976

Capital Punishment
Moore sentenced 1-15, 23G1
Sup Ct to review 5 cases 1-22, 87G2
Simants sentncd in Neb 1-29, 492C1
Ford endorses 2-14, 130A1
527 rptd awaiting executn 3-29, 262C1
Sup Ct hears arguments 3-30, 3-31, 261G3
Sup Ct upholds Tex, Fla, Ga laws, voids NC, La 7-2, 491F1
Oklahoma law voided 7-6, new law enacted 7-24, 568B3
State laws, doomed prisoners rptd 491C3
Powell stays 3 executns 7-22, 568F2
GOP platform text 8-18, 604F1
Sup Ct reaffirms ruling; remands 2 Ark cases, OKs Ga rape review 10-4, 746E1
Gilmore sentncd 10-7, asks executn 11-8, 890E3
Sup Ct to review police killer law 11-29, 900F2
Gilmore executn stayed 12-3, 920A3
White executn stayed 12-6, 920G2
Sup Ct curbs anti-death juror exclusion 12-6, 920B3
Gilmore stay vacated 12-13, death date set 12-15, 952F1

Firearms—*See FIREARMS*
Gambling—*See GAMBLING*
Hearst Case—*See HEARST, Patricia*
Intelligence Issues—*See SECURITY*
Juvenile Delinquency—*See YOUTH*
Kidnapings
FBI-backed rt-wing abductns chrgd 1-11, 42C1
DC truck co exec's son 1-12—1-17, 159F3
Williams freed 1-16, 79A1
Provenzano, others indicted 6-23, 460A1
Chowchilla schlchildren 7-15, suspects arrested 7-23, 7-29, 560A1
Tullers sentncd in '72 hijacking 7-16, 544C1
DC exec son's kidnapers sentncd 7-21, 544D1
Harrises convicted 8-9, 595B3; sentenced 8-31, 679B3
GOP platform text 8-18, 604G1
Murphy abductor sentncd 9-17, 796E3
Harrises indicted 9-29, 735E2
Provenzano chrgs dismissed 10-29, 972B1
Chowchilla trial moved 11-10, 876E3
2 acquitted in Bronfman case 12-10, 952A3

1977

Teamsters insurnc deal probed 11-1—11-2, 837B1
Truckers sued by ICC 11-3, 861A1
'76 bank embezzlemt, insurnc fraud costs rptd 11-17, 919C1
3 Navy ex-officers acquitted for Iran contract fraud 11-24, 942E2
NY vet indicted in horse-switch scandal 12-2, 971A1
Transport Dept aide sentncd 12-21, 1009F1

Capital Punishment
Gilmore delays sought 1-11—1-17; executed 1-17, 40E1
Student survey released 1-14, 157E1, A2
Ct delays Jurek executn 1-17, 40B3
Dvpts in 11 states 2-2—7-12, 594C1-G2
Harris Survey results rptd 2-7, 594G2
ABA unit rejcts repeal resolutn 2-15, 594C3
Sup Ct delays Dobbs executn 2-25, 174B3
Sentencing on secret info curbed 3-22, 230D3
Sup Ct declines Jurek case review 3-28, 276D3
Darden convictn review denied 4-19, 342B2
White case review declined 4-25, 342A3
'76, '77 death row populatn rptd 5-5, 6-7, 593F3
Justice Dept backs uniform fed standards 5-18, 594D3
Sup Ct curbs mandatory sentncs 6-6, 478C2
Fla retroactive sentnc upheld 6-17, 518F1
Calif veto overridden 8-11, 652D2
Sup Ct declines 9 case reviews 10-3, 760D3
NY law sectns voided 11-15, 919B3
Utah law upheld 11-26, 919E3

Child Abuse—*See CHILDREN*
Espionage—*See under 'E'*
Firearms—*See under 'F'*
Gambling—*See under 'G'*
Hearst Case—*See HEARST, Patricia*
Intelligence Issues—*See U.S. GOVERNMENT, subheads CENTRAL Intelligence Agency and FEDERAL Bureau of Investigation*
Juvenile Delinquency—*See YOUTH—Crime*
Kidnapings
Ind mortgage co exec seized 2-8—2-10, 162G1
Cincinnati couple seize 8 2-11, chrgd 2-13, 163F1
US issues terrorism rpt 3-2, 484A1
Ohio man takes hostages 3-7—3-8, arraigned 3-9, 178B3
Hanafi Muslims seize 134 3-9—3-11, 192F2
Hare Krishna indictmts dropped 3-17, 287A2
Va death penalty bill signed 3-29, 594E1
Edgar Smith sentenced 4-25, 396E1
Hanafis indicted 5-3, 396A1
Croats held on US chrgs 6-16, 497D2
Bus hijacked, 2 slain 7-4, 568D3
Hanafis convicted 7-23, sentncd 9-6, 711D1
'76 Chowchilla kidnapers plead guilty 7-25, 642D1
Ohio man sentencd 9-12, 712G1
Secretariat's missing mare rptd found 12-9, 971A2
Chowchilla kidnapers convicted 12-15, 992D1

1978

Franklin bank ex-offcls indicted 7-13, 681B1
New film indus probe set, Deluxe Gen fraud suit cited 7-14, 599F2-A3
Insurnc promoter indicted 7-18, 599D1
HEW asks welfare loopholes closed 7-20, 684E3
Lloyd Carr execs indicted 8-3, 665C2
Admin linked to Vesco 'pol fix,' denials issued 9-1—9-15, 719G3
Calif woman wins Synanon suit 9-19, 841D3
NY vet convicted in '77 horse switch 9-21, sentncd 11-3, 1028F1
Litton indictmt rule refused by Sup Ct 10-2, 751G1
Stirling Homex convictns review denied by Sup Ct 10-2, 751E2
Houston U ex-aide chrgd by SEC 10-5, 770B3
Estes pleads guilty 10-18, 886E3
Govt witness in racketeering case slain 10-25, pornographer arrested 11-9, 971D2
Ala ex-sheriff, 18 others chrgd 10-27, 992A2
Fruehauf Corp convictn review denied by Sup Ct 11-6, 874D1
Stockbroker liability case refused by Sup Ct 12-4, 959C1
Conn A-sub plot wire fraud chrgd 12-6, 2 convicted 12-14, 12-19, 992E1
HEW anti-fraud drive launched 12-13, 984G2
Houston ex-police chief convctd 12-14, 991A2
Calif woman sentncd in welfare fraud 12-28, 1029C1
Continental Grain pleads guilty 12-28, 1029D1

Capital Punishment
NJ bill pocket-vetoed 3-3, 388E3
Jan death row populatn rptd 3-6, 388D1
Sentencing study finds bias 3-6, 389A1
Md restores death penalty 3-10, 388F3
NYS death penalty bill clears legislature 3-20; Carey vetoes 4-11, veto override fails 5-2, 388G2-B3, D3
NYC policemen slain, Carey '76 Attica pardon scored 4-5, 388C3
Ala death penalty upheld 5-19, 388G3
Secret evidence convictn case declined by Sup Ct 5-30, 430C3
Ohio law voided; NY, Pa cases refused by Sup Ct 7-3, 552D1-B2
Tex executn filming case declined by Sup Ct 7-3, 552D2
NYS restoratn appeal declined by Sup Ct 10-16, 789C2
ACLU hails expanded death penalty defeat 10-20, 981C3
Ore, Calif referenda OKd; NYS campaign cited 11-7, 847A2, 849F1, 856A3, 857C2, 920C2

Child Abuse—*See CHILDREN*
Embezzlement—*See 'Bribery' above, 'Robbery' below*
Espionage—*See ESPIONAGE*
Firearms—*See FIREARMS*
Forgery
Prosecutors' plea-bargaining power expanded 1-18, 64E3
Columbia Pictures pres quits in scandal 2-9, indicted 3-31, 251C1
Oberlander, 4 others sentncd in London 5-31, 824C3
Columbia Pictures ex-pres fined 6-28, 599B2
Gambling—*See GAMBLING*
Hearst Case—*See HEARST, Patricia*
Intelligence Issues—*See U.S. GOVERNMENT, subheads CENTRAL Intelligence Agency and FEDERAL Bureau of Investigation*
Juvenile Delinquency—*See YOUTH—Crime*
Kidnaping
'76 Chowchilla kidnapers sentncd 2-17, 232C3
Fla involuntary servitude chrgd 3-2, 396E3
NYS death penalty bill clears legislature 3-20; Carey vetoes 4-11, override fails 5-2, 388A3
Colo banker's wife ransomed 4-6, 396C3
Pulitzer awarded for Ind '77 photo 4-17, 314G2
3 arrested in Tenn abductn 5-3, 5-4, 396A3
Calif woman wins Synanon suit 9-19, 841D3
Harrises sentncd 10-3, 823F3

1979

Fla law firm chrgd in visa fraud 6-1, 491D3
Moon church bank fraud chrg setld 6-6, 547E2
Provenzano, 3 others sentenced 7-10, 548E1
Bagley acquitted 8-1, 578D2
Estes sentenced 8-6, 604E3
Sindona rptd kidnaped 8-6, 635A3
Scientology church loses fraud suit 8-15, 640E2
Penn-Dixie ex-pres convicted 8-29, 655F3
Mail fraud crackdown set 9-19, 921B3
Cook settles chrgs, Miss R Grain case cited 9-26, 727G2-C3
SBA minority-aid abuse rptd 9-28, 947A3
Newark ex-mayor paroled 10-2, 891F1
Horizon land sales scored by FTC 10-3, 903E1
NYU prof indicted in drug case 10-4, 839G3
Cornfeld acquitted 10-15, 817F3
2 in FBI rptd removed 10-17, 1 kills self 10-18, 787B2; other pleads guilty 11-15, 906G1*
'Hillside Strangler' sentncd 10-19, 10-22, accomplice chrgd 10-19, 818F2
Thevis, 2 others convicted 10-21, 818A2
Pauline Fathers probe rptd 11-9, 905E3
Scotto convicted 11-15, 890A1
Pensn safeguards urged 11-26, 905C1
Gulf+Western, execs sued 11-26, 923D1
Travel Act bribery convictn upheld by Sup Ct 11-27, 919E3
U of New Mex basketball scandal detailed 12-13–12-21, 1003F1
Smith damage judgement rptd 12-24, 991G3

Capital Punishment
Cuevas sentenced in Tex 1-26, 400B2
Ill law declared illegal 1-30, 400A2
ABA seeks free counsel in Sup Ct cases 2-13, 130B2
RI law overturned 2-19, 188B2
Spenkelink appeal refused by Sup Ct 3-26, 230F2
NM restores death penalty 4-1, 400B2
Evans death delay refused by Sup Ct 4-13, executn stayed in Ala 4-20, 400F1
Spenkelink death warrant signed, stays denied 5-19–5-25, executed in Fla 5-25; Young comment draws fire 5-25–5-26, 399G3, 400D1
Darden death warrant signed 5-19, executn stayed 5-22, 400A1
Smith Va challenge declined by Sup Ct 5-21, 400E3
Green sentnc vacated by Sup Ct 5-29, 421E3
Mass bill signed 8-14, 989G1
ABA vs death penalty reinstatemt 8-15, 768E3
Neb slayer acquitted in retrial 10-17, 890F3
Bishop executn stay denied 10-21, dies in Nev gas chamber 10-22, 817G1-F2
Neb 'cancer' murderer sentncd 11-7, 891A1
State death row figures rptd 11-25, 989E3
Amnesty Intl scores US 12-9, 980B2
Counterfeiting
Currency offset printing urged 9-25, 727E2
Embezzlement—*See 'Bribery' above, 'Robbery' below*
Espionage—*See ESPIONAGE*
Firearms—*See FIREARMS*
Forgery
Begelman named MGM movie pres 12-18, 1007D1
Gambling—*See GAMBLING*
Hearst Case—*See HEARST, Patricia*
Intelligence Issues—*See U.S. GOVERNMENT, subheads CENTRAL Intelligence Agency and FEDERAL Bureau of Investigation*
Juvenile Delinquency—*See YOUTH—Crime*
Kidnaping
Gacy indicted in Chicago 1-8, 24A3
Verbal rights waiver backed by Sup Ct 4-24, 364A2
Niehous rescued 6-30, 505B3
NJ bank exec's wife abducted 7-20–7-22; suspects seized, ransom recovered 7-22, 7-26, 604F3
Fla child abducted 7-28, parolee arrested in SC 7-30, 604G3
Bundy sentncd in Fla 7-31, 604G1
Sindona rptd missing in NY 8-6, 635A3
Mass death penalty bill signed 8-14, 990A1
Harris convictns review declined by Sup Ct 10-1, 768B1
3 held in NH re Iran crisis 11-23–11-24, 898D2
Murphy abductor parole rptd set 12-18, 1005E3
Baker urges '1st Brigade' 12-19, 983C1

1980

Lance cleared on fund misuse, mistrial declared on 3 counts 4-30, 332D3
'Charlie's Angels' fraud probe rptd 5-1, 376F2
Mass prof indicted 5-13, 414D3
la grain fraud probe rptd 5-14, 414E2
'Pyramid' schemes rptd growing 5-17, Calif collapses rptd 6-18, 655G2-E3
Errico convicted 5-19, 447A3
Ala black dist judge nominee accused 5-19, withdraws 9-17, 744G2, B3
U of NM coach, 2 others indicted 5-23, 469C3
SEC fraud intent proof required by Sup Ct 6-2, 512A3
Lance case dropped 6-9, 459F2-A3
Ohio judge acquitted 6-13, 503A2
Lloyd Carr chief sentenced 6-20, 503C1
NY Mafia boss indicted 6-30, 502E3
FBI bribe plotters convicted 7-3, 655D2
SE road builders guilty pleas rptd 7-5, 655E1
Pfeiffer resigns as NBC chrmn, RCA dir 7-10, 582F1
UNM coach acquitted of US chrgs 7-20, 875G3
De Angelis sentncd in pork swindle 7-21, 655B1
Ariz ex-football coach, others indicted 7-24, state probe asked 10-16, 875G2
Commonwealth Ed, 2 offcls acquitted 8-8, 649D1
Eastn hijacker chrgd with extortn 8-18, 667A2
Hell's Angels sentenced 8-18, 714B1
Revlon heir, financier indicted 8-19, 713F3
Extortionists bomb Nev casino 8-27, 833F3
Pa lottery fraud chrgs rptd 9-19, 786B3
Ore U indictmts cited 10-15, 875C3
Offshore bank fraud indictmts 10-20, 860G2-E3
Eagleton niece, atty convicted 10-24, 890C1
ERA advocate fined in Ill bribe case 11-7, 997A3
Ga 'death row' escape extortn chrg 11-8, 927A1
NY Mafia boss convicted 11-21, 971D2
LA DA ends 'Charlie's Angels' probe 12-2, 1002E2
Methodists settle retiremt home fraud suit 12-10, 963C3
NY businesswoman, partner convicted 12-21, 997F2

Capital Punishment
Viet-era Marine ct-martial asked 2-1, 115C3
Bolles killers convictns overturned 2-25, 214B3
Gacy sentenced in Chicago 3-13, 214C1-2
Collier, Dix appeals declined by Sup Ct 3-24, 265C2
Ga law applicatn narrowed by Sup Ct 5-19, 439E3
Md ct backs death penalty law, voids Tichnell sentnc 6-10, 869F1
Ala death penalty struck down by Sup Ct 6-20, 555C1
Potts executn stay issued 6-28, Sup Ct continues stay 6-30, 511F1
GOP platform adopted, Hook scores plank 7-15, 535B1, C3, 537E1
Ala death row inmates ordrd retried 10-15, 869A1
Calif ct upholds Jackson death sentnc 10-23, 868F3-869A1
Mass law struck down 10-28, 868D3
Judy murder convictn appeal discharge OKd 10-28, 869E1
Bolles killer sentenced 11-14, 926B3-927A1
Counterfeiting
Female white-collar crime rptd up 1-21, 215F3
NY record co, 2 execs indicted in tape fraud 2-28, 237C3
Female Secret Svc agent slain 6-5, 503F2
Espionage—*See ESPIONAGE*
Firearms—*See FIREARMS*
Forgery
NY businesswoman, partners indicted 1-10, 216B1
Female white-collar crime rptd up 1-21, 215E3
NY businesswoman, partner convicted 12-21, 997F2
Gambling—*See GAMBLING*
Juvenile Delinquency—*See YOUTH--Crime*
Kidnaping
Beatrice Foods liability barred 1-6, 18A1-B2
Bundy sentenced again 2-12, 136C2
2 Calif boys found 3-1, 3 chrgd 3-2, 238C2
Sindona convicted of bank fraud 3-27, 237G1
FALN execs hit list siezed 4-8, 309E1
Religious deprogrammer convicted 8-29, 727B1; sentncd 9-26, 857B3

1976

Labor Corruption—*See LABOR*
Libel
Sup Ct limits 'public figures' rule 3-2, 169E2
State, local offcls win fed immunity 3-23, 218C3
Sup Ct bars review of Church case 4-5, 262A2
Sup Ct bars review of LA Times case 10-4, 807D2
Murders
Fine arrested 1-7, 32E2
US health rpt issued 1-12, 32C1
Simants sentncd in Neb 1-29, 492C1
'74 death rates rptd 2-3, 123G3 ★
1 chrgd in Ill nursing home fire 2-3, 271A3
Carson, 5 others acquitted '74 convictn cited 2-6, 124E1
Ford backs capital punishmt 2-14, 130A1
'63 Ala bomb probe reopened 2-18, 159D3
Sup Ct grants prosecutors immunity 3-2, 169D3
'68-74 increase rptd 3-2, 336E3
'57 Alabama suspects indicted 3-5, freed 4-14, 316D2
Carter, Artis get new trial 3-17; bail posted 3-19, 256D3
'75 decrease rptd 3-25, 336A3
4 sentncd in 'Zebra' killings 3-29, 292F3
Edgerly chrgs in '74 Mass case pending 4-1, 287F1
Ray appeal denied 5-10, 384F2
NJ MD indicted re curare 5-19, 384A3
2 convicted in Knight killing 5-20, 6-14, 503G3
Ex-NYC aide slain 6-6, 442D3
Starkweather companion paroled 6-8, 442C3
Fine pleads guilty 6-8, 776A3
Ariz reporter dies 6-13, 483G2; **see BOLLES, Don**
2 chrgd in '75 Mich VA Hosp deaths 6-16, 503D3
Provenzano, 3 others indicted 6-23, 460A1
Neb pretrial press gag order voided 6-30, 491D3-492C1
Sup Ct upholds capital punishmt 7-2, 491F1
7 killed on Calif campus 7-12, 860G1
Tullers' Tex chrgs pending 7-16, 544D1
2 cleared in SD '75 FBI deaths 7-16, 640E2
'75 death rates rptd 7-31, 911F1
Means acquitted 8-6, 640D2
San Quentin 6 verdict 8-12, 656B1
Van Houten wins new trial; Manson, Atkins, Krenwinkel denied 8-13, 640B3
Cleaver freed on bail 8-13, 640C3
Ray changes prisons 8-13, 640G3
Yablonski slayers sentncd 9-3, 816A3
Croats face chrgs re NYC policeman 9-13, 685B1
Speck denied parole 9-15, 860A2
Sup Ct reaffirms capital punishmt rule 10-4, 764E1
Gilmore sentncd to die 10-7; asks executn 11-8, 890E3; executn stayed 12-3, 920A3
Carter, Artis retrial opens, judge replaced 10-12—11-11, 860B1
Saxe mistrial declared 10-13, 816B2
Kallinger gets life 10-14, 972E1
Mistrial declared in Ariz rptr's death 10-21, 859E2
Cuba exile killed in PR 10-25, 844C3
New judge OKd in Ariz trial 11-19, venue chng ordrd 12-7, 971C3
Sup Ct stays gag order in Okla youth case 11-24, 901C2
Gilmore stay vacated 12-13, death date set 12-15, 952F1
Carter, Artis convicted 12-21, sentencing set 12-23, 1015C3

1977

Labor Corruption—*See LABOR*
Libel—*See under 'L'*
Murders (& manslaughter)—*See also ASSASSINATIONS under 'A'*
Cuban exile ldr slain 1-7, 163D1
Gilmore death delays sought 1-11—1-17; executed 1-17, 40E1
Bolles murder suspect pleads guilty 1-15, 161D3
Sup Ct delays Jurek executn 1-17, 40B3
Saxe pleads guilty 1-17, 140E1
Boyle convictn upset 1-28, 95D3
Longet sentncd re Sabich 1-31, 102E3
Carter nurse pardoned 2-3, 354D2
Death penalty survey rptd 2-7, 594A3
Carter, Artis sentenced 2-9, 140C1
Bompensiero slain 2-10, 568D2
New Rochelle (NY) man kills 5, self 2-14, 162E2
Dobbs executn delayed 2-25, 174B3
Raped Calif woman acquitted 3-4, 262B1
Okla youth ct gag order voided 3-7, 211B2
Hanafis shoot radio rptr 3-9, 192F2
Missing Nev unionist found slain 3-17, 261C3
Fla death sentence on secret info remanded 3-22, 230E3
Miranda rule review sidestepped 3-23, 275A3
Chesimard convicted, sentncd 3-25, 288B3
Jurek case review denied 3-28, 276D3
Va death penalty bill signed 3-29, 594E1
Darden convictn review denied 4-19, 342B2
Manson convictn review denied 4-25, 342G2
White case review declined 4-25, 342A3
Edgar Smith sentenced 4-25, 396E1
Hanafis indicted 5-3, 396A1
Indianapolis heiress shot 5-7, 492F1
Sodomist linked to '73 Tex murders 5-15, 432A3
Justice Dept backs uniform fed procedures 5-18, 594D3
Calif death penalty vetoed 5-27, 594A2
NC death penalty in effect 6-1, 594C2
Peltier sentncd in '75 FBI case 6-2, 491G3
Sup Ct curbs mandatory death sentences 6-6, 478D2
Wis U '70 bomber sentncd 6-8, 6-10, 492C1
3 Girl Scouts slain in Okla 6-13, 492E1
Croats face NYS chrgs 6-16, 497E2
Fla retroactive death sentnc upheld 6-17, 518F1
Ill death penalty bill signed 6-21, 594E2
San Fran homosexual slain 6-22, 560D2
Newton to face '74 Calif chrgs 6-24, 531G3
Son of Sam sought 6-26, 532C1; **for subsequent developments, see BERKOWITZ, David R.**
Bus hijacked, 2 slain 7-4, 568D3
2 convicted in '75 Mich VA Hosp deaths 7-13, 568F2
Calif mass murder suspect indicted 7-13, 603F2
Sacco, Vanzetti vindicated 7-19, 652E2-A3
Conn family slain 7-22, suspect indicted 9-7, 712E1
Hanafis convictd 7-23, sentncd 9-6, 711D1
French Connectn drug figure slain 7-26, 642B1
Diamond dealer deaths probed 7-28—10-19, 871B3
Van Houten mistrial declared 8-6, 3d trial planned 9-1, 711C2
Escaped convict sought in Girl Scout deaths 8-22, 711E3
NJ sniper kills 6 8-26, 807A3
San Fran Chinatown gang slayings 9-4, 9-11, 711G2
US Open spectator shot 9-4, 787C2
NC sniper kills 2, self 9-5, 848G2
Alice Crimmins paroled 9-7, 848D1
'76 FBI data rptd 9-27, 847E3
Polygamists chrgd 9-27, 847F3
Youth guilty in Fla TV trial 10-7, 807F2; sentncd 11-7, 907F3
Contempt convictn review in Little '75 case barred 10-17, 797G3
Battered wife acquitted in Mich 11-3, 928E1
'73 Hanafi massacre figure cleared 11-5, 871G2
2 convicted in Bolles case 11-6, 871B2
NY death penalty provisn voided 11-15, 919C3
Texas millionaire acquitted 11-17, 928A1
Ala '63 church bomber convicted 11-18, 907G2
LA music promoter slain 11-21, 952G3
Utah death penalty law upheld 11-26, 919F3
Black life expectancy linked 12-13, 962C3
11th found strangled in Glendale (Calif) 12-14, 992B1
Dawson 5 chrgs dropped 12-19, 991B2
Mich VA Hosp convictns overturned 12-19, 991G2
Calif trashbag suspect sentncd 12-21, 991A3

1978

Labor Corruption—*See under LABOR*
Libel—*See LIBEL*
Murder (& manslaughter)—*See also ASSASSINATIONS*
Lyle chrgd in shooting 1-6, 56C1
Boyle gag-order case remanded 1-9, 13G1
Bolles killers get death 1-10, 24B2
Hunter fined in FBI aide's death 1-14, 69B2
Criminal code revisn OKd by Sen 1-30, 64C3
'75 Mich VA Hosp chrgs vs 2 nurses dropped 2-1, 116C2
Speck confesses '66 Ill slayings 2-6, 172D2
NYC '76 soc club arsonist sentenced 2-7, 380G3
Ga stocking strangler victim found 2-12, 232E3
Amer Chicle '76 blast chrgs dismissed 2-15, 212D3
Boyle convicted again 2-18, 129A1
Tex marshal sentenced 2-18, 991E3
Calif trash bag killer pleads guilty 2-21, 232B3
Death sentencing bias rptd 3-6, 389A1
Md restores death penalty 3-10, 388F3
NYS death penalty bill clears legislature 3-20; Carey vetoes 4-11, override fails 5-2, 388G2-B3, D3
Hoffa, Castellito murder suspect killed 3-21, 232G2
3 Houston ex-cops sentncd in Torres case 3-28, appeal rptd 12-14, 991B3
NYC policemen slain, Attica ex-inmate arrested 4-5, 388C3
Okla girl scout slaying suspect arrested 4-6, 380D3
Actress killed in Mich auditn 4-10, 380E2
Ga inmate slain, probe opens 4-10, 396G2
IBM heir convicted in plot 4-26, 380F2
Calif MD mistrial in abortn death 5-5, 369C2
'Son of Sam' pleads guilty 5-8, sentenced 6-13, 500F2
Newton arrested 5-11, chrgs dropped 7-13, 971G2
5 youths sentenced in '76 NYC racial assault 5-12, 380E3
Tex boy kills teacher 5-18, 396A2
Ill father convicted of slaying children 5-22, 396D3
2 AIM activists acquitted in Calif 5-24, 396B2
Calif man sentenced 5-24, 396F2
Secret evidence convictn case declined by Sup Ct 5-30, 430C3
4 Houston ex-cops chrgd in '77 Webster death cover-up 6-7, 991F2
Provenzano, Konigsberg convicted 6-14, sentenced to life 6-21, 480B2
Murder scene search warrants backed by Sup Ct 6-21, 509D2
TV actor found slain in Ariz 6-29, 540E2
NJ MD curare case press freedom controversy 6-30—8-30, 678C2
US drops dual prsecutn of Dallas cop in '73 Rodriguez case 7-14, 991C3
Utah widow kills self, 6 children 8-3, 685C3
Phila radicals chrgd in cop killing 8-8, 645D1
Soledad Brother chrgd in Calif slaying 8-25, 886G3
Arsonist convicted in NYC '74 disco fire 9-7, 824F2
Chicago rptr shoots wife, self 9-11, 777G3
Ford indicted in Ind Pinto deaths 9-13, 718F3-719A1
FBI informant indicted in '65 Liuzzo death 9-20, 720D2
Atlanta prison inmate slain 9-21, 771B1
Angels outfielder slain 9-23, 777G3
Fla youth loses TV violence suit 9-26, 759F2
2 Croatians slain 9-29, 11-22, 933E3
Hypnosis-related case refused by Sup Ct 10-2, 751C2
2 convicted in NYC '77 diamond dealers death 10-6, 824D2
Calif atty attacked by rattler 10-10, 2 Synanon members chrgd 10-17, 841G2
Van Houten sentncd 10-11, 824F2
US, Canada exchng prisoners 10-12—10-13, 794E3
Punk rock star accused 10-12, 842C1
NYT rptr's jailing scored by IAPA 10-13, 829F1
NYS death penalty restoratn plea refused by US Sup Ct 10-16, 789C2
Gig Young kills bride, self 10-19, 888G3
NJ MD acquitted in curare case, NYT rptr wins release 10-24, 841F1-F2
Govt witness in racketeering case slain 10-25, pornographer arrested 11-9, 971B2
Ruppert retrial case refused by Sup Ct 11-6, 874E1
Ore, Calif death penalty referenda OKd; NYS campaign cited 11-7, 847A2, 849F1, 856A3, 857C2
San Fran mayor, supervisor slain 11-27; ex-supervisor chrgd 11-29, 920G1-D3
NYT press freedom case declined by Sup Ct 11-27, 937F1
Synanon founder chrgd in rattler attack 12-3, 971F1
Bolles state witness jailed 12-9, 992D2
NJ sentencing system upheld by US Sup Ct 12-11, 981C1
2 Houston ex-cops chrgd in '75 Joyvies cover-up 12-14, 991D2
Lyle acquitted 12-16, 1028D2
'77 Tenn jail arsonist sentncd 12-20, 992A2
'74 Houston sex slayer's sentnc reversed 12-20, 992B2

1979

Labor Corruption—*See under LABOR*
Libel—*See LIBEL*
Murder (& Manslaughter)—*See also ASSASSINATIONS*
Gacy indicted in Chicago mass murder 1-8, pleads not guilty 1-10, 24F2
Pa abortn control law voided by Sup Ct 1-9, 14F1
Tex industrialist freed in mistrial 1-22, 64D3
Buckley admits misled in '57 Smith case 1-22, 78G3
Punk rock star freed on bail, ODs 2-2, 156B3
3 Houston ex-cops win Torres case appeal 2-6, 156B2
FBI informant's extraditn OKd 2-7, 120D1
Wyo police chief chrgd in '78 shooting 2-7, 156A1
Mineo killer convicted 2-13, 119E2
Wichita TV rptr contempt convictn review refused by Sup Ct 2-21, 128C3
Paramount resumes 'Warriors' ads 2-22, 174G1-A2
'Son of Sam' pre-arrest evidence rptd 2-26, 156F2
SLA '75 convictn reversed 2-27, 156C1
SC abortn prosecutn ban voided by US Sup Ct 3-5, 185B1
Calif nurse sentnd to 'house arrest' 3-6, 316A2
Mineo killer sentenced 3-15, 240D2
MacDonald trial challenge declined by Sup Ct 3-19, 203G2-A3
Polygamists acquitted 3-20, 240A2
Newton case ends in mistrial 3-24, 239C1
Fla death penalty appeal refused by US Sup Ct 3-26, 230F2
Easter killed in holdup 3-29, 1002E3
Md nurse freed 3-29, 291F1-A2
Okla Girl Scout slaying suspect acquitted 3-30, 291E2; dies 6-4, 508A3
Tenn slayings tied to pardon scandal 4-14, 4-17, 309A3
Conn armored car guards killed 4-16, 4 arrested 4-17, 316E1
Calif newspr loses libel case 4-18, 334C2
Evans executn stayed in Ala 4-20, 400G1
4 slain in Bedford Hills (NY) 5-10, 2 chrgd 7-19, 548F1
Darden death warrant signed 5-19, executn stayed 5-22, 400A1
Smith Va death penalty challenge declined by Sup Ct 5-21, 400F3
San Fran ex-supervisor convicted in Moscone-Milk slaying, gays protest 5-22, 385G3
NJ indicts 8 in Genovese 'family' 5-23, 508G1
Spenkelink executed in Fla 5-25, 400A1
Green death sentnc vacated by Sup Ct 5-29, 421E3
Co-defendant confessns allowed by Sup Ct 5-29, 422A1
Attica inmate slain in racial brawl 6-3, 548F2
'Probable cause' in detentns backed by Sup Ct 6-5, 464C2
Provenzano, Konigsberg '78 murder convictns upset; new trial ordrd 6-7, 491F3
Little paroled 6-9, 527D3
Mont homicide convictn reversed by Sup Ct 6-18, 499F1
Calif KKK member sentncd 6-19, 492G1
Ala trucker shot 6-20, 479D2
Juvenile 'Miranda rights' case remanded by Sup Ct 6-25, 540B2
Houston sex slayer convicted again 6-27, 819C1
Evidence standard eased by Sup Ct 6-28, 558D2
Ctroom pub access curbed by Sup Ct 7-2, 515B2
Power to void state convictns backed by Sup Ct 7-2, 558E3
San Fran ex-supervisor sentenced in Moscone-Milk slaying 7-3, 547E3
FBI sued over '65 Liuzzo slaying 7-5, 521C1
Galante slain 7-12, 548A1
Bundy gets death penalty for '78 Fla slayings 7-31, 604C2
3 FBI agents slain 8-9, suspect chrgd 8-16, 727E3
Mass death penalty bill signed 8-14, 990A1
NC MD gets life for '70 slayings 8-29, 817F2
FBI sets '70 Black Panther convictn probe 9-24, 886E2
Ex-Mafia informant sues US 9-26, 840F2
Newton case ends in 2d mistrial, chrgs dropped 9-27, 818B3
Calif schl sniper pleads guilty 10-1, 819E2
Neb 'cancer' murderer convicted 10-5, gets death penalty 11-7, 891A1
Ky convictn vacated by Sup Ct 10-9, 784C1
Motorist 'Miranda rights' case declined by Sup Ct 10-9, 784D1
2d 1/4 rise rptd 10-9, 819B3
Boyle sentncd again re Yablonski 10-11, 840B1, C1*
Coppolino paroled in Fla 10-16, 839G2
Neb slayer acquitted in retrial 10-17, 890E3
Phoenix (Ill) mayor slain 10-18, 840C2
'Hillside Strangler' gets life 10-19, 10-22, accomplice chrgd 10-19, 818D2

1980

Labor Corruption—*See LABOR--Corruption*
Libel—*See LIBEL*
Murder (& Manslaughter)—*See also ASSASSINATIONS*
Ex-Army gay activist chrgd 1-2, 18C3
Parole offcls immunity upheld by Sup Ct 1-15, 51F1
Okla slaying spurs racial violence 1-20, murder chrg filed 1-21, 94E1
Indian activist sentenced 1-23, 349E1
Tex witches' priest acquitted 2-1, 238E1
New Mexico prison riot 2-2—2-3, 112B2
Adamson slaying suspect chrgd 2-2, 238B3
Fla drug trial plot disclosed 2-4, 270G3
Ex-Black Panther denied parole 2-5, 215A2
Bundy gets 3d death sentence 2-12, 136C2
'63 KKK church bombing prosecutn rptd blocked 2-18, 227D2
Bolles killers convictns overturned 2-25, 214G2
Calif slayers sentenced 2-27, 238C3
8 Galante slaying probe figures indicted 3-3, 215C1
'Scarsdale Diet' MD slain 3-10, suspect chrgd 3-11, 214E3
San Fran Chinatown gang ldr convicted 3-10, 238A2
Gacy convicted in Chicago mass murder 3-12, gets death sentence 3-13, 214C1-C2
Ford acquitted in Ind Pinto case, evidence rptd restricted 3-13, 185B3-186D1
Ex-Rep Lowenstein slain 3-14, suspect chrgd 3-18, 214C2
Pa Mafia ldr slain 3-21, 237B2
Racketeer law cases declined by Sup Ct 3-24, 265D1
2 Ga death penalty pleas declined by Sup Ct 3-24, 265C2
Mandatory sentncs rptd up 3-29, 359E1
GI chrgd in parachute death 4-1, acquitted 5-27, 460B3
Multiple sentencing curbed by Sup Ct 4-16, 328B3
2 convicted for '79 Haitian drownings 4-18, 336B1; sentncd 6-5, 503A3
Thevis firearm convictn case refused by Sup Ct 4-21, 344B2
Phila radicals convicted in '78 cop killing 5-8, 414A1
Police interrogatn defined by Sup Ct 5-12, 386B2
4 Miami cops acquitted in black exec's '79 death 5-17, 382F2
Ga death penalty applicatn narrowed by Sup Ct 5-19, 439F3
Miami riot arrests 5-26, 5-27, 401E3
Polygamist ldr convicted 5-28, sentenced 6-2, 502A3
Jordan shot in Ft Wayne (Ind) 5-29, 410D2; case stymied 6-1—6-12, 442G1
Nev nurse cleared 5-30, 656A1
Jacobson flees jail 5-31, sentenced 6-3, 502A2
Female Secret Svc agent slain 6-5, 503E2
'Son of Sam' Soc Sec benefits rptd 6-5; insanity plea faked 8-4, 639E2
Pre-arrest silence testimony backed by Sup Ct 6-10, 512C1
Md ct backs death penalty law, voids Tichnell sentnc 6-10, 869F1
NY gun control bill signed 6-13, 470C3
Ala death penalty struck down by Sup Ct 6-20, 555C1
Tex church shooting 6-22, 5 dead 6-23, 568D2
Potts executn stay issued 6-28, Sup Ct continues stay 6-30, 511F1
Hell's Angels mistrial declared 7-2, 568C2
'70 Weatherman fugitive surrenders 7-8, plea bargain rptd 7-18, 576A3
Jacobson recaptured 7-9, 997D2
Synanon founder, 2 aides convicted 7-15, 655E3
US, Canada rates compared 7-16, 562C3
KKK members acquitted in Chattanooga shooting 7-22, 575F3
NYC violinist found slain 7-24, 654A1
Ga convicts escape 7-28, recaptured in NC 7-30, 654E1
Atkins denied parole 7-29, 639D2
Calif 'freeway murder' suspects chrgd 7-29, 654B2
NC MD convictn voided 7-30, 654F3
PR Navy ambush suspects murdered 8-11, 9-11, 1 rptd missing 9-8; natists plan probe 9-19, 786A2
'Playmate of Yr' found slain 8-15, 713D3
4th chrgd in 'freeway murders' 8-22, 727E1
Ga rptr, 2 others indicted in 'death row' escape 8-27, 712F2-D3
NYC stagehand arrested in violinist slaying 8-30, indicted 9-7, 713B1
Synanon founder gets probation 9-3, 860D2
Buffalo area blacks slain 9-22—9-24; police, FBI probes rptd 10-13, 997C1
'79 US data rptd 9-24, 971E1, F1
Navy sailor convicted of Kenya murder 9-30, sentence rptd scored 10-13, 10-20, 859C3
Evans wins Ala retrial order 10-15, 869C1
Calif 'alphabet bomber' convicted 10-16, sentncd 11-24, 927A2
Boles killer convicted 10-17, 860E3
Calif ct upholds Jackson death sentnc 10-23, 868F3-869A1
Judy convictn appeal discharge OKd 10-28, 869E1
'70 Weatherman bomber sentncd 10-28, 928D1

1976

Narcotics—*See NARCOTICS*
Organized Crime (including Mafia)
IRS-Justice probe agrmt issued 1-10, 41E3
Link to Ariz land deals rptd 6-2, 483C3, 484C1-F1
Emprise '75 convictn ruling cited 483D3
Dem platform text 6-15, 474B1
Mickey Cohen dies 7-29, 716G2
Press probes Ariz crime 10-2, 849C2
Carlo Gambino dies 10-15, 932D3
Paul Carbo dies 11-9, 970D1
Parole—*See 'Prisons & Prisoners' below*
Police—*See under 'P'*
Political Assassinations—*Note: Initial incident only listed; for subsequent developments, see country, personal names*
Duvalier attempt rptd 267A3
'75 attempt on Afars pres rptd 1-6, 86A1
FBI backed rt-wing plots chrgd 1-11, 42C1
Moore gets life term 1-15, 23F1-D2
Bokassa attempt fails 2-3, 204B2
Basque mayor 2-9, 144F2
House intelligence com offers reforms 2-10, 150A2
Gen Mohammed in Nigeria 2-13, 141C3
Ford bars foreign role 2-17, 2-18, 127F1, A3
Boonsanong in Thailand 2-28, 176E3
Kodama attempt fails 3-23, 286B2
Malloum attempt fails 4-13, 270E3
Qaddafi attempt rptd 4-19, 334F1
Alleged slayers of Iran Islam leader rptd arrested 5-17, 365B3
Guinea pres attempt rptd 6-6, 503A3
Amin attempt fails 6-10, 502C2
Chile's Letelier killed in DC 9-21, 710C2
Spain royal adviser 10-4, 774G2
Iran envoy shot in Paris 11-2, 1002F2-A3
Makarios plot foiled 11-10, 963C3
French centrist 12-24, 1002D2
Political Corruption—*See 'Corruption Issues' under POLITICS*
Political Payments Issues—*See under BUSINESS*
Pornography—*See under 'P'*
Presidential Election
Ford speech in Fla 2-14, 129G3
Reagan: law aids defendant 5-26, 391A2
Dem platform text 6-15, 473D3-474F1, 477B2
Carter pledge 7-15, 507F1, 510B3
Mondale pledge 7-15, 511B3
Carter queried on nephew 7-26, 551F1
GOP platform text 8-18, 604E1-E2
Ford acceptance speech 8-19, 611E3
Ford lists as top issue 8-27, 645D1
Carter, Mondale for firm law enforcemt 9-13, 9-14, 686G2, 687G1
Ford vows actn vs recidivists 9-15, 686A1
Ford, Carter debate 9-23, 702B1—A2
Ford urges 'crusade' 9-27, 723D3
Mondale, Dole debate 10-15, 782E3
Carter speaks on issue 10-15, 785E1
Ford, Carter debate 10-22, 801C3, 802C2
Prisons & Prisoners
Ala prison reform ordrd 1-13, 25G2
Ford State of Union message 1-19, 38B2, 39C3
AEC tests on Ore, Washn prisoners confrmd 2-28, 316C2
Parole bill clears Cong 3-2, 3-3, 181D2; Ford signs 3-15, 982D1
'74 US job training rpt issued 3-9, 271D2
Fed prison populatn up 3-14, 336F3
Sup Ct rejects right to silence in disciplinary hearings 4-20, 331E2
Black Dems draft plank 5-1, 343E3
Sup Ct rules on trial garb 5-3, 359G1
Dem platform text 6-15, 473G3
Sup Ct upholds transfers 6-25, 552A2
'77 fed prison funds signed 7-14, 534E2
San Quentin 6 verdict 8-12, 656B1
Ray transferred 8-13, 640D3
Manson cultist escapes jail 8-14, 640A3
GOP platform text 8-18, 604D2
Attica strike 8-23—8-28, 656E1
Parole comm alters ratings 10-4, 796F3
H Rap Brown wins parole 10-21, 912C3
Sup Ct bars immediate parole-revocatn hearings 11-15, 882D2
DeMent gets Rockefeller award 11-16, 911D3

1977

Narcotics—*See under 'N'*
Organized Crime (including Mafia)
Hustler publisher convicted 2-8, 118A2
Bompensiero slain 2-10, 568D2
Chemical Bank indicted 2-24, 155E2
Chem Bank, 2 ex-offcls plead guilty 3-3, 4-14, 540A3
Teamsters to revise pensn posts 3-13, 195D1
Legitimate business infiltratn; South, Westn operatns rptd 3-13—7-3, 568B1
Trafficante at JFK probe 3-16, 228E2
Ariz press probe rpt 4-3, 332G3
San Fran ex-mayor wins libel suit 5-3, 532B2
Child porno, prostitutn role rptd 5-15, 432A2
Zicarelli linked to laetrile operatn 5-16, 508A3
NYC ldrship struggle rptd 5-16, 568C1
2 ICC offcls suspended in trucking probe 6-8, 500C3
Vincent Papa slain 7-26, 642D1
Md Gov Mandel, 5 others convicted 8-23, 652A1
Mandel, 5 others sentncd 10-7, 807D2
Bufalino sentenced 10-21, 991D3
Zerilli dies 10-30, 872B3
Provenzano kickback chrg dropped 11-11, 928E1
Salerno mistrial declared 12-15, 992G1
Provenzano reindicted 12-19, 991B3
Police—*See under 'P'*
Political Corruption—*See POLITICS*
Political Payments—*See under BUSINESS*
Pornography—*See under 'P'*
Prisons & Prisoners
Death penalty survey rptd 2-7, 594A3
Dual prosecutn OKd re civil rights violatns 2-11, 821B1
US-Canada exchng treaty 3-2, 200B1
US issues terrorism rpt 3-2, 484B1
Fla, Tex penal inst judgmts upheld 3-21, 230A3
Va death penalty bill signed 3-29, 594E1
Cook County (Ill) conditns scored 4-4, 288F3
Mil incarceratns rptd down 4-6, 343B2
ABA inmate rights rpt issued 4-26, 383C2
Inmate legal aid ordrd 4-27, 383D1
Plea-bargaining review backed 5-2, 406D2
'76, '77 death row populatn rptd 5-5, 6-7, 593F3
Burger cites '69-76 prisoner rights cases 5-17, 419A3
Ray escapes 6-10, recaptured 6-13, 459A1
Inmate union curbs upheld 6-23, 539C2
42 die in Tenn jail fire 6-26, 508E3
Ala prison employe standards voided 6-27, 538E3

1978

Narcotics—*See NARCOTICS*
Obscenity—*See PORNOGRAPHY & Obscenity*
Organized Crime (including Mafia)
Bolles killers sentncd 1-10, 24C2
Criminal code revisn OKd by Sen 1-30, 64F2
Provenzano convicted 3-25, 232B2
Italy ldrs threaten Red Brigades 3-28, 247B2
Colombo dies 5-22, 440D2
ICC fires Kyle 6-7, 570B2
FBI agent indicted 9-15, 11-6; resigns, pleads guilty 11-9, 886C3
ICC ex-offcl indicted 9-22, 770F2
Trafficante, 2 others cited at JFK death hearings 9-26, 9-27; Trafficante testifies 9-28, 750B1-C2
Palmeri indicted in NJ 10-5, 770F3
Govt witness in racketeering case slain 10-25, pornographer arrested 11-9, 971D2
Mafia link to King murder rptd probed 11-22, 938F2
Bolles state witness jailed 12-9, 992D2
2 convicted in A-sub plot wire fraud 12-14, 12-19, 992F1
ICC ex-offcl acquitted 12-21, 1007G3
House com discounts JFK murder role 12-30, 1002C2
Perjury
Ex-Texas judge sentncd 1-27, 232A3
Criminal code revisn OKd by Sen 1-30, 64B3
Gurney trial press-curbs review declined by Sup Ct 4-17, 308D2
Brooke admits false loan disclosure 5-26, 506B1
4 Houston ex-cops chrgd in '77 Webster death cover-up 6-3, 991F2
Goodwin legal immunity case declined by Sup Ct 6-19, 492E2
Flood indicted 9-5, 685B1
Ex-rep Clark indicted 9-5, 685E1
Houston ex-police chief convctd 12-14, 991B2
Calif woman sentcnd in welfare case 12-28, 1029C1
Police—*See POLICE*
Political Corruption—*See POLITICS, WATERGATE*
Political Payments—*See under BUSINESS*
Pornography—*See PORNOGRAPHY*
Prisons & Prisoners
Criminal code revisn OKd by Sen 1-30, 64C2
Tenn prison bldg ordrd closed 1-30, 440E1
Tex marshal sentncd in '75 Morales slaying 2-18, 991E3
Limited immunity for prison offcls backed 2-22, 126C2
NY gov orders Little extradited 2-23, appeals ct backs 5-9; Marshall delays 5-30, Sup Ct declines appeal 6-5, 431A2
Md restores death penalty 3-10, 388F3
NYS death penalty bill clears legislature 3-20; Carey vetoes 4-11, override fails 5-2, 388A3
NYC policemen slain, Carey '76 Attica pardon scored 4-5, 388C3
Ga inmate slain, probe opens 4-10, 396G2
'Boxcar' cells ruled illegal 4-19, 440F1
NY 'strip-frisk' searches ordrd ended 4-22, 440G1
Va inmate parole hearings case declined by Sup Ct 4-24, 322E2
Ehrlichman freed in Ariz 4-27, 320A2

1979

Conn mass murderer convicted 10-19, 819B2
Bishop executn stay denied 10-21, dies in Nev gas chamber 10-22, 817G1-F2
Thevis, 2 others convicted 10-21, 818G1
Papa slayers convicted 10-23, 840A2
Mass jury approval case refused by Sup Ct 10-29, 884B2
3 Houston ex-cops resentncd 10-30, 839B3
Chesimard escapes NJ prison 11-2, 953C2
NC anti-KKK rally, 5 slain 11-3, 864C2-F3
Cuyohoga cmdr sentncd for '78 collisn 11-3, 887A3
Tex industrialist acquitted 11-9, 890D2
Cuban refugee ldr slain in NJ 11-25, FBI probe rptd 11-28, 906B1-D1
Manson parole denied 11-27, 953D3
San Diego schl sniper sentenced 11-30, 953F3
Conn mass murderer sentenced 11-30, 954A1
Cleaver chrgs rptd dropped 12-3, 1006E1
2 sailors slain in PR 12-3, 924G2
14 indicted in NC anti-KKK rally deaths 12-13, 991E3
Narcotics—*See NARCOTICS*
Obscenity—*See PORNOGRAPHY & Obscenity*
Organized Crime (including Mafia)
Justice probe of JFK death role asked 1-1, Ruby link rptd unproven 1-3, 4D1
Johnny Dio dies 1-12, 176F2
NYC airport theft arrest 2-17, 155D3
NJ casino granted license 2-26, 152A1
Galante release ordrd 2-27, 156F1
Galante returns to jail 3-7, gets bail 3-23, 240F2
2 sentncd in A-sub plot wire fraud 3-15, 3-20, 240E2
Nev takes over casino 3-16, 209B1
House com suspects JFK death link 3-16, 204E3
Calif bank wire-transfer setup rptd 3-20, 239B2
FBI informant loss rptd 3-22, 232C2
Alleged Mafia chief indicted 4-27, 368F1
CIA '63 Castro death plot rptd confrmd 5-2, 367E3, 368A1
NJ indictmt details Mafia 5-23, 508E1
Aladdin loses gambling license, underworld ties cited 6-15, 520G1
Caesars World opens in Atlantic City, Perlman associatn barred 6-26, 520D1
Galante slain 7-12, 548A1
NJ ex-Mafia informant sues US 9-26, 840E2
Priest-penitent case declined by Sup Ct 10-1, 767G3
Newark ex-mayor paroled 10-2, 891A2
Hell's Angels trial opens 10-4, 840E1
Thevis, 2 others convicted 10-21, 818G1
Scotto convicted 11-15, 890C2
Travel Act bribery convictn upheld by Sup Ct 11-27, 919E3
NM newspapers libel case refused by Sup Ct 12-3, 964B2
Argent buyer probe rptd 12-12, 965C1
Aladdin sale bid rejected 12-15, 965D1
Perjury
FBI ex-agent sentenced 1-17, 92B3
ITT-Chile case dropped 2-8, 88C1; 3-7, 188A2
Franklin Bank ex-offcl convicted 1-23, 205B3; sentncd 3-27, 291E3
Police—*See POLICE*
Political Corruption—*See POLITICS-Corruption; WATERGATE*
Political Payments—*See BUSINESS-Payments*
Pornography—*See PORNOGRAPHY*
Prisons & Prisoners
Tenn parole-selling probe continues 1-4, 36F1-B3; **for subsequent developments, see TENNESSEE**
Va convict gets abuse award 1-5, 24A2
Ray parole deal rptd too costly 1-18, escape convictn upheld 2-21, 156D2
Mitchell paroled 1-19, 176D1
Tex inmate gets death sentnc 1-26, 400B2
Amnesty Intl scores Pa, Ala conditns 2-1, 85F2
Ala prisons put in receivership 2-2, 112A3
Moore escape try fails 2-5, 156A2
Burger notes bail crime rise 2-11, 130E1
Attica riot convict paroled 2-21, 156E1
Cuban defector released in NY 2-21, 442G1
Ill prison gang rule broken 2-24; arms, drugs rptd seized 3-3, 196D3
Galante release ordrd 2-27, 156F1
Calif experimts with 'house arrest' 3-6, 316A2
Galante returns to jail 3-7, gets bail 3-23, 240F2

1980

Atlanta child slayings probe continues 11-6, 927C3-928A1
Bolles killer sentenced 11-14, 926B3-927A1
6 Klansmen acquitted in '79 NC slayings 11-17; reactn 11-17—11-18, 898D2-C3
Ga 'death row' escape extortn chrg 11-18; rptr, wife cleared 11-12, 927A1
Polish ex-track star found slain 12-4, 1004F3
Halberstam slain 12-5, suspect chrgd 12-6, 934F3
Lennon slain in NYC, ex-mental patient chrgd 12-8; reactn 12-9, 933D2-943A3
FBI informant cleared 12-15, 990B1
Calif MD insulin-slaying chrgs reduced 12-29, 997G1
Narcotics—*See NARCOTICS*
Obscenity—*See PORNOGRAPHY*
Organized Crime (including Mafia)
FBI Brilab probe rptd 2-8—2-13, 111D2-112C1; for subsequent developments, see U.S. GOVERNMENT—FEDERAL Bureau of Investigation—Brilab Probe
Reagan tells ethnic joke 2-16, apologizes 2-18, 128B2
Bolles killers convictns overturned 2-25, 214B3
8 Galante slaying probe figures indicted 3-3, 215C1
Pa Mafia ldr slain 3-21, 237B2
George Wolf dies 3-23, 280G2
Racketeer law cases declined by Sup Ct 3-24, 265C1
Waterfront racketeer convicted 5-2; 7 sentncd 5-20, 927E2
NY Mafia boss indicted 6-30, 502E3
Calabria murders linked 6-30; constructn co bars Mafia paymts 7-11, 564B3
Hell's Angels mistrial declared 7-2, 568G1
FBI bribe plotters convicted 7-3, 655D2
Falcones indicted 7-31, pizza indus ties probed 8-24, 714D1
Bonanno, nephew convicted 9-2, 712E3
Myers Abscam tapes broadcast 10-14, 781G2
2 NJ casinos granted gambling licenses, crime links rptd severed 10-25, 12-29, 988G2-C3
NY Mafia boss convicted 11-21, 971E2
Lenient sentence appeal backed by Sup Ct 12-9, 936A3
Presser's Reagan transitn role defended 12-15, 12-18, 955E3
Perjury
8 convicted in Fla pot ring 2-4, 270E3
Sindona convicted 3-27, 237E1
Bonanno's nephew convicted 9-2, 712F3
NYU prof sentenced 11-13, 997D3
Police—*See POLICE*
Political Corruption—*See POLITICS--Corruption, WATERGATE*
Political Payments—*See BUSINESS--Payments Issues*
Pornography—*See PORNOGRAPHY*
Prisons & Prisoners
State of State messages 1-2—2-6, 269C1, E2, G3, 270C3; 1-9, 1-15, 403A3, 404F1; 1-15 483B2, 484A2
Estes '83 parole rptd 1-3, 64F3
Scott convictn appeal refused 1-14, 320F3
Parole offcls immunity upheld by Sup Ct 1-15, 51E1
Inmate escape justificatn curbed by Sup Ct 1-21, 92E3
Boyce escape rptd 1-22, 55E1
Indian activist sentenced for '79 escape 1-23, 349D1
Attica prison violence, overcrowding rptd 1-31, 2-1, 112D3
NM prison riot 2-2—2-3, 112B2
Burger 'State of Judiciary' address 2-3, 114F2
Ex-Black Panther denied parole 2-5, 215A2
Hayes paroled 2-6, released 2-27, 175F2
Carter's nephew reimprisoned 2-13, 200D2
Job project gains rptd few 2-27, 228E3
State legislators' immunity curbed by Sup Ct 3-19, 249E3

1976

Sup Ct affirms med care right 11-30, 920E3
Attica ex-inmates pardoned 12-30, 995C2

Prostitution—*See under 'P'*
Rape
Ford backs limited abortns 2-3, 88B1
Sup Ct bars 'proof' rule review 3-1, 170D1
'75 rate rise rptd 3-25, 336A3
Dem platform text 6-15, 474E1
Detroit youth gangs chrgd 8-15, 776G1
GOP platform text 8-18, 604C2
Sup Ct OKs Ga death penalty review 10-4, 746G1
'Scottsboro Boy' pardoned 10-25, 859G3-860B1
Sup Ct bars review of jury bias questioning rule 11-1, 867D3

Robberies—*See also HEARST, Patricia*
CIA bars data on Hughes LA office robbery 1-5, 24E2
FBI backed rt-wing burglaries chrgd 1-11, 42C1
Soliah freed on bail 1-15, 70A2
LA warrantless arrest upheld 1-26, 87B2
Soliah defense motns denied 2-9, 114F3
'75 rate rise rptd 3-25, 336A3
Menominee Indian ldr convicted 4-21, 316G3
Carter queried on nephew 7-26, 551F1
Harrises convicted 8-9, 595C3; sentenced 8-31, 679B3
Detroit youth gangs chrgd 8-15, 776G1
Sup Ct bars review of Tex juvenile evidence case 10-4, 766C1
Saxe mistrial declared 10-13, 816B2
H Rap Brown wins parole 10-21, 912D3
Riviera bank robbers arrested 10-27, 876F3
Chowchilla trial moved 11-5, 876F3
Stock Manipulations & Frauds—*See STOCKS*

1977

Fire preventn study begun 6-27, 604G1
Conn blaze kills 5 7-7, 604F1
NYS death penalty bill vetoed 7-12, 594F2
Sen ratifies Mex prisoner exchng 7-21, 746F2
Papa slain in Atlanta jail 7-26, 642B1
CIA mind-control tests revealed 8-1—8-9, 610C3
Barnes released 10-14, 870F2
Little escapes 10-15, seized 12-7, 992A1
Young cleared in Thevis aid chrg 10-19, 861D3
4 ex-Houston police indicted re Torres 10-20, 820F3
Ray sentenced for escape 10-27, 848C1
US-Mex, Canada exchng bill signed 10-28, 834E1
Amnesty Intl probes US 11-5, 942G3-943A1
Va bond referendum OKd 11-8, 879C2
Felony probatn-loss case review declined 11-14, 878B3
Correctns officer firing case remanded 11-14, 878C3
NY death penalty provisn voided 11-15, 919C3
US, Mex exchng 1st prisoners 12-9, 957A2

Prostitution—*See under 'P'*
Rape—*See under SEX Crimes*

Robberies—*See also HEARST, Patricia*
Saxe pleads guilty 1-17, sentncd 2-11, 140E1
NY coffee thefts rptd 3-6, 169A1
Indian ldr convictn review denied 3-21, 230F2
Va death penalty bill signed 3-29, 594E1
Woolbright convicted 4-22, 396G1
Slain Indianapolis heiress robbed 5-7, 492F1
NYC blackout arrests 7-13—7-14, 537G2
Diamond dealer robberies probed 7-28—10-19, FBI in gem hunt 10-3, 871C3, F3
'76 FBI data rptd 9-27, 847E3
Dual fed-state prosecutns curbed 11-7, 857A2
Youth sentncd in Fla TV trial 11-7, 907F3
'76 cost to business rptd 11-17, 919B1
LA music promoter slain 11-21, 952G3
Sports players' agent sentenced 11-28, 1021A2
NL pres robbed 11-30, 990F2

1978

Pornographer flees Ind jail 4-28, 971C2
Carter plans policy review 5-4, 320B3
'77 state, natl inmate populatn rptd 6-3, 440B1
Little extradited to NC 6-9; indicted 6-18, sentenced 7-12, 560E3
Ark reform, attys fees backed by Sup Ct 6-23, 566D1
Press data access curbed by Sup Ct 6-26, 566G2-D3
DC escapes win retrials 7-12, 627C3
US, Canada prisoner exchng ratified 7-19, 572B1
Pontiac (Ill) riot, 3 guards slain 7-22, 627E2
Reidsville (Ga) prison riot, 3 killed 7-23; prisoner slain 8-16, 627G2
Md overcrowding ordrd cut 8-4, 627A3
Mass prison riot 8-8, 627A3
Chatham Cnty, Atlanta jail violence 9-9, 9-21; Reidsville probe indictmts 9-14, 770G3
US, Canada exchng prisoners 10-12—10-13, 794D3
Alaska, Ala bond issue results 11-7, 915C2, D2
FBI urges file disclosure delay, prisoner misuse cited 11-8, 877F3-878A1
Inmate suits judicial-aid case refused by Sup Ct 11-13, 874B3
US bureau ex-dir dies 11-19, 972E2
Tenn gov's aides arrested in parole payoff 12-15; pardons voided 12-20, defended 12-22, 12-24, 1011E1-E2
Extraditn probes barred by US Sup Ct 12-18, 981F1
'77 Tenn jail arsonist sentncd 12-20, 992A2
Haldeman freed in Calif 12-20, 1011G2

Prostitution—*See PROSTITUTION*
Rape—*See under SEX Crimes*
Riots & Civil Disorders—*See also 'Prisons' above*
Abortn clinic violence rptd 3-7, 5-17, 744B2
Phila radicals blockaded 3-8, surrender 5-7, 410D1-C2
Phila radicals routed; cop killed, 12 chrgd 8-8, 645D1
White House anti-war protesters seized 9-4, 947C2
Grand Coulee generator sabotaged 10-30, 963C1
Black ldrs warn Carter on urban unrest 12-4, 936A3, C3

Robbery—*See also HEARST, Patricia*
St Louis museum sculptures stolen 1-21, 2-20, 335C1; Byers implicated 6-26, 589G3
NE blizzard looting, arrests 2-7, 105D2
Columbia Pictures pres quits in embezzlemt scandal 2-9, indicted 3-13, 251C1; fined 6-28, 599A2
NY gov orders Little extradited 2-23, appeals ct backs 5-9; Marshall delays 5-30, Sup Ct declines appeal 6-5, 431A2
Chaplin's body stolen 3-2, 232D3; recovered 5-17, 380D1
DEA ex-agents convicted 3-10, 380B1
NYS death penalty bill clears legislature 3-20; Carey vetoes 4-11, override fails 5-2, 388A3
Ark convictns reversed by Sup Ct 4-3, 309B1
NY '77 blackout rpt issued 4-23, 396F1
Chicago bank offers reward in '77 theft 5-1, 380C1
Diamond recovered in autopsy 5-4, 380E1
Mitsubishi unit indicted 5-9, 404B2
2 AIM activists acquitted in Calif 5-24, 396B2
Little extradited to NC 6-9; indicted 6-18, sentenced 7-12, 560E3
2 convicted for Washn, Ore bank robberies 7-11, 824A3
New film indus probe set; Screen Gems, Deluxe Gen cases cited 7-14, 599F2-A3
House minority whip mugged 7-21, 843B3
Memphis blackout looting, arrests 8-16, 644G2
Soledad Brother chrgd in Calif 8-25, 887A1
Arsonist convicted for NYC '74 disco fire 9-7, 824F2
Conn A-sub theft foiled 10-4, 824F1; chrgs chngd 12-6, 992E1
Inner city survey rptd 10-16, 842A2
LA bank robbed by phone 10-25; Rifkin arrested 11-5, chrgd 11-20, 991G3-992D1
Atlantic City rate up 25% 11-10, 920F1
Ray's brother arrested in St Louis 11-27, 938F1
La tornado looting 12-3, 972B2
Police auto search power broadened by Sup Ct 12-5, 959D2
NYC airport theft 12-11, 1028G2
2 Houston ex-cops chrgd in '75 Joyvies cover-up 12-14, 991D2

1979

Va inmate gets rape setlmt 3-17, 316D2
Va inmate threat case refused by Sup Ct 4-16, 302E3
Sup Ct worker fired re news leaks 4-20, 302A3
Washington prison riots 548D2
Pretrial detentn curbs backed by Sup Ct 5-14, 383F1
FALN suspect escapes in NY 5-21, 431E1
Marshall decries pretrial detentn ruling 5-27, 422D1
States given parole discretn by Sup Ct 5-29, 421D1-B3
Attica inmate slain in racial brawl 6-3, 548F2
NJ ex-offcls subject to rejailing by Sup Ct 6-4, 438G3
Jewish inmate rights case refused by Sup Ct 6-4, 439F1
Little paroled 6-9, 527D3
Moore sentenced 6-12, 492E1
'Catonsville 9' fugitive surrenders 6-19, 492E1
'78 inmate totals rptd 6-21, 548A2
Phila police brutality chrgd 8-13, 610G1
ABA com rejects inmate rights 8-15, 768E3
Priest-penitent case declined by Sup Ct 10-1, 767F3
US Marshals to track escapees 10-1, 771B1
Newark ex-mayor paroled 10-2, 891F1
Coppalino paroled 10-16, 839G2
2 Atlanta inmates convicted in Papa slaying 10-23, 840A2
Chesimard escapes NJ jail 11-2, 953C2
Ray jail break fails 11-5, 891E2
US Helsinki com asks improvemt 11-7, 981B1
Sirhan parole hearing denied 11-7, 953B3
PR protester found dead in Fla jail 11-11, probes ordrd 11-18, 11-23, 904A3
Cepeda hired by White Sox; early release cited 11-20, 1002F3
Phila inmate '60s drug tests rptd 11-25, 947E1
Manson parole denied 11-27, 953D3
Murphy abductor parole rptd set 12-18, 1005E3
Carter nephew paroled 12-24, 1006B1
Prostitution—*See PROSTITUTION*
Rape—*See under SEX Crimes*

Robbery—*See also HEARST, Patricia*
FBI seizes stolen films in Ohio 1-8, intl probe rptd 1-10, 102D2
'73-77 survey rptd 1-18, 119A1
Cowboys quarterback robbed 1-30, 175A3
GE worker chrgd in uranium theft 2-1, 119F3
NY Met museum sculpture stolen 2-9, recovered 2-14, 119D1
Art security symposium held in Del 2-12—2-14, 119A2
NYC airport theft arrests 2-17, 2-20, 155B3
Baltimore looting 2-18; curfew imposed 2-19—2-20, arrests rptd 2-22, 176B2
LEAA projct cuts Hartford burglaries 2-25, 156C3
Right-to-counsel doctrine clarified by Sup Ct 3-5, 185A2
2d LA bank wire-transfer theft 3-25, 239C2
Rifkin sentncd in '78 LA bank phone theft 3-26, 239G1
Easter killed in holdup 3-29, 1002E3
Conn armored car depot robbed 4-16, 4 arrested 4-17, 316E1
Covert 'bugging' entry upheld by Sup Ct 4-18, 346C1
Evans executn stayed in Ala 4-20, 400G1
Verbal rights waiver backed by Sup Ct 4-24, 364A2
Smith convicted in San Diego 5-7, sentncd 5-31, 442C2
NJ indicts 8 in Genovese 'family' 5-23, 508G1
Flemish art stolen from Rome convent 6-3, 656F1
Warrantless phone surveillnc upheld by Sup Ct 6-20, 516D1
2 chrgd in Bedford Hills (NY) 7-19, 548G3
Trial speedup for offenders urged 7-22, 655D3
NYC subway receipts rptd stolen 7-23, 656E1
Bundy sentncd in Fla 7-31, 604F2
NYC record bank robbery 8-3, 2 suspects arrested 8-8, 8-9, 656C1
Bank robberies rise sharply 8-12, 619G2
Priest cleared in Penna 'gentleman bandit' case 8-20, look-alike sentncd 11-30, 953F2
13 NYC banks robbed, 2 suspects arrested 8-21—8-22; police protectn ordrd 8-22, 656A1
Karpis dies 8-26, 671E2

1980

Class actn 'moot' standard redefined by Sup Ct 3-19, 250E1
Inmate mental health hearings backed by Sup Ct 3-25, 265D2
NJ prison riot 3-25—3-26, 370G3
Chicago strip search suit setld 3-26, 404C2
Mandatory, determinate sentncing gains; impact rptd 3-29, 359D1
Ex-convict Braly dies 4-7, 360C1
Prisoners right to sue broadened by Sup Ct 4-22, 343B3
Jacobson flees 5-31, DeRosa indicted 6-4, 502B2, D2
'Son of Sam' Soc Sec benefits rptd 6-5; insanity plea faked 8-4, 639E2
Informant use curbed by Sup Ct 6-16, 511B3
'79-80 Sup Ct term ends, decisns cited 7-2, 540E2
Jacobson recaptured 7-9, 997D2
Idaho prison riot coverage seized in TV statn raid 7-26, 582B2
Ga convicts escape 7-28, recaptured in NC 7-30, 654E1
Atkins denied parole 7-29, 639D2
Idaho prosecutor sued over TV tapes raid 8-1, 732B3
Cuban refugees jailed at Lewisburg 8-5, 591B3
Ga rptr, 2 others indicted in 'death row' escape 8-27, 712F2-D3
Ga prof released 9-30, 890B3
Parole violator freed by Cuba, arrested in Miami 10-27, 828D3
W Sutton dies 11-2, 928E3
Inmate cell crowding case accepted by Sup Ct 11-3, 856E2
NJ constructn bond issue OKd 11-4, 847G3
Ga 'death row' escape extortn chrg 11-8; rptr, wife cleared 11-12, 927A1
Inmate legal fees ruling upset by Sup Ct 11-10, 868C1
Calif probe of Ark prisons curbed by Sup Ct 12-8, 937C1
Prostitution—*See PROSTITUTION*
Rape—*See SEX Crimes*
Riots & Civil Disorders
Alamo occupied by radicals, other protests rptd 3-20, 485A2
Miami racial riots erupt 5-17—5-19, 382E2; for subsequent developments, see FLORIDA—Crime
Cuban refugees riot at Eglin, Chaffee 5-24—5-26, 395F3-396B1; 6-1, 419G3-420C1
Chattanooga racial disorders erupt 7-22—7-26, 575F3
Youths riot at Pa refugee cntr 8-5, 591G2
Moslems in DC pro-Khomeini marches 8-7, 8-8, 635F1
Wis refugee cntr riots 8-13, 27 arrested 8-14, 631F3
Wis, Pa refugee cntr riots continue 8-28, 9-9—9-10, 684E3
6 Klansmen acquitted in '79 NC slayings 11-17; reactn 11-17—11-18, 898D2-C3
Buffalo racial incidents prompt probe 12-13, 997F1
Robbery
Prosecutn disparities rptd 1-6, 24B3, C3
NY-NJ Customs corruptn probed 1-11, 2-13, 359C2-B3
Scott convictn appeal refused 1-14, 320F3
'Miranda rights' waiver proof backed 1-21, 93B3
FBI 'Miporn' probe rptd 2-14, 136C1
Galante slaying probe figures indicted 3-3, 215E1
Racketeer law cases declined by Sup Ct 3-24, 265D1
Car box search case refused by Sup Ct 3-24, 265C2
Mandatory sentncs rptd up 3-29, 359E1
Ctroom cameras case accepted by Sup Ct 4-21, 344E1
Hearst probation rptd ended 5-9, 471E3
Jail informant use curbed by Sup Ct 6-16, 511B3
Illegal search protectn narrowed by Sup Ct 6-25, 541B1
Chattanooga looting 7-22—7-24, 575G3
Hispanic crime study rptd 7-28, 654C3
Ariz alien case mistrial declared 7-29, retrial sought 8-29, 713E2
8 FALN suspects convicted 7-30; 2 others sentncd 8-4, 601C1, E1
Calif Brink's truck robbed 8-15, 654G2
'79 US data rptd 9-24, 971E1-A2
Ore U indictmts cited 10-15, 875C3
Ctroom cameras case argued in Sup Ct 11-12, 882A2
PR gang steals $2.4 mln 11-21, 971G2
Halberstam slaying suspect, DC thefts rptd linked 12-7, 940A1
Calif insulin-slaying chrgs reduced 12-29, 997C2

1976

Supreme Court Rulings—*See appropriate subheads in this section and under U.S. GOVERNMENT—SUPREME Court*
Tax Evasion—*See under U.S. GOVERNMENT—INTERNAL Revenue Service*
Watergate Issues—*See WATERGATE*

1977

Sex Crimes—*See under 'S'; also PROSTITUTION*
Supreme Court Rulings—*See appropriate subheads in this section and under U.S. GOVERNMENT—SUPREME Court*
Tax Evasion—*See under U.S. GOVERNMENT—INTERNAL Revenue Service*
Watergate—*See under 'W'*
Wiretapping—*See under 'W'*

1978

Cleveland mayor's brother arrested 12-18, 1008G3
NYC armored truck heist 12-19, 1028E2
Chicago, San Fran art thefts 12-25, 12-27, 1028E3-1029A1
Sex Crimes—*See SEX Crimes*
Supreme Court Rulings—*See appropriate subheads in this section and under U.S. GOVERNMENT—SUPREME Court*
Watergate—*See WATERGATE*
Wiretapping—*See WIRETAPPING*

1979

Amer Express travelers check TV ad chngd 8-29, 903C1
D Kennedy robbed in NYC 9-12, 859G3
Canadian sentncd in Calif bank wire theft 9-24, 840C3
Harris convictns review declined by Sup Ct 10-1, 768B1
'Exclusionary rule' case refused by Sup Ct 10-1, 768A3
2d 1/4 rise rptd 10-9, 819B3
Carter nephew paroled 12-24, 1006B1
Sex Crimes—*See SEX Crimes*
Supreme Court Rulings—*See appropriate subheads in this section and under U.S. GOVERNMENT-SUPREME Court*
Tax Evasion—*See under TAXES*
Vandalism
NYC outdoor sculpture smashed 5-6, 375C1; rededicated 9-15, 892G2
Va A-plant sabotage probed 5-8, 5-10, 386D2
Va A-plant sabotage chrgs rptd 6-18, 466E1
Student violence rptd 7-5, 786E1, A2
Va A-plant saboteurs convicted 10-16, 807D1; sentenced 11-27, 925B2
Watergate—*See WATERGATE*
Wiretapping—*See WIRETAPPING*

1980

Sex Crimes—*See SEX Crimes*
Tax Evasion—*See TAXES--Tax Evasion (& other irregularities)*
Vandalism
Va sterilization program rptd 2-23, 158E3
FALN raids Carter, Bush campaign hqs 3-15, 208A3-209A1
NYC sculpture smashed again 3-24, 472D3
Watergate—*See WATERGATE*
Wiretapping—*See WIRETAPPING*

1976

CRIPPEN, Curtiss E.
SEC sues, settles 6-29, 984B2
CRISTOL, Jose
Lauds SEATO 2-20, 148D1
CRISWELL, Rev. W. A.
Backs Ford 10-10, 763C2
CROATIA—*See YUGOSLAVIA*
CROCIANI, Camillo
Indictmt rptd 3-24, 298D1
CROCKER National Corp.
Crocker National Bank (San Francisco)
'73 San Diego bank failure cited 1-12, 111E1
Soliah trial motns denied 2-9, 114G3
Hamilton Natl fails 2-16, 166F3
Hearst info on '75 robbery rptd 4-14, 4-16, 368C1
CROCODILES—*See WILDLIFE*
US files consent decree 11-16, 989D1
CRONIN, Jeremy
Arrested 7-29, 592D1
Chrgd in S Africa 9-7, 662B2
Sentenced 9-29, 733G3
CRONJE, Rowan
On Sovt role in Africa 8-20, 661D1
CRONKITE, Walter
Interviews Ford 2-3, 88A1
Carter, Ford debate 10-22, 800E3
Interviews Carter 11-29, 897D3
CROOK, William
Chrgs Duvalier bribe request 3-2, 267C3
CROSBIE, John
Elected 10-18, 808C2
CROSLAND, Anthony
Bids for prime min 3-17, fails 3-25, 239G1
UK foreign min 4-8, 266E3
Meets Kissinger 4-23—4-24; lauds Rhodesia statemt 4-28, 293D2, G2
In Iceland talks, signs cod pact 5-31—6-1, 389B3
Denies Italian loan ban 7-19, 530F3
Announces Uganda ties cut 7-28, 547G3
Meets Kissinger 8-5, 580D3
Retains Cabt post 9-10, 694A1
Sees Kissinger re Rhodesia 9-24, 717C2
Smith OKs Rhodesia conf 9-30, 738C2
Disputes Smith on conf aim 10-5, 10-7, 781B2
Asked to chair conf 10-17, 781F1
Confs with Richard 843D1
Meets Richard 11-22, 879G1
Scores Warsaw Pact A-proposal 12-9, 933E2
Sees Kissinger on Rhodesia 12-10—12-11, rpts to Parlt 12-14, 935E1
CROSS, Bert S.
Tax fraud chrgs dismissed 7-27, 566C2
CROSS Jr., Norman C.
Acquittal rptd 12-22, 1016F2
CROSSAN, Terry
Detained 2-8, 146C2
CROUCH, Andrae, and the Disciples (music group)
Wins Grammy 2-28, 460C3
CROWDER, Richard
Kunstler to ask chrgs dropped 1-17, 79E1
CROWE, Judge Guthrie F.
Dismisses Panama Canal talks suit 12-18, 1008F2
CROWE, Marshall
Rpts oil export cuts 11-23, 945F2
CROWN Central Petroleum Corp.
Indicted 6-1, 412D3
CROWNED Heads (book)
On best-seller list 12-5, 972F2
CROWTHER-Hunt, Norman
Named UK home-rule min 1-23, 73E1
Resigns post 4-8, 266G3
CRUICKSHANK, Jorge
Wins seat in Mex Sen 7-4, 677C2
CRUM & Foster Insurance Cos.
Industrial Indemnity Co.
Johnson to head unit 2-1, 80E2

1977

CRIMINAL Justice Standards & Goals, National Advisory Committee on—*See 'Law Enforcement Assistance Administration' under U.S. GOVERNMENT—JUSTICE*
CRIMMINS, Alice
Paroled 9-7, 848D1
CRISOLOGO, Manuel
Sentenced 2-10, 100B1
CRISTOFER, Michael
Wins Pulitzer Prize 4-18, 355D2
CROATIA—*See YUGOSLAVIA*
CROCKER National Corp.
'73 US Natl Bank failure cited 3-11, 194F2
UM&M's United Factors sale OKd 7-25, 612G1
CROISSANT, Klaus
Arrested in France 9-30, extradited to W Ger 11-16; leftists protest 11-17, 968F2
Suicide denial published 11-17, 968F3
Protests W Ger jail conditns, razor blades found 11-23, 969A1
France defends extradtn, denies brutality 11-25—11-28, 969C1
CROMARTIE, Warren
NL batting ldr 10-2, 926D3
CRONJE, Rowan
To head manpower board 2-15, 123A2
Sets increased call-ups 2-28, 144G2
CRONKITE, Walter
Carter call-in moderator 3-5, 171B1, E3
Interviews Sadat, Begin 11-14, 873D1
CROSBY, Bing (Harry Lillis)
Dies 10-14, 872D1
CROSLAND, Anthony
On Japan-EC trade talks 1-18, 73A3
Warns Smith 1-24, 1-25, 49B2
In talks with Young, Richard 2-2, 105B1
Warns Czech re dissidents 2-2, 114G3
Dies 2-19, 164E2
Replaced as forgn secy 2-21, 200F3
Grimsby seat filled 4-28, 374B1
CROSSE, Howard D.
Pleads guilty 6-21, 540G2
CROWDER, Randy
Put on waivers 8-1, sentncd for drug sale 8-10, 659A2
CROW Dog, Leonard
Convictn review denied 3-21, 230F2
CROWE, Guthrie F.
In TV campaign vs Canal pacts 10-29, 912C1
CROWLEY, Dr. Brian
Ex-CIA man convicted 5-5, 409A3
CROWN Central Petroleum Corp.
Crown-Seadock superport backing rptd 7-19, 559F2
Gulf wins Kewanee control 8-9, 612F2
Acquitted on trust chrgs 8-30, 691B3
CROWN Cork & Seal Co.
Steelworkers OK new pact 10-31, 837E1
CROWN Publishers Inc.
Sues Haley 5-24, 643D1
CROWN-Seadock Pipe Line Corp.—*See CROWN Central Petroleum Corp.*
CROWN Zellerbach Corp.
Reed Hunt dies 11-26, 952E2
CRS Design Associates Inc.
Rpts forgn paymts 6-23, 503G2
CRUGUET, Jean
Seattle Slew wins Triple Crown 6-11, 491B1, D1
CRUISE MISSILE—*See ARMAMENTS—Missiles*

1978

CRIMEA—*See USSR*
CRIMINAL Code—*See U.S. CODE*
CRISCUOLO, Lou
Contessa of Mulberry St opens 1-4, 887E1
CRIST v. Bretz
Double jeopardy protectn lengthened by Sup Ct 6-14, 468G3
CRITICAL Mass Energy Project
A-waste storage rpt scored 3-15, 184A1
Scores Admin A-plant licensing revisn bill 3-17, 205A3
CROATIA—*See YUGOSLAVIA—Croation Issues*
CROCE, Gerard
Once In Paris released 11-9, 970E2
CROCKER National Bank—*See under CROCKER National Corp.*
CROCKER National Corp.
Crocker National Bank (San Francisco, Calif.)
FDIC paymt case declined by Sup Ct 10-16, 789D1
CROCKETT, Frederick E.
Dies 1-17, 96E1
CROFT, Chancy
Leads in Alaska primary for gov 8-22, 682F3
Primary win official 10-20, 831E2
Loses electn 11-7, 856B2
CROISSANT, Klaus
Trial delayed over searches 3-6, 3-21, adjournmt granted 4-3, 250A3
French ct upholds '77 extraditn 7-7, 649B3
Groenewold given suspended sentence 7-10, 651G2
CROMWELL (play)
Opens 7-12, 887E1
CRONJE, Rowan
Sets Rhodesia vote 7-25, 615E1
On electn delay 11-1, 867D2
CROSS, James Richard
Kidnapers ask amnesty 1-3, 7D1
6th kidnaper hunted 11-2, 880B1
Cossette-Trudels return to Canada 12-13, 964B2
CROSSE, Howard D.
Named Franklin co-conspirator, '77 guilty plea cited 7-13, 681D1
CROSSED Swords (film)
Released 3-2, 619C1
CROWN Zellerbach Corp.
Harold Zellerbach dies 1-29, 96G3
DSMO OKd for cystitis 3-20, 231F2
CRUCIFER of Blood, The (play)
Opens 9-28, 1031C1
CRUISE Missile—*See ARMAMENTS—Missiles*
CRUS, Lorenzo J.
Pl vs electn coverage 4-11, 269D1
CRUTCHFIELD, Bishop Finis A.
Scores WCC rebel grants 11-4, 907B1
CRUYFF, Johann
World Cup soccer odds listed 6-1, 519G3
CRUYWAGEN, Willem
S Africa black educ min 1-25, 55C1
To study student protests 2-1, 92E2
S Africa educ min 11-14, 904C3

1979

CRIMEA—*See USSR*
CRINKLEY, Richmond
Elephant Man opens 1-14, 292D1
CRISTALDI, Franco
Wifemistress released 1-6, 174G3
CRITCHLOW, Paul
On cattle deaths near 3 Mile I 5-20, 382F1
CRITICAL Mass (anti-nuclear group)
Pollock on 3 Mile I comm final rpt 10-30, 826E1
CROCAMO, Abraham
Panama coup plot alleged 10-24, 836D3
CROCIANI, Camillo
Convicted 3-1, 155D2
CROCKETT, James
Dies 7-11, 588E2
CROFT, Michael
Good Lads opens 3-27, 711E3
CROMARTIE, Warren
NL batting ldr 9-30, 955F2
CROMBIE, David
Canada health, welfare min 6-4, 423G3
CROSBIE, John
Canada finance min 6-4, 423F3
Sees '79 trade deficit 7-24, 613D1
Inflation comm disbanded 7-25, 581D1
Sees econ slowdown 7-26, 612E3
Sets mortgage tax credits 9-17, 706A1
Introduces budget 12-12; scores defeat 12-13, 936B3, E3
CROSBY, James
Atlantic City casino license granted 2-26, 152B1
CROSLAND, David
INS revives gay alien curb 12-26, 992B1
CROSS, Charles T.
Heads Amer Inst in Taiwan 4-21, 299E2
CROSS, James Richard
Lanctot returns to Canada, arrested 1-6, 19G1
Lanctot chrgd, bail set 1-11, 37B2
Cossette-Trudels sentenced 8-7, 632B3
Lanctot sentncd 11-8 872D1
CROSS, Staf' Sgt. Ricky L.
Marines suspend 6-27, beating incident probed 7-7, 520B1
CROSSE, Howard D.
Sentncd 3-26, 291F3
CROTHERS, Sam
Father's Day opens 6-21, 711A3
CROWDER, Eddie
On Colo U-Fairbanks deal 4-3, 335A3
CROWELL, McLin
Hitting Town opens 1-6, 292F1
CROWLEY, Cpl. Steven
Killed in Pak Emb raid 11-21, 893B1, C2
CROWLEY, Terry
In World Series 10-10—10-17, 816C3
CROWNED Heads (book)
Fedora released 4-14, 528B2
CROWN Publishers Inc.
Krantz paperback rights sold for record sum 9-12, 755E3
CROWN Zellerbach Corp.
Paper workers strike ends 2-20, 345G2
Price violatn chrgd 4-27, 385E1
CROZIER, William M.
On '77 FRB withdrawal, reserve requiremt cost 4-9, 303B2
CRUCIBLE Alloy Division—*See under COLT Industries Inc.*
CRUEL Shoes (book)
On best-seller list 6-3, 432B2; 7-1, 548B3; 8-5, 620C3; 9-2, 672B3; 10-14, 800C3
CRUISE Missile—*See ARMAMENTS—Missiles*
CRUISIN' (recording)
On best-seller list 2-14, 120F3
CRUMB, Ann
Madman and Nun opens 1-18, 292B2
CRUYFF, Johan
Signs with Aztecs 5-22, plays 1st game 5-23, 655B1
Named NASL top offensive player 8-25, NASL MVP 9-5, 776B1
Named to NASL All-Star team 8-27, 776E1

1980

CRIMES of Passion (recording)
On best-seller list 10-8, 796C3; 12-3, 948C3
CRIMINOLOGY
Sheldon Glueck dies 3-10, 279B3
CRIMMINS, Craig S.
Arrested in opera murder 8-30, confessn rptd 9-5; indicted 9-7, 713B1
CRINKLEY, Richmond
Tintypes opens 10-23, 892F3
CRISIS Investing (book)
On best-seller list 9-14, 716B3 10-12, 796D3; 12-7, 948E3
CRISP, Mary D.
GOP hq bugging suspected 6-21, 6-24, 480D3
Protests platform planks 7-9, 506E2
Heitman gets GOP post 7-18, 549F2
CRITICAL Mass (antinuclear group)
'79 A-plant mishap rptd 7-14, 551D2
CRITTENBERGER, Lt. Gen. Willis D. (ret.)
Dies 8-4, 676B1
CROCIANI, Massimo
Soccer scandal rptd 3-6, 194F2
CROCKER National Corp.
Midland sets takeover 7-15, 557G1
Forgn bank takeovers debated 8-28, 9-17, 806A3, E3
CROCKETT Jr., George W.
Wins Mich US House primaries 8-5, 682A3
Elected to US House 11-4, 843F1, 846C2, E3, 851D1
CROHN, Frank T.
Named Beneficial deputy chrmn 9-28, 959B3
CRONIN, James W.
Wins Nobel Prize 10-14, 889B3
CRONKITE, Walter
Rather to replace 2-15, 198E3
Mudd gets NBC post 7-1, 638F2
Interviews Ford 7-16, 530C1, E1
On CBS electn projectns lag 11-5, 866C1
CRONSON, Robert
Scores Chicago schl bd fscl policies 4-2, 292B1
CROSBIE, John
Scores Ottawa budget, energy plan 10-29, 858C2
CROSBY, Mary
'Dallas' TV episode aired 11-21, viewing record rptd 11-25, 905G3
CROSS, Christopher
Ride Like the Wind on best-seller list 4-30, 359G3
Sailing on best-seller list 8-13, 640B3; 9-10, 716E3
Christopher Cross on best-seller list 8-13, 640C3; 9-10, 716F3
CROSS, Julie Y.
Slain 6-5, 503E2
CROUCH, Andrea
Wins Grammy 2-27, 296E3
CROUSE, Lindsay
Twelfth Night opens 12-16, 1003F3
CROWN Central Petroleum Corp.
'79 price violatns chrgd 3-7, 248E2
CROWN Simpson Pulp Co. v. Costle
Case decided by Sup Ct 3-17, 226F1
CROWN Zellerbach Corp.
Fine paper trust suit rptd setld 9-29; acquittal rptd in 2d suit 12-3, 917A2, B2
CRUCIANI, Massimi
Rptd fined in soccer scandal 12-22, 12-24, 995F1
CRUEL Shoes (book)
On best-seller list 1-13, 40C3
CRUISE Missile—*See ARMAMENTS--Missiles*
CRUISING (film)
Opens, draws gay protests; Gen Cinema contract dispute cited 2-15, 216D2, 239F2
Top-grossing film 2-27, 200G3
CRUM, Denny
Louisville wins NCAA basketball title 3-24, 240E1-D2
CRUYFF, Johan
Signs with Diplomats 2-26, Jansen joins team 3-6, 770A3, B3
Rights revert to Cosmos 12-5, 1001E1

1976

CSAPO, Geza
Wins Olympic medal 7-31, 574F1
CSCE—*See 'Security and Cooperation in Europe, Conference on' under EUROPE*

1977

CRUZ, Hector
Traded to Cubs 12-8, 990E1
CRYPTOGRAPHY
Callimahos dies 10-28, 872D1
CRYSTAL Palace (race Horse)
3d in Arc de Triomphe 10-2, 971A2
CSA—*See COMMUNITY Services Administration under U.S. GOVERNMENT*
CSCE—*See EUROPE—Security and Cooperation*

1978

CRUZ, Jose
NL batting ldr 10-2, 928D2
CRUZ, Julio
AL stolen base ldr 10-2, 928F3
CRYDER, Bob
In NFL draft 5-2, 336F2
CRYPTOGRAPHY
Intell reorgn bill introduced 2-9, 107C1
US issues WWII secret documts 9-10—9-18, 744D2-G3
CSCE—*See EUROPE—Security and Cooperation*
CUADROS, Victor
Miners strike broken 9-8, 775C3

1979

CRUZ, Arturo
On Nicaragua bank reserves, govt debts 7-25, 603B2, E2
CRUZ, Hector
Traded to Reds 6-28, 1002A3
CRUZ, Julio
AL stolen base ldr 9-30, 955F3
CRUZ Cuenca, Miguel
Assassinated 1-9, buried 1-10, 60D3, 61B1
CRYSTAL, Lester
Replaced as NBC News pres 8-28, 756G1
CRYSTAL River Plant—*See FLORIDA—Atomic Energy*
CSONKA, Larry
Contract with Dolphins rptd 2-22, 175F2
CSX Corp.
Shareholders back Chessie-Seaboard merger 2-13, 205F3
CTI International Inc.—*See under RELIANCE Group Inc.*
CUADRA, Joaquin
Tours US mil bases 11-11—11-21, 910B1
CUADROS Paredes, Victor
Arrested 3-16, freed 3-17; Assemb bars immunity waiver 3-20, 255E2

1980

CRUZ, Arturo J.
Resignatn rptd 4-22, 315D2
Joins junta 5-18, 390C1
CRUZ, Jose
NL batting ldr 10-6, 926E2
CRUZ, Julio
AL stolen base ldr 10-6, 926F3
CRYPTOGRAPHY
Elizabeth Friedman dies 10-31, 928E2
CSCE—*See CONFERENCE on Security and Cooperation in Europe*
CSONKA, Larry
NFL '79 touchdown ldr 1-5, 8B2
CSX Corp.
Chessie, Seaboard merge 9-24, 745C3

CUBA

1976

CUBA—*See also COMECON, NONALIGNED Nations Movement, SELA*
'71 defns budget, mil force rptd 1-2, 60G2
Listed as 'not free' nation 1-19, 20D3
Const OKd in referendum 2-15, 137G3-138B1
Constitution enacted 2-24, 251E3
Quits oil effort, plans A-plants 3-2, 251G3
Castro on econ ills 9-27, 771G3-772E1
Munic assembs elected 10-11, 858C1
Castro cites visit plan 10-15, 780F1
Natl, prov assembs elected 11-2, 1001A1
Natl Assemb meets, elects Castro pres 12-2—12-3, 1000C3

Angola Issue
US refugee mercenary training rptd 1-3, 3C2
Nigeria repudiates US plea 1-7, 2B3, 3A1
MPLA battle role in S rptd, Unita shows prisoners 1-7, 3A2
OAU deadlocks on Angola role 1-10—1-13, 15D3
Delegatn at OAU summit 1-10—1-13, 16G1
Azores refueling ban defied 1-10—1-15; Portugal, US protest 1-13, 1-19, 53C2
MPLA troop support rptd 1-11, 16D3
Cuba vows contd MPLA aid, admits June '75 entry 1-11, 1-15, 16E3, 138F1 ★
Javits: US-Cuba ties 'aborted' 1-11, 52F2
Zaire chrgs Dilolo rocketing 1-15, 16C3
Fighting rages along southn front 1-15—1-23, 35B2, C3
US estimates Cuba MPLA forces 1-16, 35E3
Zaire protests Dilolo raid to UN Cncl 1-16, warns Cuba 1-17, 36B1
Tanzania backs Angola role 1-18, 36D1
Halts troop airlift 1-21; Azores, Canada refueling 1-28, 1-30, 106B2
Troops aid MPLA drive south 1-23—1-27, 57C1
Venez, Carib natns vs role 1-24, 138G1
Unita hints Cuba exit 1-25, 57G2
S Africa defends Angola role 1-26, 57D2
Zambia scores Angola role 1-28, 77F3
S Africa chrgs peace threat 1-31, 103F2
Troops take Lobito 2-2, 82G1
Canada prime min on Cuba visit 2-3, 116D2
Domestic dissent rptd 2-4, 138C2
Kissinger scores role 2-5, 138C1
Troops lead Huambo drive 2-9, 105A2
Ford scores Cong aid bar 2-10, 109G2-B3
Kissinger, Latin ldrs discuss 2-16—2-23, 177E2, 178B1, E1
UN Cncl meets; Cuba, US trade chrgs 2-26—3-31, 228D2
Ford calls Castro 'outlaw' 2-28, 165G2-A3
Tito lauds MPLA aid 3-6, 251B3
Guyana denies refueling stops 3-6, 253B2
Austria vs interventn 3-12, 380E2
Kissinger warns anew 3-22, 214C3
Sovt-UK talks end 3-25, 228G3
Portugal emb bombing rptd 4-26, 371F1
US for Angola troop exit 4-30, 318A2
Troop exit set; US Sweden informed 5-21—5-26; US for faster exit 5-25, 370B2
Angola confirms pullout 5-25, 370D3
Troops rptdly mass 6-3, 455C2
US rpts troop data, NATO sees no exit 6-13, 467D1
US-Zaire talks re Sovt, Cuba roles 6-17—6-19, 467B1
US vetoes Angola UN membership 6-23, 455E1
Castro vows aid 7-26, Neto ends visit 7-29, 649E2
Troop exit rptd 9-22, 862A2
S Africa chrgs massacre 9-28, 734A3
US scores interventn 9-30, 719E1
Angola-Portugal ties restored 9-30, 812D2
Troops rptd in drive vs Unita 11-10, denied 11-14, 862G1, A2
US vs Angola mil role 11-22, 879D1
US shuns UN vote on Angola entry 12-1, 895C1
S Africa rpts refugee shootings 12-10, 995F3

1977

CUBA—*See also COMECON, NONALIGNED Nations Movement*
Aeroflot jet crashes 5-27, 604D1
Natl Assembly holds 1st sessn 7-12—7-14, 654C2
Amb to Malaysia dies in jet crash 12-4, 992D2

African Relations
S Africa rpts Angola war role 1-3, 85C2
Cabinda fighting rptd 1-8, 86E1
Angola war role detailed 1-9, 18F3; Moss rpt disputes 1-31, 86A1
Canada chrgs Rhodesia spy plan 1-10, 17E2; Cuba admits Angola operatn, 4 expelled 1-12, 42D3
Young on Angola role 1-25; State Dept comments 1-31, 2-2, 105F1
Angola troop cut rptd 2-15, 110G1; 2-16, 180G2
US links Angola to ties 2-16, 110A1, 180G2
Mil delegatn arrives in Uganda 2-26, 141F2
Castro tours 8 Arab, black natns; signs trade pacts, backs Djibouti independnc, vows contd Angola aid 3-1—4-2, 249F1
Uganda advisers rptd 3-3, denied 4-2, 4-7, 308B2, C2
Cabrera Uganda visit cited 3-3, 308C2
Carter on Africa role 3-5, 171B2
Amin denies troops in Uganda 3-8, 170D2
Ethiopia aid request rptd 3-8, 239B1
Ethiopia coup backed 3-11, 238A3
Zaire rebel role denied 3-16, 207E3
Zaire invasn chrgs disputed 3-21—4-11, 249G2, 261D1, 265C2, G2, 283B1
Angola civilian killings rptd 3-30, 424B2
Zaire breaks ties 4-4, 261C1
Angola troop cuts confrmd 4-8, 283B1
Young defends Angola statemt 4-11, 271F3
Ethiopia mil advisers rptd 4-17, 328A1
Morocco chrgs Zaire role 4-18, 317G1
Zaire POWs claim Angola training 4-20, 4-26, 317D1
Senegal scores Africa role 5-3, 394E1
US Africa ambs on Cuba role 5-9—5-24, 398C3
Rhodesia chrgd re Botswana raid 5-18, 399B2
Carter scores Angola role 5-22, 397F1
Castro denies Ethiopia advisers 5-24; US rpts arrival, warns Cuba 5-25, 427E1
US on advisers in Ethiopia 5-26, 417A3
US rep rpts assurances on Ethiopia 6-1, 456C2
Ford, GOP ldrs link US ties, Cuba exit 6-3, 6-5, 455F3
Castro again denies Ethiopia role, confirms Angola exit end 6-9, 456F1
Mobutu warns re presence 6-9—6-10, 490F1
US Sen OKs compromise amendmt 6-16, 478B1
Angola rebelln aid rptd 6-20, 484B2
OAU vs interventn 7-1—7-5, 512D1, G1
Vance rejects arms race 7-1, 535D3
Zambia accepts aid 7-8, 536F1
US poll backs Cuba troop pullout 8-8, 654A2
Castro, Church discuss Cuba role 8-10, 653G3
Young calls US fears irrational 8-11, 646D3
E Ger role noted 8-21, 684G3
US, Cuba exchng 'interest' offices 9-1, 685F3
Angola troop increase rptd 9-11, 779A1
Ethiopia rpts med aid 9-16, 715F2
Ethiopia denies troop role 9-18, 715E2
US sees increased Ethiopia role 11-4, 11-14; troop chrg denied 11-5, 875E1
Somalia ends ties 11-13, 874D3
US warns vs mil buildup, Sovt role feared; NSC study issued 11-17, 896C1
Castro rejcts US pullout call 12-5; Young scores 12-6, Castro reaffirms stands 12-24, 1011F2
Angola rebels rpt attacks 12-14, 1009B2
Ethiopia troop aid rptd up 12-16, 998E1
Jamaica defends Angola role 12-16, 1019G1
US OKs Sudan jet sale 12-23, 1019C2

1978

CUBA—*See also COMECON, GATT, NONALIGNED Nations Movement*
Interest rates on loans set 5-1, new acctg system for state cos urged 5-26, 687C2

African Policy
Castro: troop role 'moderate' 1-2, 22E1
Carter scores Cuba, Sovt role 1-12, 12E1
Adviser total, R Castro visit rptd by US 1-12, 43F3
Ethiopia rebels rpt troop capture 1-15, 100B2
Ethiopia troops denied 1-18, 43E3
US, allies meet re Ethiopia role 1-21, 43E2
Ethiopia Ogaden offensive gains 1-22—2-14, 99C2
Equatorial Guinea aid rptd 1-25, 152A3
Angola rebels rpt death toll rise, mutiny 1-25—3-2, 165A1
Somalia displays prisoner 1-29; Ogaden buildup, bombings rptd 2-8, 99E2
Vance asks Ogaden troop exit 2-10, 99B3
Angola troop total rptd 165D1
Troop move from Angola rptd 2-10, 165D1
US hikes Ethiopia troop estimate 2-17, 2-24, 137F1
Eritrea troop arrivals rptd 2-27, 3-16, 215B3
Ethiopia admits troops 3-2, Cuban newspr acct rptd 3-15, 178D3
Ethiopia exit backed by US, Yugo 3-7—3-9, 194A1
Ethiopia troop cut plan rptd 3-10, 178A3
Rhodesia rebel role rptd 3-12, 210C3
US on USSR vow re Ethiopia troop cut 3-15, 215G3
Carter, Venez pres score role 3-28, 4-1, 233D1, G2
Arab League scores moves 3-29, 215D1
Ethiopia troops estimated 3-31; Eritrea offensive launched, US scores 5-16, 372D2
Angola anti-rebel drive rptd 4-4, 265B2
UK scores troop role 4-5, govt protests 4-7, 259C1
Ogaden fighting, death toll rptd 4-15, 372D3
Ethiopia ldr visits, Castro hedges on troops 4-21—4-27, 372B3 ★
Eritrea talks rptdly sought 4-27, 372G2
Zaire chrgs Shaba invasn aid 5-14, 359A2
Rhodesia rebels rptd trained in Zambia 5-14, 395B3
Zambia pres fears Rhodesia role 5-16, urges pol solutns 5-19, 395E2, A3
Castro sees US envoy, denies Zaire role 5-17, 382A1
Angola deaths rptd 5-17, 5-20; anti-rebel drive launched 6-4, rptd repulsed 6-16, 645C3
Zaire advisers rptd seen by France 5-19, 382C1
Carter scores US curbs 5-19; Young rebuts 5-21, 383A1, F1
Carter gets CIA evidence on Zaire role 5-19, 442A1
US offcls dispute Zaire role, seek clarificatn 5-24, 5-26, 418A2
Carter chrgs Zaire role 5-25, 5-30; Rodriguez denies 5-30, 418A1, E1
Ethiopia amb exit rptd 5-25, 5-26, rift denied 5-25, 584C3
Brzezinski chrgs Zaire role 5-28, USSR responds 5-30, 399B1
NATO debates role 5-30—5-31, 397E1
Ethiopia oppositn ldr backing rptd 5-30, 584E3
USSR scores NATO re Zaire role 5-31, 423B2
US evidence on Zaire role doubted 6-2—6-9, 442D1
Zaire advisers rptd by captured rebels 6-5, 418G1
Rhodesia rebel ldr rpts advisers in Zambia 6-6, 455D2
Carter chrgs USSR proxy role 6-7, 423C3
Zaire role scored by China 6-7, 441D2
Tanzania defends Africa role 6-8, 442A1
Angola denies Zaire role 6-10, 441A2
Hungary backs Africa role 6-10, 534F2

1979

CUBA—*See also COMECON, DISARMAMENT—Geneva Committee, GATT, NONALIGNED Nations Movement, OAS*

African Relations
US cites as obstacle to full ties 1-2, 20G1, A2
US GOP seeks SALT linkage 2-3, 86B1
US response to Sovt surrogates urged 2-8, 89B2
China scores interventn 2-27, 141E2
US rpts S Yemen advisers 2-28, 144E2
S Yemen troop role rise rptd 3-8, denied 3-14, 179E1
Ethiopian troops shifted to Ogaden 3-2, 271C1
US fears Cuba escalatn re Rhodesia sanctns end 5-15, 359C2
E Ger role detailed 5-23, 406G2
Carter: USSR warned at SALT talks 6-18, 449E2, 459A3
Ethiopia troop reductn rptd 8-3, mil aid lauded 8-23, 791B1
Southn Africa rebel support backed 8-28—9-1, 674C1
US on Sovt troops in Cuba 8-31, 657E1; 9-12, 673E2
Angola, Ethiopia troop totals rptd 9-12, 673E2
Young scores US 'fear' re Angola 9-16, 721B1
Castro scores US role in S Africa 10-12, 778G2
African children rptd trained 12-4, 12-10, 981B2

Atomic Energy & Safeguards
A-plant constructn plans rptd 11-8, 872B2

Economy & Labor
Monthly wage rptd doubled from '58 3-16, 238B2
Castro scores worker performance 7-4, 685E3

Exiles—*See also CHILE—Letelier*
US House com asks JFK death role probed 1-1, 4D1
Muniz slain in PR 4-28, other exiles rptd threatened 5-3, 350G2
Refugee ldr slain in NJ 11-25, FBI probe rptd 11-28, 906B1-D1

1980

CUBA—*See also COMECON, GATT, GENEVA Committee, NONALIGNED Nations, OAS*
Hurricane Allen hits 8-7, 621D2
Illiteracy study rptd 12-4, 953A3

African Relations
Angola, Ethiopia cited in US pres hopeful's 'basic speech' 2-29, 207B3
Algeria quake aid rptd 10-11, 776E1
Castro admits Angola, Ethiopia troop role 12-17, 12-20, 993B1

Economy & Labor
'79 tobacco crop damaged 1-1, '80 sugar crop threatened 1-11, 38F2
'79 growth rptd, '80 target trimmed 1-1, 38A3
'79 econ performance scored 1-1; Castro restructures govt 1-11, tightens security 1-12, 38B3
Sugar price hits 5 1/2-yr high 10-9, 777D2
Castro outlines '81-85 policy, admits '80 setbacks 12-17, 12-20, 992G3

1976

Exiles

Exiles blamed for Latin terrorism 8-17, 8-18, 8-22, 791B1
Exile plot to kill Castro rptd 8-17—8-18, 791F1
Sovt containership bombed 9-17, 908A1
Bombed jet crashes 10-6, 16 seized in Trinidad, Venez 10-7—10-15, exile confessn rptd 10-18, 779A3
Anti-Castro exile coalitn rptd 10-11, 779D3
Castro ties CIA to jet crash, other terrorism; US denies 10-15, 779B3, 780A1-C2
Castro lists Apr-Aug anti-Cuba attacks 10-15, 780G1-C2
Rpt FBI to probe Letelier case in Venez; exile-DINA ties chrgd 10-18; exiles deny murder role 10-20, 10-21, 844C2
Exile intl terrorist plans, Letelier murder role rptd 10-19, 779B3, 780C2
Venez trial re jet crash set 10-21—10-22; Trinidad deports 2 10-26; 4 indicted 11-4, 843F2
FBI Venez contact with crash suspects confrmd 10-25, 844A2
Vera Serafin killed in PR 10-25, 844C3
Rpt Venez ousts 3 US rptrs 11-1, 844F1
Air office bombed in Spain 11-7; CORU claims credit 11-9, 844A3
Nicaragua denies base chrg 11-16, 926F1

Foreign Relations (misc.)—*See also 'Exiles' above*

Torrijos sees Castro, signs pacts 1-10—1-15, 52C2
Mil advisers in Africa, Mideast, Algeria rptd 1-10, 138F1
Uruguay bans youth group 1-20, 208B1
Venez fears troops in Guyana 1-24, 138A2
Sahara Polisario aid rptd 1-25, 58F2
Canada prime min visits 1-26—1-29, '75 trade data rptd 1-30, 116D2
'75 Guyana rice sales rptd 1-30, 252F3
Guatemala rejects quake aid 2-11, 120D3
Backs UN rights comm resolutn vs Israel 2-13, 125E2
Colombia trade pacts rptd 2-20, 251F3
Namibia aid offer rptd 2-23—3-2, 206D1
Guyana denies mil presence, weighs refueling stops 2-23—3-10, 253B1
UN Palestine com member 2-26, 162C1
Aide in bombed Cambodian town 3-2—3-4, 238B2
Castro tours E Eur, Africa 3-6—3-16, 251G2-E3
Pope receives Cuba amb 3-25, 252A1
Troops rptd in Red Sea area 4-5, 242F1
Portugal emb bombed 4-22, 367B2
Backs Algeria UNCTAD attack vs Israel, S Africa 5-5, 320D2
Iran guerrilla link rptd 5-10, 365D2
US seen vs Jamaica ties 5-14, 522A2
Castro vs Africa, Latin 'crusader' role 5-21, 371C1
OAS scores pol prisoner abuse 6-11, 465G1
Africa mil presence rptd 6-13, 467C1
Snubs Fraser in China 6-20, 481C1
Rpt Libya trains terrorists 7-15, 531B2
Emb aides vanish in Argentina 8-9; kidnap feared 8-10, 'desertn' rptd 8-16, 672F1
Portugal seizes emb blast suspects 8-9, 733D1
Libya seen vs Sovt ties 8-18, 622A1
Castro agents blamed for Latin terrorism 8-18, 8-22, 791B1
SWAPO seeks arms 8-22, 654G2
Silent on Mao death 9-9, 657G2
Portugal trade pact rptd 9-14, 811G3
OAS re-entry rejected 9-14, 832G3
World sugar prices down 9-23; E Eur imports up in '75 9-30, 771G3, 772D1

1977

Angola Issue—*See 'African Relations' above*

Exiles

US anti-Castro ldr slain 1-7, 163D1
Linked to '71 swine fever 1-9, 19A3
Vance sees ldrs 2-25, Castro scores 2-26—2-27, 180B3, F3
Spain police infiltrate exile groups 3-5, 307F2
Prio Soccarras dies 4-4, 356F3
US cruise to Cuba protested 5-15, 390A2
Miami airline office bombed 5-25, 456F2
Venez pres sues Bosch 7-4, 868B1
2 commandos freed after US, forgn pleas 8-2, 654A2
US giving Cuba terrorist info 8-3, Miami-based raid foiled 8-15, 654E1
CIA link to '76 jet crash cited 646A3
Venez AF jet bombed in Miami 8-14, 868A1
Miami exiles vow more attacks 8-31, 686C1
US, Cuba exchng 'interest' offices 9-1, 685G3
Letelier murder probe implicates 9-7—9-10, 743E2
Venez mil trial for Bosch, 3 others re '76 jet bombing rptd 10-10, 867F3-868C1

Foreign Relations (misc.)—*See also 'Exiles' above, 'UN Policy' below*

Canada fines fishing boats 1-4, 7F1
Canada chrgs spy plan 1-10, 17E2; Cuba admits operatn, 4 expelled 1-12, 42D3
Canada rpts '76 spy surveillnc 1-16, 61C1
UK sees Rhodesia interventn 1-25, 49B2
Mex offers aid re US ties 2-15, 110D1
'77 Spain trade protocol signed 2-20, 242C3
Chile rights abuse resolutn backed 3-9, 219F1
Castro in E Ger 4-2—4-4, USSR 4-4—4-6, 249G1, E2
'66-75 arms transfers table 4-8, 415A2
Malta ties rptd 4-11, 309G2
Renewed OAS natn ties cited 4-14, 295F3
El Salvador prisoner haven sought 4-19, 373C2
Guatemala pres cites Castro 5-20, 414B3
Guatemala chrgs rebel arms aid 7-4, 673F1
Chile hijackers get asylum 7-5, 537B2
Belize oppositn fears Price ties 7-11, 553D2
Venez rptdly urged early US Panama Canal treaty 7-27, 590C1
Haiti to expel Cuba-trained pol prisoners 9-21, 767E2
Intl sugar pact OKd, world mkt share cited 10-7, 855D1
Canal pact interest disputed in US 10-10, 792G1
Sweden lets debts stand 10-12, 904A1
Castro in Jamaica, vows aid 10-16—10-21; reactn 10-16, 10-23, 883E3-884E1
Nicaragua rebels deny Cuba aid 10-26, Somoza disputes 11-7, 864B2
CIA plots vs Jamaica ldr rptd 11-2, 884G1
Malta premr provokes walkout in Peking 11-3, 925G2
USSR role in Africa buildup feared 11-17, 896E1, B2
Jamaica defends Cuba Angola role, asks US renew Cuba ties 12-16, 1019G1

1978

Carter asked Brazil, Venez exit pressure 6-11, 443C1
Castro denies Zaire role 6-13; US disputes denial 6-12—6-14, 442F2, 443A1
Castro chrgs CIA aids Angola rebels 6-18, 645E3
Castro: Brzezinski misleads Carter 6-18, 687B2
Vance: US concerned re Africa role 6-19, 490D3
US will not mirror activities 6-20; Tass rebuts 6-22, 487D1, C3
US Angola recognitn dispute cited 6-21, 487G3
Carter silent on Africa role at OAS 6-21, 489A3
Eritrea mil role rptd ended 6-21, 7-29, 584A3
USSR backs Africa role 6-22, 487C3
Zaire claims prisoners 6-22, US doubts 6-23, 652G1
Tanzania backs Africa role 6-25, 487E3
Eritrea negotiatns seen backed 6-26, 584C3
Rhodesia forgn min: US lacks 'guts' 6-30, 615E2
OAU ldrs debate role 7-18, 561G1-A2
1,500 troop deaths since '75 rptd 7-18, 603C3
Angola backs troops 7-21, US bars Angola ties 7-22, 562G1
Nonaligned conf scores role 7-25—7-30, 583A2-A3
Somalia scores mil role 8-14—8-26, 676C2
China, Yugo vs African role 8-25—8-27, 675G2
US: troops block better ties 8-31, 687D1
Angola, S Africa swap prisoners 9-2, 742A2
Eritreans rpt Cuba troops 9-11, 922G3
Castro in Ethiopia 9-12—9-19; Libya, Algeria 9-19, 776G3
Anti-UNITA offensive rptd 10-10, 925A3
Rhodesia Patriotic Front backing cited 10-25, 906F3
Uganda chrgs troops aid Tanzania invasn 10-27, 830A3
US cites mil role as obstacle to ties 11-13, 880G3
Ethiopia role rptd 'decisive' 12-2, 1016E2
Castro scores US chrgs 12-9, 1016E1
Angola pro-West trend 12-10, 985C1
Angola cites S Africa threat re troops 12-13, 985A1

Exiles—*See also CHILE—Letelier Murder Probe*

Nixon memoir excerpt links Watergate break-in 4-30, 319F3
Exile editors visit Havana 9-7, 687E1
UN mission bombed by anti-Castroists 9-9, 777B1
Miami exiles see Castro, fly ex-prisoners to US 10-21; ask faster screening 11-13, 880D2-B3
US exiles split on Castro ties 10-24, invited for pol talks 11-4, 880C3
Exile ldrs, Castro meet; prisoner exodus set 11-21—11-22, 12-8—12-9; 177 fly to US 12-12, 100 to Venez 12-24, 1016B1
US House com discounts JFK murder role 12-30, 1002C2

Foreign Relations (misc.)—*See also 'African Policy' above, 'UN' below*

Ecuador hijacked plane lands 1-18, 212A3
DR leftist ldr sees ties 5-20, pres-elect rebuffs 5-21, 414F2
Guatemala scores guerrilla aid 6-1, 497C1
Latin A-ban treaty cited 6-21, 489C3
S Yemen denies troop dominatn 7-2, 522C2
Eur rights ct rejcts Baader chrgs vs W Ger 7-19, 651A3
Nicaragua pres accuses Castro 7-22, 593F1
World Youth Festival held 7-28—8-5, 831B1
Colombia rebels rptdly merge 8-24, 814E3
Nicaragua freed prisoners arrive 9-1, 690F3
Spain premr visits, firms trade ties 9-9—9-10; natlizatn paymts; Venez, USSR oil pact rptd 9-15, 821E3, G3
USSR MiG-23 delivery rptd 11-14, Kosygin defends 11-16, 905F1
USSR: MiGs purely defensive 11-20, 1016F1
Trade boycott set by forgn unions 11-24, 1014C2
Guyana death ritual tape cites Cuba emigratn plan 12-8, 955A1
Quebec terrorists return 12-13, 964B2

1979

Foreign Relations (misc.)—*See also 'African' above, 'UN' below*

Castro scores China, Egypt; reps quit rite 1-1, 20A1
Canada '69 hijacker expelled 1-14, 37A2
Trade boycott dropped by ORIT 1-15–1-16, 28D3
Teng vs US stand 2-7, 84B1
China scores Africa, Mideast role 2-27, 141E2
Grenada prime min's visit defended 3-16, 236E3
12 Cubans gain Venez asylum 5-13, 7 fail 5-25, 411C2
Castro visits Mex; trade, other issues discussed 5-17–5-18, 372D2
Nicaragua interventn opposed 6-21, 461B1
Nicaragua given aid 7-25, 574B2
Nicaragua junta ldrs visit 7-26, 574C2
China, Egypt, Westn natns scored; Heng Cambodia govt backed 8-28–9-1, 9-3, 674C2-675B1
Nicaragua seeks arms aid 8-31; educ, mil training progrms rptd 9-1, 689B3
Leb hijackers chng flight plan 9-7, 677D3
Burma quits nonaligned movemt 9-28, 742D2
Castro scores 3d World econ disparities, Mideast peace; asks $300 mln aid fund 10-12, 778F2, A3
El Salvador proposes ties 10-18, 813E1
Matos, 26 others flown to CR 10-22, 812E2
Guatemala rebel ties rptd 10-26, 813G3
Swiss bond sale abandoned 11-8, 872G1
'77-78 trade deficit, debt rptd 11-14, 872B2
Canada FLQ exile leaves 12-23, 992F3

1980

Foreign Relations (misc.)—*See also 'UN Policy' below*

Venez, Peru asylum seekers rptd shot 1-18; Venez, Peru recall ambs 1-19, 103C1, 261A2
Tito sends detente plea 2-21, 139B3
DR Emb captors in Colombia offered asylum 3-18, 211C3
Afghan-Pak feud mediatn sought 3-25—3-27, 271C2
El Salvador rebel aid chrgd 3-27, 220C2
French trade accord reached, Antilles non-interventn pledge cited 4-1, 253F2
7,000 seek Peru Emb asylum 4-1—4-6; Castro vows safe passage 4-7, Andean Group debates resetlmt 4-9—4-10, 261G1
Peru Emb refugees get exile support 4-7, 261A3
CR refugee flights suspended 4-10, 10,000 offered asylum 4-20; marchers rally 4-19, flights resume 4-24, 300C2-D3
Peru Emb refugees offered asylum by 11 natns 4-14—4-17, flights to CR begin 4-16, 285B1
Peru Emb refugee curbs imposed 4-15, Lima scores 4-16, 285F1
Morocco severs ties over Polisario 4-23, attacks 2 tankers off Africa 7-12; Spain escorts to Canaries 7-14, 563C2
Colombia DR Emb captors arrive, hostages freed 4-27, 335E1
Greek freighter fired on by Cuban gunboats 5-1, 326F1
Swiss Emb attacked, 386 take refugee 5-2, 339F2
Tito funeral held 5-8, 339A1
CR hosts intl refugee conf 5-8, 361B1, A2
Cuban MiGs sink Bahamas patrol boat, buzz island 5-10; talks open 5-12; UN protest filed 5-13, 371A2-B3
4-natn refugee talks rejctd 5-23, 396G1
450 remain in Peru Emb, talks rptd underway 5-29, 397B1
442 leave Peru Emb 6-2, 33 detained 6-5, 420D2
S Yemen mil activity rptd 6-9, 468G2-B3
Amb to Grenada escapes assassinatn 6-19, 498C2
Bahamas convicts 8 of poaching, patrol boat compensatn rptd 7-9, 563E2

1976

Castro on trade prospects 9-27, 772A1
Rpt US execs visit via Mex, Jamaica 9-27, 791C2
Nujoma visits 10-5, 794B1
Uruguay pres scores Kennedy 10-8, 814G1
Burma ties set 10-11, 832G3
Canada seizes fishing boats 11-8, 888F3
Nicaragua chrgs guerrilla training 11-16, 926E1
UK orders US rptr ousted 11-17, 946E2
Venez signs Sovt oil pact 11-26, 929F3
Soclst Intl seeks US sanctns end 11-27, 935F3
Castro vs OPEC price hikes 12-2, 1000E3
Castro ties Jamaica electn issue 12-15, Cuba hails Manley win 12-16, 965A2, D2, F3
Chile Matos-Montes exchng rejctd 12-18, 955D3, 963C1

Soviet Relations—*See also 'Angola' above*
Sovt trade pact signed 2-6, 138E2
Castro addresses Sovt CP Cong 2-25, 196E1
Sovt oil imports rptd 3-2, 252A1
'75 Sovt trade rptd 5-5, 340G3
Libya seen vs ties 8-18, 622A1
Cuba role in Sovt space program set 9-14, 684D1
Sovt containership bombed in US 9-17, 908A1
Castro on Sovt aid 9-27, 772A1
Sovt '75 sugar imports, oil price rise rptd 9-30, 772D1
USSR, Venez sign oil pact 11-26, 929F3

Sports
Olympic results 7-18—7-31, 573C3, 574A1-C1, 574G3, 575G3, 576A1, B1, C2

U.S. Relations—*See also 'Angola' and 'Exiles' above*
US vetoes baseball series 1-7, 23E1
Castro, Torrijos confer on Panama canal talks 1-10—1-15, 52C2
Javits: US-Cuba ties aborted 1-11, 52F2
Russell ct scores '61 'mil aggressn' 1-17, 61C2
Kissinger: 'exports revolutn' 2-5, 138C1
Ford calls Castro 'outlaw' 2-28, 165F2-A3
Rpt Warren Comm told of attempts vs Castro 3-1, 217E2
Castro rejcts US warnings 3-14, 251D3
CIA memos on Oswald link rptd 3-20, 3-21, 217A2
Kissinger warns vs Africa role 3-22, 3-23, 214C3
Reagan scores Ford policy 3-31, 232E3
Duvalier treatmt at Guantanamo rptd 4-1, 267A3
CIA blamed in Portugal emb blast 4-24, 367B2
US seen vs Jamaica ties 5-14, 522A2
US Dem platform text cites 6-15, 478A3
Ford warns re PR 6-26, 462A3
US sentncs '72 jet hijackers 7-16, 544C1
US GOP platform text cites 8-18, 609F3, 610A2, C2
Kennedy scores re prison access 8-28, 791G1-B2
Castro scores re sugar 9-27, 772D1
US execs visit rptd 9-27, 791B2
Uruguay pres scores Kennedy 10-8, 814G1
US occidental immigratn revisn signed 10-20, 835D1
United Brands linked to Bay of Pigs 10-21, 844D3
'76 US loan default cited 11-11, 915G2
UK orders US rptr ousted 11-17, 946E2
Soclst Intl seeks US sanctns end 11-27, 935F3
US panel urges renewed dialogue 12-14, 975A1
Jamaica pledges normalizatn role 12-15, 965C2

1977

Human Rights (including political prisoner issues)
4000 pol prisoners rptd 1-1, 3G1
Vance sets dialogue terms 1-27, 180C2
Carter presses dialogue terms 2-12, 2-16, 2-23, 110A1, 126G2, 180A3
Castro scores US pressure 2-26—2-27, 180C3
US envoys sees jailed natls 4-28—5-2, 390B1
US sen vs renewed ties 6-3, 455F3
US pleas for jailed natls 6-3, 10 freed 6-12, 456C1
Castro estimates 2000-3000 held; US disputes 6-9, 456E1
OAS rejcts rights abuse rpt 6-17, 494D2
OAS rejcts rights abuse rpt 6-17, 494D2
2 exile commandos freed 8-2, 654A2
Young scores rights abuse 8-11, 647A1
US natls, kin allowed to leave 8-11, 653B3
US, Cuba 'interest' offices open 9-1, 685F3
Amnesty Intl rpts prison abuse, better conditns 9-17, 781E3
US natls, kin fly to US 9-22, 781B2
US prisoner release confrmd 10-13, 896F2
US bars intl bank loans 10-19, 815A2
Castro: almost all US jailed natls freed, US offcl visits 2 10-26, 896E2
US prisoner to be freed 12-13, 1011C3

Obituaries
Artime, Manuel 11-18, 952B2
Garcia Imchaustegui, Mario

UN Policy & Developments
UN Assemb member 3F3
UN comm scores Israel occupatn rule 2-15, 107F2
UN comm rejcts Argentine rights probe 3-4, 198E1
Assemb condemns hijacking 11-3, 852E3

U.S. Relations—*See also 'African Relations' and 'Exiles' above*
US trade, other overtures continue; Castro backs talks, scores rights pressure 1-27—3-4, 180A2
Cuba rptd ready for tourists 2-8, 181D1
Bingham arrives 2-10, rpts 2-15, 110E1
Carter on key to normal ties 2-12, 2-16, 110A1, 180G2
Mex offers aid re normal ties 2-15, 110D1, 136F3
Carter on prisoners, other issues 2-23, 126G2
US sets 200-mi fishing limit 3-1, 147G1
Carter answers call-in questns 3-5, 171F1, B2
US OKs sports games 3-5, 3-8, 181B1
Carter sets travel ban end 3-9, 172F3, 173D1
US probes mobster on plots vs JFK, Castro 3-16, 228E2
US fishing talks 3-24—3-29, 283B2
US eases currency curbs 3-25, 283E2
'74-75 secret talks disclosed 3-28, 283D2
US basketball team, offcls visit 4-4—4-9; McGovern rpts, says trade embargo end demanded 4-11, 282B3
'Venceremos Brigade' volunteers arrive 4-8—4-11, 283F2
Carter on Latin A-ban pact, ties 4-14, 295F2, F3
Minn businessmen visit 4-18—4-22, 390D1
Fishing talks 4-24—4-27, pacts signed 4-27; delegates see US prisoners 4-28—5-2, 390A1
US Sen com backs embargo ease 5-10, Castro scores 5-11, 389C3
US OKs group tours 5-13, cruise ship departs 5-15, 390F1; 5-19, 456D2
Fishing pact published 5-25, 456D2
Miami airline drops svc plan 5-25, 456E2
Carter signs Latin A-pact 5-26, 415E3
US rep sees Castro 5-28, briefs Carter 6-3, 456C2
Mrs Carter, Manley confer 5-30—5-31, 454C2
'Interest' offices set 5-30, GOP ldrs score 6-3, 6-5, 455G2, F3
Castro-Walters TV interview; prisoners, ties discussed 6-9, 456D1-B2
Pol prisoner estimate rptd 6-9, 456D1
US to challenge Sovt role 6-10, 460D2

1978

Human Rights—*See 'Political Prisoners' and 'Press & Censorship' below*

Political Prisoners
Emmick freed, flies to Canada 1-2, 22D1
Lunt swap rptd discussed 4-24, 318F2
US dual citizens to be freed, Castro asks concessns 8-17, 687E1
Pol offenders offered to US 8-31, 687B1
Nicaragua freed prisoners arrive 9-1, 690F3
Dual natls fly to Miami 9-14, 10-3, 776G3; 11-14, 880B3
2 US prisoners freed 10-3, 777A1
IAPA seeks rptrs' release 10-13, 829D1
Ex-prisoners, kin fly to US 10-21; faster screening asked 11-13, 880C2-B3
US exiles invited for pol talks 11-4, 880C3
Castro meets US exile reps, sets prisoner release terms 11-21—11-22, 12-8—12-9; 177 fly to US 12-12, 100 to Venez 12-24, 1016A1
US to admit more refugees 11-28, 934F1
US pres hopeful scores Castro 11-29, 938E3
Carter vows refugee aid 12-6, 934E1

Press & Censorship
Press curbs scored by IAPA 10-13, 829A2

Sports
Boxers dominate World Amateur matches 5-6—5-20, 600C2
Marathon swimmers depart for Fla 7-11, 8-13, 653E1-B2

UN Policy & Developments
US ouster of Viet amb protested 2-9, 103A3
Rights comm res condemns Israel 2-14, 99A2
Rodriguez addresses disarmamt sessn 5-30, 418F1
Missn bombed by exiles 9-9, 777B1
PR called US colony 9-13, 979C3
Assemb member 713D3

U.S. Relations—*See also 'African Policy', 'Exiles' and 'Political Prisoners' above*
Guantanamo troop strength rptd 1-2, 5D2
Reps in Havana; Castro hints partial embargo end OK 1-2, 22E1
US Sen debates Panama Canal pact 2-8, 120F1
US ouster of Viet UN amb protested 2-9, 103A3
Castro receives US envoy 5-17, 382A1
Carter chrgs nonaligned movemt subverted 6-7, 423D3
Castro lauds Carter, scores Brzezinski 6-18, 687B2
US mayors visit, Castro asks Carter mtg 6-22—6-27, 687A2
CIA ex-aide, Cubans chrg CIA misdeeds 8-1—8-24, 831B1
JFK death hearings 9-13—9-18, Castro tape played 9-19, 749F2-F3, 750A2
PR called US colony by UN panel 9-13, 979C3
US: ties improved, problems remain 11-13, 880F3
USSR MiG-23 delivery rptd 11-14; US, USSR dispute impact 11-16, 905F1
US backs interest paymts on frozen forgn assets 11-14, 977G1
US resumes spy photo flights 11-16, 1016F1
US pres hopeful scores Carter 11-29, 938E3
Castro: US ties 'bad' 12-9, 1016E1
Trade boycott backed by US unions 12-10, 1014C2
US House com discounts JFK murder role 12-30, 1002C2

1979

Political Prisoners
Castro offers US-PR prisoner trade 1-7, 40F3
CR to take 130 2-2, 238F1
400 prisoners pardoned, '79 total rptd 8-27, 685F3
US commutes sentncs of 4 PR natlsts, Cuba prisoner trade denied 9-6, 666F1
4 US pol prisoners freed 9-17, 706C3
Matos, 26 others freed 10-21; flown to CR 10-22, 812E2

Soviet Relations
USSR role, SALT linkage sought by US GOP 2-3, 86B1
Sovt sub, torpedo boats delivered 2-10, 109B3
2d Sovt sub rptd delivered 3-30, 334B1
US, Mex in troop talks 6-28—6-29, 753B2
US confrms Sovt troop presence, Cuba denies 8-31, 657A1, C2
Cuba backs at nonaligned summit 9-3—9-9, Sovts laud conf 9-9, 674B2, 675B1, C2
SALT pact endangered re Cuba troop issue 9-5, 657F1; 9-6, 674B1
Carter warns USSR re troops 9-7, vs SALT linkage 9-8; statemt text 673A1-A2
Vance sees Dobrynin re troops 9-10, 9-12, 673D1
Pravda denies troop presence 9-10, US sees Africa training missns 9-12, 673A2-674A1
'76-79 Sovt mil buildup cited 9-10, 674A1
Vance sees Dobrynin, Gromyko 9-14—9-30, 738A2
Sovt troops stall Panama Canal treaty implementatn 9-20, 723B1
Carter on USSR troops 9-25, 723E2
Gromyko scores 'lies' 9-25, 738B2
US blocks USSR computer sale, troop issue cited 9-27, 775E1
Castro denies Sovt combat brigade 9-28, 737G2
US sets surveillance, maneuvers program; Carter speech text 10-1; US Sen, Sovt, Eur reactn 10-1—10-3, 737A1-739D2
SALT II additn re troops proposed by US sen 10-11, 822B3
Castro ignores troop issue in UN speech 10-12, sees 2 US reps 10-13, 778G2-A3, 779F1
US Marines begin Guantanamo maneuvers 10-17, 781C2
US mil activity scored at OAS mtg 10-23, 10-24, 824B2-C2
Sovt UN missn in NYC bombed 12-12, 965C3

Sports
World Cup wrestling results 4-1, 507G3
Pan Am Game results, 3 defect 7-1—7-15, 798F2, C3

UN Policy & Developments
Sihanouk scored in Cncl debate 1-11, 10E2
UNCTAD rptd vs Palestinian resolutn 6-3, 417B3
Membership listed 695F2
Castro addresses Assemb, asks 3d World aid 10-12, 778B2-D3
UN mission in NYC bombed 10-27, 852D1; 12-7, 947B3

U.S. Relations—*See also 'African', 'Exiles' and 'Soviet Relations' above*
Castro scores US, rep quits rite 1-1; US cites obstacles to full ties 1-2, 20A1
Agee '78 mtg cited 1-4, 17C3
Castro sees US reps, asks trade embargo eased 1-7, 40E3
Debt to US rptd past due 2-5, 84C3
Teng vs US stand 2-7, 84B1
US rights rpt omits 2-10, 107A2
Student enrollmt in US rptd 167E2
US musicians visit 3-1—3-4, 238D2
Minn Univ exchng rptd 3-27, 238C2
CIA '63 Castro death plot rptd confrmd 5-2, 367E3-368A1
US jet hijacked to Havana 6-11, 442A1
US interventn in Nicaragua opposed 6-21, 461B1
US House com final rpt clears in JFK death 7-17, 538C1

1980

Castro in Nicaragua, marks Somoza downfall; CR protests refugee policy, shuns fete 7-18—7-19, 565G2
Mex pres visits, signs cooperatn agrmts 7-31—8-3, 605B3
Nicaragua arms shipmts rptd 8-1, 709F2
83 in Swiss Emb surrender 8-7, 618E3
Surinam coup backing rptd 8-18, 653A3
Refugees storm jet in Lima, demand flight to US 8-29; surrender 8-30, 672B2
Afghan mil role rptd 9-15, 705C1
Swiss Emb occupatn ends 9-23, 749D2
Venez acquits '76 jet bombing suspects 9-26; diplomats withdrawn, chrgs traded 9-29, 794G2
Nicaragua presence spurs riot 9-30, 792F1
Jamaica electn issue 10-5, 791G3
El Salvador guerrillas flee Honduras 10-14, 873A1
5 Cubans defect in Lisbon 10-18, 828E3
Manley defeated in Jamaica 10-30, 854E1
Iran-Iraq war mediatn attempted 11-11—11-14, 894D3
Uruguayan hijacks plane to Argentina 11-12, surrenders 11-13, 888C3
Castro scores Polish workers' movemt 12-17, 12-20, 992F3

Government & Politics—*See also other appropriate subheads in this section*
Castro tightens rule, assumes key ministries 1-11, 38E2, C3
2d CP Cong held 12-17—12-20, 992C3

Political Prisoners
Padilla allowed to leave for US 3-16, 231A3
US revises refugee policy 5-14, 361C1
Castro frees US natls 10-27, 828B3
Boniato hunger strike begins 11-12, Matos asks UN probe 12-4, 965C2

Soviet Relations
Econ dependence rptd, aid estimated 1-11, 38F2
UN Afghan resolutns opposed 1-14, 25G1; 2-14, 123E3
3d Sovt sub deployed; 5-yr costs rptd, US threat seen 1-17, 192E1
Reagan suggests US blockade 1-27, 91B3
Kennedy scores Admin re Sovt troop stand 1-28, 74B3
Sovt brigade resumes maneuvers 2-29, 192D1
US pres hopeful's 'basic speech' scores US-Sovt detente 2-29, 207B3
Soyuz team in space 9-18—9-26, 737D2
5 Cubans defect at Lisbon airport 10-18, 828E3
Castro backs Afghan invasn 12-17, 12-20, 992E3

Sports
US baseball team signs refugee 6-3, 637C1
Moscow Olympic results 7-20—8-3, Stevenson wins 3d gold medal 8-2, 588A3, 589E1, 622E1-624F2

UN Policy & Developments
Mex elected to Cncl 1-7, 12A2
Afghan resolutns opposed 1-14, 25G1; 2-14, 123E3
UN missn protest 4-19, 300A3
Bahamas files Cncl protest 5-13, 371B3
UN refugee involvmt barred 6-5, US processing aid rptd 6-9, 435A2
Women's conf racism motion withdrawn 7-28, 587G2
Attache assassinated in US, Omega 7 takes credit 9-11, 685A2
Cncl seat try ended 10-20, CR seat oppositn rptd 11-12, 896D1
UNESCO illiteracy study rptd 12-4, 953A3
Matos asks Boniato hunger strike probe 12-4, 965C2

U.S. Relations—*See also 'African Relations', 'Soviet Relations' above*
Carter cites missile crisis 1-23, 42G1
Delta jets hijacked to Havana 1-25, 7-22, Amer flight in LA 4-9, 617A3
Reagan suggests blockade 1-27, 91B3
'67 Army defector sentenced for desertn 1-30, 94E3; overturned 2-28, 189E1
US issues rights rpt 2-5, 87A3
Reagan, Connally 'basic speeches' cite 2-29, 207B3; 3-7, 184G3
El Salvador rebel aid chrgd 3-27, 220C2
Vance on 3d world role 3-27, 243C3
Exiles rally in Miami, other cities 4-7, 261A3
Peru Emb refugees offered sanctuary 4-10, 261F2
3,500 Peru Emb refugees offered asylum 4-14, press blames CIA 4-16, 285A1
Bay of Pigs marked 4-19, 300G2-B3
CR refugee flight pressure pledged 4-20, 300F2
US hikes Honduras aid 4-20, 314A1
US flotilla picks up refugees 4-21—4-24, 300E3
Castro drama opens in NY 4-23, 392G2
Refugee exodus hampered by storms 4-25—4-28; total hits 6,000, 55 rptd detained 5-1, 326A1
US announces refugee processing cntr 5-1, 326G1
Refugee flow slowed by storm, Swiss Emb interest office attack 5-2; visa procedures suspended 5-4, 339E2
Carter offers refugees 'open arms', 3,500 more arrive in US 5-5, 339D2
Carter declares emergency, refugee influx at 17,636 5-6, 339B3
CR hosts intl refugee conf 5-8, 361B1, A2
Hispanic immigrants in US surveyed 5-11—5-20, 396A3

1976

1977

10 US natls freed 6-12, 456C1
Sen OKs compromise amendmts 6-16, 477D3, G3
Newton leaves to face US chrgs 6-25, 531G3
2 seized in Fla for espionage 7-20, 576B3
Aid bar signed 8-4, 668B2
Church visits, sees Castro 8-8—8-11; US natls, kin allowed to leave 8-11, 653B3-654D1
US poll on Cuba ties, Bay of Pigs reparatns rptd 8-8, 654G1
101 Haitians reach Guantanamo 8-10, US returns 97 9-6, 706C3
Young sees improved ties, scores rights abuse 8-11, 646C3, 647A1
Emb repair costs compared 8-16, 686B1
'Interest' offices open 9-1, 685E3-686C1
US ends forgn ships 'blacklisting' 9-7, 781D3
Reagan on Panama role 9-8, 699B1
US natls, kin leave for US 9-22, 781A2
Castro sees US thaw 'long, slow'; cites embargo, naval base 9-29, 781F2 ★
Trade min in US, sees execs 10-3, 781A3
Cuba aid to '60s, '70s US radicals rptd 10-9, 896A3
Canal pact interest disputed in US 10-10, 792G1
US prisoner release confrmd 10-13, 896F2
Castro sees US amb in Jamaica, Manley asks embargo end 10-16, 884B1
US Cong bars intl bank loans 10-19, 815A2-C2
Oil products reach US 10-20, 896B3
US execs visit 10-24—10-28; see Castro on trade, CIA, prisoners 10-26, 896C2
US offcl sees jailed US natls 10-26, 896F2
CIA plots vs Jamaica ldr rptd 11-2, 884G1
Cuba, US profs mtg rptd 11-9, 896C3
FBI Cointelpro campaign detailed 11-21, 940E3
US reps visit 12-5, 1011F2
FBI releases JFK assassinatn files 12-7, 943G1
US prisoner to be freed 12-13, 1011C3
Jamaica asks US renew Cuba ties 12-16, 1019G1

1978

1979

'60s CIA agent pardoned 8-27, 686A1
Castro scores nonaligned policy, death plots 9-3, 674C2
US-PR prisoner trade denied 9-6, 666F1*
4 US pol prisoners freed 9-17, 706C3
Israel cites US 'weakness' 9-18, 694B1
US ups Guantanamo, Carib mil activity 10-1, 737G1, 739A1
Castro in NYC amid tight security 10-11–10-14; addresses UN, asks 3d World aid 10-12, sees 2 black congressmen 10-13, 778B2-779F1
Marines begin Guantanamo maneuvers 10-17, 781C2
UN mission in NYC bombed 10-27, 852D1; 12-7, 947B3
'67 Army defector returns to US 11-21, 924F1
US sets counter Carib policy 11-29, 960B3
'67 Army defector charged as deserter 12-19, 965G3

1980

US rescue copter buzzed by MiGs 5-12, 371C3
Carter curbs 'open arms' policy, orders flotilla end; 5-pt progrm detailed 5-14, 361A1
US personnel withdrawn, protests feared 5-14, 361D2
US refugee total at 46,000, 400 deported 5-15, 361G1, B2
US amends refugee finance regulatns 5-15, 361A2
Cuba regrets copter buzzing 5-15, 380B2
US turns back Cuban flotillas 5-17—5-21; refugee flow slows, total at 67,000 5-21, 379F3
Refugee boat capsizes, US blames Cuba 5-17, 5-18; sealift deaths at 24 5-21, 380F1
Havana anti-US protest draws 1 mln 5-17, 380G1
US opens 3d refugee processing cntr 5-18, 2 others rptd filled 5-21, 380D1
US grants refugees pol asylum 5-21, 380B1
CBS blocked from satellite broadcast, previous transmissns cited 5-22; policy review rptd 5-23, 397C1
Refugee talks barred 5-23, 396G1
US processing camps hit by unrest, resetlmt delays rptd 5-24—5-26; security tightened 5-26—5-27, 395F3-396C1
Refugee resetlmt costs estimated 5-25, 396D1
US opens Wis refugee processing cntr 5-25; security checks rptd complete, resetlmt lags 6-1—6-2, 420D1
Cuban flotilla boat seizures protested 5-28, 700 face fines 5-29, 396F1
US refugee total at 87,995, 300 vessels stalled in Mariel 5-29, 396E1
450 Cubans remain in Peru Emb 5-29, 397B1
Refugees riot at Ft Chaffee 6-1; processing suspended, troops enforce calm 6-2, 419G3-420D1
CBS satellite broadcasts cleared 6-1, 420G2
US freighter, 34 other vessels arrive in Fla; refugee influx hits 101,476 6-3, 420B2
US baseball team signs refugee 6-3, 637C1
Carter consults Cong ldrs on refugees 6-4, orders criminals expelled 6-7, 435A1
Flotilla end seen 6-5, US expands blockade 6-10, 435B2
Carter in Miami 6-9, 439F1
Refugees granted 6-mo reprieve, get pub assistance 6-20, 484B3-485D1
Bay of Pigs invasn scored 6-20, 498E2
US backs homosexual entry bar repeal 6-20, 2000 await processing 7-7, 514G2-D3
US expels 18 criminals, Havana blocks return 6-24; 1,395 jailed 6-30, 514C2
US Cong OKs refugee aid bill 7-2, Carter signs 7-8, 515F1
Marines alerted; mystery freighter intercepted, no refugees found 7-4, 514G3, 515B1*
US releases Cuban flotilla boats 7-7, 514E3
Reagan pres nominatn acceptance speech 7-17, 533A1, 534G3
Castro lauds Carter, scores Reagan 7-18—7-19, 565A3
Mex vows aid vs US trade embargo 8-1, 605B3
256 arrive in Key West, refugee total rptd 8-2, 591C3
Youths riot at refugee camp 8-5, troops quell violence 8-6, 591G2
83 in Swiss Emb interest office surrender 8-7, 618E3
Refugees hijack Air Fla jets to Havana, '80 total rptd 8-10, 8-13, 617A2
US refugee resetlmt problems grow 8-12—9-10, 14,000 remain in camps 8-29, 684E3
US budgets $16.8 mln for refugee relief 8-13, 617E1
Refugees riot at Wis camp 8-13, 27 arrested 8-14, 631F3
Carter pres renominatn acceptance speech 8-14, 613C1
Refugees hijack 4 jets, 2 attempts foiled 8-14—8-17; FAA tightens security 8-15, 631B3
Eastn hijack attempt foiled 8-18, 667F1-A3
Refugees continue US hijack attempts 8-26—9-17; Havana issues strong warning 9-16, returns 2 9-18, 704B1-B2
Refugees in Peru storm Braniff jet, demand flight to Miami 8-29; surrender 8-30, 672B2
UN attache assassinated in NY, Omega 7 takes credit 9-11, 685A2
Carter sets 3-pt refugee resetlmt plan 9-18, 742G1
'81 refugee quota cut 9-19, 883A3
Carter quotes Reagan blockade proposal 9-23, 722D3
PR refugee resetlmt camp to be opened 9-23, 725E3-726A1
Swiss Emb interest office occupatn ends, 11 surrender 9-23, 749D2
'Hard-core' refugees transfered to Ark camp 9-25, 725C3
Refugee aid to states clears US Cong 9-25, 10-1, Carter signs 10-10, 785B1
Mariel harbor closed, flotilla ends; refugee total at 125,000 9-26, 742C1, B2

1980

PR sues US to block refugee camp 9-30, 742E2
PR refugee camp blocked by legal battles 10-1—10-24, 825B3
US prisoners to be freed 10-13, 788G3
Carter assails Reagan plan 10-16, 802F2
30 US prisoners freed, 3 remain 10-27, 828B3
PR refugee camp ban lifted 11-3, 869C2
Reagan electn deplored 11-5, 841E2
US FBI convicts 2 ex-offcls 11-6, 884E2
US curbs French steel imports 11-17, 886B1
Airlift of 600 begins, 120 reach Fla 11-19, 883E2
Reagan Latin policy scored by US amb 12-11, 942E1
Castro warns US on emigratn rift, other policy differences 12-17, 12-20, 992E3, F3, 993B1

1976

CUBAN Americans—*See SPANISH Americans*
CUBBON, Brian
Injured 7-21, 538F2
CUEVAS, Mario
2d in Boston Marathon 4-19, 292E3
CULLEN, Jack Sydney George ("Bud")
Sworn manpower, immigratn min 9-15, 692D1
On immigratn drop 11-2, 851F1
CUNHAL, Alvaro
Urges unrest curbed 1-23, 76B1
Scores electoral change 1-24, 76C1
Scores govt econ, forgn policy 8-5, 774E2
CUNNINGHAM, Imogen
Dies 6-24, 524D2
CUNNINGHAM, John
On North Sea oil productn 10-3, 791G3
CUNNINGHAM, Patrick J.
Indicted 5-26, 6-7, 442E2
Nadjari dismissed 6-25, 1016D1
Indictmts dismissed 12-22, 1016E1
CURARE—*See 'Drugs' under MEDICINE*
CURCIO, Renato
Seized 2-18, 141B1
CURME Jr., George O.
Dies 7-28, 716A3
CURRAN, Richard P.
Indicted 9-14, arrested 9-17, 859F3
CURRIE, Malcolm R.
On US-Sovt arms research 2-15, urges US actn 2-26, 182A3
Censured 3-16, 200A3
Rockwell bias chrgd 10-14, 982G3
CURRY, John
Wins Olympic medal 2-11, 159B1
CURTAIN (book)
On best seller list 1-25, 80B3; 2-29, 208E3; 12-5, 972E2
CURTIS, Sen. Carl (R, Neb.)
Com ends Scott probe 9-15, 980A1

1977

CUELLO, Miguel
'77 boxing champion 12-17, 970A3
CUETO, Mario
Jailed 3-8, 261D2
CUEVAS, Jose
'77 boxing champion 12-17, 970A2
CULBRO Corp.
Havatampa merger blocked 6-28, 520E3
CULLEN, Jack Sydney George ("Bud")
Vs immigratn power-sharing 5-18, 425D2
CULTS—*See RELIGIOUS Cults*
CULTURE—*See ARTS & Culture*
CULVER, Sen. John C. (D, Iowa)
Votes vs Bell 1-25, 52G2
Chrgs Sen subcom SALT leaks 11-7, 11-8, 996F2
CUMBACEA, Vasile
Rptd ousted 11-23, 948A2
CUMBERLAND Packing Corp.
Saccharin ban scored 3-9, layoffs set 3-10, 177A1
CUMBERLAND River (Ky., Tenn.)
Floods rptd 4-3—4-6, 311G2
CUMMINGS, John
Rpts CIA plots vs Jamaica ldr 11-2, 884F1
CUMMINS Engine Co.
Haynes confrmd amb to Algeria 5-9, 418E1
CUNHA, Joao
Scores prisoner abuse 8-31, 741A2
CUNHAL, Alvaro
Backs USSR, scores Eurocommunism 10-28, 886F3
CUNNINGHAM, Billy
Hired as 76er coach 11-4, 991B1
CUNNINGHAM, Rep. Jack (R, Wash.)
Wins US House seat 5-17, 382F1
Rebuts Carter energy plan 6-2, 443G1
CUNNINGHAM, Patrick J.
NYS pol penalty voided 6-13, 517B2
CUNY (City University of New York)—*See NEW York, City University of*
CUOMO, Mario M.
NY mayoral primary 9-8; Koch wins runoff 9-19, 723A2
Loses mayoralty electn 11-8, 855E2
CUPOZ, Victor
Gets death sentence 11-25, 947B1
CURACAO—*See NETHERLANDS Antilles*
CURARE (Pavulon)—*See MEDICINE—Drugs*
CURCIO, Renato
Turin trial postponed 5-3, sentenced in Milan 6-23, 1014A2
CURRENCY—*See MONETARY Developments*
CURTIS, Sen. Carl T. (R, Neb.)
Votes vs Young 1-26, 52C3
Vs Sen ethics code 4-1, 251F3
Scores Soc Sec bill 12-15, 957D3

1978

CUBAN Film Institute
Battle of Chile released 1-12, 618C3; Teacher 5-13, 620A1
CUBIE, Jim
Scores NRC A-reactor safety test 12-10, 961A2
CUBILLO, Antonio
Wounded in Algiers 4-5, blames Spain 4-20; 2 tried, sentncd 5-6—5-7, 576C3
CUBILLOS, Hernan
Sworn Chile forgn min 4-21, 350G3
Scores US amb recall 6-23, 496B1
New Beagle Channel talks fail 12-12, blames Argentina 12-13, 979D2
CUELLO, Miguel Angel
Parlov KOs 1-8, 56C1
CUERVO Gomez, Maj. Gen. Antonio
DR 1st mil brigade cmdr 10-2, 881C1
CUESTA, Tony—*See CUESTA Valle, Antonio*
CUESTA Valle, Antonio (Tony Cuesta)
Flies to Miami 10-21, 880D2
Asks faster Cuba ex-prisoners screening 11-13, 880A3
CUEVAS, Jose
TKOs Weston 3-4, 379B2
CULLEN, Jack Sydney George ("Bud")
On US RCMP informer's entry 2-27, 166B2
Sets new immigratn rules 3-8, 188A2
Reveals jobless overpaymts 5-5, 350G2
Eases jobless paymt curbs 10-10—10-11, 813E3
Econ Dvpt Bd member 11-24, 921B3
CULLUM, John
On 20th Century opens 2-19, 887D2
Zinnia opens 3-22, 760G3
Wins Tony 6-4, 579G2
CULTURE—*See ARTS & Culture*
CULVER, Sen. John C. (D, Iowa)
Votes for Panama Canal neutrality pact 3-16, 177D2
Votes for 2d Canal pact 4-18, 273B1
Vs A-carrier funds 7-11, 526F2
Endangered Species Act revised 7-19, 551D2
Issues USSR civil defns study 7-19, 564D1
CUNHAL, Alvaro
Scores Socialist-CDS pact 1-20, 92D1
CUNNINGHAM, Imogene
Kanaga dies 2-28, 196C3
CUNNINGHAM, Rep. John E. (R, Wash.)
Loses reelectn 11-7, 857B3
CUNNINGHAM, Keith
New evidnc rptd in uranium case 4-20, comments 4-24, 346G2-A3
CUNNINGHAM, Roger
Thread of Scarlet opens 12-8, 1031B3
CUNNINGHAM, Sam
NFL '77 rushing ldr 1-1, 56B3
CUNNINGHAM, William D.
Timbuktu opens 3-1, 760E3
CUNY—*See NEW York, City University of*
CURARE—*See MEDICINE—Drugs*
CURB, Mike
Elected Calif lt gov 11-7, 856F2
CURCIO, Renato
Turin trial halted 3-10, 191F1
Ejected from Turin trial 5-10, 338B2
Sentenced 5-18, 393B3
Prosecutn asks 15-yr jail term 5-29, 453B3
Given 15-yr term in Turin trial 6-23, 516E3, 517C1
Asinara prison transfer rptd 9-7, 724D1
Red Bridgades successor sentncd 9-20, 724B1
Mantovani arrested 10-1, 817E1
CURIEL, Henri
Murdered 5-4, 352D2
Murder weapon linked to rightists 5-11, 474A1
CURREN, Kevin
Loses NCAA tennis title 5-29, 419E2
CURRENCY—*See ECONOMY (U.S.)—Monetary Policy & Developments; MONETARY Developments, International*
CURRIE, Austin
SDLP backs Brit exit 11-4—11-5, 923B3
CURTIS, Sen. Carl T. (R, Neb.)
Votes vs Panama Canal neutrality pact 3-16, 177G2
Vs Soc Sec funding from Treas 4-5, 241A1
Votes vs 2d Canal pact 4-18, 273B1
Scores Carter forgn policy 5-3, 342F2
Not standing for reelectn 5-9, 363F1
Exon wins seat 11-7, 846F1, 854F3

1979

CUBA (film)
Released 12-21, 1007B3
CUBAN-American Committee for the Normalization of Relations
Negrin slain 11-25, 906B1
CUBELAS Secades, Rolando
Pardoned in Cuba 8-27, 685G3
CUBILLOS, Hernan
Says Letelier extraditns unlikely, US ties strained 2-7, 114A3
Scores US re aid reductn 11-30, 927A3
CUEVAS, Ignacio
Gets death sentence 1-26, 400B2
CULLEN, Jack Sydney George ("Bud")
Govt papers found in garbage 5-26, 444A3
CULLERTON v. Fulton Market Cold Storage Co.
Case declined by Sup Ct 1-15, 32D1
CULLMAN, Joan
Carmelina opens 4-8, 711A2
CULP, Robert
Goldengirl released 6-15, 820C1
CULTURE—*See ARTS & Culture*
CULVER, Sen. John C. (D, Iowa)
Conservative PAC plans drive 8-16, 627G3
CUMMINGS, Constance
Wings opens 1-28, 292G3
CUNHAL, Alvaro
Communists gain in municipal electns 12-16, 968A3
CUNNINGHAM, Gary
Brown succeeds as UCLA coach 3-27, 291E1
CUNNINGHAM, John
Dancing in Dark opens 1-21, 292D1
CUOCOLO, Fausto
Wounded 5-31, 426E3
CUOMO, Lt. Gov. Mario M. (D, N.Y.)
Scotto convicted 11-15, 890A2
CURARE—*See MEDICINE-Drugs*
CURB, Lt. Gov. Mike (R, Calif.)
Gubernatorial powers upheld re Brown state absence 12-27, 983D3
CURBISHLEY, Bill
Kids Are Alright released 6-15, 820E1
Quadrophenia released 11-2, 1008C1
CURCIO, Renato
Milan trial opens, warns attys 2-15, 212A2
Letter scores dissidents 8-10, 635C2
Sentenced for trial behavior 10-17, 793E2
CURRAN, Joseph
Told to repay NMU benefits 7-27, 744G2
CURRAN, Paul J.
Named Carter peanut probe spec counsel, GOP scores limits 3-20, 203A1
Gains new probe power 3-23, 301G2-C3
Questions B Carter re family business 5-18, 381A1
Carter peanut business documts rptd subpoenaed 5-27, 5-28, 401B2
Blocks Lance witness plea bargain 6-6, 500A3
Gets '76 Carter campaign ad financing rpt 6-22, 500C2
Clears Carter family peanut business 10-16, 782F2-783A1
CURREN, Kevin
Wins NCAA tennis title 5-28, 570A2
CURRENCY—*See ECONOMY (U.S.)-Monetary Policy & Developments; MONETARY Developments, International*
CURRLIN, Lee
Named NBC-TV program chief 3-5, 334G3
CURTIN, Valerie
And Justice for All released 10-19, 1007G2
CURTIS, Bruce Cohn
Roller Boogie released 12-19, 1008C1

1980

CUBAN Community, Coordinating Committee of the
Refugee airlift funded 11-19, 883G2
CUBILLAS, Teofilo
Cosmos win NASL title 9-21, 770G1
CUBILLOS, Hernan
Dismissed 3-25, 255G3
CUE New York (magazine)
Sale agreemt rptd 3-4, 239G1
CUEVA, Pio
Shot in Ecuadoran cong debate 9-30, 789D2
CUEVAS, Jose (Pipino)
KOs Volbrecht 4-6, 320D3
Hearns TKOs for WBA welterwgt title 8-2, 907F2
CUISINARTS Inc.
Fined in trust case 12-19, 986B1
CULHAM Laboratory (Great Britain)
Tokamak fusion advance rptd 7-17, 715B3
CULLEN, Susan
On 'doomsday clock' 1-1, 12D3
CULTURE—*See ARTS & Culture*
CULTURE of Narcissism, The (book)
Wins Amer Book Award 5-1, 692D2
CULVER, Sen. John C. (D, Iowa)
Unopposed in primary 6-3, 439E3
Small business aid signed 9-19, 784D2
Loses reelection 11-4, 837D2, 845A2, 851A1
CUMBERLAND—*See RHODE Island*
CUMBY, George
In NFL draft 4-29, 336G2
CUNHAL, Alvaro
CP loses 7 Assemb seats 10-5, 760B1
CUNNINGHAM, Billy
Lakers win NBA title 5-16, 432F1
CUNNINGHAM, Mary E.
Bendix controversy, resignatn rptd 9-28—10-9, 958D3
CUNNINGHAM, Sean S.
Friday the 13th released 5-10, 675F2
CUOMO, Lt. Gov. Mario M. (D, N.Y.)
Carter loses NY vote 3-25, 221B3
CURLEY, Thomas
CPU strikes Abitibi mills 6-27, 497C2
CURRENCY—*See ECONOMY--Monetary Policy, MONETARY Developments, International*
CURRIE, Bob
Wins Polk award 2-25, 692F3
CURRY, Tim
Amadeus opens 12-17, 1003G2
CURTIN, Jane
How to Beat the High Cost of Living released 7-11, 675A3
CURTIN, Richard T.
Credit card use study rptd 1-30, 92A3
CURTIN, Valerie
Inside Moves released 12-19, 1003A2

1976

CURTIS, Thomas B.
On Morton campaign role 1-14, 21C3
Pacified on Morton role 1-19, Strauss objcts 1-22, 41C2, F2
Submits FEC resignatn 4-30, 346C3
Springer gets FEC post 5-21, 391A3
CURTO, Marcelo
Portugal labor min 7-23, 558F1
CUSTERS, Peter
Sentenced 9-20, deported 9-23, 734C3
CUTOV, Simon
Wins Olympic medal 7-31, 574B1
CUTTER, Bowman
Carter budget aide 11-23, 881G2
CYANIDE
Calif weapons cache found 12-4—12-11, 952E3
CYCLAMATES—*See SWEETENERS, Artificial*
CYCLING
Olympic results 7-18—7-26, 574A2
CYCLONES—*See STORMS*
CYPRUS—*See also COMMONWEALTH of Nations, NONALIGNED Nations Movement*
Total IMF oil loan rptd 1-7, 4-1, 340A1, C2
Clerides quits peace talks 1-13, withdraws resignatn 1-18, 48D2
Peace talks resumptn set, UN role rptd 1-18, 48E2
Listed as 'partly free' 1-19, 20C3
Sampson arrest asked 1-28, faces Makarios plot chrg 2-3, 155D1
Famagusta populatn shift chrgd 1-28, 155F1
Backs UN rights comm resolutn vs Israel 2-13, Medit pollutn pact 2-16, 125E2, C3
Communal talks 2-17—2-21, 155C1
UN Palestine com member 2-26, 162C1
Sampson arrested 3-16, sentncd 8-31, 858E1
Leb Christians seek refuge 3-28, 226D1
Clerides admits secret pact, replaced as negotiator 4-8; Onan replaces Denktash 4-15, 311A2
IMF OKs SDR purchase 4-29, 457F1
Yugo, Greece back talks 5-13, 543D3
Islamic Conf backs Turks 5-15, 373D1
UK rpt scores '74 policy 5-19, 457D1
Greek Cypriot expulsns chrgd, UNFICYP mandate extended 6-16, 457B1
Waldheim urges talks resume 6-16, 457D1
Turk Cypriots elect Denktash pres, Greeks rejct 6-20, 456G3
Dem Rally Party formed, Clerides heads 7-5, 772A2
Israel arms to Leb rptd 7-20, 527D3
Makarios vs compromise 7-20, 772B2
Papadopoulos named parlt pres 7-22, 772G1
Israel seizes ship 8-5, 578F1
Makarios backers win parlt electns 9-5, 772E1
Anthimos dies 9-19, 1015B1
Greeks in Turkish sector rptd 11-1, 12-4, 963A3
3 held in Makarios plot 11-10, 963C3
UN asks Turkey to quit 11-12, 863D1
Greece vs NATO mediatn 11-12, 897A3
UN commander resigns 11-19, 963C3
Rpt Palestinians flee Leb to Iraq 12-2, 894D3
UN rpts looting, Greek expulsns 12-4—12-13, 963G2
Turks, UN erect Nicosia posts 12-16, 963B3
U.S. Relations
US role in coup, Davies death probe rptd scored 1-20, 93F2
US to resume mil aid to Turkey 3-26, Nicosia emb attacked 4-6, 244A2, D3
Greek Cypriots storm emb again 4-12, 259F2
US, Greece letters exchng released 4-15, 259A2
Reagan scores Ford policy 6-3, 410G1
US Dem platform text cites 6-15, 478F1
Refugee aid authorized 6-30, 532G3
US GOP platform text cites 8-18, 609G1
Kissinger asks UN talks, Turkish troop exit 9-30, 719E2
Greek reactn to Carter electn 11-3—11-4, 826F1
Carter's view rptd 12-1, 916C3

1977

CURTIS, Kenneth M(erwin)
Carter picks as Dem chrmn 1-6, 14D2
Dem com endorses 1-21, 53A2
Resigns as Dem chrmn 12-7, 960A3
White named Dem chrmn 12-28, 1005D3
CUSSLER, Clive
Titanic on best-seller list 2-6, 120E3; 3-6, 184E3; 4-3, 264G1; 11-6, 872E3; 12-4, 1021A3
CUSTOMS and Patents Appeals, U.S. Court of—*See under U.S. GOVERNMENT*
CUSTOMS Service, U.S.—*See under U.S. GOVERNMENT—TREASURY*
CUTLER, Dave
Montreal wins Grey Cup 11-27, 950A3
CUTLER-Hammer Inc.
I I Industries offcls sentncd 3-14, 203E2
CUYAHOGA River
Frozen 1-19, 54G2
CWA—*See COMMUNICATIONS Workers of America*
CYANIDE
Laetrile overdose death 6-11, 508G1
42 die in Tenn jail fire 6-26, 508E3
CYCLONES—*See STORMS*
CYCLOTRONS—*See ATOMIC Energy*
CYLINDER Forming Ltd.
NATO orders revealed, bankruptcy cited 8-19, 700A2
CYPRIOT Orthodox Church—*See EASTERN Orthodox Churches—Greek Orthodox Church*
CYPRUS—*See also COMMONWEALTH of Nations, NONALIGNED Nations Movement*
'76 Eur Cncl pact vs terror cited 9G2
1,000 Turk troops to leave 1-24, 109C1
Greek, Turk Cypriot ldrs meet, set talks 1-27, 2-12, 108A3
Makarios resignatn pledge rptd 2-16, 147B1
Greek-Turk talks 3-31—4-8; Waldheim rpts to UN 5-2, 394E2
Luns sees NATO threat 5-9, 359D1
Turkey vows Greek solutn 6-5, 451C2
Makarios seeks Greek-Turk compromise 6-8—6-15, 487D1
'76 Turk Cypriot trade rptd 6-15, 467D1
UN peacekeeping mandate extended 6-16, 476G1
2 EOKA-B members sentncd 6-21, Papadopoulos given life 8-11, 764D2
Erbakan vs Greek federatn 7-5, 530D2
Demirel forms new govt 7-21, 565D1
Denktash: Famagusta to reopen, Makarios scores 7-22, 764B2
Makarios dies, successors named 8-3; reactn 8-4—8-12; funeral 8-8, 616F3-617B2
Facts on Makarios 617F1
Kyprianou named interim pres 8-13; Denktash asks Turkish independence 8-16, 636B2, C2 ★
Kyprianou sworn pres 8-31, rptd ill 9-21, 764B2
Eur Cncl to study Turkey rights abuses 9-8, 764G1-A2; rpt shelved, Greece protests 11-3, 946E3
Finnish troops to leave 9-16, 764F3
Waldheim sees contd deadlock 9-19, 713F1
Denktash splits with Turkey over independnc 9-24, 946D3
Greece, Turkey back new talks 10-2, 764E1
W Ger jet hijackers refuel 10-13, 789D1
Chrysostomos elected archbp 11-12, ordained 11-13; pol role seen 11-14, 924C1
Greek electn results 11-20, 925B1, C1
UK base bombed 11-31, 946B3
Kyprianou's son abducted 12-14, freed 12-18, 983F3-984B1
Clerides drops pres bid 12-16, 984B1
Helsinki Agreement—*See EUROPE—Security and Cooperation*
UN Policy & Developments
Assemb member 3F3
Rights comm scores Israel occupatn rule 2-15, 107F2
UNCTAD shipping study rptd 4-17, 337E2
Waldheim rpts to Cncl on Greek-Turk talks 5-2, 394E2
Peacekeeping mandate extended 6-16, 476G1
Cncl urges talks renewal 9-15, 764A2
Denktash splits with Turkey over independnc 9-24, 946D3
Pollutn conf ends, Medit pact reached 10-21, 876B2
Kyprianou chrgs Turks ignore resolutns 11-19, 946C3
Peacekeeping mandate extended 12-15, 984C1
U.S. Relations
US aid to Turkey rptd delayed 2-13, 109B1
US envoy on fact-finding missn 2-17—2-26, 122F1, 146G3
CIA paymts to Makarios rptd 2-19, 124F1
US sets Turkey arms aid terms 4-19, 351F1
Carter sees Caramanlis, Demirel 5-10, 359C1
Davies murder trial ends 6-3, 466F3-467C1

1978

CURTIS, Charles
Notes Con Ed improvemts since '77 blackout 7-6, 530B1
CURTIS, Kenneth
Successor installed 1-27, 87A3
CURTIS, Tony
Bad News Bears released 7-14, 969C3
CURTISS-Wright Corp.
Kennecott takeover sought; suit filed, denunciatns exchngd; prelim tally fails 3-13—5-24, 402A1-403D1
'77 profits, assets cited 5-24, 402C1
Kennecott victory voided, new electns ordrd 9-28, 752D2
Kennecott dispute settled 12-15, 1004G3
CUSHING, Dr. Harvey (deceased)
2d daughter dies 11-4, 972B3
CUSHMAN, Austin T.
Dies 6-12, 540E2
CUSTER, Roberta
Bleacher Bums opens 4-24, 760E1
CUSTOMS Service, U.S.—*See under U.S. GOVERNMENT—TREASURY*
CUTLER, Dave
Edmonton wins Grey Cup 11-26, 1025E1
CUTLER, Elliot R.
Water projects proposed 6-9, 446A3
CUTLER, Rupert
On US sci missn to China 7-17, 564B3
CUTLER Hammer Inc.
Leeds stake sold, Tyco foiled 6-22; Eaton takeover backed 6-26, 553F1, C2
CUTUGNO, Lorenzo
Killed 4-11, 329C3
CUYAHOGA (U.S. Coast Guard cutter)
Chesapeake Bay collisn 10-20, 908C3
CWA—*See COMMUNICATIONS Workers of America*
CYCLAMATES—*See SWEETNERS, Artificial*
CYPHER, Rev. Michael Jerome (d. 1975)
Murderers sentenced 2-2, 194C2
CYPRUS—*See also COMMONWEALTH of Nations, COUNCIL of Europe, GATT, NONALIGNED Nations Movement*
Nicosia expenses rated 1-14, 28B3
Kyprianou wins new pres term 1-26, 74G3
EOKA-B announces dissolutn, govt probes 2-10, 147E3
Denktash asks joint econ projcts 2-15, 148D1
Kyprianou takes office 3-1, 148A1
Kyprianou names new Cabt 3-8, 189E1
Price hikes protested; Konuk sees Denktash, resigns 3-24, 226C2
Anti-govt plotters arrested 4-11, 287G3
Orek replaces Konuk 4-22, 329A1
Prison siege by EOKA-B 9-15—9-19, 894C3
Turk Cabt mins resign 11-28, 922F2-B3
Foreign Relations (misc.)—*See also 'UN' below*
Ecevit stresses Cyprus solutn 1-4, 8C2
Denktash, Ecevit in settlmt talks 1-19, 148E1
Caramanlis-Ecevit mtg agreed 1-23, 2-9, 170C2
Turkey to withdraw 500 troops 1-24, 226F2
Kyprianou visits Greece 2-14, 148B1
Egypt recalls aides 2-20, cuts ties 2-22, 118G1
Kyprianou seeks Egypt ties renewal 2-23, 138F2; 3-1, 148A1
Caramanlis-Ecevit summit 3-10—3-11, 216A3
Ecevit chrgs US summit pressure 3-10, stand rptd hardened 3-12, 216D3
Ecevit sees 2 communities in setlmt 3-24, 230F2
Greeks postpone Turkish talks 4-11, 277D1
Turks present separatn plan 4-13, text issued 4-21; Kyprianou rejects 4-19, 4-27, 328A3
USSR reassures on Turkish arms aid 5-5, 477F1
Ecevit, Caramanlis link setlmt, NATO role 5-17, 5-27, 398B3
Ecevit, Caramanlis meet; more talks set 5-29, 398B2
NATO urges settlemt 5-31, 397C2
USSR shifts policy, backs direct talks 6-25, 595F2
Israel sentncs Cypriot for PLO link 7-7, 547G1
Turkey withdraws 2250 troops 7-10, 595A3
Leb war refugees flee to 10-7, 761D2
Helsinki Agreement—*See EUROPE—Security and Cooperation*
Palestinian Terrorist Attack—*See MIDDLE EAST—PALESTINIAN Developments—Cyprus Terrorist Attack*
UN Policy & Developments
Turkey warns US vs peace role 1-20, 170G2
Rights comm res condemns Israel 2-14, 99A2
Waldheim gets Turkish plan 4-13, 328B3
Ecevit scores Waldheim 5-16, 398G2
Assemb member 713D3
US plan calls for Varosha role 11-28, 922E2
U.S. Relations
US rights rpt scored 2-5, 148C1
Vance links setlmt, Turkey arms aid 3-9; Ecevit scores 3-10, 216C3
Davies death terms cut protested 3-21, 226E2
US moves to lift Turkish arms embargo 3-29—4-6; Greeks, Cypriots condemn 4-2—4-16, 276A2-277A2

1979

CURTIS, Thomas B.
Nixon Admin pub TV moves disclosed 2-24, 194D2
CURVE of Binding Energy, The (book)
H-bomb letter cites Taylor interviews 9-16, 9-18, Taylor denies chrgs 9-17, 714B1, C2; text of letter 717G1
CUSTER, George Armstrong (1839-76)
Sioux awarded $100 mln 6-13, 464F3
CUSTOMS Service, U.S.—*See under U.S. GOVERNMENT-TREASURY*
CUTLER, Dave
Edmonton wins Grey Cup 11-25, 1001G1
CUTLER, Lloyd N.
US-Canada fishing talks progress seen 1-10, 37B1
Named Carter counsel 8-17, 623E1
CUTLER, Walter
On US concern re Iran executns 5-15, 357D2
Iran arrival delayed 5-20, 388B3, F3
Iran bars as US amb 6-4; Africa, Zaire role cited 6-5, 425F2
Laingen named amb to Iran 10-2, 752G2
CUTSINGER, Pfc. Roger
Challenges army gay policy 10-1, 850E3
CUVILLER, Phillipe
French Emb seige in El Salvador ends 6-1, 424C3
CUYAHOGA (U.S. Coast Guard cutter)
'78 collisn rpts issued 1-20, 140F3; 2-26, 3-2, 240E3
Cmdr convicted for '78 collisn 11-3, sentncd 11-5, 887A3
CYANIDE
Laetrile treatmt for 3-yr old ordrd ended 1-23, 1-30, 139C1; blood test rptd 3-7, 196B1
Laetrile deaths rptd 2-1, 138G3
Laetrile testing delayed 3-13, 196A1
FDA laetrile ban upheld by Sup Ct 6-18, 498E2
Laetrile rptd lethal to rats 7-13, 571C1
CYCLE, The (film)
Released 2-12, 174C2
CYCLONES—*See STORMS & Floods*
CYPRUS—*See also COMMONWEALTH of Nations, COUNCIL of Europe, GATT, NONALIGNED Nations Movement*
Intercommunal talks set 5-19, 387C2
Foreign Relations (misc.)—*See also 'UN' below*
2 PLO aides slain 12-15, 980F1
Helsinki Agreement—*See EUROPE—Security and Cooperation*
UN Policy & Developments
Waldheim visits 5-17, announces new intercommunal talks 5-19, 387C2
UN rep's antiquities seized 9-14, resigns 9-15, 751E2
Membership listed 695G2
U.S. Relations
Carter State of Union Message 1-23, 48F1
US hails new talks accord 5-19, 387B3

1980

CURTIS, Gustavo
Loses kidnap suit 1-6, 18B1
CURTIS, Jamie Lee
Prom Night released 8-15, 675C3
CURTIS, Kenneth
Carter wins Me caucus vote 2-10, 109D1
CURTIS, Pam
On Reagan mtg 7-15, 533E3
CURTIS, Tony
Little Miss Marker released 3-21, 216C3
Mirror Crack'd released 12-18, 1003C2
CURTISS-Wright Corp.
GE suit partial setlmt upheld 4-22, 344C1
CUSSLER, Clive
Raise the Titanic released 8-1, 675D3
CUSTOMS Service, U.S.—*See under U.S. GOVERNMENT--TREASURY*
CUTLER, Lloyd N.
On Olympic alternate games 3-18, 206C1
On Olympic boycott effect 5-24, 420F3
Testifies in B Carter probe 9-10, 701E1
CUTLER, Lynn
Wins Ia US House primary 6-3, 439E3
CUTSINGER, Roger
Charged in murder 1-2, 18C3
CUYLER v. Sullivan
Case decided by Sup Ct 5-12, 426G2
CYANIDE
Memphis area illness probed 4-2, 331B3
CYCLAMATES—*See SWEETNERS, Artificial*
CYCLING—*See BICYCLING*
CYCLONES—*See STORMS & Floods*
CYCLOPS Corp.
Reagan visits Pittsburgh mill 10-2, 738C2
CYPRUS—*See also COMMONWEALTH of Nations, COUNCIL of Europe, CSCE, GATT, NONALIGNED Nations*
Kyprianou sets unity bid 1-14, 96B3
Kyprianou shuffles Cabt 9-9, 749E2
Foreign Relations (misc.)—*See also 'UN Policy' below*
Greek terrorist plot vs emb chrgd 2-15, 150D3
Greece, Turkey end Aegean air dispute 2-22, 2-23, 150G2
Armenian, Greek Cypriots linked to Turkey attack vs envoys 3-1, 197E2
Greece rejoins NATO mil wing 10-20, 800D1
Turkish zone at Islamic econ conf 11-4—11-6, 865D1
UN Policy & Developments
Rights Comm Sovt Afghan res abstensn 2-14, 123E3
Waldheim rpts intercommunal talks fail 4-3, 273C2
Intercommunal talks resume 8-9, 633C2

1976

CYRILLE, Odoutan
Sentenced 2-1—2-2, 404D1

CZECHOSLOVAKIA—*See also COMECON, DISARMAMENT—Geneva Committee, WARSAW Pact*
Portugal forgn min visits 1-14—1-16, 143B1
Pilot fined for '75 E Ger airlift 1-14, 158B1
Listed as 'not free' nation 1-19, 20D3
Austrian chancellor visits, pacts OKd 2-17—2-19, 289D2
Chile rptdly bought Sovt arms 2-25, 288E3
To join A-safeguards group 4-1, 243G2
15th CP Cong, Sovt support stressed 4-12—4-16; Husak reelected, gives 5-yr econ plan 4-12; Presidium, Secretariat chngs 4-16, 289B1
Yugo sentences Cominformists 4-14, 542G3
Shuns China fete for Egypt vp 4-19, 275G2
Yugo paper shuts news bureau 4-30, 341A3
Zdenek Fierlinger dies 5-2, 368F2
'75 Sovt trade rptd 5-5, 340G3
Quake tremors rptd 5-6, 352B3
Arms sales to Ethiopia rptd 5-19, 364A3
Addresses E Ger SED Cong 5-19, 381A2
'68 Sovt invasion cited at Eur CP conf 6-30, 461E1
Rock musicians trial opens 7-7; sentncs reduced 9-3; 4 others sentncd 9-23, 851E3
Jet crashes 7-28, 560G3
Husak vows no '77 food price rise 8-28, 750B3
Poor harvest, grain imports rptd 9-13, 750A3
Role in Sovt space program set 9-14, 684D1
Agri min, dep premrs fired; Nagr named agri min 9-15, 750G2
Prague editor censured 9-17, 852C1
Student defects to Italy 9-27, 852C1
E Ger border wall constructn rptd 9-29, 772F2
USSR cuts oil export 10-4; energy curb rptd 10-18, 851B3
Bars playwright's Austria visit 10-9; natns trade chrgs 10-12—10-14, 852A1
Parlt elected 10-22—10-23, 946A2
W Ger to try hijacker 10-29, 946F1
Pavel Reiman dies 11-1, 932F3
Acad ousts Prague editor 11-5, 1012B3
Suicide rate rptd 11-17, 944F3
Iran pipeline pact rptd 11-22, 946A2
Dubcek backers freed 12-10, 1012B3

European Force Reduction Issues—*See under EUROPE*

Obituaries
Fierlinger, Zdenek 5-2, 386F2
Reiman, Pavel 11-1, 932F3
Vilim, Blazy 9-23, 1015A3

Sports
Winter Olympics results 2-4—2-15, 159A2, B2
Summer Olympic results 7-18—7-31, 573D3, 574C2, 575B1, B2, 576B2, A3
Olympic athlete disqualified 7-30, 563B2
Canada Cup hockey results 9-15, 736F3

U.S. Relations
US '68 invasn info rptd scored 1-20, 93B3
Dubcek-CIA-RFE link chrgd 3-10, 289E2
Byrne confrmd amb 4-28, 412E1
Travel curbs eased 11-3, 946E1

1977

Turkey vows improved US ties 6-5, 451C2
2 sentncd in Davies murder 6-21, 530E2
US security aid signed 8-4, 668D1
Carter urges talks renewal 8-25; Greece, Turkey agree 10-2, 764A1
Denktash splits with Turkey over independnc 9-24, 946D3
Eur Cncl rights abuse rpt shelved, Greece protests 11-3, 946F3

CYPRUS, UN Force In—*See under UNITED Nations*

CYPRUS Mines Corp.
'76 Fortune 500 list drops 341D1

CZECHOSLOVAK Airlines
Jet hijacked to Frankfurt 10-11, 848F3

CZECHOSLOVAKIA—*See also COMECON, DISARMAMENT—Geneva Committee, WARSAW Pact*
Ex-min arrested as spy 1-4, 19E3
Spy trial opens 1-10, 82F3; 4 sentncd 2-3, 115C1
'76 econ growth rptd 6-14, 513C2
Single party-state ldr cited 6-16, 469F2
Tomasek '76 cardinal apptmt revealed 6-27, 768B3
Price hikes, reductns set 7-22, 675E1
Jet hijacked to W Ger 10-11, 848F3
Ex-min rptd sentenced 12-20, 1018G3

Foreign Relations (misc.)—*See also 'Human Rights' and 'Monetary, Trade & Aid' below*
UN Assemb member 3G3
Forgn spy operatns rptd 1-6, 1-7, 19F3; trial opens 1-10, 82F3; 4 sentncd 2-3, 115C1
UK denies spy chrgs 1-23, 82G3
Spain ties renewed 2-9, 242C2
Simko defects, reveals spy network 2-24, 220B3
Dutch forgn min visits 2-28—3-2; sees Patocka 3-1, 220G2
W Ger sentences '76 hijacker 3-31, 380B2
US, Cuba envoy exchng agreed 5-30, 455A3
Carrillo Eurocommunism scored 7-8; Carrillo book popularity rptd 7-24, 590B3
Cuba 'interest office' opens in US 9-1, 685B3
UN Cncl elects member 10-24, 852F3
Malta premr provokes walkout in Peking 11-3, 925G2
Austria cooperatn pact signed 11-22, 936F2
Egypt closes consulates, cultural cntrs 12-7, 929B1, 930B1

Helsinki Agreement—*See EUROPE—Security and Cooperation*

Human Rights
Dissidents issue manifestos 1-6, 1-8, detained 1-7—1-12, 20A1
Charter '77 dissidents gain US, intl support 1-19—1-31; rejct Austria emigratn 1-28, 82D2-E3
French CP ldr scores repressn 1-25, 63B2
Norway cancels trade visit 1-30, 99C3
Dissidents gain more support; govt disputes tactics 2-2—2-10; Sovt offcl arrives 2-8, 114D3
US, W Ger rptrs detained; US protests 2-4—2-14, 114G2, B3 ★
Rumania dissidents back Charter 77 2-8, 314B2
Dubcek denies anti-Charter 77 stand 2-10, 115B1
Waldheim scores press detentns 2-16, rpts disputed 2-17, 220G3
Rumania actn vs dissidents compared 2-26, 315G1
Patocka detained 3-1—3-2; dies 3-13, buried 3-16, 220F2, A3, 264C3
US papers returned 3-1, 3-16, 220E3
2 French journalists expelled 3-2; 2 others attacked 3-3, 220D3, E3
Spain rptr held 4-1—4-3, Canada rptr's belongings seized 4-24, 314A3
Dissident reprisals rptd 4-7, 4-25, 314B2
Forgn rptr censorship set 4-8, 314F2
More charters rptd 4-29, 5-4, 437D1
Charter 77 spokesman freed 5-20, 437B1
Charter 77 issues new chrgs 6-7, 513B1
Mlynar in Vienna 6-13, backs movemt 6-16, 513A1
Amnesty for '68 refugees set 6-30, 512F3
Charter 77 lists banned writers 7-11, individual support planned 9-28, 752E2
Charter 77 signers rptd jailed 9-28, 752D2
Huebl's wife chrgs educ bias 10-4, 812A2
Charter 77 signers, other dissidents sentncd 10-18, more trials seen 10-19; France, US reactn 10-18, 10-19, 812B1

Monetary, Trade & Aid Issues (including all foreign economic developments)
Sovt oil price rise seen 1-6, 67D3
Air Canada to end svc 1-26, 43D2
'76 OECD trade gap rptd 1-26, 123D2
Norway cancels trade visit 1-30, 99C3
UN chrgs Rhodesia sanctn violatns 2-10, 123A1
Westn debt rptd mounting 2-13—4-13, 335C3
A-supplier natns meet 4-28—4-29, 403F1-A2
'76 trade data rptd 6-14, 513B2
Egypt curbs cotton trade 8-14, 636A3
Egypt bans cotton exports 10-26, 811F3
Austria trade talks open 11-22, 936G2

Obituaries
Patocka, Jan 3-13, 220F2

1978

US set back in moves to lift Turkish arms embargo 5-3, 5-11; reactn 5-12, 378C1
Ecevit bars mediatn role 5-16, 398G2
Carter sees Ecevit, Caramanlis 5-31, 398D2
Turkish arms embargo end gets Cong OK 8-1, reactn 8-2, 587D2-588B1
Carter signs refugee aid 9-26, 734G1
US negotiatn proposal revealed 11-28, 11-29, 922G1-E2

CYPRUS Airways
2 Palestinians hijack jet in Cyprus 2-18—2-19, 117F1

CYPRUS Wire & Cable Co.
Sued re price fixing 9-21, 769C1

CYSTITIS—*See MEDICINE—Diseases*

CZECHOSLOVAKIA—*See also COMECON, DISARMAMENT—Geneva Committee, GATT, WARSAW Pact*
RC church ldr named, admin boundaries revised 1-10, 17C3
'77 econ data rptd 2-7, 115D2
3-yr econ experimt set 2-14, 189B2

European Force Reduction Talks—*See under EUROPE*

Foreign Relations (misc.)—*See also 'Human Rights', 'Monetary, Trade, Aid & Investment' and 'UN' below*
At USSR maneuvers 2-6—2-10, 103C2
Jet hijacker, 3 others get W Ger asylum 2-6, 212D2
Cosmonaut joins USSR space flight 3-2, 157E2
Husak visits W Ger 4-10—4-14, detente support pledged 4-11, 332F3
Brezhnev visits 5-30—6-2, 423A2
Afghans name new amb 7-10, 538A1
W Ger sentncs Czech hijacker 10-4, 776E3
Rumania neutrality re '68 invasn cited 11-25, 913B3

Helsinki Agreement—*See EUROPE—Security and Cooperation*

Human Rights
Charter 77 asks open debate 1-1, 17F3
2 Charter 77 activists held 1-28; 4 Hungarians rptd exiled 3-7, 180E2, G2
Husak defends rights policy 4-11, 333D1
US rptr ousted for Charter 77 interview 5-1, 439B3
Dissidents held re Brezhnev visit 5-30, 504E1
Grusa arrested re underground novel 5-30, 504F1
Charter 77 prison rpt cited 5-30, 504A2
Writers fear crackdown, underground press cited 6-7, 504E1
W Ger rptr ousted for '68 Sovt invasn expose 7-4, 635E1
Belgian rptr ousted 8-10, min cancels visit 8-11, 691B3
Charter 77, Polish dissidents mark '68 Sovt invasn 8-15, 635F1
Prague vigil marks '68 Sovt invasn 8-21, 691G2
Gottwald statue blast marks '68 Sovt invasn, 2 arrested 9-2, 868F3
Sabata arrest near Polish border rptd 10-7, 868G3
Kohout leaves for Austria 10-28, 885E2
Charter 77 plea to Waldheim, Helsinki natns rptd 11-8, 885D2

Monetary, Trade, Aid & Investment
A-export safeguard pact detailed 1-11, 11B2
EC imposes steel dumping levies 1-23, 80B2
3-yr econ experimt set 2-14, 189C2
Australia joins A-suppliers' group 2-24, 129C2
Husak in W Ger talks 4-10—4-14, 332G3, 333C1
W Ger probes terrorist aid 6-22, 500F1
US bars clothespin import curbs 10-2, 805E1

Sports
World hockey title lost 5-14, 458C3
Navratilova wins Wimbledon, press plays down 7-7, 540B1

UN Policy & Developments
Abstains on UN Leb force 3-19, 197C1
Abstains on UN Leb force expansn 5-3, 340F1
Abstains re Namibia plan 7-27, 562B1
Abstains on Unifil extensn 9-18, 713B1
Assemb member, named to Cncl 9-19, 713A3, D3
Abstains re Namibia plan 9-29, 819E2
Waldheim gets Charter 77 plea 11-8, 885D2

U.S. Relations
AP rptr ousted 5-1, 439B3
Pan Am to end Prague svc 9-7, 701G1
US bars clothespin import curbs 10-2, 805E1

1979

CYPRUS Mines Corp.
Indiana Standard to buy 4-11, 560B3

CYROCKI, John
Chicago DC-10 crash rpt issued 7-10, 538F3

CZARAVICH (race horse)
3d Woodward Stakes 9-23, 876E3

CZECHOSLOVAKIA—*See also COMECON, DISARMAMENT-Geneva Committee, GATT, WARSAW Pact*

Economy & Labor
'78 natl income, agri output rptd 1-31, 117D1
Bad weather cripples econ 1-31, 120C2
Price increases ordered 9-20, 9-23, 741F3

European Force Reduction Talks—*See under EUROPE*

Foreign Relations (misc.)—*See also 'UN' below*
China invasn of Viet scored 2-19, Rumania stand denounced 2-21, 122F2
Kosygin visits, urges energy measures 5-24, 397B1
Caths see Pope in Poland 6-2, 413B2; Pope cites 6-8, 435A2
Iran drops gas pipe plans 7-28, 583A1
Rumania travel ban set 8-1, 645F3
Rumania eases gas paymt rules 9-3, 741G3-742A1
USSR troop deploymt rptd 761F2
Kohout citizenship revoked; Austria exile, Westn contacts cited 10-8, 838A2

Helsinki Agreement—*See EUROPE-Security and Cooperation*

Human Rights
Sabata sentenced 1-11, 62C2
Charter 77 picks new ldrs 2-8, 126F3
Bible availability cited 3-13, 238E1
Sabata sentence extended 5-10, 782F1
Kohout citizenship revoked 10-8, 838G1
Havel, 5 other dissidents arrested 5-9; trial opens 10-21, sentncd 10-23; US, others score 10-23, 802G1

Obituaries
Kadar, Jan 6-1, 508B3
Svoboda, Ludvik 9-20, 756E3

Sports
Sovts retain world ice hockey title 4-25, 448E1
US wins Federatn Cup 5-6, 391E2
Navratilova wins Wimbledon 7-6, 7-7, 570B1
US wins Davis Cup 12-16, 1003B3

UN Policy & Developments
Cambodia issues Cncl plea vs Viet 1-11, 10G1
Cncl action on Cambodia-Viet war opposed 1-15, 28F1
Unifil extension opposed 1-19, 51D1
Unifil renewal abstentn 6-14, 436A3
Membership listed 695G2
Zimbabwe sanctns vote abstentn 12-21, 976C3
Iran sanctns res abstentn 12-31, 974G2

U.S. Relations
'57 spy chrgs vs Sterns dropped 3-22, 232D1
US A-accident media coverage rptd 4-11, 323C1
US protests dissident trial 10-23, 802D2

1980

CZECHOSLOVAKIA—*See also COMECON, CSCE, GATT, GENEVA Committee, MBFR, WARSAW Pact*

Economy & Labor
'79 data rptd 1-24, 166F1
'78 factory reform extended 3-11, 391A1
'81 austerity budget set 4-11, 390G3-391A1
ILO scores work laws 5-12, 381E2
Factory coms warned on worker interests 8-25, 642A2

Foreign Relations (misc.)—*See also 'UN Policy' below*
USSR Afghan invasn backed 1-10, 11A1
W Ger visit rptd cancelled 1-30, 103F1
UK prof deported 3-9, 262D2
2d UK prof ousted 4-13, UK protests 4-21, 326D3
Zimbabwe gains indepndnc 4-18, 301F1
Iran hostage rescue try scored 4-25, 324E1
E Ger gas cash purchases barred 6-1, 431D3
Poland strike setlmt denounced 9-2, 658G3
Afghan mil role rptd 9-15, 705C1
Poland 'antisocialist forces' condemned 9-30, 753C1; 10-9, 761E1
Poland warned, mil intervention hinted 10-8, 10-19, 831E1
Cuba to free US prisoners 10-13, 789B1
Poland criticism rptd 11-5, 860G1-A2
Iraq seeks arms 11-11—11-12, 879A3
Sovt role defended 11-13, 863F1
Polish currency exchng, travel curbed 11-20, 879C1
Polish govt warned 11-27; Sovts echo 11-30, 910G1, C2
Sovt Poland invasn preparatn rptd complete 12-7, 930C1
Poland solidarity stressed 12-8, 929D2

Government & Politics—*See also other appropriate subheads in this section*
Husak addresses CP com 10-9, 761F1

Human Rights
Lederer rptd freed 1-13, 40B1
Tomin lectures disrupted 3-9, 3-19, 4-2, 262C2
Theater couple defects 3-17, 262E2
Tomin arrested 4-9, 4-12, 326D3
ILO scores work law, Charter 77 dismissals 5-12, 381E2
15 Charter 77 signers arrested 6-1, 431B3
Lederer expelled 9-2, 680F1
US scores Sovt role; USSR defended 11-13, 863E1, F1

Sports
Lake Placid Olympics results 2-12—2-24, 154F2, 155F2-156D1
Canada Cup hockey tourn cancelled 4-30, 488F3
US wins Federatn Cup 5-25, 607B1
Moscow Olympic results 7-20—8-3, 588A3, 622A2, F2, F3, 623B1-G1, E2,
David Cup won 12-7, 946C3

UN Policy & Developments
ILO scores work laws 5-12, 381E2
Cncl replacemts seated 395A2

U.S. Relations
Iran hostage rescue try scored 4-25, 324E1
Cuba to free US prisoners 10-13, 789B1
US scores Sovt rights curbs; Czechs defend 11-13, 863E1, F1
US rpts Sovt Poland invasn preparatn complete 12-7, 930C1

1976

CZIURA, Grzegorz
Wins Olympic medal 7-19, 576D2

1977

Husak, Viera 10-20, 872C2
Zrzavy, Jan 10-13, 872C3
Sports
Keeps ice hockey title 5-8, 430A2
U.S. Relations—*See also 'Human Rights' above*
Ex-CIA agent rpts US spy role 1-7, 19G3
US soldier permit request rptd 1-14, 82G3
A-supplier natns score Carter plans 4-28—4-29, 403F1-A2
Brzezinski '68 Dubcek aid scored 6-13, 512G3
Cuba 'interest office' opens in US 9-1, 685B3
CZECHOSLOVAK Refugees Inc., American Fund for—*See AMERICAN Fund etc.*

1979

CZINKOCZY, Zsuzsa
Just Like At Home released 4-19, 528F2

1980

CZOPEK, Agnieszka
Wins Olympic medal 7-26, 623E3
CZYREK, Josef
Visits Moscow 12-26, 976A3

D

1976

DABLANC, Christian
Bans Afars demonstratns 1-3, 86A1
D'ABO, Lady Ursula
Named in Getty will 6-8, 444D2
DACKO, David
Named Bokassa adviser 9-17, 858B1
DACRON
DuPont sets price hike 11-30, 898G1
DAFINOIU, Costica
Wins Olympic medal 7-31, 574D1
DAFT, Lynn
Carter transition aide 11-23, 881A3
DAHLBERG, Kenneth
Ford donatn rptd 10-22, 938G3
DAHLGREN, Anders
Named to Swedish Cabt 10-8, 794C2
DAHLUL, Ahmed Dib
Soldier convicted in death 10-1, 799D1
DAHOMEY—*See BENIN, People's Republic of*
DAILY News, The (N.Y. newspaper)
Vs gag order 1-13, 124A2
Carter interview 4-4, 260E2
Kennedy denies pres bid rpt 5-20, 357D2
Ford endorsement rptd 10-30, 831F2
Backs Gilmore death plea 11-12, 891B2
DAIMLER-Benz A.G.
US ends car dumping probe 5-4, 321D2
DAIRY Products
France scores EC milk policy 1-16, 139B1
Dec, '75 CPI 1-21, 90A2
Milk price supports vetoed 1-30, veto upheld 2-4, 88D1
Australia-Japan talks 2-4—2-15, 137E3
W Ger hit by lira drop 2-10, 140E2
Milk price supports raised 3-3, 186B1
EC sets milk-feed plan 3-6, OKs revisn 4-14, 276F2
US foreign milk aid set 3-8, 186C1
Ford, Dems on price supports 4-2, 4-3, 245F1, G2
EC agri comr quits 4-9, 276B2
Pacific Commodities Exchng closes 5-10, 348C2
Sup Ct bars Jacobsen plea-bargaining review 5-19, 393D3
US files Mid-Amer Dairymen consent decree 5-28, 989B2
Quebec farmers riot 6-3, 416F2
EEC farmers ask drought aid 6-19, 548D3
Jacobsen gets 2 yrs probatn 8-20, 1016A1
Aug CPI rptd 9-21, 708F2
Mondale on price supports 9-22, 725A1
EPA: milk contaminated by China A-blast 12-27, 992G1
DALE (U.S. warship)
In Intl Naval Review 7-4, 488D3
DALE, William N.
Replaced as amb to CAR 2-4, 110C2
DALEY, Mayor Richard J. (Chicago, Ill.)
Facts on 969E3-970B1
Ill primary results 3-16, 196F2, A3, 197D1, F1
Endorses Carter 6-9, 408G3
Patronage ousters barred 6-28, 468B3
Carter visits 7-1, 490D2
Walker endorses Howlett 7-6, 493A1
Dem Conv speaker 7-13, 509B3
Mondale visits 8-25, 645E2
Carter sees, lauds 10-11, 762G2
Ford scores Carter 10-15, 784F1
Howlett loses electn 11-2, 820E3, 823B2
Misses mayors mtg 11-7—11-8, 845F3
Dies 12-20, funeral 12-22, 969B3
Successors selected 12-28, 12-29, 994A1

1977

DACH, Leslie
Harvard DNA resrch halted 12-15, 1022E2
DADE County, Fla.—*See FLORIDA*
DAHDAH, Col. Antoine
Replaced as security chief 4-11, 297A3
DAHLBERG, Edward
Dies 2-27, 164E2
DAHOMEY—*See BENIN, People's Republic of*
DAIGNEAULT, Rene
'72 RCMP raid rpt cited 10-26, 841G1
DAILY American (Rome newspaper)
Closes 8-23, 729C2
DAILY Express, The (London newspaper)
Sold 6-30, 526G3
DAILY Mail, The (London newspaper)
Leyland bribery chrgs stir controversy 5-19—5-25, 526C1, D1 ★
DAILY Nation (Kenyan newspaper)
Editor quits 5-3, 393F1
DAILY News, The (N.Y. newspaper)
Batchelor dies 9-5, 787F3
DAIMLER-Benz AG
Air bag test program set 1-18, 213E2
Schleyer kidnaped 9-5, 695F1
DAIRY Products
Ford '78 budget proposal 1-17, 32B3
NY storm losses rptd 1-27—2-1, 76D1
ARA Svcs rpts rebates 1-28, 94E1
'76 cong contributns rptd 2-15, 128E1
EC butter sale to USSR spurs dispute 3-1, E Eur sales curbed 3-2, 269E1-A2
Interstate United rpts rebates 3-16, 215F2
Milk price supports raised, product cost hikes seen 3-22, 213E3
Canada raises price supports 4-4, 304D1
Kraft rpts milk discounts 5-22, 503E2
June milk price rptd up 7-8, 554G1
Rhodesia subsidies rptd 8-25, 730E3
Farm bill signed, target prices detailed 9-29, 736D2, D3
DAISAGEN, Poul
Danish agri min 2-25, 373E1
DALAI Lama
Invited to end exile 5-1, 347D1
China chrgs India aids rebels 8-6, 616E3
DALEY, Richard J. (1902-76)
Chicago police spying rptd 5-11, 388D2
Bilandic elected mayor 6-7, 446B3
DALEY, Robert A.
CBS Entertainmt pres 10-17, 846A2
DALKON Shield—*See BIRTH Control*
DALLA Riva, Peter
Montreal wins Grey Cup 11-27, 950G2

1978

DA (play)
Opens 3-13, 887E1
Wins Tony 6-4, 579F2 ★
DABADIE, Jean-Loup
We Meet Paradise released 5-22, 620B1
Da COSTA, Alfredo Nobre (Portugal premier)
Named Portugal premr-designate; Soares, leftists score 8-9, 632F2
Sworn premr 8-28, Cabt sworn 8-29, 671F3
Sets govt program 9-7, rejected 9-11; govt falls 9-14, 757D3-758C1
New electoral law passed 10-2, 777C3
Mota Pinto named premr 10-25, 830C2
DADE Christian Schools v. Brown
Schl integratn challenge refused 2-21, 126C1
DADE County, Fla.—*See FLORIDA*
DADE County Medical Society
Westmoreland addresses 12-6, 960D3
DADZIE, Kenneth
Named UN econ dvpt dir gen 3-8, 401D3
DAEDALUS Enterprises Inc. (Ann Arbor, Mich.)
US bars China sale 5-8; OKs 6-9, 436D2
DAHLIN, Ernest W.
Wins US House Dem primary 3-21, 207F1
DAHOMEY—*See BENIN, People's Republic of*
DAHRENDORF, Ralf
Resigns 6-6, 592D3
DAILEY, Dan
Dies 10-16, 888A3
DAILEY, John D.
Suspends Calif bond ratings 6-8, 426E1
DAILY News, The (N.Y. newspaper)
Struck by Guild 6-13—6-17, 625A2
WPIX-TV license renewed 6-16, 672E1
Strike halts publicatn 8-9, 625G1
Strike ends, impact rptd 11-6, 864D3-A2
DAIMLER-Benz AG
Brazil Mercedes workers strike 5-16—5-18, 412B1, C1
DAIRY Products
Humphrey illegal gifts cited 33E1
Australia vs EC import curbs 1-24, 69D2, G2
Nigeria milk import ban rptd 4-4, 248C1
Australia threatens EC cheese export curbs 4-6, talks delayed 4-14, 310D3
Japan, NZ trade accord rptd 5-23, 498A1
Assoc Milk Producers Com ranked 9th-top PAC fund-raiser 9-7, 753C2
Mich cattle feed contaminated by PBBs 10-8, 769E2
Mich PBB suit dismissed 10-27, 834C1
Hershey to buy Friendly Ice Cream 12-26, 1005G1-A2
DAKO, Toshiwo
Vs US fiscal policy 8-28, 695B2
DAKOV, Mako
Loses Bulgaria agri post 4-29, 530G3
DALBOKOV, Sava
Loses Bulgaria agri post 4-29, 530G3
DALE, Elaine
Bears child 10-13, 948G3
DALI, Salvatore
Paintings destroyed in Brazil museum fire 7-8, 579A2

1979

DACH, Leslie
Asks sleep aid, nose spray ban 5-1, 354C3
DACKO, David (Central African Republic president)
Deposes Bokassa 9-20, rpts on French aid 9-22, Libya threat 9-23, 720E1-C2
DADDAH, Moktar Ould
Mauritania sets Polisario talks 5-3, 324B1
DADE County, Fla.—*See FLORIDA*
DAFFLON, Roger
Mayoralty of Geneva assured 5-25, 428D3
DAGNINO, Giancarlo
Shot 4-24, 331C3
DAHLBERG Electronics Inc. v. Kievian
Case refused by Sup Ct 3-19, 203B3
DAHOMEY—*See BENIN, People's Republic of*
DAI Han-chao
Taiwan wins Little League title 8-25, 797A3
DAI-Ichi Kangyo Bank Ltd. (Tokyo bank)
Ranked '78 world's 8th biggest bank 6-19, 476B2
DAILY Californian, The (Berkeley) (newspaper)
Judge bans H-bomb letter publicatn 9-15, Justice Dept drops suit 9-17, 714C1, A2
DAILY News, The (N.Y. newspaper)
Morales phone tip rptd 5-27, 431C2
Daily, Sunday circulatn listed 6-6, 431B1, C1
Wall St Journal daily circulatn lead rptd 11-7, 1007F1
DAILY Oklahoman, The (newspaper)
UAW wins GM organizing dispute 7-19, 598A2
DAIMLER-Benz AG
Brazil metalworkers strike 3-13–3-27, 328C3
US Mercedes truck plant plan rptd 7-26, 663F3
DAIRY Products
Borden price compensatn case declined by Sup Ct 1-22, 54B2
Connally announces pres bid 1-24, 70A3
A&P milk price actn backed by Sup Ct 2-22, 150F2
Milk rptd contaminated by 3 Mile I A-accident 3-29–4-3, 242C3, 244E2, 245F3
Price guidelines tightened 3-29, 264A2
3 Mile I milk contaminatn denied 4-8, 4-9, 261F1, A2
NC PCB dumping chrgd 6-4–6-13, disposal disputed 6-5, 597C3
Yellow No 5 labeling ordrd 6-26, 571B2
PCB limits cut 6-28, 571C2, E2
Foreign Developments (including U.S. international news)
US hikes Australia cheese quota 1-8, 36F2, D3
EC milk surplus tax urged 1-31, 85A2
Rumania '78 output rptd short 2-6, 170G3
UK '78 aid to Portugal rptd 2-20, 212F3
GATT pact signed 4-12, 273F2
Australia-EC accord set 5-29, 404G3, 405A1
Denmark chrgs 10 in Unilever margarine case 7-2, 563F3
Wis Sens vote vs trade bill 7-23, 646G3
EC import curbs on Australia, NZ cited 8-21, 632A1
China hikes egg prices 11-1, 854D3
DAJANI, Burhan
Scores Iran assets freeze 11-14, 862A1
DALAI Lama
Teng support rptd 6-14, 445A1
China invites back 7-18, refuses 7-19, 563A3
Arrives US for visit 8-3, 685A3
People's Cong electns, Tian Bao gets top post 8-6–8-14, 685D3
DALE, David L.
Chrgd in GE uranium theft 2-1, 119G3
DALE, Grover
King of Schnorrers opens 11-28, 956C3
DALEY, Richard J. (1902-76)
Byrne wins mayoral primary 2-27, 149E3
Byrne elected Chicago mayor, '75 win cited 4-3, 252A1
Chicago bond rating drops 9-19, 920D3
Chicago-Cook Cnty patronage ruled illegal 9-24, 770D3
2d salary disclosed 12-4, 946G3
DALIA v. U.S.
Case decided by Sup Ct 4-18, 346B1
DALLA Chiesa, Gen. Carlo Alberto
Aide murdered 7-13, 584B1
Cited as Milan carabinieri head 12-17, 995A2

1980

DA VINCI, Leonardo (1452-1519)
Crack in 'Last Supper' rptd 6-16, 472E3
Ms sold for $5.28 mln 12-12, 997E3
DACKO, David
Obote wins Uganda electn 12-13, 968B3
DADA Hirezi, Hector
Joins El Salvador junta 1-9, 19G3-20A1
Quits junta, flees to Mex 3-4, 172E1
Duarte succeeds 3-9, 191E2
DADE County—*See FLORIDA*
DAHNE, Heike
Wins Olympic medal 7-27, 623D3
DAHOMEY—*See BENIN*
DAILY News, The (N.Y. newspaper)
Felker staff post rptd 8-27, 732G3
DAIMLER-Benz, A.G.
Kuwait 14% interest rptd 6-25, 562E1
DAINGERFIELD—*See TEXAS*
DAIRY Products
Dec '79 CPI rise rptd 1-25, 75A3
USDA 'junk food' rules rptd 1-27, 157F3
US dietary guidelines issued 2-4, 157A3
Mar producer prices rptd 4-4, 263C1
Cholesterol rpt issued 5-27, 432A3
Mafia, cheese indus ties probed 8-24, 714D1
Sept farm prices rptd up 9-30, 741C2
Oct farm prices rptd 10-31, 883C1
Foreign Developments (including U.S. international news)
EC suspends USSR export licenses 1-7, 9C2
Peru drought halves milk productn 2-8, 234E3
Zimbabwe ends margarine tax 4-20, 301B2
Poland sees butter shortage, EC trade suspensn blamed 7-9, 566F1
USSR 1st 1/2 milk productn drop rptd 7-16, 711G2
USSR milk shortage rptd 10-21, 10-22, 797G2, 798G1
Poland butter rationing set 11-19, 878G2
DAKIN, Roland
Judges middlewgt title bout, decisn scored 3-16, 320D2
DALAI Lama
Sees China moderatn 4-22, controls eased 5-31, 4-22, 462D1
Supporters Tibet visit spurs demonstratns 7-29; China curbs visit, backs return 7-31, 603E3-604A1
DALE, Jim
Barnum opens 4-30, 392D2
Wins Tony 6-8, 692C3
DALEY, Richard J. (1902-76)
Byrne scores 'past admins' 1-30, 186G2
DALEY, Richard M.
Wins Ill primary 3-18, 206B3
Elected Cook Cnty state atty 11-4, 850D3
DALISERA, Joe
Missing in Carib copter crash 11-13, 869F3

1976

DALLAS, Tex.—*See TEXAS*
DALLAS News
Ford endorsement rptd 10-30, 831F2
DALLAS Times Herald (newspaper)
Rpts Connally barred GOP post 8-22, 631D1
Ford endorsement rptd 10-30, 831F2
DALLA Tea, Gen. Carlos
To head mil legis comm 3-25, 236D1; Vannek to head 4-2, 264B1
DALTON, Judge Thomas F.
Sentences Kallinger 10-14, 972F1
DALY, Lar
Ill primary results 3-16, 196D2
DAL Zotto, Fabio
Wins Olympic medal 7-21, 574E2
DAM, Henrik
Dies 4-17, 368E2
D'AMOURS, Rep. Norman E. (D, N.H.)
Reelected 11-2, 830C1
DAMS
New River projects upheld 3-24, 219B3
Ganges dam protested 5-16—5-17, 365F1
Idaho dam collapses 6-5, 423B1
Ford OKs Teton victims aid 7-12, 517E3
Interior Dept, cong com on Teton collapse 7-15, 9-25, 736C1
New River dams blocked 9-11, 689D1
Mex dam collapse kills 630 10-1, 840D2
DAN, Uri
90 Minutes at Entebbe publshd 7-26, 547G1
DANCE
Obituaries
Berkeley, Busby 3-12, 240D3
Blair, David 4-1, 484C3
DANFORTH, John Clagett
Wins Mo Sen primary 8-3, 565F2
Elected 11-2, 820B1, 823A3, 828B2
DANGE, S. A.
Says followers arrested 1-9, 29C1
DANG Seng
Cambodia asks Thais return 9-4, 734F3
DANIEL, Price
William Blakely dies 1-5, 56A3
DANIEL Jr., Rep. Robert W. (R, Va.)
Reelected 11-2, 830G3
DANIEL, Rep. W.C. (Dan) (D, Va.)
Reelected 11-2, 830G3
DANIELS, Dale H.
Andreotti payoffs rptd 9-1, 684F3
DANIELS, Rep. Dominick (D, N.J.)
LeFante elected 11-2, 821C2
DANIELS, Wilhelm
Bonn OKs electn aid 4-21, 404B1
DANIELSON, Rep. George E. (D, Calif.)
Reelected 11-2, 829D1
DANJANOVIC, Jozo
Held in 'mistaken identity' shooting 6-8, 542E3
DANKERT, Piet
Dutch Dassault bribe case opens 2-10, 141G2
DANMARK (Danish sailing ship)
In Operation Sail 7-4, 488A3
DANNA, Anthony A.
Indicted 1-19, 44E1
DANNEBERG, Jochen
Wins Olympic medal 2-7, 159E1
DANSON, Barnett J.
Stays urban affairs min 9-14, 692C2
Named acting defense min 10-13, 790G1
Confirmed defense min 11-3, 851E2
DANTE, Nicholas
Chorus Line wins Pulitzer 5-3, 352C3
DANTZIG, George B.
Awarded Science Medal 10-18, 858D3
DAPCEVIC, Vladimir
Sentenced 7-5, 559A3
DAPHNE (tanker)
Runs aground off PR 12-28, 1014A2
D'AQUINO, Iva Toguri (Tokyo Rose)
Files pardon petition 11-17, 892C2
DARCH, William
On Alaska pipeline completn 9-5, 690G2
DARLINGTON, S.C.—*See SOUTH Carolina*
DARMAN, Richard G.
Commerce asst secy 1-27; confrmd 2-26, 186F1
DARNISH, Jabbar
In Damascus raid 9-26, executed 9-27, 720C3, 721A1
DAR Pomorza (Polish sailing ship)
In Operation Sail 7-4, 488A3
DARTMOUTH College (Hanover, N.H.)
Louis Morton dies 2-12, 160F3
Da SILVA, Manoel Santiago
Tortured by police 10-22, 836G1
DATA Lease Financial Corp.
Rptd on FRB 'problem' list 1-22, 111B2
Miami National Bank
Rptd on comptroller's 'problem' list 1-26, 113E1
DATA Processing—*See ELECTRIC & Electronics Industry*
DATE, Jiichiro
Wins Olympic medal 7-31, 576D3
DATSUN—*See NISSAN Motor Corp.*
DATTEL, Dany
Arrested in Herstatt fraud 8-26, 679A1

1977

DALLAS, Tex.—*See TEXAS*
DALLAS Power & Light Co.
Settles Westinghouse suit 12-26, 1003C3
DALTON, Harry I.
Named Brewer gen mgr 11-20, 990B2
DALTON, John N.
Nominated for gov 6-4, 465C1
Elected 11-8, 855E1, C2
DAMASH, Ahmad
Vs govt-sheikh agrmt 784C1
D'AMBROSIO, Anthony
Indicted 2-24, 155F2
DAMON Corp.
Unit chrgd re Arab boycott 1-7, 167A2
DAMSON Oil Corp.
Sells gas field 1-27, 76B2
DAMS & Reservoirs
Teton collapse rpt issued 1-6, 120B3
Endangered fish halts Tellico constructn 1-31, 95G2-C3
Carter proposes fund cuts 2-22, 126E1
Sen backs water projcts 3-10, 174C2
More fund cuts studied 3-23, 209D3
Fed water rights in Calif upheld 4-4, 253C1
USDA bureaucracy scored 4-12, 365B1
Carter eases fund cut request 4-18, 299E2
Carter energy plan 4-20, 293F2
Cong bars '77 funds impoundmt 5-3, 365C2
Cong OKs Meramec funds cut 5-3, 365D2
Cong OKs funds for 9 water projects 7-25, 592G2
Brazil, Paraguay, Argentina in hydroelec talks 9-22—9-23, 794F3
India-Bangladesh dispute cited 11-5, 896E3
Ga dam burst kills 39 11-6, 888E2 ★
Clean-water bill revised 11-10, 900G2
US to inspect high-risk dams 11-30, 914E1
Ga burst laid to seepage 12-21, 1023E3
Garrison Diversion Unit (including Lonetree Reservoir)
IJC bd scores 1-7, 60C3
Project halted 2-18, 133A1
Carter proposes fund cut 2-22, 126E1
Carter on fund cut 3-16, 210C1
IJC rpt scores projct, asks moratorium 9-19, 725G3
DANBURY, Conn.—*See CONNECTICUT*
DANBURY Federal Correctional Institution—*See CONNECTICUT*
DANCE
US hosts Sovt exhibit 11-12, 988D2
Obituaries
Duncan, Irma 9-20, 788A1
Eglevsky, Andre 12-4, 1024E1
Roslavleva, Natalia 1-2, 84E3
Shankar, Uday 9-26, 788E2
Soloviev, Yuri 1-16, 84G3
DANDAVATE, Madhu
Released 1-5, 45D3
Named rail min 3-26, 240B1
DANFORTH, Sen. John C. (R, Mo.)
Rebuts Carter energy plan 6-2, 443G1
DANIEL Martin (book)
On best-seller list 11-6, 872D3; 12-4, 1021G2
DANSON, Barnett
Admits spying 11-14, 945D3
Sets Navy modernizatn 12-22, 1010F1
DANTLEY, Adrian
Named NBA rookie-of-yr 5-16, 584E3
Traded to Pacers 9-1, to Lakers 12-13, 990G3
DAO, Oumarou
Named Upper Volta educ min 1-14, 183A2
DAOUD, Abu
France arrests 1-7, frees, expels to Algeria 1-11; intl reactn 1-9—1-12, 9A1-10E1
France defends release, protests continue 1-13—1-18, 27B2-28D1
Sees Israel death plot 1-14, OKs Bonn trial 1-15, 27E3
Israel, France reconcile ties 2-8, 87B1
DAPCEVIC, Vladimir
Pro-Sovt Yugo exiles rptd seized 11-22, 12-17, 1018C3
DAPHNE, MTS (U.S. ship)
Sails for Cuba 5-15, 390G1
Completes Cuba visit 5-19, 456D2
D'AQUINO, Iva Toguri (Tokyo Rose)
Ford pardons 1-19, 36B2
DARDEN, Willie Jasper
Sup Ct bars convictn review 4-19, 342B2

1978

DALLAS, Tex.—*See TEXAS*
DALLAS County, Ala.—*See ALABAMA*
DALLAS Morning News (newspaper)
JFK murder film assessed 11-26, 916G1, C2
House com asks JFK film review 12-30, 1002D1
DALLAS Museum of Fine Arts
Meadows dies 6-10, 540C3
DALTON, Gov. John N. (R, Va.)
Declares state of emergency 3-7, 160D2
DALY, Gerry
On NASL All-Star team 8-20, 707B3
DALY, James
Dies 7-3, 620F2
DALY, Lar
Loses Sen GOP primary 3-21, 207G1
DAMAS, Leon
Dies 1-22, 96E1
DAMEREL, Myrtle Vail (Myrt)
Dies 9-18, 778A1
DAMIEN-Omen II (film)
Released 6-8, 619D1
DAMONTE, Humberto
Deportatn rptd 6-2, 475A2
D'AMOURS, Rep. Norman E. (D, N.H.)
Reelected 11-7, 847F3, 851F2
DAM-Phuong, Tran Thi
Rpts father's '76 death 7-10, 692G1
DAMS & Reservoirs
GOP attacks Carter budget 1-31, 63C1
Pak, India to resume talks 2-6—2-7, 113B1
Kenya dam contracts rptd 4-9, 479D1
Pulitzer awarded for safety study 4-17, 315A2
TVA member resigns, cites Tellico constructn halt 5-5, 390F2
EPA bars Denver permit 5-25, 409A1
Tellico constructn halt backed by Sup Ct 6-15, 468G1-D2
Tellico cited re Endangered Species Act revisn 10-15, 834C2; 11-10, 1003B1
Brazil, Paraguay divert Parana waters for hydro project 10-20, 829F2
Grand Coulee generator sabotaged 10-30, hydro projct delayed 11-10, 963C1
US-China Yangtze dam constructn deal rptd 11-6, 871C2
DANAIR (Danish airline)
UK air pact OKd 12-22, 1017B2
DANCE
Baryshnikov joins NYC Ballet 4-26, 335E3
Obituaries
Bailey, Bill (rptd) 12-17, 1032C2
Karasavina, Tamara 5-26, 440G2
Luahine, Iolani 12-11, 1032C3
DANCIN' (play)
Opens 3-27, 887F1
Fosse, Fisher win Tonys 6-4, 579A3
DANELO, Joe
NFL '77 kicking ldr 1-1, 56F2
DANFORTH, Sen. John C. (R, Mo.)
Votes for Panama Canal neutrality pact 3-16, 177F2
Votes for 2d Canal pact 4-18, 273B1
Personal finances rptd 5-19, 385D3
Sen votes conditl end to Rhodesia sanctns 7-26, 588F1
DANIEL, Beth
2d in Women's Intl 5-8, 580D3
DANIEL Jr., Rep. Robert W. (R, Va.)
Reelected 11-7, 852D3
DANIEL, Rep. W. C. (Dan) (D, Va.)
Reelected 11-7, 852D3
DANIEL International Corp.
A-worker firing to be probed by NRC, GAO review sought 3-29, 242G1
DANIEL Martin (book)
On best-seller list 1-8, 24D3
DANIELS, Robert
Fined in FBI aide's death 1-14, 69B2
DANIELSON, Rep. George E. (D, Calif.)
Reelected 11-7, 850A2
DANNEMEYER, William E.
Wins US House seat 11-7, 850B2, 856G3
DANON, Raymond
'First Time' released 3-28, 619A2
DAN River Inc.
Discriminatn suit settled 9-28, 811C3
DANSON, Barnett Jerome
Rpts USSR satellite search cost 2-3, 103E1
Hints air regimt breakup 7-6; Painchaud scores 7-10, transferred 7-12, 556A3
DANTE, Joe
Piranha released 8-4, 970F2
DANTE, Ron
Mighty Gents opens 4-16, 760E2
DANTIN, Maurice
Faces US Sen primary runoff in Miss 6-6, 448B1
Wins runoff 6-27, 510C1
Loses electn 11-7, 852F2
DANZANSKY, Steve
NASL Diplomats sale rptd 10-5, 969G2
DARAKHSHANI, Brig. Gen. Ali Akbar
Arrested as spy, dies 3-27, 289A1
DARBY Creek Road (race horse)
3d in Belmont Stakes 6-10, 539G3
DARE to Love (book)
On best-seller list 4-2, 272D3; 4-30, 356B2
DARK, Alvin
Fired as Padres mgr 3-21, 355B2
DARKNESS On the Edge of Town (recording)
On best-seller list 7-5, 580A1

1979

DALLAS, Tex.—*See TEXAS*
DALLAS/Ft. Worth Airport
Concorde svc begins 1-12, 35A3
DALLAS Museum of Fine Arts
Church painting donatn rumored 10-25, 892B1
DALLAS Times Herald (newspaper)
Rozelle admits Super Bowl officiating error 2-22, 175C3
DALTON, Gov. John N. (R, Va.)
Sends troops to quell shipyd violence 4-16, 561C1
DALTON, Timothy
Agatha released 2-8, 174C2
DALTREY, Roger
Kids Are Alright released 6-15, 820E1
DALY, James (1919-78)
Companion sues estate 3-16, 289G1
DALY, Judge T. F. Gilroy
Orders Galante release 2-27, 156F1
Returns Galante to jail 3-7, grants bail 3-23, 240F2
DALYELL, Tom
Vs devolutn efforts 3-2, 169E1
D'AMICO, Quinto
Arrested 5-27, 426F2
D'AMICO, Suso Cecchi
Innocent released 1-11, 174G2
DAMM, Carl
AWACS deal threatened 8-1, 8-3, 586G1
DAMS & Reservoirs
'79-81 budget outlays table 42F2
Carter asks cost-sharing 5-16, 365A3
China offcl tours Brazil hydro projct 5-22, 443C3
India dam collapse kills 15,000 8-11, 620B1
Tellico Dam completn authorized 9-26, 766G2
Argentina, Brazil, Paraguay accords signed 10-19, 845A1
Fla dam breaks 10-31, 912A3
Tellico Dam suit by Cherokees dismissed 11-2, 990B1
Teton dam defects rptd 11-28, 954A3
Tellico Dam completed 11-29, 990A1
DANARO, Giovanni
Killed 1-4, 21G1
DANCE
Baryshnikov named Amer Ballet dir 6-20, 527E3
Bolshoi's Godunov defects to US 8-23; US detains wife 8-24, releases 8-27, 8-23, 644D3-645F1
Bolshoi's Kozlovs defect to US 9-16, 697C2
Godunov ABT resigntn rptd 11-21, 1005E3
Amer Ballet dancers OK pact 12-20, 987G1-B2
Obituaries
Joos, Kurt 5-22, 432A3
Massine, Leonide 3-16, 272B3
DANCING In The Dark (play)
Opens 1-21, 292D1
DANDRIDGE, Bob
Sonics win NBA title 6-1, 506F3
DANELO, Joe
NFL '78 kicking ldr 1-6, 80F1
DANFORTH, Sen. John C. (R, Mo.)
Finances disclosed 5-18, 383E2, F3
Tours Cambodia refugee camps in Thailand 10-21—10-23; in Cambodia, proposes food convoy 10-24; rpts to Carter 10-26; Cambodia vs plan 10-27, 823C3-824E1
D'ANGELO, Beverly
Hair released 3-13, 528D2
DANIEL, Beth
2d in Westn Union Intl 8-13, Columbia Savings Classic 9-9; wins Patty Berg Classic 8-26, 970A1, B1, D1
LPGA top money winner 11-30, 969G2
DANIEL, John (d. 1978)
SEC role in pensn plans barred by Sup Ct 1-16, 32F1-D2
DANIELE, Graciela
Most Happy Fella opens 10-11, 956D3
DANIELS, Jack
New JFK murder film rptd 2-8, 166F1
DANIELS, Jeff
Minnesota Moon opens 1-31, 292B2
DANIELS, Phil
Quadrophenia released 11-2, 1008C1
DANIELS, Sharon
Most Happy Fella opens 10-11, 956E3
DANIELSON, Gary
NFL '78 passing ldr 1-6, 80D1
D'ANNUNZIO, Gabriele
Innocent released 1-11, 174G2
DANON, Marcello
Cage aux Folles released 5-12, 528F1
DANSON, Barnett Jerome
Female mil role widened 1-29, 95F2
Loses electn 5-22, 377D2
DARDEN, Thom
NFL '78 interceptn ldr 1-6, 80C1
DARDEN, Tony
Shares indoor sprint medley mark 2-23, 911E2
DARDEN, Willie Jasper
Death warrant signed 5-19, executn stayed 5-22, 400A1
DARE, Michael
Reveals emb bugging plan 7-4, 522F2
On '72 APLQ break-in 7-4, 522B3
DARIO Rosado, Arnaldo (d. 1978)
Death disputed 4-30—5-3, probe ordrd 5-2, 350A2
Natlst ambush kills 2 US sailors 12-3, 924B3
DARK at the Top of the Stairs, The (play)
Opens 11-29, 956G2
DARKE, Rev. Bernard
Slain 7-15, 814G1
DARKIN, Michael
Victim opens 5-3, 712C3

1980

DALLAS (TV series)
'79-80 Nielsen rating rptd 4-22, 376C1
'Who shot J.R.?' episode aired 11-21, viewing record rptd 11-25, 11-21, 905A3
DALLAS, U.S.S. (Coast Guard cutter)
Cuban gunboat incident rptd 5-1, 326F1
DALLAS Morning News
Reagan pres endorsemt rptd 11-1, 841G3
DALLAS Times-Herald (newspaper)
Hagler wins Pulitzer 4-14, 296G2
DALTON, Gov. John (R, Va.)
State of State message 1-9, 404D1
DALTON v. California
Case refused by Sup Ct 3-24, 265D2
DALY, Robert
Named Warner Bros chrmn 12-1, 959E3
D'AMATO, Alfonse M.
Wins NY US Sen primary 9-9, 682E1
Elected to US Sen 11-4, 840F2, 845A3, 846A1, 848A3
DAMDIN, Tsendying
Wins Olympic medal 7-31, 623B1
DAMILANO, Maurizio
Wins Olympic medal 7-24, 623G3
DAMME, Jorg
Wins Olympic medal 7-22, 623C2
DAMN The Torpedoes (recording)
On best-seller list 2-6, 120G3; 3-5, 200F3
DAMON, Cathryn
Wins Emmy 9-7, 692C1
D'AMOURS, Rep. Norman E. (D, N.H.)
Reelected 11-4, 843F2, 848F2
DAMS & Reservoirs
Carter budget outlays, table 1-28, 70F1
TVA challenge declined by Sup Ct 3-24, 265B2
Appropriatn clears Cong 6-25, 9-10, signed 10-1, 803D2, E2
Calif OKs water projct 7-18, 632B2
NJ bond issue OKd 11-4, 847A1
Pacific NW power bill clears Cong 11-19, signed 12-5, 981A2
DANA, Bill
Nude Bomb released 5-9, 675B3
DAN Air (British airline)
Jet crashes in Canary I 4-25, 392C1
DANCE
USSR's Stefanov defectn rptd in Rome 1-23, 88F1
Bolshoi's Messerers defect to US 2-6, 88D1
Stefanov returns to USSR 4-1, 262A2
E Ger's Giersche defectn in Australia rptd 4-22, 327A1
Vlasova seeks US return 8-1, 638B2
Reagan's son makes NY ballet debut 10-10, 908A3
ABC, CBS in cable-TV deals 12-2, 12-10, 1003A1
Obituaries
Champion, Gower 8-25, 676A1
Fernandez, Royes 3-3, 279F2
Van, Bobby 7-31, 608F3
DANCIGERS, Georges
Incorrigible released 3-3, 416B3
DANCING Wu Li Masters: An Overview of the New Physics, The (book)
Wins Amer Book Award 5-1, 692F2
D'ANDREA, Paul
Trouble with Europe opens 1-28, 136F3
DANIEL, Beth
2d in Birmingham Classic 4-27, 412E3
Wins Golden Lights 6-1, 2d in WUI 7-27, 715A1, E1
Wins Patty Berg Classic 8-17; Women's World Series, breaks LPGA earning mark 9-7; ties for 2d in Inamori Classic 10-12, 972B1, F1, D2
LPGA top money winner 10-12, 971F3
Named LPGA top golfer 11-19, 971B3
DANIEL Jr., Rep. Robert W. (R, Va.)
Reelected 11-4, 844D3
DANIEL, Rep. W. C. (Dan) (D, Va.)
Reelected 11-4, 844D3
DANIELPUR, Albert
Executed 6-5, 644B3
DANIELS (U.S. missile crusier)
Trible says unfit, scores deploymt 6-30, 517F3
DANIELS, Derick J.
Playboy audit, repayments revealed 2-12, 558B2
DANIELSON, Rep. George E. (D, Calif.)
Reelected 11-4, 842A2
DANNEMEYER, Rep. William (R, Calif.)
Reelected 11-4, 842B2
DANTE, Ron
Children of a Lesser God opens 3-30, 392E2
DANTLEY, Adrian
In NBA All-Star Game 2-3, 279B1
NBA scoring, field-goal ldr 3-30, 278C3, D3
DAOUDY, Adib
On UN comm to probe shah 2-17, 122C1
To resume Iran hostage mission 5-17; Waldheim briefs 5-22; in Iran 5-26, 393D2, 394A1
Ends Iran visit 6-16, mission failure confirmed 6-19, 464F1
DARDEN, Tony
Sets indoor sprint medley relay mark 2-29, 892F1
DARE, Michael
'70s sabotage unit rptd 4-20, 350E3
D'AREZZO, Bernardo
Italy tourism min 4-4, 275G3
DARIDA, Clecilo
Italy communicatns min 4-4, 275G3
DARIO Rosado, Arnaldo (d. 1978)
Cops cleared in slaying 4-25, 348A3

1976

DAUGHTERS of the American Revolution (DAR)
Ford addresses conv 4-21, 281C2
DAVENPORT, Ia.—*See IOWA*
DAVENPORT, Chester
Carter transition aide 11-23, 881C3
DAVENPORT, Willie
Wins Olympic medal 7-28, 576A1
DAVIDIAN, Nelson
Wins Olympic medal 7-24, 576A3
DAVIDSON, Ronald
Vs Israel Gaza resettlemts 11-23, 878A3
DAVIES, John
Thatcher changes shadow Cabt 11-19, 1004G1
DAVIES, Rodger P. (d. 1974)
US role in death probe rptd scored 1-20, 93G2
DAVIES, Rupert
Dies 11-22, 970E1
DAVIGNON, Viscount Etienne
Europn Comm meets 12-22—12-23, 977G1
D'AVILA, Gen. Ednardo
Plot vs Geisel aborted 1-9, 98B2
Fired 1-19, 97G3
DAVIS, Alan
'72 campaign gift listed 4-25, 688C1
DAVIS, Colin
Wins Grammy 2-28, 460D3
DAVIS, David Brion
Wins Natl Book Award 4-19, 292D3
DAVIS 3rd, Edward Charles
Loses libel suit vs cop 3-23, 218D3
DAVIS, Gene
Wins Olympic medal 7-31, 576D3
DAVIS, Hallowell
Awarded Science Medal 10-18, 858D3
DAVIS, Howard
Wins Olympic medal 7-31, 574B1
DAVIS, J. E.
Ford campaign donatn rptd 10-22, 938G3
DAVIS, Lanny J.
Wins Cong primary 5-18, 357A2
DAVIS, Rep. Mendel J. (D, S.C.)
Reelected 11-2, 830G3
DAVIS, Meyer
Dies 4-5, 272F3

1977

DART Industries Inc.
Thatcher Glass Division
Strike ends 10-14, 818G3
DARNTON, John
Nigeria ousts 3-12, 258E1
DASCA, Maria Jesus
Freed from prison 7-17, 582B3
DASHOWITZ, Leo
'74 murder rptd 10-4, 871E3
DASSAULT, Marcel
Cleared on corruptn chrgs 4-21, 597F3-598B1
Co natlizatn plan cited 5-17, 543B1; set 6-8, 597D3
DATA Processing—*See COMPUTERS*
DATSUN—*See NISSAN Motor Corp.*
DAUGHTERS Of the American Revolution (DAR)
1st black member rptd 12-3, 1021D2
DAVANT, James W.
On Dean Witter-Reynolds merger 10-3, 799F3
DAVENPORT, Chester
Confrmd Transport asst secy 2-10, 148E3
DAVENPORT, J. D.
Murder chrg dropped 12-19, 991F2
DAVES, Delmer
Dies 8-17, 696F2
DAVIDSON, Gordon
Wins Tony 6-5, 452C1
DAVIDSON, John
Safe in Ky nightclub blaze 5-28, 429F2
DAVIDSON (N.C.) College
Tenure policy changed 5-6, 471F3
DAVIES, Rodger P. (d. 1974)
Cyprus murder trial ends 6-3, 466F3—467C1
2 Greek Cypriots sentenced 6-21, 530E2
2 EOKA-B members sentncd 6-21, 764E2
DAVIGNON, Etienne
Gets Eur Comm post 1-7, 74B2
Vs voluntary US steel trade curbs 10-11, 775F1
DAVIS, Al
Rozelle gets new contract 2-17, 163C3
DAVIS, Angela
Powell defends Sakharov letter 2-18, 137F2
Wilmington 10 denied retrial 5-20, 531F3
Shcharansky trial observers asked 12-15, 1017B2
DAVIS, Bette
Gets Amer Film Inst award 3-1, 354G1
DAVIS, Bettina
Dies 10-9, 872E1
DAVIS, Brad
In NBA draft 6-10, 584B2
DAVIS, Chester C.
Ousted as Summa dir 5-28, sues Lummis 6-8, 472G2
DAVIS, Clinton
Scores Concorde decisn delay 3-7, 212A3
DAVIS, Edward M.
On Calif pot decriminalizatn 3-14, 332C2
DAVIS, Joseph Ell
NY ct voids death penalty 11-15, 919C3
DAVIS, Marvin
Buys Oakland A's, sets Denver move 12-14, 989A2

1978

DARROW, Clarence (1857-1938)
Scenes From Country Life opens 3-13, 887A3
DART Industries Inc.
Mallory OKs takeover 11-17, 1005C2
DARWAISH, Abdullah
Financial Gen sues 2-17, 204B3
SEC chrgs 3-18, settles 3-19, 204B2
DASCHLE, Thomas A.
Loses US House electn 11-7, 855C1
Wins cong seat on recount 12-19, 1008F1
Da SILVA, Luis Inacio (Lula)
On May striker reprisals, scores anti-strike decree 8-15, 772C2
Govt OKs collective bargaining 10-27, 879D2
DASSLER, Adolf (Adi)
Death rptd 9-18, 778B1
DATA Bases—*See INFORMATION Services*
DATA Processing—*See COMPUTERS*
DATING—*See FRATERNIZATION*
DAUD Khan, Lt. Gen. Mohammad (Afghan president, premier; replaced Apr. 27)
Killed in coup 4-27, 317A1
Taraki denies heavy coup toll 5-6, 349C2
Pak cites border agrmt 5-19, 391B2
Shah loses citizenship 6-14, 538B1
DAUPHIN, Claude
Dies 11-17, 972G2
DAVEY, Maj. Christopher
Atlantic balloon flight fails 7-30, 653B1
DAVID, Immanuel (Bruce Longo)
Suicide rptd 8-2, 685D3
DAVID, Rachel (Margit Ericsson)
Kills self, 6 children 8-3, 685C3
DAVIDSON, Jack
In Recovery Lounge opens 12-7, 1031B2
DAVIDSON, Martin
If I See You released 5-24, 619D2
DAVIDSON, Richard M.
Approaching Zero opens 11-30, 1031A1
DAVIE, Fla.—*See FLORIDA*
DAVIES, Rodger P. (d. 1974)
US protests shortened terms in murder case 3-21, 226E2
DAVIGNON, Viscount Etienne
EC Comm orders fiber cartel modificatn 11-9, 871C3
DAVILA, Alberto
Zarate KOs 2-25, 379B2
Lujan decisns 9-15, 726D2
DAVIS, Angela
Joins SF State U faculty 1-26, 172B2
DAVIS, Anthony
Traded to Oilers 4-30, 336A2
DAVIS, Benjamin O.
Vs mil pensn revisn plan 4-10, 281E1
DAVIS, Lt. Gen. Bennie L.
On AF pilot drain 12-13, 984C2
DAVIS, Bette
Return From Witch Mt released 7-14, 970G2
Death On Nile released 9-29, 970B1
DAVIS, Bill
Accepts Kerr resignatn 9-9, 721D3
DAVIS, Brad
Midnight Express released 10-6, 970C2
DAVIS, Cleveland (Eric [Jomo] Thompson)
Arrested in NYC police slayings, '76 Attica pardon scored 4-5, 388C3
DAVIS, E. Lawrence
Loses US Sen primary 5-2, 342B3
DAVIS, Edward M.
Loses primary for Calif gov 6-6, 447D3
DAVIS, Francis W.
Dies 4-16, 356E2
DAVIS, Gary
NFL '77 kick return ldr 1-1, 56C3
DAVIS, Hal
Dies 1-11, 96F1
DAVIS, Jack
Resigns prov seat 9-17, fined for fraud 9-18, 739E2
DAVIS, Jefferson (1808-89)
US citizenship restored 10-17, 843B3
DAVIS, John
Traded to Pacers 6-8, 457C2
DAVIS, Capt. Leon T.
Dismissed from Army, fined 11-4, 877A3
DAVIS, Lloyd
Verandah opens 5-4, 760F3
DAVIS, Luther
Timbuktu opens 3-1, 760E3
DAVIS, Marvin
A's sale fails, scores Finley 3-27, 354F3
DAVIS, Rep. Mendel J. (D, S.C.)
Reelected 11-7, 852B2
DAVIS, Renn
At Solomons independnc fete 7-7, 549E1

1979

DaRONCH, Carol (d. 1974)
Bundy sentncd in Fla 7-31, 604G2
DARRA Hirezi, Hector
Named El Salvador forgn min 10-22, 813A1
DART Containerline Co. Ltd.
Indicted re price fixing 6-1, 423E2; pleads no contest, fined 6-8, 442B2
UK trust legis proposed 10-31, 855F3
DARTMOUTH College (Hanover, N.H.)
Wins NCAA hockey match 3-24, 356E1
Kemeny named to 3 Mile I probe 4-11, 275C1
Goldsmith says FDR possible cancer victim 12-2, 925A3
Kemeny lauds Carter response to 3 Mile I rpt 12-7, 940D2
DARVISH, Sakher
Denies PLO mediatn try in Iran 11-8, 842D1
DARVON (propoxyphene)—*See MEDICINE-Drugs*
DASBURG, Andrew
Dies 8-13, 671A2
Da SILVA, Luis Inacio (Lula)
Metalworkers strike 3-13–3-27, 328B3
Reinstated as union ldr 5-15, 399G1
Backs Belo Horizonte strike 7-31, 612D2
Addresses striking metalworkers 11-8, 871B2
DATA General Corp.
On '78 Fortune 500 list 5-7, 305B2
DATA Processing—*See COMPUTERS*
DATELLE, Brenda
Loudspeaker opens 4-30, 712C1
DAUBBERTIN, Rolf
Arrested as E Ger spy 1-28, 77D3
DAUER, Rich
In World Series 10-10–10-17, 816E2
DAUGHERTY, William
Hostage status disputed 11-30–12-1, spy trial threatened 12-1, 12-4, 914A2
DAVID, Donald K.
Dies 4-3, 356C3
DAVIDOW, Jeffrey S.
Named unoffcl Zimbabwe envoy 6-25, 490C2
DAVIDSON, Gordon
Zoot Suit opens 3-25, 712G3
DAVIDSON, Jack
Winter Signs opens 3-11, 712F3
DAVIDSON, John
Montreal wins Stanley Cup 5-21, 447D3
DAVIDSON, John (singer)
Concorde Airport '79 released 8-3, 820A1
DAVIDSON, William
Wounded 5-10, 565D1
DAVIE County, N.C.—*See NORTH Carolina*
Da VINCI, Leonardo (1452-1519)
'Last Supper' restoratn rptd 2-27, 173B3
Mural believed found 11-1, 892E1
DaVINCI Trans-America (balloon)
Flight falls short 10-2, 992A3
DAVIS, Angela
Seeks FBI files preservatn 6-26, 520G3
DAVIS, Benny
Dies 12-20, 1008D2
DAVIS, Bette
Wins Emmy 9-9, 858E2
DAVIS, Chester C.
SEC suit vs Hughes settled 1-19, 88B2
DAVIS, Frances B.
Loses Sup Ct case 6-11, 478F1
DAVIS, Gary
US rejects passport 12-19, 1006A1
DAVIS, Gwen—*See MITCHELL, Gwen Davis*
DAVIS, Jack
Reelected to BC parlt 5-10, 369D1
DAVIS, Larry
Leave It to Beaver opens 4-3, 712B1
DAVIS, Mac
North Dallas Forty released 8-1, 820D2
DAVIS, Oliver
NFL '78 interceptn ldr 1-6, 80D1
DAVIS, Ossie
Take It From The Top opens 1-19, 292D3
DAVIS, Owen
Whoopee opens 2-14, 292F3
DAVIS, Priscilla Childres (Mrs. T. Cullen)
Divorce case judge withdraws, declares mistrial 3-25, 271G3
Wins divorce setlmt 4-20, 392D3
Divorce rptd final 5-25, 527C3
Ex-husband acquitted in kill-for-hire case 11-9, 890E2
DAVIS, Richard Beale
Wins Natl Book Award 4-23, 356B2
DAVIS, Rick
Named NASL top N Amer player 9-5, 776D1

1980

DART Industries Inc.
Kraft merger set 6-5, 557D1
Mullaney resigns 7-23, 600B3
DARTMOUTH College (Hanover, N.H.)
'79 endowmt earnings rptd 3-24, 319C2
Kemeny 3 Mile I study cited 7-2, 550F3
DARVILLE, Desiree (d. 1977)
Murderer hanged 1-29, 132B2
DARVON (propoxyphene)—*See MEDICINE--Drugs & Health-Care Products*
DARWAISH, Abdullah
Financial Gen deal set 7-25, 600E3
DASCHLE, Rep. Thomas A. (D, S.D.)
Reelected 11-4, 844B2, 851F2
Da SILVA, Luis Inacio (Lula)
Issues metalworker demands 4-1, 272F2
Arrested 4-19, 310B1
Ends hunger strike 5-11, 388C2
Freed 5-19, 405E3
DAS Lusitania Songspiel (play)
Opens 1-10, 136B3
DATA Resources Inc.
Econ rpt issued 2-28, 168B3
DAUB, Hal
Elected to US House 11-4, 845E2, 851A2
D'AUBUISSON, Robert
Accused in death of atty gen 2-23, 149A2
Rightist coup attempt fails 5-2, arrested 5-7, 372A3
Freed 5-13, 389E2
Visits US illegally 6-30—7-3, 521C3
El Salvador presence rptd 12-9, 942A1
DAUGHERTY, William
Hostages' letters publshd 1-18—1-20, 47B3
Fellow hostage calls spy 4-9, 282C3
DAUMAN, Anatole
Tin Drum released 4-11, 416F3
DAUSSET, Dr. Jean
Wins Nobel 10-10, 889F3
DAVAADALAI, Ravdan
Wins Olympic medal 7-25, 623C1
DAVAALAV, Jamtsying
Wins Olympic medal 7-30, 624D3
DAVALOS, Pablo
Shot in Ecuadoran cong debate 9-30, 789D2
DAVENPORT, Lt. Col. Robert L.
Attacked in PR 3-12, 190D1
DAVENPORT, Willie
On US Olympic bobsled team 2-24, 154C3
DAVIA, Howard R.
Testifies on GSA abuses 1-19, 112B2
DAVIDSON, Daniel
FDA cyclamate ban rptd upheld 2-7, 317D2, A3
DAVIDSON, Gordon
Children of a Lesser God opens 3-30, 392E2
Division St opens 10-8, 892B3
DAVIDSON, I. Irving
Indicted in Brilab probe 6-17, 454D3, 455B1
DAVIDSON, Jon
Airplane released 7-2, 675G1
DAVIDSON, Martin
Hero at Large released 2-8, 216F2
DAVIDSON, Ralph P.
Named Time chrmn 5-15, 456E2
DAVIES, Dennis Russel
Wins Grammy 2-27, 296F3
DAVIES, Jack
Ffolkes released 4-18, 416F2
DAVIES, Roger
NASL scoring ldr 8-24, 770D3
Named NASL MVP 9-16, 1001G2
DAVIES, Sharron
Wins Olympic medal 7-26, 623E3
DAVIGNON, Etienne
Warns vs US steel curbs 2-28, US talks failure seen 3-14, 204C2, F2, A3
EC OKs steel cutback plan 10-30, 822D1
DAVIS, Al
NFL OK needed for Raiders LA move 1-18, 62C1
DAVIS, Angela
Marries 7-5, 639A1
DAVIS, Bette
Watcher in the Woods released 4-16, 416G3
DAVIS, Brad
Small Circle of Friends released 3-9, 216F3
DAVIS, Christopher
Rpts Sovt '71-76 infant mortality rates 6-25, 525F2
DAVIS, Colin
Wins Grammy 2-27, 296F3
DAVIS, Ernie (d. 1962)
Brown fined for autobiography chrgs 1-22, 175C3
DAVIS, George
Pleads guilty in US Customs probe 2-13, 359C2
DAVIS, Gerry
Final Countdown released 8-1, 675E2
DAVIS, Howard
Watt decisns 6-8, 1000F3
DAVIS, John
Named La gas tax case fact-finder by Sup Ct 3-3, 210G1
DAVIS, John H. P.
Really Rosie opens 10-12, 892E3
DAVIS, John W.
Dies 7-12, 608E1
DAVIS, Judy
My Brilliant Career released 2-1, 216C3
DAVIS, Rep. Mendel J. (D, S.C.)
Hartnett wins House seat 11-4, 850E1
DAVIS, Monti
In NBA draft 6-10, 447G1
DAVIS, R. G.
We Won't Pay! opens 12-17, 1003G3
DAVIS, Richard J.
Ties Fla banks to drug trade 6-5, 502B1
DAVIS, Ricky
Cosmos win NASL title 9-21, 770D2

1976

DAVIS, Shane
'72 campaign gift listed 4-25, 688C1
DAVIS, Sterling Blake
Finances Mex jailbreak 3-12, 420F1
DAVIS, W. Jack
Elected Rotary Intl pres 6-14, 484D2
DAVIS, Willie
NL batting ldr 10-4, 795G3
DAYAN, Moshe
Time rpts '73 Israel A-bombs; Israel denies 4-5, 243E1
Mission to Uganda vetoed 7-10, 515D1
DAY Care Issues—*See under CHILDREN*
DAY Co., Martin E.
Arab boycott noncompliance rptd 10-28, 986A3
DAYLIGHT Saving Time—*See TIME*
DAYS in the Trees (play)
Opens 9-26, 1014E3
DAYTON, O.—*See OHIO*
DAYTONA Beach, Fla.—*See FLORIDA*
DAYTON News (newspaper)
Carter endorsement rptd 10-30, 831B3

1977

DAVIS, Shirley
Sex-bias suit vs Passman OKd 1-3, 59D3
DAVIS, T. Cullen
Acquitted 11-17, 928A1
DAVIS, Walter
Marquette wins NCAA title 3-28, 262B2
In NBA draft 6-10, 584A2
DAVIS, William Grenville
PC wins legis electn 6-9, 466F2
Scores Levesque language offer 7-27, 596E3
On Asia tour 9-22—10-4, 780F2
DAVIS Cup—*See TENNIS*
DAVIS Oil Co.
Chrmn buys Oakland A's 12-14, 989C2
DAVIS Walker Corp.
Chrgs Canada steel dumping 11-3, 836F3
DAWIT Wolde Ghiorgis
Chrgs Sudan, Somalia send troops 6-24, 547D3
DAWKINS, Darryl
Fined for NBA playoff brawl 5-27, 490C3
DAWSON, Andre
Named NL rookie-of-yr 11-23, 927G1
DAWSON, Dennis
Wins election 5-24, 410C3
DAWSON Five—*See GEORGIA*
DAYAN, Moshe
Vs land return to Jordan 2-25, 143E3
OKs Begin Cabt bid 5-25, 401E2
Quits Labor Party 5-27, 450G1
Begin delays appointment 5-29, 450A2
Likud clarifies W Bank stand 6-17, 474A3
Israel forgn min 6-20, 474C2, D2
Bars ceding W Bank 6-22, 495A3
US presses Israel on exit 6-27, 495G2
Defends Begin peace plan 7-19, 550A1
Begin: Rabin violated secret memo 7-25, 570D3
Sadat on Israel-Arab pre-Geneva mtg plan 8-2, 588D2
Meets Vance 8-9, 605F1
Vance meets W Bank ldrs 8-10, 605B2
Sees pacts with Egypt, Jordan, Leb 8-11, 623B3
US vs new Bank setlmts 8-18, 623A1
On W Bank sharing plan 8-19, 648D2
Sees NATO chief 9-15; in Paris 9-16, mtg with Jordan premr rptd 9-20, 713F2-714A1
Accused re '67 US ship raid 9-18, 715A1
Meets Carter, other US offcls; submits peace plan, US presses compromise 9-19, 713G1
Carter urges Leb restraint 9-19, 714B3
Sees Geneva talks agrmt 9-20, 713E2
At US House com hearing, backs Haifa base 9-20; US rules out 9-22, 714A1
On PLO at peace talks 9-25, 9-27, 733D2, G2
2 W Bank setlmts barred 9-25, 9-28, 734G2
Meets Vance 9-26, 733F2
Meets Carter, Geneva conf plan OKd 10-4—10-5; urges Israel Cabt OK 10-5, 749C1-A2
Gives 4-pt peace plan 10-10, PLO vs 10-11, 769A2
Reveals secret US-Israel Geneva working paper 10-13, 769B1-A2
Says US, Israel accord bars PLO at Geneva 10-13, US denies 10-14, 793D1
Vs Egypt Geneva plan 11-6, 850A2
Greets Sadat, in talks 11-19, 889C1
Asks Egypt policy review 11-23, 909G2
Heads pol com in Egypt talks 12-26, 993E1
DAY-Care—*See CHILDREN*
DAYS 3rd, Drew S.
Asst atty gen 2-16, confrmd 3-4, 211E1
Wilmington busing backed 3-18, 216D2
Heads FBI break-in probe 12-7, 940G1
DAYTON, O.—*See OHIO*
DBCP (dibromochloropropane)—*See PESTICIDES*
DBI (phenformin)—*See MEDICINE—Drugs*
DDT (dichloro-diphenyl-trichloroethane)—*See PESTICIDES*

1978

DAVIS, Robert W.
Wins US House primary in Mich 8-8, 626B1
Elected 11-7, 851E1, 854B1
DAVIS, Sammy
Stop the World opens 8-3, 887C3
DAVIS, Sylvia
My Old Friends opens 12-2, 1031E2
DAVIS, Tom (Cook Islands prime minister)
Sworn Cook I prime min 7-25, 591G2
DAVIS, Walter
NBA scoring ldr 4-9, 271E2
Named NBA top rookie 5-9, 457A3
DAVIS, William
Denies tax cuts aid Ontario 5-18, 391G3
Vs Quebec constructn worker curb 6-22, 571C3
DAVIS Cup—*See TENNIS*
DAVISON, Jon
Piranha released 8-4, 970F2
DAWIT Wolde-Ghiorgis, Maj.
Denies USSR, Cuba troops, Somali invasn plan 1-18, 43E3
DAWKINS, Darryl
NBA field-goal ldr 4-9, 271E2
DAWKINS Jr., Sam
Foiled in hijack attempt 1-28, 212C2
DAWN (recording)
Wins Grammy 2-24, 316B1
DAWOOD, Taha Ahmed al-
Escapes death try 7-28; Iraq Paris emb raid linked 7-31, 2 suspects held 8-2, 582D2
DAYAN, Moshe
Meets Pope on Jerusalem status 1-12, 10G2
In Egypt pol talks, confirms impasse 1-17, 25F1
Denies '77 settlmt vow to Carter 2-1, 60F2
Reveals Ethiopia arms sales 2-6, 100A1; Ethiopia expels Israelis 2-18, 138B1
In US feud over setlmts 2-7, 78F1; text of US statemt 79B1-B2
In US, questns mediator role 2-12, 98D1
Vs US jets to Egypt, Saudis 2-14, 97C2
Sees Carter, Vance; vs US jets to Saudis 2-16, 139G1
Denies US-Israel feud on Res 242 3-6, 156G2
Meets Ceausescu 4-3—4-4; lauds talks 4-5, 235D3
On Res 242 stand 4-16, 275A1
Sees Waldheim on Israeli Leb role 4-18, 274G2
Carter vs jet pkg halt 4-25, 307E1
Meets Vance on Egypt talks renewal; vs US jet pkg deal 4-26—4-27, 299D2
Begin meets Carter 5-1, 339B2
US asks peace talks renewal 5-19, 424D2
UN assures on PLO Leb infiltratn 5-22, 383D2
Calls Egypt peace plan to US 'impossible' 5-24, 424E2
Chrgs Unifil soft on PLO 6-13, Waldheim denies 6-14, 462F1
UK lauds Rumania peace role 6-14, 515C3
Sees contd US-Israel feud 6-18, 461E1
Defends W Bank, Gaza views 6-19; US vs 6-21, 461G1, C2
Weizman denies plan to quit 6-23, 489E1
Begin OKs UK mtg with Egypt forgn min 7-2, 502A1
Vs Kreisky-Brandt plan 7-13, 521D2
At Egypt forgn min mtg in UK 7-18—7-19, 546C1
Egypt vs W Bank, Gaza compromise 7-23, 563G1, B2
Offered softened W Bank, Gaza stand 7-24; Egypt rejects 7-25, 563A2
Sadat scores W Bank plan 7-30, 581G2
Tells US of Egypt mil moves 602E1
Tells US aide of Leb crisis 8-30, 674D2
Warns Syria on Leb clashes 8-31, 674B2
In Camp David summit talks 9-7, 673E1
On Israeli gunboat raid on west Beirut 10-8, 762B1
In Egypt pact talks 10-12—10-18; sees snag 10-17, US denies 10-18, 782C2, G2
Meets Carter in Egypt pact talks, recalled for consultatn 10-21, 802A3
Says setlmt expansn does not violate Camp David agrmt, Saunders remarks provoked Israel 10-26, 802D2, F2
Sees Vance, says Israel vs Egypt pact-W Bank linkage 11-8, 858B3
Sees Vance, new Egypt pact plan set 11-12, 892G2
Defends pact text release 11-25, 931A1
Carter cites W Bank-Gaza vote deadline 12-13, 951D1
Sets terms for Egypt talk renewal 12-18, 978F3
Meets Vance, Khalil; pact talk revival fails 12-24, 997E3
DAY Care—*See under CHILDREN*
DAYLIGHT Saving Time—*See TIME*
DAYLIN Inc.
Bids for Dymo, withdraws 5-24, 404D1
DAYS of Heaven (film)
Released 9-13, 970A1
DAYTON Hudson Corp.
To acquire Mervyn's 1-23, 66C2
DBCP (dibromochloropropane)—*See PESTICIDES*

1979

DAVIS, Russell
Breaks Shrine Game records 1-6, 8C3
DAVIS, Shirley
Passman ruled liable to sex-bias suit by Sup Ct 6-5, 464A1
Wins sex bias suit settlmt 8-23, 649F3
DAVIS, T. Cullen
Freed after kill-for-hire mistrial 1-22, 64D3
Divorce case judge withdraws, declares mistrial 3-25, 271G3
$3.3 mln divorce setlmt ordrd 4-20, 392D3
Divorce rptd final, remarries 5-25, 527C3
Acquitted in kill-for-hire case 11-9, 890D2
DAVIS, Walter
NBA scoring ldr 4-8, 290E2
DAVIS, William
Vs oil price rise plan 11-12, 889A1
DAVIS-Besse Nuclear Power Station—*See OHIO—Atomic Energy*
DAVISON, Charles H.
Loses Peat Marwick electn 10-10, 851F3
DAVIS v. Passman
Case decided by Sup Ct 6-5, 463G3-464F1
Sup Ct workforce data rptd 6-11, 464F1
DAWES Laboratories Inc.
DES banned in animal feed 6-28, 571B3
DAWN of the Dead (film)
Released 4-19, 528A2
Top-grossing film 5-2, 356F2
DAWSON, Andre
NL batting ldr 9-30, 955E2
DAWSON, Anthony M.
Killer Fish released 12-7, 1007F3
DAY, Edmund
Deadly Delilah opens 7-6, 711D2
DAY, Gerry
Black Hole released 12-21, 1007A3
DAYAN, Moshe
Threatns to expel W Bank, Gaza pro-PLO Arabs 1-23, 50G3
Sees PLO Mideast role, denies policy shift 2-13, 144C1
Regrets Iran tie break 2-19, 126C1
Meets Vance, Khalil in prelim pact talks 2-22—2-25; briefs Cabt, parlt; backs Begin talks with Carter, Khalil 2-26—2-28, 142F2, A3, C3
Signs separate Israel-US agrmt 3-26, 221B1, G2
Vs Begin Palestinian autonomy plan 5-17, drops oppositn 5-21, 394E2, A3
Says Egypt wants open border delayed 5-23, 394D2
Votes vs Nablus setlmt plan 6-3, 415F1
In Egypt, travel agrmt set 6-4—6-6, 415E2
On Elon Moreh oppositn 6-18, 461F3
Rejects EC setlmt protest 6-20, 462C1
Hospitalized 6-23, cancer rptd 6-28, 527G2
Chrgs US oil-peace link 8-7, 591E2
Says US OKs raids on PLO in Leb 8-13, 625C2
Meets PLO backers 8-29, comments 8-30, 9-4; contacts scored by Israel 9-4, lauded by US 9-5, 658C3
'78 mtgs with PLO backers disclosed 9-6, 676G3
Meets W Ger forgn min 9-10, scores Palestinian rights stand; Bonn denies tilt 9-11, 677B1
At Camp David anniv rites 9-17, 695E1
Israel, Egypt, US Sinai pact set 9-19, 694D1
Vetoes Jesse Jackson mtg 9-20, 694F2
Young says aired Terzi mtg 9-24; Young meets, absolves 9-26, 763G2
Offers resignatn 10-2; proposes autonomy talks concessns 10-18, quits in policy dispute 10-21, leaves office 10-23, 801A1
Back from Eur Socialist conf 10-11, warns vs setlmt expansn plan 10-14, 780D1
Joins govt in no-confidence votes 10-23, 801A2
Yadin rejects forgn min post 10-29, 856C2
DA Ya Think I'm Sexy (recording)
On best-seller list 2-14, 120E3; 3-7, 174D1; 4-4, 271D2
DAY Care—*See under CHILDREN*
DAYLIN Inc.
Grace takeover OKd, Narco bid dropped 1-24, 88E3
DAYS 3d, Drew S.
Argues govt minority constructn grants case in Sup Ct 11-27, 944G3
DAYS of Heaven (film)
Almendro wins Oscar 4-9, 336A2
DAYS of Sorrow and Pain (book)
Baker wins Pulitzer 4-16, 336G2
DAYTON, O.—*See OHIO*
DAYTON (O.), University of
Paxson in NBA draft 6-25, 507B3
DAYTONA Beach, Fla.—*See FLORIDA*
DAYTON Board of Education v. Brinkman
Case decided by Sup Ct 7-2, 539E2
D.C. Coalition in Solidarity with the Nicaraguan People
IMF loan protested 4-25, 332E1
DC-10 Plane Series—*See AVIATION*

1980

DAVIS, Rep. Robert (R, Mich.)
Reelected 11-4, 843F1
DAVIS, Ronnie
We Won't Pay! opens 12-17, 1003G3
DAVIS, William
Chrgs Sovt auto dumping 8-7, 618C1
Backs Canada const 'patriatn' 9-18, 728G1
Mitchell wins Ontario by-electn 11-20, 900C3
DAVIS Cup—*See TENNIS*
DAVIS v. Passman
Case cited by Sup Ct 4-22, 343G3
DAVYDOVA, Yelena
Wins Olympic medals, Rumania contests 7-24, 7-25, 589E2, A3, 622G3
DAWKINS, Darryl
Lakers win NBA title 5-16, 432B2
DAWSON, Andre
NL batting ldr 10-6, 926D2-F2
Wins Golden Glove Award 12-6, 926E1
DAWSON Chemical Co. v. Rohm & Haas Co.
Case decided by Sup Ct 6-27, 511D2
DAY, Dorothy
Dies 11-29, 928C2
DAY, Raymond
Arrested 1-2, 94B3
DAYAN, Moshe
Shamir named forgn min 3-9, 179B3
Votes no-confidence vs Begin govt 11-19, 880B2
Vs new pol role 11-22, 902A1
DAYCARE—*See CHILDREN*
DAY in Hollywood/A Night in the Ukraine, A (play)
Opens 5-1, 392E2
3 win Tonys 6-8, 692C3
DAYTON—*See OHIO*
DAYTON, University of
Wins NCAA Div II football title game 12-6, 999G2
DAYTON Daily News
Carter interviewed 10-2, 762D2
Carter endorsemt rptd 11-1, 841G3
DDT (dichloro-diphenyl-trichloroethane)
See PESTICIDES

1976

DEAF-Blind Youths and Adults, National Center for
Cong OKs rehabilitatn act extensn 2-17, 3-2, 182F1
DEAK & Co.
Lockheed payoffs role probed 3-5, 191E1
DEAN, David
On US evacuatn from Peking 8-1, 561E2
DEAN 3rd, John W.
Butz resigns 10-4, 743F3-744B1
Ford on Watergate coverup chrg 10-14, 761A3
De ANCHORENA, Manuel
On indefinite leave from UK post 1-14, 96E3
DEANE, Martha—*See McBRIDE, Mary Margaret*
DEARBORN, Mich.—*See MICHIGAN*
DEASON, Willard
Succeeded as ICC member 3-18, 232C1
DEATH Issues—*See under MEDICINE*
DEATH Penalty—*See 'Capital Punishment' under CRIME*

1977

DEACON, Gladys Marie—*See MARLBOROUGH, Duchess of*
DEAD Sea
New scroll analyzed 11-12, 1022F3
DEAFNESS—*See MEDICINE—Handicapped*
DEAN 3rd, John W.
Blind Ambition on best-seller list 2-6, 120F3
Nixon-Frost interview 5-4, 366D3-367A1
DEAN, Robert W.
Replaced as amb to Peru 5-25, 500B1
DEANE, Philip
On dieback fungus 2-14, 132F2
DEAN Witter Organization Inc.
Reynolds merger set, reactn 10-3, 799G2
DEARY, John
Rhodesia jails 8-30, frees 9-4, 811C2
DEATH Issues—*See under MEDICINE*
DEATH Penalty—*See CRIME—Capital Punishment*
DEATH Penalty, National Coalition Against
'77 death row populatn rptd 6-7, 594B1

1978

DEA—*See U.S. GOVERNMENT—JUSTICE—Drug Enforcement Administration*
DEAD End (play)
Opens 5-4, 760G1
DEAFNESS—*See HANDICAPPED*
DEAKIN, George
Arrested in murder plot 8-4, 614C2
Murder-conspiracy trial ordrd 12-13, 987E3
De ALMEIDA, Luis
Angola mobilizes vs S Africa 11-7, 925B3
DEAN, James (1931-55)
'Sept 30 1955' released 3-31, 619E3
DEAN 3rd, John W.
Cited in Nixon memoir excerpts 4-30, 5-1, 320B1, F1
DEAN, Kenneth
On '68 Dem conv FBI role 7-1, 507F3
DEAN, Phillip Hayes
'Paul Robeson' opens 1-19, 760A3
DEAN, R. Hal
Backs Carter wage-price plan 11-1, 863B3
DEAN, Stephen O.
Fusion research advance rptd 8-12, 653F2
DEAR Detective (film)
Released 4-24, 619D1
DEATH Issues—*See under MEDICINE*
DEATH On the Nile (film)
Released 9-29, 970A1
Top-grossing film 10-4, 800G3
DEATH Penalty—*See CRIME—Capital Punishment*

1979

DEA—*See U.S. GOVERNMENT-JUSTICE-Drug Enforcement Administration*
DEADLY Delilah (play)
Opens 7-6, 711C2
DEAD Sea Scrolls
Temple Scroll contents told 3-2, 217G2
DEAD Zone, The (book)
On best-seller list 10-14, 800A3; 11-4, 892D3
DEAFNESS—*See HANDICAPPED*
DEAKIN, George
Acquitted 6-22, 485E3
DEAN, John Gunther
Leb asks halt to Israel raids 8-24, 643D1
DEANE, Hamilton
Dracula released 7-13, 820A1
DeANGELO v. U.S.
Case declined by Sup Ct 2-26, 164F3
DEATH Instinct, The (book)
Mesrine slain 11-2, 890E3
DEATH Issues—*See under MEDICINE*
DEATH on the Nile (film)
Powell wins Oscar 4-9, 336A2
DEATH Penalty—*See CRIME-Capital Punishment*

1980

DE VARGA, Pierre
Poniatowski impeachmt sought 4-14, 312B3
DE VINCENZO, Roberto
Wins US Senior Open 6-29, 715C1
DEA (Drug Enforcement Administration)
See under U.S. GOVERNMENT--JUSTICE
DEAD End Kids (play)
Opens 11-18, 1003A3
DEAD Sea
Israel plans Medit canal, map; Jordan role asked 8-24, 643F2
Jordan Red Sea canal plan rptd 8-30, 661G1
DEAD Zone, The (book)
On best-seller list 8-17, 640G3; 9-14, 716C3
DEAN Jr., Charles D.
Scores 'test-tube baby' clinic 1-8, 24B2
DEAN, John Gunther
Condemns Israel Leb raid, US disavows 8-21, 644A1
Escapes assassinatn 8-28, 643F3
Sees Leb forgn min, rpts peace moves 8-28, 643G3
DEAN 3rd, John W.
Discounts Liddy, Agnew claims 4-23, 333E3
DE ANGELIS, Anthony (Tony)
Sentncd in pork swindle 7-21, 655B1
DEAN Witter Reynolds Inc.
NYSE halts trading 3-27, 223C2
Intercapital money mkt fund listed 3-31, 223F3
DEARBORN—*See MICHIGAN*
DEATH Issues—*See under MEDICINE*
DEATH of a Princess (TV film)
UK telecast strains Saudi ties 4-10, 294B1
Australia bars telecast 4-15, 309F3
Saudi orders UK envoy to leave 4-23, visits cancelled 4-25, 313F2
US telecast protested 5-8, PBS airs 5-12; Nielsen rating rptd 5-13, 375E2
US cts rule on telecast 5-9, 5-12, 375F3
UK regrets airing 5-22, 407A3
UK-Saudi ties restored 7-28, 578A3
DEATH Penalty—*See CRIME--Capital Punishment*

DEATHS

1976

DEATHS—*Note: Persons whose deaths are recorded in Facts on File are listed alphabetically below.*
US health rpt issued 1-12, 32B1
'74 rates rptd 2-3, 123D3
'20-73 female data rptd 4-27, 379F3, 380A1
'75 US rate rptd 7-31, 911E1
Smoking-health study rptd 9-14, 875F3
Top natl suicide rates rptd 11-17, 944E3
IUD abortn deaths rptd 11-18, 931E2
'75 job-related deaths rptd 12-9, 950F2
'75 heroin deaths rptd 12-12, 972B3, D3

Aalto, Alvar 5-11, 404E1
Abdala, Carlos 6-9, 542D3
Actis, Omar 8-19, 672B1
Albers, Joseph 3-25, 240C3
Ali, Abu 7-5, 485F2
Allen, Ward 12-17, 1015A1
Alvariza, Carlos (rptd) 3-5, 207D3
Amaya, Mario Abel 10-19, 996G1
Anaya, Joaquin Zenteno 5-11, 350D3
Anda, Geza 6-13, 524C2
Angelelli, Enrique 8-4, 672E1
Anthimos 9-19, 1015B1
Araluce y Villar 10-4, 774G2
Aram, Bahran 11-16, 910F2
Archbold, Richard 8-1, 816D3
Arja, Jayel Al- 7-5, 485F2
Arlen, Richard 3-28, 240C3
Armstrong, Barbara 1-18, 56G2
Arnold, William 9-30, 1015B1
Arpels, Louis 3-20, 240D3
Arrostito, Norma 12-3, 996B2
Arzamendia, Mario (rptd) 6-9, 557D3
Arzumanyan, Grigory 11-28, 932C3
Atrash, Linda 5-27, 385D2
Auchincloss Sr, Hugh 11-20, 970B1
August, Jan 1-17, 56A3
Azzawi, Ahmed al- 7-10, 679A3
Bachauer, Gina 8-22, 892F2
Baddeley, Angela 2-22, 192C3
Badi, Aquiles 5-8, 368D2
Bailey, Pearce 6-23, 524C2
Baker, Milton G 8-7, 892F2
Baldovinos, Carlos 9-12, 996D1
Ballard, Florence 2-22, 192C3
Bankhead, Dan 5-2, 368D2
Barker, John 7-10, 519A3
Barqani, Mohammed 9-27, 721A1
Barrett, Mark 8-18, 618C3
Barrett, William A 4-12, 305B1, 315F3
Baukhage, Hilmar 2-1, 124C3
Beber, Sam 8-25, 656E3
Beecher, Henry K 7-25, 680F3
Belkin, Samuel 4-18, 315G3
Bellah, James Warner 9-22, 1015B1
Bender, Albert 2-16, 160C3
Bergonetti, Carlos Antonio 8-19, 672B1
Berhanu, Haile 7-25, 674B2
Berkeley, Busby 3-14, 240D3
Betachew, Nadew (rptd) 7-13, 523D3
Beyen, Johan 4-29, 368E2
Beyene, Seleshi 8-12, 674C2
Bhashani, Abud Hamid 11-17, 970B1
Bilski, Jean 5-14, 381C3
Bisalla, Iliyasu 3-11, 222C2
Bjoerneboe, Jens 5-9, 404F1
Blair, David 4-1, 484C3
Blakely, William 1-5, 56A3
Bloomgarden, Kermit 9-20, 970C1
Bodnaras, M Emil 1-24, 160C3

1977

DEATHS—*Note: Persons whose deaths are recorded in Facts On File are listed alphabetically below.*
US lifestyle reflected 2-25, 183F3
Drug-related deaths rptd 2-28, 224C2
'76 US data rptd 7-25, 12-13, 962B3
Barbiturate deaths rptd 11-27, 972E3

Abdullahi Yousuf 7-30, 649C1
Abernathy, Roy 2-28, 164B2
Abusaid, Carlos 11-3, 1011A2
Addinsell, Richard 11-15, 952A2
Adrian, Edgar Douglas 8-4, 696B2
Aguero Echeverria, Carlos (rptd) 4-9, 476C1
Aguirre Salinas, Osmin 7-12, 580B3
Ahmed, Fakhruddin Ali 2-11, 116A1
Alemayehu Haile 2-3, 98D2
Alfaro Castillo, Carlos 9-16, 747E1
Alia, Queen 2-9, 87D1
Allende, Beatriz 10-12, 871G3
Allison, Wilmer 4-20, 356F2
Allred, Rulon 5-10, 847F3
Altmeier, Peter 8-28, 696B2
Amanrich, Gerard 4-19, 312E3
Amaury, Emilien 1-2, 84F2
Ames, Elizabeth 3-28, 264B2
Anderson, Eddie (Rochester) 2-28, 164B2
Andreski, Mitchell 1-20, 65G3
Anick, Betty 3-22, 264C2
Arauz, Pedro 10-17, 802E2
Arriaga Bosque, Rafael 9-29, 805B3
Artime, Manuel 11-18, 952B2
Arun Thavathasin 3-26, 243F1
Arvey, Jacob 8-25, 696C2
Ashbee, Barry 5-12, 452D2
Asmar, Sali al- 995F2
Astor, Gertrude 11-9, 952B2
Atkins, Ollie 1-9, 84F2
Atnafu Abate 11-13, 875C2
Ato Tewodros Legesse 2-25, 238D3
Baader, Andreas 10-18, 790D2
Baden-Powell, Olave 6-25, 532E2
Barbour, George 7-11, 604E2
Barlow, Perry 12-26, 1023G3
Barnes, George 9-4, 787F3
Barnes, Robert 10-24, 872A1
Barrett, Edith 2-22, 164C2
Barrett, Edward 4-4, 356F2
Bashir, Mohammed el- 2-9, 87D1
Batchelor, C D 9-5, 787F3
Bautista, Teodulfo 10-10, 803F2
Bayona Jimenez, Rafael 2-13, 255B1
Beale, Edith Bouvier 2-25, 164C2
Beams, Jesse 7-23, 604E2
Beel, Louis 2-11, 164C2
Ben-Ami, Jacob 7-22, 604E2
Benoist, Emil Pierre 8-26, 807A3
Bettanin, Leonardo 1-1, 16D3
Bhaktivendanta, A C 11-14, 952C2
Biayenda, Emile Cardinal 3-23, 220C2
Bibring, Grete L 8-10, 696C2
Biddle, Katherine 12-30, 1023G3
Bierman, Bernard 3-7, 264C2
Biggs, E Power 3-10, 264D2
Bijedic, Dzemal 1-18, 48G2
Biko, Steven 9-12, 707C3
Bissell, Richard 5-4, 452D2
Black, Douglas M 5-15, 452D2
Bliven, Bruce 5-27, 452E2
Bloch, Ernst 8-3, 696D2
Boehm, Franz 9-26, 872A1

1978

DEATHS—*Note: Persons whose deaths are recorded in Facts On File are listed alphabetically below.*
Acker, Jean 8-16, 708A2
Adnan, Hammad 8-3, 582D3
Adoula, Cyrille 5-24, 440D2
Agulla, Horacio 8-28, 792F3
Ahn, Philip 2-28, 196B2
Alexander, Eben Roy 10-30, 888D2
Alikhanian, Artemi 2-25, 196B2
Allen, Clifford R 6-18, 540D2
Allen, James B 6-1, 432E1
Alvarez, Walter Clement 6-18, 540D2
Amador, Salvador (rptd) 11-6, 883A2
Amos, Sharon 11-19, 890D3
Andersen, Anar 6-27, 519E1
Arguello, Gustavo (rptd) 9-14, 705A3
Ascoli, Max 1-1, 96C1
Ashqar, Samin 11-1, 828B2
Atkinson, Walter 1-6, 96C1
Awar, Salem 6-26, 499B1
Bacioglu, Basir 6-2, 476D3
Bailey, Bill (rptd) 12-17, 1032C2
Bakunas, A J 9-22, 777E3
Baldwin, Faith 3-19, 252C2
Balopoulos, Michael 3-3, 252C2
Barrera, Ernesto 11-29, 987A1
Barrie, Wendy 2-2, 196B2
Baugham Jr, U E 11-6, 972E2
Bedson, Henry 9-6, 927A2
Begle, Edward 3-2, 252D2
Belmar, Innocent 1-5, 94F2
Bennett, James V 11-19, 972E2
Berardi, Rosario 3-10, 191G1
Bergen, Edgar 9-30, 777E3
Bertoia, Harry 11-6, 972F2
Best, Charles H 3-31, 252D2
Betz, Carl 1-18, 96C1
Bieber, Margarete 2-25, 196C2
Bierwirth, John E 4-3, 356B2
Blair Jr, Charles F 9-2, 777F3
Blaisdell, George G 10-3, 888D2
Bliss, George 9-11, 777F3
Bobst, Elmer Holmes 8-2, 708A2
Bolin, Wesley 3-4, 186F3
Bonnet, Henri 10-25, 888D2
Borland, Hal 2-22, 196C2
Bostock, Lyman 9-23, 777G3
Boumedienne, Houari 12-27, 1012B2
Bowles, Robert (rptd) 8-25, 887A1
Boyer, Charles 8-26, 708B2
Boyle, John 7-11, 630B3
Braden, Spruille 1-10, 96D1
Bradford, Alex 2-15, 196D2
Bradshaw, Robert 5-24, 440D2
Bray, John R 10-10, 888E2
Breech, Ernest Robert 7-3, 620E2
Brel, Jacques 10-9, 888E2
Briguglio, Salvatore 3-21, 232F2
Brooks, Edward H 10-10, 888F2
Brown, George S 12-5, 1032C2
Brown, Robert I 11-18, 889F2
Brown, Zara Cully 2-28, 196D2
Brugnon, Jacques 3-20, 252D2
Bryan, Frederick van Pelt 4-17, 356C2
Burch, Preston M 4-4, 356C2
Burden, Wm Douglas 11-14, 972F2
Burgess, W Randolph 9-16, 778A1
Burns, W Sherman 1-5, 96D1
Bushuyev, Konstantin D 10-26, 888F2
Busia, Kofi 8-28, 708C2
Busic, Bruno 10-16, 805A2
Butler, John M 3-16, 252E2

1979

DEATHS—*Note: Persons whose deaths are recorded in Facts On File are listed alphabetically below.*
A'Alam, Jamshid 9-24, 814B3
Acheampong, Ignatius Kutu 6-16, 468D3
Adler, Samuel 11-12, 932A2
Afrifa, Akwasi A 6-26, 485E2
Ager, Milton 5-6, 432D2
Ahmed, Ali Salem 12-15, 980F1
Akuffo, Fred W K 6-26, 485E2
Alessandrini, Emilio 1-29, 98B1
Allbritton, Louise 2-16, 176E2
Allen, Frank A 11-20, 932A2
Allen, Levin C 9-27, 756A2
Almond, Edward M 6-11, 508D2
Alphand, Nicole 2-15, 176E2
Amini-Afshar, Parviz 2-20, 125E1
Andraca Roca, Manuel 2-14, 237E1
Anglin, Ernie 3-14, 309A3
Aplin, Billy Joe 8-3, 660D1
Araqi, Hessam 8-26, 653A3
Araqi, Mehdi 8-26, 653A3
Ardizzone, Edward 11-8, 932B2
Arguello, Ariel 6-20, 461E2
Arzner, Doris 10-1, 860G1
Austin, Bernard L 8-21, 671F1
Ayesh, Mohammed 8-8, 602F2
Aziz, Ibrahim Abdul 12-15, 980F1
Azmoun, Manuchehr 4-9, 276B3
Badri, Abdul Ali 2-11, 105G1
Baires, Jaime 3-4, 235B1
Barbour, Clifford E 1-10, 104E2
Baroody, Jamil M 3-4, 272A2
Barr, John A 1-16, 104E2
Barth, Alan 11-20, 932B2
Bartlett, Dewey F 3-1, 272A2
Barzani, Mustafa al- 3-1, 272B2
Batasuna, Herri 9-28, 754E2
Bayh, Marvella 4-24, 356B3
Beglari, Mohammed Amin 2-12, 105A2
Behbahani, Seyyed Mohsen 7-21, 565D3
Belmont, Eleanor 10-24, 860A2
Beltran Espantoso, Pedro 2-16, 176E2
Bengsch, Alfred 12-13, 1008A2
Bennett, Harry H 1-4, 104F2
Bennett, W(illiam) A C 2-23, 176F2
Berenjian, Hashem 4-13, 276D3
Berkowitz, Martin 1-15, 26D1
Berlanga Robles, Francisco 1-2, 40F1
Bernac, Pierre 10-17, 860B2
Bernstein, Theodore M 6-27, 508D2
Bhutto, Zulfikar Ali 4-4, 247A1
Bishop, Elizabeth 10-6, 860B2
Bishop, Jesse Walter 10-22, 817G1-F2
Blodgett, Katharine 10-12, 860B2
Blondell, Joan 12-26, 1008B2
Bolton, Guy R 9-5, 756A2
Borromeo Mata, Carlos 3-3, 234E3
Bouceif, Ahmed Ould 5-27, 412E1
Boulanger, Nadia 10-22, 860C2
Boulin, Robert 10-30, 834F3
Brabourne, Lady (dowager) 8-28, 641C1
Breckinridge, John B 7-29, 588D2
Brent, George 5-26, 432D2
Brodie, Israel 2-13, 176F2
Brown, John N 10-9, 860D2
Brundage, Percival F 7-16, 588D2
Buchanan, Edgar 4-4, 356C3
Burrell, Berkeley G 8-31, 671G1
Cain, Harry Pulliam 3-3, 272B2
Canistracci, Paul 6-3, 548G2
Cansino, Jose 6-10, 445B3

1980

DEATHS—*Note: Persons whose deaths are recorded in Facts On File are listed alphabetically below.*
Abecassis, Snu 12-4, 923E1
Abu-Wardeh, Mohammed 11-18, 880B3
Adams, Gerald Williams 8-4, 621D1
Adams, Theodore 2-27, 175C3
Adamson, Joy 1-3, 104D1
Adorno Maldonado, Jose Juan 8-11, 786B2
Agar, Herbert 11-24, 928F1
Albanese, Alfredo 5-12, 408C1
Ali, Chaudhri Mohammed 12-1, 1003G3
Allon, Yigal 2-29, 175D3
Alsop, Mary 10-14, 876A1
Alter, Louis 11-3, 928G1
Alvarez Cordoba, Enrique 11-27, 921E1
Amalrik, Andrei A 11-11, 928G1
Amaro da Costa, Adelino 12-4, 923D1
Amato, Mario 6-23, 564G2
Amato, Pino 5-19, 408E2
Amendola, Giorgio 6-5, 528A1
Amerasinghe, Hamilton 12-4, 1004A1
Amin, Abdullah 6-8, 475D2
Amin, Assadullah 6-8, 475D2
Andersch, Alfred 2-21, 279C1
Anderson, Glenn M 6-25, 528A1
Andrews, Gould A 7-1, 608B1
Anne, Princess 9-27, 755A2
Anson, Jay 3-12, 279C1
Ardrey, Robert 1-14, 104E1
Ariyak, Sarik 12-17, 991C2
Arnaldi, Eduardo 4-19, 408G1
Arnold, Elliot 5-13, 448B1
Aronson, Boris 11-16, 928B2
Arrese, Jaime 10-23, 832D2
Ashford, Emmett 3-1, 279D1
Avery, Fred (rptd) 9-1, 755B2
Azar, Abraham el- 1-2, 136A1
Bachelet, Vittorio 2-12, 151A2
Badylak, Walenty 3-20, 262F3
Bailey, Jack 2-1, 175E3
Baittiner, Jou 9-17, 697G2
Bakke, Richard 4-24, 321E2
Ballantrae, Baron 11-28, 928B2
Banghart, Charles K (rptd) 5-31, 528B1
Baroody Sr, William J 7-29, 608B1
Barrera, Enrique 11-27, 921F1
Barry, Donald 7-17, 698C1
Barry, Tom 7-2, 608C1
Barthes, Roland 3-25, 279D1
Bates, Lucias C 8-22, 676A1
Bateson, Gregory 7-4, 608D1
Baxter, Richard Reeves 9-26, 755B2
Beaton, Cecil 1-18, 104F1
Beckman, Aldo 9-10, 755C2
Beer, Wolfgang 7-25, 581C1
Belcher, Page 8-2, 676A1
Benedictos I 12-10, 1004A1
Bennett, John C 5-4, 448C1
Berger, Samuel 2-12, 175E3
Bernays, Doris F 7-11, 608D1
Bible, Dana 1-19, 104F1
Bignard, Leon A 6-27, 528B1
Bitar, Salah el- 7-21, 567C2
Bonelli, Richard 6-7, 528C1
Bonham, John 9-25, 755C2
Boussac, Marcel 3-21, 279E1
Boyd, Julian Parks 5-28, 448C1
Braly, Malcom 4-7, 360C1
Brand, Millen 3-19, 279F1
Bright, Cyril 4-22, 353G1

1976

Bolles, Don 6-13, 484G2
Bonifas, Arthur 8-18, 618C3
Boonsanong Punyodyana 2-28, 176E3
Bosco, Henri 5-4, 368E2
Bose, Wilfred 7-5, 484G2
Boswell, Connee 10-11, 816D3
Botha, George (rptd) 12-15, 1010F2
Bourguiba, Moufida 11-14, 932C3
Bowling, Roy H (rptd) 9-6, 678B3
Bradwell, Baron 8-12, 892G2
Brailowsky, Alexander 4-25, 524C2
Brandao, Evil (rptd) 7-9, 836B2
Braun, Franziska 1-13, 56A3
Briggs, Ellis 2-21, 484C3
Britten, Benjamin 12-4, 970C1
Broumand, Garsivaz 5-4, 365D2
Bruesewitz, Oskar 8-22, 772C2
Bruns, Gunter 1-1, 11A1
Buchan, Alistair 2-4, 124D3
Bultmann, Rudolf 7-30, 816E3
Burnett, Chester 1-10, 56B3
Byrne, Donald 3-4, 484C3
Byron, Katharine 12-28, 1015B1
Calder, Alexander 11-11, 970C1
Cambridge, Godfrey 11-29, 932D3
Caouette, Real 12-16, 970D1
Capling, Elwyn Rex (rptd) 9-6, 678B3
Carbo, Paul John 11-9, 970D1
Cardozo, Cesareo 6-18, 495E3
Carey, Max 5-30, 484D3
Carpenter Jr., Walter 2-2, 124D3
Carter, Oliver J 6-14, 524D2
Casey, Richard G 6-17, 524D2
Cassidy, Jack 12-12, 1015C1
Cassin, Rene 2-20, 192C3
Castelo Soto, Eduardo 4-3, 264F1
Castiella y Maiz, F 11-25, 970D1
Cavert, Samuel McCrea 12-21, 1015C1
Chaggar, Gurdip Singh 6-4, 482D1
Chaine, Jacques 5-14, 381C3
Choi Yong Kun 9-20, 970B2
Chou En-lai 1-8, 8G2
Christie, Agatha 1-12, 56B3
Chu Teh 7-6, 520E3
Cobb, Lee J 2-11, 160C3
Cogley, John 3-28, 272E3
Cohen, Mickey 7-29, 716G2
Combs, Earle 7-21, 656E3
Contreras Escobar, Eduardo (rptd) 11-7, 926D1
Cooke, Judith 7-21, 538F2
Corghi, Benito 8-5, 589B3
Costello, John 1-5, 56B3
Costello, John M 8-28, 892F2
Cottrell, Wm 8-28, 652G1
Cowan, Louis 11-18, 970D1
Crawford, John 2-14, 160C3
Cunningham, Imogen 6-24, 524D2
Curme, George O 7-28, 716A3
Daley, Richard 12-20, 969B3
Dam, Henrik 4-17, 368E2
Davies, Rupert 11-22, 970E1
Davis, Meyer 4-5, 272F3
De Broglie, Jean 12-24, 1002D2
De Vogue, Robert-Jean 10-17, 970C3
Dennis, Patrick 11-6, 970E1
Di Rosa, Luigi 5-28, 403B1
Diamond, Stephen (rptd) 9-6, 678B3
Dimka, Bukar Suka 5-16, 366F1
Donnelly, Tom 2-10, 192D3
Dopfner, Julius Cardinal 7-24, 716A3
Douglas, Paul 9-24, 970F1
Dowling, Eddie 2-18, 160D3
Drumm, Maire 10-28, 854B3
Druzhinin, Vladimir 8-20, 892G2
Ducat, Bruce Chalmers (rptd) 9-6, 678B3
Duke, Charles 8-21, 892G2
Earnshaw, George 12-1, 1015C1
Eaton, Curtis Abbot (rptd) 9-6, 678B3
Echavarria, Octavio 3-25, 251C2
Echegoyen, Roberto 7-10, 571G1
Eckstein, Alexander 12-4, 1015D1
Edelstein, Melville 6-16, 425F2
Elazar, David 4-15, 315G3
Ellaj-Pour, Hassan 9-2, 679F1
Ernst, Max 4-1, 272F3
Ernst, Morris 5-21, 404F1
Erskine, Laurie 11-30, 1015D1
Estable, Argento (rptd) 1-13, 55E3
Evans, Edith 10-14, 970G1
Ewart-Biggs, Christopher 7-21, 538D2
Faith, Percy 2-9, 160D3
Farley, James 6-9, 444A1
Feather, Victor 7-28, 716A3
Fiel Filho, Manoel 1-17, 98B1
Fierlinger, Zdenek 5-2, 368F2
Fikre Merid 10-1, 1002E1
Fishbein, Harry 2-19, 192D3
Fishbein, Morris 9-27, 1015D1
Folsom, Marion 9-28, 932D3
Fonseca Amador, Carlos (rptd) 11-9 926D1
Ford, Paul 4-12, 316A1
Franklin, Sidney 4-26, 368F2
Friis, Harold 6-15, 524E2
Frumkin, Alexander 5-27, 404G1
Fuchida, Mitsuo 5-30, 524E2
Fukuda, Taro 6-10, 450D3
Gabin, Jean 11-15, 970F1
Gabl, Gertrud 1-18, 56C3
Gallardo, Jose 7-18, 656E3
Gallico, Paul 7-15, 716B3
Gambino, Carlo 10-15, 932D3
Gardner, George Peabody 9-18, 1015E1
Garrison, Candace M 10-26, 970G1
Gavrilovic, Milan 1-1, 56C3
Gearhart, Daniel 7-10, 519A3
Georgiou, Costas 7-10, 519A3
Getty, J Paul 6-6, 444E1
Ghosn, Raymond 2-17, 125G1
Goldberg, Lawrence (rptd) 9-6, 678B3
Goldfinger, Nathaniel 7-22, 656F3
Gonzalez Heredia, Tito (rptd) 7-2, 593A1
Gordon, Kermit 6-21, 484D3
Gorini, Luigi 8-13, 892A3
Goulart, Joao 12-6, 970G1
Granger, Lester 1-9, 56D3
Grechko, Andrei 4-27, 315E3
Gross, Ted 6-6, 442D3

1977

Bolan, Marc 9-16, 787G3
Bollinger, Elisabeth 2-22, 164C2
Bolton, Frances Payne 3-9, 264D2
Bompensiero, Frank 2-10, 568D2
Bonesteel 3d, Charles 10-13, 872B1
Borgonovo Pohl, 5-10, 373B2
Bouchard, Charles 5-11, 489D2
Bowles, Heloise 12-28, 1023G3
Boyd, Stephen 6-2, 532E2
Bramlet, Al 3-17, 261C3
Brauer, Richard 4-17, 356G2
Brazier, Eugenie 3-3, 264E2
Brooks, Geraldine 6-19, 532F2
Bruce, David 12-4, 1024A1
Bryan Jr., Blackshear 3-2, 264D2
Buback, Siegfried 4-7, 286A2
Buckner, Milt 7-27, 604F2
Budker, Gersh 7-6, 604F2
Bulter, Thomas 10-30, 872C1
Bunker, Laurence 10-10, 872B1
Burnham, Joseph 10-10, 872B1
Burns, Raymond 7-7, 604G2
Bustamante, Alexander 8-6, 696D2
Cabo, Dardo 1-6, 42C1
Cabot, Sebastian 8-23, 696E2
Cain, James 10-27, 872C1
Callas, Maria 9-16, 787G3
Callimahos, Lambros 10-28, 872D1
Camps, Alberto Miguel 9-7, 921G3
Carlson, Richard 11-25, 952C2
Carr, John Dickson 2-27, 164D2
Carrien, Jerome 6-23, 543G1
Carroll, Coleman 7-26, 604G2
Casalegno, Carlo 11-29, 1014F2
Castle, William 5-31, 452E2
Castro Olivera, Raul 10-26, 921C3
Cavanzo, Josue (rptd) 1-12, 255B1
Centeno, Norberto 7-12, 595E2
Chalard Hiranyasiri 4-21, 331E2
Chaplin, Charles 12-25, 1024B1
Cheng Chao-chang 8-30, 706G1
Chrichton, John 12-28, 1024D1
Clark, Tom 6-13, 532F2
Clouzot, Henri-Georges 1-12, 84F2
Cobham, Viscount 3-20, 264E2
Cochrane, Ralph 12-17, 1024C1
Cocke Sr, Erle 10-7, 872D1
Cohen, Manuel 6-16, 532F2
Cole, Edward N 5-2, 452F2
Coleman, John 2-23, 164D2
Colt, Ethel Barrymore 5-22, 452F2
Cone, Fairfax 6-20, 532A3
Connor, Reginald F X 8-22, 696E2
Conway, Cardinal 4-17, 356G3
Coolidge, Albert S 8-31, 696E2
Cortez, Ricardo 4-28, 356A3
Costello, Seamus 1-5, 782E3
Cotzias, George C 6-13, 532A3
Crane, Roy 7-7, 604G2
Crawford, Joan 5-10, 452F2
Crespin, Jose Leonidas 2-20, 181A2
Crosby, Bing 10-14, 872D1
Crosland, Anthony 2-19, 164E2
Dahlberg, Edward 2-27, 164E2
Daves, Delmer 8-17, 696F2
Davis, Bettina 10-9, 872E1
De Mohrenschildt, G (rptd) 3-29, 228B3
De Muralt, Bertrand 5-8, 489D3
Desmond, Paul 5-30, 452G2
Devine, Andy 2-18, 164F2
Dewey, Godfrey 10-18, 872F1
Dios, Jose Luis 9-12, 921G3
Dodds, Gilbert 2-3, 164F2
Dubingon, Robert 3-1, 288B2
DuBois, Shirley Graham 3-27, 356A3
Dufek, George 2-10, 164F2
Duncan, Irma 9-20, 788A1
Dunn, Robert 1-21, 84G2
Eccles, Marriner 12-18, 1024D1
Eda, Saburo 5-22, 452G2
Eden, Anthony 1-14, 84G2
Eghbal, Manouchehr 11-25, 952C2
Eglevsky, Andre 12-4, 1024E1
Eiseley, Loren 7-9, 604A3
Elder, Ruth 10-9, 872F1
Embry, Basil 12-8, 1024E1
Ensslin, Gudrin 10-18, 790D2
Erhard, Ludwig 5-5, 452A3
Fadhel, Hafez al- 2-22, 457C3
Farag, Ahmad (rptd) 10-14, 824G1
Faulkner, Brian 3-3, 264F2
Fe, Benjamin 10-12, 824A2
Fedin, Konstantin 7-15, 604A3
Feldman, Abraham 7-21, 604B3
Ferreiros, Hector 4-5, 345E3
Ferris, Daniel J 5-2, 452A3
Fichet, France 5-1, 440A3
Fichet, Rene 5-1, 440A3
Fieser, Louis 7-25, 604B3
Finch, Peter 1-14, 84A3
Finklehoffe, Fred 10-5, 872F1
Finley, David 2-1, 164G2
Fishel, Wesley 4-14, 356B3
Fisher, Vincent 9-29, 935C1
Flowers, George 2-27, 288B2
Foley, Martha 9-5, 788A1
Ford, Mary 9-30, 788B1
Fortes, Benjamin 10-17, 847C3
Fortin, Andre 6-24, 532B3
Fourough, Kahainouri 9-13, 745F2
Fowler, Herbert 1-2, 84B3
Foy, Bryan 4-20, 356B3
Gabo, Naum 8-23, 696F2
Gabrielson, Ira 9-7, 788B1
Gaines, Cassie 10-20, 888G3
Gaines, Steve 10-20, 888G3
Gainza Paz, Alberto 12-26, 1024F1
Galich, Alexander 12-15, 1024F1
Garber, Jan 10-5, 872G1
Garcia Peralta, Aparicio 1-13, 42C1
Garner, Erroll 1-2, 84B3
Garnett, Tay 10-4, 872G1
Garst, Roswell 11-5, 952D2
Gasparoux, Andre 12-16, 981F3
Gaud Jr, William 12-5, 1024G1
Gelbard, Jose Ber 10-4, 872A2, 922A3
Gesesse, Solomon 11-13, 875E2
Ghubash, Saif ibn Said al- 10-25, 811B3
Gizew Temesgen 11-2, 875E2
Glaenzer, Jules 8-16, 696G2

1978

Buzhardt Jr, J Fred 12-16, 1032D2
Byron, Goodloe E 10-11, 888G2
Calderon Munoz, Abdon 12-9, 989D3
Caldwell, Malcolm 12-23, 997A2
Calvoso, Fedele 11-8, 1018F1
Cane, Paulos Ngolosi 7-13, 633D2
Capella, Jacques 7-31, 649D3
Capone, Roberto 11-8, 1018F1
Carita, Maria 9-5, 778A1
Carnie, Mark 7-19, 630E3
Carter, (Mother) Maybelle 10-23, 888G2
Catton, Bruce 8-28, 708C2
Cazale, John 3-12, 252E2
Chacon, Francisco Rene 2-6, 136D3
Chamorro, Pedro Joaquin 1-10, 19C3
Chamorro, Pedro Jose 5-8, 376E1
Chapman, Oscar 2-8, 196D2
Chapman, Richard D 11-15, 972G2
Chase, Ilka 2-15, 196E2
Chastenet, Jacques 2-7, 196E2
Chavez, Carlos 8-2, 708C2
Chavez, Federico 4-24, 356C2
Clapper, Aubrey 1-20, 96E2
Clark, Earl H (Dutch) 8-5, 708D2
Clark, Vernon 12-31-77, 56C1
Clay, Lucius D 4-16, 356D2
'Coggiola, Piero 9-28, 816F3
Cole, Charles W 2-6, 196E2
Colombo Sr, Joseph 5-22, 440D2
Comert, Bedrettin 7-11, 595B3
Compton, Fay 12-12, 1032D2
Conant, James B 2-11, 196F2
Corden-Lloyd, Ian 2-17, 132G2
Cowan, Patricia 4-10, 380E2
Cox, Billy 3-31, 252F2
Cozzens, James Gould 8-9, 708D2
Craig, Cleo F 4-21, 356E2
Crane, Bob 6-29, 540E2
Crockett, Frederick 1-17, 96E1
Curiel, Henry 5-4, 352D2
Cushman, Austin T 6-12, 540E2
Cutugno, Lorenzo 4-11, 329C3
Dailey, Dan 10-16, 888A3
Daly, James 7-3, 620F2
Damas, Leon 1-22, 96E1
Damerel, Myrtle Vail 9-18, 778A1
Darakhshani, Ali Akbar 3-27, 289A1
Dassler, Adolf (rptd) 9-18, 778B1
Daud Khan, Mohammad 4-27, 317A1
Dauphin, Claude 11-17, 972G2
David, Immanuel (rptd) 8-2, 685D3
David, Rachel 8-3, 685C3
Davis, Francis W 4-16, 356E2
Davis, Hal 1-11, 96F1
De Chirico, Giorgio 11-20, 972A3
De Madariaga, Salvador 12-14, 1032E2
De Rochemont, Louis 12-23, 1032E2
Denny, Sandy 4-16, 356E2
DeRosa, Carmine 1-4, 19A2
Dickinson, Edwin W 12-2, 1032F2
Diederichs, Nicolass 8-21, 708E2
Dill, Clarence Cleveland 1-14, 96F1
Docker, Bernard 5-23, 440E2
Doeg, John Hope 4-27, 440E2
Downs, Joseph Henry 9-17, 620F2
Drury, Newton B 12-14, 1032F2
Dupont, Clifford W 6-28, 540E2
DuVigneaud, Vincent 12-11, 1032F2
Eames, Charles 8-21, 708E2
Earl, Johnrae 1-10, 96F1
Eatherly, Claude R 7-1, 620F2
Echave, Rosario 7-3, 537E2
Eiler, Sally 1-5, 96F1
Emmerich Sr, John Oliver 8-17, 708F2
Erdeniz, Ahmet Cihangir 6-23, 595D3
Esposito, Antonio 6-21, 517E1
Estabrook, Howard 7-16, 620G2
Etting, Ruth 9-24, 778B1
Evans, Bergen 2-4, 196G2
Ewing, Donald M 9-2, 778C1
Fabian, Robert 6-14, 540F2
Farrell Jr, James A 9-15, 888A3
Feeney, Leonard 1-31, 96G1
Fendoglu, Hamit 4-17, 291B3
Fields, Totie 8-2, 708F2
Fine, John S 5-21, 440F2
Finney, Thomas 1-30, 96G1
Fischer, John 8-18, 708F2
Fitch, Aubrey Ray 5-22, 440F2
Flanner, Janet 11-7, 972A3
Flores Munoz, Gilberto 10-6, 818F1
Flores Munoz, Mrs Gilberto 10-6, 818F1
Flukiger, Rudolf (rptd) 4-12, 438F2
Fontaine, Frank 8-4, 708G2
Foot, Dingle 6-18, 540F2
Fosburgh, Mary Cushing 11-4, 972B3
Francois, Claude 3-11, 252F2
Francois-Poncet, Andre 1-8, 96A2
Franjieh, Tony 6-13, 463G1
Freeman, Harry 1-13, 96A2
Frick, Ford C 4-8, 356F2
Frings, Joseph Cardinal 12-17, 1032G2
Galanti, Isaac 10-25, 971E2
Galiffa, Arnold 9-5, 778C1
Garmon, William F 1-21, 96A2
Geer, Will 4-22, 356F2
Geidarov, Arif Nazar 6-29, 518G3
Genn, Leo 1-26, 96B2
Ghashmi, Ahmed Hussein al- 6-25, 498E3
Giacobbo, Placilo (Charlie) 4-25, 356G2
Gilliam, Jim (Junior) 10-8, 779F1
Gilson, Etienne 9-19, 778D1
Godel, Kurt 1-14, 196A3
Goff, Norris 6-7, 540G2
Gonzalez, Margarita 2-1, 91B2
Goodhart, Arthur Lehman 11-10, 972B3
Gorbatyuk, Yevgeny 3-5, 252F2
Gordon, Joe (Flash) 4-15, 356G2
Gordon, John 1-6, 96B2
Gordon, Max 11-2, 974C3
Goudsmit, Samuel A 1032G2
Granera, Ramiro 11-7, 883C2
Grant, Duncan 5-10, 440F2
Grayson, Wilbur Rodney 5-18, 396A2
Greenwood, Charlotte 1-18, 196A3
Grimm, Paul 12-23, 993C2
Gronchi, Giovanni 10-17, 888B3
Gunther, Rolf 9-17, 840F3

1979

Capehart, Homer E 9-3, 756B2
Capp, Al 11-5, 932C2
Carnes, Paul N 3-17, 272C2
Carroll, John 4-24, 356C3
Castillo, Jose Antonio 10-28, 834F2
Cauce, Caesar 11-3, 864D3
Cavanagh, Jerome Patrick 11-27, 932C2
Cavanaugh, John Joseph 12-28, 1008B2
Cha Chi Chol 10-26, 821G1
Chafik, Shariar Mustapha 12-7, 935B1
Chain, Ernst B 8-12, 671G1
Chalfen, Morris 11-4, 932D2
Challe, Maurice 1-18, 104F2
Chang Kuo-tao 12-4, 1008C2
Classen, Willie 11-28, 1004E3
Clore, Charles 7-26, 588E2
Colom Argueta, Manuel 3-22, 237B1
Conrad, Max 4-3, 356C3
Contreras, Rufino 2-10, 327F1
Coppolla, Leonardo 7-12, 548B1
Costello, Dolores 3-1, 272C2
Coughlin, Charles E 10-27, 860D2
Cousteau, Philippe 6-28, 508D2
Crockett, James 7-11, 588E2
Crowley, Steven 11-21, 893B1, C2
Cruz Cuenca, Miguel 1-9, 60D3
Danaro, Giovanni 1-4, 21G1
Darke, Bernard 7-15, 814G1
Dasburg, Andrew 8-13, 671A2
David, Donald K 4-13, 356C3
Davis, Benny 12-20, 1008D2
De Gaulle, Yvonne 11-8, 932E2
De Guingand, Francis 6-29, 508E2
De Klerk, Jan 1-23, 104G2
De Klerk, Theunis 9-21, 718C2
Delaunay, Sonia 12-5, 1008D2
Dempsey, James Charles 7-9, 588F2
Devers, Jacob L 10-15, 860E2
Diaz Ordaz, Gustavo 7-15, 588F2
Diefenbaker, John G 8-16, 671A2
Di Jorio, Alberto 9-5, 756B2
Dillon, Clarence 4-14, 356D3
Dioguardi, J (Johnny Dio) 1-12, 176F2
Dionne, Oliva 11-15, 932E2
Douglas, Aaron 2-2, 176G2
Draper, Christopher 1-16, 104G2
Dubs, Adolph 2-14, 106C2
Duffy, F Ryan 8-16, 671B2
Dutschke, Rudi 12-24, 1008D2
Dvorak, Ann 12-10, 1008E2
Easter, Luke 3-29, 1002E3
Eaton, Cyrus S 5-9, 432E2
Ebert, Friedrich 12-4, 1008E2
Eisenhower, Mamie Doud 11-11, 932F2
Elghanian, Habib 5-9, 353C2
Elliott, Wm Yandell 1-9, 104A3
Ellis, Bryon 11-21, 893B1
Elmore, Charles W 8-9, 727F3
Empie, Paul C 9-1, 756C2
Escobar Soto, Nicolas 1-4, 22E2
Espinoza, Juan Francisco 6-20, 461G2
Ettinghausen, Richard 4-2, 356D3
Evans, Charles 11-6, 932F2
Fahy, Charles 9-17, 756C2
Farrell, James T 8-22, 671C2
Feathers, Beattie 3-10, 272D2
Fiedler, Arthur 7-15, 588F2
Fields, Gracie 9-27, 756D2
Figueroa Cordero, Andres 3-7, 272D2
Fitzsimmons, Freddie 11-18, 1008F2
Flatt, Lester 5-11, 432E2
Fleischer, Dave 6-25, 508E2
Focke, Heinrich 2-25, 176G2
Foran, Dick 8-10, 671C2
Forssmann, Werner 6-1, 508F2
Fortson Jr, Ben 5-19, 432E2
Franke, William B(irrell) 6-30, 508F2
Frankel, Charles 5-10, 548G1
Frantz, Joseph 9-12, 756E2
Franzblau, Rose N 9-2, 756D2
Fremont-Smith, Maurice 5-4, 432E2
Fuentes Mohr, Alberto 1-25, 97E1-A2
Furey, Francis James 4-23, 356E3
Gabor, Dennis 2-8, 176A3
Gagnon, Rene 10-12, 860F2
Galante, Carmine 7-12, 548A1
Galento, Tony (Two-Ton) 7-22, 588G2
Garbisch, Bernice Chrysler 12-14, 1008F2
Garbisch, Edgar William 12-14, 1008F2
Gargan, William 2-16, 176A3
Garin, George (rptd) 5-22, 432G2
Gathings, E C (Took) 5-22, 432G2
Gehlen, Reinhard 6-8, 508F2
Giles, Warren 2-7, 176B3
Goldman, Pierre 9-20, 772E2
Gomez Hortiguela, Luis 5-25, 428D2
Gonzalez, German 10-27, 837A2
Gottlieb, Eddie 12-7, 1008G2
Granahan, Kathryn O'Hay 7-10, 588G2
Green, Chad 10-12, 905G1
Grenfell, Joyce 11-30, 932G2
Griffith, Corrine 7-13, 588A3
Grosvenor, Robert George 2-19, 176B3
Guggenheim, Peggy 12-23, 1008A3
Haekkerup, Per 3-13, 272D2
Haley Sr, Jack 6-6, 508G2
Hall, Jon 12-13, 1008A3
Hall, Leonard 6-2, 508A3
Halsman, Philippe 6-2, 508A3
Hamdani, Adnan Hussein 8-8, 602F2
Hamedanim, Hussein 2-20, 125F1
Harmon, Ernest N 11-13, 932A3
Harper, Ethel 3-31, 272E2
Harris, Jed 11-15, 932A3
Harris, Roy 10-1, 860F2
Hart, Gene Leroy 6-4, 508A3
Hartnell, Norman 6-8, 508B3
Hawkins, William 10-18, 840C2
Haworth, Leland J 3-5, 272E2
Haya de la Torre, Victor Raul 8-2, 671C2
Hayward, Max 3-18, 272F2
Hebert, F Edward 12-29, 1008B3
Herrera, Jose Maria 1-2, 40E1
Hilton, Conrad N 1-3, 104A3
Hocq, Robert 12-8, 1008C3
Hodge, Al 3-19, 272F2

1980

Britton, Barbara 1-17, 104G1
Briz Armengol, Enrique 9-2, 673G2
Brosio, Manlio Giovanni 3-14, 279F1
Browne, Virgil 1-7, 104G1
Bruno, Angelo 3-21, 237B2
Buchanan, Bessie A 9-7, 755D2
Bullard, Edward 4-3, 360C1
Burpee, David 6-24, 528C1
Burrows, Millar 4-29, 360D1
Butlin, Billy 6-12, 528D1
Buttrick, George A 1-23, 104A2
Byrd, Henry 1-30, 104A2
Caceras Lehnhoff, Eduardo 1-31, 98C2
Caetano, Marcello 10-26, 876A1
Calvaligi, Enrico 12-31, 995D1
Campora, Hector J 12-19, 1004B1
Cane, Melville H 3-10, 279G1
Carpenter, Rhys 1-2, 104B2
Casey, Joseph E 9-2, 755D2
Chacon, Juan 11-27, 921F1
Chamberlain, William 3-24, 279G1
Chami, Mohammed 2-2, 154C2
Champion, Gower 8-25, 676A1
Chekhova, Olga 3-29, 279A2
Cherif, Ezzedine 4-17, 316A3
Chervenkov, Vulko 10-21, 876B1
Chesson, Joseph 4-22, 353G1
Clarke, Maura 12-4, 921B1
Clurman, Harold E 9-9, 755E2
Cochran, Jacqueline 8-8, 676B1
Coe, Frank 6-2, 528D1
Coe, Mark 2-16, 194B1
Colean, Miles Lanier 9-16, 755F2
Collazo Araujo, Abelardo 8-29, 673A3
Collier, John 4-6, 360D1
Colmer, William M 9-9, 755F2
Connelly, Marc 12-21, 1004B1
Conway, Rose A 3-17, 279A2
Cort, Stewart 5-25, 448D1
Crittenberger, Willis D 8-4, 676B1
Cross, Julie Y 6-5, 503E2
Danielpur, Albert 6-5, 644B3
Davis, John W 7-12, 608E1
Day, Dorothy 11-29, 928C2
Decker, George 2-6, 175F3
De Lempica, Tamara 3-18, 280A1
DeLury, John J 2-12, 175G3
Demichelli, Alberto 10-12, 876C1
De Moraes, Vinicius 7-9, 608F1
Dennis Jr, Cecil 4-22, 353G1
Dennison, Robert Lee 3-14, 279B2
Denny, Cleveland 7-7, 907B3
Deutsch, Adolph 1-1, 104C2
DeVita, Teddy 5-27, 448D1
Dewey Sr, Charles S 12-26, 1004C1
Dickenson, Charles 1-29, 132B2
Dietrich, Raymond H 3-19, 279B2
Dimitri, Prince 7-7, 608F1
Dixon, Robert G 5-5, 448E1
Dodds, Harold W 10-25, 876C1
Doenitz, Karl 12-24, 1004D1
Donnell, Forrest C 3-19, 279B2
Donovan, Arthur 9-1, 755G2
Donovan, Jean 12-4, 921B1
Dornberger, Walter (rptd) 7-2, 528E1
Douek, Michelle 11-25, 921D3
Douglas, Helen G 6-28, 528E1
Douglas, William Orville 1-19, 50E3
Dragonette, Jessica 3-18, 279C2
Drew, Richard G 12-7, 1004D1
Dunn, Archibald Gardner (rptd) 10-9, 789B3
Durante, Jimmy 1-29, 104C2
Edouart, Alexander F 3-17, 279C2
Eichelberger, Clark M 1-26, 104D2
Eliot, Ray 2-24, 175G3
Emery, Katherine 2-8, 176A1
Enlow, Grayson Maynard 5-18, 448E1
Erdost, Ilhan 11-7, 923F3
Erickson, Milton H 3-25, 279D2
Erim, Nihat 7-19, 567B3
Escobar, Daniel 3-4, 172E1
Espinal Camps, Luis 3-22, 272G1
Etchebaster, Pierre 3-24, 279E2
Evans, Bill 9-15, 755G2
Evers, John W 12-5, 1004E1
Ewing, Oscar R 1-8, 104E2
Fallon, George H 3-21, 279E2
Farago, Ladislas 10-15, 876D1
Farb, Peter 4-8, 360E1
Farr, Thomas Hugh 3-17, 279F2
Farrell, Edelmiro S 10-31, 876E1
Fatha, Mounir 11-5, 873G3
Fernandez, Royes 3-3, 279F2
Fielding, Jerry 2-17, 176A1
Finletter, Thomas K 4-24, 360E1
Fischetti, John R 11-18, 928D2
Fisher, Welthy Honsiger 12-16, 1004E1
Fogerty, Anne 1-15, 104E2
Fontanet, Joseph 2-2, 97C2
Ford, Ita 12-4, 921B1
Fouche, Jacobus Johannes 9-23, 755A3
Franco, Manuel 11-27, 921F1
Frank, Otto 8-19, 676D1
Fraser, Vincent 3-4, 656B1
Friedman, Elizabeth S 10-31, 928E2
Froelich, William J 2-5, 176B1
Froman, Jane 4-23, 360F1
Fromm, Erich 3-18, 279G2
Fuller, Frances 12-18, 1004F1
Furci, Giuseppe 12-1, 944E2
Furlow, Terry 5-23, 656A2
Galindez, Victor 10-26, 876E1
Gallardo, Cesar 9-17, 697A3
Galli, Guido 3-19, 233A2
Gandhi, Sanjay 6-23, 487A2
Gantt, William 2-26, 176B1
Garcia, Eduardo 11-16, 889C1
Garcia, Sara 11-21, 1004F1
Garcia Rodriguez, Felix 9-11, 685A2
Gardiner, Reginald 7-7, 608F1
Garret, Leroy 7-21, 608G1
Garrett, Ray 2-3, 176C1
Gary, Romain 12-2, 1004G1
Gaugauin, Emile 1-6, 104F2
Gear, Luella 4-3, 360G1
Gero, Erno 3-12, 279A3
Giacumbi, Nicola 3-16, 233G1

1976

Gubbins, Colin 2-11, 160D3
Guetenet Zewde 11-9, 1002D1
Gutierrez Ruiz, H (rptd) 5-20, 399E1
Hackett, Bobby 6-7, 524F2
Haddow, Alexander 1-21, 80D3
Haile Mariam, Hassan 7-25, 674B2
Haines, Charles G 5-25, 534F2
Hale, Robert 11-30, 970A2
Halop, Billy 11-9, 970A2
Hamati, Jamil 11-23, 878D2
Hannah, Richard 1-15, 56D3
Harris, Walter 8-8, 816E3
Hart, Philip A 12-6, 1015E1
Harvel, Reginald 9-29, 776E2
Hashisha, Zueir Abou 9-26, 720D3
Hawad, Hali 11-27, 895F1
Hawi, William 7-13, 514F1
Heidegger, Martin 5-26, 404G1-A2
Heisenberg, Werner 2-1, 124D3
Henabery, Joseph 2-18, 192D3
Henderson, Vivian 1-28, 124E3
Herzberg, Joseph 2-12, 160D3
Hill, William Martin 5-18, 524F2
Hodgson, Peter C L 8-6, 892A3
Holmes, Robert D 6-6, 524G2
Hopper, Vincent 1-19, 56D3
Hornblow, Arthur 7-17, 716B3
Howe, James Wong 7-12, 716C3
Hsu Chin-chiang 7-21, 656F3
Hubbard, DeHart 6-23, 524G2
Hughes, Howard 4-5, 335B3
Hughes, Richard 4-28, 368F2
Hull, Lytle 12-11, 1015E1
Hunt, Herold 10-17, 970A2
Ingersoll, Royal 5-20, 404A2
Iselin, Philip 12-28, 1015F1
Ivanissevich, Oscar 6-5, 524G2
Jaber, Fayez 7-3, 485F2
Jaoyyoushi, Mutasem 9-27, 721A1
Jenkinson, Noel 10-9, 774A1
Jimenez Sarmiento, D 8-11, 677D1
Johnson, Guy D (rptd) 9-6, 678B3
Johnson, Malcolm 6-18, 524G2
Johnson, Mordecai 9-11, 716C3
Joseph, Richard 9-30, 970B2
Judd, Neil 12-26, 1015F1
Kahn, Ben 2-5, 124E3
Kampmann, Viggo 6-3, 524A3
Karageorgevich, Prince 9-14, 932E3
Kasahara, Masanori 8-2, 624F2
Kassa, Bewookatu 8-12, 674C2
Kearns, Carroll 6-11, 484E3
Kebede Worku 2-15, 173A1
Kempe, Rudolf 5-11, 524A3
Kenny, Robert W 7-20, 716D3
Kern, Harold 2-19, 192E3
Kerner, Otto 5-9, 368F2
Khalali, Abu Khalidai 7-5, 485F2
Khefacha, Hedi 5-25, 503C3
Kirchwey, Freda 1-3, 56E3
Kiros, Alemayehu 8-26, 674C2
Klenert, Wm Blue (rptd) 9-6, 678B3
Knud, Prince 6-14, 484E3
Kohler, Walter 3-21, 316A1
Kolstad, Thomas (rptd) 9-6, 678B3 ★
Koshevio, Pyotr 8-30, 892A3
Koulidiati, Jean-Luc 9-14, 949F3
Kris Sivara, Gen 4-23, 315E1
Krongard, Robt 8-28, 652G1
Kubitschek, Juscelino 8-23, 836F2
Kuhlman, Kathryn 2-20, 192E3
Kulski, Julian 8-18, 656F3
Kupchan, Morris 10-19, 892B3
Kuwana, Elisha 12-14, 1009C2
Lackey, Kenneth 4-16, 316A1
Laddon, I M 1-14, 80E3
LaGace, Sherry (rptd) 1-27, 80E3
Lang, Fritz 8-2, 816E3
Lanusse, Maria Caride de 2-29, 212B2
Lavon, Pinhas 1-24, 80E3
Lazarsfeld, Paul 8-30, 680F3
Leaf, Munro 12-21, 1015G1
Lehmann, Lotte 8-26, 892B3
Leighton, Margaret 1-13, 56E3
Lentz, Roger Lyle 4-19, 383E3
Lercaro, Giacomo 10-18, 970B2
Leslie, Edgar 1-22, 80E3
Letelier, Orlando 9-21, 710C2
Leventhal, Albert 1-6, 56E3
Levy, Gustave 11-3, 970B2
Lhevinne, Rosina 11-9, 970C2
Li Ta-chang 5-3, 368G2
Limb, Ben 9-21, 1015G1
Lin Yutang 3-26, 316D1
Lippincott, Joseph 10-22, 970C2
Lippisch, Alexander 2-11, 160E3
Lisagor, Peter 12-10, 1015A2
Litton, Jerry (& family) 8-3, 565C2
Liu Wen-hui (rptd) 6-24, 524G3
Loening, Grover 2-29, 192E3
Loftus, John 3-23, 484F3
Long, Herman 8-8, 816F3
Lowry, Judith 11-29, 932E3
Lowry, Laurence 2-23, 192F3
Lozano, Domingo 10-10, 996F1
Lukonin, Mikhail 8-5, 892C3
Lyons, Leonard 10-5, 970C2
Lysenko, Trofim 11-20, 970D2
Macdonald, Torbert 5-21, 404A2
MacInnes, Colin 4-22, 524A3
MacMillan, H R 2-9, 160E3
Madekurozwa, E (rptd) 4-14, 428C2
Maeno Mitsuyasu 3-23, 286B2
Mainbocher 12-27, 1015A2
Mallios, Evanghelos 12-15, 1004A2
Malraux, Andre 11-23, 970D2
Maluf, Chafic 12-27, 1015A2
Manolescu, Gersce 7-12, 649F2
Mantilla, Carlos 7-20, 680F3
Mao Tse-tung 9-9, 657A1
Mariano, Frank 8-8, 892C3
Marin, Edison (rptd) 3-5, 207D3
Marine, David 11-26, 970E2
Martinon, Jean 3-1, 192F3
Mauze, Abby R 5-27, 404B2
McBride, Katherine 6-3, 484F3
McBride, Mary Margaret 4-7, 272F3
McClintock, Robert 11-2, 970E2
McCoy, George Braidwood 12-22, 1015A2

1977

Godfrey, Isidore 9-12, 872A2
Goldblatt, Harry 1-6, 84B3
Goldmark, Peter 12-7, 1024A2
Gonzalez, Ana Maria 1-19, 197E3
Goscinny, Rene 11-5, 952D2
Graiver, David (rptd) 345D2
Grande Garcia, Rutilio 3-12, 207B1
Grauer, Ben 5-31, 452A3
Gregory, Bernard 12-25, 1024A2
Gropper, William 1-6, 84B3
Gross, Mason 10-11, 872B2
Guta Sernesa 11-2, 875E2
Guterma, Alexander L 4-5, 286E3
Guzman Alvergue, Rene 7-1, 542A3
Habe, Hans 9-30, 788C1
Haffejee, Hoosen 8-3, 640F1
Hagstrom, Andrew 10-8, 872B2
Hajari, Cadi Abdullah al- 4-10, 284D3
Hambro, Edvard 2-1, 164G2
Hamer, Fannie Lou 3-14, 264F2
Hamidi, Abdullah Mohammed 10-10, 783F3
Hamidi, Ibrahim al- 10-10, 783F3
Hannon, Thomas 10-20, 807F3
Hardy, Arthur 10-31, 872B2
Harris, Stanley 11-8, 952D2
Hawks, Howard 12-26, 1024B2
Haynes, Robert 7-13, 552F3
Heezen, Bruce C 6-21, 532A3
Hellman, Geoffrey 9-26, 788C1
Henderson, Edwin 2-3, 164A3
Herberg, Will 3-27, 264G2
Hershey, Lewis Blaine 5-20, 452B3
Hill, John 3-17, 264G2
Hillsborough, Robert 6-22, 560E2
Hobbs, Leonard 11-1, 952E2
Hobson, Julius 3-23, 264A3
Holden, David 12-7, 1019D1
Holland, Kenneth 12-9, 1024B2
Holloway, Emory 7-30, 604B3
Hourani, Mohammed Munir 6-13, 457B3
Housewright, James 9-19, 788C1
Houston, Livingston 11-22, 952E2
Howe, Quincy 2-17, 164A3
Hubbard, Cal 10-17, 872C2
Hubley, John 2-21, 164B3
Hughes, James 3-9, 928E1
Hull, Henry 3-8, 264A3
Hull Jr, William R 8-15, 696G2
Hulman Jr, Tony 10-27, 872C2
Hunt, Reed 11-26, 952E2
Husak, Viera 10-20, 872C2
Hutchins, Robert Maynard 5-14, 452B3
Hyams, Leila 12-4, 1024C2
Ilyushin, Sergei (rptd) 2-9, 164B3
Isaac, Bobby 8-14, 696G2
Jackson, Edith 6-5, 535B3
Jackson, Marjorie 5-7, 492F1
Jaffe, Saul 11-1, 952F2
Jain, Shanti Prasad 10-27, 872D2
Jalis, Ibrahim (rptd) 12-5, 967F3
Jaroslawicz, Pinchos (rptd) 9-28, 871B3
Jenan, Ali (rptd) 10-14, 824F1
Johnson, Harry G 5-8, 452C3
Johnson, Lester 4-17, 356B3
Johnson, Nunnally 3-25, 264A3
Johnston, Velma 6-27, 532B3
Jones, James 5-9, 452C3
Jumblat, Kamal 3-16, 188C1
Kabsi, Zaid el- 10-19, 824E1
Kadi, Hamdi 12-26, 995E2
Kamen, Milt 2-24, 164B3
Kaminstein, Abraham 9-10, 788C1
Kannas, Ali (rptd) 10-12, 824F1
Kantor, MacKinlay 10-11, 872D2
Kebede Gebre Michael 12-3, 998F2
Keita, Modibo 5-16, 452D3
Keller, Greta 11-4, 952F2
Keller, James 2-7, 164C3
Kennedy, Walter 6-26, 532B3
Khoram, Avi Ahmad 11-16, 969E2
Kido, Kiochi 4-6, 356C3
Kimpton, Lawrence 11-1, 952F2
King, Carleton 11-19, 952G2
Kintu, Dan (rptd) 8-17, 641A2
Kirks, Rowland 11-2, 952G2
Klein, Jose 10-8, 922A3
Kleinschmidt, Edward E 8-9, 696A3
Knorr, Nathan 6-15, 532C3
Kogler, Rudi 8-6, 624D2
Kompfner, Rudolf 12-3, 1024C2
Krech, David 7-14, 604C3
Lacerda, Carlos 5-21, 452D3
Lalique, Marc 10-26, 872D2
Langer, William 12-26, 1024D2
Langlois, Henri 1-12, 84C3
Larson Leonard (rptd) 6-8, 466E3
Laurence, William 3-19, 264B3
Legesse, Solomon 11-13, 998F2
Levy, David 3-1, 264B3
Levy, George 7-19, 604C3
Lewis, Ross 8-6, 696A3
Lilly, Eli 1-24, 84C3
Lin Li-ming 8-19, 696A3
Litvinov, Ivy 4-28, 356C3
Lollar, Sherman 9-24, 788D1
Lombardi, Ernie 9-26, 788D1
Lombardo, Guy 11-5, 952G2
Lorusso, Pierfrancesco 3-11, 1014F1
Love, Philip 8-17, 696A3
Lowell, Robert 9-12, 788E1
Lowman, Charles 4-17, 356D3
Loza, Elijah Nkwekwe (rptd) 8-1, 640G1
Lucey, Robert 8-1, 696B3
Lunt, Alfred 8-3, 696B3
Lupescu, Magda 6-29, 532C3
Luria, Aleksandr 8-16, 696C3
Luwum, Janani 2-16, 138B3
Ma Chao-chun 9-19, 788F1
Maeda, Seison 10-27, 872E2
Magruder, William 9-10, 788F1
Mahmoud, Capt 10-18, 789A1, 790A1
Makarios, Archbishop 8-3, 616G3-617B2
Malaza, Bonaventura Sipho (rptd) 11-18, 935B1
Maldonado, Osiris 7-6, 636A1
Male, John (rptd) 8-17, 641A2
Mansour, Faiz 6-12, 510F1
Marcus, Edward 4-4, 356D3
Mardersteig, Giovanni 12-27, 1024D2

1978

Haddad, Wadi 3-28, 252G2
Haddad Blanco, Jesus 3-22, 249G2
Haffejee, Hoosen 3-15, 229D3
Haines, Jesse (Pop) 8-5, 708G2
Halprin, Rose 1-8, 96B2
Hamada, Shoji 1-5, 96C2
Hammami, Said 1-4, 3F1
Harrah, William 6-30, 540G2
Harriman, E Roland 2-16, 196A3
Harris, Don 11-18, 889E2
Harris, Vic 2-23, 196B3
Harrod, Roy 3-8, 252A3
Hasatli, Recep 10-3, 822D3
Hasselblad, Victor 8-6, 708A3
Heaney, Denis 6-10, 474E3
Heber, Maria Cecilia Fontana de 9-6, 799F1
Heusler, Rudolf (rptd) 4-12, 438G2
Highet, Gilbert 1-20, 96C2
Homolka, Oscar 1-27, 96D2
Hood, Clifford F (rptd) 11-27, 972C3
Hoshino, Naoki 5-29, 440G2
Humphrey, Hubert 1-13, 32E2
Ibrahim, Mohammed Ahmed 11-15, 885C3
Ivy, Andrew 2-7, 196B3
Jacobs, Paul 1-3, 96D2
Jacopucci, Angelo 7-21, 600B2
James, Charles 9-23, 778D1
James Jr, Daniel 2-25, 196C3
Janhu, Abdul-nur 2-8, 99F1
Jennewein, Carl Paul 2-22, 196C3
Johannesson, Eve Helen 6-27, 519E1
Johannesson, Henry 7-3, 519E1
John Paul I, Pope 9-28, 746B3
Johnson, Sam Houston 12-11, 1032A3
Jones, Blanche Calloway 12-16, 1032A3
Jones, Jim 11-18, 890E1
Kaid, Ahmed 3-5, 252A3
Kanaga, Consuelo 2-28, 196C3
Kappler, Herbert 2-9, 114C3
Kapuuo, Clemens 3-27, 229C2
Karamessines, Thomas 9-4, 778D1
Karasavina, Tamara 5-26, 440G2
Katayama, Tetsu 5-30, 440A3
Katsaris, Maria 11-18, 890G2
Keldysh, Mstislav 6-24, 540A3
Kelso, James L 6-28, 540A3
Kenny, Bill 3-23, 252B3
Kenyatta, Jomo 8-22, 639D1
Ketchum, William M 6-24, 540B3
Khachaturian, Aram 5-1, 440A3
Khaibir, Mir Akbar 4-17, 317E1
Kiernan, Walter 1-8, 96D2
King, Cyril Emanuel 1-2, 96E2
Kipnis, Alexander 5-14, 440A3
Knoll, Michael 10-7, 884G3
Koch, John 4-19, 356A3
Koussevitzky, Olga 1-5, 96E2
Krag, Jens Otto 6-22, 540B3
Kuhne, Marie Peary 4-16, 356A3
Kulakov, Fyodor D 7-16, 620G2
Kuneralp, Nekia 6-2, 476D3
Kuo Mo-jo 6-12, 540B3
Kyazimov, Saladin 6-29, 519A1
Lacy, William S B 12-11, 1032B3
Lamberz, Werner 3-6, 228D1
Lanham, Chas (Buck) 7-20, 620A3
Lapointe, Louis (rptd) 6-29, 515A1
Lasswell, Harold D 12-18, 1032B3
Lawrence, Josephine 2-22, 196D3
Leake, Chauncey 1-11, 96E2
Lear, William Powell 5-14, 440B3
Leavis, Frank Raymond 4-14, 356B3
Leibowitz, Samuel 1-11, 96F2
Linder, Richard 4-16, 356B3
Lo Jui-ching 8-3, 708A3
Lopez, Hermogenes 6-30, 722C2 ★
Lourie, Arthur 10-4, 888B3
Love, Nicholas 3-27, 596A1
Luahine, Iolani 12-11, 1032C3
Lubin, Isador 7-6, 620A3
Lyng, John 1-18, 96F2
MacArthur, John 1-6, 96G2
Maguire, Brian 5-10, 373F2
Mahmoud, Taha 8-2, 582D3
Mahmud, Nusa 6-28, 543A2
Mallowan, Max 8-19, 708B3
Mangena, Alfred 6-28, 594A3
Margain Jr, Hugo 8-29, 690C2
Markov, Georgi Ivanov 9-11, 748C3
Markowski, Paul 3-6, 228D1
Marsters, Joe 5-15, 440B3
Martinez Montenegro, Roberto 2-15, 289F3
Martinson, Harry E 2-11, 196D3
Mason, F van Wyck 8-28, 708B3
Matobako, Jankie Maklomola 3-19, 633C2
Matsumoto, Fujio 10-13, 881C3
McAllister, Miller 4-22, 373D2
McCarthy, Joseph V 1-14, 96G2
McCoy, Tim 1-29, 96G2
McEntee, Patrick 6-25, 630G2
McFall, Robert 8-10, 708B3
McGinley, Phyllis 2-22, 196D3
McGrath, Paul 4-13, 356B3
McKenzie, Bruce 5-24, 479B1
McKerrow, Gavin 1-27, 96A3
Mead, Margaret 11-15, 972D3
Meadows, Algur Hurtle 6-10, 540C3
Meir, Golda 12-8, 1032D1
Mejia Duque, German 9-8, 814A3
Mendes, Francisco 7-7, 620A3
Meneses Cantarero, Edmundo 9-16, 777F1
Menzies, Robert Gordon 5-14, 440B3
Mercader, Ramon 10-18, 888B3
Messel, Oliver 7-13, 620B3
Messerschmitt, Willy 9-15, 778E1
Metcalf, Lee 1-12, 96A3
Metcalfe, Ralph H 10-11, 853B2, 888C3
Mikoyan, Anastas Ivanovich 10-22, 888C3
Milk, Harvey 11-27, 920G1
Miller, Izetta Jewel 11-15, 972D3
Miller, Millie (rptd) 3-2, 167F2
Misha Abdul Aziz, Princess (rptd) 2-1, 172F3
Montoya, Joseph M 6-5, 540C3

1979

Hollister, John Baker 1-4, 104B3
Holmberg, Helena 1-11, 117B1
Hom, William 9-23, 729E2
Hoveida, Amir Abbas 4-7, 276E2
Hughes, Albert W 3-22, 272G2
Hunt, Walter 6-22, 508B3
Hussendair, Hasham 6-1, 414F2
Hutton, Barbara 5-11, 432A3
Ipecki, Abdi 2-1, 117A1
Jacoby, Neil H 5-31, 432A3
Jafari, Fazollah 4-20, 297C3
Jafarian, Bjorkat 2-11, 105G1
Jahanbani, Nader 3-13, 179G3
Jalil, Ghanem Abdul 8-8, 602F2
Jones, Preston 9-19, 756E2
Joos, Kurt 5-22, 432A3
Jouhandeau, Marcel 4-7, 356E3
Jumaa, Saad 8-19, 671E2
Kadar, Jan 6-1, 508B3
Kahn, Albert E 9-15, 756E2
Kahnweiler, Daniel-Henry 1-11, 104B3
Kapler, Aleksei Y (rptd) 9-15, 756F2
Kardelj, Edvard 2-10, 176B3
Karpis, Alvin 8-26, 671E2
Kauffman, Draper L 8-18, 671F2
Kelly, Emmett 3-28, 272G2
Kenton, Stan 8-25, 671F2
Khajenouri, Mohsen 9-24, 814B3
Khalatbari, Abbas Ali 4-11, 276C3
Khalil, Mahmoud Shihadi (rptd) 9-1, 710G3
Khorram, Hassan 5-9, 353D2
Khosrodad, Manucher 2-16, 125E1
Kiewit, Peter 11-2, 932B3
Kleberg Jr, Richard M 5-8, 432B3
Knatchbull, Nicholas 8-27, 641B1
Knowles, John H 3-6, 272A3
Kuznetsov, Anatoly V 6-13, 508C3
La Malfa, Ugo 3-26, 254A3
Lang, Edgar 4-16, 332D1
Larsen, Roy E 9-10, 756F2
Lawrence, Marjorie 1-13, 104C3
Leach, Bernard 5-6, 432B3
Leemans, Alphonse 1-19, 104C3
Leib, Hans Joachim 10-14, 814C3
Leonetti, Tommy 9-15, 756F2
Lessing, Gottfried 6-1, 429B2
Levison, Stanley 9-12, 756G2
Liebes, Ernesto 3-21, 234B3
Lloyd, Sherman P 12-15, 1008C3
Lovelady, Billy Nolan 1-14, 93C2
Lynen, Feodor 8-8, 671G2
Lyon, Ben 3-22, 272A3
Mackay, Donald (rptd) 11-6, 870F2
Mahar, William Ross 8-20, 818B2
Mahjub, Mohammed 8-8, 602F2
Mahlangu, Solomon 4-6, 270B3
Malik, Manucher 2-20, 125F1
Maloney, James 8-9, 727F3
Manion, Clarence E 7-28, 588A3
Marcuse, Herbert 7-29, 588B3
Marques, Rene 3-22, 272B3
Martin-Artajo, Alberto 9-1, 756A3
Marx, Zeppo 11-30, 932B3
Mashambanhaka, Terence 9-16, 718B2
Masie Nguema Biyogo 9-29, 742E1
Massine, Leonide 3-16, 272B3
Matbui, Iraj 9-24, 814B3
Maudling, Reginald 2-14, 176C3
Maxwell, Paul 8-27, 641B1
Maze, Paul 9-17, 756G2
McClusker, Marilyn 10-2, 860G2
McCoy, Van 7-6, 588B3
McDonald, David J 8-8, 671G2
McIntyre, James Francis 7-16, 588B3
McMillan, John L 9-2, 756A3
McNeil, Wilfred 8-30, 671A3
Melnik, Mikhail 3-6, 238D1
Merritt, H Houston 1-9, 104D3
Mesrine, Jacques 11-2, 890A3
Meyer, Andre 9-9, 756B3
Michaux, Andre 3-22, 228B3
Miller, Don C 7-28, 588C3
Minetti, Jean Kerr 12-15, 1008C3
Mingus, Charles 1-5, 104D3
Mini, Adel 4-11, 488F1
Mistrali-Guidotti, Luisa 7-6, 546G3
Mofateh, Mohammed 12-18, 958F2
Moghadam, Nasser 4-11, 276D3
Mohsen, Zahir 7-26, 551G3
Monnet, Jean 3-16, 272C3
Monsarrat, Nicholas 8-7, 671A3
Moriarty, Joseph Vincent 2-24, 176D3
Morris, Joe Alex 2-10, 105B2, 176D3
Morton, Rogers 4-19, 356E3
Motahari, Morteza 5-1, 321D1
Motemadi, Nematollah 2-20, 125F1
Mountbatten, Earl 8-27, 641A1
Mowrer, Elizabeth Hadley 1-22, 104D3
Muir, Malcolm 1-30, 104E3
Muniz, Carlos 4-28, 350G2
Munoz Vazquez, Agustin 3-5, 191E3
Munson, Thurman 8-2, 671A3
Murchison, John D 6-14, 508C3
Murdock, Abe 9-15, 756C3
Murphy, Gardner 3-19, 272D3
Muse, Clarence 10-13, 860G2
Mussolini, Rachele 10-30, 860G2
Nagy, Ferenc 6-12, 508D3
Narayan, Jayaprakash 10-8, 860A3
Nassiri, Nematollah 2-16, 125D1
Nathan, Michael 11-3, 864D3
Natta, Giulio 5-2, 432C3
Nazemi, Fazollah 5-7, 353A2
Nazih, Riza 2-16, 125E1
Neave, Airey 3-30, 254E1
Negrin, Eulalio Jose 11-25, 906B1
Nervi, Pier Luigi 1-9, 104E3
Neto, Agostinho 9-10, 705A2
Newhouse, Samuel I 8-29, 671B3
Novaes, Guiomar 3-7, 272D3
Nuri, Khajeh 4-9, 276B3
Oberon, Merle 11-22, 932C3
Ohlin, Bertil 8-3, 671B3
Oliver, Johnnie L 8-9, 727G3
O'Malley, Walter F 8-9, 671C3
Ortin Gil, Constantino 1-3, 40F1
Ortiz, Octavio 1-20, 59E1
Ottaviani, Alfredo 8-3, 671C3
Pallais Checa, Marcel 10-4, 793F3

1980

Gifford, William 3-9, 279B3
Gil-Robles, Jose Maria 9-14, 755A3
Gimbel, Bruce A 10-7, 876F1
Giri, Varahagiri V 6-24, 528F1
Glenn Jr, B. Duke 12-4, 959F3
Glueck, Sheldon 3-10, 279B3
Golan, Moshe 6-25, 547C2
Goldman, Richard F 1-19, 104F2
Golikov, Filipp (rptd) 7-31, 676E1
Gordon-Walker, Patrick 12-2, 1004A2
Gorman, Patrick E 9-3, 755C3
Gosnjak, Ivan 2-8, 176C1
Gottlieb, Michael 4-8, 360G1
Goubau, Georg 10-17, 876G1
Gouveia, Antonio Patricio 12-4, 923E1
Grayzel, Solomon 8-12, 676E1
Gregg, Peter 12-15, 1004A2
Gregg, Troy Leon 7-30, 654G1
Griffin, John Howard 9-9, 755C3
Griffin, L Francis 1-18, 104F2
Griffith, Hugh 5-14, 448F1
Grubb, David Alexander 7-24, 608A2
Gruen, Victor 2-14, 176D1
Grunwald, Levi Y 4-12, 360A2
Gunning, Robert 2-29, 279C3
Habash, Bassam Mohammed 6-29, 547C2
Haggerty, Patrick E 10-1, 876G1
Hagnes, Helen 7-24, 654A1
Halberstam, Michael J 12-5, 934F3
Hall, Paul 6-22, 528G1
Hardin, Tim 12-29, 1004B2
Harsh, George 1-25, 104G2
Hart, Winsette 1-29, 132B2
Harvey, John 4-24, 321E2
Hass, Eric 10-2, 876A2
Hassan, Baba 6-7, 491D3
Hatam, Hushang 7-14, 545F2
Hayden, Robert 2-25, 176E1
Hayler, Robert W 11-17, 928E2
Haymes, Dick 3-28, 279C3
Hays, Paul 2-13, 176E1
Healey, Giles G 2-29, 279D3
Healy Jr, George W 11-2, 928E2
Heindorf, Ray 2-2, 176F1
Heller, Raymond 1-31, 237A1
Heneries, Richard 4-22, 353A2
Henriquez, Maria Magdalena 10-7, 789D3
Hernandez, Donoteo 11-27, 921F1
Herrington, William 11-15, 888A2
Hicks, Sue Kerr 6-27, 528A2
Hill, Lawrence D 3-26, 460C3
Hill, Ralph L 6-15, 528A2
Hires Jr, Charles E 3-19, 279D3
Hitchcock, Alfred 4-29, 360A2
Hobgood, Norman 3-10, 279E3
Hoffa, Josephine 9-12, 755D3
Hollander, Louis 1-3, 104A3
Holmes Jr, George N 4-24, 321E2
Hoosier, Harlan 1-18, 907E3
Hoskins, Allen 7-26, 608B2
Howard, Elston 12-14, 1004B2
Hurleigh, Robert F 8-10, 676F1
Hurley, Ruby 8-10, 676F1
Ibraimov, Sultan 12-4, 945C3
Ingelfinger, Franz J 3-26, 279E3
Irurzin, Hugo Alfredo 9-18, 697C3
Iturbi, Jose 6-28, 528B2
Jaabari, Mohammed Ali 5-29, 448G1
Jackson, Eddie 7-16, 608B2
Janney, Leon 10-28, 876B2
Janssen, David 2-13, 176F1
Jantar, Anna 3-14, 214B1
Jara, Jose Eduardo 8-2, 603F2
Jarman, Walton Maxey 9-9, 755D3
Jenkins, Ray H 12-26, 1004B2
Jerbo, William (rptd) 5-15, 381F3
Johnson, Dewey L 4-24, 321E2
Johnson, Gerald W 3-23, 279F3
Johnson, Tom 3-14, 214A1
Johnson, Willie 5-3, 448G1
Jones, Howard Mumford 5-11, 448A2
Jones, Lawrence 2-12, 176G1
Jordan, Ralph 7-28, 608C2
Jordan, Wilbur 6-3, 528C2
Joseph, Bernard (Dov) 1-6, 104A3
Journiac, Rene 2-8, 176A2
Jumbaz, Hisham 8-16, 673D3
Kaitcher, Leonard (rptd) 2-9, 194G1
Kaminska, Ida 5-21, 448B2
Kandinsky, Nina 9-3, 755E3
Kaufman, Boris 6-23, 528C2
Kaufman, Walter 9-4, 755E3
Kazel, Dorothy 12-4, 921B1
Kean, Robert Winthrop 9-21, 755F3
Keeney, Barnaby C 6-18, 528C2
Keeton, William 8-17, 676G1
Kendrick, Pearl L 10-8, 876B2
Kennedy, George C 3-18, 279F3
Kenney, Douglas (rptd) 9-1, 755F3
Khama, Seretse 7-13, 562A1
Kim Jae Kyu 5-24, 395F1
King, Charles 4-22, 353A2
King Jr, Richard 3-30, 279G3
Kintner, Robert E 12-20, 1004C2
Kirkus, Virginia 9-10, 755G3
Kokoschka, Oskar 2-22, 176A2
Koksaloglu, Abdurrahman 7-15, 544F3
Koppler, Heinrich (rptd) 5-11, 390E3
Kostelanetz, Andre 1-13, 104A3
Kotelawala, John 10-2, 876C2
Kronenberger, Louis 4-30, 360C2
Labaree, Leonard W 5-5, 448B2
Laker, Edwin Francis 3-1, 279G3
Latham, John 2-21, 176B2
Lauck, Chester 2-21, 176B2
Lavasani, Abbas 5-5, 337F1
Lawzi, Selim al- 3-4, 179F3
Laye, Camara 2-4, 176C2
Leftwich, James T 7-6, 608C2
Leger, Jules 11-22, 928F2
Lennon, John 12-8, 933D2
Lessage, Jean 12-11, 1004D2
Lesser, Sol 9-19, 755G3
Levene, Sam 12-28, 1004D2
Levenson, Sam 8-27, 676G1
Levitt, Arthur 5-6, 448C2
Lewis, Alfred 10-30, 876C2

1976

McDevitt, Ruth 5-27, 524B3
McDonald, Henry 6-12, 524B3
McGuire, John A 5-28, 524B3
McKelway, Benjamin 8-30, 680G3
McKenzie, Andrew 7-10, 519A3
McLaughlin, Charles 2-5, 124E3
McLeod, Fred 5-8, 524B3
McLure, Lynn 3-13, 378A1
Mduli, Joseph 3-19, 428E3
Meinhof, Ulrike 5-9, 383G1
Meloy Jr, Francis 6-16, 425A1
Menshikov, Mikhail 7-21, 716D3
Menzel, Donald 12-14, 1015B2
Mercado, Jose Raquel 4-19, 311C1
Mercer, Johhny 6-25, 524C3
Merchant, Livingston 5-15, 404B2
Metz, James (rptd) 9-6, 678B3
Michelini, Zelmar (rptd) 5-20, 399E1
Mielziner, Jo 3-15, 240D3
Miller, Ruby 4-2, 524C3
Miller, William E 4-12, 316B1
Millet, Fred 1-1, 56F3
Mineo, Sal 2-12, 160F2
Mitchell, Martha 5-31, 404C2
Moffitt, Ronni Karpen 9-21, 710C2
Moghrabi, Zoheir 6-16, 425A1
Mohammed, Murtala 2-13, 141C3
Mohammed, Sidi 4-21, 483D2
Mohapi, Mapetla 8-5, 591G3
Mojuntin, Peter 6-6, 419E1
Monnington, Thomas 1-7, 56F3
Monod, Jacques 5-31, 404D2
Montgomery, Field Marshal 3-24, 240E3
Morand, Paul 7-23, 970E2
Morgan, Gerald 6-15, 484F3
Morison, Samuel 5-15, 368G2
Morton, Louis 2-12, 160F3
Moss, Robert V 10-25, 970E2
Moudour, Ahmed 4-21, 483D2
Moulay Mohammed Ben Arafa, Sidi 7-17, 716E3
Moulder, Morgan Moore 11-12, 1015B2
Moussa, Bayere 4-21, 483D2
Mueller, Frederick H 8-31, 680G3
Murtagh, John 1-13, 56F3 ★
Murtaugh, Danny 12-2, 932F3
Muskhelishvili, Nikolai Ivanovich 7-15, 716E3
Najeimy, Robert 2-17, 125G1
Nash, Dorothy 3-5, 484F3
Nethanyahu, Yehonathan 7-3, 485C1
Neuman, Herman 5-4, 524C3
Nevers, Ernie 5-3, 368A3
Newman, Ceil 2-7, 160G3
Nichols, Barbara 10-5, 970F2
Nikon, Archbishop 9-4, 1015C2
Noe, James 10-18, 970F2
Nordberg, William 10-3, 970F2
North, Joseph 12-20, 1015C2
O'Brien, Henry 7-23, 656F3
O'Malley, Brian 4-6, 267B1
Obrou, Fidel 2-14, 288E2
Occorsio, Vittorio 7-10, 539B1
Ochs, Phil 4-9, 272G3
Odlum, Floyd 6-17, 524C3
Oliva, Chris Ana Olson de 10-20, 996A2
Omar, Khayri Tewfik 12-18, 954A3
Onsager, Lars 10-5, 970G2
Osman, Hassan Hussein 1-23, 502E1
Ospina Perez, Mariano 4-14, 316B1
Packard, Reynolds 10-15, 970G2
Pages, Jean 10-21, 970A3
Panagoulis, Alexandros 5-1, 351D3
Parma, Jimmy (rptd) 10-21, 874B2
Patman, Wright 3-7, 240E3
Pavon, Guillermo 3-29, 264F1
Pedenovi, Enrico 4-29, 333A3
Peive, Jan 9-17, 970A3
Penfield, Wilder 4-5, 316C1
Penido Burnier, Joao Bosco 10-12, 836C1
Pereira da Silva, Armenio 1-1, 11A1
Perrini Guala, Aldo (rptd) 3-5, 207D3
Peterson, Charles 8-4, 892D3
Phillips, Robert 9-20, 1015D2
Piatigorsky, Gregor 8-6, 892D3
Piccioni, Attilio 3-10, 240F3
Pimsleur, Paul 6-22, 524D3
Piston, Walter 11-12, 970A3
Plummer Jr, Chester 7-25, 860E1
Polanyi, Michael 2-22, 192F3
Ponce, Camilo 9-14, 1015D2
Pons, Lily 2-13, 160G3
Pontes, Paulo 12-28, 1015D2
Qazi Nazrul Islam 8-29, 1015F1
Radziwill, Stanislas 6-27, 524D3
Rajaonah, Pierre 7-30, 926C1
Rakotomalala, Joel 7-30, 926A1
Ranucci, Christian 7-28, 588E3
Rascovich, Mark 12-10, 1015D2
Rathbone, Monroe 8-2, 816F3
Ray, Man 11-18, 970A3
Razak, Abdul 1-14, 55F2
Rebelo Teixeira, Celestino 1-1, 11A1
Redfield, William 8-17, 892D3
Reed, Carol 4-25, 368A3
Reichmann, John 2-2, 124F3
Reiman, Pavel 11-1, 932F3
Rethberg, Elisabeth 6-6, 444G2
Reyes, Rafael 2-11, 212E1
Reynolds, Milton 1-23, 80F3
Richter, Hans 2-1, 124F3
Roark, William (rptd) 9-6, 678B3
Robeson, Paul 1-23, 80F3
Roche, Josephine A 7-29, 716E3
Rodriguez, Fernando 6-15, 522C2
Rodriguez, Jorge Antonio 7-25, 592B3
Rodriguez, Jose (rptd) 8-6, 874A3
Rodriguez de Valcarcel, A 10-22, 1015E2
Rodriquez Fabregat, E 11-21, 970B3
Rolfe, Sidney 3-10, 240F3
Roos, J L 7-15, 539F2
Rose, Alex 12-28, 1015E2
Rosebury, Theodor 11-25, 1015E2
Rosenstiel, Lewis 1-21, 80G3
Rosenthal, Harold 8-11, 578B3
Roy, Mike 6-26, 524E3
Ruggieri, Pasquin 9-25, 773A1
Ruggieri, Xavier 9-25, 773A1

1977

Mark, Julius 9-7, 788F1
Markel, Lester 10-23, 872E2
Marlborough, Duchess of 10-13, 872E2
Marschak, Jacob 7-27, 604D3
Marshall, SLA 12-17, 1024E2
Martinez, Jose 10-26, 921C3
Marx, Groucho (Julius) 8-20, 696D3
Marx, Gummo (Milton) 4-21, 356D3
Massamba-Debat, Alphonse 3-25, 282G2
Masterman, John 6-6, 532D3
Matthews, Herbert 7-30, 604D3
Matti, Rodolfo 10-26, 921C3
McCarroll, Marion C 8-4, 696D3
McClellan, John 11-27, 952A3
McClure, Don 3-27, 328F1
McCulloch, Robert 2-25, 164C3
Mehu, Delorme 7-3, 583C2
Melville, Ward 6-5, 532D3
Meusel, Bob 11-28, 952B3
Miles, Joseph 7-13, 552F3
Miller, Eric 9-22, 788G1
Miller, Harry Willis 1-1, 84C3
Milstone, Jacob 1-27, 164D3
Mingas, Saidi V D (rptd) 5-29, 424A2
Mobutu, Marie 10-22, 872F2
Molina Canas, Raul 11-12, 969G3
Molokwana, Nicholas 9-26, 825C3
Moqarrebi, Ahmed 12-25, 1019F1
Moran, Lord 4-12, 356E3
Morehouse, Clifford 2-17, 164D3
Morgenstern, Oskar 7-26, 604D3
Morton, Wm Hastings 3-10, 238E3
Moskowitz, Stacy 7-31, 641D3
Mostel, Zero 9-8, 788G1
Mowrer, Edgar Ansel 3-2, 264C3
Moyo, Jason 1-22, 49D2
Mulugetta Alemu 8-3, 649C1
Murayama, Nagataka 8-7, 696E3
Murphy, Charles 9-20, 788A2
Muschenheim, Carl 4-27, 356E3
Musial, Joe 6-6, 532E3
Nabokov, Vladimir 7-2, 604E3 ★
Nairac, Robert (rptd) 5-16, 487F2
Nangolo, Filemon 5-30, 457E2
Nash, John 9-23, 788B2
Negussie Negassa 4-8, 328D1
Ngouabi, Marien 3-18, 220A2
Nin, Anais 1-14, 84D3
Nobadula, Mzukisi (rptd) 12-26, 1016C3
Novillo, Horacio 1-18, 197F3
Noyes, Eliot 7-17, 604E3
Noyes, Nicholas 12-25, 1024E2
Nyabadza, Basil 4-1, 297C1
O'Brien, Davey 11-18, 952B3
O'Donnell, Kenneth 9-9, 788B2
O'Neill, Shane 6-23, 1024F2
Oboth-Ofumbi, ACK 2-16, 138C3
Ofer, Avraham 1-4, 8E1
Oryema, Erenaya 2-16, 138C3
Palmedo, Roland 3-15, 264C3
Papa, Vincent 7-26, 642B1
Pardo Leon, Alberto 12-22, 1011A2
Patocka, Jan 3-13, 204C3, 220F2
Patterson, Russell 3-17, 264D3
Paul, Alice 7-9, 604E3
Paul, William 12-19, 1024F2
Pawley, William 1-7, 84D3
Payne, Paul 12-2, 1024G2
Payne, Virginia 2-10, 164D3
Pedro, Purificacion (rptd) 7-31, 618E3
Peer, Lyndon 10-8, 872F2
Pellicer, Carlos 2-16, 164E3
Perdue, Arthur 6-27, 532E3
Persons, Wilton 9-5, 788C2
Petrie, Charles 12-13, 1024G2
Petrovic, Dusan 7-21, 604F3
Pi Ting-chun (rptd) 7-25, 706A2
Pignatari, Francisco 10-27, 872F2
Pistolesi, Angelo 12-28, 1014E2
Pitts, Robert 6-6, 532E3
Pollack, James 3-15, 264D3
Poma, Roberto (rptd) 2-25, 182B1
Ponto, Jurgen 7-30, 601A3
Powell, Clilan 9-22, 788C2
Powers, Francis Gary 8-1, 696E3
Powers, John 7-19, 604F3
Presley, Elvis 8-16, 695C3
Prevert, Jacques 4-11, 356F3
Prinze, Freddie 1-29, 84E3
Prio Soccarras, Carlos 4-4, 356F3
Pyjas, Stanislaw 5-7, 436F3
Rabbo, Jaber Abed 1-6, 2D2
Radcliffe, Viscount 4-2, 356G3
Rapoport, Miguel 2-5, 197G3
Raspe, Jan-Carl 10-18, 790D2
Rattigan, Terence 11-30, 952B3
Rayi, Hassan 1-6, 2E2
Razouk, Abdul Hamid 6-18, 496E2
Richardson, Ronald J (rptd) 3-26, 373G3
Ritchard, Cyril 12-18, 1024G2
Roberts, Clifford 9-29, 788D2
Robinson, Jacob 10-24, 872G2
Rocca, Antonino 3-15, 264D3
Rodriguez, Santos (rptd) 9-29, 821D1
Romm, May 10-15, 872G2
Rootes, Reginald 12-20, 1024A3
Roque, Julio 5-29, 522F3
Roschmann, Eduard (rptd) 8-11, 670D3
Rosendahl, Charles E 5-14, 452E3
Roslavleva, Natalia 1-2, 84E3
Ross, Nellie 12-19, 1024A3
Rossellini, Roberto 6-3, 532F3
Rossi, Walter 9-30, 1014C2
Rostand, Jean 9-3, 788D2
Rubenstein, Jorge (rptd) 12-10, 982C1
Rubio Diaz, Jose M (rptd) 3-1, 223G2
Ruiz, Julian 8-4, 696F3
Rupp, Adolph 12-10, 1024B3
Russell Jr, Arthur 12-4, 1024B3
Russo, Giuseppe 8-21, 1014C3
Sabah al-Salem al-Sabah 12-31, 1019A2
Saleh, Mahmoud 1-3, 9C1
Salgado, Salomon 2-11, 182B1
Sampson, William 2-15, 160E2
Sanchez, Manuel Antonio 2-17, 182B1
Sandburg, Lillian 2-18, 164E3 ★
Sanguyo, Benjamin 9-1, 747A1
Saypol, Irving 6-30, 532F3
Scanlon, Robert (rptd) 10-9, 805F1
Schermerhorn, Willem 3-12, 264E3

1978

Moon, Keith 9-7, 778F1
Moore, Henry 3-12, 252B3
Moreell, Ben 7-30, 620B3
Moro, Aldo 5-9, 337A2
Morris (the cat) 7-7, 620B3
Morrison, Bret 9-25, 778F1
Mortimer, Charles G 12-25, 1032C3
Moscone, George 11-27, 920G1
Moureu, Henri (rptd) 7-20, 620C3
Mughrabi, Dalal 3-11, 175C3
Mujia, Mario 7-22, 722B2 ★, 723E2-F2
Mullin, Willard 12-21, 1032C3
Muqbil, Abdul Salam 11-15, 885C3
Murphy, Robert 1-9, 96A3
Murphy, William 1-29, 96B3
Mustafa, Shukri Ahmed 3-19, 211E2
Nabokov, Nicholas 4-6, 356C3
Nahury, Elias 6-10, 454E3
Naif, Abdul Razak al- 7-10, 522E2
Nebel, Long John 4-10, 356C3
Nikodim, Metropolitan 9-25, 778G1
Nobile, Umberto 7-29, 620C3
Noble, Ray 4-3, 356C3
Norrish, Ronald G W 6-7, 540D3
O Dalaigh, Cearbhall 3-21, 252B3
O'Neill, C William 8-20, 708C3
Obenshain, Richard 8-2, 645A3
Obolensky, Serge 9-29, 778G1
Orsini, Dominique 4-10, 396G2
Osorio, Guillermo (rptd) 3-8, 189C1
Oswald, Barbara Ann 5-24, 1029F1
Ottolina, Renny 3-16, 231A1
Oz, Dogan 3-24, 230G1
Padilla, Miguel Tobias 4-11, 285A3
Paisley, John (rptd) 10-1, 835D3
Paley, Barbara (Babe) 7-6, 620D3
Palma, Riccardo 2-14, 133D1
Paolella, Alfredo 10-11, 817B1
Pardo Buelvas, Rafael 9-12, 814B3
Parks, Patricia 11-18, 889E2
Paul VI, Pope 8-6, 601A1
Payne, Frederick George 6-15, 540D3
Pei, Mario 3-2, 252C3
Perez Rodriguez, Juan 7-21, 575E3
Perez Vega, Reynaldo 3-8, 192A2
Pervukhin, M G (rptd) 7-25, 620D3
Peterson, Ronnie 9-11, 778A2
Philippe, Claudius C 12-25, 1032D3
Pierson, Warren Lee 1-12, 96C3
Pillay, Moonsamy (rptd) 1-2, 20F2
Pineda, Robert 5-3, 539C3
Pi Shu-shih, Ignatius 5-16, 440C3
Pittman, Portia 2-26, 196E3
Pollak, Emile 1-6, 96C3
Portell, Jose Maria 6-28, 537D2
Portes Gil, Emilio 12-10, 1032D3
Poulter, Thomas C 6-14, 540E3
Poynter, Nelson 6-15, 540F3
Prescott, Robert W 3-3, 252C3
Prima, Louis 8-24, 708C3
Prouvost, Jean 10-17, 888D3
Purtell, William A 5-31, 440C3
Quick, Armand J 1-26, 96C3
Ramirez Lima, Samuel Humberto 6-20, 497G1
Rankin, Jacob 7-4, 630B3
Rattner, Abraham 2-14, 196E3
Ray, Joie 5-13, 440D3
Reid, Rose Marie 12-18, 1032D3
Reutershan, Paul 12-14, 984D1
Rich, Lorimer 6-2, 540F3
Ritter, Willis 3-4, 252C3
Roberts, Gilbert 1-1, 96D3
Robertson, James R 8-1, 708D3
Robinson, Gregory 11-18, 889E2
Robson, Mark 6-20, 540F3
Rockefeller 3d, John D 7-10, 620D3
Rockwell, George L 3-3, 252D3
Rockwell, Norman 11-8, 972E3
Rockwell, Willard F 10-16, 888D3
Rodriguez, Carlos Alberto 9-18, 823A3
Rodriguez, Ruben Alfonso 9-16, 823G2
Romero, Juan de Jesus 7-30, 620E3
Rosen, Pinhas 5-3, 440D3
Ross, Roy 1-8, 96D3
Rothermere, Viscount 7-12, 620F3
Rubaya Ali, Salem 6-26, 498E3
Rubicam, Raymond 5-8, 440D3
Rubin, Gail 3-11, 175A2
Rubirosa Fermin, Guillermo 3-26, 292C2
Rueda Sierra, Agustin 3-13, 249A3
Rueff, Jacques Leon 4-23, 356D3
Ryan, Leo J 11-18, 889A1
Saikhanov, Aziz 6-29, 519A1
Saleh, Jasem 6-26, 499B1
Sanchez Ramos, Juan 7-21, 575E3
Santoro, Antonio 6-6, 453D2
Saqqaf, Salem al- 11-15, 885C3
Sawyer, Ralph A 12-6, 1032E3
Sayed, Abu 3-8, 157C2 ★
Schwendler, William 1-14, 96E2
Scott, Paul 3-1, 252E3
Searle, John 1-21, 96E3
Sebai, Youssef el- 2-18, 117C1
Selwyn-Lloyd, Lord 5-17, 440E3
Serly, Tibor 10-8, 888E3
Shabangu, Samuel 6-29, 633G2
Shaer, Musieh (rptd) 2-1, 172F3
Shaw, Robert 8-28, 708D3
Shay, Dorothy 10-22, 888E3
Sheekman, Arthur 1-12, 96E3
Shevchenko, Leongina I 5-8, 440E3
Shishkin, Julius 10-28, 888E3
Shiyanga, Toivo 2-7, 114B1
Siegbahn, Manne 9-26, 778A2
Sigcau, Botha 12-1, 1032E3
Simeonov, Vladimir 10-2, 749A1
Smith, W Eugene 10-15, 888F3
Sobukwe, Robert 2-27, 196E3
Soilih, Ali 5-29, 445B2
Sonnenberg, Benjamin (rptd) 9-18, 778A2
Sporn, Philip 1-24, 96F3
Sproul, Allan 4-9, 356D3
Spungen, Nancy 10-12, 841C1
Steiger, William A 12-4, 1032E3
Steinberg, William 5-16, 440E3
Stevens, Ann 12-4, 1032A1
Still, William 12-3, 1032F3
Stone, Edward Durell 8-6, 708E3

1979

Paray, Paul 10-10, 860B3
Park Chung Hee 10-26, 821A1
Parks Jr, Gordon 4-3, 356F3
Parsons, Talcott 5-8, 432C3
Partridge, Eric 6-1, 508D3
Payne-Gaposhkin, Cecelia 12-6, 1008D3
Peach, Blair 4-24, 313B1
Perelman, S J 10-17, 860C3
Perez Alfonzo, Juan Pablo 9-3, 756C3
Piasecki, Boleslaw 1-1, 104F3
Pickford, Mary 5-29, 432D3
Pinilla, Jose M 8-10, 671D3
Pious, Minerva 3-16, 272D3
Porter, J Robert 8-9, 727F3
Pospelov, Pyotr 4-24, 356F3
Potofsky, Jacob S 8-5, 671D3
Potter, Charles Edward 11-23, 932D3
Power, Donald C 3-11, 272E3
Prokes, Michael 3-13, 220C1
Qaraneh, Mohammed Wali 4-23, 297C1
Rabii, Amir Hussein 4-9, 276B3
Rabinowitz, Yehoshua 8-12, 671E3
Radzievsky, Alexei 9-3, 756D3
Rahimi, Amir 2-16, 125E1
Rand, Sally 8-31, 671E3
Randolph, A Philip 5-16, 432E3
Ratia, Armi 10-3, 860C3
Ray, Nicholas 6-1, 508D3
Reitsch, Hanna 8-30, 671E3
Renoir, Jean 2-13, 176D3
Revercomb, Wm Chapman 10-6, 860C3
Rhys, Jean 5-4, 432E3
Richards, I A 9-7, 756D3
Richards, James P 2-21, 176E3
Riperton, Minnie 7-12, 588C3
Robb, Inez 4-4, 356F3
Rockefeller, Nelson Aldrich 1-26, 103E3
Rodgers, Richard 12-30, 1008D3
Rodriguez Cristobal, Angel 11-11, 904B3
Rolf, Ida P 3-19, 272E3
Roman, Jo 6-10, 521B2
Romero, Jose Ernesto 2-10, 234D3
Romero, Jose Javier 9-6, 686B1
Roosevelt, Archibald 10-13, 860D3
Rosenbloom, Carroll 4-2, 356G3
Rosenwald, Lessing J 6-24, 508E3
Rossa, Guido 1-24, 98C1
Rotton, Alan H 10-18, 787C3
Rovere, Richard H 11-23, 932D3
Rudolph, Marvin (Mendy) 7-4, 588C3
Ryall, George Francis 10-8, 860D3
Ryan, Elizabeth 7-6, 570C1
Saadatmand, Hassan 5-9, 353D2
Salameh, Ali Hassan 1-22, 51A1
Saltonstall, Leverett 6-17, 508E3
Sampson, William 11-3, 864D3
Saville, Victor 5-8, 432F3 .
Sawyer, Charles 4-7, 356G3
Schenken, Howard 2-20, 176E3
Schettini, Italo (rptd) 3-30, 269F1
Schultz, Henry E 5-5, 432F3
Seaton, George 7-28, 588D3
Seberg, Jean (rptd) 9-8, 704G3
Seeger, Charles L 2-7, 176F3
Seiberling, Henrietta Buckler 12-6, 1008E3
Serrano, Apolinaro 9-30, 790B3
Sheen, Fulton J 12-9, 1008E3
Shimada, Mitsuhiro 2-1, 98E2
Short, Dewey 11-19, 932E3
Shumlin, Herman 6-14, 508E3
Sibeko, David 6-12, 476G3
Simonov, Konstantin 8-28, 671F3
Simons, Arthur D 5-21, 432F3
Singer, John 1-18, 94B1
Sirt, Walid Mahmoud 8-8, 602F2
Skinner, Cornelia Otis 7-9, 588D3
Slovik, Antoinette 9-7, 756D3
Smith, Charlie 10-5, 860E3
Smith, Sandy 11-3, 864D3
Soderberg, C Richard 10-17, 860E3
Soldati, Francisco 11-13, 906E2
Solovyev-Sedov, Vasily 12-2, 1008F3
Sorg, Herbert Peter 3-11, 272E3
Speranzo, Dimicius 4-4, 266F2
Stafford, Jean 3-26, 272F3
Stakman, Elvin Charles 1-22, 104F3
Stewart, Bill 6-20, 461F2
Straub, Karel 3-22, 228E2
Strauss, Anna Lord 2-23, 176F3
Strong, Ken 10-5, 860E3
Sugiufa, Kanematsu 10-21, 860F3
Svoboda, Ludvik 9-20, 756E3
Sykes, Richard 3-22, 228E2
Tabanero Perez, Pedro 8-14, 670F2
Taghi, Mohammed 4-20, 297C3
Taheri, Monir 2-23, 144B3
Taleghani, Mahmoud 9-10, 687G3-688C1
Taraki, Nur Mohammad 10-9, 787D2
Tarkani, Taghi Haj 7-8, 525E1
Tate, Allen 2-9, 176G3
Teekah, Vincent 10-24, 838B2
Teitelbaum, Joel 8-19, 671F3
Templer, Gerald Walter 10-25, 860F3
Terranova, Cesare 9-25, 793C2
Tikhonov, Nicolai S 2-8, 176G3
Tiomkin, Dimitri 11-11, 932F3
Tolstoy, Alexandra 9-26, 756E3
Tomonaga, Shinichero 7-8, 588E3
Tongogara, Josiah 12-29, 976A1
Travis, Robert 11-19, 932F3
Tugwell, Rexford Guy 7-21, 588E3
Turano, Giuseppe 7-12, 548B1
Unsoeld, Willi(am F) 3-4, 272F3
Utuka, E K 6-16, 468D3
Valles, Lorenzo Gonzales 9-23, 754G1
Vance, Vivian 8-17, 671F3
Van Slyke, Helen 7-3, 588F3
Vargas Garayar, Julio 1-20, 51G3
Varisco, Antonio 7-13, 584A1
Velasco Ibarra, Jose Maria 3-30, 272G3
Velikovsky, Immanuel 11-17, 932F3
Viansson-Ponte, Pierre 5-7, 432G3
Vicious, Sid 2-2, 156B3
Villot, Jean Cardinal 3-9, 272G3
Vlasenko, Y 3-28, 237E3
Von Dyck, Elisabeth 5-4, 374E2

1980

Lewis, Harold 4-24, 321E2
Libby, Willard F 9-8, 756A1
Lieb, Fred 6-3, 528D2
Linge, Heinz 3-17, 280A1
Livingston, David 9-19, 765C2
Loden, Barbara (rptd) 9-22, 756B1
Longley, James B 8-16, 676A2
Longo, Luigi 10-16, 876D2
Longworth, Alice 2-20, 176C2
Lowenstein, Allard 3-14, 214C2
Ludman, Anna Maria 3-28, 255B1
Lundvall, Bjoern (rptd) 9-22, 756C1
Lye, Len 5-15, 448C2
MacAusland, Earle 6-4, 528D2
Mackey, Bernard 3-5, 280B1
Macon, Robert C 10-27, 876E2
Maguire, Anne 1-21, 59D1
Malik, Yakov 2-11, 176D2
Mallory, Walter H 6-17, 528E2
Mandelstam, Nadezhda 12-29, 1004E2
Mann, Katharina 4-18, 360C2
Mann, Marty 7-22, 608D2
Mantovani, Annunzio Paolo 3-29, 280B1
Marini, Marino 8-6, 676B2
Marquard, Richard 6-1, 528E2
Martin, Strother 8-1, 676B2
Martin Jr, William T 10-13, 876F2
Martinez, Maria 7-20, 608D2
Mattarella, Piersanti 1-6, 20B3
Matthias, Bernd T 10-27, 876F2
Mauchly, John W 1-8, 104B3
Mayo, Joel C 4-24, 321F2
McCarty, Mary 4-5, 360D2
McCormack, John W 11-22, 928G2
McCoy, Andre 3-14, 214A1
McCulloch, William 2-22, 176E2
McDonnell Jr, James S 8-22, 676C2
McEwen, John 11-20, 928A3
McFarlane, William 2-18, 176E2
McGann, Roy 10-14, 791D3
McGinn, Hugh 12-28, 994E1
McIntosh, Lynn D 4-24, 321F2
McKelway, St Clair 1-10, 104C3
McLean, Robert 12-5, 1004F2
McLuhan, Herbert Marshall 12-31, 1004F2
McMillan, Charles T 4-24, 321F2
McQueen, Steve 11-7, 928B3
McWilliams, Carey 6-27, 528F2
Meany, George L 1-10, 14G2
Medford, Kay 4-10, 360E2
Meeker, Richard C 10-15, 890A2
Mehdiyan, Sayed 8-15, 644E2
Mendoza, Humberto 11-27, 921F1
Mercer, David 8-8, 676C2
Milestone, Lewis 9-25, 756C1
Miller, Henry 6-7, 528F2
Mills, Al 2-26, 190A3
Mills, Daphene 2-27, 190A3
Mills, Jeannie 2-26, 190A3
Minervini, Giroloma 3-18, 233G1
Mingo, Norman 5-8, 448D2
Mohammed, Faiz 9-14, 727G2
Mohammed, Nazar 9-14, 727G2
Molina Orantes, Adolfo 1-31, 98C2
Monroney, Mike 2-13, 176F2
Morgenthau, Hans J 7-19, 608E2
Mosley, Oswald 12-2, 1004A3
Mueller, Merrill 12-1, 1004B3
Muhlenberg, Frederick A 1-19, 104C3
Munoz Marin, Luis 4-30, 360E2
Murray, Stuart S 9-19, 756D1
Nafa, Mahmoud 4-25, 353A3
Narimisa, Ismail 6-29, 507B1
Neal, David 4-22, 353G1
Nenni, Pietro 1-1, 104C3
Neumann, Emanuel 10-26, 876G2
Newell, Charles 1-17, 907E3
Ngoyi, Lillian 3-12, 280C1
Nielsen, Arthur C 6-1, 528A3
Niles, John Jacob 3-1, 280D1
Nolan, Bob 6-16, 528A3
Nugent, Elliott 8-9, 676D2
O'Connell, John F 2-27, 176G2
Ohira, Masayoshi 6-12, 434C3
Okun, Arthur 3-23, 280D1
Olivier, George Borg 10-29, 876A3
O'Neil, Barbara 9-3, 756D1
O'Neill, Ralph A 10-23, 876A3
Orellana, Melvin Rigoberto 10-10, 829D2
Ormskerk, Frits 5-2, 410G2
Owen, Johnny 11-3, 907A3
Owens, Jesse 3-31, 280E1
Ozmen, Jalip 7-31, 606A1
Paasio, Rafael 3-17, 280F1
Page, Joe 4-21, 360F2
Pahlevi, Mohammed Riza 7-27, 571B1
Pak Hung Ju 3-6, 195E3
Pal, George 5-2, 448D2
Paleckis, Justas 1-26, 176G2
Pallotto, Marino (rptd) 8-1, 605G1
Paoletti, Paolo 2-5, 99C1
Paputin, Viktor S 1-3, 26B2
Parker, Clarence 4-22, 353A2
Parsa, Farrokhrou 5-8, 373E1
Partsalides, Dimitrios 6-22, 528B3
Patrick, Gail 7-6, 608F2
Patterson, William A 6-13, 528C3
Patterson, William L 3-5, 280F1
Pehrson, Wilfred R 10-14, 876B3
Peshkin, M Murray 8-17, 676D2
Peter, Prince 10-16, 876C3
Petri, Louis 4-7, 360G2
Petrou, Pandelis 1-16, 150D3
Petrov, Boris N (rptd) 8-26, 676E2
Pezzoli, Roberto 12-11, 966C3
Phillip, Strachen 6-20, 498D2
Phillips, Dayton 10-23, 876C3
Phillips, James 4-22, 353G1
Piaget, Jean 9-16, 756E1
Pierre, James 4-22, 353A2
Pignedoli, Sergio 6-15, 528C3
Plambeck, Juliane 7-25, 581C1
Poe, James 1-24, 176A3
Pollan, Clayton 9-13, 756F1
Portella Nunes, Petronio 1-6, 104E3
Porter, Katherine Anne 9-18, 756G1
Powers, John A (Shorty) 1-1, 104E3

1976

Rukhin, Yevgeny 5-24, 404D2
Rupp 3d, Paul 8-3, 565D2
Rupp Jr, Paul 8-3, 565D2
Russell, Rosalind 11-28, 932F3
Ruzicka, Leopold 9-26, 932G3
Ryle, Gilbert 10-6, 932G3
Saab, Edouard 5-16, 354D3
Saeed, Mohammed Nur 8-5, 592D2
Safaie, Kohsrow 5-4, 365E2
Salinas, Cesar Augusto 6-25, 926G1
Sammarraye, Abdel 7-3, 484F2
Sanjuan, Pedro 10-18, 970B3
Sansom, William 4-20, 524E3
Santucho, Mario Roberto 7-19, 571E1
Satyukov, Pavel 11-17, 970B3
Savloff, Guillermo 1-21, 96A2
Sayed, Abdel Wahab al- 12-24, 973F2
Scherer, Mario (rptd) 6-9, 557D3
Schmitt, Adolf Gregor 12-15, 1009D2
Schoene, Lester 7-19, 656G3
Schoonmaker, Frank 1-11, 56G3
Schuts, Ruby 10-27, 1015F2
Scott, Winston 8-9, 892E3
Scudder, John 12-6, 1015F2
Sebilleau, Pierre 11-6, 910G1
Servais, Jean 2-17, 192G3
Serwaniko, John (rptd) 10-7, 874C2
Shaffer, Laurance 7-20, 716F3
Shamsabadi, Abolhassan (rptd) 5-17, 365C3
Shelly, Mary Josephine 8-6, 892E3
Sheriff, Ahmed Fuad 8-6, 892E3
Shimada, Shigetaro 6-7, 524E3
Shobek, Michaiah 10-19, 1012D2
Shtemenko, Sergei 4-23, 368A3
Silvert, Kalman 6-15, 524F3
Sim, Alastair 8-20, 892F3
Singh, Jagjit 8-7, 892F3 *
Sirit, Oscar 2-16, 125B2
Sisay Habte (rptd) 7-13, 523D3
Sissman, Louis 3-10, 316C1
Skaggs, Marion 5-8, 484G3
Smith, Donald G 8-28, 652G1
Smith, Frederick 8-14, 656G3
Smith, Gerald L K 4-15, 316C1
Smith, H Allen 2-23, 192G3
Snyder, Jerome 5-2, 524F3
Soares, Francisco 2-13, 212G1
Solano Lopez, Miguel 12-14, 1015G2
Somsak Tanthansen 12-22, 1013D3
Soria, Carmelo 7-16, 963B2
Sowinski, Rose Marie 3-15, 260A1
Stagg, Francis 2-12, 146C2
Stepanov, Sergei 10-24, 857G1
Stephens, Mohammed Fuad 6-6, 419D1
Stern, Susan 7-31, 892F3
Strand, Paul 3-31, 272F3
Streeter, Edward 3-7, 484G3
Strelsin, Alfred 8-25, 892G3
Sullivan, Frank 2-19, 192G3
Sulong, Saleh 6-6, 419E1
Symes, James 8-3, 892G3
Tarquini, Jose Miguel 2-5, 212A2
Thaler, Seymour 2-5, 124F3
Thomas, James 1-23, 80G3
Thomson of Fleet, Lord 8-4, 816G3
Thorndike, Sybil 6-9, 444G2
Thornton, Dan 1-18, 80G3
Tobey, Mark 4-24, 368A3
Tolpo, Carl 9-25, 892G3
Tolstoy, Mary 11-21, 970C3
Torres, Juan Jose (rptd) 6-2, 415D2
Travers, Howard 12-25, 1015G2
Trumbo, Dalton 9-10, 1015G2
Tshazibane, W (rptd) 12-13, 1010G2
Ugarte Roman, Marta 9-12, 963A2
Uihlein, Robert 11-12, 970C3
Unterman, Issar 1-26, 124G3
Urteaga, Jose 7-19, 571E1
Vaez-Zaden, Parviz 12-23, 1012F3
Van den Berg, Maria F 12-5, 1009D2
Varga, Laslo 8-11, 624E3
Vera Serafin, Aldo 10-25, 844C3
Vilim, Blazej 9-23, 1015A3
Villegas, Daniel Cosio 3-10, 240G3
Visconti, Luchino 3-30, 240G3
Vishniak, Mark 11-30, 1015A3
Voon, Chong Tian 6-6, 419E1
Waithayakon, Wan 9-5, 970B3
Wali, Sayed el- 6-8, 466A3
Walsh, Eric (rptd) 5-6, 524G3
Waring, Robert O 6-16, 425A1
Warneke, Lon 6-23, 524G3
Warner, Roger S 8-3, 716F3
Washington, Ned 12-20, 1015A3
Waters, Samuel E (rptd) 9-6, 678B3
Weggarten, Possenti 12-5, 1009D2
Weigle, Luther 9-2, 1015B3
Weingarten, Violet 7-17, 716G3
Wheeler, Mortimer 7-23, 716G3
Whipple, George 2-1, 124G3
White, Minor 6-24, 524G3
Whitelaw, Wm Rosario (rptd) 5-20, 399F1
Wiener, Alexander 11-6, 970D3
Wolfenstein, Martha 11-30, 1015B3
Wolfgang, Myra 4-12, 316D1
Wright, Russell 12-22, 1015C3
Yakubovsky, Ivan 11-30, 932G3
Young, John 1-12, 56G3
Zdvic, Edvin 2-7, 224E1
Zeckendorf, William 9-30, 970D3
Zukor, Adolph 6-10, 444A3

1977

Schild, Alfred 5-24, 452E3
Schippers, Thomas 12-16, 1024B3
Schleyer, Hanns-Martin 10-18, 791E1
Schoeffler, Paul 11-21, 952C3
Schorer, Mark 8-11, 696F3
Schumacher, E F 9-4, 788D2
Schumann, Jurgen 10-16, 789G1
Schuschnigg, Kurt von 11-18, 952C3
Schuyler, George 8-31, 788E2
Schwer, Francis 10-20, 921B3
Sebuliba, Mark (rptd) 8-17, 641A2
Shafizadeh, Abraham (rptd) 7-29, 871D3
Shankar, Uday 9-26, 788E2
Sharp, John 1-15, 84E3
Shashin, Valentin D 3-22, 306C3
Shaw, Lawrence Timothy 3-19, 264E3
Sheldon, William 9-19, 788F2
Shipton, Eric 3-28, 264F3
Shor, Bernard 'Toots' 1-22, 84F3
Shuster, George 1-25, 84F3
Sinatra, Natalie 1-6, 84G3
Skochilov, Anatoly 7-7, 604F3
Slesinger, Donald 10-13, 872G2
Smit, Jeanne-Cora 11-23, 934E3
Smit, Robert 11-23, 934E3
Smith, Mayo 11-24, 952D3
Smith, Oliver 12-25, 1024C3
Solar, Ricardo 10-23, 921B3
Solomon, Samuel 12-8, 1024C3
Soloviev, Yuri 1-16, 84G3
Soper, Fred 2-9, 164E3
Spencer-Churchill, Clementine 12-12, 1024C3
Staffa, Dino 8-7, 696F3
Stakhanov, Alexei 11-5, 952D3
Staley, Thomas 9-13, 788F2
Stokowski, Leopold 9-13, 788G2
Strong, S Birney 12-18, 1024D3
Stulberg, Louis 12-14, 1024D3
Stydahar, Joe 3-23, 264F3
Sullivan, William 11-9, 952D3
Szold, Robert 11-9, 952E3
Tarhil, Nashaat 1-6, 2E2
Taylor, Dean 10-16, 872A3
Teferi Bante 2-3, 98C2
Tetzel, Joan 10-31, 872A3
Thavorn, Udomleudej 4-14, 331F2
Thieriot, Charles deYoung 3-21, 264F3
Thompson, Lynn (rptd) 9-20, 871F2
Thorman, Donald 11-30, 952E3
Timakov, Vladimir D 6-21, 532G3
Timotheos, Bishop 12-14, 1024D3
Torres, Joe Campos (rptd) 5-8, 820G3
Torres, Jorge 11-10, 1011G1
Tourneur, Jacques 12-19, 1024E3
Tourtellot, Arthur 10-18, 872B3
Traglia, Luigi Cardinal 11-22, 952F3
Trottier, Edgar 2-6, 113D3
Tsegaye Debalke 2-2, 98F2
Turkawi, Rami Deeb 6-13, 457B3
Unceta Barrenechea, A 10-8, 826B2
Untermeyer, Louis 12-18, 1024E3
Van Zant, Ronnie 10-20, 888G3
Vasilevsky, Aleksandr 12-5, 1024F3
Velasco Alvarado, Juan 12-24, 1024F3
Ventura, Jose 1-5, 42B1
Vereshchagin, Leonid (rptd) 2-23, 164F3
Vidor, Florence 11-3, 952F3
Vipaowadi Rangsit, Princess 2-16, 138D1
Von Braun, Wernher 6-16, 532G3
Von Rosen, Carl Gustaf 7-13, 604G3
Vorhees, Melvin 2-6, 164F3 *
Wagner, Gerald 11-22, 952F3
Walters, Lou 8-15, 696G3
Warnecke, Frederick 2-23, 164G3
Waters, Ethel 9-1, 788A3
Watt, Donald 11-27, 952F3
Weisgal, Meyer 9-29, 788B2
Wells, Robert 7-13, 552F3
West, Sandra Ilene 3-10, 532D2
Wheatley, Dennis 11-11, 952G3
Wheaton, Anne 3-23, 264G3
White, Katherine 7-20, 604G3
Widman Jr, Michael 8-14, 696G3
Wigforss, Ernst 1-3, 84G3
Wilcox, Herbert 5-15, 452F3
Williams, Maurice 3-9, 192F2
Wilson, Kenneth 9-7, 848G2
Windham, James C 5-11, 452F3
Winslow, Ola 9-27, 788B2
Wolf, Steve 11-21, 952G3
Wolfe, Bertram 2-22, 164G3
Wolff, Robert 12-29, 1024G3
Woodham-Smith, Cecil 3-16, 264G3
Woodworth, Laurence 12-4, 1024G3
Wrigley, Philip 4-12, 356G3
Xavier, Prince of Borbon-Parma 5-7, 452G3
Yafeh, Yossi 2-28, 164G3
Yang Sen 5-15, 452G3
Ybarra y Berge, Javier de 6-18, 507C3
Yu Hui-yung (rptd) 11-8, 882D3
Zahabi, Mohammed Hussein al- 7-4, 525D3
Zerilli, Joseph 10-30, 872B3
Zrzavy, Jan 10-13, 872B3

1978

Strang, Lord 5-27, 440F3
Student, Kurt 7-1, 620F3
Swanson, Howard 11-12, 972E3
Sylvester, Victor 8-14, 708E3
Tabalaza, Lungile 7-10, 535F3
Tandy, Charles D 11-4, 972F3
Tartaglione, Giraloma 10-10, 817A1
Tate, Jackson R 7-19, 620G3
Thi, Dinh Ba 6-17, 549B2
Thien Minh, Thich (rptd) 10-26, 888F3
Thorne, Oakleigh 2-15, 196F3
Tobin, Austin J 2-8, 196G3
Torres, Antonio 6-2, 476D3
Truesdell Jr, Karl 8-22, 708F3
Trujillo, Flor de Oro 2-15, 196G3
Truman, Mary Jane 11-3, 972F3
Tsiranana, Philibert 4-16, 356E3
Tsironis, Vasilios
Tunney, Gene 11-7, 972F3
Turbitt, William 6-19, 474E2
Turner, Richard 1-8, 20D2
Turner, Thomas Wyatt 4-21, 356E3
Tuyen, Tran Van (rptd) 7-10, 692F1
Tweedsmuir, Baroness 3-11, 252E3
Underhill, Roger D 10-25, 971D2
Utely, Freda 1-21, 96F3
Vader, Artur Pavlovich 5-26, 440F3
Venuti, Joe 8-14, 708F3
Viola Sauret, Joaquin 1-25, 136A1
Von Manteuffel, Hasso 9-24, 778B2
Waddy, Joseph C 8-1, 708G3
Wallenda, Karl 3-22, 252F3
Warner, Jack L 9-9, 778B2
Webster, Donald E (rptd) 1-6, 24B3
Weicker Sr, Lowell P 11-25, 972G3
Welch, Leo D 10-22, 888G3
Wengenroth, Stow 1-22, 96G3
Wetmore, Alexander 12-6, 1032F3
Wheelock, John Hall 3-22, 252F3
Whitehead, Edward 4-16, 356F3
Williams, Jay 7-12, 620G3
Willkie, Edith Wilk 4-16, 356F3
Wills, Chill 12-15, 1032G3
Wilson, Michael 4-9, 356G3
Winston, Harry 12-8, 1032G3
Wood, Peggy 3-18, 252F3
Wrathall, John James 8-31, 708G3
Wright, Lloyd 5-31, 440G3
Wriston, Henry 3-8, 252G3
Yasin, Ali 6-15, 489A2
Young, Gig 10-19, 888G3
Youngdahl, Luther W 6-21, 540G3
Zamora, Ricardo 9-7, 778C2
Zini, Ivo 9-28, 817A1
Zukofsky, Louis 5-12, 440G3

1979

Waller, James 11-3, 864D3
Wallis, Barnes Neville 11-12, 932G3
Waltari, Mika 8-26, 671G3
Warren, Gertrude 9-6, 756F3
Wayne, John 6-11, 508F3
Wey, Hugo 5-30, 406A3
Weyland, Otto P 9-2, 756G3
Wilding, Michael 7-8, 588F3
Williams, T Harry 7-6, 588G3
Wolchok, Samuel 1-16, 104G3
Wood, John H 5-29, 431D2
Woodward, Robert Burns 7-8, 588G3
Wright, John 8-10, 671G3
Yahyahi, Bijan 4-13, 276D3
Zaim, Abdul Sattar 9-16, 755A1
Zand-Karami, Vali Mohammed 3-13, 179G3
Zanuck, Darryl F 12-22, 1008G3
Zarghani, Sadeg Mozafar 6-17, 544B3
Zeller, Andre 9-18, 756G3
Zuniga, Jose Leopoldo 3-1, 237F1

1980

Pyromaglou, Komninos 7-2, 608F2
Qadir, Abdul 9-1, 686C1
Quiroga Santa Cruz, Marcelo 7-17, 546C3
Raft, George 11-24, 928C3
Ramadan, Mohammed Mustafa 4-11, 353A3
Randall Jr, John H 12-1, 1004B3
Rappaport, Paul 4-21, 360A3
Ratebzad, Anahita 7-21, 602D1
Reed, Stanley F 4-3, 360A3
Renaldo, Duncan 9-3, 756B2
Reynolds, Julia 11-28, 1004B3
Reynolds, Richard S 10-5, 876D3
Rhine, Joseph 2-20, 176B3
Richardson, Thomas 9-27, 756B2
Rivas Rodriquez, Manuel de Jesus 11-3, 871F3
Robbins, Gale 2-18, 176B3
Roberts, Rachel 11-26, 928D3
Roberts, Richard 4-4, 360B3
Robinson, Francis 5-14, 448E2
Rodell, Fred 6-4, 528D3
Rodney, Walter 6-13, 469F1
Romero y Galdamez, Oscar Arnulfo 3-24 220E1
Ronne, Finn 1-12, 104F3
Rosenberg, Jakob 4-7, 360B3
Rosenstein, Nettie 3-13, 280G1
Roth, Lillian 5-12, 448F2
Rubin, Morris H 8-8, 676E2
Rukeyser, Muriel 2-12, 176B3
Rumbough, William S 12-2, 1004C3
Runnels, Harold L 8-5, 676F2
Sa Carneiro, Francisco Manuel Lumbrales de 12-4, 923D1
Sadr, Mohammed al-Bakr (rptd) 4-15, 300A2
Salazar Aguello, Jorge 11-17, 887G1
Samadzadeh, Ali Akbar 5-5, 337C1
Sanders, Harland 12-16, 1004C3
Sandrini, Luis 7-5, 608G2
Sands, Dorothy 9-11, 756C2
Sanyama, Oliver 1-22, 80C2
Sartre, Jean-Paul 4-15, 360C3
Sauer, Louis 2-10, 176C3
Saxon, James J 1-28, 104F3
Sayegh, Fayez A 12-9, 1004D3
Sazak, Gun 5-27, 445B3
Schaper, W H 9-8, 756C2
Schary, Dore 7-7, 608A3
Schwab, Jack 3-17, 280A2
Sebald, William J 8-10, 676G2
Sebastian, John 8-18, 676A3
Sebastiani, August 2-16, 176C3
Seif, Juseiman bin 1-9, 22C1
Sellers, Peter 7-24, 608B3
Selvin, Benjamin B 7-28, 608C3
Semenenko, Serge 4-24, 360E3
Serasino, Roberto 12-11, 966C3
Sever, Engin 12-17, 991C2
Shaib, Musa 7-28, 579A3
Sharaf, Abdul Hamid 7-3, 608C3
Shea Jr, George E 4-27, 360E3
Shelkov, Vladimir 1-27, 87G3
Shelley, Norman 8-22, 676A3
Sherman, John 4-22, 353A2
Sherrill, Henry Knox 5-11, 448F2
Shoumatoff, Elizabeth 11-30, 928D3
Shukairy, Ahmed 2-26, 176D3
Sierra Torres, Manuel de la 8-1, 605E3
Simpson, William H 8-15, 676B3
Sisler, Frederick D 3-2, 280B2
Slack, John M 3-17, 280C2
Smythe, Conn 11-18, 928E3
Snider, Paul 8-15, 713D3
Snow, C P 7-1, 608D3
Somoza Debayle, Anastasio 9-17, 697F2
Steeples, Lemuel 3-14, 214A1
Stein, William 2-2, 176D3
Stender, Fay 5-21, 448G2
Stern, Edith R 9-11, 756D2
Stewart, Donald Ogden 8-2, 676B3
Stewart, Ella Winter 8-5, 676C3
Stewart, Frank 4-22, 353A2
Stewart, George R 8-22, 676C3
Still, Clyfford 6-23, 528E3
Stoloff, Morris 4-16, 360E3
Stone, Milburn 6-12, 528E3
Storr, Vernall 1-29, 132B2
Stratten, Dorothy 8-15, 713D3
Strong, Michael 9-17, 756E2
Summerskill, Edith 2-4, 176E3
Sundstrom, Frank L 5-23, 448A3
Sutherland, Graham 2-18, 176F3
Sutton, Willie 11-2, 928E3
Symonette, Roland (rptd) 3-17, 280C2
Tabatabai, Ali Akbar 7-22, 545B1, B2
Taha, Riad 7-23, 579F2
Talmon, Jacob L 6-16, 528F3
Tarnower, Herman 3-10, 214E3
Tauber, Maurice F 9-21, 756F2
Taylor, Lee 11-13, 1002A2
Teale, Edwin Way 10-18, 876D3
Temple, George F 9-30, 756F2
Thomas, Lord 2-8, 176F3
Thomas, Billy 10-11, 876E3
Thomas, Tony 1-1, 907E3
Thompson, Joe 4-21, 360F3
Tishman, David 6-18, 528F3
Tito, Josip 5-4, 338G1-339C2
Tobagi, Walter 5-28, 408A2
Tobias, George 2-27, 176F3
Tolbert, Frank 4-22, 353A2
Tolbert, William 4-12, 284A3
Ton Duc 3-30, 280D2
Tovorov, Orin 8-16, 676D3
Townsend, E Reginald 4-22, 353A2
Trask, Willard R 8-10, 676D3
Travers, Ben 12-18, 1004D3
Truman, Harry 5-18, 382G1, 504D3
Tuckner, Howard 8-2, 676E3
Turkler, Kemal 7-22, 580D3
Turnley, John 6-4, 619D2
Tynan, Kenneth 7-26, 608E3
Tyrer, James 9-15, 756G2
Ulloa, Felix Antonio 10-29, 871G3

1980

Vagnozzi, Egidio 12-26, 1004E3
Valentine, Alan 7-14, 608E3
Valladares, Ramon 10-26, 829C2
Van, Bobby 7-31, 608F3
Van Vleck, John 10-27, 876E3
Vance, Nina 2-18, 176G3
Velasco Zuazo, Jesus Maria 1-10, 101E2
Verbano, Valerio 2-22, 151A3
Vergara Campos, Roger 7-15, 563A1
Vodopyanov, Mikhail V (rptd) 8-14, 676E3
Von Schlabrendorff, Fabian 9-3, 756G2
Vysotsky, Vladimir 7-24, 580C2
Waccher, William 2-7, 151C2
Wagner, Gustov Franz 10-3, 810E1
Wagner, Winnifred 3-5, 280D2
Wallenberg, Jacob 8-2, 676F3
Walsh, Stella 12-4, 1004F3
Walters, Albert 10-20, 876F3
Ward, Robert E 4-9, 360F3
Warren, Shields 7-1, 608G3
Watts, George 3-29, 280E2
Weltfish, Gene 8-2, 676F3
West, Mae 11-22, 928F3
Westheimer, Irvin F 12-30, 1004F3
Whitaker, Frederic 3-9, 280E2
Wilder, Alec 12-24, 1004G3
Wiley, Bell I 4-4, 360G3
Wilhemina 3-1, 280F2
Wolf, George 3-23, 280G2
Wood, Mae C Ryan 10-14, 876F3
Wright, James 3-25, 280G2
Wyndham-White, Eric 1-27, 104G3
Yacoub, Moran 6-25, 528G3
Yahya Khan, Agha Mohammad 8-8, 676G3
Yuga Xona, Gregaria 2-2—2-3, 98E2
Zambrano, Jorge Marcos 2-14, 335E2
Zamora, Efrain 5-16, 464B1
Zamora Rivas, Mario 2-23, 149G1
Zayan Candal, Jorge 9-11, 786B2
Zhao Dan 10-10, 876G3
Zimin, Aleksandr A (rptd) 3-14, 280G2
Zouni, Darwich el- 12-27, 996G2-A3
Zubicaray, Jesus Maria 2-3, 101E3

1976

DEATH Valley National Monument (Calif.)
Sen votes mining halt 2-4, 135A2, C2
Mining curbs signed 9-28, 834B2, C2
De BANE, Pierre
Air pact talks cited 7-1, 496A3
To represent Quebec air group 8-3, 587G2
De BEER, Cedric
Acquitted 12-2, 927G1
De BELLEVAL, Denis
Named treas bd vp, pub svc min 11-26, 903A3
DEBERNARD, Daniele
Wins Olympic medal 2-13, 158E3
DeBLASIO, Ralph
Ford wins pres nominatn 8-19, 597F1
De BORCHGRAVE, Arnaud
S Africa bar rptd 10-26, 927G2
DEBRE, Michel
Gaullist rptd for Eur defns group 1-15, 126E2
De BROGLIE, Jean
Killed in Paris 12-24, 1002D2

1977

DeBARTOLO Jr., Edward J.
49er team acquisitn OKd 3-29—4-1, Thomas rptd signed 3-29, 263F2
DeBARTOLO Corp., Edward J.
NFL OKs 49er team buy 3-29—4-1, 263F2
DEBRE, Michel
Vs defense budget cuts 11-18, 924G1
De BROGLIE, Jean
Police versn of murder questnd 1-5—1-9, 43G3
DEBS, Eugene V. (1855-1926)
FBI surveillance rptd 6-19, 481E1
DEBT, Public—*See under U.S. GOVERNMENT—BUDGET*
DeBUTTS, John D.
On AT&T record '76 earnings 2-1, 93C3
De CASTRO, Federico
World Ct member 4F1
DECENT Interval (book)
Viet evacuatn scored 11-18, 897G3
De CLERQ, Willy
Liberals slip in electns 4-17, 326F2
DECOIN, Didier
Wins Prix Goncourt 11-21, 927F2
DeCROW, Karen
ERA rescissn validity questnd 3-26, 279F3
Succeeded as NOW pres 4-24, 532G1
DEEGAN, Judge Leo
Convicts Chowchilla kidnapers 12-15, 992D1
DEEP, The (book)
On best-seller list 6-4, 452B2; 7-3, 548F3

1978

DEATH Trap (play)
Opens 2-26, 760A2
De BANE, Pierre
Canada supply min 11-24, 921E3
DeBARR, Dennis
Traded to Indians 3-15, 195A1
De BAYONA, Gaston
Scores US border fence plan 10-24, 818C1
De BEERS Consolidated Mines Ltd.
Diamond surchrg set 3-28, 4-27, 319A1
London diamond price hiked 8-8, 622F2
De BROCA, Philippe
Dear Detective released 4-24, 619D1
King of Hearts opens 11-22, 1031C2
DEBT, External
Defined 50D2
DEBT, Public—*See under U.S. GOVERNMENT—BUDGET*
DeBUTTS, John D.
Announces AT&T retiremt 10-18, 808D3
Vows AT&T price compliance 12-1, 934D3

1979

DEAVER, Michael K.
Reagan campaign resignatn cited 11-14, 982E2
De BANE, Pierre
Asks security clearance review 2-23, 189C2
De BEAUVOIR, Simone
Leftist writer slain 9-20, 772B3
DEBRE, Michel
Scored at UDF parley 2-10–2-11, 135D1
DEBT, Foreign
External debt defined 33C2
Nicaragua delays debt paymt 2-1, 101F2
Fiscal '78 debt to US rptd up 2-5, 84A3
Brazil '78 debt rptd 3-15, 210B1
Polish '78 debt to West rptd 3-16, 3-20, 200E3, 212A2
Sovt-bloc '78 Westn debt estimated 3-20, 200C3
Canada '78 record debt rptd 4-7, 311E3
Chile '78 debt rptd, Israel cited 5-21, 369F3
Venez '79 debt at $7.41 bln 5-28, 429E3
Nicaragua paymts in doubt 9-28, 753D2
Venez revised debt at 12.2 bln 10-6, 837A3
Economists fear rise 10-29, 11-1, 826D2, 827A1
Bolivia '79 debt estimated 11-16, 888G2
Peru prepaymt agreed, '80 external debt forecast 11-26, 951C2
Nicaragua paymts rescheduled 11-27, 909C3-910A1
Brazil '79 debt, '80 forecast rptd 12-7, 948A3
Zaire debt rescheduled 12-12, 999E1
DEBT, Public—*See under U.S. GOVERNMENT–BUDGET*

1980

DEATH Ship (film)
Released 4-25, 416F2
DEAVER, Michael K.
Named Reagan aide 12-17, 955C3
DeBAKEY, Dr. Michael
Examines Tito 1-5, 49D2
In Panama med dispute 3-21—3-23, follows shah to Cairo 3-26, 217F1, B2
Removes shah's spleen, Egypt honors 3-28; goes to Jordan 3-29, 242E1
DEBANE, Pierre
Canada regional econ expansn min 3-3, 171B2
DEBARTOLO Sr., Edward J.
White Sox purchase OKd by bd 8-23, 795A3
AL owners rejct White Sox purchase bid 10-24, 12-11, 1000E1
DEBAYLE Somoza, Salvadora
At son's funeral 9-17, 721D1
DE BEAUVOIR, Simon
Sarte dies 4-15, 360D3
DEBERG, Steve
NFL '79 passing ldr 1-5, 8E2
DEBOER, Lieuwe
Wins Olympic medal 2-15, 155G3
DE BORCHGRAVE, Arnaud
Spike on best-seller list 7-13, 568B3; 8-17, 640E3; 9-10, 716B3
DEBRE, Michel
Announces pres bid 6-30, 522C1
DE BROCA, Philippe
Incorrigible released 3-3, 416A3
DE BROGLIE, Jean (d. 1976)
Poniatowski impeachmt sought 4-14, 312E2
DEBT, Foreign
External debt defined 34E2
Venez '79 debt rptd 1-14, 103B1
Jamaica '79 debt rptd 1-17, 99F1
Turkey debt cited 1-24, 61B1
Turkey sets debt plan 1-28, 80D1
'79 Sovt bloc debt to West estimated 2-4, 166B3; 4-1, 285A3
Norway repaymt seen 2-5, 100F2
USSR '79 Westn debt down 3-26, 235E3
Canada '79 debt rptd up 4-11, 310A3
Jamaica accord reached, default averted 4-15, 314C2
Zaire estimates 4-24, 356A2
Brazil repaymts revised 5-24, 406C1
Jamaica refinancing plan advances 6-4, 465B1
Turkey revised plan rptd 6-6, 445G3
Turkey '79 debt rptd 6-19, 468E1
IMF sees poor natn problems 6-24, 477D2
Argentina '66, '79 debt compared 7-11, 561B3
Turkey debt rescheduled 7-24, 568A1
Mex 1st 1/2 debt at $32 bln 9-1, 729G3
Bolivia debt paymts postponed 9-3, 686E2-B3
Poland '79 Westn debt chrgs rptd 9-4, 659D2
Nicaragua debt rescheduled 9-5, 689C2-A3
Poland pledges Westn paymts 9-8, 679E1
IMF role in oil debt studied 9-15, 695D2
Brazil sets '81 paymt 12-17, 991F3
DEBT, Public—*See under U.S. GOVERNMENT--BUDGET*
DEBUS, Chuck
Denies Anderson steroid use 6-28, 891E2
DEBUTTS, John D.
Carter names to Synfuels Corp bd 9-13, Sen panel OKs 9-25, 725F2
Carter names to interim Synfuels Corp 10-5, 786F2

1976

DECKER Jr., Andrew J.
Cited re FBI break-ins 8-18, 634G2
De CLERQ, Willy
On Jamaica monetary accord 1-8, 14F2
DECONCINI, Dennis
Wins Ariz Sen primary 9-7, 687A3
AFL-CIO donatn rptd 10-22, 938D3
Elected 11-2, 820A1, 824B1, 828B1
De CROVO, Maria Elena
Quits Cabt 10-10, 924F3
DeCROW, Karen
Dem conv rule debated 7-13, 513C1
Scores pregnancy coverage ruling 12-7, 920A2
DeCUBAS, Jose L.
Denies anti-Allende offer 12-23, 999D2
DEEP, The (book)
On best-seller list 12-5, 972E2
DEERE & Co.
UAW strike 10-1—11-9, 847D3
Boycott rpt released 10-18, 785G3
DEERING, Fred
McCloy rpt scores 133E2
Ousted from Gulf post 1-15, 132C3, 133A1
DEFALCO, Luciano
Sworn Italy health min 7-30, 573G1
De FARIA, Carl M.
Sentenced 11-30, 921A3
DEFENSE—*See ARMAMENTS, ATOMIC Energy, DISARMAMENT, SECURITY, U.S.; for military strength issue, see DEFENSE under U.S. GOVERNMENT; also country names*
DEFENSE Manpower Commission (Washington, D.C.)
Armed forces study scored 6-7, 454E1
DEFFERRE, Gaston
Scores Marseilles oil case 5-16, 537F3
DeFREEZE, Donald D. (Cinque) (d. 1974)
US MD claims Hearst 'brainwashed' 1-29, 70F1
Cited in Hearst jury selectn, trial 2-3—2-9, 113A3-114C2
Cited in Hearst trial, Harrises article 2-17, 2-20, 2-22, 201C2-C3
DEFRENNE, Gabrielle
Wins EC sex bias case 4-8, 276C3
De GAULLE, Gen. Charles Andre Joseph Marie (1890-1970)—*See 1970 p. 817E2 for biog. data*
Chalandon rptd for Eur defns group 1-15, 126D2
Sanguinetti dismissed 7-7, 521E2
Would-be assassin killed 8-11, 624F3
Andre Malraux dies 11-23, 970D2
De GRANDPRE, Philippe
Vs inflation plan ruling 7-12, 554F3
De GUIRINGAUD, Louis
PLO seating disputed 5-4, 320D1
Israeli settlemts scored 5-26, 406D3
Named foreign min 8-27, 650D3-F3
DEHEZA, Jose
Argentina justice min 1-15, 71C2
DEKALB AgResearch Inc.
Heinhold sued 5-27, 397E3
De KLERK, William
Asks race reform 11-8, 928D2
De KOONING, Willem
Mark Tobey dies 4-24, 368B3

1977

DEEP, The (film)
Top-grossing film 7-6, 548G3
DEEP Throat (film)
Sup Ct bars retroactive porno prosecutns 3-1, 175F1
DEERE & Co.
Rpts forgn paymts 2-1, 94G1
DeFELITTA, Frank
Audrey Rose on best-seller list 2-6, 120G3
DEFENSE—*See ARMAMENTS, ATOMIC Energy, DISARMAMENT; for military strength issue, see DEFENSE under U.S. GOVERNMENT; also country names*
DEFENSE, Department of—*See under U.S. GOVERNMENT*
DEFENSE Contracts—*See U.S. GOVERNMENT—DEFENSE, Department of*
De GAULLE, Gen. Charles Andre Joseph Marie (1890-1970)—*See 1970, p. 817E2 for biog. data*
Dassault cleared 4-21, 598B1
Levesque visits tomb 11-1, 862C2, E2
De GUIRINGAUD, Louis
Israel ties reconciled 2-8, 87B1 ★
Warns US vs Concorde ban 3-8, 212G2
Named foreign min 3-30, 239A2
Scores Algeria re Polisario raid 5-3, 440B3
Chad mil aid rptd 7-18, 597F1
Warns S Africa vs A-test 8-17, 663D3
Tanzania protest halts African tour 8-18, 662E2
Warns S Africa vs A-test 8-22, 656F3
Sahara kidnap prompts Cabt mtg 10-27, 831A3
DeJESUS, Estaban
KOs Saldivar 6-27, 828B1
'77 boxing champion 12-17, 970A3
De JONGH, T. W.
Small bank aid set 2-22, 160E3
De KOCK, Wickus
Quits Parlt 7-1, 536A3
De KONING, Jan
Named Dutch cooperatn, dvpt min 12-19, 986B1

1978

De CASTRO, Sergio
Meany firm on trade boycott 12-10, 1014B2
DECENCY, National Federation for
Sears withdraws TV ads 5-12, 599D3
DECENT Interval (book)
US sues Snepp 2-15, 129C1
US wins Snepp suit, to get profits; Random House scores 7-7, 527A3
De CHIRICO, Giorgio
Dies 11-20, 972A3
DeCINCES, Doug
AL batting ldr 10-2, 928E3
DECKARD, H. Joel
Wins US House seat 11-7, 850B4, 853A3
DECKER, Gerald
Coal Policy Project study issued 2-9, 184B2
DECKER, Mary
Sets 1000-yd run mark 2-4, 692E3
DECOLONIZATION Committee—*See under UNITED Nations*
DeCONCINI, Sen. Dennis (D, Ariz.)
Canal pact vote sought 3-9, deals rptd 3-13, 3-16; neutrality pact OKd 3-16, 177F1-B3
Panama govt, other oppositn to reservatn threatens pacts 3-14—4-14, 255F1-E3
Seeks 2d reservatn, OKs 'understanding'; Moynihan, Haskell threaten vote vs pact 4-13, 255E3-256A1
OKs Canal Treaty reservatn compromise 4-17, votes for pact 4-18, 273B1, B2
Torrijos OKs pact reservatn 4-17, Panamanians score 4-19—4-20, 273F1, 274D1
Personal finances rptd 5-19, 385D3
Burger vs bankruptcy bill 9-28, 788E3
Burger defends judicial lobbying 10-25, 832F3
Visits USSR 11-11—11-18, 905A2
DeCONCINI, John
Named Bakery, tobacco union ldr 8-16, 700A2
DEDERICH, Charles
Arrested in rattler attack 12-2, freed on bail 12-11, 971F1
DEELEY, Michael
Deer Hunter released 12-14, 1030F2
DEEP Throat (film)
Children excluded from porno rule by Sup Ct 5-23, 405D3
DEER Hunter, The (film)
Released 12-14, 1030F2
DEFENSE—*See ARMAMENTS, ATOMIC Energy, DISARMAMENT, U.S. GOVERNMENT—DEFENSE; country names*
DEFENSE, Department of—*See under U.S. GOVERNMENT*
DEFENSE Civil Preparedness Agency—*See under U.S. GOVERNMENT—DEFENSE*
DEFENSE Contracts—*See U.S. GOVERNMENT—DEFENSE; country names*
DEFENSE Intelligence Agency (DIA)—*See under U.S. GOVERNMENT—DEFENSE*
DEFENSE Systems Acquisition Review Council—*See under U.S. GOVERNMENT—DEFENSE*
DEFOLIANTS—*See HERBICIDES*
DEGAS, (Hilaire Germain) Edgar (1834-1917)
In Front of a Mirror stolen 7-30, 1029B1
De GAULLE, Gen. Charles Andre Joseph Marie (1890-1970)—*See 1970, p. 817E2 for biog. data*
France in UN Leb peace force 3-19, 197F2
Chablan-Delmas wins Assemb post 4-3, 245G2
Rueff dies 4-23, 356D3
USSR-France tensns rptd 10-29, 830F3
DeGAZON, Fred
Elected Dominica pres 12-21, 1021F2
De GEER, Lars
Swedish defense min 10-18, 822G2
De GUIRINGAUD, Louis
Scores Carter-Mitterrand mtg 1-10, 54E1
At Namibia conf 2-11—2-12, sees progress 2-13, 113G3
Renamed French forgn min 4-5, 245F2
Defends Zaire rescue 5-19, 381F2
US, France seek Leb peace 10-3, 745A2
Blames Chamoun for Leb clashes 10-16; Chamoun blames Syria 10-17, 783D1
Backs S Africa sanctns if Namibia plan rejected 10-23, 819D3
Sees Gromyko 10-25—10-28, 830E3-831A1
Quits 11-27, 1017C1
DEJA Vu for Percussion Quartet and Orchestra (musical composition)
Colgrass wins Pulitzer 4-17, 315C1
DeJESUS, Esteban
Duran TKOs for lightwgt title 1-21, 55F3
DeJESUS, Ivan
NL batting, stolen base ldr 10-2, 928F2
DeJONG, David
Loses Quebec by-electn 7-5, 514B3
De JONGH, James
Do Lord Remember Me opens 4-4, 887F1
De KLERK, F. Willem
Viljoen-Motlana mtg rptd 8-17, 669D3
Adds S Africa sports portfolio 11-14, 904C3

1979

DECATUR, Ala.—*See ALABAMA*
DeCINCES, Doug
In World Series 10-10—10-17, 816C1
DeCONCINI, Sen. Dennis (D, Ariz.)
Sen income limit stayed 3-8, 185G2
Finances disclosed 5-18, 383D2
De CONCINI, Ennio
Last Romantic Lover released 10-5, 1007G3
De COTRET, Robert Rene
Canada econ dvpt, trade min 6-4, 423G3
Metric review study ordered 6-6, 444C2
DeCOURCEY, Richard
Indicted 6-28, 647F1
DEDRICK, Joan
Kidnaped 7-20—7-22; suspects seized, ransom recovered 7-22, 7-26, 604F3
DEDRICK, William
Wife kidnaped 7-20—7-22, 604F3
DEE, Pham Van
On sunk boat 8-8, 626G1
DEE, Ruby
Take It From The Top opens 1-19, 292C3
DEERE & Co.
UAW strike setlmt cited 12-19, 987G1
DEER Hunter, The (film)
Wins Oscars 4-9, 336G1-B2
Top-grossing film 5-2, 356F2
DEES, Morris
Named Kennedy campaign finance dir 10-24, 847G1
DEFENSE, Department of—*See under U.S. GOVERNMENT*
DEFENSE Intelligence Agency—*See under U.S. GOVERNMENT—DEFENSE*
DEFENSE Systems Management College—*See under U.S. GOVERNMENT—DEFENSE*
DEFOLIANTS—*See HERBICIDES*
DeFRANK, Robert
Madman & Nun opens 1-18, 292B2
De GAULLE, Gen. Charles Andre Joseph Marie (1890-1970)—*See 1970, p. 817E2 for biog. data*
Gen Challe dies 1-18, 104F2
'67 Quebec statemt cited 2-9, 2-13, 133G3, 134A1
Zeller dies 9-18, 756G3
Widow dies 11-8, 932E2
De GAULLE, Yvonne (Mrs. Charles)
Dies 11-8, 932E2
DEGNAN, John J.
Resorts Intl granted casino license 2-26, 151G3-152A1
Details Mafia evidence 5-23, 508F1, A2
De GUINGAND, Maj. Gen. Francis
Dies 6-29, 508E2
De HAAN, Dale S.
UN-Viet refugee plan set 3-1, 181D1
De HAVILLAND, Olivia
5th Musketeer released 9-7, 820C1
DEIGHTON, Len
SS-GB on best-seller list 5-6, 356C2
DEKKER, Eduard Douwes
Max Havelaar released 1-20, 174A3
De KLERK, Jan
Dies 1-23, 104G2
De KLERK, Theunis
Killed 9-21, 718C2
DeKOVEN, Roger
Strider opens 5-31, 712G2
De KRETSER, Chris
Ousted from Iran 9-1, 670D2

1980

DECARLO, Yvonne
Silent Scream released 2-2, 216E3
DECATUR—*See ALABAMA*
DECENT Interval (book)
CIA disclosure limits upheld by Sup Ct 2-19, 130C3
Snepp novel rptd submitted for CIA OK 6-13, 517B1
DECKARD, Rep. H. Joel (R, Ind.)
Reelected 11-4, 842B4
DECKER, Gen. George Henry (ret.)
Dies 2-6, 175F3
DECKER, Mary
Sets 5 track marks 1-1—7-12, 891A1
DECKERT, Manfred
Wins Olympic medal 2-17, 155D3
DeCONCINI, Sen. Dennis (D, Ariz.)
Interviews Vesco 7-27, B Carter role discounted 7-30, 570D1
US halts drug enforcemt progrms 8-13, junta trafficking chrgd 8-15, 668B1
Judicial discpline bill signed 10-15, 918F3
El Salvador alien deportatn proceedings begin 10-18, 826A1
DECRANE Jr., Alfred C.
Saudi completes Aramco takeover, retains bd seat 9-4, 662A2
DEDERICH, Charles
Convicted in rattler attack 7-15, 655E3
Granted probation 9-3, 860D2
DEER Hunter, The (film)
Heaven's Gate withdrawn from theaters 11-19, 906B1
DEERING Milliken Inc.
Darlington Mfg '56 labor dispute setld 12-3, workers OK 12-14, 962D2
DEFENSE, Department of—*See under U.S. GOVERNMENT*
DEFENSE Intelligence Agency—*See under U.S. GOVERNMENT--DEFENSE*
DE FILIPPO, Eduardo
Filumena opens 2-10, 392G2
DEFOLIANTS—*See HERBICIDES*
DEGAS, Hilare Germain Edgar (1834-1917)
Painting sold for record sum 5-13, 472G1
Painting stolen in Argentina 12-25, 991E1
De GAULLE, Gen. Charles Andre Joseph Marie (1890-1970)—*See 1970, p. 817E2 for biog. data*
Debre enters pres race 6-30, 522C1
DE GEUS, P. B. R.
US scores Dutch mil spending 10-3, 737D1
DEGEYTER, Marc Andre
Arrested as Sovt trade spy 5-18, sentenced 8-1, 598B2
DE GRACA Machungo, Mario
Mozambique planning min 4-3, 278D2
DE GRUENECK, Harald
Visits US hostages in Iran 4-14, rpts 4-14, 4-15, 282B2
DE GUZMAN, Jossie
West Side Story opens 2-14, 136G3
DEIGHTON, Len
SS-GB on best-seller list 4-6, 280D3
DEJA Vu (recording)
Warwick wins Grammy 2-27, 296C3

1976

De la CIERVA, Ricardo
Scores press censorship 7-11, 523A3
De la FLOR, Gen. Miguel Angel
Sees Kissinger 2-18, 177G2
Loses Cabt post 7-16, 590A3
De la GARZA, Rep. Eligio (D, Tex.)
Reelected 11-2, 830D4
DELANEY, Daniel G.
Sentenced 2-4, 135F3
DELANEY, Rep. James J. (D, N.Y.)
Reelected 11-2, 830G1
Carter meets cong ldrs 11-17, 864B2
DELANEY, Steve
Denies W Bank riot link 5-9, 338A3
De la PUENTE Radbill, Jose
Peru forgn min 7-17; nonaligned natns mtg boycott rptd 8-4, 590C3
On Sovt plane deal 8-23, 652C3
DELARGEY, Msgr. Reginald
Appointed cardinal 4-27, 336C2
De LARROCHA, Alicia
Wins Grammy 2-28, 460D3
De la TORRE, Juan de Dios
Kidnaped 3-8, ransomed 3-16, 419B2
DELAWARE
Farmers Bank rpts loss 1-29; state, FDIC bailout dvpts 2-4—6-10, 437F2
Food stamp ineligibility rate rptd 2-11, denied 2-12, 129B1
Southern-Delmarva talks fail 3-23, Conrail takes over tracks 4-1, 235E2-A3
Wilmington schl integratn plan ordrd 5-19, 453C2
7 oil cos, trade assn indicted 6-1, 412F3
Ford to get 13 delegates 6-19, 450F2
Dem conv women delegates, table 508B2
Dem conv pres vote, table 7-14, 507B2
GOP pre-conv delegate count 8-14, 583B3
GOP conv pres, vp vote tables 8-18—8-19, 8-19, 599B1, B3
Dole campaign visit 8-31, 646A1
Football lottery starts 9-1, 736D3
Fscl '75 per capita income, tax burden rptd 9-15, 10-12, 959G1, B2
Election results 11-2: pres 818A1, E1, 819B2; cong 820D1, 821A1, 828D1, 829A2; state 817E1, 820F2, 821B1, 831D1
US Sup Ct refuses Wilmington busing case 11-29, 900A3
DELAWARE River
Oil spill 12-27, 1014E1
DeLEEUW, Dianne
Wins Olympic medal 2-13, 159A1
DELGADO, Nelson
CIA memo on Cuba-Oswald link cites 3-20, 3-21, 217D2
De LIPKOWSKI, Jean
French cooperation min 1-12, 49B2
DELJANA, Thoma
Purge rptd 4-30, 331E3
DELL, Edmund
UK trade min 4-8, 266F3
Sees Australia envoy 8-12, 623A2
Named UK commerce secy 9-10, 694A1
Dell'ACQUA, Msgr. Angelo
Rptd Vatican spy 2-14, 140E3
DELL Publishing Co. Inc.
US files consent decree 7-27, 989G1
DELLUMS, Rep. Ronald V. (D, Calif.)
Declines pres bid 3-20, 214F2, A3
Nominated for vp at conv 7-15, 506B3
Reelected 11-2, 829A1
DELLWO, Karl-Heinz
Trial opens 5-6, 503F1
DEL Monte Corp.
SEC rpts paymts probe 5-12, 727B1
Calif cannery strike ends 7-31, 570C1
DELTA Airlines
Swiss pact rptd ended 1-9, 31G1
'75 zero tax paymt rptd 10-2, 847F1
Ford rejcts transatlantic route 12-28, 992C2
DELTA Weighing and Inspection Bureau, Inc.
Chief inspector pleads guilty 3-5, 247G2
DELTONA Corp.
Fla wetlands dvpt denied 4-16, 284A3
DEMACI, Adam
Sentenced 2-8, 224B1
DEMARCO, Anibal
Sought for arrest 3-26, 236E3
Rights revoked, arrest ordrd 6-23, 520C1
De MARTINO, Francesco
Socialists quit Moro support 1-7, 10A2
Softens Socialist demand 1-9, 29C2
Shuns socialist mtg 1-24—1-25, 120D1
At Soclst Party Cong 3-3—3-7, 254B2
At Europn socialist mtg 3-13—3-14, 222F3
Soclsts back gen electns 4-9, 296C3
On elections 6-21, 445A2
Resigns 7-13, 539A1
DeMENT, Ira
Wins Rockefeller award 11-16, 911D3
DEMERS, Roger
Air controller slowdown 7-1, 496C3

1977

De la GARZA, Rep. Eligio (D, Tex.)
On Argentina civil rights 8-20, 670B2
Wife testifies on Korean lobbying 10-19—10-21, 816F2
De la GARZA, Mrs. Eligio
On Korean lobbying 10-19—10-21, 816F2
De la MELENA, German
Sees US bankers 8-19, IMF ldrs 8-22—8-23, 785F1
Negotiated Peru-IMF pact 9-30, 785A2
DELANEY, Rep. James J. (D, N.Y.)
'76 special interest gifts rptd 2-4, 128G3, 129G1, D2
FDA sets saccharin ban 3-9, 176C3
Offshore leasing bill blocked 10-25, 833A3
De la PUENTE Radbill, Jose
On Videla visit 3-8, 259E2
Sees Mrs Carter 6-3, lauds 6-5, 455B1
De las CASAS Grieve, Angel
Social property deemphasized 1-7, 46G3
De LAURENTIS, Antonio
Escapes prison 11-10, 1014C2
DELAWARE
Legislature schedule rptd 6D2
US backs Wilmington busing 3-18, 216C2
US antifraud rules expansn barred 3-23, 276G2 ★
'76 per-capita income table 5-10, 387D2
Wilmington busing upheld, quotas barred 5-18, 446C2
Sup Ct backs US fishing laws 5-23, 444A2
Laetrile use legalized 6-21, 508E1
Stock seizure law voided 6-24, 539C3
Wilmington desegregatn delayed, busing plan rejctd 8-5, 630D3
Ct OKs '77 football lottery, state postpones 8-12, 659F1
Offshore lease sale OKd by ct 8-25, 650B1
5 indep oil cos convicted 8-30, 691A3
'76 per capita income, tax burden table 9-13, 10-18, 821B2
5 indep oil cos fined 9-16, 918F2
Wilmington busing case review declined 10-3, 760F1
DELEZA, Wadson Bini
Named Malawi labor min 7-8, 772C1
DELGADO, Gen. Humberto (d. 1965)
Ex-secret police chrgd 10-19, 887C1
DELL, Edmund
Hails US air svc pact 6-22, 500D2
Signs US air svc pact 7-23, 593C1
DELLACROCE, Aniello
Mafia ldrship struggle rptd 5-16, 568D1
DELL Books—*See DOUBLEDAY & Co.*
DELLEPIANE Ocampo, Rear Adm. Jorge (ret.)
Expelled 1-8, 46B3
DELLUMS, Rep. Ronald V. (D, Calif.)
Troop cut amendmt fails 4-25, 324D1
Sees Castro 5-28, rpts Ethiopia assurances 6-1; briefs Carter 6-3, 456C2
DELTA Air Lines Inc.
Atlanta-London svc OKd 12-21, 1006C2
DELTA-Democrat Times (Greenville, Miss. newspaper)
Carter named to US post 1-17, 53F1
DELTA of Venus (book)
On best-seller list 8-14, 643F1; 9-4, 712D3; 10-2, 808D3
DELURY, Bernard E.
Replaced as Labor asst secy 3-18, 272F2
DeMARCO, Frank
Challenges NFL labor pact 4-25, 491F2
De MARCO, Guido
Adami elected oppositn ldr 1-16, 136D2
DeMARCO, Ralph
Sup Ct refuses case 10-3, 760C3
DEMAURO, Paschal
Indicted 2-24, 155F2

1978

De la GARZA, Rep. Eligio Kika (D, Tex.)
Cleared by ethics com re Park gift 7-13, 527A2
Reelected 11-7, 852A3
De la MALENE, Christian
Loses French legis seat 10-1, 815B2
De LANCEY, William
Minn plant to continue 7-7, 553D3
DELANEY, Rep. James J. (D, N.Y.)
Not standing for reelectn 9-12, 716C2
De la RIVA, Rear Adm. David (ret.)
Argentina defense min 11-6, 865E2
De LAROSIERE, Jacques
Quota hike compromise set 9-24, 731G3
At IMF mtg, asks growth rate convergence 9-25; Blumenthal backs 9-26, 731A3
De las ROSAS, Jesus
Named DR sports min 8-16, 648D2
De la TORRE, Manuel
2d in PGA Senior tourn 2-5, 355A3
De LAURENTIIS, Federico
King of Gypsies released 12-19, 1030B3
De LAURENTIIS, Dino
Serpent's Egg released 1-27, 619F3
DELAWARE
Legislature schedule rptd 14E3
No state sales taxes rptd 1-5, 15C3
Wilmington busing ordrd 1-9, 15F2-A3
State govt tax revenue table 1-9, 84C2
Gannett buys 2 Wilmington papers 1-30, 109D3
Carter at Biden dinner 2-20, 123C3
Wilmington busing plan OKd 7-24, 611F1
DC voting rep amendmt ratificatn delayed 878A3
Primary results 9-9, 736G1
Wilmington schls open calmly 9-11, 698F2
Election results 11-7: cong 846G1, 848A1, D1, 850E2
FCC orders NYC, Phila TV statn studios in NJ 11-9, 1030D2
Guyana cult victims arrive Dover air base, prepared for burial 11-24—11-30, 909D1-910C2
592 Guyana victims identified 12-8, 1st bodies leave Dover base 12-9, 955F2
Rape law revisn cited 12-27, 1028D3
DELAWARE, University of (Newark)
Wins NCAA Div II football title 12-9, 1025B2
DELAWARE River
Phila sued on sewage pollutn 5-24, 409G1
House votes parks bill 7-12, 526D3
US parks bill cleared 10-13, 834A3
DELGADO, Gen. Humberto (d. 1965)
Murder trial opens 10-9, 799D1
DELGADO, Julian
Kidnaped 6-4, 792D3
De LIAGRE Jr., Alfred
Death Trap opens 2-26, 760A2
DELIGNE, Pierre
Wins Field Medal 8-15, 1023F2
DELL, Edmund
Japan to curb UK car exports 3-3, 168A1
DELLENBAUGH, Cornelia
Vietnam frees 1-5, 8E2
DELLIBOVI, Alfred A.
Wins cong primary in NY 9-12, 716C2
DELLUMS, C. L.
Union merges with BRAC 2-28, 185C2
DELLUMS, Rep. Ronald V. (D, Calif.)
Scores seabed mining bill 7-26, 589B1
Defense veto upheld by house 9-7, 677D2
Scores '67 PR status vote 9-15, 979D3
Reelected 11-7, 850E1
Del MONTE Corp.
Reynolds seeks merger 8-3, offer OKd 9-25, 752A3
DeLOACH, Cartha
Mtg with black ldr cited in FBI '64 memo on King 5-29; reactn 5-30, 410A3, G3
De Los REYES, Rupert
Apollo wins ASL title 9-10, 707E3
DELTA Air Lines, Inc.
Boston '73 crash suit refused review 2-21, 126A2
IATA membership end set 11-11, 894C3
France sentences '72 hijackers 11-23, 926F3
DELTA Air Lines v. U.S.
Boston '73 crash suit refused review 2-21, 126B2
DeLUCA, Robert N.
Named acting US Phila atty 1-24, 62D2
DeLUGO, Ron
Loses electn for VI gov 11-7, 915E3
DELUISE, Dom
'End' released 5-10, 619G1
DELUXE General Inc.—*See TWENTIETH Century Fox Film Corp.*
Del ZIO, Doris & John
Embryo implant trial begins 7-17, 597G1
Wins damages 8-18, 770G1
De MADARIAGA, Salvador
Dies 12-14, 1032E2
DeMAIN, John L.
Hello Dolly opens 3-5, 887A2
DeMARTINO, Guido
15 sentncd for '77 kidnap 1-10, 133G2-A3
DeMASCIO, Judge Robert
Rules NHL compensatn clause illegal 9-18, 990D3
DEMBELE, Lt. Col. Karim
Arrested 2-28, 250F3
DEMERS, Jacques
Resigns as WHA Stingers coach 6-7, 656G3

1979

De La PAZ, Danny
Boulevard Nights released 3-22, 528E1
De la PUENTE Radbill, Jose
Replaced as Peru forgn min 2-2, 101A3
De la RENTA, Oscar
'79 fashion roundup rptd 1006B2
De LAROSIERE, Jacques
Addresses IMF-World Bank mtgs 10-2, 10-5, 779G2, A3
DELAUNAY, Sonia
Dies 12-5, 1008D2
De LAURENTIIS, Dino
Hurricane released 4-11, 528E2
DELAWARE
Legislature schedule rptd 5C3
Justice Dept bars Jonestown bodies transfer 1-6; Calif group to oversee 2-1; 588 rptd unclaimed at Dover 2-1, 117E2
GE worker chrgd in Wilmington A-plant theft 2-1, 119F3
Art theft symposium held in Newark 2-12-2-14, 119A2
Pub schl cost share rptd 3-5, 282E3
Random car checks by police barred by Sup Ct 3-27, 263E1
546 Jonestown bodies rptd unclaimed at Dover, Calif transfer set 4-21, 336D1
Biden '78 labor gifts rptd 6-13, 595D1
Priest cleared in Penna 'gentleman bandit' case 8-20, look-alike sentncd 11-20, 8-23, 953F2
Odd-even-gas rules lifted 9-5, 683F1
Hurricane David hits 9-7, 690B1
'78 per capita income rptd 9-16, 746A2, C2
Ft Dix (NJ) to stay open 10-10, 809E1
DELAWARE, University of (Newark)
Wins NCAA Div II football title 12-8, 1001F2
DELAWARE River
Phila sewage suits settled 5-30, 704E2
DELAWARE v. Prouse
Random car checks by police barred by Sup Ct 3-27, 263D1
DELFIM Netto, Antonio
Brazil agri min designate 1-19, 95B1*
Named Brazil planning min 8-10, outlines anti-inflatn plan 8-15, 612B3
Econ policy, reforms rptd 8-15—10-31, 870E3-871F1
Metalworkers strike continues 11-6, 871G1
Brazil announces new econ policy 12-7, 948G2
DELIVER Unto Satan (book)
Bear acquitted 12-4, 932F1
Della CHIESA, Gen. Carlo Alberto
Scored in intellignc rpt 2-14, 136F1
DELLINGER, David
Arrested in NYC A-protest 10-29, 827E2
DELLON, Alain
Concorde Airport '79 released 8-3, 820A1
DELLUMS, Rep. Ronald V. (D, Calif.)
DC Com chrmn 1-24, 71C1
Chrgs Navy recruiting bias 6-14, 519C3
Sees Castro 10-13, 779E1
Del MONTE Corp.—*See REYNOLDS Industries*
DELP, Grover (Bud)
Spectacular Bid loses Triple Crown 6-9, 448B2
DELSENER, Ron
Gilda Radner Live opens 8-2, 711C3
DELTA Air Lines Inc.
Fuel shortage forces flight cuts 3-6, 162B2
Jet hijacked to Cuba 6-11, 442A1
DELTA Meat Packing Co.
Settles '78 beef-price suit 10-22, 985E3
DELTA Queen (U.S. steamboat)
Carter boats down Mississippi 8-17—8-24, 622F1-623D1
De MENIL, Christophe
Southern Exposure opens 2-27, 292B3
DEMEROL (meperidine)—*See MEDICINE—Drugs*
DEMERS, Roger
Lauds bilingual air control rule 8-22, 651B1
DEMIC, Larry
In NBA draft 6-25, 507A2

1980

DE la GARZA, Rep. E. Kika (D, Tex.)
Reelected 11-4, 844A3
DE la GUARDIA, Adm. Jose Maria
Dismissed 11-15, 903B3
DE la JARA, Jose Maria
In Cuban refugee exit talks 8-29—8-30, 672E2
DE la PENA, George
Nijinsky released 3-20, 216D3
DELAPORTE, Maj. Jean-Jacques
Rptd jailed by Libya 9-9, 709C1
DE la RENTA, Oscar
'80 fashion roundup rptd 998F1
DE la RICA, Jose Miguel
On SEAT investmt 6-4, 467A3
DE LAROSIERE, Jacques
Meets Jamaican prime min 1-15, 99E1
Addresses World Bank-IMF mtg 9-30, 761A2
DE LAURENTIIS, Dino
Flash Gordon released 12-5, 972E3
DELAWARE
US Iran envoys at Dover base 1-30—1-31, 88D3
'Unfit' parent case accepted by Sup Ct 3-24, 265G1
Fla circus tax case refused by Sup Ct 3-24, 265A2
Wilmington busing case declined by Sup Ct 4-28, 368E3
FCC proposes VHF TV statn expansn 9-18, 732A1
New Castle Cnty, Stauffer toxic waste suits filed 10-9, 825B1
Law schl libel case declined by Sup Ct 11-10, 868B3
Water shortage rptd, comm issues warning 12-1, 947B3
Politics & Government
Legislature schedule rptd 18D1
Carter wins Dem caucus vote 3-12, 209B1
Mondale in New Castle 10-9, 780G2
Election results 11-4: pres 838A1, 839A1, D3; cong 840D1, 842E2, 848E1; state 845D2, 847E1
'80 census rptd 12-31, 983D1
DELAWARE Board of Education v. Evans
Case declined by Sup Ct 4-28, 369A1
DELAWARE River Basin Commission
Water warning issued 12-1, 947B3
DELAWARE State College (Dover)
Job bias suit filing time limit upheld by Sup Ct 12-15, 957B2
DELAWARE State College v. Ricks
Case decided by Sup Ct 12-15, 957B2
DELCHEV, Stoyan
Wins Olympic medals 7-24, 7-25, 622E3
DE LEMPICA, Tamara
Dies 3-18, 280A1
DELEON, Carlos (Sugar)
Decisns Camel for WBC cruiserwgt title 11-25, 1001A1
DELERUE, George
Wins Oscar 4-14, 296G1
DELFIM Netto, Antonio
Rischbeiter quits in dispute 1-15, 95D2
Urges export hike, cites import costs 3-5, 191G1
Dockers, metalworkers strike 3-17—4-7, 272B3
In Argentina trade talks 5-15—5-17, 405E2
Survey shows unemploymt rising 5-23, 405G3
Ortiz reelected IDB pres 11-1, 864E3
'81 budget set 12-17, 991C3
DELIS, Luis
Wins Olympic medal 7-28, 624C1
DELLACROCE, Aniello
Galante slaying probe figures indicted 3-3, 215F1
DELLACROCE, Armond
Indicted 3-3, 215D1
DELLA FEMINA, Jerry
Mets fined for ad campaign 5-1, 637D1
DELLUMS, Rep. Ronald V. (D, Calif.)
Addresses Dem conv, makes token challenge 8-13, 611D3
Reelected 11-4, 842E1, 846E3
DELP, Bud
Named top trainer 12-17, 1002C2
DELTA Airlines Inc.
Chicago flight hijacked to Cuba 1-25, NY-Atlanta run 7-22, 617A3
Jet lands at wrong field 6-21, pilot suspended 6-22, 519C2
'70 hijacker jailed in US 6-30, 514D2
Miami flight hijacked to Cuba 8-16, 631C3
N Orleans-Atlanta flight diverted to Cuba 9-13; Charleston flight commandeered 9-17, Havana returns 2 hijackers 9-18, 704B1, B2
DELTORN, Jose
Claims rightists infiltrate police 10-4, 767F2
DEL TREDICI, David
Wins Pulitzer 4-14, 296F2
DEL TUFO, Robert
On NJ chem dump suit 1-30, 93F3
DE LUCA, Allessandra
Arrested 5-20, 523A3
DELUISE, Dom
Fatso released 2-1, 216E2
DELURY, John J.
Dies 2-12, 175G3
DEMBONCZYK, Tadeusz
Wins Olympic medal 7-21, 624E2
DE MERODE, Prince Alexandre
On Olympic drug use rpt 8-3, 590A3
DEMETRIADES, Andreas
Named Cyprus justice min 9-9, 749G2
DEMIANENKO, Viktor
Wins Olympic medal 8-2, 622F1

1976

DEMICHELI, Alberto
Assumes Uruguay pres 6-12, vows dem rule 6-14, 440D3, 441D1
Replaced as pres 7-14, 542A1
Lauds armed forces 8-31, 678E2
DEMICHEV, Pyotr N.
Politburo alternate member 3-5, 195D2
DEMIREL, Suleyman (Turkish premier)
On student unrest 1-9, 192G2
Vs text change in US pact 4-1, 259F2
Accepts Greek peace bid 4-17, 278D2
Addresses Islamic Conf 5-12, 373A2
Tito visits 6-8—6-10, 543D3
Aegean oil search delay rptd 7-13, 538F1
Greece vs in Aegean feud 8-20, cites intl pacts 8-24, 643C3
Assures US on quake 11-28, 897D1
De MITA, Ciriaco
In new Italy Cabt 7-30, 573F1
DEMLEITNER, Elisabeth
Wins Olympic medal 2-7, 159A2
DEMOCRATIC Francaise (book)
Published 10-11, 852C3
DEMOCRATIC Mayors, National Conference of—*See MAYORS, U.S.*
DEMOCRATIC Party—*See under POLITICS*
DEMOCRATS Abroad
Votes at Dem conv OKd 6-29, 490A1
Conv women delegates, table 508E2
Pres votes, table 7-14, 507E2
DEMPSEY, Jack
Ali decisns Norton 9-28, 756F2
DENIAU, Jean-Francois
Dropped from French govt 1-12, 49E2
DENIZ, 'Cacho'
Identified as Diaz abductor 7-6, 7-7, 542A3
DENKTASH, Rauf
In new communal talks 2-17—2-21, 155C1
Replaced as Cyprus negotiator 4-15, 311B2
Elected Turk Cypriot pres 6-20, 456G3
UN votes vs debate role 11-9, 863E1

DENMARK—*See also ADB, EUROPEAN Community, IEA, NATO, OECD*
CP dep bugged in '58 1-9, 48D3
SDR rate rptd 1-15, 14A3
Listed as 'free' nation 1-19, 20B3
Obscenity, drug crackdown 1-26, 101A1
'Free city' to be razed 2-29, 252F1
VAT increased 3-1, 252G1
WHO cancer studies rptd 6-3, 484B3
Austerity plan adopted 8-19, workers strike 8-19—8-23, 637G2-C3
Jorgensen shuffles Cabt 9-9, 712F1
Central Bank ups discount rate 10-5, lowers 12-6, 1001A2
Greenland mineral rights kept 11-8, 949B2
Truck drivers strike 11-18—11-26, 905B1
'74 tax rate rptd 11-18, 905F1
Mid Oct-Nov jobless rate up 11-29, 935C2
Wage, price freeze imposed 12-5, 1001F1-A2
European Force Reduction Issues—*See under EUROPE*
Foreign Relations (misc.)
Sovt agents '75 ouster rptd 1-11, 101C1
Europn socialists meet 1-18—1-19, 48F2
Spanish soclst aid set 1-24, 120G1
Vs World Bank Chile loan 2-3, 99G2
Angola MPLA recognized 2-18, 163B1
Coastal defns steps set 2-27, 252C1
France quits currency 'snake' 3-15, 229A2
Viet orphans allowed to stay 3-16, relocated 3-19, 3-21, 252D1
Firms taken off Arab blacklist 3-24—4-3, 242C1
Vs WHO anti-Israel stand 5-19, 355D2
Jorgensen at intl soc dems mtg 5-23—5-25, 449B3
IDB entry set 6-3, 465D3
Lauds Israel Uganda raid 7-4, 486G1
French, E Ger constructn deal rptd 7-12, 889C2
EC entry pattern cited 7-27, 853E3
Trade deficit forces record loan 8-5, 588D2

1977

DEMIREL, Suleyman (Turkish premier)
Student clashes rptd 2-3, 138D2
Gen scores govt 2-10, responds 2-11, coalitn divisns rptd 2-16, 138B2
Sees US envoy 2-20—2-22, 122C2
Scores US arms aid delays 4-29, 351A2
Forgn reserves crisis 5-24—7-4, 565D2
Ecevit wins electns 6-5, 451D1
Asked to form new govt 7-4, Erbakan backs 7-5, 530A2
Forms govt 7-21, 565D1
Wins confidence vote 8-1, 641C1
Munic electns weaken govt 12-11, resigns 12-31, 1018E1
DEMOCRATIC Institutions, Center for the Study of (Santa Barbara, Calif.)
Hutchins dies 5-14, 452B3
Mitchell succeeds Hutchins 11-21, 927F2
DEMOCRATIC Party—*See under POLITICS*
De MOHRENSCHILDT, George
Found dead 3-29, CIA link rptd 3-31, 228B3
De MURALT, Bertrand
Commits suicide 5-8, bank fails 5-9, 489D3
DENIAU, Jean-Francois
Named forgn affairs min 9-26, 744F2
DENISON Mines Ltd.
Uranium cartel role rptd 4-25, 479F2
Scores Canada cartel probe 10-19, 895B3
TVA sues re uranium 11-18, 895G1
DENKTASH, Rauf
Sees Makarios, sets talks 1-27, 2-12; press conf 2-13, 108B3
Makarios plans resignatn 2-16, 147C1
Meets US envoy 2-23—2-26, 147A1
To reopen Famagusta, Markarios scores 7-22, 764B2
Asks Turk Cypriot independnc 8-16, 636B2
Splits with Turkey over independnc 9-24, 946D3

DENMARK—*See also EC, ESA, IDB, IEA, NATO, OECD*
Armed forces subversn rptd 1-31, 426E2
Heroin addictn rptd up 10-17—10-21, 971E3
Gang battle kills youth 11-6, 883A1
Economy & Labor (domestic)
Shipyard decline predicted 1-17, 62A1
Electn called, econ problems cited 1-22, 61D3
Labor dispute closes newspapers 1-31, 115D2
Dec '75-76 inflatn rate rptd 2-7, 87B2
Newspaper strike dvpts 2-17—5-23, 426B3
'76 econ growth rate rptd 2-22, 146C2
Unemplymt rate estimated 3-1, 373F1
Tax package OKd 3-8, 373E1
Defense budget passed 3-29, 426A2
Wage agreemt passed 4-15, 373F1
SAS strike setld 5-9—5-20, 469G3
PVC plants blocked 7-7, 672E1
Govt asks tax hike, other govt aims rptd 8-22; jobless rate at 7%, rptd rising 8-31, 672D2-A3
1st in '75 world pay, buying power 11-6, 853C3
Foreign Relations (misc.)—*See also 'Monetary, Trade & Aid' below*
UN Assemb member 3G3
Polish consul ousted 1-10, 62B1
'76 Eur Cncl pact vs terror cited 9G2
Poll shows EC support wanes 1-19, 62C1
In 14-natn sulphur-dioxide pact 1-19, 109B3
Austria jails '76 Pole hijacker 2-15, 425A2
Sovt radio jamming rptd 2-23, 426A3
USSR mocks defense chiefs 3-23, 426B3
NATO concerned re budget; Warsaw Pact maneuvers cited 426D2-A3
Poles ask W Ger asylum 5-3, 427D1
Spain exiles Basque prisoners 6-9, 454B1
Yugo ousts newsman 6-15, 473A2
To take Indochina refugees 8-31, 685E2
Eur Cncl to study Turkey rights abuses in Cyprus 9-8, 764G1-A2; rpt shelved, Greece protests 11-3, 946E3

1978

De MICHELI, Adriano
Viva Italia released 7-9, 970C3
DEMIREL, Suleyman
Ecevit named premier 1-1, 8B2
Vs Ecevit talks with Greece 3-12, 216C3
Ankara prosecutor assassinated 3-24, 230A2
Blames govt for riots 12-26, 1021F1
De MITA, Ciriaco
Italy southn regions min 3-11, 191B1
DEMOCRATIC Kampuchea—*See CAMBODIA*
DEMOCRATIC Majority, Coalition for—*See COALITION for a Democratic Majority*
DEMOCRATIC Party—*See under POLITICS*
DEMONE, Michael
Cuba frees 10-3, 777A1
DEMPSEY, Jack
Gene Tunney dies 11-7, 972F3
DEMPSEY, William H.
RR coal carrying capacity backed 1-18, 49F1
On record rail industry losses 5-9, 433E3
De MUNN, Jeffrey
Prayer For My Daughter opens 1-17, 760B3
DEN, Hideo
China denies chrg re Senkaku 4-15, 278A2
DENARD, Bob
Comoro govt cncl ouster rptd 7-23, 596D1
Quits Comoro army 9-26, leaves 9-27, 798B3
DENEAU Trophy, Paul—*See HOCKEY—Awards*
DENGLER, Michael Herbert
Denied name chng 2-13, 172C3
DENIAU, Jean-Francois
Named French external trade min 4-5, 245G2
Signs China-France trade pact 12-4, 986A2
De NIRO, Robert
Deer Hunter released 12-14, 1030F2
DENKTASH, Rauf
See Ecevit on Cyprus solutn 1-19, 148E1
Asks joint Greek econ projcts 2-15, 148D1
Konuk resigns 3-24, 226D2
Hails US on Turkey arms embargo end 8-2, 588B1
Turk Cypriot Cabt mins resign 11-28, 922G2-B3

DENMARK—*See also COUNCIL of Europe, EC, GATT, IDB, IEA, NATO, OECD*
Free City squatters lose claim 2-2, 89D3; get reprieve 2-9, 131B1
Energy conservatn progress seen 6-5, 449E3★, 450E1
Economy & Labor (domestic)
Higher educ applicatns rptd up 1-25, 89G3
'77, Dec jobless rates rptd 1-31, 89F3
'73-77 wage gain rptd 2-27, 189B3
Fishermen protest Baltic quotas, block Zealand traffic 5-5, 371D2
Fishermen renew Zealand port blockades; demonstrate in Copenhagen, ask Jakobsen resignatn 5-10, 436A3
Fishermen loan legis rptd introduced 5-18, 436D3
6-mo price, profit freeze; VAT tax set 8-30, 687G2, C3
Jorgensen proposes wage-price controls, tax hikes, spending curbs 10-3, 774A1
European Force Reduction Talks—*See under EUROPE*
Foreign Relations (misc.)—*See also 'Monetary, Trade, Aid & Investment' and 'UN' below*
Amb ends Cambodia visit 1-21, calls Pnompenh 'ghost city' 1-22, 43A2; Thai min disputes 2-2, 61E1
France, W Ger OK ESA rocket launcher 2-6—2-7, 122B1
Jorgensen's remarks on French electn spur dispute 2-23—3-1, 167G1
S Africa culture, sports ties banned 3-11, 193C3
USSR spy trawlers rptd in Baltic 3-11, 391A3
USSR denies use of spy trucks 3-15, 291F2
Eur conservative group formed 4-24, 424C3
ESA communicatns satellite launched 5-12, 384D3
Ugandan envoy loses libel suit re murder chrg 6-18, 688B1
Bulgarian aide given asylum 7-26, 688D1

1979

De MICHELI, Adriano
Till Marriage Do Us Part released 7-20, 820E3
De MILLE, Agnes
Oklahoma opens 12-13, 1007D2
DEMIREL, Suleyman (Turkish premier)
Ecevit govt censure motion fails 1-4, 8B1
At Milliyet editor's funeral 2-4, 117A1
Predicts Ecevit overthrow 3-29, 333D2
Oppositn to U-2 flights rptd 5-16, 397E3
Parlt recesses after oppositn moves fail 6-28, 488G1, B2
Chrgs re Kurdish unrest rptd 8-24, 795F3
Lockheed bribe cover-up chrgd 9-20, 775F1
Party wins parlt electns 10-14, asks gen electns 10-15; Ecevit govt resigns 10-16, 795A3
Forms govt 11-12, 876B1
Confrmd in office by confidence vote 11-25, 929G2-A3
Meets Pope 11-28, 930C3
DEMME, Jonathan
Last Embrace released 5-3, 528F2
DEMOCRATIC Majority, Coalition for—*See COALITION for a Democratic Majority*
DEMOCRATIC Party—*See under POLITICS*
DEMPSEY, Rear Adm. James Charles
Dies 7-9, 588F2
DEMPSEY, John
Named NASL top defensive player 8-25, 776C1
DEMPSEY, Rick
In World Series 10-10—10-17, 816E2
DEMPSTER, Curt
Welfare opens 5-10, 712D3
DEMY, Jacques
Umbrellas Of Cherbourg opens 2-1, 292E3
DENEAU Trophy, Paul—*See HOCKEY—Awards*
DENHAM, Mary
Candida opens 3-6, 711A2
DENISON Mines Ltd.
Reserve Oil accepts bid 8-14, ends agrmt 10-31, 986B3
DENKTASH, Rauf
New intercommunal talks set 5-19, 387D2
DENMAN, Roy
On EC-China textile pact 6-18, 554G3

DENMARK—*See also COUNCIL of Europe, EC, GATT, IDB, IEA, NATO, OECD*
Atomic Energy & Safeguards
Swedish plant protests 4-1, 4-3, 246D1
A-plants deferred 4-9, 276B2
A-power referendum planned 8-22, 668D1
Sweden issues study 11-19, 910F3
Economy & Labor
'78 living standards ranked 2-2, 109G1
'78 per capita GNP ranked 3d 7-24, 575E3
'80 budget rptd, oil impact noted 8-28, 668A1
OECD study rptd 9-7, 668F1
Govt coalitn end linked 10-23, 751C3
Soc Dems gain in electns 10-23, 812D3
Heinesen replaced as finance min 10-26, 855B1
Wage-price freeze, loan curbs set 11-4, 855C1
Jorgensen outlines legis progrm 11-6, 855F1-A2
Energy—*See also 'Atomic' above*
Iran oil cutoff impact assessed 2-20, 126A3
Gasoline conservatn urged, 15% cut seen 5-22, 396C3
Budget, oil prices linked 8-28, 668A1
Govt coalitn end linked 10-23, 751C3
European Force Reduction Talks—*See under EUROPE*
Foreign Relations (misc.)—*See also 'Atomic' above, 'Monetary' and 'UN' below*
Chile refugee relocatn rptd 5-7, 369B3
USSR vs A-missiles 10-13–10-16, 880A3
Sovt-bloc A-arms talks seen 12-7, 938A2
Government & Politics—*See also other appropriate subheads in this section*
Eur Parlt electns 6-7, 433A1, 434E1
Jorgensen resigns, calls electns 9-28, 751A3
Soc Dems gain in electn 10-23, 812A3
Jorgensen forms new govt 10-26, 855A1

1980

DE MICHELIS, Gianni
Italy state participatn min 4-4, 275G3
DEMICHELLI, Alberto
Dies 10-12, 876C1
DE MILLE, Agnes
Brigadoon opens 10-16, 892A3
DEMIREL, Suleyman (Turkish premier)
Mil warns pol ldrs, urges unity; comments 1-2, 7C2, F2
Ecevit backs coalitn govt 1-9, 22D3
Sets new econ measures 1-25, 80A1
Sets debt plan 1-28, 80D1
Ecevit chrgs repressn 2-14, violence scored 2-15, 135D2
Sees $3 bln forgn aid 3-8, OECD pkg deferred 3-26, 236C2
Labor unrest mounts 3-13, 197A2
Pres electn deferred 3-22, 236F1
US bases, aid pact signed 3-29, 255B3
OECD OKs $1.16 bln aid 4-15, 295B3
IMF econ proposals rptd 5-6, 446C1
Bars sanctns vs Iran 5-22, 393B2
Pres voting chng barred 5-24—5-25, 410G3-411B1
On Apr inflatn drop 5-28, 410E3
Ecevit vs re terrorism 5-30, 445C3
IMF OKs $1.6 bln loan 6-18, 468A2
Wins confidence vote 7-2, 500E2
Clarifies U-2 flight stance 7-4, 526C1
Ecevit scores Fatsa move 7-11, 544D3
Erim death deplored 7-19, 567D3
Anti-terrorist bills set 7-24, comments 7-25, 580A3, B3
Mil coup ousts govt 9-12, 679F2
Arrested 9-12; coup ldrs back econ plan 9-15, 696E2, B3
New premr named 9-20, 720B3
Freed 10-11, 793C3
DEMOCRATIC Party—*See under POLITICS*
DE MORAES, Vinicius
Dies 7-9, 608F1
DENARDIS, Lawrence J.
Elected to US House 11-4, 842D2, 848D1
DE NELO, Eurico
Sworn Portugal interior min 1-3, 21E3*
DENGLER, Michael
Name chng case dismissed by Sup Ct 5-19, 440D2
DENGLER v. Minnesota
Case dismissed by Sup Ct 5-19, 440D2
DENG Xiaoping (Teng Hsiao-ping)
US amb's pol gaffes rptd 1-30, 200D2
Quits as army chief 2-25, 172A1
Politburo promotes 2 followers 2-29, 171G3
New party guidelines issued 3-15, 231G1
Addresses Italy rptrs; scores USSR, affirms US ties 4-17, 314G1
On govt reorganizatn 4-17, 351F1
Delivers eulogy for Liu 5-17, 388F3
Meets with Bush 8-22, 646E1
Hua quotes Mao philosophy 9-7, 678B1
Zhao becomes premr 9-10, 677C1
Zhao vows govt reforms 9-11, 706D3
Giscard visits China 10-15—10-22, 829B3
Wang, Yao admit plot vs appointmt 11-24, Jiang denies plot 11-26, 975G1-A2
Hua scored in press 12-16, 12-30, 975E3
DE NIRO, Robert
Raging Bull released 11-14, 972G3
DENKER, Henry
Horowitz & Mrs Washn opens 4-2, 392C3
DENKIN, Marty
Pintor KOs Owen 9-19, Owen dies 11-3, 907B3
DENKTASH, Rauf
UN-sponsored talks resume 8-9, 633F2
DENMARK—*See also ADB, COUNCIL of Europe, CSCE, EC, GATT, IDB, IEA, MBFR, NATO, OECD*
TB vaccine study rptd 1-20, 632C2
Princess Anne dies 9-27, 755A2
Atomic Energy & Safeguards
A-plant decisn deferred 1-26, 96D3
Economy & Labor
Armed forces cut proposed 1-21, 96F3
Discount rate hike rptd 2-29, 153D3
Overtime curbs planned 3-13, 256A1
Austerity plan rptd 4-10, 273F2
New econ plan proposed 5-5, 351A2
Labor costs rptd 8-12, 698D1
Foreign Relations (misc.)—*See also 'Monetary', 'UN Policy' below*
Moscow Olympic boycott rejected 1-22, 68D1
Mex emb occupied 2-18, 152A1
USSR May Day parade shunned 5-1, 354G2
ESA rocket test fails 5-23, 397G2
ESA plans comet probe 7-15, 548A1
Westn labor costs compared 8-12, 698D1
Monetary, Trade, Aid & Investment
'79 trade deficit rptd up 1-29, 96G3
Trade deficit linked to austerity plan 4-10, 273F2
Paymts deficit spurs plan 5-5, 351C2
IMF revises SDR valuatn method 9-17, 695C2
IEA sets oil buying curb, stocks called 'adequate' 12-9, 932D1
Norway orders fishing halt 12-10, 969C3
Sports
Moscow Olympic boycott rejected 1-22, 68D1
Moscow Olympic results 7-20—8-3, flag controversy 7-24, 588E1, B3, 622F2, 623D2, B3, 625F3, G3
UN Policy & Developments
Women's parly, alternate conf held in Copenhagen 7-14—7-30, 587E1-D3
Assemb Palestinian state res abstentn 7-29, 572F1
U.S. Relations
US scores mil spending 10-3, 737D1

1976

Taiwan opera rptd barred 8-21, 712G1
Argentina violence scored 8-26, 672E2
Tito cancels Margrethe visit 9-13, 734G2
N Korean diplomats expelled 10-15, 799A3
W Ger mark revalued 10-17, 782B1, C1
Deportee hijacks Polish plane, surrenders 11-4, 907A2
Crown devaluatn vs W Ger mark cited 12-6, 1001B2
Rpt grain imports planned 12-31, 977E3
Greenland—*See GREENLAND*
Obituaries
Dam, Henrik 4-17, 368E2
Kampmann, Viggo, 6-3, 524A3
Knud, Prince 6-14, 484E3
Sports
Olympic results 7-18—7-31, 573E3, 574B2, 576F3
U.S. Relations
'58 CIA bugging rptd 1-9, 48E1
Ship in US Bicentennial event 7-4, 488A3, D3
DENNIS, Patrick
Dies 11-6, 970E1
DENT, Frederick B.
On steel import quotas 3-16, 212E3, 213E1
Named to payoff probe 3-21, 262F2
Ford bars shoe import curb 4-16, 322A1
US sets steel quotas 6-7, Japan OKs pact 6-9, 430F3, 431E1
Rpts brandy duty hike 11-26, 976G2
DENT, Rep. John H. (D, Penn.)
Backs black-lung bill 3-2, 182B1
US ends car dumping probe 5-4, 321B2
Reelected 11-2, 830F3
DENT, Phil
Wins US Open mixed doubles 9-12, 716D1
DENTISTRY—*See under MEDICINE*
Den TOON, Willem
Bernhard role in '71 W Ger jet buy rptd 9-2, 684G2
Den UYL, Joop
At Denmark socialist conf 1-18—1-19, 48A3
Confrms Bernhard bribe, sets probe 2-9, 131E2
At Portugal socialist mtg 3-13—3-14, 222F3
Confrms '51 Argentina bribe 3-18, 254G3
On Eur Parlt enlargemt 7-15, 529F2
Sees royal couple on probe rpt 8-23, 626A3
Details Bernhard probe rpt to parlt 8-26, 626F2; text excerpts 627A1
Parlt vs Bernhard prosecutn 8-30, 642D2
Rpts 3 legislators approached by Lockheed 9-1, 684B2
DENVER, Colo.—*See COLORADO*
DENVER Post (newspaper)
Breaks Callaway story 3-12, 197A2
Carter endorsement rptd 10-30, 831G2
DENVER Rocky Mountain News (newspaper)
Ford endorsement rptd 10-30, 827F3
De OLIVIERA, Joao
Wins Olympic medal 7-30, 576C1
De OTEIZA, Jose Andres
Mex natl resources min 12-2, 907A1
De PAULA Chavez, Francisco
On Lockheed probe delay 8-23; ct scores 9-1, 740G1
De POIX, Vice Adm.
Named as Rockwell guest 3-17, 200G3
DePREE, Willard A.
Amb to Mozambique 1-20; confrmd 2-4, 110A2
DERAIN, Andre (1880-1954)
Works donated to France 1-31, 124F2

1977

W Eur heroin conf 10-17—10-21, 971E3
Nigeria pirates raid ship 11-21, govt scores 11-22, 986E2
Abstains from UN Israel occupatn res 11-25, 910D2
Government & Politics—*See also other appropriate subheads in this section*
Parlt dissolved, electn set 1-22, 61D3
Soc Dems make electn gains 2-15, 115D1
Cabt named 2-25, 372G3
Jorgensen on electn results 3-1, 373D1
Secret svc probe ordered 7-8, 672G1
Cabt chngs announced 10-1, 10-3, 882E3
Greenland—*See under 'G'*
Helsinki Agreement—*See EUROPE—Security and Cooperation*
Monetary, Trade & Aid (including all foreign economic developments)
UK fishing limits protested 1-29, 115G2-A3
'76 trade deficit rptd 2-1, 115F2
UK-Irish Rockall dispute 2-3, 329C2
IMF SDR defined 87G2
GATT to probe US ruling on Japan elec duties 5-23, 416C2
IWC cuts whaling quotas 6-24, 496F3
'77 paymts deficit forecast 7-31, 586D2
North Sea gas line OKd 8-1, 872C1; delay rptd 12-9, 967D3
Sweden quits 'snake' 8-29, 709A1
Krona devalued 5% 8-29, 709B1
Jan-June paymts deficit, trade data rptd 8-31, 672F2-A3
S Africa investmt bar backed 9-20, 771B1
UK bans some SAS flights 10-30, 882G3
U.S. Relations
US F-16 sale review set 1-17, 70D3
US-ESA flight set 2-16, 170C3
US F-16 pact set 5-5, 441A2
GATT to probe US ruling on Japan 5-23, 416C2
ESA satellite launching aborted 9-13, 735G3
DENSEN-Gerber, Dr. Judianne
Testifies on child abuse 5-23, 432E3
DENSON, Terry W.
Indicted re Torres 10-20, 820G3
DENT, Bucky
In World Series 10-11—10-18, 806B3
DENT, Frederick B.
Replaced as trade rep 3-29, 272D3
DENT, Harry
SBA minority aid abuse chrgd 7-8, 577C3
DENT, Rep. John H. (D, Pa.)
'76 special interest gifts rptd 2-15, 128F2
Admin asks $2.50 min wage 3-24, 229F2
Minimum wage bill signed 11-1, 834C1
DENT, Phil
Australia wins Davis Cup 12-4, 970E2
DENTAL Association, American
FTC sues 1-14, 156G2
DENTISTRY—*See under MEDICINE*
Den UYL, Joop (Netherlands premier)
Govt resigns 3-22, 221A3
Fails to form govt 5-25—8-25, resignatn accepted 8-25, 656B1
On attack to free hostages 6-11, 467E3
Parties heal rift over abortn 9-2, Queen names mediator 9-5, 729F2
DENVER, Colo.—*See COLORADO*
DENVER, University of
Mitchell to head study center 11-21, 927F2
DEOXRIBONUCLEIC Acid (DNA)—*See GENETICS*
DEPARTMENT & Variety Stores
2d ¼ profits rptd 7-28, 668B3, C3
Burnham dies 10-10, 872B1
Abercrombie closing planned 11-12, stores rptd closed 12-14, 980D3
Marshall Field vs Carter Hawley bid 12-14, 1004A2

1978

Policy shift barred by new coalitn govt 8-30, 687G3
USSR physicist arrives 10-10, 946F3
Government & Politics—*See also other appropriate subheads in this section*
Death penalty for terrorism rejctd 2-10, 131D1
Glistrup fined in tax case 2-17, 130B3
Soc Dem gain in local electns 3-7, 189D2
Death penalty in wartime abolished 4-29, 333C3
Greenland home rule proposed 5-15, 371F2
Glistrup wins tax case appeal 5-23, 436F2
Anderson quits Cabt, sets parlt bid 6-2, 596E1
Soc Dems weigh broader coalitn 6-2, 596F1
Coalitn govt formed 8-30, 687G2-688A1
Jorgensen opens parlt, outlines legis goals 10-3, 774A1, D1
Greenland home rule voted 11-17, 902D1
Greenland—*See GREENLAND*
Helsinki Agreement—*See EUROPE—Security and Cooperation*
Monetary, Trade, Aid & Investment
Iran lifts trade ban 1-11, 55F2
'77 trade, paymts deficits rptd 2-6, 2-14, 2-22, 130G3
S Africa investmt banned 3-11, 193C3
'77 forgn loans record rptd 3-14, 189D3
Krone dropped from new SDR basket 4-3, 300E3
US OKs uranium exports 4-9, 278G3
US F-16 review urged 4-24, 407D2
Fishermen protest Baltic quotas 5-5, 371E2
W Ger fishermen join protest 5-10, 436C3
Paymt deficit measures set 8-30, 687E3
Forgn dvpt aid level proposed 10-3, 774D1
W Ger mark revalued up 10-16, 798C2
At Brussels monetary summit, EMS entry backed 12-4—12-5 952C2
Ireland to join EMS 12-15, 979F1
UK air pact OKd 12-22, 1017F1
Obituaries
Krag, Jens Otto 6-22, 540B3
UN Policy & Developments
Hartling heads refugee post 1-1, 62B1
Leb peace force (Unifil) formed 3-19, 197D2; **for peacekeeping developments, see MIDDLE EAST—LEBANON**
Sea Law Conf talks continue 5-23—7-15, 8-21—9-16, 732E3
Racism conf boycotted 8-26, 676B2
Assemb member 713E3
Dvpt aid quota funding proposed 10-3, 774D1
U.S. Relations
US alerts to Sovt satellite fall 57E1
Jorgensen in US 2-23, 167A2
Jorgensen backs US energy legis 4-8, 257G3
US OKs uranium exports 4-9, 278G3
GAO urges F-16 review 4-24, 407D2
US launches ESA satellite 5-12, 384D3
US seabed mining bill debated at UN conf 8-21—9-16, 732E3
DENNY, Sandy
Dies 4-21, 356E2
DENSON, Terry W.
Sentncd in Torres case 3-28, appeal rptd 12-14, 991C3
DENT, Bucky
Yankees win AL East playoff 10-2, 778E2
In World Series 10-10—10-17, named Series MVP 10-17, 799F2
DENT, Rep. John H. (D, Pa.)
Not standing for reelectn 5-16, 389E3
Bailey wins seat 11-7, 849F2
DENTAL Association, American
Dental insurnc coverage rptd up 5-21, 578C2
DENTISTRY—*See under MEDICINE & Health*
D'ENTREMONT, Francois
Rpts RCMP '72 FLQ infiltratn 1-10, 35A2
Den UYL, Joop
Soclsts slip in local electns 5-31, 454B3
DENVER, Colo.—*See under COLORADO*
DEOXYRIBONUCLEIC Acid (DNA)—*See GENETICS*
DEPAKENE (valproate)—*See MEDICINE—Drugs*
DEPARDIEU, Gerald
Barocco released 4-7, 618B3
Get Out Handkerchiefs released 12-17, 1030A3
DEPARTMENT of Revenue v. Association of Washington Stevedoring Cos.
State tax OKd by Sup Ct 4-26, 344C1
DEPARTMENT & Variety Stores
Marshall Field to buy Liberty House stores 1-20, plans Houston store 2-7, 185F1
Dayton Hudson to buy Mervyn's; Grace to buy King's 1-23, 66C2
Carter Hawley drops Marshall Field bid 2-22, Wanamaker merger planned 3-8, 185E1
BAT Industries US retail divisn cited 5-5, 345D3
Montgomery Ward warranty violatn chrgd 10-11, 942B1
3d ¼ profits rptd up 10-30, 919G2
Radio Shack chrmn dies 11-4, 972F3
DePAUL University (Chicago, Ill.)
Corzine in NBA draft 6-9, 457G3

1979

Greenland—*See GREENLAND*
Monetary, Trade, Aid & Investment
Iran oil cutoff impact assessed 2-20, 126A3
Sweden seeks joint coal progrm 3-13, 214A1
Unilever trust chrgs filed 7-2, 563F3
OECD study rptd 9-7, 668F1, A2
EMS currencies realigned 9-24, 719A1
Paymts deficit rise forecast, wage-price freeze linked 11-4, 855C1, D1
Obituaries
Haekkerup, Per 3-13, 272D2
UN Policy & Developments
Membership listed 695G2
U.S. Relations
US A-accident sparks Swedish plant protests 4-1, 4-3, 246D1; plant deferral 4-9, 276A2, B2
US air base unaffected by Greenland electn 4-4, 286D1
Mondale visits Eur 4-11–4-22, 299C2
Denmark backs 6-mo A-missile delay 12-7, 938G1
DENNEHY, Brian
Says I, Says He opens 2-20, 292G2
DENNY, John
Traded to Indians 12-7, 1002F2
DENSON, Terry W.
Wins Torres case appeal 2-6, 156C2
Resentenced 10-30, 839C3
DENTAL Association, American (ADA)
Dental ad accord reached 4-27, 596D1
DENTISTRY—*See under MEDICINE*
DENTON, Harold R.
On NRC A-plant closing order 3-13, 186F1
On 3 Mile I A-accident 3-31–4-3, 244E1, 245A1, E2-G3
On 3 Mile I clean-up 4-4, 4-5, declares crisis over 4-9, 259D2, 260B1, D2, 261A2, F2
3 Mile I NRC transcripts released 4-12, 275G3
On Babcock plant closings 4-25, 4-27, 321E3, 322B1
Testifies on 3 Mile I accident 4-30, Met Ed disputes chrgs 5-7, 344E1-A2
Delays reactor licensing, reorganizes staff 5-21, 381D3
Lifts NRC reactor freeze 8-22, reverses decision 8-23, 665A1
DENVER, Colo.—*See COLORADO*
DENVER, University of
NCAA rejcts Brody reforms 1-9, 102G3
DENVER Post, The (newspaper)
New JFK '63 murder film rptd 2-8, 166C1
DENZER, Judge Richard
Sentences Holzer 5-3, 431A3
DEOXYRIBONUCLEIC Acid (DNA)—*See GENETICS*
DEPARTMENT & Variety Stores
Sony video recorder copyright trial opens 1-22, 120F2
Sears sues US re bias laws 1-24, 92B1
Penney's ex-chrmn dies 3-22, 272G2
Mays chrmn convctd of IRS bribe 3-26, 239E3
Alexander's sentncd re TV rebate fraud 3-29, 298C3
Woolworth sought by Brascan 4-9, spurns bid 4-11; holds Revco merger talks, other dvpts 4-12–4-23, 303B3-304C2
Sears ends fed contract work 4-24, 366A1
Sears sets price rollback 4-27, 4-30, 363C1
Sears suit vs US dismissed 5-15, 365A3
Woolworth bid setbacks for Brascan 5-25; offer dropped, suits setld 5-29, 440C2
Montgomery Ward settles FTC credit chrg 5-29, 596A2
City Stores files bankruptcy 7-27, 648F3
Sears TV repair recall set 8-31, 903D1
Mail order finance chrg case refused by Sup Ct 10-1, 768B2
US sues Sears re job bias 10-22, 885B3
3d 1/4 profit drop rptd 10-31, 923B1
DePAUL University (Chicago, Ill.)
NCAA basketball tourn results 3-26, 238F2, A3
Meyer in basketball HOF 4-30, 526C3

1980

DENNIS Jr., C. Cecil
Executed 4-22, US asylum bid denial rptd 4-29, 353G1, C2
DENNISON, Adm. Robert Lee
Dies 3-14, 279B2
DENNISTON, Leslie
Happy New Year opens 4-27, 392A3
DENNIS v. Sparks
Case decided by Sup Ct 11-17, 882B1
'Mr Justice' title dropped by Sup Ct 11-17, 882A3
DENNY, Cleveland
KOd by Hart 6-20, dies; Canada launches probe 7-7, 907B3
DENT, Phil
Loses South Pacific tourn 10-12, 947A2
DENTED (play)
Opens 8-11, 756C3
DENTON, Harold R.
38 A-plants fail NRC safety rules 1-2, 16G3-17A1
3 Mile I gas venting proposed 3-12, 248D3
DENTON, Jeremiah
Wins Ala US Sen primary 9-2, 682G2
Elected to US Sen 11-4, 840C1, 846A1, 849E1
DENUNZIO, Ralph D.
Named Securities Indus Assn chrmn 11-6, 959B2
DEN UYL, Joop
Govt censure vote fails 6-27, 499F1
DENVER—*See COLORADO*
DENVER Post, The (newspaper)
Times Mirror Co to buy 10-22, 857C1
DE OLIVIERA, Joao Carlos
Wins Olympic medal 7-25, 624A1
DEPARTMENT of Education v. Seattle University
Case accepted by Sup Ct 12-1, 918B2
DEPARTMENT of Energy v. Mobil Oil
Case refused by Sup Ct 5-12, 426D2
DEPARTMENT & Variety Stores
Sears appliance performance claim order rptd 5-19, 703D2
Woolworth's ex-chrmn dies 7-6, 608C2
Korvettes financial dvpts, closings 8-22—10-9, 985C3
Bruce Gimbel dies 10-7, 876F1
Kress liquidatn set 11-6, 986B1
Boston transit system shuts down 12-6, resumes svc 12-7, 939E2
DEPAUL University (Chicago, Ill.)
Aguirre named top coll basketball player, Meyer named top coach 3-21, 240E3, F3
NCAA basketball tourn results 3-24, 240A2

1976

De ROULET, Vincent W. (d. 1975)
Alcoa claims solicited funds 7-16, 690E1-C2
DEROW, Peter A.
Newsweek pres, publisher 10-5, 892A2
DERR, Dr. John
On Turkish quake 11-24, 897F1
DERRICK Jr., Rep. Butler C. (D, S.C.)
Reelected 11-2, 830A4
DERRIEN, Patt
Dem conv rule debated 7-13, 513D1
DERSU Uzala (film)
Wins Oscar 3-29, 240A3
DERWINSKI, Rep. Edward J. (R, Ill.)
Reelected 11-2, 829F2
DES (diethylstilbestrol)—*See 'Drugs' under MEDICINE*
DESAI, Hitendra
On Gujarat unrest 2-4, 101C3
Named works min 12-22, 1006C1
DESAI, Makarand
Scores Gandhi rule 4-24, 313A2
De SANTIAGO, Lt. Gen. Fernando
Replaced 9-22, 753A1
DeSAPIO, Carmine G.
Pleads not guilty 5-24, 442B3
Indictmt dismissed 12-17, 1016B2
DESCHENES, Jules
Judicial probe rpt issued 2-12, 220E3 *
Trudeau vs judicial interfernc probe 3-3, 187F3 *
OKs bilingual pilots 9-7, 692D2
De SEQUEIRA, Erasmo
Chrgs 100,000 detained 2-4, 101D3
DESERET (Utah) News
On Gilmore case 11-13, 891B2
DESERTS—*See RESOURCES, Natural*
DES Journees Entieres Dans les Arbres (play)
Opens 5-6, 1014D3
DES Moines, Ia.—*See IOWA*
DES Moines Register (newspaper)
Risser wins Pulitzer 5-3, 352E3
Carter interview 8-25, 632E2
Carter endorsement rptd 10-30, 831D3
DESTREMAU, Bernard
In Australia 2-4, 116A2
DESYR, Luc
Cited re Cabt shuffle 4-6, 4-9, 267F2
DETENTE—*For Soviet-U.S. relations, see 'U.S. Relations' under USSR*
EC rpt urges detente with USSR 1-7, 20G1
W Ger defends 'Ostpolitik' 1-29, 157G3
Brezhnev terms detente 'leading trend', accuses Peking 2-24, 193F2, 194C2
Ford vs word 'detente' 3-1, 165E3
Kreisky lauds 3-12, 380E2
US Sen thwarts resolutn 3-22, 245F3
Senegal pres on 4-19, 356C1
Giscard visits US 5-17—5-22, 372G1, C2
E Ger affirms W Ger detente 5-18, 381E1
USSR scores US, W Ger, China 5-19, 381F1
NATO stresses 5-21, 353B1
Fraser anti-Sovt talk scored 6-1, 438A3
US Dem platform text 6-15, 476E1
Kissinger on E-W ties 6-25, 466A2, C2
E, W Eur CP conf backs 6-30, 461D1
Fraser stresses limits 7-29, 554A2
US GOP platform com OKs plank 8-13, 582C3
US GOP conv platform plank OKd 8-18, 600F3
Soclst Intl topic 11-26—11-28, 935A3
DETROIT, Mich.—*See MICHIGAN*
DETROIT Edison Co.
Sup Ct allows trust suit 7-6, 569F1
DETROIT Free Press (newspaper)
Carter endorsement rptd 10-30, 831G2
DETROIT News, The (newspaper)
Ariz crime probed 10-2, 849D2
Ford endorsement rptd 10-30, 827G3
DEUTSCHE Bank AG (Frankfurt)
Buys IMF gold 9-15, 739D3
DEVCON Corp.
Boycott rpt released 10-18, 786B1

DEVELOPING Nations—*See also regional headings (e.g., AFRICA); specific country and organization names*
IMF Jamaica accord on aid, gold sale trust fund planned 1-8, 1-9, 13B1, 14C1; text excerpts 1-9, 15A1

1977

DEPROGRAMMING—*See under RELIGIOUS Cults*
DEREGULATION of Industry—*See industry names*
DERIAN, Patricia
In Argentina 8-7—8-10, 670C1
De RIBEMOND, Patrick
Police versn of de Broglie murder questnd 1-5—1-9, 44D1
De RUDDER, Dr. Jean
Antiviral drug rptd 8-10, 675B3
De RUITER, Johan
Named Dutch justice min 12-19, 986B1
DERWINSKI, Rep. Edward J. (R, Ill.)
Probe re KCIA defector rptd 10-28, 816F3
DES (diethylstilbestrol)—*See MEDICINE—Drugs*
DESAI, Morarji Ranchodji (Indian prime minister)
Released 1-18, 45E2
Party wins electns 3-16—3-20, named prime min 3-24, 205A1
Forms Cabt; Ram, 2 others balk, relent; Cabt sworn 3-26, 3-27; policy address read 3-28, 239E3
Probe of son asked 4-1, 283D3
Meets Gromyko 4-26, 348F1
On arrest of 4 ex-Gandhi aides 8-15, 637D2
Forced birth control dropped 10-3, 842A3
Gandhi chrgs govt abuse 10-10, 801E2
In Moscow 10-21—10-26; Sovts vow aid 10-26, 842F2
Ordrs A-blast probe 12-6, 966D2
DESEGREGATION—*See EDUCATION—School Integration*
DESERTS
UN conf held, spec fund set 8-29—9-9, 770B1
DESHMUKH, Nanaji
Chrgs Gandhi re chaos plot 10-13, 801C2
DES Moines, Ia.—*See IOWA*
DESMOND, Paul
Dies 5-30, 452G2
DETENTE—*Note: Only general material listed here. For U.S.-Soviet relations, see USSR—U.S. Relations; see also other country names*
Brezhnev, Giscard stress 6-21—6-22, 494D3-495D1
Trudeau, Schmidt pledge commitmt 7-7, 566G2
Andreotti scores Giscard US criticism 7-19, 581E2
Yugo, China views compared 8-30—9-8, 710B1
Schmidt stresses small natn role 11-22, 926B2
DETROIT, Mich.—*See under MICHIGAN*
DETROIT Edison Co.
Canadian oil imports cited 1-19, 54A1
DETROIT News, The (newspaper)
Slam Marshall dies 12-17, 1024E2
DETROIT River
Detroit sued on pollution 5-6, 422D2
DEUTSCH, Alejandro
Kidnaped with family 8-27; army admits arrest 9-6, 922D2
DEUTSCHE Airbus
Eastern to lease Airbus 5-24, 441D2
DEUTSCHE Bank AG (West Germany)
Mex gets $1.2 bln intl loan 11-18, 967C1
De VALERA, Eamon (1882-1975)
Party wins Irish electn 6-16, 475E2
De VARGA, Pierre
Police versn of de Broglie murder questnd 1-5—1-9, 44C1
De VATHAIRE, Herve
Dassault cleared 4-21, 598A1

DEVELOPING Nations—*See also regional headings (e.g., AFRICA); specific country and organization names*
OPEC allocates funds 1-10, 12A3
6th IMF gold auctn 1-26, trust loans set 2-4, 87D2
Uganda probe by UN comm blocked 2-7—3-11, 207F1

1978

De PINA, Miguel
Returns from Guyana to US 11-27, 910C2
DEPROGRAMMING—*See under RELIGIOUS Cults*
DEREGULATION of Industry—*See industry names (e.g., GAS, Natural)*
DERIAN, Patricia
Scores Argentina rights abuse; forgn min, press rebuke 8-20, 792E2
DERN, Bruce
Driver released 7-28, 970B1
De ROBURT, Head Chief Hammer (Nauruan president)
Takes over as Nauru pres 5-15, 439F3
De ROCHEMONT, Louis
Dies 12-23, 1032E2
De ROSA, Carmine
Slain 1-4, 19A2
De ROULET, Lorinda
Becomes Mets chrmn 11-18, 1026E2
DERRICK Jr., Rep. Butler C. (D, S.C.)
Reelected 11-7, 852B2
DERRYBERRY, Larry
Faces Okla primary runoff for gov 8-22, 683C1
Loses runoff 9-19, 737A1
DERSU Uzala (film)
Released 1-13, 619E1
De RUITER, Jacob
On Moluccan-held bldg assault 3-14, 192A1
Cabt OKs liberalized abortn bill 11-16, 965F1
DERWINSKI, Rep. Edward J. (R, Ill.)
Reelected 11-7, 850D3
DESAI, Morarji Ranchodji (Indian prime minister)
Carter visit; A-issues highlighted 1-1—1-3, 1C2-2A1
Commonwealth ldrs' hotel bombed 2-12, 110E1 *, A2; blames Indian terrorists 2-14, 121C3
Commonwealth conf meets 2-13—2-16, asks A-test ban 2-15, 121G2
Vs Sikkim annexatn 3-7, 3-10, 227B3, D3
States vs econ plan 3-18—3-19, 227A3
On prohibition drive 3-31, 246B1
Confrms loss of '65 US A-device 4-17, 288B2
US bars uranium sale 4-20, 288C3
Warns US vs uranium ban 4-23, 4-24, 313A2
Singh quits Janata posts, party split seen 4-29, 374D3
Wins confidence vote 5-11, 374F3
Backs Gandhi rule condemnatn 5-15, 374B3
Sees Carter, A-cooperatn pledged 6-13—6-15, 466C3
On Gandhi prosecutn 6-17, 516B2
2 Cabt mins vs handling of Gandhi case 6-28; resignatn asked 6-29, 2 quit 6-30, 516F1, D2
Lal fired for anti-Janata remark 7-4; restored in party compromise 7-9, 631E3
Mishra quits over Singh ouster 7-6, 631E3
Assures Indian minorities 10-12, 797F1
Gandhi elected to Parlt 11-5, 861F2
DESCHENES, Jules
Rules Quebec language law invalid 1-24, 70C2
DESEGREGATION—*See EDUCATION—School Integration*
DESERT Locust Control Organization for East Africa (Dlcoea)
Locust plague aid appeal issued 6-6, 465C2
DeSIMONE, Bob
Hopkins wins NCAA title 5-27, 540B2
DETENTE—*Note: Only general material listed here. For U.S.-Soviet relations, see USSR—U.S. Relations*
France urges in SE Asia 1-19, 71F1
US, Yugo back 3-7—3-9, 194B1
Czech, W Ger pledge support 4-11, 332G3
USSR, W Ger affirm commitmt 5-4—5-7, 417A1, D1
China, Yugo talks rptd 8-21—8-22, 675E2
France: Sovt ties central to E-W detente 10-29, 830G3
Hungary, France affirm support 11-17, 894F2
DETROIT, Mich.—*See MICHIGAN*
DETROIT, University of
Vitale named Pistons coach 5-1, 656B1
De TROYES, Chretien
Perceval released 10-6, 1030D3
DETTINGER, Maj. Gen. Garth
Denies Agent Orange health damage 10-11, 984A2
DEUKMEJIAN, George
Elected Calif atty gen 11-7, 856G2
DEUTCH, John M.
A-waste storage study issued 3-15, 183B3
On fusion advance 8-14, 653D3
US, Japan plan joint energy research 9-6, 695B3 *, D3 *
Rpts NM A-waste burial plan 11-15, 961D2
DEUTSCHE Bank AG (Frankfurt)
4th in '77 world ranking 11-8, 914A1, D1
Nigeria loan cited 11-30, 934A2
DEVELOPING Nations—*See also regional headings (e.g., AFRICA); country and organization names*
Dutch aid hike proposed 1-16, 90A3
UK ends propaganda unit 1-27, 71F2

1979

DEPRESSION—*See MEDICINE—Mental Health*
DEREGULATION of Industry—*See industry names (e.g., GAS, Natural)*
DEREK, Bo
10 released 10-5, 1008A2
DeROCHE, Everett
Patrick released 9-7, 820F2
DERRICK, Michael & Karl
In Israel W Bank riot 5-2; ordrd deported 5-10, leave 5-14, 360G1
DERRICKS, Cleavant
But Never Jam Todays opens 7-31, 711A2
DES (diethylstilbestrol)—*See MEDICINE—Drugs*
DESAI, Morarji Ranchodji (Indian prime minister; resigned July 15)
Singh sworn dep prime min 1-24, 97G2
Scores China invasn of Viet 2-18, 123D1
Kosygin in India 3-9—3-15, USSR aid agrmts signed 3-14, 200A2
Bangladesh accords reached 4-18, 328C2
Gandhi bars parlt race 5-20, 411E2
Vs Sovt Afghan aid request 6-14, 443E1
Threatens violence curbs 6-25, 503B2
Janata feud rptd, Narain quits party 6-26, 503B2, 544G1
Cabt mins quit 7-12—7-15, Fernandes urges resignatn 7-14; resigns 7-15, retains Janata post 7-17, 544D1
Quits as Janata ldr, Ram replaces 7-27, 573G1
Singh sworn prime min 7-28, 573A1, F1
Birth control problems rptd 8-13, 687D3
Singh reverses A-arms stand 8-15, 646D1
DESERET News (Salt Lake City, Utah)
Utah '50s leukemia study rptd 2-14, 112A2
DESHLER, Col. R. C.
Recommends Pearce desertn charge 12-19, 965G3
De SILVA, Juan
Assaulted by US basketball coach 7-8, 798E3
DeSIMONE, Thomas
Sought in Lufthansa cargo theft, '78 murder; death presumed 1-14, 155C3
DES Moines, Ia.—*See IOWA*
DES Moines Register, The (newspaper)
Risser wins Pulitzer 4-16, 336A3
Invites Brown to debate 12-4, 962A3
Carter declines forum 12-28, chng of site offered 12-31, 983G2
DES Moines Tribune, The (newspaper)
Invites Brown to debate 12-4, 962A3
Carter declines debate 12-28, bars chng of site offer 12-31, 983G2
DESPAIR (film)
Released 2-15, 174D2
DETENTE—*Note: Only general material listed here. For U.S.-Soviet relations, see USSR-U.S. Relations*
4-natn Guadeloupe summit backs 1-6, 12E2
Rumania: Cambodia invasn threatens 1-10, 11G1
USSR, Yugo back 5-18, 380A1
French pres vows Eur committmt 10-29, 835B2
DETROIT, Mich.—*See MICHIGAN*
DETROITBANK Corporation
Columbia U sells stock 3-23, 271A1
DETROIT Edison Co.
Job-testing data disclosure reversed by Sup Ct 3-5, 184B3
Shareholders defeat A-power delay 4-23, 322G3
DETROIT Edison v. National Labor Relations Board
Case decided by Sup Ct 3-5, 184A3
DETROIT Free Press, The (newspaper)
Daily, Sunday circulatn listed 6-6, 431C1, D1
DETROIT News, The (newspaper)
Daily, Sunday circulatn listed 6-6, 431C1, D1
DETROIT Symphony Orchestra
Paul Paray dies 10-10, 860B3
DEUTSCHE Babcock AG (Frankfurt)
US bank attaches Iran assets 11-28, 896F2
DEUTSCHE Bank AG (Frankfurt)
Iran banks natlzd 6-7, compensatn vowed 6-10, 469A2
DEVANE, William
GR Point opens 4-16, 711E3
Yanks released 9-19, 820G3
De VARENNE, Michel
Sentncd re Marion kidnap 4-6, 267D1
De VEAUX, Alexis
Season To Unravel opens 1-25, 292G2

DEVELOPING Nations—*See also regional headings (e.g., AFRICA); country and organization names*
USSR '74-77 heavy arms sales compared 1-7, 13G1
UK dvpt aid budgeted 1-17, 59A3
W Ger shipbldg competitn cited 1-21, 77F3

1980

DEPLEY, Roger
Le Monde chrgd re revelatns 11-7, 872G1; France frees 11-29, 921F2
DEPOSIT Guaranty National Bank v. Roper
Case decided by Sup Ct 3-19, 250D1
DEPOSITORY Institutions Deregulation Committee—*See under U.S. GOVERNMENT*
DEREGULATION of Industry—*See AVIATION, GAS, Natural, RAILROADS, TRUCKS (& Trucking)*
DEREK, Bo
Change of Seasons released 12-17, 1003G1
DERIENZO, Jim
2d in 6,000-m Penn Relays 4-25, 892D2
DEROSA, Anthony
Indicted 6-4, 502D2
DERRICK Jr., Rep. Butler C. (D, S.C.)
Reelected 11-4, 844B2
DERWINSKI, Rep. Edward J. (R, Ill.)
Reelected 11-4, 842D3
DES (diethylstilbestrol)—*See MEDICINE—Drugs & Health-Care Products*
DESHAZO, Walter Anthony
Chrgd in Okla slaying 1-21, 94A2

DE SILVA, David
Fame released 5-16, 675D2
DES Moines—*See IOWA*
DES Moines Register, The (newspaper)
GOP pres debate held; poll cited 1-5, 4C2, E2
Poll results 1-11, 33D1-A2
Privacy case refused by Sup Ct 2-25, 188A1
DES Moines Tribune, The (newspaper)
GOP debate held 1-5, 4C2
D'ESTAINVILLE, Kim
Heartaches of a Pussycat opens 3-19, 392A3
DETENTE—*Note: Only general material listed here. For U.S.-Soviet relations, see USSR-U.S. Relations*
US official, W Ger chancellor meet, detente backed 1-16, 28A2
West warns on Sakharov treatmt 1-23—2-5, 85G3
Brezhnev backs 2-4, 84E3
France, W Ger: more difficult 2-5, USSR reacts 2-6, 84F2, C3
China denounces USSR 2-5, 108B1
USSR warns W Eur on Afghan reactn effect 2-7, 106C3
Poland backs 2-11, 152B2
Italy CP: USSR, US threaten 2-17, 134E1
Tito in intl appeal 2-21, Carter replies 2-25, 139B3
E Ger affirms commitmt 3-19, W Ger seeks talks 3-20, 236C3, E3
Warsaw Pact backs 5-15, 377F2
France, USSR back world summit 5-19, 378A3
French-Vatican talks 5-31, 476D3
NATO condemns Afghan invasn 6-26, 489F2
Warsaw Pact reaffirms commitmt, asks Eur conf 10-19—10-20, 800C2, E2
Sovt troop movts called threat at NATO, CSCE mtgs 12-12, 12-19, 949A1, 950G1
DETJEN, Jim
Wins Polk award 2-25, 692F3
DETOLEDANO, Ralph
Nader libel case declined by Sup Ct 2-19, 131E1
DETOLEDANO v. Nader
Case declined by Sup Ct 2-19, 131F1
DETROIT—*See MICHIGAN*
DETROIT Free Press
Carter endorsemt rptd 11-1, 841F1
DETROIT Metropolitan Airport
DEA detainmt procedure backed by Sup Ct 5-27, 453G1
DEUTSCH, Adolph
Dies 1-1, 104C2
DEUTSCH, Stephen
Somewhere in Time released 10-3, 836F3
DEUTSCHE Bank AG (Frankfurt)
Brazil oil loan rptd 3-5, 191F1
Nicaragua debt rescheduled 9-5, 689A3
Earnings, assets rptd up 12-10, 969G1

DEVELOPING Nations—*See also regional headings (e.g., AFRICA); country and organization names*
India's new head backs close ties 1-6, 11G3
NATO rejects united actn re Afghan 1-15, 28F1

1976

OPEC aid debated at Jamaica IMF conf 1-8, aid data rptd 1-12, 14B3
SELA meets 1-12—1-15, 60E2
Freedom House survey rptd 1-19, 20D2-E3
OPEC sets funds 1-26—1-28, 62B2
PLO joins UNCTAD Group of 77 1-27, 85A2
UNESCO literacy drive fails 2-4, 85A2
UNCTAD sets trade guidelines 2-10, 107G3
Intl econ conf 2-11—2-20, 148B1
'60-74 defense spending up 2-29, 182E3
Japan vs eased import curbs 3-3, 191G2
Austria backs liberatn 3-11—3-13, 380D2
Bordaberry rptd vs ties 3-12, 4-11, 382A3
IMF ends oil loan program 4-1, 340B2
Arab-African mtg 4-19—4-22, 355G3
UNCTAD conf opens 5-5, 320E1
'75 Sovt trade rptd 5-5, 340C3, 341A1
Kissinger addresses UNCTAD 5-6, 317A1-318G1
France proposes Africa aid plan 5-10—5-11, 355F3
OPEC aids UN agri fund 5-11, 389E1
WHO rejects Israel rpt 5-17, 355G1
Giscard in US 5-17—5-22, 372A2, D2
Venez urges new econ order 5-18, 465F3
OECD OKs multinatl code 5-21, 430C3; adopts code 6-21, 450D1
USSR, Mozambique stress unity 5-23, 403E3
Eur, Latin soc dems meet 5-25, 449F2, A3
UNCTAD OKs commodity fund 5-30, 388E2
UN Habitat conf held 5-31—6-11, 431E2
IMF gold auction held 6-2, 430B2
ILO World Employmt Conf 6-2—6-18, 449D3
World Food Cncl stockpile plan stalled 6-14—6-16, 450B1 *
7-natn econ summit discusses UNCTAD demands 6-27—6-28, 462C2
EC aid set 7-8, 529G2
Intl econ conf deadlocked 7-8—7-10, 7-12—7-17, 530D1
2d IMF gold auctn held 7-14, 530F1
OPEC meets on aid 8-5—8-6, 643G1
Nonaligned natns conf 8-16—8-20, 621G2
Barbados cites policy 9-3, 673D1
3d IMF gold auctn held 9-15, 739D3
IMF group drops debt moratorium demand 10-2, 778F1
Issue at IMF-World Bank mtgs 10-4—10-8, 777B1, A2
China scores Eur 'oppressn' 10-5, 760A1
World Bank poverty data chart 778A1
UN world econ rpt issued 10-13, 760E1
4th gold auction held 10-27, 832C2
UNESCO shelves Sovt press plan 11-6, 842D2
'75-76 US bank loans rptd up 11-10; NYC bank data 915E1, C2
UNESCO comm OKs news plan 11-22, 879B1
Soclst Intl topic 11-27, 11-28, 935D3, E3
Castro scores OPEC 12-2, 1000F3
OPEC responsibility seen 12-9, 935A1
'76 intl borrowing rptd 12-22, 976G1
OPEC OKs loans to 6 12-23, 975E3
U.S. Relations
Major banks on 'problem' list 1-11, 110F3, 111C1
Ford State of Union message 1-19, 38B3
Dem policy rptd 1-21, 40G2
US House com rpt on pol payments leaked 1-26, 92E1, F3
US urges intl resources bank, econ dvpt plan 5-6, 317A1-318G1
Carter urges energy conf 5-13, 375A1
US Dem platform text 6-15, 476E1, G2, A3, 477A3, 478B1, C1, C3
Kissinger addresses OECD 6-21, 450F1
Carter vs arms sales, trade curbs 6-23, 451F3
Carter airs views 6-24, 490B2
Carter pledges help 7-15, 510F3
Carter backs trade aid 8-17, 617C2
US: Sovt aid minimal 9-30; reactn 10-1, 719B2
US vows debt renegotiatn aid, scores Sea Law Conf tactics 9-30, 719G2
Carter, Ford debate 10-6, 741D2
Forgn paymts rptd accepted 12-20, 985A3

DEVI, Gayatri
Paroled 1-9, 29E1
DEVINE, Rep. Samuel L. (R, Ohio)
Scored by environmt group 3-25, 220A1
Reelected 11-2, 830A3
DEVITT, Judge Edward J.
Fines Reserve Mining 5-4, 379C2
Sets Reserve Mining deadline 7-7, 570D3
DEVLETOGLOU, Evangelos
Sets '77 budget 11-29, 1004A3
De VOGUE, Comte Robert-Jean
Dies 10-17, 970C3
De VRIES, Klaus
Rptd approached by Lockheed 9-1, 684B2
DEXTER, Dr. Keith
Advises farmers on drought 8-19, 630A3

1977

OPEC fund allotmt set 2-28, 227E3
7th IMF gold auction 3-2, 145E3
IMF gold auctions 3-2, 4-6, 5-4, 335G3
UN rights comm block votes seen weaker 3-5, 207G1
Afro-Arab summit pledges aid 3-7—3-9, 170F1, A2
'76 trade data rptd 3-8, 188A3
Sovt '76 trade surplus rptd 3-21, 285A2
IMF paymts debt managing role rptd 3-28, com backs lending facility 4-29, Saudis rpt role 5-3, 5-4, 362E3-363D1
UN Sri Lanka energy experimt rptd 3-30, 298E3
Canada to lower tariffs 3-31, 254A2
Jamaica buys Reynolds assets 3-31, 257G3
UNCTAD commodity talks deadlocked 4-3, 297D3
WHO launches immunizatn drive 4-7, 287C3
UNCTAD shipping study rptd 4-17, 337A3
UNESCO press parley 4-18—4-20, 319F2
Bilderberg conf 4-21—4-24, 359B3
Salzburg A-conf debates plant safety 5-3, 403B1
7-natn econ summit backs aid 5-7—5-8, 357A2-E2, 358D1, B2
WHO sets 7-yr cancer study 5-10, 431B2
Intl bankers conf on debt 5-22—5-25, 437D3
External debt total cited 6-3, 437A3
'74-76 bank loans rptd 6-5, 438B1
Commonwealth conf aid talks 6-8—6-15, 487C1
World Food Cncl conf 6-20—6-24, 513C3
Brazil bank ranked in top 10 6-21, 578A2
OAS urges econ aid 6-22, 494A1
Venez urges multinatl regulatn 6-28, 546B2
Albania scores China 3-worlds theory 7-8, 540D3
UN Sea Law Conf adjourns 7-15, 572B3
3-worlds theory explained 595D1
IMF, World Bank bias vs chrgd 8-31, 9-8, 785D1
IMF rpts '76 paymts deficit, '77 forecast 9-11, 700F2
Econ growth rptd 9-18, 717A3
UN Assemb '76 N-S conf debate ends 9-19, 713D1
Commonwealth finance mins discuss poor natn aid 9-21—9-24, 936D2
McNamara asks trade hike, links '76 econ growth rate, scores rich natns' forgn aid level 9-26, 754E1
Hong Kong scores Canada textile duties 10-4, 780D3
Canada import quotas scored 10-4, 780D3
IMF gold auctn; total sale proceeds rptd 10-5, 792G3
Sweden cancels 8 natns' debts 10-12, 903F3
USSR '76 arms sales rptd 10-13, 949B2
IMF auctns gold 11-2, 12-7, total proceeds rptd 12-7, 933E3
Unctad common-fund commodity talks fail 12-1, 974E2
'78 debt servicing costs, '77 debts rptd 12-6, 998A1
OPEC plans investmt hike 12-7, 997E3
Brandt intl dvpt comm meets 12-9—12-11, 997G3
Solar energy investmt urged 12-11, 975G2
Debt rise data cited by Venez pres, OPEC aid urged 12-20, 973B2
North-South Conference—*See ECONOMIC Cooperation, Conference on International*
U.S. Relations
'75 Ford Foundatn grants cited 1-11, 56E1
US modifies duty-free list 2-28, 189F2
FRB asks OPEC lending role 3-10; US bank aid rptd 3-28, 362E3-363D1
Water dvpt fund barred 3-14—3-25, 250E1
Austria-US talks on N-S conf 3-14, 425F1
Carter addresses UN 3-17, 185C2
Carter vows Latin trade, econ aid 4-14, 296A1, B1
Aid backed, N-S conf cited at 7-natn summit 5-8, 357B2, 358D1
Carter stresses aid 5-22, 397E2
N-S conf aid plan backed 5-30, 437E2
'76 bank loans outstanding rptd 6-5, 438E1
Sen OKs aid-rights link 6-14, 477F2
Young tours Carib region, vows econ aid 8-5—8-17, 646G1
'76 US investmts rptd up 8-29, 669D1
Imports blamed for US copper industry woes 10-31, 859A1
Latins seen part of 3d World 11-24, 913C1
DEVINE, Adrian
Traded to Braves 12-8, 990B1
DEVINE, Andy
Dies 2-18, 164E2
DEVINE, Rep. Samuel L. (R, Ohio)
'76 special interest gifts rptd 2-15, 128F2
DEWEY, Godfrey
Dies 10-18, 872F1
DEWEY, John (1859-1952)
FBI surveillance rptd 6-19, 481E1
DEWEY, Melvil (1851-1931)
Son dies 10-18, 872F1
DEXTRAZE, Gen. Jacques
Asks defns forces hiked 1-15, 82F1
DHAN, Ram
Released 1-5, 45D3
Protests Desai selectn 3-24, 205E1
DHARIA, Mohan
Freed 1-12, 45C3
Named commerce min 3-26, 240B1
Import curbs eased 4-28, 392D2

1978

Commonwealth regional conf ends 2-16, 121E2
UN econ post dir gen named 3-8, 401F3
Unctad talks on debt relief, '77 debt estimates cited 3-11, 301A1
Canada urges indl natn concern 3-21, 225D3
USSR '77 trade rptd 3-28, 230B1
Venez pres, Carter in aid talks 3-28, 3-29, 233E1
Arab aid rise rptd 4-9, 257B2
Intl commodity fund planned 4-23, 391D2
Japan to increase aid 5-3, 341G2
UN Sea Conf ends in deadlock 5-19, 401A3
UN Sea Conf talks resume 5-23—7-15, 8-21—9-16, 732C3
USSR '77 trade rptd 6-28, 634E3
Dutch cancel 4 natns debts, Sweden '77 moves cited 7-10, 575E1
Arms sales policy assessed 7-16, 564F1
Bonn summit backs aid, Japan doubles commitmt 7-17, 544C2, F2
Nonaligned ask more indl natn aid 7-30, 583D3
UK cancels 17 natns debts 7-31, 592C1
Swiss debt cancelatn rptd 8-1, 592F1
ASEAN-US commodities program set 8-4, 603G2
World Bank poverty, income table 732A2
World Bank head asks trade curbs end 9-25, 732G2
Denmark proposes forgn aid level 10-3, 774D1
Norway budgets '79 aid 10-5, 884C1
W Ger debt cancelatn rptd 10-6, 776F2
Mex, China in raw material price talks 10-24—10-30, 903D3
'73-77 oil consumptn rptd up 11-14, 871A2
Common fund talks fail 11-30, 998F1
U.S. Relations
Carter urges US-Eur aid 1-4, 2E1
US $ strategy to spur econ recovery rptd 1-23, 27G2
Asia, Pacific mil commitmt affirmed 2-20, 126D3
Debt relief proposals rejctd 3-11, 301C1
Carter, Venez pres in aid talks 3-28, 3-29, 233E1
OPIC extensn signed 4-24, 323D2, F2
UN Sea Conf ends in deadlock 5-19, 401A3
Mondale backs arms funds for econ dvpt 5-24, 421E1
US-ASEAN commodities program set 8-4, 603G2
UN Sea Conf debates US seabed mining bill 8-21—9-16, 732C3
Vance sets '79 priority 11-25, 925E1

DEVESI, Baddeley (Solomon Islands governor-general)
Sworn Solomons gov-gen 7-7, 549E1
DEVILLE, Michel
Dossier 51 released 12-12, 1030F2
DEVINE, Bing
Quits as Cardinals gen mgr 10-18, 1026A3
DEVINE, Dan
Notre Dame ranked 1st 1-3, 8F2
DEVINE, Rep. Samuel (R, Ohio)
King assassinatn hearings 8-14—8-18, 641F3
Reelected 11-7, 851E3
DeVITO, Karen
Piano Bar opens 6-8, 887E2
DEWAERE, Patrick
Get Out Handkerchiefs released 12-17, 1030A3
DEWAR, Donald
Wins Scottish by-electn 4-14, 288D1
DeYOUNG, John
On Bikini I radiatn hazard 4-12, 278G2
De YOUNG Memorial Museum, M. H. (San Francisco, Calif.)
4 Dutch paintings stolen 12-25, 1028G3-1029A1
DHARSONO, Gen. Hartono
Ousted as ASEAN head 1-23, 72E1
Formally quits ASEAN post, scores govt 2-18, 122B2

1979

'78 trade, paymts rptd 2-8, 161D1
UN rights comm res vs Israel backed 2-21, 148E1
UK: EC farm policy biased 2-21, 154F2
WHO sees alcoholism as econ threat 3-9, 218C3
Pope presents 1st encyclical 3-15, 217C1
Seabed mining spurs indl natn split 3-19—4-27, 360D3
UNCTAD fund set 3-20, 200D2
Wheat pact extended 3-23, 274B2
USSR '78 trade surplus cited 3-28, 237C3
GATT pact signing boycotted 4-12, 273B1
Abortn death data rptd 4-29, 547C3, D3
UNCTAD mtg in Pl 5-7—6-3, 417E2
IMF gold sales profits rptd 5-14, 435D3
Lome pact talks collapse 5-26, 398E3
SALT II communique backs struggle 6-18, 458D1
Lome pact extensn set 6-27, 512D3
Ecuador to back democracy 8-10, 613B3
Nonaligned movemt draft scores West 8-28—9-1; Iraq OKs aid 9-4, 675C1, G1
IISS notes mil buildup 9-4, 825A3
IMF sees '79 paymts gap widening 9-16, 720D1
World radio conf held 9-27—12-6, 1006B3
Mex proposes energy plan 9-27, 753F1
Pope scores rich natns, deplores gap 10-2, 757F2, 758A1, A2
IMF scored re oil loans 10-3, 779C3
Castro addresses UN; scores econ disparity, asks $300 bln aid 10-12, 778E2, A3
2 economists win Nobel 10-17, 858G1-B2
Lome pact extensn signed 10-31, 845E1
Hungary opens E-W bank 11-9, 882B3
'78 smoking rise rptd 11-22, 970E2, F2
OPEC sets aid 12-20, 977A2
U.S. Relations
'74-77 heavy arms sales rptd 1-7, 13G1
Carter budget proposals 1-22, 41C2
'78 trade gap rptd 1-30, 71F3
Sovt surrogate response urged 2-8, 89D2
US seabed mining legis opposed 3-19—4-27, 360E3
Carter urges science aid 4-23, 300B3
SALT II communique backs struggle 6-18, 458D1
Carter addresses Cong on SALT II 6-18, 459A3
US weighs land reform aid 7-20, 554E1
Castro scores US, asks aid 10-12, 778E2, B3

DEVERS, Gen. Jacob L.
Dies 10-15, 860E2
De VICENZO, Roberto
Wins Legends of Golf title 4-29, 2d in PGA Sr 7-8, 587D2
De VILLIERS, Jacobus Wynand
Denies S Africa A-test 10-26, 824D3
DEVIL Went Down to Georgia, The (recording)
On best-seller list 9-5, 672E3
DEVINE, Adrian
Traded to Rangers 12-7, 1002F2
DEVINE, Frank J.
El Salvador Emb attacked 10-30, 834A3
DEVINE, Rep. Samuel L. (R, Ohio)
Challenges JFK findings 1-26, 91A2
DEVITT, Judge Edward J.
Sentncs Chippewas for Minn violence 7-22, 630G3
DEVOS, Richard M.
Amway price-fixing end ordrd 5-23, 985F3
DEVOUR the Snow (play)
Opens 5-13, 711D2
DEVRIES, Jon
Devour the Snow opens 5-13, 711D2
DEWAERE, Patrick
French Detective released 3-10, 528C2
DEWHURST, Colleen
Taken in Marriage opens 2-26, 292D3
DeWITT, Hugh
Cited in H-bomb letter 9-16, 9-18, 716G3-717G1
DHARIA, Mohan
Asks Desai quit Janata post, backs Ram 7-18, 544C2

1980

OECD sees more grain re US Sovt embargo 1-23, 49G3
China scores USSR 'aggressn' 2-5, 108B1
UN dvpt aid disputed 2-9, 124A2
N-S study urges aid plan 2-12, 124G2
OPEC backs supply guarantees, financial aid 2-22, 142G1
UN rights comm postpones Sakharov debate 3-11, 181A3
USSR, Cuba roles cited by US 3-27, 243C3
French ldr urges OPEC aid 4-14, 312E2
IMF $ support plan shelved, 1st 1/4 loans rptd 4-24, 302F1
Dutch queen urges more ties 4-30, 353E3
French-W Ger TV satellite pact signed 4-30, 356F1
OECD backs free trade 6-3, 422G1
Venice summit urges aid; food, populatn curb efforts 6-23, 473G2-474C1
IMF econ forecast grim 6-24, 477D2
W Ger sees Sovt Afghan invasn impact 6-30, 489G1
Populatn, food forecast gloomy 7-23, 573A2
UN Sea Law Conf yields draft accord 7-29—8-29, 660C1, E1
W Ger pol asylum rules rptd tightened 7-31, 581C2
Saudis, Kuwait freeze World Bank loans 8-2, 592C2, D2
World Bank '80 econ forecast grim 8-17, 628G2
UN special sessn hears Muskie, Rao on aid 8-25; Kuwait oil focus warning rptd 8-27, 642G2-643D1
UN special sessn hears McGuigan on aid 8-26, Canada rpt sees survival threatened 8-27, 669B1, E1
GATT sees global trade lag; oil prices, inflatn cited 9-16, 695D3
UN Assemb scores intl aid agrmt failure 9-16, 736F1
World Bank issues annual rpt; '80 loans, disbursmts rptd 9-22, 720B1-B2
World Bank-IMF mtg sets aid goals 9-30—10-3, 761A2
OPEC postpones 3d World aid mtg 10-6, 759D1
UNESCO world info order backed, Westn news coverage scored 10-25, 821G2
Press coverage study rptd 11-29, 914B1
IMF Jan-Oct loans rptd 12-1, 914B1
Sovt, E Eur, China '79 arms sales rptd 12-10, 933A2
U.S. Relations
Carter notes improved ties 1-23, 42C3, 43D1
OECD sees more grain re Sovt embargo 1-23, 49G3
Vance on Sovt, Cuban roles 3-27, 243C3
Latin influx to US surveyed 5-11—5-20, 396C2
Carter vows aid in World Bank-IMF address 9-30, 762G3
Haig stresses role 12-22, 980D1

DEVILLIERS, Jean-Paul
Australia A-plant backing rptd 3-3, 171B1
DEVIL'S Alternative, The (book)
On best-seller list 2-10, 120B3; 3-9, 200A3; 4-6, 280B3; 5-4, 359C3; 6-8, 448B3
DEVIL Went Down to Georgia, The (recording)
C Daniels band wins Grammy 2-27, 296D3
DEVINE, Rep. Samuel L. (R, Ohio)
Loses reelectn 11-4, 846G1, 851D2
DEVITA, Teddy
Dies 5-27, 448D1
DEVLIN, Don
My Bodyguard released 8-1, 675B3
DEVO (singing group)
Whip It on best-seller list 12-3, 948B3
DEVORE, Christopher
Elephant Man released 10-3, 836E2
DEWAERE, Patrick
Coup De Tete released 1-21, 216D2
DEWEY Sr., Charles S.
Dies 12-26, 1004C1
DEWEY, Thomas Edmund
O'Connell dies 2-27, 176G2
Vote turnout cited 11-4, 838B3
DG Bank (Deutsche Genossenschaftsbank) (Frankfurt)
Brazil oil loan rptd 3-5, 191F1
Chrysler rescue plan backed 6-20, 481A3

1976

DIA, Mamadou
Pardoned 4-3, 591D3
DIABETES—*See 'Diseases' under MEDICINE*
DIAKITE, Moussa
Rpts plotters arrested 7-15, 1005B2
DIALLO, Moctar
Guinea rural dvpt min 12-11, 1005G1
DIALOGUE Behind Walls (book)
Nasser cleared of theft chrg 2-4, 119C1
DIAMOND, Lt. Stephen W.
Vietnam rpts killed 9-6, 678B3
DIAMOND International Corp.
Antitrust suit dvpts 2-18—10-5, 886C1; 11-30, 921F2
SEC lists paymts 5-12, 727B1
DIAZ, Elena Quintero de
Seized in Venez emb 6-28, 542G2
Husband rptd kidnaped 7-19, 571A3
DIAZ, Jose Felix
Kidnaping rptd 7-19, 571A3
DIAZ, Raul J.
On US-based Cuban terrorism 8-22, 791C1
DIAZ Bessone, Gen. Ramon
Hard-line generals retired 12-3, 996C3
DIAZ Chavez, Ricardo
Rptd expelled re Peru strike 6-25, 499A3
DIAZ Estrada, Gen. Nicanor
Quits Cabt 3-5, replaced 3-8, 288G2
DIAZ Redondo, Regino
Named Excelsior dir 7-8; campaign vs Scherer rptd 7-11, 620D1
DIBA, Vasile
Wins Olympic medals 7-30, 7-31, 574E1, F1
DIBIASI, Klaus
Wins Olympic medal 7-27, 563B1, 575D3
DICHTER, Misha
Lhevinne dies 11-9, 970C2
DICKINSON, Rep. William Louis (R, Ala.)
Reelected 11-2, 828F2
DICKMAN, Francois M.
Named United Arab Emirates amb 8-25; confrmd 9-23, 807F3
DICKS, Norman D.
Elected 11-2, 825F1, 831A2
DIDRIKSEN, Jorn
Wins Olympic medal 2-12, 158F3
DIEDERICHS, Nicholaas
Transkei gets independnc 10-26, 813B1
DIEFENBAKER, John
Scores Trudeau econ remarks 1-11, 27F3
PC elects Clark ldr 2-23, 188C2
Accuses JFK 10-4, 837C1
DIEGO Garcia (British territory)
Australia backs US role 1-12, 26E2
India, USSR vs Indian O bases 6-13, 440D1
Nonaligned conf vs US base 8-20, 621C3
DIETHYLSTILBESTROL—*See 'Drugs' under MEDICINE*
DIETRICH, Noah
Hughes will names executor 4-27, 335E3
Hughes estate dvpts 7-16, 596F3
Hughes will forgery chrgd 12-13, 971D2
DIEZ Alegria, Lt. Gen. Manuel (ret.)
Army officers sentenced 3-10, 314G2
DiFALCO, Samuel
Indictmt dismissed 11-4, 1016A2
DIGGS Jr., Rep. Charles C. (D, Mich.)
At OAU summit, scores US Angola policy 1-10—1-13, 16G1
Black leaders meet Carter 7-12, 513B2
Reelected 11-2, 829E4
DIGRAZIA, Robert J.
Vs violent busing protests 2-16, 203B1
DILLON, Reed & Co. Inc.
Rptd disciplined re boycott 8-11, 747C2
DILNO, Gordon
Sentenced 11-30, 921A3
DILWORTH, James
Chrgs Hughes will forged 12-13, 971A2

1977

DHAWAN, R. K.
Arrested 8-15, 637D2
DIABETES—*See MEDICINE—Diseases*
DIABETES Association, American
FDA saccharin ban scored 3-10, 177D1
DIAFERIA, Lourenco
Arrested for insulting army 9-21, 741E1
DIAMOND, Billy
On language bill 8-26, 671D3
DIAMONDS
W Australia find rptd 2-1, 96A3
Dealer murders probed 7-28—10-19, FBI in gem hunt 10-3, 871B3, F3
Angola sets domestic mine shares natlzatn 9-1, 779B1
US-Sovt 1st ⅓ trade rptd 9-12, 766B2
Central African Empire exports cited 946A3
DIARRHEA—*See MEDICINE—Diseases*
DIAS, Col. Erasmo
On arrested author's novel 7-27, 633C2
Backs police raids on univ 9-27, 840B2
DIAYBASS, Nadia Shehade
Identified as Lufthansa hijacker 10-27, 868F2
DIAZ, Charles J.
Indicted 3-3, 204D1
DIAZ Ordaz, Gustavo
Named amb to Spain 4-7, controversy ensues 4-7—5-11, 529F1
DIAZ Serrano, Jorge
On oil reserves 3-18, 240C3
DIBBS, Eddie
Tourn results 2-13, 4-3, 4-24, 430G2-431A1
US beaten in Davis Cup 4-29—5-1, 353E3
DIBROMOCHLOROPROPANE (DBCP)—*See PESTICIDES*
DICARLO, Joseph J. C.
Convicted 2-25, sentenced 3-23, 252G3
Expelled from Mass Sen 4-4, 253A3
Reelectn bid fails 5-24, 446F3
DICHLORO-diphenyl-trichloroethane (DDT)—*See PESTICIDES*
DICKMAN, James
E Coast dock protest ends 4-18, 324F2 ★
DICKSON, Carr (or Carter)—*See CARR, John Dickson*
DIEDERICHS, Nicolaas
Opens Parlt 1-21, 66G3
DIEGO Garcia (British territory)
Australia denies chrgs on US bases 1-25, 81B2
USSR urges US base end 3-24, 247C3
US base build-up observed 4-6, 270C2
DIEHL, Woodrow Wilson
Carter a guest at farm 10-21, 817C1
DIELDRIN—*See PESTICIDES*
DIEM, Ngo Dinh (1901-63)
CIA payments rptd 2-19, 124F1
Wesley Fishel dies 4-14, 356B3
DIEN, Ngo
Plans US MIA search 3-17, 206B2
DIETHYLSTILBESTROL (DES)—*See MEDICINE—Drugs*
DIETRICH, Noah
Hughes 'heir' admits lying 1-11, 120E1
DIETS & Dieting—*See FOOD*
DIEZ Benjumea, Gen. Salvador
Quits Cortes 4-19, 307C1
DIEZ Urzua, Sergio
Vs UN rights abuse res 12-16, 983F1
DIGREGORIO, Ernie
NBA final standings 4-10, 331D3
DIHIGO, Martin (d. 1971)
Inducted into baseball HOF 8-8, 644B1
DILLARD, Hardy Cross
World Ct member 4F1
DILLIN, Judge S. Hugh
Indianapolis busing plan voided 1-25, 79F3-80A1
DILLINGHAM Corp.
Australia compensatn offer rejctd 9-22, 762B2
DIMAS, George
Pregnant women warned vs alcohol 5-31, 472G1

1978

DIA—*See U.S. GOVERNMENT—DEFENSE—Defense Intelligence Agency*
DIABETES—*See MEDICINE—Diseases*
DIALYSIS—*See MEDICINE—Diseases*
DIAMOND, Jerry
WTA ends Va Slims pact 4-21, 419C2
DIAMOND, Neil
You Don't Bring Me Flowers on best-seller list 11-8, 888D1
DIAMONDS
Prices rptd inflated; inflatn, Israel speculatn blamed 3-17, 319D1
De Beers sets surchrg 3-28, 4-27, reactn 4-27, 319A1
De Beers hikes prices 8-8, 622E2
2 convicted in NYC '77 dealer's death 10-6, 824D2
LA bank robber arrested after Sovt deal 11-5, 992C1
Harry Winston dies 12-8, 1032G3
DIAMOND Shamrock Corp.
To buy Falcon Seaboard 11-2, 1005A2
DIARRHEA—*See MEDICINE—Diseases*
DIARY of Anne Frank, The (play)
Opens 12-18, 1031C1
DIAZ, Bo
Traded to Indians 3-30, 779C3
DIAZ Chavez, Ricardo
Rpts home bombed 8-29, 776A1
DIAZ Estrada, Gen. Nicanor (ret.)
Scores govt on dissent, Leigh dismissal 8-24; Leigh agrees 8-31, 796C1
DIAZ Serrano, Jorge
Claims new oil reserves 11-13, 903E2
DIBBS, Eddie
USTA ranks 7th 1-5, 22E3
Connors wins Grand Prix Masters 1-8, 22B3
Loses St Louis WCT 2-12, WCT singles title 5-14, Italian Open 5-27, 418E2-419A1
Loses Washn Star Intl 7-23; wins Volvo Intl 8-6, Canadian Open 8-20, 1027A2, B2
DIBROMOCHLOROPROPANE (DBCP)—*See PESTICIDES*
DI CICCO, Bobby
Wanna Hold Your Hand released 4-21, 619E2
DICKER, Richard
Named Penn Central chrmn 10-24, 875G3
DICKERMAN, Leland
Vietnam frees 1-5, 8E2
DICKEY, Curtis
Texas A&M wins HoF Bowl 12-20, 1025D2
DICKEY, Eldridge
Williams in NFL draft 5-2, 336B2
DICKINSON, Edwin W.
Dies 12-2, 1032F2
DICKINSON Jr., Fairleigh S.
Sun Oil buys Becton Dickinson shares 1-17, 65F3
DICKINSON, Gardner
Wins Legends of Golf title 4-30, 356B1
DICKINSON, Rep. William Louis (R, Ala.)
Reelected 11-7, 850A1
DICKS, Rep. Norman D. (D, Wash.)
Reelected 11-7, 852B4
DICTAPHONE Corp.
OKs Pitney-Bowes takeover bid 12-21, 1005E1
DIEDERICHS, Nicolaas (South African president)
Dies 8-21, 708E2 ★
DIEGO Garcia (British territory)
US troop presence rptd 1-2, 5E2
DIEM, Ngo Dinh (1901-63)
Chinese flee Vietnam 5-1, 341B1
Tuyen '76 death rptd 7-10, 692F1
DIETS & Dieting—*See under FOOD*
DIETZ, S. Marie
Wins cong primary in Vt 9-12, 716E2
DIFFERENT Story, A (film)
Released 6-13, 619E1
DIGGS Jr., Rep. Charles C. (D, Mich.)
Indicted 3-23, 220C2
Wins renomination 8-8, 626A1
Convicted 10-7, 791D3
Reelected 11-7, 846E2, 851F1, 854B1
Sentenced 11-20, 900A2
Dem ethics chmg threatens subcom chair 12-6, 958C2
DI GREGORIO, Eduardo
'Celine & Julie' released 2-24, 618G3
DILL, Clarence Cleveland
Dies 1-14, 96F1
DILLIN, Judge S. Hugh
Indianapolis busing ordrd 6-2, 611D1
DILLINGHAM Corp.
To close Australia mines 1-17, 34F2
DILLMAN, Bradford
Amsterdam Kill released 3-30, 618B3
DILLON, C(larence) Douglas
Named Met Museum bd chrmn 4-18, 335C3
DILONE, Miguel
AL stolen base ldr 10-2, 928F3
DILS, Steve
Stanford wins Bluebonnet 12-31, 1025F2
DIMAGGIO, Joe
Rose hits in 44 straight games 6-14—8-31, 618E2
DIMETHYL Sulfoxide (DMSO)—*See MEDICINE—Drugs*

1979

DIA—*See U.S. GOVERNMENT-DEFENSE-Defense Intelligence Agency*
DIABETES—*See MEDICINE-Diseases*
DIABLO Canyon Nuclear Power Plant—*See CALIFORNIA–Atomic Energy*
DIAGHILEV, Sergei Pavlovich (1872-1929)
Massine dies 3-16, 272B3
Chinchilla opens 6-4, 711B2
DIAMOND, Neil
You Don't Bring Me Flowers on best-seller list 1-10, 80E3
DIAMOND, Sigmund
Kissinger-FBI '50s link rptd 11-3, 870B2
DIAMONDS
Bokassa gifts to Giscard alleged 10-10, 791D1
Australia find rptd 10-20–10-21, 852B3
Bokassa gifts to Giscard alleged again 12-4, 993D3
DIAMOND Shamrock Corp.
Viet Agent Orange suit filed 2-1, 90C1
2d Agent Orange suit filed 11-26, 904A3
DIAZ Bruzual, Leopoldo
Venez Investmt Fund pres 3-10, 192D3
DIAZ Ordaz, Gustavo
Dies 7-15, 588F2
Conservatives laud 10-29, 874G3
DIAZ Serrano, Jorge
On Mex oil blowout 7-26, 635F3
Questnd on Pemex oil blowout, OKs audit 9-20, 718E3
Bars US oil export hike 11-23, 909B3
DIBA, Faridah
Iran urges assassinatn 5-13, 357E1
DIBBS, Eddie
Loses Birmingham WCT 1-21, Tulsa Grand Prix 4-15, 391F2, B3
Wins Forest Hills Invitatn 7-17, loses Ohio Grand Prix 8-12; US Open results 9-9, 734C1, A2, C2
DIBENSOFURAN (PCDF)—*See CHEMICALS*
DIBONA, Charles J.
Vs oil co pipeline divestiture 1-4, 55G2
On '78 oil demand 1-18, 36A1
Meets with Carter 5-31, 418E1
Vs price controls 10-17, 831F2
Defends 3d 1/4 oil profits 10-25, 804E2
DICHIERA, DAVID
Most Happy Fella opens 10-11, 956D3
DICK, Raymond
Washn Star renegotiates pacts 1-1, 5G1
DICKENS, Charles (1812-1870)
Comin' Uptown opens 12-20, 1007C2
DICKENS Hill (race horse)
2d in English Derby 6-6, 448B3
2d in Irish Derby 7-1, 876E3
DICKERSON, Glenda
Season To Unravel opens 1-25, 292G2
Glorious Monster opens 7-10, 711C3
DICKINSON Jr., Fairleigh S.
Absolved re Sun stock sale 7-9, 541G2
DICKSON, Larry
3d in Pocono 500 6-24, 491E1
DIECKAMP, Herman
On 3 Mile I A-accident 5-7, 344B2
DIEFENBAKER, John G.
Dies 8-16, 671A2
NDP wins seat 11-19, 907F3
DIEGO Garcia (British territory)
US mil base cited 4-16, 314A1
DIEM, Bui
Nixon '73 peace treaty pressure rptd 1-7, 29F1
DIENSTBIER, Jiri
Named Charter 77 ldr 2-8, 126F3*
Arrested 5-29, sentncd 10-23, 802B2
DIESEL Fuel—*See PETROLEUM*
DIETHYISTILBESTROL (DES)—*See MEDICINE–Drugs*
DIETZ, Howard
Dancing in Dark opens 1-21, 292D1
DIGGS Jr., Rep. Charles C. (D, Mich.)
Bars subcom reelectn bid 1-23, 71G2
Expulsn rejctd, ethics com to study case 3-1, 165E2
Admits funds misuse, accepts censure 6-29, 515D1
Censured by House, bars resignatn 7-31, 578D1
Sued by US 8-16, 649G3-650B1
Conviction upheld 11-14, 900F2
DI JORIO, Cardinal Alberto
Dies 9-5, 756B2
DILEO, Philip F.
Case declined by Sup Ct 4-23, 346E2
DILEO v. Board of Regents
Case declined by Sup Ct 4-23, 346D2
DILLON, C. Douglas
Father dies 4-14, 356D3
DILLON, Clarence
Dies 4-14, 356D3
DILLON, Mia
Once A Catholic opens 10-10, 956F3
DILLON Read & Co.
Clarence Dillon dies 4-14, 356D3

1980

DIA (Defense Intelligence Agency)—*See under U.S. GOVERNMENT--DEFENSE*
DIAKOV, Lubtcho
Wins Olympic medal 7-20, 623C2
DIAMOND, Jerry
Women end US Open boycott threat 11-12, 947B1
DIAMOND, M. Jerome
Wins primary for gov 9-9, 700C3
Loses Vt gov electn 11-4, 849D1
DIAMOND, Neil
Jazz Singer released 12-19, 1003B2
DIAMOND, Stuart
Wins Polk award 2-25, 692E3
DIAMOND Crystal Salt Co.
La lake 'swallowed' in salt-mine collapse 11-20, 970B3
DIAMONDS
Australia major find seen 1-11, 18E2
Anglo-Amer buys Consolidated Gold 2-12, 398A3
Australia Aborigines protest mining 5-8, 371B1
Australia mining projct OKd 7-27, 602C2
Bokassa confirms Giscard gifts 9-17, 728G3
Le Monde chrgd re Bokassa-Giscard revelatns 11-7, 872G1; France frees key figure 11-29, 921A3
DIAMOND Shamrock Corp.
Ohio toxic waste suit filed 10-7, 825F1
DIAMOND v. Bergy
Upjohn case remanded by Sup Ct 1-14, 37D1
DIAMOND v. Chakrabarty
Case decided by Sup Ct 6-16, 452E3
DIAZ Serrano, Jorge
On Mex '80 oil productn, long-term supply 1-15, 60G1-A2
On oil field discovery 1-15, 60B2
DIBA, Vasile
Wins Olympic medal 8-1, 622B2
DIBBS, Eddie
Loses Louisville Intl tourn 5-18, 607D3
Wins US Pro Outdoor 7-20, loses NH Grand Prix 8-3, 691G2, A3
DIBERNARDO, Angelo
Cosmos win NASL title 9-21, 770B2
DIBLEY, Colin
Australian Open results 1-2, 213F1
DICHLORO-diphenyl-trichloroethane (DDT)—*See PESTICIDES*
DICK Cavett Show (TV series)
Hellman sues Cavett, McCarthy 2-15, 199E2
DICKENSON, Charles
Hanged 1-29, 132B2
DICKENSON, Russell E.
Named Park Svc dir 5-1, 333D2
DICKERSON, Glenda
Reggae opens 3-27, 392F3
DICKEY, Curtis
Wins NCAA indoor 60-yd dash 3-15, 891F3
In NFL draft 4-29, 336E2
DICKEY-Lincoln Dam (Maine)
Study funds clear Cong 6-25, 9-10, signed 10-1, 803E2
DICKINSON Jr., Fairleigh S.
SEC drops ct damages action 2-14, 558A2
DICKINSON, Rep. William Louis (R, Ala.)
Reelected 11-4, 842A1
DICKS, Rep. Norman D. (D, Wash.)
Joins open-conv move 7-28, 570A2
Reelected 11-4, 844B3
DICU, Petre
Wins Olympic medal 7-22, 624B3
DIDC (Depository Institutions Deregulation Committee)—*See under U.S. GOVERNMENT*
DIEGO Garcia (British territory)
OAU denounces US base 7-1—7-4, 509G1
USSR, India vs US mil base 12-11, 930D2
DIEHL, Terry
2d in Texas Open 9-21, 972B2
DIE Laughing (film)
Released 5-23, 675B2
DIERS, Ines
Wins Olympic medals 7-21—7-27, 623C3, D3
DIETHER, Anton
Night Games released 4-11, 416D3
DIETHYISTILBESTROL (DES)—*See MEDICINE--Drugs & Health-Care Products*
DIETRICH, Raymond H.
Dies 3-19, 279B2
DIETS & Dieting—*See under FOOD*
DIFILIPPI, Jack
Convicted 9-2, 712F3
DIFRANCESCO, Eugene
Lenient sentence appeal backed by Sup Ct 12-9, 936B3
DIGGS Jr., Rep. Charles C. (D, Mich.)
Convictn cited re Abscam 2-21, 143G3
Sup Ct refuses convictn review 6-2, resigns 6-3, 428A1
Wilson censured 6-10, 438D2
Enters prison 7-24, Justice Dept drops suit 8-4, 908D3
Mich primary results 8-5, 682B3
Crockett wins seat, Preyer loses reelectn 11-4, 846C2, 850A1, 85AD1
DI GIOVANNI Jr., Cleto
S America visit scored by US Nicaragua amb 12-11, 942D3
DILL, William R.
May to replace at NYU 3-18, 224E3
DILL-Bundi, Robert
Wins Olympic medal 7-24, 622F2
DILONE, Miguel
AL batting, stolen base ldr 10-6, 926D3, F3
DI LORENZO, Edward
Idolmaker released 11-14, 972F3
DIMARIA, Leonard
Indicted 3-3, 215E1

1976

DIMITRIEV, Roman
Wins Olympic medal 7-31, 576C3
DIMKA, Lt. Col. Bukar Suka
Mohammed slain 2-13; police seek 2-15, 141E3
Mtg with UK envoy rptd 2-17, 2-18, 191E3
Arrested 3-5, 191C3
Rpts Gowon coup counsel 3-11, 222D2
Executed 5-16, 366F1
DINESEN, Erling
Resignatn prompts Cabt shuffle 9-9, 712F1
DINGELL, Rep. John D. (D, Mich.)
Scores Albert on gas bill 2-3, 109A1
On Alaska pipeline probe 7-6, 690E3
Reelected 11-2, 829E4
DINITZ, Simcha
Vs US criticism of Israel occupatn policies 3-24, 211C2
Sees Kissinger on Leb crisis 6-14, 430B1
US protests oil drilling curb 9-6, 663D2
Tells US of Leb border fears 11-23, 877B2
US ousts PLO aide 11-23, 878B2
DINSTEIN, Zvi
US oil deal OKd 5-6, 338D3
DIONNE, Jean
Accused 10-12, 999A1
DIOP, Mahjenout
Returns from exile 1-23, pardoned 4-3, 591E3
DIOP, Sheikh Anta
Scores multiparty amendmt 6-11, 591G2
DIPLOCK, Lord Kenneth
Angola mercenary probe set 2-10, 106A1
DIPLOMAT National Bank (Washington, D.C.)
S Korea probe rptd 11-14; Anderson resigns 11-21, 899A2, C2
DIRKSEN, Everett McK. (1896-1969)
Cited in Ford biog sketch 614A1
Di ROSA, Luigi
Slain by rightists 5-28, 403A1

1977

DINGELL, Rep. John D. (D, Mich.)
On missing A-material 8-8, 717F1
DINH Ba Thi
Cncl OKs Viet UN entry 7-20, 572F2
DINI Ahmed, Ahmed (Djibouti premier)
Named Djibouti premier 7-12, picks Cabt 7-15, 583B2
Resigns 12-17, 1018G3
DINITZ, Simcha
Sees Vance on Rabin resignatn 4-8, 267F2
Sees Vance, vs Carter on UN resolutns 5-28, 440G1
US repeats ban on jet sale to Ecuador 7-6, 511D1
US vs legalizatn of 3 W Bank towns 7-26, 570C1
Gives Vance copy of Begin invitatn to Sadat 11-15, 873F1
DIOR, House of
'77 fall fashions rptd 7-29, 1022C1
DIOS, Jose Luis
Killed by soldiers 9-12, 921G3
DIPLOMAT National Bank (Washington, D.C.)
Ex-chrm named KCIA agent 6-5, 442B1
SEC chrgs, consent accord filed 9-28, 774B1
DIPTHERIA—*See MEDICINE—Diseases*
DIRNHOFER, Karl
Arrested for Traube affair 12-1, 968E2
DIROSA, Joseph V.
Loses mayoral race 11-12, 879C1
DISABLED—*See MEDICINE—Handicapped*

1978

DIMONA, Joseph
Ends of Power on best-seller list 4-2, 272B3
DIN, Salah el-
Arms bid for Iran revolt rptd 12-29, 993F2
DINEEN, Bill
Named top WHA coach 7-6, hired as Whalers coach 7-17, 656D3, F3
DINGELL, Rep. John D. (D, Mich.)
On Energy Dept emergency preparedness rpt 9-11, 701D2
Reelected 11-7, 851F1
Subcom staff rpt chrgs 'middleman' oil price fraud 12-10, 983C3
DINNIS, Richard
Fired as Fury coach 6-14, 707D3
DION, Michel
WHA goaltending ldr 4-11, 296G2
DIOR, House of
'78 high chic fashion rptd 8-4—8-11, 10-27—11-3, 1029D2
DIOXIN—*See CHEMICALS*
DIPHENHYDRAMAMINE Hydrochloride (Benylin)—*See MEDICINE—Drugs*
DIRKS, Raymond I.
SEC censures re Equity Funding 9-4, 681A2
DISABLED—*See HANDICAPPED*
DISARMAMENT, U.N. Conference of the Committee on (CCD)—*See DISARMAMENT—Geneva Committee*

1979

DIMITRIOS I, Patriarch (Istanbul)
Meets Pope 11-29, 11-30, joint statemt issued 11-30, 930F3-931B1
DINCA, Ion
Named Rumania dep premr 1-31, 171C1
DINNEGAR, Robert
On Shroud of Turin tests 11-21, 931G2
DINOSAURS
Extinctn, extraterrestial event linked 5-28, 691B3
DIO, Johnny—*See DIOGUARDI, John*
DIOGUARDI, John (Johnny Dio)
Dies 1-12, 176F2
DIONNE, Jean
Cleared re Giguere case 12-7, 949C1
DIONNE, Oliva
Dies 11-15, 932E2
DIOXIN—*See CHEMICALS*
DI PALMA, Carlo
Teresa the Thief released 5-5, 528F3
DI PIRAMO, Renzo
Convicted on banking chrgs 3-1, 155A3
DIPLOMAT National Bank (Washington, D.C.)
Moon church fraud chrgd, '77 complaint cited 5-1, 376D2
Moon church fraud chrg settld 6-6, 547E2
DIRE Straits (recording)
On best-seller list 3-7, 174E1; 4-4, 271E2
DIRE Straits (singing group)
Dire Straits on best-seller list 3-7, 174E1; 4-4, 271E2
DIRT (film)
Top-grossing film 8-29, 672G3
DISARMAMENT, U.N. Conference of the Committee on (CCD)—*See DISARMAMENT-Geneva Committee*

1980

DIMITRI, Prince (Russia)
Dies 7-7, 608F1
DIMITROV, Stefan
Wins Olympic medal 7-22, 624E2
DIMMITT—*See TEXAS*
DIMSKI, Henryk
Arrested in W Ger 9-9, 889E1
DINEEN, Gerald P.
False A-alerts traced to failed component 6-17, 458D1
DINGELL, Rep. John D. (D, Mich.)
On Energy Mobilizatn Bd defeat 6-27, 515C2
Reelected 11-4, 843F1
DINNAN, James A.
Released from jail 9-30, resumes teaching 10-6, 890C3
DINOSAURS
Extinctn, asteroid collision linked 1-1, 415F1
Swimming carnivor evidence rptd 3-14, 415G2
DIONNE, Jean
Acquittal appeal set 1-4, 6A2
DIONNE, Marcel
NHL scoring ldr, clinches Ross Trophy 4-6, 295F3, G3, 296D1
DIOXIN—*See CHEMICALS*
DI PRINZIO, Robert A.
Hijacks Argentina jet 6-30—7-1, 519G2
DIRKS, Mayor A. Stephen (Ogden, Utah)
Loses Sen primary 9-9, 700A3
DIRTY Work I & II (books)
Justice Dept suit vs Agee OKd 4-1, 268E2

DISARMAMENT & ARMS CONTROL

1976

DISARMAMENT & Arms Control
Brezhnev policy speech 2-24, 194C1
S Pacific Forum backs A-free zone 3-8—3-9, 179B2
Sovt surprise attack capability, Europn unpreparedness rptd 3-15; NATO disavows 3-16, 3-19, 297B2
Italy CP urges NATO A-free role 4-18, 297C1
NATO warns on E-W arms race 5-21, 353E1
US warns on A-arms spread 7-29, 739D2; 9-30, 719F2
USSR sets UN resolutn 9-28, 719A3
Venez scores US, USSR 11-26, 929G3-930A1
Warsaw Pact asks A-weapon 1st use ban 11-27, 896B3
NATO vetoes 1st A-use ban 12-10, 933E2
US vows progress 12-22, 955B1

Geneva Committee (U.N. Conference of the Committee on Disarmament) (formerly ENDC) (Argentina, Brazil, Bulgaria, Burma, Canada, Czechoslovakia, East Germany, Egypt, Ethiopia, France, Great Britain, Hungary, India, Iran, Italy, Japan, Mexico, Mongolia, Morocco, Netherlands, Nigeria, Pakistan, Peru, Poland, Rumania, Sweden, USSR, U.S., West Germany, Yugoslavia, Zaire)
'76 conf 2-17—4-22, 761C2
Summer sessn opens 6-22, 761C2
US-Sovt weather-war pact OKd 9-3, 761B2

Nuclear Nonproliferation Treaty
Japan premr to spur parlt OK 1-9, 51C2
Japan ratifies 5-24, documents deposited 6-9, 418E3
US-Sovt undergrnd A-pact reaffirms 5-28, 387C1
US Dem platform text cites 6-15, 476G2
IAEA conf opens, warns re non-signatories 9-21, 760D3
French ratificatn seen 10-11, 1002B3
Australia issues uranium rpt 10-28, 835D2

1977

DISARMAMENT & Arms Control
Carter inaugural 1-20, 26C1, F1, 27F1
Carter statemt to world 1-20, 26F1, C2
Carter budget revisions 2-22, 125C1
Carter addresses UN 3-17, 185C1, D1, F2
Salzburg intl conf 5-2—5-13, 402F2
NATO backs realistic cuts 5-11, 359F3
Trudeau, Giscard meet 5-13, 389B2
Carter sets arms-sales policy 5-19, 380D2
Carter forgn policy address 5-22, 397F2
France vs Sovt global conf plan 6-22, 495E1
US, USSR, UK A-talks set 7-28, 574E2
US agency '78 funds OKd 8-2, 8-17, 689G1, C2
French drive announced 8-26, 1012G3
Yugo, China views compared 8-30—9-8, 710B1
French, US talks 9-15—9-16, 1012E3
US, USSR, UK A-test talks 10-3—10-4, 12-5—12-10; USSR backs ban 11-2, 996F3-997C1
Carter stresses at UN 10-4, 751G2, G-3
US M-X dvpt seen problem 10-7, 10-8, 777E1
UK, USSR sign accidental A-war pact 10-10, 812G3
Atomic Plant Issues—*See 'Industrial Use' under ATOMIC Energy*
Geneva Committee (U.N. Conference of the Committee on Disarmament) (formerly ENDC) (Argentina, Brazil, Bulgaria, Burma, Canada, Czechoslovakia, East Germany, Egypt, Ethiopia, France, Great Britain, Hungary, India, Iran, Italy, Japan, Mexico, Mongolia, Morocco, Netherlands, Nigeria, Pakistan, Peru, Poland, Rumania, Sweden, USSR, U.S., West Germany, Yugoslavia, Zaire)
'77 sessn opens, USSR asks A-test ban 2-15, 147C1
Weather-war pact signed 5-18, 400B3
US rejcts USSR total arms ban call; Japan asks curbs vs A-treaty non-signers 8-11, 686A3
'77 sessn ends; US, USSR note chem arms, A-test ban progress 8-30, 686G2

Nuclear Nonproliferation Treaty
Canada presses Brazil, Argentina ratificatn 1-28, 190F1
Argentina rejection cited 259G1
Japan ratificatn cited 3-22, 209A3
Australia safeguards proposed 3-29, 253A3
A-fuel licensing terms cited 268B2
Intl A-energy conf ends 4-13, 334G2
US A-export curbs proposed 4-27, 334F1
Australia sets uranium export curbs 5-24, 465B3
Japan asks curbs vs non-signers 8-11, 686B3
US asks S Africa safeguards 8-20, 657B1

1978

DISARMAMENT & Arms Control
US-India declaratn vows A-arms curb; Desai scores A-powers 1-3, 1D2
Humphrey stand cited 32G3
Carter State of Union Message 1-19, 31D2
France offers negotiatn plan 1-25, reactn 1-31, 61D2-D3
US A-material ban rptd debated 4-3, 277B2
NATO reactn to neutron bomb deferral 4-7, 254D2
Hungary scores US stance 6-10, 534F2
US vows A-weapon restraint 6-12, 445F1
Rumania, UK talks 6-13—6-16, 515D3
Carter lauds Latin A-ban pact 6-21, 489C3
USSR, UK join US A-weapon restraint vow 6-30, 523C1
Carter admits US spy satellite use 10-1, 861B2
Gromyko: France, USSR discussed Eur conf 10-29, 831A1
Force Reduction Talks, Mutual and Balanced (MBFR)—*See under EUROPE*

Geneva Committee (U.N. Conference of the Committee on Disarmament) (CCD) (formerly ENDC) (Argentina, Brazil, Bulgaria, Burma, Canada, Czechoslovakia, East Germany, Egypt, Ethiopia, France, Great Britain, Hungary, India, Iran, Italy, Japan, Mexico, Mongolia, Morocco, Netherlands, Nigeria, Pakistan, Peru, Poland, Rumania, Sweden, USSR, U.S., West Germany, Yugoslavia, Zaire)
France asks end, offers new com plan 1-25, 61E2
'78 session opens: US, USSR score French plan; others back 1-31, 61B3
Brezhnev visits W Ger 5-4—5-7, 417E1
France, China hint role 5-25, 5-29, 421C2-422A1
Membership rise, rotating chrmnshp OKd by UN sessn 6-30, 522G2
Sovts score Huang speech 10-10, 796C2
USSR-France tensns cited 10-29, 830F3
Nuclear Nonproliferation Treaty
India scores A-powers 1-3, 1F2
India bars ratificatn 1-9, 37F1
Humphrey role cited 33A1
India ratificatn terms rptd 6-13, 466F3
US urges S Africa ratificatn 6-25—6-29, 536G3
US cancels S Africa uranium contracts, ratificatn refusal cited 11-4, 904C2
Nuclear Safeguards Issue—*See ATOMIC Energy—Industrial*
Nuclear Test Ban Developments—*See also 'Nuclear Nonproliferation Treaty' above, 'U.S.-Soviet' below*
Humphrey stand on A-test ban cited 33A1
India links safeguards OK, test-ban pact 1-9, 37E1
Carter State of Union Message 1-19, 31D2
India asks A-test ban 2-15, 121G2
US to seek 5-yr test ban 5-20, 996E2
India A-test ban proposal cited 6-30, 523C1

1979

DISARMAMENT & Arms Control
Carter State of Union Message 1-23, 47C3
US blocks H-bomb article 3-9, 193C3-194A1
Pope presents 1st encyclical 3-15, 217F1
USSR bars Eur conventnl arms cut talks 4-28, 323C3
USSR, Yugo back controls 5-18, 380A1
Conv arms talks backed in SALT II communique 6-18, 457F3
Pope, Carter joint statemt backs curbs 10-6, 759D3
USSR offers E Ger troop cut, Eur missile freeze 10-6; Westn natns score 10-7, 10-9, 761E1, A3-F3
USSR offers Eur troop, missile cuts 10-13—11-6, 880G2
Warsaw Pact asks arms reductn talks 12-6, 938C3

Force Reduction Talks, Mutual and Balanced (MBFR)—*See under EUROPE*

Geneva Committee (U.N. Conference of the Committee on Disarmament) (CCD) (formerly ENDC) (Algeria, Argentina, Australia, Belgium, Brazil, Bulgaria, Burma, Canada, China, Cuba, Czechoslovakia, East Germany, Egypt, Ethiopia, France, Great Britain, Hungary, India, Indonesia, Iran, Italy, Japan, Kenya, Mexico, Mongolia, Morocco, Netherlands, Nigeria, Pakistan, Peru, Poland, Rumania, Sri Lanka, Sweden, USSR, U.S., Venezuela, West Germany, Yugoslavia, Zaire)
'79 sessn begins; France joins, China bars attendance 1-27, 625G2
SALT II communique backs cooperatn 6-18, 457F3, G3, 458A1
'79 sessn ends; chem, A-arms bans proposed, '78 A-tests discussed 8-14, 625F2-D3

Nuclear Nonproliferation Treaty
Carter lauds Mex support 2-14—2-16, 124F2
IAEA safeguards stressed in SALT II communique 6-18, 457D3

Nuclear Safeguards Issues—*See ATOMIC Energy—Industrial Use*
Nuclear Test Ban Developments—*See also 'Nuclear Nonproliferation' above, 'U.S.-Soviet' below*
Test ban treaty progress cited in SALT II communique 6-18, 457C3
US, USSR, UK rpt on talks 7-31, 625C3

1980

DISARMAMENT & Arms Control
US, W Ger back controls 1-16, 28A2
Soviet-French talks held 4-24—4-25, 351F3
Europn CPs seek confs 4-29, 327C3
USSR vs NATO missile offer 5-19, 378B3
UK Labor Party disputes position 5-31, 429D2, G2
USSR rejected W Ger A-missile freeze offer 6-9; Schmidt gets Carter letter vs 6-16, seeks mtg 6-18, 450B3-451D1
US, Italy back NATO stand 6-20, 474C2
NATO backs E-W Eur conf 6-26, 489F2
Schmidt, Brezhnev in A-missile talks, negotiatns seen 6-30—7-1, 489B1
W Ger backs NATO A-missiles 7-15, 540E1
UK Labor Party backs unilateral move 10-2, 768B3
Warsaw Pact asks Eur conf 10-19—10-20, 800E2
UK rally held 10-26, 886G3
Carter scores Reagan nonproliferatn stance 10-29, 816C2
Israel for Mideast A-ban 11-13, 864A2
Carter urges Latin A-arms treaty 11-19, 881A3
NATO studies Sovt talks curb 12-12, 949F1
Beagle Channel 'zone of peace' proposed 12-12, 978E3
Force Reduction, Mutual and Balanced—*See MUTUAL and Balanced Force Reduction*
Geneva Committee—*See GENEVA Committee*

Nuclear Nonproliferation Treaty
NRC bars India uranium sale 5-16, 440E3
Carter OKs India uranium sale 6-19, 495F2
Geneva review conf ends; Sri Lanka cites implementatn failure 9-7, 696A1
US Cong fails to block India uranium sale 9-24, 723G1

1976

Strategic Arms Limitation Talks (SALT)—*See 'U.S.-Soviet Developments' below*

U.S. Presidential Election (& transition)
Reagan scores US policy, Ford rebuts 2-10, 109A2
Ford defends policy 3-5, 179E3
Reagan scores on-site pact 4-9, 281C3
Ford defends policy 4-21, 281D2
Carter scores US-Sovt A-pact 5-13, 375C1; 5-14, 390F3
Rpt Sovt admits SALT violatn 5-24, 386A3
US Dem platform plank 6-15, 432E3
US Dem platform text cites 6-15, 476G2, 477B1, F1, 477D2, F2
Carter vs 'bargaining chips' 6-24, 490G1
US GOP platform com actn 8-13, 582C3
US GOP platform text cites 8-18, 610D2
Reagan GOP pres conv remarks 8-19, 613B3
Mondale stresses issue 8-30, 645C3
Ford scores Carter stand 9-9, 665C2
Ford, Carter debate 10-6, 741A3, 742D1
Carter hopeful re SALT 11-15, 864B1
Vance stresses priority 12-3, 916G1
Carter to push SALT talks 12-3, 916B3
Carter for A-arms curbs 12-27, 978A3

U.S.-Soviet Developments—*See also 'U.S. Presidential Election' above*
Kissinger sets Sovt SALT trip 1-14, 17A1
Ford State of Union message 1-19, 38B3, E3
Kissinger in Moscow; SALT progress rptd 1-21—1-23, 61A3
Rumsfeld on SALT talks 1-27, 68C2
Kissinger defends policy 2-3, 88G2
Ford hopeful re SALT 2-10, 109B3
Brezhnev cites SALT accord aim, Sovt Trident proposal 2-24, 194C1
Underground test curbs drafted 4-9, 242C2-C3
Ford asks more missile $ 4-26, 307C3
SALT talks adjourn 5-5, resume 6-2, 408E1
Undergrnd A-pact initialed; US stays signing 5-12; pact signed 5-29, 371C2, 386B3; text 387A1
Rpt Sovt admits SALT violatn 5-24, 386A3
Australia stresses US-Sovt ties 6-1, 438E2
USSR chrgs US SALT stall 6-5, 408D1
US arms control rpt cites Sovt A-weapons 7-29, 739E2
Sovt MIRV buildup cited 8-31, 739D1
SALT talks resume 9-21, 739B1
USSR asks test ban, SALT accord 9-28, 719C3
Sovt OKs A-blast inspectn 10-4, 739C1
Brezhnev scores Westn pressure 10-5, 739F1
Sovt undergrnd A-tests rptd near limit 10-15, 948D2
Secret missile, A-accident pacts rptd 11-4, 948F2
NATO warned re SS-20 11-18, 879G2
SALT talks adjourn 11-20, 916B1
Brezhnev asks SALT renewal 11-30, 947A3
Brzezinski on arms levels 12-16, 936C3

1977

Strategic Arms Limitation Talks (SALT)—*See 'U.S.-Soviet Developments' below*

U.S.-Latin Developments
Carter backs Latin A-ban pact 4-14, 295F2
Carter signs Latin A-ban pact 5-26, 415D3
Carter Ecuador arms policy clarified 6-1—6-3, 454D3
Mrs Carter in Peru, Andean pact backed 6-3, 455A1
Nicaragua anti-Sovt stance cited 6-21, 656B3
Carter, Venez pres joint communique 7-1, 546D2
Argentina to sign A-ban pact 11-21, 912A3
Vance in Brazil A-talks 11-22, 912C3

U.S.-Soviet Developments
Ford State of Union message 1-12, 12F3, 13D3
Brezhnev asks SALT II pact, scores mil aims rpt 1-18, 70F1
Carter to seek A-test ban, cuts 1-24, 51G2
Carter to seek early SALT II pact 1-27, 70D1
Warnke named US negotiator 2-2, Carter defends 2-4, 2-8, 88F3; confrmd 3-9, 171G3
Carter asks quick arms accord, other proposals 2-8, 88A2
US discounts Sovt rift 2-18, 137A3
Carter: Sovt stance unchngd 3-9, 172D3
Carter addresses UN 3-17, 185F2
Ford on Sovt buildup, SALT failure 3-23, 3-26, 236E2, F1
Podgorny asks Indian O demilitarizatn 3-24, 247C3
US delegatn arrives USSR 3-26; SALT talks open 3-28, working groups set 3-29, 225G1
US vs Sovt fishing ship seizures re SALT talks 3-28—4-4, 270E1
USSR rejcts US SALT bids, Geneva talks agreed 3-30, 225A1, E2
Carter vows arms limitatn fight 3-30, 225E2
Gromyko scores US offer; Carter stands firm 3-31, 4-2, 246D2, E3
Vance defends US proposals 3-31—4-3, US reactn 3-31—4-4, 247A1
Kissinger sees agrmt 'achievable'; Jackson, Ford vs pre-talk rhetoric 4-5, 4-6, 247A2-F2
Brezhnev sees SALT compromise 4-5, reassures Carter 4-8, 400D3
US, USSR reps meet on SALT 4-7—4-15, 400B3
Pravda hits US proposals 4-14, Carter rebuff 4-15, 400F3
Carter optimistic on SALT talks 4-15, 299A2
China doubts talks 'serious' 4-17, 298C2
IISS scores Carter policy 4-28, 401D1
US orders more ICBMs 5-3, 343C3
Brown sees limited SALT agrmt 5-6, 401C1
US, USSR OK SALT framework 5-18—5-20, stress differences 5-21, 400D2-A3
Carter sees cong arms experts 5-18, 401A1
Carter assesses SALT talks 5-26, 417F1
US defends new warhead deploymt 6-1, 6-2, 462B1
Vance-Gromyko SALT talks delayed 6-15, Warnke comments 6-27, 530B1
France stresses US-USSR progress 6-22, 495E1
Indian O demilitarizatn talks 6-22—6-27, 530C1
Carter kills B-1, backs cruise missile 6-30; USSR reactn 7-3, 514D3
Carter bars SALT, rights link; asks Brezhnev prelim talks 6-30, 515A1, D1
Brezhnev rejcts prelim talks 7-5, 529F3
Carter defends policy, defers neutron bomb 7-12, 533D1, F1
Carter sees Schmidt 7-13—7-14, 566B2
Carter on SALT aims, Eur troop cuts, missile deploymt 7-21, 550B3
Giscard scores US proposals 7-25, 551A1
US, USSR, UK A-test talks set 7-28, 574E2
Arbatov chrgs US obstacles 8-3, 590G1
CIA sees Sovt arms cuts in '80s 8-8, 949B1
US vs USSR total arms ban call 8-11, 686A3
Brezhnev backs SALT initiative 8-16, 640E2
Chem arms, A-test ban progress noted 8-30, 686G2
Gromyko-Vance mtg delayed 8-31, cruise missile debate cited 9-11, 751C2
Strategic weapons compared 751A3
Waldheim sees SALT progress 9-19, 713F1
Gromyko sees Vance 9-22—9-23, Carter 9-23, 9-27; progress rptd, Carter-Brezhnev summit seen 9-23, 9-29, 10-1, 750D3
US, USSR extend '72 SALT pact 9-23, 9-25, 750A3
US SALT extensn debate seen, Sen role asked 9-26, 9-30; res set aside 10-3, 751C1

1978

US treaty delay re SALT rptd, 3-yr test-ban order cited 10-5, 996D2
A-arms reliability questnd 11-3, 877F1-B2

Security and Cooperation in Europe, Conference on (CSCE)—*See under EUROPE*

Strategic Arms Limitation Talks (SALT)—*See 'U.S.-Soviet Developments' below*

UN Developments—*See also 'Geneva Committee' above*
France plans proposal 4-24, 313D1
Assemb special sessn opens 5-23; US, USSR affirm A-test ban commitmt regional agrmts 5-24, 5-26, 421A1
France, China hint Geneva role 5-25, 5-29, 417F3, 421C2-422A1
Canada ends A-arms role 5-26, 422B1
Cuba vp addresses sessn 5-30, 418E1
Brezhnev scores NATO members 5-31, 423C2
Fraser urges A-arms curb 6-5, 450D3
Cambodia chrgs Viet aggressn 6-9, 490E1
Assemb sessn ends, proposals adopted 6-30, 522G2

U.S.-Soviet Developments
Carter vows NATO consultatn 1-6, 1D1
Carter State of Union Message 1-19, 29B1, A3, 31B2
Carter urges satellite A-ban 1-30, 57E2, 62A3
UN sessn opens, French conf plan opposed 1-31, 61B3
Sovts score US indecisn 2-11, 3-28, 4-7, 297C2
W Ger asks neutron bomb limitatn talks 2-23, 140A2
Brezhnev scores SALT delays 2-24, US links Horn of Africa interventn 2-25, 3-2, 137B1, 140E2
US confident re SALT monitoring 2-24, 298F1
US rpts USSR '72 SALT pact adherence 2-28, 298B1
US links SALT delay, Horn of Africa interventn 3-1; USSR scores 3-2, 178F3
US links neutron bomb halt, Sovt arms restraint 3-10; USSR reactn 3-11, 4-4, 254F1
Carter warns USSR vs mil buildup, interventn; Tass scores 3-17, 202G1-A3
US A-material ban debated 4-3, 277C2
Brown urges Turkish arms embargo end 4-6, 276F2
Carter defers neutron bomb productn 4-7, 253B1
NATO talks on neutron bomb deploymt rptd 4-9, 253E2
NATO backs neutron bomb deferral, vs cruise missile limits 4-19, 298C2, D2
Vance in Moscow talks, communique issued 4-20—4-22; progress rpt 4-23, 4-25, 297A1
USSR asks joint neutron bomb restraint; Carter: no significance 4-25, 297A2, 307A2
Shevchenko book contract rptd 4-26, 302B3
A-ceiling, allied aid limits set 5-1, 5-4, 423D1, E1 *
Carter lauds USSR effort 5-5, 342F1
USSR seeks cruise missile limits on 747s, B-52s 5-7, US rejcts 5-26, 422D3-423C1
UN spec sessn opens 5-23, US scores USSR re SS-20 missile deploymt, Indian O role 5-24; Gromyko replies 5-26 5-26, 421C1
Mondale pledges A-test ban, affirms SALT commitmt 5-24, 421C1
Carter warns USSR on Africa 5-25, 418C1
Gromyko sees Vance, Carter 5-25—5-31; Zaire exchng causes tensn 5-27, ICBM snag rptd 6-3, 422C1-E2
Gromyko for SALT agrmt, total A-test ban 5-26, 421A2
China briefing by Brzezinski rptd 5-27, 399G1
Brzezinski evaluates US SALT offer 5-28, 422C3
W Ger backs US warning on Africa 5-31, 397A2
Brezhnev backs mutual agrmt ban 5-31, 423C2
Schmidt rpts Carter SALT briefing 6-1, 519A2
US SALT 'freeze' rptd by Washn Post, Carter denies 6-2, 422F2
Carter rpts SALT progress, bars conditns; Tass replies 6-7, 423D2, 424A1, E1
Vance vows A-arms restraint 6-12, 445F1
USSR urges US effort for SALT treaty OK 6-17, 464F3
Vance stresses SALT priority, denies Africa policy 'linkage' 6-19, 490B3, C3, D3
SALT impact on USSR arms spending discounted 6-27, 563B3
UN spec sessn chngs Geneva chrmn rules; US, USSR bar India test ban proposal, vow A-arms restraint 6-30, 522B3, 523C1
US congressmen score SALT mtg, link Shcharansky trial 7-10—7-12; Vance defends 7-10, 542D1, 543G2-B3
US land-based missile plan rptd 7-12, 529C1
Young on Shcharansky, Ginzburg trials, SALT link 7-12, 542E2

1979

Strategic Arms Limitation Talks (SALT)—*See 'U.S.-Soviet Developments' below*

UN Developments—*See also "Geneva Committee" above*
Assemb sessn cited in SALT II communique 6-18, 458A1
Pope addresses Assemb, urges curbs 10-2, 757F2, 758A1

U.S.-Soviet Developments
UK, W Ger back proposed SALT pact 1-6, 12E2
US mil ex-ldrs warn of Sovt challenge 1-12, 15D1
Vance backs re China tie 1-15, 27D2
Carter denies SALT security threat 1-17, 29G3
US monitor in Iran rptd closed 1-18, 26F2
Carter State of Union Message notes SALT 1-23, 46C2, D2, 47G2-E3, 48C1
Brown on SALT agrmt 1-25, 52G2
USSR warned re data encoding 1-31, 258F2
Tass: Teng trip to US undermines SALT 2-1, 84F1
USSR long-range cruise missile tests rptd, SALT cited 2-1, 99E3
GOP seeks open SALT debate 2-3, 86A1
Teng rptd vs US SALT signing 2-5, 65G1
US '78 protesters sentncd, 21 arrested 2-12, 133A2-B3
Carter on SALT linkage, emerging pact 2-20, 123F2, F3-124B1
NATO concerned re SS-20 2-20, 148D1
Kennedy backs SALT 2-20, other Sen reactn 3-4, 4-5, 258D1
Iran bans intell posts, US personnel flee; SALT monitoring rptd unaffected 2-21—2-28, 145C2
US confrms arms dvpt restraint if SALT fails, denies exec agrmt rpt 2-23, 258B2
Haig doubts on SALT cited 2-28, 147E3
Brezhnev sees SALT agrmt 3-2, 172C1
Baker urges SALT criticism 3-10, 186B1
USSR 14-MIRV SS-18 '78 test rptd 3-13, 258G2
Mondale briefs Brazil pres on SALT 3-22, 248A1
U-2 use for SALT verificatn seen 4-3, 258D2
US SALT ratificatn pressed; Brzezinski, Brown back 4-4, 4-5, 257F2
US mil ex-ldrs score SALT 4-11, 294D3-295A2
US sen vs SALT, asks amendmts 4-11, 295A2
SALT missile verificatn gap seen by CIA 4-16, Brown disputes 4-17, 279D2
China bid to monitor SALT 4-19, 312C1
USSR ldrs assure US reps re SALT verificatn 4-20, 314A2
Mondale briefs Dutch on SALT 4-21—4-22, 299D2
Carter urges scientists back SALT 4-23, 300F2
Carter promotes SALT pact ratificatn 4-25, 294A2
USSR tactical A-arms feared 4-25, 340C1
SALT motive seen in dissident-spy swap 4-27, 317F1
US spy satellite data rptd compromised 4-28, 318F2
USSR seeks French role in SALT III 4-28, 323B3
Carter: would uphold SALT terms without Sen ratificatn 4-30, 319A1
Turkey-US controversy re bases, U-2 flights 5-7—5-8, 5-14—5-29 397G2, B3
US, USSR '72, '79 strategic weapons compared 338E3
SALT draft announced in US 5-9, USSR 5-10; Carter-Brezhnev summit planned; SALT II proposed limits, terms 338B3-339G3
US sens score SALT II 5-10—5-17, Jackson chrgs 'appeasemt' 6-12, 6-17, 449F2, 459F2-460C1
Admin stresses SALT debate 5-15, 365D2
NATO mins back SALT 5-16, 359G2; 5-31, 415D3
Carter on MX deploymt 5-29, 402D1
SALT cited re lower USSR warhead yield estimates 5-31, 410G1
Brezhnev backs SALT summit 6-1, 417B1
French forgn min on SALT treaty 6-5, 485E1
Carter OKs MX dvpt 6-8; Sovts score, SALT pact cited 6-10, 438B1-D1

1980

Strategic Arms Limitation Talks (SALT)—*See 'U.S.-Soviet Developments' below*

U.S.-Soviet Developments
Nuclear 'doomsday clock' moved forward 1-1, 12D3
US to delay pact for Sovt Afghan invasn 1-2, 1B2
USSR rejects Eur A-missile talks 1-3, 4A3
Kennedy seeks firm US stand 1-14, 32D3
Carter reaffirms goal, cites SALT 1-23, 41C2, 42A2
Gromyko reaffirms Sovt interest 2-18, 124B1
Carter confirms SALT support 2-25, 139C3
Reagan 'basic speech' scores SALT 2-29, 207F2, G2
Carter hints SALT renunciatn, doubts Sen ratificatn 3-14, 209D1
Reagan stresses arms talks 3-17, 208G1-B2
USSR '72 biological ban adherence questnd 3-18, 235C2*
USSR bars SALT II implementatn talks 3-19, sets ABM dismantling 3-20, 219B2
Europn CPs back SALT ratificatn 4-29, 327C3
Vance urges SALT OK 6-5, 421C3
Carter vs E-W A-missile freeze 6-16, 450B3-451D1
US sets Sovt conf terms 6-26, 489G2
US chrgs Sovt anthrax cover-up, '72 treaty upheld 6-29, 500D1
Carter briefed on W Ger-USSR A-missile talks 7-2, 489C1
Turkey bars USSR consultatn re U-2 7-4, 526C1
Carter weighs Sovt A-weapon talks proposal 7-5, 506A1
US evangelicals vs SALT 7-11—9-15, 819B1
Kissinger-Dobrynin '77 SALT mtg cable rptd 7-14, 754B1
US GOP platform adopted 7-15, 536G1
Carter pres renominatn acceptance speech; text 8-14, 612D1, F3, 613B1, A3
Reagan urges US strength 8-18, 8-20, 629B1, F1
Brezhnev asks talks 8-22, US denies delay 8-26; Muskie indicates US ready, hints SALT ratificatn 9-7, 679D3-680B1
Anderson platform offered 8-30, 665C1, G1, B2
Carter blasts Reagan on A-arms race 9-2, 664B3
Sovt A-test rptd 9-14, US protests 9-15, 730F1
Sovt ABM system rptd updated 9-14, 730A3
Carter cites arms talks 9-18, 698B3
US rep chrgs Sovt SALT violatns, US denies 9-18, 730C2
Muskie praises SALT, scores Reagan oppositn 9-18, 10-16, 776G1
Mondale hits Reagan stand 9-23, 780F2
Missile force data traded 9-26, 776G3
Reagan would redo SALT 9-30, Carter assails 10-1, 738E3, 739B2; 10-2, 10-6, 762B2
Carter attacks Reagan on arms control, SALT 10-8—10-10, 778B2, F2, D3
US Navy sub total rptd at 13-yr low 10-11, 986E3
Brezhnev urges talks resume 10-14, 776C3
Carter assails Reagan, sees 'nuclear precipice' 10-16, 10-19, 802D2
Reagan pledges SALT III talks 10-19, 801C2, 802A1
Mondale hits Reagan SALT stance 10-26, 816D3
Carter, Reagan TV debate 10-28, 813A1, E1, A2, 814F2, B3, 815G2
Anderson answers TV debate questns, backs SALT II 10-28, 816C1
Carter hits Reagan SALT stance 10-29, 816D2
Carter hits issue 10-30, 841B1
Reagan plans policy shift 11-6, 839D2
Carter on Reagan policy support 11-12, 865A3
Kennedy urges SALT pact 11-19, 881D1
Schmidt, Carter stress accords 11-20; Schmidt reaffirms 11-24, 904A1, G1
Percy in Moscow, forsees SALT talks 11-26—11-28; Reagan pleased 11-28, Meese optimistic 11-30, 914F3-915A2
Percy 'confident' of talks 12-12, Arbatov cool 12-15, 950A3

1976

1977

Gromyko at UN, backs A-test ban 9-27, 770B1
US, USSR, UK A-test talks 10-3—10-4, 12-5—12-10; USSR backs ban 11-2, 996F3-997C1
NATO fears cruise missile SALT compromise 10-11—10-12, 956C3
SALT draft text rptd 10-11, cruise missile concessns confrmd 11-17; talks recess 12-16, 996A1
Brzezinski sees better USSR ties 10-18, 866E1
Carter sees SALT accord in 'few wks' 10-21, 817C1
Carter on SALT progress 10-27, 813A3, G3
US SALT critic leaks details 11-1; Defns Dept rebuts 11-6, Sen subcom accused 11-7, 11-8, 996D2-B3
ABM accord OKd 11-21, 997E1
USSR ABM violatns chrgd 11-23, 997C1
NATO reassured on security needs, backs SALT pact 12-8—12-9, 956F3
Carter sees Brezhnev visit after SALT accord 12-28, 1002C1
Carter optimistic in Warsaw 12-30, 1001D1

1978

Vance sees Gromyko in Geneva 7-12—7-13; delivers Shcharansky trial protest 7-12, sees wife 7-13, 543D2
USSR scores MAP 7-23, Warnke backs 8-24, 747A3
US cong pro-defns coalitn formed 8-8, 604C3
Brezhnev rptdly wants Carter mtg 8-25, 670B2
US-Sovt A-balance seen in mid-'80s 8-29, 677A1
USSR detains 7 US protesters 9-4, 947C2
Warnke sees Gromyko, rpts progress 9-7—9-8, 747D2
Kennedy, Brezhnev confer on SALT 9-9, 743A1
US reps protest MAP missile plan 9-22, 737F3
Vance-Gromyko talks 9-27—9-28, Carter mtg 9-30—10-1, 747F2
Carter sees SALT success, Sen treaty OK 9-27, 751E3
Warnke to quit after SALT talks 10-10, 766G3
Carter prefers SALT pact as treaty 10-10, 766G3
Warnke quits as SALT, ACDA head 10-10; Earle, Seignious replacemts set 10-20, 804F1
Vance, Gromyko resume talks in Moscow; revised cruise missile limits proposed, Backfire, MIRV, other issues cited 10-22—10-23, 803C3-804F1
USSR SALT concessns linked to anti-cruise missile success 10-23, 877D2
USSR scores US neutron parts productn order 10-26, 833E2
Gromyko hints SALT expansn 10-29, 831A1
Carter cites priority 11-6, 862E1
Kosygin denies Cuba MiGs threaten talks 11-16, 905F1
Brezhnev stresses SALT, blames US for delay 11-17, 905E1
Warsaw Pact summit topic 11-22—11-23, 913E2
Vance: SALT agrmt still possible in '78 11-25, 925D1
US critics, backers on upcoming SALT pact 11-27—12-20, 996D1
Brezhnev links trade to SALT pact 12-6, 966D2
NATO assured re US support 12-9, 954A3
US, Rumania discuss topic 12-9, 965F3
Carter on SALT pact delay, summit 12-12, 957C1, D1
Carter: SALT unaffected re US-China tie 12-19, 976G1
Vance, Gromyko meet, SALT pact completn delayed 12-21—12-23, US-China ties linked 12-26, 995F2, 996B1

1979

Carter, Brezhnev hold Vienna summit 6-15–6-18; Backfire dispute resolved 6-17; **SALT II pact signed 6-18,** 449A1-C2; texts of treaty, Backfire statemt, US-Sovt communique 450A1-458E2
Carter addresses Cong on SALT II 6-18, 449C2; text 458F1-459E3
SALT II verificatn talks rptd 6-21, U-2 substitutes sought 6-28, 497B1
Toon: 'confident' on SALT II verificatn 6-22, 496F3
Turkey mil chief, Ecevit vs U-2 flights 6-24, 6-27, 488C2
Gromyko warns vs SALT chngs 6-25, Goldwater scores 6-26, 496G2
Baker favors SALT amendmts 6-27, Seignious opposes 6-30, 496C3
France backs SALT II 6-28, 497A1
Gov Brown backs SALT II 6-29, 496G3
Byrd in USSR 7-1–7-5, sees Brezhnev 7-4; warns vs SALT amendmts 7-8, 510B3
SALT ratificatn debated in US Sen com 7-9–7-11, 510D1-A2
US Sen com continues SALT hearings 7-12, 7-17, 7-18, 536D1
Australian Labor Party backs SALT monitoring base 7-19, 542G1
US Sen com gets SALT testimony 7-24–8-1, 643G2
Toon, Amer Legion back SALT pact 7-26, 8-22, H Byrd vs 7-30, 644B1-D1
Norway SALT monitor role denied 7-26, 762F1
Carter vs arms budget link to SALT 7-27; Kissinger backs 7-31, 8-2; US sens react 8-2, 8-3, 590G2, E3
A-test ban talks progress rptd 7-31, 625C3
USSR scores US SALT opponents 8-2, 644D1
AFL-CIO backs SALT pact 8-7, 591D1
VFW scores SALT treaty 8-21, 628D1
US sens in USSR re SALT, get Backfire pledge 8-28–8-30, 657E2
SALT hearing stayed 9-4; pact endangered re USSR troops in Cuba 9-5, 657F1; 9-6, 674B1
Carter chooses 'racetrack' MX deployment plan; diagram 9-7, 677F2, 678A2
Carter bars SALT-Cuba troop link 9-8, 673C1
Pravda scores US re Cuba troop rpt 9-10, 673D2
U-2 use in SALT verificatn dropped 9-12, 762D1
Reagan scores SALT 9-15, 739D3
W Ger defense paper cites SALT 9-24, 733G1
Ex-Pres Ford opposes SALT II 9-26, Brzezinski rebuts 9-27, 739D2, A3
Carter urges SALT ratificatn despite Cuba troops; speech text 10-1; Sen, Sovt, Eur reactn 10-1–10-3, 737A1-739D2
Pope backs SALT II 10-2, 758B1
SALT verificatn assessed by Sen Intellignc Com 10-5, 761G3
US Turkish base extensn set 10-8, 796B1
Carter scores USSR missile freeze offer 10-9, 761A3
US Sen Forgn Relatns Com ends SALT hearings 10-10, reservatns voted 10-15–10-31, 822A2-B3
Church proposes SALT 'understanding' re Cuba troops 10-11, 822B3
Byrd backs SALT pact 10-25, 822C3
'63 A-test-ban treaty cited re mystery A-blast 10-26, 824D3
Baker cites Sen SALT debate 11-1, 828F3
US Sen Forgn Relatns Com OKs SALT pact 11-9, 864A1
W Ger backs Eur A-missile talks 12-6, 938E2
SALT Sen debate delayed till '80 12-6, 938E3
US vows Eur A-missile talks committmt, SS-20s cited 12-7, 938F1, B2
NATO seeks A-weapon talks 12-12, 959G1, A2
USSR negative on Eur A-arms talks 12-13–12-16, 959F2
Carter defense budget, SALT linked 12-13, 963A2-E2
19 sens ask SALT treaty vote delay, Carter rejcts 12-16, 979A2
Carter, UK prime min discuss SALT 12-17, 968A2
Sen Armed Svcs Com rejcts SALT 12-20, 979D1

1980

DISASTERS—*See also ACCIDENTS, DROUGHTS, EARTHQUAKES, FAMINES, STORMS & Floods, VOLCANIC Eruptions*
Cong clears added funds 5-19, 411E3; signed 6-1, 982F1
US relief aid authorized 6-30, 532G3
Ford signs aid funds 6-30, 533D2
EC aid set 7-8, 529A3
US GOP platform text 8-18, 603E1, 610F3
Australia rpts fly, locust plagues 12-30, 997D3
DISCIPLES of Christ—*See CHRISTIAN Church*
DISCRIMINATION—*See MINORITIES; specific groups (e.g., BLACK Americans, INDIANS); also REVERSE Discrimination*

DISASTERS—*See also ACCIDENTS, DROUGHT, EARTHQUAKES, FAMINES, STORMS & Floods*
Small business loans broadened 8-4, 689D3
US funds signed 10-4, 796F3
DISCIPLES of Christ—*See CHRISTIAN Church*
DISCRIMINATION—*See MINORITIES, RELIGION; specific groups (e.g., BLACK Americans, INDIANS); also REVERSE Discrimination*

DISASTER Assistance Administration, Federal—*See U.S. GOVERNMENT—HOUSING & Urban Development—Federal Disaster Assistance Administration*
DISASTERS—*See also ACCIDENTS, DROUGHT, EARTHQUAKES, STORMS & Floods*
US added funds signed 4-4, 261C3
Carter proposes emergency agency 6-19, 466D2-B3
LNG safety measures urged 7-31, 610A1
Budget cleared after Cong dispute 9-23, 734A1
'79 funds signed 9-30, 750F2-A3
DISCIPLES of Christ—*See CHRISTIAN Church*
DISCOTHEQUES—*See RESTAURANTS & Nightclubs*
DISCRIMINATION—*See MINORITIES; specific groups (e.g., WOMEN)*

DISASTERS—*See also ACCIDENTS, DROUGHT, EARTHQUAKES, STORMS & Floods, VOLCANIC Eruptions*
US Cong OKs victims funds bill 7-17, 7-20, Carter signs 7-25, 700A2
DISCIPLES of Christ—*See CHRISTIAN Church*
DISCOTHEQUES—*See RESTAURANTS & Nightclubs*
DISCRIMINATION—*See MINORITIES; specific groups (e.g., WOMEN)*

DISASTERS—*See also specific kinds (e.g., STORMS)*
State of State messages 1-15, 2-12, 484A2, A3
DISCRIMINATION—*See MINORITIES*

1976

DISGUSTING, Dirty and Mean (film)
Dir wins Cannes award 5-28, 460F1
DISEASE Control, Center for—*See under U.S. GOVERNMENT—PUBLIC Health Service*
DISEASES—*See under MEDICINE & Health*
DISNEY World (Orlando, Fla.)
Lockheed Venez bribe rptd 2-7, 147E3
DISTRICT of Columbia—*See WASHINGTON, D.C.*
DITIATIN, Alexander
Wins Olympic medal 7-23, 574C3
DIVERSIFIED Industries Inc.
SEC lists paymts 5-12, 727C1
DIVING—*See SWIMMING & Diving*
DIVORCES
'75 Australia law in effect 1-5, 7D3
French attys protest law 1-21—1-24, 120D2
Hinshaw divorce rptd 1-26, 95G3
Australia petitns rptd filed 1-29, 97G2
Firestone libel suit ruling 3-2, 169E2
W Ger bill OKd 4-8, 4-9, 270G1
Linked to cigaret smoking 6-15, 875D3
Rev Franzoni defrocked 8-4, 951B2
GOP platform text 8-18, 604B3
Cong OKs alimony tax revisns 9-16, 705F3
US Cath conf seeks reform 10-21—10-23, 859D1
Tenn bishop grants gen absolutn 12-5, 12-12, 951E1-B2
Sup Ct bars Soc Security paymts to divorced mothers 12-13, 940C3
DIXON, George H.
Treas dep secy 2-9; confrmd 3-2, 196G1
DIXON, James P.
Replaced 4-12, 504G2
DIXON, Paul Rand
Named acting FTC chrmn 1-6, 68C1
DIXON (Ill.) Telegraph (newspaper)
Anderson endorsement rptd 10-30, 827E3
DJIBOUTI—*See AFARS & Issas*
DLIMI, Col. Maj. Ahmed
Rpts Amgala casualties 2-1, 107B3
Promoted 4-26, 342B1
DNA (deoxyribonucleic acid)—*See GENETICS*

1977

DISEASE Control, Center for—*See under U.S. GOVERNMENT—PUBLIC Health Service*
DISEASES—*See under MEDICINE & Health*
DISNEY, Walt
Stokowski dies 9-13, 788G2
DISTRICT of Columbia—*See WASHINGTON, D.C.*
DITTER Jr., Judge J. William
Clears 2 in Penn rail scheme 3-11, 491E3
DIVESTITURE—*See ANTITRUST*
DIVIDENDS—*See STOCKS, INCOMES*
DIVINE Comedies (book)
Wins Pulitzer Prize 4-18, 355D2
DIVORCES & Separations
Trudeau separatn rpts 4-8, 4-11, 281C3; confrmd 5-27, 426F1
Baptist coll prof chrgs bias 5-2, 472C1
US RC excommunicatn rule dropped 5-4, 375B1
Brazil legalizes divorce 6-23, 524F3
Soc Sec revisns OKd by House 10-27, 814D3
RC excommunicatn for remarried ends in US 11-10, 906D3
New Brazil law cleared 12-4, 964D3
Soc Sec revisn clears Cong 12-15, 958B2; signed 12-20, 1001C2
DIXON, Paul Rand
Slurs Nader 1-17, 2-2, 95G3
DIZDAR, Vladimir
Invades UN missn 6-14, held 6-16, 497D2
DJANDOUBI, Hamida
Guillotined for murder 9-10, 728B2
DJIBOUTI, Republic of (formerly Afars & Issas)—*See also ARAB League, OAU*
French-Somali pact rptd agreed 1-7, 88C1
Police, leftist students clash 1-30, 88B1
Afro-Arab summit backs blacks 3-7—3-9, 170G1
Castro urges S Yemen-Somalia-Ethiopia alliance 3-10—3-16, 249C2
Independence set, French defns pledged 3-19, 221E2
Pol factns set Assemb slate 3-28—4-2, 363A3
Ethiopia-Somalia strife rptd 4-16, 328C1
At French-African summit 4-20—4-21, 316F3
Independnc voted, Assemb slate OKd; UN, OAU, Arab League observe 5-8, 363A2-B3
Map 363C2
FLCS '75, '76 terrorism cited 5-8, 380A2
Somalia rejcts alliance 5-18, 428E2
Ethiopia rail line cut 6-1—6-21, Somalia chrgd 6-16, 486D1
OAU member 6-27, 512F2
Dini named premr 7-12, picks Cabt 7-15, 583B2
Ethiopia fighting threatens RR 7-14—7-17, 562C2
Colonial history cited 587F3
Ogaden cited re econ troubles 8-8, 608F1
Ethiopia food cutoff rptd 8-23, 684F3
Joins Arab League 9-4, 685E1
US-Somalia deal rptd 9-19, 715F3
UN entry OKd 9-20, 713A1
Cafe bomb kills 2 12-15, 1019A1
Dini, 4 Cabt members resign; tribal tensn cited 12-17, 1018G3
DJILAS, Milovan
Issues human rights plea 2-8, 139A3
Backs Carter rights stand 3-13, 226G1
Cousin jailed 5-6, 437E1
DJILAS, Vitomir
Jailed 5-6, 437E1
DJURANOVIC, Veselin
Named Yugo premier 3-15, 223G3
DNA (deoxyribonucleic acid)—*See GENETICS*

1978

DISEASE Control, Center for—*See under U.S. GOVERNMENT—PUBLIC Health Service*
DISEASES—*See under MEDICINE & Health*
DISENGAGEMENT Observer Force, UN—*See MIDDLE EAST—UN—UNDOF*
DISINI, Herminio T.
Westinghouse paymt rptd 1-13; probe, Herdis group sale ordrd 1-16, 38D2
US probes Westinghouse payoff 2-8, 134E3
DISNEY Productions Inc., Walt
House votes parks bill 7-12, 526E3
US parks bill cleared 10-13, 834A3
DISSIDENTS, Political—*See HUMAN Rights; country names*
DISTANT Mirror, A: The Calamitous Fourteenth Century (book)
On best-seller list 10-9, 800C3; 11-6, 887G3; 12-3, 971B1
DISTRICT of Columbia—*See WASHINGTON, D.C.*
DITCHBURN, Anne
Slow Dancing released 11-8, 970B3
DITERLIZZI, Michael
Pleads guilty to conspiracy 8-28, 725E1
DIVERSIONS and Delights (play)
Opens 4-12, 887F1
DIVESTITURE—*See ANTITRUST*
DIVIDENDS—*See STOCKS*
DIVINE (female impersonator)
Neon Woman opens 4-16, 760G2
DIVINE Light Mission
Argentina arrests 87 2-15, 208C1, D1
DIVORCE & Separation
Wallace suit settled 1-4, 96A1
Carter pol aide rptd separated 1-9, 96B1
Mandel ordrd to pay back alimony 2-15, 172B3
New CPIs described 222F2
Catholic views polled 3-2, 295A1
1st female Episc priest files 4-4, 420B3
Haley files vs Minnelli 4-19, 420C3
Mormon women vs ERA 5-5, 907E2
Calif jurisdictn in child-support case denied by Sup Ct 5-15, 387F3
Iowa press info order review refused by Sup Ct 5-15, 388B1
Bianca Jagger files 5-15, 420C3
Guaranteed income study rptd 5-19, 720E3
Princess Margaret, Lord Snowdon divorced 5-24, 420D3
Brooke admits false depositn disclosure 5-26, 406B1
Ehrlichman separatn rptd 6-1, 420E3
New Pope elected, views cited 8-26, 658B1
Quebec Premr Levesque divorced 9-8, 844G3
Bellow alimony, child-support ordrd 9-10, 844F3
Brooke loses reelectn 11-7, 845E1, D2, 846E1, 847G2
DIXON, Edward F.
Flood influence-selling probe rptd 2-19, 240F1
DIXON, Harvey Douglas
Arrested 5-4, 396B3
DIXON, John P.
Flood influence-selling probe rptd 2-19, 240F1
DIXON, Joseph
Scores CORE conv, Innis 9-18, 810C1
DIXON, Julian C.
Wins US House seat 11-7, 850A2, 856E3
DIXON, William Andrew
Arrested 5-3, 396A3
DJIBOUTI, Republic of (formerly Afars & Issas)—*See also ARAB League, NON-ALIGNED Nations Movement, OAU*
Freedom House lists as free 44E1
New Cabt named 2-5, 115F2
Cyprus jet hijackers refuel 2-19, 117B2, 118E1
Ethiopia demands Somalia renounce all land claims 3-10, 178B3
Ethiopia RR rptd open 3-12, 178C3
7 freed in '77 grenade attack 4-5, 292A2
French mil aid rptd 5-24, 382C3
Locust spraying begun 6-6, 465F2
UN Assemb member 713E3
Cabt dismissed, new premr named 9-21, 840E3
DLCOEA—*See DESERT Locust Control Organization of East Africa*
DNA (deoxyribonucleic acid)—*See GENETICS*

1979

DISEASE Control, Center for—*See under U.S. GOVERNMENT–PUBLIC Health Service*
DISEASES—*See under MEDICINE*
DISENGAGEMENT Observer Force, United Nations (UNDOF)—*See under MIDDLE EAST–U.N.*
DISHY, Bob
Murder at Howard Johnson's opens 5-17, 712F1
DISPATCHES (play)
Opens 4-18, 711D2
DISTANT Mirror, A: the Calamitous Fourteenth Century (book)
On best-seller list 1-7, 80B3; 2-4, 120C3; 3-4, 173E3
DISTRIBUTIVE Workers of America, National Council of
Boston U strike ends 4-22, 326G3
DISTRICT of Columbia—*See WASHINGTON, D.C.*
DITIATIN, Alexandr
Wins world gym title 10-5–10-9, 1005C2
DITTER Jr., Judge J. William
Dismisses Phila police brutality suit 10-30, 831C3
DIVINE Nymph (film)
Released 10-12, 1007B3
DIVORCE & Separation
Rideout, spouse reconciled 1-6, 79D1
Califanos separate 1-19, 79A2
Luci Johnson Nugent files 1-19, 79B2
Sup Ct excludes rail pensn in Calif divorce case 1-22, 53G3
Hearst legal separatn rptd 1-25, 79G1
Eisenhower '45 rumor debunked 1-28, 79E1
Farrow divorces Previn 1-31, 79B2
Tito '78 divorce rptd 2-4, 176C1
Greece issues eased law 2-19, 135F3
Dead Sea Scroll barred 3-2, 217C3
Single-sex alimony barred by Sup Ct 3-5, 184C2
Willy Brandt files 3-8, 271F3
Pope presents 1st encyclical 3-15, 216G3
Sen Kassebaum divorced 3-17, 271F3
Alimony rule in NYS child custody case backed by Sup Ct 3-19, 203F2
Brooke cleared of wrongdoing 3-20, 208F2
Davis case judge withdraws, declares mistrial 3-25, 271G3; $3.3 mln setlmt ordrd 4-20, 392D3
Blumenthal separatn rptd 4-14, 392F3
Rideout divorced 4-20, 392E3
Davis divorce rptd final 5-25, 527C3
Steiger pre-nuptual agrmt upheld 7-5, 527D3
Canada Indian women protest bias 7-20, 601F2
ABA backs armed forces pensn law chngs 8-15, 769A1
Luci Johnson Nugent divorced 8-31, 859B3
Pope in US, affirms oppositn 10-3–10-5, 758B3, 759B2, D2
Jagger divorce final 11-2, 1006C2
Spain rally denounces 11-18, 952B2
DJAM, Gen. Feridun
Rejects Iran war min post 1-6, 11G2
DJAVADI, Ahmad Sadr Haj Sayed
Named Iran interior min 2-13, 105G2
DJIBOUTI, Republic of (formerly Afars & Issas)—*See also ARAB League, NONALIGNED Nations Movement, OAU*
3 US warships arrive 3-6, 157F2
UN membership listed 695G2
DJILAS, Milovan
Warned vs dissent 4-8–4-9, 334F1
Fined re unoffcl writings 10-15, 838D2
DNA (deoxyribonucleic acid)—*See GENETICS*

1980

DISEASE Control, Center for—*See under U.S. GOVERNMENT--PUBLIC Health Service*
DISEASES—*See MEDICINE--Diseases*
DISNEY, Walter Elias (1901-66)
Watcher in the Woods released 4-16, 416G3
DISTANT Mirror: The Calamitous 14th Century, A (book)
Wins Amer Book Award 5-1, 692E2
DISTILLERY, Wine and Allied Workers International Union (DWAW) (AFL-CIO)
Calif 17-day strike ends 9-22, 747A3*
DISTRICT of Columbia—*See WASHINGTON, D.C.*
DISTRICT of Columbia v. Bishop
Case declined by Sup Ct 5-27, 454A1
DITYATIN, Alexandr
Wins 8 Olympic medals 7-24, 7-25, 588D3, 622E3, F3
DIVINE Madness (film)
Released 9-25, 836E2
Top-grossing film 10-1, 796G3
DIVING—*See SWIMMING & Diving*
DIVISION Street (play)
Opens 10-8, 892B3
DIVORCE & Separation
Calif pension case declined by Sup Ct 1-14, 37B1
Ford setlmt rptd 2-20, 200F2
W Ger ct upholds law 2-28, 197F2
C Carter divorce final 2-29, 199G1
Canada woman awarded 1/2 ex-spouse's stock 3-26, 273A2
DC Christian rally held 4-29, 348E3
Summary alimony case dismissed by Sup Ct 5-12, 426C3
Bryant files 5-22, 471D3
Pope affirms traditionalism 6-1, 476F3
Sovt '71-76 infant mortality rise rptd 6-25, 525F2
Reasoner files 6-30, 639A1
Evangelical Christian pol actn profiled 7-11—9-15, 818E3
US, Canada rates compared 7-16, 562C3
Teinowitz $6.8 mln setlmt rptd 8-15, 639D1
Bryant divorce rptd 8-21, 639C1
Jerry Lewis sued 9-5, 908F1
China eases requiremts 9-10, 677C2
RC bishops family life conf opens, Pope affirms oppositn 9-26, 810D2, C3
Princess Caroline divorced 10-9, 890D3
Unwed couples child custody case refused by Sup Ct 10-20, 807A1
Mil pensns case accepted by Sup Ct 10-20, 807A3
DIX, Horace William
Death penalty appeal declined by Sup Ct 3-24, 265C2
DIXON, Alan J.
Wins Ill US Sen primary 3-18, 206C3
Elected to US Sen 11-4, 840F1, 845B2, 850B3
DIXON, Rep. Julian C. (D, Calif.)
Reelected 11-4, 842A2
DIXON Jr., Robert G.
Dies 5-5, 448E1
DIX v. Georgia
Case declined by Sup Ct 3-24, 265C2
DJIBOUTI, Republic of (formerly Afars & Issas)—*See also ARAB League, NONALIGNED Nations, OAU*
Olympic boycott OK rptd 2-2, 85C1
Ethiopia, Kenya urge Somali end land claims 12-4, 933E1
DNA (deoxyribonucleic acid)—*See GENETICS*

1976

DOBRIANSKY, Lev
Scores Ford E Eur remark 10-8, 762D3
DOCTOROW, E. L.
Ragtime on best seller list 1-25, 80B3; 2-29, 208E3; 12-5, 972F2
DOCTORS—*See 'Physicians' under MEDICINE*
DODBIBA, Piro
Purge rptd 4-30, 331E3
DODD, Rep. Christopher J. (D, Conn.)
Reelected 11-2, 829G1
DOG Day Afternooon (film)
Dec '75 top-grossing film 32G3
Top-grossing film 1-28, 104E3; 2-25, 208G3
Pierson wins Oscar 3-29, 240A3
DOHERTY, Liam
'IRA' carved on leg 9-28, 855A1
DOHERTY, Margaret
Son mutilated 9-28, 855A1
DOLANC, Stane
Addresses Sovt CP Cong 2-27, 196D1
DOLE, Mary Elizabeth Hanford (Mrs. Robert J.)
Dole biog sketch 614B2
With husband in NC 9-1, 646A1
Home town honors 9-2, 666C1
To take leave of absence from FTC 9-4, 666C1
DOLE, Sen. Robert J. (R, Kan.)
Addresses Mo conv for Ford 6-12, 432D2
In Iowa for Ford 6-18, 451D1
Rptd Ford vp prospect 8-10, 584C1
Addresses GOP conv as chrmn 8-16, 615B1
Wins GOP vp nominatn, accepts 8-19, 598B2-599F1, C2; speech text 612E1
GOP conv vp vote table 8-19, 599A3
Ford acceptnc speech cites 8-19, 611F1
Biog sketch 614G1, D2 ★, C3 ★
Nixon rptdly favors Connally for vp 8-19, 616C1
Dow falls 8-19—8-20, 846E3
Photo with Ford 597A1 ★
Visits hometown with Ford 8-20, 631B2
Willing to debate 8-20, 632F3
On Face the Nation 8-22, 631C2
Fed funds OKd 8-24, 688A3
Scores Carter on amnesty, grain embargoes 8-25, 8-26, 632B2
Ford denies 'hatchet' role 8-27, 645A1, D1
In Md, Del, Ga, NC 8-30—9-1, 645F3-646A1
TV debate with Mondale set 9-1, 644B1
In South, Midwest, NE 9-2—9-9, 665C3-666C1
Denies fund irregularities 9-6, 9-8, 665D3
In Tex, Ky, Utah, Calif, NY 9-10—9-16, 686F3-687C1
In farm belt 9-17—9-28, 724B3
Hits Carter tax remark 9-18—9-19, 703C3
Scores Ford fund probe 9-27, 723F2
Attacks Carter on forgn policy, church taxatn 10-1—10-5, 743E1-E2
Scores Butz 10-2, 744A2
Mondale scores on Watergate 10-5, 743C3
Scores Carter, admits GOP slump 10-6, 10-8, 763E3-764A1
On Ford's E Eur remark 10-7, 10-8, 762E3, 763G3
Debates Mondale 10-15, 782E1-784E1
Mondale chrgs misleads 10-16, 803B3
Stumps across US 10-16—10-27, 804C1
Ford, Carter debate 10-22, 801B2
Mondale vs wars statement 10-26, 804B1
Mondale on Watergate 10-29, 827C2
Final campaign swing 10-29—11-1, 827F2
Carter, Mondale elected 11-2, 817G1
Caddell: vp choice hurt Ford 11-11, 845E2
Warns GOP vs narrow appeal 11-30, 917A3
Electoral Coll votes 12-13; final tally rptd 12-18, 979B1, C1
DOLGIKH, Vladimir
CP Secretariat member 3-5, 195F2
DOLLINGER, Rudolf
Wins Olympic medal 7-18, 575A2
DOLORES (book)
On best-seller list 12-5, 972E2
DOLPHIN International Inc.
Copter crash kills workers 4-23, 736A3
DOLSEN Sr., Harry O.
Sentenced 2-4, 135F3
DOMBECK, Carola
Wins Olympic medal 7-22, 574E3
DOMENICI, Sen. Peter V. (R, N.M.)
Rptd Ford vp prospect 8-10, 584C1
GOP conv vp vote table 8-19, 599F3
DOMESTIC Workers
Jobless benefits revisn signed 10-20, 788D1
DOMINGUEZ, Antonio
Arrested 1-15, exiled 1-20, 121A3
DOMINGUES, Gen. Oswaldo Ignacio
Denies Death Squad exists 7-9, 836A2
DOMINICA—*See CARIBCOM*
DOMINICAN Republic—*See also IDB, OAS, SELA*
'74 defns budget, mil force rptd 1-2, 60G2
Russell ct scores rights abuse 1-17, 61D2
Listed as 'partly free' 1-19, 20C3
Chile emb refugees to get safe-conducts 1-25, 100C1
Rojas named cardinal 4-27, 336A2
Spain king, queen visit 5-31—6-1, 459B2
Haiti assassins stop over 8-27, 1005E3
Cuba exile coalitn rptd 10-19, 779E3
Illegal Haitians expelled 10-24, 1001B3
Oppositn groups coalesce 11-12, 1001A3
Govt to buy more Rosario equity 12-15, 1001E2

1977

DOBBERT Jr., Ernest John
Fla death sentnc upheld 6-17, 518G1
DOBBERT v. Florida
Death sentence upheld 6-17, 518F1
DOBBS, Wilburn W.
Sup Ct delays executn 2-25, 174B3
DOBRONSKY, Gen. Fernando
Rejects labor amnesty 9-21, 823G3
DOBRYNIN, Anatoly Fedorovich
Scores US Sakharov statemt 1-27, sees Carter 2-1, 84B1, D1
Vance sees on Krimsky ouster, dissidents 2-4, 101G1, B2
Sees Hartman, scores US rights stand 2-17, 137D2
Carter defends arms proposals 4-2, 246C3
Sees US reps on SALT 4-7—4-15, 400B3
US doubts PLO eases stand on Israel 5-9—5-11, 360F2
Bennett visa bid denied 6-1, 436F2
Us protests Toth detentn 6-14, 475F1
Sees Vance re Shcharansky 10-31, 955A2
Sees Carter, delivers Brezhnev note 11-18, 894E3
DOBSON, Richard
Talks to business group 9-27; bias chrgd 10-20; resigns 10-21, 863G3
DOCTOROW, E. L.
Nation magazine sold 12-22, 1004G3
DOCTORS—*See 'Physicians' under MEDICINE*
DODD, Rep. Christopher J. (D, Conn.)
On proposed King hearing 3-3, 149E1
Clinch R A-breeder compromise rejected 9-20, 758D3
DODDS, Rev. Gilbert L. (Gil)
Dies 2-3, 164F2
DOKES, Phil
In NFL draft 5-3, 353B2
DOLE, Sen. Robert J. (R, Kan.)
Cong declares Carter winner 1-6, 14G2
Spec interest gifts rptd 3-7, 232G2
Scores Admin farm plan 3-23, 214D1
Scores US-Cuba thaw 6-3, 455F3
Sen OKs Indochina aid amendmt 6-14, 477C3
Sen rejcts Cuba amendmt 6-16, 477G3
Vs US-Sovt Geneva plan 10-2, 750E1
Releases pvt US cable on Panama Canal treaty interpretatns 10-4; scored 10-5, 754F3
Canal cable release probe asked 10-5; chrgs State Dept harassmt 10-6, 792B1
Cites Torrijos drug trade rpts 10-13, 792C1
On Carter-Torrijos Canal pact statemt 10-15, 792A1
To get Torrijos kin drug files 11-16, 912C2
DOLORES (book)
On best-seller list 6-4, 452B2; 7-3, 548F3
DOME Petroleum Ltd.
Canada operatn cited 6-4, 466D3
DOMESTIC Council—*See under U.S. GOVERNMENT*
DOMESTIC Surveillance—*See PRIVACY Issue*
DOMINGUES, Antonio
Sentncd 1-5, leniency scored 1-6, 21D2
DOMINICA (British colony)
Independnc talks rptd ended 6-5, 567B1
OAS fails to act on entry 6-21, 494B3
John asks govt workers end strike 10-11, independnc delay seen 10-14, 949C2
DOMINICAN Republic—*See also IDB, OAS*
UN Assemb member 3G3
'75-76 trade, paymts data; table 3-11, 189B1, A2 ★, B2
'66-75 arms transfers table 4-8, 415A2
Water rationing rptd 4-12, 312F2
'61-75 GDP variatns table 5-30, 439A1
Young visits; sees oppositn, Balaguer, gets rights conv vow 8-13—8-14, 646E1, 647E1
Balaguer frees leftist rebels 9-2, 710D2
Balaguer at Panama Canal pact signing 9-7, 678C1
Lajara sets pres bid, vows forgn cos natlzatn, cites Gulf + Westn 9-11, 767E1
Gulf + Westn appeals sugar paymt order 9-16, 767F1

1978

DNEPROVSKY, Gell A.
Promoted by UN despite US, UK spy chrgs 8-29, 676E1
DOAR, John
Perkins pleads guilty 9-21, sentncd 10-17, 808E2
DOBLER, Conrad
Traded to Saints 1-31, 172D1
DOBRYNIN, Anatoly Fedorovich
Sees Brzezinski on Sovt satellite fall 1-12, 1-17, 57B1, F2
Sees Vance 3-12; US on USSR troops in Ethiopia 3-15, 215G3
Meets Shevchenko 4-9, 302D2
Crawford arrest scored 6-16, 476E2
US releases spy suspects into custody 6-26, 506E1
Vance sees re US rptrs slander chrg, other issues 7-1, 518E2
Brzezinski reassures re US-China tie 12-15, 976G1
DOBUTAMINE Hydrochloride (Dobutrex)—*See MEDICINE—Drugs*
DOBUTREX (dobutamine hydrochloride)—*See MEDICINE—Drugs*
DOBY, Larry
Named White Sox mgr 6-30, 560E1
Fired as White Sox mgr 10-19, 1026A2
DOCKER, Bernard
Dies 5-23, 440E2
DOCTOROW, E. L.
Drinks Before Dinner opens 11-23, 1031D1
DOCTORS—*See MEDICINE—Physicians*
DR. X Case—*See JASCALEVICH, Dr. Mario*
DODD, Rep. Christopher J. (D, Conn.)
Says Conn sub-base secure 10-5, 824D2
Reelected 11-7, 850D2
DOEG, John Hope
Dies 4-27, 440E2
DOENITZ, Adm. Karl (ret.)
WWII secret documts rptd decoded 9-10—9-18, 744C3, D3
DOGAN, Lutfu
Named Turkey state min 1-5, 21D2
DOGOLOFF, Lee I.
Rpts armed forces drug abuse up, backs random tests 4-27, 368B2
DOGS of War (book)
Episode rptd staged 4-16, 335A3
DOG Soldiers (book)
Who'll Stop Rain released 8-25, 1030G3
DOLAN, Anthony R.
Wins Pulitzer Prize 4-17, 315A2
DOLANC, Stane
Yugo CP secy gen 6-23, 519C3
DOLE, Sen. Robert J. (R, Kan.)
Raises Torrijos drug link 2-10; Sen debates 2-21—2-22, Canal votes rptd unchngd 2-22, 120B2, D3
Votes vs Panama Canal neutrality pact 3-16, 177G2
Sen votes farm aid 3-21, 218C3
House defeats farm bill 4-12, 261D1, F2
Votes vs 2d Canal pact 4-18, 273B1
Sen OKs oil import fee bar 6-27, 511B3
Pro-defns cong coalitn formed 8-8, 604A3
Vs new China policy 12-20, 976A1
DOLLAR—*See MONETARY Developments, International; country names*
DO Lord Remember Me (play)
Opens 4-4, 887F1
DOMECQ, Pedro
Daughter kidnaped 10-30, rescued 11-12, 926C3
DOMENICI, Sen. Peter V. (R, N.M.)
Votes vs Panama Canal neutrality pact 3-16, 177G2
Votes vs 2d Canal pact 4-18, 273B1
Unopposed in primary 6-6, 448C2
Reelected 11-7, 848E2, 855C2
DOMESTIC Surveillance—*See PRIVACY Issue; also U.S. GOVERNMENT—FEDERAL Bureau of Investigation*
DOMESTIC Workers
Black female job exit cited 5-8, 810D3
DOMINICA (British colony)—*See CARIBBEAN Community*
UK sets independence date 7-21, 573F3
Independence effected, USSR recognizes 11-2; facts on 861G2
DeGazon elected pres 12-21, 1021F2
DOMINICAN Republic—*See also GATT, IDB, OAS*
Amnesty bill vetoed 9-3 enacted 9-8; 33 freed 9-11, 774E1-A2
Labor ldr arrested 9-3, 774A2
Univ budget hiked, Guzman at graduatn 10-29, 881F1
Foreign Relations (misc.)—*See also 'Monetary, Trade, Aid & Investment' below*
Carib 'social catastrophe' warned by Balaguer 1-22, 100D3
PRD ldr sees Cuba ties 5-20; Guzman rebuffs, sees closer Latin ties 5-21, 414F2
Latin ldrs consulted on DR electn 5-21, 414C2
Amer rights conv enacted, ct formed 7-18, 828E3, 829C1

1979

DOBELL, Sir William
Paintings rptd stolen 1-3, 18F2
DOBELLE, Evan
Cited as Carter campaign com head 4-25, 300B1
Carter early primary losses feared 8-2, 593A1
Carter campaign com treasurer 8-10, 608F2
Backs Jordan cocaine denial 8-25, 647A2
Strauss named Carter campaign com head 11-6, 961B2
DOBRYNIN, Anatoly Fedorovich
Vance assures on China-US talks 2-1, 65D2
Gets US protest on Kabul shootout 2-14, 106F2
Regrets Dubs death 2-16, 147E2
Dissident-spy swap talks rptd 4-27, 317D1
Vance mtgs cited re SALT 5-9, 339C1
Cited in SALT II summit communique 6-18, 457D1
Vance sees re Sovt troops in Cuba 9-10, 9-12, 673D1
Vance mtgs on Cuba issue continue 9-14—9-30, 738A2
Toon scores US reliance 10-16, 794F3-795A1
US protests statemt on Iran 12-5, 913G2
US warns vs UN veto on Iran sanctns 12-22, 974B3
DOCTORS—*See MEDICINE—Physicians*
DODD, Thomas J. (1907-71)
'67 censure cited 10-10, 769C1
DOLAN, John (Terry)
PAC Sen campaign announced 8-16, 627G3-628A1
DOLANC, Stane
Demoted 5-16, 430A3
DOLE, Sen. Robert J. (R, Kan.)
Scores Carter forgn policy 2-16, 124E1
Talks to Midwest GOPs, offcls rate 3-10, 185G3, 186D1
Asks Carter peanut loan probe 3-13, 184B2
Backs new powers for Carter probe spec counsel 3-23, 301B3
Scores SALT treaty 4-5, 258F1
Enters pres race 5-14, 363B3
Pres campaign fund rptd 7-12, 594A1
On Carter statemt re Sovt Cuba troops 10-1, 737F2
Scores Connally Mideast peace plan 10-12, 783E2
Staff resignatns rptd 12-6, 983C2
Scores Carter re Iran 12-26, 983B2
DOLKART, Joel
Gulf+Western fraud probe aid rptd 11-26, 923B2
DOLLAR—*See MONETARY Developments, International; country names*
DOLLARD, James F.
Rpts rise in wood use for fuel 20, 6G2
DOLLEZHAL, Nikolai A.
A-safety article rptd publshd 10-14, 815C2
DOMENICI, Sen. Peter V. (R, N.M.)
Scores SALT treaty 4-5, 258G1
DOMESTIC Workers
Illegal alien issue detailed 1-29, 127E1
DOMINICA—*See also CARIBBEAN Community, COMMONWEALTH of Nations, OAS*
Freedom House lists as free 12F3
OAS admits as member 1-19, 101F1
Riot leaves 3 dead 5-29; gen strike called, govt resignatn asked 5-30, 424G2-A3
Parlt dissolved, new electns asked 6-15; Cabt quits amid unrest 6-16—6-18, 468D2
Seraphine replaces John; vows govt probe, Grenada ties 6-29, 502C3
Hurricane David wrecks havov 8-30, US relief hampered 9-3, 690B3, E3
151st UN member 9-18, 695A2, G2
US sets Carib policy 11-29, 960E3
DOMINICAN Republic—*See also GATT, IDB, OAS*
Treasure ship rptd found 1-1, 24F1
Guzman stresses agri dvpt 3-2, 256D3
Gas price protests spur violence 8-1, 575G3
Hurricane David wreaks havoc; 600 die, 150,000 left homeless 8-31, 690C3
Foreign Relations (misc.)—*See also 'Monetary' below*
Balaguer backers get forgn mil posts 1-12, 62D2
Nicaragua plebiscite plan rejctd by Somoza 1-19, 76D2
Pope visits 1-25—1-26, 67A3
Mex-CR missn on Nicaragua dispatched 5-21, 409B1
Spain premr visits 8-14, 654G2

1980

DOBROFSKY, Neal
Bronco Billy released 6-11, 675A2
DOBRYNIN, Anatoly Fedorovich
Aeroflot flight data tampering probed 1-31, 115E1
Vance sees re Afghan 2-29, 165E1
US asks Viet Thai raid halt 6-26, 508C2
'77 Kissinger SALT mtg cable rptd 7-14, 754C1
Sovt soldier seeks asylum in US Emb in Kabul 9-15, 704G2
Sees US offcl, gets A-test protest 9-15, 730B2
DOBY, Larry
Wills hired as Mariners mgr 8-4, 926A2
DOCHTERMANN, Rudy
Fiendish Plot of Dr Fu Manchu released 8-8, 675E2
DOCTORS—*See MEDICINE—Physicians*
DOCUMENTS on Australian Defense and Foreign Policy, 1968-75 (book)
Australia blocks publicatn 11-9, 885D1
Ban upheld by High Ct 12-1, 919E2
Newspapers publish articles 12-2, 991G2
DODD, Rep. Christopher J. (D, Conn.)
Wins US Sen nomination 9-9, 700C2
Elected to US Sen 11-4, 840D1, 845B2, 848B1, D1
DODDS, Harold Willis
Dies 10-25, 876C1
DOE, M. Sgt. Samuel Kanyon (Liberian head of state)
Ousts Tolbert 4-12, names Cabt 4-13, 284A3
Barred from CEAO mtg 5-28, 469G1-A3
DOENITZ, Karl
Dies 12-24, 1004D1
DOE v. Delaware
Case accepted by Sup Ct 3-24, 265A2
Case cited by Sup Ct 10-6, 782B3
DOE v. Irwin
Case declined by Sup Ct 10-6, 782G2
DOHERTY, Lawrie (deceased)
Borg wins 5th Wimbledon title 7-6, 606A2
DOHRN, Bernadine
Weatherman fugitive surrenders 7-8, 576E3
Surrenders 12-3, 928A1
DOLANC, Stane
Urges pvt enterprise 6-5, 468C3
DOLE, Elizabeth Hanford (Mrs. Robert Dole)
Named pres asst 12-20, 980C2
DOLE, Sen. Robert J. (R, Kan.)
Urges embargo vs Iran 1-3, 5F1
In Ia GOP debate, scores Reagan absence 1-5, 4F2, G3
Ia poll results 1-11, 33F1, G1
Last in Ia caucus vote 1-21, 50F1
Asks Miller-Textron spec prosecutor 2-11, 145A2
Quits PR primary 2-13, Bush wins 2-17, 130B1, E1
NH gun control forum 2-18, GOP pres debate 2-20, 129B3, G3
NH debate exclusn spurs controversy 2-23, 143D1
NH primary vote results 2-26, 142E3, G3
Mass primary results 3-4, 166F2, E3
Scores Miller-Textron spec prosecutor rejectn 3-11, 185G2
Loses matching funds 3-13, 209D1
Quits pres race 3-15, 208C1
Reagan wins Kan primary, endorsemt cited 4-1, 246B2
Backs Reagan tax cut 6-25, 480B2
Nominates Bush for vp 7-17, 529E2
Wins Kan US Sen primary 8-5, 682E3
Scores Civiletti re B Carter probe 8-7, 595C2
Reelected 11-4, 840F1, 845B3, 851B1
Wife named pres asst 12-20, 980C2
DOLGOV, Vladimir
Wins Olympic medal 7-21, 623E2
DOLGOWICZ, Jan
Wins Olympic medal 7-24, 624B3
DOLLAKU, Kristap
Replaced as industry min 5-2, 356F2
DOLLAR—*See MONETARY Developments, International*
DOLLOUS, Louis
On arrest of Tolbert's son 6-14, 499D1
DOLPH, Robert N.
Saudi completes Aramco takeover, retains bd seat 9-4, 662A2
DOMBROWSKI, Lutz
Wins Olympic medal, sets long jump mark 7-28, 589B1, 624B1
DOMINICA—*See also COMMONWEALTH of Nations, OAS*
Freedom Party wins electn, woman prime min named 7-21, 635G3
DOMINICAN Republic—*See also GATT, IDB, OAS*
Economy & Labor
Fuel prices hiked, other austerity measures decreed 5-28; taxi drivers strike, violence erupts 5-29—6-3; PRD rift rptd 5-31, 462F1
Foreign Relations (misc.)—*See also 'UN Policy' below*
Colombia Emb seized; amb, other forgn diplomats held 2-27, 140F3
Colombia, emb captors talk 3-2—3-13, 180B2
Uruguay amb escapes Colombia Emb, Venez amb suffers 2d heart attack 3-17, 211G2-B3
Colombia rejcts emb captors demands, urges more talks 3-18, 211C3

1976

U.S. Relations
Russell ct scores '65 'mil aggressn' 1-17, 61C2
Kissinger visits 6-6—6-7, 465E2
Ship in US Bicentennial event 7-4, 488C3
Dole legis record cited 614C2
Sugar duties tripled 9-21, 721D3
To buy more Rosario equity 12-15, 1001E2
Philip Morris payoffs rptd; Balaguer denies 12-28, 1001B2
DOMINICK, Peter
Carter disavows dumping memo 8-13, 616F3
DOMITIEN, Elizabeth
Out as CAR premier 4-7, 288D2
DONAHEY, Gertrude W.
Pres primary vote 6-8, 409D1
DONAT-Cattin, Carlo
Lists failing firms 1-6, 29D3
Named CIA aid recipient 1-31, 140C3
DONCHEV, Dobri
On China quake casualties 8-1, 562C1
DONEGAN, Patrick
Attacks O Dalaigh 10-18, regrets 10-19, 837D3
DONG, Pham Van
In Laotian talks 2-11, 121F1
Premier of united Vietnam 7-3, 502D3
For US ties 8-17, 621E3
Presents 5-yr plan 12-16, 968A1
In Politburo 12-19, 967F3

1977

Evening rallies banned, oppositn parties score 9-24, 844C3
Wessin sets pres bid 9-30; Balaguer, mil chiefs vs return 10-2, 786E1
Backs Brazil coffee policy 10-21, 876C3
Exxon admits paymts 10-25, 818A2
CP legalized 10-26, 844D3
Hardliner gets key army post 11-4, backs Balaguer reelectn 11-5, 969D3
PRD nominates Guzman for pres 12-2, 969E3
Bauxite base price OKd 12-7, 975E1
DOMINICK, Peter H.
Replaced as amb to Switz 6-7, 500D1
DOMINO Principle, The (film)
Top-grossing film 4-6, 264E1
DONAHUE, Robert W.
Replies to Carter attack 10-13, 773A1
DONALDSON, Lufkin, & Jenrette Inc.
Buys Pershing, Wood Struthers 10-11, 799G3
DONEGAN, Patrick
Sets fishing vessel curbs 2-15, 146B3
DONEGAN, Thomas
Gets Allon protest on Syria 2-6, 106B2
DONG, Pham Van (Vietnamese premier)
Meets US MIA missn 3-17, 206C2
US OKs talks on ties 3-23, 206A1
Visits France 4-25—4-28, 329A1
In Laos 7-15—7-18, 553A1
Admits food shortages 10-1, 998F3
DON King Productions
Boxing scandal rpt issued 9-3, 828C1-D2

1978

Perez y Perez named Spain amb 9-3, 774B2
Nicaragua oppositn weighs mediatn 9-14, 705C3
UN Assemb member 713E3
Nicaragua crisis mediatn OKd 9-30, 757G2; intl team arrives 10-6, 777D2
Nicaragua pol talks suspended 10-21, rptd stalled 10-27, 839D1; impasse continues 11-5, 883E2
Perez y Perez gets UK post 11-9, 881D1; retiremt forced 11-17, 989B3
Nicaragua plebiscite OKd 11-30, terms disputed 12-8—12-22, 1018D2, G2, D3
Government & Politics—*See also other appropriate subheads in this section*
Gen Perez lauds Balaguer, electoral bd bars pol statemts 1-20, 94C2
PRD-PR shootout 1-26, 94D2
CP picks pres candidate 1-27, 94C2
Lora accepts pres nominatn 2-10, 136C3
2 die in campaign violence 2-19, 152C2
Wessin, Fernandez end pres bids, back Lora 3-3, 292D2
Balaguer, PRD ldrs sign 'non-agressn pact' 3-10, 230D3
Guerrilla ldr killed 3-26, 292C2
PRD, Balaguer trade vote fraud chrgs 4-26, 354A3
Balaguer vp nominee replaced 5-5, 354F2
Oppositn coalitn talks fail 5-6, 354A3
PRD harrassmt by PR, police rptd 5-12—5-13; polls rptd divided 5-14, 372F1
Electns held 5-16, army suspends vote count 5-17; Balaguer pledges fair electn, vote count resumes 5-18, 371G2, B3★, C3★-372F1
PRD ldr sees soclist govt 5-20, Guzman rebuffs 5-21, 414F2
PR, PRD trade vote fraud chrgs 5-21, 414E2
Guzman reassures mil ldrs 5-21, 414F2
Vote count halted again 5-23, resumed 5-24, 414D2
PRD wins electns 5-26; Balaguer concedes to Guzman, mil ldrs vow acceptnc 5-27, 414F1
Final electn results 6-2, 456G3-457A1
Guzman electn confrmd; PR wins Sen majority, PRD to appeal 7-8, 558E3
Pres power curbed 7-19, 617A3
PRD appeal rejected 7-20, 617F2
Guzman sworn pres, scores Balaguer govt; Cabt sworn, mil ldrs replaced 8-16, 648C1
Guzman kin get govt posts 8-23, 671F2
Balaguer admin offcls replaced 8-25, 774C2
Army chief fired, named Spain amb 9-3, 774B2
Guzman presses mil ldrship shift 10-2, 10-16, 881B1
Guzman assets: $1 mln 10-9, 774F2
Press freedom rptd by IAPA 10-13, 829A2
Security forces image shift rptd 10-29, 881D1
Sen rejcts Guzman amb apptmts 11-9, 880G3
Army chief gets UK post 11-9, 881D1; retiremt forced 11-17, 989A3
Monetary Trade, Aid & Investment
Carib conf on US ties rptd 1-22, 100D3
Coffee exports to be withheld 3-10, 181B3
'77 trade deficit rptd 3-10, 230F3
US aid, investmts cited 5-19, 414C2
Guzman reassures multinatls 5-21, 414A3
Electn troubles hurt tourism 5-23, 5-25, 414A3
Obituaries
Trujillo, Flor de Oro 2-15, 196G3
U.S. Relations
Carib conf on econs ties rptd 1-22, 100D3
US scores vote count suspensn, cites Carter pledge 5-17; Balaguer shuns amb, reassures Vance 5-18, 371D3-372C1
Carter consults Latin ldrs, warns vs vote fraud 5-19; prompts Guzman victory acceptance 5-27, 414B2
Guzman sees closer ties 5-21, 414F2
Hotel owners score US electn coverage 5-23, tourism rptd down 5-25, 414A3
Rights abuse chrgd by US panel 6-24, 490C1
Guzman sees Gen McAuliffe 8-15; Vance, Young at inaugural 8-16, 648C1, A2
Labor ldr seized at Gulf + Westn 9-3, 774B2

DOMINIGUEZ, Berta
'Crossed Swords' released 3-2, 619C1

DONA Flor and Her Two Husbands (film)
Released 2-26, 619F1

DONAT-Cattin, Carlo
Named Italy indus min 3-11, 191C1
On business rescue bill 8-1, 724A2

DONEN, Stanley
Movie, Movie released 11-22, 970C2

DONG, Pham Van (Vietnamese premier)
Urges Cambodia peace talks 1-5, 42D3
Denies federatn plan 201B3
Closer US ties rptd asked 8-7, 603E2
Meets US reps, drops reparatn demand 8-22, 660G2
In Thailand; econ, refugee agrmts reached 9-6—9-10, 696E1-A3
In USSR 11-2, signs friendship pact 11-3, 859E2
DONKER, Georgina
Disputes Menten immunity claim 12-7, 965D2

1979

Haitian worker 'slavery' rptd 8-17, 804A3
Mil attache to Colombia arrested 9-25, 751G3
Argentina rights abuse cited in OAS electn 10-24, 824D2
UN membership listed 695G2
Government & Politics—*See also other appropriate subheads in this section*
Freedom House lists as free 12F3
Guzman names forgn mil attaches 1-12, 62D2
Guzman state-of-natn speech rptd 3-2, 256D3
Finance min, econ coordinator fired 3-9, 256B3
Army plot foiled 9-25—9-26, 751D3
Monetary, Trade, Aid & Investment
Intl bank loan OKd 3-20, 256B3
US hurricane relief efforts hampered 9-3, 690E3
U.S. Relations
US natl treasure ship find rptd 1-1, 24F1
US issues rights rpt 2-10, 107E3
US aide confers on Nicaragua 7-5, 504B1
Textron pleads guilty to currency violatns 7-10, 923E2
Gulf+Western sugar probe rptd 8-16; land expropriatn urged 8-19, 632D3
US hurricane relief efforts hampered 9-3, 690E3
DOMINION Bridge Co.
AMCA International Corp.
Bendix wins Warner & Swasey bid 12-17, 986F2
DONA Flor and Her Two Husbands (film)
Savara opens 2-11, 292F2
DONAHUE, Thomas
Elected AFL-CIO secy-treas 11-19, 885F1
DONALDSON, Walter
Whoopee opens 2-14, 292F3
DONDENNE, Michel
Seized in El Salvador emb raid 5-4, 370F3, 371B1
Freed 6-1, 424B3
DONG, Pham Van
Singapore scores SE Asia policy 1-13, 28G1
In Pnompenh 2-16—2-20, friendship pact signed 2-18, 123D2
Vs Waldheim mediatn 5-1, 340B2
DONGIER, Maurice
Admits LSD experiments 1-29, 96B1
DON Juan Comes Back from the War (play)
Opens 4-15, 711E2

1980

Castro offers Colombia Emb captors asylum 3-18, 211C3
Colombia Emb talks resume 3-24, 3-26, 3 more hostages freed 3-25, 231D2-G2
Colombia Emb captors free more hostages 3-30, resume talks 4-1, 253D2-F2
Secy held as suspect in Colombia Emb seizure 4-6, 293C3
Colombia Emb captors ask govt mtg, free CR envoy 4-19; govt bars 'dialogue' 4-21, 311F2-D3
Colombian Emb siege ends, hostages freed 4-27, 335D1
Mex, Venez sign oil supply guarantee 8-3, 605D3
22 drown on Panama freighter 9-5, crew detained 9-9, 687C3
Jerusalem emb shift rptd set 9-7, 800E3
Columbia amb slain by aide 11-16, 889C1
Cuba ex-offcl asks UN probe prison hunger strike 12-4, 965D2
Bolivia coup condemned by Santa Marta conf 12-17, 992A3
Government & Politics—*See also other appropriate subheads in this section*
Vice pres demoted 6-6, 462E2
UN Policy & Developments
Assemb res backing Palestine state opposed 7-29, 572F1
Cuba ex-offcl asks prison hunger strike probed 12-4, 965D2
U.S. Relations
Mafia ldr slain 3-21, 237E2
Hispanic immigrants in US surveyed 5-11—5-14, 396G2
US $ purchases barred, central bank dir quits 5-28, 462G1
Gulf & Westn sugar dispute setld 9-5, 687F2
22 stowaways drown on Panama freighter 9-5, smuggling ring uncovered 9-9, 687C3
US aid rptd 11-1, 854E2
DONAHUE (book)
On best-seller list 3-9, 200C3; 4-6, 280C3; 5-4, 359D3
DONAHUE, Edward M.
Loses US House electn 11-4, 848C1
DONAHUE, Phil
Donahue on best-seller list 3-9, 200C3; 4-6, 280C3; 5-4, 359D3
Marries 5-22, 471A2
DONA Rosita (play)
Opens 3-20, 392F2
DONAT-Cattin, Carlo
Son sought as terrorist 5-13, 408D1, E1
Testifies in terrorist tipoff probe 5-29, resigns 5-31, 430B1
Cossiga innocence upheld 7-27, 579A1, D1
DONAT-Cattin, Marco
Sought as terrorist 5-13, 408C1
Parlt com probes tipoff; Cossiga cleared, father resigns 5-29—5-31, 430B1
Cossiga innocence upheld 7-27, 579A1, D2
Arrested in Paris 12-18, 995E1
DONATI, Antigone
Bank fraud chrgs rptd 4-2, 254G3
DONDERO, Robert
On Hell's Angels mistrial 7-2, 568B2
DONELON, James J.
Loses cong runoff in La 5-17, 404E3
DONEN, Stanley
Saturn 3 released 2-15, 216D3

1976

DONNELLY, Tom
Dies 2-10, 192D3
DON'T Step on My Olive Branch (play)
Opens 11-1, 1014F3
DOOLING Jr., Judge John F.
Voids Medicaid abortn funds curb 10-22, Sup Ct bars stay 11-8, 848G1, C3
DOPFNER, Julius Cardinal
Dies 7-24, 716A3
DORIS Day (book)
On best seller list 2-29, 208F3; 12-5, 972B2
DORNAN, Robert K.
Elected 11-2, 829D1
D'ORNANO, Michel
Named industry, resrch min 8-27, 650G3
Gaullists vs as Paris mayor 11-18, 872G3
DORRONSORO, Alvarez
Freed 5-25, 422F2
DORSETT, Tony
Wins Heisman award 11-30, 969D2
DORSEY, Bob R.
McCloy rpt details paymts role 133A2-134C1
Ousted from Gulf post 1-15, 132A3-133A1
Gulf shareholder suits settled 11-18, 939A2, C2
DORSEY, Jasper
'70 Carter campaign donor 10-17, 805C1
DORTICOS, Osvaldo
On Angola troop withdrawal 5-26, 370D3
Loses presidency 12-3, 1000D3
DOS Santos, Johnny Eduardo
MPLA offers S Africa guarantees 2-13, 162C3
Vs US, China re UN Angola vote 12-1, 895C3
DOUBLEDAY & Co. Inc.
US files consent decree 7-27, 989G1
DOUGLAS, Paul H.
Dies 9-24, 970F1
DOUGLAS, Justice William O(rville)
Sen intelligence com cites as target 4-28, 330F1
'72 vote vs death penalty cited 7-2, 491A2
DOUMIT, Michael
Leb planning min 12-9, 913E2
DOURADO, Wolf
Denies torture chrg 10-19, 1013C3
DOURDAH, Abu Zaid Omar
Mediates Syria-PLO feud 8-19, 628C3
DOUWES-Dekker, Loet
Banned 11-16, 927B3
DOW Chemical Co.
$700 mln Yugo oil deal 3-26, 256G1
Product picketing rule vacated 10-4, 807A2
E Ger pact rptd 11-26, 1001G3
DOW Jones & Co.
Index climbs, hits 1,000 1-2—3-11, 184C2-185C1
Index hits high, stalls 3-11—5-28, 413A2
Index closings 6-1—11-10, 846G2
Index ends year up 11-10—12-31, 984B1

1977

DOODY, C. W.
Sets budget 4-28, 372A3
DOOLING Jr., Judge John F.
'76 Hyde Amendmt stay vacated 6-29, 557B3
Lifts '76 Hyde Amendmt stay 8-4, 786A2
DORFMAN, Allen
Sen panel probes Teamsters insurnc deal 10-31—11-2, 837B2
DORNAN, Rep. Robert K. (R, Calif.)
Scores Panama Canal pact 8-17, 622D2
D'ORNANO, Michel
Chirac to run for Paris mayor 1-19, 63D1
Munic electns 3-13, 3-20; in Chirac pact 3-15, loses Paris mayoral bid 3-20, 221D1 *
Named culture min 3-30, 239A2
DORNBERG, John
USSR ousts Krimsky 2-4, 101F1
DORSEN, Norman
Sets ACLU abortn rights drive 10-6, 786A3
DORSETT, Tony
Sets Sugar Bowl record 1-1, 8F3
In NFL draft 5-3, 353G1-D2
In disco brawl 6-30, assault chrgs dropped 8-18, 659C2
Campbell wins Heisman 12-8, 950C2
DORSEY, Bob R.
Gulf sales rptd unhurt by bribery crackdown 2-28, 233E1
Convicted by Bolivia 12-23, 1010A3
DORSEY Corp.
Chattanooga Glass Co.
Strike ends 10-14, 818F3
Dos PASSOS, John (1904-70)
FBI surveillance rptd 6-19, 481E1
Dos SANTOS, Marcelino
At Frelimo cong 2-3—2-7, econ program rptd 2-8, 137B1, D1
DOTSON, Dick
Traded to White Sox 12-5, 990C1
DOUBLEDAY & Co. Inc.
Haley sues, Dell paperback rights cited 3-16, 356G1
Walker sues re Roots 4-22, 356D1
Douglas Black dies 5-15, 452D2
Haley sued 5-24, 643E1
DOUBLE Dipping—*See PENSIONS*
DOUBLEY, Larry
Sets long jump mark 6-3, 603C1
DOUGAN, William
Charges dropped 3-21, 520B3
DOUGLAS, Paul (1892-1976)
Arvey dies 8-25, 696C2
DOUGLAS-Home, Sir Alexander Frederick (Earl of Home)
25th Bilderberg conf 4-21—4-24, 359B3
DOUGLAS Oil Co.—*See CONTINENTAL Oil*
DOUGLAS v. Seacoast Products Inc.
Fed fishing laws backed 5-23, 444B2
DOW Chemical Co., The
Sup Ct backs EPA authority 2-23, 150A3
Questionable paymts rptd 3-28, 233D2
Branch, Merszei pay rptd 5-23, 408D3
Seadock backing rptd 7-19, 559F2
DBCP productn suspended 8-11, 723E2
DOW Corning Corp.
On '76 Fortune 500 list 341C1
DOW Jones Industrial Average—*See under STOCKS*

1978

DONNE, Gaven
Ousts Henry over electn fraud, swears Davis 7-25, 591F2
DONNELLY, Brian J.
Wins US House primary in Mass 9-19, 736C3
Elected 11-7, 847D3, 851D1
DONNELLY, Donal
My Astonishing Self opens 1-18, 760F2
DONNER, Richard
Superman released 12-14, 1030E3
DONOGHUE, Kevin
Admits CIA security lax 11-9, 940C2
DONOVAN, Hedley
Synanon threats probed 10-15, 842A1
DONOVAN Leisure Newton and Irvine
Perkins pleads guilty 9-21, sentncd 10-17; Doar role cited 808D2
DON'T It Make My Brown Eyes Blue (song)
Wins Grammys 2-24, 316A1
DON'T Leave Me This Way (recording)
Houston wins Grammy 2-24, 315G3
DON'T Look Back (recording)
On best-seller list 9-6, 708F1; 10-11, 800F3
DOOLING Jr., Judge John F.
Orders Queens schl desegregatn 5-16, 369G1-C2
DORE, Gordon
Cited in Passman indictmt re Korea 3-31; disputes Park testimony 4-5, 239F1, C3
DORFMAN, Allen M.
US sues to bar contract 10-16, 792F1
US set back in Teamster suit 11-1, 11-7, 899D1
DORN, William Jennings Bryan
Loses primary for SC gov 6-13, 467D1
DORNAN, Rep. Robert K. (R, Calif.)
Mil abortn curb passes House 8-9, 604F2
Reelected 11-7, 850A2
D'ORNANO, Michel
Named French environmt min 4-5, 245F2
DORSEN, Norman
On Sup Ct Bakke ruling 6-28, 482G2
DORSETT, Tony
NFL '77 touchdown, rushing ldr 1-1, 56E2, E3
Cowboys win Super Bowl 1-15, 39A3
Named NFL top rookie 1-23, 171E3
DORSEY, Larry
Traded to Chiefs 5-3, 336B2
Dos SANTOS, Manuel
Named Mozambique internal trade min 4-22, 331D1
Dos SANTOS, Marcelino
Renamed Mozambique econ min 4-22, 331E1
DOSSEE, Judge Robert L.
Dismisses sex abuse suit vs NBC 8-8, 635B2-A3
DOSSIER 51 (film)
Released 12-12, 1030F2
DOUALE, Hussein Haji Ali
Rpts anti-Barre plot 2-28, 269G1
DOUBLEDAY & Co., Inc.
Onassis becomes assoc editor 2-13, 172C2
Farber book deal scored 8-11, 678C3
Benchley book sets record film price 9-1, 759E2
Courlander suit settled 12-14, 1029E3
DOUBLE-Dipping—*See PENSIONS*
DOUBLE Eagle II (balloon)
3 Amers cross Atlantic 8-11—8-17, 652D3
DOUBLE Vision (recording)
On best-seller list 8-2, 620F1; 9-6, 708F1; 12-6, 971F1
DOUGHERTY Jr., Alfred
Backs ownership ceilings on coal, uranium reserves 4-5, 282D2
DOUGHERTY, Charles F.
Wins US House seat 11-7, 849D2, 852C1
DOUGHERTY County, Ga.—*See GEORGIA*
DOUGHERTY County v. White
Schl bd pol rule struck down by Sup Ct 11-28, 937E3
DOUGLAS, Michael
'Coma' released 2-1, 619B1
DOUGLAS, Paul H. (1892-1976)
FBI probe rptd, files detailed 11-14, 877C3
DOUGLAS-Home, William
Kingfisher opens 12-6, 1031B2
DOUGLAS Oil Co.—*See CONTINENTAL Oil*
DOUGLASS, Dale
Ties for 2d in Greater Hartford Open 7-30, 672D3
DOUKARA, Lt. Col. Kissima
Arrested 2-28, 250F3
DOVER, Del.—*See DELAWARE*
DOW, Richard
International Stud opens 5-22, 887A2
DOW Chemical Co., The
In USSR pact 2-28, 151F3
Exec changes announced 5-3, 809F1
Moscow rep refused exit 11-7, 884B3
Moscow rep cleared 12-1, 966E1
Agent Orange critic dies 12-14, 984E1

1979

DONNELLY, Terry
Mich State wins NCAA basketball title 3-26, 238D3
DONOVAN, Hedley Williams
Quits Time, replaced 6-21; named Carter adviser 7-25, 556E1
DON'T Stop 'Til You Get Enough (recording)
On best-seller list 10-3, 800E3
DOOBIE Brothers (singing group)
Minute By Minute on best-seller list 3-7, 174E1; 4-4, 271D2; 5-2, 356A3
What a Fool Believes on best-seller list 4-4, 271D2; 5-2, 356A3
DOOLEY, Allan
Perfect Couple released 4-5, 528C3
DOOLEY, Paul
Breaking Away released 7-17, 819F3
DORIN, Francoise
Your Turn, My Turn released 1-27, 174G3
DORNEY, Keith
In NFL draft 5-3, 335F1
DORON, Yacov
Israel recalls re Arafat visit 7-8, 511C3
DOROTHEE
Love On The Run released 4-5, 528A3
DORSETT, Tony
NFL touchdown, rushing ldr 1-6, 80E1, E2
Steelers win Super Bowl 1-21, 62E3-63A2
DORST, Tankred
On Mount Chimborazo opens 5-21, 712A2
Dos SANTOS, Jose Eduardo (Angolan president)
Named Angola interim pres 9-10, 705B2
Named offcl pres 9-20, 796F2
DOUBLEDAY & Co. Inc.
Novelist libel case refused by Sup Ct 12-3, 964F1
DOUBLEDAY v. Bindrim
Case refused by Sup Ct 12-3, 964A2
DOUCET, Staff Sgt. Freeman A.
Convicted of assault 8-18, 868E3
DOUGHERTY, Dr. Ralph
Links sterility, toxic chems 9-11, 736F1
DOUGLAS, Aaron
Dies 2-2, 176G2
DOUGLAS, Kirk
Villain released 7-20, 820E3
DOUGLAS, Melvyn
Joe Tynan released 8-17, 820C3
DOUGLAS, Michael
China Syndrome released 3-16, A-accident impact rptd 3-29, 4-1, 246D3, G3, 528G1*
Running released 11-2, 1008D1
DOUGLAS Oil Co. v. Petrol Stops Northwest
Case decided by Sup Ct 4-18, 346C2
DOUWES-Dekker, Loet
'76 ban lifted 9-17, 732F2
DOVER, Del.—*See DELAWARE*
DOW, Charles Henry
Dow average described 72G1
DOW, Richard
Tunnel Fever opens 5-10, 712B3
DOW Chemical Co., The
Viet Agent Orange suit filed 2-1, 90B1
Australia petrochem plans seen unlikely 2-8, 94E3
Weed killer ban protested 3-1, 167B2
US troops Agent Orange exposure rptd 11-24, Mass vets sue 11-26, 904E2-A3
DOWD, Nancy
Wins Oscar 4-9, 336A2
DOW Jones Industrial Average—*See under STOCKS*

1980

DONNELL, Forrest C.
Dies 3-19, 279B2
DONNELLY, Rep. Brian J. (D, Mass.)
Reelected 11-4, 843D1
DONNENFELD, Charles R.
Replaces Cohn in Benson Ford suit 3-12, 225E3
DONNER, Clive
Nude Bomb released 5-9, 675B3
DONNER, Richard
Inside Moves released 12-19, 1003A2
DONOHUE, Martin Henry
Jamaica sues US grain shippers 2-4, 99F2
DONOVAN, Anne
Old Dominion wins AIAW basketball title 3-23, 240B3
DONOVAN, Arthur
Dies 9-1, 755G2
DONOVAN, Brian
Wins Polk award 2-25, 692E3
DONOVAN, Jean
Found slain in El Salvador 12-4, 921B1
DONOVAN, Raymond J.
Named Labor secy 12-16, 955F2
DON'T Answer the Phone (film)
Released 8-9, 675C2
DON'T Stop 'Till You Get Enough (recording)
Jackson wins Grammy 2-27, 296C3
DOOBIE Brothers (singing group)
Win 4 Grammys 2-27, 296A3
One Step Closer on best-seller list 10-8, 796B3
DOOLING Jr., Judge John F.
Voids Medicaid abortn aid ban 1-15, 35B3
Marshall stays Medicaid abortn aid order 2-14, Sup Ct lifts stay, accepts case 2-19, 130G2-B3
Medicaid abortn funding limits upheld by Sup Ct 6-30, 491F3
DOOR, Marvin Dean
Sentenced for murder 2-27, 238D3
DOORN, Robert
Phoenix Foundatn, New Hebrides separatists linked 6-8, 436C2
DOPAMINE—*See CHEMICALS*
DORGAN, Byron L.
Elected to US House 11-4, 843C4, 851B2
DORIA Medina, Col. Arturo
Pledges mil regime support 8-5, 602D3
DORIC Petroleum Inc.
Sale to Petro-Lewis rptd 8-26, 745F2
DORMAN, Rep. Robert K. (R, Calif.)
Reelected 11-4, 842A2
DORNBERGER, Walter
Death rptd 7-2, 528E1
DORONJSKI, Stevan
Succeeds Tito as CP ldr 5-4, 338D2
Named Yugo top CP leader 6-12, 487G2
Replaced as Yugo CP chief 10-20, 810C1
DORSEN, David M.
On women bindery workers suit 5-20, 442E1
DORSET, Tony
Cowboys win playoffs 12-28, 999D1
DOS SANTOS, Manuel
Ousted in Mozambique Cabt shuffle 3-21, 234E2
DOS SANTOS, Marcelino
Ousted from Mozambique Cabt 4-3, 278D2
DOST, Shah Mohammed
Afghan aide defects 2-22, 139E1
In Moscow, Sovts vs UK neutrality plan 3-14, 205C1
Scores UN Afghan res 11-21, 900A1
DO That To Me One More Time (recording)
On best-seller list 2-6, 120F3
DOTRICE, Roy
A Life opens 11-3, 892A3
DOUBLEDAY, Abner (1819-93)
Great-grand nephew buys NY Mets 1-24, 795A3
DOUBLEDAY Jr., Nelson
Buys NY Mets 1-24, 795A3
DOUBLEDAY & Co. Inc.
NY Mets purchased 1-24, 795G2
DOUBLE Fantasy (recording)
Lennon slain 12-9, 934B1, E3
DOUEK, Michelle
Killed 11-13, 921C3
DOUGALL, William
Harrah's gets temp NJ gambling license 11-1, 988D3
DOUGHERTY Jr., Alfred F.
Resigns from FTC 5-27, 703A1
DOUGHERTY, Rep. Charles F. (R, Pa.)
Reelected 11-4, 844B1
DOUGLAS, Helen Gahagan (Mrs. Melvyn)
Dies 6-28, 528E1
DOUGLAS, Kirk
Saturn 3 released 2-15, 216E3
Final Countdown released 8-1, 675F2
DOUGLAS, Melvyn
Wins Oscar 4-14, 296G1
Wife dies 6-28, 528F1
Tell Me a Riddle released 12-17, 1003E2
DOUGLAS, Peter Vincent
Final Countdown released 8-1, 675E2
DOUGLAS, William O(rville)
Dies 1-19, 50E3
DOUKOV, Mikho
Wins Olympic medal 7-29, 624D3
DOVER—*See DELAWARE*
DOW, Charles Henry
Dow average described 76D1
DOW Chemical Co., The
Anti-cholesterol drug risk rptd 2-17, 159A3
Accuses EPA of spying 3-25, 387C2
La chem-dump suit names 7-15, 558G3
Texas chem plant cancer cases rptd 7-24, 584D2, G2
Richardson-Merrell unit bought 11-3, 985E2
DOW Jones Industrial Average—*See under STOCKS*

1976

DOWLING, Eddie
Dies 2-18, 160D3
DOWNEY, Rep. Thomas J. (D, N.Y.)
Questns Pentagon credibility 1-27, 68G1
Questions AWACS offer 3-2, 183E2
Reelected 11-2, 830F1
DOWNING, Rep. Thomas N. (D, Va.)
On Kennedy, King deaths 9-17; heads assassinatn panel 9-21, 729G1
Trible wins seat 11-2, 823C1
DOWNS, Hector
Arrested 9-17, 792B2
DOYCHINOVIC, Vladimir
Rptd in Yugoslav jail 7-27, 559G2
DOYLE, John C.
Arrest warrant rpt issued 1-14, 28B1
DOZIER, Bishop Caroll T.
Grants gen absolutn 12-5, 12-12, 951F1-B2
DRABANT, Herbert
Sentenced 8-9, 772E2
DRAGOYCHEVA, Tsola
On Bulgaria Politburo 4-2, 250C1
DRAME, Alioume
Arrested 8-10, 1005B2
DRANE, Noel
Named to econ advisory bd 9-14, 730F1
DRAPEAU, Jean
Vs Olympic debt for Montreal 12-19, 998F3
DREIFKE, Joachim
Wins Olympic medal 7-25, 575D1
DRESDNER Bank AG (N.Y.)
Buys IMF gold 9-15, 739D3
DRESSER Industries Inc.
SEC lists paymts 5-12, 727C1
DREW, Elizabeth
Pres debate panelist 9-23, 700G3
DREYFUS, Jack
'72 campaign gift listed 4-25, 688C1
DREYFUS Corp., Louis—*See under SOCIETE Anonyme Louis-Dreyfus et Cie*
DRIBERG, Tom—*See BRADWELL, Baron*
DRIESSEN, Dan
In World Series, 1st Series DH 10-16—10-21, 815D2
DRINAN, Rep. Robert F. (D, Mass.)
Scores com gun control vote 3-2, 170F1
Oil import fees upheld 6-17, 452C3
Asks boycott compliance halt 10-20, 786F2
Reelected 11-2, 829B4
Probes Argentine rights abuse 11-5—11-15, 996C2
DRIVER, Dick
Forced retiremt protested 2-20, 154F3
DROGOU (French warship)
In Intl Naval Review 7-4, 488C3

DROUGHT
Brazil NE food airlift rptd 1-16, 98E2
Argentina crop losses rptd 1-17, 96B3
West Coast drought ends 2-5, 271C3
Niger seeks urgent food aid 2-9, 205A3
US proposes Sahel aid program 5-1, 318C2
EC farmers seek aid 6-19, 7-19, 548C3
French drought effects rptd 7-23, 555D3
9 die in southn Ethiopia 8-4, 674B3
UK, Belgium act; Dutch study proposals 8-15—8-24, 630D1-B3
GOP platform text 8-18, 603E1
France sets farm aid 8-25, 675C1
Australia study issued, relief set 9-8, 709E2-E3
France rpts trade deficit 9-17, more relief set 9-22, 772E3, F3
Cuba sugar crop, agri hurt 9-27, 772A1
Australia drought ends 10-5, 770D3
2 win Rockefeller award re Africa aid 11-16, 911F3
UK water stocks up 11-16; Eur losses rptd 12-16, 977C3
EC grain harvest hurt 11-18, 935E2
French trade deficit rises 11-18, 964D2

1977

DOWNING, Brian
Traded to Angels 12-5, 990C1
DOWNTOWN Athletic Club
Awards Heisman, Downtown AC trophies 12-8, 950B2
DOXIADES, Spyros
Named Greek social svc min 11-28, 925B2
D'OYLY Carte Opera
Isidore Godfrey dies 9-12, 872A2
DOZIER, Bishop Carroll T.
Scored re gen absolutn 3-25, defends 4-26, 375D2
DRAFT, Military—*See U.S. GOVERNMENT—SELECTIVE Service*
DRAGONS of Eden, The (book)
On best-seller list 7-3, 548E3; 8-14, 643G1; 9-4, 712E3; 10-2, 808E3; 11-6, 872E3
DRAYTON, Jerome
Wins Boston Marathon 4-18, 602G3
DREISER, Theodore (1871-1945)
FBI surveillance rptd 6-19, 481E1
DREIZA, Mustafa
Denies aid to PI rebels 10-17, 824F2
DRESSER Industries Inc.
Forgn paymts rptd, '76 disclosure cited 2-17, 233B3
Antiboycott bill ad rptd 4-14, 323B3
DRESSES—*See CLOTHING*
DREYFUS Corp., Louis—*See under SOCIETE Anonyme Louis—Dreyfus et Cie*
DRINAN, Rep. Robert (D, Mass.)
'76 harassmt in Argentina cited 8-20, 670A2
DROST, Willem (1630-1678)
Painting defaced 10-7, men arrested 10-8, 848F2

DROUGHT
Ford budgets Sahel aid 1-17, 31G1
Calif, Colo get fed aid 1-20, 1-29, 79G3
Calif cnty rations water 2-1, 76C3
Calif rationing spreads 2-8, 2-19, 153A1
BPA asks 10% power cut 2-11, 244D3
Western drought continues 2-15, Andrus meets govs 2-20, 152E3
Colo, Washn cloud-seeding efforts 2-21, 2-28, 153E1
Science group topic 2-21, 183D2, G2
Dust storm hits Colo 2-23, 153F1
LA groundwater pumping cut 3-1, water rationing voted 5-12, 492D3
Carter call-in topic 3-5, 171C1
Calif estimates losses 3-7—3-8, 244E2
River flow decline rptd 3-8, 244G2
Blizzard hits Midwest 3-10—3-12, 204B3
Denver water use drops 3-15, San Fran conservatn set 3-22, 244B3
Carter asks Cong for aid 3-23, 210A2
'78 budget deficit projectns cited 3-23, 228F3
Texas High Plains hit 3-24, 244F3
Carter signs emergency aid 4-7, 273E1
Calif econ losses scaled down, new wells rptd 4-9, 376D3
Bergland tours Calif 4-14—4-18, briefs Carter 4-18, 365D1, 376E3 365D1
'76 SD cattle loss rptd 4-18, 376F3
Spring runoff in West rptd 4-19, 376C3
West Coast record 5-4, 376B3
More emergency aid clears Cong 5-5, 365F2; Carter signs 5-13, 380D3
Carter visits Calif farm 5-17, 381B3
Carter signs 3d emergency aid bill 5-23, 405A3
Santa Catalina cuts water use 5-25, 492F3
Marin Cnty water pipe laid 6-7, 492A3
Westn drought persists 6-16, 492G2
Drought conditns plague natn 6-23—8-9; 34 states, PR, VI to get fed aid 8-24, 659D3
Forest fire data rptd 8-23, 660A2
ND dam projct scored 9-19, 726B1
Foreign Developments
China drought rptd 3-11, 200A3
UN Water Conf held 3-14—3-25, 250F1
China drought spreads 3-18—3-25, 238A1
Haiti hit; Jamaica, DR water rationing rptd 4-12, 312E2
Hong Kong water rationing rptd 7-7, 660F1
Mex farming regions rptd dry 8-8, 660D1
Gambia crop loss projctd 8-22, 660E1
Haiti econ crippled 9-6, 706D3
Australia '77-78 wheat crop loss forecast 11-28, 945A1

1978

DOWD, Nancy
Coming Home released 2-15, 619B1
DOWDESWELL, Colin
Loses S African Open 4-10, 419C1
DOW Jones Industrial Average—*See under STOCKS*
DOWLING, Kathyrn
Spring Awakening opens 7-13, 887B3
DOWNER, Herb
Verandah opens 5-4, 760F3
DOWNEY, Rep. Thomas J. (D, N.Y.)
Reelected 11-7, 851C3
DOWNS, Joseph Henry
Dies 7-13, 620F2
DOWNTOWN Athletic Club (N.Y., N.Y.)
Heisman awarded to Sims 11-28, 1025A2
DOYLE, Sir Arthur Conan (1859-1930)
Crucifer of Blood opens 9-28, 1031C1
DOYLE, Brian
In World Series 10-10—10-17, 800D2
DO You Turn Somersaults? (play)
Opens 1-9, 760A2
DPF Inc.
'77 record sales rise rptd Interstate Brands buy cited 5-8, 325B2
DRABINSKY, Garth H.
Broadway Musical opens 12-21, 1031B1
DRACH, Michel
Replay released 7-10, 970F2
DRACULA (play)
Wins Tony 6-4, 579A3
DRAFT, Military—*See U.S. GOVERNMENT—SELECTIVE Service; country names*
DRAGANESCU, Emil
Named Rumania sports min 3-7, 193C2
DRAGONS of Eden, The (book)
Sagan wins Pulitzer 4-17, 315C1
On best-seller list 6-4, 460D3
DRAKE, Dieter
Sentenced 1-12, 36B2
DRAKE Jr., W. Homer
Tonelli indicted 7-19, 599B1
DRAMA—*See THEATER*
DRAPER, Laurence
S Australian police chief 1-19, 53B2
DREAMS Die First (book)
On best-seller list 9-4, 708D1
DRESDNER Bank AG (Frankfurt)
10th in '77 world ranking 11-8, 914B1
Nigeria loan set 11-30, 934A2
DRESSER Industries Inc.
USSR contracts rptd 6-1, 499F3
USSR oil sales review set 7-18, 542G1; 9-6, 743D1
USSR sale OKd 8-9, 634D2
DREYFUS, Lee Sherman
Wins primary for Wis gov 9-12, 736G1
Elected 11-7, 846C3, 853F3, 854G1
DREYFUSS, Richard
Wins Oscar 4-3, 315C3
Big Fix released 10-6, 969C3
DRINAN, Rep. Robert F. (D, Mass.)
Consumer group lauds 3-4, 183D1
Gets Cong Watch top rating 10-28, 865A3
Reelected 11-7, 851C1
DRINKS Before Dinner (play)
Opens 11-23, 1031D1
DRISCOLL, John
3d in Mont Sen primary 6-6, 448B2
DRIVAS, Robert
Cheaters opens 1-15, 760F1
DRIVER, The (film)
Released 7-28, 970B1
DROLLINGER, Ralph
Rejects Nets offer 3-15, 272E2
DROUGHT
Westn drought end rptd near 1-8, 24C1
Mondale tours Westn states 1-9—1-13, 34D1
Aid extensn clears Cong 1-31, 107A3; signed 2-7, 218A2
Drought declared over 3-5, 207A2
Calif cnty rejects A-plant re water needs 3-7, 184D1
Foreign Developments
Sub-Sahara drought feared 1-3, 24G1
Australia financial losses rptd 1-11, 16B1
Australia brush fires 1-13—1-18, 145G1
Sub-Sahara relief rptd sought 2-1, 3-8, 237F1
Peru drought rptd 4-28, 353D2
Poland '77 econ linked 5-15, 535A2
Ethiopians face famine, aid rptd 6-4—6-12 465G2
Haitian econ growth effect rptd 6-9, 479A1
Senegal gets IMF loan 10-30, 885D3
Ethiopia asks aid 12-20, 1016A3

1979

DOWN, Lesley-Anne
Great Train Robbery released 2-1, 174F2*
Hanover Street released 5-17, 528E2*
DOWNEAST Airlines
Maine commuter plane crashes 5-30, 412E2
DOWNING, Brian
NL wins All-Star Game 7-17, 569D1
AL batting ldr 9-30, 955D3
DOWNS, Stephen
Festival opens 5-7, 711A3
DOWNTOWN Athletic Club (N.Y., N.Y.)
Heisman awarded to White 12-3, 1001D2
DOYLE Dane Bernbach Inc.
Sony video recorder copyright trial opens 1-22, 120F2
Video recorder use upheld 10-2, 858F2
DRABINSKY, Garth H.
Silent Partner released 5-10, 528E3
DRACULA (film)
Released 7-13, 820A1
Top-grossing film 8-1, 620G3
DRACULA (play)
'78-79 success rptd 11-4, 956E2
DRACUP, Charlotte
Improper PCB storage chrgd 3-9, 206F3
DRACUP, Daniel
Improper PCB storage chrgd 3-9, 206F3
DRACUP and Co., Daniel J.
Named in PCB suit 3-9, 206F3
DRAFT, Committee Against Registration and the
House rejects draft registratn 9-12, 724B3
Lynn scores registratn 11-13, 868G2
DRAFT, Military—*See U.S. GOVERNMENT-SELECTIVE Service System*
DRAGOSAVAC, Dusan
Yugo CP secy gen 5-16, 430B3
DRAGOTI, Stan
Love At First Bite released 4-12, 528G2
DRAMA—*See THEATER*
DRAPER, Christopher
Dies 1-16, 104G2
DRAPER, Morris
Rpts N Yemen arms shipmt speedup 2-26, 144E2
DRED Scott Case, The (book)
Fehrenbacher wins Pulitzer 4-16, 336G2
DRESS Gray (book)
On best-seller list 3-4, 173D3
DREYFUSS, Richard
Othello opens 8-8, 712A2
DRINAN, Rep. Robert F. (D, Mass.)
Tours refugee camps, visits Hanoi 8-4—8-9; scores Viet rule 8-5, 607C2, E2

DROUGHT
Senegal gets IMF loan 3-30, 411G2
Fla drought ends 4-25, 472A3
Australia farmers hit 8-28, 650F2
Zambia drought cited 11-5, 844A3
Mex '79 rainfall down 18% 12-12, 950G2

1980

DOW Jones v. U.S. Postal Service
Case declined by Sup Ct 1-7, 15F3
DOWNEY, James
Rpts drought eased 7-3, 520B2
DOWNEY, Robert
Up the Academy released 6-6, 675F3
DOWNEY, Rep. Thomas J. (D, N.Y.)
Joins open-conv move 7-25, 7-28, 570F1, A2
Reelected 11-4, 843C3
DOWNTOWN Athletic Club (N.Y., N.Y.)
Rogers wins Heisman Trophy 12-1, 999E2
DRABINSKY, Garth H.
Changeling released 3-28, 416E2
Tribute released 12-13, 1003F2
DRACUP & Co., Daniel S
Pa PCB dumping suit filed 10-9, 825B1, D1
DRAGONETTE, Jessica
Dies 3-18, 279C2
DRAIN, Geoffrey
Scores public sector pay lid 11-8, 886D3
DRAKE, T. Y.
Terror Train released 10-3, 836G3
DRAPEAU, Jean
Blamed for '76 Olympic debt 6-5, 444C1
Scores '76 Olympic debt rpt 6-14, 461A3
Iran barred from cultural exhibitn 7-3, 520F3-521B1
Aide chrgd in '76 Olympic fraud 10-2, 788E1
DRAWINGS And Digressions (book)
Wins Amer Book Award 5-1, 692B2
DREIER, Dave
Elected to US House 11-4, 842B2, 852A2
DRESDNER Bank A.G.
Kaufhof shares rptd sold 12-12, 969E1
DRESSED To Kill (film)
Top-grossing film 8-6, 640C3
DRESSER Industries Inc.
SEC parallel probe case refused by Sup Ct 11-17, 882E1
DRESSER Industries v. SEC
Case refused by Sup Ct 11-17, 882E1
DREW, Larry
In NBA draft 6-10, 447G1
DREW, Richard G.
Dies 12-7, 1004D1
DREXEL Burnham Lambert Inc.
Sunshine Mining silver bonds offered 4-11, 265C3
DREYER, Peter
Titian forgeries chrgd 2-26, 472B3
DREYFUS, Gov. Lee Sherman (R, Wis.)
State of State message 2-6, 270A3
DREYFUS Corp.
Money mkt fund unit listed 3-31, 223F3
DREYFUSS, Richard
Competition released 12-3, 972D3
DRINAN, Rep. Robert F. (D, Mass.)
Priests barred from politics 5-4, drops reelectn bid 5-5, 341D2
Frank wins primary seat 9-16, 724E2
DROEGE, Wolfgang
Opens KKK hq in Canada 6-26, 497C1

DROUGHT
Peru crops hit 2-8, 234D3
Australia threat rptd 4-7, 271G3; aid planned 4-14, 309F2; threat ends 4-24, 334E1
Pope asks Upper Volta aid 5-10, 363D3
Mex cattle, crops threatened 6-13; US blamed 6-19, 7-1, 524B2
Midwest, South hit; death toll rptd 6-23—8-15; Carter declares disaster 7-16, 616C1-D2
Canada drought eased by rain, haylift 6-27, 7-3, 520B2
Reagan cites Africa drought in pres nominatn acceptance speech 7-17, 534G3
Carter in Dallas 7-21, 549E3
USSR harvest threat rptd 8-6, 711B3
US Aug farm prices rptd 8-29, 666E1
Midwest, South death toll final rpt 9-7, 857G1-B3
Northeast hit 9-12—12-1; NJ emergency declared 10-19, water warning issued 12-1, 947A3

1976

DRUGS—*See under MEDICINE & Health; also NARCOTICS & Dangerous Drugs*
DRUMGO, Fleeta
Acquitted 8-12, 656B1
DRUMM, Maire
Arrested 8-9, 590D1
Released 8-27, 679A2
Slain 10-28, buried 11-1, 854B3
DRUMMOND, William
Sues vs Panama Canal talks 10-26; car bombed 10-31; suit thrown out 12-18, 1008G2-A3
DRURY, Charles M.
Ontario OKs inflatn program 1-13, 46F3
Judicial interference chrgd 2-20, denied 3-3, 3-4, 187G3
Resignatn rejectd 3-12, 220D3-221B2
Fed cleaning contracts probed 4-5, 265B3
Resigns 9-14, replaced 9-15, 692E1
On '73 A-sale mtg 12-2, 923E3
DRUT, Guy
Wins Olympic medal 7-28, 576A1
DRUZHININ, Vladimir N.
Dies 8-20, 892G2
DRY Ridge, Ky.—*See KENTUCKY*
DUAN, Le
In Laotian talks 2-11, 121F1
Addresses Sovt CP Cong 2-25, 196D1
Opens party congress 12-14, 968C1
In Politburo 12-19, renamed party leader 12-20, 967D3, E3
DUBAI—*See UNITED Arab Emirates*
DUBCEK, Alexander
CIA link chrgd 3-10, 289E2
Husak offer to supporters 4-12, 289C1
Backers freed 12-10, 1012B3
DuBOIS Gervasi, Rear Adm. Jorge
Peru integratn min 7-17, 590G2
DUBRUL Jr., Stephen
On new export credit terms 6-9, 529F3
DUCAT, Lt. Bruce Chalmers
Vietnam rpts killed 9-6, 678B3
DuCHESSI, William M.
Clothing, textile unions merge 6-3, 436G1
DUCRAY, Gerard
Dropped from French govt 1-12, 49E2
DUFF, Antony
At mtg re Rhodesia fund 10-5—10-7, 781B3
DUFFEY, Joseph D.
Platform discussn rejctd 7-13, 509B2
DUGA Kugbeto Lo
Zaire trade min 2-4, 270C2
DUGAN, James P.
Carter criticizes 4-27, 324B1
Humphrey bars campaign 4-29, 305C3
Carter sees 6-30, 468F1
DUGWAY, Utah—*See UTAH*
DUHAIME, Yves
Named tourism min 11-26, 903A3
DUHE, Camille
Yr of Beauty on best-seller list 12-5, 972B2
DUISENBERG, Willem
Submits '77 budget 9-21, 732A2
DUKAKIS, Gov. Michael S. (D, Mass.)
Heads platform panel 5-17, 358A1
NE govs meet 11-13—11-14, 864B3
Signs anti-boycott law 8-19, 987A2
Asks spill relief 12-22, 969D1
DUKE, Gen. Charles M.
Dies 8-21, 892G2
DUKE, David
Chrgs marines harassed 11-28, 983A2
DUKE University (Durham, N.C.)
Sanford ends '76 pres bid 1-23, 95D1
Kreps named Commerce secy 12-20, 956F1
DULLES, Allan W(elsh) (1894-1969)—*See Vol. 1969, p. 64F1 for biog. data*
Olson files made public 1-10, 25C1
Strauss Lockheed letter termed forgery 9-22, 740B1
DULLES International Airport (Virginia)
Concorde landing hearing 1-5, 5C2
Concorde test OKd 2-4, 94 D3
Giscard in 1st Concorde landing 5-17, 372F1
Concorde runs inaugurated 5-24, 378C2-C3
Sup Ct bars review of Concorde landing OK 11-15, 882B2
DULUTH, Minn.—*See MINNESOTA*
DUMBARTON Methodist Church (Washington, D.C.)
Cheek, 3 others form Episc unit 5-9, 755C3
DUMMAR, Melvin
Hughes will names 4-27, 335F3
Will forgery chrgd 12-13, 971B2
DUMONT, Claude
Libya binocular fraud rptd 12-25—12-30, 1007A1
DUNCAN Jr., Charles William
Named Defense dep secy 12-21, 978F3
DUNCAN, D. K.
Wins Jamaica House seat 12-15, 965B2
DUNCAN, Rep. John James (R, Tenn.)
Reelected 11-2, 830B4
DUNCAN, Rep. Robert (D, Ore.)
Reelected 11-2, 830C3

1977

DROUGHT Coordinating Committee, Interagency—*See under U.S. GOVERNMENT*
DROUIN, Jude
Agent admits theft 9-20, sentenced 11-28, 1021A2
DRUG Abuse, National Institute on (NIDA)—*See U.S. GOVERNMENT—PUBLIC Health Service—Alcohol, Drug Abuse & Mental Health Administration*
DRUG Abuse Council (Washington, D.C.)
Mitchell named Carter asst 1-14, 35C3
Falco named to US post 1-21, 53D1
DRUG Abuse Policy, Office of—*See under U.S. GOVERNMENT*
DRUG Enforcement Administration—*See under U.S. GOVERNMENT—JUSTICE*
DRUG Enforcement Association, International
W Eur heroin traffic conf 10-17—10-21, 972A1
DRUGS—*See under MEDICINE & Health; also NARCOTICS & Dangerous Drugs*
DRUM, Donald E.
Arrested 7-27, 627F3
DRUMMOND, William
Panama detains 2-11, 2-12, US protests 2-14, 379C2
DRYDEN, Ken
NHL season ldr 4-3, 262B3, G3
DUAN, Le
In Laos 7-15—7-18, 553A1
USSR revolutn anniv fete photo 11-7, 865C2
DUBAI—*See UNITED Arab Emirates*
DUBCEK, Alexander
On Charter 77 stand 2-10, 115B1
Brzezinski aid chrgd 6-13, 512G3
DUBE, Normand
Quebec wins WHA title 5-27, 430C1
DUBINGON, Robert
Dies 3-1, 288B2
DuBOIS, Rev. Albert J.
Dissident Episcopalians unite 1-14, 119C3
DUBOIS, Chantal
Daily American closes 8-23, 729C2
DuBOIS, Shirley Graham
Dies 3-27, 356A3
DUCAUD-Bourget, Msgr.
Paris church occupied 2-27, 471B1
DUC de Brabant Hotel (Brussels, Belgium)
Fire kills 15 5-22, 429B3
DUCHATEAU, Philippe
USSR censors photo exhibit 8-18, 657F2
DUCKETT, George (d. 1972)
Killers' sentences confrmd 5-2, 374E2
Burrows executed 12-2, 935G2
DUCKS—*See WILDLIFE*
DUDKA, Stan
On 200-mi limit enforcemt 1-4, 7A2
DUFALA, Robert F.
Mistrial declared 3-10, 261F2
DUFEK, Rear Adm. (ret.) George J.
Dies 2-10, 164F2
DUFFEY, Joseph D.
Named State asst secy 1-21, 53C1
DUFFY-Mott Co. Inc.—*See AMERICAN Brands Inc.*
DUGAN, James P.
Loses renomination bid 6-7, 446E3
DUGAN 3rd, Judge Michael T.
Bars bio text in Indiana 4-14, 471D3
DUHE, Adam
In NFL draft 5-3, 353B2
DUISENBERG, Willem
Warns on EEC loans 3-14, 269E2
DUKAKIS, Gov. Michael S. (D, Mass.)
Lauds Carter energy plan 4-20, 320E2
Sacco, Vanzetti vindicated 7-19, 652E2-A3
Govs' panel visits DC 11-29, 960A1
DUKE Power Co.
A-plant accident liability limit voided 3-31, 277D2
DUKE University (Durham, N.C.)
Kreps rpts '76 income 2-25, 148B1
Armstrong in NBA draft 6-10, 584B3
DULLES, Alan W(elsh) (1894-1969)
CIA mind-control tests revealed 8-1—8-9, 611A1
DULLES International Airport (Virginia)
Concorde Issue
FAA issues noise rpt 4-14, 368G2
GAO rpt scores FAA study 9-16, 739A1
Test svc to continue 9-23, 738C2
DUMITRESCU, Sorin
UNESCO protests treatmt 10-8, 948E1
DUMMAR, Melvin
Admits lying re Hughes will 1-11, testifies 1-25—1-27, 120D1
Hughes will called fake 4-15, 354C3
DUMPING—*See FOREIGN Trade; also commodity names (e.g., STEEL)*
DUNAWAY, Faye
Wins Oscar 3-28, 264C1
DUNCAN Jr., Charles William
Confrmatn recommended 1-13, 34D3; confrmd 1-31, 148F3 ★
DUNCAN, D. K.
Named mobilizatn min 1-4, 46B1
Quits Cabt, PNP posts 9-18, 884D2
DUNCAN, Irma
Dies 9-20, 788A1
DUNCAN, Isadora
Daughter dies 9-20, 788A1
DUNCAN, Rep. John James (R, Tenn.)
'76 specl interest gifts rptd 2-15, 128F2; 3-7, 232B3
DUNCAN, Peter
To challenge uranium mining 11-14, 901E1
DUNCAN, Judge Robert M.
Orders Columbus (O) integratn plan 3-8, 217A1
Rejcts Columbus schl integratn plans 7-29, 631C1
DUNCAN, Verne
On Ore schl funding 1-13, 16D2

1978

DRUCKMAN, Jacob
Elected to Arts Institute 2-7, 316E1
DRUG Abuse, National Institue on (NIDA)—*See U.S. GOVERNMENT—PUBLIC Health Service—Alcohol, Drug Abuse & Mental Health Administration*
DRUG Enforcement Administration (DEA)—*See under U.S. GOVERNMENT—JUSTICE*
DRUGS—*See under MEDICINE & Health; NARCOTICS*
DRUGS, Bureau of—*See U.S. GOVERNMENT—FOOD & Drug Administration*
DRUM, Leonard
Gay Divorce opens 3-9, 760C2
DRURY, Newton B.
Dies 12-14, 1032F2
DRYDEN, Ken
Wales Conf wins NHL All-Star game 1-24, 76D3
NHL goaltending ldr 4-9, 296E1, E2
DSMO (dimethyl sulfoxide)—*See MEDICINE—Drugs*
D'SPAIN, Jim
November People opens 1-14, 760A3
DUAN, Gen. Le
Laos backs Viet in China feud 7-22, 603B2
In USSR 11-2; signs friendship pact, scores China 11-3, 859E2, A3
DUBAI—*See NONALIGNED Nations Movement, United Arab Emirates*
DUBCEK, Alexander
Husak visits W Ger 4-10—4-14, 333A1
Du BOISROUVRAY, Albina
Woman at Her Window released 6-9, 620C1
DuBOSE, Winston
Cosmos win NASL title 8-27, 707C2
DUBROVSKAYA, Silva
Rptd Shcharansky lawyer 2-24, 179G3
DUCHARME v. Merrill-National
Case refused by Sup Ct 12-4, 959C2
DUDMAN, Richard
In Cambodia 12-9, escapes gunman 12-23, quotes govt offcls on attack 12-24, 997A2
DUEL, The (book)
Film versn released 1-14, 619F1
DUELING
Miss ban repealed 11-7, 852F3
DUELLISTS, The (film)
Released 1-14, 619F1
DUFFEY, Thomas J.
Named in US Teamster fund suit 2-1, 83F1
DUFFY, Sharon
Penn State wins women's lacrosse title 5-28, 540C2
DUGDALE, Bridget Rose
Married 1-24, 172E2
DUKAKIS, Gov. Michael S. (D, Mass.)
Blizzard hits Mass 2-5—2-7, orders roads closed 2-8, 105A2, B2
Welfare compromise prepared 6-7, 446B2
Defeated in primary 9-19, 736F2
DUKAKIS, Olympia
Starving Class opens 3-2, 887C3
DUKE Power Co. v. Carolina Environmental Study Group
A-accident liability law backed by Sup Ct 6-26, 567B1
DUKE University (Durham, N.C.)
Med cntr heart victim hosp study rptd 2-2, 578A2
Loses NCAA basketball title 3-27, 272A1
Herpes virus linked to colon cancer 5-6, 1023A2
DULUTH, Minn.—*See MINNESOTA*
DULZIN, Arye
Sees Jewish emigratn rise 9-28, 947B1
DUMA, Enoch
Acquitted 5-29, 456C1
DUMITRESCU, Florea
Out as Rumania finance min 3-7, 193C2
DUMITRESCU, Sorin
Rptd back at UNESCO post 5-18, 360A2
DUMMAR, Melvin
Hughes Mormon will ruled fake 6-8, 458G3
DUMPING—*See FOREIGN Trade; commodity names (e.g., STEEL)*
DUNAWAY, Faye
Eyes of Laura Mars released 8-4, 970C1
DUN & Bradstreet Companies Inc.
Moody's Investors Service Inc.—*See separate listing*
DUNCAN Jr., Charles William
Repeal of combat bar for women rptd sought 3-4, 162A2
Nerve gas productn order rptd 10-19, 833G2
DUNCAN, Rep. John James (R, Tenn.)
Reelected 11-7, 852C2
DUNCAN, Rep. Robert (D, Ore.)
Reelected 11-7, 852B1

1979

DRUG Abuse, National Institute on—*See U.S. GOVERNMENT–PUBLIC Health Service–Alcohol, Drug Abuse & Mental Health Administration*
DRUG Enforcement Administration—*See under U.S. GOVERNMENT–JUSTICE*
DRUGS—*See under MEDICINE & Health; NARCOTICS*
DRURY, Lt. Col. Peter
On Ft Dix sex scandal 12-3, 924B1
DRURY College (Springfield, Mo.)
Wins NAIA basketball title 3-17, 239B1
DRYDEN, Dave
Brother leads NHL goaltenders 4-8, 356D1
WHA goaltending ldr 4-18, 355G2, 356D1
Named WHA MVP, top goalie 5-16, 470E2
DRYDEN, Ken
Sovts win Challenge Cup 2-11, 118D2-F2
NHL goaltending ldr, wins Vezina Trophy 4-8, 355E2, 356B1
Brother leads WHA goaltenders 4-18, 356D1
Montreal wins Stanley Cup 5-21, 447B3
Laroque shares top goalie award 6-12, 470D2
Announces hockey retiremt 7-9, 655A3
DUAN, Le
Viet defector assails rule 8-8, 604F1
DUARTE, Jose Napoleon
Returns to El Salvador, riots mar downtown rally 10-25, 834E2
DUBAI—*See UNITED Arab Emirates*
DUBIN, Lawrence
Queries Townley re Letelier murder 1-24, 58D2
DUBS, Adolph
Kidnaped in Kabul, dies in shootout 2-14, 106C2
USSR regrets death, denies blame 2-16—2-17, 147D2
Afghan rejcts US protest, denies Sovt role 2-19, 147E2
US cuts Afghan forgn aid 2-22, 147C1
US secret cable details death 2-22, 147E1
DUDLEY Station Corp.
FCC doubts RKO Gen license fitness 7-18, 618A2
DUFF, Sir Anthony
Starts Rhodesia talks 5-16, 359F2
DUFFY, F. Ryan
Dies 8-16, 671B2
DUFFY, Terry
Urges govt to aid BL 9-10, 686B3
Scores lockout policy 9-19, 730A1
Hails engineers' pact 10-4, 773B1
DUGUAY, Ron
Montreal wins Stanley Cup 5-21, 447C3
DUKE, Daryl
Silent Partner released 5-10, 528E3
DUKE, David
KKK activity rptd 7-22, 865E2
At Columbus (Ga) KKK rally 8-18, 866E1
DUKE Power Co.
NRC orders SC A-plant closings 4-27, 322D1
DUKE University (Durham, N.C.)
Spanarkel in NBA draft 6-25, 507B3
DULUTH, Minn.—*See MINNESOTA*
DULZIN, Arye
Warns Iran vs Jews mistreatmt 5-15, 357B2
DUMAS, Alexander (1802-1870)
5th Musketeer released 9-7, 820B1
DUMPING—*See FOREIGN Trade; commodity names (e.g., STEEL)*
DUNAWAY, Faye
Champ released 4-3, 528G1
DUNAWAY, Irving
'Probable cause' in detentns backed by Sup Ct 6-5, 464C2
DUNAWAY v. New York
Case decided by Sup Ct 6-5, 464C2
DUN & Bradstreet Companies Inc.
Moody's Investors Service Inc.—*See MOODY'S Investors Service*
DUNCAN, Andrew
Shame of Jungle released 9-14, 820C3
DUNCAN Jr., Charles William
Named Energy secy 7-20, 529D1; confrmd 7-31, 627B2; sworn 8-24, 623E1
Claytor confrmd Defense dep secy 7-27, 577D1
Reassures NE govs on heating fuel 8-28, 703G1-C2
Plans energy policy review 9-14, 702F3
DUNCAN, Judge Robert
Columbus busing order upheld by Sup Ct 7-2, 539G2
Reissues Columbus busing order 8-2, 596A3
DUNCAN, Sandy
Peter Pan opens 9-6, 956G3

1980

DRUDZHEV, Sabit
Urengoy gas dvpt lag noted 3-6, 235A3
DRUG Abuse, National Institute on—*See under U.S. GOVERNMENT--PUBLIC Health Service*
DRUG Enforcement Administration—*See under U.S. GOVERNMENT--JUSTICE*
DRUGS—*See MEDICINE--Drugs & Health-Care Products, NARCOTICS*
DRUMMON, Kevin
Backs Quebec referendum 3-19, 230G1
DRUMMOND, Edwin
In Statue of Liberty protest 5-11, 667D1
DRURY, C. M.
Rpt vs NWT prov status 3-6, 273C1
DUARTE, Jose Napoleon
Sees El Salvador civil war 1-3, 6E2
Joins El Salvador junta 3-9, 191E2
Blames left for Romero funeral violence 3-30, 253E3
On coup attempt 5-2, 372F2
Coup ldr's release spurs junta rift 5-13—5-14, 389A3
Son foils kidnap in Guatemala 10-17, 829E2, 830F1
Warns of rightist coup 12-5, urges end to violence 12-7, 941A3, C3
Named El Salvador pres 12-13, sworn 12-22, 993C1
DUBAI—*See UAE*
DUBCEK, Alexander
Cited in Czech warning vs Polish unrest 11-27, 910A2
DUBIN, Robert N.
Charged in GSA scandal 1-15, 112F1
DUBOIS, Marie
Soupcon released 3-26, 416E3
DUBS, Adolph (d. 1979)
US releases death probe rpt 2-20, 140B1
DUDAR, Helen
Agnew interview publshd 4-20, 333C3
DUDKO, Rev. Dmitri
Arrest rptd 1-15, 46F3
Recants on TV 6-20, 500E1
DUDLEY Station Corp.
FCC blocks WNAC-TV purchase 1-24, 119B3
DUERKSEN, Larry D.
Cutsinger charged in murder 1-2, 18C3
DUET (recording)
Burton, Corea win Grammy 2-27, 296E3
DUFFY, James
Electronic mail plan OKd, conflict of interest chrgd 4-8, 347B3
DUFFY, Judge Kevin Thomas
Backs Iran assets freeze 11-13, 861E2-862A1
DUKE Astin, Patty
Wins Emmy 9-7, 692D1
DUKES of Hazzard, The (TV series)
'79-80 Nielsen rating rptd 4-22, 376C1
DUKE University (Durham, N.C.)
Ape-human ancestor rpt discovered 2-7, 416F1
Pot cancer aid study rptd 3-24, 357F3
Simulated dive depth record rptd 4-12, 415E3
Exercise, blood clot dissolutn linked 5-1, 674A1
Gminski in NBA draft 6-10, 447F2
DULLES International Airport (Virginia)
Teamsters boycott Sovt plane 1-22, 45F1
Aeroflot jets land at Kennedy 2-3, 2-10, 115A1, C1
DULZIN, Arye
Begin vs Sovt Jews in US 4-2, 262D3
DUNAWAY, Faye
First Deadly Sin released 10-24, 836G2
DUNCAN Jr., Charles William
In Saudi oil talks, reserve purchases barred 3-1—3-4; US stockpiling stalled 3-5, 165B3
Sets Canada gas price pact 3-24, 229G3
In Mex for energy talks 4-2—4-3, 315G1
Rescinds Sohio price hike order 5-1, 366F1
Scores OPEC price hikes 6-11, 435D3
Energy conservatn acceptance seen 7-24, 553D1
Aug oil imports show record drop; Jan-Aug decline rptd 9-6, 785A3
In Yamani secret talks 9-18, oil stockpiling rptd resumed 10-27, 826E1
DUNCAN, Graham Bowie
Sentenced 4-17, 301B3
DUNCAN, Rep. John James (R, Tenn.)
Reelected 11-4, 844C2
DUNCAN, Rep. Robert (D, Ore.)
Loses primary 5-20, 404B3

1976

DUNG, Col. Van Tien
Surprised by '75 victory 4-26, 315A3
DUNHAM, Richard L.
Moss threatens impeachmt 9-1, 868A3
DUNHAM Bush International
Boycott rpt released 10-20, 786A2
DUNLAP, Max A.
Linked to Bolles murder 7-15, 859B3, C3
DUNLAP, Tom
Wins primary runoff 9-21; defeated 11-2, 822A3
DUNLOP, John T.
Constructn picket bill vetoed 1-2, union ldrs quit Ford com 1-8, 3E3, G3
Quits Ford cabt 1-14, 23B1
Replaced as Labor secy 1-22, 40E3
At Carter econ briefing 12-1, 898F2
Marshall named labor secy 12-21, 957F3
DUNN, J. M.
Named to payoff probe 3-21, 262F2
DUNN, Richard
Ali defends title 5-25, 424B3
DUNN Jr., Willie
Bronfman trial verdict 12-10, 952C3
DUNNE, George W.
Gets Daley's party post 12-29, 994B1
DUNPHY, John
Resigns, pleads guilty 8-13, 666F3
DUPERRE (French warship)
In Intl Naval Review 7-4, 488D3
Du PLESSIS, A. H.
Vs Namibia indepndnc 8-9, 654B1
Conf com OKs const plan 10-22, 832F1
DUPONT, Clifford
Replaced as Rhodesia pres 1-14, 53D3
Du PONT 4th, Rep. Pierre Samuel (R, Del.)
Elected 11-2, 817E1, 820E3, 821B1, 831D1
DuPONT, Robert L.
NIDA rpts most abused drugs 7-9, 524A2
DuPONT de Nemours & Co., E. I.
Grimble in Mex talks 1-26, 75F1
Walter Carpenter dies 2-2, 124D3
US files consent decree 11-16, 989C1
Shapiro named Carter aide 11-19, 881D3
Dacron price raised 11-30, 898G1
DUPREE, Judge Franklin T.
Ordrs J P Stevens end bias 6-25, 944C1
DURACK, Peter
Named repatriatn min 7-4, 520G2
DURAFOUR, Michel
On indl reform bill 4-13, 312B2
Finance min-delegate 8-27, 650C3, F3
DURAN Arcentales, Gen. Guillermo
Rodriguez hands over power 1-9; junta role scored 1-9, 1-11, 1-12, 28E1, C2
Vasconez, Puma amnestied 1-28, 363D3
DURKIN, Sen. John A. (D, N.H.)
Queries Usery re Teamsters 7-1, 492C2
DURNING, Marvin
Loses Dem gov primary 9-21, 804C3
DURRANT, Patricia
Scores OAS rights resolutn 6-18, 464D2
DURRER, William
CIA favor rptd 1-13, 24E3
DUTCH Reformed Church
S Africa synod res on mixed marriages rptd 8-18, 8-19, 639E3
DUVAL Corp.—*See PENNZOIL Corp.*
DUVALIER, Francois (Papa Doc) (1907-71)
Son shuffles Cabt 4-1, 267D2
Embezzlment rptd 4-9, 267G2
DUVALIER, Jean-Claude (Haitian president)
US co chrgs bribe request 3-2, 267B3
Shuffles Cabt 4-1, 267D2
Assassinatn attempt rptd 4-1, 267A3
Embezzlment rptd 4-9, 267G2
Siclait fired 9-7, expelled 9-24, 1005B3
Sets amnesty 9-30, 1005F3
DUVALIER, Simone (Mrs. Francois)
Cited re Cabt shuffle 4-6, 4-9, 267F2
DUVALON, Ramon
Wins Olympic medal 7-31, 574A1
DVOINIKOV, Valeriy
Wins Olympic medal 7-28, 575A1

1977

DUNHAM, Richard L.
To administer emergency gas act 2-2, orders supply shifts 2-3, 2-5, 91G2-B3
Sees summer shortages 2-3, 91D3
Backs Alcan Alaska gas route 5-2, 369D3
DUNLAP, Max A.
Arrested 1-15, Adamson testifies 1-26—1-27, 161F3-162F1
Convicted 11-6, 871B2
DUNLEAVY, Steve
'Elvis' sets order record 8-20, 696D1; 10-2, 808F3
DUNN, Robert W.
Dies 1-21, 84G2
DUNSTAN, Donald
On S Australia gas tax 2-1, 96G1
Party wins S Australia electns 9-17, personal triumph rptd 9-24, 740E1
Du PLESSIS, Abraham
Reelected Namibia party ldr 9-27, 770A3
DuPONT, Dr. Robert L.
Urges home-grown pot reforms 2-4, 332E2
'Angel dust' danger rptd 11-1, 972E2
Rpts on barbiturate abuse 11-27, 972F3
DuPONT de Nemours & Co., E. I.
Sup Ct backs EPA authority 2-23, 150G2
On '76 Fortune 500 list 340F1
Christiana merger OKd 6-16, 518A1
NIOSH med data access OKd 12-22, 1008F2
Shapiro rptdly backs Miller as FRB chrmn 12-28, 1000B3
DUPUIS, Brother Arthur
Rhodesia jails 8-30, frees 9-4, 811C2
DUPUY, Michel
Defends Canada forgn aid progrm 11-3, 863D1
DUQUESNE Light Co.
Westinghouse settlemt rptd 3-3, 177D2
Westinghouse formally ends dispute 3-30, 252G1-B2
Westinghouse setlmt cited 12-26, 1003B3
DUQUESNE University (Pittsburgh, Pa.)
Nixon in NBA draft 6-10, 584B3
DURACK, Peter
Named Australia atty gen 12-19, 982B2
DURAFLEX Corp.
Mex guerrillas kill Andreski 1-20, 65G3
DURAN, Hector
Denies Letelier murder testimony 9-10, 743B3
DURAN, Roberto
KOs Fernandez 1-29, 263C2
Decisions Muniz 5-16, 395D1
Decisns Viruet 9-17, 827G3
'77 boxing champion 12-17, 970A2
DURNING, Marvin
Loses US House electn 5-17, 382F1
DURR, Francoise
Loses Bridgestone tourn 4-10, 430D3
DUST Storms—*See STORMS & Floods*
DUTCH Guiana—*See SURINAM*
DUTSON, Roger
Dummar admits lying 1-11, 120D1
DUVAL Corp.—*See PENNZOIL*
DUVALIER, Francois (Papa Doc) (d. 1971)
Son frees 'last' pol prisoners 9-21, 767F2
DUVALIER, Jean-Claude (Haitian president)
Sees US envoy Young 8-15, 647D2
Civilian pol court set 8-23, 707A1
Frees 'last' pol prisoners 9-21, 767F2
DWG Corp.
Sharon Steel drops Foremost takeover bid 4-5, 275D1

1978

DUNLAP, Louise
Scores indus-environmt coal study 2-9, 184C2
DUNLAP, Max A.
Sentenced 1-10, 24B2
DUNLOP, John T.
Fraser quits labor-mtg panel 7-19, 611B2
DUNN, Richard
Holmes KOs Evangelista 11-10, 969C1
DUNNE, George
Cook Cnty bd pay hike vote rptd 11-29, Carter angry 12-1, Kahn asks rollback 12-4, 935A1
DUNSTAN, Donald
Fires police chief 1-17, names successor 1-19, 53F1
DUNSTAN, Roberts
Denies Jennings chrgs vs Holding 9-14, 771G1, D2
DUPOIS, Starletta
Mighty Gents opens 4-16, 760E2
DUPONT, Clifford W.
Dies 6-28, 540E2
DUPONT, Laura
Loses Kent championshp 6-10, 540C1
DuPONT de Nemours & Co. Inc., E.I.
In Dow Jones indl avg 66E2
Pigment mkt monopoly chrgd 4-10, 345G3
Shapiro sees Carter, backs inflatn plan 4-20, 361G3
On '77 Fortune 500 list 5-8, 325F1
EC Comm orders fiber cartel modificatn 11-9, 871F3
News-Journal Co.
Gannett buys Wilmington papers 1-30, 109E3
Remington Arms Co.
Air gun recall rptd, record setlmt cited 10-25, 942D1
DuPONT Glore Forgan Inc. v. AT&T
Centrex case refused by Sup Ct 11-13, 874D2
DURAN, Jose
Mattioli KOs 5-14, 379E2
DURAN, Roberto
TKOs DeJesus for lightwgt title 1-21, 55E3
DURAN Ballen, Sixto
Rightists nominate for pres 1-30, 148D2
2d in pres vote 7-16; Roldos runoff set 7-18, 556G3
Cotopaxi pres votes rptd annulled 8-8, 671A3
Pres runoff set for Apr '79 10-5, 881C2
To face Roldos in runoff 11-15, 989C3
DURANG, Christopher
History of Amer Film opens 3-30, 760C2
DURBANO, Steve
WHA penalty minutes ldr 4-11, 296G2
DURENBERGER, David
Wins US Sen primary in Minn 9-12, 716B1
Tax-cut proposal cited 9-21, 735A1
Elected 11-7, 846F1, 854A3, 858D2
DURER, Albrecht (1471-1528)
Watercolor auctioned 6-21, 579B1
DURKIN, Sen. John A. (D, N.H.)
Backs Panama Canal pacts 2-1, 58E1
Scores Energy Dept in cancer-radiatn inquiry 2-28, 164D3
Votes for Panama Canal neutrality pact 3-16, 177D2
Votes for 2d Canal pact 4-18, 273B1
Vs Calif fuel oil export 6-16, 471B1
Visits USSR 11-11—11-18, 905A2
DuROSS, Kathleen
Cited in Ford suit 5-16, 390F3
DURYEA, Perry B.
Unopposed in primary for NY gov 9-12, 716B2
Loses electn 11-7, 849D1
DUSSART, Philippe
Dossier 51 released 12-12, 1030F2
DUST Bowl—*See SOUTHWEST*
DUTCH Reformed Church
S Africa church breaks ties re anti-racism stand 4-4, 269G2
DUTTON, Frederick G.
Named as lobbyist for Saudis 237B1
DUVALIER, Francois (Papa Doc) (d. 1971)
Ex-Tontons sentncd 3-21, 292B3
UN panel probes Haiti rights 8-18—8-25, 691B3
DUVALIER, Jean-Claude (Haitian president)
Repressn rptd eased 2-3, 94C3
UN panel probes rights 8-18—8-25, 691C3
Replaces mil, police chiefs 9-15, 777A2
DUVALL, Robert
'Betsy' released 2-9, 618C3
DuVIGNEAUD, Vincent
Dies 12-11, 1032F2
DWYER, Jim
Carew rejcts Giants trade 12-7, 1026A1
DWYER, Mary
Ties for 2d in Eur LPGA 8-6, 672E3
DWYER, Richard
Visits Guyana cult commune with US delegatn 11-17, aids wounded 11-18, 889F1, 890D1
DWYER, William F.
Scores HEW anti-smoking plan 1-11, 23B3

1979

DUNDON, Donna
Light Shines opens 1-11, 292G1
DUNG, Gen. Van Tien
In Pnompenh 2-16—2-20, friendship pact signed 2-18, 123D2
DUNGY, Tony
NFL '78 interceptn ldr 1-6, 80D1
DUNLOP, John T.
Pay Advisory Com chrmn 9-28, members named 10-16, 1st mtg held 10-17, 829E2
DUNN, Archibald Garner
Kidnaped in El Salvador 11-28, 908G1-A2
DUNN, James
On E Timor famine 11-3, 856A2
DUNN, Reed
Backs commodity options trading resumptn 9-5, 681B2
DUNNE, George
2d Daley salary confrmd 12-4, 946G3
DUNN v. U.S.
Case decided by Sup Ct 6-4, 439E1
DUNSTAN, Don
Quits as S Australia premr 2-15, 153A1
DUNWOODY, Gwyneth
Scores budget 6-12, 445A2
DUPLAT, Carlos
Accuses mil of torture 3-12, 993C1
Du PLESSIS, Commodore Willem N.
US ousts 4-13, 287C1
DUPONT, Rene
Murder By Decree released 2-8, 174B3
Du PONT de Nemours & Co. Inc., E.I.
In Dow Jones indl avg 72E1
Dow Jones index revised 6-28, 481B3
Shapiro scores Carter re Cabt shake-up 7-19, 531B2
Monopoly case dismissed 9-17, 810C1
DuPRE, Pat
Wimbledon results 7-6, 7-7, 569E3
Loses Hong Kong Grand Prix 11-11, 1003F3
DUPREE, Billy Joe
Steelers win Super Bowl 1-21, 63G1
DUPREE Jr., Judge Franklin T.
Sentences MacDonald 8-29, 817F2
DUQUESNE Light Co.
Pa A-plant ordrd shut 3-13, 186E1
Uranium supply suit setlmt cited 5-15, 366B2
DURAL, Nezih
Lockheed spy role chrgd 9-20, 775A2
DURAN, Roberto
Abandons world lightwgt title 2-1, 412G3
DURANG, Christopher
Nature & Purpose opens 2-23, 292C2
DUREN v. Missouri
Mo women jury exclusn law voided by Sup Ct 1-9, 14A3
DURER, C. S.
Madman & Nun opens 1-18, 292A2
DURI, Izzat Ibrahim al-
Elected to Iraqi Cmnd Cncl 7-16, 544F3
DURKIN, Sen. John A. (D, N.H.)
Offers energy plan 7-25, 557C3
DURNING, Charles
North Dallas Forty released 8-1, 820D2
When A Stranger Calls released 10-12, 1008A2
DURNING, Marvin B.
Texaco fined in gas-switching 4-26, 301D2
DUTSCHKE, Rudi (Red Rudi)
Dies 12-24, 1008D2
DUTTO, Attilio
Injured by car bomb 3-21, 269E1
DUVAL, Leon-Etienne Cardinal
Sees hostages 12-24—12-25, Iran forgn min 12-27, 975B1-B2
DUVALIER, Francois (Papa Doc) (d. 1971)
Son praises security group 9-22, 874F1
DUVALIER, Jean-Claude (Haitian president)
Praises security group 9-22, 874E1
Shuffles Cabt 11-13, 874F1
DUVALL, Robert
Apocalypse Now released 8-15, 819D3
DVORAK, Ann
Dies 12-10, 1008E2
DVORAK, Dr. Harold & Ann
Cancer cocoon discovery rptd 8-20, 735G1
DWORKIN, Sidney
On Woolworth Revco bid 4-23, 304A2

1980

DUNDEE, Angelo
Holmes KOs Ali 10-2, 772D1
DUNG, Gen. Van Tien
Named Viet defense min 2-7, 90G1
DUNLAP, Max A.
Murder convictn overturned 2-25, 214A3
Adamson convicted 10-17, 860G3
DUNN, Archibald Garner
Ex-educ min joins kidnapers 1-8, 20B1
El Salvador church ldr appeals to kidnapers 4-8, 351A3
Rptd alive 6-23, 497C3
Rptd dead 10-9, 789B3
DUNN, Jim
Elected to US House 11-4, 843E1, 851C1
DUNN, Read
Testifies on commodity futures trading curbs 4-15, 290C1, C2
DUNNE, Griffin
Coming Attractions opens 12-3, 1003A3
DUPONT, Chaney
Postell, wife cleared 11-12, 927B1
DUPONT, Norman
Indicted 3-3, 215E1
DU PONT, Gov. Pierre Samuel (Pete) (R, Del.)
Reelected 11-4, 845D2, 847E1, 848E1
DU PONT de Nemours & Co. Inc., E. I.
In Dow Jones indl avg 76E1
IRS tax dispute declined by Sup Ct 4-14, 307E1
Nader coalitn attacks 4-17, 308B2
On '79 Fortune 500 list 5-5, 290F1
EC textile duties rptd 5-6, 412A1
Shapiro named to Econ Revitalizatn Bd 8-28, 663C2
Monopoly case dismissal upheld 10-27, 916F3
New England Nuclear merger set 12-8, 985A2
DURACK, Peter
Press articles on US ties banned 11-8, 885C1
DURAN, Roberto
Decisns Leonard for WBC welterwgt title 6-20, 772D2
Hart KOs Denny 6-20, Denny dies 7-7, 907C3
Leonard TKOs for WBC welterwgt title 11-25, 907B2
Fined 11-26, rejcts retiremt 11-28, 1000A3
DURANG, Christopher
Lusitania Songspiel opens 1-10, 136B3
DURANTE, Jimmy
Dies 1-29, 104C2
Eddie Jackson dies 7-16, 608B2
DUREN, John
In NBA draft 6-10, 447G1
DURGAN, Jeff
Named NASL top rookie 9-13, 1001A3
Cosmos win NASL title 9-21, 770B2
DURHAM, Roy
Soupcon released 3-26, 416E3
DURKIN, Sen. John A. (D, N.H.)
Wins primary 9-9, 700F2
Loses reelectn 11-4, 837D2, 845A2, 848E2
D'URSO, Giovanni
Kidnaped by Red Brigades 12-12, 966D2
Trani prisoners revolt 12-28, 995B1
DUST Commander (race horse)
Hunts bailout loan collateral listed 5-28, 426C1
DUTCH Reformed Church
S African split re apartheid rptd 5-10, 374F1
DUTTON, John
NFL free agent rule upheld by arbitrator 5-16, 998G2
DUVALIER, Francois (Papa Doc) (d. 1971)
Son marries 5-27, 471G1
DUVALIER, Jean-Claude (Haitian president)
New law stifles press criticism 4-11, 294E2
Haitians seek refuge in US 4-13, 294D2
Chngs Cabt, consolidates power 4-26, 335F3-336A1
Marries 5-27, 471F1
US refugees win suit, deportatns halted 7-2, 514G1
OKs stranded refugees return 11-13, 869C3
400 critics arrested 11-28—11-30, 922E2
Defends arrests 12-4, 942A3
Scores forgn interference, 9 prisoners released 12-5, 942D2, G3
DUVALIER, Simone
Son consolidates power 4-26, 335G3, 336A1
DUVALL, Shelley
Shining released 5-23, 675D3
Popeye released 12-12, 972G3
DWYER, Bernard
Wins NJ US House primary 6-3, 439A3
Elected to US House 11-4, 843B3
DWYER, Charles Breen
Jamaica sues US grain shippers 2-4, 99F2
DWYER, Cynthia
Arrested in Iran 5-6, 434B1

1976

DYCKES, Shirley
Plans to wed Kelley 9-4, 680F2
DYER, Masu K.
Seconds Ford nominatn 8-18, 598A1
DYER, Wayne W.
Erroneous Zones on best-seller list 12-5, 972C2
DYKE, William
Amer Indep Party vp nominee 8-27, 666F1
DYKES Jr., William R.
Freed in Beirut 2-25, 145C2
DYLAN, Bob
Wins Grammy 2-28, 460B3
Carter, Artis get new trial 3-17, 256G3
Carter quotes 7-15, 511A1
DYSON Shipping Co.
Boycott rpt released 10-19, 10-20; warned 10-20, 786C1, F1, B2
DYSON-Smith, Desmond
Sanctions banned masses 8-31, 691F3
DZHEMILEV, Mustafa
Trial, Sakharovs detained 4-14; sentncd 4-15, 292C1, F1
DZIEDZIC, Stan
Wins Olympic medal 7-31, 576D3

1977

DYER, Wayne W.
Erroneous Zones on best-seller list 2-6, 120F3; 3-6, 184F3; 4-3, 264G1; 5-1, 356C2; 6-4, 452A2; 7-3, 548E3; 8-14, 643G1; 9-4, 712D3; 10-2, 808E3; 11-6, 872E3; 12-4, 1021A3
DYES—*See CHEMICALS*
DYNALECTRON Corp.
Rpts forgn paymts 2-4, 94F1
DYNASTY (book)
On best-seller list 10-2, 808D3
DYSENTERY—*See MEDICINE—Diseases*
DZERZHINSKY, Felix Edmundovich (1877-1926)
100th birthday feted 9-9, 753F1
DZHEMILEV, Mustafa
Rptd freed 12-22, 1017B2

1978

DYER, Wayne W.
Erroneous Zones on best-seller list 1-8, 24F3; 3-5, 195F3; 4-2, 272D3; 4-30, 356B2
Pulling Your Own Strings on best-seller list 6-4, 460C3; 8-6, 620B2; 9-4, 708C1
DYES—*See CHEMICALS*
DYLAN, Bob
'Renaldo & Clara' released 1-25, 619D3
DYMALLY, Lt. Gov. Mervyn (D, Calif.)
Loses reelectn 11-7, 856F2
Guyana cult visit cited 11-21, 891G1
DYMO Industries Inc.
Pricel takeover foiled 5-12; Esselte, Daylin bid 5-15, 5-24, Esselte bid OKd 5-26, 404B1
DYNASTY (book)
On best-seller list 10-9, 800D3
DZHANIBEKOV, Lt. Col. Vladimir
Soyuz 27 docks with Salyut 1-11, 11C2
Returns to Earth 1-16, 157A3
DZUNDZA, George
Prayer For My Daughter opens 1-17, 760B3

1979

DYER, Jack
Teacher strike ends 3-12, 187C3
DYER, Wayne W.
Pulling Your Own Strings on best-seller list 10-14, 800D3; 11-4, 892D3
DYKSTRA, John
Battlestar Galactica released 5-17, 528C1
DYMSHITS, Mark Y.
Freed in spy swap 4-27; honored in NY, leaves for Israel 4-29; facts on 317B1, B2, E2
DZHEMILEV, Mustafa
Internal exile rptd 3-6, 172F2

1980

DYER, Wayne
Sky's the Limit on best-seller list 12-7, 948E3
DYLAN, Bob
Wins Grammy 2-27, 296B3
Lennon slain 12-8, 934D3
DYMALLY, Mervyn
Wins Calif US House primary 6-3, 439A2
Elected to US House 11-4, 842A2, 846B2, E3
DYSON, Royden
Elected to US House 11-4, 843B1, 848C2
DZHUMANAZAROV, Setymkul
Wins Olympic medal 8-1, 624E1

E

1976

EAC—*See EAST African Community*
EAGLE (U.S. sailing ship)
In Operation Sail, photo 7-4, 488F1, A3
EAGLEBURGER, Lawrence S.
2 censured for leaks 3-12, 198E2
Refutes Reagan chrg 3-31, 232F2
Criticizes GAO Mayaguez probe 10-5, 749G2
EAGLE Has Landed, The (book)
On best-seller list 12-5, 972G2
EAGLES (music group)
Wins Grammy 2-28, 460A3
EAGLETON, Sen. Thomas F. (D, Mo.)
Carter support slips 5-25, 373E3

EANES, Gen. Antonio Ramalho
Army to cut manpower 1-23, 143B3
Rpt backed Soares for pres 5-2, 366F3
Soares backs for pres 5-12, confrms candidacy 5-14, 366D3
Campaign dvpts 5-27—6-27, elected pres 6-27, to name Soares premr 6-28, 482B3-483C2
CP backs 7-7, 558E2
Sworn pres 7-14, mil chief 7-15; installs Soares, minority Cabt 7-23, 558A1
Swears army chief, warns vs mil politics 7-19, 558F2
Torture, pol arrests since '74 coup rptd 8-1, 733A2
Rpt leftists fear Spinola link 8-11, 733A1
Cncl sets membership rules 8-12, 733C2
Lourenco keeps mil post, cncl seat 8-12, 733E2
Blasts precede Oporto visit 9-3, 733D1
At Azores, Madeira assemb inaugurals 9-4, 10-23, 812F1, C2
EARHART, Walden Charles
Wins Nev Cong primary 9-14, 705C1
EARLY, Rep. Joseph D. (D, Mass.)
Reelected 11-2, 829B4
EARLY, Joseph P.
Ariz crime probe opens 10-2, 849D2
EARNSHAW, George
Dies 12-1, 1015C1
EARP, Brig. Dennis
Rpts 15 SWAPO killed 7-30, 654B3
EARTH
Ford State of Union message 1-19, 37G3, 39D2
US research budgeted 1-21, 64D2, A3
Dem platform text cites geothermal energy 6-15, 474B3, 475D1
Ford OKs geothermal funds 7-12, 517F2
GOP platform text 8-18, 607D2
GAO urges geothermal funding 8-24, 649B2, D2
EARTH, Wind and Fire (music group)
Wins Grammy 2-28, 460B3
EARTHQUAKE Information Service, National
Guatemala quake analysis rptd 2-7, 121A1
EARTHQUAKES
Quake hits Guatemala, Honduras, El Salvador, Mex 2-4, 81A1-D2
Guatemala tremors continue, death toll at 17,000 2-6—2-9, 120F2
Guatemala quake analysis rptd 2-7, 121A1
Guatemala death toll passes 22,000 2-11—2-22, 155F2
US vows more Guatemala aid 2-24, 178F1
US Cong clears Guatemala aid 4-13, 283B3
Ford signs relief aid 4-21, 982E1; 6-30, 533E2
Italy hit, Eur tremors rptd 5-6—5-11, 352F2
USSR Uzbek Republic hit 5-17, 404F2
Indonesia quakes kill 1,000 6-26—6-28, 7-14, 544G2
PI hit, thousands die 8-17, 619G1; death toll rptd 8-22, 638B3
Italy, Yugo hit 9-11—9-16, 756E1
New Guinea hit 10-29, 931E3
Iran, Philippines hit 11-7, 931F3
Cited re Sovt A-waste blast 11-17, 948D3
Turkey hit, US offers aid 11-24—11-28, 896F3; map 897A1
'76 activity evaluated 11-24, 897F1
'76 death toll rptd 11-27, 931G3

1977

EAC—*See EAST African Community*
EAGLEBURGER, Lawrence
Named amb to Yugo 5-13, confrmd 6-7, 499E3
EAGLE Forum
Rallies vs women's conf 11-19, 917G3
EAGLE Has Landed, The (film)
Top-grossing film 4-6, 264E1
EAGLETON, Sen. Thomas F. (D, Mo.)
On AF computer project cost 5-10, 421E3
Sen bars abortn amendmt 9-16, 738C1

EANES, Gen. Antonio Ramalho (Portuguese president)
Technocrats join Cabt 3-25, 330E2
Warns Soares re econ crisis 4-25, 330G2
Sees Mondale 5-16, 398A2
Land reform law OKd 9-17, 886B3
Oppositn ldr quits 11-7, 886D3
Soclst govt falls 12-8, 947F1
EARTH—*See GEOTHERMAL Energy*

EARTHQUAKES
'76 China deaths rptd 1-5, 120F2
'76 death toll rptd 1-20, 120E2
Richter scale revised 2-14, 161B3
Palmdale (Calif) bulge chng rptd 3-3, 288A2
Rumania hit 3-4, 204E1
Carter on water prjct cut 3-16, 210C1
Iran hit 3-22—3-23, 4-6, 312C2
Eastern Turkey hit 3-25, 286D3
Calif dam projct dropped 4-18, 299C3
Developing natns A-safety debated 5-3, 403B1
NRC vs Calif A-plant reopening 8-5, 838C2
Indonesian islands struck 8-19, 747A3
Italy quake relief scandal 8-27—9-8, 783B1
Va A-plant safety cover-up rptd 9-30, 838E1
Indian Pt (NY) A-plant found safe 10-12, 838F2
Argentina hit 11-23, 928D2
Iran hit 12-20, 1023C1

1978

E-Plane Series—*See ARMAMENTS—Aircraft*
EAGLES, The (singing group)
Wins Grammy 2-24, 315E3
EAGLETON, Sen. Thomas F. (D, Mo.)
Votes for Panama Canal neutrality pact 3-16, 177E2
Vs Turkish arms embargo end 4-5, 276E3
Votes for 2d Canal pact 4-18, 273B1
Backs Saudi plane deal 5-15, 357C2
Visits USSR 11-11—11-18, 905A2
EAMES, Charles
Dies 8-21, 708E2

EANES, Gen. Antonio Ramalho (Portuguese president)
Asks econ austerity, pvt sector recovery role 4-25, 331G2
Scores govt on soc, econ advances 5-28, 594B1
CDS asks anti-fascist bill veto 6-19, 593F3
Ends Neto mtg, OKs Angola cooperatn 6-26, 562A2
Soc Dems vow contd criticism 7-3, 594A1
Sees Giscard in Lisbon 7-19—7-21, 667B2
Fires Soares 7-27, seeks new govt 7-28—7-30, warns pol ldrs 8-1, 593E2-C3
Names da Costa premr designate 8-9, 632F2
Agrmt on Angola refugees rptd 8-10, 645F3
Da Costa sworn premr 8-28, 672A1
Da Costa govt falls 9-14; warns new electns 9-22, meets pol ldrs 9-26, 757E3
New electoral law passed 10-2, 777C3
Names Mota Pinto premr 10-25, 830C2
EARL, Johnrae
Dies 1-10, 96F1
EARLE 2nd, Ralph
Named chief SALT negotiator 10-20, 804A2
EARLY, Rep. Joseph D. (D, Mass.)
Reelected 11-7, 851C1
EARLY Dark (play)
Opens 4-25, 760A2
EARTH (planet)—*See also GEOTHERMAL Energy*
Moon mass rptd 623B2
Asteroid orbits rptd 3-12, 293D3
EARTH Day (1970)
Sun Day celebrated 5-3, 321C3

EARTHQUAKES
Japan hit 1-13—6-21, 479E3
2 jailed in Italy relief scandal 1-28, 103F3
'77 death toll rptd 1-29, 480G1
Calif, Wash, Aleutian I hit 3-11—6-3, 480F1
Greece hit 5-24, 6-19—6-21, 480A1
US disaster program ready 6-4, 480F1
US detectn equipmt sale to China rptd 6-9, 436G1
San Andreas Fault shift rptd 6-18, conclusn challenged 6-20, 480C1
Guatamala hit 7-29, 759C1
LNG safety measures urged 7-31, 610A1
Chile hit 8-3, 759B1
Ore, Calif A-plant protests 8-6—8-7, 609C3, E3
Santa Barbara (Calif) hit 8-13, 759B1
El Salvador hit 8-18, 759C1
Taiwan hit 9-1—9-6, '78 total rptd 9-6, 759C1
W Ger hit; tremors felt in France, Austria, Switz, E Ger 9-3, 758G3
Iran hit, 25,000 die 9-16, 9-26, 758D3

1979

E-Plane Series—*See ARMAMENTS–Aircraft*
EAGLE (U.S. Coast Guard sailing ship)
Coast Guard safety training faulted 1-20, 140F3
EAGLES (singing group)
Heartache Tonight on best-seller list 11-7, 892E3
Long Run on best-seller list 11-7, 892F3
EAGLETON, Sen. Thomas F. (D, Mo.)
Chrysler aid compromise set 12-19, 981G2

EANES, Gen. Antonio Ramalho (Portuguese president)
Links econ sacrifices to EC entry 1-1, 22D3
Accepts Mota Pinto resignatn 6-7, 427B2
Dissolves parlt, asks electns 7-13; names Pintassilgo caretaker premr 7-19, 545F2
Socialists lose assemb electns 12-2, 916G3
EARLE, Ralph
Cited in SALT II summit communique 6-18, 457D1
EARTH (planet)
Black hole at galaxy cntr seen 3-31, 290D1
EARTHLINE Corp.
US sues re NJ pollutn 2-7, 130B1

EARTHQUAKES
Iran hit 1-16, 140D2
'78 death toll rptd 1-25, 140F2-A3
5 US A-plants ordrd shut 3-13, 186E1-C2
Mexico City hit 3-14, 316G3
Yugoslavia, Albania hit 4-15, 316D3
NE quake, Maine A-plant unhurt 4-17, 323E1
Calif hit 5-7, 8-6, 619D3
Mex, Guatemala hit 6-23, 619F3
China quake kills 11 7-9, 619G3
Japan hit 8-12, 619G3
Indonesia hit 9-13, 800E2
Southn Calif, Mex hit 10-15, 799A2
Iran quake kills 248 11-14, 918B1
Midwest quake threat rptd 11-15, 954B1
Colombia quake kills 60 11-23, 912F2-A3

1980

EAGLEBURGER, Lawrence
On Carter absence from Tito funeral 5-7, 338C3
EAGLES (singing group)
Long Run on best-seller list 1-2, 40F3
Win Grammy 2-27, 296C3
EAGLESON, Alan
Canada Cup hockey tourn cancelled 4-30, 488B3
NHL players reject overtime 10-8, 1000E2
EAGLETON, Sen. Thomas F. (D, Mo.)
Wins Mo primary 8-5, 682E3
Niece, atty convicted in extortn scheme 10-24, 890C1
Reelected 11-4, 840D2, 845A3, 851F1
MX funds cut proposal rejected 11-21, 896D3

EANES, Gen. Antonio Ramalho (Portuguese president)
Clashes with Sa Carneiro 3-4—4-1, 277A2-C3
Vetoes new econ laws 4-11, 315G2
Soares gets AD pres nod 4-11, 315C3
Vetoes revised econ laws 5-21, 410A2
Carter sees 6-26, 475C1
Moves to end pilots' strike 7-14, 580E1
AD wins Assembly electn 10-5; Sa Carneiro sees defeat, responds 10-6, 760G1
Scores leftist policies 10-14; Soares quits Soclst post 10-19, 809C2
Stresses pol stability, Sa Carniero scores 11-21; Oporto hq stormed as pres campaign starts 11-22, 902G3
Suspends campaign re Sa Carneiro death 12-4, 923G1
Reelected 12-7, AD govt resigns, comments 12-8, 944A1, A2, D2
Names Pinto Balsemao premr 12-22, 995G3
EARLY, Rep. Joseph D. (D, Mass.)
Reelected 11-4, 843C1
EARNHARDT, Dale
Wins NASCAR Gr Natl title; top $ winner 11-15, 1002D1
2d in top driver vote 12-5, 1002E1
EARTH (planet)
Core study rptd 6-19, 715A2
EARTH Day '80
Celebrated natnwide 4-22, 307E3
EARTHLINE Corp.
NJ dump suit partly setld 1-30, 93G3

EARTHQUAKES
Azores Islands quake kills 52 1-1, 24E2
Northern Calif hit 1-24—1-27, 80E2
Washn volcanic quakes rptd 3-26, 252F1
US OKs PI A-reactor 5-6, 440F3
Mt St Helens erupts 5-18, 382D2
Algeria hit 10-10, 20,000 rptd dead 10-14, 775G3, 776F1
Mex hit 10-24, death toll rptd 10-26, 874F3—875B1
Southern Italy hit, map 11-23; death toll, devastatn rptd 11-24—11-28, 893A1-C2
Italy relief effort detailed, controversy sparked; death toll disputed 11-26—12-11, 943B2-944E1

1976

UN vs environmt manipulatn 12-10, 955D1
China—*See under CHINA*

EAST African Community (EAC) (Kenya, Tanzania, Uganda)
IBRD suspends loans; Uganda cited 5-11, 371F3
Kenya closes Nairobi RR hq 8-4, 974B3
Ry project rptd near collapse 9-12, 974A3
Tanzania, Kenya feud 12-7, 974E2-A3
Tanzania, Uganda OK airline paymts 12-14—12-16, 974A3
EAST Brunswick, N.J.—*See NEW Jersey*
EASTERN Airlines
'74 NC crash damages awarded 1-19, 80A2
'75 NY crash rpt 5-1, 736D2
'72 hijackers sentenced 7-16, 544C1
Borman heads honor code study 8-23, 670E2
'74 zero tax paymt rptd 10-2, 847G1

EASTERN Orthodox Churches
Hoxha upholds 'Albanianism' 3-17, 332A1
Coptic Orthodox Church
Ethiopia deposes patriarch 2-18, arrest rptd 3-1, 173D1
Greek Orthodox Church
Israel bars Capucci release 9-6, 662A3
Russian Orthodox Church
Archbp Nikon dies 9-4, 1015C2
Serbian Orthodox Church
Sup Ct rejects Ill ruling 6-21, 553B1
EASTEX Packaging Inc.—*See TIME Inc.*
EAST Germany—*See GERMAN Democratic Republic*
EAST Haddam, Conn.—*See CONNECTICUT*
EASTLAKE, O.—*See OHIO*
EASTLAND, Sen. James O. (D, Miss.)
Backed Bentsen in caucuses 1-24, 95A1
With Carter in Miss 9-17, 704E1, G2
EAST Rutherford, N. J.—*See NEW Jersey*
EAST Timor—*See TIMOR*
EASTWICK, Rawley
NL pitching ldr 10-4, 796A1
Reds win pennant 10-12, 796F1
EATON, Maj. Curtis Abbot
Vietnam rpts killed 9-6, 678B3
EBERT, Friedrich
E Ger Politburo enlarged 5-22, 381E2
EC—*See EUROPEAN Community*
ECCENTRICITIES of a Nightingale, The (play)
Opens 11-23, 1014F3

ECEVIT, Bulent
Blamed for student unrest 1-9, 192G2

1977

EAST African Airways
Folds 2-2, 88D1
Tanzania closes Kenya border 2-4, 106B1

EAST African Community (EAC) (Kenya, Tanzania, Uganda)
Airline dispute grows 1-18—1-31, flights end 2-1, 88D1
Kenya suspends Tanzania sports events 1-31, plans air svcs 2-3, 88F1
Tanzania closes Kenya border 2-4, 106C1
Tanzania shuts Kenya border permanently 4-18; Kenya cuts aviatn svcs 4-19, 392E3
Kenya-Tanzania mtgs rptd 5-18, 393B1
Kenya quits 6-30; Uganda, Tanzania set 3-mo funding 7-2, 573B1, A2 ★
Uganda employes ordrd home 7-30, 200 in Tanzania refuse 8-17, 641B2
Uganda repudiates debts, scores Kenya, Tanzania re assets 10-9, 805B2
EAST Cleveland, O.—*See OHIO*
EASTERN Air Lines Inc.
Attendants' weight standards OKd 3-3, 279F1
To lease European Airbus 5-24, 441B2
No-smoking seats to be added 6-14, 593G1
EASTERN College Athletic Conference (ECAC)—*See specific sport (e.g. HOCKEY, Ice)*
EASTERN Orthodox Churches
Dimitrios I, Coggan dispute women priests 5-1, 374D3
Uganda permits freedom 9-20, 805D2
Coptic Orthodox Church
Pope visits US, Canada 4-14, 471F2
Greek Orthodox Church
Makarios dies, Chrysostomos of Paphos named archbp 8-3, 616G3-617B2
Bishop Timotheos dies 12-14, 1024E3
Maronite Church
Makhlouf canonized 10-9, 845F3
Orthodox Church in America
Trifia suspended from NCC 2-4, 119F3
Conv picks 1st US ldr 10-24, 906F3
Rumanian Orthodox Church
Gafton rptd held in Rumania 3-3, 314E2
Russian Orthodox Church
Vs ordinatn of women 9-25, 845B3
EASTERN Provincial Airways
Pilots fined for '76 strike 2-16, 133E1
EAST Germany—*See GERMAN Democratic Republic*
EASTLAND, Sen. James O. (D, Miss.)
'76 special interest gifts rptd 1-15, 128F3, 129D1
Internal Security panel dies 3-31, 251G3
EASTMAN Kodak Co.
Kreps to quit post 1-10, 34B3
EAST River (N.Y.)
NYC clean-air case review declined 10-17, 797D3
EAST Tennessee Natural Gas Co.
FPC OKs emergency gas purchase 1-20, 54C1
EAST-West Shrine Game—*See FOOTBALL—Collegiate*
EASTWICK, Rawly
Traded to Cardinals 6-15, 644E2 ★
Signs with Yankees 12-9, 989F3
EASTWOOD, Edwin John
Kidnaps 15, arrested 2-14—2-15, 163C1
EATON, Col. Curtis A.
Body misidentified 3-23, 206G1
EATON, Gordon
Rpts on Kilauea volcano 9-28, 747E2
EATON Corp.
Seeks Carborundum purchase 10-28, Kennecott bid OKd 11-16, 880C1
EBAN, Abba
To run for premier 1-24, quits race 2-3, 135F1
Faces currency probe 4-23, denies misdeed 4-24, 329A3
EBERHART, Richard
Wins Natl Book Award 4-11, 355A2
EC—*See EUROPEAN Community*
ECCLES, Marriner S.
Dies 12-18, 1024D1
ECEVIT, Bulent
Sees US envoy 2-22, 122C2
Pol violence 4-28, 351D1
Party wins electn 6-5, 451C1
Forms govt 6-21; loses confidence vote, resigns 7-3, 530A2
Demirel forms govt 7-21, 565D1
Regrets Makarios death 8-4, 617B1
Demirel resigns 12-31, 1018F1

1978

EARTH, Wind, and Water (singing group)
All 'N' All on best-seller list 2-4, 116G3
EARTHWORMS—*See INSECTS*
EASTABROOK, Christine
City Sugar opens 6-5, 887D1

EAST African Community (EAC) (Kenya, Tanzania, Uganda)
Kenya, Uganda seek improved ties 2-8, 3-8—3-10, 289D2
EAST Dayton Tool & Die Co.
Union wins right to job data 11-3, 899B1
EASTERLY, Jamie
McCovey hits 500th homer 6-30, 560A1
EASTERLY, Tom
Wins US House primary in Ky 5-23, 406D2
Loses electn 11-7, 853B3
EASTERN Air Lines Inc.
'76 tax nonpaymt rptd 1-27, 65G2
Buys European Airbuses 4-6, 264B3
Mutual strike-aid pact quit 7-14, 681A1
Boeing 757s ordrd 8-31, 684F1
Natl merger sought 12-11, 1007B3
EASTERN Central Motor Carriers Association v. ICC
Case refused by Sup Ct 10-10, 789D3
EASTERN Europe—*See COMMUNISM & Communist Countries, EUROPE; also country, organization names*
EASTERN Illinois University (Charleston)
Loses NCAA Div II foootball title 12-9, 1025B2
EASTERN Michigan University (Ypsilanti)
Johnson in NFL draft 5-2, 336G3
EASTERN Orthodox Churches
'64 papal mtg cited 8-6, 601B2
Greek Orthodox Church
Turkey eases curbs 3-9, 216F2
Russian Orthodox Church
Nikodim dies 9-5, 778G1
EASTEX Inc.—*See under TIME Inc.*
EASTEX Inc. v. NLRB
Union pol organizing backed by Sup Ct 6-22, 508A3
EAST Germany—*See GERMAN Democratic Republic*
EASTLAND, Sen. James O. (D, Miss.)
Votes vs Panama Canal neutrality pact 3-16, 177F2
Votes vs 2d Canal pact 4-18, 273B1
Not standing for reelectn 6-6, 448C1
Dantin wins Sen nominatn 6-27, 510D1
Cochran wins seat 11-7, 582F2
Carter backs judges merit selectn 11-8, 873A3
EASTMAN Kodak Co.
In Dow Jones indl avg 66E2
Berkey wins trust suit 1-21, 67C1
Berkey damages awarded 3-22, 205B1
Berkey award reduced 7-3, 808E2
Lawyer pleads guilty 9-21, sentncd 10-17, 808C2
EAST Pakistan—*See BANGLADESH*
EAST Stroudsburg (Pa.) State College
Loses women's lacrosse title 5-28, 540C2
EAST Timor—*See INDONESIA*
EASTWICK, Rawly
Traded to Phillies 6-14, 779B3
EATHERLY, Claude R.
Dies 7-1, 620F2
EATON, William Orville (d. 1966)
Rowe indicted for '65 slaying 7-20, 720E2
EATON Corp.
Buys Tyco stake in Cutler 6-12, seeks takeover 6-26, 553A2, C2
EBASCO Services Inc.—*See ENSERCH Corp.*
EBEID, Fikry Makram
Egypt deputy premier 10-5, 774B3
EC—*See EUROPEAN Community*

ECEVIT, Bulent (Turkish premier)
Named premier 1-1; wins independents backing 1-2, plans Cabt expansn 1-5, 8A2
Announces govt priorities 1-4, 8C2
Names new Cabt 1-5, 21C2, D2
Speech sparks parlt unrest 1-15, 74G1
Wins confidence vote 1-17, 74E1, A2
Sees Denktash on Cyprus solutn 1-19, 148E1
Caramanlis OKs talks 1-23, 2-9, 170C2
Currency devalued 23% 3-1, 170A3
Eases curbs on Greek community 3-9, 216F2
In Caramanlis summit talks 3-10—3-11, oppositn scores 3-12, 216D2
Scores Vance arms aid, Cyprus link 3-10, summit stand rptd hardened 3-12, 216D3
Scores pol terrorism 3-24, 230B2
Warns US on defense ties 3-24, 230E2
Threatens NATO exit 3-29, US moves to lift arms embargo 3-29—4-6, 276B2
Greeks postpone talks 4-11, 277E1
Malatya mayor, family killed in bombing 4-17, 291E3
Supporters attacked at Igdir 4-23, 378E2
USSR proposes arms aid 4-26, 477F1
Scores US setback in moves to lift arms embargo 5-11, 378E1
In W Eur: gets W Ger aid pledge; bars Cyprus mediatn, warns NATO 5-15—5-17, 398E2, A3
Demirci party hq burned 5-27, 477A1
Backs USSR visit, goodwill treaty 5-29, 397D2

1979

EARTH, Wind and Fire (singing group)
Best of Earth, Wind & Fire on best-seller list 1-10, 80F3
Wins Grammy 2-16, 336F3
I Am on best-seller list 7-4, 548F3
EASON, William Edward
Sentncd in GSA kickback scandal 4-7, 367B3
EAST Baton Rouge School Board v. Davis
Case refused by Sup Ct 1-15, 32E1
EASTER, Luke
Killed in holdup 3-29, 1002E3
EASTERLING, Rita
East wins WBL All-Star game, named game MVP 3-14, 507G1
EASTERN Air Lines Inc.
Natl Airlines merger bids OKd 7-10; TXI quits race 7-28, Pan Am buys TXI shares in Natl 8-2, 578G3
Canada discount fares halted 8-30, 667F2
Natl merger bid rejected 9-27, 830B1
EASTERN Kentucky University (Richmond)
Wins NCAA Div 1-AA football title 12-15, 1001F2

EASTERN Orthodox Churches
Baptism rites agrmt reached 3-31, 375F2
Runcie named Anglican ldr 9-7, 755G2
Pope in US, holds ecumenical prayer svc 10-7, 760A1
Pope in Turkey, seeks RC reunificatn 11-28—11-30; sees Dimitrios I 11-29, joint statemt issued 11-30, 930A3
Greek Orthodox Church
Eased divorce law opposed 2-19, 135G3
Zimbabwe archbp's home attacked 7-4, 546F3
Russian Orthodox Church
US groups rptd backing emigratn 2-26, 172F2
Priest arrested in Moscow 11-1, 856A3
EAST Grand Forks, Minn.—*See MINNESOTA*
EASTMAN Kodak Co.
In Dow Jones indl avg 72E1
Berkey award reversed 6-25, 517C2-A3
Antitrust suit filed by Argus 8-28, 986C1
EASTMAN School of Music (Rochester, N.Y.)
Hanson in Arts Institute 12-7, 1005A3
EASTON, Md.—*See MARYLAND*
EAST Pakistan—*See BANGLADESH*
EAST Texas State University (Commerce)
Johnson in NBA draft 6-25, 507B3
EAST Timor—*See INDONESIA*
EASTWOOD, Clint
Escape from Alcatraz released 6-21, 820B1
EASTWOOD, Jayne
One Man released 7-27, 820E2
EATON, Cyrus S.
Dies 5-9, 432E2
EBAN, Abba
Vs Nablus mayor deportation 11-14, 881C3
EBENEZER Baptist Church (Atlanta, Ga.)
Carter marks King death anniv 1-14, 31A3
EC—*See EUROPEAN Community*

ECEVIT, Bulent (Turkish premier; resigned Oct. 16)
Interior min resigns; cites forgn origins of terrorism 1-2, 8C1
Censure motion fails 1-4, 7G3
Defense min quits; new defense, interior mins named 1-14, 40F2
At Milliyet editor's funeral 2-4, 117A1
Martial law extended 2 mos 2-25, 214G2
Econ rescue plan announced 3-16, goals listed 3-21, 214D1
On govt strike ban 3-29, 333D2
Cabt dispute resolved 4-17, 287D3
3 MPs quit party 4-23, 397D2
Martial law renewed, extended 4-25, 333E1
In US base talks 5-7, 5-8, 397A3
Rebuts businessmen's chrgs 5-13, 398E1
On US U-2 flights 5-15, 397C3
Union ldrs rptd freed 5-22, 398G1
Reelectn as party chrmn rptd 5-28, 397G3-398B1
Turkey aid package set 5-30, 397D2
Devaluatn, other austerity steps set 6-12, 447A1
Opposes U-2 flights 6-27, 488E2
Parlt recesses after oppositn moves fail 6-28, 488F1-B2
In Egypt Emb raid talks 7-13, 536F2
Martial law extended 8-21, 637B2
Probes Kurdish unrest 8-23, 795E3
Mins chrgd re Lockheed bribe role 9-20, 775A2

1980

EARTH Resources Co.
Mapco merger set 12-5, 985E1
EARTH Wind and Fire (singing group)
Win Grammys 2-27, 296D3
EAST, John P.
Elected to US Sen 11-4, 840F2, 845A2, 849F3
EAST African Community (EAC) (Kenya, Tanzania, Uganda)
Mtg fails to revive 1-2, 90E1
EASTERN Air Lines Inc.
Coast-to-coast svc set 6-1; fares cut 6-6, hiked 7-1, 516B2, C2
Jet hijacked to Cuba 8-16, 631C3
Cuban hijack attempt foiled 8-18, 667F1-A3
EASTERN Associated Coal Corp.
W Va miners strike 2-21—3-3, 170A1
EASTERN Illinois University (Charleston)
Loses NCAA Div II football title game 12-13, 999G2
EASTERN Kentucky University (Richmond)
Loses NCAA Div I-AA football title game 12-20, 999B3

EASTERN Orthodox Churches
Greek Orthodox Church
Benedictos I dies 12-10, 1004A1
Russian Orthodox Church
Moscow priest rptd arrested 1-15, 46F3
Moscow priest recants 6-20, 500E1
Syrian Orthodox Church
Patriarch Yacoub dies 6-25, 528G3
EASTERN Virginia Medical School (Norfolk, Va.)
'Test-tube baby' clinic OKd 1-8, 24F1, A2
EASTLAND, James O.
5th judicial circuit split 10-14, 918D3
EASTMAN Kodak Co.
In Dow Jones indl avg 76E1
Film product prices hiked 1-8, 31A1
Berkey trust appeal refused by Sup Ct 2-19, 130F3
EC textile duties rptd 5-6, 412A1
EC polyester duties set 9-1, 662F2
EAST Timor—*See INDONESIA*
EASTWOOD, Clint
Bronco Billy released 6-11, 675A2
Any Which Way You Can released 12-17, 1003F1
EATON, Rev. David
Scores conservative Christian ldrs 4-29, 349B1
EATON, Linda
Wins breast-feeding case 3-20, 442A1
EATON-Merz Laboratories
FTC chrgs misleading birth control ads, complaint setld 2-28, 358F2
EAVES, Jerry
Louisville wins NCAA basketball title 3-24, 240C2
EBAN, Abba
Visits Egypt 11-7—11-9, 863F2
EBENEZER Baptist Church (Atlanta, Ga.)
Carter addresses members 9-16, 698A2
EBERLE, Emilia
Wins Olympic medal 7-25, 623A1
EBERT, Joyce
Watch on the Rhine opens 1-3, 136F3
EBONY (magazine)
Reagan sees editors 8-5, 597B3
EC—*See EUROPEAN Community*
ECCLESTONE, Bernie
Rival Gr Prix circuit set 10-31, 1002C1

ECEVIT, Bulent
Mil warns pol ldrs, urges unity 1-2, 7C2
Backs coalitn govt 1-9, 22D3
Scores govt 2-14, 135E2
Pres electn deferred 3-22, 236F1
Pres voting chng barred 5-24—5-25, 411A1
Scores govt re terrorism 5-30, 445C3
Party offcl killed 6-17, 468C2
Demirel clarifies U-2 stand 7-4, 526D1
Scores govt re Fatsa move 7-11, 544C3
Lauds Erim 7-19, 567D3
Backs coalitn govt 7-21, 567G3
Anti-terrorist bills set 7-24, 580A3, C3
Arrested 9-12, 696E2
Freed 10-11, 793D3
Resigns party post 10-30, 832B3

1976

ECHAVARRIA, Octavio
Kidnaped 3-20, found dead 3-25, 251C2
ELN scores murder 4-18, 311G1
ECHEGOYEN, Vice Commodore Roberto
Kidnap rptd 5-5, 399A1
Killed 7-10, 571G1
ECHEVERRIA Alvarez, Luis
'75 Ford letter on drugs rptd 1-19, 61G1
Sees Canada prime min 1-24—1-26, 116E2
Lopez Portillo elected pres 7-4, 498G1
Cited re Excelsior ousters 7-11, 7-14, denies role 7-14, 620D2, G2
Carter disavows dumping memo 8-13, 616F3
Sets anti-inflatn measures 9-1, defends peso float 9-7, 694D2, C3
Orders La Paz dam probe 10-1, 840E2
UN post chances rptd 10-5, sets bid 11-29, 906D3; loses bid 12-7, 914D2
Signs peasant land deeds 11-30, 906D3
Lopez Portillo sworn pres 12-1; Reyes Heroles, interior min 12-2, 906C3, F3
ECKERSLEY, Dennis
AL pitching ldr 10-4, 796D1
ECKERT, Baerbel
Wins Olympic medal 7-28, 576G1
ECKHARDT, Rep. Bob (D, Tex.)
Reelected 11-2, 830C4
ECKSTEIN, Alexander
Dies 12-4, 1015D1
ECLIPSE, Solar
Observed from Australia 10-23, 808B2
ECONOMIC Club (Pittsburgh)
Ford scores Carter 10-26, 802G3
ECONOMIC Club of Detroit (Mich.)
Bailar addresses 3-8, 186C3
Ford addresses 5-12, 343D1
Reagan addresses 5-14, 356F3
Carter addresses 10-15, 785F1
ECONOMIC Community of West African States (ECOWAS)(Benin, Gambia, Ghana, Guinea, Guinea-Bissau, Ivory Coast, Liberia, Mali, Mauritania, Niger, Nigeria, Senegal, Sierra Leone, Togo, Upper Volta)
Ratification rptd 11-6, 974D2
ECONOMIC Cooperation, Conference on International (North-South conference)
4 comms map plans 2-11—2-20, 148B1
Talks deadlocked 7-8—7-10, 7-12—7-17, 530C1
Venez scores Sovt absence 11-26, 929G3
Delays meeting 12-9, 976F3
ECONOMIC Priorities, Council on (N.Y.)
Issues business payoffs rpt 12-18, 985E1
ECONOMIST, The (magazine)
On US, Sovt naval comparisons 5-15, 394C3
ECONOMY (non-U.S.)—*See also COMMODITIES, MONETARY Developments and other economic headings; also specific country, group (e.g., EC) and commodity names*
OECD issues Italy econ rpt 1-26, 74A3
Balkan natns meet 1-26—2-5, 213E3
UNCTAD Manila conf ends 2-10, 107G3
27-natn conf 2-11—2-20, 148B1
Ford seeks curbs on CIA spying 2-18, 127A2
Johan Beyen dies 4-29, 368E2
UNCTAD Nairobi conf opens 5-5, 320E1
Kissinger addresses UNCTAD 5-6, 317A1-318G1
France for new world order 5-19, 372D2
Eur, Latin soc dems meet 5-23—5-25, 449F2-C3
OPEC holds price freeze 5-28, 389D1
UNCTAD OKs commodity fund 5-30, 388E2
2d 7-natn summit set 6-1, 6-3, 388F3
7-natn export credit terms tightened 6-9, 6-15, 529C3
OECD sets growth rate goal 6-22, 450B2
7 natn summit 6-27—6-28, 461F2-482C3; repercussns 7-16—7-19, 530D3; 7-20, 557A1
Nonaligned conf warns rich natns 8-20, 621F2
Mondale campaign topic 9-26, 725A1
IMF-World Bank mtgs stress inflatn fight, poor natn aid 10-4—10-5, 777A1
UN rpt sees world econ growth 10-13, 760D1
OECD sees '77 growth slowdown 11-22—11-23, 975F3
Soclst Intl cong 11-26—11-28, 935B3, E3
Giscard asks 3d summit 12-2, 964D1
OECD rpts Oct '75-76 prices, inflatn rate 12-6, 976A1
UN Assemb pres warns 12-22, 955A1
'76 intl borrowing peak rptd 12-22, 976F1
U.S. Presidential Campaign Issue
US Dem platform text 6-15, 476G1, 478B1
US GOP platform text 8-18, 611B1
Carter briefed 8-18, 617B2

1977

ECHAZU, Col. Jorge
Anti-Banzer plot foiled 12-9, 1009F3
ECHEVERRIA, Juan Martin
Venez justice min 1-7, 23F2
ECHEVERRIA Alvarez, Luis
Cts to resolve land dispute 1-3, 65G2, E3
CIA payments rptd 2-19, 124F1
'76 land seizures backed 5-4, 528F1
Named roving amb 5-16, 529A3; UNESCO envoy 7-8, 563A1
Rpt Lopez eased US tension 8-28, 746C2
ECHEVERRI Correa, Fabio
Scores govt econ policies 9-30, 1011E1
ECKERD, Jack M.
Replaced at GSA 2-15, 148F3
ECKERSLEY, Dennis
Pitches no-hitter 5-30, 644F1
AL pitching ldr 10-2, 927A1
ECKHARDT, Rep. Bob (D, Tex.)
On assassination com 2-1, 77F1
ECLA—*See UNITED Nations—Latin America, Economic Commission for*
ECOLOGY—*See ENVIRONMENT*
ECONOMIC Advisers, President's Council of—*See under U.S. GOVERNMENT*
ECONOMIC Club of New York
Levesque addresses 1-25, 81D3
ECONOMIC Cooperation, Conference on International (North-South conference)
Schmidt-Andreotti talks 1-17—1-18, 65A1
Saudis tie oil prices, conf progress 2-6, 107D3
Austria-US talks 3-14, 425F1
UNCTAD talks impasse rptd 4-4, 298B1
7-natn summit backs talks 5-7—5-8, 357C2
Talks end, summary 6-3, 437F1
UN Assemb '76 mtg debate ends 9-19, 713C1
Waldheim sees contd deadlock 9-19, 713F1
Sweden cancels poor natn debts 10-12, 903F3
ECONOMIC Development Administration—*See under U.S. GOVERNMENT—COMMERCE*
ECONOMIC Policy Group—*See under U.S. GOVERNMENT*
ECONOMICS & Econometrics
Oskar Morgenstern dies 7-26, 604D3
Jacob Marschak dies 7-27, 604D3
E F Schumacher dies 9-4, 788D2
ECONOMIC & Social Council—*See under UNITED Nations*
ECONOMIST, The (magazine)
Singapore correspondent arrested 2-15, 223D3
ECONOMY (non-U.S.)—*See also MONETARY Developments and other economic headings; also specific country, group (e.g., EC) and commodity names*
Mondale plans summit talks 1-8, 14E2
Mondale on W Eur, Japan trip 1-23, 2-1, 2-2, 69E1, F1-B2
'77 EC growth rate forecast 1-28, 74D1
OECD rpts Dec '75-76 inflatn 2-7, 87A2
UN rpts '76 commodity price rise 2-14, 145F3
Asia '76 growth rptd up 2-16, 147A2
IMF '76 lending sets record 3-7, 209A1
Carter addresses UN 3-17, 185C1, B2, 186F1
Bilderberg conf 4-21—4-24, 359B3
7-natn London summit 5-7—5-8, 357A1-358B2
Carter hails London summit 5-12, 381G1
Mil spending, GNP data rptd by NATO 5-17, 379F3
BIS rpts on intl situatn 6-12, 502E1
'76 US investmts abroad rptd up 8-29, 669D1
IMF annual rpt 9-11, 700C2
Rich, poor nations' econ growth rptd 9-18, 717A3
IMF, World Bank mtgs stress econ recovery, world trade 9-26—9-30, 753C2
Energy conservatn seen compatible with econ growth 10-5—10-6, 794C1
Nobel won by Ohlin, Meade 10-14, 951E3
'75 world pay, buying power survey rptd 11-6, 853C3
OECD urges stimulus, sees '78 slowdown 12-27, 999A1

1978

Sees Caramanlis in US, more talks set 5-29; confers with Carter 3-31, 398B2
In Moscow, signs pacts 6-21—6-23; West reassured 6-24, 6-30, 595F1
USSR shifts Cyprus policy 6-25, 595F2
Aegean talks resume 7-4—7-6, 624B1
Praises Comert 7-11, 595D3
Police assns dissolutn order rptd overturned 7-20, 595E3
On US arms embargo end 8-2, 587G3
Warns West on aid rise 11-4, 905G2
Says right foments riots 12-26, 1021F1
ECHAVE, Juan Jose
Wounded in ambush, wife killed 7-3, 537E2
ECHAVE, Rosario
Killed 7-3, rioters protest 7-5, 537E2, G2
ECHAZU, Jorge
Bolivia mines min 11-24, 913E1
ECHEVERRIA, Juan Jose
Named CR interior min 3-4, 171A1
ECHEVERRIA Alvarez, Luis
Ex-aide seized for corruptn 3-21, 289A3
Ex-aide free on bail 4-21, 518B1
Mex pres in China 10-24—10-30, 903D3
ECKERD, Jack M.
Wins primary for Fla gov 9-12, 736D1
Loses electn 11-7, 849C3
ECKERSLEY, Dennis
Traded to Red Sox 3-30, 779C3
AL pitching ldr 10-2, 928G3
ECKHARDT, Rep. Bob (D, Tex.)
Reelected 11-7, 852A3
ECOLOGY—*See ENVIRONMENT*
ECONOMIC Advisers, President's Council of—*See under U.S. GOVERNMENT*
ECONOMIC Club of New York
Trudeau addresses 3-23, 225F2
ECONOMIC Community of West African States (ECOWAS) (Benin, Gambia, Ghana, Guinea, Guinea-Bissau, Ivory Coast, Liberia, Mali, Mauritania, Niger, Nigeria, Senegal, Sierra Leone, Togo, Upper Volta)
6 W African natns back 3-18, USSR scores 3-20, 237E1
ECONOMICS & Econometrics
Pupil competency tests rptd 5-9, 348A3
Simon wins Nobel 10-16, 886C1, G2-B3
Obituaries
Harrod, Roy 3-8, 252A3
Lubin, Isador 7-6, 620A3
Rueff, Jacques Leon 4-23, 356D3
Shiskin, Julius 10-28, 888E3
ECONOMIC & Social Council (ECOSOC)—*See under UNITED Nations*
ECONOMOU, Arthur N.
US offcls' legal immunity defined by Sup Ct 6-29, 567B2
ECONOMY (non-U.S.)—*See also MONETARY Developments and other economic headings; also country, group (e.g., EC) and commodity names*
Glossary of terms 50A1
Carter State of Union Message 1-19, 29B2, A3, 31A1, F2
UK prime min urges Bonn summit plan 3-14, sees Carter 3-23, 226G2
EC sets united econ policy, 4-5% growth rate 4-7—4-8, 257G2
Japan asks US inflatn curbs 5-3, 341B3
Oil shortage link studied 6-5, 449E3 ★, G3, 450A2, F2
Australia urges intl cooperatn 6-5, 450D3
OPEC maintains price freeze, '79 hike seen 6-19, 465F1, A2
Comecon forced econ integratn proposal fails 6-27—6-29, 504G3
7-natn Bonn summit 7-16—7-17, 543B3-544C3, 546A1
'77 top per capita GNPs ranked 7-18, 624C1
Latin '77 econ rated poor by IDB 9-10, 828D2-A3
June '77-78 world inflatn rates ranked 10-18, 914E1

1979

Housing min resigns 9-29, 775C2
US base extensn set 10-8, 796A1
Loses electns 10-14, resigns 10-16, 795G2
Demirel govt formed 11-12, 876D1

ECHANDIA, Dario
Scores mil power 11-14, 993F1
ECHEVERRIA, Juan Jose
Defends Civil Guard arms 3-23, 238G1
US AF unit lands 7-8, ordrd out 7-10, 512G2, A3
ECHOCARDIOLOGY—*See MEDICINE–Heart*
ECK, Theodore R.
On US gas shortfall 5-7, 343D1
ECKERSLEY, Dennis
AL pitching ldr 9-30, 955F3, G3
ECKHARDT, Rep. Bob (D, Tex.)
Wins Commerce oversight subcom chair 1-30, 86F3
On chem dump sites 11-1, 886B1
ECKSTEIN, Otto
McGraw-Hill buys Data Resources 8-28, 682G3
ECOLOGY—*See ENVIRONMENT*
ECONOMIC Advisers, Council on—*See under U.S. GOVERNMENT*
ECONOMIC Club of Chicago
Kahn scores business on prices 3-13, 182B1
ECONOMIC Research, National Bureau of
Recessn defining role cited 33C3
ECONOMICS & Econometrics
2 win Nobel Prize 10-17, 858G1-B2
Obituaries
Jacoby, Neil H 5-31, 432A3
Ohlin, Bertil 8-3, 671B3
Tugwell, Rexford Guy 7-21, 588E3
ECONOMIC & Social Council (ECOSOC)—*See under UNITED Nations*

ECONOMY (non-U.S.)
GDP, other econ terms defined 33A1
EC rpts '78 inflatn 7.3% 1-8, 13B1
EC '78 living standards ranked 2-2, 109G1
Carter Westn econ summit warning rptd 2-10, rpt disputed 2-15, 160E1
W Eur growth forecast 3-13, 180A2
Pope presents 1st encyclical 3-15, 217B1, D1
7-natn indicators index rptd 6-11, 513G1
Tokyo 7-natn summit, OPEC price hike impact feared 6-28–6-29, 493D1
OECD predicts slowdown 7-19, 554E2
'78 GNP per capita ranked 7-24, 575C3
OECD rpts 1st 1/2 inflatn 8-9, 627B1
IMF sees stagflatn, paymts problems in '79, '80 9-16, 719F3-720D1

1980

ECHANDIA, Dario
Leftists ask Panama mtg 4-19, 311G2
ECHEVERRIA, Gen. Hugo
Coup plot fails, retains command 3-23, 272A2
ECKERT Jr., J. Presper
Mauchly dies 1-8, 104B3
ECKHARDT, Rep. Bob (D, Tex.)
Scores SEC natl securities mkt plan failure 9-12, 806E1
Loses reelectn 11-4, 837E1, 846F1, 850A2
ECLIPSE Awards—*See HORSE Racing*
ECOLOGY—*See ENVIRONMENT*
ECONOMIC Advisers, Council of—*See under U.S. GOVERNMENT*
ECONOMIC Alternatives, National Center for
Small business study rptd 1-13, 455B3
ECONOMIC Club of Detroit
Reagan addresses 5-15, 383B1
Bush addresses 9-19, 781B1
ECONOMIC Development Administration (EDA)—*See under U.S. GOVERNMENT--COMMERCE*
ECONOMIC Research, National Bureau of
Recessn since Jan rptd 6-3, 424F3
ECONOMICS & Econometrics
Economists react to Carter anti-inflatn plan 3-17, 202G1
Nobel announced 10-15, 890A1
Obituaries
Colean, Miles Lanier 9-16, 755F2
Okun, Arthur 3-23, 280D1
ECONOMIC & Social Council (ECOSOC)
See under UNITED Nations
ECONOMIC & Social Research, National Institute of
UK econ downturn predicted 3-3, 172E2
ECONOMIST, The (magazine)
Spooner arrested in Bolivia 8-6, Harvey negotiates release 8-12, 668D1

ECONOMY (non-U.S.)
GDP, other econ terms defined 34B1
Pacific orgn studied 1-20, 78B2
World wide purchasing power rated 2-12, 125D3
OECD rpts '79 inflatn 2-13, 125B3
OECD issues '80 forecasts; backs inflatn curbs, free trade 6-3—6-4, 422D1
Venice 7-natn summit 6-22—6-23, 473A1-474E1
IMF rpts grim econ outlook 6-24, 477D2
World Bank '80 forecast grim; Africa, S Asia seen hardest hit 8-17, 628E2
GATT links inflatn, global trade lag 9-16, 695C3
World Bank, IMF set more poor natn aid 9-30, 761B2-762A1
Islamic econ conf 11-4—11-6, 865B1
Beagle Channel accord proposed 12-12, 978E3

ECONOMY (U.S.)

1976

ECONOMY (U.S.)—*See also AGRICULTURE, BANKS, BUSINESS, COMMODITIES, LABOR, TAXES; BUDGET and other economic headings under U.S. GOVERNMENT; also industry names*
Ford record cited 614F1
'33 depressn emergency ended 9-14, 689B2
Clean air amendmts not cleared 10-2, 883C2
Friedman wins Nobel 10-14, 839G3
'60-75 consumer spending rptd 11-23, 959F1

1977

ECONOMY (U.S.)—*See also BUSINESS, LABOR, TAXES; BUDGET and other economic headings under U.S. GOVERNMENT; also industry names*
Nov-Dec '76 consumer confidence rptd 1-9, 38F1
CEA rpt to Cong 1-18, 35E3
Dec '76 indicators index rptd; index described 1-28, 92F2, C3; **for subsequent data, see BUSINESS—Statistics**
Giaimo proposes budget 3-23, 228D3
Carter studies local dvpt reorganizatn 6-29, 499G2

1978

ECONOMY (U.S.)—*See also BUSINESS, LABOR, TAXES; also BUDGET and other economic headings under U.S. GOVERNMENT; also industry names*
Glossary of terms 50A1
London Times scores Carter policies 1-4, 27B3
Black-white gap rptd widening 8-8, 810E3-811A1
Carter Anti-Inflation Plan
Carter readies anti-inflatn program 10-10, 766F2

1979

ECONOMY (U.S.)
Glossary of terms 33A1
Carter Econ Message, CEA rpt 1-25, 48C2-49A2
Economists on '29 Depression, '80s forecast 10-29, 11-1, 826D3-827D2
Connally campaign themes cited 11-15, 983A1
Carter Anti-Inflation Plan
Final rules set, Wage-Price Stability Cncl surveillance broadened 1-3, 4E3
Gulf oil workers settle within guides 1-11, 87B1

1980

ECONOMY (U.S.)
Glossary of terms 34B1
Carter Econ Message, CEA rpt 1-30, 74B1
Carter Anti-Inflation Plan
Carter unveils 5-pt plan, stresses fed spending cuts, bars wage-price controls 3-14; Cong, other reactn 3-14—3-18, 201A1-203C3
FRB money mkt rule contested 3-20, 223F2, 224A1
Russel sees continued inflatn 3-25, 222C2

1976

Gross National Product (GNP)
'75 health cost share rptd 1-15, 32F1
'46-75 GNP revised 1-16, 89B3-90E1; tables 89F1, 90A1
'75, 4th ¼; 3d ¼ revised 1-20, 89D1
'77 budget forecast 1-21, 63A1, D3
Ford Econ Rpt 1-26, 67C1, E1
'75 4th ¼ revised 2-19, 168E1
Cong com scores Ford econ plans 3-10, 230A3
4th ¼ '75 real GNP revised 3-19, 1st ¼ rptd 4-19, 278F3-279G1
Cong OKs '77 US budget targets 5-12, 5-13, 358G1
1st ¼ data revised 5-20, 396C1
Dem platform text 6-15, 469B2
Admin forecast updated 7-16, 535G3
2d ¼ rate, 1st ¼ revised 7-20, 536D1-A2
Carter seeks tax share stabilizatn 7-28, 551A1
Dow reactn to 2d ¼ revisn 8-19—8-20, 846F3
3d ¼ rate, 2d ¼ revised 10-19, 805E1-E2
Ford, Carter debate 10-22, 800F1
3d ¼ rate revised down 11-18, 866G1

1977

Gross National Product (GNP)
Ford '78 budget proposals 1-17, 30B2, F2
CEA projcts '77 growth rate 1-18, 36E1
'76, 4th ¼ rptd, 3d ¼ revised 1-18, 56F1
Blumenthal on hike as intl aid 1-28, 92D2
CBO questns Carter goals 2-15, 126F1
Carter budget revisions 2-22, 124F3
Giaimo proposes budget 3-23, 228F3
1st ¼ rptd, '76 4th ¼ revised 4-20, 299G3
'77 real GNP forecast revised 4-22, 408A1
'77 growth goal set 5-7—5-8, 357C1
Mil spending, GNP data rptd by NATO 5-17, 379F3
'77 real GNP forecast revised 7-1, 518F3
2d ¼ rate rptd, 1st ¼ revised 7-21, 553F2
Cong forecasts re '78 budget levels 9-15, 719F2
3d ¼ rate rptd, 2d ¼ revised 10-19, 798B1

1978

Carter unveils anti-inflatn plan, voluntary controls 10-24, names Kahn to head 10-25; reactn 10-24—10-26, 805B2-807B1
ABC-Harris poll rptd 10-24, 807B1
Carter seeks progrm cooperatn 10-26, 831A2
Meany scores Carter plan, backs mandatory controls 10-31, 11-5; Marshall, Kahn comment 10-31, 11-5, 863G1-G2
Costle to head Carter Regulatory Cncl 10-31, 863A3
Carter advisers hold St Louis forum 11-1, 863G2-C3
Carter gives priority 11-2, 11-6, 862D1, E1, A2
Carter bars mandatory controls 11-6, 862F1
Carter defends plan, scores Hershey price hike 11-9, 875B1
Steel cos back price guidelines 11-9, US Steel hikes prices 11-14, 1006C1
Kahn sees depressn if plan fails 11-15, Carter comments 11-16, 11-30, 917C3
OECD backs plan 11-17, 918A1
Carter asks business price compliance 11-19, 934C3
Hershey price hike OKd 11-20, 917G3
Plan off to slow start; guidelines, mgt problems cited 11-21, 11-30, 917E2
Oil, machinists union ldrs rptd vs wage curb 11-21, 917B3
Women's group protests impact 11-22, 915E1
RRs trim rate hike request to 7% 11-24, ICC OKs 6½% hike 12-11, 1007A3
Carter seeks mayors cooperatn 11-27, support pledged 11-29, 914C3, F3
Trucking freight-rate hike voided 11-27, 1007E2
Ill, Ohio pay hikes voted 11-29; Carter angry 12-1, Kahn asks rollback 12-4, 934F3-935C1
Carter prefers 1 term to plan failure 11-30, 917F3
Paper union sues to void plan 12-1, 934B2
AT&T, GM vow price compliance 12-1, 934G2
Schultze: VAT fuels inflatn 12-3, 962E2
Blacks score budget plans 12-4, 936A3
Dem midterm conf debate 12-8—12-10, plan backed 12-10, 956D1-B3
CWA pres scores Meany 12-11, 960F3
Carter vs consumer boycotts of wage-price violators 12-12, 957B1
Wage-price rules revised 12-13, 957E1-C3
Chicago offcls OK pay hike cut 12-13, 957C3
Kahn scores OPEC price hike 12-17, 978B1
Fastener indus price compliance cited 12-26, 999A1
Hospital cost guide set 12-28, 1012F1

Gross National Product (GNP)
GNP, GDP defined 50D2
'77, 4th ¼ rptd; 3d ¼ revised 1-19, 49C3-50G1
Carter budget forecast 1-23, 44E3, 46B2
1st ¼ GNP rptd, '77 4th ¼ revised 4-19, 303A3
'77 link to energy use rptd down 4-20, 282B2
'75-78 GDP income rank rptd 5-12, 384E3
'78, '79 real growth forecast revised 7-6, 506D2
CBO rpts on Propositn 13 impact 7-6, 525F2
Economists see slowed '78, '79 growth 7-7, 506E3
'77 per capita GNP ranked 5th 7-18, 624E1
2d ¼ GNP rptd, 1st ¼ revised 7-21, 606E2
IMF asks slower rise 9-25, Blumenthal backs 9-26, 731C3
Trade % of GNP rptd 9-26, 804D2
Humphrey-Hawkins bill cleared, sets goal re fed share 10-15, 808F1
3d ¼ rptd, 2d ¼ revised 10-20, 863D3
Carter vows to cut fed spending share 10-24, '76 share cited 805C3
Muskie sees Carter budget problems 12-14, 980C1

1979

Rail clerk setlmt exceeds guides 1-13, 87A2
State of Union Message 1-23, 46D3, F3, 47F1, A2
Carter vs controls 1-23, 47D1
'Real wage insurnc' credit plan opposed in Cong 1-23, 55C3
Paper mill setlmts rptd 1-30–5-9, 345A3
URW bars wage-guide contract limit 2-2–5-9; seeks ct ruling 5-2, hearing set 5-4, 344B1-345A2
Farmers protest in DC 2-5–2-6, 109G2
GAO, Library of Cong call contract denial illegal 2-5, 2-12; Admin vs 2-5, 127B3
Compliance vow by 207 big cos rptd 2-6, gen business reactn noted 2-12, 127F3
Carter sees success, urges hosp cost curbs, 'real wage insurnc' 2-12, 109D3
Hosp cost plan faces cong hurdles 2-13, 110D1; bill sent to Cong 3-5, 163A2; **for subsequent developments, see MEDICINE–Hospitals**
AFL-CIO maps plans 2-19–2-22, 148E2-E3
NYSE employe setlmt within guides 2-21, 23D1
Insurnc guidelines disputed 2-24, 264A3
Teamsters issue demands 3-6, Kahn warns 3-15; guidelines strike called, industry locks out 4-1, 251D1
Bosworth sees noncompliance 3-8, 182E3
Kahn scores business on prices 3-13, 182A1
AFL-CIO files wage-guide suit 3-13, 182B2
Price hike deferral set, Alcoa agrees 3-15, 182G1
Bank guidelines set; insurnc, utility rules revised 3-16, 264C2-B3
Kahn scores '78 4th 1/4 profit rise 3-20, 201B2
Carter vows firmer price watch 3-24, 3-25, 230A2
Carter poll rating drops 3-29, 231F3
Price rules tightened; noncompliance, inflatn surge noted 3-29, 264A1
GM price hike OKd 3-31, 305F2
Teamsters pact seen within guides 4-10, 262D1, A2
Carter stresses wage-price guides, bars mandatory controls 4-10, 263C3, 264B1, B2
Scott rolls back prices 4-16, 385G1
UAW pres discounts, cites Teamsters pact 4-17, 280A1
Carter: best solutn 4-25, 300C1
Sears sets price rollback 4-27, 4-30, 363C1
2 paper co price violators chrgd 4-27; Hammermill cleared, 5 other cos chrgd 5-17, 385E1, G1
AFL-CIO calls guidelines 'flop' 5-8, 345A2
Blumenthal ups inflatn forecast 5-8; Schultze, Bosworth defend wage hike limit 5-10, 362B2
Ideal Basic price violatn chrgd, Giant Food rolls back prices 5-9, 385A2
Carter cites 'real wage insurnc' plan defeat by House panel 5-25, 401B2
Bosworth on UAL pact 5-28, 402E2
Carter defends 5-29, 402C1
Amerada Hess price violatns chrgd, other refiners warned; Jan-May hikes noted 5-30, 396C1
ILGWU gets 25%, 3-yr pact 5-30, 402G1
Ct bars wage-guide contract denial; Admin, other reactn 5-31, 399A2-F3
Rail dispatchers accord set 5-31, 598A3
Carter rptd vs Bosworth controls remark 6-4, Bosworth resignatn plan rptd 6-16, 463E1
URW pacts exceed guides 6-15, 6-18, 480E1
Appeals ct backs wage-guide contract denial 6-22, 480B2
Wage-price penalty upheld 6-22, case refused by Sup Ct 7-2, 498C2
UAW warns Admin 6-30, Big 3 contract talks begin 7-16, 598A1
UAW reaches accord with GM 9-14, Kahn lauds 9-15, 698D1, D2
Pay Advisory Com set 9-28, 829C2-B3
Interim price rule set 9-28, chngs barred 11-1, 829B3

Gross National Product (GNP)
GNP, GDP defined 33C2
'78, 4th 1/4 rise rptd; 3d 1/4 revised 1-18, 72A1-73A1
Carter budget forecasts 1-22, 41E1, F1; table 43A2, B2
Carter gives '80 budget deficit as % 1-23, 47G1
'79 real growth rate forecast, '78 cited 1-25, 48B3, C3, G3
Spending limit amendmt urged 1-30, 86A3
'78 GNP, profit rise linked 3-20, 201E2
'78, 4th 1/4 revised 3-20, 202F3
1st 1/4 rise rptd 4-19, 280G1-F2
Carter links energy efficiency 6-28, 7-1, 494B1, D2
OECD sees econ slowdown 7-19, 554A3
2d 1/4 drop rptd; 1st 1/4, '78 4th 1/4 revised 7-20, 556F2-C3
'78 per capita GNP ranked 8th 7-24, 575D3
3d 1/4 rise rptd, 2d 1/4 revised 10-19, 805D1-E2

1980

Credit rptd tightened 3-27, 3-28, 222D2; **for subsequent developments, see** CREDIT, Consumer
Carter Economic Renewal Plan
Carter plans program 8-6, 597C2; offers plan; tax cuts, investmt incentives stressed; reactn 8-28, 663A1-D3

Gross National Product (GNP)
Small businesses' contributn estimated 455E3
GNP, GDP described 34E1
'76-79 real growth chart 51C3
'79, 4th 1/4 rise rptd; 3d 1/4 revised 1-18, 51F3-52C1
Carter budget forecasts 1-28, 69D2, E3; table 71A2
'80 real growth rate forecast, '79 cited 1-30, 74B2
'79 4th 1/4 revised 3-19, 305G2
Carter revised budget forecasts 3-31, 243E3
1st 1/4 rise rptd 4-18, 305F2
2d 1/4 drop rptd 7-18, 555E3
Admin revises forecast 7-21, 550F1-A2
3d 1/4 rise rptd 10-17, 804G2

1976

Inflation & Recession—*See also 'Presidential Election' and 'Wage-Price Developments' below*
Dow rise linked to econ pickup 1-2—3-11, 184F2
'46-75 inflatn revised 1-16, 89C3, 90D1
State of Union message 1-19, 36G2, 37F2, 39D1
'75 4th ¼ inflatn rate rptd 1-20, 89A2
Muskie rebuts Ford 1-21, 40B2
Ford '77 budget charts moderate pace; summary 1-21, 62G1-66G2
Ford Econ Rpt 1-26, 66G2, 67E1; excerpts 67A1
House OKs pub works bill 1-29, 93C3; **for subsequent developments, see PUBLIC Works**
'75 4th ¼ inflatn rate revised 2-19, 168F1
Cong panels score Ford econ policies 3-10, 3-15, 230D2-231D1
Inflatn, stock mkt retreat linked 3-11—5-28, 413G1, C2
Consumer confidnc rptd up 3-26, 230A2
Greenspan: Teamsters pact not inflationary 4-5, 249A1
1st ¼ inflatn rate down 4-19, 279A1
Mar consumer credit rptd up 5-6, 375F3
Cong OKs '77 US budget targets 5-12, 5-13, 358G1
1st ¼ inflatn data revised 5-20, 396D1
Admin sees trade deficit as recovery sign 5-26, 5-30, 396G1, E3
Dow Jones closings 6-1—11-10, 846A3-847D1
Corp borrowing rptd up 6-4, 436D3, E3
Ford at 7-nation summit 6-27—6-28, 461F2-462E1
Admin forecast updated 7-16 535G3
2d ¼ inflatn, 1st ¼ revised 7-20, 536D1
Reagan lauds Schweiker 7-26, 550F1
Cong Budget Office sees contd recovery 8-2, 647A2
Sen OKs prelim embargo ban 8-27, 746F2
Greenspan sees 'pause' in recovery 8-30, 647F1
Pub Health Svc cites costs 9-7, 680E1, F1 ★
NE govs meet 10-1, 743A1
3d ¼ inflatn rate rptd, 2d ¼ revised 10-19, 805E1-A2
Rptd top electn issue 11-2, 818B3
Caddell: issue decondary 11-5, 845C2
Mayors ask anti-recessn plan 11-8, 845D3
Burns vs stimulative policies, rpts lower M1 target 11-11; denies Carter rift 11-12, 865E1
Burns on 10% OPEC price hike effect 11-11, 865D3
3d ¼ inflatn rate revised down 11-18, 866A2
Fed Reserve eases curbs 11-19, 12-17, 939G2
OECD rpts Oct '75-76 inflatn rate 12-6, 976B1

Labor—*See under 'L'*

1977

Inflation & Recession
Carter plans 2-yr, $30 bln pkg 1-7, 5C1
Carter plan scored 1-10, 14C1
Ford State of Union message 1-12, 12F2, 13B1, F2
Ford '78 budget estimates 1-17, 30B2
CEA rpt to Cong 1-18, 35E3, 36F1
'76, 4th ¼ inflatn rptd, 3d ¼ revised 1-18, 56F1
Carter revises aid plan 1-27, 51G3-A2; submits to Cong 1-31, 75A2
Cong debates Carter plan 1-27—2-4, GOP offers alternative 2-2, 89A2
Carter defends recovery plan 2-2, 75A2
Fuel bills drain on econ rptd 2-2, 76A1
Dec '75-76 inflatn rate rptd 2-7, 87A2
Carter on Cong plan 2-8, 88C3
CBO questns Carter goals 2-15, 126E1
Carter budget revisions 2-22, 124G3
Fed spending lag rptd 3-2, 174A3
Cong sets new '77 budget levels 3-3, 174B1
Ford concerned, scores Carter budget 3-26, 236D2
Carter poll standings 4-4, 251D1, F1
Carter pushes plan 4-7, drops rebate, tax cut proposals; business reactn 4-14, 270F2, 271C1
Carter outlines inflatn plan 4-15, 298F2
Carter concedes energy plan inflationary 4-15, 299E1
Welfare study issued 4-15, 302G1
Ford scores Carter inflatn plan 4-16, 321G3
Carter energy plan 4-18, 4-20, 289B2, 290B2, 295A1, A2; fact sheet 291A2
1st ¼ inflatn, '76 4th ¼ revised 4-20, 300C1
Lance discounts energy plan impact 4-21, 294G1
Carter defends energy plan 4-22, 321F2
Admin forecasts revised 4-22, 407G3
Carter scored by AFL-CIO, McGovern 5-4, 5-7, 364E2, B3
Stimulus, other funds clear Cong 5-5, 365E2; Carter signs 5-13, 380D3
Carter at 7-natn summit 5-7—5-8, 357A1
Cited re Soc Sec deficits 5-9, 363G3
'76 per-capita income rptd 5-10, 387B3
Urban business confidence rptd, chart 5-16, 384A2, D2
Carter environmt message 5-23, 404C2
Home purchases seen as inflatn hedge 5-24, 554C3
Carter warns re vetoes 5-26, 417E1
'77 capital spending upturn seen 6-7, 6-24, 6-27, 518A3
'77 inflatn forecast revised 7-1, 518F3
Carter cites stimulus legis 7-12, 534E1
2d ¼ inflatn up, 1st ¼ revised 7-21, 553A3
Carter town mtg topic 7-21, 575D1
Poll finds COL, inflatn top worries 8-10, 632C2
Sagging stock mkt linked 8-29, 691E1, D2
Finished-goods index unveiled, June-Aug rptd 9-1, 692C1
Inflatn spurs housing boom, data analyzed 9-12, 9-20, 721F3
Cong forecasts re '78 budget levels 9-15, 719F2
Min wage indexing provisn killed in House 9-15, 759B1, D1
Aug indl output drops 9-16, 722D1
Carter: will meet '77, '78 growth goals 9-26, 753E2
'75, '76 income, inflatn compared 10-3, 821G3-822B1
Wage-price panel rpts on steel industry 10-7, 776E2
3d ¼ inflatn rptd, 2d ¼ revised 10-19, 798D1
Admin fears tight money impact on recovery 10-20, 798B3
Burns asks 'bold' Admin moves 10-26, 817D2-A3
Carter cites gains vs inflatn 10-27, 813F3
Merger activity, inflatn linked 11-4, 879D3
Carter vs high oil imports 11-8, 854D2
AFL-CIO urges stimulus program 12-12, 960C1
Business sees recessn, faults Admin 12-14, 962E1
Carter: top priority in '78 12-14, 976E3; 12-28, 1002A1
Carter tax program curbs proposed 12-20, 976C2
Miller to succeed Burns 12-28, Carter-Burns policy dispute examined 12-28, 12-29, 1000D1, C3

1978

Inflation & Recession—*See also 'Carter Anti-Inflation Plan' above*
Cost of living, inflatn rate defined 50C2
Carter warns steel industry on quotas 1-18, 80D3
Carter State of Union Message 1-19, 29F1, 30G1, A2, C2, F2, D3, 31A1, G3
'77, 4th ¼ inflatn rptd; 3d ¼ revised 1-19, 49E3
Carter Econ Message 1-20, 48E2
Carter budget shows restraint, few new programs 1-23, 44C2-48E2
Carter urges proposals kept intact 1-30, 62B3
Burns warns vs inflatn danger 1-30, 161D3
GOP attacks Carter budget 1-31, 62F3
Carter: top priority for '78 2-17, 123A2
AFL-CIO offers stimulus plan 2-20, 141E3
Higher inflatn, $ drop linked 3-7, 234B2
Fed Reserve chrmn backs anti-inflatn drive 3-15, 181D1
Humphrey-Hawkins bill clears House 3-16, 182D3
Food inflatn forecasts 3-28, 5-30, 428B2
Carter: steel price hike inflationary 3-30, 262G3
Burns links 'credible anti-inflatn policy', $ defense 3-31, 235E2
Consumer confidence rptd down, inflatn named chief worry 4-6, 260C3
Carter sets anti-inflatn plan: curbs fed, White House exec salaries; names Strauss coordinator 4-11, 259C2
Carter plan reactn 4-11, 4-12, 260E2
1860-1978 consumer price table 427E1
Carter poll standings rptd down 4-12, 260A3
1st ¼ inflatn rptd; '77, 4th ¼ rate revised 4-19, 303B3
Inflatn fights aimed at sagging $, weakness persists 4-19—7-14, 523F1, C2
Business ldrs see Carter, back inflatn plan 4-20, 5-11; Admin scores critics 5-8, 361A3, G3
Carter poll drop linked 4-24, 308B1
Carter vows contd inflatn fight 4-25, 307C3
'76, '77 living costs rptd 4-26, 349E1
GM, Ford hike prices; Strauss backs 4-28, 5-9, Meany scores 5-10, 361C3, E3, 362B2
'78 inflatn forecast revised 5-2, 362D1
Carter urges legal-fee lid 5-4, 320C3
Carter bars wage-price controls 5-4, 321C2
FRB tight $ policy scored 5-9, 361E2
Meany, labor ldrs see Carter; rejct wage-restraint plea 5-10; Bosworth backs stand 5-11, 361F2, D3
Carter scales down tax-cut plan 5-12, 361B1, F1
Wage cncl asks TVA rate hike moderatn 5-15, increase scaled down 5-17, 362A2
Builders vow 6-mo profit freeze, back other measures 5-16, 362F1
Cong '79 budget target res cleared 5-17, 385F2
Carter orders govt-purchasing controls 5-18, 405E1
Admin jawboning rptd successful 5-19—6-1, campaign stepped up 6-6, 427B3-428B1
Pernicious inflatn seen, govt blamed 5-22, 6-12, 6-19, 427D1-A3
Apr CPI called 'disaster' 5-22, 428C3
US Steel vs Carter price restraint plea 5-24; Strauss, Bosworth score 5-31, 6-19, 428D1
Carter plans budget cuts 5-25, 404F2
Oil demand linked to recess 5-26, 408A1
Bethlehem holds price hike to 3%, Admin lauds restraint 6-12; 'Big 3' follow suit 6-13—6-15, 470B2
Cotton dust rules issued 6-19, 471D3
Natl health plan delay seen 6-26, 491E2
Oil import fee seen inflationary 6-29, 512A1
FRB hikes discount rate, Admin scores 6-30, 679G1
Kemp notes tax-cut benefits 7-3, 735C1, F1
'78, '79 inflatn forecast revised 7-6, 506C2-F3
CBO rpts on Propositn 13 impact 7-6, 525G2
Carter vows inflatn fight at Bonn summit 7-16—7-17, 554A1, E1
Carter cautions Cong 7-20, 549E3
2d ¼ inflatn rptd, 1st ¼ revised 7-21, 606F2
'77 median family income, 'real' gain rptd 7-24, 8-9, 679G3-680B1
Productivity, inflatn linked 7-27, 606D3
Carter health plan outlined 7-29, 586B1
Cong study sees '79 tax hikes 8-2, 587B2
Mondale addresses Urban League 8-7, 811C1
Meany warns re depressn, denies wages role 8-8, 624A3
Black jobless, recessn linked 8-8, 810F3
Capital gains inflatn 'indexing' OKd by House 8-10, 604F1
EPA to ease clean-water rules 8-10, 644F1
Poll finds growing pessimism re inflatn, Carter policies 8-13, 679E2
Carter urges farmers fight 8-14, 626D1
Carter links price hikes, $ drop 8-16, 622B2
Car price hikes, inflatn fears linked 8-18, 664G3, 665F1-A2
GM hikes '79 model prices, deceleratn vow cited 8-18, 665F1-A2
FRB hikes discount, fed funds rate 8-18, 679A1-B2
Tax-cut proponents back 'indexing' 8-21, 735B3

1979

Inflation & Recession—*See also 'Carter Anti-Inflation Plan' above*
Cost of living, inflatn, recessn defined 33B2, E2, C3
Carey holds up NY example 1-1, 13G2
Carter aide warns Dems on 'new realities' 1-4, 3E2
Brown: US govt culprit 1-8, 13E2
Carter sees oil-price rise 1-17, 30B1
Urban League dir concerned 1-17, 35E1
'78, 4th 1/4 inflatn up; 3d 1/4 revised 1-18, 73A1
Anti-pollutn rule costs rptd 1-19, 129C3
Carter budget proposals 1-22, 41A1, A2, 44B3
Carter State of Union Message 1-23, 46C2, E2-F3, 47D1-B2
Greenspan sees '79 recessn, inflatn worsening 1-24, 48B2
Carter Econ Message, CEA rpt see inflatn easing; '79, '80 rates forecast 1-25, 48C2, C3
Miller, Rivlin vs Admin '79 econ forecasts 1-25, 48E3
Carter sends Cong legis agenda 1-25, 70B2
Carter scored on oil-profits remark 1-26, 70A2
GOP urges tax indexing 2-4, 86B2
AFL-CIO urges govt actn 2-19, 148D2
Oil price effect warned by GAO 3-7, 182F2
'78 hosp costs rise rptd 3-8, 194G2
Crane links monetary policy 3-10, 186C1
Admin revises budget forecast 3-15, 183D3
Regulatn Q, inflatn hedges linked 3-16, 264F2
'78, 4th 1/4 inflatn rate revised 3-20, 203A1
Mar-May car sales drop, recessn fears linked 4-4, 5-3, 6-5, 441D2
Carter admits oil price decontrol inflatnary 4-5, 250F2
Mar employmt rpt, inflatn linked 4-6, 280A3
Carter stresses problem 4-10, 263C3, 264D1
1st 1/4 inflatn rise rptd 4-19, 280A2
Carter sees contd inflatn 4-25, 300C1
Soc Sec COL hike rptd 4-26, 310F1
'78 profits, inflatn linked by Fortune 5-7, 305E1
Blumenthal sees 8-8.5% rate 5-8, 362B2
Carter warns Dems vs inactn 5-25, 401D1
Carter: inflatn top priority 5-29, 402A1
Carter sees consumerists 5-31, Dems re inflatn 6-1–6-2, 418A1, G1, F2
Carter econ team rptd revamped 6-4, 463D1
Rep Anderson scores Carter 6-8, 439E2
7-natn indicators index rptd, US growth lags 6-11, 513G1
Productivity, inflatn fight linked 6-13, 6-19, 463G1-A2
ADA scores Carter 6-24, 982D2
Carter on OPEC price hike impact 7-1, 494C2
Carter poll rating low 7-1, 497G1
Soc Sec, vet paymts hiked 7-1, 622A1
Prop 13 impact rptd 7-2, 499G2, B3
Carter reviews policy, sees US ldrs, resets natl speech 7-6–7-12, 513C2
Cabt shake-up impact seen 7-19, 7-20, 530C1, 531E3
2d 1/4 inflatn rise rptd, 1st 1/4 revised 7-20, 556G2
Food inflatn forecast hiked 7-26, 578B1
Retail slowdown linked 7-27, 648G3
Productivity decline linked 7-30, 577D3
Chrysler sales drop, recessn linked 7-31, 576B3
Citizens Party platform backs price controls 8-1, 595A1
Miller, Volcker on inflatn 8-6, 627E2
Record industry slump rptd 8-8, 618G1
Bank robbery rise linked 8-12, 619A3
Kennedy links inflatn, '80 pres bid 9-6, 9-11, 680A1, F1
Miller on recessn 9-14, 701E2
IMF sees recessn 9-16, 720C1
'69-78 inflatn, income growth compared 9-16, 746B2
Carter links inflatn, OPEC price hikes 9-25, 723G2
Miller at Belgrade mtg vows inflatn fight 10-3, 779B3, D3
FRB hikes discount rate, sets monetary policy 10-6; Carter backs, other reaction 10-6–10-12, 764C1-766B1, 767E1
Carter: job losses no inflatn cure 10-11, 807F2
Gold speculatn, inflatn linked 10-16, 780B1
Volcker sees living standard drop 10-17, 10-28, 940C3
3d 1/4 inflatn rise rptd 10-19, 805G1
Natl Agenda Comm created 10-24, 810A1
Urban fscl policy chngs predicted 10-24, 920A2
Kahn calls '79 inflatn goal unattainable 10-26, 828B1
Economists on '29 Depression, '80s forecast 10-29, 11-1, 826D3-827D2
Calif OKs spending-CPI link 11-6, 846E3
Kennedy scores Carter 11-7, 847F1
Brown sees stagflatn 11-8, 847F2
Reagan scores Admin 11-13, 866E2
Reagan campaign themes cited 11-14, 982G1
Meany vs Admin policies 11-15, 885A1
Brown offers 'new order' 11-9, stresses inflatn 11-20, 962E2, A3
Income tax bite rptd up 11-28, 925B1
Carter cites inflatn issue 12-4, 918C2

1980

Inflation & Recession
Cost of living, inflatn, recessn defined 34D2, G2, D3
Volcker bars policy change 1-2, 52C2
State of State messages 1-2—2-6, 269E1-F2, 270E1, A2, D2; 1-7—1-15, 2-19, 403C2; 1-9—4-8, 482F3-484A3
'79, 4th 1/4 inflatn up; 3d 1/4 revised 1-18, 52A1
Carter State of Union proposals 1-21, 1-23, 41D1, F2, 43C2, D2, B3
Carter, Kahn on '79 inflatn rise 1-25, 75B3
Carter budget forecasts, proposals 1-28, 69B2-D2
Carter Econ Message, CEA rpt see moderate recessn, persistent inflatn: '80 rates forecast 1-30, 74B1
Urban purchasing power rptd tops 2-12, 125D3
'79 inflatn rptd up by OECD 2-13, 125C3
FRB hikes discount rate 2-15, prime hike follows, Volcker vows tight money policy 2-19, 126A1-A2
AFL-CIO stresses inflatn 2-18, 146C3
Bond price drop, inflatn linked 2-21, 127F3
Carter: inflatn at crisis stage 2-25, 144G2
Schultze on inflatn rise 3-7, 182D2
Inflatn, money mkt funds growth linked 3-21, 223G2
Russell sees continued inflatn 3-25, 222C2
Carter revised budget forecasts 3-31, 243E3
Recessn, Mar jobless rate linked 4-4, 263F1
Miller sees mild recessn 4-15, 286C3
Carter sees short recessn 4-17, 285G2
Tamm sees recessn start 4-30, 329F2
FRB ends discount rate surchrg 5-6, 344C2
FRB eases credit controls 5-22, 399F3
Kahn sees contd inflatn 5-23, 400A3
Pensn revisn urged 5-23, 404A2
Carter calls recessn steeper 6-1, 424E3
UAW head scores Carter 6-1, 457E2
Recession since Jan rptd 6-3, 424F3
Carter, Miller on inflatn 6-6, 437F2
Mil recruiters to stress recessn 6-11, 458C2
Pvt anti-inflatn com sets policy 6-21, 481D1
IMF econ forecast grim 6-24, 477D2, A3
Sen Dems name task-force 6-26, 480B3
Cox sees contd recessn 6-30, 492C2
Dems vow contd fight 7-1, 493A1
FRB ends credit controls 7-3, 513E1
Russell: inflatn not over 7-8, 513E3
Admin budget review pessimistic 7-21, 550D1-C2
Forgn investmt, inflatn linked 8-7, 601F3
AFL-CIO cncl backs reindustrializatn bd 8-21, 647D3
Middle-class tax burden rptd 9-12, 747A2
'79 median family income rptd 10-23, 823G3
'80 budget deficit doubles 10-29, 824E3
ITC bars Japan auto imports curbs 11-10, 866E3
FRB hikes discount rate, sets surchrg 11-14, 882D3
New scenic area air rules issued 11-25, 898A2
Fed deficit estimate rises 12-2, 916F2
Eizenstat cites inflation 12-4, 938E3
O'Neil vows Dem cooperatn 12-8, 936F2
Amer Enterprise Inst study issued 12-24, 980C3

1976

Monetary & Fiscal Developments—
See also BALANCE of Payments, BANKS, U.S. GOVERNMENT, subheads BUDGET, FEDERAL Reserve and TREASURY; for U.S. role in international money market, see MONETARY Developments
Ford Econ Rpt 1-26, 67E1, C2
Dec '75 money supply down 1-28, 91A1
Money supply growth targets changed 2-3, growth rptd 2-18, 167F3-168B1
Money-growth targets cut, credit tightened 5-3, 347E2
Dem platform text 6-15, 470C1
GOP platform text 8-18, 602A3
Burns warns vs stimulating econ, rpts M1 target lowered, M2, M3 widened 11-11; denies Carter rift 11-12, 865E1
Dow climb, eased credit policies linked 11-18—12-31, 984D1
Fed Reserve eases curbs 11-19, 12-17, 939G2
Presidential Election (& transition)
Shriver issues econ plan 1-7, 22F2
Wallace scores big govt 1-9, 22D2
Ford stresses 'econ discipline' 2-6—2-8, 109B1
Ford cites inflation drop 2-17, 129C3
AFL-CIO scores Admin 2-21, 149C1
Ford: on crusade vs inflatn 2-28, 165B3
Ford notes good signs 3-5, 3-9, 180B1, C1
Reagan scores Admin 3-31, 232B2
Carter issues policy paper 4-23, 305A2
Ford scores Cong 4-26, 307A3
Ford cites upturn 5-8, 342A3
AFL-CIO issues warning 5-19, 391C1
Dem platform text 6-15, 469F1-F3, 470A1-E1, 473C2
Mrs. Ford cites upturn 6-18, 451B1
Dole lauds Ford, vs govt interventn 6-19, 612F3-613D1
Carter sees mayors 6-29, 468A1
Humphrey scores GOP 7-13, 509E2
Muskie hails Dem plank 7-13, 509A3
Carter for free system 7-15, 507E1, 510C3, 511A1
Mondale cites inflatn 7-15, 507G2, 511B2
Carter outlines goals 7-28, 550G3
Mondale scores GOP 8-15, 617B3
GOP platform text 8-18, 602A1, E2, 606B3, 607A1
Ford acceptance speech cites 8-19, 611G3, 612B2, D2
Reagan vs govt interventn 8-19, 613A3
Ford legis record cited 614E1-G1
Carter scores Ford vetoes 8-23, 631C3
Ford urges as debate topic 8-24, 632G3
Mondale scores Admin 8-28, 645B3
Set as TV debate topic 9-1, 644B1
Carter stresses inflatn curb 9-3, local actn 9-6, 664D1, B2
Mondale scores Admin 9-6, 665E2
Mondale scores mismanagmt 9-13, 687F1
Carter scores GOP policies 9-15, 686D3
Ford, Carter debate 9-23, 701E1, 702D2, C3
Carter scores GOP 9-24—9-27, 724F1, A3
Ford on inflatn battle 9-26, 723B3
Carter on Aug indicator drop 9-27, 768D1

1977

Monetary & Fiscal Developments—
See also BALANCE of Payments, BANKS, U.S. GOVERNMENT, subheads BUDGET, FEDERAL Reserve and TREASURY; for U.S. role in international money market, see MONETARY Developments
Econ indicator index described 1-28, 92E3; **for data, see 'Statistics' under BUSINESS**
Fed spending lag rptd 3-2, 174A3
Tight money policy affects Dow 3-17—5-25, 408B1
Apr money growth, FRB tight credit policy cited 5-13, 5-30, 407F1
Apr, May money supply cited 6-29, 502D2
FRB hikes discount rate, money growth targets cited 8-29, 703D3
Prime rate rise, money supply growth rates linked 10-4, 10-10, 798E2-B3
Admin warns FRB re rate rise 10-20, 798B3
FRB hikes discount rate 10-25, 817B3
Burns on Admin criticism 10-26, 817G2-A3
Miller to replace Burns 12-28, Carter-Burns policy dispute examined 12-28, 12-29, 1000G1, C3

1978

Natl health plan urged by Kennedy 8-28, 682B1
Strauss sees inflatn peaking 8-29, 682C1
Calif enacts tax 'indexing' 8-30, 735F2
Carter asks 5.5% fed pay hike 8-31, 681E2
Business spending rptd up, consumer spending down 9-15, 717E1
Meany notes inflatn causes, urges interest rate cuts 9-18, 715D2
Business spending lag, econ fears linked 9-18, 716B3-717B1
Carter plans new anti-inflatn proposals 9-20, 715E1
Carter vows inflatn fight, IMF dir links growth rate 9-25, 731G2, C3
Inflatn, weak $ linked by Swiss offcl 9-27, 732C2
Carter asks tougher FRB anti-inflatn role 9-27, 9-28, 751E1
Carter scores 5 bills, threatens pub works veto 9-28, 751F3
'78 underlying inflatn rate seen worsening 10-4, 789F3
$ drop seen inflatn cause, symptom 10-4, 790E1
Pub works veto upheld 10-5, 765D1, C2
FRB hikes discount rate, disunity cited 10-13, 791A2
Tax-cut bill cleared 10-15, 785G1, E2, B3
Humphrey-Hawkins bill cleared, sets inflatn rate goals 10-15, 808E1
FRB Open Mkt Com debate on high interest rates rptd 10-16, 791C2
Dow drops on inflatn fears, Carter plan 10-16—10-31, rebounds on $ aid steps 11-1—11-3, 826E1-827A1
June '77-78 inflatn rate ranked 10-18, 914F1
Carter vs ITC on copper imports curb, cost cited 10-20, 804G3-805A1
3d ¼ inflatn rate rptd, 2d ¼ revised 10-20, 863F3
3d ¼ profits rise, '79 recessn fears linked 10-30, 919E2
Md voters link cnty spending, CPI 11-7, 849A1
Admin stresses tight '80 budget 11-13—11-14, 875E1, F1
Carter budget problems seen 11-28, 12-14, 980E1
Fed anti-recessn funds loss linked to Newark, Detroit econ woes 12-11, 12-27, 1012D1, F1
Schultze, FRB, others assess OPEC price hike impact 12-17—12-19, 978C1, B2
Monetary Policy & Developments—
For U.S. dollar role in international currency market, see MONETARY Developments, International
Econ indicator index described 128B1
Discount rate hiked 1-6, Partee issues dissent 1-9; reactn 1-23, 28A1
Fed funds rate hiked 1-9, 28B2
Carter on interest rates 1-12, 12B1
Carter inflatn plan avoids money supply issue 4-11, 260F2
Stock mkt reacts to FRB credit moves 4-14, 4-27—4-28, 303C1, C2
Higher prime, fed funds rate linked 4-28, 326C2
Admin vs tight $ policy 5-9, FRB hikes discount rate 5-11, 361C2
Carter scales down tax-cut plan 5-12, 361F1
Prime rate hiked, FRB moves cited 5-25, 403G2
EPA plans econ analyses 6-28, 512C3
Carter revises secrecy rules 6-29, 508F1
FRB hikes discount rate; Miller, Admin score 6-30, 679G1
Economists see tight $ policy 7-7, 506E3
HUD-White House disagreemt over FRB policy cited 8-7, 605B2
Regulatory overhaul asked by ABA 8-8, 626E2
Fed funds rate hiked 8-16, 622A2
FRB hikes discount, fed funds rate 8-18, 679A1-B2
OMB cash flow savings rptd 8-19, 715E3
Prime rate hiked 9-15, 9-25, 752B1
Business cash holdings, spending lag linked to tight $ fears 9-18, 716D3, F3
Fed discount rate hiked to 8% 9-22, 731D2
Swiss score money policy, rate strategy failure cited 9-27, 732C2
Carter scores FRB rate hike, asks tougher anti-inflatn role 9-27, 9-28, 751C3
Suffragette $ coin bill signed 10-10, 788B2
FRB hikes discount rate 10-13, 791A2
FRB Open Mkt Com debate on high interest rates rptd 10-16, 791C2
M1 rapid growth rptd 10-19, 791B3
FRB Oct credit tightening cited 10-30, 864A3
FRB hikes discount, fed funds rate to aid $ 11-1, 825B1, D1, 827B1
Meany scores discount rate hike 11-1, 863E2
Carter vows responsible progrm 11-2, 862A2
Prime rate hiked 12-20, 1003D3
Nov indicators drop, money supply shrinkage linked 12-28, 1003C3

1979

Monetary Policy & Developments
Discount, prime rates explained 621E1
Carter Econ Message cites restraint 1-25, 48E2
Dec indicators down, tight money policy cited 1-31, 111B2
Crane links to inflatn 3-10, 186C1
Default crisis 4-1—4-2, debt ceiling bill OKd 4-2, 251F2
Indicators index revised, money supply chngs cited 4-1, 252A2
FRB membership, reserve problems rptd 4-9; aid bill abandoned 4-24, 303E1
FRB Open Mkt rpt disclosure delay backed by Sup Ct 6-28, 558C3
Blumenthal fired, Miller replaces 7-19, 529C1, 530C1; Volcker replaces Miller 7-25, 555C2
FRB hikes discount rate, tight money shift seen 7-20, 531E3; 8-16, 621A1
Volcker links high rates, inflatn fight 9-7, 680C3
Discount rate hike, Canada bank rate increase linked 9-7, 684A3
FRB hikes discount rate, short-term rates cited 9-18, 701C2
Bentsen asks interest rate hike halt 9-20, Proxmire backs Volcker policies 9-26, 745A2
$1 bill replacemt urged 9-25, 727A2
FRB hikes discount rate, **sets monetary policy 10-6;** Carter, financial mkts react 10-6—10-12, 764C1-766B1, 767E1
Discount rate hike, Canada bank rate hike linked 10-9, 771G2
FRB admits money supply errors 10-25, 10-30, NY bank takes blame 10-26; Reuss scores FRB 10-30, 828C2-C3
Greenspan, Galbraith on '80s forecast 10-29, 826D3
Discount rate hike, Swiss lending fee increase linked 11-2, 875F3
Brown notes weak $ 11-8, 847F2
Brown seeks strong $ 11-9, 962E2

1980

Monetary Policy & Developments
Volcker bars tight money policy change 1-2, 52C2
'79 money supply growth rptd 1-10, 52G1
Tight money, small business hardships linked 1-13, 5-15, 5-29, 455E2
Carter Econ Message backs restraint 1-30, 74D1
FRB chngs money supply terms 2-7, 113C3
FRB hikes discount rate 2-15; prime hike follows, Volcker vows tight money 2-19, 126A1-A2
AFL-CIO berates Admin 2-18, 146F3
Tight money, bond price drop linked 2-19, 127B1
Cong com asks new policies 2-28, 168G2-D3
FRB discount rate hike speculatn rptd 3-13, 182G2
FRB sets discount rate surchrg 3-14, 201A2
Credit rptd tightened 3-27, 3-28, 222D2-A3
FRB modifies credit controls 4-2, 263D2
FRB ends discount rate surchrg 5-6, 344C2
FRB eases credit controls 5-22, 399F3
FRB cuts discount rate to 12% 5-28, 400B2
FRB cuts discount rate to 11% 6-12, 438E1
FRB ends credit controls 7-3, 513E1
GOP platform adopted; text 7-15, 535G3, 536D1, A2
FRB cuts discount rate to 10% 7-25, 574F3
FRB vows '81 tight money targets 7-31, House com backs 8-4, 616A3
FRB hikes discount rate to 12%, sets surchrg 11-14, 882B3
Money supply growth rptd 11-18, 882D3
Presidential Election (& Transition)
Kennedy warns vs decline 1-14, 32C3
Kennedy cites inflation 1-20, 50D2
Bush attacks Carter 1-20, 50E2
Kennedy seeks wage-price controls, GOP scores 1-28, 74E2, F3
Kennedy issues econ paper 2-6, 90F3-91C1
Kennedy stages mock debate with Carter 2-7, 91G1, C2
Connally scores inflation 2-14, 129F1
Kennedy wage-price call cited 2-15, 126E2
GOP candidates debate in NH 2-20, 129G2, A3, D3
Reagan 'basic speech' excerpts 2-29, 207B2
Bush 'basic speech' excerpts 3-3, 208C2
Kennedy links inflatn, Mass primary win 3-4, 167A1
Kennedy calls Carter policy intolerable 3-9, 206E3
Kennedy 'basic speech' excerpts 3-10, 183B1, E1, B2, E2
Ford attacks Carter 3-12, 207G1
Reagan links forgn policy 3-17, 208G1
NY primary issue 3-25, 221C2, A3
Kirkland scores Carter 3-31, 247A2
Brown scores Carter policies, ends pres bid 4-1, 246C3

1976

Mondale topic 9-29, 725C1
Carter stresses inflatn 9-30, 10-1, 742E3, 743A1
Ford scores Carter on inflatn 10-8, 763B2
Mondale topic 10-10, 763D3
Ford on 'pause' 10-14, 762A1
Dole, Mondale debate 10-15, 782F2, D3, F3-783B3
Mondale discusses 10-16—10-26, 803B3
Carter sees GNP rise as 'downward slide' 10-19, 805F1
Ford, Carter debate 10-22, 799F3, 800E1-G2, F3, 802G2
Ford issue 10-23—10-28, 802G3, 803F1-A3
Mondale hits inflatn rate 10-30—10-31, 827D2
Carter scores Ford inflatn record 10-31, 827A2
Inflatn rptd top electn issue 11-2, 818B3
Stock mkt reactn to electn 11-3—11-4, 826B1
Carter on inflatn goal 11-15, 863E2-864A1
Carter meets cong ldrs 11-17, 864F1
Carter plans early program 11-23, 881B2
Carter on steel price hike impact 11-29, 897D3, G3
Carter sees top advisers 12-1, 898B2
Carter; econ 'will need help' 12-3, 917E1, B2
Carter, staff offer econ aid plans 12-9—12-14, 937C2-938A1
Schultze: top priority 12-16, 937A1
Carter sees improvemt 12-27, 978C2
Carter Cabt unit set up 12-29, 978E2

Prices—*See also 'Wage-Price Developments' below; also specific industry, commodity names*
CPI described 90E2
Dec '75 WPI down 1-9, 21C2
Dec, '75 CPI rptd 1-21, 90E1
Jan WPI, CPI rptd 2-13, 2-20, 168B1, B2
Ford notes CPI drop 2-17, 129C3
Feb WPI rptd 3-4, 199B1; CPI 3-19, 215D1
March WPI rptd 4-1, 262F3
March CPI, 1st ¼ data rptd 4-21, 306E1
April WPI rptd 5-6, 347C1
April CPI rptd 5-21, 375D1
May WPI rptd 6-4, 412A3
May CPI rptd 6-22, 453G2
June WPI rptd 7-9 519B1
'76 CPI forecast revised 7-16, 536B1
June 2d ¼ CPI rptd 7-21, 536C2
July WPI rptd 8-12, 635A2
July CPI rptd 8-20, 635E1
Aug WPI rptd 9-2, 667B3
Aug CPI rptd 9-21, 708D2
Sept WPI rptd 10-7, 769B3
Sept CPI rptd 10-21, 805F2-A3
Oct WPI rptd 11-4, 846B2
Oct CPI rptd 11-19, 884F3
Nov WPI rptd 12-3, 918F3
Nov CPI rptd 12-21, 958F1

1977

Prices—*See also 'Wage-Price Developments' below; also specific industry, commodity names*
CPI described 78C1
Nov '75-76 consumer rise rptd 1-7, 29C3
Dec, '76 WPI rptd 1-12, 38E2
'76, Dec CPI rptd 1-19, 77E3-78B1
Econ indicator index described 1-28, 92D3; **for data, see BUSINESS—Statistics**
Jan WPI rptd 2-11; calculatn table 111A1, B1 ★, A2
Jan CPI rptd 2-18, 129G2
Carter '78 CPI projectn 2-22, 124G3
Feb WPI rptd 3-10, 176C2
Feb CPI rptd 3-18, 214F3-215D1
Mar WPI rptd 4-7, 273G3
Mar CPI rptd 4-21, 324G1
'77 CPI forecast revised 4-22, 408A1
Apr WPI rptd 5-5, 383F2
Apr CPI rptd 5-22, 406G2
May WPI rptd 6-3, 445G1
May CPI rptd 6-22, 481F3
WPI, CPI indexes early release set 6-28, 554D2
June WPI rptd 7-8, 554F1
June CPI rptd 7-21, 554B2
July WPI rptd, June revised 8-11, 628F3
July CPI rptd 8-19, 651C1

1978

Price Indexes—*See also 'Inflation' above; also specific industry, commodity names*
WPI, CPI, finished goods indexes described 51E2, A3, C3
Econ indicator index described 128B1
'77, Dec WPI, finished-goods index rptd 1-12; CPI 1-20, 51C2, A3, C3
Carter budget assumptns, projectns 1-23, 46B2, C2
CPI labor pact escalator clauses rptd 1-27, 128E2
Jan finished-goods index, WPI rptd 2-10, 128E1, G1
New CPIs described 222A2
New CPIs released; Jan, Feb inflatn up 2-27, 3-28, 222B1
Feb finished-goods index rptd 3-9, 222B3
Mar finished-goods index, Jan-Mar intermediate goods index, WPI rptd 4-6, 262E2
1860-1978 consumer price table 427E1
Mar CPIs rptd 4-28, 344F3
Apr finished-goods index rptd 5-4, 344C3
Apr CPIs rptd 5-31, 428A3
May wholesale finished, intermediate, crude goods index rptd 6-2, 428E3
May CPIs 6-30, 506F3-507A1
CBO rpts on Propositn 13 impact on CPI 7-6, 525E2

1979

Price Indexes
Producer price indexes described 32D3
CPI described 73C2
'78, Dec producer prices 1-11, 32B3
'77-84 budget assumptns, projectns 1-22, 43A2, B2
Dec '78 CPI 1-24, 73D1-C2
'79 CPI rise forecast, '78 cited 1-25, 48C3
Jah producer prices 2-9, 111D1
Jan CPI 2-23, 151G1
Feb producer prices 3-8, 3-13, 182E1, D3
Feb CPI 3-25, 252D1
Mar producer prices 4-5, 252A1
Mar CPI 4-26, 324D3
Apr producer prices 5-3, 325B1
Apr CPI 5-25, 402C3
May producer prices 6-7, 422F1
May CPI 6-26, 480A3
June producer prices 7-6, 516F3-517A1
June CPI 7-26, 556D3
July producer prices 8-9, 621B2
July CPI 8-25, 646B2
Aug producer prices 9-7, 680G3
Aug CPI 9-25, 725B2
Sept producer prices 10-4, 766C1
Sept CPI 10-26, 827E3
Oct producer prices 11-1, 828B1
Oct CPI 11-27, 903E2

1980

Carter urges wage restraint, vows tough price monitoring, scores Kennedy 4-1, 247C1
Bush, Reagan, Kennedy attack Admin 4-7—4-10, 264C2, F2, B3
Citizens' Party hits inflatn 4-13, 288B3, D3
Simon heads Reagan panel 4-17, 304C3
Carter, Kennedy Pa campaign theme 4-18—4-23, 304F1, A2
Carter on inflatn prospects 5-9, 367G1, F2
Kennedy scores Carter 5-21, 383F1
Jackson: Reagan may win 5-22, 399E3
Reagan on inflatn 5-29, 6-3, 423C3, G3
Carter sees lower inflatn 5-29, 423F3
Kennedy on public anguish 6-5, 423F1
Reagan, Anderson score Carter 6-6, 437A3
Carter addresses mayors 6-10, 438E2
Kennedy on Dem goals 6-14, 480F1
Dem platform drafted 6-24, 479G2, F3
Reagan scores Carter 6-25, 480B2
Hooks sees black vote for Dems 7-6, 515B3
GOP plank scores Carter 7-10, 506G2-A3
Ford, Vander Jagt score Carter 7-14, 7-16, 534A2-F2
GOP platform adopted; text 7-15, 535B3, G3, 536A1, A2
Reagan accepts nominatn 7-17, 531D1, B2, G2, 532A1, C1, A2, D2
Urban League hears pres candidates 8-5, 8-6, 597B2, C2
Kennedy plans conv speech 8-6, 596D2
Dem conv keynote speech 8-11, 612A2*, C2
Kennedy Dem conv speech 8-12, 609D1, 610G1, 613F2, 614E1, G1
Kennedy wins platform planks, wage-price controls defeated 8-12; Carter accepts intent, conv OKs 8-13, 609D1, 610E2, 611F1-612A2; text excerpts 614C2
Carter accepts renominatn 8-14, 612F1, F3, 613A2
Carter, Kennedy confer 8-25, 646G2
Reagan sees 'Carter depressn' 8-27; defends remark, vows action 9-1, 664A2, C2
Carter offers econ renewal plan; Reagan scores; Carey vows support; other reactn 8-28, 663A1-D3
Anderson platform offered 8-30, 665B1, D1
Bush stresses issue 9-1—9-26, 780B3, E3, 781C1, F1
Reagan hits issue 9-8, 699B3
Reagan proposes 5-yr plan 9-9, 699A2
Carter sees 'encouraging' signs, vs 'quick-fix' approach 9-18, 698C3, G3
Reagan, Anderson TV debate 9-21, 721E2, 722F1
Reagan scores 'killer inflation' 9-30, 738B3
Reagan attacks Admin 10-1, 738B1
Carter hits Reagan ideas 10-6, 762G2-B3
Reagan: govt data doctored 10-6, 763A3
Carter vows 'renaissance' 10-12, 10-14, 779A1, E1
Bush scores Carter policies, vows fewer govt regulatns 10-15, 10-16, 817E2
Carter sees 'full recovery' 10-20, 803A1
Carter hits Reagan policies, denies CPI tampering 10-24, 816F2
Reagan hits Carter record, gives 8-pt plan 10-24, 10-29, 817G1-E2
Mondale: Reagan weak on issues 10-26, 816D3
Carter, Reagan TV debate 10-28, 813B1, 814B1, 815G2, E3
Anderson answers TV debate questns 10-28, 816A1
Libertarian candidate cites stance 10-28, 818F2
Reagan finishes strong 10-29—11-3, 840A1
Carter sees electn impact, exit-poll rptd 11-4, 837F1, 838F1, E3
Reagan aides stress inflatn controls 11-23, 897D2
Reagan declares 1st priority 12-1, 914D2
Reagan considers emergency action 12-17, 956B1
Schultze attacks Reagan advisers 12-19, 980D3
Emergency act opposed by Carter, Burns 12-24; Reagan aide says unlikely 12-28, 980G2-A3, B3

Price Indexes
Producer price indexes described 15B1
CPI described 75F3-77E1
'79, Dec producer prices 1-10, 14F3
Dec, '79 CPI 1-25, 75B2
'71-79 CPI rise 1-25, 75D2
'78-85 budget assumptns, projectns table 1-28, 71B2
'80 CPI rise forecast, '79 cited 1-30, 74B2
Jan producer prices 2-15, 126B2
Jan CPI 2-22, 144E1
Feb producer prices 3-7, 182A2
Feb CPI 3-25, 222A2
'79-81 revised budget projectns 3-31, 243F3
Mar producer prices 4-4, 263A1
Mar CPI 4-22, 305G1
Apr producer prices 5-9, 367D2
Apr CPI 5-23, 400F2
May producer prices 6-6, 437B3
May CPI 6-24, 480F3
June producer prices 7-8, 513B3
June CPI 7-23, 556C1
July producer prices 8-15, 630G2
July CPI 8-22, 648A3
Aug producer prices 9-5, 684D1
Aug CPI 9-23, 741A1
Sept producer prices 10-3, 783F1

1976

Wage-Price Developments—*For price data, see 'Prices' above*
Shriver for guidelines 1-7, 22G2
US cncl scores Ford price hike 1-12, 280A3
Mail delivery competitn backed 1-19, 44F3
Muskie for US cncl creatn 1-21, 40C2
Dem platform text 6-15, 470D1-E1
Muskie on cncl role 7-13, 509B3
GOP platform text 8-18, 602G2
Ford, Carter debate 9-23, 701E1
Ford, Carter debate 10-22, 800E1
Carter to seek restraint 11-15, 863E3
Carter renounces controls 12-3, 917E1

1977

Aug WPI rptd 9-1, 692A1
Finished-goods index unveiled, June-Aug rptd 9-1, 692C1
'70-76 CPI rptd 9-12, 722A1
Aug CPI rptd 9-21, 722G1
Sept WPI rptd 10-6, 776D3
Sept finished goods index rptd 10-6, 776G3
Sept CPI rptd 10-21, 817C3
Oct WPI rptd 11-3, 836C2
Oct finished-goods index rptd 11-3, 836D2
Oct CPI rptd 11-22, 898D3
Nov WPI rptd 12-8, 961D2
Nov finished goods index rptd 12-8, 961F2
Nov CPI rptd 12-21, 977D1

Wage-Price Developments—*For price data, see 'Prices' above; for wages, see under LABOR*
Ford energy message to Cong 1-7, 14A3
OECD urges crude oil, gas decontrol 1-11, 169E3
Ford orders end to gas price controls 1-19; Carter rescinds 1-24, 55D1
Carter: US to firm up monitoring; asks business-labor notice on wage rises 1-31, 89E3
Meany vs notice to US 2-21, backs US advisory com role 2-24, 153F2
Carter seeks voluntary control 2-23, 126C3
Carter seeks anti-inflatn effort 4-15, 298G3
Carter plans hosp cost curbs, business scores 4-15, 299C1, E2
Carter energy plan bars gas, oil deregulatn 4-20, 390B2, C2, 292C2-D3
Carter energy plan reactn 4-20, 293G3, 320D2
Carter affirms gas, oil deregulatn bar 4-22, 321C2
Carter urges hosp cost curbs 4-25, reactn 4-25—4-26, 322A1, G1
Steel price prenotificatn cited 5-11, 385C2
US cncl rpts on steel indus 10-7, 776F1
US panel rpts on steel indus 10-7, 776E2

1978

June producer price indexes (wholesale finished, intermediate, crude goods) rptd 7-7, 552B3
June CPIs 7-28, 607D1
July producer prices 8-10, 607B2
July CPIs 8-29, 679G2
Aug producer prices 9-8, 717F1
Aug CPIs 9-26, 752B1
Jan-Aug CPI analyzed; food, housing, health care costs cited 10-4, 789F3
Sept producer prices 10-5, 790F1
Sept CPI 10-27, 864C1
Oct producer prices 11-2, 864F1-D2
Oct CPI, prices double '67 level 11-29, 918F1, E2
Nov producer prices 12-7, 957E3
Nov CPI 12-22, 1003F1

Wage-Price Developments—*See also 'Carter Anti-Inflation Plan' above; also commodity names*
Carter State of Union Message 1-19, 29A2, 30E3
Carter Econ Message 1-20, 48E2
Schultze outlines policy, Meany scores 1-20, 48D3
GOP rebuts Carter State of Union proposal 1-26, 63G1
Carter inflatn plan bars mandatory controls 4-11, 259D2
Business ldrs see Carter, back plan 4-20, 5-11; Admin scores critics 5-8, 361A3, G3
Carter bars controls 5-4, 321C2
Meany, labor ldrs see Carter; rejct wage-restraint plea 5-10; Bosworth backs stand 5-11, 361F2, D3
Wage cncl asks TVA rate hike moderatn 5-15, increase scaled down 5-17, 362A2
Admin jawboning rptd successful 5-19—6-1, campaign stepped up 6-6, 427B3-428B1
US Steel vs Carter price restraint plea 5-24; Strauss, Bosworth score 5-31, 6-19, 428D1
Bethlehem holds price hike to 3%, Admin lauds restraint 6-12; 'Big 3' follow suit 6-13—6-15, 470B2
Carter links curbs, budget restraint 6-14, 446C3
Strauss on deceleratn compliance 8-29, 682C1
Carter links curbs, interest rate cuts 9-27, 751D1
'71 controls, Greenspan cited re $ rescue plan 11-1, 825D1, 826G1, C3

1979

Nov producer prices 12-6, 921D3
Nov CPI 12-21, 984B2

Wage-Price Developments—*See 'Carter Anti-Inflation Plan' above*

1980

Sept CPI 10-24, 823B3
Oct producer prices 11-7, 866G3
Oct CPI 11-25, 897A3
Nov producer prices 12-5, 937B3
Nov CPI 12-23, 983C3

Wage-Price Developments
Pay Advisory Com backs high raises 1-22, 52C1
Brookings economists back controls 2-6, 2-7, 126G2
Business ldrs back controls 2-21, 2-22, 144E3
Kirkland warns of guidelines breakdown 2-22, 144E2
Carter controls resistance rptd 2-25, 2-27, 144G2
11 oil cos cited for '79 abuses, Mobil chrgd 2-25, 189C3
Miller, Kahn vs controls 3-2, 168F1
Schultze: no controls planned 3-7, 182E2
UAW-Ford contract said to violate guidelines 3-7, sanctions imposed 3-26, 225F2
Pay Advisory Com recommendatns OKd 3-13, 182G2
Wage-Price Cncl seeks '79 4th 1/4 price reports 3-18, 209D2
USW pact termed within guidelines 4-23, 385C1
Kirkland says guidelines no curb, scores Admin on natl accord 5-6, 385E1
AFL-CIO exec cncl backs natl accord 5-6, 385B2
Guidelines revised 9-19, 764E3
Wage-Price Cncl ends guidelines 12-16, 983A2

1976

ECOWAS—*See ECONOMIC Community of West African States*

ECSE—*See EUROPEAN Communities*

ECUADOR—*See also ANDEAN Group, IDB, LAFTA, OAS, OPEC, SELA*
'73 mil force rptd 1-2, 60G2
'73 defns budget rptd 1-2, 60G2
Transport fare hike causes strikes, riots 1-4—1-10; rescinded 1-10, 28G1, C2
TV statn closed, mgrs seized 1-4; freed 1-8, 28E2
Rodriguez Lara ousted 1-11, Civil Junta scores coup 1-12, 28D1
Censorship set 1-12, lifted 1-15, 49C1
Junta scores 1-12, 49D1
New cabt sworn 1-14, 48F2
Wage hikes, price freeze asked 1-14, 49F1
Levoyer vows partial pol amnesty 1-16, 49C1
Listed as 'partly free' 1-19, 20C3
'75 plotters, others amnestied 1-21—4-10, Gonzalez exclusn scored 4-13, 363B3
Govt, parties hold talks 2-3—3-16, 363D2
Civilian state govs named 3-8, 363G2
Conservative Party split 3-8, 363A3
Labor protests smashed 4-8, 363F3
Govt min replaced 6-12, 693B1
Students riot, strike 6-15—6-21, 693G1
Agri workers strike 6-20, 600 fired 6-29, 693F1
Transport workers strike 6-21—6-26, 693F1
Police strike 7-15, 13 ldrs seized 7-16, 693E1
Mantilla dies 7-20, 680F3
Electn plan oppositn rptd 8-8, 693C1
Ponce dies 9-14, 1015D2
Parties get charter role 10-11, 872E2
Quito gen strike fails 10-14, 872C2
Gen strike, riots in Riobamba 10-19—10-28, 872G1
Quito students riot 10-28, 872D2
Esmeraldas strikes, riots 11-18—11-23, 1002A1

Foreign Relations (misc.)
Dutch reporter ousted 1-13, 28F2
Anglo yields oil installatns 1-16, 49F1
Vargas vows oil exports hike 1-17, 49B1
Panama exiles dissidents 1-20, 121B2
Chile emb refugees to get safe-conducts 1-25, 100C1
UNESCO literacy drive fails 2-4, 85C2
Forgn bishops seized, expelled; govt, clerics trade chrgs 8-12—8-25, 692B3-693B1
At nonaligned conf 8-16—8-20, 622C1

U.S. Relations
UPI reporter ousted 1-13, 28F2
Brewster quits as amb 3-17, 232F1
Bloomfield confrmd amb 4-1, 262C3
OAS vs US trade curbs 6-18, 464F2
Transport strikers ask US co abolished 6-21—6-26, 693F1

1977

ECOSOC—*See UNITED Nations—Economic & Social Council*

ECUADOR—*See also ANDEAN Group, IDB, OAS, OPEC*
Christmas amnesty rptd 1-1, 3D1
Rightists score junta transitn plan 2-11, 348B1
Velasco scores Bucaram 3-3, Bucaram challenges 3-4; Velasco asks junta revolt 3-25, 348A1
Civiln rule delayed 4-5, anti-Bucaram move seen 4-22, 347C3
Bucaram begins pres bid 7-18; Calderon, Acosta rptd running 8-26, 842F1
Leftist parties coalesce 8-26, 842A2
Mil-civiln pol mtg raided 8-31, pol ldrs score 9-1, 842B2
Const referendum set 9-13, 842E1

Economy & Labor (domestic)
Teachers strike 5-18—6-16, 485B3
Natl gen strike fails 5-18, 485C3
'61-75 GDP variatns table 5-30, 439B1
May strike ldrs rptd sentncd 7-8, 823G3
Teacher, gen strike amnesty rejctd 9-21, 823F3
Labor repressn scored by bishop 10-5, 823E3
Sugar strikers die in police raid 10-18; arrests rptd 10-19; scored 10-25, 823A3
Sugar strike deaths protested 10-26, 10-28; strike continues 11-4, 842A1

Foreign Relations (misc.)—*See also 'Monetary, Trade & Aid' below*
UN Assemb member 3G3
Poveda at Panama Canal pact signing 9-7, 678C1

Monetary, Trade & Aid Issues (including all foreign economic developments)
Gulf assets bought 1-1, 7G2
Israel rptd prime arms seller 1-15, 28E3
US bars Israel jet sale 2-7, 87A3
'75-76 trade, paymts table 3-11, 189A2★, C2
'66-75 arms transfers table 4-8, 415A2
Peru to cut oil imports 5-25, 427G3
US Israel jet sale bar protested, Peru mil buildup cited 6-1—6-3, 454C3
US repeats Israel jet sale ban 7-6, 511C1
Backs Brazil coffee policy 10-21, 876C3

U.S. Relations
Gulf assets bought 1-1, 7G2
US bars Israel jet sale 2-7, 87A3
'66-75 arms transfers table 4-8, 415A2
Mrs Carter visits; Israel jet sale, trade discussed 6-1—6-3; students demonstrate 6-2, 454E1, B3
Carter lauds democratizatn plan 6-3, 455A1
Mrs Carter visit cited 7-5, US repeats Israel jet sale ban 7-6, 511C1
Poveda at Panama Canal pact signing 9-7, 678C1

1978

ECOSOC—*See UNITED Nations—Economic & Social Council*

ECOWAS—*See ECONOMIC Community of West African States*

ECU (European Currency Unit)—*See EUROPEAN Community*

ECUADOR—*See also ANDEAN Group, IDB, OAS, OPEC*
Briz '77 murder arrests rptd 1-20, 112C1
Christian Dem ldr shot at by terrorists 2-22, 194A2
Press curbs rptd by IAPA 10-13, 829B2

Economy & Labor (domestic)
Guayas sugar strike ends 2-17, 148E2
Riots follow bus fare hike 4-3—4-18, 557G1
VP econ role cited 7-16, 557F1
Oil boom rptd over 10-9, 798D3

Foreign Relations (misc.)—*See also 'Monetary, Trade, Aid & Investment' below*
Plane hijacked to Cuba 1-18, 212A3
Peru chrgs border attacks 1-18; mil chiefs meet, declare amity 1-20, 216A2
Israel consul shot at by terrorists 2-22, 194B2
Amazon 8-natn pact signed 7-3, 829C2
Amer rights conv enacted, ct formed 7-18, 828E3, 829C1
UN Assemb member 713E3
8 US natls held on art contraband chrgs; Roldos murder chrg dropped 12-22, 1021C3

Government & Politics—*See also other appropriate subheads in this section*
Rightist parties coalesce 1-6, center-left coalitn formed 1-13, 111F3
Pol parties back const, Velasco urges boycott 1-14, 111E3
Bucaram backs new const 1-14, 111G3
New const approved, armed forces hail 1-15, 111F2
Bucaram, other pol ldrs arrested 1-15; freed 1-30, 2-4, 112A1
Right-wing, Liberal, Dem Left pres candidates rptd 1-30, 2-13, 2-21, 148D2
Const final vote results 2-9, 148E2
Bucaram, 2 other pres candidates barred; pol parties score move 2-20, 148F1
Mil man to be defense min 6-23, 557E1
Pres vote held 7-16; runoff set for Roldos, Duran, vp 7-18, 556F3
Roldos home fired on 7-17, 557D1
Cotopaxi pres votes rptd annulled, slow recount continues 8-8, 671A3
Electoral ct quits, chrgs vote fraud; new count, early runoff set 9-22, 777B1
Local offcls take office 9-29, 777D1
Roldos backers bombed 9-29, 777E1
Pres runoff, cong vote set for Apr '79 10-5; Roldos scores lateness 10-13, 881G1
Liberals split 10-20, 881D2
Pres runoff to pit Roldos vs Duran 11-15, 989C3

1979

ECOSOC—*See UNITED Nations–Economic & Social Council*

ECUADOR—*See also ANDEAN Group, IDB, OAS, OPEC*

Economy & Labor
Min wage hiked 3-2, 256F3
Econ reforms, oil exploratn pledged 8-10, 613G2-C3

Foreign Relations (misc.)—*See also 'Monetary' and 'UN' below*
Papal attack on 'liberatn theology' denied 2-1, 108C3
Ayala visits Nicaragua 6-11, 446E3
Spain premr visits 8-9—8-13, 654D2
Latin ldrs, Spain premr at Roldos inaugural 8-10, 613C2
El Salvador rebels kidnap exec 9-21, 729D2

Government & Politics—*See also other appropriate subheads in this section*
Freedom House lists as partly free 13A1
Ex-min tied to Calderon death 1-12, 62E2
3 parties lose offcl recognitn 1-12, 62G2
Reformed electn law publshd 1-19, vote delayed 2-2, 117E1
11 parties to run cong candidates 3-9, 256D3
Calderon murder suspect caught; Jarrin to be tried in mil ct 3-12, 256E3
Roldos wins pres electn, cong majority 4-29, 329D3*
Roldos sworn pres, outlines policies 8-10, 613C2-C3
Cabt resigns 11-29; Roldos, Bucaram meet 12-4, new Cabt named 12-9, 967A3-968A1

Monetary, Trade, Aid & Investment
Forgn bank loan set 1-30, 101G1
Forgn investmt rules planned 8-10, 613B3
Oil price per barrel rptd 12-21, 977B2

Obituaries
Velasco Ibarra, Jose Maria 3-30, 272G3

UN Policy & Developments
Membership listed 695G2
Pol Pot govt seat upheld 9-19, 695C2

U.S. Relations
8 US prisoners freed 1-5, 62G2
US issues rights rpt 2-10, 107E3
Mrs Carter, Vance at Roldos inaugural; US rights stand praised 8-10, 613D2, C3

1980

ECOSOC—*See UNITED Nations--Economic & Social Council*

ECUADOR—*See also ANDEAN Group, IDB, OAS, OPEC*

Economy & Labor
Soc Sec debate spurs cong shooting 9-30, 789D2

Foreign Relations (misc.)
200 Cuban refugees offered asylum 4-16, 285C1
Bolivia coup condemned 7-29, 577D1
Israel Emb shift rptd 8-26, 643E2
Brazil oil sales rptd 10-2, 759A2
OPEC postpones Quito mtg 10-6, 759D1
Amazon pact signed 10-28, 865D2
Cuba ex-offcl asks UN probe prison hunger strike 12-4, 965D2
Bolivia coup condemned by Santa Marta conf 12-17, 992A3

Government & Politics—*See also other appropriate subheads in this section*
Freedom House lists as free 87D3
Roldos calls plebiscite on const reforms, sets new party 4-11, 312A1
Roldos gains parlt support, cancels plebiscite 5-19, 462G2
Ex-pres shoots 2 in cong 9-30, 789D2

U.S. Relations
Hispanic immigrants in US surveyed 5-11—5-14, 396G2
Carter quotes Reagan on '75 fishing war 9-23, 722D3

1976

4 bishops seized, expelled; clerics protest 8-12—8-16, 692C3
Texaco pays back taxes 8-20, 872E1
Govt to buy Tex-Gulf pipeline 9-17, 872E1
Gulf pays back taxes 9-30; sellout talks begin 10-25, 872A1

EDDE, Raymond
Meets US mediator 4-3, 241E2
Shuns parlt meeting 4-10, 257C2
Nominated for pres 4-26, 296B1
Moslems back for pres 4-30, 319B1
Assad seeks new candidate 319C1
Loses Leb election 5-8, 337B1
US denies Leb is Syria 'satellite' 5-11, 337D2
Charges Phalangist death plot 5-23, wounded 5-25, 369F2
In Natl Union Front 7-11, 514D3
Escapes assassination 11-11, 861C1
Escapes death try 12-11, protests to Sarkis 12-13, 953C1

EDDEN, Mike
Sees guerrilla setback 11-3, 855E2

EDEL, Leon
Gets Arts & Letters medal 5-19, 504C3

EDELMAN, Marian Wright
Named Carter adviser 11-19, 881E3

EDELSTEIN, Julius
Cited as Carter adviser 4-23, 305F2

EDELSTEIN, Melville
Killed 6-16, 425F2

EDEN, John W.
Commerce asst secy 7-2; confrmd 8-3, 807F3

EDENTON (U.S. warship)
In Intl Naval Review 7-4, 488D3

EDEY, Marion
Sees Carter 12-16, 937C2

EDGERLY, George O.
Convicted 4-1, 287E1
Conspiracy convictn 12-23, 988F1

EDITH Wharton: A Biography (book)
Lewis wins Pulitzer 5-3, 352C3

EDGAR, Rep. Robert W. (D, Pa.)
Reelected 11-2, 830D3

EDITOR & Publisher (magazine)
Rpts pres endorsemts 10-30, 827D3

EDMONDS, Walter D.
Wins Natl Book Award 4-19, 292D3

EDMONDSON, Ed
Senate seats Bellmon 3-4, 180C2

EDMONSON, Mark
Wins Australian Open 1-4, 31E3

1977

EDA, Saburo
Dies 5-22, 452G2

EDDY, John A.
Links sunspots to weather 2-21, 183D2

EDDY, Paul
Chrgs Israel torture 6-19, Israel denies 7-3, 511B2

EDELMAN, Marian Wright
In missn to Viet, Laos 3-16—3-20; Carter gets rpt 3-23, 206B1

EDEN, Sir Anthony (Earl of Avon)
Dies 1-14, 84G2

EDENFIELD, Judge Newell
Backs Kuhn power vs Turner 5-19, 567D3

EDEY, Marion
Sen com defers nomination 10-17, 800G1

EDGE, Maj. Gen. Robert L.
AF computer project scored 4-27, 421G2

EDISON Electric Institute
Carter energy plan reactn 4-24, 320A1

EDITOR and Publisher (magazine)
Most reliable govt news sources listed 12-10, 1009A1

EDLER, Dr. Inge G.
Wins Lasker Award 11-16, 927A3

EDLINGER, Bernard
Chrgs Israel beatings 7-7, 511F2-A3

1978

Calderon shot 11-29, dies 12-9, suspect rptd seized 12-13, 989D3
Interior min, police chief replaced, Calderon murder probe cited 12-20, 1021B3

Monetary, Trade, Aid & Investment
Forgn exchng reserves, SDRs explained 1-10, 148G2
'77 trade deficit posted, forgn exchng reserves at record high 2-3, 148F2
Colombia to press econ border projects 8-7, 629A3
Forgn financing down 10-9, 798E3

ECUMENISM—*See ROMAN Catholic Church—Ecumenical Developments*

EDELBAUM, Maurice
Provenzano convicted 3-25, 232E2

EDELMAN, Marian Wright
Vs Head Start shift 4-14, 279A2

EDELSTEIN, Judge David
On IBM trust case 4-26, 510D2

EDELSTEIN, Julius
Scores Sup Ct Bakke ruling 6-28, 482G2

EDGAR, Rep. Robert W. (D, Pa.)
Reelected 11-7, 852C1

EDGINGTON Oil Co.—*See PENN Central Corp.*

EDMONDSON, Ed
Faces Sen primary runoff in Okla 8-22, 683A1
Loses runoff 9-19, 736G3

EDMUND Fitzgerald (ore boat)
Hatch covers blamed for '75 sinking 4-20, 460A1

1979

ECUMENISM—*See under ROMAN Catholic Church*

EDDOWES, Michael H.B.
Files Oswald exhumatn suit 1-9, wins med data access 2-23, 166A3
Oswald substitutn theory discounted 10-22, 905A3

EDELIN, Dr. Kenneth C.
Gets Boston U med schl post, '75 convictn reversal cited 3-15, 272B1

EDELMAN, Harlan
Rpts Laetrile lethal to rats 7-13, 571C1

EDELSTEIN, Judge David
IBM calls for ouster 7-19, 610F2

EDENFIELD, Judge B. Avant
Sentences wildlife refuge protesters 5-4, 368E1

EDGAR, Rep. Robert W. (D, Pa.)
Challenges JFK findings 1-26, 91A2

EDISON Electric Institute
Lewis on 3 Mile I comm final rpt 10-30, 826D1

EDMONDSON, Mark
•Loses Australian Hard Ct tourn 1-7, 391F2

EDMONDSON, William B.
S Africa, US oust envoys 4-12, 4-13, 287F1

EDMONDS v. Compagne Generale Transatlantique
Case decided by Sup Ct 6-27, 558C2

EDPER Equities Ltd.
Brascan tender offer 4-9, reneges 4-11; Ontario blocks new offer 4-20, 303C3, G3, 304B2
Brascan stock purchased 4-30–5-1, takeover effort renewed 5-30, 440D2, G2
Brascan takeover completed 6-14, 6-29, 542D3

1980

ECUMENISM—*See under ROMAN Catholic Church*

EDDY, Col. Gerald A.
On Rift Valley Fever vaccines 3-2, 318G2, A3

EDELSTEIN, Judge David
IBM ouster call rejected 2-25, 266C2

EDGAR, Rep. Robert W. (D, Pa.)
Reelected 11-4, 844C1

EDISON—*See NEW Jersey*

EDITOR & Publisher (magazine)
3d World press coverage study rptd 11-29, 914C1

EDMONDS, Louis
Interview opens 4-24, 392D3

EDMONSON, Mark
Loses Wimbledon mixed doubles 7-5, 606A3

EDOUART, Alexander F.
Dies 3-17, 279C2

EDUCATION

1976

EDUCATION—*See also under BLACK Americans; country names*
House com asks CIA contacts bar 2-10, 150B2
Sen OKs copyright revisn 2-10, 152D2
US, Venez see more cooperatn 2-17, 177F2
New IQ test rptd 2-18, 203G1
Boston attendance up 2-25, 203D1
US prison job training rpt issued 3-9, 271D2
NCES rpts on '75-76 spending, enrolmt, minority access 3-15, 203E2
Sup Ct bars review of sex ed suit 4-5, 262B2
Declining SAT scores rptd 9-11, 993C1
'74-75 city SAT average rptd below natl 9-13, 993E1
'71-75 reading study released 9-21, 993B2
Cong clears copyright revisns 9-30, 764G3 765D1
Vocatnl, lifelong learning aid signed 10-12, 788E3, 789A1
Sup Ct accepts Phila sex-segregatn case 10-18, 867C3
State PBE programs rptd 10-21, 993D3
'76 HS drug use up 11-23, 931D3
Women get 1st Rhodes scholarships 12-19, 993E3

Busing—*See 'School Integration' below*

Colleges & Universities—*See also 'Federal Aid' and other appropriate subheads in this section; college names*
Pratt bequests rptd 1-9, 80C2
House com rpt on CIA contracts leaked 1-26, 93E1
Ford asks CIA research role 2-18, 127C3
NCES rpts '75-76 enrolmt up 3-15, 203G2
'74-75 gifts rptd down 3-20, 263F2
West Pt cheating scandal rptd 4-12, 4-22, 286G3
Sup Ct backs mil acad honor-code disclosures 4-21, 331B3
CIA acad contacts rptd 4-26, 299G1
Female '50-75 enrolmt, degrees data 4-27, 379G2, 380A1
West Pt cheating scandal spurs honor code review 5-19—6-3, 394E3
Dem platform text 6-15, 472C3
Ford signs options tax bill 9-3, 708D1

1977

EDUCATION—*See also U.S. GOVERNMENT—HEALTH, Education & Welfare*
Ohio, Ore pub schls reopen 1-3, 1-11, 16C2
'75 Ford Foundatn grants cited 1-11, 56E1
Cold weather, fuel shortages force schl closings 1-18—1-31, 53C3, 54A2-C2; 2-8, 92B1
HEW chrgs NYC bias 1-18, 112C2
'76 NEA cong gifts rptd 2-15, 128G1
Cleaners end NYC schl strike 2-28, 153C3
Columbus (O) schls reopen 3-7, 196G2-A3
NYC debt repaymt plan detailed 3-10, 193F2
Conn schl funding held unconst 4-18, 302G2
Colo alien voting law review barred 4-18, 342D1
'60-61, '72-73 family spending compared 5-10, 423E2
Intercity bus fare hiked 5-15, 423C2
Burger cites '69-76 student rights cases 5-17, 419A3
B Graham fund disclosed 6-26, 731F3-732A1
China bars US exchngs 6-28, 505E3
Privacy panal submits rptd 7-12, 632B1
Poll on top US concerns 8-10, 632D2
Pa schl funding OKd 8-20, 666D1
Graham fund assn gifts rptd 10-21, 845G1
Cleveland schls kept open by US cts, Ohio legis 10-21—12-7, 939E2
Ohio tax referenda results 11-8, 879E2
Women's studies urged by natl conf 11-19—11-21, 917D3
Ohio financing ruled illegal 12-5, 939D3
Me voters repeal tax law 12-5, 939F3

Busing—*See 'School Integration below*

Colleges & Universities—*See also other appropriate subheads in this section; college names*
Campuses rptd more conservative 1-14, 157E1-E2
HEW guidelines for 6 states ordrd 1-17, 112B2
Tenn univs ordrd merged 1-31, 112G2
Anti-bias compliance data ordrd 2-17, 156G3
Carter sees officials 2-28, 148B3
Carter vs student draft defermt 3-1, 148A3; 3-5, 171G2
HEW warns on sex bias rpt non-compliance 3-15, 279G3
Califano endorses quotas 3-17, 217C3; backs down 3-31, 235B2
'77-78, '70-77 costs rptd 3-27, 483C1
Califano backs down on quotas 3-31, 235B2
HEW guidelines for 6 states reordrd 4-1, 446C1

1978

EDUCATION—*See also U.S. GOVERNMENT—HEALTH, Education & Welfare; also country names*
FCC cable-TV access rules voided 2-24, 195F2
Student sex survey case review denied by Sup Ct 3-20, 206C1
Suspended students damages curbed by Sup Ct 3-21, 220G2
Carter proposes Cabt-level dept 4-14, 279A1-B2
Black-white wage gap down 5-8, 810B3
Pupil competency testing rptd 5-9, 348F2
Bilingual progrm scored 5-9, 348F3-349A1
Intellectual performance study rptd 7-8, 1023E2
FCC to renew children's TV probe 7-28, 672B2
Watts jobless linked 8-8, 811G1
Gas bill OKd by Sen 9-27, 733D3
US-China acad exchng set 10-22, 814E1
Asbestos danger inspectns in schls urged 12-21, 1009G1

Busing—*See 'School Integration' below*

Colleges & Universities—*See also other appropriate subheads in this section; also SPORTS and sport names; college names*
Carter budget proposals 1-23, 47D1, F1, 48C2
Covert intell contracts barred 1-24, 49G2; legis introduced 2-9, 107B1
Pa ex-state sen begins jail term 2-20, 172A3
NYS denies Unification Seminary charter 2-22, 295G2
Med student ouster upheld 3-1, 143D2
Divinity schl female enrollmt rptd 3-23, 295B2
'78-79 cost rise rptd 4-10, 264A2
Med schl '78-79 applicant decline rptd 4-13, 597D2
Cabt-level dept proposed 4-14, 279C1
Md U social-actn group case refused by Sup Ct 5-1, 364B1
Burger: improve law students' skills 5-16, 388D2

1979

EDUCATION
Carter State of Union Message asks govt reorg 1-23, 46G3
China pact signed 1-31, 65D1
Carter proposes Cabt-level dept 2-8, 110F2
Bell & Howell to reimburse home-study students 3-26, 308D3
Lead level impact study rptd 3-29, 266E1
Cable TV pub-access rule upset by Sup Ct 4-2, 281G1
Sen OKs Educ Dept, rejcts sex educ amendmt 4-30, 326B2
'78 enrollmt rptd down 5-12, 367F1-C2
Carter sees ldrs at Camp David 7-6—7-11, 513F2; thanks 7-30, 608F3-609A1
House OKs Educ Dept bill 7-11, 514C3
Califano firing linked to Educ Dept oppositn 7-18, 529G2
Mich HS voter turnout law signed 8-14, 724D2
Adult literacy progrms scored 9-8, 785G3
Math achievemt scores decline 9-13, 785D2
Educ Dept bill signed 10-17, 782A2
TV networks children's programs scored 10-30, NAB responds 11-1, 858B3-E3
USSR exchng progrm benefits mil 11-8, 857A1, C1
HS system criticized 11-27, 925D1-A2
Children's TV plan modified 12-19, 1006G1

Bilingualism
Bilingual progrm oppostn rptd 1-29; '68, '79 costs compared 1-30, 127G1
HEW proposes new program rules 6-29, 596F3
Ann Arbor standard English teaching plan ordrd 7-12, 597B1
Spanish-Eng programs ordrd in NY 7-18, 7-20, 597C1, D1
Ann Arbor OKs 'Black English' teacher progrm 8-15, 650A3

Colleges & Universities—*See also other appropriate subheads in this section*
Carter budget proposals 1-22, 43G2, 44B2, F2, 46B2
Forgn students surveyed, visa probe planned 1-29, 93F2
Peabody, Vanderbilt merge 3-19, 209D1
SAT coaching schl study issued 5-29, 785A2
NYS admissn test disclosure law enacted 7-14, 785A3
ABA panel backs law schl chngs 8-15, 768F3
SAT, Achievemt Test scores rptd down 9-8, 785E1; 10-4, 810G1
Black woman wins Rhodes scholarship 9-9, 1005F2
SAT decline, '50s A-fallout linked 9-17, 747A2
Calif lawyer survey rptd 9-17, 787E1
NYU prof indicted in drug case 10-4, 839G3

1980

EDUCATION
Female math interest increase rptd 4-15, 559D2
Educ Dept begins operatn 5-4, 369G3
Ia schools to buy White House uniforms 5-16, 460A3
Schl censorship power upheld 6-13, 582G3
US Families Conf meets in Minn 6-19—6-21, LA 7-10—7-12, 601C2, E2
High schl grads spur June unemploymt rise 7-3, 513E2
UNESCO rpts world illiteracy 12-4, 953E1
Reagan aide, Sowell address black conf 12-14, 956G2

Bilingualism
Hispanic immigrants surveyed 5-11—5-14, 396D2

Colleges & Universities
State of State messages 1-10, 2-19, 403D3, 404A1; 2-12, 4-8, 483F1, 484G2
Aptitude test study disputed 1-14, 36G1
Freshmen survey rptd 1-20, 319C3-320B1
Black enrollmt rptd up 1-22, 94E2
Enrollmt decline seen 1-22, 319D2
Transcript scandal spreads; FBI, NCAA probes rptd 1-23—5-23; U of NM ex-coach indicted 5-23, 469B2-D3
Carter budget proposals 1-28, 69E3, 72G2-A3, E3
ABA tables law schl affirmative actn proposal 2-5, 114E3
Photocopy co sued 2-5, 119F3
Pvt coll faculty unions curbed by Sup Ct 2-20, 146C1-B2
Kennedy 'basic speech' excerpts 3-10, 183D1
Photocopy suit rptd setld 3-21, 376D3

1976

Grade dip rptd 9-7, 993A3
Sup Ct stays Calif U reverse bias ruling 11-15, 882C1
Calif U to appeal bias ruling 11-19, 995F2
Enrolmt rptd at standstill 11-22, 993E2-A3

Federal Aid—*See also 'Presidential Election' below*
Ford State of Union message 1-19, 36G2, 37B2, 38G2, 39G2
House votes Viet refugee aid 1-19, 69F2
House OKs broadcast funds 1-20, 94B2
Muskie rebuts Ford 1-21, 40A2
'77 budget proposals 1-21, 62B3, 63F1, 65C1, C2, 66B2
Ford rpts govs back budget plan 1-22, 41C2
HEW funds veto overridden 1-27, 1-28, 69A2
Ford to up budget request 2-16, 166D3
NJ TM grant cited 2-25, 203E2
Energy dvpt loans urged 2-26, 149E2
Ford asks block-grant program for states 3-1, 166F2-D3
Md HEW funds cutoff barred 3-8, 203D1
'75-76 spending peak seen 3-15, 203F2
Fscl '77 Ford, House com budgets table 231B1
Sen OKs food-stamp reform 4-8, 282A1
Cong OKs MD incentives 4-12, 282G2
Cong OKs '77 budget target 5-12, 5-13; Ford, OMB, Cong budgets table 358F1, C2; signed 5-27, 982F1
Cong clears ACTION funds 5-13, 393D1
Cong clears added funds 5-16, 411E3
Cong OKs broadcast aid 5-25, 434B3; Ford signs 6-5, 982F1
Sup Ct OKs some church-coll aid 6-21, 452D3
HEW father-son, mother-daughter rule suspended 7-7, 535E2-C3
Sen OKs student tax credits 8-6, 586D1
Cong sets '77 budget levels, table 9-16, 706C2
Cong OKs HEW inspector-gen bill 9-29, 765G2
'77 HEW funds veto overridden 9-30, 727A3; signed 10-19, 482G1
Cong OKs vet benefits 10-1, 807B1; signed 10-15, 982G1
Block grant bill not cleared 10-2, 882G3, 883B2
Vocational, higher educ aid signed 10-12, 788E3
Health manpower aid signed 10-13, 788E2
Mayors urge spending 12-14, 937A3

Non-Public Schools
Va bias ruling backed 1-5; Justice Dept disputes 4-9, 263C2
Caths back parochial schls 3-23, 443G3
Sup Ct bars pvt schl bias 6-25, 479B1
Ford vows tax aid 9-15, 686B1
Pres candidates dispute taxatn 10-2, 743E2, G2

Obituaries
Armstrong, Barbara 1-18, 56G2
Belkin, Samuel 4-18, 315G3
Buchan, Alistair 2-4, 124D3
Haines, Charles 5-25, 524F2
Henderson, Vivian 1-28, 124E3
Hopper, Vincent 1-19, 56D3
Johnson, Mordecai 9-11, 716C3
McBride, Katherine 6-3, 484F3
Millet, Fred 1-1, 56F3
Pimsleur, Paul 6-22, 524D3
Shaffer, Laurance 7-20, 716F3
Silvert, Kalman 6-15, 524F3

Presidential Election (& transition)
Wallace downplays busing issue 1-9, 22D2
Reagan for shift to states 1-12, 22E1
Mass primary issue 3-2, 166C1, F1
Carter, Jackson at odds 3-3, 166F1
Wallace upset in Fla 3-9, 179G2
Black Caucus drafts plank 5-1, 343E3
Dem platform disputed 5-14, 5-20, 357E3
Ford defends stand vs busing 5-26, 391D1
Reagan, Ford views 6-2—6-6, 410D2

1977

Food-stamp chngs sought 4-5, 250E2
US-Cuba exchng sought 4-11, 283A2
Califano backs minority admissn goals 6-5, 445F3
NYS alien tuitn law voided 6-13, 517E2
HEW issues 6-state desegregatn plan 7-5, 630F2
CIA mind-control tests revealed 8-1—8-9, 610C3
Pa budget cuts OKd 8-20, 666A2
'63-77 SAT score drop rptd 8-23; '77-freshmen scores hit low; study, SATs criticized 8-24, 739C1-C2
Bakke brief filed 9-19; Sup Ct hears arguments 10-12, orders more briefs 10-17, 834F2-835G1
Food stamp eligibility tightnd 9-29, 737G1-A2
Utah State U broker dispute review declined 10-11, 774A3
NJ, Va referenda OKd 11-8, 879C2
Idaho student jobless benefits law upheld 12-5, 939C1
Curriculum reform urged 12-15, 1009C1

Federal Aid
Carter plans job-training 1-7, 5A2
Boston aid request rptd 1-16, 112C3
Ford '78 budget proposals 1-17, 30B1, 32B2, F2, B3, 33B1
HEW plans cutoffs re integratn, bias; orders Tex, Ark reviews 2-17, 156C3
Ct orders Chicago cutoff 2-17, 157A1
Welfare cost rptd 2-19, 176C1
Carter budget revisions 2-22, 124C3, 125A2, 126A1
HEW reorganizatn effected 3-9, 175C3
HEW warns on bias rpt non-compliance 3-15, 279G3
Giaimo urges 'impact aid' end 3-23, 229A1
Handicapped ask HEW rule chngs 4-5, 301B3
Educ Office reorganized 4-11, 301D3
Carter energy plan 4-20, 290G1; fact sheet 292C1
Handicapped rules signed 4-28, 338E3
Vocational, handicapped schl bias suit filed 5-11, 446D2
Cong sets '78 target 5-17, 405A1
Carter vs impacted aid 5-26, 417C1
Califano backs admissn goals 6-5, 445G3
House curbs HEW busing, quota enforcemt 6-16, 6-17, 478C1
NYC minority aid withheld 7-5, 631E1
Carter rebuts black criticism 7-25, 573F1
House OKs Carter energy pkg 8-5, 609B3, 610A1
Loan default collectn by pvt groups set 9-8, 739D2
NC, Tenn church coll aid backed 10-3, 760E3
Vets benefits review signed 10-8, 773A2
Energy conservatn credit bill OKd by Sen 10-31, 832G2
Vet benefits, schl admin aid cleared 11-4, 877D2, B3; signed 11-23, 1001F2
Career guidance authorizatn clears Cong 11-29, 959A2; signed 12-13, 1001G2
Busing curb clears Cong 12-7, 958D3; signed 12-20, 1001A3
Forgn-trained med student transfer rule eased 12-7, 959C2

Non-Public Schools
Sup Ct backs limited state aid 6-24, 539F2

Obituaries
Dewey, Godfrey 10-18, 872F1
Eiseley, Loren 7-9, 604A3
Gross, Mason 10-11, 872B2
Hardy, Arthur 10-31, 872B2
Henderson, Edwin 2-3, 164A3
Herberg, Will 3-27, 264G2
Holland, Kenneth 12-9, 1024B2
Houston, Livingston 11-22, 952E2
Hutchins, Robert 5-14, 452B3
Johnson, Harry 5-8, 452C3
Kimpton, Lawrence 11-1, 952F2
Payne, Paul 12-2, 1024G2
Shuster, George 1-25, 84F3
Winslow, Ola Eliz 9-27, 788B3

1978

MD specializatn rptd too high 5-19, 597E2
Law schl female enrollmt rise rptd 5-31, 554F2
Bakke med schl admissn ordrd, race-based affirmative actn principle upheld by Sup Ct; reactn, opinion excerpts 6-28, 481A1-483A1, E1-487C2
Harvard admissns program described 483A1
NC Univ minority rep case sent back by Sup Ct 7-3, 552C1
Cigaret smoking rptd down 7-5, 727D1
Med schl cutbacks forecast 7-23, 577C3
Burger renews trial lawyer attack 8-9, 626A3
SAT verbal scores stabilize 9-16, 754G1
HEW suit vs Md refused by Sup Ct 10-2, 751F2
Business aid grows 10-4, 754B2
'77 black med, law schl enrollmts down 10-8, 811C2
State college aid up 10-10, 770C2
New med schls opposed 10-24, 948C3
Army 2-yr enlistmt plan rptd 11-10, 895E2
Job-bias ruling voided by Sup Ct 11-13, 874F1-C2
Harvard-CIA secret ties revealed 12-1, 962F2

Federal Aid
NCAA suit vs Title IX dismissed 1-9, 40E2
Carter State of Union Message 1-19, 29F2, 30G1, 31B1, E1, G3
Carter budget proposals 1-23, 44E2, 46F1, F3, 47D1, 48C2; table 45E2
Coll student aid plan unveiled 2-8, 84A2
Carter scores coll loan defaulters 2-17, 123F2
Ct-ordrd desegregatn fund bar review denied 2-27, 143F1
Carter submits plan to Cong 2-28, 141A3
NYC local bd suspended in ethnic data dispute 3-10, 264A2
House rebuffs Carter plan 3-20, 202B3
VA curbs backed by Sup Ct 3-20, 205E3
Black vote issue seen 4-10, 568F2
Tuitn tax credit OKd by House com, Carter vs 4-11, 260G3, 261B1
Cabt-level dept proposed 4-14, 279A1-B2
Energy conferees in accord 4-21, 304G3, 305G1
Sen votes budget targets 4-26, 305A3
Cong '79 budget target res cleared 5-17, 385F1, A2, C2
Carter plans budget cuts 5-25, 404A3
Tuitn tax credits OKd by House, Califano scores 6-1; Carter threatens veto 6-8, 431G2, F3
Tuitn aid cut defeated in House 6-8, 445D2
Coll racial quotas barred by House 6-13, 445G3
Mil educ, training cited in US '79 forgn aid bill 9-26, 734D1
Carter vs tuitn tax credit bill 9-28, 751G3
Carter asks Viet vet progrm, reactn 10-10, 878D1, G1
Educ Dept bill dies 10-15, 785B1
Tax-cut bill cleared, tuitn credit out 10-15, 785G1, 786C1, E1, 807B2
Energy bill clears 10-15, 787C2
Coll student aid expansn cleared 10-15, 807G1; Carter signs 11-2, 873E1
HEW vs new med schl grants 10-24, 948C3
Higher-educ groups protest Carter budget plans 12-14, 980G1
Carter hikes '80 budget funds 12-22, 1002E3

Non-Public Schools
Fla Baptist schl integratn challenge refused by Sup Ct 2-21, 126D1
Carter submits aid plan 3-2, 141D3
House rebuffs Carter aid plan 3-20, 202C3
RC enrollmt drop halted 3-20, 348C3
Tuitn tax credit OKd by House com, Carter vs 4-11, 261A1, B1
Tuitn tax credits OKd by House 6-1, Carter threatens veto 6-8, 431G2, F3
Coll student aid expansn, tuitn tax credit rejectn cleared 10-15, 785G1, 807G1

Obituaries
Ascoli, Max 1-1, 96C1
Begle, Edward 3-2, 252D2
Cole, Charles W 2-6, 196E2
Conant, James B 2-11, 196F2
Evans, Bergen 2-4, 196G2
Goodhart, Arthur Lehman 11-10, 972B3
Highet, Gilbert 1-20, 96C2
Pei, Mario 3-2, 252C3
Turner, Thomas Wyatt 4-21, 356E3
Wriston, Henry 3-8, 252G3

1979

Pope in US, backs academic freedom 10-7, 760B1
NJ bond issue loses 11-6, 846C2, 847A1
Forgn-language study urged 11-7, 944G1
Emory U gets $100 mln gift 11-8, 902C2
Greenville coll suspends Iranians 11-21, 898E2
Title IX sports guidelines issued 12-4, 1000F2
'78 enrollmt decline rptd 1-29, 5-12, 367B2
Forgn student abuses detailed 3-2, visa crackdown announced 3-8; enrollment chart 167C2, E2
Pvt debt collectn for US urged 3-10, 208E3
Pvt coll decrease rptd 3-19, 282A3
Minn U, Cuba exchng rptd 3-27, 238C2
Ethics decline seen 4-2, 4-18, 282A2-A3
Southn bd survey excludes 4-9, 307A2
Tenn univ merger upheld 4-13, 326G2-C3
'Italian Bakke case' declined by Sup Ct 4-23, 346D2
Yale provost quits in fund dispute 5-2, 392D2
Wilson Coll closing barred 5-26, 482C1
Prop 13 effects reviewed 6-3, 499E3
Antioch averts bankruptcy 6-4, 482G1-B2
Right to bar disabled backed by Sup Ct 6-11, 478E1
Tenn univ merger stay denied by Sup Ct 6-18, 499B2

Federal Aid
Carter restores some '80 budget cuts 1-5, 3D3
Carter budget proposals 1-22, 41C2, 44G1-B2, F2, 46C1, B2; table 42E2
Cabt-level dept proposed 2-8, 110F2
US desegregatn actn urged 2-13, 110D2
Job-training aid cuts scored 2-26, 149A1
Aid shift to states rptd 3-5, 282C3
MD, nursing schl fund cuts trimmed 3-6, 163D3
Pvt debt collectn for US urged 3-10, 208E3
Pvt Title IX suit allowed by Sup Ct 5-14, 382C3
Schls right to bar disabled backed by Sup Ct 6-11, 478E1
HEW bars Chicago desegregatn funds 9-15, 944B1
Carter proposes expanded indl research grants for univs 10-31, 829G3
Title IX job bias funds cutoff bar declined by Sup Ct 11-26, 919D2
NYC schl funds denial upheld by Sup Ct 11-28, 944A2
Title IX sports guidelines issued 12-4, 1000F2

Non-Public Schools
Church schl labor interventn barred by Sup Ct 3-21, 231D2
NYS reimbursemt bar voided by Sup Ct 4-2, 281A3
'78 enrollmt rptd down 5-12, 367G1-A2
NJ tax break ban affirmed by Sup Ct 5-29, 421F3
Pa transport law challenge dismissed by Sup Ct 6-25, 540C2

Obituaries
David, Donald K 4-13, 356C3
Cavanaugh, John Joseph 12-28, 1008B2
Elliott, Wm Yandell 1-9, 104A3
Parsons, Talcott 5-8, 432C3
Tugwell, Rexford Guy 7-21, 588E3
Williams, T Harry 7-6, 588G3

1980

'79 endowmt earnings rptd 3-24, 319C1
SAT data to be disclosed 4-7, 318E3
Freshmen math experience rptd 4-15, 559A3
NCAA wins Title IX appeal 4-19, 469D3
LaSalle Extensn U ads ruled misleading 5-12, 703G1
Buckley cancels Vassar commencemt appearance 5-19, 471B2
UNM ex-coach acquitted of US chrgs 6-20, 875E3
Grads spur June unemploymt rise 7-3, 513E2
Berkeley Barb folds 7-3, 582F3
US, Canada enrollmt compared 7-16, 562D3
NYU prof convicted in drug case 7-16, 607F3-608A1
Ariz ex-football coach, others indicted 7-24, state probe asked 10-16, 875G2
NCAA probe of UCLA basketball team 'rewards' rptd 7-27, 875D3
ABA backs law schl minority 'opportunities' 8-6, 744D1
Pac-10 punishes 5 schls in transcript scandal 8-11, 875C1
Kennedy Dem conv speech 8-12, 614G1
Natl Student Marketing liquidates 9-10, 985F3
Higher educ authrzn clears Cong 9-18, 9-25, Carter signs 10-3, 803A3
Motorola settles job bias suit 9-23, 746E3
USC reveals faulty athletic admissns 10-13, coaches comment 10-15, 10-29, 875C2
Ore U athletic dept probe delay chrgd 10-13, denied 10-15, 875B3
Scientific literacy lag rptd 10-22, 990D1
Del Law Schl case declined by Sup Ct 11-10, 868B3
Patent law revisn clears Cong 11-21, 915F3
Faculty sex-bias Title IX case accepted by Sup Ct 12-1, 918B2

Federal Aid
$2 bln youth training progrm asked 1-10, 16B2
Carter State of Union proposals 1-21, 1-23, 43A2, F2, D3
USDA 'junk food' rules rptd 1-27, 157E3
Carter budget proposals 1-28, 69E3, 72C3, 73E2; table 70E1
US dietary guidelines issued 2-4, 157B3
Black Caucus vs Carter budget 2-5, 94G2
Kennedy 'basic speech' excerpts 3-10, 183F1
Reagan admits gaffe on Viet vet GI benefits 4-10, 288E2
NCAA wins Title IX appeal 4-19, 469E3
Land-grant exchng ban upheld by Sup Ct 5-19, 440A2
Cuban, Haitian refugee assistance set 6-20, 485A1
Summer Head Start progrm rptd 6-30, 496A1
Carter addresses NEA 7-3, 505C2
Cuban, Haitian refugee funds budgeted 8-13, 617E1
Carter pres renominatn acceptance speech 8-14, 613A1, B2
Higher educ authrzn clears Cong 9-18, 9-25, Carter signs 10-3, 803A3
Refugee aid to states clears Cong 9-25, 10-1, Carter signs 10-10, 785B1
Vet aid clears Cong 9-25, 9-26, signed 10-17, 856F2
Reagan backs parochial schl tax credits 10-1, 738F1
NYC parochial schl remedial aid case refused by Sup Ct 10-6, 782F2
Reagan vs 'federalized' role 10-13, 780A1
Faculty sex-bias Title IX case accepted by Sup Ct 12-1, 918B2

Non-Public Schools
NYS reimbursemt upheld by Sup Ct 2-20, 146B2
RC bishops family life conf opens 9-26, 810C3
Reagan backs tax credits 10-1, 738F1
NYC remedial aid case refused by Sup Ct 10-6, 782F2

Obituaries
Dodds, Harold W 10-25, 876C1
Fisher, Welthy Honsiger 12-16, 1004E1
Jordan, Wilbur 6-3, 528C2
Keeney, Barnaby C 6-18, 528C2
McLuhan, Marshall 12-31, 1004F2
Randall Jr, John H 12-1, 1004B3
Rodell, Fred 6-4, 528D3
Valentine, Alan 7-14, 608E3

1976

Carter backs PS prayer ruling 6-6, 411A1
Dem com OKs platform plank 6-15, 432D3
Dem platform text 6-15, 471F2, G2, 472C2, F2, C3, 473A2, F3, G3, 474E2, 475A2
Ford speaks vs busing 6-22, 452E2
Carter pledge 7-15, 507E1, 510D2, F2, 511A1
Mondale asserts commitmt 7-15, 511D3
Carter legis record cited 512D1, F1, C2
Mondale record cited 512B3, C3
Carter sees limited busing 8-3, 564B3
Reagan: Schweiker compatible 8-4, 564G1
GOP delegate educ level rptd 8-7, 8-8, 616C2
Reagan urges anti-busing platform plank 8-8, 583C1
GOP platform com OKs anti-busing, other planks 8-13, 582E3, 583F1
Mondale scores GOP, cites Carter priority 8-16, 617C3
GOP platform text 8-18, 602E3, 603E3, 604A3, D3-605C1, B2, G3, 606F4, G2, 607C1
AFT endorses Dem ticket 8-18, 617D3
Ford acceptance speech cites 8-19, 611D3, 612C2, D2
Mondale scores Admin 8-25, 8-28, 645G2, B3
Indep Party vs busing 8-27, 666F1
Dole: Mondale 'Mr Busing' 9-11, 687A1
Ford on tax aid, job-training 9-15, 686B1
Ford, Carter debate 9-23, 702F1, A2
Tax on church-owned institutns disputed 10-2, 743E2, G2
Carter sees Utah group 10-7, 762C1
Mondale, Dole debate 10-15, 782G3, 783C1, A2
Ford, Carter debate 10-22, 800F3, 801C3, D3, 802C1, D1
Dole backs schl prayer 10-31, 827A3
NAACP vs Bell as atty gen 12-20, 956G2, C3

Religion Issues
Religious class time off rule review denied 1-19, 43C1
Suit seeks bar to TM in NJ schools 2-25, 203C2
Caths back parochial schls 3-23, 443G3
Carter backs PS prayer ruling 6-6, 411A1
Prayer amendmt cited re Passman vote defeat 8-26, 633B1
Carter, Ford debate 10-22, 802C1, D1
Sup Ct refuses Mo tuitn aid case 12-13, 960A3

School Integration & Busing—*See also 'Presidential Election' above, 'Teachers' below; also 'Boston' under MASSACHUSETTS*
Pvt schl integratn ban backed 1-5; Justice Dept disputes 4-9, 263C2
NAACP loses Cleveland schl constructn plea 1-6, 6C2
Sup Ct declines Denver rule review 1-12, 24E1
Milwaukee integratn ordrd 1-19, 42B3
Chicago study rptd 1-25, 95B2
Detroit busing starts 1-26, 95E1
Cong overrides HEW funds bar 1-28, 69E2
Md HEW funds cutoff barred 3-8, 203D1
Court sets Dallas plan 3-10, 203A3
Penn anti-busing bill vetoed 3-19, 203B3
Omaha plan accepted 4-27, 453D2
Justice Dept, Ford seek Sup Ct busing review 5-14, 5-18, 5-19; Levi assigned 5-18, 377E2-D3
Wilmington plan ordrd 5-19, 453C2
US holds Louisville hearings 6-14—6-16, 453F1
'70-75 data released 6-19, 992C3
Ford proposes busing curbs; Wilkins denounces 6-24, 452G1, D2
Sup Ct bars pvt schl bias 6-25, 479B1
Sup Ct bars contd rezoning 6-28, 468F3
Sup Ct declines Chattanooga plan review, 6-30, 552A3 ★
'60s anti-black strategy chrgd 8-12, 671F2
NAACP offcl scores GOP, Dem planks 8-24, 8-25, 666A2
Fall in local conflicts rptd 9-14, 992F3
Antibusing bills not cleared 10-2, 883B2
Sup Ct stays Calif U reverse bias rule, to review Detroit plan 11-15, 882C1, E2; refuses Wilmington case 11-29, 900A3; vacates Austin busing plan 12-6, 920B2
Calif U to appeal bias ruling 11-19, 995F2
Bell atty gen apptmt scored 12-20, 956G2, G3

1977

Religion Issues
Coll student survey issued 1-14, 157A2
Ind ct bars biology text 4-14, 471D3
RC-NLRB dispute case refused 5-2, 406C2
Baptist coll divorce dismissal chrgd 5-2, 472C1
Davidson Coll drops tenure curbs 5-6, 471F3
Sup Ct backs limited state aid 6-24, 539F2
Bishops synod theme 9-30—10-29, 906A1
NC, Tenn church coll aid backed 10-3, 760E3
TM banned by NJ ct 10-20, 845D3
Bishops on women's roles 11-15, OK new catechism 906E1, G2
NYS schl aid law voided 12-6, 938A3

School Integration & Busing
Sup Ct bars Boston receivership case review 1-10, 57D1
Boston HS violence 1-10, 112D3
Boston rpts instructn decline 1-16, 112C3
HEW guidelines for colls in 6 states ordrd 1-17, 112B2
Cleveland busing plan proposed 1-18, 112F2
Sup Ct voids Indianapolis plan 1-25, 79D3-80C1
Sup Ct bars Louisville busing plan review 1-25, 80D1
Syracuse OKs voluntary plan 1-25, 112A3
Tenn univs ordrd merged 1-31, 112G2
Bused Chicago blacks show improvemt 2-14, 157C1
US comm backs city-suburb busing 2-15, 112C1
HEW plans aid cutoffs, orders Tex, Ark reviews 2-17, 156C3
Anti-bias compliance data ordrd 2-17, 156G3
Chicago ruled in violatn 2-17, 157A1
LA student boycott 2-18; busing plan OKd by bd 3-3, 216D3
Columbus (O) plan ordrd 3-8, 217A1
Milwaukee goal set 3-11, 216F3
HEW warns on sex bias rpt non-compliance 3-15, 279G3
Califano backs quotas, busing 3-17, 217B3; backs down 3-31, 235B2
Wilmington (Del) busing backed 3-18, 216C2
Austin integratn plan asked 3-18, 216A3
HEW guidelines for colls in 6 states reordrd 4-1, 446C1
Phila sex bias affirmed 4-19, 342C2
Dayton (O) busing backed 4-22, 446D1
HEW sued re vocational, handicapped bias 5-11, 446D2
Boston HS violence 5-12—5-16, 446A2
Wilmington busing upheld, quotas barred 5-18, 446C2
Kansas City (Mo) seeks Interstate integratn 5-26, 446E1
House curbs HEW busing, quota enforcemt; OKs anti-pairing amendmt 6-16, 6-17, 478C1
Dayton busing ruling vacated 6-27, 538F2
Dayton busing rule remanded 6-27, 538F2; voided 12-15, 978B3
Detroit remedial bias progrms upheld 6-27, 538A3

1978

Religion Issues
Fla Baptist schl integratn challenge refused by Sup Ct 2-21, 126D1
House rebuffs Carter aid plan 3-20, 202C3
RC enrollmt drop halted 3-20, 348C3
Tuitn tax credit OKd by House com, Carter vs 4-11, 261A1, B1
Tuitn tax credits OKd by House, Califano scores 6-1; Carter threatens veto 6-8, 431D3
Tuitn tax credit dies in Cong 10-15, 785G1, 807B2

School Integration & Busing
LA plan set for Sept 1-3, 5E1-A2
Wilmington plan ordered 1-9, 15F2-A3
Carter State of Union Message 1-19, 30G2
US rejcts Va, Ga, NC coll plans; OKs Ark, Okla, Fla proposals 2-2, 85C1
Fla Baptist schl integratn challenge refused by Sup Ct 2-21, 126D1
Fed fund bar for ct-ordrd desegregatn denied review 2-27, 143F1
Carter submits aid plan 2-28, 141D3
US OKs Ga, Va, NC coll plans 3-8—5-12, 368G3
NYC school bd suspended in ethnic data dispute 3-10, 264G1-A2
Chicago OKs voluntary plan 4-12, state objects 4-13, 263E3
LA enters mandatory phase 4-14, 309E2
Dallas plan upset 4-24, 309B2
Chicago plan OKd by Ill 5-11, 611C1
NYC schl desegregatn ordrd 5-16, 369G1-C2
Indianapolis plan ordrd 6-2, 611E1
Coll racial quotas barred by House 6-13, 445G3
Bakke med schl admissn ordrd, race-based affirmative actn principle upheld by Sup Ct; reactn, opinion excerpts 6-28, 481A1-483A1, E1-487C2
Harvard admissns progrm described 483A1
NC Univ minority rep case sent back by Sup Ct 7-3, 552C1
Columbus (O) plan OKd 7-14, 611E1
Wilmington (Del) busing plan OKd 7-24, 611F1
Dayton (O) busing plan upheld 7-27, 610G3
LA busing appeals rejctd 8-3—9-9; busing starts peacefully, 10,000 boycott 9-12, 698D2, B3-699A1
Cleveland busing deadline cited 8-23, 663G2
Cleveland plan deferred 8-25, 699C1
HEW suit vs Md refused by Sup Ct 10-2, 751F2
'77 black med, law schl enrollmts down 10-8, 811C2
ACLU hails anti-busing bill defeat 10-20, 981C3
Mass, Washn, Miss referenda results 11-7, 847A2, D3, 852F3, 857C3
Ga, Tex integratn cases declined by US Sup Ct 12-4, 959A2

1979

Religious Issues
Utah Mormon shot, '73 child educ issue cited 1-18, 94C1
Church schl labor interventn barred by Sup Ct 3-21, 231D2
NYS pvt schl reimbursemt bar voided by Sup Ct 4-2, 281A3
Sen OKs prayer amendmt 4-5, 326D2
Carter vs pro-schl prayer legis 4-10, 263F3
NJ pvt schl tax break ban affirmed by Sup Ct 5-29, 421F3
Pa transport law challenge dismissed by Sup Ct 6-25, 540C2
House OKs prayer amendmt 7-11, 514E3
Va expulsn upheld 8-23, 650A2
Calif teacher firing case dismissed by Sup Ct 12-10, 988F1

School Integration & Busing
La segregatn case refused by US Sup Ct 1-15, 32E1
Sears sues US on bias laws 1-24, 92D1; suit dismissed 5-15, 365B3
US comm rpts desegregatn lags 2-13, 110B2
Racial attitudes surveyed 2-20, 307C1
St Louis busing order denied 4-12, 596C3
Tenn univ merger, higher educ plans upheld 4-13, 326G2-C3
DiLeo case declined by Sup Ct 4-23, 346D2
Milwaukee desegregatn case setld 5-4, 596E2
Integratn study rpts Southn gains 5-9, 650D1
Carter links black vote, bias 5-20, 384G2
Washn anti-busing initiative overturned 6-15, 596D3
Tenn univ merger stay denied by Sup Ct 6-18, 499B2
Ohio busing orders upheld by Sup Ct 7-2, 539E2
Anti-quota, busing amendmts OKd by House 7-11, 514D3; 2d anti-busing amendmt defeated 7-24, 559E2
Fla HS literacy test voided 7-12, 785C3
Columbus busing ordered 8-2, 596A3
Wallace upholds integratn 8-2, 656F1
KKK protesters arrested in Ala 8-12, 631C1
LA busing plan challenged 8-27, Calif referendum rptd set 9-2, 679C3
Chicago compulsory busing ordrd 8-31, 679A3
6 states rpt busing progrms set 9-2, 679E3
Dayton, Columbus busing begins peacefully 9-4, 9-6; Cleveland protests staged 9-9, plan effected 9-10, 679G1-A3
HEW bars Chicago desegregatn funds 9-15, seeks suit 10-29, 944B1
IRS tax power curb clears Cong 9-26, Carter signs 9-29, 883E2
Carter backs 'minimized' busing 10-16, 807C3
Boston violence erupts 10-17–10-19, 850G1
NAACP sues vs Calif measure 11-14, 991A2
NYC schl aid denial upheld by Sup Ct 11-28, 944A2

1980

Religious Issues
Chicago Jehovah's Witness firing case declined by Sup Ct 1-7, 15D3
Mass schl prayer law in effect 2-5, stay denied 2-13; House com studies legis 2-6, 156D1
NYS pvt schl reimbursemt upheld by Sup Ct 2-20, 146B2
Ex-atheist apologizes in schl prayer dispute 5-9, 471F2
Voluntary prayer debated at US Families Conf in Minn 6-19—6-21, LA 7-10—7-12, 601A2, F2
Evangelical Christian pol actn profiled 7-11—9-15, 818E3, 819B1, B2, C2
GOP platform adopted 7-15, 535C3, 537E1
Reagan notes evolutn 'flaws', backs teaching chngs 8-22, 646D2
Reagan backs tax credits 10-1, 738F1
NYC parochial schl remedial aid case refused by Sup Ct 10-6, 782F2
Reagan backs voluntary prayers 10-8, 763E2
Sioux Falls (SD) case refused by Sup Ct 11-10, 868G1
Ky 10 Commandmts law upset by Sup Ct 11-17, 881B3

School Integration & Busing
Austin busing plan OKd 1-3, 5B3
US rights comm rpts desegregatn lag, lauds Sup Ct rulings 1-14, 36G2, E3
Dallas case refused by Sup Ct 1-21, 93D2
ABA tables law schl affirmative actn proposal 2-5, 114E3
South Bend desegregatn plan set 2-8, 112C2
Cleveland busing challenge refused by Sup Ct 3-17, 225F3
Chicago desegregatn dispute cited 4-2, 292F1
Wilmington (Del) case declined by Sup Ct 4-28, 368E3
Atlanta integratn ruling upheld by Sup Ct 5-12, 386B3
Houston desegregatn suit filed 5-15, 559C1
LA busing plan ordered 5-19, 426E3
St Louis desegregatn ordered 5-21, 559A2
Tex aliens schooling ordered 7-21, 576G1
ABA backs law schl minority 'opportunities' 8-6, 744D1
Dem platform plank adopted 8-13, 615A1
St Louis, LA busing begins peacefully 9-3, 9-16; Chicago OKs integratn agrmt 9-24, 9-24, 723F3
Detroit, Indianapolis busing challenges declined by Sup Ct 10-6, 782G2
Chicago black quotas case dismissed by Sup Ct 10-20, 807B2
Busing, housing integratn rptd linked 11-16, 989A3
Reagan backs antibusing measure 11-18, 880F3
Antibusing rider clears Cong 12-3, Carter vows veto 12-4, vetoes 12-16; 2d rider deleted 12-12, 953D3
Reagan reaffirms busing oppositn 12-11, 965E2

1976

State Aid
Reagan backs aid shift 1-12, 22E1
NJ schls ordrd shut 7-1, income tax bill signed 7-8, 995B2
NM bond issue OKd 11-2, 824F2
Student Unrest, Foreign—*For complete listing of student incidents, see country names in entries*
Libya students rptd killed 1-4—1-5, 205D2
Ecuador riots 1-5—1-10, 28G1, C2
Turkey violence 1-8—3-8, 192D2
Colombia strikes 1-19—2-3, 118D1
Bolivia strikes 1-27—3-6, 237C3
Pl Univ demonstratn 1-30, 103C2
Zambia shuts univ 2-9, 503E2
Latin riots 2-16—2-24, 177C1, 178C1
Spain unrest 3-3, 3-12, 207D2
France unrest 3-17—4-23, 311D3
Mex unrest 4-20—5-4, 419E2
Tunisia protests cited 503C3
Nigeria univ closed 5-15, 366E2
S Africa riots 6-16—6-19, 425F1
Peru riots re austerity 7-1, 499G1
Uganda protest 7-10, 874F1
Tanzania protest 8-9, 874G1
Thais vs Viet refugees 8-17—8-27, 678A1
Australian protest 8-23, 650B1
Panama students riot 9-10, 9-15, 9-20, 792B1
Sri Lanka student killed 11-12, 890F1
UK marchers vs spending cuts 11-17, 889G2
Student Unrest, U.S.—*See also 'School Integration' above; also 'Boston' under MASSACHUSETTS*
Violence study released 3-18, 263E1

Teachers (& other staff issues)
Pratt bequests rptd 1-9, 80C2
Race quotas for NY principals voided 1-19, 42G1-C2
Chicago integratn study rptd 1-25, HEW orders new plan 2-8, 95D2
Pittsburgh strike ends 1-26, 95G2
Strike in Newark 2-3—2-8, 153G2-A3
Boston admin quota set 2-24, 202E3
HEW rejects Chicago integration plan 3-31, 263G1
LA staff sues vs desegregatn plan 5-22, 435E2
Sup Ct upholds strike firings 6-17, 552D3
Sup Ct rules on min wage laws 6-24, 468A2
AFT endorses Dem ticket 8-18, 617D3
Sup Ct bars review of transsexual firing 10-18, 867B3
Jobless benefits revisn signed 10-20, 788E1
HEW charges NYC bias 11-9, 921D3
Greenwich strike setld 11-24, 991G1
Louisville strike 11-30—12-13, 991F1

1977

Sen rejcts HEW affirmative actn curbs, schl dist pairing 6-28, 515D3
Omaha, Milwaukee busing orders vacated 6-29, 557G2
Columbus KKK rally disrupted 7-4, 540F1
HEW issues 6-state coll plan 7-5, 630F2
LA plan rejected 7-6, 8-8, 630G3-631C1
Columbus integratn plans rejctd 7-29, 631C1
Wilmington desegregatn delayed, busing plan rejctd 8-5, 630D3
Kan City plan challenged 8-15, 631D1
Louisville term opens calmly 8-30; anti-busing rally 9-5, 838B1
Columbus (O) KKK rally 9-5, 838C1
Chicago busing plan begins, protested 9-7—9-14, 837C3
Boston, KC (Mo), Bayonne, Dayton schls open calmly 9-7, 837G3-838B1
Bakke brief filed 9-19; Sup Ct hears arguments 10-12, orders more briefs 10-17, 834F2-835G1
Wilmington case review declined 10-3, 760F1
NYC plan ordrd by HEW 10-6, 838C1
Louisville busing review declined 10-31, 835A3
Legal scholar scores Sup Ct rulings 10-31, 878G3, 879B1
Hicks loses Boston reelectn 11-8, 855D3
Busing curb clears Cong 12-7, 958D3
Cong busing curbs challenged 12-9, 978D3
LSC curbs clarified 12-28, 1002D2, F2
School Meals—*See under FOOD*
State Aid
NYS alien tuitn law voided 6-13, 517E2
Calif financing rule review rejctd 6-20, 517D1
Limited aid for church schls backed 6-24, 539F2
Fscl '76 spending rptd up 9-2, 740E1
Student Unrest, Foreign—*For complete listing of student incidents, see country names in entries*
Brazil protest 5-1—6-4, 447B2
Guatemala deaths rptd 9-17, 805C3
Panama studnts burn US amb's car 10-4, 755G1
S Korea demonstratn 10-7, 804C3
Swaziland riot 10-13, 869C2
Colombia protests 2-17—3-10, 254A3
Ecuador protests 5-20—6-4, 485E3
Egypt univ protest 2-12, 115B3
Ethiopians rptdly occupy Moscow emb 5-4—5-8, 391B1
Ghana protests rptd 7-1, 598C2
Italy protests 2-1—2-17, 135F2
Mex Oaxaca clashes 2-22—3-3, 240F1
Peru protests 6-13—6-21, 488F2
S Africa riots 4-27—4-28, 350C1
Sierra Leone protest 1-30, 139G3
Tunisia protesters sentncd 1-24, 140B1
Turkish violence rptd 2-3, 138D2
Venez riots 5-5—5-12, 547A2
Student Unrest, U.S.
Boston HS closed 1-10, 112D3
Campus attitudes study rptd 1-14, 157B2
Rudd, other '60s Weathermen surrender 3-25—9-15, 839C1
Boston HS violence 5-12—5-16, 446A2
Kent State protestors arrested 7-12, 560E1
Kent protests continue 7-29—10-25, 820E2-A3
Kent '75 damage suit retrial ordrd 9-12, 820B3
Chicago HS walkout 9-13, 837D3

Teachers (& other staff issues)
Sup Ct upholds free speech right 1-11, 57F3
'69-75 faculty views rptd 1-14, 157D2
Boston rpts instructn decline 1-16, 112C3
Strikes in Racine 1-25—3-17; KC 3-21—5-8; Milwaukee, 4-7—5-10; Cincinnati 4-13—5-10, 481C2
Carter on draft options 3-5, 171G2
Teacher of yr honored 3-22, 354A2
Sup Ct backs spankings 4-19, 342E1
RC-NLRB dispute case refused 5-2, 406C2
Baptist coll divorce dismissal chrged 5-2, 472C1
Davidson Coll drops sectarian tenure curbs 5-6, 471F3
Sup Ct backs agency shops 5-23, 444D1
Hazelwood (Mo) job bias suit vacated 6-27, 538F3
Sen rejcts HEW affirmative actn curbs 6-28, 515E3
NYC loses aid re assignmt bias 7-5, 631F1
NYC union fined for '75 strike 7-20, 558D2
Natl Educ Assn scores SATs 8-24, 739B2
Salary hikes, property tax boosts linked 9-12, 722B1
Mandatory retiremt curb voted by House 9-23, 737G2
Gay cases review refused 10-3, 760D1
Chicago assigns by race 10-11, 837E2
NYC assignmt by race challngd 10-31, 837A3
RC women's policy-making roles rptd 11-15, 906G2
Cleveland strike 11-29—12-8, 939B3

1978

State and City Fund Issues
Cleveland crisis 1-6—4-6, state advances funds 4-13, 279B2
Ohio rescues Cleveland schls 4-13, 279B2
Cleveland, Columbus, other Ohio levy, bond issues defeated 6-6, 425B1
Calif aid to localities seen 6-6, 6-8, 425C3, 426B1
Calif property-tax revenue drop voted 6-6; cutbacks set, other reactn 6-7—6-8, 425D2-426D1
NY property tax ruled illegal 6-23, 526F1
NEA conv discusses Propositn 13 7-5, 525G3
Cleveland crisis grows 7-10—8-23, 663G2
Cleveland gets state loan 8-28, 699B1
Propositn 13 upheld by Calif ct 9-22, 735C2
Ohio, Mich, Alaska, Ala referenda results 11-7, 854C1, F1, 915C2-E2
Student Unrest, Foreign—*For complete listing of student incidents, see country names in entries*
Bolivia protests 4-27, 411E3
Brazil protests 10-15, 794C1
Chile hunger strike backed 5-31, 453G2
Colombia riots 5-30, 413F3
Cyprus students protest 4-4—4-5, 277A2
Czechs mark '68 Sovt invasn 8-21, 691G2
El Salvador protests 4-11—4-18, 723B3 ★
Gabon univ shut 2-4, 94E2
Guatemala protests 6-1, 6-8, 497D1
Indonesia dissent suppressed 1-21, 1-26, 71F3
Iran student protests 2-27, 152E3
Italy student unrest 2-25—2-26, 191F2
Malagasy riots vs standards 5-29—5-30, 479D2
Mex riots 6-26, 6-28, 517C2, F2
Nicaragua demonstratns 1-30, 73E2
Nigerians vs tuitn rise 4-28, 479E1
Panama leftists 4-19, 274F1
Papua New Guinea strike 5-7—5-11, 395D3
Peru riots 5-15, 5-16, 394B1
Rhodesia protests 4-24, 318B1
Tanzania protest 3-5, 169F3
Turkey univ closed 4-21, 378D2
Student Unrest, U.S.
Tenn Davis Cup protests 3-17, 3-19, 251E3, G3
Stanford U '71 press office search backed by Sup Ct 5-31, 429F3
Teachers (& other staff issues)—*See also personal names*
Cleveland (O) payroll crisis 1-6—4-6, state advances funds 4-13, 279B2
SC teacher tests backed 1-16, 33D2
'53, '78 cong membership compared 1-30, 107G2
NJ transsexual wins disability pay 2-16, 327D2
Ga, NC coll integratn plans OKd by US 3-8, 5-12, 369A1, C1
NYC local bd suspended in ethnic data dispute 3-10, 264G1-A2
Mandatory retiremt hike deferred 4-6, 238F3
NY ends assignmt by race 4-7, 264C1
Women show few gains in coll jobs 4-7, 554A3
Brunswick (O) teachers jailed 4-8—4-14, Toledo schls struck 4-10, 279G2-A3
Ala State Univ white bias ruled 5-1, 348A3
PTA gets Sears aid re TV programming 5-12, 599E3
Tex boy kills teacher 5-18, 396A2
Calif tax-cut OK spurs layoffs, teachers assn challenges 6-7, 425C3, 426C1
Coll hiring quotas barred by House 6-13, 445G3
'Reverse check-off' pol gifts barred 7-21, 565A3
Strikes mar fall term 8-30—9-11, 698D2-A3, 699A1
Cleveland strike ends 10-16, 1008E3
DC pensn reform vetoed 11-4, 897F2

1979

State and City Fund Issues—*See also other appropriate subheads in this section*
Prop 13 effects reviewed 6-3, 6-5, 499D3, F3
Reagan seeks program shift to states, localities 11-13, 866E2
Chicago schls in fscl crisis 11-13—12-7, 943D3-944A1; 12-21, 991E1
Hufstedler backs state, local primacy 11-27, 946A3
Student Unrest—*See also country names*
Kent State '75 damage suit settled 1-4, 5C2
Atlanta protests 1-14, 31A3
Boston violence erupts 10-17—10-19, 850G1

Teachers (& other staff issues)
Pub employe free speech backed by Sup Ct 1-9, 14G2
St Louis strike 1-16—3-12, 187A3
Okla dismissal backed by US Sup Ct 2-26, 164G3
Levich gets City Coll post 3-2, 272E1
Edelin gets Boston U post 3-15, 272B1
8 NJ colleges struck 3-20, 207D1
Church schl labor interventn barred by Sup Ct 3-21, 231D2
Minn U, Cuba exchng rptd 3-27, 238C2
DC 23-day strike ends 3-29, 262G2
Baton Rouge strike ends 4-2, 599D1
Boston U strikes 4-5—4-22, 326D3
NYS alien ban backed by Sup Ct 4-17, 325E3
Coll ethics decline seen 4-18, 282D2
Yale provost quits in fund dispute 5-2, 392D2
'77 staffing hike rptd 5-12, 367E2
Waggoner quits as Wilson Coll pres 5-27, 482F1
Prop 13 effects reviewed 6-3, 499E3
Antioch May pay deferrals cited 6-4, 482A2
Kennedy named Stanford provost 6-16, 527F3
Teacher 'burn-out' rptd 7-5, 786E1
Ann Arbor OKs 'Black English' progrm 8-15, 650A3
Strikes in 14 states mar schl openings 8-27—9-13, 679A1
Test scores of future teachers drop 10-4, 810G1

1980

State and City Fund Issues
State of State messages 1-8—1-10, 2-19, 403D3, 404A1, E1; 1-9—4-8, 483A1-484G2; 1-10—1-16, 269A2, F2, 270B2, F2
Chicago schls virtually closed, City Cncl OKs aid fund plan 1-28, 77F2-D3
NYS pvt schl reimbursemt upheld by Sup Ct 2-20, 146B2
Fla property tax cut voted 3-11, 184G1
Chicago schl bd fscl policies scored 4-2, 292B1
Reagan Calif record noted 7-16, 534E1
Tex aliens schooling costs seen 7-21, 576C2
Fla to get refugee funds 8-13, 617E1
Immigratn econ impact rptd 9-22, 826F3
Refugee aid to states clears Cong 9-25, 10-1, Carter signs 10-10, 785B1
Alaska bond issue OKd 11-4, 847A2
Student Unrest
Dade Cnty schls shut in Miami rioting 5-18, 382C3

Teachers (& other staff issues)
'67-77 elected offcls, schl dist drop rptd 1-2, 5E3
Cleveland strike ends 1-3, 5A3
Sovern named Columbia U pres 1-7, 200C1
2 Calif sex harassmt cases rptd; '79 sex survey cited 1-9, 77D3-78C1
State of State messages 1-9, 2-19, 404B1, E1; 1-9, 1-15, 483E2, 484D1
Chicago schl teachers protest 1-28, 77F2-A3
Chicago bond rating drop linked 1-31, 186C2
South Bend (Ind) desegregatn plan set 2-8, 114D2
Chicago teachers return 2-11, 114G1
Pvt coll faculty unions curbed by Sup Ct 2-20, 146C1-B2
CIA admits use of professors 2-21, 189A3
Commoner to accept Queens post 3-17, 471C3
May to become NYU business school dean 3-18, 224E3
Chicago teachers pact renegotiatn dispute seen 4-2, 292E1
CIA use of academics backed by Turner 4-10; Sen OKs intell oversight bill 6-3, 458E3, 459B1
'Good faith' schl bd immunity ended by Sup Ct 4-16, 328D2
NYC pact setld 5-18, 518C1, E1
USC pres named 5-21, 471A1
Cornell business schl dean named 5-21, 456F2; 9-29, 959D2

1976

1977

1978

Calif rejcts gay ban 11-7, 847A3, 857A1
College sex-bias ruling voided by Sup Ct 11-13, 874F1-C2
Ga schl bd pol rule struck down by Sup Ct 11-28, 937E3
AFT to organize nurses 11-29, 961A1
Newark layoffs scheduled 12-11, 1012D1
Vocational Schools—*See also other appropriate subheads in this section*
Age bias in vocational rehabilitatn progrms rptd 1-10, 14C1
Flood trade schl paymt chrg rptd, Elko convictn cited 2-15, 240C2
Flood indicted 9-5, 685C1
Flood indicted again 10-12, 792C1
Rules issued 12-13, 963B1

1979

Ariz State fires Kush 10-13, Kush sues univ 11-9, 1001C3
San Fran strike ends 10-23, 850F1
Hawaii strikes shut schls 10-26–11-16, 922B3
Title IX job bias funds cutoff bar declined by Sup Ct 11-26, 919D2
Chicago schl offcls quit 11-28–12-4, 943G3
NYC schl aid denial upheld by Sup Ct 11-28, 944B2
Calif religious firing case dismissed by Sup Ct 12-10, 988F1
Chicago schls miss payday 12-21, 991E1

1980

Barnard pres resigns 5-28, 471B1
Mathews resigns as Ala pres 6-11, 638E2
Marxist historian denied Md faculty post 6-12, 638C3
Kennedy named Stanford pres 6-13, 638D2
DC fscl recovery plan proposed 7-19, 742D3
Carter gets AFT endorsemt 8-21; addresses conv, sees clear choice 8-22, 646E2
Strikes in 10 states mar schl openings 9-1—9-8, 723G2
Detroit budget woes, teacher layoff plan rptd 9-8, 743E2, G2
Jordan gets Cornell post 9-29, 959D2
Ga prof released from jail 9-30, resumes teaching 10-6, 890B3
Scientific literacy lag rptd 10-22, 990D1
Job bias suit filing time limit upheld by Sup Ct 12-15, 957B2

1976

EDUCATIONAL Progress, National Assessment of (Denver, Colo.)
Rpts reading study findings 9-21, 993B2
EDUCATIONAL Testing Service (Princeton, N.J.)
Boston bars schl admin tests 2-24, 202F3
'74-75 city SAT, natl averages rptd 9-13, 993E1
EDUCATION Association, National—*See NATIONAL Education Association*
EDUCATION, Inc., Council for Financial Aid to
College Entrance Examination Board
Rpts on '74-75 coll gifts 3-20, 263F2
Rpts declining SAT averages 9-11, 993C1
On Minneapolis SAT scores 9-13, 993A2
EDWARDS, Rev. Bruce
Church bars blacks 10-31, 826F3
Retained as pastor 11-14, 864D2
EDWARDS, Rep. Don (D, Calif.)
Reelected 11-2, 829B1
EDWARDS, Gov. Edwin W. (D, La.)
Endorses Brown 6-10, 432G1
Signs MD malpractice bill 7-2, 1016E3
Other Dem govs back Carter 7-6, 492C3
Wife endorses Ford 9-26, 723C3
Admits Park gifts 10-25, 900D1
EDWARDS, Elaine (Mrs. Edwin W.)
Endorses Ford 9-26, 723C3
Park gifts admitted 10-25, 900D1
EDWARDS, Rep. Jack (R, Ala.)
Reelected 11-2, 828F2
EDWARDS, Gov. James B. (R, S.C.)
Schweiker visits 7-29, 7-30, 564G1
Asks conv pre-ballot addresses 8-9, 582G1
Addresses GOP conv 8-16, 615F1
GOP conv vp vote table 8-19, 599F3
Links Butz, Carter remarks 10-3, 744D2
EDWARDS, Mickey
Elected 11-2, 822A3, 830C3
EDWARDS Jr., Willie (d. 1957)
Murder suspects freed 4-14, 316D2
EEC—*See EUROPEAN Community*
EFAW, Fritz
Speaks at Dem conv 7-15, 506C3
Draft evasn chrgs dropped 8-11, 680G2
Schrump addresses GOP conv 8-17, 615A2
EFIMOV, Mihail
Chrgs Olympic anti-Sovt campaign 7-31, 562G2
EGAN, William
Former asst indicted 7-8, 816G2
EGELAND, Kjoley
Norway defense min 1-12, 30A2
EGERVARI, Marta
Wins Olympic medal 7-22, 574F3
EGGS—*See DAIRY Products*
EGLI, Rev. Paul
Arrest rptd 12-8, 1010C1

1977

EDUCATION, Institute of International
Kenneth Holland dies 12-9, 1024B2
EDUCATIONAL Development, Academy for
Ford named chairman 1-28, 236C3
EDUCATIONAL Testing Service
'77-78, '70-77 coll costs rptd 3-27, 483D1
College Entrance Examination Board
'63-'77 SAT score drop rptd 8-23; '77-freshmen scores hit low; study, SATs criticized 8-24, 739D1, A2
EDUCATION Association, National—*See NATIONAL Education Association*
EDWARDES, Michael
Heads Leyland 10-25, 864A1
EDWARDS, Danny
Wins Greensboro Open 4-3, 311E1
EDWARDS, Rep. Don (D, Calif.)
Questns FBI domestic surveillnc 11-9, 861B3
Wilmington 10 pardon sought 12-4, 943B1
EDWARDS, Eddie
In NFL draft 5-3, 353A2
EDWARDS, Gov. Edwin W. (D, La.)
Scores Carter energy plan 4-20, 320D2
Cited in Park indictmt 9-6, 688C1
EDWARDS, James
Traded to Pacers 12-13, 991A1
EDWARDS, Gov. James B. (R, S.C.)
Signs death penalty bill 6-8, 594D2
Vs Carter welfare plan 9-9, 719A2
EDWARDS Air Force Base, Calif.—*See CALIFORNIA*
EEC—*See EUROPEAN Community*
EEOC—*See U.S. GOVERNMENT—EQUAL Employment Opportunity Commission*
EGER, John
'75 USSR tap warning cited 7-10, 551A2
EGHBAL, Dr. Manouchehr
Dies 11-25, 952C2
EGLEVSKY, Andre
Dies 12-4, 1024E1
EGLI, Rev. Paul
Sentenced 1-12, 11F2
Sentence cut 4-6, 297B1
EGLY, Judge Paul J.
Rejects LA desegregatn plan 7-6, 8-8, 630G3-631C1
EGUREN, Alicia
Kidnaping rptd 2-25, 198B1

1978

EDUCATION, American Council on
Peltason on Bakke ruling 6-28, 482A3
EDUCATION, Council for Financial Aid to Education
Rpts on college aid 10-4, 754B2
EDUCATION, Office of—*See under U.S. GOVERNMENT—HEALTH, Education & Welfare*
EDUCATIONAL Testing Service
'77 black law schl applicant data rptd 10-8, 811D2
College Entrance Examination Board
Coll Scholarship Svc cost survey rptd 4-10, 264B2
SAT verbal scores stabilize 9-16, 754G1
EDUCATION Association, National—*See NATIONAL Education Association*
EDWARDES, Michael
Callaghan backs 1-26; sets reorganizatn, job cuts 2-1, 112D1-D2
On BL labor troubles, profits 9-11, 9-14, 739A3-F3
EDWARDS, Blake
Revenge of Pink Panther released 7-19, 970A3
EDWARDS, Clancy
Sets 100-mtr, 200-mtr dash marks; AAU outdoor champ MVP 6-1—6-4, 6-8—6-10, 600A3, F3
EDWARDS, David
Sues Citibank re dismissal, tax evasn 7-24, 717B3
EDWARDS, Don
NHL goaltending ldr 4-9, 296E2
EDWARDS, Rep. Don (D, Calif.)
Reelected 11-7, 850E1
EDWARDS, Gov. Edwin W. (D, La.)
Korean gifts rptd 1-14, 63D3
Cited in Passman indictmt re Korea 3-31, 239E1
EDWARDS, Glen
Traded to Chargers 8-22, 1025A1
EDWARDS, Gus
Black Body Blues opens 1-24, 887B1
EDWARDS, Henry
Sgt Pepper's released 7-21, 970B3
EDWARDS, Herman
NFL '77 interceptn ldr 1-1, 56G2
EDWARDS, Rep. Jack (R, Ala.)
Reelected 11-7, 850A1
EDWARDS, Gov. James B. (R, S.C.)
Primary results 6-13, 467E1
Riley elected SC gov 11-7, 853B1
EDWARDS, Rep. Marvin H. Mickey (R, Okla.)
Reelected 11-7, 852A1
EDWARDS, Dr. Robert G.
'Test-tube' baby delivered 7-25, 596F3, 597F1
EDWARDS, Ronnie Claire
Patio/Porch opens 4-13, 887D2
EDWARDS v. Carter
Panama Canal treaty stay denied 4-17, 308G2
Panama Canal treaty challenge refused by Sup Ct 5-15, 388A1
EDWIN Hawkins Singers (singing group)
Win Grammy 2-24, 316A1
EDZEL, Salip Phang
Surrenders 3-1, 248F1
EEC—*See EUROPEAN Community*
EEOC—*See U.S. GOVERNMENT—EQUAL Employment Opportunity Commission*
EFTA—*See EUROPEAN Free Trade Association*
EGAN, Patrick
Henry IV opens 11-27, 1031A2
EGENBERGER, Joseph
Sentenced 5-24, 396F2
EGGERT Economic Enterprises Inc.
Fscl '78, '79 econ growth forecast 7-7, 506E3
EGGS
Nigeria import ban rptd 4-4, 248C1
PCB contaminated eggs destroyed 4-12, 727D3
US-Japan quota talks fail 9-5—9-7, 695B1
FTC ad case declined by Sup Ct 10-2, 751D2
EGLIN, Colin W.
Scores govt re scandals 12-7, 989F1
EGLY, Judge Paul J.
Sets LA busing plan 1-3, 5E1-A2
Bars LA busing stay 8-3, 698C3
EGUINO, Antonio
'Chuquiago' released 4-18, 619A1

1979

EDUCATION, Department of—*See under U.S. GOVERNMENT*
EDUCATION, Office of—*See under U.S. GOVERNMENT–HEALTH, Education & Welfare*
EDUCATIONAL Testing Service
College Entrance Examination Board
SAT coaching schl study disputed 5-29, 785B2
SAT, Achievemt Test scores rptd down 9-8, 785F1
SAT decline, '50s A-fallout linked 9-17, 747A2
Test scores of future teachers drop 10-4, 810G1
EDUCATION Association, National—*See NATIONAL Education Association*
EDWARDES, Michael
Bars strike concessions 2-12, 115D3
Honda-BL productn planned 5-17, 388E2
On BL job cut plans 9-10, 686E2
BL workers back cutbacks 11-1, 855B3
Fires BL union militant 11-19, 994A2
BL aid promised 12-20, 994D1
EDWARDS, Blake
10 released 10-5, 1008G1
EDWARDS, Dr. Charles C.
Replaces spinal column 8-31, 736E2
EDWARDS, Rep. Don (D, Calif.)
Chrgs Navy recruiting bias 6-14, 519C3
On anti-busing amendmt defeat 7-24, 559G2
Scores FBI audit on informants, urges GAO probe 8-22, 747A3
EDWARDS, Gov. Edwin W. (D, La.)
Treen elected gov 12-8, 946E3
EDWARDS, Gus
Old Phantoms opens 2-8, 292D2
EDWARDS, Herman
NFL '78 interceptn ldr 1-6, 80G1
EDWARDS, Rep. Jack (R, Ala.)
On AF F-15, F-16 engine trouble 10-23, 852A2
EDWARDS, James B.
Endorses Connally 12-27, 982F2, G2
EDWARDS, Nicholas
UK Wales secy 5-5, 338G1
EEC—*See EUROPEAN Community*
EEOC—*See U.S. GOVERNMENT-EQUAL Employment Opportunity Commission*
EEOC v. Burlington Northern Inc.
EEOC data curb upheld by Sup Ct 2-21, 128F3
EERT, Friedrich
Dies 12-4, 1008F2
EGAN, Michael J.
Supports refugee bill 3-14, 308A1
EGAN, Patrick
Wild Oates opens 1-8, 292G3
EGGS
PCB contaminated eggs destroyed 9-17, 704D3
EGLESON, Jan
Billy released 1-31, 174C2
EGLIN, Colin W.
Replcd as oppositn ldr 9-3, 733A1
EGLY, Judge Paul J.
LA busing plan challenged 8-27, 679C3
NAACP sues vs Prop 1 11-14, 991C2

1980

EDUCATION, American Council on
Coll freshmen survey rptd 1-20, 319D3-320B1
EDUCATION, Department of—*See under U.S. GOVERNMENT*
EDUCATION, National Consortium of Public Policy
Mathews named ldr 6-11, 638E2
EDUCATIONAL, Scientific, and Cultural Organization, UN—*See UNITED Nations--UNESCO*
EDUCATIONAL Broadcast Corp.
Hellman sues 2-15, 199E2
EDUCATIONAL Testing Service
College Entrance Examination Board
Test study disputed 1-14, 36G1
SAT data to be disclosed 4-7, 318E3
College freshmen math experience rptd 4-15, 559A3
SAT coaching rptd helpful 5-15, 559B3
SAT decline continues 10-4, 786C2
Scientific literacy study rptd 10-22, 990F1
EDUCATION Association, National—*See NEA*
EDWARD and Mrs. Simpson (TV series)
Wins Emmy 9-7, 692D1
EDWARDES, Michael
BL pay pact rejected 2-12, 117B3
Strike re unionist rejected 2-20, 150F1
BL workers take 7% pay deal 11-18, 886E2
EDWARDS, Benjamin F.
DeNunzio replaces as chrmn 11-6, 959B2
EDWARDS, Dan
Wins Natl Team Championship 10-19, 972E2
EDWARDS, Dave
Wins Natl Team Championship 10-19, 972E2
EDWARDS, Don
NHL goaltending ldr, clinches Vezina Trophy 4-6, 296A1
EDWARDS, Rep. Donald (D, Calif.)
Joins open-conv move 7-25, 570G1
Reelected 11-4, 842E1
EDWARDS, Rep. Jack (R, Ala.)
House OKs '81 defns appropriatn 9-16, 741B3
Reelected 11-4, 842A1
EDWARDS, James B.
Named Energy secy 12-22, 979G2, F3
EDWARDS, Jimmy
NFL '79 kick return ldr 1-5, 8G3
EDWARDS, Rep. Marvin H. (Mickey) (R, Okla.)
Reelected 11-4, 844A1
EDWARDS, Dr. Robert G.
US 'test-tube baby' clinic OKd 1-8, 24G1
EDWARDS, Wallace
Sovt 13-yr debt dispute rptd settled 10-22, 828B2
EDWARDS & Son, A. G.
Hunt silver debt repaid 4-16, 345F1
EDWARDS v. Service Machine Corp.
Ruling affirmed by Sup Ct 10-20, 807A3
EEOC (Equal Employment Oppprtunity Commission)—*See under U.S. GOVERNMENT*
EGGLETON, Arthur
Elected Toronto mayor 11-11, 900D3
EGGS
US dietary guidelines issued 2-4, 157B3
Mar CPI rise rptd 4-22, 305C2
Cholesterol rpt issued 5-27, scored 6-1, 432A3, D3
EGIDI, Egidio
Grandi named ENI head 5-6, 408G3
EGLY, Judge Paul J.
Orders LA busing plan 5-19, 426E3

1976

EGYPT, Arab Republic of—*See also AFRICAN Development Bank, ARAB League, NONALIGNED Nations Movement, OAU;*
Nasser cleared of '67 theft chrg 2-4, 119B1
Sadat to reorganize press cncl, OKs 'forums' in pol party 3-14, 193E1
Newspapers reorganized 3-14, 3-19, 3-28, 333E1
Sheriff dies 8-6, 892E3
Train blast kills 8 8-14, 629D3
Jet hijacked 8-23, 629B2; hijackers sentncd 9-18, 700C1
Sadat renominated 8-25, reelected 9-16, 734F3
Bus drivers strike ends 9-20, 734G3
Sadat sworn for 2d term 10-16, 852E1
Parlt electns 10-28, 11-4, 852F1
New Cabt sworn 11-10, 852D1
Multiple parties restored 11-11, 852A2

Foreign Relations (misc.)
French Mirage purchase cited 1-16, 36C2
Greek oil tanker order rptd 1-16, 73C2
Sadat seeks Sahara setlmt 1-27, 58C2
Sahara diplomatic efforts continue 2-1—2-6, 107A3
At intl econ conf 2-11—2-20, 148B1
EC trade talks rptd 2-12, 164B3
Angola MPLA recognized 2-13, 163E2
Aide in bombed Cambodia town 3-2—3-4, 238C2
IMF oil loans rptd 3-5, 4-1, 339F3, G3 340C2
Tunisian detained 3-9, 205A2
Ends Sovt friendship treaty 3-15, 193A1, 194B2; **for subsequent developments, see 'Egypt' under MIDDLE EAST—ARAB Policies**
Gamasy ends French visit 3-26, 275F1
Sadat in Eur 3-29—4-12, 274E3-275E2
Mubarak in China, arms pact signed 4-18—4-21, 275E2
'75 Sovt trade rptd 5-5, 341A1
Sovt mil presence rptd 6-13, 467C1
Sudan defense pact 7-13—7-14, 531D2
In Saudi, Sudan alliance 7-18—7-19, 531B2
Olympic withdrawal rptd 7-21, 528B3
Sadat chrgs Libya re Sudan coup 7-22, 547B3
Kuwait confrms troop mass 7-25, 547C3
Libya recalls Saudi amb 7-25, 547D3
Dependents quit China quake area 8-1, 561E2
Moslem extremists arrested 8-6, 588A3
Gets Arab aid fund 8-21, 630A1
Israel lauds hijack recovery 8-24, 629C3
French missile deal rptd set 8-27, 675A1
Sovt backs Libya in Egypt feud 8-30, 682B3
IAEA dir cites 9-21, 760F3
Ramses mummy flown to Paris for repair 9-26, scientists challenge need 11-8, 912F2
Sadat meets Assad, Syrian union set 12-18—12-21, 954D2

1977

EGYPT, Arab Republic of—*See also ARAB League, DISARMAMENT—Geneva Committee, NONALIGNED Nations Movement, OAU*
Food price hikes set 1-17, rioters force recall 1-18—1-19; Sadat returns Cairo 1-20, 43A3
CP blamed for riots 1-21, press scores 1-23, 62A2, D2
Rpt riot troops left Sinai line 1-21, 62G2
Riot curfew lifted 1-22, 62G2
Leftist riot role chrgd 1-29, 2-3; denied 1-30, 83E1
Campus politics banned 1-30, 83B1
Cabt shift tied to riots 2-1, 83F1
Political curbs decreed 2-3, 83B1
Hussein vs plebiscite 2-5, expelled from Assemb 2-14, 115D3
Leftist party vs curbs 2-8, 115C3
Plebiscite OKs curbs 2-10, law effected 2-11; students protest 2-12, 115A3
5-yr dvpt plan, other reforms urged 5-11—5-12, 390A3
Moslem sect abducts ex-min 7-3, slays 7-4, body found 7-7, 525D3
Moslem sect bombings 7-6, vows 'war' vs Sadat 7-7, 526A1
Moslem sect arrests 7-8, 7-11; army cell smashed 7-12, 542G1
Food rioters sentenced 7-28, 619B2
Moslem fanatics indicted 8-11, 636E2
Law vs Copts sought; Copts protest, plan dropped 9-12, 863E2
Cholera outbreak rptd 9-26, 748A1
Moslem-Copt strife confrmd 9-28, 863D2
Sadat changes Cabt 10-25, 824A1
Forgn min, dep resign 11-17, chief adviser 11-18, 890B2
Sadat addresses parlt 11-26, 909A1
Kamel named forgn min 993E1
Arab-Israeli Conflict—*See MIDDLE EAST*

Foreign Relations (misc.)—*See also 'Libyan Relations', 'Monetary, Trade & Aid' and 'UN Policy' below*
French defense min visits 1-5—1-9, 10G2
Sovt ties deterioratn cited 1-9, 24C1
Sudan activates defns pact 1-15—1-16, 62D3
Tito visit canceled 1-20, 43F3
Sovts score CP riot chrgs 1-22; press assails Sovts 1-23, 62B2
Khaddam visits Sadat 2-3, pol cmnd formed 2-4, 87A1
Sovts score Sadat memoirs 2-19, Egypt replies 2-22, 144A2
Saudi held CIA link to Sadat 2-22, 124A3
Sudan joins Egypt-Syria cmnd 2-27—2-28, 143F2
Afro-Arab summit held 3-7—3-9, 170D1
Ethiopian amb defects 3-9, 238F2
Cuba proposal on Djibouti opposed 3-10—3-16, 249D2
Sadat in Paris 4-3, 245B2
Zaire mil missn rptd 4-9, 265F2
Sadat assesses Rabin resignatn 4-9, 267G2
Morocco fears Zaire interventn 4-18, 317A2
Zaire gets pilots, concern re USSR influence cited 5-2, 394A1
Pilots to leave Zaire 5-25, 490E1
Ethiopia shuts defns office 5-28, 486C1
Fahmy in USSR 6-9—6-10, joint statemt 6-11, 457F2
Brezhnev, Fahmy meet 6-15; Brezhnev visit set 6-22, Cairo denies 6-24, 496B2
Rpts 'no progress' in Moscow talks 6-24, 496A2
Ethiopia army strength compared 6-25, 547D3
USSR plan to subvert Egypt, Sudan rptd 7-25, 569C2
Somali ldr visits 8-31, 684C3
Anti-Copt plan dropped, Canada, Australia protests cited 9-12, 863F2
Yugo visit by Sadat delayed 10-27, 844E2
Sadat ends Rumania, Iran, Saudi visit 11-3, 850A2
Israel visit by Sadat discussed 11-9—11-15, set 11-17, 873A1; **for subsequent developments, see MIDDLE EAST—EGYPT-Israel Peace Moves**
Sadat in Syria talks 11-16, 873G1
Greece emb violence 11-18, 890F2
Amb to Yugo quits 12-1, 930F2
Ambs to 4 Arab states recalled 12-4, ties cut 12-5, 929A1, C2
Sovt bloc cntrs closed 12-7, 929B1, 930B1
UK newsman found slain 12-7; 3 Arabs seized 12-15; spy group link hinted 12-31, 1019D1
Sadat meets Hussein, on PLO peace role 12-8—12-9, cites Rabat decisn 12-10, 953G2
Lebanon Civil Strife—*See under LEBANON*

1978

EGYPT, Arab Republic of—*See also ARAB League, DISARMAMENT—Geneva Committee, GATT, NONALIGNED Nations Movement, OAU*
A-bomb seen unlikely before '84 1-26, 61C2
5 Moslem extremists hanged 3-19, 211D2
'76 jet crash in Thailand laid to pilot 5-12, 460A1
Bus plunges into Nile, 56 die 7-17, 636B3
Arab-Israeli Conflict—*See MIDDLE EAST*
Cyprus Terrorist Attack—*See under MIDDLE EAST—PALESTINIAN Developments*
Economy & Labor (domestic)
Econ min removed 5-7, 392G2
Sadat notes rising prices, econ stagnatn 5-14, 392D2

Foreign Relations (misc.)—*See also 'Monetary, Trade, Aid & Investment' and 'UN' below*
Sadat chrgs USSR, Cuba raids vs Somali 2-6, 99F3
Sadat tours 6 Eur natns 2-9—2-13, 98C2-C3
Chad rebels rpt troops killed 2-15, 130C2
Kenya downs Somalia-bound plane 2-15, 137D2
Cyprus aides recalled 2-20, ties cut 2-22, 118G1
Cyprus urges ties renewal 2-23, 138F2; 3-1, 148A1
Forgn terror group rptd smashed, 24 seized 4-22, 4-24, 4-26, 300C2
Uganda vp rptd in hosp 4-24, 331C3
CP founder murdered in France 5-4, 352D2; murder weapon linked to rightists 5-11, 474A1
Journalists ordrd home; Libya, Iraq financing chrgd 5-26, 414D3
Sadat warns forgn newsmen 6-7, 473E2
Ghali visit to Zaire rptd 6-13, 441G1
Amb to Portugal suspended, scores Sadat policies 6-19, refuses return 6-20, 473A2
Arab press group scores Sadat crackdown 6-21, 473D2
Austria visit ended by Sadat 7-14, 546C2
Athletes attacked at Algiers games 7-22; team leaves 7-23; 5 Arab states boycotted 7-24, 573C1
Hardline Arab states end ties 9-24, 729F2
Sadat sends Meir condolences 12-8, 1032G1
Rumania ties cited 12-9, 965F3

Government & Politics—*See also other appropriate subheads in this section*
New Wafd Party reinstated 2-3, ldr named 2-17; assemb clash rptd 2-15, 131D1
Sadat asks Cabt shift 5-1; Kaissouni, 2 others ousted 5-7, 392G2
Sadat sets referendum to curb oppositn 5-14, voters back plan 5-21, 392F1
Leftist press issues seized 5-17, 392F2; 5-24, 415C1
Sadat scores pol parties, leftist press 5-23, 392D2
30 journalists ordrd home in crackdown 5-26, 150 others under investigatn 5-28; Sadat defends 5-30, 414D3
Assemb enacts pol curbs 6-1; New Wafd dissolves 6-2, Progressive Union suspends activities 6-5, 436E3
Leftist press issue seizure overturned by ct 6-7, 437C1
Al Ahaly ceases publicatn 6-14, 573A2

1979

EGYPT, Arab Republic of—*See also ARAB League, DISARMAMENT-Geneva Committee, GATT, OAU*
Arab-Israeli Conflict—*See MIDDLE EAST*
Arab Relations—*See also 'Monetary' below*
Centers attacked in Iran, Kuwait, Syria 3-25, 222D2
Jordan withdraws amb, Egypt recalls aides 3-29, 248B3
Arab League to cut ties 3-31, 248B2
Envoys from 7 Arab states recalled, Arab League hq shift barred 4-7, 278D1
Iraq halts Sudan oil shipmts 4-10, 278A2
OAPEC ousts, imposes oil embargo 4-17; Arab Monetary Fund, sci group suspends 4-18, 278G1-B2
Kuwait, Saudi cut ties 4-22, 4-23; Cairo retaliates 4-23; Mauritania, Qatar, UAE cut ties 4-24, 296D1
Syria terror plot chrgd 4-24, 296E1
Tunisia, Morocco cut ties 4-27, 319C2
Sadat assails Saudi 5-1, Riyadh refutes 5-2, 319E1
Sadat gave Hassan plea re Jerusalem 5-3, 360G1
US-Saudi talks on jet funds rptd 5-8, 341C2; Sadat doubts Saudi aid 5-12, 360A1
Arab arms plant to close 5-14, 359E3
US role to end Saudi feud confirmed 5-20, 5-21, 378B3
Syria links to Moslem extremists 6-28, 505A3
Emb in Turkey raided 7-13; siege ends 7-15, Arab ldrs blamed 7-16, 536D2
PLO aide's murder, Turkey Emb attack linked 7-26, 552B1
Sadat chrgs Saudi 'hate campaign', fears Libya link; Faud denies accusatns 10-10, 801E2-802A1
Saudis capture mosque raiders 12-4, 916B1

Foreign Relations (misc.)—*See also 'Monetary' and 'UN' below*
Cuba pres scores, rep quits rite 1-1, 20A1
Aides in Cambodia flee to Thailand 1-8, 10A1
Iran shah visits Sadat 1-16, 25C1; leaves 1-22; vacatn plan rptd 1-23, 49C3
Moslems vs Sadat for backing shah 161F3
Sadat in W Ger 3-29, 250A1
Iran ties severed 4-30, 408A2
Sadat may offer shah asylum 5-24, 408G1
Sadat offers shah asylum 6-23, 486A3
Emb in Turkey raided 7-13-7-15, 536C2
Turkey Emb attack, PLO aide's murder linked 7-26, 552B1
Israel blamed for Young resignatn 8-16, 606F2
Nonaligned natns split re expulsn 8-28-9-1, 9-3; stays member 9-9, 674F2, 675A1, E1
Shah offered asylum, Khomeini scored 11-9, 862B3
Iran denounced for US Emb seizure 11-24, 895D3
Shah's asylum offer affirmed 11-30; oppositn ldr scores 12-4, bid ruled out 12-5, 914D1
Vs Sovt Afghan invasn 12-31, 974E2

Government & Politics—*See also other appropriate subheads in this section*
Freedom House lists as partly free 13B1
Sadat warns Islamic radicals 3-1, 161C3
Referendum OKs electns 4-19; parlt ended, vote date set 4-21, 295B3
Govt party wins parlt electns 6-7, 6-14; new Khalil Cabt sworn 6-21, 468G2
60 plotters, 23 Progressive Party men arrested 8-16; Sadat scores exploiters 8-17, 633F1

1980

EGYPT, Arab Republic of—*See also ARAB League, GATT, GENEVA Committee, NONALIGNED Nations, OAU*
Ape-human ancestor rptd discovered 2-7, 416E1
Jurists vs 'law of shame' 2-15; law aired 2-21, 148F3
'77 Rift Valley Fever epidemic cited 3-2, 318B3
Meat sale banned for 1 month 9-1, 691D1
Arab-Israeli Conflict—*See MIDDLE EAST*

Foreign Relations (misc.)—*See also 'UN Policy' below*
Sovts chrg Afghan rebel training 1-1, 1E2
Saudis execute 10 mosque raiders 1-9, 22B1
Islamic conf boycotted 1-27—1-29, 67D2, E2
Sovt emb staff cut, experts ousted 1-28, 69E1
Olympic boycott OK rptd 2-2, 85C1
Afghan rebel training confrmd 2-13, 123D1
Colombia amb seized in DR emb raid 2-27, 141B1
Shah arrives, gets permanent asylum 3-24; enters hosp, Sadat discounts protests 3-25, 217A2
Iran warns vs shah's asylum 3-25, 217D2
Shah's spleen removed 3-28; student protests continue 3-28, 3-31, 242D1
Arab states, PLO back anti-Sadat front 4-2, 273C3
PLO gunman dies in Israel raid 4-7, 260E2
Shah leaves hospital 4-9, 283E1
Iran says Kissinger helped shah quit Panama 4-16, 283D1
Iran hostage rescue role denied 4-24, 297A2; try backed 4-25, 324F1
Colombia DR Emb siege ends, amb freed 4-27, 335F1
Medit pollutn pact signed 5-17, 381D3
Libya warns dissidents 6-7, 451B3
Sadat-Iran exiled gen mtg rptd 6-11, 434A1
Libya rptdly backs anti-Sadat move 6-11, Egypt reimposes martial law near border 6-16, 451C3
US anti-Khomeini broadcasts rptd 6-29, 490G2
Shah has lung surgery 6-30, 490D3
Iran protests Canada pavillion rental 7-3, 520G3-521B1
Shah dies 7-27, Sadat leads state funeral 7-29; intl reactn 7-27—7-28, 571B1-E2
Libya mutiny rpt denied 8-18, 652B3
Libya, Syria to merge; '73 pact cited 9-2, 660G3
Khomeini scores US-Sadat link 9-12, 693E1
World Bank '80 loans rptd 9-22, 720E1
Iran calls 'prime supplier' of Iraq 10-17, 798F2
Shah's son claims title 10-31, 859F2
Iran govt recognized; Iraq, Syria, Libya scored 11-1, 859A3
Islamic League meets 11-10, 895A2
Turkey sentncs 4 Palestinians to die for '79 emb raid 12-23, 997A1

Government & Politics—*See also other appropriate subheads in this section*
Copts chrg Moslem persecutn 3-30, govt assures 3-31; Moslems protest vs Sadat 4-4, 273D3
Anti-Sadat front formed; Shazli heads 4-2, 273B3
30 dissenters indicted 4-17, 20 sentenced for '77 riot role 4-19, 312F1
Khalil govt quits 5-12; Sadat plans Cabt shift, announces econ steps, scores Copts 5-14; Cabt revamped, Sadat takes premrshp 5-15, 389G1
Charter chng voted, Sadat pres term limit lifted 5-22; final results 5-23, 406E3
NDP wins Consultative Cncl electn 9-25, 769F1
Human rights record scored 12-10, 978B3

1976

Libyan Relations—*See also 'Egypt' under MIDDLE EAST—ARAB Policies*
Libyan students occupy emb 1-8—1-9, 205C2
Libyan saboteurs seized, Tunisian detained 3-6, 3-9, 3-11; Qaddafi chrgd 3-9, 205G1-B2
Libya expulsns rptd, denied 3-11, 205B2
More Libya plotters seized 3-11, travel banned 3-13; more expulsns rptd 3-18, 239F2-A3
Libya envoy denies chrgs re students 4-19, 334C1
Rpts Libya bomb attempts 5-9, arrests 6-9, 467E1
Qaddafi on 'tenuous' ties 5-25, 467B2
Libyan amb ousted 6-30, 547E3
Joins Saudis, Sudan vs Libya 7-18—7-19, 531B2
Libya ties strained, Sudan coup role chrgd 7-22, 547A3
Libya chrgs troop mass, Kuwait confrms 7-25, 547C3
Libya recalls Saudi amb 7-25, 547D3
Govt bldg bombed, Libya blamed 8-8, 588F2
Troops massed on Libya border, Libya sabotage drive chrgd 8-13; Libya asks Arab League meet 8-15, 629E3
Libya tied to train blast, other bombings 8-15, 629D3
Qaddafi scores 8-18, 622A1
Libya blamed for hijack try 8-23, Libya denies 8-24, 629B2-B3
Egypt, Libya ask forgn missns closed 8-23, 8-24, 629B3
2 Egyptians seized in Libya 8-24, 629B3
USSR backs Libya 8-30, 682B3
Qaddafi denies bombings, hijack 9-2, 682D3, 683A1 ★
4 seized re train blast 9-6, 683A1
Hijackers acquitted of Libya link 9-18, 700D1

Middle East Conflict—*See MIDDLE EAST*

UN Policy & Developments—*See also UN DEVELOPMENTS under MIDDLE EAST*
OKs Medit pollutn pact 2-16, 126C3

U.S. Relations—*See also 'Egypt' under MIDDLE EAST—ARAB Policies*
Fulbright award rptd 1-28, 160D2
Boeing payoff to Egyptair probed 2-19, 138F2
US studies C-130 sale 3-3, 161D1
US House OKs arms aid, sales 3-3, 181A2
C-130 deal gets tacit OK 4-14, 275A2
'76, '77 arms aid authorized; '76 funds signed 6-30, 532E3, 533C2
Ship in US Bicentennial event 7-4, 488D3
Libya scores ties 8-18, 622A1
US '77 aid funds signed 10-1, 806C3
Reactn to Carter electn 11-3—11-4, 826B2
US sens, reps visit: A-proliferatn studied, arms asked 11-11—11-17, 877G2

1977

Libyan Relations
Consulates raided 4-10, 361D2
Egypt, Libya natls curbed, Qaddafi protests 4-13, 361E2
Egypt smashes 'plot' 4-13, 361F2
USSR note chrgs mil plans vs Libya 4-24; Egypt protests 4-27—4-29; note withdrawn 5-5, 361G2
Qaddafi chrgs mil designs 5-1, 361D3
Egyptians rptd deported 5-2; more ousters set, Libya denies 5-3, 361E3
Border incidents 7-12, 7-16, 7-19, 569B1
Major border clashes 7-21—7-24; Sadat asks truce 7-24, combat stops 7-25, 569A1, C1-B4, D2
Sadat scores Qaddafi, Sovt 7-22, 569E1
Arab mediatn efforts 7-22—7-25, 569E2
Egypt pre-emptive strike plans described 7-25, 569C2
Carter lauds US, USSR restraint 7-28, 574B3
Egypt Moslem sect linked 8-11, 636F2
Libya vs Sadat Israel visit 11-15, 11-16, 874B1
Libya ends ties 11-19, 890A3
Fahmy discloses Libya arms vow 12-3, 930E2
Egypt recalls amb 12-4, cuts ties 12-5, 929A1, C2

Monetary, Trade & Aid Issues (Including all foreign economic developments)
OPEC allocates loan funds 1-10, 12A3
France jet deal set, US reactn 1-12, 10G2
EEC trade pact signed 1-18, 73E3
Saudis vow econ aid 1-22; Sudan gives food 1-23, 62F2
US to up import loan 2-1, 390E2
To get 50 Sovt MiG-21s 2-27, 144F1
Gulf group assistance rptd 3-25, 390C3
Arab monetary fund created 4-18, 318C1
Ford plant agrmt OKd 5-10, other US deals rptd 5-16, 390A2
Intl consortium vows aid 5-11—5-12, 390F2
Forgn investmt rules rptd eased 5-16, 390C2
China arms deal rptd 6-25, 496C2
Sadat: USSR cut mil contracts, Saudis to finance defense 7-16, 550B1
US backs plane sales 7-26, Israel vs 7-27, 570G2-B3
Sovt, Czech cotton trade curbed 8-14, 636A3
Somalia arms aid rptd 9-1, 684G2
US backs MiG-21 repairing, other jet sales 9-15, 698C1
US '78 security aid funds cleared 10-19, 815G2; signed 11-1, 834D1
USSR debt paymt suspended; cotton sales to USSR, Czech banned 10-26, 811F3
Ford truck agrmt signed 10-29; Coca-Cola, AMC pacts cited 863G1, B2

UN Policy & Developments
UN Assemb member 3G3
Waldheim visits 2-2—2-4, 86D2; 2-11—2-12, 107D1
Cncl bars PLO Geneva conf role 3-25, 3-28—3-29, 226F3
Fahmy vs Israel peace stand 9-28, 734E1
Not in Medit pollutn pact 10-21, 876B2
Meguid UN post noted 10-25, 824B1
Anti-Israeli res OKd 10-28, 830F2
Envoy walks out on Syria 11-22, 894F1
Meguid meets Israel envoy 11-27, 909E2

U.S. Relations—*See also 'Monetary, Trade & Aid' above; for Arab-Israeli conflict, see MIDDLE EAST, subheads EGYPT-Israel Peace Moves and U.S. DEVELOPMENTS*
Vance visits 2-17, lauds Sadat plan for PLO-Jordan link 2-18, 121G1, C2
Carter plans visit 3-8, 165A2
Amb to US mediates Hanafi surrender 3-11, 192A3
Young asked UN Cncl mtg adjournmt 3-28, 3-29, 227B1
Sadat sees Carter 4-4—4-5, rpts differences 4-6, 245A1
Young vs US 'cold war' policy 4-11, 271D3
Egypt returns 2 Israeli spies hanged in '55 4-14, 297B2
Carter sees Libya conflict restraint 7-28, 574B3
Vance meets Sadat 8-1—8-2, 588G1
US security aid signed 8-4, 668D1
Vance briefs on Israel talks 8-11, 605G2
Anti-Copt plan dropped, protests cited 9-12, 863F2
Fahmy sees Carter in NY 10-4, 749A3
Vance visits 12-9, Sadat vows overall peace setlmt 12-10, 953E2
Carter to visit Sadat 12-31, 1000F3, 1001E1

1978

Dissident crackdown defended 6-29, 573B2
Al Ahaly resumes publicatn; seized, seizure overturned 7-12, 573F1
Sadat premrshp takeover plan rptd 7-12, 573G1
Sadat plans new party 7-22, 563D1
Kamel, Ghorbal quit posts 9-18, 710F3, 712C1
Salem quits, Khalil named premr 10-2; war min, staff chief removed 10-3, 746C2
New Cabt takes office, chngs listed 10-5, 774G2-B3
16 plotters chrgd 10-25, 838A1
Ex-dep prime min named Westinghouse payoff recipient 10-26, 961G2, B3
Sadat wins Nobel Peace Prize 10-27, 886D1
Sadat to shun Nobel rites 11-30, aide accepts 12-10, 950B3

Libyan Relations
Sadat asks US F-5Es 2-7, 78B1; US OKs sale 2-14, 97E1
Journalists ordrd home 5-26, others probed 5-28, 414F3
Libya athletes attack Egyptians in Algiers 7-22, 573D1
Ties severed 9-24, 729G2
Sadat scores hangings 10-2, 746B2

Monetary, Trade, Aid & Investment—*See also MIDDLE EAST—ARMAMENTS*
US A-export controls clear Sen 2-7, 82B3
Oil pact with 2 US cos signed 2-16, 139A3, B3 ★
France signs AIO arms pact; US, UK deals cited 3-14, 237C1 ★
Islamic, Arab poor-natn aid rise rptd 4-9, 257F2
Zaire aid rptd pledged 6-7, 6-13, 441G1
USSR '54-76 credits cited 595F2
Boeing chrgd re payoffs 7-28, 642G3
UK cancels debts 7-31, 592D1
Arab fund loan to Sudan rptd 8-17, 925F3
US econ aid authorzn signed 9-26, 734E1
US econ aid funds signed 10-18, 862D2

Press & Censorship—*See also 'Government' above*

Sports
Athletes attacked at Algiers games 7-22; team leaves 7-23; 5 Arab states boycotted 7-24, 573C1

UN Policy and Developments—*See also MIDDLE EAST—UN*
Assemb member 713E3

U.S. Relations—*See also MIDDLE EAST, subheads ARMAMENTS and EGYPT-Israel Peace Moves*
Carter sees Sadat 1-4, 1C1, 2A2
CIA sees no A-bomb before '84 1-26, 61C2
Sadat in US; seeks arms, food 2-3—2-8, 77A1-78C1
US proposes A-export controls 2-7, 82B3
Rights rpt released 2-9, 102A2
Oil pact with 2 US cos signed 2-16, 139A3, B3 ★
Carter lauds Egypt raid in Cyprus 2-23, Vance affirms neutrality 2-26, 138G2
AIO arms pact cited 3-14, 237C1 ★
Boeing chrgd re payoffs 7-28, 642G3
Carter signs econ aid authorzn 9-26, 734E1
Carter signs econ aid funds 10-18, 862D2
Westinghouse payoff figure named 10-26, fined 11-20, 961G2

1979

Monetary, Trade, Aid & Investment
Australia wheat deal rptd 1-22, 56F3
US arms requested 2-16—2-18, 143B3
Sadat seeks W Ger econ aid 3-29, 250A1
OAPEC imposes oil embargo, trade curbs 4-17; Arab Monetary Fund suspends 4-18, 278G1-B2
US trade group visits 4-17, 296C1
Arab aid group disbands, 3 others oust 4-27, 319D2
Arab econ aid discounted 5-1, 319G1
US-Saudi talks on Egypt jet funds rptd 5-8, 341C2
Sadat: Saudis to renege on US jet sale 5-12, 360A1
China arms deal set 6-5, 415A3
US arms coproductn sought 6-5, 415C3
China jet exchng rptd 6-22, 475C1
US delays F-5 jet sale re Saudi finance halt, OKs F-4s 7-6, 512A1
US arms experts en route 8-9; shipmts start, displayed 10-6, 762C3
Morocco gets aid vow 9-2, arms 9-8, 697G1
US aid talks 9-11, 677A2
Bahrain offered Iran annexatn threat aid 9-28, rejected 10-2, 752C3

UN Policy & Developments—*See also MIDDLE EAST—U.N.*
Membership listed 695G2
WHO hq move bid fails 5-24, 398G2

U.S. Relations—*See also MIDDLE EAST—EGYPT-Israel headings*
CIA alleged agent named 1-4, 17C3
US issues rights rpt 2-10, 107C3
Defns Secy Brown visits, Egypt asks US arms 2-16—2-18, 143B3
US-Israel separate agrmt scored, US offers similar pact 3-28, 222B1
US trade group visits 4-17, 296C1
US neutral on Saudi feud 5-2, 319B2
US House com hearing on aid 5-8, 341B2
Atherton named US amb 5-8, 347B3
US-Saudi talks on Egypt jet funds rptd 5-8, 341C2
Sadat sees no Saudi aid to buy US jets 5-12, 360A1
US role to end Saudi feud confrmd 5-20, 5-21, 378B3
Egypt seeks arms coproductn 6-5, 415C3
Carter address Cong on SALT II 6-18, 459A3
US delays F-5 jet sale re Saudi finance halt, OKs F-4s 7-6, 512A1
US arms experts en route 8-9; shipmts start, displayed 10-6, 762C3
Mubarak sees Vance, US aid discussed 9-11, 677A2
Jesse Jackson visits, meets Sadat 9-30—10-1, 763E1
Iran US Emb seizure denounced 11-24, 895D3

1980

Israeli Relations—*See MIDDLE EAST*

Sports
Olympic boycott OK rptd 2-2, 85C1

UN Policy & Developments
Sovt Afghan invasn opposed 1-5, 2B2
Cncl res scores Israel Jerusalem moves 6-30, 491B2
Women's conf in Denmark 7-14—7-30, 587B2

U.S. Relations—*See also MIDDLE EAST, subheads ARMAMENTS and EGYPT-Israel Peace Moves*
Bases offered to US 1-4, 1-7; US refuses 1-9, 11E1-G1
Joint US air exercises rptd 1-8, 11C1
US issues rights rpt 2-5, 87F2
US to sell F-16s, tanks; F-15 buy deferred; Israel concerned 2-25, 140B2
US MDs to attend to shah 3-26, 217B2
DeBakey honored 3-30, 242F1
Iran hostage rescue role denied 4-24, 297A2; try backed 4-25, 324F1
US vs Begin E Jerusalem office move 6-26, 476A2
US anti-Khomeini broadcasts rptd 6-29, 490G2
Egypt F-4E problems rptd 7-8, US squadron deployed for joint war games 7-10, 548A2
Anderson visits 7-11—7-12, 549G3
Khomeini scores US-Sadat link 9-12, 693E1
Reagan electn reactn 11-5, 841B2
US announces mil maneuvers 11-7; US transport plane crashes, 13 die 11-13; air, ground games held 11-18—11-28, 914B2
US Cong clears '81 aid authrzn 12-3, signed 12-16, 981C3
Haig apptmt praised 12-17, 955E2

1976

EGYPTAIR
Govt probes Boeing payoff 2-19, 138F2
Iraq airport blast 12-14, 954A1
EHRENBERG, Herbert
W Ger labor min 12-15, 968A2
EHRLICHMAN, John D(aniel)
FBI to destroy '69 files on Kraft 3-30, 235D1
Named in wiretap suit 5-10, 349G2
Cited in Dole biog sketch 614B3
Watergate convictn upheld 10-12, 770E1-C2
Ford denies pardon rumor 10-20, 784E3
Enters prison 10-28, 849F2
Cleared re Halperin tap 12-16, 981A1
1876 (book)
On best-seller list 12-5, 972E2
EILBERG, Rep. Joshua (D, Pa.)
Reelected 11-2, 830D3
EILTS, Hermann F.
In talks on Leb crisis 6-22, 448B2
EISENBERG, Bill
Wins world bridge title 5-8, 352G3
EISENBERG, Shaul
Canada probes A-sales 11-30, 923C3
On A-sale expenses 12-4, AECL rpts paymts 12-8—12-9, vows reimbursemt 12-9, 962C3
Canada audit OKd 12-21, 998D1
EISENHOWER, Dwight David (Ike) (1890-1969)—*See 1969, p. 178E1 for biog. data*
Ford State of Union message cites 1-19, 39A2
Field Marshal Montgomery dies 3-24, 240E3
Reagan cites Lebanon role 6-3, 410G1
Gerald Morgan dies 6-15, 484F3
GOP platform text cites 8-18, 607F1, 608G2
Ford on Arab boycott 10-20, 784B3
EIZENSTAT, Stuart
Dem com OKs platform 6-15, 432G2, 433A1
At NE govs mtg 11-13—11-14, 864C3
Carter policy aide 11-23, 881F2
EKANDEM, Dominic Cardinal
Appointed cardinal 4-27, 336D2
EKLUND, Sigvard
Addresses IAEA conf 9-21, 760D3
EL—*Arabic names bearing this prefix are indexed by surname (e.g., QADDAFI, Col. Muammar el-)*
ELAZAR, Lt. Gen. David
Dies 4-15, 315G3
ELDERLY—*See AGED Persons*
ELECTIONS—*See under POLITICS*
ELECTRICAL, Radio and Machine Workers, International Union of (IUE) (AFL-CIO)
Settles with GE 6-27, 536G3
Strikes Westinghouse 7-18—7-20, 536C3
ELECTRICAL, Radio and Machine Workers of America, United (UE) (unaffiliated)
Settles with GE 6-27, 536F3
Strikes Westinghouse 7-18—7-20, 536C3

1977

EGYPT, Consultative Group for the Arab Republic of—*See CONSULTATIVE Group for the Arab Republic of Egypt*
EHRLICH, Simcha
Israel finance min 6-20, 474E2
Announces austerity plan 7-17, 563G2
Vs US-Sovt Geneva plan 10-2, 749F2
Announces econ policy 10-28, 842E3
EHRLICHMAN, John D(aniel)
Sup Ct bars convictn review 2-22, 150A1
Liddy's term commuted 4-12, 325E3
Sup Ct coverup appeal decisn leaked 4-21, defense motion denied 5-2, 382C2; appeal denied 5-23, 406D1
Nixon-Frost interview 5-4, 366G1, 367B1-A3
Disputes Nixon re firing 5-16, 368A1
Nixon-Frost interview 5-25, 420A2
Haldeman, Mitchell enter prison 6-21, 6-22, 483A3
Sentnc cut after apology 10-4, 762A1
Sup Ct disbars 10-31, 835A3
EICHELBERGER, Dave
Wins Milwaukee Open 7-3, 676G1
EILBERG, Rep. Joshua (D, Pa.)
On illegal alien hiring 4-30, 370G2
EILTS, Hermann F.
Sadat gets Israel invitatn 11-15, 873F1
Given Egypt peace plan 12-31, 995A1
EINSTEIN, Albert (1879-1955)
Relativity evidence rptd 1-7, 170E3
EIRE—*See IRELAND*
EISELEY, Loren C.
Dies 7-9, 604A3
EISENBERG, Shoul
Macdonnell rejects UDI books 2-1, 114G1
EISENHOWER, Dwight David (Ike) (1890-1969)—*See 1969, p. 178E1 for biog. data*
Anne Wheaton dies 3-23, 264G3
Nixon disputed re Adams firing 5-4, 5-5, 367C1
Carter vs impacted aid 5-26, 417C1
Wilton Persons dies 9-5, 788C2
EISENHOWER Exchange Fellowships
Ford assumes presidency 2-1, addresses 3-23, 236F2-A3
EISENSTADT, Marvin
Scores saccharin ban 3-9, 177A1
EIZENSTAT, Stuart E.
Named Carter domestic asst 1-14, 35A3
Carter submits reorganizatn plan 7-15, 555F3
Cargo preference stand cited 8-1, 719D3
Vets benefits review signed 10-8, 773A2
EKLUND, Sigvard
Scores US plutonium ban 4-17, 334A3
EKUKINAM, A. E.
Nigeria Cabt drops 3-15, 393D2
EL—*Arabic names bearing this prefix are indexed by surname (e.g., QADDAFI, Col. Muammar el-)*
ELAHI Choudhry, Fazal (Pakistan president)
Rejcts Bhutto foes demands 3-27, 259B1
Bhutto overthrown, to remain head of state 7-5, 509C1
EL Al Israel Airlines
US bars charter flights 8-1, 589C1
CAB acts on NY-London budget fare 9-9, 9-15, Carter overrules 9-26, 860E2
ELDER, Lee
Loses Crosby Pro-Am 1-23, 104B1
ELDER, Nan
On Korean lobbying 10-19—10-21, 816E2
ELDER, Ruth
Dies 10-9, 872F1
ELDERLY—*See AGE and Aged Persons*
ELEANOR and Franklin: The White House Years (TV film)
Wins Emmy 9-11, 1022A1
ELECTIONS—*See under POLITICS*
ELECTORAL College—*See under U.S. GOVERNMENT*

1978

EHLERS, Federico
Arrest rptd 1-20, 112C1
EHRENBERG, Herbert
Retains W Ger labor post 2-3, 93A3
EHRET, Gloria
2d in Orange Blossom Classic 2-20, 355C3
2d in Lady Tara tourn 4-30, 356B1
EHRLICH, Simcha
Backs Weizman on setlmts 3-7, 157G1
EHRLICHMAN, Jeanne
Rpts separatn 6-1, 420E3
EHRLICHMAN, John D(aniel)
Freed from prison 4-27, 320A2
Cited in Nixon memoir excerpt 4-30, 320C1
Wife rpts separatn 6-1, 420E3
EICHMANN, Adolf (1906-62)
Wagner arrested 5-30, 477B2
EILBERG, Rep. Joshua (D, Pa.)
Marston dismissal controversy 1-12, 12F2; Bell ousts 1-20, 32A2
Carter, Bell cleared on Marston ouster 1-24, Carter defends ouster 1-30, 62D1, A2, C2
DeLuca named Marston temp successor 1-24, 62E2
House probe announced 2-8; Marston probe re Hahnemann Hosp cited, denies chrgs 3-9, 240A1-F1, F2
Sen com finds no Marston affair cover-up, Mathias disputes 4-24, 309A3
Civiletti confirmed 5-9, 342E3
Wins primary 5-16, 389E3
House panel chrgs ethics violatns 9-13, 697F1-C2
Indicted 10-24, pleads not guilty 11-1, 835C2
Loses reelectn 11-7, 846D2, 849D2
EILER, Sally
Dies 1-5, 96F1
EILTS, Hermann F.
Reassures Egypt on Palestine stand 5-1, 339G2
Gets Egypt protest on Israel W Bank, Gaza stand 6-19, 461F2
EIRE—*See IRELAND*
EISENBERG, Shoul
Canada probe asks paymt halt 2-27, 166B3
EISENHOWER, David
1st child born 8-15, 844F3
EISENHOWER, Dwight David (Ike) (1890-1969)—*See 1969, p. 178E1 for biog. data*
Cong support rating cited 1-7, 12B3
John Fine dies 5-21, 440F2
'47 Nev A-test site oppositn rptd 12-18, 1012C1
EISENHOWER, Jennie
Born 8-15, 844F3
EISENHOWER, Julie Nixon (Mrs. David)
1st child born 8-15, 844F3
EISSA, Salah
Egypt probes, exit barred 5-28, 415A1
EIST, Alexander A.
Ray confessn alleged, credibility attacked 8-18; scores 8-19, 641C3
Testifies on Ray confessn 11-9, 898G1-B2
EITAN, Lt. Gen. Rafael
Installed staff chief 4-16, 359C1
OKs more Leb pullbacks 4-18, 274F2
Doubts Egypt peace motives, for holding Arab lands 5-11; Cabt upholds 5-14, 358D3-359C1
EIZENSTAT, Stuart E.
On Carter urban-aid plan 3-24, 217E2
Rpts on Carter Westn tour 5-6, 342D2
Scores FRB tight money policy 5-9, 361E2
Costanza TV spot canceled 7-25, 606A1
Tax-cut bill cleared 10-15, 785E1
Carter praise of 95th Cong rptd 10-16, 784F2
Tight budget stressed 11-14, 875E1, A2
Defends natl health policy at Dem midterm conf 12-9, 956D2
EL—*Arabic names bearing this prefix are indexed by surname (e.g., SADAT, Anwar el-)*
EL Al Israel Airlines
3 Arabs slain in Paris airport raid 5-20, 383E3
US, Israel reach air svc pact 7-15, 640B2
Bus attacked in London, 2 die 8-20; UK laxity chrgd 8-21, 638B1
Office in Iran attacked 12-31, 993E2
ELBOW Room (book)
McPherson wins Pulitzer 4-17, 315C1
EL Capitan (Yosemite National Park, Calif.)
1st woman climbs alone 10-26, 843A3
ELDER, Lee
Wins Milwaukee Open 7-9, Westchester Classic 8-20; 2d in Greater Hartford Open 7-30, 672B3-D3
ELDERLY—*See AGE & Aged Persons*
ELDJARN, Kristjan (Icelandic president)
Coalitn govt attempts fail 7-12—8-24, crisis resolved 8-31, 688E3
El DORADO, Ark.—*See ARKANSAS*
ELECTIONS—*See under POLITICS; country names*
ELECTRICAL, Radio & Machine Workers, International Union of (IUE) (AFL-CIO)
NLRB backs right to job data 11-3, 899B1

1979

EHLER, Ursula
On Mount Chimborazo opens 5-21, 712A2
EHRLICH, Simcha
Vs subsidy cut, Liberals ask resignatn 7-18, 566D1
Reverses subsidy stand, urges abolitn 7-30, 583D2
Replaced as finance min, gets new post 10-29, 856B2
EHRLICH, Willie
Named ASL top coach 9-15, 776F2
Forecasts Cousey ASL ouster 11-19, 1004A3
EICHELBERGER, Dave
Wins Mixed Team tourn 12-9, 969C3
EICHMANN, Adolf (1906-62)
'60 abductn in Argentina cited 8-8, 617A1
EIDSON, Judge Joe
Barron quits Davis divorce case 3-25, 272A1
Davis acquitted in kill-for-hire case 11-9, 890E2
EILBERG, Joshua
Pleads guilty in plea-bargain 2-24, 152C2
Pa law practice suspended 3-29, 272A1
EILTS, Hermann F.
Mediates Israel-Egypt pact feud 4-25, 295G2
Atherton to succeed 5-8, 347B3
Prince Fahd mtg rptd 5-20, 378C3
EINSTEIN, Albert (1879-1955)
A-scientists 'doomsday clock' unchngd 1-1, 13F1
Monument unveiled 4-22, 392E2
Relativity cited re quasar study 5-17, 691F2
EISENHOWER, Dwight David (Ike) (1890-1969)
Rockefeller dies 1-26, 104A1
Marshall letter disclosed, divorce rumor debunked 1-28, 79E1
Richards dies 2-21, 176E3
Anna Strauss dies 2-23, 176F3
CIA '63 Castro death plot rptd confrmd 5-2, 368A1
Jacoby dies 5-31, 432A3
Cited in Carter SALT address 6-18, 458G2
Brundage dies 7-16, 588D2
WWII secret diary rptd disclosed 9-16, 9-17, 748A1
Anthony coin oppositn rptd 9-25, 727C2
White House tapes revealed 10-21, 868G3-869C1
Widow dies 11-11, 932F2
Short dies 11-19, 932E3
Allen dies 11-20, 932B2
EISENHOWER, Mamie Doud (Mrs. Dwight David)
Divorce rumor debunked 1-28, 79E1
Dies 11-11, 932F2
EISENHUT, Darrell
Lists 3 Mile I A-accident errors 4-4, 259E3
On A-plant pipe leaks 5-2, 322C3
On A-plant cooling system hazard 11-2, 849B2
EITAN, Lt. Gen. Rafael
On Israeli raid vs Leb 1-19, 50G2
Offcr's prison term rptd cut 7-4, 496F2
Ct bars Elon Moreh 10-22, 801C2
EIZENSTAT, Stuart E.
Warns Dems face 'new realities' 1-4, 3C2
Welfare plan presented 5-23, 384F1
Carter econ team rptd revamped 6-4, 463E1
Bosworth reprimand rptd 6-4, 463G1
ADA opts for Kennedy 6-24, 482F2
Carter consults re energy 7-5, 497D3
On Carter speech cancelatn 7-6, 513G2
Energy memo leaked 7-7, 513C3
Forgn-language study urged 11-7, 944F1
Library conf resolutns to be studied 11-15—11-19, 901A2
EKETEBI Moyindiba Mondjolomba
Named in McDonnell Douglas paymts chrg 11-9, 886D2
EKSTEEN, J. Adriaan
Scores UN ouster 5-24, 409G3
EL Al Israel Airlines
Iran airport strikers ask ban 1-1, 3A1
Brussels PLO raid thwarted 4-16, 278A3
2 W Gers sentncd for '76 plot 9-11, 677A3
ELAM, Jack
Villain released 7-20, 820E3
Apple Dumpling sequel released 8-31, 819E3
EL Centro, Calif.—*See CALIFORNIA*
ELDAR, Ephraim
Escapes ambush 11-13, 882B1
ELDERLY—*See AGE & Aged Persons*
ELDREDGE, Carleton
Drops '77 NH A-protest chrgs 7-3, 519C1
ELDSON, Judge Joe
Davis case withdrawal cited 3-25, 272A1
ELECTIONS—*See under POLITICS; country names*
ELECTORAL College—*See under U.S. GOVERNMENT*
ELECTRICAL, Radio & Machine Workers, International Union of (IUE) (AFL-CIO)
GE, Westinghouse talks cited 5-31, 399D3
GE contract ratified 7-11, 598C2
Westinghouse struck 7-16–9-2, pact ratified 9-3, 744C2
ELECTRICAL, Radio & Machine Workers of America, United (UE) (unaffiliated)
GE contract ratified 7-11, 598C2
Westinghouse struck 7-16–9-2, pact ratified 9-3, 744C2

1980

EHRENBERG, Herbert
USSR visit cancellatn cited 1-30, 103F1
Sworn W Ger labor min 11-5, 925E1
EHRENFREUND, Judge Norbert
Sentences religious deprogrammer 9-26, 857C3
EHRLICH, Simcha
Vs Carter explanatn of US UN vote 3-4, 163D3
Vs Hebron setlmt vote 3-24, 218C3
EHRLICH, Willie
Named ASL top coach 9-8, 771F1
EHRLICHMAN, John D.
Calif bar resignatn accepted 1-19, 199D1
Parole ended 10-27, 890E1
EICHELBERGER, Clark M.
Dies 1-26, 104D2
EICHELBERGER, Dave
Wins Bay Hill Classic 3-2, 412F2
Ties for 2d in Southern Open 10-5, 972D2
EIDENBERG, Eugene
Named Carter intergovt asst, Cabt secy 6-11, 439B1
E.I. du Pont v. U.S.
Case declined by Sup Ct 4-14, 307E1
8:30 (recording)
Weather Report wins Grammy 2-27, 296E3
EIKENBERRY, Jill
Hide in Plain Sight released 3-21, 216G2
Onward Victoria opens 12-14, 1003E3
EILAN, Arieh
Israel offers Mideast A-ban 11-13, 864A2
EINSTEIN, Albert (1879-1955)
You Know Al opens 11-13, 892G3
EISENHOWER, Dwight David (Ike) (1890-1969)
Ikle on defns spending 1-15, 32B2
Bush on GOP missn 7-17, 529F2
Carter pres renominatn acceptance speech 8-14, 613B1
Carter cites in TV debate 10-28, 815F2
EITAN, Rafael
On Israeli raids in Leb 5-8, 341A1
EIZENSTAT, Stuart E.
Carter coal-fired utilities plan presented 3-6, 169G3
Fears US mil action vs Iran 4-22, 298G2-A3
Sees House Dems re taxes 6-26, 480C3
In Detroit re auto aid 7-7, 505A2
Econ plank compromise fails 8-12, 610A3
Urges Dem Party reform 12-4, 938B3
EKAI, Paul Nakware
Chrgd in Adamson slaying 2-2, 238B3
EKWUEME, Alex
Signs US trade pact 7-23, 620C2
EL Al Israel Airlines
Turkey rep killed 1-2, suspects arrested 2-13, 135G3, 136A1
Direct Tel Aviv-Cairo flights start 3-3, 180A2
ELAM, Chief Justice Harry J.
'Caligula' ruled not obscene in Boston 8-1, 640B2
ELASS, Majed
Saudi completes Aramco takeover, retains bd seat 9-4, 662A2
ELBOAR, David
Commonwealth Ed, 2 offcls acquitted 8-8, 649F1
ELDERLY—*See AGE & Aged Persons*
ELDJARN, Kristjan (Icelandic president)
New govt bid set 1-16, 39C3
ELECTORAL College—*See under U.S. GOVERNMENT*
ELECTRICAL & Electronics Engineers, Institute of
USSR barred from US mtg 2-22, 135G1; exchngs suspended 2-24, 181G2

1976

ELECTRICAL Workers, International Brotherhood of (IBEW) (AFL-CIO)
Pillard quits Ford panel 1-8, 4C1
Strikes Westinghouse 7-12—7-20, 536C3
ELECTRIC Boat Division—*See under GENERAL Dynamics*

ELECTRIC & Electronics Industries
US equipmt to Morocco rptd 1-7, 36D2
Finnish-Japanese deal rptd 1-27, 104E2
'75 4th ¼ profits rptd 2-3, 215A3
NYS accuses GE re PCBs 2-9, 171E3
'75 top 500 US indls ranked 437B1, D1, F2
US computer sale to S Africa rptd 5-26, 388A2
E Ger gets Eur$ loan 6-4, 417C2
Dem platform text 6-15, 471F2
Paul Pimsleur dies 6-22, 524D3
Westinghouse, GE strikes end 6-27, 7-19, 7-20, 536B3
Steel price hike canceled 8-30, 646G3
IBM Sovt sale OKd 9-2, 752C2
NYS, GE sign PCB pact 9-8, 691F2-B3
Sup Ct bars review of Ampex class-action ruling 10-4, 807B3
'60 antitrust suit cited 10-5, 886A1
US rpts Sovt mil lag 10-5, 961C1
Science Medals awarded 10-18, 858C3-F3
US computer sales to China, USSR rptd 10-28, 11-1, 832F2-C3
3d ¼ profits rptd up 10-28, 866G2
Pa plant illness identified 11-5, 911A2
France, UK set cooperatn 11-21, 880C2
Steel prices hiked 11-24—11-29, 897C2
Sup Ct refuses computer-evidence case 11-29, 900E3
GE, Westinghouse trust suits dropped 12-10, 988C2
Utah Intl, GE merge 12-16, 984G3

ELECTRIC Light & Power—*See also ATOMIC Energy, ENERGY; company names*
Dec '75 output rptd up 1-16, 92A1
'77 budget tax proposal 1-21, 62C2
New River dam prjct upheld 3-24, 219B3
San Fran electricians strike 3-31—5-8, 348C3
Utah power projct dropped 4-14, 284B2
Dem platform text 6-15, 475A1
Oil import fees upheld 6-17, 452C3
Trust suits vs state-regulated cos upheld 7-6, 569F1
Ford OKs '77 funds 7-12, 517E1
May, June CPI rptd 7-21, 536D2
GOP platform text 8-18, 603A1, F1, 607A2
New River dams blocked 9-11, 689E1
Elec car bill vetoed 9-13, overridden 9-17, 707D3
Clean air amendmts not cleared 10-2, 883D2
Mo, Ohio vote results 11-2, 823C3, G3
Foreign Developments (including U.S. foreign developments)—*See also country names*
Guatemala IDB hydro loan rptd 1-9, 55A2
Greek-Sovt deal rptd 1-12, 73C2
France-India pact signed 1-22—1-26, 139F2
France-Bahrain pact 3-2, 204G3
S Africa rpts Angola hydro plant pledge 3-25, 228A1

1977

ELECTRIC Boat Division—*See under GENERAL Dynamics*

ELECTRIC & Electronics Industries—*See also COMPUTERS*
Racal wins Milgo takeover 2-17, 275A1
GE Utah Intl purchase cited 2-18, 274F2
US modifies duty-free list 2-28, 189E3
E-Systems Korean paymts rptd 3-10, 233B3
2 US execs sentncd for Sovt sales 3-14, 203D2
Carter energy plan for appliances 4-20, 290A2; fact sheet 292F1
1st ¼ profits rptd up 4-28, 668E3
Raytheon to buy Falcon Seaboard 6-22, 519C1
Sylvania TV sales rules upheld 6-23, 539G1
Lilly buys Ivac 7-20, 650E3
House OKs Carter energy pkg 8-5, 610C1
July appliance productn rptd up 8-15, 628F3
Sen OKs home appliance rules 9-13, 703F1
Zenith cost-cutting plans rptd 9-27, 974D2
Nobel Prizes announced 10-11, 951A3
Aluminum wire makers sued re safety 10-27, 900C3
Wiring device makers indicted re prices 10-27, 918G3-919A1
Israel-Rumania trade rptd 12-10, 987C3
Time plans cable-TV purchase 12-22, 1004C3
Japan
TV imports injury ruled 3-8, tariff hike asked 3-14; '76 data rptd 3-18, 208G2
US-Japan TV trade talks 3-21, 209B3
Solitron case review denied 3-21, 230G2
Motorola forgn paymts rptd 3-23, 233G2
Japan color TV export probe OKd by US 3-23, 318C3
Japan Feb TV exports to US rptd 3-23, 318D3
Japan mfrs study US investmt rise 3-28; Mitsubishi plans rptd 4-14, 318F3
Carter faces TV import decisn 248E1, E3-249E1
US ups Japan TV bond requiremt 4-7, 318G2-B3
US trade rep ends Japan TV talks 4-8, 318E3
Japan electronics import duties ordrd 4-12; opposed 4-13, 4-14, 318G1
'76 Japan exports to US rptd 318E2
US TV coalitn vs Japan export level 5-18, 416C1
Japan OKs export-limit pact 5-20; reactn 5-20—5-23, 415E3
TV antitrust probe rptd 5-20, 416F1
GATT probes electronics duty order 5-23, 416B2
Apr TV exports to US rptd 5-30; '76 data 416A1, E1
1st ¼ June color TV exports rptd 6-14, 7-28, 587G1
US ends color TV probe, OKs consent pact 7-14, 587E1
GATT warns US re duties order 7-16, 587C1
US duties order reversed 7-28, 586D3
Witteveen scores trade curb pacts 9-26, 753E3
Zenith cost-cutting plans rptd 9-27, 974D2
Hitachi-GE TV venture planned 12-7, 974B2
Toshiba plans Tenn plant, other US operatns cited 12-14, 974A2
Obituaries
Goldmark, Peter 12-7, 1024A2
Kompfner, Rudolf 12-3, 1024C2

ELECTRIC Light & Power—*See also ATOMIC Energy; company names*
Ford energy message 1-7, 14C3
Ford proposes energy dept 1-11, 14F3
US Nov '76 prices rptd 1-14, 37E2
Dec '76 CPI rise rptd 1-19, 78B1
Utility stocks hit 3-yr high 1-24, 54E3
Calif cnty rations water 2-1, 76C3
US acts to free Tex gas 2-5, 91A3, C3
Jan indl output, CPI rptd 2-15, 2-18, 129D3, F3
Westn US drought cutbacks rptd 2-15, 152E3
Carter budget revision 2-22, 125D2
Regional power systems urged 2-23, 277G2
Carter asks energy dept 3-1, 148B2, C2
Westinghouse, 3 utilities settle 3-3, 177B2
24-hr power watch ended 3-11, 277C2
Peak-load pricing urged 3-11, 277D3
'76 energy use rptd 3-13, 196A2, 132
Feb CPI rise rptd 3-18, 215C1
Calif to test voltage cuts 3-18, 278A1
Ariz conflict-of-interest cited 3-21, 210A2
US '76, '71-76 data rptd 3-23, 3-25, 277E1
Babcock vs United Tech purchase 4-4, 274C3
'75 Colo bombing convictn reversed 4-5, 484E1

1978

ELECTRICAL Workers, International Brotherhood of (IBEW) (AFL-CIO)
AT&T bias case declined by Sup Ct 7-3, 552A1
ELECTRIC Boat Division—*See GENERAL Dynamics Corp.*

ELECTRIC & Electronics Industries—*See also COMPUTERS*
FBI favoritism toward US Recording rptd 1-10, 15B2
Wiring device makers sentncd 2-3, 142F1
'64-78 spending pattern chngs reflected in new CPIs 222E2
United Tech to buy Ambac 3-2, 185D1
Seatrain pleads guilty on Tenna rebates 3-16, 184C3
PCB ban formally proposed 6-7, 513B1
Appliance energy-cost labels OKd 6-28, 702A3
Leeds-Gen Signal merger ends Tyco, Cutler bidding battle 7-7, 553E1
Cable makers sued 9-22, 768G3
Fuse product makers, execs indicted 9-28, 769C1
Aluminum wire dispute refused by Sup Ct 10-2, 751E1
Energy bill authorizes appliance efficiency standards 10-15, 787B2
Oreck trust damage award case refused by Sup Ct 10-30, 832G2
Space indus possibilities rptd 11-3, 861D1
US sues vs United Tech-Carrier merger 11-13, 896B2
Mallory OKs Dart takeover bid 11-17, 1005C2
Borg-Warner, Firestone to merge 11-28, 935D1
US agencies scored on microwave safety 12-11, 936B3
Reliance Elec to buy Fed Pacific Elec 12-18, 1005A2
Foreign Developments (including U.S. international news)
USSR cuts TV prices 3-1, 151A3
US hikes CB radio tariffs 3-28, 443C3
Dutch name 3 Sovts as spies 3-30, 247F3
Japan to curb US TV exports 5-3, 341F2
Siemen exec in Italy shot 5-12, 393A2
Zenith import duty rebuffed by Sup Ct 6-21, 491G2
Japan TV export curbs affirmed 7-17, 544A2
UK, Japan cos set joint plant 8-23, 667C3
Japan Apr-June TV exports rptd down 9-8, 694C2
US-China hydro power talks rptd set 11-6, 871D2
France-China trade pact signed 12-4, 986A2
Obituaries
Sporn, Philip 1-24, 96F3
ELECTRIC Light Orchestra (singing group)
Out of the Blue on best-seller list 2-4, 116G3

ELECTRIC Light & Power—*See also ATOMIC Energy, SOLAR Energy; company names*
Indl output index described 52F1
NW hydro power restored 1-10, 24E1
Ohio, Mich blizzard outages 1-25—1-26, Boston blackout 2-7—2-9, 195D2, C3
PR strike, sabotage rptd 1-29, 2-2, 115G3
Coal strike threatens 9-state area 2-10—2-16; Ind, W Va order cutbacks 2-13, 104C1, E3
Feb income, shortages linked 3-17, 223D1
Cities trust law liability upheld by Sup Ct 3-29, 280F1-E2
Cong conferees OK conservatn measures, rate-setting provisn 4-21, 305F1, A2
NYC '77 blackout rpt issued 4-23, 396F1
W Va power plant scaffold collapses 4-27, 459F2
Mar CPI rptd up 4-28, 345B1
Utility customer hearings backed by Sup Ct 5-1, 364A1
Fortune ranks '77 top 500 indls 5-8, 325E1, F1
Energy study sees hydroelec power growth 5-8, 366E2
Waste combustn seen as energy source 5-11, 367C1
TVA scales down rate hike 5-17, 362G1

1979

ELECTRICAL Workers, International Brotherhood of (IBEW) (AFL-CIO)
St Regis Paper struck 5-15, pact ratified 6-23, 598B3
Punitive damages vs unions barred by Sup Ct 5-29, 421C3
Westinghouse struck 7-16, settles 8-17, 744C2
ELECTRICAL Workers v. Foust
Case decided by Sup Ct 5-29, 421B3
ELECTRIC & Electronics Industries
'78 color-TV sales hit high 1-9, 160F2
UV Industries to liquidate 1-18, 131G3
Fedders OKs heat pump repairs 2-22, 308A3
Bell & Howell to reimburse home-study students 3-26, 308D3
Price guidelines tightened 3-29, 264A2
Alexander's sentncd re TV import rebates 3-29, 298C3
Thompson settles dishwasher ad chrg 4-15, 308F3
PCB rules issued 4-19, 281G3
Voluntary hair dryer recall asked 4-19, 308D2
GM car-radio trust suit settled 5-14, 441F3-442A1
Hair dryer recall praised 5-17, 595E3
GE, Westinghouse IUE talks cited 5-31, 399C3
GE contract ratifed by 2 unions 7-11, 598C2
Westinghouse struck 7-16—9-2, unions ratify pact 9-3, 744C2
Corning percolator recall set 9-4, 902D3
Borg-Warner develops motor-control device 10-2, 770E2
Sears dishwasher ads faulted 10-16, 903A2
Postal Svc electronic mail plan rejected 10-18, 921F2
Franchise terminatn case refused by Sup Ct 10-29, 884B1
Shure Brothers-Korvettes patent case refused by Sup Ct 11-5, 884D3
Foreign Developments (including U.S. international news)—*See also 'Mergers' below*
Taiwan, S Korea OK color-TV export limits; '78, Japan data rptd 1-9, 1-17, 160A2
GATT pact signed 4-12, 273A2, 274F1
US demands color-TV dumping paymt 4-13, Japan mfrs score 4-26, 298F2
Canada sets research grants 4-17, 311B3
US-Japan NT&T dispute cited 5-2, 320C2
Taiwan indl dvpt projcts rptd 11-6, 952D3
Telefunken rescue plan rptd 12-4, 998F2
Mergers & Acquisitions
White buys Frigidaire from GM 1-31, 131A3
GE, Cox merger agreed 2-21, 188C2-A3
GCE buys Generale Occidentale share 3-16, 236B2
United Tech-Carrier merger set 3-30, 349E3-350A1
Fairchild rejcts Gould merger bids 5-4, 5-8, suits filed 5-8, 5-9, 350D1
Exxon unveils motor-control device, seeks Reliance merger 5-18, 404G1
Schlumberger to acquire Fairchild, Gould drops bid 5-21, 440D3
Hoover sale to Fuqua blocked 6-11, 560A3
SEC faults United Tech-Carrier merger 6-25, shareholders back 7-5, 541A3
Allied Chem to buy Eltra 6-28, 560G1
RCA seeks CIT 7-5, bid fails 7-10, 517E1
McGraw-Edison to acquire Studebaker-Worthington 7-24, 682F2-A3
RCA reaches CIT accord 8-17, 682A2
Hoover purchase bid by Fuqua dropped 8-20, 664A2
EMI-Paramount deal called off 9-12, 942F2
United Tech buys 21% of Mostek 9-17, 986G2-A3
Exxon purchases Reliance 9-24, 770F1
Raytheon to acquire Beech Aircraft 10-2, 785A1
ELECTRIC Horseman, The (film)
Released 12-21, 1007C3
ELECTRIC Light & Power
Carter cuts research budget 1-22, 45F2
Carter orders fed agency cuts 2-6, 82C3
Gulf States to buy Central La Energy 2-12, 132G1
Carter seeks conservatn powers 2-26, 145C3
Cleveland votes Muny Light retentn 2-27, 150A1
Solid hydrogen rptd formed 3-2, 290D1
Utility cost pass-through OKd 3-16, 264B3
Met Ed rate hike suspended 3-22, 274D3
NY, Calif, Mich utility shareholders defeat A-power delays 4-3, 4-18, 4-23, 322F3
NM tax voided by Sup Ct 4-18, 346B2
GPU cuts dividend, salaries 4-26, 322B2
Carter asks hydro power projct cost-sharing 5-16, 365F2
Exxon unveils energy-saving device 5-18, 404G1
Utilities get coal-use rules 5-25, 403G2-404B1
GPU gains credit line, NJ rate hike 6-19, 519A1
NYS utility cases accepted by Sup Ct 10-1, 919A3
NM suit vs Texas refused by Sup Ct 10-9, 784D1

1980

ELECTRICAL Workers, International Brotherhood of (IBEW) (AFL-CIO)
AT&T pact reached 8-9, 648C1

ELECTRIC & Electronics Industries
Lafayette Radio files for bankruptcy 1-4, 131E3
Copper futures trading limited 1-24, 69C1
Electronic mail plan OKd 2-22, 4-8, conflict of interest chrgd 2-27, 4-8, 347D2-E3
Organic superconductor rptd 4-5, 415C3
PCB rules publshd 5-9, 387A2
Sears appliance performance claim order rptd 5-19, 703D2
Rayfield named GTE Communicatns pres 7-2, 600G2
Pay-TV lobbying group formed 7-15, 640A1
Conrac stock manipulatn indictmt 8-19, 713G3
PCB cleanup methods rptd 8-21, 9-11, 747B2
Motorola settles job bias suit 9-23, 746E3
Foreign Developments (including U.S. international news)
Japan semi-conductor research cited 2-16, 160B3
Sears indicted on Japan TV rebates 2-26, 251G3
'79 forgn investmt in US rptd 4-8, 329C1
US sets Japan typewriter duties 4-22, 368B1
Japan TV dumping case setld 4-28, US ct blocks 5-9, 368C1
Taiwan, S Korea TV import curbs extensn asked, Japan quota end said OK 5-13, 368A2
Argentina-Brazil accords signed 5-15—5-17, 405D2
Mex-Sweden projcts agreed 5-24, 409A3
UK Labor backs limited natlzn 5-31, 429E2
Carter eases Taiwan, S Korea TV quotas; ends Japan curbs 6-30, 515C3
Taiwan '79 sales rptd up 7-4, 567A3
US, Canada TV purchases compared 7-16, 562E3
UK plans monopoly curbs 7-21, 563G3
Mergers & Acquisitions
Racal to acquire Decca 2-14, 132D3
Signal to buy Ampex 2-19, 385F3-386A1
Schlumberger OKs Unitrode divestiture 3-4, 558A1
Cox drops GE merger plans 4-25; FCC OKs merger 4-28, 386E1
Dart sets Kraft merger 6-5, 557D1
GK Technologies, Penn Central agree 7-7, 745E3
Gould, Systems Engineering agree 9-8, 746A1
UV Industries, Sharon Steel deal final; SEC probe, Reliance suits cited 9-26, 746B2
Signal, Ampex deal revised 10-13; signed 10-29, 985F1
Westinghouse to acquire Teleprompter 10-15, 836E1
GK Technologies, Penn Central deal dropped 11-25, 985G1
ELECTRIC Horseman, The (film)
Top-grossing film 1-9, 40G3; 1-30, 120A3

ELECTRIC Light & Power
State of State messages 1-9, 484D2; 1-10, 270E2
NAS backs A-power, coal generatn 1-14, 53D3
Carter seeks more coal-fired utilities 3-6, 169B3
Fla ct review voted 3-11, 185B1
TVA dam constructn challenge declined by Sup Ct 3-24, 265B2
Mar CPI rise rptd 4-22, 305C2
Cleveland Elec air rule firmed 6-17, 494B3
Antipollutn costs overestimated 6-18, 494E2
Utilities' free speech upheld by Sup Ct 6-20, 555F1-C2
Tex heat wave strains svc 6-23—8-15, 616D1
Reagan pres nominatn acceptance speech 7-17, 532C2
Calif OKs water projct 7-18, 632B2
Heat wave use final rpt 9-7, 857B2
Maine votes to keep A-plant 9-23, 723F2
GE OKs Hudson R dump site cleanup 9-24, 825E2
Pa, New England snowstorms cut svc 11-17, 947G3
Vepco cancels N Anna 4 A-plant 11-25, 961B2

1976

IDB OKs Bolivia loan 6-19, 456B3
Uganda cuts Kenya power 7-24, 548F2
Eximbank sued re Zaire loan 8-9, 621C2
Uganda restores power to Kenya 8-23, 874C1
Suit vs Eximbank re Zaire dropped 10-13, 890A3
Guatemala IDB loan set 10-13, 1005E1
Canada co natlzd by Venez 11-12, 875F2
ELECTRONIC Associates Inc.
SEC lists paymts 5-12, 727C1
ELECTRONIC Surveillance—*See WIRETAPPING*
ELEPHANTS—*See WILDLIFE*
ELF-Erap (Elf Acquitaine Group)
Norway oil cleanup sought 11-17, 873E2
ELIAV, Aryeh
Scores Kadum closure move 5-9, 338G1
ELIFAS, Chief Filemon (d. 1975)
Assassin sentncd 5-12, 386A2
ELIZABETH, N.J.—*See NEW Jersey*

ELIZABETH II, Queen (Elizabeth Alexandra Mary) (Great Britain)
Names knights 1-1, 80E2
Wilson quits 3-16, 239C1
Margaret, Snowdon separate 3-19, 252B3
Callaghan elected prime min 4-5, 252B2
Knights Wilson 5-19, 368B3
Pleads for Angola mercenaries 7-5, 517D3
Arrives US 7-6, 489E2
Opens Montreal Olympics 7-17, 528D2
Trinidad becomes republic 8-1, 714B3
Govt policy speech read 10-12, 771E2
ELIZAROV, Aleksandr
Wins Olympic medal 2-6, 159F1
ELIZUR, Yuval
On W Bank anti-riot moves 5-18, 354D2
ELK Hills, Calif.—*See CALIFORNIA*
ELKIN, Richard
Wins ND gov primary 9-7, 687E3
Loses election 11-2, 820B3, 823E3
ELLAJ-Pour, Hassan
Slain 9-2, 679F1

1977

Carter energy plan 4-18, 4-20, 290A2, 294E3; fact sheet 291D2, 292G1-C2, 293F2
March CPI rptd 4-21, 324C2
Carter energy plan reactn 4-24, 320A1
Sen votes energy dept 5-18, 405C2, E2
Carter energy plan scored 5-18, 443E2
TVA sued on air pollution 6-22, 521A3
United Tech Babcock takeover blocked 7-5, 520F1
NYC blackout 7-13—7-14, 537C2
June CPI rptd 7-21, 554D2
US Energy Dept created 8-4, 591F2, G2
McDermott wins Babcock bidding war, United withdraws 8-25, 666E3
Sen OKs conservatn bill 9-13, 703E1
Sen com vs fed rate-setting 9-14, 757C2
Westinghouse settles Ala Power suit 9-21; utilities suit proceeds 11-9, 895G1-C2
Columbus (O) voters OK coal-, trash-fueled plants 11-8, 879D2
Coal strike begins 12-6, 937D1
McDermott to buy remaining Babcock shares 12-8, 1004C2
Cong energy conf com OKs elec rate sectn 12-22, 1002B2
Westinghouse, 3 Tex utilities settle suit 12-26, 1003A3
Foreign developments (including U.S. foreign Developments)—*See also country names*
Canada loan to Ghana rptd 1-13, 48G1
US OKs Canada gas exchng 2-5, 91C3
French oust Sovt indl spy 2-11, 159D3
UN Sri Lanka experimt rptd 3-30, 298D3
Quebec gets US hydro loan 9-13, 742D1
Montreal, Quebec blackouts 9-20, 742A3
Brazil, Paraguay, Argentina in hydro talks 9-22—9-23, 794D3
W Ger seeks Berlin link 10-5, 984E1
Paraguay vs grid frequency chng 11-11, 976B1
Pl power outage 11-13—11-14, 928F3
Westinghouse denied Rio Tinto evidence by UK 12-1, 1003C3
ELECTRIC Power Research Institute (Palo Alto, Calif.)
Breeder reactor called safe 3-26, 234G3
ELECTRONICS Industry—*See ELECTRIC & Electronics Industries*
ELECTRONIC Surveillance—*See WIRETAPPING*
ELEGANT, Robert S.
Dynasty on best-seller list 10-2, 808D3
ELENA, Princess—*See LUPESCU, Magda*
ELF-Erap (Elf Acquitaine Group)
Signs Saudi deal 1-24, 50G1
Viet oil agrmt rptd 4-28, 329C1
ELIAS, Taslim
World Ct member 4F1
ELIAV, Aryeh
In Israel peace group 10E2

ELIZABETH II, Queen (Elizabeth Alexandra Mary) (Great Britain)
Visits NZ, names Holyoake gov-gen 2-22—3-7, 222A2
Arrives Australia 3-7; monarchy ties protested 3-7—3-13, 199C1
In Papua New Guinea 3-23—3-26, ends Australia tour 3-30, 280D2, 309A3
Daughter rptd pregnant 4-8, 396A3
Silver Jubilee held 6-5—6-11, 486F2
Canada bills await OK 7-25, 596D2
Jubilee visit to Ulster 8-10—8-11, 638A3
In Canada, promotes unity 10-14—10-19, 822A2
Opens Bahamas Parlt 10-20, 844G2
Grandson born 11-14, christened 12-22, 1021E2
Canada govt duties end 12-30, 1010D1
ELLE (magazine)
Czechoslovakia expels 2 3-2, 220E3

1978

New TVA chrmn takes over 5-19, 390G1-G2
Carter urges broader TVA role, lauds rate restraint 5-22, 386G2-A3
Ind & Mich utility suit rule review refused by Sup Ct 5-22, 388C2
Power plant size, efficiency studied 6-2, 408C3
Carter proposes hydro projcts 6-6, 426D3
Calif residual fuel oil exports set 6-15, 470D3
SC pool light accident electrocutes 4 6-27, 636F3
Small business loan aid signed 7-4, 512A2
Con Ed blamed in '77 NY blackout 7-6, 529F3
Memphis blackout 8-16, 644G2
Cleveland utility debt cited 8-23, 663E3
Renewable energy study issued 8-25, 718B2
Energy Dept emergency plans faulted 9-11, 701F2
'80s shortages seen 9-11, 701F3
'77 consumer bills rptd up 9-17, 718C3
Public works veto upheld 10-5, 765C1
Southn Calif Edison refund case refused by Sup Ct 10-16, 789A2
Boston Edison rate limit case refused by Sup Ct 10-30, 832G2
Grand Coulee generator sabotaged 10-30, hydro projct delayed 11-10, 963C1
Energy Dept fuel rules unveiled 11-15, 919F3-920B1
NRC plant safety progrm scored 11-25, 940F3
Solar cell advance claimed 11-30, scientists cautions 11-30, 12-1, 983D1-D2
TVA OKs clean-air pact 12-14, 982G2-C3
Cleveland Muny Light sale issue dvpts 12-15, 12-19, 12-22, 1008F2-C3
OPEC oil price hike to raise '79, '80 rates 12-19, 978D2
Foreign Developments (including U.S. International news)—*For foreign domestic news, see country names*
Japan plans US trade missn 1-13, 27A1
USSR, Turkey sign trade pact 4-5, 477D1
Indonesia loan OKd by US 5-6, 360G3
Argentina Eximbank hydro loan blocked 7-19, OKd 9-26, 792D2
Brazil, Paraguay divert Parana waters for hydro project 10-20, 829F2
French blackout 12-19, 1016B3
ELECTRIC Power Research Institute (Palo Alto, Calif.)
New A-fuel reprocessing method rptd 2-27, 144A3
Study discounts oil shortage 6-5, 449E3 ★, 450B1
ELECTRIC Reliability Council, National
Elec shortages in '80s seen 9-11, 701F3
ELECTRONICS Industry—*See ELECTRIC & Electronics Industry*
ELECTRONIC Surveillance—*See WIRETAPPING*
ELEGANT, Robert S.
Dynasty on best-seller list 10-9, 800D3
ELENI V (Greek tanker)
Split by collision 5-6, 524A2
ELFVIN, Judge John T.
Lifts AHL ban on 1-eyed player 2-2, 296F3
ELIADES, Marios
Named Cyprus communicatns, works min 3-8, 189A2
ELIAS, Maj. Abel
Bolivia pres secy gen 11-24, 913E1
ELICI, Serafettin
Named Turkey pub works min 1-5, 21E2
ELI Lilly & Co.
FDA Dobutrex OK rptd 10-3, 948E2 ★
ELI Lilly and Co. v. Staats
Case refused by Sup Ct 11-6, 873G3
ELIOT, T. S.
Nayatt School opens 5-12, 887B2
ELIZABETH II, Queen (Elizabeth Alexandra Mary) (Great Britain)
Argentina disputes Beagle Channel arbitratn 1-6—2-10, 101A1-A3
Quebec language law ruled invalid 1-24, 70E2
Prince Andrew is 18 2-19, 172D2
Extends Hong Kong gov term 3-23, 259B3
Argentina, Chile fail in Beagle Channel talks 5-22—11-2, 860D2
Views English Derby 6-7, 539B2
Hosts Ceausescu 6-13—6-16, 515G2
Cousin married 6-30, 580F1
Solomons independnc feted 7-7, 549E1
Visits Canada 7-26—8-6, 647B2
Canada debates role curbs 8-10, 8-16, 647E1, G1
Canada const plan sent to Sup Ct 9-13, 754G3
Outlines govt progrm 11-1, 838C1
Dominica becomes independent 11-2, 861A3
OKs Schreyeras Canada gov gen 12-7, 963D3
ELKHART County, Ind.—*See INDIANA*
ELKINS, Stephanie
Upset in 400-m freestyle 8-2, sets relay mark 8-26, 780C1, G1, E2
ELKO, Stephen B.
Flood, Eilberg probed, testimony vs detailed; '77 bribery convictn cited 1-27—3-9, 240D1, G1
Flood indicted 9-5, 685C1
Flood indicted again 10-12, 792B1
ELLEINSTEIN, Jean
Scores Marchais 4-27, 352C1

1979

Met Ed license challenged, rate hike asked 11-1, 826E2
Westchester rejects Con Ed takeover 11-6, 846F3
Foreign Developments (including U.S. International news)
S Africa hydro energy cited 1-4, 22D1
Swedish energy bill rptd 3-13, 213E3, 214A1
EC comm backs coal use 6-13, 437G1
W Ger energy plan detailed 7-4, 506G1
US-China power dvpt pact signed 8-28, 644C2
Norway protests 10-8—10-12, 796G3
Argentina, Brazil, Paraguay hydro accords signed 10-19, 845A1
Canada James Bay generator started 10-27, 833D3
Canada prime min backs coal use 11-12, 888F3
USSR urges oil conservatn 11-27, 928C3
China, Japan sign pact 12-7, 939E3
US co in USSR tech deal 12-14, 997E2
ELECTRONIC Data Systems Inc.
Perot claims Iran prison rescue 2-19, 125F3
ELECTRONIC Surveillance—*See WIRETAPPING*
ELECTROSHOCK Therapy—*See MEDICINE-Mental Health*
ELEKDAG, Sukru
Denies USSR OK sought in U-2 use 9-12, 762E1
ELEPHANT Man, The (play)
Opens 1-14, 292D1
ELFICK David
Newsfront released 5-30, 820D2
ELFVIN, Judge John T.
Fines Olin 12-10, 947B1
ELGHANIAN, Habib
Executed 5-9, 353C2
US sens query executn 5-15, 357B2, F2
ELIAS, Michael
Frisco Kid released 7-6, 820C1
Jerk released 12-14, 1007E3
ELI Lilly & Co.
HEW rejcts Darvon ban; orders FDA hearing, MD warning 2-15, 138G2
ELISSA, Omar Salih
Denies Uganda invasn plans 8-9, 637C3

ELIZABETH II, Queen (Elizabeth Alexandra Mary) (Great Britain)
Canada panel urges prov lt gov apptmts 1-25, 74E2
Canada bars role chng 2-5—2-6, 113G2
Tours Arab states 2-12—3-2, 190A1
Lauds St Lucia independnc 2-21, 181B2
Conservatives win electn 5-3; Callaghan resigns, Thatcher apptd 5-4, 337E1
Outlines Tory legis progrm 5-15, 358D2
Dressmaker dies 6-8, 508B3
Canada Indians protest Const patriatn 7-2, 522E3
Canada Indians see gov gen 7-19, 632G2
At Lusaka Commonwealth conf 8-7, 589E1
IRA kills Mountbatten 8-27, 641A1, D1
Attends Mountbatten funeral 9-5, 669C1
St Vincent gets indepndnc 10-27, 825D1
Blunt named 4th spy 11-15, foreknowledge uncertain 11-21, 908C2-E3
ELKO, Stephen
Head convicted 10-12, sentncd 10-24, 906E1
ELK River Resources Co.
Sun Co purchase set 7-31, 986B3

1980

Foreign Developments (including U.S. international news)
Spain hydro projects budgeted 1-8, 22C2
US-China hydro pact signed 3-15, 231A2
French-Cuba accord rptd 4-1, 253A3
USSR-Argentine '79 trade rptd 4-15, 336A2
DR hikes chrgs 5-28, 462G1
French workers strike 6-12, 463A1
Australia workers strike 6-24, 496C2
OECD warns vs A-plant delays 7-8, 509B3
Canada's Atco bid for Calgary Power stalled 7-16, 543F2
Guyana hydro project set 7-25, 791D2
Australia statn builders strike 8-18, 650A3
Israel sets Medit-Dead Sea hydro plan 8-24, 643F2
Jordan Red Sea-Dead Sea hydro plan rptd 8-30, 661G1
Sovts pledge COMECON export rise 10-1, 753D3
Norway sets tax hike 10-6, 792G3
Venez fuel-oil price rise impact on US utility costs cited 10-27, 822G1
Iran sets austerity measures 11-9, 879D3
ELECTRONIC Surveillance—*See WIRETAPPING*
ELEPHANT Man, The (film)
Released 10-3, 836E2
ELEPHANTS
Mammoth link rptd 7-11, 715F3
ELIAS, Michael
Serial released 3-28, 416E3
ELIASON, Joyce
Tell Me a Riddle released 12-17, 1003E2
ELI Lilly & Co.
Ind pesticide plant case declined by Sup Ct 2-19, 131D1
US to curb Darvon 4-24, 358A2, C2
ELI Lilly & Co. v. Costle
Case declined by Sup Ct 2-19, 131E1
ELIOT, Ray
Dies 2-24, 175G3

ELIZABETH II, Queen (Elizabeth Alexandra Mary) (Great Britain)
Canada parlt opens 4-14, 292F3
Visits Australia 5-23—5-28, 405D3
Charts govt programs 11-20, 900F3-901F1
Jules Leger dies 11-22, 928F2
Ballantrae dies 11-28, 928B2
ELK Hills—*See CALIFORNIA*

1976

ELLICE Islands—*See TUVALU*
ELLICOTT, Robert
Trades chrgs with Whitlam 3-4, 187D2 ★
Rpts on Iraq fund probe 3-25, 237C1
US antitrust actn blocked 11-18, 997C2
ELLINGTON, Duke
Record wins HOF award 2-28, 460E3
ELLIOTT, A. H.
3 seized in Lockheed case 6-22, 450C3
ELLIOTT, Osborne
Quits Newsweek for NYC post 10-5, 892G1
ELLIS, Diane
Escapes jail 8-14, 640A3
ELLIS, Dock
AL pitching ldr 10-4, 796D1
Yankees win pennant 10-14, 796A2
In World Series 10-16—10-21, 815B2, B3
ELLSBERG, Daniel
Ehrlichman verdict upheld 5-17, 379C1
Nixon disbarred in NY 7-8, 493E3
Ehrlichman enters prison 10-28, 849G2
ELLSWORTH, Robert F.
Replaced in Defense post 5-3, 412G1
Asks Sen OK F-16s for Iran 9-16, 773G2
ELOCUTIONIST (horse)
3d in Kentucky Derby 5-1, 336F2
Wins Preakness 5-15, 368G3
EL Paso, Tex.—*See TEXAS*
EL Paso Co.
Ford submits Alaskan plan 2-26, 149A2
El Paso Natural Gas Co.
Vows no boycott compliance 3-18, 747B2
EL Paso County Bank (Colo.)
Buys Woodmoor bank 1-12, 167C2
EL Salvador—*See also CACM, IDB, OAS, SELA*
Listed as 'free' nation 1-19, 20B3
Earthquake hits 2-4, 81A1, D2
Kissinger sees forgn min in CR 2-24, 177B1
Bombs exploded 2-26—3-13, 289E3
Molina scores oppositn 3-8, 289D3
Govt sweeps electns 3-14, 289G2
Total IMF oil loan rptd 4-1, 340C2
New ERP split rptd 4-4, 289F3
Rodriguez, 6 others seized in US gun plot 5-15, 5-16; new mil chief named 5-22, 401E1-E2
Romero PCN '77 pres candidate 7-5, 1012D3
Honduras border clashes 7-14—7-22; DMZ OKd 8-12, arbitratn set 10-6, 975F2
Lozano confrmd US amb 8-4, 808B1
At nonaligned conf 8-16—8-20, 622C1
US sentencs Rodriguez 11-23, 1012C3
Listed as partly free 12-22, 977B3

1977

ELLER, Karl
Folds WHA Phoenix team, sells 3 stars 4-1, 263A1
ELLICOTT, Robert
Quits re Whitlam probe 9-6, 693D1
Named Australia home affairs min 12-19, 982B2
ELLIOTT, Carless
Cited re Houston police indictmt 10-20, 821B1
ELLIS, Bo
Marquette wins NCAA title 3-28, 262A2
In NBA draft 6-10, 584B2
ELLIS, Dock
Traded to Rangers 6-15, 644F2
ELLSBERG, Daniel
Sorensen withdraws CIA nominatn 1-17, 35D1
Nixon calls a 'punk' 5-19, 406B1
ELLSWORTH, Robert F.
Replaced in Defense post 1-31, 148F3
EL Paso, Tex.—*See TEXAS*
EL Paso Alaska Co.—*See EL Paso Co.*
EL Paso Co.
Califano backs hiring quotas 3-17, 217B3
El Paso Alaska Co.
FPC splits on gas pipe route 5-2, 369D2
Trudeau, Carter OK Alcan line 9-8, 687A2

EL Salvador—*See also IDB, OAS*
Poma abducted 1-27, found dead 2-25, 182B1
UNO chrgs pre-electn fraud 2-8, 181F1
Orden members killed 2-11, 2-17, 182B1
Romero elected 2-20; vote fraud protests 2-20—3-4, seige imposed 2-28, 181E1-182A1
'75-76 trade, paymts data; table 3-11, 189B1, A2 ★, B2
Priest killed 3-12, church asks probe 3-17, 207B1
Post-electn death toll rptd 3-18, 207B1
Anti-govt violence continues 4-8, 373C3
Guerrillas kidnap, slay forgn min 4-19, 5-10, 373A2
Zamora, wife seized 4-22, 373D3
Church asks priest torture end 4-23, 373B3
8 die in May Day clashes 5-1, 373F2
Terrorists attack priest, youth killed 5-11, 373B3
Rightists threaten Jesuits 6-21; Jesuits defy, govt takes precautns 7-17—7-21, 580B1
Santa Ana bomb blasts, state of seige lifted 6-30; ex-offcl assassinated 7-1, 542A3
Romero inaugural 7-1; archbp boycotts, chrgs rights abuses 7-1, 7-3, 543D2-A3
Ex-pres slain, leftists claim credit 7-12, 580B3
Alvarez Geoffrey kidnaped 8-11, freed 8-19, 710F2
27 bombs explode 8-21, rebels claim credit 8-22, 710E2
3 Cath youths killed 8-26; church asks 'persecutn' end 9-1, 710D2
Malaria upsurge rptd 9-4, 747D3
Univ rector killed 9-16; police seek guerrillas 9-17, 747D1
Guerrilla attacks 9-21; police, mil alerted 9-22, 767G1
Bishop chrgs priests re Marxism 10-4, Vatican rebukes 10-8, 844E3
2 coffee workers die in San Salvador protest 10-27, 844D3
2 die in funeral shootout 10-28, 905D2
Workers, peasants seize Labor Min bldg, take hostages 11-10—11-13, 969F3
Exec killed in kidnap try 11-12, 969G3
Jail terms for protesters enacted 12-6, 969G3
Economy (domestic)
Newspaper shut down 3-4, 181E3
'61-75 GDP variatns table 5-30, 439B1
Land ownership data rptd 580A3
Foreign Relations (misc.)—*See also 'Monetary, Trade & Aid' below*
UN Assemb member 3G3
Israel rptd prime arms seller 1-15, 28E3
Molina backs Panamanian Canal demands 1-18, 46G1
Claramount exiled to CR; Morales, 2 others take emb Asylum 2-28, 181A3
Panama priest deported 5-6, 373A3
Guatemala leftists kidnap amb before IDB mtg 5-29, free 6-1, 438G1-F2
Romero at Panama Canal pact signing 9-7, 678D1 ★
Spanish king visits 9-14—9-15, 804G3
UN Assemb condemnatn of Israel occupatn opposed 11-25, 910D2

1978

ELLICE Islands—*see TUVALU*
ELLICOTT, Robert
Offers Norfolk I home rule 5-8, 369D3
Announces Cocos Is purchase 7-2, 514D1
Gets sports portfolio 11-30, 944A1
ELLINGHAUS, William
Named AT&T pres 10-18, 808E3
ELLISVILLE, Miss.—*See MISSISSIPPI*
ELLIS, Allan
NFL '77 interceptn ldr 1-1, 56G2
ELLIS, Msgr. John Tracy
Awarded Laetare Medal 3-6, 172F3
ELLSBERG, Daniel
At Dutch neutron bomb protest 3-18—3-19, 255D1
Ehrlichman freed 4-27, 320B2
Convicted in Rocky Flats A-protest 11-29, 941B2
ELMONT, N.Y.—*See NEW York State*
ELMORE, Steve
Piano Bar opens 6-8, 887E2
ELON (N.C.) College
Loses NAIA Div I football title 12-16, 1025C2
El PASO, Tex.—*See TEXAS*
EL Paso Co.
Natural gas diversn curbed by Sup Ct 5-31, 430G3
EL Paso Natural Gas v. Southland Realty
Natural gas diversn curbed by Sup Ct 5-31, 430F3-431D1

EL Salvador—*See also IDB, OAS*
UK cancels armored cars sale; rights abuses, Belize cited 1-19, 75A1
Christian Dems to boycott Mar electns 1-29, 136D3
Immigratn ex-chief slain 2-6, 136D3
Nicaragua emb bombed 2-14, 115G2
Archbishop chrgs rights abuse 2-26, 152E2
Coffee exports to be withheld 3-10, 181B3
Govt wins electns 3-12, 245G1
5 dead in San Salvador clash 3-17, 245F1
29 die in rural clashes 3-22—3-28, 245A1
Forgn embs, cathedral occupied by peasants, students; govt, church trade chrgs 4-11—4-18, 723B3 ★
Guerrillas kidnap coffee merchant, 2 forgn execs 5-17—8-25, 722E1-B2, 723F2 ★
Carter hopeful on Honduras border setlmt 6-21, 489C3
Rights abuse chrgd by US panel 6-24, 490C1
Amer rights conv enacted, ct formed 7-18, 828E3, 829C1
US aides find rights abuse worse 8-5, 723G2 ★
Honduras junta vows contd border talks 8-8, 614C3
Quake, tidal wave hits 8-18, 759C1
Cong ex-pres killed, US emb fired on 9-16; 2 cops, univ dean killed, rector fired on 9-18, 823G2
PCN offices bombed 9-18; Const suspensn warned 9-21, 823A3
UN Assemb member 713E3
Rights abuse chrgd by ICJ 9-20, 823B3
Press curbs rptd by IAPA 10-13, 829B2
Univ police chngs set 10-13, offcls seized in dean's murder 10-21, 881E2
Prisoner torture rptd, 715 seized 10-13, 881G2
Japan kidnaped exec found dead 10-13, 881C3
Nicaragua refugees arrive 11-6, 883D2
Cities bombed 11-7, elec plant 11-17, W Ger chem plant; 11-24, 986F3
4 forgn business execs kidnaped 11-24—12-7; cos move execs out 12-21, 986A3; Dutch exec ransomed 12-30, 1021G3
Priest, 3 others killed by police 11-29, archbp denies guerrilla chrg 12-19, 987A1
UK panel scores govt repressn 12-10, 987C1
Arrests, disappearances continue 12-21, 987B1
Radio, TV statns raided, 2 die 12-21, 1021D3
Nicaragua pres sees mil ldrs 12-29, 1018D3

1979

ELLENBERGER, Norm (Stormin' Norman)
Fired by U of New Mex in basketball scandal 12-17, 1003E1
ELLIOT, Sam
Legacy released 9-28, 820F1
ELLIOTT, Denholm
Saint Jack released 4-26, 528E3
ELLIOTT, Patricia
Wine Untouched opens 6-22, 712F3
ELLIOTT, William Yandell
Dies 1-9, 104A3
ELLIS, Bob
Newsfront released 5-30, 820D2
ELLIS, CWO Bryon
Killed in Pak Emb raid 11-21, 893B1
ELLIS, Dock
Traded to Pirates 9-21, 1002B3
ELLIS, Frank N.
Sentncd in GSA kickback scandal 4-24, 367B3
ELLSBERG, Daniel
Rocky Flats A-protesters sentncd 1-8, 17E3
Arrested in Colo A-protest 4-29, 322E3
Convicted for Colo A-protest 6-22, 743D1
Seeks FBI files preservatn 6-26, 520G3
Arrested in NYC A-protest 10-29, 827E2
ELMORE, Charles W.
Slain 8-9, 727F3
EL Paso, Tex.—*See TEXAS*
EL Paso Co.
Calif-Tex pipe bar denied 3-14, 183A2
Mex natural gas purchased 10-18, 814F3

EL Salvador—*See also IDB, OAS*
Economy & Labor
Food prices cut 11-8, 872C3
Workers' wages raised 29% 11-18, 908B2
Businessmen strike 12-10, 968C1
35 slaughterhouse strikers slain 12-18, 993B2
San Salvador rent cut agreed 12-21, 993E2

Foreign Relations (misc.)—*See also 'UN' below*
Mex emb, OAS offices seized 1-16; leftists gain Mex asylum 1-18, 59F1
Israel consul kidnaped 1-17, killed 3-21; UK, Japan execs threatnd 3-19, 234B3
OAS panel chrgs rights abuse 1-22, 58E3-59C1
Latin bishops back Romero 2-12, 108D3
Bolivia migratn pact rptd 2-12, 235A2
Japan trade missn relocates 3-1, businessmen exit 3-9, 235E1
Dutch exec '78 ransom rptd 3-23, 235G1
French, CR, Venez embs seized 5-4, 5-11; CR amb escapes 5-7, 370F3
Venez amb, aides flee emb 5-20, BPR rejct safe-conduct 5-21, 5-20, 387E3
Mex dispatches Latin missn on Nicaragua 5-21, 409C1
Swiss diplomat slain 5-30, 406A3
Panama, Mex asylum offered militants 5-31; emb sieges end; French amb, 5 others freed 6-1, 424B3
Nicaragua arms aid chrgd 6-2, 427F1
200 leave emb in Nicaragua, 72 held 7-26, 574G1
Red Cross, OAS rights role asked 8-16, 652B2
Nicaragua rebel role chrgd 9-24, 731E3
Romero seeks refuge in Guatemala 10-15, 790A2
Nicaragua, Cuba ties proposed 10-18, 813E1
S African amb kidnapped 11-28, 908G1-A2

Government & Politics—*See also other appropriate subheads in this section*
Romero deposed in coup 10-15; state of seige imposed 10-16, pol amnesty set 10-17, 790F1
3 civilns join junta 10-17, 790E2
Junta outlines progrm 10-18; names Cabt, seeks leftist support 10-22, 812G3
Junta lifts state of seige 10-24, 813D2
Duarte returns 10-25, 834E2
Human Rights—*See also 'Unrest' below*
Freedom House lists as partly free 13B1
OAS panel chrgs abuses 1-22, 58E3-59C1
US issues rights rpt 2-10, 107C2

1980

ELLENBERGER, Norman (Stormin' Norman)
Indicted for fraud 5-23, 469C3
Acquitted 6-20, 875E3
ELLENDER, Rich
NFL '79 kick return ldr 1-5, 8D3
ELLENSTEIN, Jean
Scores Marchais 1-8, 57C3
ELLER, Karl
Charter Media formed, buys Phila Bulletin 4-10, 376G3
Charter Media dissolved 9-30, 836B2
Turns over Phila Bulletin, San Fran radio statn to Charter Co 11-6, 907G1-A2
ELLINGHAUS, William M.
AT&T settles ITT trust chrgs 2-27, 240D1
AT&T begins reorgn, managemt realigned 8-20, 648G1
ELLINGTON, Duke (Edward K.)
Wins Grammy 2-27, 296E3
ELLIS, Harry
Carter, Reagan TV debate panelist 10-28, 813F1
ELLIS, Ron
Wins Oscar 4-14, 296A2
ELMENDORF, Dave
Steelers win Super Bowl 1-20, 61E3-62C1
ELON (N.C.) College
Wins NAIA Div I football title game 12-20, 999B3
EL Paso—*See TEXAS*
ELROD v. Burns
Case cited by Sup Ct 3-31, 291A2

EL Salvador—*See also IDB, OAS*
Economy & Labor
Leftists disrupt econ, coffee crop impact noted 1-17, 39B1
Teachers strike 2-4, 97A2
Bank natlizatn, agrarian reform announced 2-11, 117D2
Agrarian, other reforms disavowed; security stepped up 2-20, 149F1
Land reforms decreed 3-6, 172B1
Banking system natlized, compensatn set 3-7, 192G1-B2
Junta curbs econ power of oligarchy 3-12, 191C2
Coffee plantatn natlzatn violence 3-17, 211F3
Sharecropping abolished, land sale set 4-29, 351B3
MDs strike 5-21, 444C2
Teachers strike 6-5—6-6, 444G2
Leftists call 2-day strike, San Salvador paralyzed 6-24—6-25, 497F2
Leftists call 3-day strike, San Salvador unaffected 8-13—8-15, 633G2
Sugar price hits 5 1/2-yr high 10-9, 777D2
Business groups score govt re 'econ crisis' 10-13, 829B2
Vieytez on coffee crop, warns on credit, materials lack 10-15, 829G1-A2
Leftists burn 4 mln lbs of coffee, crop destructn vow cited 11-22, 921B2
Foreign Relations (misc.)—*See also 'Monetary', 'Unrest' below*
Panama emb seized 1-11; Panama, CR ambs, 4 others exchngd for 7 leftists 1-14, 38G3
Spanish emb seized, amb taken 2-5, 96G3
Guatemala emb clashes 2-12, 117B2
Spanish amb freed 2-12, demands met 2-17, emb vacated 2-18, 149C1
Panama emb seized again, amb taken hostage 2-13, 117C2
Panama emb occupatn ended, amb freed 2-14, 149D1
Colombia amb seized in DR emb raid 2-27, 141B1
Emb in Panama occupied 2-28, 152D1
Junta member flees to Mex 3-4, 172F1
Cuban rebel aid chrgd 3-27, 220C2
Latin church ldrs at Romero funeral 3-30, 253C3
Pope lauds Romero 4-3, 341D3
Leftist in Mex, seeks forgn support 5-26, 444G2
Panama AF plane crashes 6-15, gunrunning denied 6-16, 462C3
CR Emb occupied by leftists 7-11, 563G2
CR Emb refugees granted asylum 7-25, 203 flown to San Jose 7-26, 633D3
Guerrillas seek refuge in Honduras 8-1, 604C1
Mex withdraws amb 8-14, hints leftist ties 8-18, 633B3
Rebel leader captured in Honduras 10-14, 872G3
Duarte's son foils kidnap in Guatemala 10-17, 829E2, 830F1
Honduras, Mex refuge from violence sought by peasants 10-25, 829D1
Honduras ties restored 10-30, 872C3
Government & Politics—*See also other appropriate subheads in this section*
Junta, Cabt mins, 25 others resign 1-3, 6B2
Duarte sees civil war 1-3, 6E2
3 civilns join junta 1-9, 19F3-20A1
Civilian quits junta 3-4, 172E1
Duarte joins junta 3-9, 191E2
Junta strategy described 3-12, 191C2
Moderates organize, back leftists 4-2, 351D2
Economics dep min resigns 4-9, 351G2
Rightist coup thwarted 5-2; planning min resigns 5-2, mil chief replaced 5-12, 372E2
Rightist coup ldr freed 5-13; junta rift grows, Christian Dems meets 5-14, 389E2

1976

1977

1978

Monetary, Trade & Aid Issues
'75-76 trade, paymts data; table 3-11, 189B1, A2★, B2
'66-75 arms transfer table 4-8, 415A2
Brazil coffee policy backed 10-21, 11-9, 876C3, D3

1979

US mission completed 6-5, 427G1
PEN scores abuses 7-21, 554B1
Red Cross, OAS role asked 8-16, 652B2
Pol prisoner amnesty declared 10-17, 790E2
Pol prisoner probe vowed 10-18, 813D1
UN Policy & Developments
Membership listed 695G2

Unrest
Leftists seize Mex emb, OAS offices 1-16; gain Mex asylum 1-18, 59F1
Israel honorary consul kidnaped 1-17, killed 3-21; UK, Japan execs threatened 3-19, 234B3
Priest, youths killed 1-20; archbp scores govt 1-21, sets mourning 1-22, 59D1
Guerrilla bombs kill 16 2-1, 117F1
Guerrilla assassinatns, violence mount 2-10–3-13, 234E3
Security law repealed 3-1; govt violence, repressn continue 3-4–3-22; businessmen voice concern 3-9, 234F3-235F1
Electricity workers strike 3-19–3-20, 235C1
Guerrilla ransom rptd at $36 mln 3-23, 235G1
Guerrillas seize munic cathedral, 3 forgn embs; unions strike; govt frees 2 BPR ldrs, bars negotiatns 5-4–5-12, 370F3
Romero calls for natl forum 5-18, 388A1
Venez amb, aides flee emb 5-20; BPR rejct safe-conduct 5-21, 387E3
14 protesters killed 5-22, educ min assassinated 5-23, 387C3
State of siege decreed 5-24, 387G3
Natl forum opens, BPR barred; oppositn boycotts 5-24, 406D3
Munic cath occupation ends 5-25, 406C3
Swiss diplomat slain 5-30, 406A3
Emb sieges end, militants get safe conduct; French amb, 5 others freed 6-1, 424B3
UK bank execs ransomed 7-2, 547G1
State of siege lifted 7-24, 601C3
Rebels occupy 2 cathedrals 7-25, 601D3
Army put on alert 7-25, 601E3
Metal workers protest wages, stage hunger strike 7-25; 150 RC priests join 8-19, 652B3
Gen amnesty called; Red Cross, OAS rights role asked 8-16, 652G1
Right-wing vigilantes kill 8 auto workers 8-16, 652A3
Workers seize 2 US-owned factories, detain mgr 8-17–8-18, 652F2
US mgr escapes 8-24, 668B2
Romero's brother slain 9-6; violence ensues, 11 die 9-8–9-9, 686B1
Rebels end cathedral occupatn, 2,500 march in San Salvador 9-11, 686E1
Leftist gains seen 9-13, 707D1
Teachers march marred by violence 9-14, 707C1
Independnc Day festivities canceled 9-15, 707B1
2 US execs kidnaped 9-21, rebel group takes credit 9-24, 729D2
Romero's residence raided, US citizen killed 9-23, 729E2
Nicaragua rebel role chrgd 9-24, 731E3
4 peasant ldrs slain 9-30, 12,000 march in protest 10-4, 790B3
Leftists seize radio statns, urge insurrectn 10-12, 790C3
Romero deposed in coup 10-15, state of seige declared 10-16; violence continues 10-16–10-17, 790F1, A3
Leftist violence continues 10-18–10-22, 2 guerrilla groups declare truce 10-19, 813G3
Leftists seize 2 ministries, demand pol prisoners freed 10-24, 813C2
San Salvador pro-govt march, junta lifts state of seige 10-24, 813D2
Leftists resume violence 10-25–10-28, cops clash 10-29; attack US Emb, take 3d ministry 10-30, 834B2-B3
Leftist demands met, Cabt mins freed 11-6, 872A3
BPR calls 30-day truce 11-6, 908B2
US execs freed 11-7, 872E2
S African amb kidnaped 11-28, 908G1-A2
Leftists disrupt peace march 12-10, 968A1
Peace Corps volunteer, 12 others held 12-13–12-21; guerrilla demands rejctd 12-14, met 12-21, 968D1, 993E2
Troops kill 35 strikers 12-18; 500 protest, 5 wounded 12-19, 993B2

1980

Majano-Gutierrez rift threatens junta 8-31, reassurances issued 9-4, 669G2-C3
Christian Dem spokesman slain 10-10, 829D2
Electns set in '82, '83 10-15, 789G2
Duarte warns of rightist coup 12-5; Majano leaves junta 12-7, 941A3-E3
Rightist coup plotter's return rptd 12-9, 942A1
Duarte named pres, Gutierrez vp 12-13; sworn 12-22, 993C1
Monetary, Trade, Aid & Investment
Forgn trade curbs announced 2-11, 117E2
US weighs aid pkg 2-22, 149B2; 3-27, 220C2
Forgn banks exempt from natlizatn; deposits barred, currency debts assumed 3-7, 192B2
US aid pkg signed, '80 total rptd 3-28, 254A1
Panama denies leftist arms aid 6-16, 462D3
Junta aid requests rptd blocked, US $90 mln aid scored by rights groups 10-15, 829E1
Coffee sales, ICO quota cited; Vieytez warns on forgn exchng, credit lack 10-15, 829G1-A2
US bishops urge aid cutoff 11-8, 872A1
US suspends aid 12-5, 941E2
US restores aid 12-17, IDB OKs loans 12-18, 993F1
Unrest
Leftist violence sparks govt resignatns 1-3, 6B2
Leftists seize radio statns 1-3, Natl Guard hq attacked 1-4, 6D2
Ex-educ min joins rebels 1-8, 20B1
Leftists form coalition 1-10, 38E3
Panama emb seized 1-11; Panama, CR ambs, 4 others exchngd for 7 leftists 1-14, 38G3
Leftists overrun San Salvador suburbs, urge revolutn 1-15, 39A1
Leftists disrupt econ 1-17, 39B1
20 die in San Salvador protest march 1-22; leftists retaliate, Natl Univ closed 1-23; violence spreads 1-24, 97D1
Christian Dem hq seized, Colindres' wife held 1-29, 97D1
San Miguel violence, 2 teachers killed 2-2, 18,000 strike 2-4, 97C1, A2
Death toll at 164 2-3, 97C2
San Salvador church occupatn violence 2-4, 97B2
Spanish emb seized, amb taken 2-5; demands issued, 7 leftists freed 2-6, 96G3
Educ Ministry seized, Colindres taken hostage 2-5, 97C1
Christian Dem hq stormed, Educ Min occupatn ended 2-12, 117G1
Police, leftists clash outside Guatemala emb 2-12, 117B2
Spanish amb freed 2-12, demands met 2-17, emb vacated 2-18, 149C1
Panama emb seized again, water admin offices occupied 2-13, 117C2
Panama emb occupatn ended 2-14, 149D1
Leftists free 220 hostages, hold march 2-19; junta disavows reforms, steps up security 2-20, 149E1
Atty gen slain, right-wing blamed 2-23, 149G1
Emb in Panama occupied 2-28, 152D1
Christian Dem ldr slain, party member quits junta, flees to Mex 3-4, 172E1
State of siege declared 3-6, 172D1
Family of kidnaped exec buys ad 3-12, 191A3
Kidnaped exec freed 3-14, 212C1
50 die in widespread clashes 3-17, 2 guerrilla ldrs found dead 3-18, 211E3
Archbishop Romero assassinated 3-24; violence erupts, US Emb kin evacuated 3-25, leftists threaten strike 3-26, 220E1
Violence mars Romero funeral 3-30, US amb blames left 3-31, 253C3
Peace Corps office attacked 3-30, 254B1
State of siege extended 4-2, 351F2
US pres candidate cites 4-7, 264D2
Romero's successor offers leftist mediatn, pleas for S Africa amb 4-8, 351A3
Romero-backed coup fails 5-2, right-wing ldr arrested 5-7; junta, mil ldrs meet 5-10—5-11, 372E2
US amb's home besieged 5-10—5-12, emb machine gunned 5-12, 372E3
Right-wing ldr freed 5-13; Christian Dems, US score 5-14, 5-15, 389E2
Leftists seize 15 radio statns 5-17, 389E2
100 leftists slain in heavy fighting 5-18, 389D2
Hosp murders continue 5-21, 444C2
Ex-educ min arrested 5-27, chrgs rptd 6-7, 444E2
Death toll mounts, Jan-May casualties hit 2,065; Honduras, Guatemala cooperatn rptd 6-13, 462E3
Junta member's son arrested as rebel 6-19, 497D3
Leftist guerrilla ldr captured 6-23, 497B3
S Africa amb rptd alive 6-23, 497C3
Leftists call 2-day strike, 15 killed 6-24—6-25, 497F2
Natl Univ stormed, leftist stronghold uncovered 6-26; admin bars transfer, asks church role 6-30, 521D2
CR Emb occupied by leftists 7-11, 563G2; granted asylum 7-25, flown to San Jose 7-26, 633D3
Right-wing violence leaves 68 dead 7-12—7-13, 563B3
Major battles in NE rptd, 170 slain 7-29—8-1, 604B1

1976

ELSMAN, James
Loses Mich Sen primary 8-3, 565G2
ELWYN-Jones, Lord
Retains Cabt post 9-10, 693G3
EMBEZZLEMENT—*See 'Bribery' under CRIME*
EMBRY, Judge Frank
Frees 3 in '57 Ala murder 4-14, 316E2
EMERSONS Ltd.
Admits beer co paymt 2-13, 360G2
SEC sues, settles 5-11, 359D3, 360F2-D3
SEC sues Foremost 7-7, 669B2
EMERY, Rep. David F. (R, Me.)
Reelected 11-2, 821D1, 829G3
EMMY Awards—*See 'Awards' under BROADCASTING*

1977

1978

U.S. Relations
US probes vote fraud 3-9; US mil aid rejected 3-16, 206G2
US ties deteriorate, Richardson disappearnc cited 3-26, 373F3
'66-75 arms transfer table 4-8, 415A2
US delays police sales 7-17, mil supplies continue 7-25, 572F3-573A1
US concerned re Jesuit threats 7-20, Cong panel opens probe 7-21, 580A2
Exec's wife kidnaped 9-6, 710F2
Romero at Panama Canal pact signing 9-7, 678D1 *
US bars mil credit sales 10-19, 815A3; 11-1, 834D1

ELUKI Mongo Aundu, Col.
Replaced 3-31, 260D3
ELVIR Sierra, Col. Cesar
Replaced as staff chief 1-3, 45E1
ELVIS: What Happened (book)
Record single order rptd 8-20, 696D1; 10-2, 808F3
EMBEZZLEMENT—*See 'Bribery' under CRIME*
EMBRY, Sir Basil Edward
Dies 12-8, 1024E1
EM Camara Lenta (In Slow Motion) (book)
Brazil arrests author 7-27, 633C2
EMERGENCY Coalition to Stop the Concorde—*See CONCORDE, Emergency Coalition to Stop the*
EMERGENCY Force, UN—*See MIDDLE EAST—UN DEVELOPMENTS—UNEF*
EMERSON, Ralph Waldo (1803-82)
Brook Farm destroyed 3-27, 396B2
EMERY, Rep. David F. (R, Me.)
On Indian land claims 2-28, 197B1
EMERY Industries Inc.
Natl Distillers plans merger 12-19, 1004B3
EMHART Corp.
Rpts forgn kickbacks 4-6, 503E2
EMIGRATION—*See country names*
EMMICK, Frank
Cuba to free 12-13, 1011C3
EMMINGER, Otmar
Rptd vs $ drop, US trade deficit-reducing strategy 8-8, 585G2
Says mark overvalued 12-8, 933B1
EMMY Awards—*See BROADCASTING—Awards*

1979

Mounting violence spurs US staff cuts 12-26, 993E2
US bank branch, 3 cos bombed 12-27, 993G2

U.S. Relations
US issues rights rpt 2-10, 107C2
Coffee price squeeze chrgd 3-13, 348G1
US rights missn completed 6-5, 427G1
Vaky visit rptd, mil aid reviewed 8-2, 652B2
2 factories seized, mgr held 8-17—8-18, 652F2
US mgr escapes 8-24, 668B2
Leftists protest US policies 9-14, 707D1
US urges early electns 9-14, 707E1
2 US execs kidnaped 9-21, 729D2
US citizen killed in rebel raid 9-23, 729E2
Nicaragua rebel role chrgd 9-24, 731E3
US firm runs ads to free 2 execs 10-10, 790D3
Coup reactn favorable, mil aid seen 10-16, 790G2
US coup role denied 10-18, 813F1
Bank of Amer bldg bombed 10-28, US Emb attacked 10-30, 834G2, A3
2 US execs freed 11-7, 872E2
Peace Corps volunteer seized by leftists 12-13, 968D1; freed 12-21, 993E2
US cuts diplomatic staff 12-26, 993F2
Citibank branch, 3 US cos bombed 12-27, 993G2-A3

EL Super (film)
Released 4-28, 528B2
ELTER, Peter
Loses Indian Grand Prix 11-25, 1003G3
ELTRA Corp.
Allied Chem to buy 6-28, 560G1
ELYTIS, Odysseus
Wins Nobel Prize 10-18, 857G3-58A1
EMAMI, Jaffar Sharif
Iran urges assassinatn 5-13, 357F1
Khomeini rptdly backs executn 5-22, 389C1
EMBEZZLEMENT—*See CRIME, subheads 'Bribery' and 'Robbery'*
EMERGENCY Relief Committee
To oversee Jonestown bodies transfer 2-1, 117E2
EMIGRATION—*See country names*
EMI Ltd.
Paramount deal called off 942F2
EMMINGER, Otmar
Central bank tightens credit 1-18, 62E1
Rpts interest rate hikes 7-12, 586D1
Bundesbank successor named 9-19, 733G2
On interest rate hikes 10-31, 838D1
EMMY Awards—*See BROADCASTING—Awards*
EMORY University (Atlanta, Ga.)
Birth pill-hypertensn study rptd 5-7, 355F1
KKK analysis rptd 7-22, 865C1
Carter speech 8-30, 661B2
$100 mln gift donated 11-8, 902C2

1980

Leftists call 3-day strike, 129 deaths rptd 8-13—8-15, 633G2
Troops end 24-hr power blackout, 17 union reps arrested 8-22; mil trials set 8-25, 669C3
Rebels occupy San Martin, 2 die in gun battle 9-2, 669F3
Leftist coalitn splits 9-12, 749A3
US Emb hit by rocket grenades 9-16, OAS offices seized 9-17, 708C1, D1
San Salvador bomb blasts mark leftist offensive 9-19, 749C3
Rights activist kidnaped 10-3, slain 10-7, 789D3
S Africa amb rptd dead 10-9, 789B3
Christian Dem spokesman slain 10-10, 829D2
Leftists offered amnesty 10-15, 789A3
Army drive uproots 25,000 peasants in north 10-25, 829B1
Rights chief assassinated 10-26, 829C2
Univ rector, 41 others slain 10-29, 871G3
State of siege extended, '80 death toll rptd 11-1, 871G3-872A1
Junta member escapes assasinatn, trade fair dir slain 11-3, 871F3
US bishops ask aid cutoff 11-8, 872A1
Leftists occupy Verapaz, burn coffee warehouse 11-22, 921B2
OAS cites poor rights record 11-27, 913D3
6 leftist ldrs slain, govt blamed 11-27, Met Cathedral blast 11-28, 921E1
3 US nuns, lay worker rptd missing 12-3, found slain 12-4, 921A1
US aid suspended 12-5, nuns murder probe begins, church links govt 12-6—12-7, 941E2
Right-wing ldr's return rptd 12-9, 942A1
Amnesty Intl scores rights record 12-10, 978A3
Leftists launch major offensive in North 12-26; troops repel guerrillas, stall drive 12-28, 993A2
Leftists plan revolutionary govt 12-26, 993E2

U.S. Relations
Citibank, Bank of Amer natlzatn set 2-11, 117F2
Armed forces warned vs coup, aid pkg weighed 2-22, 149B2
Police storm occupied Beckman plant 3-18, 212A1
US Emb kin evacuated 3-25, 220G1
House studies aid pkg, Cuba rebel role rptd 3-27, 220C2
US amb scores left, right violence 3-28, 3-30; Chacon denies death rumor 3-28, 253F3
Aid pkg signed, '80 total rptd 3-28, 254A1
Peace Corps office attacked 3-30, 254B1
Bush cites terrorism 4-7, 264D2
Land reform aid rptd 4-29, 351D3
Amb's home besieged 5-10—5-12, US Emb machine-gunned 5-12, 372E3
Rightist coup ldr's release denounced 5-15, 389B3
Leftist scores interventn 5-26, US visit rptd planned 6-4, 444B3
Teacher arrested 5-27, release rptd 6-7, 444F2
D'Aubuisson visits US illegally 6-30—7-3, 521C3
14 aliens rescued in US desert 7-4—7-9, 518D2-C3; 4 held 7-11, 7-19, 560E2
US Emb hit by rocket grenades 9-16, 708C1
US $90 mln aid scored by intl rights groups 10-15, 829E1
Alien deportatn proceedings begin 10-18, 2 smugglers convicted 10-20, 825F3, G3
US refuge from violence sought by peasants 10-25, 829B1
3d alien smuggler sentncd 11-4, 870B1
Reagan electn welcomed 11-5, 841F2
US bishops urge aid cutoff 11-8, 872A1
Carter urges 'pluralistic' policy 11-19, 881G2
3 nuns, lay worker rptd missing 12-2, found slain 12-4, 921B1
Aid suspended 12-5, nuns murder probe begins 12-6—12-7, 941E2
Reagan policy scored by US amb; rightist's return rptd 12-9, 941F3
Aid restored 12-17, 993F1
ELSON, Gordon Ray
Convicted 4-23, 372B1
ELSTON, Terry
Houston wins Cotton Bowl 1-1, 23F1
ELTON John (Reginald Dwight)
Little Jeannie on best-seller list 7-9, 568E3
ELVIR Sierra, Cesar
Signs Honduras, El Salvador peace pact 10-13, 872C3
ELY, Ron
Named Miss America emceee 3-5, 198G3
EMERSON, Bill
Elected to US House 11-4, 843D2, 851G1
EMERY, Rep. David F. (R, Me.)
Reelected 11-4, 843A1, 848G1
EMERY, Katherine
Dies 2-8, 176A1
EMIGRATION—*See IMMIGRATION & Refugees*
EMILIANO, Vittorio
Rptrs hold protest strike 5-26, 408C3
EMIRZYAN, Servard
Wins Olympic medal 7-26, 623F3
EMIZH, Aramby
Wins Olympic medal 8-1, 623B1
EMMY Awards—*See BROADCASTING—Awards & Honors*
EMORY University (Atlanta, Ga.)
Wiley dies 4-4, 360G3

1976

EMPIRE State (U.S. warship)
In Intl Naval Review 7-4, 488D3
EMPLOYMENT—*See under LABOR*
EMPRISE Corp.
'60 probe, '75 Sup Ct rule cited 483C3
EMRICH, Donald
Sentenced 3-9, 271C2
ENCINOSO, Carmen Romero de
Dismisses Occidental chrgs 11-16, 930D1
ENCYCLOPAEDIA Britannica Inc.
FTC rules vs sales practices 3-26, 235E3
ENDER, Kornelia
Sets world swim marks 6-1—6-5, 424F3
Wins Olympic medals 7-18—7-25, 562D3, 575A3, B3
ENDERS, Thomas O.
Replaced as State asst secy 1-28, 186G1
On IEA accord 1-31, 108F1
Warns Canada vs ties cut 6-13, 438F3
Urges Canada up NATO budget 12-8, 933C1
ENDO, Sumio
Wins Olympic medal 7-26, 575A1
ENERGY Action Committee
Vs superports decision 12-17, 992D1

1977

ENERGY, Department of—*See under U.S. GOVERNMENT*
ENERGY Conservation, Alliance for
Kissinger to head 2-12, 110E3
ENERGY Conversion Devices Inc.
Solar cell advance rptd 7-5, 558E3

1978

EMPLOYE Stock Ownership Plans (ESOPs)—*See LABOR*
EMPLOYMENT—*See under LABOR*
ENDANGERED Species—*See WILDLIFE, specific kinds*
ENDRIN—*See PESTICIDES*
EMAMI, Jaffar Sharif (Iranian premier; replaced Nov. 5)
Named Iranian premr, appeases Moslems 8-27, 667E3
Riot curb scored 9-10, 9-12, 693B2
New govt OKd; policies outlined, CP plot chrgd 9-16, 740A1
Announces Cabt change 10-30, 827E3
Vs oil strike, wins confidence vote 10-31, 827B2
Resigns 11-5, 857E2
EMBEZZLEMENT—*See CRIME, subheads 'Bribery, Fraud & Extortion' and 'Robbery'*
EMBRY, Robert C.
Carter presents urban-aid plan 3-27, 217D2
EMBRYO Implants—*See CHILDBIRTH*
EMERSON, Gloria
Wins Natl Book Award 4-10, 315D2
EMERSON, Roy
Lobsters lose WTT title 9-21, 1027F1
EMERY, Rep. David F. (R, Me.)
Reelected 11-7, 847F2, 851A1
EMIGRATION—*See country names*
EMMERICH Sr., John Oliver
Dies 8-17, 708F2
EMMICK, Frank
Freed, flies to Canada 1-2, 22D1
EMMINGER, Otmar
On US-Bonn $ swap 3-13, 234C3
EMMY Awards—*See BROADCASTING—Awards*
EMOTION (recording)
On best-seller list 3-8, 196A1; 4-5, 272F3
EMPAIN, Baron Edouard-Jean
Kidnaped 1-23; ransom transfer foiled 3-24, freed 3-26, 232D1-A2
EMPLOYMENT—*See under LABOR*
EMPLOYMENT Standards Administration—*See under U.S. GOVERNMENT—LABOR*
EMPORIA (Kan.) State University
Wins NAIA baseball title 6-1, 560A2
EMPRISE Corp.
Bolles killers sentenced 1-10, 24C2
EMS (European Monetary System)—*See EUROPEAN Community*
ENAHOU, Mohammed el Hafed Ould
Ousted as Mauritania info min 1-26, 95D1
ENCEPHALITIS—*See MEDICINE—Brain*
END, The (film)
Released 5-10, 619G1
Top-grossing film 5-31, 460E3
ENDANGERED Species—*See WILDLIFE; specific kinds*
END Measles Inc. (Indianapolis, Ind.)
Armed forces rptd major source, immunizatn asked 11-10, 927A3
ENDS of Power, The (book)
Excerpts scooped by Washn Post 2-16, publicatn plans upset; installmts highlighted 2-16—2-17, 124G1-125E1
Haldeman legal fees to exceed profits 8-17, 844C1
ENERGY, Department of—*See under U.S. GOVERNMENT*
ENERGY Action
Flug scores energy bill 11-9, 873D1
ENERGY Conversion Devices Inc.
Solar cell breakthru claimed 11-30, 983E1

1979

EMPIE, Rev. Dr. Paul C.
Dies 9-1, 756C2
EMPIRE Airlines—*See EMPIRE Gas Corp.*
EMPIRE Gas Corp.
Airline in near-collisn 2-11, FAA updates NY area radar improvemt 3-12, 206C2; rpt issued 4-9, 412D2
Okla gas tank blast injures 3 6-7, 572A3
EMPLOYMENT—*See under LABOR*
EMPLOYMENT Research Associates
US mil spending inequities rptd 11-18, 904F1
EMS (European Monetary System)—*See EUROPEAN Community*
ENCHANTED Pig, The (play)
Opens 4-23, 711E2
ENCYCLOPEDIA Americana
H-bomb letter cites Teller article 9-16, 9-18, Teller denies chrgs 9-17, 714A1, B2; text of letter, diagram 714D1-717E3
ENERGY, Department of—*See under U.S. GOVERNMENT*
ENERGY Action Educational Foundation
Carter remark scored 1-26, 70G1-A2
ENERGY Coalition, Citizen/Labor
Oil industry protested 10-17, 831B2
ENERGY Conversion Devices Inc.
Solar dvpt accord with Atlantic Richfield rptd 5-2, 419C1

1980

EMOTIONAL Rescue (recording)
On best-seller lists 8-13, 640B3; 9-10, 716F3
EMPIRE Strikes Back, The (film)
Released 5-21, 675D2
Top-grossing film 5-28, 448G3; 7-2, 568G3; 8-6, 640D3; 9-3, 716G3
Book on best-seller list 7-13, 568D3
US summer boxoffice gross rptd 9-10, 732D2
EMPLOYMENT—*See LABOR--Employment & Unemployment*
ENCYCLOPAEDIA Britannica Inc.
Sales practices case refused by Sup Ct 3-17, 226E1
ENCYCLOPAEDIA Britannica Inc. v. FTC
Case refused by Sup Ct 3-17, 226E1
ENERGY, Department of—*See under U.S. GOVERNMENT*
ENERGY and Environmental Research, Institute for (Heidelberg, West Germany)
3 Mile I gas venting danger seen 6-18, 550D3

ENERGY & POWER

1976

ENERGY & Power—*See also specific sources (e.g., PETROLEUM); country names*
UNECE rpt issued 2-10, 164G1
Intl econ conf 2-11—2-20, 148B1
US, Venez see more cooperatn 2-17, 177F2
US stays joint Sovt talks 3-16, 196G1
E Ger to hike USSR investmt 5-21, 381C2
Intl econ conf deadlocked 7-8—7-10, 7-12—7-17, 530D1
US: USSR only self-sufficient indl natn 10-5, 961D1
Venez, UK pact signed 11-23, 929D3

1977

ENERGY & Power—*See also specific sources (e.g., ATOMIC Energy, GAS, PETROLEUM); country names*
Ford message to Cong 1-7, 14A3
20th Century Fund scores US 1-11, 170B1
Ford State of Union message 1-12, 13D1, E1, B2, A3
Record cold taxes heating fuel supplies 1-14, 37E1-E2
'76 fuel price rises cited 37D2
Ford '78 budget proposals 1-17, 31C2, 32F2
Cold weather, fuel shortages persist; emergency actns taken 1-18—1-26, 53B3-54E3
Carter urges thermostats lowered 1-21, 53D3, F3
Fuel emergencies declared 1-27—1-29, 75B3
OECD rptd on world outlook, stresses US use cut 1-27, 169A3
Carter in Pittsburgh, warns on permanent shortage 1-30, 75B3
Layoffs, fuel cost to consumers rptd 1-30, 2-2, 75F3-76B1
Sen creates new com 2-4, 90F1, D3, 91C1
Kissinger to head nongovt panel 2-12, 110E3
ASEAN trade pact signed 2-24, 145G2
Cong sets '77 budget levels 3-3, 174E1
'76 use rptd up 4.8% 3-13, 196F1-C2
Carter addresses UN 3-17, 185E2
White House conf 3-25, 234C2
UN Sri Lanka experimt rptd 3-30, 298D3
Fuel shortages eased 4-1, 252D1
NE-Midwest House coalitn vs fed spending policy 423D3

1978

ENERGY & Power—*See also specific sources (e.g., ATOMIC Energy, GAS, Natural, PETROLEUM);*
Research authorizatn clears Cong 2-8, 107G1; signed 2-25, 218B2
Adams issues transportatn policy statemt 2-8, 109D1
Humphrey-Hawkins bill clears House 3-16, 182C3
Alcohol productn backed in farm bill 3-21, 218A3
Oil, gas cos' lid on coal, uranium reserves seen competitn aid 4-5, 282D2
Environmtal Cncl backs renewable sources 4-12, 281F3
GNP '77 link to use rptd down 4-20, 282B2
Mar CPI rptd up 4-28, 345B1
Experimental fuel (gasohol) provisn in farm bill clears Cong 5-4, 343G1; signed 5-15, 465D3
Energy Dept issues annual rpt 5-8, 366A2
Waste combustn seen as energy source 5-11, 367C1
Cong '79 budget target res cleared 5-17, 385E1
Carter urges broader TVA role 5-22, 386A3
Ocean thermal energy use seen remote 6-7, 512B2
Energy Dept authorzn bill rptd by Sen com 6-11, 469B3
Solar, other renewable-energy business loan aid signed 7-4, 512E1
Calif energy-saving law, housing permits surge linked 7-19, 7-31, 607G2, G3
GAO urges new fed agency 7-31, 610E1, A2

1979

ENERGY & Power
Alcoa false ad chrgs settled 1-10, 91A3
Adams outlines urban-aid policy 2-13, 129A3
Environmt cncl sees use cut 2-20, 132C2
Jan CPI rise rptd 2-23, 151B2
Dole backs decontrol 3-10, 186D1
Business rpts US rule compliance costs 3-14, 230A3
Price guidelines tightened 3-24, 264B2
Crisis discounted in poll 5-4, 343F1-B2
Exxon unveils energy-saving device 5-18, 404G1
Calif plan offered by Brown 5-31, 418F3
Connally at Mayors Conf 6-11, 439E3-440A1
May CPI rise rptd 6-26, 480C3
Eizenstat memo leaked 7-7, 513C3
Govs Assn topic 7-8—7-10, 517B3
Kennedy-Durkin plan revealed 7-25, 557B3
Citizens Party platform backs natlztn 8-1, 594G3
UAW holds energy job action 8-22, 831G2
Mail fraud crackdown 9-19, 921C3
Aug CPI rise rptd 9-25, 725C2
Mobilizatn bd clears Cong 10-4, 11-1, 961D1
Natl Agenda Comm created 10-24, 810A1
Energy Dept authrzn clears House 10-24, 848G3
Urban fscl policy chngs predicted 10-24, 920G1
Sept CPI rise rptd 10-26, 827G3

1980

ENERGY & Power
State of State messages 1-2—2-6, 268F3, 269C1-A3, 270B1-C3; 1-7—1-15, 403B2-404E1; 1-9—4-8, 482F3-484A3
CEA ex-chrmn stresses 1-14, 32E1
NAS rpt issued 1-14, 53D3
Carter State of Union proposals 1-21, 1-23, 41D2, 43F1, F3
Carter budget proposals 1-28, 71E3-72C1, G3; table 70F1
AFL-CIO proposals issued 2-18, 146D3
Carter links Cong inactn, inflatn 2-25, 144G2
Feb producer prices rptd 3-7, 182B2
Windfall oil profits tax clears Cong 3-13, 3-27, Carter signs 4-2, 244B2-E3
Carter revised budget proposals 3-31, 243G2, 244D1
Mar producer prices rptd 4-4, 263B1
Mar CPI rptd 4-22, 305C2
Apr producer prices rptd 5-9, 367F2
Apr CPI rptd 5-23, 400B3
Synfuel dvpt clears Cong 6-19, 6-26, 479A2; Carter signs 6-30, 494G1-A2
May CPI rptd 6-24, 481B1
Energy appropriatn clears Cong 6-25, 9-10, signed 10-1, 803A2
Energy Mobilizatn Bd defeated by House 6-27, 515G1-D2
June producer prices rptd 7-8, 513C3
June CPI rptd 7-23, 556D1
Wheelabrator-Huyck merger set 7-30, 745E3
July producer prices rptd 8-15, 630B3
July CPI rptd 8-22, 648C3
Home improvemt tax credit claims rptd 9-12, 747A2

1976

International Energy Agency—*See separate listing*
U.S. Developments (domestic)—*See also 'U.S. Presidential Election' below*
Dec '75 output rptd up 1-16, 92A1
Ford State of Union message 1-19, 37E3, 39C2
'77 budget proposals 1-21, 62E3, 63F1, 64E2
'74, '75 food mktg rpt cites energy cost rises 2-11, 216G1
Ford message to Cong 2-26, 149F1
Fscl '77 budget estimate tables 231A1, 358B2
Cong 'dirty dozen' listed, Rhodes scores 3-25, 219F3
'75 energy use data rptd 4-4, 285A1
ERDA re-aims at conservatn 4-19, 284E3
Sup Ct backs broad FPC powers 6-7, 435F1
Cong clears '77 funds 6-29, Ford signs 7-12, 517E1
Ford urges Cong action 7-19, 532C1
May, June CPI rptd 7-21, 536D2
Sen OKs tax benefits 8-6, 586F1
FEA extensn, conservatn incentive bill signed 8-14, 622F2
Appeals Ct OKs Atlantic offshore lease sale 8-16, 648C3
GAO vs synfuel program, ERDA scores 8-24, 649F1, D2
Cong '77 budget levels, table 9-16, 706B2
Indl output index revised 9-16, 709E1
Synfuel loan bill defeated 9-23, 883A3
NE govs meet 10-1, 743A1; 11-14, 864E3
Clean air amendmts not cleared 10-2, 883D2
U.S. Presidential Election (& transition)
Jackson urges dvpt progrm 1-6, 22B3
Shriver issues plan 1-7, 22G2
Muskie rebuts Ford 1-21, 40C2
Reagan scores Admin 3-31, 232C2
Carter urges world conf 5-13, 375A1
Reagan scores '75 bill 5-14, 356F3
Dem com OKs platform plank 6-15, 432C2
Dem platform text 6-15, 469A2, C2, 470A2, 473A3, 474B3-475A2, 476F2
Boren on Carter task force 7-6, 492G3
Muskie on Dem plank 7-13, 509A3
Carter, Brown agree on conservatn 8-13, 617A1
Carter briefed 8-17, 617G1
GOP platform text 8-18, 603F1, 607B2, F3
Connally scores Carter 8-27, 645C1
Carter proposes Cabt-level dept 9-21, 704F1, E2
Ford, Carter debate 9-23, 702E2
Carter topic 9-30, 10-1, 742E3, 743A1
Mondale, Dole debate 10-15, 782G3
Mondale address 10-18, 803D3
Solid waste research signed 10-21, 833A3
Ford, Carter debate 10-22, 800D1, 801E2, A3
Mass voters vs power authority 11-2, 821G1
Carter rep addresses mayors 11-7, 845B3
Carter names transitn aide 11-23, 881B3
Carter Cabt unit set up 12-29, 978E2

1977

US crisis polled 4-15, 320A3
Cong hikes housing aid 4-28, 339C1
'76 fuel tax revenues rptd 5-4, 388F1
7-natn summit backs conservatn 5-7—5-8, 357D2, 358D1, B2
McGovern scores Carter 5-13, 381D2
Urban business confidence rptd 5-16, 385B1
Cong sets '78 budget target 5-17, 405A1
Carter environment message 5-23, 404B2
Intl Inuit conf 6-13—6-17, 619F2
Technology dvpts 7-5—7-17, 558D3
ERDA funds signed 7-26, 592E3; 8-8, 609D2
Mil constructn bills signed 8-1, 8-15, 668D2
Poll on top US concerns 8-10, 632D2
Sagging stock mkt linked 8-29, 691D2
Research authorizatn OKd by House 9-20, 758D2
Intl Fuel Cycle Evaluatn Conf 10-19, 794F1
Research authorizatn cleared by Cong 10-20, 832G3
Syn-fuel waste conversn OKd by Cong 10-20, 833F1
Ore bond issue rejected 11-8, 879A2
NZ prime min in US talks 11-9—11-10, 925F3
14 scientists issue statemt 11-16, 939F3
3d World renewable source dvpt urged 12-11, 975A3
Carter cites as world tour issue 12-28, 1002D1
Carter National Plan
Carter fireside chat: on program, energy dept, conservatn need 2-2, 75C1
Carter sees sacrifices, undue profits curb 2-8, 88B3
Carter budget revisns 2-22, 125G1, A2
Carter proposes energy dept 3-1, 148F1
Carter town mtg topic 3-16, 190E3
Carter at W Va seminar 3-17, 190G3
Carter drops tax rebate plan 4-14, 270B3
Carter concedes plan inflationary 4-15, 299E1
Carter presents natl policy plan to natn 4-18, addresses Cong 4-20, 289A1-290B1
Carter address to natn text 4-18, 294D2-295C1
Cong reactn 4-20, 290B3, 293F1
Fact sheet 4-20, 291A1-293F3
Domestic, forgn reactn 4-20—4-24, 319A3-320F3
Castro lauds plan 4-20—4-21, 390E1
Lance discounts econ impact, estimates cost 4-21, 294G1
US House forms panel 4-21, 321B1
USDA sees food price hike 4-21, 324B2
Carter defends plan 4-22, 321D1
GOPs score taxes 4-25, 320F3
Cong, labor, consumer, business criticism continues 4-30—6-8; GOP TV rebuttal 6-2, 443D1-G2
Labor scores plan 5-4, 364D3
Sen votes Cabt-level dept 5-18, 405E1
UAW pres scores car proposals 5-19, 408F2
Cong legis tussle 6-9—6-14, 460E1-C2
Carter cites Cong action 7-12, 534E1
Carter Miss town mtg topic 7-21, 575E1
Carter reaffirms policy 7-28, 574C3
Energy Dept created, Schlesinger confrmd secy 8-4, 591C2
Carter sees crisis 8-4, 591E3
House OKs legis package 8-5, 609E2-610C1
Sen OKs coal-conversn bill, bars Kennedy amendmt 9-8, 702A3, F3
Govs assured of conf 9-8, 719A2
Sen OKs gas guzzler ban, homeowner provisns 9-13, 703C1
Sen sets back 9-14—10-4, 757A1
Seen IEA oil-use goal key 10-5—10-6, 794B1
Carter scores oil industry; reactn 10-13, 772E2, F3
Research authorizatn cleared by Cong 10-20, 832G3
Carter topic in Iowa 10-21, 817C1
Burns links business fears 10-26, 817D2
Carter delays tax pkg 10-27, 813A1, A3-E3
Carter on poll rating drop 10-27, 814B1
Tax bill OKd by Sen 10-31, 832C1-F3
A-plant delays not linked to licensing 11-5, 917D2
Carter cancels forgn trip; TV appeal for legis support 11-8, 854A1
Schlesinger comments re legis compromise draw fire from House 11-21—11-23, 916B3-917C1
Carter reschedules forgn trip 11-29, 12-1, 914B2
Carter sees Cong conf com compromise 11-30, 914B1
Carter: major failure of '77 12-15, 976G3
Cong com adjourns without compromise bill 12-22, 1002E1
Carter: top priority in '78 12-28, 1002A1, D1
International Energy Agency—*See separate listing*

1978

Energy Dept emergency plans faulted 9-11, 701B2-A3
Carter National Plan
London Times scores Carter 1-4, 27C3
NAACP scores re jobs 1-11, 68C1
Carter pleas for legis 1-12, 11F3
State of Union Message 1-19, 29C1, D1, 30G1, A2, 31A1, F2
Carter Econ Message 1-20, 48B3, D3
Budget proposals 1-23, 44E2, D3, 46E1; table 45D2
GOP ldrs attack State of Union, budget proposals 1-26, 1-31, 63C1, F1
Burns asks plan passage 1-30, 161D3
Legis logjam, $ weakness linked 2-24—3-6, 119A1
Govs see Schlesinger, Carter; urge more fed funding 2-26—2-27, 145A1
Carter links to poll drop 3-2, 141E1
Cong deadlock persists 3-7—3-22, 219F2-220B2
Coal industry problems linked 3-25, 217B2
Burns links enactmt, $ defense 3-31, 235E2
London press rpts energy bill delay, $ drop link 4-7, 235E1
EC scores legis passage failure 4-8, 257G3
Carter anti-inflatn plan vows oil import cut, asks plan passage 4-11, 260D1
Carter, key Cong conferees meet in pvt sessns 4-11, 4-12; House protests 4-13, 304F1-A3
Anniv marked by Cong mock celebratns, Carter appeal 4-20, 304A3
Cong conferees end gas price deadlock, compromise detailed 4-21, 304E1, B3-305A2
Carter bars admin actn, cites Cong progress 4-25, 307A3
Carter marks Sun Day, plans renewable fuel project funds 5-3, 321C3-322B1
CIA study on Sovt-bloc assessed 5-21, 384E1, A2
Gas price compromise OKd by conf com 5-23, 5-24, other provisns 6-13, 446A1-
IEA, Trilateral Comm study scores inactn 6-5, 6-13, 449E3 ★, 450F1, C2
Carter topic in Tex 6-23—6-24, 509G3
CBO crude oil tax study rptd 6-29, 511G3
Coal conversn bill clears Sen, program status rptd 7-18, 549G3-550F1
Coal slurry pipeline bill defeated 7-19, 550G1
Carter links bill, inflatn, $ drop 8-16, 622D2
Canada gas pipe delay, Cong inactn linked 8-16, 647F2
Govs conf backs enactmt; set Carter, cong talks 8-28, 682F1
Carter to lobby for gas bill 8-30, 664G1
Business spending lag, energy debate linked 9-18, 716C3
Delays, weak $ linked by Swiss offcl 9-27, 732C2
Gas compromise OKd by Sen; bill terms 9-27, 733A1-D3
Carter vows cong cooperatn 10-5, 765E1
Carter stresses legis 10-10, 766G2
Cong energy bill actn completn cited 10-15, 784E2; Carter signs 11-9, 873A1
Cong clears revised 5-part bill 10-15, 786A2-787F2
Cong 95th sessn rated 10-28, 865A3
Foreign Developments (including U.S. international news)—*See also country, organization names*
Commonwealth regional conf sets study 2-16, 121D2
UK prime min urges Bonn summit plan 3-14, sees Carter 3-23, 226B3
Trilateral Comm study scores govts, urges summit 6-13, 450B2
US, Japan plan joint research 9-6, 695B3
US natl security progrm authorzn signed 10-25, 833C2
US-China talks 10-25—11-5, US aid offer rptd 11-6, 871C2
Norway, Sweden sign cooperatn pact 12-8, 965G2

1979

Me conservatn bond issue OKd 11-6, 847B1
Brown stresses A-optns 11-8, 847G2
'80 Energy Dept funds clear Cong 11-9, 883E1; Carter signs 11-27, 920C1
Brown seeks 'selective credit' 11-9, stresses issue 11-20, 962F2, A3
Reagan campaign themes cited 11-14, 982G1
Carter Domestic Actions—*For Energy Security Fund plan, see PETROLEUM—Carter Decontrol*
Budget proposals 1-22, 45B2; table 42F2
Admin drafting dvpt legis 1-25, 70D2
Carter on '78 profits 1-26, 70G1
Fed agency fuel-saving ordrd 2-6, 82C3
Conservatn urged 2-12, 109C3
Domestic price controls ended; profits tax, conservatn, other measures asked 4-5, 250B2-251A1
Carter on plans; notes, 'horizontal divestiture' 4-10, 263C2
Carter vows farm supplies 5-4, 346C3
Carter scores Cong inactn 5-5, 347D1
Carter warns vs Dem inactn 5-25, 401D1, G1
Carter sees House, Ind Dems 6-1—6-2, 418A1, B2, F2
Conservatn measures in Cong 6-5, 8-1, 595C2
Carter urges dvpt funds 6-28, 473A2
Carter poll rating low 7-1, 497G1
Carter plans progrm, address 7-2, 7-3, cancels speech 7-4; reactn 7-5, 497F1
Carter reviews policy; sees US ldrs at Camp David, resets natl speech 7-6—7-12, 513C2
Admin policy previewed 7-8, 513G3, 517B3
Carter orders temp controls 7-10, 514G1
TV address on new 6-pt program 7-15, text; details plan in KC, Detroit speeches 7-16; domestic, forgn reactn 7-15—7-17, 532A1-535C1
Carter accepts Cong energy plan delay 7-24, 557C2
Carter thanks Camp David participants 7-30, 608F3-609A1
Carter defends plan in Miss R boat trip 8-17—8-24, 622F1-623D1
Carter asks program passage 9-3, 661F1
Carter agrees to plan modificatns 9-11, 702D2
Carter predicts plan passage 9-25, 723B3
Kennedy scores 11-2—12-13, 962B1, E1, A2
Carter sees environmentalists 11-7, 961A3
Carter signs '80 Energy Dept funds 11-27, 920C1
Carter cites issue 12-4, 918C2
Foreign Developments (including U.S. international news)
US, Mex sign cooperatn pact 2-16, 124D3
Swedish bill rptd 3-13, 213D3-214A1
GATT pact signed, tariff cuts seen 4-12, 273G1
US-Japan research pact 5-2, 320E2
Spain vows actn re crisis 5-16, 428C1
Sovt-Hungary trade cited 5-30, 417C1
Schmidt, Carter in talks 6-6, 430A1
EC comm proposes plan 6-13, 437E1
Lome pact extensn set 6-27, 513A1
Tokyo summit, tech group set 6-28—6-29, 493A1-F2
Comecon shortage denied 6-29, 497B2
Australia measures set 7-3, 522C1
Greece conservatn pkg rptd 7-3, 543E3
W Ger program detailed 7-4, 506A1
OECD sees econ slowdown 7-19, 554G2, C3
Canada seeks Carter environmt commitmt 7-20, 581D3
WCC issues statemt 7-24, 640F1
Canada vs N Amer common mkt 7-26, 581A2
Spain energy plan OKd 7-30, 585C2
France plans conservatn 8-29, 652E3
Dutch plan conservatn progrms 9-18, 9-19, 730B3, 731B1
Mex pres proposes 9-pt plan 9-27, Carter lauds 9-28—9-29, 753D1, B3
Canada seeks energy bank, more investmt 11-12, 888E3, G3
UN energy conf gets Venez rpt 11-21, 953A1
Intl conf in Paris 12-10, 933C2
EC Parlt rejects '80 budget 12-13, 960F2
US co in USSR tech deal 12-14, 997E2

1980

Aug CPI rptd 9-23, 741C1
Wheelabrator buys Pullman control 9-25, 784G2
Sept CPI rptd 10-24, 823E3
Pacific NW power bill clears Cong 11-19, signed 12-5, 981G1
New scenic area air rules issued 11-25, 898A2
Alaska lands bill signed 12-2, 916C1
Wood fuel bill clears Cong 12-8, 953E2; signed 12-19, 982C1
Calif desert plan issued 12-22, 987B1
Foreign Developments (including U.S. international news)
Canada's Trudeau vows self-sufficiency 1-12, 38C1
Australia, Japan discuss 1-16, 78F1
W Ger urges more steps 1-18, 103B2
Belgium conservatn steps rptd 3-24, 237C1
US-Mex talks 4-2—4-3, 415G1
Greece-US pact signed 4-22, 352F2
Venice summit sets '90 goal 6-22—6-23, 473A1-474D1
Japan research, dvpt urged 8-17, 628F2
Muskie addresses UN aid talks 8-25, 642C3
3d World aid called matter of survival 8-27, 669F1
World Bank '80 loans rptd 9-22, 720D1
Islamic econ conf 11-4—11-6, 865C1
Polish shortage rptd 11-12; govt retains productn control 11-19, 878F2, C3
U.S. Presidential Election (& Transition)
GOP pres debate topic 1-5, 4D3
Kennedy issues position papers 2-2, 2-6, 91B1, C1
Kennedy cites as major issue 2-7, 91C2
Reagan 'basic speech' excerpts 2-29, 207E3
Connally 'basic speech' excerpts 3-7, 184F2
Kennedy 'basic speech' excerpts 3-10, 183B1, C2, E2
Ford attacks Carter 3-12, 207G1
Carter scores Kennedy on controls 4-1, 247C1
Citizens' Party hits issue 4-13, 288B3, C3
Carter sees 'security' 5-29, 423E3
Reagan seeks deregulatn 5-29, 424B1
Dem platform drafted 6-24, 479A3, 480A1
GOP platform backs deregulatn 7-10, 506C3
Ford, Kissinger score Carter 7-14, 7-15, 534F2, E3
GOP platform adopted; text 7-15, 535C3, 536D3, 537A1, F1
Reagan acceptance speech 7-17, 531D1, 532A1, A2, B2
Carter attacks GOP 7-17, 532E1
Dem conv keynote speech 8-11, 611A2*, D2
Kennedy Dem conv speech 8-12, 610E2, 614F1
Dem platform planks adopted 8-13, 615F1
Carter acceptance speech 8-14, 612E1, F3, 613F1, B3
Anderson platform offered 8-30, 665C2
Bush hits Admin policy 9-10, 780F3
Carter attacks Reagan 9-22, 722G2
Reagan, Anderson TV debate 9-21, 721E2, F3-722A1
Reagan hits issue 9-10, 9-11, 699D3
Carter hails fed progrm results 9-18, 698D3
Carter cites efforts 10-12, 10-14, 779B1, F1
Reagan offers 8-pt econ plan 10-24, 817D2
Carter, Reagan TV debate 10-28, 813D1, 815E1
Anderson answers TV debate questns 10-28, 816A1

1976

ENGINEERING
Boston GSA contracting violatns rptd 1-20, 71F1
Sup Ct voids PR alien bar 6-17, 552E3
ENGINEERS, International Union of Operating (AFL-CIO)
Wharton quits Ford panel 1-8, 4D1
ENGLAND—*See GREAT Britain*
ENGLES, Friedrich (1820-95)
China quotes obedience dictum 11-23, 905A1
ENGLISH, Rep. Glenn (D, Okla.)
Reelected 11-2, 830C3
ENGMAN, Lewis A.
Replaced as FTC chrmn 1-6, 68C1
Succeeded as FTC comr 3-18, 232D1
ENNALS, David
UK social services secy 4-8, 266F3; UK soc svcs secy 9-10, 694A1
ENOMOTO, Toshio
Arrested 7-27, 557G1
Indicted 8-9, out on bail 8-17, 624A2, C2
ENRIQUEZ, Edgardo
Rptd arrested 4-10, 399B1
Echegoyen killed 7-10, 571A2
ENSSLIN, Gudrun
Meinhof found hanged 5-9, trial adjourned 5-13, 383A2
ENTEBBE Airport Incident—*See 'Air France Jet Hijacking' under MIDDLE EAST—AVIATION Incidents*
ENTERTAINER, The (recording)
Wins Grammy 2-28, 460C3
ENTERTAINMENT—*See also specific industries*
MCA to aid minority, women businesses 8-20, 944B1
ENVIRONMENTAL Action Inc.
Lists Cong 'dirty dozen' 3-25, 219E3
ENVIRONMENTAL Defense Fund
Files suit vs Concorde 2-4, 94C3
Utah power project dropped 4-14, 284E2
Fla wetlands dvpt denied 4-16, 284D3
Ct votes porpoise protectn 5-11, 398E2
Concorde decision upheld 5-19, 378G2
Urges DNA research curbs 11-11, 891G3
ENVIRONMENTAL Policy Center (Washington, D.C.)
Scores Ford park plan 8-29, 644B3

1977

ENERGY Research & Development Administration—*See under U.S. GOVERNMENT*
ENERGY Resources, Committee for
Mobil Irvine takeover bid opposed 5-6, 519F1
ENERGY Resources Council—*See under U.S. GOVERNMENT*
ENGELHARD Mineral & Chemical Corp.
TVA sues re uranium 11-18, 895F1
ENGELS, Friedrich (1820-95)
USSR scores Eurocommunism 6-23, 507B2
ENGINEERING
Dynalectron rpts pol paymts 2-4, 94F1
NSF '78 authorizatn signed 8-15, 689E1
'75 world pay, buying power ldrs ranked 11-6, 853C3
ENGINEERS, Corps of—*See under U.S. GOVERNMENT—ARMY*
ENGINEERS, International Union of Operating (AFL-CIO)
Cleaners end NY schl strike 2-28, 153D3
ENGLE, Col. Joe
Lauds 2d shuttle test 9-13, 731A2
ENGLISH Channel
UK-French boundary dispute setld 7-18, 625C1
France rejcts boundary chng 9-29, UK appeals 10-12, 772F1-B2
ENOMOTO, Toshio
Lockheed bribe trial opens 1-27, 83D2
ENRIGHT, Judge William B.
Laetrile smugglers sentncd 5-16, 508F2
ENRILE, Juan Ponce
On casualty toll 10-20, 824D2
ENSSLIN, Gudrun
Sentenced 4-28, 352G1
Hunger strike ends 9-2, Schleyer kidnapers ask release 9-6, 9-8, 695B2
Baader atty arrested 9-30, extradited 11-16, 968E3
Release barred 10-16; Schleyer body found 10-19, 791F1, B2
Hijacked jet freed; found dead 10-18, reactn 10-18—10-20, 789B1, 790D2-791E1
Suicide rpt issued 10-26, buried 10-27, 868D1
Lufthansa jets threatened 11-5, 868A3
More explosives found 11-11, 888C2
ENTEBBE Airport Incident—*See MIDDLE EAST—INTERNATIONAL Developments*
ENTE Nazionale Idrocarburi (ENI)
Extra Saudi oil purchases rptd 2-16, 108B1
Agip SpA
Qatar completes takeover 2-9, 108F2
ENTERPRISE (U.S. space shuttle)—*See ASTRONAUTICS—Space Shuttle*
ENTERPRISE, U.S.S. (aircraft carrier)
Ends Kenya good-will visit 2-23, 141E2
ENVIRONMENTAL Action
Carter energy plan reactn 4-21, 320B2
ENVIRONMENTAL Defense Fund (EDF)
Sleepwear flame-retardant banned 4-7, 302F2 ★
House limits porpoise kill 6-11, 443B1
LI ocean dumping upheld 9-19, 724A1
Schardt vs Concorde policy 9-23, 738G2, B3
Wins coal-leasing rule 9-27, 1007D2
Hudson R found toxic 9-28, 762A2
Fyrol FR-2 warnings rptd 9-29, 820B2
Hair dye linked to cancer 10-17, 962D3
Harvard DNA resrch halted 12-15, 1022E2
ENVIRONMENTAL Liaison Center
Sudan canal oppositn rptd 9-7, 844C1
ENVIRONMENTAL Protection Agency—*See under U.S. GOVERNMENT*
ENVIRONMENTAL Quality, Council on—*See under U.S. GOVERNMENT*

1978

ENGAARD, Knud
Named Danish interior min 8-30, 688A1
ENGER, Valdik
Arrested as Sovt spy 5-20, 409B3
Dobrynin takes custody 6-26, 506G1
Crawford sentence suspended 9-7, 742E3
Convicted as spy 10-13, sentncd 10-30, 835A2
USSR demands return, denounces sentnc 11-4, 863E1
ENGINEERING
Sir Gilbert Roberts dies 1-1, 96D3
Society fee code ruled illegal by Sup Ct 4-25, 323A1
Ocean thermal-energy use discounted 6-7, 512E2
W Va scaffold negligence chrgd 6-8, 459B3
Hartford arena rpt issued 6-15, 460C1
Solar, other renewable-energy loan aid signed 7-4, 512G1
Cotton dust controls ordrd 9-16, 472C1
Black opportunities seen rising in '77 10-8, 811E2
ENGINEERS, Corps of—*See under U.S. GOVERNMENT—ARMY*
ENGINEERS, International Union of Operating (AFL-CIO)
Turner on '77 top-paid labor ldrs list 5-15, 365F1
ENGINEERS, National Society of Professional
Fee code ruled illegal by Sup Ct 4-25, 323A1
ENGLAND—*See GREAT Britain*
ENGLAND, Mike
On NASL All-Star team 8-20, 707A3
ENGLEHORN, Shirley
Lopez ties tourn win mark 6-11, 580A3
ENGLISH, Alex
NBA field-goal ldr 4-9, 271E2
ENGLISH, Rep. Glenn (D, Okla.)
Rpts E Ger heroin smuggling 6-1, 433G2
Reelected 11-7, 852A1
ENGLISH Channel
Supertanker spill fouls French coast 3-17, 201G3
Supertanker spill spreads 3-23—3-29, 238B1
UK offers new offshore sites 8-2, 592C1
ENLUND, Eric
Swedish agri min 10-18, 822A3
ENNALS, David
Implicated in Thorpe cover-up 12-4, 945C2
ENNTEX Oil & Gas Co. v. State of Texas
Case refused by Sup Ct 11-13, 874C3
ENRILE, Juan Ponce
Announces drive vs CP rebels 4-15, 290C2
ENSERCH Corp.
Ebasco in A-plant constructn accord 4-18, 281B3
ENSLIN v. Wallford
NC anti-gay rule review declined by Sup Ct 5-15, 387E3
ENSSLIN, Gudrun
Experts confirm suicide 1-23, 115A1
Parlt rpt affirms suicide 2-23, 152A2
Stuttgart prosecutor's office affirms suicide 5-8, 354D1
Eur rights ct rejcts jail abuse chrgs 7-19, 651A3
64 arrested at mem'l rally 10-18, 885G1
ENTERTAINMENT—*See also specific industries*
Presley offer to aid FBI rptd 7-14, 553F3-554B1
Aug CPI rise rptd 9-26, 752D1
ENVIRONMENTAL Defense Fund
Carter gets high rating 12-20, 1009F1
Cites asbestos danger in schls 12-21, 1009G1
ENVIRONMENTAL Policy Center
Carter gets high rating 12-20, 1009F1
ENVIRONMENTAL Protection Agency—*See under U.S. GOVERNMENT*

1979

ENGEL, Georgia
Tip Toes opens 3-26, 712A3
ENGELBERG, Mort
Villain released 7-20, 820E3
ENGER, Valdik
Freed in dissident exchng 4-27, 317B1
ENGINEERING
Pensn paymts case refused by Sup Ct 2-26, 164D3
5 US A-plants ordrd shut 3-13, 186A2
Lake Placid Olympic facilities rptd faulty 4-24, 798C2
ISC accused of forgn paymts 7-9, 541E3
Coll test score rise rptd 10-4, 810D2
Obituaries
Nervi, Pier Luigi 1-9, 104E3
Soderberg, C Richard 10-17, 860E3
ENGINEERS, Corps of—*See under U.S. GOVERNMENT-ARMY*
ENGINEERS, International Union of Operating (AFL-CIO)
Pensn paymts case refused by Sup Ct 2-26, 164D3
ENGLE, Dave
Traded to Twins 2-3, 619E1
ENGLISH, Ind.—*See INDIANA*
ENGLISH Channel
UK, France plan tunnel 2-9, 135A3
ENNALS, David
Releases UK smallpox rpt 1-3, 7D2
Sees hosp strike perils 1-30, 75G3
ENRIGHT, James
In basketball HOF 4-30, 526D3
ENTEBBE Airport Incident—*See MIDDLE EAST-AVIATION Incidents*
ENTEZAM, Abbas Amir
Named Iran dep premr 2-12, 105F2
Rpts US listening post taken over 3-1, 161D2
Iran ousts US activist 3-5, 199C2
Shah to be tried in absentia 3-6, 161F1
Admits Motahari in ruling cncl 5-1, 321F1
Seized, US ties cited 12-19, 975G3
ENTWISTEL, John
Kids Are Alright released 6-15, 820E1
ENVIRODYNE Industries Inc.
Wis Steel Corp fed aid cited 8-28, 682F1
ENVIRONMENTAL Defense Fund (EDF)
2 herbicides total ban urged 3-1, 167C2
Tenn-Tombigbee projct upheld 3-13, 188B3
Hair dryer recall sought 4-19, 308F2
Sleep aid, nose spray ban asked 5-1, 354B3
EPA coal-use rule opposed 5-25, 404B1
Ohio air rule revisn opposed 6-6, 423B1
ENVIRONMENTAL Policy Center
Carter scored re Tellico Dam bill 9-26, 766D3
ENVIRONMENTAL Protection Agency—*See under U.S. GOVERNMENT*
ENVIRONMENTAL Quality, Council on—*See under U.S. GOVERNMENT*
ENVIRONMENT Information, Center for International
Brazil alcohol use for auto fuel rptd 6-4, 430G1

1980

ENGELBERG, Mort
Hunter released 8-1, 675A3
ENGELHARD Minerals & Chemicals Corp.
Hunts use oil assets to cover silver losses, NYSE halts trading 3-31, 244F3
Canada clears Hunts oil property transfer 4-28, 345D1
NN Corp purchase set 6-24, 557D3
NN Corp bid lost 8-20, 745G3
ENGELS, Friedrich (1820-95)
China orders portrait removed 8-16, 651F2
ENGINEERING
College freshmen study rptd 4-15, 559B3
Saudis bar US co contracts to UK 5-21, 407B3
Wheelabrator buys Pullman control 9-25, 784G2
US scientific literacy lag rptd 10-22, 990E1
Obituaries
Gifford, William 3-9, 279B3
Gruen, Victor 2-14, 176D1
ENGINEERS, Corps of—*See under U.S. GOVERNMENT--ARMY*
ENGL, Barbara
Scores RC traditionalism 11-19, 905F2
ENGLISH, Rep. Glenn (D, Okla.)
Reelected 11-4, 844A1
ENGLISH Channel
Pvt tunnel plan rptd 3-4, 193F3
UK OKs tunnel concept, bars funding 3-19, 212A2
ENGST, Syd
In China govt post 231D2
ENIWETOK Atoll (U.S. trust)
Resettled 4-9, 349A3
ENKE, Karin
Wins women's sprint skating title 2-10, 470A2
Wins Olympic medal 2-14, 156A1
ENLOW, Grayson Maynard
Dies 5-18, 448E1
ENN, Hans
Wins Olympic medal 2-19, 155F2
ENRIGHT, Judge William B.
Upholds Smith jury award 1-18, 55D2
ENVIRONMENTAL Protection Agency—*See under U.S. GOVERNMENT*
ENVIRONMENTAL Quality, Council on—*See under U.S. GOVERNMENT*

ENVIRONMENT & POLLUTION

1976

ENVIRONMENT & Pollution—*See also country names*
Muskie rebuts Ford 1-21, 40A2
Cong 'dirty dozen' listed 3-25, 219E3
Cancer-agent unit set 3-29, 384B2
Ford OKs '77 funds 7-12, 517F2
Fla ecologist dies 8-1, 816D3
Geneva conf OKs weather-war pact 9-3, 761B2
Cong '77 budget levels, table 9-16, 706B2
UN world econ rpt issued 10-13, 760D1, A2
Venez, UK pact signed 11-23, 929D3
Sup Ct bars Miss hwy constructn case 11-29, 901C1
UN vs manipulatn 12-10, 955D1
Mayors urge US spending 12-14, 937A3

Air & Water—*See also other appropriate subheads in this section; also 'SST' under AVIATION*
Judge removed in Minn iron plant case 1-6, 25C2
WMO urges limited SST fleet 1-17, 104A3

1977

ENVIRONMENT & Pollution—*See also country names*
Carter statemt to world 1-20, 26G1, A3
Sen creates new com 2-4, 90F1, D3, 91C1
Govt regulatn, merger rise linked 2-18, 274C2
Carter budget revision 2-22, 125A2
NAS rpt scores EPA 3-21, 252B2
Odum wins Tyler Ecology Award 4-15, 354F1
WHO sets 7-yr cancer study 5-10, 431G1
Carter forgn policy address 5-22, 397F2
Carter message to Cong, reactn 5-23, 404G1-G2
Mil constructn bills signed 8-1, 8-15, 668D2
Panama, US sign canal treaty 9-7, 680C3
White House cncl nominee rejected 10-17, 800G1
Burns links Admin policy, business fears 10-26, 817D2

Air & Water—*See also other appropriate subheads in this section*
5 toxic chemicals curbed 1-3, 95A2
Ford urges eased air curbs 1-7, 14C3
US-Canada rpt vs ND dam project, Canada cites harm 1-7, 60C3

1978

ENVIRONMENT & Pollution—*See also country names*
Carter budget proposals 1-23, 44E2, 47B2, E3, 48G1; table 45D2
US '77 environmental decline rptd 85G1
Lobbying bill passes House 4-26, 232A2
Sun Day marked, '70 Earth Day cited 5-3, 321C3
Cong '79 budget target res cleared 5-17, 385F1
EPA plans econ analyses 6-28, 512C3
Regulatory overhaul asked by ABA 8-8, 626F2
Carter halts forgn impact statemts 9-26, 804F2
Tax credit rise for pollutn control clears 10-15, 786B1
Carter rated 'outstanding' 12-20, 1009D1

Air & Water—*See also other appropriate subheads in this section*
US Steel to close Youngstown plants 1-3, 4B3
EPA curbed on asbestos rule 1-10, 13E2
NJ cancer rate link studied 1-12, 23E3

1979

ENVIRONMENT & Pollution
US projcts forgn impact rpts ordrd 1-5, 16F3
Business rpts EPA rule compliance costs 3-14, 230G2
Fed impact statemts curbed by Sup Ct 6-11, 478E3
Admin briefing planned 7-12, 513E2
'80 EPA funds clear Cong 10-24, Carter signs 11-5, 883G2
Carter meets with ldrs 11-7, 961F2
Brown stresses protectn 11-8, 847A3
Connally campaign themes cited 11-15, 983B1

Air & Water
GAO rpt scores EPA efforts 1-9, 16E2
Diesel exhaust rule proposed 1-10, 16A3
Ohio EPA sulphur-dioxide emissns case refused by Sup Ct 1-15, 32B1

1980

ENVIRONMENT & Pollution
State of State messages 1-2—1-25, 269D1-F3; 270F1; 1-7—1-15, 403D2, B3-F3, 404F1; 1-9—1-16, 403D2, B3, D3, F3, 404F1
Impact ct reviews limited by Sup Ct 1-7, 15A3
Earth Day '80 celebrated 4-22, 307E3
Park Svc dir fired 4-24, 333B2, C2
UN Environmt Progrm ends S Africa ties 4-28, 374G1

Air & Water
Truck pollutn rule set 1-2, 5F2
State of State messages 1-7, 1-9, 403E2, 404F1; 1-10, 1-15, 483C1, 484G1
GAO rpt scores sewer projects 1-9, 54F1-D2

1976

Wildlife Federatn rpt issued 1-18, 45B1
'77 budget proposals 1-21, 66D1
House OKs pub works bill 1-29, 93E3; Ford vetoes 2-13, 127E3
UN conf opens 2-2, Medit pact signed 2-16, 126A3
NYS accuses GE re Hudson R PCBs 2-9, closes part of Hudson 2-25, 171E3
EPA urges toxic chem law, cites Kepone cases 2-26, 171E2
US cncl rpts pollution down, costs up 2-27, 171G1
Fscl '77 US budget estimate tables 231A1, 358B2
Sen OKs sewage treatmt plants 4-13, 283D1
Utah power prjct dropped 4-14, 284C2, D2
Sewage treatmt funds enacted 4-15, 282C2
Engineer Corps denies Fla wetlands dvpt 4-16, 284G2-D3
NY clean-air plan upheld 4-26, 308B1
Asbestos found in 5 water supplies 4-30, 349F1
Minn ore plant fined 5-4, 379C2
Allied Chem indicted, other Kepone suits pending 5-7, 349A1
Govt spending up 5-11, 414E3
Sup Ct frees US bases from state permits 6-7, 435C2
Dem platform text 6-15, 469A2, 474E2, 475B1-D1
LI (NY) shore declared disaster area 6-23, 454F2
Gene research curbed 6-23, 7-7, 735F3, 736A1
Fed ct review of state plans barred 6-25, 552C2
Ford vetoes water treatmt funds 7-6, 518E2
Minn ore plant deadline set 7-7, 570D3
Water treatmt funds veto overridden 7-22, 533G2
EPA bars NY ocean sewage-dumping 7-23, 570F3
Eased clean-air rules OKd 8-2, 570E2
GOP platform text 8-18, 602G3, 607C3
Chem barge spill off Va 8-18, 796F2
Standard air-quality index proposed 8-23, 671G1
NYS, GE sign PCB pact 9-8, 691F2-B3
New River dams blocked 9-11, 689E1
Aerosol curb urged 9-13, 691C2
Cong OKs water treatmt funds 9-22, 727G3; signed 10-1, 982F1
Markley-Ford talk on legis cited 9-30, 723A2
Water pollutn authorizatn bill not cleared 10-2, 883A1, E2
Allied Chem fined re Kepone 10-5, 767D3
Toxic chem bill PCB ban signed 10-12, 764E2
Canada vs US reservoir 10-12, 945G3
Aerosol curbs, warning labels urged 10-15—11-23, 901F3
NATO programs lauded 10-16, 934D1
Resource-planning bill vetoed 10-19, 919B2
Coke oven emissns curb set 10-20, 847E3-848A1
NJ bond issue voted 11-2, 821D2
3 seized re Phila water threat 11-3, 972D1
EPA to OK new plants 11-10, 869A1
DNA research curbs urged 11-11, 891G3
Rhine pollutn pacts signed 12-4, 977A2
EPA rpts '70-75 air quality improvemt 12-8, 943A1
US vs ozone penetratn 12-10, 955D1

Automobile Pollution
Calif fines AMC, bans 3 models 1-5, 5D3
US sues NY on taxis 2-20, 154C1
US cncl rpt notes Calif 2-27, 171D2
EPA curb on lead in gas upheld 3-19, 219D2

1977

Ford '78 budget proposals 1-17, 31B3, 32F2
EPA bars PCB dischrg 1-19, GE finds replacemts 2-7, 95E1
14-natns set sulphur-dioxide watch 1-19, 109F2
Minn plant wins dump site 1-31, 95D2
Sludge-gasificatn plant set 2-3, 278D1
ND project halted 2-18, 133A1
Carter-Trudeau talks 2-21—2-23, 132C3
Aerosols, dioxides linked to weather 2-21, 183G2
Carter budget revisn 2-22, 126D1
Carter proposes ND projct $ cut 2-22, 126E1
EPA water pollutn curbs upheld 2-23, 150D2
St Louis METROMEX study rptd 2-24, 184B1
Sovt Soyuz 24 lands 2-25, 170F2
Ore aerosol ban takes effect 3-1, 323B2
New coal-burning process set 3-4, 278B1
FMC plant shut 3-9, EPA pact set 3-15, 196A3, D3
Sen OKs sewage plants 3-10, 174B2
UN Water Conf held 3-14—3-25, 250F1
NAS rpt scores EPA 3-21, 252D2
UN Sri Lanka energy experimt rptd 3-30, 298F3
NH A-plant constructn halted 3-31, 344D3
Carter energy plan 4-18, 4-20, 289G1, 295A1, C1, E1, A2; fact sheet 291B1, F1, 293A2-B2
Admin views given 4-18, 322F2, C3
Water pollutn control deadline upheld 4-18, 342A1
Corn refiners appeal rejctd 4-18, 342D1
Carter energy plan reactn 4-20—4-24, 319G3-320B1, A2
FDA orders fluorocarbon aerosol warning 4-26, 323E1
House OKs strip-mining curbs 4-29, 365G2
Coal use impact studied 4-30, 5-31, 499C1
'75 coal-related deaths rptd 5-2—5-13, 402G3
3 EPA appeals cases remanded 5-2, 406F2
Sewage plant authorizatn dropped 5-3, 365F1
Airlines act on ozone threat 5-6, 369G1
US sues Detroit on water pollutn 5-6, 422D2
FEA proposes indl plant coal conversn 5-9, 370B1
Fluorocarbon ban proposed 5-11, 387E1
UN weather-war pact signed 5-18, 400B3
Carter message to Cong 5-23, 404A2-G2
House weakens '70 Clean Air Act 5-26, 418B2
Sen amends '70 Clean Air Act 6-10, 461B1
US Steel settles 2 Ind EPA cases 6-16, 461E1
EPA stresses water cleanup deadline 6-21, 483B3
TVA sued on air pollution 6-22, 521A3
Coal slurry bill deferred 6-27, 516C1
Steel cos OK Mahoning R pacts 6-30, 521C3
Seafarer funds authorized 7-14, 576C1
UN Sea Law Conf adjourns 7-15, 572A3
Coal use health threat rptd 7-17, 559F1-A2
Strip-mine bill cleared 7-21, 575D2-D3
Milwaukee ordrd to end L Mich pollutn 7-29, 595B1
Amended Clean Air Act clears Cong 8-4, Carter signs 8-8, 610D1-F2
EPA sues LA on sewage 8-12, 724C1
LI ocean dumping upheld 9-19, 723G3
US-Canada com scores ND projct 9-19, 725G3
Fed facility violatns rptd 9-19, EPA warns US agencies 10-20, 800A2
Bethlehem Steel to clean up Md plant 9-22, 762E1
Hudson R found toxic 9-28, 762A2
Sup Ct remands air quality cases 10-3, 760G2
E-W Ger talks set 10-5, 984E1
Steel indus cost rise seen 10-7, 776G2
Va parking ban backed 10-11, 774A3
US Steel: Carter backs controls easing 10-13, 775G2
US Steel plant closes, cost cited 10-13, 775A3
NYC clean-air case review declined 10-17, 797C3
UN pollutn conf ends, Medit pact reached 10-21, 876A2
NC votes sewer projcts 11-8, 879B2
NJ votes harbor cleanup 11-8, 879C2
Pittsburgh OKs pro-steel referendum 11-8, 879A3
Clean-water bill revised 11-10, 900B2
US facilities cited for abuses 11-25, 944B2
Winter fuel shortage plan suspends clean-air rules 12-1, 942B3
Steel indus rule chngs planned 12-6, 932A1
Lead-pollutn rule proposed 12-12, 1007G2
Clean water revisn, city sewage aid cleared 12-15, 958G3; signed 12-28, 1001A3
Seafarer studies released 12-15, Mich voters opposed 12-16, 977D3—978B1
Clean-air progress rptd 12-21, 1007E2
Chemical inventories ordrd rptd 12-22, 1007A2

Automobile Pollution
Ford energy message 1-7, 14C3
EPA orders Ford halt productn 2-8, 113B1
Cadillac recall ordered 3-22, 252A3

1978

4MMPD, tetrachloroethylene curbs urged 1-13, 86A1
Acrylonitrile rule issued 1-16, 85F3
Coal slurry impact studied 1-18, 49C1
Carter State of Union Message 1-19, 31G3
Carter budget proposals 1-23, 47C2
EPA asks cancer chem water filtratn 1-25, 86B1
'77 environmental decline rptd 85A2
Mich sues Ford Motor 2-1, 163C3
Benzene exposure rule issued, API scores 2-2, 85G2, C3
Adams issues transportation policy statemt 2-8, 109E1
Coal Policy Project rpt issued 2-9, 184G1
Ohio, Ind curbs suspended 2-11, 2-16, 104F1
EPA sulfur dioxide rules for Ohio upheld 2-13, 109G1
103 areas violate air rules 2-23, 144C3
Chem-spill fines set 3-3, 163E3
Atlantic sludge sites OKd 3-3, 164A1
Sewage treatmt '78 supplemental funds signed 3-7, 160F2
Fluorocarbon aerosols banned 3-15, 186G1-C2
New fuel standards for light trucks issued 3-15, 284F1-B2
Ill firm sued on PCB 3-17, 243B1
Sulfur, lime, paper plant rules set 3-22, 263F2
Olin indicted on mercury dischrg 3-23, 243E1
Aircraft rules revised 3-27, 263C2
GM agrees to $170,000 fine 3-27, 263B3
Chrysler remedy ordrd 4-20, 349C1
TVA-pollutn setlmt scored 5-5, 5-18; new TVA chrmn backs 5-19, 390C2
Ocean pollutn study bill signed 5-8, 343B2
AMC '76 cars recalled 5-10, 349A1
Helsinki naval conf 5-16—5-18, 424F3
Phila sued on sewage pollutn 5-17, 5-24, 409G1
AMC expands recall 5-19, 409F2
VW dealers sued by US 5-24, 409C2
EPA bars Denver dam permit 5-25, 409E1
Coal gasificatn plan submitted 6-2, 471F2
PCB ban formally proposed 6-7, 513A1
Smog regulation eased 6-13, 512F2
New-plant air rules issued 6-13, 512A3
Asbestos rule amended 6-15, 512D3
EPA sets indl water-dischrg rule re city sewers 6-20, 512F3
Coast Guard '79 authrzn signed 6-30, 525C2
Bad-air cities rated 7-5, 513C1
Ohio sulfur-dioxide rule stay denied 7-6, 513E1
Minn plant to continue mining 7-7, 553E2
Bad-air cities rpt corrected 7-19, 644B2
Allis-Chalmers to buy American Air Filter 7-28, 718F1
EPA to ease clean-water rules 8-10, 644F1
DC funds clear Cong 8-17, 697G2
Coal-fired power plant scrubber installatns proposed 9-11, 703F1
Acrylonitrile final rule set 9-29, 753G3
Lead-pollutn rule issued 9-29, 754C1
Solar energy study rptd 12-12, 983C1
TVA OKs pollutn pact 12-14, 982G2-C3
Toxic-waste rules proposed 12-14, 982C3
Flexible air rule proposed 12-21, 1009A1
Asbestos danger in schls cited 12-21, 1009G1

Atomic Waste Issues—*See ATOMIC Energy—Industrial*
Automobile Pollution—*See 'Air & Water' above*

1979

Anti-pollutn inflatn costs, jobs gains rptd 1-19, 129C3
Carter budget proposals 1-22, 45A3; table 42F2
US cncl cites cleanup gains 1-25, 90G1
US Steel, Erie Coke sued re Ohio plants 1-25, 2-5, 90E2-G2
Smog standard eased 1-26, 90D1
NJ cos sued re hazardous wastes 2-7, 129G3-130B1
Truck exhaust rule tightnd 2-15, 187C1
Carter backs rule enforcemt 2-27, 149G2-A3
'Last Supper' restoratn rptd 2-27, 173B3
Pa co sued re PCB storage 3-9, 206D3
Auto use threat seen 3-10, 187E3, G3
2d Ohio EPA sulphur-dioxide emissns case refused by Sup Ct 3-19, 203B3
EPA proposes new fines 3-21, 206E2
Ohio coal co sues vs air rules 3-22, 206A3
EPA sues Ford Motor 3-22, 206C3
Carter hints rules delay 4-5, 250G3
3 Mile I water contaminatn denied 4-9, 261A2
Chem dump hearings, Hooker held aware of NY seepage in '58 4-10, 4-11, 281B3
PCB rules issued 4-19, 281G3-282A1
EPA upheld re Ohio coal use 5-7, 351C1
Pittsburgh area cleanups set by Colt unit 5-7, US Steel 5-22, 385B2-B3
Marine accord set by UN Sea Law Conf 5-13, 360F3
PR suit against Navy rptd 5-16, 385G3
Utilities get coal-use rules, controversy ensues 5-25, 403G2-404B1
Phila sewage suits settled 5-30, 704C2
Air-quality standards relaxed to spur no-lead gas output 6-4, 418B3
GM emissns dispute setld 6-5, 441F2
NC PCB dumping chrgd 6-4-6-13, disposal disputed 6-5, 597G2-E3
EPA eases air rule for Cleveland utility 6-6, 422D3-423C1
Carter proposes hazardous waste cleanup 6-13, 441E1
SALT II communique backs conservatn 6-18, 458D1
Hooker Calif chem dumping, well pollutn rptd 6-18; US, state probe 6-19, 6-21, 597F1
Hooker sued for Mich clean-up 6-22, Fla abuses rptd 8-5, 597C2
Stratospheric ozone levels studied 6-22, 692D1
FDA cuts PCB limits 6-28, 571F2
Canada seeks US commitmt 7-12, 7-20; agrmt set 7-26, 581D2, C3
West mounts 'Sagebrush Revolt' 7-13-9-7, 704C1
Pittsburgh area cleanup suit settd by US Steel 7-23, 704F2
Chrysler links deficit, rules cost; seeks emissns rule delay 7-31, 576B1, D1
Tellico Dam funds clear Cong 8-1, 9-10, Carter signs 9-26, 766F2
3 Mile I water purificatn method urged 8-14, 629B3
Olin convicted for mercury dumping 8-16, 704E1
NJ Meadowlands mercury cleanup ordrd 8-26, 704A2
Wheeling-Pittsburgh gets fed aid 8-28, 681G3
Hooker chrgd in NY pollutn 8-31, 665G1
Interior Dept seeks to protect 47 areas 9-7, 703B3
Army sued on San Fran '50 germ warfare test 9-16, 727B1
Army '64 Utah BZ test rptd 9-24, 727F1
US Steel settles SEC suit 9-27, 941F2
Hooker settles Mich dump suit 10-24, 808E3
Australia auto curbs disputed 10-31, 888A1
Chem dump sites listed 11-1, 886B1
Mo bond issue approved 11-6, 847A1
Eur, US, Canada OK pact 11-13, 864A3
Halocarbon aersol risk estimate revised up 11-17, 1000E2
US Steel links rules cost, econ woes 11-27, 941D2
Jones & Laughlin plans control equipmt 11-28, 941G3
EPA revises clean-air rule 12-3, 924D3
Olin fined re mercury dumping 12-10, 947A1
US sues Occidental, Olin re NY pollutn 12-20, 990E1

Atomic Waste Issues—*See ATOMIC Energy—Industrial*
Automobile Pollution—*See 'Air & Water' above*

1980

Carter budget proposals 1-28, 72B1, 73E2; table 70F1
Amazon pact signed 1O-28, 865C2
NJ waste suit partially setld, Edison dump to be covered 1-30, 93D3
GM to close 2 plants, costs cited 1-31, 287B2
Airline ozone measures rptd 2-12, 159A1
Lilly Ind pesticide plant case declined by Sup Ct 2-19, 131D1
US cncl details problems 2-19, 145C2
Diesel exhaust rules set 2-21, 145G3
Carter seeks more coal-fired utilities 3-6, 169E3
Minn plant ends Lake Superior dumping 3-16, 227A1
EPA dischrg permit ct reviews backed by Sup Ct 3-17, 226F1
EPA sewage permit extensn power backed by Sup Ct 3-18, 226D3
Dow chrgs EPA spying 3-25, 387C2
US rpt sees control benefits 4-21, 307G3
Eliz (NJ) chem dump burns 4-22, 331B2
US sues Union Corp 4-24, 331E3
NY sues Occidental, Hooker re Love Canal dumping 4-28, 331C3
Clean air rules review rptd 5-14, 384G1
Love Canal dump health defects rptd 5-16, US sets evacuatn 5-21, 386D3-387D1
Medit pollutn pact signed 5-17, 381G2
Mt St Helens damage assessed 5-24—7-4, 503E3, 504A3
EPA guidelines appeals ct review backed by Sup Ct 5-27, 453E3
Detergent carcinogen OKd 5-27, 526C3
Calif zoning ordinances backed by Sup Ct 6-10, 512F1
Milwaukee city, cnty bond ratings lowered 6-13, 743G3
EPA firms Cleveland utility rule 6-17, 494B3
Antipollutn costs overestimated 6-18, 494A2-F2
Canada scores US acid rain policy 6-23, 486F2
Energy Mobilizatn Bd defeated by House 6-27, 515B2
Carter seeks eased auto emissn curbs 7-8, 505B1-E1
La chem-dump suit filed 7-15, 558F3
US global forecast gloomy 7-23, 573C2
UN Sea Law Conf yields draft accord 7-29—8-28, 660B2
Wheelabrator-Huyck merger set 7-30, 745D3
US, Canada sign acid rain pact 8-5, 603E1
NRC staff backs 3 Mile I cleanup 8-14, 649D2
PCB cleanup methods rptd 8-21, 9-11, 747B2
Shenango OKs Pa plant pollutn curbs 8-22, 825C2
Reagan scores fed auto regulatns 9-2, EPA disputes 9-3, 664G2
Reagan releases steel indus plan 9-16, 699G2
Acid rain rptd centuries old 9-18, 726E2
House passes toxic waste clean-up funds 9-19, 9-23; Sen OKs 'superfund' 11-24, 897G3-898G1
GE OKs Hudson R dump site cleanup 9-24, 825E2
Carter asks steel indus deadlines delayed 9-30, 740B3
Anaconda to close 2 Montana units 9-30, 825F2
Love Canal relocatn aid enacted 10-1, 739E1
Carter dam support scored 10-1, 803A3
Clean water amendmts clear Cong 10-1, signed 10-21, 981E1
EPA toxic waste suits filed 10-7, 10-9, 825A1-A2
Beaufort Sea leases upheld 10-14, 960C3
US Steel OKs Utah plant controls 10-16, 825A2
EPA scored re toxic waste policy 10-31, 869B2
Washn, NJ, Alaska bond issues OKd 11-4, 847F3, 848A1, A2
FMC pleads guilty 11-10, 869G1-C2
New scenic area rules issued 11-25, 898G1-C2
PPG accused of fuel-switching 11-25, 899C3
EPA Chrysler recall order challenge refused by Sup Ct 12-1, 318E2
Alaska lands bill signed 12-2, 916C1
EPA clean water enforcemt backed by Sup Ct 12-2, 918A1
EPA airborne lead standards challenge refused by Sup Ct 12-8, 937F1
EPA halts Calif, Ky funds 12-11, 963B1
US Steel fined $345,000 12-22; Clairton coke site deadline extended 12-30, 987C1, E1
Diesel emissns rule set 12-24, 987E2

1976

NY clean-air plan upheld 4-26, 308B1
Elec car bill vetoed 9-13, overridden 9-17, 708A1
EPA fuel-econ ratings, table 9-22, 766G1-770C2
Lead curb deadlines eased 9-24, 767B3
Chrysler sued 9-27, 729E3
Research bill veto sustained 9-29, 745G3
Clean air amendmts not cleared 10-2, 883A1, C2
Ford, Carter debate 10-22, 801E2
'70-75 air quality progress rptd, Calif stressed 12-8, 943C1
EPA orders Chrysler recall 12-10, 942D3

Land-Use Planning—*See RESOURCES, Natural*

Natural Resources—*See RESOURCES, Natural*

Noise Abatement—*See also 'SST' under AVIATION*

'77 budget proposals 1-21, 66F1
Cong clears '76-77 funds 5-20, 412C1; signed 5-31, 982F1
Airport aid authorizatn signed 7-12, 567C1
US rule extended to old planes 10-21, 849C1
Ford boosts control 10-25, 802E3
Airlines get US timetable 11-18, 868B3

Oil & Gas Issues—*See also ALASKA*

'77 budget proposals 1-21, 64E3
EPA curb on lead upheld 4-26, 308B1
Spanish tanker explodes 5-12, 384C1
St Lawrence Seaway spill 6-23, 859D2
Coastal states aid signed, local control backed 7-26, 566G2
Atlantic offshore lease sale challenged 8-13—8-17, opens 8-17, 648G2-C3
Colo oil shale leases suspended 8-23, 649A1, D1
Bacteria use re spills cited 9-22, 860E3
Lead curb deadlines eased 9-24, 767B3
Clean air amendmts not cleared 10-2, 883D2
Sup Ct bars review of spill liability case 10-4, 807C3
Pipeline safety aid signed 10-11, 834C3
Tanker sinks off France 10-14, 912E2
Nantucket spill 12-15—12-22, 968D3; hearing 12-28—12-31; suit delayed 12-30, 1013E3
LA harbor spill 12-17, 969F1
Coleman to OK 2 superports 12-17, 991G3
Gasoline spill in Australia 12-18, 997B3
Delaware R spill 12-27, 1014E1
Thames R oil leak 12-28, 1014G1

Pesticides—*See under 'P'*

Presidential Election (& transition)

Carter urges US jobs 4-23, 305D2
Dem platform text 6-15, 469A2, 473B2, 474E2, B3, 475B1-E1, B3, 476F3
Carter pledge 7-15, 507E1, 511A1
Carter record cited 512C2
GOP platform text 8-18, 602A2, G3, 603G1, 607C1, D2, C3, 608F1
Mondale cites crisis 9-26, 725A1
Mondale, Dole debate 10-15, 782G3
Ford, Carter debate 10-22, 799F3, 801D2-B3
Ford backs airplane noise controls 10-25, 802E3
Carter sees group reps 12-16, 937B2
Carter Cabt unit set up 12-29, 978E2

Radiation Hazards—*See also 'Environmental Hazards' under ATOMIC Energy*

Sovt microwave threat in US emb rptd 2-6—2-10, 122D2
Cosmic, solar threats cited 2-27, 171E2
Sovt microwave level in US emb rptd down 7-7, 540C3

Resources, Natural—*See under 'R'*

Sewage—*See 'Air & Water' above*

Solid Wastes

'77 budget proposals 1-21, 66F1
Govt spending up 5-11, 414E3
Dem platform text 6-15, 475E1
GOP platform text 8-18, 608E1, D2
GAO urges energy research 8-24, 649B2
Funds, EPA office signed 10-21, 833F2
4 states vote on container deposits 11-2, 821D1, 823F2, 824F1, 825B3

Wildlife—*See WILDLIFE*

1977

GM drops rotary engine projct 4-12, 409D1
EPA rpts Admin views on emissn standards 4-18, 322E2
EPA asks free car repairs 5-13, 422G2
House weakens '70 Clean Air Act 5-26, 418B2
Sen amends '70 Clean Air Act 6-10, 460F3
Intl Inuit conf 6-13—6-17, 619F2
Amended Clean Air Act clears Cong 8-4, Carter signs 8-8, 610D1-F2
Suit vs Chrysler dismissed 8-22, 723E3
Bus, truck exhaust rules set 9-5, 739D3
Swiss defeat lead gas cuts 9-25, 766F3
NYC clean-air case review declined 10-17, 797D3
Elec-car tax credit OKd by Sen 10-31, 832A3
Lead-pollutn rule proposed 12-12, 1007B3

Land-Use Planning—*See RESOURCES, Natural*

Natural Resources—*See RESOURCES, Natural*

Noise Abatement—*See AVIATION—SST/Concorde*

Oil & Gas Issues—*See also ALASKA—Oil & Gas, CANADA—Environment*

Oil spills rptd 1-5—3-3, 214F2
Panama tanker sunk off Cape Cod 1-11, 104E3, 214D3
OECD, 20th Century Fund rpts on energy outlook 1-11, 1-27, 169E3, 170C1
DOT rpt urges controls vs oil spills; Coleman scores Cong 1-15, 58E3
Ship safety rules tightnd 1-31, 214D2
Carter plans oil-spill bill 2-2, 75E1
Liberia tanker fails US inspectn 2-7, 214E3
Carter asks spill bill 3-18, 214G1-D2
Japan tanker collision 4-6, 1000B1
North Sea oil blowout capped 4-30; OECD urges safety rules 5-1, 336D1-C3
Carter on fuel crisis 5-17, 381B3
Offshore oil sales delayed 5-17, Andrus defends 5-19, 6-3, 498G3
'78 Coast Guard authorizatn clears Cong 6-21, 501B1
Cargo preference backers see benefit 720F1
Superport oil spill liability cited 7-29, 724D3
Danes OK North Sea gas line 8-1, 672C1
E Coast offshore lease sale OKd by ct 8-25, 650B1
North Sea blowout blamed on human error 10-10, 967B3
Offshore leasing bill blocked in House 10-25, 833C2
Cleanup liability extended in revised bill 11-10, 900A3
Carrier spill liability extended to 200 mi-limit 12-15, 959F1; signed 12-28, 1001A3
Supertankers collide off S Africa 12-16, 999E3-1000A1
Chemicals inventories ordrd rptd 12-22, 1007B2

Pesticides—*See under 'P'*

Radiation Hazards—*See RADIATION*

Resources, Natural—*See under 'R'*

Sewage—*See 'Air & Water' above*

Solid Waste—*See WASTE, Solid*

Waste, Solid—*See under 'W'*

1978

Natural Resources—*See RESOURCES, Natural*

Noise Abatement

Carter budget proposal 1-23, 47D2
EPA asks motorcycle rules 3-15, 186D2
Aircraft bill clears House 9-14, stalled in Sen 10-3, 765C3

Oil & Gas Issues

LI Sound spills rptd 1-10, 3-16, 524F1, A2
Carter budgets Coast Guard fund 1-23, 47E3
Atlantic offshore lease sale delayed 1-30, 108D2
Gulf of Mex spill rptd 1-31, 524G1
Benzene exposure rule issued 2-2, 85C3
Portland (Me) tanker leak 2-6, 524G1
Salem Sound (Mass) spill 2-6, 524A2
Alaska pipe blast spill 2-15, 108E3
NJ offshore drilling challenge refused 2-21, 125E2-B3
Oil-eating bacterium patent upheld 3-2, 187G1
States curbed on tanker regulatn 3-6, 161G3
Liberia tanker spill fouls French coast 3-17, 201C3
EPA sets sulfur-recovery plant rules 3-22, 263G2
Liberia tanker spill spreads 3-23—3-29, 238B1
Liberia warned by US re tankers 4-3, 234E1
Italy completes Adriatic poison cargo recovery 4-25, 330E3
Greek tanker spill off Great Yarmouth (UK) 5-6, 524A2
UK coal carrier rams Mobile R oil dock 5-26, 524C2
France acts to curb spills 6-4—7-5, 524A1-F1
Offshore leasing bill clears Cong 8-22, 662F2, D3, F3
Amoco sued on Liberia tanker spill 9-13, 749C1
Australia warns re Antarctic exploitatn 9-17, 900D3
Tanker safety law signed 10-17, 807B3
Calif voters OK Sohio lease 11-7, 857B1
2 oil cos begin gas rationing 12-1, 3 others seek OK 12-3, 939D1

Parks & Recreation Areas—*See PARKS & Recreation Areas*

Pesticides—*See PESTICIDES*

Radiation Hazards—*See ARMAMENTS—Tests, ATOMIC Energy—Industrial Use, MEDICINE—Cancer*

Resources, Natural—*See RESOURCES, Natural*

Sewage—*See 'Air & Water' above*

Solid Waste—*See WASTE, Solid*

Waste, Solid—*See WASTE, Solid*

Wildlife—*See WILDLIFE*

1979

Noise Abatement

RR-yard rules proposed 4-16, 282A1
Concorde program ended 9-21, 721G2

Oil & Gas Issues

Greek tanker spill off Spain rptd 1-1, 201A1
French tanker splits in Irish port 1-8, 201C1
US sues NJ cos 2-7, 130A1
Mass offshore lease ban lifted 2-20, 186F3
Liberia tanker '78 spill rpt issued 3-8, 162C2, A3, 163A1
UK tanker splits off Nova Scotia 3-15, 201D1
Oil Spill Conf held in LA; tanker inspectn progrm rptd effective 3-20, 200F3
Carter sees reps 6-1, 417G3
Mex oil well blows out 6-3–6-16, 462A2, A3
Carter asks spill cleanup 6-13, 441F1
Greek, Liberian tankers collide off Tobago, Carib Sea fouled 7-19, 553G2; Greek tanker sinks off Barbados 8-2, 592A3
Mex oil blowout reaches Tex beaches 8-9, 608G1; Pemex scored, Sedco role noted 8-21, 635E3-636B1
'74-78, 1st 1/4 '79 oil spill data; tanker safety records rptd 8-15, 608A1
US asks blowout damages, cleanup costs rptd 8-23; Mex bars liability 8-24, 688E3, 689B1
US-Mex blowout talks agreed 9-28–9-29, 753A2
Va refinery OKd by Army 10-4, 770E1
Mex cones blowout 10-14, total spill estimated 10-16, 782B1
Tex supertanker port OKd 10-15, 769D3
US, Tex file Mex blowout suits 10-18, 10-23, 809D2

Sewage—*See 'Air & Water' above*

Solid Waste—*See WASTE, Solid*

Wildlife—*See WILDLIFE*

1980

Noise Abatement

US cncl notes problem 2-19, 145D2
OSHA cites Va shipyd 2-27, 147F3
LA airport nuisance award case refused 10-6, 782A2
Motorcycle rules set 12-24, 987D2

Oil & Gas Issues

Mex spill continues 1-10, 60D2
Canada tanker spill feared 1-17, 56D3
Carter budget proposals 1-28, 70A2, 73G2
Chesapeake Bay oil spills cited 2-19, 145G2
Mex caps blowout, total spill rptd 3-24, 233C3
Calif offshore leasing pressed, oppositn rptd 3-28, 330E3
NC train collisn spill 4-2, 392B1
US sues Union Corp 4-24, 331E3
US offshore leasing speedup OKd 6-17, 552E2
Antipollutn costs overestimated 6-18, 494C2
Venice summit concerned 6-23, 473F2
Oil spill rpts backed by Sup Ct 6-27, 511A2
Alaska offshore lease curbs lifted 7-3, 7-8, 552F3
ND synfuel plant loan OKd 7-18, 553C2
House passes clean-up funds 9-19, 9-23; Sen omits 11-24, 898D1, F1
La rig punctures salt mine, lake 'swallowed' 11-20, 970C2
PPG accused of fuel-switching 11-25, 899C3
Clean-up legis promised 12-3, 935F3

Presidential Election (& Transition)

Reagan 'basic speech' excerpts 2-29, 207D3
Connally 'basic speech' excerpts 3-7, 184F2
Kennedy 'basic speech' excerpts 3-10, 183G2
Reagan vs auto regulatn 5-15, 383B1
Anderson urges sewer aid 6-9, 438G3
GOP platform adopted; text 7-15, 535C3, 536F3, 537B1, G1
Reagan acceptance speech 7-17, 532C2
Kennedy Dem conv speech 8-12, 610B2, D2, 614C1
Dem platform planks adopted 8-12, 8-13, 611A1, 615G1
Carter acceptance speech 8-14, 613F1
Reagan backs eased rules 9-2, 664G2
Reagan backs NYC Westway projct 10-1, 738D1
Reagan remarks disputed 10-7—10-9, 779B2-D3
Carter optimistic 10-12, 779D1
Carter ridicules Reagan on 'tree' pollutn 10-22, 802F3
Carter, Reagan TV debate 10-28, 815F1-A2
Anderson answers TV debate questns 10-28, 816D1
Carter plans to speak out 11-12, 865F2

Solid Waste—*See WASTE, Solid*

Wildlife—*See WILDLIFE*

1976

EPIDEMICS—*See 'Diseases' under MEDICINE*

EPISCOPAL Church, Protestant

Cheek rejcts compromise 4-4, forms separate unit 5-9, 755C3
Beebe '75 convictn reversed 4-9, new trial denied 6-11, 755A3
Bittner quits 4-9, 755E3
Schiess sues central NY bishop 7-8, 755E3
Pope, Coggan dispute female ordinatn 8-20, 756D1
65th Gen Conv: ordinatn of women, prayer bk revisn OKd 9-11—9-23, 755G1
Colo parish secedes 11-28, 932F1
US Polish Church cuts ties 11-29, 932D1
Canada ordains women 11-29, 932D1

EPPLER, Erhard

SPD loses state vote 4-4, 270F1

1977

ENVIRONMENT Program, UN—*See under UNITED Nations*

EPA—*See U.S. GOVERNMENT—ENVIRONMENTAL Protection Agency*

EPISCOPAL Church, Protestant

1st woman priest ordained 1-1, 119B3
Lesbian ordained 1-10, 845C2
Dissidents form unit 1-14, 119C3
Morehouse dies 2-17; Warnecke 2-23, 164D3, G3
Hispanic comm linked to FALN 3-21, 261D2
Vermilye porno arrest rptd 5-15, 432E2
Charismatic conf held 7-20—7-24, 620D3
LA priests deposed, parishes sued 8-5, 731G2
Dissidents plan schismatic church 9-14—9-16, 731C2
Walker installed DC bishop 9-24, 845F2
House of Bishops meet; Allin resignatn rejctd, dissident issues discussed 9-30—10-7, 845G1
Female ordination data 9-30, 845B2

Anglican Church of North America—*See separate listing*

EPLEY 3rd, Marion J.

Settles Natl Student Mkting suit 5-2, 520A1

EQUAL Employment Opportunity Commission—*See under U.S. GOVERNMENT*

1978

ENVIRONMENTAL Policy Center (EPC)

Scores Coal Policy Projct rpt 2-9, 184C2
Carter water plan discounted 6-6, 427A1

ENVIRONMENTAL Quality, Council on—*See under U.S. GOVERNMENT*

ENYU Island (U.S. trust)

Bikini islanders relocatn set 4-12, 278C2

EPA—*See U.S. GOVERNMENT—ENVIRONMENTAL Protection Agency*

EPIDEMICS—*See MEDICINE—Diseases & Epidemics*

EPILEPSY—*See MEDICINE—Diseases*

EPISCOPAL Church, Protestant

Female clergy survey rptd 3-23, 295B2
Female canon preaches in Westminster 4-2, 294E2
Means files for divorce 4-4, 420B3
Gen Theological Seminary sells Gutenberg Bible 4-7, 295E2

EPPLER, Maria

Wins world skiing title 2-4, 316G2

EPPS, Dwain

Asks US oust Nicaragua pres 11-8, 883E3

EPSTEIN, Pierre

Bright Golden Land opens 4-3, 760E1

EQUAL Employment Opportunity Commission—*See under U.S. GOVERNMENT*

1979

EPA—*See U.S. GOVERNMENT–ENVIRONMENTAL Protection Agency*

EPIDEMICS—*See under MEDICINE*

EPISCOPAL Church, Protestant

Traditionalists advised vs successn 5-12, 375D3
Hispanic comm not questnd on Morales escape 5-27, 431D2
66th Natl Conv: prayer book revisn OKd, gay ordinatn barred 9-12–9-18, 755D1-E2

EPP, Jason

Canada Indian affairs min 6-4, 423F3
Alberta tribes to administer fed funds 8-13, 632D2
Grants Yukon cncl more power 10-10, 833F3

EPSTEIN, Benjamin R.

Awards ADL Freedom Prize 6-17, 467F1

EQUAL Employment Opportunity Commission—*See under U.S. GOVERNMENT*

1980

EPA (Environmental Protection Agency) *See under U.S. GOVERNMENT*

EPA v. National Crushed Stone Association

Case decided by Sup Ct 12-2, 918B1

EPHLIN, Donald

Named UAW vp 6-4, 457B2

EPIDEMICS—*See MEDICINE–Diseases*

EPISCOPAL Church, Protestant

Protestant unity mtg ends, common ministry OKd 1-24, 156G2
Intercommunion poll rptd 4-4, 413A3
Sherrill dies 5-11, 448F2

EPPLE, Irene

Wins Olympic medal 2-21, 155A3

EPSTEIN, Dasha

Children of a Lesser God opens 3-30, 392E2

EQUAL Employment Opportunity Commission (EEOC)—*See under U.S. GOVERNMENT*

1976

EQUAL Rights Amendment—*See 'Politics & Government' under WOMEN*
EQUATORIAL Guinea—*See also NONALIGNED Nations Movement, OAU*
Nigeria chrgs repressn 1-7, evacuates contract labor 1-26, 62A1
Listed as 'not free' nation 1-19, 20D3
100,000 rptd in exile 1-24, 62F1
US severs ties 3-15, 238G3
EQUESTRIAN—*See HORSEBACK Riding*
EQUITABLE Life Assurance Society of the U.S.
To buy Peabody Coal shares 12-14, 985C1
EQUITY Funding Corp. of America—*See ORION Capital Corp.*
EQUUS (play)
Reopens 10-5, 1014E3
ERAMERICA
Defends day care proposals 2-13, 172A2
Opens DC office, scores foes 2-25, 172F1
ERASMUS, George
On Indian land claim 10-25, 851A3
ERB, John D.
Daughter kidnaped 9-15; in jail 10-2, 996E1
ERB, Patricia
Kidnaped 9-15; in jail 10-2, 996E1
EREK, Ali Sevki
On student clashes 4-8, 315A2
EREZ, Oded
On US agri deal delay 10-18, 811A1
ERFAN, Gamal
Quits as Egyptair head 138G2
ERGENEKON, Yilmaz
Sets '77 budget, defns hike 12-1, 1011G3
ERGIN, Lt. Gen. Cemal
Named Turkey AF cmdr 3-5, 192D2
ERIE, Pa.—*See PENNSYLVANIA*
ERIE Lackawanna Railway Co.
Chessie drops out of Conrail 3-23, 235E2
Conrail begins operations 4-1, 235E1
ERKEL, Gunther
W Ger Lockheed files rptd missing 9-17, 740F1
ERSKINE, Laurie York
Dies 11-30, 1015D1
ERLENBORN, Rep. John N. (R, Ill.)
Reelected 11-2, 829G2
ERLICH Jr., Dr. S. Paul
Vs WHO anti-Israel stand 5-19 355E2
ERNST, Max
Dies 4-1, 272F3
ERNST, Morris
Dies 5-21, 404F1
ERNST & Ernst
Fraud damage suit upheld 3-30, 262F1
ERRATH, Christine
Wins Olympic medal 2-13, 159A1
ERTEL, Allen E.
Elected 11-2, 830F3
ESCH, Rep. Marvin L. (R, Mich.)
Wins Sen primary 8-3, 565F2-A3
AMA donatn rptd 10-22, 938E3
Loses electn 11-2, 823E2
ESCOVAR Salom, Ramon
Sees Kissinger 2-16—2-17, 177B2
ESKIMOS
Canada land claim cited 10-25, 851A3
ESMERALDA (Chilean sailing ship)
In Operation sail 7-4, 488A3
ESPINO, Gen. Romeo
Retired 3-27, 255B3
ESPINOZA, Gustavo
Arrest rptd 7-30, 591A1

1977

EQUAL Rights Amendment (ERA)—*See WOMEN—Politics & Government*
EQUATORIAL Guinea—*See also NON-ALIGNED Nations Movement, OAU*
UN Assemb member 3G3
28 rptd executed 7-11, 658F2
Cuba mil, other aides cited 11-17, 896F1
EQUITABLE Life Assurance Society of the U.S., The
Teamster fund fiduciary 6-17, 558C2
Peabody Holding Co.—*See separate listing*
EQUITY Funding Corp. of America—*See ORION Capital Corp.*
ERA (Equal Rights Amendment)—*See WOMEN—Politics & Government*
ERBAKAN, Necmettin
Coalition divisns rptd 2-16, 138B2
Ecevit wins electns 6-5, 451E1
Backs Demirel 7-5, 530D2
Demirel wins confidence vote 8-1, 641D1
ERDA—*See U.S. GOVERNMENT—ENERGY Research & Development Administration*
ERDMAN, Paul E.
Crash of '79 on best-seller list 2-6, 120E3; 3-6, 184E3; 4-3, 264F1; 5-1, 356C2; 6-4, 452G1; 7-3, 548D3; 8-14, 643F1; 9-4, 712C3; 12-4, 1021A3
ERHARD, Ludwig
Dies 5-5, 452A3
ERIE, Lake
Frozen 1-19, 54F2
Detroit sued on pollution 5-6, 422D2
St Lawrence Seaway tolls hiked 12-16, 982E3
ERITREA—*See under ETHIOPIA*
ERLENBORN, Rep. John N. (R, Ill.)
Vs Sovt computer deal 6-5, 469A3
House backs re minimum wage 9-15, 758G3
ERNST & Ernst
Sen subcom staff rpt scores 1-17, 78C3
FDIC suit rptd 2-9, 155C3
Big 8 acctg firms ranked 8-22, 650G2
ERVIN Jr., Sam J.
Nixon 'still covering up' 5-4, 367D3
ERVING, Julius (Dr. J)
Phila '76ers lose NBA title 6-5, 490B3, D3
ERYTHROMYCIN—*See MEDICINE—Drugs*
ESA—*See EUROPEAN Space Agency*
ESB Inc.—*See under INCO Ltd.*
ESCALERA, Alfredo
KOs Garvey 3-17, 263F1
KOs Becerril 5-16, 395D1
ESCH, Marvin L.
'76 specl interest gifts rptd 2-15, 128E2
ESCOBAR Bethancourt, Romulo
Lauds Linowitz 3-3, 379A1 ★
Suspends new Canal talks 5-11, 378G2 ★
Asks Canal treaty compensatn 7-29, 589B3 ★
Optimistic on Canal treaty 8-5, 607B1 ★
Rpts Canal accord 8-10, defends 8-12, 621D1, 622A3
Disputes US treaty interpretatns 8-19; controversy ensues 9-26—10-5, 754A3
ESCOBAR Garcia, Roberto
Workers, peasants take hostage 11-10, freed 11-13, 969F3
ESCOVAR Salom, Ramon
Venez forgn min 1-7, 23E2
Cites Carter letter to Perez 2-22, 124A2
Addresses OAS assemb 6-14, 494C1
Replaced as forgn min 7-15, 566A1
ESKIMOS—*See INUIT; also CANADA—Indians*
ESMARK Inc.
Carrier buys Inmont 8-11, 629B3
ESOPs (Employe Stock Ownership Plans)—*See LABOR*
ESPADAS, Guty
'77 boxing champion 12-17, 970A2
ESPALDON, Rear Adm. Romulo
Urges rebels to give up 6-11, 468B3
ESPINOZA, Gustavo
Arrest rptd 3-11, 241F2

1978

EQUAL Rights Amendment (ERA)—*See WOMEN—Politics & Government*
EQUATORIAL Guinea—*See also NON-ALIGNED Nations Movement, OAU*
Freedom House lists as not free 44A2
Rights abuses rptd 1-25, UN rep denies 2-16, 152G2, A3 ★
USSR, China, Cuba aid rptd 1-25, 152A3
RC Church rptd banned 6-30, Vatican murder chrgs cited 7-24, 596F1
2,000-4,000 prisoners, torture, chrgd 7-25, 596G1
UN Assemb member 713D3
EQUITABLE General Corp.
Great Southern merger planned 4-17, 283G1-A2
Gulf United merger bid OKd 6-26, 553D2
EQUITY Funding Corp. of America—*See ORION Capital Corp.*
ERA (Equal Rights Amendment)—*See WOMEN—Politics & Government*
ERASMUS, Rudolf
Heads Info Dept probe 11-6, 868G1
Info Dept probe mandate extended 12-1, rpt issued 12-5, 946D1
ERDAHL, Arlen
Wins US House seat 11-7, 851A2, 854D3
ERDENIZ, Ahmet Cihangir
Slain 6-23, 595D3
ERDMAN, Paul E.
Crash of '79 on best-seller list 1-8, 24F3
'Silver Bears' released 4-20, 619G3
ERGOT (grain fungus)—*See GRAIN*
ERICSSON, Margit—*See DAVID, Rachel*
ERLENBORN, Rep. John N. (R, Ill.)
Reelected 11-7, 850E3
Defends House com illegal alien plan 12-20, 1010G2-A3
ERITREA—*See under ETHIOPIA*
ERLICHMAN, Martin
'Coma' released 2-1, 619B1
ERNST & Ernst
Cleveland deficit rptd 8-22, 663C3
ERSKINE, Maj. Gen. Emmanuel Alexander
Heads UN force in Leb 3-19, 197E2
Arafat vows cooperatn in Leb 3-28, 213B1
On Unifil total in Leb 4-11, 256E2
Arafat vows truce cooperatn 5-5, 340C1
Meets Arafat on PLO infiltratn 5-16, 383G2-A3
Says Haddad has Leb govt OK 6-13, Leb denies 6-14, 462E2
Asks Israel to get Leb Christns to stop attacks 8-8, 638B3
Says Unifil missn lags 11-19, 951D1
ERSOY, Bahir
Named Turkey labor min 1-5, 21F2
ERTEL, Rep. Allen E. (D, Pa.)
Submits res for Park testimony 1-23, 64D1
Reelected 11-7, 852D1
ERTL, Josef
Retains W Ger agri post 2-3, 93A3
ERVING, Julius (Dr. J)
East wins NBA All-Star game 2-5, 271D3
On NBA all-star team 6-13, 457C3
ESA—*See EUROPEAN Space Agency*
ESAKI, Masumi
Japan trade min 12-7, 945F2
OPEC price hike to hurt econ recovery 12-18, 978A2
ESCALERA, Alfredo
Arguello TKOs 1-28, 379A2
ESCOBAR Bethancourt, Romulo
Hints treaty chngs OK 3-16, 178B2
Treaty chng OK buys time 3-16; pol ldrs, execs ask renegotiatn 4-6, 255B2
ESCOBAR Sierra, Hugo
Colombia justice min 8-7, 629C3
ESHKOL, Levi (1895-1969)
Golda Meir dies 12-8, 1032F1
ESKIMOS—*See INUIT; also CANADA—Indians & Inuit*
ESKIND, Jane
Wins Tenn US Sen primary 8-3, 606B2
Loses electn 11-7, 853D1
ESMAIL, Sami
Israel convicts 6-6, sentncs 6-12, 489C2
Israel paroles 10-18, expels 10-20, 783C2
ESMARK Inc.
In Dow Jones indl avg 66E2
Low '76 tax paymt rptd 1-27, 65A3
Carrier '77 merger fight cited 9-25, 896G1
ESPAILLAT Namita, Leopoldo
Named DR pres tech secy 8-16, 648D2
ESPALDON, Rear Adm. Romulo
Rpts on anti-rebel drive 1-27, 73F3
ESPINOZA, Lt. Col. Pedro
US indictmt in Letelier case seen 5-23, 452D1
US indicts; arrested 8-1; 'proof' asked re extraditn 8-2, 613F3-614E1
Townley admits link 8-11, 647D3
US asks extraditn 9-20, held in mil hosp 9-29, 755G2, E3
Queried by Sup Ct pres 10-19, 1014C3

1979

EQUATORIAL Guinea—*See also NONALIGNED Nations Movement, OAU*
US rights rpt omits 2-10, 107A2
Masie ousted in coup 8-3; border fighting rptd, surrender demanded 8-7, 613E3*
Spain sets ties, pledges aid 8-5, 614B1
Pol prisoners granted amnesty 8-6, 613G3
Spain defends nonaligned conf plans 8-10, 8-13, 654E2
Masie captured 8-18, 638G2
UN membership listed 695G2
Masie convicted, shot 9-29, 742E1
ERA (Equal Rights Amendment)—*See WOMEN—Politics*
ERASMUS, Rudolf
Comm clears Vorster 4-2, 270B1
Natl Party expels Mulder 4-6, 270F1
Final comm rpt issued, Vorster resigns 6-4, 427B3
ERC Corp.
Spurns Conn Gen bid 10-18, Charter Co plans offer 12-21, 986C3
ERDELATZ, Edward
Wins libel case 4-18, shares award 4-19, 334B2
ERHARDT, Ron
Named Patriots head coach 4-6, 335A3
ERIE Coke & Chemical Co.—*See MERCIER Corp.*
ERKMAN, Hayrettin
Named Turkey forgn min 11-12, 876E1
ERSBOELL, Niels
US oil import subsidy scored 6-1, 417A2
ERSKINE, Maj. Gen. Emmanuel Alexander
Says PLO, Leb leftists infiltrate UN zone in Leb 8-26, 643C1
ERVIN, Dr. Frank
Cleared in malpractice suit 2-9, 139E3
ERVING, Julius (Dr. J)
West wins NBA All-Star game 2-4, 175B1
ERWIN, Tenn.—*See TENNESSEE*
ERXLEBEN, Russell
In NFL draft 5-3, 335F1
ESCALERA, Alfredo
Arguello TKOs 1-29, 412D3
ESCAPE from Alcatraz (film)
Released 6-21, 820A1
Top-grossing film 6-27, 548G3
ESCOBAR, Numa
Arrest protested 5-4, 371A1
ESCOBAR Soto, Nicolas
Killed by guerrillas 1-4, 22E2
ESHLEMAN, Clayton
Wins Natl Book Award 4-23, 356B2
ESHRAGHI, Hojatoeslam Sahab
On Nazih's ouster 9-24, 752E2
ESKANDARIAN, Andranik
Gets 1-game suspensn 8-29, 775F3
ESMARK Inc.
In Dow Jones indl avg 72E1
Dow Jones index drops listing 6-28, 481E2
Vickers Energy Corp.
Fairbanks Colo U football deal leaked 4-2, 335D2
ESP—*See EXTRASENSORY Perception*
ESPAILLAT Nanita, Leopoldo
Fired by Guzman 3-9, 256C3
ESPANA, Ernesto
TKOs Lira 8-4, 839B1
ESPINOSA, Nino
Traded to Phillies 3-27, 1002G2
ESPINOZA, Gustavo
Arrest rptd 1-8, 39F1
ESPINOZA, Juan Francisco
Slain 6-20, 461G2
ESPINOZA, Manuel
Rpts progress in US talks 7-12, 512F1
ESPINOZA Bravo, Lt. Col. Pedro
US submits more data in Letelier case 1-8; freed for mil ceremony 1-11, 19B3
Townley on Letelier murder role 1-18, 58D1, F1, A3
Extraditn seen unlikely 2-7, 114B3
3 Cubans convictd re Letelier 2-14, 114E2
Avoids US extraditn 5-14, 369C2
Ct bars extraditn, frees 10-1, 750G1
ESPINOZA-Ortiz, Osvaldo
Arrested in alleged Carter death plot 5-5, 404D1

1980

EQUAL Rights Amendment (ERA)—*See WOMEN--Politics*
EQUATORIAL Guinea—*See also NONALIGNED Nations, OAU*
USSR fishing depot withdrawal rptd, US ties rptd restored, pro-West tilt cited 1-28, 119C1
US issues rights rpt 2-5, 87E2
EQUESTRIAN—*See HORSEBACK Riding*
EQUITABLE Life Insurance Co.
Savage named to Synfuels Corp bd 9-13, Sen panel OKs 9-25, 725F2
Savage named to interim Synfuels Corp bd 10-5, 786F2
ERA (Equal Rights Amendment)—*See WOMEN--Politics*
ERB, Walter
Arrested as spy 11-10, 925G2
ERBAKAN, Necmettin
Pres voting chng barred 5-24—5-25, 411A1
Demirel wins confidence vote 7-2, 500G2, B3
Arrested 9-12, 696E2
Arrested again 10-15, 793G3
ERC Corp.
Getty bid OKd 6-5, 557G2
ERDAHL, Rep. Arlen (R, Minn.)
Reelected 11-4, 845A2
ERDEM, Kaya
Named Turkey finance min 9-21, 720C3
New budget announced 12-1, 924A1
ERDOST, Ilhan
Arrested 11-5, dies in jail 11-7, 923F3
EREN, Orhan
Rpts martial law extensn, violence toll 4-18, 316B2
ERICKSON, Milton H.
Dies 3-25, 279D2
ERIE—*See PENNSYLVANIA*
ERIM, Nihat
Slain 7-19, 567B3
Murder suspects rptd arrested 10-3, 794B1
ERISA (Employee Retirement Income Security Act)—*See PENSIONS & Retirement*
ERKMEN, Hayrettin
EC membership bid planned 2-7, 102C3
Aegean Sea air dispute ended 2-22, 2-23, 150G2
Signs US bases, aid pact 3-29, 255A3
On EC entry goal 7-1, 526A2
ERLENBORN, Rep. John N. (R, Ill.)
Reelected 11-4, 842E3
ERNOTTE, Andre
Coming Attractions opens 12-3, 1003A3
EROLA, Judy
Canada mines min 3-3, 171C2
ERRICHETTI, Mayor Angelo J. (Camden, N.J.)
Linked to bribery in Abscam probe 2-2, 2-3, 81B2
Indicted in Abscam probe 5-27, 5-28, 402E2, F2
Abscam judge quits case 8-7, 599F3
Convicted in Abscam trial 8-31, 684B2
Appeals ct backs Abscam tapes broadcast 10-1; Sup Ct refuses stay, tapes aired 10-14, 781D2
Indicted again in Abscam probe 10-30, 824E2
ERRICO, Con
Convicted of race fixing 5-19, 447A3
ERROL Flynn: The Untold Story (book)
Higham sued 8-1, 639E1
ERSBOELL, Niels
On IEA import quotas 2-19, 142D1
ERSIN, Gen. Nurettin
In Turkey mil junta 9-21, 720C3
ERSKINE, Maj. Gen. Emmanuel
Meets Christn militia, Israeli cmdrs 4-14, 284B1
E. R. Squibb & Sons v. Sindell
Case declined by Sup Ct 10-14, 781G3
ERTEL, Rep. Allen E. (D, Pa.)
Reelected 11-4, 844D1
ERTL, Joseph
On SPD-FDP coalition electn win 10-5, 759D3
Sworn W Ger agri min 11-5, 925E1
ERUZIONE, Mike
US Olympic hockey team beats Sovts 2-22, wins gold medal 2-24, 155A2
ERVIN Jr., Sam J.
Reveals cancer 9-12; scores ct system 10-22, 908G1
ERVING, Julius (Dr. J)
NBA scoring ldr 3-30, 278C3
Lakers win NBA title 5-16, 432B1
2d in NBA MVP vote 5-29, 656B3
On NBA all-league team 6-2, 656D3
ERWIN—*See TENNESSEE*
ESCAPE (recording)
On best-seller list 1-2, 40E3; 2-6, 120F3
ESCOBAR, Daniel
Slain 3-4, 172E1
ESCOBAR, Elixzan
Convicted 7-30, 601D1
Indicted 12-10, 963G3
ESCONDIDO—*See CALIFORNIA*
ESFAHANI, Abbas
Denies Iran funded US protests 8-9, 635D2
ESMARK Inc.
Vickers Energy Corp.
3 units sold 8-26, 745E2-A3
ESPALDON, Adm. Romulo
Says Moslem rebellion ending 10-31, 902D3
ESPERANZA, Antonio
Arrested 11-14, 888A3
ESPINAL Camps, Rev. Luis
Slain 3-22, 272G1
ESPINO, Gen. Romeo
27 chrgd in Pl plot 10-28, 874F2

1976

ESPIONAGE—*See also SECURITY; also U.S. GOVERNMENT, subheads CENTRAL Intelligence Agency and FEDERAL Bureau of Investigation*
Canada ex-prime min diary cites '45 Sovt case 1-1, 8F1
Algeria arrests 3 1-8; France denies chrg 1-9, links spies to anti-Basque unit 1-11, 45B2-E3
ABA forms Rosenberg unit 1-8, 70F2
Denmark '75 expulsn of Sovt agents rptd 1-11, 101C1
US judge to see Rosenberg papers 1-13, 70B2
French press rpts 2 named Sovt spies 1-19, 50A1
Ex-Israel defns min dies 1-24, 80E3
E Ger seeks Guillaume visit 1-25, 158A2
E Ger jails refugee smuggler 1-26, 85E1-A2
Sovt microwave taps in US emb rptd 2-6—2-10, 122D2
Ford backs capital punishmt 2-14, 130A1
Sovts tie microwaves to US bugging 2-26, 196C2
Algeria sentncs 7 in French-linked ring 3-3, 454F3-455A1
Yugo upholds US citizen's '75 arrest 3-17, 256F1
Hiss book review rptd 3-18, 217E3
Yugo holds Sovt offcl 4-6, 256B1
Poland sentences Pawlowski 4-10, 268B3
Yugo sentences Cominformists 4-14, 542F3
Data on Sovt spies in US rptd 4-26, 304F1
Japan chrgs Sovt newsman re US fleet 5-12—5-14, 356E1
W Ger secy arrested 5-14; CDU, intellignc officials suspended 5-17, 5-19, 383D1
Japan frees alleged Sovt spy 5-22, 373B2
US newsmen in USSR chrgd 5-25, 5-26, 371G2
Yugo sentences Sovt spy 5-25, 542C3
W Ger arrests more suspects 6-2—6-14, 441E3
US Dem platform text 6-15, 474F1
Yugo pardons US citizen 7-23; other arrests rptd 7-26, 7-27, 559A2
Yugo scores US amb re Toth 7-31, 594D1
Uganda arrests 2 Britons, frees 1 8-3, 581A1
FBI restructure set 8-11, 633C3
Swiss arrest officer 8-16; expel Sovt, Rumania envoys 8-22, 640A1
2 arrested in W Ger 8-16, 640B2
US GOP platform text 8-18, 610B3
Uganda frees 2d Briton 8-25, 874E1
Rumania sentences 2 for indl spying 8-29, 907A3
Swiss deport Iranian 8-30, Swiss envoy recalled 8-31, 735E1
US spy device sale to Sweden rptd 9-14, 734D1
France expels Sovt as spy 10-14, 852F2
S Korea rpts N Korea spy surrenders, 12 seized 10-30, 910B3
Swiss chrg 4 as Sovt spies 11-10, 11-24, 1011A3
US amb to Yugo resigns 11-17, 910B2
Thais return 26 Cambodia refugees 11-23, 929B2
S Yemen downs Iran jet 11-24; chrgs spying, bans overflights 11-25—11-29, 913F2-914C1

1977

ESPIONAGE—*See also U.S. GOVERNMENT—CIA*
CIA ex-employe arrested 12-22-76, 41A2
Australia asks Sovt ship exit 1-4, 17G1; USSR complies 1-5, 42C3
Czech ex-min arrested 1-4, 19E3; trial opens 1-10, 82F3; sentncd 2-3, 115C1
US seizes Sovt immigrant 1-7, 41A3
Canada orders 5 Cubans expelled 1-10, 17E2
Denmark ousts Polish consul 1-10, 62B1
Cuba admits Canada recruiting 1-12, 42D3
Boyce, Lee arrested as Sovt spies 1-16, 41D2-A3
UK denies Czech chrgs 1-23, 82G3
Norway expells 6 Sovt spies 1-28, 99A3
USSR ousts AP newsman 2-5, 101D1
French oust Sovt UNESCO offcl 2-11, 159C3
Sovt training of Spain refugees cited 2-14, 242F2
USSR expels 2 Norway envoys 2-14, 967A3
UK sets Agee, Hosenball expulsns 2-16, 134A2
Canada deports Sovt scientist 2-24, 159E1
Czech defector reveals spy network 2-24, 220B3
USSR chrgs US dissident recruiting 3-4, 226B3
Singapore rearrests journalist 3-12, 223C3
Agee prosecutn barred 3-18, 212A2
Greece jails 5 Britons 3-18, 256C3
French arrest 4 as Sovt spies 3-22, 255B3
Ethiopia ousts 2 US natls 3-30, 327D3
Egypt returns 2 Israeli spies hanged in '55 4-14, 297F1, A2
Zaire accuses USSR 4-20, 317F1
CIA Australia union infiltratn chrgd 4-27, 326D1-A2
Boyce convicted, Lee trial begins 4-28, 344A2; Lee convctd 5-15, 409B3; gets life 7-18, 576E3; Boyce sentncd 9-12, 732E3
W Ger arrests Ger spies 5-4—6-28, 602F1-B2
Ex-CIA employee convicted 5-5, 409D2
Zaire ousts newsmen 5-6, 394G1
Justice Dept backs uniform fed procedures 5-18, 594D3
UK chrgs 3 5-24; Hosenball, Agee expelled 5-27, 6-3, 526C3
CIA ex-employe sentenced 6-1, 462G2
Greece releases Britons 6-4, 487E3
John Masterman dies 6-6, 532D3
USSR detains US rptr 6-11—6-15, 474D3
Syria executes 2 Iraqis 6-13, 457B3
Swiss gen convicted 6-17, 489C2
Ethiopia frees US natl 7-1, 562F2
Spain expels Sovt agent 7-4, 546A1
Danish secret svc probe ordrd 7-8, 672G1
USSR chrgs US rptr 7-12, 564E1
US double agent's release from USSR sought 7-14, 564B2
Central African Empire holds US, UK rptrs 7-14—8-15, 634E3
Amer, W Ger seized in Fla 7-20, 576A3
Canada accuses USSR envoy 7-20, 579F3
Tanzania ex-agent sentencd 7-29, 806A1
Francis Gary Powers dies 8-1, 696E3
USSR blames US in double agent's disappearance 8-17, 640D3
France expels Agee 8-18, 654D2
Callaghan denies Wilson bugged 8-23, 745D2
E-W Ger spies sentncd 9-23—12-6, 968D2
Cambodia links to evacuatn 10-2, 779E3
USSR tries to blackmail US envoy 10-19; US protests 10-19—10-31, 866C2-B3
Australia agency to widen role 10-27, 862G1
Swiss gen's case reviewed 10-27, 904B3
US Sovt-blackmail attempt chrgd 11-7, 866B3
Australia advertises for spies 11-12, 923B1
Manuel Artime dies 11-13, 952B2
Guinea halts Sovt flights 11-19, 989F1
CIA bars news media contacts 11-30, 941C1
Agee asked to leave Holland 12-2, 986E2
W Ger Defns Min spy scandal disclosed 12-12; NATO, US, other reactn 12-12—12-15, 968C1
Czech ex-min rptd sentenced 12-20, 1018G3
Iran executes Sovt spy 12-25, 1019F1

ESPOSITO, Phil
NHL season ldrs rptd 4-3, 262A3

1978

ESPIONAGE
E Ger bars W Ger rptr 1-4, closes press office 1-10, 11B3
W Ger arrests 2 in Netherlands 1-4, 21E3
Uruguay frees Mex newsman 1-5, 136F3
Israel sentences US woman 1-9, 10B3
IRA forces UK agent pullout 1-9, 18F2
E Ger rpts arrests, sentences 1-9—1-14, 36A2
Taiwan sentences 6 1-17, 38C1
US rpts Sovt offcl ousted 1-19, 39G1
S Australia police chief fired 1-19, 53G1
USSR satellite falls in Canada 1-24, 57C1; **for subsequent developments, see ASTRONAUTICS—Satellites**
W Ger defns min linked to new tap scandal 1-24, 74A3
Agee Dutch residency rejctd, W Ger bar cited 1-25, 90E3
E Ger sentncs W Ger natl 1-26, 61F3
US arrests 2 as spies for Viet 1-31, 68G2
French sentnc 5 as spies for USSR 2-1, 71B2
W Ger defns min resigns 2-3, 93D2
US ousts Viet UN amb 2-3; Viet, others protest 2-3—2-9; stay issued, amb leaves 2-10, 103E2
Canada chrgs 13 Sovts 2-9, 110D3
W Ger convicts 3 as E Ger spies 2-13, 115C1
Austria protests W Ger secret svc surveillnc 2-14, 110B3
W Ger Defns Min scandal probed 2-24, 210D3
W Ger parlt curbs secret svcs 3-9, 210G3
USSR trawlers rptd in Baltic 3-11, 291A3
USSR chrgs Canada frame-up 3-15, 209E1
USSR denies Scandinavian spy trucks 3-15, 291E2
Toronto newspr chrgd re USSR spy rpt 3-17, 208F3-209E1
Iran rpts Sovt spy ring smashed 3-27, 4-16, 288G3
Dutch name 3 Sovts as spies 3-30, 247E3
USSR sentences 2 as spies 4-10, 5-15, 416G2, A3
US, E Ger prisoner exchng talks rptd 4-24; 3-way swap completed 5-1, 318A2
S Korea claims N Korea spy boat sunk 4-28, 340F3
Mitsubishi unit chrgd in US 5-9, 404B2
US convicts 2 as spies for Viet 5-19, 389F3-390F1
US arrests 2 Sovt UN employes 5-20, 409G2
USSR seizes US businessman Crawford, retaliatn vs US cited 6-12, 476B2; Carter scores 6-26, 491E1
USSR bares Peterson expulsn 6-12, 476A3
Sovt UN employes, US businessman freed 6-26, 506E1-A2
US sentences 2 Viet spies 7-7, 555A1
French war hero jailed as Sovt spy 7-12, 649G3
USSR sentences Shcharansky, link with US rptr cited 7-14, 541A1
USSR sentences Filatov 7-14, 541E2
France ousts Sovt diplomat 7-15, 649F3
Greece, US implicated in UK rptr's '71 death 7-24, 631A3
2 Sovt aides to UN ousted 7-31, 3d aide promoted despite US, UK protests 8-29, 676C1
W Ger natls rptd jailed by E Ger 8-11, 622B3
CIA ex-employe seized by FBI 8-17, 645D2
NATO U-2 missns rise rptd 8-22, 748A3
Rumanian defector implicates W Ger offcls in spy scandal, chrgs disputed 8-31—9-6, 725C2, D2 *
Rumanian defector triggers purges 9-1, 9-6, 741C3
Crawford gets suspended sentnc 9-7, 742B3
US issues WWII secret documts on Ger, Japanese decoded messages 9-10—9-18, 744D2-G3
Bulgarian defectors slain in UK 9-11, 10-2; attacks rptd in France, US 9-14, 748C3
W Ger drops spy probe 9-26, 868G2
CIA ex-offcl found dead 10-1, Sovt link denied 10-5—10-26, 835F3
Carter admits spy satellite use 10-1, 861B2
W Ger sentences Schmidt ex-aide 10-5, 776D3
US convicts 2 Sovt UN employes 10-13, sentncd 10-30, 835A2; USSR demands return 11-4, 863E1
UK drops major chrgs vs 3 10-23, 838A3; convicts, suspends sentncs 11-17, 924E1
USSR bars Dow exec's exit, sentncs cited 11-7, 884B3
FBI probe of Douglas rptd 11-14, 877E3
Australia chrgs USSR bugged Moscow emb 11-14, 878C3
CIA ex-employe convicted 11-18, manual said to help USSR 11-23, 940F1, G2
US emb study discounts Sovt microwave harm 11-20, 924E3
CIA-Harvard secret ties revealed 12-1, 962F2
CIA ex-employe sentncd 12-22, 1011C3

ESPOSITO, Antonio
Slain 6-21, 517E1

1979

ESPIONAGE—*See also RECONNAISSANCE*
CIA alleged agents abroad listed 1-4, 17B3
FBI head warns of Chinese spies 1-7, 17G2
Oswald exhumatn suit filed 1-9, med data access agreed 2-23, 166A3
Peru executes Chilean spy 1-20, 51F3
W Ger arrests 5 E Ger spy suspects 1-20, NATO offcl defects 1-21, 61B3
Taiwan oppositn ldr arrested 1-21, 116E1
'50s CIA files made public, 'disposal' problems detailed 1-22, 55G1-C2
Paisley death probe urged by US Sen com 1-24, 54G3
France arrests 2 as E Ger spies 1-28, 77D3
W Ger continues E Ger arrests 1-31, 77C3
US spy satellite photo release urged 1-31, 89F2
Fuchs retiremt in E Ger rptd 2-1, 78E3
US WWII secret files released 2-3, 2-6, 93F1
Italy expels US offcl re critical intellignc rpt 2-14, 136E1-A2
E Ger sentnces W Ger natl 2-15, 181B1
Iran bans intell posts 2-21; US personnel flee, secrets safety disputed 2-24–2-28, 145F1
CIA resignatns, new security measures rptd 2-22, 132G3
CIA ex-agent Angleton cleared of Sovt spy chrg 2-27, 152D3
US missile info leak alleged 3-1, 207E2
NATO secy defects 3-5, 180E3
W Ger CDU infiltratn, E Ger spy data rptd 3-6–3-13, 180G2
Australia surveillance bill proposed 3-8, 209F2
CIA considered ESP spies in '50s 3-11, 208D2
US drops '57 spy chrgs vs Sterns 3-22, 232C1
US FBI informant loss rptd 3-22, 232C2
US intell on China-Viet War praised 3-25, 231F3
Brecht '43-56 FBI surveillnc rptd 3-29, 367C3
S Africa ousts 3 US envoys 4-12, US retaliates 4-13, 286E3, 287C1
Paisley death probe dropped by Justice Dept 4-18, 283F3; Sen panel sets probe 4-30, 368A1
CIA-disputed Uganda acct publshd 4-19, 309B3
Toronto paper avoids trial re USSR spy rpt 4-23, 311B2
US swaps 2 Sovt spies for 5 dissidents 4-27, 317A1
CIA '63 Castro death plot rptd confrmd 5-2, 367E3-368A1
Julius Rosenberg article publshd 6-16, 466A1
Lutzes, Gerstners sentncd in W Ger 6-18; 3 others arrested 6-21, 489E3, 490A1
Sovt spy suspected in FBI 6-24, 521B1
US Sup Ct broadens libel suit rights 6-26, 540C3
Paisley death questioned 6-27, CIA scored on probe 7-8, 520B2-G2
Syria calls Moslem extremists agents 6-28, 505A3
Israel paroles US woman 6-29, deports 6-30, 496F1
CIA spying on antiwar activists rptd 7-16, 561A2
E-W Ger prisoners exchngd 7-20, 586C2
S Korea sinks N Korea spy ship 7-21, 567C3
FBI charter proposed 7-31, 599C2, C3
Swedish envoy '45 USSR disappearance case reopened 8-4, 690D2
US GOP asks intell overhaul 8-6, 610C3
Admin denies forgn spies aided in US 8-9, 664B2
US newsman linked to KGB 8-11, 611E1
US yeoman chrgd in secrets sales 8-14, 611D1
W Ger rptr chrgd 8-16, 742E2
Sovt '77 equipmt delivery to Cuba cited 9-10, 674A1
Cuba frees 4 US prisoners 9-17, 706D3
Turkey exec chrgd as Lockheed spy 9-20, 775A2
US yeoman pleads guilty 9-25, 747E3; sentncd 10-26, 831F3
Oswald KGB substitutn theory discounted 10-22, 905A3
USSR rptr defects in Japan, flies to US 10-24, 856D3
UK spy ring scandal reopened 10-28, 10-29, 873F3; art historian named 4th man 11-15, controversy ensues 11-15–11-21, 908C2-909F1
NSA upheld on withholding data 10-29, 945C3
Iran accuses US hostages, trial threatened 11-18–11-20, 877F1; **for subsequent developments, see IRAN–U.S. Embassy Takeover**
UK secrets legis withdrawn 11-20, 909A1
E Ger sentences W Ger rptr 12-14, 980F3
US revokes Agee passport 12-22, 991D2

ESPOSITO, Phil
NHL scoring mark cited 4-8, 355G3

1980

ESPINOZA, Julian
Captured 6-23, 497B3
Vows rebel offensive 8-22, 669E3

ESPIONAGE
Canada comm asks Secrets Act revisn, accuses Treu 1-11, 78F2, E3
S Africa domestic spying chrg spurs Natl Security Dept reorgn 1-15, 60D3
Japan arrests 3 as Sovt spies 1-18, 60A1
Canada expels 3 Sovts re US spying 1-21, 56F2
Boyce prison escape rptd 1-22, 55E1
Sovt spy case prompts Japan mil resignatns 1-28, 2-3, 99C3
French catch Sovt spy 2-9, 141F2
Spain arrests Sovt as spy 2-14, another leaves for Moscow 2-16, 141A3
Swiss allege 200 Sovt spies 2-18, 141B3
CIA admits press, clergy, academics use 2-21, 189A3
US ouster of 5 Sovt bloc diplomats rptd 2-29, 189C2
Soviet double agent introduced 3-3, 189F1
CIA alleged agents abroad listed 3-7, 189F2
Poland sentncs UN employe 3-7, 220G3
Finns sentence spy 3-18, 212B1
Afghan govt arrests US natl 3-19, 271F2; release rptd 5-16, 443D1
US, Turkey sign bases pact 3-29, 255C3
Poland upholds UN employe's sentnc 4-14, 326G3
Iran arrests US woman 5-6, 434B1
Libya expels 25 US natls 5-12, detains 2 5-13, 373E3
Sovt trade spy arrested in US 5-18, sentenced 8-1, 598B2
Iran executes Jew 6-5, 644B3
E Ger rpts UNESCO aide's arrest 6-10, sentenced 9-6, 708A1
Iran expels Sovt diplomat 6-30, 491B1
S Korea chrgs North infiltratn 6-30, 525B2; N Korea denies 7-18, 547C1
Iran executes 2 7-14, 545G2
Trigon-Kissinger controversy rptd 7-14—10-4, 753F3
USSR honors Philby 7-15, 566G2-B3
China sentences 3 Sovt spies 7-20, 563G1
Argentina intell operatns scandal disclosed 7-28, 580D1
W Ger arrest of E Ger spy rptd 7-31, 606D1
France arrests E Ger ex-mil chief 8-19, chrgs rptd 9-6, 707F3
Blunt quits British Academy 8-18; controversy rptd 8-24, 652D1
Portugal ousts 4 Sovt diplomats 8-20, 689A3
W Gers arrest Pole 9-9, 889D1
Filatov USSR death sentence rptd commuted 9-23—9-24; ID controversy rptd 10-4, 753E3
CIA ex-agent indicted 10-24, pleads guilty 10-29, 855G2
Le Monde chrgd re Libya spy revelatns 11-7, 872G1; France frees alleged spy 11-29, 921F2
W Ger arrests 3 11-10, 925F2
French NATO spy arrested, 2 Sovt Emb aides expelled 11-13, 921B3
Carter aide cleared in spy leak 12-5, 940B2
W Ger secy sentncd 12-12, 969A2
Iran Hostage Issue—*See IRAN--U.S. Hostage Issue*

ESPOSITO, Tony
NHL goaltending ldr 4-6, 296E1

1976

ESQUIRE (magazine)
Richard Joseph dies 9-30, 970B2
Venez ousts Branch 10-22, 844F1
ESSEX International Co.
Pa plant closed 10-7—10-27, illness identified 11-5, 911A2
ESSO Standard (Near East)—*See EXXON*
ESTABA Moreno, Delia
Indicts Cuba exiles 11-2, 843F2
ESTABLE, Argento
'75 torture death rptd 1-13, 55E3
ESTIER, Claude
At French CP congress 2-4—2-7, 119F2
ESTONIAN Soviet Socialist Republic—*See 'Republics' under USSR*
ESTROGEN—*See 'Cancer' under MEDICINE*
ETCHEVERRY, Tabare
Rptd detained 3-4, 207F3
ETEKI Mboumoua, William
OAU warns S Africa 6-18, 447G2
ETHICS, Political (U.S.)—*See under POLITICS*

ETHIOPIA—*See also AFRICAN Development Bank, DISARMAMENT—Geneva Committee, NONALIGNED Nations Movement, OAU*
Listed as 'not free' nation 1-19, 20D3
6 mil cncl members arrested 1-28, 173C1
Interests in Afars cited 85D3
'Reactionaries' arrested 2-15—2-28, ex-cmdr slain 2-15, 172G3
Tewoflos deposed 2-18, rptd arrested 3-1, 173D1
7 cabt mins ousted 2-23, 173B1
Mengistu natl address 4-20, 311G2
Political progrm announced 4-21, 311D2
Artists protest quelled 4-22, 311A3
May Day violence 5-1, 335G1
Unrest in 7 provs rptd 5-7, 364F2
Rpt Selassie smothered 6-21, 457A3
Econ crimes decree issued 7-6, 523F3
2 named to Dergue 7-16, 8-17, 674D2
Officer deaths rptd 7-25, 8-12, 8-26, 674B2
Drought in south rptd 8-4, 674B3
Mengistu attacked 9-23, 2 offcls slain 10-1, 11-9, 4 executed 11-2, 1002D1
Local cncls get educ control 9-26, 1002C2
Birr replaces $ 10-14, 1002B2
27 dissidents executed 11-18; pol prisoners freed 12-23, 1002E1

Eritrean Developments
ELF frees 2 Americans 1-9, 31C1
Senegal, Zaire threaten ties 1-11, 1-13, 16A1
ELF chrgs Um Berami massacre 3-22, 311C3
Govt chrgs Arab aid 4-11, 311B3
Rebels free 2 Americans, 1 Briton 5-3, 335F1
Govt prepares major offensive; rebels get Christian aid, hamper advance 5-11—5-18, 364A1, B2
Teferi makes conciliatn bid 5-16, 364C2
Special mil unit rptd 5-18, 364G2
Govt envoys in Sudan 5-31, min sees US amb 6-9, 457D2
PLF claims attacks on peasants, govt forces 5-31, 457G2
Last US hostage freed 6-3, 457B3
Peasant march halted, peace progress cited 6-19, 457A2
Betachew, Sisay, 17 others rptd executed 7-13, 523D3
Rpt Libya gives rebels arms 7-15, 531F1
Rebels free French teacher 8-17, UK newsman 9-6, UK family 9-7, 674F2-B3
87 prisoners rptd freed 9-2, 674E2
Somalia blamed re unrest, talks asked 9-12, 1002G1
3 Britons freed 10-2, 1002B2
Fighting, govt casualties rptd 12-26, 1002A2

1977

ESQUIRE Inc.
Esquire (magazine)—*See separate listing*
ESQUIRE (magazine)
Sold to Felker group 8-26, 695G2
ESTES, Elliott M.
On GM engine exchng 4-25, 326C1
E-SYSTEMS Inc.
S Korean paymts rptd 3-10, 233B3
SEC probes vp re Korea 11-29, 915D3
ETEKI Mboumoua, William
On Smith UK plan rejectn 1-25, 49C2
Sees Young, lauds US policy 5-18, 399A2
ETEMAD, Akbar
On Iran A-program 11-10, 926C2

ETHIOPIA—*See also DISARMAMENT—Geneva Committee, NONALIGNED Nations Movement, OAU*
Dergue reorganized 1-7, 62E3
Famine preventn plan rptd 1-15, 62G3
EDU gains claimed 1-22, 62B3
Begemder culture min assassinated 2-2, 98F2
Teferi, 6 Dergue members slain; anti-govt plot chrgd 2-3, 98C2
Mengistu asks support 2-4, sets govt role 2-6, 98G2
Arrests, killings rptd 2-9, 98B3
Mengistu gains sole power 2-11, 238C2
Union ldr killed 2-25, 238D3
Econ rptd stable 2-27, 328F1
Urban squads get arms 3-5, 238E3
Cabt named 3-11, 238E2
Lutheran radio natlized 3-12, 238C3
Mounting unrest detailed 3-22, 238F3
6 offcls executed 4-2, 328E1
Dergue member killed 4-8, 328D1
Peasant drive vs rightists rptd 4-30; Begemder death toll rptd 5-17, 427B2
500 students rptd killed 5-3, 427G1
Rightists yield Begemder 6-14, setback seen 6-16, 486A2
Peasant army paraded 6-25; sent to Eritrea, Ogaden 6-28, 547C3
Rightist exiles granted amnesty 7-1, 562D2
2 offcls assassinated 8-4, 649C1
Royal family escapes 8-5, 649D1
Food shipmts rptd blocked 8-23, 684E3
Mil command restructured 8-29, 684D2
Factional strife detailed 9-9, 716B1
Extra mobilizatn set, total armed forces rptd 9-17, 756C2
Cholera rptd 9-19, 748C1
Dergue members, urban rep assassinated 11-2, 11-13, 875E2
Identity papers set 11-12, 875F2
Dergue vice chrmn executed 11-13, 875C2
Addis Ababa violence rptd; Dergue adviser, union offcl killed 11-13, 12-3, 998F2

Eritrean Developments
Govt deaths rptd 1-4, 20B2
Rebels free UK family 1-5, 20A2
Soldiers flee to Sudan 1-7, 20G1
Fighting continues 1-22; ELF claims 75% control 1-24, 62A3
Sudan backs separatists 1-30, Ethiopia scores 2-2, 98B3
Rebel advances rptd 2-3, 98D3, F3 ★
Saudi, Sudan rebel aid chrgd 2-4, 98A3
Sudan refugee total rptd 2-25, 238C3
Afro-Arab policy statemt scored 3-3—3-5, 170B2
Rebels chrg Cuba aid asked 3-8, 239B1
Cuba, Libya score rebels 3-10, aid sought 3-17, 249B2, E2
Dist capital captured 3-22, 239A1
Rebels capture Tessenei 4-5, set fire to Assab oil tanks 4-20, 328D2
Cuban mil advisers arrive 4-17, 328B1
US, Sudan, 4 W Eur consulates closed 4-23, 327F2
2 ELF hijackers killed 4-26, 328D1
Peasant training by govt rptd 4-30, 427C2
2 factns in unity pact 5-31, 486F1 ★
Rebels rejct USSR federatn offer 6-9, 486G1
Militia dispatched 6-28, 547D3
Rebels advance; Asmara threatened, prisoners freed 7-6—7-18, 562G1
Rebels take Agordat 7-27; encircle Massawa, threaten Asmara 8-25, 684C3
UN offcl links food cutoff 8-23, 684E3
Civiln govt factn rptd pro-independnc 9-9, 716F1

1978

ESSELTE AB
Dymo take over bids 5-15, 5-24, bid OKd, 5-26, 404B1
ESSEX Group Inc.
Sued re price fixing 9-21, 769C1
ESSO Exploration & Production Australia—*See EXXON Corp.*
ESSO Minerals Canada Ltd.—*See IMPERIAL Oil Ltd.*
ESTABA, Luis
Netrnoi TKOs 7-29, 600A2
ESTABROOK, Howard
Dies 7-16, 620G2
ESTATES—*See WILLS & Estates*
ESTEBAN, Enrique
Kidnaped 7-23, freed 9-30, 792C3
ESTES, Billy Sol
Ordrd to pay back taxes 2-10, grand jury probes new chrgs 2-27, 172B3
Pleads guilty to fraud 10-18, 886E3
ESTES, Elliott M.
Sets GM S Africa plant integratn 8-29, 742A3
UAW southn plant pact set 9-11, 699C3, 700B1
ESTONIAN Soviet Socialist Republic—*See USSR—Republics*
ESTRADA, Gen. Jaime
Chile housing min 12-26, 1014E2
ESTRELLA Sadahala, Cesar
Named DR labor min 8-16, 648D2
ESZTERHAS, Joe
F.I.S.T. released 4-26, 619A2
ETCHEBERRY, Alfredo
Barred from Letelier extraditn hearings 9-22, US protests 9-28, 755B3
ETCHISON, Lenore
Loses Sen primary in Neb 5-9, 363F1
ETEMAD, Akbar
Replaced in atomic post 10-22, 816D3
ETHERINGTON, Gary
Named NASL top rookie 8-17, 707G2

ETHIOPIA—*See also DISARMAMENT—Geneva Committee, NONALIGNED Nations Movement, OAU*
Freedom House lists as not free 44A2
Terror campgn vs dissent defended, deaths rptd 2-8, 100B2
Army, militia strength rptd 2-11, 99E3
Right-wing executns, other terrorism rptd 3-23—4-12; executn toll at 477 3-25, 372F3
Workers protest unemploymt 4-5, 258F2
Trade unionist arrest rptd 5-29, 585F1
Locust plague rptd, emergency declared 6-6—6-8, 465F2
Mengistu death tries rptd 6-28, 585D1
Wollo prov drought aid sought 12-20, 1016A3

Eritrean Developments
Facts on 215D3
Sudan border town attacked 1-2, 3F3
Rebels rpt Asmara airport closure 1-3, 3E3
USSR, Cuba troops rptd captured 1-15; mil actn noted 2-2, 100A2
Cuban troops rptd 2-27, 3-16, 215B3
USSR backs Ethiopia US on USSR troop cut vow 3-15, 215E3, F3
Rebels ask Western aid 3-20, 215C3
UK warns USSR re Cuba role 4-5; Sovt, Ethiopia ambs protest 4-6, Cuba scores 4-7, 259E1, F1
Cuba hedges on troop aid 4-21—4-27, backs rebel talks 4-27, 372G2, B3 ★
ELF, EPLF merge commands; troop total, Saudi funding rptd 4-27, 372F2
Govt launches Asmara offensive, Cuban aid rptd; US scores 5-16, 372B2
Iraq warns Sovts vs rebel aid 5-25, 416D1
Mengistu offers rebel amnesty 6-7, 584G2
S Yemen rptd vs mil role 6-7, 584D3
US backs peaceful solutn 6-20, 487G1
Cuba mil role rptd ended 6-21, 7-29, 584A3
ELF ldr rptd in USSR 6-22, 584F2
Tessenei, Mendefra, Massawa retaken 6-23—6-26; rebels deny 6-27, 584E2
S Yemen pres executed 6-26, 499D1
ELF, EPLF offer talks 6-29, 584E2
Ethiopia offensive rptd foiled 7-2, 584D2
Cuba troop reductn rptd 7-6, 584B3
OAU asks Sudan tensn end 7-22, 561F1

1979

ESQUIRE (magazine)
Sale to Tenn firm rptd 5-1, 334D2
ESQUIVEL Valverde, Julio
Seized in El Salvador Emb raid 5-4, escapes 5-7, 370F3, 371A1
ESSER, Otto
Worker codeterminatn upheld 3-2, 172E3
ESTABLISHMENT, The (book)
On best-seller list 11-4, 892A3
ESTATES of the World Inc.
Colo land sale refunds set 5-8, 596A1
ESTERMAN, Laura
Teibele and Her Demon opens 12-16, 1007F2
ESTES, Billie Sol
Indicted 2-22, 156G1
Convicted 7-11, sentncd 8-6, 604E3
ESTES, Elliott M.
Protests diesel exhaust rule 1-10, 16D3
ESTROGEN—*See MEDICINE–Drugs*
ETCHEGARAY, Cardinal Roger
Installed cardinal 6-30, 640D2
ETHAN Allen Inc.
Interco to acquire 8-13, 664B1
ETHER—*See MEDICINE–Drugs*
ETHERIDGE, John R.
Jenrette denies drug role probe 8-8, 650C1

ETHIOPIA—*See also DISARMAMENT–Geneva Committee, NONALIGNED Nations Movement, OAU*
New hominid species claimed 1-18, 137G3
Refugee total rptd 2-22, 201F1
Tigre rebels rpt govt defeat 4-23, 638F2

Eritrean Developments
Cuban troops shifted to Ogaden, Sovt soldiers remain 3-2, 271C1
Army offensive launched 7-14, 638E2
Army offensive rptd failure 7-31, 790F3

1980

ESTABLISHMENT, The (book)
On best-seller list 10-12, 796F3; 12-7, 948F3
ESTES, Billie Sol
'83 parole rptd 1-3, 64G3
'65 Sup Ct case cited 11-12, 882F2
ESTES, Elliott M.
Bars more layoffs 1-14, 35B2
Pledges '85 GM fuel-efficient cars 7-9, 556D3
GM retiremt, replacemt set 9-9, 701G3
ESTES v. Dallas NAACP
Case refused by Sup Ct 1-21, 93E2
ESTONIAN Soviet Socialist Republic—*See UNION of Soviet Socialist Republics–Republics*
ESTRADA, Lt. Col. Carlos
Gueiler assault attempt fails 6-7, 443B3
ESTRADA Kalaw, Eva
Chrgd in Pl plot 10-28, 874D2
ETCHEBASTER, Pierre
Dies 3-24, 279E2

ETHIOPIA—*See also GENEVA Committee, NONALIGNED Nations, OAU*

Eritrean Developments
Rebel Dec '79 battle win, USSR evacuatn aid rptd 1-12, 40C1
Connally cites Sovt threat 3-7, 184E3
Rebels chrg depopulatn effort 3-8, 274D1

1976

Foreign Relations (misc.)—*See also 'Eritrean Developments' above*
Angola MPLA displays S Africa, Portugal mercenaries 1-12, 16G2
Angola MPLA recognized, US pressure denied 1-15, 15G3
UNESCO literacy drive fails 2-4, 85C2
China pact signed 3-22, 311D3
Arms shipmts rptd from US 5-14, Israel 5-18, Turkey, Czech, Yugo 5-19, 364G2
OAU backs re Afars 7-6, 487E3
Mercenary role in Sudan coup chrgd 7-6, 501E3
Olympic withdrawal rptd 7-21, 528B3
Somali terrorists attack hotel 8-4, 581B1
Anti-US stand hit 8-7, 674E2

1977

Agordat capture confrmd 9-15, 716A1
Troop mobilizatn ordrd 9-17, 756C2
Cholera rptd at POW camp 9-19, 748C1
2 rebel factns merge 10-20, 830G1
Assab-Addis Ababa link rptd cut 12-5, 998A2
Rebels besiege Massawa 12-9, Adi Caieh rptd taken 12-18, 998G1

Foreign Relations (misc.)—*See also 'Eritrean' above, 'Ogaden' below*
UN Assemb member 3G3
Sudan chrgs subversn 1-1; alerts border 1-2, recalls amb 1-5, 24A3
Sudan activates Egypt defns pact 1-15—1-16, 62D3
Mil defectns to Sudan rptd 1-22, 62B3
Sudan amb recalled; chrgs exchngd re rebel support 1-25, 62C3
US, UK cultural cntrs stoned 1-28; govt calls rally 1-30, 98F2
Saudi, Sudan EDU ties chrgd 2-4, 98A3
Pro-Sovt policy seen; Mengistu backing rptd, ambs received 2-11, 238A3
US to cut aid re rights abuse 2-24, 142E1
Sudan refugee total rptd 2-25, 238C3
Sudan joins Egypt-Syria cmnd 2-28, 143A3
Forgn min, 3 ambs defect 3-9—3-11; ambs recalled 3-11, 238F2
UK natl killed 3-10, 238E3
US issues rights rpt 3-12, 187B1, G1
Castro visits, backs federatn re Djibouti 3-14—3-16, 249C2
Djibouti independnc set 3-19, 221F2
Red Sea summit scores Israel aid 3-22—3-23, 208E2
US missionary killed 3-27, 328F1
Amnesty Intl accuses 3-28, 238B3
2 US natls ousted 3-30, 327D3
Sudan attacks disputed, mobilizatn urged 4-2, 4-11—4-13, 328B2
Egypt seeks US arms vs Sovt threat 4-5, 245C1
Sovt arms shipmt rptd 4-16, '76 secret pact noted 4-24, 327G3
US, Sudan, other forgn offices closed; US natls' exit ordrd 4-23, 327F2
3 Westn rptrs ousted 4-25, 327B3
US notes weakening ties 4-25, 327E3
US halts arms, all natls out 4-30, 390F3
Mengistu in USSR, signs aid pact 5-4—5-8, 390E3
Young discounts Sovt ties 5-12, 398C3
Somalia scores USSR aid 5-15, 428F2
Nimeiry scores Sovt role 5-17, 450E1
Somalia bars federatn, Djibouti dispute cited 5-18, 428E2
US natl arrested 5-22, freed 7-1, 562E2
Sudan asks US arms 5-24, 400C1
Cuba denies mil advisers 5-24, US rpts arrival, warns Cuba 5-25, 427E1
Mondale, Young on Cuban advisers 5-26, 417A3
Castro reassures US on aid 5-28, denies sending troops 6-9, 456F1, C2
US emb staff cut ordrd; US, Egypt, UK defns offices ordrd shut 5-28; natls in US ordrd home 6-2, 486C1
Djibouti rail line cut 6-1—6-21, Somalia chrgd 6-16, 486D1
US sen scores Cuba troops 6-5, 456A1
Students in USSR score govt 6-13, 486B2
Somalia, Sudan troop role chrgd 6-24, 547D3
Djibouti Repub proclaimed 6-27, 506F2
Sudan infiltratn chrgd 7-2—7-5, 512E1
Horn of Africa alliances shift 7-6, 588F1
Saudi amb defects 7-17, 562E2
Kenya-Somalia border pact set 7-20, 588D1
Israel, Libya, USSR mil aid rptd 7-26, 588B1
Royal family asks Sweden asylum 8-5, 649D1
USSR arms deal rptd 9-1, 684C3
Breaks Somali ties 9-7; Somalia retaliates 9-8, 715B2
Cuba medical aid rptd 9-16, 715F2
US ties rptd improving, newsman's reentry rptd 9-23, 830D1
Royal family arrives US 9-24, 808E1
US bars mil aid, credits 10-19, 815G2; signed 11-1, 834D1
USSR to supply arms 10-19, 829G2
Sweden cancels debts 11-8, 904A1
Cuba mil, medical aides cited 11-17, 896F1
USSR aid vow worries US 11-17, 896B2
Kenya OKs port use 11-30, 998B2
2 US reps see Mengistu 12-13; rpt terror, urge aid vs USSR influence 12-16, 998C2
USSR, Cuba arms, aides rptd hiked 12-16, 998E1

Ogaden Developments
Facts on 587E3
Somalia clashes 2-22, 3-22, 239A1
Somalia territorial disputes rptd 4-16, 328B1
Somali ties worsen 5-18, force data rptd 5-24, 428F2
Somalia troop role chrgd 6-24, 547D3
Militia dispatched 6-28, 547E3
Kenya chrgs Somalia raids 6-30, 512E2
Somali battle rptd 7-14—7-17, 562C2
Fighting intensifies; Somali-backed rebels claim gains, US jets downed 7-18—7-31, 587A3
US arms offer to Somalia scored 7-27, 588A1
Somali amb OKs US, UK arms aid 7-28, 608A2
Somalia rebels plan union talks, rpt troop data 8-1, 608C1

1978

Asmara siege lifted 7-28; Decamere retaken 7-31; advances on Adi Caieh rptd 8-2, 584A2
Smallpox cases rptd 8-2, 636B1
Agordat retaken 8-9; Keren attack fails, army losses rptd 8-18, 8-25, 667C1
Cuba troops rptd 9-11, 922G3
Asmara retaken 11-22, Keren 11-28, 922E3-923A1
EPLF admits Sovt, Cuba role 'decisive' 12-2, 1016C2
Troops recapture Keren, refugees flee 12-11, 1016E2

Foreign Relations (misc.)—*See also 'Eritrean' above, 'Ogaden' below*
USSR aid total cited 1-18, 43A3
Egypt asks for US arms 2-7, 78B1
Cyprus jet hijackers denied landing 2-18, 117A2
Heyerdahl protests entry bar 4-4, 420A2
Amnesty Intl scores 'red terror' 4-12, 372F3
Mengistu in Cuba 4-21—4-27, 372B3 ★
Somalia invasn of Kenya rptd foiled 5-8, 758B2
Saudis note Sovt role 5-13, 358E2
Zambia pres urges pol solutns 5-19, 395A3
Cuba, S Yemen ambs exit rptd 5-25, 5-26; rift denied 5-25, 584C3
Cuba support of oppositn ldr rptd 5-30, 584E3
UN food aid rptd 6-4, 6-9, 465A3
USSR proxy role chrgd 6-7, 423C3
Tanzania defends Cuba role 6-8, 442B1
Zaire pan-Africa force rptd opposed 6-8, 442D1
USSR defends aid 6-22, 487C3
Comecon observer 6-27—6-29, 504G3
Cuba death toll rptd 7-18, 603D3
Castro visits 9-12—9-19, 776G3
UN Assemb member 713D3
USSR signs cooperatn pact 11-20, 922C3
Intl drought aid sought 12-20, 1016A3

Ogaden Developments
Iran warns vs Somalia invasn 1-2, 43G3
USSR airlift rptd halted 1-5, 3C3
Carter scores Sovt role 1-12, 12E1
USSR, Cuba adviser total, Castro visit rptd by US 1-12, 43F3
Somalia backs talks, Ethiopia bars 1-14, 43F2
Somalia chrgs invasn plan 1-16, Ethiopia denies 1-18, 43F3
US bars Somali aid 1-17, Somali scores 1-18, 43A3
USSR, Cuba troops denied 1-18, 43E3
US scored by Ethiopia 1-20, 43G2
Africa natl border problem cited 43B3
OAU warns Iran 1-20, presses mediatn drive 2-9, 100E1
US, allies meet re war, USSR, Cuba role 1-21, 43E2
W Ger amb ousted re Somali loan 1-22, 44A1
Somalia loses ground in counteroffensive 1-22—2-14; total deaths estimated 99C2
US warns USSR 1-25, 43D3
Egypt, Sudan offer Somalia aid; USSR, Cuba role scored 1-26, 2-6, 99F3
Kenya rpts Somali rebel raid 1-26, 137G2
Cuba soldier displayed 1-29; buildup, bombings rptd 2-8, 99E2
Ethiopia denounces Westn, Arab aid to Somali 2-1, 2-14, 100C1
Somalia asks Westn aid 2-4, gets French tanks 2-8, 99G3
Israel discloses Ethiopia aid 2-6, 100A1; Israelis ousted 2-18, 138B1
USSR pledge vs Somalia invasn rptd 2-8, 2-10, 99A3
Cuban troops from Angola rptd 2-10, 165D1
Somalia orders gen mobilizatn 2-11, troop strength compared 99D3
Kenya downs Egypt plane 2-15, Egypt retaliates 2-16, 137D2

1979

Foreign Relations (misc.)—*See also 'Eritrean' above, 'Ogaden' and 'UN' below*
E Ger mil aid rptd 5-23, 406G2
Cuba troop cuts, USSR adviser totals rptd 8-3; Mengistu lauds mil aid 8-23, 8-3, 791B1
Army rptd Africa's largest 9-4, 825B3
Cuba troop total rptd 9-12, 673E2
Cuba rptd training children 12-4, 981B2, C2

Ogaden Developments
Civilian reprisals rptd, refugees flee to Somalia 1-14, 271D1
Somalia hints better USSR ties 1-21, 85G3
Somalia chrgs air attacks 2-7, 193B2
Cuban troop transfer rptd 3-2, 271D1
Rebels rpt govt defeat 4-23, 638F2
Rebels rpt govt ambush 8-31–9-2, 791A1
Somalia refugee total rptd 9-21, 791B1

UN Policy & Developments
Membership listed 695G2

U.S. Relations
US issues rights rpt 2-10, 107E2
Israel says US 'lost' 9-18, 694B1

1980

Foreign Relations (misc.)—*See also 'Eritrean Developments' above, 'Ogaden Developments', 'UN Policy' below*
Sovt-Cuba ties cited by Reagan 2-29, 207B3
USSR combat copters sent 6-13, 509B2
W Ger pol asylum rules rptd tightened 7-31, 581E2, F2
Sovt arms stockpiles rptdly sent to Iran 10-6, 757C1

Ogaden Developments
Fighting intensified 3-18, 274A1
Somali refugee problem noted 4-6, 274B1
USSR combat copters sent 6-13, 509C2
Somalia mil convoy ambushed, 1300 rptd killed 8-8, 653D3
US, Somalia sign mil base pact 8-21, 645C3
Somali invasn chrgd 8-27, denied 8-28; US rptrs shown bodies 8-30, 661D2
US House subcom scores Somali mil pact 8-28, 661E3
Mengistu scores US-Somali mil pact 9-12, 735G3-736B1
US House subcom conditionally OKs Somali pact 9-30, 735D3
Somali land claims end asked, arms shipmt ban urged 12-4, 933E1
Castro admits Cuban troop role 12-17, 12-20, 993B1

Sports
Moscow Olympic results 7-20—8-3; Yifter wins 'distance double' 7-27, 8-1, 588B3, 589D1, 624B1-E1

UN Policy & Developments
Afghan resolutns opposed 1-14, 25G1; 2-14, 123E3

U.S. Relations
Reagan 'basic speech' cites Sovt-Cuban ties 2-29, 207B3
US reps on Somali refugee problem 4-6, 274C1
US amb expelled; Ethiopia $34.5 mln debt cited 7-29, 661G2
Chem weapons use suspected 8-7, 628D3
US House subcom scores Somali mil pact 8-28, 661E3
Mengistu scores Somali mil pact 9-12, 735G3
US House subcom OKs Somali mil sales 9-30, 735D3
Muskie warns of Reagan's 'endless' wars 10-11, 776B3

1976

ETZIONI, Moshe
2 Arabs deported 3-27, 227D2
EUCHARISTIC Congress, International—*See ROMAN Catholic Church*
EUGENE (Ore.) Register-Guard, The (newspaper)
Ariz crime probed 10-2, 849D2
EURATOM—*See EUROPEAN Community*
EUROPE—*See also COMMUNISM, International; COMMUNIST Countries; specific country, organization names*
'66 UN rights covenant effected 1-4, 36E3
Socialists meet in Denmark 1-18—1-19, 48F2
Freedom House survey rptd 1-19, 20E2
Equatorial Guinea exiles rptd 1-24, 62B2
Southn socialists meet in Paris 1-24—1-25, 120B1
Independent Program Group meets 2-2, 2-9, 297B3
UNECE energy rpt issued 2-10, 164G1
Austria lauds detente 3-12, 380E2
Socialists meet in Portugal 3-13—3-14, 222D3
ILO rpts '75 jobless total up 3-13, 297E3
Liberals meet in W Ger 3-26—3-27, 260C3
'75 Sovt trade rptd 5-5, 340B3
France urges US back joint Africa aid 5-17—5-18, 372A2
Soc dems meet 5-23—5-25, 449E2-C3
French dispute defns strategy 6-1—6-3, 417B3
E Eur ambs snub Fraser in China 6-20, 481C1
Cunhal vs Portugal ties with capitalists 8-5, 774F2
E Eur silent on Mao death 9-9, 658A1
Portugal seeks more W Eur aid 9-9, 774D1
China scores West re 3d World 'oppressn' 10-5, 760A1

1977

Somalia rebels, Ethiopia trade massacre chrgs 8-1, 608D1
OAU mediatn asked 8-2; com meets, Somalia quits talks 8-5—8-9, 608D1
Ethiopia admits Somalia rebel gains 8-4; casualties, equipmt losses rptd 8-6, 608A1
USSR rptdly urges Somalia cease-fire 8-4, 608G1
Djibouti econ trouble seen 8-8, 608F1
Somalia warns vs forgn troop role 8-10, 608E1
Westn rptrs tour, see Somali PWs 8-13—8-14, 648B3
USSR chrgs Somalia invasn, backs Ethiopia 8-14, 8-16; Somalia scores 8-19, 648F3
Somalia chrgs aid raids 8-15, 648C3
Major Diredawa battle, map 8-16—8-19, 648G2, D3
China arms aid offer to Somalia rptd 8-16, 649B1
Somalia guides Westn rptrs 8-20—8-24, 684D2
Ethiopia calls gen mobilizatn 8-21, 648C3
E Ger presence rptd 8-21, 684F3
Mengistu asks gen mobilizatn 8-24, 684C2
Somali ldr in USSR 8-29—8-31, 684A3
US, France, UK cancel Somalia arms sales, Arab offers rptd 8-31—9-2, 684F2
Arab League shuns Somali aid request 9-4, 685F1
Jijiga attackers beaten back 9-6, 684G1
Ethiopia breaks ties 9-7; Somalia retaliates 9-8, 715B2
Somalia vs Sovt arms halt 9-7, 715B3
Kenya offers Ethiopia aid 9-9, 715G2
Forgn rptrs see Diredawa; shown Somali arms 9-14, 714C2
Somalia gets Saudi aid offer, scores Ethiopia 9-14, 715A3
Troop mobilizatn ordrd 9-17, 756C2
Jijiga fall to rebels rptd 9-18, 715F1
Ethiopia scores UN, OAU, US; denies Cuba troop role 9-18, 715D2
Somalia chrg of US aid deceptn rptd, US denies 9-19, 715C3
Somali offcl backs truce 9-20, rebels disavow 9-24, 756E2
Rebels cut refinery access 9-21, oil shipmts continue 9-26, 756D2
Marda Pass rebel buildup 9-23, Harar clashes rptd 9-25, 756A2
Rptrs tour Jijiga 9-27, rpt rebels take Marda Pass 9-29, 756G1, B2
Brezhnev vs rebel backing 9-28; USSR cuts Somalia arms 10-19, 829G2
Jijiga mutiny confrmd 10-9, Mengistu morale trip rptd 10-13, 875B2
Kenya-Somalia ties worsen 10-15—10-20, 830A2
Ethiopia offensive halts Somalis 10-31, 875G1
US sees increased Cuba role 11-4, 11-14; Cuba denies troop chrg 11-5, 875E1
Somalia ousts USSR aides, breaks Cuba ties 11-13, 875A1
Ethiopia holds Harar 11-23—11-28, 998C1
Somalia chrgs Ethiopia air attacks 12-10, 12-28, 998F1
Mengistu bars Somalia invasn 12-13, 998E2
Carter, Shah seek end to conflict 12-31, 1001A1
ETNIER, David A.
Endangered fish halts dam constructn 1-31, 95B3
EUBANK, Judge Luther
Orders record back pay in bias suit 10-11, 819B1
EUROCOMMUNISM—*See COMMUNISM and Communist Countries*
EUROCOMMUNISM and the State (book)
USSR scores 6-23, 507G1
EUROFER (EC steel producer group)—*See EUROPEAN Community*
EUROGAS
Union Bank dir chrgd with fraud 8-15, 658D1
EUROPE—*See also specific country, organization names; also COMMUNISM and Communist Countries*
14-natns set sulphur-dioxide watch 1-19, 109F2
Socialst ldrs meet 1-29—1-30, 82D3
Mid-'75 populatn rptd 1-30, 123G2
Soclst ldrs at Frelimo cong 2-3—2-7, 137D1
W Eur oil import rise seen 4-18, 294E1
Gerovital use cited 5-20, 508B3
Maputo UN conf reps bar S Africa, Rhodesia embargo 5-21, 399F2
Australia trade decline rptd 6-22, 504F2
English Channel boundary setld 7-18, 625C1
West vs UN desert fund 9-9, 770F1
S Korea textile import cuts seen 10-5, 804D3
W Eur heroin traffic conf 10-17—10-21, 971B3
'76 oil-use rise rptd 11-24, 999C1

1978

US hikes USSR, Cuba troop estimates 2-17, 2-24; warns USSR vs interventn 2-25, USSR defends aid 2-26, 137A1
US delegatn visits 2-17—2-18; Carter warns vs Somalia invasn 2-17, Mengistu vow rptd 2-21, 137G1-A2
Iran breaks Kenya ties 2-18, 137F2
Somali pres sees Italy CP rep, denies USSR peace proposal 2-20—2-22; scores Ethiopia border, US exit call 2-21, 138A1
US links SALT delay, USSR role 3-1; USSR scores 3-2, 178F3
Carter warns USSR 3-2, 140E2
Cuban troops acknowledged 3-2, press account rptd 3-15, 178D3
Ethiopia advances, recaptures Jijiga 3-5—3-13; Djibouti RR reopened 3-12, 178B3
US, Yugo back USSR, Cuba exit 3-7—3-9, 194A1
Rebels vow to continue struggle 3-8, 178D3
Somalia orders troop exit, sets terms 3-9; Ethiopia presents counter-demands 3-10, 178D2, A3
US lauds Somali exit 3-9; rpts USSR troop cuts, cease-fire plan 3-10, 178F2
Somalia: exit complete 3-15; army seen weakened 3-17, 215G2
US envoy in Somalia 3-18—3-23, 215D2
Ethiopia claims total control 3-24, 215B3
US use of Israel Sinai base for USSR surveillnc rptd 3-26; US denies 3-27, 215F1
Arab League urges USSR, Cuba exit, vows aid 3-29, 215D1
Kenya gets US planes 3-31, 289F2
Cuban troops, USSR advisers estimated 3-31, 372D2
Somalia chrgs jet attack 3-31, 372E3
UK scores USSR, Cuba role 4-5; USSR, Ethiopia ambs protest 4-6, Cuba scores 4-7, 259E1
Somali army revolt crushed 4-9, 269F1
Somali secessionists rpt heavy fighting 4-15, defectn of prov offcl 4-24, 372D3
Mengistu warns Somalia vs rebel support 5-12, 372B3
Cuban troops rptd moving north 5-16, 372D2
S Yemen troop total rptd 6-7, 584D3
Somali troops rptdly reinvade, US doubts 6-7, 584F3
US backs talks 6-20, 487G1
Somalia rpts towns bombed 6-22—6-25, 7-13, 585D1
Rebels claim casualties, govt names study comm 7-3, 585B1
OAU asks border solutn 7-22, 561E1
Somalia dispute at nonaligned conf 7-25—7-30, 583B3
Rebel fighting rptd 12-27, 1016G2
U.S. Relations—*See also 'Eritrea' and 'Ogaden' above*
Ethiopia amb to US resigns, asks US residence 1-29, 137B2
US info leaks cited in Viet spy chrgs 1-31, 68E3
Egypt asks for US arms 2-7, 78B1
US rights rpt released 2-9, 101E3
US delegatn visits, ties discussed 2-17—2-18; non-mil equipmt deliveries OKd 2-22, 137G1-C2
Rebel aid plan rptd 5-24, 383A2, 443D1
US food aid rptd 6-4, 465A3
Charter chrgs USSR proxy role 6-7, 423C3
ETHIOPIAN Airlines, S. C.
Asmara airport rptd closed 1-3, 3E3
ETTING, Ruth
Dies 9-24, 778B1
EUBIE (play)
Opens 9-20, 1031E1
E.U.E.-Screen Gems—*See COLUMBIA Pictures Industries Inc.*
EUGENE, Ore.—*See OREGON*
EURATOM—*See EUROPEAN Community*
EUREKA, Calif.—*See CALIFORNIA*
EUROCOMMUNISM—*See COMMUNISM and Communist Countries*
EUROPE—*See also country, organization names (e.g., EC, NATO); also COMMUNISM and Communist Countries*
Begin cites re Egypt talks breakdown 1-23, 41F2
Begin sees Jewish ldrs 2-8, 78D1
Sadat 6 natn tour, seeks backing 2-9—2-13, 98C2-C3
'77 oil output rptd up 2-14, 158D3
Fascists meet in Antwerp 3-4—3-5, 238D3
Bank loans to Brazil rptd 3-10, 311A2
Workers protest unemploymt 4-5, 258F2
Israel: terrorists train in Leb 4-7, 256D3
Conservative parties form group 4-24, 424B3
Iran shah's visit postponed 5-11, 352F3
Waste combustn as energy source rptd 5-11, 367D1
Trilateral Comm rpt scores energy inactn 6-13, 450B2
China backs Spain policy 6-18, 576E2
ILO rpts '77 jobless rise 7-28, 677D1
Chile trade boycott set by forgn unions 11-24, 1014G1
Japan affirms ties 11-28, 912D3
OPEC oil price hike impact assessed 12-18, 978D1

1979

ETRA, Donald
Seeks Carter death plot chrgs dismissed 5-29, 404C1
ETTINGHAUSEN, Richard
Dies 4-2, 356D3
EULESS, Tex.—*See TEXAS*
EURATOM—*See EUROPEAN Community*
EUROCOMMUNISM—*See COMMUNISM and Communist Countries*
EURODIF (Belgium, France, Iran, Italy)
France freezes Iranian stake 10-24, 976E2
EUROPE—*See also country, organization names (e.g., EC, NATO); also COMMUNISM and Communist Countries*
Iran oil cutoff impact assessed 2-13, 2-20, 126E2-A3
Iran Air cuts svc 2-25, 144E3
Swiss animal rabies vaccine experimt rptd 2-28, 196E1
UN sees higher W Eur econ growth, notes '78 inflatn, paymts 3-13, 180A2
Baptism rites agrmt reached 3-31, 375F2
30-natn A-conf opens 5-7, 373F3-374C1
African natns back closer ties 5-21–5-22, 398B3
Zimbabwe meat exports cited 7-8, 547C1
China backs closer ties 9-22, 751C2; premr tours 10-15—11-6, 789E2, 853D3-854F2
W Eur heroin use rptd up 11-11, 972C3
Amnesty Intl reviews '79 rights 12-9, 980B2

1980

ETHOLOGY
Kin recognitn study rptd 6-19, 715C2
ETHYL Corp.
La chem-dump suit names 7-15, 558G3
ETUDE de Nu (Study of a Nude) (painting)
Sold for record sum 5-13, 472G1
EUGENE—*See OREGON*
EUGENE, Gregoire
Arrested 11-28, 922G2
In US exile 12-5, 943A1
EURATOM—*See EUROPEAN Community*
EUROCHAMP, M/V (Greek freighter)
Cuban gunboat incident rptd 5-1, 326F1
EURODIF (Belgium, France, Iran, Italy)
France freezes Citibank funds 1-16, 48F1
Italy plans share cut 5-2, 409D1
EUROPE—*See also country, organization names*
Canada exports up in '79 2-2, 96B2
Space industry research rptd 2-16, 160G2, A3
Australia wool strike setld 3-21, 229G2
Zaire debt rescheduled 4-23, 356G1
OPEC sets pricing plan 5-7—5-8, 364C3
Libyan students occupy embs 5-10, 373A3
'79 terrorism rptd 5-11, 365E3
Tech sales to USSR cited 5-22, 431A1
Oil glut cuts prices 7-4—8-12, 628F1-B2
Giscard stresses role 7-7, 7-9, 520G3
Schmidt backs world role 7-11, 540B1
Canada immigratn records rptd found 8-20, 651F1-C2
Nicaragua debt rescheduled 9-5, 689G2-A3
World Bank '80 loans rptd 9-22, 720F1
Canada Aug sales drop rtpd 10-4, 788A2
E-W Eur conf asked by Warsaw Pact 10-19—10-20, 800E2
Eastern Europe—*See COMMUNISM and Communist Countries*

1976

Air quality improvemt rptd 10-16, 934D1
EEC-Rumania textile pact rptd 11-12, 907F2
'75 E Eur trade deficit rptd 11-18, 977D1
W Eur abstains re UNESCO res vs Israel 11-22, 879A1
US rpts Portugal loan plan 11-23, 966C3
'75 oil imports down 12-6, 936B1, A2
Italy denies E Eur benefit from Libya Fiat deal 12-10, 965E1
Schmidt for eased E Eur tensn 12-16, 968C3
Lebanon war refugees fled to 974F1
E Eur hails Sovt-Chile prisoner exchng 12-18, 955D3
Albania bars Westn, Sovt bloc pacts 12-30, 1012C2

Force Reduction Talks, Mutual and Balanced (MBFR)
Sovt bloc rejects NATO bid 1-30, offers new plan 2-19; Brezhnev cites 2-24, 194E1 *
NATO mins cite 5-21, 353F1
US Dem platform text cites 6-15, 477A3
Sovt rpts troop levels 7-10, 9th sessn ends 7-21, 761B1-A2
US GOP platform text cites 8-18, 609F1
10th sessn 9-10, 761C1
Recesses, troop buildup cited 12-16, 978A2

Security and Cooperation in Europe, Conference on (CSCE) (Helsinki)
USSR to allow more Westn dailies 1-21, 76A3
French adm ousted re criticism 1-22, 139F1
Nixon scores '75 conf 2-22, 189D3
Reagan scores Helsinki pact 3-31, 232D3
USSR chrgs US violatn 4-18, US denies 4-19, 277B1
Sovt dissidents to monitor USSR compliance 5-13, 408F1
US Cong clears monitoring panel 5-21, 392D3; signed 6-3, 982E1
USSR chrgs US violatns 5-25—5-38, 407G3
US Dem platform text cites 6-15, 477C3
US researcher chrgs Sovt visa violatn 7-3, 540B3
Eur Parlt chrgs Sovt rights violatn 7-9, 540B3
US GOP conv platform plank OKd 8-18, 600F3
US GOP platform text cites 8-18, 608D3, 610G2
China denounces agrmt 10-5, 760A1
Carter, Ford debate 10-6, 741A3
Warsaw natns bar US fact-finders 11-5—11-21, 880F1
Warsaw Pact asks A-weapon 1st use ban 11-27, 896C3
US issues progress rpts 12-2, 12-8, 934E1
Bukovsky scores '75 pact 12-19, 955A3

Soviet Relations—*See other appropriate subheads in this section*

U.S. Relations—*See also other appropriate subheads in this section*
'70 CIA media manipulatn rptd 1-16, 92C3
US defns needs outlined 1-27, 68D2
Kissinger backs Sovt confrontatn 1-29, 88F3
Marine Corps reorganizatn urged 2-2, 95C3, E3
Lockheed payoffs rptd 2-4, 2-6, 130E2, D3, 131C1
Bilderberg Conf canceled 3-5, 254C3
Kissinger scores US critics 3-11, 197G3

1977

Force Reduction Talks, Mutual and Balanced (MBFR)
US on NATO defens cuts 1-24, 69E2
Schmidt, Carter OK new initiatives 7-14, 566B2
Carter Miss town mtg topic 7-21, 550B3
Schmidt asks NATO, Warsaw Pact equality; vs natl ceilings 11-22, 926B2
Talks adjourn; Westn offers, deadlock rptd 12-15, 996B3

Helsinki Conference—*See 'Security and Cooperation in Europe' below*

Monetary Developments—*See under 'M'*

Security and Cooperation in Europe, Conference on (CSCE) (Helsinki Agreement) (Austria, Belgium, Bulgaria, Canada, Cyprus, Czechoslovakia, Denmark, East Germany, Finland, France, Great Britain, Greece, Hungary, Iceland, Ireland, Italy, Liechtenstein, Luxembourg, Malta, Monaco, Netherlands, Norway, Poland, Portugal, Rumania, San Marino, Spain, Sweden, Switzerland, Turkey, U.S., USSR, Vatican, West Germany, Yugoslavia)
US bars Sovt editor 1-12, 22D1
US chrgs Czech violatns 1-26, 82E2
UK warns Czech 2-2, 115A1
USSR arrests unoffcl monitors 2-5, 2-10, 117B1; US sees crackdown 2-14, 101C2
Rumanians issue rights plea 2-8, 137E1
Spain, USSR renew ties 2-9, 242D2
Yugo scores dissident coverage 2-13, 139G2
Sovt bloc dissident activities continue 2-20—4-27, 314D1
Sovt dissident urges US stand 2-23, 142C3
Eurocommunists ask 'full applicatn' 3-3, 242G3
US to end travel bans 3-9, 172G3
Sovt unionists denied US visas 4-16, 306B3
Irish-UK torture case hearings 4-19—4-22, 315E3
NATO warns USSR on Berlin 5-9, 358D2
Sovt dissident treason chrgd 6-1, 436E1
US chrgs Sovt bloc non-compliance 6-6, USSR scores Carter 6-8, 473C1
Croats raid Yugo UN missn 6-14, 497D2
Belgrade conf opens 6-15, 473A1
US Cong backs rights talks 6-15, 501C1
USSR to get Indian chrgs vs US 6-17, 473B2
Yugo ousts protesters 6-28, 7-7, 606D2
W Eur observers at USSR mil exercises 7-11, 551D1
Carter sees Schmidt, eases Belgrade conf rights stand 7-13, 566E2
US OKs Italy CP press bur 7-20, 581G2
Belgrade conf ends, Helsinki conf agenda set 8-5, 606B1
US panel scores Sovt bloc re rights 8-5, 606B2
Sovt dissident emigratn rptd 8-8, 606G2
US eases visa curb 8-17, 667E2
Sovts arrest pact monitors 8-24, 684C1
B Graham in Hungary 9-3—9-14, 732D1
Sovt envoy at NATO war games 9-13, 700C1
Formal review conf opens 10-4, 752G1
Formal review conf debates rights, trade, other issues; sets '78 agenda, adjourns 10-6—12-22, 997F1
Czech dissident trial scored 10-18, 812G1
Sakharov invitatn tampering chrgd 12-1, 955B3

Soviet Relations—*See also other appropriate subheads in this section*
E Eur-OPEC oil cartel rptd sought 1-24, 108F1
USSR sub exercise rptd 7-28, 591E1
US focused mil buildup need seen 9-26, 858B1, E1

U.S. Relations—*See also other appropriate subheads in this section*
Mondale visit announced 1-8, 14E2
Ford State of Union message 1-12, 13F3
Rumsfeld urges conventional force buildup 1-18, 39A2
Mondale in W Eur 1-23—1-29, 69A1
Carter budget revisns 2-22, 125C1
US sets new air fares 3-9, 325B1
US rights rpts exclude W Eur 3-12, 186D3
Carter trade policy pressure rptd 3-23, 249A1

1978

Force Reduction Talks, Mutual and Balanced (MBFR)
France proposes disarmament talks reorganizatn 1-25, 61A3
Neutron bomb talks urged by Dutch 2-23, 140A3
NATO offers concessns, demands troop parity 4-19; USSR agrees to common troop ceiling 6-7; ground force total disputed 6-15, 488E1
Brezhnev offers mutual force cuts 5-2, in W Ger 5-4—5-7, 417B1
Warsaw proposes troop replacemt plan, W Ger force hike OKd 6-22, 488C2
USSR asks West OK proposal 6-25, 488C3
Carter optimistic 6-26, 491F1
Talks end, troop data conflict cited 10-25, 913C3
Warsaw Pact summit topic 11-22—11-23, 913D2

Helsinki Conference—*See 'Security and Cooperation in Europe' below*

Monetary Developments—*See MONETARY Developments, International*

Security and Cooperation in Europe, Conference on (CSCE) (Helsinki Agreement) (Austria, Belgium, Bulgaria, Canada, Cyprus, Czechoslovakia, Denmark, East Germany, Finland, France, Great Britain, Greece, Hungary, Iceland, Ireland, Italy, Liechtenstein, Luxembourg, Malta, Monaco, Netherlands, Norway, Poland, Portugal, Rumania, San Marino, Spain, Sweden, Switzerland, Turkey, U.S., USSR, Vatican, West Germany, Yugoslavia)
Formal review conf debates rights, Medit conf, adopts statemt 1-17—3-8; conf ends 3-9, 179C1
France asks Eur disarmamt com 1-25, 61G2
US scores Rostropovich citizenship rescissn 3-16, 179D3
USSR monitors rptd sentncd 3-30, 275B3
USSR sentences Orlov, US scores 5-18, 359B3
USSR defends Orlov sentnc 5-18, 5-21; West protests 5-19—5-30, 401C1
USSR chrgs UK violatns 5-18, 401C2
USSR sentences 2 Georgian monitors 5-19, 401D2
20 USSR monitors rptd jailed 6-12, 504A1
Yugo chrgs Bulgaria violated '75 agrmt 6-23, 531F1
USSR holds maneuvers, Westn observers barred 7-3—7-7, 648D3
Lithuanian monitor sentncd 7-13, 541E2
San Marino asks rights agrmt enforced 7-18, 575B2
Czech dissident plea rptd 11-8, 885D2
USSR monitors rptd sentncd 12-5, 947F1

Soviet Relations—*See also other appropriate subheads in this section; also ARMAMENTS—Neutron Bomb; COMMUNISM and Communist Countries*
US sees Sovt edge in conventional warfare 1-6, 5B3
SS-20 seen greater threat than neutron bomb by UK 2-21, 140F1
US chrgs USSR mil buildup 3-17, 202E1
Carter notes Sovt tank strength 4-25, 307B2
SS-20 deploymt scored by US 5-24, 421D1
Giscard scores conv arms threat 5-25, 421F2
Brzezinski scores mil buildup 5-28, 399D1
China sees Sovt threat 5-29, 422A1
Brezhnev lauds ties 6-25, 488C3
Kosygin compares indus growth 7-5, 518D3
China scores Sovt hegemony, seeks to counter role 8-16—8-29, 674G2-675A3
Sovt bloc shipping rate-cutting scored 9-11, 9-13, cargo share rptd 9-17, 820F2-C3
France-USSR ties seen vital re detente 10-29, 830G3
Gromyko: USSR, France discussed Eur disarmamt 10-29, 831A1
E-W balance rptd threatened by Finnish-Sovt mil link 11-15, 894D2

U.S. Relations—*See also other appropriate subheads in this section; also ARMAMENTS—Neutron Bomb*
Carter vows US commitmt 1-4, 2E1
US sees Sovt edge in conventional warfare 1-6, 5B3
Carter State of Union Message 1-19, 31B2
Carter chrgs USSR mil buildup 3-17, 202E1

1979

Force Reduction Talks, Mutual and Balanced (MBFR)
SALT II communique backs talks 6-18, 457E3
Vance warns US vs SALT rejectn 7-10, 510D2
NATO vs USSR proposed E Ger cuts 10-7, 761E3
NATO offers troop reductn 12-14, 959B2

Security and Cooperation in Europe, Conference on (CSCE) (Helsinki Agreement) (Austria, Belgium, Bulgaria, Canada, Cyprus, Czechoslovakia, Denmark, East Germany, Finland, France, Great Britain, Greece, Hungary, Iceland, Ireland, Italy, Liechtenstein, Luxembourg, Malta, Monaco, Netherlands, Norway, Poland, Portugal, Rumania, San Marino, Spain, Sweden, Switzerland, Turkey, U.S., USSR, Vatican, West Germany, Yugoslavia)
SALT II communique backs results 6-18, 458E1
USSR bars monitor 8-23, 689G3
USSR offers mil maneuvers cut 10-6, 761E1
US com assesses US compliance 11-7, 980G3
USSR arrests monitor 12-7, 939F1

Soviet Relations—*See also other appropriate subheads in this section*
US mil ex-ldrs warn of Sovt challenge 1-12, 15C1
US A-target chng urged 1-13, 52E3
SALT scored by US ex-mil ldr 4-11, 295F1
USSR bars conventnal arms cut talks 4-28, 323C3
USSR hints E-W cable link 6-27, 497D2

U.S. Relations—*See also other appropriate subheads in this section*
AMC, Renault sign sales pact 1-10, 131F2
US mil ex-ldrs warn of Sovt challenge 1-12, 15C1
US A-target chng urged 1-13, 52E3
Carter budget proposals 1-22, 42F1
US Jan trade surplus rptd 2-28, 159C2
US Feb trade surplus rptd 3-28, 252A3
SALT scored by US ex-mil ldr 4-11, 295F1
US Mar trade surplus rptd 4-27, 325D2

1980

U.S. Relations
US bank deposits rptd down 1-18, 48A2
Persian Gulf defense steps seen 1-29, 65B1
US Dec '79 trade surplus rptd 1-29, 77E2
USSR seen seeking split 2-4, 84F3
US issues rights rpt 2-5, 87A3
US Jan trade surplus rptd 2-28, 167F3
Connally backs troops in 'basic speech' 3-7, 184G3
US urges sanctns vs USSR 3-12, 205E1, F1
Air fare hikes OKd by CAB 3-12, 346E2

1976

Reagan scores E Eur policy 3-31; Kissinger, Ford rebut 4-1, 4-2, 232G2, 233B1, 245B2
Kissinger warns vs CP govts 4-7, 4-13, 259A3
Eastern bloc, Italy score US critics 4-9—4-18, 276E3
Giscard on joint Africa aid, free Eur govts 5-17—5-18, 372A2
US Cong backs IDB entries 5-20, 392B3
US Dem platform text cites ties, Sovt forces, CPs in govts 6-15, 476C2, 477B1, E2, 478B1, E1
Carter urges partnership 6-23, 451F2, A3, E3
Kissinger urges W Eur unity, on E-W relations, E Eur independnc 6-25, 466D1
US inefficiency in Eur rptd 7-8, 760F2
W Ger vs US troop cuts 7-17, 530G2
Ikle scores A-aid 7-23, 739G2
US GOP conv platform cites E Eur-Sovt ties, US ties 8-18, 600F3, 609D1, 610A3, 612B1
Ford pres acceptance speech cites ties 8-19, 612B1
US cites Sovt E Eur MIRV buildup 8-31, 739D1
Ford, Carter debate 10-6, 740E2, E3, 741B3
Ford debate 'blunder' on E Eur scored by Carter, Mondale, ethnic groups 10-7—10-10; Ford clarifies, admits error 10-12, 10-14, 761E3, 762A1-763F1, A3
Dole, Mondale debate Ford E Eur statemt 10-15, 783E3
Ford scores Carter 10-26, 803B1
Rpt hits NATO sales to USSR 11-4, 880B1
Carter pollster minimizes Ford debate error 11-11, 845E2
US-Rumania econ pact 11-21, 907C2
US vows AWACS contracts 933E1
US corp paymts study rptd 12-20, 985C2
Ford rejcts air route chngs 12-28, 992A2

EUROPE, Council of (Austria, Belgium, Cyprus, Denmark, France, Great Britain, Iceland, Ireland, Italy, Luxembourg, Malta, Netherlands, Norway, Sweden, Switzerland, Turkey, West Germany)
Ulster rights study scores UK, full disclosure urged 2-11—2-12, 147C1
Ulster rights study issued 9-2, 675E1-F2
Admits Portugal 9-22, 733F2
Support of US rptr in UK cited 11-25, 946D3

EUROPE, Economic Commission for—*See under UNITED Nations*

EUROPEAN-American Banking Corp. European-American Bank & Trust Co. (N.Y.)
Franklin Natl '74 failure cited 1-12, 111E1
2 ex-Franklin offcls plead guilty 1-20, 78F2
Hamilton Natl fails 2-16, 166F3
6 ex-Franklin offcls sentncd 3-9, 271B2
House com scores US comptroller re Franklin collapse 10-6, 940B2

EUROPEAN Atomic Energy Community (Euratom)—*See EUROPEAN Community*

EUROPEAN Coal & Steel Community—*See EUROPEAN Community*

EUROPEAN Commission on Human Rights—*See EUROPE, Council of*

1977

Investmt sought by US states 4-11, 385B3
US A-fuel export delays rptd 4-14, 268C2
Bilderberg conf 4-21—4-24, 359B3
Eastern to lease Airbus 5-24, 441B2
US focused mil buildup need seen 9-26, 858B1, E1
US, Canada OK uranium exports 11-15, 913D1

EUROPE, Council of (Austria, Belgium, Cyprus, Denmark, France, Great Britain, Iceland, Ireland, Italy, Luxembourg, Malta, Netherlands, Norway, Sweden, Switzerland, Turkey, West Germany)
'76 pact vs terrorism cited 9G2
UK MPs urge Daoud protest 1-13, 28A1
Irish torture chrgs vs UK heard 4-19—4-22, 315E2
Cyprus chrgs Turkey rights abuses 9-8, 764G1-A2; rpt shelved, Greece protests 11-3, 946E3

EUROPE, Economic Commission for—*See under UNITED Nations*

EUROPEAN-American Banking Corp. European-American Bank & Trust Co. (N.Y.)
FDIC suit vs Franklin auditors rptd 2-9, 155C3
Franklin Natl takeover cited 3-1, 155C2
Franklin Natl failure cited 3-11, 194F2
Gilpatric interest conflict chrgd 5-24, 407C1
Franklin ex-offcl pleads guilty 6-21, 540G2

1978

US conv force upgrading cited 3-24, 223C3
Carter notes Sovt tank strength 4-25, 307B2
A-tech transfer limit rptd 5-1, 423F1
US '78 arms sales forecast 5-19, 387B1
USSR SS-20 deploymt scored 5-24, 421D1
Brzezinski scores USSR mil buildup 5-28, 399D1
Vance vows A-arms restraints 6-12, 445A2
Brown affirms US mil superiority, notes Sovt troop threat 6-23, 493G2
Citibank sued re tax evasn 7-24, 717B3
Peugeot to buy Chrysler units 8-10, 623C2
Carter vetoes '79 arms authorzn 8-17, 621D1
Pan Am to end svc to 9 cities 9-7, 701F1
US shipping malpractice bill vetoed 11-4, 897G2
Firestone losses cited 11-28, 935B2
Steel plate dumping probed; Natl, Armco chrgs withdrawn 12-28, 1005G3-1006B1

EUROPE, Council of—*See COUNCIL of Europe*

EUROPE, Economic Commission for—*See under UNITED Nations*

EUROPE, Jim
Eubie opens 9-20, 1031E1

EUROPEAN-American Banking Corp.
Franklin bank ex-offcls indicted 7-13, Bordoni pleads guilty to '75 chrgs 9-5, 681B1

European-American Bank & Trust Co (N.Y.)
Sindona ordrd extradited to Italy 5-19, 454B2
Bordoni extradited to US 6-2, arraigned 6-5, 454C2
Societe Gen-FDIC case declined by Sup Ct 10-16, 789F1

EUROPEAN-American Bank & Trust Co.—*See under EUROPEAN-American Banking Corp.*

EUROPEAN Atomic Energy Community (Euratom)—*See EUROPEAN Community*

EUROPEAN Commission on Human Rights—*See COUNCIL of Europe*

1979

GM expansn plans detailed 6-11, 555F1, A3
Carter addresses Cong on SALT II 6-18, 459E2
FDA Laetrile ban upheld by Sup Ct 6-18, 498F2
Carter energy plan assessed 7-16, 534E3
US June trade surplus rptd 7-29, 577B3
US July trade surplus rptd 8-28, 646C3
Nixon on China tie 9-22, 751C2
US Aug trade surplus rptd 9-27, 745E2
Sovt-Cuba troop issue reactn rptd 10-3, 738A1
US Sept trade surplus rptd 10-30, 828B2
US mil heroin use rptd 11-11, 972C3, E3
US Oct trade surplus rptd 11-29 10-4, 922D1
Missn on Iran set, econ moves sought 12-5, 913C2
Vance in W Eur, seeks econ sanctns vs Iran 12-10—12-11, 933B1, B2
Carter reaffirms defns commitment 12-12, 963C1
US Nov trade surplus rptd 12-28, 984G3

EUROPE, Council of—*See COUNCIL of Europe*

EUROPE, Economic Commission for—*See under UNITED Nations*

EUROPEAN-American Banking Corp.

European-American Bank & Trust Co. (N.Y.)
Treas ex-secy discloses Sindona loan 1-9, 205D3
3 Franklin ex-offcls convicted 1-23, 205G2-D3
Sindona, Bordoni indicted 3-19, 205C2
Franklin ex-offcls sentncd 3-26, 3-27, 291E3
Sindona rptd kidnaped 8-6, 635D3
Sindona reappears 10-16, 793F2

EUROPEAN Commission on Human Rights—*See COUNCIL of Europe*

1980

US tank detector system rptd 3-21, 267F1
Olympic coms rejct Moscow boycott 3-22, 259B3
US Feb trade surplus rptd 3-27, 247D3
Steelmakers resume US orders 4-2, 262B3
Iran crisis support asked 4-6, 257D2
US allies withhold support on Iran 4-10, 4-11, plead for hostages 4-12, 281G2, 282E1
Carter presses allies on Iran sanctns 4-13, 281D2
Iran econ, diplomatic sanctns voted 4-22, US lauds 4-23, 298C1, D2
US Mar trade surplus rptd 4-29, 329A1
CIA rpts '79 terrorism 5-11, 365E3
Air fare hikes OKd by CAB 5-15, 516E1
3 socialists visit Iran re hostages 5-25—5-26, 394C1
US Apr trade surplus rptd 5-28, 401D1
Sovt purchase of US soy meal rptd 6-2, 431B1
Army cuts overseas duty time 6-6, 458A3
UAW asks auto import curbs, '75-79 Japan trade data cited 6-12, 457A3
Carter visits 6-19—6-26, backs Eur-Sovt ties 6-23, 473C1-475C1
US May trade surplus rptd 6-27, 492A3
Anderson tours 7-13—7-18, scores Reagan 7-20, 549F3
US GOP platform adopted; text 7-15, 536G1, D2
Reagan pres nominatn acceptance speech 7-17, 533B1
US June trade surplus rptd 7-29, 574A3
US July trade surplus rptd 8-27, 666B2
Anderson platform offered 8-30, 665G1
US Army sgts recalled 9-5, combat divsn drain cited 9-8, 683D3
US record oil inventories rptd 9-5, Admn assured vs shortfall 10-3, 785E3
US Aug trade surplus rptd 9-26, 741A2
US Sept trade surplus rptd 10-29, 824G1
US Oct trade surplus rptd 11-28, 916A2
US Nov trade surplus rptd 12-30, 984A2

EUROPE, Council of—*See COUNCIL of Europe*

EUROPEAN-American Banking Corp. European-American Bank & Trust Co. (N.Y.)
Franklin Natl fraud appeals refused by Sup Ct 2-19, 131A1; 3-17, 228G1
Sindona convicted 3-27, 237D1
Sindona fraud suit ruling refused by Sup Ct 4-21, 344A2
Bordoni sentenced 4-23, 415B1

EUROPEAN Channel Tunnel Group
Channel plan rptd 3-4, 193F3

EUROPEAN COMMUNITY

1976

EUROPEAN Community (EC) (including EEC, ESCE, Euratom) (Belgium, Denmark, France, Great Britain, Ireland, Italy, Luxembourg, Netherlands, West Germany)
Tindemans rpts on Europn unity, '2-tier' econ dvpt urged 1-7; Ortoli scores 1-8, 20C1
New French-Italian wine dispute 1-7—2-5, 138B3-139A1
UNESCO conv postponed 1-15, 36A3
Rpt French Gaullist for Eur defns group 1-15, 126D2
France scores dairy, beef policies 1-16, 139B1
Potato import duties lifted 1-20; crop shortage, price rise rptd 1-26, 1-29, 84C1
Ban on Spanish talks lifted 1-20, 84D3
ECSC backs minimum steel price scale 1-20, 85A1
Japan curbs steel exports 1-20, 85B1
Jobless rise rptd slowing 1-28, 84E3
Portugal min confs 1-28; aid pledge cited 2-5, 143B1
French socialists score Tindemans rpt 1-29, 119D3
Schmidt defends detente 1-29, 158A1
200-mile fishing zone backed 1-30, 85C1
Argentina beef exports down 80% 2-2, 96C3
40 ACP natns OKd Lome conv 2-3, 164D3
Tindemans rpt debated, '2-tier' concept rejctd 2-5—2-8, 164A1
Italy farm border tax OKd 2-6, 163C3
Bonn urges compulsory border import taxes 2-10, 140E2
At intl econ conf 2-11—2-20, 148B1
Dutch curb potato exports 2-12, 2-16, 141A3
Italy loan set, austerity urged 2-16, 140G3
Ireland loan set 2-16, 157B1 ★
Agri mins open talks 2-16, OK potato export tax 2-17, 164A1

1977

EUROPEAN Community (EC) (including EEC, ESCE, Euratom) (Belgium, Denmark, France, Great Britain, Ireland, Italy, Luxembourg, Netherlands, West Germany)
UK fishing zone in effect 1-1, 21A1
Comm posts distributed 1-7, 74F1
UK '76 car imports rptd 1-8, 45D1
Bonn backs Italy credits 1-18, 64G3
Denmark support drops 1-19, 62C1
Ireland econ study rptd 1-20, 64C2 ★
'77 growth rate forecast 1-28, 74D1
'76 trade deficit rptd 1-31, 74B1
Dec '76 jobless rptd 2-7, 109C2
Fish stock protectn agreed, Ireland sets ship curbs 2-15, 146F2
'76 indl output rptd up 2-22, 146B2
NZ sets UK lamb trading 2-22, 258G1
Jan jobless rate up 2-25, 146E2
Dutch warn on EEC loans 3-14, 269E2
Lawyer mobility OKd 3-23, 269D3
Commodity fund plan backed 3-27, 297E3
UK blocks farm-price rise 3-29, 269A3
PNG Lome Conv entry rptd 3-30, 309A3
Italy loan OKd 4-15, 527D2
Sugar pact talks 4-18—5-27, 458A1
'68 high seas uranium loss confrmd 5-2, 335B2
Jenkins 7-natn summit role disputed 5-7—5-8, 358F1
GATT to probe US ruling on Japan elec duties 5-23, 416C2
'68 uranium loss rptd Israeli plot 5-30, 416C3, F3
N-S talks end, aid plan backed 6-3, 437D2, E2
Belgian Cabt crisis resolved 6-3, 466D1
French Socialists dispute W Ger role 6-17—6-19, 542D3
ASEAN backs ties 6-27—6-29, 537E1
Ldrs meet, defer JET decisn 6-29—6-30, 624G2-A3
Andreotti sees Barre 7-18, 581F2
NZ scores farm import curbs 7-21, 638D2

1978

EUROPEAN Community (EC) (including EEC, ESCE, Euratom) (Belgium, Denmark, France, Great Britain, Ireland, Italy, Luxembourg, Netherlands, West Germany)
Finland pres electn delay cited 1-16, 36D2
Steel dumping levies vs 7 suppliers imposed, 6 others probed 1-23, 80A2
Belgian A-plant leak disputed 1-25, 69F3
UK vetoes fishing policy 1-30—1-31, members score 2-14, 158F3
France, W Ger score UK fishing zone stand 2-6—2-27, 122C1
Helsinki review conf statemt OKd 2-14, 179B2
Commonwealth regional conf scores 2-16, 121E2
Shorter work hours, overtime curbs urged 2-16, 258E2
French-Danish electn dispute 2-23—3-1, heads of state mtg rptd threatened 3-1, 167B2
EFTA OKs steel export curbs; '76, 9-mo '77 sales rptd 2-28; other restraint pacts sought 3-2, 158F1
'78 growth rate forecast 3-16, 257C3
Heads of state meet in Copenhagen: united econ policy, W Ger stimulatn role agreed; rights, other issues debated 4-7—4-8, 257G2-258F1
Youth job program announced 4-7, 258D2
Europn conservative group formed 4-24, 424D3
EFTA '77 trade deficit rptd 5-2, 319A2
Danish fishermen protest Baltic quotas 5-5, 371D2
UN Sea Law Conf talks continue 5-23—7-15, 8-21—9-16, 732E3
Monetary zone OKd by Schmidt, Giscard 6-23, plan presented at Bremen summit 7-6—7-7; UK, others wary 7-7, 7-8, 545D1-G3
Jenkins at 7-natn Bonn summit, monetary plan debated 7-16—7-17, 543D3, 544D2

1979

EUROPEAN Community (EC) (including EEC, ESCE, EURATOM) (Belgium, Denmark, France, Great Britain, Ireland, Italy, Luxembourg, Netherlands, West Germany)
'78 inflatn rptd 7.3% 1-8, 13B1
Italy CP oppositn to EMS cited 1-18, 38C3
W Ger urges shipbldg aid 1-21, 77G3, 78A1
'78 unemployment rptd 1-22, 85C2
Farm price freeze backed, EMS linked; milk surplus tax urged 1-31, 85D1
'78 trade deficit down 1-31, 85B2
'78 living standards ranked 2-2, 109G1
Ireland claims highest '78 growth rate 2-7, 155A1
French Gaullists, UDF debate ties 2-10—2-17, 135E1
W Ger '78 net contributn down 2-20, 137G1
French job measures urged 2-21, 134G3
UK scores farm policy 2-21, 154D2
Greece on '79 growth rates 2-23, 154D3
Farm price accord reached 3-6, France drops EMS oppositn 3-7, 160A3
Summit mtg; oil import cuts OKd, EMS begins 3-12—3-13,
Jean Monnet dies 3-16, 272C3
Wheat pact extended 3-23, 274B2
Ireland ends UK £ parity re EMS 3-30, 268E3
Greece EMS entry vowed 4-4, 268D3
UK Labor Party seeks reforms 4-6, 267F3
UK Tories back surplus agri-product price freeze 4-11, 268E1
GATT pact signed, tariff cuts seen 4-12, 273F1, B2, E2, 274D1
Irish farm income hike cited 4-24, 371F3
UK role increase seen 5-5, 338D2
UK Tories affirm commitmt; to seek agri reform, weigh EMS role 5-15, 358A3

1980

EUROPEAN Community (EC) (including EEC, ESCE, EURATOM) (Belgium, Denmark, France, Great Britain, Ireland, Italy, Luxembourg, Netherlands, West Germany)
UK urges Ulster parallel talks 1-7, 39D2
W Ger seeks energy coordinatn 1-18, 103B2
UK curb on US fibers OKd 2-5, UK widens request 2-7, 125E1
'79-83 A-fusion funds OKd 2-5, 125B2
Forgn mins mtg 2-6, 84A3
French-UK lamb dispute continues 2-14—2-20, 125A1
Ireland asks intl parley re Ulster 2-17, 133A2
English Channel tunnel plan rptd 3-4, 193G3
France vs UK budget proposal 3-12, 3-17, 3-19; UK stresses EC policy reform 3-20, 3-24; W Ger backs UK 3-28, 242B2
UK OKs Channel tunnel concept 3-19, 212C2
Summit deferred; Italy pol crisis, UK budget issue cited 3-24, 242G1
French, W Ger steelmakers fined 4-3, 262F2
Turkey aid OKd 4-15, 295B3
Auto research backed 4-23, 303C3
Summit held; farm price, UK budget impasses remain 4-27—4-28, 327B1-A2
French set farm price hike 4-30, 327A2
W Ger fund hike unlikely 4-30, 355G3
Medit pollutn pact signed 5-17, 381A3
Red Brigades threaten mtg 5-17, 408G2
UK budget, French lamb dispute resolved 5-29—5-30; Thatcher OKs 6-2, 421C2
Spanish-French produce dispute spurs violence, truckers block border 6-16—6-20, 525B3
Dutch to probe S Africa sanctns 6-27, 499A2
Turkey aid pact set 7-1, 526F1
'80 budget set 7-9, 548D1

1976

COMECON talks open 2-16, 164E1
Angola MPLA recognized 2-17—2-20, aid offered 2-23, 162D3
Backs southn Africa states' independnc 2-23, 163A1
African self-determinatn backed 2-23, 164C3
France-Italy wine talks 2-24, 163D3
Japan Jan-Sept '75 auto exports rptd 2-24, 191F2
New A-plant study asked 2-26, 164B2
'76-77 farm policy set 3-6, milk-feed plan revisn agreed 4-14, 276E2
France-Italy wine pact drafted 3-6, 276A3
Canada talks open 3-11, 204E1
Europn soclsts urge aid to Portugal 3-13—3-14, 222G3
Italy, Ireland loans OKd 3-15, 253G3
EEC vs US steel import quotas 3-17, 213B2 ★
Spain rightists vs EEC entry 3-21, 269G1
British Steel loan OKd 3-25, 529A3
Cncl deadlocks on Tindemans rpt, econ issues; reaffirms Rhodesia policy 4-1—4-2, 275G3
'77 EEC budget debated; France, W Ger differ 4-5, 276E1
Zaire, Zambia, Malawi aid set 4-6, 276C2
Argentina rpts EEC beef import ban cost 4-9, 264C3
UK, Italy food import subsidies forecast 4-14, 276B2
Italy CP backs EEC role 4-18, 297C1
Center-right party formed 4-30, 389G1
2d Italy loan authorized 5-12, 529B3
Asks S Africa for SWAPO mercy 5-17, 386C2
Canada ups UK, Ireland tariff 5-25, 400E3
Spain min asks EEC entry 6-3, 459G2
EEC farmers seek drought aid 6-19, 7-19, 548C3
EEC sees S Africa 'responsibility' re Rhodesia peace 6-22, 447A3
EEC-Canada pact signed 7-6, 496D3
Developing natns aid pact 7-8, 529G2
Spain reaffirms EEC entry bid 7-13, 541C3
7-natn summit scored 7-20, 557B1
EEC OKs 200-mi sea limit; UK, Dutch compromise 7-27, 563A3
Cunhal vs Portugal entry 8-5, 774F2
Australia scores trade curbs 8-12, 623A2
Argentina agri sales expected 8-20, 649D3
Denmark bars Taiwan opera 8-21, 712A2
UK signs EURATOM pact 9-6, 936B2
Callaghan meets Trudeau 9-16, 730B2
Portugal seeks membership 9-20, 812F2
Cncl of Eur admits Portugal 9-22, 733F2
IMF takes no actn on gold sales 10-8, 778E2
Rumania-EEC textile pact rptd 11-12, 907E2
EEC vs COMECON trade plan 11-15, 955E1
Jan-June Austria-EEC trade rptd 11-17, 923C2
Drought cut grain harvest 11-18, 935D2
US ups brandy duties, poultry war cited 11-26, 976F2-C3
Mid-Oct—mid-Nov jobless up 11-29, 935B2
France asks 3d 7-natn summit 12-2, 964D1
Rhine pollutn pacts signed 12-4, 977G1
Bonn seeks closer ties 12-16, 968C2
MD mobility OKd 12-20, 977B2

European Commission

Tindemans rpt urges reforms 1-7, 20A2
Minimum oil-import price asked, UK demand cited 1-16, 85A1
Opposes French border tax plan 1-16, 138D3; shifts stand 2-6, 163C3
Lardinois mediates Italy-French wine dispute 1-20, 138E3
US steel quota role rptd asked 1-21, 85C1
China talks rptd set 1-27, 84B3
Affirms Greek entry, urges delay 1-29, 84B2-E2 ★; delay overruled 2-9, 164E2
Backs 200-mi fishing zone 1-30, 85C1; sets fishing policy 2-18, 164D1
Tunisia, Morocco protest EC bias 2-3, 164F2 ★
Ulster rights study scores UK, full disclosure urged 2-11—2-12, 147A1
Parlt urges farm measures; UK, Ireland border tax end 2-12, 163E3
Lardinois quits, scores budget curbs 4-9, 276A2
OKs Italy import controls 5-5, 366B1
Spinelli rptd on Italy CP ticket 5-17, 5-30, 402D3
7-natn export credit terms tightened 6-9, 6-15, 529E3
Canada pact signed 7-6, 496E3
Jenkins to become pres 9-10, 693C3
New Comm, Jenkins meet 12-22—12-23, 977E1

European Court of Justice

'75 French wine tax rule pending 163D3
6-natn export credit pact rptd 2-25, 164D2
Sex bias in pay banned 4-8, 276B3

European Investment Bank

Loans to Tunisia, Morocco set 1-13, 84G2
Portugal aid set 4-6, 276E2

European Parliament

Tindemans rpt urges wider role 1-7, 20B2
Brandt to seek seat 2-6, 158B2
Urges farm measures 2-12, 163E3
UK electns 'green paper' issued 2-14, 174F2
Vs milk-feed plan 3-6, 276G2
Cncl deadlocks on direct electns 4-1—4-2, 276A1, C1

1977

Jobless youth problem rptd 8-9, June-Aug data 9-24, 9-26, 771G1-C2
GATT scores steel import curbs 9-12, 717F2
France curbs worker immigratn 9-27, 744D2
W Ger, UK set JET vote 10-18; UK site chosen 10-25, 852G3
UN pollutn conf ends, Medit pact reached 10-21, 876B2
Eur Cncl rpt on Cyprus rights abuses shelved, Greece protests 11-3, 946E3
Korea, Hong Kong textile pacts 12-2, 12-3, 998C1
Multifiber pact protectnist clause OKd, job layoffs cited 12-13, 974C3-975A1
UK defeats proportional representatn 12-13, 1013C2
Canada footwear import curbs protested 12-14, 983B1
Steel, textile imports curbed 12-20, 998B1
Canada uranium pact signed 12-20, 1010G1

African Relations

Zaire interventn condemned 4-18, 317E2
EEC cancels Uganda loan 6-21, 508C1
S Africa ethics code adopted 9-20; invstmts, exports rptd 9-23, 770C3
S Africa policies protested 10-27, rejctd 10-28, 853B2

Australian Relations

Australian beef import levy set 1-5, 60C2
Australian energy talks 3-14, 3-16, 218C1
Australia scores protectionism, threatens uranium export ban 6-1, 7-4, 595D3
ASEAN backs ties 6-27—6-29, 537E1
Australia farm import demands rejctd 10-30, 862D1

Eastern European Relations

USSR fishing licenses OKd 2-18, 146D3
USSR butter sale spurs dispute 3-1, E Eur trade curbed 3-2, 269E1-A2
Comecon OKs formal talks 9-21, 771C2
USSR curbs Barents fishing 9-24, 9-27, EC bans Sovt trawlers 9-31, 771F2

European Court of Justice

Ireland fishing boat curbs ordrd lifted 7-13, 771A3

European Investment Bank

Israel loans set 2-8, 146D1
Euro-yen bond issue made 4-19, 318C1

European Parliament

Jenkins wins no-confidence vote 3-23, 269E1-A2
French OK direct electns 6-16, 6-22, 598C3
N Sea herring fishing banned 9-16, 771B3
UK OKs proportional rep vote 9-28, 745B1

1978

UN racism conf boycotted 8-26, 676B2
W Ger mark revalued up vs snake countries 10-16, 798F2
Italy chem indus rescue plan proposed 10-26, 817C2
Synthetic fiber cartel modificatn ordrd 11-9, 871B3
Denmark offers Greenland home rule 11-17, 902F1
France backs confederatn 11-21, 902C2
Monetary system (EMS) OKd at Brussels summit, currency unit (ECU) set 12-4—12-5, 951A3
UK bars EMS entry; Italy, Ireland defer 12-5; French vs eased terms 12-7, 951B3, F3
France OKs VAT harmonizatn 12-8, 987F2
Norway bars EMS entry 12-11, quits snake 12-12, 952B2
Italy backs EMS entry despite CP oppositn 12-12—12-13, 952D1
Ireland to join EMS 12-15, 979D1
Brunner deplores OPEC price hike 12-18, 978F1
French delay EMS start 12-29, 999B1

African Relations

S Africa steel export agrmt sought 3-2, 158C2
Belgium backs Zaire force 5-24, 417D3
Comm at Zaire aid mtg 6-13—6-14, 478A1
Schmidt to seek Zambia, Zaire copper aid 6-30, 584D1
S Africa Zulus back labor code 7-13, 633F1

Asian Relations

China lauds French role 1-20, 71G1
Japan, S Korea steel dumping levies imposed 1-23, 80B2
China 5-yr trade pact initialed 2-3, USSR scores 2-6, 2-9, 102F2-D3
Japan, S Korea steel export agrmts sought 3-2, 158C2
China 5-yr trade pact signed 4-3, USSR denounces 4-4, 302E3
Japan, UK cos set joint plant 8-23, 667C3

Australian Relations

Australia scores import curbs, boycott warned 1-24—1-26, 69D2-D3
Fraser fails to win Commonwealth support 2-15, 121E2
Australia steel duty imposed 2-16, 129C2
Australia scores trade curbs 3-1, 3-7, 265F2
Fraser threatens curbs 4-6, trade talks delayed 4-14, 310D3
Wool imports rptd down 4-14, 411A2
Coal import cuts barred, uranium talks sought 6-13, 494F3-495A1
Auto, beef import link sought 7-13, 530B2
UK-Australia uranium pact halted 7-27, 666E1

Canadian Relations

Canada '75 investmt rptd 1-10, 70C3
Canada lifts uranium ban; UK, W Ger shipmts, inspectn set 1-16, 102D3
Steel dumping levy imposed 1-23, 80B2
Steel dumping measures rptd 2-21, 244G2-B3
Quebec backs separate currency 5-16, 412D3

Eastern European Relations

Steel dumping levies vs Poland, Czech, Bulgaria imposed; E Ger, Rumania, Hungary probed 1-23, 80B2
USSR scores China trade pact 2-6, 2-9, 102C3; 4-4, 302G3
Comecon steel export agrmt sought 3-2, 158C2
Sovt-bloc shipping competitn rptd 7-11, 670B3
Sovt-bloc rate-cutting scored 9-11, cargo share rptd 9-17, 820B3

European Court of Justice

United Brands '75 fine upheld 2-14, 159C1

European Parliament

'79 direct electns set 4-7, 258A1
France opposes expansn, discounts W Ger control 11-12, 11-21, 902G1-G2

1979

Lome pact talks collapse 5-26, 398E3
Energy plan proposed 6-13, 437E1
Farm prices hiked, green currencies revised 6-21, 513D1
Leaders meet; back oil import lid, EMS, UN conf on Indochina refugees 6-22, 476C1
Lome pact extensn set 6-27, 512D3
Tokyo summit sets oil import targets 6-28–6-29, 493F1, C3
France seeks Euratom revisn 7-24, 633B2
Italy to protest French knitwear import curbs 8-20, 668F3
NZ import curbs cited 8-21, 632A1
UK '80 budget contributn projctd tripled 9-4, Howe protests hike 9-17, 719G1
'80 draft budget OKd; regional aid cut, farm spending hiked 9-12, 719D1
EMS currencies realigned 9-24, 718G3
Comm reforms proposed 9-24, 719B3
UK Tories hear Thatcher re budget 10-12, 791F3
Lome pact extensn signed 10-31, 845E1
French-UK lamb dispute progress rptd 11-14, 873B1
Summit mtg; UK cost contributn cut rejected 11-29–11-30, 917B3
Intl sugar agrmt exclusn cited 11-30, 987E2

African Relations

UK Tories set policy 4-11, 285D3
Uganda aid pledged 5-23–5-24, 429D2

Asian Relations

Japan '78 trade deficit up 1-24, 98B2
BL-Honda productn planned 4-11, 388C2
Japan imports rise backed 6-22, 476F1
Indochina refugee conf backed 6-22, 476G1
China textile pact initialed 7-18, 554E3
Japan ball bearing dumping probe opened 9-20, 719E2

Australian Relations

Trade accord set 5-29, 404F3-405C1
UK A-pact OKd by EC panel 7-5, 522E1; signed 7-24, 562F2
Import curbs cited 8-21, 632A1

Eastern European Relations

E Eur ball bearing dumping probe opened 9-20, 719E2

European Court of Justice

Hoffman-La Roche '76 ruling upheld 2-13, 137B1
French-UK lamb dispute progress rptd 11-14, 873B1

European Parliament

French UDF scores Gaullist remarks 2-17–2-18, 135D1
Italy candidate shot 5-29, 426E3
Electns held 6-7, 6-10; pol lineup rptd 6-12, 433A1-434C2
Thorn to seek presidency 6-10, 469E2
Mitterrand quits re French vote 6-20, 485A2

1980

Steel output cut rptd OKd, Italy bars 7-29, 628F3
Turkey coup response 9-16, 696E3
Sheepmeat policy set 9-30, 737E2
Cattle feed hormone use banned 10-1, 737B3
France to seek agri mkts 10-1, 749F3
Steel productn cutback plan OKd, W Ger oppositn cited 10-30, 821F3-822D1
W Ger wine scandal rptd 11-3, 11-18, 925D2
Italy puts quake costs at $12 bln 12-1, 943F3
Norway orders fishing vessels out 12-10, 969C3

Asian Relations—*See also 'Soviet-Afghan' below*

Japan cited re auto research plans 4-23, 303C3
Japan dumping chrgs cited 5-6, 412B1
Nissan, Alfa Romeo project OKd 9-20, 751D3

Australian Relations

Steel accord rptd set 2-5, 132A1
Sheepmeat talks founder 7-15, 561C3
Airbus deal OKd, sheepmeat agreemt cited 9-29, 748B1

Eastern European Relations—*See also 'Soviet Relations' below*

Rumania pact rptd initialed 2-12, 109A2
Yugo 5-yr trade pact signed 4-2, 365A3; cited by OECD 6-6, 468E3
Poland butter exports suspended 7-9, 566F1
USSR warned vs Poland mil interventn; aid to Poland vowed 12-2, 910D3, 911A1

European Investment Bank

Turkey aid pact set 7-1, 526A2

European Parliament

English Channel tunnel plan rptd 3-4, 193G3
UK censure for Iran sanctns reversal sought 5-21, 378E2
'80 budget OKd 7-9, 548D1

1976

Center-right party formed 4-30, 389A2
W Ger, France conf on electns 7-6, 521F1
Chrgs Sovt CSCE rights violatn 7-9, 540B3
Expansn, direct electns set 7-12, 529C2 ★
Parlt vote accord signed 9-20, 721F3
UK Laborites oppose electns 9-29, 791F2

Greek Membership
Comm 'OKs' entry, urges delay 1-29; Greece scores 1-31, 84B2-E2 ★
Greek entry delay rejctd 2-9, 165E2
Talks open 7-27, 853D3
EC convenes 10-11, mtg schedule agreed 10-19, 853E3
Entry assurance rptd 11-3, 853F3

Middle East Relations
Tunisia, Morocco pacts rptd 1-13, 84E2
Algeria pact rptd 1-21, 84A3
Tunisia, Morocco protest Algeria pact 2-3, delay signing 2-4, 164F2 ★
Egypt, Syria, Jordan talks rptd 2-12, 164B3
Arab League talks end 5-20, 529B3

Ministers, Council of
Van de Stoel signs Canada pact 7-6, 496E3

Monetary Issues—*See 'European' under MONETARY Developments*

U.S. Relations
Tindemans rpt stresses detente 1-7, 20G1
Rpt French Gaullist for Eur defns group 1-15, 126E2
Steel group scores US policy 1-21, 85C1
Hinton confrmd US amb 1-28, 186A2
Vs milk-feed plan 3-6, 276G2
EEC rptd vs US car dumping probe 5-4, 321G1
US sets steel quotas 6-7, EEC scores 6-14, 430G3, 431C1
US GOP platform text cites EEC ties 8-18, 609A2

EUROPEAN Economic Community—*See EUROPEAN Community*

1977

Helsinki Agreement—*See EUROPE—Security and Cooperation*

Japanese Relations
Japan rejcts shipbldg plan 1-17, trade talks rptd stalled 1-18; comm issues study 1-24, 73F2
Japan fined for ball-bearing dumping 2-7, plans appeal 2-8, 109D1
Japan ball-bearing duty dropped 7-27, 624B3
'75 Japan steel trade curb pact cited 9-19, 775A2
US steel export growth compared 9-19, 776D1
Mutual limits on US steel exports asked 10-4, 775E1

Latin American Relations
'76 exports to Venez rptd 1-6, 23C2
Argentina increases trade 7-25, 614A3
EEC to close Chile office 9-7, 743B2

Membership
Turkey stalled entry talks cited 2-13, 109C1
Portugal entry backed 3-13, applicatn filed 3-28, 269B2
Spain asks full membership 7-28, 582D2
Spain King's Venez trip cited re EC entry bid 9-16, 805E1
Spain Soclsts back entry 9-23; premr sees ldrs 11-3, 11-4, 867G1, B2
UK membership backed by UK Labor 10-5, 863G2
Spain, Greece, Portugal entry concern rptd 11-6, 837A2
Greek electn results 11-20, 925B1, C1

Middle Eastern Relations
Egypt, Syria, Jordan pacts signed; Israel pact set 1-18, 73E3
'70-75 trade data rptd 1-18, 74A1
Israel signs pact, vs terms 2-8, 146C1
EEC in Arab League talks, bars PLO recognitn 2-10—2-12, 146G1
Lebanon pact initialed 2-16, 269B3
Intl consortium OKs Egypt aid 5-11—5-12, 390B3
Palestine homeland, Geneva conf role backed 6-29; Begin scores 6-30, 510C1
Sadat Israel trip backed, French oppositn cited 11-22, 894G3
OPEC price freeze hailed 12-21, 973G1

Monetary Developments—*See MONETARY Developments—European*

U.S. Relations
Mondale sees comm officials in Brussels 1-23—1-24, 69B1, 70C1
'76 trade deficit with US rptd 1-31, 74C1
US fishing limits accepted 2-15, 109D2
US fishing agrmt signed 3-3, 173D3
Carter energy plan reactn 4-21, 320D3
US Steel countervailing duty request refused 7-10, 587D1
US warned vs extra duties 7-19, tariff-cutting formula agreed 9-23, 853F1
Japan steel export growth compared 9-19, 776D1
Japan asks mutual limits on US steel exports 10-4, 775E1
US wage-price panel on steel competitn 10-7, 776C2
Eurofer backs US steel export limit 10-10, Davignon asks talks 10-11, 775E1
US probes French steel dumping 10-19, 933G2
US' Armco chrgs UK steel dumping 12-5, 932C1, 933A3
US offers Japan steel import curb plan 12-6, 931D3

EUROPEAN Court of Justice—*See under EUROPEAN Community*
EUROPEAN Currency Cooperation Agreement (Snake)—*See MONETARY Developments—European*
EUROPEAN Economic Community—*See EUROPEAN Community*

1978

Latin American Relations
Paraguay '77 meat exports cut 2-17, 292F3
Brazil steel export agrmt sought 3-2, 158C2

Membership
Greek premr in UK, Belgium, France, W Ger for entry talks 1-25—2-1, 149G1
Portugal premr vows talks renewal 1-30, 92B1
Greek entry backed by France, W Ger 2-6—2-7, 122C1
Spain names negotiator 2-10, entry review delayed 2-14; Jenkins in Spain 4-27—4-28, 395C1
Nondemocratic states entry, expulsn debated 4-7—4-8, 258C1
Greek Cabt shuffled 5-10, 373D3
Greece entry moves rptd 6-9, 6-18, 631D1
Giscard backs Spain entry 6-29, 649F1
Giscard backs Portuguese entry 7-19—7-21, 667B2
Spain entry asked by UK oppositn ldr 10-21, 821F2
Greek entry terms set 12-21, 1017A3

Middle Eastern Relations
Sadat on Mideast role 2-9, 98D2
OPEC warned on oil-refining role 10-9, 871F1

Turkish Relations
Turkey seeks aid, tariff cut, investmt 10-12—10-26, 840E1, D2
Turkey rejcts austerity demands 11-4, 905A3

U.S. Relations
Carter visits hq, reassures 1-6, 1D1
Steel trigger plan scored in US rpt 1-7, 80B3
US '77 steel imports rptd 2-14, 158E1
A-export contract renegotiatn disputed; France blocks response, deadline expires 4-4—4-9, 258D1
Independent econ policy set; US $ drop, weak ldrshp cited 4-7—4-8, 257A3
US OKs uranium exports 4-9, 278F3
Uranium export renegotiatn scored by W Ger 4-12, 255B1
Schmidt reviews Carter talks 6-1, 519C2
EC monetary zone proposed 7-7, plan linked to $ weakness 7-8; Carter reservatns rptd 7-18, 545A2, E2, G3
US seabed mining bill debated at UN Conf 8-21—9-16, 732E3
France vs fed structure, cites US influence 11-21, 902D2
US backs EMS 12-7, 952F2
GATT talks rift over duty waiver, textile stands 12-22, 998B1

EUROPEAN Court of Justice—*See under EUROPEAN Community*
EUROPEAN Currency Unit (ECU)—*See EUROPEAN Community*
EUROPEAN Democratic Union (EDU)
Formed 4-24, 424B3
EUROPEAN Economic Community—*See EUROPEAN Community*
EUROPEAN Free Trade Association (EFTA) (Austria, Iceland, Norway, Portugal, Sweden, Switzerland; associate member: Finland)
EC steel export curbs agreed; '76, 9-mo '77 sales rptd 2-28, 158F1
'77 trade deficit rptd 5-2, 319F1

1979

W Berlin delegates electn cited 6-28, 513D1
Veil elected pres 7-17, 537B2
UK Liberals protest exclusn 7-18, 537A3
Veil scores Czech trial 10-23, 802E2
Olesen named Danish forgn min 10-26, 855B1
'80 budget rejected 12-13, 960C2-B3

Latin American Relations
France backs Mex bond float 4-1—4-4, 372C2
Andean Group names trade rep 5-26—5-28, 398B2

Membership
Portugal sees econ sacrifices 1-1, 22D3
Greek '81 entry date set 4-4, 268B3
Greenland exit seen possible 4-4, 286C1
Greek entry treaty signed 5-28, 407B2
Greece ratifies entry treaty 6-28, sets new bank hrs 7-3, 543B3, F3
Comm reforms proposed 9-24, 719C3
Spain entry talks in France 11-26—11-27, 952E1

Middle Eastern Relations
Iran oil cutoff impact assessed 2-13, 126E2
OPEC price hike scored 3-28, 227F3
Israel setlmt policy opposed 6-18, Israel rejects 6-20, 462C1
Iran urged to free US Emb hostages 11-20, 895D3

U.S. Relations
US oil import subsidy attacked 5-30—6-2, 417G1
US $ drop vs mark re EMS realignmt seen 6-24, 719D1
Carter energy plan praised 7-16, 534G3

EUROPEAN Court of Human Rights—*See COUNCIL of Europe*
EUROPEAN Court of Justice—*See under EUROPEAN Community*
EUROPEAN Economic Community—*See EUROPEAN Community*

1980

Iran Hostage Issue
Iran ties weighed 3-20, 204C1
Iran urged to free hostages 3-31, 242C1
Iran scored, sanctns withheld 4-10; Cncl of Eur, Japan endorse 4-10, 4-11, 281G2
Iran asks non-support of US policy 4-11, 282G1
Iran gets US plea, ambs recalled 4-12, 282E1
Iran econ, diplomatic sanctns voted 4-22; US lauds 4-23, 298C1, D2
Iran hostage kin seek support 4-23, 299D2
Muskie warns Waldheim on UN missn renewal 5-17, 393F2
Iran limited sanctns imposed, US lauds 5-18; UK modifies stand 5-19, Bonn, US deplore 5-20, 5-21; Bonn, Paris implement 5-21, 378F1-E2
UK modifies Iran sanctns further 5-29, 393F1
Iran parlt ldr rebuffs appeal 8-17, 634D3
Iran sanctns end on hostage freedom vowed 11-4, 879C3

Membership
Turkey initiative launched, assured re Greek role 2-5, formal applicatn seen 2-7, 102A3
Spain entry, Gibraltar talks linked 2-6, 133B1
France asks expansn slowdown; Spain, Portugal entry delay seen 6-5, Spain reactn 6-6, 435E3-436D1
Spain mil poll on entry rptd 6-12, 436C1
Carter backs Spain entry 6-25, 474C3
Turkey assoc status renewed, membership aim reaffirmed 7-1, 526F1, A2
Spain shuffles Cabt, entry talks cited 9-8, 690E2
UK Labor Party backs exit 10-1, 768E2
UK Tories affirm backing 10-10, 790G2
UK govt stresses commitmt 11-20, 901B1
UK Labor exit plan spurs rift 11-28, 922A1

Middle East Relations—*See also 'Iran' above*
Giscard tours Arab states 3-1—3-10, 180E1
France vows peace initiative 5-30; Dutch assure Israel 6-4, 418C1-E1
US cautns vs UN Cncl Res 242 chng 5-31, 417F2
Summit backs PLO peace role, vs Israel setlmts 6-12—6-13; US, PLO, Israel reactn 6-13—6-15, 449A1, F1
Thorn starts peace missn, meets Begin 7-31—8-1, Arafat 8-4, 585E2-586C1
Israel scores re terrorist violence 10-7, 767B3
8 vote vs UN res on Israeli pullout; France abstains 12-15, 952F2

Soviet-Afghan Issue
US grain embargo backed 1-7, 9B2; US call for sanctns rejected 1-10, no increase in exports to USSR vowed 1-12, 27E3
France, W Ger conf 1-9, 10G2
Afghan neutrality plan offered, Olympics issue barred from mins' final statemt 2-19, 123F3
Brezhnev Afghan offer cited 2-22, 139G2
USSR gets neutrality plan 2-28, scores 3-2, 165B1
USSR barley sales to resume 10-23, 832B1

Soviet Relations—*See also 'Soviet-Afghan' above*
Sakharov exile protested 1-24, 86A1
USSR warned vs Poland mil interventn 12-2, 910D3

U.S. Relations—*See also 'Iran' above*
Sovt grain embargo backed 1-7, 9B2; US call for trade sanctns vs USSR rejected 1-10, no sales increase vowed 1-12, 27E3
US backs Afghan neutrality plan 2-28, 165C1
US warned vs steel curbs 2-28, talks failure seen 3-14; '78, '79 data 204C2
Comm bars trade war, rejects US Steel suits 3-27, 242C3
EC fines French, W Ger steelmakers 4-3, 262G2
Comm backs Europn auto research 4-23, 303C3
US steel import ruling scored 5-1, 456G1
US polyester fiber dumping probed 5-5, duties on acrylics set 5-6, 411F3
Carter cautns vs UN Cncl Res 242 chng 5-31, 417F2
Carter backs Spain membership 6-25, 474D3
US polyester duties set 9-1, 662E2
USSR barley sales to resume 10-23, 832B1

EUROPEAN Economic Community—*See EUROPEAN Community*

1976

EUROPEAN Investment Bank—*See under EUROPEAN Community*
EUROPEAN Parliament—*See under EUROPEAN Community*
EUROPEAN Steel Producers, Association of
Vs US steel import quotas 1-21, 85C1
EUTHANASIA—*See MEDICINE*
EVANGELISM
Kathryn Kuhlman dies 2-20, 192E3
EVANS, Billy Lee
Elected to US House 11-2, 822E1, 829D2
EVANS, Colin
Angola sentences 6-28, 480B2
EVANS, Gov. Daniel J. (R, Wash.)
Ford lists as potential vp 1-22, 41A2
Govs OK welfare plan 7-6, 492A3
VP prospect cited 8-10, 584C1
Scores Carter tactics 10-11, 763E2
Spellman loses electn 11-2, 825E1
EVANS, Rep. David W. (D, Ill.)
Reelected 11-2, 829B3
EVANS, Dwayne
Wins Olympic medal 7-26, 575G3
EVANS, Dwight
AL batting ldr 10-4, 796C1
EVANS, Dame Edith
Dies 10-14, 970G1
EVANS, Capt. Eugene G.
On '75 Marine dropouts 6-9, 435C3
EVANS, Rep. Frank Edwards (D, Colo.)
Reelected 11-2, 824E1, 829F1
EVANS, Robert
At Bronson trial 6-17, 493D2
EVANS, Rowland
Rpts Sonnenfeldt '75 remarks on E Eur policy 3-22; rpt disputed 3-29—4-2, 232G2, 233B1, 245B2
E Eur press scores Sonnenfeldt rpt 4-9—4-14, 277D1, F1
EVANS, Stephen
Sentence rptd 7-20, 860F2
EVANS Jr., Thomas B.
Seconds Ford nominatn 8-18, 598A1
Elected 11-2, 821A1, 829A2
EVANS, William
On Australia coal-mining project 7-7, 496A2
EVANSVILLE, Ind.—*See INDIANA*
EVELEIGH, Sir Edward
Sentences Stonehouse 8-6, 589C1
EVENSEN, Jens
Norway law of sea min 1-12, 30A2
EVERT, Chris
Wins L'eggs world series 1-11, 31D3
Named '75 top female athlete 1-15, 31F3
Tourn results 1-18, 1-25, 123A3
Wins Sarasota Va Slims 2-29, 716C2
Wins Wimbledon title 7-2, 504F1
Wins US Open 9-11, 716C1
Named athlete of yr 12-3, 969A3
EVINS, Rep. Joe L. (D, Tenn.)
Gore elected 11-2, 822E3
EWART-Biggs, Christopher T. E.
Killed 7-21, 538D2-B3
Ireland declares state of emergency 9-1, 676B2
EX-Cell-O Corp.
'75 Cadillac arms sales listed 2-6, 147C3
EXCHANGE National Bank & Trust (Atchison, Kan.)
Buys IMF gold 9-15, 739D3
EXIMBANK—*See EXPORT-Import Bank under U.S. GOVERNMENT*
EXNER, Judith Campbell
Sells JFK story 1-13, 80G2

1977

EUROPEAN Investment Bank—*See under EUROPEAN Community*
EUROPEAN Migration, Intergovernmental Committee for
Viet refugees arrive US 9-20, 739F3
EUROPEAN Parliament—*See under EUROPEAN Community*
EUROPEAN Space Agency (ESA) (Belgium, Denmark, France, Great Britain, Ireland, Italy, Netherlands, Spain, Sweden, Switzerland, West Germany)
Joint US mission planned 2-16, 170C3
Satellite missn postponed 6-16, aborted 9-13, 735G3
Sun-earth study satellites launched 10-22, 908C3
EUTHANASIA—*See MEDICINE—Death Issues*
EVANGELISM
B Graham fund disclosed 6-26, 731E3-732A1
Charismatics meet, hail ecumenical gains 7-20—7-24, 620A3
Ethel Waters dies 9-1, 788A3
Graham in Hungary 9-3—9-14, 732A1
Graham assn rpts finances 10-21, 845C1
Catholic evangelizatn urged 11-14, 906A3
New RC catechism stresses 11-17, 906A2
EVANGELISTA, Alfredo
Ali decisions 5-16, 395A1
EVANGELISTIC Association, Billy Graham—*See BILLY Graham Evangelistic Association*
EVANGELISTIC & Christian Education Fund, World—*See BILLY Graham Evangelistic Association*
EVANS, Rep. Billy Lee (D, Ga.)
In South Korea 4-12, 305F3
EVANS, Brock
Lauds Carter energy plan 4-21, 320A2
EVANS, Rev. Joseph H.
Replaced as Church of Christ pres 7-4, 642G2
EVANS, Moss
Elected TGWU head 4-21, 392F1
EVANS, Rowland
Scores cruise missile 10-29, 857D3
SALT leaks in article cited 11-8, 996A3
EVANS v. Hills
Sup Ct refuses review 1-17, 58D1
EVANSVILLE (Ind.), University of
Basketball team dies in plane crash 12-13, 1023C2
EVE, Arthur O.
Loses mayoral vote 11-8, 855C3
EVENING Standard, The (London newspaper)
Sold 6-30, 526G3
EVERARD Baths (N.Y.)
Fire kills 9 5-25, 429G2-A3
EVERGREEN (Song)
Wins Oscar 3-28, 264D1
EVERGREEN Marine Corp. U.S.A. Ltd.
Rebates cited 1-5, 6C3
EVERT, Chris
Va Slims tourn results 1-6, 1-9, 103G3
Tourn results 2-6—4-17, 430C3-431E1
Wade wins Wimbledon 7-1, 548A2
Apples win WTT title 8-27, 787E3, F3
Wins US Open 9-11, 787C1
EVERT, Miltiadis
Named Greek industry min 11-28, 925B2
EVERTSZ, Juan
Loses electn 6-17, 567E1
EVOLUTION—*See BIOLOGY*
EWART-Briggs, Christopher
Lynch vs anti-terrorist measures 5-26, 475F2
Lynch drops detentn law 10-6, 782D3
EXECUTIVE Branch, U.S.—*See under U.S. GOVERNMENT*
EXECUTIVE, Legislative and Judicial Salaries, Commission on—*See under U.S. GOVERNMENT*
EXECUTIVE Office of the President—*See under U.S. GOVERNMENT*
EXIMBANK—*See EXPORT-Import Bank under U.S. GOVERNMENT—EXPORT—Import Bank*

1978

EUROPEAN Migration, Intergovernmental Committee for
Jan-June USSR Jewish emigratn rptd 8-5, 634C2
EUROPEAN Monetary System (EMS)—*See EUROPEAN Community*
EUROPEAN Parliament—*See under EUROPEAN Community*
EUROPEAN Southern Observatory (La Silla, Chile)
Asteriod find near Earth rptd 3-12, 293D3
EUROPEAN Space Agency (ESA) (Belgium, Denmark, France, Great Britain, Ireland, Italy, Netherlands, Spain, Sweden, Switzerland, West Germany)
France, W Ger OK launcher constructn 2-7, 122B1
Communicatn satellite launched 5-12, 384D3
EUROPEAN Trade Union Confederation
Workers protest unemploymt 4-5, 258F2
EUSTACHE de St. Pierre (sculpture)
Stolen 2-20, 335C1
EVANGELISM
Laity ldrship role cited 2-19, 294C3
Oral Roberts gets hosp OK 5-25, 577A3
EVANGELISTA, Alfredo
Holmes KOs 11-10, 969A1
EVANS, Bergen
Dies 2-4, 196G2
EVANS, Rep. Billy Lee (D, Ga.)
Reelected 11-7, 850B3
EVANS, Rep. David W. (D, Ind.)
Reelected 11-7, 850B4
EVANS, Don
Mahalia opens 6-5, 887A2
EVANS, Dwight
Wins Golden Glove Award 11-21, 928A3
EVANS, Rep. Frank E. (D, Colo.)
Kogovsek wins seat 11-7, 855G3
EVANS 3rd, John Louis
Ala death penalty upheld 5-19, 388G3
EVANS, Acting Gov. John V. (D, Ida.)
On Carter natl water plan 6-7, 427D1
Unopposed in primary 8-8, 625D3
Elected Ida gov 11-7, 853E2, 856A1
EVANS, Melvin
Elected VI delegate to US House 11-7, 915F3
EVANS, Mike
In NBA draft 6-9, 457G2
Draft rights traded to Kings 6-26, 656A1
EVANS, Mostyn
Scores 5% pay hike policy 10-1, 763D1
EVANS, Ray
On NASL All-Star team 8-20, 707A3
EVANS Jr., Rep. Thomas B. (R, Del.)
Reelected 11-7, 848A1, 850E2
EVANSVILLE (Ind.) University of
'77 plane crash blame fixed 8-18, 758C3
EVENING News Association
FCC OKs WWJ-TV swap 5-18, 599G3
EVEN Now (recording)
On best-seller list 3-8, 196C1; 4-5, 272G3
EVENT 1000 (book)
Film versn released 3-10, 619C2
EVERETT, Tom
Winning Isn't Everything opens 12-3, 1031C3
EVERGREEN (book)
On best-seller list 9-4, 708B1; 10-9, 800A3; 11-6, 887F3
EVERGREEN (song)
Wins Grammy 2-24, 315E3
EVERINGHAM, John
Rescues Laotian girlfriend 5-27, 420D2
EVERINGHAM, Paul
N Terr granted partial self rule 7-1, 570B3
EVERS, Mayor Charles (Fayette, Miss.)
Loses US Sen electn 11-7, 582F2
EVERS, Medgar Wiley (1926-63)
Brother loses US Sen electn 11-7, 582G2
EVERT, Chris
Loses Boston Va Slims 3-19; wins Phila Va Slims 3-26, Family Circle Cup 4-16, 419A2
Loses Eastbourne Intl 6-24, Wimbledon 7-7, 539E3, 540A1, D1
Wins US Open 9-10, 707A1, E1
Strings win WTT title, named playoff MVP 9-21, 1027F1, G1
Wins Atlanta Women's Classic 10-2, Series Championship 11-18, 1027B2, C2
US wins Federatn Cup 12-3, 1026G3, 1027A1
EWART-Biggs, Christopher T. E. (d. 1976)
Ireland death probe rptd 1-4, 1-13, 37C3
EWBANK, Weeb
Enters Pro Football HOF 7-29, 1025B1
EWING, Donald M.
Dies 9-2, 778C1
EXCLUSIVE Native (race horse)
Affirmed wins Triple Crown 6-10, 539A2
EXECUTION of Charles Horman, The (book)
Links CIA, Horman's death 9-12, 795E3
EXECUTIVE Branch, U.S.—*See under U.S. GOVERNMENT*
EXECUTIVE Orders—*See under CARTER*
EXILE (singing group)
Kiss You All Over on best-seller list 9-6, 708F1; 10-11, 800E3; 11-8, 888C1
EXIMBANK—*See U.S. GOVERNMENT—EXPORT-Import Bank*

1979

EUROPEAN Migration, Intergovernmental Committee for
Chile refugee relocatn rptd 5-7, 369A3
EUROPEAN Monetary System (EMS)—*See EUROPEAN Community*
EUROPEAN Nuclear Conference
Opens in Hamburg; Schmidt, Carter back A-power 5-7, 373F3-374C1
EUROPEAN Parliament—*See under EUROPEAN Community*
EVANGELISM
Graham assn rpts finances 9-21, 755A3
EVANGELISTA, Alfredo
Zanon decisns for Eur heavywgt title 4-18, 412G3
EVANS, Amon Carter
Sells Tennessean 7-5, 618B3
EVANS, Rep. Billy Lee (D, Ga.)
In Viet 2-21, visits war zone 2-24 141A2
EVANS, Bruce A.
Man, Woman & Bank released 9-28, 820G1
EVANS, Charles (Chick)
Dies 11-6, 932F2
EVANS, Dwight
Wins Golden Glove Award 11-20, 956C1
EVANS, Gwynfor
Vs govt devolution effort 3-2, 169C1
Loses Parlt seat 5-3, 337B2
EVANS, Harold
Hails Eur rights ct ruling vs UK censorship 4-26, 331C1
EVANS, Jeanette
Convicted 10-21, 818A2
EVANS 3rd, John Louis
Death delay refused by Sup Ct 4-13, exectn stayed 4-20 400F1
EVANS, Gov. John V. (D, Ida.)
Nez Perce dispute setld 6-7, 465A1
Scores Forest Svc policies 8-8, 620G1
EVANS, Joseph
State age bias filings required by Sup Ct, time limit barred 5-21, 400D2
EVANS, Lee
AAU clears for US meets 11-29, 956G1
EVANS, Peter
Don Juan opens 4-15, 711E2
EVANS, Silliman (deceased)
Family trust sells Tennessean 7-5, 618B3
EVERGREEN (book)
On best-seller list 8-5, 620D3; 9-2, 672D3; 10-14, 800D3
EVERGREEN Cemetery (Oakland, Calif.)
Peoples Temple burials set 4-19, 336D1
EVERS, Charles
Labor '78 campaign gifts rptd 6-13, 595C1
EVERS, Dianne
Australian Open results 1-3, 103E2
EVERT, Chris—*See LLOYD, Chris Evert*
EVERY Good Boy Deserves Favour (play)
Opens 7-30, 711F2
EVERY Which Way But Loose (film)
Top-grossing film 1-10, 80G3; 2-7, 120G3
EVITA (play)
Opens 9-25, 956A3
EVOLUTION
New hominid species claimed 1-18, Leakey disputes 2-17, 137F3-138D1
EVREN, Gen. Kenan
U-2 flights oppositn rptd 6-24, 488C2
Probes Kurdish unrest 8-21, 795E3
EVRON, Ephraim
Sees Vance on UNTSO, US tanks to Jordan; assured on PLO 7-27, 574F2-A3, 575B1
Meets Carter on US-Israel feud 8-8, 591F1
Protests Young-PLO contact 8-14, 605D2
Sees Vance, asks more US aid 9-11, 677B2
Weizman, US aide in dispute 9-18, 693F2
EWART-Biggs, Christopher T. E. (d. 1976)
UK amb to Holland killed 3-22, 228F2
EXCEDRIN P.M.—*See MEDICINE—Drugs*
EXECUTIVE Branch, U.S.—*See under U.S. GOVERNMENT*
EXECUTIVE Orders—*See under CARTER*
EXIT House (book)
Roman kills self 6-10, 521C2
EXNER, Judith Campbell
Giancana-Ruby links detailed 7-17, 538A2

1980

EUROPEAN Investment Bank—*See under EUROPEAN Community*
EUROPEAN Space Agency (ESA) (Belgium, Denmark, France, Great Britain, Ireland, Italy, Netherlands, Spain, Sweden, Switzerland, West Germany)
Rocket test fails 5-23, 397G2
Halley's Comet probe planned 7-15, 548A1
EUSTIS, Rich
Serial released 3-28, 416E3
EVANGELISM
Airwave symposium held 2-6—2-7; broadcast growth rptd, TV revenues listed 2-25, 413C1-D2
Bryant files for divorce 5-22, 471D3
Pol role profiled 7-11—9-15; voters surveyed, Falwell ministry detailed 9-15, 818C3-819F3
Reagan addresses fundamentalists 8-22, 646B2
Baptist ldr disparages Jewish prayers 8-22, religious ldrs denounce 9-18, 9-19, 811B1
Jerusalem unified capital status backed 9-22, 9-30, 800C3
Faith Center TV license revoked 10-10, 907C1
Falwell reverses Jewish prayer stance 10-11, 811F1
EVANGELISTI, Franco
Quits Italy Cabt post 3-4, 173A2
EVANS, Bill
Dies 9-15, 755G2
EVANS, Rep. Billy Lee (D, Ga.)
Reelected 11-4, 842B3
EVANS, Charles
Pleads guilty 7-31, 639C3
Gets probation 10-7, 890F1
EVANS, Cooper
Wins Ia US House primary 6-3, 439E3
Elected to US House 11-4, 842C3, 851B1
EVANS, Rep. David W. (D, Ind.)
Reelected 11-4, 842B4
EVANS, Edward P.
Elected Macmillan bd chrmn 2-11, 225A1
EVANS, Gov. John (D, Idaho)
State of State message 1-7, 403C2
EVANS 3rd, John Louis
Wins retrial order 10-15, 869A1
EVANS, Johnny
NFL '79 punting ldr 1-5, 8B3
EVANS, Mostyn
BL strike ends 4-21, 313B2
EVANS, Peter
Wins Olympic medal 7-22, 623F2
EVANS, Robert
Urban Cowboy released 6-11, 675F3
Pleads guilty 7-31, 639B3
Gets probation 10-7, 890E1
Popeye released 12-12, 972F3
EVANS, Robert L.
Cancels Beatrice merger 12-29, 985D1
EVANS, Judge Terence T.
Orders Army lesbian reinstated 5-20, 428A3
EVENING News, The (newspaper)
Evening Standard merger set 10-1, 750D3
EVENING Standard, The (newspaper)
Evening News merger set 10-1, 750D3
EVERS, Charles
Endorses Reagan 10-22, 802C2
Visits Reagan 12-9, 956B2
EVERS, John W.
Dies 12-5, 1004E1
EVERT Lloyd, Chris (Mrs. John Lloyd)
Avon tourn results 1-13, 1-27, 607C2
Wins Women's Italian Open 5-11, Chichester 6-14, 607C3, E3
US wins Federatn Cup 5-25, 607B1
Wins French Open 6-7, 606B3
Loses Wimbledon 7-4, 606G1
Wins US Clay Cts 8-10, 691B3
Wins US Open 9-6, 691F1, D2
Wins English Women's Grand Prix 10-26; Lions Cup results 11-23, 947C2, G2
US wins Wightman Cup 11-1, 947A1
EVERY Child (film)
Wins Oscar 4-14, 296A2
EVERY Which Way But Loose (film)
'79 top domestic rental film 2-6, 120G2
EVITA (play)
Wins Tonys 6-8, 692A3
EVREN, Gen. Kenan
Mil warns pol ldrs, urges unity 1-2, 7C2
Asks more mil powers 2-15, 135A3
Impatient re terrorism 7-21, 567G3
Mil coup ousts govt 9-12, 679D2-A3
Coup consolidated, sees return to civilian rule 9-12; junta sworn 9-18, 696C2-A3
Named Turkey junta chrmn 9-21, 720C3
Mil affirms powers 10-27, 832G2
Insists terrorist policy impartial 11-18, 888B2
EVRON, Ephraim
Protests US plan to vote vs Israel at UN 3-1, 163A3
Vs extra gear for Saudi F-15s 6-17, 450C2
Fears Jordan war aid to Iraq 10-8, 757F1
Settles '67 Liberty attack case 12-18, 966C2
EWING, Oscar R.
Dies 1-8, 104E2
EXECUTIONER'S Song, The (book)
On best-seller list 1-13, 40B3
Mailer wins Pulitzer 4-14, 296D2, E2
EXECUTIVE Orders—*See under CARTER*
EXECUTIVE Woman (magazine)
Ex-publisher indicted 1-10, 216G1
EXETER—*See NEW Hampshire*
EXIMBANK (Export-Import Bank)—*See under U.S. GOVERNMENT*

1976

EXPLOSIONS—*See 'Fires & Explosions' under ACCIDENTS*
EXPRESS Forwarding & Storage Co.
Boycott rpt released 10-18, 786B1
EXTORTION—*See 'Bribery, Fraud & Extortion' under CRIME*
EXXON Corp. (formerly Standard Oil Co. of N.J.)
Venez oil natlzd 1-1, pact signed 1-6, 12B3
Ireland oil finds rptd 2-1, 157C1
1st UK Auk shipmt rptd 2-25, 173D3
NY dismisses '74 trust case 3-10; 2d case rptd pending 3-11, 413C1
Italy paymts fund rptd 4-11, 267B2
In Viet oil talks 4-24, 352B2
On '75 Fortune 500 list 437A1, D1, G1
SEC lists paymts 5-12, 727D1
UK invites for N Sea talks 7-1, 522A1
Rathbone dies 8-2, 816F3
Esso Standard quits Leb 8-25, 629A2
Atlantic offshore bids accepted 8-25, 648F2
Kauffmann vs House Arab boycott bill 9-19, 746D3
Norske Esso oil cleanup sought 11-17, 873D2
Nigeria unit natlized 12-23, 1007E3
EYADEMA, Gen. Gnassingbe
Benin, Togo reopen border 3-27, 372C1
At France-Africa summit 5-10—5-11, 355A3
EYEGLASSES
UAW seeks benefits 3-18, 220D1
EYZAGUIRRE, Jaime
Protest of lawyers' chrgs re DINA rptd 6-12, 465E1

1977

EXORCIST II-The Heretic (film)
Top-grossing film 7-6, 548G3
EXPLOSIONS—*See FIRES & Explosions*
EXPORT-Import Bank of the United States—*See under U.S. GOVERNMENT*
EXPORTS—*See FOREIGN Trade; commodity, country names*
EXTORTION—*See 'Bribery, Fraud & Extortion' under CRIME*
EXXON Corp. (formerly Standard Oil Co. of N.J.)
In UK N Sea pact 1-5, 20E3
On Venez, Saudi purchases 1-6, 23G1
Paymts total cited 1-21, 79G1
Age-bias judgment reversed 1-30, 279A1
To mkt extra Saudi oil 2-16, 108C1, D1
Gulf of Mex gas probe set 2-17, 151F3
On '76 Fortune 500 list 340D1, 341A1
Employe stock plan cited 5-6, 409G1
Saudi fire forces sale cut 5-19, 402C2
Imperial Oil Canada drilling rptd 6-4, 466D3
FTC info order review rejctd 6-13, 517G1
Alaska pipeline opens 6-20, 476B1, B2
B Graham fund holding rptd 6-26, 732A1
ICC sets Alaska pipe rates 6-28, 498F1
Seadock superport project dropped 7-12, 559A2
Washington sues 8-16, 691E3
Replies to Carter attack 10-13, 773B1
Sup Ct OKs Alaska pipe interim rate rise 10-20, upholds order 11-14, 878E2
Settles SEC paymts chrgs 10-25, 818D1-A2
Overchrgs rptd, denied 12-27, 1008C2
Chile copper mine buy rptd 12-28, 1019B1
Exxon Nuclear Co.
Laser uranium enrichmt rptd, US classifies 12-14, 975F1
EXXON Nuclear Co.—*See EXXON Corp.*
EXXON Pipeline Co. v. U.S.
Sup Ct upholds Alaska pipe rate order 11-14, 878E2
EYADEMA, Etienne Gnassingbe (Togo President)
UK foils assassinatn plot 10-13, 988F2
EYES & Eyesight
Sup Ct bars review of Va optometry bd ruling 2-22, 150G1
EYZAGUIRRE, Jose Maria
Chrgs DINA blocks disappearnc probes, sees Todman 8-11, 635E2

1978

EXON, Gov. J. James (D. Neb.)
Unopposed in US Sen primary 5-9, 363F1
Elected 11-7, 846E1, 848D2, 854F3
EXORCISM
4 convicted in W Ger death 4-21, church curbs rites 5-1, 379D3
Obituaries
Burden, William Douglas 11-14, 972F2
Crockett, Frederick 1-17, 96E1
EXPLOSIONS—*See FIRES & Explosions*
EXPORT Administration Review Board—*See under U.S. GOVERNMENT—COMMERCE*
EXPORT-Import Bank of the United States—*See under U.S. GOVERNMENT*
EXPORTS—*See FOREIGN Trade; commodity, country names*
EXTORTION—*See CRIME—Bribery, Fraud & Extortion*
EXXON Corp. (formerly Standard Oil Co. of N.J.)
In Dow Jones indl avg 66E2
Overchrg claim repeated, denial issued 1-11, 14B2
Rebates to consumers barred 1-20, 109A1
Chile copper mine purchased 1-24, 312C2
Belize drilling cited 1-25, 94A2
Low '76 tax paymt rptd 1-27, 65A3
Offshore lease sale delayed 1-30, 108A3
Coal, uranium holdings lid backed by FTC aide 4-5, 282F2, G2
Garvin sees Carter, backs inflatn plan 4-20, 361G3
On '77 Fortune 500 list 5-8, 325D1
Garvin on '77 top-paid execs list 5-15, 364G3
Conoco well off NJ rptd dry 6-2, 6-5, 449C3
ICC Alaska pipe rates backed by Sup Ct 6-6, 447B2
Energy Dept sues on overchrg 6-8, 450A3
Md refiner-run gas statn ban upheld by Sup Ct 6-14, 492C1
Pipeline divesture urged by Sen subcom, Garvin scores 6-21, 471E1, G1
UK hikes offshore oil tax 8-2, 591G3
2d-ranked cash-rich US co 9-18, 716E3
Australia oil find rptd 9-21, 738D3
Kauffman scores Carter 'export consequences' order 10-10, 804B3
Welch dies 10-22, 888G3
Overchrg suit filed, denial issued 11-1, 900D1
NJ offshore well rptd dry 12-6, 1010B1
Barrow rptd Kennecott chrmn 12-15, 1005B1
EXXON Corp. v. Governor of Maryland
Md refiner-run gas statn ban upheld by Sup Ct 6-14, 491F3
EXXON Pipeline Co. v. U.S.
ICC Alaska pipe rates backed by Sup Ct 6-6, 447B2
EYEN, Tom
Neon Woman opens 4-16, 760G2
EYE of the Needle (book)
On best-seller list 9-4, 708B1
EYES & Eyesight—*For blindness, see HANDICAPPED*
AHL ban on 1-eyed player lifted 2-2, 296E3
NM OKs marijuana use for glaucoma 2-22, 598D3
Vision dvpt study rptd 4-15, 334B3
Glaucoma victim wins marijuana case 5-19, 728F3
FTC adopts eyewear ad rule 5-24, 434C1
Fungal keratitis drug OKd 11-1, 948A3
Microwave safety scored 12-11, 936C3
EYES Of Laura Mars (film)
Released 8-4, 970B1
EYUBOGLU, Orhan
Named Turkey dep premr 1-5, 21D2

1979

EXPORT-Import Bank of the United States—*See under U.S. GOVERNMENT*
EXTORTION—*See CRIME—Bribery, Fraud & Extortion*
EXTRASENSORY Perception (ESP)
CIA considered spies in '50s 3-11, 208D2
EXXON Corp. (formerly Standard Oil Co. of N.J.)
In Dow Jones indl avg 72E1
US consolidates overchrg suits 1-5, 17B1
Iran oil crisis forces sales curbs 2-6, 83A1
Canada deliveries rptd cut 2-15, 153B2
Crude oil sales curbed 3-13, 183G2-A3
Canada oil imports ordrd 3-13, 210G2
Canada oppositn ldr scores 3-27, 266E3
Australia offshore drilling rptd 3-28, 233D1
2d NJ offshore well rptd dry 4-10, 361E3
1st 1/4 oil profits rptd 4-27, 301B2
May gas allocatn rptd cut 5-7, 343B1
On '78 Fortune 500 list 5-7, 304E1, 305A1
Australia record profits rptd 5-8, 352A1
Australia oil shortages seen 5-18, 368D2
Elec motor-control device unveiled, Reliance merger talks rptd 5-18, 404G1
June gas supplies cut 5-30, 395C3
Reliance purchase bid set 6-21; ct OKs, limits control 8-17, Reliance drops suit 9-19, purchase completed 9-24, 770F1-D2
3d NJ offshore well rptd dry 7-6, 518E2
UK OKs Scottish gas plant 8-10, 614A2
'79 heating oil price freeze attempt seen 9-19, 703E1
4th NJ offshore well rptd dry 9-27, 867D2
Borg-Warner develops motor-control device 10-2, 770E2
Tex supertanker port OKd 10-15, 769F3
US overchrgs alleged 10-18—10-19, 849B3, D3; 11-8, 905F2
3d 1/4 profits rptd up 10-22, 10-25, 804D2, F2, C3
UK orders N Sea cutback 10-29, 836F1
Australia field reclassified; tax break seen, exploratn permit granted 11-27, 925F2, 926A1
UK prime min at NJ unit 12-18, 968C2
EYE of the Needle (book)
On best-seller list 8-5, 620D3
EYES & Eyesight
Optometrists' use of corp names curbed by Sup Ct 2-21, 128D2
More states OK pot use for glaucoma 6-1, Ore law signed 6-18, 492B3
Long-wear contact lenses OKd 6-13, 572D1
Disabled nurse firing case refused by Sup Ct 6-18, 499D2
Hallucinogen tested by Army in '64 9-24, 727G1
Pot use for glaucoma cited 10-14, 972E1
EYES on the Harem (play)
Opens 4-24, 711F2
EYUBOGLU, Orhan
Turkey interior min role asked 1-2, 8C1

1980

EXON, Sen. J. James (D, Neb.)
Joins open-conv move 7-30, 570B2
EXPLORERS
Ronne dies 1-12, 104F3
EXPORT-Import Bank—*See under U.S. GOVERNMENT*
EXPRESS Newspapers Ltd.
Evening News, Evening Standard to merge 10-1, 750D3
EXTON, Clive
Awakening released 10-31, 972C3
EXTORTION—*See CRIME—Bribery, Fraud & Extortion*
EXXON Corp. (formerly Standard Oil Co. of N.J.)
In Dow Jones indl avg 76F1
US '79 gas selling lead rptd 1-2, 90D3
Venez '80 oil sale cut, '79 purchases rptd 1-16, 103A1
'79 profits rptd 1-25, 90F2, G2
Nader coalitn attacks 4-17, 308B2
1st 1/4 profit sets record 4-23, 331B1, D1
On '79 Fortune 500 list 5-5, 290D1, 291A1
Solar production rptd 5-5, 554D1
Arco shale oil project bought 5-13, 553G2
Saudi hikes prices 8% 5-14, 365B1
Wis out-of-state earnings tax backed by Sup Ct 6-10, 511E3
Australia-Esso shale oil accord set 7-7, 520B1
La chem-dump suit names 7-15, 558G3
Wholesale gas price cut rptd 8-8, 666D3
UK gasoline prices cut 8-11, 628G1
Saudi completes Aramco takeover, bd members listed 9-4, 662B1, A2
OPEC pricing agrmt impact seen 9-18, 695B1
Gasoline price cut rptd 9-23, 786C1
Beaufort Sea oil find rptd 10-3, 785E2-A3
Canada oil sands operatn suspended 11-18, 920F3
Australia unit pay accord scored 11-26, 940C2
EXXON v. Wisconsin
Case decided by Sup Ct 6-10, 511E3
EYADEMA, Gen. Gnassingbe (Togolese president)
Proclaims 3d republic, frees prisoners; '79 reelectn cited 1-13, 61C2
In Chad truce attempt 4-5, 311E1
EYES & Eyesight
Japan optics research rptd 2-16, 160B3
Africa Rift Valley Fever epidemic rptd 3-2, 318F2-D3
EZRA, Derek
On UK coal indus 7-30, 578E2

F

1976

F-Plane Series—*See 'Aircraft' under ARMAMENTS*
FABIANO Sobrinho, Nelson
Loses post, pol rights 1-6, 27B2
FABRE, Robert
Joint '77 electn drive stalled 5-21, 381A3
FABRI, Francesco
Sworn Italy navy min 7-30, 573G1
FACIO, Gonzalo
Hails Kissinger 2-23, 178E1
Cited as Vesco lawyer 10-29, 1000G2
FAHD Ibn Abdel Aziz Al Saud, Crown Prince (Saudi Arabia)
Egypt, Syria talks called off 5-19, 370A2
Gets Arafat plea vs Syria 10-13, 758D2

1977

F-Plane Series—*See ARMAMENTS—Aircraft*
FAA—*See U.S. GOVERNMENT—TRANSPORTATION—Federal Aviation Administration*
FABIEW, Serge
Held as Sovt spy 3-22, 255D3
FACE the Nation—*See CBS Inc.*
FACETTI, Carlo
2d in Daytona endurance 2-6, 531E2
FACIO, Gonzalo
Abandons pres bid, reassumes min post 1-9, 48E1
Latin ldrs back Panamanians 1-18, 46F1, G1
Sees Mrs Carter 5-31, lauds 6-1, 454F2
FADANA, P.
3 party members freed 2-25, 160C3
FADELL v. Minneapolis Star & Tribune Co.
Libel case refused 11-28, 919A3
FADHEL, Hafez al-
Killed 2-22, 457C3
FAHD Ibn Abdel Aziz Al Saud, Crown Prince (Saudi Arabia)
Meets Vance, says flexible on Geneva 2-19, 121G2
Sees Perez 4-25—4-27; rptd firm on oil prices 4-28, 362B1
On Palestine state plan 5-10, 360A3
Meets Carter, bars oil embargo, for Geneva conf 5-24—5-25, 401F3
Carter note from Arafat cited 7-20, 550B2
W Ger asks help re hijacking 789F2
Vs Israel recognitn 12-10, 954G2
Meets Vance 12-14, 954C2

1978

F-Plane Series—*See ARMAMENTS—Aircraft*
FAA—*See U.S. GOVERNMENT—TRANSPORTATION—Federal Aviation Administration*
FABIAN, Robert
Dies 6-14, 540F2
FABIEW, Serge
Sentenced as spy 2-1, 71C2
FABIOLA, Queen (Belgium)
Greets Carters 1-6, 1E1
FABRE, Dominique
Servant & Mistress released 6-6, 619F3
FABRE, Robert
Confers with Carter 1-6, 2F1
Quits left-wing alliance 3-20, resigns ldrship 3-22, 201C2
FACES Of Love (film)
Released 7-7, 970C1
FACE the Nation—*See under CBS Inc.*
FAHD Ibn Abdel Aziz Al Saud, Crown Prince (Saudi Arabia)
Sees Carter 1-3, comments 1-4, 1C1, 2A3
Calls Israel intransigent 582C1
Meets Sadat 7-30—7-31, 582D1
Vance sees on summit pact 9-21, 713A1
FAHEY, Bill
Traded to Padres 10-25, 1026B1

1979

F-Plane Series—*See ARMAMENTS-Aircraft*
FAA—*See U.S. GOVERNMENT-TRANSPORTATION-Federal Aviation Administration*
FABBIANI, Oscar
NASL scoring ldr 8-12, 654F3, 655A1
Named NASL top scorer 8-13, 776D1
Whitecaps win NASL title 9-8, 775G2, C3
FABER, Peter
Max Havelaar released 1-20, 174A3
FABIUS, Lauren
Chrgd re pirate broadcasts 8-24, 653C1
FABRE, Robert
Job creatn plans proposed 2-21, 134D3
FABREGA, Edwin
Panama Canal Comm member 12-6, 939D1
FACE The Nation—*See under CBS Inc.*
FADEL, Mohammed
Iraqi housing min 7-16, 544F3
FAERIES (book)
On best-seller list 1-7, 80C3
FAHD Ibn Abdel Aziz Al Saud, Crown Prince (Saudi Arabia)
Carter offers Khalid talks 2-11, 143D2
Cancels trip to US 2-22—2-24, 143F1
US mtg re Egypt feud rptd 5-20, 378C3
Strauss sees 7-7, 511D2
Assures Carter on oil output hike 7-9, 536D3
Saudi to maintain '79 oil productn 9-26, 781E1
Denies Egypt chrgs 10-10, 801G2-802A1

1980

FAA (Federal Aviation Administration)—*See under U.S. GOVERNMENT--TRANSPORTATION*
FABIAN, Robert
Rpts on Peoples Temple assets 2-6, 170E3
FABRE, Rene
Murder sentence rptd 5-27, 463B2
FABRE, Robert
Giscard names ombudsman 7-31, 652B1
FABRIKANT, Max
Sues Columbia Pictures 10-7, 906C3
FACE The Nation—*See CBS Inc.*
FADE to Black (film)
Released 10-17, 836F2
FAFIAN, Joseph
Named Beneficial pres 9-28, 959B3
FAHD Ibn Abdel Aziz Al Saud, Crown Prince (Saudi Arabia)
Lauds Carter Persian Gulf vow 1-26, 65D1
US briefs on Palestine autonomy talks 2-2, 89D2
US briefs on Pak talks, Persian Gulf 2-4—2-5, 83A2
In US oil talks 3-1—3-4, 165B3
UK amb ordrd to leave 4-23, 313D2
Proposes Mideast peace role 5-25; Begin invites to Israel 5-27; reactn 5-28, 395A2
Urges holy war vs Israel 8-14, 627F2

1976

FAHMY, Ismail
Backs PLO at Geneva conf 1-5, 18F3
Vs Syria Leb invasion 6-3, 406F1
US thanks PLO for Leb evacuatn aid 6-21, 448E1
In Syrian talks 6-23—6-24, 449D1
Vs attacks on Leb refugee camps 6-25, asks forgn mins meet 6-29, 463G3
Scores Israel Uganda raid 7-4, 486D2
Egypt offers tanks to Leb 7-11, 514E2
Meets Sovt forgn min 11-3—11-4, 841F2
Mediates Syria-Iraq border feud 11-24—11-25, 895B1
For new Geneva conf 12-2, 894A3
Syria, Egypt plan union 12-21, 954E2
FAINBERG, Viktor
USSR chrgs UK internmt 2-4, 122C2
FAIR, Maj. Gen. Robert L.
Resigns after losing command 1-5, 43C2 ★
FAIRCHILD Industries, Inc.
Sikes conflict of interest chrgd 4-7, 286G2
SEC rpts paymts probe 5-12, 727D1
Sikes reprimanded 7-29, 551F3
FAIRCO Inc.
Boycott rpt released 10-20, 786A2
FAIRFAX County, Va.—*See VIRGINIA*
FAITH, Percy
Dies 2-9, 160D3
FALKLAND (Malvinas) Islands (British colony)
Argentina asks UK remove amb 1-13, 26F1
Argentina amb to UK on indefinite leave 1-14, 96F3
UK cultural institute in Cordoba bombed 1-15, 96C2
OAS com backs Argentina claim 1-15, 96G3
Argentines score Arauz dismissal 1-17, 71A3
UK withdraws Argentina amb 1-19, 96E3
Argentina fires on UK research ship, UK protests 2-4; ship resumes research 2-21, 220D2
FALLACI, Oriana
On Panagoulis death 5-2, 352A1
FALLDIN, Thorbjorn
Center wins elections 9-20, 714E1
Facts on 714E2
Names Cabt, delivers nuclear speech 10-8, 794F1, B2
FALSTAD, William
Seconds Ford nominatn 8-18, 598A1
FALSTAFF Brewing Co.
Ballantine merger cited 5-11, 360F2
SEC sues Emersons 5-11, 360F2

FAMILIES & Family Life—*See also CHILDREN, BIRTH Control*
Eucharistic Cong topic 8-1—8-8, 596D2
Ford pres acceptance speech cites 8-19, 612C2
Jobless benefits bill signed 10-20, 788A2
FAMILY Planning—*See BIRTH Control*
FAMILY Practice, American Board of
Gives 1st proficiency exam 10-29, 972F3
FAMINES
Guatemala quake famine denied 2-8, 121A1
Niger seeks intl aid 2-9, 205A3
US Dem platform text 6-15, 475F2
Linked to populatn growth decline 10-28, 863F1, A2

1977

FAHMI, Sayed Hussein
Out as interior min 2-1, 83F1
FAHMY, Ismail
Sees war if peace try fails 1-11, 10B2
Meets Waldheim 2-3, 86D2
Vs Sovt note chrging plot vs Libya 4-27; note withdrawn 5-5, 361B3
Warns oil embargo vs US 5-22, Saudi ldr denies 5-24—5-25, 401F3
Sees Sovt forgn min 6-9—6-10, joint statemt issued 6-11, 457F2
Meets Brezhnev 6-15; rpt better ties set 6-22, 496B2
On Hussein-Sadat talks 7-10, 534F3
Sadat on Moscow visit 7-16, 550B1
For PLO peace talks role 7-20, 549C2
Sadat on Israel-Arab pre-Geneva mtg plan 8-2, 588D2
Vs W Bank settlmts 8-19, 648C2
Sees Carter, Vance 9-21; says Arabs 'to accept Israel' 9-22, 714D1
Vs Geneva conf without PLO 9-26; vs Israel peace stand 9-28, 734C1
Sees Carter in NY 10-4, 749A3
For PLO at Geneva conf 10-19, 793A1
Quits re Sadat Israel trip 11-17, 890B2
Kamel becomes foreign min 993E1
Scores Sadat Israel visit 12-3, 930D2
FAHMY, Lt. Gen. Mohammed Ali
Rpts Egyptian, Israel 'shooting' 5-4, 361C2
FAHOUM, Khaled
Jordan, PLO link OKd 2-22—2-23, 122E1
Reelected to Palestine Natl Cncl 3-13, 208D1
FAIR Campaign Practices Committee
'76 electn complaints rptd 1-4, 59F2
FAIRCHILD Industries Inc.
Wernher von Braun dies 6-16, 532G3
FAIRFAX, Beatrice—*See McCARROLL, Marion*
FAIR Play for Cuba Committee
FBI Cointelpro papers released 11-21, 940E3
FAISAL, Prince Saud al- (Saudi Arabia)
Meets Vance 12-14, 954C2
FAISAL Malik Faisal ibn Abdel Aziz, King (Saudi Arabia) (d. 1975)
Cited in Begin Knesset speech 11-20, 894C1
FALCAO, Armando
Sets forgn censorship 5-28, 524B3
FALCO, Mathea
Named to State drug post 1-21, 53D1
FALCONER (book)
On best-seller list 4-3, 264G1; 5-1, 356B2; 6-4, 452G1; 7-3, 548D3; 8-14, 643F1
FALCON Seaboard Inc.
Raytheon purchase set 6-22, 519C2
FALKLAND (Malvinas) Islands (British colony)
Falkland, UK, Argentina talks rptd 12-18, 1018E3
FALLDIN, Thorbjorn
On price freeze, austerity plan 4-4, 429D1
On krona devaluatn 8-29, 708D3
FALN (Armed Forces of Puerto Rican National Liberation)
Torres probe arrests 3-1, 3-8, 261D2
NYC FBI hq, other blasts linked 3-21, 261A2
Chicago blast claimed 6-4, 464E3
2 NYC office bldgs bombed 8-3, 3d bomb found 8-8, 613D3, G3
Figueroa pardoned 10-6, 808A2
FALSTAFF Brewing Corp.
Bribery chrgd 2-16, 215D2
FAMILIES & Family Life—*See also BIRTH Control, BIRTHS, CHILDREN, YOUTH*
House subcom sets TV family hour hearings, '76 ruling cited 2-9, 158A1
Carter stresses stability 2-10, 110E2
'60-61, '72-73 expenses rptd 5-10, 423D2
Ohio nuclear family zoning rule upset 5-31, 461F3
Carter on stability 6-30, 515C2
Adoptn subsidies proposed 7-12, 628F2-C3
Planning funds authorized 8-1, 689A3
'63-77 SAT score drop linked 8-23, 739E1
Sup Ct upholds disability benefits loss 11-8, 857A1
TV viewing decline rptd 12-6, 1021E3
Carter on urban aid 12-14, 960C1
Helsinki review conf adjourns 12-22, 997D2
FAMILIES of Missing in Action, National League of—*See MISSING in Action, etc.*
FAMILY Planning—*See BIRTH Control*
FAMILY Planning Coalition, Great Lakes
Abortn alternatives proposed 7-19, 786D3
FAMILY Planning Forum, National
Abortn alternatives proposed 7-19, 786D3
FAMINES
Ethiopia preventn plan rptd 1-15, 62G3
Carter statemt to world 1-20, 26G1, A3
Haiti hit 4-12, 312F2
Cambodia problems rptd 5-2, 337A1
Carter forgn policy address 5-22, 397F2
New Sahel famine seen 9-19, 770G1-A2

1978

FAHMY, Hussein
Says party newspr to republish 7-11, 573A2
FAHMY, Lt. Gen. Mohammed Ali
Removed as staff chief 10-3, 746D2
FAINA, Carlo
Indicted 4-3, 330D3
FAIRBANKS, Alaska—*See ALASKA*
FAIRBANKS, Chuck
Suspended by Patriots, U of Colo job offer cited 12-18; reinstated 12-20, 1024D2
FAIRCHILD Industries Inc.
Co, chrmn indicted 9-8, 9-10, 808A3
FAIRLEIGH Dickinson University (Rutherford, N.J.)
Jacobs sets indoor high jump record 1-27, 76A3
FAISON, Frankie R.
Black Body Blues opens 1-24, 887B1
FAISON, George
Blacks opens 5-24, 887C1
FALCONE, Pete
Traded to Mets 12-5, 1026C1
FALCON Rodriguez, Mario (d. 1977)
Sinoloa rptr killed 2-13, 290A1
FALCON Seaboard Inc.
Diamond Shamrock to buy 11-2, 1005B2
FALK, Peter
Cheap Detective released 6-22, 619A1
FALKLAND (Malvinas) Islands (Brilsh colony)
Argentina, UK hold new talks 2-15—2-17, 208C2
FALLDIN, Thorbjorn (Swedish premier; replaced Oct. 13)
Deputy premier quits govt 1-31, 93D1
At 26th Bilderberg Conf 4-21—4-23, 302D3
Panel backs A-power 6-14, govt split rptd 6-15, 691F1-A2
Quits in A-power dispute 10-5, 764F2
Ullsten becomes premr 10-13, 822E2
FALLON, Seamus
Vs UK Parachute Regimt recall 4-3, 268A2
FALLON, Walter A.
Berkey wins trust suit vs Kodak 1-21, 67F1
FALLS, Adm. R. H.
Orders Painchaud transfer 7-12, 556B3

FAMILIES & Family Life—*See also BIRTH Control, CHILDBIRTH, CHILDREN, YOUTH*
Helsinki review conf ends 3-9, 179C2
Guaranteed income study rptd 5-19, 720E3
NYC 'runaway' father crackdown rptd 7-3, 685A1
Grandparent child care tax credit clears Cong 10-15, 786D1
Carter gets Mormon award 11-27, 914G3
NYS illegitimate child inheritance law upheld by US Sup Ct 12-11, 981B1
FAMILY Business (play)
Opens 4-12, 760B2
FAMILY Planning—*See BIRTH Control*
FAMINES
Sahel relief rptd sought 2-1, 3-8, 237F1
Ethiopia locust plague, food aid rptd 6-4—6-12, 465G2

1979

FAHRINGER, Herald
Lawyers' interstate rights limited by Sup Ct 1-5, 31D3
FAHY, Charles
Dies 9-17, 756C2
FAIRBANKS, Chuck
Patriots release 4-2, 335D1
FAIRBANKS, Douglas (1883-1939)
Mary Pickford dies 5-29, 432D3
FAIRCHILD Camera & Instrument Corp. (of Schlumberger Ltd.)
Gould merger bids rejctd 5-4, 5-8, suits filed 5-8, 5-9, 350D1
Schlumberger purchase set, Gould drops bid 5-21, 440D3
FAIRCHILD Industries Inc.
Acquitted of tax chrgs 2-7, 88A1
Complaint vs IRS refused by Sup Ct 3-26, 231B1
FAIRCHILD Industries v. Harvey
Case refused by Sup Ct 3-26, 231C1
FAIRFAX Ltd., John
Acquires Herald interest 11-26, 966A3
FAIRPORT, O.—*See OHIO*
FAISAL Malik Faisal ibn Abdel Aziz, King (Saudi Arabia) (d. 1975)
Sadat lauds, notes warning 5-1; Saudi denies 5-2, 319A2
FAITH Healer (play)
Opens 4-4, 711G2
FALCO, Mathea
Rpts on W. Eur heroin use 11-11, 972C3
FALDO, Nick
US wins Ryder Cup Matches 9-16, 969F3
FALK, Peter
In-Laws released 6-15, 820D1
FALKLAND (Malvinas) Islands (British colony)
UK-Argentina amb exchng set 11-16, 906D2
FALLDIN, Thorbjorn (Swedish premier)
Ullsten energy plan rptd 3-13, 213G3
Urges A-plant shutdown 3-31, 246G1
A-plant fueling OKd 6-25, 505B2
Named premier 10-9, confrmd 10-11, 795E1-A2
FALLOWS, James
Calls Carter 'arrogant' 4-22, 300B3
Scores Carter staff 5-18, 627F2
FALN (Armed Forces of National Liberation)
Morales convicted 3-9, sentncd 4-20; escapes 5-21, 431E1
NYC bomb hoax, Indian Pt threatened 10-17—10-18; Chicago, PR blasts 10-18, 786A2
PR ambushers named 12-3, 924C3
FALS Borda, Orlando
Colombia detains 1-24, 115A2

FAMILIES & Family Life
Foster care benefits backed by Sup Ct 2-22, 151B1
Unwed fathers adoptn, damage suit rights defined by Sup Ct 4-24, 364A1
Unwed mothers denied survivors' aid by Sup Ct 6-27, 558F1
'78 median income, poverty data, '60-78 income growth rptd 11-24, 965E1-G2
FAMILY Planning—*See BIRTH Control & Family Planning*
FAMINES
Zaire food shortages rptd 2-6, 137A3
Zaire situatn worsening 2-15, 215E1
Pope presents 1st encyclical 3-15, 217C1
FAO hunger conf held in Rome 7-13—7-20, 554B1
E Timor populatn down, US probes 12-4, 12-15, 994F3-995B1
Cambodia—*See CAMBODIA–Famine*

1980

FAHNER, Tyrone C.
Named Ill atty gen 7-29, 654G2
FAIR, T. Willard
Warns re Miami rioting 12-6, 963G1
FAIRBAIRN, Jay Randall
Missing in Carib copter crash 11-13, 869E3
FAIRCHILD Industries Inc.
VSI Corp merger set 8-26, 746C1
FCC OKs satellite launchings 12-4, 990E3
FAIRLEIGH Dickinson University Rutherford Campus
2d in IC4A indoor champ 3-8—3-9, 892C2
FAISON, Sandy
Charlie & Algernon opens 9-14, 892B3
FAITH Center (Glendale, Calif.)
FCC revokes KHOF-TV license 10-10, 907C1
FAKOURI, Col. Javad
Named Iran AF cmdr 6-19, 464E2
Iranian defense min 9-7, 689B1
FALCO, Louis
Fame released 5-16, 675D2
FALCONE, Joseph
Indicted 7-31, 714A2
FALCONE, Vincent
Indicted 7-31, 714A2
FALLAH, Gen. Valiollah
Iran army staff chief 6-19, 464D2
FALLDIN, Thorbjorn (Swedish premier)
Referendum backs A-power, govt seen endangered 3-23, 219C3, F3, G3
Bars labor dispute interventn 5-2, 355B3
Labor pact set 5-11, 365C1
Sees Mex pres 5-24, 409G2
VAT hike set 8-19, 653C3
Budget cuts set 9-16, 730F3
Wins confidence vote 10-22, 822F3
On Reagan US electn 11-5, 841A3
FALLING in Love Again (film)
Released 11-21, 972D3
FALLON, George Hyde
Dies 3-21, 279E2
FALN (Armed Forces of National Liberation)
Carter, Bush campaign hqs raided 3-15, 208A3-209A1
11 suspects arrested 4-4; houses raided, execs hit list seized 4-7, 4-8, 308F3-309E1
8 suspects convicted 7-30; 2 others sentncd, 1 rptd extradited 8-4, 601C1
11 indicted for '75-79 Chicago bombings 12-10, 963F3
FALWELL, Jerry
TV revenues rptd 2-25, 413A2
Political role profiled 9-15, 818F3, 819A1, A2, B3
Reagan disavows prayer stand 10-3, 763F2
Reverses Jewish prayer stance 10-11, 811F1
FAME (film)
Released 5-16, 675D2
FAMILIES, White House Conference on
Opens in Baltimore 6-5, 442E2; meets in Minn 6-19—6-21, LA 7-10—7-12, 601G1

FAMILIES & Family Life
'70-77 credit card use rptd 1-30, 92G2
LA adults-only housing barred 1-31, 115C2
Spouse testimony upheld by Sup Ct 2-27, 188B2
Del 'unfit' parent case accepted by Sup Ct 3-24, 265G1
Retarded youth surgery case refused by Sup Ct 3-31, 291B3
White House Conf opens in Md 6-5, 442E2; meets in Minn 6-19—6-21, LA 7-10—7-12, 601G1
GOP drafts platform 7-9, 506C2
Evangelical Christian pol actn profiled 7-11—9-15, 818E3, 819E1
GOP platform adopted; text 7-15, 535D2, E2, E3
Reagan pres nominatn acceptance speech 7-17, 531C1, E2, F3, 532B3, 533C2
Ukrainian youth granted asylum in US 7-21, 560C1
Reagan, Anderson TV debate 9-21, 722B2
RC bishops conf opens 9-29; birth control, annulmt, other issues debated 9-29—10-6, 810C2
Mich contraceptive distributn case declined by Sup Ct 10-6, 782G2
Stepfather adoptn rights case accepted by Sup Ct 10-6, 782B3
Unwed couples child custody case refused by Sup Ct 10-20, 807A1
'79 median income, poverty data rptd 10-23, 823E3
Pope in W Ger, affirms traditionalism 11-15—11-19, 905D1
Stepfather adoptn right ruling vacated by Sup Ct 11-17, 882F1
Domestic violence victims bill dropped 11-17, 982A2
FAMILY Liaison Action Group
US hostage kin seek W Eur support 4-13, 299C2
FAMILY Planning—*See BIRTH Control*
FAMINES
Zaire food aid rptd diverted 2-28, 356C2
Reagan pres nominatn acceptance speech 7-17, 534G3
World Bank '80 econ forecast grim 8-17, 628B3
Cambodia—*See CAMBODIA (Democratic Kampuchea)--Famine*

1976

FANALI, Duilio
Arrested 3-22, indictmt rptd 3-24, 298D1
FANALE, Raser P.
On Mars atmosphere 7-21, 526G2
FANFANI, Amintore
CD chrmn 4-14, 297G1
Campaigns vs CP 6-11, 445E2
Hails election 6-21, 445G1
Elected Senate pres 7-5, 497G1
Vs CP Cabt formatn role 7-25, 556F3
Replaced as CD pres 10-14, 890C3
FANNIN, Sen. Paul J. (R, Ariz.)
DeConcini wins seat 11-2, 820C1, 824C1
FARAH, Abdulrahima
Disputes US OAU summit role 1-28, 67E3
FAR Eastern Economic Review, The (magazine)
Faces Thai censorship 10-11, 775E3
FARGO, N.D.—*See NORTH Dakota*
FARHAT, Abdallah
Tunisia defense min 5-31, 503C3
FARKAS, George
'72 campaign gift listed 4-25, 688B1
FARKAS, Ruth
'72 campaign gift listed 4-25, 688B1
Quits as amb to Lux 5-4, replaced 5-20, 412E1, B2
FARLEY, James A.
Facts on 444C1
Dies 6-9, 444A1
FARM Bureau Federation, American
Ford addresses 1-5, 2B2, 3E1-B3
Sugar industry lobbying cited 9-21, 721C3
FARMER, James
Quits CORE 2-19, 163A3
FARMERS Bank of the State of Delaware
Rpts loss 1-29; bailout dvpts 2-4—6-10, 437F2
FARMERS & Farming—*See AGRICULTURE*
FARMERS Union, National
Mondale, Humphrey ratings cited 512D3
FARM Workers of America, United—*See UNITED Farm Workers of America*
FARR, William T.
Wins 5-yr ct test 12-21, 995C1
FARRAGUT (U.S. warship)
In Intl Naval Review 7-4, 488D3
FARROW, Mia
Sinatra marries Marx 7-11, 640G3
FARY, Rep. John G. (D, Ill.)
Reelected 11-2, 829F2
FASCELL, Rep. Dante B. (D, Fla.)
On US Korea mil buildup 9-1, 641G1
Reelected 11-2, 829C2
On Helsinki progress rpt 12-8, 934G1
FASCISM
Spain bookstore attacks rptd 11-12, 909D2
FASHION—*See CLOTHING*
FASSER, Paul J.
Replaced in Labor post 5-12, 412A2
FATZER, Justice Harold
Cited in Dole biog sketch 614C2
FAULKNER, (Arthur) Brian (Deane)
Quits as Protestant party ldr 8-19, 638E2
FAULKNER, Harry D.
Charges Marine bias 6-4, 435A3
FAULKNER, James H.
Sworn Canada sci min 9-15, 692E1
FAUNTROY, Del. Walter E. (D, D.C.)
Reelected 11-2, 821C1, 825C2, 829A2
FAVA, Maria
Sought in Lockheed probe 2-17, 132C2
Indictmt rptd 3-24, 298D1

1977

FANFRELUCHE (race horse)
Vanishes 6-25, rptd found 12-9, 971A2
FANG YI
Chen replaces in econ post 1-14, 61G2
In Politburo 8-21, 645F2 *
FANNIE Mae—*See U.S. GOVERNMENT—HOUSING & Urban Development—Federal National Mortgage Association*
FANS (Fight to Advance the Nation's Sports)
Formatn planned 9-27, 820F1
FAN Yuan-yen
Defects to Taiwan 7-7, describes China conditions 7-8, 536E3-537C1
FAO—*See UNITED Nations—Food & Agriculture Organization*
FARAG, Maj. Ahmad
Assassination rptd 10-14, 824F1
FARBER, Barry
Koch wins mayoral primary 9-8, 723B2
Koch elected mayor 11-8, 855E2
FAR Eastern Economic Review (magazine)
Singapore correspondent rearrested 2-12, 223C3
FARHAD, Mohammed
Arrested 10-13, 805G2
FARIS, Mustapha
Named Morocco agri min 10-10, 772F1
FARKAS, Judge Leonard
Suppresses Dawson 5 confessn 9-29, overturned 11-8, 991D2
FARLEY Jr., James A.
Quits NYS Athletic Comm 6-3, ABC rpt clears 9-3, 828A2
FAR-Mar-Co.
Farmland merger set 2-11, 408E3
FARMER, Karen
DAR membership rptd 12-3, 1021D2
FARMER, Millard
Dawson 5 murder chrgs dropped 12-19, 991E2
FARMER, Thomas L.
Named to Intell Oversight Bd 5-5, 462E2
FARMERS (& Farming)—*See AGRICULTURE*
FARMERS Export Co.
Grain elevator blast 12-27, 1023G1-B2
FARMLAND Industries Inc.
Far-Mar-Co merger set 2-11, 408E3
FARM Workers of America, United—*See UNITED Farm Workers of America*
FASCELL, Rep. Dante B. (D, Fla.)
US bars Sovt editor 1-12, 22E1
Bukovsky urges Sovt rights stand 2-23, 142B3
Vance testifies on Shcharansky 6-6, 436G1
Cong backs Helsinki rights talks 6-15, 501D1
FASHION—*See CLOTHING*
FASI, Mayor Frank (Honolulu, Hawaii)
Bribery charges dismissed 12-27, 1008E1
FAST, Howard
Immigrants on best-seller list 11-6, 872D3
FATAH, Zakaria Abdul
On EC trade pacts 1-18, 73G3
FAUCHEUX, Ron
Defeats Tonry 6-25, 501E1
Loses to Livingston 8-27, 693C1
FAULKNER, (Arthur) Brian (Deane)
Dies 3-3, 264F2
FAULKNER, James Hugh
Canada Indian affairs min 9-16, 725A3
James Bay land pact becomes law 11-1, 862E3 *
FAUMUINA, Wilson
In NFL draft 5-3, 353B2
FAUNTROY, Del. Walter E. (D, D.C.)
Vs Sprague firing 2-10—2-21, 127A1
Chrgs press-CIA links 4-24, backs down 4-28, 339C2
FAURE, Edgar
Loses Radical ldrship bid 5-15, 449G3

1978

FANFANI, Amintore (Italian president)
Assumes presidency 6-15, 516D3
FANG YI
Named China dep premr 2-26—3-5, 153E1
Issues 8-yr sci plan 5-28, 436D1
Signs French tech science pact 10-20, 814B1
FANJUL, Roberto
Peru rightists kidnap 9-3—9-10, 776B1
FANNIE Mae—*See U.S. GOVERNMENT—HOUSING & Urban Development—Federal National Mortgage Association*
FANTASIE-Stucke Op. 12 (recording)
Rubenstein wins Grammy 2-24, 316D1
FAO—*See UNITED Nations—Food & Agriculture Organization*
FARAG, Ibrahim
New Wafd Party dissolves 6-2, 436G3
FARAH, Empress (Iran)
Visits Iraq 11-18—11-19, 893G2
FARBER, Myron A.
Jascalevich case press freedom controversy 6-30—8-30; jailed for contempt 8-4, freed 8-30, 678C2
Contempt case dvpts 8-30—10-6; wins release, NY Times fine ended 10-24, 841C2
IAPA scores jailing 10-13, 829F1
Press freedom case declined by Sup Ct 11-27, 937E1
FAR East—*See ASIA; country names*
FARGO, James
Caravans released 11-1, 969F3 *
FARGO Agency, Leslie
Ford sued re fee paymt 5-16, 390F3
FARM Bureau Federation, American
House defeats farm bill 4-12, 261C2
FARMER, Ed
Traded to Rangers 12-15, 1026E1
FARMER, James
Scores CORE conv, Innis 9-18, 810C1
FARMERS (& Farming)—*See AGRICULTURE*
FARMERS' Association, Midcontinent
Carter addresses in Mo 8-14, 626D1
FARMERS Export Co.
Tex '77 grain elevator blast violatns rptd 2-23, 636E2
FARMERS Union, National
House defeats farm bill 4-12, 261C2
FARM Workers of America, United—*See UNITED Farm Workers of America*
FAROUK, King (Egypt) (1920-65)
New Wafd Party reinstated 2-3, 131B2
FAR Pavilions, The (book)
On best-seller list 10-9, 800A3; 12-3, 971A1
FARRELL, Devin
Broadway Musical opens 12-21, 1031B1
FARRELL, James
In Recovery Lounge opens 12-7, 1031B2
FARRELL Jr., James A.
Dies 9-15, 888A3
FARRELL Lines, Inc.
Farrell dies 9-15, Amer Export acquisitn cited 11-6, 888A3
FARRIS, William E.
Loses US House electn 11-7, 856G3
FARROW, Mia
Avalanche released 8-28, 969B3
Death On Nile, Wedding released 9-29, 970B1, D3
FARY, Rep. John G. (D, Ill.)
Reelected 11-7, 850D3
FASCELL, Rep. Dante B. (D, Fla.)
House OKs Turkey arms embargo end 8-1, 587C3
Reelected 11-7, 850G2
FASCISM
Eur mtg 3-4—3-5, 238D3
FASHION—*See CLOTHING*
FASI, Mayor Frank (Honolulu, Hawaii)
Loses primary for gov 10-7, 791C3
Ariyoshi elected Hawaii gov 11-7, 857C1
FASO, Nina
Working opens 5-14, 887E3
FAST, Howard
Immigrants on best-seller list 10-8, 800C3; 11-6, 888B1
2d Generatn on best-seller list 10-9, 800A3; 11-6, 887F3
FASTENERS, Industrial
ITC recommends import curbs 12-8-77; Carter bars 2-10, 181A2
ITC backs duty hike, Cong subcom veto cited 10-31; Carter OKs hike 12-26, 998D3
FAST-Food Chains—*See RESTAURANTS*
FATHERS and Sons (play)
Opens 11-16, 1031E1
FAULKNER, James Hugh
Sets Yukon dvpt halt 7-6, 531A3
Halts Indian, Metis legal funds 9-27, 866E3
FAUNTROY, Del. Walter E. (D, D.C.)
Diggs convicted 10-7, 791F3
Reelected 11-7, 848B1, 850E2
Assails Lane on FBI King plot allegatns 11-17, 938C2
FAURE, Edgar
Loses Natl Assemb pres bid 4-3, 245A3
FAURE, Roland
Quits L'Aurore 11-26, 1017A1
FAVA, Dr. Diego
Shot 5-8, 393B2

1979

FANALI, Duilio
Convicted 3-1, 155D2
FANCUTT, Michael
Loses NCAA doubles title 5-28, 570B2
FANG YI
Signs W Ger pact 6-19, 637G3
FANIA All-Stars (singing group)
Perform in Cuba 3-1—3-4, 238D2
FANNING, Gene
Brass Ring opens 7-2, 711F1
FAO—*See UNITED Nations—Food & Agriculture Organization*
FAQIR, Faqir M.
Afghan interior min 9-14, 695E3
FARABOD, Maj. Gen. Nassir
Named Iran armed forces chief 3-27, 247E2
Ousted 7-21, 565G2
FARANDA, Adriana
Arrested 5-30, 426E2
Red Brigades split revealed 7-25, 7-28, 583E3
Threatnd in Curcio letter 8-10, 635F2
FARBER, Myron A.
Jascalevich trial costs ordrd paid 8-14, 656E2
FARBOD, Gen. Nasser
Mil police cmdr defies dismissal order 7-9, 525G1
FARDUST, Gen. Hussein
Tied to death of shah's nephew 12-8, 935E1
FAR East—*See ASIA; country names*
FAR East Economic Review
Pak sentncs newsman 11-29, 951F1
FARE v. Michael C.
Case decided by Sup Ct 6-20, 516B2; cited 6-25, 540B2
FARHAT, Said
Brazil info min designate 1-19, 95E1
On Belo Horizonte strike 8-3, 612A3
FARINA, Giuliano
Red Brigades attack 3-14, 212D1
FARMERS (& Farming)—*See AGRICULTURE*
FARMERS' Union Grain Terminal Association
Strike agreement signed 9-14, 722F3
FARMINGTON, Mo.—*See MISSOURI*
FARMLAND Industries
Diesel fuel supplies rptd down 5-18, 361C3
FARM Workers of America, United—*See UNITED Farm Workers of America*
FAR Pavilions, The (book)
On best-seller list 1-7, 80B3; 9-2 672C3; 10-14, 800D3
FARRELL, James T.
Dies 8-22, 671C2
FARRELL Lines Inc.
Amer Export Lines indicted 6-1, 423D2; pleads no contest, fined 6-8, 442B2
FARRISH, Dave
In NHL expansion draft 6-13, 470A2
FARROW, Mia
Divorces Previn 1-31, 79B2
Hurricane released 4-11, 528E2
Romantic Comedy opens 11-8, 956G3
FARSHI, Hossein
Defends Tabriz seizure 12-6, 915D3
FASCELL, Rep. Dante (D, Fla.)
Releases US Helsinki rpt 11-7, 980G3
FASHION—*See CLOTHING & Fashion*
FASSBINDER, Rainer Werner
Despair released 2-15, 174D2
FAST, Howard
2d Generatn on best-seller list 1-7, 80A3; 10-14, 800C3; 11-4, 892D3
Immigrants on best-seller list 1-7, 80D3
Establishmt on best-seller list 11-4, 892A3
FAST Break (film)
Released 3-1, 174D2
Top-grossing film 4-4, 271F2
FASTENERS, Industrial
GATT pact signed, more tariff cuts barred 4-12, 274F1
FATHER'S Day (play)
Opens 6-21, 711G2
FAUNTROY, Del. Walter E. (D, D.C.)
Deplores Young UN resignatn 8-15, 606F1
With SCLC group in Leb 9-18—9-20, deplores PLO Jerusalem bombing 9-20, 694B1, D1
Drops US invitatn to Arafat 10-11, 780F3

1980

FAMOUS Potatoes (book)
Wins Amer Book Award 5-1, 692D2
FANGHANEL, Jurgen
Wins Olympic medal 8-2, 622B2
FANNY (book)
On best-seller list 9-14, 716B3; 10-12, 796D3
FARAGO, Ladislas
Dies 10-15, 876D1
FARAHMANDPUR, Eshagh
Ousted by Iran parlt 8-17, 644A3
FARB, Peter
Dies 4-8, 360E1
FARDUST, Gen. Hussein
Secret visit to US rptd 8-14, 671E3
FARER, Tom
Sees Colombia DR Emb hostages 4-22, 311E3
FARHANG, Monsour
Methodists confer on hostages 4-23, 324F3
FARKAS, Bertalan
Takes space flight 5-26, 397C3
Returns 6-3, 477C1
FARMER, Ed
NL wins All-Star Game 7-8, 636A2
AL pitching ldr 10-6, 926G3
FARR, Kimberly
Happy New Year opens 4-27, 392A3
FARR, Thomas Hugh
Dies 3-17, 279F2
FARRELL, Edelmiro S.
Dies 10-31, 876E1
FARSI, Jalaleddin
Quits Iran pres electn race 66D3
Bani-Sadr nominates premr 7-26, 571G2
FARY, Rep. John G. (D, Ill.)
Reelected 11-4, 842D3
FASCELL, Rep. Dante D. (D, Fla.)
Scores refugee progrms 6-20, 485B1
FASHION—*See CLOTHING*
FASI, Mayor Frank (Honolulu, Hawaii)
Loses primary 9-20, 745D1
FAST, Howard
Establishment on best-seller list 10-12, 796F3; 12-7, 948F3
FATHA, Mounir
Killed in Beirut 11-5, 873G3
FATSO (film)
Released 2-1, 216D2
FAUBUS, Orval
Bates dies 8-22, 676A1
FAULISO, Lt. Gov. Joseph (D, Conn.)
Becomes lt gov 12-31, 990C3
FAULKNER, Capt. Sanford W.
On GI sex harassment sentence 3-6, 189B1
FAUNTROY, Del. Walter E. (D, D.C.)
Testifies at Jenrette Abscam trial 9-22, 783A1
Reelected 11-4, 848F1
FAUVET, Jacques
Govt chrgs re ct system articles 11-7, 872D1

1976

FAY, Albert B.
Amb to Trinidad 1-20; confrmd 2-4, 110B2
FEAKES, Graham
Named Malaysia High cmr 3-23, 237B2
FEATHER, Lord Victor
Dies 7-28, 716A3
FEDERAL Paper Board Co. Inc.
Trust suit dvpts 2-18—10-5, 886B1, E2; DeFaria sentncd 11-30, 921A3
FEENEY, Patricia
Probes Argentine rights abuse 11-5—11-15, 996E2
FEHICK Tractor Co., John
Boycott rpt released 10-20, 786A2
FELDSTEIN, Martin
Cited as Carter adviser 4-23, 305F2
FELFE, Werner
Named to E Ger Politburo 5-22, 381D2
FELKER, Clay
Schorr House com rpt leak detailed 2-12, 2-26, 150G3, 151C1
House com subpoenas 8-25, testifies 9-15, released from subpoena 9-22, 748G3, 749A1
FELT, W. Mark
On FBI break-ins 8-17, 633E2, 634A2

1977

FAY, Albert B.
Replaced as amb to Trinidad 6-7, 499E3
FB-111H—*See ARMAMENTS—Aircraft*
FBI—*See U.S. GOVERNMENT—FEDERAL Bureau of Investigation*
FCC—*See U.S. GOVERNMENT—FEDERAL Communications Commission*
FDA—*See U.S. GOVERNMENT—FOOD & Drug Administration*
FDIC—*See U.S. GOVERNMENT—FEDERAL Deposit Insurance Corp.*
FE, Lt. Col. Benjamin
Slain by rebels 10-12, 824A2
FEA—*See U.S. GOVERNMENT—FEDERAL Energy Administration*
FEDERAL Aid—*See U.S. GOVERNMENT—BUDGET—Revenue Sharing; also other appropriate headings (e.g., MEDICINE—Federal Aid)*
FEDERAL Aviation Administration—*See under U.S. GOVERNMENT—TRANSPORTATION*
FEDERAL Bureau of Investigation—*See under U.S. GOVERNMENT*
FEDERAL Communications Commission—*See under U.S. GOVERNMENT*
FEDERAL Deposit Insurance Corp.—*See under U.S. GOVERNMENT*
FEDERAL Disaster Assistance Administration—*See under U.S. GOVERNMENT—HOUSING & Urban Development*
FEDERAL Election Commission—*See under U.S. GOVERNMENT*
FEDERAL Electric Co.—*See INTERNATIONAL Telephone & Telegraph*
FEDERAL Energy Administration—*See under U.S. GOVERNMENT*
FEDERAL Energy Regulatory Commission—*See under U.S. GOVERNMENT*
FEDERAL Highway Administration—*See under U.S. GOVERNMENT—TRANSPORTATION*
FEDERAL Home Loan Bank Board—*See under U.S. GOVERNMENT*
FEDERAL Home Mortgage Corp.—*See under U.S. GOVERNMENT—FEDERAL Home Loan Bank Board*
FEDERAL Housing Administration—*See under U.S. GOVERNMENT—HOUSING & Urban Development*
FEDERAL Maritime Commission—*See under U.S. GOVERNMENT*
FEDERAL National Mortgage Association—*See under U.S. GOVERNMENT—HOUSING & Urban Development*
FEDERAL Power Commission—*See under U.S. GOVERNMENT*
FEDERAL Property Council—*See under U.S. GOVERNMENT*
FEDERAL Railroad Administration—*See under U.S. GOVERNMENT—TRANSPORTATION*
FEDERAL Reserve System—*See under U.S. GOVERNMENT*
FEDERAL Trade Commission—*See under U.S. GOVERNMENT*
FEDERATED Department Stores, Inc.
Carter to sell shares 1-4, 5A1
Settles CPSC Tris complaint 8-31, Fyrol FR-2 warning rptd 9-29, 820C2
FEDERATION of Latin American Newspapermen—*See LATIN American Newspapermen, Federation of*
FEDIN, Konstantin A.
Dies 7-15, 604A3
FEED Grains—*See LIVESTOCK*
FEENEY, Charles (Chub) S.
Vs Turner mgr role 5-12, 567F3
House subcom probes TV sports 11-2, 949G3
Robbed, beaten 11-30, 990F2
FEENEY, Helen B.
Vet job preferenc law backed 10-11, 774E2
FEHRENBACHER, Don E.
Impending Crisis wins Pulitzer 4-18, 355D2
FEIGHAN, Edward
Kucinich elected mayor 11-8, 855F2
FEIN, Veniamin
Detained 2-28, 3-2, US protests 3-1, 3-3, 226D2-A3
Arrives in Israel 7-11, 551A3
FEINBERG, Judge Wilfred
Finds JP Stevens in contempt 8-31, 724B2
FELBER, Roger
Links Sovt-backed co, NATO 8-19, 700A2
FELDMAN, Abraham J.
Dies 7-21, 604B3
FELEKE Gedle-Ghiorgis, Col.
Named forgn min 3-11, 238E2
FELKER, Clay S.
Settles suit, resigns 1-7, 48B3
Group buys Esquire 8-26, 695G2
FELLOWSHIP of Concerned Churchmen—*See ANGLICAN Church of North America*

1978

FAWCETT, Novice G.
On Kennecott bd rival slate 3-27, 402G3
FAWCETT Publications Inc.—*See CBS Inc.*
FAWCETT-Majors, Farrah
Somebody Killed Her Husband released 9-29, 970B3
FAYAD, Hussein Ibrahim Mahmoud
On PLO Israel raid 3-19, 236B3
FAZIO, Vic
Wins US House seat 11-7, 850D1, 856D3
FBI—*See U.S. GOVERNMENT—FEDERAL Bureau of Investigation*
FCC—*See U.S. GOVERNMENT—FEDERAL Communications Commission*
FCC v. Pacifica Foundation
'Filthy Words' ban upheld by Sup Ct 7-3, 551F2
FDA—*See U.S. GOVERNMENT—FOOD & Drug Administration*
FDIC—*See U.S. GOVERNMENT—FEDERAL Deposit Insurance Corp.*
FDIC v. First Empire Bank-New York
Case refused by Sup Ct 10-16, 789E1
FEA—*See U.S. GOVERNMENT—FEDERAL Energy Administration*
FEBLES, Diego
3d in Daytona endurance 2-5, 538D3
FEC—*See U.S. GOVERNMENT—FEDERAL Election Commission*
FEDERAL Aid—*See U.S. GOVERNMENT—BUDGET—Revenue Sharing; other appropriate headings (e.g., MEDICINE—Federal Aid)*
FEDERAL Aviation Administration—*See under U.S. GOVERNMENT—TRANSPORTATION*
FEDERAL Bureau of Investigation—*See under U.S. GOVERNMENT*
FEDERAL Communications Bar Association
Brown scores FCC performance 10-11, 908D1
FEDERAL Communications Commission—*See under U.S. GOVERNMENT*
FEDERAL Deposit Insurance Corp.—*See under U.S. GOVERNMENT*
FEDERAL Disaster Assistance Administration—*See under U.S. GOVERNMENT—HOUSING & Urban Development*
FEDERAL Election Commission—*See under U.S. GOVERNMENT*
FEDERAL Energy Administration—*See under U.S. GOVERNMENT*
FEDERAL Energy Regulatory Commission—*See under U.S. GOVERNMENT*
FEDERAL Energy Regulatory Commission v. Southland Realty
Natural gas diversn curbed by Sup Ct 5-31, 430F3-431D1
FEDERAL Highway Administration—*See under U.S. GOVERNMENT—TRANSPORTATION*
FEDERAL Home Loan Bank Board—*See under U.S. GOVERNMENT*
FEDERAL Insurance Administration—*See under U.S. GOVERNMENT—HOUSING & Urban Development*
FEDERAL Maritime Commission—*See under U.S. GOVERNMENT*
FEDERAL Mediation and Conciliation Service—*See under U.S. GOVERNMENT*
FEDERAL National Mortgage Association—*See under U.S. GOVERNMENT—HOUSING & Urban Development*
FEDERAL Pacific Electric Co.—*See UV Industries*
FEDERAL Power Commission—*See under U.S. GOVERNMENT*
FEDERAL Preparedness Agency—*See under U.S. GOVERNMENT—GENERAL Services Administration*
FEDERAL Railroad Administration—*See under U.S. GOVERNMENT—TRANSPORTATION*
FEDERAL Reserve System—*See under U.S. GOVERNMENT*
FEDERAL Surveillance—*See PRIVACY Issue; also U.S. GOVERNMENT—FEDERAL Bureau of Investigation*
FEDERAL Trade Commission—*See under U.S. GOVERNMENT*
FEDERATION Internationale des Echecs (International Chess Federation)—*See CHESS*
FEDERATION of American Hospitals—*See HOSPITALS, Federation of American*
FEDERICI, Jose Luis
Sworn Chile transport min 4-21, 350G3
FEED Grain—*See GRAIN*
FEELS So Good (recording)
On best-seller list 5-3, 356E1; 6-7, 460G3
FEENEY, Charles (Chub) S.
A's sale fails 3-27, 355B1
FEENEY, Rev. Leonard
Dies 1-31, 96G1
FEFFERMAN, Charles
Wins Field Medal 8-15, 1023F2
FEIST, Gene
Othello opens 1-30, 887D2
Promise opens 3-8, Show-off 5-18, Pins & Needles 7-6, 760B3, C3
FEITSHANS, Buzz
Big Wednesday released 7-27, 969D3
FELDMAN, Edward S.
Other Side of Mt released 3-24, 619C3
FELDMAN, Sophie—*See FIELDS, Totie*
FELT, W. Mark
Indicted 4-10, 261F3-262A1
Dismissal motn denied 11-30, 939E3

1979

FAY, John
On OECD econ forecast 7-18, 554B3
FBI—*See U.S. GOVERNMENT-FEDERAL Bureau of Investigation*
FCC—*See U.S. GOVERNMENT-FEDERAL Communications Commission*
FCC v. Midwest Video Corp.
Cable TV pub-access rule upset by Sup Ct 4-2, 281G1
F.C.S. Industries Inc.
Kubach Trucking Co.
Offcls, Fitzsimmons' son indicted 8-2, 744D3
FDA—*See U.S. GOVERNMENT-FOOD & Drug Administration*
FDIC—*See U.S. GOVERNMENT-FEDERAL Deposit Insurance Corp.*
FDS Holding Co.
American Brands acquires 2-14, 132B2
FEATHERS, Beattie
Dies 3-10, 272D2
FEBRES Poveda, Carlos
Venez environment min 3-10, 192C3
FEC—*See U.S. GOVERNMENT-FEDERAL Election Commission*
FECTEAU, George O.
Named vp of merged union 3-6, 207C1
FEDDERS Corp.
Heat pump repairs agreed 2-22, 308A3
FEDERAL—*For U.S. departments and agencies, see under U.S. GOVERNMENT*
FEDERAL Correctional Institution (Alderson, W. Va.)
Moore escape fails 2-5, 156A2; gets 3 yrs 6-12, 492E1
FEDERAL Employees for Non-Smokers' Rights v. U.S.
Case declined by Sup Ct 10-29, 884D2
FEDERAL Energy Regulatory Commission v. McCombs
Case decided by Sup Ct 6-18, 499C2
FEDERAL Energy Regulatory Commission v. Pennzoil Producing Co.
Case decided by Sup Ct 1-16, 32F2
FEDERAL Energy Regulatory Commission v. Shell Oil Co.
Cases decided by Sup Ct 1-16, 32F2; 2-22, 150F3
FEDERAL Home Loan Bank Board v. Independent Bankers Association of America
Case declined by Sup Ct 10-15, 847D3
FEDERAL Meat Co.
Settles '78 beef-price suit 10-22, 985E3
FEDERAL Open Market Committee v. Merrill
Case remanded by Sup Ct 6-28, 558D3
FEDERAL Trade Commission—*See under U.S. GOVERNMENT*
FEDERICO, Mike
Hopkins wins NCAA lacrosse title 5-26, 507G2
FEDORA (film)
Released 4-14, 528B2
FEED Grain—*See GRAIN*
FEENEY, Charles (Chub) S.
Umpires' strike setld 5-18, 569D2, E2
FEENEY, Helen B.
Vets' job-preferenc law upheld by Sup Ct 6-5, 421E1
FEHRENBACHER, Don E.
Wins Pulitzer 4-16, 336G2
FEIN, Irving
Just You & Me Kid released 7-27, 820E1
FEINSTEIN, Mayor Dianne (San Francisco, Calif.)
Teachers strike ends 10-23, 850G1
Faces runoff 11-6, 846D3
Elected mayor 12-11, 946E3
FEINSTEIN, Martin
Kennedy Cntr resignatn set 9-17, 892E2
FEIST, Gene
Little Eyolf opens 6-29, 712B1
FEITSHANS, Buzz
Hardcore released 2-8, 174F2
1941 released 12-14, 1008B1
FEKE, Steve
When A Stranger Calls released 10-12, 1008A2
FELD, Bernard T.
Nuclear 'doomsday clock' unchngd 1-1, 13D1
FELDMAN, Harvey
US OKd Taiwan arms ban in China tie talks 1-12, 27F1
FELDSHUH, Tovah
Savara opens 2-11, 292F2
FELICIANO, Brenda
Beggars Soap Opera opens 7-23, 711E1
FELKER, Clay S.
Esquire sale to Tenn firm rptd 5-1, 334D2
FELLINI, Federico
Orchestra Rehearsal released 8-17, 820F2
FELLMAN Velarde, Jose
Role in mil coup rptd 11-1, 833D1
FELTEN, Peter
Arrested as spy 8-16, 742E2
Sentenced 12-14, 980F3

1980

FAWCETT, Farrah
Saturn 3 released 2-15, 216E3
FAZAL ul-Haq, Gen.
Warns vs Sovt attack on Pak 1-16, 27E1
FAZIO, Rep. Vic (D, Calif.)
Reelected 11-4, 842D1
FBI (Federal Bureau of Investigation)—*See under U.S. GOVERNMENT*
FCC (Federal Communications Commission)—*See under U.S. GOVERNMENT*
F.C.S. Industries Inc.
Kubach Trucking Co.
Offcls, Fitzsimmons' son rptd sentenced 2-19, 237G2
FDA (Food & Drug Administration)—*See under U.S. GOVERNMENT*
FDIC (Federal Deposit Insurance Corp.)
See under U.S. GOVERNMENT
FEC (Federal Election Commission)—*See under U.S. GOVERNMENT*
FECHTEL Jr., Vince
Cong primary runoff set 9-9, 700B2
FEDERAL—*For organizations not listed below, see key words; for U.S. departments and agencies, see under U.S. GOVERNMENT*
FEDERAL Aviation Administration—*See under U.S. GOVERNMENT--TRANSPORTATION*
FEDERAL Election Commission v. AFL-CIO
Case declined by Sup Ct 11-10, 868D3
FEDERAL Pacific Electric Co.
Sharon Steel, UV Industries deal final; suits cited 9-26, 746B2
FEDERAL Trade Commission—*See under U.S. GOVERNMENT*
FEDERATED Department Stores Inc.
Credit restrictions rptd 3-27, 222G2
Lazarus retires as chief exec, Goldfeder replaces 12-8, 959A1
FEDERATION for American Immigration Reform v. Klutznick
Injunction denied by Sup Ct 3-17, 226C1
FEED Grain—*See GRAIN*
FEENEY, Charles (Chub) S.
Phillies win NL pennant 10-12, 796F1
FEENEY, James
Indicted in offshore bank fraud 10-20, 860B3
FEIFFER, Jules
Popeye released 12-12, 972F3
FEIN, Bruce
Sup Ct '79-80 term analyzed 7-2, 540G2
FEINBERG, Alexander
Indicted in Abscam probe 10-30, 824E2
FEINSTEIN, Mayor Dianne (San Francisco, Calif.)
Marries 1-20, 199E1
San Fran faces budget crisis 3-8, 187B1
Plans city layoffs 6-4, 744A1
FEIST, Gene
Heartbreak House opens 4-29, 392B3
FELD, Irwin
Barnum opens 4-30, 392D2
FELD, Kenneth
Barnum opens 4-30, 392D2
FELDMAN, Edward S.
Last Married Couple released 2-8, 216B3
FELDMAN, Marty
In God We Trust released 9-26, 836C3
FELDON, Barbara
Past Tense opens 4-24, 392F3
FELICI, Cardinal Pericle
Affirms birth control ban 9-30, scores annulmts 10-6, 810A3
FELICIANO, Brenda
Blood Wedding opens 6-2, 756C3
FELKER, Clay S.
Tex Monthly buys New West 8-27, 732E3
FELL, Jeffrey
Private Account wins Widener Handicap 3-1, 447F3
FELT, W. Mark
Convicted 11-6, 884G1
Sentenced 12-15, 963F2

1976

FENCING
Poland sentences Pawlowski 4-10, 268B3
Olympic results 7-21—7-29, 574E2
FENDT, Joseph
Wins Olympic medal 2-7, 159G1
FENELLY, Dr. Joseph
Rptd on Quinlan case 5-30, 423G2
FENWICK, Rep. Millicent (R, N.J.)
Vs GOP conv platform on abortn 8-17, 8-18, 601D1
Reelected 11-2, 830D1
FERDINAND the Radical (film)
Wins Cannes award 5-28, 460G1
FERENCY, Zolton
Wins suit vs police unit 1-18, 45F1
FERGUSON, John
Named Ranger coach, mgr 1-7, 56E2
FERMI National Accelerator Laboratory (Batavia, Ill.)
New atomic particle observed 2-8, 124A1
FERNANDES, George
Arrested 6-10, 440D1
Indicted 9-25, 731F3
FERNANDES, Col. Jose Augusto
Portugal transport min 1-6, 11C2
FERNANDEZ, Sergio
Chile labor min 3-8, 288F2
FERNANDEZ Long, Pablo
AAA vows executn 1-26, 96D1
FERNANDEZ Maldonado, Gen. Jorge
Named Peru prime min 1-2, 55B3; sworn 1-31, 142G2
Mil revolt fails 7-9, 591B1
Loses Cabt, army posts 7-16, 590A3
Army officers rptd seized 8-13, 8-27, 652C2
FERNANDEZ Miranda, Torcuato
Legis process speeded 4-24, 314A2
Rightists score reformers 5-13, 422D1
Forced from car 12-20, 967C2
FERRARI, Giancarlo
Wins Olympic medal 7-30, 573F3
FERRARIS, Roberto
Wins Olympic medal 7-23, 575A2
FERREIRA, Jose Medeiros
Rpts Mozambique air links suspended 1-14, 52D1
FERREIRA Aldunate, Wilson
Takes asylum in Austria emb 5-24, 399D2
On Michelini, Gutierrez slayings 5-28, 441B2
Arrives France 5-31, 441B2
Arrest ordrd 8-5, loses pol rights 9-1, 678G1
Vegh vs govt persecutn 8-11, 678C2
FERRUZZI, Serafino
Named in grain fraud 3-11, 247D3
FERTILIZERS & Manure
Trinidad plants set 1-2, 55D3
China-Japan deal rptd 1-26, 100F3
US-India talks 3-25—3-26, 235A3
US potash producers indicted 6-29, 748A1
US-built plants open in China 10-25, 832D3
FIAT S.p.A.
Turin arson rptd 4-19—4-23, 297F1
US ends car dumping probe 5-4, 321D2
Argentina exec killed 5-4, 398G3
Argentina exec killed 8-19, 672B1
Turin workers strike 10-8, 10-12, 10-13, 838D2
Libya buys interest 12-1, 964F3-965E1
FIBAK, Wojtek
Wins Brit hardct tennis 5-16, 716C2
2d in US Clay Ct tennis 8-16, 656C2
FIBINGEROVA, Helena
Wins Olympic medal 7-31, 576B2
FIBREBOARD Corp.
Trust suit dvpts 2-18—10-5, 886C1, F2

1977

FEMINISM—*See WOMEN*
FERGUSON, John
Rangers name Talbot coach 8-22, 1021F1
FERGUSON, Judge Warren J.
'76 TV family hr ruling cited 2-9, 157G3
FERNANDES, George
Asks electn boycott 1-19; party ignores, protests 1-23, 1-25, 64C1
Wins Parlt seat 3-16—3-20, 205C2
Freed on bail 3-22; case dropped 3-26, 239G3
Named communicatns min, balks 3-26; relents, sworn 3-27, 239G3, 240C1
Demands Coca-Cola share 8-8, 637E2
Plans small business aid 12-23, 1013G3-1014B1
FERNANDEZ, Ismael
Young decisns Foreman 3-17, 263C1
FERNANDEZ, Vilomar
Duran KOs 1-29, 263D2
FERNANDEZ Font, Marcelo
Says Cuba wants US trade 3-4, 180G3
Sees US execs re trade 10-3, 781A3
FERNANDEZ Ordonez, Francisco
Spain finance min 7-5, 545B2
FERNANDEZ Pondal, Rodolfo
Disappears 8-5, 670F2
FERRARI, Enzo
Resignation announced 3-19, 396G2
FERREIRA, Jose de Medeiros
Quits Cabt post 10-10, 886E3
FERREIRA Neira, Hugo
Kidnaped 8-19, freed 9-16, 727C1
FERREIROS, Hector
Kidnaped 4-3, found dead 4-5, 345E3
FERRIS, Daniel J.
Dies 5-2, 452A3
FERRY, Jacques
Backs Eurofer limits on US exports 10-10, 775E1
FERTILIZERS & Manure
Beker rpts forgn paymts 1-4, 94D2
EC, 3 Arab natns sign pacts 1-18, 73G3
'75-76 Japan-China trade down 2-15, 180D1
UN Sri Lanka energy experimt rptd 3-30, 298D3
Carter energy plan 4-20, 293B1
Medit natns reach pollutn pact 10-21, 876D2
FETAL Alcohol Syndrome—*See ALCOHOLIC Beverages*
FETHERSTON, A. G.
On RCMP-OHIP link 11-29, 945C2
FEYZIOGLU, Turhan
Coalitn bickering rptd 2-16, 138A3
FHA—*See U.S. GOVERNMENT—HOUSING & Urban Development—Federal Housing Administration*
FHWA—*See U.S. GOVERNMENT—TRANSPORTATION—Federal Highway Administration*
FIAT, S.p.A.
Ferrari resigns 3-19, 396G2
Kidnaped exec ransomed 7-11, 543C2
FIBAK, Wojtek
Loses Mex City WCT 2-13, 430F2

1978

FELTER, Judge Edwin L.
Awards United Nuclear judgmt vs Gen Atomic, cites Gulf misdeeds 3-2, 144C1-F2
Gen Atomic documts rule review declined by Sup Ct 5-15, 387F3
Awards United Nuclear, Ind & Mich damages vs Gen Atomic 5-16, scored 5-17, 366G2
Gen Atomic arbitratn right interference ruled by Sup Ct 5-30, 430A3
FEMINISM—*See WOMEN*
FENDI (Italian fashion house)
'78 fur fashion rptd 8-4—8-11, 10-27—11-3, 1029E2
FENDOGLU, Hamit
Killed in bombing 4-17, 291B3
Right blamed for death 4-19, 378C2
FENSTERWALD, Bernard W.
CIA ex-offcl's suicide disputed 11-25, 917D2
FENTON, Norman
'Biko Inquest' opens 5-17, 760D1
FENWICK, Rep. Millicent (R, N.J.)
Doubts Park testimony 4-3, 239C2
Attacks Korean scandal probe 10-13, 832A1
Reelected 11-7, 851A3
FERGUSON, James
On Wilmington 10 convictn review 1-5, 24D2
Sees Carter, backs inflatn plan 4-20, 361G3
FERGUSON, Joe
In World Series 10-10—10-17, 800F2
FERGUSON, John
Replaced as Rangers gen mgr 6-1, 458B3
FERGUSON, Vagas
Notre Dame wins Cotton Bowl 1-2, 8B3
FERNANDES, Helio
Indicted 10-27, 879G1
FERNANDEZ, Benjamin
Enters '80 GOP pres race 11-29, 938G2-F3
FERNANDEZ, Jaime Manuel
Drops pres bid, backs Lora 3-3, 292D2
FERNANDEZ, Sergio
Named Chile interior min 4-12, Cabt shuffle completed 4-21, 350F3
Scores US Letelier prober's visit 5-26, 452E1
Explanatn of missing unchngd 6-23, 573A1
FERNANDEZ Larios, Capt. Armando (alias Alejandro Romeral Jara)
US seeks in Letelier murder probe 2-21, Chile: no record 2-24, 146E2
Identified as Letelier murder suspect 3-3—3-9, 188B3-189B1; 3-20, 209B3
Chile OKs US questioning, disputes Romeral Jara identity 3-23; cleared in Letelier probe 4-1, 266B3
US indictmt re Letelier seen 5-23, murder details revealed 6-2, 452A1, D1
Chile bar vs US testimony rptd 6-23, 495F3
US indicts, arrested 8-1; 'proof' for extraditn asked 8-2, 613F3-614E1
US asks extraditn 9-20, held in mil hosp 9-29, 755G2, E3
Queried by Sup Ct pres 10-17—10-18, 1014C3
Townley admits link 8-11, 647D3
FERRARI, Maurizio
Turin trial halted 3-10, 191F1
FERRARO, Geraldine A.
Wins US House primary in NY 9-12, 716C2
Elected 11-7, 846F2, 851D3
FERRIS, Charles D.
Vs WPIX-TV license renewal 6-16, 672E1
Rejects FCC censorship role 7-21, 599E1
FERTILITY—*See CHILDBIRTH*
FERTILIZERS & Manure
Grace plans King's purchase 1-23, 66C2
Zambia halves subsidies 1-27, 95D2
Tanzania port backlog blocks Zambia deliveries 3-8, 170B1
Williams fined for forgn paymts 3-26, 448D3
Ethiopia shortage rptd 6-8, 465A3
Occidental opens USSR plant 8-22, 670G1
Zambia reopens Rhodesia rail rte 10-10, 783A3
FETTIG, Lester
Named US purchasing cncl dir 5-18, 405A2
Paper union sues Admin re wage-price plan 12-1, 934D2
FEYDEAR, George
13 Rue De L'Amour opens 3-16, 760D3
FEYZIOGLU, Turhan
Named Turkey dep premr 1-5, 21D2
FHLBB—*See U.S. GOVERNMENT—FEDERAL Home Loan Bank Board*
FIASTRIAND, Iaia
Bread & Chocolate released 7-14, 969E3
FIAT S.p.A.
Exec in Turin slain 1-4, 19A2
Turin labor mgr shot 4-27, 330F1
RR carrier bombed in Milan 5-4, 393G1
Turin showroom bombed 7-10, 574F1
FIBAK, Wojtek
Wins WCT doubles title 5-7, 418A3
Loses German championship 5-21, 419D1

1979

FEMME de Jean, La (John's Wife) (film)
Released 1-8, 174E2
FENDI (Italian fashion house)
'79 fashion roundup rptd 1006D2
FENSTERWALD, Bernard
Paisley death questioned 6-27, 520C2
FERGON, Vicki
Wins Lady Stroh's Open 7-1, 587C3
FERGUSON, John W.
Arrested for Haitian drownings 8-13, 634E2
FERGUSON, Judge Warren J.
Upholds video recorder use 10-2, 858G2
FCC 'family hour' power backed 11-20, 1007C1
FERMI National Accelerator Lab (Batavia, Ill.)
Gluon existence, quantum chromodynamics confrmatn claimed 8-28, 692D3
FERNANDES, George
Asks Desai resignatn 7-14; quits Cabt, party 7-15, 544A2
FERNANDEZ, Guido
Backs Peru journalist hunger strike 3-21, 255G3
FERNANDEZ, Juan Manuel
Arrested 10-14, 795B1
FERNANDEZ Heres, Rafael
Venez educatn min 3-10, 192C3
FERNANDEZ Holmann, Ernesto
Proposed for Nicaragua junta 7-6, 504D1
FERNANDEZ Larios, Capt. Armando (alias Alejandro Romeral Jara)
US submits more data in Letelier case 1-8, 19B3
Letelier murder role cited by Townley 1-18, 58F1, G2
Extraditn seen unlikely 2-7, 114B3
Pinochet rptdly sought false '76 passport 2-9, 114E3-115B1
3 Cubans convictd re Letelier 2-14, 114E2
Avoids US extraditn 5-14, 369C2
Ct bars extraditn, frees 10-1, 750G1
FERRA, Max
Eyes on the Harem opens 4-24, 711G2
FERRAGAMO, Vince
Rams lose NFL conf title 1-7, 8G3
FERREIRA, Heitor Aquino
Brazil pres gen secy designate 1-19, 95E1
FERREOL, Andrea
Despair released 2-15, 174D2
FERRER, Jose
Carmelina opens 4-8, 711A2
Fedora released 4-14, 528C2
5th Musketeer released 9-7, 820C1
FERRIE, David
Oswald crime links detailed 7-17, 538F1
FERRIS, Charles D.
On phone competition 1-4, 15B2
On radio deregulatn 9-6, 858F3
FERRI v. Ackerman
Case decided by Sup Ct 12-4, 987E3
FERTILIZERS & Manure
NYS bird deaths laid to fertilizer 3-18, 206F3
India, Bangladesh accord set 4-18, 328E2
Turkey sets new exchng rate 6-12, 447B1
Hooker Calif dumping, well pollutn rptd 6-18; US, state probe 6-19, 6-21, 597G1
US firm in Nigeria deal 9-13, 721A1
Sovt ammonia import curbs asked 10-5, 802B3; US bars 12-11, 939F2
FESTA, Gerald (Chicken)
Sues US 9-26, 840E2
FESTIVAL (play)
Opens 5-7, 711A3
FETTIG, Lester A.
On contract denial legality 2-5, 127C3
FEUER, Cy
I Remember Mama opens 5-31, 711G3
FHA—*See U.S. GOVERNMENT–HOUSING & Urban Development–Federal Housing Administration*
FHLBB—*See U.S. GOVERNMENT–FEDERAL Home Loan Bank Board*
FIACCAVENTO, Corrado
Nominated state holding co head 1-8, 21A1
FIAD, Hussein
Convicted 10-23, sentncd 10-25, 802D1
FIALLOS Oyanguren, Mariano
Proposed for Nicaragua junta 7-6, 504C1
FIAT S.p.A.
Turin exec shot 3-14, 212D1
Polish deal signed 6-18, 487F1-A2
Argentine mkt share rptd 7-20, 562A2
Brazil alcohol fuel dvpt plan set 8-18, 871D2
Investmt plan announced 9-12, 709B2
Turin exec murdered 9-21, 793B2
61 Turin workers fired 10-10, 793B1
Terrorists attack workers, plants 12-11, 12-14, 12-21, 995C2, D2, A3
FIBAK, Wojtek
Wins Denver Grand Prix 2-25, US Natl Indoor doubles 3-4, Stuttgart Grand Prix 4-1, 391G2-B3
Loses Austrian Grand Prix 10-29, Colonge Grand Prix 11-4, 1003E3, F3

1980

FENADY, Andrew J.
Sam Marlowe released 10-3, 836E3
FENCIK, Gary
NFL '79 interceptn ldr 1-5, 8G2
FENCING
Moscow Olympic results 7-23—7-31, 622A3-C3
FENN, Michael T.
On PR navigatn statn bombings 7-14, 559F3
FENWICK, Charles
Ben Nevis wins Grand Natl Steeplechase 3-29, 448A1
FENWICK, Rep. Millicent (R, N.J.)
Reelected 11-4, 843A3
FERENCZ, George
Paris Lights opens 1-24, 136E3
FERGUS, Keith
3d in US Open 6-15, 714F2
FERGUSON, Jack
GM unit to shut plant 7-1, 543B1
FERGUSON, John W.
2 convicted for '79 Fla drownings 4-18, 336B1
FERGUSON, Vagas
In NFL draft 4-29, 336G2
FERNANDEZ, Arturo
Identified as Fla drug dealer 6-5, 502E1
FERNANDEZ, Benjamin
Contests PR GOP primary results 2-19, 130E1
Addresses GOP conv 7-14, 531D3
FERNANDEZ, Eduardo
Resigns 5-28, 462A2
FERNANDEZ, Maria
Loses AIAW doubles tennis title 6-11, 607F1
FERNANDEZ, Michael
Quits Anderson campaign 8-28, 665C3
FERNANDEZ, Royes
Dies 3-3, 279F2
FERNANDEZ Cerra, Jose
Sentncd for '77 murders 3-4, 196C2
FERNANDEZ del Valle, Rene
Arrested 1-25, 94B1
FERNANDEZ Ordonez, Francisco
Named Spain justice min 9-8, 690A3
FERNANDO, Luis
Signs with Aztecs 4-23, 770C3
NASL scoring ldr 8-24, 770D3
FERNEAU, H. Robert
Auto-Train investmt plan rptd 11-26, 958A3
FERRA, Max
Blood Wedding opens 6-2, 756C3
FERRAGAMO, Vince
Steelers win Super Bowl 1-20, 61C3-62C1
Cowboys win playoff 12-28, 999D1
FERRARA, Lidia
Birdy wins Amer Book Award 5-1, 692E2
FERRARI, Alberto
Bank fraud chrgs rptd 4-2, 254G3
FERRARI, Giancarlo
Wins Olympic medal 8-2, 622D1
FERRARO, Rep. Geraldine (D, N.Y.)
Reelected 11-4, 843D3
Named House Dem Caucus secy 12-8, 936E2
FERRE, Mayor Maurice (Miami, Fla.)
Hispanic immigrants surveyed 5-20, 396F3
FERRER, Juan
Wins Olympic medal 7-29, 623C1
FERRIER, Johan (Surinamese president; ousted Aug. 13)
Meets with mil cncl 3-3, 174G3
Ousted by mil 8-13, 653E2
FERRIGNO, Lou
Wins privacy-invasn suit 11-3, 890E2
FERRIS, Charles D.
Praises FCC cable-TV deregulatn moves 7-22, 583E1
Lauds AT&T reorgn moves 8-20, 648F2
Defends VHF TV statn expansn 9-18, 732D1
On Comsat broadcast satellite TV plan 10-2, 907A1
FERTILIZERS & Manure
OECD sees food shortages 1-23, 49E3
France-India pact signed 1-28, 97C3
French-Cuba accord rptd 4-1, 253A3
El Salvador gets IDB loan 12-18, 993A2
FESENKO, Sergei
Wins Olympic medals 7-20, 7-27, 623F2, A3
Beardsley beats Olympic swimming time 7-30, 834A3
FFOLKES (film)
Released 4-18, 416F2
FHA (Federal Housing Administration)—*See under U.S. GOVERNMENT--HOUSING & Urban Development, Department of (HUD)*
FIASTRI, Jaja
To Forget Venice released 1-28, 216F3
FIAT S.p.A.
Watchman killed in Turin 2-1, 99C1
Spain '79 SEAT losses rptd 2-21, 196F2
Research collaboratn set 4-22, 303B3
Layoff plans rptd 5-20, 408D3
SEAT acquisitn declined 6-4, 467A3
Peugeot project set 9-15; investmt, research capital sought 9-23, 751E3
Alfa Romeo, Nissan project OKd 9-20, 751B3, D3
Layoffs canceled 9-27, 751E2
Workers arrested in left-wing crackdown 10-6, 791C3
Tentative labor pact set 10-15, 791F2
FIBAK, Wojtek
Loses WCT doubles title 1-6, Grand Prix Masters 1-12, 1-6, 213B2, C2
Loses W Ger Grand Prix 7-20, 691G2
Wins Dubai Golden 11-23, 947E2

1976

FIDDLER on the Roof (play)
Opens 12-28, 1014F3
FIDRYCH, Mark
NL wins All-Star game 7-13, 544G1
AL pitching ldr 10-4, 796D1
Named rookie of year 11-30, 952E1
FIELD, A. Searle
FBI purchasing irregularities rptd 1-1, 6D1, F1
Denies com responsibility for leaks 1-26, 92G1
Backs House com intellignc rpt 2-3, 150D2
Pike cites on Rogovin threat 3-9, 217C1
FIELD Jr., Fred R.
Indicted 12-10, 986A1
FIELDEN, Donald
Frees US prisoners in Mex 3-12, chrgd 5-13, 420F1
FIELD Hockey
Olympic results 7-30, 574A3
FIELDING, Dr. Lewis J.
Ehrlichman verdict upheld 5-17, 379E1
Nixon disbarred in NY 7-8, 493F3
Ehrlichman enters prison 10-28, 849G2
FIEL Filho, Manoel
Found dead 1-17, 'suicide' scored 1-26, 1-29, 98B1
FIERLINGER, Zdenek
Dies 5-2, 368F2
FIESCHI, Jacques
Sentncd 8-31, arrest protested 9-7, 693B2
50 Ways to Leave Your Lover (song)
On best-selling list 1-28, 104G3
FIGUERES, Jose
Sued in NY re fraud 9-22, 1000G2
'Vesco Law' repealed 11-2, 1000E2
FIGUEROA, Ed
AL pitching ldr 10-4, 796D1
In World Series 10-16—10-21, 815B2, E3

1977

FICHET, France & Rene
Killed 5-1, 440A3
FIELD Jr., Fred R.
Convicted 9-29, sentencd 12-2, 937E3
FIELD, Sally
Wins Emmy 9-11, 1022A1
FIELD Research Corp.
Calif pot study cited 3-14, 332D2
FIESER, Louis F.
Dies 7-25, 604B3
FIESTA Bowl—*See FOOTBALL—Collegiate*
FIFE, Wallace
Named Australia business min 12-19, 982B2
FIGHT to Advance the Nation's Sports—*See FANS*

1978

FICO, Nino
Opera probe assests scored 6-3, 454E1
FIELD, Greg
Traded to Mets 12-8, 1026C1
FIELD, Ron
King of Hearts opens 11-22, 1031C2
FIELD Enterprises Inc.
Chicago Daily News—*See separate listing*
Chicago Sun-Times—*See separate listing*
FIELD, Sally
Hooper released 8-4, 970F1
FIELDING, Henry (1707-54)
Joseph Andrews released 4-13, 619F2
FIELDING, Dr. Lewis J.
Ehrlichman freed from jail 4-27, 320B2
FIELD Medals—*See MATHEMATICS*
FIELD-Ridley, Shirley
On Jonestown cult members 11-21, 891D2
FIELDS, J. M.—*See FOOD Fair*
FIELDS, Totie (Sophie Feldman)
Dies 8-2, 708F2
FIERSTEIN, Harvey
International Stud opens 5-22, 887A2
FIESTA Bowl—*See FOOTBALL—Collegiate*
FIFA—*See FOOTBALL, International Federation of Association*
5TH of July (play)
Opens 4-27, 760B2
52ND Street (recording)
On best-seller list 11-8, 888D1; 12-6, 971E1
FIGHT for Barbara, The (play)
Opens 11-27, 1031F1
FIGUEIREDO, Gen. Euclydes (d. 1963)
Son gets Brazil pres nod 1-5, 6A3

1979

FIDDLER on the Roof (play)
'Grease' breaks Broadway duratn record 12-8, 956F2
FIDELITY Union Life Insurance Co.
Ger firm to buy 6-25, 942C2
FIEDLER, Arthur
Conducts Boston Symphony 3-25, 272F1
Opens Boston Pops 50th season 5-1, 392A2
Dies 7-10, 588F2
FIEDLER, Melissa
Loses religious schl expulsn suit 8-23, 650G1
FIELD, Greg
Traded to Pirates 4-19, 1002G2
FIELD, Sally
Norma Rae released 3-1, 174C3
Beyond Poseidon Adventure released 5-24, 528E1
FIELD, Ted
Wins Daytona endurance 2-4, 491C1
FIELD Foundation Inc.
Malnutritn rptd down, fed food programs credited 4-30, 386B3
FIELDS, Gracie
Dies 9-27, 756D2
FIFE, Wal
Drug bur inquiry rptd 6-20, 467G2
5th Musketeer, The (film)
Released 9-7, 820B1
52ND Street (recording)
On best-seller list 1-10, 80F3; 2-14; 120E3; 4-4, 271E2
FIGGINS v. Hudspeth
Case refused by Sup Ct 4-16, 302F3

1980

FIDELITY Financial Consultants
Tex Brilab indictments 6-12, 454A3
FIDELITY Financial Corp.
Acquired by Ahmanson 7-1, 557C2
FIDELITY Mortgage Investors
Fed unincorporated business trust suits backed by Sup Ct 5-19, 440E2
FIEDLER, Arthur (d. 1979)
Williams named Boston Pops conductor 1-10, 199F2
FIEDLER, Bobbi
Elected to US House 11-4, 842G1, 846C2, 852A2
FIELD Jr., Fred B.
Sentenced 1-11, 64A2
FIELD 3rd, John
Quits CFTC post 7-22, 558E3
FIELD, Mervin
Carter trails in Calif 7-30, 570C2
FIELD, Sally
Wins Oscar 4-14, 296G1
Smokey & the Bandit II released 8-15, 675E3
FIELD, Ted
3d in Daytona endurance 2-3, 637G3
FIELDE, Rolf
John Gabriel Borkman opens 12-18, 1003C3
FIELDING, Jerry
Dies 2-17, 176A1
FIELDS, Jack
Elected to US House 11-4, 844E2, 850A2
FIENDISH Plot of Dr. Fu Manchu, The (film)
Released 8-8, 675D2
FIFTH Floor, The (film)
Top-grossing film 3-26, 280G3
FIFTH Horseman, The (book)
On best-seller list 10-12, 796D3; 12-7, 948D3
FIFTH of July (play)
Opens 11-6, 892C3
52ND Street (recording)
Joel wins Grammy 2-27, 296B3

1977

FIGUEIREDO, Gen. Joao Baptista de
Pres bid cited re Furtado ban 7-3, 541B2, C2
Barreto backs pres bid 7-12, Geisel rptd opposed 7-22; extensive press coverage rptd 7-26, 615F3
Rptd mil pres choice 9-1; Magalhaes seen pub choice 9-24, 741A1
Frota fired 10-12; Cabt mins back pres bid 10-21, 839F3
3d in execs pres poll 11-7, 964A2
Cited as Geisel pres choice 11-17, mil oppositn rptd 12-2, 964F1
FIGUERAS, Eduardo
Sentenced 2-10, 100B1
FIGUERES, Jose Marti
Named in '75 gas natlizatn scheme 6-11, 506B2
FIGUERES Ferrer, Jose
'78 PLN pres candidate named 3-13, 506D2
Chrgs Vesco pol financing scandal 4-23, 506A1
Links Monge, CIA press funds 4-23, 506D2
Named in '75 gas natlizatn scheme 6-11, 506B2
FIGUEROA, Ed
Desires trade 10-17, 806F3
FIGUEROA Cordero, Andres
Pardoned 10-6, 808A2
Cuba release of US prisoner confrmd 10-13, 896G2

1978

FIGUEIREDO, Gen. Joao Baptista de
Geisel confrms pres choice; aide quits, MDB scores 1-4—1-5, 6G2
Pres aide scores candidacy, chrgs corruptn 1-13, 165F3
Magalhaes scores selectn, asks direct electns 2-15, 165B3
Favors 'gradual' democracy, bars amnesty 2-23, 165E2
Arena nominates 4-8; front vs formed 5-29, dvpts 7-6, 7-9, 555E3-556A1
Backer loses Sao Paulo gov race 6-5, 556B1
Army capt scores, jailed 6-16, 556D1
Geisel submits const reforms 6-23, 555E2
Warns vs MDB cong victory 7-9, 556B1
Scores oppositn demands 7-27, vows to restore democracy 7-28, 646C3
Magalhaes drops pres bid 8-8, 646F2
Bentes joins MDB 8-17, pres nominatn seen 8-18, 646G2
Bentes nominated for pres 8-23, 671C2
Abreu jailed 10-2, 771F3
Elected Brazil pres 10-15, 794A1
Reaffirms dem goal 10-16, 836D2
Confirms govt taps 10-17; son implicated in corruptn 10-20, 836E2, G2
Chrgs MDB infiltrated by communists 11-14, 921D2
FIGUERES Ferrer, Jose
Loss of PLN control rptd 1-14, oppositn candidate wins electn 2-5, 89A3
Reelected PLN chief 9-29, 823F2
FIGUEROA, Ed
AL pitching ldr 10-2, 928G3
Yankees win AL pennant 10-7, 778G3
In World Series 10-10—10-17, 799A3

1979

FIGUEIREDO, Gen. Joao Baptista de (Brazilian president)
Names Cabt, vows democracy 1-19, 94G3
New econ measures set 2-2, 210B2
Metalworkers strike 3-13–3-27, 328B3
Sworn pres, vows democracy 3-15, 209F3
Hosts Mondale 3-22–3-23, 247E3
Jari projct probe set 6-8, 443G2
Spain premr visits 8-6–8-8, 654F1
Signs amnesty law 8-28, 926B2
Itaipu, Corpus dam accords signed 10-19, 845C1
Sets state cos supervisn 10-29, 871C1
Visits Venez; trade, energy discussed 11-6–11-7, 953F1
Party reform law implemented 11-30, 926D2
Announces new econ policy 12-7, 948C2
FIGUEROA Cordero, Andres
Dies 3-7, 272D2

1980

FIGUEIREDO, Gen. Joao Baptista de Oliveira (Brazilian president)
Portella Nunes dies 1-6, 104E3
Finance min quits 1-15, 95E2
Authorizes land expropriatns 2-5, 95G1
A-energy team visits Argentina 3-18, 229E2
Sabin protests stalled polio drive 4-16, 310B2
Sees Argentina pres, strengthens ties 5-15—5-17, 405C2
Greets Pope 6-30, 537F2
Greets Mex pres 7-27, scores US-Sovt arms race 7-28, 605F2-A3
Scores rightist terror, affirms reforms 8-29, 704B3, D3
Orders RC priest expelled 10-30, 871A1
At Amazon pact signing 11-28, 865C2

1976

FIJI—*See also ADB, COMMONWEALTH of Nations*
Listed as 'free' nation 1-19, 20B3
S Pacific Forum meets 3-8—3-9, 179B2
Total IMF oil loan rptd 4-1, 340C2
US triples sugar duties 9-21, 721D3
UN Assemb condemns apartheid 11-9, 842G2
FIKRE Merid
Slain 10-1, 4 executed 11-2, 1002E1
FIKRU, Col. Wolde-Tensae
Eritrea mil gov 8-17, 674D2
FILBINGER, Hans
Reelected in state vote 4-4, 270F1
FILIPIAK, Boleslaw Cardinal
Named cardinal 4-27, 336D2
FILIPOV, Grisha
On Bulgarian Politburo 4-2, 250C1
FILMS—*See MOTION Pictures*
FILMWAYS Inc.
Grosset consent decree filed 7-27, 989G1
FINAL Days, The (book)
On best-seller list 12-5, 972A2

1977

FIJI—*See also COMMONWEALTH of Nations*
UN Assemb member 3G3
New electn set 4-6, 394G2
Partl dissolved 6-1, 547E3
Sugar, dock strikes end 8-7, 8-8, 636B3
NZ to set 200-mi fishing zone 9-7, 729B3
Alliance party wins electns 9-25, 767B2
Abstains on UN anti-Israel res 10-28, 830G2
FIJII, Katsushi
Japan labor min 11-28, 932B2
FIKRE-Selassie Wogderess, Capt.
Chrgs Somalia RR bombing, Djibouti annexatn 6-16, 486F1
FILBINGER, Hans
Vs Baader gang burial 10-27, 868F1
FILIBUSTERS—*See also under U.S. GOVERNMENT—SENATE*
Tex state sen sets world record 5-4, 532G1
FILIPPI, Emilio
Ercillo rptd under govt control 2-3, new publicatns curbed 3-11, 220A1
FILMS—*See MOTION Pictures*
FINAL Days, The (book)
On best-seller list 2-6, 120G3; 3-6, 184G3
Nixon scores 5-25, 420G1
FINAN, Tom
Togo assassinatn plot foiled 12-13, 988A3
FINANCIAL Accounting Standards Board—*See ACCOUNTING Standards Board, Financial*

1978

FIJI—*See also COMMONWEALTH of Nations, SOUTH Pacific Islands*
Emperor gold mine layoffs rptd 1-5, 22F1
UN Leb force (Unifil) voted 3-5, 340F1; **for peace keeping developments, see MIDDLE EAST—LEBANON**
UN Assemb member 713E3
FILATOV, Anatoly
Sentenced 7-14, 541E2
FILBINGER, Hans
Nazi links harm pol career 5-28, 477B3
Quits post over Nazi chrgs 8-7, 616C3
Strauss asks Nazi-era amnesty 8-14, 651F3
Spaeth named successor 8-16, 725E3
Carstens' ex-Nazi membership confrmd 11-10, 872A2
FILHO, Sebastiao Miranda da Silva—*See MIRANDINHA*
FILIBUSTERS—*See under U.S. GOVERNMENT—SENATE*
FILLOL, Ubaldo
Argentina wins World Cup 6-25, 520B2
FILMS & Film Industry—*See MOTION Pictures*
FINAL Entries 1945: The Diaries of Joseph Goebbels (book)
On W Ger best-seller list, US release set 1-2, 22D1
FINANCIAL General Bankshares Inc.
Lance, Arabs sued re takeover 2-17, 204B3
SEC chrgs Lance, Arabs re takeover 3-18; complaint settled 3-19, 204F1
Lance scores press 4-12, 324F3-325A1
FINANCIAL Services—*See also kinds (e.g., INSURANCE)*
Borg-Warner, Firestone to merge 11-28, 935E1

1979

FIJI—*See also COMMONWEALTH of Nations*
2 Unifil soldiers die 2-3, 84E3
UN membership listed 695G2
In Zimbabwe peacekeeping force 12-23, 976E3
FILBY, Ian
Gold wins ASL title, named game offensive MVP 9-16, 776C2
FILIPACCHI, Daniel
Rolling Stone, Look merge 5-7, 430E3
FILMS & Film Industry—*See MOTION Pictures*
FINAL Payments (book)
On best-seller list 2-4, 120D3
FINANCIAL Services
Johns-Manville broker sentncd 3-13, 239C3
Beneficial Corp loan bias chrgd 5-8, 596F1
Banking, svcs case declined by Sup Ct 10-15, 847B3
Mergers & Acquisitions
Amer Express seeks McGraw-Hill 1-9, 15G3
Amer Express bid rejctd by McGraw-Hill 1-15, tender offer filed 1-16, 53B2-C3
Amer Express sweetened bid rejctd by McGraw-Hill 1-31; proxy battle dropped 2-23, offer expires 3-1, 151B3
Edper seeks Brascan control 4-9, 4-20, 303C3, G3, 304B2; 5-30, 440D2-A3
Shearson, Loeb Rhodes to merge 5-14, 366A3
Barclays purchase of Amer Credit OKd 5-29, 440B3
Transamerica wins Interway bidding 5-29, 560C2
HCA to buy Nev casino 6-12, drops bid 6-27, 520F1
Edper completes Brascan takeover 6-14, 6-29, 542D3
RCA seeks CIT 7-5, talks end 7-10, 517E1
Midland Bank to buy Walter Heller Corp 7-6, 682B3

1980

FIJI—*See also ADB, COMMONWEALTH of Nations*
Chile pres cancels Asian tour 3-22, 230F3
UNIFIL soldier killed in Leb 4-12, 284D1
Pacific cable planned 5-19, 387E3
Island trade pact rptd 7-24, 576G2
FILATOV, Anatoly N.
Death sentence rptd commuted 9-23—9-24; Trigon ID controversy rptd 10-4, 753E3
FILBY, Malcolm
Stoners win ASL title 9-18, 771C1
FILMS & Film Industry—*See MOTION Pictures*
FILUMENA (play)
Opens 2-10, 392F2
FINAL Countdown, The (film)
Released 8-1, 675E2
Top-grossing film 8-6, 640D3
FINANCIAL Federation Inc.
Great Western acquires 7-15, 557D2
FINANCIAL General Bankshares Inc.
Arabs sign purchase agrmt 7-25, 600D3
Forgn bank takeovers debated 8-28, 9-17, 806A3, E3
Abu Dhabi bank gets US branch OK 10-1, 806G3
FINANCIAL Services
Credit rptd tightened on FRB moves 3-28, 222A3
Itel rpts huge '79 loss 10-16, 784F1
Mergers & Acquisitions
Amer Express McGraw-Hill takeover case declined by Sup Ct 11-3, 856A2

1976

FINANCIAL Times (London) (newspaper)
USSR plans distributn 1-21, 76G2
FINANCING the 1972 Elections (book)
Excerpts published 4-25, 687G3 *
FINCH, Gov. Cliff (D, Miss.)
Miss caucus vote results 1-24, 94G3
Legis closes S&Ls 6-20, 495C1
FINCH, Robert H.
Loses Calif Sen primary 6-8, 409C2
Anti-black strategy chrgd 8-12, 671F2
FINDLEY, Rep. Paul (R, Ill.)
Vs Connally as vp 8-5, 584F2
Urges Butz resign 10-2, 744B2
Reelected 11-2, 829A3
FINDLEY, William
Testifies re Lockheed payoffs 2-4, 130B2
FINE, David Sylvan
Arrested for '70 Wis bombing 1-7, 32C2
Pleads guilty 6-8, sentncd 8-6, 776G2
FINGERS, Rollie
Sold to Red Sox 6-15, Kuhn voids sale 6-18, 444B3-F3
Contract rptd signed 12-5, 951D3

FINLAND—*See also ADB, OECD*
'75 foreign trade debt rptd 1-9, 104C2
Supplementary budget OKd 1-9, 104D2
Listed as 'free' nation 1-19, 20B3
Japan electronics deal rptd 1-27, 104E2
CP econ progrm backing rptd 2-2, 155A2
Sovt bloc trade sought 2-2, 155B2
Import deposit phase-out rptd 2-4, 155D2
Import credit fees hiked 2-4, 155E2
Union wage hike price freeze rptd 2-15, 155G1
Police strike rptd 2-18, 155C2
Angola MPLA recognized 2-20, 163D1
Police strike ends 3-1, 266G1
Seamen strike 3-9, dockers join 4-3, 266C1
Govt announces '75 progrm 3-9, 289G3
Import deposit progrm extended 3-15, 266F1
Jan-Feb trade deficit rptd 3-16, 266G1
Food workers strike 3-25—4-8, 266D1
Total IMF oil loan rptd 4-1, 339F3, 340A2
Ammunition factory blast 4-13, 404C3
Dockworkers end strike 5-3, 335A2
'75 Sovt trade rptd 5-5, 340D3
Alvar Aalto dies 5-11, 404F1
CP rejcts tax plan 5-12, govt resigns 5-13, 350F2
Kekkonen bars Cabt resignatn 5-13, coalitn restored 5-18, 364A3
Sovt oil drill deal set 7-16, 540E2
Miettunen Cabt resigns 9-17, 731E2
New Cabt sworn 9-29, 750B3
Right gains in electns 10-17—10-18, 852D2
9-mo trade deficit rptd 10-19, 852E2
Expels N Korean diplomats 10-20, 799C3
Sports
Winter Olympics results 2-4—2-15, 159C1-B2
Summer Olympic results 7-18—7-31, 573C3, 575D1, 576A1, C1, G2
Viren wins Olympic medals 7-26, 7-30, 563C2, 576A1, C1
'Blood doping' rumored re Viren Olympic wins, denied 7-29, 563C2
Canada Cup hockey results 9-15, 736G3

FINLEY, Charles O.
3 A's sold 6-15, Kuhn voids 6-18, 444B3-F3
FINLEY, Murray H.
Clothing, textile unions merge 6-3, 436G1

1977

FINANCIAL Times, The (London) (newspaper)
Singapore correspondent arrested 2-15, 223D3
Strike ends 8-24, 655E1
Leb premr interview 10-12, 793A3
FINCH, Peter
Dies 1-14, 84A3
Wins Oscar 3-28, 264B1
FINDLAY, James
FBI, ACLU surveillance rptd 6-19, 481B2
FINDLAY (O.) College
Kim Han Cho indicted 9-27, 773D3, 774A1
FINDLEY, Murray
Sees Carter on textile curbs 4-13, 271A3
FINDLEY, Rep. Paul (R, Ill.)
Farmland fund plan withdrawn 3-11, 195C1
Dayan for US naval base at Haifa 9-20, 714B1
FINE, Aaron M.
ITT suit cited 3-4, 194D3
FINEMAN, Herbert
Convicted 5-20, resigns 5-23, jailed 6-10, 484D1
FINGESI, Cmdr. O. P.
Nigeria Cabt drops 3-15, 393D2
FINISHED-Goods Index—*See 'Prices' under ECONOMY*
FINKLEHOFF, Fred F.
Dies 10-5, 872F1

FINLAND—*See so OECD*
Kekkonen asks for electn 2-1, 182C1
Meittunen govt resigns 5-11, Sorsa forms new govt 5-15, 391B1
Meningitis vaccine tests rptd 9-28, 907G1
Economy & Labor (domestic)
Jan jobless rate rptd 2-2, '77 forecast 2-10, 182A2
Dec '75-76 inflatn rate rptd 2-7, 87B2
Unions begin strikes 3-1, 182E1
Alcohol, tobacco ads banned 3-1, 182B2
Port strike 4-19, Finnair strike 4-20, strike wave ends 5-11, 391E1
Jobs progrm proposed 6-20, 764B3
Finnmark devalued 3.1% 8-31, 709B1
Devaluatn protested 9-1, 764D3
'78 budget presented 9-17—9-18, 764F2
Foreign Relations (misc.)—*See also 'Monetary, Trade & Aid' below*
UN Assemb member 4A1
In 14-natn sulphur-dioxide pact 1-19, 109B3
Ahtisaari rptd named UN Namibia comr 109D3
Socialist rep at Israel Labor Party conventn 2-22, 135F1
US amb confrmd 5-25, 500B1
Hijacked Sovt jet lands 7-10—7-12, 537F1-A2
Troops to leave Cyprus 9-16, 764F3
USSR hijackers rptd sentncd 11-10, 988E2
Nigeria pirate raid scored 11-22, 986F2
Saudis boycott ships 12-10, 955D1
Helsinki Agreement—*See EUROPE—Security and Cooperation*
Monetary, Trade & Aid (including all foreign economic developments)
UK 200-mi fishing zone in effect 1-1, 21A1
'76 paymts deficit rptd 2-2, 182G1
Kosygin in trade talks, opens A-plant 5-22—5-26, 391A2
Sports
Czechs keep hockey title 5-8, 430C2

FINLEY, Charles O.
Clashes with Kuhn over player sales 2-18—4-8, loses suit 3-17, 310A3
NHL Barons rescued 2-23, 164F1
'No-litigatn' clause upheld 8-30, 767E1
Undergoes heart surgery 9-15, 768C2
Sells A's 12-14, sued over stadium lease 12-15, 989A2
FINLEY, David
Dies 2-1, 164G2
FINLEY, James D.
Unionists jam annual mtg 3-1, 153F3
FINNAIR
Strike begins 4-20, 391G1

1978

FINANCIAL Times, The (London) (newspaper)
IRA vandalizes Dublin office 5-5, 373F2
FINANCIERE du Credit Suisse et de White Weld—*See CREDIT Suisse—Credit Suisse et de White Weld, Financiere du*
FINCH, Gov. Cliff (D, Miss.)
Faces Sen primary runoff 6-6, 448A1
Loses runoff 6-27, 510C1
On Ellisville dorm fire 12-9, 971F3
FINCH, Raymon R.
Loses primary for SC gov 6-13, 467E1
FINDLAY (O.) College
Loses NAIA Div II football title 12-9, 1025B2
FINDLEY, Rep. Paul (R, Ill.)
Queries Israel US arms use in Leb invasn 3-17, 236E2
Vs Korea aid-warning res 5-31, 432E2
On Desai mtg 6-13, 466F3
Coup cancels US missn to S Yemen 6-26, 499F1
House votes conditnl end to Rhodesia sanctns 8-2, 588C2
Reelected 11-7, 850F3
FINE, John S.
Dies 5-21, 440F2
FINE, Mort
Greek Tycoon released 5-12, 619C2
FINGERHUT Corp.
American Can outbids Interco 8-14, 718E1
FINGERS (film)
Released 3-1, 619G1
FINGERS, Rollie
NL pitching ldr 10-2, 928G2
FINISHED-Goods Index (producer price index)—*See ECONOMY—Prices*
FINK, Gerald
DNA yeast transfer rptd 1-21, 333G3
FINK, Tom
Loses Alaska primary for gov 8-22, 682D3

FINLAND—*See also EFTA, GATT, OECD*
Kekkonen reelected 1-16, 36D2
Finnair jet ransomed, hijacker arrested 9-30—10-1, 927B1
Economy & Labor (domestic)
Jan jobless rate rptd 1-30, 90C1
'77 inflatn rate, '78 forecast rptd 1-31, 90D1
June '77-78 world inflatn rates ranked 10-18, 914F1
Foreign Relations (misc.)—*See also 'Monetary, Trade, Aid & Investment' and 'UN' below*
Amb ends Cambodia visit 1-21, calls Pnompenh 'ghost city' 1-22, 43A2; Thai min disputes 2-2, 61E1
S Africa culture, sports ties banned 3-11, 193C3
USSR denies use of spy trucks 3-15, 291F2
Downed S Korean plane passengers arrive Helsinki 4-23, 302E1
Eur conservative group formed 4-24, 424C3
Naval conf in Helsinki 5-16—5-18, 424F3
USSR Finnair office shootout 5-24, 416E2
USSR defector rptd in Sweden 11-1, 947A1
USSR mil link rptd pressed, defns min denies; West rptd concerned 11-15, 894B2
Helsinki Agreement—*See EUROPE—Security and Cooperation*
Monetary, Trade, Aid & Investment
EC steel dumping probe begun 1-23, 80C2
'77 trade surplus, paymts deficit rptd 1-30, 90A1
Norway exchng rate adjustmt rptd 2-11, 133G3
S Africa investmt banned 3-11, 193C3
Australia uranium accord signed 7-20, 590C1
UN Policy & Developments
Leb peace force (Unifil) formed 3-19, 197D2; **for peacekeeping developments, see MIDDLE EAST—LEBANON**
Assemb member 713E3
U.S. Relations
US at Helsinki naval conf 5-16—5-18, 424F3

FINLEY, Charles O.
Vs Kuhn bar on Blue sale 3-3, 194F3
Calls off A's sale, Davis scores 3-27, 354G3
Kuhn upheld again on player sales 4-7, 355G1
Winkles quits as A's mgr 5-23, 560E1
Case refused by Sup Ct 10-2, 751A2
FINLEY, James D.
Forced off bank bd, union pressure cited 3-7, 163A1
Mitchell quits bd, cites union pressure 3-21, 205E1
Quits NY Life board 9-12, 699D2
FINLEY & Co. Inc. v. Kuhn
Baseball comr authority challenge refused by Sup Ct 10-2, 751B2
FINNAIR (Finnish airline)
USSR office shootout 5-24, 416E2
Jet ransomed, hijacker arrested 9-30—10-1, 927B1

1979

AEA Investors bid on Bliss rptd 8-10, 942B2
RCA reaches CIT accord 8-17, CIT ends Integon talks 8-24, 682A2, E2
Continental buys Fla Gas 8-28, 986C3
Fibic-Congoleum merger OKd 9-21, 942A2
NY group bid for Foremost-McKesson rptd 10-17, 986B3
Wein Air stock sale to HFC rptd, Alaska Air sues 11-20, 989G1
FINANCIAL Times, The (London) (newspaper)
USSR extends rptr's visa 8-3, 636G3
Iran ousts newsman 8-21, 635A2
FINCH, Gov. Cliff (D, Miss.)
Declares pres bid 12-24, 984E1
FINDLAY (O.) College
Wins NAIA Div II football title 12-8, 1001F2
FINDLEY, Rep. Paul (R, Ill.)
Vance hints Israel arms pact breach in Leb raids 8-7, 592D1
FINE, David Sylvan
Granted parole 1-11, 102F2
FINISHED-Goods Index (producer price index)—*See ECONOMY-Prices*

FINLAND—*See also GATT, IDB, OECD*
Parlt electns 3-18—3-19; left-cntr coalitn takes office, progrms outlined 5-26—5-27, 406F3-407D1
Economy & Labor
Wage pact reached 1-9, 75G2-A3
Jobless, tax plans outlined 5-27, 407C1
Helsinki Agreement—*See EUROPE—Security and Cooperation*
Monetary, Trade, Aid & Investment
'78 trade surplus, major partners rptd 2-2, 215F2
Sweden seeks joint A-progrm 3-13, 214A1
Finmark revaluation hinted 5-27, 407D1
Obituaries
Waltari, Mika 8-26, 671G3
UN Policy & Developments
Membership listed 695G2
U.S. Relations
Mondale visits Eur 4-11—4-22, 299C2

FINLEY, Murray H.
Urges shoe-import cap 3-6, 207C1
Backs Carter reelectn 7-30, 593D3
FINLEY v. Hernandez
Ill welfare overpaymts seizure curbed by Sup Ct 3-19, 203A3
FINN, Candy
Penn State wins women's lacrosse title 5-13, 507D3
FINNANE, Michael
Sinclair quits Cabt 9-27, 787D3

1980

FINANCIAL Times, The (London) (newspaper)
Yugoslav interviewed 6-5, 468C3
Spooner arrested in Bolivia 8-6, Jones negotiates release 8-12, 668D1
FINANCIAL World (magazine)
Saturday Review bought 5-20, 582D3
FINDLEY, Rep. Paul (R, Ill.)
Reelected 11-4, 842F3
FINE and Mellow (recording)
Fitzgerald wins Grammy 2-27, 296E3
FINGERS, Rollie
NL pitching ldr 10-6, 926G2
FINK, Margaret
My Brilliant Career released 2-1, 216C3
FINK, Matthew P.
Scores FRB money mkt funds reserve rule 3-20, 224A1
FINK, Rudi
Wins Olympic medal 8-2, 622F1

FINLAND—*See also ADB, CSCE, GATT, IDB, OECD*
Spy's sentnc announced 3-18, 212B1
N Sea oil platform capsizes 3-27, 256F1
Shipping strike end rptd 5-23, 407A1
Foreign Relations (misc.)
Olympic com rejcts Moscow boycott 3-22, 259C3
Iran asks non-support of US hostage policy 4-12, 282F1
Tito funeral held 5-8, 339B1
Iran hostage appeal rptd 8-16, 634G3
Government & Politics—*See also other appropriate subheads in this section*
Municipal elections held 10-19—10-20, 829F2
Obituaries
Paasio, Rafael 3-17, 280F1
Sports
Winter Olympic results 2-12—2-24, 154F2, 155F2-156D1
Olympic com rejects Moscow boycott 3-22, 259C3
Canada Cup hockey tourn cancelled 4-30, 488F3
Moscow Olympic results 7-20—8-3, 588B2, 589D1, 622D1, 623G1, 624B1, E1, B3, G3
UN Policy & Developments
Assemb Afghan invasn res abstentn 1-14, 25F2
U.S. Relations
Iran asks non-support of US hostage policy 4-12, 282F1
Iran hostage appeal rptd 8-16, 634G3

FINLAY, Frank
Filumena opens 2-10, 392G2
FINLAYSON, Jock K.
Named Royal Bank of Canada pres 9-5, 687B1
FINLETTER, Thomas K.
Dies 4-24, 360E1
FINLEY, Charles O.
Fires Marshall as A's mgr 2-13, hires Martin 2-21, 637A2
Sells Oakland A's 8-23, 795B3
FINLEY, James D.
ACTWU agreemt announced 10-19, 805C2
FINLEY, Murray
Stevens agrmt announced 10-19, 805G1, B2

1976

FINNISTON, Sir Monty
On Brit Steel losses 7-28, 589A2

FIREARMS
Ford State of Union message 1-19, 38C2, 39C3
Hearst jury selectn starts 1-27, 69C3
Handgun study backs controls 2-17, 170C2
Canada asks stiffer gun control 2-24, 250B3
Reagan vs gun controls 2-28, 166D1
House com recommits handgun ban 3-2, 170E1
US holds 7 in El Salvador plot 5-15—5-17, 401E1-E2
Nigeria rpts 2 Amers held re arms plot 6-2, Australian rptd held re illegal possessn 6-19, 498E2
Dem platform text 6-15, 474C1
Mondale legis record cited 512C3
Reagan: Schweiker compatible 8-4, 564D1
GOP platform com OKs plank 8-13, 582E3
GOP platform text 8-18, 604G1, A2
Dole legis record cited 614F2
Indep Party vs gun control 8-27, 666F1
Ford vs registratn 9-26, 723B3
Handgun ban not cleared 10-2, 884C1
H Rap Brown '68 La chrg dropped 10-21, 912C3
Ford, Carter debate 10-22, 799G3, 802C1, E1
Dole vs gun control 10-31, 827A3
Mass vs handgun curb 11-2, 821G1, 825C3
US sentncs El Salvador col 11-23, 1012C3
Calif weapons cache found 12-4—12-11, Wiggins chrgd 12-15, 952D3

FIRE and Ice (book)
On best-seller list 12-5, 972D2

FIRE Fighters
Sup Ct rules on min wage laws 6-24, 468B2
Survivor benefits signed 9-29, 834D2
Sup Ct upholds Mass unpaid duty rule 10-12, 848A3

FIRES & Explosions—*See ACCIDENTS; 'Arson' under CRIME*

1977

FINOTTO, Martino
2d in Daytona endurance 2-6, 531E2

FIREARMS
Greece cracks down vs gunrunning 1-18, 63G2
Yoshimura convicted 1-20, 59G3; sentncd 3-17, 288A3
Sup Ct broadens possessn rules 6-6, 478F3
Bus hijacker chrgd 7-5, 568D3
Canada gun-controls passed 7-18, 596A2; 7-18, 596A2
Canal Zone gun sales up 9-7—9-18, 755E1

FIRE Fighters
La cities OK job quotas 6-29; NJ sued 10-4, 819F1-B2
NYS death penalty bill vetoed 7-12, 594F2
Dayton (O) unit strikes 8-8—8-10, 613B3
Pay hikes, property tax boosts linked 9-12, 722B1
Not covered in House mandatory retirement curb 9-23, 737E2
Barnes released from jail 10-14, 870G2

FIRE Fighters, International Association of (AFL-CIO)
Dayton (O) firemen strike 8-8—8-10, 613B3

FIRES & Explosions
NYC '76 soc club indictmts 1-2, 1-11, 140A2
Pa coal mine fire 2-7—4-5, 396C2
Brook Farm destroyed 3-27, 396B2
Texas hotel blaze 4-19, 508G3
Ind heiress found dead 5-7, 492G1
Wilmington 10 denied retrial 5-20, 531C3
Fla panhandle forest fires 5-23—5-26, 660D3
NYC bathhouse fire 5-25, 429G2-A3
Ky nightclub 5-28, 429D2; faulty wiring blamed 6-10; 3 more die 6-12—7-29; suits rptd 7-29, 740A1
Wis U '70 bomber sentncd 6-8, 6-10, 492D1
N Mex forest fire 6-16—6-22, A-lab threatened 6-18, 660F3
Ariz forest fire 6-22, 660G3
US liable in Ga '71 plant blast 6-23, 604B1
Tenn jail fire 6-26, 1 chrgd 6-27, 508D3
US prison preventn study begun 6-27, 604G1
Conn prison arson 7-7, 604F1
Trans-Alaska pipeline fire 7-8, 537C3
Alaska forest fires 7-8—8-23, 660B2
NYC blackout arson 7-13—7-14, 537A3
Utah forest fire kills 3 7-16—7-19, 660A3
Montana canyon fire 7-16—7-20, 660B3
Maine state park blackened 7-17—8-2, 660C3
Wyoming forest fires rptd 7-19, 660A3
NJ forest fires, arson suspected 7-23—7-25, 660E3
Pa glass factory blast 7-25, 604B1
Calif homes, forests burn 7-26—8-23, 660B2-G2
Ore forest fires 8-4, 8-9, 660G2
Colo forest fire burns out 8-7, 660C3
Dayton (O) homes burn 8-8—8-10, 613B3
US '77 forest fire data rptd 8-23, 660F1
USSR looting in US emb rptd 9-2, 766D1
Canada jail arsonist sentncd 9-30, 848D1
CPSC sues aluminum wire mfrs 10-27, 900C3
Wilmington 10 cases probed 11-5, pardon sought 12-4, 943A1, B1
S Korea freight train blast 11-11, 928B3
Manila hotel burns 11-14, 928F3
Bermuda hotel burns 12-2, 935C3
E Coast atmospheric blasts unexplained 12-2—12-22, White House asks study 12-30, 1008D3
NJ chemical plant blast 12-8, 1023D3
RI dorm fire kills 7 12-13, 1023B3
La grain elevator blast 12-22, 1023E1
Miss grain mill blast 12-22, 1023A2
Tex grain elevator blast 12-27, 1023G1-B2

1978

FINNERTY, Michael
Fight for Barbara opens 11-27, 1031F1

FINNEY, Jack
Invasn of Body Snatchers released 12-21, 1030A3

FINNEY, Thomas D.
Dies 1-30, 96G1

FIOCCA, Francisco
Sentenced for fraud 5-31, 824C3

FIREARMS—*See also ARMAMENTS*
Gun lobby group admits false mailings 1-16, 68E2
Switzerland tightens controls 2-9, 151C2
Phila radicals blockaded 3-8, surrender 5-7, 410E1-C2
Olin indicted for S Africa sales 3-14, 193A3
Olin fined for S Africa sales 3-30, 249F2
Antique gun tax rule review declined by Sup Ct 5-22, 388B2
Houston ex-cops chrgd in '75, '77 gun plants 6-3, 12-14, 991D2, A3
Gun Owners of Amer ranked 5th-top PAC fund-raiser 9-7, 753B2
8 Ga prison guards resign 9-14, 771B1
Remington air gun recall rptd, record setlmt cited 10-25, 942D1
Newton sentncd on gun chrg 11-3, 971F2
Clark loses US Sen reelectn 11-7, 854C2
Weapons experts heard at King hearings 11-9, 898B2
Guyana cult cache found 11-18, use rptd opposed 11-21, 890A3, 891E2

FIRECRACKERS
CPSC ban review refused by Sup Ct 3-27, 241C2

FIRE Fighters
Normal (Ill) strike 3-21—5-15, 565E2
Mandatory retiremt age hike exempts 4-6, 238F3
US '75 arson deaths rptd 6-4, 440B2
LA plans layoffs 6-7, 425B3
Workweek cut vetoed 6-19, 465B3
Memphis strike 7-1—7-4, 513D2
Louisville strike ends 7-18, 565D2
Memphis strike 8-14—8-18, 644C2
Strikes in Anderson (Ind) 8-26—9-1, Wichita 9-11—9-20, Butte 9-17, Biloxi 9-18—9-20, 753C1-F1
OSHA to consolidate rules 10-24, 833G3
DC pensn reform vetoed 11-4, 897F2
Cities' power over suburbs backed by Sup Ct 11-28, 937A3, C3
Oakland (Calif) minority plan overturned 12-26, 1006F2
Cleveland layoffs canceled 12-28, 1008E3

FIRE Fighters, International Association of (AFL-CIO)
Memphis local strikes 7-1—7-4, 513D2

FIRE Prevention & Control Administration, National—*See U.S. GOVERNMENT—COMMERCE—National Fire Prevention & Control Administration*

FIRES & Explosions
Wilmington 10 denied convictn review 1-5, 24D2
Mo hotel fire kills 16 1-28, 212B3
NYC '76 soc club arsonist sentenced 2-7, 380G3
Amer Chicle '76 blast chrgs dropped 2-15, 212D3
Tex, La '77 grain elevator blast violatns rptd 2-23, 5-16, 636E2
Tenn tank car blast kills 12 2-24, 196C1
Texaco fined for '77 Tex fire 3-2, 212F3
Abortn clinic violence rptd 3-7, 5-17, 744B2
E Coast booms linked to Concorde 3-15, 187G1
NYS death penalty bill clears legislature 3-20; Carey vetoes 4-11, override fails 5-2, 388A3
RR safety measures ordrd 3-23, 4-15, 5-9, 365G2
Firecracker ban review refused by Sup Ct 3-27, 241C2
Pulitzer awarded for '77 Ky nightclub coverage 4-17, 315A2
Tex City oil blast kills 7 5-30, 460F2
Arson probe search warrant rules set by Sup Ct 5-31, 431E1
US study finds arson rise 6-4, 440A2
'Son of Sam' '74-77 arson cited 6-13, 500C3
Memphis fires break out, striking firemen deny arson 7-1—7-4, 513D2
UK train fire kills 11 7-6, 636F2
LNG safety measures urged, '44 Cleveland blast cited 7-31, 610F1
'77 Ky nightclub fire indictmts ruled out 8-2, 972C1
Anderson (Ind) block burns 8-30, 753C1
NY '74 disco fire convictn 9-7, 824F2
La oil reserve fire 9-21—9-26, 738E1
Aluminum wire dispute refused by Sup Ct 10-2, 751F1
US fire victim study rptd 10-8, 972A1
Flame retardant PBB contaminatn rptd 10-9, 769E2
OSHA drops extinguisher height rule 10-24, 833E3
Govt witness in arson case slain, Ky trial cited 10-25; pornographer arrested 11-9, 971D2, E2
PBB Mich suit dismissed 10-27, 834D1
Pa hotel arson kills 11 11-5, 971C3
Pittway OKs smoke detector fine 11-6, 942E1
NY Holiday Inn arson kills 10 11-26, 971B3
Miss dorm fire kills 15 12-9, 971E3
Toxic-waste rules proposed 12-14, 982C3
'77 Tenn jail arsonist sentncd 12-20, 992A2

1979

FIORI, Ed
Wins Southern Open 10-14, 970G1

FIREARMS
Ill prison search nets arms 3-3, 196G3
FALN suspect convicted 3-9, sentncd 4-20; escapes 5-21, 431F1
CIA seeks more armed agents 4-4, 310B2
Yoshimura '77 convictn upheld 4-5, 271A3
NY gun-in-car law upheld by Sup Ct 6-4, 438B3
Hell's Angels arrested 6-14, 492B1
Hell's Angels trial opens 10-4, 840E1
Calif Sup Ct inquiry ends 11-5, 869B2
8 Iranians seized in Md 11-15, 879F1
KKK, Nazis arrested in NJ 11-24, 991C3

FIRE Fighters
LA bias case found moot by Sup Ct 3-27, 263A2
Toledo (O) contract rejctd 7-3, 599E1

FIRES & Explosions
NJ arson kills 28 1-20, 1-22, 209F1
Tex car fire kills 2 Mex aliens 2-11, 127E2
'Son of Sam' pre-arrest evidence rptd 2-26, 156G2
Boston hotel fires 3-29, busboy chrgd 3-30, 316C3
Mo, Pa boarding home fires kill 34 4-1, 4-2, 316F2
NJ hotel destroyed 5-11, 572B3
Chippewa Minn reservatn fires 5-20, 465D1
Fla blasts injure 18 6-7, 572A2
Calif range fires 6-8—6-11, 572E2
Mich oil facility fire 6-16, 572C3
'Catonsville 9' fugitive surrenders 6-19, 492F1
Ariz fires destroy 76,200 acres 7-2, 572D3
Navy probes ship fires 7-5, 519F3
Idaho, 4 other states hit by forest fires 7-6—8-12, 620D1
Houston townhouses destroyed 7-31, 620C2
Ohio motel arson kills 10 7-31, 639F1
Miss R barge blast kills 3 8-30, 800D1
Sears TV repair recall set 8-31, 903E1
Calif brush fires 9-11—9-23, 799E2
Conn mass murderer convctd 10-19, 819C2; sentncd 11-30, 954A1
Thevis, 2 others convicted 10-21, 818A2
Liberian freighter, tanker collide off Tex 11-1; 15 rptd dead 11-9, 954F3
Ohio boarding home fire kills 14 11-11, 954D2
Conn arson 'dual sovereignty' case refused by Sup Ct 11-13, 902A2
NYC Black Muslim mosque firebombed 11-24, 898B2
Shell '70 liability case refused by Sup Ct 12-3, 964D2

1980

FINNBOGADOTTIR, Vigdis (Icelandic president)
Elected pres 6-30, 498F2

FINNEY, Sgt. Bambi Lin
Dischrgd for Playboy pose 2-21, 189C1

FIORE Jr., Vincent J.
Sentenced 1-11, 64A2

FIREARMS
Ky convictn case remanded by Sup Ct 1-14, 37G1
Reagan assails Bush on gun control 2-5, 2-6, 128G2
NH gun-control forum 2-18, GOP pres debate 2-20, 129B3, G3
Fed gun law prior convictn rule upheld 2-27, 188F2
Thevis convictn case refused by Sup Ct 4-21, 344B2
UK marksmen join indep Olympic boycott 5-17, 379E2
NY gun control bill signed 6-13, 470G2-C3
Hell's Angels mistrial declared 7-2, 5689C2
US GOP platform adopted 7-15, 535C3, 537E1
8 FALN suspects convicted 7-30, 601C1
Hells's Angels sentenced 8-18, 714B1
Yoshimura paroled 8-25, 890G1
'79 US murder data rptd 9-24, 971G1
Anderson answers TV debate questn on gun control 10-28, 816B1
NRA endorses Reagan 11-1, 844F1

FIRE Fighters
Phila layoffs take effect, pact rehiring provisn cited 3-1, 187B1
Chicago strike ends 3-8, 187E2
Ia women wins breast-feeding case 3-20, 441G3
KC strike ends 3-22, 227D3
NYC pact setld 7-3, 518B1, E1
Mobile (Ala) strike 7-14—7-20, 576D1
US trains Canadians 8-2, 633B2

FIRES & Explosions
Miami riots spur arson 5-17—5-19, 382A3, B3
Drought sparks Southwest fires 6-29, 616C2
Mobile (Ala) landmark cafe 7-20, 576E1
NJ hotel fire kills 23 7-26, 621B3
Mafia, pizza indus ties probed 8-24, 714D1
Ark A-missile silo blast kills 1 9-19, 765E1
Dutch ocean liner fire off Alaska 10-4, 769B2
Ky, W va forest fires 10-31—11-13, 971A1
Calif brush fires destroy 86,000 acres 11-15—11-30; disaster declared 948A1
Las Vegas hotel fire kills 84 11-21, probe rptd 11-25, 893C2
Wilmington 10 convictn reversed 12-4, 940C1
Harrison NY hotel fire kills 26 12-4, 948G1
Lenient sentnc appeal backed in arson case 12-9, 936F3

1976

FIRESTONE, Mary Alice
Sup Ct rules on libel case 3-2, 169E2
FIRESTONE Tire & Rubber Co.
Trust suit dropped 3-2, 988A3
Rubber workers strike 4-21, 308D3
In URW talks 8-5—8-12, strike ends 8-29, 647B3
Big 4 pacts set, boycott ends 9-8, 867A1, B1
Ford admits golf trip 9-28, 722D3
FIRMINO Miguel, Lt. Col. Mario
Portugal defense min 7-23, 558G1
Ties to Spinola cited 8-11, 733A1
FIRST Arabian Corp.
Detroit bank acquisitn OKd 12-19, 983G3
FIRST Coolidge Corp.
Rptd on FRB 'problem' list 1-22, 111B3
FIRST Georgia Bancshares Inc.
Rptd on FRB 'problem' list 1-22, 111B3
FIRST & Merchants Corp.
Rptd on FRB 'problem' list 1-22, 111B3
FIRST National Bank (Chicago)
Lowers prime 7-26, 568C2
Lowers prime rate 9-24, 846F2
Lowers prime 11-19, 939B3
FIRST National Bank (Mexico, N.Y.)
Bankers Trust acquistn barred 8-19, 667G1
FIRST National Bank of Maryland (Baltimore)
Boycott rpt released 10-19, 786C1
FIRST National Bank of Nevada
Named Hughes Nev executor 4-14, 335D3
FIRST National Boston Corp.
Rptd on FRB 'problem' list 1-22, 111B3
First National Bank of Boston
Argentina grain credits set 1-28, 96B3
Boycott rpt released 10-20, 786A2
FIRST National City Bank—*See 'Citibank' under CITICORP*
FIRST National City Bank (Houston)
Boycott rpt released 10-18, 786A1
FIRST National State Bank of New Jersey (Newark)
Buys Bloomfield bank 1-11, 167B2
FIRST Navy Bank (Pensacola, Fla.)
Sikes conflict of interest chrgd 4-7, 286A3
Sikes reprimanded 7-29, 551F3
FIRST Pennsylvania Corp.
Rptd on FRB 'problem' list 1-22, 111B2
First Pennsylvania Bank (Phila.)
Rptd on comptroller's 'problem' list 1-26, 113D1
FIRST State Bank (Hudson Co., N.J.)
Closed, sold 6-14; reopened 6-15, 495F1
FIRST State Bank of Northern California (San Leandro)
Fails 5-22; Lloyds reopens 5-23, 438B1
FIRST Tennessee National Corp. (Memphis)
Buys Hamilton Natl 2-16, reopens under new name 2-17, 167F1
FIRST Union National Bank—*See CAMERON Financial Corp.*
FIRST Wisconsin Corp.
Rptd on FRB 'problem' list 1-22, 111B2
First Wisconsin National Bank (Milwaukee)
Rptd on comptroller's 'problem' list 1-26, 113E1
Boycott rpts released 10-18, 10-20, 786B1, A2
FISCHER, Henry
Iraq fund role rptd 3-7, 187B2

FISH (& Fishing)
Peru cites low '75 catch 1-12, 142A2
EC pacts with Tunisia, Morocco rptd 1-13, 84G2
Dec, '75 CPI 1-21, 90A2
Japan seeks US talks 2-17, 141B2
GE chrgd re Hudson R PCBs 2-9, 171E3

1977

Foreign Developments (including U.S. international news)
Australia brushfires 2-12—2-13, 204G2
Moscow hotel fire 2-25, 204D2
N Sea oil-well blowout capped 4-30, 336D1-C3
Amsterdam hotel fire 5-9, 604B2
Saudi oil pipe fire 5-11—5-13, 362B2, 402B2
Brussels hotel blaze 5-22, 429B3
Canada mining town burns 5-23, 604D2
Ivory Coast nightclub fire 6-9, 604G1
Canada jail blaze 6-21, 604C2
Dutch art collector's home 7-18, 986E1
US Moscow emb fire 8-26—8-27, 673F2
Pl mental hosp blaze 12-16, 1023A3
FIRESTONE, Leonard K.
Replaced as amb to Belgium 4-29, 418D1
FIRESTONE Tire & Rubber Co., The
Beasley indicted, co paymts cited 10-25, 818C2
FIRMENICH, Mario
Spain Socist ldr backs Montoneros 7-23, 595B3
FIRST Augusta Bank & Trust Co.
Fails 5-20, 578C1
FIRST Boston Corp.
Chris-Craft damages voided 2-23, 150A2
Quebec loan rptd 9-13, 742D1
Cited in Lehman Bros, Kuhn Loeb merger 11-28, 1004G2
FIRSTHAND Report (book)
Nixon disputed re Adams firing 5-5, 367D1
FIRST International Bancshares Inc.
Bush elected dir, exec 2-23, 140F2
FIRST National Bank (Atlanta, Ga.)
1st Augusta Bank takeover 5-20, 578C1
FIRST National Bank (Chicago)
Lance cleared, US aide to probe loan 7-25, 574D1-B2
Lance cleared in govt probe 8-18, 625F2
Lance loan 'substandard' 9-8, 690D2
Abercrombie closing rptd 11-12, 980E3
FIRST Nudie Musical (film)
Top-grossing film 9-28, 808G3
FIRST Pennsylvania Bank
NFL Eagles owner loses financial control 8-8, 659A1
FIRST State Bank (Foss, Okla.)
Fails 3-10, 578C1
FIRST Western Banking Corp.
Lloyd's takeover cited 3-1, 155C2
FISCHESSER, Doug
Fought wins US Amateur golf title 9-5, 951A2
FISH, Hamilton
Group buys Nation mag 12-22, 1004F3
FISH Jr., Rep. Hamilton (R, N.Y.)
Son buys Nation mag 12-22, 1005A1

FISH (& Fishing)—*See also WHALES & Porpoises*
Md asks US aid re Chesapeake Bay freeze 1-20, 54D2
Snail darter halts Tellico Dam constructn 1-31, 95G2-C3
EC stock protectn agreed, Ireland sets ship curbs 2-15, 146F2

1978

Foreign Developments
Australia brush fires 1-13—1-18, 145G1
Burma airline explosn kills 48 3-25, 271B1
Italy Honeywell warehouse arson 5-12, 393G2
Swedish hotel fire kills 20 6-10, 460G1
Brazil museum burns 7-8, 579A2
Spanish gas truck blast kills 150 7-11, 636D1
Italy lead factory blast 7-15, 689A2
Italian panel condemns Seveso firm for '76 blast 7-27, 689E1 ★
Iran movie houses 8-18, 8-20, 639C3
Canada MP sentenced 10-6, 794G2

FIRESTONE Tire & Rubber Co., The
Beasley pleads guilty 2-28, 142C3
Retroactive jobless benefits challenge declined by Sup Ct 4-17, 308B3
Brazil factory strike rptd 5-22, 412D1
Beasley sentenced 5-31, 404D2
Tire recall sought 7-8, 8-31; suits rptd 9-22, recall set 10-20, 834E3
Borg-Warner merger planned; '77, '78 earnings woes cited 11-28, 935D1
FIRESTONE Tire & Rubber Co. v. Taylor
Retroactive jobless benefits challenge declined by Sup Ct 4-17, 308C3
FIRMENICH, Mario
Assassinatn threat chrgd 1-18, 208A2
FIRNBERG, Hertha
Says Kreisky to stay on despite A-plant vote 11-6, 879B1
FIRST Boston Corp.
Cleveland warned on default 8-23, 663E3
FIRST Chicago Corp.
Chile loans rptd undercutting US rights policy 4-11; Reuss scores 4-12, 312G1
First National Bank of Chicago
Lance loan repaymt rptd 1-17, Abedi role revealed 3-22, 204C3
Reward offered in '77 theft 5-1, 380C1
Prime rate hiked 11-13, 918D1
Nigeria Loan set 11-30, 934G1
FIRST Empire Bank-New York—*See MANUFACTURERS and Traders Trust*
FIRST Monday in October (play)
Opens 10-3, 1031F1
FIRST National Bank of Boston v. Bellotti
Corp pol free speech backed by Sup Ct 4-26, 343D2
FIRST National Bank of Chicago—*See under FIRST Chicago Corp.*
FIRST Time, The (film)
Released 3-28, 619A2
FIRST Valley Bank of Pennsylvania
Flood paymt chrg rptd 1-27, 240A2
FIRTH, Peter
Joseph Andrews released 4-13, 619F2
FISCHER, Bobby
To end retirement 10-20, 843C2
FISCHER, Erwin
Goebbels diary on W Ger best-seller list 1-2, 22C1
FISCHER, John
Dies 8-18, 708G2
FISH
Canada presses Sovt satellite search, radiatn danger cited 1-24, 57B2; 7-5, 514D3
Snail darter dispute cited in TVA resignatn 5-5, 390F2; 5-10, 436A3
Snail darter halt of Tellico upheld by Sup Ct 6-15, 468G1-D2
Wildlife program vetoed 7-10, 567F3-568B1
Snail darter cited re Endangered Species Act revisn 10-15, 834C2; 11-10, 1003B1
FISH Jr., Rep. Hamilton (R, N.Y.)
Reelected 11-7, 851F3
FISHER, Adrian S.
Scores French disarmamt plan 1-31, 61B3
FISHER, John
Pro-defns cong coalitn formed 8-8, 604B3
FISHER, Rep. Joseph L. (D, Va.)
Unopposed in primary 6-13, 467F1
Reelected 11-7, 852A4
FISHER, Jules
Dancin' opens 3-27, 887F1
Wins Tony 6-4, 579A3
FISHER, Terry
Fired as Aztecs coach 6-5, named Earthquakes coach 6-19, 707C3, D3

FISHING Industry
Swedish zones in Baltic set 1-1, 21A2
Georges Bank, other offshore lease sales delayed 1-30, 108E2
UK vetoes EC policy 1-30—1-31; France, W Ger, other EC natns score 2-6—2-7, 2-14, 122C1, 158F3

1979

Foreign Developments
Australia brush fires 1-10, 18E2
Poland bank blast kills 49 2-15, 212D2
Italian cruise liner burns 3-30, 316B3
Mex oil well blows out 6-3-6-16, 462A2, A3
Taiwan blast kills 18 6-13, 572C3
Spanish hotel fire kills 80 7-13, 572F2
India cinema fire kills 92 7-29, 639G1
French forest fires 8-14, 620B2
Canada ex-MP's sentnc hiked 9-11, 685C1
Austria fire kills 25 9-28, 918C1
Canada's Rideau Club burns 10-23, 834A1
Canada train derailmt sparks fires 11-10—11-14, 871E3-872B1
US Emb in Pak burned 11-21, 893A1, D2, 894B1
FIRESTONE Tire & Rubber Co., The
URW contract talks, wage-guides in dispute 2-2—5-9; no-strike agrmt rptd 2-12, Uniroyal struck 5-9, 344C3
'72 gold trading chrgd, Beasley allegatns cited 3-15, 202A2
Borg-Warner merger called off 4-24, 349C3
Fortune rpts '78 loss 5-7, 305F1
US indicts 5 in Nicaragua arms plot 5-14, 386D3
URW pattern pact set 6-18, 480C1
Tax fraud indictmt 7-11; pleads guilty, fined 7-26, 648B3
FIRMANI, Eddie
Fired by Cosmos 6-1, joins ASL 6-18, 655F1
Hired as Fury coach 10-9, 1004E2
FIRST Baptist Church (Calhoun, Ga.)
Maddox joins Carter staff 4-15, 300E3
FIRST Baptist Church (Washington, D.C.)
Carter discloses Park conversn effort 8-5, 639B2
FIRST Boston Inc.
First Boston Corp. Ltd.
Fibic-Congoleum merger OKd 9-21, 942A2
FIRST Chicago Corp.
First National Bank of Chicago
Poland econ monitor plan set 1-11, 59G3
Nicaragua debt paymts in doubt 9-28, 753E2
FIRST National Bank of Boston—*See under FIRST National Boston Corp.*
FIRST National Bank of Chicago—*See under FIRST Chicago Corp.*
FIRST National Bank of Newton County (Ga.)
Beasley pleads no contest re '77 loan chrg 5-14, 380F3
FIRST National Boston Corp.
First National Bank of Boston
Urban fiscal standings rptd 3-20, 204G1
A-protesters arrested 8-31, 742F3
Nicaraguan debt paymts in doubt 9-28, 753F2
FISCHER, Bobby
'76 Worldwide Church link cited 1-3, 23D3
FISCHETTI, Michael
Hitting Town opens 1-6, 292F1
FISH—*See FISHING Industry*
FISHER, Alan
Scores proposed union curbs 7-9, 524A3
Vs govt spending plans 11-1, 855E2
FISHER, J. W.
Carmelina opens 4-8, 711A2
FISHER, Rep. Joseph L. (D, Va.)
Loses Budget Com seat 1-23, 70G3
FISHER, Dr. Russell K.
Paisley death questioned 6-27, 520D2
FISHER, Terry
Fired as Earthquakes coach 5-19, 1004E2
FISHER, William & Betty
Carters visit 7-12, 513G2

FISHING Industry
Georges Bank oil-lease ban lifted 2-20, 186F3
Australia prawn arsenic levels rptd high 2-20, 188G2
Okla minnow sale ban voided by Sup Ct 4-24, 364C2

1980

Foreign Developments
Canada club fire kills 42 1-1, 24C2
Jamaica nursing home fire 5-20, 391B3
Canada forest fires rptd 5-24, 5-26, 406C2
Canada forest fire losses rptd 8-2, 633G1
Spanish radicals claim arson attacks 8-18, 653D2
Spain school blast kills 64 10-23, 948F2-A3
Reichstag arson verdict canceled 12-15, 996C3

FIRESTARTER (book)
On best-seller list 9-14, 716B3; 10-12, 796C3; 12-7, 948D3
FIRESTONE, Mr. & Mrs. Bert
Genuine Risk wins Ky Derby 5-3, 447B2
FIRESTONE Tire & Rubber Co., The
Uniroyal tire recall set 3-7, 348E2
Tex plant cited for job bias 3-21, 251G2
NHTSA fines 5-13, tire recall set 7-3, 702B2
US contracts voided 7-15, 560B2
Nevin elected chief exec 9-1, 702C1
Arab boycott data released 10-20, 801B1
FIRING Squad in Iran (photograph)
Wins Pulitzer 4-14, 296D2
FIRST BOSTON Inc.
First Boston Corp. Ltd.
Carhuff munic bond mkt comments rptd 2-28, 186G1
FIRST Charter Financial Corp.
American Savings & Loan Association
Mortgage rate hits 17.5% 3-19, 222D3
Mortgage rate cut to 12% 6-30, 514C1
Mortgage rate raised to 12.5% 7-31, 631A1
FIRST Chicago Corp.
Hunts sell shares to cover margin calls on silver 3-27, 223C2
Abboud, Kapnick ousted 4-28, 456A2
Sullivan named chrmn 6-24, 600C2
Abboud named Occidental pres 8-4, 702A1
First National Bank of Chicago
Yeo named Chicago fscl aide 1-22, 186F2
Credit restrictions rptd 3-27, 222G2
Prime rate cut to 18% 5-5, 367B3
Prime cut to 14% 5-27, 401C2
Bache loan deceptn chrgd 5-30, 425A2
Prime cut to 11.5% 7-7, 514A1
Prime cut to 11.25% 7-17, 574D3
Nicaragua debt rescheduled 9-5, 689G2
Prime hiked to 13.5% 9-12—10-1, 764E2
FIRST City Financial Corp.
Hunts' Bache stock acquired 10-21, 867B3
FIRST Deadly Sin, The (film)
Released 10-24, 836F2
FIRST Family (film)
Released 12-25, 1003G1
FIRST National Bank of Boston v. Bellotti
Case decided by Sup Ct 6-20, 555F1
FIRST National Bank of Dallas (Tex.)
Hunt silver bailout set 5-2, 344G3
Hunt bailout loan defended 5-30, 425D2
FIRST National Boston Corp.
First National Bank of Boston
Prime cut to 12% 6-11, 438D1
FIRST Pennsylvania Corp.
Mfrs Hanover to buy units 6-3, 557B2
First Pennsylvania Bank (Philadelphia)
FDIC, banks set bailout 4-28, 329D3
FIRST Wisconsin Trust Co.
Cleary named to Synfuels Corp bd 9-13, Sen panel OKs 9-25, 725F2
Cleary named to interim Synfuels Corp bd 10-5, 786F2
FIRST Women's Bank, The
Mello named pres 6-12, 600G2
FIRTH, Peter
Tess released 12-12, 1003E2
FISA (International Auto Sport Federation)—*See AUTOMOBILE Racing*
FISCHER, Brigit
Wins Olympic medal 8-1, 622D2
FISCHER & Porter Co.
Pa toxic waste suit filed 10-9, 825B1, E1
FISCHETTI, John R.
Dies 11-18, 928D2
FISH—*See FISHING Industry*
FISH Jr., Rep. Hamilton (R, N.Y.)
Reelected 11-4, 843F3
FISHBACK, Murray
Rpts Sovt '71-76 infant mortality rates 6-25, 525F2
FISHER, Anna
Husband in NASA astronaut corps 5-29, 477E1
FISHER, Carrie
Empire Strikes Back released 5-21, 675D2
FISHER, Sir Henry
Lloyd's study issued, reforms urged 6-26, 509C3
Lloyd's adopts plan 11-4, 855C3
FISHER, Rep. Joseph (D, Va.)
Loses reelectn 11-4, 850F2
FISHER, Welthy Honsiger
Dies 12-16, 1004E1
FISHER, William
Chosen to NASA astronaut corps 5-29, 477E1
FISHING Industry
Alaska State of State message 1-15, 268F3
US, Canada acid rain, pollutn perils rptd 2-2, 2-19, 145G2, B3
Whales damage Newfoundland fishing 461F2

1976

EC proposes quotas 2-18, 164D1
Cuba, Colombia sign trade pact 2-20, 251F3
Japan vs poor natns eased import curbs 3-3, 191G2
Australia forgn investmt policy outlined 4-1, 249A3
James R ban cited 5-7, 349C1
Porpoise-killing tuna fishing banned 5-11, 398B2; Ford scores 5-24, 374B1
US shrimp workers' aid urged, '75 data rptd 5-11, 431F1
Oil spill threatens Spain shellfish 5-12, 384D1
Ford urges regulatory reform 5-13, 346G3
Sup Ct acts to save Nev pupfish 6-7, 435D2
US limits porpoise kill 6-11, 570G3
US Dem platform text 6-15, 475A3
Aug CPI rptd 9-21, 708E2
Canada vs US reservoir 10-12, 945G3
Guatemala IDB loan set 10-13, 1005E1
US curbs porpoise killing 10-15, 902B1
Sept CPI rptd 10-21, 805G2
USSR curbs whale catch 11-3, 1011C2
Venez, UK pact signed 11-23, 929D3
Nantucket oil spill threatens Georges Bank 12-15—12-22, fishermen file suit 12-22, 968G3
Nantucket spill liability hearing 12-28—12-31, suit delayed 12-30, 1013F3
Iceland Issue—*See ICELAND*
International Waters Issue—*See WATERS, Territorial*

FISH Jr., Rep. Hamilton (R, N.Y.)
Reelected 11-2, 830B2
FISH, Lt. Gen. Howard M.
Says Iran seeks 300 F-16s 9-10, 773A3
FISHBEIN, Harry J.
Dies 2-19, 192D3
FISHBEIN, Dr. Morris
Dies 9-27, 1015D1
FISHER, Rep. Joseph L. (D, Va.)
Reelected 11-2, 823D1, 831A1
FISHER, Max
'72 campaign gift listed 4-25, 688B1
FISHER, William L.
Interior asst secy 2-27; confrmd 3-23, 232D1
FISHER, Co., Ray C.
Arab boycott noncompliance rptd 11-7, 986B3
FISHMAN, Rabbi Yakov
Scores Zionists 2-16, 206C3
FISKE, Richard
Guadeloupe volcano erupts 8-30, 643E3
FITHIAN, Rep. Floyd J. (D, Ind.)
Reelected 11-2, 829B3
FITT, Gerard
Vs UK troop reinforcemt 1-7, 19C3
Holds off IRA protesters 8-9, 589G3
FITZGERALD, A. Ernest
Legal costs award rptd 1-1, 6F3
FITZGERALD, Garret
UK amb killed 7-21, 538F2
FITZGERALD, Harry L.
No contest plea rptd 12-22, 1016E2
FITZGERALD, Thomas H. (d. 1975)
Wins Tony 4-18, 460E2
FITZGERALD, Thomas I.
DeSapio pleads not guilty 5-24, 442C3
FITZGERALD, Walter
Vs Trudeau econ remarks 1-11, 27F3
FITZSIMMONS, Frank E.
Quits Ford com 1-8, 4A1
Trucking pact setld 4-3, 248D3, 249A1
Pact ratified 5-10, 348G3
Dissidents demand reform 5-27, 398F1
Renamed Teamsters head, scores critics at conv 6-13—6-16, 435F3
Usery scored re conv talk 7-1, 492C2
FLAGSHIP International Inc.—*See AMERICAN Airlines*
FLAHERTY, David T.
Wins primary runoff spot 8-17, 633F1
Wins runoff 9-14, 705E1
Loses election 11-2, 820B3, 822D2
FLAHERTY, Mayor Peter (Pittsburgh, Pa.)
Carter wins primary 4-27, 305D1
FLAMBOYANTS, Les (book)
Grainville wins Prix Goncourt 11-15, 911G3
FLANNAGAN, Fionnuala
Wins Emmy 5-17, 460B2
FLANNERY, Judge Thomas A.
Dismisses suits vs Hays 10-26, 982B1
FLEISCHER, Michael
Saxe mistrial declared 10-13, 816D2

1977

EC grants USSR licenses 2-18, 146D3
French fishermen protest pollutn 3-27, 255F3
US drought aid signed 4-7, 273G1
Carter energy plan 4-20, 291E3
Peru anchovy fishing suspended 5-6, 428D1
US laws preempt state statutes 5-23, 444G1
US inflatn forecast revised 5-25, 464B2
EC orders Ireland ship curbs lifted 7-13, 771A3
UK bans herring fishing 7-18, EC OKs 9-16, 771B3
Peru export prices cited 7-28, 618E2
Peru anchovy shortage cited re fishmeal export drop 8-31, 784F3
ND dam projct scored 9-19, 726B1
USSR curbs EC fishing 9-24, 9-27, EC bans Sovt trawlers 9-31, 771F2
Medit natns reach pollutn pact 10-21, 876E2
International Waters Issue—*See WATERS, Territorial*
Oil Spills—*See ENVIRONMENT—Oil & Gas*

FISHEL, Wesley L.
Dies 4-14, 356A3
FISHER, Adrian
Notes Geneva conf progress 8-30, 686A3
FISHER, Max M.
Group wins Irvine Co 5-20, 519E1
FISHER, Dr. Vincent
Death rptd 9-29, 935C1
FISH & Wildlife Service—*See under U.S. GOVERNMENT—INTERIOR*
FISK, Carlton
NL wins All-Star Game 7-19, 567C2
AL batting ldr 10-2, 926F3, 927A1
FITCHNER, Bob
Quebec wins WHA title 5-27, 430C1
FITHIAN, Rep. Floyd J. (D, Ind.)
'76 specl interest gifts rptd 2-15, 128F2
FITZGERALD, A. Ernest
On USAF computer project 5-2, 421E3
FITZGERALD, Garret
Visits US 3-16—3-19, 329C1
Named party ldr 7-1, 530F2
FITZGERALD, Gene
Named Ireland labor min 7-5, 599A1
FITZGIBBONS 3d, Albert J.
Hughes estate appraised 3-15, 354F2
FITZPATRICK, Mary
Pardoned 2-3, 254D2
FITZSIMMONS, Frank E.
Son indicted 2-4, 102G3
UFW, Teamsters sign pact 3-10, 177E3
To resign pension post 3-13, 195C1
Carter energy plan reactn 4-21, 320C2
Resigns as pensn fund trustee 4-29, 558C2
Teamster insurnc deal probed 10-31—11-2, 837E1
FITZSIMMONS, Richard
Indicted 2-4, 102G3-103B1
FIXX, James F.
Running on best-seller list 12-4, 1021A3
FLAGG Industries Inc.
Land fraud setlmt rptd 3-11, 203D3
FLAGSHIP International Inc.—*See AMERICAN Airlines*
FLAHERTY, Peter F.
Named dep atty gen 3-9, confrmd 4-5, 272G2
Natl crime data svc under review 6-16, 480B3
LEAA regional offices to close 6-20, 630D2
Caliguiri elected mayor 11-8, 855B3
Quits to consider Pa race 11-26, 914D2
Successor named to US post 12-6, 1001D3
FLAME Retardants—*See CHEMICALS*
FLANDERS, Ed
Wins Emmy 9-11, 1022A1
FLATTO-Sharon, Shmuel
Party wins parlt seat 5-17, 377D1
FLEETWOOD Enterprises Inc.
Investors' return rise cited 340C3
FLEMING, Lady Amalia
Elected to Greek parlt 11-20, 925E1
FLEMING, Erin
Groucho Marx dies 8-20, 696D3

1978

Chile-Argentina Beagle Channel dispute cited 2-20, 216G1
Sahara rebels warn Spain on Morocco pact 2-20, 278D3
Idaho reservatn closed to non-Indians 4-22, 327D1
Danish fishermen protest Baltic quotas 5-5, 371D2
Mont fishing fee disparity backed by Sup Ct 5-23, 405F3
PCB ban formally proposed 6-7, 513B1
Turkey, USSR sign Black Sea pact 6-21—6-23, 595E2
Indians protest in DC 7-15—7-23, 568E3
NH A-plant cooling plan OKd 8-4, 609B2
Canning industry eased clean-water rules proposed 8-10, 644A2
Nitrite additives linked to cancer 8-11, FDA proposes phase-out 8-31, 727G3
Offshore leasing revisn clears Cong 8-22, 662G3
Viet, Thai agrmts reached 9-6—9-10, 696G1
Aquaculture bill vetoed 10-19, 807E3
International Waters Issue—*See WATERS, Territorial*
Oil Spills—*See ENVIRONMENT—Oil & Gas*

FISH & Wildlife Service—*See under U.S. GOVERNMENT—INTERIOR*
FISK, Carlton
NL wins All-Star Game 7-11, 559A3
AL batting ldr 10-2, 928E3
FISKE Jr., Robert B.
NYC drug dealer gets life 1-19, 95E3
F.I.S.T. (film)
Released 4-26, 619A2
FITCH, Adm. Aubrey Ray (ret.)
Dies 5-22, 440F2
FITERE, Jean-Marie
Violette released 10-9, 1030F3
FITHIAN, Rep. Floyd J. (D, Ind.)
King assassinatn hearings 8-14—8-18, 641A3
Reelected 11-7, 850A4
FITT, Gerry
Interparty talks collapse 1-9, 18B2
FITZGERALD, Garret
Scores Lynch on reunificatn 1-9, 18E3
Vs Garvey ouster 1-19, 72D2
FITZGERALD, Jerome
Wins Iowa primary for gov 6-6, 448E1
Loses electn 11-7, 854C2
FITZGERALD, William B.
Wins Mich primary for gov 8-8, 626A1
Loses electn 11-7, 854A1
FITZSIMMONS, Cotton
Named Kings coach 5-10, 656C1
FITZSIMMONS, Frank E.
Sued by US on pensn funds 2-1, 83B1
Son acquitted 4-28, 324C2
On '77 top-paid labor ldrs list 5-15, 365D1, F1
4 indicted in insurnc scheme 6-15, 560D3
PROD scores pensn funds 8-14, 625D1
US sues to bar health fund contract with Dorfman agency 10-16, 792A2
On Carter anti-inflatn plan 10-25, 806D3
FITZSIMMONS, Richard
Acquitted 4-28, 324C2
FIXX, James F.
Running on best-seller list 1-8, 24E3; 2-5, 116C3; 3-5, 195E3; 4-2, 272B3; 4-30, 356G1; 6-4, 460C3; 7-2, 579C3; 8-6, 620B2; 9-4, 708C1; 10-9, 800B3; 11-6, 888A1
FLAGG, Fannie
Patio/Porch opens 4-13, 887D2
FLAHERTY, Peter F.
Wins primary for Pa gov 5-16, 389A3
Loses electn 11-7, 846C3, 849B2
FLAMSON III, Richard J.
Sec Pacific chrmn, chief exec 10-17, 809F1
FLANAGAN, Mike
NASL scoring ldr 8-6, 655E1, C2
On NASL All-Star team 8-20; named NASL MVP, top offensive player 8-21, 707F2, G2, B3
AL pitching ldr 10-2, 928G3
FLANNER, Janet
Dies 11-7, 972A3
FLANNERY, Martin
Condemns Saudi whippings 6-15, 516B1
FLANNERY, Judge Thomas A.
Hancho Kim convicted 4-8, 279D3
Sentences Hancho Kim 5-19, 406A2
FLECKENSTEIN, Edmund A.
Indicted 4-12, 326A2
FLEENER, Terry
Israel arrests 10-25-77; sentncd as spy 1-9, 10B3
FLEETWOOD Enterprises, Inc.
'67-77 investor return rise rptd 5-8, 326A1
FLEETWOOD Mac (singing group)
Wins Grammy 2-24, 315E3
FLEISCHER, Richard
Crossed Swords released 3-2, 619C1
FLEISCHMAN, Emil
Sentenced for fraud 5-31, 824C3
FLEMING, Deryl E.
Flood influence-selling chrg rptd, Elko convictn cited 2-15, 240C2
FLEMING, Lt. Col. Harry
Army gives honorable dischrg 8-31, 843F3
FLEMING, Peter
Loses WCT Challenge Cup 12-17, 1027D2
FLEMING, Robben W.
Named CPB pres 9-14, 759E3

1979

Ga wildlife refuge protesters jailed 5-4—5-10, 368E1
Mich Indian rights upheld 5-8, 368C1
US-China pact set 5-13, 370F1
PR fishermen protest naval maneuvers 5-16, 5-19, 385C3
Mex, Cuba talks 5-17—5-18, 372F2
Nez Perce salmon dispute setld 6-7, 465A1
Oil cleanup bill asked 6-13, 441B2
PCB limits cut 6-28, 571C2, D2
Washn Indian treaties upheld by Sup Ct 7-2, 559D1
Anchovy catch in S Amer drops; '78, '79 fish-meal output data rptd 7-3, 555C1
Canada notes acid rain perils 7-17, 581G2, B3
Nicaragua plans natlztn 7-25, 574C1
Tex crabman slain, anti-Viet violence erupts 8-3, 660C1
Nicaragua export controls set, '78 trade cited 8-9, 616E1
Norway-Iceland dispute averted 8-18, 796F3
US, Canada in tuna dispute; trade data cited 8-26—9-4, 667D1
Lake Mich PCDF contaminatn rptd 9-11, 736B2
Mex oil spill suit filed 9-13, 718G2
Tellico Dam completn authorized 9-26, 766G2
Australia 200-mi zone takes effect 11-1, 832G1-A2
China hikes prices 11-1, 854D3
Me pier bond issue OKd 11-6, 847B1
Tellico Dam completed 11-29, 990B1
International Waters Issue—*See WATERS, Territorial*

FISHKO, Robert S.
GR Point opens 4-16, 711E3
FISKE, Guy W.
Vs Asbestos Corp takeover 5-9, 352G2
FISKE Jr., Robert B.
Waterfront indictmts filed 3-6, 220B2
Waterfront ldr convicted 11-15, 890D1
FITT, Gerard
Seeks parlt debate on Ulster police brutality 3-11, 190B2
Cautns vs home rule talks 10-25, 835E3
Lauds home rule plans 11-20, quits SDLP 11-22, 927F3*-928A1
FITZKEE, Scott
Penn State loses Sugar Bowl 1-1, 8F2
FITZMAURICE, David
Ct bars wage-guide contract denial 5-31, 399C3
FITZMORRIS Jr., Lt. Gov. James E. (D, La.)
Loses vote for La gov 10-27, 946D3
FITZSIMMONS, Cotton
Named NBA top coach 5-11, 526A2
FITZSIMMONS, Francis R.
Indicted 8-2, 744C3
FITZSIMMONS, Frank E.
Asks Carter to fire ICC chrmn 1-18, 111G3
Announces pact ratified 5-18, 384B3
Son indicted 8-2, 744C3
On Pay Advisory Com 10-16, 829F2
FITZSIMMONS, Freddie
Dies 11-18, 1008F2
FIUMARA, Tino
Indicted 3-6, 220C2
FLAGG, James Montgomery (1877-1960)
Dolores Costello dies 3-1, 272C2
FLAGSTAFF, Ariz.—*See ARIZONA*
FLAHERTY, Thomas M.
Subject to rejailing by Sup Ct 6-4, 439A1
FLAKES, Rev. J. J.
At Columbus (Ga) anti-KKK rally 8-18, 866G1
FLANAGAN, Mike
AL pitching ldr 9-30, wins Cy Young Award 10-30, 955C2, F3, G3
Orioles win AL pennant 10-6, 797E2
In World Series 10-10—10-17, 816A1
FLANAGAN, Pauline
Later opens 1-15, 292G1
FLANIGAN, Peter
Nixon Admin pub TV moves disclosed 2-24, 194E1
FLANNER, Janet (1892-1978)
Paris Was Yesterday opens 12-19, 1007E2
FLANNERY, Judge Thomas A.
Bars Moon church bank stock deal 6-6, 547E2
FLATT, Lester
Dies 5-11, 432E2
FLEENER, Terry
Paroled 6-29, deported 6-30, 496F1
FLEETWOOD Mac (singing group)
Tusk on best-seller list 11-7, 892F3
FLEISCHER, Dave
Dies 6-25, 508E2
FLEISCHER, Max
Brother dies 6-25, 508E2
FLEMING, Peter
Wins Grand Prix doubles 1-7, 103D3
Wins Wimbledon men's doubles 7-7, 570D1
Wins Assn of Tennis Pros 8-27, US Open doubles title 9-8, 734G1, E2
FLEMING, Robben W.
On Pay Advisory Com 10-16, 829F2
FLEMING Inc., John F.
Blake book bought for record sum 6-13, 672F1

1980

USSR rpts Caspian Sea leak plugged 3-2, 235G3
China rpts '79 rescue of Taiwan fishermen 4-9, 295F2
USSR caviar scandal rptd 4-15, 354B3
US pollutn control benefits seen 4-21, 308C1
Mar CPI rise rptd 4-22, 305C2
Norway-Iceland ocean pact set 5-10, 398C2
Antarctic pact set 5-20, 398D1
FTC ends tuna indus probe 5-22, 703E2
Mt St Helens damage assessed 5-24—7-4, 503E3, G3, 504B3
Canada raises Georges Bank quota, chrgs US overfishing 6-12, 461B2
UN Sea Law Conf yields draft accord 7-29—8-28, 660A2
French trawler crewmen strike 8-19, 633F3-634B1
France port blockade concessns offered, fishermen score 8-26; navy opens blockade 8-27, 651D3
French protests continue 9-2; Boulogne pact offer rejected 9-5, 707F2
Antarctic pact signed 9-11, 721B1
French Boulogne fishermen end strike 9-17, 750B2
Carter quotes Reagan on '75 Ecuador dispute 9-23, 722D3
Porpoise kill limit lowered 10-21, 987F2
Alaska bond issue OKd 11-4, 842A2
Aid bill clears Cong 12-4, 955B1; signed 12-22, 982C1, 995B3
Mex ends US accords 12-29, 995D2
International Waters Issue—*See WATERS, Territorial*
FISHMAN, Rabbi Yakov
Shayevich installed 4-12, 431D1
FISKE Jr., Robert B.
US Customs corruptn probed 1-11, 359A3
Waterfront ldr sentenced 1-22, 64F2
FISZBACH, Tadeusz
Named Polish Politburo alternate 12-2, 910A1
At Gdansk memorial rite 12-16, 976D2
FITCH, Bill
Named NBA top coach 5-29, 656C3
FITCH, Clyde
Hijinks! opens 12-18, 1003B3
FITCH, Val L.
Wins Nobel Prize 10-14, 889B3
FITHIAN, Rep. Floyd J. (D, Ind.)
Reelected 11-4, 842B4
FITZGERALD, A. Ernest
Nixon trial order petitn rejected by Sup Ct 5-19, 440G1
FITZGERALD, Ella
Wins Grammy 2-27, 296E3
FITZGERALD, F. Scott (1896-1940)
Clothes for a Summer Hotel opens 3-26, 392E2
FITZGERALD, Richard
Wins Theater '80 award 6-8, 692D3
FITZGERALD, Zelda (deceased)
Clothes for a Summer Hotel opens 3-26, 392E2
FITZMORRIS Jr., Lt. Gov. James E. (D, La.)
FBI Brilab probe target 2-9, 111F2
FBI Brilab indictmts 6-17, 455A1
FITZMORRIS, Louise
Navy drops lesbian chrgs 8-21, 898G3
FITZSIMMONS, Francis R.
Sentence rptd 2-19, 237F2
FITZSIMMONS, Frank E.
Son rptd sentenced 2-19, 237F2
Reagan visits 11-18, 880D3
FIUMARA, Tino
Sentenced 5-20, 927F2, A3
FLAG, U.S.—*See under U.S. GOVERNMENT*
FLAGS
Moscow Olympics controversy 7-19—8-3, 588B1
FLAHERTY, Peter
Wins Pa US Sen primary 4-22, 304D3
Loses US Sen electn 11-4, 848D3
FLAMINGO (Bahamian patrol boat)
Cuba sinks 5-10, 371C2, E2
FLAMM, Bob
Aaron boycotts awards ceremony, chrgs racism 1-28, 637G1
FLAMONT, William (Chains)
Chrgd in Ga prison escape 7-30, 654F1
FLAMSON 3rd, Richard J.
Named Security Pacific chrmn 12-16, 959F1
FLANNERY, Joseph P.
Elected Uniroyal chief exec officer 2-22, 225A1
FLAQUER, Irma
Kidnaped, son slain 10-16, 830E1
FLASH Gordon (film)
Released 12-5, 972E3
FLECKER, Clay S.
Daily News staff post rptd 8-27, 732G3
FLEER Corp.
Topps baseball card trust violatn rptd 7-2, 917F3
FLEETWOOD Realty Co.
Teinowitz divorce setlmt rptd 8-15, 639D1
FLEISCHER, Richard
Jazz Singer released 12-19, 1003B2
FLEISCHMAN, Lawrence
Buys Homer oil for $1.7 mln 10-17, 998A1
FLEMING, James
Canada multiculturalism min 3-3, 171C2
FLEMING, Mary Hodge
Guatemala Coca-Cola plant unrest, intl protests; sale pressed 4-16—5-27, 463E3, 464B1
FLEMING, Peter
Wins Grand Prix Masters doubles title 1-12, 213B2

1976

FLETCHER, Arthur A.
Seconds Dole nominatn 8-19, 598E3
FLETCHER, Cliff
Runner-up in US Open doubles 9-12, 716D1
FLETCHER, Louise
Wins Oscar 3-29, 240A3
FLINCHBAUGH Products, Inc.—*See CLABIR Corp.*
FLINT, Mich.—*See MICHIGAN*
FLINT Journal, The (newspaper)
Newhouse buys Booth chain 11-8, 901B3
FLIPPO, Ronnie G.
Elected to US Sen 11-2, 821F3, 828G2
FLOOD, Rep. Daniel J. (D, Pa.)
Reelected 11-2, 830E3
FLOODS—*See STORMS & Floods*
FLORAKIS, Kharilaos
Sovt amb warned vs mtgs 5-16, 402G1
FLORES, Brian
Resigns Guild post 7-22, 553E3
FLORES, Bishop Patrick
Ecuador expels 8-14, 692D3
FLORES Labra, Fernando
Chile frees, exiles to US 8-5, 711F2
FLORES Ortega, Alberto
Occidental bribes rptd 2-14, resignatn offered 2-19, 147G3
Arrest ordered 7-14, 593C1
Occidental chrgs dismissed 11-16, 930E1
FLORES Sanchez, Oscar
Mexico atty gen 12-2, 907A1
FLORES Troconis, Alberto
Arrest ordered 7-14, 593C1
Occidental chrgs dismissed 11-16, 930E1
FLOREZ, Luis de
Olson files released 1-10, 25B1
FLORIDA
Natl Airlines svc resumes 5B2
Cuba refugees rptd training for Angola 1-3, 3C2
Hallandale ex-mayor arrested 1-11, 160E1
Sup Ct sets death sentnc review 1-22, 87A3
AFL-CIO mtg in Bal Harbour 2-11—2-23, 148E3
Firestone libel suit ruling 3-2, 169E2
Miami revenue sharing bias cited 3-2, 187E1
Miami club bias upheld 4-15, 307G3
US bars wetlands dvpt 4-16, 284G2-D3
Lefferdink sentncd in Miami 4-26, 384G2
Anheuser-Busch Jacksonville, Tampa strike ends 6-6, 436B2
US Sup Ct upholds death penalty 7-2, 491F1
Powell stays execution 7-22, 568F2
Lake Placid ecologist dies 8-1, 816D3
Miami area held base for Cuban exile terrorism 8-18, 8-22, 791B1
Haiti refugees in Miami 8-30, 1005G3
Fscl '75 per capita income, tax burden rptd 9-15, 10-12, 959C2
Rpt exiles vs Pepsi execs Cuba visit 9-27, 791E2
Sup Ct reaffirms death penalty 10-4, 746F1
Sup Ct bars review of Miami club bias case 10-4, 766A1
Castro chrgs CIA in Apr fishing boat attack 10-15, 780G1
Cuba exile coalitn rptd 10-19, 779E3
Sues vs superport action 12-17, 992E1
Miami Beach hotels struck 12-25—12-31, 991E2
Tampa transatlantic air route rejctd 12-28, 992E2
Cape Canaveral—*For space launches, see appropriate subheads under Astronautics*
Politics
Primary date set 22A2
Reagan campaigns 1-9, 22A1
Shapp campaigns 1-20, 40A3
Reagan in Daytona Beach 2-7, 130C1
Ford in Orlando 2-13, St Petersburg, Miami 2-14, 129A3
Ford confident 2-17, 129G2
Dem primary sharpens 2-26—3-4, 166E1
Ford, Reagan campaign 2-28—3-4, 165F2; 3-4—3-7, 180D1, G1
Reagan loses equal-time bid 3-4, 180G2-A3
Pres primary results 3-9, 179D1
Sikes scored re Pensacola bank role 4-7, 286B3
Carter delegates seated 6-28, 490B1
Dem conv women delegates, table 508B2
Dem conv pres vote, table 7-14, 507B2
GOP pre-conv delegate count 8-14, 583B3
Mondale in Bal Harbour 8-16, 617A3
Ford backed on 16-C rules test 8-17, 600E1
GOP conv pres, vp vote tables 8-18—8-19, 599B1, B3
GOP conv delegates back Helms as vp 8-19, 598F2
US Cong primary results 9-7, 687B3
Carter in Hollywood 9-10, 686C2
Mondale visits 9-13—9-14, 687F1
Dole in Panama City 9-19, 703C3
Ford Orlando golf outings rptd 9-23, 722B3
Ford in Miami Beach 9-27, 723D3
Carter in Miami Beach 10-19, 785E1, E2
Gurney acquitted of final chrg 10-27, 845F3
Election results 11-2: pres 818A1, 819B2; cong 820C1, 822B1, 828D1, 829A2
Carter primary spending, contributns rptd 11-17, 938G2, A3

1977

FLETCHER Oil and Refining Co.
Settles fed trust suit 8-31, 691D3
FLEURY, Sergio
Acquitted in 3 murders 10-14, 840E2
FLOODS—*See STORMS & Floods*
FLORESCU, Ion
Rptd ousted 11-23, 948B2
FLORES Sanchez, Oscar
Says all pol prisoners freed 4-12, 528A3
On US drug offenders release 4-16, 529B1
Miami-based raid on Cuba foiled 8-15, 654E1
Cuban exiles vow more attacks 8-31, 686C1
FLORIDA
Legislature schedule rptd 6D2
Tampa Bay oil spill rptd 1-9, 214F2
'75 Miami club bias case cited 1-11—1-18, 34A2
Quebec immigratn bids rptd 1-13, 43A2
Pompano Beach sludge gasificatn plant set 2-3, 278E1
AFL-CIO ldrs meet in Bal Harbour 2-21—2-27, 153G1
Carter on Cuba ties 3-5, 171C2
Miami saccharin worker layoffs set 3-10, 177B1
De Mohrenschildt found dead in Palm Beach 3-29, 228B3
Prio Soccarras dies 4-4, 356F3
ERA defeated 4-13, 669C2
Norin Corp '76 sales rise rptd 340C1
Laetrile bill OKd by legis 5-2, 375G3
'76 per-capita income table 5-10, 387F2
Miami condominium sales up; econ data table 5-16, 384E2, B3
Apalachicola Natl Forest burns 5-23—5-26, 660D3
Carter rides A-sub 5-27, 417C3
Drought-related agri losses rptd 6-27, fed aid OKd 8-24, 659G3
Archbp Carroll dies 7-26, 605G2
State oil trust suits merged 9-12, 691G3
'76 per capita income, tax burden table 9-13, 10-18, 821D2
Amers, kin arrive from Cuba 9-22, 781A2
Episc parish secedes 10-2, 845G2-A3
Truck-train collisn 10-2, 992G2
Haitian refugees to be freed 11-8, 1019E1
ERA econ boycott rptd 11-14, 918D1
Intl A-energy forum ends, 14 back A-power 11-16, 937A1
Air Transport
Miami-London air fare kept 3-9, 325B1
Eastern to lease Airbus 5-24, 441B2
Miami landing rights for Concorde proposed 9-23, 738B2
Tampa 'gateway' air svc OKd 12-21, 1006C2
Pan Am awarded Miami-Madrid route 12-21, 1006A3
Crime—*See also 'Cuban Exiles' below*
Hunt freed from jail 2-23, 197F2
1-judge prison ruling reversed 3-21, 230A3
Death sentence on secret info remanded 3-22, 230E3
Darden convictn review denied 4-19, 342B2
'76, '77 death row populatn rptd 5-5, 6-7, 594A1, C1
Mafia operatns rptd widespread 5-16—7-3, 568E1, F1, B2, D2
Youth guilty of murder 6-4; TV trial OKd 7-5; convicted 10-7, 807F2; sentenced 11-7, 907F3
Retroactive death sentnc upheld 6-17, 518F1
Executn for rape banned 6-29, 557F2
Dual fed-state prosecutns curbed 11-7, 857A2
Cuban Exiles
Miami anti-Castro ldr slain 1-7, 163D1
'75 Miami airport bomber sentncd 3-18, 288E3
Venez AF jet bombed in Miami 8-14, 868A1
Letelier murder probed 9-7—9-10, 743E2
Fuel-Weather Crisis
Frost kills crops 1-18—1-20; Askew declares emergency, fresh fruit shipmts embargoed 1-22, 54F3
Palm Beach records 1st snow 1-19, 54G3
Frost to cost migrants jobs 1-24, 55C1
Wind shift blamed for snow 1-27, 77C1
Storm damage estimate updated 1-28, 76B1
US disaster aid rptd granted 2-5, 91A2
Layoff total rptd 2-7, 91F2
Feb food price rise linked 3-18, 215A1

1978

FLETCHER, Louise
Cheap Detective released 6-22, 619A1
FLETT, Bill
Nordiques win WHA All-Star game 1-17, 76F3
FLEURY, Sergio
Arrested re '68 murders 2-22, 166E1
Freed on bail 3-3, 412C2
FLINT, Mich.—*See MICHIGAN*
FLIPPO, Rep. Ronnie G. (D, Ala.)
Reelected 11-7, 850B1
FLOOD, Rep. Daniel J. (D, Pa.)
DeLuca named Marston temp successor 1-24, 62E2
Elko testimony vs rptd 1-27, 240G1-F2
Carter defends Marston removal 1-30, 62D1
Ethics com announces informal probe 2-8, formal probe sought 2-17, 239G3, 240G2
Marston, Justice probes re Hahnemann Hosp, Eilberg links rptd; chrgs denied 2-19, 3-9, 240C1
Gets Lions Club award 3-16, 240A3
Rabbi admits '74-76 payoffs 5-11, 363C2; sentenced 6-22, 500E3
Wins primary 5-16, 389E3
Indicted 9-5, 685B1
Eilberg chrgd by ethics com 9-13, 697C2
Indicted again 10-12, 792A1
Reelected 11-7, 846E2, 849D2, 852D1
Dems rejct ethics rule chng 12-6, 958G2
FLOODS—*See STORMS & Floods*
FLORES, Jorge
Rptdly goes underground 6-2, 475A2
FLORES Munoz, Gilberto
Slain with wife 10-6, 818F1
FLORIDA
Cowles Communicatns to liquidate 1-6, 75G3
John MacArthur dies 1-6, 96G2
State tax revenue data 1-9, 84C2, G3
Orange juice futures trading rise, '77 frost linked 1-12, 84A1
Panama Canal 'truth squad' in Miami 1-17, 58C2
Natl Airlines Miami-LA rule review barred 1-23, 65C2
College integratn plan OKd 2-2, 85D1
AFL-CIO cncl in Bal Harbour 2-20—2-24, 142A1
Baptist schl integratn challenge refused by US Sup Ct 2-21, 126D1
Miami clean-air rating rptd 2-23, 144E3
Chlorine gas from Youngstown derailmt kills 8 2-26, US rpts sabotage 3-3, 196F1
Church-bond defaults rptd 2-27, 295G3
Miami-London airfare agreed 3-17, 206D2
Press curb challenge refused by US Sup Ct 3-20, 206B1
Ct upholds gays' practice of law 3-20, 327C2
2 die in Clearwater, Gainsville tornados 5-4, 479A3
'76 AF, pvt plane collisn damages awarded 5-5, 460E1
Amtrak route cutbacks proposed 5-8, 366E1
Natl jet crashes in Pensacola Bay 5-8, 460C2
RR safety deadlines advanced 5-9, 365A3
Cape Canaveral launches ESA satellite 5-12, 384D3
Construction pact signed 5-22, 429D3
Poynter dies 6-15, 540F3
Natl Pensacola-crash pilots fired 6-16, 636E3
Klan parades in Davie 7-8, 529C2
Keys, Palm Beach elude marathon swimmers 7-13, 8-15, 653E1-A2
Haiti refugees arrive 7-18, 7-22, 671D3
Pan Am Houston-Miami svc OKd 9-1, 701E1
Cuba dual natls fly to Miami 9-14, 10-3, 777A1; 11-14, 880B3
WESH-TV license renewal voided 9-25, 907D3
IAPA ends Miami assemb 10-13, 829D1
US parks bill cleared 10-13, 834D3
Cuban ex-prisoners arrive Miami 10-21, 880C2; 12-12, 1016F1
Lufthansa to serve Miami 10-25, 831F1
Natl Pensacola crash rpt issued 11-9, 908F2 ★
Chessie, Seaboard set merger 11-16, 897B1
Westmoreland addresses Dade Cnty Med Soc 12-6, 960D3
Crime & Civil Disorders
Abrahams arrested in Tarpon Springs 1-24, 83B2
Involuntary servitude chrgd 3-2, 396E3
Death sentencing bias rptd 3-6, 389A1, C1
REA ex-chief sentenced 3-31, 310D1
Gurney trial press-curbs review declined by US Sup Ct 4-17, 308D2
Nixon memoir excerpt links Miami Cubans, Watergate break-in 4-30, 319F3
Secret evidence death convictn case declined by US Sup Ct 5-30, 430C3
'77 prison populatn rptd up 6-3, 440C1
Miami, Jacksonville ILA offcls indicted 6-7, 480F2
Union insurnc scheme chrgd 6-15, 560B3
7 indicted in oil pricing scheme 9-14, 718G2-C3
Rep Burke pleads guilty on 2 bar chrgs, no contest in 3d 9-26, 734G2
Anti-drug air patrols to be boosted 9-29, 815C1
Penn Dixie ex-offcl indicted 10-10, 808F2

1979

FLEMMING, Anne
Marries Brooke 5-12, 392C2
FLEMMING, Arthur S.
Schl desegregatn rpt issued 2-13, 110C2
Scores housing bias 4-11, 283G2
FLEMMING, Louis Constance (deceased)
Daughter marries Brooke 5-12, 392C2
FLETCHER, Louise
Magician of Lublin released 11-9, 1008A1
FLEXI-Van Corp.
Seaboard, Tiger set merger 7-18, 579F1
FLIGHT of the Gossamer Condor, The (film)
Wins Oscar 4-9, 336B2
FLINT, Mich.—*See MICHIGAN*
FLOOD, Rep. Daniel J. (D, Pa.)
Drops subcom chrmnship 1-25, 71A3
Mistrial declared 2-3, jury rptdly favored acquittal 2-5, 102A2
Head convicted of bribery 10-12, sentncd 10-24, 906E1
Sets '80 resignatn 11-7, 900C2
FLOODS—*See STORMS & Floods*
FLORENCE, Ala.—*See ALABAMA*
FLORES, Julio
Bars truce 10-22, 813B2
FLORES, Tom
Hired as Raiders coach 2-8, 175E2
FLORES Rodriguez, Irving
Sentence commuted 9-6, 666D1
Freed 9-10, returns to PR 9-12, 682G3
FLORIDA
Food Fair closes 123 supermkts 1-27, 131G2
Buckley, Sitco partners settle SEC chrg 2-7, 132C1
AFL-CIO cncl in Bal Harbour 2-19—2-26, 148C2
Laetrile shipmt recalled 3-8, 196A1
Cape Canaveral Trident sub launch fails 4-10, 307B3
Evert, Lloyd wed 4-17, 392A2
Fed job training funds challenge refused by US Sup Ct 4-30, 365A1
Miami rejcts anti-smoking law 5-8, 350C3
Emergency declared re truck strike, tomato crop impact seen 6-28, 479D2, A3
HS literacy test voided 7-12, 785C3
Somoza arrives Miami, holds news conf 7-17, 535D1
Vegetable growers withdraw Mex dumping chrgs 7-19, 553G1
'78 tomato crop rptd 7-19, 553E2
Hooker Suwannee R pollutn rptd 8-5, 509D2
6 Haitians drown off coast 8-13; illegal alien populatn data rptd 8-18, 634D2
Army recruiting fraud probed 8-19, 649G2
'78 FRB deposit growth, drug traffic linked 9-6, 840E3
Interior Dept seeks to protect primitive areas 9-7, 703C3
'78 per capita income rptd 9-16, 746E2
Tallahassee abortn trust case declined by Sup Ct 10-29, 884D2
Mex vegetable growers cleared re dumping chrgs 10-30, 831F1
Accidents & Disasters
Crestview derailmt 4-8, 472E3
Miami record rainfall; Ft Lauderdale, Homestead storms rptd 4-25, 472G2-A3
Jay, Jacksonville blasts injure 18 6-7, 572A2
SE coast evacuatns ordrd 9-2, hurricane David hits 9-3, 690F3
Hurricane Frederic hits coast 9-12; looting rptd, disaster aid OKd 9-14, 691C1
Indiantown dam breaks, 1700 stranded 10-31, 912A3
Atomic Energy
Crystal River (Red Level) A-plant safety study urged 4-1, 245F1
Crystal River A-plant '77, '78 problems rptd 4-15, 322F2
Crystal River A-plant shut by NRC 4-27, 322A1
Turkey Pt (Florida City), St Lucie (Ft Pierce) A-plant pipe leaks rptd 5-2, 322B3
Crime & Civil Disorders
Knoetze fight protested in Miami Beach 1-13, 79D2
O'Malley sentenced 1-18, 79C1
Spenkelink death penalty appeal refused by US Sup Ct 3-26, 230F2
Miami pot ring rptd broken 5-1, 492D3
5 indicted in Panama arms plot 5-14, 386C3
Spenkelink death warrant signed, stays denied 5-19—5-25, executed 5-25; Young comment draws fire 5-25—5-26, 399G3, 400D1
Darden death warrant signed 5-19, executn stayed 5-22, 400A1
NJ indictmt details Mafia 5-23, 508A2
Miami law firm chrgd in visa fraud 6-1, 491D3
Delta hijacked jet lands in Miami 6-12, 442C1
'78 inmate totals rptd 6-21, 548C2
Dayton Beach kidnap victim resued 7-30, 604G3
Bundy gets death penalty for '78 slayings 7-31, 604C2
Penn Dixie ex-offcl convicted 8-29, 655G3

1980

Wimbledon results 7-4—7-6, 606A2
Loses US Open men's doubles 9-6, 691F2
FLEMMING, Arthur S.
Urges civil rights concern 7-9, 519G1
FLIGHT Attendants, Association of (AFA)
Continental strike ends 12-20, 988G1
FLIGHTSAFETY International
Munson family sues 2-27, 637E1
FLINT—*See MICHIGAN*
FLINT (Mich.) Voice, The (newspaper)
Print shop police raid cited 7-26, 582D2
FLIPPO, Rep. Ronnie G. (D, Ala.)
Reelected 11-4, 842B1
FLOOD, Daniel J.
Resigns House seat 1-31, pleads guilty 2-26, 190F1-B2
FLOODS—*See STORMS & Floods*
FLORES, Santos Elias
Arrested in El Salvador alien case 7-11, 560F2
Convicted 10-6, sentncd 11-4, 870B1
FLOREY v. Sioux Falls
Case refused by Sup Ct 11-10, 868G1
FLORIDA
Student to get rabies shots 2-9, 200A2
AFL-CIO cncl in Bal Harbour 2-18—2-25, 146C3
Mex vegetable 'dumping' suit dismissed, growers plan appeal 3-24, 233F2
Circus tax case refused by Sup Ct 3-24, 265A2
Kid Gavilan rptd broke 4-1, 320E3
Fed unincorporated business trust suits backed by US Sup Ct 5-19, 440F2
Hunts bailout loan collateral listed 5-28, 425F3
'Parochial' banking practices curbed by Sup Ct 6-9, 512F2-A3
NAACP conv in Miami Beach 6-30—7-4, 505D2
Accidents & Disasters—*See also 'Atomic Energy' below*
Coast Guard, oil tanker collide 1-28; suit rptd filed 2-3, hearing begins 2-6, 256D2
Blizzards, tornadoes hit, citrus crop frozen 3-1—3-2, 292A2, A3
Tampa bridge collapses 5-9, disaster declared 5-14, port reopened 5-21, 391B1
News copter missing in Carib 11-13, 869F3
Atomic Energy & Safeguards
Crystal River A-plant accident 2-26, plant to stay closed 3-5, 169G1
'79 A-plant mishaps rptd 7-14, 551G2
Crime & Civil Disorders
Waterfront racketeers sentenced 1-11, 64F1-A2
8 convicted in Miami 'Black Tuna' pot ring 2-4, 270C3
Bundy gets 3d death sentence 2-12, 136C2
FBI 'Miporn' probe rptd 2-14, 136D1, F1, C2
Bahamas bank looting case rptd 3-3, 229A1
2 convicted for '79 Haitian drownings 4-18, 336B1; sentncd 6-5, 503A3
Ctroom cameras case accepted by Sup Ct 4-21, 344E1
55 Cuban refugees detained 5-1, 326C1
Miami cops cleared in black exec's '79 death 5-17, riots erupt 5-17—5-19, 382E2
Md ex-gov begins prison sentence 5-19, 471F2
Miami exec's case probed by grand jury 5-21, 401E3
Miami declared disaster area 5-22, riot death toll 5-26, 401D3
NAACP head warns of despair 5-29, 460G1-A2
Miami bank rules tightened 6-3, drug money linked 6-5, 502A1-A2
Donated porno warrants required by Sup Ct 6-20, 555A3
US comm cautns re police 7-9, 519G1
Miami violence erupts again 7-15—7-17, 560A1
Dade Cnty ex-cop indicted 7-28, 576B1
Miami riot apathy scored by blacks 8-3, 597F2
Air Fla jets hijacked to Cuba 8-10, 8-13, 617A2
4 more jets hijacked, 2 attempts foiled 8-14—8-17, 631B3
Eastn hijack attempt foiled 8-18, 667F1-A3
5 freed by Cuba arrested in Miami 10-27, 828D3
Ctroom cameras case argued in Sup Ct 11-12, 882A2
Miami riots, racism linked 12-6, 963D1
Black sentncd for Miami riot role 12-11, 990A1
Dade Cnty ex-cop acquitted 12-17, 989F3
Energy—*See also 'Atomic Energy' above*
State of State message 4-8, 483F1

1976

1977

Homosexual Rights
Bryant scores gay rights drive 3-27, 278E2
Dade Cnty homosexual rights law repealed 6-7, 446E2
Gays launch educatn campaign 6-13, 560A3
Gays protest Dade Cnty rights law repeal 6-25—6-26, 560D2, F2
Bryant citrus contract renewed 11-16, 927G2
Medicine & Health
US Sup Ct bars MD malpractice law review 1-10, 57A2
Flu outbreak rptd in Miami 1-26, 103A3
Key West, Panama City germ warfare tests rptd 3-8, 195E2
Laetrile legalizatn cited 6-23, 508E1
School Issues
Coll integratn rules ordrd 1-17, 112B2
Coll integratn rules reordered 4-1, 446D1
Schl spanking ruled legal 4-19, 342F1
Coll integratn plan issued 7-5, 630G2

1978

Rep Burke loses reelectn 11-7, 846D2, 849F3
Politics & Government
Legislature schedule rptd 14E3
'67, '77 sales-tax rates rptd 1-5, 15D3
Primary results, runoff for gov set 9-12, 734C3, 736C1
Graham wins Dem gov runoff 10-5, 769G1
Carter in Miami 10-26, 831A2
Election results 11-7: cong 846D2, A3, 848E1, 849D3, 850E2; state 847C1, G1, A2, A3, 849X3, F3, 852F1, 853E2
Black secy of state noted 11-28, 915D3

1979

Cocaine trade growth rptd 9-5, 972G2
L Blair pleads guilty to drug chrgs 9-6, 859C3
Hurricane Frederic looting rptd 9-14, 691D1
Cocaine seized, 3 arrested 10-12, 10-14, 819B3
Coppolino paroled 10-16, 839G2
Miami KKK activity cited 865B1
PR protester found dead in Tallahasse jail 11-11, probes ordrd 11-18, 11-23, 904A3
Death row populatn rptd 11-25, 989E3
Energy—*See also 'Atomic' above*
'78 per capita gas use rptd 5-27, 395G2
Politics & Government—*See also other appropriate subheads in this section*
Legislature schedule rptd 5C3
Const 'sunshine' amendmt review refused by US Sup Ct 1-22, 54F1
Miami Beach loses GOP conv bid 1-23, 70E3
Fscl '78 tax revenue rptd 2-13, 152B2
Regulatory bds rptd segregated 4-9, 307A2
Draft-Kennedy activity rptd 5-23, 384E2
Carter delegate-rule lobby failure rptd 8-2, 593D1
Hatchett joins fed appeals ct, sets precedent 8-4, 656G3
Askew named Carter trade rep 8-8, 647B1*
Landrieu to sell Key West project interest 9-12, 700G2
Dade Cnty tax cut defeated 9-18, 724B2
Carter sees Kennedy skirmish 9-25, 723B3
Key West mil hq set 10-1, 737G1, 739A1
Carter on Dem caucuses 10-9, 767B1
Dem pres caucuses 10-13, Carter win rptd 10-19, 783B1
Pres straw vote results 11-17, 11-18, 887C1
Reagan in St Petersburg 12-13, 982B2
Sports
Knoetze fight protested 1-13, 79D2
NBA bd meets at Amelia I 6-21, 526E1
Nyad completes Bahamas-Juno Beach swim 8-20, 656E3
Transportation
Delta hijacked jet lands 6-12, 442C1
Amtrak Chicago-Miami-St Pete train ordered cut 8-29, 868B1
Eastern-Natl merger rejected 9-27, 830B1
Southn Railway fined 11-12, 868A2
Carter OKs Pan Am-Natl merger 12-22, 989C1

1980

B Carter, Libyan oil deal rptd 7-14, 542D2
Environment & Pollution
Miami Beach redvpt OKd 3-11, 185B1
Hillsborough Cnty, Gulf Coast Lead toxic waste suits filed 10-9, 825C1
Public land donatn rptd 12-19, 987F1
Politics & Government—*See also other appropriate subheads in this section*
Legislature schedule rptd 18D1
Abscam probe revealed, Kelly linked, 2-2, 2-3, explains role 2-6, 81A2, 82G1
Fscl '79 tax revenue rptd 2-20, 307B3
Kelly quits House GOP conf 2-21, 143B3
Sarasota cancels bond issue 2-26, 186F1
Property tax cut, ct amendmt, other issues voted 3-11, 184G1-185C1
State of State message 4-8, 483D1
Kelley indicted 7-15, 554F1
Primary results 9-9, 700F1-B2
Stone defeated in primary runoff, other results 10-7, 807C3
5th judicial circuit split 10-14, 918A3
Election results 11-4; cong 840E1, 842F2, 846A1, G2, 849B2; state 845D2, 847B3
'80 census rptd, reapportmt seen 12-31, 983D1
Presidential Election (& Transition)
GOP platform hearing set in St Petersburg 1-14, 32A1
Connally fund shortage rptd 2-20, 129D1
Ford on GOP draft 3-6, 207D1
Carter, Reagan sweep primary 3-11, 182G3
Carter booed in Miami 6-9, 439D1
Carter stumps E coast 7-17, 532D1
Graham nominates Carter at conv 8-13, 611A3
Bush in St Petersburg, Orlando 9-2, 780C3
Reagan in Pensacola 9-23, 722B3
Carter in Tallahassee, St Petersburg 10-10, 778B3
Reagan in Tampa 10-10, 780B1
Carter in Orlando, Miami 10-21, 802C3, G3
Reagan in St Petersburg 10-23, 802A2
Mondale stop rptd 10-26, 816G3
Carter tours 10-31, 841B1
Press endorsemts rptd 11-1, 844F1
Election results 11-4, 838A1, 839B2, D3
Refugee Issues
Cuban exiles rally in Miami, Tampa, other cities 4-7, 261A3
Haitians arrive in record numbers 4-13, 294A2
Cubans clog Key West 4-24, 300E3
Cuban exodus hampered by storms 4-25—4-28; total hits 6,000, 55 detained 5-1, 326A1
Graham asks fed aid 4-29, Carter declares emergency 5-6, 339C3
Eglin AF Base processing cntr set 5-1, 326G1
Cuban flow slowed by storm, Swiss Emb interest office attack 5-2; visa procedures suspended 5-4, 339E2
Eglin airlifts begin 5-3; Natl Guard quells Key West unrest; overcrowding, disease rptd 5-6, 339E3
Carter offers Cubans 'open arms', 3,500 more arrive 5-5, 339D2
Cuban influx at 17,636, authorities detain 133 5-6, 339B3
Haitians press for pol asylum 5-7, 339G3
CR hosts intl conf 5-8, 361B1, A2
Cuban immigrants surveyed 5-11—5-20, 396A3
Carter curbs 'open arms' policy, orders flotilla end; 5-pt program detailed 5-14, 361A1
Cuba refugee total at 46,000, 400 deported 5-15, 361G1, B2
US amends finance regulatns 5-15, 361A2
Coast Guard turns back flotillas 5-17—5-21; refugee flows slows, total at 67,000 5-21, 379F3
Cuba refugee boat capsizes, US blames Cuba 5-17, 5-18; sealift deaths at 24 5-21, 380F1
Havana anti-US protest draws 1 mln 5-17, 380A2
Cubans get pol asylum 5-21, 380B1
Eglin processing cntr rptd filled 5-21, 380D1
Eglin hit by unrest, resetlmt delays rptd 5-24—5-25; security tightened 5-26, 395F3-396B1
Cuban refugee resetlmt costs estimated 5-25, 396D1
Cuban flotilla seizures protested 5-28, 700 face fines 5-29, 396F1
Cuban influx at 87,995, 300 vessels stalled in Mariel 5-29, 396E1
US freighter, 34 other vessels arrive in Key West; Cuban influx hits 101,476 6-3, 420B2
Cuban refugee signs with Tigers 6-3, 637C1
Carter consults Cong ldrs 6-4; orders criminal refugees expelled 6-7, 435B1, D1
Flotilla end seen 6-5, US expands blockade 6-10, 435B2
Carter sees black, Hispanic ldrs 6-9, 439F1
Cubans, Haitians granted 6-mo reprieve; get pub assistance 6-20, 484B3, F3, 485B1
18 criminals expelled, Havana blocks return 6-24; 1,395 jailed 6-30, 514C2
El Salvador rightist in US illegally 6-30—7-3, 521D3
Haitians win US suit, deportatns halted 7-2, 514G1

1976

FLORIDA State University (Tallahasse)
Hess rpts Mars weather 7-21, 526C3
FLORIO, Rep. James J. (D, N.J.)
Reelected 11-2, 830C1
FLOWERS, Rep. Walter (D, Ala.)
Travel expense probe ends 10-27, 981G3
Reelected 11-2, 821F3, 828G2
Meets Sadat 11-11, 878A1
FLOYD, Raymond
Wins Masters 4-11, 272G1-A2
FLU—*See 'Diseases' under MEDICINE*
FLUKE Mfg. Co., John—*See RCA Corp.*
FLUOR Corp.
To buy Peabody Coal shares 12-14, 985C1
FLUORIDATION—*See WATER*
FLUSHING National Bank (Queens, N.Y.)
NYC debt moratorium ruled unconstnl 11-19, 887C3
FLYING Tiger Line—*See TIGER International*
FLYNN, Raymond L.
On Boston anti-busing violence 2-15, 202G3
FLYNT, Rep. John James (D, Ga.)
On intelligence leak probe 3-2, 3-4, 216D3
Environmt group scores 3-25, 220B1
Reelected 11-2, 829D2
Carter meets cong ldrs 11-17, 864B2
FLY, Robin, Fly (recording)
Wins Grammy 2-28, 460C3
FMC Corp.
'75 arms sales listed 2-6, 147B3
FOCKE, Katharina
Resigns health min 10-15, 857A3
FOGARTY, Joseph R.
Named to FCC 7-21; confrmd 9-8, 807G3

1977

FLORIDA, University of (Gainesville)
Loses Sun Bowl 1-2, 8G3
FLORIDA Wire & Cable Co.
Chrgs Japan, India dumping 10-17, 836C3
US probes dumping chrg 11-22, 933B3
FLORIT, Ermenegildo Cardinal
Benelli succeeds 6-2, 768A3
FLOUR—*See GRAIN*
FLOWERS, George
Dies 2-27, 288B2
FLOYD, Ray
Wins Byron Nelson Classic 5-8, Pleasant Valley 7-17, 676C1, A2
US wins Ryder Cup Matches 9-17, 951A2
PGA top money winner 10-30, 950G3
FLU—*See 'Diseases' under MEDICINE & Health*
FLUELLEN, Ike
Boxing scandal rpt issued 9-3, 828E1
FLUOR Corp.
Peabody Holding Co.—*See separate listing*
FLUOROCARBONS—*See CHEMICALS*
FLYNN, Doug
Traded to Mets 6-15, 644D2
FLYNT, Jimmy
Acquitted 2-8, 118E2
FLYNT Jr., Rep. John J(ames) (D, Ga.)
'76 specl interest gifts rptd 2-15, 128B2
Korea probe dispute rptd 7-12—7-15, Lacovara quits 7-15, 556F1
S Africa sugar lobby sued 7-20, 614F1
FLYNT, Larry C.
Sentenced 2-8, 118A2
FMC Corp.
Sup Ct backs EPA authority 2-23, 150[illegible]
W Va plant shut 3-9, EPA pact set 3-15, 196B3, D3
FOEGE, Dr. William H.
Named CDC dir 4-5, 287D3
FOERSTER, Thomas J.
Loses mayoral electn 11-8, 855G1, A3
FOERSTER, Werner
Chesimard convctd, sentncd 3-25, 288C3
FOFANA, Kebba
Roots sources doubted 4-10, 356C1
FOGARTY, Joseph R.
On AT&T probe cost 2-24, 217G2

1978

FLORIDA, University of (Gainesville)
Chandler in NFL draft 5-2, 336E3
Tornado causes power outage 5-4, 479B3
FLORIDA A.&M. University (Tallahassee)
Wins Pioneer Bowl, NAIA Div 1-AA title 12-16, 1025C2
FLORIDA Power Corp.
Oil priceing scheme indictmts 9-14, 718A3
FLORIDA State University (Tallahassee)
NCAA basketball tourn results 3-27, 272B1
FLORIO, Rep. James J. (D, N.J.)
Reelected 11-7, 851F2
FLOURINE—*See CHEMICALS*
FLOWERS, Rep. Walter (D, Ala.)
A-breeder compromise proposal rptd 3-17, 3-23, 242A1
Faces Sen primary runoff 9-5, 699G1
Loses Sen primary runoff 9-26, 769E1
Shelby wins seat 11-7, 849B3
FLOYD, Ray
Ties for 2d in British Open 7-15, 580D2; Pleasant Valley Classic 8-13, 672E3
FLUG, James K.
Scores energy bill gas deregulatn 11-9, 873D1
FLUKIGER, Rudolf (d. 1977)
'77 death rptd 4-12, 438F2
FLUORIDATION—*See WATER*
FLUOROCARBONS—*See CHEMICALS*
FLYING Tiger Line Inc.—*See TIGER International*
FLYNN, Matthew J.
Loses US House electn 11-7, 854A2
FLYNT Jr., Rep. John J(ames) (D, Ga.)
Park subpoena set 1-4, 64B1
Flood-Eilberg probe announced 2-8, 240B1
On Kim written testimony 8-3, 605E1
Retiring; primary results 8-8, 625C3
Gingrich wins seat 11-7, 852G1
FLYNT, Larry
Shot, mistrial declared 3-6, 186G3
FM (film)
Released 4-28, 619A2
FOBBS, Larry
USC wins NCAA baseball title 6-8, 560A2
FOGARTY, Joseph R.
Vs WPIX-TV license renewal 6-16, 672E1

1979

FLORIDA, University of (Gainesville)
Sleep breathing study rptd 3-9, 196G2
FLORIDA Department of Health v. Califano
Case refused by Sup Ct 4-30, 365B1
FLORIDA East Coast Railway Co.
Seaboard cleared of trust chrgs 2-22, 206A1
FLORIDA Gas Co.—*See CONTINENTAL Group-Continental Resources*
FLORIDA Power & Light Co.
A-plant license policy case declined by Sup Ct 10-1, 768E2
Indiantown dam collapses 10-31, 912D3
FLORIDA State Prison (Starke)
Spinkelink executed 5-25, 399G3
FLORIDA State University (Tallahassee)
Jones named Sr Bowl MVP 1-13, 63B2
Bundy gets death penalty for '78 slayings 7-31, 604C2
Sterility, toxic chem link rptd 9-11, 736F1
FLORY, Dr. Paul
Cuts Sovt links re dissidents 3-1, 172D2
FLOYD, Charles
On diesel fuel supplies 5-18, 361C3
FLOYD, Jim
Disputes NRC 3 Mile I chrgs 5-7, 344A2
FLOYD, Ray
Wins Greater Greensboro Open 4-8, 587C2
FLUG, James K.
Vs Carter on oil profits 1-26, 70G1
On oil-profits tax plan 4-26, 301E1
FLUGE, Peter J.
Acquitted re price-fixing 4-29, 327C3
FLUORIDATION—*See WATER*
FLYING Blind (play)
Opens 11-15, 956A3
FLYING Paster (race horse)
Wins Santa Anita Derby 4-1, loses Ky Derby 5-5, 448E2, D3
FLYING Tiger Line Inc.—*See TIGER International*
FLYNN, Jacques
Canada justice min, atty gen 6-4, 423F3
FLYNT, Larry C.
Lawyers' interstate rights limited by Sup Ct 1-15, 31C3
Convicted in retrial 3-28, 240C1
FOCKE, Heinrich
Dies 2-25, 176G2

1980

Cong OKs resetlmt aid 7-2, Carter signs 7-8, 515F1
Mystery freighter intercepted, no refugees found 7-4, 514G3, 515B1*
Eglin gays await processing 7-7, 514G2-B3
US releases Cuban flotilla boats 7-7, 514E3
256 Cubans arrive in Key West, refugee total rptd 8-2, 591C3
Air Fla jets hijacked to Cuba 8-10, 8-13, 617A2
Miami resetlmt agencies near bankruptcy 8-12, US pledges funds 8-13; tent city closure threatened 8-30, 685C1
US budgets $16.8 mln for Cuban, Haitian aid 8-13, 617E1
4 jets hijacked to Cuba, 2 attempts foiled 8-14—8-17; FAA tightens security 8-15, 631B3
3 Haitians drown as boat capsizes 9-6; exodus accelerates, total nears 40,000 9-9, 685D1
Somoza buried in Miami, 4000 at rite 9-17, 721D1
Carter sets 3-pt refugee resetlmt plan 9-18, 742G1
Miami tent city refugees to be sent to PR camp 9-23, 725E3
Eglin 'hard-core' refugees moved to Ark camp 9-25, 725D3
Refugee aid to states clears Cong 9-25, 10-1, Carter signs 10-10, 785B1
Cuba closes Mariel harbor, flotilla ends; refugee influx at 125,000 9-26, 742C1, B2
PR camp blocked by legal battles 10-1—10-24; Miami cuts off hotel funds 10-21, 150 evicted 10-24, 825B3
PR camp ban lifted 11-3, 869C2
Bilingual progrm ended by voters 11-4, 847B3
Airlift of 600 Cubans begins, 120 arrive 11-19, 883E2
PR camp blocked again, Haitians await transfer in Miami 12-18, 988D2

School Issues
Schl prayer law cited 2-6, 156A2
State of State message 4-8, 483F1
Tampa-St Petersburg busing, housing integratn study rptd 11-16, 989E3

Sports
Tampa loses Little League finals 8-30, 796G2
Jacksonville to get NASL Tea Men 12-8, 1001F1

Transportation
ILA loads Sovt cargo 2-1, 169F1
Miami-London air svc expansn agreed 3-5, 172B3
Pan Am revives discount coupons 3-10, 346D3
Pan Am Miami-London svc retentn OKd 4-7, 346A3
Laker Miami-London svc OKd 5-15, 516D2
N&W, Southn RR merger sought 6-2, 427E2
Delta jet lands at wrong field 6-21, 519C2
Trucking deregulated 7-1, 558D2

FLORIDA, University of (Gainesville)
Loses AIAW tennis team title 6-7, 607E1
Wins Tangerine Bowl 12-20, 999C3
FLORIDA Power Corp.
Crystal River A-plant accident 2-26, plant to remain closed 3-5, 169A2
FLORIDA State University (Tallahassee)
Loses Orange Bowl 1-1, '79 rank rptd 1-2, 23C1, E1
Bundy gets 3d death sentence 2-12, 136E2
FLORIO, Rep. James J. (D, N.J.)
Names Abscam middleman 2-5, 111D1
Reelected 11-4, 843F2
Toxic waste clean-up signed 12-11, 935F3, 936C1
FLOWERS, Ellen Hunt
Acquires NM silver stake 6-24, 685D3
FLOWERS, Walter
Synfuels trade assn post rptd 9-21, 725C3
FLOYD, Ray
Wins Doral Open 3-16, 412G2
2d in World Series of Golf 8-24, 971G3-972A1
PGA top money winner 10-12, 971E3
FLUOR Corp.
Nader coalitn attacks 4-17, 308B2
FLYNN, Doug
Wins Golden Glove Award 12-6, 926E1
FLYNN, Errol (d. 1959)
Family sues biographer 8-1, 639E1
FLYNN, Laurie
Lords rule on press confidentiality 7-30, 634D2
FLYNT, Larry C.
Penthouse publisher wins libel case 3-1, 239C2
Penthouse publisher's libel award cut 4-17, 405A3
Cleveland obscenity convictn case accepted by Sup Ct 12-8, 937A2
FLYNT v. Ohio
Case accepted by Sup Ct 12-8, 937A2
FMC Corp.
Pleads guilty re water pollutn 11-10, 869G1-C2
FO, Dario
We Won't Pay! opens 12-17, 1003G3
FOEGE, Dr. William
On toxic-shock syndrome cases 6-6, 584C3
FOG, The (film)
Released 2-29, 216E2
Top-grossing film 3-26, 280G3
FOGARTY, Ken
Cosmos win NASL title 9-21, 770D2

1976

FOJTIK, Jan
In Czech Secretariat 4-16, 289B2
FOLCARELLI, Giovanni
Loses RI primary for gov 9-14, 705A1
FOLEY, Rep. Thomas Stephen (D, Wash.)
Reelected 11-2, 831A2
Voted Dem caucus chrmn 12-6, 919G1
FOLGAR, Hildo
Perez ties cited 10-24, 843E3
FOLI, Tim
NL batting ldr 10-4, 795G3
FOLSOM, Marion B.
Dies 9-28, 932D3
FOND du Lac, Wis.—*See WISCONSIN*
FONG, Sen. Hiram L. (R, Hawaii)
Primary for successor 10-2, 764D2
Matsunaga wins seat 11-2, 820C1, 825B1
FONSECA Amador, Carlos
Rptd killed 11-9, 926D1

1977

FOKKER VFW
Eastern to lease Airbus 5-24, 441D2
FOLEY, Martha
Dies 9-5, 788A1
FOLEY, Rep. Thomas Stephen (D, Wash.)
'76 special interest gifts rptd 2-4, 128G3-129F2
Cited in Park indictmt 9-6, 688C1
FOLGER Coffee Co., The—*See PROCTOR & Gamble*
FOLKERTS, Knut
Captured by Dutch 9-22, 888D1
Dutch bar extraditn 9-23, sentence 12-20, 986G1
FONS, Col. Jose
US denies visa 2-22, 351B3
FONSECA, Col. Mario Leonel
Named mil attache to Venez 1-3, 45B2
FONTAN, Antonio
Elected Spain Sen ldr 7-13, 545D2
FONTANET, Joseph
Pro-govt newspaper closes 12-17, 1013C1
FONTANNE, Lynn
Alfred Lunt dies 8-3, 696C3

1978

FOLEY, Edmund
NYS police alien ban backed by US Sup Ct 3-22, 221B1
FOLEY, Rep. Thomas Stephen (D, Wash.)
Cleared re Park gift 7-13, 527A2
Reelected 11-7, 852B4
Reelected Dem Caucus chrmn 12-4, 958A2
PAC contributns rptd 12-24, 1008C1
FOLEY v. Connelie
NYS police alien ban backed by US Sup Ct 3-22, 221A1
FOLGER Coffee Co., The—*See PROCTER & Gamble*
FOLKERTS, Knut
Dutch backers stage protest 3-14, 192G1
Drops appeal 4-13, Dutch rule on W Ger extraditn 5-8, 354C1, 454C3
Mohnhaupt arrested 5-11, 439A1 ★
Sister-in-law arrested 5-25, 439D2
Dutch broaden W Ger extraditn rule 9-7, 725E1
Extradited to W Ger 10-17, 885C1
FOLKERTS, Marion-Brigitte
Arrested in Paris 5-25, sent to W Ger 5-26, 439C2
FOLKERTS, Uwe
Wife arrested 5-25, 439D2
FOLLE Martinez, Adolfo
Named Uruguay forgn min 7-8, 577A2
FOLLETT, Ken
Eye of the Needle on best-seller list 9-4, 708B1
FONDA, Henry
1st Monday in Oct opens 10-3, 1031G1
FONDA, Jane
Coming Home released 2-15, 619B1
Presley offer to aid FBI rptd 7-14, 554A1
Comes A Horseman released 11-1, 969G3
California Suite released 12-21, 1030E2
FONSECA Amador, Carlos (d. 1976)
Widow killed in riot 2-1, 91B2
FONTAINE, Frank
Dies 8-4, 708G2
FONTEYN, Dame Margot
Ex-coach Karasavina dies 5-26, 440A3

1979

FOGELMAN, Avron
Rogues purchase OKd 10-15, 1004B2
FOGOLIN, Lee
In NHL expansion draft 6-13, 470A2
FOLEY, Dermot G.
Viet-era Marine to fight desertn chrgs 3-31, 266D1
Viet-era Marine desertn case opens 12-4, 924F1
FOLEY, Steve
NFL '78 interceptn ldr 1-6, 80D1
FOLEY, Rep. Thomas Stephen (D, Wash.)
House Dem caucus chrmn 1-15, 71A1
Agriculture Com chrmn 1-24, 71C1
Vs proposed Natural Resources Dept 3-1, 164D1
FOLEY, Tim
NFL '78 interceptn ldr 1-6, 80D1
FOLI, Tim
Traded to Pirates 4-19, 1002G2
In World Series 10-10–10-17, 816B1
FOLLETT, Ken
Eye of the Needle on best-seller list 8-5, 620D3
Triple on best-seller list 10-14, 800B3; 11-4, 892B3
FONDA, Henry
City on Fire released 9-14, 819G3
FONDA, Jane
China Syndrome released 3-16, A-accident impact rptd 3-29, 4-1, 246D3, F3, 528G1*
Wins Oscar 4-9, 336G1
At DC A-protest 5-6, 343D3
CIA surveillance rptd 7-16, 561B2
Arts cncl apptmt defeat causes furor 7-20–8-8, 593B2-B3
At NYC A-protest 9-23, 742F2, B3
Backs oil industry protest 10-17, 831D2
NSA upheld on withholding data 10-29, 945E3
Electric Horseman released 12-21, 1007C3
FONSECA, Adm. Maximiano
Brazil navy min designate 1-19, 95E1
FONTANET, Guy
Spanish plane hijackers surrender 8-5, 604B1
FONTEVECCHIA, Jorge
Disappears 1-5, 40B3
Freed by kidnapers 1-13, 117C1
FONTHAM, Michael R.
Argues Weber case in Sup Ct 3-28, 262F3

1980

FOGELBERG, Dan
Phoenix on best-seller list 2-6, 120G3; 3-5, 200F3
Longer on best-seller list 3-5, 200E3
FOGERTY, Anne
Dies 1-15, 104E2
FOGLIETTA, Thomas M.
Elected to US House 11-4, 844B1, 846D2, 848E3
FOLEY, Rep. Thomas Stephen (D, Wash.)
On oil import fee bar 6-5, 437G1
Reelected 11-4, 844B3
Named House Dem whip 12-8, 936D2
FOLEY v. U.S.
Case declined by Sup Ct 1-21, 93B3
FOLKERTS, Knut
Gets life sentence 7-31, 581B1
FOLLETT, Ken
Triple on best-seller list 1-13, 40B3; 2-10, 120C3; 12-7, 948F3
Key to Rebecca on best-seller list 10-12, 796C3; 12-7, 948D3
FOLLOWS, Sir Dennis
On UK Olympic com vote 3-25, 259F2
FOLSOM, James E. (Big Jim)
Son in Ala US Sen primary 9-2, 682G2
FOLSOM Jr., Jim
In Ala US Sen primary; runoff set 9-2, 682G2
Wins primary runoff 9-23, 745F1
Loses US Sen electn 11-4, 849E1
FONDA, Jane
Cited in Connally 'basic speech' 3-7, 184B3
NSA files case refused by Sup Ct 5-12, 426A3
Nine to Five released 12-19, 1003C2
FONDA and Hayden v. NSA
Case refused by Sup Ct 5-12, 426A3
FONDATO, Marcello
Immortal Bachelor released 2-22, 216A3
FONSEKA, M. I. B.
Cites US, UK, USSR A-treaty implementatn failure 9-7, 696C1
FONTANET, Joseph
Shot 2-1, dies 2-2, 97C2

FOOD

1976

FOOD—*See also specific types; country names*
Dec '75 output rptd up 1-16, 92A1
'75 mfg profit margins up 2-11, 216B2
Md food chain admits beer co paymt 2-13, 360G2
Ford seeks curbs on CIA spying 2-18, 127A2
HEW frees funds for aged 4-2, 249G1
FDA seeks chloroform ban 4-6, 249E2
Cong curbs FDA vitamin rules 4-12, 282B3
SEC suit vs Md food chain setld 5-11, 359D3, 360F2-D3
FDA to keep cyclamate ban 5-11, 414F3
Ford urges regulatory reform 5-13, 347A1
Mike Roy dies 6-26, 524E3
Mayer named Tufts U pres 7-1, 504D2
Ford signs '77 funds 7-12, 533C3
Pub Health Svc issues plan 9-7, 680G1
August exports rptd up 9-27, 770D1
FDA regulatn bill not cleared 10-2, 883A2
Gyorgy gets Science Medal 10-18, 858E3
Chile rejects US aid 10-19, 10-20, 871A1
Sept farm exports rptd down 10-28, 833D2
Poland-USSR pact signed 11-15, 907D1
'60-75 consumer spending rptd 11-23, 959F2
USSR-Abbott Labs pact 12-8, 948C2

Contamination Issues
FDA asks DES animal feed ban 1-9, 25E3
FDA bans Red #2 dye 1-19, 44A2
Red #2 ct challenge 1-27—2-13, FDA ban in effect 2-12, 137C1
GE chrgd re Hudson R PCBs 2-9, 171E3
EPA bans mercury pesticides 2-18, 137G1
Kepone traces rptd in Va fish 2-26, 171C3
Plastic beverage bottle challenged 4-21, 308A2
Allied Chem sued, other Kepone cases pending 5-7, 349C1
Red dye ban upheld 7-6, 571C1
Red #4, carbon black dyes banned 9-22, 729A3

1977

FOOD—*See also RESTAURANTS; also specific types, country names*
'78 Food for Peace budget proposed 1-17, 31B2
Duffy-Mott ex-pres sentncd 1-26, 103B2
ARA Svcs rpts rebates 1-28, 94D1
SEC chrgs Pertamina shakedown 2-2, 93C2
Canteen, Hilton paymts rptd 2-8, 94C2
Carter budget revision 2-22, 124E3
Pesticide use analyzed 2-22, 183E3
ASEAN trade pact signed 2-24, 145G2
Beatrice discounts, overbilling rptd 3-14, 233C2
Sharon Steel ends Foremost takeover bid 4-5, 275D1
US-Cuba trade sought 4-11, 283G1
Minn execs in Cuba 4-18—4-22, 390E1
Anderson Clayton seeks Gerber takeover 4-18, ends bid 9-19, 799F1
Norin '76 sales rise, Maple Leaf Mills purchase cited 340C1
Cuba embargo ease OKd by Sen com 5-10—5-11, 389D3
'60-61, '72-73 family spending compared 5-10, 423E2
'76 top black-owned cos rptd 6-1, 519G3
World Food Cncl conf 6-20—6-24, 513C3
'78 foreign aid authrztn signed 8-4, 668F1; domestic program funds 8-12, 688A3
Food for Peace program extended 9-29, 737B2
US forgn aid funds OKd 10-19, 815E2
Liquid protein deaths rptd 11-9, FDA proposes warning 12-1, 992A3
Child nutritn bill signed 11-10, 897D2
State police meal allowances ruled taxable 11-29, 919D1
US, Mex OK commodity pact 12-2, 976G1
US sets Mozambique aid 12-2, 1000B1
Unilever plans Natl Starch takeover 12-11, 1004F2
Black life expectancy linked 12-13, 962C3

Contamination Issues
Mich botulism outbreak 4-2—4-6, 288E1
Fluorocarbon aerosol warning ordrd 4-26, 323E1
McDonald's halts glass promotn 7-8, 7-17, sues Mass 7-12, 559G3
Australia denies exported meat diseased 8-29, 725B2
Govt seeks nitrate, nitrite data 8-31, 10-18, 820C1
DBCP pesticide curbed 9-8, 723D2
Diet supplemt recall ordrd 9-22, 820D1
Additive study ordrd by Cong 11-4, 878E1
Rabbit meat inspectn vetoed 11-10, 897B3

1978

FOOD—*See also specific types, country names*
Caricom dvpt plans fail 1-13, 100F2
Carter budgets more aged aid 1-23, 47C1
Cincinnati airlift 1-29, 105A3
Hidalgo farmers block Mex imports 3-1, 3-3, 163A2
Beatrice to buy Tropicana; Kellogg talks cited 3-5, 184F3
FDA vitamin curbs revoked 3-14, 231F3
Cath Laity pastoral role rptd 4-7, 294G3
Black, white female consumers compared 4-12, 812B1
Educ Dept child nutritn unit proposed 4-14, 279D1
Fortune data on '77 top 500 indls rptd 5-8, 325B2, D3
NY rabbi admits pol payoffs 5-11, 363E2; sentenced 6-22, 580G3
FDA calcium pangamate seizure upheld 6-14, 727G2
Canning industry eased clean-water rules proposed 8-10, 644A2
Cocaine preference by monkeys rptd 8-11, 771C1
GDV acquires Servomation 8-31, 700A3
Pillsbury to acquire Green Giant 9-18, 752C3
Cooking-related fire data rptd 10-8, 972B2
Ark sales tax exemptn loses 11-7, 855B1

Contamination Issues
Israeli orange exports poisoned 2-1, 60F3-61A1
Austria grain poisoning scandal rptd 2-8, 110G2
Somalia bans Kenya, Tanzania imports 3-24, 270E1
PCB contaminated chickens, eggs destroyed 4-12, 727D3
Nitrite-cured bacon curbed 5-15, 728F1
Nitrite additives linked to cancer 8-11; FDA proposes phase-out, botulism hazards cited 8-31, 727G3
PBBs contaminate Mich 10-9, 769C2; suit dismissed 10-27, 834C1
Infant botulism traced to honey 11-1, 948A2
Earthworm rumor hurts fast-food chains 11-16, 942F1

1979

FOOD
Labor pact bargaining backed by Sup Ct 5-14, 383B2
UNCTAD dvpt aid backing rptd 6-3, 417D3
Truckers strike 6-7–6-15, 462G3; 6-18–6-28, 479A3, 480A1
Lome pact extensn set 6-27, 512E3

Contamination Issues
Australia prawn arsenic levels rptd high 2-20, 188G2
Food-safety law revisns urged 3-2, 194G3
Milk rptd contaminated by 3 Mile I A-accident 3-29–4-3, 242C3, 244E2, 245F3
3 Mile I contaminatn denied 4-6–4-9, 260G3, 261F1, A2
Velsicol indicted for Mich PBB cover-up 4-26, pleads not guilty 5-7, 597E3
NC PCB dumping chrgd 6-4–6-13, disposal disputed 6-5, 597C3
Product coding chngs proposed 6-7, 572C1
Yellow No 5 labeling ordrd 6-26, 571A2
FDA cuts PCB limits 6-28, 571C2
US bans Nicaragua beef 8-6, 616C2
FDA drive vs lead in canned food rptd 8-30, 736G3

1980

FOOD
Meal tax case refused by Sup Ct 1-14, 36F3-37A1
TV ad rates rptd soaring 4-4, 376D2
FTC OKs ad rules 5-21, 703D2
FTC ends tuna indus probe 5-22, 703E2
Mafia, pizza indus ties probed 8-24, 714D1
Mil benefits authrzn signed 9-8, 765D1
US grain reserve authrzn clears Cong 11-17, signed 12-3, 981G1
Cuisinarts fined 12-19, 986B1

Contamination Issues
FDA ban on cyclamates upheld 2-7, 317D2
Mex tomatoes found toxic 2-20; 3 packing plants closed, border checks stiffened 3-12, 233A3
Saccharin cancer risk disputed 3-6, 317D1
USSR links meat, anthrax outbreak 3-20, 235E2
Canada convicts 6 for meat sale 4-23, 372A1
Cattle given DES in 20 states 4-24, 358D1
US sets PCB rules 5-9, 387G1
Canada radioactive vegetables found 5-22, 406G2
US banned item export curb set 8-2, 599G2
Nitrate ban rejected by US 8-19, 726C1-A2

1976

Famines—*See FAMINES*
Food Stamp Program
Reagan: shift to states 1-12, 22E1
Ford State of Union message 1-19, 38A2, 39B3
'77 budget proposal 1-21, 62B3, 66A2
Irregularities rptd 1-21—2-13, 128A1, D3-129C1
AFL-CIO defends 2-19, 149D1
Admin sets cutback 2-26, 150A1
Sen OKs reform bill 4-8, 282D3
Agri Dept orders cutbacks 5-4, 377E3
Suit blocks revisns 5-26, 5-28, estimates modified 6-15, 434D3
Dem platform text 6-15, 469E2, 471B1
Ct delays US cutback 6-19, 454B3
Vendor reform bill signed 7-6, 533E2
'77 funds signed 7-12, 533C3
GOP platform text 8-18, 606F1, A2
Dole legis record cited 614D3
Clerics sentncd in DC 9-17, 776F2
Reform bills not cleared 10-2, 883B1, 884G1
Hunger & Shortage Issues (World)—*See also FAMINES*
Intl Eucharistic hunger conf 8-2, 596D2
Global populatn growth rate rptd 10-28, 863F1, A2
Presidential Election
Shriver issues plan 1-7, 22G2
Reagan for stamp progrm shift to states 1-12, 22E1
Muskie stresses prices 1-21, 40C2
Carter stresses goal vs hunger 6-14, 433C1, E1
US Dem platform text 6-15, 469C2, E2, 471B1, 471F2; 475D2-F2, 476C3, 478C3
Hunger a GOP platform topic 6-21, 451E1
Muskie conv speech cites prices 7-13, 509A3
GOP platform text 8-18, 603E3, 606F1, A2, 610F3
Dole stamp-reform legis record cited 614D3
Mondale stresses forgn policy role 8-30, 645D3
Ford, Carter debate 10-6, 741A2, C2, 742F2
Ford vs Carter on econ boycotts 10-20, 784A3
Price Issues
Shriver campaign issue 1-7, 22G2
Dec '75 WPI rptd 1-9, 21C2
Muskie urges curbs 1-21, 40C2
Dec, '75 CPI rptd 1-21, 90G1
'75 mktg spreads rptd 2-11, 216E1
Jan WPI rptd 2-13, 168C1
Jan CPI rptd 2-20, 168D2
Jan 15-Feb 15 farm prices rptd 2-27, 216A1
Feb WPI rptd 3-4, 199E1
Feb CPI down 3-19, 215F1
March WPI rptd 4-1, 262G3
1st ¼ prices rptd 4-7, 396A1
Mar CPI rptd 4-21, 306G1, B2
'76 inflatn forecasts 5-3, 5-18, 396B1
April WPI rptd 5-6, 347D1
April CPI rptd 5-21, 375E1
Mar 15-May 15 farm prices rptd 5-28, 395E3
May WPI rptd 6-4, 412C3
Dem platform text 6-15, 469C2
May CPI rptd 6-22, 453B3
June WPI rptd 7-9, 519D1, E1
Muskie cites at Dem conv 7-13, 509A3
June CPI rptd 7-21, 536D2
July WPI rptd 8-12, 635B2
July CPI rptd 8-20, 635F1
June 15-Aug 15 farm prices rptd 8-31, 667D3
Aug WPI rptd 9-2, 667C3
Aug CPI rptd 9-21, 708E2
Mid-Sept, mid-Oct farm data 9-30, 10-29, 833D1
Sept WPI rptd 10-7, 769C3
Sept CPI rptd 10-21, 805G2
Oct WPI rptd 11-4, 846D2
Wage-Price Cncl rpts on '60-75 rise 11-9, 983E3
Oct CPI rptd 11-19, 884G3, 885A1
Nov WPI rptd 12-3, 918G3
Nov CPI 12-21, 958G1

1977

Food Stamp Program
Sup Ct upholds unequal prices 1-11, 58A1
CBO issues impact rpts 1-13, 1-17, 80B3, 81A1
Ford proposes cutback 1-17, 30B1, 32B3
Welfare cost rptd 2-19, 176C1
Carter budget revisn 2-22, 125A2, 126C1
New Carter plan presented 4-5, 250A2
Welfare study issued 4-15, 302G1
Cong sets '78 budget target 5-17, 405B1
Welfare proposal outlined 5-25, 445A3
Carter illegal alien plan 8-4, 592A1
Carter proposes abolitn 8-6, 608C3
'78 funds bill signed 8-12, 688A3
Bill signed, free stamps OKd 9-29, 736D2, 737B1
Obituaries
Brazier, Eugenie 3-3, 264E2
Butler, Thomas 10-30, 872C1
Gaud Jr, William 12-5, 1024G1
Miller Harry, 1-1, 84C3
Price Issues
'76, Dec WPI rptd up 1-12, 38F2
'76, Dec CPI rptd 1-19, 78A1
Mid-Jan farm prices, costs rise 1-31, 93B1
Jan WPI rptd 2-11, 111A3
UN rpts '76 price rise 2-14, 146A1
Jan CPI rise rptd 2-18, 129B3
Inflatn forecast revised 2-25, 154D3
Mid-Feb farm prices up 2-28, 154B3
Feb WPI rptd 3-10, 176E2
Feb CPI rise rptd 3-18, 214G3-215D1
Mar WPI rptd up 4-7, 274B1
1st ¼ inflatn rptd 4-20, 300C1
March CPI rptd, Feb revised 4-21, 324B2
USDA: Carter energy plan impact seen 4-21, 324B2
April WPI rptd 5-5, 383A3
April CPI rptd 5-22, 406G2
Inflatn forecast revised 5-25, 464G1
Mid-Oct '76-mid May farm prices, costs 5-31, 464F1
May WPI rise slows 6-3, 445C2
May CPI rptd 6-22, 482A1
June WPI rptd 7-8, 554G1
June CPI rptd 7-21, 554B2, D2
Mid-June, -July farm prices 7-29, 611F3
July WPI rptd, June revised 8-11, 628F3
July CPI rptd 8-19, 651D1, F1
Aug WPI rptd 9-1, 692B1
Aug CPI rptd 9-21, 722C2
Sept WPI rptd 10-6, 776E3
Sept CPI rptd 10-21, 817E3
Mid-July—mid-Oct farm prices rptd 10-31, 836A2
Oct WPI rptd 11-3, 836D2
'77, '78 rise forecast, '73-76 data cited 11-17, 916G2
Oct CPI rptd 11-22, 898F3
Mid-Nov farm prices rptd 11-30, 916F2
Nov WPI rptd 12-8, 961E2
Nov CPI rptd 12-21, 977E1
Mid-Dec farm prices rptd 12-30, 1003D1

1978

Diets & Dieting
Heinz to buy Weight Watchers; Foodways purchase agrmt cited 5-4, 364D2
New cholesterol treatmt rptd 5-27, 1023G1
Liquid protein hazards rptd 6-26, weight loss survey 7-23, 727G2
Saccharin, cyclamate studies rptd inconclusive 7-19, 7-28, 727B3
Calorie labeling rules set 9-21, 770B1
Famine & Hunger—*See FAMINES*
Food Stamp Program
Age bias rptd 1-10, 14C1
Carter budget proposal 1-23, 48F1
Admin acts to cut off striking miners 3-10, Meany scores 3-11, 182C2
Welfare compromise prepared 6-7, 446F1
'77 poverty level rptd 8-12, 684E2
Obituaries
Earl, Johnrae 1-10, 96F1
Price Issues
Dec '77 WPI, finished goods index rise rptd 1-12; CPI rise 1-20, 51D2, B3, D3
Jan finished-goods index rise rptd 2-10, 128F1
'64-78 spending pattern chngs reflected in new CPIs 222D2, E2
Jan, Feb CPIs rptd 2-27, 3-28, 222E1, F1
Feb farm prices 2-28, 163F2
Feb finished-goods index rise rptd 3-9, 222C3
'78 inflatn forecast revised 3-28, 219D2; 5-30, 428B2
Carter warns vs farm bill 4-6, 261D2
Mar finished-goods rise rptd 4-6, 262F2
Carter vows farm bill veto, cites inflatn threat 4-11, 260A1
Mar CPI rise rptd 4-28, 344G3-345A1
Apr finished-goods index rptd 5-4, 344D3
Bosworth cites inflatn spiral 5-11, 362D1
Apr farm income rise, price hikes linked 5-17, 389A3
'78 inflatn forecast revised 5-30, 428B2
Apr CPIs rise rptd 5-31, 428B3
May wholesale rise rptd 6-2, 428F3
Mar-June farm prices, June costs 6-30, 507C1
May CPI rise rptd 6-30, 507G3
June producer price indexes (wholesale finished, intermediate, crude goods) rptd 7-7, 552D3
June CPI rptd 7-28, 607F1
July producer prices rptd 8-10, 607D2
July CPI rptd 8-29, 679A3
Aug producer prices rptd 9-8, 717F1-B2
'73-78 hikes blamed on mktg, labor costs, weather 9-8, 717E2
Aug CPI rptd 9-26, 752C1
Jan-Aug CPI hikes rptd 10-4, 789G3
Sept producer prices rptd 10-5, 790A2
3d ¼ inflatn rate rptd, 2d ¼ revised 10-20, 863F3
Carter anti-inflatn plan to monitor 10-24, 806D1

1979

PCDF-contaminated fish rptd 9-11, 736B2
PCB contaminatn rptd in 6 Westn states 9-17, 704A3
Cancer agent found in beer, warning urged 9-19, 9-22, 735E3-736B1
Ariz radioactive tritium seized 9-26, 806D2
Mich PBB rpt issued 10-9, Velsicol setls suits 10-23, 808G2-D3
Diets & Dieting
Atkins cleared of malpractice 1-16, 78F3
Nutritn programs excluded from proposed Educ Dept 2-8, 110A3
EC '76 ruling on Hoffman-La Roche vitamins upheld 2-13, 137B1
Vitamin A variant for acne rptd 2-14, 138C2
Vegetarian diet rptd risky for children 2-22, 140F1
Strokes rptd down 2-28, 195F2
Food-safety law revisns urged, saccharin ban backed 3-2, 195D1, E1
Williams Co settles PVM chrg 3-6, 308B3
Malnutritn rptd down, fed food progrms credited 4-30, 386G2
Vitamin C anti-infectn role studied 5-5, 691D2
Diet aids approved by FDA panel 5-12, 571F3
Processing, storage rule chngs proposed 6-7, 572A1
Amphetamine ban urged, abuse detailed 7-16, 571C3
Famine & Hunger—*See FAMINES*
Food Stamp Program
Benefits rise, progrm chngs set 1-1, 18G1
Carter seeks budget rise 1-22, 46B1; table 42E2
US probe rptd 2-2, 93B3
Malnutritn rptd down 4-30, 386B3
Carter seeks cash substitute re SSI progrm 5-23, 384D1
'79 emergency funds clear Cong 7-27, 8-2, Carter signs 8-2, 700B2
'80 Agri funds clear Cong 10-26, 10-31, Carter signs 11-9, 920B1
Mergers & Acquisitions
W Ger co to buy 42% of A&P 1-16, 653C3
Daylin OKs Grace takeover, drops Narco bid 1-24, 88E3
Clerks, meat cutter unions to merge 1-26, 130G3
Amer Brands acquires FDS 2-14, 132B2
Skaggs to take over Amer Stores 3-14, 283C1
Imperial Group to buy Howard Johnson 9-10; Calif bar seen 10-12, 924B3-E3
Foremost-McKesson bid rptd 10-17, 986B3
Obituaries
Garin, Georges (rptd) 5-22, 432G2
Price Issues
'78, Dec producer prices rptd 1-11, 32C3
Dec '78 CPI rise rptd 1-24, 73G1
'79 price rise forecast, '78 rise cited 1-25, 48C3
Jan farm prices, costs rptd 1-31, 111G1-A2
Farmers protest in DC 2-5–2-6, Bergland sees no price support hike 2-6, 109C2
Wage-price noncompliance rptd 2-6, 127G3
Jan producer prices rptd 2-9, 111E1
Jan CPI rise rptd 2-23, 151A2
Feb producer prices rptd 3-8, 182F3
Cost pass-through rule cited 3-16, 264B3
Feb CPI rptd 3-25, 252E1
Guidelines tightened, USDA monitoring set 3-29, 264G1, B2
Mar farm prices rptd, Dec '78-Feb revised 3-30, 280B3
Mar producer prices rptd 4-5, 252C1
Mar CPI rise rptd 4-26, 324F3
Apr producer prices rptd 5-3, 325C1
Apr CPI rise rptd 5-25, 402E3
May producer prices rptd 6-7, 422A2
May CPI rise rptd 6-26, 480D3
June producer prices rptd 7-6, 516F3-517A1
June CPI rise rptd 7-26, 557A1
Inflatn forecast hiked 7-26, 578B1
Apr-July farm prices rptd 7-31, 578A1
July producer prices rptd 8-9, 621D2
July CPI rptd 8-25, 646D2
Hartz Mt settles FTC complaint 8-29, 903B1
Aug producer prices rptd 9-7, 681A1
Aug CPI rptd unchngd 9-25, 725C2
Sept producer prices rptd 10-4, 766D1
Sept CPI rise rptd 10-26, 827F3
Oct producer prices rptd 11-1, 828C1
Oct CPI rise rptd 11-27, 903A3

1980

Diets & Dieting
Iowa State of State message 1-15, 269B2
USDA 'junk food' rules rptd 1-27, 157E3
US issues dietary guidelines 2-4, 157G2
W Ger chrgs re Merck Vitamin B-12 pricing cited 2-12, 154C1
FTC OKs ad rules 5-21, 703E2
NAS cholesterol rpt discounts health impact 5-27, stirs controversy 6-1, 432E2
Child nutritn authrzn clears Cong 12-3, signed 12-5, 936F1, 981B1
Cong cuts '81 funds 12-4, 954C3; signed 12-15, 982B1
Famine & Hunger—*See FAMINES*
Food Stamp Program
Carter budget outlays up 1-28, 73D2; table 1-28, 70E1
Calif sailors rptd seeking food stamps 4-24, 428G1
Mass prof indicted in fraud case 5-13, 414G3
Emergency funds bill clears Cong 5-15, Carter signs 5-27, 402F3
Cuban refugees rptd ineligible 5-21, 380C1
Cuban, Haitian refugee assistance set 6-20, 484G3
Reagan pres nominatn acceptance speech 7-17, 533D1
Dem platform plank adopted 8-13, 614G3
Cong cuts '81 funds 12-4, 954D3; signed 12-15, 982B1
Foreign Developments (including U.S. international news)
OECD sees shortages in '90s 1-23, 49C3
Venice summit urges 3d World indepndnc 6-23, 474A1
Taiwan '79 sales rptd down 7-4, 567B3
US global forecast gloomy 7-23, 573B2
Muskie addresses UN aid talks 8-25, 642C3
World Bank-IMF mtg sets poor natn aid 9-30, 761D3
Poland halts exports 11-14, 879B1
US forgn policy 'weapon' backed 12-23, 980F1
Mergers & Acquisitions
Foremost-McKesson talks end 2-6, 386C1
McCormick rejects Sandoz merger offer 3-18, 386C1
Kraft sets Dart merger 6-5, 557D1
Imperial Group completes Howard Johnson deal 6-17, 557C3
Pneumo, LTV merger set 8-28, 746B1
Beatrice, Bob Evans merger cancelled 12-5, 985E1
Obituaries
Sanders, Harland 11-16, 1004C3
Price Issues
Dec '79 producer prices rptd 1-10, 15A1
Dec, '79 CPI rise rptd 1-25, 75C2
Jan farm prices rptd 1-31, 92E2
Jan producer prices rptd 2-15, 126D2
AFL-CIO urges anti-inflatn moves 2-18, 146C3
Jan CPI rise rptd 2-22, 144G1
Feb farm prices rptd 2-29, 168B1
3 retailers freeze prices 3-6, 349C1
Feb producer prices rptd 3-7, 182C2
Feb CPI rise rptd 3-25, 222C2
Mar farm price drop rptd 3-31, 263E3
Carter scores controls 4-1, 247C1
Mar producer prices rptd 4-4, 263B1
Reagan vs 'cheap food' policy 4-17, 4-18, 327E3-328A1
Mar CPI rise rptd 4-22, 305C1
Apr farm prices rptd 4-30, 329G2
Apr producer prices rptd 5-9, 367G2
Apr indl output down 5-16, 384C3
Apr CPI rptd 5-23, 400C3
May farm prices rptd 5-30, 425C1
May producer prices rptd 6-6, 437D3
May CPI rptd 6-24, 481B1
June farm prices rptd 6-30, 492C2
June producer prices rptd 7-8, 513C3
June CPI rptd 7-23, 556E1
July farm prices rptd 7-31, 575C1
July producer prices rptd 8-15, 630B3
July CPI rptd 8-22, 648C3
Aug farm prices rptd, July revised 8-29, 666D1
Aug producer prices rptd 9-5, 684E1
Drought final rpt 9-7, 857D2
Aug CPI rptd 9-23, 741B1
Sept farm prices rptd 9-30, 741A2
Sept producer prices rptd 10-3, 783B2
Sept CPI rptd 10-24, 823D3
Oct farm prices rptd 10-31, 883B1
Oct producer prices rptd 11-7, 867A1
Oct CPI rptd 11-25, 897C3
Nov farm prices rptd 11-28, 938B2

1976

Mid-Nov, Mid-Dec farm prices up 12-30, 983B3
School Meals
'77 budget proposals 1-21, 62B3, 65A2, 66B2
Child-nutritn bill not cleared 10-2, 884A2
World Food Council—*See under UNITED Nations*

FOOD For Peace—*See 'Agency for International Development' under U.S. GOVERNMENT—STATE*
FOOD Research and Action Center
HEW frees food funds for aged 4-2, 249A2
FOOT, Michael
Candidate for prime min 3-17; voting results 3-25, 3-30, 239A2; Callaghan elected 4-5, 252A2
UK Parlt leader 4-8, 266E3
Home-rule chngs rptd 5-25, 418F1
Govt wins ship natlzn ruling 5-27, 402B1
Retains Cabt post 9-10, 693F3, G3
Elected Labor deputy ldr 10-21, 853A2
Assailed by moderate Laborites 11-16, 906C1
Marchers protest spending cuts 11-17, 889E2
Spain OKs Socialist conf 11-27, 908F3

FOOTBALL
Networks win Emmy awards 5-17, 460C2
NJ Meadowlands stadium opening set 9-1, 680C3 ★
Delaware lottery starts 9-1, 736D3
Player draft ruled illegal 9-8, 736B3
Collegiate
Bowl game results 1-1, 31C3
'75 natl rankings 1-2, 31A3
Dorsett wins Heisman 11-30, 969D2
Bowl game results 12-20—12-31, 1014G2
Obituaries
Iselin, Philip 12-28, 1015F1
McDonald, Henry 6-12, 524B3
Nevers, Ernie 5-3, 368A3
Professional
Brown quits Bengals; Johnson, McCormick named 1-1, 31C2
Conf title playoff rptd, Super Bowl set 1-4, 31A2
NFL final standings rptd 1-4, 31D2, Tarkenton named AP MVP 1-13, 31A3
Steelers win Super Bowl 1-18, 56A1
Vikings, Raiders win conf titles; final standings rptd 12-26, 1014B2

1977

School Meals
Ford '78 budget proposals 1-17, 32B3
Nutritn bill, anti-fraud provisn signed 11-10, 897D2

FOOD & Agriculture Organization—*See under UNITED Nations*
FOOD & Drug Administration—*See under U.S. GOVERNMENT*
FOOD for Peace—*See 'Agency for International Development' under U.S. GOVERNMENT—STATE*
FOOD Policy Research Institute, International (Washington, D.C.)
Hathaway confrmd Agri asst secy 4-6, 272A3
FOOD Stamp Program—*See under FOOD*
FOOT, Michael
Liberal pact rptd 3-22, govt wins no-confidence vote 3-23, 239C2

FOOTBALL
5 named to Hall of Fame 1-17, 164A1
Collegiate
Bowl results 1-1, 1-2, 8D3
Heisman winner cited 1-1, 8F3
'76 natl rankings 1-2, 1-3, 8D3
NCAA conv 1-10—1-12, 104A2
Campbell wins Heisman, Downtown AC Trophies awarded 12-8, 950A2
Bowl game results 12-19—12-31, 1020B2
Arkansas players suspended 12-21, bias suit dropped 12-29, 1020D2
Obituaries
Bierman, Bernie 3-7, 264C3
Hubbard, Cal 10-17, 872C2
O'Brien, Davey 11-18, 952B3
Shaw, Lawrence (Buck) 3-19, 264E3
Stydahar, Joe 3-23, 264F3
Professional
Raiders win Super Bowl, Biletnikoff named MVP 1-9, 24C3, G3
Biletnikoff named MVP 1-9, 24G3
AFC wins Pro Bowl 1-17, 104E1
Rozelle gets new contract 1-17, 163B3
Super Bowl on TV top 10 list 2-9, 119B1
Jets to remain at Shea 2-18, 163D3
NFL labor pact signed 3-1, 163A2-B3
NFLPA labor pact OKd 3-25, class-actn suit setld 3-29, 263F3
NFL rule chngs, 49ers sale OKd 3-29—4-1, 263E2-F3
Namath waived by Jets 4-1, debuts as Ram 8-6, 659C2
NFL coaching chngs 4-6—12-23, 1020A2
NFL labor pact challenged 4-25, 491E2
NFL draft held; table 5-3—5-4, 353F1, A2
Jets-Mets dispute settled 5-26, 491A2
NFL exec dir quits, joins Jets 6-6, 659B2
NFL owners meet, Bowl sites set 6-14—6-15, 491E1-A2
Atkinson loses slander suit 7-22, 659C1
Larry Brown retires 7-26, 659B2
5 inducted into Hall of Fame 7-30, 658G3
NFLPA class-actn suit setlmt OKd 8-1, 658F3
Eagles owner loses financial control 8-8, 659A1
2 Dolphins sentncd for drug sale 8-10, 659A2
Ct OKs '77 Del lottery, state postpones 8-12, 659F1
Dorsett assault chrgs dropped 8-18, 659C2
Rozelle issues memo on violence 9-15, 1019B3
NFL officiating scored; umpire suspended, censorship denied 10-6—12-22, 1020D1
NFL record TV pact rptd 10-26, 950D1-A2
CBS wins Emmy 11-6, 1022B1
Simpson has knee surgery 11-9, 1019C3
Tarkenton sets passing accuracy mark, injures leg 11-13, 1019C3
Payton sets one-game rushing record 11-20, 1019D3
Montreal wins Grey Cup 11-27, 950E2
Tampa Bay wins 12-11, 12-18, 1019E3
NFL season ends 12-18, 1019A3
NFL final standings 12-18, 1020A3
NFL playoffs: 4 teams advance 12-24, 12-26, 1019F3

1978

Sept CPI rptd 10-27, 864D1, E1
Oct producer prices rptd up 11-2, 864A2
'79 inflatn forecast 11-14, 1003C2
Oct CPI rptd 11-28, 918C2, G2
Nov producer prices rptd 12-7, 957F3-958A1
Nov CPI rptd 12-22, 1003G1, A2
July-Dec farm prices rptd 12-29, 1003B2

FOOD & Agriculture Organization—*See under UNITED Nations*
FOOD & Drug Administration—*See under U.S. GOVERNMENT*
FOOD Fair Inc.
Bankruptcy filed, Fields blamed 10-1, 752G3
FOOD for Peace—*See U.S. GOVERNMENT—STATE—Agency for International Development*
FOOD Stamp Program—*See under FOOD*
FOODWAYS National Inc.
Heinz purchase agrmt cited 5-4, 364E2
FOOLS Die (book)
Paperback rights sale sets record 6-16, 620C2
On best-seller list 10-9, 800A3; 11-6, 887F3; 12-3, 971A1
FOOT, Sir Dingle
Dies 6-18, 540F2
FOOT, Michael
Vs Commons com on BSC papers demand 1-12, 36C3

FOOTBALL
Detroit Lions owner promoted at Ford Motor 6-8, 642G1
Collegiate
Bowl results 1-2, 8A3
'77 natl rankings 1-3, 8F2
NCAA conv 1-11—1-13, Div I realigned 1-12, 40A1-C2
Holtz named top coach 1-21, 172A1
Field-goal placemt, other NCAA rule chngs 1-21, 172E1-A2
Hadl joins U of Kan as asst coach 2-9, 171F3
Wilkinson named Cardinals coach 3-2, 171C3
Amateur sports bill clears Cong 10-15, 842F2
Roberts wins Outland Trophy 11-25, 1025A2
Sims wins Heisman Trophy 11-28, 1025F1
Bowl game results 12-9—12-31, 1025B2
Arkansas players suspended 12-14, 1025B3
Fairbanks suspended by Patriots, U of Colo job offer cited 12-18; reinstated 12-20, 1024E2
Hayes punches Clemson player 12-29, fired as Ohio State coach 12-30, 1025G2
Obituaries
Clark, Earl H (Dutch) 8-5, 708D2
Galiffa, Arnold 9-5, 778C1
Professional
Broncos, Cowboys win conf titles 1-1, 8E3
NFL '77 statistical ldrs listed 1-1, 56A2
TV contract tax value backed 1-9, 13B2
NFL coaching changes 1-9—3-2, 171C2-D3
Cowboys win Super Bowl; Martin, White co-MVPs 1-15, TV viewing record rptd 1-17, 39D2, F3
NFC wins Pro Bowl; Payton named MVP 1-23, 56D1
Payton named NFL MVP; Dorsett, top rookie; Miller, top coach 1-23, 171D3
Namath retires 1-24, 172C1
Dobler traded to Saints 1-31, 172D1
Smith suit vs NFL ends in mistrial 2-1, 172B1
Hadl retiremt rptd 2-9, 171F3
Metcalf signs with Argonauts 3-6, 171G3
NFL rule chngs, 7th official added 3-13—3-17, 336C2
Simpson traded to 49ers 3-24, other NFL trades 4-12—5-3, 336C1-C2
NFL draft held 5-2—5-3, 335G3; table 336E2
Redskins trust liability case refused by Sup Ct 6-12, 468E1
NFL player transactns 7-20—10-10; Mitchell traded to Chargers 8-23, 1024B3-1025A1
Rams plan '80 Anaheim move, LA Coliseum suit vs NFL cited 7-25, 1023F3
Ewbank, 4 others enter Hall of Fame 7-29, 1025B1
Stingley paralyzed 8-12, NFLPA seeks expanded roster 12-14, 1023G3
Allen fired by Rams 8-13, other NFL coaching chngs 9-25—12-18, 1024F2-B3
Rozelle to study NFL appeals ct 9-17, 1024A1
NFL ex-cheerleaders score managemt 11-1, 1024B1
Campbell rushes for 199 yds, 4 TDs 11-20, 1024B1
Edmonton wins Grey Cup 11-26, 1025D1
Tarkenton breaks NFL pass completn record 12-3, 1024C1
NFL season ends 12-18, 1023E3
NFL final standings 12-18, 1024A2
Fairbanks suspended 12-18, reinstated 12-20, 1024D2
NFL playoffs: 4 teams advance 12-24, 12-30, 12-31, 1024C1

1979

Aug-Nov farm prices rptd 11-30, 941A2
Nov producer prices rptd 12-6, 921E3
Nov CPI rise rptd 12-21, 984E2
'79, Dec farm prices rptd, Nov revised; '79 inflatn rptd, '80 forecast 12-31, 985A1
School Meals
Carter budget proposals 1-22, 41C2, 46C1

FOOD & Agriculture Organization—*See under UNITED Nations*
FOOD and Commercial Workers International Union, United (AFL-CIO)
Formatn set 1-26, 130F3
Established 6-6, 419F3
Carter addresses conv 6-7, 419E3
Wynn backs Carter reelectn 7-30, 593C3
FOOD & Drug Administration—*See under U.S. GOVERNMENT*
FOOD Fair Inc.
123 supermkts closed 1-27, 131G2
FOOD for Peace—*See U.S. GOVERNMENT—STATE—Agency for International Development*
FOOD Stamp Program—*See under FOOD*
FOOLS Die (book)
Krantz paperback rights sold for record sum 9-12, 755E3
On best-seller list 11-4, 892C3

FOOTBALL
Collegiate
Bowl results 1-1, 1-6, 8E2; 1-13, 1-14, 63A2
'78 natl rankings 1-2, 1-3, 8B2
Saban named West Pt coach 1-4, 175A3
NCAA vows Title IX fight, rejcts reforms 1-8—1-10, 102C3
Bruce named Ohio State coach 1-12, 175D3
Blocking below waist, other NCAA rules chngd 1-17, 175F3
Clark wins Lombardi Award 1-18, 175G2
Princeton, Rutgers to end rivalry 1-20, 175D3
Patriots release Fairbanks to Colo U post 4-2, Colo gov scores deal 4-3, 335D1
Ariz State fires Kush 10-13, Kush sues univ 11-9, 1001C3
Ritcher wins Outland Trophy 11-25, 1001E2
White wins Heisman Trophy 12-3, 1001D2
Bowl game results 12-8-12-31, 1001F2
U of New Mexico basketball scandal detailed 12-13-12-21, 1003A2
Obituaries
Feathers, Beattie 3-10, 272D2
Leemans, Alphonse 1-19, 104C3
Miller, Don C 7-28, 588C3
Rosenbloom, Carroll 4-2, 356G3
Strong, Ken 10-5, 860E3
Professional
NFL '78 statistical ldrs listed 1-6, 80A1
Steelers, Cowboys win NFL conf titles 1-7, 8D3
Michaels, Vermeil named top NFL coaches 1-14, 175B2
Campbell named NFL MVP, top rookie 1-19, 175B2
Steelers win 3d Super Bowl, Bradshaw named MVP 1-21, 62C3-63A2
NFC wins Pro Bowl, Rashad named MVP 1-29, 79D3
Staubach robbed 1-30, 175A3
Young hired as Giants operatns dir 2-14; other NFL exec, coaching chngs 1-5–2-8, 175C2
Csonka contract with Dolphins rptd 2-22, 175F2
Rozelle admits Super Bowl officiating error 2-22, 175C3
Hayes pleads guilty re drugs 3-14, sentncd 3-22, 335B3
Patriots release Fairbanks 4-2, Colo gov scores deal 4-3, 335D1
Patriots name Erhardt coach, Kilroy gen mgr 4-6, 335A3
Kapp trust damages case declined by Sup Ct 4-16, 302F3
NFL draft held; table 5-3–5-4, 335C1, E1
Hall of Fame inducts Unitas, 3 others 7-28, 1001C1
Hackbart injury suit ruling declined by Sup Ct 10-29, 884E1
Edmonton wins Grey Cup 11-25, 1001F1
NFL coaching changes 11-28–12-28, 1001D1
NFL season ends 12-16, 1000F3
NFL final standings 12-16, 1001A2
NFL playoffs: 4 teams advance 12-23–12-30, 1000G3

1980

Nov producer prices rptd 12-5, 937C3
Nov CPI rptd 12-23, 983D3
School Meals
USDA 'junk food' rules rptd 1-27, 157E3
US dietary guidelines issued 2-4, 157B3
Black Caucus vs Carter budget 2-5, 94G2
Kennedy 'basic speech' excerpts 3-10, 183F1

FOOD and Allied Workers Associations, International Union of (IUF)
Guatemala Coca-Cola plant unrest protested 4-16—5-1, 463D3
FOOD & Drug Administration (FDA)—*See under U.S. GOVERNMENT*
FOOD Stamp Program—*See under FOOD*
FOOLIN' Around (film)
Released 10-17, 836G2
FOOLS Die (book)
On best-seller list 1-13, 40D3
FOOT, Michael
Urges disarmament 6-22, 487F1
Callaghan quits as Labor Party ldr 10-15, 791E1
Elected Labor ldr 11-10, 872B2
Scores govt programs 11-20, 900F3, 901E1
Pledges Thatcher defeat 11-29, 922E1
Labor elects shadow Cabt 12-4, 942D2

FOOTBALL
Collegiate
Bowl results 1-1, 23C1; 1-5, 1-12, 1-13, 62A2
'79 natl rankings 1-2, 22G3
Ariz State fires Miller 1-3; hires Rogers as coach 1-17, settles with Kush 1-29, 175D2
NCAA conventn held 1-7—1-8, 103E3
LSU coach Rein presumed dead 1-11, Stovall replaces 1-12, 175A3
Divisn I-A rule changes set 1-17, 62C2
Transcript scandal spreads; FBI, NCAA probes rptd 1-23—5-23, 469B2-D3
Ariz ex-coach, others indicted 7-24, 875A3
Pac-10 punishes 5 schls in transcript scandal 8-11, 875D1
Ore U indictmts cited 10-15, 875C3
USC coach defends athletic admissns policy 10-29, 875F2
May wins Outland Trophy 11-20, 999F2
Rogers wins Heisman Trophy 12-1, 999D2
Bowl game results 12-6—12-31, 999G2
Obituaries
Bible, Dana 1-19, 104F1
Eliot, Ray 2-24, 175G3
Jones, Lawrence 2-12, 176G1
Jordan, Ralph 7-28, 608C2
Tyrer, James 9-15, 756G2
Professional
NFL '79 statistical ldrs listed 1-5, 8A2
Steelers, Rams win NFL conf titles 1-6, 8D1
Rozelle defends Oilers call 1-7, 23F1
Campbell named NFL MVP; Anderson, top rookie; Vermeil, Coryell top coaches 1-9, 175A1
Stingley lawyer seeks Tatum suspensn 1-10, 175G2
Disputed calls reviewed 1-16, 62G1
McCormack hired as Colts coach 1-16, 413B1
Raiders need OK for LA move 1-18, 62C1
Steelers win 4th Super Bowl, Bradshaw named MVP 1-20, 61F2-62C1
Brown fined for autobiography chrgs 1-22, 175B3
NFC wins Pro Bowl; Muncie named MVP 1-27, 175C1
Hanifan hired as Cardinals coach 1-30, 413B1
Jones arrested for rape 1-31, complaint dropped 2-1, 320E3
Hayes paroled 2-6, released from prison 2-27, 175F2
Raiders LA move attempt sparks controversy 2-22—3-5, 175E1-C2
NFL draft held; table 4-29—4-30, 336E2, B3
NFL free agent rule upheld by arbitrator 5-16, 998F2
Hall of Fame inducts 4 8-2, 999A2
NFL rookie contracts set $ mark; Sims pact cited 8-27, 998G2
McKay denies tie with USC faulty athletic admissns 10-15, 875E2
Rozelle fines players for 'unnecessary violence' 10-21, 998A3
NFL black hiring practices scored 10-27, 998C3
NFL cross-ownership ban backed 11-18, 998C3-999A1
Edmonton wins Grey Cup; Moon named game MVP 11-23, 999B2
Nolan fired as Saints coach; Stanfel named interim coach 11-25, 999G1
Fouts breaks NFL passing marks 12-13, 999A1
Saints win only '80 game 12-14, 999B1
NFL season ends; final standings 12-22, 998D2, D3
Steelers playoff hopes dashed 12-22, 999C1
NFL playoffs: Cowboys, Raiders advance 12-28, 999C1
Phillips fired as Oilers coach, gen mgr 12-31, 999F1

1976

FOOTNER & Co.
Boycott rpt released 10-20, 786B2
FOOTWEAR Industries Association, American
Trade comm rules imports hurt shoe industry 2-21, 213B3
FORCE Reduction Talks, Mutual and Balanced—*See under EUROPE*
FOR Colored Girls Who Have Considered Suicide/When the Rainbow Is Enuf (play)
Opens 9-15, 1014D3
FORD, Doug
Named to PGA Hall of Fame 1-27, 123F2

1977

FOOTE, Cone & Belding Inc.
Fairfax Cone dies 6-20, 532G2
FOOTHILL College Museum (Los Altos Hills, Calif.)
CIA mind-control tests probed 9-2—9-21, 721E1
FOOTHILLS Pipe Lines Ltd.
FPC splits on Alaska pipe route 5-2, 369C3 ★
Canada bd favors gas line 7-4, 525E1-E2
Pipe rpts issued 7-28, 8-2, 596E2-B3
US cos back route 7-29, 596C3; Canada Parlt OKs 8-8, 616B2
Carter, Trudeau OK line 9-8, 687B1
FOOTWEAR—*See SHOES*
FOOTWEAR Industries Association, American
Carter shoe import ruling scored 4-1, 248A2
FORCE Reduction Talks, Mutual and Balanced—*See under EUROPE*

1978

FOOTBALL, International Federation of Association (FIFA)
World Cup results, sidelights 6-1—6-25, 519D3-520G3
Best ban compliance rptd 10-10, 969D2
FOOTBALL Writers Association of America—*See FOOTBALL*
FOOTHILLS Pipe Lines Ltd.
Alcan gas pipe delay seen 8-16, 647F2
FOOT Loose and Fancy Free (recording)
On best-seller list 2-4, 116G3
FOOTWEAR—*See SHOES*
FORBES, Bryan
Intl Velvet released 7-19, 970G1
FORBES, George L.
Indicted for kickbacks 10-27, 1008F3
Cleveland defaults 12-16, pol squabbling scored 12-28, 1008B2
FORCE Reduction Talks, Mutual and Balanced—*See under EUROPE*
FORCE 10 from Navarone (film)
Released 12-21, 1030G2
FORD, Betty Bloomer (Mrs. Gerald)
Hospitalized for drug, alcohol abuse 4-10—5-5, 420A1
Undergoes cosmetic surgery 9-14, 844B3
Announces daughter's engagemt 10-17, 844C3
FORD, Christina
Marital separatn cited 5-16, 390F3
FORD, Dan
AL batting ldr 10-2, 928E3
FORD, Doug
Sues PGA over exemptn rule 1-23, 76G1

1979

FOOTHILLS Pipeline Ltd.
Alcan viability doubted 7-4, 522C2
FORAN, Dick
Dies 8-10, 671C2
FORBES (magazine)
State aid to schls rptd 3-5, 282C3
Pvt coll decrease rptd 3-19, 282A3
FORBES, George L.
Acquitted of bribe-taking 7-18, 580E1
FORBES, Kathryn
I Remember Mama opens 5-31, 711G3
FORCE Reduction Talks, Mutual and Balanced—*See under EUROPE*
FORD Jr., Benson
Arrested on drug chrgs 1-23; rejcts dissident stockholders role, seeks Ford bd spot 2-26, 202D3
Ford bd bid defeated, suit cited 5-10, 366B2-F2
Barred from contesting father's will 7-16, 631C1
FORD Sr., Benson (d. 1978)
Son seeks stock control 2-26, 202D3
Son barred from contesting will 7-16, 631D1
FORD, Betty Bloomer (Mrs. Gerald)
Daughter marries 2-10, 176B1
1st grandchild born 4-22, 392G3
FORD, Daniel
On '75 A-safety rpt 1-20, 54B3
On 3 Mile I comm final rpt 10-30, 826F1
FORD, Edith
Son barred from contesting father's will 7-16, 631D1
FORD, Gayle (Mrs. Michael)
Daughter born 4-22, 392G3

1980

FOOTHILLS Pipeline Ltd.
Carter OKs all-US pipe 1-17, 56C3, E3
Canada gets US assurances on Alcan pipe completn 6-27—7-17, OKs southn leg pre-bldg 7-17, 562F1-F2
Canada OKs pipe financing, constructn 7-22, 577D3
Canada filibuster vs Alcan defeated 7-23, 577B3
FORBES, Bryan
Hopscotch released 9-26, 836B3
FORD, Sen. Wendell H. (D, Ky.)
Reelected 11-4, 840G1, 845A3, 849A3
FORD Jr., Benson
Replaces lawyer in family suit 3-12, 225E3
Drops family suit 10-10, 985F2
FORD, Christina
Divorce setlmt rptd 2-20, 200F2

FORD, GERALD RUDOLPH

1976

ABORTION—*See MEDICINE & Health below*
AGED Persons
State of Union message 1-19, 36G2, 38B1, 39B2, F2
'77 budget proposals 1-21, 62B3-63C3, 64E3, 65F1, A2
Submits Medicare, Soc Sec plans 2-9, 110C1
Vows Soc Sec protectn 2-14, 129F3
On Reagan Soc Sec plans 2-17, Reagan chrgs distortn 2-18, 129F2, 130B1
Signs jobs funds bill 4-15, 282C2
Signs '77 food funds bill 7-12, 533C3
Signs housing aid bill 8-3, 566F3
Mondale chrgs apathy 9-16, 687C2
Soc Sec plan not cleared 10-2, 883A1, E3, 884C1
AGRICULTURE
Addresses Farm Bur; bars grain sales as tool vs USSR, plans estate tax chng 1-5, 3F1-B3
State of Union message 1-19, 37D3, G3, 39G1
'77 budget proposals 1-21, 63F1, B3, 66G1-D2
Vetoes milk price supports 1-30, Sen upholds 2-4, 88D1, F1
Seeks Ill farm vote: proposes estate tax chng, policy com; defends Sovt grain embargo 3-5—3-6, 179G3
'77 budgets compared 231A2
Says US to stay top producer 3-26, 231D3
Addresses farmers in Wis 4-3, 245F1
Signs '77 funds bill 7-12, 533B3
Mondale scores policy 7-31, 565C1
Acceptance speech cites 8-19, 612C2-A3
Dole cites grain embargo 9-17, 724C3
Addresses credit bank execs 9-20, 703F3
Scores Butz 10-1; Butz resigns, pol loss seen 10-4, 744C1, F1, D2
Debates Carter 10-6, 741A3, D3
Sets meat import quota 10-9, 787G3
Ups grain-support rates 10-13, 787D3
Dole, Mondale debate 10-15, 782C3
Vs Carter on govt role 10-16, 10-20, 784G1, A3
Vetoes rabbit meat inspectn 10-17, 919E2
Signs grain inspectn bill 10-21, 833B3
AMNESTY Issue—*See under DEFENSE & Armed Forces below*
APPOINTMENTS
Debates Carter 10-22, 802C2
Cabinet & Subcabinet
Baker, asst atty gen 7-27; confrmd 8-6, 807D3
Christie, FEA asst admin 2-12; confrmd 3-23, 232D1
Coleman, Interior asst secy 4-27; confrmd 5-21, 412E1
Darman, Commerce asst secy 1-27; confrmd 2-26, 186F1
Dixon, Treas dep secy 2-9; confrmd 3-2, 196G1
Eden, Commerce asst secy 7-2; confrmd 8-3, 807F3
Fisher, Interior asst secy 2-27; confrmd 3-23, 232D1
Gordon, HEW asst secy 8-23; confrmd 9-23, 807G3
Greenwald, State asst secy 1-20; confrmd 1-28, 186G1
Hughes, AF asst secy 3-1; confrmd 3-10, 232E1
Kasputys, Commerce asst admin 1-27; confrmd 2-26, 186A2
Katz, State asst secy 9-3; confrmd 9-23, 808A1
Keech, AF asst secy 8-31; confrmd 9-10, 808B1
Keuch, dep asst atty gen 1-14, 78G3
Knapp, AF asst secy 1-20; confrmd 3-10, 232F1

1977

FORD, Gerald Rudolph
Rejcts blanket amnesty, orders some discharge upgrades 1-19, 36A2
Pardons Tokyo Rose 1-19, 36B2
Joins nonprofit organizatns 1-28, 2-1, 3-25, 236A3, C3
Signs NBC deal 1-29, plans memoirs 3-9, 236C3
Visits Yale 2-6—2-8, sets USC lectures 3-25, 236B3
HEW schl aid cutoffs considered 2-17, 156D3
A-carrier funds rescinded 3-15, 195E3
Carter asks wiretap curbs 5-18, 386B3
Carter to expand wilderness, scenic river areas 5-23, 404F2
Nixon on pardon 5-25, 420C2
Young calls racist 6-3; GOP, Carter score 6-6; Young explains 6-6, 6-7, 443B3-444A1
Carter defers neutron bomb decisn 7-12, 534A3
Brown backs M-X dvpt 10-6, 10-8, 777G1
Rabbit meat inspectn vetoed 11-10, 897C3

1978

FORD, Gerald Rudolph
Cong support rating cited 1-7, 12B3
Attends Humphrey rites 1-15, 32A3
Carter backs specialty steel import quotas 1-18, 80D3
Byington resigns as CPSC chrmn 2-8, 185E2
Addresses laity conf 2-19, 294E3
Schmidt eases US $ tensns 3-9, 234E2
Shipbldg goals cut by Carter 3-24, 223F2
FBI aide chrgs pol influnc 4-13, 285B1
Kissinger testifies on Korea allegatns 4-20, 280B1
Fromme '75 trial testimony cited 4-21, 309G3
Clements wins Tex gov primary 5-6, 362E3
Poll results 5-7, 5-11; Carter discounts 5-25, 404B3, C3
China '76 computer deal cited 6-9, 436B2
US seasonal loan program for NYC expires 6-30, 609E1
Wife undergoes cosmetic surgery 9-14, 844B3
Testifies to JFK panel 9-21, 749F3
Backs Kemp-Roth bill 9-22, 734G3
Announces daughter's engagemt 10-17, 844C3
Nessen KCIA recruitmt effort rptd 11-1, 862E3
Cited in US announcemt of China ties 12-15, 275D2
Backs US-China ties 12-15, 976C1

1979

FORD, Gerald Rudolph
Rand study on S Viet '75 collapse issued 1-7, 29F1
In Jerusalem, says shah deplored US policy shift 1-21, 50A1
Rockefeller dies 1-26, at rites 2-2, 103F3, 104D2
Moore jail escape fails 2-5, 156A2
Daughter marries 2-10, 176B1
2d in Gallup GOP polls 3-4, 185E3
1st grandchild born 4-22, 392G3
'74 Brezhnev SALT mtg cited 5-9, 339D1
Weicker cites poll results 5-16, 363G3
Rules out '80 pres bid 5-25, 594D2
Moore sentenced 6-12, 492E1
Cited in Carter SALT address 6-18, 458A3
Leads Carter in poll 7-1, 514D1
Sen rejcts direct pres vote 7-10, 514C1
At All-Star Game 7-17, 568F3
Denies Sovt troops in Cuba chrg 9-8, 674A2
'76 Calif primary defeat cited 9-16, 724C1
Pres draft movements start 9-20, 10-12, 783F2
Opposes SALT II 9-26, 739D2
Dunlop chairs Pay Advisory Com mtg 10-17, 829E2
Rules out '80 pres bid again 10-19, 808D1
Secret tapes denied 10-29, 869F1
Reagan opens pres bid 11-13, 866C2
2d in GOP pres poll 11-25, 982D1
Poll results 12-11, 962D3

1980

FORD, Gerald Rudolph
Sovt grain embargo cited 1-8, 12G3
Trails Carter in poll 1-9, 13F3
Kennedy likens Carter 1-28, 74G3
A R Longworth dies 2-20, 176C2
Gets NH write-in vote 2-26, 142E3, G3
Son settles paternity suit 2-28, 199A2
Pres bid considered, Reagan challenges 3-2, 167C1-A2
Mass primary results 3-4, 166F2, D3
Contemplates pres bid 3-6—3-13, decides vs race 3-15, 207C1-208C1
Scores Carter Admin 3-12, 207G1
'76 Sup Ct oil import fee ruling cited 5-13, 366C1
Electn to GK Technologies, Shearson Loeb bds rptd 5-15, 5-22, 456G2
Sees House deciding electn 5-26, 399G2
Endorses Reagan 5-27, 399F2
Meets Reagan, pledges cooperatn 6-5, 423A2
Dem platform blames 6-24, 480A1
Electn to Tiger Intl bd rptd 6-25, 600A3
Celebrates birthday 7-14, 532G1
Addresses GOP conv 7-14, 534D2
Sees Reagan re vp spot 7-15, 7-16, reps' talks fail 7-16, Bush selectn rptd 7-17, 529D2, 530A1, 532G1
GOP platform adopted 7-15, 535B3
Photo with Reagan, Bush 7-17, 529A1
Carter scores vp 'debacle' 7-19, 549D3
Wm Baroody dies 7-29, 608B1
Carter cites '76 polls 8-4, 593E1
Hijacker demands '75 assassins released 8-18, 667A3
Elected to Amax bd 9-18, 959A3
Joins Reagan for campaign windup 11-1, 11-3, 840A2, A3
Baker gets key Admin post 11-14, 881G1

1976	1977	1978	1979	1980

Knebel, Agri acting secy 10-4, 744E3
Macdonald, Navy undersecy 9-3; confrmd 9-8, 808C1
McAuliffe, Defense asst secy 3-4; confrmd 5-3, 412G1
Moskow, Labor undersecy 5-4; confrmd 5-12, 412G1
Newman, HUD asst secy 1-27; confrmd 2-24, 186B2
Read, Labor asst secy 4-26; confrmd 5-12, 412A2
Richardson sworn Commerce secy 2-2, 110E1
Robinson, State dep secy 4-1; confrmd 4-7, 262E3
Theis, Agri dep asst secy 1-21, 40C3
Usery, Labor secy 1-22, 40E3; confrmd 2-4, sworn 2-10, 110F1
Waldman, dep asst atty gen 1-14, 78G3
Young, HUD asst secy 2-23; confrmd 3-11, 232F1

Diplomatic

Anders to Norway 3-18; confrmd 4-1, 262B3
Anderson to Morocco 1-20; confrmd 1-28, 110A2
Armstrong to UK 1-20; confrmd 1-27, 68B1
Becker to Honduras 8-21; confrmd 9-8, 807E3
Bloomfield to Ecuador 3-22; confrmd 4-1, 262C3
Boster to Guatemala 8-24; confrmd 8-26, 807E3
Byrne to Czech 3-31; confrmd 4-28, 412E1
Byrne to Mali 9-3; confrmd 9-15, 807E3
Carter to Liberia 3-22; confrmd 4-1, 262C3
Cluverius to Bahrain 9-16; confrmd 9-30, 807F3
DePree to Mozambique 1-20; confrmd 2-4, 110A2
Dickman to United Arab Emirates 8-25; confrmd 9-23, 807F3
Fay to Trinidad & Tobago 1-20; confrmd 2-4, 110B2
Gates to China 3-22; confrmd 4-1, 262C3
Ginn to Lux 5-10; confrmd 5-20, 412F1
Hargrove to Australia 1-20; confrmd 2-4, 110B2
Hinton to EC 12-19-75; confrmd 1-28, 186A2
James to Niger 9-2; confrmd 9-23, 808A1
Low to Zambia 7-14; confirmd 8-4, 808B1
Lozano to El Salvador 7-21; confrmd 8-4, 808B1
Maestrone to Kuwait 3-16; confrmd 4-28, 412F1
Masters to Bangaldesh 9-16; confrmd 9-30, 808C1
Maytag to Nepal 2-21; confrmd 3-3, 186B2
Meloy to Leb 4-26; confrmd 4-28, 412G1
Mulcahy to Tunisia 2-17; confrmd 3-3, 186B2
Palmer to Togo 9-9; confrmd 9-15, 808C1
Quainton to CAR 12-10-75; confrmd 2-4, 110C2
Reed to Sri Lanka, Maldives 4-26; confrmd 5-26, 412A2
Scranton, UN rep 2-25, 150C1; confrmd 3-3, 186C2
Smith to Sweden 3-18; confrmd 4-1, 262E3
Stearns to Ivory Coast 9-17; confrmd 9-30, 808D1
Stone to IAEA 1-20; confrmd 2-6, 110C2
Strausz-Hupe to NATO 2-23; confrmd 3-3, 186D2
Wells to Guineau-Bissau, Cape Verde 9-9; confrmd 9-15, 808D1

Miscellaneous

Aikens to FEC 5-17; confrmd 5-18, sworn 5-21, 391D3
Barnett, FDIC chrmn 3-3; confrmd 3-17, 232C1
Bensinger, DEA chief 12-9-75; confrmd 2-5, 110A2
Bush confrmd CIA dir 1-27, 68B1
Byington, Consumer Product Safety Comm chrmn 5-4; confrmd 5-26, 412D1
Casey confrmd to Fed Maritime Comm 1-21, 68C1
Christian to ICC 12-8-75; confrmd 3-18, 232C1
Collier to FTC 2-23; confrmd 3-18, 232D1
Corp payoff probe panel 3-21, 262C2
Dixon, FTC acting chrmn 1-6, 68C1
Fogarty to FCC 7-21; confrmd 9-8, 807G3
Gardner, FRB v chrmn 1-20; confrmd 1-29, 110B2
Gianturco, Eximbank vp 7-21; confrmd 7-29, 807G3
Hardesty, Postal Service gov 7-12; confrmd 8-8, 808A1
Harris to FEC 5-17; confrmd 5-18, sworn 5-21, 391C3
Herter, AID asst admin 3-16; confrmd 4-1, 262D3
Hirsch, ERDA asst admin 2-26; confrmd 3-23, 232E1
Hogue to Natl Transport Safety Bd 3-1; confrmd 4-12, 412F1
Johnson to CAB 2-2; confrmd 3-22, 232E1
Kobelinski, SBA dir 12-9-75; confrmd 2-6, 110B2
Leach to EEOC 2-10; confrmd 3-3, 186A2
Lilly to FRB 4-26; confrmd 5-28, 412F1
Martinez, Community Svcs Admin dir 3-16; confrmd 4-7, 262D3

1976 | 1977 | 1978 | 1979 | 1980

Pinkham, AID asst admin 3-17; confrmd 4-1, 262D3
Richard, Justice unit dir 1-14, 78G3
Scearce, Fed Mediatn & Conciliatn Svc dir 3-16; confrmd 4-7, 262E3
Sheldon, Civil Svc Comm v chrmn 2-3; confrmd 2-26, 186C2
Smith, Commerce counsel 1-27; confrmd 2-26, 186C2
Springer to FEC 5-17; confrmd, sworn 5-21, 391G2
Staebler to FEC 5-17; confrmd 5-18, sworn 5-21, 391C3
Thomson to FEC 5-17; confrmd 5-18, sworn 5-21, 391B3
Tiernan to FEC 5-17; confrmd 5-18; sworn 5-21, 391D3
Todd, Natl Transport Safety Bd chrmn 1-20; confrmd 2-5, 110D2
White to FCC 7-12; confrmd 9-8, 808D1
White House
Morton, Pres counselor 1-13, 21F2
Orben, speechwriter 1-21, 40C3
ASTRONAUTICS
'77 budget proposals 1-21, 63F1, 64C2
'77 budgets compared 231A2
Proclaims Space Exploratn Day 7-19, 527A2
ATOMIC Energy—*See also 'Disarmament' under FOREIGN Policy in this section below*
State of Union message 1-19, 37G3, 39D2
'77 budget proposals 1-21, 64F2
Defends A-policy 1-21, 64F2; 3-5, 179C3
Submits legis proposals 2-26, 149F2
Debates Carter 9-23, 702D2
Debates Carter 10-6, 742D1
Carter hits on safeguards 10-8, 762A2
Debates Carter 10-22, 801A3
Proposes fuel-processing curbs, Carter statemt 10-28, 848B3
AWARDS & Honors
Awards Medal of Freedom 2-10, 272C1
Gets contractors award 3-9, 180C1
Awards Medal of Freedom 4-1, 504B3
Awards Medal of Freedom 10-14, 858G3
Awards Medals of Science 10-18, 858B3
Gets AMVETS award 10-19, 784D2
Statemt at Science Medal rite scored 10-26, 840B2, C2 ★
BICENTENNIAL, American Revolution
Speaks in DC, Valley Forge, Phila, NY, Monticello 7-1—7-5, 488F3
Urges Land Heritage Act 8-31, 644E2
Debates Carter 10-22, 799G2, 800G3, 802G2
BLACK Americans—*For school busing issues, see EDUCATION in this section below*
Reprimands Butz 10-1, 744C1
Debates Carter 10-22, 799G3, 801F3
Carter church incident reactn 10-31—11-2, 826G3
BROADCASTING—*See PRESS & Broadcasting in this section below*
BUDGET—*See also other appropriate headings in this section and under U.S. GOVERNMENT*
State of Union message 1-19, 36G2, 37G2, 39E1
Briefs Cong, others on proposals 1-20, 40D1
Submits fscl '77 budget, summary 1-21, 62G1-66F2; **for reaction, see BUDGET under U.S. GOVERNMENT**
Scores Reagan plan 1-22, 41B2
Econ Rpt 1-26, 67D2, D3
On revenue sharing plans 2-7, 109D1
Scores Reagan plan 2-17, 129F2
Seeks revenue sharing extensn, scores Reagan budget 2-23, 149G2, C3
'77 Cong budgets compared, tables 231A2, 358B2
Welcomes Cong showdown 4-26, 307A3
Signs federal debt hike 6-30, 534D1
Urges revenue sharing bill 7-19, 532C1
Dole lauds position 8-19, 612G3
Carter scores vetoes 8-23, 631C3
Debates Carter 9-23, 701E1, B2 C3, 702F1-D2, C3 C3
Campaign theme 9-25, 9-26, 723A3
On HEW, Labor funds veto 9-29, 726F3
Renews tax-budget cut proposals 10-4, 742C3
Says Carter big spender 10-7—10-13, 763G1, B2, G2
Says Carter would spend more 10-14, 761F3
Carter vs chrgs 10-15; Ford replies 10-16, 785A1
Debates Carter 10-22, 800C1, 801E3, 802C1
Stresses restraint 10-23—10-28, 802G3, 803G1
Impoundment & Rescission Issues—*See under U.S. GOVERNMENT—BUDGET*
BUSINESS—*See also ECONOMY below*
Orders probe of payoffs 2-10, 134A2
Offers secret Lockheed data to Japan 3-11, 199E3
Japan accepts Lockheed data offer 3-12, 3-23, 286B1
Threatens trust bill veto 3-17, 247A1
Names payoff probe panel 3-21, 262C2
Addresses Chamber of Commerce 4-26, 307G2
Vs tuna-fishing curb 5-24, 374B1
OKs pol paymts rpts to Cong 6-30, 533G1
Submits forgn paymts legis 8-3, 668A2
Carter scores payoff proposal 8-9, 584F3
Dow reactn to electn campaign 8-17—11-10, 846E3, 847A1
GOP platform text backs pol paymts legis 8-18, 611A1
Tax incentives cited 614F1
Warns on Arab boycott compliance 9-9, 665E2

1976	1977	1978	1979	1980

1976

Signs govt in sunshine bill 9-13, 688E3
Vetoes elec car bill 9-13, overridden 9-17, 707D3
Vetoes auto research bill 9-24, 745G3
Debates Carter 10-22, 802A1
Arab Boycott
Role re killed legis disputed 9-30—10-20, 786B3
Vows disclosures in 2d debate 10-6, 740D2, 742A1
Modifies disclosure stand 10-7, 785F2
Claim re tax bill provisn scored 10-7, 787A1
Carter scores on 'discrepancy' 10-8, 762A2
Scores Carter statemts 10-20, 784F2-B3
Richardson on stand 10-20, 786A3
CABINET & White House Staff—*See also APPOINTMENTS above, RESIGNATIONS below; also specific department under U.S. GOVERNMENT; personal names*
Reagan reveals Ford bid 2-20, 148G2
Kissinger prefers to leave 5-16, 359B1
Intends to keep Kissinger 5-25, 374C1
Reprimands Butz 10-1, 744C1
CITIES & Urban Development
Mayors briefed on budget 1-20, 40D1
'77 budget proposals 1-21, 63F1, 65B3
Vows pub works-urban aid veto 1-29, 93F3
'77 budgets compared 231A2
Urges more ldrship leeway 7-17, 531F2
Urges revenue sharing bill 7-19, 532C1
Signs coastal states aid 7-26, 566A3
Debates Carter 9-23, 701C1, A2
On aid to NY 10-12, 763F2
Signs revenue sharing bill 10-13, 763A3
On aid to cities 10-14, 761G3
Mondale scores 10-19, 803E3
Debates Carter 10-22, 799G3, 801C3
CONGRESSIONAL Relations—*See also FOREIGN Policy, LEGISLATION, MESSAGES to Congress and other appropriate headings in this section; also 'Veto Action' under U.S. GOVERNMENT—CONGRESS; personal names*
Vs intelligence leaks 2-17, 127F2
Plans attack as issue 6-25, 467D3
Urges action on proposals 7-19, 532C1
Scores Cong veto concept 8-13, 646G2
Signs emergency powers curb, orders concurrent resolutn challng 9-14, 689G1-C2
Scores 94th's record 10-5, 742A3
Debates Carter 10-6, 741D1, B2
3d Carter debate 10-22, 800G3
Carter cites as vote issue 11-4, 819E2
CONSUMER Affairs
Signs credit bias ban 3-23, 233A3
Signs leasing protectn bill 3-23, 234D1
Signs product safety comm revisn bill 5-11, 345G2
Mayer becomes Tufts U pres 7-1, 504D2
Agency plan not cleared 10-2, 883A1, A2
Signs toxic substances bill 10-12, 764E2
Debates Carter 10-22, 800A2
COURTS
State of Union message 1-19, 38C2
Signs judiciary funds 7-14, 534C2
Signs 3-judge fed ct curb 8-12, 646A3
Signs civil-rights-suit fee shifting bill 10-20, 788A2
Debates Carter 10-22, 802C2
CRIME
State of Union message 1-19, 38B2, 39E2, C3
Stresses issue; for capital punishmt 2-14, 129G3
'77 budgets compared 231B2
Regrets Ariz reporter's murder 484F1
Urges Cong action 7-19, 532C1
Acceptance speech cites 8-19, 611E3
Lists as top issue 8-27, 645D1
Signs govt in sunshine bill 9-13, 688F3
Vows actn vs repeaters 9-15, 686A1
Debates Carter 9-23, 702B1, F1-A2
Vs firearms registratn 9-26, 723B3
At Chiefs of Police conv 9-27, 723D3
Carter scores 10-15, 785G1
Debates Carter 10-22, 799G3, 801C3, 802C1, E1, C2
Tokyo Rose seeks pardon 11-17, 892C2
DEFENSE & Armed Forces—*See also ATOMIC Energy above, 'Disarmament' under FOREIGN Policy below*
State of Union message 1-19, 36G3-39F3
'77 budget proposals 1-21, 62G1-63D3, 65E1, 68C3
Addresses vets in DC 2-10, 109A2
Signs '76 appropriatn bill 2-10, 109A3
'77 budgets compared 231A2, B2
Chief campaign topic 3-24—3-29, 231C3-232C1
Rebuts Reagan criticism 4-2, 245G1
Exchngs chrgs with Reagan 4-9—4-21, 280F3-281C3
Asks more missile funds 4-26, 307C3
Scores Reagan 4-28—5-2, 323G2, E3
Seeks '77 budget hike 5-4, 394D1
Signs reserves call-up powers 5-14, 982E1
Sen OKs '77 arms authorizatn 5-26, 411C2
Vetoes mil constructn bill 7-2, 517F3; Cong sustains 7-22, 533A3
Son defends 7-10, 513C3
Signs arms bill 7-14, 516F2; table 517A2
Acceptance speech cites 8-19, 611E3, 612C1
Carter TV debate topic 9-1, 644B1
Addresses Natl Guard Assn on preparedness 9-1, 645G1
Carter exchanges 9-9, 664D3, F3, 665B2
Signs govt in sunshine bill 9-13, 688E3
Stresses record budget 9-17, 9-22, 704C1
Signs '77 funds 9-22, 706F3
Campaign theme 9-25, 9-26, 723A3
Debates Carter 10-6, 740D2, C3, G3, 741C1, F1, 742F2

1977

Congress
Energy message 1-7, 14A3
State of Union message 1-12; text 12E2-14B1
'78 budget message, summary 1-17, 30A1-33G3
Urges com realignmt, pay hikes 1-17, 30D2, 33D3
Sen forms ethics panel 1-18, 77A3
Pay raises take effect 2-20, 127E2
Sees GOP ldrs 3-25, 236C2
Sen adopts ethics code 4-1, 251D2
Carter signs '78 funds 8-5, 689B1

1976

Stresses issue 10-7, 10-9, 763A2, C2
Marine recruit suit rptd 10-8, 942E2
Carter vs chrgs 10-15; Ford replies 10-16, 785A1
Scores Carter 10-16; gets AMVETS award 10-19, 784C2, D2
Vs Carter on arms boycotts 10-20, 784A3
On Brown remarks 10-20, 787E1, C2
3d Carter debate 10-22, 799F3, 800B1, 801C1, D2, G3
Stresses issue 10-23—10-26, 802G3-803C1
Visits Seattle VA hosp 10-25, 802E3
Carter appoints Schlesinger 12-23, 956G2

Amnesty Issue

ACLU chrgs clemency bd secrecy 1-6, 4A3
Dole scores Carter 8-25, 632C2
Debates Carter 9-23, 701E2
Pledges reconsideration 12-27, 980G1

Intelligence Issues

Olson widow releases CIA files 1-10, 24G3
State of Union message 1-19, 36G3, 38G3, 39F3
Lauds House censorship vote 1-29, 92A2
Offers House leak probe aid 2-12, 151E1
Revises command, asks law vs leaks 2-17, 2-18, 127A1, G2
US forgn intellignc chart 304A2 ★
Sen com issues rpt 4-26, 299C3, 304E2
GOP platform text 8-18, 609C1

DEPARTMENTS & Agencies—*See also CABINET & White House in this section above; also GOVERNMENT Reorganization, REGULATORY Agencies and department names under U.S. GOVERNMENT*

Backs Kelley on favors, gifts 9-4, 666C2
Fences with Carter re firing Kelley 9-7—9-9, 664D2, E3, 665D1
Signs govt in sunshine bill 9-13, 688C3

DEPRESSED & Disaster Areas

Declares Idaho disaster area 6-6, 423F1
Signs aid authorizatn, fund bills 6-30, 532G3, 533E2
Signs Teton Dam victims aid 7-12, 517E3; 9-7, 665C1
Declares Colo canyon disaster area 8-2, 595F2
Mass asks oil spill relief 12-22, 969D1

ECONOMY—*See also other appropriate headings in this section and under ECONOMY under 'E'; for foreign economic developments, including trade, see appropriate subheads under FOREIGN Policy in this section below*

State of Union message 1-19, 36G2-39C2
'77 budget charts moderate pace; summary 1-21, 62G1-66G2
Economic Rpt, summary 1-26, 66G2, 67E1; excerpts 67A1
To sign fishing zone bill 1-28, 94C1
Hails policies 2-6—2-8, 109B1
Vetoes pub works bill 2-13, 127E3
Notes inflation decline 2-17, 129C3
Rpts crusade vs inflatn 2-28, 165B3
Rpts econ recovery 3-9, 180C1
Says US to stay top in might 3-26, 231D3
Scores Cong policy 4-26, 307G2
Cites upturn on stump 5-8, 342A3
Vetoes public works bill 7-6, 518B2
Forecast revised 7-16, 535F3
Asks steel price hike study 8-14; revised 8-30, 646F3
Acceptance speech cites 8-19, 611G3, 612B2, D2
Dole acceptance speech 8-19, 612G3-613A1
Greenspan sees pause in recovery 8-30, 647F1
Carter TV debate topic 9-1, 644A1
Urges car-price reassessmt 9-8, 665A2
Mondale scores 'mismanagmt' 9-13, 687F1
Carter scores 'errors' 9-15, 686E3
Debates Carter 9-23, 710E1, 702D2, C3
On battle vs inflatn 9-26, 723B3
On HEW, Labor funds veto 9-29, 726G2
On Sept WPI 10-7, 769F3
On econ 'pause' 10-14, 762A1
Dole, Mondale debate 10-15, 783F1
Debates Carter 10-22, 799F3, 800E1-G2, F3, 802G2
Campaign issue 10-23—10-28, 802G3, 803F1-A2
Sept indicators rptd down 10-29, 833A1
Orders steel price study 11-24, 897G2

EDUCATION

State of Union message 1-19, 36G2, 37B2, 38G2, 39G2
'77 budget proposals 1-21, 62B3, 63F1, 65C1, C2
Rpts govs back budget plan 1-22, 41C2
Rpts budget increase plan 2-16, 166D3
Sends Cong block aid plan 3-1, 166F2
'77 budgets compared 231B2
Seeks Sup Ct busing review 5-18, denies pol motive 5-19, 377E2-A3
Defends anti-busing stand 5-26, 391D1
On Boston busing review 5-29, 392A1
Plans anti-busing legis 6-4, 410F2
On segregated private schls 6-6, 410B3
Indianapls speech vs busing 6-22, 452E2
Submits anti-busing bills 6-24, 452G1-E2
Suspends HEW schl events sex bias rule 7-7, 535E2-B3
Acceptance speech cites 8-19, 611D3, 612C2, D2
Mondale scores 8-25, 8-28, 645G2, B3
Vows tax aid, job training 9-15, 686A1, B1
Debates Carter 9-23, 702F1, A2
Block aid bills not cleared 10-2, 882G3, 883B2, 884A2
Anti-busing bills not cleared 10-2, 883B2
Debates Carter 10-22, 800F3, 801C3, D3, 802C1, D1

1977

Economy & Labor

Asks $12.5 bln tax cut plan 1-4, 5B2
State of Union message 1-12, 12F2, 13B1, C1, B2, F2, G2
Proposes airline deregulatn bill 1-13, 36F2
Submits fscl '78 budget, summary 1-17, 30A1-33G3
OKs Calif drought relief 1-20, 77A1
Brown on budget cuts 1-25, 94F2
Carter budget revisns 2-22, 124B3-126E1
AFL-CIO backs common-site picketing 2-22, 153D2
Carter asks Job Corps funds 3-9, 173G1
Milk price supports hiked 3-22, 214A1
Giaimo proposes budget 3-23, 229B1
Common-site picketing defeated 3-23, 229E1
Fears crisis, score Carter budget 3-26, 236D2
Scores Carter inflatn plan 4-16, 321G3
Cong OKs pub works jobs 5-3, 365E1
Carter Admin backs mil cutbacks 5-10—6-1, 420C3
Carter '78, '79 defns budgets compared 10-6, 857B3
Urges $68-bln tax cut 12-20, 976C3

1978

1979

1980

1976

ENERGY—*See also ATOMIC Energy in this section above; for foreign developments, see 'Energy' under FOREIGN Policy below*
State of Union message 1-19, 37E3, 39C2
'77 budget proposals 1-21, 62E3, 63F1, C2, 64E2
Special message to Cong 2-26, 149F1
'77 budgets compared 231A2
Reagan scores '75 law 5-14, 356F3
Vetoes coal leasing revisns 7-3, 518C1-A2
Orders Alaska pipeline probe 7-6, 690E3
Signs ERDA, pub works funds 7-12, 517E1
Urges Cong action 7-19, 532C1
Signs coastal states aid 7-26, 566A3
Signs oil exploratn funds 7-31, 623D1
Signs energy bill, FEA extension 8-14, 622F2
Vetoes elec car bill 9-13, overridden 9-17, 708A1
Debates Carter 9-23, 702E2
2d Carter debate 10-6, 740E2, 741D3
Debates Carter 10-22, 801E2, A3
Signs Alaska gas transport study 10-22, 834E3
Backs gas price decontrol 12-29, 991A3

ENVIRONMENT & Pollution
'77 budget proposals 1-21, 63F1, 66C1
'77 budgets compared 231A2
OKs sewage treatmt funds 4-15, 282C2
Vs tuna-porpoise ruling 5-24, 374B1
Vetoes coal leasing revisns 7-3, 518C1
Vetoes public works bill 7-6, 518E2; Cong overrides 7-22, 533G2
Signs airport noise aid bill 7-12, 567C1
Signs coastal states aid 7-26, 566G2
Vetoes pesticide bill 8-13, 646F2
Signs New River dam bar 9-11, 689D1
Vetoes elec car bill 9-13, overridden 9-17, 708A1
Vetoes auto research bill 9-24, 745G3
Vetoes resource planning bill 10-1, 919B2
Strip-mining bill not cleared 10-2, 883A1, F2
Signs toxic substances bill 10-12, 764E2
Extends noise rule to old planes 10-21, 849C1
Debates Carter 10-22, 799F3, 801D2-B3
Backs airplane-noise control 10-25, 802E3
Aircraft noise rules set 11-18, 868C3
Keeps coyote-poison ban 12-23, 980B2

FOREIGN Policy—*For Administration policy and statements, see country or subject headings in Index*
State of Union message 1-19, 36G3, 38A3, 39D3
Rebuts Reagan 2-10, 109A2; 2-13, 129E3
Defends Kissinger 3-12, 198G1
Backs Kissinger vs Reagan 4-7, 245C2
Carter sees Reagan influence 5-14, 390D3
GOP conv OKs platform 8-18, 600G2
Dole acceptance speech cites 8-19, 612F3
Biog sketch cites 614G1
Carter sees Nixon continuity 8-20, 632F1
Urges as pres debate topic 8-24, 632G3
Hits Carter inexperience 8-27, 644G3
Carter TV debate topic 9-1, 644B1
Signs govt in sunshine bill 9-13, 688E3
Campaigns on peace issue 9-17, 704D1
Debates Carter 10-6, 740B2-742G2
Scores Carter debate statemt 10-14, 761E3
Disputes Carter re world prestige loss 10-18; scientists score 10-26, 840B2, D2★
Attacks Carter 10-26, 802G3-803C1

Africa—*See also specific countries in this section*
State of Union message 1-19, 38B3
Acceptance speech cites 8-19, 612B1
On racial turmoil 9-8, 665G1
Debates Carter 10-6, 741A1, C1, D2

Aid—*See also specific country, area in this section*
'77 budget food proposals 1-21, 66D2
Vetoes authorizatn bill 5-7, 344B3-345C1
Carter: Reagan induced veto 5-14, 390E3
Signs authorizatn, Cong oversight bill 6-30, 532C3
Signs funds bill 6-30, 533B2
Signs '77 funds 10-1, 806B3

Angola
Scores Sovt role, bars grain boycott 1-5; USSR rebuffs 1-6, 2B2, 3F1
Vs Sovt grain sales as diplomatic tool re Angola 1-5, 3E1-G2
Letter to Nigeria scored 1-7, US rebuts 1-8, 2F2, D3★
Tanzania scores Angola letter 1-18, 36C1
Warns Albert vs aid cutoff 1-27, 69E1
Scores Cong aid ban 2-10, 109G2
Bars mil commitmt in south 6-6, 410C2
Signs aid authorizatn bar 6-30, 533C1
Scores mercenary execution 7-10, 519C3
Debates Carter 10-6, 741D1, G2

Asia—*See also specific countries in this section*
State of Union message 1-19, 38B3

Australia
Sees Fraser 7-27, 7-28, 554E1, G1

Botswana
Signs '77 aid funds 10-1, 806D3

Cambodia—*See 'Indochina' in this section below*

Canada
Submits oil pipe plan to Cong 2-26, 149A2

1977

Energy
Submits message to Cong 1-7, 14A3
Proposes Cabt-level dept 1-11, 14E3
State of Union message 1-12, 13D1, E1, B2, A3
'78 budget proposals 1-17, 31C2, 32F2
Orders gas price controls ended 1-19, Carter rescinds 1-24, 55D1
Carter budget revisns 2-22, 124E3, 125G1-C2
Spent A-fuel shipmt ban lifted 3-28, 235D1
Strip-mine bill cleared 7-21, 575D2

Foreign Policy
State of Union message 1-12, 12F2, E3, 13A1-E3
'78 aid, other budget proposals 1-17, 31F1, 32E2, F2, 33B1
Toon presents credentials to USSR 1-18, 47B2
SALT II talks ordrd resumed 1-27, 70E1
Carter on Rhodesia policy 2-13, 105G2
Carter drops concussn bomb sale to Israel, others 2-17, 121F1
CIA paymts to Hussein rptd 2-18, 2-23, 123F3, 124C1
Carter budget revisions 2-22, 125C1
Sugar tariff actn asked 3-3, 3-14, 189G1
On SALT talks, human rights 3-23, 3-26, 236E2
Carter denies cruise missile agrmt 3-30, 225G2
'76 shoe, steel import rulings cited 4-1, 248E1, D3
Scores arms talks rhetoric 4-6, 247E2
Latin neglect chrgd 4-17, 296C1
IISS lauds policies 4-28, 401A2
Schmidt '76 endorsemt cited 5-7, 358E1
NY Concorde ban lifted 5-11, 368F1
Brazil policy rejcted 5-11, 'consultant' pact affirmed 5-13, 414F1, C2
Scores US-Cuba thaw 6-5, 456A1
Secret US-Saudi pact rptd 6-27, 474D1
'75 USSR tap warning cited 7-10, 551A2
Double agent's release sought 7-14, Brezhnev inquiry rptd 7-15, 564D2, F2
Backs new Panama Canal accord 8-16, 622C1; Carter cites 8-23, 649B3
Teng: vowed Taiwan break 9-6; denies 9-7, 686E3-687B1
At Panama Canal pact signing, backing cited 9-7, 677E1, 678A1
PI-US base talks cited 9-22—9-23, 824B3
Kim Han Cho mtg bid, rejctn rptd 11-11, 915G1
USSR ABM violatns rptd ignored 11-23, 997C1

1978

1979

1980

1976 | 1977 | 1978 | 1979 | 1980

Trudeau visits 6-16, 481A3
Meat quota scored 10-11, 837A1

Chile
Signs aid authorizatn bill 6-30, 533C1
Debates Carter 10-6, 741D1, E2, F2
Chile rejects US aid 10-19, 10-20, 871A1

China
Chou En-lai dies 1-8, 9A2
State of Union message 1-19, 38B3
On Nixon visit 2-10, 109F3; 2-17, 129G2
On detente 3-1, 165E3
Nixon trip rpt 'useful' 3-22, 215A1
Acceptance speech cites 8-19, 612B1
Regrets Mao death 9-9, 657C2
Debates Carter 10-6, 742B1

China (Taiwan)
US force cut announced 3-11, 254F2
Vs Olympic ouster 7-12, 529B1
Debates Carter 10-6, 741E2, 742C1

Cuba
Calls Castro an 'outlaw' 2-28, 165F2
Castro rejects warnings 3-14, 251D3
Warns re PR 6-26, 462A3

Cyprus
Signs aid authorizatn bill 6-30, 532G3

Developing Countries—*See also specific countries in this section*
State of Union message 1-19, 38B3

Disarmament—*See also DISARMAMENT under 'D'*
State of Union message 1-19, 38B3, E3
Hopeful re SALT 2-10, 109B3
Defends Admin policy 3-5, 179E3
Defends SALT talks 4-21, 281D2
Asks more missile funds 4-26, 307C3
Carter on Sovt A-pact delay 5-14, 390F3
Signs Sovt underground A-pact after delay 5-28, 371C2; text 387A1
Warns vs A-arms spread 7-29, 739D2
Acceptance speech cites 8-19, 612A3
Mondale scores arms sales 8-30, 664C3
Sees Gromyko re SALT 10-1, 739B1
Debates Carter on Sovts 10-6, 741A3, 742D1
2 secret Sovt pacts rptd 11-4, 948F2

Egypt—*See 'Middle East' in this section below*

Energy—*For oil import proposals, see ENERGY in this section above*
Submits US-Canada pipe plan 2-26, 149A2
On Arab embargo 10-20, 784G2
Asks OPEC restraint 12-1; scores price rise 12-17, 934D3
Carter warns OPEC 12-14, 937F2

Europe—*See also 'NATO' and specific countries in this section*
Rebuts Reagan on Sovt role in E Eur 4-2, 245A2
Acceptance speech cites 8-19, 612B1
Debates Carter, cites Eur successes, sees no Sovt rule in E Eur 10-6, 740E2, E3, 741B1, B3
Carter attacks E Eur 'blunder' 10-7—10-12; ethnic groups, other US reactn 10-7, 10-8, 762A1, A3
Dole on E Eur remarks 10-7, 10-8, 762E3, 763G3
Admits E Eur slip 10-12, 10-14, 761E3, 762G3
Mondale, Dole debate blunder 10-15, 783E3
Scores Carter 10-26, 803B1
Carter aide minimizes debate slip 11-11, 845E2
Helsinki progress rpt issued 12-8, 934A2

France
Sees Giscard in US 5-17—5-18, 369D1, 372G1

Germany (West)
Meets Schmidt 7-15, 530E2
On Brown remarks 10-20, 787E1
Bonn reactn to electn 11-3—11-4, 826C1

Great Britain
Debates Carter 10-22, 801E1

Greece
Base pact initialed 4-15, 259E1
Signs aid funds bill 6-30, 533C2
Signs '77 aid funds 10-1, 806E3, F3

Guatemala
Sends AID relief missn 2-12, 155B3
Signs quake relief 4-21, 982E1
Signs aid funds bill 6-30, 533E2

Hungary
Cites lower exit fees 12-8, 934B2

Indochina
Vetoes forgn aid bill 5-7, 345B1; Carter chrgs pol motive 5-14, 391A1
Vs apology for US role 5-25, 374B1
Signs aid authorizatn, fund bills 6-30, 533D1, C2
Signs aid funds bill 6-30, 533D2
Acceptance speech cites 8-19, 612A1
Links Viet ties to MIA list 9-7, orders UN entry veto 9-13, 682C1, C2
Bars '77 aid funds use 10-1, 806E3
Debates Carter 10-6, 741D1, 742A2, D2
Debates Carter 10-22, 800D3, G3

Iran
Debates Carter 10-6, 742A1
On Brown remarks 10-20, 787E1

Iraq—*See 'Middle East' in this section below*

Israel—*See 'Middle East' in this section below*

Italy
CIA covert aid rptd 1-7, 10E2, D3
Signs aid authorizatn bill 6-30, 532G3
Vs CP govt role 7-19, 532E1
Andreotti visits 12-6, 947E1

Japan
State of Union message 1-19, 38A3
Offers secret Lockheed data 3-11, 199E3
Lockheed data offer accepted 3-12, 3-23, 286B1
Acceptance speech cites 8-19, 612B1
Debates Carter 10-6, 740D3, 741E3

1976	1977	1978	1979	1980

Jordan—*See 'Middle East' in this section below*
Korea (North)
On deaths of 2 US Army men 8-18, 618E3
OKs DMZ tree felling 8-20, mil buildup scored 8-22, 625E1
House com queries on mil buildup 9-1, 641G1
Korea (South)
Signs aid authorizatn bill 6-30, 533C1
OKs DMZ tree felling 8-20, 625F1
Signs arms credits 10-1, 806F3
Debates Carter 10-6, 741E2
Park Tong Sun '73 mtg cited 10-24, 899G1
Scores Carter 10-26, 803B1
Laos—*See 'Indochina' above*
Latin America—*See also specific countries in this section*
State of Union message 1-19, 38B3
Kissinger briefs on tour 2-25, 178G1
To press closer trade ties 6-9, 465C2
Acceptance speech cites 8-19, 612B1
Lebanon—*See 'Middle East' in this section below*
Libya—*See 'Middle East' in this section below*
Mexico
'75 letter on drugs rptd 1-19, 61G1
Middle East—*See also 'Arab Boycott' under BUSINESS in this section above*
Protest to Israel rptd leaked 34D3
State of Union message 1-19, 38B3
Sees Rabin 1-27—1-29, 60C1-A2
Denies rpt re borders 3-17, 198F2-A3
Hails Egypt-Sovt break 3-19, 227F3
Meets Hussein, asks Leb truce 3-30, 226B3
Threatens Israel aid veto 4-7, Rabin scores 4-8, 258A2
Lauds Syria, Israel restraint in Leb 4-20, 274C1
Leb mediator reports 319D1
Vetoes aid authorizatn bill 5-7, 344C3
France offers Leb peace force 5-21, 369D1
US amb to Leb, aide slain; calls mtg 6-16, 425B2; bodies flown to US 6-19, 448F1
Thanks PLO for Leb evacuatn 6-20; State Dept confirms 6-21, 448D1
Names Seelye amb to Leb 6-22, 448G1
Signs aid authorizatn, fund bills 6-30, 532E3, 533C2
Lauds Israel Uganda raid 7-4, 486F1
On Libya terrorist activity 7-19, 532F1
Thanks PLO for Leb evacuatn aid 7-27, 546C1
Acceptance speech cites 8-19, 612A1, B1, A3
Warns on US Arab boycott compliance 9-9, 665E2
Signs '77 aid funds 10-1, 806B3
Debates Carter 10-6, 740E2, 741A1, B2, D2, D3-742B1
Meets Allon, ends Israel arms ban 10-11, 759G1-A2
On Israel arms sale 10-14, 788A1
On Brown Israel remarks 10-20, 787E1
Scores Carter 10-26, 803B1
PLO hails electn loss 11-3—11-4, 326C2
Monetary Developments—*See also specific countries in this section*
State of Union message 1-19, 38B3
7-natn summit set 6-1, 6-3, 388F3
7-nation summit held 6-27—6-28, 462A1
Briefs Carter 11-22, 881A1
NATO
State of Union message 1-19, 38A3
Debates Carter 10-6, 741B1
Extends Haig term 11-11, 879G3
Suggests Carter mtg 11-22, 881B1
Nigeria
Letter on Angola scored 1-7, US rebuts 1-8, 2F2, D3 ★
OPEC
Asks restraint 12-1; scores price rise 12-17, 934D3
Carter warns 12-14, 937F2
Pacific Islands
Acceptance speech cites 8-19, 612B1
Pakistan
Debates Carter 10-6, 741D1
Panama Canal
Defends policy 3-6—4-19, Reagan disputes 4-13, 281C1, 291D2
Orders new ship-measuring system 3-23, 292B1
Goldwater backs stand 5-2, 324A2
Goldwater ad scores Reagan 5-8—5-9, 342B3
Immediate Canal talks asked 9-22, 792A3
Toll hike OK asked 10-5, 793D1
Debates Carter 10-6, 742F1
Torrijos scores debate stand 10-7, 792F3
Suit vs talks filed 10-26, thrown out 12-18, 1008E2
OKs toll hike 11-18; US shippers score 11-24, 1008C3
Philippines
Offers quake relief 619C2
Poland
Debates Carter 10-6, 741C3
Carter attacks Sovt-Eur debate remark 10-7—10-12; US Polish rep scores 10-7; admits error 10-12, 762C1, B3, 763A1
Portugal
OKs Portugal tariff concessns 8-31, 811F3
Debates Carter 10-6, 740G3, 741C1
Scored re 'success' claim 10-8, 812E2
Azores ldrs' US trip blocked 10-23, 812B2

1976 1977 1978 1979 1980

Rhodesia
Carter: Reagan sways chrome policy 5-14, 390F3
Scores Reagan mil stance 6-3—6-6, 410D1
Debates Carter 10-6, 741D2
Rumania
Lauded in press 4-13, 277F1
Debates Carter 10-6, 741C3
Saudi Arabia
Lauds oil price restraint 12-17, 934D3
South Africa
Fact-finding urged 8-25, 654E2
Spain
Greets king, queen 6-2, 459B2
Signs bases treaty aid 10-18, 834C3
Syria—*See 'Middle East' above*
Trade—*See also specific countries in this section*
Threatens steel quotas, asks intl trade pact 3-16, 212D3-213D2
Vows farmer protectn vs imports 4-3, 245F1
Bars shoe import curb 4-16; eases flatware, ceramics curbs 4-30, 321F3, 322D1
Shrimp industry Trade Act aid urged 5-11, 431F1
Sets specialty steel quotas 6-7, 430E3-431E1
Mondale scores arms sales 8-30, 664C3
Dole cites grain embargo 9-17, 724C3
Triples sugar import duties 9-21, 721E2
Extends Export Admin Act 9-30, 786G3
Debates Carter 10-6, 740C3, 741A2, 741A3, D3, 742F2
Sets meat import quota 10-9, 787G3
Canada scores meat quota 10-11, 837A1
Dole, Mondale debate 10-15, 782C3
Vs Carter on boycotts 10-20, 784A3
Signs grain inspectn bill 10-21, 833B3
Ups brandy duties 11-26, 976F2
Cites E Eur improvemts 12-8, 934C2
Turkey
Signs '77 aid funds 10-1, 806E3, F3
Offers quake aid 11-25, 897D1
Uganda
Lauds Israel Uganda raid 7-4, 486F1
United Arab Emirates
Lauds oil price restraint 12-17, 934D3
United Nations
Reaffirms Moynihan policy support 1-28, 67E2
No policy change planned 2-10, 109D3
Seeks IAEA aid 2-26, 149G2
Uruguay
Signs mil aid ban 10-1, 806F3, 814C1
USSR—*See also 'Angola' and 'Disarmament' in this section above*
Bars grain sales as diplomatic tool 1-5, 3F1-A3
On detente 3-1, 165E3
Defends Admin policy 3-5, 179E3
Defends '75 grain embargo 3-5, 180A1
Hails Egypt-Sovt break 3-19, 227F3
Rebuts Reagan attack 4-2, 245A2
Scores Sovt UN missn shooting 4-2, 259G3
Pravda scores re detente 4-2, 277E2
Defends defns policy, Reagan disputes 4-10, 4-21, 281B1, C2, A3
Levich scores rights stand 6-25, 540A3
GOP conv adopts platform 8-18, 600G2
Acceptance speech cites 8-19, 612B1
OKs Sovt MiG-25 pilot asylum 9-7, 696A1
Orders Viet entry veto 9-13, 682C1, E1
Signs '77 defense funds 9-22, 706G3
Debates Carter 10-6, 740E2, D3-G3, 741A3, 742A1
Carter attacks E Eur 'blunder' 10-7—10-12; ethnic groups, other US reactn 10-7, 10-8, 762A1, A3
Dole on E Eur remarks 10-7, 10-8, 762E3, 763G3
Admits E Eur slip 10-12, 10-14, 761E3, 762G3
Dole, Mondale debate E Eur blunder 10-15, 783E3
Debates Carter 10-22, 800A1, 802E2
Brezhnev scores statemts 10-25, 839B2
Scores Carter re Yugo 10-26, 803B1, D1
Yugo scores Carter debate 10-27, 910B1
Sovt reactn to electn loss 11-3—11-4, 826G1
Carter aide minimizes E Eur slip 11-11, 845E2
On emigratn policy 12-8, 934B2, D2
On Helsinki progress rpt 12-8, 934B2, D2
Venezuela
Electn defeat hailed 11-3—11-4, 826D2
Sees amb 12-1, 934D3
Vietnam—*See 'Indochina' above*
Yugoslavia
Signs aid authorizatn bill 6-30, 532F3
Jailed American freed 7-23, 559E2
Debates Carter 10-6, 741C3
Debates Carter 10-22, 800A1, 802E2; scores Carter; Carter rebuts 10-26, 803B1-D1
Yugo scores Carter debate 10-27, 910B1
Zaire
Signs '77 aid funds 10-1, 806D3, F3
Zambia
Signs aid authorizatn bill 6-30, 532F3
Signs '77 aid funds 10-1, 806D3
GOVERNMENT Regulation—*See REGULATORY Agencies (& Issues) under U.S. GOVERNMENT*
GOVERNMENT Reorganization—*See under U.S. GOVERNMENT*
HEALTH—*See MEDICINE & Health below*
HOUSING
State of Union message 1-19, 37C3, 39C2
'77 budget proposals 1-21, 62B3, 64A3, 65C3
Econ Rpt forecasts starts 1-26, 67G1
Vs 'ethnic purity' phrase 4-13, 261F2

1976 1977 1978 1979 1980

Signs '77 housing aid bill 8-3, 566D3
Signs public bldg aid 8-9, 623F1
Signs home-insulatn aid 8-14, 623B1
Mondale scores 8-25, 8-28, 645G2, B3
Lists as top issue 8-27, 645D1
Vows eased home-ownership 9-15, 685F2, 686A1
Mondale chrgs inactn 9-16, 687B2
Debates Carter 9-23, 701C1, 702F1
Carter vs Ford tax chrgs 10-15; Ford replies 10-16, 785C1
Debates Carter 10-22, 800G1, E2, F3, 801C3-802B1
INTELLIGENCE Issues—*See under DEFENSE in this section above*
ITALIAN Americans—*See MINORITIES in this section below*
LABOR
Vetoes constructn-site picketing 1-2, union ldrs quit com 1-8, 3C3, F3
State of Union message 1-19, 37B2-B3, 39F1
'77 budget proposals 1-21, 62C3-63C3, 65E2, F3, 66D2
Econ Rpt 1-26, 66A3; excerpts 67A1
Vows pub works-urban aid veto 1-29, 93C3
Vs public jobs programs 1-31, 87F3
Hails jobless rate drop 2-6, 109B1
Vetoes public jobs bill 2-13, 127E3; comments 2-17, 129B3; veto upheld 2-19, 135C2
Rpts crusade vs unemploymt 2-28, 165B3
Addresses contractors 3-9, 180C1
'77 budgets compared 231B2
Vs Hatch Act revision 4-3, 245F1
OKs pub svc, other jobs 4-15, 282C2
Scores jobs bill 4-26, 307A3
Shrimp worker aid urged 5-11; aids mushroom growers 5-17, 431F1, C2
Mayors back pub works bill 7-1, 493E1
Vetoes pub works bill 7-6, 518B2; Cong overrides 7-22, 533E2
Jobless forecast revised 7-16, 535A1
Scored by Meany 7-19, 532E2
Acceptance speech cites jobs 8-19, 612A1, D2
Lists jobs as top issue 8-27, 645D1
Vows job-training 9-15, 686D1
Debates Carter 9-23, 700F3, 701A1-B2, 702C1, 702A2, C2, A3
Orders 4.8% US pay rise 9-29, 742B3
Mondale, Dole debate 10-15, 783B3
Debates Carter 10-22, 800C1-G2, F3, 801E2, F3, 802A1, B1, A3
LEGISLATION
Plans pocket-veto curb 4-13, 284D1
Proposals & Requests—*For Congressional action, see 'Legislation' subheads under U.S. GOVERNMENT—CONGRESS*
State of Union 1-19, 36F2-39G3; text 37A1
Fscl '77 budget 1-21, 62G1-66F2
Medicare, Soc Sec plans 2-9, 110C1
Intelligence set-up, security leaks 2-17, 2-18, 127A1
Energy proposals 2-26, 149F1
Education aid plan 3-1, 166F2
Drug abuse penalties 4-9, 280G3
Missile funds 4-26, 307C3
Drug abuse program 4-27, 307B2
Regulatory reform 5-13, 346E3
Curbs vs school busing 6-24, 452G1
Watergate reform 7-19, 531G3
Forgn paymts disclosure 8-3, 668A2
$1.5 bln park plan 8-31, 644C2
Signed
Railroad aid 2-5, 109G3
'76 defense appropriatns 2-10, 109A3
Rice production 2-16, 982D1
Wildlife refuges 2-27, 982D1
Parole restructuring 3-15, 982D1
Med rehabilitatn extensn 3-15, 982E1
Drug office, funding 3-19, 233D3-234A1
Credit bias ban 3-23, 233A3
Consumer leasing protectn 3-23, 234D1
Conrail funds 3-30, 233E2
Naval Oil reserves 4-5, 982E1
Municipal bankruptcy 4-8, 982E1
Swine flu, pub svc, other funds 4-15, 282G1
200-mi fishing zone 4-15, 982E1
Guatemala relief 4-21, 982F1
Health program funds 4-22, 982E1
Highway aid authorizatn 5-5, 919A3
Peace Corps funds 5-7, 982F1
Consumer product safety comm revisn 5-11, 345G2
Science office re-creatn 5-11, 346A1
FEC revision 5-11, 346B2
Reserves call-up powers 5-14, 982E1
A-safeguard funds 5-22, 982E1
ACTION funds 5-27, 982F1
Beef Board 5-28, 982E1
Med devices regulation 5-28, 982E1
IDB aid 5-31, 982E1
Noise control 5-31, 982F1
Supplemental funds 6-1, 982F1
Helsinki monitoring panel 6-3, 982E1
NASA funds 6-4, 982F1
Educ broadcast funds 6-5, 982F1
Saline water conversn 6-22, 982F1
Disease control, health plans 6-23, 982F1
'75 tax-cut extensn 6-30, 492G1
'76, '77 arms aid authorizatn, Cong oversight 6-30, 532C3
'76 arms aid funds 6-30, 533B2
Fed debt hike 6-30, 534D1
Valley Forge natl park 7-4, 489C2
Food stamp vendor rules 7-6, 533E3
Railroad safety 7-8, 919D3
'77 ERDA, pub works funds 7-12, 517E1
'77 agri, food funds 7-12, 533B3
'77 State, other authorizatns 7-12, 534F1 ★
'76-80 airport, aviation aid 7-12, 567A1

1976	1977	1978	1979	1980

'77 arms bill 7-14, 516F2
Coastal states aid 7-26, 566G2
Interior related agency funds 7-31, 623C1
'77 housing aid 8-3, 566D3
HUD, VA, EPA, NASA, NSF funds 8-9, 623E1
3-judge court use curb 8-12, 646A3
Swine-flu liability 8-12, 982F1
Energy bill, FEA extensn 8-14, 622F2
Transportatn funds 8-14, 982F1
Options tax exemptn 9-3, 708D1
Teton Dam disaster aid 9-7, 665B1
Day-care center rules 9-7, 665C1, 689B1
New River dam bar 9-11, 689D1
Govt in sunshine 9-13, 688C3
Emergency powers curb 9-14, 689G1-C2
'77 defense funds 9-22, 704E1, 706F3
Postal subsidy 9-24, 982G1
Toxic substances 9-28, 764E2
Natl park mining curbs 9-28, 834C2
Land conservation 9-28, 982G1
Police, firemen survivor benefits 9-29, 834D2
Antitrust enforcemt 9-30, 982F1
Military constructn 9-30, 982F1
4 vet benefit bills 9-30, 10-15, 10-21, 982G1
Indian health programs 9-30, 982G1
'77 forgn aid funds 10-1, 806B3
Uruguay mil aid bar 10-1, 806E3, 814C1
'77 DC funds 10-1, 834G1
'77 Legis branch funds, pay hike bar 10-1, 834A2
Public works service 10-1, 982F1
Tax bill 10-4, 742B3
Arts & Humanities extensn 10-8, 834G2
Indian Claims Comm end 10-8, 835A1
HMO rules 10-8, 982G1
Gas pipeline safety aid 10-11, 834D3
'77 Natl Science Foundatn funds 10-11, 835A2
Vocational, higher educ aid 10-12, 788E3
Depressed areas aid 10-12, 982G1
Revenue sharing 10-13, 763A3
Med-educ-aid 10-13, 788E2
LEAA extensn, FBI dir term limit 10-15, 835G1
HEW inspector general 10-15, 982G1
Mid-decade censuses 10-17, 834F3
Indiana Dunes expansn 10-18, 834B3
Spain bases treaty aid 10-18, 834C3
Railroad aid 10-19, 834F2
Arthritis, diabetes progrms 10-19, 834A3
Copyright revision 10-19, 982G1
Jobless benefits revisn 10-20, 788D1-A2
Civil-rights-suit fees 10-20, 788B2
Occidental immigratn revisn 10-20, 835D1
Land tax compensatn for local govts 10-20, 835F1
Tax on biased soc clubs 10-20, 835F1
Solid waste aid, EPA office 10-21, 833F2
Grain inspection 10-21, 833B3
Public land use 10-21, 834F1
Emergency med care 10-21, 834A3
Forgn natn legal immunity 10-21, 835B1
Forest mgt. clear-cutting 10-22, 833F3
Alaska gas transport study 10-22, 834E3
'77-78 Army Engineer projcts 10-22, 835A2

Vetoed—*See also 'Veto Action' under U.S. GOVERNMENT—CONGRESS*

Treas secy on NSC 1-1, 4D1
Constructn site picketing 1-2, 3C3
Milk price supports 1-30, 88D1
Public jobs bill 2-13, 127E3
Day-care aid 4-6, 284C1
Hatch Act revision 4-12, 284D1
Foreign aid authorizatn 5-7, 344B3-345C1
Defense construction 7-2, 517F3
Coal leasing revisns 7-3, 518C1
Public works bill 7-6, 518A2
Humphrey scores vetoes 7-13, 509F2
Md congressmen tax exemptn 8-3, 636B3
Pesticide bill 8-13, 646F2
Acceptance speech cites 8-19, 611D3
Carter scores vetoes 8-23, 631B3
Dole defends record 9-3, 665G3-666A1
Electric car aid 9-13, 707E3
Auto research 9-24, 745G3
'77 HEW, Labor funds 9-29, 726F1
Dole, Mondale debate 10-15, 783F1
Rabbit meat inspectn 10-17, 919E2
Resource planning bill 10-19, 919B2
Duplicate forgn natn legal immunity 10-21, 835B1

MEDICINE & Health—*See also NARCOTICS in this section below*

State of Union message 1-19, 36F3, 38A1, 39E2
'77 budget proposals 1-21, 62B3, C3, 63F1, 64E3, 66E2
Backs limited abortns 2-3, 88A1
Submits Medicare plans 2-9, 110C1
Notes state aid need 2-23, 149A3
Urges flu vaccine for all 3-24, 224A2
'77 budgets compared 231B2
Signs swine flu bill 4-15, 282G1
Vaccine-maker to lose insurance 6-15, 443G1
Vows swine flu immunizatn 7-19, 532F1
Cong OKs flu vaccine liability 8-10, 586C2
Acceptance speech cites Medicare 8-19, 612C2
Health care a top issue 8-27, 645D1
Mondale scores 8-28, 645B3
Flu immunizatn delay rptd 9-1, 656B3
PHS backs cost controls 9-7, 680F1 ★
On abortn amendmt 9-8, 665E1
Bishops review abortn stand 9-10, assert neutrality 9-16, 686D1-B2
Vows health-care progrm 9-15, 686A1

1976

Debates Carter 9-23, 702F1
Ga gov scores debate reference to Medicaid 9-25, 725G1
HEW funds overridden 9-30, 726F2, G3
Medicare, natl health plans not cleared 10-2, 883D3, E3
Carter scores 10-19, 785B2
Debates Carter 10-22, 801C3, D3

MESSAGES to Congress
State of Union 1-19, 36F2-39G3; text 37A1
Fscl '77 budget, summary 1-21, 62G1-66F2
Rpts govs back budget plan 1-22, 41C2
Economic Report 1-26, 66G2, 67E1
Medicare, Soc Sec plans 2-9 110C1
Energy proposals 2-26, 149F1
Education aid plan 3-1, 166G2
Drug abuse 4-27, 307B2
Curbs vs school busing 6-24, 452G1
Arms control rpt 7-29, 739E1, D2
Proposes forgn paymts legis 8-3, 668E2

MINORITIES—*See also BLACK Americans in this section above*
Signs Indian housing aid 567A1
Vs 'ethnic purity' phrase 4-13, 261E2
Sees Polish, Italian Amers 9-24, 724A1
See GOP ethnic ldrs 10-2, 743E2
Butz resigns 10-4, 744F2
Carter debate rebuttal re E Eur groups 10-6, 740F2, 741D3
Ethnic groups deplore E Eur debate remark 10-7, 10-8, 762A3
Lauds Poles 10-7, 763A1
Admits debate slip 10-12, 763E1
Debates Carter 10-22, 799G3, 801G3

MONETARY Developments—*See ECONOMY and FOREIGN Policy in this section above*

NARCOTICS & Dangerous Drugs
State of Union message 1-19, 38D2, 39C3
Signs office, funding bill 3-19, 233D3-234A1
To seek stiffer penalties 4-9, 280G3
Special message to Cong 4-27, 307B2
Signs control authorizatn 6-30, 532G3
Acceptance speech cites 8-19, 611E3
Ford, Carter debate 9-23, 702G1

PARKS—*See RECREATION in this section below*

PERSONAL
Moore gets life term 1-15, 23F1-D2
Attends church with Cong members 1-19, 40D1
Releases financial data 2-12, answers query 2-17, 129A2, A3
At baseball All-Star game 7-13, 544G1
White House intruder killed 7-25, 860E1
Biographical sketch 613D2
Carter scores on finances 10-8, 762E1, B2
'73 IRS audit re spending, '67-72 tax returns probed 10-8, 764B1-B2
On IRS audit, spending money 10-14, 761C3
Starts vacation in Calif 11-7, 845E2
At Pocantico Hills Thanksgiving svc 11-21, 887B3
Offers papers to US 12-14, 980D2
On vacatn 12-19—12-31, 980D2
Phones Mrs Hart 12-27, 980G1

POLITICS—*See also POLITICS under 'P'; for specific issues and reaction to policies, see other headings in this section (e.g., ECONOMY above) and in Index (e.g., ECONOMY under 'E')*
Addresses Govs Conf 2-23, 149G2
Vs Hatch Act revision 4-3, 245F1
Vetoes Hatch Act revision 4-12, 284D1
Signs FEC revision 5-11, 346B2
Sees GOP natl com leaders 12-6, 938E1
In GOP unity mtg 12-9, 938A1

Assassination Issues—*See PERSONAL above*

Fund Issues
Gets US subsidy 1-2, 22D3
Releases personal assets 2-12, answers query 2-17, 129A2, A3
Fed fund total listed 3-4, 180C3
Gets $1.3 mln in fed funds 5-21, 391D3
Campaign surplus rptd 6-16; fed funds total 7-1, 491A1, D1
Still eligible for fed funds 6-23, 490G3
Ruff probes funds use 7-13, 7-16; subpoenas issued 8-19, 761D1
Ticket gets fed funds 8-24, 688A3
Nominatn costs rptd 8-28, 688E2
Com payed for Wyo trip 8-29, 644E3
'64-73 funds probe, US Steel golf trips rptd 9-21, 9-25; statemts 9-21—9-30; Justice Dept referral rptd 10-1, 722E1-723G2
Carter on chrgs 9-29, 9-30, 723D1, A2
Carter on corp favors 10-2, 743C1
Carter urges 'truth' 10-8, 762E1
Rpt on '73 IRS audit 10-8, 764B1-B2
Ruff clears Ford; Ford press conf remarks 10-14, 761D1, F2
On lobbyist-paid golf trips 10-14, 761D3
FEC lists major backers 10-22, 938F3
FEC certificatns rptd 12-31, 979E1, G2

Polls
Gallup rating drops 1-7, Callaway comments 1-8, 21G2
Trails Carter in poll 3-15, 197D1
Trails Carter, leads Reagan 4-12—8-1, 564F3
Reagan delegate profiles compared 8-7, 8-8, 8-17, 616A2
Leads Reagan in Gallup Poll 8-12, 583G3
Carter lead drops, support in South firm 8-25, 8-28, 9-1, 644G1
Wins 1st debate rating 9-30, 725E1
Carter lead down to 8% 9-30, 725A2
Carter lead up after 2d debate 10-15, 1st debate results cited 764B2
Carter ahead by 6 pts 10-21, 804B3

1977

Politics & Government
Congratulates PR gov 1-2, 16G2
Cong declares Carter winner 1-6, 14G2
NAACP vs Bell nominatn 1-10, 59C3
Callaway probe dropped 1-11, 59D2
Proposes PR statehood bill 1-14, 36C2
Final patronage apptmts rptd 1-19, 36C2
Carter lauds at inaugural 1-20, 25E1
Richardson named amb at large 1-25, 53F1
Amer Airlines gift rptd 2-9, 112B1
Govt pay raises take effect 2-20, 127E2
Sees Carter 3-24, 236C2
Sees Brock, studies '80 bid 3-25, 236D2
Carter poll ratings compared 4-4, 251F1
Scores Carter 4-16; Mondale, O'Neill rebuke 4-19, Carter discounts 4-22, 321D3-G3
FCC reverses pol ad stand 5-6, 376A2
ACLU rates Carter record 7-21, 575C2
Sees Carter 12-20, 976D3

1978

1979

1980

1976	1977	1978	1979	1980

3 give Carter edge, 1 to Ford 10-27, 10-31, 11-1, 825F3
On Carter decline 10-28, 803G1
NBC polls electn issues 11-2, 818B3
Presidential Election (including campaign & post-election developments)—*See also related subheads in this section; for specific issues, see other subject subheads under FORD*
ACLU chrgs clemency bd secrecy 1-6, 4A3
Constructn com members warn on primaries 1-8, 3F3
OKs Common Cause code 1-9, 23A1
Morton gets liaison role 1-13, Dems score appointment 1-14, 21F2, C3
Edges Reagan in Iowa straw vote 1-19, 41C1
Curtis pacified on Morton role 1-19, Strauss objcts 1-22, 41C2, F2
Govs briefed on budget 1-20, 40D1
Lists 8 potential running mates 1-22, 41G1
In Mich, Va 1-31, 87D3-88A1
Addresses NE GOP 2-6, 109C1
In NH 2-7—2-8, 109B1, D1
Discounts Reagan challenge, sees Humphrey bid 2-10, 109C3
Says Reagan too extreme to win 2-13, 2-17, 129D2, D3
In Fla 2-13—2-14, 129D3
Ends NH campaigning 2-19—2-20, 148A3
Reagan reveals Cabt bid 2-20, 148G2
Calls Reagan unrealistic 2-23, 149B3
Wins NH primary 2-24, reacts 2-25, 148E1, G1
In Fla 2-28—3-1, 165F2-E3
Wins Mass, Vt primaries 3-2, 164G3, 165G1-A2
In Ill 3-5—3-6, 179D3, G3
Wins Fla primary 3-9, 179D1, E2
Unconcerned re Reagan chrgs 3-12, 197C1
Callaway chrgd 3-12, steps aside during probe, Stuart named 3-13, 197G1
Ends Ill campaigning, backs Kissinger 3-12, 198G1
Reagan com scores Kissinger role 3-13, 198D1
Wins Ill primary, Reagan denounces tactics 3-16, 196D2-197C1
Addresses NC homemakers group 3-20, 214E1
Loses NC primary 3-23, 213G2
Stresses defns issue, in Calif 3-24—3-29, 231C3-232C1
Morton replaces Callaway 3-30, 233B1
Sees Connally 4-1, denies Cabt offer 4-19, 281B2
In Wis; rebuts Reagan TV address, backs Kissinger 4-2, 4-3, 4-7, 245F1
Large NY delegate bloc voted 4-6, 244G2
Wins Wis primary 4-6, 245C1
Delegate box score rptd 4-9, 261B1
In Tex 4-9—4-10, 280E3
Church scores as 'weak' 4-19, 282A1
Campaign vs Reagan intensifies 4-28—5-2, 323G2
Carter attacks leadership 4-30, 324D1
Reagan wins Tex primary 5-1, 3 others 5-4; reactn 5-2, 5-5, 322D2-G3, 323D1
In Ind, says Carter does 'flip-flop' 5-3, 323E3
Wins DC primary 5-4, 322F2, 323E2
In Neb 5-7—5-8, loses primary 5-11, 342D1, F2
Seeks Mich win 5-9—5-15, 343C1, 356G3
Wins W Va primary 5-11, 342B3
Wins delegates in Kan, Mo, Minn 5-11, 343A1
In Tennessee 5-14, 374F1
Carter: Reagan sways Ford 5-14, 390E3
Wins Mich, Md primaries 5-18, 356D2, 357F1
Tours West 5-22—5-25, 373G3
Gets 119 NY delegates 5-24, 374C1
Wins Ore, Ky, Tenn primaries; loses Ark, Idaho, Nev 5-25, 373D1, G1-E2, G2, 374A2
In Ohio 5-26, 391D1
Carter scores critics 5-27, 390F2
Wins RI primary; loses SD, Montana 6-1, 389F2, 390C1, A2
Winds up campaign in NJ, Ohio, Calif 6-6—6-7, 410B3
Wins Ohio, NJ primaries; loses Calif 6-8, 408F2-409E3
Primary delegates totaled 6-8, 409B3
Reagan sweeps Mo delegates 6-12, 432B2
Reagan gains 16 delegates in 5 states 6-19, 450E2
To get 20 W Va delegates 6-19, 450F3
Wife in Iowa 6-19, 451B1
Morton sees 1st-ballot win 6-22, 450G3
Reagan scores tactics 6-25, 6-28, 467B3
Hosts W Va delegates 6-25, 467C3
Minn, Mont, Ida, NM conv results 6-26, 467F1
Goldwater endorses 6-30, 467F3
Wyo delegate deal re coal bill rptd, denied 7-2, 518F1
Dems see as 'tough' opponent 7-6, 489E3
Target of Reagan TV talk 7-6, 490F2
ND, Colo conv results 7-8—7-10, 513A3
Calls Reagan qualified for pres 7-9, 513E3
Mondale cites Nixon pardon 7-15, 507G3, 511F2
Wins Conn delegates, loses Utah; Reagan struggle continues 7-17—7-20, 531D2
Scores Dem ticket 7-17, 531F2
Defends Nixon pardon 7-19, 532A1
Bars vp interviews, hints outsider 7-19, 532D1
Carter scores Nixon pardon 7-20, 532G1

1976 1977 1978 1979 1980

Delegate gains continue 7-22—7-25; Reagan names Schweiker vp choice 7-26, reactn 7-27—7-29, 549G2-550A3
Endorsed by Connally 7-27, 550B3
Visits Miss delegation 7-30, 563E3
To poll GOP re vp 7-30, 7-31, 563G3
No 'lockup' of nominatn seen before conv; delegate switches rptd 8-2—8-5, 563E2, 564B2
Carter attacks 8-3, 564E2
Connally vp selectn disputed, campaign role seen 8-5—8-10, 584A2, C2-A3
GOP platform com OKs planks 8-8—8-13, 582F2-583A2
GOP conv rules com acts on pre-ballot vp selectn, other issues 8-9—8-11, 582C1
Prospective vp nominees rptd 8-9—8-12, Reagan consultatn vowed 8-10, 584B2
More delegate gains rptd 8-10—8-14, 582A2
Carter vs condoning offcls' crimes 8-11, 585B2, E2
Miss warns vs liberal vp choice 8-12, 582E1
Pre-conv delegate count 8-14, 583A3
Seeks delegates at conv 8-15—8-18, 601E2
Press: nominatn clinched 8-16, 8-17, 601D3
Conv delegate vote bribes chrgd 8-16, 8-17, 616C1
Wins 16-C rules test 8-17, 600B1
Nominated 8-18, wins 8-19, 597E1-598E1
Conv vote table 8-18—8-19, 599A1
Reagan wins forgn policy plank, conv OKs platform 8-18, 600G2
Sees Reagan, advisers on vp 8-19, 598E1, B3
Accepts nominatn, names Dole vp, asks Carter debate 8-19, 599G1-600B1; speech text 611C1-612E3
Cited in Dole biog sketch 614D3
Nixon rptdly favors 8-19, 616A1
Photo with Dole 597A1 ★
Endorses early running mate selectn 8-20, 631G1
Carter scores re Nixon policies 8-20, 632G1
Rpt Connally vs GOP com role 8-22; sees Ford win 8-23, 631D1
Names Baker campaign chief 8-25, 631B1
Sees Dole, Rockefeller, Connally 8-26—8-27, 645A1
Says voters fear Carter 8-27, 644G3
Dole no 'hatchet man' 8-27, 645E1
Mondale cites priorities 8-28, 645A3
Stops at Rapid City (SD) 8-29, 644F3
Carter scores issue list 8-30, 645A2
Dole in Ga 9-1, 645F3, G3
Campaign kick-off delayed, pres image stressed 9-2—9-9, 664G3-E2
Carter scores leadershp 9-6, 663F2, 664A2
Opens campaign in Mich 9-15, Carter scores 9-16, 685E2, 686E3
Rockefeller disavows some platform planks 9-16, 687B1
Mondale scores turnabouts 9-16, 687C2
3d-party challenges rejctd 9-17, 9-20, 703D2
In Phila 9-24, 724A1
In Deep South 9-25—9-27, 723G2
Scores Cong 9-29, 726G2; 10-5, 742A3
Carter scores 9-30, 10-1, 10-2, 742E3, G3, 743A1
Meets with Dole 10-1, 743E1
Carter attacks 10-4, 743D1
Mondale scores on Watergate 10-5, 743A3
Dole admits GOP slump 10-8, 763G3
Carter links to Nixon 10-9, 10-10, 762C2, F2
Tex Baptist ldr backs 10-10, 763C2
Criticizes Carter 10-11, 763E2; 10-15—10-20, 784E1-D3
Carter protests chrgs 10-15; replies 10-16, 785B1
On Brown remarks 10-20, 787C2
At Al Smith fete in NYC 10-21, 785E1
Makes final swing 10-22—10-28, 802C3; 10-29—11-1, 826F2, A3
Press endorsemts rptd 10-30, 11-8, 827D3
Final TV plea 11-1, 826F2
Carter wins electn 11-2; concedes 11-3, 817D1-819D2
Popular, electoral vote table, map 818A1, 819A1
Transition work under way 11-5, 845C1
Carter aide: Dole hurt Ford 11-11, 845E2
Carter to visit 11-16, 864B2
Sees Carter on transitn 11-22, 880F2
Electoral Coll votes 12-13, 979B1
Final tally rptd 12-18; table 979C1, A2
TV Debates
Asks Carter debate, Carter agrees 8-19, 599E2
League of Women Voters sets dates 8-19, 632E3
Suggests earlier dates, Carter rep vs 8-24, 632G3-633A1
Negotiators meet 8-26, 632C3
FEC OKs debates 8-30, 644D1
Ground rules set 9-1, 644A1
McCarthy, Maddox warn suits 9-2, 644F1
Carter sees tie as victory 9-4, 664F1
More debate rules rptd 9-8, 700F3
2d, 3d debates set 703A2
Networks OK debate rules 9-18, 9-20, 703B2
1st Carter debate 9-23, 700E2-703A2
Experts rate 1st debate 9-24, 9-30, 725D1
Sound-loss cause found 9-24, 725F1
Ga gov protests reference to Medicaid 9-25, 725G1

1976 1977 1978 1979 1980

2d Carter debate 10-6, 740B2-742G2
Carter, others score 'blunder' on Sovt role in E Eur 10-7—10-12; admits error 10-12, 762A1, A3, G3; 10-27, 910B1
Refers to 'quiz show' 10-7, 763G1
Scored on Panama Canal stand 10-7, 792F3
Carter scores Arab boycott remark 10-8, 762A2
Dole admits GOP slump 10-8, 763G3
Lists Carter 'errors' 10-9, 763C2
Sup Ct bars equal-time review 10-12, 765D3
Carter poll lead up after 2d 10-15, 1st cited 764B2
Dole, Mondale debate 10-15, 782E1-784E1
3d Carter debate 10-22, 799E2-802C3
Scores Carter re Yugo; Dole scores Carter 10-26, 803C1, 804F2
Carter: key to victory 11-5, 845D1
Carter aide minimizes E Eur error 11-11, 845E2
Carter sees unifying result 11-22, 880G3

Watergate (including Nixon pardon)—*See also 'Campaign Funds' above*

Mondale cites pardon 7-15, 507G3, 511E2
Proposes Watergate reform bill 7-19, 531G3
Defends pardon 7-19, 532A1
Carter scores pardon 7-20, 532G1
Carter vs condoning exec crime 8-11, 585B2, E2
Mondale scores 10-5, 743A3
Press conf statemt on coverup chrg 10-14, 761A3
Ruff, Levi vs new probes 10-15, 10-20, 784F3
Dole rebuts Dems 10-17—10-27, 804E1-A3
Bars more pardons 10-20, 784E3
Denies coverup chrg 10-20, 784F3
Debates Carter 10-22, 799G2, 800G3, 801A1
Confronts issue 10-27, 803E1
Mondale scores Nixon pardon 10-29, 827C2
Carter on rating 11-4, 819F2

POVERTY

State of Union message 1-19, 38G1-A2, 39B3
'77 budget proposals 1-21, 62B3, 63C2, 65B1-F1, 66A2
Scores Reagan plan 1-22, 41B2
Plans food-stamp action 2-20, 150B1
'77 budgets compared 231B2
Vetoes day-care aid bill 4-6, 284C1
OKs summer jobs, recreatn funds 4-15, 282C2
Ct delays food-stamp cutback 6-19, 454C3
Signs food stamp vendor rules 7-6, 533E2
Signs '77 food funds bill 7-12, 533C3
Carter scores re welfare 8-30, 645B2
Signs day care bill 9-7, 665C1, 689B1
Debates Carter 9-23, 701F1, 702E3
Soc svc aid plans not cleared 10-2, 884A2
Carter attacks 10-4, 743D1

PRESS & Broadcasting

Interviewed in St Louis 1-5, 3G2
Holds budget briefing 1-20, 40D1
Sees NH editors 1-22, 41A2
CBS interview 2-3, 88A1
News conf, summary 2-10, 109A3
News conf, summary 2-17, 127A1, 129D2
Seeks law vs security leaks 2-18, 127D3
Fla TV interview 3-1, 165D3
Wins FCC pol ad case 3-4, 180E2-A3
Dallas news conf 4-10, 281C1
Equal-time rules upheld 4-12, 282E1
Meets editors at White House 4-13, 261F2
Harte-Hanks interview 4-19, 281A2
Goldwater ad scores Reagan 5-8—5-9, 342B3
Ohio news conf 5-26, 391D1
TV interview taped for Calif 6-4, 410F2
Nofziger vs pol ads 6-5, 410B2 ★
Reagan mgr vs ads 6-5, 410B2 ★
On Face the Nation 6-6, 410B3
News conf 7-9, 513G3
News conf, summary 7-19, 531G3
News conf on fund probe, golf trips 9-30, 723E1
TV news conf 10-14, 761F2, 787F3, 788B1
News conf, summary 10-20, 784E2
Defends pol ads re Playboy 10-20, 784D3
Carter scores TV coverage 11-5, 845F1
Nessen hosts Powell 11-16, 864D1
Rockefeller, Connally join conf 12-9, 938C1

TV Debates—*See under POLITICS above*

RECREATION & Recreation Areas

Signs youth funds bill 4-15, 282D2
Lists as top issue 8-27, 645D1
At Yellowstone, offers $1.5 bln plan 8-29; reactn 8-29—8-31, 644C2-F3
Asks $1.5 bln park plan 8-29, 8-31, 644C2
Cong OKs parkland authrzn funds 9-13, 745F2-B3; signed 9-28, 982G1
Vows parklands expansn 9-15, 686A1
Mondale scores 9-16, 687C2
Debates Carter 9-23, 702F1
Debates Carter 10-22, 801F2-B3
Dedicates Pocantico site 11-21, 887G2

1976	1977	1978	1979	1980

RELIGION
Addresses Baptists, lauds Carter 6-15, 433A2
At Intl Eucharistic Cong 8-8, 596A3
Bishops review abortn stand 9-10, assert neutrality 9-16, 686D1-B2
Tex Baptist ldr backs 10-10, 763C2
Debates Carter 10-22, 802D1

RESIGNATIONS

Cabinet & Subcabinet
Butz, Agri secy 10-4, 743F3
Dunlop, Labor secy 1-14, 23B1
Frizzell, Interior undersecy 5-27, 412B2
Pate, Commerce asst secy 1-27, 186D2
Sisco, State undersecy 2-23, 186E2

Diplomatic
Brewster, amb to Ecuador 3-17, 232G1
Bruce, NATO rep 1-30, 186D2
Cooper, amb to E Ger 5-17, 412B2
Farkas, amb to Lux 5-4, 412B2
Moynihan, amb to UN 2-2, 89B1
Silberman, Yugo amb 11-17, 910B2

Miscellaneous
Bell, Educatn comr 5-2, 412A2
Bush, CIA dir 11-24, 917C2
Gregory, Traffic Safety admin 2-26, 232G1
Hampton, Civil Svc Comm chrmn 2-10, 232G1
Low, NASA dep dir 3-19, 232A2
Nelson, CIA dep dir 4-27, 412B2
Pollard, NRC projct mgr 2-9, 115A1
Rauscher, Cancer Inst dir 9-20, 876D1
Reid, FCC member 5-27, 412B2
Sommer, SEC comr 3-6, 232A2

RESOURCES, Natural—*See also ENERGY, RECREATION in this section above*
'77 budget proposal 1-21, 63F1, 64G2
'77 budgets compared 231A2
Vetoes planning bill 10-1, 919B2
Strip-mining bill not cleared 10-2, 883A1, F2
Debates Carter 10-22, 801D2-A3

SCIENCE
Lists future goals 7-1, 488F3
Wider gene research rules urged 7-19, 9-22, 860D3
Awards Medals of Science 10-18, 858B3
Nobel laureates score claim 10-26, 840B2, D2 ★

SECURITY, Personal—*See PERSONAL above*

SPACE—*See ASTRONAUTICS in this section above*

STATE of the Union Message
Delivers 1-19, 36F2-39G3; text 37A1
Cong reactn 1-19, Muskie rebuttal 1-21, 39G3, 40E1
Shapp scores 1-20, 40A3

TAXES
Plans estate-tax change 1-5, 3B3
State of Union message 1-19, 36G2, 37G2, 39F1
'77 budget proposals 1-21, 62C3, 63C1-A2
Econ Rpt 1-26, 66B3; excerpts 67A1, A3
Submits Soc Sec plan 2-9, 110C1
Proposes estate-tax chng 3-5, 179G3
Signs '75 cuts extensn bill 6-30, 492G1
Cites in public works veto 7-6, 518B2
Urges Cong action 7-19, 532C1
Acceptance speech cites 8-19, 611D3, 612C2
Biog sketch cites 614F1
Carter scores 8-30, 645B2
Vows educ tax credits 9-15, 686B1
Disputes Carter on tax-relief proposals 9-17—9-20, 703G2-704C1
Debates Carter 9-23, 701D1, F1, A2-E3, 702G1, C3
Scores Carter on church stand 10-2, 743E2
Soc Sec plan not cleared 10-2, 883A1, 884C1
Signs tax bill, to seek more cuts 10-4, 742C3
Calls Carter big taxer 10-13, 763G2
Carter vs chrgs 10-15; replies 10-16, 785A1
Scores Carter 10-16, 784B2
Debates Carter 10-22, 800C1, F3, 801F3
Vows cuts, backs some loopholes 10-23—10-25, 802G3, 803F1, A2
Carter scores proposal 10-30, 827F1
Pledges tax cut 11-1, 826A3

TRANSPORTATION
State of Union message 1-19, 37D3, F3, 39C2, D2
'77 budget proposals 1-21, 63F1, 64A3, 65F3
Signs RR aid bill, urges other regulatory reforms 2-5, 109G3
Southern-Delmarva talks fail 3-23, 235F2
Orders new canal ship-measuring system 3-23, 292B1
'77 budgets compared 231A2
Signs Conrail funds bill 3-30, 233E2
Amtrak buys corridor 4-1, 235C2
Signs RR safety bill 7-8, 919D3
Signs '76-80 air aid authorizn 7-12, 567A1
Extends noise rule to old planes 10-21, 849C1
Debates Carter 10-22, 801E3
Airlines get antinoise rule 11-18, 868C3
Rejcts CAB transatlantic plan 12-28, 992A2

VETERANS—*See DEFENSE & Armed Forces in this section above*

WELFARE—*See POVERTY above*

WHITE House Staff—*See under APPOINTMENTS in this section above; also personal names*

WOMEN
Suspends HEW schl events bias 7-7, 535E2-C3

1976

YOUTH
Signs summer jobs bill 4-15, 282C2
Signs '77 food funds bill 7-12, 533C3
Urges actn vs crime 9-27, 723G3

FORD, Mrs. Gerald Rudolph (Betty Bloomer)
Pullen joins staff 1-21, 40D3
Greets Spain king, queen 6-2, 459B2
Visits Iowa 6-18, 451B1
Campaigns in Minn 6-25, 467A3
Campaigns in Miss 7-25, 550C2
GOP conv cheers 8-16, 615F1
Cited in Ford biog sketch 613F2
'72 spending cited 10-8, 764C1
In Buffalo 10-10, 763C3
Graham gets Freedom Medal 10-14, 859A1
Reads concession statemt 11-3, 818D3
Visits Pocantico 11-21, 887A3
Sees Mrs Carter 11-22, 880F2
Gets Mich U honorary degree 12-19, 980D2

FORD, Rep. Harold E. (D, Tenn.)
Reelected 11-2, 822D3, 830B4

FORD 2nd, Henry
Lauds Carter 5-7, 343D2
Cosponsors Carter business mtg 7-22, 550G3
Carter, Ford donatns rptd 10-22, 939C1

FORD, Jack
Campaigns for dad 7-10, 513C3

FORD, Paul
Dies 4-12, 316A1

FORD, William Clay
Named to McCarthy ticket 2-5, 95B1

FORD, Rep. William D. (D, Mich.)
Reelected 11-2, 829E4

FORD Foundation
Kalman Silvert dies 6-15, 524F3

FORD Motor Co.
Price hike in effect 1-5; wage-price cncl scores 1-12, hike rescinded 1-15, 280A3
'75, 4th ¼ profits rptd 2-19, 215D3
GM workers win Trade Act aid 4-14, 348A3
Layoffs rptd 4-15, 280G2
Sup Ct backs recall fines 4-19, 331E2
On '75 Fortune 500 list 437A1, D1, F2
US ends car dumping probe 5-4, 321C2
Ford lauds Carter 5-7, 343D2
Some workers get Trade Act aid, total cited 6-7, 431A2
UAW contract talks open 7-20, 570F1
Ford cosponsors Carter mtg 7-22, 550G3
Capri price hike set 8-16, 988D1
UAW target co 8-24, workers favor strike 8-27, 1st offer rejected 8-31, 669B2
UK strikes end 8-26, 651B3
Dow falls re strike rpts 9-1, 847A1
UAW begins strike 9-14, 689D2
EPA gas-econ ratings 9-22, 766C2-770B2
Car price hikes rptd 9-28, 747G2
Ford-Markley golf trip cited 9-30, 723G1
'74, '75 zero US tax, forgn paymts rptd 10-2, 10-14, 847F1, G1, F2
Strike cited re car sales 10-6, 747F3
UAW ratifies contract 10-12, 789B1
Strike cited re Sept indl output, indicator 10-15, 10-29, 806G1, 833D1
Spanish plant opens 10-25, 929A2
Oct sales down 11-3, 885F2
Canada plant suspensn rptd 11-16, 885C2
Strike end cited re Canada jobless drop 12-8, 945C2
Aeronutronic Ford Corp.
'75 arms sales listed 2-6, 147B3

FOREIGN Affairs (journal)
Williams on OPEC aid to poor nations 15E1
Rpts Israel troop exit plan 9-17, 699D2

1977

FORD, Mrs. Gerald Rudolph (Betty Bloomer)
Plans to write memoirs 3-9, 236C3
At Natl Women's Conf 11-19, 917E3

FORD 2nd, Henry
Quits Ford Foundatn 1-11, Bundy comments 1-12, 55E3-56D1
Irvine takeover offer 3-3, 274D3
Names 3-man chief exec panel 4-14, 409B1
Vs Carter energy plan 4-21, 320D1
Group wins Irvine Co 5-20, 519E1
'76 pay rptd 5-23, 408D3

FORD, Jack
Joins Rolling Stone staff 2-24, 354C2

FORD, John
Gertrude Astor dies 11-9, 952B2

FORD, Mary
Dies 9-30, 788B1

FORDE, Lorna
Sets 440-yd dash mark 1-14, 603A1

FORD Foundation
Ford quits 1-11, Bundy comments 1-12, 55E3-56F1
A-power study issued 3-21, disputed 3-26, 234A3, G3
LeMelle confrmd Kenya, Seychelles amb 5-9, 418F1

FORD Motor Co.
'76 productn, sales rptd up 1-3, 1-6, 38E3, 39A1
Ford quits foundatn 1-11, 55E3
Air bag test program set 1-18, 213D2
Hikes car, truck prices 2-7, 155D3
EPA acts to halt productn 2-8, 113B1
To promote S Africa equality 3-1, 160B3
Layoffs 4-11—4-15, May new-car sales 6-3, 463C3, D3
3-man chief exec panel named 4-14, 409B1
Carter energy plan reactn 4-21, 320D1
On '76 Fortune 500 list 340D1, C3
Australia plant set 5-5, 389D1
Egypt plant agreemt OKd 5-10, 390A2
Sup Ct declines claim vs FTC 5-16, 419D2
Ford, Iacocca '76 pay rptd 5-23, 408D3
Rpts forgn payoffs 6-15, 503B2
On US air bag order 6-30, 522C1
UK workers ask 15% pay hike 7-20, 581D1
2d ½ profits record rptd 8-15, 668F3
Fan, fuel tank recalls set 8-16, 651A3
GM hikes '78 prices 8-23, 722D3
Aug new-car sales rptd up 9-6, 722G2
EPA fuel-econ ratings issued 9-19, 723C3
Cuts some small car prices 10-3, hikes '78 model prices 10-5, 859B2
3d ¼ record profits, sales rptd 10-27, 11-14, 918C2
Egypt truck pact signed 10-29, Arabs vow contd boycott 10-30, 11-3, 863G1
Ford Aerospace & Communications Corp. (formerly Aeronutronic Ford Corp.)
US-UK mil info exchng OKd 5-16, 379G3

FOREGO (race horse)
Named top older horse 12-13, 970F3, G3

FOREIGN Aid (non-U.S.)—*See specific country, region, group (e.g., WORLD Bank Group) and commodity names; also DEVELOPING Nations*

1978

FORD, Rep. Harold E. (D, Tenn.)
Reelected 11-7, 852D2

FORD, Henry (1863-1947)
VW halts 'beetle' line 1-19, 74D3

FORD II, Henry
Sees Vorster 1-16, backs S Africa investmt 1-19, 38G3
Sees Carter, backs inflatn plan 4-20, 5-11, 361A3
Sued on kickbacks, bribes 4-25, 5-16; denies chrgs 5-2, 5-11, 390G2-391C1
On '77 top-paid execs list 5-15, 364F3
Promotes Caldwell, brother 6-8, fires Iacocca 7-13; rift rptd 7-17, 642D1-D2
Nader scores Pinto recall pact 8-22, rebuts 8-26, 719D1
Caldwell named Ford pres 10-16, 808F3

FORD, Phil
2d in col basketball 3-13, 272D2
In NBA draft 6-9, 457F2

FORD, Susan
Engagement announced 10-17, 844C3

FORD, Sen. Wendell (D, Ky.)
Votes vs Panama Canal neutrality pact 3-16, 177F2
Votes vs 2d Canal pact 4-18, 273B1

FORD, William Clay
Promoted at Ford Motor 6-8, Iacocca fired 7-13, 642F1, D2

FORD, Rep. William David (D, Mich.)
Reelected 11-7, 851F1

FORDE, Lorna
Sets indoor 500-mtr run record 1-15, 76A3
Sets 400-mtr dash mark 6-8—6-10, 600B3

FORD & Earl Design Associates
Named in Ford suit 5-16, 391A1

FORDHAM University (New York City)
Burger receives Stein Award, defends judicial lobbying 10-25, 832E3

FORD Motor Co.
'77 sales gain rptd 1-5, 4D3
FTC chrgs auto engine defect 1-13, 67F2
S Africa investmt backed 1-19, 38G3
Mich sues for pollution 2-1, 163C3
Pinto crash liability set at $128.5 mln 2-6, 185B3
Engine flaw notificatn rptd 2-14, 348D1
UK unit ends strike 2-20, 132C1
Pinto crash award cut 3-31, 264F3
Small car prices hiked 4-17, 283B3
Ford sees Carter, backs inflatn plan 4-20, 5-11, 361A3
Ford, 19 others sued on kickbacks, bribes 4-25, 5-16; chrgs denied 5-2, 5-11, 390G2-391C1
On '77 Fortune 500 list 5-8, 325E1
Pinto fails fed safety tests 5-8, 366B1
Prices hiked; Strauss backing rptd, pricing tactic altered 5-9, 361C3, 362E2
HMO planned 5-10, 578E1
Ford, Iacocca on '77 top-paid execs list 5-15, 364F3
Brazil factory workers strike 5-15—5-23, 412B1, F1
Small-car prices hiked 6-6, 428B2
Caldwell promoted 6-8, Iacocca fired 7-13; Ford-Iacocca rift rptd 7-17, 642D1-D2
Pintos, Bobcats recalled 6-9, deaths rptd 7-6, 7-8, 569B3
Ontario plant set 8-3, US scores Ottawa 8-4, 613B2
Argentina investmt hike seen 8-17, 793E2
Pinto recall pact reached with NHTSA 8-21; Nader, Ford trade chrgs 8-22—8-30; sales rptd up 9-14, 719B1
Transmissn hazard warned by NHTSA 8-29, 719A2
Indicted in Ind Pinto deaths 9-13, 718F3-719A1
GM cuts '79 sporty car prices 9-13, 936B2
4th-ranked cash-rich US co 9-18, 716E3
'79 model prices hiked 9-19, 936A2
UK workers strike 9-21—10-9, 763F1, D3
AMC, UAW sign 2-yr pact 9-25, 737B3
Chile facilities to be returned 10-5, 796D1
Colombia store bombed 10-9, 814C3
FTC repossessed cars complaint setld 10-14, 942C1
Caldwell named pres 10-16, 808E3
Iacocca separatn pay rptd 11-1, joins Chrysler 11-2, 936A1
UK strike ends 11-22, sanctns set 11-28; profit drop seen 11-23, 923C2-G3
Nov sales drop rptd 12-6, 935E3
More '79 model prices hiked 12-12, 1004D1

FOREGO (race horse)
Retired 6-10, 539D3

FOREHAR, Darius
Arrested 11-11, 869C2
Released 12-6, 929C2

FOREIGN Aid (non-U.S.)—*See DEVELOPING Nations; country, region, group and commodity names*

1979

FORD, Harrison
Hanover Street released 5-17, 528E2
Frisco Kid released 7-6, 820C1

FORD, Henry (1863-1947)
Harry Bennett dies 1-4, 104F2

FORD II, Henry
Greets Teng in Atlanta 2-1, 83G2
Nephew rejcts dissident stockholders role, seeks Ford bd spot 2-26, 202D3
Ford stockholders suit barred in NY 3-8, 202A3
Sets retiremt 3-14, 202G2
Hotel expenses rptd repaid 4-12, Cohn suit cited 5-10, 366D2, G2
Caldwell to succeed; B Ford feud erupts 5-10, 366B2
On '78 top-paid execs list 5-14, 347G3, 348A1

FORD, Michael
Daughter born 4-22, 392G3

FORD, Phil
NBA assist ldr 4-8, 290G2
Named NBA top rookie 5-16, 526A2

FORD, Sarah Joyce
Born 4-22, 392F3

FORD, Susan
Marries 2-10, 176B1

FORD, William Clay
Family feud marks annual mtg 5-10, 366E2

FORDE, Einar
Named Norway educ min 10-5, 774F1

FORD Foundation
Bundy sets retiremt, Thomas named pres 1-30, 78D3
Nixon Admin pub TV moves disclosed 2-24, 194E1
Adult illiteracy study issued 9-8, 785G3

FORD Motor Co.
Prices hiked 1-3, 5C1
Harry Bennett dies 1-4, 104F2
'78 sales rise rptd 1-5, 5B1
Diesel exhaust rule protested 1-10, 16D3
Spain export hike rptd 1-31, 101A1
Teng visits Atlanta plant 2-1, 83D2
BL workers reject strike 2-9, 115F3
Ford heir rejcts dissident stockholders role, seeks bd spot 2-26, 202D3
Chrysler retains ad agency 3-1, 188B1
Dissident stockholders suit barred in NY 3-8, 202A3
Brazil metalworkers strike 3-13—3-27, 328C3
Ford sets retiremt 3-14, 202G2
EPA sues 3-22, 206C3
Price hike rptd 3-31, 305E2
Trucking stoppage over 4-10, 262D2
New Europn plant barred, expansn planned 4-24, 299G2
Brandeis sells bond re S Africa 4-27, 333A1
On '78 Fortune 500 list 5-7, 304E1
Caldwell elected Ford successor; B Ford feud erupts 5-10, 366B2
Houston Astros sold 5-11, NL owners OK 5-16, 619D1
Ford, Caldwell '78 pay rptd 5-14, 347G3, 348A1
Collective bargaining on food issues backed by Sup Ct 5-14, 383A3
'Car of the future' plan set 5-18, 441C3
Spain plant cited 6-6, 428B2
Ford heir barred from contesting will 7-16, 631D1
UAW contract talks begin 7-17, 598A1
Argentina investmt planned, 1st 1/2 sales rptd 7-20, 562F1
UAW vs Chrysler wage freeze plea 8-3, 662D3
Dealer prices cut 8-22, Aug sales rptd 9-5, 663A3, D3
Brazil alcohol fuel dvpt plan set 8-18, 871D2
UAW job action scored 8-22, 831A3
Mazda maker share purchased 9-7, 745D3
UAW reaches accord with GM 9-14, 698B1
Iacocca, ex-Ford execs get top Chrysler posts 9-20, 699B3
Layoffs set 9-27, 10-22, 806F1
Sept sales rptd down 10-4, 806A2
'80 model prices hiked 10-10, 963F3
UAW contract ratified 10-22, 805G3
UAW, Chrysler reach accord 10-25, 805F2
3d 1/4 profits, sales down 10-25, 806B1
Brazil metalworkers strike 10-29, 833B2
3d 1/4 profit drop cited 10-31, 923C1
Auto makers FTC challenge declined by Sup Ct 11-5, 884F2
Oct, Nov sales slump rptd 11-6, 12-5, 963F2
Rebates set 11-16, 963B3
700 S African blacks fired 11-21, 899C3
Industry layoff total cited 12-4, 964C3

FORD Motor Co. v. National Labor Relations Board
Case decided by Sup Ct 5-14, 383C2

FOREHAR, Darius
Named Iran labor min 2-13, 105G2
Loses Iran labor post, named roving amb 9-28, 752D2

FOREIGN Aid (non-U.S.)—*See DEVELOPING Nations; country, region, group and commodity names*

1980

FORD, Rep. Harold E. (D, Tenn.)
Reelected 11-4, 844D2

FORD, Harrison
Empire Strikes Back released 5-21, 675D2

FORD II, Henry
Kickback lawsuit dropped 1-11; Cohn replaced in heir's suit 3-12, 225C3-F3
Divorce setlmt rptd 2-20, 200F2
Resigns as chairman 3-13, 224C3
W Ford named vice chrmn 4-10, 456C2
Art auctnd for record sums 5-13, 472A1, D1

FORD, Ita
Found slain in El Salvador 12-4, 921B1

FORD, Michelle
Wins Olympic medals 7-21, 7-27, 623C3, D3

FORD, Steven
Paternity suit settled 2-28, 199A2

FORD, William Clay
Cohn replaced in Benson Ford suit 3-12, 225E3
Named Ford vice chrmn 4-10, 456C2

FORD, Rep. William D. (D, Mich.)
Loses Mich primary 8-5, 682E3
Reelected 11-4, 843F1, 851D1

FORD Foundation
Job project gains rptd few 2-27, 228E3

FORD Motor Co.
Prices hiked 1-2, 14D2
Layoffs, plant closings set 1-3, 1-10, 35F1-B2
'79 sales rptd down 1-4, 14C2
S Africa strikers rehired 1-9; activist detained 1-10, 60C3, G3
Ford kickback suit settled 1-11; Ford heir chngs counsel 3-12, 225C3-F3
Jan sales rptd down 2-5, 127A3
Ford divorce setlmt rptd 2-20, 200F2
'79 profit, 4th 1/4 loss rptd 2-21; $1 bln credit line rptd added 3-24, 287D3-G3
S Africa unit scored re black pay, lauded re integratn 2-27, 195A2
Mustang passes crash test 2-28, 225A2
UAW contract said to violate wage-price guidelines 3-7, sanctions imposed 3-26, 225F2
Acquitted in Ind Pinto trial, evidence rptd restricted 3-13, 185B3-186D1
Ford resigns, Caldwell replaces; Justice Dept paymts probe rptd dropped 3-13, 224C3
Mar sales drop rptd 4-3; rebates cited for Jan, Feb sales rise 4-4, 287A3, D3
Prices hiked 4-3, 288C1
'79 top TV advertiser 4-4, 376B2
W Ford named vice chrmn 4-10, 456C2
Mahwah, 2 other plants to close; 15,000 jobs eliminated, 43,000 layoffs rpt 4-15, 287E1, B2
Brazil plant hit by metalworkers strike 4-19, 310C1
1st 1/4 losses rptd 4-28, 384D1
On '79 Fortune 500 list 5-5, 290E1, 291B1
Prices hiked 5-5, rebates offered 5-9, 384C2
Merit pay hikes, other benefits suspended 5-9, 384A1
Truck import duty lauded 5-20, 384C2
Ephlin elected to UAW post 6-4, 457B2
Spain plant productivity rptd 6-4, 467F3
May sales plunge rptd 6-5, 481E3
NHTSA determines transmissn hazard 6-11; denial issued, info suit filed 8-20, 702D1
Mex engine plant planned 6-12, 465B2
Mahwah (NJ) plant closed 6-20; worker layoffs rptd 6-21, 481F3
Supplier price cuts asked 6-21, 481G3
S Africa strike ends 6-25, 499C2
'80 price increases not seen 7-3, 556F2
Canada May, June sales down 7-5, 520A3
June sales rptd down 7-6, 556C2
Toyota productn talks revealed 7-9; rejectn rptd 7-14, 556G2-A3
GM pledges '85 fuel-efficient cars 7-9, 556F3
2d 1/4 losses rptd 7-29, 574A1, D1
Japan import curbs asked 8-4, 599C1
Worker US jobless aid OKd 8-14, 647F3
Reagan sees auto execs 9-2, 664E2
Aug sales rptd down 9-4, 701G2
Detroit tax revenue drop rptd 9-8, 743G2
Worker layoffs rptd 9-11, 701A3
AMC-UAW pact set 9-17, 725C1
Carter visits Mich plant 10-1, 739B2
Sept sales rptd down 10-6, 784G2
Auto import hearings held 10-8—10-10, 823E1
Ford heir drops family suit 10-10, 985F2
3d 1/4 loss rptd 10-28, 823A1
UK unit profits 'non-existent' 10-31, 886A3
Oct sales rptd down 11-4, 857B1, C1
ITC bars Japan import curbs 11-10, 866E3
Job-bias case setld 11-25, 899B2
W Ger unit lay-offs planned 11-27, 924C3
Subsidies offered 12-5, 938C2

FORD Motor Co. v. Milhollin
Case decided by Sup Ct 2-20, 170A3

FOREIGN Aid (non-U.S.)
World Bank '80 econ forecast grim 8-17, 628B3

1976 1977 1978 1979 1980

FOREIGN TRADE (U.S.)

1976

FOREIGN Aid—*Note: Only items involving U.S. aid are listed here. See also country, agency (e.g., WORLD Bank Group) and commodity names*
Econ aid tied to UN votes 1-9, 2A1
Food budget proposals 1-21, 66D2
Spain defns pact signed 1-24, 76E3, 77B1
Chile aid rptdly continues 1-26, 99B2
Guatemala quake aid rptd 2-4—2-11, 81E1, 120C3
India aid talks halt 2-17, 139D3
Kissinger pledges Latin aid 2-17, 2-24, 177C2, 178F1
House OKs '75 appropriatns 3-4, 181D2
Agri Dept sets milk aid 3-8, 186C1
Turkey pact signed 3-26, 244F1
Cong OKs Guatemala relief 4-12, 4-13, 283B3
Guatemala quake aid signed 4-21, 982E1; 6-30, 533E2
Cong OKs authorizatn bill 4-28, Ford vetoes 5-7, 344B3-345C1
Kissinger addresses UNCTAD 5-6, 317A1-318G1; 7-natn econ summit 6-28, 462B2
Italy quake aid OKd 5-11, 352B3
Simon for contd Chile aid 5-16, 464E3
France seeks US-Eur dvpt fund for Africa 5-17—5-18, 372A2
Spain defns pact ratified 6-21, 534F3; 7-23, 541D3
'76, '77 arms authorizatn, '76 fund bills signed 6-30, 532C3, 533B2
Mayors Conf resolution 7-1, 493D1
'75 donors ranked 7-12, 581G3
Italy loan ban disclosed 7-16, 530D3; repercusns 7-20, 557B1
Ikle scores A-aid 7-23, 739F2
Portugal pacts signed 8-13, 811E3
Rep Passman loses seat 8-14, 633B1
'77 funds signed 10-1, 806B3
Cong fails to clear Turkey pact 10-2, 883C3
AID cited re unauthorized aid 10-8, 814E1
Chile rejects US aid 10-19, 10-20, 870G3
2 win Rockefeller award 11-16, 911F3
Loan to Portugal set 11-16, Eur loan pending 11-23, 966G2
Turkey quake aid offered 11-25, 11-28, 897D1
Italy seeks credits 12-6, 947E1
UK rpts US-Bonn loan 12-15, 1003C3
US in IMF UK loan 12-21, 1004B1
Angola Aid—*See under 'A'*
Export-Import Bank—*See under U.S. GOVERNMENT*
Presidential Election
Carter on Ford veto 5-14, 390E3, G3
US Dem platform text 6-15, 476D3, 477A1
Carter proposals 6-23, 451E3
Mondale record cited 512G3
GOP platform text 8-18, 610E1, F3
Carter backs reforms 8-18, 617D2
Ford legis record cited 613F2, F3

1977

FOREIGN Aid (U.S.)—*See also commodity names*
US rpts rights abuses in 6 natns 1-1, 50E2
Ford '78 budget proposals 1-17, 31F1, 33B1
Turkey deal rptd delayed 2-13, 109B1
Portugal loan OKd 2-14; Carter urges Westn aid 4-1, sees Soares 4-20—4-22, 330B3
Carter call-in topic 3-5, 171F1
Human rights rpts issued 3-12, 186D3
Carter addresses UN 3-17, 185C2
Carter presents program 3-17, 210C3
Vance backs House rights amendmt 3-23, 210G3
Carter vs House rights amendmt 4-15, 299B2
Carter on Turkey arms aid 4-19, 351E1; 5-10, 359D1
Portugal mil aid signed 4-30, 339G1
Mondale in Portugal talks 5-16, 398B2
N-S talks end 6-3, 437B3
S Korea lobbying scheme detailed 6-5, 441D3
Sen OKs intl lending agency authorizatns 6-14, 477F2
Vance addresses OAS 6-14, 494D1
Greek mil pact signed 7-28, 617F3
'78 arms, security aid signed 8-4, 667G3
'78 economic aid signed 8-4, 668F1
'78 agri, food funds signed 8-12, 688B3
Korea cut fails in House 9-8, 774A2
Intl lending agency authorizatn, rights link cleared by Cong 9-21, 737B3
McNamara scores '76 poor natn aid level 9-26, 754G1
Food for Peace extended 9-29, 737B2
Carter, Cong in intl lending agency-rights compromise 9-30; US goals study asked 10-6, 815B2
Intl lending agency, other '78 funds cleared 10-19, 815A2; signed 11-1, 834D1
Polish credits OKd 12-30, 1001A2
Africa
Ethiopia aid cut planned 2-24, 142E1
Zaire emergency aid set 3-14, 3-16, 207G2, D3
More Zaire aid set 4-12, 265E1
Carter vs tanks to Zaire 4-22, 317A3, 321B3
Somalia arms aid offered 7-26, 587G3
Sahel region aid signed 8-4, 668G1
Somalia arms aid canceled 9-1, 684F2
Mozambique food aid set 12-2, 1000B1
Indochina
Nixon Viet vow disputed 2-22—5-23, 403E2
US missn to Viet, Laos 3-16—3-20; Carter gets rpt, OKs talks 3-23, 206C1
Carter links Viet aid, 'normal' ties 3-24, 229G2-A3
Viet asks aid 5-4, US bars 5-4, 5-5, 333C1-A3
Viet aid bid stalls talks 6-2—6-3, 441G1
Sen bars loans 6-14, 477C3
ECOSOC aid to Viet opposed 10-6, 770B2
Latin America
Argentina, Haiti, Peru rights abuse chrgd 1-1, 50E2
Argentina, Uruguay aid cuts planned 2-24; aid rejected 3-1, 142E1, B2
Brazil A-safeguards linked 3-1, 190C1
Nicaragua aid cutoff asked 3-4, 168F2
Brazil rejects mil aid 3-5, 167E3; cancels pact 3-11, 186C2
Guatemala rejcts mil aid 3-16, 187A2
El Salvador rejcts mil aid 3-16, 206G2
Nicaragua aid halt asked by Latin group 3-25, 476B1
Nicaragua aid withheld 4-7, House com backs mil aid cutoff 6-14, 475B3
Carter addresses OAS 4-14, 295C3, 296B1
Nicaragua aid cutoff defeated 6-23, 656F2
Chile loans blocked 6-28, 493A1
Chile rejects aid 6-28, 512G2
Young vows Carib aid 8-5—8-17, 646F1
Panama Canal accord rptd 8-10, Carter details 8-12, 621B1, C2
Jamaica aid resumed 9-12, 11-9, 884C2
Trinidad gets large Euro$ loan 9-19, 905F3
Mex indl dvpt aid plan rptd 9-23, 746E2
Panamanians vs Canal pact provisns 10-14, Torrijos defends 10-21, 809B2
Nicaragua rebel asks cutoff 10-26, 864G2
Panama aid pacts chrgd unconst 10-28; State Dept disputes 11-15, 912G1
Peru loan request rejected 12-15, 1015G1
Middle East
Iran rights abuse chrgd 1-1, 50E2
Israel budgets long-term aid 1-24, 99C2
Egypt import loan hike OKd 2-1, 390E2
'77 Israel aid hike rptd planned 2-7, 87A3
Egypt asks arms aid 4-4—4-5, 245A1
Leb asks arms aid 4-25, 316B3
'78 arms, security aid signed 8-4, 668A1, E1
Egypt MiG-21 repairing backed 9-15, 698C1

1978

FOREIGN Aid (U.S.)—*See also commodity names*
Carter urges 3d World aid 1-4, 2E1
Rights rpt on aid recipients released 2-9, 101C3
'79 security-related econ aid planned 2-22, 127D1, F1
Developing natn aid disputed by Carter, Venez pres 3-28, 3-29, 233E1
TV statns protest Canadian tax law 8-29, 686C3
Mil, security aid authrzn cleared 9-12, signed 9-26; provisns 734C1-G2
'79 IMF fund authrzn clears Sen, appropriatn OKd by conferees 9-22, 731E2, 732B1 ★
Mil, security aid, IMF fund bill cited in Cong roundup 10-15, 784F3
Mil, security aid funds, IMF contributn signed 10-18, 862C2, F2
Africa
S Africa aid ban asked by Nigeria 3-31, 233G2
Carter orders Africa curbs reviewed, scores Cong 5-16—5-23; Admin proposal rptd rejctd by Clark 5-24, 383A1
Carter denies knowledge of Africa proposal to Clark 5-24, 443D1
Ethiopia food aid rptd 6-4, 465A3
Africa aid stressed by Vance 6-20, 487E1
Carter signs '79 aid funds 10-18, 862E2
Asia
S Korea warned by House com 5-24, 406B2; House 5-31, 432G1
Viet World Bank loan opposed 8-8, 624F1
PI mil base-econ aid pact signed 12-31, 1000F2
Europe
Portugal gets $300 mln loan 3-2, 229G1
Admin moves to lift Turkey arms embargo 3-29—4-6; reactn 4-2—4-16 276G1-277A2
Admin moves to lift Turkey arms embargo set back 5-3, 5-11; reactn 5-12, 378B1
Turkey arms embargo end, US base reopening seen 6-28, 587C3
Turkey arms embargo end gets Cong prelim OK 8-1, reactn 8-2, 587D2-588B1
Portugal $100-mln loan released 10-4, 777D3
Greek mil aid cited 11-24, 924C2
Indochina—*See 'Asia' in this section above*
Latin America
Nicaragua aid cutoff rptd 2-1, 91D2; 2-22, 127E1
Haiti eases repressn 2-3, 94D3
Nicaragua aid resumed 5-16, 376D2, 593D2
OAS asks talks 7-1, 505C2
Argentina Eximbank hydro loan blocked 7-19; OKd 9-26, 792D2
Bolivia suspensn rptd 7-23, cutoff seen 7-26, 571B2
Bolivia mil aid resumed 8-15, 671A2
Nicaragua aid cutoff asked by 86 congressmen 10-13, 839G2
Nicaragua econ aid delay cited 11-9, 1018C3
Mex birth control, job funds urged 12-20, 1010E2
Middle East
'79 mil, security aid proposed 2-22, 127F1
Carter signs '79 aid funds 10-18, 862D2

1979

FOREIGN Aid (U.S.)
Carter budget proposals 1-22, 41C2; table 42E2
Rights rpt on 115 natns issued 2-10, 107G1, A2
Africa
Guadeloupe summit topic 1-5—1-6, 12G2
Sovt surrogate response seen 2-8, 89D2
S Africa '72-78 loans rptd 4-2, 270D2
UK Tory policy cites 4-11, 285E3
CAE aid halt planned 8-9, 601B3
Uganda vowed aid 9-19, 721F1
Asia
Thai mil credits hiked 1-21, 84E2
Afghan aid cut 2-22, 147C1
Pakistan aid cut 4-6, 277B2
Cambodia food aid plea issued 8-8—8-9, 600E3
Pak aid sanctns studied 8-11, 607F3
China aid plan disclosed 8-24, 644A3
Pak asks aid resumptn 9-22, 794E2
S Korea intl loans to be weighed 10-17—10-19, 803A3
Cambodia food aid vowed 10-24, 811F1
Europe
Poland loan OKd 1-6, 39B3
Turkey aid offer rptd 1-12, 40B2; OECD OKs role 2-6, 116E3
Turkey seeks aid 3-16, 214B2
Poland loan signed 3-30, 279G2
Hungary to seek $300 mln loan 3-30, 279B3
Turkey pkg agreed, hailed 5-30, 397E1 F2
Turkey mil aid barred by House 6-21, 488C2
Indochina—*See 'Asia' above*
Latin America
Nicaragua aid reduced 2-8, 255C1, D1
Grenada overtures rptd 3-24, 236D3
Nicaragua junta aid proposed 7-6, 503E3, 504G1
Carib aid rptd 7-6, 960F3
Nicaragua food, med aid rptd 7-19, 574A2; scored 8-4, 603A3
El Salvador mil aid review rptd 8-2, 652C2
Nicaragua seeks arms aid 8-31, 689A3
DR, Dominica relief efforts rptd 9-3, 690E3
Nicaragua aid pkg OKd 9-11, 731E2
Nicaragua junta ldrs see Carter 9-24, 731C3
Carter sets Carib aid rise 10-1, 737G1, 739A1
Castro asks 3d World aid 10-12, 778B3
El Salvador mil aid seen 10-16, 790G2
Chile aid reduced 11-30, 927E2
Bolivia food aid set 12-3, 926G1
Middle East
N Yemen aid plan rptd 2-8, 89D2; 2-11, 143C2; 2-26, 144E2; 3-12, 178B3
House com hearing on Egypt-Israel aid 5-8, 341B2
N Yemen rptdly asks more mil aid 6-12—6-13, 436G3
Egypt, Israel ask more aid 9-11, 677A2
Oman proposes Persian Gulf security aid 10-14—10-16, 804B2
Refugees—*See INDOCHINA—Refugees*

1980

FOREIGN Aid (U.S.)—*See also commodity names*
Carter budget proposals, table 1-28, 70E1
Rights rpt on world issued 2-5, 86B2
Eximbank loan offer to Australia co sparks probe 2-19; Sen com probes loan policies 5-10—5-13; GAO probe urged 10-1, 988F3
GOP platform adopted 7-15, 537A1
Muskie addresses UN sessn 8-25, 642G2
Poor-natn aid vowed by Carter at World Bank-IMF mtg 9-30, 761G3
'81 authrzn clears Cong 12-3, signed 12-16, 981C3
Stopgap funds bill clears Cong 12-15, 981A3; signed 12-16, 982C1
Africa
US to seek Kenya hike 2-22, 142B2
Zaire corruptn found 2-28, 356C2
Zimbabwe pact signed 4-18, 301C2
Somalia pact signed 8-21, 645B3
Mugabe asks Zimbabwe aid 8-27, 674F2
Somali pact scored by House subcom 8-28, 661B3
Somali pact scored by Ethiopia 9-12, 735G3
Somalia refugee aid rptd 9-21, 736D1
Somali pact OKd by House subcom 9-30, 735C3
Arms Deals—*See ARMAMENTS*
Asia
Cambodia relief aid vowed 3-26, 261F3
Europe
Turkey aid pkg set 1-9, 22A3
Turkey accord signed 3-29, 255A3
Turkey OECD aid OKd 4-15, 295A3
Turkey influence linked 5-30, 445B3
Poland asks 22% credit hike 8-27, Carter urges Westn aid 8-29; W Ger, USSR reactn 9-3, 9-4, 659C1
Poland gets $670 mln grain credit 9-12, 710F2
Poland seeks US loan, grain credit rise proposed 11-13, 879B1
Latin America
El Salvador aid pkg weighed 2-22, 149C2; House subcom holds hearings 3-27, 200D2
Bolivia aid progrm rptd 3-26, 272B2
El Salvador aid pkg signed, '80 total rptd 3-28, 254A1
Honduras '80, '81 aid hikes rptd 4-20, 314B1
El Salvador land reform funds 4-29, 351D3
Nicaragua authrzn clears Cong 5-19, 410A1
Nicaragua appropriatn clears Cong 5-31, 709F2
Nicaragua supplemental appropriatn clears Cong 7-2, Carter signs 7-8, 515E1
Bolivia aid suspended 7-17, 546D3; cut off 7-25, 577E1
Nicaragua '79-80 aid rptd 7-19, 565B3
Nicaragua funds blocked 8-1, released 9-12, 709E2-B3
Bolivia drug progrms halted 8-13, 667E3
El Salvador $90 mln aid scored by intl rights groups 10-15, 829E1
El Salvador aid suspended 12-5, 941E2
Haiti aid talks shunned; Reagan support seen 12-8, 942C3, F3
El Salvador $20 mln aid renewed 12-17, 993F1
'81 Jamaica hike, Seaga electn rptd linked 12-20, 981B3
Middle East
Israel aid request cited 1-15, 59C2
Carter pres renominatn acceptance speech 8-14, 613E1
Israel seeks $3 bln 8-20, 662F3
Israel econ, mil aid vowed 9-4, 681E3
'81 Egypt, Israel authrzn clears Cong 12-15, signed 12-16, 981C3

1976

FOREIGN Correspondents Association of the Philippines
Vs US newsman's ouster 11-5, 855E1
FOREIGN Forwarding Inc.
Arab boycott noncompliance rptd 11-2, 986A3

1977

FOREIGN Intelligence Advisory Board, President's—*See under U.S. GOVERNMENT*

1978

FOREIGNER (singing group)
Double Vision on best-seller list 8-2, 620F1; 9-6, 708F1
Double Vision on best-seller list 12-6, 971F1

1979

FOREIGN Claims Settlement Commission of the United States—*See under U.S. GOVERNMENT*

1976

FOREIGN Policy, U.S.—*See also appropriate headings under U.S. GOVERNMENT; also specific countries, organizations, subjects*
Dem platform text 6-15, 475G3-476G1, 477F3
Carter airs views 6-24, 490C1
Mondale legis record cited 512B3, C3
Reagan lauds Schweiker 7-26, 550F1
Carter briefed 7-29, 551D1
GOP platform text 8-18, 602A2, 608D2-611C3
Carter sees Nixon-Ford continuity 8-20, 632F1
Ford urges as pres debate topic 8-24, 632G3
Carter scores Admin 8-25, 632B1
Mondale for reorientatn 8-25, 645F2
Ford, Connally hit Carter inexperience 8-27, 644G3
Ford, Carter TV debate set 9-1, 644B1
Carter stresses morality 9-8, 664A3
Dole scores Carter 9-9, 666A1
Mondale scores 'expediency' 9-10, 687C1
Govt in sunshine bill signed 9-13, 688E3
Cong sets '77 budget levels, chart 9-16, 706B2
Ford stresses peace 9-17, 704D1
Mondale campaign theme 9-26, 724F3
Dole attacks Carter 10-4, 10-5, 743F1-B2
Ford, Carter debate 10-6, 740B2-742G2
Carter scores Ford 'discrepancies' 10-8, 762E1
Dole, Mondale debate 10-15, 782G2, 783G1, B3
Ford scores Carter, Carter rebuts 10-26, 802G3-803C1
Carter plans bipartisan conf 10-26, 803C2
Carter sees continuity 11-4, 819G2
Kissinger briefs Carter 11-20, 881D1
Carter stresses bipartisanship 11-23, 881G1; 12-1, 916C3
Vance on policy 12-3, 916D1

FOREIGN Policy (magazine)
Kissinger, Ford score aides on leaks to Sheehan 3-12, 3-17, 198C2
FOREIGN Policy Association (N.Y.)
Carter addresses 6-23, 451D2
FOREIGN Relations, Council on (Chicago)
Ford addresses 3-12; Carter 3-15, 198E1, A2

FOREIGN Trade—*Note: Only items involving U.S. trade are listed here. See also country, group (e.g., EC, UN) and commodity names*
Non-fed taxes on imports OKd 1-14, 23G2
SELA scores '74 Trade Act 1-15, 60E2
A-materials export ban urged 1-19, 115B3
Dec, '75 surplus 1-27, 91A1
Austria camera deal rptd 1-30, 97F3
Sweden protests import curbs 2-2, 104A1
Coleman OKs Concorde test 2-4, 94C3
Kissinger tours Latin Amer 2-16—2-24, 177A1-E3
Intl Trade Comm rpts rise in stainless flatware, shoe imports, urges tariff actn 2-21, 3-2, 213D2-D3

1977

FOREIGN Policy, U.S.—*See also appropriate headings under U.S. GOVERNMENT; also specific countries, organizations, subjects*
Ford State of Union message 1-12, 12F2, E3, 13A1, C2, E2
'77-82 Ford budget outlays table 32F2
Carter inaugural; text 1-20; 26B1, 27E1
Carter statemt to world; text 1-20, 26D1, A2
Carter fireside chat 2-2, 75B2
Carter budget revisions 2-22, 125B2
Carter defends speaking out 3-24, 230D1
Brown chrgs cong meddling 3-27, 231G3
Carter poll standings 4-4, 251E1
Kissinger on moralism 4-5, 247D2
'77 supplemental funds signed 5-4, 339E1
Nixon-Frost TV interview 5-12, 385D3
Cong sets '78 budget target 5-17, 405A1
Carter outlines new policy 5-22, 397A1
IWC cuts whaling quotas 6-24, 496G3
Carter defers world trip 11-7, 854A1
Carter begins world trip 12-29, 1000E3

FOREIGN Service—*See under U.S. GOVERNMENT—STATE*

FOREIGN Trade & Investment (non-U.S.)—*See also specific country, group (e.g., EC) names; also commodity names*
'76 trade rptd up 3-8, 188D2-C3
Japan-Zenith Radio case impact on world trade seen 4-12, 318B2
Sugar pact talks 4-18—5-27, 457G3
7-natn summit vs protectnism, backs GATT talks; Bonn, Japan OK paymts deficit move 5-7—5-8, 357G1, G2, 358B2
Japan electronics duty order probed 5-23, 416B2
Commonwealth conf talks 6-8—6-15, 487D1
ASEAN seeks West ties 6-26—6-29, 537D1
IMF sees '76, '77 protectionism rise 7-31, 586A3
'76 world trade rptd up 7-31, 586C3
GATT scores protectionism 9-12, 717E2
'75 Japan-Eur steel pact cited 9-19, 775A2
IMF, World Bank mtg stresses econ growth lag effect on trade, protectionism, poor natn trade 9-26—9-30, 753D2, 754E1
Intl sugar pact OKd, '76 top exporters cited 10-7, 855B1
Nobel won by Ohlin, Meade 10-14, 951E3
GATT sees protectnism hurting indl natns 11-28, 933C3
Unctad common-fund commodity talks fail 12-1, 974E2
Bauxite base price set by 10 natns 12-7, 975A1
Multifiber pact extended, protectnist clause added 12-13, 974C3-975A1
Helsinki review conf adjourns 12-22, 997D2

FOREIGN Trade & Investment (U.S.)
Shoe import injury ruled 1-6, 248G1
'76 purchases from Taiwan rptd 1-12, 139F3
US customs duties budget table 32E2
Rumania most-favored natn status cited 2-20, 315B1
Canada wheat-price pact agreed 2-25, 158F2
Duty-free list modified 2-28, 189F2
Sugar imports injury ruled 3-3, quota cut asked; '76 data cited 3-14, 189C1
'76 coffee imports rptd 3-10, 209E1
Carter addresses UN 3-17, 185D2
Trade policy dilemma seen, Strauss role outlined 3-22—3-23, 248E3-249D1 *, E1

1978

FOREIGN Investment, U.S.—*See BUSINESS; MERGERS & Acquisitions; country names*
FOREIGN Policy, (U.S.)—*See also under CARTER; also appropriate headings under U.S. GOVERNMENT; also country, organization names; specific subjects*
Carter ends world trip 1-6, 1B1, 12A1
Carter State of Union Message 1-19, 29F2, 31F1
Carter budget proposals 1-23, 44F2; table 45D2
Carter in S America, Africa 3-28—4-3, 233A1-234E1
Goldwater scores Carter 5-1, 321B3
GOP sens score Carter 5-3, 342E2
Carter scores Cong restraints 5-19, 5-23, 382D3; Brzezinski backs 5-28, 399D1
Carter issues 'export consequences' order 9-26, businessmen score 10-10, 804G2
Diplomatic immunity law revisn signed 9-30, 750D3
Carter lauds Cong 11-6, 862D1
Nixon: to continue speaking out 11-10, 900B3

FOREIGN Policy Association (N.Y.)
Brzezinski addresses 12-20, 975E3, 996F1
FOREIGN Relations, Council on (Chicago)
Nitze addresses 12-5, 996A2

FOREIGN Trade (non-U.S.)—*See also country, group (e.g., EC, GATT) and commodity names*
Trade balance defined 50E1
Commonwealth regional conf sets study 2-16, 121D2
Helsinki review conf ends 3-9, 179B2
Coffee to be withheld by 8 Latin natns 3-10, 181A3
'77 vol, value rptd up; $ drop linked 3-13, 443E2
UK prime min urges Bonn summit plan 3-14, sees Carter 3-23, 226G2
Trudeau backs free trade 3-21, 225C3
Intl commodity fund planned 4-23, 391D2
Sovt-bloc shipping growth rptd, West concerned 7-11—8-24, 670G2-E3
7-natn Bonn summit, GATT talks backed 7-16—7-17, 543D3, 544C2, E2
Latin export bank opens 9-8, 828C3
Latin '77 exports rptd up 9-10, 828G2
World Bank head asks trade curbs end 9-25, 732F2
Arab Boycott—*See under BUSINESS*

FOREIGN Trade (U.S.)
Trade balance defined 50E1
OPIC loses new-policy writing power 1-1, protectionism cited 1-3, 67B1
Carter reaffirms free-trade policy 1-6, 1D1
Carter State of Union Message 1-19, 29F1, 30D2, 31A1, D2
US $ strategy re Bonn, Japan rptd 1-23, 27F2
Australia farmers vs curbs 1-25, 69D3
Carter bars chrome alloy duty hike; '77 imports, Rhodesian ban cited 1-29, 80E3
Carter bars nut, bolt import curbs 2-10, 181A2
Saudi '77 trade rptd 2-11, 113E2
AFL-CIO offers legis chngs 2-21, 142A1

1979

FOREIGN Languages and International Studies, President's Commission on—*See under U.S. GOVERNMENT*
FOREIGN Policy (U.S.)—*See also under CARTER; also appropriate headings under U.S. GOVERNMENT; also country, organization names; specific subjects*
Meany scores Admin 2-19, 148D2
Bush scores Admin 3-10, 186B1
Vance, Brzezinski defend 'new diplomacy' 5-1, 347F1-F2
Reagan seeks firm stand 11-13, 866D2
Reagan campaign themes cited 11-14, 982G1

FOREIGN Policy Association (N.Y., N.Y.)
Brown addresses 4-5, 258B1
Thatcher addresses 12-18, 968C2
FOREIGN Relations, Council on (Chicago, Ill.)
Brzezinski addresses 4-4, 258B1
FOREIGN Relations, Council on (N.Y., N.Y.)
Brown addresses 4-5, 258B1
FOREIGN Service—*See under U.S. GOVERNMENT–STATE*

FOREIGN Trade (non-U.S.)
Trade balance defined 33D1
'78 record value rptd, volume up; $ drop linked 2-8, 161A1
GATT pact signed, tariff cuts seen 4-12, 273A1-274B1
Westn exporter labor costs ranked 5-1, 374A2
Lome pact talks collapse 5-26, 398F3
Lome pact extensn set 6-27, 512G3
Lome pact extensn signed 10-31, 845E1
Protectionism, '79 econ woes linked 11-1, 827A1

FOREIGN Trade (U.S.)
Trade balance defined 33D1
Carter State of Union Message 1-23, 46G3, 47B1
Textile import protectn deal set 2-15, House OKs duty waiver bill 3-1, 159C2
Carter urges world pact 2-25, 150C2
Shoe import cap urged 3-6, 207C1
'78 paymts gap widened, trade deficit cited 3-21, 252D2
Duty waiver bill cleared 3-29, signed 4-3, 298E3
Top wheat exporting natn 4-3, 253B2
GATT pact signed, reactn 4-12, 273D1, 274B1
'78 profits, protectn linked by Fortune 5-7, 305E1

1980

FOREIGN Policy (U.S.)
GOP pres candidates score Admin 1-5, 4C2, F2, E3
GOP sen scores Dems 1-14, 32B1
Kennedy attacks 1-14, 32B3; 1-20, 50E2
Bush 'basic speech' excerpts 3-3, 208F2
Ford scores Admin 3-12, 208A1
Reagan outlines position 3-17, 208F1-B2
Vance outlines goals 3-27, 243C2
Reagan sets up panel 4-20, 304C3
Muskie sees continuity, outlines policies 5-7, 343C1; sets goals 5-9, 367A2
GOP plank scores Carter 7-10, 506G2-B3
Kissinger attacks Admin 7-15, 533C3, 534C3
GOP platform adopted; text 7-15, 536D1, B2
Reagan pres nominatn acceptance speech 7-17, 532B1, D2, 533A1-B2, E2
Dem conv keynote speech 8-11, 612A2*, A3
Anderson platform offered 8-30, 665G1, B2
Mondale scores Reagan stand 9-5, 780G1
Bush scores Admin policy 9-5, 9-25, 780D3, 781C1
Sullivan scores Brzezinski '79 Iran policy 9-6, 694C1
Reagan deplores weakness 9-24, 723A1
Reagan defends firmness 10-14, 779F3
Bush scores Carter 'flipflop' 10-16, 10-19, 817C3
Reagan asserts peace priority, bipartisanship theme 10-19—10-20, 801C2-802D1
Mondale: Reagan 'dangerous' 10-26, 816D3
Libertarian pres candidate cites stance 10-28, 818G2
Electn exit poll rptd 11-4, 838F1
Reagan plans policy shift, names bipartisan advisory panel 11-6, 837F1, 839C1, D2
Haig notes setbacks 12-22, 980D1
Block stresses food role 12-23, 980F1
FOREIGN Policy Association (N.Y., N.Y.)
Mugabe addresses 8-26, 674F2
Shagari addresses 10-3, 792D2, F2
FOREIGN Policy Research Institute
Arbatov on SALT 12-15, 951A1
FOREIGN Relations, Council on (Chicago, Ill.)
Reagan addresses 3-17, 208F1
US Defns Secy Brown addresses 12-18, 950C1
FOREIGN Service—*See under U.S. GOVERNMENT–STATE*
FOREIGN Service Journal
US amb's pol gaffes rptd 1-30, 200D2
FOREIGN Trade (non-U.S.)—*See also country, region, group and commodity names*
Trade balance defined 34F1
Wyndham-White dies 1-27, 104G3
World trade forecast 1-30, 197E3
Sovt bloc '79 Westn deficit down 4-1, 285B3
OECD backs free trade 6-3—6-4, 422G1
Venice summit vs protectnism, backs export credit negotiatns 6-23, 474C1
IMF econ forecast grim 6-24, 477E2
World Bank '80 econ forecast grim 8-17, 628B3
GATT sees global lag; oil prices, inflatn cited 9-16, 695C3
Islamic econ conf 11-4—11-6, 865C1
Geneva tin talks fail 12-8, 979B3
Arab Boycott—*See under BUSINESS*

FOREIGN Trade (U.S.)
Trade balance defined 34F1
Carter signs reorganizatn plan 1-2, 94G2
State of State messages 1-10, 1-15, 403B3, E3
Raw material sea route protectn urged 1-14, 32D1
Kennedy for single agency 2-6, 91B1
Eximbank loan offer to Australia co sparks probe 2-19; Sen com probes loan policies 5-10—5-13; GAO probe urged 10-1, 988F3
Protectionism poll rptd 6-26, 515F3
Banned item export curb set 8-2, 599G2
Dem plank on farm exports adopted 8-13, 615A2
Bush bars import quotas 10-16, 817B3
Reagan offers 8-pt econ plan 10-24, 817D2

1976

Brezhnev urges intl barriers end 2-24, 194D1
6-natn export credit pact 2-25, 164C2
Ford to curb gas imports 2-26, 149D2
Jan deficit rptd 2-27, 168B3
Ford threatens steel import quota 3-16, 212D3
Exports to Latins up in '75 3-19, 466B1
Feb deficit rptd 3-26, 230E1
Ford vows farmer protectn 4-3, 245F1
Ford bars shoe import curb 4-16; eases flatware, ceramic curbs 4-30, 321F3, 322D1
VW OKs US plant 4-23, 321E2
Mar, 1st ¼ deficit rptd 4-26, 307B1
'75 Fortune 500 data rptd 437G1
Forgn car mktg probe ends 5-4; VW dumping rptd 5-6, 320E3
'75 shrimp imports rptd 5-11, 431F1
Ford urges regulatory reform 5-13, 347A1
1st ¼ capital flow, merchandise trade rptd 5-17, 396C2, D3
Apr deficit rptd 5-26, Simon comments 5-30, 396E1, A2
US uranium role in S Africa-French A-plant deal rptd 6-1, 388D1
Ford sets specialty steel quotas 6-7; Japan OKs pact 6-9; EEC scores US 6-14, 430E3-431E1
Kissinger asks close US-Latin ties 6-9, vows Mex effort 6-10—6-13, 465A2-E2
Export credit terms tightened 6-9, 6-15, 529C3
OAS vs US curbs re Venez, Ecuador 6-18, 464E2
1st ¼ merchandise deficit revised 6-18, 479G2
May surplus rptd 6-28, 494C3
June deficit rptd, '75 revised 7-27, 568A1
US-Iran pact signed 8-7, 581A2
July deficit rptd 8-26, 668A1
Portugal tariff concessns OKd 8-31, 811F3
Open govt bill signed 9-13, 688E3
Ford triples sugar duties 9-21, 721E2
Aug deficit rptd 9-27, 769G3
Export Admin Act extended 9-30, 786G3
US sets meat import quota 10-9, 787G3
US-built fertilizer plants open in China 10-25, 832D3
China, Sovt computer deals rptd 10-28, 11-1, 832F2-C3
Sept deficit rptd 10-28, 833C2
Oct auto imports rptd up 11-3, 885F2
DISC rptd ruled illegal 11-5, 976C3
E Ger grain deal OKd 11-11, 889E1
Rumania pact signed 11-21, 907C2
Yugo vows US tech safeguards 11-25—11-27, 1012C1
Sup Ct refuses '71 import surchrg challng 11-29, 901A1
Oct trade deficit rptd 11-29, 958B2
US beef suppliers to limit '77 imports 12-15, 976A2
US shoe industry rptd hurt 12-28, 976C2
Nov deficit rptd 12-28, 983C2

Arab Boycott—*See under BUSINESS*
Arms Deals—*See ARMAMENTS*

1977

Cong urges shoe-import curbs 3-29, Carter bars 4-1; reactn 4-1—4-5, 248C1
Carter, labor ldrs meet on import curbs 4-6, 4-13, 271D2
Carter energy plan 4-18, 4-20, 289C2, 290A3, 295C1, G1; fact sheet 291B1, A2, D2, A3, 293D3
Sugar pact talks 4-18—5-27, 457G3
House OKs export act 4-20, 323C3
China finance talks rptd 5-1, 333D2
Viet embargo end vowed 5-3—5-4, 333B1
Carter bars sugar quotas, OKs subsidies 5-4, 457D3
US at 7-natn summit 5-7—5-8, 357G1, 358B2
Egypt OKs Ford plant agrmt 5-10, other US deals rptd 5-16, 390A2
Protectionism, forgn investmt rise in US linked 5-11, 5-25, 385C3
Taiwan, S Korea OK prelim shoe export pacts 5-14, 5-16, 416C2
Viet talks continue 6-2—6-3, 441E1
Export control bill clears Cong 6-12, 460D1
BIS warns US re deficit 6-12, 502F1
US '76 world trade share drop rptd 6-21, 502C1
ASEAN seeks ties 6-27—6-29, 537E1
Tanker cargo preference bill debated 7-11, 538A2; 8-1—9-9, 719C3
EC warns vs extra duties 7-19, tariff-cutting formula agreed 9-23, 853F1
Copper dumping alleged 7-20, 577F2
US shoe industry gets fed aid 7-20, 587B2
US backs $ depreciatn vs mark 7-21, 552F1
VW hikes US prices, $ drop cited 7-29, 585C2
IMF sees '76, '77 protectionism rise 7-31, 586A3
Deficit-reducing strategy rptd challenged 8-8, 585D1
US shoe mfrs rptdly join importers' ranks 587F2
GATT scores protectionism 9-12, 717E2
Carter at IMF-World Bank mtgs, notes US deficit, scores Japan, Ger trade imbalance 9-26, 753F2
Witteveen scores TV, shoe pacts 9-26, 753E3
Blumenthal on '77 trade gap, capital inflow 9-27, 753F3
US farm bill calls for sugar tariff 9-29, 736D3, 737B2
Deficit effect on $ feared 9-29, 754C1
Witteveen on trade gap, $ strength 9-30, 754A1
Intl sugar pact OKd 10-7, 855D1
Carter sees intl steel woes, vs curbs 10-13, 775F1
Egypt truck pact signed 10-29, 863G1
Cheap imports blamed for copper industry woes 10-31, 858G3
Rptd 5th in China trade 11-7, 882D3
Sugar levies hiked, '77 imports estimated 11-8, 854D3
Canada uranium pact OKd 11-15, 913D1
GATT sees protectnism hurting 11-28, 933C3
VW links $ drop, export harm in US mkt 12-7, 932D3
AFL-CIO urges protectionism 12-8, 12-12, 960E3, 961D1
VW ups US prices, cites $ drop 12-14, 962D1
Carter plans export tax-break phaseout 12-20, 976B3
OECD lauds expansnism 12-27, 999A1

Arab Boycott—*See under BUSINESS*
Arms Deals—*See ARMAMENTS*

1978

$ weakness, deficit linked 2-24—3-6, 118E2, D3-119B1
Vance talks vs protectionism 2-27, 145C1
Carter links to $ policy 3-2, 140G3
Protectionism, $ drop linked 3-7, 234C2
Humphrey-Hawkins bill clears House 3-16, 182D3
Drug law revisn proposed, PMA scores 3-16, 231F1, A2
CB radio tariffs hiked 3-28, 443C3
Burns links export increase, $ defense 3-31, 235E2
Carter cites deficit, plans exports study 4-11, 260G1
Deficit cuts, gold sale aimed at sagging $; weakness persists 4-19—7-14, 523E1, E2, G2
OPEC share in '77 deficit, '74-77 trade rptd 4-28, 344F2
W Ger scores US policy 4-28, 519B2
Tris garment exports banned 5-5, 347A3
UK bank seeks US mkt 5-12, 364D2
Zinc trade relief barred 6-1, 443G2
Bosworth for protectnism, price-curb tradeoff 6-19, 428G1
Zenith import duty rebuffed by Sup Ct 6-21, 491G2
Hungary favored-natn trade status rptd, '77 data cited 7-8, 534C2
Beef import limit vowed by Carter 8-14, 626F1
Carter links $ drops, inflatn, trade gap 8-16, 622C2
ITC urges copper quotas 8-23, Carter rejects 10-20; price upturn cited 10-20, 804E3-805D1
New customs law, ups duty-free allowance 9-3, 751A1
Business spending lag, trade consequences rptd 9-18, 717A1
2d ¼ paymts gap improvemt, trade linked 9-19, 717C1
Carter links deficit cut, strong $ at IMF-World Bank mtg 9-25, 731G2
Carter unveils export promotn plan, 'export consequences' order 9-26; businessmen score 10-10, 804B2, G2
Trade % of GNP rptd 9-26, 804D2
Carter bars clothespin import curbs 10-2, 805E1
June '77-78 trade-wgtd $ drop rptd 10-4, 790E1
Hollings textile amendmt OKd 10-6, Carter vetoes 11-11, 998E1
Carter stresses deficit cut 10-10, 766G2
ITC backs nut, bolt duty rise, House subcom veto cited 10-31; Carter OKs hike 12-26, 998D3
Meany asks import regulatn 11-1, 863F2
Carter vows duty waiver extensn 11-11, Treas extends waiver power 12-29, 998E1
W Ger OKs econ stimulus to promote trade 11-24, 925E2
Value-added tax proposed 11-30, 962C2
GATT talks recess, EC dispute unresolved 12-22, 998A1

Africa
S African unit fined for Rhodesia sales 1-12, 38B3
'77 S Africa chrome imports, Rhodesia ban cited 1-29, 80F3
Uganda trade ban backed by House com 5-16, coffee boycott set 5-16—5-19, 416C3
Uganda bans OKd by Cong 6-12, 7-28, 616D2
Africa trade stressed by Vance 6-20, 487E1
Rhodesia sanctns conditnl end backed by Cong 8-2, 588B1
Uganda warns re trade ban 10-12, 822G3

Arab Boycott—*See under BUSINESS*
Arms Deals—*See ARMAMENTS*

Asia
Taiwan '77 surplus rptd 1-10, 38A2
Japan pact set 1-13, 26E2-27E1
US $ strategy re Japan rptd 1-23, 27F2
Japan nut, bolt import curbs barred 2-10, 181A3; duty hiked 12-26, 998F3
China glove-import curbs barred 3-15, 443G3
Japan vows export cuts, other agrmts rptd 5-3, 341E2
China airborne device sale agreed 6-9, 436G1
India trade talks 6-13—6-15, 466G3
Carter seeks more China trade 6-26, 491C1
Japan assuranc re export curbs rptd 7-17, 544A2
US-Japan 6-mo trade gap rptd 7-26, 607D1
Missn to ASEAN states vowed 8-4, 603A3
Japan gap rptd widened 8-29, 680E1
Japan seeks imports, missn to Japan set 9-4, 694E2
Japan talks fail; beef, citrus quotas at issue 9-5—9-7, 694D3
Japan gap rptd narrowed 9-27, 752A2; 10-26, 804E3; 11-29, 918D3; 12-18, 1003A3
Taiwan agrmts affirmed 12-15, 12-17, 973C2, 975B1, G1, C2
Japan accord reached 12-18, 998B1

1979

Film industry export probe opened 5-23, 430C3
Apparel import rate scored 5-30, 402G1
Carter submits trade bill to Cong 6-19, sets tariff cuts 6-21; House OKs bill 7-11, 541D1, A2
Carter asks trade functn reorganizatn 7-19, Sen OKs bill 7-23, Carter signs 7-26, 646E3-647C1
House bars sugar tariff hike 10-23, 808A3
Carter submits trade reorganizatn plan 10-25, 803B1
Cigaret, tobacco exports rptd 11-22, 970G2
Sen OKs intl sugar agrmt 11-30, 987E2

Africa
S Africa bribes re '77 boycott chrgd 3-21, 213F1
UK Tory policy cites 4-11, 285E3
Rhodesia sanctns end proposed 4-24, 293F2; called 'premature' 4-26, 332B2
Rhodesia urges sanctns end 4-29, 332B2
Carter affirms Zimbabwe Rhodesia sanctns 6-7, Sen votes end 6-12, 434D2, E3, 438F1
7-natn missn led by Young; trade data, deals rptd 9-5–9-21, 720F2-721C2
Zimbabwe sanctns end seen 9-19, 718A2
Zimbabwe sanctns end barred 11-14, 881B2
US cigaret exports cited 11-22, 970G2
Zimbabwe sanctns ended 12-16, 960E1

Arab Boycott—*See under BUSINESS*
Arms Deals—*See ARMAMENTS*

Asia
Businessmen assured re Taiwan trade 1-15, 27G2
China, Taiwan '78 trade total 1-15, 27A3
Taiwan, S Korea OK color-TV export limits; '78, Japan data rptd 1-17, 160B2
Japan '78 deficit rise rptd 1-24, 98B2
Carter seeks Taiwan legis 1-26, 66E2
Japan '78 deficit rptd up 1-30, 71E3
Carter warning to Japan rptd 2-10, rpt disputed 2-15, Ohira notes surplus cut 2-22, 160E1
China talks 2-24–3-1, 141D1, 146F2; Carter defends 2-27, 149D2
Japan Jan deficit rptd up 2-28, 159B2
Japan talks 3-4–3-5, 159F3-160D1
Japan Feb deficit rptd down 3-26, 252A3
Alexander's sentncd re Japan TV rebates 3-29, 298C3
Japan talks halted 3-29, 229D3
Taiwan relatns bill signed 4-10, 259B3
GATT pact signed, tariff cuts seen 4-12, 273F1, B2, 274D1
Japan color TV-dumping penalties set 4-13, mfrs score 4-26, 298B3
Japan Mar deficit rptd down 4-27, 325D2
Calif tax on Japan cargo containers voided 4-30, 364A3
Carter, Japan premr meet 5-2; US warned vs protectionism 5-3, 320F1, F2
Kreps missn arrives Peking 5-5, 352G3; talks open, pacts initialed 5-7–5-14, 369G3
Japan Apr deficit rptd up 5-30, 403B1
China textile talks collapse 5-30, US sets new quotas 5-31, 405C3
Japan sales pact signed 6-2, 416B1

1980

Special labor aid rejected 11-5, 870B2
FRB backs free-trade banking zones 11-19, 958D1

Africa
Nigeria pact signed 7-23, 620C2

Arms Deals—*See ARMAMENTS*

Asia
Most-favored-natn status for China cleared 1-24, 46E2
Japan '79 deficit rptd down 1-29, 77D2
Japan Jan deficit rptd up 2-28, 167F3
Japan Feb deficit rptd down 3-27, 247D3
US group files Japan complaint 4-4; Japan rice pact set 4-12, 314G2
Japan Mar deficit narrows 4-29, 329A1
Japan Apr deficit rptd up 5-28, 401D1
Japan May deficit rptd up 6-27, 492A3
Japan June deficit rptd down 7-29, 574A3
India talks fail 8-26, Gandhi scores 8-30, 670G3
Japan July deficit rptd up 8-27, 666B2
China pacts signed 9-17, 706G3
Japan Aug deficit rptd down 9-26, 741A2
Japan rules liberalized 9-26, 967B1
US trade talks resume 10-19, 864A3
Japan Sept deficit rptd up 10-29, 824G1
Japan Oct deficit rptd down 11-28, 916A2
Japan Nov deficit rptd down 12-30, 984A2

1976

Oil Developments—*See PETROLEUM*
Presidential Election
Carter scores Rhodesia chrome policy 5-14, 390F3
Dem platform text 6-15, 470D1, 476A2, D2
Carter proposals 6-23, 451G2, F3, 452A1
Carter backs as econ weapon 6-24, 490B2
Carter pledges support 7-22, 550D3
Mondale on crop exports 7-31, 565D1
Carter backs aid to poor 8-17, 617C2
GOP platform text 8-18, 602B3, 603A1, 609E3, 610E1, 611A2
Dole record cited 614C2
Carter scores farm export policy 8-25, Dole rebuts 8-26, 632C1, E2
Dole on grain embargoes 9-17—9-23, 724B3
Carter vows A-fuel curbs 9-25, 724B1
Ford, Carter debate 10-6, 741E3
Dole, Mondale debate 10-15, 782C3
Dole vows no grain embargoes 10-16—10-27, 804C1
Ford vs Carter on boycotts 10-20, 784A3
Trade Act Assistance—*See 'Employment & Unemployment' under LABOR*
U.S.-Soviet Developments—*See 'Foreign Economic Developments' under USSR; also GRAIN*

1977

Atomic Materials & Equipment—*See ATOMIC Energy—Industrial Use*
Japan—*See JAPAN—Monetary, Trade & Aid*
Latin America
Mex stresses US exports 2-15, 136E3
Castro urges US end embargo 2-26—2-27, Cuban, US statemts 3-4, 3-5, 180G3
Cuba asks embargo end 4-8, 4-9, McGovern backs 4-11, 282F3, 283E1
US to pursue Latin talks 4-14, 296A1
Minn businessmen visit Cuba 4-18—4-22, 390D1
Sen com eases Cuba embargo 5-10—5-11, 389C3
CR beef quota review rptd 6-1, 454F2
US to ease Ecuador curbs 6-2, 454D3
Castro rejcts eased embargo 6-9, 456B2
Venez pres, Mrs Carter discuss US curbs 6-12, 455D2
Mex 1st ¼ trade surplus down 6-13, 528D1
Police sales delayed 7-17, 572E3
Argentina cuts trade deficit 7-25, 614A3
Mexico seeks concessns 8-7—8-8, 646D2
Cuban embargo end polled 8-8, 654G1
DR rpts sugar tariff harm 8-14, 647F1
Cuba stresses embargo end re ties 9-1, 685G3
Guatemala arms sales rptd resumed 9-7, 706A3
Castro to US: lift embargo 9-29, 781F2 *
Cuba trade min in US talks 10-3, 781A3
Cuba visited by Mass execs 10-24—10-28, 896C2
Mex commodity pact OKd 12-2, 976G1
Petroleum Issues—*See Petroleum—Exports & Imports*
South Africa
S Africa sealskin imports OKd 1-3, 21F3
S Africa sactns asked 10-21, 10-24, 825C1
NCC urges S Africa boycott 11-10, 934D3
Polaroid ends S Africa sales 11-22, 934D2
S Africa investmt rptd 12-4, 934B3
Statistics
'76, Dec trade deficit 1-28, 92E1
Jan deficit 2-28, 154C1
Feb deficit, '76 revised 3-28, 233E3
Mar deficit 4-27, 339G2
Apr deficit, '77 forecast revised 5-25, 5-26, 445C1
1st ¼ paymts, trade deficits linked 6-22, 502A1
May deficit 6-27, 502G1-C2
June deficit 7-27, 585A1, 593D3
July deficit 8-25, 651F1
2nd ¼ deficit 9-21, 722F2
Aug deficit 9-26; July '76-Aug '77 graph 761F2-E3
Sept deficit 10-27, 818A1
Oct deficit 11-28, 933E1-B2
Nov deficit 12-28, 1003D1
Steel Issues—*See STEEL*
USSR—*See USSR—U.S.-Soviet Trade*

1978

Atomic Materials & Equipment—*See ATOMIC Energy—Industrial Use*
Canada
Canada tariff cuts, duty-free limit hike OKd 1-17, 53G2
Canada-US trade data rptd 1-19, 53F3
Canada-US '77 auto data rptd 8-2, 613F2
Japan—*See 'Asia' in this section above*
Latin America
Cuba asks embargo end 1-2, 22E1
Carib trade rptd over $6 bln 1-22, 100E3
OAS scores protectionism 7-1, 505C2
Cuba seeks closer US ties through exiles 11-4, 880B3
Castro scores embargo 12-9, 1016E1
Petroleum Issues—*See PETROLEUM*
Statistics
'77, Dec deficit 1-30, 127E2-B3
Jan deficit; '77, Oct-Dec revised 3-3, 221F2-B3
Feb deficit 3-31, 262E1
Mar deficit 4-26, 344B2
Apr deficit, Mar revised 5-26, 429A1
1st ¼ deficit widens 6-21, 469F3
May deficit 6-27, 507E1
June deficit 7-26, 606G3
July deficit, US-Japan gap 8-29, 680B1-E1
Aug deficit, Japan gap 9-27, 752F1-A2
Sept deficit, Japan gap 10-26, 804C3-E3
Oct deficit, Japan gap 11-29, 918B3, D3
Nov deficit, Japan gap 12-18, 1003E2, A3
Steel Issues—*See STEEL & Iron—Trade Issues*
USSR—*See USSR—U.S.-Soviet Trade*

1979

Japan May deficit rptd down 6-27, 480G3
China pact signed 7-7, 523C2
Japan June deficit rptd down 7-29, 577B3
Japan July deficit rptd down 8-28, 646C3
Japan Aug deficit rptd up 9-27, 745E2
China shirt embargo rptd 9-27, textile quotas revised 10-20, 834B1
Carter OKs China benefits 10-23, 834E1
Japan Sept deficit rptd down 10-30, 828B2
US cigaret exports cited 11-22, 970G2
Japan Oct deficit rptd up 11-29, 922C1
Japan Nov deficit rptd up 12-28, 984G3
Atomic Materials & Equipment—*See ATOMIC Energy-Industrial Use*
Australia
Beef, cheese, wool concessns granted 1-8, 36F2
Canada
Food tariffs cut 3-12, 210G3
Tariffs cut, GATT obligatn cited 7-12, 543E1
US embargoes tuna exports 9-4, 667G1
Europe
W Ger '78 deficit rptd 1-30, 71E3
W Ger, Eur data rptd 2-28, 159B2
GATT pact signed, tariff cuts seen 4-12, 273F1, B2, E2, 274D1
Mar surplus rptd up 4-27, 325D2
W Ger May deficit rptd down 6-27, 480G3
June surplus rptd down 7-29, 577B3
July surplus rptd up 8-28, 646C3
Aug surplus rptd down 9-27, 745E2
Sept surplus rptd down 10-30, 828B2
Oct surplus rptd up 11-29, 922D1
Iran trade boycott discussed 12-10-12-11, 933F2
Nov surplus rptd down 12-28, 984G3
Japan—*See 'Asia' in this section above*
Latin America
Castro asks embargo eased 1-7, 40E3
Carter in Mex talks 2-14-2-16, 124F1
Venez vs trade curbs 3-23, 248E1
Nicaragua beef boycott proposed; '78, 1st 1/4 imports rptd 6-5, 427A2
Mex '78 tomato exports rptd 7-19, 553C2
Nicaragua beef imports banned 8-6, 616C2
Chile trade boycott studied 10-1, 750D2
Castro asks embargo end 10-13, 779F1
US cigaret exports cited 11-22, 970G2
Middle East
Libya jet sales OKd 3-2, 250G1
B Carter links '78 Libya visit 4-15, 310D1
Strauss delegatn in Egypt, Israel 4-17-4-18, 296C1
Iran boycott studied 12-10-12-11, 933F2
Dole on Iran embargo 12-26, 983B2
Petroleum Issues—*See PETROLEUM*
Statistics
Japan '78 deficit 1-24, 98B2
Dec '78 deficit 1-30, 71B3
'78 deficit up with Japan, Bonn, others; surplus with communists 1-30, 71E3
Jan deficit; Jan, Nov, Dec '78 deficits revised; seasonal adjustmt method chngd 2-28, 159D1
Feb deficit; Japan, OPEC, Eur data 3-28, 252E2-A3
Mar deficit; Japan, OPEC, Eur data 4-27, 325A2
Apr deficit; Japan, OPEC data 5-30, 402F3
Nicaragua 1st 1/4 beef imports 6-5, 427A2
May deficit; Japan, Bonn, OPEC data 6-27, 480D3
Mex '78 tomato exports 7-19, 553C2
June deficit; Japan, Eur data 7-29, 577B3
July deficit; Japan, OPEC, Eur data 8-28, 646F2
Aug deficit; Japan, OPEC, Eur data 9-27, 745B2
Sept deficit; Japan, OPEC, Eur data 10-30, 828F1
Oct deficit, Japan, OPEC, Eur data 11-29, 921G3
Nov deficit, Japan, OPEC, Eur data 12-28, 984C3
Steel Issues—*See STEEL & Iron—Trade Issues*
USSR—*See USSR-U.S.-Soviet Trade*

1980

Atomic Materials & Equipment—*See ATOMIC Energy-Industrial Use*
Automobile Issues—*See AUTOMOBILES--Foreign Developments*
Canada
'79 exports strong 2-2, 96B2
US exports cited 6-3, 444C2
Canada export drop, 2d 1/4 GNP decline linked 8-29, 668F2
Electrical Appliances—*See ELECTRIC & Electronics--Foreign Developments*
Europe
W Ger, Eur, '79, Dec deficit rptd 1-29, 77E2
Jan surplus rptd up 2-28, 167F3
Feb surplus rptd down 3-27, 247D3
Mar surplus rptd up 4-29, 329A1
Apr surplus rptd up 5-28, 401D1
May surplus rptd down 6-27, 492A3
June surplus rptd up 7-29, 574A3
July surplus rptd down 8-27, 666B2
Aug surplus rptd up 9-26, 741A2
Sept surplus rptd down 10-29, 824G1
Oct surplus rptd up 11-28, 916A2
Nov surplus rptd down 12-30, 984A2
Latin America
Mex bars GATT entry 3-18, 234B1
Mex vows Cuba aid vs embargo 8-1, 605B3
Chile export fraud indictmt rptd 8-4, 603B3
Middle East
Kennedy vs Iran sanctns 1-28, 74D3
Iran sanctns imposed, Feb exports drop cited 4-7, 257A1-D2
Iran imports banned 4-17, 281C1
Statistics
'79, Dec deficit; Japan, OPEC, Eur data 1-29, 77B2
Jan deficit; Japan, OPEC, Eur data 2-28, 3-3, 167A3
Feb deficit; Japan, OPEC, Eur data 3-27, 247A3
Mar deficit; Japan, OPEC, Eur data 4-29, 328D3
Apr deficit; Japan, OPEC, Eur data 5-28, 401A1
May deficit; Japan, OPEC, Eur data 6-27, 492E2
'79 mfg exports share 7-14, 574B3
June deficit; Japan, OPEC, Eur data 7-29, 574D2-A3
July deficit; Japan, OPEC, Eur data 8-27, 666E1
Aug deficit; Japan, OPEC, Eur data 9-26, 741D1
Sept deficit; Japan, OPEC, Eur data 10-29, 824D1, F1*
Oct deficit; Japan, OPEC, Eur data 11-28, 916E1
Nov deficit; Japan, OPEC, Eur data 12-30, 984A2
Steel Issues—*See STEEL & Iron--Trade Issues*
USSR—*See GRAIN, UNION of Soviet Socialist Republics--US-Soviet Trade*

1976

FOREMAN, Carol
Named Carter advisor 11-19, 881E3
FOREMOST-McKesson Inc.
Admits business pol paymts 7-3; SEC sues, settles 7-7, 669D1
FOREST Lake Enterprises Inc.
Loses Sup Ct case 6-21, 453A1
FOSTER Lumber Co.
Sup Ct curbs tax break 11-2, 867E1
FOREST Products Association, National
Clear-cutting bill lauded 10-16, 834B1
FORESTS, National
Ford urges regulatory reform 5-13, 346G3
GOP platform text 8-18, 603G1, 608B1
Forest mgt, clear-cutting bill signed 10-22, 833F3
Smokey the Bear dies 11-9, 995G2
FORLANI, Arnaldo
Zaccagnini reelected 3-3—3-7, 254A2
Sworn Italy forgn min 7-30, 573E1, F1
Vs E Ger border shooting 8-5, 589C3 ★
FORMAN, Milos
Wins Oscar 3-29, 240G2
FORMAN, Stanley
Wins Pulitzer Prize 5-3, 352E3
FORMO, Ivar
Wins Olympic medal 2-14, 159C1
FORREST, Eva
Release asked 12-11, 967E2
FORRESTAL (U.S. aircraft carrier)
Ford lands for Intl Naval Review 7-4, 489B1
FORRESTER, Bill
Wins Olympic medal 7-18, 575D2
FORSYTHE, Rep. Edwin B. (R, N.J.)
Reelected 11-2, 830D1
FORT, Dr. Joel
Testifies vs Hearst 3-8, Bailey attacks 3-10, 202B2, D2
FORT Benning, Ga.—*See GEORGIA*
FORT Collins, Colo.—*See COLORADO*
FORT Dix, N.J.—*See NEW Jersey*
FORT Edward, N.Y.—*See NEW York State*
FORT Lauderdale (Fla.) News
Ford endorsement rptd 10-30, 827F3
FORT Pierce, Fla.—*See FLORIDA*
FORTUIN, Cecil
Angola sentences 6-28, 480B2, E2
FORTUNE (magazine)
Ranks '75 top 500 US indls 436F3
Guild begins strike 6-2, 398C1
Time ends strike 6-21, 454C2
House scores Fed Reserve make-up 8-15, 667B1
Forgn business paymts study issued 12-18, 985G1
FORT Worth, Tex.—*See TEXAS*
FOSDICK, Dorothy
Rockefeller chrgs CP ties 4-15, regrets 4-27, 305E3
FOSSATTI, Luis
Rptd missing 12-30, 996E3
FOSTER, Brendan
Wins Olympic medal 7-26, 576A1
FOSTER, George
NL wins All-Star game 7-13, 544A2
NL batting ldr 10-4, 795F3
In World Series 10-16—10-21, 815D2
FOSTER, Jack
3d in Boston Marathon 4-19, 292F3
FOUCHIER, Jacques
Wins Poitou-Charentes electn 1-6, 49C3
FOUNDATIONS—*See also organization names*
Cong OKs tax bill 9-16, 706D1
FOUNTAIN, Rep. L. H. (D, N.C.)
On HEW fraud, abuse loss 9-29, 765G2
Reelected 11-2, 830E2

1977

FOREMAN, Carol Tucker
Replaced at consumer fed 2-13, 217B2
Named Agri asst secy 3-7, confrmd 3-24, 272A3
FOREMAN, Chuck
Vikings win in playoffs 12-26, 1020A1
FOREMAN, George
Young decisions 3-17, 263C1
FOREMAN, Laura
Tied to Pa sen, quits Times 9-12, 920E3
FOREMAN, Percy
Bolles murder testimony 1-27, 162F1
FOREMOST-McKesson Inc.
Pleads no contest 3-7, 215E1
Sharon Steel ends takeover bid 4-5, 275D1
FORESTS
US plans space photos 1-17, 31F1
Sup Ct backs Calif tax powers 1-25, 80G2
Dieback fungus hits Australia 2-14, 132C2
Minn logging case review barred 3-7, 211A3
Carter proposes youth jobs 3-9, 173F1
Redwood Pk hearings 4-13, 4-14, expansn asked 4-19, 322F3
Eastn expansn urged 4-28, 323D1
Fires rage across nation 5-23—8-23, 660F1-G3
US seeks Alaska acreage 9-15, 739B3
Clean-water bill revised 11-10, 900G2
FOREST Service, U.S.—*See under U.S. GOVERNMENT—AGRICULTURE*
FORLANI, Arnaldo
In Sovt trade talks 1-10—1-13, 64A3
FORMAN, Stanley
Wins Pulitzer Prize 4-18, 355G2
FOROUGH, Kahalnouri
Killed 9-13, 745F2
FORREST, Michael
Suspended 12-21, drops bias suit 12-29, 1020E2
FORREST Jr., Dr. William H.
Amphetamine-morphine painkiller rptd 3-31, 288D1
FORSTATER, Sid
Named NFL Eagles financial chief 8-8, 659C1
FORSTER, Isaac
World Ct member 4F1
FORT Belvoir, Va.—*See VIRGINIA*
FORT Detrick, Md.—*See MARYLAND*
FORTES, Benjamin
Chimpanzee heart implant fails 10-17, 847C3
FORTIN, Andre
Dies 6-24, 532A3
FORT McPherson, Ga.—*See GEORGIA*
FORTNER Enterprises Inc.
US Steel ruling voided 2-22, 149F2
FORT Riley, Kan.—*See KANSAS*
FORTUNE (magazine)
Ranks '76 top 500 indls 340A1
FORT Worth, Tex.—*See TEXAS*
FOSSIL Fuels—*See specific kinds (e.g., COAL, GAS, PETROLEUM)*
FOSSILS—*See PALEONTOLOGY*
FOSTER, George
NL wins All-Star Game 7-19, 567B2
NL batting ldr 10-2, MVP 11-8, 926C3, D3, 927B1
FOSTER, John S.
Fired 7-7, 541E3
FOSTER Care—*See CHILDREN, subheads 'Adoption' and 'Supreme Court Cases'*
FOSTER Forbes Glass Co.—*See under NATIONAL Can*
FOTH, Judge Eberhard
Baader, others sentenced 4-28, 352F1
FOUGHT, John
Wins US Amateur golf title 9-5, 951G1
FOUKE Fur Co.
US OKs S African seal imports 1-3, 22C2
FOUNDATIONS—*See organization names*
FOUNTAIN, Judge George M.
Denies Wilmington 10 retrial 5-20, 531C3

1978

FOREMAN, Carl
Force 10 released 12-21, 1030G2
FOREMAN, Chuck
NFL '77 touchdown, rushing ldr 1-1, 56E2, E3
FOREMAN, George
Spinks decisns Ali 2-15, 171C2
Ali decisns Spinks for 3d heavywgt title 9-15, 726D1
FOREMAN, Judge James L.
Rules 'boxcar' prison cells illegal 4-19, 440G1
FOREMAN, Percy
Ray chrgs '69 guilty plea pressure 8-16, 641F1
Testifies at House com King hearings, says Ray motive racial 11-13, 898F2
FOREMAN, Richard
Stages open 3-19, 760D3
FORESTS
Timber reps assured on roadless land study 1-9—1-13, 34C2
Australia brush fires 1-13—1-18, 145G1
'77 environmental gain rptd 85G1, A2
US sales sealed-bid repeal clears Cong 2-6, 107C3; 2-20, 218A2
Redwood Park expansn clears Cong 2-9, 85E2; 3-21, Carter signs 3-27, 218E1
Carter on timber output 5-4, 320G3, 321B1
Carter protects Alaska lands 12-1, 936G3
FOREVER Yours, Marie-Lou (play)
Opens 6-21, 887G1
FORGERY—*See under CRIME*
FORLANI, Arnaldo
Named Italy forgn affairs min 3-11, 191B1
FORMA, John
Mail case refused by Sup Ct 6-26, 566F3
FORREST, George
Timbuktu opens 3-1, 760E3
FORREST, Michael
Arkansas wins Orange Bowl 1-2, 8C3
Suspended 12-14, 1025C3
FORSCH, Bob
Pitches no-hitter 4-16, 355A2
FORSCH, Ken
NL pitching ldr 10-2, 928G2
FORSTER, Arnold
Lauds Sup Ct Bakke ruling 6-28, 482C3
FORSTER, Terry
Dodgers win NL pennant 10-7, 779E1
In World Series 10-10—10-17, 799D3
FORSYTH, Frederick
'Dogs' episode rptd staged 4-16, 335A3
FORSYTHE, Rep. Edwin B. (D, N.J.)
Reelected 11-7, 851A3
FORSYTHE, Henderson
Best Little Whorehouse opens 4-17, 760D1
FORT Campbell, Ky.—*See KENTUCKY*
FORTESCUE, Priscilla Jean—*See TWEEDSMUIR, Baroness*
FORT Hall, Ida.—*See IDAHO*
FORT McPherson, Ga.—*See GEORGIA*
FORTUNE (magazine)
Ranks '77 top 500 indls 5-8, 325B1-326C1
FORT Worth, Tex.—*See TEXAS*
FORUM Communications Inc.
Loses WPIX-TV license challenge 6-16, 672D1
FOSBURGH, Mary Cushing
Dies 11-4, 972B3
FOSCO, Angelo
On '77 top-paid labor ldrs list 5-15, 365G1
FOSSE, Bob
Dancin' opens 3-27, 887F1
Wins Tony 6-4, 579A3
FOSSIL Fuels—*See specific kinds (e.g., COAL, GAS, PETROLEUM)*
FOSTER, Brendan
3000-mtr run mark broken 6-27, 600G2
FOSTER, Frances
Nevis Mountain Dew opens 12-7, 1031E2
FOSTER, George
NL wins All-Star Game 7-11, 559C3
NL batting ldr 10-2, 928E2
FOSTER, Gloria
Do Lord Remember Me opens 4-4, 887G1
FOSTER, James
Alberta RCMP probe rpts 7-25, 590G2
Bars RCMP chrgs 9-27, 837A3
FOSTER, Jodie
Candleshoe released 8-4, 969F3
FOSTER, Col. Kent
Named Canada air regimt cmdr 7-13, 556D3
FOSTER, Meg
Different Story released 6-13, 619E1
FOSTER, Smith
Leads Ga cong primary voting 8-8, 625B3
Loses primary runoff 8-29, 683E1
FOSTER Care—*See CHILDREN—Adoption & Foster Care*
FOUNDATIONS—*See also specific names*
Steel union sues 9 4-19, 309G3
College aid rptd down 10-4, 754A3
FOUNDING Church of Scientology v. U.S.
FBI raid rule review denied 3-20, 205D3
FOULKES, Bill
Resigns as Roughnecks coach 6-19, 707D3
FOUL Play (film)
Released 7-19, 970C1
FOUNTAIN, Rep. L. H. (D, N.C.)
Reelected 11-7, 851B3

1979

FOREMAN, Chuck
NFL '78 receiving ldr 1-6, 80F1
FOREMAN, John
Great Train Robbery released 2-1, 174F2
FOREMOST-McKesson Inc.
Investor group offer rptd 10-17, 986B3
FOREST Products Association, National
Lauds US timber sales order 6-11, 441D1
FORESTS
US roadless-land rpt scored 1-4, 16B2
Boise Cascade buys Stone Container 1-22, 89E1
2 herbicides banned 3-1, 167C1-E2
Carter proposes roadless-land bill 4-16, 282E1
House OKs Alaska land bill 5-16, 366F3
EPA coal-use rules scored 5-25, 404A1
More US timber sales ordrd 6-11, 441A1
Ariz fires destroy 76,200 acres 7-2, 572D3
Idaho, 4 other states hit by fires 7-6—8-12, 620D1
Nicaragua plans natlizatn 7-25, 574C1
French fires destroy 25,000 acres 8-14, 620B2
Calif fires destroy 130,000 acres 9-11—9-23, 799E2
FOREST Service—*See under U.S. GOVERNMENT—AGRICULTURE*
FORLANI, Arnaldo
Pandolfi tries to form Cabt 7-27, 583B3
FORMALDEHYDE—*See CHEMICALS & Chemistry*
FORMALDEHYDE Institute
Formaldehyde-cancer link rptd 10-18, 971D1
FORMAN, Milos
Hair released 3-13, 528D2
FORMICA Corp.
Trademark case refused by Sup Ct 6-5, 464F2
FORMICA Corp. v. Lefkowitz
Case refused by Sup Ct 6-5, 464A3
FORNES, Maria Irene
Eyes on the Harem opens 4-24, 711G2
FORRESTAL (U.S. aircraft carrier)
Navy fire probe rptd 7-5, 519G3
USSR A-powered carrier rptd 12-17, 997A3
FORSCH, Bob
Brother pitches no-hitter 4-7, 619F2
FORSCH, Ken
Pitches no-hitter 4-7, 619E2
FORSSMANN, Werner
Dies 6-1, 508F2
FORSYTH, Charles M.
Indicted on paymts chrg 11-9, 886A2
FORT Carson, Colo.—*See COLORADO*
FORT Dix, N.J.—*See NEW Jersey*
FORT Jackson, S.C.—*See SOUTH Carolina*
FORT Lauderdale, Fla.—*See FLORIDA*
FORT MacArthur, Calif.—*See CALIFORNIA*
FORT Monroe, Va.—*See VIRGINIA*
FORT St. Vrain Nuclear Generating Station—*See COLORADO—Atomic Energy*
FORTSON Jr., Ben
Dies 5-19, 432F2
FORTUNE (magazine)
Ranks '78 top 500 indls 5-7, 304D1-305C2
Reviews Prop 13 effects 7-2, 499F2
FORT Wadsworth, N.Y.—*See NEW York City*
FORT Worth Star-Telegram (newspaper)
Judge's racial slur rptd 7-14, 901B3
FORUM, The (Inglewood, Calif. arena)
Sale rptd 5-30, 527E1
FOSSE, Bob
All That Jazz released 12-20, 1007F3
FOSSIL Fuels—*See specific kinds (e.g., COAL, GAS, PETROLEUM)*
US co in USSR tech deal 12-14, 997E2
FOSTER, Alan Dean
Alien on best-seller list 7-1, 548D3
Star Trek released 12-8, 1008F1
FOSTER, David
Legacy released 9-28, 820E1
FOSTER, George
NL Wins All-Star Game 7-17, 568D3
FOSTER, Gloria
Coriolanus opens 3-14, 292C1; 6-28, 711C2
FOSTER, Greg
Ties 60-yd indoor hurdle mark 1-19, 911C1
FOSTER, Marcus A. (1923-73)
Little murder convictn reversed 2-27, 156C1
FOSTER, Robert
Boston transit line taken over 12-18, 989D3
FOSTER Care—*See CHILDREN—Adoption & Foster Care*
FOUERE, Yann
Sentncd 10-20, 835E2
FOUGHT, John
Wins Buick Open 9-16, Napa Classic 9-23, 970D1, E1
FOUNDATIONS—*See also specific names*
Steel union suit dismissed 4-19, 306A2

1980

FOREMAN, Carol Tucker
On dietary guidelines impact 2-4, 157C3
Reagan hits 'consumerism' 4-18, 327F3
FOREMAN, Laura
Marries Cianfrani 7-14, 890B2
FOREMAN, Stephen H.
Jazz Singer released 12-19, 1003B2
FOREMOST-McKesson Inc.
Investor group acquisitn rejctd 2-6, 386C1
FORER, Norman
Sees US Emb militants in Teheran 2-10, 106C1
FOREST Landscape (painting)
Forgery chrgd 2-26, 472C3
FORESTS
Calif State of State message 1-10, 483C1
Chile investmts cited 1-14, 19B3
Mt St Helens erupts 5-18, 378A1; damage assessed 5-24—7-4, 503E3, G3
Canada fires rptd 5-24, 5-26, 406C2
Mex-Canada projcts agreed 5-27, 409C3
Hunts bailout loan collateral listed 5-28, 425F3
Canada fire losses rptd 8-2, 633G1
Reagan backs more cutting 10-2, 738F2
Alaska lands bill clears House 11-12, 866A3
Calif fires destroy 86,000 acres 11-15—11-30, 948A1
$15 mln gift for land rptd 12-20, 987A2
FOREST Service—*See under U.S. GOVERNMENT--AGRICULTURE*
FORGERY—*See under CRIME*
FORLANI, Arnaldo (Italian premier)
Agrees to form govt 10-2, 751G2
Sworn; forms govt 10-18, 808G3
Govt wins confidence votes 10-25, 10-29, 873A2
Refuses Rognoni resignatn 11-27; sees quake costs at $12 bln 12-1, defends relief efforts 12-2, 943C2, G2, F3
Asinara prison closure set 12-26, 995C1
FORMANSKI, Witold
Polish Sup Ct backs unions, strike averted 11-10, 862C2
FORMICA, Salvatore
Italy transport min 4-4, 275G3
CP chrgs rptd 4-17, 314E1
FORMULA, The (film)
Released 12-19, 1003A2
FORNES, Maria Irene
Blood Wedding opens 6-2, 756C3
FORSCH, Ken
Phillies win NL pennant 10-12, 796B1
FORSHAM v. Harris
Case decided by Sup Ct 3-3, 210C1
FORSTER, Karl-Heinz
W Ger wins Eur Soccer Championship 6-22, 771E2
FORSYTH, Frederick
Devil's Alternative on best-seller list 2-10, 120B3; 3-9, 200A3; 4-6, 280B3; 5-4, 448B3
FORSYTHE, Rep. Edwin B. (R, N.J.)
Reelected 11-4, 843A3
FORT Chaffee—*See ARKANSAS*
FORT Indiantown Gap—*See PENNSYLVANIA*
FORT McCoy—*See WISCONSIN*
FORT Meade—*See MARYLAND*
FORTUNE (magazine)
Ranks '79 top 500 indls 5-5, 290D1-291G1
Loomis in pres TV debate 9-21, 721C3
FORT Wayne—*See INDIANA*
42D STREET (play)
Opens 8-25, 756D3
FOSCHI, Franco
Italy labor min 4-4, 275G3
FOSSE, Bob
All That Jazz wins Oscars 4-14, 296F1
FOSSIL Fuel
Venice summit notes environmt concern 6-23, 473F2
FOSTER, David
Wins Grammy 2-27, 296D3
FOSTER, Jodie
Foxes released 2-29, 216E2
Carny released 6-13, 675B2
FOSTER, Rod
Louisville wins NCAA basketball title 3-24, 240C2
FOSTER Care—*See CHILDREN--Adoption*
FOUCHE, Jacobus Johannes
Dies 9-23, 755A3
FOUNDATIONS
USW dissident funding suit refused by Sup Ct 3-31, 291B3
FOUNTAIN, Rep. L. H. (D, N.C.)
Reelected 11-4, 843B4

1976

FOURCADE, Jean-Pierre
On BIS gold purchases, Jamaica monetary accord 1-8, 14D1, F2
France quits currency 'snake' 3-15, 229F1
Parlt gets capital gains tax bill 4-20, 312F2
UDR backs capital gains tax 6-9, 418D1
Denies Franc devaluatn rumors 7-15, 555F3
Named French supply min 8-27, 650G3
FOURIE, Branx
At Kissinger-Vorster mtg 6-23—6-24, 446C3
FOURNIER, Pierre
Wins Grammy 2-28, 460D3
FOURTH International
Link with SWP cited 8-16, 633D3
FOWLER, Gerry
Replaced as home-rule min 1-23, 73E1
FOX, Charlie
Replaced as Expos mgr 10-4, 816A1
FOX, Francis
Sworn Canada solicitor gen 9-15, 692F1
Acts in BC prison unrest 10-7—10-11, 789E3, 790C1
FOX, Russel Walter
Issues uranium policy rpt 10-28, 835B2
Rpt debate set 11-7, uranium ban lifted 11-11, 888D1, G1
FOXBORO Co.
S Africa computer sale rptd 5-26, 388A2
FOYT, A. J.
2d in Indy 500 5-30, 424G2
FRAGA Iribarne, Manuel
On strike laws 1-1, 12C1
Visits Vitoria 3-6, 207B2
Legis eases pol mtg curbs 5-25, 422A1
Asks govt, oppositn accord 6-2; mtgs with oppositn ldrs rptd 6-4, 459D1
Suarez named premier 7-3; Fraga rejects Cabt post 7-5, 500D3, F3, 523B2
Popular Alliance formed 10-9, 908G2

1977

FOURCADE, Jean-Pierre
Named equipmt min 3-30, 239G1
Wins Sen seat 9-25, replaced in Cabt 9-26, 744F2
4MMPD (4 methoxy-m-phenylenediamine)—*See CHEMICALS*
FOUTS, Dan
Challenges NFL labor pact 4-25, 491G2
FOWLER, Dr. Herbert G.
Dies 1-2, 84A3
FOWLER, Wyche
Leads in US House vote, runoff set 3-15, 191G3
Wins runoff 4-5, 252A1
FOWLES, John
'Daniel Martin' on best-seller list 11-6, 872D3; 12-4, 1021G2
FOX, C. B.
Fined in grain probe 2-8, 113E1
FOX, Francis
Rpts '76 Cuba spy surveillnc 1-16, 61C1
Vs blacklist disclosure 1-25—1-27, 97B1, E1
Vows prison reforms 2-10, 159G1
Sovt scientist deported 2-24, 159F1
Signs US prisoner exchng treaty 3-2, 200D1
Police plead guilty in '72 break-in 5-26, 426E1
On prison rpt 6-8, 466C2
Carruthers sues, Rudnicki suit cited 6-13, 541A3
Rpts '72 break-in cover-up 6-17, 485D1
On '72 Quebec break-in 6-21, 6-23; denies blacklist 6-29, 541G2, B3
RCMP probe set 7-6, 541E2
Prison reform pledged 8-5, 634B1
Defends security suspects list 8-10, 633E3
Broadbent requests file 8-12, 633G3
Vague on Broadbent file 8-29, 705E1
Confirms legislator bugged 9-22, 742C2
Vs Quebec probe of RCMP documts 10-4, 801A1
Sees more RCMP chrgs 10-20, reveals '73 PQ office raid 10-28, 840F3, 841D2
Admits '72 arson, dynamite theft knowledge 10-31, defends PQ surveillnc 11-3, 902F3
Denies RCMP tap of PC 11-1, 902D2
Quebec RCMP probe asks documts 11-2, limits set 11-11, 903A1
NDP chrgs '72 press raid knowledge 11-2, 903E1
Confrms RCMP abuses, defends watchdog role 11-6—11-14, 882B1
Confirms 'Featherbed' 11-16, 923B2
Fails to halt Quebec probe 11-23, 11-25, 923A3, B3
RCMP curbs set 11-24, 945A3
3d bid to halt Quebec probe foiled, appeal hinted 12-11, 965A1
4th bid to halt Quebec probe foiled 12-16, 982E2
FOX, Leslie
Ethiopia frees 7-1, 562F2
FOX, Judge Noel
Backs Gerber suits vs Anderson Clayton 9-15, 799C2, D2
FOX Jr., Richard K.
Named amb to Trinidad 5-17, confrmd 6-7, 499E3
FOX, Russell Walter
Uranium environment hearings end 3-22, 253C3
Uranium comm rpt issued 5-25, 465A2
Named Australia A-envoy 10-6, 779E1
Uren leaks US A-policy rpt 11-2, 901A2
FOY, Bryan
Dies 4-30, 356B3
FOYT, A. J.
Wins Indy 500 5-29, 531F1-A2
Citicorp to drop USAC sponsorshp 6-24, 531G2
Settles Citicorp dispute, in Schaefer 500 6-26, 871B1
2d in Calif 500 9-4; final USAC standing, earnings rptd 10-31, 870F3, 871A1
Yarborough named top driver 12-8, 1020C3
FPC—*See U.S. GOVERNMENT—FEDERAL Power Commission*
FRA—*See U.S. GOVERNMENT—TRANSPORTATION—Federal Railroad Administration*
FRAGA Iribarne, Manuel
Cabt mins back new coalitn 1-21, 68B2
Scores CP legalizatn 4-9, 285F2
Arias to run for upper house 4-22, Suarez rivalry noted 4-26, 331D1
Elected to parlt, scores Suarez 6-15, 453F1, B2
FRAGUIO, Alberto
Quits Argentina Cabt 10-21, 981D2
FRAME, Richard C.
Killed 2-24, 204D3

1978

4MMPD (4 methoxym-phenylenediamine)—*See CHEMICALS*
FOUR Seasons, The (recording)
Perlman wins Grammy 2-24, 316C1
FOUST, Mary Louise
Unopposed in Ky Cong primary 5-23, 406E2
FOWLER Jr., Rep. Wyche (D, Ga.)
Reelected 11-7, 850A3
FOWLES, John
Daniel Martin on best-seller list 1-8, 24D3
FOX, The (Atlanta theater)
Rescued 3-5, 293A2
FOX, Bernard
13 Rue De L'Amour opens 3-16, 760D3
FOX, Donald T.
Rpts El Salvador prisoner torture 10-13, 881A3
FOX, Edward
Force 10 released 12-21, 1030G2
FOX, Francis
Bares fake FLQ communique, informant recruiting tactics; reaffirms documt control 1-9, 35C1
Bares non-Quebec '74 RCMP break-in 1-11, 1-12, 35C2
Resigns 1-30; text of Parlt statemt 70B1, G1
Quebec RCMP probe halted 2-21, 129F2
No chrgs brought 2-23, interview rptd 2-25, 166C2
FOX, Judge Noel
Orders Lloyd Carr offcls arrested 1-10, names receiver 1-19, 83C2, C3
FOX, Terry Curtis
Cops opens 3-28, 760F1
FOX, William B. (1889-1952)
Atlanta theater rescued 3-5, 293B2
FOXY (singing group)
Get Off on best-seller list 10-11, 800F3
FOY, Lewis
Sees Carter on coal strike 2-24, 122F3
Sees Carter, backs inflatn plan 4-20, 361G3
FOYT, A. J.
7th in Indy 500 5-29, 538E2
CART group rptd formed 12-28, 1028B2
FPC—*See U.S. GOVERNMENT—FEDERAL Power Commission*
FRA—*See U.S. GOVERNMENT—TRANSPORTATION—Federal Railroad Administration*
FRAGA, Rear Adm. Jorge (ret.)
Argentina soc welfare min 11-6, 865E2
FRAIOLI-Blum-Yesselman
Hartford arena roof collapses 1-18, 95D3
FRAMPTON, Peter
NASL Phila club ownership cited 1-5, 23C1
Sgt Pepper's released 7-21, 970B3

1979

4-H Club Program
Warren dies 9-6, 756F3
FOUST, Leroy
Punitive damages vs unions barred by Sup Ct 5-29, 421C3
FOUTS, Dan
NFL '78 passing ldr 1-6, 80A1
FOWLER Jr., William E.
OKs DC-10 flights 7-10, 538D3
FOWLER Jr., Rep. Wyche (D, Ga.)
Wins Ways & Means Com seat 1-23, 70F3
FOX, Edward
Soldier of Orange released 8-16, 820D3
FOX, Francis
Dare testifies on '72 APLQ break-in 7-4, 522B3
In Trudeau shadow cabt 7-19, 563E2
FOX, Judge Noel P.
Upholds Indian fishing rights 5-8, 368C1
FOXWORTH, Robert
Prophecy released 6-15, 820A3
FOY, Lewis
Vs Wheeling-Pittsburgh fed aid 8-28, 682C1
FOYT, A. J.
Quits CART, rejoins USAC 1-31, 491G1
2d in Indy 500 5-27, 490C3
Wins Pocono 500 6-24, 491D1
Takes 2 USAC natl titles; record earnings cited 7-29, 11-11, 1005F1
FRAGA Iribarne, Manuel
Forms rightist coalitn 1-16, 61B2
Refuses to meet Arafat 9-14, 695B1
FRAIMAN, Judge Arnold G.
Rules Graiver dead 1-8, 161B1
FRAMINGHAM, Mass.—*See MASSACHUSETTS*
FRAMPTON, Peter
'Live-in-partner' suit dismissed 4-17, 289D2

1980

FOUR Opposites (painting)
Sold for record sum 5-16, 472A2
FOUST, Mary Louise
Loses US Sen electn 11-4, 849A3
FOUTS, Dan
NFL '79 passing ldr 1-5, 8A2
Campbell named NFL MVP 1-9, 175B1
Breaks NFL passing marks 12-13, 999A1
FOWLE, Susannah
Getting of Wisdom released 8-5, 675G2
FOWLER, Henry H.
Anti-inflatn com sets policy 6-21, 481D1
FOWLER, Jack Wilson
Acquitted 11-17, 898F2
FOWLER, Norman
Rpts Channel tunnel OK 3-19, 212A2
Rpts Brit Rail sales plans 7-15, 544E1
FOWLER, Rep. Wyche (D, Ga.)
Reelected 11-4, 842B3
FOX, Francis
Canada secy of state, communicatns min 3-3, 171G1, B2
FOX, Fred S.
Oh, God! II released 10-3, 836C3
FOXES (film)
Released 2-29, 216E2
FOY, Lewis
Resignatn rptd set 1-31, 224F3
Warns vs dumping 2-28, 204G2
F-Plane Series—*See ARMAMENTS--Aircraft*
FP Publications Ltd.
Thomson Newspapers buy 1-11, 38G1
FRAGA Iribarne, Manuel
Suarez survives censure motion 5-30, 431F2
Vows police support 10-22, 832B2

FRANCE

1976
FRANCE—*See also ADB, EUROPEAN Community, NATO, OECD, SEATO*
Students protest educ reforms, univs back 3-17—4-23; govt OKs talks, bars chngs 4-12, 4-22, 311D3
Quake tremors rptd 5-6, 352B3
Lefebvre holds banned mass 9-5, 932G2
Oil tanker sinks off Brittany 10-14, 912E2
Volcanologist dismissed 10-18, 905D3
Children die in bus crash 12-21, 969C2
Afars & Issas—*See AFARS & Issas*

1977
FRANCE—*See also DISARMAMENT—Geneva Committee, EC, IDB, NATO, OECD, SEATO*
Moreau weds US film dir 2-8, 140G3
Orient Express ends svc 5-22, 458F3
Paris gay rights march 6-25, 560F2
'77 fashion wrap-up rptd 7-29, 1022C1
Picasso gifts set 9-19, 808E2
Prix Goncourt awarded 11-21, 927F2
Pro-govt newspaper closes 12-17, 1013B1
Afars & Issas—*See DJIBOUTI*

1978
FRANCE—*See also COUNCIL of Europe, DISARMAMENT—Geneva Committee, EC, GATT, IDB, NATO, OECD*
Religious groups surveyed, Moslems ranked 2d 3-24, 352G2
Film wins US Oscar 4-3, 315D3
Arts Acad '77 Wyeth inductn cited 4-24, 335D3
'74 Turkish jet crash damages awarded 5-13, 460E1
Campers killed in Spanish blast 7-11, 636E1
'78 high chic fashion rtpd 8-4—8-11, 10-27—11-3, 1029B2
Quake felt 9-3, 759A1
Blackout hits 12-19, 1016B3

1979
FRANCE—*See also COUNCIL of Europe, DISARMAMENT-Geneva Committee, EC, GATT, IDB, NATO, OECD*
Complete 'Lulu' debuts in Paris 2-25, 173G3-174C1
'79 fashion roundup rptd 1006F1
Paris on '78 world's busiest airport list 6-1, 421C1
Chevassus marries 6-15, 527E2
2 cardinals installed 6-30, 640C2
Picasso retrospective opens in Paris 10-10, 892C1
Mesrine slain by police 11-2, 890A3

1980
FRANCE—*See also ADB, COUNCIL of Europe, CSCE, EC, GATT, GENEVA Committee, IDB, MBFR, NATO, OECD*
Priest murder sentence rptd 5-27, 463B2
Assemb OKs crime bill 6-21, 497E3
Vincennes campus rptd moved 8-5, 670F1-A2
Jagger manor house buy rptd 9-18, 908A3
Alcoholism campaign set 12-10, 942F1

1976

African Relations—*See also 'Foreign Economic Developments' below; also AFARS & Issas and COMORO Islands*
Morocco premr visits; sets Hassan trip, lauds Sahara support 1-6—1-8, 36G1
Algeria arrests 3 1-8, France denies spy chrg 1-9, links spies to anti-Basque unit 1-11, 45B2-E3
Morocco summons amb re Sahara 1-28, 58B2
Sahara independnc opposed, Algeria dispute denied 1-31, 107D2
Somali-French troops clash, amb recalled 2-4, 85G2
National sentncd re CAR plot 2-14, 204C2
Angola MPLA recognized 2-17, 163A1
Algeria offices bombed 2-20, 2-22, 455A1
Mitterrand visits Algeria 2-25—2-27, 204G3
Algeria sentences 7 re spy ring 3-3, 454F3-455A1
Chirac visits Chad 3-5—3-6, 204F3
Denies US Angola aid chrg 3-9, 228D3
Algeria demands passports 3-25, 455B1
Morocco issues Sahara arrest warrants 3-26, 277C3
Abstains on UN S Africa censure 3-31, 228B2
Giscard scores Mitterrand Algeria visit 4-22, 312E3
Morocco, Mauritania boundary map corrected 4-27, 341G3
Rpt CAR expels jailed natl 4-30, 503F2
Kissinger sees Giscard 5-5, 318A3
France-Africa summit 5-10—5-11, 355F2
Galaup taken hostage in Ethiopia hotel raid 8-4, 581C1; rptd freed 8-17, 674B3
Backs US Africa policy 9-8, 681B2
Zaire names amb 10-18, 949G3
Vs black Namibia support 12-20, 955C1

Armed Forces
Army union probe documents barred 1-15, 119D3
Sanguinetti scores new mil code 1-16—1-19; ousted, Petrochilo named 1-22, 139D1
Leftists OK army union protest 1-26, 120A1
'77-81 budget hikes forecast 1-29, 139A2
1st woman general named 4-21, 316F1
Cabt OKs '77-82 budget 5-5, 417D2
Mery article sparks controversy 6-1—6-3, 417B3
Giscard, Chirac confer 6-6—6-7, 417F3
Adm Sanguinetti dismissed 7-7, 521D2
'77 defns budget hike OKd 11-9, 905E2

Arts & Culture
Rubens Visitatn stolen 1-26, 104C3
Stolen Toulouse-Lautrec returned 1-29, 104B3
Troyes gets pvt art collectn 1-31, 124F2
Avignon Picasso theft 1-31, 124G2
Cannes Film Festival 5-14—5-28, 460F1
Ramses mummy in Paris for repairs 9-26, 912F2
Prix Goncourt, Renaudot presented 11-15, 911G3

Atomic Energy & Missiles
Sub gets H-bomb warheads 1-24, 139B2
In 7-natn A-safeguards agrmt 1-27, 84A1
S Korea cancels A-plant purchase 1-29, 1-30, 103G2
Australia A-info exchng planned 2-4, 116B2
US vs Pak A-plant deal 2-23; IAEA OKs 2-24, 175C1
US cites safeguards pact stance 2-23, 243A3
Pak A-plant pact signed 3-18, 581C3
A-plant in Libya planned 3-22, 239B3
3d undergrnd test 4-2, 243C1
A-export safeguards set 4-8, 372C3
Fast-breeder reactor OKd 4-15, 372B3
Pacific atmospheric tests barred 4-16, 372E3
Cabt OKs '77-82 defense budget 5-5, 417F2
W Ger reactor pact OKd 5-18, 372F2
Giscard on A-export safeguards, S Korea deal cancelatn 5-20, 372E2
S Africa A-plant agreed 5-28, 387F1
Adm Sanguinetti dismissed 7-5, 521F2
At A-waste conf 7-12, 739G1
Signs Sovt A-safeguards pact 7-16, 540E2
US arms control rpt cites 7-29, 739E2
S Africa pact signed 8-6, 630G3
US, Pak discuss A-plant 8-8—8-9; France protests 8-9, 581G2
Carter asks breeder study 8-9, 585C1
Iran pact signed 10-6, 773E2
Sets export, control guidelines; Pak, Iran sales stand 10-11; 772B3

1977

African Relations—*See also DJIBOUTI*
Mayotte islanders in Malagasy ask repatriatn 1-7, 24B2
Congo rebels kidnap 3 natls 1-15, 48D1
Postal workers S Africa boycott fails 1-21, 67B3
Chad rebels free Claustres 1-30, 84C2
Congo releases 3 1-30, 84E2
Angola ties set 1-31, 86B2
Benin coup attempt detailed 2-1, 96F1
S Africa A-bomb capacity seen 2-17, 160C2
Zaire arms aid set 3-18, 207D3
Sahara captured arms displayed 3-28, 337B2
S Africa rejcts Namibia plan 4-7, 285C1
Zaire airlift, arms aid rptd 4-10—4-12, 265B1
Zaire troop role rptd; planes, advisers recalled 4-15—4-21, 317F2
Giscard in Senegal, at summit 4-19—4-23, 316C3
Eritrea consulate closed 4-23, 327F2
Ethiopia ousts rptr 4-25, 327C3
S Africa sees Namibia compromise 4-29, 349C2
Sahara rebels raid Mauritania; kill 2 natls, kidnap 6 5-1; France, Algeria exchng chrgs 5-3—5-8, 440G2
Zaire ousts newsman 5-6, 394A2
S Africa OKs Namibia const concessns 5-9, 400D1
Nimeiry visits; USSR, Zaire aid discussed 5-17—5-19, 450D1
Sahara rebels set release terms, score Mauritania aid 5-21, 440D3
Rhodesia office closure cited 5-27, 457F1
Castro confrms Angola pullout halted 6-9, 456G1
Mobutu thanks Giscard for aid 6-9—6-10, 490E1
S Africa OKs Namibia plan 6-10, 457B2
Algeria frees 6 natls 6-19, 566G3
Giscard, Brezhnev conf 6-21, 495C1
Mauritanian envoy shot 7-7, 543B2
Zaire debt rescheduled 7-7, 583E1
Chad mil aid rptd 7-18, 597F1
Somali history cited 587E3
Giscard evaluates USSR role 7-25, 551B1
SWAPO ldr joins Namibia talks 8-8, 639D3
US rpts S Africa A-test plan 8-17; de Guiringaud warns S Africa 8-22; Botha assures 8-30, 656F3, 663D3, 664A1
Tanzania protest cuts short de Guiringaud 4-natn tour 8-18, 662E2
Namibia compromise reached 8-19, 699D3
Somalia arms offer canceled 8-31, 684F2
Tunisian guillotined 9-10, 728C2
Namibia conf stalled 9-22—9-26, 770D2
S Africa investmts rptd 9-23, 771F1
Forgn worker immigratn curbed 9-27, 744D2
Sahara rebels kidnap 2 10-25; reactn 10-26—10-28; kidnap total rptd 10-28, 831F2
Algeria pressured on Sahara kidnap 10-30, Senegal garrison reinforced 11-1, Red Cross, Libya aid sought 11-3, 852A2
UN Namibia vote abstentns 11-4, 851E1
S Africa aircraft purchase cited 851E2
Envoy in Polisario talks, kidnap victims rptd alive 11-7, 852E2
S Africa navy sales canceled, '70-76 trade data 11-8, 883B1
Namibia tour fails to win SWAPO concessns 11-21—12-7, 1016E3
Nigeria gunboat purchase rptd 11-23, 986G2
S Africa halts phone deal 11-25, 934C2
Polisario rpts French jet hits 12-2, 12-14, 12-18, 998C3
Giscard, Callighan summit 12-12—12-13, 1013G1
S Africa oil, investmt ban abstentn at UN 12-16, 1016A2
Sahara rebels free natls, air support vs Polisario confirmed 12-23, 998G2

Atomic Energy & Safeguards
Pakistan to buy A-plant 1-3, 12B3
US urges A-export curbs 1-29, 69B2
USSR urges A-test ban 2-15, 147D1
S Africa A-bomb capacity seen 2-17, 160C2
Fessenheim A-reactor opens 3-7, protests rptd 4-11, 391C3
Vance sees Giscard on arms talks 4-1, 247A1
Carter for plutonium ban 4-7, reactn 4-8, 268B1, G1, D2
Intl A-energy conf ends, US plutonium ban scored 4-13, 334F2
Japan acts vs US plutonium ban 4-21, 335D1
Uranium cartel role rptd 4-25, 479F2
Carter proposes US A-export curbs 4-27, France fuel reliance noted 4-28, 334D2
A-supplier natns meet in London 4-28—4-29, 403F1
Suppliers conf scores Carter plans 4-28—4-29, 403F1-A2
New uranium enrichmt method rptd 5-6, 402C3
7-natn summit debates A-sales, sets study 5-7—5-8, 357D2, E2
Barre OKs 'Super Phoenix' 5-12, scientists oppose 5-30, 450A1
Trudeau on Giscard A-mtg 5-13, 389B2
Giscard sees Schmidt 6-16—6-17, 566C3
A-weapons abroad barred 6-23, 1012F3
US denies uranium cartel rpt 6-29, 624F3

1978

African Relations
Algeria pres visits Malta 1-3, 39C2
Guinea frees 3 natls 1-5, 22B2
Algeria orders import cuts, trade deficit cited 1-11, 11C3
Giscard visits Ivory Coast 1-11—1-15, 71A1
Somalia asks arms aid 1-16, 43A3
At Ogaden conf in US 1-21, 43E2
Angola troop raid chrg rptd 2-1, 87G3
Ethiopia protests Somalia aid 2-1, 100D1
Chad rebels rpt natl captured 2-2, 130C2
Somalia makes 2d aid bid 2-4, gets tanks via Saudi 2-8, 99G3
Namibia mtg 2-11—2-12, progress rptd 2-13, 133A3
UN Rhodesia pact vote abstentn 3-14, 192F3
Namibia plan backed by front-line natns 3-26, 248G2
Chad troops increased 4-6, 4-19, renewed fighting rptd 4-15, 287G1
Kenya dam contract rptd 4-9, 479D1
Chad rebels free natl 4-14, 287B2
Namibia plan OKd by Vorster 4-25, 299C1
Chad troop role confrmd 4-26, 572G1, A2
Sahara Polisario jet raids rptd 5-5, 562F2
Namibia rebel ldr cancels talks 5-7, 339D1
New Comoro govt favors ties 5-13, 371C2
Zaire rebels rptd holding Eur hostages 5-18, 359C2
Zaire rescue operatn, Belgium rift rptd 5-18—5-23, 381A1-382A1
Chad rebel drive halted 5-18—6-2, 572E1
Comoro I exiles leave 5-21, 445B3
USSR scores Zaire rescue 5-22, 382D1; chrgs massacre of whites 5-25, 417C3
Franco-African summit backs Zaire role, other mil aid 5-22—5-23, 382F2
Zaire pres arrives for Franco-African summit 5-23; sees Giscard, Tindemans; pan-African force backed 5-23—5-25, 417D3
Africa aid, troop totals rptd 5-24, 382C3
Legionnaires quit Zaire town 5-25—5-28; death toll, hostages rptd 5-30, 417E2, B3
Zaire force exit begins, US airlifts troops 6-4, 441A1
Westn natns meet on pan-Africa force; US, UK oppose plan 6-5, 441E2
Zaire defns force training rptd 6-10, 441F1
Namibia rebels OK talks 6-11, 475C3
Zaire emergency aid OKd 6-13—6-14, 478A1
Terrorism vs N Africa Arabs rptd 6-14, 474D1
Zaire role cited in Belgium govt crisis 6-15—6-19, 612F2
Zaire pullout ends 6-16, 478F1
OAU forgn mins clash re Africa role 7-7, 561E2
Mauritania aid re Sahara cited 7-10, 535F1
Namibia plan OKd by SWAPO 7-12, 547C2
Tunisia bars trial observers 7-16, 7-18, 671D1
Rptd Rhodesia arms supplier 7-23, 616D2
Giscard presses Sahara mediatn 7-27, 8-1, 676E2
Namibia contact group sees Botha, Steyn 10-16—10-18, 819G2
S Africa sanctns backed if Namibia plan rejected 10-23, 819D3
UN abstentn on Namibia electn warning 11-13, 904B2
Nigeria loan pullout cited 11-30, 934A2
Rhodesia rptd obtaining planes 12-13, 955F3
Giscard visits Guinea 12-20—12-22, 1018A1

Atomic Energy & Safeguards
'77 safeguard pact detailed 1-11, 11G1, A2
US alerts to Sovt A-satellite fall 57E1
IAEA inspectn barred, Euratom agreed 1-16, 103A1
Giscard asks disarmamt talks reorganized, US-USSR ldrshp role relinquished 1-25; reactn 1-31, 61D2-D3
S Africa enriched uranium output expanded 2-13, 135B1
Australia joins A-supplier group 2-24, 129C2
US sets A-export controls 3-10, 183D2
Giscard, Schmidt discuss Sovt uranium deal 4-7, 258C2
US OKs uranium exports 4-9, 278G3
Neutron bomb test rptd 4-17, govt denies 4-24, 312G3
Australia protests neutron bomb test 4-21, 311B1
US study backs breeder dvpt 5-10, 346G3
Japan breeder-research pact rptd 6-23, 548E3
Pacific A-test 7-19, 649D2
Pak A-contract revisn asked, US pressure cited 8-9; Pak scores 8-23, 668A2
Bhutto on US oppositn to Pak A-plant 10-5, 798F1
China science, tech pact signed 10-20, 814B1
Iran project faces curbs 10-22, 816C3

1979

African Relations
Chad rebelln rptd thwarted 2-14, 114G1
Chad civil war truce rptd 2-19, 153G3
UN rights comm res vs white-minority regimes opposed 2-21, 148G1
S Africa rejcts Namibia plan 3-5, 171B2
Chad evacuatn advised 3-9, troop exit set 3-20, 211A2
Namibia compromise proposed 3-19—3-22; Pretoria bars 5-7, extends assemb powers 5-8, 354F2
S Africa '72-78 loans rptd 4-2, 270D2
S African activist hanged 4-6, 270C3
Chad strife rptd renewed 4-6, deaths estimated 4-9, 211B2
Chad invasn by Libya fails 4-20, 329A3
Mauritania premier visits 5-3, 324A1
Debt relief vow rptd 5-4, 371C3
Franco-African summit backs Eur ties 5-21—5-22, 398B3
CAE amb asks asylum 5-22, 387B2
Uganda trade rptd 5-28, 429C2
S Africa scored in UN vote 5-31, 428B1
S Africa scandal figure arrested 7-19, 567D1; plea rejctd 8-8, extradited 8-23, 755B1
French-trained Zaire troops replace Shaba intl force 8-14, 733G3
CAE aid cut 8-17, 697F3
CAE coup aid rptd 9-20, 9-22; Bokassa refused asylum 9-21—9-24, troops to remain 9-23, 720E1-E2
Bokassa gifts to Giscard alleged 10-10, 791D1
S Africa UN vote abstentn 11-2, 875G1
Namibia UN talks reopen 11-12—11-16, 889D3
Seychelles chrgs plot 969C2
Bokassa gifts to Giscard chrgd again 12-4, 993D3

Atomic Energy & Safeguards
Nuclear 'doomsday clock' unchngd 1-1, 13F1
A-plant constructn speedup ordrd 2-7, 82D3
'78 underground tests rptd 3-6, 625D3
US A-accident sparks protests; govt sets probe, affirms commitmt 4-1—4-5, 246F1, D2
Mex agrmt signed 4-1—4-4, 372B2
A-factory, Iraq reactor sabotaged; forgn agents, US A-accident linked 4-6, 276D1
A-sales to Pak rptd 4-6, 277C2
USSR seeks French role in SALT III 4-26—4-28, 723B3
Iraq vowed replacemt reactor 5-9, 371F2
W Ger plutonium custody dispute resolved 5-16, 380B1
Dockworkers boycott A-cargo 5-17, 390G2
A-weapon policy cited 5-31, 415G3
Brittany A-protest staged 6-3, 416G1, E2
Iraq reactor agrmt rptd 7-11, 564E1
Euratom revisn sought 7-24, 633B2
A-arms priority reaffirmed 9-11, 686F1
Union, other protests delay plant fueling 10-4, 772B3
Protesters delay waste shipmt 10-9—10-10, 781G3
Iranian stake in Eurodif frozen 10-24, 976E2
Mystery A-test denied 10-26, 824D3

1980

African Relations
40 Togolese occupy emb 1-12, 61D2
Chad withdrawal negotiated 1-22, 119B1
Tunisia gets navy visit 1-27, 90C1
Libyans wreck emb, consulate 2-4, France recalls staff 2-5, 90D1
Tunisia premr hospitalized 2-26, 196G3
Cooperatn min's office attacked 3-18, 232A1
Chad fighting resumes, 3 soldiers killed 3-22—3-25; natls evacuated 3-24, 221F1
Algeria blames for Berber unrest 4-24, 334D1
Chad forces leave 5-16, 390F3
Liberia Emb stormed, Tolbert's son seized 6-14; raid protested 6-15, 499C1
UN censures S Africa, France abstains 6-27, 524F3
Bokassa confirms Giscard gifts 9-17, 728G3
US journalist expelled 10-3, 790B2
Algeria quake aid rptd 10-11, 776E1
Le Monde chrgd re Bokassa-Giscard revelatns 11-7, 872C1
UN Namibia talks schedule agreed 11-24, 967C2
Bokassa-Giscard gift figure freed 11-29, 921A3
Libya warned on Chad interventn 12-13, 965F1

Arts & Sciences
TB vaccine study rptd 1-20, 63C2
Titian forgery at Louvre chrgd 2-26, 472C3
Yourcenar elected to French Acad 3-6, 471G2
Dausset wins Nobel 10-10, 889F3
'80 fashion roundup rptd 998D1

Atomic Energy & Safeguards
'70-79 A-tests rptd 1-17, 31F3
India talks exclude 1-28, 97C3
Plogoff, Quimper A-protests 1-31, 2-9, 149A3
EC OKs A-fusion funds 2-5, 125B2
Gravelines, Tricastin A-plants OKd 2-20, 149G2
2 breeder reactors planned, Phenix, Super-Phenix facilities cited 2-26, 149D2
Iraq enriched uranium fuel, reactor shipmt OKd, US scores 2-27, 192D3
Plogoff A-protesters arrested 2-29, freed 3-17, 231C3
Australia A-plant rptd backed 3-3, 171A1
New energy measures set 4-2, 254C1
Italy cuts Eurodif share 5-2, 409D1
Uranium deposit rptd found 5-29, 407E2
Power workers strike 6-12, 463A1
7-natn Venice summit backs 6-23, 473F2
Neutron bomb research backed by Soclsts 6-25, 486F3
Neutron bomb test rptd 6-26, 486B3
OECD rpts '79 A-plant data 7-8, 509A3
W Ger backs A-arms plan 7-11, 539G3
Israel vs Iraq A-deal, US 'resigned' 7-28; Paris defends 7-29, 573A3
A-plant security rptd heightened 8-6, 670A2
Enrichmt process rptd 9-10, 707C3
A-carrier constructn rptd OKd 9-24, 750A2
A-tech dvpt set 10-1, 749E3, F3

1976

S Africa A-sales to end 11-9, 928A1
Uranium mines bombed 11-15, 1003A1
Strasbourg power plant dropped 11-20, 1002F3
Sale of reprocessing plants banned, forgn pacts hold 12-16, 1002A3

Comoro Islands—*See under 'C'*
Concorde Developments—*See 'SST' under AVIATION*
Corsica
Separatists demonstrate 1-3, bombs found 1-4, 50D2
New separatist group sets blast 5-4—5-5, 401C3
Site of violence, map 401A3
Simeoni trial opens, gen strike held 5-17, 401F2
Simeoni, others sentncd 6-22, 482A1
Wine depot dynamited 8-24, 693F2
Ferry rates protested 8-30, Fieschi sentenced 8-31, 693B2
Fieschi arrest protested, Air France jet blown up 9-7; Giscard scores 9-9, 693A2
2 farmers killed 9-25; protests 9-26—9-28, 772G3
2 TV trucks bombed 11-8, 1003B1
Crime—*See also 'Arts' above*
Assassin kills bank head, self 5-14, 381B3
Riviera bank theft 7-16, 560E2
Youth guillotined 7-28, 588F3
Death penalty poll results 7-28, 588G3
Giscard spares Benzahra 8-4, 589A1
Would-be de Gaulle killer shot 8-11, 624E3
Paris bank robbery 8-13, 674F3-675A1
7 seized in Riviera heist 10-27, 876F3
Le Pen attacked with bomb 11-2, 1002E2
Iran diplomat shot in Paris 11-2, 1002F2-A3
2 TV trucks bombed in Corsica 11-8, 1003B1
Uranium mines bombed 11-15, 1003A1
Crime rate rptd up 12-7, 1003C1
Drug dealers convicted 12-9, 971F2-C3
De Broglie killed in Paris 12-24, 1002D2
Djibouti—*See AFARS & Issas*

Economy & Labor (domestic)
Govt-wine growers mtg 1-7, 1-14, violence flares 1-19—2-5, 138B3, F3-139A1
Govt plans outlined 1-14, 49E2
Chirac in Brittany dairy, fishing talks; unions protest 1-16—1-17, 139B1
Arms industry job data rptd 1-25, 126G2
Socialists plan econ progrm 1-27—1-29, 119B3
Jobless rise rptd slowing 1-28, 84F3
Potato sales rptd halted 1-31, 84A2
Coastal oil traces rptd 1-31, 139G2
Gas, elec rate hikes rptd 2-20, 205D1
Jobless benefits hiked 2-22, 205E1
Jan price index rptd 2-27, Feb jobless 3-5, 205C1
'Wine war' clashes spread 3-1—3-4, 204A3
Environmt oversight body OKd 3-2, 204E3
Firms get tax aid 3-3, 205C1
Draft housing reforms OKd 3-4, 204D3
Public employes strike 3-9, 205E1
Educ reforms protested, labor support sought 3-17—4-23, 311F3, 312D1
Cabt OKs indl, capital tax reforms 4-13—4-14, reactn 4-15—4-22, 312A2
Cabt OKs draft 5-yr plan 4-21, 312E1
Le Monde oil correspondent fired 5-9, 537E3
Marseilles oil prosecutor's transfer scored 5-16, 537F3
Giscard modifies aims, cites data 5-25, 439F2
Capital gains tax debate opens 6-1, UDR backs bill 6-9, 418C1
Giscard, Chirac confer 6-6—6-7, 417F3
Assemb OKs capital gains tax 6-23, 481F3
Econ growth cited 6-27—6-28, 462E1
France-Soir sale set 7-5, Paris-Match 7-8, 521C2
Newspaper accord reached 7-7, 521A2
Elf-Erap, SNEA merge; Gaullists, left score 7-9, 537C3
France-Soir strike 8-16—8-27, 651C1
Chirac resigns 8-25, Barre sets inflatn fight 8-26, 637C3, 638B1
Barre, Durafour named to fight inflatn 8-25, 8-27, 8-28, 650C3, 651A1
Drought aid for farmers set 8-25, 675C1

1977

A-plant leaks radioactive gas 7-1, 543E2
4-natn 'Super Phoenix' OKd 7-5; environmentalists protest 7-31, police actn defended 8-2, 597B2-C3
Giscard visits Pierrelatte reactor site, reasserts A-policy 7-30, 597G2
Left-wing discord on A-arms 8-9, 9-14, 727F3
S Africa warned vs A-test 8-22; Botha assures 8-30, 656F3, 663D3, 664A1
Disarmamt drive announced 8-26, 1012G3
Pak A-deal confrmd 9-8, 1013A1
Open sector cyclotron constructn cited 825B3
Barre in US talks 9-15—9-16, 1012E3
Suppliers conf OKs safeguards 9-21, 717D1
USSR backs A-test ban 11-2, 997B1
A-sub funds cut from budget 11-19, 924G1
Terrorists attack power plants 11-19, 'Carlos Com' claims credit 11-21, 1011G3
Pacific A-tests rptd 11-23, 11-25, 1013B1
US uranium cartel probe jurisdictn opposed 12-1, 1003F3

Comoro Islands—*See COMORO Islands*
Concorde Developments—*See AVIATION—SST/Concorde*
Corsica
Simeoni freed 1-14, brother surrenders 9-27, 744E3, 745A1
Separatists step up bombings 8-11—8-21, threaten France 8-15, 744C3
UPC rally, non-violence urged 8-14, 744E3, F3
Corsica UPC issues bank, investmt demands 8-14, 744G3
Separatists bomb Paris station 12-26, 1011E3
Crime
Police versn of de Broglie murder questnd 1-5—1-9, 43G3
Drug dealer sntncd in US 1-21, 103B1
Ex-envoy kills family 2-1, self 4-19, 312E3
FLB bombs Brittany 2-6, 3-20, 255A3
Victim compensatn law in effect 3-5, 255G3
Riviera bank robber escapes 3-10, 288E2
Fiat exec kidnaped 4-13, ransomed 7-11, 543C2
Dassault cleared on corruptn chrgs 4-21, 598A1
Rheims shooting arrests 6-7, 728D1
Murderer guillotined 6-23, 543G1
Paris coin heist 7-28, 807B2
Forgn worker crime rate rptd 8-7, 744E2
Swiss close Hervel, seek officers 8-15, 658B1
Tunisian guillotined 9-10, 728B2
Jet hijacker seized 9-30, 807C3
Heroin addictn rptd up 10-17—10-21, 971E3
Brittany separatists explode 3 bombs 10-21, 883F1
Terrorists attack power plants 11-19, 'Carlos Com' claims credit 11-21, 1011G3
Fauchon food shop bombed 12-19, 1012B1
Paris area hit by bombings 12-25—12-27, 1011E3
Gunmen attack Marchais home 12-25, 1011F3

Economy & Labor (domestic)
'74-75 recessn job data rptd 1-3, 29E3
Wage cost hike cited 1-6, 8E2
Nov, 12-mo consumer price rise rptd 1-7, 29C3
Postal workers S Africa boycott fails 1-21, 67B3
Newspaper strike 1-21, mediatn fails 2-23, 159A3
Solar power plant opens 1-25, 159E3
Barre inflatn curbs rptd effective 1-26, unions vs contd restraints 1-26—2-1, 159D2
'76 factory wage study rptd 1-28, 158B3
Dec '75-76 inflatn rate rptd 2-7, 87B2
'76 econ growth rate rptd 2-22, 146C2
Servan-Schreiber sells L'Express shares 3-16, 255D3
Fishermen protest pollutn 3-27, 255F3
GM plant protesters evicted 4-18, 328D3
Steel industry aid set; job, output data cited 4-19, 391D2
CGT vows union actn 4-25, 328F3
Dunkirk dock strike continues 4-25, 328G3
Assemb passes econ plan 4-28, 328F2
Paris elec, garbage strike 4-28, 328C3
Dunkirk dock strike ends 5-1, 728E1
Inflatn, jobless measures pledged 5-7—5-8, 357D1, F1
Socialist-CP rift re natlizatn rptd 5-17, 543A1
Unions hold 1-day gen strike 5-24, 486D2
Rheims picket line shooting 6-5, 2 arrested 6-7, 728D1
Dassault natlizatn planned, '76 sales cited 6-8, 597D3-598B1
Retiremt plan agreed, youth jobless cited 6-13, 543E1
Air France rpts '76 losses, blames govt 6-27, 543G2
May CPI rptd 6-28, 1012E2
'77 fashion wrap-up rptd 7-29, 1022C1
Sacilor-Sollac to idle 2,500 8-3, 728B1
Aug youth jobless rate rptd 8-9, 771B2
Parisien Libere strike ends 8-16, 654B3
'78 budget presented 9-7, 744E1
Left-wing discord on natlizatn, wages 9-14, 727D3
Worker immigratn curbed 9-27, 744C2

1978

US to renew Pak econ aid 10-24, 840A1
6th A-sub set 11-2, 882A1
China A-deal OKd by US 11-24, sale set 12-4, 986G1

Comoro Islands—*See under 'C'*
Concorde Developments—*See AVIATION—SST/Concorde*
Corsica
Separatists stage bombings 1-14, 71D2
Pre-electn violence 2-11—2-12,; separatists favor left 2-12, 149B1
Belgian army resort bombed 5-6, 352E2
Ajaccio utility bds bombed, sheep herd slain 5-13—5-14; farmers protest 5-16, 496E2
Separatist bombing stirs pub anger 5-17, '78 total rptd 496D2
US rpts Zaire rescue role 6-5, 441D1
Bastia, Calvi bombings; 23 separatists seized 6-6, 6-8, 496C2
Giscard visits; vows aid, bars regional assemb 6-7—6-9, 496A2
Club Medit '77 bombings cited 6-11, 473G3
Ajaccio, Bastia bombings 7-3, 533C2
2 bombs explode near Bonafacio 7-23, '78 bomb total rptd 7-24, 649E3
Beghin castle destroyed 8-11, 649D3
Strikes hazard supply shipmts 10-23, 816C1
Truck drivers end port blockade 10-26, 882A2
Crime & Civil Disorders—*See also 'Corsica' above, 'Terrorism' below*
Govt program presented 1-7, 54C2
Industrialist kidnaped 1-23; ransom transfer foiled 3-24, freed 3-26, 232D1-A2
5 sentncd in Sovt spy ring 2-1, 71B2
Scientology founder sentenced 2-14, 232G3
3 rapists convicted 5-3, 396B1
Paris library tapestry stolen 5-12, 579G1
13 paintings stolen in Marseilles 6-20, 579F1
Delta '72 hijackers sentenced 11-23, 926F3
Paris museum art theft 12-13, 1029A1

Economy & Labor (domestic)
Govt program presented 1-7, Gaullists rptd angered 1-11, 54C2, F2
Paris expenses rated 1-14, 28A3
CP natlizatn program rptd 2-6, 148F3
CP, Soclst policy rift rptd 2-19, 148C3
Govt to acquire Dassault stock 3-8, 313E1
Tourist, fishing industries hurt by oil spill 3-22, 201G3
Giscard sees labor, business ldrs 3-26—3-31, 245D3
Barre presents econ program, retains austerity measures 4-19; Assemb OKs 4-20, 312B3
CP rift rptd, Marchais under attack 4-27, 352B1
Pub svc prices hiked 4-27, minimum wage increased 5-1, 352F1
L'Express controlling interest sold 4-27, 352A3
Lyon gets new subway 4-28, 352B3
Austerity measures spur strikes, job actions; Renault plants hit 5-25—7-4, 532G2-533G1
Boussac bankruptcy rescue refused 5-30, 473B3
Price control phase-out begins 6-1, 473F2
Air controller slowdowns 7-14—8-21, 640F2-A3
Giscard vows growth stimulus moves 7-17, 544B2
'76 arms spending rptd 7-23, 585C2
'79 budget OKd; job stimulatn, tax hikes seen 8-28, 667F1
'79 budget gets Cabt OK 9-6, 881D3
Socialist censure motion fails 10-4, 815D2
Steel rescue plan OKd by Assemb 10-11, 815B3
Oct jobless rptd 10-14, 903B1
Cabt OKs job measures 10-15, 902G3
June '77-78 world inflation rates ranked 10-18, 914F1
Dockworkers, seamen strike 10-23, 816A1
Postal strike series begins 10-24, 882G1
Corsica truckers end port blockade 10-26, 882A2
Soldiers replace striking Paris sanitatn workers 10-31, 882G1

1979

Corsica
Separatist bombings 2-27, 3-10, retaliatn 3-11, 236E1
Separatist bombings rptd 5-3, 330D2
Separatist 3d anniv bombings 5-6, 425A1
Paris hit by bomb wave 5-31, 424G3
Natlsts set off bombs 6-16, 653F1
Separatists bomb Lyons 9-13, Paris 10-25, 835C2

Economy & Labor
Barre urges contd austerity, lists econ goals 1-4, 20A2
'78 inflatn rptd 9.5% 1-8, 13C1
Steel workers stage job actns 1-12—2-6, 96F1-B2
Price decontrol to continue 1-12, 96C2
Job measures announced 1-16, 37A3
'78 living standards ranked 2-2, 109B2
Oil, gas supplier search speedup ordrd 2-7, 82D3
Job protests continue 2-8—2-21, 135B1
Jan joblessness rptd 2-15, 135C1
Job measures proposed 2-21, 134D3
Steelworker protests 2-21—2-28, govt proposes job measures 2-23, 154A1
Bourse workers strike 2-28, 189G3
Steelworker unrest continues 3-3, 3-7—3-8, reorgn plan halted 3-8, 189C3
RR workers strike 3-6—3-7, 189F3
Parlt spec sessn debates joblessness 3-14—3-16; leftist censure votes fail, probes OKd 3-16, 235C2-B3
Paris jobless protest ends in riots 3-23, CGT asks probe 3-24, 235F3
Econ study released 3-25, 236F1
Bourse workers end strike 3-30, 267G2
Chirac scores Giscard 3-31, 267C3
Indl stimulus steps OKd 4-4, 267G1-B2
'81-86 plan presented 4-4, 267B2
Soclst Party split 4-6—4-8, 267F2
Dock disputes persist 4-24—4-30, 330E1
Renault, Peugot plans rptd 4-25, 299B3
Bank rules set 4-25, 330F2
Wine mislabeling chrgd 4-25, 330A3
Paris bombings linked 5-1, 330C2
Marchais vs govt on steel 5-10, 371D2
Dockworkers boycott A-cargo 5-17, 390G2
Immigratn curbs OKd by Assemb 5-30, data rptd 5-31, 425B1
Youth jobs plan announced 5-30, 425E1
7-natn indicators index rptd 6-11, 513A3
4 banks rptd among '78 world's top 10 6-19, 476B2
Steelworker reorgn pact set 7-24, 564G1
Dockworkers sign contract 7-25, 564A1
Sacilor, Pompey to merge 7-25, 564C2

1980

China A-reactor deal set 10-17, 829A3
Iraq bars UN A-reactor inspectn 11-7, 864C2

Corsica
Separatist unrest hits Bastelica, Ajaccio 1-6—1-11, 3 die 1-9, tensns rptd eased 1-14, 58A1
Separatists demonstrate 1-26, 97F2
Ajaccio buildings bombed 3-10, 232B1
Aid promised 4-22, 312C3
Paris, Nice bombings staged 4-23, 312E3
Separatists sentncd re '78 blasts 5-13, Iran emb guards attacked 5-14, 463G1
Separatist violence continues 8-9, Simeoni disavows 8-12, 670C2
Defense & Armed Forces
'81 spending hike OKd 10-23, 886E1-A2
'79 mil spending cited 12-10, 949F2

Economy & Labor
Energy price hike, govt aid to business OKd; other price hikes rptd 1-2, 6F2, B3
Natl Front ldr links jobless, immigratn 1-4, 20C1
CFDT scores govt re Corsica 1-10, gen strike held 1-11, 58B2, D2
Budget OKd by Sen 1-16, 57D2
'79 inflatn rptd 11.8% 1-22, 97E2
Corsica separatists demonstrate 1-26, 97A3
Chirac scores Giscard 2-25, 193A1
Illegal Turkish workers protest 3-3, 193B1
Teachers protest cutbacks 3-19, 231F3
Dockers strike 3-20, 231G3
Steelmakers fined 4-3, 262F2
Chirac details plan 4-14, 312B2
Farm price hike set 4-30, 327A2
Unions strike vs health plan 5-13, 407C1
Transport workers strike 6-11, power workers 6-12, 463A1
'79 purchasing power decline rptd, GDP increase seen 6-14, 463C1
Rhone-Poulenc sells units 7-9, 522C2
Labor costs rptd 8-12, 698E1
Fishermen relax blockade 8-19, 633F3-634B1
Port blockade concessns offered, fishermen score 8-26; navy opens blockade, Seguy threatens wider strike 8-27, 651D3
Fishermen protest in Paris 9-2; Boulogne crews reject pact 9-5, 707F2
Econ stimulus plan set 9-3, 670A1
CGT-CFDT rift widens on Polish unrest 9-4, 688E1
'81 draft budget OKd 9-10, 687E3
Boulogne fishermen end strike 9-17, 750B2
Hormones in cattle feed barred 10-1, 737C3
Cabt OKs 5-year plan 10-1, 749D3
Wine scandal suspected 11-3, 11-18, 925E2

1976

Corsica ferry rates protested 8-30, 693B2
Trainmen strike 9-3—9-5, 693G2
Barre details inflatn curbs 9-22, 712B2
More drought aid set 9-22, 772F3
Bank rate hiked 9-23, 731A3
Unions call for strike 9-23, 731B3
Citroen-Peugeot merger rptd 10-1, 773B1
Gen strike re inflatn curbs 10-7, 772G2
Scores OECD incomes rpt 10-12, 964A2
Nov unemploymt up 11-16, 1003E1
Air France rpts deficit 11-18, 905B3
Austerity budget passed 11-21, 1003D1
OECD growth forecast disputed 11-23, 975G3
Mid-Oct to mid-Nov jobless rate up 11-29, 935C2
Paris newspapers strike 12-6, 964A1
Oct '75-76 inflatn rate rptd 12-6, 976B1
Business tax cut 12-8, 1003F1
Labor strikes, protests 12-14—12-15, 964E1
Margaux vineyard sold 12-18, 964F2-A3
Forest fire losses in drought rptd 12-31, 977E3

European Force Reduction Issues—*See under EUROPE*

Foreign Economic Developments
Wine growers protest Italy imports 1-7—2-5, agri mins confer 1-20, 138B3-139A1
Jamaica accord on currency reform 1-8, 14D1
SDR rate rptd 1-15, 14A3
Morocco Mirage order rptd, other purchasers cited 1-15, 1-16, 36A2
Chirac plan to cut arms sales rptd 1-15, 126E2
Zaire jet deliveries rptd 1-16, 36C1
Franc bolstered in lira crisis 1-21—1-22, 74D2
India cooperatn pacts signed 1-22—1-26, 139E2
Clerics vs arms exports, Chirac defends 1-25, 126F2
In 7-natn A-safeguards agrmt 1-27, 84A1
Mauritania compensates iron co 1-28, 104F2
S Korea cancels A-plant purchase, US pressure cited 1-29, 1-30, 103G2
Australia trade drive planned 2-4, 116A2
Le Monde launches Portugal editn 2-8, 143E2
W Ger currency accords 2-9, 2-12—2-13, 229D1
Dassault Dutch, Colombia bribe cases rptd 2-12, 2-16, 141D2, 147E3
Franc drop rptd 2-14—3-25, UK denies role 3-16, 229E1
Consortium-backed Italy loan rptd 2-16, 141A1
Jan trade deficit rptd 2-20, 205E1
US vs Pak A-plant buy 2-23; IAEA OKs plant 2-24, 175C1
Italy wine talks 2-24, 163D3
Dassault Dutch case acquittal 2-25, 158E2
6-natn export credit pact rptd 2-25, 164C2
'72 Dutch Lockheed bribe rptd 2-27, 254B3
Bahrain pacts signed 3-2, 204F3
France quits snake float 3-15, 229C1
US threatens steel quotas 3-16, 212G3
Pak A-plant pact signed 3-18, 581C3
Libya A-plant, other projects set 3-22, 239B3
Firms off Arab blacklist 3-24—4-3, 242C1
Egypt gets arms aid vows, jet deal seen 3-26—4-5, 275B1, F1
Ger, Dutch reject currency snake reform plan 4-1—4-2, 276A1, D1
A-export safeguards set 4-8, 372C3
Dutch bribe probe widens 4-13, 322C2
Fast-breeder reactor OKd 4-15, 372B3
French draft 5-yr plan OKd 4-21, 312A2
US ends car dumping probe 5-4, 321D2
'75 Sovt trade rptd 5-5, 340F3
Aid to poor natns set 5-10—5-11, 355F3
Giscard seeks US OK for Africa dvpt fund 5-17—5-18, 372A2
W Ger A-pact OKd 5-18, 372F2
S Africa A-plant pact agreed 5-28, 387F1
7-natn summit set 6-1, 6-3, 388G3
Loan to prop UK £ OKd 6-7, 407C2
IMF gold purchase rptd 6-9, 430D2
Export credit terms tightened 6-15, 529F3, 530A1
200-mil limit draft bill OKd 6-16, 481F3
Paris Club defers Zaire debt 6-17, 488A2
7-natn econ summit held 6-27—6-28, 461G2
Sovt aluminum plant deal set 7-3, 540E2
Vs Libya Mirage transfer to Uganda 7-8; 30 rptd sent 7-9, 516A3
At A-waste conf 7-12, 739G1
Danish, E Ger contructn pact rptd 7-12, 889C2
Govt acts to halt franc slide 7-15—7-27, 555E3
Italy loan ban disclosed 7-16, Giscard hedges 7-19, 530D3; repercusns 7-20, 557B1
Signs Sovt A-safeguards pact 7-16, 540E2
Israel links currency 7-18, 538D3
Libya confrms Mirage transfer to Uganda 7-18, 548C2 ★
S Africa buys 2 warships 7-31, 714C1
S Africa A-plant pact signed 8-6, 630G3
US, Pak discuss A-plant 8-8—8-9; France protests 8-9, 581G2
Carter asks breeder study 8-9, 585C1
Spain signs intl bank loan 8-9, 929A2

1977

Immigrant workers plan dropped 10-30, work force cited 1013D1
Food price controls set 11-3, gen strike called 11-8, 1012B2
Defns budget cuts debated 11-9, 11-18, Assemb OKs 11-19, 924F1
Soclst-CP compromise talks on natlizatn fail 11-9, 924A3
Baker's protest price freeze 11-9—11-10, shopkeepers rptd angry 11-15, 1012B2
Natl budget defense ratio rptd 11-11, 924A2
Cabt raises min wage, pensns 11-30, 1012G1
3 unions call 1-day gen strike; Force Ouvriere, left-wing parties disassociate 12-1, 1012C1
Giscard backs Barre econ progrm 12-8, 1012B3
Unions halt power cuts 12-12, utility co talks fail 12-14, 1012A2

1978

Seamen agree to end strike 11-4, 882C1
Truckers stage job protest 11-6, 882G1
'79 defns budget OKd by Assemb, 6th A-sub set 11-7, 882A1
L'Aurore purchase blocked 11-22, Hersant to face trust chrgs 11-29, 1016F3
L'Aurore editor quits, editorial asks govt funding 11-26, 1017A1
'78 revised budget, VAT chngs, Dassault acquisitn OKd by Assemb 12-8, 987E2
Blackout productn loss rptd $1 bln 12-19, 1016C3
Paris stock mkt rptd up; graph 12-25, 1001B3, C3

Environment & Pollution
Oil tanker spill fouls coast 3-17; tourist, fishing damage rptd 3-22, 201C3
Oil slick spreads 3-23—3-29, new safety rules ordrd 3-23, 238B1, G1
Oil-spill curb actns OKd 6-4—7-5, 524A1-F1
Amoco sued on tanker spill 9-13, 749C1

European Force Reduction Talks—*See under EUROPE*

1979

Soc Sec reforms OKd, detailed 7-25, 564D2
Oil price hike impact noted 8-2, 614C1
Science spending hike planned 8-3, 614E1
Unions attack govt 8-7, 633G2-C3
'France' sails after labor blockade 8-19, 633D3
CP, Soclst discontent rptd 8-20, 633A2
Rail workers strike 8-22, 633G3-634A1
Constructn, soc benefit pkgs rptd; union ldrs score 8-29, 652C3
Cabt OKs '80 budget 9-5, 668E2
Westn wage rates compared 9-19, 697D3
CGT, CFDT adopt joint progrm 9-19, 729G2-C3
Barre in talks with unions 10-2, 791E2
Air traffic disrupted by job disputes 10-2, 11-18, 11-12, 791D2, 872D3
'80 budget rejected by Assemb, Gaullist-UDF split cited 10-22, 834C3
MDs stage protest strike 10-23, 835F2
Giscard stresses jobless, inflatn 11-7, 873B1

Energy—*See also 'Atomic' above*
Iran oil cutoff impact assessed 3-20, 126A3
IEA boycott cited 3-2, 162C1
Mex oil agrmt signed 4-1—4-4, 372F1
Gas price rptd at $2.45 per gal 5-19, 397A1
Speed limit enforcemt set, other conservatn measures delayed 5-25, 396A3
US oil import subsidy scored 6-1, 417B2
Francois-Poncet in US talks 6-5, 485B1
Solar project rptd revived 6-18, 485F1
OPEC price hike impact seen 6-28, 473B2
Tokyo summit 6-28—6-29, 493B1-F2
Iraq to hike oil exports 7-11, 564C1
Carter plan assessed 7-16, 534F3
Oil spot mkt agrmt rptd 7-16, 494F2
Iran drops gas pipe plans 7-28, 583A1
OPEC price hike impact noted 8-2, 614C1
Research spending hike planned 8-3, 614G1
Pay hike demand linked 8-7, 633A3
Govt aid, oil prices linked; conservatn projcts planned 8-29, 652C3, E3
'80 budget seeks co surtax 9-5, 668D3
UK opposed to N Sea access 9-17, 719C2
Oil, gas exploratn incentives planned 9-21, 752B1
Iran oil import ban backed 11-13, 861F1, F2; limits pledged 11-15, 879F2
Intl conf in Paris 12-10, 933C2

Environment & Pollution
Oil tanker explodes off Ireland 1-8, 201C1
Oil tanker '78 spill rpt issued 3-8, 162A3, C3, 163A1
Forest fires destroy 25,000 acres 8-14, 620B2
Tanker fleet safety record rptd 8-15, 608F1

European Force Reduction Talks—*See under EUROPE*

1980

Energy—*See also 'Atomic Energy' above*
Oil price hikes, other govt measures OKd 1-2, 6F2
Mex oil imports seen 1-15, 60B2
'79 inflatn rptd 1-22, 97F2
Giscard gets oil guarantees from Arab states 3-1—3-10, reaches agrmt with Kuwait 3-3, 180A1
New measures set, oil use cut stressed 4-2, 254C1
Eur auto makers agree on research 4-22, 303A3
Mex trade agrmt signed 5-18, 409D2
Power workers strike 6-12, 463A1
7-natn Venice summit 6-22—6-23, 473A1-474E1
Rhone-Poulenc sells petrochem units 7-9, 522C2
Fuel prices remain high 8-12, 628A2
Port blockade concessns offered 8-26; navy opens blockade 8-27, 651D3
Algeria LNG deal rptd set 9-7, 827C3
Oil tax hike planned 9-10, 688D1
Iraq oil export cut leads to spot mkt bid 9-26, 735B1
Oil use drop set 10-1, 749G3
Saudi oil reliance cited 10-14, 790F1
Iraq resumes oil shipmts 11-20, 894B2
Oil stocks termed 'adequate' 12-9, 932D1

1976

Jet accord with US firm set 8-12, 588D3
Renault OKs US price hikes 8-16, 988D1
Australia budgets Mirage buys 8-17, 636F3
July trade defict rptd up 8-17, 675C1
Nonaligned for oil embargo 8-20, 621D3
Egypt missile deal rptd set 8-27, 675A1
Aug, 1st 8 mo trade deficit rptd 9-17, 772D3
Rpt gold returned to Poland 9-28, 907F1
UK to seek IMF loan 9-29, 721D1
Franc declines vs dollar 9-30, 721C2
Vs World Bank funds rise 10-5, 778D1
Signs Iran A-pact 10-6, 773E2
A-export guidelines set; Pak, Iran sales stand 10-11, 772B3
Sept trade deficit rptd 10-18, 852B3
Vetoes S Africa arms ban 10-19, 781D3, E3
Franc advances vs $, revalued mark 10-20, 782E1
9-mo trade deficit cited 782B2
DISC program ruled illegal 11-5, 976E3
S Africa A-sales to end 11-9, 928A1
UK IMF loan, sterling plan backed 11-12, 880B2 ★
Trade deficit rise rptd 11-18, 964D2
'75 COMECON trade gap rptd 11-18, 977D1
Strasbourg A-plant dropped 11-20, 1002F3
Iran-Czech pipeline to supply gas 11-22, 946B2
Asks 3d 7-natn summit 12-2, 964D1
Rhine pollutn pacts signed 12-4, 977A2
Sale of reprocessing A-plants barred, forgn pacts hold 12-16, 1002A3
In IMF UK loan 12-21, 1004B1
Turk auto mfr to close 12-24, 1012B1
Binocular fraud vs Libya rptd 12-25—12-30, 1006D3

Foreign Relations (misc.)—*See also 'UN Policy' below*
Mex drug agents rptd trained 1-2, 61E1
Natls quit S Vietnam 1-3, 11G3
Cambodia emb closed 1-7, 139D2
Plyushch arrives in Paris 1-12, 30E2
Rpt Chalandon backs Eur defns group 1-15, 126D2
Mitterand at soclst conf 1-19, 48C3
2 rptd named as USSR spies 1-19, 50A1
USSR to make more dailies available 1-21, 76G2
Admiral ousted re CSCE criticism 1-22, 139F1
Chirac in India 1-22—1-26, 139E2
Southn socialist meet 1-24—1-25, 120B1
Paraguay CP ldr arrest, death rptd 1-31, 2-17, 206C1
Plyushch details Sovt asylum stay 2-3, 122E1
Destremau in Australia 2-4, 116A2
CP cong scores USSR 2-4—2-7, 119D1-D2
USSR scores Comoro policy 2-5, 118G3
Brazil CP ldr addresses CP Cong 2-8, 288A1
Nazi hunter given suspended sentnc 2-9, 158D1
Accepts Chile refugee 2-16, 288D3
To represent UK in Iceland 2-19, 156G1
SEATO formally disbanded 2-20, 148C1
Rpt Chile bought Sovt arms 2-25, 288F3
Plissonier at Sovt CP Cong 2-28, 195G3
Bahrain Emir visits 3-2, 204F3
USSR protests Solzhenitsyn TV appearance 3-10, 424E1
Europn socialists meet 3-13—3-14, 222F3
Chirac in Libya 3-21—3-22, 239A3
Eur liberals meet 3-26—3-27, 260C3
Reps at Czech CP Cong 4-12—4-16, 289G1
Chile RC church atty exiled 4-12, 310D2
W Ger head cites CP 4-15, 503D1
NZ prime min visits 4-16, 372E3
Cambodia pilot seeks asylum 5-2, 335F1
Eur CPs meet, cong set 5-4—5-6, 341F1
Meinhof death protested 5-10, 383C2
Bolivian envoy slain 5-11, 350D3
France for strong deterrent vs USSR 5-18, 372C2
Pope scores Lefebvre 5-24, 424B1
Ferreira arrives 5-31, 441B2
Giscard ends UK visit, yrly mtgs set 6-24, 481C3
Marchais at E, W Eur CP conf 6-29—6-30, 461D2
Nimeiry returns from visit 7-2, 501C3
Giscard visits W Ger 7-6, 521D1
Spain premier visits 7-13, 541C3
Priests killed in Argentina 7-21, 571B2
Cambodia missn asked to leave 7-30, 572G2-B3
Portugal PIDE agents flee to 733A2
Carrillo: Spain, France CPs close 7-31, 753G1
Aides in China quake area 8-1, 561E2
Amnesty Intl rpts contd Chile repressn 8-23, 711A1
Argentina violence scored 8-26, 672E2
USSR rejcts Berlin bus protest 8-27, 678D3
Lefebvre defies papal ban 8-29, 655E3
Giscard reactn to Mao death 9-9, 657E2
Yugo pres cancels Giscard trip 9-10, 734F2
Ramses mummy in Paris for repairs 9-26, 912F2
Rpt Poland gets Danzig gold 9-28, 907F1
Brezhnev cites pressure re arms buildup 10-5, 739F1
Spain ETA holds press conf; govt protests 10-6, 774B3
W Ger troop reductn rptd 10-9, 852G2, 880D1

1977

Foreign Relations (misc.)—*See also 'Atomic Energy' above, 'Monetary, Trade & Aid' and 'UN Policy' below*
PLO rep slain 1-3, 9C1
Bourges in Egypt 1-5—1-9, 10A3
Vs E Ger Berlin visas 1-6, 7E2; protests to USSR 1-11, 20F1
Marchais scores Sovt, Czech repressn 1-6, 1-25, 63B2
Daoud arrested 1-7, freed 1-9, 9A1; **for subsequent developments, see MIDDLE EAST—INTERNATIONAL Developments—Daoud Issue**
'76 Eur Cncl pact vs terror cited 9G2
Cavaille visits Japan 1-12, 73C3
Not in 14-natn sulphur-dioxide pact 1-19, 109B3
Giscard in Saudi; oil deal signed, Mideast peace role urged 1-22—1-25, 50F1-D2
Brandt warns on W Berlin 1-24, 102A2
Greek, Turk mins meet 1-29, 122D2
Israel ties reconciled 2-8, 87B1 ★
Malta scores security talks delay 2-10, 136A3
ESA flight set 2-16, 170C3
UK Channel I dispute cited 329C2
Spain seizes rightist 2-22, 307B2
Amalrik protests Giscard policy 2-23, 2-24, 143A1
Bulgaria exiles ask CP support 2-23, 314C2
Hess amnesty denied 2-28, 298C3
Czechs oust, attack rptrs 3-2, 3-3, 220D3, E3
Marchais meets Spain, Italy CP ldrs 3-2—3-3, 242E3
4 arrested as Sovt spies 3-22, 255B3
Iraqi Kurds free 2 hostages 3-28, 256F3
Sadat in Paris 4-3, 245B2
Sovt role in Africa noted 4-12, 265D1
Viet premier visits 4-25—4-28, 329A1
Morin ends Paris visit, Chirac backs Quebec separatism 4-29, 346A3
Trudeau visits, warns on Quebec 5-11—5-14, 389G1
Sudan talks note Sovt role in Africa 5-17—5-19, 450D1
Israeli '69 gunboat seizure cited 5-30, 416E3
'75 Turkish amb death cited 6-9, 565A2
To accept Viet refugees 6-16, 497E1
Eur Parlt direct electns OKd 6-16, 6-22, 598C1
Brezhnev trip protested 6-18; tight security rptd 6-21, 495F1
Brezhnev visits, sees Giscard 6-20—6-22, 494C3-495A2
Israel asks better ties 6-21, 474D2
US-USSR mediator role denied 6-22, 495B2
Spain-USSR Eurocommunism dispute 6-23—6-27, 507G1, A3
USSR renews Carillo attack 7-6, 545D3
Yugo ousts 4 natls 7-7, 606D2
Bulgaria newsman gets asylum 7-7, 606G2
Spain leftists bomb emb bldg 7-11—7-12, 546C1
USSR mil exercises observed 7-11, 551C1
Andreotti visits; sees Giscard, Barre 7-19, 581E2
Giscard evaluates Brezhnev talks 7-25, 551A1
Spain Basque guerrilla detentn protested 8-18—8-24; vanishes after release 10-7, 826E2
Indochina refugees flow rptd 8-31, 685E2
USSR bars Airbus 9-1, 736D1
Eur Cncl to study Turkey rights abuses in Cyprus 9-8, 764G1-A2; rpt shelved, Greece protests 11-3, 946E3
Iran shah's sister escapes assassinatn 9-13, 745F2
Forgn worker immigratn curbed, Viet refugees exempt 9-27, 744C2

1978

Foreign Relations (misc.)—*See also 'Atomic Energy' above, 'Monetary, Trade, Aid & Investment' and 'UN' below*
Barre in China, urges detente in SE Asia 1-19—1-24, 71D1
At Westn natns Ogaden conf 1-21, 43E2
Greek premr visits 1-29—1-30, 149E2
Spies for USSR sentncd 2-1, 71B2
At USSR maneuvers 2-6—2-10, 103C2
Marchais calls Japan 'backward' 2-20, amb protests 2-23, 167C2
Danish premr's remarks on French electn spur dispute 2-23—3-1, 167G1
Overseas voting scandal rptd 2-25, 167A1
Spain playwright arrives 2-27, 250A2
Eur fascists meet 3-4—3-5, 238D3
USSR OKs Airbus landings 3-8, 238D2
PI rebels free Finance Min offcl 3-12, 248B2
Eur conservative group formed 4-24, 424D3
IRA links rptd sought 4-27, 373D2
Belgium army bldgs in Corsica bombed 5-6, 352E2
USSR chrgs US interventn 5-7, 349B3
ESA communicatns satellite launched 5-12, 384D3
Belgium rift re Zaire rescue rptd 5-19—5-23, 381B2, C2
USSR dissident sentence scored 5-20, 401B2
USSR scores Zaire rescue 5-22, 382D1; chrgs massacre 5-25, 417C3
Australia prime min to visit 6-1, 450E3
Westn natns meet on pan-Africa force 6-5, 441E2
Club Medit '77 robberies cited 6-11, 473F3
Giscard visits Spain 6-28—7-1, Basques protest 6-30, 649D1-C2
USSR revokes Rabin citizenship 6-30, 543A2
Laos chrgs rebel aid 6-30; diplomats ousted 7-3, 548D3
Spanish ex-terrorist ldr ambushed, wife killed 7-3, 537E2
Spain access cut off by Basque protesters 7-12, 576D1
Beaufils jailed as Sovt spy 7-12, 649G3
Air controller slowdowns delay Eur flights 7-14—8-21, 640F2-A3
USSR diplomat expelled 7-15, 649F3
Hijack pact signed at Bonn summit 7-17, 544G2-C3
Giscard visits Portugal 7-19—7-21, 667B2
Laos ties ended 8-22, 660C3
Bulgarian defector rpts stabbing 9-14, 748E3
Croat nationalist killed 10-16, 805G1
Gromyko visits, tensns rptd 10-25—10-28, 830E3-831A1
Quebec '70 kidnapers identified 11-2, 880C1
Hungary ldr visits, detente stressed 11-15—11-17, 894E2
Viet refugees accepted 11-20, 932E3
Quebec terrorists return 12-13, 964A2
China-US ties rptd discussed by Giscard, Brzezinski 12-16, 977C1
Spain terrorist killed in Anglet 12-21, 1022F1

1979

Foreign Relations (misc.)—*See also 'Atomic' above, 'Monetary' and 'UN' below*
Sovt warning re China ties cited 1-5, 12C3
Indochina refugees accepted 1-8, 51G2
Spain forgn min in ETA control talks 1-12; ETA ldr wounded 1-13, 61D1
Jesuits return to China rptd discussed 1-23, 218C1
Geneva Com joined 1-27, 625G2
23 Spain Basques arrested, future asylum barred 1-30, 100B3
Spain Basques protest deportatns to Italy 2-5, 192B1
Spain guerrillas kidnap Michelin, Citroen execs 2-5–3-1, 192C1
Barre in Canada, hedges separatism issue 2-8–2-13, 133C3
Pak pres scorns Bhutto clemency plea 2-14, 116B2
China Viet invasn scored by CP 2-19, 122A3
UK amb threatened 3-23, 228A3
Giscard USSR trip rptd canceled 4-18, 314D1
Italy Red Brigades base chrgd 4-24, 331F2
Giscard in USSR: pacts signed; space flight, arms talks unsetld 4-26–4-28, 323A3
USSR backed by CP 5-10–5-15, 371A2, E2
Immigratn curbs OKd by Assemb 5-30, 425B1
Francois-Poncet vs SALT treaty 6-5, 485E1
Thais hold Cambodian refugees for resetlmt 6-12, 436B1
Indochina refugee admissns hiked 6-26, 474C2; total rptd 6-28, 473G2
SALT II backed 6-28, 497A1
Madrid-Paris train attacked 7-2, 505C1
Indochina refugee admissns vowed at intl conf 7-20–7-21, 549D1
Spanish plane hijackers barred 8-5, 604A1
Spain Basques protest refugee status 8-30, 670G3
Socialist conf cited 10-11, 780E1
China premr arrives in Paris 10-15, meets Giscard 10-17, 789E2
Breton separatist in Ireland sentncd 10-20, 835E2
China premr ends Eur trip 11-6, 853E3, 854E1, E2
Czech dissident trial scored 10-23, 802D2
Eur detente committmt reaffirmed 10-29, 835A2
Australia drug traffic linked to natls 11-6, 870G2
Spanish premr visits; EC entry, Basque issue discussed 11-26–11-27, 952D1
Intl energy conf in Paris 12-10, 933C2
Vatican censures Dominican priest 12-18, 999B3

1980

Foreign Relations (misc.)—*See also 'Atomic Energy' above, 'Monetary', 'Soviet-Afghan Issue', 'UN Policy' below*
Immigratn, jobless linked 1-4, 20C1
Marchais in Italy 1-5, USSR 1-7, pro-Sovt stand scored 1-8—1-13, 57F2, F3
Sakharov exile scored by Soclsts, CP 1-22; Chaban-Delmas shortens visit 1-23, 46C3, 86A1, C1
Giscard in India, joint statemt signed 1-27, ends visit 1-28, 97B3
Cambodia border aid vigil staged 2-6, 108C2
Turkey envoy deaths cited 2-6, 197C2
Sovt spy discovered 2-9, 141F2
Italy fraud suspects take refuge 2-11, 151F2
CP forms rights group, issues rpt, scores Sakharov 2-20, 149C3
Sovt airline office bombed 2-24, 149F3
Illegal Turkish workers protest 3-3, 193B1
Channel tunnel plan rptd 3-4, 193F3; UK OKs 3-19, 212B2
Moro suspects seized 3-28, 255C1
Italy rejects Paris CP parley 4-2, 254C3
USSR science conf attended 4-13—4-15, 326F2
Gromyko visits 4-24—4-25, 351E3
Europn CPs meet 4-28—4-29, 327B2
Tito funeral held 5-8, 338D3, 339C1
Forgn student rules spur violent protests 5-13, 5-14, 407E1
Brezhnev meets Giscard 5-19, 378G2-379D1
Gromyko-Muskie mtg noted 5-21, 379D1
ESA rocket test fails 5-23, 397G2
Sovt Armenian immigratn estimated 5-24, 467F2
New Hebrides separatists revolt, provisional govt formed 5-28—6-3, 422A2
Pope visits 5-30—6-2, 476F2--477B1
New Hebrides rebel, forgn links chrgd 6-8; forces sent 6-11, 436E1-A3
7-natn Venice summit 6-22—6-23, 473A1-474E1
Viets capture civilian 6-25, release 6-29, 508G2
Sovt airline office bombing arrests 7-1, 522A2
Barre in Spain, receptn cool 7-2—7-3, 567G1
Eur role stressed 7-7, 7-9, 521F3; 7-11, 540B1
ESA plans comet probe 7-15, 548A1
India launches satellite 7-18, 547E3
Sovts crack down on press at Olympics 7-21, 590G1
New Hebrides force sent 7-24, presence backed 7-30, 580G3
Belgium blast kills Jewish youth 7-27, Palestinian seized 7-28, 573D2
New Hebrides independnc declared 7-30, 580E3
Olympic athletes deliver Sovt rights appeal 8-2, 590E2
Armenians attack Turk consulate 8-5, 606C1
Westn labor costs compared 8-12, 698E1
Papua New Guinea troops replace Vanuatu force 8-18; quell rebellion 8-31, 674C1
Border controls tightened, visas required 9-3, 670C1
Polish unrest widens union rift 9-4, 688E1
Dutch women injured in car blast 10-5, 768B1
Giscard visits China 10-15—10-22; warns re Sovt power monopoly 10-17, 829A3
NATO spy arrested, 2 Sovt Emb aides expelled 11-13, 921B3
Robert role in Vanuatu rebelln rptd 11-21, 903E3
Spain Basques kill 2 11-21; protest issued 11-27, 923B2

1976

Expels Sovt diplomat as spy 10-14, 852F2
USSR expels Tirat 10-21, 857E1
Journalists visit China 11-2, 871D3
Iran diplomat shot 11-2, 1002F2-A3
Canada immigratn rptd 11-3, 851E1
Yugo amb killed in mishap 11-6, 910G1
Giscard, Callaghan yrly mtg 11-11—11-12, 880B2 ★
Spain OKs Socialist conf 11-27, 908E3
Joint Eur defns rejctd 11-30, 905A3
Giscard meets Andreotti 12-2, 964E1
Giscard visits Tito 12-6—12-7, 1012A2
CP scores Sovt-Chile prisoner exchg 12-22, 955E3

Government & Politics—*See also other appropriate subheads*
Cabt family aid plan OKd 1-1, 50D1
Parlt gets 'franglais' ban bill 1-4, 50A2
Lorraine, Poitou-Charentes electn results 1-6, 49A3
Cabt reorganized 1-12, 49A2 ★
'76 programs outlined 1-14, 49E2-A3
Listed as 'free' nation 1-19, 20B3
'Totalitarian' publicatn rptd 1-20, 119A3
Attys protest divorce law 1-21—1-24, 120D2
Poll rpts CP distrust 2-3, 119G2
CP 22d cong; new line announced, Marchais reelected 2-4—2-7, 119D1
CP confrms Plyushch letter 2-4, 122D1
Socialist reactn to CP cong 2-6, 119E2
Chirac bars regional autonomy 2-24, 205B1
Left gains in local vote 3-7, 3-14, 204E2-A3
Chirac Parlt role enlarged 3-26; Giscard, Chirac score left 3-27, 4-1, 4-22, 312B3
Bord quits as UDR chief 4-9, Guena elected 4-24, 312A3
Tours by-electn 5-9, 350B3
Soclst cong, joint '77 electn drive voted 5-15—5-16; agrmt stalled 5-21, 381E2
Giscard bars resignatn with '78 left victory 5-23, 372E2
New centrist party formed 5-23, 418B1
Giscard, Chirac conf 6-6—6-7, 417E3
Const amended re pres electn 6-14, 439A3
Giscard replaces top aide 7-28, 556A1
Defense secy quits 8-4, 588B3
Chirac resigns, Barre named premr 8-25, 637C3
Barre names Cabt, takes finance post 8-27, 650A3
Cabt meets, Giscard assures Barre 8-28, 650G3
Giscard book published 10-11, 852C3
Opposition censure motion defeated 10-20, 782A2
Chirac regains Assemb seat 11-14, 872A3
Gaullists vs Giscard re Paris mayor 11-18, 872G3
Chirac forms new party 12-5, 963D3

Guadeloupe—*See under 'G'*

1977

Yugo pres visits 10-12—10-17, 844E2
Czech dissident trial scored by CP 10-19, 812F1
Quebec premr visits, gets Legion of Honor 10-23—11-4; Canada scores 11-4, 862B2, B3
Plan to bar immigrant families dropped 10-30, 1013D1
Marchais shuns USSR 60th anniv 11-2—11-7, 865G3
USSR backs A-test ban 11-2, 997B1
Rumania dissident arrives 11-20, 948C1
Yugo exiles rptd seized 11-22, 12-17, 1018B3
Malta threatens Libya defns pact 11-23, 925A3
Canada gets clarificatn re Quebec ties 12-9, 965G2
Giscard, Callaghan summit 12-12—12-13, 1013G1

French Guiana—*See FRENCH Guiana*

German Relations
Giscard in Bonn, sees Schmidt 6-16—6-17, 566C3
Anti-Ger sentimt rptd 7-28, 597E2
W Ger scored re Kappler extraditn bar 8-19, 638F1
Baader atty arrested 9-30, extradited to W Ger 11-16; leftists protest, govt defends 11-17, 11-25—11-28, 968F2, 969C1
W Ger hijacked jet rescue aided 10-17, Schmidt thanks 10-18, 789E2, 790F1
W Eur heroin conf 10-17—10-21, 971E3
W Ger terrorist suicides spur protests 10-19, 791C1
Schleyer body found 10-19, W Ger asks manhunt aid 10-20, 791E1, B2
Mendes-France at Brandt comm mtg 12-9—12-11, 998A1

Government & Politics—*See also other appropriate subheads in this section*
Servan-Schreiber wins Lorraine electn 1-6, 63A2
Chirac to run for Paris mayor 1-19, 63C1
Left gains in munic electns, Chirac elected Paris mayor 3-13, 3-20, 221A1
New Cabinet named 3-30, 239C1
Chirac on leftist '78 electn victory 4-3, 255F2
Moderate left backed in poll 5-4, CP-Socialist rift rptd 5-17, 542E3
Barre-Mitterand TV debate 5-12, 542G3
Poniatowski named Giscard amb 5-13, 391B3
Servan-Schreiber elected Radical pres 5-15, 449G3
Giscard party chngs name 5-20, 449E3
Govt wins confidence vote 6-16, 598C1
Socialist party cong, CERES disbanded 6-17—6-19, 542C3
Left-wing coalitn mtg ends in discord 9-14, 727B3
3 Cabt mins replaced 9-26, 744E2
Radical Soclsts seek Soclst alliance 10-20, 924E2
4 govt parties set electn agrmt 10-21, 924B2
CP, Soclsts trade chrgs 10-27, 10-31; left-wing compromise talks fail 11-9, 924E2, A3
Soclsts, Left Radicals electn agrmt rptd 11-11, 924D3
Left-wing party support rptd down 11-18, 924G2
Chirac sees Giscard on '78 electns 12-7; stresses unity 12-8, bars coalitn platform 12-13, 1012E2
Giscard sees major pol ldrs, backs Barre 12-8, 1012A3
Gunmen attack Marchais home 12-25, 1011F3

Helsinki Agreement—*See EUROPE—Security and Cooperation*

Latin Relations
Peru jet sales noted 1-10, 2B3
IDB joined 1-10, 438E3
Ecuador jet sale seen 2-7, 87C3
Brazil torture of minors chrgd 2-13, 168D1

1978

French Guiana—*See FRENCH Guiana*

French Polynesia—*See FRENCH Polynesia*

German Relations
Giscard, Schmidt hold summit: OK ESA rocket launcher, Greece EC entry; score UK fishing policy 2-6—2-7, 122B1
France '77 trade deficit drop rptd 2-24, 149D1
Berlin demilitarized status cited 3-14, 276B1
Giscard, Schmidt meet; Sovt uranium deal discussed 4-2, 258C2
W Ger terrorists arrested at Orly 5-11, 5-25, 439B1 ★, A2, C2
Giscard sees Schmidt in Hamburg 6-23, 545A2
Japan breeder research pact rptd 6-23, 548E3
Baader atty '77 extraditn to W Ger upheld 7-7, 649B3
Eur rights ct rejcts Baader chrgs vs W Ger 7-19, 651A3
Paris Gestapo chiefs chrgd in Cologne 7-24, 652C1
E Berlin mil displays scored 10-2, 10-7, 861F3

Government & Politics—*See also other appropriate subheads in this section*
Soclsts publish electn progrm 1-4; CP scores, rejcts Mitterrand reconciliatn offer 1-5, 54A1
CP, Gaullists, de Guiringaurd score Mitterrand-Carter mtg 1-6—1-10, 54D1
CP breaks left-wing electn accord 1-7, 54F1
Barre presents govt electn program 1-7, campaign plans 1-9; Gaullists rptd angered 1-11, 54B2
Small govt parties form electn accord 1-10, Gaullists break pact 1-11, 54G2
Barre, Chirac play down split 1-13; Giscard urges unity 1-16, 54D3
Legis candidates record seen 1-14, 54F3
Giscard urges rejectn of left, backs Barre program 1-27, 70D3
Marchais campaign proposals rptd 2-6, 148E3
Mitterrand bars CP electn deal 2-8, 148G3
Chirac speech rouses Gaullists 2-11, 149A1
Left leads in pre-electn polls 2-19, 148C3
Electn campaign officially opens 2-20, 148B3
Marchais in TV debate 2-20, 167D2
Overseas voting scandal rptd 2-25, 167A1
Govt coalitn wins legislative electns 3-12, 3-19; left renews electn pact 3-17, vote analyzed 3-20, 200F2
Chirac claims victory, Barre disputes 3-20; rift seen 3-21, 201D1
Mitterrand blames CP for electn defeat, Marchais affirms left alliance 3-20, 201G1
Radicals quit left-wing alliance 3-20, Fabre resigns ldrship 3-22, 201C2
Giscard sees leftist ldrs, Chirac 3-26—3-31, 245D3
Barre renamed premr 3-31, names Cabt 4-5, 245C2
Chaban-Delmas elected Assemb pres 4-3, 245G2
Barre Cabt gets confidence vote 4-20, 312B3
CP rift rptd, Marchais under attack 4-27, 351F1-352D1
Soclsts debate electn loss, Mitterrand scores CP 5-1, 352D1
Servan-Schreiber loses Assemb seat 6-30, 533A2
Soclists win 2 legis seats in by-electns 10-1, 815G1
Socialist censure motion fails 10-4, 815C2
Chirac calls for Gaullist-Barre truce 10-10, 815A3
'79 defns budget OKd 11-7, 882A1
De Guiringaud resigns 11-27, Francois-Poncet named 11-29, 1017C1
Chirac attacks Giscard 12-6, Gaullists quarrel 12-13—12-19, 987E1-E2
Gaullists suspend Peyrefitte 12-20, 1016D3

Helsinki Agreement—*See EUROPE—Security and Cooperation*

Latin Relations
Argentine bishops ask nuns' release 3-21, 286B1
Chile pol exile arrives 4-1, 267F1
Argentine navy cmdr visits 4-9, 285E3
Chile exiles on hunger strike 5-26, 452E2

1979

German Relations
Schmidt rptdly warns vs China sales 1-6, 12C3
2 arrested as E Ger spies 1-28, 77D3
UDF scores Gaullists 2-17—2-18, 135F1
Schmidt TV appearance rptd 3-8, 214D3
W Ger ranks labor costs 5-1, 374C2
Plutonium dispute setld 5-16, 380B1
E Ger gets credit deal 9-12—9-15, 796G2
W Ger rejects joint A-force 9-24, 733C1
Breton separatist in W Ger sentncd 10-20, 835E2
Giscard visits W Berlin 10-29, 835A2

Government & Politics—*See also other appropriate subheads in this section*
UDF parley meets, scores Gaullists 2-17—2-18, 135C1
Leftist censure votes fail, Gaullist-backed probes OKd 3-16, 235C2-B3
Left gains in local vote, cantonal electns described 3-18, 3-25, 235B3
Chirac confrmd RPR head 3-31, scores Giscard 4-3, 267B3
Soclsts hold cong 4-6—4-8, 267D2
CP cong: Marchais reelected ldr, bars Soclst pact 5-10—5-14, 371G1
Eur Parlt electns held 6-10, 433A1-B2
Mitterrand quits Eur Parlt 6-20, 485A2
Veil voted EC Parlt pres 7-17, 537B2
Mitterrand backs left alliance 8-20, 633F1
Marchais weighs Soclst ties 8-22, 652F3
Mitterrand chrgd re pirate broadcasts 8-24, 653B1
Cabt OKs party funding 9-19, 729C3
Giscard gifts from Bokassa alleged 10-10, 791D1
Giscard tax case arrest made 10-12, 791B2
'77 mil spending total rptd 10-13, 804F1
Boulin kills self, land scandal blamed 10-30, 834F3-835A2
Matteoli named Boulin successor 11-8, 872F3
Giscard denies Bokassa gift personal use 11-27; chrgs continue 12-4, 993D3
Abortn permanently legalized 11-30, 949G1-A2
Emergency budget bill passed 12-27, 12-28, 993A3

Guadeloupe—*See GUADELOUPE*

Helsinki Agreement—*See EUROPE–Security and Cooperation*

Latin American Relations
At 4-natn Guadeloupe summit 1-5—1-6, 12D2
Giscard visits Mex 4-1—4-4, 372F1
El Salvador rebels seize emb 5-4, 370F3, 371A1

1980

Sovts warned on Poland invasn 12-11, 949G1

German Relations
Giscard, Schmidt confer 1-9, 10G2
Schmidt, Giscard end semi-annual mtg, OK tank dvpt 2-5; USSR reacts 2-6, 84E2-D3, 106F2
W Ger sentncs 3 for WW2 crimes 2-11, 118E1
W Ger oppositn vs weak joint Afghan stand 3-20, 236F3
Olympic boycott decisn delay seen 3-23, 259E3
Bonn backs UK in EC budget dispute 3-28, 242B3
IOC offcl sees Olympic boycott 4-14, 283F3
Fighter jet planned 4-14, 303E1
TV satellite pact signed 4-30, 356D1
W Ger suspects arrested 5-5, 411A3
W Ger riot, Westn mil parade linked 5-18, 500F3
Franco-Sovt summit held 5-19, 378B3, C3
Giscard in W Ger 7-7—7-9, 521G3
Giscard W Ger visit ends; Schmidt backs French A-weapons, Eur role 7-11, 539G3
E Ger ex-mil chief arrested 8-19, spy chrgs rptd 9-6, 707F3
Le Monde rpt on terrorist atty extraditn cited 11-7, 872F1

Government & Politics—*See also other appropriate subheads in this section*
Natl Front ldr chrgd 1-4, 20C1
Soclsts meet, back CP alliance, '80s strategy 1-12—1-13, 57E3
CP forms rights group 2-20, 149B3
Chirac attacks Giscard 2-25, 192G3
Marchais defends war record vs L'Express chrgs 3-8, 193E1-A2
Poniatowski impeachmt sought re De Broglie murder 4-14, 312E2
Debre declares pres candidacy; Gaullist, Soclst splits seen 6-30, 522C1
Leftisit named ombudsman 7-31, 652B1
Bokassa confirms Giscard gifts 9-17, 728G3
Marchais gets CP pres nominatn 10-12, 790G1
Le Monde chrgd re ct system allegatns, Giscard gift expose cited 11-7, 872C1
Mitterrand sets pres bid, Rocard withdraws 11-8, 886A2
Giscard gift expose figure freed 11-29, 921A3
By-electns, Giscard party loses 3 Assemb seats 11-30, 921C2
Giscard cousins paid damages on Bokassa story 12-23, 996D3

Guadeloupe—*See GUADELOUPE*

Latin American Relations
Mex oil imports seen 1-15, 60B2
Cuban trade accord reached, Antilles non-interventn pledge cited 4-1, 253F2
Mex pres visits 5-16—5-18, econ agrmt signed 5-18, 409G1, C2

1976

Middle East—*See INTERNATIONAL Developments under MIDDLE EAST*

1977

Brazil mil aid request seen 3-7, 168B1
Colombia banker kidnaped 3-13, 255G1
Mexico amb resigns 4-7, 529G1
'66-67 arms transfers table 4-8, 415A3, C3
Chile exiles protest disappearances 6-14—6-23, 493G1
Panama ldr visits 10-3—10-4, 792C2
Argentina Renault workers strike 10-11—10-14, 981B1
Nicaragua emb harbors rebels 10-20, 865D1
2 nuns kidnaped in Argentina 12-8, 12-10, 981B3
Peugeot exec killed in Argentina 12-16, 981F3

Monetary, Trade & Aid Issues (including all foreign economic developments)—*See also 'Atomic Energy' above*
Andorra asks financial review 1-5, 47G3
Rossi in Canada 1-9—1-12, 43D1
Peru jet sales noted 1-10, 2B3
IDB joined 1-10, 438E3
Egypt Mirage jet deal set, US reactn 1-12, 10G2
ICFTU S Africa boycott fails 1-21, 67B3
Japan gets shipbldg plea 1-21, 73C3
Saudi oil deal signed 1-24, 50F1
'76 trade deficit rptd 1-26, 159E2
IMF SDR defined 87G2
Israel sees Ecuador jet sale 2-7, 87C3
Sovt-bloc debt rptd 2-13, 335F3
Irish ban large fishing vessels 2-15, 146C3
Brazil mil aid request seen 3-7, 168B1
Zaire arms aid set 3-18, 207D3
US asks Portugal aid 4-1, 330C3
'66-75 Latin arms transfers table 4-8, 415A3, C3
Zaire '74 arms contract cited 4-11, 265C1
Zaire troop role rptd; planes, advisers recalled 4-15—4-21, 317F2
Uranium cartel role rptd 4-25, 479F2
At 7-natn econ summit 5-7—5-8, 357A1-358B2
Intl consortium OKs Egypt aid 5-11—5-12, 390C3
Sudan talks 5-17—5-19, deals rptd 5-23, 450D1
Left seeks US co natlizatns 5-17, 543A1
Eastn to lease Airbus 5-24, 441D2
Group of 10 membership cited 438F1
Mobutu thanks Giscard for aid 6-9—6-10, 490E1
Textile import curbs imposed 6-19, 1012D2, D3
Brezhnev, Giscard sign agrmts 6-22, 495D1
In 11-natn Portugal loan 6-22, 530B3
IWC cuts whaling quotas 6-24, 496G3
Imported food prices frozen 6-28, 1012D2
Zaire debt rescheduled 7-7, 583E1
Chad mil aid rptd 7-18, 597F1
Eng Channel boundary setld 7-18, 625C1
Carter seeks arms sale curbs 7-28, 574A3, B3
'77 paymts deficit forecast 7-31, 586D2
Swiss close Hervel, seek officers 8-15, 658B1
Sweden quits 'snake' 8-29, 708G3
Somalia arms offer canceled 8-31, 684F2

1978

Giscard in Brazil; trade, tech pacts signed 10-4—10-8, 772F2
Brazil, Paraguay, 2 cos; sign hydro turbine pact 10-20, 829A3
Dominica aid hike planned 11-2, 861C3
Mex '79 oil price hike set 12-20, 978F2

Medicine & Health
Organ donatn law chngd 4-3, 597A3
Childbirth hormone study rptd 4-20, 334F3
Intellignc dvpt study rptd 7-8, 1023D2

Middle East Relations
Sadat visits, seeks peace moves backing 2-12; arms request rptd 2-13, 98A3
Egypt jet order rptd 3-1, 139B2
4 Arab natns in arms pact 3-14, 237B1
Leb asks anti-Israel actn 3-15, 174D3
Egypt protests Israel Leb invasn 3-15, 174F3
Leb peace force (Unifil) formed 3-19, Giscard on decisn 3-22, 197D2, F2; **for peacekeeping developments, see MIDDLE EAST—LEBANON**
3 Unifil soldiers slain 5-2, 339F3
Egyptian Communist slain 5-4, 352D2; murder weapon linked to rightists 5-11, 474A1
3 Arab guerrillas slain at Paris airport 5-20, 383E3
Egypt recalls journalists 5-26, 414F3
Saudi forgn min in Paris 5-31, 441A2
Leb Christn ldr asks end to Syrian attacks 7-2, 502G2
Israel chrgs PLO, Unifil infiltratn agrmt 7-4, 503C2
Malta Arab aid threat rptd discounted 7-4, 592G2
Iraq emb raided, 2 die 7-31; 3 Iraq guards expelled 8-2, 582F1-D2
2 slain in raid on PLO, Arab League offices 8-3, 582B3
Iraq emb death protested 8-3, 649D3
Leb army move to south urged 8-8, 638C3
Israel asks aid vs Syria in Leb 8-28, 674G1
Unifil extensn OKd 9-18, 713C1
US cites French 'interest' in Leb 9-28, 745D1
Leb peace asked 10-2, 10-3, Syria vs 10-3, 745A1-D2
Leb vs peace plan 10-5, reactn 10-7, 761B2
Exiled Iran govt foe arrives 10-6, 774F3
Unifil soldier slain 10-10, 783A2
Leb Christn ldr blamed for strife 10-16, denies 10-17, 783C1
Iran projct faces curbs 10-22, 816C3
Exiled Iran Moslem ldr warned 12-4, 929A2

Monetary, Trade, Aid & Investment—*See also 'Atomic Energy' above*
Algeria pres visits Malta 1-3, 39C2
Carter in poor natn aid talks 1-4—1-6, 2E1
US $ swap pact cited 1-4, 27B2
$ drop, recovery rptd 1-4, 27E3
Algeria orders import cuts, trade deficit cited 1-11, 11C3
Ivory Coast cargo ship, offshore oil pact 1-11—1-15, 71C1
Somalia asks arms aid 1-16, 43B3
'77 trade, paymts deficits rptd; US, W Ger data 1-16, 2-24, 149D1
China lauds France EC role 1-20, signs French accord 1-21; '76, '77 trade data cited 71D1
'77 $ drop rptd 1-23, 27D2
Ethiopia protests Somalia aid 2-1, 100D1
Franc falls 2-1—2-6; Giscard vows support 2-7, Mitterrand scores 2-8, 167E1
Somalia makes 2d aid bid 2-4, gets tanks via Saudi 2-8, 99G3
Giscard-Schmidt summit scores UK fishing policy, backs Greece EC entry 2-6—2-7, 122C1
Egypt Mirage request rptd 2-13, 98B3
US $ drops vs franc 2-23, 118D2
Egypt jet order rptd 3-1, 139B2
Franc value, stock prices rise 3-10—3-20, 201D2
UK prime min urges Bonn summit plan 3-14, sees Carter 3-23, 226D3
4 Arab natns in arms pact 3-14, 237B1
Renault, AMC plan joint productn, distributn; Renault US '77 sales cited 3-31, 283F3-284B1
US $ drops vs franc 4-3, 235C1
Franc in new SDR basket 4-3, 300F3
Eastern buys airbuses 4-6, 264B3
Kenya dam contract rptd 4-9, 479D1
UK financier buys control of L'Express 4-27, 352A3
US firm foils Pricel takeover 5-12, 404C1
Shell Oil boycott rptd 5-29, 474D1
US '77 thoroughbred import ban cited 539E2
Zaire aid OKd 6-13—6-14, 478A1
Rumania expansn rptd by Renault 6-14, 651A1
Border traffic blocked by strikers 6-23, 6-27, 6-28, 532C3, F3
Giscard, Schmidt meet; back EC monetary zone 6-23, 545A2
Spain rpts Mirage jet purchase 6-26, 649B2

1979

Chile refugee relocatn rptd 5-7, 369B3
El Salvador emb siege ends; amb, 5 others freed 6-1, 424B3
Renault Argentine mkt share rptd 7-20, 562G1
Martinique—*See MARTINIQUE*

Middle East Relations
Israel asks Sinai oil access 1-5, 51C2
Iran oil cutoff impact assessed 2-20, 126A3
Iran halts trial of ex-premr 3-16, 199G1
PLO disavows attack on Jewish hostel 3-27, 222F2
Iran ex-premr takes refuge 3-30, 247C3
Iraq A-reactor sabotaged, forgn agents suspected 4-6, 276D1
Iraq vowed replacemt A-reactor 5-9, 371F2
Egypt: Saudis buying Mirages 5-12, 360C1
Francois-Poncet vs Israel-Egypt treaty 6-5, 485D1
Iran banks, insurance cos natlzd 6-7, 6-25, compensation vowed 6-10, 469B2, 486E2
Iraq oil, A-reactor, arms agrmt rptd 7-11, 564C1
PLO aide arrives 7-20, shot 7-25, 551G3; suspect arrested 8-20, 625D2
Iran drops gas pipe plans 7-28, 583A1
Iran ex-premr reemerges 7-31, 582F2
Iran ousts newsman 8-21, 635A2
Leb hijackers denied refueling stop 9-7, 677D3
Jordan king on state visit 9-10, 676B3
Iran defense min quits 9-28, 752C2
Iranian stake in Eurodif frozen 10-24, 976E2
US ban on Iran oil backed 11-13, 861F1, F2; import limits pldged 11-15, 879F2
Envoy visits US hostages in Iran 11-10, 862A2
Pahlevi family fund transfers rptd 11-26, 897E2
Iran condemned for US Emb seizure 11-27, 895D3
Iran sues US bank for assets freeze 12-5, 915A2
Shah's nephew slain 12-7, 935C1
US seeks econ sanctns vs Iran 12-10, 933C2

Monetary, Trade, Aid & Investment—*See also 'Atomic' above*
Barre stresses franc strength, paymts surplus 1-4, 20B2
Israel asks Sinai oil access 1-5, 51C2
Guadeloupe summit warned vs China sales 1-6; Turkey aid offer rptd 1-12, 12C3, 40B2
Renault, AMC sign sales pact 1-10, 131E2
Dutch barge strike ends 1-10, 136B2
'78 trade balance surplus rptd; oil prices, US $ drop cited 1-17, 37D3
Spain OKs 2 banks 1-26, 100F3
EC comm backs farm price freeze 1-31, 85E1
Credit Lyonnais employes chrgd 2-5, 96F2
Turkey aid role taken by OECD 2-6, 116E3
US $ rises vs franc 2-8, 83C2
Barre in Canada trade talks 2-8—2-9, 133E3
Carter Westn econ summit warning to Japan rptd 2-10, rpt disputed 2-15, 160E1
Iran oil cutoff impact assessed 2-20, 126A3
IEA boycott cited 3-2, 162C1
EMS oppositn ends, UK rejectn of EC farm accord scored 3-7, 160A3, G3
CGE buys Generale Occidentale share 3-16, 236B2
Renault buys Mack Trucks share 3-19, 3-20, 236E2, 283B1
USSR computer sale set 3-27, 237G2
UAL orders French-US engines 3-29, 309B1
Mex oil, other trade agrmts signed 4-1-4-4, 372F1
S Africa '72-78 loans rptd 4-2, 270D2
Paymts maintenance planned 4-5, 267D2
USSR computer sale rptd under review 4-5, 287F2
Uniroyal operatns sale set 4-17, 560G3
Ford bars new plant; Renault, Peugot dispute cited 4-24, 299A3
US mislabeled wine shipmt rptd 4-25, 330A3
USSR econ pact, cooperatn agrmts signed 4-26—4-28, 723A3
US $ closes up vs franc 5-1, 321B1
W Ger ranks exporter labor costs 5-1, 374C2
Mauritania in aid talks 5-3, 324A1
Africa debt relief vow rptd 5-4, 371C3

1980

Bolivia deposed pres leaves for Paris 10-4, 787C2
US curbs Creuset Loire imports 11-17, 886B1
Cuba ex-offcl asks UN probe prison hunger strike 12-4, 963D2

Middle East Relations
Citibank funds frozen on Iran request 1-16, upheld 1-21, 48B1
Syrian emb bombed 1-29, 89C3
Iranian plan to free US hostages rptd 2-11, 2-13, 105D1
Iraq A-fuel, reactor OKd 2-27, 192D3
Giscard tours Arab states; backs Palestinian rights, gets oil guarantees 3-1—3-10, 179G3
US vs stand on Palestinians 3-31, 260F3
OPEC 3d World aid urged 4-14, 312D2
Iran hostage kin seek support 4-23, 299C2
Sovt talks held 4-24—4-25, 351F3
Iran hostage rescue missn reactn 4-25, 324A2
UN Palestinian state res abstentn 4-30, 325D1
Libyan missn bombed 5-6, 373D3
Iran emb guards attacked 5-14, 463G1, A2
Arafat warns vs pro-Israel stand 5-18, 418F1
Iran trade sanctns OKd 5-21, 378A2
Iran gold transfers rptd 6-17, 464A3
Iran takes over Rhone-Poulenc drug co unit 7-9, 546E2
Bakhtiar eludes death try; 5 seized, PLO linked 7-18; Iran warned, denies role 7-18—7-19, 545A1
Syrian ex-premr slain 7-21, 567C2
Jewish youth killed in Belgium blast 7-27, Palestinian seized 7-28, 573D2
Israel vs Iraq A-deal 7-28, Paris defends 7-29, 573A3, C3
Egypt amb at shah's funeral 7-29, 571G1
UN Palestinian state res abstentn 7-29, 572F1
Iranian visa rules set 9-3, 670D1
Leb Moslem ldr rptd jailed in Libya 9-9, 709B1
Iraq vice premier visits 9-25, 718D3
Iraq oil export cut leads to spot mkt bid 9-26, 735B1
Iran ex-premr in TV interview 9-26, 757D1
Iraq ousts journalist 10-2, 775A1
Israel scores anti-Semitism 10-13, 790A1
Saudi naval aid set 10-14, 790C1
Persian Gulf mine-sweeping force set 10-28, 821D2
Iraq bars UN A-reactor inspectn 11-7, 864C2
Le Monde chrgd re Libya spy revelatns 11-7, 872G1
Iraq seeks arms 11-11—11-12, 879A3
Iraq resumes oil shipmts 11-20, 894B2
Iraq war supplies shipped via Saudi ports 11-20, 894F2
Alleged Libya spy freed 11-29, 921F2

Monetary, Trade, Aid & Investment
See also 'Atomic Energy' above
Oil import costs estimated 1-2, 6G2
US OKs FX jet for export 1-4, 16D3
Mex '80 oil imports seen 1-15, 60B2
Citibank funds frozen on Iran request 1-16; Citibank appeals 1-17, freeze upheld 1-21, 48B2
Exports, imports predicted 1-16, 57F2
Gold reserves rptd 1-18, 30A3
'79 trade deficit rptd 1-21, 58F2
India pacts signed 1-28, 97B3
Peugot, Chrysler productn talks, finance deal rptd 2-6, 127D2
UK lamb dispute continues 2-14—2-20, 125A1
Giscard gets oil guarantees from Arab states 3-1—3-10, reaches agrmt with Kuwait 3-3, 180A1
Wine fraud re US exports disclosed 3-6, 193B2
UK scored re EC budget issue 3-12, 3-17, 3-19; W Ger backs UK 3-28, 242E2-C3
Dockers strike 3-20, 232A1
US Steel files dumping complaint 3-21, 225D1
IMF hikes SDR interest rate 3-27, 302B2
Cuba trade accord reached 4-1, 253F2
'79 US investmt rptd 4-8, 329C1
US sets steel import probe 4-10, 367F3
W Eur fighter jet planned 4-14, 303E1
Renault, Peugeot in Europn research collaboratn 4-14, 303B3
OPEC 3d World aid urged 4-14, 312D2
Turkey aid OKd 4-15, 295A3
Swiss arrest customs offcls 4-15; Swiss Bank Paris unit searched 5-7, 407B2
UK opposed on EC budget, farm prices 4-27—4-30, 327F1, A2
W Ger TV satellite pact signed 4-30, 356D1
US finds steel import damage 5-1, 456C1
Mex econ cooperatn agrmt signed 5-18, 409D2
Iran trade sanctns OKd 5-21, 378A2
Sovt trade blitz rptd 5-22, 430G3
UK lamb dispute setld 5-29, 421A3
Chrysler to sell Peugeot imports 6-2, 457C1
EC expansn delay asked 6-5, Spain scores 6-6, 435E3-436D1
Spain produce dispute spurs violence, truckers block border 6-16—6-20, 525A3
Iran gold transfers rptd 6-17, 464A3
Swiss convict customs offcls 6-18, 522F2

1976

Obituaries
Bosco, Henri 5-4, 368E2
Cassin, Rene 2-20, 192D3
De Vogue, Robert-Jean 10-17, 970C3
Gabin, Jean 11-15, 970F1
Mainbocher 12-27, 1015A2
Malraux, Andre 11-23, 970D2
Martinon, Jean 3-1, 192F3
Monod, Jacques 5-31, 404D2 ★
Morand, Paul 7-23, 970E2
Pages, Jean 10-21, 970A3
Servais, Jean 2-17, 192F3
Tolstoy, Countess Mary K 11-21, 970C3

Sports
Winter Olympics results 2-4—2-15, 158E3, 159B2
Olympic results 7-18—7-31, 573D3, 574C2-A3, 576A1, E2

1977

Barre in US, asks 'organized free trade' 9-15—9-16, 1012B3
S Africa investmts rptd 9-23, 771F1
USSR ousts Barents trawlers 9-24, curbs fishing 9-27, 771F2
IMF-World Bank mtgs see econ recovery effort 9-26—9-30, 753D3
Eng Channel boundary chng rejctd 9-29, UK appeals 10-12, 772F1-B2
Gandhi seized re oil co deal 10-3, 765A1
2d in '76 car exports 10-11, 853G2
US steel-dumping chrgs probed 10-19, 933G2
US co chrgs steel dumping 10-20, 836E3
Cuba oil products reach US 10-20, 896B3
Exxon admits paymts 10-25, 818A2
Food tariff cuts set 11-3, 1012C2
S Africa arms sales cited 851E2
S Africa navy sales canceled, '70-76 trade data 11-8, 883B1
TVA sues uranium producers 11-18, 895F1
Arms sales curb refused 11-22, 1012E3
Malta stresses econ, mil aid 11-23, 925B3
Nigeria gun boat purchase rptd 11-23, 986G2
Quebec 5-yr copper deal OKd 12-6, 965B3
$ closes up vs franc 12-8, 933C1
Mendes-France at Brandt comm mtg 12-9—12-11, 998A1
UK indus cooperatn set 12-13, 1013G1
S Africa oil, investmt ban abstentn at UN 12-16, 1016A2
$ drops 12-30, 997F2
New Caledonia—*See NEW Caledonia*

Obituaries
Amaury, Emilien 1-2, 84E2
Bollinger, Elisabeth 2-22, 164C2
Brazier, Eugenie 3-3, 264E2
Clouzot, Henri-Georges 1-12, 84F2
Goscinny, Rene 11-5, 952D2
Gregory, Bernard 12-25, 1024A2
Lalique, Marc 10-26, 872D2
Langlois, Henri 1-12, 84C3
Nin, Anais 1-14, 84D3
Prevert, Jacques 4-11, 356E3
Rostand, Jean 9-3, 788D2
Tourneur, Jacques 12-19, 1024E3

Religion
RC traditionalists occupy Paris church 2-27, Lefebvre celebrates mass 5-22, 471A1
Lefebvre preaches vs modernism in Geneva 5-30, Rome 6-6, 470E3
Lefebvre ordains priest 6-26, 620E2
2 nuns kidnaped in Argentina 12-8, 12-10, 981B3

Sports
French Open results 6-5, 548B2
Alleged wins Arc de Triomphe 10-2, 971G1-A2
Australia wins Davis Cup 12-4, 970G1

1978

Giscard in Spain 6-28—7-1, backs EC entry 6-29, 649D1-C2
Malta Arab aid threat rptd discounted 7-4, 592G2
Mauritania aid re Sahara cited 7-10, 535F1
US $ drops vs franc 7-13, 523C3
At 7-natn Bonn econ summit 7-16—7-17, 543C3, 544B2, D2, G2
US arms sales policy assessed 7-16, 564A2, B2
Giscard in Portugal; backs EC entry, OKs loans 7-19—7-21, 667B2
Peugeot to buy Chrysler units 8-10, 623C2, C3
US $ drops 8-14, 622F1
UK OKs Chrysler sale to Peugot 9-28, 764D1
Giscard visits Brazil; trade, tech pacts signed 10-4—10-8, 772F2
India to buy Anglo-French Jaguars 10-6, 10-7, 796G3-797B1
China science, tech pact signed; missile deal confrmd 10-20, 814A1
Brazil, Paraguay, 2 cos sign hydro turbine pact 10-20, 829A3
UK Airbus role agreed 10-24, 902A3
USSR warns West vs China arms deals 10-26, 814B1
US $ hits new low 10-30, rescue set 11-1, 825D2
Dominica aid hike planned 11-2, 861C3
4 banks rptd among '77 world's top 10 11-8, 914A1-D1
US OKs arms sale to China 11-9, 901F3
Nigeria loan pullout cited 11-30, 934A2
At Brussels monetary summit, EMS entry backed 12-4—12-5; eased terms opposed 12-7, 951F3, G3, 952B1, C2
China trade pact, signed 12-4, 986G1
Credit Agricole tax OKd 12-8, 987G2
Rhodesia rptd obtaining planes 12-13, 955F3
Ireland to join EMS 12-15, 979F1, C2
OPEC price hike adverse impact seen 12-18, 978F1
Mex '79 oil price hike set 12-20, 978F2
Greek EC entry terms set agri curbs noted 12-21, 1017C3, E3
US probes steel dumping chrgs 12-28, 1006B1
US $ closes down vs franc 12-29, 998E2
EMS start delayed 12-29, 999B1

Obituaries
Bonnet, Henri 10-25, 888D2
Boyer, Charles 8-26, 708B2
Brel, Jacques 10-9, 888E2
Brugnon, Jacques 3-30, 252D2
Carita, Maria 9-6, 778A1
Chastenet, Jacques 2-7, 196E2
Damas, Leon 1-22, 96E1
Dauphin, Claude 11-17, 972G2
Francois, Claude 3-11, 252F2
Francois-Poncet, Andre 1-8, 96A2
Gilson, Etienne 9-19, 778D1
Moureu, Henri (rptd) 7-20, 620C3
Pollak, Emile 1-6, 96C3
Prouvost, Jean 10-17, 888D3
Rueff, Jacques Leon 4-23, 356D3

Sports
US battles equine VD 3-15—7-13, 539F2
French Open golf results 5-15, 580E3
World Cup soccer finals, sidelights 6-1—6-25, 519F3
Renault team wins LeMans 6-11, 538F2
French open tennis results 6-11, 540D1
Hinault wins Tour de France 7-23, 692A2
2 British balloonists towed to Concarneau 7-30, 653D1
3 Amer balloonists land in Miserey 8-17, 652D3
Lancome Trophy results 10-22, 990C2

1979

China $7 bln bank loan signed 5-9, 370G1
Egypt: Saudis buying Mirages 5-12, 360C1
Renault Portugal expansn rptd 5-24, 409A3
Uganda trade rptd 5-28, 429C2
US oil import subsidy scored 6-1, 417B2
Westn natn oil import policy urged 6-5, 485B1
Iran banks natlzd 6-7, compensatn vowed 6-10, 469B2
EC green currencies revised 6-21, 513F1
Iran insurnc cos natlzd 6-25, 486E2
Oil import targets set at Tokyo summit 6-28—6-29, 493B1
Iraq oil, arms agrmt rptd 7-11, 564C1
Oil spot mkt agrmt rptd 7-16, 494F2
EC-China textile pact opposed 7-18, 554F3
Renault Argentine mkt share rptd 7-20, 562G1
Iran drops gas pipe plans 7-28, 583A1
OPEC price hike impact noted 8-2, 614C1
CAE aid cut 8-17, 733G3
'France' sails to W Ger 8-19, 633D3
Knitwear import curbs protested in Italy 8-20, 668D3
Cabt OKs '80 budget 9-5, 668B3
E Ger gets credit deal 9-12-9-15, 796G2
UK opposed on EC budget 9-17, 719C2
CAE aid cited 9-21, 720D2
EMS currencies realigned 9-24, 719A1
Renault to buy AMC interest 10-12, 784F2
China pacts signed 10-17, 789B3
US ban on Iran oil backed 11-13, 861F1, F2; import limits pledged 11-15, 879F2
UK lamb dispute progress rptd 11-14, 873B1
Pahlevi family fund transfers rptd 11-26, 897E2
Spain trade talks 11-26—11-27, 952A2
Cambodia relief rptd diverted 12-3, 917B2
Iran sues US bank for assets freeze 12-5, 915A2
US seeks econ sanctns vs Iran 12-10, 933C2
EC '80 budget backed 12-13, 960F2
Renault to buy Volvo share 12-19, 993G3-994C1
US $ closes down vs franc 12-27, 978G3
Canada prov OKs 'Michelin Bill' 12-28, 992F3

Obituaries
Alphand, Nicole 2-15, 176E2
Bernac, Pierre 10-17, 860A2
Boulanger, Nadia 10-22, 860C2
Challe, Maurice 1-18, 104F2
Cousteau, Philippe 6-28, 508D2
De Gaulle, Yvonne 11-8, 932E2
De Guingand, Francis 6-29, 508E2
Delaunay, Sonia 12-5, 1008D2
Frantz, Joseph 9-12, 756E2
Garin, George (rptd) 5-22, 432G2
Hocq, Robert 12-8, 1008C3
Jouhandeau, Marcel 4-7, 356E3
Maze, Paul 9-17, 756G2
Mesrine, Jacques 11-2, 890A3
Monnet, Jean 3-16, 272C3
Renoir, Jean 2-13, 176D3
Viansson-Ponte, Pierre 5-7, 432G3
Villot, Jean Cardinal 3-9, 272G3
Zeller, Andre 9-18, 756G3

Sports
World jr speed-skating champs 2-15, 392D1
French Open tennis results 6-9, 6-10, 570E1
Amer pedals aircraft across Eng Channel 6-12, 527F3
Hinault wins Tour de France 7-22, 655D2
Paris Open tennis results 11-4, 1003F3

1980

7-natn Venice summit 6-22—6-23, 473A1-474E1
AMC gains Renault loan 7-1, 556B3
Barre in Spain EC entry talks 7-2—7-3, 567G1
BP unit buys Rhone-Poulenc share 7-9, 522C2, D2
Iran takes over Rhone-Poulenc drug co unit 7-9, 546E2
Peugeot, Chrysler engine deal confrmd 7-17, 541E2
US urges Poland aid 8-29, strike funds rptd 8-31, 659C1, B3
Export stimulus plan set 9-3, 669G3
Algeria LNG deal rptd set 9-7, 827C3
Peugeot, Fiat project set 9-15, 751F3
IMF revises SDR valuatn method, franc gains in currency 'basket' 9-17, 695E1
US protests Sovt steel deal 9-19, 728D3
Renault increases AMC share 9-24, 724C3
Iraq oil export cut leads to spot mkt bid 9-26, 735B1
EC sets sheepmeat policy 9-30, UK ends claim 10-1, 737E2
Italy hormone raised meat import ban cited 10-1, 737C3
Algeria quake aid rptd 10-11, 776E1
Saudi naval aid set 10-14, 790C1
US curbs Creusot-Loire imports 11-17, 886B1
Iraq resumes oil shipmts 11-20, 894B2
US $ gains vs franc 12-10, 932F1; up 11% in '80 12-31, 983E2

Obituaries
Barthes, Roland 3-25, 279D1
Boussac, Marcel 3-21, 279E1
Etchebaster, Pierre 3-24, 279E2
Fontanet, Joseph 2-2, 97C2
Gary, Romain 12-2, 1004G1
Journiac, Rene 2-8, 176A2
Sartre, Jean-Paul 4-15, 360C3

Soviet-Afghan Issue
Afghan crisis reactn 1-6, 2D2; 1-9, 10F2
Marchais backs invasn 1-11, 57F2, F3
Moscow Olympics boycott opposed 1-21, 45B3; stance rptd eased 2-6, 84A3
US rpt on Persian Gulf defns issued 2-1, 84C2
Giscard, Schmidt condemn USSR 2-5, 106F2
Sovts see US pressure 2-6, 84B3
'Extreme attitude' vs USSR opposed 2-7; to boycott W Eur-US mtg 2-8; US differences cited 2-9, 106D2
US sees allied unity 2-13, 110C1
Vance in Paris, seeks policy coordinatn 2-21, 139B2
W Ger oppositn vs weak joint stand 3-20, 236F3
Olympic com vs Moscow boycott 3-22, 259C3
Olympic boycott decisn delay seen 3-23, 259E3
US rebuffs allies on Olympic boycott stand 3-31, 259G3
IOC offcl sees Olympic boycott 4-14, 283F3
Sovt talks held 4-24—4-25, 351E3, F3
Moscow May Day parade marked 5-1, 354G2
Olympic com rejcts Moscow boycott 5-13, US assails decisn 5-14, 379F2
US backed vs Afghan plan on Sovt troop exit 5-15, 362C1
Brezhnev sees Giscard 5-19, US scores mtg 5-20, 378G2-379D1
Sovt trade blitz rptd 5-22, 430G3
7-natn Venice summit seeks total Sovt exit 6-22, 473B1
Carter backs Eur-Sovt ties 6-23, 473G1
USSR bars Bastille Day broadcast, congratulates Giscard 7-14, 566B3, D3
Olympic flag controversy 7-24, 588E1
EC barley sales to resume 10-23, 832C1

Sports
Moscow Olympics boycott opposed 1-21, 45B3; stance rptd eased 2-6, 84A3
Lake Placid Olympics results 2-12—2-24, 154F2, 155F2-156D1
Olympic com vs Moscow boycott 3-22, 259C3
Olympic boycott decisn delay seen 3-23, 259E3
Nice Open tennis results 3-30, 607A3
US rebuffs allies on Olympic boycott stand 3-31, 259G3
IOC offcl sees Olympic boycott 4-14, 283F3
Olympic com rejects Moscow boycott 5-13, US assails decisn 5-14, 379F2
French Open default controversy 6-3, results 6-6—6-8, 606A3

1976

UN Policy & Developments
Cncl member 62F2; 720C1
Abstains on Cncl PLO seating 1-12, 18B1
Asks broad Mideast resolutn 1-14, 18C2
OKs Cncl pro-Palestine resolutn 1-26, 59G2
Vetoes Cncl Comoro resolutn 2-8, 118G3
Abstains on rights comm resolutn vs Israel 2-13, 125E2
OKs Medit pollutn pact 2-16, 126C3
IAEA OKs Pak A-plant deal 2-24, 175C1
IAEA signs Pak A-plant pact 3-18, 581C3
Abstains on Cncl S Africa censure 3-31, 228B2
French A-export safeguards set 4-8, 372D3
PLO UN seating disputed 5-4, 320D1
Abstains on 2 WHO anti-Israel resolutns 5-17, 5-19, 355G1, D2
Cncl scores Israeli setlmts 5-26, 406D3
WHO cancer studies rptd 6-3, 484A3
Abstains on Israel Arab land exit 6-29, 464C1
Backs anti-terror resolutn 7-14, 515F3
S Africa A-plant pact signed 8-6, 631A2
Asks Greek-Turk talks on Aegean 8-25, 643F2
Asks Viet entry vote delay 9-14, 682D1
Vetoes S Africa arms ban 10-19, 781D3
Abstains on PLO in Cncl debate 11-1, 842F1
Asked to bar aid to S Africa 11-5, 842B3
Sovt scores on press plan 11-25, 895G3
Helps soften UNDOF res 11-30, 895B2
Vs black Namibia support 12-20, 955C1

U.S. Relations—*See also 'Foreign Economic Developments' above*
Bicentennial gifts to US rptd 1-12, 80A3
Press links 44 to CIA 1-13, 1-14, US scores 1-13, 49C3
Eur defns group rptd urged 1-15, 126E2
Kissinger anti-CP lobbying rptd 2-5, 120B2
A-safeguards pact stance cited 2-23, 243A3
Denies Angola aid chrg 3-9, 228D3
Kissinger visits 5-7, 318A3
Giscard visits US 5-17—5-22, 369A1, 372E1
Ships in US Bicentennial event 7-4, 488C3, D3
US arms control rpt cites 7-29, 739E2
Giscard sees Kissinger on Vorster mtg 9-7, 660F2
US Africa policy backed 9-8, 681B2
Croats divert TWA jet to Paris 9-11, surrender 9-12, 685A2
UN Viet entry talks rptd 9-14, 682D1
Reactn to Carter electn 11-3—11-4, 826D1
Drug dealers convicted 12-9, 971F2-C3

1977

UN Policy & Developments
Assemb, Cncl member; Gros on World Ct 4A1-F1
Sovt UNESCO offcl ousted as spy 2-11, 159C3
Leb consults on troop use 3-1, 143D2
Pollutn conf ends, Medit pact reached 10-21, 876B2
Assemb asks Mayotte evacuatn 10-26, 869A1
Cncl S Africa econ sanctns vetoed, apartheid res OKd 10-31, 851F2
Assemb Namibia vote abstentns 11-4, 851E1
S Africa arms sales canceled 11-8, 883B1
Assemb condemns Israel occupatn 11-25, 910D2
S Africa oil, investmt ban abstentns 12-16, 1016A2

U.S. Relations—*See also 'Atomic Energy' and 'Monetary, Trade & Aid' above; also AVIATION-SST/Concorde*
Daoud release protested 1-11, 1-12, 10B1; France protests reactn 1-13, 27E2
Carter, Giscard talk 1-13; cooperatn vowed 1-14, 27G2
Drug dealer sentenced 1-21, 103B1
Mondale visits 1-29, 69C1, B2
US-ESA flight set 2-16, 170C3
US rights stand concern rptd 3-4, 226F1
Vance sees Giscard 4-1, 247A1; 4-2, 368B2
Giscard scores US talks with left 4-2; US assures 4-2, 4-6, 255B2
Carter TV interview 5-2, 338B2
Carter sees Giscard, summit diplomacy hailed 5-9, 5-11, 358F1, D2, F2, 359D1, G1
Hartman confrmd amb 6-7, 499E3
Brezhnev, Giscard talks stress detente 6-21—6-22; Vance briefed 6-24, 494C3-495B2
US-USSR mediator role denied 6-22, 495B2
Giscard scores Carter on detente 7-25, 550D3
US rpts S Africa A-test plan 8-17, 663D3, 664A1
Agee expelled, US pressure denied 8-18, 654D2
ESA satellite launching aborted 9-13, 735G3
Barre visits US 9-15—9-16, 1012B3
Mitterrand US visit canceled 9-16, 883D3
Carter visit scheduled 9-23, 738F1
US vs UN Mayotte res 10-26, 869A1
Carter visit deferred 11-7, 854A1; rescheduled 11-29, 914B2
Bourges in US 11-22, 1012E3
Carter expands air svc 12-21, 1006D2
Carter begins world tour 12-29, 1000G3

1978

Terrorism & Unrest—*See also 'Corsica' above; for labor unrest, see 'Economy & Labor' above*
IRA links rptd sought 4-27, 373D2
3 govt offices bombed 4-30, 352F2
Egyptian CP founder murdered 5-4, 352D2; murder weapon linked to rightists 5-11, 474A1
W Ger terrorists arrested at Orly 5-11, 5-25, 439B1 ★, A2, C2
Brittany bombings 5-12, 5-29, '78 total rptd 5-13, 474B1-D1
3 Arab guerrillas slain at Paris airport 5-20, 383E3
Club Medit hq bombed, '77 attacks cited 6-11, 473D3
Terrorism vs Jews, Arabs, blacks rptd 6-14, 474D1
Versailles bombed 6-26, Breton separatists arrested 6-27, 496C1
2 Bretons arrested for Versailles bombing 6-30, 8 chrd 7-4, 533E2
Basques protest Giscard visit 6-30, 649B2
Spanish ex-terrorist ldr ambushed, wife killed 7-3, 537E2
Baader atty '77 extraditn to W Ger upheld 7-7, 649B3
Basque protests cut Spain access 7-12, 576D1
Hijack pact signed 7-17, 544G2-C3
2 bombings in Brittany 7-22, 649C3
8 Bretons sentenced 7-25, 649F2-A3
Iraq emb raided 7-31, 3 guards expelled 8-2, 582F1-D2
2 slain in raid on PLO, Arab League offices 8-3, 582B3
Iraq emb death protested by police 8-3, 649D3
Marseilles bar shootout, 9 killed 10-3, 815F3
Croat nationalist killed 10-16, 805G1
Spain terrorist killed 12-21, 1022F1

UN Policy & Developments
IAEA inspectn barred 1-16, 103A1
Rhodesia pact vote abstentn 3-14, 192F3
Leb asks anti-Israel actn 3-15, 174D3
Leb peace force (Unifil) formed 3-19, Giscard on decisn 3-22, 197D2, F2; **for peacekeeping developments, see MIDDLE EAST—LEBANON**
Giscard plans Assemb disarmamt proposal 4-24, 313D1
3 Unifil soldiers slain 5-2, 339F3
Assemb disarmamt sessn opens 5-23, Giscard hints Geneva role 5-25, 417F3, 421G1, C2
Sea Law Conf talks continue 5-23—7-15, 8-21—9-16, 732E3
Racism conf boycotted 8-26, 676B2
Unifil extensn OKd 9-18, 713C1
Cncl, Assemb member 713A3, E3
Unifil soldier slain 10-10, 783A2
Cncl abstentn on Namibia electn warning 11-13, 904B2

U.S. Relations—*See also 'Atomic Energy' and 'Monetary, Trade, Aid & Investment' above*
Carter visits 1-4—1-6; sees Mitterrand, Fabre; declines Chirac mtg 1-6, 1B1, 2C1
Carter-Mitterrand mtg scored 1-6—1-10, 54D1
US alerts to Sovt satellite fall 57E1
At Ogaden conf in US 1-21, 43E2
Polanski seeks refuge 2-1, 116B2
'French Connection' inmate slain 4-10, 396G2
USSR chrgs US interventn 5-7, 349B3
US launches ESA satellite 5-12, 384D3
Shell Brittany hq bombed 5-29, 474C1
Zaire troop exit aided by US 6-4, role detailed 6-5, 441A1, D1
Pan-Africa force opposed 6-5, 441F2
US seabed mining bill debated at UN conf 8-21—9-16, 732E3
Pan Am to end Paris svc 9-7, 701G1
Amoco sued on tanker spill 9-13, 749C1
Carter says has 'interest' in Leb 9-28, 745D1
Giscard gives US Leb peace plan 10-2, discuss truce 10-3, 745F1
US contacts to end Leb war cited 761C1
Colby CIA book published uncut 11-19, 917F1-C2
Delta '72 hijackers sentncd 11-23, 926F3
Nixon in Paris 11-28, 942A2
US-China ties rptd discussed by Giscard, Brzezinski 12-16, 977C1

1979

Terrorism & Unrest—*See also 'Corsica' above; for labor unrest, see 'Economy & Labor' above*
23 Spain Basques arrested, future asylum barred 1-30, 100B3
Spain Basques protest deportatns to Italy 2-5, 192B1
Spain guerrillas kidnap Michelin, Citroen execs 2-5—3-1, 192C1
UK amb threatened 3-23, 228A3
Paris radicals riot 3-23, 235F3
A-factory sabotaged, forgn agents suspected 4-6, 276D1
Italy Red Brigades Paris base chrgd 4-24, 331F2
Le Monde offices, Paris, Toulouse bombed 4-29—5-3, 330B2
A-factory sabotage probe cited 5-9, 371G2
Cop's house bombed, Breton natlists linked 6-1, 425B1
PLO aide shot 7-25, 551G3; suspect arrested 8-20, 625D2
2 Moro death suspects arrested 8-18, 9-14, 709D2
Paris buildings bombed 9-15—9-16, 835D2
Jewish leftist writer slain 9-20, 772E2
Breton separatists sentncd 10-20, 835D2
Shah's nephew slain 12-7, 935C1

UN Policy & Developments
Unifil exit rptd 1-12, 84G3
Rights comm res on southn Africa opposed 2-21, 148G1
S Africa rejcts Namibia plan 3-5, 171B2
Namibia compromise proposed 3-19—3-22; Pretoria bars 5-7, extends assemb powers 5-8, 354F2
Rhodesia electn vote abstentn 4-30, 332A2
Namibia vote abstentn 5-31, 428B1
Indochina refugee conf asked 6-28, 473E2
Membership listed 695D2
S Africa vote abstentn 11-2, 875G1
Namibia talks reopen 11-12—11-16, 889D3

U.S. Relations—*See also 'Atomic' and 'Monetary' above*
Giscard at Guadeloupe summit 1-5—1-6, 12D2, F2
CP chrgs China Viet invasn role 2-19, 122A3
Renoir painting willed to LA museum 3-7, 375B2
CIA tap of Khomeini aide rptd barred 3-11, 180C1
Poncet sculpture smashed in NYC 5-6, 375D1; rededicated 9-15, 892F2
French air svc pact rptd 5-12, 465A3
Francois-Poncet in US 6-4—6-5, 485A1
Carter-Giscard ties strained 6-28, 7-2, 493F2
SALT II backed 6-28, 497A1
Carter energy plan assessed 7-16, 534F3
SALT, Cuba troop issue reactn rptd 10-3, 738B1
Envoy visits US hostages in Iran 11-10, 862A2
US informs of Iran oil ban 11-12, move backed 11-13, 861F1; 11-15, 879F2
Iran US Emb seizure condemned 11-27, 895D3
Vance in Paris, seeks sanctns vs Iran 12-10, 933C2, G2

1980

LeMans results 6-15, 637A3
Jones wins Gr Prix 6-29, 1002B1
Moscow Olympic results 7-20—8-3; flag controversy 7-24, rights appeal 8-2, 588E1, A3, 590E2, 622C2-C3, 623B1-D1
Zoetemelk wins Tour de France 7-20, 835D1
Atlantic sailing record set 8-1, 907G1
Australia wins America's Cup trials 9-5, 834G1
Lancome Trophy tourn results 10-19, 972F2

Terrorism & Unrest—*See also 'Corsica', 'Economy & Labor' above*
Ex-Cabt min shot 2-1, dies 2-2, 97C2
Sovt airline office bombed 2-24, 149F3
Cooperatn min's office attacked 3-18, 232A1
Terrorist suspects seized 3-28, 255D1
Computer facilities bombed 4-5, 4-9, 4-15, 312F3
W Ger suspects arrested 5-5, 411A3
Libyan missn bombed 5-6, 373D3
Justice bldg bombed 5-12—5-13, 463F1
Forgn student rules spur violent protests 5-13, 5-14, 407E1
Orly blast wounds 7 6-12, 463F1
Assemb OKs crime bill 6-21, 497E3
Industrialist kidnaped 6-28, freed 7-9, 522E1
Right-wing extremists arrested for Sovt airline office, other attacks 7-1, 522A2
Barre in Spain talks 7-2—7-3, 567G1
Italy suspects arrested 7-7—7-8, 523G2
Armenians attack Turk consulate 8-5, 606C1
Italy bombing suspect arrested 8-6, 620B1
Rightists held after Marseilles bombing 8-12, 634C1
Right-wing extremist group banned 9-3, 670D1
Leftist terrorists arrested 9-13, 750E1
Mil schl machine-gunned 9-19, 750F1
Jewish targets attacked 9-26, 9-28, 750A1
Paris synagogue blast kills 4 10-3, protests ensue 10-4, 10-7, militants retaliate 10-8; Giscard sets measures 10-8, 767A2-768A1
Dutch woman injured in car blast 10-5, 768B1
Rightists attacked by Jewish group 10-12; Begin scores govt 10-13, 789F3-790C1
Spain Basques kill 2 11-21; protest issued 11-27, 923B2
Jews slain in Paris 11-25, 921C3
Paris govt buildings bombed 12-3, 942B2
Italy suspect arrested 12-18, 995E1

UN Policy & Developments
Pettiti on comm to probe shah 2-17, 122B1
Palestinian state res abstentn 4-30, 325D1
Cncl abstentn on S Africa raid censure 6-27, 524F3
Assemb Palestine state res abstentn 7-29, 572F1
Iraq bars A-reactor inspectn 11-7, 864C2
Cuba ex-offcl asks prison hunger strike probed 12-4, 963D2
Israeli exit res abstentn 12-15, 952G2

U.S. Relations—*See also 'Monetary', 'Soviet-Afghan Issue' above*
US vs PLO stance 3-31, 260F3
W Europns plan fighter jet 4-14, 303F1
Iran hostage kin seek support 4-23, 299C2
Iran hostage rescue missn reactn 4-25, 324A2
Muskie sees Francois-Poncet 5-16, 379B1
US told of EC Mideast peace move 5-30, 418B1
Rabies vaccine OKd in US 6-9, 526A3
Anderson visits 7-15, 550A1
Giscard briefed on hostages in Iran 9-19, 719C3
US journalist expelled 10-3, 790B2
Giscard warns re power monopoly 10-17, 829C3
Carter cites attacks vs Jews in TV debate 10-28, 814E2
Persian Gulf mine-sweeping force set 10-28, 821E2
NATO defns input defended 12-9—12-10, 949C2
Haig apptmt praised 12-17, 955E2

1976

FRANCE, Erwin A.
Loses Cong primary 3-16, 196G2
FRANCIS, Emile
Rangers dismiss 1-6, 56E2
FRANCK, Antonio
Named forgn min 9-5, 924F2
FRANCO, Carmen Polo de
At meml mass for husband 11-20, 909A1

FRANCO, Generalissimo Francisco (1892-1975)
Backers score pol reforms; govt curbs mem'l rally, other rites 5-13—5-25, 421G3-422G1
Pol torture rptdly continues 501D2
Tacito members in new Cabt 7-8, 523D2
King drops bishop's veto 7-16, 541F1
Followers warn vs pol chng 8-31, 753B1
Ex-Cabt mins form Popular Alliance 10-9, 908G2
Rightists, Juan Carlos pay homage 11-20, 908F3-909A1
FRANCO Charais, Brig. Gen. Manuel
Quits as central mil cmdr 8-12, 733D2
FRANCOIS-Poncet, Jean
Named Giscard pres aide 7-28, 556A1
FRANJIEH, Suleiman
Karami resigns 1-18; urged to stay 1-19, 34A1
Announces truce, pol pact 1-22, 33A1
Meets Assad 2-7, PLO briefs 107F1-A2
Announces reforms 2-14, 125A1
Call for 'Arab' state opposed 162F2
Cabt meets on army crisis 3-10, 209G1
Ahdab asks resignatn 3-11, 3-14; Parlt 3-12; Christian group 3-14; Jumblat 3-24, 209A2-G2, 210F1
Rebels surround home 3-15, 210A1
Talks with Assad 3-16, 210A1
Cmnd council formed to force resignatn 3-21, 210B2
Cabt seeks successn 3-22, Syrians press move 3-23, 210D1
Flees palace after shelling 3-25, 210E1
Truce to pave way for successor 4-1, 225A1
Syria OKs removal 4-1, 225D2
Meets US mediator 4-1—4-2, 4-5, 241E2
Sadat urges resignatn 4-4, 275D1
Successor sought 241B1
Parlt OKs move to name successor 4-10, 257C1, C2
Meets French mediator 4-10, 258D1
Moslems demand resignatn 4-22, 273G1
Signs charter amendmt 4-24, electn set 4-27, 295F3
Election delayed 4-30, 319A1
Sarkis elected, delays resignatn 5-8, 337B1
France offers peace force 5-21, 369C1
Edde wounded 5-25, 370B1
Jumblat chrgs OKd Syrian invasn 6-1, 385D1
Backs Syrian invasion 6-6, 406A2
Vs Arab peace force 6-10, 405D1; 6-15, 492E2
Vs Libya in peace force 6-30, 487B2
League presses truce accord 7-26, 546B2
Christians disavow Tel Zaatar truce 7-26, 546E2
Syria, PLO talks rptd 7-27, 546F1
Offers truce 8-16, rejected 8-17, 618E2
Sees Sarkis on power shift, says Syria sets peace deadline 8-19, 628B3
Meets US aides 8-22—8-24, 628F3
In peace plan talks 8-26—8-27, 662F3
Shifts Cabt 9-15, 682E2
Scores Palestinians 9-19, 698B3
Christian rivals clash 9-20, 720A3
Sarkis replaced 9-23, 699E1
Sarkis moves into pres palace 9-24, 720G2
Sees Sarkis on Riyadh pact 10-20, 779C1
FRANKE, Maj. Gen. Karl-Heinz
Dismissed 11-1, 930E3
FRANKEL, Max
Pres debate panelist 10-6, 740F2, 741C3
FRANKLIN, Sidney
Dies 4-26, 368F2
FRANKLIN National Bank—*See 'European-American Bank' under EUROPEAN-American Banking Corp.*
FRANZONI, Rev. Giovanni Battista
CP support scored 6-17, 446B2
Defrocked 8-4, 951B2
FRASER, Rep. Donald MacKay (D, Minn.)
Chairs Uruguay aid hearing 8-4, 814D2
Reelected 11-2, 829F4
Cncl sues to see Argentina rights abuse rpt 12-19, 996G2
FRASER, Malcolm (Australian prime minister)
Devaluation rpts denied 1-5, 7B3
Backs allied defense role 1-12, 1-15, 26E2
Heads 4 cabt coms 1-14, 26G2
Coalitn wins 35 Sen seats 1-15, 46E1
In ASEAN talks 1-16—1-18, 46B1
At Razak funeral 1-16, 46C1
Forms econ advisory group 1-20, 46A2
Restores old natl anthem 1-21, 46B2
On govt spending cut, pay curbs 2-2, 2-3, 97F1
State income tax proposed 2-4, 97B2
Whitlam chrgs deceit in '75 ouster 2-9, 116E1
Announces govt job cuts 2-10, 137E2
Arbitratn Comm OKs wage hike curb 2-13, 137A3
US to OK navigation base OKd 2-17, 137C2
Orders Whitlam-Iraq electn fund probe 2-25, 172C2
Hussein visits 3-2—3-9, 204C1

1977

FRANCIS, Connie
Rape suit setlmt rptd 2-23, 140E3
FRANCO, Generalissimo Francisco (1892-1975)—*See 1975, pp. 875F3, 876G1 for biog. data*
Spain to expel extremists 1-26, 101F3
Carrillo lauds chngs 3-3, 243D1
Natl Movemt dissolved 4-1, CP legalized 4-9, 285C2, G3
Mex amb apptmt controversy 4-7—5-11, 529C2
Prince Xavier dies 5-7, 452G3
Spain holds parlt electns 6-15, 453B1, B2
Juan Carlos addresses Cortes 7-22, 582E1
Catalonia Generalitat restored 9-29, 843G1
FRANCO de Pobil, Nicolas
Ask debate on CP 4-18, 307D1
FRANJIEH, Suleiman
Vs Palestinian arms 1-10, 28A2
FRANK, Gary
Wins Emmy 9-11, 1021G3
FRANK, Joseph A.
Fined 3-21, 520B3
FRANK, Richard A.
Named NOAA dir 6-30, confrmd 7-13, 626E3
FRANKFURTER, Felix (1892-1965)
FBI surveillance rptd 6-19, 481D1
FRANKEL, Judge Marvin E.
Sentncs Stirling Homex ex-offcls 3-11, 203G2
FRANKLIN, Tony
Sets bowl record 1-2, 8G3
FRANKLIN National Bank—*See EUROPEAN-American Banking Corp.—European-American Bank*
FRANZ Joseph II, Prince (Liechtenstein)
Death sentence issued 11-26, 949F2
FRASER, Rep. Donald M(acKay) (D, Minn.)
On rights abuse rpts 1-1, 50A3
On El Salvador rights 3-9, 206D3
Rpts Carter A-safeguards exchng 3-23, 217F3
Confrms Korea plan documt 11-29; chrgs Kim testimony blocked 11-30, 914B3, F3, 915B1
FRASER, Douglas
Elected UAW pres 5-18; remarks 5-18, 5-19, 408E1-G2
Hails air bag order 6-30, 522D1

FRASER, Malcolm (Australian prime minister)
Australia denies chrgs on US bases 1-25, 81B2
Contacts US, Canada on uranium collaboratn 2-4—3-11; Carter denies cartel agrmt 6-29, 624F3-625B1
In PNG, border talks suspended 2-7, 132C1
Rpts Japan ANL ship bldg deal 2-16, 253A2
Names 1st ombudsman 3-17, 280D3
Sets pub service job cuts 4-4, 303A1
Sets CIA union infiltratn probe 4-27, 326E1
Halts CIA probe 5-3, defends ties 5-24, 410B2
Denies CIA funded Liberal Party 5-4, 372C1
Sets intellignc reorganizatn 5-5, 371F3
Warns air controllers 5-12, 389A1
Charter chngs OKd 5-21, 447E1
Wage rise OKd 5-24, 424F2, A3
Sets uranium export curbs 5-24, 465B3

1978

FRANCESCHINI, Alberto
Ejected from Turin trial 5-10, 338C2
Sentenced 5-18, 393B3
FRANCIS, Charles
Urges Lynch, Holding corruptn probe 9-14, 771F2
FRANCIS, Trevor
NASL scoring ldr 8-6, 655D2
On NASL All-Star team 8-20, 707B3

FRANCO, Generalissimo Francisco (1892-1975)—*See 1975, pp. 875F3, 876G1 for biog. data*
Secret police files ordrd destroyed 1-13, 136G2
Basques march on natl day 3-26, 250E1
Madrid rallies laud rule 11-17, 11-19, 967B2
FRANCOIS, Claude (Clo-Clo)
Dies 3-11, 252F2
FRANCOIS-Poncet, Andre
Dies 1-8, 96A2
Son named forgn min 11-29, 1017C1
French forgn min 11-29, 1017C1
FRANJIEH, Suleiman
Son slain 6-13, vows revenge 6-14, 463G1, C2
36 Christns slain 6-28, 502C2
FRANJIEH, Tony
Slain 6-13, father vows revenge 6-14, 463G1, C2
36 Christns slain 6-28, 502C2, D2
FRANK, Richard
Spring Awakening opens 7-13, 887B3
FRANKE, Egon
Retains W Ger Cabt post 2-3, 93A3
FRANKEL, Emily
Zinnia opens 3-22, 760G3
FRANKEL, Gene
Contessa of Mulberry St opens 1-4, 887E1
FRANKEL, Judge Marvin E.
Berkey wins trust suit vs Kodak 1-21, 67E1
Reduces Berkey Kodak award 7-3, 808E2
Dismisses Roots plagiarism suit 9-21, 759A3
FRANKEL, Stephen K.
Wins Provenzano case 3-25, 232E2
FRANKLAND, Herman C. (Buddy)
Loses electn for Maine gov 11-7, 847E2
FRANKLIN, Aretha
Marries 4-12, 420F2
FRANKLIN, Benjamin (1706-90)
Image on coin cited 10-10, 788C2
FRANKLIN National Bank—*See EUROPEAN-American Banking Corp.—European-American Bank*
FRANKLIN New York Corp.—*See EUROPEAN-American Banking Corp. – European-American Bank*
FRANK Lyon Co.
Tax breaks in lease-back deals OKd by Sup Ct 4-18, 309G1-B2
FRANK Lyon Co. v. U.S.
Tax breaks in lease-back deals OKd by Sup Ct 4-18, 309G1-B2
FRANKS v. Delaware
Evidence hearing rules drawn by Sup Ct 6-26, 566E3
FRASER, Rep. Donald M(acKay) (D, Minn.)
Chairs Korean lobbying probe 3-15—3-22, 203D1, F1
Rpts Moon subpoena, US exit 6-6, 433C1
Loses Sen primary 9-12, 715G3
Asks Nicaragua aid cutoff 10-13, 839G2
S Korean lobbying detailed 11-1, 862A3, F3
Sabo wins seat 11-7, 854D3
FRASER, Douglas A.
USSR trip postponed 7-14, 542B2
Quits Admin labor-mgt panel 7-19, 611G1
Scores Carter health plan 7-28, 586G1
Hails GM southn plant pact 9-11, 699F3, 700A1
Hails VW pact 10-5, pact rejctd 10-8, 809D3
On Carter anti-inflatn plan 10-26, 806F3
At Dem midterm conf anti-Carter budget res rejctd 12-10, 12-8—12-10, 956A3
FRASER, George MacDonald
Crossed Swords released 3-2, 619C1

FRASER, Malcolm (Australian prime minister)
Electn final results rptd 1-6, 53C2
EC import curbs scored 1-24, 1-26, 69D2, A3
Defends Kerr UNESCO apptmt 2-10, Kerr resigns 3-2, 165E1-A2
Orders hotel bombing probe 2-13, 110G1
Commonwealth conf meets 2-13—2-16, vs EC trade policy 2-15, 121E2
Labor Party asks immigratn curb 2-19, 129B2
Scores EC trade curbs 3-7, 265E2
Orders whaling probe 3-20, 208C3
Govt plans Aborigine rule 3-22, 225C2
Threatens EC trade curbs 4-6, EC delays talks 4-14; Hayden scores 4-16, 310D3
Meets on Queensland dispute 4-7, reaches land control compromise 4-11, 286F1
Fukuda trade talks rptd, commodity fund planned 4-23, 391C2
Defeats censure motn 5-29, 434G2

1979

FRANCE (ocean liner)
Sails to W Ger after labor blockade 8-19, 633D3
FRANCESCO, Emilio
Kidnaped 3-8, freed 3-11 212F1
FRANCIS, Trevor
Nottingham Forest wins Eur Champions' Cup 5-30, 776G2
Named to NASL All-Star team 8-27, 776E1
FRANCISCUS, James
City on Fire released 9-14, 819G3
Killer Fish released 12-7, 1007F3
FRANCO, Generalissimo Francisco (1892-1975)
Spain-Vatican Concordat ended 1-3, 61C2
Spain OKs forgn bank activities 1-26, 100F3
Dockworkers boycott A-cargo 5-17, 390B3
Martin-Artajo dies 9-1, 756A3
Rally marks death 11-18, 952B2
FRANCOIS-Poncet, Jean
Visits US 6-4—6-5, 485A1
FRANJIEH, Suleiman
Followers abducted 10-8, 5 die in rival Christn clash 10-10, 763B3
FRANK Jr., Harriet
Norma Rae released 3-1, 174C3
FRANK, Melvin
Lost & Found released 7-13, 820F1
FRANKE, Volker & Hyoon-ya
Prisoner exchange rptd 7-20, 586E2
FRANKE, William B(irrell)
Dies 6-30, 508F2
FRANKEL, Charles
Slain 5-10, 2 chrgd 7-19, 548G1
FRANKEL, Kenneth
Spokesong opens 3-15, 712F2
FRANKEL, Marvin
On Sindona letter 8-15, 635C3
FRANKEL, Richard
Magnet-synthesizing bacteria rptd 4-8, 691B2
FRANKEL, Shepherd
Dark at the Top opens 11-29, 956A3
FRANKHEIMER, John
Prophecy released 6-15, 820A3
FRANKLIN, Jon B.
Wins Pulitzer 4-16, 336C3
FRANKLIN, Matthew—*See SAUD Muhammad, Mathew*
FRANKLIN, Richard
Patrick released 9-7, 820F2
FRANKLIN, Ron
Spectacular Bid wins Fla Derby 3-6, Flamingo Stakes 3-24; loses Triple Crown 6-9, 448A2, C3
Shoemaker replaces 6-23, 876A3
FRANKLIN National Bank—*See EUROPEAN-American Banking Corp.-European-American Bank*
FRANKLIN Simon—*See CITY Stores Co.*
FRANTZ, Joseph
Dies 9-12, 756E2
FRANZBLAU, Rose N.
Dies 9-2, 756D2
FRASER, Alan
Iran cuts S Africa ties 3-4, 161B3
FRASER, Donald MacKay
Elected Minneapolis mayor 11-6, 846C3
FRASER, Douglas A.
Warns US away from talks 4-17, 280A1
Ct bars wage-guide contract denial 5-31, 399B3
Warns Admin 6-30; Big 3 contract talks begin 7-16, Chrysler gets no-strike pledge 598B1
Vs Chrysler wage freeze plea, asks natlzn 8-3, Miller bars 8-9, 662A2, B3
Scored re UAW job action 8-22, backs oil industry protest 10-17, 831D2-B3
UAW reaches accord with GM 9-14, 698A2
On Pay Advisory Com 10-16, 829F2
Chrysler accord reached 10-25, 805F2
Backs Chrysler rescue plan 11-1, 845F2
FRASER, Hugh
Purchases Iona 5-24, 407E1
FRASER, John
Canada post-master gen, environmt min 6-4, 423F3
Warns re acid rain peril 7-12, seeks US environmt commitmt 7-20, 581F2, B3

FRASER, Malcolm (Australian prime minister)
US trade concessns rptd obtained 1-8, 36F2
Aborigine mining rights probed 1-24, 94G2
Streamlines Cabt operatns 2-4, 113F1
Finance min resigns 2-22, 133C2; reinstated 2-25, 168C1
Sees econ recovery signs 2-27, 168A1
Inflatn drop doubted 3-13, 189A1
Whaling ban announced 4-4, 284C2
Scores union militants 4-22, 328F1-B2
Mineral export compromise set 4-23, 328A1
Hails EC trade accord 5-29, 404F3-405A1
Bars barrier reef oil drilling 6-4, 423F1
Announces energy measures 7-3, 522C1
Zimbabwe recognitn terms agreed with US 7-4, 501A1
Skylab aid offered, replies 7-11, 509C1
Pub employe curbs enforced 7-13, 542C1

1980

FRANCE 3, The (yacht)
Australia wins America's Cup trials 9-5, 834G1
FRANCIS, Allan
Happy New Year opens 4-27, 392A3
FRANCIS, Wallace
NFL '79 receiving ldr 1-5, 8F2

FRANCO, Generalissimo Francisco (1892-1975)—*See 1975, pp. 875E3, 876G1 for biog. data*
Moderates win upset in Catalonia 3-21, 235F1
Carter hails Spain democracy 6-25, 475A1
Thousands attend death aniv rally 11-23, 903C2
FRANCO, Manuel
Kidnaped, slain 11-27, 921F1
FRANCOIS-Poncet, Jean
On Afghan crisis 1-6, 2D2
Sees Vance, Afghan policy coordinatn sought 2-21, 139B2
Sees Gromyko 4-24—4-25, 351F3
Bars Olympic boycott stand 5-13, 379F2
Sees Muskie 5-16; Franco-Sovt summit scored 5-20, reacts 5-21, 379B1
Meets Muskie, vows EC Mideast peace move 5-30, 418B1
Warns Sovts on Poland invasn 12-11, 949G1
FRANCONA, Terry
Named NCAA baseball MVP 6-6, 796F2
FRANEK, Jan
Wins Olympic medal 8-2, 622A2
FRANEY, Pierre
Gourmet Diet on best-seller list 10-12, 796E3
FRANJIEH, Suleiman
Parlt member kidnaped 2-13; freed 3-9, 179E3
Christn rivals clash 2-17, 125D2
Backers blamed for bomb blast 2-23, 140F3
FRANK, Anne (d. 1945)
Father dies 8-19, 676D1
FRANK, Barney
Wins Mass US House primary 9-16, 724D2
Elected to US House 11-4, 843C1
FRANK, Ben
Don't Answer the Phone released 8-9, 675C2
FRANK, Otto
Dies 8-19, 676D1
FRANKE, Egon
Sworn to W Ger Cabt 11-5, 925F1
FRANKEN, Richard
Viets capture 6-25, release 6-29, 508G2
FRANKIE Inc.
McDonald's acquitted in trust suit 9-29, 917C3
FRANKLIN—*See NEW Hampshire*
FRANKLIN, Miles
My Brilliant Career released 2-1, 216C3
FRANKLIN, Roy Lee
Chrgd in extortn plot 11-8, 927B1
FRANKLIN, Tony
NFL '79 kicking ldr 1-5, 8F2
FRANKLIN Mint Corp.
Warner merger set 12-24, 985B1
FRASER, Douglas A.
Canadians bar UAW concessns 1-3, 14G1
Asks Japanese assemb plants in US 1-13, 35B2
Endorses Kennedy 1-15, 33C1
Scores Kahn on Ford-UAW ruling 3-7, 225A3
Asks Nissan US car plants 4-17, 288F1
In 'Big Business Day' protest 4-17, 308C2
On auto worker cancer rate 4-22, 356G3
Elected to Chrysler bd 5-13, 383C3
At White House mtg 5-14, 384F1
UAW conv held 6-1—6-6; addresses 6-1, reelected 6-4, 457G1, D2
Asks auto import curbs 6-12, 457G2
Sees Carter; on Reagan prospects 7-8, 505C1
Renominates Mondale 8-14, 612B1
Rpts Polish strike aid 8-31, 659A3
At ITC auto import hearings 10-8, 823G1
Urges Reagan crisis mtg 12-20, 980E2

FRASER, Malcolm (Australian prime minister)
Cautions US on Sovt grain ban 1-9, 9D2
Japan premr visits 1-16, Pacific orgn studied 1-20, 78E1-D2
Orders Sovt rutile ban 1-28, 116E1
Announces defns spending hike 2-19, 132C1
Attacks unions 3-27, 271D3
Lauds USOC boycott vote 4-14, 283G2
Plans drought aid 4-14, 309F2
Marks Zimbabwe indepndnc 4-17—4-18, 301E1
Sinclair chrgd 4-29, 334B2
China dep premr visits 5-7—5-11, 388A1
Scores Olympic com boycott rejectn 5-23, 421B1
Backs barrier reef preservatn 6-10, 460F2
Queensland rift threatns coalitn 6-16, 6-18, 486A1
Sinclair acquitted 8-14; rejoins Cabt 8-18, 650C2
Hayden scores budget 8-26, 667D2

1976

PNG aid agrmt rptd 3-4, 172D3
In NZ, at S Pacific Forum 3-8—3-11, 179C2, 187B3
Announces govt info bill 3-17, 203E3
Rpts advisory parlt coms planned 3-18, 203F3
PNG copper deal set 3-22, 237E2
OKs US navigation base 3-23, 237D1
Rockefeller visits 3-30—3-31, 249F2
Govt meets cutback goals 4-28, 332D1
Anthem for Olympics set 5-4, 349G3
Japan pact set 5-6, 349D3
On new wage policy 5-28, 415C1
Foreign policy address 6-1, 438C2
Govt lifts ban on A-ships 6-4, 455D3
Medibank expands 6-8, 456B1
Meets state premiers 6-10, 456A1
Ends Japan visit, in China 6-20, 481A1
Names new ABC head 7-4, 520E2
Chu Teh dies 7-6, 520G3
Secret papers leaked 7-17, 537F1
Visits US 7-26—7-30, 554E1
'76-77 budget introduced 8-17, 636D3
Trapped by student protest 8-23, 650B1
Whitlam scores budget proposals 8-24, 672B3
Scores political strikes 9-2, 691E3
Announces drought relief 9-8, 709E2
Arrives Indonesia 10-10, 789A2
Productivity Dept formed 11-7, 870A1
On uranium policy rpt 11-7, 888G1
Ends Fraser I mining 11-11, 888A2
Scores Stretton 11-16, 902F2
Tours Torres Strait I 11-22—11-24, 961C3
Currency devalued 11-28, 896G1
Currency revalued up 12-6, 922G3
Liberals lose Tasmania electn 12-11, 944C3

FRAUD—*See 'Bribery' under CRIME*
FRAZIER, Herman
Wins Olympic medal 7-29, 576B1
FRAZIER, Joe
Carter, Artis get new trial 3-17, 256G3
FREDA, Franco
Released from Rome jail 8-28, 676B3
FREDBORG, Niels
Wins Olympic medal 7-19, 574B2
FREDERICK, Pauline
Pres debate moderator 10-6, 740F2
FREDERICKSON, Donald S.
Testifies on gene research 9-22, 860C3
Handler letter on DNA cited 11-1, 891F3
FREEDOM House Inc.
World freedom survey rptd 1-19, 20D2 ★
World press, freedom survey rptd 12-22, 977E2
FREEMAN, Orville L.
Cited in Mondale biog sketch 512F2
FREEPORT, Tex.—*See TEXAS*
FREEPORT Minerals Co.
Firm, Natl Potash indicted 6-29, 748F1
'75 zero tax paymt rptd 10-2, 847F1
Penn Ventilator Arab boycott noncompliance rptd 11-9, 986B3
FREI Montalva, Eduardo
Rejects govt advisory role 1-2; scores Pinochet 1-3, 8E2
Pinochet scores 1-21, junta chrgs 'treason' 1-28, 99D3
Chile OKs book 1-23, bars press debate 1-31, 99B3

1977

Scores EC protectionism 6-1, 7-4, 595D3
At Commonwealth conf 6-8—6-15, 487D1
In US, sees Carter 6-21—6-23, 560C3
Labor Party conv 7-4—7-11, 541A1
Rejcts ASEAN trade criticism 7-9, 561A1
Kerr quits as gov gen 7-14, 541C1
Asks Fukuda sugar dispute role 7-16, 578C3
Japan friendship treaty ratified 7-21, 596A1
Japan sugar talks fail again 8-4, 615D2
Meets with ASEAN ldrs 8-6—8-7, 607B2
Sinclair blames strikes on UK immigrants 8-8, 632D3, F3
Pub employe strikes banned 8-19, 652E3
Lifts uranium ban 8-25, 693G1
Silent on protester surveillnc rpts 9-1, 923A1
Rejects uranium referendum 9-7, 705C1
Uranium referendum asked 9-15, 740C2
Warns Japan on trade disputes 9-23, more beef imports agreed 10-28, 862C1
Sets drug trade probe 10-5, 779B2
Names Fox A-envoy 10-6, 779E1
On US base accord renewal 10-19, 800E3
Early electns set 10-27, 839C3
Intell agency to widen role 10-27, 862G1
Labor wins Greensborough by-electn 11-5, 922E3
Accepts Lynch resignatn 11-18, 901D2
Govt reelected 12-10, party control consolidated 12-11, 963C2
Names Cabt; reappts Lynch, backs Liberal Party ldrship bid 12-19, 982D1-B2
Fires pro-apartheid min 12-21, 982B2

FRAUD—*See CRIME—Bribery*
FRAUNCES Tavern (N.Y.)
FALN seeks probe end 3-21, 261D2
FRAZIER, Walt (Clyde)
Knicks trade to Cleveland 10-8, 870G2
FREDERICK, Jane
Sets 60-yd hurdles mark 2-25, 602F3
FREDERICK & Herrud Inc.
Fortune 500 ranks 341C1
FREDRICKSON, Dr. Donald S.
Retained as NIH dir 2-3, 211B1
DNA safety debated 10-6, 846B3-E3
NIH meets on DNA rule revisn 12-15—12-16, 1022A2
FREEDOM House
Panama rights abuse rpt cited 9-8, 699D1
FREEDOM of Information—*See PRIVACY Issue*
FREEDOM of Thought Foundation (Tucson, Ariz.)
Deprogramming barred 3-28, 287C1
FREEMAN, William J.
Arrested 7-27, 627F3
FREEMASONS
Arabs boycott 6-9, 511E3
FREEPORT Fast Freight
ICC sues 11-3, 861D1
FREEPORT Minerals Co.
Firm, Natl Potash acquitted 3-9, 6-10, 483D3, E3
FREESE, Paul
Discredits Dummar 1-26, 1-27, 120G1
FRIEDERSDORF, Max
Ford, Kim Han Cho mtg bid rptd 11-11, 915A2
FREI Montalva, Eduardo
CIA payments rptd 2-19, 124F1
Denies CIA paymts 2-19, 2-21; rpts Carter apology 3-4, 219A2
Sees Mondale, Brzezinski 5-25, 493D1
Sees Todman 8-12, 635C2
At Brandt comm mtg 12-9—12-11, 998A1
FREIRE, Marcos
Scores govt rights abuse 3-22, 281A2
Scores Geisel pol reforms 303D2

1978

In US 6-1—6-5, addresses UN disarmamt sessn 6-5, 450D3
Sees inflatn rate fall 7-27, 590C2
Fires Cabt min 8-7, defends actn 8-8, 612F1
'78-79 budget presented 8-15, 628G1-E3
Budget protests; Sydney, Brisbane violence 8-17, 8-21, 646B1
Denies link to Withers scandal 8-21, no-confidence motn defeated 8-24, 703B2
Warns Telecom strikers 8-22, 721G1
Names Chaney admin svcs min 8-25, 703G2
Sees Yunupingu on uranium dvpt 9-8, 721D1
Bars Lynch, Holding corruptn probe 9-14, 771E1, F2
Sees '79 jobless peak 9-28, 812G3-813A1
Rpts Syria drops Jewish curb 10-20, 900E3
State borrowing for indl projects OKd 11-6, 878G2
Melbourne Inst scores budget 11-7, 878B2
Shuffles Cabt 11-30, 943E3
Melbourne Inst urges econ stimulus 12-19, 1012D3

FRATERNAL Association of Steel Haulers—*See STEEL Haulers, etc.*
FRATERNIZATION
US Army crackdown ordrd 12-4, 960E1
FRATIANNE, Linda
Loses world figure-skating title 3-10, 316E3
FRAUD—*See CRIME—Bribery*
FRAZIER, Herman
Sets indoor 500-mtr run record 1-7, 76G2
FRAZIER, Joe
Holmes wins WBC heavywgt title 6-9, 600F1
FRB—*See U.S. GOVERNMENT—FEDERAL Reserve*
FREBERG, Stan
Addresses laity conf 2-19, 294E3
FREDA, Franco
Rptd missing 10-4, 817A2
FREDERICK, Md.—*See MARYLAND*
FREDERICK, Jane
AAU suspends 6-23, 692E2
FREDERICK, Marica
At World Gym Championships 10-23—10-29, 928C3
FREE, Lloyd (All-World)
Traded to Clippers 10-12, 1928A1
FREEDOM House
World freedom survey rptd 44D1
FREEDOM of Information—*See PRIVACY Issue*
FREEMAN, Harry
Dies 1-13, 96A2
FREEMAN, Joseph
Ordained 1st black Mormon priest 6-11, 480E3
FREEMAN, Richard
TVA OKs clean-air pact 12-14, 982A3
FREEMAN, S. David
Named TVA chrmn 5-16, takes over 5-19, 390G1-F2
TVA OKs clean-air pact 12-14, 982A3
FREEPORT Minerals Co.
Indonesia '77 rebel raids rptd 4-15, 318D3
FREGOSI, Jim
Hired as Angels mgr 6-1, 560E1
FREIJ, Elias
Chrgs Israel Arab land takeover plan 5-23, 400E2
FREI Montalva, Eduardo
Scores plebiscite 1-2, 16E3
UN rights panel interview rptd 7-27, 591E2
Chile land reform to end 10-6, 795B1

1979

Labor Party backs US monitoring base 7-19, 542F1
Scores strikers 7-22, 562B2
Fscl yr inflatn up 7-25, 581B1
Labor wins Tasmania electn 7-28—7-29, 612E1
OECD econ survey rptd 8-3, 599G3
NZ trade union explored 8-21, 631G3
Tariff cut put off 8-24, 650C2
US ties scored by ex-amb 8-24, 650G2
Queensland anti-strike bill proposed 9-4, 706A1
Attacks ACTU wage policy 9-11, 728E2
Links Labor S Australia defeat, econ policies 9-15, 749B2
Sinclair quits Cabt post, Hayden censure motn fails 9-27, 787G3, 788B1
Scored on jobless, state aid 10-11, 832A2
Aborigine health study rptd 11-28, 906D3
Backs coal dvpt projcts 12-4, 948B1
Shuffles Cabt 12-8, 948D1

FRATERNAL Order of the Police
Birmingham slaying protested 7-20, 869F3
FRATIANNE, Linda
Wins US figure-skating title 2-4, 392A1
Regains world figure-skating title 3-17, 391D3
FRATTI, Mario
Victim opens 5-3, 712C3
FRAUD—*See CRIME-Bribery*
FRAWLEY, James
Muppet Movie released 6-22, 820C2
FRAZIER, Herman
Shares indoor sprint medley mark 2-23, 911E2
FRB—*See U.S. GOVERNMENT-FEDERAL Reserve*
FREDERICK, Jane
AAU reinstatemt cited 11-28, 956F1
FREDERICK, Lynne
Prisoner of Zenda released 5-25, 820A3
FREE, Lloyd (All-World)
NBA scoring ldr 4-8, 290D2
FREED, Kenneth
Iran bars LA Times 7-1, 525D2
FREEDMAN, Judge Frank H.
Sentences Lloyd Carr offcls 3-19, 220F2
FREEDMAN, Gerald
Grand Tour opens 1-11, 292E1
FREEDOM House
World freedom survey issued 12D3-13B1
Rhodesia electn called fair 4-20, 293C2; 5-10, 354G1
FREEDOM of Information—*See PRIVACY Issue*
FREEDOM Prize, Hubert H. Humphrey
Awarded 6-17, 467E1
FREEMAN, Alan
Wheat speculatn alleged, London optns chrgs cited 3-21, 202E1
FREEMAN, Arny
1940's Radio Hour opens 10-7, 956F3
FREEMAN, George
Vs EPA coal-use rule 5-25, 404A1
FREEMAN, Joel
Love At First Bite released 4-12, 528G2
FREEMAN, Morgan
Coriolanus opens 3-14, 292C1; 6-28, 711C2
FREEMAN Jr., Gen. Paul L. (ret.)
Warns Carter of Sovt challenge 1-12, 15B1
FREEMAN, Judge Richard C.
Rejcts Lance grand jury dismissal motn 4-13, 327F3
FREEMAN III, Rear Adm. Rowland G.
Named to head GSA 3-23, 232B2
Confirmed 6-27, 965A3
FREEPORT, Tex.—*See TEXAS*
FREIJ, Elias
Egypt talks on W Bank autonomy rptd 6-15, 475C1*
Meets US envoy, backs W Bank-Jordan federatn 9-11, 676D3
Vs Israel W Bank setlmt expansn plan 10-14, 780G1

1980

Sets electn date 9-11, 727B3
Hawke named Labor Party indl relatns spokesman 9-15, 727G3
Labor advances in polls 10-15, 787A1
Reelected 10-18, 807E2
Stock mkt rptd up on electn win 10-21, 857E3
Shuffles Cabt 11-2, 857E2
Upton criticisms re Gandhi raise concern 11-6, 870B3
Liberal coalitn loses Sen control 11-12, 885E1
Announces fed job freeze 11-18, 900D1

FRASER, Vincent
Dies 3-4, nurse cleared 5-30, 656B1
FRATIANNE, Linda
Retains US figure skating title 1-18, 470E2
Wins Olympic medal 2-23, 155F3
FRATIANNO, James Aladena
Teamster offcl sentenced 5-23, 482A3
Tieri convicted 11-21, 971F2
FRAUD—*See CRIME--Bribery, Fraud & Extortion*
FRAUNCES Tavern (N.Y., N.Y.)
FALN '75 bombing suspect seized 4-4, 308G3
FALN bombing suspect convicted 7-30, 601D1
FRAZEE, Rowland C.
Royal Bank of Canada promotn rptd 9-5, 687B1
FRAZIER, Herman
Sets indoor sprint medley relay mark 2-29, 892F1
FRAZIER, Michael
Hide & Seek opens 5-4, 392B3
FRAZIER, Tyrone
Arrested in Tabatabai slaying 7-23, 545C2
FRB (Federal Reserve System)—*See under U.S. GOVERNMENT*
FREATO, Sereno
Suspected in 'black funds' scandal 3-7, 212B3
FREDERICK, Pauline
Paul White Award rptd won 7-7, 638E2
FREDERICKSON, Donald
DNA experiment rules eased 1-29, 416B2
FREDERIKSEN, Mark
Arrested 7-1, 522B2
Arrested for Jewish attacks 9-26, released 9-28, 750B1
Paris synagogue blast link denied 10-3, 767C2
Jewish group attacks 10-12, 790A1
FREDRIK, Burry
Canterbury Tales opens 2-12, 136A3
FREE, Lloyd (All-World)
NBA scoring ldr 3-30, 278C3
FREEDMAN, Jerrold
Borderline released 10-31, 972D3
FREEDOM (yacht)
Wins America's Cup trials 8-29; 3d race finals victory upheld 9-22, retains Cup 9-25, 834E1-D2
FREEDOM House
'79 survey rptd 2-1, 87B3
Rpts on Zimbabwe electn 4-11, 301D3
FREEDOM of Information—*See PRIVACY Issue*
FREEMAN 3rd, A. Myrick
Environmt rpt released 4-21, 308A1
FREEMAN, Cynthia
Portraits on best-seller list 4-6, 280B3; 5-4, 359C3; 12-7, 948F3
Come Pour the Wine on best-seller list 12-7, 948D3
FREEMAN III, Rear Adm. Rowland G.
Clinksales demotn cited 1-19, 112A2
FREEMAN, S. David
Signs China power pact 3-15, 231B2
FREEMAN, Seth
Wins Emmy 9-7, 692C1
FREEMAN, Virginia
Charlie & Algernon opens 9-14, 892B3
FREE to Choose (book)
On best-seller list 3-9, 200B3; 4-6, 280B3; 5-4, 359D3; 6-8, 448C3; 7-13, 568C3; 8-17, 640F3; 10-12, 796E3
FREI, Eduardo
Stages anti-Pinochet rally, denounces proposed constitutn 8-27, 669B2
FREIJ, Elias
Quits as Bethlehem mayor 6-3, 417F1
Withdraws resignatn 6-5, 547C2
Begin meets on Kawasmeh, Milhem ouster 10-21, 822A3
FREI Montalva, Eduardo
Calls const plebiscite 'fraud' 9-11, 706F2
FREIMUTH, Jorg
Wins Olympic medal 8-1, 624F1

1976

FREITAS do Amaral, Diogo
Scores govt, parties 1-13, 53B1
CDS to woo Cath workers 7-24, 558A3
FREJ, Elias
Reelected Bethlehem mayor 4-12, 258A3
FREMONT, Neb.—*See NEBRASKA*
FRENCH Polio—*See GUILLAIN-Barre Syndrome*
FRENKEL, Peter
Wins Olympic medal 7-23, 575E3
FRENZEL, Rep. William E. (R, Minn.)
Seconds Ford nominatn 8-18, 597G2
Reelected 11-2, 829F4
GOP Research Com chrmn 12-8, 981E3
FRESNO, Calif.—*See CALIFORNIA*
FRESNO, Bishop Francisco
Lauds Pinochet-church ldrs mtg 1-21, 100D2
FRESNO Bee (newspaper)
4 jailed 9-3—9-17, 700C2
FRETZ, Raymond
Named in grain fraud 3-11, 247D3
Resigns, pleads guilty 11-26, 990A3
FREUHAUF Corp.
2 officials sentncd 6-30, 523G3
FREY Jr., Rep. Louis (R, Fla.)
GOP conv vp vote table 8-19, 599E3
Reelected 11-2, 829C2
Clawson wins Policy Com post 12-8, 981D3
FREY, Bishop William C.
Warns Mote vs parish secessn 11-29, 932G1
FRGIC, Ivan
Wins Olympic medal 7-24, 576G2
FRI, Robert W.
On fast breeder dvpt 1-2, 115G2
FRIDERICHS, Hans
Sovt, W Ger drop A-plant plan 3-30, 243D2
FRIEDAN, Betty
Dem conv rule debated 7-13, 513C1
FRIEDMAN, Milton
Wins Nobel Prize 10-14, 839G3
Cited re £ decline 10-24, 809F3
FRIEJ, Elias
Lauds Temple Mt ct decisn 3-21, 211D1
FRIEND, David
Bailey cleared 1-12, 271E1
FRIENDLY Jr., Alfred
Sovt press chrgs CIA link 5-25, 5-26, 371B3, E3
Sues Sovt press 6-25, suit rptd dropped 7-23, 559B1
FRIENDS of the Earth
NYC clean air plan upheld 4-26, 308F1
FRIGGEBO, Birgit
Named to Swedish Cabt 10-8, 794C2
FRIIS, Harold T.
Dies 6-15, 524E2
FRINCKE, Rev. Herman R.
Ousted as dist pres 4-2, 776C3
FRIZZELL, Dale Kent
Quits Interior post 5-27, 412B2
FROEB, Judge Donald
OKs new Bolles trial judge 11-19, 971D3
FROMME, Lynette
Sup Ct bars review of Manson film ban 4-19, 331C2
FROMMELT, Willy
Wins Olympic medal 2-14, 158D3
FRONTIER Internship
Uruguay bans 1-20, 208A1
FROST, Desmond
Addresses Rhodesia party cong 9-15, 698G1
FROSTA (Norwegian tanker)
Collides with Miss ferry 10-20, 876G1
FRUDDEN Jr., Rear Adm. Mark P.
On N Korean killings 8-19, 619B1
On N Korea DMZ plan 8-25, 626B1
On DMZ paritn plan 8-28, 641B1
Signs partitn pact 9-6, 660F1
Vs N Korea talk plan 10-9, 858B2

FRUITS & Vegetables
China-Sri Lanka deal rptd 1-2, 78D1
United Brands Panama pact 1-8, 52B3
FDA bans Red #2 dye 1-19, 44D2
Dec, '75 CPI 1-21, 90B2
UFW contracts signed 1-22, 1-31, 153B2
Tunisia, Morocco chrg EC pact 'bias' 2-3, 164A3

1977

FREJ, Elias
Shuns W Bank stand on Sadat Israel visit 12-5, 930B3
FRELINGHUYSEN, Peter
Cited in Park indictmt 9-6, 688D1
FREISLEBEN, Dave
Brock sets stolen base mark 8-29, 748E3
FREMONT National Forest (Oregon)
Fire contained 8-9, 660G2
FRENCH Connection—*See NARCOTICS*
FRENCH Guiana (French colony)
French dvpt plan rptdly fails 8-3, 728F1
FRENZEL, Rep. William E. (R, Minn.)
'76 campaign surplus rptd 5-3, 482A2
FREUD, Sigmund (1856-1939)
Bibring dies 8-10, 696C2
FRI, Robert
On coal-climate study 4-30, 499A2
On missing A-material 8-8, 717A2
FRICK, Hans
Sentenced to death 11-26, 949F2
FRIDERICHS, Hans
Quits as econ min to hd Dresdner Bank 9-9, replaced 10-7, 969B2
FRIEDEN, Bernard
Rpts new house costs soaring 3-3, 178A2
FRIEDKIN, William
Weds Moreau 2-8, 140G3
FRIEDMAN, Daniel
Sentenced 3-10, 203B3
FRIEDMAN, Howard W.
Sentenced 3-10, 203B3
FRIEDRICKS, Kurt Otto
Gets Medal of Sci 11-22, 952A1
FRIENDLY Jr., Alfred
USSR renews attack 2-2, 101D1
FRIENDLY, Judge Henry J.
Finds JP Stevens in contempt 8-31, 724B2
FRIENDS of the Earth Foundation
Uranium cartel rptd 4-25, 479D2
NYC clean-air case review declined 10-17, 797C3
FRITH, Royce
Named to Canada Sen 4-5, 281B3
FROINES, John R.
Named to OSHA 9-30, 808B2
FROMHOLTZ, Dianne
Loses Australian Open 1-9, 103F3
FRONTIER Airlines—*See GENERAL Tire & Rubber*
FROST, David
Nixon TV interviews: 5-4, 365G3-367A3; 5-12, 385D3; Carter comments 5-12, 381C2; 5-19, 405C3; 5-25, 419B3
Final Nixon interview 9-3, 692G2
Traded to Angels 12-5, 990C1
FROST, Desmond
Scores Smith on land reform 1-17, 49G2
Quits Rhodesian Front 7-2, 536F2-A3
FROSTBELT States
US urban aid debated 12-7, 959E3
FROTA, Gen. Sylvio da
Pres bid cited re Furtado ban 7-3, 541B2
Geisel rptd vs pres bid 7-22, 616A1
Rptdly to be Portugal amb 9-1, 741B1
Fired 10-12; pol activities rptd 10-14, 839E3
Bentes gains mil support 12-2, 964A2
FROWICK, Roy Halston—*See HALSTON*

FRUITS & Vegetables
Mex '76 exports to US rptd 1-3, 65D3
Frost kills Fla crops 1-18—1-20, 54F3
Midwest supplies rptd short, prices soar 1-22, 54E2
Orange-juice concentrate futures rise 1-28, 55B1; 1-31, 76C1
Fla prices soar 1-29, 76C1

1978

FRELON, Le (book)
Film version released 4-24, 619D1
FREMONT, Rob
Piano Bar opens 6-8, 887E2
FRENCH, Marilyn
Women's Room on best-seller list 7-2, 579C3; 8-6, 620A2; 11-6, 888A1; 12-3, 971C1
FRENCH Guiana (French colony)
Leon Damas dies 1-22, 96E1
FRENCH Polynesia (French territory)
Prisoners riot 1-15, captured 1-17, 71A2
FRENZEL, Rep. William E. (R, Minn.)
Reelected 11-7, 851A2
FREUDENBERGER, Daniel
City Sugar opens 6-5, 887D1
FREY Jr., Rep. Louis (R, Fla.)
Loses primary for gov 9-12, 736D1
Nelson wins seat 11-7, 849E3
FRICK, Ford C.
Dies 4-8, 356F2
FRICK Award, Ford C.—*See BASEBALL—Awards*
FRIDAY, Nancy
My Mother/My Self on best-seller list 4-2, 272C3; 4-30, 356A2; 6-4, 460C3; 7-2, 579D3; 8-6, 620B2; 9-4, 708C1; 11-6, 888A1; 12-3, 971C1
FRIDAY v. Uzzell
NC Univ minority rep case sent back by Sup Ct 7-3, 552C1
FRIED, Martin
Diary of Anne Frank revived 12-18, 1031D1
FRIED, Michael
Othello opens 1-30, 887D2
Promise opens 3-8; Show-off 5-18, Pins & Needles 7-6, 760B3-D3
FRIEDLAND, Jack
On Food Fair cash drain 10-1, 753B1
FRIEDMAN, Gary William
Platinum opens 11-12, 1031F2
FRIEDMAN, Harold
'76 earnings rptd 2-20, 365B2
FRIEDMAN, Milton
US amendmt draft drive to curb taxes, spending set 7-7, 735F3
Backs Jarvis tax-cut plan 9-26, 735E3
FRIEDMAN, Stephen R.
Working opens 5-14, 887E3
Bloodbrothers released 9-27, 969D3
FRIENDLY Ice Cream Corp.
Hershey purchase agreed 12-26, 1005G1-A2
FRIENDS, Religious Society of (Quakers)
American Friends Service Committee
S Africa stock sale set 8-15, 669G3
Collett asks US oust Somoza 11-8, 883E3
FRIENDSHIP Force
Lance named natl dir 1-17, in Eur 3-9, 204B3
FRIENDS of the Earth
Belgian A-plant leak disputed 1-25, 69F3
UK OKs Windscale A-reprocessing plant 3-22, 227D2
Carter gets high rating 12-20, 1009F1
FRIGGEBO, Birgit
Swedish housing min 10-18, 822G2
FRING, Ketti
Angel opens 5-10, 760C1
FRINGS, Joseph Cardinal
Dies 12-17, 1032G2
FRITZSCH, Ronald
Ct-apptd atty shot 5-31, 439F2
FROMHOLTZ, Dianne
Loses Detroit Va Slims 2-26, 419G1
FROMME, Lynette Alice (Squeaky)
Ford '75 trial testimony cited 4-21, 309G3
FRONDIZI, Arturo
Sees Spain king 11-28, 967G3
FRONT-Line Nations (Angola, Botswana, Mozambique, Tanzania, Zambia)—*See RHODESIA*
FROSCH, Robert
On NASA budget proposals 1-23, 46C1
FROST, J. Martin
Wins US House primary in Tex 5-6, 362G3
Elected 11-7, 852B3, 855E3
FROST, Sydney
Named whaling probe head 3-20, 208D3
FROST, Thomas
Record wins Grammy 2-24, 316B1
FROSTA (Norwegian tanker)
'76 collisn rpt issued 5-17, 460B1
FROWICK, Roy Halston—*See HALSTON*
FRUEHAUF Corp.
Convictn review denied by Sup Ct 11-6, 874D1
FRUEHAUF Corp. v. U.S.
Case refused by Sup Ct 11-6, 874D1

FRUITS & Vegetables
Hungary hikes prices 1-9, 55D2
Orange juice '77 futures trading rise rptd 1-12, 84A1
US, Japan reach trade pact 1-13, 27A1, E1
UFW ends boycotts 1-31, 83F1

1979

FREITAS Cruz, Joao
Remains Portugal forgn min 7-30, 603E3
FREMONT Hotel Inc.—*See ALKATH Corp.*
FREMONT-Smith, Maurice
Dies 5-4, 432F2
FRENCH, Marilyn
Women's Room on best-seller list 1-7, 80C3; 2-4, 120D3; 3-4, 173F3; 5-6, 356E2
FRENCH Detective, The (film)
Released 3-10, 528C2
FRENCH Postcards (film)
Released 10-19, 1007C3
FREQUENCY, The (play)
Opens 4-25, 711B3
FREUDENBERGER, Daniel
Later opens 1-15, 292F1
FREUND, Jay
American Game released 4-28, 528C1
FREY, Jane
Marriage rptd 4-4, 271C3
FREY, Jim
Hired as Royals mgr 10-24, 1002F1
FRIAS, Pepe
Traded to Rangers 12-7, 1002F2
FRIDAY, Nancy
My Mother/My Self on best-seller list 1-7, 80C3; 2-4, 120C3; 4-8, 271B2; 6-3, 432C2
FRIED, Michael
Little Eyolf opens 6-29, 712B1
FRIEDERSDORF, Max L.
Confrmd to FEC 2-21, 130B3
Named FEC vice chrmn 5-17, 401D3
Carter com billed $50,203 6-4, 419C3
FRIEDMAN, Eve
Teibele & Her Demon opens 12-16, 1007F2
FRIEDMAN, Milton
Urges US spending limit amendmt 1-30, 86G2
FRIEDMAN, Peter
Warriors opens 5-22, 712D3
FRIEDMAN, Stephen R.
Fast Break released 3-1, 174E2
Homeland opens 4-16, 711F3
Break a Leg opens 4-29, 711G1
FRIEDMAN v. Rogers
Professnal use of corp names curbed by Sup Ct 2-21, 128D2
FRIEDRICH, John
Wanderers released 7-13, 820F3
FRIEL, Brian
Faith Healer opens 4-4, 711G2
FRIENDLY Fire (TV special)
Wins Emmy 9-9, 858E2
FRIENDS (recording)
Chick Corea, group win Grammy 2-16, 336E3
FRIENDS, Religious Society of (Quakers)
American Friends Service Committee
FBI files preservation sought 6-26, 520G3
FRIENDS of the Earth Foundation
Scores US wilderness proposal 1-4, 16C2
France A-plant fueling delayed 10-4, 772E3
FRIGHTENED Country, The (book)
Fraser attack rptd 8-24, 650C3
FRISCH, Max
Biography: A Game opens 4-5, 711E1
FRISCO Kid, The (film)
Released 7-6, 820C1
FROMHOLTZ, Dianne
Wins Boston Avon tourn 3-18, 391D2
US wins Federatn Cup 5-6, 391D2
FROSCH, Robert
Rpts Carter space shuttle support 11-14, 883E3
FROST, Dave
Angels lose AL pennant 10-6, 797F2
FROUD, Brian
Faeries on best-seller list 1-7, 80C3

FRUITS & Vegetables
UFW strikes Calif lettuce farms 1-19; Chiquita banana, natl boycott set 4-26, 327A1
Vegetarian diet rptd risky for children 2-22, 140F1
Jan CPI rise rptd 2-23, 151B2

1980

FREITAS, Chagas
Orders probe of Rio bombings 8-29, 704C3
FREITAS do Amaral, Diogo
Sworn Portugal forgn min 1-3, 21D3
Backs US re Afghan crisis 1-15, 28C2
On Sovt diplomats expulsion 8-21, 689B3
Acting Portugal premr 12-4, 923A2
FRELICH, Phyllis
Children of a Lesser God opens 3-30, 392E2
Wins Tony 6-8, 692B3
FRENCH, David
Of the Fields opens 5-27, 756F3
FRENCH Guiana (French colony)
Surinam coup attempt fails 5-1—5-2, 410F2
ESA rocket launched 5-23, 397G2
ESA plans comet probe 7-15, 548B1
FRENZEL, Rep. William E. (R, Minn.)
Reelected 11-4, 843A2
FREUDENBERGER, Daniel
Trouble with Europe opens 1-28, 136F3
FREY, Jim
In World Series 10-14—10-21, 811C2-812D2
FREY Jr., Lou
Sen primary runoff set 9-9, 700G1
FREYSS, Christophe
Loses Bavarian Grand Prix 5-25, 607D3
FRICK, G. James
Auto-Train investmt plan rptd 11-26, 958B3
FRICKE, Aaron
Gay prom date OKd 5-28, 471C1
FRIDAY, Nancy
Men in Love on best-seller list 6-8, 448C3; 7-13, 568C3; 8-17, 640F3
FRIDAY the 13th (film)
Released 5-10, 675F2
Top-grossing film 5-28, 448G3
FRIED, Michael
Heartbreak House opens 4-29, 392B3
FRIEDERSDORF, Max L.
Quits FEC post 12-16; named Reagan aide 12-17, 955C3
FRIEDKIN, William
'Cruising' opens, draws gay protests; Gen Cinema contract dispute cited 2-15, 216D2, 239F2
FRIEDMAN, Bruce Jay
Stir Crazy released 12-12, 1003D2
FRIEDMAN, Elizabeth S.
Dies 10-31, 928E2
FRIEDMAN, Gary B.
Itel terminatn agrmt rptd 10-16, 784B2
FRIEDMAN, Milton
Chile econ recovery detailed 1-14, 19G1
Free to Choose on best-seller list 3-9, 200B3; 4-6, 280B3; 5-4, 359D3; 6-8, 448C3; 7-13, 568C3; 8-17, 640F3; 9-14, 716C3; 10-12, 796E3
On Reagan econ policy panel 11-16, 881D2
FRIEDMAN, Rose
Free to Choose on best-seller list 3-9, 200B3; 4-6, 280B3; 5-4, 359D3; 6-9, 448C3; 7-13, 568C3; 8-17, 640F3; 9-14, 716C3; 10-12, 796E3
FRIEDMAN, Stephen J.
Hero at Large released 2-8, 216F2
Little Darlings released 3-28, 416C3
FRIEDMAN, William F. (1891-1969)
Wife dies 10-31, 928D2
FRIENDS of the Earth
New scenic area air rules issued 11-25, 898C2
Pomerance denounces Watt apptmt 12-22, 979G3
FRIGGER, Hartmut
Escapes bank fraud arrest 7-24, 581E1
FRITSCH, Ronald
Sentenced 10-13, 833C1
FRITSCH, Tony
NFL '79 kicking ldr 1-5, 8B2
FRITSCHLER, A. Lee
Electronic mail plan OKd, conflict of interest chrgd 4-8, 347C3
FROEB, Dr. Herman F.
Smoking risk to nonsmokers rptd 3-26, 318B2
FROELICH, William J.
Dies 2-5, 176B1
FROMAN, Jane
Dies 4-23, 360F1
FROMENT-Meurice, Henri
Bastille Day broadcast barred 7-14, 566B3
FROMHOLTZ, Dianne
US wins Federatn Cup 5-25, 607B1
Loses French Open semifinals 6-6, Wimbledon mixed doubles 7-5, 606A3, D3
Loses US Women's Indoor 10-5, 947A2
FROMM, Erich
Dies 3-18, 279G2
FROMME, Lynette (Squeaky)
Hijacker's release demand foiled 8-18, 667A3
FROM the Life of the Marionettes (film)
Released 11-7, 972E3
FRONT Page, The (play)
Opens 12-22, 1003B3
FROSCH, Robert
Shuttle launch target date moved back 1-29, 71F2
FROST, David
Interviews shah 1-17, 47G1
FROST, Rep. J. Martin (D, Tex.)
Reelected 11-4, 844C3
FROWICK, Roy Halston—*See HALSTON*
FRUITS & Vegetables
Maine State of State message 1-2, 269C2
US dietary guidelines issued 2-4, 157A3
Calif crops rptd damaged 2-22, 213E3
Fla citrus crop frozen 3-1—3-2, 292B3
Mar producer prices rptd 4-4, 263C1

1976

Dutch potato exports curbed 2-12, 2-16, 141A3
EC potato export tax OKd 2-17, 164A1
Turkey export decline rptd 4-1, 315A2
Latin banana output rptd 5-7, 466C1
Mushroom grower aid OKd 5-17, 431C2
Speculators default on potato futures 5-25; suit filed 5-27, 397C1-398B1
Calif cannery strike ends 7-31, 570C1
Potato futures default penalty set 8-31, ct delays setlmt 9-27, 990E1
Aug CPI rptd 9-21, 708F2
Sept CPI rptd 10-21, 805G2
New potato futures contract OKd 11-2, trading halted 11-3, 990A1
United Brands details forgn, labor paymts 12-10, 985C3

FRUMKIN, Alexander
Dies 5-27, 404G1
FRYDENLUND, Knut
Norway foreign min 1-12, 30A2
FUCHIDA, Mitsuo
Dies 5-30, 524E2
FUCHS, Ruth
Wins Olympic medal 7-24, 576E1
FUGATE, Caril Ann
Paroled 6-8, 442C3
FUJAIRA—*See UNITED Arab Emirates*
FUJI Heavy Industries Ltd.
US ends car dumping probe 5-4, 321D2
FUJIWARA, Koichi
Arrested 7-7, 497F2
Indicted 7-28, 624D2
FUKUDA, Hajime
Japan justice min 12-24, 1006B3
FUKUDA, Takeo
Chinese oil import rise set 1-22, 208C3
Named to Lockheed probe com 2-19, 190B2
Seeks Miki ouster 5-13, 458G1
Asks Miki to quit 8-23, 626C3
Sees Miki re compromise 8-30, 676G3
To oppose Miki as LDP leader 10-20, 838G3
Miki asked to resign 10-21, 839A1
Quits Cabt, to challng Miki 11-5, 889F3
Heads LDP 12-23; elected premr, names Cabt 12-24, 1006D2
FUKUDA, Taro
Diet subpoenas 2-26, 190C3
Dies 6-10, 450D3
FULBRIGHT, J(ames) William
Registers as Emirates counsel 1-26, 160C2
Egypt award rptd 1-28, 160D2
FULLER, Keith
Named AP pres 6-3, 504E2
Denies PI chrg vs Zeitlin 11-6, 855G1

1977

Washn drought threat rptd 2-28, 153F1
Mid-Feb prices rise 2-28, 154C3
Canada import costs up 3-11, 3-15, 200F2
Feb CPI rise rptd 3-18, 215A1
Ida potato baron fined 5-20, 491D3
FTC accuses Sunkist 6-6, 520E2
NC apple labeling rule voided 6-20, 517E1
May CPI rptd 6-22, 482A1
NY commodity trading cntr opens 7-5, 521G2
Coca-Cola, Egypt in citrus grove dvpt pact 863B2
US loans to exporters curbed 10-19, 815E2
Fla Citrus Comm renews Bryant contract; orange-juice boycott cited 11-16, 927G2
Japan assures GATT on orange imports 11-29, 933E2
ILA offcl sentncd in United Brands shakedown 12-2, 937F3
US, Mex OK commodity pact 12-2, 976G1
Israel-Rumania trade rptd 12-10, 987C3

FTC—*See U.S. GOVERNMENT—FEDERAL Trade Commission*
FTOREK, Robbie
Sold 4-1, 263A1
Named WHA MVP 5-23, 430F1
FUEL—*See ENERGY; specific sources*
FUEL Cycle Evaluation Conference, International
Carter backs intl A-fuel bank 10-19, 794F1
FUENTES, Carlos
Quits France envoy post 4-7, 529G1
FUENTES Quintana, Enrique
Spain 2d dep premier 7-5, 545G1
Govt sets econ program 7-12, 545A3
FUJAIRA—*See UNITED Arab Emirates*
FUKUDA, Hajime
Resigns 10-4, 756D3
Replaced as justice min 801G3
FUKUDA, Takeo (Japanese premier)
On budget increase 1-20, 65F1
Mondale sees 1-31, 70B1
Sees Carter 3-21—3-22, 209E2
US A-policy scored 3-30, 4-2, 329C3
Carter asks Portugal aid 4-1, 330C3
At 7-natn econ summit, sees Carter 5-7—5-8, 357C1, D1, 358B1, F1
Seeks curb vs exports 6-29, 544D3
Fraser asks sugar dispute role 7-16, 578C3
US briefs on ROK troop talks 7-27, 572B2
Australia sugar talks fail again 8-4, 615D2
Meets with ASEAN ldrs 8-6—8-7, 607B2
US reflationary proposals rptd rejctd 8-8, 585B2
Awards Medal of Honor to Oh 9-5, 748G2
Govt expenditures increased 10-3, 783A2
Sees 'grave' econ situatn 11-26, 932C2
Forms new Cabt 11-28, econ task force 11-29, 932F1-F2
Vows trade surplus cut 12-19, 984E3
FULBRIGHT & Jaworski
On 5 largest law firms list 5-16, 383A2
FULL Disclosure (book)
On best-seller list 9-4, 712D3
FULLER, Keith
Scores Krimsky ouster 2-4, 101F1
FULLERTON, Lt. Col. C. Gordon
Pilots space shuttle 8-12, 627A1
FULMER, Robert
Chrgs divorce job bias 5-2, 472C1
FULTON National Bank (Atlanta, Ga.)
Lance irregularities chargd 9-6, 9-7, 690C1, F1-C2

1978

Israeli orange exports poisoned 2-1, 60F3-61A1
EC '75 fine vs United Brands upheld 2-14, 159C1
Vegetable immunizatn rptd, tomato test cited 3-2, 334G1
Tropicana purchase by Beatrice set 3-5, 184F3
Potato planting curbed in Sen farm bill 3-21, 218G2
OPIC extensn signed, citrus aid barred 4-24, 323A3
Calif crop damage, inflatn linked 5-30, 428C2
US banana cos admit Honduras payoffs 6-9, 615A1
Israeli import co in W Ger bombed 6-22, 500G1
E Ger-Brazil deal rptd 7-13, 649D1
United Brands pleads guilty re banana bribe 7-19, 643F1
Beatrice-Tropicana trust challenge rejcted 8-2, cos merge 8-7, 767E3
Reynolds seeks Del Monte 8-3, bid OKd 9-25, 752A3
Canning industry eased clean-water rules proposed 8-10, 644A2
Nitrites linked to cancer 8-11, 728E1
US-Japan citrus quota talks fail 9-5—9-7, 695A1
Pillsbury to acquire Green Giant 9-18, 752C3
DBCP pesticide curbs asked 9-19, 719C2
Chile trade boycott set by US, forgn unions 11-24; impact rptd 12-15, 1014G1
Japan US citrus pact signed 12-5, 988D2
Greek EC entry terms set; tomato, peach curbs noted 12-21, 1917E3

FTC—*See U.S. GOVERNMENT—FEDERAL Trade Commission*
FTOREK, Robbie
WHA scoring ldr 4-11, 296G2
FUCHS, Manny
Once In Paris released 11-9, 970E2
FUEL—*See ENERGY; specific kinds*
FUENTES Quintana, Enrique
Quits Cabt post 2-24, named Suarez econ aide 3-6, 394F2, E3
FUGARD, Athol
Nongogo opens 12-3, 1031F2
FUJAIRA—*See UNITED Arab Emirates*
FUKASAKU, Kinji
Message From Space released 11-17, 970B2
FUKUDA, Takeo (Japanese premier)
US trade pact scored by Soclsts 1-13, 27E1
Vs Sovt peace bid 2-22, 121D3
Scores Narita airport riots 3-28, 228C1
LDP ldrs rptd vs China peace talks 4-7, 278B2
Fraser trade talks rptd, commodity fund planned 4-23, 391C2
In US, vows export cuts 5-1—5-5, 341E2-C3
Brzezinski briefs on China talks 5-23, 384B3
Rejcts Sovt protest vs China pact 6-19, 637B2
US trade deficit poses pol problem 6-19, 695E1
At 7-natn Bonn summit; vows export curbs, aid hikes 7-16—7-17, 543C3, 544G1, F2
US export curb reassurnc rptd 7-17, 544A2
Signs anti-hijacking pact 7-17, 544A3
Asks moves vs trade surplus 7-21, 574A3
Econ stimulus plan proposed 9-3, 694B1
US, Japan, plan joint energy research 9-6, 695C3
US chrgs business opposed to trade 10-5, 798A1
Exec killed in El Salvador 10-13, 881C3
On China pact link to Korea 10-18; Sonoda corrects statemt 802B1
At China-Japan pact rites, meets Teng 10-23, 801B1, A2-802A1
Loses party electn to Ohira 11-27, 912E2
LDP feud delays Ohira confirmatn 12-6; Ohira confirmed, Cabt named 12-7, 945D2
West regrets lower growth rate goal 12-11, 988C2
FUKUNAGA, Kazuomi
Tied to Lockheed scandal 1-30, 72E3
FULAIJ, Faisal Saud al-
Financial Gen sues 2-17, 204B3
SEC chrgs 3-18, settles 3-19, 204B2
FULBRIGHT, J. William
Named as lobbyist for Saudis 237B1
FULKS, Joe (d. 1976)
In basketball HOF 5-1, 457E3
FULLAM, Judge John P.
OKs Penn Central reorganizatn plan 3-9, 185F3-186F1
FULL Disclosure (book)
On best-seller list 8-6, 620C2
FULL Employment and Balanced Growth Act of 1978 (Humphrey-Hawkins Bill)—*See LABOR—Employment*
FULLER, Alvan Tufts (1878-1958)
Cadillac dealership closes 3-1, 142F3 ★
FULLER, John G.
Ghost on best-seller list 4-2, 272D3
FULLER, Mike
NFL '77 punt return ldr 1-1, 56C3
FULLER, Peter
Cadillac dealership closes 3-1, 142G3
FULMAN v. U.S.
Personal holding co tax rate affirmed 2-22, 126G2
FULTON, Mayor Richard (Nashville, Tenn.)
Loses primary for gov 8-3, 606A2

1979

Maine potato futures trading halted 3-9, CFTC probes 5-9, 348C1
May producer price drop rptd 6-7, 422A2
Truckers strike 6-7–6-15, 462G3; 6-18–6-28, 479A3
UFW Calif lettuce strike violence 6-11, strike settled 8-31, 698G2
Foreign Developments (including U.S. international news)
Rumania '78 output rptd short 2-6, 170G3
UK '78 aid to Portugal rptd 2-20, 212F3
Canada cuts import duties 3-12, 210G3
GATT pact signed 4-12, 273F2
Sovt-Hungary trade cited 5-30, 417D1
Fla vegetable growers withdraw Mex chrgs; '78 tomato exports, crop data rptd 7-19, 553G1
Dominica banana, grapefruit crops destroyed 8-30, 690C3
US clears Mex vegetable growers 10-30, 831F1
China hikes prices 11-1, 854D3
Mex '79 bean productn down 32% 12-12, 950C2

FRYER, Robert
Sweeney Todd opens 3-1, 292C3
FTC—*See U.S. GOVERNMENT–FEDERAL Trade Commission*
FTOREK, Robbie
WHA assist ldr 4-18, 355F2, 356D1
FUCHS, Klaus Emil Julius
Retirement rptd 2-1, 78E3
Julius Rosenberg article publshd 6-16, 466E1
FUELLE, Rainer
Arrested as E Ger spy, escapes 1-20, 61C3
FUENTES Mohr, Alberto
Assassinated, facts on 1-25; Kennedy deplores 1-26, 97E1-A2
Army staff chief slain 6-10, 445D3
FUJAIRA—*See UNITED Arab Emirates*
FUKUDA, Takeo
Meets Teng 2-7, 84B1
Challenges Ohira for premier 11-2, Ohira reelected 11-6, 844B3
Ohira names new Cabt 11-8, 874F2
FULLARD-Leo, Ainsley
Vs Palmyra A-waste site 8-21, 743F3
FULL Employment and Balanced Growth Act of 1978 (Humphrey-Hawkins Bill)—*See LABOR–Employment*
FULLER, Larry
Evita opens 9-25, 956A3
FULLER, Mike
NFL '78 punt return ldr 1-6, 80C2
FULLER, R. Buckminster
Elected to Arts Institute 12-7, 1005A3
FULLER, Steve
In NFL draft 5-3, 335G1
FULLILOVE v. Kreps
Case accepted by Sup Ct 5-21, 400G3
Case argued in Sup Ct 11-27, 944F3
FULTON Market Cold Storage Co.
Tax overassessmt case declined by Sup Ct 1-15, 32C1

1980

Mar CPI rise rptd 4-22, 305C2
Hunts bailout loan collateral listed 5-28, 425F3
May farm prices rptd up 5-30, 425D1
May producer prices rptd 6-6, 437D3
Midwest, South drought damage rptd 6-23—8-15, 616C2
June farm prices rptd 6-30, 492D2
Tex hurricane losses rptd 8-13, 621B3
Sept farm prices rptd up 9-30, 741B2
Oct farm prices rptd 10-31, 883C1
Beatrice, Tropicana merger found illegal 11-28, 917F3
Nov farm prices rptd 11-28, 938B2
Foreign Developments (including U.S. international news)
CR banana workers' strike ends 1-17, 117C1
Peru potato crop hit by drought 2-8, 234E3
Mex tomatoes found toxic 2-20; 3 packing plants closed, US border checks rptd 3-12, 233A3
Connally 'basic speech' excerpts 3-7, 184B2
US dismisses Mex 'dumping' suit 3-24, 233F2
US farmers ask Canada potato import ban 3-27, 368D2
African dependence on S Africa cited 4-1, 243A2
Canada A-plant impact rptd 5-22, 406G2
Spanish-French dispute spurs violence, truckers block border 6-16—6-20, 525A3
St Lucia banana crop hit by Hurricane Allen 8-4, 621B2
USSR drought threat rptd 8-6, 711B3
Polish potato crop loss seen 11-12, 879A1
FRYDENLUND, Knut
In Moscow 12-22—12-23, 979B2
FRYE, William
Raise the Titanic released 8-1, 675D3
FTC (Federal Trade Commission)—*See under U.S. GOVERNMENT*
FTC v. Standard Oil Co. of California
Case accepted by Sup Ct 2-25, 187E3
Case decided by Sup Ct 12-15, 957E1
FUERA del Juego (Out of the Game) (book)
Padilla allowed to emigrate to US 3-16, 231B3
FUGARD, Athol
Lesson From Aloes opens 11-17, 1003D3
FUGATE, Frank B.
Saudi completes Aramco takeover, retains bd seat 9-4, 662A2
FUGITIVE, The (TV series)
Janssen dies 2-13, 176F1
'Dallas' episode viewing record rptd 11-25, 905C3
FUJAIRA—*See UAE*
FUKUDA, Takeo
Shuns Ohira confidence vote 5-16, 381B1
Party factn in Cabt 7-17, 539A3
FULAIJ, Faisal Saud al-
Financial Gen deal set 7-25, 600D3
FULLAM, Judge John P.
Cites rptr on Abscam source silence 7-10, 554B2
Dismisses Abscam convictns 11-26, 919A2
FULLER, Frances
Dies 12-18, 1004F1
FULLILOVE v. Klutznick
Case decided by Sup Ct 7-2, 510A1

1976

FULTZ, Jack
Wins Boston Marathon 4-19, 292E3
FUNADA, Naka
Scores Miki re Lockheed 8-24, 628B2
FUND For Animals
Regenstein sees Carter 12-16, 937C2
FUNNY Lady (film)
'75 top rental film 1-7, 32F3
FUNSETH, Robert L.
US halts Sovt joint talks 3-16, 196G1
Kissinger cancels speeches 5-18, 359D1
On N Korea statemt re US deaths 8-23, 625F2
FUQUA, Rep. Don (D, Fla.)
Reelected 11-2, 829B2
FUQUA, J. B.
'70 Carter campaign donor 10-17, 805B1
FURER, Julius A. (U.S. warship)
In Intl Naval Review 7-4, 488D3
FURGLER, Kurt
Elected Swiss pres 12-8, 1011F3
FURIES, The (book)
On best seller list 1-25, 80D3; 2-29, 208F3
FURIOUS Days, The (book)
Published 11-4, cyclone relief probe ordrd 11-18, 902E2
FURNISS, Bruce
Wins Olympic medal 7-19, 562D3, 575E2
FURRER, Joseph
Rptdly takes 5th in SWP case 7-14, 570B1
FURS
Ben Kahn dies 2-5, 124E3
FUSSELL, Paul
Wins Natl Book Award 4-19, 292C3

1977

FUNDAMENTALS of Ecology (book)
Odum wins ecology award 4-15, 354G1
FUND Raising—*See PHILANTHROPY*
FUNERAL Homes
FTC rpt scores practices 8-16, 651D3
FUN With Dick and Jane (film)
Top-grossing film 3-9, 184D3
FUQUA Industries Inc.
Loses Avis bid 6-27, 519C2
FURLONGER, Robert
To head intellignc office 5-5, 372A1
FURS
US OKs S Africa sealskin imports 1-3, 21F3
FURTADO, Alencar
Scores judicial reform bill 3-30, 281C1
Scores Geisel pol reforms 303D2
Scores mil govt 6-27, 523D2
Geisel bans 7-1, 541E1
Geisel bans party broadcasts 7-26, 616C1
FUSINA, Chuck
Penn St wins Fiesta Bowl, death threats cited 12-25, 1020C2
FUTURES Industry Association Inc.
Mar, 1st ¼ trading record rptd 4-18, 301A2
FYROL FR-2—*See CHEMICALS*

1978

FULTON, Wendy
Early Dark opens 4-25, 760B2
FUND Raising—*See PHILANTHROPY*
FUNGAL Keratitis—*See EYES & Eyesight*
FUNSETH, Rod
2d in Masters 4-9, 355F2
Wins Greater Hartford Open 7-30, 672D3
FUNSTON, Bob
Loses Okla primary for gov 8-22, 683C1
FUQUA, Rep. Don (D, Fla.)
Reelected 11-7, 850F2
FURIE, Sidney J.
Boys In Company C released 1-31, 618D3
FURNCO Construction Corp.
Coll sex-bias ruling voided by Sup Ct 11-13, 874B2
FURNCO Construction Corp. v. Waters
Job bias proof qualified by Sup Ct 6-29, 567D3
FURNITURE
Nigeria import ban rptd 4-4, 248C1
Quebec cuts sales tax 4-11, 286G2
Charles Eames dies 8-21, 708E2
Simmons OKs Gulf+Westn merger bid 10-15, 808A2
FURS
Aleuts win mistreatmt claim 6-21, 569F1
'78 high chic fashion rptd 8-4—8-11, 10-27—11-3, 1029D2
FURTH, George
Company opens 5-7, 887D1
FURUI, Yoshimi
Japan justice min 12-7, 945E2
FURY, The (film)
Top-grossing film 3-29, 272E3
FUSINA, Chuck
2d in Heisman vote 11-28, 1025A2
FUSION—*See ATOMIC Energy*
FUTURES Industry Association
'77 trading rise, Chicago Bd rank rptd 1-12, 83G3

1979

FUNDAMENTAL Investors Inc.
Mutual fund dirs' power backed by Sup Ct 5-14, 383B1
FUQUA, Rep. Don (D, Fla.)
Science & Tech Com chrmn 1-24, 71E1
FUQUA Industries Inc.
Hoover purchase bid blocked 6-11, 560F2
Hoover bid dropped 8-20, 664A2
FUREY, Archbishop Francis James
Dies 4-23, 356E3
FURLOW, Terry
Traded to Hawks 1-30, 526E2
FURNESS, Betty
Describes Carter mtg 6-1, 418G1
FURNITURE
GATT pact signed, tariff cuts seen 4-12, 273G1
Monaco antique auctn records rptd 6-27, 672F1
USSR hikes prices 7-2, 504D2
Sloane parent co files bankruptcy 7-27, 648F3
Ethan Allen-Interco merger deal set 8-13, 664B1
FURS
'79 fashion roundup rptd 1006C2
FUSINA, Chuck
Penn State loses Sugar Bowl 1-1, 8F2
FU Tieshan, Msgr. Michael
Elected bishop 7-25; Vatican rejcts 8-17, Chinese church scores 8-21, 639E2
FUTURES Contract—*See COMMODITIES & Commodity Trading; STOCKS*
FU Yuehua
Trial halted 10-17, backers explain 10-29, 854F2

1980

FUND for a Conservative Majority
Reagan funding drive upheld 8-28, 681A2
FUNERAL Industry
FTC funding blocked 3-15—4-30, shuts down 5-1, reopens 5-2, 348C1
FTC probe power curbed 5-28, 702F3
FUNGAROLI v. Fungaroli
Case dismissed by Sup Ct 5-12, 426C3
FUNKYTOWN (recording)
On best-seller list 6-4, 448E3; 7-9, 568E3
FUQUA, Rep. Don (D, Fla.)
Reelected 11-4, 842F2
FURCI, Giuseppe
Slain 12-1, 944G1
FURLOW, Terry
Killed in car crash, drugs found 5-23, 656A2
FURNITURE
Govt waste scored 3-18, 459D2
FUSION—*See ATOMIC Energy*
FUSTOK, Mahmoud
In Hunt silver-backed bond group 3-26, 223B1
FUTURES Contracts—*See COMMODITIES*

G

1976

GABALDON, Argimiro (d. 1962)
US exec kidnaped 2-28, 208F2
GABES, Gulf of—*See GULF of Gabes*
GABIN, Jean (Jean-Alexis Moncorge)
Dies 11-15, 970F1
GABL, Gertrud
Dies 1-18, 56C3

GABON—*See also AFRICAN Development Bank, NONALIGNED Nations Movement, OAU, OPEC*
US chrgs Sovt warships near Angola 1-7, 2A2
Listed as 'not free' nation 1-9, 20D3
Equatorial Guinea exiles rptd 1-24, 62A2
Angola MPLA recognized 2-12, 105E2
At France-Africa summit 5-10—5-11, 355G2
Olympic withdrawal rptd 7-21, 528B3
New mins named 10-19, 1003A2
Cameroon clash rptd 11-16, border closed 11-17, 1003B2
Forgn debts frozen 12-6, 1003C2
Ashland '72 Bongo paymts rptd 12-20, 985B3
GABRIEL, Rosemarie
Sets world swim marks 6-1—6-5, 424G3
Wins Olympic medal 7-19, 575A3
GADDIS, William
Wins Natl Book Award 4-19, 292C3
GADEA, Suzana
Rumania educatn min 6-15, 440C2
GADRIX Jr., Edward W.
Loses election 11-2, 822D1
GADSDEN, Henry W.
Merck panel scores 3-9, 361B2
GAF Corp.
US files consent decree 11-16, 989D1
GAFFNEY, J. Brian
Cleared in Conn scandal 1-12, 271G1
GAFNY, Arnon
Named bank gov 10-24; sworn 10-31, 854E2
GAHAGEN, Robert
Named as Spain CIA agent 1-14, 77C1
GAIRY, Eric M.
Narrowly reelected 12-7, 925C1
GAJDUSEK, Dr. Daniel Carleton
Wins Nobel Prize 10-14, 840C1
GALANENA, Crescencio
Vanishes in Argentina 8-9; 'desertn' rptd 8-16, 672F1
GALANTE, Jose
Natl Assemb scores release 7-30, 733G1
GALAUP, Alain
Taken hostage, feared dead 8-4, 581D1
Freed 8-17, 674B3
GALEANO Ramirez, Alberto
Cuba trade pacts signed 2-20, 251G3
GALGAY, Judge John J.
Rules Grant bankrupt 4-13, 984F3

1977

GABALDON, Arnoldo Jose
Venez environmt min 1-7, 23E2
GABELLAH, Elliott
Quits Muzorewa group 8-21, 662D2
GABES, Gulf of—*See GULF of Gabes*
GABO, Naum
Dies 8-23, 696F2
GABOASH, Philip Abbas
Sudan coup crushed 2-2, 117E2
GABON—*See also NONALIGNED Nations Movement, OAU, OPEC*
UN Assemb member 4A1
Cabinda rebel aid rptd 1-8, 86A2
UN issues Benin coup probe rptd 3-8, 243A3
At France-Africa summit 4-20—4-21, 316F3
Benin boycotts OAU mtgs 6-23—7-5, 512B1
2 mins replaced 7-13, 772B1
Bongo seeks UK rptr's release in CAE 8-11, 635B1
UN Cncl elects member 10-24, 852F3
GABRIELSON, Dr. Ira N.
Dies 9-7, 788B1
GADA, Elbio
Charged 5-8, 565A1
GADDIS, Bob
Montreal wins Grey Cup 11-27, 950A3
GAFTON, Very Rev. Lucian
Rptd held 3-3, 314E2
GAG Orders—*See PRESS*
GAINES, Cassie
Killed 10-20, 888G3
GAINES, Steve
Killed 10-20, 888G3
GAINZA Paz, Alberto
Dies 12-26, 1024F1
GAIRY, Sir Eric (Grenada prime minister)
Welcomes OAS delegates 6-14, 494B1
Oppositn protests dispersed 6-19, 494C3
At Panama Canal pact signing 9-7, 678C1
GAITAN Mahecha, Bernardo
Ordrs univ occupatn 4-23; students, teachers strike 4-25, 347G1
Leads Bogota anti-corruptn drive 7-8, 727G2
GALANTE, Carmine
Mafia ldrship struggle rptd 5-16, 568C1
GALE, Lauren (Laddie)
Joins basketball HOF 5-2, 490F3
GALICH, Alexander
Dies 12-15, 1024F1
GALIFIANAKIS, Nick
Cited in Park indictmt 9-6, 688D1

1978

GABELLAH, Elliott
Urges US support, scores Young 6-30, 615E2

GABON—*See also GATT, NONALIGNED Nations Movement, OAU, OPEC*
Student riots shut univ 2-4, 94E2
French overseas voting scandal rptd 2-25, 167D1
Bongo at Franco-African summit, asks joint African force 5-22, 382B3
IMF loan rptd 6-1, 596B2
Troops join Zaire peace force 6-6, 441C1
Zaire pan-Africa force rptd backed 6-8, 442D1
Benin workers ousted 7-23, 596A2
UN Assemb member, named to Cncl 9-19, 713A3, E3
U.S. Relations
Page Airways paymt to Bongo chrgd 4-13, 449B2
US aids Zaire rescue 6-5, airlifts peace force 6-6, 441C1, D1
US airline fined re Rhodesia pilot training 12-8, 955G3-956A1
GABRI, Gianvittorio
Named Turin trial defns atty 3-13, 191C2
GAF Corp.
Berkey wins trust suit vs Kodak 1-21, 67A2
GAFFIELD, Dick
Native Son opens 3-27, 760G2
GAGE, Patricia
Thread of Scarlet opens 12-8, 1031B3
GAG Rule—*See PRESS*
GAINES, Clark
NFL '77 pass receiving ldr 1-1, 56C2
GAINES, Jodie Elizabeth
Kidnaped 4-28, 3 arrested 5-3, 5-4, 396A3
GAINES, Rowdy
Sets 400-m freestyle relay mark 8-22, 780C2
GAINESVILLE, Fla.—*See FLORIDA*
GAINESWAY Farm (Ky.)
Equine VD dvpts 3-15—7-13, 539F2
GAINEY, Bob
Named NHL top defensive forward 6-12, 458F2
GALANTI, Isaac
Slain 10-25, 971E2
GALAZ, Maj. Ernesto (ret.)
Exiled to Belgium 4-15, 287F2
GALBRAITH, John Kenneth
Scores Propositn 13 6-28, 526C1
GALE, Bob
Wanna Hold Your Hand released 4-21, 619E2
GALE, David
'Biko Inquest' opens 5-17, 760D1
GALFAS, Timothy
Matilda released 6-22, 619B3
GALIFFA, Arnold
Dies 9-5, 778C1
GALIMBERTI, Rodolfo
Vows World Cup finals truce 4-7, 285D3

1979

GABELLAH, Elliott
Quits Sithole ZANU factn 3-5, 170F1

GABON—*See also GATT, NONALIGNED Nations Movement, OAU, OPEC*
Equatorial Guinea border fighting rptd 8-7, 613F3
Zaire troop exit rptd 8-14, 733G3
UN membership listed 695D2
Dacko stages CAE coup 9-20, 720G1
Oil price per barrel rptd 12-21, 977B2
GABOR, Dennis
Dies 2-8, 176A3
GABRIEL, Jim
Quits as Sounders coach 8-28, 1004E2
GACY Jr., John Wayne
Indicted 1-8, pleads not guilty in Chicago mass murder 1-10, 24F2, F3
Mrs Carter '78 photo confrmd 1-21, 79A1
GADA, Albio
Chrgd re Chiasso scandal 2-15, 137E1
Sentenced 7-3, 505E2
GAER, Paul
Electric Horseman released 12-21, 1007C3
GAESS, Anthony D.
US files pollutn suit 2-7, 130C1
GAGNON, Rene
Dies 10-12, 860F2
GAILANI, Syed Ahmed
Rebels claim victories 4-11, 284D1
GAINES, George
Wins Oscar 4-9, 336A2
GAINEY, Bob
Sovts win Challenge Cup 2-11, 118E2
Montreal wins Stanley Cup, named playoff MVP 5-21, 447D3-F3
Named NHL top defensive forward 6-12, 470D2
GAIRY, Eric
Flies to US 3-12, ousted 3-13; oppositn party rptd in control 3-14, 190F2
US recognizes rebel govt 3-22, 236G2
GAISREITER, Stefan
W Gers win world 4-man bobsled title 2-25, 392F1
GALANTE, Carmine
Prison release ordrd 2-27, 156F1
Returns to jail 3-7, gets bail 3-23, 240F2
Slain 7-12, funeral 7-16, 548A1
GALBRAITH, John Kenneth
On '29 mkt crash; scores Miller, Volcker 10-29, 826E3
GALBREATH, Tony
NFL '78 receiving ldr 1-6, 80F1
GALE, Bob
1941 released 12-14, 1008A1
GALENTO, Tony (Two-Ton)
Dies 7-22, 588G2
GALFAS, Timothy
Sunnyside released 6-1, 820D3
GALGY, Judge John H.
Food Fair closes 123 supermkts 1-27, 131A3
GALIFIANAKIS, Nick
Indicted for perjury 4-10, 283C2
Indictmt dismissed 8-3, 630A2
GALINDEZ, Fernando Mandry
Ali retires from boxing 6-26, 838G2

1980

GABON—*See also GATT, NONALIGNED Nations, OAU, OPEC*
UN Cncl replacemts seated 1-1, 12C2
Brazil oil sales rptd 10-2, 759A2
Africa oil exports vowed 11-9, 864D2
Islamic League meets 11-10, 895B2
GABOR, Pal
Angi Vera released 1-9, 216B2
GACY Jr., John Wayne
Convicted 3-12, gets death sentence 3-13, 214C1-C2
GADLEY, Jeff
On US Olympic bobsled team 2-24, 154C3
GAESS, Anthony D.
Pollutn suit partly setld 1-30, 93G3
GAFNI, Arnon
On shekel introduction 2-22, 151E1
GAGE, Dr. Stephen
On Love Canal rpt 5-17, 386G3
GAINES, Ambrose (Rowdy)
Sets 100-m freestyle, 200-m freestyle marks 4-9, 4-11, 834F3
Ties 100-m freestyle mark 8-1, 834D3
GAINES, Clark
NFL '79 rushing ldr 1-5, 8B3
GAINEY, Bob
Named NHL top defensive forward 6-6, 488C1
GALAN Mendez, Ricardo
Colombia, DR Emb captors talk 3-2—3-13, 3-2—3-13, 180C2
DR Emb talks resume 3-24, 3-26, 3 hostages freed 3-25, 231F2
Emb siege ends, freed in Cuba 4-27, 335G1
GALANTE, Carmine (d. 1979)
8 slaying probe figures indicted 3-3, 215C1
GALBRAITH, John Kenneth
In 'Big Business Day' protest 4-17, 308C2
GALE, Rich
In World Series 10-14—10-21, 812A1, D3
GALILEE, Israel
Announces Jordan-Palestine state plan 11-8, 863C3

1976

GALLAGHER, Charles D.
Freed in Beirut 2-25, 145C2
GALLAGHER, Cornelius J.
S Korea probe rptd 10-30, 11-13, 900A2
GALLAGHER, Edward
Denounces judge 1-13, 157A1
GALLAGHER, Wes
Successor named 5-3, 504F2
GALLARDO, Jorge
Rptd arrested 6-6, 415A3
GALLARDO, Jose
Dies 7-18, 656E3
GALLARDO, Samuel
Rptd arrested 6-6, 415A3
GALLEGOS, Bert A.
Replaced in Labor post 4-7, 262D3
GALLEGOS, Gen. Enrique
Loses Cabt post 7-16, 590A3
GALLEN, Hugh J.
Loses NH primary for gov 9-14, 705E1
GALLEY, Robert
Named French cooperatn min 8-27, 650F3
GALLICO, Paul
Dies 7-15, 716B3
GALLINGI, Victor
Arrested 6-29, 500D2

GALLUP Poll (American Institute of Public Opinion) (Princeton, N.J.)
'75 US church attendance 1-3, 32A3
Ford rating drops 1-7, 21G2
Carter leads Ford 3-15, 197D1
Carter leads Ford, Reagan 3-29—8-1, 564F3
Party identification 5-27, 565B1
Ford leads Reagan 7-18, 565C1
Reagan vp selectn 8-12, 583G3
Carter lead over Ford drops, Southn base firm 8-25, 8-28, 9-1, 644G1
1st debate rated 9-30, 725E1
Carter lead over Ford drops to 8% 9-30, 725B2
PC, Clark favored in Canada 10-9, 10-16, 808F2
Carter lead up 10-15, 764C2
Carter leads by 6 points 10-21, 804B3
Ford, Carter debate 10-22, 800A3
Gives Ford edge over Carter 11-1; statemt 11-3, 825G3
GALVAN Lopez, Felix
Mexico defense min 12-2, 907A1
GAMARRO, Pedro
Wins Olympic medal 7-31, 574C1
GAMASY, Mohammed Abdel Ghany el-
Ends French visit, gets arms aid vow 3-26, 275F1

GAMBIA—*See also AFRICAN Development Bank, COMMONWEALTH of Nations, NON-ALIGNED Nations Movement, OAU*
Listed as 'free' nation 1-19, 20B3
Olympic withdrawal rptd 7-21, 528B3
ECOWAS rptd ratified 11-6, 974E2
GAMBINO, Carlo
Dies 10-15, 932D3
GAMBLE, Oscar
In World Series 10-16—10-21, 815C3
GAMBLE-Skogmo Inc.
Admits shipping rebates 8-23, 690A1

GAMBLING
Leek wins NJ lottery 1-27, 160G2
Canada law review urged 3-25, 250D3
9 indicted in Alaska plot 7-8, 816F2
Delaware lottery starts 9-1, 736D3
Cong clears tax revisns 9-16, 705F3
State vote results 11-2: NJ 821D2★, E2; NY 821G2; Ga 822F1; Mich 823F2; Calif 825A1; 7 states 825C3
GAMBRELL, David H.
'70 Carter campaign donor 10-17, 805A1
GAMERO, Adolfo Martin
On labor union proposal 5-7, 422C1
GAMMAGE, Bob
Elected 11-2, 822G3★, 823A1, 830E4
GAMMAL Jr., Albert A.
Denies GSA contracting violatns 1-20, 71E1
GAMMON, Samuel Rhee
In US-Viet talks 11-12, 863A3

1977

GALINDEZ, Victor
Decisns Gregory 11-20, 970D3
'77 boxing champion 12-17, 970A2
GALLAB, Philip
Seized, riot role denied 1-23, 62E2
GALLARDO, Juan Carlos
US sci acad seeks info 4-27, 315A2
GALLEY, Robert
Named cooperatn min 3-30, 239F1
GALLO Glass Co.
Strike ends 10-14, 818F3
GALLUP Jr., George
Rpts US religious trends 4-26—4-29, 470B3

GALLUP Poll (American Institute of Public Opinion) (Princeton, N.J.)
Denmark EC support wanes 1-19, 62C1
Trudeau leads 3-5, 218D3
Pot use polled 4-1—4-4, 972F2-A3
US energy crisis 4-15, 320A3
Carter energy plan 4-20—4-21, 320A3
'76 US church attendance up 4-26—4-29, 470B3
Female ordinatn backing up 5-6, 375A2
Nixon-Frost interview 5-9, 367B3
US oil imports 6-2, 464G2-A3
UK Grunwick workers 7-20, 617E2
Cuba ties 8-8, 654F1
Econ concerns top family worries 8-10, 632C2
Chilean govt support 9-21, 743G1
Carter standing drops 10-18, 817A2
Business fears recessn, faults Admin on econ policy 12-14, 962E1
GALVESTON, Tex.—*See TEXAS*
GALVIN, Msgr. J. P.
On S Africa schl desegregatn 1-20, 67F1
GAMASY, Mohammed Abdel Ghany el-
At Sinai air exercises 5-20—5-22, 401F3
Retains war min duties 10-25, 824D1
Backs Sadat Israel trip 11-19, 890D2
Meets Israel defns min 12-20—12-21, 993G1
Heads defns com for Israel talks 12-26, 993D1

GAMBIA—*See also COMMONWEALTH of Nations, NONALIGNED Nations Movement, OAU*
UN Assemb member 4A1
IMF OKs loan, Sept '75-76 export earnings drop cited 3-16, 394B3
'Roots' sources doubted 4-10, 356C1
IMF standby loan OKd, paymts deficit cited 5-18, 710G2
Sahel dvpt plan OKd 6-1, 458E3
Cohen confrmd US amb 6-23, 626D3
Drought-related crop loss rptd, FAO aid plea 8-22, 660E1
New Sahel famine seen 9-19, 770A2
GAMBINO, Carlo (1902-76)
Mafia ldrship struggle rptd 5-16, 568C1
ICC trucking probe rptd 6-3, 500E3
GAMBINO, Joseph & Thomas
ICC trucking probe rptd 6-3, 500E3
GAMBLE, Oscar
Signs with Padres 11-23, 989E3
GAMBLE-Skogmo Inc.
Final rebates rpt cited 1-5, 6B3
GAMBLING
Sup Ct expands govt tap use 1-18, 58F1
'70-76 pol indictmts rptd 2-10, 162C3
Trafficante at JFK probe 3-16, 228E2
Mafia control rptd 5-16, 568E1
Atlantic City bill signed 6-2, 423G3
Las Vegas hotel loan from Teamsters rptd 7-18, 558B2
Ct OKs '77 Del football lottery, state postpones 8-12, 659F1
San Fran Chinatown slayings linked 9-4, 711B3
Players' agent sentenced 11-28, 1021A2
Phone surveillnc ct order backed 12-7, 939F1
Salerno mistrial declared 12-15, 992G1
GAMESMAN, The (book)
On best-seller list 4-3, 264A2; 5-1, 356C2
GAMMAGE, Rep. Bob (D, Tex.)
Paul electn challenge refused 6-6, 479A1
GAMMON, Samuel
France vs Daoud protest 1-11, 27E2
GAMSAKHURDIA, Zviad
Arrested 4-7, 314G1
GANDAPUR, Inayatullah Khan
Arrested 1-10, 66A3

1978

GALINDEZ, Victor
Decisions Lopez 5-6, 379E2
Rossman TKOs for light heavywgt title 9-15, 726C2
GALLACHER, Bernard
2d in Europn Open 10-22, 990B2
GALLACHER, Tom
Mr Joyce opens 4-23, 760F2
GALLAGHER, Cornelius J.
Park gift testimony rptd 1-14, 63C3
Aide rptd linked to KCIA in '71 FBI memo 3-21, 203E2
Park Tong Sun admits paymts 4-3, 239E2
GALLAGHER, Edward
Married 1-24, 172E2
GALLAUDET College (Washington, D.C.)
Cabt-level Educ Dept proposed 4-14, 279C1
GALLEN, Hugh J.
Wins primary for NH gov 9-12, 736F1
Elected 11-7, 847A1, F3, 853G2
Rejcts Seabrook A-plant bond guarantee 12-8, 1009G2
GALLEY, Robert
Renamed French cooperatn min 4-5, 245F2
GALLICO, Paul
Matilda released 6-22, 619B3
GALLINARI, Prospero
Turin trial halted 3-10, 191F1
Chrgd in Moro case, sought by police 6-6, 689C2
GALLO Winery, E. & J.
UFW ends boycott 1-31, 83F1
GALLUP Poll (American Institute of Public Opinion) (Princeton, N.J.)
Panama Canal pacts backed 2-2, 58D2
Catholic views polled 3-2, 294G3
Carter rating drops 4-24, 307G3
Carter poll standings 5-7, 5-11, 404C3
'77 abortn survey rptd 8-9, 744A2
Carter poll standings still bleak 8-13, 8-21, 682A2, E2
White bias vs blacks seen down 8-27, 811E3
RCMP mail-opening backed 8-30, 686C3
British troop exit from Ulster backed 9-20, 723C2
Carter rating jumps 9-22, 736B1
Canada PC lead widens 12-6, 985G2
Carter rating 50% 12-28, 1003C1
GALT, Eric S.—*See RAY, James Earl*
GALT, Thomas
Urges Sun Life move 4-25, 311D2
GALVESTON, Tex.—*See TEXAS*
GAMASY, Mohammed Abdel Ghany el-
In Israel mil talks 1-11—1-12, 10C1
Rpts no agrmt in Israel mil talks 1-13, 26G1
Vs Cyprus role in commando raid 2-27, 138A2
Meets Weizman 3-30—3-31, 235A3
Weizman told to keep contacts 6-25, 489C1
Sadat meets Weizman 7-13, 546B2
Removed as war min 10-3, 746D2
Ali takes office 10-5, 774A3
GAMBIA—*See also COMMONWEALTH of Nations, GATT, NONALIGNED Nations Movement, OAU*
At W African mtg, backs ECOWAS 3-18, USSR scores 3-20, 237E1
UK cancels debts 7-31, 592D1
UN Assemb member 713E3
GAMBINO, Carlo (1902-76)
ICC ex-offcl indicted 9-22, 770F2
GAMBINO, Thomas
ICC ex-offcl indicted 9-22, 770F2
GAMBLE, Oscar
Traded to Rangers 10-25, 1026B1

GAMBLING
Testimony thru illegal search backed by Sup Ct 3-21, 220G3
Legalizatn impact surveyed 4-2, 434D2
Ga ex-offcls acquitted, Carter testimony cited 4-21, 309E3
Atlantic City casino opens 5-26, 6-day take rptd 6-5, 434B2
World Cup soccer odds listed 6-1, 519F3
Wm Harrah dies 6-30, 540G2
Canada to continue fed lottery 7-6, Brit Columbia ban rptd 7-7, 531E2
Victimless-crime study issued 9-11, 842B2
Ali-Spinks rematch odds cited 9-15, 726F1
FBI agent indicted 9-15, 11-6; resigns, pleads guilty 11-9, 886C3
NJ casino profits rptd 10-4, violatns chrgd 10-6; crime rise linked 11-10, 920B1-G1
Stock price drop cited 11-1, 826A3
Fla, Va, NJ referenda lose 11-7, 847F1, 849D1, 852F1
Speculative stock trading rptd heavy for '78 12-29, 1004C2
Horse Racing—*See HORSE Racing*
GAMERO, Manuel
Held on drug scandal 7-5—7-10, 614G3
GAMMAGE, Rep. Bob (D, Tex.)
Loses reelectn 11-7, 855D3
GAMMON, James
Starving Class opens 3-2, 887C3
GAMSAKHURDIA, Zviad Konstantinovich
Sentenced 5-19, 401D2
2 US rptrs in slander chrg 6-28, 518C1, E2
Testifies, 2 US rptrs convctd 7-18, 575E2

1979

GALINDEZ, Victor
KOs Rossman for WBA light heavywgt title 4-14, 412F2
Johnson KOs for WBA light heavywgt title 11-30, 1004D3
GALLANT Best (race horse)
4th in Jockey Gold Cup 10-6, 876G2
GALLARDO, Edward
Simpson Street opens 3-5, 292A3
GALLEGOS, Cpl. William
NBC airs interview 12-10, 934A3
GALLEGOS Valdes, Gabriel
Named El Salvador labor min 10-22, seized by leftists 10-24, 812G3, 813C2
Leftists bar release 10-25, 834D2
Freed 11-6, 872A3
GALLEN, Gov. Hugh J. (D, N.H.)
Gets reassurance on heating fuel supply 8-28, 703C2
GALLERY, Michele
Wins Emmy 9-9, 858D2
GALLICO, Paul
Beyond the Poseidon Adventure released 5-24, 528D1
GALLINARI, Prospero
Shot, arrested 9-24, 793A2
GALLINDO, Gabriel Lewis
Shah housed at villa 12-15, 957E1
GALLO, Fred T.
Going in Style released 12-25, 1007D3
GALLONE, Giovanni
Defeated as Christian Dem whip 7-3, 525C3

GALLUP Poll (American Institute of Public Opinion) (Princeton, N.J.)
'78 church attendance rptd 1-5, 24C1
Civil defns spending hike favored 2-4, 89G1-B2
Canada Liberals lead poll 2-20, 189G1
Reagan leads GOP polls 3-4, 185E3
A-power poll rptd 4-9, 323A1
Abortion survey rptd 4-22, 315F1
Kennedy leads Carter in Dem poll 4-26, 384F2
Canada Liberals lead poll 5-12, 368G3
Carter approval rating 29% 7-1, 497G1
Reagan, Ford lead Carter 7-1, 514D1
US religious tolerance gains rptd 8-4, 639C3
Womens ordinatn survey cited 11-11, 930G2
Reagan tops GOP poll 11-25, 982D1
Carter rating up 12-5, 918E2
Carter vaults into lead 12-11, 962C3, E3
GALLUP-Silkworth Distribution Co.
Ann Arbor plant fire 6-16, 572C3
GALTIERI, Gen. Leopoldo Fortunato
Named Argentine army chief 12-7, 947F2
GALUTEN, Albhy
Wins Grammy 2-16, 336D3
GALVESTON, Tex.—*See TEXAS*

GAMBIA—*See also COMMONWEALTH of Nations, GATT, NONALIGNED Nations Movement, OAU*
UN membership listed 695D2
GAMBINO, Carlo (1902-76)
Scotto convicted 11-15, 890C2
GAMBINO, Robert W.
CIA 'interest' in Letelier killer rptd 1-11, 19D3
Seeks more CIA armed agents 4-4, 310B2
GAMBLE, Hays
On A-plant communities study 3-17, 207E3
GAMBLE, Oscar
Traded to Yankees 8-1, 1002B3
GAMBLER, The (recording)
Wins Grammy 2-16, 336F3
GAMBLING
NJ casino fined 1-3, 'card-counters' barred 2-1, 152D1, F1
Steelers win Super Bowl 1-21, 63A2
IRS exempts church bingo 1-26, 102C1
Compulsive gambling bill introduced 1-30, 152E1
Wyo '78 investigatn cited 2-7, 156B1
Joseph Moriarity dies 2-24, 176D3
NJ casino granted permanent license, 8 others pending 2-26, 151F3
Nev takes over casino 3-16, 209B1
NJ indicts 8 in Genovese 'family' 5-23, 508G1
Nev casino sale set 6-12; licenses revoked 6-15, called off 6-27, 520F1
2d NJ casino opens 6-26, 520D1
Iran executns held 7-12—7-13, 544C3
Loto Canada sale to provs OKd 8-21, 651D2; price set 9-4, 685F1-A2
Nev fines Argent, offcls for skimming 8-23, 851A1
Tax loss on illegal income estimated 8-31, 665A3
Holiday Inns to buy Harrah's 9-4, 682C3
NJ hikes tax 9-18, 851F1
NJ OKs card counters 10-24, 851A2; rescinds rule 12-13, 947C1
Mays to cut baseball ties 10-29, 1002G3
Mass arts cncl lottery set 11-15, 892G2-A3
Argent sale completed 12-10, Sachs organized crime probe rptd 12-12, 965B1
Nev casino deal rejected 12-15, 965D1
Nev casino purchase set 12-21, 992A2
GAMSAKHURDIA, Zviad Konstantinovich
Pardoned 6-29, 504B3

1980

GALINDEZ, Victor
Dies 10-26, 876E1
GALINSKI, Heinz
On W Berlin Jewish immigratn curb 9-24, 833F1
GALLAGHER, John
Postal contract ratified 6-2, 443G3
GALLARDO, Cesar
Slain 9-17, 697A3
GALLEN, Gov. Hugh J. (D, N.H.)
Wins primary 9-9, 700G2
Reelected 11-4, 845G2, 847C1, 848E2
GALLEY, Robert
Office machine-gunned 3-18, 232A1
GALLI, Guido
Slain 3-19, 233A2
GALLINARI, Prospero
Accused re Moro affair 1-2, 20G2
GALLINGHOUSE, Gerald J.
Named to Kraft probe 9-14, 700E1
Kraft probe suspended 12-12, 989G2
GALLOPS, Edgar
To take rabies shots 2-9, 200A2
GALLO Winery, E. & J.
Winery strike ends 9-22, 747A3
GALLUCCI, Domenico
Wounded 5-17, 408B3

GALLUP Poll (American Institute of Public Opinion) (Princeton, N.J.)
'79 church attendance rptd 1-4, 7F3
Carter leads Kennedy 1-8, GOP 1-9, 13F1, F3
Carter Iran support ebbs 1-10, 32G2
Bible reading survey rptd 1-18, 157F1
Pres poll results 3-31, 4-1, 246E3-247B1
Latin immigratn attitudes polled 5-16—5-18, 396D3
Pres poll rptd 5-19—6-16, 452C2; 8-17, 630C1
Evangelical Christian voters surveyed 9-15, 819A2
Pres poll standings tighten, toss-up seen 10-27, 816G1
Canada const patriatn poll rptd 12-10, 964E2
GALVEAS, Ernane
Brazil finance min quits, replacemt seen 1-15, 95E2
On Brazil forgn debt repaymt 5-24, 406C1
GALVESTON-Houston Co.
Smith Intl to acquire 3-26, 385B3
Smith deal fails 6-9, 557E2
GAMARA Perez Egana, Carlos
On Peru drought losses 2-8, 234D3
GAMBA, Ezio
Wins Olympic medal 7-25, 623C1

GAMBIA—*See also COMMONWEALTH of Nations, GATT, NONALIGNED Nations, OAU*
Moscow Olympic boycott set 4-22, 325F3
GAMBINO, Carlo (1902-76)
Galante slaying probe figures indicted 3-3, 215F1
Mafia, pizza indus ties probed 8-24, 714G1
GAMBLER, The (recording)
Rogers wins Grammy 2-27, 296D3

GAMBLING
NJ State of State message 1-8, 403F3, G3
Coll transcript scandal spreads 1-23—5-23, 469D2, B3
Me voters ban slot machines 3-11, 185C1, A2
Pa Mafia ldr slain 3-21, 237D2
Grand Met raises Liggett merger bid 5-14, Liggett OKs 5-16, 557A3
MGM to split film, hotel units 5-30, 501F2
Nev casino bombed 8-27, 833F3
Pa lottery fraud chrgs rptd 9-19, 786B3
Reagan favored in London, Vegas 11-3, 11-4, 844G2
Lottery, bingo referendums in 6 states, DC 11-4, 847C3, 848F1
Las Vegas hotel-casino fire kills 84 11-24, 893C2
'Dallas' TV episode viewing record rptd 11-25, 905F3
Nev fscl '80 casino revenue rptd 12-12, 988E3
Atlantic City Gambling—*See under NEW Jersey*
GAME, The (recording)
On best-seller list 9-10, 716F3; 10-8, 796B3
GAMIR, Luis
Named Spain commerce min 5-2, 355D1
GAMMA Rays
US solar study satellite launched 2-14, 160D2
Neutron star link rptd 5-4, 416B1

1976

GANDHI, Indira Priyadarshini
Indian Express bd revamped 1-3, 73F3
Backs rights curbs 1-5, 1-8, 28F3
Bars A-tests end 1-14, 73G2
French premr visits 1-22—1-26, 139F2
Parlt OKs electn delay 2-4, 101D3
Narayan assails emergency rule 2-13, 139G3
Party widens house majority 3-27, 253D2
Gets Bhutto peace overture 3-27, OKs talks 4-11, 278E2
Desai scores rule 4-24, 313B2
Rights group chrgs torture 6-1, 408D3
In Moscow 6-8—6-11; vs India O bases 6-13, 440A1
To continue emergency rule 6-26, 496F3
4 Indians in US lose passports 7-12, 7-18, 538A2
Says emergency rules eased 8-15, 624A1
Jethmalani gets US asylum 8-24, 676B1
Seeks wider powers 9-1, 651E3
Regrets Mao death 9-9, 657F2
5-yr plan OKd 9-25, 731E3
Mody freed 10-6, 751C2
Civil rights group formed 10-17, 810A3
Anti-Express actns scored 10-21, 837B2
Admits family-planning riots 10-27, 810F2
Charter change scored 11-2, 837G1, A2
Defends son vs critics 12-12, 1006E1
Changes Cabt 12-22, 1006C1

GANDHI, Rajmohan
Scores press curbs 8-7, 621C1
GANDHI, Sanjay
Addresses youth conv 11-19, 1006G1
Mother defends vs critics 12-12, 1006E1
GANGA, Jean-Claude
Supports Olympic boycott 7-17, 528C3
GANGES River
Bangladesh protests dam 5-16, 5-17, 365F1
GANNETT Co. Inc.
Hartford Times expires 10-20, 849G1
GANNON, James P.
Pres debate panelist 9-12, 700G3
GANNON, Sam
France protests Pak talks 8-9, 581B3
GANO, Richard C.
Named Hughes Calif executor 4-14, 335D3
Dismissal as executor denied 7-16, 596F3
GARANIN, Ivan
Wins Olympic medal 2-5, 159C1
GARAPICK, Nancy
Wins Olympic medals 7-21, 7-25, 575G2
GARBA, Col. Joseph Namvan
Scores US pressure on Angola 1-7, 3B1
On Equatorial Guinea worker evacuatn 1-26, 62C1
Aids Rhodesia guerrillas 7-6, 488A1
GARBER, Gene
Reds win pennant 10-12, 796F1
GARBER Co. Inc., The A. L.
Antitrust suit dvpts 2-18—10-5, 886C1, F2
GARBEY, Roland
Wins Olympic medal 7-31, 574C1
GARCIA, Mariano Nicolas
Named Security Directorate chief 12-23, 1011A3
GARCIA, Orlando
Perez ties cited 10-24, 843E3
GARCIA, Rogelio
Arrested 9-17, 792B2
GARCIA Calvo, Agustin
Univ chair restored 8-7, 753B3
GARCIA Cespedes, Luis
Arrest warrant rptd 3-20; amnestied 5-7, 499E3, 500C1
GARCIA Marquez, Gabriel
Russell ct meets 1-10—1-17, 61E2
GARCIA Moritan, Nino
Rpts prelim chrgs vs Peron, aides 5-6; probe transfer denied 5-19, 399E2, B3
GARCIA Pereira, Col. Luis
Bolivia air force chief 1-6, 26G3
GARCIA Trevijano, Antonio
Camaco, 2 others freed 5-25, 422F2
Freed on bail 6-12, 459G1

1977

GANDHI, Indira Priyadarshini
Letter to Mehta announces dissidents release 1-5, 45D3
Announces electns 1-18, 45C2
Gives advice to journalists 1-19, 45A3
Sri Lanka warns emergency rule 1-25, 68B3
Hears Janata complaints 1-28, 71E2
Jethmalani seeks India return 2-1, 71F2
Ram quits, vs resignatn 2-2, 71C1
Opens electn campaign 2-4, 116C1
Narain to run for seat 2-7, 116A2
Meets Carter family 2-13, 116B1
Aunt backs foes 2-14, 116E1
Party loses electns 3-16—3-20, resigns 3-22, 205A1
Replaced as Cong Party Parlt ldr 3-23, 205E2
Faces probe 4-1, 4-7, 283A3
Takes blame for electn loss 4-12, 392D2
Reddy named Cong Party pres 5-6, 392A2
Named to Cong Party exec 5-13, 392C2
Govt media stand scored 8-1, 598B3
4 ex-aides arrested 8-15, 637B2
Bansi Lal arrested 8-23, 655E2
Satpathy arrested 9-17, 801A3
Probe of rule starts 9-29, 765F1
Arrested 10-3, freed 10-4, 764G3
Forced birth control ends 10-3, 842G2
Backers riot 10-8, chaos plot chrgd 10-13, 801C2
Chrgs govt abuses 10-10, 801E2
Loses Cong pres bid 10-15, 801G1-B2
Rioters protest tour 10-29—10-30, 842C2
Shuns probe hearings 11-21, 12-2, party backs 12-5, 966D1
Quits Cong Party exec com 12-18, 984D2
Cong Party exec com splits 12-27, 1013D3
GANDHI, Sanjay
To run for Parlt 2-15, 116F1
Escapes assassin 3-14, Janata chrgs incident staged 3-15, 205F2
Loses Parlt seat 3-16—3-20, quits politics 3-22, 205B2, D2
Faces corruptn probe 4-1, 283B3
Passport taken, probe judge named 4-18, 304G1, A2
Money dealings probed 9-29, 765A2
GANESH, K. R.
Quits party 2-2, 71E1
GANGES River
India-Bangladesh pact 11-5, 896D3
Map 896E3
GANGUT, A. D.
Rpts tortured 8-4, 640F1
GANLEY, John L.
Replaced as ACTION dep dir 3-4, 211E1
GANNETT Co. Inc.
FCC OKs Okla, Mo purchases 4-14, Speidel merger Okd 5-10, 395C2
GANO Jr., Richard C.
Hughes '38 will sought 1-17, 1-26, 120C2
Will search ended 3-15, 354D3
GANTIN, Msgr. Bernardin
Inducted as cardinal 6-27, 768B3
GAO—*See U.S. GOVERNMENT—GENERAL Accounting Office*
GARAVANI, Valentino—*See VALENTINO*
GARBA, Josef
Trial opens 1-10, 82F3
Sentenced 2-3, 115C1
GARBA, Brig. Joseph
Sees Young, OKs Zaire mediation 3-22, 261A1
Backs US Africa policy 8-25, 662B1
GARBER, Jan
Dies 10-5, 872G1
GARBUZOV, Vasily Fedorovich
Outlines '78 budget 12-14, 988A1
GARCES, Raul
Uruguay detains 7-20—7-21, 601B2
GARCIA, Dave
Hired as Angel mgr 7-11, 990A2
GARCIA, Inez
Acquitted 3-4, 262B1
GARCIA, Dr. Jorge
Patient survives unusual surgery 6-2, 620A1
GARCIA, Randy
Nebraska wins Liberty Bowl 12-19, 1020B2
GARCIA Diez, Juan Antonio
Spain commerce, tourism min 7-5, 545C2
GARCIA Imchaustegui, Mario
Killed in jet crash 12-4, 992D2
GARCIA Marquez, Gabriel
Details Cuba role in Angola 1-9, 18G3
Moss disputes Angola war rpt 1-31, 86B1
GARCIA Peralta, Aparicio
Kidnaped 1-9, found dead 1-13, 42C1
GARCIA Sainz, Ricardo
Named Mex planning min 11-17, rptdly backs IMF policies 12-3, 966E3

1978

GANDHI, Indira Priyadarshini
Carter scores emergency rule 1-2, 1A2
Heads new Cong Party 1-2; regular party ousts 1-3, 7E1
Cong Party panel accepts resignatn 1-2, 7G2
UK prime min visits 1-8, 1-9, 37F1
Bars probe testimony 1-9, 1-10, faces contempt trial 1-11, 37F2
Cong Party factn stripped of electn symbol 1-31, 75C1
Party wins 2 state electns 2-25, hails victory 2-28, 168G3
Party loses Haryana electn 4-2; scores Janata 4-5, 246D1
Party becomes oppositn 4-12, 288G2-A3
Judicial comm scores rule, party chrgs pol vendetta 4-14, 374E2
Pleads not guilty re probe testimony 4-18, 374B3
Son starts jail term 5-5, 375A1
Party wins Uttar Pradesh by-electn 5-9, 374G3-375A1
Desai on prosecutn 6-17, 516B2
2 mins vs govt handling of case 6-28; Cabt asks resignatn 6-29, 2 quit 6-30, 516F1, E2
Elected to Parlt 11-5, 861E2
Parlt com condemns 11-21, debate starts 12-13; ousted, jailed 12-19, 988B1
Supporters riot, jet hijacked 12-20, released 12-21, 988E1
Released 12-26, 1018C1

GANDHI, (Mahatma) Mohandas Karamchand (1869-1948)
Carter: Rev King 'spiritual son' 1-2, 1C2
GANDHI, Sanjay
Starts 1-mo jail term 5-5, 375A1
Mother loses Parlt seat, jailed 12-19, 988C1
GANGES River
UK prime min sees India, Bangladesh ldrs 1-4—1-11; backs UK dvpt role 1-16, 37C1, A2
US A-device '65 loss in India confrmd 4-17, 288D2
GANG of 4—*See CHINA—Government & Politics*
GANN, Paul
Property-tax cut amendmt OKd 6-6; reactn 6-7—6-8, 425A1, E1
GANNETT Co. Inc.
2 Wilmington papers acquired 1-30, 109D3
Combined purchase planned; '77 profits, sales cited 5-8, 345E2, A3
To sell TV statn 8-20, 759F3
Niagara Gazette—*See separate listing*
GANS, Curtis
Rpts voter turnout down 11-7, 915G2
GANTILLON, Bruno
Servant & Mistress released 6-6, 619F3
GAO—*See U.S. GOVERNMENT—GENERAL Accounting Office*
GARBA, Brig. Joseph
Horn of Africa mediatn effort fails 2-9, 100E1
At Smith-Nkomo mtg 8-14, 740G2
GARBAGE Collectors—*See SANITATION Workers*
GARBER, Gene
Stops Rose hitting streak 8-1, 618G2
GARBO, Greta
Calls Gronowicz biog hoax 4-21, 335B3
GARCES, Rear Adm. Victor Hugo
Ecuador interior min 12-20, 1021B3
GARCIA, Dave
Fired as Angels mgr 6-1, 560E1
GARCIA, Robert
Wins US House seat 2-14, 107D2, 108B2
Reelected 11-7, 851F3
GARCIA de Paredes, Gustavo
Panama educ min 10-12, 884B2
GARCIA Marquez, Gabriel
Leftist pres candidates rebuff unity bid 4-28, 413A3
Forms human rights group 12-21, 1015B3
GARCIA Olivares, Reyes
Estate to be seized by govt 9-1, 817F3
GARCIA Parra, Jaime
Named Colombia finance min 8-7, 629C3
GARCIA Ramirez, Col. Rodrigo
Loses Natl Guard post 10-16, 884C2

1979

GANDHI, Indira Priyadarshini
Singh sworn dep prime min 1-24, 97G2
Son sentncd in censorship case 2-27, 193A1
Son arrested 4-27, 5-1, 334C1
Bars parlt electn race 5-20, 411D2
Cong-I Party ousts Urs 6-25, 503C2
Singh gets party support, bars govt role 7-26, 573C1
Angered at detractors' apptmts, balks at Singh support 7-30, 573F1
Birth control problems rptd 8-13, 687G2
Bars Parlt aid to Singh, Singh quits 8-20, 634B3
Narayan dies 10-8, 860A3
GANDHI, (Mahatma) Mohandas Karmchand (1869-1948)
Narayan dies 10-8, 860A3
Anti-US protests 11-23, 894C1
GANDHI, Sanjay
Sentncd in censorship case 2-27, 193A1
Arrested 4-27, 5-1, 334C1
Singh quits as prime min 8-20, 634B3
GANDY, Lt. Gov. Evelyn (D, Miss.)
Loses Miss Dem gov runoff 8-28, 680E2
GANN, Paul
On Prop 13 results 6-1, 500B2
Spending-curb legis sought 7-2, 499A3
GANNAWAT, Lynne
Strider opens 5-31, 712F2
GANNETT Co. Inc.
'Son of Sam' pre-arrest evidence rptd 2-26, 156F2
Neuharth scores Sup Ct 'state of mind' libel ruling 4-23, 302D2
Ctroom pub access curbed by Sup Ct, Neuharth scores ruling 7-2, 515B2, C3
Tennessean bought, Nashville Banner sold 7-5, 618B3
Burger, Powell explain trial closure rule 8-8, 8-13, 630G2
Neuharth rpts press freedom insurnc plan 9-27, 859E2
San Rafael (Calif) paper purchased, news chain circulatn lead claimed 12-12, 1007E1
GANNETT Co. v. DePasquale
Case decided by Sup Ct; reactn 7-2, 515A2, C3
'78-79 Sup Ct term ends, ruling cited 7-2, 558D1
Trial closure efforts rptd up 8-4; Burger, Powell comment 8-8, 8-13, 630C2, G2
Stevens, Blackmun comment on trial closures 9-8, 745B1
Va trial closure case accepted by Sup Ct 10-9, 784A1
Brennan criticizes press 10-17, 848E1
GAO—*See U.S. GOVERNMENT–GENERAL Accounting Office*
GAPP, Paul
Wins Pulitzer 4-16, 336C3
GARABAGHI, Gen. Abbas
Replaced as Iran staff chief 2-12, 105F2
GARAICOETXEA, Carlos
Basque home-rule bill drafted 7-17, 546A1
Scores Basque bombings 7-29, 586A1*
Scores police tactics, urges Basque self rule 9-3, 671B1
On Basque home-rule plans 10-25, 837D1
GARBERSON, Jeff
Cited in H-bomb letter 9-16, 9-18, 717C1
GARBISCH, Bernice Chrysler (Mrs. Edgar William)
Dies 12-14, 1008F2
GARBISCH, Edgar William
Dies 12-14, 1008G2
GARBUZOV, Vasily Fedorovich
Rpts '80 defense cut 11-28, 929A1
GARCES, Victor Hugo
On pres electn results 4-29, 329F3
GARCIA, Cleo
Lujan KOs 4-8, 412F3
GARCIA, Damaso
Traded to Blue Jays 11-1, 1002C3
GARCIA, Col. Jose Guillermo
3 civilns join junta 10-17, 790F2*
Named El Salvador defns min 10-22, 813A1
GARCIA, Kiko
In World Series 10-10–10-17, 816D2
GARCIA, Luis
Seized in Calderon murder 3-12, 256E3
GARCIA, Poli
Named ASL MVP 9-13, 776E2
GARCIA, Rep. Robert (D, N.Y.)
Navy chngs Hispanic recruiting policy 10-15, 850B3
Rev King holiday bill withdrawn 12-5, 945C2
GARCIA Bedoya, Carlos
Sworn Peru forgn min 2-2, 164A3
GARCIA Bustillos, Gonzalo
Venez pres secy 3-10, 192C3
GARCIA Granados, Jorge Raul
Kidnaped 10-7, 792C3
Family pays for kidnapers' ads 10-26, 813E3
GARCIA Mesa, Gen. Luis
Bars resignatn, alerts troops 11-23; Gueiler meets demands, names successor 11-25, 907D1
GARCIA Sainz, Ricardo
Ousted as Mex planning secy 5-16, 408B3
GARCIA y Garcia, Gen. Leonelo
Arrested 9-25, plot exposed 9-26, 751F3

1980

GANDHI, Indira Priyadarshini
Wins electn 1-3, 1-6, 11A3
Vs Sovt Afghan invasn, fears Pak aid 1-5, 11G3; 1-16, 27G1
Sworn prime min, names Cabt 1-14, 39E3
Cleared in 2 ct cases 1-15, 39G3-40A1
US assures on aid to Pak 1-16, 27F1
French joint statemt signed 1-27, 97D3
Sees US envoy 1-30—1-31, repeats Pak aid concern 83F2, D3
Gromyko seeks Afghan support 2-12—2-14, 108F3
Ends 9 state assembs 2-17; foes score move 2-18, 133C2
Names Patil petro min 3-7, 233A1
Asserts independnc re US A-shipmt delay 3-13, 181C1
Assam hit by unrest 3-24—4-7, 275D1
Arafat visits, lauds 3-28—3-29, 260E3
New oppositn party formed 4-6, 275D2
Ram joins Cong opposition 4-8, 275A2
Son cleared of film theft 4-11, 294A3
Seeks Assam conflict end 4-12, 4-22, 352A3, F3
Escapes assassination try 4-14, 294A3
Marks Zimbabwe indepndnc 4-17—4-18, 301E1
Janata suit dismissed, chrgs vs son dropped 5-6, 487E2
At Tito funeral 5-8, 339A1
Parlt ldr resigns re son's role 5-19, son consolidates power 6-6, 6-13, 487B2
Party wins 8 state electns 6-2, 445E1
Swears in 3 Cabt mins 6-8, 445F1
Blames forgn power for Assam unrest 6-9, 445C2
Son killed in plane crash 6-23, 487A2
Giri dies 6-24, 528F1
Lauds satellite launch 7-18, 547E3
Assam rule eased 7-26, 7-30, 578B3
Scores violence 8-15, defends police 8-18, 634A3
Denies Nehru, Mountbatten affair 8-29, 890B3
Scores US on trade talks failure 8-30, 671D1
Defends Cambodia recognitn 9-8, 680E1
Security law decreed, pol foes score 9-22, 729F2
Ousts Tamil Nadu gov, names Sismail 10-26, 873F1
Message to Reagan on electn 11-5, 841C3
Australia criticism raises concern 11-6, 870G1
Meets Brezhnev 12-8—12-9; joint declaratn 12-11, 930D2
Parlt OKs detention law 12-16, 966D1
GANDHI, Sanjay
Congress-I wins electn; gains Parlt seat 1-3, 1-6, 11E3
Mother cleared in 2 ct cases 1-15, 40A1
New oppositn party formed 4-6, 275D2
Cleared of film theft 4-11, 294G2
Riot chrgs dropped 5-6, 487E2
Govt role protested 5-19, consolidates power 6-6, 6-13, 487B2
Dies in plane crash 6-23, 487A2
GANDOIS, Jean
On Rhone-Poulenc units sale 7-9, 522E2
GANG of 4—*See CHINA—Government*
GANN, Paul
Wins Calif US Sen primary 6-3, 439G1
Loses US Sen electn 11-4, 852A2
GANNAWAY, Lynn
Ka-Boom! opens 11-20, 1003C3
GANNETT Co. Inc.
News Svc wins Pulitzer 4-14, 296B2, F2
NM paper purchase rescinded, Neuharth assails ruling 6-30, 582D2-A3
GANNETT Co. v. DePasquale
Case cited by Sup Ct 7-2, 510D2
GANTT, Dr. William Horsley
Dies 2-26, 176B1
GANT v. Union
Case refused by Sup Ct 4-28, 369G1
GANZ, Bruno
Knife in the Head released 4-23, 416B3
GAO (General Accounting Office)—*See under U.S. GOVERNMENT*
GARAICOETXEA, Carlos
Party wins Basque electns 3-9, 196C1
Basque parlt opens 4-1, Bilbao metalworkers disrupt sessn 6-26, backers march 7-3, 567C1
On Basque issues 12-11, 968D2
Basques win right to tax, expanded police power 12-30, 996E2
GARBACZ, Lori
Ties for 2d in Barth Classic 9-7, Mixed Team tourn 12-14, 972B1, A2
GARBE, Ingrid
Sentenced as spy 12-12, 969A2
GARBISCH, Bernice Chrysler (Mrs. Edgar William) (1899-1979)
Art auctnd for record sums 5-12, 472B1
GARBISCH, Edgar William (d. 1979)
Art auctnd for record sums 5-12, 472B1
GARCIA, Edmundo
Chrgs Colombia rights harrassmt 1-17, 96F2
GARCIA, Eduardo
Slain 11-16, 889C1
GARCIA, Federico Lorca (1899-1936)
Blood Wedding opens 6-2, 756B3
GARCIA, Col. Jose Guillermo
Refuses to resign 1-3, 6C2
Majano removed from junta 12-7, 941E3
Retains post in govt shakeup 12-22, 993E1
GARCIA, Manuel
Ariz alien case mistrial declared 7-29, retrial sought 8-29, 713E3
GARCIA, Rep. Robert (D, N.Y.)
Reelected 11-4, 843F3
GARCIA, Sara
Dies 11-21, 1004F1

1976

GARDERUD, Anders
Wins Olympic medal 7-28, 575B1
GARDNER, Ava
Sinatra marries Marx 7-11, 640F3
GARDNER, Colleen
Link with Young rptd 6-11, 433E3
Young cleared 8-16, 636C2
GARDNER, George Peabody
Dies 9-18, 1015E1
GARDNER, John
Scores Sikes, House Ethics Com 4-7, 286F2
GARDNER, Stephen S.
FRB v chrmn 1-20, confrmd 1-29, 110B2
Replaced as Treas dep secy 3-2, 186G1
GARDNER-Denver Co.
SEC lists forgn paymts 5-12, 727D1
GARELOCK Manufacturing Co.
Arab boycott noncompliance rptd 11-7, 986B3
GARIN, Gen. Enrique (ret.)
Quits Cabt 3-5, replaced 3-8, 288F2
GARLAND, Pvt. Charles
Shoots White House intruder 7-25, 860F1
GARLAND, Victor
Quits cabt post 2-6, chrgd 2-17, 154A3
Denied Whitlam contempt order 2-24, 172F2
Bribe case dropped 3-8, 187E2
GARLAND, Wayne
AL pitching ldr 10-4, 796D1
Signs contract 12-5, 951C3
GARMENT, Leonard
Vs UN rights comm Israel resolutn 2-13, 125G2
GARMENT Workers Union, International Ladies—*See INTERNATIONAL Ladies Garment Workers Union*
GARN, Sen. Jake (R, Utah)
Votes vs Usery confrmatn 2-4, 110F1
Named to intelligence com 5-20, 377E1
Backs Buckley candidacy 8-11, 584D3
Clean air amendmts not cleared 10-2, 883E2
GARNAC Grain Co.
Fined 3-4, 247C2
Grain abuse plan cited 3-16, 248C1
Clayton sued 5-27, 397E3
Adnac, Inc.—*See separate listing*
Midwestern Grain Co.
Exec named in grain fraud 3-11, 247D3
GARNEAU, Raymond
Olympic debt measures 5-11, 6-30, 529F1
GARNER, John Nance
House race undecided 11-2, 825F1
Loses election count 11-16, 865D1
GARNER, Phil
AL batting ldr 10-4, 796C1
GAROFALO, Andrew N.
Pleads guilty 1-20, 78G2
Sentenced 3-9, 271C2
GARON, Jean
Named agri min 11-26, 903A3
GARRAHY, John Joseph
Wins RI primary for gov 9-14, 705A1
Elected 11-2, 820B3, 821D3★, 831C2
GARRETT Jr., Ray
Cleared in Milwaukee RR case 6-29, 984C2
GARRIGUES, Antonio
Refusal of Cabt post rptd 7-6, 523B2
GARRIGUES Walker, Joaquin
Lauds Cabt policy statemt 7-18, 541E1
GARRIS, Peter
Sentenced 4-12, 316B3
GARRISON, Candace Mossler
Dies 10-26, 970G1
GARRITY Jr., Judge W. Arthur
Police cite order vs rallies 2-15, 203A1
Sets school admin quota 2-24, 202E3
GARVEY, Steve
NL wins All-Star game 7-13, 544A2
NL batting ldr 10-4, 795F3
GARY, Ind.—*See INDIANA*
GARZA, Caterino
Accuses police 3-28, 234F3
GARZA, Judge Reynaldo G.
Declined Carter post 12-16, 937B1
GAS—*See PETROLEUM*

GAS, Natural—*See also ENERGY*
Ford State of Union message 1-19, 37F3, 39C2
Sup Ct remands FPC reserves case 1-19, 43D1
'77 energy research budgeted 1-21, 64A3
House extends FPC regulatn 2-5, 108C2-109A1
Ford proposes Alaska pipe plan 2-26, 149G1
FPC gas sale rule upheld 3-3, 219D1
'75 energy use rptd 4-4, 285D1
Alaska offshore lease sale 4-26, 648E3
Dem platform text 6-15, 474B3-475D1
Oil-import fees upheld 6-17, 452C3
Winter shortage seen 6-18, 636D1
FPC hikes 'old' gas rate 7-1, 635F3
Govs for deregulation 7-6, 493A1
May, June CPI rptd 7-21, 536D2

1977

GARDENIERS-Berendsen, Mathilde
Named culture, soc welfare min 12-19, 986B1
GARDNER, Daniel Wilbur
Death sentence remanded 3-22, 230E3
GARDNER, John W.
Hails Carter conflict-of-interest code 1-4, 5C1
On Sikes subcom post loss 1-26, 53G3
Announces resignatn 2-5, 140D2
Succeeded at Common Cause 4-23, 396C3
Quits Rockefeller Fund 8-23, 927D3
GARDNER, Richard N.
Named amb to Italy 1-7, 14D2
GARDNER, Stephen
Backs Lance as bank exec 9-26, 761A2
GARFIELD, Dr. Sidney R.
HMO certified; gets LBJ Foundatn award 10-26, 870B1
GARLAND, Victor
Named Australia spec trade rep 12-19, 982B2
GARMATZ, Edward A.
Indicted 8-1, 603C3
GARMENT Workers Union, International Ladies (ILGWU)—*See INTERNATIONAL Ladies Garment Workers Union*
GARN, Sen. Jake (R, Utah)
Threatns clean-air filibuster 8-4, 610F1
On TV vs Canal pacts 10-29, 912C1
GARNER, Erroll
Dies 1-2, 84B3
GARNER, James
Wins Emmy 9-11, 1021F3
GARNETT, Tay
Dies 10-4, 872G1
GARRIGUES Walker, Joaquin
Spain pub works, housing min 7-5, 545C2
GARRISON Reservoir (N.D.)—*See DAMS & Reservoirs*
GARRITY Jr., Judge W. Arthur
Sup Ct bars review of '75 Boston receivership action 1-10, 57D1
GARST, Roswell
Dies 11-5, 952D2
GARTHOFF, Dr. Raymond L.
Named amb to Bulgaria 7-8, confrmd 7-28, 626E2
GARVEY, Ed
NFL pact OKd 3-25, 263F3
GARVEY, Ronnie
Escalera KOs 3-17, 263F1
GARVEY, Steve
NL wins All-Star Game 7-19, 567B2
NL batting ldr 10-2, 926C3, D3
In World Series 10-11—10-18, 806G1
GARZA, Rep. E. de la (D, Tex.)
Cited in Park indictmt 9-6, 688C1

GAS, Natural—*See also ALASKA—Oil & Gas; CANADA—Energy*
Ford would ease price control 1-7, 14A3
Italy-USSR trade talks 1-10—1-13, 64A3
Oct '76 price drop cited 1-12, 38A3
Nov '76 prices rptd 1-14, 37D2
Gen Dynamics wins US loan guarantee, Burmah LNG contract cited 1-19, 55E1-F2
Dec '76 CPI rise rptd 1-19, 78B1
Utility stocks hit 3-yr high 1-24, 54E3
OECD urges US price decontrol 1-27, 169E3
FPC rpts reserves drop 2-2; Dec '76, Jan usage rptd up 2-9, 91E3
Lobbyist: producers await deregulatn 2-3, 152C2
US sludge-gasificatn test set 2-3, 278E1
Jan WPI rise rptd 2-11, 111A3
Sovt, UK equipmt deal set 2-11, 134E3

1978

GARDEN City, N.Y.—*See NEW York State*
GARDIA, Mario Sottomayor
Sworn Portugal educ min 1-30, 91C3
GARDENKRANS, Keith
Sets discus mark 6-1—6-4, 600G3
GARDEN State Bowl—*See FOOTBALL—Collegiate*
GARDINER-Denver Co.
S Africa unit fined for Rhodesia sales 1-12, 38B3
GARDNER, Richard N.
Carter recalls re Italy CP crisis 1-10, 19F1
GARDNER, Stephen
Vs record discount-rate hike 10-13, 791B2
GARDNER v. Westinghouse Broadcasting Co.
Class actn certificatn appeals curbed by Sup Ct 6-21, 509G2
GARFINKLE, Louis
Deer Hunter released 12-14, 1030F2
GARLAND, Tex.—*See TEXAS*
GARLAND, Victor
Scores EC import curbs 1-24, 69D2
Protests EC trade policy 3-1, 265G2
Sees Brunner on coal, uranium imports 6-13, 495A1
GARMATZ, Edward A.
Chrgs dropped 1-9, 15G3
GARMON, William F.
Kills self 1-21, 96A2
GARN, Sen. Jake (R, Utah)
Chrgs Torrijos drug link 2-22, 120C3
Votes vs Panama Canal neutrality pact 3-16, 177G2
Votes vs 2d Canal pact 4-18, 273B1
ERA amendmt defeated 10-3, 788D1
GARNEAU, Raymond
Loses Liberal ldrship bid 4-15, 328A3
GARNER, John Nance
Wins US House primary in Washn 9-19, 736F3
Loses electn 11-7, 857B3
GARNES, Boyd
Spring Awakening opens 7-13, 887B3
GARR, Ralph
AL batting ldr 10-2, 928E3
GARRAHY, Gov. J(ohn) Joseph (D, R.I.)
Renominated 9-12, 716A3
Reelected 11-7, 847G3, 853E3
GARRETT, Tony
Tex executn filming case declined by Sup Ct 7-3, 552D2
GARRETT v. Estelle
Tex executn filming case declined by Sup Ct 7-3, 552D2
GARRISON, David
Living At Home opens 12-11, 1031C2
GARRISON, Jim
Sworn La appeals ct judge 6-15, 843G3
GARRITY Jr., Judge W. Arthur
Enjoins offshore lease sale 1-28, 108D2
GARRY, Charles
Visits Guyana cult commune with US delegatn 11-17, escapes mass murder-suicide 11-18; Guyana troops rescue 11-19, 889G1-890C3
GARSON, Greer
Playboy of Weekend World opens 11-16, 1031G2
GARTH, David
Hired by Venez pol party 5-5, 395G1
Candidate wins Venez pres electn 12-3, 953A1
GARTLEY, Markham L.
Loses electn for US House 11-7, 847F2
GARTNER, David
Confrmd to CFTC 5-17, 513A3
Carter asks resignatn 6-26; denies interest conflict, bars resignatn 6-28, 513F2
GARUDA Indonesian Airlines
Charter flight crashes in Sri Lanka 11-15, 908B2
GARVEY, Edmund
Fired 1-19, police scandals cited 1-21, 1-24, 72A2
GARVEY, Steve
NL wins All-Star Game, named game MVP 7-11, 559C3-E3
NL batting ldr 10-2, 2d in MVP vote 11-15, 928E1, D2-F2
Dodgers win NL pennant 10-7, 779A1
In World Series 10-10—10-17, 799D3
GARVIN Jr., Clifton C.
Sees Carter, backs inflatn plan 4-20, 361G3
On '77 top-paid execs list 5-15, 364G3
Vs pipeline ownership curb 6-21, 471G1
GAS (play)
Approaching Zero opens 11-30, 1031A1
GAS, Natural
Carter budgets exploratn 1-23, 47F2
Gulf Oil pipe compensatn case review refused 2-21, 126B2
Propane tank car blast in Tenn 2-24, 196C1
'76 'new' rates review refused 2-27, 143C2
Ferromagnetism in superfluid helium 3-A rptd 3-16, 293E3
FTC aide backs lid on cos' coal, uranium holdings 4-5; Justice Dept proposal rptd 4-6, 282D2, A3
Airco OKs BOC takeover 4-7, 403D3
'77 reserves rptd down, exploratn up 4-10, 282E1, F1
Oil cos cleared of '76-77 gas withholding, reserve estimates rptd high 4-27, 322C1

1979

GARDNER, Ava
City on Fire released 9-14, 819B3
GARDNER, Buddy
Ties for 2d in Tucson Open 2-18, 220E3
2d in Napa Classic 9-26, 970E1
GARDNER, Carol
Indicted 3-6, 220D2; 4-9, 298A1
GARDNER, Herb
Goodbye People opens 4-[illegible]
GARDNER, Randy
Wins world figure-skating title 3-14, 391G3
GARDNER-Denver Co.
Cooper acquires 1-22, [illegible]
1st 1/4 merger rise rptd 4-10, [illegible]
GARFEIN, Jack
Flying Blind opens 11-15, 956B3
GARGAN, William
Dies 2-16, 176A3
GARIN, Georges
Death rptd 5-22, 432G2
GARLAND, Robert
Electric Horseman released 12-21, 1007C3
GARN, Sen. Jake (R, Utah)
Sen GOP Conf secy 71B2
Vs neighborhoods panel rpt 3-15, 208B3
Clashes with Nader in Sen hearing 11-20, 1005F3
GARNER, Phil
In World Series 10-10—10-17, 816A1
GARRAHY, Gov. J. Joseph (D, R.I.)
Gets reassurance on heating fuel supply 8-28, 703C2
GARRIDO, Antonio
US wins Ryder Cup Matches 9-16, 969E3
GARRISON, Numan H.
Acquitted re price-fixing 4-29, 327C3
GARRITY Jr., Judge W. Arthur
Mass offshore oil-lease ban lifted 2-20, 187A1
GARRY, Charles
FBI papers at Jonestown to be probed 1-17, 117F3
GARSON, Greer
On Golden Pond opens 2-28, 712G1
GARTNER, David
Vs commodity options trading resumptn 9-5, 681B2
GARVEY, Ed.
NASLPA strike 4-13—4-18, 431C3
GARVEY, Steve
NL wins All-Star Game 7-17, 568D3
NL batting ldr 9-30, 955D2-F2
GARWOOD, Pfc. Robert
Denies Viet collaboratn 3-21, returns to US 3-25; plans desertn chrgs fight 3-31, 265G3
Desertn hearing opens 12-4, 924D1
GARY, Ind.—*See INDIANA*
GARY, Raphaelle (alias Crystal Gray)
Newton murder case ends in 2d mistrial, chrgs dropped 9-27, 818D3
GARY, Roman
Scores FBI '70 Seberg slander 9-14, 705D1

GAS, Natural
Energy Comm rate relief power backed by Sup Ct 1-16, 32D2
Energy Comm productn power denied by Sup Ct 2-22, 150F3
House com OKs Alaska lands bill 3-1, 187E1
Schlesinger backs as oil substitute 3-12, 183D2
El Paso denies Sohio oil pipe bar 3-14, 188A2
Utility cost pass-through OKd 3-16, 264B3
Forest land dvpt proposed 4-16, 282G1
'78 reserves rptd down 4-30, 324A3
House OKs Alaska land bill 5-16, 366G3
Diesel fuel allocatn rules adopted 5-25, 395C2
Fla tank blast injures 3 6-7, 572A3

1980

GARCIA Anoveros, Jaime
Submits Spain '81 budget 9-30, 793E2
GARCIA Diaz, Antonio
Ousted as commerce min 5-2, 355D1
GARCIA Julia, Carlos
Sentncd for '77 murders 3-4, 196C2
GARCIA Marquez, Gabriel
Leftists ask Panama mtg 4-19, 311G2
GARCIA Meza, Gen. Luis (Bolivian president)
Leads mil coup in Bolivia 7-17, 546A3
Demotes 2 army offcrs, replaces postal chief 7-30, 577C1
Decrees compulsory govt service 8-1, 602B3
Mil rival pledges support 8-5, 602D3
Gives independnc day speech; scores US, Andean Group 8-6, 602E3
Denies drug trafficking 8-12; US halts enforcemt progrms 8-13, chrgs rptd 8-15, 667F3, 668B1
Denounces La Paz archbp 8-17, church chrgs rights abuses 9-10, 686C3
Bolivia debt paymts postponed 9-3, 686B3
Gueiler in W Ger, scores regime 10-5, 787D2
Sets Santa Marta conf boycott 12-10, 992B3
GARCIA Rodriguez, Felix
Assassinated 9-11, 685A2
GARCIA y Garcia, Arturo
Scores Cuba refugee policy shift 4-16, 285F1
GARCIN, Ginette
Charles & Lucie released 5-9, 675B2
GARD, William
On Attica prison overcrowding 1-31, 113A1
GARDINER, Reginald
Dies 7-7, 608F1
GARDNER, Carol
Sentenced 5-20, 927F2
GARDNER, John W.
Cox to head Common Cause 2-2, 115E2
GARDNER, Randy
Retains US figure skating title 1-17, withdraws from world competitn 3-12, 470D2, E2
Withdraws from Winter Olympics 2-15, 154C3
GARE, Danny
NHL scoring ldr 4-6, 295G3, 296D1
GARFEIN, Jack
American Clock opens 11-20, 1003G2
GARFIELD, Brian
Hopscotch released 9-26, 836B3
GARFUNKEL, Art
Bad Timing released 9-21, 836D2
GARLAND, Victor
Leaves Cabt for UK post 11-2, 857E2
GARN, Sen. Jake (R, Utah)
Nominated for reelection 6-28, 700B3
Reelected 11-4, 840D3, 845B3, 852C1
Named Sen GOP conf secy 12-2, 915E2
GARNER, James
Assaulted 1-16, 200F1
Assailant convicted 7-19, 639A3
GARNER, Phil
NL wins All-Star Game 7-8, 636G1, A2
GARRAHY, Gov. John Joseph (D, R.I.)
State of State message 1-2, 270D1
Unopposed in primary 9-9, 700A3
Reelected 11-4, 845D3, 847D1, 848G3
GARREAU, Jacqueline
2d in Boston Marathon 4-21, awarded title 4-29, 527C2-D2
GARRET, Leroy
Dies 7-21, 608G1
GARRETT Jr., Ray D.
Dies 2-3, 176C1
GARRICK, David
Hails BC uranium ban 2-27, 148F2
GARRIPO, Judge Louis B.
Gacy convicted 3-12, gets death sentence 3-13, 214C1
GARRISON, David
Day in Hollywood opens 5-1, 392F2
GARRISON, Samuel A.
Sentenced 6-10, 460B1
GARRONE, Roberto
Wounded 2-9, 151D2
GARTNER, David
Testifies on commodity futures trading curbs 4-15, 290A2, C2
GARVEY, Cyndy (Mrs. Steve)
Magazine article reprint OKd 8-14, 637D2
GARVEY, Steve
Magazine article reprint OKd 8-14, 637D2
NL batting ldr 10-6, 926D2-F2
GARWOOD, Pfc. Robert
Court-martial asked 2-1, 115C3
GARY, Romain
Kills self 12-2, 1004G1

GAS, Natural
Miss tank blasts 2-13, 309C2
Fed leasing lottery suspended, scandal hinted 2-29; resumptn ordrd 4-7, 330B2
La tax case fact-finder named by Sup Ct 3-3, 210G1
Pipeline capacity rule challenge refused by Sup Ct 3-3, 210A2
Connally 'basic speech' excerpts 3-7, 184F2, B3
Fla ct review voted 3-11, 185B1
Hunts bailout loan collateral listed 5-28, 425C3, 426C1, E1
US intrastate sale power affirmed 6-6, 552B3
GOP platform backs deregulatn 7-10, 506C3
GOP platform adopted; text 7-15, 536F3, 537B1, F1

1976

Coastal states impact aid OKd 7-26, 566G2
FPC hikes rate 7-27, consumer coalitn vs 7-28, ct modifies 8-9, 635D2-636C1
Atlantic offshore lease sale challenged 8-13—8-17, bids accepted 8-25, 648C2-F3
GOP platform text 8-18, 607D2
GAO vs synfuel projct 8-24, 649G1
Moss scores rate hike 9-1, 10-30, 868E2, A3
FPC to reconsider rate ruling 9-2; hearings 9-16—9-17; ups cost estimate, reclassifies gas 10-20; July rate rptd reaffirmed 11-3; vote rptd 11-5, 868B1
Indl output index revised 9-16, 709E1
Ford, Carter debate 9-23, 702G2
Offshore leasing bill defeated 9-28, 883E2
Deregulatn bill not cleared 10-2, 883G2
Sup Ct bars price hike review 10-4, 807A3
Pipeline safety aid signed 10-11, 834C3
Consumer reactn to FPC rate hike 10-20, 868D2
Alaska transport study bill signed 10-22, 834D3
Nov WPI hike rptd 12-3, 918G3
Foreign Developments (including U.S. foreign developments)—*See also country names*
Austria rptd in W Ger-Iran-USSR pact 1-19, 97E3
US-Canada pipe delay rptd 1-20, treaty initialed 1-28, 116C3
US vs Siberia exploitatn 1-30, 88C3
Ford proposes US-Canada pipe, LNG import curbs 2-26, 149A2
Bolivia gets forgn pipe loan 3-12, 416F1
Dutch increase N Sea role 3-25, 255E1
US-Japan-USSR pact reached 3-31, 655C3
US utility buys N Sea gas 4-7, 521E3
Canada studies price rise 5-18, 380D3
2 W Ger cos in Sovt turbine deal 6-1, 540D2
Petro-Canada buys ARCO unit 6-7, 417C1
Canada ups price, US role cited 6-10, 417B1
US firm seeks Australia gas 8-8, 650G1
IDB OKs Argentina loan 8-27, 649C3
Canada surplus rptd 9-3, 710A1
US, Canada debate pipeline 11-1—12-22, 998A2
Iran-Czech pipeline pact 11-22, 946A2
US forgn paymt studies issued 12-18, 12-20, 985G1, D2
Sovt-UK deal rptd 12-24, 1011A2
North Sea Finds—*See NORTH Sea*
Pollution—*See 'Oil & Gas Issues' under ENVIRONMENT*

1977

Jan indl output rise rptd 2-15, 129F3
Jan CPI rise rptd 2-18, 129D3
Carter on deregulation, supply 2-23, 126D3
Carter asks energy dept 3-1, 148F1
US record exploratn budgets set 3-8, '76 drilling rptd 3-10, 196F2
Feb WPI rise rptd 3-10, 176F2
US '76 use rptd 3-13, 196B2
EC-Australia talks 3-14, 3-16, 218C1
Feb CPI rise rptd 3-18, 215C1
US '76, '71-76 power data rptd 3-23, 3-25, 277G1, B2
Dutch '76 reserves drop rptd 3-28, 412E1
Carter asks US plutonium ban 4-7, 268C1
Carter energy plan 4-18, 4-20, 289D1, F2, 290B2-D2, 294G2, 295A3; fact sheet 291E1-293E3
Cong, other reactn to Carter plan 4-20—4-24, 293G1-F3; 319A3-320F3
Mar CPI rise rptd 4-21, 324C2
Carter affirms plan, bars deregulatn 4-22, 321C2
UN unit estimates reserves 4-26, 362E2
FPC OKs Algeria LNG imports 4-29, 370B1
Carter plan scored 4-30—6-8, GOP TV rebuttal 6-2, 443E1-G2
'76 sales return rptd 340B2
FEA proposes coal conversn 5-9, 370A1
Tax deductn delay clears Cong 5-16, 382C1; Carter signs 5-23, 417F3
Sen votes energy dept 5-18, 405C2, E2
S Korea-Japan pact signed 6-8, 467G1
2 Gulf offshore leases canceled 6-8, 499C1
House subcom OKs deregulatn 6-9, Admin scores 6-10, 460G1
FTC-oil cos info rule review rejctd 6-13, 517F1
'76 FPC price hikes upheld 6-16, 464C2
FPC-Texaco dispute resolved 7-14, 559A3
'Enhanced recovery' prospects seen less 7-17, 559C1, E1
June CPI rptd 7-21, 554D2
Carter urges conservatn 7-28, 574C3
Danes OK North Sea line 8-1, 672C1
US Energy Dept created 8-4, 591F2
House OKs Carter energy pkg 8-5, 609B3
Gulf buys Kewanee 8-9, 612E2
Australia OKs NW Shelf exploratn 8-24, 704C3-705B1
Tenneco buys Phila Life 8-25, 650G3
Sen OKs weakened coal-conversn bill, bars acquisitn curbs 9-8, 702B3, F3
Sen OKs deregulatn after filibuster 9-22—10-4, 757B1, F2
Royalties dispute review refused 10-3, 760G1
Great Western Sunshine takeover OKd 10-4, 799A1
Carter scores industry, reactn 10-13, 772E2, F3
Recovery research OKd by Cong 10-20, 833F1
Offshore leasing bill blocked in House com 10-25, 833C2
Tax bill OKd by Sen 10-31, 832C1-F3
Phillips-Ashland helium dispute case declined 10-31, 11-28, 919F2
Schlesinger legis comments draw fire from House 11-21—11-23, 916G3-917A1
Mex plans US pipeline 12-1, 967E1
Carter LNG import policy faulted by GAO 12-12, 962G2
Tex agency orders Coastal States refunds 12-12, 980D1
Mex gets US pipe loans 12-15, 985C2
Energy bill delayed by deregulatn dispute 12-22, 1002E1
Shortages
FPC OKs emergency sales 1-14, 37A1
US supplies rptd depleted 1-14, 37F1
FPC rpts reserves drop 1-15, 54A3
Layoffs estimated 1-18, 1-22, 54D2
FPC OKs Canadian import 1-19; other authorizatns 1-20, 1-21, 53G3
CAB, ICC act 1-19, 1-24, 54E1
Carter asks thermostats lowered 1-21, 1-26; asks interstate reallocatn legis 1-26, 53D3
Schlesinger meets pipeline execs 1-21, 53D3
Interior Dept lifts productn limits 1-24, 54F1
Blizzard hits Midwest, emergencies declared 1-27—1-29, 75E2
FPC OKs more Canada imports 1-27; Canada OKs 1-28, 76E1
Ohio co buys own field 1-27, 76A2
Transco asks nonessential cutoffs 1-28, 75D3
'75 interstate reserves fall, price rise cited 1-28, 76A3
Carter in Pittsburgh 1-30, 75C3
Shortage eases temporarily 1-30, 75E3
Layoffs, fuel cost to consumers rptd 1-30, 2-2, 75F3-76B1
Calif restricts use 2-1, 76D1
Carter urges industry honesty 2-2, 75E1
Emergency act signed 2-2, 75C3, 76B2
US acts to ease transport 2-2, 2-3, 76F1
Dunham named emergency act admin 2-2, orders supply shifts 2-3, 91G2-B3
Summer shortages seen 2-3, 91D3
FPC OKs Mex, Algeria imports 2-4, Canada elec exchng 2-5, 91B3
Warm spell, many workers return; layoff data rptd 2-7, 91E2
Carter vs undue profits 2-8, 88B3
Ohio asks disaster status 2-8, 92B1
FPC gas-productn study rptd 2-11, 152C1
Canada gas eases crisis, East, Midwest deliveries resume 2-13—2-19, 152D2

1978

Justice Dept backs 15% lid on cos' coal holdings, 10% on uranium reserves 5-15, 471C2
Intrastate diversn curbed by Sup Ct 5-31, 430E3-431D1
Coal gasificatn plant financing plan submitted 6-2, 471E2
Calif residual fuel oil exports set 6-15, 470D3
Tenneco, Shell interstate sale probed 6-22, 471A2
Solar energy study rptd 6-23, 493F3
Tex Eastrn to buy Olinkraft 7-17, 700E3
Coal slurry pipeline bill defeated 7-19, 550A2
GAO study urges LNG safety measures, other reforms; indus, fed agencies score 7-31, 609F3
Regulatory overhaul asked by ABA 8-8, 626E2
'77 consumer bills rptd up 9-17, 718C3
Aug CPI rise rptd 9-26, 752D1
Tax law revisn clears Cong 10-15, 786E1
Plentiful '79 supplies, possible glut seen 10-29, 11-2, 899G3-900A1
Energy Dept files overchrg suit vs Exxon 11-1, 900D1
Rockwell, Textron indicted on meter price fixing 11-1, 935B3
Diamond Shamrock to buy Falcon Seaboard 11-2, 1005A2
Tex securities-regulatn case refused by Sup Ct 11-13, 874C3
Energy Dept fuel rules unveiled 11-15, 919F3-920B1
Pa coal conversn plant closed 12-1, 962G3-963A1
Alaska Developments—*See ALASKA—Oil & Gas*
Canada Developments—*See CANADA—Energy*
Carter National Plan
NAACP vs 1-11, discord rptd 1-14, 68E1, A2
Cong deadlock persists, deregulatn plans detailed 3-7—3-22, 219F2-220E1
Carter would accept deregulatn 3-9, 160D3
Carter, key Cong conferees meet in pvt sessns 4-11, 4-12; House protests 4-13, 4-20, 304F1-B23
Abourezk demands deregulatn veto 4-17, Carter assures 'open' debate 4-18, 273C2
Cong conferees break deadlock, price compromise detailed 4-21, 304E1, B3-305A2
Carter bars admin actn, cites Cong progress 4-25, 307B3
Price plan OKd by cong conferees 5-23, 5-24, other provisns 6-13, 446A1
Schlesinger on price accord effect 5-26, 408A2
Coal conversn bill clears Sen; price plan status rptd 7-18, 549G3-550F1
Compromise price plan OKd by conf com 8-17; cong coalitn, Carter A-breeder commitmt stir trouble 8-17—8-26, 677A3-678B2
Govs favor deregulatn 8-29, 682F1
Carter plans lobbying effort 8-30, 664G1
Sen OKs compromise 9-27, 733A1-D3
IMF encouraged by Sen OK 9-27, 731E2
Energy bill clears Cong 10-15, 786B2, D2, D3, 787B1, G1, E2; Carter signs 11-9, 873A1
3 states sue vs price controls 11-20, 900B1
Foreign Developments—*See also CANADA—Energy*
Dutch '77 export drop rptd 2-10, 169D3
Chile-Argentina Beagle Channel dispute cited 2-20, 216G1
China find rptd 5-6, 436E2
IEA sees smaller energy role 6-5, 449E3 *, 450F1
Spanish gas truck blast kills 150 7-11, 636D1
US issues USSR sale rules 7-31, 634F2
USSR export rise seen by US 8-13, 634F3
US co sued re Indonesian bribe 8-30, 737C1
Mex reserves rise, US price remains firm 9-1, 690B1, D1
IMF encouraged by US Sen price plan OK 9-27, 731E2
Norway '78 revenues revised down 10-5, 775F1
Trinidad dry reserves rptd 11-3, 886A1
US-China talks rptd set 11-6, 871D2
US clears equipmt sale to USSR 12-4, 966E1
US rejcts Algerian imports 12-18, 983E3
Offshore Developments (U.S.)
Atlantic offshore sale delayed 1-30, 108D2
NJ drilling challenge refused 2-21, 125E2-B3
NJ well rptd dry 6-2, 6-5, 449C3
NJ find rptd by Texaco 8-14, 665B3
Leasing chngs clear Cong 8-22, 662F2-663A1
Geological Survey reserve estimates cited 8-22, 662G2
3 NJ wells rptd dry 12-6, 12-11, 12-27, 1010B1

1979

Interstate mkt diversn curbed by Sup Ct 6-18, 499C2
House OKs synthetic fuel bill 6-26, 498G1
Tenneco fined re interstate shipmts 7-27, 629E1
NY energy plan outlined 8-7, 609G3
Calif LNG projct approved 9-27, 769C2
Alaska Developments—*See ALASKA—Oil & Gas*
Canada Developments—*See CANADA-Energy*
Carter Domestic Actions
Carter cuts research budget 1-22, 45F2
Carter on '78 profits 1-26, 70G1
Farm supplies vowed 5-4, 346D3
Foreign Developments (including U.S. international news)—*See also 'Mergers' below*
Carter on Mex prospects 1-17, 30B1
USSR '78 output rptd 1-19, 60B2
Iran shipmts to USSR rptd cut 1-23, 50B2
France supplier search speedup ordrd 2-7, 82D3
Carter, Mex pres in talks; sales negotiatns set 2-14–2-16, 124F1
Iran scores USSR deals 2-24, 145E1
Sweden seeks W Ger, Algeria LNG deal cancelatns 3-13, 213F3
Carter rpts Mex talks 4-5, 250E3
Iran shipmts to USSR resumed 4-5, 279G1
Mex 10-yr dvpt plan rptd 5-4, 354A1
IEA backs more use 5-22, 380F1
US seeks Mex deal 7-8, 517E3
UK revises N Sea estimate 7-10, 582A2
Spanish finds rptd; '79 imports, consumptn seen 7-10, 546F1
Iran cuts Sovt exports, drops pipe plans; ends US co shipmts 7-28, 582G3
UK OKs Scottish plant 8-10, 614A2
Indonesia LNG imports OKd 8-14; Calif terminal chosen 9-26, projct approved 9-27, 769C2
US-Mex talks break down 8-31, 688G3
Dutch see revenue hike 9-18, 730C3
France plans exploratn aid 9-21, 752B1
Mex sales to US set 9-21, 718D2
USSR, E Ger sign pact 10-5, 761C2
US consortium buys Mex gas 10-18, 814E3
UK orders N Sea oil cutback 10-29, 836F1
USSR rpts output 11-28, 928F3
China, Japan sign pact 12-6, 939E3
US-Mex deal finalized 12-29, 996G2
Mergers & Acquisitions
Ashland unit holdings sold 2-4, 560E3
Deutsche BP-Veba deal OKd 3-5, 214G3
Mobil bid for Gen Crude OKd 3-28, 282G3
Continental buys Fla Gas 8-28, 986C3
Offshore Developments (U.S.)
NJ (Baltimore Canyon) wells rptd dry 1-10, 17A2; 2-14, 186E3; 3-13–5-16, 361D3; 9-27, 10-3, 867C2
Baltimore Canyon finds rptd 1-17, 55C2; 5-23, 442F3; 10-22, 11-12, 867A2-C2; 11-23, 943B1
Ashland unit holdings sold 2-4, 560E3
Mass (Georges Bank) lease ban lifted 2-20, 186F3
E Coast lease bids low, reserve estimate cited 2-28, 186C3
Calif lease bids placed 6-29, 518B2; accepted 8-7, 649E1
Gulf of Mex lease bids placed 7-31, accepted 8-28, 664D3
Mass (Georges Bank) lease sale delayed 11-6, OKd 11-9, 867E1-A2
Gulf of Mex lease bids placed 11-27, 942F3; accepted 12-10, 990C2
Mass (Georges Bank) lease sale bids placed 12-18, 990G1
Price Violations
US files suit vs 8 firms, '78 Exxon suit added 1-5, 17A1
US files suit vs Mobil 6-22, 518F1
Mobil OKs refunds 11-5, 943B2

1980

Reagan pres nominatn acceptance speech 7-17, 532B2
ND synfuels plant gets $1.5 bln fed loan 11-19, ct blocks projct 12-8, 961G3
Watt sees dvpt conflict 12-22, 980A1
Alaska Developments—*See ALASKA--Oil & Gas*
Canada—*See CANADA--Energy*
Carter Domestic Actions
Budget proposals 1-28, 70B1
Foreign Developments (including U.S. international news)—*See also 'Mergers & Acquisitions' below*
Mex-US sales start 1-15, 60E1
USSR '79 output rise rptd 1-25, 79C3
Sovt-backed Afghan field opened 1-27, 85A3
USSR high prices, E Eur econ slowdown linked 2-4, 166A3
Norway econ growth seen 2-5, 100E2
Iran fields bombed 3-6—3-8, 178A2
USSR notes Urengoy troubles 3-6, 235A3
Australia labor unrest rptd 3-11, 191B1
Mex hikes US price, future increases set 3-18, 234E1
France sets new energy measures 4-2, 254D1
Mex-Canada projcts agreed 5-27, 409C3
USSR-W Ger pact set 5-29, 411C2
UK N Sea pipe OKd 6-19, 463D2
USSR, W Ger OK pipe, econ pact 7-1, 489C2, D2
Norway N Sea drillers strike 7-10, govt moves to end strike in 3 offshore fields 7-17, 565F3
Norwegian N Sea find rptd 7-16, 548D2
UK plans N Sea output cut 7-23, 563C3
Brazil seeks Bolivia deal 7-31, 577G1
France-Algeria LNG deal rptd set 9-7; Algeria cancels Dutch, W Ger plan 9-11, 827A3, C3
World Bank '80 loans rptd 9-22, 720D1
Australia NW Shelf project rptd set 10-1, 748E1
Sovts pledge COMECON export rise 10-1, 753D3
Beaufort Sea oil find rptd 10-3, 785E2-A3
Mex sets US export limits 11-19, 902C2
USSR sets 11th 5-yr plan 12-1, 945D2
NATO studies Sovt project curb 12-12, 949F1
Mergers & Acquisitions
Union Pacific, MoPac set merger 1-8, 52E3
Engelhard acquires Hunts' Beaufort Sea holdings 3-31, 244F3
Seagram accepts Sun bid for Tex Pacific 4-11, 4-11, 385B2
Alaska Interstate to buy C&K 8-18, 745F3
Sun, Tex Pacific merger completed 9-12, 985A1
Barber Oil liquidates, Petro-Lewis buys unit 10-2, 986A1
Mapco, Earth Resources merger set 12-5, 985E1
Tenneco, Houston Oil merger set 12-9, 985A1
Offshore Developments (U.S.)
Mass (Georges Bank) bids rptd accepted 1-7, 18A1
Carter budget proposals 1-28, 74A1; table 70F1
Andrus OKs leasing speedup 6-17, 552E2
Gulf coast leasing bids set records 9-30, 785G1
Exxon Beaufort Sea oil find rptd 10-3, 785E2-A3
Beaufort Sea leases upheld 10-14, 960B3
Leasing overhaul ordrd 10-31, 960G2

1976

GAS Association, American
FPC hikes 'new' gas rate 7-27, 636C1
Moss scores FPC rate hike 10-30, 868F2
GASOLINE Marketers of America, Society of Independent
Indicted 6-1, 412E3
GASPARIN, Fernando
AAB threatens 11-15, 916B2
GATES, Ronald Cecil
Named to Australia econ advisory bd 9-14, 730F1
GATES Jr., Thomas S.
Amb to China 3-22; confrmd 4-1, 262C3
GATT—*See GENERAL Agreement on Tariffs and Trade*
GATTO, Alberto Marcelo
Loses post, pol rights 1-6, 27B2
GAUS, Gunter
In E Ger border talks 8-12, 630C3
GAVRILENKO, Evgeniy
Wins Olympic medal 7-25, 575F3
GAWLIKOWSKI, Wieslaw
Wins Olympic medal 7-24, 575B2
GAWRYSIAK, Jerzy
Replaced 12-2, 926D3
GAYDOS, Rep. Joseph M. (D, Pa.)
Reelected 11-2, 830F3
GAYNAR Shipping Corp.
Boycott rpts released 10-19, 10-20, 786D1, G1
GAZELA Primeiro (U.S. sailing ship)
In Operation Sail 7-4, 488B3
GAVRILOVIC, Milan
Dies 1-1, 56C3
GAY, F. W. (Bill)
Elected Summa pres 8-4, 596D3
GAZOV, Alexander
Wins Olympic medal 7-23, 575B2
GEARHART, Daniel F.
Sentenced to die 6-28, 480F1, F2, B3
Executed 7-10, 519A3
Ford, Kissinger score executn 7-10, 519C3
Mathias refused Angola visa 7-12, 519E3
Priest helps return body 7-13, 519E3
Body arrives in US 7-26, 559C3
Jurists Comm scores trial 12-21, 995E3
GEHANI, R. K.
Loses passport 7-18, 538B2
GEIBERGER, Al
Runner-up in US Open golf 6-20, 756B3

GEISEL, Gen. Ernesto (ret.) (Brazilian president)
Fires oppositn legislators 1-6, 27A2
Mil support rptd, plot aborted 1-9, 98A2
Newsmen score Herzog 'suicide' rpt 1-13, legislators' ouster 1-23, 98G1
Fires Sao Paulo army chief 1-19, 98A1
Kissinger visits 2-19—2-22, 177D1
Fires MDB deputies 3-29, 4-1, 287D3
Media campaign rptd ordrd 6-28, 836D2
Widespread violence rptd 7-9—10-14, 835C3, 836A1, D1
Removes pol rights of 5 8-4, 850E3
Mtg with archbp re priest murder rptd 11-5, 850A3
IAPA asks 'terrorism' end 11-17, 916A2
On munic electns 11-19, 902F3

1977

Andrus sets probe; productn data cited 2-17, 151D3-152B1
FEA: 1 mln workers resume jobs 2-18, 152F2
US House com accuses Texaco, Gulf 2-22, 2-23, denied 2-23, 152E1
Utilities chrg gas withheld 2-26, 152C1
US productn drop since '73 rptd 2-26, 152B2
Tenneco questns diversns 2-28, 3-7; FPC orders probe 3-8, 196C1
Columbus (O) schls reopen 3-7, 196G2-A3
FPC staff reprisals chrgd 3-10, 196A1
24-hr fuel watch ended 3-11, 277C2
Offshore lease renewal tied to productn 3-15, 195F3
Tex costs threaten farms 3-24, 244G3
Winter plan announced 12-1, 942B3
GAS Association, American
Carter energy plan 4-20, 292E3
GASOLINE Marketers of America, Society of Independent
Convicted 8-30, 691B3
Fined 9-16, 918F2
GASOLINE & Motor Oil—*See PETROLEUM*
GASPAROUX, Andre
Assassinated 12-16, 981F3
GATES, Daryl
Testifies on child porno 5-27, 432B2
GATES of the House (prayer book)
Issued 3-7, 471A3
GATEWAY Transportation Co.
ICC sues 11-3, 861C1, D1
GATOR Bowl—*See FOOTBALL—Collegiate*
GATT—*See GENERAL Agreement on Tariffs and Trade*
GAUD Jr., William S.
Dies 12-5, 1024G1
GAUS, Gunter
Chrgs Kohl NKVD betrayal 2-8, 102A2
GAVAZZO, Maj. Nino
US denies visa 2-22, 351B3
GAY, F. W.
Hughes offcls clash over estate 5-28, 6-8, 472C3
GAYLORD, James
Sup Ct refuses case 10-3, 760D1
GAYLORD v. Tacoma School District
Sup Ct bars gay case review 10-3, 760D1
GAY Task Force, National
Sees Carter aide 3-26, 278B2
Educ campaign launched 6-13, 560G2-B3
GAZA—*See MIDDLE EAST, subheads ARAB-Israeli Occupation and EGYPT-Israel Peace Moves*
GAZIT, Mordechai
Vs Israel-PLO contacts 1-3, 10F2
Recalled from Paris 1-11, 9F2
Returns to Paris 2-8, 87C1
GAZO, Eddie
TKOs Wajima 6-7, 828B1
GDP (gross domestic product)—*See country names*
GEER, Judge Walter I.
Supresses Dawson 5 confessn 12-14, 991C2
GEERMAN, Hyacinto
Strikers end blackout 8-17, freed 8-18, 675A2
GEHRIG, Dr. Leo
Scores Admin re health costs 5-24, 479F1
GEIBERGER, Al
Wins Memphis Open 6-12, 676F1

GEISEL, Gen. Ernesto (ret.) (Brazilian president)
Strips cnclman of pol rights 2-2, 168E1
MDB backs US aid rejectn 3-6, 168C1
MDB youths arrested 3-27—3-29, 281G1
Suspends Cong, scores MDB 4-1, 281A1, D1
Decrees judicial reform 4-13, tightens mil rule 4-14, 303C1
Judicial, pol reforms scored 4-19, 4-29, 5-4, 523A3
Shuns US envoy 5-12—5-14, 414E1
Sets price freeze, controls 5-18, 524E2
Sees Mrs Carter, rights conv rejectn rptd 6-7, 455G1
Fires MDB deputy 6-14, 523E3
Cong legalizes divorce 6-23, 525B1
Bans oppositn leader 7-1, 541E1
Support for Gomes Monteiro rptd 7-22; Sen ldr sets pres bid 7-26, 615E3
Bans party broadcasts 7-26, 616B1
6 govs aks multiparty system 8-22, 8-27, 740D3
ARENA reps ask dem reforms 8-31, 740G3
Fires army min 10-12, 839E3
Calls pol system 'relative democracy', O Estado scores 11-4, 964E1
'Death squad' probe asked 11-7, 964C3
Picks Figueiredo as pres successor 11-17, mil back Bentes 12-2, 964F1
Sees Vance, A-ban talks rptd fruitless 11-22, 912C3
Backs pol reforms 12-1, MDB scores plan 12-9, 12-13, 964A1
Divorce bill cleared 12-4, 964E3; signs 12-26, 1018F3

1978

GAS Association, American
Rpts US '77 reserves down 4-10, 282F1
LNG safety study scored 7-31, 610F1
Plentiful '79 supplies seen 11-2, 900A1
GASCH, Judge Oliver
Bars 'reverse check-off' 7-21, 565F2-A3
Sentences Diggs 11-20, 900B2
GASOHOL—*See ENERGY*
GASOLINE & Motor Oil—*See AUTOMOBILES--Fuel Issues, PETROLEUM*
GASPARINO, Fausto
Wounded 7-7, 574E1
GASPERI, Alcide de
'47 CP govt role cited 3-11, 190D3
GASSER, Yves
Faces of Love released 7-7, 970C1
No Time For Breakfast released 9-15, 970D2
GASSMAN, Vittorio
Viva Italia released 7-9, 970D3
Wedding released 9-29, 970D3
GASTIL, Raymond D.
Freedom House survey issued 44B2
GATHERING, The (TV special)
Wins Emmy 9-17, 1030G1
GATO, Frank
Cuba frees 10-3, 777A1
GATOR Bowl—*See FOOTBALL—Collegiate*
GATT—*See GENERAL Agreement on Tariffs & Trade*
GAUCI, Victor J.
Demands Medit conf 3-5, 179E1
GAUGUIN, Paul (1848-1903)
Paintings stolen in Marseilles 6-20, 579F1
GAUNTLET, The (film)
Top-grossing film 1-4, 24G3
GAVRIC, Gabbo
Fired as Earthquakes coach 6-16, 707D3
GAY, F. W.
Thain indicted on drug chrg 6-6, 459A2
GAY, John
Diversions & Delights opens 4-12, 887F1
GAYAUSKAS, Balis
Rptd sentenced 4-16, 275F2
GAY Divorce, The (play)
Opens 3-9, 760C2
GAYDOS, Rep. Joseph M. (D, Pa.)
Reelected 11-7, 852E1
GAYLE, Crystal
Wins Grammy 2-24, 316A1
GAZA—*See MIDDLE EAST, subheads ARAB-Israeli Developments—Israeli Occupation Policies and EGYPT-Israel Peace Moves*
GAZETTE, The (Atlanta, Ga. newspaper)
Flynt '77 purchase cited 187B1
GAZIT, Maj. Gen. Shlomo
Warns Syria on Leb Christn attacks 7-6, 503B1, F1
GAZO, Eddy
Kudo decisns 8-9, 969E1
GDP (gross domestic product)—*See ECONOMY (non-U.S.); country names*
GDV Inc.—*See CITY Investing*
GE—*See GENERAL Electric*
GEASLAND, Jack
Twins on best-seller list 7-2, 579E3
GEER, Will
Dies 4-22, 356F2
GEHRIG, Lou (1903-41)
Jackson breaks HR record 10-10, 799C3
GEIDAROV, Lt. Gen. Arif Nazar
Killed 6-29, 518G3
GEISEL, Gen. Ernesto (ret.) (Brazilian president)
Confrms Figueiredo pres choice; aide quits, MDB scores 1-4—1-5, 6G2
Paymts to secy from US billionaire rptd 1-13, 165G3
Gomes scores govt 1-20, 165D3
Figueiredo for 'gradual' democracy 2-23, 165G2
Visits W Ger 3-6—3-10, 332D3
Carter visits 3-29—3-31, 233B2
Calls strikes 'sign of times' 5-24, 412A2
Const reforms given to Cong 6-23, 555E2
Abreu jailed 10-2, 771E3
French pres visits, pacts signed 10-4—10-8, 772F2
Govt corruptn, tap chrgs rptd 10-17, 836F2
Parana waters diverted for Itaipu dam, Eur cos sign turbine pact 10-20, 829G2
Chrgs MDB infiltrated by communists 11-14, 921D2

1979

GAS Association, American (AGA)
'78 gas reserves rptd down 4-30, 324B3
GASCH, Judge Oliver
Declares mistrial in Flood case 2-3, 102A2
GSA sentencing 5-23–6-25; controversy 5-25–5-30, 964F2-E3
Dismisses Taiwan defns treaty suit 6-6, 440F1
Rules vs Carter in Taiwan defns treaty suit 10-17, 777A1
Carter treaty ruling reversed 11-30, 919E1
GASKINS Jr., Darius W
Named ICC chrmn 10-12, 831A1
GASOHOL—*See ALCOHOL-Fuel Use*
GASOLINE Marketers Association, Independent
Calif gas shortage explained 5-7, 343C1
GASOLINE & Motor Oil—*See AUTOMOBILES--Fuel Issues, PETROLEUM*
GASSER, Yves
Your Turn, My Turn released 1-27, 175A1
GASSMAN, Vittorio
Quintet released 2-8, 174D3
GASTON, Don F.
Sued for fraud 11-26, 923D1
GATCHELL Jr., R. Tyler
Evita opens 9-25, 956A3
GATHINGS, E. C. (Took)
Dies 5-22, 432G2
GATT—*See GENERAL Agreement on Tariffs & Trade*
GAUL, Gilbert M.
Wins Pulitzer 4-16, 336E2, A3
GAUTAMA, Khrishna
Wins Kenya parlt electn 11-8, 874C3
GAVETT, Geoffrey
Wins Army guns NRA resale suit 9-4, 747A2
GAYLER, Adm. Noel
Backs SALT 7-17, 536G1
GAYLORD, Joe
On electn results 11-6, 846A2
GAYNOR, Gloria
I Will Survive on best-seller list 2-14, 120E3; 3-7, 174D1; 4-4, 271C2
GAYNOR & Ducas
CIA recruiting drive rptd 8-10, 610G3
GAY Rights Advocates
INS lifts gay alien curb 8-14, 631A3
GAZA—*See MIDDLE EAST-ARAB-Israeli Developments-Israeli Occupation Policies and EGYPT-Israel headings*
GAZZARA, Ben
Saint Jack released 4-26, 528E3
Bloodline released 6-28, 819F3
GDP (gross domestic product)—*See ECONOMY (non-U.S.); country names*
GEBHARD, Dieter
W Gers win world 4-man bobsled title 2-25, 392F1
GEE, Edwin A.
On '78 top-paid execs list 5-14, 347F3
GEFFEN, Maxwell
Drops McGraw-Hill proxy battle 2-23, 151D3
GEHLEN, Reinhard
Dies 6-8, 508G2
GEIBERGER, Al
Wins Colonial Natl 5-20, 587F2

GEISEL, Gen. Ernesto (ret.)
Simonsen, Couto e Silva remain in govt 1-19, 95B1
Figueiredo lauds admin 3-15, 210A1
Itaipu, Corpus dam accords signed 10-19, 845C1

1980

GASCH, Judge Oliver
Sentences Flood 2-26, 190B2
GASKINS Jr., Darius W.
On Rock I svc extensn 2-22, 147G3
On Santa Fe, Southn Pacific merger proposal 5-15, 427B3
On N&W-Southn RR merger proposal 6-2, 427E2
Lauds trucking decontrol bill 6-19, 479D1
GASKINS, Tangela
Navy actn on lesbian chrgs cited 899A1
GASOHOL—*See ALCOHOL--Fuel Use*
GASOLINE & Motor Oil—*See AUTOMOBILES--Fuel Issues, PETROLEUM*
GASPARI, Remo
Italy parlt relatns min 4-4, 275G3
GASSMAN, Vittorio
Immortal Bachelor released 2-22, 216A3
GATEWAY Hospital and Medical Center (Los Angeles, Calif.)
'79 women's survey rptd 1-9, 78C1
GATHERING of Days: A New England Girl's Journal, 1830-32, A (book)
Wins Amer Book Award 5-1, 692D2
GATT—*See GENERAL Agreement on Tariffs and Trade*
GAUDER, Hartwig
Wins Olympic medal 7-30, 624C1
GAUGUIN, Emile
Dies 1-6, 104F2
GAUGUIN, Paul (1848-1903)
Son dies 1-6, 104F2
Paintings sold for record sums 5-12, 5-13, 472D1, G1
GAUS, Gunter
Signs E Ger transport pact 4-30, 355D3
GAYDOS, Rep. Joseph M. (D, Pa.)
Reelected 11-4, 844D1
GAYNOR, Gloria
Wins Grammy 2-27, 296B3
GAYNOR, Janet
Harold & Maude opens 2-7, 136C3
GAZA—*See ARAB-Israeli Developments--Israeli Occupation Policies*
GAZOV, Aleksandr
Wins Olympic medal 7-24, 623D2
GEAR, Luella
Dies 4-3, 360G1
GEARON, Michael
NBA cocaine use rptd 8-19, 656A2
GEDOVARI, Imre
Wins Olympic medal 7-25, 622B3
GEHRING, Rolf
Wins Bavarian Grand Prix 5-25, 607D3

1976

GELBARD, Jose Ber
Loses pol rights, citizenship 6-23, 520D1
Indicted 10-25, US extraditn sought 11-27, 12-7, 997E1
GELDENBLOEM, Pieter
Arrest rptd 8-17, 624E3
GELDENHUYS, Gen. Michael
On journalist arrests 8-2, 592D1
GEMAYEL, Amin
On Palestinian camp blockade 1-4, 1D1
GEMAYEL, Bashir
Sees Jumblat 6-2, 385E1
Libya premier mediates 6-15, 429A3
Rpts on Palestinian moves 12-27, 973B2
GEMAYEL, Pierre
Assured on Leb sovereignty 1-25, 59G1
OKs mil pullback 1-25, 59A2
Says Phalangists rearm 2-2, 83C2
Vs cabinet enlargement 162F2
Backs new peace plan 4-17, 273F1
Chrgs Palestinian interventn 5-10, 337G1
For Syrian troop role 5-11, 337C2
Backs French peace force 5-23, 369F1
Meets Edde 5-25, 370C1
Son sees Jumblat 6-2, 385E1
Backs Syria invasion 6-6, 406B2
Vs Arab peace force 6-10, 405E1
Libya premier mediates 6-15, 429A3
League presses truce accord 7-26, 546B2
Christians disavow Tel Zaatar truce 7-26, 546E2
Jt Christian force planned, deplores rival clash 7-27, 546B3
Meets Salam 8-7, Khatib scores 8-8, 578B1
Calls partitn 'reality' 8-17, 618E1
OKs halt to civln shelling 8-18, 629B1
Meets US aides 8-22—8-24, 628G3
In peace plan talks 8-26—8-27, 662F3
Meets Al Fatah official 9-4, 663C1
Meets Syrians in Damascus 9-6, 663B1
Sees Sarkis on Riyadh pact 10-20, 779C1
Sees Sarkis, OKs Arab force 11-9, 841E1
On Palestinian arms surrender 12-5, 913D1
Chrgs Palestinian arms moves, bars surrender 12-28, 973C2
GEMINI Contenders, The (book)
On best-seller list 12-5, 972F2
GENEEN, Harold S.
Rpts on ITT Chile paymts 5-12, 361E1
GENERAL Agreement on Tariffs and Trade (GATT)
Japan vs poor natns eased import curbs 3-3, 191A3
Canada-EC talks open 3-11, 204F1
Ford asks steel pact 3-16, 212E3
US cites role in poor natn aid proposal 5-6, 318A1
7-natn econ summit cites Geneva talks 6-27—6-28, 462G2
US GOP platform text 8-18, 602B3
DISC programs ruled illegal 11-5, 976C3
US ups brandy duties, EC poultry war cited 11-26, 976B3
GENERAL Dynamics Corp.
Dutch Dassault bribe case opens 2-10, 141F2
Iran may buy F-16s 2-17, 140B1
Cruise missile dvpt suspended 3-8, 183C1
Confirms Iran jet-oil barter talks 5-11, 340B1
Top fscl '76 defns contractor 12-21, 961B3
Electric Boat Division
Defense Dept to pay Navy debt 4-8, 309B2
Navy paymt talks stalled 6-10, 453F3
Stromberg Carlson Corp.
'75 arms sales listed 2-6, 147B3

1977

GELBARD, Jose Ber
Linked to Graiver scandal 4-11, 345A3
'73 Graiver, Orfila mtg rptd 4-26, 4-28, disputed 4-29, 371D3
Army: Graiver link conclusive 5-4, 371D1, A2
Dies 10-4, 872A2, 922A3
GELDENHUYS, Gen. Michael
Denies torture rpt 4-4, 349A3
GEMAYEL, Bachir
Chrgs drive vs Christns 8-22, 647B3
GEMAYEL, Pierre
Scores hq blast 1-4, 2E1
Vs Palestinian arms 1-10, 28B2
Vs Christian strike 1-24, 72F1
Replaced as Leb Front head 3-18, 208C2
Seeks PLO curbs 4-19, 316A3
Chrgs left drive vs Christns 8-22, 647E3
Rpt sought Israel mil aid 8-22, 648F1
GENEEN, Harold S.
Replaced at ITT 2-9, 140D2
ITT-Hartford suits setld 3-4, 194C3
GENENTECH Inc.
Hormone made from bacteria 12-1, 1022A3
GENERAL Accounting Office—*See under U.S. GOVERNMENT*
GENERAL Agreement on Tariffs and Trade (GATT)
Japan vs EC ball-bearing fines 2-8, 109A2
Rpts '76 world trade rise 3-8, 188D2-C3
S Africa sets duties 3-30, 285A1
7-natn summit backs talks 5-7—5-8, 357A2
To study US ct ruling on Japan electronics duties 5-23, 416B2
Warns US re Japan duty order 7-16; ruling reversed 7-28, 587B1, C1
Trade protectionism warning issued; US, EC steel curbs scored 9-12, 717E2
US, EC OK tariff-cutting formula 9-23, 853F1
Canada considers nickel dumping chrgs vs US 10-24, 924B1
EC rejcts Australia farm import demands 10-30, 862E1
Protectnism seen hurting indl countries 11-28, 933C3
Japan assures on trade surplus 11-29, 933C2
US, Mex OK commodity pact 12-2, 976A2
Canada footwear import curbs protested 12-14, 983C1
GENERAL Atomic Co.
Suit vs United Nuclear OKd 10-31, 835B3
Allied-General Nuclear Services—*See separate listing*
GENERAL Dynamics Corp.
NATO sets F-16 sale review 1-17, 70D3
Wins fed loan guarantee 1-19, 55D1-F2
'74 Turkish jet crash settled 4-14, 312C1
Lewis '76 pay rptd 5-23, 408D3
Electric Boat Division
Trident delay, cost jump rptd 11-29, 920A1 ★

1978

GEISHA, A (film)
Released 6-1, 619B2
GEISS, Edgar Werner
Fined for Nazi salute 7-24, 652B1
GELB, Leslie
At USSR arms sales talks 12-5—12-15, Admin rift rptd 12-19, 996D3
GELBART, Larry
Movie, Movie released 11-22, 970C2
GELDENHUYS, Gellie
Wins electn 4-5, 269B3
GELDENHUYS, Michael
On Tabalaza death probe 7-21, 633E2
GELINAS, Michel
Loses Quebec by-electn 7-5, 514A3
GELLER, Henry
Named telecommunicatns agency dir 3-28, 270C2
GEMAYEL, Bashir
Disavows Phalangist attack 6-14, 463B2
Vs Unifil south Leb role 6-16, 462B3
GEMAYEL, Pierre
On Palestinians in Leb 5-15, 359E1
PLO seeks accord 11-13, 870A1
GENEEN, Harold S.
Perjury chrgs declined 3-20, CIA cover-up chrgd 3-21, 206D3
On '77 top-paid execs list 5-15, 364F3
GENENTECH Inc.
Insulin from synthetic gene rptd 9-7, 947C3
GENERAL Accounting Office—*See under U.S. GOVERNMENT*
GENERAL Agreement on Tariffs and Trade (GATT) (Argentina, Australia, Austria, Bangladesh, Barbados, Belgium, Benin, Brazil, Burma, Burundi, Cameroon, Canada, Central African Empire, Chad, Chile, Congo, Cuba, Cyprus, Czechoslovakia, Denmark, Dominican Republic, Egypt, Finland, France, Gabon, Gambia, Ghana, Great Britain, Guyana, Haiti, Hungary, Iceland, India, Indonesia, Ireland, Israel, Italy, Ivory Coast, Jamaica, Japan, Kenya, Kuwait, Luxembourg, Malagasy Republic, Malawi, Malaysia, Malta, Mauritania, Mauritius, Netherlands, New Zealand, Nicaragua, Niger, Nigeria, Norway, Pakistan, Peru, Poland, Portugal, Rhodesia, Rumania, Rwanda, Senegal, Sierra Leone, Singapore, South Africa, South Korea, Spain, Sri Lanka, Surinam, Sweden, Switzerland, Tanzania, Togo, Trinidad & Tobago, Turkey, Uganda, U.S., Upper Volta, Uruguay, West Germany, Yugoslavia, Zaire)
Japan pledges tariff cuts 1-13, 26B3
'77 world trade rptd up, $ drop linked 3-13, 443F2
EC delays Australia trade talks 4-14, 310D3
US rebuffs Zenith on import duty 6-21, 491E3
Bonn summit backs talks 7-17, 544E2
US demands farm produce agrmt 9-7, 695D1
Talks, US copper trade actns linked 10-20, 805A1
'73-77 oil consumptn, 1st ½ '78 productn rptd 11-14, 871G1-B2
US, Japan reach agrmt 12-18, 998B1
Talks recess, US-EC dispute cited 12-22, 998A1, C1
GENERAL American Oil Company of Texas
Meadows dies 6-10, 540C3
GENERAL Atomic Co.
United Nuclear wins default judgmt 3-2, 144C1
United Nuclear damage determinatn stay denied 3-20, 206D1
New evidence in United Nuclear case rptd 4-20, 346F2-A3
United Nuclear case documts rule declined by Sup Ct 5-15, 387E3
United Nuclear, Ind & Mich awarded damages 5-16, judge scored 5-17, 366G2
Judge interference re arbitratn rights ruled by Sup Ct 5-30, 430A3
GENERAL Cable Corp.
Automatn Indus purchase planned 3-15, 404F1
US sues re price fixing 9-22, 769A1
GENERAL Dynamics Corp.
'76 tax nonpaymt rptd 1-27, 65G2
8th in '77 defns contracts 3-28, 224G2
Electric Boat Division
Work stoppage on A-subs warned 3-13, temporary accord reached 3-23, 224C1
A-sub contract dispute with Navy settled 6-9, 469A1
Proxmire scores Navy contract setlmt 7-6, 528B3
Navy contract setlmt funded 10-20, 833A2
Utah Development Co.
Australia strike rptd, '77 sales down 7-13, 555C1
Australia coal deal rptd signed 12-11, 963A2

1979

GEISINGER, Elliot
Amityville Horror released 7-27, 819D3
GELBER, Jack
Seduced opens 2-1, 292A3
GELCO Corp.
Interway bid dropped 5-29, 560B2
CTI Intl purchase set 7-16, 560C2
GELL, Marilyn
Library conf held 11-15–11-19, 901E1
GEMAYEL, Bashir
Backs Haddad mil role 4-21, 296F3
GEMAYEL, Pierre
Leb Christn group co-leader 5-16, 378E2
Asks army end Beirut clashes 6-18, 462F1
GEM Packing Co.
Settles '78 beef-price suit 10-22, 985E3
GENEEN, Harold S.
Hamilton quits ITT, Araskog succeeds 7-11, 517B2
GENERAL Accounting Office—*See under U.S. GOVERNMENT*
GENERAL Agreement on Tariffs and Trade (GATT) (Argentina, Australia, Austria, Bangladesh, Barbados, Belgium, Benin, Brazil, Burma, Burundi, Cameroon, Canada, Central African Republic, Chad, Chile, Congo, Cuba, Cyprus, Czechoslovakia, Denmark, Dominican Republic, Egypt, Finland, France, Gabon, Gambia, Ghana, Great Britain, Guyana, Haiti, Hungary, Iceland, India, Indonesia, Ireland, Israel, Italy, Ivory Coast, Jamaica, Japan, Kenya, Kuwait, Luxembourg, Malagasy Republic, Malawi, Malaysia, Malta, Mauritania, Mauritius, Netherlands, New Zealand, Nicaragua, Niger, Nigeria, Norway, Pakistan, Peru, Poland, Portugal, Rumania, Rwanda, Senegal, Sierra Leone, Singapore, South Africa, South Korea, Spain, Sri Lanka, Surinam, Sweden, Switzerland, Tanzania, Togo, Trinidad & Tobago, Turkey, Uganda, U.S., Upper Volta, Uruguay, West Germany, Yugoslavia, Zaire, Zimbabwe)
Carter State of Union Message 1-23, 46G3
'78 record trade value, vol rptd 2-8, 161A1
US House OKs duty waiver bill, talks delay cited 3-1, 159E1
US-Japan talks cite 3-4–3-5, 160C1
Tariff-cutting pact signed, dvpg nations boycott; US reactn 4-12, 273A1-274F1
Carter submits trade bill to Cong 6-19, sets tariff cuts 6-21; House OKs bill 7-11, 541D1-A2
Canada tariff cuts rptd 7-12, 543D1
US Sen OKs trade bill 7-23, Carter signs 7-26, 646F3
GENERAL Assembly (race horse)
2d in Kentucky Derby 5-5, 448E2, F2
Wins Travers Stakes 8-18, 2d in Marlboro Cup 9-8, 876A3, F3
GENERAL Atomic Co.
Colo A-plant dispute rptd settled 4-3, 344E2
Arbitratn ruling declined by Sup Ct 10-9, 784E1
GENERAL Atomic Co. v. United Nuclear Corp.
Case declined by Sup Ct 10-9, 784F1
GENERAL Building Contractors of New York State
Govt minority constructn grants case argued before Sup Ct 11-27, 944G3
GENERAL Cinema Corp.
Life of Brian protests rptd 10-24, 859C2
GENERAL Corp.
Alexander's sentncd re TV import rebates 3-29, 298D3
GENERAL Crude Oil Co.
Mobil to buy 3-28, 282G3
GENERAL Dynamics Corp.
Quebec seeks asbestos unit takeover 5-2, 352E2
7th-Day Adventist firing case declined by Sup Ct 6-4, 439A2
Quebec takeover halted pending suit 6-27, 484F2
Quebec unit loses takeover suit, talks vowed 7-25, 563A1
1st in '78 defns contracts 8-1, 609A1
PQ sees as last takeover 9-6, 750D1
Quebec final offer spurned, takeover prepared 10-4, 771D3
Quebec unit wins stay 12-13, 949A1

1980

GEISSLER, Ina
Wins Olympic medal 7-21, 623C3
GEJDENSON, Samuel
Elected to US House 11-4, 842D2, 848D1
GELB, Leslie H.
Chrgs State Dept A-strategy exclusn 8-13, 630E2
GELDENHUYS, Gen. Jan
Calls Angola raids SWAPO operatn 7-2, 524G3
GEMAYEL, Bashir
Daughter killed in bomb blast 2-23, 140E3
Phalangists defeat NPL 7-7—7-8, 524E1
Rival head calls 'ruthless' 7-9, 524F1
GEMAYEL, Pierre
Philangists defeat NPL 7-7—7-8; militia merger rptd 7-9, 524E1, G1
GEMINI (play)
Screen versn released 5-2, 416G2
GENEE, Peter
Wrong Move released 1-25, 216G3
GENENTECH Corp.
Backs GE microbe patent Sup Ct ruling 6-16, 453A2
GENENTECH Inc.
Stock offer successful 10-14, 805F3
GENERAL Accounting Office—*See under U.S. GOVERNMENT*
GENERAL Agreement on Tariffs and Trade (GATT) (Argentina, Australia, Austria, Bangladesh, Barbados, Belgium, Benin, Brazil, Burma, Burundi, Cameroon, Canada, Central African Republic, Chad, Chile, Congo, Cuba, Cyprus, Czechoslovakia, Denmark, Dominican Republic, Egypt, Finland, France, Gabon, Gambia, Ghana, Great Britain, Guyana, Haiti, Hungary, Iceland, India, Indonesia, Ireland, Israel, Italy, Ivory Coast, Jamaica, Japan, Kenya, Kuwait, Luxembourg, Malagasy Republic, Malawi, Malaysia, Malta, Mauritania, Mauritius, Netherlands, New Zealand, Nicaragua, Niger, Nigeria, Norway, Pakistan, Peru, Poland, Portugal, Rumania, Rwanda, Senegal, Sierra Leone, Singapore, South Africa, South Korea, Spain, Sri Lanka, Surinam, Sweden, Switzerland, Tanzania, Togo, Trinidad & Tobago, Turkey, Uganda, Upper Volta, Uruguay, U.S., West Germany, Yugoslavia, Zaire, Zimbabwe)
US revamps trade bureaucracy 1-2, 94A3
Wyndham-White dies 1-27, 104G3
UK seeks EC curbs on fibers 2-5, 125F1
Mexico bars entry 3-18, 234A1
US-India talks fail 8-26, 670G3
'80 global trade lag seen; oil prices, inflatn cited 9-16, 695C3
Japan eases US tobacco tariffs 11-21, 902E1
GENERAL Cinema Corp.
'Cruising' contract dispute cited 2-15, 239B3
GENERAL Dynamics Corp.
FX jet for export OKd 1-4, 16D3
Cruise missile problems rptd 1-7, 16G2
SEC stock suit settled 2-27, 558C1
Boeing wins cruise missile contract 3-25, 228E1
Wins short-range cruise missile contract 4-2, 267B3
Loses Canada contract 4-16, 293D2
Quebec buys UK asbestos cos 5-8, 371F3
1st in '79 defns contracts 5-28, 403C1, E1

1976

GENERAL Electric Co.
ABP, ex-offcl found guilty 1-21, 78B3
Loses appeal on EEOC suit 1-23, 70D3
3 A-engineers quit re safety 2-3, 115A1
'75 arms sales listed 2-6, 147C2
NYS scores PCB pollutn 2-9, 171E3
On '75 Fortune 500 list 437B1, D1, F2
Seeks NRC A-licenses 5-10; protest suit rptd 5-30, 387E1
Paris group wins S Africa A-plant deal 5-28, 387F2
3-yr contract agreed 6-27, 536G3
Signs PCB pact with NYS 9-8, 691F2-B3
Wider gene research rules urged 9-22, 860E3
Med unit boycott rpt released 10-18, 785G3
B-1 contract awarded 12-2, 942E1
Sup Ct vs mandatory pregnancy benefits 12-7, 920D1
Trust suit dropped 12-10, 988C2
Merges with Utah Intl, new co set 12-16, 984G3
Top fscl '76 defns contractor 12-21, 961A3

GENERAL Foods Corp.
Bars boycott compliance 3-18, 747B2
FTC chrgs price cutting 7-16, 989B3

GENERAL Motors Corp.
Rptd vs price hikes 1-16, 280B3
'75, 4th ¼ profits rptd 2-3, 215E3
'75 arms sales listed 2-6, 147A3
US may buy Ger tank 2-12, 183C2
Bars boycott compliance 3-18, 747B2
FTC chrgs crash parts monopoly 3-22, 989E3
Wins warranty-fraud case, other suits pending 4-1, 287D1
Workers win Trade Act aid 4-14, 4-26, 348E2-A3
Layoffs rptd 4-15, 280G2
On '75 Fortune 500 list 437A1, D1, F2
US ends car dumping probe 5-4, 321C2
Total Trade Act aid rptd 6-7, 431B2
UAW contract talks open 7-19, 570F1
Hikes '77 car, truck prices 8-25, 647A1
Dow falls re prices 8-26, 846G3
UK div-Bulgaria pact rptd 9-8, 910E2
Rpts big-car price hikes 9-21, 747F2
EPA fuel-econ ratings, table 9-22, 766G1-770B2
Productn cutbacks rptd 10-25, rebates offered 11-10, 885A2
Australia GM-H to expand 10-31, 870B1
UAW sets strike deadline 11-8, 847C3
Chrysler wins tank contract 11-12, 941C3
UAW pact set after 'mini-strike' 11-19, 887C1
Nov sales rptd up 12-3, 987G2
UAW ratifies pact 12-8, 991E1
UAW wins La plant vote 12-22, 991D1
3 convicted in warranty-fraud case 12-23, 988E1

1977

GENERAL Electric Co.
US bars Israel jet sale to Ecuador 2-7, 87C3
Finds PCB replacemts 2-7, 95G1 ★
Utah Intl purchase cited 2-18, 274F2
Jones anti-inflatn role rptd 4-15, 298G3
On '76 Fortune 500 list; Utah Intl merger cited 340E1, 341A1
Utah takeover cited in merger table 880F1
US backs Egypt aircraft aid 9-15, 698D1
Hitachi joint TV venture set 12-7, 974B2
Jones on Miller selection 12-28, 1000B3

GENERAL Foods Corp.
Raises ground coffee price 1-20, 74F2
Raises coffee prices 2-19, 3-3, 168D3
Vega, Astre productn end set 3-15, 463D3
Coffee prices raised 3-16, 209G1
Mellow Roast test-mkt set 4-4, 319F1
Coffee price cut 4-14, 458D1
Coffee prices raised 4-18, 319B1
Sued on cereal ads 6-30, 613B2
Cuts coffee price 10-17, 876F2

GENERAL GMC Trucks v. General Motors Corp.
Ga franchise rule review refused 12-12, 960E2

GENERAL Mills, Inc.
Calif weight-labeling rules curbed 3-29, 277B1

GENERAL Motors Corp.
'76 productn, sales rptd up 1-3, 1-6, 38E3, 39A1
Hikes car prices 1-3, 155F3
Extends rebate 1-11, 39B1
Air bag test program set 1-18, 213D2
Action vs TV violence prgrms rptd 2-15, 157F3
To promote S Africa equality 3-1, 160G2
EPA orders Cadillac recall 3-22, 252A3
Rpts payoffs 3-31, 503A2
Drops rotary engine project 4-12, 409D1
Murphy vs Admin auto emissn stand 4-18, 322B3
Paris protesters evicted 4-18, 328D3
Murphy on Carter energy plan 4-21, 320E1
Engine switch controversy setlmt offer, NY suit resolved 4-25, 325F3
On '76 Fortune 500 list 340D1, D3
Edward Cole dies 5-2, 452E2
Australia sales slump rptd 5-4, 389E1
Brazil unit lays off 400 5-6, 524G2
Christ TV film to be shown annually 5-16, 395G2
Sup Ct declines Ford complaint vs FTC 5-16, 419E2
Murphy '76 pay rptd 5-23, 408E3
May new-car sales up 6-3, 463C3
Arabs drop boycott threat 6-19, 511D3
21 cos in S Africa equality plan 6-20, 536A1
Air bag order reactn 6-30, 522C1
Australia layoffs rptd 7-13, 560G3
2d ¼ record profits rptd 8-15, 668F3
June dividend paymt hike rptd 8-17, 629G1
'78 prices hiked 8-23, Chevette cut 9-15, 722B3
Stock price rptd down 8-29, 691A2
Aug new-car sales rptd up 9-6, 722G2
Chevrolet tops Calif June car sales 9-6, 722B3
Diesel Olds, small mid-sized cars unveiled 9-13, 722G3-723B1
EPA fuel-econ ratings issued 9-19, 723D3
Hikes '78 mid-sized car prices 9-30, 859G1
3d ¼ record profits, sales rptd 10-27, 11-14, 918C2
Ga franchise case review refused 12-12, 960E2
$40 mil engine switch paymt, warranty extensn rptd 12-17, 1007E3

1978

GENERAL Electric Co. (GE)
In Dow Jones indl avg 66E2
Gene-spliced microbe patent upheld 3-2, 187D1
5th in '77 defns contracts 3-28, 224F2
Pan Am buys Lockheed jets 4-4, 264F2
Eastn buys airbuses, gets loan 4-6, 264C3
Jones sees Carter, backs inflatn plan 4-20, 361G3
On '77 Fortune 500 list 5-8, 325E1
EEOC complaint setld 6-15, 1006B3
Utah Intl acquisitn cited 9-7, 700D2
5th-ranked cash-rich US co 9-18, 716E3
Jones backs Carter inflatn plan 10-25, 806C3

GENERALE Occidentale S.A.
Cavenham's Grand Union to buy Colonial Stores 8-1, 718A1

GENERAL Foods Corp.
In Dow Jones indl avg 66E2
Ferguson sees Carter, backs inflatn plan 4-20, 361G3
Maxwell House sets Uganda coffee boycott 5-17, 416E3
Burger Chef earthworm rumor rptd 11-16, 942A2
C G Mortimer dies 12-25, 1032C3

GENERAL Motors Corp. (GM)
In Dow Jones indl avg 66E2
'77 sales gain rptd 1-5, 4D3
John Gordon dies 1-6, 96B2
'77, 4th ¼ record profits rptd 2-6, 282F3
Chevelle crash liability set at $2.5 mln 2-9, 185E3
Argentina productn rptd suspended, mfg halt weighed 2-24, 310B2
1st Cadillac dealership closes 3-1, 142F3 ★
Small car prices hiked 3-24, 283C3
$170,000 EPA fine OKd 3-27, 263B3
Tax fraud probe ordrd ended 4-5, 284B1
Murphy sees Carter, backs inflatn plan 4-20, 361A3
Prices hiked, Strauss backs; price strategy altered 4-28, 361C3, 362B2
Chevette fails fed safety tests 5-4, 366A1
Heads '77 Fortune 500 list 5-8, 325D1
Meany scores price hike 5-10, 361E3
Murphy on '77 top-paid execs list 5-15, 364G3
Vows '78 exec pay curb 5-19, 427C3
Small-car prices hiked 5-26, 428A2
S Africa guidelines expanded 7-5, 632F3
Argentina operatns to end 8-4, 793B2
'78, '79 model price hikes rptd 8-18, 665F1-A2
S Africa plant integratn plan set 8-29, 742G2
Nader scores Vega safety 8-30, 719F1
UAW southn plant pact set 9-11, 699B3
Sues to block FTC probe 9-11, 768C1
Cuts '79 sporty car prices 9-13, 936A2
EPA fuel-econ ratings issued 9-15, 719B3
3d-ranked cash-rich US co 9-18, 716E3
AMC UAW sign 2-yr pact 9-25, 737B3
Murphy scores Carter 'export consequences' order 10-10, 804B3
Carter inflatn plan reactn 10-25, 806A3
Hikes '79 model prices 11-6, 936F1
Price compliance pledged 12-1, 934B3, F3
Calif auto franchise law upheld by US Sup Ct 12-5, 959D3
Nov sales rise rptd 12-6, 935E3
Hikes '79 model prices 12-22, 1004D1

Vauxhall Motors Ltd.
2 plants bar strike 10-23, 10-24, 816D1

1979

GENERAL Electric Co. (GE)
In Dow Jones indl avg 72E1
Wilmington uranium theft 1-26, worker chrgd 2-1, 119F3
Cox merger agreed 2-21, 188C2-A3
China Syndrome scored 3-13, 246F3
'78 microbe patent rule reaffirmed 3-29, 265F2
UAL orders French-US engines 3-29, 309B1
On '78 Fortune 500 list 5-7, 304E1, 305A1
IUE talks cited 5-31, 399D3
2 unions ratify contract 7-11, 598C2
5th in '78 defns contracts 8-1, 609C1
Spain issues A-plant permit 8-25, 670C3
Argus sues 8-28, 986C1
Microbe patent case accepted by Sup Ct 10-29, 884D1

GENERAL Energy Corp.
McCoy Elkhorn Coal Corp.
Ohio coal-use ruling issued 5-7, 351E1

GENERAL Foods Corp.
In Dow Jones indl avg 72F1
Dow Jones index revised 6-28, 481B3
FTC trust suit environmt statemt sought 10-9, 810A1

GENERAL Mills Inc.
CPG toy unit settles FTC chrg 5-23, 596G1
FTC trust suit environmt statemt sought 10-9, 810A1

GENERAL Motors Corp. (GM)
In Dow Jones indl avg 72F1
'78 sales, mkt share rise rptd 1-5, 5B1
Diesel exhaust rule protested 1-10, 16C3
Canada unit ruled liable for defects 1-25, 95D3
Frigidaire sold to White 1-31, 131A3
Australia unit rpts '78 loss, expansn plans 2-6, 94E3
Vauxhall '78 profit rptd 2-16, 135G2
Australia eases local content rule, plant constructn plans cited 2-22, 133E2
Mkt share rptd up 2-23, 188E1
Tax probe plea declined by Sup Ct 2-26, 164G2
US auto use threat seen 3-10, 188A1
Brazil metalworkers strike 3-13–3-27, 328C3
US regulatory costs rptd 3-29, 230C3
Prices hiked 3-31, 305E2
Trucking stoppage over 4-10, 262D2
Heads '78 Fortune 500 list 5-7, 304E1, D3-305A1
Car-radio trust suit settled 5-14, 441F3-442A1
'Car of the future' plan set 5-18, 441D3
Estes in Spain 6-5, plant agrmt reached 6-6, 428A2
EPA emissns dispute setld 6-5, 441F2
Eur expansn plans detailed 6-11, 555F1, A3
Dow Jones index revised 6-28, 481B3
Iran interests natlzd 7-5, 503A3
UAW opens contract talks, scores Okla City dispute 7-16, 598A1, D1
UAW wins Okla City organizing vote 7-19, 598G1
Murphy vs Chrysler aid, asks fed regulatn reform 8-2, 576G3
UAW bars Chrysler wage freeze plea 8-3, 662D3
GMAC buys Chrysler receivables 8-14, 663C2
Brazil alcohol fuel dvpt plan set 8-18, 871D2
Cash rebates barred 8-22, Aug sales rptd 9-5, 663A3, D3
UAW job action scored 8-22, 831A3
UAW stages 'ministrikes' 8-23–8-27, 698E2
UAW targets in contract talks 8-30, 9-10; accord reached 9-14, signed 9-19, 698A1
Japan interests cited 9-7, 745E3
Australia energy reserves seen abundant 9-13, 705C3
UAW pact provisn disclosed 9-18; contract rptd ratified, Kahn vs 9-30, 744F1
'80 model prices hiked 10-1, 963F3
Sept sales rptd down 10-4, 806A2
UAW, Chrysler reach accord 10-25, 805F2
3d 1/4 profits, sales down 10-25, 806B1; drop cited 10-31, 923C1
FTC challenge declined by Sup Ct 11-5, 884G2
Oct, Nov sales slump rptd 11-6, 12-5, 963F2
Rebates set 11-13, 963A3
Layoffs set 12-4, 964B3

GENERAL Public Utilities Corp.
Dividend, salaries cut 4-26, 322B2
Revolving credit line approved 6-19, 519A1

Jersey Central Power and Light Co.
Oyster Creek A-plant reopening set 5-30, 610A1
Rate hike rptd granted 6-19, 519B1

Metropolitan Edison Co. (Met Ed)
3 Mile Island accident 3-28; radiatn released; explosn, meltdown feared 3-28–4-3; Carter visits 4-1, 241A1-246C1
3 Mile I errors, clean-up detailed; crisis declared over 4-4–4-9; Carter forms probe panel 4-5, rate hike recissn urged 4-9, 259F2-261G2
3 Mile I NRC transcripts released 4-12, 275D2
3 Mile I reactor shutdown starts, suits filed 4-13–4-18; rate hike suspended 4-19, 274F2, D3, 275D1
3 Mile I No 1 x-ray flaws rptd 4-18, 275F1

1980

GENERAL Electric Co. (GE)
In Dow Jones indl avg 76F1
Upjohn microbe patents case remanded by Sup Ct 1-14, 37D1
Microbe patents case cited 3-5, 318B1
Curtiss-Wright suit partial setlmt upheld 4-22, 344C1
Cox drops merger plans 4-25; FCC OKs merger 4-28, 386E1
On '79 Fortune 500 list 5-5, 290E1
4th in '79 defns contracts 5-28, 403E1
Microbe patent upheld by Sup Ct; reactn 6-16, 452F3-453A2
Ala A-plant shutdown fails 6-28; NRC orders reactors probed 7-7, 551G1-C2
Hudson R dump site cleanup OKd 9-24, 825E2
US bars engine export to Iraq 9-25, 719B1
Arab boycott data released 10-20, 801B1
Welch to replace Jones as chrmn, chief exec 12-19, 986G2

GENERAL Foods Corp.
In Dow Jones indl avg 76F1
'79 top TV advertiser 4-4, 376A2
Coffee prices rptd soft 10-6, 777B3

GENERAL Footwear Co.
'Bionic' trademark case declined by Sup Ct 3-31, 291D3

GENERAL Footwear Co. v. American Footwear Co.
Case declined by Sup Ct 3-31, 291E3

GENERAL Mills Inc.
'79 top TV advertiser 4-4, 376B2
Atwater named chief exec 12-16, 959E1

GENERAL Motors Corp. (GM)
In Dow Jones indl avg 76F1
Prices hiked 1-2, 14D2
'79 sales rptd down 1-4, 14C2
Cadillac plant shut 1-10, more layoffs barred 1-14, 35A1
Exxon '79 profits rptd 1-25, 90B3
St Louis, Pontiac plants to close, replacemt sites set 1-31, 287B2
Jan sales rptd up 2-5, 127A3
Nader libel case declined by Sup Ct 2-19, 131F1
Eur plants set 2-20, 125A3
Diesel exhaust rule scored 2-21, 146B1, C1
Chevette, Citatn pass crash test 2-28, 225A2
Ford Pinto trial evidence cited 3-13, 186C1
Productn cuts, layoffs rptd 3-27, 4-16, 287A2
Prices hiked 4-1, 288B1
Mar sales rptd down 4-3; rebates cited for Jan, Feb sales rise 4-4, 287A3, C3
'79 top TV advertiser 4-4, 376B2
Mich plant cancer rate rptd 4-22, 357A1
1st 1/4 profits plunge 4-22, 384C1
18,000 white-collar layoffs set 4-25, 383G3
On '79 Fortune 500 list 5-5, 290E1, 291A1
Chrysler K-car plans rptd 5-10, 383F2
Bieber elected to UAW post 6-4, 457B2
May sales plunge rptd 6-5, 481E3
Worker layoffs rptd 6-21, 481F3
S Africa strike ends 6-25, 499C2
Vauxhill rpts '79 loss 7-1, 498F1
Australia unit to shut plant 7-1, 543A1
Prices hiked 7-1, 556D2
Canada May, June sales down 7-5, 520A3
June sales rptd down 7-6, 556C2
'85 fuel-efficient cars pledged 7-9, 556C3
2d 1/4 losses rptd 7-24, 574A1
FTC chrgs defect notificatn failure 8-8, 702A3
Worker US jobless aid OKd 8-14, 647F3
Reagan sees auto execs 9-2, 664E2
Aug sales rptd down 9-4, 701G2
Detroit tax revenue drop rptd 9-8, 743G2
Worker layoffs rptd 9-11, 701A3
AMC-UAW pact set 9-17, 725C1
IBH buys Terex; GM to buy shares 9-28, 746A2
Sept sales rptd down 10-6, 784F2
3d 1/4 loss rptd 10-27, 823C1
Oct sales rptd down 11-4, 857B1, C1
UK unit losses soar 11-6, 886G2
Ct blocks ND synfuels projct 12-8, 962B1

GENERAL Public Utilities Corp.
Sues Babcock & Wilcox 3-25, 249B1
3 Mile I anniv protest held 3-28, 249B1
3 Mile I cleanup aid asked, estimates revised 8-9, 649A3
3 Mile I cleanup costs revised 11-10; NRC lists aid optns 11-28, Phila Electric backs cost sharing 12-10, 961A1
$4 bln sought from NRC 12-8, 960E3-961A1

Metropolitan Edison Co. (Met Ed)
3 Mile I radioactive water leaks 2-11, 128E1
Bechtel to repair 3 Mile I 2-12, 128G1
NRC lists aid optns 11-28, 961B1

1976

GENERAL Telephone & Electronics Corp.
SEC lists forgn paymts 5-12, 727D1
GENERAL Tire & Rubber Co.
SEC sues, settles 5-10, 359B3-360E2
SEC lists paymts, probe 5-12, 726A1, 727D1
Mex unit admits payoff 5-19, 419D3
Intl Co boycott rpt released 10-19, 786D1
RKO General Inc.
SEC suit vs Gen Tire setld 5-10, 360A2
GENETIC Experimentation, Committee on
Formed 10-14, 891D3
GENETICS
Cong OKs research funds 4-12, 282F2
NIH issues research rules 6-23, 735E3
Harvard DNA research halted 7-7, 736B1
MIT rpts bacterial gene synthesis 8-28, 735F2
Wider DNA rules urged 9-22, 860B3, C3 ★
DNA research com formed 10-14, 891D3
NYS holds gene research hearing 10-21, 860E3
NIH DNA research stand cited 11-1, 891F3
Environmt attys urge DNA regulatn 11-11, 891G3
Trofim Lysenko dies 11-20, 970D2
GENSCHER, Hans-Dietrich
In Portugal 2-4—2-5, 143A1
CDU wins Lower Saxony revote 2-6, 157G2
Meets Sadat 3-29—4-2, 275A1
Sees S Africa forgn min 6-22, 447A3
Meets Kissinger 7-15, 530F2
SPD-FDP wins electns 10-3, reaffirms alliance 10-5, 754F2
GENTRY, Curt
Helter Skelter on best seller list 1-25, 80C3; 2-29, 208F3
GEO Dynamics Oil and Gas Inc.
SEC sues 6-1, 984D2
GEORGALAS, George
Arrested 12-16, 1004D2
GEORGE Prince (Mississippi ferryboat)
Norwegian tanker collisn 10-20, 876G1
GEORGETOWN University (Washington, D.C.)
Prof denied Sovt visa 10-31, 907F3

1977

GENERAL Refractories Co.
'76 Fortune 500 lists drops 341D1
GENERAL Services Administration—*See under U.S. GOVERNMENT*
GENERAL Signal Corp.
Unit chrgd re Arab boycott 1-7, 167A2
GENERAL Telephone & Electronics Corp.
Pl paymts cited in SEC suit 1-12, 79C2, F2-D3
Hughes Indonesia payoffs chrgd 1-25; govt probes 2-4, 2-14, 182A3
SEC paymts suit setld 1-27, 79G1
Sylvania Japan probe plea OKd 3-23, 318C3
Japan TV export limit OKd 5-18, 416D1
US bars Israel-Sylvania project 6-22, 511E1
Sylvania retail sales rules upheld 6-23, 539G1
Sylvania consent pact OKd 7-14, 587E1
Refunds, rate cuts ordrd 9-13, 839A2
GENERAL Tire & Rubber Co.
EEOC suit vs Frontier Air rptd 3-15, 279B2
Frontier jet hijacked 10-20, 807F3
O'Neil, others to repay illegal pol gifts 10-27, 860A2
GENETIC Research, Coalition for Responsible
Formed 3-7, 184E2
GENETICS
Herbert Fowler dies 1-2, 84A3
Cambridge ends DNA resrch ban 2-7, 103C2
DNA research curbs scored 2-22, 184F1
Jensen AAAS honors scored 2-23, 183C3
Viral DNA sequence completed 2-24, 184C1
DNA patent order lifted 2-24, 184A2
NAS forum on DNA resrch 3-7—3-9, 184D2
Research coalition formed 3-7, 184D2
NIH lab plans rptd 3-8, 184G2
EPA backs DNA resrch rules 3-8, 184B3
Admin backs DNA curbs 4-6, 451F3
USTA rejcts Richards sex test 4-12, 354D1
Insulin gene reproductn rptd 5-23, 451D3
DNA risk-assessmt mtg backs research, dispute continues; Kennedy offers compromise bill, legis rptd stalled 6-17—10-27, 846D2-847C1
1st microbe patent granted 10-6, DNA link denied 10-11, 847D1
Hormone made from bacteria 12-1, 1022G2
NIH meets on DNA rule revisn 12-15—12-16, 1022A2
Harvard DNA research halted 12-15, 1022D2
GENEVA Committee—*See under DISARMAMENT*
GENNARO, Peter
Wins Tony 6-5, 452D1
GENOCIDE
Carter to seek UN conv ratificatn 3-17, 186G1
GENSCHER, Hans-Dietrich
Meets party ldrs re Baader trial 3-18, 260A2
GEOGRAPHIC Society, National—*See NATIONAL Geographic Society*
GEOLOGICAL Survey—*See under U.S. GOVERNMENT—INTERIOR*
GEOLOGY
Calif land swell chng rptd 3-3, 288G1
George Barbour dies 7-11, 604E2
GEOMAN Services Inc.—*See GULF Oil*
GEOPHYSICAL Union, American
Coal impact on climate questnd 5-31, 499E1
GEORGETOWN Steel Corp.
Dumping chrgs probed 10-19, 933A3
GEORGETOWN Texas Steel Corp.
Dumping chrgs probed 10-19, 933A3
GEORGETOWN University (Washington, D.C.)
Coal-burning plant set 3-4, 278C1
'77-78 med student costs rptd 3-27, 483G1
Kissinger lecture 4-5, 247B2
Kissinger to teach 6-2, 532B2
CIA mind-control test revealed 8-4, 611B1

1978

GENERAL Services Administration—*See under U.S. GOVERNMENT*
GENERAL Signal Corp.
Leeds stake bought 6-22, merger planned 7-7, 553E1, B2
GENERAL Telephone Co. of California—*See GENERAL Telephone & Electronics Corp.*
GENERAL Telephone Co. of California v. California Public Utilities Commission
Case refused by Sup Ct 12-11, 981F1
GENERAL Telephone & Electronics Corp.
Berkey wins trust suit vs Kodak 1-21, 67E1
ITT wins trust suit 3-1, 510A3
Calif Gen Telephone refund case refused by US Sup Ct 12-11, 981E1
GENERAL Theological Seminary (N.Y., N.Y.)
Gutenberg Bible sold 4-7, 295E2
GENET, Jean
Blacks opens 5-24, 887C1
GENETICS
DNA yeast transfer rptd 1-21, 333F3
GE microbe patent upheld, '77 Upjohn ruling cited 3-2, 187D1
March of Dimes halts grants 3-8, 744C2
US-OKd recombinant DNA lab opens in Md 3-17, 334E3
China dvpt plan outlined 5-28, 436F1
Intellignc dvpt study rptd 7-8, 1023D2
'Test-tube baby' delivered 7-25, 597D1
US urges Sovt conf boycott 8-16, meets 8-21—8-30, 670D2
Human insulin from synthetic gene rptd 9-7, 947B3
Sickle cell anemia findings rptd 9-28, 11-4, 948C1
3 win Nobel 10-12, 886E2
Multi-parent mouse created 10-14, 1023A3
Muscular distrophy test rptd 10-19, 948B1
Mammalian gene transfer rptd 10-28, 1023B3
HEW OKs new recombinant DNA rules 12-16, advisory com expanded 12-27, 1022F3-1023E1
GENEVA Committee—*See under DISARMAMENT*
GENEVA Peace Conference—*See MIDDLE EAST—EGYPT-Israel Peace Moves*
GENEVA World Intellectual Property Organization
Patent accord takes effect 6-1, 506B3
GENN, Leo
Dies 1-26, 96B2
GENOCIDE
Carter urges Sen ratify UN conv 12-6, 934B1
GENOUD, Francois
Goebbels diary on W Ger best-seller list 1-2, 22C1
GENOVES, Andre
Barocco released 4-7, 618B3
GENSCHER, Hans-Dietrich
Retains W Ger forgn affairs post 2-3, 93A3
At Namibia mtg 2-11—2-12, sees progress 2-13, 113G3
Sees Schmidt, Baum named interior min 6-6, 456C3
GENTLEMAN Tramp, The (film)
Released 4-26, 619B2
GENTRY, John N.
Named coal-strike bd of inquiry chrmn 3-6; hearing held 3-8, deadlock rptd 3-9, 159B2, E3
GEOLOGICAL Survey—*See under U.S. GOVERNMENT—INTERIOR*
GEOLOGY
US survey device sale to China rptd 6-9, 436G1
GEORGE Jackson Brigade
2 convicted in Ore, Washn bombings, bank robberies 7-11, 824A3
GEORGE Prince (Mississippi ferryboat)
'76 collisn rpt issued 5-17, 460B1
GEORGES, George
Arrested in Brisbane protest march 10-30, 866B1
GEORGES Bank
US-Canada fishing dispute rptd 6-2—6-5, 425B2
GEORGETOWN University (Washington, D.C.)
Texas wins NIT 3-21, 272A2
Cancer treatmt with neutron beam rptd 6-13, 598F2
GEORGE Washington University (Washington, D.C.)
Students obtain Agnew papers 3-3, 164F3
Sterilization study rptd 4-15, 598D2
Cancer treatmt with neutron beam rptd 6-13, 598F2

1979

3 Mile I reaches shutdown, NRC orders other Babcock plants closed, 4-27, 321D3-322D2
NRC, 3 Mile I operators testify 4-30, 5-7; blast danger, radiatn levels rptd 5-1, 5-5, 344E1-E2
Babcock blames for 3 Mile I accident 6-5, 518B3
3 Mile I clean-up proposed 7-17, 629F2
NRC: 3 Mile I accident preventable; reactn 8-2, 609G1-D2
3 Mile I reactor No 1 shutdown extended 8-9, 629F3
NRC fines $155,000 10-26, 826F1-E2
3 Mile I comm final rpt scores, reactn 10-30, 325G3-326E1
License challenged, rate hike asked 11-1, 826E2
3 Mile I coal shift studied 11-5, 849C2
GENERAL Services Administration—*See under U.S. GOVERNMENT*
GENERALE Occidentale
CGE share acquisitn rptd 3-16, 236B2
GENERAL Telephone Co. of California v. California Public Utilities Commission
Case refused by Sup Ct 10-1, 768D1; 10-15, 848C1
GENERAL Telephone & Electronics Corp. (GTE)
Ex-chrmn Power dies 3-11, 272E3
Kodak trust award re Sylvania upheld 6-25, 517G2
Argus sues Sylvania 8-28, 986C1
Calif Gen Telephone refund stay refused by Sup Ct 10-1, 768D1; appeal denied 10-15, 848C1
GENERAL Tire & Rubber Co.
Allied Chem indicted on kickbacks 4-17, 985B3
625 S African blacks fired 11-22, 899D3, G3
RKO General Inc.
FCC doubts license fitness 7-18, 618G1
GENERIC Drugs—*See MEDICINE-Drugs*
GENETICS
MS, depressn linked 1-4, 289E3
Alcoholism linked 1-5, 289C3
Colo radium waste sites rptd 3-5, 187G1
GE, Upjohn microbe patents reaffirmed 3-29, 265F2
Low-level radiatn risks assessed 5-2, 609E2
Surviving ape hybrid rptd 7-21, 692B2
WCC issues statemt 7-24, 640F1
Mammal cloning advance rptd 7-28, 692E2
Mutatn, radiatn link disproved in mouse experimts 7-28, 692F2
Kidney cancer, linked to chromosome defect 9-13, 735B2
Pot use risks rptd 10-14, 972C1
DNA alternate structure rptd 12-13, 1000E2
GENEVA Committee—*See under DISARMAMENT*
GENGLER, Nancy
Loses natl women's intercollegiate squash title 3-4, 527D2
GENIN, Maurice
Credit Lyonnais resignatn rptd 2-3, 96G2
GENNARO, Peter
Carmelina opens 4-8, 711A2
GENOVESE, Vito
NJ indicts 8 in crime family 5-23, 508G1
GENSCHER, Hans-Dietrich
Backs common NATO policy re SALT III 5-30, 415E3
FDP backs A-power 6-16, 489B3
Meets Dayan 9-10; Palestinian rights stand scored, Bonn denies tilt 9-11, 677B1
Warns USSR on anti-missile drive 11-4, 880D3
Gromyko sees, warns vs NATO missiles 11-21-11-24, 938A3
GENT, Peter
North Dallas Forty released 8-1, 820D2
GEOFFRION, Bernie (Boom Boom)
Quits as Canadiens coach 12-12, 1004E1
GEOLOGICAL Survey—*See under U.S. GOVERNMENT-INTERIOR*
GEOPHYSICAL Union, American
Conf held 5-28—5-29, 691B3, 692A1
GEORGE, George W.
Bedroom Farce opens 3-29, 711D1
Rich Kids released 8-17, 820B3
GEORGE, Phyllis
Husband wins primary 5-29, 420D1
Husband elected gov 11-6, 846D2
GEORGES Bank
Oil-lease ban lifted 2-20, 186F3
Lease sale delayed 11-6, OKd 11-9, 867E1-A2
Lease sale bids placed 12-18, 990G1
GEORGETOWN Steel Corp.
Fed aid cited 8-28, 682F1
GEORGETOWN University (Washington, D.C.)
In Big East basketball conf 5-29, 526G3
Schlesinger gets Strategic Studies post 9-1, 859F3*
GEORGE Washington University (Washington, D.C.)
Forgn student enrollmt listed 167D3

1980

GENERAL Services Administration—*See under U.S. GOVERNMENT*
GENERAL Telephone Co. v. EEOC
Case decided by Sup Ct 5-12, 426G1
GENERAL Telephone & Electronics Corp. (GTE)
Phone industry deregulatn set by FCC 4-7, 370G1
EEOC class actn process avoidance backed by Sup Ct 5-12, 426G1
Philco, Sylvania units sold to N Amer Philips 10-2, 985E2
FCC revises phone deregulatn plan 10-28, 987A3
GTE Communications
Rayfield named pres 7-2, 600G2
GENERAL Tire& Rubber Co.
Rpts public land donatn 12-19, 987F1
RKO General Inc.
FCC lifts 3 TV licenses 1-24, 119F2
FCC backs Westinghouse unit TV license 1-30, 119D3
Cablecom merger set 9-24, 746G1
FCC backs WOR-TV move to NJ 11-6, 906F1
GENESCO Inc.
Jarman dies 9-9, 755D3
Kress liquidatn set 11-6, 986B1
GENETICS
Stuttering link rptd 1-5, 63B3
Interferon rptd produced by gene-splicing 1-16, 62G2, D3
Animal, bacteria differences rptd 1-23, 160B1
DNA experiment rules eased 1-29, 416B2
Va sterilizatn progrm rptd 2-23, 158G3
Crib death link rptd 2-28, 358C3
Shockley rpts Calif sperm bank donatns 2-28, 990D2
Chicken teeth rptd grown 3-8, 415D2
Breast cancer, enzyme link rptd 3-29, 415B3
DNA transfer between living mice rptd 4-3, 415F3
Brain chem productn rptd 5-10, 715F1
Niagara chem dump study rptd 5-16, 386F3
Alcoholism link rptd 6-7, 715G1
GE microbe patent upheld by Sup Ct; reactn 6-16, 452E3-453A2
DNA repair, lifespan link questioned 8-28, 716F1
Human X chromosome fragmts rptd cloned 8-30, 716A2
Forgn gene replicatn in mice rptd 9-13, 716D2
Nobels for medicine announced 10-10, chem 10-14, 889F2, E3
Genentech stock offer successful 10-14, 805G3
GENEVA Committee (U.N. Conference of the Committee on Disarmament) (CD) (formerly ENDC) (Algeria, Argentina, Australia, Belgium, Brazil, Bulgaria, Burma, Canada, China, Cuba, Czechoslovakia, East Germany, Egypt, Ethiopia, France, Great Britain, Hungary, India, Indonesia, Iran, Italy, Japan, Kenya, Mexico, Mongolia, Morocco, Netherlands, Nigeria, Pakistan, Peru, Poland, Rumania, Sri Lanka, Sweden, U.S., USSR, Venezuela, West Germany, Yugoslavia, Zaire)
'80 sessn opens; China joins 2-5, 108A1
'72 germ treaty reviewed 3-3—3-21, 235G2*
USSR '72 biological ban adherence questned by US 3-18, 235C2*
GENOVESE, Eugene D.
Denied Md faculty post 6-12, 638C3
GENOVESE, Vito
Clemente, Fiumara sentncd 5-20, 927F2
GENSCHER, Hans-Dietrich
Urges Sovt Afghan policy chng 1-28, 68E1
Czech visit cancellatn cited 1-30, 103F1
Backs US in Afghan crisis 2-10, 106B3
Sees Vance on Afghan policy coordinatn 2-20, 139A2
Sees Carter re Schmidt Moscow trip 7-2, 489B1
Sees no Cabt switch 10-5, 759E3
Sworn W Ger forgn min 11-5, 925E1
Greets Pope 11-15, 905C1
Warns Sovts on Poland invasn 12-11, 949G1
GENUINE Risk (racehorse)
Wins Ky Derby 5-3; 2d in Preakness 5-17, Belmont Stakes 6-7, 447A2-E2
Named top 3-yr-old filly 12-17, 1002C2
GEOFFROY, Pierre-Paul
Paroled 4-11, 310G3
GEOLOGY
Obituaries
Kennedy, George C 3-18, 279F3
GEOPHYSICS
Planetary core study rptd 6-19, 715A2
GEORGES Bank
Lease bids rptd accepted 1-7, 18A1
Mass State of State message 1-14, 483C3
GEORGETOWN University (Washington, D.C.)
Kennedy addresses 1-28, 74E2
2d in 6,000-m Penn Relays 4-25, 892D2
Duren in NBA draft 6-10, 447G2
Kirkpatrick named to Reagan Cabt 12-22, 979F2

1976

GEORGIA
Primary date set 22B2
Ft Benning mercenary training rptd 1-2, 3B2
US Sup Ct rules in Gwinnett Cnty tax case 1-14, 23G2
Sup Ct sets death sentnc review 1-22, 87A3
Hamilton files bankruptcy 2-20, 166E3
Toxic chem law urged 2-26, 171C3
Atlanta violent crime up rptd up 3-2, 336D3
Atlanta firm loses retroactive seniority suit 3-24, 218E2
Rockefeller sees GOP 4-15, 305E3
Reagan campaigns 4-21, 281B3
Still operator's convictn reinstated 4-21, 331D1
Reagan campaigns in Atlanta 4-28, 323D3
Asbestos found in Atlanta water 4-30, 349F1
Primary results 5-4, 322E2, 323B2
US Sup Ct upholds death penalty 7-2, 491F1
Dem conv women delegates, table 508B2
Dem conv pres vote, table 7-14, 507B2
Carter legis record cited 512D1-D2
Powell stays execution 7-22, 568F2
GOP pre-conv delegate count 8-14, 583B3
GOP conv pres, vp vote tables 8-18—8-19, 599B1, B3
Dole campaigns 9-1, 645F3-646A1
'74-75 Atlanta SATs rptd 9-13, 993G1
Fscl '75 per capita income, tax burden rptd 9-15, 10-12, 959C2
Carter, Ford debate record as gov 9-23, 702C1
Busbee protests Ford Medicaid remark 9-25, 725A2
Ex-gov Griffin backs Ford 9-26, 723C3
US Sup Ct reaffirms death penalty, OKs rape case review 10-4, 746F1
Carter lists '70 campaign donors 10-17, 804E3
Plains church bars black 10-31, 826D3
Election results 11-2: pres 818B1, 819B2; cong 822D1, 829D2; state 822F1
Nonprofit bingo legalized 11-2, 822F1
Carter on St Simons I 11-6—11-11, 845F2
Plains church ends black ban 11-14, 864C2
Blacks attend Plains church 11-21, 881F3
US Sup Ct curbs anti-death juror exclusion 12-6, 920B3
Atlanta heroin deaths rptd 12-12, 972D3
Bell US apptmt disputed 12-20—12-22, 956G2
Atlanta transatlantic air route rejctd 12-28, 992E2
Carter Presidential Campaign—*See CARTER Jr., Jimmy*

GEORGIA, University of (Athens)
Loses Cotton Bowl 1-1, 31C3
GEORGIAN Soviet Socialist Republic—*See 'Republics' under USSR*
GEORGIA-Pacific Corp.
Bars boycott compliance 3-18, 747B2
GEORGINE, Robert A.
Quits Ford construction com 1-8, 4B1
GEORGIOU, Costas (alias Col. Tony Callan)
Angola mercenary executn role rptd 2-8—2-10, 105G2, 106E1
UK blames re executns 2-12, 163G2
Sentenced to die 6-28, 480G1, G2
Executed 7-10, 519A3
GEOTHERMAL Energy—*See EARTH*
GEPHARDT, Richard Andrew
Elected 11-2, 823A3, 830A1
GERALDO, Raymond J.
Averted 5-15, 401D2

1977

GEORGIA
Legislature schedule rptd 6D2
Carter in Plains 1-7, 5B2
Plains church rejects black 1-9, 53C2
NAACP vs Bell 1-10, 59B3
Bell US apptmt controversy continues 1-11—1-20, 34C1
Coll integratn rules ordrd 1-17, 112B2
Peanut Special at Carter inauguratn 1-20, 26D2
Georgians at White House fete 1-21, 53A2
Winter rptd worst in 100 yrs, layoffs re fuel shortage rptd 1-22, 54C2, D2
Low temp cited 2-6, total layoffs rptd 2-7, 91D2, F2
US House seat special electn, runoff set 3-15, 191G3
College integratn rules reordered 4-1, 446D1
Southern Air crash kills 70 4-4, 286A3, 311F2
Fowler wins US House runoff 4-5, 252A1
'76 per-capita income table 5-10, 387E2
Atlanta NHL team to play in '77-78 5-12, 430G1
Shapp fund repaymt ordrd 5-12, 482C2
Atlanta, Savannah business confidence rptd; econ data table 5-16, 384E2, A3
Augusta Bank fails 5-20, 578C1
Ft McPherson cmdr assigned 5-27, 417D2
Carters vacation 5-27, 517D3
Racial adoptn curb review refused 6-20, 517B1
UK air svc pact set 6-22, 500A2
'71 Woodbine chem blast ruling 6-23, 604B1
Carter tax data issued 6-24, 499F2
Atlanta gay rights march 6-26, 560F2
Coll integratn plan issued 7-5, 630G2
Drought-related crop damage rptd 7-28, fed aid OKd 8-24, 659F3
Carter vacations in Plains 8-6, 608D2
Tanzania pres visits agri projcts 8-8—8-9, 624C1
New youth job corps center rptd open 8-31, 692E2
'76 per capita income, tax burden table 9-13, 10-18, 821D2
Overtime suit filed vs A&P 9-27, 778D2
Clifford Roberts kills self 9-29, 788C2
Atlanta reelects Jackson 10-4, 879E1
Jet hijacked 10-20, 807F3
Kelly Barnes dam bursts 11-6, 888F2 • laid to seepage 12-21, 1023E2
Right to sue natl banks affirmed 11-8, 857D1
ERA econ boycott rptd 11-14, 918D1
Farmers protest in Plains 11-25, 916E1
Motor vehicle franchise case review refused 12-12, 960D2
Farm strike backing rptd 12-21, 1003C1
Atlanta 'gateway' air svc OKd 12-21, 1006C2
Delta gets Atlanta-London route 12-21, 1006C2
Lockheed Marietta strike ends 12-29, 1005C2, E2
Crime
US Sup Ct voids search warrant system 1-10, 57E1
Carter nurse gets reprieve 2-3, 354D2
Sup Ct delays Dobbs executn 2-25, 174B3
Kidd acquitted 5-20, 424D1
'77 death row populatn rptd 6-7, 594C1
Atlanta LEAA office to close 6-20, 630E2
Executn for rape barred 6-29, 557C2
Plains KKK rally disrupted 7-2, 540A1
Atlanta Mafia operatns rptd 7-3, 568C2, D2
French Connectn drug figure slain in Atlanta jail 7-26, 642B1
CIA Atlanta prison mind-control tests rptd 8-1—8-9, 611D1
Dawson 5 murder chrgs dropped 12-19, 991B2
Lance Finances—*See LANCE, Thomas B.*

GEORGIA, University of (Athens)
Loses Sugar Bowl 1-1; '76 rankings 1-2, 1-3, 8D3
Vance addresses law schl 4-30, 338C2
GEORGIA-Pacific Corp.
Convictn overturned 1-6, 156F2
GEORGIAN Soviet Socialist Republic—*See USSR—Republics*
GEORGINE, Robert A.
Dem 'hit list' planned 11-30, 961B2
GEOTHERMAL Energy
Carter energy plan 4-20, 293C3, E3
Research authorizatn OKd by Cong 10-20, 833C1
Ownership case review declined 10-31, 835A3
GERARD, Dr. Mark J.
Indicted in horse-switch scandal, pleads not guilty 12-2, 971A1
GERBER Products Co.
Vs Anderson Clayton takeover 4-18; bid ended, stock falls 9-19, 799E1
GERDENER, Theo
Quits New Repub Party 7-22, 600G2
GEREVAS, Ronald E.
Replaced as ACTION assoc dir 8-4, 626A3

1978

GEORGIA
Legislature schedule rptd 14E3
Plains Monitor, Atlanta Gazette '77 sale cited 187B1
'67, '77 sales-tax rates rptd 1-5, 15D3
State govt tax revenue table 1-9, 84C2
Father's role in adoptns limited 1-10, 13C3
US rejcts coll integratn plan 2-2, 85C1
Lance becomes Atlanta TV commentator 2-6, 172F2
US OKs coll integratn plan 3-8, 368G3
Okefenokee Refuge expanded 3-14, 186B3
Atlanta-London air-fare agreed 3-17, 206D2
Juries of less than 6 ruled illegal by US Sup Ct 3-21, 220E3
Ft McPherson cmdr resigns 4-28, 321E2
Stevens settles NLRB suit 4-28, 324G1
Talmadge finances rptd 5-19, small cash gifts admitted 5-21, 385D3, E3
Carter ends Plains visit 5-22, 386G2
Construction pact signed 5-22, 429D3
Rap Brown rptd living in Atlanta 6-15, 844D2
Carter addresses Baptist group mtg in Atlanta 6-16, 510B1
Primary results 8-8, 625B3
Legionnaires' disease suspected in Atlanta 8-8, 635E3
Talmadge repays expense claims 8-18, denies guilt 8-19, 643G3
Carter in Plains 8-19—8-20, 664E1
GM, UAW set plant accord 9-11, 699E3
NASL OKs Colo Caribous sale, Atlanta move 10-3, 969A3
USSR scores Toon Atlanta speech 10-14, 821C1
Lufthansa to serve Atlanta 10-25, 831F1
Election results 11-7: cong 846G1, A3, 848E1, 850A3, 852G1; state 847C1, 852F1, F2, 853E2
US Sen campaign spending rptd 11-15, 898C1
Earthworm rumor hurts fast-food chains 11-16, 942G1
Baxley A-plant rating rptd 11-25, 940D3
Dougherty Cnty schl bd pol rule struck down by Sup Ct 11-28, 937E3
Valdosta schl integratn case declined by US Sup Ct 12-4, 959A2
Carter in Plains 12-21, 1003E1
Crime
Columbus stocking strangler victim found 2-12, 232E3
Flynt shot, mistrial declared 3-6, 186G3
Death sentencing bias rptd 3-6, 389A1, C1
Atlanta inmate slain, probe opens 4-10, 396G2
Kidd, Lingold acquitted; Carter testimony cited 4-21, 309F3
Gulf '70 Carter paymt rptd 6-2, 449D1
Savannah ILA offcl indicted, Atlanta probe rptd 6-7, 480F2
Paperworkers' chief indicted, atty paymts cited 7-19, 599B1
Reidsville prison riot, 3 killed 7-23; prisoner slain 8-16, 627G2
Chatham Cnty, Atlanta jail violence 9-9, 9-21; Reidsville probe indictmts 9-14, 770G3
Newsman killed in Guyana cult ambush flown home 11-21, 891B1
Thevis returned to Atlanta on '70 murder chrg 11-23, 971B2
Lance Finances—*See LANCE, Thomas B.*

GEORGIA, University (Athens)
Loses Bluebonnet Bowl 12-31, 1025F2
GEORGIA Institute of Technology (Atlanta)
Singlaub addresses ROTC 4-27, 321F2
Loses Peach Bowl 12-25, 1025E2
GEORGIAN Soviet Socialist Republic—*See USSR—Republics*
GEORGIA-Pacific Corp.
Gypsum price fixing rule upheld by Sup Ct 6-29, 567G2
GEORGINE, Robert
On A-plant constructn accord 4-18, 281D3
GEOTHERMAL Energy
Carter budgets research 1-23, 46G1
Research authorizatn clears Cong 2-8, 107A2; signed 2-25, 218B2
Govs urge more fed funding 2-27, 145A1
Energy study forecasts growth 5-8, 366E2
Renewable energy study issued 8-25, 718B2
US, Japan plan joint research 9-6, 695D3
Energy bill clears Cong 10-15, 787E2
GEPHARDT, Rep. Richard Andrew (D, Mo.)
Reelected 11-7, 851C2
GERARD, Mark
Convicted in '77 horse switch 9-21, sentncd 11-3, 1028F1
GERBER, Ella
Thread of Scarlet opens 12-8, 1031B3
GERE, Richard
Days of Heaven released 9-13, 970A1
Bloodbrothers released 9-27, 969D3

1979

GEORGIA
ITT Atlanta long-distance phone svc OKd 1-4, 15E2
Med malpractice arbitratn rptd 1-28, 139E3
Atlanta ABA mtg 2-7—2-14, 130C1
B Carter hospitalized in Americus 2-27, 149F2
Dutch firm seeks Life Insurance of Ga 3-23, 942D2
SCLC ousts Williams 4-10, 283G1
Unwed father damage suit bar upheld by US Sup Ct 4-24, 364B1
Atlanta on '78 world's busiest airport list 421C1
Child mental commitmt rules backed by Sup Ct 6-20, 515E3
Truckers' strike impact on peach crop seen 6-28, 479A3
State laws in church land dispute backed by Sup Ct 7-2, 559C1
Stevens, Milledgeville offcls sued by textile union 7-18; offcls settle 8-1, 598E3
Atlanta zoo ape hybrid rptd 7-21, 692B2
Lakewood GM plant struck 8-23—8-27, 698F2
Hurricane David hits Savannah 9-4, 690G3
'78 per capita income rptd 9-16, 746E2
Calif lawyer survey rptd 9-17, 787F1
US sues Sears re job bias 10-22, 885D3
Valdosta judge issues Life of Brian injunctn 10-29, lifts 10-30, 859D1
Atlanta real estate investmt by shah rptd 11-26, 897E3
Carter Personal Issues—*See CARTER—PERSONAL*
Crime & Civil Disorders
Child abuse data rptd 1-26, 93D3
Busbee OKs KKK informant's extraditn 2-7, 120C1
Flynt convctd in retrial 3-28, 240C1
Wildlife refuge protesters jailed 5-4—5-10, 368E1
Green death sentnc vacated by Sup Ct 5-29, 421E3
Minchew pleads guilty to fraud 7-30, 702B2
KKK, NAACP march in Columbus 8-18, 865B1, 866C1
Carswell assaulted in Atlanta 9-11, 859D3
Thevis, 2 others convicted in '78 slaying 10-21, 818G1
2 Atlanta inmates convicted in '77 Papa slaying 10-23, 840B2
Death row populatn rptd 11-25, 989F3
Lance Issues—*See LANCE, Thomas Bertram*
Politics & Government—*See also other appropriate subheads in this section*
Legislature schedule rptd 5C3
B Carter hosts Libyans in Atlanta 1-9, 31D2
Carter marks King death anniv in Atlanta 1-14, 31A3
Talmadge hospitalized for alcoholism 1-22, 176E1
Teng visits Atlanta 2-1, 83D2
Carter in Atlanta 2-20, 122C3
Atlanta fiscal status rptd 3-20, 204F1, C2
FEC clears Carter primary spending 4-2, 265D1
Regulatory bds rptd segregated 4-9, 307A2
B Carter, NBG pres deny peanut-loan, '76 campaign link 4-11, 301C3
Pastor joins Carter staff 4-15, 300E3
B Carter on Libyans' visit 4-15, 310D1
Secy of State Fortson dies 5-19, 432F2
Young press conf in Atlanta 5-25, 400D1
'71 voter statute, black registratn increase cited 8-14, 724F2
Carter speech in Atlanta 8-30, 661B2
Talmadge denounced by US Sen com 9-14, 702B1; US Sen 10-10, 769B1
R Carter campaigns 12-8, 961D3
GEORGIA Institute of Technology (Atlanta)
East wins Japan Bowl 1-14, 63C2
Carter addresses 2-20, 123E2
Morgan scores 3 Mile I A-accident 4-7, 261C1
Ivery, Hill in NFL draft 5-3, 335F2, G2
GEORGIAN, Angelo G.
Named vp of merged union 3-6, 207C1
GEORGIAN Soviet Socialist Republic—*See UNION of Soviet Socialist Republics—Republics*
GEORGIA on My Mind (recording)
Nelson wins Grammy 2-16, 336F3
GEORGIA-Pacific Corp.
Price fixing case refused by Sup Ct 10-1, 768F2
GEOTHERMAL Energy
Carter cuts research budget 1-22, 45F2
US power supplies rptd 5-9, drilling starts 5-14 361F3-362B1
Calif energy plan proposed 5-31, 419A1
Admin plans previewed 7-8, 517E3
Md drilling results poor 7-14, 787B1
GEPHARDT, Rep. Richard Andrew (D, Mo.)
Hosp cost-control amendmt passed 11-15, 883A1
GERARD, Gil
Buck Rogers released 3-29, 528E1
GERE, Richard
Yanks released 9-19, 820G3
Bent opens 12-2, 1007C2

1980

GEORGIA
Harvester strike ends 4-20, 308G2
Atlanta telecast of Saudi film cleared 5-12, 375G3
Atlanta schl integratn ruling upheld by Sup Ct 5-12, 386B3
Drought, heat wave hit; poultry losses rptd 6-23—8-15, 616A2
Carter's mother has hip surgery 10-2, 908E2
Atlanta, Augusta busing, housing integratn study rptd 11-16, 989E3
Carter Personal Issues—*See under CARTER*
Crime & Civil Disorders
Waterfront racketeers sentenced 1-11, 64B2
Lance trial opens 1-14, chrgs reduced 4-9, 291E3
State of State message 1-15, 483B2
Clarkesville mayor convicted in pot ring 2-4, 270E3
Radical protest rptd 3-20, 485A3
2 death penalty appeals declined by Sup Ct 3-24, 265C2
Black rallies spur Wrightsville violence 4-8—4-19, FBI probe rptd 4-14, 332G3
Lance cleared on fund misuse 4-30, 332D3
Death penalty applicatn narrowed by Sup Ct 5-19, 439E3
Wrightsville unrest continues 5-19, 5-22, mtg held 5-23; 18 chrgd 5-29, 490B2
Talmadge finances probe dropped 5-30, 427E3-428A1
Lance case dropped 6-9, 459G2-A3
Potts executn stay issued 6-28, Sup Ct continues stay 6-30, 511F1
Road builders bid-rigging probe rptd 7-5, 655F1
Convicts escape 'death row' 7-28, recaptured in NC 7-30, 654E1
Eastn hijack attempt foiled 8-18, 667G1-A3
Postell, 2 others indicted in 'death row' escape 8-27, 712F2-D3
Delta jet hijacked to Cuba 9-13, 704F1
Univ prof released from jail 9-30, resumes teaching 10-6, 890C3
Atlanta child slayings probe continues; curfew imposed, FBI aid set 10-20—11-6, 927C3-928A1
'Death row' escape extortn chrg 11-8; Postell, wife cleared 11-12, 927A1
Politics & Government—*See also other appropriate subheads in this section*
Legislature schedule rptd 18D1
State of State message 1-15, 483A2
Maddox pension bill fails 2-27, 200A1
Sumter Cnty ruled biased 4-7, 309A2
Voting Rights Act provision upheld by Sup Ct 4-22, 344C1
Primary results 8-5, runoff 8-26, 683B2
Election results 11-4; cong 840E1, 842A3, 845A2, 849F2; state 845E2
Cities conv in Atlanta 12-1, 914D2
'80 census rptd 12-31, 983D1
Presidential Election (& Transition)
Connally fund shortage rptd 2-20, 129D1
Carter, Reagan sweep primary 3-11, 182G3
Reagan seconded at conv 7-16, 529F1
Atlanta mayor vs open conv 8-11, 610A1
Carter in Atlanta 9-16, 698A2
Anderson ballot access challenged 9-23, 9-27, 818B2, D2
Press endorsemts rptd 11-1, 841G3
Election results 11-4, 838A1, E1, 839B2, D3
Sports
NHL club sale, transfer OKd 6-24, 488A2

GEORGIA, University of (Athens)
Dinnan released from jail 9-30, returns to campus 10-6, 890B3
Walker 3d in Heisman Trophy vote 12-1, 999F2
GEORGIAN Soviet Socialist Republic—*See UNION of Soviet Socialist Republics—Republics*
GEORGIA-Pacific Corp.
Price fixing case settled 3-3, 557F3
GEOTHERMAL Energy
France sets new energy measures 4-2, 254D1
US-Mex talks 4-2—4-3, 315A2
Hunts bailout loan collateral listed 5-28, 426D1
GEPHARDT, Rep. Richard Andrew (D, Mo.)
On tax-cut plan 6-26, 480B3
Reelected 11-4, 843D2
GERASSI, John
At anti-US conf in Iran 6-2—6-5, 418D2, 419E1
GERE, Richard
American Gigolo released 2-1, 216A2

1976

GERLOCK, Rev. Edward M.
PI deports 11-18, 890C1

GERMAN Democratic Republic (East)—*See also COMECON, DISARMAMENT—Geneva Committee, WARSAW Pact*
Listed as 'not free' nation 1-19, 20D3
Quake tremors rptd 5-6, 352B3
9th SED Cong: Honecker named secy gen; 5-yr plan OKd 5-18—5-22, 381B1
Social, labor reforms enacted 5-29, 417E1
Pastor dies in protest 8-22, clergy ask religious freedom 9-19, 772C2
Oil tanker sinks off France 10-14, 912E2
Parlt elected 10-17; Honecker named head of state 10-29, 889C1
Zero populatn growth rptd 10-28, 863G1
Poet exiled 11-16; protests 11-17—11-19, 905A2
Profs arrest denied 11-26, dissidents exit 12-10—12-12, 1001E3

Berlin—*See 'West German Relations' below*
European Force Reduction Issues—*see under EUROPE*
Foreign Relations (misc.)
Swiss refugee smuggling rptd 1-26, 85F1
Angola mercenaries rptd 2-1, 82B1
UN Palestine com member 2-26, 162C1
Guyana rpts econ advisors 3-3, 253A2
To join A-safeguards group 3-13, 243G2
USSR, Bonn abandon A-plant 3-30, 243D2
Shuns China fete for Egypt vp 4-19, 275G2
'75 Sovt trade rptd 5-5, 340F3
Cooper quits as US amb 5-17, 412B2
SED Cong lauds USSR 5-18—5-22, Sovt energy investmt rise set 5-21, 381B1, C2
Euro$ loan from US-led group 6-4, 417B2
E, W Eur CP conf 6-29—6-30, 461A1
Danish-French wire constructn pact rptd 7-12, 889C2
Rpt Libya trains terrorists 7-15, 531B2
Rues Italy border shooting 8-6, 589B3
Sovt soldier defects 9-9, 857D1
Swedish-US spy device rptd 9-14, 734G1
Sovt space progrm role set 9-14, 9-15, 684D1
Tito cancels Honecker visit 9-16, 734G2
US OKs grain deal, ships US entry 11-11, 889E1
US Jews to get reparatns 11-22, 889G1
US Jews rejct reparatns 11-23, 949D2
Dow pact rptd signed 11-26, 1001G3
Visa bids blocked 12-12, 1003G3

Nazis—*See under 'N'*
Sports
Winter Olympics results 2-4—2-15, 159A1-B2
14 swim records set 6-1—6-5, 424F3
Olympic results 7-18—7-31, 562B3, 573C3, 574B1-576G3

1977

GERIATRICS—*See AGE & Aged Persons*

GERMAN Democratic Republic (East)—*See also COMECON, DISARMAMENT—Geneva Committee, WARSAW Pact*
Cuba jet crashes, 1 hurt 5-27, 604E1
Single party-state ldr cited 6-16, 469F2
Express train crash kills 29 6-27, 888C3
Writer seized 8-23, 684E1
Riot at music festival 10-8, 782A1
Consumer price subsidies rptd 11-8, 984F1
Pol prisoners listed 11-24, 956A2

Berlin—*See 'West German Relations' below*

Foreign Relations (misc.)—*See also 'Monetary, Trade & Aid' below*
UN Assemb member 4A1
In 14-natn sulphur-dioxide pact 1-19, 109B3
US newsman detained 2-4, 114B3
Spain ties remain broken 2-9, 242G2
Sovt hotel blaze 2-25, 204D2
Danes note Warsaw Pact exercises 426G2
Castro visits 4-2—4-4, 249G1, E3
Zaire chargs rebel support 4-30, cuts ties 5-2, 394F1
USSR asserts E Berlin sovereignty 5-15, 496A3
Chile prisoner exchng 6-18, US intell link rptd 6-20, 476E1
Eurocommunism rptd scored 7-8, 590B3
UK newsman quits defectn try 7-24, 617G2
Bolen confrmd US amb 7-28, 626D2
Africa role rptd 8-21, 684F3
US rights violatns rptd chrgd 9-28, 752B3
USSR slurs spurred in riot 10-8, 782B1
Amnesty Intl chrgs pol prisoners held 10-10, 782D1
Malta premr provokes walkout in Peking 11-3, 925G2
Egypt closes consulates, cultural cntrs 12-7, 929B1, 930B1
Dissident author to visit West 12-19, 984A2
Helsinki Agreement—*See EUROPE—Security and Cooperation*

Monetary, Trade & Aid Issues (including all foreign economic developments)
UK 200-mi fishing zone in effect 1-1, 21A1
UK, US, France vs Berlin visas 1-6, 7E2; lodge USSR protest 1-11, 20F1
USSR oil price rise seen 1-6, 67D3
'76 OECD trade gap rptd 1-26, 123D2
UN chrgs Rhodesia sanctn violatns 2-10, 123A1
Westn debt rptd mounting 2-13—4-13, 335C3
US adopts fishing agrmt 2-21, 173D3
A-supplier natns score Carter plans 4-28—4-29, 403F1-A2
Guyana tech cooperatn pact rptd 7-11, 710C3
Albania air link cited 595F1
A-suppliers OK safeguards 9-21, 717D1
W Ger auto deal set 11-30, 984E1
Philippine trade pact set 12-7, 1000B2
Nazis—*See under 'N'*

1978

GERIATRICS—*See AGE & Aged Persons*
GERMAINE Monteil Cosmetiques Corp.—*See B.A.T. Industries—British-American Cosmetics*

GERMAN Democratic Republic (East)—*See also COMECON, DISARMAMENT—Geneva Committee, WARSAW Pact*
CP oppositn group rptd 1-4, 1-10, 11A3, 62A1
Schl mil drills scored by clergy 6-25, 648G2
'77 per capita GNP ranked 21st 7-18, 624E1
Youth restlessness rptd 8-1, 648C3
1st man in space 8-26, 714A1
Quake felt 9-3, 759A1
Synod rptd vs student mil training 9-21, 840G3
Salyut space visit cited 11-2, photos rptd taken from orbit 11-3, 861B1, E1

Berlin—*See 'West German Relations' below*
European Force Reduction Talks—*See under EUROPE*
Foreign Relations (misc.)—*See also 'Monetary, Trade, Aid & Investment' below*
USSR increases presence, stresses ties; CP factionalism cited 1-29, 1-31, 61G3
At USSR maneuvers 2-6—2-10, 103C2
Czech hijacks jet to W Ger 2-6, 212D2
Iranians storm emb 2-27, 152E3
Iranians, W Gers besiege missn in Bonn 2-28, 190C2
Iran to recall amb 3-2, 190B2
USSR denies use of spy trucks 3-15, 291G2
USSR amb hints neutron bomb deal 4-4, 254A2
Zaire rebel aid denied 5-22, 382F1
USSR soldier in E Berlin shootout 6-19, 549F1
USSR holds maneuvers, Westn observers barred 7-3—7-7, 648D3
UK natl jailed in escape bid 7-24, 648F3
Polish plane hijacked 8-30, 894F3
Ghana rptdly ousts envoys 9-8, 841B1
UN Assemb member 713E3
Mil parades protested by France, UK 10-2, 10-7, 861F3
Syrian Pres Assad visits 10-3, 745C2

Helsinki Agreement—*See EUROPE—Security and Cooperation*
Human Rights—*See also 'West German Relations' below*
Imprisoned rptr sentenced 1-6, 36C2
Writers cong bars 7 dissidents 4-26, 360B2
Carter on abuse 7-15, 544G3
Clergyman kills self 9-17, 840F3

Monetary, Trade, Aid & Investment
Swedish fishing zone set 1-1, 21A2
A-export safeguard pact detailed 1-11, 11B2
EC steel dumping probe begun 1-23, 80C2
Complaint vs Comecon rptd 2-21, 505D1
Australia joins A-supplier group 2-24, 129C2
Iran cuts trade ties 3-5, 190C2
Food, other import protests rptd, currency issue cited 5-11, 504F2
Cobalt purchases rptd up 5-24, 382D2
Comecon econ integratn bid fails 6-29, 505A1
'77 Westn trade rptd down, total '77 trade rptd 7-11, 649B1
Shipping competitn vs EC rptd 7-11, 670C3
Brazil trade pact rptd 7-13, 649C1
US jeans on sale 11-29, 1021A3
Nazis—*See NAZIS*
Sports
Bobsled championships 2-5, 2-12, 316F3
World figure-skating titles 3-9—3-10, 316D3
Koch sets 400-m dash mark 7-2, 692G3
Beyer sets shot-put mark 7-6, 692G3
World Swim Champnshps 8-18—8-28, 780B1, A2

1979

GERGELY, Gabor
Wins table tennis tourn 4-10, 527F1
GERHARDT, Hans-Jurgen
W Gers win world 4-man bobsled title 2-25, 392F1
GERMAIN, Dot
Ties for 2d in Greater Baltimore 7-22, 587F3

GERMAN Democratic Republic (East)—*See also COMECON, DISARMAMENT–Geneva Committee, WARSAW Pact*
Fuchs retiremt rptd 2-1, 78E3
Catholics see Pope in Poland 6-2, 413B2
20th anniv marked 10-7, 761C1, D2

Economy & Labor
Bad weather cripples econ 1-31, 120C2
W Ger mark circulatn curbed, Intershops system cited 4-16, 285F1-D2
Econ problems rptd 8-1, 741E3
Defense increase set 12-17, 959A3
European Force Reduction Talks—*See under EUROPE*
Foreign Relations (misc.)—*See also 'Monetary' and 'UN' below*
Zaire ties restored 1-20, 117A2
France arrests 2 as spies 1-28, 77D3
China invasn of Viet scored 2-19, 122F2
S Yemen advisers rptd 2-28, 144E2
NATO secy defects 3-5, E Ger spy data 3-13, 180C3, D3
Westn rptrs curbed 4-14, 285E2
USSR SS-21 deploymt rptd 4-23, 340E1; NATO error admitted 5-23, 399E1
Chile refugee relocatn rptd 5-7, 369B3
Uganda amb, wife rptd killed 6-1, 429B2
Zimbabwe guerrilla ldr visit rptd 6-19, 490F2
Brezhnev visits 10-4—10-8, sets troop cut 10-6; reactn 10-7, 10-9, 10-6, 761C1-E3
Rumania pres skips anniv fete, PLO head attends 10-7, 761E2
China premr backs Ger reunificatn 10-22, 854B1
NATO A-missiles opposed 11-1, 880E3
Cuban A-plant constructn plans rptd 11-8, 872B2
Iran takeover of US Emb backed 11-15, 878B3; scored 11-23, 895E3
USSR begins troop pullout, NATO A-missiles scored 12-5, 938C3
NATO A-missile OK spurs defns hike 12-17, 959A3
Helsinki Agreement—*See EUROPE-Security and Cooperation*
Human Rights—*See also 'West German Relations' below*
Freedom House lists as not free 13A1
Bible availability cited 3-13, 238E1
Heym, Havemann prosecutn rptd 4-25, 370C3; fined 5-22, 5-25, 406D2
Info flow curbed 6-28, 568G2
Amnesty declared 9-25, 761E2
Havemann house arrest rptd 10-14, 802A3
Amnesty completed 12-14, 980E3
Monetary, Trade, Aid & Investment
Africa mil aid rptd, role detailed 5-23, 406E2
Uganda aid cited 5-28, 429B2
Zimbabwe aid rptd sought 6-19, 490F2
W Ger oil, coal deal set 9-5, 796A3
French credit deal set 9-12—9-15, 796G2
Cambodia relief aid rptd 9-30, 741C1
USSR trade pact signed 10-5, 761C2
W Ger credit-prisoner ransom ended 11-28, 939A3

Nazis—*See NAZIS*
Obituaries
Bengsch, Alfred Cardinal 12-13, 1008A2
Ebert, Friedrich 12-4, 1008F2
Sports
Eur figure-skating title 2-1, world competitn 3-15, 391F3*, 392B1*
W Gers win world 4-man bobsled title 2-25, 392F1
Swimmer defects to W Ger 9-18, cites drug use 9-19, 721E3
UN Policy & Developments
Membership listed 695D2
W Ger prisoner ransom deals scored 11-28, 939B3

1980

GERMAN Democratic Republic (East)—*See also COMECON, CSCE, GENEVA Committee, MBFR, WARSAW Pact*
Eastern European & Soviet Relations
USSR Afghan invasn backed 1-10, 11A1; concern seen 4-17, 303B2
E Eur gas cash purchases barred 6-1, 431C3
Polish strike press coverage rptd 8-20, 626G2-A3; Gierek speech broadcast 8-25, 642B2
Poland strike setlmt denounced 8-29, 9-2, 658G3, 659A1
Warsaw Pact maneuvers hosted 9-8—9-11, 696D1
Afghan mil role rptd 9-15, 705C1
Poland warned 9-30, 753C1; 10-8, 761C1
Poland interventn hinted 10-13, 831F1
USSR backs tighter Westn currency swap rules 10-14, 789C2
Poland travel restricted 10-28, 828G3; curbs scored 10-30, 860C1; 11-20, 879E1
Poland criticism rptd 11-5, 860G1-B2
Polish union ldr scored 11-21—11-27, rail svc suspended 11-26, 910F1
Polish border shut 12-1, 910F2
Sovt Poland invasn preparatn rptd complete 12-7; US dispatches AWACS 12-9, 929G2, 930C1
Polish unions called 'counterrevolutionary' 12-8; militia alerted 12-11, 929C2, F2
Economy & Labor
'79 data rptd 1-18, 166B2
Foreign Relations (misc.)—*See also 'UN Policy' below*
Colombia amb presents credentials 2-27, 141D1
USSR Afghan invasn concern seen 4-17, 303B2
Zimbabwe gains indepndnc 4-18, 301F1
Australia asylum for dancer rptd 4-22, 327A1
Tito funeral held 5-8, 339B1
S Yemen mil activity rptd 6-9, 468G2-B3
France arrests ex-mil chief 8-19, spy chrgs rptd 9-6, 707F3
Iraq war supplies shipped via Saudi ports 11-20, 894F2
Iran resumes Kharg I oil terminal use 11-21, 894D2

Human Rights—*See also 'West German Relations' below*
E Berlin author arrested 1-4, 57C2
Dancer gets Australia asylum 4-22, 327A1

Monetary, Trade, Aid & Investment
W Ger trade expansn set 4-17, 303A2
Iran trade deal rptd 4-23, 298G1
E Eur gas cash purchases barred 6-1, 431C3
W Ger trade rptd up 8-20, 674A2
Westn hard currency swap rules tightened 10-9; USSR backs 10-14, 789F1
Algeria quake aid rptd 10-11, 776E1

Nazis—*See NAZIS*
Soviet Relations—*See 'Eastern Europe & Soviet Relations' above*
Sports
Winter Olympic results 2-12—2-24, 154F2, 155F2-156D1
2 win world figure skating titles 3-13, 3-15, 470B2
Moscow Olympic results 7-20—8-3, 588B1-589B3, 622F1-624G3
UN Policy & Developments
Cncl seat taken 1-1, 12B2
Cncl res on Sovt Afghan pullout opposed 1-7, 2G1
Afghan issue shift to Gen Assemb opposed 1-9, 25F1
Cncl sanctns vs Iran opposed 1-14, 29A1
Israel Leb incursn res abstentn 4-24, 302E3

1976

West German Relations
Forced adoptn policy ended 1-12, 1-13, 107E3
'75 trade up 1-14, 107F3
US pilot fined for '75 airlift 1-14, 158B1
Permit to see Guillaume rptd sought 1-25, 158A2
E Ger jails refugee smuggler 1-26, 85E1-A2
Schmidt defends 'Ostpolitik' 1-29, 158A1
USSR, Bonn abandon A-plant 3-30, 243D2
Bonn secy seized as spy 5-14; CDU official suspended 5-17, 383D1
Honecker affirms detente 5-18, 381E1
W Ger seizes more spy suspects 6-2—6-14, 441E3
Border shift re coal pact rptd 7-15, 889B2
Border shootings 7-28, 8-5; E-W exchng threats 8-8—8-11, hold talks 8-12, 630C3
Berlin buses halted, Schmidt protests 8-13, 630E3
Allied protest over Berlin buses rejctd, Bonn scores 8-27, 678D3
Sovt soldier defects 9-9, 857D1
Border incidents Bonn campaign issue 9-12, 754D3
Border wall constructn rptd 9-29, 772F2
Border escapes rptd 10-12—11-4, 905D2
90,000 visa bids rptd 10-20, 905C2
Poet exiled re W Ger concert 11-16; W Ger scored 11-21, 905A2
Bonn acquits ex-border guard 12-3, 931G1-B2
Dissidents exit 12-10—12-12, Bonn newsman ousted 12-22, 1001D3
Visa bids blocked 12-12, 1001G3

1977

West German Relations (including Berlin developments)
E Berlin visas asked, checkpoint guards removed 1-1; West scores 1-6, 7C2; protests to USSR 1-11, 20F1
E Ger posts guards at W Ger emb 1-11, withdraws 1-12, 20E1
Ties deteriorate 1-13—1-24, E Ger recalls amb 1-24, 62D1
Brandt warns on W Berlin econ 1-24, 102F1
E Ger '76 trade gap rptd 1-26, 123D2
Kohl NKVD betrayal chrgd 2-8, 102A2
W Berlin travel curbed 2-17, auto tolls set 2-25, 496C3
E Ger curbs travel over nationality dispute 2-22, 315D1
Cohrs defectn rptd 2-24, 315A1
2 swim to West Berlin 3-28, 315A1
E Ger emigratn policy eases anti-govt feeling 3-30, 315E1
Kunze leaves 4-14, 314D3
E Ger spies arrested 5-4—6-28, 602F1-B2
NATO warns USSR re Berlin 5-9, 358C2
Honecker statemt on E Berlin sovereignty rptd 5-12, 496B3
USSR scores NATO warning on E Berlin 5-14, rejcts 4-power pact 5-15, 496F2-B3
W Ger scored re Kappler decisn 8-19, 638F1
Bahro interview aired 8-23, 684F1
Kirsch, 5 other dissidents arrive in West 8-29, 684D1
90 pol prisoners deported 9-22, more dissident expulsns planned 9-24, 752G2
E-W Ger spies sentncd 9-23—12-6, 968D2
2 W Ger natls rptd sentncd 10-2, 752A3
E Ger workers rptdly ask 20% pay in W Ger money 10-2, 782F1
E-W Ger talks set 10-5, resume 10-26, 984D1
W Ger seeks Berlin road, power links 10-5, 984E1
Schmidt affirms unificatn aim 11-22, 926A2
Pol prisoners, Berlin Wall escape attempts rptd 11-24, 956A2
Auto deal set 11-30, 984E1
W Ger Defns Min spy scandal disclosed 12-12; NATO, US, other reactn 12-12—12-15, 968C1
Dissident author visits W Berlin 12-19, 984A2

1978

U.S. Relations
US prisoner exchng talks rptd 4-24, 3-way swap completed 5-1, 318A2
US chrgs Zaire role 5-28, 399C1
US chrgs heroin smuggling, '77 data cited 6-1, 433G2
Dresden exhibit at Natl Gallery 6-1, 578D3
Carter on rights abuse, Ger reunificatn 7-15, 544F3
Mil parades protested by US 10-2, 10-7, 861F3
US jeans on sale 11-29, 1021A3

West German Relations (including Berlin developments)
Goebbels diary on W Ger best-seller list 1-2, 22C1
W Ger newsman barred 1-4; Der Spiegel office closed, govt protests 1-10, 11G2
W Ger arrests spy couple 1-4, 21E3
Spies rptd held, sentenced 1-9—1-14, 36A2
CDU ldr barred Berlin entry 1-15, W Ger protests 1-16, 36E1
2 W Ger parlt members denied E Berlin entry, CDU mtg in W Berlin cited 1-16, 61E3
E-W tensn grows, Der Spiegel chrgs scored 1-18, 26G1-A2
W Ger defns min linked to new scandal 1-24, 74A3
W Ger natl sentncd for spying 1-26, 61F3
E-W reps meet on tensns 1-28—1-30, 61D3
W Berlin leftists, police clash 1-28—1-29, 94C1
USSR W Berlin patrols rptd increased, Der Spiegel rpts cited 1-29, 61G3
'77 narcotic deaths rptd 2-12, 211A2
W Ger convicts 3 as spies 2-13, 115C1
W Ger probes spy scandal 2-24, 210F3
W Gers, Iranians storm E Ger missn in Bonn 2-28, 190C2
E Berlin draft resisters arrest protested, Berlin demilitarized status cited 3-14, 276A1
E Ger lawyer defects 4-21, 333F1-C2
Guillaume swap rptd discussed 4-24, 318F2
Wittenberge food price protest rptd 5-1, W Ger rptrs scored 5-11, 504E2
USSR, W Ger affirm Berlin status 5-4—5-7, 417A1
Food, other imports protests rptd; currency issue cited 5-11, 504F2
Bonn rights group rpts E Ger prisoners release 5-25, Bonn paymts rptd 5-26, 504C2
US chrgs heroin smuggling, '77 data cited 6-1, 433A3
Berlin Wall escapes 6-11—6-17, 504E2
USSR soldier in E Berlin shootout, W Ger envoy injured 6-19, 549F1
Museum group buys Von Hirsch collectn 6-20—6-27, 579C1
Improved ties seen; Berlin highway, border talks cited 6-24, 622G2
Bahro sentncd re '77 interview 6-30, 585E3
E Berlin draft resister jailed 7-7, 585D3
Carter on reunificatn; Schmidt accompaniment in Berlin protested 7-15, 544F3
Berlin Wall escape rptd 7-24, 648F3
Jan-May emigratn, escape totals; '77 totals rptd 7-31, 648G3
10 W Ger natls rptd jailed as spies 8-11, 622B3
E Ger hijacks Polish plane to W Berlin 8-30, 894F3
E Berlin mil displays scored 10-2, 10-7, 861F3
Schmidt ex-aide sentncd for spying 10-5, 776D3
Transport pacts, Berlin road OKd 11-16, 905D3

1979

U.S. Relations
US rpts S Yemen advisers 2-28, 144E2
US ct frees E Ger '78 hijacker 5-28, 430E2
Carter spurns Sovt troop cut plan 10-9, 761A3
Iran takeover of US Emb backed 11-15, 878B3; scored 11-23, 895E3

West German Relations (including Berlin developments)
E Ger defects 1-18, identified 1-24; W Ger arrests 5 alleged spies 1-20, 61B3
W Ger mil offcr defectn rptd 1-21, 61E3
Spy arrests by W Ger continue 1-31, 77C3
W Ger sentncd as spy 2-15, 181B1
2 sentncd re E Ger escape aid 2-19, 250A3
NATO secy defects 3-5, 180E3
W Ger CDU infiltratn rptd, E Ger spy data 3-6—3-13, 180D3
W Ger newsmen curbed 4-14, 285F2
E Ger curbs W Ger marks 4-16, 285F1-D2
Dissident publishing rptd curbed 4-25, 370C3
TV rptr ousted re Heym interview 5-14, 370E3
E Ger '78 hijacker freed in W Berlin 5-28, 430E2
W Ger sentncs Lutzes, Gerstners 6-18; arrests 3 others 6-21, 489E3, 490A1
E Berlin reps join E Ger parlt 6-28, 513B1
Prisoner exchange rptd 7-20, 586C2
W Ger newsman arrested 8-16, 742E2
Escapes rptd rising, July total 8-17, 697A3
Oil, coal deal set 9-5, 796A3
8 flee E Ger by balloon 9-16, 697A3
E Ger swimming star defects 9-18, 721E3
Parade held 10-7, 761D2
Schmidt skeptical re Sovt troop cut plan 10-7, 761E3
Bahro, E Berlin draft resister freed 10-11, 761F2; arrive W Ger 10-17, 882G3
China premr backs reunificatn, E Ger scores 10-22, 854B1
E Ger warns vs NATO A-missiles 11-1, W Ger reacts 11-4, 880D3
W Ger prisoner ransom deals ended 11-28, 939F2
Schmidt plans '80 Honecker mtg 12-4, 938F2
W Ger newsman sentncd 12-14, 980F3

1980

Palestinian state res backed 4-30, 325D1
UNESCO protests aide's arrest 6-6, arrest confirmed 6-10; sentenced as spy 9-6, 708A1
Women's conf racism motion withdrawn 7-28, 587G2
UNIFIL mandate extensn abstentn 12-17, 977D3

U.S. Relations
W Ger warned re US policy 3-19, 236D3
US rpts Sovt Poland invasn preparatn complete 12-7; US AWACS dispatched 12-9, 929G2, 930C1

West German Relations
Schmidt-Honecker mtg postponed 1-30, 103E1
Prisoner deals resumed 3-16, 262E2
W Ger warned re US policy 3-19, seeks E Ger talks 3-20, 236B3
Mittag in W Ger, trade expansn set 4-17, 303A2
Transport pact signed 4-30, 355C3
UNESCO aide's arrest rptd 6-10, sentenced as spy 9-6, 708A1
W Ger arrest of spy rptd 7-31, 606D1
Trade rptd up 8-20, 674A2
Schmidt cancels visit 8-22, 642E2
W Ger campaign issue 9-3—9-5, 690E3
RR workers strike 9-17, W Berlin bars role 9-23, 731D1-A2
RR workers end strike 9-25, 300 rptd quit 9-29, 794G3
Hard currency swap rules tightened 10-9, 789F1
W Ger vs entry fee hikes 10-12, new projects 10-15; E Ger asks concessns, W Ger rejects 10-13, 794C3
W Ger arrests 3 as spies 11-10, 925F2
W Ger sentnces secy as spy 12-12, 969A2

1977

GERMAN Marshall Fund of the U.S.
Read confrmd State undersecy 8-3, 626D3

GERMAN Measles (Rubella)—*See MEDICINE—Diseases*

1978

GERMAN Measles (rubella)—*See MEDICINE—Diseases*

GERMAN Ribon, Miguel de
Kidnaped 3-25, abductors killed 4-14, 414B1

1980

GERMAN Requiem (recording)
Solti wins Grammy 2-27, 296F3

GERMANY

1976

GERMANY, Federal Republic of (West)—*See also ADB, DISARMAMENT—Geneva Committee, EUROPEAN Community, IEA, NATO, OECD*
42 die in Italy ski-lift crash 3-9, 384E1
Quake tremors rptd 5-6, 352B3
Countess in Getty will 6-8, 444D2
107 die in Yugo air collisn 9-10, 696D3
'Marburg' disease hits Africa 10-7, 795A3
Lefebvre holds banned mass 10-24, 932A3

1977

GERMANY, Federal Republic of (West)—*See also COMECON, DISARMAMENT—Geneva Committee, EC, ESA, IDB, IEA, NATO, OECD*
Sovt hotel blaze 2-25, 204D2
Hosp drug deaths rptd 2-28, 224E2
Ratzinger inducted as cardinal 6-27, 768B3
Art defaced 10-7, man chrgd 10-8, 848E2
Heroin addictn rptd up 10-17—10-21, 971D3

1978

GERMANY, Federal Republic of (West)—*See also COUNCIL of Europe, DISARMAMENT—Geneva Committee, EC, GATT, IDB, IEA, NATO, OECD*
Oberammergau vs revised Passion Play 1-12, 95E2; retains classic text 3-5, 295C2
Mainz, Stuttgart museums buy Gutenberg Bibles 3-10, 4-7, 295D2
Frankfurt museum paintings vandalized 4-11, 335A2
4 convicted in exorcism death 4-21, church curbs rites 5-1, 379D3
Energy conservatn progress rated 6-5, 449E3 ★, 450F1
Army strength rptd 6-22, 488D2
Campers killed in Spanish blast 7-11, 636E1
Hamburg museum art theft 7-30, 1029B1
Birth rate decline rptd 8-16, 725A3
Quake hits Swabian hills 9-3, 758G3
Krakow cardinal elected Pope 10-16, 782C1

African Relations
Somalia asks arms aid 1-16, 43B3
At Ogaden conf in US 1-21, 43E2
Somalia credits granted 1-21, Ethiopia ousts W Ger amb 1-22, 44A1

1979

GERMANY, Federal Republic of (West)—*See also COUNCIL of Europe, DISARMAMENT—Geneva Committee, EC, GATT, IDB, IEA, NATO, OECD*
Chem pollutn curbs proposed 2-20, 214E3
Schmidt at 'Lulu' premiere 2-25, 174A1
Alcohol consumptn rptd up 3-9, 218C3
Populatn drop forecast 6-26, 489D2
Chem factory peril forces Hamburg evacuatns 9-17, 796C2
Wittig wins Nobel Prize 10-16, 858B1
Environmtlsts meet 10-27—10-28, 876E1
Heroin use rptd 11-11, 972D3

African Relations
UN rights comm res vs white-minority regimes opposed 2-21, 148G1
Namibia plan fails 3-3, S Africa rejcts UN proposal 3-5, 171B2, A3

1980

GERMANY, Federal Republic of (West)—*See also ADB, COUNCIL of Europe, CSCE, EC, GATT, GENEVA Committee, IDB, IEA, MBFR, NATO, OECD*
Molsidomine use rptd 1-3, 24E1
Immense quasar rptd 4-10, 415D3
Reichstag fire verdict canceled 12-15, 996B3

1976

Berlin—*See GERMAN Democratic Republic—West German Relations*
Eastern European Policy—*See also 'West German Relations' under GERMAN Democratic Republic*
USSR to make more dailies available 1-21, 76G2
Import quotas raised 1-22, 158C2
Schmidt urges Poland pact ratificatn 1-29, 77C3
Schmidt defends 'Ostpolitik,' detente 1-29, 157G3
CDU win endangers Poland pact ratificatn 2-6, 157A3
Yugo envoy slain 2-7, 224E1
Poland emigratn pact OKd 2-19, 3-12, 260E1
Sovt A-plant plan dropped 3-30, 243C2
'75 Sovt trade rptd 5-5, 340D3
NATO concerned re Berlin, Sovt A-talks halt cited 5-21, 353F1

1977

Atomic Energy & Safeguards
Australia uranium shipmt blocked 1-2, 17C2; contracts cited 1-26, 81F2
N Rhine bans A-plants 1-13, Bavaria plant shut 1-14, 117G2
Mondale urges A-export curbs 1-25, 69F1, B2
US rptd vs Brazil A-deal 2-7, curbs hinted 2-8, 118A1
Brazil-US talks re A-deal fail 3-2, US pressure on Bonn rptd 3-11, 189F3, 190E1
Vance sees Schmidt on Brazil A-deal, SALT 3-31; pact honored 4-5, US pressure scored 4-9, 247A1, 268F2
Venez scores Brazil 4-1, 547B3
Carter proposes US plutonium ban 4-7, 268B1, G1, B2
A-policy statemt issued 4-7, 268E2
A-industry jobs estimated 4-9, 268D3
French A-reactor protests rptd 4-11, 391E3
Intl A-energy conf ends, US plutonium ban scored 4-13, 334F2
Schmidt affirms A-export policy, scores US pleas 4-21, 4-26, 334A1
Japan moves vs US plutonium ban 4-21, 335D1
A-breeder, other research funds asked 4-27, 333F2
Carter proposes US A-export curbs 4-27, W Ger fuel reliance noted 4-28, 334D2
Suppliers conf scores Carter plans 4-28—4-29, 403F1-A2
Carter OKs uranium shipmt 5-6, 403D2
7-natn summit debates A-sales, sets study 5-7—5-8, 357D2, E2, 358E1
US concedes Brazil deal 5-13, 414A2
'68 secret Israeli uranium deal rptd 5-30, 416A3
Uranium cartel probed, US pact cited 6-16, 480C1
A-data exports halted 6-17, 566C3
France bars A-weapons abroad 6-23, 1012F3
French 'Super Phoenix' OKd 7-5, environmentalists protest 7-31, 597C2, F2, C3
Schmidt sees Trudeau 7-6—7-12, A-fuel export ban eased 7-12, 566F2, A3
Schmidt sees Carter 7-13—7-14, 566B2, F2
Open sector cyclotron use cited 825B3
Suppliers conf OKs safeguards 9-21, 717D1
Iran signs A-plant deal 11-10, 926C2
US reaffirms Brazil A-deal oppositn 11-16, 896A1
Berlin—*See GERMAN Democratic Republic—West German Relations*
Eastern European Relations—*See also GERMAN Democratic Republic—West German Relations*
Czech spy trial opens 1-10, 82F3
Brandt backs Czech dissidents 1-22, 82G2
Czechs sentence spies 2-3, 115C1
'76 Sovt, E Eur trade rptd 2-9, 102C2
Sovt-bloc debt rptd 2-13, 335F3
Czechs detain newsman 2-14, 114C3
Czech defectn confrmd, spy network revealed 2-24, 220B3
Rumania blocks dissident contact 4-2, 315F1
27 Poles in Denmark ask asylum 5-3, 15 OKd 5-4, 427C1
Sovt Gers ask emigratn aid 5-18, 436G2
Observers at USSR mil exercises 7-11, 551C1

1978

Ethiopia protests Somalia aid 2-1, 100D1
Somali makes 2d aid bid 2-4, 99G3
Namibia mtg 2-11—2-12, progress rptd 2-13, 113A3
Kenyan vp ends quest for arms 3-11, 289F2
UN Rhodesia pact vote abstentn 3-14, 192F3
Namibia plan backed by front-line natns 3-26, 248G2
Kenya dam contracts rptd 4-9, 479D1
Namibia plan OKd by Vorster 4-25, 299C1
Somalia sentences '77 Lufthansa hijacker 4-25, 353F3
Zaire satellite testing site rptd 4-29, 382G1
Namibia rebel ldr cancels talks 5-7, 339D1
Schmidt backs USSR warning 5-31, 397A2
Westn natns meet on pan-Africa force 6-5, 441E2
S African blacks denied passports 6-9, 536C3
Namibia rebels OK talks 6-11, 475C3
Zaire emergency aid OKd 6-13—6-14, 478A1
S Africa race-attitude poll rptd 6-15, 6-22, 536D2
Schmidt in Nigeria, Zambia 6-26—6-30; defends S Africa ties 6-30, 584B1
Rhodesia rebels kill 2 priests 6-27, 594G2
Zambia loan cited 6-29, 617A2
Namibia plan OKd by SWAPO 7-12, 547C2
Zaire communicatns deal rptd 7-19, 652A3
Namibia electn delay barred 10-14; contact group sees Botha, Steyn 10-16—10-18, 819G2
Uganda-Tanzania border conflict 11-2—11-6, 860A2
S Africa press scandal, Springer link cited 11-2, 868F2
Canada-S Africa arms deal suspected 11-6—11-7, 904G2
UN abstentn on Namibia electn warning 11-13, 904B2
Nigeria loan set 11-30, 934A2
Atomic Energy & Safeguards
'77 A-export safeguard pact detailed 1-11, 11G1, B2
US alerts to Sovt A-satellite fall 57E1
Canada uranium shipmt set 1-16, 102D3
Dutch OK Brazil uranium sales, Urenco plant expansn 2-1; Almelo protest held 3-4, 169C2, G2
Neutron bomb in SALT pact urged, Soc Dem split cited 2-23, 140A2
Australia joins A-supplier group 2-24, 129C2
Schmidt testifies at Defns Min spy probe 2-24, 210E3
Brazil pres in talks, US A-deal oppositn cited 3-6—3-10, 332D3
Brazil scores Carter on A-deal oppositn 3-30, 233C2
Neutron bomb cancellatn by Carter rptd 4-4, W Ger deploymt stand cited 4-10, 253F1
Neutron bomb deferral reactn 4-7, Schmidt clarifies stand, warns re ties 4-12, 254A3
Schmidt, Giscard discuss Sovt uranium deal 4-7, 258C2
US OKs uranium exports 4-9, 278G3
Haig resignatn threat rptd 4-25, 298A3
Brezhnev warns vs neutron bomb deploymt 5-2, sees Schmidt 5-4—5-7, 417A1, C1
US study backs breeder dvpt 5-10, 346G3
Schmidt reviews Carter talks 6-1, 519C2
Environmtalists gain in 2 state electns 6-4, 456D2
3 A-plant accidents 6-20, 6-23, concern rptd 6-26, 500A2
Japan breeder research pact rptd 6-23, 548E3
Dutch parlt backs Brazil uranium sale 6-30, 575B1, D1
Subatomic particle mass measured 7-5, 654E2
Brazil A-plant purchases lag 10-15, 836A3
Iran work to continue 10-22, 816C3
Berlin—*See GERMAN Democratic Republic—West German Relations*
Eastern European & Soviet Relations—*See also GERMAN Democratic Republic—West German Relations*
Sovt A-satellite fall alert 57E1
At USSR maneuvers 2-6—2-10, 103C2
Czech hijacker, 3 others get asylum 2-6, 212E2
USSR '77 trade cited 3-29, 230A1
Schmidt, Giscard discuss Sovt uranium deal 4-2, 258C2
Czech pres visits 4-10—4-14, detente support pledged 4-11, 332F3
Brezhnev offers mutual force cuts 5-2; visits Bonn 5-4—5-7, trade pact signed 5-7, 417A1-B2
Yugo arrests 4 terrorists 5-11, seeks Croatn natls exchng 5-11—5-31, 438E3

1979

Namibia compromise proposed 3-19—3-22; Pretoria bars 5-7, extends assemb powers 5-8, 354F2
S Africa '72-78 loans rptd 4-2, 270D2
2 rptrs believed killed in Uganda war 4-9, 257F2
Zaire rocket tests stopped 4-27, 411A3
S Africa scored by UN vote 5-31, 428B1
Amin confirmed in Uganda 6-13, 489A1
Namibia UN talks reopen 11-12–11-16, 889D3
Atomic Energy & Safeguards
Urenco plans contd cooperatn, Gronau A-enrichmt plant OKd 2-7, 101D1
Brazil pres, Mondale confer on A-deal 3-22–3-23, 247F3, G3
US A-accident sparks protests, govt concern 3-31–4-4, 246D1, E2
A-sales to Pak rptd 4-6, 277C2
Protests rptd 4-9, sabotage attempt 4-13; US A-accident linked 276A2, C2
Schleswig-Holstein electn issue 4-29, 333A3
Eur A-Conf opens; Schmidt backs A-power, states plans 5-7, 373F3-374B1
France plutonium custody dispute resolved 5-16, 380B1
Lower Saxony blocks Gorleben reprocessing, storage facility 5-16, 410E3
Kalkar A-protest staged 6-3, 416G1, E2
FDP backs A-power 6-16, 489F2
Long-term reliance seen 7-4, 506D1
France Euratom proposal opposed 7-24, 633F2
Kraftwerk cancels Iran plant contract 7-31, 586F2
Iran demands A-plant compensatn 8-10, 634E3
Siemens gets Spain A-plant contract 8-25, 670C3
Siemens gets Argentine A-plant contract 10-1, 749C1
A-power compromise rptd 10-2, 796C2
Bonn protest held 10-14, 781F3
Environmtlsts plan anti-nuclear party 10-27–10-28, 876F1, G1
Soc Dems back 12-6, 938G2
Berlin—*For East-West German issues, see GERMAN Democratic Republic–West German Relations*
SPD-FDP gain in electn 3-18, 214A3, C3
Giscard visits; reaffirms security, Eur detente commitmt 10-29, 835A2
Eastern European & Soviet Relations
Sovt warning on China ties cited 1-5, 12C3
Shipbldg competitn cited 1-21, 77F3
USSR '78 trade rptd 3-6, 172G2
Sovt-bloc spy data cited 3-13, 180D3
Sovt-bloc '78 Westn debt estimate rptd 3-20, 200D3
USSR-Krupp steel deal rptd 3-26, 237C3
3 Volga Gers ask USSR emigratn 3-27, 238B1
USSR ousts TV rptrs 5-16, 410B2
Polish plane '78 hijacker freed 5-28, 430E2
SALT pact backed 6-6, 430D1
USSR hints cable link 6-27, 497E2

1980

Atomic Energy & Safeguards
French breeder reactor role cited 2-26, 149F2
Hesse reprocessing plant permit sought 2-27, 154A1
A-protest village dispersed 6-4, 446C3
US warned vs gas venting at A-accident site 6-18, 550C3
7-natn Venice summit backs 6-23, 473F2
A-power moratorium urged 6-26, 581G1
USSR pact signed 7-1, 489D2
OECD rpts A-plant cancellatns 7-8, 509A3
Cologne A-research office bombed 12-4, 969C2
Berlin—*See also GERMAN Democratic Republic--West German Relations*
Carter cites '60s crisis 1-23, 42G1
USSR W Berlin consulate bombed 3-7, 236B1
Leftists riot in W Berlin 5-18, 500E3
Anderson visits 7-13, 549G3
RR workers strike 9-17, city bars role 9-23, 731D1-A2
Sovt Jewish immigratn curb set 9-24, 833D1
RR workers end strike 9-25, 300 rptd quit 9-29, 794G3
Kurds attack Turkey W Berlin consulate 10-8, 794A2
Lorenz kidnapers sentenced 10-13, 833A1
Squatters arrested in protest 12-13; 3,000 riot 12-15, 969D1
Defense & Armed Forces
3% real spending hike claimed 2-25, 153D3
'80 budget supplemt OKd 4-30, 355E3
Navy curbs lifted 7-18, 540F1
Defense spending plan cited 11-20, 904B1
'79 mil spending cited 12-10, 949G2
'81 budget hike OKd, 12-17, 969B1
Eastern European & Soviet Relations—*See also 'Soviet-Afghan Issue' below*
Schmidt sees Sovt war threat 4-20, 303D1
Tito funeral held 5-8, 339B1
Gromyko-Muskie mtg noted 5-19, 378D3
Sovt trade blitz rptd 5-22, 430G3
Sovt draft trade pact set 5-29, 411A2
USSR rejected A-missile freeze offer 6-9; Schmidt gets Carter letter vs 6-16, seeks mtg 6-18, 450B3-451D1
USSR warns vs NATO A-missiles 6-12, 451D1
Schmidt vs Carter USSR trip criticism 6-21, 473E1
Schmidt rpts USSR trip plans 6-23, 474E1

1976

Sovt gas turbine deal 6-1, 540D2
Gierek visits, pacts OKd 6-8—6-11, 442D1
Sovt soldier defects 9-9, 857D1
Brezhnev visit rptd set 10-4, 754G2
Czech hijacker to face chrgs 10-29, 946F1
Signs Poland copper pact 11-2, credit deal rptd 11-4, 907E1
'75 COMECON trade gap rptd 11-18, 977D1
Rumania trade cited 12-1, 1010G1
Poland coal projct credits rptd 12-8, 966E1
Schmidt stresses Sovt, E Eur ties; confrms Brezhnev '77 visit 12-16, 968C2

East German Relations—*See 'West German Relations' under GERMAN Democratic Republic*
Economy & Labor (domestic)
'75 GNP, inflatn rate, output rptd 1-14, 157F3
Jobless rise rptd slowing 1-28, 84F3
Jan jobless total hits 20-yr high 2-5, 157D3
Jan cost-of-living rptd 2-9, 157E3
'75 bankruptcies rptd up 2-17, 157F3
Worker participatn voted 3-18, 269F3-270A1
Govt job funds progrm rptd 3-18, 270B1
Mar jobless total rptd 4-2, 270B1
Feb indl output rise rptd 4-7, 270A1
Marriage reform bill OKd 4-8, 4-9, 270A2
Printers strike 4-28, Schmidt bars mediatn role 4-30, 352D2
Printers strike ends 5-13, 383D2
1st ¼ GNP up 5% 5-25, 442G1
May jobless total down 6-3, 442A2
'76 growth rate projected 6-19, 6-22, 502G3
Econ growth cited 6-27—6-28, 462E1
Herstatt, 7 others arrested 8-26, 678G3
Aug CPI, July indl output rptd 9-2, 9-6, 734D2
2d ¼ GMP rptd up 9-20, 734A2
Jobless rate campaign issue 9-30, 754B3
Sept jobless total down 10-1, 755A1
OECD incomes rpt scored 10-12, 964C2
A-power progrm, poll rptd 11-11; Brokdorf protest staged 11-13, 931B1
Lower Saxony A-waste projct pressed 11-11, 931F1
OECD growth forecast disputed 11-23, 975G3
Oct, Nov jobless rates rptd 11-29, 935C2; 12-6, 949D1
Oct '75-76 inflatn rate rptd 12-6, 976B1
Arendt resigns in pensn dispute 12-15, 968F1, F2
Schmidt presents 4-yr progrm 12-16, 968B2
Feed crop loss from drought rptd 12-31, 977D3
European Force Reduction Issues—*See under EUROPE*
Foreign Economic Developments
Deutsche Bank group sets Mex loan 1-2, 75D1
China chem plant deal rptd 1-6, 78B1
Rptd vs liberalized IMF credit 1-8, 14C2
VW '75 US sales rptd down 1-11, 280G1
'75 E Ger trade up 1-14, 107F3
SDR rate rptd 1-15, 14A3
Zaire jets for Angola rptd 1-16, 36C1
Austria rptd in Iran-USSR gas pact 1-19, 97E3
Italy seeks $500 mln loan 1-22, 74F2
'75 Swiss arms sales rptd 1-22, 104D1
Eastn bloc, China import quotas raised 1-22, 158C2
'75 trade surplus rptd 1-26, 158D2
In 7-natn A-safeguards agmt 1-27, 84A1
Mauritania compensates iron co 1-28, 104F2
Deutschemark bond issue set 1-28, 158E1
'75 paymts deficit rptd 2-3, 158D2
Lockheed payoffs rptd 2-4—2-11, Strauss denies 2-13, 130E2-D3, 131B1, 132D2
Portugal loans pledged 2-4—2-5, 142G3-143A1
French currency accords 2-9, 2-12—2-13, 229D1
Italy lira drop hits farmers 2-10, 140E2
Nissan buys Australia VW plant 2-12, 137E3
US to consider Leopard tank 2-12, 183C2
Consortium-backed Italy loan rptd 2-16, 141A1
Poland trade credits OKd 2-19, 3-12, 260F1

1977

Sovt envoy at NATO war games 9-13, 700B1
Czech hijackers land, ask asylum 10-11, 848F3
Schmidt visits Poland 11-21—11-25, 926E1

East German Relations—*See GERMAN Democratic Republic—West German Relations*
Economy & Labor (domestic)
Wage cost hike cited 1-6, 8E2
Dec '76 jobless, forgn force rptd 1-6, 23C3
'76 GNP rise rptd 1-7, 23E3
Nov, 12-mo consumer price rise rptd 1-7, 29C3
Brandt warns on W Berlin 1-24, 102F1
Ct backs workers on bds 1-27, 118D1
'76-80 jobless forecast rptd 1-27, Jan total up 2-4, 139A2
'76 factory wage study rptd 1-28, 158B3
'76 auto output rptd up 1-31, 139C2
Dec '75-76 inflatn rate rptd 2-7, 87A2
Jan, Nov, Dec '76 COL rptd 2-9, 102B2
Cabt OKs econ stimulus pkg 3-23, 243E2
Energy research funds asked 4-27, 333F2
'77 econ growth set, jobless measures pledged 5-7—5-8, 357C1, F1
Tax pkg passes 6-16, 602C1
Aug youth jobless rate rptd 8-9, 771B2
Econ min quits to hd Dresdner Bank 9-9, 969B2
Cabt OKs '78 budget 9-14; tax cuts, stimulus progrm scored 9-15, 9-26, 969D1
1st, 2d ¼ econ growth rptd slowed 9-15, 969B2
'75 world pay, buying power rank rptd 11-6, 853D3
Lufthansa bookings fall 11-29, 969D2
Mark rise threat to growth seen 12-7, 932G3
Econ stimulus urged 12-27, 999A1

1978

Schmidt backs USSR warning re Africa 5-31, 397A2
Scientist cancels USSR trip re Orlov 6-2, 504C1
USSR, US troops compared 6-10, 534B3
Hess release plea rptd rejctd by USSR 6-11, 477E3
W Ger envoy injured by Sovt soldier in E Berlin shootout 6-19, 549F1
Bulgaria arrests, extradites 4 terrorists 6-22, 500A1
Czech, Sovt terrorist aid probed 6-22, 500F1
Czech ousts rptr for '68 Sovt invasn expose 7-4, 635E1
Rumanian offcl defects 7-28, confrmd 8-8, 650F3
Hungary opens jean factory 8-8, 882E3
Croats protest Bilandzic extraditn ruling 8-13, 706D3
2 Croats seize W Ger emb in US 8-17, 706E2
Polish plane hijacked to W Berlin 8-30, 894F3
Croat sought by Yugo flees to Sweden 8-30, 925F3
Rumanian defector implicates SPD in spy scandal 8-31—9-6, 725D2
Rumanian defector triggers purges 9-1, 9-6, 741C3
Bulgarian radio employe slain in UK 9-11, 748G3
Bilandzic, 2 other Croats extraditn ruled out 9-13, 706F3
Yugo scores Bilandzic extraditn ruling 9-13, 725F1, G1 ★
SPD spy probe dropped 9-26, 868G2
Czech hijacker sentncd 10-4, 776E3
USSR defector rptd in Sweden 11-1, 947A1
Hungary devalues forint 11-11, 906G2
Yugo bars extraditn of 4 terrorists 11-17, release rptd 11-18, 906F1
US convicts 2 Croats 12-1, 933B3
East German Relations—*See GERMAN Democratic Republic—West German Relations*
Economy & Labor (domestic)
'77, Dec jobless rates rptd 1-4, 55G1
'77 bankruptcies rptd 1-6, 55B2
Pub svc union scores US Army job plan 1-11, 55B2
'77 GNP rptd; '78 inflatn, jobless forecast 1-13, 93C3
Frankfurt rated costliest city 1-14, 28G2, A3
Westdeutsche bank chief fired, N Rhine-Westphalia finance min quits 1-17, 55D1
Volkswagen ends 'beetle' line 1-19, 74D3
Printers, journalists strike in computer dispute 1-19, 2-9, newspapers reopen 2-10, 115F1
'77 auto sales rptd 1-20, 94A1
Cabt sets '78 GNP growth rate, wage curbs 1-25, 93B3, D3
Dock strike ends 1-30, 93E3
Schmidt bars '78 growth rate hike 2-13, 119C1
Steelworkers reach accord 2-17, 152E1
Sachs takeover halted by Sup Ct 2-23, 211B1
'73-77 wage gain rptd 2-27, 189C3
Printers strike again 2-27, settle computer dispute 3-20, 250C2
Metal workers strike 3-15—4-3, 250F2
Fishermen block Kiel Canal 5-10, 436C3
Munich waste combustn rptd 5-11, 367C1
Lufthansa '77 profits rptd down 5-18, 417C2
Westdeutsche bank chief's dismissal upheld 6-1, 456F3
Schmidt vows growth rate hike 7-17, 544F1
'76 arms spending rptd 7-23, 585C2
Stimulus plan announced 7-28, 583E3-584A1
Econ factors, low birth rate linked 8-16, 725C3
'79 budget, stimulus pkg presented to parlt 9-20, 906B1
Growth rate hike backed 9-25, 9-26, 731B3
SPD to ease pub employe hiring rules 10-16, 823E1
June '77-78 world inflatn rates ranked 10-18, 914F1
4% growth in '79 seen 10-24, 823A2
Ford plant shortages cited 11-22, 923D2
$7.8 bil stimulus pkg voted 11-24, 925D2
Steelworkers strike 11-28, 925F1
Frankfurt stock index graph 12-25, 1001B2
European Force Reduction Talks—*See under EUROPE*

1979

Warsaw rally marks invasn anniv 9-1, 802F2
USSR vs NATO A-missiles 10-13—10-16, Bonn reacts 10-14, 11-1, 880G2, C3
USSR E Ger troop cut plan reactn 10-7, 761F3
Rumania expropriatn pact set 10-12, 910E2
USSR defector rptd kidnaped 10-15, 856B3
USSR detente damage feared 10-21, 853G3
Gromyko visits, warns vs NATO missiles 11-21—11-24, 938A3
Schmidt backs A-arms cut talks, plans Brezhnev '80 mtg 12-4, 938F2
Sovt Afghan invasn scored 12-28, 974C2

East German Relations—*See GERMAN Democratic Republic—West German Relations*
Economy & Labor
Steel strike widens 1-3, 8D1
Joblessness rptd down in '78 1-5, 8E1
'78 inflatn rptd 2.3% 1-8, 13C1
Steelworkers OK pact 1-10, 22F1-B2
Fed job loyalty checks eased 1-18, 61E2
Shipbldg aid proposed 1-21, 77E3
'79 growth, inflatn, jobless forecast 1-23, 61F3-62C1
Budget OKd by parlt 1-26, 77E2
'78 living standards ranked 2-2, 109A2
Publishers fined for price-fixing 2-7, 101B1
Worker codeterminatn upheld 3-2, 172B3
Bank discount, Lombard rates hiked 3-29, 333E3
London Times wkly printing set 4-20, halted 4-29, 330C3
Labor costs rptd high 5-1, 374A2
3 largest banks probed 5-17, 374E1
Banking reforms proposed 5-22, 411C1
Fed deficit cut backed by Cabt, '80 spending plan cited 5-28, 489B2
7-natn indicators index rptd 6-11, 513A3
2 banks rptd among '78 world's top 10 6-19, 476B2
Populatn drop, impact forecast 6-26, 489E2
OECD warns vs interest rate hikes 7-10, 586E1
Discount, Lombard interest rates hiked 7-13, 586B1
OECD sees econ slowdown 7-19, 554G2
'78 per capita GNP ranked 5th 7-24, 575E3
Westn wage rates compared 9-19, 697B3
Poehl named Bundesbank chief 9-19, 733G2-C3
Discount, Lombard rates hiked again 10-31, 838C1
Anti-inflatn methods cited 11-1, 827A1
Telefunken rescue plan rptd, losses cited 12-4, 998F2
Bank cartel probe dropped 12-13, 998A3
'80 budget approved 12-14, 998B3
Energy—*See also 'Atomic' above*
Iran oil cutoff impact assessed, reserve cited 2-20, 126G2
5% oil demand cut agreed 3-2, 162A1
Deutsche BP-Veba deal OKd 3-5, 214F3
Sweden seeks LNG deal cancelatns 3-13, 213F3
Auto fuel economies set 4-30, 373F2-C3
Oil conservatn steps urged 5-16, 373C3
Gas price rptd at $1.98 per gal 5-19, 397A1
US oil import subsidy reactn 6-2, 6-6, 417B2, 430C1
Schmidt, Carter in talks 6-6, 430A1
China pact signed 6-19, 637G3
Tokyo summit, oil import targets set 6-28—6-29, 493B1-F2
Schmidt policy address stresses coal; detailed 7-4, 506A1
Oil prices, inflatn linked 7-13, 586D1
Carter plan assessed 7-16, 534F3
Oil spot mkt agrmt rptd 7-16, 494F2
Iran drops gas pipe plans 7-28, 583A1
New conservatn steps rptd 9-12, 733D2
Iran oil ban backed 11-13, 861F1, F2; import limits pledged 11-15, 879F2
Iran bars US $ oil paymts 11-23, 896D3
European Force Reduction Talks—*See under EUROPE*

1980

Schmidt in USSR, discusses A-missiles 6-30—7-1; econ pact signed 7-1, 489A1-D2
Sovts bar Olympic TV broadcast 7-13, 590D1
E Ger spy rptd arrested 7-31, 606D1
Polish loan OKd 8-12, 642D2
Sovt violinist seeks asylum 8-19, 908E1
Sovts jam radio broadcasts 8-20, 626E2
Schmidt cancels E Ger trip 8-22, 642E2, 658G1
Strauss urges Polish loans withheld 8-24, 642F2
Czech dissident arrives 9-2, 680F1
Strauss scores Schmidt policies 9-3—9-5, 690E3
Polish spy rptd arrested 9-9, 889D1
Sovt Jewish immigratn curb set 9-24, 833C1
USSR backs E Ger hard currency swap rules chng 10-14, 789C2
Sovts expel Kopelev, wife 11-12, 863A2
Sovts warned on Poland invasn 12-11, 949G1

East German Relations—*See GERMAN Democratic Republic—West German Relations*
Economy & Labor
'79 GNP rise rptd 1-12—1-13, 61B2
Wage restraint urged 1-18, 103A2
Econ forecast made 1-30, 197B3
Hoffmann-La Roche tranquilizer pricing OKd, Merck chrgs cited 2-12, 154C1
Metalworkers OK pay pact 2-13, 118A2
Discount, Lombard interest rates hiked 2-29, 153A3
Merger law broadened 3-1, 197G2
Jan inflatn rate rptd up 25% 3-7, 182D2
'79 lost work days down 3-18, 236A3
Steelmakers fined 4-3, 262F2
'80 budget supplemt OKd 4-30, 355E3
Discount, Lombard rates hiked 4-30, 356A1
Canada wage hikes compared 5-27, 406C2
Pvt TV blocked by ct 5-28, 411B3
Pre-war bond redemptn set 6-3, 446F3
Lockout tactic upheld by ct 6-10, 446F2
Krupp rpts '79 profits 6-11, 446B3
Bank fraud cases rptd 7-24—7-28, 581E1
Labor costs rptd 8-12, 698C1, F1
Shipping line insolvency rptd 8-18, 674E1
RR workers strike 9-17, W Berlin bars role 9-23, 731D1-A2
Lombard rate cut 9-18, 925B2
RR workers end strike 9-25, 300 rptd quit 9-29, 794G3
Schmidt sets post-electn goals 10-7, 760A1
'81 growth drop forecast, '80 rate at 2% 10-27, 925G1
Steel productn cutback plan opposed 10-30, 822A1
Wine scandal rptd 11-3, 11-18, 925C2
Savings subsidies cut, savings maturity hiked 11-13, 904A3
Postal labor pact set 11-23, 904G2-A3
Co-determinatn legis compromise offered 11-24, 904C2
VW, Ford plan lay-offs 11-27, 924C3
Aerospace firms set merger 11-29—11-30, 925E2
Mannesman co-determinatn restructuring rptd 12-1, 924G3
Bank earnings rptd 12-5, 12-10; Dresdner, Commerzbank sell Kaufhof holdings 12-12, 969E1
'81 draft budget approved 12-17, 963G3
Energy—*See also 'Atomic Energy' above*
Oil imports estimated, new steps urged 1-18, 103B2
Coal plant projct OKd 1-30, 103E2
Econ forecast linked 1-30, 197C3, E3
Brazil oil loan rptd 3-5, 191F1
Mex trade agrmts signed 5-21, 409F2
Sovt exploratn pact set 5-29, 411C2
7-natn Venice summit 6-22—6-23, 473A1-474E1
US-Japan synfuel pact signed 7-31, 666D2
Gasoline prices cut 8-12, 628A2
Algeria LNG deal canceled 9-11, 827A3
Schmidt vs intl force to protect Gulf oil 9-26, 735E2
E Ger projects rejected 10-15, 794F3
IEA sets '81 oil buying curb, stocks called 'adequate' 12-9, 932D1
'81 gas tax hike OKd 12-17, 969A1

1976

Heckler Colombia bribe rptd 2-23, 147G2
Australia steel projct deferred 2-24, 154D3
6-natn export credit pact rptd 2-25, 164C2
Jan trade surplus rptd 3-1, 270A1
Australia loan rptd 3-4, 172A3
US Sen subcom ends payoffs probe 3-10, 200A2
Lockheed probe panel named 3-15, 270C1
US threatens steel quota 3-16, 212G3
Worker participatn voted 3-18, 269G3
Mark gains vs $ 3-25, 229B2
Sovt A-plant plan dropped 3-30, 243C2
Egypt aid pact signed 3-30, 275A1
'75 Arab exports rptd up 3-31, 270B1
French snake reform proposal rejctd 4-1—4-2, 276A1, D1
Total IMF oil loan rptd 4-1, 340F2
VW OKs US plant 4-23, 321E2
Buys UK oil 4-27, 521E3
US ends car mktg probe 5-4; VW dumping rptd 5-6, 321B1-A2, D2
'75 Sovt trade rptd 5-5, 340D3
France to join African Dvpt Fund 5-10—5-11, 355F3
French A-reactor pact OKd 5-18, 372F2
Paris consortium in S Africa A-deal 5-28, 387G2
VW plans US plant 5-28—10-5, 987C3
UNCTAD OKs commodity fund 5-30, 388G2
7-natn summit set 6-1, 6-3, 388G3
Sovt gas turbine deal 6-1, 540D2
IDB entry set 6-3, 465D3
Loan to prop UK £ OKd 6-7, 407C2
Poland econ dvpt pact 6-11, 442E1
NATO OKs Canada tank purchase 6-11, 449B2
Mil aid to Portugal cited 6-11, 449D2
Export credit terms tightened 6-15, 529F3
Paris Club defers Zaire debt 6-17, 488A2
7-natn econ summit held 6-27—6-28, 461G2
France vs joint Eurpn steel firm 7-6, 521G1
7-natn A-waste conf opens 7-12, 739G1
Brazil A-sale bar reaffirmed 7-15, 530A3
Italy loan ban disclosed 7-16, 530D3; repercusns 7-20, 557B1
Israel links currency 7-18, 538D3
Mark gain pressures float 7-29, 594A1
US tank standardizatn set 8-4, 581D1
Kohl urges E Ger trade curbs 8-8, 630E3
VW OKs US price hikes 8-16, 10-12, 988D1
Dutch study drought aid 8-24, 630F1
Bernhard role in '71 jet buy rptd 9-2, 684F2
Backs Rhodesia compensatn 9-8, 681B2
IMF auctn bidder listed 9-15, 739D3
Strauss-Lockheed letter termed forgery 9-22, files rptd missing 9-17, 740B1
VW tops US fuel-econ ratings 9-22, 766A1-769C1
Aug trade surplus rptd down 9-24, 734B2
UK to seek IMF loan 9-29, 721D1
Strauss, Schmidt trade payoff chrgs 9-29, 10-1, 754C3
Mark gains vs $ 9-30, 721D2
Schmidt bars mark devaluatn 10-4, 754G2
Aug paymts surplus rptd 10-7, 857C3
Mark revalued 10-17, Apel statemt 10-18, 782A1
Lira fall, mark revaluatn linked 10-18, 838G1
OKs Iran-Krupp pact 10-19, 782C2
Mark moves upward vs $ 10-20, 782C1
Poland copper pact 11-2, credit deal rptd 11-4, 907E1
Mark reactn to US electn 11-3, 826F2
US car import sales rptd 11-3, 885A3
Australia lifts uranium ban 11-11, 888D1
US '77 tank choice seen 11-12, 941E3-942B1
'75 COMECON trade gap rptd 11-18, 977D1
France drops Strasbourg A-plant 11-20, 1002F3
Iran-Czech pipeline pact rptd 11-22, 946B2
Iran buys shares in Krupp 11-23, 949E1
OECD growth forecast disputed 11-23, 975G3
Rumania trade cited 12-1, 1010G1
Rhine pollutn pacts signed 12-4, 977A2
Poland coal projct credits rptd 12-8, 966E1
UK rpts joint US loan 12-15, 1003C3
Schmidt presents 4-yr progrm 12-16, 968B2
In IMF UK loan 12-21, 1004B1

Foreign Relations (misc.)—*See also 'UN Policy' below*
Student killed in Portugal 1-1, 11A1
UK units moved to Ulster 1-6, 19B3
Israel premr interview aired 1-11, 18E3
Europn soclsts meet 1-18—1-19, 48G2, A3
In Iran univ deal 1-20, 102G1
Angola mercenaries rptd 2-1, 82B1
Australia consulate cutback set 2-4, 97A2
Genscher in Portugal 2-4—2-5, 143A1
Israel cntr bombed in W Berlin 2-8, 107D1
CDU delegatn in China 2-14—3-2, 189F1, 190E1
Angola MPLA recognized 2-19, 163B1
Europn socialists meet 3-13—3-14, 222F3
Denmark relocates Viet orphans 3-19, 3-21, 252E1
Eur liberals meet 3-26—3-27, 260C3
Sadat visits 3-29—4-2, 275A1

1977

Foreign Relations (misc.)—*See also 'Atomic Energy' above, 'Monetary, Trade & Aid' and 'UN Policy' below*
Rpt failed to press Daoud case 1-10, 1-17, 27C3
France denies Daoud extraditn, Bonn scores release 1-11, 9A1-A2, 10B1
'76 Eur Cncl pact vs terror cited 9G2
France defends Daoud release 1-13, 1-17; Bonn scores release 1-13, 27D2-D3
Daoud would face trial 1-15, 27E3
Italy premr visits 1-17—1-18, 64F3
In 14-natn sulphur-dioxide pact 1-19, 109B3
Rhodesia rebels slay clerics 2-6, 85A1
ESA flight set 2-16, 170C3
Socialist rep at Israel Labor Party conventn 2-22, 135F1
Brazil mil aid request seen 3-7, 168B1
Ethiopian amb seeks asylum 3-11, 238G2
'76 Czech hijacker sentncd 3-31, 380B2

1978

Foreign Relations (misc.)—*See also 'Atomic Energy' above, 'Monetary, Trade, Aid & Investment' and 'UN' below*
Spy couple arrested in Netherlands 1-4, 21E3
At Westn natns Ogaden conf 1-21, 43E2
W Eur leftists doubt Baader suicides 1-22, 114G3
Sweden jails '77 plotters 1-31, 93B1
Greek premr sees Schmidt 1-31, 149E2
Giscard, Schmidt hold summit: OK ESA rocket launcher 2-6—2-7, 122A1
Switzerland tightens gun controls 2-9, 151C2
Austria protests secret svc surveillnc 2-14, 110B3
Colombia rpts W Ger terrorist activity 2-17—2-18, 147B3
Brazilian pres visits 3-6—3-10, 332D3
Dutch protest for Baader-Meinhof 3-14, 192F1
Supertanker spill off French coast 3-17, 201G3

1979

Foreign Relations (misc.)—*See 'Atomic' and 'Energy' above, 'Monetary' and 'UN' below*
At 4-natn Guadeloupe summit 1-5–1-6, China ties cautnd 1-5, 12D2, C3
Viet refugees accepted 1-8, 51G2
Italy arrests Moro kidnap suspect 1-27–1-28, 98F1
French UDF vs Gaullists 2-17–2-18, 135F1
UK amb threatened 3-23, 228A3
Bhutto executn scored 4-4, 247A2
London Times wkly printing set 4-20, halted 4-29, 330C3
Australia sets job study missn 4-28, 351G2
Chile refugee relocatn rptd 5-7, 369B3
Viets bar refugee sea rescue 6-30, 495C3
6 slain in Afghanistan 9-7, 696C1
Neo-Nazi Dutch troop attack cited 9-13, 733D3
Dutch Shell strikers vowed union support 9-24, 731C2

1980

Foreign Relations (misc.)—*See also 'Monetary', 'Soviet-Afghan Issue', 'UN Policy' below*
Italy terrorist, RAF links seen 1-2, 20F2
Liberal theologian's ouster backed by 7 colleagues, Vatican controversy detailed 2-5, 157A1
Greek terrorist plot vs emb chrgd 2-15, 150D3
UK soldiers attacked 2-19, 3-1, 3-10, IRA linked 2-19, 194A1
English Channel tunnel plan rptd 3-4, 193G3
Chad fighting resumes 3-22, natls evacuated 3-24, 221F1
Afghan soccer players defect 3-26, 271A2
Italy CP ldr, Brandt mtg cited 4-2, 254G3
UK concerned re troop offset paymts end 4-2, 274C2
Liberal theologian setlmt reached 4-10, 364A2
Westn mil parade, riot linked 5-18, 500F3
ESA rocket test fails 5-23, 397G2

1976

Swiss probe Spinola expose 4-7, 315C1
Schmidt on Eur CPs 4-15, 503C1
India natls score curbs 4-24, 313F1
'75 Swedish emb raid trial opens 5-6, 503E1
Meinhof death stirs Paris, Rome protests 5-10, 383C2
Israel protests Cannes film 5-14—5-28, 460A2
Brandt at intl soc dems mtg 5-23—5-25, 449A3
Kissinger-Vorster mtg set 6-18, 426D1 ★, 427D1 ★; meet 6-23—6-24, 446F1, 447A1
US evacuates 20 from Leb 6-20, 448C1
Vorster sees S Africa ambs 6-21—6-22, Schmidt 6-25, 447D3 ★
Genscher sees S Africa min 6-22, 447A3
Hijackers land Uganda, ask prisoners freed 6-29, 463A1-F1; **for subsequent developments, see 'Entebbe' under MIDDLE EAST—AVIATION Incidents**
French ldr visits 7-6, 521D1
Spain rightist aid rptd 7-30, 753E1
2 spies rptd arrested 8-16, 640B2
'Carlos' rptd in Yugo 9-6—9-16, 722D1
Backs US Africa policy 9-8, 681B2
UK ship rescue aid 9-20, 713A1
Pohle extradited from Greece 10-1, 754G3
French troop reductn rptd 10-9, 852A3, 880D1
Top-level French mtgs cited 880C3
Brandt, Schmidt address Soclst Intl 11-26, 935F2, B3
Spain OKs Socialist conf 11-27, 908E3
France bars joint Eur defns 11-30, 905A3
Schmidt presents 4-yr progrm 12-16, 968B2

Government & Politics—*See also other appropriate subheads in this section*
CDU wins Lower Saxony electn, gains Bundesrat majority 1-15, 77G1
Listed as 'free' nation 1-19, 20C3
CDU wins Lower Saxony revote 2-6, FDP vetoes coalitn 2-10, 157C2
CDU wins Baden-Wurttemberg vote 4-4, 270D1
Marriage reform OKd 4-8, 4-9, 270G1
Court OKs electn aid 4-21, 403F3
Abortion bill passed 5-6, 503A2 ★
Secy arrested as spy 5-14; CDU, intellignc officials suspended 5-17, 5-19, 383D1
CDU issues campaign platform 5-20, 442B1
More spy suspects seized 6-2—6-14, 441E3
SPD campaign conv 6-18—6-19, 502G3
SPD-FDP coalitn wins electns 10-3; CDU disputes 10-4, FDP reaffirms ties 10-5, 754B2-F3
Kohl resigns prime min post; to lead oppositn 10-7, 857B3
Focke quits as health min 10-15, 857A3
Recount hikes coalitn majority 10-20, 857G2-A3
2 AF gens dismissed 11-1, CDU scores 11-8, 930D3
CSU votes break with CDU 11-19, 930B2
Nurenburg CSU votes party cong 12-6, 930C3
CDU, CSU reunite 12-12, 968D2
Carstens elected parlt pres 12-14, 968B3
Schmidt reelected, shifts Cabt 12-15; presents 4-yr progrm 12-16, 968E1
Labor min resigns 12-15, 968G1

1977

Sweden arrests plotters, links to Baader-Meinhof, deports 2 4-1—4-6, 428E3
S Africa rejcts Namibia plan 4-7, 285C1
Schmidt at Bilderberg conf 4-21—4-24, 359C3
Genscher sees Singapore ldr on rights 4-28, 394F3
S Africa sees Namibia compromise 4-29, 349C2
Senegal pres sees Schmidt 5-3, 394E1
Zaire ousts newsman 5-6, 394A2
S Africa OKs Namibia const concessns 5-9, 400D1
Schaufele, Congo min meet 6-6, 583B2
S Africa OKs Namibia plan 6-10, 457B2
Giscard visits 6-16—6-17, 566C3
Schmidt in Canada 7-6—7-12, 566G1, G2
Thai aide ends exile 7-10, 641A3
Schmidt, Carter agree on MBFR, CSCE policies 7-13—7-14, 566B2, E2
Sweden plotters indicted 7-25, 709G1
Anti-Ger sentiment in France rptd 7-28, 597E2
SWAPO ldr joins Namibia talks 8-8, 639D3
Kappler escapes Italy jail, heads of state mtg delayed 8-15; extraditn asked 8-17, 637E3
S Africa A-test plan rptd 8-17, Botha assures 8-30, 663D3, 664A1
Kappler escape causes Italy pol crisis 8-18—9-18, 728G3-729E1
Kappler asylum arouses concern 8-19—8-26, 658G1
Namibia compromise reached 8-19, 699D3
Kappler escape detailed 8-19, 9-15, 729F1
Italy asks Kappler confinemt 8-26, Bonn rejcts extraditn 9-21, 729G1
Eur Cncl to study Turkey rights abuses in Cyprus 9-8, 764G1-A2; rpt shelved, Greece protests 11-3, 946E3
Schleyer negotiator named 9-9; Dutch search 9-27; body found in France 10-19; French, Dutch manhunt aid asked 10-20, 791E1, B2, G2-A3
Namibia conf stalled 9-22—9-26, 770D2
Dutch in terrorist shootout 9-22, ask manhunt aid 9-24, 11-11, arrest 4 10-7, 888D1
Dutch bar Folkerts extraditn 9-23, 986G1
France arrests Baader atty 9-30, extradites 11-16; leftists protest, govt defends 11-17, 11-25—11-28, 968F2, 969C1
Jet hijacking dvpts 10-13—10-20, rescued in Somalia 10-18, aid deal denied 10-19, 789A1-790D2
W Eur heroin conf 10-17—10-21, 971D3
Baader gang suicides spur intl probe requests 10-18; France, Italy leftists protest deaths 10-19, 790B2, 791C1
UK mil 'offset paymt' terms agreed 10-18, 926F2
Somalia arms needs, hijack rescue aid linked 10-22, 830C1
W Ger tightens security at 13 forgn airports 10-23—10-24, Algeria flight canceled 11-8, 868C3-E3
S Africa amb recall rptd 10-25, 825C1
Dutch tycoon kidnaped 10-28, 871E1
Dutch capture 2 terrorist suspects 11-10, 887E3
Namibia tour fails to win SWAPO concessns 11-21—12-7, 1016E3
Schmidt meets Andreotti in Verona 12-1, 1014G3
Swiss capture 2 terrorists 12-20, 1017D3
Italy hunts group linked to Baader-Meinhof 12-28, 1014E2

Government & Politics—*See also other appropriate subheads in this section*
Hesse scandals harm SPD-FDP coalitn 2-23, 3-24, SPD vote 3-20, 353A1
Osswald, Arndt resignatns cited 353B1
W Berlin sen resigns 4-27, mayor quits 4-29, Stobbe named mayor 5-2, 352D3
SPD ousts youth-wing head 4-27, 353E1
Schmidt loses '73 power challenge 5-26, defeats censure motion 6-21, 601G3
Brandt warns of Nazi revival 8-19, 658G1
Friderichs quits econ post 9-9, Lambsdorff named 10-7, 969B2
Defns Min spy scandal disclosed 12-12, Kohl asks Leber resignatn 12-15, 968C1

1978

Italy terrorism linked, W Ger police join Moro kidnap search 3-20, 200C1
Schmidt sees Giscard 4-2, 258C2
Swiss host 4-natn terrorism mtg, 'hot line' set 4-8—4-9, 438B2
Eur conservative group formed 4-24, 424C3
Swiss trial of 2 terrorists opens 4-25, 353E3
Belfast seeks IRA-terrorist links 4-27, 373E2
5 arrested for Dutch arms theft 4-29, 477B3
Siemen exec in Milan shot 5-4, worker's car firebombed 5-8, 393A2, C2
Dutch arrest 3 terrorists 5-5, jail 8-21, 725C1
Dutch rule on extraditn of Folkerts, 2 other terrorists 5-8, 354C1, 454C3
Turkey premr visits 5-11, 378E1
France arrests terrorists 5-11, 5-25, 439B1 ★, A2, C2
ESA communicatns satellite launched 5-12, 384D3
Nazi arrested in Brazil 5-30, extraditn asked 5-31, 477G1
Australia prime min to visit 6-1, 450E3
Westn natns meet on pan-Africa force 6-5, 441E2
Swiss jail 2 terrorists 6-30, 558F2
French ct upholds Baader atty '77 extraditn 7-7, 649B3
Brandt, Kreisky arrange Sadat-Peres peace talks, give peace plan 7-9; plan made pub 7-10, 521B2
Hijacking pact signed 7-17, 544G2
'76 papal kidnap plot rptd 8-6, 689A3
UK Rhine army reinforcemts planned 8-16, 705F1
UK army bases bombed 8-18; terrorists linked 8-19—8-24, patrols increased 8-25, 688D1
Croat flees to Sweden 8-30, 925F3
Baum sees UK home secy 9-4—9-5, 688B2
Dutch broaden Folkerts extraditn rule 9-7, 725E1
WWII secret documts issued by US 9-10—9-18, 744D2-G3
UK arrests terrorist, extraditn asked 9-15, 725A2
Dutch extradite 3 terrorist suspects 10-13, 10-17, 885B1
El Salvador Bayer plant bombed 11-24, 986G3
Viet refugees accepted 12-2, 932E3
China-US ties lauded 12-16, 977C1

Government & Politics—*See also other appropriate subheads in this section*
Strauss tap chrgs spur controversy 1-13—1-17, 74B2
5 army officers reinstated 1-20, 114A3
Leber linked to new scandal 1-24, offers resignatn 2-1, 74F2-C3
Leber resigns, Cabt reshuffled 2-3, 93B2
Schmidt testifies at Defns Min spy probe 2-24, 210D3
Bavaria, Schleswig-Holstein electns; SPD loses Munich, Regensberg mayoralities 3-5; SPD rift blamed 3-7, 211D1
Parlt curbs secret svcs 3-9, 210G3
Oppositn asks Cabt resign 3-16, 332A3
Armed forces reorganizatn curbed 3-23, 354G1
Lower Saxony justice min resigns 3-23, 477F2
Mil svc objectors law altered 4-13, 354E1
Filbinger pres bid in doubt 5-28, 477B3
Schmidt addresses Bundestag 6-1, 519F1
Free Dems lose Lower Saxony, Hamburg state electns; environmtalists gain 6-4, 456A2
Maihofer resigns as interior min, Baum named successor 6-6, 456A3, C3
W Berlin justice min resigns 7-3, 651B2
Filbinger quits state post 8-7, 616C3
Spaeth named Filbinger successor, Rommel challenge fails 8-16, 725E3
SPD spy scandal disclosed; Brandt, Schmidt chrg smear campaign 8-31—9-6, 725C2, D2 ★
Rau named N Rhine-Westphalia premr 9-19, 725G3 ★
'79 budget presented to parlt 9-20, 906B3
SPD spy probe dropped 9-26, 868G2
Schmidt ex-aide sentncd for spying 10-5, 776D3
Schmidt coalitn wins Hesse vote 10-8, 776G2

1979

French joint A-force rejected 9-24, 733C1
France sentncs Breton separatist 10-20, 835E2
China premr arrives 10-21, backs Ger renunificatn 10-22, signs pacts 10-24, 853E3, F3
French pres visits W Berlin 10-29, 835A2
Mex conservatives score Brandt's visit 10-30, 874G3
Portugal pol party tied to CDU 12-2, 917B1
Swiss arrest terrorist 12-13, 998C3
Vatican censures liberal theologian 12-18, 999C2

Government & Politics —*See also other appropriate subheads in this section*
Fed job loyalty checks eased 1-18, 61E2
CDU infiltratn, E Ger spy data rptd 3-6—3-13, 180G2
Brandt files for divorce 3-8, 271F3
SPD-FDP gain in regional electns 3-18, 214A3
CDU wins in Schleswig-Holstein 4-29, 333F2
Carstens elected pres 5-23, 410F2
CDU-CSU alliance faces split 5-24, 5-28, 489D1
Eur Parlt electns 6-10, 433A1, D2
FDP Conv, A-power backed 6-16, 489F2
CDU, CSU unite behind Strauss 7-2, 505G3-506A1
Poehl named Bundesbank chief 9-19, 733G2-C3
SDP wins in North Rhine-Westphalia 9-29—9-30, 796A2
Strauss loses in electn dispute 10-5, 796A2
Ecologists advance in Bremen vote 10-6—10-7, 796F1
'77 mil spending total rptd 10-13, 804F1
Environmtlists plan natl 'Green Party' 10-27—10-28, 876E1
Soc Dems hold conv, Schmidt gets strong support 12-4—12-6, 938E2

1980

Amnesty Intl chgs pol prisoner abuse, Bonn scores 5-28, 441E2, 446E3
Turks, other drug arrests rptd 6-13, 517E1, G1
7-natn Venice summit 6-22—6-23, Schmidt USSR trip plans rptd 6-23, 473A1-474E1
Eur role backed 7-9, 522B1; 7-11, 540B1
NATO A-missiles backed 7-15, 540C1
ESA plans comet probe 7-15, 548A1
Navy curbs lifted 7-18, 540E1
Pol asylum rules rptd tightened 7-31, 581B2
Westn labor costs compared 8-12, 698C1
Turkey coup sympathy rptd 9-16, 696F3
Swiss sentence terrorist 9-26, 755D1
Natls flee Dutch ocean liner fire 10-4, 769A3
Kurds attack Turkey W Berlin consulate 10-8, 794A2
Viet boat people rescued 10-13, 952E1
French newspr rpt on terrorist atty extraditn cited 11-7, 872F1
Pope visits; seeks ecumenical ties, affirms traditionalism 11-15—11-19; youth ldrs denouce 11-19, 904F3-905A3
French Relations—*See FRANCE--German Relations*

Government & Politics—*See also other appropriate subheads in this section*
Environmentalists form 'Green ' party 1-12—1-13, 61E1
Divorce law upheld by ct 2-28, 197F2
Baden-Wurttemberg electns held, Greens advance 3-16, 236F3
SPD wins North Rhine-Westphalia electn 5-11, 390C3
Schmidt, Strauss campaign chrgs rptd 9-3—9-5, 690C3
RC bishops enter pol debate, Schmidt scores 9-13, 712B1
Schmidt coalition wins election, FDP advances 10-5; Schmidt sets goals 10-7, 10-5, 759G2, 760A1
Cabt sworn 11-5, 925D1
Parlt opens, Schmidt addresses 11-24, 904A2
Latin American Relations
Brazil oil loan rptd 3-5, 191F1
Cuban refugees offered asylum 4-16, 285C1
Mex pres visits 5-19—5-21, trade agrmts signed 5-21, 409G1, F2
Jamaica import credit rptd 6-4, 465D1
Brazil VW stake acquired by Kuwait 6-25, 542E3, 562C1
Nazi kills self in Brazil 10-3, 810E1
Bolivia deposed pres arrives 10-5, 787C2

1976

1977

Helsinki Agreement—*See 'Security and Cooperation in Europe' under EUROPE*

Monetary, Trade & Aid Issues (including all foreign economic developments)—*See also 'Atomic Energy' above*
Quebec bond sale 159A1
In UK sterling balances pact 1-10, 20C2
Andreotti-Schmidt talks 1-17—1-18, 64F3
UK $1.5 bln bank loan rptd 1-24, 99G1
Mondale urges econ expansn 1-25, 69A2
E Ger '76 trade gap rptd 1-26, 123D2
US links GNP hike, world trade aid 1-28, 92D2
'76 auto exports rptd up 1-31, 139C2
Indonesia, Turkey arms sales OKd 2-2, 139E2
US indicts 3 airlines 2-3, 93F2
IMF SDR defined 87G2
'76 Sovt, E Eur trade rptd 2-9, 102C2
'76 paymts surplus rptd 2-10, 118F1
Sovt-bloc debt rptd 2-13, 335F3
Irish ban large fishing vessels 2-15, 146C3
Leads West in '76 currency reserves 2-22, 260A3
'76 US central bank interventn rptd 3-2, 188G3
US execs sentncd for Sovt sales 3-14, 203F2
Feb trade surplus sets record 3-28, 260C2
US asks Portugal aid 4-1, 330C3
1st ¼ Eurobond trading rptd 4-13, 318E1
Zaire aid set 4-14, 317F3
At 7-natn econ summit, paymts deficit move OKd 5-7—5-8, 357A1-358B2
Eastern to lease Airbus 5-24, 441D2
US asks paymts deficit move 5-25, 437D3
Group of 10 membership cited 438F1
In 11-natn Portugal loan 6-22, 530B3
Lockheed cleared re paymts 6-22, 602E1
Zaire debt rescheduled 7-7, 583E1
Australia imposes car import quotas 7-12, 560F3
Schmidt, Carter agree on Eur econ aid 7-13—7-14, 566C2
Canada to buy Leopard tanks 7-13, 579E3
$ drops, US backs depreciatn 7-21, 551G3, 552F1
$ drops 4.6% vs mark 7-28, 585E2
6-mo paymts surplus rptd 7-31, 586B2
Danes OK North Sea gas line 8-1, 672D1
US trade deficit-reducing strategy, Emminger oppositn rptd 8-8, 585G1-586A1
US scores trust probe-blocking laws 8-8, 630A1
Sweden quits 'snake' 8-29, 709A1
Euroloan to Nigeria rptd 9-1, 746D3
Italy starts '74 loan repaymt 9-6, 729B2
S Africa investmts, exports rptd 9-23, 771E1
Carter scores econ growth policies at IMF-World Bank mtg, McNamara scores poor natn aid level 9-26, 753F2-F3, 754G1
E Ger shops rptd source of W Ger, other Westn currency 10-2, 782G1
US panel minimizes govt steel subsidy impact 10-7, 776D2
'76 car exports cited 10-11, 853A3
Miles Lab OKs Bayer takeover 10-17, 880A2
Canada chrgs steel dumping 10-18, 863A1
Somalia aid deal denied 10-19, 790C2; 10-22, 830C1
US unit dumping chrgs re French-produced steel probed 10-19, 933A3
US co chrgs steel dumping 10-20, 836E3

1978

Helsinki Agreement—*See EUROPE—Security & Cooperation*

Middle East Relations
Israeli oranges found poisoned 2-1, 60F3-61A1
Sadat visits, seeks Mideast peace move backing 2-9—2-10, 98E2
Iranians, W Gers storm E Ger missn in Bonn 2-28, 190C2
Egypt protests Israel Leb invasn 3-15, 174F3
'77 Lufthansa hijacker sentenced 4-25, 353F3
Egypt terror group rptd smashed 4-26, 300D2
Israel tour bus blast kills 2 4-26, 300G2
Israeli import co bombed 6-22, 500G1
Brandt, Kreisky arrange Sadat-Peres peace talks, give peace plan 7-9; plan made pub 7-10, 521B2
Hungary opens jean factory 8-8, 882E3
Klein rptd in Israel 8-17, 651D3
Iran A-plant work to continue 10-22, 816C3

Monetary, Trade, Aid & Investment—*See also 'Atomic Energy' above*
'77 trade, paymts surplus rptd 1-3, 1-4, 21C3
US $ drop, recovery rptd 1-4, 27E3
Thyssen Budd bid revealed 1-12, talks OKd 1-17, 66D1
Somalia asks arms aid 1-16, credits OKd 1-21, 43B3, 44A1
France '77 trade rptd 1-16, 149E1
Mex to continue VW 'beetle' productn 1-19, 74F3
Schmidt rejcts US econ pressure 1-19, 93E3
'77 $ drop rptd 1-23, 27D2
US $ strategy rptd 1-23, 27F2
'77 investmts in US rptd 1-24, 65D3
Finland '77 trade surplus rptd 1-30, 90C1
US picks gun for XM-1 tank 1-31, 81F3
Israeli oranges found poisoned 2-1, 60F3-61A1
Ethiopia protests Somalia aid 2-1, 100D1
Somalia makes 2d aid bid 2-4, 99G3
Giscard-Schmidt summit scores UK fishing policy, backs Greece EC entry 2-6—2-7, 122C1
Austria '77 trade deficit rptd 2-7, 110F2
Schmidt sees US Treas secy, bars growth rate hike 2-13, 119C1
Dutch '77 trade rptd 2-14, 169C3
Westdeutsche Landesbank concerned re $ crisis 2-17, 119A2
US $ drops vs mark 2-23, '77 depreciatn cited 118D2, F2
Sachs takeover by UK firm halted 2-23, 211B1
US offcls link $, W Ger econ health 3-6, 119F1
Brazilian pres visits 3-6—3-10, 332D3
Schmidt eases US $ crisis tensns 3-9; joint plan proposed 3-13, reactn 3-14, 234F1, D2
Dresdner Bank bars Peru loan refinancing 3-10, 353F1, C2
Kenyan vp ends quest for arms 3-11, 289F2
UK prime min urges Bonn summit plan 3-14, sees Carter 3-23, 226B3
Australia '77 gold imports rptd 3-15, 208F3
USSR '77 trade cited 3-29, 230A1
VW hikes US car prices, $ drop cited 3-31, 283G2
US $ hits record low 4-3, 235C1
Mark in new SDR basket 4-3, 300F3
Eastern buys airbuses 4-6, 264C3
Dresdner Bank in Chile loan 4-7, 312E1
Kenya dam contracts rptd 4-9, 479D1
Czech pres in talks 4-10—4-14, 332G3, 333C1
'77, 1st ¼ $ defns costs rptd 4-13, 523E2
ICAO picks US bad-weather landing system 4-19, 319B3
Canada gets Deutsche Bank loan 4-28, 328C1
Schmidt scores US oil imports, econ policy 4-28; sees Carter 5-30—5-31, reviews talks 6-1, 519A2
Japan seeks US pact 5-3, 341B3
USSR trade pact signed 5-7, 417F1
Fishermen join Danish protest 5-10, 436C3
E Ger protests imported food costs, currency issue cited 5-11, 504F2
Turkey aid pledge rptd 5-15, 398F2
Brazil auto workers strike 5-16—5-18, 5-22, 412B1-D1
Cobalt purchases rptd up 5-24, 382D2
US sues VW of Amer 5-24, 409C2

1979

Helsinki Agreement—*See EUROPE-Security and Cooperation*

Middle East Relations
Iran oil cutoff impact assessed 2-20, 126G2
UN rights comm res on Palestinian state opposed 2-21, 148F1
PLO scores Israel-Egypt pact support 3-25, 222B2
Sadat visits, seeks econ aid 3-29, 250A1
Palestinian rights backed 6-6, 430C1
Iran banks natlzd 6-7, compensatn vowed 6-10, 469B2; insurnc cos natlzd 6-25, 486E2
Arafat, Brandt meet 7-6–7-8, 511B3
Israel setlmts pressure rptd sought by US 7-9, 511B2
Iran drops gas pipe plans 7-28, 583A1
Kraftwerk cancels Iran A-plant contract 7-31, 586F2
Iran A-plant deal canceled 7-31, 586F2; compensatn demanded 8-10, 634E3
Iran ousts 2 newsmen 8-21, 635A2
Libyans occupy Bonn Emb 9-3, 688F2
Israeli talks 9-10; Dayan scores Palestinian rights stand, Bonn denies tilt 9-11, 677B1
Israel sentncs 2 for '76 jet plot 9-11, 677C2
Oman proposes Persian Gulf security aid 10-14–10-16, 804B2
Exec slain in Iran 10-14, 814C3
US ban on Iran oil backed 11-13, 861F1, F2; import limits pledged 11-15, 879F2
Iranian statemt issued by freed US hostages 11-21, 894F2
Iran bars US $ oil paymts 11-23, 896D3
US bank attaches Iran assets 11-28, 896E2
US missn seeks Iran sanctns 12-6; Bonn curbs Iran credit guarantees, arms exports 12-7, 934A1
US seeks econ sanctns vs Iran 12-11, 933C2

Monetary, Trade, Aid & Investment—*See also 'Atomic' above*
Guadeloupe summit warned vs China trade 1-6, Turkey aid offer rptd 1-12, 12C3, 40B2
Tenglemann Group to buy A&P share 1-16, 53C3
Central bank tightens credit, ups reserve; money supply, US $ support cited 1-18, 62C1
Shipbldg competitn cited 1-21, 77F3
'79 trade surplus drop seen 1-23, 62B1
Budget OKd by parlt 1-26, 77F2
'78 trade surplus rptd, US $ drop cited 1-26, 77G2-C3
Spain OKs 2 banks 1-26, 100F3
US '78 trade gap rptd 1-30, 71E3
EC comm backs farm price freeze 1-31, 85F1
Finland '78 trade rptd 2-2, 215G2
Turkey aid role taken by OECD 2-6, 116E3
'78 paymts surplus rptd 2-7, 137F1
US $ rises vs mark 2-8, 83B2
Carter Westn econ summit warning to Japan rptd 2-10, rpt disputed 2-15, 160E1
UK scores EC farm policy 2-21, 154F2
US Jan trade gap rptd 2-28, 159B2
EC farm accord reached 3-6, 160C3
USSR '78 trade rptd 3-6, 172G2
US $ defense rptd 3-7, 159C3, E3
Sovt-bloc '78 Westn debt estimate rptd 3-20, 200D3
USSR-Krupp steel deal rptd 3-26, 237D3
Sadat seeks econ aid 3-29, 250A1
S Africa '72-78 loans rptd 4-2, 270D2
Continental Gummi Werke to buy Uniroyal operatns 4-17, 560G3
US $ closes up vs mark 5-1, 321B1
Westn exporter labor costs ranked 5-1, 374A2
1st 1/4 trade surplus rptd 5-2, 374D1
Allianz-Versicherungs to buy 2 US insurance cos 5-11, 6-25, 942C2
Turkey aid set 5-30, 397A2
Iran banks natlzd 6-7, compensatn vowed 6-10, 469B2
China tech, raw materials pact signed 6-19, 637E3
Mineral stockpile plans rptd 6-21, 489C3
EC green currencies revised 6-21, 513F1
Iran insurnc cos natlzd 6-25, 486E2
US May trade gap rptd 6-27, 480G3
Oil prices, inflatn linked 7-13, 586D1
OECD sees paymts deficit 7-19, 554E3
VW-Chrysler Argentina plans rptd 7-20, 562A2
VW, Mercedes plan US plants 7-26, 663D3
Iran drops gas pipe plans 7-28, 583A1
US AWACS deal threatened 8-1, 586E1
'France' sails to W Ger 8-15, 633D3
French knitwear import curbs protested 8-20, 668E3
US $ down vs mark 9-13, 676D2
VW-Chrysler Argentina sale set 9-15, 699A2
IMF sees less paymts surplus 9-16, 720D1
UK EC contributn seen more 9-17, 719B2
Hong Kong import demand cited 9-17, 730F2
EMS currencies revalued, US $ drop vs mark seen 9-24, 718G3
US offcls, Schmidt meet re $, mark rates 9-29, 779E3

1980

Middle East Relations
Iran warns newsmen 1-14, 29F2
Saudi note sale set 3-24, 236E2-A3
Schmidt backs US re Iran 4-20, 303E1
Iran hostage kin seek support 4-23, 299D2
Iran hostage rescue missn backed 4-25, 324B2
Leftists back US emb takeover in Iran 5-18, 500E3
Iran trade sanctns OKd, current data cited 5-21, 378A2
Iran gold transfers rptd 6-17, 464A3
Schmidt seeks Carter mtg 6-18, 451D1
Kuwait buys 10% of Brazil VW unit 6-25, other investmts rptd 6-25, 7-15, 542E3, 562C1
Iran takes over 4 drug co units 7-9, 546A2
Iran hostage arrives Wiesbaden 7-12, 539E1
Egypt amb at shah's funeral 7-29, 571G1
UN Palestinian state res abstentn 7-29, 572F1
Iraqi diplomats held in bomb plot 8-1, 604E2
Iran trade decline, shipping line insolvency linked 8-18, 674F1
Iraqi diplomats to be deported 9-15, 712A2
Schmidt vs intl force to protect Gulf oil 9-26, 735E2
PLO, Libya linked to Munich blast 9-30, 755C1
Iranian factns clash in Bonn 11-2, 969C2

Monetary, Trade, Aid & Investment
See also 'Atomic Energy' above
Alcoa suspends USSR aluminum talks 1-3, 9A2
Gold reserves rptd 1-18, 30G2
Bank curbs on gold, other metal holdings set 1-23, 103C2
Turkey econ steps rptd 1-25, 80A1
US '79 trade gap rptd 1-29, 77E2
'79 current acct deficit, '80 deficit hike seen 1-30, 197E3
'79 US mfg investmt rptd 2-6, 92C3
VW sets 2d US site 2-12, 127B3
Swiss firm cleared in drug pricing suit 2-12, 154C1
Turkey aid role taken, Greece reassured 2-16—2-19, 135B3
US $-mark exchng rate chart 2-18—3-20, 202D1, A2
Turkey mil aid plans noted 2-25, 153E3
US linked to interest rate hikes 2-28, 153C3
Japan sets yen rescue plan 3-2, 173D2
Brazil oil loan rptd 3-5, 191F1
Pak, Turkey aid plans cited 3-10, 205E2
US $ soars vs mark, central bank intervenes 3-17; profit-taking slows surge 3-19—3-20, 202E3
US Steel files dumping complaint 3-21, 225D1
Saudi note sale set; paymts deficit, mark slippage cited 3-24, 236E2-A3
Hunt group sets silver-backed bond issue 3-26, 223D1
Turkey aid vow rptd 3-26, 236E2
IMF hikes SDR interest rate 3-27, 302B2
'79 US investmt rptd 4-8, 329C1
US sets steel import probe 4-10, 367F3
W Eur fighter jet planned 4-14, 303E1
VW in Europn auto research effort 4-14, 303B3
Turkey aid OKd 4-15, 295A3
E Ger trade expansn set 4-17, 303A2
IMF $ support plan shelved 4-24, 301G1
UK opposed on EC budget, farm prices 4-27, 4-28, 327G1, A2
Turkey aid budgeted 4-30, 355E3
EC fund hike unlikely 4-30, 355G3
French TV satellite pact signed 4-30, 356D1
Central banks rptd active in forgn exchng mkts 4-30, 436B3
US finds steel import damage 5-1, 456C1
UK shift on Iran sanctns stand scored 5-20, 378D2
Iran trade sanctns OKd, current data cited 5-21, 378A2
Mex plastics deal set, tech transfer pacts renewed 5-21, 409F2
Sovt trade blitz rptd 5-22, 430G3
US OKs mark futures trading 5-28, 481C2
Sovt draft trade pact set, '79 data cited 5-29, 411A2
Pre-war bond redemptn questnd 6-3, 446F3
Jamaica import credit rptd 6-4, 465D1
SEAT investmt talks rptd 6-4, 467C3
Iran gold transfers rptd 6-17, 464A3
Turkey '79 debt rptd 6-19, 468F1
7-natn Venice summit 6-22—6-23, 473A1-474E1
E Eur pact adherence vowed 6-23, 474G1
Kuwait buys 10% of Brazil VW unit 6-25, other investmts rptd 6-25, 7-15, 542E3, 562C1
Iran takes over 4 drug co units 7-9, 546A2
US-Japan synfuel pact signed 7-31, 666D2

1976

Nazis—*See under 'N'*

Obituaries
Braun, Franziska 1-13, 56A3
Bultmann, Rudolf 7-30, 816E3
Dopfner, Julius Cardinal 7-24, 716A3
Heidegger, Martin 5-26, 404G1-A2
Heisenberg, Werner 2-1, 124D3
Kempe, Rudolf 5-11, 524A3
Lehmann, Lotte 8-26, 892B3
Polish Relations—*See 'Eastern European Policy' above*

1977

$ drop vs mark rptd 11-1, 829D2
3d in China forgn trade 11-7, 882D3
TVA sues uranium producers 11-18, 895F1
Deutsche Bank heads Mex loan group 11-18, 967C1
Nigeria gunboat purchase rptd 11-23, 986A3
'77 mark rise vs $ rptd 11-30, 932E3
E Ger VW barter deal set 11-30, 984E1
Chrysler unveils front-drive cars 12-5—12-9, 962C1
Schmidt scores $ drop, cites EC $ purchases in '77 12-6, 932C3
Mark seen overvalued 12-6, 12-8, 933A1
VW asks currency exchng rate stability, cites export harm in US mkt 12-7, 932D3
Mark rise threat to exports, econ growth seen 12-7, 932G3
$ closes up vs mark 12-8, 933C1
Brandt intl dvpt comm meets 12-9—12-11, 997F3
VW hikes US prices, cites $ drop 12-14, 962D1
$ drops 12-30, 997F2

Nazis—*See under 'N'*

Obituaries
Altmeier, Peter 8-28, 696B2
Bloch, Ernst 8-3, 696D2
Boehm, Franz 9-26, 872A1
Erhard, Ludwig 5-5, 452A3
Mardersteig, Giovanni 12-27, 1024D2
Von Braun, Wernher 6-16, 432G3

1978

Zaire aid OKd 6-13—6-14, 478A1
Czech, Sovt terrorist aid probed 6-22, 500F1
Israel import co bombed 6-22, 500G1
US weighs oil import fee 6-22, 511A3
Schmidt, Giscard meet; EC monetary zone agreed 6-23, 545A2
Schmidt in Nigeria, Zambia 6-26—6-30; defends S Africa ties 6-30, 584B1
Zambia loan cited 6-29, 617A2
US $ up vs mark 7-14, 523B3
7-natn Bonn econ summit 7-16—7-17, 543B3-544A3
Zaire communicatns deal rptd 7-19, 652A3
Iran completes Krupp purchase paymts 7-27, 617B1
Westn econ stimulus plans urged 7-28, 583E3
US $ drops 8-15, marks sold 8-16, 622F1, A2
Comecon loan rptd 8-17, 660E3
VW tops US fuel-econ list 9-15, 719F2
IMF quota hike, SDR issue compromise agreed 9-24, 731F3
IMF asks growth rate hike 9-25, US backs 9-26, 731B3
Trade % of GNP rptd 9-26, 804D2
Swiss see trade threat from undervalued US $ 9-27, 9-28, 732G1
US $ 9-mo losses vs mark rptd 10-2, 732F1
Poor natn debts canceled 10-6, 776F2
Joint Australia coal conversn effort set 10-10, 793D3
Mark revalued up vs 'snake' countries 10-16, 798C2
Brazil, Paraguay, 3 cos sign hydro turbine pact 10-20, 829A3
US firm drops Bayer unit sale 10-24, 897F1
UK Airbus role agreed 10-24, 902A3
US air svc agrmt 10-25, 831E1
US $ hits record low 10-30, rescue plan set, $ recovers 11-1, 825B1, G1, D2, G2
Canada-S Africa arms deal suspected 11-6—11-7, 904G2
US withdraws IMF reserve marks 11-7, 998C3
2 banks ranked among world's '77 top 10 11-8, 914A1, D1
Hungary devalues forint 11-11, 906G2
E Ger transport pacts OKd 11-16, 906B1
Greece mil aid cited 11-24, 924C2
Dresdner sets Nigeria loan 11-30, 934A2
At Brussels monetary summit, EMS entry backed 12-4—12-5, 951F3, 952C2
US sells mark notes 12-13, 998G2
Ireland to join EMS 12-15, 979F1, C2
OPEC $ use seen as aid 12-17, 977F3
OPEC price hike impact disputed 12-18, 978E1-F1
Greek EC entry terms set, worker curbs cited 12-21, 1017C3, F3
US probes steel dumping chrgs 12-28, 1006B1
$ closes down vs mark 12-29, 998E2
France delays EMS start pending agri subsidy phase-out 12-29, 999D1

Nazis
Goebbels diary on best-seller list 1-2, 22A1
Anti-Semitic incidents rptd, army officers reinstated 1-7—2-5; local curbs asked 2-4, 114A2
Majdanek war crimes trial criticism rptd 1-30, 114B3
Kappler dies 2-9, 114C3
Govt denies prosecutn lag 2-22, 477D2
Scheel asks Nazis studies 3-5, 477E2
Puvogel resigns over '36 thesis 3-23, 477F2
Gypsies ask reparatns 4-11, 318A3
Maihofer rpts neo-Nazism on rise 4-29—4-30, 477G2
5 rightists arrested for arms theft 4-29, 477B3
USSR propaganda halt asked 5-4, 417G1
Filbinger links harm career 5-28, 477B3
Wagner arrested in Brazil 5-30, extraditn asked 5-31, 477G1
Frankfurt protest injures 70 6-3, 477D3
Hess release plea rptd rejctd by USSR 6-11, 477E3
Police battle neo-Nazis in Lentfoehrden, 19 seized 7-22; Kuhnen arrested 7-24, 652A1
Geiss fined for Nazi salute 7-24, 652B1
Paris Gestapo chiefs chrgd 7-24, 652C1
Baum sees neo-Nazis terror 7-25, 652D1
Kuhnen arrested again 8-4, 652D1
Filbinger quits state post 8-7, 616C3; successor named 8-16, 725E3
Strauss asks Nazi-era amnesty 8-14, 651E3
WWII secret documts issued by US 9-10—9-18, 744D2-G3
Ryan trial cited 10-30, 872E2
Carstens, Scheel confrm past membership 11-10, 11-11, 872E1, G1
Prosecutn deadline scored by Wiesenthal 11-10, MPs oppositn rptd 10-28, 11-13, 872B2

Obituaries
Dassler, Adolf (rptd) 8-18, 778B1
Frings, Joseph Cardinal 12-17, 1032G2
Kappler, Herbert 2-9, 114C3
Messerschmitt, Willy 9-15, 778E1
Student, Kurt 7-1, 620F3
Von Manteuffel, Hasso 9-24, 778B2

1979

US credit-tightening move backed 10-8, 765D3
VW US plant sales cited 10-12, 784G3
Rumania expropriatn pact set 10-12, 910E2
Oman proposes Persian Gulf security aid 10-14–10-16, 804B2
China pacts signed 10-24, 854D1
US $ decline feared re discount rate hike 10-31, 838F1
Swiss hike lending fees 11-2, 875F3
US Mannesmann unit withdraws Harnischfeger bid 11-4, 942G2
US ban on Iran oil backed 11-13, 861F1, F2; import limits pledged 11-15, 879F2
US freeze of Iran assets evaluated 11-18, 880E1
Tobacco export gains rptd 11-22, 970A3
Iran bars US $ oil paymts 11-23, 896D3
Nicaragua loans rptd 11-27, 910A1
US bank attaches Iran assets 11-28, 896E2
E Ger credit-prisoner ransom deals ended 11-28, 939A3
US missn seeks Iran sanctns 12-6; Bonn curbs credit guarantees, arms exports 12-7, 934A1
US seeks econ sanctns vs Iran 12-11, 933C2
US $ closes down vs mark 12-31, 978F3

Nazis
'Holocaust' broadcast 1-22–1-26, impact noted 1-29, 137B2
Cops raid neo-Nazis 1-29–2-1, 101E1
US WWII secret files released 2-3, 2-6, 93F1
More neo-Nazis arrested 2-10–2-11, 137B2
US releases Auschwitz photos 2-22, 193D1
Schmidt backs contd prosecutn 3-8, 214D3
Brandt death plot foiled 3-20, 271F3
4 Majdanek guards acquitted 4-19, 333C3
Carstens elected pres, past protested 5-23, 410C3
Heim convicted 6-13, 490B1
Wagner extradtn denied by Brazil 6-20, 483A3
Limitatns statute end OKd by Bundestag 7-3, 506C2
Mengele loses Paraguay citizenship, extraditn pressure cited 8-8; bounty offered 8-10, 616C3
Wagner detentn rptd; Bohne, Stangl extraditns cited 8-8, 617B1
6 neo-Nazis sentncd 9-13, 733C3
Ex-SS col arrested 11-14, 876C2

Obituaries
Bengsch, Alfred Cardinal 12-13, 1008A2
Dutschke, Rudi 12-24, 1008D2
Focke, Heinrich 2-25, 176G2
Forssmann, Werner 6-1, 508F2
Gehlen, Reinhard 6-8, 508G2
Joos, Kurt 5-22, 432A3
Lynen, Feodor 8-8, 671G2
Marcuse, Herbert 7-29, 588B3
Reitsch, Hanna 8-30, 671E3

1980

Polish loan granted 8-12, 642D2
Shipping line insolvency rptd, trade decline linked 8-18, 674F1
E Ger trade rptd up 8-20, 674A2
Strauss urges Polish loans withheld 8-24, 642F2
US urges Poland aid 8-29, Schmidt responds 9-3, 659C1, C2
Algeria LNG deal canceled 9-11, 827A3
IMF role in oil debt studied 9-15, 695E2
IMF revises SDR valuatn method, mark gains in currency 'basket' 9-17, 695E1
E Ger tightens hard currency swap rules 10-9; USSR backs 10-14, 789F1
E Ger projects rejected 10-15, 794F3
US $ gains vs mark 11-5, 845B1
Ford unit plans layoffs 11-27, 924C3
VW, Nissan projct planned 12-3, 924D3
US $ passes 2 mark level 12-10, 932E1
Norway orders fishing halt 12-10, 969C3
Swiss bank buys Kaufhof interest 12-12, 969F1
US $ up 16% vs mark in '80 12-31, 983E2

Nazis
US search deadline rptd set 1-16, 228F2
Neo-Nazi group banned 1-30, 103G1
3 sentncd for WW2 crimes 2-11, 118E1
Gypsies begin hunger strike 4-4, 316E2
Ex-Nazi arrested re war crimes 6-25, 500B3
Neo-Nazis chrgd re '77, '78 bombings 6-25, 500C3
Flynn biographer sued 8-1, 639E1
Neo-Nazi seen as Munich bomber 9-28; PLO, Qaddafi linked 9-30, 754F3, 755C1
Wagner kills self in Brazil 10-3, 810E1
Doenitz dies 12-24, 1004D1

Obituaries
Andersch, Alfred 2-21, 279C1
Doenitz, Karl 12-24, 1004D1
Dornberger, Walter (rptd) 7-2, 528E1
Koppler, Heinrich (rptd) 5-11, 390E3
Mann, Katharina 4-18, 360C2
Von Schlabrendorff, Fabian 9-3, 756G2
Wagner, Winnifred 3-5, 280D2
Soviet-Afghan Issue
USSR aluminum talks suspended 1-3, 9A2
USSR scored re Afghan invasn 1-9, 10A3
USSR cancels econ comm mtg, Gilels tour 1-9, 10A3
Schmidt sees US offcl 1-16, 28G1
Moscow Olympics stand rptd 1-21, 45C3; Sovt policy chng asked 1-28, 68E1

1976

Soviet Relations—*See 'Eastern European Policy' above*

Sports
Winter Olympics results 2-4—2-15, 158D3-159B2
Mittermaier quits skiing 5-31, 424G1
Summer Olympic results 7-18—7-31, 573C3-576G3

Terrorism and Unrest
Baader-Meinhof trial testimony 1-13, 1-27, 77G2
Parlt votes terrorist curbs 1-16, 77E2
Bundestag OKs crime compensatn 2-6, 158F1-A2
2 sentncd in Hamburg 3-16, 503F1
'75 Swedish raid trial opens 5-6, 503E1
Meinhof found hanged 5-9; protests staged 5-10, 5-15; trial adjourned 5-15, 383G1
US bases bombed 6-1, 6-2, 503G1-A2
Hijackers land Uganda, ask prisoners freed 6-29, 463A1-F1; **for subsequent developments, see 'Entebbe' under MIDDLE EAST—AVIATION Incidents**
4 women escape jail 7-7, 1 recaptured 7-21; W Berlin dep mayor quits 7-10, mayor censured 7-23, 593C3
To propose intl accord 7-16, 530A3
Parlt OKs new law 7-29, 593A3
Neo-Nazi mtg sparks violence 8-7, 624F3
Pohle extradited from Greece 10-1, 754G3
230 hurt in A-plant protest 11-13, 931B1

1977

Sports
Czechs keep hockey title 5-8, 430C2
Ger Intl tennis results 5-15, 431B1

Terrorism and Unrest
Baader trial delayed 1-20; bugging admitted, trial adjourned 3-17; Schmidt, Maihofer deny tap role 3-18, 260B1
Traube bugging rptd 2-27; Maihofer backs bug 3-1, rejcts resignatn demands 3-8; Traube cleared 3-16, 259B3
Party ldrs meet on buggings 3-18, 260A2
Sweden arrests plotters, links to Baader-Meinhof, deports 2 4-1—4-6, 428E3
Buback killed 4-7, Baader-Meinhof linked 4-9, 4-13; Schmidt reacts 286A2
Baader-Meinhof ldrs sentncd 4-28; trial, gang history 352E1
Buback suspect captured 5-3, 601E3
Baader-Meinhof members sentncd 6-2, 601F3
Sweden plotters indicted 7-25, 709G1
Bank chief slain 7-30, 601A3
Baader, 2 others end hunger strike 9-2, 695C2
Schleyer kidnaped, guards slain 9-5; Schmidt orders probe, asks talks 9-6—9-8, 695D1
Cabt OKs 3 anti-terror bills 9-8, 695D2
Dutch in terrorist shootout 9-22, ask manhunt aid 9-24, 11-11, arrest 4 10-7, 888D1
Dutch bar Folkerts extraditn 9-23, sentence 12-20, 986G1
Croissant arrested in France 9-30, extradited 11-16; leftists protest 11-17, 968F2

1978

Soviet Relations—*See 'Eastern European & Soviet Relations' above*

Sports
World Alpine ski championships 1-29—2-5, 316E2
Speed-skating record set 3-2, 316C3
Nations Cup results 5-15, 419D1
German champ tennis results 5-21, 419D1
World Cup soccer finals 6-1—6-25, goalie sets record 6-21, 519F3, 520F1, E3
World Swim Championships 8-18—8-28, 780F1, A2
Frankfurt Cup tourn results 12-10, 1027D2

Terrorism & Unrest—*See also 'Nazis' above*
Baader atty smuggled guns into prison 1-12, 21G3
Moeller denies Baader gang suicide pact 1-16, 115C1
Police dispute Baader gun smuggling 1-17, 115B1
W Eur leftists doubt Baader gang suicides 1-22, experts confirm 1-23, 114F3
W Berlin leftists, police clash 1-28—1-29, 94C1
Sweden jails '77 plotters 1-31, 93B1
Czech hijacker, 3 others get asylum 2-6, 212E2
Switzerland tightens gun controls 2-9, 151C2
'77 poll favors terrorism curbs 2-14, 151D1
Missing Strauss aide reappears 2-15, 115E1
Strict anti-terror bills passed 2-16, 151G3
W Ger terrorists rptd in Colombia; Lufthansa office bombed, 'Baader Brigade' takes credit 2-17—2-18, 147B3
Parlt com rpt affirms Baader gang suicides 2-23, 152G1
W Gers, Iranians storm E Ger missn in Bonn 2-28, 190C2
Croissant trial halted over body searches 3-6, 3-21, adjournmt granted 4-3, 250A3
Moeller lawyers protest searches 3-6, 250D3

1979

Soviet Relations—*See 'Eastern European' above*

Sports
Eur figure-skating title 2-3, world competitn 3-17, 391E3*, 393B1*
Speed-skating record set 2-17, 392D1
World-4-man bobsled champs 2-25, 392D1
Mueller signs with NASL 3-6, 655E1
Stuttgart Grand Prix tennis results 4-1, 391B3
Soccer cup results 5-2, 5-9, 5-16, 776A3
Nations Cup tennis results 5-14, Berlin Intl 5-27, 570C2
W Ger Grand Prix tennis results 7-22, 734B2
Colonge Grand Prix tennis results 11-4, 1003F3

Terrorism & Unrest—*See also 'Nazis' above*
Fed job loyalty checks eased 1-18, 61E2
Italy arrests Moro kidnap suspect 1-27–1-28, 98F1
Berster sentncd in US 2-7, release set 2-23, 119F2
Brandt death plot foiled 3-20, 271F3
UK amb threatened 3-23, 228A3
A-plant sabotage attempt rptd 4-13, 276C2
Schleyer case suspect killed 5-4, 374D2
Terrorist data given 5-10, 374E2
Schleyer suspect arrest rptd 6-10, 490E1
France sentncs Breton separatist 10-20, 835E2
Berster returns from US 11-1, 998F3
Wisniewski chrgd re Schleyer murder 11-5, 998E3
Wagner arrested by Swiss 11-20, 998C3
Speitel gets life sentence 11-30, 998G3

1980

Sovt-bloc visit cancellatns cited 1-30, 103F1
Sovt Afghan exit sought, Olympics boycott oppositn rptd eased 2-5, boycott backed 2-10, 84E2, 106F2
Sovts see US pressure 2-6, 84B3
France bars US-Eur mtg 2-8; US backed 2-10, 106E2, B3
Vance sees Schmidt, Genscher; seeks policy coordinatn 2-20, 139A2
USSR Berlin consulate bombed, Aeroflot Frankfurt office bomb found 3-7, 236B1
Baden-Wurttemberg electns linked 3-16, 237A1
Schmidt sees Carter; sets policy coordinatn, backs Olympic boycott 3-19, 205A2
Strauss vs weak Moscow Olympics, joint French stands 3-20, 236E3
Olympic boycott support hinted 3-20, 259D3
Olympic boycott endorsed 4-14, 283D3
E Ger trade expansn set, Olympic boycott reaffirmed 4-17, 303B2
E Eur trade sanctns opposed, US pressure cited 4-17, 303C2
Moscow May Day parade shunned 5-1, 354G2
US backed vs Afghan plan on Sovt troop exit 5-15, 362C1
Olympic com OKs Moscow boycott, Weyer scores IOC 5-15, 379B2
Franco-Sovt summit reactn 5-19, 378C3
Sovt trade blitz rptd 5-22, 430G3
IOC issues Olympic acceptance list, absence effect seen 5-27, 420E3
Sovt draft trade pact set 5-29, 411A2
7-natn Venice summit seeks total Sovt exit 6-22, 473B1
Carter backs Eur-Sovt ties 6-23, 473F1
Schmidt in Moscow, urges Afghan pullout; econ pact signed 7-1, 489A1-D3
Sovts bar Olympic TV broadcast 7-13, 590D1
Moscow Olympics boycotted 7-19—8-3, 587F3, 588E2
Afghan UNESCO delegate defects 10-25, 827E2
Schmidt condemns invasn 11-24, 904C2

Soviet Relations—*See 'Eastern European & Soviet Relations', 'Soviet-Afghan Issue' above*

Sports
Moscow Olympics stand rptd 1-21, 45C3
Sovt policy change re Olympics asked 1-28, 68E1
Olympics boycott oppositn softens 2-5, 84A3
US Olympic stand backed 2-10, 106C3
Lake Placid Olympic results 2-12—2-24, 154F2, 155F2-156D1
Olympics boycott backed 3-5, 205B2
World figure skating championships 3-12—3-15, 470B2
German Indoor tennis results 3-16, Frankfurt WCT 3-23, W Ger Open 5-18, Bavarian Grand Prix 5-25, 607G2, A3, D3
Strauss vs weak Moscow Olympics stand 3-20, 236E3
Olympic boycott support hinted 3-20, 259D3
Olympic boycott endorsed 4-14, 283D3
Olympic boycott reaffirmed 4-17, 303C2
Argentina wins Nations Cup 5-12, 607G1
Eur soccer cup results 5-14, 5-21, 771A3, B3
Olympic com OKs boycott, Weyer scores IOC 5-15, 379B2
US wins Federatn Cup 5-25, 607B1
IOC issues Olympic acceptance list, absence effect seen 5-27, 420E3, 421A1
Eur Soccer Championship win 6-22, 771B2
Sovts bar Olympic TV broadcast 7-13, 590D1
Moscow Olympics boycotted 7-19—8-3, 587F3, 588E2
W Ger Grand Prix tennis results 7-20, 691G2

Terrorism & Unrest—*See also 'Nazis' above*
RAF, Italy terrorist links seen 1-2, 20F2
UK soldiers attacked 2-19, 3-1, 3-10, IRA linked 2-19, 194A1
Proll sentncd, freed 2-22, 154E1
USSR Berlin consulate bombed, Aeroflot Frankfurt office bomb found 3-7, 236B1
Gypsies begin hunger strike 4-4, 316E2
French arrest suspects 5-5, 411A3
CIA rpts '79 reductn 5-11, 365F3
Anti-US leftists riot in Berlin 5-18, 500E3
Amnesty Intl chrgs prisoner abuse, Bonn scores 5-28, 411E2, 446E3
A-protest village dispersed 6-4, 446C3
Neo-Nazis chrgd re '77, '78 bombings 6-25, 500C3
Plambeck killed in crash 7-25; Folkerts sentenced 7-31, 581B1
Munich Oktoberfest blast kills 12 9-26; chrgs traded, suspects released 9-27—9-30, 754E3
Wagner sentenced by Swiss 9-26, 755D1
Munich Ocktoberfest death toll hits 13 10-1, 795B1
Alleged right-wing extremist hideout raided 10-2, 795A1
Kurds attack Turkey W Berlin consulate 10-8, 794A2
Lorenz kidnapers sentenced 10-13, 833A1
French newspr rpt on terrorist atty exdraditn cited 11-7, 872F1
Army rite protested 11-11, 904C3
Cologne A-research office bombed 12-4, 969C2

1976	1977	1978	1979	1980

1977

Lufthansa jet hijacked, Baader gang release demanded 10-13; pilot slain 10-16; lands in Somalia 10-17, W Ger raid frees 10-18, 'deal' denied 10-19, 789A1-790D2
Schleyer kidnaper demands rejctd 10-16, 791B2
Jailed Baader gang ldrs kill selves 10-18, reactn 10-18—10-20, 789C1, 790D2-791E1
Schleyer slain 10-18, manhunt begun 10-20, 789D1, 791E1
Hard line vs terrorists' release defended 10-20, 791F2
S Africa min compares situatns 10-21, 825F1
Explosives found in Baader-Meinhof jail cells 10-21, 868G1; 11-10, 888C2
Krabbe sought for Schleyer kidnap 10-21, state funeral 10-25, 868B2
Somali hijack rescue aid linked to arms needs 10-22, 830C1
Airport security tightened 10-23—10-24, Algeria flight canceled 11-8, 868C3-E3
Lufthansa hijackers identified 10-25, 10-27, 868E2
Baader deaths declared suicide 10-26, ldrs buried 10-27, 868D1
Zweibrucken bombing 10-31, 8 arrested 11-10, 888B1
Anti-terrorist unit formed 11-4, 868E3
Lufthansa jets threatnd 11-5, W Ger airports searched 11-6, 868G2
Dutch capture 2 terrorist suspects 11-10, 887E3
4th Baader-Meinhof member kills self 11-12, 888F1
Croissant publishes suicide denial 11-17, 968F3
Croissant protests jail conditns, razor blades found 11-23, 969A1
Austrian kidnapers linked 11-24, 991G1
France defends Croissant extraditn, denies brutality 11-25—11-28, 969C1
Lufthansa bookings fall 11-29, 969D2
Dirnhofer arrested in Traube affair 12-1, 968E2
Schmidt in Italy talks 12-1, 1015A1
Swiss capture 2 terrorists 12-20, 1017D3
Italy hunts group linked to Baader-Meinhof 12-28, 1014E2

1978

Schleyer hunt error admitted 3-7; pol controversy ensues 3-7—4-6, 332B2-C3
Dutch protest for Baader-Meinhof 3-14, 192F1
Terrorists linked to Italy Red Brigades, W Ger police join Moro kidnap search 3-20, 200C1
Goettingenu editors fined 4-5, 353D3
Swiss host 4-natn mtg, 'hot line' set 4-8—4-9; RAF activity rptd 4-12, 438B2
W Berlin '2d of June' terrorist trial opens 4-11, defendants disrupt proceedings 4-12, 5-1, 353A3
Anti-terror laws repassed 4-13, 332G1
W Berlin train system firebombed 4-22, 353E3
Swiss trial of 2 terrorists opens 4-25, 353E3
Lufthansa '77 hijacker sentenced in Somalia 4-25, 353F3
Sonnenberg, Becker sentncd 4-26, 353G3
Berberich sentncd for prison mutiny role 4-27, 354A1
IRA links rptd sought 4-27, 373E2
Lawyers' assn protests body searches 5-4, 354B1
USSR rights abuse protested 5-4—5-7, 417A2
Dutch arrest 3 terrorists 5-5, jail 8-21, 725C1
Dutch rule on extraditn of Folkerts, 2 other terrorists 5-8, 354C1, 454C3
Stuttgart prosecutor's office affirms Baader gang suicides 5-8, 354D1
Schleyer, Moro cases compared 5-10, 337E2
Yugo arrests 4 RAF terrorists 5-11, seeks Croatn natls exchng 5-11—5-31, 438E3
Wisniewski arrested in Paris, deported 5-11; assaults W Ger judge 5-12, 439A2
Vendor sentenced re terrorist publicatn 5-17, 439B2
Lufthansa '77 profits cut by threats 5-18, 417C2
MPs protest leftist border checks 5-19, 439B2
Folkerts arrested in Paris 5-25, deported 5-26, 439C2
Meyer escapes W Berlin jail 5-27, 438A3
Boll loses libel suit 5-30, 439E2
W Berlin ct-apptd attys threatened 5-31, 439F2
US Army hotel bombed 5-31; 3 suspects arrested in kidnap plot 6-7, 439A3
W Berlin searches, ID checks rptd up 6-1; offcls concerned 6-3, 439G2-A3
Schleyer rpt issued, police effort scored 6-3—6-4; Maihofer resigns 6-6, 456A3
3 more anti-terror laws passed 6-8, 500E2
Meyer, Rollnick, 2 other terrorists arrested in Bulgaria, extradited 6-22, 500A1
Czech, Sovt aid probed 6-22, 500F1
Israeli import co bombed 6-22, 500G1
Swiss jail 2 terrorists 6-30, 558F2
W Berlin justice min resigns 7-3, 651B2
Border police surveillnc probed 7-5, 651F2
Croissant '77 extraditn upheld by French ct 7-7, 649B3
Groenewold given suspended sentence 7-10, 651F2
Berster seized in US 7-16, arrest warrant issued 7-24, 577A1
Hijacking pact signed 7-17, 544G2
Baader jail abuse chrgs rejected by Eur rights ct 7-19, 651A3
Celle prison bomb blast 7-25, 651B3
Klein reveals '76 papal kidnap plot 8-6, 689A3
High Ct upholds terrorism law 8-8, 651C3
3 US citizens chrgd re Berster 8-12, US asylum rptd sought 8-15, 651D3
Croats protest Bilandzic extraditn ruling 8-13, 706D3
Klein rptd in Israel 8-17, 651D3
2 Croats seize W Ger emb in US, ask Bilandzic release 8-17, 706E2
UK army bases bombed 8-18; terrorists linked 8-19—8-24, patrols increased 8-25, 688D1
Stoll, 2 other terrorists elude police 8-21, 724F3
Law offices of urban terrorists in 4 cities raided 8-21, 725B1
2 US citizens plead guilty in Berster case 8-28, 8-31, 725D1
Petric flees to Sweden 8-30, 925G3
Baum sees UK home secy 9-4—9-5, 688B2
Stoll killed, 3 other terrorists arrested 9-6, 724D3
Dutch broaden Folkerts extraditn rule 9-7, 725E1
Bilandzic, 2 other Croats extraditn ruled out 9-13, 706F3
Yugo scores Bilandzic extraditn ruling 9-13, 725F1, G1 ★
UK arrests Proll, extraditn asked 9-15, 725A2
Speitel, 2d suspect wounded, captured; Baader gang link cited 9-24, 884F3-885A1
Czech hijacker sentncd 10-4, 776E3
Dutch group protests Red Army suspects treatmt 10-9, 885F1
Dutch extradite Folkerts, 2 others 10-13, 10-17, 885B1
SPD to ease pub employe security rules 10-16, 823E1
64 arrested at Baader-Meinhof rally 10-18, 885G1
Dutch guard killed at border 11-1, 885A2

1976

UN Policy & Developments
Abstains on rights comm resolutn vs Israel 2-13, 125E2
Vs WHO anti-Israel stand 5-19, 355D2
UNCTAD OKs commodity fund 5-30, 388G2
Vs World Food Cncl plans 6-14—6-16, 450C1
To propose terrorism accord 7-16, 530A3
Asked to bar aid to S Africa 11-5, 842B3
Vs black Namibia support 12-20, 955C1

U.S. Relations—*See also 'Foreign Economic Developments' above*
Fair resigns after losing cmnd 1-5, 43D2
Brandt replies to Kissinger on CP ties 1-22, 120D2
Kissinger anti-CP lobbying rptd 2-5, 120B2
Leftist wkly names CIA agents 2-9, 2-10, 158C1
US bases bombed 6-1, 6-2, 503G1-A2
NATO OKs US troop plan 6-10—6-11, 449F1
Kissinger-Vorster mtg set 6-18, 426D1 ★, 427D1 ★; meet 6-23—6-24, 446F1, 447A1
US evacuates 20 from Leb 6-20, 448C1
Kissinger-Vorster mtg protested 6-23, 446D3
Ship in US Bicentennial event 7-4, 488A3-D3
Schmidt in US, troop agrmts announced 7-15—7-17, 530E2
Kissinger cites Bonn CP ban 7-30, 753E1
Kissinger sees Schmidt on Vorster mtg 9-7, 660F2
Backs US Africa policy 9-8, 681B2
Bonn reactn to Carter electn 11-3—11-4, 826E1

1977

UN Policy & Developments
Assemb, Cncl member; Mosler on World Ct 4A1-G1
Abstains on Israel occupatn abuse resolutn 2-15, 107E2
Assemb Namibia vote abstentns 11-4, 851F1
Abstains from Israel occupatn res 11-25, 910D2
S Africa oil, investmt ban abstentns 12-16, 1016A2

U.S. Relations—*See also 'Atomic Energy' and 'Monetary, Trade & Aid' above*
Brandt warns on W Berlin 1-24, 102A2
Mondale visits 1-25, 69B1-B2
Bock role in NBC Olympic deal cited 2-6, suit vs rptd 2-14, 131D1, F1
W Berliners aid weather victims 2-7, 92D1
US-ESA flight set 2-16, 170C3
CIA paymts to Brandt rptd 2-19, 124F1; Carter rpts error 2-24, 151A2
Berlin weather aid ends 3-2, 152E3
US rights stand concern rptd 3-4, 226F1
Carter energy plan 4-18, 294E3; reaction 4-21, 320F3
Baader-Meinhof ldrs sentncd 4-28, 352A2
Carter TV interview 5-2, 338B2
Carter sees Schmidt 5-7, 358E1; summit diplomacy hailed 5-11, 359D1, B2
US gen reprimanded for speech 6-17, 482F3
Schmidt sees Trudeau on Carter rights policy 7-6—7-12, 566G2
Schmidt in US, sees Carter 7-13—7-14, 566G1
W Ger seized in US 7-20, 576A3
US rpts S Africa A-test plan 8-17, 663E3, 664A1
ESA satellite launching aborted 9-13, 735G3
Hijack rescue in Somalia aided by US 10-17, Schmidt thanks 10-18, 789E2, 790F1
Defns Min spy scandal reactn 12-13—12-14, 968B2
Carter expands air svc 12-21, 1006D2

1978

Yugo bars extraditn of 4 RAF terrorists 11-17, release rptd 11-18, 906F1
US convicts 2 Croats 12-1, 933B3

UN Policy & Developments
Rhodesia pact vote abstentn 3-14, 192F3
ICAO picks US bad-weather landing system 4-19, 319B3
Assemb disarmamt sessn opens 5-23, 421G1
Sea Law Conf talks continue 5-23—7-15, 8-21—9-16, 732E3
Racism conf boycotted 8-26, 676B2
Cncl, Assemb member 713A3, F3
Cncl abstentn on Namibia electn warning 11-13, 904B2

U.S. Relations—*See also 'Atomic Energy' and 'Monetary, Trade, Aid & Investment' above*
US troop strength rptd 1-2, 5A2, C2
US Army job plan scored 1-11, 55B2
US alerts to Sovt satellite fall 57E1
At Ogaden conf in US 1-21, 43E2
Agee Dec '77 entry bar cited 1-25, 90F3
Ryan war crimes trial rptd 1-30, 114B3
Schmidt warns re ties 4-12, 254B3, 254B1
ICAO picks US bad-weather landing system 4-19, 319B3
US Army drug abuse rptd 4-27, 368D2
US launches ESA satellite 5-12, 384D3
Schmidt visits Carter 5-30—5-31, briefs parlt 6-1, 519F1
Schmidt backs US warning to USSR 5-31, 397A2
US Army hotel bombed 5-31, 3 arrested 6-7, 439A3
GI heroin smuggling rptd, '77 data cited 6-1, 433G2
US, USSR troops compared 6-10, 534B3
Schmidt cites Carter mtg 7-7, 545G2
Carter visits, reaffirms commitmt 7-14—7-15, 542A1, 544D3-545D1
Carter scores Shcharansky trial 7-14, 542A1
Terrorist seized in US 7-16, arrest warrant issued 7-24, 577A1
US rptd questioning Rumanian defector 8-8, 650F3; SPD spy scandal disclosed 9-1, 725D2 ★
3 US citizens chrgd re terrorist 8-12, US asylum rptd sought 8-15, 651D3
2 Croats seize W Ger emb in US 8-17, 706E2
US seabed mining bill debated at UN conf 8-21—9-16, 732E3
2 US citizens plead guilty re terrorist 8-28, 8-31, 725D1
WWII secret documts issued 9-10—9-18, 744D2-G3
ITT unit linked to forgn paymts 11-2, 876E1, E2
2 Croats convicted 12-1, 933B3
Blumenthal visits 12-7—12-8, 965D3
McDonnell Douglas paymts rptd 12-15, 982F2
US-China tie lauded 12-16, 977C1

1979

UN Policy & Developments
Rights comm resolutns on Palestinian state, southn Africa opposed 2-21, 148F1
Namibia plan fails 3-3, S Africa rejcts 3-5, 171B2, A3
WHO rpts alcohol consumptn up 3-9, 218C3
Namibia compromise proposed 3-19—3-22; Pretoria bars 5-7, extends assemb powers 5-8, 354F2
Namibia vote abstentn 5-31, 428B1
Indochina refugee conf asked 6-28, 473E2
Membership listed 695D2
Namibia talks reopen 11-12—11-16, 889D3
E Ger scored re prisoner ransom deals 11-28, 939B3

U.S. Relations—*See also 'Atomic' and 'Monetary' above*
Schmidt at Guadeloupe summit 1-5—1-6, backs SALT pact 1-6, 12D2
WWII secret files released 2-3, 2-6, 93G1
US Army rescinds Spanish language ban 2-7, 89D2
Terrorist sentncd 2-7, release set 2-23, US Army deserter surrenders 5-7, 392F2
US ct frees E Ger '78 hijacker in W Berlin 5-28, 430E2
Schmidt sees Carter in US, backs SALT 6-6, 430A1
Schmidt pressure vs Israel setlmts rptd urged 7-9, 511B2
Carter energy plan assessed 7-16, 534F3
ITT unit to aid paymts probe 8-8, 648F1
US Nazi ldr's activity cited 9-13, 733C3
US criticism re defense spending rptd 9-21, 733A2
Defense ties stressed 9-24, 733D1
SALT, Cuba troop issue reactn rptd 10-3, 738B1
Terrorist returns from US 11-1, 998G3
US informs of Iran oil ban 11-12, move backed 11-13, 861F1
US hostages in Iran flown to US Air Base 11-19, 11-20, 878B1
Freed US hostages issue captors statemt 11-21, 894F2
Schmidt backs A-arms cut talks 12-4, 938E2
Vance in Bonn, seeks sanctns vs Iran 12-11, 933C2, G2
US revokes Agee passport 12-23, 991F2

1980

UN Policy & Developments
Assemb Palestinian state res abstentn 7-29, 572F1
Econ aid sessn ends in no agrmt 9-15, 736G1
Von Wechmar elected Assemb pres; facts on 9-16, 736E1
Afghan UNESCO delegate defects 10-25, 827E2
Namibia talks schedule agreed 11-24, 967C2

U.S. Relations—*See also 'Monetary', 'Soviet-Afghan Issue' above*
Schmidt, US offcl meet; detente backed 1-16, 28G1
Carter cites Berlin crisis 1-23, 42G1
Bonn 3% defns spending hike claimed 2-25, 153E3
Schmidt visits Carter 3-5, 205B2
GI sentenced for sex harassment 3-6, 189A1
Pan Am revives discount coupons 3-10, 346E3
Carter anti-inflatn plan praised 3-15, 202F2
E Ger warns re US policy 3-19, 236D3
Italian banker convicted in NY 3-27, 237A2
Agee suit OKd in US 4-1, 268E2
W Europns plan fighter jet 4-14, 303F1
Schmidt sees war threat, backs US on Iran 4-20, 303D1
Iran hostage kin seek support 4-23, 299D2
Iran hostage rescue missn backed 4-25, 324B2
CIA rpts '79 terrorism 5-11, 365F3
Anti-US leftists riot in Berlin 5-18, 500E3
Muskie-Gromyko mtg noted 5-19, 378D3
GI drug arrests rptd 6-13, '79 total 6-23; heroin use rptd down 6-18, 517D1, B2
Carter letter vs E-W A-missile freeze 6-16, Schmidt seeks mtg 6-18, 450B3-451D1
US warned vs gas venting at A-accident site 6-18, 550C3
Schmidt sees Carter, vs USSR visit criticism 6-21, 473E1
Carter sees Genscher re USSR A-missile talks, lauds Schmidt trip 7-2, 489C1
Strauss on Eur role 7-9, 522B1
Iran hostage arrives Wiesbaden 7-12, 539E1
Anderson visits 7-13—7-14, 549G3
Crane sues Stern 7-16, 890C2
Schmidt briefed on hostages in Iran 9-19, 719C3
Schmidt vs intl force to protect Gulf oil 9-26, 735E2
US mil exercise performance scored 10-11, 777D1
US scientific literacy lag rptd 10-22, 990C1
Matthoefer compares US, W Ger soldiers 11-6, 904C1
Schmidt meets Carter, Reagan re NATO, arms control 11-20; rpts to parlt 11-24, 897F2, 903G3-904A2
NATO defns input defended 12-9—12-10; Brown, Brzezinski score 12-18, 949C2, 950B1
Haig apptmt praised 12-17, 955E2
'81 budget hikes mil spending 12-17, 969C1

GERONIMO, Cesar
NL batting ldr 10-4, 795G3
In World Series 10-16—1-021, 815G2
GERRY, Martin H.
Charges NYC school job bias 11-9, 921D3
GERSHWIN, George (1898-1937)
Porgy & Bess wins music Hall of Fame award 2-28, 460E3
GERSON International Corp.
Boycott rpts released 10-18, 10-20, 786A1, A2
GERT-Dietmar, Klause
Wins Olympic medal 2-14, 159C1
GERTZ, Alejandro
Scores US, DEA 3-16, 420B1
GERULAITUS, Vitas
Beats Ashe at Wimbledon 6-26, 504F1
GESCHKE, Hans-Jurgen
Wins Olympic medal 7-24, 574C2

GERM Warfare—*See CHEMICAL & Biological Warfare*
GEROVITAL (GH3)—*See MEDICINE—Drugs*
GERSTNECKER, William R.
Acquitted 3-11, 491E3
GERULAITIS, Vitas
Tourn results 2-6—5-22, 430D2-C3
Borg wins Wimbledon 7-2, 548E1
GESCHIKTER, Dr. Charles F.
CIA mind-control tests revealed 8-1—8-9, 610G3, 611B1
Denies CIA tests on humans 9-20, 721D2
GESCHIKTER Foundation for Medical Research
CIA mind-control tests revealed 8-1—8-9, 610G3

GERMANY, Jim
Edmonton wins Grey Cup 11-26, 1025F1
GERM Warfare—*See CHEMICAL & Biological Warfare*
GERRITY Jr., Edward J.
Accused of perjury 3-20, 206C3
US drops 3 chrgs 8-18, 643B3
GERRY, Martha
Retires Forego 6-10, 539D3
GERSHWIN, George (1898-1937)
Porgy & Bess wins Grammy 2-24, 316C1
GERSTEN, Bernard
Runaways opens 3-9, Catsplay 4-16, 887C1, G2
GERULAITIS, Vitas
Wins Australian Open 12-31-77, 22G3
USTA ranks 6th 1-5, 22E3
Wins Va WCT 2-5, 418G3
Loses Scandinavian Cup 3-8, 419B1
Wins N Amer Zone Davis Cup matches 3-17, 3-19, 252B1
Loses WCT Tourn of Champs 3-26, 419B1
Loses Milan WCT 4-2, 419B1
Wins WCT singles title 5-14, 418G2
Wimbledon results 7-8, 539F3
Wins Forest Hills Invitatn 7-16; loses Smash '78 10-29, Frankfurt Cup 12-10, 1027G1, C2, D2
US Open results 9-10, 707C1
GERVIN, George
Breaks Thompson scoring mark, NBA ldr 4-9, 271E1, D2
Walton named NBA MVP 5-24, 457A3
On NBA all-star team 6-13, 457C3

GERMESHAUSEN, Bernhard
W Gers win world 4-man bobsled title 2-25, 392F1
GEROULD, Daniel
Madman and Nun opens 1-18, 292A2
GERRITY Jr., Edward J.
US drops case vs Berrellez 2-8, 88D1
US drops perjury chrgs 3-7, 188G1
GERSHWIN, George (1898-1937)
Tip Toes opens 3-26, 712A3
GERSHWIN, Ira
Dancing in Dark opens 1-21, 292D1
GERSTEN, Bernard
Bosoms & Neglect opens 5-3, 711F1
GERSTNER, Frank & Christine
Convicted on spy chrgs 6-18, 489G3
GERULAITIS, Vitas
Wins Little Rock Grand Prix 2-4; loses WCT Tourn of Champs 2-25, Monte Carlo WCT 4-15, 391G2-B3
Grand Prix dispute setld 2-10, 391F1
Wins Italian Open 5-27, French Open results 6-9, 6-10, 570F1, D2
Wins Austrian Grand Prix 7-29, loses US Open 9-9, 734D1, B2
Wins Australian Indoor 10-21, 1003E3
US wins Davis Cup 12-16, 1003G2
GERUSKY, Thomas
On 3 Mile I A-accident 3-30, 243E2
GERVIN, George
NBA scoring ldr 4-8, 290A2, D2
2d in NBA MVP vote 5-23, 526G1
On NBA all-league team 6-6, 526C2

GERO, Erno
Dies 3-12, 279A3
GERONTOLOGY Research Center (Baltimore, Md.)
Enzyme-lifespan link rptd 8-21, 716E1
GERRICK, Glo
Don't Answer the Phone released 8-9, 675C2
GERSTENMAIER, John H.
Retires from Goodyear 12-2, 959B2
GERULAITIS, Vitas
Loses Grand Prix Masters 1-13, 213A2
Loses Pepsi Grand Prix 2-10; wins Tourn of Champs 5-12, 607F2, C3
Loses French Open 6-8, 606B3
USTA, pros settle rules dispute 7-16, 691G3
Wins W Ger Grand Prix 7-20, 691G2
Loses Australian Indoor 10-19, wins Melbourne 10-26, 947B2
GERVIN, George
East wins NBA All-Star Game; named MVP 2-3, 279A1
NBA scoring ldr 3-30, 278G2, C3
On NBA all-league team 6-2, 656D3

1976

GESELL, Judge Gerhard A.
Ordrs AT&T pay reverse bias damages 6-9, 944G1
Upholds AF homosexual dismissal 7-16, 944F1
GESTRIN, Kristian
Sworn Finnish justice min 9-29, 750D3
GETTY, George Franklin
J Paul Getty dies 6-6, 444F1
GETTY, Gordon Peter
Father dies 6-6, 444A2
Elected to Getty Oil bd 7-9, 680G2
GETTY, J. Paul
Facts on 444E2
Dies 6-6, will filed for probate 6-8, 444E1-D2
Successors at Getty Oil named 7-9, 680G2
GETTY 2nd, J. Paul
Father dies 6-6, 444A2
GETTY 3rd, J. Paul
Abductors sentenced 7-29, 816B3
GETTY, Jean Ronald
Father dies 6-6, 444A2
GETTY, Louis Lynch
Named in Getty will 6-8, 444B2
GETTY Oil Co.
New Australia uranium yields rptd 1-28, 97C1
Arab boycott fine rptd 4-20, 747F1
J Paul Getty dies 6-6, 444E1-F2
Pres, bd posts filled 7-9, 680G2
GEVING, Herb
Loses ND gov primary 9-7, 687E3
GEYER, Georgie Anne
Angola ousts 6-15, 480C3
G & G Packing Co.
Named in Army meat fraud probe 5-10, 395B2
GHAFFAR Khan, Abdul
Freed from jail 8-28, 679B2

GHANA—*See also AFRICAN Development Bank, COMMONWEALTH of Nations, NONALIGNED Nations Movement, OAU*
Listed as 'not free' nation 1-19, 20D3
Awoonor arrest confirmed 2-24, 208G2
Busia assets confiscated 3-16, 503G2
Total IMF oil loan rptd 4-1, 340C2
Cancels Kissinger visit 4-28, 295G1, A2
'75 plotters rptd on trial 5-20, 543E2
EC aid set 7-8, 529A3
Olympic withdrawal rptd 7-21, 528B3
5 plotters sentncd to die 7-28; others tried 8-13, 858F1
Awoonor rptd freed 10-24, 858G1
ECOWAS rptd ratified 11-6, 974E2
Officers accused in car scandal retire 11-14—12-3, 1003C2
GHIKAS, Solon
Dropped from cabt 1-5, 73D2
Leb missn ends 11-4, 841E2
GHONEIM, Maj. Gen. Mohammed Hassan
Peace plan rejected 8-20; presses plan 8-25, 629D1
Pact eases Beirut shelling 8-25, 629G1
GHORRA, Edouard
Meets Waldheim 1-17, 34A3
Vs intl silence on Leb crisis 6-9, 406A3
Scores Palestinians at UN 10-14, 758D3
GHOSN, Raymond
Slain 2-17, 125G1

1977

GESELL, Judge Gerhard A.
DC ct reorganizatn backed 3-22, 231A2
GESESSE, Solomon
Assassinated 11-13, 875E2
GETACHEW, Mekasha
Defects to US 3-9, 238F2
GETTY Oil Co.
Mission, Skelly takeover cited in table 880G1
Washington sues 8-16, 691E3
GHALES, Murad
Quits as amb to Yugo 12-1, 930F2
GHALI, Butros
Named Egypt forgn min 11-17, 890C2
Replaced as foreign min 993E1

GHANA—*See also COMMONWEATH of Nations, NONALIGNED Nations Movement, OAU*
UN Assemb member 4A1
Civilian govt com set 1-10, 48F1
Canadian loan rptd 1-13, 48G1
Afars factns set Assemb slate 3-28—4-3, 363A3
Bishops ask civln rule, human rights 4-13, 598B2
Student strikes rptd 598C2
Young visits 5-12—5-13, 399A1
Uganda office closed 5-22, Uganda to move office to Nigeria 5-24, 429C2
Civln rule pledged 7-1, date set 7-14; prof workers end strike 7-18, 598G1
Econ problems, export smuggling rptd 7-1, 598C2
Amnesty Intl lists jailed lawmakers 9-5, 753B2
Bauxite base price OKd 12-7, 975E1
GHANAHALLAH, Ahmed Ould
Shot 7-7, 543B2
GHANI, Maj. Abdul Aziz Abdul
In N Yemen ruling cncl 10-10, 784A1
GHASHMI, Ahmed Hussein al- (North Yemeni president)
Becomes N Yemen ruler 10-10, 783G3
Escapes death try 10-19, 824D1
GHISSASSI, Abdellatif
Named Morocco finance min 10-10, 772F1
GHOLAM, Shahnaz
Identified as Lufthansa hijacker 10-25, 868G2
GHORBAL, Ashraf
Mediates Hanafi surrender 3-11, 192A3

1978

GESELL, Judge Gerhard A.
Dismisses Anderson suit vs Nixon 4-4, 265C1
Ehrlichman freed 4-27, 320C2
Rules on FTC child ad probe 11-3, 11-17, 941A3
Gays' mil dischrg ruling reversed 12-6, 960D2
GET Off (recording)
On best-seller list 10-11, 800E3
GET Out Your Handkerchiefs (film)
Released 12-17, 1030A3
GETTY Oil Co.
Crude oil price violatns chrgd 7-2, 8-4, 610A2
GHALI, Butros
On PLO raid vs Israel 3-12, 176D1
Zaire aid pledge rptd 6-13, 441G1
Remains Egypt acting forgn min 10-5, 774B3
Meets Carter on Israel pact talks 10-17, 782A3; 10-21, 802A3
Offers new pact plan 11-9, 892C3

GHANA—*See also COMMONWEALTH of Nations, GATT, NONALIGNED Nations Movement, OAU*
Freedom House lists as partly free 44F1, A2
Dadzie gets new UN econ post 3-8, 401D3
6 W African natns back ECOWAS 3-18, USSR scores 3-20, 237E1
Erskine heads UN force in Leb 3-19, 197E2
Union govt plan approved 3-30, 250D3
Govt opponents rptd arrested 4-14, 292D2
Akuffo replaces Acheampong 7-5; prisoners freed 7-6, 515C2
Akuffo ousts Acheampong aides 7-7, 596C2
Exile amnesty set 7-10, 596C2
Ex-prime min Busia dies 8-28, 708C2
Cedi devalued 8-28, 841A1
Sovt-bloc envoys rptd ousted 9-8, 841A1
UN Assemb member 713F3
Strikes rptd 11-6, outlawed 11-7, 882A2
Civil servant strike ends 11-10, 882B2
Ex-plotters freed 11-16, 1021F3
U.S. Relations
Textron '71 sales paymt queried 2-28, 161D2
CIA role in '66 coup chrgd 5-8, 367F3
Textron bribe evidence rptd destroyed 5-8, 448G3
GHANEM, Mohammed Hafez
Out as Egypt dep premr 5-7, 392G2
GHANI, Abdel Aziz Abdel (North Yemeni premier)
Takes power 6-25, 499G1
GHASHMI, Ahmed Hussein al- (North Yemeni president)
Slain, S Yemen linked 6-24; Aden denies role 6-25, 498E3, 499B2
Saudis score death 6-24, defectors role cited 6-25, 499B2
Mil cmnd takes power 6-25, 499F1
Arab League accuses S Yemen 7-1—7-2, 522F1
Saleh elected pres 7-17, 559A1
GHAZALI bin Shafie, Muhammad
On Viet refugees 12-12, 956B2
GHIRONZI, Giancarlo
Corruptn chrgs rptd 5-30, 438F1
GHORBAL, Ashraf
Quits to protest summit pacts 9-18, 710G3
GHOST of Flight 401, The (book)
On best-seller list 4-2, 272D3

1979

GESELL, Judge Gerhard A.
Guillain-Barre flu shot claims rptd stalled 6-10, 470G3
GESNER, Clark
Utter Glory opens 5-13, 712C3
GESSLER, Ernst
Banking reforms proposed 5-22, 411C1
GET Out Your Handkerchiefs (film)
Wins Oscar 4-9, 336B2
GET the Knack (recording)
On best-seller list 8-1, 620F3; 9-5, 672F3; 10-3, 800F3
GETTING Out (play)
Opens 5-15, 711B3
GETTINGS, Brian P.
On Beckwith demotn 1-26, 92G2
GETTY Oil Co.
Ashland unit offshore holdings sold 2-4, 560F3
May gas allocatn rptd unchngd 5-7, 343A1
3d 1/4 profits rptd up 10-25, 804D3
Reserve Oil accepts bid 10-31, 986B3
Overchrg setlmt agreed 12-4, 943G1-A2
More overchrgs claimed 12-9, 943E1
Nuclear Fuel Services Inc.
Tenn A-fuel plant shut re uranium loss 9-18, 809A3
NY A-waste storage protested 9-29, 742E3
GETZ, Stan
Performs in Cuba 3-1—3-4, 238D2
GHALI, Butros
Scores Arab League actn vs Egypt 4-1, 248C3
On PLO support 4-9, 295E3
Wants Israel open border delayed 5-23, 394D2
Vs Israel W Bank, Gaza policy 6-4, 415A3
Vs Castro speech on Egypt 9-3, 674F2

GHANA—*See also COMMONWEALTH of Nations, GATT, NONALIGNED Nations Movement, OAU*
Freedom House lists as partly free 13A1
State of emergency ends 1-1, 22F2, 215G2
June '77-78 inflatn estimated 1-10, 173A1
Currency exchng ordrd 3-13, 324F1
Coup attempt fails 5-15, econ exploitatn chrgd 5-28, 425A2
Akuffo ousted 6-4; Rawlings replaces; vows electns, civilian rule 6-5, 425F1
Acheampong executed 6-16, 468D3
Electns held, Limann-Owusu runoff set 6-18, 485G2-C3
Akuffo, Afrifa, 4 others executed 6-26, 485D2
Anti-corruptn drive rptd 6-26, 485F2
Limann elected pres in runoff, parlt vote rptd 7-10, 524F1
Limann inaugurated 9-24, 721C2
Foreign Relations (misc.)
IMF standby loan OKd 1-10, 172G3
S Africa UN ouster backed 5-24, 409F3
Nigeria cuts oil shipmts, other African natns protest executns 6-29—6-30; Rawlings vows halt 6-30, 524B2
UN membership listed 695D2
U.S. Relations
US issues rights rpt 2-10, 107E3
Proxmire asks Textron study 10-31, 923B3
GHARABAGHI, Gen. Abbas
Named Iran mil staff chief 1-4, 2B3
Vows to back Bakhtiar govt 1-22, 49E2
GHARAVI, Nureddin
Barred from Tabriz state house 12-8, 935G3
GHAZALI bin Shafie, Muhammed
Australia to take Viet refugees 5-7, 379F2
GHAZVINI, Yusef
Named Iran roads min 2-13, 105G2
GHEORGHIU-Dej, Gheorghe (1902-63)
Pirvulescu scores Ceausescu 11-23, 910F1
GHIO, Enrico
Wounded 5-29, 426E3
GHORBAL, Ashraf
Egypt offers shah asylum 11-9, 862B3
GHOTBZADEH, Sadegh
Iranian women protest 3-12, 179A3*
On new militia formatn 5-5, 353B3
Qualifies music ban 7-24, 565B3
US women, black hostages ordrd freed 11-17, 878B1
Named Iran forgn min 11-28, 896G1
Bars UN Cncl mtg 11-30, 913F1
Shifts hostage status stance 11-30—12-1, threatens spy trial 12-1, 12-4, 914D2
Assures Waldheim, sees hope in UN Cncl res 12-5, 913G1
Sees early hostage trial date 12-7, 934F1
Plans intl ct probe of US 'crimes' 12-8, 12-11; US protests 12-10, 934C2
Vs World Ct role on hostages 12-9, 933G1
Assures UN on hostage safety 12-9, 934F2
Bogus Kennedy letter aired 12-12, 935D3
Calls shah US exit 'victory' 12-16, 957F1
On hostage trial, Xmas release 12-16, 12-18, 958D1, G1

1980

GESELL, Judge Gerhard A.
OKs US suit vs Agee 4-1, 268F2
Refused US Agee profits denial 10-2, 990G2
Orders Matlovich AF reinstatemt 11-9, 962A2
GESTSSON, Svavar
New govt bid set 1-16, 39C3
GETTING of Wisdom, The (film)
Released 8-5, 675F2
GETTY, Gordon P.
Rejcts Kuwait bid for Getty Oil 7-18, 557B1
GETTY, J. Paul (1892-1976)
Kuwait seeks 15% of Getty Oil 7-14, 542A3
Kuwait bid for Getty Oil rejctd 7-18, 556G3
GETTY, J. Ronald
Rejcts Kuwait bid for Getty Oil 7-18, 557B1
GETTY Museum, J. Paul
Kuwait bid for Getty Oil rejctd 7-18, 557B1
GETTY Oil Co.
Pay-TV film venture set 4-22, Justice Dept to probe 4-24, 376D2
On '79 Fortune 500 list 5-5, 291B1
ERC deal OKd 6-5, 557F2
Kuwait seeks 15% interest 7-14, 542A3
Kuwait bid rejctd 7-18, 556G3
Pay-TV film plan draws trust suit 8-4, 639D3
Nuclear Fuel Services Inc.
Tenn A-fuel plant reopens despite uranium loss 1-16, 54B1
GEWENIGER, Ute
Wins Olympic medal 7-26, 623B3
GEYER, Arnold
Released, ANC links cited 10-26, 887F3
GHAFOORZAI, Abdul Rahim
Defects to US, scores Sovt Afghan invasn 2-22, 139C1
GHALI, Butros
In Palestine autonomy talks 7-13—7-15, 539A1
Begin: violates peace pact 8-8, 585G1
Israel oppositn ldrs visit Egypt 11-7—11-9, 863G2
Autonomy talks suspended 12-4, 912B3
GHANA—*See also COMMONWEALTH of Nations, GATT, NONALIGNED Nations, OAU*
Freedom House lists as partly free 87E3
Africa trade cited 4-1, 243B2
Pope visits 5-8—5-10, 363A3
GHECHEVA, Vania
Wins Olympic medal 8-1, 622D2
GHERAIEB, Abdelkarim
Visits US hostages 12-25—12-26, 974G1, C2
GHODUSSI, Hojatolislam Ali
Ghotbzadeh released 11-10, 862A2
GHOST Story (book)
On best-seller list 5-4, 359E3; 6-8 448D3

GHOTBZADEH, Sadegh
Sees Waldheim on US hostages 1-1, 1-2, 3C3
Asks Khomeini ruling on US envoy 1-5, rejctn hinted 1-8, 29G3
CBS-TV rpts slur vs Khomeini, Iran bars 29A3
Hostage compromise studied 1-11—1-12, 29D1
Connally sees Sovt role 1-11, 91F3
Asks shah extraditn 1-12; claims arrest, Panama denies 1-23; reaffirms arrest 1-24, 47C1
Says Iran backs Afghan rebels 1-14, 27E2
Warns vs sanctns 1-14, 29A2
Fears Sovt troop massing 1-19, 1-22, 44E1
Bani-Sadr elected pres 1-28, 66D3
Warns Canada on US diplomats escape 1-30, 66F2
Meets UN comm 2-24, 137F2
Vows UN comm hostage visit 2-28, 138B1
Asked to turn over hostage re Forghan link 3-2; denies request 3-4, 164G2

1976

GIAIMO, Rep. Robert N. (D, Conn.)
Angola aid cutoff passed 1-27, 69B1
On Adams' budget proposals 3-23, 231A3
Reelected 11-2, 829G1
GIANCANA, Sam
Exner sells JFK story 1-13, 80A3
GIANTURCO, Delio E.
Eximbank vp 7-21; confrmd 7-29, 807G3
GIAP, Gen. Vo Nguyen
United Viet defense min 7-3, 502F3
In Politburo 12-19, 967F3
GIBBONS, Rep. Sam M. (D, Fla.)
Reelected 11-2, 829B2
GIBBS, Arthur
Scores banning 11-30, 927D3
GIBBS, Eustace
Uganda questns UK apptmt 7-22, 548E1
GIBBS, Tim
Scores UK charter plan 3-23, 240A2
GIBLIN, E. Burke
Vaccine-maker to lose insurance 6-15, 443G1
GIBRALTAR (British colony)
Labor party wins election 9-29, 751C1
GIBSON, Cheryl
Wins Olympic medal 7-24, 575C3
GIBSON, Mayor Kenneth A. (Newark, N.J.)
US Conf of Mayors pres 7-1, 493B1
Mayors seek Carter aid 11-7, 845E3
GIENGER, Eberhard
Wins Olympic medal 7-23, 574B3
GIEREK, Edward
Hails Bonn pact ratificatn 3-12, 260A2
State Cncl member 3-25, 268D2
Visits W Ger 6-8—6-11, 442D1
CP rallies back 6-26—6-28, 482G2
At E, W Eur CP conf 6-29—6-30, 461D2
On food shortages; forms price comms 9-3; plan OKd 9-9, 811E1
In USSR, signs aid pact 11-9—11-15, 907C1
Assures farmers, workers 12-1, 926E3
On 5-yr plan 12-1, 965G3
GIETZELT, Arthur
Shadow cabt reshuffled 3-25, 237B1
GIGUERE, Louis
Arraigned 4-22, 309C3, F3
Chrgd with fraud, theft 5-5, 380G3
New chrgs filed 10-12, trial ordrd 11-26, 998G3
GILBERT, Gibby
Runner-up in Kaiser Intl golf 9-26, 756B3

1977

GHOZALI, Mohamed
Algeria energy min 4-23, 470B2
GHUBASH, Saif Ibn Said al-
Assassinated 10-25, 811B3
Slayer executed 11-16, 949B3
GIAIMO, Rep. Robert N. (D, Conn.)
On Carter econ aid plan 1-27, 52A2
'76 special interest gifts rptd 2-4, 128G3, 129A2-F2
Presents '78 budget 3-23, 228D3
Chrgs farm bill too costly 9-24, 736G3
GIAMATTI, A. Bartlett
Named Yale U pres 12-20, 1021C2
GIANCANA, Sam (d. 1975)
House assassinatn com hearing 3-16, 228F2
GIANNETTINI, Guido
Andreotti testifies at Milan trial 9-15, 1014E3
GIANT Food Inc.
Peterson named Carter adviser 4-4, 354D2
GIBBONS, David (Bermuda prime minister)
Elected prime min 8-29, names Cabt 8-31, 969B3
Executns spark riots, arson 12-1—12-3, scores oppositn ldr 12-3, 935E2, D3
GIBBONS, James
Named Ireland agri min 7-5, 599A1
GIBBS, Alan J.
Named Army asst secy 4-7; confrmd 4-25, 418D1
GIBBS, Stephen R.
Vs 2d Panama canal 7-25, 589F3
GIBION, Rita
Kidnaps 8, arrested 2-11—2-13, 163F1
GIBRALTAR (British colony)
UK asks Spain to open border 9-7, 717D3
Panama backs Spain claim 9-17, 805E1
GIBSON, Mayor Kenneth A. (Newark, N.J.)
Carter energy plan reactn 4-15, 320E2
GIBSON, Mark E.—*See NUH, Abdul*
GIBSON, Rex
Vs govt criticism of press re Biko 10-9, 804G2
GIEREK, Edward (Polish Communist Party first secretary)
Rpts bad harvest, food shortages 10-7, 885E3
Sees Wyszynski 10-29, 885F3
USSR revolutn anniv fete photo 11-7, 865C3
Schmidt visits Poland 11-21—11-25, 926E1
In Italy 11-28—12-1, sees Pope 12-1, 987B1
Welcomes Carter 12-29, 1001G1
GIFFORD, Frank
Named to HOF 1-17, 164C1
Inducted into HOF 7-30, 659A1
GIL, Pedro
Arrested re foiled Cuba raid 8-15, 654F1
GILABERT, Ricardo
Disappears 1-9, 42D1
GILBERT, Rod
Rangers release 11-23, takes PR post 12-6, 1021E1

1978

GIACOBBO, Placido (Charlie)
Dies 4-25, 356G2
GIADRESCO, Gianni
Sees Somali pres 2-20—2-22, 138A1
GIAIMO, Rep. Robert N. (D, Conn.)
Reelected 11-7, 850D2
On Carter budget plans 12-14, 980A1
GIAMBOLVO, Louis
Ballroom in St Patrick opens 12-1, 1031A1
GIANCANA, Sam
Cited at JFK death hearing 9-26, 750B1
GIANG, Vo Dong
Urges Cambodia peace talks 1-12, 43B1
GIANTS, The (recording)
Peterson wins Grammy 2-24, 315F3
GIARDINA, Anthony
Living At Home opens 12-11, 1031C2
GIBB, Andy
Love on best-seller list 2-4, 116F3; 3-8, 196B1
Shadow Dancing on best-seller list 6-7, 460F3; 7-5, 579G3, 580A1
GIBBONS, Rep. Sam M. (D, Fla.)
Reelected 11-7, 850F2
GIBSON, Edward
Lauds USSR space effort 3-4, 157D3
GIBSON, John
On '77 top-paid labor ldrs list 5-15, 365G1
GIBSON, Mayor Kenneth A. (Newark, N.J.)
Reelected 5-9, 363G1
Layoffs scheduled 12-11, 1012E1
GIEREK, Edward (Polish Communist Party first secretary)
CP members ask pol, econ reforms 1-6, 20C1
Sees price hikes, raises min wage 1-9, 20A1
Vows farmer pensn plan review 10-5, 904E1
GIGUERE, Louis
Cleared re Sky Shops 6-29, 514E3
GILA National Forest (N.M.)
NM water rights backed by Sup Ct 7-3, 552C2
GILBANE Construction Co.
Hartford arena roof collapses 1-18, 95D3
GILBERT, Ethel
Discounts Hanford radiatn-cancer link 2-25, 164G2
GILBERT, Gibby
2d in N Orleans Open 4-30, 356A1

1979

Sees clergy on hostages, vows list 12-27, 975A2
Vs Sovt Afghan invasn 12-28, 974C2

GIAIMO, Rep. Robert N. (D, Conn.)
Budget Com chrmn 1-24, 71C1
Vs more fscl '80 mil spending 9-11, 679A1
GIAMATTI, A. Bartlett
Names May Yale provost 5-4, 392D2
GIANCANA, Sam (d. 1975)
Ruby crime links detailed 7-17, 538A2
GIANELLI, John
Traded to Nets 5-30, 526F2
GIANGROSSO, In the Interest of
Case refused by Sup Ct 2-21, 128B3
GIANNINI, Giancarlo
Innocent released 1-11, 174G2
GIANT Food Inc.
Price rollback set 5-9, 385B2
GIBAVIC, Eva
On '77 NH A-protest chrgs 7-3, 519F1
GIBBONS, Edward F.
Lauds Brascan bid end 5-29, 440F2
GIBBONS, Green, Van Amerlongen Ltd.
Trailways Inc.—*See TRAILWAYS*
GIBBONS, William M.
Rock I RR bankruptcy efforts cited 9-26, 722B2
Rock I reorganizatn plan ordrd 10-10, 830E3
Files Rock I reorganizatn plan 12-28, 989D2
GIBSON, Harvey
Lands 727 in Detroit after mid-air mishap 4-4, 412A2
GIBSON, Mayor Kenneth A. (Newark, N.J.)
Sets layoffs 11-13, 921A2
Vetoes police hiring ordinance 11-15, override fails 11-20, 992F1
GIBSON, William
Miracle Worker opens 1-6, 292B2
GIDDING, Nelson
Beyond the Poseidon Adventure released 5-24, 528D1
GIDEON, Raynold A.
Man, Woman & Bank released 9-28, 820G1
GIDEON v. Wainright
Right-to-counsel doctrine clarified by Sup Ct 3-5, 185F1
GIEREK, Edward (Polish Communist Party first secretary)
Sees Pope 6-2, 413E1
GIESLER, Jon
In NFL draft 5-3, 335G1
GIGANTE, Rev. Louis R.
Case declined by Sup Ct 10-1, 767F3
GIGANTE v. Lankler
Case declined by Sup Ct 10-1, 767F3
GIGLIO, Gino
Victim opens 5-3, 712C3
GIGUERE, Louis de Gonzague
Campbell trial ordrd 4-26, 329F1
Acquitted in Liberal Party fund fraud 7-20, 563D1
Sky Shops chrg dropped 10-19, 812C2
Cleared of ad agency influence peddling 12-7, 949A1
GILBERT, Charles
Blamed for Mex City air crash 12-14, 996C3
GILBERT, Lewis
Moonraker released 6-29, 820B2
GILBERT, Ronnie
Re-Arrangements opens 3-9, 292E2

1980

Says UN comm to visit hostages, asks not to leave Iran 3-6, 164F1
In clash with militants on hostage release 3-7—3-9, 177B2
Chrgs US plot vs shah's extraditn 3-22, 217G1
Warns on hostage fate, rally protests 3-25; Islamic ldr asks trials 3-26, 217D2, F2
Cites Carter note to Bani-Sadr 3-30, 241F2
Links Iraq to US 'imperialism' 4-7, 261F1
Discounts US sanctns effect 4-8, 258G1
Threatens Iraqi coup 4-8, 300A1
Asks forgn natns non-support of US policy 4-11, 4-12, 282F1
Warns US vs port mining 4-24, 298A3
Scores Carter hostage rescue move 4-25, 322B3
Warns Iran Emb raiders 4-30, 5-1, 324G2
To limit UN comm rep role 5-17; West warning to Waldheim cited 5-23, 393F2, 394B1
At Islamic conf, backs Afghan rebels 5-18, scores US, Sovt 'aggressn' 5-19, 395D3
Meets 3 Eur socialists on hostages 5-25—5-26, 394E1
Renews stand on US hostages 6-5, 418C3
Defends Clark vs Iran critics 6-6, 433E1
Bars return of UN comm to Iran 6-16, 464F1
Orders Sovt staff cuts, scores Iran CP role 7-2, 491C1
Reassures Sovts re emb threat 7-7, 507C2
France protests Bakhtiar death try 7-18; denies role, cancels Nicaragua visit 7-18—7-19, 545D1
Asks UN role re jailed Iranians in US 8-5, 587D1
Chrgs Sovt border breach, aid to Kurds 8-12, 644D3
Successor named 8-31, 671D2
Arrested 11-7, freed 11-10, 862C1
GIACUMBI, Nicola
Slain 3-16, 233G1
GIAIMO, Rep. Robert N. (D, Conn.)
DeNardis wins seat 11-4, 848D1
'81 budget res OKd by com 11-11, 866B2
Details '81 budget res 11-20, 896B2
GIAMMALVA, Tony
Loses NCAA doubles tennis title 5-26, 607D1
GIANNINI, Giancarlo
Blood Feud released 2-22, 216C2
GIANNINI, Massimo
Italy civil service min 4-4, 275F3
GIANT Food Inc.
Retail prices frozen 3-6, 349C1
GIAP, Gen. Vo Nguyen
Replaced as Viet defense min 2-7, 90G1
GIBBONS, Rep. Sam M. (D, Fla.)
Reelected 11-4, 842F2
GIBRALTAR (British colony)
Labor party wins electns 2-6, 133B1
Spain links set by UK pact 4-10, 274G2-A3
GIBSON, Derek
Death Ship released 4-25, 416F2
GIDEON v. Wainwright
Case cited by Sup Ct 2-27, 188G2
GIELGUD, Sir John
Wins Grammy 2-27, 296G3
GIEREK, Edward (Polish Communist Party first secretary; replaced Sept. 6)
Addresses CP cong 2-11—2-15, 152F3
Vows wage hikes 7-9, 566F1, 658D1
TV speech rejects strikers' pol reform demands 8-18; USSR, Sovt bloc press rpts 8-19, 8-20, 625G1, 626B2, F2
Premier ousted, replaced 8-24, 641D1, F1
Sovt reports endorse 8-25, 8-26; E Ger TV broadcasts speech 8-25, 642C1-F1, B2
Silesia coal miners walkout 8-29, 657A2
Hospitalized 9-5, Kania succeeds as party chief 9-6, 678E2
Politburo ally ousted 9-19, 720F2
CP Central Com scores 10-4—10-6, 760E2-E3
Warsaw CP ldr quits 11-18, 878C2
Central Com ouster cited; Kowalcyk ousted from Politburo 12-2, 909G2, 910B1
GIERSCHE, Heidrum
Australia asylum rptd 4-22, 327A1
GIFFORD, William
Dies 3-9, 279B3
GIGANTE, James
PR refugee camp ban lifted 11-3, 869C2
GIGER, H. R.
Wins Oscar 4-14, 296A2
GIGUERE, Louis de Gonzague
Influence peddling acquittal appeal set 1-4, 6G1
Sky shops acquittal appeal rejctd 1-7, 57A1
Campbell, Brown convicted in Sky Shops case 2-8, 148A3; fined 3-7, 230A3
GIJSEN, Bishop Matthis
At Dutch bishops synod 1-14—1-31, 156G3
GILBERT, Bruce
Nine to Five released 12-19, 1003C2
GILBERT, Edward
Indicted 8-19, 713F3
GILBERT, Gibby
Ties for 2d in Masters 4-13, 412A2
2d in Westchester Classic 8-17, ties for 2d in Mixed Team tourn 12-14, 972B1, F1
GILBERT, Gilles
Fined over NYC brawl 1-25, 198C3

1976

GILBERT Islands (formerly Gilbert & Ellice Islands) (British colony)
Ellice Islands secede 12-31-75, 12F3
GILCHRIST, Peter N.
On Southn Bell pol paymts 10-25, 939D1
GILDER, Bob
Wins Phoenix open 1-18, 123E2
2d in BC Open golf 8-9, 656G1
GILINSKY, Victor
Vs reactor sale to Spain 6-21, 739B2
GILKES, James
IOC rejects appeal 7-22, 562F1
GILLESPIE, Alastair W.
Scores Trudeau econ remarks 1-8, 27C3
Rpts new energy plan 4-27, 332B2
Oil-price hike OKd 5-18, 380C3
Gas price rise set 6-10, 417A1
Stays Canada energy min 9-14, 692B2
Testifies re A-sales 11-24, 904F1
Rpts Marubeni Japan A-sale agent 11-29, 923G3
On '73 A-sale mtg 12-2, 923D3
Bars A-sale details 12-9, seeks Argentina agent 12-15, 962G2, C3
Rpts Argentina A-pact delay 12-22, 998G1
GILLESPIE, Dizzy
Wins Grammy 2-28, 460B3
GILLY, Paul E.
Gets life sentence 9-3, 816A3
GILMAN, Rep. Benjamin A. (R, N.Y.)
Rpts Latin, US drug drive set 1-20, 61B1
Reelected 11-2, 830C2
GILMORE, Gary Mark
Sentncd to die 10-7; asks executn 11-8, 890E3; executn stayed 12-3, 920A3
Stay vacated 12-13, death date set 12-15, 952F1
GILMORE, Kenneth
Arrested 6-8, 442E3
GILMOUR, Ian
Shadow cabt defense secy 1-15, 101B2
GILMOUR, Lloyd
Flyers beat Sovt team 1-11, 56A2
GINESTET, Pierre
Sells Margaux vineyard 12-18, 964F2
GINGA, Nicu
Wins Olympic medal 7-24, 576G2
GINN, Rep. Ronald B. (D, Ga.)
Reelected 11-2, 829D2
GINN, Rosemary L.
Amb to Lux 5-10; confrmd 5-20, 412E1
GINSBERG, Alexander
Scores Uruguay rights abuse 5-10, 441A2
In CSCE monitor group 5-13, 408B2
GIOIA, Giovanni
Mafia ties alleged 2-5, 141C1
GIOLITTI, Antonio
New European Comm meets 12-22—12-23, 977G1
GIORDANI, Claudia
Wins Olympic medal 2-11, 158E3
GIRARD, Thomas E.
Scores superports OK 12-17, 992D1
GIRAUDET, Pierre
Rpts Air France deficit 11-18, 905B3
GIRL Scouts of the U.S.A.
Ford suspends HEW rule 7-7, 535F2
GIRON, Jose Antonio
Vs EC entry 3-21, 269G1
Warns vs pol chng 8-31, 753B1
Rightists pay homage to Franco 11-20, 908F3
GISCARD d'Estaing, Ann-Aymone (Mrs. Valery)
Visits US 5-17—5-22, 372F1
GISCARD d'Estaing, Valery (French president)
Family aid plan OKd 1-1, 50D1
Reorganizes cabt 1-12, 49A2
Outlines '76 govt programs 1-14, 49E2-A3
Vs Sahara independnc, denies Algeria dispute 1-31, 107D2
Sees Schmidt 2-12—2-13, 229D1
Draft housing reforms OKd 3-4, 204D3
Left gains in electns 3-7, 3-14, 204G2
Gives Chirac Parlt role 3-26, 312B3
W Ger, Dutch reject snake reform 4-1—4-2, 276D1
Sees Sadat 4-3—4-5, 275E1
Cabt OKs indl, tax reforms 4-13—4-14, 312B2
Muldoon visits, gets Pacific A-test assurances 4-16, 372E3
News conf: scores student unrest, left 4-22, 312D1, E3
Rpt CAR expels plotter 4-30, 503F2
On '77-82 defns budget, bars NATO return 5-5; Sanguinetti scores 6-3, 417E2, G2, D3
Sees Kissinger 5-7, 318A3
At France-Africa summit 5-10—5-11, 355G2, B3
Visits US 5-17—5-22, offers peace force for Leb 5-21, 369A1, 372E1
Backs A-export safeguards 5-20, 372E2

1977

GILBERT Islands (formerly Gilbert & Ellice Islands) (British colony)
Cholera outbreak rptd 9-19, 748D1
GILBRETH, Donald
Acquitted 5-20, 424E1
GILCHRIST, Julian
Arrested 3-13, 280E2
GILLEN, Thomas J.
Indicted 6-2, 520A3
GILLESPIE, Alastair
On oil-price talks 4-7, 281F3, 282A1
Sets oil price hikes 5-12, 410F3
On oil, gas price hikes 6-23, 504E3
On home insulatn grants 6-27, 505B1
On NEB pipe route rpt 7-4, 525D2
On Foster AECL ouster 7-7, 541F3
Quebec bars fed insulatn funds 7-28, 597B1
Sees US key to IEA oil-use goal 10-5—10-6, 794A1, C1
On uranium disclosure ban 10-14, 895F3
Drops home insulatn rebate rules 12-1, 966A1
GILLESPIE, Dizzy
Sails for Cuba 5-15, 390G1
Performs in Cuba 5-18, 456E2
GILLESPIE, Irwin
'69-75 DREE aid study rptd 4-16, 327C1
GILLMAN, Peter
Chrgs Israeli torture 6-19; Israel denies 7-3, 511B2
GILMORE, Gary Mark
Death delays sought 1-11—1-17, executed 1-17, 40E1
GILMORE Steel Corp.
Steel dumping chrgs vs Japanese upheld 10-3, 774C3
GILPATRIC, Roswell L.
Reuss chrgs interest conflict 5-24, 406G3
GINJAAR, Leendert
Named pub health, environmt min 12-19, 986B1
GINN, Rosemary L.
Replaced as amb to Luxembourg 5-25, 499G3
GINNIE Mae—*See U.S. GOVERNMENT—HOUSING & Urban Development—Government National Mortgage Association*
GINSBERG, Allen
Protests dissident arrests 2-25, 226B2
GINZBURG, Alexander
Fund rptd seized 1-10, 22B2
Rpts dissident funding 2-2, arrested 2-3; US protests 2-4, 101B2
Orlov arrested 2-10, 117B1
Drive vs Helsinki monitors seen 2-14, 101C2
Chrgd 2-25, US atty named 2-28, 226C2
USSR chrgs CIA link 3-4, 226B3
US atty rpts visa denied 6-1, 436F2
Turchin arrested 7-4, 551B3
Amnesty Intl head leaves USSR 10-14, 812B2
Wife to direct dissident fund 11-6, 956C1
US bars USSR book pact 12-7, 955E2
GINZBURG, Irina
To direct dissident fund 11-6, 956C1
GIOLITTI, Antonio
Gets Eur Comm post 1-7, 74B2
GIRL Scouts of America, Inc.
3 campers slain in Okla 6-13, 492E1
Lady Baden-Powell dies 6-25, 532E2
GISCARD d'Estaing, Valery (French president)
Police versn of de Broglie murder questnd 1-5—1-9, 44E1
Andorra asks financial review 1-5, 47G3
Servan-Schreiber elected 1-6, 63A2
Saudi visit tie to Daoud case denied 1-13, 27C2
Speaks to Carter, Daoud case avoided 1-13; US offcls rpt 1-14, 27G2
US House members vs Daoud release 1-14, 28C1
Carter backs Concorde trial 1-16, 131F2
Defends Daoud release 1-17, 27B3
Chirac in Paris mayor race 1-19, 63C1
In Saudi Arabia 1-22—1-25, 50F1
Mondale visits 1-29, 69D1, C2
Visits Brittany 2-7—2-8, 255B3
Amalrik protests Sovt policy 2-23, 143A1
Warns Carter vs Concorde bar 3-4, 3-7, 212F2, B3
Left gains in munic electns, Chirac elected Paris mayor 3-13, 3-20, 221A1
Servan-Schreiber sells L'Express shares 3-16, 255E3
Instructs Barre on Cabt 3-29, 15 named 3-30, 239C1
Sees Vance on arms talks, Concorde 4-1, 247A1; 4-2, 368B2
Carter asks Portugal aid 4-1, 330C3
Scores US talks with left 4-2, 255B1

1978

GILBERT Islands (formerly Gilbert & Ellice Islands) (British colony)
Tuvalu gains independnc from UK 9-30, 1022B2
GILDER, Nick
Hot Child In the City on best-seller list 10-11, 800E3; 11-8, 888C1
GILES, Jimmy
Traded to Buccaneers 4-24, 336A1
GILLESPIE, Alastair William
Reassures cos re gas deregulatn 8-30, 739F1
Econ Dvpt Bd member 11-24, 921B3
In oil-price talks 11-27, hints price hike delay 11-30, 944F2
GILLIAM, Jim (Junior)
Brain hemmorrhage 9-15, dies 10-8; Dodgers honor 10-7, 10-8, 779E1
Yankees win World Series 10-17, 799G2
GILMAN, Rep. Benjamin A. (R, N.Y.)
Rpts E Ger prisoner exchng talks 4-24, 3-way swap completed 5-1, 318C2
Reelected 11-7, 851F3
In Northn Ireland re 'peace forum' 11-14, 923E1
GILMORE, Artis
NBA field-goal ldr 4-9, 271E2
GILMORE Steel Corp.
Japan '77 dumping ruling revised 1-9, 80D2
GILMOUR, William (Buddy)
Indicted for tax evasn 6-5, 539B3
GILPIN, Jack
Shay opens 3-7, 887B3
GILROY, Frank D.
Once In Paris released 11-9, 970E2
GILSON, Etienne
Dies 9-19, 778D1
GIMBELS Brothers Inc.—*See B.A.T. Industries—International Stores Holdings*
GIMENEZ Reyes, Rear Adm. Ramon
Stays on as DR forgn min 8-16, 648C2
GIMME Shelter (play)
Opens 12-10, 1031G1
GIN Game, The (play)
Coburn wins Pulitzer 4-17, 315C1
Tandy wins Tony 6-4, 579G2
GINGRICH, Newt
Wins US House seat 11-7, 850B3, 852F2
GINJAAR, Leendert
Cabt OKs liberalized abortn bill 11-16, 965F1
GINN, Rep. Ronald Bo (D, Ga.)
Reelected 11-7, 850A3
GINNIE Mae—*See U.S. GOVERNMENT—HOUSING & Urban Development—Government National Mortgage Association*
GINZBURG, Alexander
Trial starts 7-10, sentencd 7-13, dissident funds cited; US, other protests 7-10—7-18, 541A2-543C1
Carter rebukes Young for 'pol prisoners' remarks 7-12—7-15, 542E2
Carter deplores convictn 7-20, 549C2
GINZBURG, Arina
Ousted from ct 7-11, 541C2
GIOCOMAZZI, Franco
Shot 5-10, 393D2
GIOVANNI, Paul
Crucifer of Blood opens 9-28, 1031C1
GIOVANNI di Paolo (1403-83)
Altarpiece auctioned 6-21, 579B1
GIRALDI, Arthur
Latin export bank opens 9-8, 828D3
GIRARD Jr., George E.
Convicted in computer drug plot 3-10, 380B1
GIRARDOT, Annie
Dear Detective released 4-24, 619D1
No Time For Breakfast released 9-15, 970D2
GIRAUD, Andre
Named French industry min 4-5, 245G2
On blackout 12-19, 1016D3
GIRLFRIENDS (film)
Released 8-16, 970D1
GIRON, Jose Antonio
Scores govt at pro-Franco rally 11-19, 967B2
GISCARD d'Estaing, Valery (French president)
Carter visit 1-4—1-6, 2C1
Gaullists rptd angered over Barre electn role 1-11, 54E2
Visits Ivory Coast 1-11—1-15, 71A1
Urges govt party unity 1-16, 54E3
Asks disarmamt talks reorganizatn 1-25, 61D2
Urges rejectn of left, backs Barre program 1-27, 70D3
Sees Caramanlis, backs EC entry 1-29, 149E2
In W Ger summit mtg 2-6—2-7, 122B1
Vows to back franc 2-7, 167G1
Meets Sadat 2-12, 98B3
Scores Danish premier 2-26, 167C2
Govt coalitn wins legis electns 3-12, 3-19, 200B3, F3
Barre disputes Chirac electn claims 3-20, 201E1
Radicals quit left-wing alliance 3-20, 201C2
On UN Leb force role 3-22, 197F2
Sees leftist ldrs, Chirac 3-26—3-31, 245D3
Renames Barre premr 3-31, 245C2
Sees Schmidt, Sovt uranium deal discussed 4-2, 258C2
Chaban-Delmas wins Assemb post 4-3, 245G2

1979

GILBERT Islands—*See KIRIBATI*
GILBERTS, Dennis
On Minn A-plant leak 10-9, 786F3
GILDA Radner Live from New York (play)
Opens 8-2, 711B3
GILDEMEISTER, Hans
Loses US Pro Outdoor 8-27, 734E2
GILER, David
Alien released 5-24, 528A1
GILES, Antonio
Army drug dischrgs ordrd upgraded 11-28, 992F1
GILES, Herbert
Chinese chng transliteratn 1-1, 75D2
GILES, Warren C.
Dies 2-7, 176B3
Inducted into Baseball HOF 8-5, 618D3
GILIBERTO v. Compagnie Nationale
Case declined by Sup Ct 4-30, 365A1
GILINKSY, Victor
Votes to revoke Met Ed license 10-26, 826A2
GILL, Albert
Guilty in dredging fraud 5-5, 352B2
Sentenced 6-11, 468C2
GILLES, Clark
Sovts win Challenge Cup 2-11, 118E2, G2
GILLESPIE, Alastair William
On Exxon delivery cuts 2-15, 2-19, 153E2
Orders Petro-Canada to import oil 3-13, 210A3
On Telesat research grant 4-17, 311C3
Loses electn 5-22, 377D2
GILLETTE Co.
Schick sues over razors 6-14, 481D3
GILLIAM, Terry
Life of Brian released 8-17, 820A2
GILLILLAND, Col. William
US officers end China visit 5-15, 370C2
GILMORE, Artis
NBA scoring, field-goal, rebound ldr 4-8, 290E2, F2
GILMORE, Gary Mark (1940-77)
Spenkelink executed in Fla 5-25, 399G3
GILMOUR, Sir Ian
UK lord privy seal 5-5, 338F1
GINN, Stewart
Wins Australian PGA 11-11, 970B2
GINNANE, Antony I.
Patrick released 9-7, 820F2
GINNIE Mae—*See U.S. GOVERNMENT–HOUSING & Urban Development–Government National Mortgage Association*
GINZBURG, Alexander
Freed in spy swap 4-27, to join Solzhenitsyn 4-29; facts on 317A1, F2
GIRAUD, Andre
Proposes job measures 2-23, 154D1
Says French A-plants safe 4-1, 246E2
On oil, gas exploratn aid 9-21, 752B1
GIRL Scouts of America Inc.
Okla murder suspect cleared 3-30, 291E2; dies 6-4, 508A3
GISCARD d'Estaing, Francoise
On bank loan to China 5-9, 370B2
GISCARD d'Estaing, Valery (French president)
Orders A-plant speedup 2-7, 82D3
Gaullists scored at UDF parley 2-17–2-18, 135C1
Left gains in electns 3-18, 3-25, 235C3
Chirac scores 4-3, 267C3
UDF party offices bombed 5-1, 330D2
On forest fires 8-12, 620B2
Cabt OKs '80 budget 9-5, 668F2
Arrest made in tax case 10-12, 791B2
Boulin suicide discovered 10-30, 834G3
Names Matteoli to succeed Boulin 11-8, 872F3
Foreign Developments
At 4-natn Guadeloupe summit 1-5–1-6, 12F2, C3, 40C2
Pak pres scorns Bhutto clemency plea 2-14, 116B2
EMS oppositn dropped 3-7, 160A3
Aide rpts Bakhtiar in France 3-30, 247C3
Visits Mex; signs oil, other agrmts 4-1–4-4, 372F1
USSR trip rptd canceled 4-18, 314D1
Sees Brezhnev in USSR: pacts signed; space flight, arms talks unsetld 4-26–4-28, 323A3
Sees Mauritania premr 5-3, 324A1

1980

GILBERT, Walter
On interferon productn 1-16, 62C3
Wins Nobel Prize 10-14, 889G2
GILBERT Islands—*See KIRIBATI*
GILBRALTAR Savings & Loan Association
Mortgage rate hiked to 16% 11-6, 18% 12-16, 983F3
GILDA Live (film)
Released 3-28, 416G2
GILDER, Bob
Ties for 2d in Los Angeles Open 2-24, 412E2
Wins Canadian Open 6-22, 715B1
GILELS, Emil
W Ger concert tour canceled 1-9, 10A3
GILES, Jimmy
Plank fined for 'unnecessary violence' 10-21, 998B3
GILKESON, Robert
Backs utility cost sharing 12-10, 961E1
GILLOCK, Edgar
State legislators' immunity curbed by Sup Ct 3-19, 249E3
GILMAN, Rep. Benjamin A. (R, N.Y.)
Cuba to free US prisoners 10-13, 789C1
Reelected 11-4, 843F3
GILMORE, Artis
NBA field-goal ldr 3-30, 278D3
GILMORE, Gary Mark (1940-77)
Mailer wins Pulitzer 4-14, 296D2
GILMORE, Judge Horace
Orders census revision 9-25, 741C2
GILMOUR, William (Buddy)
Reinstated 1-30, 447C3
GIL-Robles, Jose Maria
Dies 9-14, 755A3
GILSTER 2d, Richard A.
Loses Nev, Sen primary 9-9, 700E2
GIMBEL, Bruce A.
Dies 10-7, 876F1
GIMBEL, Norman
Wins Oscar 4-14, 296G1
GIMBEL Brothers Inc.—*See B.A.T. Industries*
GINGRICH, Rep. Newt (R, Ga.)
Reelected 11-4, 842B3
GINN, Rep. Ronald B. (D, Ga.)
Reelected 11-4, 842A3
GINNIE Mae (Government National Mortgage Association)—*See under U.S. GOVERNMENT–HOUSING & Urban Development, Department of (HUD)*
GINZBURG, Alexander
Family arrives in NY 2-2, 87F3
At Cambodia border aid vigil 2-6, 108D2
GIORDANO, Joseph
Families Conf opens 6-5, 442D3
GIORDANO, Nicholas A.
Named Phila Stock Exchng pres 12-18, 959A2
GIOVANETTI, Luciano
Wins Olympic medal 7-22, 623C2
GIRAUD, Andre
Kuwait indl, oil accord reached 3-3, 180B1
GIRI, Varahagiri Venkata
Dies 6-24, 528F1
GIRL from Ipanema, The (song)
De Moraes dies 7-9, 608F1
GIRON, Carlos
Wins Olympic medal 7-23, 623E3
GISCARD d'Estaing, Valery (French president)
Sees Schmidt re Afghanistan 1-9, 10G2
In India, joint statemt signed 1-27; ends visit 1-28, 97B3
US amb's pol gaffes rptd 1-30, 200D2
Semiannual mtg with Schmidt ends, Sovt Afghan exit asked 2-5; USSR sees US pressure 2-6, 84F2-D3
Journiac dies 2-8, 176A2
Chirac scores 2-25, 193A1
Tours Arab states; backs Palestinian rights, gets oil guarantees 3-1—3-10, 179G3
Marchais defends war record 3-8, 193F1
Chirac backs hard line with UK re EC budget 3-17, 242A3
Olympic boycott decisn delay seen 3-23, 259E3
On new energy proposals 4-2, 254G1
Poniatowski impeachmt sought re De Broglie murder 4-14, 312F2
Vows Corsica aid 4-22, 312C3
US hostage kin seek support 4-23, 299C2
Farm price hike rptd 4-30, 327A2
Skips Tito funeral 5-8, 339A1
Sees Mex pres, signs trade agrmt 5-17—5-18, 409C2
Arafat warns vs pro-Israel stand 5-18, 418G1

1976

Bars resignatn with '78 left victory 5-23, 372E2
New centrist party backs 5-23, 418B1
Modifies econ aims 5-25, 439F2
US plans 7-natn econ summit 6-1, 6-3, 389A1
Confers with Chirac 6-6—6-7, 417E3
Meets Assad 6-17—6-19, 448D3
Ends UK visit 6-24, 481C3
At 7-natn econ summit 6-27—6-28, 461G2, 462E1
Visits W Ger 7-6, 521D1
Dismisses Sanguinetti 7-7, 521D2
On Italian loan ban 7-19, 531A1
Replaces top Elysee aide 7-28, 556A1
Ranucci guillotined 7-28, Benzahra spared 8-4, 588F3, 589A1
Accepts Chirac resignatn, names Barre 8-25, 628C1
Barre names Cabt 8-27, addresses mtg 8-28, 650B3, 651A1
Sees Kissinger on S Africa 9-7, 660F2
Regrets Mao death 9-9, 657E2
Scores Corsica bombings 9-9, 693E2
Tito cancels visit 9-10, 734F2
Kissinger mtg on Viet UN entry rptd 9-14, 682D1
Barre details inflatn curbs 9-22, 712B2
Signs Iran A-pact 10-6, 773F2
A-export guidelines set 10-11, 772B3
Book published 10-11, 852C3
Meets Callaghan, backs IMF loan, sterling balances plan 11-11—11-12, 880B2 ★
Chirac regains Assemb seat 11-14, 872B3
Gaullists vs re Paris mayor 11-18, 872G3
Joint Eur defns barred 11-30, 905A3
Asks 3d econ summit 12-2, 964D1
Chirac forms new party 12-5, 963G3
Parsien Libre police raid scored 12-6, 964C1
Visits Tito 12-6—12-7, 1012A2
Pakistan set on A-deal 12-16, 1002D3
Libya defrauded in binocular sale 12-25—12-30, 1006F3

GIUGNI, Henry
Wild acquitted 7-27, 566C1
GIVAUDAN Co.—*See HOFFMAN-LaRoche*
GIVE 'Em Hell Harry (record album)
Wins Grammy 2-28, 460C3
GIZIKIS, Phaidon
'67 treason chrg dropped 2-28, 221F3
GJERDE, Bjartmar
Norway industries min 1-12, 30A2
Signs UK N Sea oil pact 9-10, 832E3
GLACIER Bay National Monument (Alaska)
Sen bars new mining claims 2-4, 135A2
Mining curbs signed 9-28, 834B2
GLANZROCK, Jerome
Indicted 6-7, 442B3
GLASGOW, Earl
2 Amers seized in plot 10-25, 962E1
GLASS
US rpts sex bias suits vs Owens, Kerr 9-11, 943G3
Venez Owens natlztn stalled 11-1, 874F3
GLASS, Basil
Mason protested 9-13, 732F2
GLASS, Henry
Wins Olympic medal 2-15, 159E1
GLAUCOMA—*See 'Diseases' under MEDICINE*
GLEASON, Thomas W.
Endorses Jackson 1-6, 22B3
GLEN Burn Colliery Inc.
Indicted 11-19, 989D2
GLEN Cove, N.Y.—*See NEW York State*
GLENN, Frank
GOP conv vp vote table 8-19, 599F3
GLENN Jr., Sen. John H. (D, Ohio)
A-materials export ban urged 1-19, 115C3
Visits Carter as vp prospect 7-8, 489F3
Dem conv keynoter 7-12, 506B2, 508B1, G2
Mondale gets vp nod 7-15, 506B2
Sees Carter 12-16, 937B2
GLENN, Wayne E.
Fired 12-15, 986B1
GLICKMAN, Dan
Elected 11-2, 823D2, 829D3
GLOMAR Explorer (deep sea mining vessel)
Howard Hughes dies 4-5, 336F1
GLORIA (Colombian sailing ship)
In Operation Sail 7-4, 488A3
GLOWA, Ludwig G.
Indicted 1-27, 144E3
GLUCKSBURG (W. German warship)
In Intl Naval Review 7-4, 488C3

1977

Chirac: left will end republic 4-3, 255F2
Defends Zaire mil aid 4-12, 265D1
In Senegal, at summit 4-19—4-23, 316C3
Viet premr visits 4-25—4-28, 329A1
At 7-natn econ summit, protests Jenkins role 5-7—5-8, 357C1, F1, 358F1
Sees Carter, lauds 5-9, 358F1, D2, 359G1
At 4-power NATO talks 5-9, boycotts min mtg 5-10, 358C2, F2
Trudeau visits 5-11—5-14, 389A2
Poniatowski named envoy 5-13, 391A3
Servan-Schreiber elected Radical ldr 5-15, 450A1
Nimeiry visits France 5-17—5-19, 450D1
Party changes name 5-20, 449E3
Scientists vs A-plant 5-30, 450A1
Mobutu thanks for Shaba aid 6-9—6-10, 490E1
In Bonn, sees Schmidt 6-16—6-17, 566C3
EC policy scored 6-16, 598D1
Brezhnev in Paris 6-20—6-22; Vance briefed 6-24, 494C3-495B2
Denies US-USSR mediator role 6-22, 495B2
Child-killer guillotined 6-23, 543A2
Sees Andreotti 7-19, 581E2
Scores Carter on detente 7-25, 550D3
Visits Pierrelatte reactor site, reasserts A-policy 7-30, 597G2
S Africa A-test plan rptd 8-17, 663D3
Disarmamt drive announced 8-26, 1012G3
'78 budget presented 9-7, 744E1
Tunisian guillotined for murder 9-10, 728C2
Replaces ministers 9-26, 744F2
Tito in France 10-12—10-17, 844F2
Schmidt thanks re hijack rescue aid 10-18, 790F1
4 govt parties set electn agrmt 10-21, 924B2
Sahara kidnap prompts Cabt mtg 10-27, 831A3
Presses Algeria on kidnaped natls 10-30, sees Libya premr 11-3, rpts victims alive 11-7, 852B2, F2
Sees Levesque 11-3, 862A3
Sees Chirac on '78 electns 12-7; Chablan-Delmas, other pol ldrs; backs Barre 12-8, 1012E2
In UK summit 12-12—12-13, 1013G1
Pro-govt newspaper closes 12-17, 1013B1

GISH, John
Sup Ct refuses case 10-3, 760E1
GISH v. Board of Education
Sup Ct bars gay case review 10-3, 760D1
GITHII, George
Quits Nairobi newspaper 5-3, 393E1
GIZEW Temesgen, Lt.
Assassinated 11-2, 875E2
GLAENZER, Jules
Dies 8-16, 696G2
GLASER, Milton
Felker group buys Esquire 8-26, 695A3
GLASS
McDonald's halts promotn 7-8, 7-17, sues Mass agency 7-12, 559F3
Die makers strike 9-16—10-14, 818B3
Lalique dies 10-26, 872D2
GLASS Bottle Blowers Association of the United States and Canada (AFL-CIO)
Die makers' strike ends 10-14, 818C3
GLASS Containers Corp.—*See NORTON Simon*
GLASS Packaging Institute
Die makers' strike ends 10-14, 818C3
GLASSPOLE, Florizel (Jamaica governor general)
Greets Castro 10-16, 884A1
GLASSWARE Association, American
Mass health agency sues 7-12, 560C1
GLASS Workers' Union of North America, American Flint (AFL-CIO)
Ends 4-week strike 10-14, 818B3
GLAZER, Nathan
Scores Califano re quotas 3-31, 235E2
GLAZKOV, Lt. Col. Yuri
Soyuz 24 launched 2-7, docks 2-8, 109E3; lands 2-25, 170E2
GLEASON, John S.
Pleads guilty 6-21, 540B3
GLEASON, Thomas W.
Coast dock protest ends 4-18, 324F2
Containerships struck 10-1, 778A1
Strike ends 11-29, 916B1
GLEN Burn Colliery Inc.
Fined $20,000 3-21, 520C3
GLENDALE, Calif.—*See CALIFORNIA*
GLEYSTEEN Jr., William H.
In China money-claim talks 5-1, 333E2
GLICK, Warren A.
On '74 Eximbank Indonesia loans 1-25, 183A1
GLISTRUP, Mogens
Soc Dems make electn gains 2-15; oppositn role cited 115A2
GLOBAL Marine Inc.
Rpts forgn payoffs 6-2, 503F2
GLOVER v. Herald Co. d.b.a. Globe-Democrat Publishing Co.
Libel case refused 11-28, 919A3
GLUSHKOV, Nikolai T.
Sets price hikes, cuts 1-4, 22B1
GLUZMAN, Semyon
Amnesty Intl cites detentn 11-28, 756F2

1978

Govt denies neutron bomb test 4-21, 313B1
Inaugurates Lyon subway 4-28, 352B3
Plans Zaire troop exit 5-23, 381G1
African natns back mil aid 5-23, 382G2
Sees Mobutu 5-23, backs pan-African peace force 5-25, 417E3
Addresses UN disarmamt sessn, hints Geneva role 5-25, 417F3, 421D2
Visits Corsica 6-7—6-9, 496A2
Sees Schmidt on EC monetary zone 6-23, presents plan at Bremen summit 7-6—7-7; UK, US, others wary 7-7—7-18, 545D1-546B1
Visits Spain 6-28—7-1, backs EC entry 6-29; Basques protest 6-30, 649D1-C2
33 bombs explode in Corsica 7-3, 533E2
Cabt meets on oil spills 7-5, 524B1
At 7-natn Bonn econ summit 7-16—7-17, 543C3, 544B2
Visits Portugal, backs EC entry 7-19—7-21, 667B2
Presses Sahara mediatn 7-27, 8-1, 676E2
Sees Iraq amb on emb siege 7-31, 582C2
Asks Pak A-contract revisn, US pressure cited 8-9; Zia scores 8-23, 668A2
Corsican castle destroyed 8-11, 649E3
OKs '79 budget 8-28, 667F1
Cabinet OKs '79 budget 9-6, 881D3
Assad vs Leb peace plan 9-29, 745C2
Servan-Schreiber loses electn 10-1, 815A2
See US aide on Leb peace plan 10-2, 745F1
Gives US Leb peace plan 10-2, informs Saudis 10-3, 745F1
Visits Brazil, pacts signed 10-4—10-8, 772F2
Soclist censure motion fails 10-4, 815E2, G2
Carter contacts to end Leb war cited 761C1
Gromyko visits 10-25—10-28, 830E3-831A1
Kadar in France, stresses detente 11-15—11-17, 894F2
Vs EC Parlt expansn 11-21, 902G1-G2
L'Aurore backing sought 11-26, 1017B1
Francois-Poncet named forgn min 11-29, 1017D1
Iran Moslem ldr warned again 12-3, 929B2
Chirac attacks 12-6, Gaullists quarrel 12-13, 12-15, 987E1-D2
Vs eased EMS terms 12-7, 952C1
Hails Irish joining EMS 12-15, 979C2
Brzezinski talks re US-China tie rptd 12-16, 977C1
Gaullists suspend Peyrefitte 12-20, 1016E3
In Guinea 12-20—12-22, 1018A1
EMS start delayed 12-29, 999E1

GITTES, Harry
Goin' South released 10-6, 970D1
GIULINI, Carlo Maria
Record wins Grammy 2-24, 316C1
GIVENS, Jack
Ky wins NCAA basketball title; named tourn MVP 3-27, 272D1, F1
In NBA draft 6-9, 457G2
GLADNEY, Frank Y. (deceased)
Family OKs 7-Up sale 5-15, 364A3
GLASS
CPSC standards cited 2-8, 185A3
Toys sharp-edge tests OKd 3-10, 265A1
EPA to ease clean-water rules 8-10, 644A2
GLASS & Ceramic Workers of North America (AFL-CIO)
Canada '76 illegal strike rule upheld 3-21, 244F2
GLAUCOMA—*See EYES & Eyesight*
GLEASON, Harold V.
Indicted 7-13, 681B1
GLEASON, Jackie
Frank Fontaine dies 8-4, 708G2
GLEASON, Thomas W.
See Pinochet, says Chile labor repressn continues 5-23, 452C3
Chile trade boycott set by intl unions 11-24, 1014F1
GLEASON, William
Coolest Cat opens 6-23, 760F1
GLENN, Dan
Iowa wins NCAA wrestling title 3-18, 379G2
GLENN, Sen. John C. (D, Ohio)
Votes for Panama Canal neutrality pact 3-16, 177E2
Votes for 2d Canal pact 4-18, 273B1
Sen job-bias-bd blocked 9-20, 720B3
Gets space medal of honor 10-1, 861C2
Visits USSR 11-11—11-18, 905A2
GLICKMAN, Rep. Dan (D, Kan.)
Reelected 11-7, 850D4
GLIGORIC, Svetozar
Plan to play Fischer rptd 10-20, 843D2
GLISTRUP, Mogens
Fined in tax case 2-17, 130B3
Local electn results 3-7, 189E2
Wins tax case appeal 5-23, 436F2
GLOMAR Explorer (deep sea mining vessel)
Colby CIA book publshd uncut 11-19, 917A2
GLOVES
US bars China import curbs 3-15, 443G3
China import curb cited 10-2, 805F1
GLUSHKOV, Nikolai T.
Sets coffee, gas price hikes 3-1, 151G2
GLYNN, Carlin
Best Little Whorehouse opens 4-17, 760D1

1979

Africa debt relief vowed 5-4, 371C3
At Franco-Africa summit, asks closer African ties 5-21—5-22, 398B3
Greek EC entry treaty signed 5-28, 407C2
Eur Parlt electns held 6-10, 433G1
Mitterrand quits Eur Parlt 6-20, 485B2
At Tokyo energy summit 6-28—6-29; Carter rebuts US energy criticism 6-28; Newsweek interview publshd 7-2, 493B1
On Carter energy plan 7-16, 534F3
Veil voted EC Parlt head 7-17, 537B2
Reactn to US-Sovt conflict on SALT, Cuba troops rptd 10-3, 738B1
Bokassa gifts alleged 10-10, 791D1
Meets Hua 10-15, signs pacts 10-17, 789F2, B3
Visits W Berlin; reaffirms security, Eur detente committmt 10-29, 835A2
Sees Spanish premr in Paris 11-26—11-27, 952D1
Condemns Iran US Emb seizure 11-27, 895D3
Denies Bokassa gifts personal use 11-27, chrgs continue 12-4, 993D3
UK contributn cut to EC rejctd 11-29—11-30, 917E3
Sees Vance on Iran 12-10, 933G2

GIULINI, Carlo Maria
Wins Grammy 2-16, 336G3
GIUSSIPI, Fitzeroy
Kim decisns 6-3, 838G3
GIVENCHY, Hubert de
'79 fashion roundup rptd 1006A2, B2, F2
GIVHAN v. Western Line Consolidated District
Pub employe free speech backed by Sup Ct 1-9, 14F2
GLADSTONE Realtors v. Village of Bellwood
Case upheld by Sup Ct 4-17, 325A3
GLASHOW, Sheldon
Wins Nobel Prize 10-16, 858C1
GLASS
Venez drops Ownes-Ill takeover bid 3-13, 192D3
Roman bowl sold for record sum 6-4, 672D1
GLASS, Philip
Mercier & Camier opens 10-25, 956D3
GLAUCOMA—*See EYES & Eyesight*
GLCM (ground-launched cruise missile)—*See ARMAMENTS–Missiles*
GLEASON, Harold V.
Convicted 1-23, 205A3
Sentncd 3-27, 291E3
GLEASON Security Service
Indian Pt A-plant security said lax 10-16, 10-20, 807A2
GLENN, Sen. John C. (D, Ohio)
Meets Teng in China 1-9, 27B1
Fears secret data in Iran 'compromised' 3-2, 161A3
Scores SALT treaty 5-17, 460A1
Finances disclosed 5-18, 383D2
Cited in H-bomb letter 9-16, 9-18, 714F1, A3, 716E3, 717B1
SALT II Backfire 'killer amendmt' defeated 11-6, vs pact 11-9, 864C1
GLEN Rose, Tex.—*See TEXAS*
GLEYSTEEN Jr., William
Recalled from S Korea 10-5, 762F2
Returns to S Korea 10-17, 803A3
Asks orderly S Korea govt transitn 10-30, 822F1
S Korea army shakeup scored 12-12, 959F3
GLICK, Allen R.
Fined re casino skimming 8-23, 851B1
GLINSKY, Victor
Vs uranium sale to India 3-23, 416G2
GLOBAL International Airlines Inc.
Tunisia intercepts PLO arms for Nicaragua 7-11, 512E2
GLOBE Packing Co.
Settles '78 beef-price suit 10-22, 985E3
GLOBUS, Yoram
Magician of Lublin released 11-9, 1008A1
GLORIOUS Monster in the Bell of the Horn, The (play)
Opens 7-10, 711C3
GLOUCESTER, Duchess of
At St Vincent indepndnc rite 10-27, 825D1
GLOUCESTER, Duke of (Prince Richard Alexander Walter George)
At St Vincent indepndnc rite 10-27, 825D1
GLUSHKOV, Nikolai T.
On USSR price hikes 7-2, 504E2

1980

Sees Brezhnev on Afghan 5-19, US scores 5-20, 378G2-379D1
Meets Pope 5-31, 476C3
Asks EC expansn delay 6-5, 435E3-436D1
Spanish produce dispute flares 6-16—6-20, 525B3
Carter backs Eur-Sovt ties 6-23, 473G1
Neutron bomb test rptd 6-26, 486B3
Debre declares pres candidacy; Gaullist, Soclst splits seen 6-30, 522D1
In W Ger, stresses Eur re-emergence 7-7—7-9, 521F3
Ends W Ger visit; Schmidt backs French A-weapons, Eur world role 7-11, 539G3
Gets Brezhnev Bastille Day note 7-14, 566D3
Declines to see Anderson 7-15, 550A1
Names Fabre ombudsman 7-31, 652B1
Fishermen relax Cherbourg port blockade 8-19, 634A1
'81 draft budget OKd 9-10, 687F3
Bokassa confirms gift chrgs 9-17, 728G3
US briefs on hostages in Iran 9-19, 719C3
Meets Iraq vice premier 9-25, 718D3
Condemns synagogue bombing, sets Jewish protectn measures 10-8, 767C3
In China 10-15—10-22; warns re US-Sovt power monopoly 10-17, 829A3
Le Monde editors chrgd 11-7, 872G1
Mitterrand sets pres bid 11-8, 886C2
Party loses by-electns 11-30, 921D2
Libyan role in Chad opposed 12-13, 965F1
Cousins paid damages on Bokassa story 12-23, 996D3

GIVENCHY, Hubert de
'80 fashion roundup rptd 998E1, A2
GK Technologies
Ford electn to bd rptd 5-15, 456G2
Penn Central merger set 7-7, 745E3
Penn Central merger dropped 11-25, 985G1
GLASGOW, Nesby
NFL '79 kick return ldr 1-5, 8D3
GLASHOW, Sheldon
Cuts Sovt ties re dissidents 4-16, 326A3
GLASS, Bernhard
Wins Olympic medal 2-16, 156B1
GLASS Houses (recording)
On best-seller list 4-2, 280F3; 4-30, 360A1; 6-4, 448F3; 7-9, 568F3; 8-13, 640C3
GLASS Menagerie, The (play)
Opens 11-4, 892C3
GLEASON, Harold V.
Fraud appeal refused by Sup Ct 2-19, 131A1
GLEASON, Jackie
Smokey & the Bandit II released 8-15, 675E3
GLEASON, Theodore
At Reagan meeting 9-11, 699E3
GLEASON, Thomas W.
ILA boycotts Sovt ships 1-8, 9D1
GLEASON v. U.S.
Case refused by Sup Ct 2-19, 131A1
GLENDALE Federal Savings & Loan Association (Calif.)
Mortgage rate rptd at 16% in Calif 3-19, 222E3
GLENN Jr., B. Duke
Killed in hotel fire 12-4; Waddell gets Arrow post 12-8, 959F3
GLENN, Sen. John C. (D, Ohio)
Vs India uranium sale 9-24, 723G1
Reelected 11-4, 840G2, 845A3, 851C2
GLENN, Scott
Urban Cowboy released 6-11, 675F3
GLEYSTEEN Jr., William H.
S Korea rebels ask to set truce 5-26, 394C3
US qualifies Chun support, govt reforms asked 8-28, 673G1
At S Korea pres inaugural 9-1, 673E1
Warns vs Kim Dae Jung executn 12-6, 944B3
GLICKMAN, Rep. Dan (D, Kan.)
Reelected 11-4, 842D3
GLICKSTEIN, Shlomo
Wins Australian Hard Ct tourn 1-6, 607D2
Loses Sabra Classic 10-12, 947A2
GLOBE Newspaper Co. v. Supreme Court
Case remanded by Sup Ct 10-14, 782B1
GLORIA (film)
Released 10-1, 836A3
GLOUCESTER City—*See NEW Jersey*
GLUECK, Sheldon
Dies 3-10, 279B3
GLUT, Donald F.
Empire Strikes Back on best-seller list 7-13, 568D3

1976

GNP (Gross National Product)—*See ECONOMY; country names*
GOD Bless the Child (recording)
Wins Hall of Fame award 2-28, 460E3
GODFATHER II (film)
'75 top rental film 1-7, 32F3
GODFREY, Arthur
Palmer breaks flight record 5-19, 368F3
GODFREY, Howard B.
Testimony on FBI-terrorist ties rptd 1-11, 42C1
GODLEY, G. McMurtrie
Replaced as amb to Leb 4-28, 412G1
Meloy slain 6-16, 425B2
GODSPELL (play)
Opens 6-22, 1014D3
GODWIN Jr., Gov. Mills E. (R, Va.)
Seconds Ford nominatn 8-18, 597G2
GOENKA, Ramnath
Indian Express revamped 1-3, 73F3
Takes Express control 10-29, 837C2
GOGA, Lefter
Replaced 10-14, 949A2
GOING Up (play)
Opens 9-19, 1014E3
GOKHALE, Hari Ramachandra
Defends exec power bill 9-1, 652C1
Elections delayed 10-30, 837G2
GOKSARAN, Gen. Ihsan
Demotion rptd 3-12, 192A2
Pleads innocent 4-7, 298G1
Acquitted 4-30, 322B3

GOLD—*See also MONETARY Developments*
Portugal sells 4 tons 1-6, 11G2
IMF Jamaica accord 1-8, 13F1-14A2; text excerpts 1-9, 15A1, B2
Price plunges 1-8, 14E1
Mozambique actn spurs UK price rise 3-3, 175B3
S Africa swap deals rptd 3-17, 429C1
IMF sets sales 5-5; auction held 6-2; bidders, buyers rptd 6-3, 6-9, 430G1
London prices rptd 6-2, 430A3; 6-4—6-7, 407A3
London price rises 6-4—6-7, 407A3
2d IMF auctn 7-14, price plunges 7-14—7-22; Sovt sales rptd 7-21, 530F1
S Africa price drop moves 7-21, 540B1
French reserves rptd down 7-27, 555F3
Price slide continues; IMF auctns, other factors cited 8-23—8-31, 642A3, 654D3
S Africa holdings drop 8-27, 714A1
London price recovers 9-6—10-6, 739E3
Rpt Portugal reserves exhausted 9-9, 774D1
3d IMF auctn, buyers listed 9-15, 739C3
Rpt Poland gets Danzig gold 9-28, 907F1
IMF takes no actn on auction chngs 10-8, 778E2
4th IMF auction 10-27; gold price up 10-27, 10-28; buyers rptd 10-29, 832B2
Prices up after US electn 11-2—11-3, 826F2
UK reserves rptd down 11-2, 853B3
Prices gain 11-2—12-8, 915F3-916B1
5th IMF auction, reserves restitutn set 12-8, 915A3
DR buys more mining firm shares 12-15, 1001E2
GOLD, Eugene
Gets Moritt indictmt 8-12, 1016A2
GOLDBERG, Arthur J.
Judges sue for pay hike 2-11, 136C3
Jewish delegatn sees Spain king 6-3, 459A3
GOLDBERG, David
Named in Army meat fraud probe 5-10, 5-12, 395C2, B3
GOLDBERG, Harry
Named in Army meat fraud probe 5-10, 5-12, 395C2, B3
GOLDBERG, Capt. Lawrence H.
Rptd killed in Viet 9-6, 678B3
GOLDBERG, Norman
Indicted 6-1, 412E3
GOLDBLOOM, Victor
Olympics go-ahead set 1-28, 99F1
GOLDFINGER, Nathaniel
Dies 7-22, 656F3

1977

G.M. LEASING Corp.
Sup Ct curbs IRS tax seizures 1-12, 57A3
G. M. Leasing Corp. v. U.S.
IRS seizures curbed 1-12, 57B3
GNAVI, Adm. Pedro Alberto (ret.)
Arrested 5-4, 371B1
Freed from jail 6-13, 522D3
GNOLEBA, Maurice Seri
Ivory Coast trade min 7-30, 772C1
GNOMES (book)
On best-seller list 12-4, 1021A3
GNP (gross national product)—*See under ECONOMY*
GOAD, Roger (d. 1975)
Slayers sentenced 2-10, 222A3
GODFREY, Isidore
Dies 9-12, 872A2
GODWIN Jr., Gov. Mills E. (R, Va.)
Signs death penalty bill 3-29, 594D1
Declares drought emergency 7-7, 660A1
Vs Carter welfare plan 9-9, 719A2
Dalton elected gov 11-8, 855D2
GOENKA, Ramnath
Doubts press curb end 1-21, 64B1
GOHEEN, Robert F.
Named India amb 4-7; confrmd 4-25, 418D1
GOICO Morales, Carlos Rafael
Gulf + Westn appeals sugar paymt ordr 9-16, 767G1
GOKHALE, Hari Ramachandra
Jethmalani seeks Parlt seat 2-10, 160B1
Loses Parlt seat 3-16—3-20, 205C2 ★
On judges' demotion 9-29, 765G1
Arrested 10-3, 765C1

GOLD
Canada arsenic contaminatn chrgd 1-16, 61F1, A2
Spain-Sovt dispute unsetld 2-9, 242E2
London exchng price rptd 3-2, 145E3
London price tops $150 3-18, 336C1
Portugal reserves depleted 4-25, 330E3
Canada arsenic rpt issued 6-6, 447G3
'77 fashion wrap-up rptd 6-6, 1022G1
Futures contract trading cited 7-5, 521F2
S Africa black miners get pay hike 7-28, 600B2
Australia revalues reserves 8-11, 725C2
Anglo-Amer productn cited 8-16, 657E2
S Africa mine cave-ins 9-3, 768G3
US OKs gold payment for long-term business contracts 10-14, 815D3
Hits 2-yr high 10-19, 792F3
Price rise rptd 11-3, 829F2
London exchng rate rptd 12-8, 933D1
London price rptd 12-30, 997F2
IMF Sales
IMF auction 1-26, trust loans set 2-4, 87F1-G2
IMF auctions, new schedule set 3-2, 4-6, 5-4, 145D3, 335G3
IMF total sales proceeds rptd 10-5, 792F3
IMF auctns held 11-2, 12-7, total proceeds rptd 12-7, 933E3

GOLD, Vladimir
Hughes Indonesia kickback rptd 1-25, 182F3
GOLDBERG, Arthur J.
Scores Czech dissident trial 10-18, 812G1
GOLDBERG, Capt. Lawrence H.
Body misidentified 3-23, 206G1
GOLDBLATT, Dr. Harry
Dies 1-6, 84B3
GOLDEN, Colo.—*See COLORADO*
GOLDEN Eagle Refining Co. Inc.—*See ULTRAMAR Co.*
GOLDEN Gate, The (book)
On best-seller list 7-3, 548F3
GOLDEN Jason (Liberian tanker)
Fails US inspectn 2-7, scrapped 3-10, 214E3
GOLDENSON, Leonard H.
'76 pay rptd 5-23, 408D3
GOLDEN Triangle—*See BURMA, LAOS, THAILAND*
GOLDFARB, Herman
On testimony vs Provenzano 11-3, 928C1

1978

GM—*See GENERAL Motors*
G.M. Leasing Corp. v. U.S.
IRS agent liability case review denied by Sup Ct 3-20, 206C1
GNOMES (book)
On best-seller list 1-8, 24E3; 3-5, 195E3; 4-30, 356A2; 12-3, 971B1
GNP (gross national product)—*See under ECONOMY*
GOBLE, Robert
Power plan size, efficiency study rptd 6-2, 408E3
GOCHMAN, Len
Bright Golden Land opens 4-3, 760E1
GODDARD Space Flight Center—*See U.S. GOVERNMENT—NATIONAL Aeronautics & Space Administration*
GODEL, Kurt
Dies 1-14, 196A3
GODFATHER, The (book)
Paperback rights sold for record sum 6-16, 620D2
GODFREY, Lynnie
Eubie opens 9-20, 1031E1
GODOY Urrutia, Cesar
Chile Bars reentry 4-27, 5-2, 351E2
GOEBBELS, Dr. Joseph (1897-1945)
'45 diary on W Ger best-seller list 1-2, 22A1
GOERING, Hermann (1893-1946)
Goebbels diary on W Ger best-seller list 1-2, 22B1
GOETTEL, Judge Gerard L.
Sentences Abrahams 4-20, 283D1
GOFF, Norris
Dies 6-7, 540G2
GOGOL, Nikolai Vasilievich (1809-52)
Inspector Gen revived 9-21, 1031A2
GOICO Morales, Carlos Rafael
Replaces Balaguer vp nominee 5-5, 354G2
Alvarez Bogaert loses sugar post 8-25, 774E2
GOIN' South (film)
Released 10-6, 970D1

GOLD
London price rptd 1-3, 1-5, 27F3
Fiji mine layoffs 1-5, 22F1
London price hits $183.20 2-23, 118E2
USSR price hiked 3-1, 151A3
Australia '77 productn rptd 3-15, 208D3
Burns urges sale to defend $ 3-31, 235B2
IMF abolishes offcl price 4-1, 300G3
London price rises 4-3, 235D1
Stock mkt gains, gold sale rpt linked 4-19, 303G1
US sets sales to aid $ 4-19, auctns held 5-23, 6-20 523D1, C2, G2
Apr jewelry price rise rptd 5-4, 344D3
Peru sets exploratn incentives 5-11, 353D1
London price rptd 7-14, 523C3
London price soars on $ drop 7-28, 8-16, 622D2
London price passes $200 7-28, hits record high 9-25, 732F2
Base-metals price upturn cited 10-20, 805D1
Sept US exports up 10-26, 804D3
London price soars 10-30, falls on $ rescue plan 11-1, 826B1
US hikes sales to aid $, Nixon '71 move cited 11-1, 825B1, F1
US ups sale 12-19, 998D3
'78 futures vol rptd up 1004B3

GOLD, Jack
Medusa Touch released 4-14, 619B3
GOLDA (play)
S Africa showing rptd scored 7-19, 633C3
GOLDBERG, Arthur J.
On Helsinki review conf 3-9, 179E2
Sadat blames for peace impasse 7-22, 563D1
Cited in Camp David summit letter 9-22, 730E3
GOLDBERG, David
Backs Nazi defense role 1-27, 69C1
GOLDBERG, Dick
Family Business opens 4-12, 760B2
GOLDBERG, Marvin L.
Named Caltech pres 3-6, 172E3
GOLDBERGER, Judge Kim
Rocky Flats A-protesters convicted 11-29, 941C2
GOLDBLUM, Jeff
City Sugar opens 6-5, 887D1
Invasn of Body Snatchers released 12-21, 1030A3
GOLDEN, Colo.—*See COLORADO*
GOLDEN Guernsey Dairy Cooperative
McKerrow dies 1-27, 96A3
GOLDENSON, Leonard H.
On '77 top-paid execs list 5-15, 364F3
GOLDFARB, Bernard S.
Named in US Teamster fund suit 2-1, 83F1
GOLDFARB, Herman
Provenzano, Bentrovato convicted 3-25, 232D2

1979

GM v. U.S.
Case declined by Sup Ct 2-26, 164G2
GNOMES (book)
On best-seller list 1-7, 80B3; 2-4, 120C3
GNP (gross national product)—*See under ECONOMY*
GOD Bless You Mr. Rosewater (play)
Opens 5-20, 711D3
GODDU, David
Marries sister 5-25, sentncd for incest 7-31, 656B2
GODOY, Virgilio
Outlines farm works progrm 9-18, 732F1
GODREAU, Miguel
Sancocho opens 3-28, 712C2
GODUNOV, Alexander
Defects to US 8-23; wife detained 8-24, released 8-27, 644D3-645F1
Kozlovs defect to US 9-16, 697C2
ABT resigntn rptd 11-21, 1005E3
GOFFREDO, John
Chinchilla opens 6-4, 711B2
GOFMAN, Dr. John
Testifies in Silkwood A-suit 5-18, 381E2
GOHEEN, Robert
India vs US assurance to Pak 12-31, 974B2
GOHR, Marlies Oelsner
Ashford sets Amer 100-m dash mark 6-16, 911B2
GOING After Cacciato (book)
Wins Natl Book Award 4-23, 356G1
GOING In Style (film)
Released 12-25, 1007D3
GOLAN, Menahem
Magician of Lublin released 11-9, 1007G3

GOLD
London price soars 2-7, falls 2-8, 83C1-F1
S Africa reserve rise rptd 2-8, 171D3
London dealers named, mkt explained 2-18, 83G1
US '78 USSR imports rptd 3-6, 172G1
S Africa miners protest 3-7, 171F3; end walkout 3-14, 191A2
Firestone '72 trading chrgd 3-15, 202A2
US inflatn 'hedge' demand cited 3-16, 264G2
S Africa oil import paymts rptd 3-26, 270A3
US auctn supply cut set 4-18, 435B3
IMF auctn cutback set, profits rptd 5-14, 435D3
London price soars; oil, inflatn fears cited 5-27–6-11, 435D2
USSR hikes jewelry prices 7-2, 504D2
London price tops $300 7-18, 531C3
London price rises 7-26, drops 8-7, hits record high 8-30, 645E2-C3
BP to join Australia mining project 7-27, 580G2
Canada Maple Leaf coin on sale 9-6, 684C3
S Australia mining dvpt seen 9-16–9-17, 749D2; projct OKd 10-9, 811A1
London price tops $400 10-1, hits $437 10-2; oil money linked 10-3, 739F3
London, NY prices react to FRB credit move 10-8–10-11, 764E1, 765B3
US alters sale procedures, record auctn price bid 10-16, 779F3
London price tops $400 again 11-28, $500 12-26; closes '79 at $534 12-31, 978A1
USSR coin sales pushed 11-29, 929E1
'70s trade dvpts detailed 12-31, 978D1
'79 London price chart 12-31, 978A2
GOLDBERG, Dan
Meatballs released 7-3, 820A2
GOLDBERGER, Judge Kim
Sentences Rocky Flats A-protesters 1-8, 17D3
GOLDBERGER, Paul
Queries Townley in Letelier case 1-22, 58F2
GOLDE, Judge Stanley
On 'house arrest' experiment 3-17, 316A2
GOLDEN Act (race horse)
3d in Ky Derby 5-5; 2d in Preakness 5-19, Belmont Stakes 6-9, 448B2, G2
GOLDENGIRL (film)
Released 6-15, 820C1
GOLDENSON, Leonard H.
Pierce promoted to ABC vp 4-30, 334F3

1980

GMINSKI, Mike
In NBA draft 6-10, 447F1
GNAUCK, Maxi
Wins Olympic medals 7-24, 7-25, 589G2, 622G3, 623A1
GNOMON Corp.
Sued by 7 publishers 2-5, 119F3
Publishers suit rptd setld 3-21, 376C3
GNOSTIC Gospels, The (book)
Wins Amer Book Award 5-1, 692F2
GNP (gross national product)—*See ECONOMY--Gross National Product (GNP)*
GODARD, Alain
Coup De Tete released 1-21, 216D2
GODEL, Escher, Bach: An Eternal Golden Braid; A Metaphorical Fugue on Minds and Machines in the Spirit of Lewis Carroll (book)
Hofstadter wins Pulitzer 4-14, 296E2
Wins Amer Book Award 5-1, 692F2
GODFATHER, The (film)
FBI 'Miporn' probe rptd 2-14, 136B2
GODFREY, Paul
Vs KKK in Toronto 6-26, 497E1
GODFREY, Robert Franklin
Ga death penalty applicatn narrowed by Sup Ct 5-19, 439F3
GODFREY v. Georgia
Case decided by Sup Ct 5-19, 440B1
GOD Save The Queen (anthem)
Proclaimed royal anthem 7-1, 497B1
GODUNOV, Alexander
Wife seeks US reunion 8-1, 638C2
GOERNER, Hugh H.
Saudi completes Aramco takeover, retains bd seat 9-4, 662A2
GOETHE, Johann Wolfgang von (1749-1832)
Charlotte opens 2-27, 392D2
GOHEEEN, Robert
US assures India on aid to Pak 1-16, 27G1
GOHR, Marlies
Wins Olympic medal 7-26, 624G1
GOIZUETA, Roberto C.
Named Coca-Cola pres 5-30, chrmn 8-6, 600D2
GOJACK, Mary
Unopposed in Nev US Sen primary 9-9, 700E2
Loses US Sen electn 11-4, 852A1
GOLACINSKY, Allan
Mother sees Giscard 4-23, 299D2
GOLACINSKY, Pearl
Sees Giscard 4-23, 299C2
GOLAN, Moshe
Slain 6-25, suspect killed in shootout 6-29, 547C2
GOLD
Prices soar 1-2—1-18; top $800 in NY 1-17, Hong Kong, London 1-18; US, W Eur reserves rptd 1-18, 30F1-C2
Round-the-clock trading detailed 1-7, 30D2
Australia stock gains linked 1-18, 56D1
S Africa '80 productn, income seen 1-21, 101B1
Prices hit record $875 1-21; London, NY prices plummet below $478 3-17; trading erratic 3-18—3-19, 203A1
W Ger sets bank curbs 1-23, 103C2
Mex levies 40% tax on sales 1-25, 68F3
Anglo-Amer buys Consolidated Gold 2-12, 398A3
London price chart 2-18—3-20, 202A3
USSR exports to US cited 2-20, 134G3
Reagan 'basic speech' cites price rise 2-29, 207B2
Papua New Guinea conditionally OKs consortium dvpt 3-10, 194G3
S Africa budget, income hike linked 3-26, 277D3, F3
Occidental profits from futures trading hedge 3-31, 245D1
Portugal revalues reserves 4-2, 277A3
Zimbabwe rpts reserves 4-11, 301E2
IMF $ support plan shelved 4-24, 302C1
Iran withdraws Eur deposits 6-17, 464A3
June producer price rise rptd 7-8, 513D3
Calif deposit found; '79 US, forgn productn rptd 8-27, 685F2
USSR sales rptd resumed 9-24, 730D3
Canada reserves rptd 9-30, Sept sales rptd 10-3, 767E1
Price surges, drops on Reagan electn 11-5, 845C1
Price drops on higher US interest rates 12-10, 932G1
US '80 futures trading up 12-31, 984G3
GOLD, Col. Harold
USSR expels 1-31, 95E3
GOLDBERG, Leonard
'Charlie's Angels' fraud probe rptd 5-1, 376B3
ABC ties rptd probed by SEC 8-7—8-8, 640D1
LA DA ends 'Charlie's Angels' probe 12-2, 1002E2
GOLDEN, Soma
Panelist in pres TV debate 9-21, 721C3
GOLDEN Gate Quartet (singing group)
Johnson dies 5-3, 448A2
GOLDEN Nugget Inc.
Atlantic City casino opens 12-12, 988F2
GOLDFEDER, Howard
Named Federated chief exec 12-8, 959A1
GOLDFIELD Corp.
NM silver mining venture rptd, stake sold to Hunt daughter 6-24, 685D3

1976

GOLDMAN, Bo
Wins Oscar 3-29, 240A3
GOLDMANN, Nahum
Rejects E Ger reparatns 11-23, 949D2
GOLDWATER, Sen. Barry M(orris) (R, Ariz.)
Testifies for Concorde 1-5, 5A3
Reagan's Soc Sec stand clarified 2-18, 130B1
Scranton named UN amb 2-25, 150D1
Intelligence com issues rpt 4-26, 304C3
Scores Reagan Canal stand 5-2, 5-4, 324G1
Ford ad scores Reagan 5-8—5-9, 342B3
Named to intelligence com 5-20, 377E1
Chrgd re Ariz land deal 6-2, denies 6-14, 483B3, 484A1
Ford cites '64 pres defeat 6-7, 410D3
Endorses Ford 6-30, 467F3
Addresses GOP conv 8-16, 601F3, 615B1, E1
Cited in Dole biog sketch 614E3
Steiger wins Sen primary 9-7, 687A3
GOLDWATER Jr., Rep. Barry M(orris) (R, Calif.)
Holds Mex prison abuse hearing 1-15, 75B2
Reelected 11-2, 829C1

GOLF
Nicklaus named top '75 player 1-16; Burke, Ford named to HOF 1-27, 123F2
Crenshaw leads '76 $ winners 2-1, 123E2
Mercury pesticides banned 2-18, 137G1
Fred McLeod dies 5-8, 524B3
Winners
Amer Golf Classic, D Graham 8-29, 656B2
BC Open, Wynn 8-9, 656G1
Bing Crosby, Crenshaw 1-25, 123E2
British Open, Miller 7-10, 716E2
Hawaiian open, Crenshaw 2-1, 123F2
Kaiser Intl, Snead 9-26, 756A3
LPGA, Burfeindt 5-30, 424C3
Masters, Floyd 4-11, 272G1-A2
PGA, Stockton 8-16, 656A2
Phoenix open, Gilder 1-18, 123E2
Tucson open, Miller 1-11, 123D2
US Open, Pate 6-20, 756B3
Westchester Gold Classic, Graham 7-18, 716E2

1977

GOLDIN, Harrison J.
SEC rpt chrgs '74-75 financial deceptn 8-26; reactn 8-28, 665C2, G3
NYC cancels pub note sale 11-10, bars new sale 11-13, 881F1
GOLDMAN, Leslie J.
Named FEA asst admin 4-7; confrmd 5-12, 418E1
GOLDMAN, Philip
Testifies on CIA gadgetry 9-20, 721C2
GOLDMAN Sachs & Co.
Cited in Lehman Bros-Kuhn Loeb merger 11-28, 1004G2
GOLDMARK, Peter
Gets Medal of Sci 11-22, 952A1
Dies 12-7, 1024A2
GOLDSMITH, Sir James
Buys L'Express shares 3-16, 255E3
Drops Pvt Eye libel suit 5-16, 527B1
Beaverbrook chain purchased 6-30, 527B1
GOLDSMITH, Jerry
Wins Oscar 3-28, 264D1
GOLDSMITH, Michael
Zaire ousts 4-4, 261B1
Detained in CAE 7-14—8-15, 634E3
GOLDSTEIN, Richard
DNA safety concern rptd 10-6, 846E3
GOLDWATER, Sen. Barry (Morris) (R, Ariz.)
Scores Viet pardon action 1-21, 51D2
Vs Warnke nomination 2-23, 172G2
Mafia ties alleged 3-13—3-20, 568A2
Water projct interest conflict chrgd 3-21, 210G1
Vs Sen ethics code 4-1, 251F3
Nixon 'dead' politically 5-5, 367E3
Scores Carter forgn policy 7-29, 593A1
Opposes Panama Canal pacts 9-11, 698G2
Backs US Concorde proposal 9-23, 738C3
GOLDWATER, Robert
Mafia ties alleged 3-13—3-20, 568A2
GOODPASTER, Gen. Andrew J.
Named West Point head 4-4, 354B2

GOLF
Watson sets tourn marks 1-23, 1-30, 104A1
Lietzke leads '77 $ winners 2-6, 104E1
4 inducted into HOF 8-23, 675E3
Stacy sets LPGA record 9-5, 951D1
PGA top money winners listed 10-30, 950G3
LPGA top money winners listed 11-27, 951E1
Obituaries
Roberts, Clifford 9-29, 788C2
Winners
Andy Wms-San Diego, Watson 1-30, 104A1
Atlanta Classic, Irwin 5-29, 676E1
Australian Open, Graham 11-20, 950F3
Bing Crosby tourn, Watson 1-23, 104A1
British Open, Watson 7-9, 659G2
Byron Nelson Classic, Floyd 5-8, 676C1
Canadian Open, Trevino 7-24, 676A2
Colgate Far East, Bertolaccini 11-13, 951E1
Colgate Triple Crown, Blalock 1-15, 104C1
Colgate Winners Circle, Whitworth 4-3, 951B1
Colonial Natl tourn, Crenshaw 5-15, 676C1
Doral Open, Bean 3-13, 311A2
Fla Citrus Open, Koch 3-6, 311D2
Gleason-Inverrary, Nicklaus 2-27, 311C2
Greater Greensboro Open, Edwards 4-3, 311E1
Hall of Fame tourn, Irwin 8-28, 675D3
Hartford Open, Kratzert 8-7, 676B2
Hawaiian Open, Lietzke 2-6, 104E1
Heritage Classic, Marsh 3-27, 311B2
Hope Desert Classic, Massengale 2-13, 311C2
Houston Open, Littler 5-1, 676B1
Irish Open, Green 8-28, 676C2
Kemper Open, Weiskopf 6-5, 676E1
LA Open, Purtzer 2-20, 311G1
LI Charity Classic, Austin 8-14, 951D1
LPGA Championship, Higuchi 6-12, 951C1
LPGA Classic, Whitworth 5-22, 951C1
Masters, Watson 4-10, 311C1
Memorial Classic, Nicklaus 5-23, 676D1
Memphis Open, Geiberger 6-12, 676F1
Milwaukee Open, Eichelberger 7-3, 676G1
Mixed Team, Pate-Stacy 12-4, 950C3
Muscular Dystrophy Open, Stacy 9-5, 951D1
New Orleans Open, Simons 4-24, 676B1
Pensacola Open, Thompson 10-30, 950F3
PGA Championship, Wadkins 8-14, 659D2
PGA Seniors, Boros 1-30, 104D1
Phila Classic, McGee 7-31, 676B2
Phoenix Open, Pate 1-9, 104C1

1978

GOLDIN, Harrison J.
Role in NYC fiscal crisis 86A3
Reactn to Sen Banking Com rpt on NYC 2-9, 87D1
GOLDIN, Marilyn
Barocco released 4-7, 618B3
GOLDMAN, William
Magic released 11-18, 970A2
GOLDMANN, Nahum
Meets Sadat 7-10, 521A2
GOLDSHTEIN, Grigorii
Jailed 3-20, 275C3
GOLDSMITH, Sir James
Buys control of L'Express 4-27, 352A3
Grand Union, Colonial Stores to merge 8-17, 718C1
GOLDSTEIN, Lawrence
Rpts on GNP-energy link 4-20, 282C2
GOLDSTEIN, Judge Leonard
Cuts Pinto crash award 3-31, 264F3
GOLDWATER Jr., Rep. Barry M. (R, Calif.)
Reelected 11-7, 850F1
GOLDWATER, Sen. Barry M(orris) (R, Ariz.)
Votes vs Panama Canal neutrality pact 3-16, 177G2
Votes vs 2d Canal pact 4-18, 273B1
Backs Singlaub, scores Carter 5-1, 321A3
Scores Carter China policy, plans suit vs Taiwan tie cut 12-15, 12-18, 974B3; files 12-22, 995C2

GOLF
PGA seniors sue over exemptn rule 1-23, 76E1
Player wins 3 consecutive tourns 4-9, 4-16, 4-23, 355D2
Lopez sets win record, rookie-earnings mark 5-14—6-18, 580D2, C3
Amateur sports bill clears Cong 10-15, 842F2
PGA, LPGA top $ winners listed 10-31, 11-20, 990B3
Lopez honored as LPGA top player, rookie 12-11, 990F2
Nicklaus named top sportsman 12-20, 990A3
Obituaries
Chapman, Richard D 11-15, 972G2
Winners
Amer Cancer Society, Austin 2-13, 355B3
Amer Defender Classic, Alcott 4-23, 356A1
Atlanta Classic, Heard 5-28, 580E3
Australian PGA, Irwin 11-12, 990D2
Australian Open, Nicklaus 11-19, 990D2
Bankers Trust Classic, Lopez 6-18, 580B3
BC Open, Kite 9-4, 990G1
Bent Tree Classic, Lopez 2-26, 355D3
Birmingham Classic, Stacy 4-16, 355G3
Borden Classic, Carner 7-16, 672C3
British Open, Nicklaus 7-15, 580B2
Buick Open, Newton 6-18, 580F3
Byron Nelson Classic, L Watson 5-7, 580D3
Canadian Open, L Wadkins 8-20, 672F3
Canadian PGA, Lietzke 6-25, 580G3
Canadian Women's Amateur, Sherk 8-12, 990F1
Colgate Triple Crown, Carner 1-29, 76E1
Colonial Natl, Trevino 5-14, 580D3
Crosby Classic, Little 3-19, 355F3
Crosby Pro-Am, L Watson 1-23, 76B1, C1
Doral Open, Weiskopf 3-12, 355E3
Dunlop Phoenix, Bean 11-26, 990D2
Eur LPGA, Lopez 8-6, 672E3
Europn Open, B Wadkins 10-22, 990B2
Far East Open, Lopez 11-12, 990D2
Fla Citrus Open, McLendon 3-5, 355D3
French Open, Hayes 5-15, 580E3
Garden State PGA, L Wadkins 10-22, 990B2
Greater Baltimore Classic, Lopez 5-14, 580E2
Greater Greensboro Open, Ballesteros 4-2, 355G3
Greater Hartford Open, Funseth 7-30, 672D3
Hall of Fame Classic, L Watson 8-27, 672G3
Hawaiian Open, Green 2-5, 355B3
Heritage Classic, Green 3-26, 355F3
Hoosier Classic, Bradley 7-30, 672E3

1979

GOLDIN, Harrison J.
Doubts NYC long-term borrowing 10-28, 920C2
GOLD Institute, The (Washington, D.C.)
Rpts on USSR gold coins 11-29, 929F1
GOLDMAN, Bo
Rose released 11-17, 1008C1
GOLDMAN, Pierre
Slain 9-20, 772E2
GOLDMAN, Sherwin M.
Most Happy, Fella opens 10-11, 956D3
GOLDMAN, William
Butch & Sundance released 6-15, 819F3
GOLDREICH, Peter
Uranus ring theory rptd 1-11, 289G3
GOLDSCHMIDT, Neil Edward
Named Transportatn secy 7-27; facts on 577B1, B2
Drops mass transit, highway agencies merger; sees Trust Fund shortfall 9-17, 726F1
Vs Rock I reorganizatn plan 10-10, 830F3
Warns Chicago aid loss 11-20, scored 11-20—12-6; OKs road funds 12-4, 983F3
Air safety panel formed 12-19, 988E3
GOLDSMITH, Dr. Harry S.
Says FDR possible cancer victim 12-2, 925A3
GOLDSMITH, Sir James
CGE buys Occidentale share 3-16, 236B2
GOLDSTEIN, Abraham
Quits as Yale Provost 5-2, replaced 5-4, 392D2
GOLDSTEIN, Allan
Vitamin C anti-infectn role studied 5-5, 691D2
GOLDSTEIN, Manny
Resigns from U of New Mex in basketball scandal 12-13, 1003F1
GOLDSTONE, John
Life of Brian released 8-17, 820A2
GOLDWATER, Sen. Barry Morris (R, Ariz.)
Teng invites to Peking 1-2, 2G1
Taiwan defns treaty suit dismissed 6-6, 440F1
Scores Gromyko re SALT warning 6-26, 496B3
Harcourt Brace sues 9-14, 859G3
Wins Taiwan defns treaty suit 10-17, 777B1, F1
Econ policies cited 11-1, 827B2
Taiwan defns treaty abrogatn upheld 11-30, 919D1
Taiwan defns treaty case refused by Sup Ct 12-13, 940B1
GOLENBOCK, Peter
Bronx Zoo on best-seller list 5-6, 356D2*; 6-3, 432B2*; 7-1, 548C3; 8-5, 620C3

GOLF
2 herbicides banned from courses 3-1, 167F1
Warsham sets hole-in-one record 4-1, 587B2
Trevino career earnings top $2 mln 6-24, 587B3
Snead shoots round below age 7-22, 587E3
PGA, LPGA top $ winners listed 11-30, 969F2
Lopez named LPGA top player 12-12, 970C2
Obituaries
Evans, Charles 11-6, 932F2
Winners
Arden Classic, Alcott 2-18, 220E3
Atlanta Classic, Bean 6-10, 587B3
Australian Open, Newton 11-18, 970C2
Australian PGA, Ginn 11-11, 970B2
Barth Classic, Little 8-20, 970B1
Bent Tree Classic, Little 3-5, 220G3
British Open, Ballesteros 7-21, 586G3
Buick Open, Fought 9-16, 970D1
Byron Nelson Classic, Watson 5-13, 587F2
BC Open, Twitty 9-2, 970C1
Canadian Open, Trevino 6-24, 587B3
Canadian PGA, Trevino 9-2, 970C1
Citrus Classic, Byman 3-4, 220F3
Coca Cola Classic, Lopez 5-20, 587G2
Colonial Natl, Geiberger 5-20, 587F2
Columbia Savings Classic, Little 9-9, 970D1
Corning Classic, Pulz 5-27, 587A3
Crosby Pro-Am, Hinkle 2-4, 220D3
Doral Open, McCumber 3-18, 587G1
Europn Championship, Lyle 9-9, 970C1
Europn Open, Lopez 8-5, 970A1
Golden Lights, Lopez 6-3, 587A3
Greater Baltimore Classic, Meyers 7-22, 587F3
Greater Greensboro Open, Floyd 4-8, 587C2
Greater Hartford Open, McGee 8-14, 970A1
Greater Milwaukee Open, Peete 7-15, 587E3
Hall of Fame, Classic, Watson 8-26, 970B1
Hawaiian Open, Green 2-11, 220E3
Heritage Classic, Watson 4-1, 587B2
Honda Civic Classic, Carner 3-18, 587A2
Hope Desert Classic, Mahaffey 1-14, 220C3
Houston Open, Levi 5-6, 587E2
Inverrary Classic, Nelson 3-11, 220A3
Italian Open, Barnes 5-6, 587F2
Japan Open, L Wadkins 10-28, 970A2
Kemper Open, McGee 6-3, 587A3
KC Classic, Post 9-20, 970E1
Lady Citrus Classic, Blalock 4-22, 587D2

1980

GOLD Kist Inc.
US to buy Sovt shipmt 1-21, 44C3
GOLDMAN, Hal
Oh, God! II released 10-3, 836C3
GOLDMAN, Richard Franko
Dies 1-19, 104F2
GOLDSCHMIDT, Neil Edward
Asks Rock I svc extensn 2-14, 131B2
Rock I svc extended 2-22, 147F3
Sees auto execs, notes concern 5-14, 384G1
FAA overhaul asked 6-26, 519B1, D1
In Detroit re auto aid 7-7, 505A2
Disputes Reagan on auto regulatns 9-3, 664G2
GOLDSMITH, Barbara
Little Gloria on best-seller list 8-17, 640F3; 9-14, 716C3
GOLDSTEIN, Fania Fenelon
Protests Redgrave TV role 1-13, 120B2
GOLDSTEIN, Manny
Ellenberger acquitted 6-20, 875F3
GOLDWATER Jr., Rep. Barry M. (R, Calif.)
Reelected 11-4, 842F1
GOLDWATER, Sen. Barry Morris (R, Ariz.)
Ford cites '64 press bid 3-2, 167D1
Warns vs Iran mil action 4-24, 298A1
Paisley cleared by Sen comm 4-24, 459D1
Addresses GOP conv 7-15, 531D3, F3
Unopposed in primary 9-9, 700D2
'64 press endorsemnts cited 11-1, 841F3
Reelected 11-4, 840C1, 845B3, 851A3
Carter aide cleared in spy leak 12-5, 940A3

GOLF
Nicklaus, Trevino career earnings rptd 3-23, 412A3
Watson penalized for advising Trevino at Tourn of Champs 4-20, 412D3
Alcott wins US Women's Open 7-13, 714B3
Daniel breaks LPGA earnings mark 9-7, 972B1
Trevino clinches Vardon Trophy 9-21, 971C3
Watson, Daniels named top golfers 10-18, 11-19, 971B3
Hallberg, Van Hoose named top rookies 11-18, 12-9, 971D3
Alcott wins Vare Trophy 12-9, 971D3
Winners
Amer Defender Classic, Alcott 4-13, 412C3
Arden Classic, Blalock 2-10, 412D2
Atlanta Classic, Nelson 6-8, 715A1
Barth Classic, Spuzich 9-7, 972A2
Bay Hill Classic, Eichelberger 3-2, 412F2
BC Open, Pooley 8-31, 972G1
Bent Tree Classic, Carner 2-24, 412E2
Birmingham Classic, Barrow 4-27, 412E3
Boston Five Classic, Lundquist 6-15, 715B1
Brazil Open, Pate 11-24, 972G2
British Open, Watson 7-20, 714G2
Buick Open, Jacobsen 8-25, 972F1
Busch Classic, Crenshaw 9-28, 972C2
Byron Nelson Classic, Watson 5-11, 412F3
Canadian Open, Gilder 6-22, 715B1
Coca-Cola Classic, White 5-18, 413A1
Colonial Natl, Lietzke 5-18, 412G3
Corning Classic, Young 5-26, 714G3
Crosby Pro-Am, Burns 2-3, 412C2
Curtis Cup, US 6-7, 715A1
Dallas Classic, Britz 9-29, 972C2
Doral Open, Floyd 3-16, 412G2
ERA Real Estate Classic, Young 9-21, 972B2
Golden Lights, Daniel 6-1, 715A1
Greater Baltimore Classic, Bradley 7-20, 715D1
Greater Greensboro Open, Stadler 4-6, 412B3
Greater Hartford Open 7-27, 715D1
Greater Milwaukee Open, Kratzert 7-13, 715D1
Greater New Orleans Open, Watson 4-27, 412E3
Hall of Fame, Hancock 9-14, 972A2
Hawaiian Open, Bean 2-10, 412D2
Honda Civic Classic, Carner 3-16, 412A3
Hope Desert Classic, Stadler 1-14, 412B2
Houston Open, Strange 5-4, 412F3
Inamori Classic, Alcott 10-12, 972D2
Inverrary Classic, Miller 3-9, 412F2
Japan Classic, Ohsako 11-9, 972F2

1976

GOLF Writers Association of America (GWAA)—*See GOLF*
GOLLAN, John
Scores Sovt ties 2-7, 174A3
GOMES da Silva, Sergio
Torture rptd 4-15, 288D1
GOMES Monteiro, Gen. Dilermando
Named Sao Paulo army chief 1-20, 98C1
Gets letter bomb 10-14, 836A1
GOMEZ, Jose Luis
Wins Cannes film award 5-28, 460F1
GOMEZ, Brig. Julio
Argentina justice min 3-29, 236C1
GOMEZ Estrada, Cesar
Colombia justice min 11-19, 925C1
GON, Francois
Named energy min 9-5, 924E2
GONCALVES, Guilhermo Maria
In UN Timor debate 4-12, 334G3
GONCOURT, Prix (literature award)
Presented 11-15, 911G3
GONZALES, Robert
Kidnaped 7-15, 560F1
GONZALEZ, Ana Maria
Named in Cardozo murder 6-18, 495F3
GONZALEZ, Antonio
On Cuban agents in Miami, anti-Castro plot 8-18, 791E1

1977

Pleasant Valley Classic, Floyd 7-17, 676A2
Ryder Cup Matches, US 9-17, 951A2
Southern Open, Pate 10-23, 950E3
Tallahassee Open, Sneed 4-17, 675G3
Texas Open, Irwin 10-16, 950E3
Tourn of Champs, Nicklaus 4-17, 676A1
Tourn Players, Hayes 3-20, 311D2
Tucson Open, Lietzke 1-16, 104D1
US Amateur Championship, Fought 9-5, 951G1
US Open, Green 6-19, 659B3
US Womens Open, Stacy 7-24, 951A1
Walker Cup, US 8-27, 951F1
Westchester Classic, North 8-21, 675F3
Western Open, Watson 6-26, 676F1
Women's Intl, Palmer 4-17, 951B1
World Series, Wadkins 9-5, 950B3

GOLF Writers Association of America
Graffis inducted into HOF 8-23, 675E3
GOLTZ, Dave
AL pitching ldr 10-2, 927A1
GOMA, Paul
Manifesto signers emigrate 315E1
Chrgs rights curbs 3-13, arrest rptd 4-13, 314G1
Freed 5-9, 437A1
Rights movemt rptd abating 9-3, 752F3
In Paris 11-20, asks Westn rights pressure 11-24, 948C1
GOMES, Severo
Asks full democracy 1-21, 2-2; quits Cabt 2-8, replaced 2-9, 281B2
GOMES Monteiro, Gen. Dilermando
Prisoner torture exam rejctd 2-16, 186C3
Geisel rptdly backs for pres 7-22, 616A1
GOMES Peres, Glenio
Rpts torture schls 2-1, loses pol rights 2-2, 168E1
GOMEZ Sandoval, Fernando
Named Oaxaca univ rector 3-3, 240A3
GONE With the Wind (movie)
On TV top 10 list 2-9, 119B1
GONZALEZ, Ana Maria
Killed 1-19, 197E3
GONZALEZ, Carlos Hank
On police campaign vs rebels 1-21, 66A1

1978

Hope Desert Classic, Rogers 2-13, 355B3
Houston Exchng Clubs Classic, Young 10-22, 990C2
Houston Open, Player 4-23, 355G2
Inverrary Classic, Nicklaus, 2-26, 355D3
Irish Open, Brown 8-27, 672G3
Kemper Open, Bean 6-4, 580E3
Kent Golden Lights, Lopez 5-29, 580F2
LA Open, Morgan 2-19, 355C3
Lady Keystone Open, Bradley 6-25, 580G3
Lady Stroh's Open, Post 8-24, 672F3
Lady Tara, Coles 4-30, 356B1
Lancome Trophy, Trevino 10-22, 990C2
Legends of Golf, Snead, Dickinson 4-30, 356B1
LI Classic, Rankin 8-13, 672F3
LPGA Championship, Lopez 6-11, 580G2
LPGA Classic, Lopez 5-21, 580F2
Masters, Player 4-9, 355E2
Mayflower Classic, Blalock 7-3, 672B3
Memorial Tourn, Simons 5-21, 580E3
Memphis Classic, Bean 6-11, 580F3
Mexico Cup, Graham 12-10, 990E2
Milwaukee Open, Elder 7-9, 672C3
Mixed Team, Hinkle-Bradley, 12-3, 990D1
N Orleans Open, Hinkle 4-30, 356A1
Orange Blossom Classic, Blalock 2-20, 355C3
Pacific Club Masters, Morgan 10-8, 990A2
Pensacola Open, McLendon 10-30, 990C2
Peter Jackson Classic, Carner 6-4, 580F3
PGA Championship, Mahaffey 8-6, 672E2
PGA Senior, Jimenez 2-5, 355A3
Phila Classic, Nicklaus 7-23, 672D3
Phoenix Open, Barber 1-16, 76D1
Pleasant Valley Classic, Mahaffey 8-13, 8-13, 672E3
Rail Charity Classic, Bradley 9-4, 990G1
San Diego Open, Haas 1-29, 76E1
Sarah Coventry Open, Young 9-17, 990G1
Southern Open, Pate 9-10, 990G1
Sunstar, Lopez 3-12, 355E3
Tallahassee Open, Jaeckel 4-16, 356A1
Texas Open, Streck 9-17, 990A2
Tourn of Champs, Player 4-16, 355G2
Tourn Players, Nicklaus 3-19, 355E3
Tucson Open, L Watson 1-8, 76B1
US Amateur, Cook 9-3, 990F1
US Open, North 6-18, 580G1
US Women's Open, Stacy 7-23, 672G2
US Women's Amateur, Sherk 8-19, 990E1
Victorian Open, Wolstenholme 2-19, 355C3
Westchester Classic, Elder 8-20, 672B3
Western Open, Bean 7-3, 672C3
Wheeling Classic, Blalock 7-9, 672C3
Winners Circle, Post 4-2, 355F3
Women's Intl, Stephenson 5-8, 580D3
World Cup, US (Mahaffey-North) 12-3, 990E2
World Ladies, Moriguchi 4-16, 355G3
World Match Play, Aoki 10-16, 990A2
World Series, Morgan 10-1, 990B1

GOLIKOV, Vladimir
USSR wins world hockey title 5-14, 458D3
GOLTZ, Dave
AL pitching ldr 10-2, 928F3
GOMES, Antonio Sousa
Sworn Portugal housing min 1-30, 91C3
GOMES, Severo
Backs Magalhaes for pres, scores Geisel 1-20, 165D3
Deserts Magalhaes, backs Bentes pres bid 7-6, 556B1
GOMEZ, Jose
Wins World Amateur Boxing tourn 5-6—5-20, 600E2
GOMEZ, Juan Carlos
Arrest re '77 kidnap-murder rptd 1-20, 112C1
GOMEZ, Victor J.
7th in Colombia pres vote 6-4, 443E2
GOMEZ, Wilfredo
KOs Zarate 10-28, 969F1
GOMEZ Izquierdo, Luis
Arrested 1-15, freed 1-30; previous arrest cited 1-20, 112B1
GONELHA, Antonio Maldonado
Sworn Portugal labor min 1-30, 91C3
GONELLA, Sergio
Argentina wins World Cup 6-25, 520F2
GONORRHEA—*See MEDICINE—Diseases*

1979

Lady Keystone Open, Lopez 6-24, 587C3
Lady Michelob, Post 5-13, 587F2
Lady Stroh's Open, Fergon 7-1, 587C3
Lancome Trophy, Miller 10-28, 970B2
LA Open, L Wadkins 2-25, 220F3
Legends of Golf, Boros, De Vicenzo 4-29, 587D2
LPGA Championship, Young 6-10, 587E1
LPGA Match-Play, Carner 2-4, 220D3
LPGA Team, Lopez-Washam 9-16, 970E1
Mary Kay Classic, Lopez 9-30, 970F1
Masters, Zoeller 4-15, 587B1
Mayflower Classic, Stacy 7-8, 587D3
Memorial Tourn, Watson 5-27, 587G2
Memphis Classic, Morgan 7-1, 587C3
Mixed Team, Eichelberger-Breer 12-9, 969C3
Mizuno Classic, Alcott 11-3, 970B2
Napa Classic, Fought 9-23, 970E1
Natl Team Championship, Crenshaw-Burns 10-28, 970A2
NCAA Championship, Ohio State 5-26, 587F1
New Orleans Open, Green 4-29, 587D2
Orange Blossom Classic, Blalock 2-26, 220F3
Otey Crisman Classic, Blalock 4-29, 587E2
Patty Berg Classic, Daniel 8-26, 970B1
Pensacola Open, Strange 10-21, 970G1
Peter Jackson Classic, Alcott 7-29, 587F3
Phoenix Open, Crenshaw 1-22, 220C3
Pleasant Valley Classic, L Graham 9-9, 970D1
PGA Championship, D Graham 8-6, 969E2
PGA Senior, O'Connor 7-8, 587D3
Philadelphia Classic, Graham 7-29, 587F3
Quad Cities Open, Weibring 7-22, 587E3
Rail Charity Classic, Washam 9-3, 970C1
Ryder Cup Matches, US 9-16, 969E3
Sahara Natl Pro-Am, Lopez 3-25, 587A2
San Diego Open, Zoeller 1-28, 220D3
Sarah Coventry Open, Blalock 6-17, 587B3
Southern Open, Fiori 10-14, 970G1
Sunstar Classic, Lopez 3-11, 220G3
Texas Open, L Graham 10-7, 970F1
Tourn of Champs, Watson 4-22, 587C2
Tourn Players, Wadkins 3-25, 587A2
Tucson Open, Lietzke 2-18, 220E3
United Va Bank Classic, Alcott 10-14, 970F1
US Amateur, O'Meara 9-2, 969D3
US Open, Irwin 6-17, 587A1
US Women's Open, Britz 7-15, 587D1
US-Japan Championship, Japan, Purtzer 11-11, 970B2
Walker Cup, US 5-31, 587A3
West Lakes Classic, D Graham 10-28, 970A2
Westchester Classic, Renner 8-19, 969F3
Western Open, Nelson 7-8, 587D3
Westn Union Intl, Rankin 8-13, 970A1
Wheeling Classic, Massey 10-7, 970F1
Winners Circle, Post 4-8, 587C2
Women's Intl, Lopez 5-6, 587E2
Women's Kemper Open, Carner 4-1, 587B2
World Cup, US (Irwin-Mahaffey) 11-11, 970C2
World Match Play, Rogers 10-14, 970G1
World Series, Hinkle 9-30, 969A3
GOLIATH, Inge
Defectn to E Ger rptd 3-12, 180B3
GOLIKOV, Aleksander
Sovts win Challenge Cup 2-11, 118E3
GOLIKOV, Vladimir
Sovts win Challenge Cup 2-11, 118E2, F2, C3
GOLTZ, Dave
Signs with Dodgers 11-14, 1001F3
GOM, Lt. Col. Alfred
Israel arrests 6-15, PLO arms smuggling admitted 6-22, 551F3
Israel sentncs, expels 12-24, 980C1
GOMA, Paul
Releases workers manifesto 3-5, 334E1
GOMEZ, Leroy
Rpts PCB feed grain contaminatn 9-17, 704C3
GOMEZ, Luis
Traded to Braves 12-5, 1002E2
GOMEZ, Wilfredo
KOs Jiminez 3-9, 412D3
TKOs Mendoza 9-28, 838E3
GOMEZ Hortiguela, Lt. Gen. Luis
Assassinated 5-25, 428D2
GOMEZ Quesada, Ruben
Disappearance rptd 40C3
Freed by kidnapers 1-11, 117C1
GONE With the Wind (film)
FBI seizes stolen copy 1-8, 102F2
'Jaws' viewed on TV by 80 mln 11-4, 1006F3
GONORRHEA—*See MEDICINE–Diseases*
GONZAGA, Octavio
Orders police action on strike 11-6, 871A2
GONZALES, Jose Esteban
Alleges illegal executns 12-3, 951D1
GONZALEZ, Betulio
Draws with Oguma 1-29, 412C3
KOs Oguma 7-6, 839A1

1980

Japan Open, Rogers 9-7, 972G1
Kemper Open, Mahaffey 6-1, 714G3
Lady Citrus Open, White 4-20, 412D3
Lady Keystone Open, Carner 6-22, 715B1
Lady Michelob, Higgins 5-11, 412G3
Lancome Trophy, Trevino 10-19, 972F2
Las Vegas Natl Pro-Am, Young 3-23, 412B3
Legends of Golf, Bolt, Wall 4-27, 412E3
Los Angeles Open, Watson 2-24, 412E2
LPGA Championship, Little 6-8, 714B3
LPGA Team, Whitworth, Young 10-5, 972C2
Masters, Ballesteros 4-13, 412G1
Mayflower Classic, Alcott 7-6, 715C1
Memorial Tourn, D Graham 5-25, 714A3
Memphis Classic, Trevino 6-29, 715B1
Mixed Team, Strange, Lopez-Melton 12-14, 972A1
Natl Team Championship, Edwards, Edwards 10-19, 972E2
NCAA individual title, Blake 5-31, 714F3
NCAA team title, Okla State 5-31, 714F3
Patty Berg Classic, Daniel 8-17, 972F1
Pensacola Open, Halldorson 10-12, 972D2
Peter Jackson Classic, Bradley 8-10, 972F1
PGA Championship, Nicklaus 8-10, 714B2
PGA Seniors, Palmer 12-7, 972G2
Phila Classic, Tewell 8-3, 972E1
Phoenix Open, Mitchell 1-20, 412B2
Pioneer Cup, US, Alcott 11-2, 972F2
Pleasant Valley Classic, Levi 9-7, 972G1
Quad Cities Open, Hoch 7-20, 715D1
San Diego Open, Watson 1-27, 412C2
Sarah Coventry, Lopez-Melton 6-29, 715B1
Southern Open, Sullivan 10-5, 972D2
Sun City Classic, Stephenson 3-2, 412F2
Sunstar Classic, Carner 3-9, 412G2
Tallahassee Open, Pfeil 4-21, 714F3
Texas Open, Trevino 9-21, 972B2
Tourn of Champs, Watson 4-20, 412D3
Tourn Players, Trevino 3-23, 412A3
United Va Bank Classic, Young 9-14, 972B2
US Amateur, Sutton 8-31, 714D3
US-Japan Championship, US, Japan, Pate 11-9, 972F2
US Open, Nicklaus 6-15, 714D2
US Senior Open, De Vincenzo 6-29, 715C1
US Women's Amateur, Inkster 8-17, 714E3
US Women's Open, Alcott 7-13, 714A3
Westchester Classic, Strange 8-17, 972F1
Western Open, Simpson 7-6, 715C1
Wheeling Classic, Post 8-3, 972E1
Whirlpool Championship, Carner 2-3, 412D2
Winners Circle, Young 4-6, 412C3
Women's Intl, Stacy 5-4, 412F3
Women's Kemper Open, Lopez-Melton 3-30, 412B3
Women's World Series, Daniel 9-7, 972B1
World Amateur Team, US, Sutton 10-12, 972E2
World Cup, Canada (Halldorson-Nelford) 12-14, 972G2
World Match Play, Norman 10-14, 972E2
World Seniors Invitatnl, Littler 9-28, 972C2
World Series, Watson 8-24, 971G3-972A1
WUI Classic, Little 7-27, 715E1

GOLIKOV, Gen. Filipp
Death rptd 7-31, 676E1
GOLOVANOV, Vladimir
Iran expels, calls spy 6-30, 491B1
GOMA, Lameck
Named Zambia forgn min 12-4, 969F2
GOMEZ, Jose
Wins Olympic medal 8-2, 622A2
GOMEZ, Preston
Fired as Cubs mgr 7-25, 926A2
GOMEZ, Rodolfo
2d in NYC Marathon 10-26, 890G3
GOMEZ, Wilfredo
KOs Valdez, sets consecutive KO mark 2-3, 320A3
GOMEZ Fyns, Fernando
Escapes from DR Emb in Colombia 3-17, 211G2-A3
Colombia Emb attack thwarted 4-14, 294A1
GOMEZ v. Toledo
Case decided by Sup Ct 5-27, 454C1
GOMULKA, Wladyslaw
Gdansk workers strike 8-14—8-22, 625B1
GONE With The Wind (film)
McQueen sues Greyhound 1-4, 199A3
GONG Show Movie, The (film)
Top-grossing film 5-28, 448G3
GONORRHEA—*See MEDICINE–Diseases*

1976

GONZALEZ, Felipe
At Europn socialist confs 1-18—1-19, 48A3; 3-13—3-14, 222F3
At intl soc dems mtg 5-23—5-25, 449B3
Rpt met with US amb 6-8, 459E3
Sees Suarez 8-11, 752E3
Lauds defns min apptmt 9-22, 753A1
Addresses Soclst Intl 11-28, 935D3
Govt talks rptd set 12-9, 967B2
GONZALEZ, Gerardo
On US role in student unrest 9-19, 792D2
GONZALEZ, Rep. Henry B. (D, Tex.)
Reelected 11-2, 830E4
GONZALEZ, Adm. Hugo
Replaced as navy cmdr 3-5, 205F3
GONZALEZ, Julio Cesar
Peron shuffles cabt 1-15—1-16, 71D2
Lopez Rega extraditn asked 3-8, 211G3
Arrested 3-24, 211G2
Govt questns 4-30; prelim chrgs filed 5-6, 399G2
Goods frozen 7-1, 520A2
GONZALEZ Alvear, Gen. Raul
Backers demand amnesty 4-13, 363D3
GONZALEZ de la Lastra, Carlos
Scores Apede hq raids 1-25, 1-29, Torrojos 1-26, 121D3
GONZALEZ Heredia, Tito
Rptd killed 7-2, 593A1
GONZALEZ Videla, Gabriel
Accepts govt advisory role 1-2, 8D2
GOOD, Ernst
Wins Olympic medal 2-10, 158D3
GOODELL, Brian
Wins Olympic medals 7-20, 7-22, 575E2
GOODELL, Charles E.
Issues clemency bd final rpt, urges revival 1-15, 43F1
GOODIN, Carl V.
Sentenced 7-6, 524C1
GOODLING, Rep. William F. (R, Pa.)
Reelected 11-2, 830F3
GOODLOW, Marie
Charges bribe bid 8-16, 616D1
GOODMAN, E. S.
Loses election 11-2, 823F1
GOODRICH Co., B. F.
Rubber workers strike 4-21, 308D3
SEC lists forgn paymts 5-12, 727D1
Firestone, Goodyear strikes end 8-28, 8-29, 448B1
URW pact set 9-8, 866G3
GOODWILL Zwelithini, King (Zulu)
Zulu pol struggle setld 1-15—1-19, 76A2
GOODYEAR Tire & Rubber Co.
Trust suit dropped 3-2, 988A3
Rubber workers strike 4-21, 308D3
FTC probes chrgs vs Gen Tire 4-27, 360C2
SEC lists paymts 5-12, 727D1
URW strike ends 8-28, 647A3
Big 4 pacts set 9-8, 867A1
GOOLAGONG, Evonne (Mrs. Roger Cawley)
Tourn results 1-4, 1-11, 31D3
2d in Sarasota Va Slims 2-29, 716C2
Loses at Wimbledon 7-2, 504G1
Loses Federatn Cup tennis 8-29, 716A2
2d in US Open 9-11, 716C1
GOONETILLAKE, Sir Oliver
Convicted in absentia 2-4, 123B2
GORANOV, Kamen
Wins Olympic medal 7-24, 576B3
GORCH Fock (W. German sailing ship)
In Operation Sail 7-4, 488A3
GORDIEVSKY, Stanislav
Denies chrgs vs Aeroflot 7-27, 908B1
GORDIMER, Nadine
On S Africa banning of Meer 7-24, 592G1
GORDON, Kermit
Dies 6-21, 484D3
GORDON, Susan B.
HEW asst secy 8-23; confrmd 9-23, 807G3
GORE Jr., Albert
Elected 11-2, 822E3, 830B4
GOREN, Rabbi Shlomo
Urges Hebron peace 10-6, 799C1
GORI, Dr. Gio B.
Urges less cigaret toxins 10-28, 876B1
GORINI, Luigi
Dies 8-13, 892A3
GORMAN, Chester
New Bronze Age date set 5-13, 504F3
GORMAN, Tom
Wins Baltimore intl indoor 1-25, 123G2
GORMLEY, Joseph
Scores UK wage curbs 1-23, 72D2
Miners reject NCB offer 11-23, 906A1
GORSE, Georges
Sent to Leb 4-8, opens talks 4-10, 258D1
GORSHKOV, Alexander
Wins Olympic medal 2-9, 159B1
GORTAT, Janusz
Wins Olympic medal 7-31, 574D1

1977

GONZALEZ, Felipe
Elected to parlt 6-15, 453F1, C2
Claims PSOE 'victory', sets goals 6-23, 506E3-507A1
Gets econ program briefing 7-12, 545B3
Backs Argentine guerrillas 7-23, 595B3
In Chile, sees rights improvemt 8-28—8-31, 743C2
Visits EC hq, sees Jenkins 9-23, 867B2
Pol, econ pacts OKd by govt, oppositn 10-8—10-9, Soclst union 11-4, 867C1, F1
GONZALEZ, Gerardo
On US Panama Canal interventn rights 9-30, 754E3
GONZALEZ, Rep. Henry B. (D, Tex.)
Heads assassinatn com 2-2, 77A2
Fires Sprague, com balks 2-10—2-21, 126G3-127D2
Quits com 3-2, 149A1
House accepts resignatn 3-8, 228D2
GONZALEZ, Jose Napoleon
Police close newspaper 3-4, 181F3
GONZALEZ, Virgilio R.
Nixon com to pay $50,000 2-22, 157G2
GONZALEZ Marten, Jorge
CR pres candidate 9-2, 710B2
GONZALEZ Revilla, Nicolas
Named Panama forgn min 2-9, 379B1
Scores canal talks bugging rpt 9-16, 716F2
GONZALEZ Salazar, Roque
Asks Argentine refugees safe conduct 1-18, 66C2
GOODELL, Charles
Scores Concorde ruling delay 3-7, 212E2
GOODMAN, Dr. Howard M.
Rpts insulin gene reproductn 5-23, 451D3
GOODMAN, Roy M.
Wins mayoral primary 9-8, 723B2
Koch elected mayor 11-8, 855E2
GOODYEAR Tire & Rubber Co.
Egypt contract rptd 5-16, 390E2
SEC paymts chrgs setld 12-21, 1005A1
GOP—*See POLITICS—Republican Party*
GORBACH, Dr. Sherwood
DNA reassurnc to NIH rptd 10-6, 846B3
GORBATKO, Col. Viktor V.
Soyuz 24 launched 2-7, 109E3; lands 2-25, 170E2
GORDIAN Associates Inc.
Regional power systems backed 2-23, 277A3
GORDON, Kim
On Natl Front riots 8-17, 637E1
GORE Jr., Rep. Albert A(rnold) (D, Tenn.)
Named to Intell Oversight Bd 5-5, 462E2
Gulf uranium cartel hearings 6-16—6-17, 480C1, G1
Scores TV violence rptd 10-24, 921A2
GOREN, Rabbi Shlomo
Sees Carter 6-15, 474A1; US denies Palestine pledge 6-16, 496G1
GORMAN, Miki
In Boston Marathon 4-18, 603A1

1978

GONZALEZ, Felipe
PSOE drops 'Marxist' label 5-22, 821D3
Sees Giscard in Madrid 6-30, 649A2
Scores gen's assassinatn 7-21, 576A1
Backs new const on TV 12-5, 967A1
GONZALEZ, Gusatavo
Panama planning, econ policy min 10-12, 884B2
GONZALEZ, Rep. Henry B. (D, Tex.)
Reelected 11-7, 852B3
GONZALEZ, Margarita
Killed, funeral spurs riot 2-1, 91B2
GONZALEZ, Tomas
Last Supper released 5-5, 619G2
GONZALEZ Martin, Cardinal Marcelo
Spain const OKd in referendum; Toledo 'no' vote large 12-6, 966C3
GONZALEZ Revilla, Nicolas
Leads Torrijos pol party 10-12, 884C2
GONZALEZ Videla, Gabriel
UN rights panel interview rptd 7-27, 591E2
GOODALL, Jane
Rpts violent chimpanzee behavior 4-19, 335A1
GOODBYE Girl, The (film)
Top grossing film 2-1, 116E3; 3-1, 196A1; 3-29, 272E3; 4-26, 356C1
Dreyfuss wins Oscar 4-3, 315C3
GOODHART, Arthur Lehman
Dies 11-10, 972B3
GOODLING, Rep. William F. (R, Pa.)
Reelected 11-7, 852E1
GOODMAN, Lord (Arnold Abraham)
Denies Thorpe plot role 11-21, 945C1
GOODMAN, Benny
Louis Prima dies 8-24, 708C3
GOODMAN, Julian
Pfeiffer replaces at NBC, RCA 9-13, 759D3
GOODRICH, Frances
Diary of Anne Frank revived 12-18, 1031D1
GOODRICH Co., B.F.
Slush fund tax fraud chrgd 9-13, 737F1
GOODWIN, Guy
Legal immunity case declined by Sup Ct 6-19, 492D2
GOODWIN, Richard
Death on Nile released 9-29, 970B1
GOODWIN v. Briggs
Goodwin legal immunity case declined by Sup Ct 6-19, 492E2
GOODYEAR Tire & Rubber Co.
In Dow Jones indl avg 66E2
Chile tire co purchased 2-9, job cuts set 3-29, 312C2
Pilliod sees Carter, backs inflatn plan 4-20, 361G3
'77 sales ranking cited re Firestone, Borg-Warner merger plan 11-28, 935G1
GOODYEAR Tire & Rubber Co. v. FTC
Case refused by Sup Ct 11-6, 873D3
GOOLAGONG, Evonne (Mrs. Roger Cawley)
Wins Australian Open 1-1, 22F3
Wins Fla Va Slims 1-15, 419G1
Loses Chicago Va Slims 2-5, 419F1
Wins Brinker tourn 3-12, 419A2
Wins Boston Va Slims 3-19, 419A2
Loses Va Slims title 4-2, 419D1
Wins Kent championship 6-10, 540C1
Wimbledon results 7-7, 540A1
GOP—*See POLITICS—Republican Party*
GORBACHOV, Mikhail
Promoted to USSR CP Secretariat 11-27, 924D3
GORBATYUK, Gen. Yevgeny M.
Dies 3-5, 252F2
GORDON Jr., Angus
Scores NE A-plant delays 9-11, 702B1
GORDON, Joe (Flash)
Dies 4-15, 356G2
GORDON, John F.
Dies 1-6, 96B2
GORDON, Judith
History of Amer Film opens 3-30, 760C2
GORDON, Keith
Gimme Shelter opens 12-10, 1031G1
GORDON, Lawrence
Driver released 7-28, 970B1
GORDON, Max
Dies 11-2, 974C3
GORDON, Judge Myron
Backs SEC on paymt disclosure power 6-8, 642E3
GORDON, Stuart
Bleacher Bums opens 4-24, 760E1
GORDON, Col. William
On Guyana suicide survivors 11-26, 909E2
GORE, Rep. Albert (D, Tenn.)
Rpts drug mislabeling 9-8, 727E2
Reelected 11-7, 852D2
GORENSTEN, Friedrich
Slave of Love released 8-14, 1030D3
GOREY, Edward
Wins Tony 6-4, 579A3
GORI, Gio Batta
Rpts 'tolerable' cigaret hazards 8-9, 726F2
GORING, Butch
Named NHL best sportsman 6-12, 458F2
GORMAN, Leo
Fuel delivery strike ends 11-15, loses arbitratn 11-20, 921A1
GORMAN, Michael
Gets life sentence 5-26, 474A3
GORONWY-Robert, Lord
Brunei independence set 6-30, 533F3

1979

GONZALEZ, Felipe
PSOE runs 2d in Cong electns 3-1, 191A3
Quits PSOE ldrship 5-20, 390C2
Reelected PSOE ldr 9-30, 754F2
GONZALEZ, German
ETA slays 10-27, 837A2
GONZALEZ, Godofredo
Scores US on trade curbs 3-23, 248E1
GONZALEZ, Manuel
Kudo decisns 3-14, 412E3
Kudo KOs 6-20, 839A1
GONZALEZ, Pancho
McEnroe wins US Open 9-9, 734B1
GONZALEZ Malave, Alejandro
Testimony on soclsts '78 deaths rptd 5-3, 350D2
GONZALEZ Pacheco, Juan Antonio
5 Grapo guerrillas escape jail 12-17, 998A1
GOOD as Gold (book)
On best-seller list 4-8, 271A2; 5-6, 356C2; 6-3, 432G1
GOODBYE People, The (play)
Opens 4-30, 711D3
GOODE, W. Wilson
Defends 3 Mile I Met Ed rate hike suspensn 4-19, 275A1
On Met Ed license challenge 11-1, 826E2
GOODFELLOW Air Force Base, Tex.—*See TEXAS*
GOOD Guys Wear Black (film)
Top-grossing film 4-4, 271F2
GOOD Lads at Heart (play)
Opens 3-27, 711E3
GOODMAN, Julian
NBC retiremt plan rptd 3-8, 334G3
GOODPASTER, Lt. Gen. Andrew J.
Names West Pt brigade cmdr 8-11, 609D1
On West Pt hazing scandal 11-9, 868B3
GOODRICH Co., B. F.
URW contract talks, wage-guides in dispute 2-2—5-9; Uniroyal struck 5-9, 344C3
URW pact reached 6-15, 480B1
GOOD Times (recording)
On best-seller list 8-1, 620E3; 9-2, 672E3
GOODYEAR Tire & Rubber Co.
In Dow Jones indl avg 72F1
URW contract talks, wage-guides in dispute 2-2—5-9; Uniroyal struck 5-9, 344C3
URW sets pattern pact 6-18, 480C1
GOOLAGONG, Evonne (Mrs. Roger Cawley)
Wins Chichester tourn 6-17, Wimbledon results 7-6, 7-7, 570A1, D2
Loses US Clay Cts 8-12, Toray Sillock 9-16; US Open results 9-9, 734E1, C2, E2
GOPAYEGHANI, Ayatollah Mohammed Riza
Listed in Moslem hierarchy 297A3
GORBACHOV, Mikhail
Alternate Politburo member 11-27, 929D1
GORDON, Lawrence
Warriors released 2-9, 174F3
GORDON, Mary
Final Paymts on best-seller list 2-4, 120D3
GORDON, Ruth
Wins Emmy 9-9, 858D2
Boardwalk released 11-14, 1007A3
GORING, Butch
NHL scoring ldr 4-8, 355E2
GORRILL, Maggy
Peter Pan opens 9-6, 956G3
GORSHKOV, Adm. Sergei Georgievich
A-powered carrier rptd 12-17, 997A3
GORTNER, Marjoe
When You Comin' Back released 2-8, 174F3
GOSSAMER Albatross (pedal aircraft)
Allen crosses Eng Channel 6-12, 527F3
GOTODA, Masaharu
Japan home affairs min 11-8, 874G2

1980

GONZALEZ, Felipe
Socialists suffer setback in Catalonia 3-21, 235G1
Calls Suarez censure motion 5-21, 431B2
Carter sees 6-25, 475B1
Suarez Cabt shift scored 9-9, 690G2
Sees Suarez, Andalusian autonomy set for '81 10-23, 832E1
GONZALEZ, Francisco
Loses Assn of Tennis Pros tourn 8-24, 691C3
GONZALEZ, Gerardo—*See KID Gavilan*
GONZALEZ, Rep. Henry B. (D, Tex.)
Reelected 11-4, 844B3
GONZALEZ, Oscar Alfredo
Describes Argentina detentn 2-4, 95B1
GONZALEZ Malave, Alejandro
PR cops cleared in '78 deaths 4-25, 348A3
GOODBYE Fidel (play)
Opens 4-23, 392G2
GOODELL, Brian
Sets 800-m freestyle mark 7-29, 834C3
GOODHEW, Duncan
Wins Olympic medal 7-22, 623F2
GOODHILL Foundation
$10 mln gift for endangered sites rptd 12-20, 987B2
GOODLING, Rep. William F. (R, Pa.)
Reelected 11-4, 844D1
GOODMAN, Ellen H.
Wins Pulitzer 4-14, 296G2
GOOD Morning America—*See AMERICAN Broadcasting Cos.*
GOODRICH Co., B. F.
Trust case setlmt 12-15, 986C1
GOODSPEED Opera House of East Haddam (Conn.)
Wins Tony 6-8, 692D3
GOODWIN, Richard
Mirror Crack'd released 12-18, 1003C2
Inside Moves released 12-19, 1003A2
GOODY Inc., Sam
Co, 2 offcls indicted 2-28, 237B3
GOODYEAR Tire & Rubber Co.
In Dow Jones indl avg 76F1
S Africa strikers fired 6-25, 499B2
PCB cleanup method rptd 8-21, 747B2
Gerstenmaier retires, Mercer replaces 12-2, 959B2
GOOLAGONG, Evonne (Mrs. Roger Cawley)
Loses Avon tourn 2-24, Chichester 6-14; wins Wimbledon 7-4, 606G1, 607D2, E3
Lions Cup results 11-23, 947F2
GORBACHOV, Mikhail
Named full Politburo member 10-21, 798C1
GORBATKO, Viktor
Launched into space 7-23, 547G3
Returns to Earth 7-31, 592D1
GORDON, Dr. Glenn
Arrested, freed by S Korea 6-28, 499F3
GORDON, Judy
Barnum opens 4-30, 392D2
GORDON, Mark
Act of Kindness opens 9-11, 756B3
GORDON, Dr. Navvin
Sentenced in Koch assault 6-6, 639G2
GORDON, Robert
Canada E Eur immigratn records rptd found 8-20, 651G1
GORDON-WALKER, Patrick
Dies 12-2, 1004A2
GORDY, William J.
Loses Del gov electn 11-4, 848E1
GORE, Rep. Albert (D, Tenn.)
Memphis area illness probed 4-2, 331G2
Reelected 11-4, 844C2
GORE, Chester
Horowitz & Mrs Washn opens 4-2, 392C3
GORE, Christopher
Fame released 5-16, 675D2
GOREN, Rabbi Schlomo
Calls Israeli reform rabbi ordinatn invalid 2-19, 134A1
GORLEKU, George
Named ASL MVP 9-8, 771F1
Stoners win ASL title 9-18, 771B1
GORMAN, Patrick E.
Dies 9-3, 755B3
GORMLEY v. Connecticut
Case declined by Sup Ct 12-1, 918G2
GOROSTIZA, Felipe
Blood Wedding opens 6-2, 756C3
GORTON, Slade
Wins Washn US Sen primary 9-16, 724B2
Elected to US Sen 11-4, 840E3, 845A2, 852G2
GORYL, John
Hired as Twins mgr 8-24, 926B2

1976

GOSNY, Don R.
Link to Hays rptd 6-12, 433D3
GOTTLIEB, Dr. Sidney
Olson files made public 1-10, 25E1
GOULART, Joao
Dies 12-6, 970G1
US '64 coup aid rptd 12-29, 998A1
GOULD, Bryan
Calls for £ devaluatn 10-26, 809F3
GOULD, William R.
Utah power projct dropped 4-14, 284C2
GOUZENKO, Igor
Mackenzie King diaries publshd 1-1, 8A2
GOVERNMENT Employes—*See under LABOR; CIVIL Service under U.S. GOVERNMENT*

GOVERNORS, U.S.—*See also specific names*
Ford budget briefing 1-20, 40D1
Ford rpts budget plan support 1-22, 41B2
Natl Conf 2-23—2-24, 149G2
Sup Ct rules on fed min wage law 6-24, 468G2
Natl Conf backs welfare plan, Dems endorse Carter 7-5—7-6, 492G2
Carter vows campaign aid 7-16, 532A3
Ford sees GOP govs at conv 8-18, 601C3
Southern Conf meets 9-1, 671G2-A3
Carter at NE govs mtg 10-1, 743A1
Electn results 11-2; govs listed 817E2, 820E2, 825A2, 831B1
Ark salary hike OKd 11-2, 822A1
NE govs draft aid plan 11-13—11-14, 864A3
GOP govs meet 11-29—11-30, 917F2-D3
NE govs sees Carter 12-9, 937F3
GOWON, Gen. Yakubu
Mil govs corruptn chrgd 2-3, 102D3
Mohammed slain 2-13, 142B1
Denies coup role 2-13, Lagos implicates 2-18, 191F3, 192B1
30 executed for coup role 3-11, Nigeria asks extraditn 3-12, 222D2, F2
Army ouster, UK extraditn bar rptd 5-16, 366G1
GOYER, Jean-Pierre
On Lockheed contract delay 4-1, 250F2
Signs Lockheed contract 4-30, 332C3
Vs Lockheed financing 5-17, 363F1
Lockheed Cabt repercussns 6-1—6-8, 416A2
Signs revised Lockheed deal 7-21, 555A1
Stays Canada supply min 9-14, 692B2
GRAAFEILAND, Judge Ellsworth Van
Voids race quotas for NY principals 1-19, 42B2
GRAAFF, Sir de Villiers
Vs Xhosa citizenship bill 5-26, 428A3
Scores govt re riots 6-24, 447F1
GRACE, Marshall
On Colo canyon flood 8-10, 756A2
GRACE, William E.
Sentenced 6-30, 523G3
GRACE Church (Syracuse, N.Y.)
Schiess sues central NY bishop 7-8, 755F3
GRADISON Jr., Rep. Willis D. (R, O.)
Reelected 11-2, 830F2
GRADY, Dr. John L.
GOP conv vp vote table 8-19, 599E3
Wins Fla Sen primary 9-7, 687B3
AMA donatn rptd 10-22, 938E3
Defeated 11-2, 822B1

1977

GOSCINNY, Rene
Dies 11-5, 952D2
GOSSAGE, Rich
NL wins All-Star Game 7-19, 567F2
Signs with Yankees 11-22, 989D3
GOTTFRIED, Brian
Grand Prix results 2-27—4-24; US Indoor 3-6, SW Pacific tourn 4-3, 430C3, D3, 431A1
US beaten in Davis Cup 4-29—5-1, 353C3
Loses French Open 6-5, 548B2
Loses US Open doubles match 9-9, 787B2
GOTTLIEB, Dr. Sidney
Testifies on CIA mid-control tests 9-21, 721D2
GOTZ, Fidel (deceased)
'69 Penn rail scheme rulings 3-11, 3-30, 491G3
GOUDSMIT, Samuel A.
Gets Medal of Sci 11-22, 952A1
GOUGLEMANN, Tucker P. E. (deceased)
Viets return body 9-30, 795E1
GOULD, R. Gordon
Awarded laser patent 10-11, 860A1
GOULED Aptidon, Hassan (Djibouti president)
Coalitn slate backing rptd 5-7, 363B3
Elected Djibouti pres 6-24, on policy 6-27, 506F2
Names Dini premr 7-12, 583C2
GOULEM, Pierre
On prison reforms 2-10, 159A2
GOURAD, Sarkat
Djibouti independnc set 3-19, 221A3
GOURIET, John P.
Ct upholds S Africa boycott injunctn 1-27, 98G3
S Africa boycott ruling upset 7-26, 617B3
GOVERNMENT by Judiciary (book)
Published 10-31, 878E3
GOVERNMENT Employees, American Federation of (AFGE) (AFL-CIO)
Mil fears unionizatn 3-18—4-19, 343A1
Mil organizing plan rejected 9-7, Sen vs mil union 9-16, 760A1, C1
GOVERNMENT Employment—*See under LABOR*
GOVERNMENT National Mortgage Association—*See under U.S. GOVERNMENT—HOUSING & Urban Development*
GOVERNMENT Reorganization—*See U.S. GOVERNMENT, subheads CONGRESS, EXECUTIVE Branch and JUDICIARY*

GOVERNORS, U.S.—*See also specific names*
Natl Conf gets pot rpt 3-31, 332G2
Natl Conf: name chngd, Carter welfare progrm backed 9-8—9-9, 719F1
Carter sees Westn govs in Denver 10-22, 817D1
NJ, Va electn results 11-8, 855E1, A2
NC OKs 2d consecutive term 11-8, 879G2
Amer Samoa elects gov 11-22, 943E3
Urban policy panel in DC 11-29, 960A1
GOVERNOR Skipper (race horse)
Wins harness award 12-13, 970G3
GOYER, Jean-Pierre
'71 blacklist revealed 1-26, 97A1
Carruthers sues, Rudnicki suit cited 6-13, 541A3
'72 break-in cover-up chrgd 6-17, 485D1
Denies '72 raid cover-up 6-21, 541B3
Denies blacklist 6-29, 541G2
GRAAFF, Sir De Villiers
Gerdener quits party 7-22, 600G2
Asks probe re Biko death 9-14, 707G3
Quits politics 10-5, 826C1
GRACE, Princess (Monaco) (Grace Kelly)
Daughter's engagemt announced 8-25, 808B3
GRACE, Anthony
Crimmins paroled; marriage noted 9-7, 848D1
GRADY, Judge John F.
Orders Milwaukee end Lake Mich pollutn 7-29, 595B1
GRAFFIS, Herb (deceased)
Inducted into golf HOF 8-23, 675E3
GRAFFITI
Carter backs cleanup 5-17, 381C3

1978

GOSPEL Hump Area (Idaho)
Wilderness area clears Cong 2-9, 109D2; Carter signs 2-24, 218A2
GOSSAGE, Rich
NL wins All-Star Game 7-11, 559D3, E3
AL pitching ldr 10-2, 928F3
Yankees win AL pennant 10-7, 779B1
In World Series 10-10—10-17, 799F3
GO Tell the Spartans (film)
Released 9-23, 970E1
GOTTFRIED, Brian
USTA ranks 3d 1-5, 22E3
Connors wins Grand Prix Masters 1-8, 22B3
US wins World Cup 3-9—3-12, 252C1
Wins Volvo Classic 3-18, 419B1
Wins Houston WCT 4-23, 419C1
US Open results 9-10, 707C1
US wins Davis Cup 12-10, 1026E3, F3
GOTTLIEB, Carl
Jaws 2 released 6-16, 619E2
GOTTLIEB, Melvin B.
Fusn research advance rptd 8-15, 653A3
GOTTLIEB, Morton
Tribute opens 6-1, 887D3
Same Time Next Yr released 11-22, 970A3
GOTTWALD, Klement (1896-1953)
Statue blown up 9-2, 868F3
GOUDSMIT, Samuel A.
Dies 12-4, 1032G2
GOULART, Joao (1918-76)
Figueiredo elected pres 10-15, 794C1
GOULD, Elliott
Capricorn One released 6-2, 618E3
Matilda released 6-22, 619B3
GOULD, Heywood
Boys From Brazil released 10-5, 969D3
GOUSSELAND, Pierre
Socal bid for Amax rptd made 9-4, rejctd 9-7; eavesdrop conversatn rptd 9-8, 700E2, G2
GOUTMAN, Christopher
Promise opens 3-8, 760C3
GOVE, Harry E.
Rpts Turin shroud carbon test set 11-14, 926F1
GOVERNMENT Employment—*See under LABOR; also U.S. GOVERNMENT—CIVIL Service System*
GOVERNMENT National Mortgage Association—*See under U.S. GOVERNMENT—HOUSING & Urban Development*
GOVERNMENT Printing Office—*See under U.S. GOVERNMENT*
GOVERNMENT Regulation—*See U.S. GOVERNMENT—REGULATORY Agencies*
GOVERNMENT Reorganization—*See U.S. GOVERNMENT—EXECUTIVE Branch—Reorganization*
GOVERNMENT Surveillance—*See PRIVACY; U.S. GOVERNMENT—FEDERAL Bureau of Investigation*
GOVERNORS (U.S.)—*See also personal names*
Mondale meets 13 Westn govs 1-13, 34E1
Carter sees 12 Midwest govs on coal strike 2-16, 104D2; 3 coal-state govs 2-23, 122E3
Natl Assn meets: water, energy main topics 2-26—2-28; Carter, Vance address 2-27, 144G3-145C1
Carter asks coal strike restraint 3-6, govs vow cooperatn 3-7, 160C2
Carter vows water policy talks 5-4, 321A1
Westn govs on Carter water plan 6-6—6-7, 427A1
Natl Assn meets: govt spending, energy resolutns OKd; Dems back Carter 8-28—8-29, 681D3-682A2
Carter lobbies for gas compromise 8-31, 678F1
Electn results 11-7, 845C1-E3, 846B3, 847B2-849C3, 852F1-857G1; govs listed 853D2
GOP govs meet; minorities, cities stressed 11-27—11-28, 915F3
Carter sees 7, backed on budget 12-20, 980C2, D2
GOVERNORS Association, Republican
Williamsburg mtg 11-27—11-28, 915F3
GOYER, Jean-Pierre
Sets resignatn 4-6, 287E1
Stopforth awarded libel damages 4-13, 287A1
RCMP documts rptd destroyed 4-26, 328E2
Held aware of RCMP illegalities 10-24, 837B2
Replaced by De Bane 11-24, 921E3
GRABERT, Horst
Regrets Austria secret svc incident 2-14, 110C3
GRABURN, Judge Lloyd K.
Suspends Rolling Stone's heroin sentnc 10-24, 842F1
GRACE, Princess (Monaco) (Grace Kelly)
Daughter married 6-28, 6-29, 580D1
GRACE, William E.
Convictn review denied by Sup Ct 11-6, 874D1
GRACE & Co., W. R.
King's purchase planned 1-23, 66C2
GRADE, Lord Lew
Autumn Sonata released 10-8, 969B3
GRADISON Jr., Rep. Willis D. (R, O.)
Reelected 11-7, 851D3
GRADY, Wayne
2d in golf World Cup 12-3, 990E2

1979

GOTTESMAN, Michael H.
Argues Weber case in Sup Ct 3-28, 262F3, 263B1
GOTTFRIED, Brian
Loses Volvo Tennis 2-18, Volvo Classic 3-17, 391G2, A3
Loses Wimbledon men's doubles 7-7, 570D1
Wins Dublin (O) Grand Prix 8-12, 734C2
Wins Swiss Indoor 10-21, 1003E3
GOTTFRIED, Dr. Kurt
Scientists cut Sovt links 3-1, 172B2
GOTTLIEB, Carl
Jerk released 12-14, 1007E3
GOTTLIEB, Eddie
Dies 12-7, 1008G2
GOTTLIEB, Morton
Faith Healer opens 4-4, 711G2
Romantic Comedy opens 11-8, 956G3
GOTTLIEB, Paul
In Praise of Older Women released 2-8, 174A3
GOUGH, Michael
Bedroom Farce opens 3-29, 711D1
GOULART, Joao (1918-76)
Brazil amnesty law signed 8-28, 926B2
GOULD, Elliott
Silent Partner released 5-10, 528F3
GOULDEN v. Oliver
Case refused by Sup Ct 6-4, 439F1
GOULD Inc.
Fairchild merger bids rejctd 5-4, 5-8, suits filed 5-8, 5-9, 350D1
Fairchild bid withdrawn 5-21, 440D3
United Tech buys Mostek interest 9-17, 986A3
GOULET, Jean
On Giguere acquittal 7-20, 563D1
GOURGE, Gerard
Beaten at human rights mtg 11-9, 874D1
GOVERNMENT Employees, American Federation of (AFL-CIO)
Carter pay plan scored 6-6, 419F2
GOVERNMENT Employment—*See under LABOR; also U.S. GOVERNMENT–CIVIL Service System*
GOVERNMENT National Mortgage Association—*See under U.S. GOVERNMENT–HOUSING & Urban Development*
GOVERNMENT Printing Office—*See under U.S. GOVERNMENT*
GOVERNMENT Regulation—*See U.S. GOVERNMENT–REGULATORY Agencies*
GOVERNMENT Reorganization—*See U.S. GOVERNMENT- EXECUTIVE Branch–Reorganization*
GOVERNMENT Surveillance—*See PRIVACY; U.S. GOVERNMENT–FEDERAL Bureau of Investigation*

GOVERNORS (U.S.)
GOP conf held in Md 2-3–2-4, 86C1
Natl Assn meets: US balanced budget, revenue-sharing backed; Carter addresses 2-25–2-27, 150G1
Carter calls NE govs re gas 7-2, 497C3
Carter sees ldrs 7-6–7-11, 513F2
Natl Assn meets 7-8–7-10, 517B3, 518B1
Carter urges oil conservatn aid 11-16, 879A3
GOP group meets in Austin, Baker addresses 11-18, 983F1
GOVERNORS, Coalition of Northeast
Energy secy reassures re heating fuel 8-28, 703B2
GOYER, Jean-Pierre
Role in RCMP taps, other illegalities rptd 3-28–3-30, 253F2-C3
Wins libel appeal 3-30, 253F3
Dare testifies on '72 APLQ break-in 7-4, 522C3
GOYKE, Gary R.
Loses Cong election 4-3, 265A2
GRACE & Co., W. R.
Daylin OKs sweetened takeover bid 1-24, 88E3
GRADUATE Record Exam (GRE)
Test scores of future teachers drop 10-4, 810B2
GRADY, Judge John F.
Stays CFTC wheat trading order 3-18, 202C1
Abortn funding cases accepted by Sup Ct 11-26, 919C2
GRAFFTEY, Heward
In Canadian Cabt 6-4, 423G3
Shifted to Canada sci post 10-8, 789A1

1980

GOSNEY, Vern
Layton acquitted of attempted murder 5-22, 407F3-408B1
GOSNJAK, Gen. Ivan (ret.)
Dies 2-8, 176C1
GOSSAGE, Rich (Goose)
AL pitching ldr 10-6, 926G3
Royals win AL pennant 10-10, 796A1
GOTSMAN, Dr. Mervyn
On Begin heart attack 6-30, 498A3
GOTTA Serve Somebody (recording)
Dylan wins Grammy 2-27, 296B3
GOTTFRIED, Brian
Wins WCT doubles title 1-6, 213B2
Loses French Open men's doubles 6-7; wins Surrey Grass Cts 6-21, 606F3, 607E3
Wimbledon results 7-4—7-6, 606A2
Wins Washn Star Intl 7-27, 691A3
Wins Vienna Grand Prix 10-26, Paris Open 11-2 947B2, D2
GOTTLIEB, Michael
Dies 4-8, 360G1
GOUBAU, Georg
Dies 10-17, 876G1
GOUDAZI (Forghan leader)
Arrested 1-8, 20C2
GOULD, Elliott
Falling in Love Again released 11-21, 972E3
GOULD, William R.
South Calif Edison chrmn 4-18, 456C2
GOULD Inc.
Systems Engineering merger set 9-8, 746A1
GOURDINE, Simon
Warns NBA players on drug use 8-20, 656G2
GOURMET Magazine
MacAusland dies 6-4, 528D2
GOUT—*See MEDICINE--Diseases*
GOUVEIA, Antonio Patricio
Dies in Lisbon plane crash 12-4, 923E1
GOVERNMENT National Mortgage Association—*See under U.S. GOVERNMENT--HOUSING & Urban Development, Department of (HUD)*
GOVERNMENT Printing Office—*See under U.S. GOVERNMENT*
GOVERNMENT Regulation—*See under U.S. GOVERNMENT*
GOVERNMENT Reorganization—*See under U.S. GOVERNMENT--EXECUTIVE Branch*

GOVERNORS (U.S.)
State of State messages 1-2—2-6, 268B1-270C3; 1-7—1-15, 2-19, 403B2-404F1; 1-9—4-8, 482F2-484A3
Judge loses Mont primary 6-3, 439G2
Natl Assn meets; Dem politics dominate, fed ties scored; Anderson assaulted 8-3—8-5, 595F3-596D1, F3
7 Southn govs score Reagan Klan remark 9-2, 664A1
Election results 11-4, 837D1, 847A1, 848B1-852G3; govs listed 845C2
Reagan calls GOP group, Bush visits 11-17, 880G1
Greater Dem party role urged 12-4, 938B3
Conn's Grasso resigns 12-31, 990A3
GOYAN, Jere
Issues FDA caffeine warning 9-4, 726C2
GOYER, Jean-Pierre
RCMP '71 suspect list rptd sent abroad 2-28, 192B1
GRAANOOGST, Lt. Ivan
Named to Surinam mil council 8-18, 653A3
GRABSKI, Tadeusz
Scores Gierek, associates 10-6, 760G2
Named to Polish Politburo 12-2, 910A1
GRADE, Lord Lew
Saturn 3 released 2-15, 216D3
Marionettes released 11-7, 972F3
GRADISON Jr., Rep. Willis D. (R, Ohio)
Reelected 11-4, 843D4
GRADY, Judge John F.
MCI wins $1.8 bln AT&T suit 6-13, 456C3
Medicaid abortn funding limits upheld by Sup Ct 6-30, 491F3

1976

GRAHAM, Billy
Angels on best seller list 1-25, 80C3; 2-29, 208F3; 12-5, 972B2
Dole cites Jeff Carter remark 10-6, 763F3
GRAHAM, Lt. Gen. Daniel O.
Rpts China ICBM projct dropped 2-24, 190C1
GRAHAM, David
Wins Westchester Gold Classic 7-18, 716E2
Wins Amer Golf Classic 8-29, 656B2
GRAHAM, Lou
2d in Amer Golf Classic 8-29, 656B2
GRAHAM, Martha
Awarded Freedom Medal 10-14, 858G3
GRAHAM, Thomas C.
Urges Carter meeting 11-30, 897E3

1977

GRAHAM, Billy
Assn fund disclosed 6-26, 731E3-732A1
Ethel Waters dies 9-1, 788A3
Preaches in Hungary 9-3—9-14, 732A1
Assn financial rpt filed 10-21, gift fund OKd 10-26, 845C1
GRAHAM, Daniel
Defends Sovt mil study 3-11, 212A1
GRAHAM, David
2d in Doral Open 3-13, 311B2
Wins Australian Open 11-20, 950F3
GRAHAM, John
Tours Southn Africa 5-17—6-1, 457C1
In Zambia, Rhodesia 7-5—7-10, 536A1
GRAHAM, Lou
2d in US Open 6-19, 659B3

1978

GRAHAM, David
2d in Fla Citrus Open 3-5, 355D3
Wins Mexico Cup tourn 12-10, 990E2
GRAHAM, Lou
2d in Tourn Players 3-19, 355E3
Ties for 2d in Atlanta Classic 5-28, 580E3
GRAHAM, Robert (Bob)
Faces primary runoff for Fla gov 9-12, 736C1
Wins nomination 10-5, 769A2
Elected Fla gov 11-7, 849C3, 853E2

1979

GRAHAM, Billy
Urges financial disclosure law 1-17, 102E1
Assn finances rptd 9-21, 755A3
GRAHAM, Lt. Gen. Daniel O. (ret.)
Criticizes SALT treaty 4-11, 295C1
GRAHAM, David
Wins PGA Championship 8-6, West Lakes Classic 10-28; 2d in Westchester Classic 8-19, 969E2, G3, 970A2
GRAHAM, Donald
Named Washn Post publisher 1-10, 78C3
GRAHAM, Katharine
Steps down as Washn Post publisher, son succeeds 1-10, 78C3
GRAHAM, Lou
Wins Philadelphia Classic 7-29, 587F3
Wins Pleasant Valley Classic 9-9, Tex Open 10-7, 970D1, E1
GRAHAM, Robert
Book cited in suit vs shah, wife 11-28, 897G2
GRAHAM, Gov. Robert (Bob) (D, Fla.)
Signs Spenkelink, Darden death warrants 5-19, 400A1
Young draws fire on Spenkelink executn comment 5-26, 400F1
Orders Hurricane David evacuatns 9-2, 690F3
Coppolino paroled 10-16, 839B3

1980

GRAHAM, Billy
TV revenues rptd 2-25, 413A2
GRAHAM, David
Wins Memorial Tourn 5-25, 714F3
GRAHAM, Gov. Robert (Bob) (D, Fla.)
State of State message 4-8, 483D1
Asks Cuban refugee aid 4-29, Carter declares emergency 5-6, 339C3
Declares Tampa disaster 5-14, 391A2
Sends Guardsmen to Miami 5-18, 382B3
Tours Miami riot area 5-22, 401F3
Renominates Carter at Dem conv 8-13, 611A3
Miami riots, racism linked 12-6, 963D1
GRAHAM, Robert K.
Rpts sperm bank donatns 2-28, 990F2
GRAHAM, Tony
Wins Austrian Indoor championship 3-23, 607G2

1976

GRAIN—*See also specific types*
'75 China wheat purchase goals exceeded 1-22, 100B3
Australia sales to China, India rptd 1-29, 97F2
Australia-Pak wheat deal OKd 2-11, 137F3
Canada-China deal set 2-27, 190G1
Australia-SE Asia wheat deals rptd 3-11, 187D3
World Food Cncl stockpile plan stalled 6-14—6-16, 450B1 ★
China crop rptd up 9-1, 809A3
Drought hurts Australia crop 10-5, 770E3
Albania sufficiency rptd 11-1, 850A1
EC harvest rptd low 11-18, 935D2
Canada-Poland deal set 11-24, 889B1
Poland forecasts '77 imports 12-1, 966A1
Canada-China sale rptd 12-8, 946B1
Export Probe Developments
Justice Dept seeks Rametta contempt chrg 1-7, 43D3
Mulloy sentenced 1-9, 43E3
USDA inspects Polish ship cargo 1-17—1-19, 44A1
3 La inspectors indicted 1-19, 44D1
Agri Dept vs La comm inspectn role 1-22, 136A1
Agri Dept sets inspectn chngs 1-23, 2-3, 2-11, 136B1, F1
House com accuses Agri Dept on inspectn 1-29, 136C1
6 ex-Bunge employes sentncd 2-4, 135E3
GAO study issued, fed inspectn control backed, Humphrey comments 2-16, 136F1
Cook disputes Polish cargo grade, sues Agri Dept 2-26, 3-12, 247E3
GAO study chrgs subsidy abuses 3-2, 247E2
3 La cos fined 3-4, 247B2
Delta inspector pleads guilty 3-5, 247G2
Sen Agri subcoms hold hearings 3-11—3-16, 247B3, D3 ★
Agri Dept in Cargill agrmt, begins inspector training 3-16, 248A1
India sues 5 cos 5-3, 333D1
Risser wins Pulitzer 5-3, 352E3
Indictmts handed up, sentences rptd 5-4—11-26, 990E2
Carter scores cheating 8-25, 632C1
Grain inspectn bill signed 10-21, 833B3
Feed Grains—*See LIVESTOCK*
Latin Developments—*See also 'U.S. Developments' below*
Argentina-Brazil wheat smuggling rptd 1-9, 96A3
Argentina-Venez trade pact 1-14, 96D3
Argentina drought damage rptd 1-17, 96B3
Maize output rptd 5-7, 466C1
Soviet Developments
Ford on Angola issue 1-5, 3F1-G2
Ford defends '75 embargo 3-5, 180A1
Hungary barter pact rptd 4-1, 543A3
US sales rptd 4-28—5-4, 321G2
'75 US trade rptd 5-5, 340E3
US CIA doubts self-sufficiency 5-24, 856G2
US sees low '76 harvest 6-8, 421F1
US Dem platform text cites 6-15, 477C3
More US sales rptd 7-2—7-14, 540A2
US protests shipping methods 8-17, 655E2
US GOP platform text cites 8-18, 610F2
Gold sales denied 8-23, 643C1
US sale total rptd 8-31, 655D2
US revises '76 crop estimate 9-9, 752C2
Dole defends '75 embargo 9-17, 724C3
Cuba sale price rptd low 9-27, 9-30, 772C1
US shipping talks 9-30—10-7, 856A3
US sales rptd 10-1, 10-6, 752B2
Ford, Carter debate 10-6, 741A3, D3
US sees higher harvest 10-8, 839G1
US sale rptd 10-13, 856G2
Brezhnev sees record yield, 5-yr investmt rise 10-25, 839F1
'72 India famine linked to US-Sovt trade 10-28, 863A2
US sale rptd 12-3, 948B1
US shipping talks fail 12-8, 947F3

1977

GRAIN
Australia ups '76-77 forecast 1-3, 17E1
UN rpts '76 wheat price drop 2-14, 146B1
Ethiopia '76 imports rptd 2-27, 328G1
China-Australia wheat pact signed, '76 sales cited 3-6, 178F3
'76 world productn rptd 3-8, 179A1
China wheat shortage feared 3-11, 200A3
Australia scores EC protectionism 6-1, 595F3
World Food Cncl asks reserves 6-24, 513D3, F3
China record Australia wheat buy 7-4, 578E2
Uruguay crisis rptd 7-8, 601C2
Record worldwide wheat, corn crops seen 7-29, 611G3-612A1
Gambia projcts drought losses 8-22, 660E1
Total world stocks rptd 8-29, 666B3
New Sahel famine seen 9-19, 770F1-A2
China on harvest 10-23, 823A2
Canada-Poland sale rptd 11-9, 987B2
Australia '77-78 wheat output, exports forecast; Egypt accord rptd 11-28, 945C1
Argentina wheat exports set record 12-2, 981E2
St Lawrence Seaway toll hike set 12-16, 982E3
Export Probe Developments
4 firms fined 2-8, 113D1
Feed Grains—*See LIVESTOCK*
Soviet Developments
Record '76 harvest rptd; US imports to continue 1-5, 21G3
US shipping pact terms set 2-7, 161A1
US shipping pact OKd 3-30, 306C2
Record crop, US exports seen 7-7, 619D1
Sovt tap cited re '72 US purchase 7-10, 551G1
Australia wheat deal rptd 8-2, 596B1
US sales announced 8-9, 8-12, 640B3
US 1st ½ trade rptd 9-12, 766A2
US lifts ceiling 10-6, shipping rate pact extended 10-17, USSR purchases rptd 10-31—11-15, 948G2
Shortfall rptd 11-2, ship charters hiked 11-21, 948D2, F2
Poor crop, US sales cited 11-15, 916F2
US mid-Nov prices rptd up, Sovt purchases cited 11-30, 916G2
Harvest total revised down 12-14, 988B1
US grain purchase total cited 12-14, 1017A3
U.S. Developments—*See also 'Export Probe' and 'Soviet Developments' above*
Far-Mar, Farmland merger set 2-11, 408F3
Carter-Trudeau talks 2-21—2-23, 132C3
Dust storm hits Colo crop 2-23, 153F1
Canada wheat-price pact agreed 2-25, 158F2
Washn drought threat rptd 2-28, 153F1
Australia backs wheat-price pact 3-1, 179C1
Midwest blizzard eases drought 3-10—3-12, 204A3
Cargill forgn paymts rptd 3-18, 233D2
Carter farm plan outlined 3-23, 214D1
Tex drought threat rptd 3-24, 244F3
Flour wgt-label rules curbed 3-29, 277B1
Mar exports rptd up 4-27, 339C3
Cook rpts payoffs, confirms fraud chrgs 5-5, 503C2
Western wheat crop rptd 6-16, 492A3
ICC curbs rail car deals 8-1, 612G3
Kan wheat farmers' debts rptd 8-8, 612B1
Carter cuts wheat acreage, asks reserves; ups corn price supports 8-29, 666B2
US stocks at 80 mln tons 8-29, 666B3
Farm bill signed, target prices detailed 9-29, 736E2, A3, F3
Rail shipping price policy curbed 10-3, 760D2
'77 disaster aid ceiling lifted by Cong 10-25, 833C3
Mid-Oct price rise cited 10-31, 836B2
Carter cuts '78 acreage; bumper crops seen 11-15, 916C2

1978

GRAIN
Austria poisoning scandal rptd 2-8, 110G2
Tanzania port backlog blocks Zambia deliveries 3-8, 170B1
Australia port strike setld 4-9—4-10, 350B1
PCB contaminated animal feed recalled 4-12, 727C3
Colombia '77 trade data rptd 5-19, 414F1
Ethiopia rptd hit by ergot 6-8, 465G2
Argentina, China sign pact 6-9, 793A3
Chile imports up 9-15, 795E1
Spain-Argentina wheat trade talks 11-26—11-30, 967A3
Intl wheat talks fail 12-20, 998A2
Soviet Developments
US order canceled, delays studied 2-28; remaining orders rptd 3-2, 151E2
US-Sovt '77 trade down 3-29, 229F3
US aide tours 5-9; purchases rptd 5-22, crop estimated 6-12, 499D2
Turkey trade agrmt signed 6-21—6-23, 595E2
US purchases rptd 8-3; Sovt record crop seen 8-9, import drop feared 8-10, 634G2
USSR record crop seen 11-4, 884C3
Brezhnev rpts record harvest 11-27, 966E2
Record '78 harvest rptd 11-29, 1020B2
US purchases rptd 12-26, 1020A3
U.S. Developments—*See also 'Soviet Developments' above*
Dec '77 feed grain WPI rptd 1-12, 51D2
Wheat target paymts hike Dec '77 income 1-18, 52B2
Acreage set-aside participatn rptd small 2-8, Bergland tours farm states 2-21, 163C2, E2
Pesticide sales curbed 2-15, 163B3
Tex, La '77 blast violatns rptd, fines proposed 2-23, 5-16; grain dust blamed 3-30, 636E2
Set-aside paymts, target prices clear Sen 3-21; reactn 3-21, 3-22, 218F2-219A1
Carter farm aid plan revised, Mondale warns cong bill veto 3-29, 219C1-D2
Farm bill defeated in House 4-12, 261C1
Farm bill compromise clears Cong 5-4, 343C1-A2; signed 5-15, 465D3
Cook rptd selling operatns 5-8, 325C2
Viet gets US wheat 5-22, 500G1
Ethiopia ergot aid rptd 6-4, 465A3
Rail lines fined in freight-car shortage 6-15, 7-3, 569D2
Gartner bars resignatn re Archer gift 6-28, 513E3
OSHA eases grain elevator checks 7-18, 636C2
Mich feed grain contaminated by PBBs 10-9, 769C2; suit dismissed 10-27, 834C1
US sees more China sales 11-14, 901G3
Continental Grain pleads guilty 12-28, 1029D1

1979

GRAIN
Australia wheat deals rptd with China, 4 other natns 1-22, 56G2-F3, 253G1
Rumania '78 output rpt short 2-6, 170G3
Wheat pact extended 3-23, 274G1
Australia-Canada wheat accord 4-3, 253A1
Top wheat exporters rptd 4-3, 253B2
China rpts '78 output rise 6-18, '79 price estimate 6-21, 484G2
Australia alcohol fuel projct rptd 8-30, 666D3
Zimbabwe bars Zambia shipmts 11-5, 844E2-A3
Mex '79 productn down, '80 imports seen 12-12, 950C2
Zimbabwe lifts Zambia embargo 12-17, 960G1
Soviet Developments
US '78 trade rptd 3-6, 172F1
'79 corn, wheat purchases rptd 3-15, 237D3
US wheat, corn prices rise; Sovt crop cited 7-2, 567E3
US rpts on orders, purchases 7-2—7-22, 567G3
US cuts '79 crop estimate 7-12, 567D3
US hikes '79, '80 sale limits 8-1, 636B3
'79 crop shortfall rptd 9-28, 774E3
US OKs '79-80 record sale limit, '78-79 sales totaled 10-3, 774B3, F3
Low harvest rptd 11-27, 928B3
US rpts wheat, corn purchases 11-28, 928C3
Australia sales detailed 11-28, 948B1
US wheat, corn purchases rptd 12-20, 997F2
U.S. Developments—*See also 'Soviet Developments' above*
Adams rail deregulatn plan criticism rptd 1-15, 35F3
Jamaica offcl fired re US kickbacks 1-29, 101B2
Farm income drop, subsidy paymt end linked 2-16, 151D2
CFTC halts Chicago wheat trading 3-15, cts stay 3-18—3-19; trading ends, speculators named 3-21, 201C3
Wheat pact extended 3-23, 274B2
ITT bread fiber chrg setld 3-25, 308C3
Top wheat exporting natn 4-3, 253B2
Mich feed grain contaminatn chrgd 4-26, 597E3
Rail decontrol bill scored 6-6, 579G2
ICC rail rate suspensn power backed by Sup Ct 6-11, 478E3
Antibiotics in animal feed rptd risky 6-25, 734F3
Handlers strike 7-6; pact set 9-14, setlmt reached 9-23, ratified, farmers losses estimated 9-25, 722C1, D3-723A1
China pact signed 7-7, 523G2
Wheat acreage, loan rate increased, support price reduced 8-1, 636E3
Continental Grain unit fined 8-27, 648G2
Rock Island RR struck 8-28, 8-29, Carter orders return 9-20; transport system overload, '78-79 record harvests cited 9-21, ICC orders takeover 9-26, 722A1-C3
Cook settles export fraud chrgs, Miss R Grain case cited 9-26, 727G2-C3
Harvest total noted 10-3, 774D3
Rock Island RR svc resumes 10-5, 830E3
Army '50 cereal blight tests rptd 10-7, 770G3
Mich feed grain contaminatn rpt issued 10-9, Velsicol settles suits 10-23, 808G2-D3
Handlers strike impact rptd 11-29, 922C1
Ammonia import curbs barred 12-11, 939E2
'79 record corn crop rptd 12-31, 985B1

1980

GRAIN
Peru crop hit by drought 2-8, 234E3
China '79 harvest rptd, '80 target set 5-1, 521E1
China vows contd Australia purchases 5-7—5-11, 387F3
Mex crops threatened by drought; 1st 1/2, May imports rptd 6-13, 524B2
Canada drought damages crops 6-27, 520C2
Poland sees food shortage, '79 harvest blamed 7-9, 566F1
China '79, '80 output data 9-1, 678D1
Australia crop seen reduced 10-13, 827E3
Polish harvest loss rptd 11-12, 879A1
Panama Canal clogged by shipmts 11-24, 895C1, E1
Soviet Developments—*See also 'Soviet Embargo' below*
USSR orders, total purchases rptd 1-3; US suspends futures trade 1-6, 2B1
'79 harvest rptd down 1-25, 79D3; stockpiling cited 6-13, 467G1
US '79 trade rise rptd 2-20, 134F3
Canada sale, '79 data rptd 2-29, 171E2
US pres candidate's 'basic speech' excerpts 2-29, 207A3
Argentine deal signed, 1st 1/4 purchases rptd 4-15, 336G1
US embargo exempt sales rptd 8-20, 9-7, 711E2, C3
'80 productn forecast rptd dropped 9-7, 711B3
'80 shortfall rptd, '81 target set 10-21, 10-22, 797F2, 798F1
11th 5-yr plan set 12-1, 945F2
Soviet Embargo (& reaction)
Carter sets ban for Afghan invasn 1-4, 1B1
Carter to ease farmer burden 1-4, 1B1, F1; US agri groups score embargo 1-6, 10C1, D1
Kennedy vs embargo; trades chrgs with Powell, Mondale 1-5—1-10, 12G2-13F1
US GOP ldrs reactn 1-5, 4G2-C3; 1-7, 1-10, 13G2
EC, Canada, Australia back US embargo 1-7, 1-9, 9B2
Bergland sees farm groups in Ia 1-8, 1-9, 10E1
EC backs US embargo, rejects trade sanctns 1-10; UK backs sanctns, Argentina rejects 1-10, Brazil rejects 1-14, 27G3-28D1
Gasohol, embargo link denied 1-11, 33C2
Brezhnev assures natn re bread 1-12, 26A3
Exporters vow no Sovt sales increase 1-12, 27E3, 28B1
Mondale defends embargo; kennedy, Brown score 1-12, 32F2
Mondale hits issue 1-16, 50G2-A3
US crop 'diversn' paymts studied 1-18, 44F3
US to buy corn in ports 1-19, 45B1
Mondale on grain hardship 1-19, 50A3
Carter State of Union topic 1-23, 41B2, 42D2
OECD sees more grain for 3d World natns 1-23, 49G3
Carter budget affected 1-28, 73B2
ILA loads Sovt ship 1-29, 169B1
US Jan farm prices rptd down 1-31, 92F2
Argentina cooperatn sought by US 2-5, 87G1
Ia elevator scandal linked 2-25, 238B1
US crop 'diversn' paymt plan dropped 2-29, 168F3
USSR need seen met 4-9, 315G3
US rpts farm purchases end 4-14, 316B1
Ia grain fraud probe rptd 5-14, 414B3
US soy meal purchased in W Eur 6-2, 431B1
Sovt auto workers strike 6-13, 467G1
Australia sale hike rptd 6-17, 460E2
Australia sets '80-81 sale limit 6-24, 496A2
Carter reaffirms stand 7-4, 505F2
US GOP platform proposed 7-10, 506C3; adopted 7-15, 537D1
Sovt milk productn drop linked 7-16, 711A3
Canada lifts embargo 7-24, 577F3

1976

U.S. Developments—*See also 'Export Probe' and 'Soviet Developments' above*
Food budget proposals 1-21, 66C2
Argentina export credits set 1-28, 96B3
Sen OKs rice output bill 2-3, 135D2
'75 record harvest seen 2-27, 216E1
Exports rptd down 3-26, 230F1
GOP platform text 8-18, 603B1
Dole legis record cited 614C2
Carter scores US export policy 8-25, Dole rebuts 8-26, 632C1, E2
Dole scores Carter embargo policy 9-22—9-23, 724D3
Record crops rptd 10-12, 787E3
Ford hikes support rates 10-13, 787D3
Dole vows no embargoes 10-16—10-27, 804C1
Vogel gets Science Medal 10-18, 858F3
Fed Grain Inspectn Svc created 10-21, 833B3
E Ger deal OKd 11-11, 889E1
Record '76 wheat, corn crops rptd 12-10, 983D3

GRAINVILLE, Patrick
Wins Prix Goncourt 11-15, 911G3
GRAMMY Awards—*See 'Awards' under MUSIC*
GRAND, Lucien
Loses Poitou-Charentes electn 1-6, 49C3
GRANDAL Segade, Col. Carlos
Suspended 10-27, paymt rptd 11-6, 909E1
GRAND Isle, La.—*See LOUISIANA*
GRAND Rapids, Mich.—*See MICHIGAN*
GRAND Rapids Press, The (newspaper)
Newhouse buys Booth chain 11-8, 901B3
GRANELLI, Luigi
Asks Chile democracy restored 1-3, 47D2
GRANET, Paul
Rpts new environmt com 3-2, 204E3
GRANGER, Lester
Dies 1-9, 56D3
GRANITE (magazine)
Sup Ct bars review of funding curb 10-18 867A3
GRANT, Lee
Wins Oscar 3-29, 240A3
GRANT Co., W. T.
Adjudged bankrupt 4-13, 984F3
GRANUM, Rex
Lance slated for Cabinet 11-24, 898D2 *
GRANVIK, Ragnar
Sworn Finnish traffic min 9-29, 750D3
GRAPHIC Arts
Jerome Snyder dies 5-2, 524F3
GRASSLEY, Rep. Charles E. (R, Iowa)
Scored by environmt group 3-25, 220A1
Reelected 11-2, 829D3

1977

Farmers protest, seek parity prices; wheat price cited 11-25, 916F1
Mid-Nov price rise rptd 11-30, 916F2
St Lawrence Seaway toll hike set 12-16, 982E3
Striking farmers block deliveries, trading impact rptd small 12-21, 1003A1, C1
La, Tex, Miss blasts 12-22, 12-27; US probe asked 12-28, safety rules planned 12-29, 1023E1-B2

GRAIVER, David (rptd. d. 1976)
Rptd killed in '76 air crash 345D2
Guerrilla financing scandal breaks 4-11, 345B2; **for subsequent developments, see ARGENTINA—Graiver Scandal**
Gelbard dies 10-4, Klein 10-8, 922A3
La Opinion owner loses rights 11-10, 922F2
GRAIVER, Eva
Gets 4-yr jail term 12-9, 982B1
GRAIVER, Isidoro
Arrested 4-14, 345F2
Faces trial re rebel ties 10-15, 922G2
Gets 15-yr jail term 12-9, 982B1
GRAIVER, Juan
Guerrilla financing scandal breaks 4-11; arrested 4-14, 345B2, F2
Anti-Semitism linked 7-7, 614G3
Faces trial re rebel ties 10-15, 922G2
Gets 15-yr jail term 12-9, 982B1
GRAIVER, Lidia
Arrested 4-14, 345E2
Faces trial re rebel ties 10-15, 922G2
Gets 15-yr jail term 12-9, 982B1
GRAIVER, Pedro
Arrested 4-23, 371A2
GRAMLEY, Lyle E.
Named to CEA 1-18, 52E3
GRAMMAS, Alex
Brewers confirm firing 11-20, 990C2
GRANADOS, Enrique
Scores US prisons 12-13, 957F2
GRAND Calumet River
US Steel settles EPA case 6-16, 461G1
GRANDE Garcia, Rev. Rutilio
Murdered 3-12, 207B1
GRAND Juries—*See COURTS*
GRAND Prix (tennis circuit)—*See TENNIS*
GRAND Union Co.
Butler dies 10-30, 872C1
GRAND Zenith (Panamanian tanker)
Sinking rptd, crew lost 1-11, 104E3, 214D3
GRANT, M. Donald
Jets dispute setld 5-26, 491A2
Trades Seaver 6-15, 644B2
Denies NYC Olympic loss blame 9-26, 828D3
GRANT Co., W. T.
'75 bankruptcy, '76 liquidatn cited 7-12, 612E2
Back-tax case review refused 10-3, 760F2
GRANTS-in-Aid—*See 'Revenue Sharing' under U.S. GOVERNMENT—BUDGET*
GRANUM, Rex
Liddy's term commuted 4-12, 325D3
Singlaub recalled 5-19, 404A1
Carter supports Young 5-23, 444B1
On Carter-Jordan meeting 7-25, 573E2
GRAPHS—*See 'Tables, Charts & Graphs' under ILLUSTRATIONS*
GRASHOF, Manfred
Sentenced to life 6-2, 601F3
GRASS Is Always Greener Over the Septic Tank, The (book)
On best-seller list 3-6, 184F3; 10-2, 808F3

1978

GRAIVER, David (rptd. d. 1976)
Indicted for embezzlemt 4-12, death questnd 4-12, 4-13, 326C1
GRAIVER, Juan
Son, 4 others indicted 4-12, 326F1
GRAMBLING (La.) College
Williams in NFL draft 5-2, 336B1, F3
GRAMERCY, La.—*See LOUISIANA*
GRAMM, Phil
Wins US House seat 11-7, 852E2, 855D3
GRAMMY Awards—*See MUSIC—Awards*
GRANAI, Edwin P.
Wins primary for Vt gov 9-12, 716D2
Loses electn 11-7, 847G3
GRAND Canyon College (Phoenix, Ariz.)
Wins NAIA basketball title 3-18, 272B2
GRAND Central Terminal (N.Y. railroad station)
Office complex barred by Sup Ct 6-26, 566G3
GRAND Coulee (Wash.) Dam
Generator sabotaged 10-30, hydro projct delayed 11-10, 963C1
GRAND Juries—*See COURTS*
GRAND Prix (tennis circuit)—*See TENNIS*
GRAND Teton National Park (Wyo.)
Carters vacation 8-24, 664F1
GRAND Union Co.—*See GENERALE Occidentale S.A.*
GRANERA, Ramiro
Killed by guerrillas 11-7, 883C2
GRANICK, Harry
Bright Golden Land opens 4-3, 760E1
GRANT, Barra
Slow Dancing released 11-8, 970B3
GRANT, Duncan
Dies 5-10, 440F2
GRANT, Lee
Damien released 6-8, 619D1
GRANT, M. Donald
Resigns as Mets chrmn 11-8, 1026E2
GRANT, Mick
Working opens 5-14, 887E3
GRANIER-Deferre, Pierre
Woman at Her Window released 6-9, 620C1
GRANTS-in-Aid—*See U.S. GOVERNMENT—BUDGET—Revenue Sharing*
GRANUM, Rex
Costanza resigns 8-1, 605G3
Rpts Kirbo to monitor GSA probe 9-7, 715D1
GRAPHIC Scanning Corp.
FCC to probe Western Union 3-9, 270F2
GRAPHS—*See ILLUSTRATIONS—Charts, Graphs & Tables*
GRAS, Col. Yves
Sets Zaire stay scores Belgium 5-23, 381B2
GRASS
DBCP pesticide curbs asked 9-19, 719D2
GRASSHOPPERS—*See INSECTS*
GRASSLEY, Rep. Charles E. (R, Iowa)
Reelected 11-7, 850C4

1979

GRAIN Millers, American Federation of (AFL-CIO)
Duluth, Superior struck 7-6; pact set 9-14, setlmt agreed 9-23, ratificatn vote 9-25, 722D3
GRAIVER, David (rptd d. 1976)
NYS judge rules dead, dismisses chrgs 1-8, 163B1
Argentina expels Timerman 9-25, 728C1
GRAIVER, Lidia (Mrs. David)
Husband ruled dead, Argentina jailing rptd 1-8, 161D1
GRAMERCY, La.—*See LOUISIANA*
GRANAHAN, Kathryn O'Hay
Dies 7-10, 588G2
GRAND Coulee (Wash.) Dam
Canada project compared 10-27, 833E3
GRAND Juries—*See COURTS*
GRAND Tour, The (play)
Opens 1-11, 292E1
GRANGER, Farley
Month in the Country opens 12-11, 1007D2
GRANIER-Deferre, Pierre
French Detective released 3-10, 528C2
GRANITE
Low-level radiatn risk assessed 5-2, 609F2
GRANT, Cary
Ex-wife Hutton dies 5-11, 432A3
GRANT, Christine
Elected AIAW pres 1-10, 103C2
GRANT, David Marshall
Table Settings opens 3-23, 712G2
Bent opens 12-2, 1007C2
GRANT, John
Scores trade union reforms 12-7, 949F2
GRANT, Lee
When You Comin' Back released 2-8, 174F3
GRANTS-in-Aid—*See U.S. GOVERNMENT-BUDGET-Revenue Sharing*
GRAPEFRUITS—*See FRUITS & Vegetables*
GRAPHIC Scanning Corp.
Graphnet Systems Inc.
FCC ends Westn Union telegram monopoly 1-25, 78A2
GRAPHS—*See ILLUSTRATIONS-Charts, Graphs & Tables*

1980

Carter cites sale suspensn in pres renominatn acceptance speech 8-14, 613B1
US exempt sales rptd 8-20, 9-7, 711E2, C3
ILA affirms loading ban 9-18, 826D3
Reagan scores US 'grandstanding' 9-30, 738A3
EC to resume barley sales 10-23, 832B1
Mondale hails Carter stance 10-26, 816E3
Carter chrgs Reagan 'flipflop' 10-27, 816B3
Carter says hurting USSR 11-12, 865E3
US Sen OKs fund cutoff 11-17, 880G3
Australia affirms embargo 11-18; Canada ends support, US-China pact cited 11-20, 900B2, F2
US Cong drops fund cutoff 11-20, 953F3
US agri secy favors review 12-23, 980G1
U.S. Developments—*See also 'Soviet Developments' above*
Admin to hike storage loan paymts 1-8, 10B1
Grain trading prices stabilize 1-19, 44G3
Jamaica sues US shippers for fraud 2-4, 99B2
US dietary guidelines issued 2-4, 157A3
Kenya aid planned 2-22, 142C2
Ia elevator scandal rptd 2-25, consumer suit filed 3-25, 237F3
Ethanol productn to cut exports 20% 3-15, 251C1
Mar farm prices rptd 3-31, 263F3
CFTC emergency order case declined by Sup Ct 4-28, 369E1
Apr farm prices rptd 4-30, 329A3
PCB rules publshd 5-9, 387G1
Ia grain fraud probe rptd 5-14, 414E2
Mt St Helens damage assessed 5-24—7-4, 503G3
Hunts bailout loan collateral listed 5-28, 426D1
Midwest drought damage rptd 6-23—8-15, 616B2
Canada barley, corn imports rise 6-27, 520D2
Carter orders crop price support increase 7-28, 575E1
Poland seeks credits 8-27, 659B2
Aug farm prices rptd 8-29, 666E1
Drought damage final rpt 9-7, 857A3
Poland granted $670 mln credit 9-12, 710F2
Sept farm prices rptd up 9-30, 741B2
China trade pact signed 10-22, 801G1
Shortage fears spur price jumps 10-28, '81 stockpiles seen down, Mideast, N Africa '80 imports rptd 11-4, 855C1
Oct farm prices rptd 10-31, 883C1
Poland credit rise proposed 11-13, 879B1
Reserve authrzn clears Cong 11-17, signed 12-3, 981G1
Canada ends Sovt embargo support, China pact cited 11-20, 900B2
Panama Canal clogged by shipmts 11-24, 895E3
'80 wheat futures trading up 12-31, 984G3
GRAIVER, David (d. 1976)
Family wins death damages 10-15, 826G3
GRAIVER, Lidia (Mrs. David)
Wins damages for husband's '76 death 10-15, 826G3
GRAMM, Rep. Phil (D, Tex.)
Reelected 11-4, 844E2
GRANDI, Alberto
Named ENI head 5-6, 408F3
GRAND Island—*See NEBRASKA*
GRAND Metropolitan Ltd.
Liggett merger bid raised 5-14, OKd 5-16, 557A3
GRAND Rapids—*See MICHIGAN*
GRAND Union Co.
Wood replaces Scott as A&P chrmn 4-29, 456D2
GRANGER, Robert
Ctroom cameras case argued in Sup Ct 11-12, 882A2
GRANITZA, Karl-Heinz
NASL scoring ldr 8-24, 770D3
GRANT, Bill
On Calif offshore leasing 3-28, 330E3
GRANT, Christine
Scores NCAA women's title tourn move 1-8, 103F3
GRANT, James
Says Cambodia famine 'disaster' averted 2-10, 108D1
Warns re Cambodia famine 3-21, 261D3
GRANT, Lee
Little Miss Marker released 3-21, 216C3
Tell Me a Riddle released 12-17, 1003E2
GRANT, Leonard
'79 suspensn cited in US Customs probe 2-13, 359E2
GRANT, Roger
Wins Emmy 9-7, 692C1
GRANT, Ulysses S. (1822-85)
Hijinks! opens 12-18, 1003B3
GRANTS—*See under U.S. GOVERNMENT--BUDGET*
GRANVILLE, Maurice F.
To quit Texaco bd 6-30, 600B3
GRAPHS—*See ILLUSTRATIONS--Charts, Graphs & Tables*
GRASS, Gunter
Tin Drum released 4-11, 416F3
GRASSBY, Albert
Sees rising Aborigine-white tensns 12-3, 964F1-A2
GRASSLEY, Rep. Charles E. (R, Iowa)
Wins US Sen primary 6-3, 439D3
Elected to US Sen 11-4, 840F1, 845A2, 851A1

1976

GRASSO, Gov. Ella T. (D, Conn.)
Jackson 3d in pres voting 5-11, 342G3
Ray elected Wash gov 11-2, 820C3
Ford wins state 11-2, 821A1
NE govs seek aid 11-13—11-14, 864B3
GRAUBARD, Seymour
ADL meets 11-16—11-24, sees Pope 11-24, 912C1
GRAVEL, Sen. Mike (D, Alaska)
Charge of sex with Ray rptd 6-12, 434B1
GRAIVER, Juan
Amer Bank & Trust fails 9-15, 940B1
GRAVITT, T. O.
Ashley wins tap suit 12-17, 995F1
GRAY, Kenneth J.
Ray sex chrg rptd 6-12, 434B1
GRAY 3rd, L. Patrick
'70s burglaries role chrgd 8-17, 8-18; denies 8-17, 633E2, 634B2-A3
GRAY, Lorne
Macdonald on A-sales 11-29, 923F3
GRAYSON, Ernset C.
On resegregatn chrg 6-16, 453B2
GRAZE, Stanley
Indicted 1-14, 78C2
GREASE (play)
Long run listed 12-31, 1014G3
GREAT (film)
Wins Oscar 3-29, 240B3
GREAT Atlantic & Pacific Tea Co. (A&P)
'75 profits rptd down 2-11, 216B2

1977

GRATT, Thomas
Arrested 11-23, 991G1
GRAUER, Ben
Dies 5-31, 452A3
GRAVEL, Sen. Mike (D, Alaska)
Spec interest gifts rptd 3-7, 232G2, A3
On Alcan financing 11-2, 856E3
GRAVES, John
Wins Daytona endurance 2-6, 531D2
GRAVITT, T. O.
Widow wins Southwestn Bell slander suit 9-12, 724B2
GRAY Jr., Judge Frank
Orders Tenn coll merger 1-31, 112G2
GRAY, Hanna Holborn
Named Chicago U pres 12-10, 1021A2
GRAY, Tony
Hartwick wins NCAA soccer title 12-4, 1020F3
GRAY, Harry J.
Rptd top-paid '76 exec 5-23, 408C3
GREAT Atlantic & Pacific Tea Co., Inc. (A&P)
US files overtime suit 9-27, 778C2

1978

GRASSO, Gov. Ella T. (D, Conn.)
Fears Navy sub work stoppage 3-13, 224A2
Wins primary 9-12, 716E2
Reelected 11-7, 847B2, 853E2
GRAVEL, Sen. Mike (D, Alaska)
Votes for Panama Canal neutrality pact 3-16, 177E2
Votes for 2d Canal pact 4-18, 273B1
House OKs Alaska lands bill 5-19, 386C2
Helps kill Alaska land bill 10-15, 785A1
Carter protects Alaska lands 12-1, 937B1
GRAVES, Charles L.
McDermott slush fund cited 2-22, 142B3
GRAVITT, T. O. (d. 1974)
SW Bell slander suit appeal cited 2-16, 142F3
SW Bell slander judgmt reversed 11-29, 963F1 ★
GRAVITY Is My Enemy (film)
Wins Oscar 4-3, 315D3
GRAVITY Waves—*See PHYSICS*
GRAY, David
Borg quits Grand Prix bonus chase 6-2, 540G1
GRAY, Eugene
Arrested 5-5, jailed 8-21, 725D1
GRAY, Harry J.
Launches United Tech bid for Carrier 9-18, 896D1
GRAY, John
On breeder dvpt study 5-10, 346D3
GRAY 3rd, L. Patrick
Indicted 4-10, 261E3-262A1
Dismissal motion denied 11-30, 939E3
GRAY, Lily (d. 1972)
Ford assessed $128.5 mln in car crash case 2-6, 185B3
Ford crash award cut 3-31, 264F3
GRAY, S. M.
Rhodesia oil-sanctions violatn study released 9-19, 755G3-756A1
GRAY, Simon
Rear Column opens 11-19, 1031A3
GRAY, Spalding
Nayatt School opens 5-12, 887B2
GRAY III, Rev. William H.
Wins US House primary in Pa 5-16, 389D3
Elected 11-7, 849E2, 852B1
GRAY Lady Down (film)
Released 3-10, 619B2
GRAYSON, Wilbur Rodney
Killed 5-18, 396A2
GREASE (film)
Released 6-16, 619C2
Top-grossing film 7-6, 579F3; 7-26, 620D1; 8-30, 708A2
GREASE (recording)
On best-seller list 8-2, 620E1; 9-6, 708E1
GREASE Soundtrack (recording)
On best-seller list 7-5, 580A1; 8-2, 620F1; 9-6, 708F1; 10-11, 800F3

1979

GRASSO, Gov. Ella T. (D, Conn.)
Gets reassurance on winter heating fuel supply 8-28, 703C2
Attends Carter dinner 10-24, 961F2
GRASSONI, Giovanni
Scored in intellignc rpt 2-14, 136G1
GRAU Pelegri, Enrique
On Cuban exile's death 5-3, 350B3
GRAVEL, Sen. Mike (D, Alaska)
House OKs Alaska land bill 5-16, 367D1
GRAVEL Neck, Va.—*See VIRGINIA*
GRAY, Bruce
Winter Signs opens 3-11, 712F3
GRAY, Gordon
Madman & Nun opens 1-18, 292B2
GRAY, Harry J.
On '78 top-paid execs list 5-14, 347F3
Haig named United Tech pres 12-26, 984A2
GRAY, Herbert
Scores govt re econ 7-26, 613C1
On July jobless drop 8-16, 612D3
GRAY, Junius
Chrgd in Bedford Hills (NY) slayings 7-19, 548F1
GRAY, Mike
China Syndrome released 3-16, 528G1*
GRAY, Nellie J.
Rejects NOW abortion conf 1-22, 63F2
GRAY, Tim
NFL '78 interceptn ldr 1-6, 80D1
GRAY Panthers
Kuhn joins Citizens Party 8-1, 594F3
GREASE (film)
Top-grossing film 5-23, 448G3
GREASE (play)
Longest-running Broadway show 12-8, 956E2
GREAT American Federal Savings v. Novotny
Case decided by Sup Ct 6-11, 479A1
GREAT Atlantic & Pacific Tea Co. Inc. (A&P)
W Ger co buys share 1-16, 53C3
Milk price actn backed by Sup Ct 2-22, 150F2
GREAT Bank Hoax, The (film)
Released 3-22, 528C2

1980

GRASSO, Gov. Ella T. (D, Conn.)
State of State message 2-6, 269E1
Carter loses primary vote 3-25, 221C3
Backs Carter in conv rules fight 8-11, 610A1
Ill health forces resignatn 12-31, 990A3
GRATIOT County—*See MICHIGAN*
GRAVEL, Sen. Mike (D, Alaska)
Filibuster cut off 8-18, 631D2
Loses Alaska primary 8-26, 683E1-B2
Murkowski wins seat 11-4, 846A1
GRAVEL Neck—*See VIRGINIA*
GRAVES, John Earl
Kin vs US Iran policy 3-4, 164D2
GRAY, Andy
Wolverhampton wins English League Cup 3-15, 771E3
GRAY, Fred D.
Named US dist judge 1-10; controversy ensues 5-19—9-17, withdraws 9-17, 744B2
GRAY, Hamish
On N Sea gas pipe 6-19, 463E2
GRAY, Herb
In Japan for auto talks 8-2—8-11, 618G1
Massey-Ferguson aid plea rejected 9-4, 728F2
GRAY, John
Billy Bishop opens 5-29, 756B3
GRAY 3rd, L. Patrick
2 FBI ex-offcls convicted 11-6, 884C2
Charges dropped 12-11, 940G1
GRAY, William
Changeling released 3-28, 416E2
Prom Night released 8-15, 675C3
GRAY III, Rep. William H. (D, Pa.)
Reelected 11-4, 844B1
GRAYDON, Jay
Wins Grammy 2-27, 296D3
GRAYZEL, Solomon
Dies 8-12, 676E1
GREASE Soundtrack (recording)
NY record co indicted 2-28, 237D3
GREAT Atlantic & Pacific Tea Co. Inc. (A&P)
Retail prices frozen 3-6, 349C1
Wood replaces Scott as chrmn 4-29, 456D2

GREAT BRITAIN & NORTHERN IRELAND

1976

GREAT Britain & Northern Ireland, United Kingdom of (UK)—*See also ADB, COMMONWEALTH of Nations, DISARMAMENT—Geneva Committee, EUROPEAN Community, IEA, NATO, OECD, SEATO*
5 Armada ships found 1-11, 124C3
London subway bomb defused 2-13, 146F2
Hume named archbp 2-17, cardinal 4-27, 336G1, E2
Train robber paroled 3-15, 316F3
Margaret, Snowdon separate 3-19, 252A3
2 Britons in Getty will 6-8, 444B2, D2
'69 Derbyshire blast cited 7-25, 560D3
USAF transport crashes 8-28, 859B2
Riot erupts at London fair 8-30, probe sought 8-31, 651F1
Warships collide off Dutch coast 9-20, 712G3
Penicillin-resistant gonorrhea rptd 10-7, 815C1
Govt wins debate limit on hosp, educ bills 11-8, 853A1
Lefebvre holds banned mass 11-14, 932A3
Black gets Lasker 11-17, 910E3
Rpt MDs seek mobility 12-19, 977D2
1st women Rhodes Scholars named 12-19, 993F3

African Relations—*See also 'Foreign Economic Developments' below; also RHODESIA*
Briton killed in Namibia 1-2, 11D3
Thorpe chrgs Sovt African bribe 1-3, USSR denies 1-6, 2E2
Libyans occupy London emb 1-12, 205D2
Thatcher scores Sovt Angola role 1-19, 101D1
Morocco summons amb re Sahara 1-28, 58B2
Mercenaries rptd in Angola 1-28—2-3, UK deplores 1-30, 81E2
US denies Angola recruitmt rpt 2-2, 82E1
Mercenaries in Angola executed 2-8; UK sets probe, detains 44 2-10, 105F2
Angola recruitmt continues 2-8, 106D1
Angola mercenary chrgs ruled out 2-12, 163F2
Zambia rptdly arrests lecturer 2-14, expels 3-27, 503E2

1977

GREAT Britain & Northern Ireland, United Kingdom of (UK)—*See also CENTO, COMMONWEALTH of Nations, DISARMAMENT—Geneva Committee, EC, ESA, IDB, IEA, NATO, OECD, SEATO*
Lady Churchill bars aid 2-22, 140D3
Scientific curbs scored 2-22, 184G1
Princess Anne rptd pregnant 4-8, 396A3
11 die in Aeroflot Cuba crash 5-27, 604E1
'77 Punk fashion rptd 1022F1
London gay rights march 6-25, 560F2
Woman breaks Channel swim record 9-8, 808B3
Mott, Meade win Nobels 10-11, 10-14, 951G2, E3
Queen's grandson born 11-14, christened 12-22, 1021E2

African Relations—*See also RHODESIA, subheads 'British Relations' and 'Majority Rule'*
S Africa rptr visa denial cited 1-5, 3E3
Ethiopian rebels free family 1-5, 20A2
ICFTU to boycott S Africa 1-13, 1-15, 29A2; boycott fails 1-21, 67A3
Ct upholds S Africa boycott injunctn 1-27, 98F3
Ethiopia cultural cntr stoned 1-28, 98F2
16 rescued from downed Uganda plane 2-1, 102C3
Anti-Amin plot chrgd 2-16, 138E3
UN rights comm bars Uganda probe 3-1, 142A1
Uganda claims invasn threat 3-2, 141C2
Ethiopia urban squad kills natl 3-10, 238E3
Uganda pilot defects 3-13, 308D2
US Amb Young: UK 'racist' 4-5; Carter reactn 4-7; OAU 4-8, 272D1-E2
S Africa rejcts Namibia plan 4-7, 285C1

1978

GREAT Britain & Northern Ireland, United Kingdom of (UK)—*See also COMMONWEALTH of Nations, COUNCIL of Europe, DISARMAMENT—Geneva Committee, EC, GATT, IDB, IEA, NATO, OECD*
Churchill '54 portrait rptd destroyed 1-11, 335D2
Scottish Highlands hit by blizzards 1-28—1-30, 132G3
Prince Andrew is 18 2-19, 172D2
Vegetable immunizatn rptd 3-2, 334G1
Oil spill off Great Yarmouth 5-6, 524B2
Princess Margaret divorced 5-24, 420D3
Energy conservatn progress rated 6-5, 449E3 ★, 450F1
Sotheby auctns Von Hirsch collectn 6-20—6-27, Patino 6-29, 579E1, 587D3
Unified field theory rptd confrmed 6-22, 7-8, 654A2
Westminster mass protested 7-6, 557D3
Train fire kills 11 7-6, 636F2
London populatn drop rptd 8-4, 631B1
Seal kill off Scotland canceled 10-16, 816A2
Mitchell wins Nobel Prize 10-17, 886C2

African Relations—*See also RHODESIA*
S Africa editor plans residence 1-3, 8F1
Somalia asks arms aid 1-16, 43A3
At Ogaden conf in US 1-21, 43E2
Angola mercenary recruitmt bared 1-27, 87F3
Ethiopia protests Somalia aid 2-1, 100D1
Somalia makes 2d aid bid 2-4, 99G3
Namibia mtg 2-11—2-12, progress rptd 2-13, 113A3
Kenyan vp ends quest for arms 3-11, 289F2
Nigeria withdraws Barclays funds in S Africa dispute 3-22; '76, '77 data cited 237A2
Midland Bank S Africa loan policy rptd 3-25, 237C2
Namibia plan backed by front-line natns 3-26, 248G2
UK student killed 3-27, Botswana clears of chrgs 5-17, 596A1

1979

GREAT Britain & Northern Ireland, United Kingdom of (UK)—*See also COMMONWEALTH of Nations, COUNCIL of Europe, DISARMAMENT-Geneva Committee, EC, GATT, IDB, IEA, NATO, OECD*
English, Welsh populatn down 1-11, 38F1
Heath at 'Lulu' premiere 2-25, 174A1
Iona rptd for sale 3-23, 268C2; purchased by Scottish millionaire 5-24, 407E1
Queen Victoria secret marriage alleged 5-22, 388F2
Heathrow on '78 world's busiest airport list 6-1, 421C1
Irish Sea storm, 18 yachtsmen drown 8-14, 799F3; rpt issued 12-10, 955C1
Tanker fleet safety record rptd 8-15, 608F1
Environmt cntr grant ended 9-17, 730A2
2 win Nobels 10-12, 10-17, 858E1, A2
Jagger divorce final 11-2, 1006C1

African Relations—*See also ZIMBABWE Rhodesia*
Namibia plan fails 3-3, S Africa rejcts UN proposal 3-5, 171B2, A3
Namibia compromise proposed 3-19—3-22; Pretoria bars 5-7, extends assemb powers 5-8, 354F2
S Africa pol bribes chrgd 3-21, 213E1, G1
S Africa '72-78 loans rptd 4-2, 270D2
S African activist hanged 4-6, 270C3
Tories set policy 4-11, 285B3
Uganda govt recognized 4-15, 288C2
Uganda High Comm reopened 4-21, 314D3
Uganda aid rptd 5-28, 419C2
Dora Bloch's body found 5-30, 429D1
Nigeria warns vs Zimbabwe recognitn, bars contract bid 5-31, 393G1-B2
S Africa scored by UN vote 5-31, 428B1
Uganda ex-pres arrives 7-8, 637G2

1980

GREAT Britain & Northern Ireland, United Kingdom of (UK)—*See also ADB, COMMONWEALTH of Nations, COUNCIL of Europe, CSCE, EC, GATT, GENEVA Committee, IDB, IEA, MBFR, NATO, OECD*

Accidents & Disasters
N Sea oil platform capsizes 3-27, 256F1
Jet crashes in Canary I 4-25, 392B1

African Relations—*See also ZIMBABWE*
S Africa ex-agent bares spying 1-15, 60E3
Anglo-Amer buys Consolidated Gold 2-12, 398A3
UN censures S Africa, UK abstains 6-27, 524F3
S Africa names amb 8-26, 689G3-690A1
UN Namibia talks schedule agreed 11-24, 967C2

Antigua—*See ANTIGUA*

Arts & Sciences
Sanger wins 2d Nobel 10-14, 889G2
Da Vinci ms sold for $5.28 mln 12-12, 997E3

1976

UK envoy implicated in Nigeria coup, Nigeria protests 2-16—2-20; envoy recalled 3-4, 191D3
Nigeria ousts Reuters rptr 2-16, 192A1
Angola MPLA recognized 2-18, 163B1
US rpts covert Angola aid 3-9, 228D3
S Africa implicated in Thorpe scandal 3-9—3-13, 252E2-A3
Nigeria asks Gowon extraditn 3-12, 222F2
UK-Sovt talks on forgn role in southn Africa 3-15—3-19, 229A1
S Africa, Angola mediatory role rptd 3-21, 3-25, 3-26, 228A1
UK-Sovt talks on Angola end 3-25, 228G3
Abstains on UN Cncl S Africa censure 3-31, 228B2
S African plot vs Hain chrgd 3-31—4-9, 351E1
Eritrean rebels free Briton 5-3, 335F1
Denies Gowan extraditn 5-16, 366G1
Goans arrive UK 5-16; UK warns Malawi 5-18, 382B2
More expelled Goans arrive UK 5-23, 497C3
Angola mercenary trial begins 6-11, 3 Britons to die 6-28, 480E1
Amin threatens BBC rptr 6-14, 502E2
Angola ousts journalist 6-16, 480C3
Paris Club defers Zaire debt 6-17, 488A2
Queen pleads for Angola mercenaries 7-5, mercenaries executed 7-10, 519G2, D3
Uganda ousts envoys 7-13—7-22, UK cuts ties 7-28, 547F3
Uganda chrgs mercenaries in Kenya 7-17, 548B2
Uganda lauds Kenya crisis aid 7-20, 548D2
Angola mercenaries executn analyzed 7-26, 559C3
Uganda seizes 2 Britons; frees Tully 8-3, 581A1
Sudan exile interviewed 8-4, Sudan warns BBC re UK ties, protests staged 8-6—8-9, 592D2, G2, 857D2
Uganda frees Clegg 8-25, 874E1
Ethiopia rebels free newsman 9-6, 674F2-A3
S Africa accuses 8 9-7, 662B2
Ethiopia rebels hold family 9-7, 674A3
Vorster accord on US-UK Rhodesia plan rptd 9-9, 660B2
S Africa sentences 3 9-29, 733F3
Rowlands in Tanzania, Mozambique 10-1—10-2, 738D3
Eritrean rebels free 3 10-2, 1002B2
Brezhnev scores re southn Africa 10-7, 856E3
Amin vows better ties 10-7, 874B1
Vetoes S Africa arms ban 10-19, 781D3, E3

Associated States & Colonies—*See ANGUILLA, BELIZE, BERMUDA, FALKLAND Islands, GILBERT Islands, HONG Kong, SEYCHELLES, TUVALU, WEST Indies*

Concorde Developments—*See 'SST' under AVIATION*

1977

Zaire denies mercenary bid 4-7, 317E3
Kenya ousts rptr 4-13, 393E1
Eritrea consulate closed 4-23, rptr ousted 4-25, 327F2, C3
S Africa sees Namibia compromise 4-29, 349C2
Zaire ousts newsman 5-6, 394G1
S Africa OKs Namibia concessns 5-9, 400D1
Callaghan, Owen briefed on Mondale-Vorster mtg 5-22, 398E1
Ethiopia shuts defnse office 5-28, 486C1
Uganda curbs natls 6-8, 487A1; 6-10, 508B1
Uganda ex-min rpts Bloch death ordrd 6-8, 487A1
S Africa OKs Namibia plan 6-10, 457B2
Seychelles govt recognized 6-13, 489B1
Amin plot rpts scored 6-23, 507G3
Uganda lifts natls curbs 7-1, 600C3
Uganda min defectn rptd 7-2, 600D3
Zaire debt rescheduled 7-7, 583E1
CAE holds natl 7-14—8-15, 634E3
Ethiopia diplomat defects 7-17, 562E2
Somali history cited 587E3
S Africa boycott ruling upset 7-26, 617C3
Somalia OKs arms aid 7-28, 608A2
SWAPO ldr joins Namibia talks 8-8, 639D3
S Africa A-test rptd 8-17, Botha assures 8-30, 663E3, 664A1
Namibia compromise reached 8-19, 699D3
Owen sees S African business, labor reps 8-29, 661C2
Chase unit in Nigeria loan 9-1, 746C3
Somalia arms sale postponed 9-2, 684G2
Uganda exiles ask UK trade boycott 9-12, 805G1
S Africa sanctns feared 9-20; investmts, exports rptd 9-23, 771D1
Namibia conf stalled 9-22—9-26, 770D2
Uganda rpts UK natl escape 9-22; rptd dead 10-9, 805F1
Sudan oppositn ldr returns 9-27, 843F3
Tanzanian sentncd as spy 10-5, 806A1
Togo assassinatn plot foiled 10-13, 988F2
Somalia blames re Kenya border 830E2
UN Namibia vote abstentns 11-4, 851E1
Namibia tour fails to win SWAPO concessns 11-21—12-7, 1016E3
Nigeria arms purchases cited 11-23, 986A3
UN abstentn on S Africa oil, investmt bans 12-16, 1016A2

Associated States & Colonies—*See ANGUILLA, BELIZE, BERMUDA, DOMINICA, FALKLAND Islands, GIBRALTAR, GILBERT Islands, HONG Kong, St. LUCIA, WEST Indies*

Atomic Energy & Safeguards

Brazil URENCO safeguards rptd asked 3-11, 190F1
US OKs Japan spent A-fuel export 3-28, 235D1
Vance sees Callaghan re arms talks 3-31, 247A1
Carter proposes US plutonium ban 4-7, 268B1, G1, E2
Japan moves vs US plutonium ban 4-21, 335D1
Carter proposes US A-export curbs 4-27, UK fuel reliance noted 4-28, 334D2
Suppliers conf scores Carter plans 4-28—4-29, 403F1-A2
7-natn summit debates A-sales, sets study 5-7—5-8, 357D2, E2
A-test talks with US, USSR set 7-28, 574E2
S Africa A-test rptd 8-17, Botha assures 8-30, 663E3, 664A1
Suppliers conf OKs safeguards 9-21, 717D1
In A-test talks with US, USSR 10-2—10-3, 12-5—12-10; USSR backs ban 11-2, 996F3-997C1

Concorde Developments—*See AVIATION—SST/Concorde*

Crime

12 bomb blasts hit London 1-29, 222B3
'75 London slayers sentenced 2-10, 222F2
Goldsmith drops Pvt Eye libel suit 5-16, 527B1
Forgery, libel cloud Leyland bribery disclosures 5-19—5-25, 526C1, D1 ★
Newsman arrested 6-23, 7-24, 617G2
Ed fined for blasphemy 7-12, 617E3
Black festival ends in brawl 8-28—8-29, ban urged 8-31, 672A3
Newsman fined for Grunwick violence 9-28, 864F1

1978

Owen scores Sovt, Cuban role 4-5; ambs, Cuba protest 4-6, 4-7, 259C1
Namibia plan OKd by Vorster 4-25, 299C1
Namibia rebel ldr cancels talks 5-7, 339D1
Zambian pres visits, econ aid hiked 5-15, 395D2
Zaire gets transport planes 5-18, 381B1
Tanzania ousts Lonrho 6-2, 479B2
Westn natns meet on pan-Africa force, UK vs French plan 6-5, 441E2
Namibia rebels OK talks 6-11, 475C3
Zaire emergency aid OKd 6-13—6-14, 478A1
Zambia loan cited 6-29, 617A2
Namibia plan OKd by SWAPO 7-12, 547C2
S Africa Natl Front link cited 7-19, 633B3
Facts on Walvis Bay 562B1
Poor natns debts canceled 7-31, 592D1
Kenya pres eulogized by Callaghan 8-22, 639B3
UK study detailing Rhodesia oil-sanctions violatn released 8-31, 9-19; UK, Zambia reactn 9-2—9-28, 755G3-756G3
Namibia electn delay barred 10-14; contact group sees Botha, Steyn 10-16—10-18, 819G2
Zambia gets missiles 10-27, 10-28, 829E3-830A1
Uganda-Tanzania border conflict 11-2—11-6, 860A2
Canada-S Africa arms deal rptd probed 11-7, 904F2
UN abstentn on Namibia electn warning 11-13, 904B2
Botswana soldier cleared in UK student's death 11-13, 906D2
Zambia to hike arms outlay 11-20, 912D1
Nigeria loan set 11-30, 934G1

Associated States & Colonies—*See BELIZE, BERMUDA, BRUNEI, CAYMAN Islands, DOMINICA, FALKLAND Islands, GILBERT Islands, HONG Kong, St. LUCIA, SOLOMON Islands, TUVALU*

Atomic Energy & Safeguards

Callaghan in India talks on A-curbs 1-6—1-11, 37D1
'77 A-export safeguard pact detailed 1-11, 11A2
US alerts to Sovt A-satellite fall 57E1
Canada uranium shipmt set 1-16, 102D3
Dutch OK Brazil uranium sales, Urenco plan expansn 2-1; Almelo protest held 3-4, 169C2, F2
Callaghan defends neutron bomb 2-21, 140D1
Australia joins A-supplier group 2-24, 129C2
New fuel reprocessing tech rptd 2-27, 144A3
Parker rpt backs Windscale reprocessing plant 3-6, Parlt OKs constructn 3-22, 227G1
Carter neutron bomb deferral backed 4-7, 254E2
US study urges joint breeder effort 5-10, 346B3
Windscale funds OKd 5-15, Japan reprocessing contracts rptd signed 5-25, 437F2-A3
US to seek 5-yr test ban 5-20, 996E2
UN disarmamt sessn opens 5-23, 421G1
UN disarmamt sessn ends, A-arms restraints vowed 6-30, 523C1
Dutch parlt backs Brazil uranium sale 6-30, 575B1, D1
A-sub workers strike 7-7—8-13, 650A1
EC halts UK-Australia uranium pact 7-27, 666E1
Plutonium contaminatn found at Aldermaston 8-16, facility closed 8-24, 667D2
Australia A-waste issue; UK negligence denied, aid offer accepted 10-5—10-10, 771A3, C3
A-test ban talks rptd delayed, US 3-yr test-ban order cited 10-5, 995E2
Aldermaston safety study released 11-21, 964E3

Belize—*See BELIZE*

Bermuda—*See BERMUDA*

Brunei—*See BRUNEI*

Cayman Islands—*See CAYMAN Islands*

Concorde Developments—*See AVIATION—SST/Concorde*

Crime & Civil Disorders

'77 crime rate rise rptd 3-20, 227E2
Natl Gallery painting slashed 4-3, 335D1
'Hungarian Circle' forgers sentncd 5-31, 824B3
London race riot 6-11, 452D3
Protesters throw manure in Commons, demonstrate outside Buckingham 7-6, 533A3
Thorpe arrested in murder plot 8-4, 614A2
Thorpe faces 2d murder chrg 9-2, 688B2
Prison probe ordrd 11-2, 867G1-B2

1979

Nigeria cuts BP oil, S Africa sales cited 7-12, 545A2
Nigeria nationalizes BP assets, govt protests 7-31, 584D2-D3
S Africa atty to seek asylum 8-10, 617E2
S Africa UN vote abstentn 11-2, 875G1
Zambia pres visits 11-8—11-10, Nigeria envoy 11-15, 881E1
Namibia UN talks reopen 11-12—11-16, 889D3
Zambia contacted re raids 11-20, 899E2
Zambia raid compensatn barred 11-20, high comm stormed 11-22—11-23, Allinson recalled 11-24, 899F2
S Africa Zimbabwe accord impact seen 12-18, 968C2

Associated States & Colonies—*See BELIZE, FALKLAND Islands, HONG Kong, St. VINCENT*

Atomic Energy & Safeguards

Nuclear 'doomsday clock' unchngd 1-1, 13F1
Urenco plans contd cooperatn, W Ger A-enrichmt plant 2-7, 101D1
'78 underground tests rptd 3-6, 625D3
US A-accident sparks reassurnc 4-3, 246G2
Labor bars A-weapon ban, seeks reactor hearings 4-6, 267F3, G3
A-sales to Pak rptd 4-6, 277C2
Test ban treaty cited in SALT II communique 6-18, 457C3
Heysham plant financing OKd 6-27, 524B3
Australia pact OKd by EC panel 7-5, 522E1; signed 7-24, 562F2
BP to join Australia uranium mining project 7-31, 580G2
A-test ban talks progress rptd 7-31, 625C3
Film stars' deaths tied to '53 US A-test 8-4, 630B1
Mystery A-test denied 10-26, 824D3
'56 US air crash rptd 11-5, 845G1
Westinghouse pressurized water reactor OKd, A-needs detailed 12-18, 994B2

Belize—*See BELIZE*

Concorde Developments—*See AVIATION—SST/Concorde*

Crime & Civil Disorders

Stolen film probe rptd 1-10, 102E2
IRA bombs fuel depots 1-17, 96G3
IRA bomb blasts in Yeovil 2-23, 190D2
S Africa pol bribes chrgd 3-21, 213F1
Tory MP slain, IRA linked 3-30, 254E1
Cops suspended in corruptn probe 4-6, 268D2
Natl Front protest spurs violence 4-23, 313A1
Tory programs outlined 5-15, 359A1, D1
Thorpe, 3 others acquitted 6-22, 485D3-486C1
Death penalty ban upheld 7-19, 543E2

1980

Associated States & Colonies—*See ANTIGUA, HONG Kong*

Atomic Energy & Safeguards

Uranium-enrichmt plant planned 1-9, 39G2
'70-79 A-tests rptd 1-17, 31F3
A-weapon plans revealed 1-24, 79F1
Sovt A-superiority detailed 6-4, 450F2
Cruise missile sites set 6-17, 486G3
A-weapons protested 6-22, 487E1
7-natn Venice summit backs 6-23, 473F2
Trident purchases slated; Labor Party scores, defns debate cited 7-15, 544A2
A-nonproliferatn treaty review conf ends, Sri Lanka cites implementatn failure 9-7, 696C1
Disarmament backed by Labor Party 10-2, 768B3
Disarmament rally held 10-26, 886G3

Crime & Civil Disorders

Soldiers injured in Netheravon blasts 3-7, 194E1
Police svc spending hike planned 3-26, 232E2
Blacks, cops clash in Bristol 4-2, 274B3
Libyan exiles slain 4-11, 4-25, 353A3; suspects arrested 5-12, 373D3; envoy expelled 6-13, 463F2
A-weapons protested 6-22, 487E1
'75 London bombing organizer sentncd 6-25, 619B3
Turkey airline office bombed 10-12, 794G1*

1976

Diego Garcia—*See DIEGO Garcia*
Economy & Labor (domestic)
Chrysler bailout plan signed 1-5; layoffs, terms rptd 1-14, 1-23, 72F2
'75 strike, indl disputes rptd 1-6, 174D1
Burmah Oil govt loan rptd 1-13, 173F3
Defns budget cut talks, Mason resignatn threat 1-14—1-15; cuts OKd 1-15, 101E1
Gulf-Conoco N Sea oil find rptd 1-19, govt buys 51% interest 2-26, 173A3
Mid-Dec—mid—Jan jobless up 1-20, Healey vows actn 1-26, 72B2
3d ¼ '75 coal output rptd 1-21, 174D1
Unions score wage curbs 1-23, 72D2
Civil svc job cuts planned 1-26, 72F2
'75 jobless rise rptd slowing 1-28, 84F3
Potato price rises rptd 1-29, 84A2
Chrysler Linwood strike ends 2-3, 174A2
Brit Aircraft rpts layoffs 2-10, 174E1
Voluntary price curbs proposed 2-11, 173F1
Indl output, jobless forecast 2-12, 173A2
TUC urges more jobless aid 2-12, 173A2
Jobless aid, incentives proposed 2-12, 173B2
Jan steel output rptd down 2-17, 174F1
'77-79 spending cuts proposed 2-19, 173D2
Mine ldrs end overtime ban 2-19, 700 continue job actn 2-23, 174B1
Metal exchng prices rise 3-3, 175B3
Parlt rejcts spending cuts 3-10, govt wins no confidence vote 3-11, 239F1
'77-80 jobless forecast rptd 3-10, 267E1
Govt buys interest in Ninian Field 3-10, 521D3
Mid-Feb—mid-Mar jobless down 3-23, 267D1
Parlt gets '76-77 budget; Thatcher, CBI score 4-6, 266A2
TUC rejcts pay curbs 4-14, Scottish unit backs 4-20, 312F3
Mar inflatn rate rptd 4-15, 313C1
Mid-Mar—mid-Apr jobless down 4-22, 313D1
Leyland strikes rptd 4-22, 4-23, 365D1
A-fuel productn set 4-27, 4-28, 351F2-B3
Bank staff probed 4-28, 458A1
TUC, govt reach pay accord; CBI backs 5-5, 351G1
Leyland rpts 6-mo profit 5-17, 365C1
Govt wins ship natlzn ruling 5-27, 401E3
4 N Sea finds rptd 5-28, 7-9, 521B3
Mine workers OK pay curbs 6-7, 407B3
Callaghan defers natlzn plans 6-7, 407B3
TUC ldrs back pay curbs 6-16, 439E3
May inflation rate down 6-18, 458C1
Econ turmoil cited 6-27—6-28, 462E1, G1
BP, govt to share N Sea fields 7-1, 521F3
June inflatn rate down 7-16, 556F2
Mid-May—mid-June jobless up 7-20, 556D1
Leyland loan set 7-21, 556F2
Spending cut, tax hike set 7-22; TUC, left protest 7-22, 7-26, 556D1, B2
TUC OKs spending cuts, tax hike 7-28, Commons votes 8-2, 572B3
Brit Steel loss rptd 7-28, 589G1
Labor, TUC ratify social contract 7-29, 572E3
Leyland strikes, layoffs rptd 8-10, 8-11, 638F1
BP rpts Irish Sea well dry 8-13, 638A2
July inflatn rate down 8-13, 651F2
Drought hits agri, industry; govt acts 8-15—8-24, 630D1-B2
July 8-Aug 12 jobless record 8-24, 651A3
Ford strikes end 8-26, 651B3
Br Airways rpts 1st ¼ losses 8-26, 675B3
Lending rate raised 9-10, 694B1
Leyland strikes end 9-10, 712B3
Aug CPI rptd up 9-17, 712F2
Mid-Aug—mid-Sept jobless down 9-21, 712G2
Seamen's strike averted 9-22, 750E3
Job measures set 9-23, 773A2
Labor Party Conf 9-27—10-1, 791B3
North Sea oil productn rptd 10-3, 791G3
Tory-union accord vowed 10-6, 791F3
Healey hikes lending rate, Parlt OKs 10-11, 773C1
OECD incomes rpt scores 10-12, 964C2
'76 inflatn target raised 10-14, Sept CPI rptd up 10-15, 810G1
Courtaulds to shut 3 plants 10-22, 889E3
Callaghan backs soc policies 10-25, Conservatives score 10-26; Labor res vs spending cuts 10-27, 810D1
Mid-Sept—mid-Oct jobless down 10-26, 810F1
'76 inflatn rate 'unsatisfactory' 10-27, 853G2
Labor loses 2 by-electns 11-4, 853G1
Bank special deposits deferred 11-5, 853C3
Spending curb plan cited re £ rise 11-7, 853C2

1977

Heroin addictn rptd up 10-17—10-21, 971E3
Scott murder plot alleged 10-19, Thorpe denies link 10-27, 883G1

Diego Garcia—*See under 'D'*
Economy & Labor (domestic)
Newspr publicatn stalled 1-3, 7G3
Rubery Owen job actn end agreed 1-4, 44F3
Shell, Exxon N Sea pact signed 1-5, 20E3
Increased worker effort asked 1-5, 44C3
CBI sets econ targets 1-6, Healey backs tax reform 1-14, 44G3
'76 business failures rptd 1-7, 21B1
Nov 12-mo consumer price rise rptd 1-7, 29C3
Sterling balances accord set 1-10, 20A3
Callaghan to supervise indl, sterling policies 1-12, 1-13, 44B2
Miners accept NCB compromise 1-12, 44D3
'76 COL rptd up, '77 forecast 1-20, 99E1
Ct upholds boycott injunctn, scores Silkin 1-27, 98F3
'76 factory wage study rptd 1-28, 158B3
'76 strike total rptd 2-2, 134C3
Dec '75-76 inflatn rate rptd 2-7, 87B2
'75 indl profitability falls 2-8, 201D1
Union wage dispute spurs £ fall 2-11, 134G2
Jan inflatn rise rptd 2-18, 134A3
Leyland strikes idle 21,000 2-18—2-28, 201C1
'76 econ growth rate rptd 2-22, 146D2
Jan jobless total rptd 2-25, 146F2
Shipbldg, aircraft natlizatn clears Parlt 3-15; takeovers formalized 4-29, 7-1, 526C2-B3
Leyland rpts record 15-mo profit 3-17, 256B2
Leyland strikers return to work 3-21, 256B1
Healey presents budget 3-29, 256C2
Govt suspends Leyland investmt 3-30, 256B2
Evans elected TGWU head 4-21, 392F1
Airline strike ends 4-27, 392B1
Mar strike record rptd 4-28, TUC scores Port Talbot steel strikers 5-18, 392D1
Inflatn, jobless measures pledged 5-7—5-8, 357D1, F1
Grunwick dispute dvpts '76-77 543B3
Newsman arrested on Grunwick picket line 6-23, 617G2
Leyland investmt freeze lifted 6-29, loan OKd 7-25, 695B1
Beaverbrook newspr chain sold 6-30, 526F3-527B1
Ryder quits Natl Enterprise Bd 7-1, 526G1
Lucas strike threatens Leyland productn 7-4, 695B1
26 postmen suspended re Grunwick job actn 7-5, 543F3
Grunwick strike violence, 70 arrested; '76-77 dispute detailed 7-11, 543A3
Grunwick strikers backed by ct 7-12; Gallup polls workers 7-20, 617B2
Unions end wage restraint 7-13, 544A1
Anti-inflatn pkg presented 7-15, Commons OKs 7-20, 580D3
Purchasing power rpt issued 7-20, 581C1
Ct boycott ruling upset 7-26, 617B3
Aug jobless rates rptd 8-9, 9-26, 771A2, C2
Financial Times strike ends 8-24, 655E1
Leyland workers rejct strike 8-29, 694F3
TUC backs once-a-yr raises, rejcts spending cuts 9-7, 745A2
Natlzd industry 1st ½ profits rptd down 9-20, 883A3
Leyland Chrmn Dobson address 9-27; bias chrgd 10-20; quits post 10-21, Edwardes named 10-25, 863G3
Liberal-Labor pact backs wage curbs 9-28, 745E1
Grunwick violence renewed 10-17, 864E1
Brit Steel Apr-Sept record losses rptd 10-20; TUC, Parlt comment 11-11, 883D2
Inflatn rate, N Sea revenues, £ float linked 11-1, 829B2
Air traffic controllers end strike 11-1, 1013C3
'75 engineers' pay rptd low 11-6, 853D3
Firemen strike, troops battle fires 11-14—12-12; TUC bars support 12-21, 1013G2
Grunwick strikers lose appeal 12-14, 1013E2
OECD sees '78 growth, cites N Sea oil 12-27, 999C1

1978

Thorpe pretrial hearings 11-20—12-4, 944G3-945C2
Thorpe trial ordered 12-13, 987D3
IRA bombs explode in 6 cities 12-17, 12-18, 1017F2
'73 train robber freed 12-18, 1028B3
Defense & Armed Forces—*See also 'Atomic Energy' above*
'73-77 armed forces manpower cuts rptd 4-17, 298B3
Army morale rptd low despite pay hike 5-18, 705G1
Army increased by 4000, BOAR reinforcemts set; Feb hike cited 8-16, 705E1
Gurka unit cutbacks canceled 8-18, 705G1
Diego Garcia—*See DIEGO Garcia*
Dominica—*See DOMINICA*
Economy & Labor (domestic)
Firemen in contract talks 1-3—1-5, vote to end strike 1-12, 17G3
BSC rpts '77 losses 1-10, scored 1-11; govt cuts annual investmt 1-17, 36G2
Journalists end 32-wk strike 1-10, 90D2
Jobless rate rptd 1-12, 18G2
Birmingham expenses rated 1-14, 28B3
'77 strike toll trebled 1-26, 90C2
Callaghan warns Leyland workers 1-26; Edwardes sets reorganizatn, job cuts 2-1, 112D1-D2
Holliday Hall workers vote to strike over pay hike suspensn 2-3; govt withdraws sanctns, increase effected 2-6, 131E2
Swan Hunter ship contract reassigned 2-5; layoffs, severance pay rptd 2-6, 2-8, 112A3
Sanctns vs excess pay hikes backed 2-7, 131B2
Coal miners OK wage limits 2-8, 90B2
Leyland assemb operatn to close, 3000 layoffs seen 2-15, 132B1
Elec engineers OK pay hike within guidelines 2-17, 131C3
Ford strike ends, job rotatn set 2-20, 132C1
'73-77 wage gain cited 2-27, 189C3
Callaghan addresses London bankers 3-14, 226B3
Leyland massive '77 losses rptd 3-20; loan granted 3-23, cost cuts pledged 3-28, efficiency study rptd 3-30, 267C3-G3
North Sea oil revenue plans announced; Callaghan, Thatcher comment 3-21, 227B1
NEB '77 losses rptd 4-6, 267G3
Spillers closing costs 8,000 jobs 4-7, 415F2
'78-79 stimulus budget presented, tax cuts detailed 4-11, 267C2
Tories amend finance bill, force tax cuts 5-8, 5-10; Labor bars confidence vote 5-11, 415E1, C2
Liberals to end Labor pact 5-25, 453A1
Econ upturn, Labor popularity linked 6-2, 437C2
Labor narrowly wins confidence vote 6-14, 496A3
Britsh Rail pensn fund buys art 6-22, 579B1
Shipbldg losses rptd 6-27, limit set 7-10, 573A3
A-sub workers strike 7-7—8-13, 650A1
Grunwick dispute ends 7-12, 557G2
GNP 1% fscl stimulus noted 7-17, 544C2
Pay-increase curbs extended, TUC scores 7-21, 573C2-A3
Inflatn rate rptd down 7-21, 573G2
Offshore oil tax hiked, new sites offered 8-2, 591D3
BL ex-exec jailed 8-11, 667G2
TUC rejcts 5% pay-hike policy 9-6; Labor Party split, unions score 10-1—10-6; Tories back free mkt 10-10, 763B1-C3
Gen electn delayed 9-7; tax cuts, other econ policy results awaited 9-8, 704B1
BL labor troubles persist 9-11, 9-14, rpts 1st ½ profits 9-14, 739G2
Ford workers strike 9-21—10-9, 763F1, D3
Pay accord breaks down, TUC rejcts policy statemt 10-14, 903C1
June '77-78 world inflatn rates ranked 10-18, 914F1
2 Vauxhall plants bar strike 10-23, 10-24, 816D1
Poll rpts Callaghan 5% wage curb backing 10-28, 867E1
Labor outines legis program 11-1, 838G1
Bakers strike, bread supplies cut 11-7, 882B3
Bank lending rate hiked 11-9, 882D2
Healey cautions vs wage hikes 11-12, 882F2
1st ½ '78 oil productn rptd up 11-14, 871B2
Ford strike ends 11-22, sanctns set 11-28, 923C2
Times suspends publicatns 11-30, 923G3-924E1
Tories score pay sanctns 12-13; Callaghan renounces, wins confidnc vote 12-14, 964E2
Bakers strike ends 12-13, 987G3
BBC job actn, 'blackout' ends 12-24, 1017D1

1979

'Yorkshire Ripper' kills 12th victim 9-3, 839D1
Fscl '81 crime control spending hike planned 11-1, 855C2
Dover letter bomb blast, IRA linked 12-17, 994E3
Defense & Armed Forces—*See also 'Atomic' above*
Malta troops withdrawn 4-1, 269C2
Armed forces pay hikes rptd 4-18, 331D1; 5-10, 388A2
Tory programs outlined 5-15, 358G2, 359D1
Sr officer pay hikes OKd 6-5, 425D2
Govt workers strike 9-10, 686D3
Fscl '81 spending hike planned 11-1, 855C2

Economy & Labor
Truckers strike 1-3, 7F1
'78 inflatn rptd 9.5% 1-8, 13C1
Rolls-Royce plant continues strike 1-8, 20C3
N Sea oil workers' strike expands 1-8, 20D3
Natl rail strike threatened 1-9, 20C3
Truckers' strike sanctned by union 1-11; layoffs, other effects felt 1-11, 1-12, 20D2-A3
Oil tank drivers end strike 1-11, 20B3
Engineers, miners prepare pay claims 1-11, 20C3
'78 steel output rptd down 1-11, 38D1
Manchester sewage workers strike 1-12, 20E3
Wage policy revised, detailed 1-16, 37G3
Callaghan scores truckers 1-16, 38D1
Prov journalists' strike ends 1-17, 38G1
Govt spending plans unveiled 1-17, 59E2
City workers strike 1-22, rail engineers; truck layoffs rptd 1-23, 59A2
Secondary picketing curbed 1-26, 96A3
Truckers end strike 1-29, 75B3
Callaghan sees TUC ldrs 1-29, 76C1
Callaghan bars wage-price freeze 1-30, 75E3
Pub worker strikes scored by Callaghan 2-1, impact rptd 2-2, 75F3
'78 living standards ranked 2-2, 109B2
Conservatives lead poll 2-6, 116A1
BL Longbridge workers strike 2-7–2-14, co-wide strike rejected 2-9, 115B3-F3
Minimum lending rate hiked 2-8, 116B1; cut 3-1, 154G2; 4-5, 286A1; 6-12, 445G2
Water, sewage workers settle 2-9, 211C3
TUC-govt accord announced 2-14, 115D2
'78 earnings rise rptd 2-14, 135E2
British Airways Concorde debt canceled 2-22, 154B2
More civil svc workers strike 2-23, 2-25, 3-21, 211F2
Miners OK 9% pay hike 2-27, 211B3
Local-govt manual workers OK 9% pact, health employes rejct 3-6, 211C2
Callaghan, Thatcher spar 3-28, 228B2, C2
Health worker pay pact set 3-28, 3-29, 268E2
Miners ratify accord 3-28, 268F2
Civil svc workers strike 4-2, 268G2
Caretaker budget presented 4-3, 268B2
Labor Party issues manifesto 4-6, Tories issue 4-11, 268A1, B1
BL hit by wildcat strike 4-9, 285F3-286A1
Times labor negotiatns continue 4-16–4-18, 330G3-331A1
Mil pay hikes rptd 4-18, 331D1; 5-10, 388A2
Times intl wkly planned 4-20, printing halted 4-29, 330C3
£ strength, N Sea earnings linked 5-1, 321C1
Civil svc pay dispute setld 5-2, 388C1
Callaghan cites strikes re defeat 5-4, 337G1, E2
Tory programs outlined, Callaghan scores 5-15, 358E2, B3, 359E1
BL sees job gains in Honda plan 5-17, union concern rptd 5-18, 388D2, E2
Teachers' pay pact set 5-21, 388E1-A2
Civil svc, other govt spending cuts rptd planned 5-24–5-25, 407F1
PO workers strike 6-1, 425C2
Pub sector top salaries hike OKd 6-5, 425D2
Laker charter svc halted 6-6, 421A1
Civil svc cost review rptd 6-11, 468F3
Constructn workers OK wage pact 6-11, 469C1
7-natn indicators index rptd 6-11, 513A3
Budget presented, detailed 6-12, 445E1-B3
Rail workers warn vs rail cuts 6-25, pay accord rptd 6-26, 486D1
Thatcher sees union chiefs 6-25, TUC scores govt 6-27, 502F3
Union curbs proposed by govt; reactn 7-9, 524E2-B3
Brit Steel plans plant closings, losses cited; TUC offcl protests 7-12, 543F1
Depressed area indl aid cut announced 7-17, 543A2
Econ slowdown seen 7-19, 554A3
Brit Airways, Aerospace share sales set 7-20; Brit Shipbldrs denatlzn deferred 7-23, 564A3
Health offcls' revolt squelched 8-1, 582C2
Power workers OK pay pact 8-3, 634C2
Engineers strike 8-6, 8-13, 8-20, 634F1

1980

Scottish terrorists sentncd 10-15, 808F2
'Yorkshire Ripper' kills 13th victim 11-17, 927D1
Defense & Armed Forces—*See also 'Atomic Energy' above, 'Foreign' below*
Soldiers hurt in Netheravon blasts 3-7, 194E1
Spending hike planned 3-26, 232E2
Defense white paper issued 4-2, 2741
Spending cuts backed by Labor, disarmamt rift rptd 5-31, 429D2
Armor purchases set 7-14, 564E1
Disarmament backed by Labor Party 10-2, 768B3
Svcwomen to be armed 12-2, 922F1-A2
'79 mil spending cited 12-10, 949F2

Economy & Labor
Steelworkers strike 1-2, 6D3
Nurses pay hiked 20% 1-4, 20F1
Brit Airways workers strike 1-10, 59F1
Current acct deficit linked 1-16, 59F1
'Quango' paring set 1-16, 79E2
Pvt steelworkers join strike 2-1—2-3, 97E3
BL bars reinstatemt of fired steward 2-7, 117B3
Pub housing sale plan rptd 2-7, 149G3
BL sets layoffs 2-11, pay pact rejected 2-12, 117G2
'79 inflatn rptd up 2-13, 125C3
Racal to acquire Decca 2-14, 132D3
Union immunities curb asked 2-19, 150G1
BL workers rejct strike 2-20, 150D1
'79 wages rptd up 19.6% 2-20, 150E2
Econ recovery seen slow, Feb jobless hike rptd 2-26, 150C2
Labor censure vote defeated, Thatcher defends policies 2-28, 172G1
BBC announces cutbacks 2-28, 172F3
Econ downturn seen in 4 rpts 3-3, 172D2
Steel strike mediator urged 3-3, 193A3
British Steel annual 1 bln pound loss seen 3-6, 193B3
Steelworkers OK vote on pay offer 3-9, 193D2
Thatcher admits problems 3-12, 212G1
By-electn results linked 3-13, 212F1
New budget presented, detailed; reactn 3-26, 232C1-G2
Steel strike settled, loss estimated 4-1, 254B2
Defns budget estimated 4-2, 274B2
BL unions bar strike 4-2, 274E2
BL workers walk out 4-11, strike ends 4-21, 313E1
Rail worker pay pact set 4-17, 313D1
Rail pact revisn OKd 4-29, 335C3
New Brit Steel chrmn named 5-1, 352E1
'Day of Actn' strike fails 5-14, 373A1
MD pay hike set 5-19, 389C3
Natlzn backed by Labor 5-31, 429D2
Austerity opposed by business 6-2, 445B1
Howe urges pay restraint 6-6; wage curbs rptd rejected 6-7, 444C3
Interest rate cuts seen 6-6, 444F3
Civil Svc cutback rptd set 6-19, 487F1
June jobless rate hits post-war high 6-24, 498C1
Vickers, Rolls-Royce to merge 6-25, 498G1
Min lending rate cut to 16% 7-3, 523F1
BP plans Selectn Trust takeover 7-7, 523A2
Miners seek 35% wage hike 7-8, 523C2
Brit Rail plans sales 7-15, 544E1
State utility, mail monopolies to be curbed 7-16, 7-21, 563F3
Docks Bd to sell shares 7-21, 564D1
Thatcher wins no-confidence vote 7-29, 578C1-B2
British Steel record loss rptd 7-30, 578B2
Coal Bd, Brit Shipbldrs, Brit Airways rpt fscl '80 performance 7-30, 7-31, 578E2
Lords rule on Granada TV-BSC case 7-30, 634G1-E2
BBC cutbacks rptd modified 7-31, 670D3
Labor costs rptd 8-12, 698E1, F1
Observer wage accord reached 8-16, 670B3
Times journalists strike 8-22, 652G1; settle 8-29, 670F2
TUC conf; Thatcher scored, Polish trip canceled 9-1—9-5, 688A2-B3
Liberal econ plan proposed 9-12, 708E2
Local authorities' funds cut 9-18, 729C1
Brit Steel aid hike set 9-26, 750D2
Labor Party backs 35-hr week, private educ ban 9-29, 768D3
BSC drops Granada case 9-30, 750F3
Hormones in cattle feed barred 10-1, 737C3
23 London newspapers to merge 10-1, 750D3
Thatcher affirms policies 10-10, 790F2
TUC econ plan rejected 10-14, 790C3
London Times offered for sale 10-22, 808A3
BL seeks more govt aid 10-27; strike threatened 11-3, workers accept 7% pay deal 11-18, 886D2
Econ outlook remains grim 10-28, 859G1
Pub sector 6% pay lid set 11-6; oppositn, unions denounce 11-7—11-8, 886B3
Thatcher maintains econ policy 11-20, 901D1
Interest rate, govt spending cuts, new oil levy set 11-24, 901F1
Jobless protest in Liverpool 11-29, 922D1
Coal miners OK 13% pay hike 12-1, 922B1
Brit Steel recovery plan outlined 12-10; wage curbs sought 12-11, layoffs set 12-12, 965E2

1976

Govt wins debate limit votes on natlzn, farm homes, dock worker jurisdictn 11-8, jurisdictn chng defeated 11-10, 852G3
Healey rpts borrowing underestimate 11-8, 853D2
Oct raw material cost up 11-8, 853A3
Shares plunge 11-8, up 11-10, 853C3
105 Labor MPs vs spending cuts 11-10, 853F2
Longshoreman strike rpt hurts £; rpt denied 11-11, 853E2
Concern rptd re IMF loan effects 11-11, 880D2
Oct inflatn rptd 11-12, 889B3
Rains renew water stocks 11-16, drought losses rptd 12-31, 977C3, E3
40,000 protest spending cuts 11-17, 889D2-B3
'74 tax rate rptd 11-18, 905A2
Miners rejct NCB offer, £ falls 11-23, 905E3
Oct '75-76 inflatn rate rptd 12-6, 976B1
Spending cuts, tax hikes set; BP stock sold 12-15, 1003F2
'76 budget deficit rptd 12-17, 1003B3

European Force Reduction Issues—*see under EUROPE*

Falkland Islands—*See FALKLAND Islands*

Foreign Economic Developments

Mauritius drops £ sterling link 1-5, 104G2
Australian SAM deal rptd 1-6, 7E3
Norway to buy BP unit 1-7, 30D2
SDR rate rptd 1-15, 14B3
Anglo yields Ecuador oil unit 1-16, 49F1
Brazil bauxite operatn begun 1-16, 98G2
Gulf-Conoco N Sea oil find rptd 1-19, govt buys 51% interest 2-26, 173A3
Argentina vs Falkland oil exploitatn 1-20, 96F3
In 7-natn A-safeguards agrmt 1-27, 84A1
Mauritania compensates iron co 1-28, 104F2
'75 auto exports rptd up 1-29, 174G1
BP rpts oil traces off Brittany 1-31, 139G2
Vs World Bank Chile loan 2-3, 99G2
Italy Leyland layoffs completed 2-4, 141C1
N Sea oil Euroloans rptd 2-4, 2-5, 173E3
Lockheed payoffs cited 2-6, 131B1
US-Israel ship co default threatens UK deals 2-9, 173G3
2 Iran aides ousted in sugar fraud 2-10, 156D3
Guatemala rejcts quake aid 2-11, 120C3
Guatemala accepts pvt quake aid 2-12, 155D3
Kuwait buys tanks 2-16, 126B2
Consortium-backed Italy loan rptd 2-16, 141A1
US bank files bankruptcy 2-20, 167D1
Guyana sets Booker unit natlizatn 2-23, 252B3
6-natn export credit pact rptd 2-25, 164C2
1st Auk oil shipmt rptd 2-25, 173D3
'75 Mozambique aid offer rptd 3-4, 175G2
£ falls 3-5—3-25, franc-run role denied 3-16, 339F1, B2
Canada refinery bankrupt 3-12, 221A3
Bolivia oil co gets bank loans 3-12, 4-14, 416E1
US threatens steel quotas 3-16, 212G3
Firms off Arab blacklist 3-24—4-3, 242C1
Sovt trade credit use vowed 3-25, 229B1
Total IMF oil loan rptd 4-1, 340A2
£ drops 4-4—4-22, 313B1
£ gains 4-6, hits new low 4-9, 266C3
US utility buys N Sea gas 4-7, 521E3
BP, Shell confirm Italy bribes 4-13, 267F1
Mar paymts surplus rptd 4-14, 313B1
A-fuel productn set, effect on US dealings rptd 4-27, 4-28, 351F2-B3
W Ger buys N Sea oil 4-27, 521E3
Australia oil dvpt projct set 4-29, 332C1
Paraguay paper, cellulose investmt set 4-30, 403B3
Mine ownership in Australia rptd 5-2, 350A1
US ends car dumping probe 5-4, 321D1
'75 Sovt trade rptd 5-5, 340F3
N Viet vows oil cooperatn 5-7, 367A3
£ drop continues 5-14—5-17, 365E1
Warns Malawi of aid cutoff 5-18, 382E2
£ hits record lows 5-21, 5-28, 383F2
Canada sets tariff rise 5-25, 400E3
Govt wins ship natlzn ruling 5-27, 401G3 ★
UNCTAD OKs commodity fund 5-30, ?88G2
7-natn summit set 6-1, 6-3, 388G3
£ dips lower 6-3—6-4; intl loan OKd, £ rises 6-7; IMF loan terms rptd 6-8, 407A2-B3
IMF gold purchases rptd 6-3, 6-9, 430F2, G2
IDB entry set 6-3, 465D3
May trade deficit up 6-14, 458C1
Export credit terms tightened 6-15, 529F3
£ drop linked to OPEC 6-16, 457C3
Paris Club defers Zaire debt 6-17, 488A2
US scores econ policies 6-22, 457G3
7-natn econ summit held 6-27—6-28, 461G2
Hungary devalues vs £ 7-6, 925C2
Australia-Japan coal-mining projct set 7-7, 496A2
7-natn A-waste conf opens 7-12, 739G1
June trade deficit rptd 7-14, 556E2
Italy loan ban disclosed 7-16, denied 7-19, 530D3; repercusns 7-20, 557B1
Israel links currency 7-18, 538D3
EC entry pattern cited 7-27, 853E3
US files consent decree vs major publishers 7-27, 989D1

1977

Falkland Islands—*See FALKLAND Islands*

1978

European Force Reduction Talks—*See under EUROPE*

Falkland Islands—*See FALKLAND Islands*

1979

Commercial TV shut by strike 8-11, 634B2
Scotland shipyd closings, job cutbacks planned; protests sparked 8-16, 634B1
Police reach pay pact 8-16, 634C2
TUC conf: govt scored 9-3–9-7, 707C2-A3
BL plans job cuts, 1st 1/2 profits rptd 9-10, 686D2
Govt workers strike 9-10, 686C3
Engineers strike again 9-10, 686D3
Commercial TV strike continues 9-10, 686E3
Journalists seek pay hike 9-11, 686E3
PO reform proposed 9-12, 687B1
Westn wage rates compared 9-19, 697B3
Rolls-Royce locks out workers 9-19, 729G3
Bank of England sees slump 9-20, 730D1
Engineers' strike continues 9-24, 729E3
Miners seek 65% wage hikes 9-24, 730B1
Labor Party links electn loss 10-1–10-5, backs renatlzn 10-3, 10-3, 773D2, G2-B3
Engineers' pact set 10-4, 772F3
Thatcher addresses Tories on unions, strikes 10-12, 791D3
Lewis wins Nobel 10-17, 858A2
Times labor pact reached 10-21, 813E2
Commercial TV strike setld 10-23, 836C2
Unionists dominate Labor Party inquiry com 10-24, 873A3, E3
Thatcher praise by China premr scored 10-31, 854B2
Tory paper outlines fscl '81 spending plans; reactn 11-1, 855A2
BL employes endorse cutbacks, Thatcher hails 11-1, 855F2-B3
Times resumes publicatn 11-13, 874B1
Lending rate hiked, other money curbs adopted 11-15, 889C2
BL union militant fired, strikes ensue 11-19, interim pact OKd 11-27, 994G1
NEB members quit over Rolls-Royce transfer 11-20, new members named 11-21, 11-20, 949C3
Trade union reforms proposed; reactn 12-7, 949B2
BSC '80 strike called, 1st 1/2 losses cited 12-7, 949G2
Jan-mid Nov inflatn at 17.4%, VAT hike cited 12-14, 968D2
BL aid vowed 12-20, signs Honda accord 12-27, 994C1

Energy—*See also 'Atomic' above*

N Sea oil workers' strike expands 1-8, 20C3
Texaco UK oil tank drivers end strike 1-11, 20B3
Iran oil cutoff impact assessed, N Sea access cited 2-20, 126A3
Tanker spill off Nova Scotia 3-15, 201D1
£ strength, N Sea earnings linked 5-1, 321C1
Gas price rptd at $1.53 per gal 5-19, 397A1
Oil consumptn curbs barred 5-24; gas, diesel shortages rptd 5-26–5-29, 396F3
US oil import subsidy scored 6-2, 417B2
Gas tax hike, BP shares sale set 6-12, 445E2, G2
Tokyo summit, oil import targets set 6-28–6-29, 493B1-F2
N Sea oil estimate revised 7-10, 582A2
Nigeria cuts BP oil 7-12, 545A2
BP share sales planned 7-24, 564F3
USSR oil export freeze rptd 7-18, 568F1
BNOC cutbacks, increased N Sea exploratn planned 7-26, 582B1
BP natlzd by Nigeria 7-31, 584D2-D3
Exxon Scottish gas plant OKd 8-10, 614A2
BP profits soar 9-6, 686F3
BL job cut plans, oil prices linked 9-10, 686F2
N Sea oil assets sale barred 9-14, 707G1
France N Sea access, EC budget contributn opposed 9-17, 719D2, E2
Shortages, import needs forecast 9-18, 752D1-A2
Econ slump, oil linked 9-20, 730E1
BP stock sale plan announced 10-16, 792D2
N Sea oil cutback ordrd 10-29, 836F1
BNOC sets price hike 11-6, 864B2
Iran export cut confirmed 11-8, 843G1
US ban on Iran oil backed 11-13, 861F1, F2
Inflatn, oil price hikes linked 12-14, 968E2

European Force Reduction Talks—*See under EUROPE*

Falkland Islands—*See FALKLAND Islands*

1980

Jobless rise, deeper recessn seen in '82 12-21, 994D2
Jobless rate at post-war high 12-23, 994C2
BL strike end urged by Thatcher 12-31, 994F1

Energy—*See also 'Atomic Energy' above*

Oil productn legis plans rptd; '79, '80 output estimated 1-4, 7B1
Tax hikes planned 3-26, 232E1, G1
Iran oil purchase barred 4-22, 298F1
Saudis weigh trade curbs 4-22, 313E2
Libya threatens oil cutoff 5-9, 373B3
N Sea oil natlzn asked by Labor 5-31, 429E2
N Sea gas pipe OKd 6-19, 463D2
7-natn Venice summit 6-22—6-23, 473A1-474E1
Gasoline prices cut 7-4, 8-11, 628G1
BP plans Selectn Trust takeover 7-7, 523A2
BP unit buys Rhone-Poulenc share 7-9, 522C2, D2
State elec monopolies to be curbed 7-21, 563F3
N Sea oil, gas output cuts planned 7-23, 563C3
N Sea oil profits to aid indus backed by Labor 7-29, 578G1
'80 coal productn rptd 7-30, 578E2
OPEC drops planned 10% cut 9-26, 735B1
New oil levy planned 11-24, 901F1, B2
N Sea oil bolsters pound 12-10, 932G1

1976

Carter asks A-breeder study 8-9, 585C1
July trade deficit up 8-13, 675G3
Br Airways orders 12 Lockheed jets 8-18, 675D3
Oil found off Scotland 8-19, 675F2
Pound drops in intl mkt 8-25, 630F2
Ex-min rptd bribed by Lockheed, Conservatives deny 8-30, 642F2-A3
A-safeguard, pacts signed 9-6, 936A2
Bulgaria truck pact rptd 9-8, 910E2
Lending rate boost spurs £ 9-10, 694C1
Norway N Sea oil pact signed 9-10, 832E3
IMF auctn bidders listed 9-15, 739D3, G3
Callaghan sees Trudeau 9-16, 9-18, 730B2
Morgan Grenfell in Venez finance co 9-17, 875E1
Rpt gold returned to Poland 9-28, 907F1
IMF loan plan rptd 9-29, gains after record low 9-30, 721B1
Healey vs stringent tariffs 9-30, 791B3
Backs World Bank funds rise 10-5, 778D1
Lending rate hike boosts £ 10-7, 773G1
IMF takes no actn on loan request 10-8, 778D2
Sept trade deficit rptd up, £ falls 10-14, 810B2
£ declines vs $, revalued mark 10-20, 782D1
£ falls to new low; IMF, US, other factors listed 10-24—10-28, 809C3
IMF lending funds rptd low 10-26, 915D1
Barclays, Vickers on Arab blacklist 10-29, 889D3
Oct reserves rptd down 11-2, 853B3
US hits China jet sales 11-4, 880B1
£ edges up 11-7, fluctuates 11-8—11-11, 853C2
EC aid to £ seen 11-8, 853E2
US stock prices fall, UK finances linked 847C1
US FRB chrmn sees IMF loan 11-11, 853F2
Australia lifts uranium export ban 11-11, 888F1
France backs IMF loan, sterling plan 11-12, 880B2 ★
US balks on sterling balances 11-16—11-17, 880C3
BAC, Iran oil-arms deal 11-18, 906F1
Venez pres in talks 11-22; pact signed 11-23, 929D3
Pound falls 11-23, 905F3
Australia cuts tariffs 12-7, 944E2
Trade deficit up, £ falls 12-14, 946E3
Poland econ pact signed 12-15—12-17, 966D1
Healey rpts IMf loan support 12-15; OECD panel OKs loan 12-21, 1003A3, F3
US, W Ger loan extensn rptd 12-15, 1003C3
Group of 10 OKs IMF loan 12-21, 1004A1
US ct blocks London opt rule 12-22, 990B2
Sovt gas deal rptd 12-24, 1011A2
US rejcts air route chngs 12-28, 992B2

Foreign Relations (misc.)—*See also 'UN Policy' below*

Europn soclsts meet 1-18—1-19, 48G2
Thatcher scores detente, backs strong defns 1-19; Wilson statemt 1-28; USSR, China reactn 1-22—1-30, 101C1-A2
Laos ICC disbands 1-21, 55E2
USSR to make more dailies available 1-21, 76G2
USSR chrgs emigre internmt 2-4, 122C2
CP scores Sovt ties 2-7, 174A3
Rpt 100,000 Pak residents 2-8, 121A2
Australia rocket range to close 2-18, 154C3
SEATO formally disbanded 2-20, 148C1
McLennan addresses Sovt CP Cong 3-1, 196C1
Trudeau seeks Canada Const repatriatn 3-5, 238A3; outlines proposals 4-1, 4-9, 265C2 ★
Callaghan sees Sovt amb 3-15—3-19, 229A1
Airs Solzhenitsyn warning vs communism 3-24, 424F1
Gromyko ends visit 3-25, 228G3
Spain seizes oppositn ldrs 4-3, 269D1
India natls score curbs 4-24, 313F1
Canada defers Const issue 5-6, 380F3 ★
Parlt com scores '74 Cyprus stand 5-19, 457D1
Japan ratifies A-pact 5-24, deposits documents 6-9, 419C1
Powell fears race war 5-24, 482F1
Asian immigrants attacked, 2 killed 6-2—6-21, Callaghan deplores 6-15, 482B1
Giscard ends visit, yrly mtgs set 6-24, 481C3
W Ger lauds UK-France mtg plans 7-6, 521F1
Portugal to seek closer ties 7-19, 558E1
To quit Oman bases 7-19, 594E2
In Dutch sea limit compromise 7-27, 563C3
USSR cuts Wilson drug sentnc 7-30, 655B2
Dependents quit China quake area 8-1, 561E2
BBC closes New Delhi office 8-5, 621D1
Cambodia links restored 8-9, 589B2
Australia dep prime min visits 8-12, 623A2
USSR rejcts Berlin bus protest 8-27, 678D3
2 sentncd in Sovt drug case 9-9, 857F1
Callaghan visits Canada 9-11—9-18, 730G1
Tito cancels Thatcher visit 9-16, 734G2
W Ger, Dutch aid ship rescue 9-20, 713A1
Malta forgn policy cited 9-20, 713E1, F1
USSR scores Rhodesia plan 9-28, 719D1

1977

Foreign Relations (misc.)—*See also 'Monetary, Trade & Aid' and 'UN Policy' below*

Vs E Ger Berlin visas 1-6, 7E2; lodges USSR protest 1-11, 20F1
India lifts BBC ban 1-6, 45G3
'76 Europe Cncl pact vs terror cited 9G2
Norway sulphur-dioxide chrgs disputed 1-17, monitoring pact rejctd 1-19, 109C3
CP defends Czech dissidents 1-19, 82F2
Czech spy chrgs denied 1-23, 82G3
Brandt warns on W Berlin 1-24, 102A2
Czechs warned re dissidents 2-2, 114G3
Malta scores security talks delay 2-10, 136A3
Canada drops 'subject' status 2-15, 133A3
French Channel I claim cited 329C2
Czech defects, reveals spy network 2-24, 220B3
Hess amnesty denied 2-28, 298C3
Queen Eliz arrives Australia 3-7; monarchy ties protested 3-7—3-13, 199C1
Greece jails 5 for spying 3-18, 256C3; releases 6-4, 487F3
NZ prime min visits 3-31, 258B2
Sweden arrests terrorist 4-1, 429A1
Thatcher in China 4-11, 282B2
Canada '76 emigratn rptd 4-13, 389D2
Pak protests BBC role 4-28, 349A2
Australia urges envoy cuts 6-2, 484D3
Viet refugees rptd accepted 6-16, 497E1
Australia gov gen quits 7-14, 541C1
Newsman quits E Ger defectn try 7-24, 617G2
A-test talks with US, USSR set 7-28, 574E2
At Makarios funeral 8-8; Turkey warns re successor 8-12, 617E1
Owen visits Spain 9-6—9-7, asks Gibraltar border opening 9-7, 717D3
USSR bars books 9-6, 766A1
Eur Cncl to study Turkey rights abuses in Cyprus 9-8, 764G1-A2; rpt shelved, Greece protests 11-3, 946E3
BMA backs Maltese MDs 9-9, 925C3
In A-test talks with US, USSR 10-2—10-3, 12-5—12-10; USSR backs ban 11-2, 996F3—997C1
Owen in USSR; Rhodesia plan backed, A-war pact signed 10-10—10-11, 812F3
Queen, Philip in Canada 10-14—10-19, 822A2
W Ger hijack rescue aided 10-17, Schmidt thanks 10-18, 789E2, 790F1
W Eur heroin conf 10-17—10-21, 971E3
W Ger mil 'offset paymt' terms agreed 10-18, 926F2
Queen opens Bahamas Parlt 10-20, 844G2

1978

Foreign Relations (misc.)—*See also 'Atomic Energy' above, 'Monetary, Trade, Aid & Investment' and 'UN' below*

Callaghan visits Bangladesh, India, Pak 1-3—1-13; backs Ganges R dvpt role 1-16, 37B1, A2
At Westn natns Ogaden conf 1-21, 43E2
China-US ties lauded 12-16, 977B1

1979

Foreign Relations (misc.)—*See also 'Atomic' above, 'Monetary' and 'UN' below*

At 4-natn Guadeloupe summit 1-5–1-6, Sovt warning on China ties cited 1-5, 12D2, B3
Canada arrests alleged envoy kidnaper 1-6, 19G1; bail set 1-11, 37B2
Brunei independnc pact signed 1-7, 40D3
Canada panel urges prov lt gov apptmts 1-25, 74D2
Canada bars monarchy role chng, debates const amendmt process 2-5–2-6, 113G2, E3
Channel tunnel planned 2-9, 135A3
Forgn emb contacts blocked by strike 2-25, 211A3
Amb to Holland killed 3-22, IRA linked; other ambs warned 3-23, 228E2-D3
Malta troops withdrawn 4-1, 269C2
Bhutto executn scored 4-4, 247G1
W Ger printing of Times wkly set 4-20, halted 4-29, 330C3
USSR abuse chrgd by British rptr 4-20, 390F1-A2
Greek premier visits 1-25, 149B2
3d world propaganda unit disbanded 1-27, 71E2
France, W Ger OK ESA rocket launcher 2-6—2-7, 122B1
Sardina '74 bombing cited 2-11, 133F2
USSR travel bar rptd 2-17, 230E1
USSR campaign vs neutron bomb scored, SS-20 missile threat seen 2-21, 140D1
Cyprus presses chrgs vs UK rptr 2-22, drops case 2-24, 138E2
Eur fascists meet 3-4—3-5, 238D3
Berlin demilitarized status cited 3-14, 276B1
Australia defns research pact signed 4-18, 391E2
USSR dissidents called sane 4-20, 360C1
Eur conservative group formed, Thatcher addresses 4-24, 424C3
Defns chief in China, remarks on USSR cause uproar 5-1, 329F2
Dutch arrest terrorist in W Ger plot 5-5, jail 8-21, 725C1
Afghan ties to continue 5-6, 349A3
ESA communicatns satellite launched 5-12, 384D3
Orlov trial protested 5-15, 360A1; 5-25, USSR counterchrgs 5-18, 401A2, C2
Turkish premr visits 5-15, 398F2
Australia prime min to visit 6-1, 450E3
Natl Front opens Australia branch 6-3, 495A1
Rumania pres visits; detente, disarmamt discussed 6-13—6-16, 515F2

1980

Foreign Relations (misc.)—*See also 'Atomic Energy' above, 'Monetary', 'Soviet-Afghan Issue', 'UN Policy' below*

Gromyko visit canceled 1-5, 2D2
Carrington in Pak, India 1-16, 27E1, A2
Sakharov exile condemned 1-22, 46C3
Sovt ABM penetratn sought 1-24, 79A2
McCartney deported from Japan 1-26, 200E2
UK soldiers attacked in W Ger 2-16, 3-1, 3-10; IRA claims credit, notes Dutch amb's death 2-19, 194A1
W Ger ex-terrorist seeks return 2-22, 154F1
Channel tunnel plan rptd 3-4, 193F3
Czechs deport Oxford prof 3-9, 262D2
Carrington in Rumania 3-13—3-14, 205G1
Channel tunnel concept OKd, funding barred 3-19, 212A2
Defns white paper cites Sovt threat, W Ger offset paymts end 4-2, 274F1, C2
Spain accord sets Gibraltar links 4-10, 274G2-A3
USSR science conf attended 4-13—4-15, 326F2
Czech ousts 2d prof 4-13, protest issued 4-21, 326D3
Canada parlt opens 4-14, 292F3
Europn CPs meet 4-28—4-29, 327C2
Tito funeral held 5-8, 339A1
W Ger riot, Westn mil parade linked 5-18, 500F3
ESA rocket test fails 5-23, 397G2
Queen in Australia 5-23—5-28, 405D3
New Hebrides separatists revolt; natls flee, provisional govt formed 5-28—6-3, 422A2
Independent forgn policy backed by Labor 5-31; 429A3
New Hebrides rebel, forgn links chrgd 6-8; forces sent 6-11, 436E1-A3
7-natn Venice summit 6-22—6-23, 473A1-474E1
Viets capture civilian 6-25, release 6-29, 508G2
ESA plans comet probe 7-15, 548A1
USSR honors Philby 7-15, 566G2
New Hebrides force sent 7-24, presence backed 7-30, 580G3
Belgium blast kills Jewish youth 7-27, Palestinian seized 7-28, 573D2
Tibet exiles in China 7-29, 603F3
New Hebrides independnc declared 7-30, 580E3
Westn labor costs compared 8-12, 698E1, F1
USSR spy quits academy 8-18, controversy rptd 8-24, 652D1

Rpt Poland gets Danzig gold 9-28, 907F1
Canada Const talks 10-1—10-2, 749G3
Brezhnev scores re southn Africa 10-7, 856E3
Canada immigratn rptd 11-3, 851E1
'58 Sovt A-waste blast rpt disputed 11-7, 948B3
Callaghan, Giscard yrly mtg 11-11—11-12, 880B2 *
Spain OKs Socialist conf 11-27, 908F3
France bars joint Eur defns 11-30, 905A3
Poland prime min visits 12-15—12-17, 966C1
CP scores Sovt repressn 12-22, 955F3

1977

Cambodia ties barred 10-24, 11-9, 864F1
SAS flights banned 10-30, 882G3
Malta threatens Libya defns pact 11-23, 925A3
Cyprus base bombed 11-31, 946F3
USSR expels Shcharansky atty 12-4, 956C1
Giscard, Callaghan summit 12-12—12-13, 1013G1
Queen ends Canada govt duties 12-30, 1010D1

1978

Indonesia, Malaysia back Brunei independnc 6-30, 533F3
Malta premr's daughter arrested 7-6, 533B3
Malta bans rptrs 7-9, closes radio statn 7-16, 592A3
USSR Shcharansky, Ginzburg trials scored 7-10, 542B3
French controller slowdowns delay Eur flights 7-14—8-21, 640A3
Hijacking pact signed in Bonn 7-17, 544G2
Cambodia denies rights breach 7-21, 660C1
E Ger jails natl in escape bid 7-24, 648F3
Queen visits Canada 7-26—8-6, 647B2
Greek ct questns '71 UK murder case convictn 7-31, 631F2
Canada debates monarchy role 8-10, 8-16, 647E1, G1
Rhine army reinforcemts planned 8-16, 705F1
Rhine army bases bombed 8-18; IRA, W Ger terrorists linked 8-19—8-24, patrols increased 8-25, 688D1
Air Canada shutdown strands travelers in London 8-25—9-5, 686F2
Canada monarchy role dispute continues 8-30—9-25, 754G3, 755E1
Rees sees W Ger min on terrorism 9-4—9-5, 688B2
USSR detains natls 9-4, 947C2
Bulgarian defector dies 9-11, ruled murder 9-29; 2d defector found dead 10-2; Paris incident rptd 9-14, 748C3
W Ger terrorist arrested, extraditn asked 9-15, 725A2
Chrgs Cambodian cruelty 9-20, 748G1
Tuvalu independence effected 9-30, 1022B2
E Berlin mil displays scored 10-2, 10-7, 861F3
China forgn min visits 10-10—10-13, 796G1
Thatcher at Spain party cong, asks EC entry 10-21, 821F2
6th Cross kidnaper alleged 11-2, 880B1
Briton in Cambodia 12-9, slain 12-23, 997A2

Australia sets job study missn 4-28, 351G2
Thatcher electn reactn 5-4—5-5, 338A2
USSR frees drug smugglers 5-6, 390B3
Quebec language law const case argued 6-11, 484F1
Canada RCMP plans emb. bugging 7-4, 522A3
USSR extends rptr's visa 7-10, 636G3
Gilbert Islands gain independnc, chng name 7-12, 526B1
Canada Indians see gov gen 7-19, 632G2
USSR rptd questnd on fate of missing Swedish envoy 8-4, 690C2
Canada sentncs 2 re envoy kidnap 8-7, 632B3
Japan excluded from Mountbatten funeral 9-5, 669A1
Dutch Shell strikers vowed union support 9-24, 731C2
China ties linked to Hong Kong gov reappt 9-25, 730C2
USSR vs A-missiles 10-13—10-16, 880G2
Canada's Rideau Club burns 10-23, 834B1
China premr arrives 10-28, accords OKd 11-1, 854E1-B2
USSR spy ring scandal reopened 10-28, 10-29, 873F3; 4th man identified 11-15, controversy ensues 11-15—11-21, 908C2-909F1
Canada sentncs 3d envoy kidnaper 11-8, 872D1
Pak mobs sack library 11-21, 893F1
Pol Pot govt ties ended 12-6, 978G3
SALT noted in Thatcher, Carter talks 12-17, 968A2
Sovt Afghan invasn opposed 12-28; Thatcher protests to Brezhnev 12-29, 974C2

1979

1980

Papua New Guinea troops replace Vanuatu force 8-18; quell rebellion 8-31, 674B1
Sovts jam BBC broadcasts 8-20, 626E2
Sovt A-sub aided off Japan 8-20, 653C1
Nehru, Mountbatten affair alleged 8-27; Gandhi denies 8-29, 890A3
Poland visit canceled by TUC 9-5, 668F2
Sri Lanka cites A-treaty implementatn failure 9-7, 696C1
Trudeau seeks const patriatn 9-8—9-13, 705F3
Turkey coup sympathy rptd 9-16, 696F3
British soccer fans riot in Madrid 9-17, 771E3
Canada Parlt recalled for patriatn 9-18, 728E1; plan rptd opposed in poll 12-10, 964F2
Turkey airline office bombed 10-12, 794G1

Gibraltar—See GIBRALTAR
Government & Politics—See also other appropriate subheads in this section
Queen names knights 1-1, 80E2
Parlt debates Scot, Wales home-rule; 'takes note' of '75 white paper 1-13—1-19, 72C3
Shadow cabt reshuffled 1-15, 101B2
Scottish Labor Party meets 1-18, 73D1
Listed as 'free' nation 1-19, 20C3
Home-rule min replaced 1-23, 73D1
Thorpe denies financial, sexual chrgs 1-29; Liberals back 1-30, 2-5, 174B2
'71 Thorpe probe rptd 2-6, coverup chrgd 2-14, 174E2
New anti-bias bill proposed 2-18, 174C3
Thorpe bars resignatn 3-7, Liberals back 3-17; S Africa implicated in scandal 3-9—3-13, 252D2-A3
Govt wins no-confidence vote 3-11, 239F1
Wilson quits 3-16, 5 bid for post 3-17—3-30, 239C1
Callaghan elected prime min 4-5, 252G1
Stonehouse quits, Labor loses Parlt majority 4-7, 267B1
Callaghan names Cabt 4-8, 266D3-267A1
Liberal youth ldr cleared of bank theft 4-9, 351D1
Stonehouse trial begins 4-27, 313D1
Tories gain in local electns 5-7, 351B3
Thorpe controversy continues 5-8—5-9, resigns 5-10, 350G3
Grimond gets interim Liberal post 5-12, 364E3
Thorpe 'coverup' detailed 5-12, 364F3
Wilson knighted 5-19, 368B3

Gibraltar—See GIBRALTAR
Government & Politics—See also other appropriate subheads in this section
Ct curbs atty gen's power 1-27, 98F3
Owen named forgn secy 2-21, 200F3-201A1
Labor loses Scot, Wales home rule vote 2-22, 239B3
Conservative wins London dist by-electn 2-24, 201A1
Labor rpts Liberal pact 3-22, wins no-confidence vote 3-23, 239A2
Tories win Stechford by-electn 3-31, 239A3
Tories win Ashfield, lose Grimsby by-electns 4-28; win local electns 5-5, 373G3, 374C1
Labor loses Scot local electns 5-3, 374G1
Jay appointmt scored 5-11, 391F3
Queen holds Silver Jubilee 6-5—6-11, 486F2
Tories win Saffron Walden by-electn 7-8, 544C1
MP quits over Poulson scandal 7-22, 2 others scored 7-26, 581D1
Atty gen ruling upset 7-26, 617B3
Liberals extend pact with Labor 7-26, 637G1
Riots, racial tension mark Natl Front marches 8-13, 8-15; facts on Front rptd 8-17, 636E3, 654G3
Labor wins Birmingham by-electn 8-18, 654G2
Callaghan denies Wilson bugged 8-23, 745D2
Natl Front march banned 9-20, police guard protesters 10-16, 864G1

Gilbert Islands—See GILBERT Islands
Government & Politics—See also other appropriate subheads in this section
Judge defends racial slurs, MPs demand resignatn 1-6, 18D1
Labor govt reliance on Ulster MPs cited 1-11, 19A1
Covert propaganda unit disbanded 1-27, 71E2
Bolton campaign violence 2-10; Ilford march banned 2-22, police keep order 2-25, 167E3
Scot home rule passed; Shetlands, Orkney provisn cited 2-22, 131D3
Tories win Ilford North by-electn 3-2, voting analyzed 3-3—3-6, 167E2-D3
Lords revisn proposed by Home rpt 3-20, 226E3
Parlt sessns broadcast 4-3, 268A1
Labor rpts Scottish by-electn 4-14, party moral bolstered 4-17, 288C1
Labor loses 2 of 3 by-electns, Liberal setbacks rptd 4-27, 4-29, 329B1-F2
Local electns held; Natl Front, Scot Natls fare badly 5-4, 392D3
Labor bars confidence vote 5-11, 415C2
Liberals to end Labor pact 5-25, 452G3
Labor wins Hamilton by-electn 6-1; SNP decline seen, Conservatives rptd heartened 6-1—6-2, 437E1
Labor narrowly wins confidence vote on Healey's salary 6-14, 496F2
Commons disrupted by manure throwing 7-6, 533A3
Paisley, Ulster MP protest Westminster mass 7-6, 557D3
Labor wins 2 by-electns 7-13, 557C2
Thorpe arrested in murder plot 8-4; sets reelectn bid, Liberals score 8-5, 614A2

Government & Politics—See also other appropriate subheads in this section
Spending plans unveiled 1-7, 59E2
Conservatives lead poll 2-6, 115G3
Callaghan backs Scottish, Welsh devolutn 2-12, 2-21, 135G1
Callaghan backs fall electn 2-26, 154F1
Scottish, Welsh devolutn set back in vote 3-1, 168F3
Conservatives win Knutsford, Clitheroe by-electns 3-1, 169A2
MP bribery chrgd 3-21, 213F1
Labor backs delayed Scottish, Welsh home rule actn 3-22, 228F1
Labor loses confidence vote 3-28, May electns set 3-29, 228C1
Tory MP slain 3-30, 254E1
Labor issues electn manifesto 4-6, Tories issue 4-11, 267D3-268B1
Liberals stress electn reform 4-10, 285G2
Natl Front protest spurs violence 4-23, 313A1
Conservatives win electn 5-3; Callaghan resigns, Thatcher apptd prime min 5-4; Cabt named 5-5; forgn reactn 5-4, 5-5, 337A1-338C2
Thatcher photo, facts on 338A1, D2
Callaghan reelctd Labor head 5-9, 359F1
Tory programs outlined, Callaghan scores 5-15, 358D2-359E1
Eur Parlt electns held 6-7, 433A1, B2
Thorpe, 3 others acquitted 6-22, 485D3-486C1
Min, MP salaries hiked 7-6, 543G2
Liberals protest EC Parlt exclusn 7-18, 537A3

Gibraltar—See GIBRALTAR
Government & Politics—See also other appropriate subheads in this section
Labor rpt on Trotskyist penetratn debated 1-7—1-17, 58G2; publicatn barred 1-23, 79C2
'Quango' paring announced 1-16, 79E2
Labor censure vote defeated 2-28, 172G1
Tories win Southend by-electn 3-13, 212D1
Lords reject school transport chrgs 3-13; govt statemt 3-18, 254G2
Labor wins local electns 5-1, 352B1
Labor outlines progrm, asks Lords' abolitn 5-31, 429C2
Thatcher wins no-confidence vote 7-29, 578C1-B2
Citizenship plan proposed 7-30, 604D1
Liberals meet; Steel addresses, woos Labor dissidents 9-12, 708G1
Labor Party conf, Lords' abolitn urged 9-29—10-3, 768D1-769A1
Tories meet; policies affirmed 10-7—10-10, 790D2
Callaghan quits as Labor ldr 10-15, 790F3
Foot chosen Labor ldr 11-10, 872B2
Queen opens Parlt, charts govt programs 11-20, 900E3-901F1
Williams bars Labor candidacy, scores left 11-28, 921E3-922B1
Labor electn shadow Cabt 12-4, 942C2

1976

Home-rule changes rptd 5-25, 418F1
No-confidence motion loses 6-9, 458D1
Liberals name head 7-7, 521F2
Judicial Com backs special schools 8-2, 572F3
Stonehouse, secy sentncd 8-6, 589A1
Stonehouse quits Parlt 8-27, 676A1
Callaghan reshuffles Cabt 9-10, 693C3
Labor conf 9-27—10-1; EC electns opposed 9-29, 791F2
Heath, Thatcher address Tories 10-6, 10-8, 791D3
Foot elected Labor dep ldr 10-21, 853A2
Labor loses by-electns 11-4, 853D1
Govt wins 3 key votes 11-8, loses 2 11-10, 852F3
Moderate Laborites assail leftists 11-16, etiquette studies voted 11-17, 11-18, 906B1
Left wing oppositn grows 11-17, 889F2
Thatcher chngs shadow Cabt 11-19, 1004G1 ★
Tories vs devolutn bill 12-9, 1004D1
Devolutn bill OKd, referendum set 12-16, 1004C1
Prentice quits as overseas min, Judd named 12-21, 1004F1

Iceland Relations—*See 'Fishing Issues' under ICELAND*

Latin American Relations—*See also 'Foreign Economic Developments' above; for Argentina Falkland dispute, see FALKLAND Islands*
MD torture chrg backed 1-1, Chile denies 1-5, 8C2
'75 Jamaica gun ct ruling cited 51A1
Mex drug agents rptd trained 1-2, 61E1
Writ filed for Argentina prisoners 1-12, 26A2
MD testifies on Chile torture 1-19, 47G1
Chile leftist linked to MD arrest 1-24, 100B1
Argentina actn on prisoners urged 2-27, 220F2
Argentina frees couple 4-8; police scored 4-11, 264A2
Argentina refugee asylum rptd 7-19, 571F2
Belize independnc talks continue 9-21—9-22, 977E3
Cuba contact ordrd ousted 11-17, 946E2
Venez pres visits 11-21—11-24, 929D3

Middle East—*See also INTERNATIONAL Developments under MIDDLE EAST*
Lebanon interventn plea rptd 2-2, 83F1
To quit last bases 7-1, 594F2

1977

Liberals back Labor pact 9-28, 745A1
Labor Party conf 10-4—10-6, 863F2
Conservative Party conf 10-11—10-14, 863D3
Thorpe scandal revived 10-19—10-27, Steel welcomes probe 10-20, 883G1
Thatcher shifts oppositn spokesmen 11-4, 883B3
Scot, Wales home rule motion passes Commons 11-16, 903D2
Scot devolutn bill intro defeated 11-22, Liberal support falters 11-23, 1013A2
EC proportional representatn defeated 12-13, Liberal defectn averted 12-15, 1013C2

Helsinki Agreement—*See EUROPE—Security and Cooperation*

Irish Relations—*See also NORTHERN Ireland, subheads 'Anglo-Irish' and 'Unrest'*
Irish dispute Rockall oil rights 2-3, arbitratn set 2-17, 329B2

Latin American Relations—*See also FALKLAND Islands*
Peru ship sales, Chile arms embargo cited 1-10, 2B3
Jamaica to natlize radio statn 1-19, Barclays unit 3-23, 257A2, D2
Brazil A-safeguards rptd asked 3-11, 190F1
'66-75 arms transfers table 4-8, 415A3, C3
Guatemala aid re Belize pact seen 7-6—7-9, 553A2
Bolivia loan cancelled 8-9, 902B2
Peru police questn newsman 9-6, 784E2
Trinidad gets Euro$ loan 9-19, 905F3
Chile-Argentina Beagle Channel setlmt cited 11-4, 944C3
Lloyds Bank heads Mex loan group 11-18, 967C1

Medicine & Health
Viral gene sequence completed 2-24, 184C1
Scot hosp drug deaths rptd 2-28, 224E2
Ulcer drug gets US OK 8-23, 748E2
BMA backs Maltese MDs 9-9, 925C3
Vane gets Lasker Award 11-16, 927B3

Middle East Relations
MPs vs Daoud release, Govt bars actn 1-13, 28A1
UN abstentn on Israel occupatn abuses 2-15, 107E2
N Yemen ex-premr slain 4-10, 284D3
Egypt intl consortium aid set 5-11—5-12, 390C3
Leb gunman hijacks jet 6-29, 535B2
Palestinian hijackers free 3 Britons 7-10, 535C1
UN abstentn on Israel occupatn 11-25, 910D2
Israeli premr visits 12-2—12-7, 930C3
Newsman found slain in Egypt 12-7, 1019D1
Saudis boycott ships 12-10, 955D1

1978

Thorpe faces 2d murder chrg 9-2, 688B2
Callaghan delays gen electn; Thatcher, Steel score 9-7; Healey defends decisn 9-8, 704D3
Labor Party conf 10-2—10-6, 763B1
Major secrets chrgs vs 3 dropped 10-23, 838A3; convicted, sentncs suspended 11-17, 924E1
Labor wins 2 by-electns 10-26, 867C1
Poll on Callaghan, party performance rptd 10-28, 867E1
Labor legis progrm outlined; Scot, Wales actn vowed 11-1, 838D1
Callaghan wins legis confidence vote 11-9, 866F3
Thorpe pretrial hearings 11-20—12-4, 944G3-945C2
Thorpe trial ordered 12-13, 987D3
Callaghan wins confidence vote 12-14, 964E2

Helsinki Agreement—*See EUROPE—Security and Cooperation*
Hong Kong—*See HONG Kong*

Immigration
Thatcher urges immigratn cutoff 1-30; Parlt scores, '77 total rptd 1-31, 90D1
Heath warns vs entry bar 2-13, 167D3 ★
Tory policy linked to by-electn win 3-2—3-6, 167E2, B3

Irish Relations—*See NORTHERN Ireland, subheads 'Anglo-Irish Relations' and 'Unrest'*

Latin American Relations
Argentina, Chile dispute Beagle Channel islands ownership 1-6—2-10; map 101A1, E1
El Salvador armored car sale canceled 1-19, 75A1
Chile UN rights abuse res backed 3-6, 210F1
Cuba role in Africa scored by Owen 4-5, reactn 4-7, 259C1
Guyana OKs constitutnl reform bill 4-10, 378C3
Chile pol exile arrives 4-15, 287F2
Guyana prime min visits 5-6, 354C2
Dutch parlt backs Brazil uranium sale 6-30, 575B1, D1
Bolivia vote fraud chrgd 7-12, 571F1
Dominica independence set 7-21, 573E3
DR Sen rejects Perez y Perez as mil attache 11-9, 881B1, D1; Perez retired 11-7, 989B3
Lloyds Bank execs kidnaped in El Salvador 12-1, release talks rptd 12-21, 986C3
El Salvador repressn scored 12-10, 987C1

Medicine & Health
Early pregnancy, breast cancer immunity study rptd 1-19, 334A1
Natl Health Svc '78-79 budget proposed 4-11, 267G2
Dialysis data rptd 4-27, 578A2
Labor narrowly wins confidence vote 6-14, 496A3
'Test-tube baby' born, reactn 7-25, 596D3
Smallpox death 9-11; lab virus destructn asked 10-27, eradicatn countdown continues 11-7, 927F1-D2
'Test-tube baby' born in India 10-3, 824E3
Thalidomide victim bears child 10-13, 948F3

Middle East Relations
2 Syrian emb aides slain 12-31-77, 3B2
Algeria pres visits Malta 1-3, 39C2
PLO aide slain 1-4, 3F1
Iran denies students harassed 1-30, 190F2
Sadat visits, seeks peace moves backing 2-9, 98D2
UN rights comm OKs res on Israel 2-14, 99B2
PLO raiders sought amb hostage 3-12, 175F2
Arab group arms pact cited 3-14, 237C1 ★
Leb asks anti-Israel actn 3-15, 174D3
Egypt protests Israel Leb invasn 3-15, 174F3
Saudis whip 2 workers 5-15; other natls rptd arrested, sentenced 6-15—6-21, 515E3
Egypt recalls journalists 5-26, 414F3
Rumania peace role lauded 6-14, 515C3
Leb Christn ldr asks end to Syrian attacks 7-2, 502G2
Leb pres asked to stay 7-6, 502B3
Iraqi ex-Premr Naif shot 7-9, dies 7-10, 522E2
Naif murder suspects held 7-12, 582A3
Saudi workers fired 7-17, 631A1
Iraq missn ousted, terror chrgd; Iraq ousts UK missn 7-27, 582F2
Iraq amb escapes murder 7-28; 2 held 8-2, 582G1, D2

1979

Mountbatten slain by IRA 8-27, 641A1; funeral held 9-5, 669A1
PO reform proposed 9-12, 687B1
57 quangos abolished 9-17, 730F1
Liberals hold conf 9-25–9-29, 792D1
Labor Party conf, leftists gain 10-1–10-5, 773D1-B3
Tories meet; Thatcher, Carrington backed 10-9–10-12, 791F2
Left to dominate Labor Party inquiry com 10-24, Callaghan scores 10-31, 11-2, 873E2-E3
Philby spy ring scandal reopened 10-28, 10-29, 873F3
Blunt revealed as spy ring member 11-15, controversy ensues 11-15–11-21; statemt issued 11-20, 908C2-909F1
Secrets legis rptd withdrawn 11-20, 909A1
Fitt quits SDLP 11-22, 928A1
Jenkins urges center coalitn, proportional representatn 11-22, 950A1
Churchill admits liaison 12-15; Thatcher backs MP re security 12-17, 994G2

Helsinki Agreement—*See EUROPE—Security and Cooperation*
Hong Kong—*See HONG Kong*

Immigration
Asian fiancee virginity tests ended 2-2, 96D3
Tories back new curbs 3-11, 268E1
Tory programs outlined 5-15, 359C1
Indochina refugee conf asked 6-18, 6-28, 473E2, 474A1
Indochina refugee admissns vowed at intl conf 7-20–7-21, 549D1
China curbs re Hong Kong sought 11-1, 854A2
New curbs proposed 11-14, 873F1-E2

Irish Relations—*See NORTHERN Ireland subheads 'Anglo-Irish Relations' and 'Unrest'*

Latin American Relations
At 4-natn Guadeloupe summit 1-5–1-6, 12D2
DR names Lluberes mil attache 1-12, 62D2
St Lucia gains independnc 2-21, 181A2
El Salvador FARN seek ransom 3-19, 234C3
Grenada rebel regime recognized 3-24, Commonwealth ties affirmed 3-25, 236A3
Nicaragua ties reduced 3-29, 255A2
Chile refugee relocatn rptd 5-7, 369B3
Lloyds Bank execs freed in El Salvador 7-2, 547G1
St Vincent independnc set 7-9, 568B3
Nicaragua bank operatns curbed 7-25, 574B1
Argentina amb exchng set 11-16, 906C2

Medicine & Health
Birmingham smallpox outbreak rpt released 1-3, 7A2
'Test-tube baby' born in Scotland 1-14, 79C2
Hosp admissns halted by strikes 2-2, 75G3
Health workers rejct pact 3-6, 211E2
Welsh black lung disease legis cited 3-28, 228A2
Health worker pay pact set 3-28, 3-29, 268E2
Labor backs more funding 4-6, 267D3
Thalidomide article censorship scored by Eur rights ct 4-26, 331A1
Tory programs outlined 5-15, 359C1
MD, dentist pay hikes OKd 6-5, 425D2
Test-tube baby marks 1st birthday 7-25, 656B2
Health offcls' revolt squelched 8-1, 582C2
Film stars' deaths tied to '53 US A-test 8-4, 630B1
Hounsfield wins Nobel 10-12, 858E1
Fscl '81 cuts planned 11-1, 855B2

Middle East Relations
Queen tours Arab states 2-12–3-2, 190A1
Iran oil cutoff impact assessed 2-20, 126A3
Iran halts trial of ex-premr 3-16, 199G1
PLO scores Israel-Egypt pact support 3-25, 222B2
Iran banks natlzd 6-7, compensatn vowed 6-10, 469A2; insurnc cos natlzd 6-25, 486E2
Iraq lifts business embargo, trade pact weighed; to review Briton's life sentnc 7-5, 583A2
Iran ousts 2 newsmen 8-21, 635A2
Israel tank use cited 8-28, 643C2
Libyans occupy London Emb 9-3, 688F2
Oman proposes Persian Gulf security aid 10-14–10-16, 804B2
Natls alerted in Iran 10-14, 814D3
Iran occupies emb, chrgs Bakhtiar asylum 11-5, 841G1
Iran oil export cut confirmd 11-8, 843G1
US ban on Iran oil backed 11-13, 861F1, F2
Iran sues US banks for assets freeze 11-30, 915A2
Iran assets freeze upheld 12-5, 915F1
US seeks econ sanctns vs Iran 12-10, 933C2
Churchill admits affair with Saudi arms dealer's ex-wife 12-15, 994A3

1980

Hong Kong—*See HONG Kong*

Irish Relations—*See NORTHERN Ireland--Anglo-Irish Relations*

Latin American Relations
Colombia residents kidnaped 1-5, 19D3
Chile relatns to be restored 1-16, 57G1
Bahamas prime min visits 5-10, 371F2
Cuba bars refugee talks 5-23, 397A1
Webster elected Anguillan prime min 5-28, 469E1
Chile detains UK natl 7-16—7-18, torture chrgs disputed 7-29, 8-6, 749E1
Chile arms embargo lifted 7-22, Amnesty Intl protests 9-8, 749E1
Journalist detained in Bolivia 8-6—8-12, 668D1
Colombia residents freed by guerrillas 8-10, 707D2
Nicaragua debt rescheduled 9-5, 689G2-A3
Nicaragua rioters linked 10-1; Anglican mins deportatns seen 10-2, 792G1
Uruguay arrests rptr 11-7, frees 1-10, 888B3
Cuba ex-offcl asks UN probe prison hunger strike 12-4, 965D2
Guyana electn observed 12-15, declared 'fraudulent' 12-19, 994A3

Medicine & Health
Nurses pay hiked 20% 1-4, 20F1
Schizophrenia, dopamine link rptd 1-10, 415E1
VD epidemic rptd, NGU rise blamed 2-5, 158A1, D1
Pro-abortn demonstratn held 2-8, 132F3-133B1
Spending hike planned 3-26, 232E2
Sneezing record rptd 4-29, 471D1
MD pay hike set 5-19, 389C3
Drug natlzn backed by Labor 5-31, 429E2

Middle East Relations
Iran warns newsmen 1-14, 29F2
Iran trade cut cited 1-16, 59E1
Iran chrgs newsmen took gifts from shah 2-9, 122B3
Persian Gulf stockpiling weighed 4-2, 274A2
Saudi ties strained by TV film, '79 trade cited 4-10, 4-11, 294B1
Libyan exiles killed 4-11, 4-25, 353A3
Iran sanctns vowed 4-14, 282C1
Iran oil purchase barred 4-22, 298F1
Saudis order UK amb to leave, weigh trade curbs 4-22; visits cancelled 4-25, 313C2-B3
Iran hostage kin seek support 4-23, 299D2
Iran hostage rescue missn backed 4-25, 324G1
Iran Arabs seize London Emb 4-30, Ghotbzadeh denounces 4-30, 5-1; deadlines pass 5-2, 324E2-C3
UN Palestinian state res abstentn 4-30, 325D1
Iran Arabs slay 2 London Emb hostages; UK commandos storm emb; 19 rescued, 5 killed 5-5, 337A1
Libya threatens oil cutoff 5-9, 373B3
4 Libyans ousted, 3 arrested 5-12, 373C3
Iran sanctns move reversed 5-19; EC, US deplore 5-20, 5-21, 378C2
Saudis bar US co contracts 5-21, 407B3
Saudi TV film regretted 5-22, 407B3

1976

1977

Monetary, Trade & Aid Issues (including all foreign economic developments)—*See also 'Atomic Energy' above*
200-mi fishing zone in effect 1-1, 20G3
IMF loan set 1-3, £ up 1-5, 7C3
Reserves fall, US loan repaymt cited 1-5, 7F3
'76 car imports rptd up 1-8, 45B1
Peru ship sales, Chile arms embargo cited 1-10, 2B3
Sterling balances pact set, £ up 1-10, 20B2-C3
Callaghan to supervise sterling balances 1-12, 44D2
ICFTU to boycott S Africa 1-13, 1-15, 29A2; boycott fails 1-21, 67A3
Dec '76 trade gap narrows, £ rises 1-18, 44G2
Swiss '76 currency interventn rptd 1-18, 84A2
Jamaica to natlize radio statn 1-19, Barclays unit 3-23, 257A2, D2
$1.5 bln intl bank loan rptd 1-24, 99G1
Bank of Amer group cancels IBEC loan 1-26, 123E2
Ct upholds S Africa boycott injunctn 1-27, 98F3
Denmark protests fishing limit 1-29, 115G2-A3
BAC rpts Concorde sales lag 2-1, 99E1
Irish dispute Rockall oil rights 2-3, arbitratn set 2-17, 329B2
IMF SDR defined 87G2
Sovt bloc Rhodesia sanctn violatns chrgd 2-10, 123A1
Sovt gas equipmt deal set 2-11, 134E3
Jan trade, paymts deficits rptd; £ falls 2-14, 134D2
Irish ban large fishing vessels 2-15, 146C3
NZ sets lamb-trading 2-22, 258E1
Bank of Calif takeover rejctd 3-1, 155A2
'76 forgn exchng mkt tensn rptd 3-2, 188D3
Callaghan sees Carter 3-10—3-11, 213B1
Tin price swing rptd 3-16—4-18; Bolivia sets pact ratificatn 3-29, 398D1, G1
IMF paymts debt managing role rptd, loan cited 3-28, 362F3, 363D1
US asks Portugal aid 4-1, 330C3
'66-75 Latin arms transfers table 4-8, 415A3, C3
At 7-natn econ summit 5-7—5-8, 357A1-358B2
Intl consortium OKs Egypt aid 5-11—5-12, 390C3
Leyland bribery chrgs stir controversy 5-19—5-25, Ryder retires 7-1, 526C1, D1 ★
Rhodesia sanctn breakers sued by Lonrho 5-31, 413C2
Turkey exports rptd barred 6-2, 451B2
BP admits overseas paymts 6-3, 526A2
Group of 10 membership cited 438F1
'76 Turkish Cypriot trade rptd 6-15, 467D1
London banking center rptd growing 6-21, 578B2
Australia trade data rptd 6-22, 504F2
In 11-natn Portugal loan 6-22, 530B3
IWC cuts whaling quotas 6-24, 496G3
Sears loses Avis bid 6-27, 519C2
Guatemala aid re Belize pact seen 7-6—7-9, 553A2
Zaire debt rescheduled 7-7, 583E1
Australia imposes car import quotas 7-12, 560F3
Channel boundary settled 7-18, 625C1
N Sea herring fishing banned 7-18, 771B3
Carter seeks arms sales curbs 7-28, 574A3
Somalia OKs arms aid 7-28, 608A2
'77 paymts deficit forecast 7-31, 586D2
Danes OK North Sea gas line 8-1, 672E1
Australia blames immigrants for econ problems 8-5; Tebbit refutes, cites UK export data 8-8, 632B3
US scores trust blocking laws 8-8, 630A1
Bolivia loan cancelled re miner abuse 8-9, 902B2
Sweden quits 'snake' 8-29, 708G3
Chase unit in Nigeria loan 9-1, 746C3
Somalia arms sale postponed 9-2, 684G2
£ closes at '77 high 9-7, 745C2

1978

Egypt debts canceled 7-31, 592D1
Leb army move to south urged 8-8, 638C3
Arabs attack El Al bus, 2 die 8-20; UK laxity chrgd 8-21, 638B1
Shah gets UK support 10-22, 827G3-828B1
Iran emb burned 11-5, 857F2

Monetary, Trade, Aid & Investment—*See also 'Atomic Energy' above*
Callaghan in Bangladesh, India, Pak talks on aid, trade; cites '77 India trade surplus 1-3—1-13, 37B1
US $ swap pact cited 1-4, 27B2
$ drop, recovery rptd 1-4, 27E3
Canada '75 investmt rptd 1-10, 70C3
'77 paymts surplus rptd 1-17, 132D1
El Salvador armored car sale canceled 1-19, 75A1
Finland '77 trade surplus rptd 1-30, 90C1
US rejcts gun for XM-1 tank 1-31, 82A1
Ethiopia protests Somalia aid 2-1, 100D1
Somalia makes 2d aid bid 2-4, 99G3
Polish ship order reassigned 2-5, 112B3
Japan bars auto export curbs; '77, Jan sales rptd 2-8, 112E2
US $ drops vs £, gold price up 2-23, 118D2
Guest takeover of W Ger firm halted 2-23, 211B1
Japan to curb car exports 3-3, 168A1
Unctad debt relief stand cited 3-11, 301D1
Callaghan urges Bonn summit plan 3-14, sees Carter 3-23, 226G2
Arab group arms pact cited 3-14, 237C1 ★
Nigeria withdraws Barclays funds in S Africa dispute 3-22; '76, '77 data cited 237A2
Midland Bank S Africa loan policy rptd 3-25, 237C2
£ rises vs US $ 4-3, 235C1
£ in new SDR basket 4-3, 300F3
Pan Am buys Rolls-Royce engines 4-4, 264F2
Hong Kong-based bank to buy US bank 4-5, 263E1-A2
London optns sales suspended 4-5, 283B1
BOC bid to buy Airco OKd 4-7, 403D3
IMF loan repaymt, money supply measures budgeted 4-11, 267F2
ICAO picks US bad-weather landing system 4-19, 319B2-C3
BAT Industries plans NCR purchase 5-5, 345B3
IMF budget limit threatened by tax votes 5-8, 5-10, 415B2
NatWest to buy US bank 5-12, 364F1
Zambia econ aid increased 5-15, 395D2
Tenneco offers Albright & Wilson purchase 5-23, 404F1
US '77 thoroughbred import ban cited 539E2
Tanzania expels Lonrho 6-2, 479B2
Standard Chartered to buy Calif bank 6-8, 553B1
Zaire aid OKd 6-13—6-14, 478A1
Rumania pres visits 6-13—6-16, jet deal signed 6-15, 515F2
Rumania '77 trade rptd 6-15, 515B3
US Sen ratifies tax pact 6-27, 588E2
Zambia loan cited 6-29, 617A2
US $ down vs £ 7-14, 523C3
At 7-natn Bonn econ summit 7-16—7-17, 543C3, 544C2, G2
US arms sales policy assessed 7-16, 564B2
Gold price passes $200 7-28, hits record high 9-25, 732F2
17 poor natns debts canceled 7-31, 592C1
Offshore oil tax hiked, new sites offered 8-2, 591G3
Chrysler to sell UK unit to Peugeot, Varley miffed; '76, '77 losses, '78 Linwood walkout cited 8-10, 623C2-B3
£ tops $2 mark 8-15, 622F1
Japan co sets joint plant 8-23, 667C3
Brit Airways orders Boeing 757s, Airbus Industrie scores 8-31, 684A2
Rhodesia oil-sanctions violatn study released 8-31, 9-19; UK, Zambia reactn 9-2—9-28, 755G3-756G3
Australia blocks Brooke Bond tea co takeover 9-7, decisn analyzed 9-29, 754F2
Chrysler sale to Peugeot OKd 9-28, 764D1

1979

Thatcher backs Carter re Iran crisis 12-17, 968G1

Monetary, Trade, Aid & Investment—*See also 'Atomic' and 'Energy' above*
Asian oppositn to Australia air policy rptd 1-5, 6C1
China jet, indl pkg revealed; W Ger warning cited 1-5, 12B3
Poland econ to be monitored by bank 1-11, 59F3, G3
Portugal sets farm seizure compensatn 1-11, 212E3
Guadeloupe summit aid offer to Turkey rptd 1-12, 40B2
Forgn dvpt aid rise slated 1-17, 59A3
Spain OKs 2 banks 1-26, 100F3
EC comm backs farm price freeze 1-31, 85G1
Finland '78 trade rptd 2-2, 215G2
Credit Lyonnais employe chrgd 2-5, 96F2
Turkey aid role OKd by OECD 2-7, 116E3
£ falls vs US $ 2-8, 83C2
Imperial Chem Australia unit plans petrochem expansn 2-8, 94C3
Channel tunnel planned 2-9, 135A3
Carter Westn econ summit warning to Japan rptd 2-10, rpt disputed 2-15, 160F1
Vauxhall Motors '78 profit rptd 2-16, 135G2
Portugal agri min visits, aid sought; '78 credits cited 2-20, 212E3
Deutsche BP-Veba deal OKd 3-5, 214F3
EC farm accord rejctd 3-6, France scores 3-7, 160D3
Stocks rise, Labor confidence-vote defeat linked 3-29, 228D2
Poland loan signed 3-30, 279G2
Ireland ends £ parity re EMS 3-30, 268E3-269A1
S Africa '72-78 loans rptd 4-2, 270D2
IMF loan repaymt rptd 4-3, 268G1
Tories back tight money supply control 4-11, 268D1
Tories set Africa policy 4-11, 285C3
Uniroyal operatns sale set 4-17, 560G3
NY gov urges N Ireland role 4-22, 312B3
£ falls vs US $, campaign cited 5-1, 321B1
W Ger ranks exporter labor costs 5-1, 374C2
Tories weigh EMS role 5-15, 358A3
BL-Honda productn planned 5-17, 388B2
Uganda trade rptd 5-28, 429C2
Barclays purchase of Amer Credit OKd 5-29, 440B3
US oil import subsidy scored 6-2, 417B2
Iran banks natlzd 6-7, compensatn vowed 6-10, 469A2
Forgn exchng controls eased 6-12, 445A3
EC farm prices hiked 6-21, 513F1
Iran insurnc cos natlzd 6-25, 486E2
Denmark files Unilever trust chrgs 7-2, 563G3
£ above $2.20 7-3, 503C1
Iraq trade pact weighed 7-5, 583B2
Midland Bank to buy Walter Heller Corp 7-6, 682B3
Intl Whaling Comm conf 7-11, 554B2
EC Parlt agri com chrmnship assured 7-17, 537E2
Brit Airways share sales set 7-20, 564F3
Nicaragua bank operatns curbed 7-25, 574B1
BP to join Australia mining project 7-31, 580G2
French knitwear import curbs protested 8-20, 668E3
Israel tank use cited 8-28, 643C2
USSR bars book entry 9-4, 690E1
EC '80 budget contributn seen tripled 9-4, scores 9-17, 719G1
Exports, £ strength linked 9-10, 686G2
Imperial Group to buy Howard Johnson 9-10, Calif bar seen 10-12, 924B3-E3
EC draft budget cuts aid 9-12, 719E1
Zimbabwe econ sanctns cited re talks 9-16, 718C1
Australia OKs BP mining projct 10-9, 811A1

1980

Iran sanctns modified further 5-29, 393E1
UN Res 242 chng to aid Palestinians asked 5-31, 418B1
Libya envoy threatens exiles 6-12, expelled 6-13, 463F2
Iran gold withdrawn, forgn exchng holdings ordrd returned 6-17, 464A3, C3
3 TV rptrs flee Iran 7-25, 572B1
Jewish youth killed in Belgium blast 7-27, Palestinian seized 7-28, 573D2
Saudi ties restored 7-28, 578A3
Egypt envoy at shah's funeral 7-29, 571G1
UN Palestinian state res abstentn 7-29, 572F1
Iranians demonstrate in London 8-4, police brutality chrgd 8-9, 635B2
Iran arrests 3 missionaries 8-8, 8-9, 671C3
Iran emb closed 8-17, 634D1
Iran scores student detentns 9-4, 671A3
Iran emb aides withdrawn, arrested Iranians deported 9-9, 689C1
Iran-Iraq war prompts OPEC to drop planned 10% cut 9-26, 735B1
Iraq use of Oman in Iran war rptd blocked 10-3, 758F1
Iraq, Iran arms rejctd 11-4; Iraq arms missn rptd 11-11—11-12, 879A3
Parsons ask Iran-Iraq war end 11-5, 894C3
Iran ends forgn press ban 11-15, 879E3

Monetary, Trade, Aid & Investment
Gold prices soar above $800 1-2—1-18, round-the-clock trading rptd 1-7, 30F1-E3
Futures contracts detailed 1-2, 94D3
US OKs FX jet for export 1-4, 16D3
USSR trade sanctns favored 1-10, 28A1
Thomson buys FP publicatns 1-11, 38G1
'79 current acct deficit rptd 1-16, 59E1
Eur deposits in US banks rptd down 1-18, 48A2
Australia stocks make gains 1-18, 56C1
Sovt credit curbs set 1-26, 67C3
US fiber import curbs sought 2-5, 2-7, 125E1
'79 US mfg investmt rptd 2-6, 92C3
Anglo-Amer buys Consolidated Gold 2-12, 398A3
French lamb dispute continues 2-14—2-20, 125A1
Gold price closings 2-18—3-20; prices plummet below $478 3-17, trading erratic 3-18—3-19, 2-18—3-20, 202A3, 203A1
Turkey aid sought 2-19, 135D3
French wine fraud disclosed 3-6, 193B2
US Steel files dumping complaint 3-21, 225D1
Money supply growth goals rptd 3-26, 232D1
IMF hikes SDR interest rate 3-27, 302B2
NY Insurnc Exchng opens; Lloyd's financial losses, liability cited 3-31, 266A1
'79 US investmt rptd 4-8, 329C1
US sets steel import probe 4-10, 367F3
Saudi '79 trade cited, strained ties seen 4-11, 294G1
Iran sanctns vowed 4-14, 282C1
W Eur fighter jet planned 4-14, 303E1
BL in Europn auto research effort 4-14, 303B3
Marsh & McLennan to buy Bowring 4-14, 386B1
Zimbabwe sanctns violators amnestied 4-15, 301B3
Australia to end tariff breaks 4-16, 309D3
Iran oil purchase barred, US support cited 4-22, 298F1
Saudis weigh trade curbs 4-22, 313E2
EC budget, farm price impasses continue 4-27—4-30, 327B1-B2
W Ger EC funding hike unlikely 4-30, 355G3
Lazard Freres compensatn for MacGregor set 5-1, 352F1
US finds steel import damage 5-1, 456C1
Quebec buys Turner & Newall asbestos units 5-8, 371D3
Libya threatens oil cutoff 5-9, 373B3
Grand Met raises Liggett merger bid, Standard Brands quits 5-14; bid accepted 5-16, 557A3
Iran sanctns move reversed 5-19; EC, US deplore 5-20, 5-21, 378F1-E2
Saudis bar US co contracts 5-21, 407B3
US OKs pound futures trading 5-28, 481C2
Iran sanctns modified further 5-29, 393E1
EC budget, French lamb dispute resolved 5-29—5-30; Thatcher OKs, Labor Party scores 6-2, 421C2
Import curbs backed by Labor 5-31, 429E2
US cruise missile shipmt set for '83 6-3, 450A3
Thatcher stresses strong pound 6-6, 444G3
Iran gold withdrawn, forgn exchng holdings ordrd returned 6-17, 464A3, C3
Imperial Group completes Howard Johnson deal 6-17, 557C3
7-natn Venice summit 6-22—6-23, 473A1-474E1
Vauxhall rpts '79 loss 7-1, 498F1
BP unit buys Rhone-Poulenc share 7-9, 522C2, D2
Eur Parlt OKs EC budget 7-9, 548G1
US Trident acquisitns set 7-15, 544A2
Midland Bank sets Crocker takeover 7-15, 557G1
Chile arms embargo lifted 7-22, Amnesty Intl protests 9-8, 749E1
Exxon, Shell cut gasoline prices 8-11, 628G1

1976

Northern Ireland—*See NORTHERN Ireland*

Obituaries

Baddeley, Angela 2-22, 192C3
Bradwell, Baron 8-12, 892G2
Britten, Benjamin 12-4, 970C1
Buchan, Alstair 2-4, 124D3
Christie, Agatha 1-12, 56B3
Davies, Rupert 11-22, 970E1
Evans, Dame Edith 10-14, 970G1
Feather, Victor 7-28, 716A3
Gubbins, Colin Mcvean 2-11, 160D3
Haddow, Alexander 1-21, 80D3
Hughes, Richard 4-28, 368F2
Laurence, Lowry 2-23, 192E3
Leighton, Margaret 1-13, 56E3
MacInnes, Colin 4-22, 524A3
Miller, Ruby 4-2, 524C3
Monnington, Thomas 1-7, 56F3
Montgomery, Field Marshal 3-24, 240E3
O'Malley, Brian 4-6, 267C1
Radziwill, Stanislas 6-27, 524D3
Reed, Sir Carol 4-25, 368A3
Sansom, William 4-20, 524E3
Sim, Alastair 8-20, 892F3
Thomas, James 1-23, 80G3
Thomson of Fleet, Lord 8-4, 816G3
Thorndike, Dame Sybil 6-9, 444G2
Wheeler, Mortimer 7-22, 716G3

Sports

Winter Olympics results 2-4—2-15, 159A1, B2
Wimbledon results 7-2, 7-3, 504E1
Brit Open results 7-10, 716E2
Queen opens Summer Olympics 7-16, 528E2
Summer Olympic results 7-18—7-31, 562D3, 573D3, 574B1, 575A1-F2, 576A1, F3
Brit hardct results 8-31, 716C2
Chess olympiad results 11-10, 969B3

1977

Australia min clarifies immigrant chrgs 9-12, 762A3; scores immigrants again 10-9, 880A3
Uganda exiles ask UK trade boycott 9-12, 805G1
Trinidad gets large Euro$ loan 9-19, 905F3
S Africa sanctns feared 9-20; investmts, exports rptd 9-23, 771D1
USSR ousts Barents trawlers 9-24, curbs fishing 9-27, 771F2
IMF-World Bank mtgs see econ recovery effort 9-26—9-30, 753D3
France rejcts Channel boundary chng 9-29, UK appeals 10-12, 772F1-B2
'76 car exports cited 10-11, 853A3
Steel dumping chrgd by US co 10-20, 836E3
£ floated 10-31; inflatn fears cited 11-1; Oct forgn funds inflow rptd up 11-2, 829G1
US Sup Ct declines '74 commodity law challenge 11-7, 857F1
TVA sues uranium producers 11-18, 895F1
Lloyds Bank heads Mex loan group 11-18, 967C1
Australia livestock banned 11-23, 922G3
Nigeria arms purchases cited 11-23, 986A3
'77 £ rise vs $ rptd 11-30, 932E3
Westinghouse denied Rio Tinto evidence 12-1, 1003C3
US Armco chrgs steel dumping 12-5, 932C1, 933A3
$ closes up vs £ 12-8, 933C1
Heath at Brandt comm mtg 12-9—12-11, 997F3
Saudis boycott ships 12-10, 955D1
Unilever plans Natl Starch takeover 12-11, 1004C2
French indl cooperatn set 12-13, 1013G1
$ drops, '77 £ gain cited 12-30, 997F2

Northern Ireland—*See under 'N'*

Obituaries

Adrian, Edgar Douglas 8-4, 696B2
Baden-Powell, Olave 6-25, 532E2
Biggs, E Power 3-10, 264D2
Bolan, Marc 9-16, 787G3
Cabot, Sebastian 8-23, 696E2
Cobham, Viscount 3-20, 264E2
Cochrane, Ralph 12-17, 1024C1
Crosland, Anthony 2-19, 164E2
Eden, Anthony 1-14, 84G2
Embry, Basil Edward 12-8, 1024E1
Finch, Peter 1-14, 84A3
Godfrey, Isidore 9-12, 872A2
Litvinov, Ivy 4-28, 356C3
Marlborough, Duchess of 10-23, 872E2
Masterman, John 6-6, 532D3
Miller, Eric 9-22, 788G1
Moran, Lord 4-12, 356E3
Nash, John 9-23, 788B2
Petrie, Charles 12-13, 1024G2
Radcliffe, Viscount 4-2, 356G3
Rattigan, Terence 11-30, 952B3
Rootes, Reginald 12-20, 1024A3
Schumacher, E F 9-4, 788D2
Sharp, John 1-15, 84E3
Shipton, Eric 3-28, 264F3
Spencer-Churchill, Clementine 12-12, 1024D3
Wheatley, Dennis 11-11, 952G3
Wilcox, Herbert 5-15, 452F3
Woodham-Smith, Cecil 3-16, 264G3

Sports

Wimbledon results 7-1—7-2, 548D1
US wins Walker Cup 8-27, Ryder Cup 9-27, 951F1, A2
Nastase barred from '78 Davis Cup 10-3, 1020B3

1978

India to buy Anglo-French Jaguars 10-6, 10-7, 796G3-797B1
Australia air fare cut set 10-11, 793A3
Rhodesia sanctns violatn denial chngd by BP 10-22, 838E2
France OKs Airbus role 10-24, 902A3
USSR warns vs China arms sales 10-26, 814C1
US $ drops 10-30; rescue plan set, $ recovers 11-1, 825B1, E2, 826A1
IMF repaymt made 10-30, 838D3
Bank regulatn cited in govt progrm 11-1, 838C2
Dominica aid grants cited 11-2, 861C3
US OKs tech, arms sales to China 11-7, 11-9, 901F3, G3
Canada-S Africa arms deal rptd probed 11-7, 904F2
Banks dropped from '77 world top 10 list, £ devaluatn linked 11-8, 914C1
Bank lending rate hiked to 12.5% 11-9, 882D2
Zambia to hike arms outlay 11-20, 912D1
Ford sanctns imposed 11-28, 923G2
Natwest sets Nigeria loan 11-30, 934G1
At Brussels monetary summit 12-4—12-5, EMS entry barred 12-5, 951B3, F3
NATO sets Nimrod planes purchase 12-5—12-6, 954C2
Australia top-investors ranked 12-13, 985C2
Ireland to join EMS 12-15, 979D1, G1
Rhodesia oil sanctn violatns probe urged by Callaghan 12-15, 987A3
N Sea oil seen as OPEC price hike hedge 12-18, 978E1
Scandinavia air pacts OKd 12-22, 1017F1
US probes steel dumping chrgs 12-28, 1006B1
US $ closes down vs £ 12-29, 998E2
France delays EMS start 12-29, 999C1

Northern Ireland—*See NORTHERN Ireland*

Obituaries

Compton, Fay 12-12, 1032D2
Corden-Lloyd, Ian 2-17, 132G2
Denny, Sandy 4-21, 356E2
Docker, Bernard 5-23, 440E2
Dupont, Clifford W 6-28, 540E2
Fabian, Robert 6-14, 540F2
Foot, Dingle 6-18, 540F2
Genn, Leo 1-26, 96B2
Grant, Duncan 5-10, 440F2
Harrod, Roy 3-8, 252A3
Highet, Gilbert 1-20, 96C2
Leavis, Frank Raymond 4-14, 356B3
Mallowan, Max 8-19, 708B3
Messel, Oliver 7-13, 620B3
Miller, Millie (rptd) 3-2, 167E2
Moon, Keith 9-7, 778F1
Moore, Henry 3-12, 252B3
Noble, Ray 4-3, 356C3
Norrish, Ronald George 6-7, 540D3
Roberts, Gilbert 1-1, 96D3
Rothermere, Viscount 7-12, 620F3
Scott, Paul 3-1, 252E3
Selwyn-Lloyd, Lord 5-17, 440E3
Shaw, Robert 8-28, 708D3
Strang, Lord 5-27, 440F3
Sylvester, Victor 8-14, 708E3
Tweedsmuir, Baroness 3-11, 252E3
Utely, Freda 1-21, 96F3
Whitehead, Edward 4-16, 356F3

Rhodesian Relations—*See RHODESIA*

Solomon Islands—*See SOLOMON Islands*

Sports

US battles equine VD 3-15—7-13, 539E2
World Cup soccer finals 6-1—6-25, Scottish player suspended 6-5, 519F3, 520B3
Shirley Hgts wins English Derby 6-7, 539A2
James sails solo around world 6-8, 653D2
Wimbledon results 7-7, 7-8, 539E3-540C1
British Open results 7-15, 580B2
FIFA to ban Best 10-10, 969D2

1979

Oman proposes Persian Gulf security aid 10-14—10-16, 804B2
Forgn exchng controls ended, £ drops 10-23, 813A3
Zimbabwe sanctns end, Muzorewa OK of transitn plan linked 10-27, 844A2
Trust bill proposed, US legis targeted 10-31, 855C3
China jet sales seen 11-1, 854G1
Fscl '81 aid cuts planned 11-1, 855C2
French lamb dispute progress rptd 11-14, 873B1
Zimbabwe '65 sanctn law lapses 11-14, 881G1
Tobacco export gains rptd 11-22, 970A3
Iran sues US banks for assets freeze 11-30, 915A2
Iran assets freeze upheld 12-5, 915F1
US seeks econ sanctns vs Iran 12-10, 933C2
Zimbabwe sanctns ended 12-12, 960E1
EC '80 budget rejected 12-13, 960A3
Zimbabwe oil sanctns violatn probe ended 12-19, 976D3
BL-Honda accord signed 12-27, 994E1
US $ closes down vs £ 12-31, 978F3

Obituaries

Ardizzone, Edward Jeffrey Irving 11-8, 932B2
Bolton, Guy R 9-5, 756A2
Brodie, Israel 2-13, 176F2
Chain, Ernst B 8-12, 671A2
Clore, Charles 7-26, 588E2
Draper, Christopher 1-16, 104G2
Fields, Gracie 9-27, 756D2
Gabor, Dennis 2-8, 176A3
Grenfell, Joyce 11-30, 932G2
Grosvenor, Robert George 2-19, 176B3
Hartnell, Norman 6-8, 508B3
Hayward, Max 3-18, 272F2
Leach, Bernard 5-6, 432B3
Maudling, Reginald 2-14, 176C3
Monsarrat, Nicholas 8-7, 671A3
Mountbatten, Lord 8-27, 641A1
Rhys, Jean 5-14, 432E3
Richards, I A 9-7, 756D3
Saville, Victor 5-8, 432F3
Templer, Gerald Walter 10-25, 860F3
Vicious, Sid 2-2, 156B3
Wallis, Barnes Neville 11-12, 932G3
Wilding, Michael 7-8, 588F3
Woodcock, George 10-30, 860G3

Sports

World figure-skating competitn 3-15, 391F3
Soccer cup results 3-17, 5-1, 5-30, 776F2, A3
Best suspensn lifted 3-28, 655C2
Soccer teams cleared in drug probe 3-28, 655D2
Grand Natl steeplechase 3-31, English Derby 6-6, 448A3
WBC lightwgt title bout 4-17, 412F3
US wins Walker Cup 5-31, 587A3
Amer pedals aircraft across Eng Channel 6-12, 527F3

1980

US urges Poland aid 8-29, strike funds rptd 8-31, 659C1, B3
Nicaragua debt rescheduled 9-5, 689G2-A3
IMF revises SDR valuatn method, pound gains in currency 'basket' 9-17, 695E1
EC sets sheepmeat policy 9-30, claim vs France dropped 10-1, 737E2
Sovt barley sales opposed 10-23, 832D3
GM, Ford units rpt losses 10-31, 11-6, 886G2
Money supply rptd high 11-4, 859C2; growth curb seen 11-24, 901G1
Norway orders fishing halt 12-10, 969C3
Pound remains strong vs US $ 12-10, 932G1; up 7% in '80 12-31 983F2, A3

Northern Ireland—*See NORTHERN Ireland*

Obituaries

Ballantrae, Baron 11-28, 928B2
Beaton, Cecil 1-18, 104F1
Bullard, Edward 4-3, 360C1
Butlin, Billy 6-12, 528D1
Collier, John 4-6, 360D1
Dimitri, Prince 7-7, 608F1
Gardiner, Reginald 7-7, 608F1
Gordon-Walker, Patrick 12-2, 1004A2
Griffith, Hugh 5-14, 448F1
Hitchcock, Alfred 4-29, 360A2
Lennon, John 12-8, 933D2
Mercer, David 8-8, 676C2
Mosley, Oswald 12-2, 1004A3
Owens, Johnny 11-3, 907A3
Roberts, Rachel 11-26, 928D3
Sellers, Peter 7-24, 608B3
Shelley, Norman 8-22, 676A3
Snow, C P 7-1, 608D3
Summerskill, Edith 2-4, 176E3
Sutherland, Graham 2-18, 176F3
Thomas, Lord 2-8, 176F3
Travers, Ben 12-18, 1004D3
Wyndham-White, Eric 1-27, 104G3

Soviet-Afghan Issue

Sovts chrg Afghan rebel training 1-1, 1D2
Gromyko visit canceled 1-5, 2D2
USSR trade sanctns backed 1-10, 28A1
Navy ships shifted to Medit 1-14, 46A2
Carrington in Pak, India 1-16, 27E1, A2
USSR Olympics shift sought 1-17, US move backed 1-21, 45A3; boycott sympathy noted 1-18, 28C3
Olympic site offered 1-22, 68C1
Sovt invasn protest moves set 1-26, 67B3
US rpt on Persian Gulf defns issued 2-1, 84C2
US support cited 2-5, 125A2
France bars US-Eur mtg 2-8, 106E2
Afghan neutrality plan offered 2-19, 123G3
Vance sees Carrington, seeks policy coordinatn 2-21, 139C2
Afghan subversn chrgd 2-22, 138F2
USSR gets neutrality plan, US backs 2-28; USSR, China score 3-2, 165B1
USSR vs Afghan neutrality plan 3-11, 3-14, 205A1
Rumania in joint Sovt criticism 3-14, 205G1
Olympic com OKs participatn 3-25, 259E2
Defns white paper issued 4-2, 274A2
Europn CPs meet 4-28—4-29, 327A3
USSR May Day parade shunned 5-1, 354G2
US backed vs Afghan plan on Sovt troop exit 5-15, 362C1
Indep Olympic boycott spreads 5-17, 379E2
Franco-Sovt summit reactn 5-19, 378C3, 379A1
Sovt invasn scored by Labor, exit asked 5-31, 429F2
Olympic flag controversy 7-19, 588D1
Afghan wrestler denies defectn plan 7-21, 590B2
EC barley sales to resume 10-23, 832D1

Sports

Thatcher to seek Moscow Summer Olympic shift 1-17, backs Carter move 1-21, 45A3; boycott sympathy noted 1-18, 28C3
Summer Olympic site offered 1-22, 68C1
Cousins wins Eur figure skating title 1-24, 470F2
Lake Placid Winter Olympic results 2-12—2-24, 154F2, 155F2-156D1
Wolverhampton wins English League Cup 3-15, 771E3
Minter wins world middlewgt title 3-16, 320B2

1976

UN Policy & Developments
Cncl member 62F2; 720C1
Rpt Belize seeks independnc guarantee 1-8, 55B2
Abstains on Cncl PLO seating 1-12, 18B1
UK MD testifies on Chile torture 1-19, 47G1
Mideast amendmt rejctd, abstains on pro-Palestine resolutn 1-26, 59G2, C3
Abstains on rights comm resolutn vs Israel 2-13, 125E2
Israel protests Cncl occupatn vote 3-27, 227C3
Backs Cncl role in Leb 3-30, 226D2
Abstains on Cncl S Africa censure 3-31, 228B2
Vs UN rights stand 4-30, 320D3
Vs WHO anti-Israel stand 5-19, 355D2
UNCTAD OKs commodity fund 5-30, 388G2
WHO rpts no swine flu 6-3, 423F3
Abstains on Israel Arab land exit 6-29, 464C1
Cncl vs anti-terror resolutn 7-14, 515F3
Asks Greek-Turk talks on Aegean 8-25, 643F2
IAEA pact signed 9-6, 936A2
Vetoes S Africa arms ban 10-19, 781D3
Abstains on PLO in Cncl debate 11-1, 842F1
Asked to bar aid to S Africa 11-5, 842B3
Sovt scores on press plan 11-25, 896A1
Helps soften UNDOF res 11-30, 895B2
Vs black Namibia support 12-20, 955C1
U.S. Relations—*See also 'Foreign Economic Developments' above; also 'Majority Rule Issue' under RHODESIA*
Natl Airlines Svc resumes 1-6, 5B2
CIA agents named 1-15, 1-22, 50B1
Seychelles independence set 1-22, 270G3
Armstrong confrmd US amb 1-27, 68B1
US denies Angola recruitmt rpt 2-2, 82E1
US rpts covert Angola aid 3-9, 228D3
US Cong clears Magna Carta trip 4-5, 283G2
Kissinger visits 4-23—4-24, 293G2
Pope-Hennessey gets Met Museum post 5-25, 504D2
Ship in US Bicentennial event 7-4, 488C3
Queen Eliz arrives US 7-6, 489E2
UK cited in US arms control rpt 7-29, 739E2
Joint US A-test 8-26, 663D3
Carter trip disclosed 9-29, 723D2
US Gen Brown remarks rptd 10-17—10-18, 787C1, A2, F2
Ford, Carter debate Brown remark 10-22, 801E1
US scores China sales 11-4, 880B1
US rptrs ordrd ousted 11-15, 11-17; Labor MPs, others dispute 11-17—11-25, 946B2

1977

UN Policy & Developments
Assemb, Cncl member; Waldock on World Ct 4C1-G1
Sovt bloc Rhodesia sanctn violatns chrgd 2-10, 123A1
Abstains on Israel occupatn abuses resolutn 2-15, 107E2
Rights comm bars Uganda probe 3-1, 142A1
Rights comm ends sessn 3-11, 207F1
UN desert fund opposed 9-9, 770F1
UN Rhodesia rep urged 9-26, OKd 9-29, 809F2-810A1
S Africa econ sanctns vetoed, apartheid res OKd 10-31, 851F2
Namibia vote abstentns 11-4, 851E1
Abstains from Israel occupatn res 11-25, 910D2
S Africa oil, investmt ban abstentns 12-16, 1016A2
U.S. Relations—*See also 'Atomic Energy' and 'Monetary, Trade & Aid' above; also AVIATION-SST/Concorde, RHODESIA-Majority Rule Issue*
Mondale visits 1-27, 69C1, F2, 70C1
Agee, Hosenball expulsns set 2-16, 134A2
US-ESA flight set 2-16, 170C3
Zuckerman at US sci conf 2-22, 184G1
Clifford visits re Cyprus missn 2-26—2-28, 147B1
US keeps Miami-London air fare 3-9, 325C1
Callaghan in DC, air treaty talks rptd 3-10—3-11, 213A1
Young calls racist 4-5; apologizes, Carter reactn 4-7, 272D1
Carter energy plan reactn 4-21, 320E3
Brewster confrmd amb 4-29, 418C1
Carter TV interview 5-2, 338B2
Carter visits; tours NE, sees Thatcher 5-5—5-8; visit hailed 5-8, 358F1, 359C2
Jay named US amb, opposed 5-11, 391F3
Mil info exchng OKd by US 5-16, 379G3
Mondale sees Callaghan, Owen 5-22, 398A1, E1
Eastern to lease Airbus 5-24, 441D2
3 chrgd under Secrets Act 5-24; Hosenball, Agee expelled 5-27, 6-3, 526C3
Carter OKs Laker 'Skytrain' svc 6-13, 500F2
Air service pact set 6-22, 500E1
Air service pact signed 7-23, 593C1
Pan Am, TWA, Brit Airways seek lower US-UK fares 7-24, 7-29, 8-1, 593D1
US rpts S Africa A-test plan 8-17, 663E3, 664A1
US wins Walker Cup 8-27, Ryder Cup 9-27, 951F1, A2
Ulster peace aid pledge reactn 9-1, 729G3
ESA satellite launching aborted 9-13, 735G3
Thatcher sees Carter 9-13, ends US visit 9-15, 883C3
UK OKs Laker svc requests 9-14, 9-29; 'Skytrain' begins 9-26, profit rptd 10-24, 860B2
Carter OKs NY-London budget air fares 9-26, 860D2
Carter expands air svc 12-21, 1006C2

1978

World Match Play results 10-16, Europn Open 10-22, 990A2, B2
Benson & Hedges tennis results 11-19, 1027C2
US wins Federatn Cup 12-3, 1026G3
US wins Davis Cup 12-10, 1026D3
Tuvalu—*See TUVALU*

UN Policy & Developments
Rights comm OKs res on Israel 2-14, 99B2
Callaghan on UN disarmamt conf 2-21, 140E1
Chile rights abuse res backed 3-6, 210F1
Unctad debt relief stand cited 3-11, 301D1
Rhodesia pact vote absentn 3-14, 192F3
Leb asks anti-Israel actn 3-15, 174D3
ICAO picks US bad-weather landing system 4-19, 319B2-C3
Assemb disarmamt sessn opens 5-23, 421G1
Sea Law Conf talks continue 5-23—7-15, 8-21—9-16, 732E3
Sovt ILO aide quits, Geneva aide defects 676D1, G1
Assemb disarmamt sessn ends, A-arms restraint vowed 6-30, 520C1
Cambodia scores rights com probe request 7-21, 660C1
Racism conf boycotted 8-26, 676B2
Sovt aide promoted despite spy chrgs 8-29, 676E1
Cncl, Assemb member 713A3, F3
Cncl abstentn on Namibia electn warning 11-13, 904B2
U.S. Relations—*See also 'Atomic Energy' and 'Monetary, Trade, Aid & Investment' above; also AVIATION—SST/Concorde, RHODESIA—Majority Rule*
US troop presence rptd 1-2, 5C2
US alerts to Sovt A-satellite fall 57E1
Carter State of Union Message 1-19, 31D2
At Ogaden conf in US 1-21, 43E2
Burger defends US trial lawyer criticism 2-12, 107G3
US air-fare dispute flares 2-28, 3-7, agrmt reached 3-17; Braniff London svc starts 3-18, 306E1
US, Dutch air svc accord 3-10, 206G2
US Dems score Ulster rights abuses 3-16, 373A3
Callaghan sees Carter in US 3-23, 226G2
Female canon preaches in Westminster 4-2, 294D2
ICAO picks US bad-weather landing system 4-19, 319B2-C3
US news show chngs set 4-19, 419B3
LA to get 'Skytrain' 5-5, 2-carrier London svc 6-9, 570D1
US launches ESA satellite 5-12, 384D3
CIA implicated in UK rptr's '71 death 7-24, 631A3
CAB waives charter rules for stranded air travelers 8-4, 640B3, D3
Ray confessn alleged by ex-cop, credibility attacked 8-18, 641C3
US seabed mining bill debated at UN conf 8-21—9-16, 732E3
Secrets chrgs vs 3 dropped 10-23, 838A3
Ray confessn affirmed by ex-cop 11-9, 898G1-B2
Nixon at Oxford 11-30, 942B2
Owen lauds US-China tie 12-16, 977B1

1979

Chichester tennis tourn results 6-17, Stella Artois 6-18, Eastbourne Intl 6-23, 570D2
Wimbledon results 7-6, 7-7, 569C3
British Open golf results 7-21, 586G3
10-ft craft completes N Atlantic crossing 7-24, 656C3
Fastnet yachting disaster 8-14, 799F3; rpt issued 12-10, 955C1
US wins Ryder Cup 9-16, 969E3
US wins Wightman Cup 11-4, 1003C3
Coe expense paymts probe rptd 11-12, named to Olympic team 11-13, 956A2
London Grand Prix tennis results 11-18, 1003G3
Eng Women's Grand Prix tennis results 11-25, 1004A1

UN Policy & Developments
Namibia plan fails 3-3, S Africa rejcts 3-5, 171B2, A3
Namibia compromise proposed 3-19—3-22; Pretoria bars 5-7, extends assemb powers 5-8, 354F2
W Bank setlmt res abstentn 3-22, 178F2
Tories urge Namibia rebel support end 4-11, 285E3
Rhodesia electn vote abstentn 4-30, 332A2
Namibia vote abstentn 5-31, 428B1
Indochina refugee conf asked 6-18; US, Viet OK 6-19, 6-20; Tokyo summit backs 6-28, 473E2, 474A1
Membership listed 695B3
S Africa vote abstentn 11-2, 875G1
Namibia talks reopen 11-12—11-16, 889D3
E Ger prisoner ransom deals scored 11-28, 939B3
World Ct gets US plea on Iran 12-10, 933F1
Thatcher vows US Cncl support re Iran 12-17, sees UN offcls 12-18, 968A2, C2
Zimbabwe sanctns end scored by Assemb 12-18, 960F1
U.S. Relations—*See also 'Atomic', 'Energy' and 'Monetary' above*
Callaghan at Guadeloupe summit 1-5—1-6, backs SALT pact 1-6, 12D2
Airline '72 crash case refused by US Sup Ct 1-15, 32D1
Pan Am, TWA warned on London fares 1-23, 87G3
Student enrollmt in US rptd 167E2
Tory Africa policy cites 4-11, 285D3
US House speaker, NY gov fault re N Ireland; MPs score 4-19—4-24, 312E2
US protests Sovt abuse of rptr 4-20, 390F1-A2
Carter congratulates Thatcher, Young warns re Rhodesia 5-4, 338A2
Scientology Church documts seizure by US upheld 5-14, 383A3
Vance, Carrington conf on Rhodesia 5-21—5-23, 393E2
US grounds DC-10s, forces Laker shutdown 6-6, 421A1
Anglicans bar US svcs by women priests 7-27, 640A3
Carter lauds Commonwealth Zimbabwe plan 8-6, 590G1-C2
US lifts gay alien curb 8-14, 631A3
US delegatn at Mountbatten funeral 9-5, 669E1
Black woman wins Rhodes scholarship 9-9, 1005G2
US Sen aides' Zimbabwe conf role questnd 9-20, 718F1
Princess Margaret in US 10-13, 860B1
Church painting sold for record sum 10-25, 892A1
UK seeks protectn vs US trust laws 10-31, 855C3
US informs of Iran oil ban 11-12, move backed 11-13, 861F1
Zimbabwe transitn plan acceptance lauded 11-14, 881B1
Zimbabwe peace force transport OKd 12-6, 937D1
Vance in London, seeks sanctns vs Iran 12-10, 933C2, G2
Thatcher in DC, visits Carter 12-17, in NY, NJ 12-18, 968G1
Carter OKs Pan Am-Natl merger 12-22, 989C1
Zimbabwe Rhodesian Relations—*See ZIMBABWE*

1980

Olympic alternate games backed 3-18, 206C1
Olympic com rebuffs US on Moscow boycott 3-22, OKs participatn 3-25, 259E2, C3
Eur soccer cup results 5-7, 5-21, 771A3
West Ham United wins English FA Cup 5-10, 771C3
Indep Olympic boycott spreads 5-17, 379E2
US wins Curtis Cup 6-7, 715A1
Watt retains WBC lightwgt title 6-8, 1000F3
Chichester tennis results 6-14, Queen's Club 6-15, Surrey, BMW 6-21, 607E3
Thatcher's son crashes at LeMans 6-15, 637C3
Coe sets 1000-m mark 7-1; Ovett tops mile record 7-1, ties 1500-m mark 7-15, 589G1-A2
Wimbledon results 7-4—7-6, 606F1-A3
Jones wins Gr Prix 7-13, 1002B1
Moscow Olympic results, flag controversy 7-19—8-3; Thompson wins decathlon 7-26; Coe, Ovett compete 7-26, 8-1, 588D1, A3, 589B1, F1, 622G1-624C2
Brit Open results 7-20, 714G2
Afghan wrestler denies defectn plan 7-21, 590B2
Atlantic sailing record set 8-1, 907G3
Woman sets distance running record 8-15, 638B3
Ovett breaks 1500-m mark 8-27, 892G1
Soccer fans riot in Madrid 9-17, 771E3
Owen KOd by Pintor 9-19, dies 11-3, 907A3
Minter loses world middlewgt title, fans riot 9-27, 772A2
World Match golf results 10-14, 972E2
US wins Wightman Cup 11-1, 946G3
UN Policy & Developments
Spain accord sets Gibraltar links 4-10, 274A3
Palestinian state res abstentn 4-30, 325D1
UN Res 242 chng asked 5-31, 418B1
Cncl abstentn on S Africa raid censure 6-27, 524F3
Assemb Palestinian state res abstentn 7-29, 572F1
Special econ dvpt sessn ends in no agrmt 9-15, 736G1
UN Namibia talks schedule agreed 11-24, 967C2
Cuba ex-offcl asks prison hunger strike probed 12-4, 965D2

U.S. Relations—*See also 'Monetary', 'Soviet-Afghan Issue' above*
UK plans uranium plant 1-9, 39B3
US-UK air svc expanded 1-24, 347A2; 3-5, 172A3; pact revised 2-1, 346A2
Carter anti-inflatn plan praised 3-15, 202F2
Mafia ldr slain 3-21, 237E2
World Air Boston-London svc OKd 4-10, 346C2
Thatcher vows support on Iran 4-14, 282C1
W Europns plan fighter jet 4-14, 303F1
Iran hostage kin seek support 4-23, 299D2
Iran hostage rescue missn backed 4-25, 324G1
US condemns Iran Emb seizure 4-30, 324C3
Laker Miami-London svc OKd 5-15, 516D2
Independent forgn policy backed by Labor 5-31, 429A3
UK cruise missile sites set 6-17, 487A1, C1
Anderson visits 7-16—7-17, 550B1
Iranians demonstrate at US Emb 8-4, police brutality chrgd 8-9, 635B2
Thatcher briefed on hostages in Iran 9-19, 719C3
Labor Party backs A-arms exit 10-2, 768B3
US mil exercise performance scored, praised 10-11, 777D1, F1
Reagan favored for pres by gamblers 11-3, 844G2
Reagan electn reactn 11-5, 841B3
'Dallas' TV episode viewing record rptd 11-25, 905F3
Lennon slain in NYC, ex-mental patient chrgd 12-8; reactn 12-9; background, photos 12-8, 933D2-943F3
NATO defns input defended 12-9—12-10, 949C2
Haig apptmt praised 12-17, 955E2

Zimbabwe Relations—*See ZIMBABWE*

1976

GREATER Baton Rouge Port Commission
3 inspectors indicted 1-19, 44D1
Agri Dept vs grain inspectn role 1-22, 136A1
GREAT Contractor (race horse)
3d in Belmont 6-5, 424E3
GREATER Jersey Bancorp.
Buys First State 6-14, reopens under new name 6-15, 495F1
GREAT Falls (Mich.) Tribune (newspaper)
Ford endorsemt rptd 10-30, 831F2
GREAT Lakes—*See also specific lake name*
Air quality progress rptd 12-8, 943B1
GREAT War and Modern Memory, The (book)
Wins Natl Book Award 4-19, 292C3
GREAT Western Bank & Trust Co.—*See PATAGONIA Corp.*
GREAT Western Sugar Co.—*See GREAT Western United Corp.*
GREAT Western United Corp.
Yugo frees sugar exec 7-23, 559A2
GRECHKO Andrei Antonovich
Named to Politburo 3-5, 195B2
Dies 4-27, 315E3
Replaced as defense min 4-29, 334F2
GRECU, Danut
Wins Olympic medal 7-23, 574C3

GREECE—*See also NATO, OECD*
Newspaper owner, publisher sentncd 1-21, 73E2
Knossos tomb, Athens cemetery excavatns rptd 1-31, 160F1
Socrates' jail identified 2-1, 124A3
Minimum wage raised 2-19, 382C1
Pollutn threatens Acropolis 3-11, 333C2
'75 GNP, inflatn rptd 4-28, 402E2
Labor strikes 5-24, 1 dies 5-25, 381D3-382C1
Olympic crash kills 50 11-23, 912D2
Pilots bar night flights 11-30, 1004C3
Cyprus—*See under 'C'*
European Force Reduction Issues—*See under EUROPE*
Foreign Economic Developments
Sovt oil, elec deals rptd 1-12, 1-19, 73B2
French Mirage purchase cited 1-16, 36C2
Egypt oil tanker order rptd 1-16, 73C2
EC entry affirmed, delay urged; Caramanlis scores 1-29, 84B2-E2 ★
EC entry delay rejctd 2-9, Caramanlis welcomes 2-10, 164E2
Northrop rpts payoffs 2-20, 362C3
Yugo trade pact 3-16, 333C2
Total IMF oil loan rptd 4-1, 340B2
Lockheed data exchng set 5-20, 402C2
EC entry talks open 7-27; Comm convenes 10-11; assurance rptd 11-3, 853D3
IMF loan OKd, export earnings rptd 9-9, 854A2
Iran bank rptd OKd 9-29, 854G1
Lockheed rptd cleared 11-2, 854A1
Rumania oil search rptd 11-3, 854F1
Hydrocarbon search rules rptd eased 11-3, 854F1
World Bank loan rptd OKd 12-10, 1004B3
Foreign Relations (misc.)
Sovt anchorage sites rptd 1-19, 73A2
Balkan natns meet 1-26—2-5, 213E3
Australian consulate closed 2-4, 97A2
OKs UN Medit pollutn pact 2-16, 126C3
Recalls US base delegatn 3-30, 244C3
Athens protests to US backed 3-31, Caramanlis call cited 4-12, 259E1, C2
New Sovt amb appointed 4-2, warned re pol mtgs 5-16, 402F1, A2
Ceausescu visit rptd 4-8, 333B2
Zhivkov visits 4-9—4-11, 333A2
US base pact initialed, letters exchng on Cyprus released 4-15, 259C1-C2
Tito visits 5-10—5-13, 543C3
Welch probe ends 5-21, 402D2
Rhodes ship visit protested 5-24—5-25, 402B2
US presses on NATO ties 6-15, 449F1
US Dem platform text cites 6-15, 478D1
US evacuates 10 from Leb 6-20, 448C1
Leb evacuees arrive in Athens 6-29, 546A1
US '76 arms aid funds set 6-30, 533C2
World Ct gets Greek plea on Aegean 8-10, 622C3
UN debates Aegean dispute 8-12—8-13, US mediates 8-14, 622D2
Ger terrorist extradited 10-1, 754G3
'77 US aid signed 10-1, 806E3, F3
US reporter sentncd 10-4, 873D1
US Sup Ct bars review of TWA '73 case 10-12, 848B3
12 sentncd re anti-US protests 10-31, 873D1
Greek reactn to Carter electn 11-3—11-4, 826E1
Leftists linked to Welch death 12-18, 1004C2
Government & Politics—*See also other appropriate subheads in this section*
2 cabt mins shifted 1-5, 73D2
Ioannides gets further sentences 1-10, 73E1
Listed as 'free' nation 1-19, 20B3
Educ reforms, Demotic Greek language enacted 1-31, 221G3
'67 treason chrgs vs 89 dropped 2-28, 221F3
Ioannides sentncd re '75 plot 3-16, 221C3
'75 torture sentncs cut 4-22, 333G1
Panagoulis killed in car crash 5-1, murder suit filed 5-5, 351D3

1977

GREATEST, The (film)
Top-grossing film 6-1, 452C2
GREAT Lakes—*See also specific lake names*
Carter-Trudeau talks 2-21—2-23, 132C3
Detroit sued on pollution 5-6, 422F2
GREAT Lakes Family Planning Coalition—*See FAMILY Planning Coalition, etc.*
GREAT Western United Corp.
Settles FTC land fraud case 1-26, 156D1
Land fraud setlmt rptd 3-11, 203D3
Hunts seek Sunshine Mining takeover 3-21, 275C1
Hunt sugar, silver trading cited 4-28, 341B3
Bid-cutting strategy rptd 8-12; Sunshine Mining takeover OKd 10-4, 798F3
GRECHKO, Georgi
Soyuz launched 12-10, docks with Salyut 12-11, 999E1
GREDAL, Eva
Danish welfare min 2-25, 373E1

GREECE—*See also NATO, OECD*
Tanker splits off Midway I 1-17, 214G2
Gunrunning crackdown begins 1-18, 63G2
Stamatis attack foiled 1-18, 182E2
Athens pol bombings 2-4, 2-5, 182F2
Rumania quake felt 3-4, 204F1
Floods hit Athens, Piraeus 11-2—11-3, 888D3
Tomb of King Philip found 11-24, 952D1
Cyprus—*See under 'C'*
Economy & Labor (domestic)
Unions warned on wage demands 1-18, 63E2
Dec '75-76 inflatn rate rptd 2-7, 87B2
'76 GNP, indl output up 2-10, 135B1
Strikers protest wage restraint 3-2, 182C2
Collective labor pact rptd 3-3, 182D2
Petrochem plant set 3-14, 203A2
Shopkeepers strike for siesta 3-21, 256E3
Siesta ban eased 4-24, 547F3
Air controllers strike 5-13—5-23, 487E3
Luxury taxes, energy cuts set 5-18, 487B3
Foreign Relations (misc.)—*See also 'Monetary, Trade & Aid' below*
UN Assemb member 4A1
Ethiopian amb gets asylum 3-10, 238G2
5 Britons jailed as spies 3-18, 256C3; released 6-4, 487F3
UN pollutn conf ends, Medit pact reached 10-21, 876B2
Palestinians storm Egypt emb 11-18, 890F2
Government & Politics—*See also other appropriate subheads in this section*
126 army cols retired 6-23, 618A1
Early electns planned 9-19, 728D2
3 mins replaced 10-21, 925C2
Caramanlis, party win electn 11-20, offcl results 11-23; Cabt named 11-28, 924E3, 925F1
Mavros quits as DCU head 11-27, 925C2

1978

GREATEST Hits Vol. 2 (recording)
On best-seller list 12-6, 971E1
GREAT Lakes
US bans Canada fishing 6-4, 435G1
PCB ban formally proposed 6-7, 513B1
GREAT Meadow Correctional Facility (Comstock, N.Y.)
'Strip-frisk' searches ordrd ended 4-22, 440A2
GREAT Plains—*See MIDWEST*
GREAT Slave Lake (Canada)
USSR A-satellite falls 1-24; radiatn detected, debris found 1-25—2-1, 57E1; 2-4, 103B1
GREAT Southern Corp.
Equitable Gen merger planned 4-17, 283G1
Equitable cancels merger 6-26, 553D2
GREAT Southwest Corp.—*See PENN Central Corp.*
GREAT Western Sugar Co., The—*See GREAT Western United Corp.*
GREAT Western United Corp.
'74 sugar co trust chrgs settled 6-12, 511C1
Idaho corp takeover law ruled unconst 8-10, 700F3
GRECHKO, Georgi
Soyuz 27 docks with Salyut 1-11, 11E2
Breaks US space endurance record 3-4, 157D2
Returns to Earth 3-16, 180D3

GREECE—*See also COUNCIL of Europe, GATT, IEA, NATO, OECD*
Tanker spilt by collisn 5-6, 524A2
Salonika area hit by quakes 5-24, 6-19—6-21, 480A1
Christina Onassis weds Sovt citizen 8-1, 844E3
Cyprus—*See CYPRUS*
Economy & Labor (domestic)
Unions rejct minimum wage hike offer 1-17, ct sets 22% increase 2-8, 149E3
'78 budget presented 2-16, 149F2
1-day gen strike in Athens 3-1, 149F3
Workers protest unemploymt 4-5, 258F2
Econ measures announced 6-18, 631D1
'79 budget presented 11-24, 924B2
European Community Relations
Caramanlis in 4 EC natns for entry talks 1-25—2-1, 149G1
EC entry backed by France, W Ger 2-7, 122C1
EC entry gains support 5-10, 373D3
EC entry moves rptd 6-9, 6-18, 631D1
EC entry terms set 12-21, 1017A3
European Force Reduction Talks—*See under EUROPE*
Foreign Relations (misc.)—*See also 'European Community' above, 'Monetary, Trade, Aid & Investment' below*
Caramanlis in 4 W Eur capitals 1-25—2-1, 149G1
Cyprus jet hijackers denied landing 2-18, 117A2
Amnesty Intl holds torture conf 3-10—3-11, 180B3
Soviet film show bombed 3-11, 374E1
Panagiotopoulos in Albania, tours ethnic areas 3-28—3-30, 374B2
Viet refugees arrive in Kenya 4-17, 341B2
Italy abortn reform enacted 5-18, 375G1
Corfu Club Medit '77 robbery cited 6-11, 473F3
UK rptr's '71 death case convictn questnd 7-31, 631F2
UN Assemb member 713F3
Government & Politics—*See also other appropriate subheads in this section*
DCU split rptd 3-16, Mavros resigns 4-11, 374B1
Caramanlis shuffles Cabt 5-10, woos DCU 5-11, 373C3
Oppositn wins mayoral electns 10-22, 816D2
'79 budget presented 11-24, 924B2

1979

GREAT Canadian Oil Sands Ltd.
Sun Oil merger agreed 8-22, 651A2
GREATER Cleveland Growth Association
City cash shortage noted 2-27, 150E1
GREATER Harrisburg Board of Realtors
3 Mile I property values rptd unaffected 8-20, 743A3
GREATER New York Conference on Soviet Jewry
Rally honors Dymshits, Kuznetsov 4-29, 317B2
GREATEST Hits Vol. 2 (recording)
On best-seller list 1-10, 80F3
GREAT Gilly Hopkins, The (book)
Wins Natl Book Award 4-23, 356B2
GREAT Lakes
Weather Svc rpts unnavigable 2-20, 176C2
Huron A-plant safety scored in Canada rpt 4-27, 352A3
Indian Lake Mich fishing rights upheld 5-8, 368C1
GREAT Neck, Va.—*See VIRGINIA*
GREAT Southern Corp.
NLT acquires 1-17, 88G3
GREAT Train Robbery, The (film)
Released 2-1, 174E2*
GREAT Western Packing Co.
Settles '78 beef-price suit 10-22, 985E3
GREAT Western United Corp.
Idaho takeover law challenge rejctd by Sup Ct 6-26, 540F3

GREECE—*See also COUNCIL of Europe, IEA, NATO, OECD*
Tanker hull crack rptd 1-1, 201A1
Divorce law eased 2-19, 135F3
Bus, Yugo gas truck collisn kills 30 3-14, 240E3
Niarchos daughter marries 6-15, 527E2
Atlantic Empress collides off Tobago 7-19, 553A3; sinks 8-2, 592A3
Tanker fleet safety record rptd 8-15, 608E1
Elytis wins Nobel 10-18, 857G3
Cyprus—*See CYPRUS*
Economy & Labor
10% pay hike curb proposed, income growth cited 2-22, 135B3
Price freeze ordered, pay curbs cited 2-23, 154B3
Gas price rptd at $2.93 per gal 5-19, 397A1
Energy measures announced 7-3, spur bank strike 7-4—7-12, 543D3
Bank workers return ordrd 8-14, new strike rptd voted 9-11, 708E1
Anti-inflatn steps announced 8-21, 708A1
Caramanlis on energy, inflatn problems 9-8, 707E3
OECD rpt stresses investmt, cites inflatn, GNP 9-12, 707A3
European Community Relations
'79 growth rates seen 2-23, 154D3
'81 entry date set 4-4, 268B3
Membership treaty signed 5-28, 407B2
Membership treaty ratified 6-28, 543B3
Bank hrs revised 7-3, 543F3
European Force Reduction Talks—*See under EUROPE*
Foreign Relations (misc.)—*See also 'Monetary' and 'UN' below*
Libyans occupy Athens Emb 9-3, 688F2
Sovt ship accord rptd signed 9-11, 708C1
Government & Politics—*See also other appropriate subheads in this section*
Caramanlis attacks critics 9-8, 707G3

1980

GREATE Bay Corp.
Atlantic City casino operatn cited 988E3
GREAT Escape The (film)
George Harsh dies 1-25, 104G2
GREATEST Hits (recording)
On best-seller list 12-3, 948B3
GREATEST Hits on the Radio (recording)
On the best-seller list 1-2, 40F3; 2-6, 120G3
GREATHOUSE, Pat
Replaced as UAW vp 6-4, 457B2
GREAT Lakes
Acid rain rptd 2-2, 145C3
GREAT Western Financial Corp.
Financial Federation deal set 7-15, 557D2
Great Western Savings & Loan Association
Mortgage rate raised to 12.25% 7-23, 575B1
Mortgage rate raised to 13.5% 8-18, 631B1
GREBEY, Ray
Baseball strike averted 5-23, 402A1
GRECO, Hector
Arrest ordered 4-25, 349F3
GREDLER, Wilfried
Loses Austria pres electn 5-18, 388F1

GREECE—*See also COUNCIL of Europe, CSCE, IEA, MBFR, NATO, OECD*
Acropolis rescue plan set 4-15, 285D2
Hann icons sold for record sum 4-17, 472A3
Cyprus—*See CYPRUS*
Economy & Labor
Shopowners close in profit control protest 1-21, 98F1
Bank workers end strike 2-23, 150A3
Price, profit freeze, inflatn cut linked 3-4, 173C1
Labor costs rptd 8-12, 698E1
Civil servants strike 10-31—11-1; govt offers 5-day workwk 11-6, natl strike 11-10, 872G2
European Community Relations
Turkey EC initiative launched 2-5, 102D3
Fiber dumping chrgs dismissed 5-6, 412B1
France asks EC expansn delay 6-5, 436A1
Foreign Relations (misc.)—*See also 'Monetary' below*
Caramanlis to seek permanent Olympic site 1-18, 45C3
Terrorist plot vs forgn embs chrgd 2-15, 150B3
Iran ties cut weighed 3-20, 204C1
Iran asks non-support of US hostage policy 4-12, 282F1
Cuban gunboats fire at freighter 5-1, 326F1
USSR May Day parade marked 5-1, 354A3
Close Westn ties vowed 5-23, 407E3
Armenians kill Turk diplomat 7-31, 606A1
Westn labor costs compared 8-12, 698E1
Iran hostage appeal rptd 8-16, 634G3
NATO mil re-entry, US bases linked 8-20, 652C2
Libya-Iran airlift rptdly uses airspace 10-10, 774D2
NATO mil wing rejoined 10-20, 800C1
Government & Politics—*See also other appropriate subheads in this section*
Caramanlis elected pres 5-5, Rallis premr 5-8, 352B2
Caramanlis sworn 5-15, 407E3
Rallis wins confidence vote 5-23, 407D3
Center Party formed 11-16, 901E3
Publishers sentncd re Caramanlis article 12-30, 996E3

1976

Mrs Papadopoulos sentncd 6-28, 873C1
Rt-wing group implicated in Panagoulis death 7-9, 538B1
Bill dissolves Andreadis holdings 8-31; Niarchos, Andreadis, Latsis face chrgs 11-2, 854B1
Ex-police offcrs sentncd; retrial asked 10-12—10-14, 873A1
Monarchist party formed 11-27, 1004F2
'77 budget presented 11-29, 1004G2
Govt sets oil refinery takeover 12-4, 1004A3
Ex-police chief slain; pro-rightist violence, police disciplined 12-14—12-18, 1004A2
Mrs Papadopoulos acquitted 12-15, 1004E2

Turkish Relations
EC urges Greek settle differences 1-29, 84D2
Athens recalls envoy 3-30, 244C3
US letters exchng on Aegean released 4-15, 259B2
Athens offers peace bid, Ankara accepts 4-17, 278D2
Aegean oil dispute flares 6-27—7-13, 538D1
Turk research ship enters Aegean 7-29, chrgs traded 8-7—8-11; UN debates 8-12—8-13, US mediates 8-14, 622D1
World Ct gets Greek plea 8-10, 622C3
Turks to continue sea research 8-16, 622B3
Greece vs Turkey on Dodecanese stand 8-20; Turks cite intl pacts 8-24, 643B3
Turk research ship returns 8-24, 643A3
UN asks Aegean talks, World Ct role 8-25, 643D2
Turkey lauds UN talks call 8-25, vs ct role 8-26, 643G2
Turk ship back to Aegean, Greece alerts navy 9-1; Caramanlis asks talks 9-4; World Ct rejects pleas 9-11, ship returns Izmir 9-25; talks resume 11-2, 845A1-B2
Aegean talks OKd, study set 11-11, 897G1
AF ties to reopen 11-28, 897A3
Greek '77 defns budget presented 11-29, 1004A3
Turkey hikes '77 defns budget 12-1, 1011G3
AF link reopened 12-11, 936B2

GREEK-Americans
Turkey base pact oppositn seen 3-29, 244B3
Carter sees Chicago group 10-10, 762F2
GREEK Orthodox Church—*See under EASTERN Orthodox Churches*
GREEK Treasure, The (book)
On best seller list 1-25, 80B3; 12-5, 972F2
GREEN Jr., Arthur J.
Baxtrum role in SWP burglaries rptd 7-29, 570A1
GREEN, Ernest
Wins Rockefeller award 11-16, 911E3
GREEN, Judge June
To see Rosenberg papers 1-13, 70B2
GREEN, Larry C.
Convicted 3-13, sentncd 3-29, 292F3
GREEN, Marshall
Replaced as amb to Australia 2-4, 110B2

1977

Helsinki Agreement—*See EUROPE—Security and Cooperation*
Monetary, Trade & Aid Issues (including all foreign economic developments)
Rpt Israel sells US-made arms 1-6; Israel denies 1-7, 28C3
UNESCO asks Acropolis aid 1-10, 63C3
'76 paymts gap narrows 2-10, 134G3
Albania air link set 7-18, 595F1
'77 paymts deficit forecast 7-31, 586D2
EC natns uneasy re entry 10-6, 867A2
Saudis boycott ships 12-10, 955D1

Turkish Relations
Forgn mins meet re Aegean 1-29, 122D2
US envoy Clifford sees Greek, Turk ldrs 2-17—2-22, 122F1
Ecevit seeks better ties 6-5, 451C2
Demirel forms new govt 7-21, 565G1
Greece rejects US envoy 7-22, 598F2
Makarios dies 8-3, reactn 8-4—8-12, 616F3-617B2
Caramanlis wins electn 11-20, 925B1

U.S. Relations
Rpt Israel sells US-made arms 1-6; Israel denies 1-7, 28C3
US envoy visits 2-17—2-19, 122F1
Carter sees Caramanlis 5-10, 359C1
64 US CIA agents rptd 6-11, 618B1
Schaufele confrmd US amb 7-13, 626E3
Anti-US incidents rptd 7-14, 618D1
Schaufele rejctd as US envoy 7-22, 598F2
US defense pact signed 7-28, 617F3
Arms aid signed 8-4, 668C1
Caramanlis scores US in campaign 10-25, 925D1
Anti-US feeling used in campaign 11-20, 925C1

GREEK Orthodox Church—*See under EASTERN Orthodox Churches*
GREEN, David
Wins Emmy 9-11, 1021G3
GREEN, Gary
In NFL draft 5-3, 353B2
GREEN, Hubert
2d in Mem'l Classic 5-23, wins Irish Open 8-28, 676D1, C2
Life threatened, wins US Open 6-19, 659B3
3d in British Open 7-9, 659A3
US wins Ryder Cup Matches 9-17, 951A2
PGA top money winner 10-30, 950G3
GREEN, Judge June L.
Sentences Hastings 1-31, 103E1
GREEN, Rickey
In NBA draft 6-10, 584B2

1978

Helsinki Agreement—*See EUROPE—Security and Cooperation*
Monetary, Trade, Aid & Investment
'77 trade, paymts deficits rise 2-6, 149C3
Albania trade pact signed 3-28—3-30, 374B2
US asks aid hike 4-6, 276A3
Japan imports halted 6-23, forgn exchng credit curbed 7-18, 631G1
Boeing chrgd re payoffs 7-28, 642G3
Obituaries
Balopoulos, Michael 3-3, 252C2

Terrorism & Unrest—*For labor unrest, see 'Economy & Labor' above*
55 injured in Patras riot 3-21, 8 arrested 3-22, 6 sentncd 3-29, 374F1
Terrorism death penalty OKd 4-17, 374C1
Athens newspaper office firebombed 5-31, 631A2
Tsironis killed in police raid 7-11, 631C2
Athens, Piraeus bomb blasts 7-24, 8-6, 631E2
9 rightists chrgd under terrorism law 8-2, 631A2
World Ct bars Aegean dispute actn 12-19, 1000E3
Turkish Relations
Ecevit scores US role in Greek-Turkish dispute 1-4, 8C2
Turkey warns US vs peace role 1-20, 170G2
Caramanlis OKs Ecevit talks 1-23, 2-9, 170C2
Turkey eases curbs on Greeks 3-9, 216F2
Caramanlis, Ecevit hold summit 3-10—3-11; oppositn scores 3-12, 216D2
Ecevit chrgs US pressure 3-10, summit stand rptd hardened 3-12, 216D3
US moves to lift Turkish arms embargo 3-29—4-6; Greeks angered by US actn 4-2—4-16, postpones Turkish talks 4-11, 276G1-277E1
Turkey bars Aegean arbitratn 4-25, 398A3
Aegean talks resume 7-4—7-6, 624A1
Turkey ex-offcl questns UK rptr's '71 death 7-24, 631A3
US OKs Turkey arms embargo end 8-1, reactn 8-2, 587G2, F3
Greece protests boat sinking 11-1, 905B3
U.S. Relations
US troop presence rptd 1-2, 5C2
Papandreou asks US mil exit 1-4, 22G1
US alerts to Sovt satellite fall 57E1
US moves to lift Turkish arms embargo, increase Greek aid 3-29—4-6; Greeks angered 4-2—4-16, 276G1-277E1
US set back in moves to lift Turkish arms embargo 5-3, 5-11; reactn 5-12, 378G1
CIA implicated in UK rptr's '71 death 7-24, 631A3
Boeing chrgd re payoffs 7-28, 642G3
US OKs Turkish arms embargo end 8-1, reactn 8-2, 587G2, F3
US ends Turkey arms embargo 9-26, 734C2
CIA ex-aide convicted as spy 11-18, 940G1

GREECE, N.Y.—*See NEW York State*
GREEK Orthodox Church—*See under EASTERN Orthodox Churches*
GREEK Tycoon, The (film)
Released 5-12, 619C2
Top-grossing film 5-31, 460E3
GREEN, Adolph
On 20th Century opens 2-19, 887C2
Wins Tony 6-4, 579A3
GREEN, Dave
NFL '77 punting ldr 1-1, 56F3
GREEN, Gerald
'Holocaust' aired 4-16—4-19, NBC rpts 120 mln viewers 4-20, 316A2
Wins Emmy 9-17, 1030F1
GREEN, Hubert
Wins Hawaiian Open 2-5, Heritage Classic 3-26, 355B3, F3
Player wins 3 consecutive tourns 4-9, 4-16, 4-23, 355D2
2d in Masters 4-9, 355F2
3d in Westchester Classic 8-20, 672B3
2d in World Series of Golf 10-1, 990B1
PGA top money winner 10-31, 990B3
GREEN, Mark
Questns oil lobbyist links to Energy Dept 5-15, 408F2-C3
Rates 95th Cong 10-28, 865B2
GREEN, Paul
Native Son opens 3-27, 760G2
GREEN, Reuben
Twilight Dinner opens 4-18, 760F3
GREEN, Roosevelt
In World Amateur Boxing tourn 5-6—5-20, 600D2
GREEN, S. William
Elected to US House 2-14, 107D2, 108F1-B2
Reelected 11-7, 851E3
GREEN, Walt
Hooper released 8-4, 970F1

1979

Helsinki Agreement—*See EUROPE—Security and Cooperation*
Monetary, Trade, Aid & Investment
EMS entry vowed 4-4, 268D3
Intl bank loan set 9-7, 708C2

Sports
Pinto swims Strait of Otranto 7-14, 656F3

Terrorism & Unrest
13 chrgd in '78 bombings 1-22, 201F1
Police expansn announced 2-10, 135G3

Turkish Relations
Tourism accord signed 6-5, 447A2
UN Policy & Developments
Membership listed 695E2

U.S. Relations
CIA alleged agent named 1-4, 17C3
Time Inc to sponsor art show 7-19, 672D2

GREEK Orthodox Church—*See under EASTERN Orthodox Churches*
GREEN, Chad
Laetrile treatmt ordrd ended 1-23, 1-30, parents flee 1-25, 139C1
Cyanide rptd in blood 3-7, 196B1
Dies 10-12, autopsy rptd 10-21, 905G1
GREEN, Cliff
Picnic At Hanging Rock released 2-22, 174D3
GREEN, Dallas
Hired as Phillies mgr 10-18, 1002F1
GREEN, Dave
NFL '78 punting ldr 1-6, 80F2
GREEN, Dennis
God Bless You Mr Rosewater opens 5-20, 711D3
GREEN, Earl
Radiatn tests questnd 7-28, 692G2
GREEN, Gary
Hired as Caps coach 11-13, 1004F1
GREEN, Hubert
Wins Hawaiian Open 2-11, 220E3
Wins N Orleans Open 4-29, 587D2
US wins Ryder Cup 9-16, 969F3
GREEN, Judge June L.
Dismisses Sears suit 5-15, 365A3
Fines shippers, execs 6-8, 442A2
Drops Park indictmt 8-16, 630F1
Refuses Soul City injunctn 8-27, 665C2*
Orders Iranian student probes halted 12-11, 935F2*
GREEN, Lorne
Battlestar Galactica released 5-17, 528C1
GREEN Jr., Roosevelt
Death sentnc vacated by Sup Ct 5-29, 421E3
GREEN, Tony
NFL '78 punt, kick return ldr 1-6, 80F2, G2
GREEN Jr., William E.
Plea bargain blocked 6-6, 500A3

1980

Monetary, Trade, Aid & Investment
Import curbs protested 1-21, 98G1, A2
W Ger finance min in Athens, reassures ldrs on Turkey mil aid 2-16, 135E3
Voluntary import curbs, price freeze rptd 3-4, 173A1
US cooperatn pact signed 4-22, 352E2
Albania trade increase rptd 5-2, 356F2
EC fiber dumping chrgs dismissed 5-6, 412B1
Obituaries
Partsalides, Dimitrios 6-22, 528B3
Peter, Prince 10-16, 876C3
Pyromaglou, Kominos 7-2, 608F2
Sports
Caramanlis to seek permanent Olympic site 1-18; US backs 1-20, 45E2, C3
Moscow Olympic results 7-20—8-3, 588B3, 624A3, D3, F3
Terrorism & Unrest
Police offcl slain 1-16, 150D3
Forgn emb plotters rpt arrested 2-15, 150C3
Student uprising anniv marked, 2 die 11-16—11-17, 901C3

Turkish Relations
Turkey EC initiative launched 2-5, 102D3
Greek, Armenian links re Turkey envoy attacks cited 2-6, 197E2
Turkey mil aid reassurances rptd 2-16, 135E3
Aegean Sea air dispute ended 2-22, 2-23, 150F2
Forgn mins meet, pledge cooperatn 6-28, 500C2
Turkey coup response 9-12, 696G3
Greece rejoins NATO mil wing 10-20, 800D1, A2

U.S. Relations
US backs permanent Olympic site 1-20, 45E2
Terrorist plot vs US Emb, mil installatns chrgd 2-15, 150D3
Iran asks non-support of US hostage policy 4-12, 282F1
Cooperatn pact signed 4-22, 352E2
Iran hostage appeal rptd 8-16, 634G3
US bases, NATO mil re-entry linked 8-20, 652C2
Anti-US protest, 2 die 11-16—11-17, 901C3

GREEK Orthodox Church—*See under EASTERN Orthodox Churches*
GREELEY, Horace (1811-72)
Hijinks! opens 12-18, 1003B3
GREEN, Alan
NASL scoring ldr 8-24, 770D3
GREEN, Dallas
In World Series 10-14—10-21, 811C2-812D3
GREEN, Davey (Boy)
Leonard KOs 3-31, 320E2
GREEN, Hugh
2d in Heisman Trophy vote 12-1, 999F2
GREEN, Jacob
In NFL draft 4-29, 336F2
GREEN, Mark
Cong Watch ratings issued 1-12, 53B3
GREEN, Peter J. F.
Backs Lloyd's reforms 6-26, 509F3
GREEN, Roy
NFL '79 kick return ldr 1-5, 8G3
GREEN, Rep. S. William (R, N.Y.)
Reelected 11-4, 843E3
GREEN, Stuart H.
Vs US-China textile pact 9-18, 707E1

1976

GREEN, Rep. William Joseph (D, Pa.)
Wins Sen primary 4-27, 305B1
Loses Sen race 11-2, 821A3
GREEN Bay, Wis.—*See WISCONSIN*
GREENE, Robert
Heads Ariz crime probe 10-2, 849B2
GREENER, William
Campaign staff realigned 8-25, 631B1
GREENGLASS, David
Judge to see Rosenberg papers 1-13, 70E2
GREEN Haven State Correctional Facility (Stormville, N.Y.)
H Rap Brown paroled 10-21, 912D3 ★
GREENHILL, Lord (Sir Denis Arthur)
In Rhodesia talks 2-24—2-27, 176B2
GREENLAND (Danish possession)
Dutch study drought action 8-24, 630F1
USAF transport crashes 8-28, 859B2
Denmark to keep mineral rights 11-8, 949B2
GREENPEACE Foundation (Canada)
Cancels seal-hunt protest 3-24, 250E3
GREEN River
Colo oil shale leases suspended 8-23, 649E1
GREENSPAN, Alan
On Econ Rpt 1-26, 66E3
On Teamsters pact 4-5, 249A1
7-natn econ summit set 6-1, 389A1
On Ford econ summit remarks 6-27, 462C1
Sees Australia prime min 7-27, 554F1
Sees recovery pause 8-30, 647F1
On Aug jobless rate 9-3, 667D2
Ford campaign donatn rptd 10-22, 938G3
On women in job market 12-5, 917F3
GREENWALD, Barry
Wins Cannes film award 5-28, 460G1
GREENWALD, Joseph A.
State asst secy 1-20; confrmd 1-28, 186G1
Replaced in EC post 1-28, 186A2
In India econ talks 3-25—3-26, 253A3
Replaced as State asst secy 9-23, 808A1
GREENWICH, Conn.—*See CONNECTICUT*
GREENWOOD, Ivor
Retires 7-4, 520F2
GREENWOOD Stripping Corp.
Indicted 11-19, 989E2
GREGG, Hugh
Charges Ford distortion 2-18, 130B1
GREGG, Steven
Wins Olympic medal 7-18, 575D2
GREGOR, Jan
Dismissed 9-15, 750G2
GREGORY, James B.
Quits Transportatn post 2-26, 232G1
GRENADA—*See also CARIBCOM, COMMONWEALTH of Nations, OAS*
Listed as 'partly free' 1-19, 20C3
Total IMF oil loans rptd 4-1, 340C2
At nonaligned conf 8-16—8-20, 622C1
Cited in Barbados campaign 8-28, 673C1
Gairy, GULP reelected 12-7, 925D1
E Carib $ falls, deficit rptd 12-7, 925G1
US prosecutns rptd barred, atty gen deported 12-7, 925G1
Police supt rptd fired, runs for House seat 12-7, 925B2
GRENDYS, Michal
Polish State Cncl member 3-25, 268D2
GRESZKIEWICZ, Jerzy
Wins Olympic medal 7-23, 575B2
GREY, Anthony
Rpts new Australia uranium yields 1-28, 97C1
GREYHOUND Corp.
Bars boycott compliance 3-18, 747B2
GRIBBLE Jr., Lt. Gen. William C.
On Fla wetlands dvpt 4-16, 284A3
GRIBKOV, Col. Gen. Anatoly I.
Warsaw Pact staff chief 10-12, 858G2
Named general 10-30, 908G3
GRICH, Bobby
AL batting ldr 10-4, 796C1
Contract rptd signed 12-5, 951E3
GRIDIRON Club of Washington, D.C.
2d woman elected member 3-5, 272A1
SWP suit dvpts 8-3, 8-15, 634C3
GRIESA, Judge Thomas P.
Sentences 6 ex-Franklin offcls 3-9, 271B2
Delays Nantucket oil spill suit 12-30, 1013G3
GRIFFEY, Ken
NL wins All-Star game 7-13, 544B2
NL batting ldr 10-4, 795E3, F3
In World Series 10-16—10-21, 815D2
GRIFFIN, Desmond
Museum neglect rptd 1-16, 26D3
GRIFFIN, Marvin
Endorses Ford 9-26, 723C3
GRIFFIN, Sen. Robert P. (R, Mich.)
Backs Ford 5-12, 343D1
Helps Ford in Iowa 6-18, 451D1
Vs Connally vp 8-5, 584G2
GRIFFITH, Leon
Loses election 11-2, 820A3, 821G3
GRIFFITHS, Edgar H.
Named RCA head 9-16, 708B2

1977

GREEN, William Joseph
'76 specl interest gifts rptd 2-15, 128C2
GREEN Bay & Western Railroad
ICC OKs BN purchase 7-15, 613D1
Brae Corp seeks 11-22; ICC OKs BN bid 11-30, BN drops offer 12-1, 1007B1
GREENBERG, Sanford
NHL Barons sale OKd 5-12, 430G1
GREENBERG'S Express Inc.
ICC probe rptd 6-3, 500D3
GREENLAND (Danish possession)
Danish Cabt min named 2-25, 373E1
Eskimos at intl conf 6-13—6-17, 619D2
GREENSPAN, Alan
On CEA econ rpt 1-18, 35F3, 36A1
GREEN Speed (race horse)
Wins harness award 12-13, 970G3
GREENSPUN, Herman (Hank)
Wins Summa damage suit 6-3, 472C2
GREENWOOD Stripping Corp.
Fined 3-21, 520C3
GREGG, Forrest
Named to HOF 1-17, 164B1
Inducted into HOF 7-30, 659A1
Fired as Browns coach 12-13, 1020A2
GREGG, Lawrence T.
Testifies on uranium cartel 6-17, 480B2
GREGG, Peter
3d in Le Mans 6-12, 531B2
GREGORIO, Maria Elena
Arrested at rights rally 9-18, 740C3
GREGORY, Bernard
Dies 12-25, 1024A2
GREGORY, Eddie
Galindez decisions 11-20, 970D3

GRENADA—*See also COMMONWEALTH of Nations, OAS*
UN Assemb member 4A1
Belize independnc backed 6-16, 494G2
Anti-Gairy protests dispersed 6-19, 494B3
Ortiz confrmd US amb 7-13, 626C3
Gairy at Panama Canal pact signing 9-7, 678C1
Chile ties called threat to Carib 10-26, 869A1
GREYHOUND Corp.
Intercity bus fare hiked 5-15, 423A2
Del stock seizure law voided 6-24, 539C3
GRIEVE, Tom
Traded to Mets 12-8, 990B1
GRIFFEY, Ken
NL batting ldr 10-2, 926C3, D3
GRIFFIN, Archie
Campbell wins Heisman 12-8, 950C2
GRIFFIN, James
Elected Buffalo mayor 11-8, 855C3
GRIFFIN, John Wesley
Cleared 11-5, 871G2
GRIFFIN, Sen. Robert P. (R, Mich.)
Baker elected minority ldr 1-4, 6E1, A2
Scores Warnke 3-4, 172C1
Issues FTC cargo preferne rpt 9-9, 720D1
GRIFFIN, Robert T.
Named Gen Services admin 2-15, 148F3

1978

GREENBELT National Park (Va.)
Indians encamp 7-15—7-23, 568E3
GREENE, David
Gray Lady Down released 3-10, 619B2
GREENE, Graham
Human Factor on best-seller list 4-30, 356G1; 6-4, 460B3
GREENE, Ken
In NFL draft 5-2, 336F2
GREENE, Richard
Family Business opens 4-12, 760B2
GREENE, Tony
NFL '77 interceptn ldr 1-1, 56D2
GREENE v. Massey
Double jeopardy evidence rule backed by Sup Ct 6-14, 468F3
GREENFIELD, Meg
Wins Pulitzer Prize 4-17, 315A2
GREEN Giant Co.
Pillsbury acquisitn agreed 9-18, 752C3
GREENLAND (Danish possession)
Danish home rule proposed 5-15, 371F2
Jorgensen backs local autonomy 10-3, 774D1
Danish parlt offers home rule 11-17, 902D1
GREENPEACE (ecology organization)
Seal kill off Scotland canceled 10-16, 816B2
GREENSPAN, Alan
Carter inflatn plan, $ drop linked 11-1, 826B3
GREENWOOD, Charlotte
Dies 1-18, 196A3
GREGG, Peter
Wins Daytona endurance 2-5, 538C3
3d in LeMans 6-11, 538A3
GREGORY, Dick
At Davis Cup protests 3-18, 251F3
At Seabrook A-plant protest 6-24—6-26, 494E1
GREGORY, Don
Paul Robeson opens 1-19, 760A3

GRENADA—*See also CARIBBEAN Community, COMMONWEALTH of Nations, OAS*
Agri Min aide shot 1-4; dies, 3 suspects held 1-5, 94F2
Amer rights conv enacted, ct formed 7-18, 828E3
UN Assemb member 713F3
GRENDEL, Frederic
Violette released 10-9, 1030F3
GRESHAM, Ore.—*See OREGON*
GREY Advertising Inc.
Dental ad complaint rptd setld 8-31, 702E2
GREYHOUND Corp.
IBM trust case review denied 1-16, 33E2
Mt Hood trust award curbed by Sup Ct 6-19, 492A3
GRIESA, Judge Thomas P.
Orders Sindona extraditn 5-19, 454F1
FBI informant case declined by Sup Ct 6-12, 468E1
Cites Bell for contempt in FBI informants case 7-6, 507A2; ordr stayed 7-7, 525A1
GRIESE, Bob
NFL '77 passing ldr 1-1, 56A2
GRIEVE, Tom
Traded to Cardinals 12-5, 1026C1
GRIFFIN, Mike
Traded to Yankees 11-10, 1026B1
GRIFFIN, Sen. Robert P. (R, Mich.)
Votes vs Panama Canal neutrality pact 3-16, 177G2
Votes vs 2d Canal pact 4-18, 273B1
Wins renomination 8-8, 625G3
Loses reelectn 11-7, 845E1, D2, 846E1, 854A1
GRIFFIN, Robert T.
Firing strains O'Neill-White House ties, new post found 7-28—8-7, 605E2
GRIFFIN, Rod
In NBA draft 6-9, 457G2
GRIFFITH, Calvin
Remarks on blacks, players cause furor 9-28—10-2, 779B2
GRIFFITH, Kristen
Rib Cage opens 5-28, 887G2

1979

GREEN 3rd, William J.
Wins Phila mayoral primary 5-15, 363C2
Campaigns with Kennedy 10-22, 808B1
Elected 11-6, 846A3
GREEN Jr., William J. (deceased)
Son wins electn 11-6, 846B3
GREENBERG, Richard
Colo land sale refunds set 5-8, 596A1
GREENBURG, Mark
Hopkins wins NCAA lacrosse title 5-26, 507G2
GREENE, Ellen
Nature & Purpose opens 2-23, 292C2
Teeth 'n' Smiles opens 8-13, 712A3
GREENE, Graham
Human Factor on best-seller list 3-4, 173F3
GREENE, Judge Harold H.
Upholds FEC apptmt 1-8, 130E3
AT&T proposes speedy trust trial date 1-11, 88A3
Upholds Uniroyal contract ban 7-20, 885B3
Rules vs NRA in Army gun resale suit 9-4, 747F1
GREENE County Nuclear Power Plant—*See NEW York State–Atomic Energy*
GREENHOLTZ v. Inmates
Case decided by Sup Ct 5-29, 421E2-B3
GREENLAND (Danish possession)
Home rule backed in referendum 1-17, 40F3
Soclsts win 1st home-rule electn, EC exit seen 4-4, 286C1
Eur Parlt electns 6-9, 433A1, 434F1
GREENSBORO, N.C.—*See NORTH Carolina*
GREENSPAN, Alan
On State of Union Message, budget 1-24, 48A2
On Prop 13 natl impact 6-3, 500D1
On '79 econ problems 10-29, 826D3
GREENSPUN, Herman
SEC suit vs Hughes settled 1-19, 88B2
GREEN v. Georgia
Case decided by Sup Ct 5-29, 421E3
GREENVILLE, S.C.—*See SOUTH Carolina*
GREENVILLE (S.C.) Technical College
104 Iranians suspended 11-21, 898E2
GREENWALD, Gerald
Named Chrysler exec vp 9-20, 700A1
GREENWOOD, David
In NBA draft 6-25, 507A2
GREGG, Forrest
Named Bengals coach 12-28, 1001E1

GRENADA—*See also CARIBBEAN Community, COMMONWEALTH of Nations, NONALIGNED Nations Movement, OAS*
Gairy flies to US 3-12, overthrown 3-13; oppositn party rptd in control 3-14, 190F2
New regime makes diplomatic overtures; US, UK, Caricom recognize 3-15–3-24, 236G2-F3
Govt aides named 3-23, 237A1
Const suspended, Commonwealth ties affirmed 3-25, 236F3
Dominica pledges ties 6-29, 502D3
Nonaligned movemt joined 9-3, 675E1
UN membership listed 695E2
Oppositn paper closed 10-15, 792A3
20 arrested in plot 10-16, 792G2-A3
Coup plot fails 11-3, 855G3-856A1
US sets Carib policy 11-29, 960E3
GRENFELL, Joyce
Dies 11-30, 932G2
GRETZKY, Wayne
Named WHA top rookie 5-16, 470F2
GREVEY, Kevin
Sonics win NBA title 6-1, 506E3, 507A1
GREY, Dr. Jerry
Backs solar power satellites 1-10, 36D1
GREY, Joel
Grand Tour opens 1-11, 292F1
GREY Cup—*See FOOTBALL*
GREYHOUND Corp.
ICC intercity bus svc expansn suit filed 7-13, 579C2
GRGUREV, Fred
MISL top scorer 3-18, 432E1
GRICH, Bobby
Angels lose AL pennant 10-6, 797F2
GRIESA, Judge Thomas P.
Seeks FBI ex-agent's statemt in SWP trial 1-16, 92B2
Bell contempt citatn overturned 3-19, 207E1
Sentences Franklin Bank ex-offcls 3-26, 3-27, 291E3
GRIESE, Bob
NFL '78 passing ldr 1-6, 80A1
NFC wins Pro Bowl 1-29, 79E3
GRIFASI, Joe
On The Yard released 1-18, 174C3
Says I opens 2-20, 292G2
GRIFFI, Guiseppe Patroni
Divine Nymph released 10-12, 1007B3
GRIFFIN, Alfredo
Named AL co-top rookie 11-26, 955B3
GRIFFIN, Col. John
Cited in H-bomb letter 9-16, 9-18, 714F1, 716E3-717A3
GRIFFIN, Robert T.
Muellenberg named GSA inspector gen 1-30, 92E3
O'Neill cites '78 firing 7-18, 531B2
GRIFFITH, Calvin
Carew traded to Angels 2-3, 619F1
GRIFFITH, Corinne
Dies 7-13, 588A3
GRIFFITH, James
Scores shipyd strike 4-11, 306B3
GRIFFITHS, Edgar H.
On RCA-CIT merger 8-17, 682B2

1980

GREEN 3rd, Mayor William J. (Phila., Pa.)
Phila Journal strike ends 1-25, 115A3
Sets police, fire layoffs 2-4, effected 3-1, 187C1
Kennedy wins primary 4-22, 304D1
Rpts refined oil tax dropped, co 'contributns' set 6-10, 743F3
Carter tours Phila 9-3, 699A1
GREEN Bay—*See WISCONSIN*
GREENBERG, Daniel
Panelist in pres TV debate 9-21, 721C3
GREENBERG, Harold
Death Ship released 4-25, 416F2
Terror Train released 10-3, 836G3
GREENE, Bob
Bryant files for divorce 5-22, 471D3
Bryant divorce rptd 8-21, 639C1
GREENE, Graham
Human Factor released 2-8, 216G2
GREENFELD, Josh
Oh, God! II released 10-3, 836C3
GREENHUT, Robert
Stardust Memories released 9-26, 836F3
GREENLAND, Chris
Zimbabwe min freed in murder case 12-8, 946C2
GREENPEACE (U.S. environment group)
Spain impounds ship 6-18, escape prompts Adm's dismissal 11-15, 903B3
GREEN Ripper, The (book)
Wins Amer Book Award 5-1, 692E2
On best-seller list 6-8, 448D3
GREENSPAN, Alan
At GOP platform hearings, stresses energy 1-14, 32E1
Meets Reagan reps re Ford vp spot 7-16, 530B1
On Sept CPI 10-24, 823B3
GREENVILLE—*See CALIFORNIA, NORTH Carolina, SOUTH Carolina*
GREER, Curtis
In NFL draft 4-29, 336E2
GREGG, Judd
Elected to US House 11-4, 843F2, 848F2
GREGG, Peter
Kills self 12-15, 1004A2
GREGG, Troy Leon
Escapes prison 7-28, found slain 7-30, 654G1
GREGOREK, John
2d in 6,000-m Penn Relays 4-25, 892D2
GREGORY, Eddie
TKOs Johnson for WBA light-heavywgt title 3-31, 320E1
GREGORY, Rodgers
Admits S Africa arms sales 3-25, 278F1
GREISMAN, Alan
Heart Beat released 4-25, 416A3
GRENADA—*See also COMMONWEALTH of Nations, NONALIGNED Nations, OAS*
Freedom House lists as partly free 87D3
Peoples Temple assets located 2-6, 170F3, G3
Bishop assassinatn try foiled, suspect slain 6-19; war alert called 6-20, 498B2
Foreign Relations (misc.)
UN res vs Sovt Afghan invasn opposed 1-14, 25G1
Bishop in Nicaragua, marks Somoza downfall 7-19, 565F2
GRETZKY, Wayne
NHL scoring, assist ldr 4-6, 295F3, 296D1
Named NHL MVP, top sportsman 6-6, 488B1
GREY Cup—*See FOOTBALL--Professional*
GREYHOUND Corp., The
Film actress sues 1-4, 199A3
Bus plunges into Tampa Bay 5-9, 391C1
Fla ends busing regulatn 7-1, 558F2
Mt Hood trust case declined by Sup Ct 10-6, 782C2
Swanson resigns 10-7, Batastini named pres 11-20, 959C1
GREYHOUND Corp. v. Mount Hood Stages Inc.
Case declined by Sup Ct 10-6, 782D2
GRIESA, Judge Thomas P.
Sindona convicted 3-27, 237G1
Sentences Sindona aide 4-23, 415C1
GRIFFEY, Ken
NL wins All-Star Game, named MVP 7-8, 636F1, B2, D2
NL batting ldr 10-6, 926E2
GRIFFIN, Alfredo
AL batting ldr 10-6, 926E3
GRIFFIN, John Howard
Dies 9-9, 755C3
GRIFFIN, L. Francis
Dies 1-18, 104F2
GRIFFIN, Robert T.
Named to Chrysler post 3-13, 199B3
GRIFFITH, Darrell
Louisville wins NCAA basketball title, named tourn MVP 3-24, 240E1, B2, D2
In NBA draft 6-10, 447B1, E1
GRIFFITH, Hugh
Dies 5-14, 448F1
GRIFFITHS, Edgar H.
Valente becomes RCA pres 1-1, fired 6-18, 582G1
NBC drops Olympic telecast plans, estimates loss 5-6, 379D3
Announces Carson contract 5-6, 470G3
Pfeiffer resigns as NBC chrmn, RCA dir 7-10, 582E1

1976

GRIGORENKO, Pyotr
In CSCE monitor group 5-13, 408B2
GRILLO, Gustavo
Angola sentences 6-28, 480B2, G2
GRIMBLE, Robert
In Mex talks 1-26, 75F1
GRIMOND, Jo
Gets interim Liberal post 5-12, 364E3
New Liberal head named 7-7, 521F2
GRISHIN, Viktor V.
Named to Politburo 3-5, 195B2
GRIVAS, Gen. George (1898-1974)
Sampson arrest asked 1-28, 155E1
GROBAN International Inc.
Boycott rpt released 10-19, 786D1

GROMYKO, Andrei A.
In Japan peace treaty talks 1-10—1-13, 29G3-30C1
Japanese fishermen freed 1-19, 52C1
In Kissinger SALT talks 1-21—1-23, 61A3
Named to Politburo 3-5, 195B2
Ends UK visit 3-25, Angola vows rptd 3-26, 228C1, F3
Signs French A-safeguards pact 7-16, 540E2
Addresses UN Assemb 9-28, sees Kissinger 9-29, 10-1, 719B1, A3
Sees Ford re SALT 10-1, 739B1
China rebuffs proposals 10-5, 759G3
Meets Egypt forgn min 11-3—11-4, 841F2

GRONOUSKI, John
Milwaukee schl integratn ordrd 1-19, 42B3
GROS, Piero
Wins Olympic medal 2-14, 158D3
GROSS, Manvela
Wins Olympic medal 2-7, 159B1
GROSS, Nelson G.
Sup Ct bars conviction review 10-4, 766D1
GROSS, Robert E.
Cited in Bernhard probe rpt 8-26, 628A1
GROSS, Ted
Slain 6-6, 442D3
GROSSET & Dunlap Inc.—*See FILMWAYS Inc.*
GROSSMAN, Lawrence K.
Elected PBS pres 1-8, 80F2
GROSS National Product (GNP)—*See ECONOMY; country names*
GROSSO, Kevin
Arrested 11-3, 972D1
GROTON, Conn.—*See CONNECTICUT*
GROUP of 77—*See 'Trade and Development, U.N. Conference on' under UNITED Nations*
GROUP of 10—*See INTERNATIONAL Monetary Fund*
GROVE Valve & Regulator Co.
Boycott rpt released 10-19, 786D1
GRUENEBERG, Gerhard
E Ger Politburo enlarged 5-22, 381E2
GRUMMAN Corp.
Japan Lockheed role chrgd 3-9, 191A2
Rpt CIA had '50s Lockheed bribe data 4-2, 286E2
Bid for Nixon donatn chrgd 9-13, denied 9-15, 9-16, 979G1-E3
'74 Iran F-14 sale probed 9-26, 979D3, F3
Top fscl '76 defns contractor 12-21, 961B3
Grumman Aerospace Corp.
'75 arms sales listed 2-6, 147B2
Iran drops jet order, commissn disputed 2-17, 140B1
GRUNER, George F.
Jailed 9-3—9-17, 700B3
GRUNKE, Klaus-Jurgen
Wins Olympic medal 7-19, 574B2

1977

GRIGORENKO, Pyotr G.
Leaves on 6-mo US visit 11-30, 956D1
GRIMOND, Jo
Liberals extend pact with Labor 7-26, 637A2
GRINAKER Precast Ltd.
US contract bid rptd 10-17, 979E1
GRISHIN, Boris A.
FBI cites re espionage 1-16, 41F2
GRISHIN, Viktor Vasilevich
Revolutn anniv fete photo 11-7, 865D2
GROCERY Manufacturers of America Inc.
Dixon slurs Nader 1-17, 96A1
GROH, Viktor
Sentence rptd 10-19, 812E1
GROHMAN, Josef
Arrest rptd 1-4, 19E3
Trial opens 1-10, 82F3
Sentenced 2-3, 115C1
Rptd sentenced 12-20, 1018G3

GROMYKO, Andrei Andreevich
Sees Vance on arms limits 3-29, 225G1
Scores US arms proposals 3-31; Carter replies 3-31, 4-2, 246D2
Vance defends US proposals 4-1, 247B1
In India 4-25—4-27, 348D1
OKs SALT framework 5-18—5-20, stresses differences 5-21, 400D2-A3
Sees Egypt forgn min 6-9—6-10; joint statemt issued 6-11, 457F2
Vance mtg delayed 6-15, 530B1
To visit Cairo 6-24, 496C2
India drops steel plant aid 8-24, 655C2
Meets Arafat 8-30—8-31, 663C1
Vance mtg delayed 8-31, 751C2
Meets Vance, Carter on SALT; sees Carter-Brezhnev summit 9-22—10-1, 750D3, 751B1
Addresses UN 9-27, 750G3, 769G2
Warns US on rights stand, backs A-test ban 9-27, 769G2
Meets Vance 9-30; joint statemt on Geneva 10-1, 749B2; text 750A1
Sees Owen re Rhodesia, detente 10-10—10-11, 812F3
Bars Cairo conf 11-29, 910E1

GROOM, Raymond
Named environment, housing, community dvpt min 12-19, 982B2
GROPPER, William
Dies 1-6, 84B3
GROS, Andre
World Ct member 4F1
Lockheed payoffs rpt cites 5-26, 502C3
GROSS, Courtlandt S.
Lockheed payoffs rpt cites 5-26, 502C3
GROSS, Mason Welch
Dies 10-11, 872B2
GROSS, Robert E. (deceased)
Lockheed payoffs rpt cites 5-26, 502C3
GROSS National Product (GNP)—*See under ECONOMY*
GROTON Pacific Carriers
Tanker explodes off Hawaii 2-24, 214C3
GROUP of 10—*See IMF*
GRUBBS, Victor
Survives Pan Am-KLM crash 3-27, 244E1
GRUENSTEIN, Peter
Nader sports-fan group planned 9-27, 820G1
GRUMMAN Corp.
US funds Israeli boat, copter productn 7-22, 570C3
Iran comm settlmt rptd 12-15, 978B1
GRUNDMANN, Wolfgang
Sentenced 6-2, 601G3
GRUNERT, Rolf
Arrested for spying 5-22, 602A2
GRUNFELD, Ernie
In NBA draft 6-10, 584A2
GRUN Moss, Gabriel
Asks return to rule of law 8-13, 633B2

1978

GRIGG, Charles L. (deceased)
Family OKs 7-Up sale 5-15, 364A3
GRIGORENKO, Pyotr G.
Citizenship stripped 2-13, scores 3-13, 179F2
Gets US asylum 4-19, 275E2
Leads Sovt rights protest in Bonn 5-4—5-7, 417A2
GRIGSON, A. C.
Loses Sen primary in Ark 5-30, 426A2
GRIMAU, Julian (d. 1963)
Book chrgs Carrillo aided arrest, executn 2-24, 136E2
GRIMM, Paul
Slain in Iran 12-23, 993C2
GRIMM & Co., W. T.
'77 merger activity rptd down 1-11, 65E3
GRIMSHAW, Richard
Ford assessed $128.5 mln in car crash case 2-6, 185B3
Ford crash award cut 3-31, 264F3
GRIMSLEY, Ross
NL pitching ldr 10-2, 928G2
GRIPP, Helga
On W Ger birth rate decline 8-16, 725D3
GRISHAM, Wayne
Wins US House seat 11-7, 850B2, 856F3
GRISSOM, Virgil (d. 1967)
Wife accepts space medal 10-1, 861C2
GRIZZARD, George
Man & Superman revived 12-17, 1031D2
GROCERY Trade—*See SUPERMARKETS & Chain Stores*
GRODEN, Robert L.
Analyzes JFK murder film, plans House panel presentatn 11-26, 916E1-E2
GROENDAL, Benedikt
Fails to form Icelandic govt 7-12—7-12, named forgn min in Progressive coalitn 8-31, 688E3
GROENEWOLD, Kurt
Given suspended sentence 7-10, 651F2
GROLEAU, Pierre
Begelman chrgd with forgery 3-31, 251E1
GROMYKO, Andrei Andreevich
In Japanese peace talks 1-9, 28D3
Sees Vance on SALT 4-20—4-21, 297B1
Shevchenko defects 4-26, 302A3
SALT A-arms transfer limits rptd agreed 5-1, 423E1
Sees Vance, Carter on SALT 5-25—5-31; scores Zaire chrgs Africa propaganda 5-27, 6-4, 422C1-C2
Addresses UN disarmamt sessn; backs SALT agrmt, A-test ban 5-26, 421G1
Spy warning to Vance cited 6-15, 476G2
Young US 'pol prisoners' remark spurs controversy 7-12—7-15, 542D2
Sees Vance on SALT 7-12—7-13, gets Shcharansky trial protest 7-12, 543D2
Denounces Camp David summit 9-6, 673G2
Sees Warnke on SALT 9-7—9-8, 747E2
Sees Vance on SALT 9-27—9-28, meets Carter 9-30—10-1, 747F2
Sees Vance on SALT 10-22—10-23, revised cruise limit plan rptd 10-24, 803C3-804F1
In France 10-25—10-28, 830E3-831A1
Meets Arafat 10-30, 828F1
Sees US sens, gets emigratn requests 11-15, 905C1, G1
Sees Vance, SALT pact delayed 12-21—12-23, 995F2
GRONCHI, Giovanni
Dies 10-17, 888B3
GRONOWICZ, Antoni
Garbo calls book hoax 4-21, 335B3
GROOM, Ray
Australia housing, constructn min 11-30, 943G3
GROSBARD, Ulu
Straight Time released 3-18, 619G3
GROSPIRON, A. F.
Rptd vs Carter wage curb 11-21, 917B3
GROSS, Ernest A.
Shevchenko defects 4-26, 302D2
GROSS Domestic Product (GDP)—*See ECONOMY (non-U.S.); country names*
GROSSET & Dunlap Inc.
Nixon memoir excerpts published 4-30, 5-1, 319E2
GROSSMAN, Paula Miriam (nee Paul Monroe)
Wins disability pay 2-16, 327E2
GROSS National Product (GNP)—*See under ECONOMY*
GROTE, Jerry
In World Series 10-10—10-17, 800B1
GROUP of 77
US seabed mining bill opposed 8-21—9-16, 732D3
GRUBMAN, Patty
Dancin' opens 3-27, 887F1
King of Hearts opens 11-22, 1031C2
GRUENEWALD, Thomas
Living At Home opens 12-11, 1031C2
GRUMMAN Corp.
Wm Schwendler dies 1-14, 96E2
7th in '77 defns contracts 3-28, 224F2
SEC sues Page Airways 4-13, 449C2
To fly out kin from Iran, hq firebombed 12-8, 954D1
GRUNDMAN, Irving
Named Canadiens managing dir 9-6, 991B1
GRUNFELD, Jorge
Sentncd for fraud 5-31, 824C3
GRUNOW, John E.
On Kennecott bd rival slate 3-27, 402G3

1979

GRIMALDI, Dan
Victim opens 5-3, 712C3
GRIMES, Brian
On 3 Mile I A-accident 3-30, 243F3-244A1
GRIMES, Tammy
Father's Day opens 6-21, 711A3
Month in the Country opens 12-11, 1007D2
GRIMM & Co., W. T.
1st 1/4 merger rise rptd 4-10, 349F2
GRINESLAND, N.C.—*See NORTH Carolina*
GRIVELET, Bernard
Chrgd re wine mislabeling 4-25, 330B3
GRODEN, Robert F.
JFK autopsy photo forgery claim denied 7-9, 520A3
GRODIN, Charles
Real Life released 3-1, 174E3

GROMYKO, Andrei Andreevich
In Italy 1-22-1-26, sees Pope 1-24, 60E2
Gets US protest on Iran broadcasts 2-16, 125D3
Says China Viet invasn imperils US ties 2-26, 141G2
Meets Assad in Damascus 3-24; Israel-Egypt pact scored 3-26, 222D2
Assures US reps re SALT 4-20, 314A2
In Hungary with Brezhnev 5-30—6-1, 417A1
At SALT II summit 6-15—6-18, 449F1; communique text 457C1
Warns Sen vs SALT chngs 6-25, US scores 6-26—6-30, 496G2-F3
Ogarkov vs SALT opponents 8-2, 644E1
Sees Vance re Cuba troop issue 9-24, 9-27, UN statemt chrgs 'lies' 9-25, 738B2
Visits W Ger, warns vs NATO missiles 11-21—11-24, 938A3
GROSBARD, Ulu
Woods opens 4-25, 712F3
GROSPIRON, A. F.
Gulf contract reached 1-11, 87F1
GROSS, Kathy
Describes ordeal as hostage 11-18, freed 11-19, 878A1, E1, B2
GROSS, Shelly
Murder at Howard Johnson's opens 5-17, 712F1
GROSS Domestic Product (GDP)—*See ECONOMY (non-U.S.), country names*
GROSS National Product—*See under ECONOMY*
GROSVENOR, Robert George (Duke of Westminster)
Dies 2-19, 176B3
GROUND-Launched Cruise Missile (GLCM)—*See ARMAMENTS–Missiles*
GROUND Saucer Watch (organization)
CIA UFO probe detailed 1-12, 93A1
GROUP Against Smokers' Pollution (GASP)
Miami rejcts anti-smoking law 5-8, 350D3
GROUP Health Cooperative of Puget Sound
Uterine cancer study rptd 1-31, 139G1
GROUP Life and Health Insurance Co. v. Royal Drug Co.
Drug plan trust rule upheld by Sup Ct 2-27, 165A1
G.R. Point (play)
Opens 4-16, 711E3
GRUBER, Lee
Murder at Howard Johnson's opens 5-17, 712F1
GRUENAWALD, Peter
Held in Lufthansa theft 2-17,
GRUHL, Herbert
Natl 'Green Party' planned 10-27—10-28, 876F1
GRUMMAN Corp.
SEC sues re paymts, case settled 1-4, 16D1-A2
Japan probes SEC payoff rpt 1-9, Nissho exec kills self 2-1, 98E2
Forgn payoffs disclosed, Japan bribes denied 2-8, 305G2
4 indicted in Japan bribe scandal 4-5, 5-15, 389G2
Aerospace unit sued by textile union 7-18, settles 8-1, 598F3
10th in '78 defns contracts 8-1, 609C1
GRUNDMAN, Irving
Bowman resigns as Canadiens coach 6-10, 470A3

1980

GRIMES, Tammy
42d Street opens 8-25, 756D3
GRIMM, Willard T.
On 1st 1/4 merger activity 4-8, 386F1
On 1st 1/2 merger activity 7-9, 557D1
GRIMM, Yuri
Sentenced 10-11, 863B2
GRIMM & Co., W. T.
'79 merger rise rptd 1-15, 52E2
1st 1/4 merger activity slows 4-8, 386F1
1st 1/2 merger activity slows 7-9, 557C1
GRIMSHAW, Don
Wins Calif US House primary 6-3, 439B2
GRISHAM, Rep. Wayne (R, Calif.)
Reelected 11-4, 842B2
GRIVNINA, Irina
Arrest rptd 9-17, 863E2
GRIZZARD, George
Wins Emmy 9-7, 692D1
GROBBELAAR, Bruce
NASL goalkeeping ldr 8-24, 770D3
GROGAN, Steve
NFL '79 passing ldr 1-5, 8A2

GROMYKO, Andrei Andreevich
UK cancels visit re Afghan invasn 1-5, 2E2
In Syria, vows arms 1-27—1-29, 140D3
In Rumania, India re Afghan support 1-31—2-2, 108F3
Reaffirms arms talks 2-18, 124B1
Vs UK Afghan neutrality plan 3-14, 205B1
Visits France 4-24—4-25, 351E3
Muskie mtg planned 5-7, 343B1
Sees Muskie in Vienna 5-16; W Ger, French reactn 5-19, 5-21, 378A1, D3, 379D1
Iran chrgs border breach, aid to Kurds 8-12, 644D3
Meets Waldheim on Iran-Iraq war 9-23, meets Muskie 9-25, 718E3, 719A2
Meets Japan forgn min in NY 9-24, 752D1
In Poland for Warsaw Pact mtg 10-19—10-20, 800E2
Sees US Sen Percy 11-26, 11-28, 915D1, G1
Meets Norway forgn min 12-22—12-23, 979B2
Meets Polish forgn min 12-26, 976A3

GROOM, Ray
Ousted from Australia Cabt 11-2, 857F2
GROSS, Volkmar
NASL goalkeeping ldr 8-24, 770D3
GROSSMAN, Lawrence K.
Plays down RCTV BBC deal 12-11, 1002E3
GROSS National Product (GNP)—*See under ECONOMY*
GROUP of 77
UN dvpt fund asked 2-9, 124B2
GROVENOR, Linda
Die Laughing released 5-23, 675C2
GRUBB, David Alexander
Dies 7-24, 608A2
GRUDZIEN, Zdzislaw
Ousted from Poland CP post 9-19, 720F2
GRUEN, Victor
Dies 2-14, 176D1
GRUENING, Clark S.
Wins Alaska US Sen primary 8-26, 683F1-B2
Loses US Sen electn 11-4, 852F1
GRUENING, Ernest (1887-1974)
Grandson wins US Sen primary 8-26, 683G1
GRUEN v. U.S.
Case declined by Sup Ct 1-21, 93B3
GRUMMAN Corp.
Navy grounds A-6 planes after crashes 2-27, flights resumed 3-4, 228F1
Nader coalitn attacks 4-17, 308B2
8th in '79 defns contracts 5-28, 403F1

1976

GUADAGNO, Gennaro
Rptd on CP ticket 5-17, 5-30, 402C3
GUADELOUPE (French overseas department)
Soufriere volcano eruptn forecast, islanders evacuated 8-16, 643G3
Soufriere volcano erupts 8-30, 643C3
Volcano evacuatn scored 9-2, 674C3
Volcanologist dismissed 10-18, 905D3
GUAM (U.S. territory)
Air Manila jet crashes 6-4, 736A2
Dem conv women delegates, table 508E2
US Dem conv pres vote, table 7-14, 507B2
GOP pre-conv delegate count 8-14, 583B3
Ford, Reagan seek conv delegates 8-16, 8-17, 601A3, B3
GOP conv pres, vp vote tables 8-18—8-19, 8-19, 599B1, B3
GOP platform text 8-18, 605E3
US House Dem ldrs elected 12-6, 919C1
GUARDO, Ricardo
Loses defense post 2-23, 211F3

GUATEMALA—*See also CACM, IDB, OAS, SELA*
'76 record budget rptd 1-9, 55G1
Russell ct scores rights abuse, '54 US coup aid 1-17, 61C2
Listed as 'partly free' 1-19, 20C3
Earthquake hits 2-4, relief operatns begin 2-4—2-5, 81A1-B2
Tremors, relief aid continue 2-4—2-11; death toll at 17,000 2-9, 120F2
Quake analysis rptd 2-7, 121A1
Tremors, relief aid continues; death toll passes 22,000 2-11—2-22, 155F2
Alleged looters shot 2-14, vigilantes rptd 2-16, 155G3
Kissinger Latin tour, more quake aid pledged 2-16—2-24, 177A1, 178F1
Quake econ damage rptd light 2-24, 155E3
US Cong clears relief bill 4-13, 283B3; Ford signs 4-21, 533E2; 6-30, 982E1
Lopez elected Cong pres 6-25, rightists assume control 7-18, 1005B1
Guerrillas stage attacks 7-9—11-20, Amnesty Intl rpts executns 12-13, 1004D3
Boster confrmd US amb 8-26, 807E3
US sugar duties tripled 9-21, 721D3
Vs UNESCO res vs Israel 11-22, 879A1
Belize Issue—*See BELIZE*

GUAY, Joseph-Philippe
Named min of state 11-3, 851E2
GUBBINS, Maj. Gen. Sir Colin Mcvean (ret.)
Dies 2-11, 160D3
GUDE, Rep. Gilbert (R, Md.)
Steers wins seat 11-2, 821E1
GUDGER, Lamar
Elected to US House 11-2, 822F2, 830F2
GUENA, Yves
Elected UDR chief 4-24, 812A3
Scores govt defense policy 6-2, 417C3
Lauds Chirac resignatn 8-25, 638A1
On US election results 11-3—11-4, 826D1
Chirac forms new party 12-5, 963G3
Scores Parisien Libere raid 12-6, 964A1
GUENTHER, Detlef
Wins Olympic medal 2-7, 159G1

1977

GRUSON, Sidney
Disputes NY Times-CIA link 9-12, 720D3
GRUTKA, Most Rev. Andrew G.
NLRB dispute case refused 5-2, 406C2
GSA—*See U.S. GOVERNMENT—GENERAL Services Administration*
GTE Sylvania Inc.—*See GENERAL Telephone & Electronics*
GUAM (U.S. territory)
Sup Ct jurisdictn curbed 5-23, 444A1
GUARDIAN, The (British newspaper)
Kenya ousts rptr 4-13, 393E1

GUATEMALA—*See also IDB, OAS*
190 pol prisoners rptd 1-1, 3G1
Coffee crop damage cited 74B3
'66-76 disappearances, executns rptd 2-21, 168A3
'61-75 GDP variatns table 5-30, 439B1
Montes rptd leftist rebel ldr 7-4, 673D1
Spreading violence, rights abuse protested 7-14—8-23, congressman killed 8-23, 672F3
2 new right-wing terror groups rptd 7-20, 7-21, 673B1
Malaria upsurge rptd 9-4, 747D3
Pol kidnaps, violence rptd 9-5, 706B3
Guatemala City rioters killed 9-15, 805C3
Ex-defns min killed 9-29, 'extreme left' blamed 9-30, 805B3
Rightists threaten teachers, students 10-10, 869E1
Police kidnap student; 2 held hostage 10-14, 869E1
'78 electns set, candidates cited 10-16, 869D1
June-Aug pol murders examined 11-2, 905E2
Belize Issue—*See BELIZE*
Foreign Relations (misc.)
UN Assemb member 4A1
'75-76 trade, paymts table 3-11, 189A2 ★, B2
'66-75 arms transfers table 4-8, 415A2
Venez scores Orfila re '76 quake funds 4-27, 371F3
El Salvador amb kidnaped 5-29—5-30, 438G1-F2
Barbados seizes Israel arms shipmt 6-25; Israel sale rptd 7-6, 553E2
Laugerud at Panama Canal pact signing 9-7, 678D1
Spanish king visits 9-10—9-13, 804G3, 805C1
Brazil coffee policy backed 10-21, 876C3
Abstains on UN anti-Israel res 10-28, 830G2
U.S. Relations
US modifies duty-free list 2-28, 189E3
US rights stand scored 3-12, mil aid rejctd 3-16, 187A2
US delays arms sales 7-17, 572F3
Arms sales resumptn rptd 9-7, 706A3
US bars mil credit sales 10-19, 815A3; signed 11-1, 834D1

GUAY, Joseph-Philippe
Canada natl revenue min 9-16, 725F2
RCMP tax data use rptd 12-2, 945F2

1978

GRUSA, Jiri
Arrested 5-30, 504F1
GSA—*See U.S. GOVERNMENT—GENERAL Services Administration*
GSCHEIDLE, Kurt
Retains W Ger transport post 2-3, 93A3
GTE—*See GENERAL Telephone & Electronics*
GUAGLIARDO, Vincenzo
Protests jail conditns 5-28, 453A3
GUAM (U.S. territory)
US troop presence rptd 1-2, 5D2
GUANDIQUE, Felix Esteban
Shuns Chamorro death probe panel 4-6, 376C2
GUANTANAMO (U.S. naval base)—*See CUBA—U.S. Relations*
GUARINI, Frank J.
Wins US House seat 11-7, 849C1, 851B3
GUASCO, Guido
To prosecute Il Messaggero editor 5-22, 393E3

GUATEMALA—*See also IDB, OAS*
Guerrillas, troops clash in 2 rural areas 1-18, 152D3
Ex-forgn min ransomed from guerrillas 1-30, 152B3
FAR guerrillas killed 2-7, attacks resume 2-24, 168E3
Peralta Mendez scores climate of violence 2-15, 168A3
'77 pol deaths, kidnaps rptd 2-22, 168B3
Gen electns 3-5; violence, fraud chrgs delay count 3-5—3-9, 168F1
Govt, far right rift rptdly grows 3-9, 168F2
Electn results disputed 3-10—3-11, offcl figures rptd 3-14, 190F1
Lucas named pres-elect by Cong 3-13, 190D1
Final electn results rptd 4-28, 354B3
Peasants die in Panzos clashes 5-29; govt blames guerrillas; students, church accuse landowners 6-1—6-9, 496G3-497E1
Guerrillas kill 17 soldiers 6-13, 497F1
Ex-army chief killed 6-20, 497G1
Panzos peasant deaths called govt massacre 6-24, 722A3 ★
Priest killed 6-30; RCC, Mormons protest 7-21, 722C2 ★
'Death squad' acknowledged by govt 6-30, blamed for 30 murders 7-1, 722G2 ★
Lucas inaugurated as pres 7-1, 538E1
Guerrillas attack rural towns 7-7, 7-9, ambush soldiers 8-24, 722E2 ★
Civilns dominate Cabt 7-21, 722B3 ★
Union ldr slain 7-22; exec blamed 7-23; murder protested 7-22—7-23, 8-4, 722B2 ★, 723E2-F2
Earthquake hits 7-29, 759C1
Bus fare riots, 12 die 10-2—10-4, 777E1
Strikes follow bus fare protests 10-6—10-10, 796A3
Press curbs rptd by IAPA 10-13, 829B2
Belize—*See BELIZE*
Foreign Relations (misc.)—*See also 'Monetary, Trade, Aid & Investment' below*
Nicaragua troops beat 2 TV rptrs 2-1, 91C2
Amer rights conv enacted, ct formed 7-18, 828E3, 829C1
El Salvador guerrilla manifesto publshd 8-25, 722B2, 723F2 ★
Panama ties resumed 8-29, 798A3
Nicaragua amb killed by guerrillas 9-16, 777F1
UN Assemb member 713F3
Nicaragua crisis mediatn OKd 9-30, 757G2; mediators in Nicaragua 10-6—10-7, 777D2
Somoza restaurant burned 10-6, 796B3
Nicaragua pol talks suspended 10-21, rptd stalled 10-27, 839D1; impasse continues 11-5, 883E2
Nicaragua plebiscite OKd 11-30, terms disputed 12-17—12-29, 1018D2, G2, D3
Monetary, Trade, Aid & Investment
'77 export earnings up, trade surplus posted 1-13, 168F3
Coffee exports to be withheld 3-10, 181B3
Islamic bank poor-natn aid rise rptd 4-9, 257F2
Cuba guerrilla aid chrgd 6-1, 497C1
U.S. Relations
Carter hopeful on Belize setlmt 6-21, 489C3
Rights abuse chrgd by US panel 6-24, 490C1
GUATHIER, Hubert
Replaced as Francophone ldr 9-7, 721F3
GUBAREV, Col. Alexei
In joint Czech flight 3-2, docks with Salyut 3-3, 157E2
Returns to Earth 3-10, 181B1
GUDGER, Rep. Lamar (R, N.C.)
Reelected 11-7, 851C3
GUENA, Yves
On govt electn program 1-11, 54F2
GUENTHNER, Louis R.
Wins US Sen primary in Ky 5-23, 406F2
Loses electn 11-7, 853B3

1979

GRUNWALD, Henry Anatole
Named Time ed in chief 6-21, 556G1
GSA—*See U.S. GOVERNMENT–GENERAL Services Administration*
GUADELOUPE (French overseas department)
4-natn summit held 1-5–1-6, 12D2-C3, 40C2
Hurricane David hits 8-30, 690C3
GUADELOUPE Summit
4 natns meet 1-5–1-6; SALT accord, detente backed 1-6, 12D2-C3
Turkey aid offer rptd 1-12, 40C2
OECD OKs Turkey aid role 2-6, 116E3
GUANTANAMO (U.S. naval base)—*See CUBA–U.S. Relations*
GUARD, Dominic
Picnic At Hanging Rock released 2-22, 174D3
GUARDADO, Facundo
Arrest protested 5-4, freed 5-11, 371A1, C1
GUARDINO, Harry
Goldengirl released 6-15, 820C1
GUARE, John
Bosoms & Neglect opens 5-3, 711F1

GUATEMALA—*See also IDB, OAS*
Freedom House lists as partly free 13B1
Quake strikes 6-23 619F3
PEN scores on rights 7-21, 554B1
Foreign Relations (misc.)—*See also 'UN' below*
Nicaragua plebiscite plan rejctd by Somoza 1-19, 76D2
Mex troops aid fight vs guerrillas 1-26, 97C2
Mex dispatches Latin missn on Nicaragua 5-21, 409C1
Nicaragua arms aid chrgd 6-2, 427F1
Nicaragua relief convoy set 7-21, 574B2
El Salvador deposed pres seeks refuge 10-15, 790A2
Cuba guerrilla ties rptd 10-26, 813G3
Unrest
'Death squad' kills 18 1-15–1-17, 97C2
Fuentes Mohr slain 1-25, 97E1-A2
Guerrillas raid Nebaj 1-26, 97B2
Right, left-wing violence rptd 2-14–3-1, 237E1
Colom slain 3-22, right-wing terror mounts 3-24, 237B1
Army staff chief slain 6-10, 445B3
Amnesty Intl puts '78-79 pol deaths at 2000 9-12, 708D2
Lucas Garcia's nephew kidnaped, 3 others killed 10-7, 792C3
Leftists take credit for army staff chief's death 10-7, 792D3
Garcia kin buy ads for leftist kidnapers 10-26, 813E3
UN Policy & Developments
Membership listed 695E2
U.S. Relations
Kennedy deplores Fuentes Mohr assassination 1-26, 97F1
US rights missn completed 6-5, 427G1
US exec flees El Salvador 8-24, 668C2

GUBERMAN, Igor
Arrested 8-13, 980B3
GUEILER Tejada, Lidia (Bolivian president)
Meets Natusch re peace plan 11-3, 853A1
Cong elects president 11-16, 888A2
Cabt sworn 11-19, 907G1
Army cmdr rebels 11-23; demands met, successor named 11-25, 907D1
Sets econ measures 12-3, 926C1
GUERRA, Lynne
Wine Untouched opens 6-22, 712F3
GUERRA Jimenez, Eduardo
Released from prison 2-21, criminal record cited 442F1
Hijacks jet to Cuba 6-11, 442B1
GUERREIRO, Ramiro Saraiva
Brazil forgn min designate 1-19, 95E1

1980

GRUNTHAL G.m.b.H.
Iran unit takeover rptd 7-9, 546E2
GRUNWALD, Levi Yitzhak
Dies 4-12, 360A2
GRUPP, Bob
NFL '79 punting ldr 1-5, 8B3
GSA (General Services Administration)—*See under U.S. GOVERNMENT*
GSCHEIDLE, Kurt
Sworn W Ger post min 11-5, 925F1
GTE Sylvania v. Consumers Union
Case decided by Sup Ct 3-19, 250B1
GUADELOUPE (French overseas department)
French-Cuban trade accord rptd, interventn pledge linked 4-1, 253B3
Terrorist bomb blast kills 1, destroys Air France jet 9-17, 769G1
Terrorist bombings continue 11-16—11-17, 896E1
GUAM (U.S. territory)
Carter sets econ plan 2-14; govs meet, set projects 2-19—2-22, 495B1
N Marianas lose US citizenship 3-7, 495F1
Reagan gains pres conv delegates 5-3, 342D3
GUARDSMAN, The (play)
Opens 1-3, 136B3
GUARINI, Rep. Frank (D, N.J.)
Reelected 11-4, 843B3
GUASCO, Guido
Rpt accuses 21 re Moro affair, backs separate probe of intellectuals 1-2, 20E2-A3

GUATEMALA—*See also IDB, OAS*
Foreign Relations (misc.)—*See also 'UN Policy', 'Unrest' below*
Spanish ties severed 2-1, 98B2, F2
El Salvador Emb clashes 2-12, 117B2
Colombia DR Emb siege ends; amb, envoy freed 4-27, 335G1
El Salvador border patrol rptd 6-13, 462G3
El Salvador rightist arrives 7-3, 521E3
Jerusalem Emb shift rptd set 9-7, 800E3
El Salvador junta member's son foils kidnap 10-17, 829E2, 830F1
Government & Politics—*See also other appropriate subheads in this section*
VP resigns in rights protest 9-2, 670F3
Sports
Moscow Olympic results 7-20—8-3, 622G2
UN Policy & Developments
Assemb res backing Palestine state opposed 7-29, 572F1
Unrest
Spanish Emb seized 1-31; survivor abducted 2-1, slain 2-2—2-3, 98B2, E2
Spain severs ties 2-1, 98F2
Coca-Cola plant union ldr, 3 others slain; intl protests launched 4-16—5-27, 463B3
Nestle exec kidnaped 6-17, ransom demand rptd 6-20, 487F2
Palace plaza bomb kills 7, 3 others defused 9-5, 708E3
Leftists attack northn army post, 10 die 9-6; patrol defuses RR bridge bomb 9-8, 708G3
Nestle exec freed 9-10, 731B3
Rights activist kidnaped, son slain 10-16, 830E1
El Salvador junta member's son foils kidnap 10-17, 829E2, 830F1
Amnesty Intl scores rights record 12-10, 978A3
U.S. Relations
Spanish amb takes refuge 2-1, 98A3
Coca-Cola plant labor unrest, intl protests; US sale pressed 4-16—5-27, 463B3
Reagan electn welcomed 11-5, 841F2

GUCCIONE, Robert (Bob)
Caligula released 2-2, 216C2
Wins libel case vs Flynt 3-1, 239B2; award cut 4-17, 405A3
GUCWA, Stanislaw
Warns vs Poland interventn 12-13, 976F1
GUDGER, Rep. Lamar (D, N.C.)
Loses reelectn 11-4, 850A1
GUEILER Tejada, Lidia (Bolivian president; ousted July 17)
Receives US amb 3-26, 272B2
Swears new Cabt, gives mil 2 posts 4-7, 272E1
Coup rumors intensify 5-30—6-10, mil asks electn delay, US amb's ouster 6-9, delay denied 6-10, 443B2
Assault attempt fails 6-7, 443B3
Scores Santa Cruz riot, bars electn delay 6-19, 496D3
Electns held 6-29, Siles leads 7-3, 508E3
Ousted in mil coup 7-17, 546E2
Coup protested by women at UN conf 7-18, 587C3
Seeks refuge with papal nuncio 8-1, 602C3
Debt paymts postponed 9-3, 686F2, A3
Gets OK to leave Bolivia 9-15, 728A1
Leaves Bolivia 10-4, scores Garcia regime 10-5, 787C2
GUERIN, Dr. Camille (1872-1961)
TB vaccine cited 1-20, 63B2

1976

GUEST, Judith
Ordinary People on best-seller list 12-5, 972F2
GUEST, Raymond P.
'72 campaign gift listed 4-25, 688A1
GUETENET Zewde
Slain 11-9, 1002D1
GUEVARA, Maj. Ernesto 'Che' (1928-67)
'75 OAS embargo end cited 138C2
Death controversy grows 4-14—5-17 415B3
Bolivian envoy slain 5-11, 350E3
GUEVARA, Nacha
Theater bombed; resumes exile 1-2, 26A1
GUGLEMAN, Tucker
Rptd in Hanoi jail 593B2
GUI, Luigi
Named in Lockheed scandal, quits cabt 2-11—2-12, 132G1
Successor sworn 2-13, 140B2
Payoff probe set 4-2, 298F1
GUICHARD, Olivier
Named French justice min 8-27, 650E3, F3
GUIGA, Driss
Ousted 5-31, 503C3
GUILFOYLE, Margaret
Rpts Indochina refugee aid 3-22, 237B2
GUILLAIN-Barre Syndrome—*See 'Diseases' under MEDICINE & Health*
GUILLAUME, Christel
E Ger seeks visit 1-25, 158A2
GUILLAUME, Gunter
E Ger seeks visit 1-25, 158A2
GUILLEN, Nicolas
Elected to Natl Assemb 11-2, 1001A1
GUIMARAES, Ulysses
On municipal electns 11-19, 902F3

GUINEA—*See also AFRICAN Development Bank, NONALIGNED Nations Movement, OAU*
Listed as 'not free' nation 1-19, 20D3
UNESCO literacy drive fails 2-4, 85C2
UN Palestine com member 2-26, 162C1
Castro visits 3-14—3-16, 251D3
Benin, Togo reopen border 3-27, 372B1
Total IMF oil loans rptd 4-1, 340C2
Toure rpts May assassinatn try, arrests 6-9, 503A3
Sovt, Cuba mil presence rptd 6-13, 467C1
More Toure plotters arrested 7-15, 8-10; min chrgs CIA link 8-24, 1005A2
ECOWAS rptd ratified 11-6, 974E2
Cabt shuffled, amb to Algieria named 12-11, 1005F1
OPEC loan set 12-23, 975F3
GUINEA, Equatorial—*See EQUATORIAL Guinea*
GUINEA-Bissau, Republic of (formerly Portuguese Guinea)—*See also NON-ALIGNED Nations Movement, OAU*
Listed as 'not free' nation 1-19, 20D3
Freezes Portugal bank assets, Lisbon suspends paymt 3-1, 543F2
Cabral sees Castro 3-15—3-16, 251E3
At France-Africa summit 5-10—5-11, 355A3
Wells confrmd US amb 9-15, 808D1
ECOWAS rptd ratified 11-6, 974E2
GULF of California
Mex enforces 200-mi limit 6-6, 420A2
GULF of Gabes
Tunisia-Libya oil dispute 3-22, 239F2
GULF of Mexico
Oil rig sinks 4-15, 544D3
Copter crash kills 12 4-23, 736G2
US to OK 2 superports 12-17, 991G3
GULF Oil Corp.
McCloy rpt on paymts detailed 133E1
3 Dutch officials admit link 1-11, 134G1
Rpts Bolivia '66 bribe, Bolivia denies 1-14, 147G1
Dorsey, 3 others ousted; McAfee named chrmn 1-15, 132A3-133E1
N Sea oil find rptd 1-19, UK buys controlling interest 2-26, 173A3
Jones pleads guilty 1-29, 134E1
Angola operatns halt cited 1-30, 82D2
US OKs Angola operatns 2-21, 163E1
NY dismisses '74 trust case 3-10; 2d case rptd pending 3-11, 413C1
Angola gets '75 royalties 3-11, Cabinda operatns to resume 4-5, 287E2
Wild indicted 3-12, acquitted 7-27, 566A1
Copter crashes in Gulf of Mex 4-23, 736A3
On '75 Fortune 500 list 437B1, D1, G1
N Viet vows forgn cooperatn 5-7, 367A3
SEC lists paymts 5-12, 725G3, 727E1
North Sea find rptd 5-28, 521D3
Job Bias setlmnt rptd 7-16, 943C3
Viglia sentenced 8-4, 566A2
Rpts Angola output 8-19, 649G2
Colo oil shale leases suspended 8-23, 648G3
Dole denies fund irregularities 9-6, 9-8, 665D3
Scott gifts probe 9-15, 980A1
Ecuador to buy pipeline 9-17, 872E1
Pays Ecuador back taxes 9-30; sellout talks begin 10-25; 872A1
'75 US tax paymt rptd 10-2, 847A2
Cannon reelected 11-2, 824D2
On S Korea deals 11-2, 899C1
Shareholder suits setld 11-18, 939E1

1977

GUEST, Judith
Ordinary People on best-seller list 9-4, 712F3
GUEVARA, Ernesto (Che) (1928-67)
'65 Cuba role in Congo cited 1-9, 19B1
GUEYE, Boubacar
Senegal conservative party ldr 9-9, 710F3
GUGGENHEIMER, Elinor
Coffee boycott role cited 1-11, 74G2
Rpts NYC coffee consumptn down 4-26, 319E1
GUGGENHEIM Foundation
Gross dies 10-11, 872B2
GUI, Luigi
Indicted 1-29, 116B3
Claims innocence 3-8, trial set 3-10, 284B1
GUICHARD, Olivier
Ousted from Cabinet 3-30, 239D1
GUIDRY, Ron
AL pitching ldr 10-2, 927A1
In AL playoff 10-5—10-9, 807E1
In World Series 10-11—10-18, 806A3
GUILFOYLE, Bishop George
Fires newspaper editor 2-11, 471E1, G1
GUILFOYLE, Margaret
Named Australia soc sec min 12-19, 982A2
GUILLAIN-Barre Syndrome—*See MEDICINE—Diseases*
GUILLAUME, Gunter
W Ger Defns Min scandal rptd 12-12, 968F1
GUILLEMIN, Dr. Roger C. L.
Wins Nobel Prize 10-13, 951C3
Gets Medal of Sci 11-22, 951G3
Somatostatin made from bacteria 12-1, 1022A3
GUILLEN, Capt. Fernando
Bolivia housing min 10-13, 902D1
GUIMARAES, Ulysses
Scores mil govt 6-27, 523C2
Acquitted on electn chrgs 11-30, 964B2
Scores Geisel pol reform plan 12-9, 964B1

GUINEA—*See also NONALIGNED Nations Movement, OAU*
UN Assemb member 4A1
Amin on Toure death plot 7-4, 512A2
Cuba mil, other advisers cited 11-17, 896G1
USSR spy flights rptd halted, bid for US ties stalled 11-19, 989F1
Bauxite base price OKd 12-7, 975E1
GUINEA, Equatorial—*See EQUATORIAL Guinea*
GUINEA-Bissau, Republic of—*See also NONALIGNED Nations Movement, OAU*
UN Assemb member 4A1
IMF, World Bank entry rptd 3-24, 309C2
At France-Africa summit 4-20—4-21, 316F3
Cuba mil, other advisers cited 11-17, 896G1
GUINESS Mahon Holdings Ltd.
Kaiser confrmd amb to Hungary 6-30, 626F2
GUINNESS Book of Records, The (book)
McWhirter slayer sentenced 2-10, 222A3
GUISE, Sir John
Resigns as gov-gen 2-8, 203B3
Somare elected prime min 7-12, 639G1
GULAG Archipelago, The, 1918-1956 (book)
Royalties aid dissident fund 2-2, 101C2
GULF of Aden
Djibouti strategic role cited 506A3
GULF of Gabes
Italy oil rig withdrawn 497F2
US oil rig protested by Tunisia 5-27, 497G2
World Ct to hear Libya-Tunisia dispute 6-10, 497F2
GULF of Mexico
Gas rptd withheld 2-11, 2-22, 2-26, 152C1
'76 gas reserves data cited, US sets probe 2-17, 151D3-152B1
FPC gas testimony reprisals chrgd 3-10, 196C1
Offshore oil sales delayed 5-17, 499A1
2 offshore leases cancelled 6-8, 499C1
Carter visits oil rig 7-22, 575A2
Oil rig copter crashes 12-8, 1023F2
GULF Oil Corp.
Ecuador buys local assets 1-1, 7G2
Montana coal option revoked 1-13, 59A1
Jones guilty plea cited 2-16, 112A1
Gas withholding chrgd, denied 2-23, 152G1
Sales unaffected by paymts crackdown 2-28, 233E1
IRS ex-employe sentenced 3-31, 288G2
US amb: Cubans protect Angola plants 4-11, 271G3
Uranium cartel role chrgd 4-25; NYS, US probes rptd; McAfee role denied 6-9—6-17, 479A2-480E2
On '76 Fortune 500 list 340E1, C3
Sup Ct declines Wild waiver case 5-16, 419A2
Canada unit to halt Mackenzie drilling 6-4, 466B3
Indicted for IRS gifts 6-15, 504A1
Quits superport project 7-12, 559B2
FTC asks Kewanee purchase delay 8-3; buys Kewanee 8-9, 612E2
Kewanee takeover cited in merger table 880F1
Washington sues 8-16, 691E3
Peru to pay re '75 natlzatn 8-24, 785C2
India rejctd Geoman low bid 10-3, 765B1
United Nuclear trial opens 10-31, 895D2
Fined re laundered pol gifts 11-13, 881D2
TVA sues re uranium 11-18, 895F1
Pleads guilty, fined on IRS gifts 11-22, 944A1

1978

GUEST, Ron
Blue Collar released 2-9, 618D3
GUEST, Keen & Nettlefolds Ltd.
Sachs takeover halted by W Ger ct 2-23, 211B1
GUIDOLIN, Aldo (Bep)
Hired as Rockies coach 11-23, 991C1
GUIDON, Bobby
Named WHA playoff MVP 7-6, 656D3
GUIDRY, Ron
AL pitching ldr 10-2; wins CY Young Award 11-1, 2d in MVP vote 11-7, 928D1, G1, F3-G3
Yankees win AL pennant 10-7, 779B1
In World Series 10-10—10-17, 800A1
GUILLAUME, Christel
Prisoner swap rptd discussed 4-24, 318F2
GUILLAUME, Gunter
Prisoner swap rptd discussed 4-24, 318F2
GUILLERMIN, John
Death on Nile released 9-29, 970B1

GUINEA—*See also NONALIGNED Nations Movement, OAU*
Pol prisoners, 3 French natls rptd freed 1-5, 22B2
At W African mtg; backs ECOWAS, upgrades ties 3-18; USSR scores 3-20, 237D1
Islamic bank poor-natn aid rise rptd 4-9, 257F2
Senegal ties restored 5-5, 445A2
200 prisoners rptd freed, pvt enterprise OKd, travel curbs eased 6-9, 596E2
2,000-4,000 prisoners rptd held 6-21, 596D2
UN Assemb member 713F3
Giscard visits, Westn thaw noted 12-20—12-22, 1018A1
GUINEA, Equatorial—*See EQUATORIAL Guinea*
GUINEA-Bissau, Republic of—*See also NONALIGNED Nations Movement, OAU*
6 W African natns back ECOWAS 3-18, USSR scores 3-20, 237E1
Angola, Portugal ldrs meet 6-24—6-26, 562A2
Mendes killed 7-7, 620A3
UN Assemb member 713F3
Polisario recognitn cited 11-10, 999G2
GUINN, Vincent
Testifies at JFK assassinatn hearing 9-8, 698F1
GULF of Aden—*See ADEN, Gulf of*
GULF of Aqaba—*See AQABA, Gulf of*
GULF of Mexico—*see MEXICO, Gulf of*
GULF of Suez—*See SUEZ, Gulf of*
GULF Oil Corp.
Rebates to consumers barred 1-20, 109A1
Low '76 tax paymt rptd 1-27, 65A3
Gas pipe co contract compensatn challenge refused 2-21, 126B2
United Nuclear wins uranium suit; impact on other Gulf suits seen 3-2, 144E1, B2
Bolivia compensatn paymt rptd 4-14, 478A3
New United Nuclear evidence revealed 4-20, 346F2-A3
Wild gives SEC depositn 4-26, settles paymt chrgs 5-11; gift recipients rptd 6-2, 449B1
On '77 Fortune 500 list 5-8, 325E1, A2
US files uranium cartel chrgs 5-9, 346D1-D2
Westinghouse suit filed 5-9, 346D2
Lee on '77 top-paid execs list 5-15, 364F3
Natural gas diversn curbed by Sup Ct 5-31, 430F3-431D1
Pleads no contest in uranium cartel case fined 6-2, 449G2-A3
Crude oil pricing suit setld 7-27, 610F2
Canadian unit urges US gas exports increased; graph 9-1, 704A2, D2
8th-ranked cash-rich US co 9-18, 716E3
IRS offcl's bribery convictn review refused by Sup Ct 11-27, 937C2
General Atomic Co.—*See separate listing*
Pittsburg & Midway Coal Mining Co. (P&M)
Coal agrmt reached, UMW cncl OKs 2-20, 122G3
Pact rejected by miners, Marshall cites 2-26, 160A1

1979

GUEST, Christopher
Shame of Jungle released 9-14, 820C3
GUEVARA Arze, Walter (Bolivian president; replaced Nov. 1)
Bolivia interim pres 8-6; facts on 600A2
Army rebelln put down, control assured 10-11, 811E1*
OAS address stresses access to Pacific, US tin sales 10-22, 824F1
Overthrown in mil coup 11-1, 832E3
Loyal troops plan offensive 11-3, sends Cong message 11-6, 852F3
Gueiler replaces Natusch 11-16, 888B2
Army chief rebels, Gueiler relents 11-23—11-25, 907F1*
GUGGENHEIM, Peggy
Dies 12-23, 1008A3
GUI, Luigi
Acquitted 3-1, 155C2
GUIDELLA, Vittorio
On Fiat investmt plan 9-12, 709C2
GUIDRY, Ron
NL wins All-Star Game 7-17, 569D1
AL pitching ldr 9-30, 955F3, G3
GUILES, Paul
On Giscard-Bokassa gift chrg 10-11, 791G1
GUILLAIN-Barre Syndrome—*See MEDICINE—Diseases*
GUILLAUME, Robert
Wins Emmy 9-9, 858D2
GUILLEN Murillo, Humberto
Ecuador health min 12-9, 967E3
GUILMARTIN, Ken
Nasty Rumors opens 4-12, 712F1

GUINEA—*See also NONALIGNED Nations Movement, OAU*
Liberia gets troops vs riots 4-17, 279G3
Tchidimbo freed, improved rights climate noted 8-6, 796A3
Toure in US, gets aid pledge 8-8—8-15, 796C3
UN membership listed 695E2
GUINEA-Bissau, Republic of—*See also OAU*
UN membership listed 695E2
Iran takeover of US Emb opposed 11-16, 878D3
Cuba rptd training children 12-10, 981B2, C2
GUINNESS Book of World Records, The (book)
Snake sitting record set 5-13, 392C3*
Rafferty completes Death Valley run 7-15, 656D3
GUITTARD, Laurence
Umbrellas Of Cherbourg opens 2-1, 292E3
Oklahoma opens 12-13, 1007D2
GULCIGIL, Mustafa
Named Turkey interior min 11-12, 876E1
GULF Air
Entebbe hijack case declined by US Sup Ct 4-30, 364G3
GULF Oil Corp.
US files overchrg suit 1-5, 17B1
NJ offshore well rptd dry 1-10, 17A2
Oil workers OK pact within Carter guidelines 1-11, 87B1
Iran oil crisis forces sales curbs 2-6, 83A1
Carter cites oil worker pact 2-12, 109E3
Oil sales curb announced 3-8, 183B3
Gen Crude merger bid rejctd 3-28, 283A1
2d NJ offshore well rptd dry 4-2, 361E3
1st 1/4 oil profits rptd 4-27, 301G1, B2
US overchrg claims denied 5-2, 343B2
On '78 Fortune 500 list 5-7, 304E1, 305A1
June gas supplies cut 5-29, 395B3
McAfee on Carter mtg 5-31, 418C1
US clears re Vepco overchrg 6-12, 580A3
July gas supplies rptd 6-27, 479F1
Vs Carter heating oil price freeze request 9-17, 703E1
Tex supertanker port OKd 10-15, 769F3
3d 1/4 oil profits rptd up 10-25, 804D3
US overchrgs alleged 11-6, 849G2; 11-14, 905G2-A3; 11-18, 12-11, 943B1, F1; 12-10, 990G2
General Atomic Co.—*See separate listing*

1980

GUEST, Judith
Ordinary People released 9-19, 836D3
GUEVARA Arze, Walter
Electns held 6-29; Siles leads, lacks majority 7-3, 508E3
GUGLIELMO, Tony
Loses US House electn 11-4, 848D1
GUIDICE, Raffaele
Arrested re oil tax evasn 10-24, 873F2
GUIDRY, Ron
AL pitching ldr 10-6, 926G3
Royals win AL pennant 10-10, 795G3
GUILBAULT, Jacques
Says Liberal MPs 'bullish' on const 'patriatn' 9-7, 728G1
GUILTY (recording)
On best-seller list 10-8, 796B3; 12-3, 948B3
GUIMARES de Carvalho, Hervasio
In Argentina for A-talks 3-18, 229C2
GUINAN, Texas
Froelich dies 2-5, 176B1

GUINEA
Chad peacekeeping force arrives 1-18, 119B1
Laye dies 2-4, 176C2
Tito sends detente plea 2-21, 139B3
Tito funeral held 5-8, 339B1
Toure assassinatn foiled 5-14, 431E3
Chad peace conf fails 10-18—10-19, 810G1
Libyan role in Chad opposed 12-23—12-24, 979E1
GUINEA-Bissau, Republic of—*See also NONALIGNED Nations, OAU*
Islamic conf boycotted 1-27—1-29, 67C2
Vieira seizes power 11-14, Cabral safety assured 11-18, 887B1
GUINNESS, Alec
Raise the Titanic released 8-1, 675D3
GULABZOI, Sayed Mohammed
Links Amin to rebels, CIA 1-21, 44G1
GULCIGIL, Mustaga
Resigns 7-21, 567E3
GULF Coast Lead Co.
Fla toxic waste suit filed 10-9, 825B1, D1
GULF Oil Corp.
'79 profit rptd 1-24, 90F2, C3
Natl park drilling rights affirmed by Sup Ct 3-31, 291A3
1st 1/4 profit rptd 4-24, 331D1, G1
On '79 Fortune 500 list 5-5, 290E1, 291B1
Phila refining tax dropped, 'contributn' set 6-10, 743F3
Gasoline prices cut 7-9, 553F1
US, W Ger, Japan synfuel pact signed 7-31, 666E2
Wholesale gas price cut rptd 8-1, 666D3
Nigeria disputes oil-take 8-8, 620F1
Mobil halts Newfoundland Ben Nevis drilling 8-22, 668D3
Gasoline price cut rptd 9-23, 786C1
Canada oil sands operatn threatnd 11-19, 920G3

1976

GULF & Western Industries Inc.
Simon & Schuster consent decree filed 7-27, 989A2
Kayser Roth boycott rpt released 10-18, 786A1
GULLETT, Don
Reds win pennant 10-12, 796F1
In World Series 10-16—10-21, 815C2
Signs contract 12-5, 951D3 ★
GULLION, Edward P.
Indicted 7-14, 796B3
GULLOTTI, Antonio
Sworn Italy works min 7-30, 573F1
GUNDELACH, Finn Olav
Europn Comm meets 12-22—12-23, 977G1
GUNEY, Yilmaz
Sentenced re '74 murder 7-13, 873G3
GUNN, Hartford
Named PBS vice chrmn 1-8, 80G2
GUNS—*See FIREARMS*
GUNTHER, John
Scores revenue sharing critics 3-2, 187F1
GUR, Lt. Gen. Mordechai
Details Uganda raid 7-8, 514F3
GURA, Larry
Yankees win pennant 10-14, 796G1
GURENEWALD, Armin
Clarifies Italian loan ban 7-19, 530F3
GURIRAB, Theo-Ben
On Cuban aid offer 3-2, 206E1
On S Africa arms ban veto 10-19, 781F3
GURNEY, Edward J.
Acquitted of final chrg 10-27, 845F3
GUSTAVSSON, Rune
Named to Swedish Cabt 10-8, 794C2
GUTHRIE, Perry Eugene
Arrest rptd 6-2, Lockheed link cited 6-19, 498E2
GUTIERREZ, Jose
Letters on Colombia bribes publshd 2-8, 147E2
GUTIERREZ, Nelson
Chile asks Vatican emb release 1-9, 47F2
Linked to UK MD arrest 1-24, 100B1
Gets safe-conduct, Sweden offers refuge 1-28, 100A1
Exiled to Sweden 2-21, vows return 2-22, 288B3
GUTIERREZ Mellado, Lt. Gen. Manuel
Promoted, named regional cmdr 3-28, 314B3
Spain defns min, 1st dep premr 9-22, 753A1
GUTIERREZ Ruiz, Hector
Kidnaped 5-18, body found 5-20, 399F1-D2 ★
Mourners seized at funeral 5-25, 441C2
Govt linked to death 5-28, 441B2
GUTTUSO, Renato
Rptd on CP ticket 5-17, 5-30, 402C3
GUY, Dortha
EEOC complaint deadline upheld 12-20, 960D1

GUYANA—*See also CARIBCOM, COMMONWEALTH of Nations, NONALIGNED Nations Movement, SELA*
Listed as 'partly free' 1-19, 20C3
Venez: Cuba planes to Angola refuel 1-24, 138A2
Alcan unit purchase rptd set 1-30, 252E3
'75 rice output, sales rptd 1-30, 252F3
PPP backs PNC govt 2-21, 252F3
Booker unit natlizatn set 2-23, 252B3
Cuba, China mil presence denied 2-23—3-10; Venez anti-govt drive continues 3-12, 253B1
Reynolds admits pol paymts 6-2, 690E2
Olympic withdrawal rptd 7-21, 528B3
Sprinter's bid to remain rejctd 7-22, 562F1
Cited in Barbados campaign 8-28, 673C1
Govt schl takeover OKd 10-1, 1005C2
Accuses US 10-17; US scores, ties deteriorate 10-20—10-21, 844D2
Cuban exile terrorism rptd 10-19, 780D2
Cuba jet crash trial set in Venez 10-21—10-22, 843G2, C3
Canada immigratn rptd 11-3, 851E1
Grenada deports atty gen 12-7, 925A2
UN Policy & Developments
Cncl member 62F2; 720C1
US delays aid re UN votes 1-9, 2B1
OKs pro-Palestine resolutn 1-26, 59G2
OKs Israel Arab land exit 6-29, 464C1
Shuns vote on anti-terror 7-14, 515G3
S Africa arms ban vetoed 10-19, 781D3
GUYER, Rep. Tennyson (R, O.)
S Korea probe rptd 10-30, 11-13, 900G1
Reelected 11-2, 830G2
GUYS and Dolls (play)
Opens 7-21, 1014D3

1977

Supertankers collide 12-16, 999G3-1000A1
Bolivia convicts Dorsey 12-23, 1010A3
General Atomic Co.—*See separate listing*
GULF Organization for the Development of Egypt (Kuwait, Qatar, Saudi Arabia, United Arab Emirates)
$1.5 bln Egypt loan rptd set 3-25, 390C3
Intl consortium OKs Egypt aid 5-11—5-12, 390B3
GULF + Western Industries Inc.
DR pres candidate vows natlzatn 9-11; sugar paymt order appealed 9-16, 767F1
Madison Square Garden Corp.—*See separate listing*
GULLETT, Don
In World Series 10-11—10-18, 806F1
GUMBS, Emile
Named Anguilla chief min 2-2, 190D2
GUNDELACH, Finn Olav
Gets Eur Comm post 1-7, 74C2
GUNDERSEN, Gen. Herman Fredrik Zeiner
Named NATO mil com chrmn 4-15, 360F1
Urges Turkey mil aid hike 12-6, 957E1
GUNS—*See FIREARMS*
GUPALOV, Alexander
Fined 5-2, 363C3
GUPTA, Kanwarlal
Govt sets corruptn probe 4-1, 283D3
GUR, Lt. Gen. Mordechai
Doubts copter crash sabotage 5-11, 396F2
Warns Arab natns on war 5-21, 440F2
On air raid vs PLO bases 11-9, 849D1
Chrgs Egyptian buildup 11-15, 873B2
GUTA Sernesa
Assassinated 11-2, 875E2
GUTERMA, Alexander L.
Dies 4-5, 286E3
GUTERMA, Marc
Survives air crash 4-5, 286E3
GUTHRIE, Janet
Indy 500 results 5-29, 531A2
GUTIERREZ, Elsa (Elsa Suarez)
IRS rptd cleared in Miami probe 1-6, 16A2
GUTIERREZ, Rodrigo
CR pres candidate 9-2, 710B2
GUTIERREZ Mellado, Lt. Gen. Manuel
Spain 1st dep premr 7-5, 545F1
GUTOWSKY, H. S.
Gets Medal of Sci 11-22, 952A1
GUTTMACHER Institute, The Alan
Rpts state funding of abortns 10-12, 786G3
GUY, Ray
Raiders win Super Bowl 1-9, 24D3

GUYANA—*See also COMMONWEALTH of Nations, NONALIGNED Nations Movement*
UN Assemb member 4A1
US effort vs Cuba planes to Angola cited 1-9, 19G1
CIA paymts to Burnham rptd 2-19, 124F1
'75-76 trade, paymts table 3-11, 189B1, A2 ★, C2
'61-75 GDP variatns table 5-30, 439B1
USSR, E Ger cooperatn pacts rptd 7-11, 710C3
Young visits, vows more econ aid 8-9—8-10, 646E1, G2
Nkomo visits, sees Young 8-9, 646B3
Sugar strike begins 8-24—8-30; govt search, arrest powers OKd 9-1, 710A3
Chinese help build textile plant 9-2, 710B3
Burnham rejects coalitn plan 9-9, 767C2
Sugar strike ldrs seized 9-9, 767D2
Trinidad workers boycott oil shipmts; govt ends sugar strikebreaking 11-4, 869F1
Sugar strikers' food seizure chrgd 11-4, 869G1
Bauxite base price OKd 12-7, 975E1
GUYER, Rep. Tennyson (R, Ohio)
Denies Korea lobbying link 9-27, 773F3 ★
Ford, Kim Han Cho mtg bid rptd 11-11, 915A2
GUYTON, Robert P.
On stockholders dividends 7-5, 574E2

1978

GULF United Corp.
Equitable merger set 6-26, 553D2
GULF + Western Industries Inc.
Talcott purchases planned 5-7, 404E1
DR arrests labor ldr 9-3, 774B2
Simmons OKs merger bid 10-15, 808B2
Madison Square Garden Corp.—*See separate listing*
Simon & Schuster Inc.
Garbo calls biography hoax 4-21, 335B3
GULLIKSON, Tim
Loses US Natl Indoor 3-5, 419A1
Loses Stockholm Open 11-14, Benson & Hedges tourn 11-19; wins S Africa Grand Prix 12-4, 1027C2, D2
GULLOTTI, Antonio
Named Italy posts min 3-11, 191C1
GULPILIL
Last Wave released 12-18, 1030B3
GUN Owners of America
5th-leading PAC fund-raiser 9-7, 753B2
GUNS—*See ARMAMENTS—Firearms; FIREARMS*
GUNTHER, Pastor Rolf
Kills himself 9-17, 840F3
GUR, Lt. Gen. Mordechai
Gives Israeli Sinai plan 1-12, 10E1
On Egypt mil talks 1-13, 26F1
On Israel invasn of Leb 3-15, 173C2
Confrms Israel abandons security belt 3-18, 198E1
Says Leb villages ask Israeli invaders in 3-19, 198A2
Gets Leb truce order 3-21, 198A1
Gives Leb pullback plan 4-6, 236A1
Replaced as staff chief 4-16, 359C1
Says Israel used cluster bombs vs PLO in '76 4-21, 300A2
GUR, Ugur
Wounded in assassinatn attempt 3-16, 230C2
GURA, Larry
Royals lose AL pennant 10-7, 778G3
Re-signs with Royals 11-13, 1025E3
GURFEIN, Judge Murray I.
Stays Bell contempt order 7-7, 525A1
Upholds CIA mail-opening damages 11-9, 940D1
GURNEY, Dan
CART group rptd formed 12-28, 1028B2
GURNEY, Edward J.
Trial press-curbs review declined by Sup Ct 4-17, 308D2
Wins US House primary in Fla 9-12, 736D1
Loses electn 11-7, 849E3
GUSCOTT, Kenneth
Defends NAACP energy plan statemt 1-14, 68B2
GUSHIKEN, Yoko
KOs Vargas 1-29, 379A2
KOs Chung 10-15, 969E1
GUTENBERG Bible (book)
W Ger museums buy copies 3-10, 4-7, 295D2
GUTH, Bill
Guides Carter raft-trip 8-22, 664E1
GUTH, Norm
Guides Carter raft-trip 8-22, 664E1
GUTHRIE, Arlo
At Seabrook A-plant protest 6-24—6-26, 494E1
GUTHRIE, Janet
9th in Indy 500, pre-race injury rptd 5-29, 538E2
GUTIERREZ, Alesio
Fired by Somoza 8-18, 659B3
GUTIERREZ Apea, Tomas
Last Supper released 5-5, 619G2
GUY, Ray
NFL '77 punting ldr 1-1, 56B3

GUYANA—*See also CARIBBEAN Community, COMMONWEALTH of Nations, GATT, NONALIGNED Nations Movement*
Sugar strike ends 1-6; '77 productn, earnings rptd 1-27, 94G2
Budget, paymts deficits cited 1-13, 100G2
'77 forgn exchng deficit rptd 1-27, 94B3
Belize defns aid agreed 3-10, 211C2
'78 budget announced 3-24, 292G2-B3
Const reform bill passed 4-10, 378A3
Burnham ends USSR visit, communique 4-22, 301G3
Burnham in UK, backs Belize independnc 5-6, 354C2
Const referendum set, Burnham sees '78 electns stay 5-15; PNC const draft rptd, oppositn scores 6-9, 478E3
Amazon 8-natn pact signed 7-3, 829C2
Govt wins const referendum 7-10, Assemb extends term 7-21, 688D2
IMF loan, terms accepted 8-8, 688A3
UN Assemb member 713F3
Press curbs rptd by IAPA 10-13, 829B2
Peoples Temple—*See separate listing*
GUYER, Roberto
Meets Leb pres on Unifil role 5-20—5-21, 383E2
Assures Israel on PLO Leb infiltratn 5-22, 383D2
GUYER, Rep. Tennyson (R, O.)
Reelected 11-7, 851D3

1979

GULF States Utilities Co.
Central La Energy purchase agreed 2-12, 132G1
GULFSTREAM American Corp.
Grunman pleads guilty re forgn paymts 1-3; SEC sues, case settled 1-4; '78 sale cited 16D1
GULF+Western Industries Inc.
Paramount resumes 'Warriors' ads 2-22, 174F1-A2
DR sugar probe rptd 8-16, land expropriatn urged 8-19, 632D3
Paramount-EMI deal called off 9-12, 9-12, 942F2
SEC files fraud suit 11-26, 923D1
Simon & Schuster Inc.
'Brethren' publicatn stirs controversy 12-2, 988A2
GULLIKSON, Tim
Wimbledon results 7-6, 7-7, 569E3
GUMBLETON, Msgr. Thomas
Sees hostages 12-24—12-25, Iran forgn min 12-27, 975B1-B2
GUMEDE, Josiah Zion (Zimbabwe Rhodesian president)
Elected pres 5-30, 393F1
GUNDELACH, Finn-Olav
Sets Australia trade accord 5-29, backs ties 5-30, 405B1
GUNES, Hasan Fehmi
Named Turkish interior min 1-14, 40G2
On martial law extensn 8-21, 637C2
Probes Kurdish unrest 8-23, 795E3
Resigns 10-5, 795D3
GUNS of August, The (book)
Tuchman elected Arts Inst pres 2-27, 176G1
GUNTON, Bob
Evita opens 9-25, 956A3
GURFEIN, Judge Murray I.
Dies 12-16, 1008A3
GUSHIKEN, Yoko
KOs Lopez 4-8, 412F3
GUTHRIE, Gay
Rocky Flats A-protesters sentncd 1-8, 17E3
GUTIERREZ, Eugene J.
Resigns Chicago schl post 12-4, 943G3
GUTIERREZ, Col. Jaime Abdul
Leads El Salvador coup 10-15, 790B2
GUTIERREZ, Gen. Julio
Proposed for Nicaragua junta 7-6, 504C1
GUTIERREZ, Mario
Bolivia pres bid rptd 3-16, 233G2
GUTIERREZ Mellado, Gen. Manuel
Opponents score 1-4, king backs 1-6, 60G3-61B1
GUTMAN, James C.
Short of Paradise released 10-5, 1008F1
GUTWILLIG, Bob
Rolling Stone, Look merge 5-7, 430F3
GUY, Ray
NFL '78 punting ldr 1-6, 80B2

GUYANA—*See also CARIBBEAN Community, COMMONWEALTH of Nations, GATT, IDB, NONALIGNED Nations Movement*
Freedom House lists as partly free 13B1
Bauxite strike ends 2-3, 299F3
Const formatn slowed by Jonestown, bauxite strike, govt scandal 3-2, 299E3
'78 econ growth rptd zero 3-23, 299G3
Oppositn party protests; ldrs arrested, priest slain 7-10—7-15, 814F1
Bauxite, other strikes prompt pol crisis; econ impact noted 7-23—8-28, 687G1
Burnham postpones electns amid pol crisis 10-22, 814B1, B2
Educ min slain 10-24, 838B2
Foreign Relations (misc.)
Grenada rebel regime recognized 3-21, 236A3
UN membership listed 695E2
Peoples Temple—*See PEOPLES Temple*
GUYLER, Lydia
Bolivia Chamber of Deps pres 8-4, 600D2
GUYON, Melvin B.
Arrested, chrgd re murder 8-16, 727G3
GUYTON, Robert P.
Bars Lance, Carter repaymt 1-23, 55E3
Denies Carter peanut loan, '76 campaign link; false bank rpts 4-12, 301E3

1980

GULF Resources & Chemical Corp.
Placid Oil offer rejctd 2-26, 385A3
Hunts sell shares to cover margin calls on silver 3-27, 223C2
GULF & Western Industries Inc.
Brown sale to James R Corp agreed 2-1, 3-27, 385E3
Paramount in Getty Oil pay-TV film venture 4-22, Justice Dept to probe 4-24, 376E2
Elec car dvpt claimed 6-5, 541F2
GM sets elec car battery test 7-9, 556E3
Paramount pay-TV film plan draws trust suit 8-4, 639F3
DR sugar dispute setld 9-5, 687F2
Madison Square Garden Corp.—*See MADISON Square Garden Corp.*
GULLICKSON, Bill
2d in NL top rookie vote 12-1, 926A1
GULLIKSON, Tim
Loses Baltimore Grand Prix 1-20, 607E2
GULLIKSON, Tom
Loses World Super tourn 11-2, 947C2
GUMBLETON, Msgr. Thomas
Knew Canada hid Iran envoys 1-29, 89A1
GUMBS, Emile
Webster elected prime min 5-28, 469E1
GUNBA, Saida
Wins Olympic medal 7-25, 624G1
GUNDELACH, Finn Olav
Australia sheepmeat talks founder 7-15, 561D3
GUNDELACH, Renee
Left-Handed Woman released 4-2, 416B3
GUNDERSON, Steven
Elected to US House 11-4, 844C4, 851A3
GUNNING, Robert
Dies 2-29, 279C3
GUNTER Jr., William (Bill) D.
Fla US Sen primary runoff set 9-9, 700F1
Wins primary runoff 10-7, 807C3
Loses US Sen electn 11-4, 849D2
GUNTHARDT, Heinz
Wins Rotterdam WCT tourn 3-16, 607G2
GUNTHER, Curt
BYU wins Holiday Bowl 12-19, 999B3
GUNTHER, Gerald
Sup Ct '79-80 term analyzed 7-2, 540B3
GUNTHER, John
Scores Carter revised budget 3-31, 244F1
GURA, Larry
AL pitching ldr 10-6, 926F3
Royals win AL pennant 10-10, 795G3
In World Series 10-14—10-21, 811C3, 812E2
GURANDOU-N'Diaye, Louis
Elected IOC vp 7-16, 590E3
GURNEY, Edward
Williams indicted in Abscam probe 10-30, 824B3
GURNEY, Rachel
Major Barbara opens 2-26, 392D3
GUSBERG, Dr. Saul B.
Urges fewer cancer tests 3-20, 317A1, C1
GUTHKE, Karin
Wins Olympic medal 7-21, 623F3
GUTIERREZ, Col. Jaime Abdul
3 civilns join junta 1-9, 20A1
Named mil chief 5-12, 372D3
Rift with Majano threatens junta 8-31, 669A3
Sets '82 electns, offers leftists amnesty 10-15, 789A3
Majano removed from junta 12-7, 941B3
Named El Salvador vp, army chief 12-13; sworn 12-22, 993C1
GUTIERREZ Mellado, Lt. Gen. Manuel
Suarez shuffles Cabt 5-2, 355E1
GUTIN, Marvin
Act of Kindness opens 9-11, 756B3
GUTTMACHER Institute, Alan
'78 abortn data rptd 1-9, 23B3
GUY, Ray
NFL '79 punting ldr 1-5, 8B3
GUYANA—*See also COMMONWEALTH of Nations, GATT, IDB, NONALIGNED Nations*
Colonial stamp sold for record sum; photo 4-5, 472C2, D2
Leftist ldr killed by bomb 6-13, 469F1
Leftist's brother arrested 6-24, controversy continues 10-6, 791A2
Burnham assumes presidency, names Reid prime min 10-6, 791E1
Burnham, PNC win reelectn 12-15; intl observers chrg fraud 12-19, 994F2
Foreign Relations (misc.)
IMF-World Bank loans OKd, hydro plan set 7-25, 791C2
Amazon pact signed 10-28, 865C2
Peoples Temple—*See PEOPLES Temple*
Sports
Moscow Olympics results 7-20—8-3, 588C3, 622E1
GUYANA, Cult of the Damned (film)
Released 1-25, 216F2
GUYANA Tragedy: The Story of Jim Jones (TV film)
Aired 4-15, 4-16, Nielsen rating rptd 4-22, 376D1
GUYER, Rep. Tennyson (R, Ohio)
Reelected 11-4, 843D4

1976

GUZZETTI, Rear Adm. Cesar
Argentina forgn min 3-29, 236C1
Scores US rights hearings 10-6, 996E2
GWINNETT County, Ga.—*See GEORGIA*
GYGER, Walter
Expelled from Iran 8-31, 735E1
GYMNASTICS
Olympic results 7-18—7-23, 563B1, 574A3
US team to visit S Africa 7-20, 528E3
GYMNASTICS Federation, International
US confrms S Africa trip 7-20, 528E3
GYONG, Margaret Ann (Mrs. Paul)
Husband wins Science Medal 10-18, 858E3
GYORGY, Paul (1893-1975)
Awarded Science Medal 10-18, 858E3
GYPSIES
Albania ethnic name-chng decree rptd 2-26, 332A1

1977

GUZMAN, Antonio
PRD nominates for pres 12-2, 969E3
GUZMAN, Leonardo
Uruguay expels 9-29, 905D1
GUZMAN Alvergue, Rene
Assassinated 7-1, 542A3
GUZZETTI, Rear Adm. Cesar
Scores US on rights 2-28, 142D2
Guerrillas wound 5-7, 388F2
GWEDE, Martin
Sentenced 2-14, 309E2
GWINNET Industries Inc.
Cited in Lance banking probe 8-18, 625A3
GYPSUM
4 co convictns overturned 1-6, 156E2

1978

GUZMAN, Antonio (Dominican president; sworn Aug. 16)
Rpts Balaguer, PRD 'non-agressn pact' 3-10, 230E3
Rptd shot at during campaign 5-12; final polls divided 5-14, 372G1
Electns held 5-16, army halts vote count 5-17; claims victory 5-17—5-18; count resumes 5-18, 371A3-372F1
Rebuffs PRD ldr, sees closer US, Latin ties 5-21, 414F2
Declared pres-elect 5-26; Balaguer concedes, mil ldrs vow acceptnc 5-27, 414G1
Final vote count rptd 6-2, 456G3-457A1
Electn confrmd; PR wins Sen majority, PRD to appeal 7-8, 558E3
Power curbed by mil statutes 7-19, 617A3
PRD appeal rejected 7-20, 617G2
Sworn pres, scores Balaguer govt; Cabt sworn, mil ldrs replaced 8-16, 648C1, C2, D2
Kin get govt posts; daughter defends 8-23, 671F2
Replaces Balaguer admin offcls 8-25; fires army chief, names as Spain amb 9-3, 774B2, C2
Amnesty bill enacted after veto 9-8, 774E1-A2
More mil ldrship chngs made 10-2, 881C1
Lists assets at $1 mln 10-9, 774F2
Hikes univ budget, at graduatn 10-29, 881F1
Sen rejects amb apptmts 11-9, 880G3
Retires army chief 11-17, 989A3
GUZMAN, Patricio
Battle of Chile released 1-12, 618C3
GUZZI, Paul
Loses Sen primary in Mass 9-19, 736B3
GWERTZMAN, Bernard
Vance interview publshd 11-25, 925B1
GYLLENHAMMAR, Pehy
Hails Volvo deal 12-8, 965C3
GYMNASTICS
AIAW chngs scholarship rules 1-7—1-11, 40B3
Olga Korbut marries 1-7, 95G3
World Championship results 10-23—10-29, 928B3
GYORGYEY, Clara
Catsplay opens 4-16, 887C1
GYPSIES
2d world cong held; Nazi reparatns, UN recognitn asked 4-8—4-11, 318G2
GYPSUM
Price fixing ruling upheld by Sup Ct 6-29, 567F2

1979

GUZMAN, Antonio (Dominican president)
Gives forgn mil posts to Balaguer backers 1-12, 62D2
Greets Pope 1-25, 67A3
Fires finance min, econ coordinator 3-9, 256B3
Gulf+Westn sugar probe rptd 8-16, 632B1
Army plot foiled 9-25–9-26, 751D3
GUZMAN, Gen. Jaime Nino de
Remains Bolivia AF chief 11-25, 907G1
GWYN, Althea
WBL rebound ldr 4-7, 507F1
GYLLENHAMMAR, Pehr
Volvo sale to Norway barred 1-26, 77B2
GYMNASTICS
Shaposhnikova wins Spartakaide title 7-26, 799E1
World Championships held 10-5–10-9, 1005B2
GYPSUM
Price fixing case refused by Sup Ct 10-1, 768F2

1980

GUZA Jr., Robert
Prom Night released 8-15, 675C3
GUZMAN, Antonio (Dominican president)
Orders fuel price hike, other austerity measures 5-28; taxi drivers strike 5-29—6-3, party regulars score 5-31, 462F1
Demotes vice pres 6-6, 462E2
Gulf & Westn sugar dispute setld 9-5, 687F2
Attends Santa Marta conf 12-17, 992A2
GWYNNE, Fred
Salt Lake City opens 1-23, 136E3
GYMNASTICS
Soviets dominate Moscow Olympics 7-20—8-3; disputes mar women's competitn 7-21—7-25, Dityatin wins 8th medal 7-25, 588F2, D3, 589D2-B3, 622D3-623A1
GYPSIES
W Ger hunger strike begun 4-4, 316E2
GYPSUM
Price fixing case settled 3-3, 557F3

H

1976

HAACK, Robert W.
Named to Lockheed probe 2-5, 131C2
Named Lockheed chrmn 2-13, 131E1
In Canada talks 2-29, 250A3
Lockheed settles SEC chrgs 4-13, 285F3
Signs Canada contract 4-30, 332C3
Signs Canada deal 7-21, 555A1
On UK Lockheed buy 8-18, 675F3
HABASH, George
Rpts PLA move into Leb 1-20, 34F1
Meets Arafat 3-30, 225C2
Iran guerrilla tied to PFLP 365F2
Denies PFLP hijack role 7-11, 515C2
PFLP tied to Uganda hijack 8-13, 629G3
HABIB, Philip C.
Says Viets renege on agrmt 7-21, 593C2
Asks Sen OK F-16s for Iran 9-16, 773G2
'74 Korea bribe bid rptd 10-29, 900B2
HABY, Rene
Students protest educ reforms 3-17—4-23, 311G3, 312B1
Named French educ min 8-27, 650F3
HABYALIMANA, Maj. Gen. Juvenal
Sees Amin re oil blockade 4-7, 502F2
At France-Africa summit 5-10—5-11, 355A3
HACKEL, Stella B.
Wins Vt primary for gov 9-14, 705B2
Loses election 11-2, 820D3, 821E3, 825B2
HACKENSACK, N.J.—*See NEW Jersey*
HACKETT, Bobby (musician)
Dies 6-7, 524E2
HACKETT, Bobby
Wins Olympic medal 7-20, 575E2
HADDAD, Rev. Antonio
Scores prisoner 'suicide' 1-26, 98D1
HADDAD, Dr. Wadi
Rptd in Libya terrorist network 7-15, 531G1

1977

HAACK, Robert W.
Denies Lockheed overbilled Navy 6-14, 482C3
Chase admits overbilling chrg overstated 8-22, 650D1
Says US made money on Lockheed guarantee 9-28; retires 9-29, 858C3
HAAG, Siegfried
Chrgd re Buback murder 4-9, 286C2
HAAS, J. Eugene
On US drought measures 2-21, 183A3
HAAS, Wilhelm
Giscard defends Daoud release 1-17, 27C3
HAAVIK, Gunvor Galtung
Norway expels 6 Sovt spies 1-28, 99B3
HABASH, George
Says PFLP may quit PLO 3-6, 166A2
Mansour slain 6-12, 510F1
At Tripoli anti-Sadat mtg 12-2—12-5, 929B2
HABE, Hans
Dies 9-30, 788C1
HABER, Joyce
Users on best-seller list 3-6, 184E3; 8-14, 643A2
HABIB, Philip C.
Carter retains in post 1-7, 14A2
Singlaub loses Korean cmnd 5-21, 403G2
Sees Korean ldrs on US troop exit, oppositn ldrs 5-24—5-26, 440G3
Hails US-Cuba thaw 9-1, 685D3
In Sovt Mideast talks 12-5—12-6, 930G1
HABY, Rene
Named educatn min 3-30, 239G1
HABYALIMANA, Juvenal
Young sees 2-4, 105D1
HACKETTSTOWN, N.J.—*See NEW Jersey*
HADDAD, Maj. Saad
Chrgs Palestinian atrocities, scores Sarkis 4-18, 297E2
Asks Israel mil aid 7-7, 571B2
Chrgs Syrian support vs Christns 8-5, 648B1
Denies PLO pullout rpt 10-10, 793D3

1978

HAACK, Dieter
Named W Ger housing min 2-3, 93A3
HAAPKYLAE, Jorma
Chairs Helsinki naval conf 5-16—5-18, 424G3
HAARS, Elberta
Red Army suspects extradited to W Ger 10-13, 10-17, 885B1
HAAS, Jay
Wins San Diego Open 1-29, 76E1
HABASH, George
Scorns Leb truce 3-30, 236B2
Castro favors Eritrea talks 4-27, 372A3
HABEAS (human rights organization)
Founded by Garcia Marquez 12-21, 1015B3
HABELER, Peter
Climbs Everest without oxygen 5-8, 420C2
HABIB, Ahmed
150 probed in pol crackdown 5-28, 414D3, G3
HABIB, Philip C.
Kissinger cites in Korea testimony 4-20, 280C1
HABRE, Hissene (Chadian premier)
Cease-fire rptd 2-5, 89G1
Named premier 8-29, 732G3
HACKBERRY, La.—*See LOUISIANA*
HACKER, Larry Ed
Tenn gov's aides arrested 12-15, 1011A2
HACKETT, Albert
Diary of Anne Frank revived 12-18, 1031D1
HACKMAN, Gene
Superman released 12-14, 1030E3
HADAR, Samir Mohammed
In Cyprus terror raid, hijacks jet 2-18; surrenders 2-19, 117D1
Trial starts 3-9, gets death sentnc 4-4, 236E3
Death sentnc commuted 11-14, 870G1
HADASSAH
Rose Halprin dies 1-8, 96B2
HADDAD, Naim
Says 21 CP members executed 6-7, 439C3
HADDAD, Maj. Saad
Forces get Israeli posts in south Leb 6-13, 462C1
Unifil says Leb OKs south Leb role 6-13, Leb denies 6-14, 462D2
Christn factns clash 6-15, 462A3
Arrest by Christns rptd 6-16, confrmd 6-19, 462G2
Ordrd back to Beirut 7-31; refuses 8-1, 581D1

1979

HAAS, Jay
2d in Phoenix Open 1-22, 220C3
HAAS, Mark
Stamp collectn sold for record sum 8-14, 672G1
HABASH, George
Group tied to Iran Arab unrest 6-3, 446D1
HABER, Joyce
FBI admits '70 Seberg slander 9-14, 705C1
HABIB, Philip C.
Retiremt end rptd 7-6, sets Carib policy 11-29, 960D3
HABRE, Hissene (Chadian premier)
Rebelln rptd thwarted 2-14, 114A2
Nigeria mediatn rptd OKd 3-1, 153F3
Signs peace pact 3-20, 211F1
HACK, Dick
Lovely Sunday opens 1-21, 292A2
HACKBART, Dale
NFL injury suit ruling declined by Sup Ct 10-29, 884E1
HACKETT, Gen. Sir John
3d World War on best-seller list 6-3, 432A2; 7-1, 548B3; 8-5, 620B3; 9-2, 672B3
HACKFORD, Taylor
Wins Oscar 4-9, 336C2
HACKLER, Lloyd W.
Labor rptd vs trade rep selectn 8-3, 647C1
HADARY, Jonathan
God Bless You Mr Rosewater opens 5-20, 711D3
HADDAD, Maj. Saad
Bars Leb troops in south 4-15; Israel OKs, Weizman briefs 4-17; sets 'free' zone 4-18, govt scores 4-19, 277B3
Begin denies orders issued 4-19, 278B1
To lift UN base siege, reneges 4-21, 296C3
Christn ldrs back mil role 4-21, 296F3
On PLO S Leb base sites 6-6, 415D1
Says Unifil lax vs PLO Leb raids 7-27, 592B1
Warns PLO vs attacks 8-30, 658B3

1980

HAACK, Dieter
Sworn W Ger pub works min 11-5, 925F1
HAAS, Helen
Scores US nitrite decision 8-19, 726G1
HAAS Jr., Walter
Buys Oakland A's 8-23, 795B3
HABBERSTAD, John
Testimony in Ford Pinto trial rptd 3-13, 186A1
HABERMAN, Rex
Neb rejects DC voting amendmt 2-11, 147B3
HABIBI, Hassan
Bani-Sadr nominates premr 7-26, 571G2
HABICHY Ralacio, Edgardo
Recalled from Cuba 1-18, 261A2
HABRE, Hissene (Chadian premier)
Factional fighting resumed 3-22—3-25, 221E1
Truce efforts fail, fighting intensifies 4-9, 311F1
Peace conf fails 10-18—10-19, 810G1
Libyans occupy Chad capital; flees to Cameroon, signs cease-fire 12-16, 965D1
HACKETT, Gen. Sir John
3d World War on best-seller list 5-4, 359F3
HACKFORD, Taylor
Idolmaker released 11-14, 972F3
HACKIN, Dennis
Bronco Billy released 6-11, 675A2
HACKS, Peter
Charlotte opens 2-27, 392D2
HADDAD, Maj. Saad
Israel says PLO gets Sovt tanks 2-12, 107F3
Chrgs Irish UNIFIL pro-PLO bias 4-11; meets UNIFIL, Israeli cmdrs 4-14, 284B1
Ireland asks Israel drop backing 4-20, 302C3
Injured by mine 4-29, blames UNIFIL 4-30, 363A1

1976

HADDOW, Alexander
Dies 1-21, 80D3
HADJIRACLEOUS, Eraclis
Asks Sampson arrest 1-28, 155E1
HADLUMAGID, Mustafa
Surrenders in hijacking 7-6, 539A2 *
HAEKKERUP, Per
Named Danish commerce min 9-9, 712F1
HAFERKAMP, Wilhelm
Europn Comm meets 12-22—12-23, 977F1
HAGEDORN, Rep. Tom (R, Minn.)
Reelected 11-2, 829F4
HAGER, Kurt
E Ger Politburo enlarged 5-22, 381E2
HAGER, Nina
Exiled 12-10, 1001F3
HAGOEL, Gen. David
Apologizes for Hebron incident 10-2, 737F2
HAHM Suk Hon
Sentenced 8-28, 655D1
HAI, Lt. Ho Kim
Defects to Thailand 3-8, 223A2
HAIDAR, Ghassan
Rpts Moslem-Christian truce 12-10, 953B1
HAIDAR, Mohammed
Out of Syrian Cabt 8-8, 594G2

HAIG Jr., Gen. Alexander M(eigs)
Cites Warsaw Pact improvemts 9-25, 760F2
On NATO problems 10-13; term extended 11-11, 879F3
Cleared in Halperin tap suit 12-16, 981A1
HAILE Mariam, Col. Hassan
Rptd executed 7-25, 674B2
HAILEY, Arthur
Moneychangers on best seller list 2-29, 208F3
HAIN, Peter
Cleared of bank theft 4-9, 351D1
HAINES, Charles G.
Dies 5-25, 524F2
HAITHAN, Mohammed Ali
Plotter release sought 8-23, 629A3

HAITI—*See also IDB, OAS, SELA*
Russell ct scores rights abuse 1-17, 61D2
Listed as 'not free' nation 1-19, 20D3
US co chrgs Duvalier bribe request 3-2, 267B3
Kennecott copper pact signed 3-24, 267A3
Cabt shuffled 4-1; liberal purge, Duvalier plot rptd 4-6, 4-9, 267D2-A3
Total IMF oil facility drawings rptd 4-1, 340C2
Amnesty Intl scores jail conditns 6-23, 1005F3
Adolphe named Tontons head 8-17, 1005E3
Gunmen kill Tontons, flee 8-27, 1005E3
Refugees reach Miami 8-30, 1005G3
Siclait dismissed 9-7, rptd ousted 9-24, 1005B3
Trade min replaced 9-7, 1005D3
Duvalier sets amnesty 9-30, 1005F3
DR expels illegal immigrants 10-24, 1001B3

1977

HADEN 2d, Judge Charles H.
Orders FMC plant shut 3-9, reopened 3-15, 196B3, D3
HADIBROTO Jr., Udaya
Tied to Hughes kickback 1-25, 182E3
HAEKKERUP, Per
Danish econ min 2-25, 373E1
HAENE, Bishop Alois
Successor installed 2-22, 375A3
HAFERKAMP, William
Gets Eur Comm post 1-7, 74C2
HAFFEJEE, Hoosen
Dies 8-3, 640F1
HAGE, Jorge
Removed as Salvador mayor 4-11, 303F2
HAGGART, Elinor
Murdered 6-4; Zamora convicted 10-7, 807G2
HAGSTROM, Andrew
Dies 10-8, 872B2
HAGSTROM Map Co.—*See under MACMILLAN Co.*
HAHN Joo Kyung, Gen
Denies N Korea ambush 5-9, 411B3

HAIG Jr., Gen. Alexander M(eigs)
Mondale sees 1-24, 70C1
Revises Sovt attack warning time 9-2, 700E1
Korea scandal cover-up rptd 9-5, 688F1
Meets Dayan 9-15, 713G2
Sees Sovt tank, hovercraft threat 12-8, 941D3
HAILE Fida
Disappearance rptd 9-9, 716C1
HAILSTORMS—*See STORMS*
HAIR Dyes—*See COSMETICS*
HAISE, Fred W.
Pilots space shuttle 8-12, 627A1

HAITI—*See also IDB, OAS*
UN Assemb member 4A1
IMF loan set 2-4, 87E2
'75-76 trade, paymts table 3-11, 189A2 *, B2
Drought, famine kill 300 4-12, 312E2
'61-75 GDP variatns table 5-30, 439B1
Amb to Brazil slain 7-3, aide held 7-12, 583C2
Illegal emigratn to Bahamas cited 7-19, 579E1
Civilian pol court set 8-23, 707A1
Pol prisoner dies 9-2, 707B1
Drought cited re emigratns 9-6, 706D3
Govt frees 'last' pol prisoners 9-21, 767E2
Exiles claim pol prisoners still held 9-30, 805D3
Ex-interior min freed, exiled 10-14, 905G2
Amnesty Intl: pol arrests, torture continue 10-21, 905G2
Canada forgn aid scandal cited 863D1
Bauxite base price OKd 12-7, 975E1

1978

Asks attacks halted 8-3, vs Leb army in south 8-4, 638G2
To be tried for aiding Israel 10-22, 803D1
Christns to build airport, seaport 12-2, 951A2
HADDAD, Maj. Gen. Sobhi
Named Syrian AF head 3-27, 269F3
HADDAD, Dr. Wadi
Dies 3-28, 252G2
Egypt terror group rptd smashed 4-26, 300D2
'76 papal kidnap plot veto rptd 8-6, 689B3
PLO says Iraqis murdered 8-24, 674C1
HADDAD Blanco, Jesus
Assassinated by guerrillas 3-22, 249G2
10 murder suspects seized 7-27, 706A2
HADDON-Cave, Philip
Presents '78 Hong Kong budget 3-1, 189G3
HADEN, Pat
NFL '77 passing ldr 1-1, 56D2
NFC wins Pro Bowl 1-23, 56F1
HADJISTEFANOU, Costas
Named Cyprus state secy 3-8, 189A2
HADL, John
Retiremt from pro football rptd 2-9, 171F3
HAEKKERUP, Per
Named to Danish econ post 8-30, 688A1
HAFERKAMP, Wilhelm
On China-EC trade pact 4-3, 302F3
HAFFEJEE, Hoosen
Death ruled suicide 3-15, 229D3
HAFT, Judge Robert M.
Sentences 5 in '76 NYC racial assault 5-12, 380F3
HAGAN, Cliff
In basketball HOF 5-1, 457E3
HAGAR, Ray
In barroom brawl 11-11, Martin chrgd 11-12, 1026E2
HAGEDORN, Rep. Tom (R, Minn.)
Reelected 11-7, 851A2
HAGEN, Herbert
Chrgd for war crimes 7-24, 652C1
HAGMAN, Matti
Nordiques win WHA All-Star game 1-17, 76E3, G3
HAGOEL, Brig. Gen. David
Replaced as W Bank mil govt cmdr 5-2, 340G1
HAHNEMANN Medical College and Hospital of Philadelphia (Pa.)
Flood, Eilberg influence-selling rptd probed 2-8—3-9, 240C1
Eilberg chrgd by ethics com 9-13, 697A2
Eilberg indicted 10-24, pleads not guilty 11-1, 835D2
HAIG Jr., Gen. Alexander M(eigs)
At 26th Bilderberg Conf 4-21—4-23, 302D3
Resignatn threat rptd, denies 4-25, 298E2-B3
To remain NATO chief 5-19, popularity rptd 5-23, 398D3-399B1
Korea '74 paymt offer rptd 6-1, 433C1
Apel backs NATO maneuvers 9-27, 748A3
HAIKALA, Eino
Kekkonen reelected 1-16, 36G2
HAINES, Jesse (Pop)
Dies 8-5, 708G2
HAIRDRESSING
Hair-dye warning proposed 1-4, workers exposure curbs urged 1-13, 86A1
Obituaries
Carita, Maria 9-6, 778A1
HAIR Dyes—*See HAIRDRESSING*

HAITI—*See also GATT, IDB, OAS*
Repressn rptd eased; US pressure, forgn aid needs cited 2-3, 94B3
Ex-Tontons sentncd re '77 assault 3-21, 292B3
'77 econ growth 1%, drought blamed 6-9, 479A1
Bahamas order out illegal aliens 6-29, 538C1
Refugees arrive US from Bahamas 7-18, 7-22, 671C3
Amer rights conv enacted, ct formed 7-18, 828E3, 829C1
UN panel probes rights 8-18—8-25, 691B3
Mil staff chief, police chief replaced 9-15, 777G1
UN Assemb member 713F3
Press curbs rptd by IAPA 10-13, 829A2

1979

HADDAM Neck, Conn.—*See CONNECTICUT*
HADDON, Dayle
Last Romantic Lover released 10-5, 1007G3
HADDON-Cave, Philip
Proposes budget 2-28, 169B2
On Hong Kong GDP revisn 9-17, 730E2
HADEN, Pat
Rams lose NFL conf title, injury cited 1-7, 8F3
HAEKKERUP, Per
Dies 3-13, 272D2
HAFFNER, The (symphony)
NYC library buys manuscript 7-16, 672G2
HAGAR, Ray
Martin settles battery chrg 5-24, 619B2
HAGLER, Marvin
Draws with Antuofermo 11-30, 1004D3

HAIDALA, Lt. Col. Mohammed Khouna Ould (Mauritanian premier)
Appointed premier 5-31, 417F1
HAIG Jr., Alexander Meigs
Sets NATO, Army resignatn 1-3, 3A2
Rogers named successor, SALT doubts cited 2-28, 147C3
Army 'quick-strike' force planned 6-21, 482D3
Assassinatn try fails 6-25, 476D2
Backs SALT ratificatn delay 7-26, 643G2
Pres draft com forms 9-10, 680C2
Decides vs pres bid 12-22, 984G1, A2
Named United Tech pres 12-26, 984F1
HAIGHT Jr., Judge Charles S.
Dismisses trust suit vs Stevens 8-6, 598D3
HAILEY, Arthur
Overload on best-seller list 2-4, 120B3; 3-4, 173D3; 4-8, 271G1
Concorde Airport '79 released 8-3, 820A1
HAILEY, Oliver
Father's Day opens 6-21, 711G2
Just You & Me Kid released 7-27, 820D1
HAILSHAM, Lord
UK lord chancellor 5-5, 338E1
Salary hike rptd rejected 7-7, 543A3
HAINES, Chris
Notre Dame wins Cotton Bowl 1-1, 8A3
HAIR (film)
Released 3-13, 528D2
HAIR (play)
Holzer convicted of grand larceny 3-15, 239G2
HAIRDRESSING
Safeway firing case declined by Sup Ct 2-21, 128D3
Voluntary dryer recall sought 4-19, 308D2
Hair dryer recall praised 5-17, 595E3
HAITI
6 drown off coast, 3 arrested 8-13, 634D2
DR worker 'slavery' rptd 8-17, 804A3
Populatn, per-capita income rptd 8-18, 634F2
UN membership listed 695E2
Duvalier lauds security group 9-22, rights mtg disrupted 11-9, 874D1
Cabinet shuffled 11-13, 874F1

1980

HADDON-Cave, Philip
Proposes new budget 2-27, 193C3
HADEN, Pat
Steelers win Super Bowl; injury cited 1-20, 61A3-62C1
HADI, Moslem
Ties Iraq plotters to Iran 4-9, 300D1
HADJICOSTAS, George
Named Cyprus communicatns min 9-9, 749G2
HADJILOANNIDIS, Georges
Wins Olympic medal 7-29, 624D3
HAFTEL, Rep. Cecil (D, Hawaii)
Reelected 11-4, 842C3, 852D2
HAGAN, James
Lodges UN appeal 9-3, 686G1
HAGEDORN, Rep. Tom (R, Minn.)
Reelected 11-4, 843A2
HAGEL, Raymond C.
Resigns Macmillan post 2-11, 225A1
HAGEN, Herbert
Sentncd for WW2 crimes 2-11, 118F1
HAGEN, Uta
Charlotte opens 2-27, 392D2
HAGEN, Walter (1892-1969)
Nicklaus ties PGA title record 8-10, 714C2
HAGGARD, Piers
Fiendish Plot of Dr Fu Manchu released 8-8, 675E2
HAGGERTY, Patrick E.
Dies 10-1, 876G1
HAGLER, Erwin H.
Wins Pulitzer 4-14, 296G2
HAGLER, Marvin
TKOs Minter for world middlewgt title 9-27, 772A2
HAGMAN, Larry
'Dallas' TV episode aired 11-21, viewing record rptd 11-25, 905D3
HAGNES, Helen
Found slain 7-24, 654A1
Stagehand arrested 8-30, indicted 9-7, 713B1

HAIDALA, Lt. Col. Mohammed Khouna Ould (Mauritanian president)
Deposes Luly, named pres 1-4, 21A1
HAIDER, Donald
Quits as Chicago Budget Dir 1-11, 186A3
HAIG Jr., Alexander Meigs
Agnew death fears rptd 4-20, 333D3
Iran ties to post-shah plot, denies link 6-2, 418G2
Reagan Cabt post seen 12-6, 12-9, 935F1
Named secy of state 12-16; US, forgn reactn 12-16—12-17, 955G1
Hires atty for confirmatn hearings 12-22, 980B1
HAIGH, Kenneth
Clothes for a Summer Hotel opens 3-26, 392E2
HAIGHT, Judge Charles S.
Backs NFL cross-ownership ban 11-18, 998D3-999A1
HAILEY, Arthur
Overload on best-seller list 2-10, 120D3

HAITI—*See also GATT, IDB, OAS*
New law stifles press criticism 4-11, 294E2
Duvalier chngs Cabt, consolidates power 4-26, 335F3-336A1
Duvalier marries 5-27, 471F1
Hurricane Allen kills 220, destroys coffee crop 8-5, 621C2
400 govt critics arrested 11-28—11-30; econ crisis rptd 11-30, 922E2, D3
Duvalier defends arrests 12-4, 942A3
9 prisoners released to US exile 12-5, 942G3-943A1
Foreign Relations (misc.)
Colombia amb seized in DR Emb raid 2-27, 141B1
Colombia DR Emb siege ends, amb freed 4-27, 335G1
Refugees rptd stranded in Bahamas 10-9; Bahama evicts, Duvalier OKs return 11-13, 869F2
64 refugees reach Bahamas 11-21; refugee rptd on Cayo Lobos 11-22, 920C1-E1
OAS cites poor rights record 11-27, 913D3
Forgn reserve shortage rptd 11-30, 922D3

1976

HAJEK, Jiri
Name removed from masthead 9-17, 852C1
Science Acad ousts 11-5, 1012B3
HAJJ, Col. Ahmed al-
Cmnds Arab Leb force 11-4, 841D1
HALAMANDARIS, Val J.
On US health program kickbacks 2-16, 128B2
On Medicaid fraud prosecutns 8-30, 715G2
HALDEMAN, Donald
Wins Olympic medal 7-20, 575A2
HALDEMAN, H(arry) R(obbins) (Bob)
Files wiretap depositn 3-11, 184A2
Named in wiretap suit 5-10, 349G2
Cited in Dole biog sketch 614B3
Watergate convictn upheld 10-12, 770E1-C2
Ford denies pardon rumor 10-20, 784E3
Held liable in Halperin tap suit 12-16, 980C3-981B1
HALE, Robert
Dies 11-30, 970A2
HALEY, Alex
Roots on best-seller list 12-5, 972D2
HALEY, Rep. James A. (D, Fla.)
Ireland elected 11-2, 822C1
HALL, Gary
Wins Olympic medal 7-21, 575D2
HALL, Gus
Addresses Sovt CP Cong 3-1, 196E1
Charges vs Young rptd 6-11, 434B1
Final pres vote tally 12-18, 979B2
HALL, Paul
Ford fund probe rptd 9-25, 722G3
HALL Jr., Rep. Sam B. (D, Tex.)
Reelected 11-2, 830C4
HALL, Rep. Tim L. (D, Ill.)
Loses reelectn 11-2, 823G1
HALL, Ulysses
Testifies for Hearst 2-20, 201E2
HALLANDALE, Fla.—*See FLORIDA*
HALLECK, Charles A.
Cited in Ford biog sketch 613E3, G3
HALLGRIMSSON, Geir
UK fishing talks set 1-19, 50D3
In UK talks 1-24—1-27; Wilson proposals rejctd 2-4, 155B1-E1 ★
HALLINAN, Patrick
Posts Cleaver bail 8-13, 640C3
HALL of Fame (music)—*See 'Awards' under MUSIC*
HALLOWELL, Burton C.
Replaced as Tufts U pres 7-1, 504D2
HALOP, Billy
Dies 11-9, 970A2
HALPERIN, Morton H.
Kissinger, Haldeman tap depositns filed 1-12, 3-11; Nixon depositn released 3-10, 184B1, B2
Colby vs CIA budget disclosure 3-17, 217E1
Nixon, 2 aides held liable in tap suit 12-16, 980A3-981B1

1977

U.S. Relations
US reports rights abuses 1-1, 50D3
Jones named US amb 8-3, 626E2
101 refugees reach Guantanamo 8-10; US returns 97 9-6, 706C3
Young visits, scores rights abuse 8-14—8-15, 646E1, 647A2
Young cited re new civilian ct 8-23; pol prisoner dies 9-2, 703A1
Young visit cited re pol prisoner releases 9-21, 767F2
Exiles claim pol prisoners still held 9-30, 805D3
Rights 'progress' seen by Todman 10-21, 905F2
US to free 120 refugees 11-8, 1019E1
HAJARI, Cadi Abdullah al-
Slain 4-10, 284D3
HAJEK, Jiri
Detained 1-7, 20D1
Austria offers asylum 1-25, rejcts 1-28, 82C3
Rpts Charter 77 support 2-7, 114E3
2 French rptrs attacked 3-3, 220D3
HAJIM, Abu
Denies buildup, Israeli raid 6-6, 439D3
HAJJ, Col. Ahmed al-
Gets new cmnd post 4-11, 297B3
HALDEMAN, H(arry) R(obbins) (Bob)
Liddy's term commuted 4-12, 325E3
Sup Ct appeal decisn leaked 4-21, defense motion denied 5-2, 382C2; appeal denied 5-23, 406D1
Nixon-Frost interview 5-4, 366F1, D3, 367B1-B2, 368A1; 5-25, 420A2
Challenges Nixon's story 5-26, 420B3
Jail delay refused 5-31, 461F3
Enters prison 6-21, 483F2
Sup Ct denies 2d appeal 6-27, 538F3
Halperin awarded $5 in tap suit 8-5, 652C2
Nixon-Frost interview 9-3, 692A3
Sentence reduced after apology 10-4, 762A1
HALE Observatories (Pasadena, Calif.)
'Mini-planet' discovery rptd 11-8, 908C2
HALEVY, Binyamin
Loses parlt speaker race 6-13, 474F2
HALEVY, David
On Israel Leb role 8-22, 648E1
HALEY, Alex
Roots sets TV record 1-23—1-30, 118B3; table 2-9, 119B1
Roots on best-seller list 2-6, 120F3; 2-20, 118E3; 3-6, 184F3; 4-3, 264G1; 5-1, 356C2; 6-4, 452A2; 12-4, 1021A3
Sues Doubleday 3-16, 356G1
Roots sources doubted 4-10, 4-22, 356B1
Gets Natl Book Award citatn 4-11, 355B2
Wins special Pulitzer 4-18, 355B3
Courlander sues 5-24, 643D1
HALL, Asaph H.
Replaced as Fed RR admin 6-23, 626F3
HALL, Del
Phoenix owner sells 4-1, 263A1
HALL, Dolores
Wins Tony 6-5, 452D1
HALL, Gus
Powell defends Sakharov letter 2-18, 137F2
HALL, Marquette A.—*See MUZIKIR, Abdul*
HALL, Judge Peirson M.
Rules on Calif damages law 1-4, 312D1
HALL, Richard O.
Kidnaped 2-8, freed 2-10, 162G1
HALLBERG, Gary
US wins Walker Cup 8-27, 951G1
HALL of Fame (HOF)—*See specific sport (e.g., FOOTBALL)*
HALL of Fame Bowl—*See FOOTBALL—Collegiate*
HALPERIN, Dan
Israel combats Arab boycott 3-7, 167A2
HALPERIN, Morton H.
UK sets Agee ouster 2-16, 134C2
Awarded $5 in tap suit 8-5, 652A2
HALSTON (Roy Halston Frowick)
'77 fall fashions rptd 6-6, 1022F1
HAMAD, Brig. Mohammed al-
Hijackers release 7-10, 535B2

1978

HALABI, Mohammed Ali al- (Syrian premier)
Named Syrian premier 3-27, forms Cabt 3-30, 269F3
HALABY, Elizabeth (Lisa)—*See NOOR al-Hussein, Queen*
HALABY, Najeeb
Daughter to wed Hussein 5-15, 420A3
HALDEMAN, H(arry) R(obbins) (Bob)
Book excerpts scooped by Washn Post 2-16, syndicatn plans upset; Nixon accused on cover-up, break-in 2-16—2-17, 124G1-125E1
Ends of Power on best-seller list 4-2, 272B3
Ehrlichman freed 4-27, 320D2
Nixon memoir excerpts cite Watergate role 4-30, 319E3, G3, 320C1
Legal fees to exceed book profits 8-17, 844C1
Released on parole 12-20, 1011G2
HALEY, Alex
Alexander plagiarism suit dismissed 9-21, 759A3
Settles Courlander plagiarism suit 12-14, 1029E3
HALEY Jr., Jack
Files for divorce 4-19, 420C3
HALINKA, Ivan
Czechs lose world hockey title 5-14, 458D3
HALL, Anthony
Loses Tex Cong primary runoff 6-3, 426G2
HALL, Carol
Best Little Whorehouse opens 4-17, 760D1
HALL, Charles
Hails US Venus mission 12-9, 968D2
HALL, David
Released from prison 5-22, 420G3
HALL, Joe B.
Kentucky wins NCAA basketball title 3-27, 272G1
HALL, Paul
On '77 top-paid labor ldrs list 5-15, 365G1
HALL, Richard O.
Pulitzer awarded for '77 kidnap photo 4-17, 314G3
HALL Jr., Rep. Sam B. (D, Tex.)
Reelected 11-7, 852D2
HALL, Tony P.
Wins US House seat 11-7, 851D3, 854E1
HALLGRIMSSON, Geir (Icelandic premier)
Electn losses spur resignatn 6-26, 497G1
Fails to form coalitn govt 7-25—8-10, Progressives end govt crisis 8-31, 688D3
HALL of Fame (HOF)—*See specific sport (i.e., BASEBALL)*
HALL of Fame Bowl—*See FOOTBALL—Collegiate*
HALLOWEEN (film)
Released 10-15, 970E1
HALLOWEEN Bandit, The (play)
Opens 12-18, 1031G1
HALPERIN, Morton
On CIA press operatns 1-4, 14A3
HALPRIN, Rose
Dies 1-8, 96B2
HALS, Dirk
Painting smeared 4-11, 335A2
HALSTENBERG, Friedrich
Quits over Poullain firing 1-17, 55D1
HALSTON (Roy Halston Frowick)
'78 high chic fashion rptd 8-4—8-11, 10-27—11-3, 1029F2
HAMADA, Shoji
Dies 1-5, 96C2

1979

HAJEK, Jiri
Charter 77 picks new ldrs 2-8, 126F3
HAJJ-Sayed, Ahmed Sadir
Bazargan rptdly vs komitehs 4-12, 297E2
HALBERSTAM, David
Powers That Be on best-seller list 6-3, 432B2; 7-1, 548C3
HALDEMAN, H(arry) R(obbins) (Bob)
Discloses '75 TV interview fee 1-27, 176C1
Nixon Admin pub TV moves disclosed 2-24, 194G1
Ruled liable in tap suits 7-12, 611D2
HALE Jr., Alan
5th Musketeer released 9-7, 820C1
HALEY Sr., Jack
Dies 6-6, 508G2
HALFPENNY, John
Scores wage guidelines 9-10, 728C2
HALL, Celeste
Big Bad Burlesque opens 8-14, 711E1
HALL, James Norman
Hurricane released 4-11, 528E2
HALL, Jon
Dies 12-13, 1008A3
HALL, Leonard
Dies 6-2, 508A3
HALL, Paul
Backs Carter reelectn 7-30, 593D3
HALL, Peter
Bedroom Farce opens 3-29, 711D1
HALL Jr., Rep. Sam B. (D, Tex.)
Loses Ways & Means Com seat 1-23, 70G3
HALL, William
Rowe extradition OKd 2-7, 120D1
HALLBERG, Gary
Wins NCAA golf title 5-26, 587G1
HALLER, Daniel
Buck Rogers released 3-29, 528E1
HALLINAN, Richard
Portrait of the Artist released 4-21, 528D3
HALL of Fame (HOF)—*See specific sport*
HALLORAN, Richard
S Korea bars 10-13, OKs entry 10-14, 803B3
HALLOWEEN (film)
Top-grossing film 10-31, 892G3
HALPERIN, Morton
Nixon, aides held liable in tap suit 7-12, 611A3
HALSMAN, Philippe
Dies 6-2, 508A3
HALSTED, David
Uganda emb rptd reopened 6-21, 489D1
HALVONIK, Deborah
Arrested on drug chrgs 9-20, 748F1
HALVONIK, Judge Paul N.
Arrested on drug chrgs 9-20, 748F1

1980

IMF OKs aid 12-5, 943A1
U.S. Relations
Refugees reach Fla in record numbers 4-13, 294A2
2 convicted for '79 Fla drownings 4-18, 336B1; sentncd 6-24, 503A3
Refugees press for pol asylum 5-7, 339G3
Cuban refugees granted pol asylum 5-21, 380D1
Refugees granted 6-mo reprieve, get pub assistance 6-20, 484B3-485D1
Refugees in US suit, deportatns halted 7-2, 514E1
US refugee aid clears Cong 7-2, Carter signs 7-8, 515F1
Reagan pres nominatn acceptance speech 7-17, 534G3
US budgets $16.8 mln for refugee relief 8-13, 617E1
3 drown as boat capsizes 9-6; exodus accelerates, total nears 40,000 9-9, 685D1
17 jailed for ship hijacking 9-17, 726B1
Carter sets 3-pt refugee resetlmt plan 9-18, 742G1
'81 refugee quota cut 9-19, 883A3
PR refugee resetlmt camp to be opened 9-23, 725E3-726A1
PR sues US to block refugee camp 9-30, 742E2
PR camp delayed by legal battles 10-1—10-24, 825B3
US rpts refugees stranded in Bahamas 10-9; US news copter missing 11-13, 869F2, C3
Refugee aid to states signed 10-10, 785B1
PR camp ban lifted 11-3, 869C2
9 in US exile 12-5, 942G3-943A1
US shuns aid talks, '80 total rptd; Reagan support seen 12-8, 942C3, F3
HAJDENBURG, Daniel
Jewish targets attacked 9-26, 9-28, 750C1
HALABI, Mohammed Ali al- (Syrian premier)
Ousted 1-6, 22E2
HALBERSTAM, David
Brother slain 12-5, 940C1
HALBERSTAM, Dr. Michael J.
Slain 12-5; suspect chrgd 12-6, area thefts rptd 12-7, 939F3
HALDEMAN, H(arry) R(obbins) (Bob)
Taps case accepted by Sup Ct 5-19, 440D1
Taps case argued in Sup Ct 12-8, 937B2
HALES, Jonathan
Mirror Crack'd released 12-18, 1003C2
HALEY, William
US backs UNESCO world info res 10-25, 821C3
HALL, Allen
Wilmington 10 convictn reversed 12-4, 940F1
HALL, Dino
NFL '79 punt return ldr 1-5, 8C3
HALL, Emmett
Study scores Canada MDs 9-3, 687A2
HALL, Gus
Poland strike setlmt rptd scored 8-29, 659A1
HALL, Harold H.
Named Southn Rail chief exec 9-29, 959C2
HALL, Jim
Rutherford wins Indy 500 5-25, 637F2
HALL, Paul
Dies 6-22, 528G1
HALL, Peter
Amadeus opens 12-17, 1003G2
HALL, Ralph
Elected to US House 11-4, 844E2, 850B2
HALL, Randy
Sets NCAA pole vault record 6-7, 892A1
HALL, Robert
Recession since Jan rptd 6-3, 425B1
HALL Jr., Rep. Sam B. (D, Tex.)
Reelected 11-4, 844D2
HALL, Rep. Tony P. (D, Ohio)
Reelected 11-4, 843D4
HALL, Willis
Filumena opens 2-10, 392F2
HALLBERG, Gary
2d in Lancome Trophy tourn 10-19, 972F2
Named PGA top rookie 11-18, 971D3
HALLDORSON, Don
Wins Pensacola Open 10-12, Canada wins World Cup 12-14, 972D2, A3
HALLEY, Edmund (1656-1742)
ESA plans comet probe 7-15, 548C1
HALLEY'S Comet
ESA plans satellite probe 7-15, 548A1
Sovt mission rptd planned 11-23, 933E1
HALLGRIMSSON, Geir
Gestsson govt bid set 1-16, 39D3
HALLQUIST, Barbara
Loses US Open quarterfinal 9-4, 691E2
HALPERIN, Morton
Nixon taps case accepted by Sup Ct 5-19, 440E1
Taps case argued in Sup Ct 12-8, 937B2
HALSTON (Roy Halston Frowick)
'80 fashion roundup rptd 998F1
HALVONIK, Deborah
Sentenced 5-5, 414G1
HALVONIK, Judge Paul N.
Resigns, sentenced 5-5, 414F1
HAMADA, Koichi
Chrgd with corruptn 5-16, 381B1

1976

HAMAMSSI, Galal Eddin el
Nasser cleared of '67 theft chrg 2-4, 119C1
HAMATI, Jamil
Dies 11-23, 878D2
HAMED, Mohammed Salaheddin
In Egypt finance post 11-10, 852F1
HAMER, Rupert J.
Reelected Victoria premr 3-20, 237A1
On Nissan plant deal 8-15, 650F1
HAMEX—*See KAYEX Corp.*
HAMID, Sherif Abdul
Demands Israeli withdrawal 1-13, 18B2
HAMILL, Dorothy
Wins Olympic medal 2-13, 159A1
HAMILL, Pete
Wins Grammy 2-28, 460B3
HAMILTON, Alexander (1757-1804)
Murdoch to buy NY Post 11-19, 887E2
HAMILTON, Charles L.
Sentenced 11-30, 921G2
HAMILTON, Denis
Knighted 1-1, 80F2
HAMILTON, Fred
Wins world bridge title 5-8, 352G3
HAMILTON, Rep. Lee Herbert (D, Ill.)
Reelected 11-2, 829C3
HAMILTON Bancshares Inc.
Rptd on FRB 'problem' list 1-22, 111B2
Sells Nashville, Memphis banks 2-19; files bankruptcy 2-20, coal venture cited 2-21, 166E3, 167A1
3 non-banking units file bankruptcy 2-20, 166G3
Hamilton National Bank (Chattanooga)
Ruled insolvent, sold 1-16, 166F3, 167E1
Rptd on comptroller's 'problem' list 1-26, 113E1
HAMIS, Abdul Razzq al-
Kuwait buys UK tanks 2-16, 126B2
HAMLISCH, Marvin
Chorus Line wins Pulitzer 5-3, 352C3
HAMM, Hillard
Sentenced 6-21, 860C2
HAMMER, Armand
Case transferred 2-5, pleads guilty again 3-4, 180D3
Babcock sentence upheld 2-10, 144G3
Sentenced 3-23, 442B2
Scores Venez payoffs rpt 6-10, protests arrests 7-14, 593E1
Signs Iran deal 6-20, 450C2
Watson pleads guilty, fined 9-23, 725D2
Sees Brezhnev on trade 10-20, 947E3
HAMMER, Zevulun
Vs Avineri appointment 2-15, 126A1
On W Bank electn results 4-12, 258C3
Removed form Cabt 12-19, 964C3
HAMMERBERG, Judge Jack L.
Moves Chowchilla trial 11-10, 876E3
HAMMERSCHMIDT, Rep. John Paul (R, Ark.)
Reelected 11-2, 828G3
HAMMOND, Wallace
Acquitted, '74 convictn cited 2-6, 124F1
HAMOUZ, Frantisek
Dismissed 9-15, 750G2
HAMPTON, Fred (d. 1967)
FBI role in death raid rptd 5-6, 344D2
HAMPTON, Millard
Wins Olympic medal 7-26, 575G3
HAMPTON, Robert E.
Quits Civil Svc Comm 2-10, 232G1
HAMPTON, William
Acquitted, '74 convictn cited 2-6, 124F1
HAMRICK, Rev. Albert R.
Pleads guilty 8-6, sentncd 9-17, 776F2
HAMTRAMCK, Mich.—*See MICHIGAN*
HANAHAN, Thomas
Court rules on immunity 1-5, 7B1
HANDBALL
Olympic results 7-28, 574F3

HANDICAPPED—*See under MEDICINE*
HANDLER, Philip
DNA research stand cited 11-1, 891E3
HANFORD, Wash.—*See WASHINGTON*

1977

HAMADI, Ibrahim Mohammed al-
At Red Sea summit 3-22—3-23, 208F2
HAMBRO, Edvard Isak
Dies 2-1, 164G2
HAMDI Ould Mouknass
Named Mauritania forgn min 8-4, 772E1
HAMER, Fannie Lou
Dies 3-14, 264F2
HAMER, Rupert J.
Scores power strike 10-18, 822G1
HAMIDI, Col. Abdullah Mohammed al-
Assassinated 10-10, 783F3
Other slayings rptd 10-12, 10-14, 824F1
Ghashmi escapes death try 10-19, 824E1
HAMIDI, Ibrahim Mohammed al- (North Yemen president; assassinated Oct. 10)
Assassinated 10-10, 783F3
Other slayings rptd 10-12, 10-14, 824F1
Ghashmi escapes death try 10-19, 824E1
HAMILTON, Carl Edwin
Ethiopia ousts 3-30, 327D3
HAMILTON, Leonard D.
At Salzburg A-conf 5-2—5-13, 402G3
HAMILTON Jr., Lyman C.
Named ITT chief exec 2-9, 140C2
HAMILTON Bancshares Inc.
Trustees sue auditors 2-11, 155A3
HAMILTON Brothers Petroleum Corp.
Gulf wins Kewanee control 8-9, 612F2
HAMILTON-Fairley, Gordon (d. 1975)
Slayers sentenced 2-10, 222A3
HAMMADI, Saadoun
Signs Japan aid pact 1-21, 65E2
HAMMARSTROM, Judge Everett J.
Bars Chicago fed schl aid 2-17, 157A1
HAMMER, Armand
US-Rumania coal deal set 5-30, 468E3
HAMMER, Zevulum
Israel educatn min 6-20, 474E2
HAMMOND, Richard
Ethiopia ousts 3-30, 327D3
HAMPTON, Fred (d. 1969)
Police win Panther suit 6-21, 540E2
HAN Byung Ki
Named KCIA agent 6-5, 442A1
HANAFI Muslims—*See ISLAM*

HANDICAPPED—*See under MEDICINE*
HANDLER, Philip
Asks Shcharansky trial observers 12-24, 1017F1

1978

HAMANI, Mohamed
Named Mali indus min 1-7, 75F1
HAMBURGERS—*See MEAT*
HAMELI, Dr. Ali
On Guyana death certificates 11-27, 910B2
HAMER, Rupert
Scores chrgs vs Lynch, Holding 9-14, 771E2
HAMIDI, Ibrahim Mohammed al-(d. 1977)
Ghashmi assassinated 6-24, 499D2
Saleh elected pres 7-17, 559A1
HAMILL, Mark
Corvette Summer released 8-4, 970A1
HAMILTON, Archibald
Wins Epsom, Ewell by-electn 4-27, 329F1
HAMILTON, Guy
Force 10 released 12-21, 1030G2
HAMILTON, Rep. Lee Herbert (D, Ind.)
Reelected 11-7, 850B4
HAMILTON, Richard
Buried Child opens 11-6, 1031B1
HAMMAMI, Ahmed
Arrested in Iraq emb raid 7-31, 582D2
HAMM, Rear Adm. Warren C.
Says N Korea dug DMZ tunnel 10-27, 860D3
HAMMAMI, Said
Slain 1-4, 3F1
Egypt terror group rptd smashed 4-24, 300E2
PLO ties Iraq, Nidal to death 7-4, 546G2
Brother seized in Iraq emb raid 7-31, 582D2
Arab summit scores Camp David accords 11-5, 859D1
HAMMER (play)
Actress killed in auditn 4-10, 380F2
HAMMER, Armand
Mead vs Occidental takeover bid 8-18, 767E2
Opens USSR ammonia plant 8-22, sees Brezhnev 8-25, 670F1
HAMMER, Zevulun
Bans '48 war film 2-6, ban lifted 2-13, 112F3
HAMMERSCHMIDT, Rep. John Paul (R, Ark.)
Reelected 11-7, 850D1, 855A2
HAMMERSTEIN, James
Rear Column opens 11-19, 1031A3
HAMMOND, Bob
NFL '77 punt return ldr 1-1, 56F3
HAMMOND, Gov. Jay (R, Alaska)
House OKs land bill 5-19, 386C2
Leads in primary vote 8-22, 682D3
Primary win official 10-20, 831E2
Reelected 11-7, 853D2, 856A2
HAMPSHIRE College (Amherst, Mass.)
S Africa stock divestiture rptd 6-18, 633D1
HAMROUSH, Ahmed
Egypt probes, exit barred 5-28, 415A1
HANCE, Kent
Bush to oppose for US House 6-3, 426F2
Elected 11-7, 852B3, 855D3
HANCOCK, Phil
2d in Southern Open 9-10, 990G1

HANDICAPPED
Suits vs HEW rptd setld 1-4, 5C1
HEW anti-bias rules issued 1-13, 14G1
Carter State of Union Message 1-19, 32A1
Carter budgets SSI; rehabilitatn, educ aid 1-23, 46F3, 47B1-E1
AHL ban on 1-eyed player lifted 2-2, 296E3
PR SSI benefits exclusn upheld by Sup Ct 2-27, 143A1
Expedited disability benefits rule review declined by Sup Ct 2-27, 143E1
ERA boycott scored 3-20, 494A3
Electrode implant paralysis treatmt rptd 5-6, 1023F1
AMC to end bus productn, fed rules cited 5-31, 665B2
Eagle Scout honored at White House 7-21, 844G1
Viet vet jobless rptd high 10-10, 878C1
Jobs tax credit clears Cong 10-15, 785D3
HANDLER, Philip
Scores USSR human rights 5-20, 401E1
HANDLER, Ruth
Indicted 2-16, 116D2
HANDY Man (recording)
Taylor wins Grammy 2-24, 315F3
HANES Corp.
Consolidated Foods purchase agreed 9-14, 717G3
HANFORD Atomic Reservation (Richland, Wash.)
Radiatn-cancer hazard disputed 2-17, 2-25, 164D1, B2
HANFT, Lt. Col. John W.
Dismisses Army MD, scores recruiters 11-4, 877B3

1979

HAMADI, Saadun
On Arab League actn vs Egypt 3-31, 248D2
HAMATA, Frank
Guilty in dredging fraud 5-5, 352B2
Sentenced 6-11, 468C2
HAMBLETON, T. Edward
Later opens 1-15, Says I 2-20, 292F1, F2
HAMBURGER, Richard
Hitting Town opens 1-6, 292F1
HAMDANI, Adnan Hussein
Iraqi vice premr 7-16, 544E3*
Arrested as plotter 7-28, 583E1*
Sentenced 8-7, executed 8-8, 602F2
HAMDI, Omar al-
Scores Carter, Begin, Sadat 5-10, 341F2
HAMEDANIM, Brig. Gen. Hussein
Executed 2-20, 125F1
HAMER, Rupert
Liberals win Victoria electns 5-5, fed job funding sought 5-8, 387B1
HAMILTON, Billy
Brocks breaks stolen base mark 9-23, 1003E1
HAMILTON, George
Love At First Bite released 4-12, 528G2
HAMILTON Jr., Lyman C.
Quits ITT 7-11, 517A2
HAMILTON, Roy
In NBA draft 6-25, 507A2
HAMLISCH, Marvin
They're Playing Our Song opens 2-11, 292E3
HAMMERMILL Paper Co.
Price violatn chrgd 4-27, cleared 5-17, 385E1
HAMMERSTEIN 2nd, Oscar (1895-1960)
Oklahoma opens 12-13, 1007D2
Richard Rodgers dies 12-30, 1008D3
HAMMERSTEIN, William
Oklahoma opens 12-13, 1007D2
HAMMIL, John
Songs From City Streets opens 4-9, 712E2
HAMMOND, Frank
US Open results 9-9, 734C1
HAMPSHIRE College (Amherst, Mass.)
S Africa stock divestiture OKd 3-10, 271B1
HAMPTON, Va.—*See VIRGINIA*
HAMPTON, Christopher
Don Juan opens 4-15, 711E2
HAMPTON, Dan
In NFL draft 5-3, 335E1
HAMPTON Roads, Va.—*See VIRGINIA*
HAMPTON Roads Energy Co.
Army OKs Va oil refinery 10-4, 770A1
HAMTRAMCK, Mich.—*See MICHIGAN*
HAND, Judge W. B.
Stays Evans executn 4-20, 400F1

HANDICAPPED
Carter budget proposals 1-22, 43G2, 44A2
Sears sues US on bias laws 1-24, 92D1
Monkeys rptdly aid quadriplegics 3-19, 219C2
SSI COL hike rptd 4-26, 310G1
Calif odd-even gas rationing exemptn 5-9, 342F3
Sears suit vs US dismissed 5-15, 365B3
Carter seeks SSI food stamp plan chng 5-23, 384D1
Schls right to bar entry backed by Sup Ct 6-11, 478E1
Carter unveils natl health plan 6-12, 438D2
Nurse firing case refused by Sup Ct 6-18, 499D2
Bilingual program rules proposed 6-29, 597A1
Amtrak funding bill signed 9-29, 867G3
Cong OKs heating aid bill 11-9, 883B2
Library outreach urged 11-15—11-19, 901G1
VA malpractice ruling reversed by Sup Ct 11-28, 944D3
HANDMAN, Wynn
Seduced opens 2-1, 292A3
HANEL, Rudolf
Jupiter comments rptd 3-17, 216E2
HANEY, Lt. Connie
Vs 'sexist' language review 1-19, 89F3
HANFORD, Wash.—*See WASHINGTON*

1980

HAMADI, Saadun
On Iraq oil exports; Turkish, Syrian pipelines 9-27, 735C1
Meets Muskie, limited war stressed 9-30, 733C2
Defends Iraq invasn at UN 10-15, 774D1
Defends stand on '75 Iran-Iraq pact 10-17, 798B3
Warns US vs arms to Iran 10-25, 10-26, 820F2
HAMADY, Ron
Fade to Black released 10-17, 836F2
HAMBRECHT & Quist Inc.
Genentech stock offer success rptd 10-14, 806A1
HAMER, Rupert
Victoria pay pact rptd scored 12-2, 940G2
HAMILL, Mark
Empire Strikes Back released 5-21, 675D2
HAMILTON, Frank
Heartbreak House opens 4-29, 392B3
HAMILTON, Guy
Mirror Crack'd released 12-18, 1003C2
HAMILTON, Rep. Lee Herbert (D, Ind.)
Scores Myers expulsn proceedings 10-2, 740E1
Reelected 11-4, 842B4
HAMILTON, Norm—*See WELCH Jr., Bernard Charles*
HAMILTON, Pat
Loses US House electn 11-4, 850A3
HAMILTON Jr., Maj. Thomas B.
Asks Garwood ct-martial 2-1, 115C3
HAMLIN, Shelley
2d in ERA Real Estate Classic 9-21, 972B2
HAMMED, Gen. Mohammed Saleh
Named Saudi chief of staff 1-1, 22D1
HAMMER, Armand
Sees Brezhnev 2-27, 165F1
Rpts gold, silver futures trading profits 3-31, 245D1
Meets Brezhnev 10-14, 776C3
Buys Da Vinci ms for $5.28 mln 12-12, 997E3
HAMMER, Robert
Don't Answer the Phone released 8-9, 675C2
HAMMERMILL Paper Co.
Fine paper trust suit rptd setld 9-29; acquittal rptd in 2d suit 12-3, 917B2
HAMMERSCHMIDT, Dr. Dale E.
Heart disease curb rptd 5-22, 527F1
HAMMERSCHMIDT, Rep. John Paul (R, Ark.)
Reelected 11-4, 842C1
HAMMETT, Dashiell (1894-1961)
Sam Marlow released 10-3, 836E3
HAMMOND, Gov. Jay S. (R, Alaska)
State of State message 1-15, 268C3
Alaska OKs income tax break, shares wealth 4-15, 307B3
Income tax break overturned 9-5, signs income tax repeal 9-24, 747A1
Says lands bill 'not ideal' 12-2, 916D1
HAMPTON, Fred (d. 1969)
Panther Chicago shootout retrial order declined, legal fees voided by Sup Ct 6-2, 513A1
HAM Sok Hun
Sentncd 1-25, spared 1-29, 101E1
HANCE, Rep. Kent (D, Tex.)
Reelected 11-4, 844B3
HANCHAR, Cheryl
Jackson hits 400th homer 8-11, 636A3
HANCOCK, Phil
Wins Hall of Fame tourn 9-14, 972A2
HANDAL, Shafik
Salvadoran leftists launch offensive 12-26, 993C2
HANDBALL
Moscow Olympic results 7-29, 7-30, 623A1
HANDELSKREDITBANK A.G.
Offcls arrested 7-24, bank closed 7-26—7-27, 581E1
HANDICAPPED
Stuttering, genetics link rptd 1-5, 63B3
State of State messages 1-7, 1-8, 2-19, 404E2, G3, 404B1; 1-15, 484D1
Carter budget proposals 1-28, 72B3, D3
Fla property tax cut voted 3-11, 184G1
US Families Conf urges sensitivity 7-12, 601C2
Vet educ aid clears Cong 9-25, 9-26, signed 10-17, 856A3
HANDKE, Peter
Wrong Move released 1-25, 216G3
Left-Handed Woman released 4-2, 416B3
HANFORD—*See WASHINGTON (state)*
HANFORD, George H.
On SAT data disclosure 4-7, 318G3

1976

HAN Ju Kyong, Maj. Gen.
Blames US for DMZ attack 8-19, 619D1
Asks Panmunjom partition 8-28, 641C1
Sings partition pact 9-6, 660F1
HANK Gonzalez, Carlos
Mexico fed dist regent 12-2, 907A1
HANLEY, Rep. James Michael (D, N.Y.)
Reelected 11-2, 830C2
HANNA, Richard T.
Admits Park partnership 11-9, 900F1
HANNAFORD, Rep. Mark W. (D, Calif.)
Reelected 11-2, 829E1
HANNAH, Richard (Dick)
Dies 1-15, 56D3
HANNAY, Judge Allen B.
Fines 9 steel firms 4-10, 988D3
HANNUN, Hilmi
Warns on Tulkarm riots 5-20, 407E1
HANSEL, Helen S.
Loses Fla Sen primary 9-7, 687C3
HANSEN, Sen. Clifford P. (R, Wyo.)
Denies Ford delegate deal 7-2, 518F1
Backs Buckley candidacy 8-11, 584D3
HANSEN, Rep. George V. (R, Ida.)
Reelected 11-2, 824A2, 829E2
HANSEN, Irwin R.
Tax fraud chrgs dismissed 7-27, 566C2
HANSEN, Rolf
Norway defense min 1-12, 30A2
HAO, Gen. Song
Heads inspection com 12-20, 967E3
HARALAMBIE, Ivan
Defects to Canada 7-29, 562E2

1977

HAN Hsu
In US financial talks 5-1, 333E2
HANKS, Nancy
Successor sworn 11-30, 927G3
HANNA, Arthur
Retains Bahamas Cabt posts 7-29, 675D1
Salary increased 10-29, 844B3
HANNA, Richard T.
Named Park co-conspirator, denies chrgs 9-6, 687F2, A3
Indicted 10-14, 815F3
HANNA Mining Co.
USW ore-range strike ended 12-16, 977B3
HANNON, Thomas M.
Hijacks jet, kills self 10-20, 807F3
HANRAHAN, Edward V.
Released 4-15, 540F2
HANSEN, Sen. Clifford P. (R, Wyo.)
Elected conf secy 1-4, 6A2
Sues vs Linowitz in Panama Canal talks 3-16, 379E1
Vs Sen ethics code 4-1, 251F3
HANSEN, Rep. George V. (R, Ida.)
Campaign fund guilty plea cited 2-16, 112A1
Personal use fund-raising OKd 3-24, 233A1
HANSEN, Hal
Fasi trial folds 12-27, 1008E1
HANSEN, Joergen
Danish church min 2-25, 373E1
HANSEN, Kent
Sen com rejects nominatn 10-17, 800E1
HARB, Nabile Ibrahim
Identified as Lufthansa hijacker 10-27, 868F2
HARBI Farah, Ibrahim
Named Djibouti finance min 7-15, 583C2

1978

HAN Ju Kyong, Gen.
Denies N Korea dug DMZ tunnel 10-27, 860E3
HANLEY, Edward T.
On '77 top-paid labor ldrs list 5-15, 365F1
HANLEY, Rep. James Michael (D, N.Y.)
House retains vets job preference 9-11, 696D2
Reelected 11-7, 851G3
HANLON, Paul
Named to RR strike bd 9-28, 809C2
HANNA, Arthur
In Bahamas Cabt com on investmt 3-6, 194A2
HANNA, Kenneth (d. 1970)
Thevis arrested for murder 11-9, 971B2
HANNA, Richard T.
Park gifts testimony rptd 1-14, 63E2, C3
Pleads guilty in Korea bribery scandal 3-17, 202E3
Passman indicted 3-31, Park testifies on paymts 4-3, 239G1, E2
Sentenced, scores Justice probe 4-24, 323F3-324A1
Korea indictmts seen ended 6-1, 432A3
Loses reelection 11-7, 856C3
HAN Nianlong
In Japan peace talks 7-21—8-12, 637C1
HANNON, Joseph
Chicago bd OKs desegregatn plan 4-12, state objects 4-13, 263G3
HANSEN, Asger (Boots)
Puts out oil reserve fire 9-26, 738G1
HANSEN, Sen. Clifford P. (R, Wyo.)
Votes vs Panama Canal neutrality pact 3-16, 177G2
On Redwood Park extensn bill 3-21, 218G1
Votes vs Canal pact 4-18, 273B1
Mocks Carter energy plan 4-20, 304B3
Coal conversn bill clears Sen 7-18, 550B1
Vs gas compromise 8-31, 678A2
Not standing for reelectn 9-12, 736C2
Simpson wins seat 11-7, 856F1
HANSEN, Rep. George V. (R, Ida.)
Wins renomination 8-8, 625F3
Reelected 11-7, 850C3, 856C1
HANSEN, Ivan
Named Danish pub works min 8-30, 688A1
HANSEN, Joergen
Named Greenland min 8-30, 688A1
HANSEN, Robert V.
Loses Neb gov primary 5-9, 363E1
HANSSON, Bertil
Swedish cnty affairs min 10-18, 822A3
HANTASH, Yousuf Abu
Escapes death try, blames Iraq 8-5, 602E2
HAN Yu-tang
'Gang of 4' spared executn 2-21, 130G2-A3
HAO Kuang-teh
Arrested 4-11, 287B3
HAPPY Days (TV series)
Silverman to head NBC 1-20, 75F2

1979

HANG Gliding
1st transcontinental flight 7-9—8-16, 656C3
HANGSLEBEN, Alan
In NHL expansion draft 6-13, 470B2
HANIKA, Sylvia
Loses Women's Italian Open 5-14, 570B2
US Open results 9-9, 734E1
HANLEY, Rep. James Michael (D, N.Y.)
Post Office Com chrmn 1-24, 71E1
HANNA, Richard T.
Park indictmt dropped 8-16, 630F1
HAN Nianlong
Offers Vietnam peace plan 4-26, 298F1
Blames Viets re impasse 5-18, 379B3
Vs Viet peace proposal 6-28, 537A1
On China Viet war role 7-20, 575F2
Asks Viets quit Cambodia 8-29, 660A2
Chrgs Sovt war threat 9-27, 741B2
HANNON, Joseph
Quits Chicago schl post 11-28, 943G3
HANOVER Street (film)
Released 5-17, 528D2, E2*
HANSCOM, Daniel H.
Sears dishwasher ads faulted 10-16, 903A2
HANSEN, Charles R.
Judge bans H-bomb letter publicatn 9-15; Wis, Chicago papers defy ban 9-16, 9-18; Justice Dept vows probe 9-17, 713B1, G1, B2; text of letter, diagram 714D1-717E3
3 scientists deny H-bomb letter chrgs 9-17, 714B2
HANSEN, Rep. George V. (R, Ida.)
Canal treaty implementatn bill clears House 6-21, 481E1, A2
In Iran 11-20—11-28; sees hostages 11-25; O'Neill, others score 11-26, 895E2
HANSEN, Lisa & Elisa
Separated 5-30, 527F2
Leave hospital 7-17, 656C2
HANSON, Harry
Seeks Jourdain ouster 5-20, arrested 5-5, 465E1
Sentncd for Chippewa violence 7-22, 630F3
HANSON, Howard
Elected to Arts Institute 12-7, 1005A3
HANSON, Stephanie
Red Lake violence flares 5-20—5-25, 465E1
HANSON, Walter E.
Peat Marwick rejects nominee as chrmn 10-10, 851E3
HANTA Yo (book)
On best-seller list 6-3, 432A2
HAPAG-Lloyd A.G.
Indicted re price fixing 6-1, 423D2; pleads no contest, fined 6-8, 442B2

1980

HAN-Gyong Si
Wins Olympic medal 7-20, 624D2
HANIFAN, John
Hired as Cardinals coach 1-30, 413B1
HANIGAN, Patrick
Mex alien case mistrial declared 7-29, retrial sought 8-29, 713F2
HANIGAN, Thomas
Mex alien case mistrial declared 7-29, retrial sought 8-29, 713E3
HANISCH, Wolfgang
Wins Olympic medal 7-27, 624B1
HANKIN, Ray
Cosmos win Challenge Cup 5-26, 771A1
HANLEY, Rep. James M. (D, N.Y.)
GOP wins seat 11-4, 848C3
HANN, George R.
Icons sold for record sum 4-17, 472A3
HANNA, Arthur D.
On Cuban patrol boat attack 5-11, 371F2
HANNAFORD, Mark
Loses Calif US House primary 6-3, 439A2
HANON, Mario
Arrest rptd 11-18, 887C2
HANRAHAN, Edward V.
Panther Chicago shootout retrial order declined by Sup Ct 6-2, 513B1
HANRAHAN v. Hampton
Case declined by Sup Ct 6-2, 513C1
HANSA, D.D.G.
Insolvency rptd 8-18, 674E1
HANSEL, Herbert
Cautns press at autonomy talks 7-15, 539C1
HANSEN, Rep. George V. (R, Ida.)
Reelected 11-4, 851G3
HANSEN, James V.
Elected to US House 11-4, 844C3, 852D1
HANZLIK, Bill
In NBA draft 6-10, 447G1
HAPAG-Lloyd A.G.
Hansa insolvency rptd 8-18, 674G1
HAPPY Birthday Gemini (film)
Released 5-2, 416G2-A3
HAPPY New Year (play)
Opens 4-27, 392A3

1976

HARBORS & Ports—*See also SHIPS & Shipping*
S Africa opens new port 4-1, 429E1
NE govs seek port dvpt 11-14, 864F3
Chile rejects Bolivia seaport plan 11-26, 975G1
Coleman to OK 2 superports 12-17, 991G3
HARCOURT Brace Jovanovich Inc.
US files consent decree 7-27, 989A2
HARDESTY Jr., C. Howard
Continental Oil cites paymts abuses 12-16, 986C1
HARDESTY, Robert L.
Postal Svc gov 7-12; confrmd 8-8, 808A1
HARDISON, Larry E.
Swine flu rptd 11-22, unconfrmd 11-27, 911D1
HARGROVE, James W.
Amb to Australia 1-20; confrmd 2-4, 110B2
Arrives Australia 2-18, 155B1
HARGUINDEGUY, Brig. Gen. Albano
Argentina interior min 3-29, 236B1 *
Sees church ldrs 7-14, 571E2
HARKIN, Rep. Thomas R. (D, Ia.)
Chrgs grain scandal cover-up 1-29, 136D1
In Chile 3-11—3-15; chrgs rights abuse 3-17, 310C2
Reelected 11-2, 829D3
HARLAN County (U.S. warship)
In Intl Naval Review 7-4, 488E3
HARLE Services Inc.
Boycott rpt released 10-20, 786A2
HARLEY Corp.
Indicted 10-29, 886C3

1977

HARBORS & Ports—*See also SHIPS & Shipping*
Bechtel-Saudi projct cited 1-10, 78G2-A3
Seadock superport threatnd 7-12, 559A2
Seadock pres scores govt controls 7-26, Tex aid seen 7-27, 724G3-725A1
Loop superport license signed 8-1, 724E3
NJ, Va referenda OKd 11-8, 879C2, D2
HARDISON, Larry G.
Religious rights limited 6-13, 517C3
HARDY, Arthur C.
Dies 10-31, 872B2
HARE Krishna—*See KRISHNA Consciousness, International Society for*
HARELSON, Judge Gilbert
Edgar Smith sentenced 4-25, 396G1
HARGAN, Steve
Traded to Braves 6-15, 644F2
HARGROVE, James W.
Replaced as Australia amb 4-29, 418C1
HARGUINDEGUY, Gen. Albano
Scores pol parties 7-24, 615A2
HARKNESS, Ned
Quits as Union Coll coach 12-23, 1021G1
HARLAN County, U.S.A. (film)
Wins Oscar 3-28, 264D1
HARLEM River
NYC clean-air case review declined 10-17, 797D3
HARLEY Corp.
No contest plea cited 11-23, 918B3
HARMAN, Sidney
Named Commerce undersecy 1-6, 14F1
US shoe industry gets fed aid 7-20, 587D2
HARNESS Racing—*See HORSE Racing*
HARNETT, Joel
Koch wins mayoral primary 9-8, 723B2

1978

HARBORS & Ports—*See also SHIPS & Shipping*
Australia ports hit by job actns 4-9—5-2, 349F3-350B1; congestn continues 5-22, 411A2; dock setlmt rptd 6-5, 450F3
HARBOR View Farm
Affirmed wins Triple Crown 6-10, 538G3-539A2
HARD Again (recording)
Wins Grammy 2-24, 316A1
HARDEMAN, Don
Traded to Buccaneers 4-30, 336A2
Traded to Colts 8-13, 1024D3
HARD to Bet (race horse)
McHargue sets earnings mark 12-31, 1028F1
HARDWICK, Steve
NASL goalkeeping ldr 8-6, 655D2
HARDY, James
In NBA draft 6-9, 457F2
HARE Krishna—*See KRISHNA Consciousness, International Society for*
HAREWOOD, Doran
Mighty Gents opens 4-16, 760E2
HARGROVE, Mike
Traded to Padres 10-25, 1026B1
HARGUINDEGUY, Gen. Albano
Scores pol parties 4-26, 611D3
Retained in Cabt shuffle 11-6, 865E2
HARKIN, Rep. Thomas (D, Iowa)
Asks Nicaragua aid cutoff 10-13, 839G2
Israel frees US Arab 10-18, 783E2
Reelected 11-7, 850C4
Asks Chile disappearances probe 12-8, 1014C1
Backs Chile trade boycott 12-8, 1014B2
HARLEY Corp.
Fined 10-2, 768A3
HARMAN, Barry
Wins Emmy 9-17, 1030F1
HARMATZ, Joel
Rules vs J P Stevens 3-26, 243C2
HARMEN, Cpl. Paul (d. 1977)
IRA forces pullout of UK agents 1-9, 18G2
HARMSWORTH, Vere
Leasy elected Trib chrmn 1-17, 75E3
HARO, Nassar
Calls slain rptr criminal 4-20, 517A3

1979

HARBORS & Ports—*See also SHIPS & Shipping*
St Lucia free-port zone planned 2-21, 181E2
US-China pact rptd 2-23, 146G2
Floods shut N Orleans port 3-15, 288F3
Mex 10-yr dvpt plan rptd 5-4, 354A1
Tex supertanker port OKd 10-15, 769B3
China, Japan sign pact 12-7, 939E3
HARCOURT Brace Jovanovich Inc.
Goldwater sued 9-14, 859G3-60A1
Author in aerial protest 10-11, 860F1
HARDCORE (film)
Released 2-8, 174F2
Top-grossing film 2-28, 174B2
HARDEN, Richard
Vesco case perjury rptd 8-30, Heymann denies 8-31, 725G2
Carter to videotape Vesco testimony 12-5, 943E2
HARDWARE
Dealers shift conv to Memphis 4-4, 260B2
HARDWICK, Elizabeth
Book awards protest rptd 8-9, 755F3
HARDY, Joseph
Romantic Comedy opens 11-8, 956G3
HARE, David
Teeth 'n' Smiles opens 8-13, 712A3
HARE, Mayor Robert C. (Passaic, N.J.)
Layoff threat rptd 11-26, 921G1
HARE Krishna—*See KRISHNA Consciousness, International Society for*
HARKIN, Rep. Thomas (D, Iowa)
Ends Latin rights missn, asks Nicaragua beef ban 6-5, 427G1-A2
Seeks Chile loan disclosures 10-1, 750D2
On E Timor starvatn 12-4, 995A1
HARKINS, Jerry
On Crane pres bid 5-16, 363D3
HARLAN, Charles
On Skylab descent 7-11, 509F2
HARLECH, Lord
On African recogntn of Zimbabwe 7-10, 546D3
HARLOW, Larry
Angels lose AL pennant 10-6, 797F2
HARMAN, David
Scores adult literacy progrms 9-8, 786D1
HARMON, Maj. Gen. Ernest N.
Dies 11-13, 932A3
HARNISCHFEGER Corp.
Paccar seeks 6-11, Mannesmann withdraws offer 11-4, 942G2

1980

HARBORS & Ports
NY-NJ Customs corruptn probed 1-11, 2-13, 359C2-B3
US territories set projects 2-19—2-22, 495E1
Australia harbor pilot strike rptd 5-16, 371F1; ends 5-21, 405C3
Mex in French, Swedish, Canadian agrmts 5-18, 5-24, 5-27, 409D2, A3, C3
Tampa port reopened 5-21, 391F1
Mt St Helens damage assessed 5-24—7-4, 504B3
UK Docks Bd to sell shares 7-21, 564D1
French port blockade eased 8-19, 633F3-634B1
French port blockade concessns offered, fisherman score 8-26, navy opens blockade 8-27, 651D3
NJ, Alaska bond issues OKd 11-4, 847A1, A2
HARDEMAN, Buddy
NFL '79 punt return ldr 1-5, 8F3
HARDEN, Richard
Vesco grand jury ends 4-1, 251C3
HARDIN, Tim
Dies 12-29, 1004B2
HARDY, Jim
Australia wins America's Cup trials 9-5, Freedom retains Cup 9-25, 834G1
HARDY, Robin
Wicker Man released 3-26, 416G3
HARDY, Thomas (1840-1928)
Tess released 12-12, 1003E2
HARIMOTO, Isao
Gets 3000th hit 5-31, 637D1
HARKIN, Rep. Tom (D, Iowa)
Reelected 11-4, 842C4
HARMAN, Rodney
Wins NCAA doubles tennis title 5-26, 607D1
HARMENBERG, Johan
Wins Olympic medal 7-28, 622B3
HARNESS, Edward G.
Retires from Procter & Gamble 12-9, 959B1
HARNEY, Paul
2d in PGA Seniors 12-7, 972G2
HAROLD and Maude (play)
Opens 1-7, 136B3

1976

HARPER & Row Publishers Inc.
US files consent decree 7-27, 989A2
HARMER, John
Loses Senate primary 6-8, 409D2
HARMS, Kenneth
Files honor code suit 7-1, 670G2
HARRAH'S
SEC lists paymts 5-12, 727E1
HARRELL, James
Eritrea rebels free 5-3, 335G1
HARRIGAN, Dan
Wins Olympic medal 7-24, 575C2
HARRIMAN, Leslie O.
Submits Transkei resolutn 10-26, 799A2
HARRIMAN, W. Averell
Supports Carter 6-14, 432C1
Tito cancels visit 9-16, 734A3
Sees Brezhnev 9-20, comments 9-29, 752B1
Confers with Carter 11-29, 898B3
HARRINGTON, Rep. Michael J. (D, Mass.)
Rpts Chile aid continues 1-26, 99C2
Reelected 11-2, 829B4
HARRIS, Donald M.
Bolles mistrial declared 10-21; dismissed from case 10-22, seeks files return 10-26, 859F2-A3
HARRIS, Emily M. and William T.
ACLU suit filed 1-5, 70G1
Soliah freed on bail 1-15, 70B2
Cited in Hearst trial 2-4—2-10; issue denial 2-5, 113D3-114E3
Cited in Hearst trial 2-11—3-18, 201E1-202B2
Article on Hearst rptd 2-22, 201C3
Hearst agrees to testify 4-14; in ct with Hearst 5-12, 367F3, 368B1
Article rpts on break with Hearst 4-25, 368E1
Hearst 'mute' at hearing 5-28, 423B2
Convicted re LA robbery, kidnap 8-9, mistrial request denied 8-10, 595B3
Sentenced 8-31, 679B3
Indicted for Hearst, Benenson kidnap 9-29, 735D2
Hearst retrial petitn filed 9-29, denied 11-19, 891C3
HARRIS, Fred Roy
Gets US campaign subsidy 1-2, 22E3
Common Cause rpts code backing 1-9, 23A1
3d in Iowa precinct vote 1-19, 41A1
Miss caucus vote results 1-24, 94G3, 95A1
2d in Okla caucuses 2-7, 129E1
4th in NH primary 2-24, 148F1, B3
5th in Mass primary 3-2, 165A1
3d in Vt primary 3-2, 165A2
Fed fund total listed 3-4, 180C3
Gets 8% in Ill primary 3-16, 196E2
Gets 1% vote in NC 3-23, 214B1
Wins 1% of Wis vote 4-6, 245D1
Ends natl campaign effort 4-8, 261G2
Loses Sup Ct funds plea 4-23, 306C1
Md primary results 5-18, 357G1
Gets more FEC funds 5-21, 391E3
Idaho, Tenn, Ore primary results 5-25, 374E2-E3
SD primary results 6-1, 390D2
Calif primary results 6-8, 409B1
Primary delegates totaled 6-8, 409B3
FEC ends fed funds 6-23, 490F3
Fed fund total rptd 7-1, 491A1
Dem conv pres vote, table 7-14, 507E3
FEC certificatn total rptd 12-31, 979G2
HARRIS 2nd, Rep. Herbert E. (D, Va.)
Reelected 11-2, 823D1, 831A1
HARRIS, James
Scores Ramses restoratn 11-8, 912A3
HARRIS, Patricia Roberts
Named Carter adviser 11-19, 881E3
Named HUD secy 12-21, 956G1, 957F2
Photo 956C3
Biog sketch 957F2
HARRIS, Ray
Becomes uncommitted delegate 8-3, 564C2
HARRIS, Rosemary
Wins Emmy 5-17, 460C2
HARRIS, Thomas E.
Renamed to FEC 5-17; confrmd 5-18, sworn 5-21, 391C3
HARRIS, Walter (Slide)
Dies 8-8, 816E3
HARRISBURG, Pa.—*See PENNSYLVANIA*
HARRISBURG News
Ford endorsement rptd 10-30, 831F2
HARRIS Corp.
RF Communicatns boycott rpt released 10-19, 786D1
HARRISON, Antonio
Carter meets black leaders 7-12, 513A2
HARRISON, Mrs. Charles
Testifies on Mex prisoner abuses 1-15, 75A2
HARRISON, Karen
Mex prisoner abuse hearing 1-15, 75A2
HARRIS Survey (Louis Harris & Associates, Inc.)
Carter leads Ford, Reagan 7-26, 564G3
Ford leads Reagan 7-28, 565C1
Reagan vp selectn 8-12, 584A1
Predicts Carter over Ford 10-31, 826A1
HARRY, Ralph
UN tin pact OKd 4-28, 380F1
HARSCO Corp.
'75 arms sales listed 2-6, 147C3
HARSHA, Rep. William H. (R, Ohio)
Reelected 11-2, 830G2
HARSHILADZE, Ramaz
Wins Olympic medal 7-28, 575A1
HART, Sen. Gary W. (D, Colo.)
Intellignc com issues rpt 4-26, 304D3
Named to intelligence com 5-20, 377E
HART Jr., Judge George L.
Babcock jail term set aside 6-4, 442D2
HART, Judith
'75 Mozambique aid offer rptd 3-4, 175A3

1977

HARPER, Michael
S Africa detains 6-10, 496A2
HARPER & Row Publishers Inc.
Record paperback sum rptd 3-1, 356A2
At USSR book fair 9-6—9-14, 765E3
Knowlton on USSR book pact 12-7, 955D2
Lippincott purchase set 12-23, 1004D3
HARRIMAN, Leslie O.
Scores Young speech 5-19, 399E2
HARRINGTON, Rep. Michael J. (D, Mass.)
Chrgs inequities in defns spending 4-10, 4-26, 423B3
HARRIS, Emily M. and William T.
Hearst pleads no contest 4-18, 302C2
HARRIS, Kenton L.
Nigeria holds 2-16, frees 3-7, 393E2
HARRIS, Patricia Roberts
Confrmatn hearings 1-10; confrmatn recommended 1-18, confrmd 1-20, 34B1, E2
Says budget 'starved' 2-14, 110C3
On Carter budget revisn 2-22, 125F2
Rpts personal finances 2-25, 148A1
Details new grant program 3-7, 178B1
Carter tours South Bronx 10-5, 761A1
At League of Cities conf 12-7, 959B3, 960A1, D1
Sees Carter, black ldrs 12-14, 960D1
HARRIS, Stanley R. (Bucky)
Dies 11-8, 952D2
HARRIS, Ted
Fired as North Stars coach 11-24, 1021F1
HARRISBURG, Pa.—*See PENNSYLVANIA*
HARRIS Savings and Trust of Chicago
Treas Dept threatens on bias 8-25, 669G2
HARRIS Survey (Louis Harris & Associates, Inc.)
Poll on death penalty rptd 2-7, 594G2
Carter ratings high 4-4, 251C1
Carter energy plan poll rptd 4-23, 320B3
Carter standing drops 10-10, 817F1
HARNETT, Joseph D.
Scores ICC Alaska pipe rates 6-28, 498C1
HART, Sen. Gary W. (D, Colo.)
Moves vs AT&T 2-24, 217A3
On intell com watch 2-26, 151D1
Relays word on Warnke 2-27, 172A3
Scores Micronesia surveillnc 5-3, 387D1
Asks NATO overhaul 9-10, 700C1
Scores Mondale, Byrd re filibuster end 9-22—10-3, 758C1
NRC nominee rejected 10-17, 800F1
Scores NRC A-plant safety 11-19, 917B2
HART, Gene Leroy
Chrgd with murder 6-23, sought 8-22, 711E3
HART Jr., Judge George
Orders Tris recall cost sharing 4-28, 5-3, 483C2
Dismisses EPA suit vs Chrysler 8-22, 723E3
HART, Gerry
NFL suspends 10-7, 1020D1

1978

HARPER, Bruce
NFL '77 kick return ldr 1-1, 56C3
HARPER'S (magazine)
John Fischer dies 8-18, 708G2
HARPER Valley PTA (film)
Top-grossing film 5-31, 460E3
HARRAH, Toby
Traded to Indians 12-8, 1026D1
HARRAH, William
Dies 6-30, 540G2
HARRELL, Willard
NFL '77 punt return ldr 1-1, 56F3
HARRELSON, Bud
Traded to Phillies 3-23, 779C3
HARRIER B—*See ARMAMENTS—Aircraft*
HARRIMAN, E. Roland
Dies 2-16, 196A3
HARRIMAN, Edward Henry (1848-1909)
Son dies 2-16, 196B3
HARRIMAN, W. Averell
Brother dies 2-16, 196B3
HARRINGTON, Rep. Michael J. (D, Mass.)
Not standing for reelectn 9-19, 736B3
Mavroules wins seat 11-7, 847C3
HARRIS, Bill
GOP switches Sen electns 10-2, 769G1
HARRIS, Don
Arrives Guyana 11-15, visits cult commune 11-17; killed 11-18, body flown home 11-21, 889A1-F2, 891C1
HARRIS, Emily M. and William T.
Plead guilty 8-31, convicted 10-3; Hearst reactns 9-1—10-8, 823F3-824F1
823F3-824F1
HARRIS, Franco
NFL '77 touchdown, rushing ldr 1-1, 56B2, B3
HARRIS II, Rep. Herbert E. (D, Va.)
Renominated 6-13, 467F1
Reelected 11-7, 852A3
HARRIS, Ike
Traded to Saints 1-31, 172D1
HARRIS, Joseph
Working opens 5-14, 887E3
HARRIS, Julie
Record wins Grammy 2-24, 316B1
HARRIS, Lagumot (Nauruan president; replaced May 15)
Replaced as Nauru pres 5-15, 439F3
HARRIS, Luisa
Unsigned by WBL 12-9, 1027A3
HARRIS, Nan
Porch opens 11-14, 1031G2
HARRIS, Patricia Roberts
Housing bias rptd 4-17, 285D2
Cancels cong testimony, White House disagreemt re Fed policy cited 8-7, 605F1
Issues Fannie Mae rules 8-14, 627D3
HARRIS, Ronnie
Corro decisns 8-5, 969D1
HARRIS, Sheson
Elected Chamber of Commerce chrmn 4-29, 420G1
HARRIS, Vic
Dies 2-23, 196B3
HARRISBURG, Pa.—*See PENNSYLVANIA*
HARRIS Corp.
Americans in Uganda warned 10-12, 823A1
HARRISON, George
Sgt Pepper's released 7-21, 970B3
HARRISON, Rex
Kingfisher opens 12-6, 1031B2
HARRIS Survey (Louis Harris & Associates, Inc.)
Carter rating low 3-30, 308B1
US backs Panama Canal Treaty 4-3, 256B1
Carter trails Ford 5-24, 404C3
Carter, Cong ratings rptd 8-27, 682B2
Poll on wage-price controls rptd 10-24, 807B1
HARROD, Roy
Dies 3-8, 252A3
HARROP, William C.
Says PLO not terror group 6-27, 503B3
HARSHA, Rep. William H. (R, Ohio)
Reelected 11-7, 851D3
HART, Sen. Gary W. (D, Colo.)
Votes for Panama Canal neutrality pact 3-16, 177E2
Votes for 2d Canal pact 4-18, 273B1
On '79 arms authorzn 7-12, 526D2, G2
HART, Gene Leroy
Arrested in Okla Scout slayings 4-6, 380D3
HART Jr., Judge George L.
Fines AFL-CIO $10,000 6-12, 509D3
ITT denied stay on sealed data 10-30, 832D2
Orders SEC suit vs ITT unsealed 11-2, 816D1, C2
HART, Jim
NFC wins Pro Bowl 1-23, 56F1

1979

HARPER, Bruce
NFL '78 punt return ldr 1-6, 80C2
HARPER, Ethel
Dies 3-31, 272E2
HARPER, Malcolm
On blocked Cambodia aid 12-20, 978G2
HARPER, Steven Roy
Convicted in 'cancer' murders 10-5, gets death penalty 11-7, 891A1
HARPER, Valerie
Chapter Two released 12-14, 1007B3
HARPER, Wally
Grand Tour opens 1-11, 292E1
HARPER & Row Publishers Inc.
Exhibits Random House books at USSR fair 9-4—9-10, 690A1
HARRAH Independent School District v. Martin
Okla teacher dismissal backed by US Sup Ct 2-26, 165A1
HARRAH'S
Holiday Inns to buy 9-4, 682C3
HARRELL, Willard
NFL '78 punt return ldr 1-6, 80F2
HARRIER B—*See ARMAMENTS—Aircraft*
HARRIMAN, N.Y.—*See NEW York State*
HARRIMAN, Leslie O.
Scores Westn loans to S Africa 4-2, 270E2
HARRIMAN, W. Averell
Rockefeller dies 1-26, 104B1
Attends Mountbatten funeral 9-5, 669D1
HARRIS, Al
In NFL draft 5-3, 335F1
HARRIS, Ann
Sky High opens 6-28, 712D2
HARRIS, Barbara
N Amer Irregulars released 4-12, 528B3
Joe Tynan released 8-17, 820C3
HARRIS, Berkeley
Devour the Snow opens 5-13, 711D2
HARRIS, Eloise
Sky High opens 6-28, 712D2
HARRIS, Emily M. and William T.
Convictns review declined by Sup Ct 10-1, 768B1
HARRIS, Franco
NFL '78 rushing ldr 1-6, 80B2
Steelers win Super Bowl 1-21, 63E1
HARRIS, Jayne Anne
Sky High opens 6-28, 712D2
HARRIS, Jed
Dies 11-15, 932A3
HARRIS, Joseph P.
1940's Radio Hour opens 10-7, 956F3
HARRIS, Julie
Bell Jar released 3-20, 528D1
Break a Leg opens 4-29, 711G1
HARRIS, Lulu Belle
Sky High opens 6-28, 712D2
HARRIS, Patricia Roberts
Scores mortgage bias vs women 3-9, 209A1
US comm vs housing bias 4-11, 283B3
Named HEW secy 7-19, 529D1
Addresses Urban League 7-25, 560C1
Confrmd HEW secy 7-27, 577C1
Seeks black-Jewish reconciliatn 8-29, 661G2
Chicago desegregatn funds barred 9-15, suit sought 10-29, 944B1
Title IX sports guidelines issued 12-4, 1000G2
HARRIS, Robert
Mediates UAL strike 5-24, 402B2
HARRIS, Roy
Dies 10-1, 860F2
HARRISBURG, Pa.—*See PENNSYLVANIA*
HARRIS Neck Wildlife Refuge (Ga.)
Protesters jailed 5-4—5-10, 368D1
HARRISON, Rex
5th Musketeer released 9-7, 820C1
HARRIS Survey (Louis Harris & Associates Inc.)
Racial poll optimistic 2-20, 306D3
Carter poll rating low 7-9, 514D1
Reagan tops GOP poll 11-25, 982E1
HARRIS v. California
Case declined by Sup Ct 10-1, 768B1
HARRIS v. Isleboro School Committee
Case declined by Sup Ct 11-26, 919E2
HARROLD, Tex.—*See TEXAS*
HART, Alberto
Freed by leftists 11-6, 872B3
HART, Sen. Gary W. (D, Colo.)
Meets Teng in China 1-9, 27B1
On Sen income limit delay 3-28, 281E1
On 3 Mile I A-accident cleanup 4-2, 245G2
On Armed Svcs Com SALT vote 12-21, 979G1
HART, Gene Leroy
Acquitted in Okla Scout slayings 3-30, 291E2
Dies 6-4, 508A3
HART Jr., Judge George L.
Named to wiretap ct 5-18, 442B3
Fines Tenneco 7-27, 629G1, A2
HART, Gerry
In NHL expansion draft 6-13, 470B2

1980

HARPER, Dr. Alfred E.
Cholesterol rpt issued 5-27, 432G2
HARPER, Chris
Expelled from Iran 2-28, 138A2
HARPER & Row Publishers Inc.
Basic Books Inc.
Photocopy co sued 2-5, 119G3
Photocopy suit rptd setld 3-21, 376D3
HARPER'S (magazine)
Publicatn to end 6-17, 501A1
Sold to philanthropies 7-9, 582A3
HARRELL, Willard
NFL '79 kick return ldr 1-5, 8G3
HARRELL Jr., Jack
Loses US House electn 11-4, 849A3
HARRIMAN, W. Averell
Marks Zimbabwe indepndnc 4-17—4-18, 301F1
At Tito funeral 5-8, 338B3
HARRINGTON, Michael
At DC draft protest 3-22, 228A1
HARRIS, Alicia
Navy actn on lesbian chrgs cited 899B1
HARRIS, Denny
Silent Scream released 2-2, 216E3
HARRIS, Don (d. 1978)
Layton faces murder chrgs 5-22, 407G3
HARRIS, Emmylou
Wins Grammy 2-27, 296D3
HARRIS, Franco
NFL '79 rushing ldr 1-5, 8B3
Steelers win Super Bowl; TD record cited 1-20, 61D3-62C1
HARRIS, Fred Roy
Wife chosen vp candidate 4-12, 288E3
HARRIS II, Rep. Herbert (D, Va.)
Loses reelectn 11-4, 850E2
HARRIS, James
Defends Boise TV statn raid 7-28, sued 8-1, 732A3
HARRIS, Jane Gary
Complete Critical Prose wins Amer Book Award 5-1, 692G2
HARRIS, Jean S.
Chrgd in Tarnower slaying 3-11, 214E3
HARRIS, Jeff
Hopkins wins NCAA lacrosse title 5-31, 638B1
HARRIS, Joseph P.
Roast opens 5-8, 392G3
HARRIS, LaDonna (Mrs. Fred Roy)
Citizens' Party vp nominee 4-13, 288E3
HARRIS, Neil
Bull Pen opens 6-12, 756C3
HARRIS, Patricia Roberts
Warns DES violators 4-15, 358G1
Health & Human Svcs begins operatn 5-4, 370C1
Reagan chrgs Klan link attempt 9-2, 664E1
Medicaid abortn funding review denied by Sup Ct 9-17, 703B3
HARRIS, Robert
On banned item export curb 8-2, 599A3
HARRIS, Rosemary
Sea Gull opens 11-11, 892F3
HARRIS, William
'Scarsdale Diet' MD slain 3-10, 214G3
HARRISBURG—*See PENNSYLVANIA*
HARRISON, Benjamin (1833-1901)
A R Longworth dies 2-20, 176D2
HARRISON, George
Lennon slain 12-9, 934A2, B3
HARRISON, Rex
Rachel Roberts dies 11-26, 928D3
HARRISON, Stafford
Reggae opens 3-27, 392F3
HARRISON v. PPG Industries
Case decided by Sup Ct 5-27, 453F3
HARRIS Survey (Louis Harris & Associates Inc.)
Pres poll rptd 3-9, 208B1
Reagan takes poll lead 6-17, 452B2
Carter rating at new low 7-30, 570B2
Post-debate pres polls rptd 9-23, 9-25, 739G2, A3
Pres poll standings tighten, toss-up seen 10-27, 816A2
HARRIS v. McRae
Case accepted by Sup Ct 2-19, 130A3
Case argued in Sup Ct 4-21, 306B2
Case decided by Sup Ct 6-30, 491F2
HARRIS v. Rosario
Case decided by Sup Ct 5-27, 453C3
HARSH, George
Dies 1-25, 104G2
HARSHA, Rep. William A. (R, Ohio)
McEwen wins seat 11-4, 851D2
HART, Gaetan
KOs Racine 5-17, Denny 6-20; Denny dies, Canada launches probe 7-7, 907B3
HART, Sen. Gary W. (D, Colo.)
Scores Cong override of oil import bar veto 6-6, 437B2
Issues 3 Mile I rpt, backs gas venting 7-2, 551D1
Unopposed in primary 9-9, 700D2
Reelected 11-4, 840D1, 845A3, 846B3, 851C3
HART Jr., Judge George
Backs Iran assets seizure damages 7-10, 546F1
HART Jr., John N.
Onward Victoria opens 12-14, 1003E3

1976

HART, Sen. Philip A. (D, Mich.)
Backs patent reform bill 2-26, 181D3
Intellignc com issues rpt 4-26, 304D3
Primary results for seat 8-3, 565F2
Riegle wins seat 11-2, 820C1
Asst named Carter adviser 11-23, 881B
Dies 12-6, 1015E1
Ford to reconsider amnesty 12-27, 980G1
HART, William L.
Named Detroit police chief 9-28, 776C2
HART, William S.
Sentenced delayed 11-30, 921B3
HARTE-Hanks Newspapers, Inc.
Ford interview 4-19, 281A2
HARTFORD, Conn.—*See CONNECTICUT*
HARTFORD, Ian—*See TENDLER, Stewart*
HARTFORD Courant (newspaper)
Ford endorsement rptd 10-30, 827F3
HARTFORD Times (newspaper)
Ceases publication 10-20, 849F1
HARTKE, Sen. Vance (D, Ind.)
Wins primary 5-4, 323A2
Sup Ct lets stand FCC ruling 5-24, 393F2
AFL-CIO donatn rptd 10-22, 938D3
Loses reelection 11-2, 819D3, G3, 823G2
HARTLEY, Fred L.
Sup Ct bars libel suit review 10-4, 807D2
HARTLEY, William
Censured re Iraq fund 3-7, 187A2
HARTMANN, Robert T.
Speechwriters shifted 1-21, 40D3
HARTWICK College (Oneonta, N.Y.)
In NCAA soccer playoff 12-5, 969G2
HARTZENBERG, F.
Named Bantu dvpt dep min 1-22, 76F1
HARVARD University (Cambridge, Mass.)
Kistner changes view on pill 1-10, 32A2
Moynihan quits UN post 2-2, 89B1
Samuel Morison dies 5-15, 368G2
DNA research barred 7-7, 736B1
Australia prime min dedicates chair 7-30, 554B2
'75 animal gene synthesis cited 735D3
Lipscomb wins chem Nobel 10-18, 840E1
Wilson gets Science Medal 10-18, 858G3
Donald Menzel dies 12-14, 1015B2
HARVEL, Reginald
Found shot to death 9-29, 776E2
HARYONO, Maj. Gen. Piet
Heads Pertamina 3-4, 176G3
HASHIMOTO, Tomisaburo
Arrested 8-21, 628E2
Indicted 9-10, 740B2
HASHISHA, Zuheir Abou
Dies in Damascus raid 9-26, 720D3
HASKELL, Sen. Floyd K. (D, Colo.)
Carter meets cong ldrs 11-17, 864A2
HASKELL Jr., Harry G.
Abercrombie plans bankruptcy plea 8-6, 984E3
HASLEHURST, Brian
Captured 5-2, freed 10-2, 1002B2
HASNEN, Nabil
Leads raid vs Syria emb 10-11, 759E1
HASSAN II, King (Morocco)
French visit set 1-8, 36G1
Arab natns seek Sahara settlmt 1-27—1-29, 58C2
Kissinger sees Lamrani 1-29, more mil aid pledged 1-30, 107G2
Promotes Sahara officers 4-26, 342A1
'73 plotters tried 7-8, 6 sentncd 7-20, 559F3
HASSAN, Hassan Mohammed
Egypt housing min 11-10, 852F1
HASSAN, Sir Joshua
Labor wins Gibraltar electns 9-29, 751C1
HASSAN, Syed Fida
Assumes amb post in India 7-21, 538G1
HASSANALY, Mohammed
Comoro vp 1-2, 119B1
HASSANIEN, Ali Mahmoud
Arrested 7-7, 501G3
HASSLER, Andy
Yankees win pennant 10-14, 796A2
HASTINGS, James F.
Resigns House seat 1-20, 68D3
Dems win House seat 3-2, 166F2
Convicted 12-17, 982C1
HASUMI, Kikuko
Nishiyama '74 acquittal reversed 7-20, 539F1
HATCH, Orrin G.
Wins Utah Sen primary 9-14, 705F1
Elected 11-2, 819D3, 824G2, 828C3

1977

HART, William
Reverse bias chrgd re police 1-4, 278B3
HARTFORD Fire Insurance Co.—*See INTERNATIONAL Telephone & Telegraph Corp.*
HARTKE, Vance
'76 spec interest gifts rptd 2-15, 128G1, C2, E2; 3-7, 232G2, A3
HARTLEY, William
Accuses US Labor conv observer 7-5, 541B1
HARTLING, Poul
Soc Dems make electn gains 2-15, 115G1
HARTMAN, Arthur A.
Dobrynin hits US rights stand 2-17, 137D2
Named amb to France 5-13, confrmd 6-7, 499E3
HARTWICK College (Oneonta, N.Y.)
Wins NCAA soccer title 12-4, 1020E3
HARUNA, Maj. Gen. Ibrahim
Nigeria Cabt drops 3-15, 393C2
HARVARD University (Cambridge, Mass.)
Champion, Nye get US posts 1-19, 53A1, D1
DNA research ban ended 2-7, 103C2
AAAS conf; Jensen apptmt protested, Wallace quits 2-21—2-25, 183C3, C3, 184A2
Urban cntr rpts on house costs 3-3, 178B2
Wald backs DNA resrch halt 3-7, 184F2
Glazer scores quotas 3-31, 235E2
Smoking-menopause link rptd 6-25, 620D1
Richmond confrmd HEW undersecy 6-28, 626D3
Goldstein DNA concern rptd 10-6, 846E3
Van Vleck wins Nobel 10-11, 951G2
Barghoorn fossil find rptd 10-15, 908G1
Legal scholar scores Sup Ct rulings 10-31, 878E3
Wilson gets Medal of Sci 11-22, 952C1
DNA research halted 12-15, 1022D2
Rosovsky barred Yale pres post 12-20, 1021D2
HARYONO, Gen. Piet
Pertamina debt settled 8-11, 637D3
HASAN, Mubashir
Quits ruling party post 4-13, 305G2
HASBRO Industries Inc.
Rebates rptd 1-19, 94E2
HASHEM, Jawad
Named Arab fund dir 4-18, 318B1
HASHIMOTO, Teiichi
Scores Canada econ policies 9-27, 780G2
HASHIMOTO, Tomisaburo
Lockheed bribe trial opens 1-31, 83E2
HASHISH—*See NARCOTICS & Dangerous Drugs*
HASKINS & Sells
Sen subcom staff rpt scores 1-17, 78C3
Big 8 acctg firms ranked 8-22, 650G2
HASSAN II, King (Morocco)
Press curbs lifted 3-8, 467E2
Chrgs Cuban role in Zaire, fears escalatn 4-18, 317G1
Electns back 6-3, 467C2
Cabt dismissed 10-5, replaced 10-10, 772E1
Opens parlt 10-14, 869A2
Warns Algeria on Polisario 11-6, 852G2
Cited in Begin Knesset speech 11-20, 893D3
HASSAN, Hatimil
Chrgs govt massacre 10-12, 803F2
HASSAN, Khalid al-
For talks with US 9-13, 697F1
HASSAN, Syed Fida
Quits Pak ruling party 4-8, 305F2 ★
HASSAN Ahmed, Ahmed
Named Djibouti defns min 7-15, 583C2
Resigns 12-17, 1019A1
HASSAN Gouled Aptidon (Djibouti president)
Coalitn slate backing rptd 5-7, 363B3
Elected Djibouti pres 6-24, on policy 6-27, 506F2
Names Dini premr 7-12, 583C2
HASSAN Khan, Lt. Gen. Gul
Quits amb post 4-14, 305E2
HASSETT, Gen. Sir Francis
Retires 4-20, 302F3
HASTINGS, James F.
Sentenced 1-31, 103D1
HATALSKY, Morris
2d in Milwaukee Open 7-3, 676G1
HATCH, Sen. Orrin G. (R, Utah)
Scores Panama Canal talks 7-29, 590A1
Clean-air bill passed 8-4, 610F1
Plans Canal treaty oppositn 8-18, 622A1
In Canal Zone 8-19—8-20, vows pacts defeat 9-7, 678E1

1978

HART, Judith
Cancels 17 poor natns debts 7-31, 592C1
HART, Mike
Traded to Rangers 12-8, 1026D1
HART, Moss (1904-61)
Once in a Lifetime opens 6-15, 887C2
HART, Samuel
Hears Israel plea on Leb 8-30, 674D2
HART, Warren
Admits solicitor gen, MP taps 2-22; informant role noted 2-27, 166G1
HARTFORD, Conn.—*See CONNECTICUT*
HARTLEY, Neil
Joseph Andrews released 4-13, 619F2
HARTLING, Poul
Heads UN refugee post 1-1, 62B1
Australia to accept Indochina refugees 3-15, 187F2
Seeks more Indochina refugee funds 4-18, 341D2
On Indochinese refugees 11-10, 870A3
HARTMANN, Hans-Peter
Confirms Baader gang suicides 1-23, 114G3
HARTNACK, Michael
Scores forgn press censorship 1-8, 20C2
HART Trophy—*See HOCKEY—Awards*
HARVARD University (Cambridge, Mass.)
Early mammals held nocturnal, cool-blooded 3-23, 334D3
Curriculum revised 5-2, 348A2
Solzhenitsyn addresses commencemt, text excerpts 6-8, 444A2 ★ -G3
Bakke case brief describes admissns program, Powell cites as model in decisn 6-28, 382C1, 483A1, 484G2
Stendahl to quit in '79 7-3, 844E1
Cigaret smoking rptd down 7-5, 727D1
Healy named postal mediator 8-29, 766D1
US emb study discounts Sovt microwave harm 11-20, 924G3
CIA secret ties revealed 12-1, 962F2
Urban Studies cntr rpts on redlining 12-7, 942F2-A3
Braunwald on artery spasm research 12-7, 992C3
HARVEY, Lt. Gov. W. Brantley (Dem, S.C.)
Faces primary runoff for gov 6-13, 467D1
Loses runoff vote 6-27, 510D1
HARWELL, Samuel A.
Indicted 5-15, 380A3
Chrgd by SEC 10-5, guilty plea cited 770B3, C3
HASANI, Ali Nassar Mohammed (South Yemeni head of state)
Takes power in S Yemen 6-27, 499C1
HASATLI, Recep
Slain 10-3, leftists blamed 10-4, 822D3
HASHIMOTO, Tomisaburo
Tied to Lockheed scandal 1-30, 72E3
HASKELL, Sen. Floyd K. (D, Colo.)
Votes for Panama Canal neutrality pact 3-16, 177E2
Threatens vote vs Canal pact 4-13, 256A1
Votes for 2d Canal pact 4-18, 273B1
Scores Andrus, Bergland 5-2; greets Carter 5-3, 342A2
Unopposed in primary 9-12, 736D2
Loses reelectn 11-7, 846B1, 855F3
HASSAIN, Saeed
Wounded in Pak hijack attempt 3-2, 212G2
HASSAN II, King (Morocco)
Sadat seeks peace backing 2-2, 60F1
On Zaire peace force role 5-28, 417G3
OKs Zaire defense force 6-2, 441B1
Sadat briefs on summit pact 9-20—9-23, 730A3
Protest re Algerian attack rptd 10-3, 999F2
HASSAN, Crown Prince (Jordan)
Named Hussein successor 6-8, 580C1
Cites Carter vow to Sadat on E Jerusalem, W Bank-Gaza 11-10; US denies 11-12, 892E3-893B1
Shah refuses aid 11-18, 894A1
HASSAN, Abdel Fattah
New Wafd Party dissolves 6-2, 436G3
HASSAN, Salem
Held in Naif murder 7-12, 582A3
HASSANAL Bolkiah, Sultan Sir Muda (Brunei)
Brunei independence set 6-30, 533F3
HASSAN Gouled Aptidon (Djibouti president)
Dismisses Cabt, names premr 9-21, 840E3
HASSELBLAD, Victor
Dies 8-6, 708A3
HASSETT, Marilyn
Other Side of Mt released 3-24, 619C3
HATCH Jr., Francis W.
Wins primary for Mass gov 9-19, 736A3
Loses electn 11-7, 847C2
HATCH, Sen. Orrin G. (R, Utah)
Votes vs Panama Canal neutrality pact 3-16, 177G2
Votes vs 2d Canal pact 4-18, 273B1
Vs DC voting amendmt 8-22, 661A2
Vs new China policy 12-20, 976A1

1979

HART, Lorenz (Larry) (1896-1943)
Richard Rodgers dies 12-30, 1008D3
HART, Roxanne
Loose Ends opens 6-6, 712C1
HARTFORD, Conn.—*See CONNECTICUT*
HARTFORD Institute of Criminal & Social Justice
Crime-control progrm rptd 2-25, 156C3
HARTIGAN, Brian
Suicide In B Flat opens 3-13, 292B3
HARTLEY, Mariette
Wins Emmy 9-9, 858D2
HARTLING, Poul
Malaysia vs plea on Viet refugees 6-15, renews plea 6-16, 460F1, 474E1
On Geneva conf aid to Indochina refugees 7-21, 549C1
HARTMAN, Arthur H.
At 'Lulu' debut in Paris 2-25, 174A1
HARTMAN v. Virginia
Case declined by Sup Ct 10-1, 768A2
HARTNELL, Norman
Dies 6-8, 508B3
HARTSEL Ranch Corp.
Colo land sale refunds set 5-8, 596A1
HARTSFIELD, Roy
Fired as Blue Jays mgr 9-30, 1002F1
HARTSVILLE, S.C.—*See SOUTH Carolina*
HART Trophy—*See HOCKEY—Awards*
HARTZELL, Paul
Traded to Twins 2-3, 619E1
HARTZ Mountain Corp.
FTC complaint setld 8-29, 903B1
HARVARD University (Cambridge, Mass.)
Peabody to sell Inman portraits 2-9, 173F2
Adams outlines urban-aid policy 2-13, 129A2
Wald on 3 Mile I radiatn 3-29, 242G3
Needleman lead study rptd 3-29, 266G1
Forgn student enrollmt listed 167D3
Black hole at galaxy cntr seen 3-31, 290E1
Moroz teaching offer rptd 4-29, 318A1
Woodward dies 7-8, 588G3
Puritan site found near Wadsworth Gate 8-9, 631B3
McGraw-Hill buys Data Resources 8-28, 682G3
H-bomb letter cites Rotow 9-16, 9-18, 717A2
2 physicists win Nobel 10-16, 858C1
Dunlop chairs Pay Advisory Com 10-17, 829E2
Kissinger-FBI '50s link rptd 11-3, 870B2
Cecelia Payne-Gaposhkin dies 12-6, 1008D3
HARVEY, Raymond Lee
Arrested in alleged Carter death plot 5-5, dismissal sought 5-29, 404C1
HARWYN Industries Corp.
HCA unit interest purchased 6-12, 520F1
HASKELL, Floyd
Labor '78 campaign gifts rptd 6-13, 595D1
HASON, Curtis
Silent Partner released 5-10, 528E3
HASSAN II, King (Morocco)
Vs Hussein PLO rapproachmt 4-15, 278G2
Got Sadat plea re Jerusalem 5-3, 360G1
Warns Mauritania vs Sahara pullout, US studies arms sale 8-2, 592B2, D2
Morocco annexes Tiris el-Gharbia 8-11; vows defns, scores Mauritania 8-19, 626D3
US Admin OKs arms sale 10-22, 803G3, 804B1
HASSAN, Abdi Kassim Salad
Scores US re arms delay 2-7, 193A2
HASSAN, Abu—*See SALAMEH, Ali Hassan*
HASSAN, Hani al-
Stresses PLO-Iran ties 2-26, 144F1
HASSAN Morales, Moises
Named to Nicaragua provisional junta 6-17, 461A2
Visits Cuba 7-26, 574C2
Sees Nicaragua electns in '82 8-8, 636A2
Announces natl health plan, other reforms 8-9, 616A1, C1
HASSETT, Marilyn
Bell Jar released 3-20, 528D1
HATCH, Sen. Orrin G. (R, Utah)
Votes vs trade bill 7-23, 646G3
Votes vs Talmadge denunciatn 10-10, 769G1

1980

HART, Warren
Rpts tape on Allmand 4-24, 350F3
HART, Winsette
Hanged 1-29, 132B2
HARTFORD Courant, The (newspaper)
Times Mirror divestiture ordered 1-24, 120A1
HARTLING, Poul
Somalia asks more refugee aid 9-21, 9-21, 736C1
HARTNACK, Carl E.
Retires as Security Pacific chrmn 12-16, 959F1
HARTSBURGH, Craig
In NHL All-Star game 2-5, 198A3
HARTSFIELD International Airport (Atlanta, Ga.)
Bid-rigging probe rptd 7-5, 655C2
HARTSTEIN, Bernd
Wins Olympic medal 7-23, 623D2
HARTUNG, Brig. Gen. Paul
On Israel base constructn lag 6-12, 498C3, E3
HARTWICK College (Oneonta, N.Y.)
4th in NCAA soccer 12-14, 1001C3
HARTZENBERG, Ferdie
S Africa schl normalizatn steps set 9-5; 77 boycotted schls closed 9-23, 753C2
HARVARD University (Cambridge, Mass.)
Interferon rptd produced in lab 1-16, 62C3
D Kennedy MD found guilty on drug chrgs 1-18, 199G3
Buttrick dies 1-23, 104A2
Cox to head Common Cause 2-2, 115E2
New drug rptd effective vs heroin addictn 2-2, 160C2
Kennedy addresses 2-12, 109C2, F2, 110F1
Saccharin cancer risk study rptd 3-6, 317F1
Sheldon Glueck dies 3-10, 279B3
'79 endowmt earnings rptd 3-24, 319B2
Rosenberg rptd dead 4-7, 360C3
Jones dies 5-11, 448A2
SAT coaching rptd helpful 5-15, 559C3
Vance addresses graduates 6-5, 421D3
Shields Warren dies 7-1, 608G3
Carnesale named NRC chrmn 7-9, 551A3
Aquino plans Pl return 8-20, 672E3
Bencerraf, Gilbert win Nobels 10-10, 10-14, 889G2, F3
Van Vleck dies 10-27, 876E3
T Leary Calif radio statn firing rptd 11-1, 890E2
HARVEY, Doug
Phillies win NL pennant 10-12, 796E1
HARVEY, James R.
Transamerica apptmt cited 12-12, 986A3
HARVEY, Sgt. John Davis
Killed in Iran rescue mission 4-24, 321E2
HARVEY, Judge John R.
Clears Postell, wife 11-12, 927A1
HARVEY, Robert
Negotiates Spooner release in Bolivia 8-12, 668F1
HARVEY'S Resort Hotel-Casino (Lake Tahoe, Nev.)
Extortionists bomb explodes 8-27, 833F3
HARWELL, Hicks
Loses US House primary runoff 6-24, 496G1
HASANI, Ali Nasser Mohammed al- (South Yemeni president)
Becomes S Yemen pres 4-23, 315E3*
N Yemen guerrilla war escalatn rptd 6-1, 468E2
HASBIU, Maj. Gen. Kadri
Rptd Albania defns min 5-2, 356E2
HASS, Eric
Dies 10-2, 876A2
HASSAN II, King (Morocco)
Briefed on Palestine autonomy talks 2-4, 89E2
Vs Sihanouk Cambodia plan 2-22, 141D2
Backs Iraq in Iran war 9-23, 719E2
HASSAN, Baba
Dies 6-7, body misplaced 6-17, 491C3
HASSAN, Joshua
Labor wins Gibraltar electns 2-6, 133B1
HASSAN Morales, Moises
In USSR, signs Sovt trade accord 3-19; starts E Eur tour 3-22, 234G2
HASTINGS, Jeffrey
Convicted for '79 Fla drownings 4-18, 336B1*
Sentenced 6-24, 503A3
HATAM, Lt. Gen. Hushang
Executed 7-14, 545F2
HATCH, Clifford
Named Hiram-Consumers chrmn 4-8, 310E3
HATCH, Sen. Orrin G. (R, Utah)
Asks Miller-Textron spec prosecutor 2-11, 145B2
Labor breaks filibuster 4-22, 333F2
Interviews Vesco 7-27, B Carter role discounted 7-30, 570D1
Leads fair-housing bill filibuster 12-4—12-9, 954A2

1976

HATCH Act—*See 'Government Employment' under LABOR*
HATCHER, Mayor Richard (Gary, Ind.)
Carter meets black leaders 7-12, 513E1, B2
HATFIELD, Charles
Arrest ordered 7-14, 593D1
Indictmt rpts in error 11-16, 930E1
HATFIELD, Sen. Mark (R, Ore.)
Named to intelligence com 5-20, 377E1
Sup Ct lets stand FCC ruling 5-24, 393E2
Scott campaign gift rptd 8-30, 980E1
HATHAWAY, Sen. William D. (D, Maine)
Named to intelligence com 5-20, 377E1
HATTA, Mohamad
Arrested, released 9-14, 735B1
HATEM, Hunen
Held hostage, freed 10-11, 759D1
HATOYAMA, Iichiro
Japan foreign min 12-24, 1006B3
HATTERSLEY, Roy
On EC Rhodesia policy 2-23, 164D3
On Dutch seabed compromise 7-27 563D3
Named UK consumer affairs secy 9-10, 693E3, 694A1
HATZIZISIS, Maj. Nikolaos
Sentence cut 4-22, 333A2
HAUBEN, Lawrence
Wins Oscar 3-29, 240A3
HAUGHTON, Daniel J.
Lockheed testimony cited 2-6, 131B1
Quits Lockheed post 2-13, 131D1
Settles SEC suit 4-13, 285G2
HAUSER, Ernest F.
Diary rpts Strauss bribe 2-8, 2-11, 132E2
Chrgs US AF payoffs 2-29, 3-1; Pentagon sets probe 3-2, 200D2
US ends Bonn payoff probe 3-10, 200B2
Quote on Lockheed bribe to UK ex-min rptd 8-30, 642F2
Andreotti payoffs rptd 9-1, 685A1
Dulles-Strauss letter termed forgery 9-22, 740C1
Andreotti probe dropped 10-13, 858A2
HAUSER, Rita E.
Ford, Carter TV debates set 9-1, 644C1
HAVEL, Vaclav
Austria trip barred 10-9, 852A1
HAVEMANN, Robert
Arrest rpt denied 11-26, 1001F3
HAVLIN, Josef
Named to Czech Secretariat 4-16, 289B2
HAWAD, Hall
Killed 11-27, 895F1

HAWAII
Dem conv women delegates, table 508B2
Dem conv pres vote, table 7-14, 507B2
GOP pre-conv delegate count 8-14, 583B3
Ford, Reagan seek conv delegates 8-16, 8-17, 601A3, B3
GOP conv pres, vp vote tables 8-18—8-19, 8-19, 599B1, B3
MD malpractice law in effect, Argonaut insurnc rates hiked 9-1, 1016E3 ★
Fscl '75 per capita income, tax burden rptd 9-15, 10-12, 959G1, E2
Revenue sharing funds cleared 9-30, Ford signs 10-13, 763A3, 764C3
Primary results 10-2, 764D2
Election results 11-2: pres 817D2, 818B1, F1, 819B1; cong 820A1, 825B1, 828D1, 829E2
9 hotel firms indicted 11-17, 989E2

HAWAII, University of (Honolulu)
Methane ice on Pluto rptd 4-2, 443A3
HAWATMEH, Nayef
New Leb peace plan proposed 4-16, 273E1
HAWI, William
Killed 7-13, 514F1
HAWKE, Robert J.
On Iraq fund charges 3-7, 187B2
Gen strike vs Medibank chngs 7-12, 520C2
HAWKINS, Rep. Augustus F. (D, Calif.)
Carter backs jobs bill 4-8, 261G1
Mayors back jobs bill 7-1, 493E1
Udall urges jobs bill 7-14, 506D1
GOP platform text cites 8-18, 602A3
Ford, Carter debate jobs bill 9-23, 701G1
Full employmt bill not cleared 10-2, 883B1, G3
Reelected 11-2, 829D1
HAWLEY, Donald
Powell fears race war 5-24, 482A2

1977

HATCH Act—*See LABOR—Government Employment*
HATCHER, Mayor Richard G. (Gary, Ind.)
Blacks meet re govt 'neglect' 8-29, 702E1
HATFIELD, Sen. Mark O. (R, Ore.)
Vs neutron bomb 7-1, 534D3
Sen campaign financing killed 8-2, 592C2
Backs Panama Canal pacts 8-20, 679A1
HATFIELD, Richard Bennett
On Levesque language offer 7-27, 596G3
Language educ study OKd 8-19, 653E1
HATHAWAY, Dale E.
Named Agri asst secy 3-24, confrmd 4-6, 272A3
HATOYAMA, Iichiro
Signs Iraq aid pact 1-21, 65E2
Vs US A-policy 3-30, 329C3
Replaced as forgn min 11-28, 932B2
HATZEIRA, Aharaon abu-
Israel religious min 6-20, 474E2
HAUGHEY, Charles
Named Ireland health min 7-5, 598G3
HAUGHTON, Daniel J.
Lockheed payoffs rpt accuses 5-26, 502A3
HAUK, Judge A. Andrew
Fines Simplot 5-20, 491E3
Challenges minority constructn quota 10-31, 978G3-979C1
HAUSER, Ernest
Lockheed cleared re paymts 6-22, 602E1
HAUSER, Joseph
Teamsters deal probed 10-31—11-2, 837F1
HAVATAMPA Corp.
Culbro merger blocked 6-28, 520E3
HAVEL, Jelena
Detained 1-7, 20C1
HAVEL, Vaclav
Detained 1-7, 20C1
Arrest rptd 1-17, Austria offers asylum 1-25, 82B3, F3
Freed 5-20, backs Charter 77 5-22, 437B1
Gets suspended sentence 10-18, 812D1
HAVLICEK, John
3d all-time NBA scorer 11-14, 991D1

HAWAII
Legislature schedule rptd 6D2
Oil tanker explodes 2-24, 214A3
Carter call-in 3-5, 171C1
'76 per-capita income table 5-10, 387G2, B3
4 hotels fined for rate-fixing 5-11, 504C2
Honolulu econ data table 5-16, 384G2
Washington sues 10 oil cos 8-16, 691E3
Kilauea erupts 9-13—9-28, 747D2
'76 per capita income, tax burden table 9-13, 10-18, 821F2
Honolulu landing rights for Concorde proposed 9-23, 738B2
Free abortions continued 10-12, 787A1
Westn Union mailgram svc case review declined 10-17, 798A1
HMO unit certified 10-26, 870A1
Sugar workers strike 11-2—11-22, 899D2
Air cargo deregulatn bill signed 11-9, 899B3
Honolulu loses '78 Dem conv bid 12-9, 960D3
Viet MIA missn agreed 12-19—12-20, 975F3
Fasi trial folds 12-27, 1008E1
HAWAIIAN Patriot (Liberian tanker)
Explodes off Honolulu 2-24, 214A3
HAWAII Hotel Association
Fined for rate-fixing 5-11, 504D2
HAWATMEH, Nayef
Scores Sadat on Palestine stand 12-25, 995B2
HAWKE, Robert (Bob)
In Tokyo talks 1-28; shipbldg plea rejctd 2-16, job actn urged 2-17, 253F1, C2
For wage freeze 4-19, rise OKd 5-24, 424F2
On pub employe strike ban 8-19, 652D3
Asks uranium ban referendum 8-26, 693E2; Fraser vs 9-7, 705C1
ACTU cong 9-12—9-15, uranium referendum asked 9-15, 740D2
Scores power workers pay hike bar 10-18, 822F1
Backs Hayden for Labor Party ldrship 12-10, 963E3
HAWKER Siddeley Group Ltd.
2 units nationalized 4-29, 526B3
Eastern to lease Airbus 5-24, 441D2
HAWKINS, Rep. Augustus F. (D, Calif.)
Carter vows jobs action 9-7, 702C1
Carter backs compromise jobs bill 11-14, 876F3
HAWKINS, Roger
Named mil operatns min 3-7, 223F2
Assumes Rhodesia defns post 9-18, 824E3
HAWKS, Howard
Dies 12-26, 1024B2

1978

HATCHER, John
Sentenced 1-19, 95F3
HATCHER, Mayor Richard G. (Gary, Ind.)
Refuses White House job 6-6, 568B3
Martin named Carter aide 8-11, 663G3-664A1
On HEW anti-fraud drive 12-13, 984C3
HATFIELD, Sen. Mark O. (R, Ore.)
Votes for Panama Canal neutrality pact 3-16, 177F2
Votes for 2d Canal pact 4-18, 273B1
Wins primary 5-23, 406A3
Vs '79 arms authorzn 7-11, 526B3
Carter A-breeder deal threatens gas compromise support 8-26, 678C1
Reelected 11-7, 848G2, 857C2
HATFIELD, Sen. Paul G. (D, Mont.)
Named to Metcalf Sen seat 1-22, 52A3, 107C2
Votes for Panama Canal neutrality pact 3-16, 177F1, E2
Votes for 2d Canal pact 4-18, 273B1
Defeated in primary 6-6, 448A2
Baucus win seat 11-7, 856D1
HATFIELD, Richard Bennett
Scores Lang re const plan 8-10, 647D1
HATHAWAY, Sen. William D. (D, Me.)
Carter backs reelection 2-17, 123E1
Votes for Panama Canal neutrality treaty 3-16, 177E2
Votes for 2d Canal pact 4-18, 273B1
Unopposed in primary 6-13, 467B1
Loses reelectn 11-7, 846B1, C1, 847C2
HATSKIN Trophy, Ben—*See HOCKEY—Awards*
HATTON, John
Asks transport agency probe 11-30, 963E2
HAUFF, Volker
Named W Ger tech min 2-3, 93A3
HAUGAN, Gregory T.
Resigns as NE rail project dep dir 1-30, 225C1
HAUGE, Gabriel
S Africa held credit risk 4-23, 377G1-A2
To retire as Mfrs Hanover chrmn 10-17, 809E1
HAUSER, Joseph
Indicted 6-15, 560G2-D3
HAUSER, Thomas
Book links CIA, American's death in Chile 9-12, 795E3
HAUSNER, Siegfried (deceased)
Dutch jail 3 terrorists 8-21, 725C1
HAVASI, Ferenc
Named Hungary SWP Central Com chrmn 4-20, 534C2
HAVE a Little Walk With Jesus (recording)
Oak Ridge Boys win Grammy 2-24, 315G3
HAVEL, Vaclav
Held 1-28, 180E2
HAVLICEK, John
Sets retiremt 1-29, plays last game 4-9, 271B3

HAWAII
Legislature schedule rptd 14E3
'67, '77 sales-tax rates rptd 1-5, 15D3
NASL '77 club move cited 1-5, 23A1
State govt tax revenue table 1-9, 84C2
Honolulu meets clean-air rules 2-23, 144D3
Honolulu '77 living costs rptd 4-26, 349F1
Va judicial inquiry law voided by US Sup Ct 5-1, 363E3
Tidal power plant planned 5-3, 321E3
'77 prison populatn rptd up 6-3, 440D1
US Sup Ct voting alignmt shift noted 7-3, 566C1
Primary results 10-7, 791C3
Election results 11-7: cong 848E1, 850C3, 857C1; state 847C1, E1, 853E2, 857B1
Iolani Luahine, dies 12-11, 1032C3

HAWAIIAN Sound (race horse)
2d in English Derby 6-7, 539B2
HAWAII v. Consumer Product Safety Commission
Firecracker ban review refused by Sup Ct 3-27, 241D2
HAWKE, Robert
On uranium export curbs 1-16, 110D1
Scores '78-79 budget 8-15, 628A3
Mediates Telecom strike 8-26, sees tech impact 9-3, 721F1, B2
HAWKER Siddeley Group Ltd.
NATO sets Nimrod purchases 12-5—12-6, 954C2
HAWKINS, Rep. Augustus F. (D, Calif.)
Full employmt bill OKd by House 3-16, 182F2
Full employmt bill cleared 10-15, 784F3, 808A1; Carter signs 10-27, 873A2
Reelected 11-7, 850A2
HAWKINS, Edwin
Wins Grammy 2-24, 316A1
HAWKINS, Roger
Defends Muzorewa rebel photos 8-16, 650E3
Quits Cabt 11-18, 912D2
HAWKINS, Trish
Lulu opens 2-17, 760D2
HAWN, Goldie
Foul Play released 7-19, 970D1

1979

HATCH, Richard
Battlestar Galactica released 5-17, 528C1
HATCHER, Mayor Richard G. (Gary, Ind.)
Wins primary 5-8, 363F2-A3
On UN Amb Young resignatn 8-19, 624A2
HATCHETT, Judge Joseph W.
Joins fed appeals ct in Fla, sets precedent 8-4, 656G3
HATFIELD, Sen. Mark O. (R, Ore.)
Scores SALT treaty 3-4, 258G1
Deplores go-ahead for MX 6-11, 438A1
On Talmadge denunciatn 9-14, 702G1
HATHAWAY, Dale
Rpts Sovt grain sale agrmt 10-3, 774D3
HATHAWAY, William
Labor '78 campaign gifts rptd 6-13, 595D1
HATIRAII, Mostafa
Named Iran housing min 2-13, 105G2
HATSKIN Trophy, Ben—*See HOCKEY-Awards*
HATZIPETROS, Paskalis
Flown to Tex after tanker collisn 7-19, 553E3
HAUER, Rutger
Soldier of Orange released 8-16, 820D3
HAUFRECHT, Marcia
Welfare opens 5-10, 712D3
HAUGHEY, Charles (Irish prime minister)
Elected prime min 12-7, 950E1
HAUGHTON, Daniel J.
US drops paymts probe 2-15, 306D1
Lockheed pleads guilty, fined 6-1, 422B3
HAUK, Judge A. Andrew
Dismisses Kerkorian trust case 8-14, 756C1
Dismisses OPEC trust suit 8-23, 647C3
HAUSER, Joseph
Pensn safeguards urged 11-26, 905C1
HAUSMAN, Michael
Rich Kids released 8-17, 820B3
HAVEL, Vaclav
Charter 77 picks new ldrs 2-8, 126F3
Arrested 5-29, sentncd 10-23, 802A2
HAVEMANN, Robert
Prosecutn rptd 4-25, house arrest lifted 5-10, 370C3
Fined 5-25, 406D2
Placed under house arrest 10-14, 802A3
HAVENS, Brad
Traded to Twins 2-3, 619E1

HAWAII
Legislature schedule rptd 5C3
Honolulu air quality monitored 1-26, 90F1
Pub schl cost share rptd 3-5, 282E3
Carter vacatn canceled 7-1, 497G2
Indochina refugees strain US health svcs 7-18, 550F2
Police end 'sickout' 7-18, 599F1
Palmyra A-waste site disputed 8-21, 743E3
'78 per capita income rptd 9-16, 746A2, G2
Mil personnel assaults rptd up 9-21, 809F1
Schls shut by strikes 10-26—11-16, 922B3
Methodist legal immunity cases declined by Sup Ct 11-26, 919E2
Public workers end strike 12-3, 922G2
Pub access to waterways curbed by Sup Ct 12-4, 988A1
Honolulu '79 living costs ranked 12-28, 990F3

HAWKE, Robert
Scores Fraser 4-22, 328A2
Scores pub employe curbs 7-13, 542C1
Vs govt on econ policy 9-10, 728C2
To run for Parlt 9-23, 771A2
Wins ALP preselectn test 10-14, 832D2
HAWKINGS, Geoffrey
Deplores engineers' strike 10-4, 773C1
HAWKINS, Rep. Augustus F. (D, Calif.)
Sponsors jobs bill 5-23, 384A2
HAWKINS, Trish
Talley's Folley opens 5-3, 712A3
HAWKINS, William
Shot 10-16, dies 10-18, 840C2
HAWORTH, Leland J.
Dies 3-5, 272E2

1980

HATCHER, Charles
Elected to US House 11-4, 842B3, 849A3
HATCHER, Mayor Richard G. (Gary, Ind.)
Black conf held 2-29—3-2, 190F2
Econ plank compromise fails 8-12, 610A3
Meets with Reagan 12-11, 956F2
HATCHETT, Derrick
In NFL draft 4-29, 336G2
HATFIELD, Sen. Mark O. (R, Ore.)
Brown discounts A-war 6-9, 458A1
Draft registratn filibuster fails 6-10—6-12, comments 6-12, 478D1, D2
Blocks Sawhill Synfuels Corp confirmatn 10-1, 786A3
Votes vs '81 defns appropriatn 11-21, 12-5, 896C3, 935A3
HATFIELD, Richard
Admits PC paymts 3-22; repaymt rptd 3-25, 253B2
Backs Canada const 'patriatn' 9-18, 728G1
HATHAWAY, Dale
Denies China grain pact violates Canada deal 11-20, 900E2
HATHAWAY, William
Vs anti-Anderson moves 6-24, 493A3
HATTERSLEY, Martin
Named Socred pres 11-3, 885E3
HATTERSLEY, Roy
Labor wins local electns 5-1, 352D1
Scores local authorities' funds cut 9-18, 729F1
Scores pub sector pay lid 11-7, 886E3
HATZLACHH Supply Co. v. U.S.
Case decided by Sup Ct 1-21, 93A3
HAUFF, Reinhard
Knife in the Head released 4-23, 416B3
HAUFF, Volker
Sworn W Ger transport min 11-5, 925F1
HAUGHEY, Charles (Irish prime minister)
Urges Ulster solutn 2-16, backs intl parley; reactn 2-17, 133D1
Meets Thatcher re Ulster 5-21, 389E3
Scores US groups aiding IRA 7-27, 604B3
Natl wage pact set 9-18, 751D1
Meets Thatcher in Dublin 12-8, 942F2
HAUSER, Joseph
FBI Brilab probe role rptd 2-8—2-9, 2-13, 111D3, 112B1
Tex Brilab indictmts 6-12, 454G2
La Brilab indictmts 6-17, 454F3
3 acquitted in Tex Brilab case 10-23, 971C2
HAVARD, Lezley
Hide & Seek opens 5-4, 392B3
HAVENS, J. Lee
'Exclusionary rule' narrowed by Sup Ct 5-27, 453C2

HAWAII
World Air cuts fares 4-9, 346B3
Gonorrhea epidemic cited 4-9, 584F3
Pacific cable planned 5-19, 387E3
DC-9 engine fails in Honolulu take-off 6-15, 667C1
NY-Peking air svc sets Honolulu stopover 9-17, 707C1
Crime & Civil Disorders
FBI 'Miporn' probe rptd 2-14, 136F1
Chapman chrgd in Lennon slaying 12-8, 933F2
Methodists settle retiremt home fraud suit 12-10, 963D3
Politics & Government—*See also other appropriate subheads in this section*
Legislature schedule rptd 18D1
ACU '79 voting survey rptd 1-18, 53C3
Island territories get econ plan 2-14; govs meet, set projects 2-19—2-22, 495D1
Carter wins Dem caucus vote 3-11, 209B1
DC voting rep amendmt OKd 4-17, 576F1
Sen, mayoral primary results 9-20, 745D1
Election results 11-4: pres 838B1, E1, 839A2, D3; cong 840E1, 842C3, 845A3, 846F3, 852C2; state 845E2
'80 census rptd 12-31, 983D1

HAWAII, University of (Honolulu)
Loses NCAA baseball title 6-6, 796E2
HAWES Jr., Alexander B.
Wins Pulitzer 4-14, 296F2
HAWKE, Robert
Named Labor Party indl relatns spokesman 9-15, 727G3
Scores govt labor policy 9-18, 766E2
HAWKINS, Rep. Augustus F. (D, Calif.)
Reelected 11-4, 842A2
HAWKINS, John
Canterbury Tales opens 2-12, 136A3
HAWKINS, Paula
Sen primary runoff set 9-9, 700G1
Wins runoff 10-7, 807D3
Elected to US Sen 11-4, 840E1, 846A1, G2, 849B2
HAWN, Goldie
Seems Like Old Times released 12-19, 1003D2

1976

HAYA de la Torre, Victor Raul
At intl soc dems mtg 5-23—5-25, 449B3
HAYAKAWA, S. I.
Wins Senate primary 6-8, 409C2
Wins election 11-2, 817E1, 819D3, 824F3, 828C1
HAYDEN, Tom
Loses Senate primary 6-8, 409B2
HAYDEN, William
Shadow cabt reshuffled 3-25, 237B1
Rebuts govt defns chrgs 5-25, 399G3
Scores navy re fire 12-7, 922G3
HAYES, Judge Keith
Delays Hughes will trial 12-14, 971D2
HAYES, Rep. Philip H. (D, Ind.)
Loses Sen primary 5-4, 323A2
Cornwell elected 11-2, 823B2
HAYMAN, Rollo
Named Rhodesia agri min 1-13, 53E3
HAYMOUR, Mohammed
Seized in Canada emb siege 2-23, 145G2
HAYNES, George
Rules vs Miss NAACP boycott 8-9, 671C2
HAYNSWORTH, Judge Clement F.
Cited in Ford, Dole biog sketches 614C1, D2 ★
HAYS, Rep. Wayne L. (D, O.)
Rptd vs CIA Italy aid 1-7, 10B3
On Turkey base pact 3-29, 244B3
Admits affair with aide, asks House probe 5-25, 392B2
House com votes probe 6-2, 433A2
Asked to quit posts 6-2, to quit Dem party post 6-3, 433F2
Wins renomination 6-8, 409D3
Enters hosp in coma 6-10, 433B3
Gosney link rptd 6-12, 433D3
Quits com post, leaves hosp 6-18, 551F2
Quits reelection race 8-13, 636F1
Resigns, Ethics Com cancels hearings 9-1, 646D1
Suits dismissed 10-26, Justice Dept drops chrgs 12-8, 982B1
Applegate wins seat 11-2, 823F3
O'Neill oppositn cited 12-6, 919E1
HEALD, D. W.
On air safety comm 6-28, 481F2
HEALEY, Denis W.
Defense cut talks 1-14—1-15, 101E1
Sees union ldrs, vows jobless actn 1-26, 72C2, E2
Rpts jobless aid measures 2-12, 173B2
On proposed spending cuts 2-19, 173E2
Rejects franc-run blame 3-16, 339A2
Bids for prime min 3-18, 3-25, eliminated 3-30, 239A2
Callaghan to retain 4-5, 252C2
Parlt gets '76-77 budget 4-6, 266A2
Retains Cabt post 4-8, 266D3
TUC urges expanded wage talks 4-14, 313A1
TUC, govt reach pay accord 5-5, 351C2
On spending cut, tax hike 7-14, 7-22, 556E1
Commons OKs spending, tax pkg 7-28, 572B3
Retains Cabt post 9-10, 694A1
UK to seek IMF loan 9-29, 721B1
Addresses Labor conf 9-30, 791B3
Hikes lending rate 10-7, Parlt OKs 10-11, 773C1
Resignatn rpts linked to £ fall, denied 10-25—10-27, 809G3
Borrowing underestimate cited 11-8, 853D2
On EC aid to £ 11-8, 853E2
Announces spending cuts, tax hikes, IMF loan support 12-15, 1003F2
HEALTH—*See MEDICINE & Health*
HEALTH Maintenance Organizations (HMOs)—*See 'Insurance' under MEDICINE*
HEALTH Research Group
Seeks cockpit smoking ban 4-20, 308A2
HEALTH Spas—*See RECREATION*

1977

HAWTHORNE, Nathaniel (1804-64)
Brook Farm destroyed 3-27, 396B2
HAY
Ga drought crop damage rptd 7-28, 659F3
HAYA de la Torre, Victor Raul
Lauds pol, econ plan 2-25, 241B2
HAYAKAWA, Sen. S. I. (R, Calif.)
'76 spec interest gifts rptd 2-15, 128E2
Vs Sen ethics code 4-1, 251F3
Sen backs HEW affirmative actn 6-28, 515D3
Backs Panama Canal pacts 8-20, 679A1
HAYAT, Shaukat
Ousted from Parlt 4-16, 305G1
HAYDEN, William G. (Bill)
Sets Whitlam challenge 3-9, 218G1
Loses Labor Party ldrship bid 5-31, 465D3
Labor Party conv 7-4—7-11, 541A1
To seek Labor Party ldrship 12-10, 963E3
Elected Labor Party ldr 12-22, facts on 1009C2
HAYES, Dale
2d in Fla Citrus Open 3-6, 311D2
4th in World Series of Golf 9-5, 950C3
HAYES, Denis
Urges solar energy for 3d World 12-11, 975G2
HAYES, Elvin
Named to NBA all-star team 6-13, 584G3
HAYES, Frank
Convicted 9-29, 821C1
HAYES, Judge Keith
Accuses Dummar 1-25—1-27, 120G1
Hughes will called fake 4-15, 354B3
HAYES, Mark
Wins Tourn Players title 3-20, 311D2
HAYNES, Sgt. Robert
Killed 7-13, body returned 7-16, 552F2, F3
HAYNES, Tommy
Wins long jump, triple jump 2-25, 602F3
HAYNES Jr., Ulric St. Clair
Named amb to Algeria 4-27; confrmd 5-9, 418E1
HAYNSWORTH, Judge Clement F.
Byrd wins Sen majority post 1-4, 6A1
HAYS, Wayne L.
Cong pub funds bill asked 3-16, 232G3
HAYWARD, Brooke
Haywire on best-seller list 5-1, 356D2; 6-4, 452A2; 7-3, 548E3
HAYWIRE (book)
On best-seller list 5-1, 356D2; 6-4, 452A2; 7-3, 548E3
HAYWOOD, Hurley
Wins Daytona endurance 2-6, 531D2
HAZELWOOD, Mo.—*See MISSOURI*
HEALEY, Denis
On sterling balances accord 1-11, 20C3
Callaghan plans industry policy supervisn 1-12, 1-13, 44F2
Backs tax reform 1-14, 45B1
Rpts $1.5 bln intl bank loan 1-24, 99G1
Owen named forgn secy 2-21, 200F3
Presents budget 3-29, 256C2
Presents anti-inflatn pkg 7-15, 580F3
At Commonwealth finance mins conf 9-21, 936D3
HEALTH—*See MEDICINE & Health*
HEALTH Care Financing Administration—*See under U.S. GOVERNMENT—HEALTH Education & Welfare*
HEALTH, Education & Welfare, Department of—*See under U.S. GOVERNMENT*
HEALTH Maintenance Organizations (HMOs)—*See U.S. GOVERNMENT—HEALTH, Education & Welfare*
HEALTH Research Group—*See PUBLIC Citizen Inc.*
HEALY, James (1830-1900)
Miss black bishop installed 6-6, 471D2

1978

HAYA, Maria Eugenia
Last Supper released 5-5, 619G2
HAYA de la Torre, Victor Raul
Party registered for June electns 2-3, 134D2
Constituent Assemb elected 6-18, APRA leads vote 6-22, 475C1
Leftists win 30 Assemb seats 7-15, 668D3
Elected Constituent Assemb pres 7-27, Assemb opens 7-28, 668G2
HAYAKAWA, Sen. S. I. (R, Calif.)
Redwood Park expansn bill OKd 1-31, 85G2
Votes for Panama Canal neutrality pact 3-16, 177F2
Threatens vote vs 2d Canal pact 4-14; sees Carter 4-17, votes for pact 4-18, 273D2, G2
Vs DC voting amendmt 8-22, 661E1
Petitns for Hearst pardon 9-26, 824B1
Opposes ERA extensn 10-6, 788F1
Rhodesia prime min visits US 10-7—10-20, 818E3
HAYDEN, Sterling
King of Gypsies released 12-19, 1030B3
HAYDEN, William G.
On Fraser EC policy 4-16, 310G3
Submits govt censure motn 5-29, 434B3
Scores Fraser on Withers' firing 8-8, 612D2
Scores '78-79 budget 8-15, 628A3
Scores Fraser on budget 8-21, 646C1
No-confidence motn vs Fraser defeated 8-24, 703G2
Urges Maralinga A-waste probe 10-9, 771G2
HAYES, Dale
Wins French Open 5-15, 580E3
HAYES, Elvin
NBA rebound ldr 4-9, 271F2
HAYES, Frank
Sentenced 2-18, 991E3
HAYES, Helen
Candleshoe released 8-4, 969F3
HAYES, Mark
Ties for 2d in Kemper Open 6-4, 580F3
2d in Westchester Classic 8-20, 672B3
2d in BC Open 9-4, 990G1
HAYES, Paul L.
Prosecutors' plea bargaining power expanded 1-18, 64E3
HAYES, Woody
Alabama wins Sugar Bowl 1-2, 8D3
Fired by Ohio State 12-30, 1025G2
HAYMAN, Rollo
Sees Rhodesia indep delay 9-6, 741E1
Quits, scores internal setlmt 12-27, 1019G2
HAYS, Renfro
Alibi for Ray retracted 8-19, 642C1
HAYWARD, Jack
Testifies at Thorpe hearing 11-24, 945E1
HAYWARD, Adm. Thomas B.
Named naval operatns chief 4-5, 281A2
HAYWOOD, Hurley
3d in LeMans 6-11, 538A3
HAZELTINE Corp.
ICAO picks US bad-weather landing system 4-19, 319C3
HCI Holdings Ltd.
Backs Abitibi takeover of Price 9-29, 772E3
HEAD, Murdock
Flood, Passman influence-selling rptd 1-27, 3-9; denied 3-7, 240A2, B2 ★
HEAD Start—*See U.S. GOVERNMENT—HEALTH, Education & Welfare—Child Development, Office of*
HEALEY, Denis
Analyzes Ilford by-electn 3-1, 167C3
Presents '78-79 budget 4-11, 267C2
Condemns tax cuts 5-8, 415B2
Rebuts Howe, govt narrowly wins confidence vote on salary 6-14, 496G2
Calls govt pay policy success 7-21, 573G2
Defends Callaghan electn delay 9-8, 705B1
On TUC pay, price rebuff 10-14, 10-15, 903C2
Defends bank lending rate hike 11-9, 882D2
Cautions vs wage hikes 11-12, 882F2
Pay talks with labor ldrs set 12-14, 964D3
HEALTH—*See MEDICINE & Health*
HEALTH-Care Management Institute (Williamsburg, Va.)
Rural MD shortage seen despite '85 surplus 7-23, 577C3
HEALTH, Education & Welfare, Department of—*See under U.S. GOVERNMENT*
HEALTH Evaluation Systems Inc.
Stockbroker liability case refused by Sup Ct 12-4, 959D1
HEALTH Insurance Association of America
Carter health plan backed 7-29, 586F2
HEALTH Maintenance Organizations (HMOs)—*See MEDICINE—Insurance*
HEALTH Research Group—*See under PUBLIC Citizen*
HEALTH Services Administration—*See under U.S. GOVERNMENT—PUBLIC Health Service*
HEALY, James
Revises postal contract 9-15, 766D1-A2
HEANEY, Denis
Killed 6-10, 474E3
HEAO (High Energy Astronomy Observatory)—*See ASTRONAUTICS—Satellites*

1979

HAWTHORNE, Greg
In NFL draft 5-3, 335G1
HAY, Alexandre
Scores Rhodesia war 3-20, 286B3
HAYA de la Torre, Victor Raul
Ill with cancer in US 3-12, 255A3
Dies 8-2, 671C2
HAYAKAWA, Sen. S. I. (R, Calif.)
Woodcock confrmd China amb 2-26, 146E1
Sees Carter on gas shortage 5-16, 361B2
Finances disclosed 5-18, 383E2
Votes vs Talmadge denunciatn 10-10, 769G1
HAYDEN, Sterling
Winter Kills released 5-17, 528G3
HAYDEN, Tom
At DC A-protest 5-6, 343D3
Fonda arts cncl apptmt defeat causes furor 7-20—8-8, 593B2-B3
At NYC A-protest 9-23, 742G2, B3
Backs oil industry protest 10-17, 831D2
NSA upheld on withholding data 10-29, 945E3
HAYDEN, William G.
Scores Fraser re Robinson resignatn 2-22, 133D2
Scores govt austerity measures 5-24, 404F3
Backs US monitoring base 7-19, 542G1
Details budget plans 8-28, 684A1
On Labor S Australia defeat 9-15, 749B2
Fraser censure motion fails 9-27, 788A1
Hawke wins ALP preselectn 10-14, 832E2
HAYES, Bob
Pleads guilty on drug chrgs 3-14, sentncd 3-22, 335B3
HAYES, Dale
2d in Italian Open 5-6, 587F2
2d in Eur Championship 9-9, 970D1
HAYES, Elvin
Sonics win NBA title 6-1, 506G3, 507B1
On NBA all-league team 6-6, 526B2
HAYES, Jimmy
Carter peanut loan scheme alleged 3-11—3-13, spec prosecutor sought 3-13, 183F3-184B2
B Carter denies false bank rpts 4-11, 301D3
Carter peanut business cleared 10-16, 782E3
HAYES, Adm. John B.
Plans Coast Guard training upgrade 1-20, 140G3
HAYES, Mark
Ties for 2d in Crosby Pro-Am 2-4, 220D3
HAYES, Woody
Bruce named Ohio State coach 1-12, 175D3
HAYLING, Patricia
Glorious Monster opens 7-10, 711D3
HAYNES, Mike
NFL '78 interceptn ldr 1-6, 80C1
HAYWARD, Max
Dies 3-18, 272F2
HAYWARD, Susan
Death tied to '53 A-test 8-4, 630B1
HAYWARD, Adm. Thomas B.
Orders anti-racist policy 8-29, 664E2
HAYWOOD, Hurley
Wins Daytona endurance 2-4, 491C1
HAYWOOD, Spencer
Traded to Jazz 1-5, 526D2
HAZELHOFF, Erik
Soldier of Orange released 8-16, 820D3
H. B. ROBINSON S. E. Plant—*See SOUTH Carolina—Atomic Energy*
HCA Inc.
Nev casino purchase planned 6-12; casino licenses revoked 6-15, drops bid 6-27, 520F1
HEAD, Freddy
3 Troikas wins Arc de Triompe 10-7, 876B3
HEAD, Helaine
Second Thoughts opens 5-4, 712C2
HEAD, Murdock
Convicted 10-12, sentenced 10-24, 906D1
HEAD Over Heels (film)
Released 10-19, 1007D3
HEAD Start—*See U.S. GOVERNMENT—HEALTH, Education & Welfare—Child Development, Office for*
HEALEY, Denis
Early IMF repaymt announced, caretaker budget revealed 4-3, 268G1
Vs govt spending plans 11-1, 855D2
Scores lending rate hike 11-15, 889G2
HEALTH—*See MEDICINE*
HEALTH, Education & Welfare, Department of—*See under U.S. GOVERNMENT*
HEALTH Research Group—*See under PUBLIC Citizen*

1980

HAYA de la Torre, Victor Raul (d. 1979)
Peru electn results rptd 5-18, 390E2
Peru munic electns held 11-23, 923C1
HAYDEN, Robert E.
Dies 2-25, 176E1
HAYDEN, Tom
Brown quits pres race 4-1, 246D3
NSA files case refused by Sup Ct 5-12, 426A3
HAYDEN, William G.
Scores wage hike 1-8, 37E2
Scores bond rate hike 3-2, 211B1
Job plan announced 3-23, 271G2
Scores govt re Saudi princess film 4-15, 310A1
Vs metalworkers' demand 5-8, 338C1
Offers alternative budget 8-26, 667B2
Outines indl relatns policy, names Hawke spokesman 9-15, 727E3
Labor advances in polls 10-15, 787B1
Govt wins natl electns 10-18, 807G2
HAYDON, Julie
Glass Menagerie opens 11-4, 892D3
HAYES, Bob
Paroled 2-6, released from prison 2-27, 175F2
HAYES, David S.
Pretrial press exclusn case refused by Sup Ct 11-17, 882F1
HAYES, Elvin
NBA scoring ldr 3-30, 278C3
HAYES, Helen
Wins Langer award 6-8, 692D3
HAYES, Lester
NFL '79 interceptn ldr 1-5, 8C2
HAYES, Patti
Ties for 2d in Inamori Classic 10-12, 972D2
HAYES, Robert C.
Indicted in welfare fraud 5-13, 414D3
HAYES, William
ABC ties to Spelling-Goldberg rptd probed by SEC 8-7—8-8, 640G1
HAYES v. Pennsylvania
Case refused by Sup Ct 11-17, 882F1
HAY Fever—*See MEDICINE—Diseases*
HAYLER, Vice Adm. Robert W.
Dies 11-17, 928F2
HAYMES, Dick
Dies 3-28, 279C3
HAYNES, Harold J.
Retires from Socal 9-24, 959A3
HAYNES, Mark
In NFL draft 4-29, 336F2
HAYS, Judge Paul R.
Dies 2-13, 176E1
HAYS, Robert
Airplane released 7-2, 675G1
HAYWARD, Adm. Thomas B.
Praises female Naval Acad grads 5-28, 428E1
Backs draft 6-19, 478F3
MX distortn rptd 10-5, 897C1
HEAD Start—*See under U.S. GOVERNMENT—HEALTH, Education & Welfare, Department of*
HEALD, Anthony
Glass Menagerie opens 11-4, 892D3
HEALEY, Denis
Left advances at Labor Party conf 9-29—10-3, 768D2, F2
Callaghan quits as Labor ldr 10-15, 791C1
Foot elected Labor ldr 11-10, 872B2
Scores new govt econ measures 11-24, 901A3
Labor elects shadow Cabt 12-4, 942D2
HEALEY, Giles G.
Dies 2-29, 279D3
HEALEY, Robert
On Chicago teachers walkout 1-28, 77A3
HEALTH—*See MEDICINE*
HEALTH, Education & Welfare, Department of—*See under U.S. GOVERNMENT*
HEALTH & Human Services, Department of—*See under U.S. GOVERNMENT*
HEALTH Research Group—*See PUBLIC Citizen*
HEALY Jr., George W.
Dies 11-2, 928E2

1976

HEARD, Anthony
On journalist arrests 7-29, 592E1
HEARING Aids
Jackson for Medicare coverage 1-22, 41B3
HEARN, George Henry
Successor confrmd 1-21, 68C1
HEARNES, Warren E.
Fed probe cited, Mercantile pol costs rptd 2-27, 181B1
Loses Senate primary 8-3, 565E2
Named Sen nominee 8-21, 633D1
Loses electn 11-2, 823A3
HEARST, Patricia C.
Mental exams disputed 1-7—1-23, 69D3
Jury selectn starts 1-27, 69C3
UK MD claims SLA 'brainwashed' 1-29, 70D1
Jury selectn ends 2-3, 113G2
Trial opens 2-4, testifies 2-9; Matthews disputes 2-10, 113E2, D3
Trial dvpts, testimony disputed 2-11—3-17; trial ends 3-18, 201B1-202E3
Convicted 3-20, 220C2
Provisional sentence imposed 4-12; begins mental tests 5-4; 'mute' in state ct 5-12, 367B3
Article on pre-arrest life, ties with SLA, Soliah publshd 4-25, 368E1
'Mute' in state hearing, judge enters plea 5-28, 423G1
Judge Carter dies 6-14, 524D2
LA robbery, kidnap trial delayed 7-26, 596B1
Harrises convicted 8-9, 595D3
Harrises sentenced 8-31, 679D3
Final sentence imposed 9-24, 735G1
Testifies re kidnap 9-27, Harrises indicted 9-29, 735E2
Freed on bail; retrial denied 11-19, 891C2
HEARST, Randolph A.
Homes bombed 2-12, 3-11, comments 3-12, 201B3
Wife testifies 3-17, 202G2
HEARST Corp.
Kern dies 2-19, 192E3
Carter sees editorial bd 7-22, 551E1
Brezhnev interview rptd 12-29, 978C3
HEART—*See under MEDICINE & Health*
HEATH, Edward
New shadow cabt excludes 1-15, 101B2
Moves to unite Tories 10-6, 791D3
HEBER, Mario
Seized 5-25, freed 5-29, 441C2
HEBERT, Rep. F. Edward (D, La.)
Primary runoff for seat set 8-14, 633D1
Tonry wins seat 11-2, 822A2
HECHLER, Rep. Ken (D, W. Va.)
3d in primary for gov 5-11, 342D3
Defeated 11-2, 823F1
HECHT, Rev. Harold L.
Ousted as dist pres 4-2, 776C3
HECKLER, Rep. Margaret M. (R, Mass.)
Travel expense probe ends 10-27, 981G3
Reelected 11-2, 829C4
HEDDERICH, Heinz
Arrested in Herstatt fraud 8-26, 679A1
HEENAN, John Cardinal
Replaced as Westminster archbp 2-17, 336E2
HEFNER, Rep. W. G. (Bill) (D, N.C.)
Reelected 11-2, 830E2
HEFTEL, Cecil
Elected to US House 11-2, 825C1, 829E2
HEHN, Jurgen
Wins Olympic medal 7-23, 574F2
HEIDAR, Mohammed
Sahara missn rptd 1-29, 58C2
HEIDEGGER, Martin
Dies 5-26, 404G1-A2
HEINEMAN, Judge Frederic W.
Declares Bolles mistrial 10-21, 859E2
Replaced in Bolles slaying trial 11-19, 971D3
HEINESEN, Knud
Signs record loan 8-5, 588E2
HEINHOLD Commodities Inc.—*See DEKALB AgResearch*
HEINZ 3rd, Rep. H. John (R, Pa.)
Wins Senate primary 4-27, 305A1
Elected to Sen 11-2, 817E2, 820B1, 821A3, 828B3
HEIRESS, The (play)
Opens 4-20, 1014C3
HEISENBERG, Werner
Dies 2-1, 124D3

1977

HEAPS, Alvin
Joins AFL-CIO exec cncl 12-12, 961G1
HEARD, Alexander
Ford quits foundatn 1-11, 55E3
HEARING Aids
FDA sets sales rules 2-13, 217F1
HEARST, Patricia C.
Yoshimura convicted 1-20, 60A1
Yoshimura sentenced 3-17, 288A3
Pleads no contest 4-18, 302B2
Gets probation, ordrd to pay restitutn 5-9, 370E3
Bank robbery convictn upheld 11-2, 838G3
HEARST Corp.
Avon pays record sum for paperback 3-1, 356A2
Baltimore trust suit setld 5-26, 504B2
CIA links charged 9-12, 720B3
HEART—*See under MEDICINE & Health*
HEATH, Edward
At Brandt comm mtg 12-9—12-11, 997G3
HEATING Oil—*See PETROLEUM*
HEBENTON, Clay
Phoenix owner sells 4-1, 263A1
HEBLER, Dave
Presley book sets order record 8-20, 696E1
HECHINGER v. Martin
DC Home Rule provisn upheld 1-10, 57B2
HECK, L. Douglas
Named amb to Nepal 5-3, confrmd 5-25, 499F3
HEDBERG, Anders
Final WHA standings 4-7, 310E2
HEDGE, K. S.
India lower house speaker 7-21, 637A3
HEEZEN, Bruce C.
Dies 6-21, 532A3
HEIFETZ, Jascha
Ex-wife dies 11-3, 952F3
HEIGHT, Dorothy I.
Blacks meet re govt 'neglect' 8-29, 702E1
HEIMANN, John G.
To probe Lance loan 7-25, 574B2
Rpt clears Lance in banking probe 8-18, 625F1-626F1
Carter on Lance probe 8-23, 649G1
2d report on Lance 9-7, testifies 9-8, 690E1, D2
Testifies on Lance banking abilities 9-26, 761A2
HEINESEN, Knud
Danish finance min 2-25, 373D1
HEINSOHN, Tommy
Celtics trade Scott 12-27, 1021B1
HEINZ 3rd, Sen. H. John (R, Pa.)
Votes vs Bell confrmatn 1-19, 34D1
Rebuts Carter energy plan 6-2, 443G1
Poses neutron bomb issue 7-1, 534E3
HEISER, Carl J.
Arrested 7-20, 576A3

1978

HEARD, Jerry
2d in Colonial Natl 5-14, wins Atlanta Classic 580D3, E3
HEARNES, Warren E.
Nominee for state auditor 8-8, 626B1
HEARST, Patricia
Rehearing appeal rejected 1-4, 24F2
Convictn review declined by Sup Ct 4-24, 322F1
Returns to prison 5-15, 379A3
Harrises plead guilty 8-31, sentncd 10-3; father reacts 9-1, 823F3, 824A1
Pardon petitioned to Justice Dept 9-26, 824B1
Hearst press launches release drive 10-8, 824C1
FBI break-in case refused by Sup Ct 12-4, 959F1
HEARST, Randolph A.
On Harrises' guilty plea 9-1, 824A1
Murphy editorial seeks daughter's release 10-8, 824D1
HEARST, William Randolph
Launches drive to free niece 10-8, 824C1
HEARST Corp.
Puzo paperback rights sale record set 6-16, 620D2
P Hearst release drive launched 10-8, 824C1
San Francisco Examiner—*See separate listing*
HEART—*See under MEDICINE*
HEATH, Edward
Warns Thatcher vs immigratn bar 2-13, 167D3 ★
Rhodesia sanctns-breaking debate set 9-28, 756G3
Callaghan urges Rhodesia oil sanctn violatns probe 12-15, 987D3
HEATH, Mike
Traded to Rangers 11-10, 1026B1
HEAT Wave—*See WEATHER*
HEAVEN Can Wait (film)
Released 6-27, 619D2
Top-grossing film 7-6, 579F3; 7-26, 620D1; 8-30, 708A2
HEAVEN'S Just a Sin Away (recording)
Kendalls win Grammy 2-24, 316A1
HEAVERLO, Dave
Traded to A's 3-15, 194G3
HEBER, Maria Cecilia Fontana de
Poisoning death rptd 9-6, 799F1-A2
HEBER, Mario
Wife rptd poisoned 9-6, 799F1-A2
HECHLER, Ken
Loses Cong primary in W Va 5-9, 363D1
HECHT, Rabbi Abraham B.
Opposes gay rights 5-18, 410B1
HECHT, Ben (1894-1964)
On 20th Century opens 2-19, 887C2
Chicago Daily News ceases publicatn 3-4, 195G1
HECKLER, Rep. Margaret M. (R, Mass.)
Reelected 11-7, 851D1
HECTOR, Kevin
NASL scoring ldr 8-6, 655D2
HEDBERG, Anders
Nordiques win WHA All-Star game 1-17, 76F3
Signs with NHL Rangers 3-20, 296F1
WHA scoring ldr 4-11, 296A2, G2
Winnipeg wins WHA title 5-22, 458C2, D2
HEFLIN, La.—*See LOUISIANA*
HEFLIN, Howell T.
Faces US Sen primary runoff in Ala 9-5, 699G1
Wins runoff 9-26, Martin to oppose Stewart 10-2, 769E2, F1
Elected 11-7, 846G1, 848C1, 849G2
HEFNER, Rep. W. G. (Bill) (D, N.C.)
Reelected 11-7, 851C3
HEFTEL, Rep. Cecil (D, Hawaii)
Reelected 11-7, 850C3, 857C1
HEIDEN, Eric
Wins speed-skating title 2-26, sets records 3-2, 3-12, 316A3
HEILEMAN Brewing Co., G.
Miller 'Lite' trademark case review barred 1-9, 13D1
HEIMANN, John G.
Graiver indicted 4-12, 326F1
HEINE, Edward J.
Charges vs Garmatz dropped 1-9, 16A1
HEINESEN, Knud
Named Danish finance min 8-30, 688A1
HEINRICHSHON, Ernst
Chrgd for war crimes 7-24, 652C1
HEINSOHN, Tommy
Fired as Celtic coach 1-3, 40F3
HEINZ 3rd, Sen. H. John (R. Pa.)
Votes for Panama Canal neutrality pact 3-16, 177E2
Votes for 2d Canal pact 4-18, 273B1
Personal finances rptd 5-19, 385D3
HEINZ Co., H. J.
Weight Watchers purchase planned, Foodways agrmt cited 5-4, 364D2
HEISMAN Trophy—*See FOOTBALL—Collegiate*
HEJDANEK, Ladislav
US rptr ousted re interview 5-1, 439B3

1979

HEARD, John
On The Yard released 1-18, 174C3
Head Over Heels released 10-19, 1007E3
HEARN, George
I Remember Mama opens 5-31, 711G3
HEARST, Catherine (Mrs. Randolph A.)
Legal separatn rptd 1-25, 79G1
HEARST, Patricia Campbell
Parents legal separatn rptd 1-25, 79A2
Released from prison 2-1, 79F1
Little murder convictn reversed 2-27, 156C1
Marries 4-1, 271G2
Yoshimura '77 convictn upheld 4-5, 271G2
Harris convictns review declined by Sup Ct 10-1, 768B1
HEARST, Randolph A.
Legal separatn rptd 1-25, 79G1
HEARST Corp.
UPI press partnership sale rptd 10-4, 859G2
HEART—*See under MEDICINE*
HEARTACHE Tonight (recording)
On best-seller list 11-7, 892E3
HEART Association, American
Annual conf; heart disease preventn, alcohol use linked 3-19, 219A1
HEART Of Glass (recording)
On best-seller list 5-2, 356G2; 5-30, 448E3
HEATERS, Water—*See WATER Heaters*
HEATH, Edward
At 'Lulu' debut in Paris 2-25, 174A1
Thatcher wins UK electn 5-3, 338F2
Excluded from Thatcher Cabt 5-5, 337G2
HEATHCOTE, Jud
Mich State wins NCAA basketball title 3-26, 238A3
HEATON, Pfc. Jonathan
Coronado dismissed on gay chrg 10-15, 850D3
HEAVEN Can Wait (film)
Oscars presented to 3 4-9, 336A2
HEBERT, F. Edward
Dies 12-29, 1008B3
HEBNER, Richie
Traded to Mets 3-27, Tigers 10-31, 1002G2, C3
HEDBERG, Anders
Montreal wins Stanley Cup 5-21, 447C3
HEDRICK, Frank E.
On Beech Aircraft-Raytheon merger 10-2, 785C1
HEEFNER, David Kerry
Lovely Sunday opens 1-21, 292A2
HEFLIN, Sen. Howell T. (D, Ala.)
Named Sen Ethics Com chrmn 10-31, 945A3
HEFLIN, Marta
Perfect Couple released 4-5, 528C3
HEGMAN, Mike
Steelers win Super Bowl 1-21, 63A1
HEIDEN, BETH
Wins world speed-skating title 2-4, jr title 2-15, 392B1
HEIDEN, Eric
Wins world speed-skating title 2-11, sets world marks 2-11, 2-17, 392B1
HEIM, Aribert
Convicted of war crimes 6-13, 490B1
HEIMANN, John G.
FDIC lists '78 problem banks 1-30, 113A2
Warns banks re credit over extensn 9-13, 681D1
HEIM Gallery (London)
Antique purchase record rptd 6-27, 672G1
HEINESEN, Knud
'80 draft budget rptd 8-28, 668B1
Replaced as finance min 10-26, 855A1
HEINTS, Manuel
Named El Salvador econ min 10-22, seized by leftists 10-24, 812G3, 813C2
Leftists bar release 10-25, 834D2
Freed 11-6, 872A3
HEINZ 3rd., Sen. H. John (R, Pa.)
Elected GOP Sen Campaign Com chrmn 1-15, 30C2
Finances disclosed 5-18, 383D2, F3
Financial disclosure statemt studied 9-1, 701G3
HEINZ Co., H. J.
Heinz finances rptd 5-18, 383F3
Heinz' financial disclosure statemt studied 9-1, 701G3
HEISSLER, Rolf
Arrest rptd 6-10, 490E1
HEITZLER, Joseph
Announces WTT demise 3-8, 391D3

1980

HEARD, John
Heart Beat released 4-25, 416A3
HEARN, George
Watch on the Rhine opens 1-3, 136F3
HEARNS, Thomas (Hit Man)
TKOs Cuevas for WBA welterwgt title 8-2, 907E1
HEARSE, The (film)
Released 6-7, 675G2
HEARST, Patricia Campbell
Probatn rptd ended 5-9, 471E3
Yoshimura paroled 8-25, 890G1
HEARST Corp.
UPI financing plan fails 1-31, 120C1
HEART—*See MEDICINE--Heart & Lungs*
HEARTACHES of a Pussycat (play)
Opens 3-19, 392A3
HEARTACHE Tonight (recording)
Eagles win Grammy 2-27, 296C3
HEART Beat (film)
Released 4-25, 416A3
HEARTBREAK House (play)
Opens 4-29, 392B3
HEATH, Edward
A-weapon plans revealed 1-24, 79G1
HEAVEN'S Gate (film)
Withdrawn from theaters 11-19, 906A1
HECHINGER, John
At Reagan DC fete 11-18, 880E3
HECHINGER, Judge John F.
Jails union head 2-21, 187A3
HECHT, Ben
Front Page opens 12-22, 1003B3
HECKLER, Rep. Margaret M. (R, Mass.)
Reelected 11-4, 843D1
HEED The Call (recording)
Imperials win Grammy 2-27, 296E3
HEFFER, Eric
Vs publicatn of Labor rpt on Trotskyist penetratn 1-16, 58C3
Labor backs EC exit 10-1, 768E2
Not in Labor shadow Cabt 12-4, 942E2
HEFFERNAN, Sister Esther
Female white-collar crime data disputed 1-21, 216A1
HEFFRON, Richard T.
Foolin' Around released 10-17, 836G2
HEFLIN, Sen. Howell T. (D, Ala.)
US dist judges named 1-10; controversy ensues 5-19—9-17, drops Gray support 8-12, 744C2, C3
HEFNER, Hugh M.
Playboy audit, repayments revealed 2-12, 558B2
HEFNER, Rep. W. G. (Bill) (D, N.C.)
Reelected 11-4, 843C4
HEIDEN, Beth
2d in world speed skating 1-13, 470E1
Wins Olympic medal, scores press 2-20, 155D1, 156B1
HEIDEN, Eric
Sets 2 world speed records 1-13, 1-19; retains men's sprint title 2-10, loses world title 3-2, 470C1, F1, A2
Wins 5 Olympic gold medals, sets records 2-15—2-23, 155A1, G3-156A1
Sister wins Olympic medal, scores press 2-20, 155D1
HEIGHT, Dorothy I.
Meets with Reagan 12-11, 956F2
HEILFORT, Hellfried
Wins Olympic medal 7-21, 623C2
HEIM, Alan
Wins Oscar 4-14, 296A2
HEINDORF, Ray
Dies 2-2, 176F1
HEINEMAN, Ben W.
Named First Chicago chrmn 4-28, 456B2
HEINKE, Harald
Wins Olympic medal 7-29, 623C1
HEINRICHSOHN, Ernst
Sentncd for WW2 crimes 2-11, 118F1
HEINZ 3rd, Sen. H. John (R, Pa.)
Defeated for Sen GOP post 12-2, 915E2
HEISKELL, Andrew
Replaced as Time chrmn 5-15, 456F2
HEISMAN Trophy—*See FOOTBALL--Collegiate*
HEITMAN, Betty
Named GOP co-chrmn 7-18, 549F2
HE Knows You're Alone (film)
Released 9-26, 836A3

1976

HELBING, Karl-Heinz
Wins Olympic medal 7-24, 576A3
HELICOPTERS—*See AVIATION*
HELLER, Walter
At Carter econ mtd 12-1, 898F2
HELLICKSON, Russ
Wins Olympic medal 7-31, 576E3
HELM, Lewis M.
Replaced at HEW 9-23, 808A1
HELM, Rudiger
Wins Olympic medals 7-30, 7-31, 574E1, F1
HELLMAN, Lillian
Scoundrel Time on best-seller list 12-5, 972B2
HELMS, Sen. Jesse A. (R, N.C.)
Anti-abortn amendmt tabled 4-28, 346G1-A2
Promotes Buckley 8-11, 8-12, 584A3
Vs platform com planks 8-13, 582G2, 583A1, D1
Reagan meets 8-16, 601G2
Schrump addresses GOP conv 8-17, 615A2
Seconds Reagan nominatn 8-18, 598B1
Vs vp nominatn, wins delegate support 8-19, 598E2
GOP conv vp vote table 8-19, 598E2, 599E3
Cited re Hunt victory 11-2, 822E2
HELMS, Richard M.
Olson files made public 1-10, 25D1
Named as Iran terrorist target 365G2
Nixon on '72 tape transcript 3-11, 183E3
Va break-in ruling cited 5-17, 379B2
HELSINKI Agreement—*See 'Security and Cooperation in Europe' under EUROPE*
HELSTOSKI, Rep. Henry (D, N.J.)
Indicted 6-2, 414C3
Leads primary tally 6-8, 410A1
Wins primary revote 9-21, 725B2
Loses reelectn 11-2, 820B2, 821B2
HELTEN, Inge
Wins Olympic medal 7-25, 576F1
HELTER Skelter (book)
On best seller list 1-25, 80C3; 2-29, 208F3
HEMISPHERIC Affairs, Council on
Argentina abuse rpt suit rptd 12-19, 996G2
HEMMAN, Paul
On Carter undocumented spending 8-8, 585E3
HEMMI, Heini
Wins Olympic medal 2-10, 158D3
HEMPSTEAD, N.Y.—*See NEW York State*
HENABERY, Joseph
Dies 2-18, 192D3
HENCKEN, John
Wins Olympic medals 7-20, 7-24, 575C2
HENDERSON, Rep. David N.
Whitley wins seat 11-2, 822E2
HENDERSON, Dr. Donald A.
Accepts Lasker award 11-17, 910G3
HENDERSON, Maxwell
'73 letter re Polysar rebates cited 11-26, 904G1
Trudeau defends Polysar; probe OKd 11-30, 924B1
HENDERSON, Thomas H.
Heads new Justice unit 1-14, 78E3
HENDERSON, Vivian
Dies 1-28, 124E3
HENDRICK, George
AL batting ldr 10-4, 796C1
HENDRICKS, Sterling Brown
Awarded Science Medal 10-18, 858E3
HENDRICKSE, Alan
Rptd detained 8-27, 653F1
Detentn protested 9-4, 662G1
HENDRIX, Harold V.
Charged in ITT case 11-5, 869E2
HENNESSEY, James
Meets Amin on missing hostage 7-8—7-9, 515G2
HENNING, Joel
Testifies on busing 6-14, 453G1
HENRY, Dr. Aaron
Backed Shriver in caucuses 1-24, 95A1
Greets Carter in Miss 9-17, 704A3
HENRY, Michel
Wins Prix Renaudot 11-15, 911G3
HENRY, Paul
On Ford fund probe 9-21, 722F2
HENRY, William L.
McCloy rpt scores 133E2
Ousted from Gulf post 1-15, 132C3, 133B1
HEPATITIS—*See 'Diseases' under MEDICINE*

1977

HELICOPTERS—*See ACCIDENTS—Aviation; ARMAMENTS—Aircraft; AVIATION*
HELIUM—*See GAS, Natural*
HELLER, Mark J.
Named Berkowitz atty 8-16, 642A1
Quits Berkowitz case 9-15, 848E3
HELLMAN, Geoffrey T.
Dies 9-26, 788C1
HELLMAN, Dr. Louis
Rpts '76 abortn figures 6-1, 787B1
HELMAN, Justice Nathaniel T.
Fines teachers union 7-20, 558D2
HELMICK, Dave
Wins Daytona endurance 2-6, 531D2
HELMS, Sen. Jesse A. (R, N.C.)
Votes vs Young 1-26, 52C3
Vs Linowitz in Canal talks 2-21, 379C1
Cuba prisoner rpt released 5-13, 390C1
Vs antiboycott bill 6-10, 460A1
Sen backs HEW affirmative actn 6-28, bars strict abortn fund curb 6-29, 515A3, D3
Plans canal treaty oppositn 8-18, 622A1
In Canal Zone 8-19—8-20, vows pact defeat 9-7, 678F1
Scores urban aid grant formula 10-8, 796D2
In TV campaign vs Canal pacts 10-29, 912C1
HELMS, Richard
Suits vs US re spying rptd 5-22, 422C3
Replaced as amb to Iran 5-25, 500C1
Carter: no decisn re indictmt 10-27, 814C1
Pleads no contest re '73 Chile testimony; Carter, Church reactn 10-31, 838A3
Fined, prison term suspended 11-4, 861E1
Carter backs setlmt 11-10, 877F1
US prisoner in Cuba admits link 12-7, 1011D3
Settlemt scored by US rep 12-9, 979F3
HELSINKI Agreement—*See EUROPE—Security and Cooperation*
HEMISPHERIC Affairs, Council on
Argentina abuse rpt issued 12-22, 1018E3
HENDERSON, Edwin
Dies 2-3, 164A3
HENDERSON, Maxwell
Polysar admits illegal rebates 2-8, 114D2
Scored re Polysar rebates 7-7, 542B1
HENDERSON, Dr. Ralph H.
WHO launches immunizatn drive 4-7, 287C3
HENDERSON, Steve
Traded to Mets 6-15, 644D2
Dawson named NL top rookie 11-23, 927A2
HENDERSON, Zac
Wins Downtown AC Trophy 12-8, 950E2
HENDRICK, George
NL batting ldr 10-2, 926C3
HENDRICKSON, Craig
Traded to Reds 6-15, 644E2
HENDRIE, Joseph M.
Vs A-plant licensing halt 10-3, 794D3
HENLEY, Nadine
Hughes '38 will sought 1-12, 120D2
Hughes offcls clash over estate 5-28, 6-8, 472B3
HENNING, Lorne
NHL season ldr 4-3, 262F3
HEPTACHLOR—*See PESTICIDES*

1978

HELANDER, Wendy Joy
Patrick deprogramming suit rptd 4-16, 295E3
HELDT, Henning
Indicted 8-15, 645A1
HELFELD, David M.
Rpts Paraguay rights 'crisis' 1-10, 113B2
HELGEMOE v. Meloon
NH rape law case refused by Sup Ct 6-5, 431B2
HELICOPTERS—*See ARMAMENTS—Aircraft, AVIATION*
HELIUM—*See GAS, Natural*
HELLER, Mayor Max M. (Greenville, S.C.)
Loses US House electn 11-7, 853C1
HELLMAN, Jerome
Coming Home released 2-15, 619B1
HELLO Dolly (play)
Revival opens 3-5, 887G1
HELMS, Sen. Jesse A. (R, N.C.)
Says Sen Canal vote unchngd by Torrijos drug chrgs 2-22, 120D3
Votes vs Panama Canal neutrality pact 3-16, 177G2
Votes vs 2d Canal pact 4-18, 273B1
Unopposed in primary 5-2, 342B3
Ingram wins Dem runoff 5-30, 426E2
Sen votes conditnl end to Rhodesia sanctns 7-26, 588F1
Carter at Ingram rally 8-5, 605F3
Reelected 11-7, 848F2, 852F3
Tops US Sen electn spending list 11-15, 898B1, D1
Attacks Carter re China 12-15, 974B3
HELMS, Richard
'77 no contest plea re Chile testimony cited 3-20, 206F3
Snepp book ruling scored 7-7, 527D3
On CIA 'mole' issue 10-2, 940E2
HELSINKI Agreement—*See EUROPE—Security and Cooperation*
HEMINGWAY, Ernest (1899-1961)
Lanham dies 7-20, 620A3
HEMISPHERIC Affairs, Council on
US rights drive praised, Latin abuses scored 6-24, 490A1
HENDERSON, Ken
Traded to Mets 3-15, 195A1
HENDERSON, Kenneth Lynn
Charged by SEC 10-5, 770C3
HENDERSON, Luther
Ain't Misbehavin opens 5-9, 760A1 ★
Mahalia opens 6-5, 887B2
HENDRIE, Joseph M.
Seabrook A-plant constructn OKd 1-7, 242E3

HENG Samrin
Heads Cambodian rebel front 12-3, 933G1 ★
HENLEY Jr., Elmer Wayne
'74 convictn overturned 12-20, 992B2
HENLEY, Judge J. Smith
Ark prison reform, attys fees backed by Sup Ct 6-23, 566E1
HENRY IV: Part I and II (play)
Opens 11-27, 1031A2
HENRY VIII, King (Great Britain) (1491-1547)
Westminister Mass protested 7-6, 557G3
HENRY, Aaron
On '68 Dem conv FBI role 7-1, 507G3
HENRY, Albert (Cook Islands prime minister; replaced July 25)
Ousted over electn fraud 7-25, 591F2
HENRY, Buck
Heaven Can Wait released 6-27, 619D2
HENRY, Geoffrey
Ousted over electn fraud 7-25, 591C3
HENRY, Paul-Marc
Israel cites UNESCO rpt 11-13, 931A2
HENRY, Trupul A.
Ousted over electn fraud 7-25, 591C3
HENSLEY, Judge J. T.
Awards A-worker mental health damages 3-15, 242F3
HEPATITIS—*See MEDICINE—Diseases*

1979

HELD, Irving
Indicted 4-9, 292A1
HELDT, Henning
Sentenced 12-6–12-7, 1000D1
HELICOPTERS—*See ARMAMENTS-Aircraft*
HELLER, Joseph
Good as Gold on best-seller list 4-8, 271A2; 5-6, 356C2; 6-3, 432G1
HELLER, Paul
Promise released 3-7, 528D3
HELLER & Co., Walter E.
Cited in Lance banking practices rpt 1-15, 31D1
HELLMAN, Jerome
Promises in the Dark released 11-2, 1008B1
HELL'S Angels (motorcycle gang)
32 arrested 6-14, 492B1
18 tried 10-4, 840E1-A2
HELLWIG, Klaus
Your Turn, My Turn released 1-27, 175A1
HELMS, Sen. Jesse A. (R, N.C.)
Sees Teng, scores re Taiwan 1-30, 65G2, 66B1
Woodcock confrmd China amb 2-26, 146E1
Sen OKs schl prayer amendmt 4-5, rejcts sex educ legis 4-30, 326D2
Asks Rhodesia sanctns end 4-24, 293F2
Schweiker Rhodesia res passed 5-15, 359A2
HUD withdraws Soul City support 6-28, 665B2
Muzorewa visits US 7-9–7-11, 546D2
Aides' Zimbabwe conf role rptd 9-19, denies influence chrg 9-21, 718G1
Votes vs Hufstedler 11-30, 946G2
HELPERN Jr., David
Short of Paradise released 10-5, 1008F1
HELSEL, Thomas
On 3 Mile I property values 8-20, 743A3
HELSINKI Agreement—*See EUROPE-Security and Cooperation*
HELSINKI Watch Committee, American
USSR bars Bernstein 8-23, 689G3
HELSTOSKI, Henry
Cong immunity broadened by Sup Ct 6-18, 498C3
Indictmt rule backed by Sup Ct 6-18, 499A1
HELSTOSKI v. Meanor
Case decided by Sup Ct 6-18, 499A1
HEMINGWAY, Ernest (1899-1961)
First wife dies 1-22, 104D3
HEMINGWAY, Mariel
Manhattan released 4-24, 528B3
HEMOPHILIA—*See MEDICINE-Blood*
HENDERSON, Thomas (Hollywood)
Cowboys win NFL conf title 1-7, 8G3
Steelers win Super Bowl 1-21, 63A1
HENDERSON, Tom
Sonics win NBA title 6-1, 506F3, 507A1
HENDERSON State University (Arkadelphia, Ark.)
Loses NAIA basketball title 3-17, 239B1
HENDRIE, Joseph M.
Hedges on A-plant shutdown 1-26, 90B3
On 3 Mile I A-accident 3-29, 3-31, 242B3, 243C1, 244D1
Testifies on 3 Mile I A-radiatn 4-4, OKs Babcock reactors 4-6, 260F1, D3
Plans NRC A-safety rules review 4-10, 275G1
3 Mile I NRC transcripts released 4-12, 275G2, C3, 276A1
Backs Met Ed license 10-26, 826B2
On A-plant cooling system hazard 11-2, 849B2
On NRC reactor licensing freeze 11-5, 848G3-849F1
Replaced as NRC chrmn 12-7, 940G1, E2
HENG Samrin (Cambodian president)
Heads Cambodia governing Cncl, '78 activities cited 1-8, 10A1
Chrgs Pol Pot massacres, lauds Viet aid 1-25, 68E3
Concedes guerrilla resistance 2-6, 142D1
Signs Viet friendship pact 2-18, 123B2
Pol Pot-Khieu Samphan mtg rptd 5-14, 360F2
Viets: China seeks Pol Pot comeback 6-1, 474F2
Nonaligned mtg bars rep 6-4, 437D1
US, China vs peace role 8-28, 644F2
Nonaligned natns split re recognitn 8-28–9-9, 674B3
Viet challenges Pol Pot govt UN seat 9-18, seat upheld 9-19, 695C2
Sihanouk discloses exile group formatn 10-4, 811B2
UK ends Pol Pot govt ties, vs Pnompenh recogntn 12-6, 978G3
HENLEY Jr., Elmer Wayne
Convicted again 6-27, 819C1
HENRY, Sir Albert
US co fined for '78 electn fraud role 6-2, 648B2
HENRY, Justin
Kramer vs Kramer released 12-19, 1007F3
HENSLEE, James N.
Sentenced in GSA scandal 5-23, 964A3
HENSLEY, Pamela
Buck Rogers released 3-29, 528E1
HENSON, Everett Michael (d. 1978)
Slayer sentncd 6-19, 492G1
HENSON, Jim
Muppet Movie released 6-22, 820C2
HEPATITIS—*See MEDICINE-Diseases*
HEPBURN, Audrey
Bloodline released 6-28, 819F3

1980

HELICOPTERS—*See ARMAMENTS--Aircraft*
HELIN, Eila
Espionage sentence rptd 3-18, 212B1
HELLER, Raymond
Kills self 1-31, grain scandal rptd 2-25, consumer suit filed 3-12, 237A1
Grain fraud probe rptd 5-14, 414F2
HELLMAN, Lillian
Watch on the Rhine opens 1-3, 136F3
My Mother, My Father opens 1-9, 136D3
Emery dies 2-8, 176A1
Sues Mary McCarthy 2-15, 199E2
HELL'S Angels (motorcycle gang)
Mistrial declared 7-2, 568G1
HELM, Rudiger
Wins Olympic medal 8-2, 622C2
HELMS, Sen. Jesse A (R, N.C.)
Protests Carter forgn policy, votes vs Muskie confrmatn 5-7, 343F1
Evangelical Christian pol role rptd 7-11—9-15, 819G1
Gets votes as vp nominee, addresses GOP conv 7-17, 529G1, E2
Reagan ties scored by Lucey 8-25, 646F3
East wins US Sen seat 11-4, 849F3
Sponsers antibusing rider, sees '81 legis 11-20—12-10, 953G3, 954D1
HELSINKI Agreement—*See CONFERENCE on Security and Cooperation in Europe (CSCE)*
HELSTOSKI, Henry
Cleared of '76 charges 2-27, 228B1
HEMPSTEAD—*See New York*
HENBIT (race horse)
Wins English Derby 6-4, 448B1
HENDERSON—*See KENTUCKY*
HENDERSON, Rickey
AL batting, stolen base ldr 10-6, 926F3
HENDON, William
Elected to US House 11-4, 843C4, 850A1
HENDRICK, George
NL wins All-Star Game 7-8, 636G1
NL batting ldr 10-6, 926E2
HENDRICKSE, Rev. Alan
On S Africa unrest 6-19, 466E1
HENDRIE, Joseph M.
Carnesale named NRC chrmn 7-9, 551B3
HENDRIX, Dr. Stephen
Rpts faster hay fever treatmt 2-18, 159F3
HENERIES, Richard
Executed 4-22, 353A2

HENG Samrin (Cambodian president)
Gandhi support cited 1-6, 11G3
Brezhnev backs detente 2-4, 84E3
Sihanouk scores rule 2-22, 141C2
HENNESSEY, Barbara
Birthday of Infanta wins Amer Book Award 5-1, 692B2
HENNING, Lorne
Islanders win Stanley Cup 5-24, 487E3
HENRIK Ibsen (oil platform)
N Sea accident kills 123 3-27, 256A2
HENRIQUEZ, Maria Magdalena
Kidnaped 10-3, slain 10-7, 789D3
HENRY, Billy Gale
Jail informant use curbed by Sup Ct 6-16, 511B3
HENRY, Buck
Nude Bomb released 5-9, 675B3
First Family released 12-25, 1003G1
HENRY, Wally
NFL '79 punt return, kick return ldr 1-5, 8F3, G3
NFC wins Pro Bowl 1-27, 175D1
HENRY 3rd, William A.
Wins Pulitzer 4-14, 296G2
HENSON, Jim
Wins Grammy 2-27, 296G3

1976

HERBSTEIN, Denis
S Africa ousts 11-7, 927G2
HERCE, Fernando
Lockheed paymt rptd 11-6, 909F1
HERCULES, Inc.
'75 arms sales listed 2-6, 147B3
HEREDITY—*See GENETICS*
HERLY, Jean
Lauds Israel Uganda raid 7-4, 486A2
HERNANDEZ, Jorge
Wins Olympic medal 7-31, 574A1
HERNANDEZ, Olivia Ledesma de
Wounded 8-11, rptd seized 8-20, 677F1
HERNANDEZ Acosta, Valentin
Asks Flores quit 2-17, 147G3
On OPEC price increases 12-9, 12-10, 12-17, 934E2, 935A1
HERNANDEZ Colon, Gov. Rafael (D, P.R.)
Loses reelection 11-2, 825G1
Reelectn defeat linked to tap scandal 11-27, 995B1
On PR statehood proposal 12-31, 994C3
HEROIN—*See NARCOTICS & Dangerous Drugs*
HERRARA, Angel
Wins Olympic medal 7-31, 574B1
HERREMA, Tiede
Kidnaper in ct exchng 1-13, 157A1
HERRERA, Fortunato
Seized re US exec kidnap 8-3, 592D3
Sup Ct voids arrest, OKs mil probe 8-25; immunity lifted 8-26, 874D2
HERRERA, Juan Manuel
Arrested 1-20, freed 1-21, 118C1
HERRERA, Leon
On press censorship 7-13, 523C3
HERRERA Latoja, Gen. Francisco (ret.)
Quits Cabt 3-5; replaced 3-8, 288F2
HERRERAS, Casildo
Scores Peron cabt shift 1-18, 1-21, 71D2
Negotiates wage hike 1-22, 96D2
Gets Mex emb asylum 3-31, safe-conduct 4-9, 382B3
Escape to Uruguay cited 5-15, 399D3
Rights revoked, arrest ordrd 6-23, 520D1
HERREROS Robles, Capt. Antonio
Arrested 2-26, 314B3
HERRMANN, Edward
Wins Tony 4-18, 460D2
HERSANT, Robert
France-Soir sale protested 8-13, 8-16, 8-27, 651C1
HERSHBERGER, Freddy
Seconds Ford nominatn 8-18, 597G2
HERSHEY, Pa.—*See PENNSYLVANIA*
HERSTATT, Iwan D.
Arrested 8-26, 678G3
HERSTATT, Bankhaus I. D.
Herstatt, 7 others arrested 8-26, 678G3
HERTER, Christian A.
AID asst admin 3-16; confrmd 4-1, 262D3
Vs anti-Israel resolutns at Habitat conf 6-11, 431C3
HERTZBERG, Rabbi Arthur
Rpts 22 cos bar boycott compliance 3-18, 747G1
HERTZ Corp.—*See under RCA Corp.*
HERZBERG, Joseph G.
Dies 2-12, 160D3
HERZL (play)
Opens 11-30, 1014F3
HERZOG, Chaim
Boycotts UN Cncl debate, scores Arab stand 1-12, 18B1, E1
Vs UN Palestine committee 2-26, 162A1
Lauds US UN Cncl veto 3-25, 211A2
Vs Vorster visit criticism 4-29, 320C3
PLO UN seating dispute 5-4, scores Egypt 5-5, 320C1
Says Arabs paid for W Bank riots 5-7, 338G2
On Cncl statemt vs setlmt policy 5-26, denies US feud 5-27, 407B1
Fears Syria Leb invasion 6-9, 406G2
Vs resolutn on occupatn 6-29, 464E1
Ties Uganda to hijackers 7-9, 7-13, 516B1, F1
Walks out on PLO speaker 11-1, 842G1
Scores UN vote vs Israel 11-11, 842D1
Vs Assemb call for Palestine state 11-24, 895B3
Asks Geneva conf 12-6, vs Palestinian role 12-9, 914F1, A2
HERZOG, Vladimir (d. 1975)
Govt 'suicide' rpt scored 1-13; torture, death denounced 1-26, 1-29, 98E1

1977

HERALD Co.
Glover libel case refused 11-28, 919A3
HERBERG, Will
Dies 3-27, 264G2
HERBERT, Anthony B.
Journalists' thoughts protected 11-7, 920A3
HERBST, Dr. Arthur L.
DES cancer risk found less 5-3, 432C1
HERBST, Hilda
ITT suit cited 3-4, 194D3
HERBST, Robert L.
Named Interior asst secy 3-3, confrmd 4-1, 272A3
HERCULES (U.S. transport plane)—*See ARMAMENTS—Aircraft*
HERCULES, Inc.
Chrgd re Arab boycott 1-7, 167A2
Sup Ct backs EPA authority 2-23, 150A3
To buy Warren-Teed 7-19, 650F3
HERD, Bishop Brian
Uganda ousts 3-4, 308C3
HEREDITY—*See GENETICS*
HERLY, Jean
Israel vs Daoud release 1-11, 1-12, 9G2
HERMAN, James R.
Named ILWU candidate 4-23, 324A3
Elected ILWU pres 6-23, 481E3
HERMAN, Judge R. Dixon
Sentences coal firms 3-21, 520B3
HERMANSDORFER, Judge H. David
Mining widows' suit dismissed 9-12, 900F3
HERMES (newsletter)
Child porno network rptd 5-15, 432B3
HERNANDEZ, Keith
NL batting ldr 10-2, 926D3
HERNANDEZ, Michael B.
EEOC bias ruling rptd 1-20, 278F3
HERNANDEZ, Plutarco
Denies Cuba aid, communist goals 10-26, 864C3
HERNANDEZ Acosta, Valentin
Venez energy, mines min 1-7, 23F2
HERNANDEZ Colon, Rafael
Ties statehood to oil deposits 1-5, 16A3
HERNANDEZ Cuesta, Santo
Canada expels 1-12, 42F3
HERNANDEZ Gil, Antonio
Named Spain parlt pres 6-15, 453E1
HEROES (film)
Top-grossing film 12-7, 1021B3
HEROIN—*See NARCOTICS & Dangerous Drugs*
HERPES Encephalitis—*See MEDICINE—Diseases*
HERRERA, Trinidad
Arrested 4-25; chrgs torture, freed 5-13, 468D2
HERRERA Campins, Luis
Minor pres candidates announce 7-30, 8-20, 8-26: Copei nominates 8-18, 674F1, C2
HERRING—*See FISH & Fishing*
HERRIOT, James
All Things Wise on best-seller list 10-2, 808D3; 11-6, 872D3; 12-4, 1021G2
HERRZE, Martin F.
Replaced as amb to Bulgaria 7-28, 626E2
HERSHEY, Gen. Lewis Blaine (ret.)
Dies 5-20, 452B3
HERSKOWITZ, Mickey
'Camera' on best-seller list 9-4, 712E3
HERTEL, Rob
USC wins Bluebonnet Bowl 12-31, 1020D2
HERTZ, Dr. C. Hellmuth
Wins Lasker Award 11-16, 927A3
HERVEL, Serge
Bank closed, arrest ordrd 8-15, 658C1
HERVEL, Theodore
Bank closed, arrest ordrd 8-15, 658C1
HERVEL & Co.
Scandal closes, officers sought 8-15, 658B1
HERZOG, Chaim
Meets Sovt UN rep on PLO peace role 2-3, 86D3
Vs Jordan plan on occupatn 3-25, 226G3
Vs Egypt for calling UN mtg 3-28, 227A1
Vs Waldheim on W Bank stand 8-18, 623C1
Vs Fahmy on peace stand 9-28, 734E1
Vs UN anti-setlmts res 10-28, 830A3
Explains Leb raid to UN 11-12, 874C3
Meets Egypt UN envoy 11-27, 909E2
Vs UN Palestine 'rights' drive 12-2, 931F1

1978

HERBICIDES
Paraquat peril in marijuana warned 3-10, rptd exaggerated 8-3, 728B2
500 Viet vets claim Agent Orange disabilities 10-11, critic dies 12-14, 984D1-A2
HERDIS Management and Investment Corp.
Westinghouse A-contract fee rptd 1-13; co sale, probe ordrd 1-16, 38D2
HEREDITY—*See GENETICS*
HERFNER, Jack
Patio/Porch opens 4-13, 887D2
HERITAGE Foundation
Seabrook A-plant shutdown costs rptd 10-10, 941F1-A2
HERMAN, Jerry
Hello Dolly opens 3-4, 887A2
HERMASZEWSKI, Maj. Miroslaw
1st Pole in space, docks with Salyut 6-28, 506A1
Ends Soyuz 30 flight 7-5, 623C3
HERNANDEZ, Emilio
Zarate KOs 6-9, 600G1
HERNANDEZ, Jose Maria
Sworn DR pres admin min 8-16, 648D2
Wife gets DR post 8-23, 671F2
HERNANDEZ, Keith
Wins Golden Glove Award 11-21, 928A3
HERNANDEZ, Sonia Guzman de
Gets DR post, defends father 8-23, 671F2
HERNANDEZ Acosta, Valentin
On oil productn decline, US demand 4-16, 331G3
HERNANDEZ Agosto, Miguel
Elected PDP pres 7-25, 627B1
HERNANDEZ Colon, Rafael
Quits as PDP pres 7-19; won't bar '80 gov race 7-25, 627A1
HERNANDEZ Sancho, Plutarco
Seized in CR 4-13, 376A2
HERNDON, Walter S.
Hooper released 8-4, 970F1
HERNES, Rainieri
Car firebombed 5-8, 393C2
HERNU, Charles
Scores budgeting of A-sub 11-7, 882C1
HEROIN—*See NARCOTICS*
HEROUX, Denis
Violette released 10-9, 1030F3
HERPES Simplex Virus—*See MEDICINE—Diseases*
HERRERA, Angel
Wins World Amateur Boxing tourn 5-6—5-20, 600E2
HERRERA, Efren
NFL '77 kicking ldr 1-1, 56F2
Cowboys win Super Bowl 1-15, 39A3
NFC wins Pro Bowl 1-23, 56G1
Traded to Seahawks 8-14, 1025A1
HERRERA, George Ralph
Indicted 6-15, 560G2
HERRERA Campins, Luis
Tied in Venez pres poll 3-24, campaign opens 4-1, 270A1
URD backs pres bid, Pinerua leads poll 7-15, 559C2
Ties Pinerua in pres poll 9-29, 799B2
Elected 12-3, Pinerua concedes 12-5, returns incomplete 12-8, 952G2
Declared pres-elect in final vote count 12-11, 989G3
HERRERA Ibarguen, Roberto
Ransomed from guerrillas 1-30, 152B3
HERRING, Edmund
Confrms wartime hangings 5-8, 350D1
HERRIOT, James
All Things Wise on best-seller list 1-8, 24D3; 3-5, 195E3; 4-2, 272C3; 10-9, 800C3; 12-3, 971C1
HERRITY, John F.
Wins Cong primary in Va 6-13, 467F1
HERSANT, Robert
L'Aurore purchase blocked 11-22, to face trust chrgs 11-29, 1016F3
HERSCHLER, Gov. Edward (D, Wyo.)
On govs' role in water plan 6-7, 427B1
Wins renomination 9-12, 736B2
Reelected 11-7, 853F3, 856G1
HERSHEY Foods Corp.
Carter vs candy bar price hike 11-9, 875C1
Candy bar price hike OKd 11-20, 917G3
To buy Friendly's 12-26, 1005G1-A2
HERSHMAN, Michael
Denies NSA curbed Korea lobbying probe 3-21, 203B3
HERTZ Commercial Leasing Corp.
Parking ticket case refused by Sup Ct 10-30, 832F2
HERTZ Commercial Leasing Corp. v. Chicago
Case refused by Sup Ct 10-30, 832F2
HERZOG, Barbara
Beasts opens 2-8, 760C1
HERZOG, Chaim
Doubts effective UN force for Leb 3-16, 174A3
Defends Israel invasn of Leb 3-17, 197B2
Israel to stay in Leb Christn villages 4-6, 236B1
HERZOG, Clarice (Mrs. Vladimir)
Govt blamed in husband's '75 death 10-28, 879E1
HERZOG, Vladimir (d. 1975)
Prison death marked 10-25; judge blames govt, asks probe 10-28, 879D1

1979

HERALD and Weekly Times Group
Murdoch ends takeover bid 11-22, 906G2
Fairfax acquires interest 11-26, 966A3
HERBEIN, John G.
On 3 Mile I A-accident 3-28–3-31, 241D2, 242E3, 243D2, E3, 244E1
HERBERT, Anthony B.
'State of mind' libel queries backed by Sup Ct 4-18, 301G3, 302E2
HERBERT v. Lando
'State of mind' libel queries backed by Sup Ct 4-18, 301G3
Marshall decries ruling 5-27, 422C1
Brennan criticizes press 10-17, 848E1
HERBICIDES
Viet Agent Orange suit filed 2-1, 90A1
2,4,5-T, Silvex banned; reactn 3-1, 167E1-C2
Carter vows Viet vet study 5-30, 419B2
Mex pot paraquat peril cited 10-29, 972A2
GIs Agent Orange exposure rptd 11-24; 5 mfrs sued 11-26, 904B2-A3
HERBST, Kathleen
Settles Guillian-Barre flu shot claim 8-14, 771F1
HERBST, Robert (deceased)
Widow settles Guillian-Barre flu shot claim 8-14, 771F1
HERCULES Inc.
Agent Orange suit filed 2-1, 90B1
2d Agent Orange suit filed 11-26, 904A3
HERE You Come Again (recording)
Parton wins Grammy 2-16, 336F3
HERLIHY, Ed
God Bless You Mr Rosewater opens 5-20, 711D3
HERMAN, Jerry
Grand Tour opens 1-11, 292E1
HERMANN, Mitchell
Sentenced 12-6–12-7, 1000D1
HERMANNSSON, Steingrimur
To form Icelandic govt 12-4, 928C1
HERMANSDORFER, Judge H. David
Upholds EPA re Ohio coal use 5-7, 351C1
HERMITAGE Museum (Leningrad)
Control Data to sponsor art show 7-19, 672E2
HERMOSA, Maj. Jaime
Links ex-min to Calderon death 1-12, 62F2
HERNANDEZ, Keith
NL batting ldr 9-30, named co-MVP 11-13, wins Golden Glove Award 11-20, 955F1, D2-F2, 956C1
HERNANDEZ, Rubin
Coastal wins Belmont Stakes 6-9, 448C2
Coastal 3d in Jockey Gold Cup 10-6, 876G2
HERNANDEZ Juarez, Francisco
Offers phone strike compromise 5-1, 372A3
HEROIN—*See NARCOTICS*
HEROLD, Horst
Gives terrorist data 5-10, 374E2
HEROUX, Claude
City on Fire released 9-14, 819G3
HERPES Simplex Virus—*See MEDICINE–Diseases*
HERR, Michael
Dispatches opens 4-18, 711E2
HERRERA, Maj. Jose Maria
Assassinated 1-2, 40E1
HERRERA Campins, Luis (Venezuelan president)
Names Cabt 3-10; sworn pres, scores Perez 3-12, 192C2, B3
Hosts Mondale 3-23–3-24, 247E3, 248E1-A2
Army chief resigns 5-22, 429B3
At Andean Group mtg, OKs Colombia oil talks 5-26–5-28, 398C2
Pledges fscl restraint 5-28, 429C3
Party wins munic electns 6-3, 429A3
Roldos sworn Ecuador pres 8-10, 613F2
Vs union wage bill 10-4, 837F3
Brazil pres visits; trade, energy discussed 11-6–11-7, 953F1
HERRERA Rebollo, Carlos Antonio
Assassinated 5-23, 387C3
HERRING, Robert L.
Vesco jury foreman resigns 8-29, 647E2
Bell comments on Vesco case 12-5, 943A3
HERRIOT, James
All Things Bright & Beautiful released 3-8, 528A1
HERSHEY, Pa.—*See PENNSYLVANIA*
HERSHEY Foods Co.
3 Mile I A-accident impact feared 4-9, 261E2
HERSHEY Medical Center, M.S. (Hershey, Pa.)
Sex seen as pregnancy risk 11-29, 971C3
HERZFELD, John
Voices released 3-13, 528F3
HERZOG, Werner
I Am My Film released 4-19, 528E2
Woyzeck released 8-24, 820F3
HERZOG, Whitey
Fired as Royals mgr 10-2, 1002F1

1980

HERARD, Gabriel
Arrested 11-28, 922A3
HERARD, Jean-Robert
Arrested 11-28, 922G2
HERBICIDES
Carter vetoes dioxins study 1-2, 17G2
Australia study blames Agent Orange in birth defects 1-3, 6A1
Australia Viet defoliant study ordrd 1-8, 37E2
HERBIE Goes Bananas (film)
Released 9-12, 836A3
HERBST, Dr. Arthur
DES, problem pregnancies rptd linked 1-25, 63E2, G2
HERCULES Inc.
US files Ark chem-dump suit 3-4, 190E3
HERITAGE Foundation
'Big Business Day' countered 4-17, 308A2, D2
HERITAGE of Michael Flaherty, The (book)
Outsider released 6-3, 675C3
HERMANSSON, Steingrimur
Gestsson govt bid set 1-16, 39D3
HERMASSI, Elbaki
Suspended re sex harassmt 1-9, 77F3
HERMENING, Kevin
Letter describes emb takeover 1-19, 47G2, D3
Mother visits 4-21, 299E1
HERNANDEZ, Donoteo
Kidnaped, slain 11-27, 921F1
HERNANDEZ, Juan
Wins Olympic medal 8-2, 622E1
HERNANDEZ, Keith
NL wins All-Star Game 7-8, 636A2
NL batting ldr 10-6, 926D2-F2
Wins Golden Glove Award 12-6, 926E1
HERNANDEZ Colon, Rafael
Wins PR gov electn 11-4, recount called 11-5, 852D3
Loses electn recount 12-18, 988A2
HERNDON, Larry
NL batting ldr 10-6, 926E2
HERO at Large (film)
Released 216F2
HEROIN—*See NARCOTICS*
HERRARA, Emil
Blood Wedding opens 6-2, 756C3
HERRERA, Angel
Wins Olympic medal 8-2, 622F1
HERRERA, Bernabe
Ariz alien case mistrial declared 7-29, retrial sought 8-29, 713E3
HERRERA, Efren
NFL '79 kicking ldr 1-5, 8B2
HERRERA Campins, Luis (Venezuelan president)
Perez censured in shipping scandal 5-8, 411G1
Condemns Bolivia coup 7-29, 577D1
Meets Mex pres in CR, signs Latin oil supply guarantee 8-3, 605C3
Attends Santa Marta conf 12-17, 992A3
HERRING, Eric
Houston wins Cotton Bowl 1-1, 23E1
HERRINGTON, Sgt. William C.
Killed in Turkey 11-15, 888A2
HERRIOT, James
Yorkshire on best-seller list 1-13, 40C3; 2-10, 120D3
HERRMANN, Mark
Purdue wins Liberty Bowl 12-27, 999D3
HERRMANN, Rudolph Albert
Introduced as Soviet double agent 3-3, 189F1
HERRON, John
Queensland rift threatens fed coalitn 6-16, 485G3
HERSCHLER, Gov. Edward (D, Wyo.)
State of State message 2-12, 484E2
HERSEY, David
Wins Tony 6-8, 692B3
HERSH, Dr. Colin
Biko probe squashed 6-29, 525E1
HERTZBERG, Hendrik
Fears US mil action vs Iran 4-22, 298G2
HERZALLAH, Khader
Named to Aramco bd 7-8, 662F1
HERZOG, Maurice
Sees French Olympic boycott 4-14, 283F3
HERZOG, Raymond H.
Replaced as 3M chrmn 5-13, 456E2
HERZOG, Whitey
Hired as Cardinals mgr 6-8, 637B2
Quits as Cardinals mgr, becomes gen mgr 8-29, field mgr 10-24, 926B2

1976

HESBURGH, Rev. Theodore M.
Named Carter adviser 11-19, 881D3
HESELTINE, Michael
In new UK shadow Cabt 11-19, 1004A2
HESS, Leon
'72 campaign gift listed 4-25, 688B1
HESS, Seymour L.
Reports Mars weather 7-21, 526C3
HESS, W. Dale
Nephew implicated in Pallotine Fathers' fund-raising scheme 6-18, 951B1
Mistrial in Mandell case 12-7, 922C3
HESSEN (W. German warship)
In Intl Naval Review 7-4, 488D3
HETTICH, Urban
Wins Olympic medal 2-9, 159E1
HEWITT, Sir Lenox
Rpts Qantas '75 losses, admits price cutting 9-23, 749D3
HEYKAL, Mohammed Hassanien
Criticized by Sadat 3-14, 193F1
HIBBETS, Melvin
Named in grain fraud 3-11, 247D3
Pleads guilty 9-27, probatn rptd 11-4, 990G2
HIBBITT, Richard
Arrested, freed 1-22, 159G3
HIBERNIA Bank (San Francisco, Calif.)
Hearst Case—*See HEARST, Patricia*
HICKS, Rep. Floyd V. (D, Wash.)
Dicks wins seat 11-2, 825F1
HICKS, Louise Day
Lauds US actn re busing review 5-15, 377E3
Sup Ct bars busing review 6-14, 452G2 ★
HIEN, Phan
Hints Nixon aid note airing 2-2, 103A2
HIEU, Nguyen Van
Warns political foes 4-22, 367F2
HIGGINBOTHAM Jr., Judge A. Leon
Upholds AT&T affirmative actn plan 8-27, 944B2
HIGGINS, George V.
Cleaver defns fund announced 2-17, 272F1
HIGGINS, Jack
Eagle Has Landed on best-seller list 12-5, 972G2
Storm Warning on best-seller list 12-5, 972A3
HIGHTOWER, Rep. Jack (D, Tex.)
Reelected 11-2, 830D4
HIGHWAYS—*See ROADS*
HIJACKINGS—*See under AVIATION; also AVIATION Incidents under MIDDLE EAST*
HILDENBRAND, Klaus-Peter
Wins Olympic medal 7-30, 576C1
HILL, Clarence
Wins Olympic medal 7-31, 574D1
HILL, Jesse
Endorses Carter 4-13, 261C2
HILL, Sir John
Discounts Sovt A-disaster rpt 11-7, 948B3
HILL, William Martin
Dies 5-18, 524F2
HILLEL, Shlomo
Assures Arabs on prayer rights 2-28, 161G1
On Galilee violence 3-30, 227F1
HILLERS, Harlan
Hijacker killed 4-19, 383F3
HILLERY, Patrick J.
Facts on 873G1
Named Ireland pres-elect 11-9, 873E1
HILLIS, Rep. Elwood (R, Ill.)
Reelected 11-2, 829B3
HILLS, Carla Anderson
Scores Reagan proposal 1-8, 22A1
Reviews urban aid program 1-8, 25E1
Backs Ford in Calif 5-24, 374A1
Rpts HUD low-interest mortgages 9-9, 709B2
Rpts FHA loan rate reduced 10-15; Sept. housing starts up 10-19, 805D3
Ford campaign donatn rptd 10-22, 938G3
HILLS, Denis Cecil
UK cuts Uganda ties 7-28, 548B1
HILLS, Roderick M.
Rpts Lockheed SEC setlmt 4-13, 285G2
Testifies on forgn paymts disclosure bill 5-18, scores Richardson 6-16, 668D3, 669A1
On SEC boycott rules 6-4, 747E2
Sen OKs anti-bribery bill 9-15, 708D1

1977

HESS, Rudolf
Attempts suicide 2-21, amnesty denied 2-24, 298B3
HESS, W. Dale
Convicted 8-23, 652F1, A2
Sentenced 10-7, 807D2
HESS, Wolf Ruediger
Father attempts suicide 2-21, 289B3
HESTER, W. E. (Slew)
Scores US Open racial remark 9-8, 787F2
HETLER, Hans
Danish secret svc probe ordrd 7-8, 672A2
HEUNIS, J. Christiaan
On productn powers assumptn 11-9, 887A3
HEW—*See U.S. GOVERNMENT—HEALTH, Education & Welfare*
HEWITT, Bob
Wins US Open doubles title 9-9, 787B2
HICKS, Louise Day
Loses reelectn 11-8, 855D3
HIDALGO, Edward
Named Navy asst secy 4-1, confrmd 4-25, 418E1
HIDALGO Sola, Hector
Kidnaped 7-18; pol views rptd 7-22, 595G1
HIEN, Phan
In US talks 12-19—12-20, 976B1
HIGGINS, Jack
Storm Warning on best-seller list 2-6, 120F3
HIGGINSON, Dr. John
On WHO 7-yr cancer study 5-10, 431A2
HIGHWAYS—*See ROADS*
HIGUCHI, Chako
Wins LPGA Championship 6-12, 951C1
HIGUERAS, Jose
US Open fans sit-in 9-5, 787D2
HIJACKINGS—*See under AVIATION*
HILAL, Ahmed Ezzedin
Egypt oil, mining, indus min 10-25, 824C1
HILL, Dave
US wins Ryder Cup Matches 9-17, 951A2
HILL, David Douglas
Surrenders 7-1, released 7-14, 603F2
HILL, James
Seattle Slew wins Triple Crown 6-11, ownership probe rptd 6-16, 491E1
HILL, John
Seeks Hughes inheritnc tax 4-15, 354E3
HILL, Rev. Mel
Sees Rhodesia missionary exodus 4-3, 297C1
HILLEL, Shlomo
Meets Rabin on Ofer probe 1-1, 8G1
Loses parlt speaker race 6-13, 474F2
HILLEMAN, Dr. Maurice
Pneumonia vaccine gets FDA OK 11-21, 907B1
HILL and Knowlton Inc.
John Hill dies 3-17, 264G2
HILL-Norton, Adm. Sir Peter
Retires 4-15, 360G1
HILLS, Carla Anderson
At PR gov inaugratn 1-2, 16G2
Elected to IBM bd 2-22, 140G2
HILLS, Roderick M.
Quits as SEC chrmn 3-2, 211A2
Replaced at SEC 7-7, 272D3
HILLSBOROUGH, Robert
Slain 6-22, 560D2
HILLS Brothers Coffee Inc.—*See COPERSUCAR*

1978

HESS, Rudolf
Beasts opens 2-8, 760C1
Scheel release plea rptd rejctd by USSR 6-11, 477E3
HESTER, W. E. (Slew)
Backs US-S Africa Davis Cup matches 1-31, 251B3
HESTON, Charlton
Gray Lady Down released 3-10, 619C2
HETHERINGTON, Anthony
Gets Rhodesia sanctns-breaking rpt 8-31, 756E2
HEUSLER, Rudolf
Death rptd 4-12, 438F2
HEW—*See U.S. GOVERNMENT—HEALTH, Education & Welfare*
HEWITT, Bob
Wins N Amer Zone Davis Cup match 3-18, 252B1
HEYERDAHL, Thor
Burns boat in protest 4-4, 420G1
HEYKAL, Mohammed Hassanien
Says Sadat peace moves failed 415C1
Faces probe 5-28, denies wrongdoing 5-29; Sadat scores 5-30, 415A1
HEZEMANS, Antoine
Wins Daytona endurance 2-5, 538C3
HFC—*See HOUSEHOLD Finance Corp.*
HIBERNIA Bank (San Francisco, Calif.)
Hearst Case—*See HEARST, Patricia*
HICKEL, Walter J.
Trails in Alaska primary for gov 8-22, 682D3
Primary loss official 10-20, 831E2
HICKLIN v. Orbeck
Alaska oil job preference law voided by Sup Ct 6-22, 509A1
HICKMAN, Maj. Tim
On Guyana cult death toll 11-24, 909F1
HICKS, John
Traded to Steelers 4-17, 336G1
HIDALGO, Tex.—*See TEXAS*
HIDALGO Villavicencio, Ignacio
Leads Liberal Party factn 10-20, 881D2
HIEN, Phan
Discounts China aid cutoff 7-4, 504E3
Meets US reps 8-21, 660G2
HIGDON Construction Co.
'Prehire' union picketing curbed 1-17, 34A1
HIGGINS, Colin
Foul Play released 7-19, 970D1
HIGGINS, Joel
Angel opens 5-10, 760C1
HIGGINS, Pam
Ties for 2d in LI Classic 8-13, 672F3
HIGGITT, William
On RCMP illegalities 10-24, 10-25, 837B2, F2
HIGH Blood Pressure—*See MEDICINE—Blood*
HIGH Energy Astronomy Observatory (HEAO)—*See ASTRONAUTICS—Satellites*
HIGHET, Gilbert
Dies 1-20, 96C2
HIGHLAND Park, Mich.—*See MICHIGAN*
HIGHTOWER, Rep. Jack (D, Tex.)
Reelected 11-7, 852A3
HIGHWAYS—*See ROADS*
HIGUERAS, Jose
Loses Italian Open 5-27, 418E2
Loses US Clay Courts title 8-13, 1027A2
HIJACKINGS—*See under AVIATION*
HILAIRE, Gen. Jean-Baptiste
Retired as mil staff chief 9-15, 777G1
HILL, Calvin
Quits football 9-7, signed by Browns 9-27, 1024G3
HILL, Debra
Halloween released 10-15, 970E1
HILL, Dick
AABA debuts 1-6, folds 2-4, 271F3
HILL, Henry
Sun vibratn rptd measured 8-3, 654F2
HILL, John L.
Wins primary for Tex gov 5-6, 362D3
Loses electn 11-7, 846B3, 855A3
HILL, Mike
2d in Mixed Team tourn 12-3, 990D1
HILL, Phil
Andretti wins world driving title 9-10, 968C3
HILL, Walter
Driver released 7-28, 970B1
HILLES Associates Inc.
2 indicted 9-29, plead guilty in GSA probe 10-4, 753C3, E3
HILLIS, Rep. Elwood (R, Ind.)
Reelected 11-7, 850B4, 853A3
HILLIS, Margaret
Record wins Grammy 2-24, 316C1
HILLMAN, Darnell
Traded to Kings 6-26, 656A1
HILLS, Patrick
On New South Wales coal find 9-1, 686A1
HILLS Bros. Coffee Inc.—*See COPERSUCAR*

1979

HESELTINE, Michael
UK environment secy 5-5, 338F1
Rpts quango abolitn 9-17, 730G1
HETU, Herbert
CIA ex-agent cleared of Sovt spy chrg 2-27, 152D3
On Blahut ouster 6-17, 466B3
HEUNIS, J. Christiaan
Plans oil info ban 2-20, 126B3
Supports Riekert rpt 5-8, 373E2
Named transport min 6-14, 469B3
HEW—*See under U.S. GOVERNMENT-HEALTH, Education & Welfare*
HEWITT, Bob
Wins Wimbledon mixed doubles 7-7, 570D1
Wins US Open mixed doubles title 9-9, 734G1-A2
HEYM, Stefan
Prosecutn rptd 4-25, W Ger rptr ousted re interview 5-14, 370C3, E3
Fined 5-22, 406D2
HEYMANN, Philip B.
Carter peanut probe spec counsel named 3-20, 203C1
Denies Vesco probe cover-up 8-29, 647B3
Vesco case perjury comments rptd 8-30, denies 8-31, 725F2
HICKEY, Eddie
In basketball HOF 4-30, 526E3
HICKEY, Robert J.
Argues govt minority constructn grants case in Sup Ct 11-27, 944G3
HICKOK, Lorena (d. 1968)
E Roosevelt friendship rptd 11-5, 860C1
HICKSON, Joan
Bedroom Farce opens 3-29, 711D1
HIDALGO, Edward
Named Navy Secy 9-13; Nixon link rptd 9-18, 700B3
On Hispanic recruiting policy 10-15, 850A3
Confirmed 10-19, 965B1
HIDALGO-Gato, Raymond
El Super released 4-28, 528B2
HIDAYATULLAH, Mohammed
Elected India vp 8-9, 634C3
HIEN, Phan
To correct Viet refugee abuse 2-26, 181G1
Offers China peace plan 4-18, 298C1
Blames China re impasse 5-18, 379C3
Denies Viet blame for refugees 7-20, 549F1
HIERRO Chomon, Fernando
Escapes Spain jail 12-17, 997E3
HIGGENBOTHAM Jr., Judge A. Leon
Named to wiretap ct 5-18, 442C3
HIGGINS, James
On 3 Mile I A-accident 3-29, 243B2
HIGGINS v. Marshall
Case declined by Sup Ct 4-30, 364D3
HIGGITT, William
Testifies on RCMP 3-29, 253B3
Allmand cites '76 letter re RCMP '72 break-in 4-3-4-5, 311A3
HIGGS Jr., W. Otis
Loses Memphis mayoral vote 11-15, 904E3
HIGUCHI, Chako
2d in Women's Kemper Open 4-1, 587B2
HIGUERAS, Jose
Wins Houston WCT 4-22, 391C3
Wins W Ger Open 5-20, 570C2
Wins US Pro Outdoor 8-27, 734E2
HIJACKINGS—*See under AVIATION*
HIKEN, Gerald
Stider opens 5-31, 712F2
HILBIG, John
On Hurricane Frederic losses 10-5, 954G2
HILBISH, John
On 3 Mile I A-accident 4-2, 245A2
HILL, Rev. Albert Fay
N Amer Irregulars released 4-12, 528B3
HILL, Drew
East wins Japan Bowl 1-14, 63C2
HILL, George Roy
Little Romance released 4-27, 520F1
HILL, Jack
City on Fire released 9-14, 819G3
HILL, John
Granted parole 2-21, 156E1
HILL, Kent
In NFL draft 5-3, 335G2
HILL, Judge Robert
Sentences Estes 8-6, 604E3
HILL, Ruth Beebe
Hanta Yo on best-seller list 6-3, 432A2
HILL, Tony
Steelers win Super Bowl 1-21, 62G3-63A2
NFC wins Pro Bowl 1-29, 79F3
HILL, Walter
Warriors released 2-9, 174F3
Alien released 5-24, 528A1
HILLER, Arthur
In-Laws released 6-15, 820D1
HILLERY, Patrick (Irish president)
Greets Pope 9-29, 760E1
HILLMAN, Larry
Fired as WHA Jets coach 2-28, 470B3
HILLMAN, Stanley E.G.
Milwaukee Rd borrowing OKd 5-4, svc cut denied 6-1, 465A2
Quits as Milwaukee Rd bankruptcy trustee 6-15, 867F2
HILLMAN Co.
Trailways Inc.—*See TRAILWAYS*
HILLS, Carla Anderson
Backs IBM case judge's ouster 7-19, 610A3
HILL v. Western Electric Co.
Case refused by Sup Ct 10-29, 884C2
HILTON, Conrad N.
Dies 1-3, 104A3

1980

HESBURGH, Theodore M.
Immigratn panel issues prelim rpt 12-7, 939A1, F1
HESELTINE, Michael
Seeks pub housing sale 2-7, 150A1
Local authorities' funds cut 9-18, 729C1
HESS, Erika
Wins Olympic medal 2-23, 155A3
HESS, Rudolf
UPI admits error in Clark story 6-27, 507E2
HESS, W. Dale
Appeal refused by Sup Ct 4-14, 307B1
HESTON, Charlton
Awakening released 10-31, 972C3
HEUBLEIN Inc.
United Vintners strike ends 9-22, 747A3
United Vintners divestiture order rptd overturned 10-15, 917C1
HEUKRODT, Olaf
Wins Olympic medal 8-1, 622B2
HEUSER, Jurgen
Wins Olympic medal 7-30, 624G2
HEUSSER, Sharris
Navy drops lesbian chrgs 8-21, 898G3
HEW (Health, Education & Welfare)—*See under U.S. GOVERNMENT*
HEYMANN, Philip B.
Nazi search deadline rptd set 1-16, 228D2
Defends Abscam probe vs entrapmt chrgs 2-6, 82G2
Pregerson letter revealed 2-8, organized crime summit rptd canceled 2-13, 111G3
HICKS, Sue Kerr
Dies 6-27, 528A2
HIDE and Seek (play)
Opens 5-4, 392B3
HIDE in Plain Sight (film)
Released 3-21, 216G2
HIGGINS, Colin
Harold & Maude opens 2-7, 136B3
Nine to Five released 12-19, 1003C2
HIGGINS, Pam
Wins Lady Michelob 5-11, 412G3
HIGGS, Richard
Scores BC uranium ban 2-27, 148G2
HIGHAM, Charles
Flynn family sues 8-1, 639E1
HIGHTOWER, Rep. Jack (D, Tex.)
Reelected 11-4, 844A3
HIGHTOWER, Stephanie
Sets 60-yd hurdles mark 2-8, 892E2
HIJACKINGS—*See AVIATION--Hijackings & Bombings*
HIJINKS! (play)
Opens 12-18, 1003B3
HIKMATYAR, Gulbaddin
Amin linked to rebel ldr 1-21, 44G1
Denies Kunar prov rout 3-6, 205C3
HILDGARTNER, Paul
Wins Olympic medal 2-16, 156C1
HILER, John P.
Elected to US House 11-4, 842B4, 846D1, 850G3
HILL, Carolyn
Ties for 2d in Barth Classic 9-7, 972A2
HILL, Charles
Remains in Cuba 10-27, 828D3
HILL, David
Purdue transcript scandal rptd 1-23, 469E2
HILL, Debra
Fog released 2-29, 216E2
HILL, Jaime
Family buys ad to secure release 3-12, 191A3
Freed 3-14, 212C1
HILL, Joe (1879-1915)
Salt Lake City opens 1-23, 136E3
HILL, Capt. Lawrence D.
Killed in parachute jump 3-26; rigger chrgd 4-1, acquitted 5-27, 460B3
HILL, Ralph Lee
Dies 6-15, 528A2
HILL, Richard
Canterbury Tales opens 2-12, 136A3
HILL, Tony
NFC wins Pro Bowl 1-27, 175D1
HILLIARD, William
Carter, Reagan TV debate panelist 10-28, 813F1
HILLIS, Rep. Elwood (R, Ind.)
Reelected 11-4, 842B4
HILLS, Carla Anderson
At GOP platform hearings, urges fed responsibility shift 1-14, 32A2
HILLSBOROUGH County—*See FLORIDA*

1976

HILTON Hotels Corp.
Moon buys New Yorker 5-12, 971D1
Indicted 11-17, 989F2
HINDENBURG, The (film)
Dec '75 top-grossing film 32G3
Top-grossing film 1-28, 104F3
HINDI, Sharif Hussein al-
Cited in Sudan plot 592E2
Sentenced to die 9-30, 857C2
HINSHAW, Rep. Andrew J. (R, Calif.)
Divorce reported 95G3
Convicted 1-26, 95E3
Loses primary 6-8, 807F1
House expulsn blocked 10-1, 807E1
HINTON, Deane R.
EC amb 12-19-75; confrmd 1-28, 186A2
HINZMAN, Gabriele
Wins Olympic medal 7-29, 576A2
HIPOLITO, Bishop Adriano
Attacked 9-23, 835E3
HIRAI, Kazumasa
Wins Olympic medal 7-19, 576D2
HIRAYAMA, Noichiro
Wins Olympic medal 7-24, 576G2
HIREMUTH, S. R.
Loses passport 7-18, 538B2
HIROHITO, Emperor
Marks 50-yr reign 11-10, 890A1
Fukuda forms Cabt 12-24, 1006B3
HIRSCHFELD, Abraham
Loses NY Sen primary 9-14, 687E2
HIRSCH, Robert L.
ERDA asst admin 2-26, confrmd 3-23, 232E1
HIRSCHFELD, Burt
Aspen on best seller list 2-29, 208F3
HIRSCHFELDER, Joseph O.
Awarded Science Medal 10-18, 858E3
HISCOCK, Harry
Charges Marine cruelty 4-25, 435F2
HISPANIC Americans—*See also MEXICAN Americans, PUERTO Ricans*
Quotas set for Chicago police 1-5, 6B2, C2
Ford seeks Fla Cuban vote 2-28, 165G2
Ford wins Fla primary 3-9, 179E2
Merrill Lynch OKs job quotas 6-4, 414F1
Schl desegregatn data rptd 6-19, 992D3
Carter visits Houston group 7-1, 490E2
San Quentin 6 verdict 8-12, 656B1
GOP platform text 8-18, 605B3
Carter visits LA area 8-23, 631E2
Dems launch voter-registratn 8-23, 631F2
NY constructn union quota ordrd 9-1, 943F3
Carter visits Mich group 9-16, 686E3
Occidental immigratn bill cites Cubans 10-20, 835D1
HEW chrgs NYC school job bias 11-9, 922A1
Braniff job bias setlmt OKd 11-23, 943G2
US sues Boston on job bias 11-26, 944E1
Dole urges GOP seek vote 11-30, 917B3
HISS, Alger
Attacked in book review, denies chrgs 3-18, 217E3
HISTORIC Buildings and Sites
Valley Forge made natl park 7-4, 489C2
Ford urges $1.5 mln park plan 8-29, 644C2
Cong authorizes parkland funds 9-13, 745A3; Ford signs 9-28, 982G1
Dedicatn at Pocantico (NY) 11-21, 887G2
HISTORY & Historiography
MacKenzie King diaries publshd 1-1, 8C1
Louis Morton dies 2-12, 160F3
Daniel Villegas dies 3-10, 240G3
Davis wins Natl Book Award 4-19, 292D3
Horgan wins Pulitzer 5-3, 352D3
Samuel Morison dies 5-15, 368G2
HITLER, Adolf (1889-1945)
Franziska Braun dies 1-13, 56A3
'Mein Kampf' circulated in Argentina 8-15—8-30, 672B2 *
Spain neo-fascist attacks rptd 11-12, 909F2

1977

HILTON Hotels Corp.
Hawaii unit fined 5-11, 504D2
HILTON International Co.—*See under TRANS World Airlines*
HINDI, Sharif Hussein al-
Pardoned 8-13, 711C1
HINDUISM
TM banned in NJ schls 10-20, 845D3
HINES, Earl (Fatha)
Sails for Cuba 5-15, 390A2
Performs in Cuba 5-18, 456E2
HINKLE, Lon
2d in Tallahassee Open 4-17, 676A1
HINZ Jr., Judge Edward A.
Van Houten mistrial called 8-6, 711D2
HIRSCH, Arthur (Buzz)
Wins 1st Amendmt protectn 9-23, 921D2
HIRSCH, Phoebe
Surrenders 3-25, sentncd 9-13, 839E1
HISLE, Larry
AL batting ldr 10-2, 926F3
Signs with Brewers 11-18, 989E3
HISPANIC Americans—*See also MEXICAN Americans, PUERTO Ricans*
NYC school bias chrgd 1-18, 112C2
Chicago police hiring goals accepted 2-6, 279B3
Chicago fed schl aid barred 2-17, 157B1
Sup Ct bars NYC compensatn case review 2-28, 175C2
Sup Ct backs racial voter redistricting 3-1, 174E3-175D1
Frontier Air job-bias suit rptd 3-15, 279B2
Illegal alien plan proposed 4-27, 370A3
Pre-'64 seniority bias upheld 5-31, 461C2
LA, NYS, NJ sued re police, fire dept job bias 6-2, 9-8, 10-4, 819B2, D2
'77 death row populatn rptd 6-7, 594B1
Chicago busing plan begins 9-7, 837F3
Chicago police quota case review refused 10-3, 760A3
Sup Ct hears Bakke case arguments 10-12, 834D3
Natl Women's Conf OKs minority res 11-19—11-21, 917C3
HISTORY & Historiography
Howe wins Natl Book Award 4-11, 355G1
Potter wins Pulitzer 4-18, 355D2
Obituaries
Langer, William 12-26, 1024D2
Marshall, Slam 12-17, 1024E2
Masterman, John 6-6, 532D3
Petrie, Charles 12-13, 1024G2
Robinson, Jacob 10-24, 872G2
Tourtellot, Arthur 10-18, 872B3
Woodham-Smith, Cecil 3-16, 264G3
HITACHI Ltd.
Plans GE joint TV venture 12-7, 974B2
HITE, Shere
Hite Rpt on best-seller list 2-6, 120F3; 3-6, 184F3; 5-1, 356D2; 6-4, 452B2; 7-3, 548F3
HITE Report, The (book)
On best-seller list 2-6, 120F3; 3-6, 184F3; 5-1, 356D2; 6-4, 452B2; 7-3, 548F3
HITLER, Adolf (1889-1945)
Hess attempts suicide 2-21, 298B3
USSR photo censorship rptd 8-18, 657C3
Brandt warns of Nazi revival 8-19, 658G1
Franz Boehm dies 9-26, 872A1
HITLER: A Career (film)
Brandt warns of Nazi revival 8-19, 658C2

1978

HILTON Head Island, S.C.—*See SOUTH Carolina*
HILTON International Co.—*See TRANS World Airlines Inc.*
HIME, Rex
Loses US House electn 11-7, 856D3
HINAULT, Bernard
Wins Tour de France 7-23, 692A2
HINDI, Sharif Hussein al-
Nimeiry, Natl Front sign pact 4-12, 293C1
HINERFELD, Ruth
Backs DC voting amendmt 8-22, 661C2
HINGA, Bernard
Quits re corruptn probe 11-1, 885A3
HINKLE, Lon
Wins N Orleans Open 4-30, 356A1
2d in Tex Open 9-17, wins Mixed Team tourn 12-3, 900D1, A2
HINSON, Jon C.
Wins US House seat 11-7, 851C2, 852G2
HIROHITO, Emperor (Japan)
Meets China's Teng 10-23, 801A2
HIRSCH, Burkhard
On Schleyer hunt error 3-7, Schmidt defends 3-13, 332E2
HIRSCHFIELD, Alan J.
Fired as Columbia Pictures pres 7-20, 599C2
HISLE, Larry
AL batting ldr 10-2, 928E3
HISPANIC Americans
Carter State of Union Message 1-19, 29C2, 30A3
'53, '78 cong membership compared 1-30, 107E2
3 Houston ex-cops sentncd in Torres case 3-28, appeal rptd 12-14, 991B3
Bilingual educ scored 5-9, 348F3-349A1
5 sentncd in '76 NYC racial assault 5-12, 380D3
Guaranteed income study rptd 5-19, 720F2
Carter job apptmt data rptd 6-15, 811E1
Harvard admissns progrm described 483B2
'77 poverty level data rptd 8-12, 684E2
Covered in US minority business contract ruling 9-23, 811F2
Cong action vs Roybal scored 10-12, 831G3-832A1
Minority-white female earnings gap rptd filled 10-19, 812B3
Carter backs judges merit selectn 11-8, 873C3
Fernandez enters pres race 11-29, 938A3
US House com illegal alien plan scored 12-20, 1010F2
HISTORIC Buildings & Sites
Coates Hotel razed by fire 1-28, 212B3
Atlanta theater rescued 3-5, 293A2
Radio City Music Hall saved 4-13, 293C1
Grand Central office complex barred by Sup Ct 6-26, 566G3
Parks bill cleared 10-13, 834G2
HISTORY & Historiography
Lincoln letter donated to Rochester U 4-15, 335G2
Nixon data access to historians upheld 12-21, 1011B3
Awards
Chandler, Bate win Pulitzers 4-17, 315C1
Obituaries
Bieber, Margarete 2-25, 196C2
Catton, Bruce 8-28, 708C2
Chastenet, Jacques 2-7, 196E2
Gilson, Etienne 9-19, 778D1
HISTORY of the American Film, The (play)
Opens 3-30, 760C2
HITLER, Adolf (1889-1945)
Goebbels diary on W Ger best-seller list 1-2, 22B1
Volkswagen 'beetle' productn halted 1-19, 74D3
Ill Nazi rally swastika display OKd 1-27, 68F3
Vogel asks Nazis curbs 2-4, 114D2

1979

HILTON Hotels Corp.
Conrad Hilton dies 1-3, 104A3
HIMALAYAS, The
Venus mts compared 5-29, 692A1
HINAULT, Bernard
Wins Tour de France 7-22, 655D2
HINDMAN, Earl
Dark at the Top opens 11-29, 956A3
HINES, Gregory
Comin' Uptown opens 12-20, 1007C2
HINES, Tommy Lee
SCLC protests '78 rape convctn 6-9, 865G3
HINKLE, Lon
Wins Crosby Pro-Am 2-4, 2d in LA Open 2-25, 220D3, F3
Wins World Series of Golf 9-30, 969A3
PGA top money winner 11-30, 969F2
HINTON, Alan
Fired as Roughnecks coach 8-31, 1004E2
HINTON, Deanne
Oil import subsidy scored 5-30, 417A2
HIROHITO, Emperor (Japan)
Hosts Carter 6-25, 494A2
HIRSCH, Judd
Talley's Folley opens 5-3, 712A3
HIRSCHFELD, Abraham
Nixon agrees to buy apartment 8-11, 656A3
HISPANIC Americans
AT&T cleared re job bias 1-17, 92B2
Illegal alien issue detailed 1-29, 127G1
3 Houston ex-cops win Torres case appeal 2-6, 156C2
US Army rescinds Spanish language ban 2-7, 89D2
Illegal alien policies protested, pol activism seen 2-12, 127F2
NYC Transit Auth ex-addict ban backed by Sup Ct 3-21, 231C2
San Antonio city cncl shifts to whites 4-7, 265B2
'Italian Bakke case' declined by Sup Ct 4-23, 346F2
Mex border fence dropped by US 4-26, 327F2-B3
Carter at LA fete 5-5, 346C1, 347B1
Bonilla chosen LULAC head 6-17, 810E1
Weber case Sup Ct ruling lauded 6-27, 477B3
Suffolk Cnty, Brentwood bilingual programs ordrd 7-20, 597D1, E1
Castillo quits as INS head 8-10, 630D3
Torres named Carter spec asst 8-10, 608F2
Phila police brutality chrgd 8-13, 610G1
Viet refugee violence in Denver 8-20—8-24, 660B1
Cranston vs Carter '80 nominatn support 8-20, 627B3
City hosp closings rptd 9-2, 970G3, 971A1
Hidalgo, Valdez get Navy, State Dept posts 9-13, 700B3
Pope in NY 10-2, Chicago 10-5, 758G1, 759G2
Navy chngs recruiting policy 10-15, 850A3
Chicago schl bd rejects HEW desegregatn guides 10-17, 944C1
Hidalgo, Valdez confirmed 10-19, 11-5, 965B1
US sues Sears re job bias 10-22, 885C3
Phila police brutality suit dismissed 10-30, 831E3
3 Houston ex-cops resentncd 10-30, 839B3, F3
Houston cncl member voted 11-6, 904E3
'78 median family income, poverty data rptd 11-24, 965F2
INS neighborhood raids curbed 11-26, 924C1
Govt constructn grants case argued before Sup Ct 11-27, 945B1
HISPANICS for Nixon
Hidalgo link rptd 9-18, 700D3
HISQUIERDO v. Hisquierdo
Sup Ct excludes rail pensn from divorce pact 1-22, 54A1
HISTORIC Buildings & Sites
Iona island rptd for sale 3-23, 268C2; purchased 5-4, 407E1
Rome Palace of Sens bombed 4-20, 313F1-C2
Baker Hotel in Dallas closes 8-31, 887B2
Biddle sets preservatn trust retiremt 9-12, 892C2
US seeks pollutn protectn 9-7, 703B3
Canada's Rideau Club burns 10-23, 834A1
HISTORIC Preservation, National Trust for
Biddle sets retiremt 9-12, 892C2
HISTORY & Historiography
Awards & Honors
Davis wins Natl Book Award 4-23, 356B2
Pulitzer Prizes Awarded 4-16, 336C2
Obituaries
Elliott, Wm Yandell 1-9, 104A3
HITLER, Adolf (1889-1945)
W Ger arrests more neo-Nazis 2-10—2-11, 137B2
Apartheid compared 8-1, 617E1, A2
USSR seizes US books 9-4, 690D1

1980

HIMALAYAS, The
Acid rain rptd centuries old 9-18, 716E2
HINAULT, Bernard
Drops out of Tour de France 7-9, 835E1
HINDS, Lennox S.
At anti-US conf in Iran 6-2—6-5, 418D2, 419D1
HINERFELD, Ruth
On pres debate controversy 9-10, 680E3
HINES, Henry
TAC OKs paid amateur meets, ATFA formatn cited 6-28, 891C3
HINES, Tommy Lee
Rape convictn overturned 3-18, 215E2-A3
Declared unfit for retrial 11-21, 927E1
HINKLE, Lon
3d in US Open 6-15, 714F2
3d in PGA Championship 8-10, 714C2
HINSON, Rep. Jon (R, Miss.)
Reelected 11-4, 843C2
HINTON, Alan
Named NASL top coach 9-6, 1001A3
HINTON, Joan
In China govt post 231D2
HIPOLITO, Bishop Adrinao
'76 attack cited 1-11, 95B3
HIRAM Walker Gooderham & Worts Ltd.
Consumers Gas merger set 1-9, 19D1; OKd 4-8, 310E3
HIRES Jr., Charles E.
Dies 3-19, 279D3
HIRES Root Beer Co.
Charles Hires Jr dies 3-19, 279D3
HIRSCHHORN, Joel
Argues ctroom cameras case in Sup Ct 11-12, 882B2
HISPANIC Americans
Austin busing plan set 1-3, 5C3
Lee Way settles job bias suit 1-10, 17D2
US rights comm rpts jobless rate 1-15, 36D3
Tex witches' priest acquitted of murder 2-1, 238E1
US illegal populatn rptd 2-4, 147G1
Alamo occupied by radicals 3-20, 485A2
Amoco settles credit bias suit 4-29, 370B3
Latin immigrants to US surveyed 5-11—5-20, 396A2
Houston schl desegregatn suit filed 5-15, 559E1
2 die in Miami riots 5-17—5-19, 382B3
LA school busing plan ordered 5-19, 427E1
Sears Ala bias suit dropped 5-22, 485D1
Carter sees Fla ldrs re Cuba refugees 6-9, 439F1
Govt constructn grants upheld by Sup Ct 7-2, 510C1
June jobless rate rptd 7-3, 513A3
Tex aliens schooling ordered 7-21, 576C2
Crime study rptd 7-28, 654C3
Ariz alien case retrial declared 7-29, retrial sought 8-29, 713E2
Aug jobless rate rptd 9-5, 684A1
NY Times settles '74 job bias suit 9-17, 746B3
EEOC suits setld vs CF&I 9-22, Motorola 9-23, 746D3, F3
Chicago '79-80 schl enrollmt rptd 9-24, 724G1
Sept jobless rate rptd 10-3, 783E2
'79 median family income rptd 10-23, 824B1
Oct jobless rate rptd 11-7, 867D1
LA settles job bias suit 11-21, 962B3
Nov jobless rate rptd 12-5, 938D1
Boston settles US job bias suit 12-5, 962B3
Presidential Election (& Transition)
Kennedy visits Mex 4-28, 327D3
Dem platform planks adopted 8-13, 614F2, 615C1
Mondale notes support 9-18, 780D2
Mondale campaigns in Calif 10-3, Tex 10-26, 816G3-817B1
Kennedy stumps Tex for Carter 10-22, 817C1
Carter, Reagan TV debate 10-28, 814B2
Election results 11-4: cong 846B2, F3; state 11-4, 847B3
HISS, Alger
Dodds dies 10-25, 876C1
HISTORIC Buildings & Sites
Carter asks tax change 1-28, 70B2
Okla State of State message 2-19, 404C1
Acropolis rescue plan set 4-15, 285D2
Italy plans preservatn 5-20, 409A1
Fire destroys Mobile (Ala) landmark cafe 7-20, 576E1
Natl Historic Preservatn Act Amendmts clear Cong 11-19, signed 12-12, 981C2
Calif desert plan issued 12-22, 987C1
HISTORY & Historiography
Marxist denied Md faculty post 6-12, 638C3
Obituaries
Boyd, Julian Parks 5-28, 448C1
Johnson, Gerald W 3-23, 279F3
Jones, Howard Mumford 5-11, 448A2
Labaree, Leonard W 5-5, 448B2
Talmon, Jacob L 6-16, 528F3
Wiley, Bell I 4-4, 360G3
Zimin, Aleksandr A (rptd) 3-14, 280G2
HITACHI Ltd.
Canada min in Japan 8-2—8-11, 618B2
US unit convicted 11-5, 957C3
HITCHCOCK, Alfred
Dies 4-29, 360A2
HITLER, Adolf (1889-1945)
Ex-butler dies 3-17, 280A1
Assassinatn plotter dies 9-3, 756A3

1976

HIYAMA, Hiroshi
Quits as Marubeni chrmn, retained 3-3, 191B1
Arrested 7-13, Tanaka linked 7-27, 557D1
Indicted 8-16, freed on bail 8-17, 624A2
H.M.S. Pinafore (play)
Opens 5-16, 1014D3
HOAN, Tan
In US-Viet talks 11-12, 863A3
HOAN, Tran Quoc
United Vietnam interior min 7-3, 502E3
HOBART (Australian warship)
In Intl Naval Review 7-4, 488D3
HO Chi Minh (1890-1969)
Party post left vacant 12-20, 967D3

HOCKEY, Ice
Rangers dismiss Francis 1-6, Stewart 1-7, 56E2
Sovt tour ends 1-12, 56E1
Winter Olympic results 2-14, 159A2
NHL pres arraigned 4-22, 309B3
Canadiens win Stanley Cup 5-16, 404E3
Final NHL standings 5-16, 404E3
Canada wins Canada Cup 9-15, 736F3

1977

HIYAMA, Hiro
Lockheed bribe trial starts 1-27, 83D2
HMOs (Health Maintenance Organizations)—*See U.S. GOVERNMENT—HEALTH, Education & Welfare*
HOAN, Nguyen Cong
Rpts Viet jailings 5-3, 470G1-A2
HOBBS, Leonard S.
Dies 11-1, 952E2
HOBSON, Butch
AL batting ldr 10-2, 926F3
HOBSON, Julius W.
Dies 3-23, 264A3
HOCKEY, Field
Black elected to USOC post 4-29, 491A3

HOCKEY, Ice
NHL final standings, league leaders 4-3, 262G2-G3
WHA final standings 4-7, 310D2
Awards & Honors
Bowman named NHL coach of yr 5-13, 429G3
Lafleur named playoff MVP 5-14, 429G3
Ftorek named WHA MVP 5-23, 430F1
Bernier named playoff MVP 5-27, 430C1
Lafleur named Canada top male athlete 12-19, 1021E1
Collegiate
Union Coll coach resigns 12-23, players quit 12-27, 1021G1
Obituaries
Asbee, Barry 5-12, 452D2
Player & Executive Developments
Fighting Saints fail 164G1
Cleveland Barons rescued 2-23, 164D1
WHA Phoenix team folds, stars sold 4-1, 262G3
NHL Barons sale OKd 5-12, 430F1
Howe, sons sign with Whalers 5-23, 430D1
WHA to play intl teams 5-23, 430E1
Ziegler named NHL pres 6-22, 548B3
NHL-WHA 'expansn' proposed 6-24, 603D1
NHL rejects WHA merger 8-9, 644D3
WHA Oilers '76-77 losses rptd 8-17, 644G3
WHA 7-team schedule rptd 8-18, 644G3
Murdoch arrested on drug chrg 8-18, 1021E1
Baldwin named WHA pres 8-22, 1021D1
Rangers name Talbot coach 8-22, 1021F1
Rangers release Gilbert 11-23, takes PR post 12-6, 1021E1
Harris fired as North Stars coach 11-24, 1021F1
Players' agent sentenced 11-28, 1021A2
Records & Achievements
Esposito ranks 2d in NHL goals 11-30, 1021D1
Howe scores 1,000th goal 12-7, 1021C1
Winners
Wales Conf wins NHL All-Star 1-25, 104F1
Czechs retain world title 5-8, 430A2
Montreal wins Stanley Cup 5-14, 429C3
Quebec wins WHA title 5-27, 430A1

1978

HMOs (Health Maintenance Organizations)—*See MEDICINE—Insurance*
HOBAN, Russell
Mouse & His Child released 7-7, 970C2
HOBBIT, The (book)
On best-seller list 2-5, 116D3
HOBBS, Donald W.
Wins US Sen primary in Alaska 8-22, 682G3
Loses electn 11-7, 856B2
Electn spending disparity rptd 11-15, 898C1
HOCHHUTH, Rolf
Rpts Filbinger Nazi links 5-28, 477B3

HOCKEY, Ice
NHL final standings, statistical ldrs 4-9, 296C1, B2
WHA final standings, statistical ldrs 4-11, 296G1, F2, A3
Czechoslovakia ousts US rptr 5-1, 439C3
Awards & Honors
Lafleur wins Ross Trophy (NHL top scorer) 4-9, 296D1
Dryden, Larocque win Vezina Trophy (NHL top goalies) 4-9, 296E1
Kromm named top NHL coach 4-19, 458F2
Robinson wins Smythe Trophy (playoff MVP) 5-25, 458G1
Lafleur wins Hart Trophy (NHL MVP) 6-12, 458D2
Bossy wins Calder Trophy (NHL top rookie) 6-12, 458E2
Potvin wins Norris Trophy (NHL top defenseman) 6-12, 458E2
Gainey wins Selke Trophy (NHL top defensive forward) 6-12, 458F2
Goring win Lady Byng Trophy (NHL sportsmanship) 6-12, 458F2
Smith wins Hatskin Trophy (WHA top goalie) 7-6, 656C3
Tardif wins Howe Trophy (WHA MVP) 7-6, 656C3
Dineen named top WHA coach 7-6, 656D3
Guidon named WHA playoff MVP 7-6, 656D3
Keon wins Deneau Trophy (WHA sportsmanship) 7-6, 656D3
Nilsson wins Kaplan Award (WHA top rookie) 7-6, 656D3
Sjoberg wins Murphy Trophy (WHA top defenseman) 7-6, 656D3
Collegiate
Boston U wins NCAA title 3-25, 296B3
Obituaries
Clapper, Aubrey 1-20, 96E2
Player & Executive Developments—*See also 'Awards' above*
AHL ban on 1-eyed player lifted 2-2, 296E3
Blues fire Boivin, hire Plagar 2-16, 458B3
WHA OKs NHL entry bids 2-22, 296B3
Sanderson makes NHL comeback 3-15, scores 200th goal 3-16, 296D3
NHL Rangers sign WHA's Nilsson, Hedberg 3-20, 296F1
NHL top paid players listed 4-6, 296F3
Kings fire Stewart 4-20, hire Berry 4-21, 458B3
Murdoch fined on drug chrg 4-24, suspended by NHL 7-24, 656D3
Islanders owner sued 5-2; ct names fscl mgr 6-6, NHL OKs refinancing plan 8-10, 656B2
Shero quits as Flyers coach 5-22, OKs Rangers contract 6-1, 458G2
Neale quits as WHA Whaler coach, joins Canucks 5-26; replcd by Dineen 7-17, 656F3
Demers quits as WHA Stingers coach 6-7, replaced by Smith 7-27, 656G3
NHL North Stars, Barons merge; divisn shifted 6-14, 656F2
Howell named NHL North Stars coach 7-5, 656G3
WHA Aeros fold 7-6, 656G2
NHL Canadiens sold 8-3, 656A3
NHL OKs Rockies sale 8-9, 656B3
Pollock quits as Canadiens gen mgr vp, Grundman named 9-6, 991A1
NHL compensatn clause ruled illegal 9-18, 990D3
McVie fired as Caps coach, Belisle replaces 10-9, 991B1
Hull, Orr retire; careers cited 11-1, 11-8, 991D1-A2
Howell quits as North Stars coach, Sonmor named 11-18, 991C1
Kelly fired as Rockies coach, Guidolin replaces 11-23, 991C1
Sabres fire gen mgr Imlach, coach Pronovost 12-4; Inglis named interim coach 12-6, 991D1
WHA Racers fold 12-16, 990G1
Winners
Nordiques win WHA All-Star game 1-17, 76E3
Wales Conf wins NHL All-Star game 1-24, 76C3
Boston U wins NCAA title 3-25, 296B3
WHA playoffs 5-12—5-22, Winnipeg wins Avco Cup 5-22, 458G1
NHL playoffs 5-13—5-25; Montreal wins Stanley Cup, Robinson named MVP 5-25, 458A1
USSR wins world title 5-14, 458B3

1979

HITTING Town (play)
Opens 1-6, 292F1
HNATYSHYN, Ramon
In Canadian Cabt 6-4, 423F3
Vs N Amer energy mkt 7-26, 581A2
Petro-Canada breakup studied 9-5, 684E3
Warns US of oil export cuts 9-11, 706F2
On gas export price hike 10-5, 788G3
Grafftey gets science post 10-8, 789B1
Petro-Canada stock giveaway urged 10-14, 812C1
Alberta oil price hike accord rptd near 10-22, 853A3
HOAD, Lew
Borg named '78 top player 1-18, 103G2
HOAN, Hoang Van
Defects to China 7-5; Hanoi, Peking confirm 8-6, 8-8, 604C1
HOANG, Vu
On Viet refugee policy 5-16, 379F1
HOBARD, Rick
GR Point opens 4-16, 711E3
HOBBY, Lt. Gov. Bill (D, Tex.)
'Killer Bees' disrupt Sen, pres primary chng in doubt 5-18—5-22, 594A3
HOBGOOD, William
Addresses UMW for Carter 12-13, 987D1
HOBOKEN, N.J.—*See NEW Jersey*
HOCH, Scott
US wins Walker Cup 5-31, 587A3
HO Chi Minh (1890-1969)
Hoan defects to China 8-2, 604D1
HOCKE, Jean-Pierre
Rpts Cambodia aid blocked 12-17, Pnompenh refutes 12-24, 977D3
HOCKEY, Ice
NHL, WHA final standings, statistical ldrs 4-8, 4-18, 355B2, F3-356E1
Awards & Honors
Trottier wins Ross Trophy (NHL top scorer) 4-8, 355G3
K Dryden wins Vezina Trophy (NHL top goalie) 4-8, 356B1
D Dryden wins Howe Trophy (WHA MVP), Hatskin Trophy (WHA top goalie) 5-16, 470E2
Gretzky wins Kaplan Award (WHA top rookie) 5-16, 470F2
Ley wins Murphy Trophy (WHA top defenseman) 5-16, 470F2
Nilsson wins Deneau Trophy (WHA sportsmanship) 5-16, 470F2
Brophy named WHA top coach 5-16, 470G2
Preston named WHA playoff MVP 5-20, 470G2
Gainey wins Smythe Trophy (NHL playoff MVP) 5-21, 447F3
Trottier wins Hart Trophy (NHL MVP) 6-12, 470B2
Potvin wins Norris Trophy (NHL top defenseman) 6-12, 470C2
Gainey wins Selke Trophy (NHL top defensive forward) 6-12, 470D2
Laroque shares Vezina Trophy (NHL top goalie) 6-12, 470D2
MacMillan wins Lady Byng Trophy (NHL) sportsmanship) 6-12, 470D2
Arbour named top NHL coach 6-12, 470E2
Smith wins Calder Trophy (NHL top rookie) 6-12, 470E2
Player & Executive Developments
West Pt recruiting abuses probed 1-4, 175B3
Hillman fired as Jets coach, McVie replaces 2-28, 470B3
NHL-WHA merger set 3-22, details OKd 3-30, 355G1, A3
NHL ex-pres faces Canada trial 4-26, 329F1
Creighton fired as Flames coach 5-3, McNeil replaces 6-7, 470C3
NHL reserve clause upheld 5-22, 448F1*
Cherry released as Bruins coach 5-24, signs with Rockies 5-29, 470C3
Kings, Forum arena rptd sold 5-30, 527E1
Johnstone replaces Pulford as Black Hawks coach 6-9, 470D3
Bowman quits as Canadiens coach 6-10, signs as Sabres gen mgr 6-11, hires Neilson to coach 6-20, 470G2
NHL expansion draft held 6-13, 470E1
K Dryden announces retiremt 7-9, 655A3
Imlach named Maple Leafs operatns dir 7-4, 655C3
Creighton named Bruins coach 7-5, 655B3
NHL entry draft held 8-9, 655F2
Belisle fired as Caps coach, Green replaces 11-13, 1004F1
Plager quits as Blues coach 12-8, Berenson replaces 12-10, 1004F1
Geoffrion quits as Canadiens coach, Ruel replaces 12-12, 1004E1
Bruins, fans brawl in NYC 12-24, 1004C1
Records & Achievements
Flyers break winning mark 12-22, 1004B1
Winners
Minn U wins NCAA title 3-24, 356E1
NHL playoffs 5-13—5-21; Montreal wins Stanley Cup, Gainey named MVP 5-21, 447E2
Sovts win Challenge Cup 2-11, 118F1
Sovts retain world title 4-25, 448D1
WHA playoffs 5-11—5-20; Winnipeg wins Avco Cup 5-20, 447F3

1980

HITZE, Dr. Karl-Ludwig
Scores TB vaccine study 1-20, 63A2
HITZIG, Rupert
Happy Birthday Gemini released 5-2, 416A3
HJORT, Howard W.
Scores planting amendmt 12-4, 954F3
H.L. v. Matheson
Case accepted by Sup Ct 2-25, 187G3
HOBGOOD, Norman
Dies 3-10, 279E3
HO-Bong Choi
Wins Olympic medal 7-20, 624D2
HOCH, Scott
Wins Quad Cities Open 7-20, 715D1
HOCKEY, Field
NCAA OKs women's title tourns 1-8, 103C3
Afghan team rptd ambushed 5-3, 349F2
UK indep Olympic boycott spreads 5-17, 379E2
Australia fed bars Olympic participatn 5-28, 421D1
Afghan team ambush detailed 7-15, 561G1-B2
Moscow Olympic results 7-29, 7-31, 622D3

HOCKEY, Ice
Winter Olympic results 2-24, 155E3
NHL final standings, statistical ldrs 4-6, 295D3, 296B1
Canada Cup tourn cancelled 4-30, 488B3
9 NHL teams' lost money in '79-80 5-7, 488B2
NHL adopts fight curbs 6-9, overtime rules 6-23, 488E1
Awards & Honors
Leach named NHL All-Star game MVP 2-5, 198A3
Dionne clinches Ross Trophy (NHL top scorer) 4-6, 295G3
Sauve, Edwards clinch Vezina Trophy (NHL top goalies) 4-6, 296A1, E1
Gretzky wins Hart Trophy (NHL MVP), Lady Byng (NHL sportsmanship) 6-6, 488B1
Gainey wins Selke Trophy (NHL top defensive forward) 6-6, 488C1
Bourque wins Calder Trophy (NHL top rookie) 6-6, 488C1
Robinson wins Norris Trophy (NHL top defenseman) 6-6, 488C1
Quinn named top NHL coach 6-6, 488D1
Obituaries
Smythe, Conn 11-18, 928E3
Player & Executive Developments
Ziegler suspends Bruins over NYC brawl 1-25, suspensns upheld 1-30, 198B3
NHL ex-press convicted in Canada 2-8, 148A3; sentncd 3-7, NHL compensatn rptd 3-13, 230G2
Mikita retires 4-14, 488G2-A3
Howe retires 6-4, 488E2
Stoughton declared free agent 10-3, 1000F2-A3
NHL players reject overtime 10-8, 1000D2
NHL '81-82 realignmt approved 12-10, 1000F1
Records & Achievements
Flyers undefeated streak ends 1-7, 198D3
Howe sets NHL All-Star point record 2-5, 198B3
Jets set NHL winless record 12-16, 1000E2
Winners
NHL playoffs 5-13—5-24; Islanders win Stanley Cup, Trottier named MVP 5-24, 487A3
U of ND wins NCAA title 3-29, 488G3
US Olympic team upsets Soviets 2-22, wins gold medal 2-24, 155E1
Wales Conf wins NHL All-Star game, attendance record set 2-5, 198F2

1976

HO Dam
On DMZ clash 8-18, 621C3
HODGES, John
Rpts export racket 7-8, 537D1
HODGETTS, John
Oppositn asks probe 11-25, 924B2
HODGSON, Peter C. L.
Dies 8-6, 892A3
HOEFLIGER, Jean
Tel Zaatar to evacuate wounded 8-2, 561C1
HOERNER Waldorf Corp.
Antitrust suit dvpts 2-18—10-5, 886C1, F2; Allen sentncd 11-30, 921F2
HOEVEN, Charles
Cited in Ford biog sketch 613F3
HOFF, Dierk
Testifies at Baader-Meinhof trial 1-27, 77B3
HOFFA, James R.
Teamsters pass resolutn 6-14, 436D1
Provenzano, Briguglio chrgd 6-23, 460E1
O'Brien indicted 7-7, 570D2
HOFFMAN, Maj. Gen. Carl
On Camp Pendleton KKK transfers 11-29, 983G1
HOFFMANN, Heinz
E Ger Politburo enlarged 5-22, 381E2
HOFFMAN, Karel
Named to Czech Presidium 4-16, 289A2
HOFFMAN, Martin R.
Studies W Ger tank purchase 2-12, 183C2
Reconsiders honor code review 6-2, 394E3, G3
US-W Ger tank accord set 8-4, 581D1
Offers expelled cadets readmissn, sets honor code review 8-23, 670D1
Chrysler wins tank contract 11-12, 941E3
HOFFMANN-La Roche & Co. A. G. F.
Milan chem plant blast area evacuated 7-10—7-28, 560C3
Milan blast dvpts 8-11—10-11, 840B3
Givaudan pays blast damages 12-2, 932A1
HOFFMEISTER, Gunhilde
Wins Olympic medal 7-30, 576A2
HOFSTRA University (Hempstead, N.Y.)
Carter rally 10-28, 803A3
HOGAN, Fred W.
Carter, Artis convicted 12-21, 1015E3
HOGAN, Warren
Named to Australia econ advisory bd 9-14, 730F1
HOGE, James
Moderates pres debate 10-15, 782B3
HOGUE, Philip A.
Transport Safety Bd member 3-1; confrmd 4-12, 412F1
HOHENBERG, John
Gets Pulitzer citation 5-3, 352F3
HOHN, Siegfried
Signs Pa VW pact 9-15, 987F3
HOIST (U.S. warship)
In Intl Naval Review 7-4, 488D3
HOLBORN Oil Co.—*See COASTAL States Gas Corp.*
HOLBROOK, Hal
Wins Emmy 5-17, 460C2
HOLBROOKE, Richard
Sees Carter 11-29, 898C3
HOLCOMB, Luther
Succeeded in EEOC post 3-3, 186A2
HOLIDAY, Anthony
Arrested 7-29, 592D1
Bail denied 10-8, 794F1
Sentenced 11-19, Mashabela freed 11-21, 927E2
HOLIDAY, Billie
Record wins Hall of Fame 2-28, 460E3
HOLIDAYS & Special Events
US Space Exploratn Day proclaimed 7-19, 527A2
HOLLAND (Dutch warship)
In Intl Naval Review 7-4, 488C3
HOLLAND, Rep. Kenneth L. (D, S.C.)
Reelected 11-2, 830A4
HOLLAND, Robert C.
Replaced on FRB 5-28, 412F1
HOLLAND, Stephen
Wins Olympic medal 7-20, 575F2
HOLLANDER, Eugene
Pleads guilty 2-2, sentncd 5-4, 5-18, 384C3
HOLLENBECK, Harold C.
To face Helstoski 9-21, 725C2
Elected 11-2, 821B2, 830E1
HOLLINGS, Sen. Ernest Fritz (D, S.C.)
Seeks Sen majority post 3-5, 181F1
HOLLOMAN III, John H.
Moss threatens impeachmt 9-1, 868A3
HOLLOWAY III, Adm. James L.
On US, Sovt naval strength 5-5, 394F1

1977

HODGES Jr., Sen. Kaneaster (D, Ark.)
Apptd to Sen 12-10, sworn 12-12, 1005A3
HODGSON, James D.
Replaced as amb to Japan 4-21, 418G1
HOENLIEN, Malcolm
On conversion of Jews 5-13, 492E2
HOERNER Waldorf Corp.
Champion Intl takeover cited in table 880G1
HOF (Hall of Fame)—*See specific sport (e.g., FOOTBALL)*
HOFFA, James R.
Zerilli dies 10-30, 872B3
HOFFMAN, Henry L.
Sentenced 3-10, 203B3
HOFFMAN, Martin R.
Rules on cheating scandal 1-5, 40G3
Replaced as Army secy 2-11, 148C3
HOFFMAN, Paul F.
Scores Velsicol indictmt 12-12, 1007E3
HOFFMANN-La Roche & Co. A. G., F.
DNA patent order lifted 2-24, 184C2
HOFHEINZ, Mayor Fred (Houston, Tex.)
To retire, successor elected 11-22, 900B3
HOFMANN, Paul
Czechs detain 2-12—2-13, 114G2
Disputes Czechs 2-17, papers returned 3-1, 3-16, 220E3
HOFSTADTER, Robert
Endorses A-power 11-16, 936G3
HOFSTEDE, Albert
Elected Minneapolis mayor 11-8, 855F1, A3
HOFSTRA University (Hempstead, N.Y.)
Laurel in NBA draft 6-10, 584B3
HOGAN, Lawrence
Cited in Park indictmt 9-6, 688D1
HOGAN & Hartson
Suit urged re Vesco representatn 11-29, 980B3
HOGSHEAD, Nancy
Sets swim record 8-18—8-21, 828F3
HO Kwon Ping
Rearrested 2-12, 223C3
Released 4-29, 394F3
HOLBROOKE, Richard C.
In Hanoi talks 5-3—5-4, 333D1
In new US-Viet talks 6-2—6-3, 441G1
On Cambodia death toll 7-26, 590D2
Briefs Taiwan, S Korea on Vance Peking trip 8-26, 8-27, 664E2
In US-PI base talks 9-22—9-23, 824B3
In Viet talks 12-19—12-20, 976B1
HOLDEN, David
Found slain 12-7; 3 seized 12-15; spy group link hinted 12-31, 1019D1
HOLIDAY Inns Inc.
Trailways bus fares rise 5-15, 423A2
HOLLADAY, Thomas L.
US office opens in Cuba 9-1, 686A1
HOLLAND—*See NETHERLANDS*
HOLLAND, Kenneth
Dies 12-9, 1024B2
HOLLINGS, Sen. Ernest Fritz (D, S.C.)
Byrd elected majority ldr 1-4, 5F3
Votes vs Marshall 1-26, 52B3
FCC network probe suspended 6-30, 583F2-A3
In Argentina, rpts 'free govt', scores Admin 8-30, 670C2
Backs Panama Canal treaties 9-20, 755B3
HOLLOMAN 3rd, John H.
Backs Arctic Gas Alaska plan 5-2, 369D3
HOLLOWAY, Emory
Dies 7-30, 604B3
HOLLOWAY III, Adm. James L.
Sees unionizatn threat 4-19, 342E3

1978

HOD, Mordechai
Chrgs UK laxity in El Al bus attack 8-21, 638E1
HODGES Jr., Sen. Kaneaster (D, Ark.)
Votes for Panama Canal neutrality pact 3-16, 177E2
Votes for 2d Canal pact 4-18, 273B1
Sen primary results 5-30, 426B2
Pryor wins seat 11-7, 855G1
HODGES Jr., Luther H.
Faces Sen primary runoff in NC 5-2, 342A3
Loses NC runoff vote 5-30, 426C2
HODGES, Michael
Damien released 6-8, 619D1
HOEDEMAN, Co
Film wins Oscar 4-3, 315D3
HOEFFNER, Joseph Cardinal
3 arrested in kidnap plot 6-7, 439A3
HOERNER Waldorf Corp.
Indicted for price fixing 1-25, 67C2
Fined 10-13, 1005G2
HOEVELER, Judge William
Dismisses Zamora TV violence suit 9-26, 759F2
HOF (Hall of Fame)—*See specific sport (i.e., BASEBALL)*
HOFFA, James Riddle
Provenzano convicted in kickback case 3-25, 232F2
F.I.S.T. released 4-26, 619A2
Cited at JFK death hearing 9-27, 750F1
HOFFBERGER, Jerold C.
Vs Kuhn bar on Blue sale 3-3, 194F3
HOFFENSTEIN, Samuel
Gay Divorce opens 3-9, 760C2
HOFFMAN, Dustin
Straight Time released 3-18, 620A1
HOFFMAN, Jan
2d in world figure-skating title 3-9, 316D3
HOFFMAN, Sieglinde Gutrun
Arrested in Yugo 5-11, 439B1
Yugo bars extraditn 11-17, release rptd 11-18, 906G1
HOFFMANN-La Roche & Co. A. G. F.
Seveso '76 chem plant blast condemned by Italian panel 7-27, 689E1 *
HOGSHEAD, Nancy
Sets 200-yd butterfly mark 4-6, 780C1, A3
HOHENEMSER, Christoph
Power plant size, efficiency study rptd 6-2, 408E3
HOHLA, Dietmar
Shot 5-31, 439F2
HOLBROOKE, Richard C.
Says US neutral in Indochina feud, cites refugee problem 10-25, 830D1
HOLCROFT Covenant, The (book)
On best-seller list 4-30, 356F1; 6-4, 460B3; 7-2, 579C3; 8-6, 620A2
HOLDEN, John V.
Lynn convicted of extortn 12-14, 991A2
HOLDEN, William
Damien released 6-8, 619D1
HOLDER, Geoffrey
Timbuktu opens 3-1, 760E3
HOLDING, Clyde
Pol corruptn, land-deals chrgd; denials issued, probe barred 9-14, 771D1
HOLDING Companies—*See BUSINESS; company names*
HOLGATE, Danny
Eubie opens 9-20, 1031E1
HOLIDAY Inn (Greece, N.Y.)
Arson kills 10 11-26, 971B3
HOLIDAYS & Special Events—*See also country names*
NH flag lowerings stayed by Sup Ct 3-24, 221A2; stay extensn denied 4-24, 322G2
HOLLAND—*See NETHERLANDS*
HOLLAND, Judith
Mushier elected AIAW pres 1-11, 40C3
HOLLAND, Rep. Kenneth L. (D, S.C.)
Reelected 11-7, 852B2
HOLLE, Gary
Traded to Rangers 12-15, 1026E1
HOLLENBAUGH v. Carnegie Free Library
Case declined by Sup Ct 12-11, 981B1
HOLLENBECK, Rep. Harold C. (R, N.J.)
Reelected 11-7, 851B3
HOLLINGS, Sen. Ernest F. (Fritz) (D, S.C.)
Votes for Panama Canal neutrality pact 3-16, 177E2
Votes for 2d Canal pact 4-18, 273B1
Misgivings re FTC children's TV ad curbs rptd 4-27, 347A3
Textile trade amendmt OKd 10-6, Carter vetoes 11-11, GATT talks rift cited 12-22, 998E1
HOLLINGSWORTH, Marvin J.
Loses primary for Oregon gov 5-23, 406G2
HOLLOMAN, Frank
Rejcts King murder conspiracy 11-11, 898C2
HOLLOWAY, Barry
Rpts currency revaluatn 1-9, 192C3
Presents '78 PNG budget 2-22, 192G2
HOLLOWAY III, Adm. James L.
Backs 20-yr pensn optn 1-18, 53E1
Backs Nimitz-class carriers 2-23, 127B2
Replaced as naval operatns chief 4-5, 281A2
HOLLOWAY, Jean
Magic of Lassie released 8-3, 970B2
HOLLOWAY, Randy
In NFL draft 5-2, 336F2
HOLLOWAY v. Arkansas
Robbery, rape convictns reversed by Sup Ct 4-3, 309C1

1979

HOCQ, Robert
Dies 12-8, 1008C3
HODGE, Al
Dies 3-19, 272F2
HODGE, Martha
Deadly Deilah opens 7-6, 711D2
HODGES, Bill
Named top coll basketball coach 3-24, 290F3
Mich State wins NCAA basketball title 3-26, 238G2
HOEFS, Ursula
Arrested as spy 3-6, 180B3
HOFFA, James Riddle
House com suspects JFK death link 3-16, 204C3
House com cites final rpt 7-17, 538B1
HOFFBERGER, Jerold C.
Sells Baltimore Orioles 8-2, 619B1
HOFFMAN, Alexander
Scores USSR book seizures 9-4, 690G1
HOFFMAN, Dustin
Agatha released 2-8, 174C2
Kramer vs Kramer released 12-19, 1007F3
HOFFMAN, Jan
Wins Eur figure-skating title 2-1, 392B1*
3d in world figure skating 3-15, 391F3*
HOFFMANN-La Roche & Co. A. G. F.
EC comm '76 ruling upheld 2-13, 137B1
Vitamin A variant for acne rptd 2-14, 138D2
NJ unit ups women's pay 5-13, 482G3
Valium promotn scored 9-10, 734D3
HOFFMANN, Heinz
Acknowledges mil aid to Africa 5-23, 406E2
HOFSISS, Jack
Elephant Man opens 1-14, 292D1
HOGAN, Bosco
Portrait of the Artist released 4-21, 528D3
HOGAN, Marty
Wins natl paddleball title 3-18, 527B2
HO-Kwang Mao
Solid hydrogen rptd formed 3-2, 290C1
HOLBROOKE, Richard C.
Assures S Korea dissidents re rights 3-7, 389G3
China rptd vs plea on Viet refugees 6-16, 460G2
On slowed Viet tie talks 8-3, denies renewal 8-9, 607A3
Says Cambodia faces starvation 9-27, 741D1
Tours Cambodia refugee camps in Thailand 10-21—10-23, 824A1
On E Timor starvatn 12-4, 995A1
HOLCOMB, Sarah
Walk Proud released 6-15, 820F3
HOLCROFT Covenant, The (book)
On best-seller list 3-4, 173F3; 4-8, 271C2
HOLDEN, William
Fedora released 4-14, 528C2
HOLDER v. NRC
Case declined by Sup Ct 10-1, 768E2
HOLEVILLE (play)
Opens 12-4, 956B3
HOLGATE, Ron
Grand Tour opens 1-11, 292F1
HOLIDAY Inns Inc.
Trailways summer svc expansn OKd 7-12, 579B2
Ohio fire kills 10 7-31, 639F3
Trailways sale completed 8-21, Harrah's purchase set 9-4, 682C3-F3
HOLIDAYS & Special Events
Carter asks natl day for Rev King 1-14, 31G2
Kennedy backs day for Rev King 7-23, 560D1
ACLU sues vs Iowa cnty papal holiday 9-24, 760D3
Rev King bill withdrawn 12-5, 945B2
HOLLAND—*See NETHERLANDS*
HOLLAND, Brad
In NBA draft 6-25, 507B2
HOLLAND, Col. Leland
Hostage status disputed 11-30—12-1, spy trial threatened 12-1, 12-4, 914D2
HOLLEY, R. Eugene
Agrees to consent order 4-9, 305E3-306C1
HOLLINGS, Sen. Ernest F. (Fritz) (D, S.C.)
Votes vs Talmadge denunciatn 10-10, 769F1
HOLLISTER, John Baker
Dies 1-4, 104B3

1980

HODGERS, Silvia Mercedes
Sought in Somoza death 9-18, 697C3
HODGES Jr., Luther
Elected Natl Bank of Washn bd chrmn 11-15, 959C3
HODGES, Mike
Flash Gordon released 12-5, 972F3
HODGMAN, Michael
Australia home affairs min 11-2, 857F2
HOECHST A.G.
Iran unit takeover rptd 7-9, 546E2
HOEVELER, Judge William
Sentences ILA offcls, businessmen 1-11, 64F1
HOFFA, James Riddle
Fitzsimmons sentence rptd 2-19, 237A3
Wife dies 9-12, 755D3
HOFFA, Josephine
Dies 9-12, 755D3
HOFFMAN, Abbie (alias Barry Freed)
Interviewed by ABC, autobiog publshd 9-2, 713E2
Surrenders in NY; fugitive yrs recapped 9-4, 713G1
HOFFMAN, Dustin
Wins Oscar 4-14, 296G1
HOFFMAN, Sieglinde
Arrested 5-5, 411A3
HOFFMANN, Falk
Wins Olympic medal 7-28, 623F3
HOFFMANN, Jan
Wins Olympic medal 2-19, 155F3
Wins world figure skating title 3-13, 470B2
HOFFMANN, Karl-Heinz
Neo-Nazi group banned 1-30, 103A2
Detained re Munich bombing 9-29, 754F3
HOFFMANN-La Roche & Co. A.G., F.
Canada convicts re price-cutting 2-6, 116E2-C3
W Ger OKs tranquilizer prices 2-12, 154C1
'76 Italy blast accord rptd 3-26, 233B1
US unit gets tranquilizer warnings 7-11, 584G1
New Italy damage accord set 12-19, 995F1
HOFFNER, Cardinal Joseph
Greets Pope 11-15, 905C1
HOFSTADTER, Douglas R.
Wins Pulitzer 4-14, 296E2
Godel, Escher, Bach wins Amer Book Award 5-1, 692F2
HOFSTRA University (Hempstead, N.Y.)
ASL club moves to Shea 5-28, 771E1
Carter holds town mtg 10-16, 802D2
HOGAARD, Vern
Orders occupied Mex emb guarded 2-18, 152B1
HOGAN, Ben
Nicklaus wins PGA Championship 8-10, 714D2
HOGAN, Jonathan
Sunday Runners opens 5-4, 392G3
HOGAN & Hartson
Prettyman hired as Abscam spec counsel 2-13, 143F2
HOGOBOOM, Judge William
Synanon founder, aides convicted in rattler attack 7-15, 655F3
Grants Synanon founder probatn 9-3, 860D2
HOHL, Norma
Navy drops lesbian chrgs 8-21, 898G3
HOLBROOK, Hal
Fog released 2-29, 216E2
HOLBROOKE, Richard C.
In talks on S Korea 5-28, 430B3
Sees E Timor revolt over 6-10, 604D2
US to screen visits to ROK 6-12, 467E1
Mtg with PI oppositn ldr scored 9-20, 752B3
HOLD Out (recording)
On best-seller list 8-13, 640C3; 9-10, 716F3
HOLIDAY Hills
Hunts interest rptd 5-28, 426E1
HOLIDAY Inns Inc.
Harrah's gets temp NJ gambling license 11-1, 988D3
HOLIDAYS & Special Events
USSR bars US, French independnc day speeches 7-4, 7-14, 566B3
Sioux Falls (SD) schls case refused by Sup Ct 11-10, 868G1
HOLLAND—*See NETHERLANDS*
HOLLAND, Rep. Kenneth L. (D, S.C.)
Reelected 11-4, 844B2
HOLLAND, Michael
UN comm visit rptd 3-12, 178D1*
HOLLAND America Cruises
470 flee ocean liner fire 10-4, 769F2
HOLLANDER, Louis
Dies 1-3, 104A3
HOLLENBECK, Rep. Harold C. (R, N.J.)
Reelected 11-4, 843B3
HOLLINGS, Sen. Ernest Fritz (D, S.C.)
Scores Carter budget stand 5-28, 424C2
Reelected 11-4, 840C3, 845A3, 850D1
Defends '81 budget res 11-20, 896D2
HOLLINS, Lionel
Lakers win NBA title 5-16, 432G1
HOLLOWAY, Adm. James L.
On US hostage rescue missn 8-23, 644F1

1976

HOLLYWOOD, Fla.—*See FLORIDA*
HOLMES, David
Thorpe 'coverup' detailed 5-12, 365A1
HOLMES, Robert D.
Dies 6-6, 524G2
HOLSHOUSER, Gov. James E. (R, N.C.)
Hunt elected 11-2, 822D2
HOLT, Rep. Marjorie S. (R, Md.)
Reelected 11-2, 829A4
Loses Research Com post bid 12-8, 981E3
HOLT & Co. Inc., T. J.
Buys IMF gold 9-15, 739D3
HOLTROP, Marius
'51 Argentina bribes rptd 3-12, 254E3
HOLTZMAN, Rep. Elizabeth (D, N.Y.)
Dem conv rule debated 7-13, 513D1
Ford probe rejcted 10-15, 10-20, 784G3
Reelected 11-2, 830A2
HOLTZMAN, Ken
Traded to Orioles 4-2, 444B3
Martin vs Series scheduling 10-21, 815B2
HOLYOAKE, Sir Keith
On curbs vs S Africa sports 10-16, 910G2
HOME Builders, National Association of
Local-zoning referendum upheld 6-21, 453E1
HOME-Stake Production Co.
Trippet, others rptd fined 12-22, 1016D2
HOME Sweet Homer (play)
Opens 1-4, 1014B3

HOMOSEXUALITY
Anchorage anti-bias law passage rptd 1-3, 7D1
Vatican condemns 1-15, 124B2
Sup Ct bars review of NC convictn 3-29, 261E3
Sup Ct upholds Va ban 3-30, 261B3, C3 ★
Methodists rejct membership 5-5, 951G2
Dems reject platform plank 6-15, 432F3
Baptists vs ordinatn 6-15—6-18, 951E2
Rights rally in Phila 7-4, 489C1
Demonstratn at NY Dem conv site 513D1
AF sgts dismissal upheld 7-16, 944F1
Tenn bishop grants absolutn 12-5, 12-12, 951F1-B2

1977

HOLMAN, M. Carl
Blacks meet re govt 'neglect' 8-29, 702E1
HOLMES, Cheryl
Testifies on Korea lobbying 10-19—10-21, 816G2
HOLMES, John
Summa dismissal rptd 5-28, 472A3
HOLMES Trujillo, Carlos
Affirms '78 primary plan 8-17, 727E2
HOLT, Rep. Marjorie S. (R, Md.)
Backs budget target resolutn 5-17, 404F3
HOLT, Victoria
Pride of the Peacock on best-seller list 8-14, 643A2
HOLTAN, Richard Dean
Executn set 3-18, 594D1
HOLT, Rinehart & Winston Inc.
Rinaldi libel case refused 11-28, 919A3
HOLTZ, Lou
Suspends football players 12-21, bias suit dropped 12-29, 1020E2
HOLTZMAN, Rep. Elizabeth (D, N.Y.)
Scores budget targets 5-17, 405C1
HOLYOAKE, Sir Keith
Named NZ gov-gen 3-7, 222A2
HOLY Spirit Church (West Palm Beach, Fla.)
Secedes from Episc Church 10-2, 845G2-A3
HOLZER, Adela
Indicted 7-12, 10-13, 848F1
HOMAYOUN, Daryoush
Iran info min 8-7, 618F1
HOMESTEAD, Pa.—*See PENNSYLVANIA*
HOMICIDE—*See CRIME—Murder*

HOMOSEXUALITY
Sup Ct voids Washn dismissal ruling 1-10, 57A1
Episc lesbian ordained 1-10, 845C2
Rights group sees Carter aide 3-26, 278B2
Miss State U ad case review refused 4-25, 342C3
Navy ensign's dischrg upgraded 4-27, 344F1-A2
Child porno, prostitutn arrests rptd 5-15—5-27, 432G1
9 die in NY bathhouse fire 5-25, 429G2-A3
Miami rights law repealed 6-7, 446E2
Educ campaign launched 6-13, 560G2-B3
Gay slain in San Fran 6-22, 560E2
Rights marches in US, Eur 6-25—6-26, 560C2
Church of Christ scores bias 7-5, 642E2
UK editor fined for blasphemy 7-12, 617E3
Calif mass murder suspect indicted 7-13, 603F2
Dissident Episcs plan new church 9-14—9-16, 716D2
Gay teacher cases review refused 10-3, 760D1
Episcs condemn, ban ordinatn 10-3, 845B2
Milk elected San Fran supervisor 11-8, 855D3
US bishops score RC study 11-16, 906E2
Fla citrus comm renews Bryant contract 11-16, 927G2
Natl Women's Conf backs rights, conservatives rally vs lesbianism 11-19—11-21, 917B3, G3
Calif mass murderer sentncd 12-21, 991A3

1978

HOLLY, Buddy (1939-59)
Buddy Holly Story released 7-21, 969E3
HOLLY Sugar Corp.
'74 trust chrgs settled 6-12, 511C1
HOLM, Melvin C.
Spurns United Tech merger bid for Carrier 9-25, 896F1
HOLMES, David
Arrested in murder plot 8-4, 614C2
Thorpe faces 2d murder chrg 9-2, 688C2
Murder-conspiracy trial ordrd 12-13, 987E3
HOLMES, Ernie
Traded to Buccaneers 5-3, 336C2
HOLMES, John M.
Indicted on drug chrg 3-16, 459G1
HOLMES, Larry
Decisns Shavers 3-25, decisns Norton for WBC heavywgt title 6-9, 600A1
Ali decisns Spinks for 3d heavywgt title 9-15, 726C1
KOs Evangelista 11-10, 969A1
HOLMES, Robert
Named in US Teamster fund suit 2-1, 83E1
HOLMES, Tommy
Rose ties game hit record 7-24, breaks mark 7-25, 618F2
HOLMS, John Pynchon
Taudshow opens 3-24, 887D3
HOLOCAUST (TV film)
Broadcast 4-16—4-19, NBC rpts 120 mln viewers 4-20, 316F1
Bantam paperback sales figures rptd 316D2
Wins Emmy 9-17, 1030G1
HOLSTON, Rand
FM released 4-28, 619A2
HOLT, Ala.—*See ALABAMA*
HOLT, Fritz
Platinum opens 11-12, 1031F2
HOLT, Rep. Majorie S. (R, Md.)
Reelected 11-7, 851B1
HOLT, Will
Platinum opens 11-12, 1031F2
HOLT Civic Club v. City of Tuscaloosa
Cities' power over suburbs backed by Sup Ct 11-28, 937A3
HOLTON, Linwood
Loses Sen nominatn in Va 6-3, 467A2
HOLTZ, Lou
Named top coll football coach 1-21, 172A1
HOLTZ, Uwe
Accused of spying, smear compaign chrgd 8-31—9-6, 725C2
Spy probe dropped 9-26, 868A3
HOLTZMAN, Rep. Elizabeth (D, N.Y.)
Gets top consumer ratings 3-4, 183D1; 11-8, 981G2
Vs mil abortn fund curb 8-9, 604G2
Gets Cong Watch top rating 10-28, 865A3
Nazi deportatn bill passed 10-30, 872D2
Reelected 11-7, 851E3
HOLTZMAN, Ken
Traded to Cubs 6-10, 779B3
HOLZMAN, Red
Named Knicks coach 12-11, 1027E2
HOME, Alexander
Proposes revisn of House of Lords 3-20, 226E3
HOME Builders, National Association of
6-mo profit freeze vowed, other anti-inflatn measures backed 5-16, 362E1
HOMEMAKERS—*See also DOMESTIC Workers*
Mormon role for women affirmed 4-1, 907E2
Black, white female consumers compared 4-12, 812B1
HOMES, David
Newton testifies 11-27, 945F1
HOME Where I Belong (recording)
Thomas wins Grammy 2-24, 316A1
HOMICIDE—*See CRIME—Murder*
HOMINIDS—*See ANTHROPOLOGY*
HOMOLKA, Oscar
Dies 1-27, 96D2
HOMOSEXUALITY
Mo univ Gay Lib status challenge refused 2-21, 125C3
Fla upholds practice of law 3-20, 327C2
St Paul repeals rights law, 4 other city votes pending 4-25, 327A2
Wichita, Eugene repeal rights law 5-9, 5-23, 409D3
NC anti-gay rule review declined by Sup Ct 5-15, 387E3
Rabbinical ldr vs rights 5-18, 410B1
Presbyterian study backs ordinatn, Assemb bars 5-22, 409E3-410B1
UK MP arrested in murder plot 8-4, 614A2; **for subsequent developments, see THORPE, Jeremy**
Mil-dischrg policy chng rptd 8-21, 683E2
Okla gov denies campaign chrg 8-23, 683B1
Australia backers, police clash 8-27, 686C1
VD epidemic rptd 11-6, 992G2
Fla, Calif, Wash rights referenda results 11-7, 847A3, 849F3, 857A1, C3
Rev Jones sexual tyranny rptd 11-24, 911F1-D2
San Fran supervisor slain 11-27, 920A3
Mil dischrgs held unfair, review ordrd 12-6, 960A2
'74 Houston slayer's sentnc reversed 12-20, 992B2

1979

HOLM, Celeste
Utter Glory opens 5-13, 712C3
Paris Was Yesterday opens 12-19, 1007E2
HOLM, Ian
Alien released 5-24, 528A1
HOLM, Maj. Gen. Jeanne M. (ret.)
On female combat role 11-13, 868E2
HOLMAN Station, Ala.—*See ALABAMA*
HOLMBERG, Helena
Found dead 1-11, new autopsy ordrd 1-12, 117B1
HOLMER, Paul
Murder attempt seen 3-22, 228C3
HOLMES, David
Acquitted 6-22, 485E3
HOLMES, Jake
Songs From the City Streets opens 4-9, 712E2
HOLMES, Larry
TKOs Ocasio 3-23, 412A3
KOs Weaver 6-22, 838B3
TKOs Shavers 9-28, 838C3
HOLMES, Walter
Sees Natl Bank takeover hitch 3-19, 205E1
HOLMES Jr., Walter S.
CIT-RCA merger set 8-17, 682C2
HOLMESBURG Prison (Philadelphia, Pa.)
Inmates '60s drug tests rptd 11-25, 947E1
HOLOCAUST (TV film)
Broadcast in W Ger 1-22—1-26, impact noted 1-29, 137B2
Cited in Heim convictn 6-13, 490D1
HOLOGRAPHY
Gabor dies 2-8, 176A3
HOLSINGER, Joe
Loses US House electn 4-3, 265F1
HOLT, Rep. Marjorie S. (R, Md.)
Anti-busing amendmt defeated 7-24, 559B3
HOLTON, Thomas L.
Elected Peat Marwick chrmn 10-10, 851F3
HOLTZMAN, Rep. Elizabeth (D, N.Y.)
In Viet 2-21, visits war zone 2-24, 141A2
Chrgs Viet refugee bribe racket 2-26, 181F1-A2
In Pnompenh 11-12, 863F2
HOLZ, Ernest
Installed Salvatn Army natl cmdr 3-28, 272D1
HOLZER, Adela
Convicted of grand larceny 3-15, 239E2
Sentncd to 6 yrs 5-3, 431A3
HOM, William
Killed 9-23, 729E2
HOME, Lord
Blunt ID as ex-spy spurs controversy 11-15—11-21, 908E3
HOMELAND (play)
Opens 4-16, 711E3
HOMESTEAD, Fla.—*See FLORIDA*
HOMICIDE—*See CRIME—Murder*

HOMOSEXUALITY
Chicago man indicted in mass murder 1-8, 24G2
Daly companion sues estate 3-16, 289G2
Va inmate gets rape setlmt 3-17, 316E2
Masters & Johnson rpt 'reverse' therapy 4-16, book publshd 4-23, 315E3-316D1
Gay couple attend SD prom 5-3, 392C3
Thorpe loses Parlt seat 5-3, 337B2
Milk slayer convicted, San Fran protests 5-22, 386B1
Houston sex slayer convicted again 6-27, 819C1
Milk slayer sentenced 7-3, 547G3
FBI dir calls security risk 7-22, 561G3
Vatican criticism of sexual ethics book rptd 8-11, 640F2
INS lifts alien curb 8-14, 631G1
Calif judge sworn 9-17, 748C2-A3
Episcopalians bar ordinatn 9-17, 9-18, 755A2
Yeoman pleads guilty to espionage 9-25, 748A1; sentncd 10-26, 831A3
Army policy challenged 10-1, 850E3
Pope in US, affirms church stand 10-5, 759B2, E2
AF capt discharged 10-15, 850C3
Methodists uphold pastor 11-1, 931F3
UK ex-spy denies link 11-20, 909E1
Feinstein San Fran mayoral win, Scott endorsemt linked 12-11, 946F3
INS revives alien curb 12-26, 992B1
HOMOSEXUALITY in Perspective (book)
Published 4-23, 315F3

1980

HOLLYWOOD—*See CALIFORNIA*
HOLLYWOOD Knights, The (film)
Top-grossing film 5-28, 448G3
HOLMERTZ, Per
Wins Olympic medal 7-27, 623G2
HOLMES Jr., Cpl. George N.
Killed in Iran rescue mission 4-24, 321E2
HOLMES, Dr. King K.
Rpts VD-linked diseases 2-5, 158B1
HOLMES, Larry
TKOs Zanon 2-3, Jones 3-31, 320F1
TKOs LeDoux 7-7, 1000D3
KOs Ali, sets heavywgt KO mark 10-2, 771F3
HOLMES, Rupert
Escape on best-seller list 1-2, 40E3; 2-6, 120F3
HOLMGREN, Paul
Islanders win Stanley Cup 5-24, 487E3
HOLMS, John Pynchon
You Know Al opens 11-13, 892G3
HOLT, Rep. Marjorie S. (R, Md.)
On female draft registratn rejectn 3-6, 188D3
Reelected 11-4, 843B1
HOLT, Victoria
Tiger on best-seller list 6-8, 448D3
HOLTZ, Fritz
Perfectly Frank opens 11-30, 1003E3
HOLTZMAN, Rep. Elizabeth (D, N.Y.)
Refused UN Mideast vote info 3-12, Vance reaffirms exec privilege 3-21, 218A3
Wins NY US Senate primary 9-9, 682C2
Loses US Sen electn 11-4, 846A3, 848B3
HOLYOKE (Mass.) Geriatric Center
Life aid ordrd in 'Right-to-Die' case 1-24, 158E2
HOME (play)
Opens 5-7, 392B3
HOME Builders, National Association of
US aid moves scored 4-17, 286G1
HOMER, Winslow (1836-1910)
Painting sold for $1.7 mln 10-17, 997G3-998A1
HOME Savings & Loan Association—*See under AHMANSON & Co.*
HOMESTAKE Mining Co.
Calif gold deposit found; '79 US, forgn productn rptd 8-27, 685F2
HOMICIDE—*See CRIME--Murder*
HOMMOLA, Ute
Wins Olympic medal 7-25, 624G1

HOMOSEXUALITY
Ex-Army activist chrgd in murder 1-2, 18C3
FBI 'Miporn' probe rptd 2-14, 136A2
'Cruising' opens, draws protests; Gen Cinema contract dispute cited 2-15, 239F2
Penthouse publisher wins libel case 3-1, 239C2
Gacy convicted 3-12, gets death sentence 3-13, 214C1-C2
Methodists reaffirm stand 4-21, 413B3
DC Christian rally held 4-29, 348E3, 349A1
Navy sets lesbian probe 5-15, probe scored 6-13, 6-15; 6 rptd chrgd, '79 dismissal total 6-28, 517A3-E3
Army lesbian ordered reinstated 5-20, 428C2
Bryant files for divorce 5-22, 471D3
RI prom date upheld 5-28, 471C1
San Jose, Santa Clara voters reject housing, jobs referenda 6-3, 439F2
US Families Conf opens in Baltimore 6-5, 442C3; meets in Minn 6-19—6-21, LA 7-10—7-12, 601A2, E2
US backs entry bar repeal 6-20, 2000 Cubans await processing 7-7, 514G2-D3
Evangelical Christian pol actn profiled 7-11—9-15, 818E3, 819B1
Calif 'freeway murder' suspects chrgd 7-29, 654D2
Flynn biographer sued 8-1, 639F1
ABA rejects alien rights proposal 8-6, 744G1
San Fran OKs at-large vote 8-19, 632B3
Bryant divorce rptd 8-21, 639C1
Navy drops lesbian chrgs vs 4 8-21; actn vs 4 others cited 898F3
Eagleton niece, atty convicted of extortn 10-24, 890C1
Navy dismissals upheld 10-24, 898D3
Bauman loses reelectn 11-4, 846B2
Matlovich AF reinstatemt ordered 11-9, setlmt reached 11-24, 962G1
Gay rights stand cited re Toronto mayor's defeat 11-11, 900D3

1976

HONDA Motor Co., Ltd.
US ends car dumping probe 5-4, 321D2
Oct US sales rptd 11-3, 885A3
HONDURAS—*See also IDB, OAS, SELA*
Pol parties back '79 const rule 1-6, internal disputes rptd 1-11, 55B2
Listed as 'partly free' 1-19, 20C3
Earthquake hits 2-4, 81A1, C2
Forgn min sees Kissinger in CR 2-24, 177B1
Total IMF oil loan rptd 4-1, 340C2
El Salvador border clashes 7-14—7-22; DMZ OKd 8-12, arbitratn set 10-6, 975F2
Becker confrmd US amb 9-8, 807E3
Hosts Guatemala-Belize talks 10-26—10-28, 977G3
United Brands details '74 bribe 12-10, 985C3

HONECKER, Erich
Addresses SED Cong 5-18, named secy gen 5-22, 381C1, E2
In W Ger border talks 8-12, 630C3
Tito cancels visit 9-16, 734G2
Elected state head, Defns Cncl chrmn 10-29, 889C1

HONEST Pleasure (race horse)
2d in Kentucky Derby 5-1, 336F2
HONEY (record album)
Wins Grammy 2-28, 460B3
HONEYWELL Inc.
SEC lists paymts 5-12, 727F1
'74 zero tax paymt rptd 10-2, 847G1
HONG Kong (British colony)—*See also ADB*
Natls quit S Vietnam 1-3, 11G3
Airways dir quits re Lockheed bribe 2-11, 132G2
Canada immigratn rptd 11-3, 851E1
Canada Anglicans ordain women 11-29, 932C1

HONI, Maj. Abdul Moneim al-
Italy seized Libyan plotters 3-6, 205B2
HONORIO Bareto (Portuguese warship)
In Intl Naval Review 7-4, 488C3
HOOGENDIJK, Ferry
Admits Gulf paymts 1-11, 134A2

1977

HONDA Motor Co., Ltd.
1st ¼ US import rank, '76 sales rise rptd 4-11, 463E3
Plans Ohio motorcycle plant 10-11, 859E2
Hikes US prices 11-24, 932F3
HONDURAS—*See also IDB, OAS*
UN Assemb member 4A1
100 pol prisoners rptd 1-1, 3G1
Mil staff shuffled 1-3, coup threat disputed 1-6, 1-8, 45E1
US disputes Israel arms sales 1-14, deal OKd 1-16, 28G2
Melgar backs Panamanian Canal demands 1-18, 46F1
'75-76 trade, paymts data; table 3-11, 189B1, A2★, B2
'66-75 arms transfers table 4-8, 415B2
'61-75 GDP variatns table 5-30, 439B1
Malaria upsurge rptd 9-4, 747D3
Melgar at Panama Canal pact signing 9-7, 678D1
Spanish king visits 9-13—9-14, 804G3
Nicaragua guerrillas begin offensive 10-12, 10-16, 802E1, E2
Brazil coffee policy backed 10-21, 876C3
Civilian 'plot' rptd smashed 10-29, 949E2
Oct plotters get amnesty 12-6, 970C1

HONECKER, Erich (East German head of state)
Backs travel curbs 2-22, 315D2
W Ger arrests spies 5-4—6-28, 602B2
E Berlin sovereignty statemt rptd 5-12, 496B3
USSR revolutn anniv fete photo 11-7, 865C2
HONEGGER, Fritz
Elected Swiss econ min 12-7, 1018E1
HONEYWELL Inc.
French left seeks natlizatn 5-17, 543B1
On Arab boycott list 6-19, 511D3
HONGISTO, Richard D.
Police dispute ends 12-16, 1005G1

HONG Kong (British colony)
'76 Taiwan trade data rptd 1-12, 139F3
'76 econ growth rptd 2-16, 147C2, G2
US modifies duty-free list 2-28, 189E3
Canada '76 emigratn rptd 4-13, 389D2
Viet refugees barred 6-8, 497A2
US-UK air svc pact set 6-22, 500F1
Drought, water rationing rptd 7-7, 660F1
'76 China trade cited 8-11, 635F3
Marcos plotters escape 10-1, 803B3
Canada textile quotas scored 10-4, 780C3
Police corruptn probe spurs violence, strike threats 10-28—12-7; limited amnesty granted 11-5, UK scores 11-24, 936B1
2d in China forgn trade 11-7, 882D3
Australia livestock banned 11-23, 922G3
EC textile pact 12-3, 998C1

HONOLULU, Hawaii—*See HAWAII*
HONOURABLE Schoolboy, The (book)
On best-seller list 11-6, 872C3; 12-4, 1021G2
HON Sui Sen
Backs ASEAN-West econ ties 6-29, 537E1
HOOD, Robin
Wins Pulitzer Prize 4-18, 355A3
HOOK, Sidney
Scores Califano on quotas 3-31, 235E2

1978

HONDA Motor Co. Ltd.
'78 US import price hike rptd 7-17, 665E1
HONDURAS—*See also IDB, OAS*
Pol parties resume activities, score electn law 1-1; peasant ldr sets pres bid 1-20, 94D3
Army officers sentncd in '75 land reform murders 2-2, 194C2
Drug scandal breaks, mil ldrs linked; Interpol chief, others arrested 4-24—7-10, 614E3
Mil role in '75 Olandro massacres rptd 4-28, 614D3
2 new pol parties OKd, rightists rptd angered 4-28, 614D3
Army chief, 'mafia' head linked in land deal 6-9, 615B1
Melgar distributes campgn song 7-21, 615C1
Melgar ousted 8-7; junta vows to continue policies, respect liberties 8-8, 614A3
Junta retains 7 of 11 in Cabt 8-9, 691D3
Press freedom rptd by IAPA 10-13, 829A2
Foreign Relations (misc.)
Coffee exports to be withheld 3-10, 181B3
Amer rights conv enacted, ct formed 7-18, 828E3, 829C1
UN Assemb member 713F3
OAS Nicaragua censure vote abstentn 10-17, 839A3
Nicaragua guerrilla camp raided 10-26, 839D3
Nicaragua refugees arrive, UN unit vows aid 11-6, 883D2
Nicaragua pres sees mil ldrs 12-29, 1018D3
U.S. Relations
Melgar in US for med treatmt 4-24, 614D3
US banana cos admit payoffs 6-9, 615A1
Carter cites El Salvador border dispute 6-21, 489C3
United Brands pleads guilty re '74 bribe 7-19, 643F1
Boeing chrgd re payoffs 7-28, 642G3
HONECKER, Erich (East German head of state)
CP oppositn rptd 1-4, 1-10, 11B3
Comecon complaint rptd 2-21, 505D1
Lamberz killed in copter crash 3-6, 228E1
Seiffert defects to W Ger 4-21, 333A2
Churches score schl mil drills 6-25, 648B3
HONESDALE, Pa.—*See PENNSYLVANIA*
HONEY
Infant botulism from honey rptd 11-1, 948A2
HONEYWELL Inc.
Italy warehouse fire 5-12, 393G2
HONGISTO, Richard D.
Ouster as police chief prompts mayoral recall move 3-24, 663B2
HONG Kong (British colony)
Chinese urged to visit China 17B3
Freedom House lists as 'partly free' 44F1
Ex-policeman jailed, 9 disciplined 1-23, UK corruptn probe rptd 1-24, 189E3
US info leaks cited in Viet spy chrgs 1-31, 68E3
Laos, Viet reopen air lane 2-11, 140C1
US-Taiwan textile pact rptd 2-27, 140C3
'78 budget presented 3-1, 189G3
GNP '77 growth rate rptd, '78 forecast 3-1, 190C1
Australia '77 gold imports rptd 3-15, 208F3
Governor's term extended 3-23, 259B3
Hongkong Bank to buy Marine Midland 4-5, 263E1-A2
118 policemen dismissed 4-7, 19 indicted 4-10, 259G1
Canton flights to resume 4-9, 259B3
China OKs 'capitalist' bank methods 7-6, 532E1
Trade missn rptd in Japan 10-18, 798D1
Chinese emigratn up 11-11, 902C1
Bars Viet refugees 12-23, some land for treatmt 12-25, 997E2
Stock index graph 12-25, 1001E1

HONGKONG & Shanghai Banking Corp.
Marine Midland purchase agreed 4-5, 263E1-A2
HONOLULU, Hawaii—*See HAWAII*
HONORABLE Men (book)
Published in US 5-22, French versn appears uncut 11-19, 917F1-C2
HONOURABLE Schoolboy, The (book)
On best-seller list 1-8, 24D3; 2-5, 116B3; 3-5, 195D3
HOOD, Clifford F.
Death rptd 11-27, 972C3

1979

HONDA Motor Co. Ltd.
BL joint productn planned 5-17, 388B2
BL accord signed 12-27, 994E1
HONDURAS—*See also IDB, OAS*
Foreign Relations (misc.)
Nicaragua calls 'friendly' 1-9, 21G3
Nicaragua border clashes continue 1-19, 76B3
Nicaragua border fighting rptd 4-8, 269F2
Mex dispatches Latin missn on Nicaragua 5-21, 409C1
1,200 Somoza soldrs seek refuge 7-21, Nicaragua invasn plan chrgd 7-28, 573F2
UN membership listed 695E2

HONECKER, Erich (East German head of state)
Warns W Ger vs A-missiles 11-1, 880D3
Schmidt plans '80 mtg 12-4, 938F2
HONEST Pleasure (race horse)
Gen Assemb sets Travers Stakes records 8-18, 876G3
HONEYWELL Inc.
French unit, USSR in computer deal 3-27, 237A3

HONG Kong (British colony)
Budget proposed, GNP predicted 2-28, 169B2
Student enrollmt in US rptd 167D2; 5-11, 379E2
US-China direct mail svc set 5-25, 406B1
Chinese efforts vs illegal emigratn rptd 7-4, 524C1
Mondale visits 9-1-9-2, 660D2
Nixon stops over 9-15, 751G1
GDP growth estimate revised up, China immigratn cited 9-17, 730E2
MacLehose reapptd gov 9-25, 730C2
Aug trade surplus rptd 9-25, 730D2
UK seeks China emigratn curbs 11-1, 854A2
Indochina Refugees
Viet boat people admitted 1-19, land 1-20–1-23, 51D2
Viet refugee boat capt chrgd on passenger overload 2-4; ship gold cache found 2-7, 109C1
More Viet boat people arrive 2-6–2-7, 109E1
US refugee worker quits re morals chrg 2-12, 109E1
Viet ethnic Chinese asylum rptd 5-11, 379D2
Refugees arrive, total at 50,000 5-19, 37C2; 5-26–6-10, 436F1
2,600 refugees land 6-30, 495C3
Refugees seen aided by merchant ships 8-2; Viet origin shift rptd 8-5, smugglers sentncd 8-9, 626C1, G1, C2
US reps visit refugee camps 8-4–8-5, 607G1, C2
532 refugees arrive 8-20, 659B3
Mondale in refugee relief talks 9-1–9-2, 660A3
79 Viets land, total rptd 9-8, 764A1
HONGKONG & Shanghai Banking Corp.
US OKs Marine Midland purchase 3-16, 205C1
HONG Seun Hwan
Ousted as bank pres 4-13, 287C2
HONG Soon Yup
Ousted as bank pres, arrested 4-13, 287C2
HONICKER v. U.S. Nuclear Regulatory Commission
Case refused by Sup Ct 4-16, 303B1
HONOLULU, Hawaii—*See HAWAII*
HONOLULU Heart Study
Heart disease preventn study rptd 3-19, 219E1
HOOD, Bart
Convicted 10-21, 818A2

1980

HONDA Motor Co. Ltd.
US car plant set 1-11, 35F2
US prices hiked 7-2, 556E2
Canada min in Japan 8-2—8-11, 618B2
HONDURAS—*See also IDB, OAS*
Foreign Relations (misc.)
Cuban aid to El Salvador rebels rptd 3-27, 220D2
IOC rpts Olympic boycott 3-28, 259F3
El Salvador border patrol rptd 6-13, 462G3
El Salvador guerrillas seek refuge 8-1, 604C1
OAS office occupied 8-15, 708F1
El Salvador rebel ldr captured 10-14, 872G3-873A
El Salvador ties restored 10-30, 872C3
Government & Politics—*See also other appropriate subheads in this section*
Liberals win upset in assemb vote 4-20, 313E3
Paz cedes power to assembly; Suazo named chrmn, electns set 7-20, 564C2
U.S. Relations
US backs civiln electns; '80, '81 aid hikes rptd 4-20, 314B1
US lauds return to civiln rule 7-20, 564D2

HONECKER, Erich (East German head of state)
Mtg with W Ger chancellor postponed 1-30, 103E1
Warns W Ger re US policy 3-19, Schmidt seeks talks 3-20, 236B3
At Tito funeral 5-8, 339B1
Schmidt cancels visit 8-22, 642D2
Poland warning rptd 10-8, 761C1
Asks W Ger concessns, rejected 10-13, 794D3
Hints Poland interventn 10-13, 831F1
At Moscow summit on Poland 12-5, 929E1
HONEYWELL Inc.
US defense computer system rptd unreliable 3-10, 210B2

HONG Kong (British colony)—*See also ADB*
Gold prices soar above $800 1-2—1-18, round-the-clock trading rptd 1-7, 30F1-E3
'79 trade deficit rptd 1-28, 193E3
New budget proposed, current fscl budget surplus seen 2-27, 193C3
Chile pres cancels Asian tour 3-22, 231A1
Stock exchng merger set 5-27, 398B3
Viet refugees arrive 6-10, 476C1
Chinese illegal immigrant ban set 10-23, 855D2-C3

HONOLULU—*See HAWAII*
HONORAT, Jean-Jacques
Arrested 11-29, 922C3
HONORAT, LaMartiniere
Arrested 11-29, 922C3

1976

HOOKER Jr., John Jay
Loses Sen primary 8-5, 633G1
HOOKS, Benjamin L.
To head NAACP 11-6, 892A2
HOOVER, Herbert C. (1874-1964)
Carter cites '32 race 9-6, 664A2
Ford, Carter debate 10-22, 800C2
Carter cites slogan 10-29, 827F1
HOOVER, J(ohn) E(dgar) (1895-1972)
FBI counterintellignc cuts rptd 2-27, 248G2
Nixon tap depositn released 3-10, 184A1-E1
Sen com cites cong testimony 4-28, 330C3
Oppositn to Rev King rptd 5-5, 344A1
Callahan fired 7-16, 634B1
Kelley announces FBI reforms 8-11, 633B2, 634E1
FBI favors cited 9-1, 666E2
HOOVER, Mike
US team climbs Mt Everest 10-8, 876D3
HOPE (Ark.) Star (newspaper)
Ford endorsemt rptd 10-30, 827F3
HOPEWELL, Va.—*See VIRGINIA*
HOPI Indians—*See INDIANS, American*
HOPPE, Harley
Loses GOP gov primary 9-21, 804D3
HOPPER, Vincent
Dies 1-19, 56D3
HOPSON, Eben
Loses electn 11-2, 824E3
HORGAN, Paul
Wins Pulitzer 5-3, 352D3
HORI, Shigeru
Named house speaker 12-24, 1006A3
HORI, Taro
Rptd vs World Bank policies 11-22, 976E1
HORN, Kurt
Named in grain fraud 3-11, 247D3
HORN, Willie E.
Sentenced 2-4, 135F3
HORNBLOW Jr., Arthur
Dies 7-17, 716B3
HORNER, Jack
Loses PC ldrship bid 2-23, 188F2
HORNIG, Donald F.
Resigns 6-30, replaced 8-14, 640G3
HOROWITZ, David
Rockefellers on best-seller list 12-5, 972C2
HORROCKS, James
Uganda asks ouster 7-13, 515A3
Expelled from Uganda 7-17, 548E1
HORSEBACK Riding
Olympic results 7-25—8-1, 574C2
Meadowlands track opens in NJ 9-1, 680C3

HORSE Racing
John Loftus dies 3-23, 484F3
Eric Walsh buried 5-6, 524G3
3 fraud suspects rptd in Grenada 12-7, 925A2
Philip Iselin dies 12-28, 1015F1
Winners
Belmont, Bold Forbes 6-5, 424E3
Hambletonian, Steve Lobell 9-4, 716F2
Kentucky Derby, Bold Forbes 5-1, 336F2
Preakness, Elocutionist 5-15, 368G3

1977

HOOKER Jr., Roger W.
Replaced as Transport asst secy 2-10, 148C3
HOOKS, Benjamin L.
Leaves FCC 7-27, 583F2-A3
Blacks meet re govt 'neglect' 8-29, 702E1
Addresses AFL-CIO 12-13, 961E1
HOOPER, Capt. James (ret.)
Acquitted re Iran contract fraud 11-24, 942F2
HOOTON, Burt
NL pitching ldr 10-2, 926E3
In NL playoff 10-4—10-8, 807F1
In World Series 10-11—10-18, 806B2
HOOVER, J(ohn) Edgar (1895-1972)
Feminist surveillance rptd 2-6, 423E1
Chile loans blocked 6-28, 493A1
Wm Sullivan dies 11-9, 952D3
Cointelpro papers released 11-21, 940G3
JFK assassinatn files released 12-7, 943D1
HOPE, Bob
Bing Crosby dies 10-14, 872E1
HOPKINS, Bob
Fired as Sonics coach 11-30, 991C1
HOPSON, Eben
Scores bowhead whale quota 12-7, 936E3
HORMONES
Nobel won by Yalow, Guillemin 10-13, 951C3
Medal of Sci won by Guillemin 10-13, 951G3
Somatostatin made from bacteria 12-1, 1022G2
HORNBLOWER, Weeks, Noyes & Trask Co.
Plans Loeb Rhoades merger 10-27, 1004A3
HORNER, John Henry (Jack)
Joins Liberals 4-20, 304A1
Named Canada industry min 9-16, 725G2-A3
Bars Arab boycott list disclosure 12-15, 1010B2

HORSE Racing
Gulf + Westn plans Madison Sq Garden takeover bid 3-7, 275D1
Seattle Slew wins Triple Crown 6-11, NYS ownership probe rptd 6-16, 490G3
Secretariat's mare vanishes 6-25, rptd found by FBI 12-9, 971A2
Md Gov Mandel convicted 8-23, 652F1
Cauthen sets earning marks 10-24, 12-10; named top jockey 12-10, sportsman of yr 12-14, 970F2
Players' agent sentenced 11-28, 1021A2
NY vet indicted in horse-switch scandal 12-2, 971A1
Seattle Slew named top horse, other Eclipse Awards 12-13, 970F3
Obituaries
Levy, George Morton 7-19, 604C3
Winners
Arc de Triomphe, Alleged 10-2, 971G1-A2
Belmont Stakes, Seattle Slew 6-11, 490G3, 491D1
Kentucky Derby, Seattle Slew 5-7, 491A1
Preakness Stakes, Seattle Slew 5-21, 491C1

1978

HOOKER Chemical Co. (of Occidental Petroleum Corp.)
Hooker Chemicals and Plastics Corp.
Niagara chem dump site drainage aid offered 8-7, 703C1, E1
HOOKS, Benjamin L.
At Davis Cup protests 3-18, 251F3
On Sup Ct Bakke ruling 6-28, 482D2
Addresses GOP Natl Com 7-21, 568A2
On Carter mtg re budget 12-11, 980A2
HOOPER (film)
Released 8-4, 970E1
HOOTERS (play)
Opens 4-30, 760D2
HOOTON, Burt
NL pitching ldr 10-2, 2d in Cy Young vote 10-24, 928F1, G2
Dodgers win NL pennant 10-7, 779A1
In World Series 10-10—10-17, 799D3
HOOVER, J(ohn) Edgar (1895-1972)
Corruptn described 1-10, 15F1
Memos to Nixon offcls on Korea lobbying probed 3-21, 203C2
Kissinger: no memory of Korea memos 4-20, 280D1
Black ldr cited in FBI '64 memo on anti-King effort 5-29, 410G2
Presley offer to aid FBI rptd 7-14, 553G3-554A1
Cited at King hearings 11-11, 898E2
HOPKINS, Anthony
Magic released 11-18, 970A2
HOPKINS, Larry J.
Wins US House seat 11-7, 850E4, 853B3
HORMAN, Charles E. (d. 1973)
Book links CIA to death 9-12, 795E3
HORMONES
Brain protein study rptd 2-18, 334D1
Relaxin in males rptd 4-20, 334F3
Progestin pregnancy-risk warning ordrd 10-12, 948D2
HORNER, Bob
1st pick in baseball draft 6-6, 779G3
Named NL top rookie 11-20, 928A2
HORNER, John Henry (Jack)
MP retracts C$ speculatn chrg 5-24, 412G3, 413B1
Sets Arab boycott disclosure 5-30, 435C2
Econ Dvpt Bd member 11-24, 921B3
HORNER, Richard
Crucifer of Blood opens 9-28, 1031C1
HORN of Africa—*See DJIBOUTI, ETHIOPIA, SOMALI Republic*
HOROWITZ, Charlotte
Sup Ct upholds med schl ouster 3-1, 143D2

HORSE Racing
Canada sets metric conversn 1-16, 89C1
Seattle Slew syndicated as stallion 2-18, 539C3
Ky battles equine VD 3-15—7-13, 539D2
REA ex-chief sentncd 3-31, 310D1
Pineda killed, 2 other jockeys hurt at Pimlico 5-3, 539C3
Gilmour indicted for tax evasn 6-5, 539B3
Affirmed wins Triple Crown 6-10, 538G3-539A2
Forego retired 6-10, 539D3
NY vet convicted in '77 horse switch 9-21, sentncd 11-3, 1028F1
Va betting referendum rejctd 11-7, 847G1, 853F1
Affirmed named top horse, other Eclipse Awards 12-12—12-13, 1028B1
Obituaries
Burch, Preston M 4-4, 356C2
Winners
Belmont Stakes, Affirmed 6-10, 539F1
English Derby, Shirley Heights 6-7, 539A2
Kentucky Derby, Affirmed 5-6, 539B1
Marlboro Cup, Seattle Slew 9-16, 1028D1
Preakness, Affirmed 5-20, 539E1

1979

HOOKER Chemical Co. (of Occidental Petroleum Corp.)
Mich sues for pollutn clean-up 6-22, Fla abuses rptd 8-5, 597C2
USSR phosphorous deal rptd 8-5, 597F2
Mich dump suit settled 10-24, 808E3
Hooker Chemicals and Plastics Corp.
Niagara chem dump hearings, seepage known in '58 4-10, 4-11, 281B3
Niagara chem dump probes rptd 6-18, 597A2
NY chrgs in LI dumping 8-31, 665G3
Occidental Petroleum Co.
Calif chem dumping, well pollutn rptd 6-18; US, state probe 6-19, 6-21, 597F1
HOOKS, Benjamin L.
Sees Kennedy win, grudging Dem support 6-24; maps NAACP pol activism 6-25, 559D3
Backs Weber case Sup Ct ruling 6-27, 477G2
Maps NAACP intl role 9-9, closer black-Jewish ties 9-11, 677G1
Warns blacks vs PLO support 10-11, urges debate halt 10-17, 780F2, B3
Vs Connally on affirmative actn 11-26, 983A1
HOOTON, Burt
NL pitching ldr 9-30, 955G2
HOOVER, Clair
Cattle deaths near 3 Mile I rptd 5-20, 382G1
HOOVER, Herbert C. (1874-1964)
Phone monitoring claimed 10-21, 869C1
HOOVER, J(ohn) Edgar (1895-1972)
'63 death threat vs Oswald revealed 2-18, 166G2
FBI personnel rules rptd dropped 7-22, 561F3
Cited re FBI reorganizatn 8-8, 611C1
FBI admits '70 Seberg slander 9-14, 705B1
FBI hq name chng proposed 10-30, 886D3
Kissinger-FBI '50s link rptd 11-3, 870C2
Malcolm X neutralizatn plan rptd 11-5, 886B3
HOOVER Co.
Fuqua purchase bid blocked 6-11, 560F2
Fuqua drops bid 8-20, 664A2
HOPCRAFT, Arthur
Agatha released 2-8, 174C2
HOPE, Anthony
Prisoner of Zenda released 5-25, 820A3
HOPE, Capt. Herbert A.
On Navy 'sexist' language review 1-19, 89G3
HOPKINS, John
Murder By Decree released 2-8, 174B3
Losing Time opens 9-30, 956C3
HOPPER, Wilbert
Announces Arctic gas find 5-15, 405B2
HORGAN, Daniel W.
Quits in NJ HFA scandal 8-9, 747B3
HORIZON Corp.
Land sales scored by FTC 10-3, 903E1
HORMONES
Estrogen, uterine cancer link rptd 1-4, 23F1-A2; 1-31, 139E1
Anti-estrogen drug for breast cancer rptd 9-11, 736D1
Estrogen use linked to uterine cancer 9-14, 735A3
Pot use risks rptd 10-14, 972C1
HORMUZ, Strait of
Persian Gulf states meet on security 10-14—10-16, 804A2
HORNER, Bob
Contract dispute settled 6-4, 1003B1
NL batting ldr 9-30, 955D2, E2
HORNER, John Henry (Jack)
Scores Ontario anti-boycott law 3-20, 267B1
Loses electn 5-22, 377D2
HORN of Africa—*See DJIBOUTI, ETHIOPIA, SOMALI Republic*
HOROWITZ, Ronald
Peter Pan opens 9-6, 956G3
HORSE Racing
Spectacular Bid loses Triple Crown 6-9, 448G1
NYS license suspensn voided by Sup Ct 6-25, 540E1
Pincay, Barrera set earning records 10-6, 876F2
Affirmed retired to stud 10-22, named top horse; other Eclipse Awards 12-11, 1005B1
Obituaries
Minor, Audax 10-8, 860E3
Winners
Arc de Triomphe, Three Troikas 10-7, 876B3
Belmont Stakes, Coastal 6-9, 448B2
English Derby, Troy 6-6, 448B3
Flamingo Stakes, Spectacular Bid 3-24, 448C3
Florida Derby, Spectacular Bid 3-6, 448C3
Grand National, Rubstic 3-31, 448A3
Irish Derby, Troy 7-1, 876D3
Jockey Gold Cup, Affirmed 10-6, 876E2
Kentucky Derby, Spectacular Bid 5-5, 448A2, D2
Marlboro Cup, Spectacular Bid 9-8, 876G2
Preakness, Spectacular Bid 5-19, 448A2, F2
Queen's Plate, Steady Growth 6-30, 876C3
Santa Anita Derby, Flying Paster 4-1, 448D3
Santa Anita Handicap, Affirmed 3-4, 448C3

1980

HOOKER Chemical Co. (of Occidental Petroleum Corp.)
Hooker Chemicals and Plastics Corp.
NY sues re Love Canal dumping 4-28, 331C3
Love Canal dump health defects rptd 5-16; denies responsibility 5-21, 386D3-387D1
EPA proposes lindane curbs 7-3, 519C3
Love Canal relocatn aid enacted 10-1, 739E1
HOOKS, Benjamin L.
Warns re blacks' despair 5-29, 460F1-A2
Opens NAACP conv 6-30, 515D2
Sees black vote for Dems 7-6, 515B3
Addresses GOP conv 7-15, 533F3, 535A1
Addresses Dem conv 8-13, 611E3
On electn results 11-4, 846G3
Meets with Reagan 12-11, 956C2, E2
HOOSIER, Harlan
Dies from boxing injury 1-18, 907E3
HOOVER, Herbert C. (1874-1964)
Named in Kennedy ad 4-22, 304E1
Jackson warns Dems 5-22, 399E3
Anderson likens Carter 6-6, 437B3
Carter pres nominatn acceptance speech 8-14, 613A3
Carter precedent cited 11-4, 837G1
HOOVER, J(ohn) Edgar (1895-1972)
'63 KKK church bombing prosecutn rptd blocked 2-18, 227C2
2 FBI ex-offcls convicted 11-6, 884C2
HOOVER, Orval
Ohio judge acquitted of sex-bartering 6-13, 503D2
HOOVER, Dr. Robert
On saccharin cancer risk 3-6, 317G1, B2
HOPE, Bob
Joins Reagan campaign windup 11-3, 840A3
HOPKINS, Anthony
Elephant Man released 10-3, 836F2
Change of Seasons released 12-17, 1003G1
HOPKINS, Rep. Larry J. (R, Ky.)
Reelected 11-4, 842E4
HOPPER, Wilbert
On Canada oil plan oppositn 11-5, 871B3
HOPSCOTCH (film)
Released 9-26, 836B3
Top-grossing film 10-1, 796G3; 12-3, 948G3
HO Pyong Li
Wins Olympic medal 7-31, 624D3
HORMONES
Long jump champ denies steroid use 6-28, 891E2
EC bans cattle use 10-1, 737B3
HORMUZ, Strait of
Iran warns vs blockade 1-11, 29D2; for subsequent developments, see IRAN—Oil
Carter cites US defns policy 1-23, 42F2
HORNER, Bob
NL batting ldr 10-6, 926E2
HORNER, Richard
A Life opens 11-3, 892G2
HORODINCA, Christina
Hospitalized 3-3, asks US asylum 3-6, 221C1
HORODINCA, Nicolae Ion
Defects 2-24, 142A3
Wife hospitalized 3-3, asks asylum 3-6, 221C1
HOROVITZ, Israel
Sunday Runners opens 5-4, 392G3
HOROWITZ, Vladimir
Wins Grammy 2-27, 296F3
HOROWITZ and Mrs. Washington (play)
Opens 4-2, 392C3
HOROWITZ Concerts 1978/79, The (recording)
Horowitz wins Grammy 2-27, 296F3
HORROCKS, Ray
BL strike ends 4-21, 313G1
HORSEBACK Riding
UK indep Olympic boycott spreads 5-17, 379E2
Moscow Olympic results 7-27—8-3, 622F2-A3
HORSE Racing
Gilmour reinstated 1-30, 447C3
Spectacular Bid sets stud price, winnings marks 3-11, 6-8, 447E3
Splendid Girl sets speed record 5-14, 447D3
Errico convicted of race fixing 5-19, 447A3
Hunts bailout loan collateral listed 5-28, 425D3, 426B1
Jacobson flees jail 5-31, sentenced for murder 6-3, 502A2
Jacobson recaptured 7-9, 997D2
Spectacular Bid named top horse; other Eclipse Awards 12-17, 1002C2
Winners
Belmont Stakes, Temperance Hill 6-7, 447E2
English Derby, Henbit 6-4, 448A1
Flamingo Stakes, Superbity 3-5, 447F3
Grand Natl Steeplechase, Ben Nevis 3-29, 448A1
Kentucky Derby, Genuine Risk 5-3, 447A2
Preakness, Codex 5-17, 447C2
Santa Anita Derby, Codex 3-30, 447G3
Widner Handicap, Private Account 3-1, 447F3
Wood Memorial, Plugged Nickle 4-19, 448A1

1976

HORTA, Jose Ramos
In UN Timor debate 4-12, 334G3
HORTON, Rep. Frank (R, N.Y.)
Reelected 11-2, 830D2
HORTON, Jack
Named to Lockheed probe 2-5, 131D2
HORWOOD, Owen
Presents budget 3-31, 429A1
HOSENBALL, Mark
UK orders expulsn 11-15, 946B2
HOSPITAL Association, American (AHA)
'75 hospital admissns down 1-14, 32G1
HOSPITAL Corp. of America
SEC lists forgn paymts 5-12, 727F1
HOSPITAL and Health Care Employees, National Union of (AFL-CIO)
NYC strike 7-7—7-17, 553E2
HOSPITALS—*See under MEDICINE*

HOSS, Selim al-
Named premr 12-8, forms Cabt 12-9, 913C2
Newspaper seizure protested 12-17, 953D2
Parlt OKs decree rule 12-24, 974B1

HOSSAIN, Shah Moazzem
Arrested 11-29, 923E2
HOTCHNER, A. E.
Doris Day on best seller list 208F3; 12-5, 972B2
HOT Chocolate (song group)
You Sexy Thing on best-selling list 1-28, 104G3
HOTEL and Restaurant Employees and Bartenders International Union (AFL-CIO)
Myra Wolfgang dies 4-12, 316D1
Miami Beach hotels struck 12-25—12-31, 991E2
HOTELS & Motels
Neb hotel blast 1-10, 80F1
Moon buys New Yorker 5-12, 971D1
9 cos indicted 11-17, 989E2
Miami Beach strikes 12-25—12-31, 991E2
HO Tsu-cheng
Cited in Mao biog 659G1
HOUCK, F. Bryan
Indictment dropped 10-25, 939D1
HOUGHTON, Maj. Gen. Kenneth J.
Drops chrgs in McClure death 8-18, 942A2
HOUGHTON, Robert
Meets Leb Christn ldrs 8-22—8-24, 628E3
HOUGHTON Mifflin Co.
US files consent decree 7-27, 989A2
HOUMAYYAD, Vice Marshal Outhman al-
OKs Saudi Golan exit 10-3, 738B2

HOUPHOUET-Boigny, Felix
Shuffles Cabinet 3-4, 594D2
At Zambia mtg on Rhodesia 3-24—3-25, 240E2
At France-Africa summit 5-10—5-11, 355G2
HOUSEHOLD Finance Corp.
National Car Rental System Inc.
FTC trust suit setld 7-12, 989A3

1977

HORVITZ, Wayne L.
Coal strike begins 12-6, 937E1
HORWOOD, Owen
Sets sales tax hike 3-7, 242F1
Presents S Africa budget 3-30, 284G3
Backs A-bomb 8-30, 663F3
HOSENBALL, Mark
UK confirms ouster 2-16, 134A2
Leaves for US 5-27, 526C3
HOSPITAL Association, American (AHA)
Carter cost-cutting plan scored 4-26, 322G1
Gehrig scores Admin cost policy 5-24, 479F1
HOSPITALS—*See under MEDICINE*

HOSS, Selim al-(Lebanese premier)
Sees Sarkis on Christn hq blast 1-4, 2F1
On war reconstructn 1-10, 28D2
Moscow hotel blaze 2-25, 204C2
Iran, Pak, Turkey sign pact 3-12, 190C2
Asks calm in Jumblat death 3-16, 188F1
Sees US amb; vs Israel shelling, PLO troop mass 6-16, 510C2
Sees US aide on fighting 9-17, 714B3
Asks Israel halt interventn 10-12, 793G2
Scores Israeli raid 11-10, 849B2

HOSSAIN, Shah Moazzem
Arrested 10-13, 805G2
HOTEL and Restaurant Employees and Bartenders International Union (AFL-CIO)
Bramlet found slain 3-17, US sues to protect pensn fund 3-30, 261C3
HOTELS & Motels
Tex hotel fire 4-19, 508G3
Amsterdam hotel blaze 5-9, 604B2
4 Hawaii hotels fined for rate-fixing 5-11, 504C2
Mafia infiltration rptd 5-16, 568E1
Brussels fire kills 15 5-22, 429B3
Miami gay rights law repealed 6-7, 446F2
USSR hotel blast arrest rptd 7-7, 564G2
Las Vegas hotel Teamster loan rptd 7-18, 558C2
Flood hits Kansas City hotel 9-12—9-13, 768D3
Manila (Pl) hotel burns 11-14, 928E3
HOT Rod Association, International—*See AUTOMOBILE Racing*
HOUGHTON, Brenda (Brenda Jones)
Kenya ousts 4-13, 393E1
HOUGHTON, Phillip W.
Age bias case refused 11-28, 919D2

HOUPHOUET-Boigny, Felix (Ivory Coast president)
Meets PLO reps 1-25; briefs Rabin 2-4, Rabin rpts 2-5, 86B3
Sees Young 5-12, 398C3
Sees Vorster 5-22, 398F1
HOURANI, Mohammed Munir
Convicted 6-2, executed 6-13, 457B3
HOUSE of Representatives—*See under U.S. GOVERNMENT*
HOUSEWRIGHT, James T.
Dies 9-19, 788C1

1978

HORTA, Adolfo
Wins World Amateur Boxing tourn 5-6—5-20, 600E2
HORTA, Basilio
Sworn Portugal trade, tourism min 1-30, 91C3
Quits Cabt 7-24, govt falls 7-27, 593F2
HORTON, Rep. Frank (R, N.Y.)
Sees consumer agency goal dead 2-8, 82E2
Reelected 11-7, 851A4
HORTON, John
Rear Column opens 11-19, 1031A3
HORVITZ, Wayne L.
Postal pact reached 7-21, 564F2
Postal talks resumed 8-28, 766C1
HORWITZ, Murray
Ain't Misbehavin opens 5-9, 760A1 ★
HORWOOD, Owen
Presents '78 budget 3-29, 249B2
HOSHINO, Naoki
Dies 5-29, 440G2
HOSIERY
Hanes purchase by Consolidated Foods set 9-14, 717G3
HOSPITAL Association, American (AHA)
Rpts surplus beds 3-21, 577G2
Carter health plan backed 7-29, 586E2
HOSPITAL Corp. of America
MacNaughton named chrmn, chief exec 6-28, 809A1
SEC sues re paymts, setld 10-26, 876E3-877C1
HOSPITAL & Health Care Employees, National Union of (AFL-CIO)
S Africa investmt barred 1-29, 135G1
HOSPITALS—*See under MEDICINE*
HOSPITALS, Federation of American
US cost guideline scored 12-28, 1012G1
HOSS, Selim al-(Lebanese premier)
Meets Arafat 3-31; Leb truce vowed 4-1, 236G1
Vs Israel Leb pullback plan 4-8, 256F2
Resigns 4-19, 299E3
Renamed premr to form unity govt 4-28; rpts failure, old Cabt reinstated 5-15, 359D1
Negotiates PLO exit pact 5-24, 400A3
Moslems vs Leb troops in south 6-4, 462D3
Vs Haddad role in south 6-14, 462D2
Heads Arab summit delegates 11-4; Egypt press scores 11-5, 859D2
HOSTETLER, Dave
USC wins NCAA baseball title 6-8, 560A2
HOT Child in the City (recording)
On best-seller list 10-11, 800E3; 11-8, 888C1
HOTEL California (recording)
Wins Grammy 2-24, 315E3
HOTEL, Hospital, Nursing Home and Allied Health Services Union (of Service Employes International Union)(AFL-CIO)
NYC nursing home strike 4-4—4-7, 284F3-285A1
HOTEL and Restaurant Employees and Bartenders International Union (AFL-CIO)
Top-paid US labor ldrs rptd 2-20, 5-15, 365F1, G1, A2
HOTELS & Motels
Mo hotel fire kills 16 1-28, 212B3
ERA boycott scored 3-20, 494A3
Teamster convicted in kickback case 3-25, 232C2
Brittany oil spill suit filed 749F1
Quebec cuts sales tax 4-11, 286B3
Loews buys 3 NYC hotels 5-31, 404G1
S Africa apartheid eased 6-4, 536A2
Sweden fire kills 20 6-10, 460G1
Pa arson kills 11 11-5, 971C3
NY newspaper strike ends 11-6, 865G1
NY Holiday Inn arson kills 10 11-26, 971B3
Philippe dies 12-25, 1032D3
HOTEL Woodstock (N.Y., N.Y.)
Teamster convicted in kickback case 3-25, 232C2
HOT Springs, Va.—*See VIRGINIA*
HOUCHINS, Sheriff Thomas L.
Press prison-data access curbed by Sup Ct 6-26, 566A3
HOUCHINS v. KQED
Press prison-data access curbed by Sup Ct 6-26, 566G2-D3
HOUGH, John
Return From Witch Mt released 7-14, 970G2
Brass Target released 12-21, 1030E2
HOUK, Ralph
To retire as Tigers mgr 9-21, 1026G1
HOULE, Rejean
Montreal wins Stanley Cup 5-25, 458F1
HOUPHOUET-Boigny, Felix (Ivory Coast president)
Giscard in Ivory Coast 1-11—1-15, 71C1
Backs French mil support 5-23, 382G2
HOURS—*See LABOR—Wages, Hours & Productivity*
HOUSE Calls (film)
Top-grossing film 4-26, 356C1
HOUSEHOLD Finance Corp. (HFC)
FTC chrgs lending violatns 7-7, 589F1
HOUSE of Representatives—*See under U.S. GOVERNMENT; for legislation, see U.S. GOVERNMENT—CONGRESS*
HOUSE on the River (painting)
Stolen from Chicago museum 12-27, 1028F3

1979

Travers Stakes, General Assembly 8-18, 876F3
Wood Memorial, Instrument Landing 4-21, 448C3
Woodward Stakes, Affirmed 9-23, 876E3
HORSES—*See WILDLIFE*
HORVITZ, Wayne
Mediates grain handlers strike 9-23, 722E3
HORWOOD, Owen
Sets rand float 1-24, 99G1
Presents '79 budget 3-28, 270F1
Erasmus comm clears Vorster 4-2, 270D1
Erasmus comm rpt clears 6-4, 427F3
HOSEA, Bishop Addison
Urges traditionalists vs successn 5-12, 375D3
HOSIERY
Sup Ct rules in Parklane case 1-9, 14B2
HOSPITAL Association, American (AHA)
Hosp cost-control bill scored 3-6, 163C3
'78 cost rise rptd 3-8; Sen hearings open, McMahon scores bill 3-9, 194F2
City hosps decline rptd 9-2, 970E3
HOSPITALS—*See under MEDICINE*
HOSPITALS, Federation of American
Bromberg scores cost control bill 3-9, 194A3
Carter cost-control bill defeated 11-15, 883C1

HOSS, Selim al- (Lebanese premier)
Christns chrg Syrians shell to undermine talks 1-13, 85C1
Arafat OKs Leb shelling halt 1-23, 69A2
Vs Christn militia 'secessn' 4-19, 277E3
Leb vs Israel peace bid 5-7, 341E1
Resigns as premr 5-16, 378F2
Asked to form new govt 7-2, announces Cabt 7-16, 671D1
Asks US press Israel on Leb raids 8-24, 643D1
Meets Jesse Jackson 9-28, 763D1
Sees Iran emissaries at Arab League summit 11-21, 916E2

HOSSEINI, Ayatollah Ezzedin
Kurd autonomy demands rptd 3-1, 145E2
HOSTY Jr., James
Reveals '63 death threat vs Oswald 2-18, 166E2
HOTCHNER, A. E.
Sophia on best-seller list 4-8, 271A2; 5-6, 356D2
HOTELS & Motels
Hilton dies 1-3, 104A3
CAB adopts new charter rules 3-1, 166C3
2 Boston hotel fires 3-29, busboy chrgd 3-30, 316C3
NJ hotel destroyed by fire 5-11, 572B3
Pl constructn in China set 7-8, 567D1
Spanish fire kills 80 7-13, 572F2
Ohio Holiday Inn arson kills 10 7-31, 639F1
Holiday Inns completes Trailways sale 8-21, to buy Harrah's 9-4, 682C2-F2
Nev casino skimming fines imposed 8-23, 851B1
Historic Dallas hotel closes 8-31, 887B2
Imperial Group to buy Howard Johnson 9-10; Calif bar seen 10-12, 924B3-E3
HOT Stuff (recording)
On best-seller list 5-30, 448E3, 7-4, 548E3; 8-1, 620E3
HOU Chia-mou
Taiwan wins Little League title 8-23, 797A3
HOUDAILLE Industries
Investor group to buy 4-2, 283B1
HOUGHTON Jr., Arthur A.
Sells Blake book for record sum 6-13, 672F1
HOULE, Rejean
Montreal wins Stanley Cup 5-21, 447E3
HOUNSFIELD, Godfrey Newbold
Wins Nobel Prize 10-12, 858E1
HOUSEHOLD Finance Corp. (HFC)
Chrysler receivables purchased 8-10, 663C2
Wien Air merger bid cited 10-4, 830A2
Wien Air stock purchase rptd 11-20, 998A2
HOUSEMAN, John
Voice of My Own opens 5-2, 712D3
HOUSE of Representatives—*See under U.S. GOVERNMENT; for legislation, see U.S. GOVERNMENT-CONGRESS*

1980

HORTA, Adolfo
Wins Olympic medal 8-2, 622F1
HORTA, Basilio
Sworn Portugal commerce min 1-3, 21E3
HORTICULTURE
Burpee dies 6-24, 528C1
HORTON, Rep. Frank (R, N.Y.)
Reelected 11-4, 843A4
HORTON, Jack K.
Resignatn set 4-18, 456C2
HORVATH, Stephen
Australia plans hydrogen cars 6-22, 496C2
HORWOOD, Owen
Presents budget 3-26, 277D3
HOSKINS, Allen
Dies 7-26, 608B2
HOSPITALS—*See MEDICINE--Hospitals*

HOSS, Selim al- (Lebanese premier)
Asks Syrians to stay in Beirut 2-13, 125G2
Quits 6-7; resignatn accepted, Sohl named 7-20, 579C3
Scores Israel raid 8-19, 628A1
Wazan named premr 10-22, 874A1

HOSSEIN, Bir
Visits US hostages 12-25—12-26, 974D2
HOST, Reinhold
2d in LeMans 6-15, 637B3
HOTEL and Restaurant Employees and Bartenders International Union (AFL-CIO)
San Fran 27-day strike ends 8-12, 648A1
HOTEL Conquistador Inc.
Meal tax case refused by Sup Ct 1-14, 36G3
HOTEL Conquistador Inc. v. U.S.
Case refused by Sup Ct 1-14, 36G3
HOTELS & Motels
Meal tax case refused by Sup Ct 1-14, 36G3
Miami Beach redvpt voted 3-11, 185C1
Grand Met raises Liggett merger bid 5-14, Liggett OKs 5-16, 557A3
Mt St Helens damage assessed 5-24—7-4, 504C3
MGM to split hotel, film units 5-30, 501F2
Spain beach resorts bombed 6-25, 500G1
Brit Rail plans sales 7-15, 544E1
ABA urges sex bias end 8-6, 744A2
San Fran 27-day strike ends 8-12, 647G3-648B1
Nev casino bombed 8-27, 833F3
US-Canada tax treaty signed 9-26, 748C2
Miami cuts off refugee funds 10-21, 150 evicted 10-24, 825C3
Las Vegas hotel fire kills 84 11-21, 893C2
Harrison NY hotel fire kills 26 12-4, 948G1
Golden Nugget opens in Atlantic City 12-12, 988F2
HOT Stuff (recording)
Summer said born-again 1-25, 199G2
Summer wins Grammy 2-27, 296B3
HOUDAILLE Industries
Canada auto plant closing set 6-9; UAW workers stage sit-in 8-8—8-21, return 8-25, 650C3
HOUGH, John
Watcher in the Woods released 4-16, 416G3
HOUGH, Richard
Alleges Nehru, Mountbatten affair 8-27; Gandhi denies 8-29, 890A3
HOUK, Ralph
Hired as Red Sox mgr 10-28, 926A3
HOUPHOUET-Boigny, Felix (Ivory Coast president)
Meets Pope 5-10, 363G3
Son-in-law seized 6-14, 499E1
HOUSEHOLD Finance Corp. (HFC)
Chrysler Financial Corp deal fails 4-11, 287A1
HOUSEMAN, John
Fog released 2-29, 216E2
HOUSE of Representatives—*See under U.S. GOVERNMENT*

1976

HOUSING (U.S.)
HUD to offer low-interest mortgages 1-7, 25B2
Ford State of Union message 1-19, 37C3, 39C2
'77 budget proposals 1-21, 62B3, 64A3, 65C3
Ford Econ Rpt 1-26, 67G1
Pa agency devault averted 2-2, 994C2
Savings & loan problems, mortgage defaults rptd 2-17, 185A2
FHA, VA mortgage rates lowered 3-30, 375D3
US files home-loan bias suits 4-15, 4-16, 285G1
US stresses energy conservatn 4-19, 284G3
Cross-district low-income housing upheld 4-20, 308C2
4 US agencies sued on bias 4-26, Sen com issues rpt 5-31, 413E2-C3
Chicago Trib wins Pulitzer 5-3, 352E3
House OKs FRB reform bill 5-10, 345F1
Ford urges regulatory reform 5-13, 347A1
Cong clears added funds 5-19, 411E3
Ill zoning case cited 6-7, 435E1
Nader group scores bank diversificatn 7-5, 495C2
'77 aid signed 8-3, 566D3
Pub constructn funds signed 8-9, 623F1
Energy bill signed 8-14, 622G3
HUD to offer low-interest mortgages 9-9, 709B2
Sup Ct bars review of 2 bias cases 10-4, 766B1, 807G2
Dow fall rptd 10-12, 847C1
NJ bond issue OKd, Calif rejected 11-2, 821D2, 825A1
Ohio planner wins Rockefeller award 11-16, 911E3
Sup Ct declines to review Pa tax bias ruling 11-29, 900G3
US constructn aid urged 12-9, 937D3
Presidential Election
Reagan scores HUD 1-9, for program shift to states 1-12, 22B1, E1
Carter 'ethnic purity' remark evokes criticism 4-4—4-13, 260D2-261F2
Carter proposes jobs progrm 4-23, 305D2
Black Dems draft plank 5-1, 343D3
Carter stresses goal 6-14, 433C1
Dem platform text 6-15, 469G1, C2, 470C1, A2, 473D2, F3, 474E2
Carter urges low-interest loans 6-29, 468E1
Mondale legis record cited 512C3
Mondale on depressn, asserts commitmt 7-15, 507G2, 511C2, D3
Carter pledge 7-15, 510D2
GOP conv delegates' views on sales to blacks rptd 8-17, 616G2
GOP platform text 8-18, 605G3, 606G2, F3, 607A1, 608B1
Ford legis record cited 614A1
Mondale scores Admin policy 8-25, 8-28, 645G2, B3
Ford lists as top priority 8-27, 645D1
Indep Party vs pub housing 8-27, 666F1
Ford vows easier home-ownership 9-15, 685F2
Mondale scores Ford 9-16, 687B2
Ford, Carter debate 9-23, 701C1, 702F1
Carter vows redlining end 9-25, 724F1
Mondale, Dole debate 10-15, 782F2, G3, 783A2
Carter rebuts Ford tax chrgs 10-15, Ford replies 10-16, 785C1
Ford, Carter debate 10-22, 800G1, E2, F3, 801C3, 802B1
NJ bond issue OKd, Calif rejected 11-2, 825A1
Carter considers jobs plan 11-23, 881C2
Statistics
Dec, '75 rent up 1-21, 90D1
Jan starts, Dec '75 revised 2-18, 153D1
Feb starts, permits; Jan revised 3-16, 199C2
Mar starts, permits; Feb revised 4-16, 279A3
Feb new-house costs 5-12, 375B3
Apr starts, permits 5-18, 375E2
May starts, permits; Apr revised 6-16, 479F3
June starts, permits; May revised 7-19, 568E1
2d ¼ 6-yr price rise 8-16, 647G2-A3
July starts, permits; June revised 8-17, 647D2
Aug mortgages rates 9-16, 709C2
Aug starts, permits rptd; July revised 9-17, 709F1
FHA, VA loan rates reduced 10-15, 805D3
Sept starts, permits 10-19, 805A3
Sept new, used house costs 10-20, 805E3
Oct starts, permits, Sept revised 11-16, 866G2
Oct '75-76 CPI rise cited 11-19, 885A1
Nov starts, Oct revised 12-16, 958D2
Nov '75-76 CPI costs 12-21, 958A2

1977

HOUSING (U.S.)
Simon vetoes tax shelter ban 1-5, 36E2
Ill restrictive suburban zoning upheld 1-11, 14G3
'75 Ford Foundatn grants cited 1-11, 56E1
CBO issues poverty rpt 1-13, 80B3
Ford '78 budget proposals 1-17, 31E2, F3
Sup Ct bars review of New Castle (NY) grants 1-17, 58C1
Sup Ct voids Indianapolis busing plan 1-25, 80A1
Sup Ct voids Toledo restrictive zoning rule 1-25, 80D2
Sup Ct backs Calif Forest Svc taxes 1-25, 80G2
Stirling Homex ex-offcls convicted 1-29, 103F1 ★; sentncd 3-11, 203F2
AFL-CIO on Carter econ plan 2-4, 89F2
Welfare cost rptd 2-19, 176C1
Carter budget revisions 2-22, 125E2
New house costs seen soaring 3-3, 178A2-A3
HUD pledges NYC aid 3-3, debt repaymt plan detailed 3-10, 193C2, D3
Harris details grant progrm, low-income aid 3-7; Carter comments 3-9, 178B1
Califano on integratn 3-17, 217E3
US drive vs home-mortgage bias rptd 3-24, 279E2
Carter energy plan 4-18, 4-20, 289E2, 290E1, 295A2; fact sheet 291F3-292F1
Carter energy plan reactn 4-20, 290C3; 4-21, 4-23, 320G2, B3
Rent subsidy bill cleared 4-28, 339A1; Carter signs 4-30, 380E3
'For sale' sign ban lifted 5-2, 406G1
1-family sales boom, Calif speculatn rptd 5-2—6-2, 554A3
'60-61, '72-73 family spending compared 5-10, 423E2
Urban business confidence rptd 5-16, 384B3, 385B1
ICC to curb movers 5-23, 423D3
Kansas City chrgs state segregatn 5-26, 446G1
Atlantic City low-income effort rptd set 5-27, 424C1
Ohio nuclear-family zoning rule upset 5-31, 461F3
GOP energy plan TV rebuttal 6-2, 443E1
Miami gay rights law repealed 6-7, 446F2
Consumer spending, starts upturn linked 6-7, 518B3
Carter rebuts black criticism 7-25, 7-28, 573E1, A3
Energy Dept created 8-4, 591G2
House OKs Carter energy pkg 8-5, 609B3, 610A1
Inflatn spurs buying boom, land-price data analyzed 9-12, 9-20, 721F3
Sen votes energy conservatn bill 9-13, 703E1
'78 HUD funds signed 10-4, 796G2, D3
'78-80 urban aid bill signed, NE-Midwest grants hiked 10-12, 796G1
Tight money impact feared by Admin 10-20, 798D3
Energy conservatn tax credits clear Sen 10-31, 832A3
Redlining curb set, S&Ls score 11-9, 898C2
Appraisers agree to rule out bias 11-11, 898A3
S&L interest rates extended 11-16, 878G1
Toledo (O) rule review declined 12-5, 939C1
US urban policies scored 12-7, 959G3
Black life expectancy linked 12-13, 962C3
Central cities to get fed aid 12-27, 1008B3
Statistics
CEA projcts '77 starts 1-18, 36A2, 111G1-F2
'76, Dec starts, permits 1-18, 111G1
Econ indicator index described 1-28, 92F3; **for data, see 'Statistics' under BUSINESS**
'76 mortgage lending 2-1, 155G1
Dec '76, Jan new house costs 2-14, 178D2
Jan starts, permits; Dec '76 revised 2-16, 130F1
Feb starts, permits; Jan revised 3-17, 194A2
Mar starts, permits; Feb revised 4-18, 300D2
Apr starts, permits; Mar revised 5-17, 384D1
May CPI rptd 6-22, 482C1
June starts, permits; Mar-May revised 7-19, 554F2
June CPI 7-21, 554D2
July starts, permits; June revised 8-16, 629C1
July CPI 8-19, 651F1
'70-76 ownership costs 9-12, 722A1
Aug starts, permits 9-19, 721D3
Aug CPI 9-21, 722D2
Sept starts, permits; Aug revised 10-19, 817G3-818A1
'69-Sept '77 lumber prices 10-21, 817F3
Oct starts, permits; Sept revised 11-16, 898G3
Nov starts, permits; Oct revised 12-16, 977F1-A2

1978

HOUSING (U.S.)—*See also CONSTRUCTION Industry, REAL Estate, TAXES*
State, local govt policies linked to segregatn 1-8, 13F3
Carter State of Union Message 1-19, 30G2, 31G3
Carter budget proposals 1-23, 46F1, 47F3, 48A1; table 45E2
Carter unveils urban-aid plan, 3-27, reactn 3-27—3-30, 217D3, 218A1, C1
Carter anti-inflatn plan cites higher costs 4-11, 260A1
S Bronx offered fed aid 4-12, 285G1
Coll progrm included in proposed Educ Dept 4-14, 279D1
Survey finds widespread bias 4-17, 285C2
Cong energy conferees OK insulatn provisn 4-21, 305D1, G1
Denver utility settles FTC credit chrg 5-3, 434A2
Mobile home mfr tops '67-77 investor-return list 5-8, 326A1
Indian conditns rptd by GAO 5-13, 569G1
Builders vow 6-mo profit freeze, back other anti-inflatn measures 5-16, 362E1
Cong '79 budget-target res cleared 5-17, 385F2
Solar energy study rptd 6-23, 493E3
Kaufman FTC complaint rptd setld 7-7, 702C2
Anti-crime plan unveiled by Carter 7-10, 525A2
Petaluma (Calif) developers fee rptd 7-21, 611D2
Home sale tax exemptn OKd by House com 7-27, 586B3, 587G1
HUD secy cancels Cong testimony, White House disagrmt cited 8-7, 605F1
Improvemt for blacks cited by LA mayor 8-8, 811G1
'77 poverty level data rptd 8-12, 684E2
HUD issues Fannie Mae rules 8-14, 627D3
Gallup poll: black bias down 8-27, 811F3
CORE Arab-financed NY dvpt projct plans cited 9-18, 810G1
Sen OKs gas bill 9-27, 733D3
'79 funds signed 9-30, 750C2-A3
Residential fire victim data rptd 10-8, 972A1
Flood indicted again 10-12, 792C1
Tax cut, energy plan clear Cong 10-15, 784F3, 785A2, 786A1, E1, 787C2, D2
Carter inflatn plan to monitor costs 10-24, 806D1
Carter signs tax cut 11-6, energy bill 11-9, 873A1, E1
Seattle gay rights repeal fails 11-7, 857C3
Calif OKs vet loans 11-7, 915D2
Cities' power over suburbs backed 11-28, 937D3
Mortgage Rate Issues
May mortgage rates 6-18, 470E1
Variable rate mortgages OKd, HUD secy vs 7-24, 605D2
June CPI, mortgage rates 7-28, 607F1
Meany seeks mortgage rate cut 9-18, 715D2
Mortgage lending rptd strong, new 6-mo certificate use cited 10-18, 790E3
Mortgage rates, house costs rise rptd 11-2, 919C1
Calif, NY mortgage rates hiked; usury ceilings cited 11-6—11-17, 919C1
Redlining study rpts on usury ceilings 12-7, 942A3
NYS ups rate lid 12-8, 962F1
3 new mortgages OKd, '75 Cong actn cited 12-14, 962A1
Redlining
S&L redlining curbed 5-18, 410D2
Ill case refused by Sup Ct 10-30, 832C3
NYS study finds race bias 12-7, 942E2-A3
NYS ban signed 12-8, 962F1
Statistics—*See also 'Mortgage Rate Issues' above*
'77, Dec starts, permits 1-18, 52D2
Jan starts, permits; Dec '77 revised 2-17, 106C2
'64-78 spending pattern chngs reflected in new CPIs 222E2, F2
Jan, Feb CPIs rptd 2-27, 3-28, 222E1, F1
Feb starts, permits; Jan revised 3-16, 222E3
Mar starts, permits; Feb revised 4-18, 304C1
Mar CPI up 4-28, 345A1
Apr starts, Mar revised 5-16, 389B2
Apr CPI up 5-31, 428D3
May starts, permits; Apr revised 6-16, 470D1
May CPI 6-30, 507A1
June starts, permits; May revised 7-19, 607E3
June indicators rise, Calif permit surge linked 7-31, 607F2, E3
July starts, permits; June revised 8-16, 680D2
July CPI 8-29, 679B3
June bldg surge, Propositn 13 linked 8-31, 680G1
Aug starts, permits; July revised 9-19, 717G2-A3
Aug CPI 9-26, 752D1
Jan-Aug CPI hikes 10-4, 790A1
Sept starts, permits; Aug revised 10-18, 790D3
Sept CPI 10-27, 864D1
Oct starts, permits; Sept revised 11-17, 919A1
Oct CPI 11-28, 918C2, G2
Nov starts, permits; Oct revised 12-18, 982G1
Nov CPI 12-22, 1003G1, A2

1979

HOUSING (U.S.)
'76-77 home values double 1-11, 18D1
Carter budget proposals 1-22, 42C1, A2, 44E3, 45D2
Sears sues US on bias laws 1-24, 92D1
Carter seeks bias curbs 1-25, 70C2
Boston Navy Yd renovatn set 2-1, 94A1
Kerr-McGee OKs fuel price refund 2-8, 113B1
HUD rpts on city revitalizatn impact 2-13, 132G2-C3
US, Mex sign cooperatn pact 2-16, 124D3
Racial attitudes surveyed 2-20, 307E1
Carter seeks oil conservatn powers 2-26, 145C3
Inflatn 'hedge' demand cited 3-16, 264G2
Insulatn lag rptd 3-28, 228A1
Carter asks fuel-saving measures 4-5, 250F3
US rpt scores bias 4-11, 283F2-C3
St Louis busing order refused 4-12, 596D3
Carter links black vote, bias 5-20, 384G2
Prop 13 impact reviewed 6-1-7-2, 499G2, 500C1, G1
Carter orders timber sales 6-11, 441A1
Carter proposes solar energy plan 6-20, 498A1
Condominium, co-op conversn growth rptd 6-23, 482F2-B3
HUD withdraws Soul City support 6-28, 665E1, C2*
HUD ends Newfields (O) project 6-28, 665D2
Tex disaster relief authorized 7-28, 638E3
Houston townhouses destroyed by fire 7-31, wooden shingles curbed 8-2, 620C2
NJ HFA kickback scandal rptd, Carter aide quits 8-9, 747C3
Insulatn rating rule OKd by FTC 8-23, 903A1
Calif drug profit investmt cited 9-5, 972F2
Aug purchase price rptd up 9-6, 701B3
Improvemt projcts, literacy progrm link urged 9-8, 786C1
Mail fraud crackdown set 9-19, 921C3
Mobile home warranty problems rptd 10-4, 903G1
NY bond prices fall on FRB credit moves 10-11, 765C1
Formaldehyde-cancer link rptd 10-18, 971E1
'80 HUD funds clear Cong 10-24, Carter signs 11-5, 883G2
Baltimore, San Fran, Me referenda results 11-6, 846B2, F3, 847B1
Mortgage Rate Issues
Carter budget proposals 1-22, 44G3
'78 CPI rise rptd 1-24, 73G1
Chase REIT files for bankrupcy 2-22, 131G1-E2
HUD scores bias vs women 3-9, 208G3-209B1
Mar rate record rptd 4-6, 281D1
Carter asks variable rates 5-22, FHLBB OKs 5-30, 403F1, E2
Carter proposes solar energy bank 6-20, 498C1
June CPI rise rptd 7-26, 557A1
July CPI rise rptd 8-25, 646C2
July, Aug rate rise rptd 9-6, 701A3
Sept CPI rise rptd 10-26, 827F3
Oct CPI rise rptd 11-27, 903G2
Nov rates up 1.9% 12-21, 984D2
Statistics—*See also 'Mortgage Rate' above*
'78, Dec starts; Nov revised 1-17, 35B1
Dec '78 CPI rise, Prop 13 impact cited 1-24, 73F1
Jan starts, permits; Dec '78 revised 2-16, 151F2
Admin '79 starts forecast 2-16, 151A3
Feb starts, permits 3-16, 252B3
Feb CPI rise 3-25, 252F1
Mar starts, permits 4-17, 281B1
Mar CPI rise 4-26, 324G3
Apr starts, permits; Mar revised 5-16, 363A1
Apr CPI rise 5-25, 402E3
May starts, permits; Apr revised 6-18, 463C3
May CPI rise 6-26, 480D3
June starts, permits 7-18, 557E1
June CPI rise 7-26, 556G3-557A1
July starts, permits 8-16, 622B1
July CPI rise 8-25, 646D2
Aug starts, July revised 9-19, 701G2
Aug CPI rise 9-25, 725C2
Sept starts, permits; Aug revised 10-17, 784D2
Sept CPI rise 10-26, 827F3
Oct starts, Sept revised 11-19, 922C2
Oct CPI rise 11-27, 903G2
Nov starts, permits 12-18, 964D1
Nov CPI rise 12-21, 984D2
Supreme Court Cases
Govt relocatn aid curbed 4-17, 325G3
Racial 'steering' suits allowed 4-17, 352G2
Ohio busing orders upheld 7-2, 539B3

1980

HOUSING (U.S.)
State of State messages 1-8, 1-15, 403B3, 404A1; 1-9, 1-15, 269B2, 270C1; 1-9—1-16, 483A1, G3, 484D2
US rights comm rpt scores 'widespread' bias 1-14, 36G2, A3, D3
'70s black home owners rpt up 1-22, 94F2
Carter budget proposals 1-28, 69D3, 70A2, 73E1; table 70F1
LA adults-only housing barred 1-31, 115C2
Standard Oil settles price case 2-14, 190A1
AFL-CIO urges anti-inflatn moves 2-18, 146C3
Fla property tax cut, Miami Beach redvpt voted 3-11, 184G1, 185C1
'79 property tax collectns rptd 4-17, 307D2
Carter backs mil compensatn 5-26, 403A2
Calif rent-control repeal, San Jose, Santa Clara gay rights referenda rejected by voters 6-3, 439E2, F2
Vanderbilt drops River House suit 6-12, 639G1
US summer jobs progrm rptd 6-30, 496A1
Rental shortage not linked to condos 7-2, 518A2
FHLBB proposes S&L loan plan 7-31, 600A1
Mil benefits authrzn signed 9-8, 765D1
Home improvemt tax credit claims rptd 9-12, 747A2
Housing, community dvpt authrzn clears Cong 9-30, signed 10-8, 763A2, 804B2
Carter names 2 panels, issues white paper 10-8, 763B2
Miami cuts off refugee funds 10-21, 150 evicted 10-24, 825C3
IRS revokes bond tax exemptns 11-10, 989C2
Integration rptd linked to busing 11-16, 989A3
Fair-housing legis debated 12-4—12-9, dropped 12-9, 954F1
Budget reconciliatn signed 12-5, 936G1
Mortgage Rate Issues
Mortgages defined 266B3
Rate hikes rptd 2-8—2-28, 145B1
Jan CPI rise rptd 2-22, 144G1
Rates rptd 'astronomical' 3-7, 3-19, 222A3
Banking deregulatn bill signed 3-31, 246D1
Renegotiated-rate mortgages OKd 4-3, 266E2, F3
FHA, VA rates rise to 14% 4-3, 266F3
Carter backs subsidized mortgages, unsold home financing set 4-17, 286D1
Rates reduced 4-28, 5-1, 329B2
Rates drop, hit 12.75% 5-6—5-19, 384F3
FHA, VA rates cut to 11.5% 5-15, 384E3
Rates continue to fall 5-22—7-9, 514B1
FHA, VA multifamily rates cut to 12% 7-7, 513G3
Fannie Mae 2d 1/4 loss rptd 7-10, 576D2
NY bank drops rate to 12% 7-15; Calif rates hiked to 12.25% 7-23, 575A1
FHLBB proposes S&L loan plan 7-31, 600D1
Calif rate hikes continue 7-31—8-19, 631A1
Rates continue to rise 9-25—10-7, 867B2
Housing, community dvpt authrzn clears Cong 9-30, signed 10-8, 804B2
Reagan vows lower rates 10-2, 738E3
FHA, VA rate rise delay scored 10-24, 823C3
Calif rates rise to 18% 11-7—12-16, 983F3
FHA, VA rates hit 13.5% 11-24, 984A1
'81 HUD appropriatn clears Cong 12-3, 954A3; signed 12-15, 982B1
Presidential Election (& Transition)
Kennedy urges rent controls 1-28, 74F3; 2-6, 90G3
Kennedy urges energy conservatn incentives 2-2, 91E1
Kennedy 'basic speech' excerpts 3-10, 183D1, G1, F2
Bush cites falloff 4-7, 264D2
Reagan backs 'urban homesteading' 8-5, 597G1
Kennedy Dem conv speech 8-12, 610E2, 614D1
Dem platform planks adopted 8-13, 614D2
Carter renominatn acceptance speech 8-14, 612G1
Carter offers econ renewal plan 8-28, 663B2
Anderson, Reagan TV debate 9-21, 722A1, D1
Reagan gives aid plan 10-2, 738E2
Reagan assails Carter policies 10-2, 763C1
Mondale denounces Reagan tax cuts 10-16, 817C1
Statistics
'79 Nov new, used home sales 1-9, 15E2
'79, Dec housing starts; Nov revised 1-17, 35D1
'79 CPI 1-25, 75A3
Jan starts; Dec '79 revised 2-19, 126C3
Jan CPI 2-22, 144G1
Feb starts; Jan revised 3-18, 209E2
LA prices 3-29, 248A1
Mar starts, Feb revised 4-16, 286A1
Mar CPI 4-22, 305D1
Apr starts, Mar revised 5-16, 384G2-A3
Apr indl output down 5-16, 384C3
Apr CPI 5-23, 400C3
May starts, Apr revised 6-17, 455G1
May CPI 6-24, 481C1
June starts, May revised 7-17, 542A1

1976

HOUSTON, Tex.—*See TEXAS*
HOUSTON Chronicle (newspaper)
Ford endorsement rptd 10-30, 831F2
HOUSTON Symphony Orchestra
Gets grant 1-12, 32E3
HOUT, Shafik al-
Wounded 1-31, 83A1
HOVEIDA, Amir Abbas
On budget deficit financing 2-3, 102B1
HOWARD, Rep. James J. (D, N.J.)
Reelected 11-2, 830D1
HOWARD, John
Rpts jobs plan 9-21, 770A3
HOWARD, Kathy
S Africa tour confrmd 7-20, 528E3
HOWARD, Percy
In Super Bowl 1-18, 56D1
HOWARD University (Washington, D.C.)
Mordecai Johnson dies 9-11, 716C3
HOWE, Rep. Allan Turner (D, Utah)
Arrested 6-12, denies chrg 6-13, pressed to drop 2d term bid 6-14, 434G1-B2
Convicted, affirms reelectn bid 7-23, staff resignatns rptd 7-25, 552A1
Conviction upheld 8-24, 636E2
Aide arrested 8-24, 636A3
Unopposed in primary 9-14, 705G1
Loses reelection 11-2, 820B2, 824A3
HOWE, Sir Geoffrey
Scores UK IMF loan plan 9-29, 721A2
Scores govt econ policy 10-26, 810D1
Scores defense cuts 12-15, 1003E3
HOWE, Irving
World of Our Fathers on best-seller list 12-5, 922A2
HOWE, James Wong
Dies 7-12, 716C3
HOWELL, Denis
Named water use overseer 8-24, 630D1
Rpts water stocks replenished 11-16, 977C3
HOWIE, Libby
Named Sotheby auctioneer 1-27, 272B1
HOWLAND International, T. G.
Chrgd re Arab boycott 10-19, 786E1
HOWLETT, Michael J.
Wins primary for gov 3-16, 196F2
Boren endorses 7-6, 493A1
Loses election 11-2, 820E3, 823A2
HOXHA, Enver
Backs 'Albanianism' as natl religion 3-17, 332A1
On anti-China plot purge 4-30, 331C3
At CP cong 11-1—11-2; reelected 11-7, 849E2
HOYER-Boots, Nadja
Testifies on Army meat fraud 5-10, 395E2
HOYOS Arango, Samuel
Resigns 10-13, 924G3
HRUSKA, Sen. Roman L. (R, Neb.)
GOP conv OKs platform plank 8-18, 600C3
Lobbying disclosure bill not cleared 10-2, 883D1
Zorinsky wins seat 11-2, 820C1, 823C3
HRUSKO, Miloslav
Named to Czech Presidium 4-16, 289B2
HSU Chia-Tun
Attacked in Nanking posters 7-19, 555D2
HSU Chin-chiang
Dies 7-21, 656F3
HSU Shih-yu
Listed in China ldrship 9-10, 712B1

HUA Kuo-feng
Chou En-lai dies 1-8, 8E3, 9B1
Rumania trade pact signed 1-29, 117D1, E3
Named 'acting' premier 2-7, 117C1
Sees visiting Venez offcl 2-7, 117D1

1977

HOUSING Conference, National
Harris addresses 3-7, 178E1
HOUSING & Urban Development, Department of—*See under U.S. GOVERNMENT*
HOUSTON, Tex.—*See TEXAS*
HOUSTON, Livingston W.
Dies 11-22, 952E2
HOUSTON, University of
Wins Cotton Bowl 1-1, '76 rank rptd 1-2, 1-3, 8E3, F3
Loses NIT basketball tourn 3-20, 262E2
Whitley in NFL draft 5-3, 353A3
Birdsong in NBA draft 6-10, 584A3
HOUSTON Pipe Line Co.
FPC OKs emergency gas sales 1-14, 37A1
HOVARD Jr., John F.
Returns to Moon sect 4-11, 310D1
HOVE, Ove
Danish building min 2-25, 373C1, E1
HOVEIDA, Amir Abbas (Iranian premier; resigned Aug. 6)
Denies pub trial prompted by US rights policy 4-11, 527A2
Quits as premr 8-6, Amouzegar replaces 8-7, 618E1
HOWARD, Rep. James J. (D, N.J.)
Adams backs mass-transit fund 10-12, 860B3
HOWARD, John
Outlines royal comm RCMP probe 12-6, 965D1
Retained as Australia treas 12-19, 982G1, A2
HOWARD, John Winston
On EC farm import demands 10-30, 862D1
Replaces Lynch as treas 11-18, 901D2
HOWARD, Robert T.
NBC to limit violence 2-14, 157E3
NBC cancels Emmy broadcast 4-15, 355B3
Fired as NBC-TV pres 8-22, 658A3
HOWARD Johnson Co. Inc.
Francis rape suit rptd setld 2-23, 140E3
HOWARD University (Washington, D.C.)
Pierre confrmd Army asst secy 5-9, 418G1
Nigeria ldr addresses 10-12, 797A2
HOWE, Chris
Jackson assault case dismissed 11-1, 927C2
HOWE, Gordie
Signs with WHA Whalers 5-23, 430D1
Esposito ranks 2d in goals 11-30, 1021D1
Scores 1,000 on goal 12-7, 1021C1
HOWE, Irving
Wins Natl Book Award 4-11, 355G1
HOWE, Mark
Signs with WHA Whalers 5-23, 430D1
HOWE, Marty
Signs with WHA Whalers 5-23, 430D1
HOWE, Quincy
Dies 2-17, 164A3
HOWELL Jr., Henry E.
Wins primary for gov 6-14, 465A1
Carter stumps in Va 9-24, 761C1
Loses electn for gov 11-8, 855E1, C2
HOW to Save Your Own Life (book)
On best-seller list 5-1, 356C2
HOWZE, Rev. Joseph Lawson
Named bishop 3-8, installed 6-6, 471B2
HOXHA, Enver
Anti-China purge rptd 9-9, 731B1
HOYT, Mary Finch
On Mrs. Carter's surgery 4-28, 322E2
HRABOSKY, Al
Traded to Royals 12-8, 990F1
HSIAO Hua, Gen.
Heads Lanchow rail post 6-22, 505A3
HSIEN Heng-han
Ousted as Kansu head 6-22, 505G2
HSIN Chun-chieh
Urges Kiangsi purge 6-6, 505C3
HSU Hsiang-chien
In Politburo 8-21, 645G2 *
Urges army discipline 9-19, 743E3
HSU Shih-yu
In Politburo 8-21, 645F2

HUA Kuo-feng (Chinese premier)
Asked to act vs '76 Peking rioters 1-10, 61D2
Anti-Chiang drive seen weak 2-5, 98D1
Defense meetings held 2-6, 134G1
Greater discipline urged 2-7, 98B1

1978

Supreme Court Cases
Arlington Hts zoning case review barred 1-9, 13D2
Hartford suits vs suburbs case review refused 1-16, 33G2
State emergency welfare standards backed 6-6, 447E2
Stirling Homex convictns review refused 10-2, 751E2
SC Mobile Homes case refused 10-10, 789G2
United Methodist Calif immunity case refused 10-16, 789E2
Ill redlining case refused 10-30, 832D3

HOUSING, National Committee Against Discrimination in
Survey finds widespread housing bias 4-17, 285D2
HOUSING & Urban Development, Department of—*See under U.S. GOVERNMENT*
HOUSTON, Tex.—*See TEXAS*
HOUSTON, Thelma
Wins Grammy 2-24, 315G3
HOUSTON, University of
Admin shuffled 4-3, ex-aide indicted 5-15, 380A3
SEC chrgs ex-aide 10-5, univ losses rptd 10-5, 770B3
HOUSTON Grand Opera
Wins Grammy 2-24, 316C1
HOUSTON Oil & Minerals
NJ offshore wells rptd dry 12-6, 12-11, 12-27, 1010E1
HOVE, Byron Reuben Mtonhadzi
Ousted 4-28; govt split threatened, probe set 4-28—5-2, 317E1, 318A1
Ouster upheld 5-9, UANC scores 5-14, 376E3
UANC expels 8-13, 650C3
HOVEIDA, Amir Abbas
Arrested 11-8, 858B1
HOVING, Walter
On diamond price rise 3-17, 319D1
HOWARD, Rep. James J. (D, N.J.)
Carter effort to win energy bill votes rptd 10-16, 786G3
Reelected 11-7, 851A3
Asks ICC deregulatn halt 12-7, O'Neal rejcts 12-21, 1007C2
HOWARD, John
On 1st ¼ GDP 6-16, 472E2
Rpts budget deficit 50% above forecast 7-7, 530E1
Presents '78-79 budget, sees inflatn rate drop 8-15, 628F1, D3
HOWARD Jr., Rev. M. William
Elected NCC pres 11-4, 907F1
HOWARD University (Washington, D.C.)
Cabt-level Educ Dept proposed 4-14, 279C1
HOW Deep Is Your Love (recording)
Bee Gees win Grammy 2-24, 315F3
HOWE, Sir Geoffrey
Scores Healey in confidnc vote debate 6-14, 496F3
Lauds Vauxhall anti-strike votes 10-25, 816F1
Scores Healey econ actions 11-12, 882A3
HOWE, Gordie
Hull retires from hockey 11-1, 991F1
HOWE, Julia Ward (1819-1910)
Arts Institute honors 8 2-7, 316E1
HOWE, Mark
Nordiques win WHA All-Star Game 1-17, 76F3
HOWELL, Harry
Named NHL North Stars coach 7-5, 656G3
Quits as North Stars coach 11-18, 991C1
HOWES, Libby
Nayatt School opens 5-12, 887C2
HOWE Trophy, Gordie—*See HOCKEY—Awards*
HOWSAM, Bob
Vs Kuhn bar on Blue sale 1-30, 3-3, 194D3, F3
HOWSER, Dick
Jackson suspended 7-17, 618E1
HRABOSKY, Al
Jackson suspended 7-17, 618E1
HSIEH Fu-chih
Poster criticizes 11-23, 949B2
HSU Hsiang-chien, Marshal
Named China defense min 2-26—3-5, 153C1
HTIEN Lien, U
Gets death sentence 2-23, 145C2

HUA Kuo-feng (Chinese premier)
Signs accord with Barre 1-21, 71F1
Ordrs Sinkiang ldrshp change 1-29, 89B2
Cites improved conditns 2-23, 154E2
Reelected premier 2-26—3-5, 153A1
Announces econ goals 2-26, 154B1

1979

HOUSING & Urban Development, Department of—*See under U.S. GOVERNMENT*
HOUSTON, Tex.—*See TEXAS*
HOUSTON, University of
Loses Cotton Bowl 1-1, '78 rank rptd 1-3, 8E2, A3
Forgn student enrollmt listed 167D3
Adams in NFL draft 5-3, 335G2
HOUSTON Chronicle (newspaper)
Eisenhower secret diary rptd 9-16, 9-17, 748B1
Eisenhower tapes revealed 10-21, 868G3
HOUSTON Oil & Minerals Corp.
NJ offshore well rptd dry 2-14, 186F3
HOUT, Shafik al-
In US 4-1—4-21, House scores 4-24, 319E2; Begin protests 5-2, 320B1
HOUWER, Rob
Soldier of Orange released 8-16, 820D3
HOVEIDA, Amir Abbas
Justice min quits re trial plan 1-17, 25D2
Trial 3-14—3-15, suspended 3-16, 199G1
Trial reopens 4-4, executed 4-7, 276E2
Mrs Javits lobby role bared 5-30, 408C2
HOWARD, Rep. James J. (D, N.J.)
Softens trucking deregulatn stand 1-9, 111E3
HOWARD, John
Banking inquiry rptd 1-23, 74A1
'78 4th ¼ inflatn rptd 1-31, 94E2
Currency futures market set 2-1, 74C1
Dropped from Coordinatn Com 2-4, 113D2
Interest rates hiked 4-23, 311B1
Proposes austerity measures 5-24, 404G2
Budget deficit underestimated 5-30, 443G1, B2
Presents Australian budget 8-21, 631E2
HOWARD, Marc
Utter Glory opens 5-13, 712C3
Getting Out opens 5-15, 711B3
HOWARD, Ron
More Amer Graffiti released 8-17, 820B2
HOWARD, Sidney
Most Happy Fella opens 10-11, 956D3
HOWARD, Trevor
Hurricane released 4-11, 528E2
HOWARD, Rev. William
Sees hostages 12-24—12-25, Iran forgn min 12-27, 975B1-B2
HOWARD Johnson Co.
Imperial group to buy 9-10, Calif bar seen 10-12, 942B3-E3
HOWE, Sir Geoffrey
UK chancellor of Exchequer 5-5, 338D1
Presents budget 6-12, 445E1-B3
Sees union ldrs 6-25, 502F3
Backs £ value increase 7-3, 503D1
TUC scores govt 9-3—9-7, 707D2
Scores EC budget 9-17, 719G1
Forgn exchng controls ended 10-23, 813A3
HOWE, Mark
WHA scoring ldr 4-18, 355G2
HOWELL, David
UK energy secy 5-5, 338G1
Heysham A-plant financing OKd 6-27, 524B3
On BNOC cutback, N Sea exploratn 7-26, 582B1, F1
N Sea oil assets sale barred 9-14, 707B2
On A-power safety 12-18, 994C2
HOWELL, James Allen
Indicted in arms plot 5-14, 386E3
HOWE Trophy, Gordie—*See HOCKEY-Awards*
HOWIE, Robert
In Canadian Cabt 6-4, 423G3
HOWSER, Dick
Hired as Yankee mgr 10-28, 1002B1
HOW To Prosper During the Coming Bad Years (book)
On best-seller list 4-8, 271A2; 5-6, 356D2; 8-5, 620C3; 9-2, 672C3; 10-14, 800B3; 11-4, 892C3
HOXHA, Enver
Chrgs US-China plot 1-27, 69C3
HO Xuan Dich
Canada expels 3-29, 267E1
HOYLE, Douglas
Backs renatlzn measure 10-3, 773A3
HRABOSKY, Al
Signs with Braves 11-20, 1001G3
HSU Shih-yu
Identified as Viet invasn cmdr 2-21, 122D1
HSU Wen-hien, Capt.
Chrgd re passenger overload 2-4, 109D1

HUA Kuo-feng (Hua Guofeng) (Chinese premier)
Protesters barred from mtg 1-14, 58C3
At new yr rite with Liu's widow 1-28, 75F1
Invited to visit US 1-29, 65A2

1980

June CPI 7-23, 556E1
July starts, June revised 8-18, 631C1
July CPI 8-22, 648C3
Aug starts, July revised 9-17, 701C3
Aug CPI 9-23, 741C1
Sept starts, Aug revised 10-17, 804E3
Sept CPI 10-24, 823D3
Oct starts, Sept revised 11-19, 882F3
Oct CPI 11-25, 897B3
Nov starts, Oct revised 12-16, 957G2
Nov CPI 12-23, 983E3
Supreme Court Cases
Environmental impact ct reviews limited 1-7, 15B3
Black Jack (Mo) low income case refused 2-25, 188A1
Calif redlining law curbed 3-17, 226C1
HOUSING & Urban Development, Department of—*See under U.S. GOVERNMENT*
HOUSTON—*See TEXAS*
HOUSTON, University of
Wins Cotton Bowl 1-1, '79 rank rptd 1-2, 23B1, E1
Stuttering, physical abnormality link rptd 1-5, 63E3
Saudi film telecast ordrd 5-9, overturned 5-12, 375G3
Wins Garden State Bowl 12-14, 999A3
HOUSTON Chronicle (newspaper)
Reagan pres endorsemt rptd 11-1, 841G3
HOUSTON Oil & Minerals Corp.
Tenneco merger set 12-9, 985A2
HOUTS, Peter S.
3 Mile I health study rptd 4-17, 332A3
HOVE, Richard
Zimbabwe public svc min 3-11, 198D1
HOVING, Walter
Retires from Tiffany 11-17, 959D2
HOWARD, Elston
Dies 12-14, 1004B2
HOWARD, Rep. James J. (D, N.J.)
Names Abscam middleman 2-5, 111D1
Reelected 11-4, 843A3, 848A3
HOWARD, John
Announces bond rate hike 3-2, 210G3
Rpts budget moves, tax cuts 3-6, 210E2
Rpts interest rates hiked 12-2, 964A1
HOWARD, Rev. M. William
Knew Canada hid Iran envoys 1-29, 89A1
Scores Citibank re S Africa aid 3-24, 278A1
HOWARD, Marc
Watch on the Rhine opens 1-3, 136F3
Lady From Dubuque opens 1-31, 136C3
Charlotte opens 2-27, 392D2
HOWARD Johnson Co.
Imperial Group completes purchase 6-17, 557C3
HOWARD v. Des Moines Register
Case refused by Sup Ct 2-25, 188A1
HOWE, Art
Astros win NL West playoff 10-6, 795E2
Phillies win NL pennant 10-12, 796E1
HOWE, Sir Geoffrey
Sees slow econ recovery 2-26, 150C2
Presents new budget 3-26, 232C1-D2
Urges wage restraint 6-6, 444C3, 445D1
Tory conf affirms policies 10-7—10-10, 790E2
Rpts interest rate cut, new oil levy 11-24, 901F1
HOWE, Gordie
Sets NHL All-Star point record 2-5, 198A3
Retires 6-4, 488E2
HOWE, Steve
Named top NL rookie 12-1, 926A1
HOWELL, David
Rpts N Sea gas pipe OKd 6-19, 463D2
Elec monopoly to be curbed 7-21, 563G3
Plans oil, gas output cut 7-23, 563C3
Says OPEC drops 10% cut plan 9-26, 735B1
HOWLAND, Michael
Prelate visits 12-25, 974A2
HOWSER, Dick
Quits as Yankee mgr 11-21, 926E1
HOW to Beat the High Cost of Living (film)
Released 7-11, 675A3
HOW to Prosper During the Coming Bad Years (book)
On best-seller list 2-10, 120E3; 3-9, 200D3
HOXHA, Enver
Cabt shuffle rptd 5-2, 356E2
HRUBESCH, Horst
W Ger wins Eur Soccer Championship 6-22, 771D2
HRUSINSKY, Rudolf
Magicians released 12-26, 1003B2
HSIE Fu-chih—*See XIE Fuzhi*
HSUEH, Thomas
On Taiwan Olympic rejectn 2-13, 154G3

HUA Guofeng (Hua Kuo-feng) (Chinese premier; resigned Sept. 7)
Vows aid to Cambodia guerrillas 3-9, 181E1
Power shift seen 4-16, 351E1
At Tito funeral 5-8, 339B1

1976

Mao ties rptd 2-8, 117E2
Rptd at Tibetan fete 2-8, 117A3
USSR doubts improved ties 2-10, 117B3
Campaign vs Teng launched 2-10, 189A1, B2
Sees Nixon; scores detente, 'capitalist roaders' 2-21—2-26, 189A3, C3
Nixon calls 'impressive' 3-22, 215D1
Named premier 4-7, 243B3
Rallies, press back 4-8—4-28, 332F3-333D1
Hails Egypt-Sovt break 4-19, 275A3
Meets Egypt vp 4-21, 275G2
Radical strength rptd 4-27, 333E1
May Day CP unity rptd 5-2, 332E3
Meets Fraser 6-20, 481D1
Chu Teh buried 7-11, 521A1
Tours quake site 7-30, 561G2
In Cambodia 8-7, 588D2
Scores 'class enemies' 9-1, 673G2
Cited as possible Mao successor 9-9—9-10, 658D1
Heads China ldrship list 9-10, 712A1
Addresses Mao meml rally 9-18, 711B3
Radical plot, purge rptd 10-7—10-14, 757F1; confrmd 10-22, 790A2
Named Mao successor 10-7, 871E2
Appointmts announced 10-12; oppositn rptd 10-14, 757A1, D2
Facts on 757B1-758D1
Army vows support 10-17, 10-19, 790D3
Rallies honor, Mao support rptd 10-23, 10-24, 809E1-A2
Sovt congratulatns rejected 10-28, 871F3
Rpt plot thwarted 10-30, 11-8, 871D2
Hoxha speech ignores 11-1, 849F3
Troops quell Fukien unrest 11-23, 904D3
'Gang of 4' accused 12-18, 999G3
Sees '77 purge, blames 'gang of 4' 12-24, 999G2

HUANG Chen
Sees Kissinger 8-19, 619A1

HUANG Hua
Scores Sovt Angola policy 3-26, 228D2
Named foreign min 12-2, 904D2-A3

HUBBARD, Cal
Named to Hall of Fame 8-9, 816D1

HUBBARD Jr., Rep. Carroll (D, Ky.)
Reelected 11-2, 829E3

HUBBARD, DeHart
Dies 6-23, 524G2

HUBBARD, Richard B.
Resigns GE A-post 2-3, 115C1

HUBER, Antje
W Ger health min 12-15, 968A2

HUBER, Robert
Loses Senate primary 8-3, 565A3

HUCKABY, Jerry
Wins House primary 8-14, 633A1
Elected 11-2, 822G1, B2, 829F3

HUCKLEBERRY Finn (TV special)
Wins Emmy 5-17, 460C2

HUDDLESTON, Sen. Walter (D, Ky.)
Drops CIA disclosure request 2-17, 150E2
Named to intelligence com 5-20, 377E1

HUDSON Falls, N.Y.—*See NEW York State*

HUDSON River
NYS accuses GE re PCBs 2-9, curbs fishing 2-25, 171E3
NYS, GE sign PCB pact 9-8, 691G2-B3

HUEBL, Milan
Freed 12-10, 1012B3

HUGESSEN, Judge James
Rules Ouellet in contempt 1-23, 72E1
Drury contact rptd 3-12, 220G3-221E1

HUGHES, Francis
AF asst secy 3-1; confrmd 3-10, 232E1
Replaced as AF asst secy 9-10, 808B1

1977

Yunnan CP shifts rptd 2-12, 134C1
Army urged to stress skills 2-26, 180B1
Chekiang offcls disgraced 3-2, 179C3
Kweichow progress lauded 3-5, 179F3
Hangchow foes executed 3-12, 238A2
Liaoning offcl arrested 3-14, 220E1
US congressmen in China 4-9—4-17, 298C2
Econ recovery plan outlined 4-11, 282E1
Opens industrial conf 4-20, 449C2
Sadat thanks for arms 6-25, 496D2
Teng rehabilitated 7-22, 571E2
CP Cong held, addresses 8-20—8-23, 646C1
In ruling triumvirate 8-21, 645E2
Asks end to US-Taiwan ties 8-22, 645F1
Meets US Secy Vance 8-25, 645C1
Greets Tito 8-30, 710A1
At Mao mausoleum rites 9-9, 706B1
Kwangsi dissent hinted 9-22, 744B1
Greets Pol Pot 9-28, 741A3
Natl People's Cong set for '78 10-23, 823E1

HUANG Chao-chi
Scored at rally 6-29, 562A1

HUANG Hua
US congressmen in China 4-9—4-17, 298C2
Meets US Secy Vance 8-22, 8-23, 645E1, A2
In Canada 10-4—10-7, 801D1

HUANG Ko-cheng
Rehabilitated 8-1, 8-2, 616C3

HUANG Shang
China culture min 1-29, 98C2

HUBACKER, Helmut
Asks bank probe 5-3, 564E3

HUBBARD, L. Ron
FBI raids on Scientology offices ruled illegal 7-27, 628C2

HUBBARD, Robert Calvin (Cal)
Dies 10-17, 872C2

HUBLEY, John
Dies 2-21, 164B3

HU Chi-wei
Named Jenmin Jih Pao editor 3-7, 179G3

HUD—*See U.S. GOVERNMENT—HOUSING & Urban Development, Department of*

HUDDLESTON, Sen. Walter (D, Ky.)
In Panama; links pact support, rights 11-9—11-12, 911C2, E3

HUDSON Pharmaceutical Corp.
Vitamin ads to children barred 2-7, 217D1

HUDSON River
Oil barge spill 2-4, 214G2
Study finds toxic chemicals 9-28, 762A2

HUEBL, Eliska
Bias vs children chrgd 10-4, 182A2

HUEBL, Milan
Austria offers asylum 1-25, rejcts 1-28, 82C3
Bias vs children chrgd 10-4, 812A2

HUECK, Cornelio
Quits as Cong pres 10-21, 865F1

HUFF, Floyd A.
St Louis environment study rptd 2-24, 184B1

HUGESSEN, James K.
Rejects Quebec probe halt 11-25, 923C3
Rejcts 3d bid to halt Quebec probe 12-11, 965B1

HUGHES, David
Protests UK monarchy ties 3-13, 199C1

HUGHES, Francine
Acquitted 11-3, 928E1

1978

Posters rptdly torn down 4-9, 287F3
In N Korea; sees Kim on reunificatn, US mil presence 5-5—5-10; S Korea scores 5-11, 340D2
Meets Brzezinski 5-22, 384A3
Greets Spain king 6-16; lauds forgn policy 6-18, 576C2
Zaire receives mil delegatn 6-24, 652A3
Lauded for openness 7-3, 532D2
Urges econ, trade growth 7-7, 532B1
USSR assails Rumania, Yugo, Iran trip 8-5, 8-21, 8-27; Rumania pres reassures Brezhnev 8-7, 675D3-676A1
At Japan pact signing 8-12, 637C1
Visits Rumania, Yugo, Iran; seeks to counter Sovt influence, signs agrmts 8-16—9-1, 674G2-675D3
Albania scores trip, chrgs Balkan war plot 9-3, 676B1
On econ progress 10-1, 773B3
In raw materials talks with Mex pres 10-24—10-30, 903D3
Meets Schlesinger 11-4, 871F2
Posters criticize 11-20, 11-25, 949A1-C2
Rumania visit cited 11-25, 913B3
Teng denies break 11-27, 949G2
Appears with Teng in pub 12-1, 950C1
US ties agreed 12-14; announces, cites Taiwan ties 12-16, 973C1, A2, G2
Text of China statemt on US ties 12-17, 975F1

HUANG Chen
Gets China CP post 1-2, 54A1
Replaced as US envoy 5-19, 384C3

HUANG Hua
Vs Cambodia-Viet mediatn 2-1, 80G1
Sees Brzezinski 5-20, 5-21 384E2; SALT briefing rptd 5-27, 399B2
Addresses UN disarmamt sessn; hints Geneva role, scores USSR 5-29, 421G2-422A1
Ends Zaire visit, pledges support 6-7, 441D2
Signs Libya pact 8-9, 691F2
Signs Japan peace pact 8-12, 637C1
Anti-Sovt stand cited 8-12, 637C2
With Hua in Rumania, Yugo, Iran 8-16—9-1, 674D3
Visits UK, scores Sovts 10-10—10-13, 796G1
Sovts say blocks arms pact 10-10, 796C2
Japan pact implemented, text states role 10-23, 801B1, F1

HUA Yao-pang
Gets China CP post 1-2, 54A1

HUBBARD Jr., Rep. Carroll (D, Ky.)
Reelected 11-7, 850E4

HUBBARD, L. Ron
Sentenced, fined 2-14, 232G3
Indicted 8-15, 644C3, G3, 645C1

HUBBARD, Mary Sue
Indicted 8-15, 644C3

HUBBARD Broadcasting v. Ammerman
NM press info order review refused by Sup Ct 5-15, 388B1

HUBBART, Tony
Held by Saudis 6-15, 516D1

HUBER, Antje
Retains W Ger youth min 2-3, 93A3

HUBER, Dieter
Kidnaped 2-13, reappears 2-15, 115E1

HUBNER, Nico
Arrested 3-14, 276A1
Jailed 7-7, 585D3

HU Chiao-mu
Named China dep premr 2-26—3-5, 153F1

HUCKABY Rep. Jerry (D, La.)
Reelected 11-7, 850F4

HUD—*See U.S. GOVERNMENT—HOUSING & Urban Development*

HUDDLESTON, Sen. Walter (Dee) (D, Ky.)
Votes for Panama Canal neutrality pact 3-16, 177E2
Votes for 2d Canal pact 4-18, 273B1
Wins primary 5-23, 406E2
Reelected 11-7, 848G1, 853B3

HUDOCK, Robert P.
Loses US House electn 11-7, 849D2

HUDSON, Alan
Signs with Sounders 10-16, 969D2

HUDSON, Rock
Avalanche released 8-28, 969B3

HUDSON Bay of Canada Co.—*See CONTINENTAL Oil Co.*

HUDSON River
PCB ban formally proposed 6-7, 513B1

HUDSPETH, Tommy
Fired as Lions coach 1-9, 171C2

HUECK, Cornelio
Chamorro murder role chrgd 1-22, 73G1

HUERTA, Raul Clemente
Runs 3d in pres electn 7-16, 556G3-557A1
Cotopaxi pres votes rptd annulled 8-8, 671A3
Pres runoff set for Apr '79 10-5, party splits 10-20, 881C2
Out of '79 pres runoff 11-15, 989D3

HUERTA Montalvo, Francisco
Liberals nominate for pres 2-13, 148D2
Expelled from Liberal Party 10-20, 881D2

HUFFMAN, Phillip
Traded to A's 3-15, 195A1

HUGHES, Barnard
Da opens 3-13, 887E1
Wins Tony 6-4, 579F2 ★

HUGHES, Cledwyn
New UK Rhodesia envoy 11-23, starts trip 11-28, 911F3

HUGHES, Harry R.
Wins primary for Md gov 9-12, 716E1
Elected 11-7, 848B2, 853F2

1979

Pak pres scorns Bhutto clemency plea 2-14, 116B2
Meets Waldheim on Viet conflict 5-1, 340A2
Teng rptd scored by Hunan radio 5-29, 406C1
Admits econ errors, rpts '78 data 6-18, 484E2
Meets Mondale, signs pacts 8-27—8-28, 644B2
Nixon visits China 9-17—9-22, 751F1
Poster criticisms rptd 9-22, 751E1
Visits 4 W Eur natns, signs pacts 10-15—11-6, 789E2, 853D3-854F2
Sees Japan premr, econ pact signed 12-5—12-7, 939D3

HUANG Hua
Signs US consulate pact 1-31, 65C1
Protests US-Taiwan ties 3-16, 312D1
Links Viet moves, Sovt world strategy 10-18, 789A3

HUBAY, Dr. Charles
Rpts new drug for breast cancer 9-11, 736C1

HUBBARD Jr., Rep. Carroll (D, Ky.)
Loses primary for gov 5-29, 420D1

HUBBARD, L. Ron
Wife sentenced 12-6—12-7, 1000D1

HUBBARD, Mary Sue
Sentenced 12-6—12-7, 1000D1

HUBBARD, Phil
In NBA draft 6-25, 507B2

HUBER, Antje
Proposes chem pollutn curbs 2-20, 214E3

HUBIN, Fernand
A-plant closure reversed 4-8, 276B2

HUBLEY, Season
Hardcore released 2-8, 174F2

HUBNER, Nico
Freed 10-11, 761F2
Arrives in W Ger 10-17, 882G3

HUD—*See U.S. GOVERNMENT-HOUSING & Urban Development*

HUDDLESTON, Sen. Walter (Dee) (D, Ky.)
Votes present on Talmadge denunciatn 10-10, 769G1

HUDNUT, Mayor William (Indianapolis, Ind.)
Reelected mayor 11-6, 846D3

HUDSON, Hugh
Dunstan quits as Australia premr 2-15, 153B1

HUDSON County Bus Owners Association
6 Iranian drivers fired 11-22, 898C2

HUDSPETH, James
Threat case refused by Sup Ct 4-16, 302F3

HUERTEMATTE, Robert
Panama Canal Comm member 12-6, 939D1

HUFF, Frederick E.
Acquitted re price-fixing 4-29, 327C3

HUFSTEDLER, Shirley M.
Named Educ secy 10-30, 829F1
Confrmd 11-30, sworn 12-6, 946F2

HUGHES, Albert W.
Dies 3-22, 272G2

HUGHES, Cledwyn
UK abandons Rhodesia conf plan 1-17, 39D3

HUGHES, Gov. Harry R. (D, Md.)
Sworn gov 1-17, 56E1
Abstains in gov vote on Carter '80 support 7-8, 518D1

1980

Visits Japan 5-27—6-1, 421G3
At Ohira rites 7-9; meets Carter, USSR scores 7-10, 506B1, F1
Scores Mao 8-10, 651A3
Submits resignatn as premr to Natl People's Cong 8-30, addresses 9-7; Cong accepts, names Zhao 9-10, 677A1-678C1
On resignatn as premier 9-27, 788B3
Giscard visits China 10-15—10-22, 829B3
Kang purged 10-31, 859G1
Scored in press 12-16, 12-30, 975C3

HUANG Hua
In Pak, vows aid vs Sovt threat 1-18—1-21, 44G2
Meets with Bush 8-21, 646B1
Named deputy premier 9-10, 677F1

HUANG Yungsheng
Trial set 9-27, delayed 11-1, 859C1
Admits Lin plot role to kill Mao 11-25, 975B2

HUBACHER, Ulrich
200 Sovt spies alleged 2-18, 141C3

HUBBARD Jr., Rep. Carroll (D, Ky.)
Reelected 11-4, 842E4

HUBBARD, Hugh J.
Onward Victoria opens 12-14, 1003E3

HUBBARD Jr., Ira Chase
Kidnaped 8-16, 707B2

HUBBARD, John R.
Zumberge named replacmt 5-21, 471B1

HUBBLE, Philip
Wins Olympic medal 7-20, 623F2
US swimmers beat Olympic time 7-30, 834B3

HUBER, Antje
Sworn W Ger health min 11-5, 925F1

HUCKABY, Rep. Jerry (D, La.)
Wins primary 9-13, 724A3
Reelected 11-4, 842F4

HUD (Housing & Urban Development, Department of)—*See under U.S. GOVERNMENT*

HUDAK, Harald
Ovett breaks 1500-m mark 8-27, 892A2

HUDNUT 3rd, Mayor William H. (Indianapolis, Ind.)
Elected cities league pres, reads Reagan message 12-1, 914D3

HUDSON, Ray
Cosmos win NASL title 9-21, 770G1

HUDSON, Rock
Mirror Crack'd released 12-18, 1003C2

HUDSON Bay Mining & Smelting Co. Ltd.
Seeks Rosario 1-10; Amax to buy Rosario 2-4, 385D3

HUERGUEDAS, Gloria
Sentncd for '77 murders 3-4, 196C2

HUFF, Richard H.
Loses US House electn 11-4, 851B3

HUFSTEDLER, Shirley M.
Names transitn aides, Smith sworn educ comr 1-9, 18B2, D2
On Educ Dept goals 5-7, 370D1
On Carter's last cabt meeting 12-3, 935G2

HUGEL, Charles E.
Named AT&T Intl chrmn 8-20, 648A2

HUGHES, Conrado
Arrested 11-14, 888A3

HUGHES, Gov. Harry R. (D, Md.)
State of State message 1-16, 269E2-A3
Heads China delegatn 6-15, 452D3

1976

HUGHES, Howard R(obard)
Facts on 336B1
CIA bars data on office burglary 1-5, 24E2
Leventhal dies 1-6, 56E3
Hannah dies 1-15, 56D3
Dies 4-5, buried 4-7; purported will found 4-27, 335B3-336B1
Will disputed 7-13, 7-16, 596E3
Summa electns held 8-4, 596C3
Relatives file pact 8-27; will forgery rptd 12-13, trial delayed 12-14, 971A2
HUGHES, Richard
Dies 4-28, 368F2
HUGHES, Judge Richard J.
Rules on Quinlan case 3-31, 292E2
HUGHES, Royston C.
Replaced in Interior post 5-21, 412E1
HUGHES, Rep. William J. (D, N.J.)
Reelected 11-2, 830D1
HUGHES Aircraft Co.
'75 arms sales listed 2-6, 147D2
Hughes dies 4-5, 336D1
Hughes Aircraft Co.—*See separate listing*
HUGHES Medical Institute, Howard
HUGHES Tool Co.—*See SUMMA Corp.*
HULA, Vaclav
Named to Czech Presidium 4-16, 289A2
HULL, Lytle
Dies 12-11, 1015E1

HUMAN & Civil Rights—*Note: General material pertaining to freedom and privacy is listed here. See also AMNESTY International; UNITED Nations—Human Rights, Commission on; also country names*
Rpt WCC chrgs Latin abuses 1-9, 61F2
Russell ct scores US, 11 Latin govts 1-17, 61B2
Latin, Eur soc dems score dictatorships 5-25, 449F2
Dominates OAS mtg 6-4—6-18, 464B2
Soclst Intl cong 11-26—11-28, 935A3, E3
Helsinki progress rpts issued 12-2, 12-8, 934F1, C2
Freedom House rpt on world press, freedom issued 12-22, 977E2
U.S. Developments (domestic)—*See also areas of abuse (e.g., EDUCATION, HOUSING, LABOR, POLICE, WIRETAPPING); subjects of abuse (e.g., MINORITIES, WOMEN); also U.S. GOVERNMENT subheads (e.g., CIA, IRS, SOCIAL Security, SUPREME Court)*
Russell ct scores US 1-17, 61C2
Freedom House survey rptd 1-19, 20D2-E3
US privacy comm hearings 2-11—2-13, 151A2
Credit bias ban signed 3-23, 233A3
Hatch Act repeal clears Cong 3-31, 234A2
Govt access to bank records upheld 4-21, 331C1
Groups sue vs food stamp revisns 5-26, 434E3
Carter urges intl standards 6-23, 451B3
Arms aid, sales curb signed 6-30, 533B1
Open govt bill signed 9-13, 688F3
Revenue sharing bias bar clears 9-30, Ford signs 10-13, 763A3, 764D3
Ford, Carter debate 10-6, 741E1, F2; 10-22, 801F3, 802C2
Rights-suit fee shifting signed 10-20, 788A2

1977

HUGHES, Howard R(obard) (1905-76)
Mormon will 'heir' admits lying 1-11, testifies 1-25—1-27, 120C1
'38 will sought 1-12, 1-17, 120B2
Estate appraised 3-15, 354E2
Family ends will search 3-15, 354D3
Calif, Ariz, Nev land holdings rptd 4-14, 354A3
Mormon will called fake 4-15, 354B3
Sanity affirmed, Tex seeks inheritanc tax 4-15, 354E3
Nixon-Frost interview 5-25, 420B2
Greenspun wins Summa damage suit 6-3, 472C2
HUGHES, James
Murdered 3-9, wife acquitted 11-3, 928E1
HUGHES Aircraft Co.
Indonesia payoffs chrgd 1-25, govt probes 2-4, 2-14, 182G2
Hughes Aircraft Co.—*See separate listing*
HUGHES Medical Institute, Howard
Files petitn for '38 will 1-12, 120D2
Family ends will search 3-15, 354E3
Offcls clash over Hughes estate 5-28, 6-8, 472C3
HUGHES Television Network Inc.—*See SUMMA Corp.*
HUGO, Carlos
Prince Xavier dies 5-7, 452G3
HULL, Bobby
Esposito passes in NHL goals 11-30, 1021D1
HULL, Henry
Dies 3-8, 264A3
HULL Jr., William R.
Dies 8-15, 696G2
HULL House
Addams surveillance rptd 6-19, 481E1
HULMAN Jr., Anton (Tony)
Dies 10-17, 872C2

HUMAN & Civil Rights—*Note: General material is listed here. See also specific areas of abuse (e.g., MAIL Surveillance, PRIVACY, WIRETAPPING) and subjects of abuse (e.g., MINORITIES, WOMEN); also AMNESTY International; country and region headings*
US issues rpts on forgn abuses 1-1, 50D2
'75 Ford Foundatn grants cited 1-11, 56E1
Carter inaugural 1-20, 25G2, 27E1
Carter statemt to world 1-20, 26F1, A3
Carter fireside chat 2-2, 75C2
Carter reaffirms commitmt 2-8, 88F2
US OKs dual prosecution 2-11, 821B1
FBI curbs proposed 2-15, 157A3
Carter backs civil rights acts 2-16, 110D2
Carter explains US stand 2-23, 126B2, G2
US aid cuts planned 2-24, 142E1
US Sen intell com watch scored 2-26, 151D1
Castro chrgs US abuses 2-26—2-27, 180E3
Carter reaffirms commitmt 3-1, 142A3
Carter to lift US travel bans 3-9, 172F3
Carter for world ldrship role 3-9, 173A1
US submits rpts to Cong 3-12, 186D3
Fannie Lou Hamer dies 3-14, 264F2
Carter town mtg 3-16, 190F3
Carter addresses UN 3-17, 185A1, 186E1-A2
Carter presents forgn aid progrm 3-17, 210C3, F3
US role in state civil actns curbed 3-22, 231G2
Vance backs aid bill amendmt 3-23, 210G3
58 sens back Carter stand 3-25, 226G2
Ford evaluates Carter stand 3-26, 236F2
Vance defends US stand 3-28, denies SALT link 3-30, 225B2, C2
Poll backs Carter stance 4-4, 251F1
Kissinger evaluates US policy 4-5, 247C2
Carter stresses in OAS address 4-14, 295C2
Carter vs aid bill amendmt 4-15, 299B2
US natl ID stand polled 4-24, Carter panel examines 4-27, 370B3, D3
IISS scores Carter stance 4-28, 401D1
Vance for US 'realistic' stand 4-30, 338C2
Carter topic on Europn TV 5-2, 338A2
7-natn summit discusses Carter stand 5-7—5-8, 357F2, 358E1
Carter addresses NATO reps 5-10, 359B1
Burger disputes critics 5-17, 419E2-B3
Carter forgn policy address 5-22, 397B2, E2
Blumenthal urges IDB stand 5-30—5-31, 438E3
Mrs Carter on Latin tour 5-30—6-12, 454G1
US rpt scores Sovt bloc 6-6, reactn 6-8, 6-13, 473E1
Sen backs Carter vs intl lending agency authorizatn amendmt 6-14, 477F2
Vance addresses OAS 6-14, 494D1
Helsinki preparatory conf opens 6-15, 473A1
US Cong backs Helsinki talks 6-15, 501C1
Giscard-Brezhnev talks 6-21, 495D1
Carter defends stance 7-12, 533D1
House sets intell panel 7-14, 557C1
US delays police arms sales to Latins 7-17, 572E3-574A1
ACLU: Carter record 'poor' 7-20, 575C2
Carter town mtg topic 7-21, 575F1

1978

HUGHES, Howard (R(obard) (1905-76)
Calif, Tex dispute domicile 2-13, 3-29, 459C1
Haldeman versn of Watergate rptd 2-16—2-17, 124A3
3 ex-aides indicted on drug chrgs 3-16, 6-6, 459F1
Autopsy, toxicology rpts revealed 3-16, 6-11, 459D2
Meier ordrd to repay Summa 3-29, 459F2
Nev ct rules Mormon will fake, 'lost will' rule pending 6-8, 458E3
Estate tax dispute interventn refused by Sup Ct 6-22, 509A1
Ex-aide cleared on drug chrgs 9-21, 1011A1
Med Inst breaks secrecy 12-7, 1010C3-1011A1
HUGHES, Randy
Cowboys win Super Bowl 1-15, 39G2
HUGHES, Sean Patrick
Captured 3-16, 268C1
HUGHES, Rep. William J. (D, N.J.)
Reelected 11-7, 851F2
HUGHES Aircraft Co.
9th in '77 defns contracts 3-28, 224G2
IRS probe of med inst noted 12-7, 1010E3, F3
HUGHES Medical Institute, Howard
Mormon will ruled fake, 'lost will' rule pending 6-8, 458F3, 459B1
Operatn secrecy broken, IRS probe noted 12-7, 1010C3-1011A1
Hughes Aircraft Co.—*See separate listing*
HUGHES Tool Co.—*See SUMMA Corp.*
HUGUET, Pierre
Freed by PI rebels 3-12, 248B2
HULL, Bobby
2 WHA stars sign with NHL Rangers 3-20, 296G1
Winnipeg wins WHA title 5-22, 458C2
Quits hockey, career cited 11-1, 991D1
HUMANA Inc.
Amer Medicorp OKs purchase, Hilton bid withdrawn 1-10, 66D2

HUMAN & Civil Rights—*Note: General material is listed here. See also specific areas and subjects of abuse (e.g., PRIVACY, WOMEN); also country, organization and region headings*
Carter theme on world tour 1-1—1-4, 1F1, 2D1
Freedom House survey issued 44B2
Humphrey role cited 32E3, 33A1
Carter State of Union Message 1-19, 29F2, 31G1, C3
Carter reorganizes intell agencies, sets curbs; ACLU, others score 1-24, 49A2
US Sen criminal code revisn scored by ACLU 1-30, 64A2
US issues rpt on 105 natns 2-9, 101C3-102F2
US intell agency bill introduced 2-9, 106D3
US plans '79 arms aid cuts 2-22, 127E1
Helsinki review conf ends 3-9, 179F1
Amnesty Intl holds torture conf 3-10—3-11, 180B3
EC adopts rights res 4-7, 258C1
Carter sees rights effort impact 4-11, 260E3
OPIC extensn bars aid to violators 4-24, 323A3
Carter appeals to Latins 6-16, 463A3
Young US 'pol prisoners' remark spurs controversy; Carter rebukes 7-12—7-15, 7-20, 542C2, 549E2
UK cancels poor natn debts 7-31, 592E1
US '79 forgn aid bill bars arms, police equipmt for offenders 9-26, 734D2
Carter states goals 11-13, 914C2
Carter defends policy 11-30, 936A3
Carter reaffirms policy 12-6, 933G3-934F1
Colombia novelist forms rights group 12-21, 1015B3

1979

HUGHES, Howard R(obard) (1905-76)
SEC suit settled 1-19, 88G1
Seduced opens 2-1, 292G2
HUGHES, Wendy
Newsfront released 5-30, 820D2
HUGHES Aircraft Co.
8th in '78 defns contracts 8-1, 609C1
HUGHES Air West—*See SUMMA Corp.-Air Holdings Corp.*
HUGHES Tool Co.—*See SUMMA Corp.*
HUGHES v. Oklahoma
Case decided by Sup Ct 4-24, 364D2
HULCER, Larry
Named NASL top rookie 8-30, 776D1
HULL, Bobby
NHL scoring mark cited 4-8, 356A1

HUMAN & Civil Rights—*See also specific areas and subjects of abuse (e.g., PRIVACY, WOMEN); also country, organization and region headings*
Freedom House survey issued 12D3-13B1
Carter State of Union Message 1-23, 47E2, E3
Amnesty Intl reviews '78 2-1, 85C2
US issues rpt on 115 natns 2-10, 107F1-108D2
Pope presents 1st encyclical 3-15, 217F1
SALT II summit topic 6-15–6-18, 449D1
Carter addresses Cong on SALT II 6-18, 459A3
FBI files preservatn sought by activists 6-26, 520F3
PEN chrgs 6 Latin natns 7-21, 553G3
Landrieu, Goldschmidt records cited 7-27, 577E1-D2
Carter likens Palestinian issue, US civil rights drive 7-31; scored 8-1, 575C1
Citizens Party platform 8-1, 595A1
Admin denies forgn spies aided in US 8-9, 664C2
Pope addresses UN 10-2; sees Carter, joint statemt issued 10-6, 757D1, F2, 758E1, 759D3
US com assesses Helsinki compliance 11-7, 980F3
Amnesty Intl issues '79 rpt 12-9, 980G1

1980

HUGHES, Howard R(obard) (1905-76)
Flying boat to be dismantled 5-22, 560G2
HUGHES, Wendy
My Brilliant Career released 2-1, 216C3
HUGHES, Rep. William J. (D, N.J.)
Names Abscam middleman 2-5, 111D1
Reelected 11-4, 843A3
HUGHES Aircraft Co.
6th in '79 defns contracts 5-28, 403F1
HUGHES v. Rowe
Case decided by Sup Gt 11-10, 868C1
HUGILL, Randy
Canterbury Tales opens 2-12, 136A3
HUHTALA, Mikko
Wins Olympic medal 7-23, 624B3
HULL, Bobby
'61-62 NHL scoring title tie cited 4-6, 295F3
HUMAID, Gen. Othman
Resignatn as staff chief cited 1-1, 22E1

HUMAN & Civil Rights—*See also specific areas and subjects of abuse; also country, organization and regional headings*
Meany backed civil rights 1-10, 14D3
US rights comm sees 'drift' in '79 1-14, 36G2
Carter reaffirms goal 1-23, 41C2, 43D1
King Peace Prize award rptd 1-28, 200B1
Freedom House '79 survey issued 2-1, 87B3
US issues rpt on world 2-5, 86A2-87B3
French CP issues world rpt 2-20, 149D3
Reagan 'basic speech' excerpts 2-29, 207E3
NYS suit filing limit upheld by Sup Ct 5-19, 440F2
Ill non-labor picketing rights affirmed by Sup Ct 6-20, 555D2
Carter stresses 6-21, 474D2
Dem platform drafted 6-24, 480A1
Pope calls for 'just society' 6-30—7-11, 537A2-538F2
US comm cautns re police 7-9, 519G1
Carter cites campaign issues 8-15, 629D3
Canada min urges UN role 9-22, 749B1
Perez awarded Nobel Peace Prize 10-13, 889A2
Carter, Reagan TV debate 10-28, 814A2, 815D3
Reagan backs consistency 11-6, 839E2
Carter plans to speak out 11-12, 865F2
Sovts scored at Helsinki conf 11-12, 11-13, 863C1; 11-14—12-19, 950E1
Pope affirms Helsinki agrmt 11-16, 905G1
Sup Ct bars extended judicial immunity from civil suits 11-17, 882A1
Pope issues social justice encyclical 12-2, 969G3
Defendants fed ct suits curbed by Sup Ct 12-9, 937B1
Amnesty Intl issues '80 rpt; US scored 12-10, 978E2

1976

HUMANE Legislation Inc., Committee for—*See COMMITTEE for, etc.*
HUMAN Life Amendment Group
Sup Ct bars Quinlan case review 11-1, 867G3
HUMAN Rights, International League for—*See INTERNATIONAL League for Human Rights*
HUMBOLDT, Ciro
Rptd arrested 6-6, 415A3
HUMBOLDT'S Gift (book)
Bellow wins Pulitzer 5-3, 352C3
HUME, Basil Cardinal
Named Westminster archbp 2-17, cardinal 4-27, 336G1, F2
HUMMELL Jr., Arthur W.
Sees Ethiopia forgn min 6-9, 457D2
Rpts on Korean crisis 9-1, 641D1
HUMPHREY, Sen. Hubert H. (D, Minn.)
Ford sees Dem bid 2-10, 109D3
On GAO grain report 2-16, 136G1
Meany: 'more electable' 2-16, 148G3
Backs arms sales disclosure 2-17, 151F3
Gets write-in vote in NH 2-24, 148F1
Asks cruise missile test halt 2-25, 183D1
Sen Mansfield to retire 3-4, 181F1
Gallup poll results 3-15, 197E1
Gets 6 Ill delegates 3-16, 196E3
Scores anti-DC talk 3-24; Carter, Udall clash 3-25—3-31, 233D1
Upstages candidates in NY 4-1, 233C2
Favored by 16 NY delegates 4-6, 244G3
Carter backs jobs bill 4-8, 261G1
Dem delegate box score 4-9, 261B1
Carter offers health plan 4-16, 282A1
'72 election costs rptd 4-25, 688G1
Pa 'Stop Carter' drive fails 4-27, 305C1
Carter would like backing 4-28, 324D1
Rules out campaign 4-29, 305F2
Byrne backs Carter 4-29, 324C1
Ala primary results 5-4, 323D2
Deplores forgn aid veto 5-7, 345C1
Gets 7% vote in Neb 5-11, 342G1
Platform com testimony 5-18, 357B3
Kennedy denies pres ticket bid 5-20, 357D2
Idaho, Ore primary results 5-25, 374E2-D3
NJ delegate slate backs 5-27, 390C3
SD primary results 6-1, 390B1
Reagan: ready to take on 6-1, 391C2
On pres bid 6-3, 6-8; sees Carter lead, frees delegates 6-9, 409G1, G3
Primary delegates totaled 6-8, 409A3
NJ delegate slate wins 6-8, 409E3
Sen Dems endorse Carter 6-24, 490D2
Mayors back jobs bill 7-1, 493E1
Rpts US NATO inefficiency 7-8, 760G2
Dem conv speaker 7-13, 505E1, 509D2; nominates Mondale for vp 7-15, 506A3
Udall urges jobs bill 7-14, 506D1
Dem conv pres vote, table 7-14, 507E3
Cited in Mondale biog sketch 512F2, A3-F3
Scores US arms sales to Iran 8-1, 581G2
GOP platform text cites 8-18, 602A3
Wins renomination 9-14, 705B1
With Carter in Minn 9-15, 686D3
Asks Letelier murder probe 9-21, 710E2
Carter, Ford debate jobs bill 9-23, 701F1
Full emplymt bill not cleared 10-2, 883B1, G3
Sup Ct bars Chestnut convictn review 10-4, 766D1
Reelected 11-2, 820D1, 823G2, 828B2
Carter meets cong ldrs 11-17, 864A2
Aide named Carter adviser 11-23, 881B3
HUMPHREYS, Burrell I.
Carter, Artis convicted 12-21, 1015F3
HUNDTOFTE, Virgil A.
Indicted 5-7, 349D1
Sentenced 10-5, 767F3
HUNGARY—*See also COMECON, DISARMAMENT—GENEVA Committee, WARSAW Pact*
Admin jobs frozen 1-1, 101C2
Portugal forgn min visits 1-12—1-14, 143B1
Sovt oil price up 1-15, 101D2
Listed as 'not free' nation 1-19, 20D3
Lekai named Esztergom archbp 2-12, cardinal 4-27, 336C2, D2
UN Palestine com member 2-26, 162C1
Refugees leave Chile emb 3-6, 288E3
Yugo sentences 4 3-12, 223C3
Sovt barter pact rptd 4-1, 543A3
Press scores Kissinger 4-9, 277G1
Yugo sentences Cominformists 4-14, 542G3
Shuns China fete for Egypt vp 4-19, 275G2
'75 Sovt trade rptd 5-5, 340G3
Addresses E Ger SED Cong 5-19, 381A2
Ratifies intl tin pact 6-11, 543G2
Eurocurrency loan rptd 7-2, 925D2
Meat prices raised 7-5, 925B2
Forint revalued vs Swiss franc, devalued vs £ 7-6, 925C2
Sovt space progrm role set 9-14, 684D1
Lekai urges church-state dialogue 9-18, 947B1
Secretariat hard-liner replaced 10-27, 947A1
Suicide rate rptd 11-17, 944F3
US rpts exit fees lowered 12-8, 934B2
Forint revalued vs $ 12-14, 1012E3
US WWI debt paymt rptd 12-24, 1012D3
European Force Reduction Issues—*See under EUROPE*
Sports
Olympic results 7-18—7-31, 573D3, 574E1-575B1, 576A1-E3

1977

Helsinki preparatory conf ends 8-5, 606B1
Young Carib tour 8-5—8-17, backs UN comr 8-8—8-9, 646F1, G2
US eases visa curb 8-17, 667E2
Latin dictators arrival protested 9-6—9-7, 678B1
Intl lending agency authorizatn, rights amendmt cleared by Cong 9-21, 737C3
Intl lending agency authorizatn signed 10-3, 834D1
Helsinki formal review parley opens 10-4, 752A2; US, USSR debate 10-16—10-22, 997C2
Carter signs UN pacts 10-5, 769D2
Forgn aid appropriatns clear Cong 10-19, 815A2; Carter signs 11-1, 834D1
Mondale reaffirms US commitmt 11-20, 955F1
NATO scores USSR 12-9, 957B1
AFL-CIO hears Sovt pleas 12-12, 12-13, 961D1
Carter remark in Warsaw 12-29, 1001G1
HUMAN Ecology Inc., Society for the Investigation of
CIA mind-control tests revealed 8-1—8-9, 610G3
HUMAN Life Amendment, National Committee for a
On abortn funding curb 12-7, 958C3
HUMAN Rights, American Convention on
Carter backs ratificatn 4-14, 295D2
Jamaica, Peru pledge ratificatn; Brazil bars 5-30—6-7; Venez signs 6-12, 454E2, 455B1, A2, E2
DR vows ratificatn 8-14, 647F1
HUMAN Rights, Commission on—*See under UNITED Nations*
HUMAN Rights, International Court of—*See EUROPE, Council of*
HUMAN Rights, Vietnamese Committee for—*See VIETNAMESE Committee for Human Rights*
HUMAN Sexuality: New Directions in American Catholic Thought (book)
US bishops score 11-16, 906C2
HUMBOLDT Bay, Calif.—*See CALIFORNIA*
HUMMEL Jr., Arthur W.
Named amb to Pak 5-23, confrmd 6-7, 499F3
HUMPHREY, Sen. Hubert H. (D, Minn.)
Byrd elected majority ldr 1-4; special post voted 1-5, 5E3, 6C1
Carter econ plan disclosed 1-7, 5B2
'68 effort vs Allende chrgd 1-9, 18F2
On Sovt mil buildup 1-18, 40B1
'76 spec interest gifts rptd 2-15, 128C2
Defends Warnke 3-8, 172F1
Minn execs in Cuba 4-18—4-22, 390F1
'76 campaign surplus rptd 5-3, 482G1
S Korea gifts alleged 6-5, 6-6, 442D1
Backs Carter Mideast moves 6-29, 496C1
Carter vows job action 9-7, 702C1
HEW hq named in honor 10-23, 817E1
Returns to DC with Carter 10-23, 817E1
Carter backs compromise jobs bill 11-14, 876F3
HUMPHREY, Prof. John
Chrgs Pl rights violatns 7-31, 618G3
HUMPHREY-Hawkins Bill—*See LABOR—Employment*
HUNDLEY, William
Rpts Park immunity offer 9-17, says return unlikely 9-21, 774E1, G1
Park diaries rptd sought by IRS 11-29, 915A3
HUNGARY—*See also COMECON, DISARMAMENT—Geneva Committee, WARSAW Pact*
UN Assemb member 4B1
Sovt oil price rise rptd 1-6, 67C3
In 14-natn sulphur-dioxide pact 1-19, 109B3
Intellectuals back Czech dissidents 1-22, 82G2
'76 OECD trade gap rptd 1-26, 123D2
Spain ties renewed 2-9, 242C2
Westn debt rptd mounting 2-13—4-13, 335C3
Pope Paul sees bishops 5-2, Kadar 6-9, 492B2
Lefebvre vs Kadar-Pope mtg 6-29, 620D2
Eurocommunism, Spain CP backed 6-30, 513E2
Kaiser confrmd US amb 6-30, 626F2
Eurocommunism stand reversed 7-3, 7-24, 590D3
Albania air link cited 595F1
Billy Graham visits 9-3—9-14, 732A1
Jamaica loan rptd 9-27, 884E3
Hans Habe dies 9-30, 788C1
Malta premr provokes walkout in Peking 11-3, 925G2
Egypt closes consulates, cultural cntrs 12-7, 929B1, 930B1
Helsinki Agreement—*See EUROPE—Security and Cooperation*

1978

HUMAN Factor, The (book)
On best-seller list 4-30, 356G1; 6-4, 460B3
HUMAN Rights, American Convention on
Carter vows ratificatn effort 6-21, 489D3
Enacted 7-18, 828E3-829C1
HUMAN Rights, Commission on—*See under UNITED Nations*
HUMAN Rights, European Commission on—*See also COUNCIL of Europe*
HUMAN Rights, Inter-American Commission on—*See under ORGANIZATION of American States*
HUMAN Rights, Inter-American Court of (Colombia, Costa Rica, Dominican Republic, Ecuador, El Salvador, Grenada, Guatemala, Haiti, Honduras, Panama, Venezuela)
Established 7-18, 828E3
HUMAN Rights, International Court of—*See also COUNCIL of Europe*
HUMAN Rights, International League for—*See INTERNATIONAL League for Human Rights*
HUME, Basil Cardinal
Scores El Salvador armored car sale 1-13; sale canceled 1-19, 75B1
HUMPHREY, Gordon J.
Wins US Sen primary in NH 9-12, 736E1
Elected 11-7, 846B1, 847E3, 848E2
HUMPHREY, Sen. Hubert H(oratio) (D, Minn.)
Cyril King dies 1-2, 96E2
Dies 1-13; DC rites 1-15, funeral 1-16; facts on 32E2
Carter State of Union Message 1-19, 29C3, 31D3
Widow to fill Sen seat 1-25, 52F2, 107C2
Full employmt bill OKd by House bill 3-16, 182F2
Sen ethics com rpts Park gift disputed 6-19, 527E2
Gartner under fire for Andreas gift 6-26, 6-28, 513A3
FBI informants rptd at '68 Dem conv 7-3, 507F3
Primary results for seat 9-12, 716C1
Full employmt bill cleared by Cong 10-15, 784F3 808A1; Carter signs 10-27, 873A2
Aides' testimony re Park queried 10-16, 832D1
Durenberger wins seat 11-7, 854A3
HUMPHREY, Muriel Buck (Mrs. Hubert H.)
Husband dies 1-13, 32D3
Named to husband's seat 1-25, 52F2, 107C2
Votes for Panama Canal neutrality pact 3-16, 177E2
Votes for 2d Canal pact 4-18, 273B1
Primary results for seat 9-12, 716C1
HUMPHREY, Ronald L.
Arrested as Viet spy 1-31, 68B3
Asks Thi ouster barred 2-8, stay issued 2-10, 103B3
Convicted 5-19, 389F3-390F1
Sentenced 7-7, 555A1
HUMPHREY-Hawkins Bill—*See LABOR—Employment*
HUNGARY—*See also COMECON, DISARMAMENT—Geneva Committee, GATT, WARSAW Pact*
4 dissidents rptd exiled 3-7, 180F2
SWP mtg ends; party shuffled, Nemeth promoted 4-20, 534G1
Kadar rpts church curbs eased 6-10, 534C3
'74 Mindszenty dismissal cited 8-6, 601D2
Travel curbs eased, '77 tourist total rptd 10-31, 841B1
Economy & Labor (domestic)
Price hikes set, CPI rise rptd 1-9, 55D2
'77 indl output, GNP, other data rptd 2-9, 534E1
Price controls end set, '77 costs cited 4-20, 534B1
Kadar explains price reforms 6-10, 534C3
Alcohol price hike rptd 7-24, 691E3
Average monthly wage rptd 8-8, 882F3
June '77-78 world inflatn rates ranked 10-18, 914F1
European Force Reduction Talks—*See under EUROPE*
Foreign Relations (misc.)—*See also 'Monetary, Trade, Aid & Investment' below*
Rumania minority bias chrgd 1-24, 3-1, 180A2
Rumania-Hungary CP ldrs meet 2-16—2-19, tensns rptd 2-23, 180D2
Rumania pleas on minority bias rptd 4-25, dissident poet scored 5-7, 360E1 ★
'Hungarian Circle' bank forgers sentncd in UK 5-31, 824B3

1979

HUMAN Factor, The (book)
On best-seller list 3-4, 173F3
HUMAN Justice, International League for
Iran executns scored 4-13, 276F3
HUMAN Rights, Commission on—*See under UNITED Nations*
HUMAN Rights, Inter-American Commission on—*See under ORGANIZATION of American States*
HUMAN Rights, Society for the Protection of
Haitian 'slavery' in DR rptd 8-17, 804A3
HUMAN Sexuality: New Directions in American Catholic Thought (book)
Vatican criticism rptd 8-11, 640F2
HUME, John
Named SDLP head 11-28, 928A1
HUME, Tom
NL pitching ldr 9-30, 955G2
Reds lose NL pennant 10-5, 797C2
HUMMEL, Anton
Spy arrest announced 6-21, 490A1
HUMMEL Jr., Arthur W.
Pak fears A-projct covert actn 8-14, 607G3
US Emb in Pak sacked 11-21, 893E2
HUMPHREY, Sen. Gordon J. (R, N.H.)
Vs SALT treaty 4-5, 258G1
HUMPHREY, Hubert Horatio (1911-78)—*See 1978, p. 32C3 for biog. data*
Nixon cancer gift rptd 7-11, 527B3
HUMPHREY-Hawkins Bill—*See LABOR—Employment*
HUMPHREYS, Roger
Pardoned by Gov Blanton 1-16, 36A2
HUMPHRIES, David
Quadrophenia released 11-2, 1008B1
HUMPHRIES, Capt. Michael G.
AF plane lost 4-12, feared dead 5-5, 404B3
HUNDLEY, William
On Tongsun Park testimony 4-16, 283E2
HUNERWADEL v. Baird
Case decided by Sup Ct 7-2, 559G1
HUNGARY—*See also COMECON, DISARMAMENT—Geneva Committee, GATT, WARSAW Pact*
Catholics see Pope in Poland 6-2, 413B2
Economy & Labor
Price hikes set, '79 CPI predicted 1-8, 101A2
'78 econ data rptd 2-9, 256G3
Econ dvpt praised 5-30, 417C1
Econ reorganizatn rptd 9-3, 741G2
European Force Reduction Talks—*See under EUROPE*
Foreign Relations (misc.)—*See also 'Monetary' and 'UN' below*
Cambodia downfall rptd lauded 1-10, 11B2
China invasn of Viet scored 2-19, Rumania stand denounced 2-21, 122F2
Brezhnev visits 5-30-6-1, 416F1
Swedish envoy '45 USSR disappearance case reopened 8-4, 690C2
USSR troop deploymt rptd 761F2
Helsinki Agreement—*See EUROPE—Security and Cooperation*
Monetary, Trade, Aid & Investment
US loan rptd sought 3-30, 279B3
USSR trade talks 5-30-6-1, 417C1
Rumania travel ban set 8-1, 645F3
Free exchng rate rptd sought 9-3, 741A3
East-West bank opens 11-9, 882A3
US bank branch opens 11-15, 882B3
Obituaries
Nagy, Ferenc 6-12, 508D3
Sports
Men's table tennis champs 4-30, 527E1

1980

HUMAN Factor, The (film)
Released 2-8, 216G2
HUMAN Freedom Center
Founders slain 2-26, 190D3
HUMAN Rights, Commission on—*See under UNITED Nations*
HUMAN Rights, Inter-American Commission on—*See under ORGANIZATION of American States*
HUMBARD, Rex
TV revenues rptd 2-25, 413A2
HUME, John
Home rule talks begin 1-7, 39A2
On home rule plan 7-2, 523D1
HUME, Tom
NL pitching ldr 10-6, 926G2
HUMPHREY, Sen. Gordon J. (R, N.H.)
Votes vs Muskie confrmatn 5-7, 343F1
Evangelical Christian pol role rptd 7-11—9-15, 819C2
HUMPHREY, Hubert Horatio (1911-78)
Ex-aide named in Jamaican grain fraud case 2-4, 99A3
HUMPHRIS, Barry
Getting of Wisdom released 8-5, 675G2
HUNG, Pham
Named Viet interior min 2-7, 90G1
HUNGARY—*See also COMECON, CSCE, GATT, GENEVA Committee, MBFR, WARSAW Pact*
Economy & Labor
'79 data rptd 2-8, 166G1
CP cong notes problems 3-24—3-28, 274D3-275A1
Foreign Relations (misc.)—*See also 'Monetary' below*
USSR Afghan invasn rptd 1-10, 11A1
USSR backed, Afghan cited 3-24, 274G3
Sovt rabbi completes study 4-12, 431D1
Zimbabwe gains indepndnc 4-18, 301F1
Soyuz 36 launched 5-26, 397B3
Polish strike press coverage rptd 8-18, 626G2
Polish govt chngs rptd 8-25, 624B2
Poland strike setlmt praised 8-31, 659B1
Poland criticism rptd mild 10-21, 831B2
Sovt role defended 11-13, 863F1
Poland summit warning rptd stressed 12-10, 929D2
Government & Politics—*See also other appropriate subheads in this section*
12th CP cong held, Politburo shuffled 3-24—3-28, 274D3-275A1
Monetary, Trade, Aid & Investment
$250 mln Westn loan confrmd 2-18, 142B3
Westn debt, Sovt raw material price hikes cited 3-24, 274E3
Ukraine electric grid cited 10-1, 753D3
Obituaries
Gero, Erno 3-12, 279A3
Sports
Lake Placid Olympic results 2-12—2-24, 154F2, 155F2-156D1

1976

HUNGATE, Rep. William L. (D, Mo.)
Volkmer wins seat 11-2, 823B3
HUNGER—*See FAMINES, FOOD*
HU Nim
Says Sihanouk hails charter 1-5, 8B1 *
Announces election date 2-4, 98C3
Chrgs US jet raid 2-27, 172E3
Rpts People's Assembly list 3-22, 238A2
HUNT Jr., E. Howard
Ehrlichman verdict upheld 5-17, 379D1
Nixon disbarred in NY 7-8, 493D3
HUNT, Herold C.
Dies 10-17, 970A2
HUNT Jr., James B.
Wins primary for gov 8-17, 633E1
To face Flaherty 9-14, 705E1
Elected gov 11-2, 820B3, 822D2, 831G1
HUNT, Ralph J.
Medibank expands 6-8, 456B1
HUNTER, Daniel S.
Bronson ct-martial starts 6-14, 435D3
Outlines Bronson defense 6-18, 493D2
HUNTER, Jim (Catfish)
NL wins All-Star game 7-13, 544A2
AL pitching ldr 10-4, 796E1
Yankees win pennant 10-14, 796G1, A2
In World Series 10-16—10-21, 815F2
HUNTING—*See WILDLIFE*
HUNT Oil Co.
Scotland find rptd 8-19, 675A3
HUPP, Rev. Robert P.
Vs UN anti-apartheid stand 11-9, 842B3
HURFORD, Christopher
In Australia shadow cabt 1-29, 116E1 *
Scores monetary curbs, 11-7, 850D1
Scores currency system 12-14, 944B3
HURLEY, Most Rev. Francis T.
Named archbp of Anchorage 5-4, 424C1

1977

HUNGER—*See FAMINES*
HUNT, Douglas
Chrgd re soybean futures 4-28, 341E1
Soybean trading ruled illegal 9-28, 858E3
HUNT Jr., E. Howard
Paroled 2-23, 140A3
Released from prison 2-23, 197F2
Nixon-Frost interview 5-4, 366F1-C3
HUNT, H. L.
Heirs seek Sunshine Mining takeover 3-21, 275C1
HUNT, James
Wins US, Japan Grand Prix 10-1, 10-23; final standing 10-23, 870D3, E3
HUNT Jr., Gov. James B. (D, N.C.)
Wilmington 10 pardon sought 12-4, 943B1
HUNT, Lamar
Oil suit case declined 12-5, 938E3
HUNT, Nelson Bunker
Great Western settles FTC case 1-26, 156F1
Seeks Sunshine Mining takeover 3-21, 275C1
Sued on soybean futures 4-28, 341E1
Countersues 5-4, ct lifts trading ban 5-6, 464B1
Soybean trading ruled illegal 9-28, 858E3
Sunshine takeover OKd 10-4, 798G3
Oil suit case declined 12-5, 938E3
HUNT, Ralph
Named Australia health min 12-19, 982A2
HUNT, Reed O.
Dies 11-26, 952E2
HUNT, Sam
NFL officiating scored 12-18, 1020F1
HUNT, Steve
Cosmos win NASL title, named game MVP 8-28, 676E2, F2
HUNT, William Herbert
Great Western settles FTC case 1-26, 156F1
Seeks Sunshine Mining takeover 3-21, 275C1
Sued on soybean futures 4-28, 341E1
Countersues 5-4, ct lifts trading ban 5-6, 464B1
Soybean trading ruled illegal 9-28, 858E3
Sunshine takeover OKd 10-4, 798G3
Oil suit case declined 12-5, 938E3
HUNTER, Alan
Arrested in terrorist plot 4-1, 429A1
HUNTER, Billy
Hired as Ranger mgr 6-27, 644B3
HUNTER Jr., Judge Edwin F.
Cities Svc bias accord rptd 3-2, 279E1
HUNTER, Jim (Catfish)
In World Series 10-11—10-18, 806B2
HUNTER College (N.Y.)
George Shuster dies 1-25, 84F3
HUNTING—*See WILDLIFE*
HUNT Oil Co.
Sup Ct declines case 12-5, 938E3
HUNT v. Mobil Oil Corp.
Sup Ct declines case 12-5, 938G3
HURLEY, Archbishop Denis
Backs S Africa COs 2-9, 100F2

1978

Kadar defends USSR, Cuba role in Africa; scores arms race, backs Eurocommunism 6-10, 534F2
UN Assemb member 713F3
Kadar in France, detente stressed 11-15—11-17, 894E2
Helsinki Agreement—*See EUROPE—Security and Cooperation*
Monetary, Trade, Aid & Investment
EC steel dumping probe begun 1-23, 80C2
'77 trade rptd 2-9, 534G1
Jamaica alumina refinery aid rptd 2-28, 194E2
US favored-natn status granted, '77 trade rptd 7-8, 534C2
US jean factory opens 8-8, 882D3
Forint devalued vs W Eur currencies, revalued vs US $ 11-11, 906G2
Obituaries
Serly, Tibor 10-8, 888E3
Sports
World Cup soccer finals, sidelights 6-1—6-25, 519F3
U.S. Relations
US returns St Stephen crown 1-6, facts on 7G1
Kadar interviewed by US rptr, stresses ties 6-10, 534E2
US grants favored-natn trade status, '77 data rptd 7-8, 534C2
US jean factory opens 8-8, 882D3
Pan Am to end Budapest svc 9-7, 701G1
Forint revalued vs US $ 11-11, 906G2
HUNKE, Father Heinz
Ousted from Namibia 7-14, 547B3
HUNT Jr., E. Howard
Denies JFK murder role before House subcom 11-3, scores 'memo' 11-4, 898D3
HUNT, Guy
Nominated for Ala gov 9-5, 699C2
Loses electn 11-7, 849G2
HUNT Jr., Gov. James B. (D, N.C.)
Wilmington 10 denied convictn review 1-5, 24D2
Cuts Wilmington 10 sentences 1-23, 560C2
HEW OKs coll integratn plan 5-12, 369E1
Govs OK budget resolutn 8-29, 682D1
HUNT, Lamar
Stars defy 'Super Grand Prix' 4-23, 418C3
HUNT, Leslie
US Open results 9-10, 707D1
HUNT, Linda
Tennis Game opens 11-5, 1031B3
HUNT, Steve
Cosmos win NASL title 8-27, 707C2
HUNT, Ruth
Pregnancy, cancer immunity link rptd 1-19, 334A1
HUNTER, Billy
Fired as Rangers mgr 10-1, 1026G1
HUNTER, James
NFL '77 interceptn ldr 1-1, 56G2
HUNTER, Jim (Catfish)
Yankees win AL pennant 10-7, 779B1
In World Series 10-10—10-17, 799D3
HUNTER, Oakley
HUD outlines authority 8-14, 628B1
HUNTER, Robert
Lauds hosp cost lid rejectn 7-18, 551A1
HUNTING—*See WILDLIFE*
HUNTINGTON, Samuel P.
China SALT briefing rptd 5-27, 399B2
HUNTLEY, Joni
Sets indoor high jump record 1-14, 76F2
HUPPERT, Isabelle
No Time For Breakfast released 9-15, 970D2
Violette released 10-9, 1030F3
HURAULT, Bertrand
Near & Far Away released 3-24, 619B3
HURLBERT, Gordson C.
Denies wrongdoing in PI contract 1-16, 38A3

1979

UN Policy & Developments
Membership listed 695E2
U.S. Relations
$300 mln loan rptd sought 3-30, 279B3
US A-accident media coverage rptd 4-11, 323D1
US bank branch opens 11-15, 882B3
HUNGER—*See FAMINES*
HUN Sen
Cambodian forgn min 1-8, 10B1
Gets US plan on emergency aid 10-24, 824B1
US congresswomen get relief aid vow 11-12, 863F2
HUNT Jr., Gov. James B. (D, N.C.)
PCB disposal plan rejctd by EPA 6-5, 597C3
HUNT, Nelson Bunker
Oil suit ruling declined by Sup Ct 12-10, 988G1
HUNT, Ralph
Prawn arsenic levels rptd high 2-20, 188G2
Sees Liberal-NCP coalitn threat 9-24, 771C2
HUNT, Walter (Pee Wee)
Dies 6-22, 508B3
HUNTER, The (painting)
Willed to LA museum 3-7, 375G1
HUNTER, Carman St. John
Scores adult literacy progrms 9-8, 786D1
HUNTER Jr., Dr. Conway
Rpts Valium abuse 9-10, 734C3
HUNTER, Judge Edwin F.
Braniff pays trust fine 2-23, 206D2
HUNTER, Judge Elmo
Upholds ERA conv boycott 2-21, 128F1
HUNTER, Evan
Walk Proud released 6-15, 820F3
HUNTING, Earl W.
Scores judge on drug arrest 9-20, 748B2
HUNTINGTON, Ronald
In Canadian Cabt 6-4, 423G3
HUNTINGTON, Samuel P.
USSR bars book entry 9-4, 690E1
HUNT v. Coastal States
Case declined by Sup Ct 12-10, 988G1
HURD, Mayor Gordon (Davy, W. Va.)
Rpts Davy flood damage 5-16, 472G2
HURON, Lake—*See GREAT Lakes*

1980

Moscow Olympics results 7-20—8-3, 588A3, 622E1-624G3
Chess Olympiad results 12-7, 972A3
U.S. Relations
Mfrs Hanover confrms loan 2-18, 142B3
US rights 'violatns' chrgd 11-13, 863F1
HUNGER—*See FAMINES*
HUNT, Annette
Dona Rosita opens 3-20, 392F2
HUNT Jr., E(verette) Howard
Liddy book excerpts reveal death plot 4-21, 333B3
HUNT, Elizabeth
Father's bailout loan collateral listed 5-28, 425D3
HUNT, H. L. (1889-1974)
Comex moves to curb silver speculatn by heirs 1-8, 31C1
Gulf Resources rejects Placid Oil offer 2-26, 385B3
Heirs bailout loan collateral listed 5-28, 426F1
HUNT, Houston Bunker
Father's bailout loan collateral listed 5-28, 425D3
HUNT Jr., Gov. James B. (D, N.C.)
Assaulted in Denver 8-5, 596G3-597A1
Warns vs econ platform plank 8-12, 611A1
Reelected 11-4, 845C3, 847C1, 849G3
HUNT, Lamar
$1.1 bln silver bailout set 5-2, 344F3
Bailout loan paid 5-27, collateral listed 5-28, 424E2, B3-426F1
Sen com probes bank deals, weighs FRB regulatn 5-29—5-30; legal actn threatened 5-30, 425D1-B3
HUNT, Nelson Bunker
Sets silver-backed bond issue 3-26, 222F3
Margin calls shake empire; silver prices plunge, stock mkt in turmoil 3-26—3-27, 223E1
Uses oil assets to settle Engelhard debt 3-31, 244F3
Silver trading, Bache ties probed 3-31—4-2; additional debts rptd, shakeup seen 3-31, 245G1-B3
Silver trading debts repaid 4-8, 4-16; Canada OKs Engelhard setlmt 4-28, 345D1
Sunshine Mining offers silver-backed bonds 4-11, 265F3
Regulators debate commodity trading curbs, seek testimony 4-14—4-15, 290B2
Gets contempt warning 4-29; testifies at House, Sen probes 5-2, 345F1
$1.1 bln silver trading bailout set 5-2, 344F3
Bailout loans paid 5-27, collateral listed 5-28, 425E2, B3-426F1
Sen com probes bank deals, weighs FRB regulatn 5-29—5-30; legal actn threatened 5-30, 425D1-B3
Daughter acquires NM silver stake 6-24, 685D3
Columbia sues Kerkorian 10-2, 906A3
Liquidates Bache stock 10-21, 867B3
CFTC sets tighter commodity trading rules 11-25, 899C1
HUNT, Ralph
OKs more US-Australia flights 7-30, 617F2
Airbus deal OKd 9-29, 748B1
HUNT, W. Herbert
Asks Merrill Lynch margin call delay 3-27, 223D2
Uses oil assets to settle Engelhard debt 3-31, 244F3
Silver trading, Bache ties probed 3-31—4-2; additional debts rptd, shakeup seen 3-31, 245G1-B3
Silver trading debts repaid 4-8, 4-16; Canada OKs Engelhard setlmt 4-28, 345D1
Regulators debate commodity trading curbs, seek testimony 4-14—4-15, 290B2
Gets contempt warning 4-29, testifies at House, Sen probes 5-2, 345F1
$1.1 bln silver trading bailout set 5-2, 344F3
Bailout loans paid 5-27, collateral listed 5-28, 425E2, B3-426F1
Sen com probes bank deals, weighs FRB regulatn 5-29—5-30; legal actn threatened 5-30, 425D1-B3
Liquidates Bache stock 10-21, 867B3
CFTC sets tighter commodity trading rules 11-25, 899C1
HUNTER, Duncan
Elected to US House 11-4, 842C2, 852B2
HUNTER, Minnie
Indicted 8-27, 712B3
HUNTER, Oakley
Maxwell replaces at Fannie Mae 9-24, 960A1
HUNTER, The (film)
Released 8-1, 675A3
HUNTER, Thomas
Final Countdown released 8-1, 675E2
HUNT Stephens Investments Co.
Hunts bailout loan collateral listed 5-28, 425G3
HUPP, Debbie
Wins Grammy 2-27, 296D3
HURD, W. Michael
Wins Mich US House primary 8-5, 682D3
HURDLE, Clint
In World Series 10-14—10-21, 811F2, 812G2
HURLEIGH, Robert F
Dies 8-10, 676F1
HURLEY, Ruby
Dies 8-10, 676F1

1976

HURRICANES—*See STORMS*
HURRIYA (Egyptian warship)
In Intl Naval Review 7-4, 488D3
HURTADO, Hector
Signs Argentina econ pact 1-14, 96D3
HUSAK, Gustav
CP Cong reelects, rpts 5-yr econ plan 4-12, 289B1, C2
Vows no '77 food price rise 8-28, 750B3
HUSCHKE, Thomas
Wins Olympic medal 7-22, 574B2
HUSSEIN, Sadam
Seeks Sahara setlmt 1-29, 58C2
Halts Kurd deportatns 7-5, 547F2
Gets Arafat plea vs Syria 10-13, 758D2
Named bomb blast target 12-15, 954A1

HUSSEIN ibn Talal ibn Abdullah el Hashim, King (Jordan)
Secret Rabin talks rptd 1-12, 19D1
Joint Syria war games rptd 1-18, 35D1
Decree bars electns 2-4, reconvenes Parlt 2-5, 83F2
PLO scores re W Bank policy 2-15, 126D1
Visits Australia 3-2—3-9, 204B1
Meets Ford on Leb crisis 3-30, 226B3
Asks Syrian troops in Leb 3-31, 4-1, 225C3 226F2-D3
Ends US visit, sees missile sale delay 4-4, 242E1
Confirms seeks Sovt arms, US warns 6-16, 464A2
In Moscow, seeks arms 6-17—6-28, 464F1
Names Badran premr 7-13, 949A3
Moscow visit cited 7-31, 561A2
W Bank Arabs assail 9-12, 9-16, 699D3, G3
Meets Leb Christns 11-1, 841G1
Amman raiders crushed 11-17, 861A2
Meets Assad on merger 12-7—12-8, 913A2
Sadat backs Palestine state tie 12-29, 973B1

HUSSEIN Onn
Malaysia premier 1-15, 55F2
In ASEAN-Australia talks 1-16—1-17, 46D1
Signs ASEAN pact 2-24, 148D2
HUSTLE (film)
Dec '75 top-grossing film 32G3
Top-grossing film 1-28, 104F3
HUSTLE, The (recording)
Wins Grammy 2-28, 460B3
HUTCHINSON, James D.
Testifies on Teamster probe 7-1, 492D2
HUTCHISON, Ray
Reagan sweeps Tex vote 5-1, 322F3

1977

HURRICANES—*See STORMS*
HURTADO, Hector
Venez finance min 1-7, 23E2
Venez state min, Investmt Fund pres 7-15, 566A1
HURVITZ, Igael
Rumania trade expansn rptd 12-10, 987B3
HURWITZ, Yigal
Israel commerce min 6-20, 474E2
HUSAK, Gustav
US authors back dissidents 1-19, 82A3
Cancels van der Stoel mtg 3-2, 220A3
Wife dies 10-20, 872C2
USSR revolutn anniv fete photo 11-7, 865C3
HUSAK, Viera
Dies 10-20, 872C2
HUSSAIN, Chief Justice Mushtaq
Bhutto chrgs bias, loses plea 11-20, 987B1
HUSSEIN, Abdel Aziz
US oil co nationalized 9-19, 805G3
HUSSEIN, Abdirizak Haji
US blamed re arms, Ogaden 9-19, 715D3
HUSSEIN, Kamal Eddin
Vs plebiscite 2-5, loses Assemb seat 2-14, 115D3
Meets Arafat 3-8, 170C2
Sees war possibility 5-31, 496E1
Begin asks peace talks 6-21, 474C2
Begin asks Israel visit 11-20, 893F3
On Sadat Israel trip 11-28, 909D2

HUSSEIN bin Dato Onn (Malaysian prime minister)
At ASEAN summit 8-4—8-5, 607A2

HUSSEIN ibn Talal ibn Abdullah el Hashim, King (Jordan)
Daoud arrested 1-7, freed 1-11, 9E2
Meets Sadat, PLO peace role backed 1-14—1-15, 50C1
Meets Waldheim 2-8—2-9, 86F2
Queen killed in air crash 2-9, 87D1
Meets Vance 2-18—2-19; reactn to Sadat plan for PLO-Jordan link rptd 2-19, 121D2
CIA paymts rptd, Jordan assails; US, PLO statemts 2-18—2-23, 123A3, 124C2; 2-24—2-28, 151E1, G2
Defends CIA paymts 2-28, 151D2
For Geneva conf delay 4-2, 245D2
Sees Carter, for Geneva conf delay 4-25—4-26, 315G3-316B1
Peres says impedes peace 4-25, 316F1
PLO chrgs US plot 5-8, 360C3
Meets Sadat, PLO-Jordan link backed 7-9—7-10, 534G2
Carter rpts Palestinian view 7-12, 533F2
Scored by PFLP 7-14, 535A1
Meets Vance 8-5—8-6, sees Mideast agrmts 8-7, 605B1
Sharaf meets Carter 9-28, 734B1
Begin to invite 11-15, 873G1
Sees Assad, Sadat on Arab rift 12-7—12-8, 930B2
Begin hints concessns 12-7, 931C1
Meets Sadat, on PLO peace role 12-8—12-9, 953G2
Meets Vance, backs Sadat peace moves 12-12, 954C1
Carter: PLO 'negative' 12-15, 954C3
PLO says would bar Begin W Bank plan 12-19, 995B3
Carter sees in Iran 12-31, 1000F3

HUSTLER (magazine)
Flynt sentenced 2-8, 118A2
HUSTLER Magazine Inc.
Fined 2-8, 118B2
Hustler (magazine)—*See separate listing*
HUSTON, Margo
Wins Pulitzer Prize 4-18, 355E2
HUSTON, Tom Charles
Nixon cites spy plan 5-19, 405D3
HUTCHESON, Rick
Named 'paper flow' dir 7-15, 556A1
HUTCHINS, Robert Maynard
Dies 5-14, 452B3
Successor announced 11-21, 927F2
HUTCHINSON, Fred(erick Charles) (1919-64)
McCovey wins Hutch Award 11-14, 990E2

1978

HURRICANES—*See STORMS*
HURT, Marybeth
Interiors released 8-2, 970F1
HURT, William
5th of July opens 4-27, 760C2
HURTADO, Osvaldo
Arrested 1-15, freed 1-30, 112A1
HURVITZ, Yigal
Vs Sinai settlmnt exit 9-18, 712F3
Vs Camp David summit pact, quits Cabt 9-24, 9-28, 729C1
HUSAIN, Ghulam
Arrested 10-4, 775D2
Wattoo arrested 10-12, 818C3
HUSAK, Gustav
Visits W Ger 4-10—4-14; detente support vowed, rights policy defended 4-11, 332F3
HUSKY Oil Ltd.
Petro-Canada, Occidental in bidding war; collusn chrgd, bd member quits 6-10—7-27; Alberta Gas wins control 6-27, 628E3-629E2
Occidental takeover bid cited 8-18, 767D3
Petro-Canada buys Phillips unit 11-10, 11-20, 901D2
HUSS, Erik
Swedish indus min 10-18, 822G2
HUSSAINI, Hatim I.
Heads info office in Washington 5-1, 340C2
HUSSEIN, Abdel Aziz
Lauds PLO raid vs Israel 3-13, 176E1
HUSSEIN bin Dato Onn (Malaysian prime minister)
Party wins electns 7-8, forms new Cabt 7-27, 592C2
Warns China vs interference 11-10, cites differences 11-12, 894E1

HUSSEIN ibn Tal Abdullah el Hashim, King (Jordan)
Meets Carter 1-1—1-2; vs Israel W Bank plan 1-2; Begin scores 1-3, 2E2-D3
US aide briefs on peace moves 1-27—1-28, 60E1
Jordan freed Palestinian prisoners 3-3, 157A2
Meets US aide 3-5, vs mediatn 3-6, 156G3-157C1
Israeli Leb invasn protested 3-21, 198D3
Engagement announced 5-15, 420A3
Names successors 6-8, 580C1
Marries 6-15, 580B1
Vance summit pact missn set 9-18, 709E2
Sadat may seek W Bank pact alone 9-19, 710E3
Vance sees on summit pact 9-20, 712G3
Hardliners asks summit pact rejctn 9-22, 9-26, fears separate Israel-Egypt setlmt 9-23, 730C1
Sadat stand on Jerusalem cited 9-22, 892G3
Warns vs separate Egypt-Israel pact 10-1, 762G1
US aide answers W Bank queries 10-17—10-19, 802A2

HUSSEY, Marmaduke, J.
Suspends Times publicatns 11-30, 924B1, E1
HUSTLER (magazine)
Flynt shot, mistrial declared 3-6, 186G3
HUSTLER Magazine Inc.
Plains Monitor, Atlanta Gazette '77 purchase cited 187B1
Hustler (magazine)—*See separate listing*
HUTCHISON, Ray
Loses primary for Tex gov 5-6, 362E3
HUTTER, Erhard
Expelled by USSR 9-30, 821E1 *
HUTTO, Earl D.
Wins US House seat 11-7, 849D3, 850E2
HUTTO v. Finney
Ark prison reform, attys fees backed by Sup Ct 6-23, 566D1

1979

HURRICANE (film)
Released 4-11, 528E2
HURRICANES—*See STORMS*
HURT, John
Alien released 5-24, 528A1
HURT, Mary Beth
Head Over Heels released 10-19, 1007E3
HURTADO Larrea, Osvaldo
Wins Ecuador vp bid 4-29, 330E1
Ecuador Cabt shuffled 12-9, 967G3
HURVITZ, Yigal
Named Israel finance min 10-29, 856B2
HUSKY Oil Ltd.
Alberta Gas sets takeover 5-13, 405F2
HUSS, Erik
Indl stimulus pkg proposed 3-9, 287B3
HUSSEIN, Haled
Convicted 10-23, sentncd 10-25, 802D1
HUSSEIN, Mohye Abdul
Arrested as plotter 7-28, 583E1
HUSSEIN, Saddam (Iraqi president)
In Syrian talks 1-28—1-30, sees unity delay 1-30, 69F2
Named Iraq pres, shifts Cabt 7-16, 544D3
Plotters arrested 7-28, Syria linked 7-30, 583E1, G1
Ties Assad to plot 8-5, 602A3
Offers poor natns aid 9-4, 675G1
Saudi denies Egypt chrgs 10-10, 801G2-802A1
Arab League vs oil as weapon 11-20, 916C2

HUSSEIN bin Dato Onn (Malaysian prime minister)
Bars Viet refugees 1-5, 51A3
Gets UN plea on Viet refugees 6-15, drops threat to shoot 6-18, 460D2

HUSSEIN ibn Tal Abdullah el Hashim, King (Jordan)
Sees Canada oppositn ldr in Jordan 1-17—1-18, 57B3
Sees Arafat, vs Egypt-Israel treaty 3-17, 198C2
US missn seeks support for Israel-Egypt pact 3-18; chrgs 'arm-twisting' 3-20, 197F2, 198B1
Brother rptd vs PLO rapproachmt 4-15, 278G2
Rejcts Begin peace talk bid 5-19, 379B1
Sees Strauss 7-7, 511D2
PLO critic shot 7-25, 552D1
At Qaddafi coup anniversary 9-1, 688C3
In France, bars autonomy talks role 9-10, 676B3
At UN, vs Egypt-Israel peace talk role 9-24, 741E2
Arab League OKs peace plan 11-22, 916B2

HUSSENDAIR, Sheik Hasham
Slain 6-1, PFLP takes credit 6-2, 414F2
HUSTLER (magazine)
Flynt convctd in retrial 3-28, 240D1
HUSTLER Magazine Inc.
Lawyers' interstate rights limited by Sup Ct 1-15, 31C3
Hustler (magazine)—*See separate listing*
HUSTON, John
Winter Kills released 5-17, 528G3
HUTCHINSON, Ron
Says I opens 2-20, 292F2
HUTCHINSON, Ronald R.
Libel suit rights broadened by Sup Ct 6-26, 540F2
HUTCHINSON v. Proxmire
Case decided by Sup Ct 6-26, 540E2
HUTTON, Barbara
Dies 5-11, 432A3
HUTTON, Bill
Festival opens 5-7, 711A3
HUTTON & Co., E. F.
SEC censures re optns trading 2-6, 349G1

1980

HURRICANES—*See STORMS & Floods*
HURT, John
Elephant Man released 10-3, 836F2
HURVITZ, Yigal
'79 inflatn at 111.4%, austerity efforts cited 1-15, 59A2, D2
Defends austerity plan, credit freeze 1-23, 133B3
On shekel introduction 2-22, 151F1
Weizman quits, mil budget dispute cited 5-25, 429C3
Israel plans Medit-Dead Sea canal 8-24, 643D3*
HUSAK, Gustav (Czechoslovakian president)
Scores Poland 'antisocialists' 10-9, 761E1
At Moscow summit on Poland 12-5, 929E1
HUSSAIN, Ghasi
Austria gives special status 3-13, 206A1
HUSSEIN, Abdel Aziz
Vs Carter Persian Gulf vow 1-25, 65C1
HUSSEIN, Saddam (Iraqi president)
Defies Iran overthrow threat 4-8, 300A1
Disclaims A-weapon plan 7-20—7-21, 573B3
Ends Iran border pact 9-17, 694G1-B2
Khomeini seeks overthrow 9-22, 717C2
Jordan king backs Iraq vs Iran 9-23, 9-24, 719D2
Asks truce 9-28; Iran vs 9-29, 9-30, 733C1
Claims Khurramshahr capture 9-28, 734D2*
Meets Jordan King Hussein 10-4—10-5, 757D1
Syria scores for war vs Iran 10-7, 757C2
Waldheim proposes truce 10-10, 774F1
King Hussein visits 10-27—10-28, 820F3
Sadat scores 11-1, 859B3
Threatens increased peace demands 11-4, 854G3-855C1
Vows 'holy war' vs Iran 11-9, renews truce bid 11-10, 879D2
Iraqi foes in Syria seek ouster 11-13, 895B1
Meets Cuban peace mediator 11-14, 895A1
Meets UN peace missn delegate 11-23—11-24, 894A3
Rpts Iraqi drive into Kurdistan, urges Iran accept demands 12-25, 977E3
HUSSEIN ibn Tal Abdullah el Hashim, King (Jordan)
US aide asks Palestine autonomy backing 1-26, 89C2
Arab hardliners seek aid in raids vs Israel 4-15—4-16, 284F2
Vs Israel Labor Party W Bank plan 4-23, Peres for talks 4-24, 325A1
Begin confirms W Bank talks 6-4, 434G1
Fatah seeks Jordan base vs Israel 6-9, 434D2
In US; sees Carter, vs autonomy talks role 6-17—6-18; US to sell 100 tanks 6-19, 450A1, F1
Sharaf dies 7-3, 608C3
Backs Iraq in Iran war 9-23, 9-24, 719C2
Visits Iraq 10-4—10-5; plans war aid 10-6, denies troop presence 10-8, 757A1, A2
Iran, US, Israel score aid to Iraq 10-7, 757F1
Visits Saudis, asks aid for Iraq 10-11—10-12; rpt Saudis vs direct aid 10-13, 774G2
Moscow visit canceled 10-11, 774B3
Visits Iraq, renews support 10-27—10-28, 820F3
Warns US vs arms to Iran 10-29, 820B3
Addresses Arab summit 11-25, 11-27, 911E1, G1
Defies Syria border threat 11-29, 11-30; seeks US arms 12-1, 911D2, B3
Cites Syrian threat, seeks US arms 12-1, 911B3
Gets Syria setlmt terms 12-2, rejcts 12-3, 911F2
Accepts Syria feud talks 12-5, 931A3
Says Iraq slows drive in Iran 12-8, 931E3
Syria chrgs foment war 12-10, 931B3
HUSTLER (magazine)
Penthouse publisher wins libel case vs Flynt 3-1, 239C2
Libel award vs Flynt cut 4-17, 405A3
Flynt Cleveland obscenity case accepted by Sup Ct 12-8, 937A2
HUSTON, Tom Charles
2 FBI ex-offcls convicted 11-6, 884B2
HUTCHINSON, Rep. John G. (D, W. Va.)
Elected to US House 6-3, 439C3
Loses reelectn 11-4, 850A3
HUTCHINSON, Ronald
Proxmire settles libel suit 3-24, 470D3
HUTCHISON, Mavis
Sets UK distance running record 8-15, 638C3
HUTTO, Rep. Earl D. (D, Fla.)
Reelected 11-4, 842F2
HUTTON, Brian
First Deadly Sin released 10-24, 836F2
HUTTON, Lauren
American Gigolo released 2-1, 216A2
HUTTON, Timothy
Ordinary People released 9-19, 836D3
HUTTON & Co., E. F.
Peru silver futures losses rptd 2-15, 152G1
Interferon investmt rptd 3-5, 318A1
HUTTO v. Davis
Case remanded by Sup Ct 3-31, 291G2
HUXLEY, Aldous (1894-1963)
GE microbe patent upheld by Sup Ct; reactn 6-16, 453G1

1976

HWANG San Duk
S Korea educ min 12-4, 928A3
HYDE, Rep. Henry J. (R, Ill.)
Reelected 11-2, 829F2
Medicaid abortn stay barred 11-8, 848A2
HYNES, Charles J.
Blumenthal case dismissed 4-13, 271C1
HYONG Ik Ki
Rejcts US peace conf plan 7-23, 557F2
HYPERTENSION—*See 'Blood' under MEDICINE*
HYUNG Chang
Wins Olympic medal 7-30, 574G3

1977

HUYGEN, Wil
Gnomes on best-seller list 12-4, 1021A3
HWANG San Duk
Replaced in S Korea Cabt 12-20, 1017D1
HYAMS, Leila
Dies 12-4, 1024C2
HYDE, Rep. Henry J. (R, Ill.)
Abortn amendmt stay lifted 8-4, 786A2
HYDE Amendment—*See ABORTION*
HYDROELECTRIC Power—*See ELECTRIC Light & Power*
HYDROTHERMAL Energy
Carter energy plan 4-20, 293F3
HYSTERECTOMIES—*See MEDICINE—Surgery*

1978

HU Yao-pang
In China politburo 12-22, 1015F1
HUYGEN, Wil
Gnomes on best-seller list 1-8, 24E3; 3-5, 195E3; 4-2, 272C3; 4-30, 356A2; 12-3, 971B1
HYAMS, Peter
Capricorn One released 6-2, 618E3
HYDE, Rep. Henry J. (R, Ill.)
Backs abortn funding curb 6-13, 445E3
Reelected 11-7, 850D3
HYDEN, Ky.—*See KENTUCKY*
HYDROELECTRIC Power—*See ELECTRIC Light & Power*
HYDROGEN
Fuel potential, storage study rptd 4-18, 293G3 *
Solar cell advance claimed 11-30, 983G1
HYDROGEN Bomb—*See ARMAMENTS—Atomic Weapons, RADIATION*
HYMAN, Earle
Othello opens 1-30, 887D2
HYPERTENSION—*See MEDICINE—Blood*
HYPNOSIS
Calif murder case refused by Sup Ct 10-2, 751C2
HYUN, Montgomery K.
Calls Anacin ads misleading 9-16, 769F3

1979

HU Yao-pang
Gets top China party posts 1-4, 6D3
Anti-corruptn speech rptd 7-31, 651E3
HUYCK, Willard
French Postcards released 10-19, 1007D3
HUYCK, William
More Amer Graffiti released 8-17, 820B2
HUYGEN, Wil
Gnomes on best-seller list 1-7, 80B3; 2-4, 120C3
HUYN, Montgomery
Finds Kroger ads deceptive 6-21, 596C2
HUYSER, Gen. Robert E.
Contacted Iran mil ldrs 1-8, 12G1
Ends Iran mission 2-6, 82E2
HYAMS, Peter
Hanover Street released 5-17, 528D2
HYATT Hotel Corp.
Shah chrgd with embezzlemt 12-11, 935D2
HYDE, Rep. Henry J. (R, Ill.)
Abortn funding cases accepted by Sup Ct 11-26, 919A2
HYDE, R.
Beneath the Valley of Ultravixens released 5-11, 528D1
HYDE Amendment—*See ABORTION*
HYDEN, Lee
Sentncd for extortn 1-26, 156E2
HYDE Park, N.Y.—*See NEW York State*
HYDROELECTRIC Power—*See ELECTRIC Light & Power*
HYDROGEN Bomb—*See ARMAMENTS—Atomic Weapons*
HYOSCINE (scopolomine)—*See MEDICINE—Drugs*
HYSAN, Lloyd
Washn Star pacts renegotiated 1-1, 5A2
HYUN, Montgomery K.
Assails Bristol-Myers ads 10-12, 902F3

1980

HU Yaobang (Hu Yao-pang)
Politburo promotes, heads CP 2-29, 171G3
Wang named propaganda chief 3-7, 231A2
Tibet, Tsinghai reforms set 5-31, 6-8, 462A1, E1
Scores Mao 7-8, 651G2*
Hua scored in press 12-16, 12-30, 975E3
HUYCK Corp.
Wheelabrator merger set 7-30, 745E3
HUYSER, Gen. Robert E.
Iran airs post-shah plot role 6-2, 418F2
US ex-amb scores Brzezinski '79 Iran policy 9-6, 694E1
HYAMS, Peter
Hunter released 8-1, 675A3
HYDE, Rep. Henry J. (R, Ill)
Medicaid abortn funding limits upheld by Sup Ct; reactn 6-30, 491G2, 492G1
Reelected 11-4, 842D3
HYDE Amendment—*See ABORTION*
HYDROELECTRIC Power—*See ELECTRIC Light & Power*
HYDROGEN Bomb—*See ARMAMENTS--Atomic Weapons & Tests*
HYPNOSIS
Dr Erickson dies 3-25, 279D2

I

1976

IAN, Janis
Wins Grammy 2-28, 460G2
IBAGNES, Eugene
France denies spy chrg 1-9, 45D2
IBANEZ, Lt. Gen. Antonio
Spain Civil Guard chief 12-23, 1011G2
IBARRURI, Dolores (La Pasionaria)
Asks return to Spain 1-22, 77F1
Raimon audience cheers 2-5, 144E2
Spain denies passport 8-26, 753A3
I CAN'T Help It (If I'm Still in Love With You) (recording)
Wins Grammy 2-28, 460A3
ICB Corp.
Rptd on FRB 'problem' list 1-22, 111B3
Intl City Bank fails 12-3, sold 12-5, 939E3-940A1
ICBM (intercontinental ballistic missile)—*See 'Missiles' under ARMAMENTS*
ICE Hockey—*See HOCKEY, Ice*

1977

IACOCCA, Lee A.
On Ford chief exec panel 4-14, 409C1
IAEA—*See UNITED Nations—International Atomic Energy Agency*
IAPA—*See INTER-American Press Association*
IATA—*See AIR Transport Association, International*
IBANEZ O'Brien, Gen. Gaston
Econ min quits 5-13, 427D2
Govt sets austerity program 6-10, 488D2
Oppositn to Morales econ policies rptd 7-15, 563A3
IBARRA Munoz, David
Named Mex finance min 11-17, rptdly backs IMF policies 12-3, 966F3
'78 budget announced 12-15, 985A2
IBARRA Vasquez, Carlos
Cuba frees 8-2, 654B2
IBARRURI, Dolores (La Pasionaria)
Seeks Spain return 2-18, heads CP candidates list 2-21, 285C3
Elected to parlt 6-15, 453F1
Rejcts Sovt criticism of Carrillo 6-25, 507F2
Julian Ruiz dies 8-4, 696F3
IBEC—*See COMECON—International Bank for Economic Cooperation*
IBERIA Air Lines
Italian hijacks jet 3-14—3-16, 224A3
IBM—*See INTERNATIONAL Business Machines*
IBRAHIM, Abdul Wahab
Named Sudan interior min 2-11, 117F2
ICALLA Iarraga, Gen. Jose
Quits Cortes 4-19, 307C1
ICAO—*See UNITED Nations—International Civil Aviation Organization*
ICART, Fernand
Named regional dvpt min 9-26, 744F2
ICBM (intercontinental ballistic missile)—*See ARMAMENTS—Missiles*
ICC—*See U.S. GOVERNMENT—INTERSTATE Commerce Commission*
ICE Hockey—*See HOCKEY, Ice*

1978

IACOCCA, Lee A.
On '77 top-paid execs list 5-15, 364F3
Ford fires 7-13, 642D1-D2
Caldwell named successor 10-16, 808G3
Ford separatn pay rptd 11-1, named Chrysler pres 11-2, 936A1
IAEA—*See UNITED Nations—International Atomic Energy Agency*
IAM—*See MACHINISTS and Aerospace Workers, International Association of*
IANNONE, John
Links to Energy Dept scored 5-15, 408F2-C3
IAPA—*See INTER-American Press Association*
IATA—*See AIR Transport Association, International*
IBANEZ O'Brien, Gen. Gaston
Replcd 5-15, 394E2
IBEW—*See ELECTRICAL Workers, International Brotherhood of*
IBM—*See INTERNATIONAL Business Machines*
IBRAHIM, Mohammed Ahmed
Executed 11-15, 885C3
ICAO—*See UNITED Nations—International Civil Aviation Organization*
ICBM (intercontinental ballistic missile)—*See ARMAMENTS—Missiles*
ICC—*See U.S. GOVERNMENT—INTERSTATE Commerce Commission*
ICE Cream
Hershey to buy Friendly Ice Cream 12-26, 1005G1-A2
ICE Hockey—*See HOCKEY, Ice*

1979

IACOCCA, Lee A.
Cafiero resignatn rptd 3-1, 188E1
H Ford, Chrysler scored 5-10, 366F2
'78 Ford, Chrysler pay rptd 5-14, 348B1
Chrysler marketing tactics cited 7-31, 576F2
UAW rejects wage freeze plea 8-3, 662C3
Salary cut 8-30, 662G3
Named Chrysler chrmn, sets rebate end 9-20, 699B3, 700E1
On 3d 1/4 loss 10-30, 846A1, F1
IAEA—*See UNITED Nations–International Atomic Energy Agency*
I Am (recording)
On best-seller list 7-4, 548F3
I Am My Films: A Portrait of Werner Herzog (film)
Released 4-19, 528E2
IBERIA (Spanish airline)
Ground employes stage slowdown 2-20, 192G1
Jet hijacked 8-4, 3 surrender to Swiss 8-5, 603F3
Spain, France in air traffic talks 11-26—11-27, 952A2
IBM—*See INTERNATIONAL Business Machines Corp.*
IBRAHIM, Abdel Kassim Mohammed
Ousted as Sudan vp 8-12, 617G3
IBRAHIM, Youssef
Iran ousts 7-22, US regrets 7-23, 565F3, 566B1
IBSEN, Henrik (1828-1906)
Little Eyolf opens 6-29, 712B1
ICBM (intercontinental ballistic missile)—*See ARMAMENTS–Missiles*
ICC—*See U.S. GOVERNMENT–INTERSTATE Commerce Commission*
ICEBERGS (painting)
Sold for record sum 10-25, 891F3
ICE Castles (film)
Top-grossing film 2-7, 120G3; 2-28, 174B2
Released in NY 2-22, 174F2
ICE Hockey—*See HOCKEY, Ice*

1980

IACOCCA, Lee A.
Optimism disputed 2-13, 2-19, 127A2
Lauds Chrysler loan guarantees 5-10, defends Fraser bd electn 5-13, 383G2, E3
Sinatra offers Chrysler aid 6-11, 457F1
Predicts 4th 1/4 profit 6-25, 481B3
Sees Chrysler 4th 1/4 profit 7-31, 573G3
IAEA—*See UNITED Nations--International Atomic Energy Agency*
IBANEZ Freire, Gen. Antonio
Ousted as interior min 5-2, 355E1
IBARRA, Luis
Kim KOs for WBA flywgt title 2-17, 320B3
IBH Holding
Buys GM unit, GM buys shares 9-28, 746A2
IBM—*See INTERNATIONAL Business Machines Corp.*
IBM v. Greyhound Computer Corp.
Case refused by Sup Ct 4-28, 369G1
IBRAHAMI, Asghar
Named Iran oil min 8-31, 671D2
IBRAIMOV, Sultan
Slain 12-4, 945D3
IBSEN, Henrik (1828-1906)
John Gabriel Borkman opens 12-18, 1003C3
ICBM (intercontinental ballistic missile)
See ARMAMENTS--Missiles
ICC (Interstate Commerce Commission)
See under U.S. GOVERNMENT
ICEBERGS (painting)
Homer oil sold for $1.7 mln 10-17, 998A1

1976

ICELAND—*See also NATO, OECD*
Listed as 'free' nation 1-19, 20C3
Unions launch gen strike 2-17, 156A2
Total IMF oil loan rptd 4-1, 340B2
WHO cancer studies rptd 6-3, 484B3
Croats divert TWA jet 9-10, 685F1
Oct '75-76 inflatn rate rptd 12-6, 976B1
Fishing Issues
Iceland-UK incidents 1-3—1-9; Iceland asks NATO role 1-8, 50A3
Iceland warns UK 1-8, 1-13, 1-19; UK withdraws boats 1-19, 50F2
NATO meets 1-12; Luns in talks with Iceland 1-14—1-15, UK 1-19, 50D3
UK '74-75 cod catch up 1-17, 50E3
UK sets Hallgrimsson mtg 1-19, 50E3
UK trawlers harrassed 1-23—2-19; Wilson protests, warships return 2-5, 156C1, E1
Hallgrimsson, Wilson talks 1-24—1-27, UK proposals rejctd 2-4, 156B1-E1 *
Luns mediation fails 2-12, 156C1
Iceland unions vow cooperatn 2-18, 156B2
UK ties cut 2-19, 156A1
Iceland-UK incidents continue 2-19, 2-23, 156G1
NATO mins discuss 5-20—5-21, 353B2
UK withdraws warships 5-30, 389B3
UK talks, interim pact OKd 5-31—6-1; UK ties restored 6-3, 389D2

1977

ICELAND—*See also NATO, OECD*
'76 jobless rate, COL rptd 1-3, 102G2
Dec '75-76 inflatn rate rptd 2-7, 87C2
Wage accord reached, job actns end 6-27; oppositn role rptd 7-5, 728G2
Krona devalued 2.5% 8-30, 709B1
Civil servants strike ends 10-25, 984B2
Foreign Relations (misc.)
UN Assemb member 4B1
UK 200-mi limit in effect 1-1, 21A1
'76 Eur Cncl pact vs terror cited 9G2
Mondale refueling stopover 1-29, 69D1
IWC cuts whaling quotas 6-24, 496F3
Eur Cncl to study Turkey rights abuses in Cyprus 9-8, 764G1-A2; rpt shelved, Greece protests 11-3, 946E3
Nigeria pirate raid scored 11-22, 986F2
Helsinki Agreement—*See EUROPE—Security and Cooperation*

1978

ICELAND—*See also COUNCIL of Europe, EFTA, GATT, NATO, OECD*
Krona devalued 13%; '77 inflatn rate, wage hikes cited 2-8, 94F3
Left gains in local electns 5-28, inflatn measures blamed 5-31, 437A3
Govt set back in gen electn, inflatn blamed 6-25; Cabt to resign 6-26, 497G1
Coalitn govt attempts fail 7-12—8-24, Johannessen forms Progressive coalitn 8-31, 688B3-689B1
Amers '77 balloon ditching cited 652F3
Currency transactns halted 8-28, krona devalued 15% 9-4, 689B1
European Force Reduction Talks—*See under EUROPE*
Foreign Relations (misc.)
US alerts to Sovt satellite fall 57E1
S Africa investmt, other ties banned 3-11, 193C3
Eur conservative group formed 4-24, 424C3
UN Assemb member 713F3
Helsinki Agreement—*See EUROPE—Security and Cooperation*

1979

ICELAND—*See also COUNCIL of Europe, GATT, NATO, OECD*
US VP Mondale visits Eur 4-11—4-22, 299C2
Norway fishing dispute averted 8-18, 796F3
UN membership listed 695E2
Progressives gain in electns, Hermannsson asked to form govt 12-4, 928C1
European Force Reduction Talks—*See under EUROPE*
Helsinki Agreement—*See EUROPE–Security and Cooperation*

1980

ICELAND—*See also COUNCIL of Europe, CSCE, GATT, NATO, OECD*
Eldjarn to try govt bid 1-16, 39C3
Thoroddsen forms govt 2-8, 117E3
USSR May Day parade marked 5-1, 354A3
Norway ocean accord set 5-10, 398B2
Finnbogadottir elected pres 6-30, 498F2

1976

ICE Skating—*See SKATING, Ice*
ICHORD, Rep. Richard Howard (D, Mo.)
Reelected 11-2, 830B1
IDA—*See 'International Development Association' under WORLD Bank Group*
IDAHO
Primary date set 22B2
Reagan in Twin Falls 5-11, 343B1
Primary results 5-25, 373F1, G1, F2, 374A3
Teton R Dam bursts 6-5, 423B1
Reagan gets more delegates 6-26, 467F2
Dem conv women delegates, table 508B2
Ford OKs dam victims aid 7-12, 517E3; 9-7, 665C1
Dem conv pres vote, table 7-14, 507B2
Teton Dam probe rpts 7-15, 9-25, 736C1
GOP pre-conv delegate count 8-14, 583B3
GOP conv pres, vp vote tables 8-18—8-19, 8-19, 599B1, B3
Fscl '75 per capita income, tax burden rptd 9-15, 10-12, 959E2
Election results 11-2: pres, 818B1, 819A1; cong 824G1, 829E2
IDAHO Statesman, The (newspaper)
Ariz crime probed 10-2, 849D2
IDB—*See INTER-American Development Bank*
I.D. Corp.
Cited in Lockheed payoff rpt 2-4, 130D2, E3
Lockheed paymts probed 2-24, 2-26, 190F2, G2
IDEAL Basic Industries
Potash divisn indicted 6-29, 748F1
IDO, Ichitaro
Named to Lockheed probe com 2-19, 190B2
IDOYAGA, Hugo
Rpts Rhodesia raid 8-20, 661A2
IEA—*See INTERNATIONAL Energy Agency*
IENG Sary
Retains Cabt post 4-14, 265D1
In Peking, meets Hua 8-7, 588D2
IENG Thirith
Cambodia social action min 4-14, 265E1
IGARTUA, Francisco
Amnestied 5-7, 500C1
IGLESIAS, Enrique V.
On '75 Latin econ decline 1-13, 60C3
On Latin food output 5-7, 466C1
IGNATOVIC, Dragoljub S.
Lawyer sentenced 3-10, 224A1
IGOLHO, Lt. Col. Jacques
Replaced 10-19, 1003A2
I HAVE a Dream (play)
Opens 9-20, 1014E3
IKARD, Frank N.
Crude oil reserves down 3-30, 285F1
IKLE, Fred C.
Testifies on A-safeguards pact 2-23, 175C1, 243A3
Scores US A-aid 7-23, 739F2
Cites Sovt MIRV buildup 8-31, 739D1
IKOLA, Heikki
Wins Olympic medal 2-6, 159F1
ILLINGS Ltd.—*See ANGLO-American Corp.*
ILLINOIS
Cicero nursing home fire 2-4, 271A3
US Sup Ct bars review of flag mutilatn ruling 4-26, 359C2
Arlington Hts zoning case cited 6-7, 435E1
US Sup Ct voids Serbian Church rule 6-21, 553A1
Sen rpt chrgs medicaid fraud 8-30, 715B1
Joliet integratn praised 9-14, 993A1
Speck denied parole 9-15, 860A2
Fiscal '75 per capita income, tax burden rptd 9-15, 10-12, 959G1, B2
Richardson vows boycott info 10-20, 786G2
Fiscal '76 bankruptcies rptd 10-20, 984C3
US Sup Ct bars review of Lake Mich A-plant OK 11-8, 882C3
Anti-boycott law cited 12-1, 987B2
10% get swine flu shots 12-2, 911B1
US Sup Ct bars review of legis immunity appeal 12-6, 920C3

1977

IC4A (Intercollegiate Association of Amateur Athletes of America)—*See specific sport (e.g., TRACK & Field)*
ICG (Illinois Central Gulf Railroad Co.)—*See IC Industries*
IC Industries Inc.
ICC curbs ICG rail grain-car deals 8-1, 613A1
ICJ—*See INTERNATIONAL Commission of Jurists*
ICKX, Jacky
Wins Le Mans 6-12, 531A2
IDA—*See WORLD Bank Group—International Development Association*
IDAHO
Legislature schedule rptd 6D2
Teton Dam collapse rpt 1-6, 120B3
Andrus confrmd Interior secy 1-20, 34B1, G3
ERA rescinded 2-8, 112G3
Drought continues, conservatn urged 2-15, 152E3
Andrus rpts net worth 2-25, 147C3
Right to die law cited 3-31, 355D1
'76 per-capita income table 5-10, 387G2
Boise econ data table 5-16, 384E2
Simplot fined for tax evasn 5-20, 491D3
Drought persists 6-16, 492A3
'76 per capita income, tax burden table 9-13, 10-18, 821E2
GM cuts '78 Chevette price 9-15, 722F3
Abortn funding curbed 10-12, 787A1
Secret news source case review refused 10-31, 835E2
ERA rescission cited 11-14, 918E1
Student jobless benefits law upheld 12-5, 939C1
IDAHO National Engineering Laboratory
Breeder reactor called safe 3-26, 235A1
IDB—*See INTER-American Development Bank*
IDEAL Basic Industries, Inc.
Potash chrgs dismissed 2-25, 483E3
IDENTITY Card, National—*See IMMIGRATION*
IEA—*See INTERNATIONAL Energy Agency*
IENG Sary
In China, CP post cited 9-28, 741A3
Identified as Cambodia dep premr 10-3, 780B1
IENG Thirith
Identified as Cambodia social affairs min 10-3, 780C1
IFALPA—*See AIRLINE Pilots Associations, International Federation of*
IFC—*See 'International Finance Corp. under WORLD Bank Group*
IFV (Infantry fighting vehicle)—*See ARMAMENTS—Tanks*
IGNACIO-Pinto, Louis
World Ct member 4F1
IGUINI Ferreira, Luis
Torture rptd 2-15, 352A1
I.H.T. Corp.—*See under WHITNEY Communications*
I. I. INDUSTRIES—*See CUTLER-Hammer*
IISS—*See INSTITUTE for Strategic Studies, International*
IKARD, Frank
On 2d ¼ oil well drillings 7-28, 628B1
IKONIKOF, Ignacio
Disappears 6-25, 595E2
ILA—*See LONGSHOREMEN'S Association, International*
ILGWU—*See INTERNATIONAL Ladies Garment Workers Union*
ILLEGAL Aliens—*See IMMIGRATION*
ILLINOIS
Legislature schedule rptd 6D2
Arlington Hts zoning upheld 1-11, 14G3
NYS stock transfer tax amendmnts ruled illegal 1-12, 57F2
Podiatrist group chrgd 2-15, 156B3
ERA set back 3-9, 279C3
Cook Cnty prisons scored 4-4, 288F3
Edward Barrett dies 4-4, 356F2
Fed spending inequities chrgd 4-6, 423D3
Carter energy plan reactn 4-20, 320E2
US Sup Ct backs illegitimate children's rights 4-26, 382A3
'76 per-capita income table 5-10, 387D2
US Sup Ct backs driver's license law 5-16, 419F1
Property attachmt case refused 5-31, 462A1
ERA defeated 6-6, 669C2
Price-fixing suit dismissed 6-9, 501E2
Obscenity convictn upheld 6-9, 501B3
Skokie Nazi rally ban upset 6-13, 617G2
Death penalty bill signed 6-21, 594E2

1978

ICELANDIC Airlines
Leased plane crashes in Sri Lanka 11-15, 908B2
ICE Skating—*See SKATING, Ice*
ICFTU (International Confederation of Free Trade Unions)—*See TRADE Unions, International Confederation of Free*
ICHORD, Rep. Richard Howard (D, Mo.)
House votes conditnl end to Rhodesia sanctns 8-2, 588B2
Reelected 11-7, 851D2
IC Industries Inc.
Boyd named Amtrak pres 4-25, 349B2
Abex Corp.
RR high-carbon wheels curbed 3-23, 365E3
ICJ—*See INTERNATIONAL Commission of Jurists*
ICKYX, Jackie
2d in LeMans 6-11, 538G2
IDA—*See WORLD Bank Group—International Development Association*
IDAHO
Legislature schedule rptd 14E3
'67, '77 sales-tax rates rptd 1-5, 15D3
Mondale tours Westn states 1-9—1-13, 34E1
State govt tax revenue table 1-9, 84C2
Gospel-Hump wilderness area clears Cong 2-9, 109D2; signed 2-24, 218A2
'Right-to-die' law rptd 3-18, 597F3
Ft Hall reservatn closed to non-Indians 4-22, 327C1
OSHA warrantless searches curbed by US Sup Ct 5-23, 405C2
ERA '77 rescissn cited 494D2
US ratifies UK tax pact 6-27, 588B3
Extended jobless aid rptd 7-10, 552A3; ends 8-4, 607D3
Primary results 8-8, 625D3
Corp takeover law ruled unconst 8-10, 700E3
ERA rescissn amendmt rejected by US House 8-15, 661G2
Carter vacations 8-21—8-30, 664D1
ERA rescissn amendmts rejected by US Sen 10-3, 788C1
Election results 11-7: cong 846A2, 848F1, 850C3, 855C1; state 847C1, E1, 853E2, 855A1, D1, 897C3
A-reactor safety test called success 12-9, 961E1
IDAHO v. Vance
Panama Canal treaty challenge refused 1-16, 33G2
IDB—*See INTER-American Development Bank*
IEA—*See INTERNATIONAL Energy Agency*
IENG Sary
Scandinavian ambs end visit 1-22, 43D2
In Thai talks 1-30—2-2, 61C1
Chrgs Hanoi aggressn 6-9, 490E1
Chrgs US, Viet plots 6-13, 548E2
In Cambodia, OKs border pact, scores Viet 7-14—7-17; rpt China arranged visit 7-14, 548F2
Defends '75 border closure, urban ousters 7-28, 593B3
For Viet peace treaty 10-12, 794F1
Asks West observers, Waldheim to visit Cambodia; on Viet issue 10-13, 794D1
In Pl, chrgs Sovts aid Viets 10-19, 803E2
Rebel front scores 12-3, 12-4, 933F1, B2
On slaying of UK visitor 12-23, 997B2
IFC—*See WORLD Bank Group—International Finance Corp.*
IF Ever I See You Again (film)
Released 5-24, 619D2
IF Life Is a Bowl of Cherries—What Am I Doing in the Pits? (book)
On best-seller list 4-30, 356G1; 6-4, 460B3; 7-2, 579C3; 8-6, 620A2; 9-4, 708B1; 10-9, 800C3; 11-6, 887G3; 12-3, 971B1
IGNATIUS, Paul
Urges greater reliance on mil 7-12, 528A3
IKARD, Frank N.
Rpts US '77 oil, gas exploratn rise 4-10, 282F1
Says gas supplies adequate 12-1, 939A1
ILA—*See LONGSHOREMEN'S Association, International*
ILGWU—*See INTERNATIONAL Ladies Garment Workers Union*
ILHAN, Vecdi
Named Turkey forestry min 1-5, 21F2
ILIEV, Pavel
Given asylum by Danes 7-26, 688D1
I'LL Find a Way (film)
Wins Oscar 4-3, 315D3
ILLINOIS
Arlington Hts zoning case review barred 1-9, 13D2
Blizzard hits, O'Hare airport closed 1-25—1-26, 105G2, B3
ABA defeats anti-Burger resolutn 2-13, 108B1, E1
Chicago, Aurora-Elgin areas violate clean-air rules 2-23, 144D3
Daily News ceases publicatn 3-4, 195E1
Chicago-London air fare agreed 3-17, 206D2
US sues Outbd Marine on PCB pollutn 3-17, 243B1
Chicago suspended student damages curbed by US Sup Ct 3-21, 220G2
Chicago OKs schl integratn plan 4-12, state bd objects 4-13, 263E3
Abortn law struck down 4-13, 744A1
ABC news show chngs set 4-19, 419B3
Northwestern U tax dispute review refused by Sup Ct 5-1, 364E1
Begin visits Chicago 5-3, 339E2

1979

ICE Skating—*See SKATING, Ice*
ICFTU—*See TRADE Unions, International Confederation of Free*
ICHASO, Leon
El Super released 4-28, 528B2
IC Industries Inc.
Midas muffler assn denied tax break by Sup Ct 3-20, 203D3
Ill Central takeover of Rock Island set 9-26, 722C3
Ill Central, Amtrak collisn 10-13, 800G1
IDAHO
Legislature schedule rptd 5C3
DC voting rep amendmt rejectn rptd 3-19, 204B3
Nez Perce fishing dispute setld 6-7, 465A1
Takeover law challenge rejctd by Sup Ct 6-26, 540E3
Forest fires destroy 130,000 acres, US policies questnd 7-6-8-12, 620D1
Interior Dept seeks to protect primitive areas 9-7, 703C3
'78 per capita income rptd 9-16, 746F1, F2
PCBs contaminate food 9-17, 704A3, D3
Teton dam defects rptd 11-28, 954A3
Intl sugar agrmt OKd by US Sen 11-30, 987G2
IDEAL Basic Industries Inc.
Price violatn chrgd 5-9, 385A2
IDLE, Eric
Life of Brian released 8-17, 820A2
IDRIS Al-Mahdi as-Sanusi, Mohammed
Libyans occupy forgn embs 9-3, 688A3
IEA—*See INTERNATIONAL Energy Agency*
IENG Sary
Asks UN interventn in Viet war 1-2, 1E1
On Pol Pot right-wing alliance bid 5-31, 6-2, 443D3
Gets death sentnc 8-19, 666F3
Retains UN Assemb seat 9-21, 741G1
IF Life Is a Bowl of Cherries—What Am I Doing in the Pits? (book)
On best-seller list 4-8, 271B2; 5-6, 356E2; 6-3, 432C2
IGARASHI, Tsutomu
Park decisions 5-20, 838G3
IISS—*See INSTITUTE for Strategic Studies*
IJC—*See INTERNATIONAL Commission of Jurists*
IJIMERE, Obotunde
Plays From Africa opens 1-14, 292D2
ILGWU—*See INTERNATIONAL Ladies Garment Workers Union*
ILLINOIS
ITT Chicago long-distance phone svc OKd 1-4, 15E2
Allied fluorocarbon suit settled 1-5, 56A2
Blizzards hit, O'Hare airport closed 1-12-1-14, 1-24-1-27, 120F1
Tax overassessmt case declined by US Sup Ct 1-15, 32C1
Med malpractice arbitratn rptd 1-28, 139E3
Foster care benefits backed by Sup Ct 2-22, 151C1
Welfare overpaymts seizure curbed by Sup Ct 3-19, 203A3
Peoria, Kampville floods 3-24-3-27, 288F3
Chicago drinking age cited 4-16, 309F3
Racial 'steering' suits allowed by US Sup Ct 4-17, 325A3
Medicaid, welfare cuts set 6-19, 561G1
Chicago condominium growth rptd 6-23, 482F2, A3

1980

ICHORD, Rep. Richard H. (D, Mo.)
Bailey wins seat 11-4, 851F1
ICKX, Jacky
2d in LeMans 6-15, 637B3
IDABELL—*See OKLAHOMA*
IDAHO
Milwaukee Rd RR svc cut set 2-25, track sale rptd 4-1, 346B1, E1
Asarco tax case remanded by Sup Ct 3-24, 265B2
Govt desert land retentn backed by Sup Ct 4-16, 328D3
DES in cattle rptd 4-24, 358F1
Mt St Helens erupts 5-18, 382E1
Mt St Helens damage assessed 5-24—7-4, 503E3
Sunshine Mining strike ends 11-8, 883D3
Crime & Civil Disorders
Boise TV statn raided by police, prison riot coverage seized 7-26, 582A2
Ada Cnty prosecutor defends tapes raid 7-28, sued by Boise TV statn 8-1, 732A3
Politics & Government—*See also other appropriate subheads in this section*
Legislature schedule rptd 18D1
State of State message 1-7, 403C2
Pres primary results 5-27, 399G1, C2
GOP pres delegates picked 6-28, 506A2
Reagan tours farm area, pledges price supports 10-14, 780B1
Election results 11-4: pres 838B1, 839A1, D3; cong 837D1, 840E1, 842C3, 845A2, 851E3; state 845E2
'80 census rptd 12-31, 983D1
IDAHO State Penitentiary
Boise TV statn riot coverage seized in police raid 7-26, 582B2
Prosecutor sued over TV tapes raid 8-1, 732B3
IDB—*See INTER-American Development Bank*
IDOLMAKER, The (film)
Released 11-14, 972F3
IDRIS, Maj. Seyyed
Libya mutiny rpt denied 8-18, 652A3
IEA—*See INTERNATIONAL Energy Agency*
IENG Sary
Refutes Pol Pot excesses 2-28, 181F1
Blames Viets for relief aid halt 7-9, 591E2
On Pol Pot ouster, exile govt reform plan 11-29, 913E2-A3
IKLE, Fred C.
At GOP platform hearings, on defense spending 1-15, 32B2
ILAKUT, Ben-Bella
Arrested 1-23; freed 2-10, 125F3
ILGWU—*See INTERNATIONAL Ladies Garment Workers Union*
I'LL Be Thinking of You (recording)
Crouch wins Grammy 2-27, 296E3
ILLINOIS
Union Pacific, MoPac set merger 1-8, 52C3
Chicago hay fever study rptd 2-18, 159G3
NY abortn funding case accepted by US Sup Ct 2-19, 130A3
Schaumburg charity solicitatn limit voided by Sup Ct 2-20, 170B2
Tornadoes hit 4-7—4-8, 391G2
Abortn funding cases argued in Sup Ct 4-21, 306B2
Earth Day marked 4-22, 307G3
DES in cattle rptd 4-24, 358F1
Saudi film telecast 5-12, Nielsen rating rptd 5-13, 375F3
N&W, Southn RR merger sought 6-2, 427E2
Ukrainian youth granted asylum 7-21, 560D1
Teinowitz record divorce setlmt rptd 8-15, 639D1
Heat wave road damage rptd 9-7, 857C2

1976

Largest US coal mine identified 12-15, 985D1
Chicago
Racial quotas for police set 1-5, 6G1
Transit trains collide 1-9, 80G1
Reagan cites '75 speech 1-12, 22C1
Schl integratn study rptd 1-25, 95B2
Nursing home fire 1-30, arson chrgd 2-3, 271G2
FCC rules on WGN-TV pol ads 3-4, 180E2
Teacher integratn plan rejctd 3-31, 263G1
Teamsters pact 4-3, 248C3
Metcalfe probe dropped 4-15, 286E3
Sup Ct upholds cross-district housing 4-20, 308D2
Asbestos not found in water 4-30, 349G1
FBI efforts vs Panthers rptd 5-6, 344C2
Daley endorses Carter 6-9, 408G3
Carter visits 7-1, 490D2
Kissinger speech 7-6, 535C3
'74 bank theft cited 7-16, 560G2
Mondale sees Daley 8-25, 645E2
Indep Party conv 8-26—8-27, 666G1
Carter at Dem State Conv 9-9, 664C1
Mondale campaigns 9-16, 687B2
Carter 'whistlestop' ends 9-21, 704D3
Carter visits 10-10—10-11, 762F2
Ford campaigns 10-26, 803C1
US Mayors conf held 11-7—11-8, 845G2
'75 heroin use cited 12-12, 972C3
Mayor Daley dies 12-20, 969B3
Acting mayor, Cook Cnty head named 12-28, 12-29, 994A1
Politics—*See also 'Chicago' above*
Primary date set 22A2
State legislators granted some immunity 1-5, 7A1
Reagan campaigns 1-12, 22C1
Bensinger confrmd to DEA 2-5, 110A2
Ford campaigns 3-5—3-6, 179D3, G3
Reagan campaigns 3-8—3-10, 180F1, A2
Ford ends campaign 3-12, 198G1
Primary results 3-16, 196D2-D3
Ex-Gov Kerner dies 5-9, 368F2
Sex chrg vs Gray rptd 6-12, 434B1
US Sup Ct bars Cook Cnty patronage ouster 6-28, 468A3
Walker backs Howlett 7-6, 492G3
Dem conv women delegates, table 508B2
Dem conv pres vote, table 7-14, 507B2
GOP pre-conv delegate count 8-14, 583B3
GOP conv delegate bribes chrgd 8-16, 8-17, 616C1
Ford, Reagan seek conv delegates 8-17, 601A3
GOP conv pres, vp vote tables 8-18—8-19, 8-19, 599B1, E1, A3
Mondale in Morton Grove 8-28, 645A3
Carter in Peoria 9-9, 664C1
Dole campaigns 9-27—9-28, 724E3
Mondale campaigns 10-6, 763D3
Dole at Cicero festival 10-10, 764A1
Ford in central Ill, Lincoln 10-16, 784A2, 785B1
Mondale campaigns 10-16, 803B3
Carter campaigns 10-26, 803C2
Mondale in Aurora 10-30, 827D2
Dole stumps 11-1, 827B3
Election results 11-2: pres 818B1, G1, 819B2; Cong 820D2, 823G1, 829F2; state 820F2, D3, 823A2, 831E1
Mikva declared winner 11-19, 882A1
Mayor Daley dies 12-20, 969B3

1977

Skokie rule review ordrd 6-23, swastika display barred 7-12, 560A2
GM back-pay award case refused 6-29, 557C3
Vendo contract dispute award ordrd 6-29, 557D3
Milwaukee ordrd to end Lake Mich pollutn 7-29, 595B1
'76 per capita income, tax burden table 9-13, 10-18, 821C2
Police break-in case review declined 10-3, 760B3
Free abortions continued 10-12, 787A1
ICC sues trucking firms 11-3, 861A1
US facilities cited for pollutn 11-25, 944C2
Moore rape convictn reversed 12-12, 960G2
Chicago
Train crash 1-4, 104F2-A3
Police hiring resolved, impounded funds released 1-11—3-25, 279G2
Blizzard hits 1-28—1-29, 75F2
Record low temp rptd 2-6, 91D2
'70-76 indictmt of pub offcls rptd 2-10, 162D3
Bused blacks show improved tests 2-14, 157C1
US rights comm backs city-suburb busing 2-15, 112E1
US educ aid cutoff ordrd 2-17, 157A1
FALN seeks blast probe end 3-21, 261C2, E2
'69 anti-war protesters surrender 3-25, 6-21, 9-15, 839E1
Chessie S Bend run contd 4-8, 325F2
On '75 10 largest cities list 4-14, 388A1, C1
FCC reverses pol ad stand 5-6, 376A2
Police spying disclosed 5-11, 388D2
Child porno ring rptd 5-15, bookstore crackdown 5-20, 432A3, C3
Law business boom rptd 5-16, 383G1, A2
Business confidence rptd, econ data table 5-16, 384F2, 385A1
Train crash probe rpt 5-16—5-18, 412E3
PR riots 6-4—6-5; Bilandic sees ldrs 6-6, jobs set 6-7, 464A3
Bilandic wins mayoral electn 6-7, 446B3
Fairfax Cone dies 6-20, 532G2
LEAA office to close 6-20, 630E2
Police win Panther suit 6-21, 540E2
Gays march for rights 6-26, 560F2
Venez pres visits 7-1, 546C2
Mafia operatns rptd 7-3, 568D2
Jacob Arvey dies 8-25, 696C2
US Steel South Works closing feared 8-26, 775C3
Schools open with limited busing plan 9-7, protests lessen 9-14, 837C3
FRA to buy C&NW stock 9-9, 778B3
Mass transit funds OKd 9-19, 778D3
Concorde landing rights proposed 9-23, 738B2
Police quota case review refused 10-3, 760A3
Teachers assigned by race 10-12, 837E2
ERA econ boycott rptd 11-14, 918D1
Bilandic fires accuser 11-21, 944C2
Marshall Field vs Carter Hawley bid 12-14, 1004A2

1978

'70-77 Fortune 500 hq shift rptd 5-8, 326C1
Amtrak Chicago route cutbacks proposed 5-8, 366E1
Chicago schl integratn plan OKd 5-11, 611C1
Emergency welfare standards backed by Sup Ct 6-6, 447E2
New marijuana test rptd 8-29, 728C3, E3
NCC ends Chicago bank ties re S Africa 9-21, 742F2
US parks bill cleared 10-13, 834C3
Abortn law appeal, United Meth Calif cases refused by US Sup Ct 10-16, 789D2, E2
US, W Ger air svc pact expanded 10-25, 831F1
Auto rental parking ticket, redlining cases refused by Sup Ct 10-30, 832F2, C3
Chessie, Seaboard set merger 11-16, 897B1
Chicago populatn ranked 12-6, 942D3
Crime & Civil Disorders—*See also 'Nazi Demonstrations' below*
Speck confesses '66 slayings 3-6, 172D3
Marion prison 'boxcar' cells ruled illegal 4-19, 401G1
Juvenile suspect-rights case review refused by US Sup Ct 4-24, 322G2
Chicago bank offers reward in '77 theft 5-1, 380C1
Chicago student chrgd in welfare fraud 5-8, 684F3
Father convicted of slaying children 5-22, 396D3
Pontiac prison riot, 3 guards slain 7-22, 627E2
Ray '67 Alton bank robbery cited 8-17, 641A3; 11-15, 898A3; Ray's brother denies role 11-30, 938D1
2 Croats seize W Ger emb in Chicago 8-17, 706E2
Chicago rptr shoots wife, self 9-11, 777G3
Croatian factory rptd bombed 11-29, 933F3
Serbs indicted in Tito murder plot 12-1, 933D3
Police auto search power broadened 12-5, 959D2
TWA jet hijacked in Marion, youth surrenders 12-21, 1029F1
Chicago museum art theft 12-27, 1028E3
Energy Issues
Coal Policy Project issues rpt 2-9, 184E2
Carter sees gov on coal strike 2-16, 104D2
Morris A-plant ratings rptd 11-25, 940D3
NRC A-plant safety progrm scored 11-25, 940F3
Commonwealth Edison orders 2 A-plants for Carroll Cnty 12-20, 1009G3
Labor
Miners return to work delayed 3-28, 217F1
Coal strike utility billing probe set 5-10, 366F3
Firemen in Normal end strike 5-15, 565E2
Extended jobless aid rptd 7-10, 552A3; ends 8-4, 607D3
Chicago postal pact oppositn rptd 7-21, 565A1
Chicago Teamster fund scored 8-14, 625E1
Chicago sex bias suit setld 11-17, 1006G2
Nazi Demonstrations
Skokie Nazi rally swastika display OKd 1-27, 68F3-69A1
ACLU split on Skokie defns role 1-27, 69B1
Carter deplores Skokie march, bars interventn 1-30, 62E1, D3
Skokie rally ordinances struck down 5-23; Nazi rally delay sought 6-9, Sup Ct denies stay 6-12, 447F2
Skokie Nazi march canceled, Chicago rally OKd 6-20—7-7; rally, counter-demonstratns held 7-9, 529E1
Skokie rally ordinances case refused by US Sup Ct 10-16, 789B2
Politics & Government
Legislature schedule rptd 14E3
'67, '77 sales-tax rates rptd 1-5, 15D3
State tax revenue data 1-9, 84C2, F3
Ex-Rep Murphy dies 1-29, 96B3
Primary results 3-21, 207E1-A2
Cnty clerk electn-ballot case refused by US Sup Ct 3-27, 241E2
Carter in Chicago, Springfield; backs ERA 5-25—5-26, 404B3, 418B1, 494C2
Chicago ERA boycott losses rptd 5-26, 494A3
ERA defeated by legis 6-7, 6-22, 494A2
Dems bar pres 'loophole primary' 6-9, 448A3
FBI informants rptd at '68 Dem conv 7-3, 507E3
GOP tax-cut tour in Chicago 9-21, 734F3, G3
Rep Metcalfe dies 10-11, 853B2, 888C3
Carter in Chicago, Skokie 11-2, 862A2
Election results 11-7: cong 846A2, A3, 848F1, 850C3, 853G1-A2, B2; state 847C1-E1, 853A2, C2, E2
Douglas FBI file detailed 11-14, 877C3
Black controller noted 11-28, 915D3
State offcls pay hikes voted, city hikes cited 11-29; Carter angry 12-1, Kahn asks rollback 12-4, 934F3-935C1
Forgn Relatns Cncl hears Nitze 12-5, 996A2
Chicago offcls OK pay hike cut 12-13, 957C3

1979

AMA chrgd in NY chiropractors suit 7-5, 570A3
Chicago Army recruiting fraud probed 8-19, 649G2
'78 Chicago FRB funds cited 9-6, 840G3
Chicago Navy recruiting probed 9-7, 904B1
'78 per capita income rptd 9-16, 746D2
Chicago bond rating drops, deficits predicted 9-19, 920C3, F3
Chicago bond ratings listed 9-20, 920E3
Mail order finance chrg case refused by Sup Ct 10-1, 768B2
Pope in Chicago; addresses bishops, holds masses 10-4—10-5, 757D1, 759B2-A3; photo 757A1; visit cost estimate 10-4, 761A1
Princess Margaret in Chicago 10-13, 860B1
Chicago papal mass crowd figures disputed 10-21, 931C2
Ward Foods settles '78 price suit 10-22, 985F3
Midwest quake threat rptd 11-15, 954C1
Abortn funding cases accepted by Sup Ct 11-26, 919A2
Iran consulate staff in Chicago ordrd cut 12-12, 933C1
Chicago '79 living costs ranked 12-28, 991A1
Atomic Energy
Chicago radium waste sites alleged 3-5, 187B2
A-reactor review ordrd 4-2, 261A3
Carter rejcts A-plant closings 5-7, 344A1
Marble Hill protesters arrested 6-3, 416D2
NRC studies plant site rules, Zion dangers cited 9-17, 743A2
Zion protest rptd 9-29, 742E3
La Salle (Seneca) reactor licensing delayed 11-5, 849C1
Zion shutdown possible 11-5, 849E1
Crime & Civil Disorders
Chicago man indicted in mass murder 1-8, 24F2, F3
Chicago bank embezzler convicted 2-7, 119A3; sentncd 2-25, 156A2
Death penalty law declared illegal 1-30, 400A2
Rosemont arms exhibit spurs protest 2-18—2-19, 152F3
Joliet prison gang rule broken 2-24; arms, drugs rptd seized 3-3, 196D3
Right-to-counsel doctrine clarified by US Sup Ct 3-5, 185F1-D2
REA vp indicted for funds misuse 3-8, 239F3
Entebbe hijack case declined by US Sup Ct 4-30, 364G3
Truckers' strike sparks protests, violence 6-18—6-28, 479C2
Serbian hijacks jet in Chicago 6-20, surrenders 6-21; sentncd for '75 bombings 6-22, 491E2
Phoenix mayor shot 10-16, dies 10-18, 840C2
FALN bomb Chicago govt offices, naval training cntr 10-18, 786A2
Iranians march in Carbondale 11-8, 842A3
Extended searches curbed by Sup Ct 11-28, 944E2
Energy—*See also 'Atomic' above*
'78 per capita gas use rptd 5-27, 395G2
US oil prices cited 11-12, 889A1
Labor & Employment
Collective bargaining on food issues backed by Sup Ct 5-14, 383A3
Truckers strike 6-18—6-28, 979C2
AFL-CIO meets in Chicago 8-6—8-7, 591E1, 629D2*
LaGrange GM plant targeted for UAW strike 9-10, 698D1
Teachers' strikes rptd 9-12, 679B1
Chicago-Cook Cnty patronage ruled illegal 9-24, 770G3
Chicago job reductn rptd 11-16, 921A1
Chicago transit strike 12-17—12-20, 987C2
Caterpillar strike ends 12-19, 987E1
Nazi Demonstrations
'78 Skokie Nazi activity cited 1-19, 102B1
Politics & Government—*See also other appropriate subheads in this section*
Legislature schedule rptd 5D3
Fscl '78 tax revenue rptd 2-13, 152B2
3d party electn law struck down by US Sup Ct 2-22, 150D1
Chicago mayoral primary results 2-27, 149E3-150A1
Stevenson bars reelectn bid 3-30, 265D2
Byrne elected Chicago mayor 4-3, 251G3
Forgn Relatns Cncl hears Brzezinski 4-4, 258B1
Scott indicted on tax evasn 4-9, 291B3
Vance addresses Chicago coll assn 5-1, 347F1-B2
Anderson enters pres race 6-8, 439C2
Peoria mayor heads Mayors Conf 6-13, 440C1
Chicago all-white club judicial membership surveyed 9-19, 901F2
Chicago-Cook Cnty patronage ruled illegal 9-24, 770C3
Judge retiremt law challenge refused by Sup Ct 10-9, 784F1
Kennedy seeks Byrne support; Carter in Chicago, Byrne lauds 10-15, 807A3
Carter holds Dolton town mtg 10-16, 807C3

1980

Unwed couples child custody case refused by Sup Ct 10-20, 807A1
Atomic Energy & Safeguards
Carter outlines A-waste storage plan, Morris site studied 2-12, 128B1
Commonwealth Ed, 2 offcls indicted re Quad-Cities (Cordova) A-plant security 3-26, 249D1
Zion A-plant '79 dischrg data rptd 4-7, revised 4-27, 441A2
Commonwealth Ed, 2 offcls acquitted re Quad Cities plant security 8-8, 649D1
Crime & Civil Disorders
Neo-Nazi ex-ldr arrested on sex chrgs 1-10, 55D3
Chicago Delta flight hijacked to Cuba 1-25, 617A3
Gacy convicted 3-12, gets death sentence 3-13, 214C1-C2
FALN raids Carter hq 3-15, 208B3-209A1
Scott convicted of tax evasn 3-19, 215A3
Commonwealth Ed, 2 offcls indicted 3-26, 249D1
Chicago strip search suit setld 3-26, 404C2
11 FALN suspects seized in Evanston 4-4, 308F3
'Pyramid' money schemes rptd 5-17, 655A3
Panther shootout retrial order declined, legal fees award voided by Sup Ct 6-2, 513A1
Chicagoan indicted in ERA bribe probe 6-5, chrgs denied 6-6 441C3
Weatherman fugitive surrenders in NYC 7-8, 576E3
Scott sentenced 7-29, 654F2
8 FALN suspects convicted 7-30; 2 others sentncd, 1 rptd extradited 8-4, 601C1
Nazi rally in Evanston 10-19, 884E3
'70 Weatherman bomber sentncd in NYC 10-28; '69 fugitive surrenders 12-3, 928A1, D1
ERA advocate fined in bribe case 11-7, 997A3
Inmate legal fees ruling upset by Sup Ct 11-10, 868C1
11 FALN members indicted for '75-79 bombings 12-10, 963F3
Energy—*See also 'Atomic Energy' above*
State of State message 1-9, 483A3
Fiscal Issues
State of State message 1-9, 483F2
Chicago budget dir resigns 1-11, City Cncl backs tax error levy 2-14, 186G2
Chicago budget deficit rptd 1-12; Byrne names Yeo chief fscl aide 1-22, assails 'past admins' 1-30, 186D2-G2
Chicago bond, note rating lowered by Moody's 1-31, 186A2
Chicago purchasing power rptd high 2-12, 125D3
Fscl '79 tax revenue rptd 2-20, 307B3
Chicago OKs emergency borrowing 9-10, 743D3
Labor & Employment
State of State message 1-9, 483A3
Chicago firemen strike 2-14—3-8, 187E2
Chicago bank uniform case declined by Sup Ct 3-17, 226F1
Harvester strike ends 4-20, 308G2
Non-labor picketing rights affirmed by Sup Ct 6-20, 555D2
Bush scores Carter 'failure' 9-9, 780E3
Politics & Government—*See also other appropriate subheads in this section*
Legislature schedule rptd 18D1
'66-77 elected offcls drop rptd 1-2, 5G3
Byrne appts spouse press secy 1-9, 199F1
State of State message 1-9, 483D2
GOP wins Mikva cong seat 1-22, 50D3
Carter budget cut delay scored 3-17, 201F2
State primary results 3-18, 206G2
ERA fails in House 6-18, 482C3
Detroit census revisn ordrd, Chicago suit cited 9-25, 741F2
Election results 11-4; cong 840F1, 842D3, 845B2, B3, 846C3-E3, 850B3; state 845E2, 847G, C3, 850D3
Block named agri secy 12-23, 980E1
Ex-rep Dewey dies 12-26, 1004C1
'80 census rptd, reapportmt seen 12-31, 983E1
Presidential Election (& Transition)
Reagan campaigns 1-10, 13F2
GOP platform hearing set in Chicago 1-14, 32A1
Anderson strategy detailed 2-15, 129F2
Mrs Reagan makes racial gaffe in Rosemont 2-17, 128D2
Connally fund shortage rptd 2-20, 129D1
Kennedy campaign said troubled 3-4, 167B1
FALN raids Carter hq 3-15, 208B3-209A1
Carter, Reagan win primary 3-18, 206B2-F3
Jackson at Cook Cnty fete 5-22, 399E3
Reagan sees Chicago blacks 8-5, 597B3
Reagan, Anderson address VFW conv 8-18, 8-20, 629A1, G3-630A1
Reagan in Chicago 9-8, 9-9, 699C2, C3
Byrne joins Mondale in Chicago 9-9, 780A2
Bush in Moline 9-9, Joliet 9-23, 780E3, 781C1
Carter visits Springfield, sees Dem offcls 9-22, 722G2
Carter in Addison, Chicago 10-6, 762E2, G2, B3
Carter visits W Frankfort coal mine 10-13, 778F3
Bush addresses bankers in Chicago 10-15, 817E2
Muskie in Chicago 10-20, 799D1

1976

ILLINOIS, University of (Champaign-Urbana)
Mondale visits 9-14, 687F1
ILLINOIS Car & Truck Renting & Leasing Association
Cited in ct ruling on immunity 1-5, 7C1
ILLITERACY
UNESCO literacy drive fails 2-4, 85A2
ILLUECA, Jorge Enrique
Gets UNDOF compromise 11-30, 895D2
ILLUSTRATIONS
Pres primary dates 22A2
'77 Ford, OMB, Cong budgets table 358B2
Latin mil data table 1-2, 60F2
NFL final standings 1-4, 31D2
Official SDR rates 1-15, 14A3
'46-75 GNP, inflatn tables 1-16, 89F1, 90A1
'75-77 US budget receipts, outlays table 63E1
'77 US budget $ table 63A2
'77 Ford, House com budgets table 231A1
'74, '75 IMF oil facility drawings, loans 4-1, 340A2
Dem, GOP delegate box score 4-9, 261A1; 6-8, 409A3
'72 pres electn donor list 4-25, 688A1
US forgn intelligence chart 304A1
Map of Corsica 401A3
'75 data on 10 top corporatns 437A1
'65-75 Sovt forgn trade table 5-5, 341A1
SEC corporate paymts list 5-12, 726A2-729F2
'70-Apr '76 indl output graph 5-14, 375A2
Final NHL standings 5-16, 404F3
Pres primary results tables 5-25, 374A2; 6-1, 390A2; 6-8, 409A1
Map of S Africa riot area 6-16—6-19, 426A2
Italy electn results 6-20—6-21, 446A1
Fed electn fund grants list 7-1, 491A1
Photo of Operatn Sail in NY 7-4, 488C1
Dem conv women delegates table 508A2
Dem conv pres vote table 7-14, 507A2
'77 arms authorizatn table 7-14, 517A2
Carter, Mondale photo after nominatn 7-15, 505A1
Diagram of Viking 1 525A1
Viking 1 photo of Mars 7-21, 526A1
Revised '75, '76 productivity, labor costs 7-26, 567A2
GOP pre-conv delegate count table 8-14, 583A3
Ford, Dole photo after nominatn 8-16, 597A1 ★
GOP conv pres, vp vote tables 8-18—8-19, 8-19, 599A1, A3
Korean DMZ partitn map 9-6, 660A1
Fscl '75 state per capita income, tax burden table 9-15, 10-12, 959A2
Admin, Cong '77 budget levels table 9-16, 706A2
Jan '73-May '76 indl output table 9-16, 709A1
EPA gas-econ ratings table 9-22, 766A2-770C1
World Bank poverty data chart 778A1
Baseball final standings table 10-4, 795C3-796E1
Jean Pages dies 10-21, 970A3
Carter, wife after electn 11-2, 817A1
Popular, electoral pres vote table, map 818A1, 819A1
Election returns 11-2, 828A1-831A3
Diagram of F-14 recovery 11-11, 941A1
Turkey quake map 11-24, 897A1
Leading econ indicators graph 918A2
Final pres vote table 12-18, 979A2
Carter Cabinet photo 956A1
Total FEC certificatns 12-31, 979F3

1977

ILLINOIS, University of
Solaun confrmd amb to Nicaragua 7-28, 626E3
New form of life rptd 11-2, 908A1
Gutowsky gets Medal of Sci 11-22, 952A1
ILLINOIS Brick Co.
Price-fixing suit dismissed 6-9, 501E2
ILLINOIS Brick Co. v. Illinois
Sup Ct curbs trust suits 6-9, 501E2
ILLINOIS Central Gulf Railroad Co. (ICG)—*See IC Industries*
ILLINOIS v. Polito
Sup Ct bars police identificatn rule review 10-3, 760B3
ILLINOIS Wesleyan University (Bloomington)
Sikma in NBA draft 6-10, 584A3
ILLUSIONS (book)
On best-seller list 8-14, 643F1; 9-4, 712C3; 10-2, 808D3
ILLUSTRATIONS
Canary I jet collisn diagram 3-27, 244A1
Charts, Graphs & Tables
State legis schedule 6C2
'76, '77 big co mergers table 880F1
Dow closings, vol 1-3—1-21, 38A2
US '77-82 budget receipts, outlays 32D2
US '78 budget $ 32A2
Dow closings, vol 1-24—2-11, 93A2
'76 econ indicators index 92A2
Cong ldrship, coms, chrmn 90A2-E3
OECD Dec '75-76 inflatn 2-7, 87A2
TV top 10 viewing list 2-9, 119A1
Jan WPI calculatn 2-11, 111A1
Dow closings, vol 2-14—3-4, 154A2
Carter '78 budget revisns 125A2
Dow closings, vol 3-7—3-25, 215A2
Latin paymts balance 3-11, 189A2
Dow closings, vol 3-28—4-15, 274A2
WHA final standings 4-7, 310F2
'66-75 Latin arms transfers 4-8, 415A2
NBA final standings 4-10, 331F3
US '71-77 indl output 4-14, 300A1
US '75 10 largest cities 4-14, 388A1
Dow closings, vol 4-18—5-27, 408A2
US Cong '78 budget target 405A1
Fortune '76 top 20 indls data 340D1
NFL draft 1st round 5-3, 353A2
US '76 per-capita income 5-10, 387C2
Oct '74-May '77 prime rate 407A1
Largest US law firms 5-16, 383A2
US urban econ data 5-16, 384D2
IDB '73-76 lending 5-30, 438A2
Latin '61-75 GDP variatns 5-30, 439A1
Dow closings, vol 5-31—6-17, 464A2
NBA college draft 6-10, 584A2
Dow closings, vol 6-20—7-8, 521A2
Dow closings, vol 7-11—8-5, 593B3
'77 indl output 7-15, 553E3
NASL final standings 8-7, 676C3
Dow closings, vol 8-8—8-26, 651A2
WTT final standings 8-16, 787C3
Dow closings, vol 8-29—9-23, 722A2
Brock stolen base record 8-29, 748F3
US-USSR strategic weapon totals 751A3
'76 state per capita income, tax burden table 9-13, 10-18, 821A2
July '76-Aug '77 US trade gap 9-26, 761A3
Dow closings, vol 9-26—10-21, 799A2
Baseball final standings 10-2, 767E3
PGA top money winners 10-30, 950G3
Dow closings, vol 11-21, 941E2
LPGA top money winners 11-27, 951E1
Dow closings, vol 12-12—12-30, 1004A1
'77 boxing champions 12-17, 970A2
NFL final standings 12-18, 1020A3

1978

ILLUSIONS (book)
On best-seller list 1-8, 24D3; 2-5, 116B3
ILLUSTRATIONS
Charts, Graphs & Tables
State legis schedule 14D3
NFL '77 statistical ldrs 1-1, 56A2
US troops abroad 1-2, 5C2
Dow closings, vol 1-3—1-31, 66E1
'67, '77 state sales-tax rates 1-5, 15D3
State govt tax revenue 1-9, 84B2
Costliest cities 1-14, 28A3
US '77-79 budget receipts, outlays 45B2
Federal budget dollar 63A1
US '76-83 budget assumptns, projectns 1-24, 46A2
'53, '78 cong compositn compared 1-30, 107D2
Dow closings, vol 2-1—2-28, 142A2
NATO, Warsaw Pact force comparison 2-20, 162C3
Dow closings, vol 3-1—3-31, 223A2
Panama Canal neutrality pact roll call vote 3-16, 177C2
US '77 top 10 defns contractors 3-28, 224F2
Dow closings, vol 4-3—4-28, 303E2
NBA final standings, statistical ldrs 4-9, 271C2
Hockey final standings, statistical ldrs 4-9, 4-11, 296B2
1860-1978 consumer prices 427E1
Dow closings, vol 5-1—5-31, 403A2
NFL coll draft 5-2—5-3, 336E2
Fortune '77 top 20 indls data 5-8, 325D1
'77 top-paid corp execs 5-15, 364E3
'77 top-paid labor ldrs 5-15, 365F1
Cong '79 budget targets 5-17, 385E1
Dow closings, vol 6-1—6-30, 493E1
NBA coll draft 6-9, 457F2
Dow closings, vol 7-3—7-31, 606B2
Laffer Curve 735D1
Baseball mid-yr standings 7-11, 560A1
Dow closings, vol 8-1—8-31, 664A2
NASL final standings, statistical ldrs 8-6, 655A2
WTT final standings 8-14, 1027C1
Canada-US gas export graph 9-1—9-8, 704A2
Dow closings, vol 9-1—9-29, 737A2
US top 10 cash-rich firms 9-18, 716D3
UN members listed 713B3
World Bank proverty, income table 732A1
Baseball final standings 10-2, 778B3
Dow closings, vol table 10-2—10-31, 826A2
'74-78 prime, discount, fed fund rates 791D1
World chess championship final game 10-16—10-17, 843B1
'72-78 indl output chart 10-17, 790C2
PGA, LPGA top $ winners 10-31, 11-20, 990B3
Dow closings, vol table 11-1—11-30, 918A2
Election results 11-7: cong 848B1, 850A1-852E3; govs 853D1
'77 world top-ranked banks table 11-8, 914A1
Dow closing, vol 12-1—12-29, 1004E2
US 20 largest cities table 942D3
NFL final standings 12-18, 1024A2
World stock mkt activity graphs 12-25, 1001B1

1979

Byrne endorses Kennedy 10-19, 847B2
Baker seeks '80 primary win 11-1, 829A1
Kennedy in Chicago 11-8, 962C1
Goldschmidt warns Chicago aid loss 11-20, scored 11-20–12-6; OKs road funds 12-4, 983F3
2d Daley salary disclosed 12-4, 946G3
Mondale stumps state 12-6, 961D3
School Issues
Chicago church schl interventn barred by US Sup Ct 3-21, 231D2
Integratn study rpts urban lag 5-9, 650F1
Pvt Title IX suit allowed by US Sup Ct 5-14, 382D3
Chicago compulsory busing progrm ordrd 8-31, 679A3
Teachers' strikes rptd 9-12, 679B1
HEW bars Chicago desegregatn funds 9-15, seeks suit 10-29, 944B1
Chicago schls in fscl crisis 11-13–12-7, 943D3-944A1
Chicago schls miss payday 12-21, 991E1
Transportation
Blizzard closed O'Hare airport 1-14–1-16, 120F1
Chicago DC-10 crash kills 275 5-25, 411C3; DC-10s grounded 6-6, 420E2
O'Hare on '78 world's busiest airport list 421C1
FAA lifts DC-10 flight ban 7-13, 538A3
Amtrak Chicago-Houston, Seattle trains ordrd cut 8-29, 868B1
Amtrak collisn kills 2 10-13, 800F1
Milwaukee Rd embargoes track 11-1–11-5, 867G2
Chicago transit strike 12-17–12-20, 987C2
ILLINOIS Brick Co. v. Illinois
Case cited by Sup Ct 6-11, 478G2
ILLINOIS Central Gulf Railroad Co.—*See IC Industries Inc.*
ILLINOIS River
1000s flee floods 3-24–3-27, 288F3
ILLINOIS State Board v. Socialist Workers Party
Ill 3d party electn law struck down by Sup Ct 2-22, 150E1
ILLMENSEE, Karl
Mammal cloning advance rptd 7-28, 692E2
I'LL Never Love This Way Again (recording)
On best-seller list 9-5, 672E3
ILLUSTRATIONS
Charts, Graphs & Tables
State legis schedule 5B3
Federal budget dollar 42A1
US '79-81 budget receipts, outlays 42C2
US '77-84 budget assumptns, projectns 43A2
Cong ldrship, com chrmn 71A1
US illegal aliens apprehensn 127A2
Dow Jan closings, vol 1-2–1-31, 72A1
NFL '78 statistical ldrs 1-6, 80A1
Dow Feb closings, vol 2-1–2-28, 166A2
US forgn student enrollmt 167C2
Dow Mar closings, vol 3-1–3-30, 230C3
3 Mile I A-plant diagrams 242A1, 243A3
Dow Apr closings, vol 4-2–4-30, 325D2
NBA final standings, statistical ldrs 4-8, 290B2
Hockey final standings, statistical ldrs 4-8, 4-18, 355B2, F3-356E1
1st 1/4 oil profits 301A2
Dow May closings, vol 5-1–5-31, 402A3
NFL coll draft 5-3–5-4, 335E1
Fortune '78 top 20 indls data 5-7, 304D1
US, USSR strategic weapons comparison 338E3
SALT II treaty proposed limits 339A2
'78 top-paid corp execs 5-14, 347E3
US Sen millionaires 5-18, 383C2
Canada vote breakdown 377A2
'78 top 10 states per capita gas use 5-27, 395F2
'78 world's busiest airports 421C1
Dow June closings, vol 6-1–6-29, 481C2
US top circulatn papers 6-6, 431B1
NBA coll draft 6-25, 507A2
Dow July closings, vol 7-2–7-31, 578B2
White House staff evaluatn form 530C2, 531C1
Dow Aug closings, vol 8-1–8-31, 648D2
US '78 top 10 defns contractors 8-1, 609C1
NASL final standings, statistical ldrs 8-12, 654C3
US 2nd 1/4 mil recruiting 8-20, 649E2
Dow Sept closings, vol 9-3–9-28, 745A3
MX 'racetrack' deployment diagram 9-7, 678A2
H-bomb cross-section 716C1
'78 state per capita income 9-16, 746B2
UN members listed 695D2
Municipal bond ratings 9-20, 920E3
Baseball final standings 9-30, 797E1
Dow Oct closings, vol 10-1–10-31, 827A3
USSR E Eur troop deploymt 761F2
3d 1/4 oil profits 10-25, 804C3
Dow Nov closings, vol 11-1–11-30, 903B2
'60-78 median family income 11-24, 965A2
PGA, LPGA top $ winners 11-30, 969F2
Dow Dec closings, vol 12-3–12-31, 985A2
NFL final standings 12-16, 1001A2
OPEC prices 12-21, 977A2
'79 gold price rise 12-31, 978A2

1980

Reagan in Williamson Cnty 10-21, 802F1
Reagan winds up campaign 10-31, 11-3, 840A2, B2
Press endorsemts rptd 11-1, 841F3, G3
Mondale, Carter wind up campaign 11-2, 11-3, 841C1, D1
Election results 11-4, 838B1, 839A2, D3
School Issues
Chicago teacher firing case declined by Sup Ct 1-7, 15D3
State of State message 1-9, 483E2
Chicago schls virtually closed, City Cncl OKs aid fund plan 1-28, 77F2-D3
Chicago bond rating down 1-31, 186C2
Chicago schls reopen 2-11, 114G1
Chicago schl bd fscl policies scored, desegregatn dispute cited 4-2, 292B1
Teachers strike in 10 districts 9-3, 723D3
Chicago OKs integratn agrmt 9-24, 724F1
Chicago black quotas case dismissed by Sup Ct 10-20, 807B2
Sports
Chicago White Sox sale OKd by bd 8-23, 795A3
AL owners rejct DeBartolo White Sox purchase 10-24, 12-11, 1000E1
ILLINOIS, University of (Urbana)
NIT results 3-20, 240E2
GE microbe patent upheld by Sup Ct 6-16, 452G3
ILLINOIS Brick Co. v. Illinois
Case cited by Sup Ct 10-14, 782A1
I'LL Never Love This Way Again (recording)
Warwick wins Grammy 2-27, 296C3
ILLUSTRATIONS
Charts, Graphs & Tables
State legis schedule 18C1
US '76-79 GNP 51C3
Dow Jan closings, vol 1-2—1-31, 76A1
Federal Reserve System bank defectns 1-23, 113D1
'71-79 CPI rise 1-25, 75D2
Federal budget dollar 69G3
US '79-81 budget receipts, outlays 70C1
Cancer risks 357B1
US '78-85 budget assumptns, projectns 71A2
'79 oil profits 1-31, 90F2
Dow Feb closings, vol 2-1—2-29, 167C2
Lake Placid Olympic results 2-12—2-24, 155F2-156D1
Canada vote breakdown chart 2-18, 121F1
Dow closing, $ exchng, gold price charts 2-18—3-20, 202A1
Olympic medal standings 2-24, 154F2
TV evangelist revenues 2-25, 413A2
NH primary vote 2-26, 142E2, G3
'77-80 prime rate 2-29, 144A1
Dow Mar closings, vol 3-3—3-31, 248C1
Mass, Vt pres primary results 3-4, 166C2-G3
Canada '76-80 CPI 3-13, 230C2
Ill primary vote 3-18, 206C2, D3
Cancer test guidelines 3-20, 316D3
'79 univ endowmt earnings 3-24, 319A2
NY, Conn pres primary results 3-25, 221B2-D3
Money mkt funds 3-31, 223F3
Wis, Kan pres primary results 4-1, 246G1-A3
Dow Apr closings, vol 4-1—4-30, 329A3
'79 top 10 TV advertisers 4-4, 376A2
La primary vote 4-5, 264G3, 265A1
NHL final standings, statistical ldrs 4-6, 296B1
1st 1/4 oil profits 4-21—4-30, 331C1
Pa pres primary results 4-22, 304B1, F2
NFL coll draft 4-29, 336E2
Dow May closings, vol 5-1—5-30, 401A2
Tex pres primary results 5-3, 342B2
Fortune '79 top 20 indls 5-5, 290D1
Tenn, Ind, NC, DC pres primary results 5-6, 342B1
Md, Neb pres primary results 5-13, 366E2
Mich, Ore pres primary results 5-20, 382G3, 383E1
Ark, Ida, Ky, Nev pres primary results 5-27, 399C2
US '79 top 10 defns contractors 5-28, 403E1
Dow June closings, vol 6-2—6-30, 495D3
Calif, Mont, NJ, NM, Ohio, RI, SD, W Va pres primary results 6-3, 423A2
Dem pres delegate count 6-4, 596A2
NBA coll draft 6-10, 447E1
GOP pres delegate count 6-28, 506A2
Dow July closings, vol 7-1—7-31, 575A2
AL, NL midseason standings 7-8, 636E2
Moscow Olympic results 7-20—8-3, 588A3, 622C1-624G3
Dow Aug closings, vol 8-1—8-29, 666A3
NASL final standings, statistical ldrs 8-24, 770B1, C3
Dow Sept closings, vol 9-1—9-30, 764A2

1976

ILYICHEV, Leonid F.
Returns Peking 11-27, talks resume 11-30, 908C1
IMAGES (record album)
Wins Grammy 2-28, 460B3
I'M Easy (song)
Wins Oscar 3-29, 240A3
IMF—*See INTERNATIONAL Monetary Fund*
IMMERFALL, Dan
Wins Olympic medal 2-10, 158F3

IMMIGRATION & Refugees—*See also country names*
US House votes Viet educ aid 1-19, 69F2
US Sen OKs Laos refugee aid 2-16, 182C1
Rival Viet groups in US split 2-20, 176F2
Sup Ct upholds state jobs curb 2-25, 169F1
Ford vows Cuban naturalizatn speedup 2-28, 165A3
Denmark allows Viet orphans stay 3-16, 252D1
Civil svc jobs bar voided 6-1, 414G1-B2
Medicare benefits bar upheld 6-1, 414B2
Rep Helstoski indicted 6-2, 414C3
Jury duty bar upheld 6-7, 414D2
Dem platform text 6-15, 472B2
Viet refugee funds use extended 6-30, 533C2
Warrantless alien interrogatn upheld 7-6, 534G3
Lennon gets US residency 7-27, 640F3
US '75 populatn growth rptd 7-31, 911G1
More SE Asia refugees arrive US, total rptd 8-16, 696A3
GOP platform text 8-18, 606D1, F1
Canada curb urged 8-22, decline rptd 11-3, 851D1
Haiti refugees in Miami 8-30, 1005G3
US hikes crime rating 10-4, 796G3
Jobless benefits for illegal aliens barred 10-20, 788F1
US revises rules re occidentals 10-20, 835C1
Thais return 26 to Cambodia 11-23, 929B2
Helsinki progress rpts issued 12-2, 12-8, 934G1, B2

1977

Maps
Zaire 207A3
Leb battle zone 266A2
Southern Philippines 330D1
N Sea Ekofisk oil slick map 336A2
Afars & Issas 363C2
Alaska pipeline 476D2
Legalized Israel W Bank settlemts 570A2
Ogaden battle 8-16—8-19, 648D3
Mid-Atlantic offshore drilling sites 650A2
Panama Canal Zone 9-7, 678A2
Catalonia province 843A2
Nicaragua rebel offensive 802C2
Ganges R boundary 896E3
North Israel, south Leb battle zone 849D1
Photographs
Carter swearing-in 1-20, 25A1
USSR revolutn 60th anniv fete 11-7, 865A2

ILO—*See UNITED Nations—International Labor Organization*
ILWU—*See LONGSHOREMEN'S and Warehousemen's Union, International*
ILYICHEV, Leonid F.
Ends China border talks 2-28, 161D1
ILYUSHIN, Sergei V.
Death rptd 2-9, 164B3
IMF—*See INTERNATIONAL Monetary Fund*
IMMIGRANTS, The (book)
On best-seller list 11-6, 872D3
IMMIGRATION & Naturalization Service—*See under U.S. GOVERNMENT—JUSTICE*

IMMIGRATION & Refugees—*See also country, region names*
Miami rpts Quebec bids 1-13, 43A2
US pardons draft evaders 1-21, 51C2
US speeds Sovt Jews' visas 1-30, 117A2
Gay rights group sees Carter aide 3-26, 278D2
Colo schl voting law review declined 4-18, 342D1
Poll on illegal aliens rptd 4-24, 370B3
Sup Ct rules on alien fathers' illegitimate children 4-26, 382C3
Carter gets illegal alien plan, ID proposal studied 4-27, 370E1-B3
Kennedy on Carter wiretap curb proposal 5-18, 386D3
NYS alien tuitn law voided 6-13, 517E2
Carter illegal alien plan; reaction 8-4, 591F3
Young, Mex ldrs discuss alien plan 8-7—8-8, 646D2
Cuba OKs US natls' kin exit 8-11, 653B3
Mex expert scores Carter plan 8-28, 746A2
US natls' kin leave Cuba 9-22, 781A2
Food stamp eligibility tightnd 9-29, 737A2
US to admit more Sovt Jews 12-14, 956E1
Indochina
Indochina postwar rpt 5-1—5-3, 336D3-338G1
Indochina refugee flow increases 6-12—6-26, 497B1, G1
US OKs 15,000 for resetlmt 8-11, 1st wave arrives 9-20, 739E3
Indochina refugee pleas by US, UN rptd 8-25, 685G2
Indochina refugee flow data 8-31, 685D2
Refugee aid signed 10-28, 834B2
Viets hijack boat 11-7, 157 reach Australia 11-29; Handi denied return 11-30, 1018D2
Viet total in Australia 11-23, 1018E2
Thais to bar Viets, UN role cited 11-25, 1018F2-A3
32 Viets reach Thailand 12-23, 1018C2
Viet govt blocks escapes 12-25, 1018B2

1978

Maps—*See also Facts On File Atlas*
Cambodia-Viet battle 9F1
Beagle Channel islands 101E1
PLO raid on Israel, 3-11, Israeli invasn of Leb 3-15, 174B1
Transkei 258E3
Zaire, Shaba prov 359D2
Beirut battle zone 503C1
Mideast summit accord 710A2
Nicaragua cities where revolts crushed 757A2
Tanzania-Uganda conflict 860C1
Guyana murder, suicide sites 11-18, 889C1
Photographs
2 Pulitzer winners 4-17, 4-21, 314D2, 315D1
Solzhenitsyn Harvard speech excerpts 6-8, 444A2 ★ -G3
Von Hirsch enamels 6-22, 578F2
World Cup championship 6-25, 520C1
Bakke Sup Ct ruling 6-28, 482A1
Pope Paul VI 8-6, 601E1
Kenya Pres Kenyatta 639D2
Pope John Paul I 8-26, 657C1
Shroud of Turin 926A2
Sadat, Carter, Begin sign summit pact 9-17, 709A1
Pope John Paul II 10-16, 781C1
US Rep Ryan 891A2
Rev Jim Jones 890A1
Guyana cult bodies 909A1
ILLYES, Gyula
Rumania scores minority protest 5-7, 360F1
ILO—*See UNITED Nations—International Labor Organization*
ILYICHEV, Leonid Fyodorovich
Returns to China 4-26, 360A3
ILYUKHIN, Mikhail
Asks suspended sentence for Crawford 9-6, 742C3
IMBERT McGregor, Maj. Gen. Alfredo
Sworn DR AF staff chief 8-16, 648E2
IMF—*See INTERNATIONAL Monetary Fund*
IMITATION of Christ (book)
Pope John Paul I dies 9-28, 746C3 ★
IMLACH, George (Punch)
Fired as Sabres gen mgr 12-4, 991D1
IMMIGRANTS, The (book)
On best-seller list 10-9, 800C3; 11-6, 888B1
IMMIGRATION & Naturalization Service—*See under U.S. GOVERNMENT—JUSTICE*
IMMIGRATION & Refugees
Unificatn Church '77 deportatn moves cited 2-22, 295C3
State police alien ban backed by Sup Ct 3-22, 221A1
US rep scores Rumania emigratn curbs 4-11, 291G1-A2
NYS alien MD rule review declined by Sup Ct 5-15, 388A1
Alien deportatn trial backed by Sup Ct 6-6, 447E3
Haiti refugees arrive Fla 7-18, 7-22, 671C3
Cuba dual natls arrive Miami 9-14, 10-3, 776G3; 11-14, 880B3
Cuban ex-prisoners arrive Miami 10-21, 880C2
Mex border fence set by US 10-24, 818B1
US OKs ex-Nazi deportatn 10-30, 872C2
Unificatn Church abuses chrgd by House subcom 11-1, 862C3
Cuba, Leb refugee entry to double 11-28; Carter vows aid 12-6, 934F1
US House com seeks illegal alien curbs, scores Carter plan 12-20, 1010B2-B3
Indochina—*See INDOCHINA—Refugees*
Soviet Issues—*See USSR—Human Rights*

1979

Maps—*See also Facts On File Atlas*
Cambodia battle 9A1
Amtrak route cutback plan 1-31, 129C1
China-Viet battle zone 121A1
Israel Sinai exit schedule 249A1

Photographs
Ayatollah Khomeini 82A1
Teng Hsiao-ping 83D3
Jupiter 2-13, 3-4, 162D2
Auschwitz death camp 2-22, 193D1
Margaret Thatcher 5-3, 338A1
Joseph Clark 5-23, 377E1
Saturn 8-29, 696A2
Pope in US 10-5, 10-6, 757A1, 758C1
Park Chung Hee 821D1

I Love Lucy (TV series)
Vivian Vance dies 8-17, 671F3
I Love My Wife (play)
Opens 5-15, 711F3
IMAGE Carrier Corp. v. Koch
Case refused by Sup Ct 4-2, 281F2
IMAMURA, Yojiro
Indicted 4-5, 389G2
IMF—*See INTERNATIONAL Monetary Fund*
IMLACH, George (Punch)
Named Maple Leafs hockey dir 7-4, 655C3
IMMIGRANTS, The (book)
On best-seller list 1-7, 80D3
IMMIGRATION & Naturalization Service—*See under U.S. GOVERNMENT-JUSTICE*
IMMIGRATION Policy, Commission on—*See under U.S. GOVERNMENT*

IMMIGRATION & Refugees
US surveys forgn students, visa probe planned 1-29, 93F2
US-Mex illegal alien issue detailed 1-29; Carter, Lopez Portillo in talks; comr named 2-14–2-16, 124G1, 127A1
US '64-78 illegal alien deportatn data 127A2
US rpts Mex record Jan crossings 2-11; entry policies protested, pol activism seen 2-12, 127D2-A3
US forgn student abuses detailed 3-2, visa crackdown set 3-8; enrollmt chart 167C2, E2
US refugee bill proposed 3-8, Sovt paroles extended 3-26, 307E3-308D1
US Mex deportatn spurs protests 3-9, 3-10, 308E1
NYS alien teacher ban backed by Sup Ct 4-17, 325E3
Mex border fence dropped by US 4-26, 327F2-B3
Carter vows Mex aliens protectn 5-5, 347B1
Chile refugee relocatn rptd 5-7, 369G2
Portugal '78 remittance rise rptd 5-25, 409G2
Fla law firm chrgd in visa fraud 6-1, 491D3
Cong immunity broadened by Sup Ct 6-18, 498C3
US-Mex vegetable growers rift setld 7-19, 553D2
Latin pol refugees occupy Swedish consulate in Rio, protest Argentina repressn 8-6; UN responds 8-8, 627D1, F1
Castillo quits as INS head 8-10, 630D3
INS lifts gay alien curb 8-14, 631G1
Calif KKK clash 8-19, 866B2
Jamaica '75-78 emigratn to US rptd, '79 forecast 9-30, 996F1
US Helsinki com scores policies 11-7, 981A1
US orders status review for Iranians 11-13, 863F1; 11-15–11-17, 879D1; visa checks rptd 11-23, 898F1; probes ruled illegal 12-11, 935F2
INS neighborhood raids curbed 11-26, 924B1
Amnesty Intl scores US on Mex illegal aliens 12-9, 980B2
US sees '80 Mex alien rise 12-12, 950G2
Davis passport denied 12-19, 1006A1
INS revives gay alien curb 12-26, 992B1
US check on Iranians upheld; deportatns, other data rptd 12-27, 975B2
Indochina—*See INDOCHINA–Refugees*

1980

Ark A-missile silo blast diagram 9-19, 765C2
Dow Oct closings, vol 10-1—10-31, 824A2
Baseball final standings 10-6, 795C3
PGA, LPGA top money winners 10-12, 971E1
Dow Nov closings, vol 11-3—11-28, 916A3
US popular, electoral pres vote tables 838A1, 839D3
Election returns 11-4: US Sen 840B1*; House 842A1*-844E4; gov 845C2
La 'swallowed' lake 11-20, 970E2
Dow Dec closings, vol 12-1—12-31, 984B3
NFL final standings 12-22, 998D3
'80 census figures 12-31, 983C1
Maps
Afghanistan, surrounding nations 25A1
Federal Reserve System 1-23, 113B1
Israeli raid into Lebanon 4-9, 260A2
US rescue mission in Iran 322A1
Venus 5-28, 477E2
Jerusalem 585A2
Israel Medit-Dead Sea canal 8-24, 643A3
Libya-Syria merger 9-10, 697A1
Iran-Iraq war zone 718D1
US electoral vote 839A1
Italy quake 11-23, 893E1
Photographs
Mugabe 161C1
British Guiana stamp 4-5, 472C2
Iranian firing squad 4-14, 317E2
Tito '79 Cuba visit 338A2
Reagan, Ford, Bush at GOP conv 7-17, 529A1
Carter, Kennedy at Dem conv 8-14, 609A1
Chinese Premr Zhao 9-10, 677C1
Reagan, wife after electn 11-4, 837A1
John Lennon 934B1
IMAMURA, Yujiro
Gets suspended sentnc 7-24, 605D2
IMF—*See INTERNATIONAL Monetary Fund*
IMIRIE Jr., Scott F.
Charged in GSA scandal 1-15, 112F1
IMMIGRATION & Naturalization Service—*See under U.S. GOVERNMENT--JUSTICE*
IMMIGRATION Reform, Federation for American
Illegal alien census suit dismissed 2-26, 147A2

IMMIGRATION & Refugees
US prosecutn disparities rptd 1-6, 24B3
Carter seeks more aid 1-28, 72D2
US illegal aliens rptd at 6 mln 2-4, 147D1
US 'guest worker' study rptd 2-13, 147C2
Refugee reform bill clears Cong 2-25, 3-4, Carter signs 3-17, 249A2
US illegal alien census suit dismissed 2-26, 147A2
Ex-Rep Helstoski cleared of '76 chrgs 2-27, 228B1
N Marianas loses US citizenship 3-7, 495F1
Iran immigratn data since emb takeover rptd 3-12, 178F1
Carter defends Iranian entries 3-14, 209G1
US census postponemt denied by Sup Ct 3-17, 226B1
Iranian student deportatn ban denied by Sup Ct 3-31, 291G2
Latin influx to US surveyed 5-11—5-20, 396A2
Iranian student case refused by Sup Ct 5-19, 440B2
Venice summit notes concern 6-22, 473D1
KKK opens Canada office 6-26, 497D1
Nicaraguans get 3-mo extensn in US 6-30, 495B2
El Salvador rightist in US illegally 6-30—7-3, 521C3
El Salvador aliens rescued in Ariz desert 7-4—7-5; search continues 7-7, arrests rptd 7-9, 518D2-C3; 4 held 7-11, 7-19, 560E2
UN women's conf topic 7-14—7-30, 587G1
US, Canada data compared 7-16, 562B3
Ukrainian youth granted asylum 7-21, 560C1
Tex aliens schooling ordered 7-21, 576A2
Mex alien case mistrial declared 7-29, retrial sought 8-29, 713F2
UK proposes new citizenship plan 7-30, 604A2
W Ger pol asylum rules rptd tightened 7-31, 581B2
Iranian jailed protesters freed 8-5, 586D2
ABA rejects alien gay rights proposal 8-6, 744G1
Canada E Eur records rptd found 8-20, 651F1-C2
DR stowaways drown on Panama freighter 9-5, smuggling ring uncovered 9-9, 687C3
US cuts '81 quota 9-19, 883A3
US econ impact rptd 9-22, 826D3
US tightens Japan visas 10-6, 870C1-B2
El Salvador alien deportatn proceedings begin 10-18, 2 smugglers convicted 10-20, 815F3, G3
Hong Kong sets China ban 10-23, 855D2-C3
Brazil law controversy rptd 10-30, 871A1
Canada '81 refugee total rptd cut 10-31, 871E2
3d El Salvador smuggler sentenced 11-4, 870B1
107-yr-old W Va women votes 11-4, 890G2*
US higher quotas, amnesty for illegal aliens backed 12-7, 939A1

1976	1977	1978	1979	1980

Ct bars US House deportatn res 12-24, 989G1
Afghanistan —*See AFGHANISTAN—Soviet Military Intervention*
Cuba
Refugees offered asylum 4-14—4-17, 285C1
Cuba flights to CR suspended 4-18, 10,000 offered asylum 4-20; marchers rally 4-19, flights resume 4-24, 300C2-D3
Refugees picked up by US flotilla, granted conditional entry 4-21—4-24, 300E3
Refugee exodus hampered by storms 4-25—4-28; US total hits 6,000, 55 detained 5-1, 326A1
Fla gov asks fed aid 4-29, Carter declares emergency 5-6, 339C3
US sets Eglin AF Base processing cntr 5-1, 326G1
US flow slowed by storm, Swiss Emb interest office attack 5-2; visa procedures suspended 5-4, 339E2
Eglin airlifts begin 5-3; overcrowding, disease rptd 5-6, 339E3
Carter offers 'open arms', 3,500 more arrive in US 5-5, 339D2
US refugee influx at 17,636, authorities detain 133 5-6, 339B3
CR hosts intl policy coordinatn conf 5-8, 361B1, A2
US immigrants surveyed 5-11—5-20, 396A3
Carter curbs 'open arms' policy, orders flotilla end; 5-pt progrm detailed 5-14, 361A1
US refugee total at 46,000, 400 deported 5-15, 361G1, C2
US amends finance regulatns 5-15, 361A2
US turns back Cuban flotillas 5-17—5-21; refugee flow slows, total at 67,000 5-21, 379F3
Refugee boat capsizes, US blames Cuba 5-17, 5-18; sealift deaths at 24 5-21, 380F1
Havana anti-US protest draws 1 mln 5-17, 380A2
Pa processing cntr opens 5-18; Eglin, Chaffee rptd filled 5-21, 380D1
US grants refugees pol asylum 5-21, 380B1
Cuba bars 4-natn talks 5-23, 396G1
Eglin, Chaffee hit by unrest, resetlmt delays rptd 5-24—5-26; security tightened 5-26—5-27, 395F3-396C1
Refugee resetlmt costs estimated 5-25, 396D1
Wis processing cntr opens 5-25; US security checks rptd complete, resetlmt lags 6-1—6-2, 420D1
Cuban flotilla seizures protested 5-28, 700 face fines 5-29, 396F1
US refugee total at 87,995, 300 vessels stalled in Mariel 5-29, 396E1
450 remain in Peru Emb, talks rptd underway 5-29, 397B1
Refugees riot at Chaffee 6-1; processing suspended, troops enforce calm 6-2, 419G3-420D1
442 Cubans leave Peru Emb 6-2, 33 detained 6-5, 420D2
US freighter, 34 other vessels arrive in Fla; refugee influx hits 101,476 6-3, 420B2
US baseball team signs refugee 6-3, 637C1
Carter consults Cong ldrs 6-4; orders criminal refugees expelled 6-7, 435A1
Cuba bars UN involvmt 6-5, UN processing aid rptd 6-9, 435A2
Flotilla end seen 6-5, US expands blockade 6-10, 435B2
Carter sees Fla black, hispanic ldrs 6-9, 439F1
Refugees granted 6-mo reprieve, get pub assistance 6-20, 484B3-485D1
US backs homosexual entry bar repeal 6-20, 2000 await processing 7-7, 514G2-D3
US expels 18 criminals, Havana blocks return 6-24; 1,395 jailed 6-30, 514C2
US Cong OKs aid bill 7-2, Carter signs 7-8, 515F1
Marines alerted; mystery freighter intercepted, no refugees found 7-4, 514G3, 515B1*
US releases Cuban flotilla boats 7-7, 514E3
CR protests refugee policy, shuns Nicaragua fete 7-15, 565A3
256 arrive in Key West, refugee total rptd 8-2, 591C3
Youths riot at Pa camp 8-5, troops quell violence 8-6, 591G2
83 in Swiss Emb interest office surrender 8-7, 618F3
Refugee resetlmt problems grow; crime, violence rampant 8-12—9-10; 14,000 remain in camps 8-29, 684E3
US budgets $16.8 mln for Fla 8-13, 617E1
Wis refugee cntr riots 8-13, 27 arrested 8-14, 631F3
4 jets hijacked to Cuba, 2 attempts foiled 8-14—8-17, FAA tightens security 8-15, 631B3
Refugees continue hijack attempts 8-26—9-17; Havana issues strong warning 9-16, returns 2 9-18, 704B1-B2
Braniff jet stormed at Lima airport 8-29, refugees surrender 8-30, 672B2
Carter sets 3-pt resetlmt plan 9-18, 742G1
US '81 refugee quota cut 9-19, 883A3
PR camp to be opened 9-23, 725E3-726A1

1976

IMMUNIZATION—*See 'Diseases' under MEDICINE*
IMPERIAL Bancorp.
Rptd on FRB 'problem' list 1-22, 111B2
INABA, Osamu
Issues Lockheed probe rpt 10-15, 838G2, C3
IN Chhou Deth, Col.
Cambodia asks Thais return 9-4, 734F3
INCLAN, Hilda
Arrives Venez 10-21, ousted 10-22, 844F1

INCOMES (U.S.)
Medical insurnc data rptd 1-12, 32E1
Dec, '75 income; Oct, Nov, '73, '74 revised 1-19, 91A2
Jan income rise rptd, Dec '75 revised 2-17, 168E3
Feb income rise rptd, Jan revised 3-17, 215F3
'77 Ford, House com budgets table 231B1
Mar rise rptd, Feb revised 4-15, 279A2
Male-female, black-white data rptd 4-27, 379B3, 380B1
Cong OKs '77 budget target 5-12, 5-13; Ford, OMB, Cong budgets table 358F1, C2
'60-74 disposable income rise rptd 7-11, 582A1
'75 intl rank rptd 7-12, 581F3
Apr-June incomes rptd 7-20, 568A2
Incomes of GOP conv delegates compared 8-7, 8-8, 616D2
Cong sets '77 budget levels, table 9-16, 706C2
World Bank chart 778A1
Sept income rptd; July, Aug revised 10-15, 806B2
'60-75 consumer income rptd 11-23, 959F1

1977

IMMUNIZATION—*See 'Diseases' under MEDICINE*
IMPENDING Crisis, The (book)
Wins Pulitzer Prize 4-18, 355D2
IMPERIAL Oil Ltd.—*See EXXON*
IMPORTS—*See FOREIGN Trade; commodity names*
IMPOUNDMENTS, Fund—*See U.S. GOVERNMENT—BUDGET—Impoundment & Recission*
INCEST—*See SEX Crimes*
INCO Ltd.
ESB acquisitn OKd 11-11, 918E3

INCOMES (U.S.)
Transfer paymts described 56D3
CBO issues poverty rpts 1-13, 1-17, 80A3, 81B1
'76, Dec income rise rptd; Nov revised 1-17, 56G2
Jan growth rptd slowed; Dec '76 revised 2-17, 130B2
Feb income rptd; Jan revised 3-17, 194C1
Poverty level raised 4-1, 302A2
Mar rise rptd, Feb revised 4-19, 300B3
'76 per-capita income up, table 5-10, 387B2, C2
Cong sets '78 budget target 5-17, 405B1
Apr income; Feb, Mar revised 5-18, 384C1
May, June income; Apr revised 7-20, 555D1
July income; May, June revised 8-17, 629E1
'76 state per-capita data revised, table 9-13, 821E1
Aug income, July revised 9-16, 722E1
'75, '76 real family incomes up 10-3, 821G3-822B1
Sept income, Aug revised 10-18, 798B2
Oct income 11-16, 898F3
Nov rise rptd; Aug-Oct revised 12-16, 977A2

1978

IMMUNIZATION—*See MEDICINE—Diseases*
IMPERATO, Anthony
Runaways opens 3-9, 887G2
IMPERATORE, Arthur
NHL OKs Rockies purchase 8-9, 656B3
IMPERIAL Oil Ltd.
Canada unit rpts uranium find 9-13, 722B1
IMPERIALS (singing group)
Win Grammy 2-24, 315G3
IMPORTED Steel, American Institute for
Orban scores US trigger prices 1-4, 3B3
IMPORTS—*See FOREIGN Trade; commodity, country names*
IMS International Inc.
CBS seeks purchase 2-15, rejctd 2-22, 185B1
INA Corp.
Stockbroker liability case refused by Sup Ct 12-4, 959C1
INCEST—*See SEX Crimes*
INCHAESTEGUI Cabral, Hector
Sworn DR min without portfolio 8-16, 648D2
INCO Ltd.
In Dow Jones indl avg 66E2
Copper strike cited 10-20, 805C1
INCOMES (U.S.)—*See also LABOR—Wages*
Income index described, transfer paymts cited 52C2
'77, Dec income rise rptd 1-18, 52G1, A2 ★
Carter budget assumptns, projectns 1-23, 46B2, C2
'76 median family income revised, '73-75 cited 2-10, 128E3
Jan incomes; Nov, Dec '77 revised 2-20, 128G2
Feb income up, Jan revised 3-17, 223B1
Carter cites real income rise 4-11, 260B2
Mar income rptd, Dec '77-Feb revised 4-18, 303F3-304A1
'76, '77 family incomes, living costs rptd 4-26, 349E1
Mar CPI rptd up; Soc Sec, other transfer paymts linked 4-28, 345C1
Per capita income rank rptd 5-12, 384E3
Apr income up; Mar, Feb revised 5-17, 389F2-A3
Guaranteed income study rptd 5-19, 720E3
May income up; Apr, May transfer paymts rptd 6-16, 470F1-A2
June income; Apr, May revised 7-19, 607G3 ★ -608A1
'70-78 2-income families rptd 7-24, 679F3
Black-white '72-76 gap rise rptd 8-8, 810E3
'77 median family income, 'real' gain rptd 8-9, 680A1
July income up; June, May revised 8-17, 643D3
Aug incomes rptd 9-18, 717B2
Carter rpts on Viet vets 10-10, 878B1
Sept income up 10-18, 790B3
Oct income up, Sept revised 11-17, 918F3
Nov income up 12-18, 982B2

1979

IMMOBILAIRE New England
Boston Navy Yd renovatn set 2-1, 94B1
IMMUNIZATION—*See MEDICINE-Diseases*
IMPERIAL Chemical Industries Ltd.
ICI Australia petrochem plans rptd 2-8, 94C3
IMPERIAL Group Ltd.
Howard Johnson purchase set 9-10, Calif bar seen 10-12, 942B3-E3
I'M Ready (recording)
Wins Grammy 2-16, 336G3
INCER Barquero, Roberto
Sees forgn debt paymt delay 2-1, 101F2
INCEST—*See SEX Crimes*
INCO Ltd.
In Dow Jones indl avg 72F1

INCOMES (U.S.)
Carter State of Union Message 1-23, 46E2, 47B1
Dole backs farmers 3-10, 186D1
'64, '79 incomes compared 11-28, 925C1
Statistics
Black-white gap 1-17, 35F1, G1
Income index described, transfer paymts cited 34D3
'78, Dec income gains 1-17, 34A3
Jan income, Dec '78 revised 2-16, 151C2
Feb income up; Oct-Dec '78, Jan revised 3-19, 252C3
Mar income rptd; Jan, Feb revised 4-18, 280G3
Apr income rptd, Mar revised 5-17, 362G3
May income rptd, Apr revised 6-19, 463G2
June income; Apr, May revised 7-19, 557ZZ
July income; May, June revised 8-16, 621G2-622B1
'78 per capita state income 9-16, 746C1
Aug income up, June July revised 9-18, 701E1
Sept income; July, Aug revised 10-17, 784B2
Oct income, Sept revised 11-19, 922A2
'78 median family income, '60-'78 real growth 11-24, 965E1-G2
Nov income, Oct revised 12-18, 964B1

1980

Ft Chaffee gets 'hard-core' refugee transfers 9-25, 725C3
Refugee aid to states clears Cong 9-25, 10-1, Carter signs 10-10, 785B1
Mariel harbor closed, flotilla ends; refugee influx at 125,000 9-26, 742C1, B2
PR sues US to block camp 9-30, 742E2
PR camp blocked by legal battles 10-1—10-24; Miami cuts off hotel funds 10-21, 150 evicted 10-24, 825A3
PR camp ban lifted 11-3, 869C2
Fla voters end govt bilingualism 11-4, 847B3
Airlift of 600 begins, 120 reach Fla 11-19, 883E2
Castro threatens to reopen Mariel over emigratn rift 12-17, 12-20, 992E3
PR camp blocked again 12-18, 988B2
Haiti
Haitians reach Fla in record numbers, status delayed by suits 4-13, 294A2
Haitians press for US pol asylum 5-7, 339G3
Haitians granted 6-mo reprieve, get pub assistance 6-20, 484B3-485D1
Haitians win US suit, deportatns ordrd halted 7-2, 514E1
Haitian resetlmt aid clears US Cong 7-2, Carter signs 7-8, 515F1
US budgets $16.8 mln for Fla 8-13, 617E1
3 drown as boat capsizes 9-6; 400 reach US; exodus accelerates, total nears 40,000 9-9, 685D1
17 jailed for ship hijacking to Fla 9-17, 726B1
Carter sets 3-pt resetlmt plan 9-18, 742G1
US '81 refugee quota cut 9-19, 883A3
PR camp to be opened 9-23, 725E3-726A1
Refugee aid to states clears Cong 9-25, 10-1, Carter signs 10-10, 785B1
PR sues US to block camp 9-30, 742E2
PR camp blocked by legal battles 10-1—10-24, 825B3
Refugees rptd stranded in Bahamas 10-9; Bahama evicts, Duvalier OKs return 11-13, 869F2
PR camp ban lifted 11-3, 869C2
US news copter missing 11-13, 869C3
64 refugees reach Bahamas 11-21, refugee rptd on Cayo Lobos 11-22, 920C1-E1
PR camp blocked again 12-18, 988B2
Indochina—*See INDOCHINA--Refugees*
U.S. Presidential Election (& Transition)
Kennedy visits Mex City 4-28, 327G2
Reagan acceptance speech 7-17, 534G3
Dem conv keynote speech 8-11, 612A2*, A3
Dem platform plank adopted 8-13, 615C1
Reagan urges eased Mex entry rules 9-16, 699F3
IMMORTAL Bachelor, The (film)
Released 2-22, 216A3
IMMUNIZATION—*See MEDICINE--Diseases*
IMPERIAL Group Ltd.
Howard Johnson deal completed 6-17, 557C3
IMPERIAL Irrigation District v. Yellin
Case decided by Sup Ct 6-16, 511E2
IMPERIAL Oil Ltd. (of Exxon Corp.)
Oil sands operatn suspended 11-18, 920F3
IMPERIALS (singing group)
Win Grammy 2-27, 296E3
IMPERIAL Valley—*See CALIFORNIA*
IMPOSIMATO, Ferdinando
Sees Rome Red Brigadists nearly eliminated 7-3, 523G2
INA Corp.
Iran asset damages backed by US court 7-10, 546E1
Insurance Co. of North America
Mutual fund fraud case refused by Sup Ct 3-24, 265F1
INCO Ltd.
In Dow Jones indl avg 76F1
INCOMES (U.S.)
Family income, aptitude test scores linked 1-14, 36D2
Carter cites net rise 1-20, 50D2
'78-85 budget assumptns, projectns table 1-28, 71B2
Hispanic immigrants surveyed 5-20, 396E3
Canada median income compared 7-16, 562G2
Statistics
Income index described, transfer payments cited 35B1
'79, Dec income gains 1-17, 35A1
'70s black-white gap 1-22, 94D2
Jan income up 2-19, 145D1
Feb incomes up 3-18, 209G2-B3
Mar income up 4-17, 286C3
April income gains 5-19, 384C3
May income, Apr revised 6-17, 455C2
June income, May revised 7-17, 542E1
July income, June revised 8-18, 631A2
Aug income; July, June revised 9-18, 725B2
Sept income, Aug revised 10-16, 783E2
'79 median family income 10-23, 823E3
Oct income, Sept revised 11-18, 883C1
Nov income, Oct revised 12-22, 984B1

1976

INDEPENDENCE, Mo.—*See MISSOURI*
INDEPENDENCE Examiner (newspaper)
Ford endorsement rptd 10-30, 827G3
INDEPENDENCIA (Peruvian warship)
In Intl Naval Review 7-4, 488B3
INDEPENDENT Freedom Party
Black candidacy planned 3-20, 214F2
INDEPENDENT Order of Odd Fellows
'74 Phila fever rptd 8-9, 656A3

INDIA—*See also ADB, COMMONWEALTH of Nations, DISARMAMENT—Geneva Committee, NONALIGNED Nations Movement*
'75 mine blast search ended 1-19, 80A2
Picachy named cardinal 4-27, 336C2
US jet sets world mark 5-2, 912F3
Naga guerrillas freed 5-15, 365C2
Jet crashes in Bombay 10-12, 840F2
'72 starvatn deaths rptd 10-28, 863C2
Religious ldr gets life term 11-29, 952G3

Atomic Energy
Gandhi bars A-tests end 1-14, 73G2
'74 US info rptd scored 1-20, 93C3
US reports Tarapur plant leak 1-30, India denies 2-7, 156D2
Canada cites '74 incident 2-25, 175B1
Canada bars A-sales 5-18, India scores 5-20, 363A2
A-plant expansn underway 6-19, 538C2
US OKs fuel sale 7-21, 739D2
US arms control rpt issued 7-29, 739E2
US admits A-blast aid 8-2, 581D3
USSR heavy water sale rptd 12-8, 955A2

Economy & Labor (domestic)
Strikers protest bonus ban 1-6, 29B1
CP joins bonus ban protest 1-22, 73B3
Equal pay law adopted 1-30, 101E3
5-yr econ plan OKd 9-25, 731D3

Family-Planning Developments
Birth-control plan 4-16, New Delhi riots 4-19, 290B1, E1
Civil svc birth-control plan 9-6, 676E1
Riot deaths rptd 10-17, 10-27; Gandhi admits 10-27, 810C2
Moslems score sterilizatn riot deaths 10-28; law chief shifted 11-1, 837A3

Foreign Relations (misc.)—*See also 'Atomic Energy' above, 'UN Policy' below*
Natls quit S Vietnam 1-3, 11G3
Tanzania pres visits 1-18, 36D1
French premr visits, pacts signed 1-22—1-26, 139E2
Aid to Bangladesh rebels denied 1-26, 156B2
2 Australian consulates closed 2-4, 97A2
At intl econ conf 2-11—2-20, 148B1
Egypt rpts MiG parts ban 3-14, 193C1
Confrms Egypt MiG parts ban 3-17, 275C3
Firms taken off Arab blacklist 3-24—4-3, 242C1
Pak makes peaceful overtures 3-27, Gandhi OKs talks 4-11, 278E2
Fears forgn arms to Pak; cites China aid to Pak 3-31, 278B3, C3
Total IMF oil loan rptd 4-1, 340C2
To exchng ambs with China 4-15, 278D3
Bangladesh clashes 4-19—4-20, 290F1
'75 Sovt trade rptd 5-5, 341A1
Renewed Pak ties set 5-12—5-14, 5-18, 356C2
Bangladesh protests dam 5-16—5-17, 365F1
B Desh chrgs border raid 5-18, 382A2
At Timor Assemb meeting 5-31, 423A1
Gandhi in Moscow, ties bolstered 6-8—6-11; Indian O bases opposed 6-13, 440A1
Amnesty Intl asks emergency rule end 6-24, 497A1
Amb takes post in China 7-7, 538C2
Developing natns OK press pool 7-13, 619A3
Pak amb exchng 7-21, rail svc renewed 7-22, 538F1, G1
BBC closes New Delhi office 8-5, 621D1
S Africa seizes 3 students 8-12, 624C3
Gandhi reactn to Mao death 9-9, 657F2
Jet hijacked 9-10; Pak recaptures 9-11, 685C3
Forgn press curbs lifted 9-18, 700C3
Bangladesh chrgs rebel aid 9-25, India denies 9-26, 755B1
Canada immigratn rptd 11-3, 851E1
Australia probes airline food 12-6, 962C1

1977

INDEPENDENT Petroleum Association of America—*See PETROLEUM Association of America, Independent*
INDERAL (Propranolol)—*See MEDICINE—Drugs*

INDIA—*See also COMMONWEALTH of Nations, DISARMAMENT—Geneva Committee, NONALIGNED Nations Movement*
Birth curb program eased 4-2, 283F3
Train falls into river, 44 die 5-30, 992G2
Malaria upsurge rptd 9-4, 747F3
Japan jet hijacked 9-28, 756A3
Forced birth control dropped 10-3, 842G2-B3
Express train crash kills 61 10-10, 888B3
Cyclones hit 11-12, 11-19, 928A2
Sabotage acts suspected 11-23, 11-25, security tightened 11-27, 966E2
Ananda Marga tied to diplomat attacks 11-28, 12-1, 966F2-A3
A-plant blast 12-3, probe ordrd 12-6, 966C2

Economy & Labor (domestic)
CP launches price protests 1-1, 8B1
'76 econ growth rptd 2-16, 147C2
Interim budget announced 3-28, 240E1
Record wheat crop seen 7-29, 612A1
Solar energy obstacles cited 12-11, 975D3
Small business aid planned; per capita income, indl output cited 12-23, 1013G3-1014B1

Foreign Relations (misc.)—*See also 'Monetary, Trade & Aid' and 'UN Policy' below*
Pak frees hijackers 1-5, India protests 1-6, 45F3
BBC ban lifted 1-6, 45G3
Bangladesh Ganges talks fail 1-23, 64D1
Gromyko visits 4-25—4-27, 348D1
Dalai Lama exile end sought 5-1, 347D1
Pak chrgs mil threat 5-11, 378A2
China chrgs Tibet rebel aid 8-6, 616E3
Envoy assaulted in Australia 9-15, 779F1
Desai in Moscow 10-21—10-26; Sovts vow contd aid 10-26, 842F2
W Ger asks more Bombay airport security 10-23, 868D3
Bangladesh Ganges R pact 11-5, map 896D3

1978

INCOME Tax—*See TAXES*
INDEPENDENCE, Mo.—*See MISSOURI*
INDEPENDENT (St. Petersburg, Fla. newspaper)
Poynter dies 6-15, 540F3
INDEPENDENT Cosmetic Manufacturers & Distributors Inc. v. HEW
Case refused by Sup Ct 10-10, 789E3
INDERAL (propranolol)—*See MEDICINE—Drugs*
INDEY, Amos
PNG confrms detentn 2-27, 192D3

INDIA—*See also COMMONWEALTH of Nations, DISARMAMENT—Geneva Committee, GATT, NONALIGNED Nations Movement*
Air India 747 crashes off Bombay 1-1, 23F3-24A1
Liquor prohibitn drive rptd 3-31, 246B1
Uttar Pradesh deaths, Bihar riots rptd 4-2, 245G3-246B1
28 die in sectarian clashes 4-13, 415F3
Tornadoes hit Orissa, W Bengal 4-16, 479C3
Locust spotted in westn area 6-14, 465F2
8 die in caste clashes 7-27—8-6, 631F3
Malaria rptd on increase 8-6, 635G3
Floods kill 450 8-13, 655C1
Floods kill 1,200 9-19, 759D1
'Test-tube baby' born in Calcutta 10-3, 824D3
Hindu-Moslem riots 10-6, 10-11; Desai assures minorities 10-12; rpt on Aligarh riot 10-15, 797E1
W Bengal cholera outbreak rptd 10-8, 927E2
Encephalitis virus kills 480 10-29, 992G3
AF plane crash in Kashmir kills 78 11-19, 908B2

Atomic Energy & Safeguards
Carter in safeguards talks, OKs uranium sale 1-2, declaration issued 1-3, 1D2
UK prime min in A-safeguard talks 1-6—1-11, 37D1
US Sen OKs A-export controls 2-7, 82B3
Desai asks A-test ban 2-15, 121G2
US A-device loss in '65 confrmd 4-17, 288B2
US bars uranium sale 4-20, 288A3
Desai vs US uranium sale bar 4-23, 4-24, Carter OKs sale 4-27, 313G1
US A-fuel export license deferral rptd 5-20, 408B2
UN disarmamt sessn opens 5-23, 421G1
Desai sees Carter; A-cooperatn pledged, nonproliferatn treaty terms rptd 6-13—6-15, 466C3
UN disarmamt sessn ends, A-test ban rptd proposed 6-30, 523C1
US uranium sale OKd by House 7-12, 551D1

Economy & Labor (domestic)
States vs econ plan 3-18—3-19, 227G2
Labor protests, 15 die 4-9, 4-13, 415E3
IBM halts operatns, employes take over 6-1, 415B3
Delhi electricians strike 6-6, 479D3

Foreign Relations (misc.)—*See also 'Atomic Energy' above, 'Monetary, Trade, Aid & Investment' and 'UN' below*
UK prime min visits; sees Desai, Gandhi 1-6—1-11, 37D1, A2
Pak talks on ties 2-6—2-7, 112G3
Ananda Marga terrorists linked to Commonwealth conf bombing 2-14, 121C3
USSR talks, joint projcts set 3-1—3-6, 169C1
Bomb found at home of amb to Australia, Ananda Marga denies blame 3-22, 225D2
Ananda Marga members arrested in Australia emb bomb plot 4-21, 211B1
Desai sees Carter on Afghan coup 6-13—6-15, 466G3
Australia Ananda Marga hq raided 6-17, 495D1
'64 papal visit cited 8-6, 601B2
Karachi, Bombay consulates open 796G3

1979

INCOME Tax—*See TAXES*
INDEPENDENT Salaried Unions, Federation of
Westinghouse contract reached 7-25, 744D2
INDEPENDENT Truckers Association (ITA)
Strike begins 6-7–6-15; ICC orders surcharge 6-15, 462D3-463B1
INDEPENDENT Truckers Unity Coalition
Strike end voted 7-7, 516F2

INDIA—*See also COMMONWEALTH of Nations, DISARMAMENT–Geneva Committee, GATT, NONALIGNED Nations Movement*
Naga attacks in Assam, 50 die 1-5, 97E2
Anti-conversn bill scored 4-14, 376D3
Jamshedpur relig riots, 110 die 4-18, 314E3
Floods kill 600 5-17, 472A3
Mizoram violence 6-13–6-17, 503D2
Tucitorin cinema fire kills 92 7-29, 639G1
Space launch fails 8-10, 626G2
Morvi flood kills 15,000 8-11; relief efforts hampered, probe asked 8-12, 620A1
Birth control problems described, populatn data cited 8-13, 687G2
Mother Teresa wins Nobel Peace Prize 10-17, 857E3

Atomic Energy & Safeguards
Nuclear 'doomsday clock' unchngd 1-1, 13F1
US OKs uranium sale 3-23, 416F2
Pak bars A-inspectn 4-6, A-race cited 4-16, 277D2, B3
A-bomb barred in response to Pak threat 4-20, concern voiced 5-3, 323D3
USSR A-plant bid rejctd 5-2, 323F2
US delays uranium shipmt 8-4, 646D1
US seeks Pak A-projct halt 8-11, 607C3
A-arms race vs Pak warned 8-15, 646C1
Mystery A-test ruled out 10-26, 824D3

Economy & Labor
Fiscal '79 budget announced 3-1, 169F2
Striking police, troops clash, 26 die; Desai threatens curbs 6-25, 503F1
Singh vows reform 7-28, 573E1

Foreign Relations (misc.)—*See also 'Atomic' above 'Monetary' below*
Canada oppositn ldr visits 1-11–1-14, 57F2
China backs Pak on Kashmir feud 1-22, 59D3
UK ends fiancee immigrant virginity tests 2-2, 96D3,, F3
Teng fears Iran chain reactn, Cambodia recognitn 2-7, 84C1
Vajpayee ends China visit, Viet invasn scored 2-18; ties rptd unaffected 2-21, 123D1
Kosygin visits 3-9–3-15, 200G1
Bangladesh accords reached 4-18, 328C2
Sovts ask Afghan role 6-14, 443D1
Singh vows contd nonalignmt 7-28, 573E1
UK's Mountbatten's death mourned 8-27, 641A2
Sovt consulate attacked 11-23, 894C1

1980

INCOME Tax—*See TAXES*
INCOMPARABLE Max (play)
Revival opens 6-15, 756D3
INCORRIGIBLE (film)
Released 3-3, 416A3
INCREDIBLE Hulk (TV series)
Ferrigno wins suit 11-3, 890F2
INDEPENDENCE—*See MISSOURI*
INDEPENDENT Commission on International Development
N-S study urges more aid 2-12, 124A3
INDEPENDENT Insurance Agents of America
Bush addresses Gen Assemb 9-29, 781G1

INDIA—*See also ADB, COMMONWEALTH of Nations, GATT, GENEVA Committee, NONALIGNED Nations*
2 TB vaccines rptd ineffective 1-20, 63E1
'79 dowry murders rptd 4-9, 275D2
Satellite launched 7-18, 547D3
Galaxy formatn study rptd 8-14, 716B1
Illiteracy study rptd 12-4, 953G1

Atomic Energy & Safeguards
Canada PCs cite '74 aid cutoff 1-8, 38F1
'70-79 A-tests rptd 1-17, 31F3
France talks exclude 1-28, 97C3
US delays uranium fuel shipmts, Gandhi affirms indepndnc 3-13, 181G3
US uranium sale blocked 5-16, 440B3
Carter OKs uranium sale 6-19, 495F2
US Cong fails to block uranium sale 9-24, 723C1

Economy & Labor
Gandhi wins electn 1-3, 1-6, 11F3, 12B1
Defns-GNP ratio rptd 2-19, 132G1
Assam hit by unrest 3-24—4-7, 275D1, E1
Assam unrest intensifies 4-12—4-29, 352B3-G3
Assam strike 5-21—5-30, unrest spreads 6-5, 6-9, 445B2
Assam unrest renewed 10-19—11-2, activists strike 10-27, 873A1
Bihar gen strike 12-3—12-4, police threaten statewide actn 12-5, 966A1

Foreign Relations (misc.)—*See also 'Atomic Energy' above, 'Monetary', 'UN Policy' below*
USSR Afghan pullout backed 1-1; Afghan exiles protest invasn 1-2, 2E2, D3-3A1
US mil aid to Pak opposed 1-1, 1-5, 2F2, 12B1; US assures India 1-16, 12A1
Gandhi vs Sovt Afghan invasn 1-5; Cambodia govt, 3d World ties support cited 11G3; 1-16, 27G1
UK forgn secy meets Gandhi 1-16, 27A2
French pres signs joint statemt 1-27, ends visit 1-28, 97B3
Gandhi fears US arms aid to Pak, vs Sovt Afghan role 1-30; US reassures 1-30—1-31, 83A3
Gromyko visits, seeks Afghan support 2-12—2-14, 108F3
Tito sends detente plea 2-21, 139C3
Bengali-Assamese unrest 3-24—4-7, 275B1
PLO recognized 3-26; Arafat visits 3-28—3-29, 260D3
USSR Kunar prov battle rpt issued 3-29, 271E1
Bengali-Assamese unrest intensifies 4-12—4-29, 352G2
Zimbabwe gains indepndnc 4-18, 301E1
Iran hostage rescue missn scored 4-25, 324G1
Afghan student riots rptd 5-1, 349D2
Tito funeral held 5-8, 339A1
Bengali-Assamese unrest spreads 5-21—6-9, Gandhi blames 'forgn power' 6-9, 445G1
Cambodia ties set; ASEAN, US, China score; USSR lauds 7-7, 547F2
Burma ex-premr ends exile 7-29, 617D3
W Ger pol asylum rules rptd tightened 7-31, 581F2
Burma citizenship law rptd proposed 8-13, 617G3
Mountbatten, Nehru affair alleged 8-27; Gandhi denies 8-29, 890A3
Commonwealth conf hosted 9-4—9-8; Gandhi defends Cambodia ties 9-8, 680B1
Supply ships for Iraq rptd at Jordan port 10-6, 757C1
Iran attacks ships 10-7, 758G2
Australia criticisms re Gandhi raise concern 11-6, 870E2
Brezhnev visits 12-8—12-11; meets Gandhi 12-8—12-9, joint declaratn 12-11; addresses parlt 12-10, 930D1-A3
Afghans stage Sovt emb protest 12-27, 991B1

1976

Government & Politics—*See also other appropriate subheads in this section*
Tax evaders get amnesty 12-31-75, 29E1
Cong Party OKs rights curbs 1-1; Parlt debates 1-5—1-8, 28C3
Tamil Nadu CP members seized 1-2, 29D1
Oppositn plans Parlt boycott 1-4, 28G3
7 charter articles suspended 1-8, 28B3
CP ldr says followers seized 1-9, 29C1
Devi paroled 1-9, 29E1
Listed as 'partly free' 1-19, 20C3
Parlt OKs wider arrests 1-22, 73A3
Govt takes over Tamil Nadu 1-31; Dravidian members seized, oppositn denounces 2-2, 101E2
Gujarat chaos chrgd 2-2, 101B3
Parlt OKs electn delay 2-4, 101C3
Narayan vs emergency rule 2-13, 139G3
Gujarat takeover 3-12, arrests 3-13, 222B1
Oppositn parties plan merger 3-26, 253E2
Cong Party widens house majority 3-27, 253D2
Sup Ct upholds jailings 4-28, 313B2
Mehta released 5-15, 365B2
Govt foe Fernandes arrested 6-10, 440D1
Detention period extended 6-16, 440E1
Emergency rule to stay 6-26, 496F3
Jagjit Singh dies 8-7, 892F3 ★
Patel, others arrested 8-9, 624B1
Gandhi: emergency rules eased 8-15, 624A1
Govt bill seeks wider powers 9-1, 651E3
Parlt votes Swamy probe 9-2, 676C1
Fernandes, 24 others indicted 9-24, 731F3
Mody freed 10-6, 751C2
Rally vs charter changes 10-16, 810B3
Civil rights group formed, Narayan heads 10-17, 810A3
Parlt convenes, oppositn boycotts 10-25, 837G1
Electns postponed 10-30, 837G2
Lower house OKs charter chng 11-2, 837F1
Youth Cong hears S Gandhi 11-19, 1006G1
Gandhi defends son vs critics 12-12, 1006E1
Govt takes Orissa rule 12-16, 1006D1
Minor Cabt shift 12-22, 1006C1
Govt yields Gujarat rule 12-24, 1006B1

1977

Government & Politics—*See also other appropriate subheads in this section*
Dissidents freed 1-5, 1-12, 45C3
Gandhi-Mehta exchng made public 1-5, 45D3
Mar electns set; Desai, Advani freed 1-18, 45C2
Gandhi advises journalists 1-19, 45A3
Parlt dissolved 1-19, 45B3
Fernandes asks electn boycott 1-19; party ignores, quits 1-23, withdraws resignatn 1-25, 64C1
States ordrd to free prisoners 1-20, 45E2
4 anti-govt parties to merge 1-20, 45A3, B3 ★
Narayan returns to Delhi 1-22, 63G3
Govt foes open electn drive 1-23, 63E3
Janata doubts dissidents release 1-23, 64A1 ★
Beg opposed as chief justice 1-25, named 1-28, sworn 1-29; ct boycotted 1-31, 71A3
Janata chrgs dissidents held 1-27; Gandhi meets 1-28, says detainees freed 2-1, 71D2
Desai scores govt at rally 1-30, 71B2
CP to join Janata in electn 1-30, 71C2
2 defectors seek return 2-1, 71F2
6 quit Cong Party, form new group; Ram quits Cabt 2-2, 71C1 ★ -B2
Gandhi opens electn drive 2-4, 116C1
Narain, Limaye freed; Narain to run for Gandhi seat 2-7, 116G1
Janata Party airs platform 2-10, 116D1
Pres Ahmed dies, Jatti named 2-11; funeral 2-13, 116A1
Gandhi aunt joins govt foes 2-14, 116E1
Sanjay Gandhi to run for Parlt 2-15, 116F1
Jethmalani, Swamy return 2-20, 160B1
Rpt govt foes still held 2-20, 160C1
Cong for Democracy vows end to curbs 2-21, 159G3
2 defect Cong Party 3-2, 3-3, 205G2
Sanjay Gandhi escapes murder try 3-14, Janata says incident staged 3-15, 205F2
Cong Party loses electns 3-16—3-20, Gandhi resigns 3-22; Desai named prime min 3-24, 205A1, B2
Emergency powers ended 3-21, 205B1
Chavan named Cong Party Parlt ldr 3-23, 205E2
Desai forms Cabt; Ram, 2 others balk, relent; Cabt sworn 3-26, 3-27, 239E3
Desai policy address read 3-28, 240C1
Gandhi, son, others face probe 4-1, 4-7, 283G2
Emergency rule jailings listed 4-5, 283E3
State, natl assemb term cuts sought 4-7, 304E2
Corruptn probe judges named 4-8, 304A2
Janata forms Gujarat govt 4-11, 304B2
Gandhi takes blame for electn loss 4-12, 392D2
Barooah quits Cong Party post 4-13, Singh named interim pres 4-15, 392B2
Sanjay Gandhi, Lal passports lifted 4-18, 304G1
State assemb electns asked 4-18, 304C2
9 state assembs dissolved 4-30, 348F1 ★
CDP joins Janata Party 5-1, 348C2, D2 ★
Cong Party elects Reddy pres, 2 offcls quit 5-6, 392A2
Gandhi named to Cong Party exec 5-13, 392C2
State assemb electns 6-10—6-14, 487F3-488B1
Natl Conf Party wins Kashmir electn 6-30, 7-3, 544F1
Reddy nominated for pres 7-7; chosen 7-21, 637G2
Hedge named lower house speaker 7-21, 637A3
4 ex-Gandhi aides arrested 8-15, 637B2
Lal arrested, son sought; Aggarwal arrested 8-23, 655E2
Satpathy arrested 9-17, 801G2-A3
Gandhi rule probe starts 9-29, 765F1
Gandhi, others arrested on corruptn chrgs 10-3; Gandhi freed 10-4, 764G3
Gandhi backers riot 10-8, Gandhi chaos plot chrgd 10-13, 801C2
Gandhi chrgs govt abuses 10-10, 801E2
Gandhi loses Cong Party pres race 10-15, 801G1-B2
Anti-Gandhi riots 10-29—10-30, 842C2
Gandhi shuns probe hearings, defends rule 11-21, 12-2; party backs boycott 12-5, 966D1
5 Andhra Pradesh mins quit 12-1, 966C1
Gandhi quits Cong Party panel 12-18, 984D2
Cong Party suspends Urs 12-26, exec com splits 12-27, 1013D3

Monetary, Trade & Aid Issues (including all foreign economic developments)
OPEC allocates loan funds 1-10, 12A3
Sweden budgets aid 1-10, 23B1
Sea zone limits set 1-15, 64F1
Sovt oil-trade deal signed 2-19, 161E1
USSR pacts set 4-25—4-27, 348D1
Import curbs eased 4-28, 392D2
US sells Pak 2 warships 5-19, 450E3
US bars jet sale to Pak 6-2, 450C3
Coca-Cola share demanded 8-8, 637E2
USSR steel plant aid dropped, US replaces 8-24, 655B2
Sweden cancels debts 11-8, 904A1
IBM to halt operations 11-15, 984E2
US probes steel-dumping chrgs 11-22, 933B3

Obituaries
Ahmed, Fakhruddin Ali 2-11, 116A1
Bhaktivendanta, A C 11-14, 952C2
Jain, Shanti Prasad 10-27, 872D2
Shankar, Uday 9-26, 788E2

1978

Government & Politics—*See also other appropriate subheads in this section*
Gandhi, backers form new Cong Party 1-1—1-2; defectors scored 1-2, 7F2
Freedom House lists as free 44E1
Cong Party panel accepts Gandhi resignatn 1-2, 7G2
CP wins Tripura electn 1-2, takes power 1-5, 37B3
Gandhi ousted from Cong Party 1-3, 7E2
Reddy vows to retain pres 1-3, ousted by rebel Cong factn 1-4, 7F2, C3
Gandhi bars probe testimony 1-9, 1-10, faces contempt trial 1-11, 37F2
Cong Party factn stripped of electn symbol 1-31, 75C1
Gandhi party wins 2 state electns 2-25, hails victory 2-28, 168G3
Reddy, Karnataka party ldr quit 2-27, 169B1
Desai vs Sikkim annexatn 3-7, 3-10, 227B3
Gandhi party loses Haryana electn 4-2, Gandhi scores Janata 4-5, 246D1
Gandhi party becomes oppositn 4-12, 288G2-A3
Gandhi pleads not guilty in judicial probe testimony bar 4-18, 374B3
Singh quits Janata posts, party split seen 4-29, 374C3
Sanjay Gandhi starts 1-mo jail term 5-5, 375A1
Cong Party-I wins Uttar Pradesh by-electn 5-9, 374G3-375A1
Desai wins confidence vote 5-11, 374F3
Judicial comm scores Gandhi rules, party chrgs pol vendetta 5-15, 374E2
Desai on Gandhi prosecutn 6-17, 516C2
Singh, Narain vs govt handling of Gandhi case 6-28, 516G1
Cabt asks Singh, Narain resign 6-29, quit 6-30; Janata gen secy quits 7-2, 516F1, B2, D2
Haryana State chief min purged 7-4; restored in Janata compromise, Singh calls off rally 7-8, 7-9, 631C3
Janata dep ldr quits over Singh ouster 7-6, 631F3
Gandhi elected to Parlt 11-5, 861E2
Parlt com condemns Gandhi 11-21, debate starts 12-13; ousted, jailed 12-19, 988B1
Pro-Gandhi riots, 5 dead 12-20; plane hijacked 12-20, released 12-21, 988E1
Gandhi released 12-26, 1018C1

Monetary, Trade, Aid & Investment—*See also 'Atomic Energy' above*
UK prime min in aid, trade talks; cites India '77 trade surplus 1-6—1-11, 37D1
US ct OKs drug trust suit 1-11, 33D3
Pak trade talks 2-6—2-7, 113A1
USSR joint projects set 3-1—3-6, 169C1
Rupee revalued 5-24, 415C3
IBM halts operatns, employes take over 6-1, 415B3
Desai in US trade talks 6-13—6-15, 466F3
USSR '54-76 credits cited 595F2
UK cancels debts 7-31, 592D1
Anglo-French Jaguar jet purchase set 10-6, 10-7, 796G3-797B1
US denies F-5E deal with Pak 10-6; rpt India said Pak rejctd US bid, assured Pak on Jaguars 10-16, 797B1
Pak trade talks fail 10-7—10-9, 796E3

1979

Government & Politics—*See also other appropriate subheads in this section*
Singh sworn dep prime min, other Cabt changes 1-24, 97G2
Sanjay Gandhi, ex-info min sentncd in censorship case 2-27, 193A1
Sanjay Gandhi arrested 4-27, 5-1, 334C1
Gandhi bars parlt race 5-20, 411D2
Cong-I Party ousts Urs 6-25, Narain quits Janata Party, scores Desai 6-26, 503B2, 544F1
Cabt mins resign 7-12–7-15; Desai quits as prime min 7-15, keeps Janata post 7-17; Chavan asked to form govt 7-18, 544D1-C2
Desai asked to quit Janata post 7-18, 544C2
Chavan, Ram end Cabt bid 7-22; Singh asked 7-26; sworn prime min 7-28; names Cabt 7-28, 7-30, 573A1
Desai quits as Janata Party ldr, Ram replaces 7-27, 573G1
Hidayatullah named vp 8-9, 634C3
Singh quits 8-20; Parlt dissolved, electns set 8-22, 634G2

Monetary, Trade, Aid & Investment—*See also 'Atomic' above*
USSR aid agrmts signed 3-14, 200G1
OPEC oil price hike scored 3-27, 227G3
Bangladesh accords set 4-18, 328E2
US religious group aid rptd 9-21, 755C3

Obituaries
Narayan, Jayaprakash 10-8, 860A3

1980

Government & Politics—*See also other appropriate subheads in this section*
Electn-related violence 1-1—1-4, 12B1
Cong-I wins electn 1-3, 1-6, Gandhi asked to form govt 1-10, 11A3
Gandhi sworn prime minister, names Cabt 1-14, 39E3
Gandhi cleared in 2 ct cases 1-15, 39G3-40A1
Gandhi ends 9 state assembs 2-17, foes score move 2-18, 133C2
Ram quits Janata Party 3-7, 232E3
Patil named petro min 3-7, 233A1*
Hindu group leaves Janata, forms new party 4-6, 275C2
Ram joins Cong oppositn 4-8, 275A2
Gandi's son cleared of film theft 4-11, 294A3
Gandhi escapes assassinatn 4-14, 294A3
Gandhi suit dismissed, chrgs against son dropped 5-6, 487E2
Parlt ldr resigns 5-19, Gandi's son 487B2
State electns 5-28, 5-31; Congress-I Party wins 8 states 6-2, 445E1
3 Cabt mins sworn 6-8, 445F1
Gandi's son killed in plane crash 6-23, 6-23, 487A2
Security law decreed, Gandhi foes score 9-22, 729D2
Tamil Nadu gov removed, Sismail named 10-26, 873F1
Parlt OKs detention law 12-16, 966C1

Monetary, Trade, Aid & Investment
UN indl dvpt fund disputed 2-9, 124E2
US delays uranium fuel shipmts 3-13, 181G3
US uranium sale blocked 5-16, 440B3
USSR arms pact signed 5-28, US concerned 5-29, 398A1
US OKs uranium sale 6-19, 492F2
Cambodia aid planned 7-7, 547G2
US trade talks fail 8-26, Gandhi scores 8-30, 670G3
World Bank '80 loans rptd 9-22, 720E1
US Cong fails to block uranium sale 9-24, 723C1
US uranium arrives 10-7, 830C2
USSR trade ties expanded 12-11, 930E2

Obituaries
Fisher, Welthy Honsiger 12-16, 1004E1
Gandhi, Sanjay 6-23, 487A2
Giri, Varahagir V 6-24, 528F1

1976

Press & Censorship
2 Socialist weeklies closed 621B1
Indian Express revamped 1-3, 73F3
Govt-proposed news agency merger set 1-7, 1-20, 73C3 ★
Newspr head loses passport 1-24, seeks return 2-16, 139C3
Parlt OKs more press curbs 1-28—1-29, 74A1
Permanent censorship OKd 1-28, 2-2, 101E3
Narayan scores press curbs 2-13, 140A1
40 newsmen lose certificatn 2-14, 139A3
Overseas Indians vs curbs 4-24, 313F1
7,000 arrests rptd 5-17, 382E1
Developing natns OK press pool 7-13, 619A3
Statesman censored 7-20, 620G3
2 anti-govt journals rptd closed 7-25, 620F3
BBC closes office 8-5, 621D1
Curbs scored 8-7, 621B1
Case vs Statesman dropped 9-14, 696C2
Forgn press curbs lifted 9-18, 700C3
Indian Express power cut 9-30, restored 10-2; padlocked 10-4, ct orders reopened 10-6, 751F1
Express credits end 10-14; curbs protested 10-21; 5 ousted, Goenka regains control 10-29; property sold 10-31, ct acts 11-1, 837B2
Himmat asks contributns 837D2
Times ed arrested 10-25, 837E2
Mainstream closes 12-28, 1006A1

UN Policy & Developments
UNESCO literacy drive fails 2-4, 85C2
Backs rights comm resolutn vs Israel 2-13, 125E2
Palestine com member 2-26, 162C1
Pak offers to drop ICAO case 3-27, 278F2
Submits WHO anti-Israel resolutn rpt 5-17, 355G1
Rights group chrgs torture, asks UN probe 6-1; India denies 6-7, 408B3
Offers Assemb Geneva conf amendmt 12-6, 914B2

U.S. Relations
'74 A-bomb info rptd scored 1-20, 93C3
US rpts Tarapur A-plant leak 1-30, India denies 2-7, 156D2
US halts aid talks 2-17, 139D3
US econ talks 3-25—3-26, 253G2
'75 arms embargo lift cited 3-31, 278C3
Sues 5 US grain cos 5-3, 333D1
'75 shrimp import data rptd 5-11, 431G1
Emergency rule protested in NY 6-26, 496G3
4 in US lose passports 7-12, 7-18, 538A2
US OKs A-fuel sale 7-21, 739D2
US arms control rpt issued 7-29, 739E2
US admits A-blast aid 8-2, 581D3
Grain co indictmt rptd 8-23, 990D3
Gandhi foe gets US asylum 8-24, 676B1

INDIANA
Primary date set 22B2
US House votes Dunes park expansn 2-17, 171A1
Carter campaigns 4-6, 260F2
Ford campaigns 5-2—5-3, 323E3
Primary results 5-4, 322E2, 323E1
Carter at Lafayette relig conv 6-19, 452B1
Ford in Indianapolis 6-22, 452E2
Dem conv women delegates, table 508B2
Dem conv pres vote, table 7-14, 507B2
Job bias actn vs Uniroyal rptd 8-6, 944C2
GOP pre-conv delegate count 8-14, 583B3
Reagan seeks conv delegates 8-16, 601G2
GOP conv pres, vp vote tables 8-18—8-19, 8-19, 599B1, B3
Fscl '75 per capita income, tax burden rptd 9-15, 10-12, 959B2
Carter in Indianapolis 9-16, 686E3
Carter in Evansville 9-27, 724B2
Carter in South Bend 10-9, 762D2
Ford signs Dunes expansn 10-18, 834B3
Dole in Terre Haute 10-27, 804A3
Ford in Indianapolis 10-28, 803F1
Mondale in Gary 11-1, 827E2
Election results 11-2: pres 818B1, 819B2; cong 819D3, 820D2, 823B2, 828E1, 829B3; state 820E3, 823C2, 831E1
US Sup Ct bars review of Lake Mich A-plant OK 11-8, 882C3
US Sup Ct bars review of car passenger suit ruling 11-8, 882D3
US Sup Ct upholds MD office abortns 11-29, 900C3

1977

Press & Censorship
Press curbs lifted 1-20, 45C2
Editor doubts censorship end 1-21, 64B1
Gandhi govt media stand scored 8-1, 598B3
Gandhi backers chrg bias 10-8, 801D2

UN Policy & Developments
Assemb, Cncl member; Singh World Ct vp 4B1, E1, F1
Scores Israel occupatn rule 2-15, 107F2

U.S. Relations—*See also 'Monetary, Trade & Aid' above*
2 defectors seek return from US 2-1, 71F2
Carter mother, son at Ahmed funeral; meet Gandhi 2-13, 116B1
Goheen confrmd amb 4-25, 418D1
Nixon on '73 Pak war 5-12, 385E3, 386B2
Nutrition aid signed 8-4, 668A2
Carter visit scheduled 9-23, 738F1
Carter visit deferred 11-7, 854A1; rescheduled 11-29, 914B2
Carter begins world tour 12-29, 1000G3

INDIANA
Legislature schedule rptd 6D2
US Sup Ct bars ct structure appeal review 1-10, 57A2
US Sup Ct rules on Terre Haute steelworker electns 1-12, 57E3
FTC sues dental groups 1-14, 156A3
Indianapolis rpts record low 1-16, 54F2
ERA ratified 1-18, 59A2
US Sup Ct voids Indianapolis busing plan 1-25, 79D3-80C1
US Sup Ct affirms abortn rule on minors 1-25, 80F2
Laetrile legalized 2-1, 375F3, 508E1
US declares emergency status 2-5, 91B2
Lafayette, Indianapolis rpt low temps 2-6, 91D2
Gas, weather layoffs rptd 2-7, 91F2
Indianapolis mortgage exec kidnaped 2-8—2-10, 162G1
US rights comm cites Indianapolis busing plan bar 2-15, 112F1
ERA '75 ratificatn cited 3-15, 279E3
Fed spending inequities chrgd 4-6, 423D3
S Bend-Chicago Chessie operatns contd 4-8, 325F2
Ct bars biology text 4-14, 471D3
Saccharin legalized 5-1, 375F3
US Sup Ct refuses RC-NLRB dispute case 5-2, 406C2
Heiress slain, $3 mln stolen 5-7, 492F1
'76 per-capita income table 5-10, 387D2
NBA aids Pacers 6-15, 583E3, 584B1
US Steel settles 2 Gary EPA cases 6-16, 461E1
'76 per capita income, tax burden table 9-13, 10-18, 821C2, G2
Anti-abortn amendmt rptd sought 10-6, 786B3
ICC sues trucking firms 11-3, 861A1
US facilities cited for pollutn 11-25, 944C2
Jet crash kills 29 12-13, 1023C2

1978

UN Policy & Developments
Rights comm OKs res vs Israel 2-14, 99A2
Assemb disarmamt sessn opens 5-23, 421G1
Assemb disarmamt sessn ends 6-30, 523C1
Cncl, Assemb member 713A3, F3

U.S. Relations—*See also 'Atomic Energy' and 'Monetary, Trade, Aid & Investment' above*
Carter visits 1-1—1-3, 1E1
Carter State of Union Message 1-19, 31B3
US columnist's suit vs Nixon dismissed 4-4, 265C1
Desai sees Carter, communique issued 6-13—6-15, 466C3
Press reactn to Guyana cult deaths 11-30, 911F2

INDIANA
'67, '77 sales-tax rates rptd 1-5, 15D3
Marrieds tax law case review barred 1-9, 13A2
'Prehire' union picketing curbed 1-17, 33G3
Blizzard hits 1-25—1-26, losses estimated 2-11, 105G2, B3, D3
Coal Policy Project issues rpt 2-9, 184E2
Coal strike threatens power shortage 2-10—2-11, cutbacks ordrd 2-13; Carter declares energy emergency, sees gov 2-16, 104C1-D2, E3
Coal truck convoy protectn ordrd 2-14, 160D2
Miners return to work delayed 3-28, 217F1
Judicial immunity in sterilizatn case backed by US Sup Ct 3-28, 241F2
Pulitzer awarded for Indianapolis '77 kidnap photo 4-17, 314G2
Auto Club charter crashes in Rushville 4-23, 460E2
Pornographer flees New Albany jail 4-28, 971C2
Coal strike utility billing probe set 5-10, 366F3
Lykes Ind Harbor shutdown warned 5-24, 492G3
Legionnaires' disease rptd in Bloomington 5-28, 635D3
Indianapolis busing ordrd 6-2, 611E1
Evansville team '77 air crash blame fixed 8-18, 758C3
Anderson firemen strike 8-26—9-1, block destroyed by fire 8-30, 753C1
Elkhart Cnty grand jury indicts Ford in Pinto deaths 9-13, 718F3-719A1
Baseball player slain in Gary 9-23, 77G3
Marble Hill A-plant protesters arrested 10-7, 941E2
Steel haulers strike 11-11, 1006G1-A2
Earthworm rumor hurts fast-food chains 11-16, 942G1
Indianapolis populatn ranked 12-6, 942F3
Indianapolis WHA club folds 12-16, 990G3
Schl inspectn for asbestos danger asked 12-21, 1009C2

Politics & Government
Legislature schedule rptd 14E3
State govt tax revenue table 1-9, 84C2
Cong primary results 5-2, 342C3
Hatcher refuses White House job 6-6, 568B3
Electn results 11-7: cong 846A3, 848F1, 850A4, 853C2, A3; state 897B3

1979

Sports
Indian Grand Prix tennis results 11-25, 1003G3

UN Policy & Developments
Membership listed 695E2

U.S. Relations
Student enrollmt in US rptd 167D2
US OKs uranium sale 3-23, 416F2
Carter address Cong on SALT II 6-18, 459E2
Uranium shipmt delayed 8-4, 646D1
US seeks Pak A-projct halt 8-11, 607C3
Calcutta consulate attacked 11-23, 894C1
Anti-US protest in Calcutta 11-30, 915C1, D1
Protests US aid assurance to Pak on Afghan coup 12-31, 974B2

INDIANA
Blizzards hit 1-12–1-14, 1-24–1-27, 120F1
Bloomington fiscal status rptd 3-20, 204G1
Church schl labor inventn barred by US Sup Ct 3-21, 231E2
A-power protest staged 4-1, 261G3
Integratn study rpts urban lag 5-9, 650F1
Gasohol sales test set in Indianapolis 8-10, 649G1
Indianapolis teachers stage walkout 9-4, 679B1, F1
'78 per capita income rptd 9-16, 746D2
Uniroyal Mishawaka plant suit setld 10-23, 885G2
Pregnancy jobless pay case refused by Sup Ct 11-13, 902A2
Midwest quake threat rptd 11-15, 954D1
Krishna solicitatn rights case refused by Sup Ct 11-26, 919F2

Politics & Government
Legislature schedule rptd 5D3
GOP meets in Indianapolis 3-10, 185F3
Hatcher renominated in Gary 5-8, 363F2-A3
Carter sees Indianapolis Dems 6-2, 418E2
Carter visits English 7-31, 592G2
Ex-Sen Capehart dies 9-3, 756B2
Hudnut reelected Indianapolis mayor 11-6, 846D3

1980

Sports
Moscow Olympic results 7-20—8-3, 588C3, 622D3

UN Policy & Developments
Assemb Sovt Afghan invasn res effort fails 1-13, abstains 1-14, 25E2-G2
Indl dvpt aid fund disputed 2-9, 124E2
Rights comm Sovt Afghan res abstentn 2-14, 123E3
Rao addresses aid talks 8-25, 642D3
UNESCO illiteracy study rptd 12-4, 953G1

Unrest
Caste groups clash, 13 die 1-17, 2-7, 2-8, 133G2
Harijans attacked, 14 killed 2-26, 232G3
Assam hit by unrest 3-24—4-7, 275B1
Assam unrest intensifies 4-12—4-29, violence hits Imphal 4-28, 352G2
Assam strike 5-21—5-30, unrest spreads to Tripura 6-5, more troops sent 6-9; Gandhi blames forgn power 6-9, 445G1
350 Bengalis slain in Tripura 6-7—6-8, no survivors found 6-9, 464C1; massacres alleged 6-22, 578E3
Assam rule eased 7-26, 7-30, 578B3
Moradabad mosque riot, 86 die 8-13, 619E3
Uttar Pradesh rioting death toll mounts 8-13—8-17, 634E2
Gandhi scores violence 8-15, defends police 8-18, 634A3
Kashmir violence, 4 killed 8-16, 634G2-A3
Assam anti-Bangladeshi drive renewed 9-7, 729C2
Uttar Pradesh rioting renewed 9-8, 9-10, 729A2
Bihar state violence 9-8, 729C2
Security law decreed 9-22, 729D2
Police kill 12 Naxalites 10-11, 830G1
Assam protests renewed 10-19—11-2, 873A1
Bihar police blind prisoners 11-22, 14 arrested 12-1; protests staged, strike threatened 12-3—12-5, 965G3
Detentn law approved 12-16, 966C1

U.S. Relations
Pak arms sale opposed 1-1, 1-5, 2F2, 12B1; anti-US rally 1-9, US assures India 1-16, 27F1
US envoy in talks, reassures on US aid to Pak 1-30—31; US to sell mil gear 2-1, 83C2, A3
Gandhi fears US arms to Pak 1-30, 83D3
US delays uranium fuel shipmts, Gandhi affirms indepndnc 3-13, 181G3
Iran hostage rescue missn scored 4-25, 324G1
US uranium sale blocked 5-16, 440B3
US concerned re Sovt arms pact 5-29, 398C1
CIA role in Assam unrest hinted 6-9, 445C2
Carter OKs uranium sale 6-19, 492F2
US scores Cambodia ties 7-7, 547G2
Trade talks fail 8-26, Gandhi scores 8-30, 670G3
US Cong fails to block uranium sale 9-24, 723C1
US uranium arrives 10-7, 830C2
Gandhi message to Reagan on electn 11-5, 841C3

INDIANA
Lafayette pesticide plant case declined by US Sup Ct 2-19, 131E1
Allis-Chalmers pact set 3-15, 308A3
Methodist conv in Indianapolis 4-2, 324D3
Tornadoes hit 4-7—4-8, 391A3
Harvester strike ends 4-20, 308G2
Strip mining case accepted by Sup Ct 10-6, 782E1

Crime & Civil Disorders
Ford acquitted in Pinto trial 3-13, 185B3
Prisoners right to sue broadened by Sup Ct 4-22, 343D3
KKK rally in Kokomo 4-26, 333F1
V Jordan shot in Ft Wayne, 5-29, 401D2; case stymied 6-1—6-12; enters NY hosp 6-12, 442A2
Judy murder convictn appeal discharge OKd 10-28, 869E1

Politics & Government—*See also other appropriate subheads in this section*
Legislature schedule rptd 18D1
State ct jurisdictn narrowed by Sup Ct 1-21, 93C2
Election results 11-4: cong 837D1, E2, 840F1, 842A4, 845A2, 846D1, 850F3; state 845E2, 847E1, 851A1
'80 census rptd, reapportmt seen 12-31, 983E1

Presidential Election (& Transition)
Indianapolis GOP platform hearing set 1-14, 32A1
Pres primary results 5-6, 341F2, 342C1
Reagan in Kokomo 9-8, 699B3
Election results 11-4, 838B1, 839A2, E3

School Issues
South Bend desegregn plan set 2-8, 114C2
Indianapolis busing challenge declined by Sup Ct 10-6, 782A3

1976

INDIANA, University of (Bloomington)
Loses NCAA soccer title 12-5, 969G2
INDIANA Dunes National Lakeshore
House OKs enlargement 2-17, 171A1
Expansn authorizatn signed 10-18, 834B3
Sup Ct bars review of A-plant OK 11-8, 882C3
INDIAN Airlines
Jet hijacked 9-10, Pak recaptures 9-11, 685C3
Bombay crash 10-12, 840F2
INDIANAPOLIS, Ind.—*See INDIANA*
INDIANAPOLIS Star and News
Early on Ariz crime probe 10-2, 849C2
Ford endorsement rptd 10-30, 827G3
INDIAN Movement, American—*See AMERICAN Indian Movement*
INDIAN Ocean
Australia, NZ score Sovt buildup 3-8—3-11, 187C3
China scores Sovt buildup 3-13, 265C3
US assures Australia on Sovt buildup 3-30—3-31, 249F2
USSR, Mozambique vs mil bases 5-23, 403E1
Australia: USSR impedes neutral zone 6-1, 438F2
India, Sovts vs forgn bases 6-13, 440C1
Australia scores Sovt buildup 6-20, 481D1
Australia asks stronger US force 7-29, 554B2
Nonaligned conf vs US base 8-20, 621D3
USSR asks forgn mil cutback 9-28, 719C3
Australia ups defns spending, cites Sovt bldup 11-4, 850B2
INDIAN Point, N.Y.—*See NEW York State*
INDIANS, American
Nov '75 Ore gun incident, Banks indictmt cited 7G1
Explosives found near Ariz BIA office 1-1, 7E1
Sup Ct bars review of mining suit 3-29, 261F3
Paraguay abuse chrgd, US scored 4-5, 403E2
Menominee ldr convicted 4-21, 316G3
Sup Ct backs tax suit rights 4-27, 359F1
Thomas Means shot 5-5, 384E2
Sup Ct backs Cheyenne mineral rights 5-19, 394A1
Dem platform text 6-15, 472A2
Rights rally in Phila 7-4, 489C1
FBI queried re AIM harassmt 7-7, 640F2 *
2 cleared in '75 FBI deaths 7-16, 640E2
'77 health funds signed 7-31, 623D1
At Intl Eucharistic Cong 8-1—8-8, 596F2
Ford signs housing aid 8-3, 567A1
Means acquitted 8-6, 640D2
GOP platform text 8-18, 605C3
Ecuador murder chrgd 8-25, 693B1
Cong clears health aid 9-16, 745D3; signed 9-30, 982G1
Claims Comm end signed 10-8, 834G3
File Canada land claim 10-25, 851G2
Brazil bishops score abuses 11-16, 903E1, C2
Dole urges GOP seek vote 11-30, 917B3
FPC backs Canada pipeline 12-7; Indians lose moratorium suit 12-22, 998C2, E2
Canada to extradite Peltier 12-17, 999B1

INDOCHINA—*See CAMBODIA, LAOS, VIETNAM headings*
Amnesty Issue—*See under U.S. GOVERNMENT—ARMED Forces; also country names*
Missing In Action—*See under U.S. GOVERNMENT—ARMED Forces*
Refugees—*See IMMIGRATION & Refugees*

1977

INDIANA, University of (Bloomington)
Benson in NBA draft 6-10, 584A3, D3
INDIAN Affairs, Bureau of—*See under U.S. GOVERNMENT—INTERIOR*
INDIAN Airlines
Pak frees hijackers 1-5, India protests 1-6, 45F3
INDIANAPOLIS, Ind.—*See INDIANA*
INDIAN Head Inc.
Strike ends 10-14, 818F3

INDIAN Ocean
Australia denies Sovt chrgs on US bases 1-25, 81B2
USSR chrgs ASEAN mil plans 2-24, 145B3
Carter seeks arms accord 3-9, 172E3
Carter for Sovt-US restraint 3-17, 186B1
Podgorny asks demilitarizatn 3-24, 247C3
US, USSR OK working group 3-30, 225A2
US base buildup observed 4-6, 270D2
Warnke in Moscow talks 6-22—6-27, 530D1
Carter cites USSR demilitarizatn controversy 6-30, 515C1
Carter cites USSR talks 7-21, 550B3
Severe quake strikes 8-19, 747A3
US, USSR ship deploymt rptd 9-26, talks end 12-10, 999A2
Maldives vs Sovt base bid 10-2, 844G3
Carter rpts Sovt restraint 10-4, 751G3
US-Australia base pact OKd 10-19, 800F3
Cyclones hit India 11-12, 11-19, 928A2
Somalia ousts USSR 11-13, 875C1
INDIAN Point, N.Y.—*See NEW York State*
INDIANS, American—*See also CANADA—Indians & Inuit*
Herbert Fowler dies 1-2, 84A3
Maine land dispute setlmt sought 1-11—1-21, 59C1-A2
Mont coal leases revoked 1-13, 58F3
Sen forms com 2-4, 90G2, F3
Mass, RI, Conn, NY, SC land claims rptd 2-7, 197D1
Navajo ldr, ex-aide indicted 2-9, 162E3
Justice Dept backs Maine claims, Carter to appt mediator 2-28, 196E3
Carter call-in topic 3-5, 171C1, E1
US rpt on Brazil abuses cited 3-7, 168A1
5 tribes vs Ariz water projct 3-21, 210G1
Sioux ldr '73 convictn review denied 3-21, 230F2
Sioux reservatn land laws upheld 4-4, 341G3
Welfare study issued 4-15, 302E1
Mohawks get NY land 5-13, 632D2
Burger cites '69-76 cases 5-17, 419A3
Navajo fraud case dismissed 5-17, 492A1
Peltier sentncd in '75 FBI deaths 6-2, 491G3
'77 death row populatn rptd 6-7, 594B1
Inuit conf in Alaska 6-13—6-17, 619D2
USSR to get rights chrgs 6-17, 473A2
Comanches, Utes end feud 7-24, 619A3
US health funds signed 7-26, 592F3
Natl Women's Conf OKs minority res 11-19—11-21, 917C3
Amnesty Intl chrgs rights abuses 12-8, 956D2
INDIAN Treaty Council, International
USSR to get rights chrgs 6-17, 473B2

INDOCHINA—*See CAMBODIA, LAOS, VIETNAM*
Refugees—*See IMMIGRATION & Refugees*

1978

INDIAN Affairs, Bureau of—*See under U.S. GOVERNMENT—INTERIOR*
INDIANA Harbor, Ind.—*See INDIANA*
INDIANA & Michigan Electric Co.—*See AMERICAN Electric Power Co.*
INDIANAPOLIS, Ind.—*See INDIANA*
INDIANA State University (Terre Haute)
Bird 3d in coll basketball 3-13, 272E2
Bird in NBA draft 6-9, 457C2, F3
INDIANA University (Bloomington)
Legionnaires' disease rptd 5-28, bacterium isolated 8-11, 635D3
Loses NCAA soccer title 12-10, 969G1
Basketball players disciplined for pot use 12-12, 1028A1

INDIAN Ocean
US to delay Sovt demilitarizatn agrmt 2-10, 99B3
US links SALT delay 3-1, 179A1
US surveillnc flights from Israel Sinai base rptd 3-26; US denies 3-27, 215F1, G1
US scores USSR buildup 5-24, 421D1
Seychelles warns US, USSR vs mil expansn 8-7, 8-20, 692C1
US, USSR clash on arms sales, talks stalled 12-5—12-15, 996E3

INDIAN Point, N.Y.—*See NEW York State*
INDIANS, American—*See also CANADA—Indians & Inuit*
Mass land claim set back 1-6, 6C1-B2
Mondale meets SW tribe ldrs 1-10, 34D2
'Longest Walk' 2-11—7-15, DC demonstratns 7-15—7-23; ldrs see Mondale, Andrus 7-18, 568C3
RI settles Narragansett land claim 3-2, 326E3
Tribal ct trials of non-Indians barred 3-6, 162D1
Rape retrial backed by Sup Ct 3-22, 221D1
Mass dismisses Wampanoag land claim 3-24, 327A1
Cabt-level Educ Dept proposed 4-14, 279D1
Calif bars Banks extraditn to SD 4-19, 327E1
Idaho reservatn closed to non-Indians 4-22, 327C1
Washn Quileutes ask Canada fishing ban 5-5, 350D2
GAO says housing worsens 5-13, 569G1
Tribal authority backed by Sup Ct 5-15, 387A3
2 AIM activists acquitted in Calif 5-24, 396B2
Aleuts win mistreatmt claim 6-21, 569F1
Harvard admissns progrm described 483B2
Amazon pact vows protectn 7-3, 829E2
US minority business contracts ruling 9-23, 811E2
Maine electn results 11-7, 847D2
Obituaries
Romero, Juan de Jesus 7-30, 620E3

INDOCHINA—*See also CAMBODIA, LAOS, VIETNAM*
Refugees
Singapore urges Westn refugee aid 2-17, 121G2
Australia to accept refugees 3-15, 187E2
US, Australia asylum asked 4-9, 265B3
Pulitzer awarded for expose 4-17, 315A2
Malaysia gives Viets temp asylum 4-17, 341B2
51 Viets arrive Kenya 4-17, 341B2
UN seeks more funds 4-18, 341D2
Cambodians sent to Thai camps 4-30, 341C2
Mondale vows Thai resetlmt aid 5-4, 360E3
Australia to admit 9,000 refugees 5-17, 369A3
Australia to increase coast patrols 7-9, 530B2
Calif welfare cuts protested 8-2, 844E2
UK kin leave Viet 8-7, 603C2
Viet-Thai refugee agrmts reached 9-6—9-10, 696F1, A3
Viet boat refugee flow up 10-11, 776B2
Viet, Cambodia, Laos land escapes at 9,000 a month 10-11, 776C2
US: flow a problem for West 10-25, 830F1
Thais, Viet impasse over refugees in Thailand 10-29, 830G1-B2
UN rpts flow up, plans conf 11-10, 870G2
US says more Viets flee 11-14, 870C3
Viet 'boat people' stranded off Malaysia; provisns OKd 11-14, 871A1
US to admit more boat people 11-17, 11-28, 932F3-933D1, 934F1
France, Canada, W Ger take boat people 11-20, 11-26, 11-29, 12-2; Malaysia takes remaining 12-2, 932D3
Over 300 Viets die in boat mishaps off Malaysia 11-22, 12-2, 12-3, 932G2-C3
Malaysia lifts ban on Viet boat people 12-4, 932G1
Taiwan rescues stranded Viets 12-4, 932C3
Carter vows aid 12-6, 934E1

1979

INDIANA Employment Security Board v. United Auto Workers
Case refused by Sup Ct 11-13, 902A2
INDIAN Affairs, Bureau of—*See under U.S. GOVERNMENT-INTERIOR*
INDIANAPOLIS, Ind.—*See INDIANA*
INDIANA State University (Terre Haute)
Bird named top basketball player 3-12, 290E3
Loses NCAA basketball title 3-26, 238F2
Bird signs with Celtics 6-8, 507E2
INDIANA University (Bloomington)
Wins NIT 3-21, 238E3
Knight arrested in Pan Am Games assault 7-8, convctd 8-22, resignatn rejctd 8-24, sentncd 9-10, 798E3
Wins Holiday Bowl 12-21, 1001A3
INDIAN Ocean
USSR, US naval increase rptd 4-12, 4-16, 313E3-314A1
SALT II communique backs talks 6-18, 457G3
Skylab comes down 7-11, 509B1
Whaling banned, sanctuary set 7-11, 554B2
Carter orders mil buildup 10-1, 739C1
US rpts unknown A-blast 10-25, 824B3

INDIANS, American—*See also CANADA-Indians & Inuit*
Schls excluded from proposed Educ Dept 2-8, 110A3
Peabody to sell Inman portraits 2-9, 173F2
Cherokee acquitted in Okla Scout slayings 3-30, 291A3; dies 6-4, 508A3
'Italian Bakke case' declined by Sup Ct 4-23, 346F2
House com seeks progrm shift to proposed Educ Dept 5-2, 326F2
Mich Chippewa fishing rights upheld 5-8, 368C1
Chippewa Minn reservatn violence flares 5-20, 465D1
Nez Perce Ida fishing dispute setld 6-7, 465A1
Calif Morongo reservatn fire rptd 6-11, 572F3
Sioux awarded $100 mln re Black Hills 6-13, 464D3-465A1
Child custody case refused by Sup Ct 6-18, 499A2
State laws in land cases backed by Sup Ct 6-20, 516G1
Brazil lands protected 6-22, 483G1-G2
Washn salmon fishing treaties upheld by Sup Ct 7-2, 559D1
Black Hills A-protest held 7-7, 743C1
Chippewas sentned for Minn reservatn violence 7-22, 630F3
Calif LNG projct opposed 9-27, 769B3
Cherokee suit vs Tellico Dam dismissed 11-2, 990C1
US Helsinki com reviews status 11-7, 981B1
Feathered artifact sale ban upheld by Sup Ct 11-27, 919G3
Sioux Black Hills compensatn case accepted by Sup Ct 12-10, 988F1
INDIANTOWN, Fla.—*See FLORIDA*
INDOCHINA—*See also CAMBODIA, LAOS, VIETNAM*
US, China discuss 8-28, 644E2
Refugees—*See also CAMBODIA-Famine*
Malaysia bars Viets 1-5, 51A3
PI removes Viet boat people; US, France, W Ger, Israel to accept 1-8; 100 arrive Israel 1-24, 51F2-A3
Hong Kong to admit Viet boat people 1-19, land 1-20-1-23; to join kin 1-22, 51D2
Hong Kong chrgs Viet boat capt on passenger overload 2-4, ship gold cache found 2-7, 109C1
Hong Kong gets more refugees 2-6—2-7, 109E1
US pledge to Thailand 2-7, 84C2
US, Canada, Australia to accept Viet refugees from PI 2-12, 109A1
US Hong Kong aide quits re morals chrg 2-12, 109E1
2 US reps in Viet 2-21, 141A2
US rep chrgs Viet bribe racket 2-26, 181F1-A2
UN-Viet exodus plan agreed 3-1, 181C1
250,000 Laotians rptd in Thailand 3-24, 331E3
US extends paroles 3-26, 308B1
Canada expels Viet diplomat 3-29, 267E1
Indonesia, PI OK UN resetlmt plan 3-30, 299G1
104 Viets drown off Malaysia 3-31, UN protests 4-2, 299D1
Japan to accept 500 Viets 4-3, 299A2
261 Viets in PI flown to Canada; US, Canada to take more 4-5, 299F1
Cambodia civilns, troops flee to Thailand; forced back, shelling chrgd 4-16—4-29, 318B1-B2
US rpts on Viet, Cambodia, Laos setlmts 4-25, 379F2
Australia to take 12,000 from Malaysia 5-7, 379E2
Waldheim in Indonesia, Singapore, Thai talks 5-9—5-13, 379C2
Viet ethnic Chinese total in Hong Kong, Macao rptd 5-11, 379D2

1980

INDIAN Affairs, Bureau of—*See under U.S. GOVERNMENT--INTERIOR*
INDIANAPOLIS—*See INDIANA*
INDIANA State University (Terre Haute)
Nicks in NBA draft 6-10, 447G2
INDIANA University (Bloomington)
Woodson in NBA draft 6-10, 447F2
3d World press coverage study rptd 11-29, 914C1
Loses NCAA soccer title game 12-14, 1001C3
INDIAN Medical Sciences, Journal of
TB vaccine study rptd 1-20, 63E1

INDIAN Ocean
US air, naval buildup rptd 1-19, 1-20, 46
Carter cites US policy 1-23, 42F2, C3
Brezhnev backs detente 2-4, 84F3
USSR naval squadron approach rptd 2-5, 84E2
US assault force dispatched 2-12, 106B2
Australia sets mil buildup 2-19, 132E1
Kenya pres in US 2-20—2-22, 142B2
OAU denounces US base 7-1—7-4, 509G1
US, Somalia sign mil base pact 8-21, 645B3, D3
US House subcom OKs Somali mil sales 9-30, 735F3
Zimbabwe scores US bases 10-9, 795C1
USSR, India vs forgn mil bases 12-11, 930D2

INDIANS, American
Peltier sentenced 1-23, 349D1
Penobscot tribe OKs Me land setlmt, Passamaquoddy approval cited 3-15, 210A3
Land 'inverse condemnatn' barred by Sup Ct 3-18, 226F3
Windfall oil profits tax bill exempts 4-2, 244B3
Harris chosen vp candidate 4-13, 288E3
Govt land managemt liability limited by Sup Ct 4-15, 306F1
Constructn contract prefernc barred by Sup Ct 5-27, 454B1
Sioux Black Hills compensatn upheld by Sup Ct 6-30, 511B1
Govt constructn grants upheld by Sup Ct 7-2, 510C1
Pope meets Brazilian ldrs 7-10, 538D2
Oglala Sioux seek Black Hills compensatn award 7-18, 560F1-B2
Oglala Sioux Black Hills compensatn suit dismissed 9-11, 704B2
Bush addresses Pueblos 9-30, 781A2
Obituaries
Martinez, Maria 7-20, 608D2
Pehrson, Wilfred 10-14, 876B3

INDOCHINA
Refugees
Cambodian camp conquered by Khmer Rouge, 1000s cross into Thailand 1-4—1-6, 12B3
Thai pirates kill 167 Viets 1-10, 49A2
US to take refugees in Malaysia 1-12, 49G1
Cambodia-Viet clashes rage near Thai camps 1-25—1-31, US fears Viet drive threat 1-26, 68C2, F2
Carter seeks more aid 1-28, 72D2
US rights rpt scores Viet 2-5, 87A2
US-bound refugees arrive in PI 2-22, 141B2
Vietnamese escape via Cambodia rptd 2-24, 141E1
Indonesia rptd seizing Viet boats 2-25, 141G1
Reagan's 'basic speech' excerpts 2-29, 207G3
Connally cites boat people in 'basic speech' 3-7, 184E3
Cambodia refugee camp rivals battle, 46 die 3-19; refugees return from Thailand 3-21, 262B1
Somali problem compared 4-6, 274C1
Viet malaria outbreak rptd 5-31, 478A3
Viet refugee tide continues 6-10, 476C1
UN asks Thais delay Cambodia repatriatn 6-15; 823 sent back to Cambodia 6-17—6-18, 475D3
Venice summit concerned 6-22, 473D1
Viets capture 4 Westn civilians 6-25, release 6-29, 508F2
ASEAN conf notes Cambodia refugee repatriatn 6-26, 508G1
US Cong OKs Cambodia aid 7-2, Carter signs 7-8, 515F1
Reagan pres nominatn acceptance speech 7-17, 534G3
Malaysia rpts less Viet refugees 8-10, 645D1
US Navy rescues 109 Viets 8-21, 645F1
Viet-US emigration plan seen failing 8-24, 645A1
Refugee aid to states clears Cong 9-25, 10-1, Carter signs 10-10, 785B1

1976

1977

1978

UN conf 12-11—12-12; US eases entry 12-11, Malaysia urges central camp 12-12, 956A1
Viets barred in Malaysia, Hong Kong, Brunei, PI 12-13—12-27, 997D2

1979

24-state Jakarta conf; Viet problem, US asylum aid cited 5-15–5-16, 379E1
Viet flow to Malaysia, Indonesia, Hong Kong rptd; Laotian, Viet flow to Thailand 5-19, 379B2
Viets flee to Hong Kong 5-26–6-10, 436F1
Viet armed resistance seen 5-31, 547A2
Thais rpt ousted Cambodians killed 6-4, 436A1
US health team dispatched 6-5, San Fran svcs rptd strained 7-18, 550C2
Viet-UN agrmt set 6-8, 436D1
Thais turn back Cambodians 6-11; permit 1,430 temporary stay, asked Pol Pot stop flow 6-12, 435E3, 436B1
US concerned re Thai policy 6-11, 6-12, 435F3, 436C1
Thais ask China accept Cambodians 6-12, 436C1
Malaysia threatens to oust, shoot Viets 6-15; shooting threat dropped after intl pleas 6-18, 460D1
500-800 Viets land in Malaysia 6-16, expelled 6-17, 460F2
China vs US plea to take more Viets, demands Viet halt flow 6-16, 460G2
UN plea to Malaysia 6-16, 474E1
Japan to accept more Viets 6-18, 460C3
UK asks UN conf 6-18; US, Viet OK 6-19, 6-20, 474A1
Malaysia denies UN access to Viets 6-19, 474D1
UN rpts June 1-15 data, total admissns 6-21, 473G2
Canada, Sweden, Israel to take more 6-21; France 6-26, 474B2
Taiwan bars asylum, gives aid 6-21, 474C2
Cambodia: Thais kill refugees 6-22, 474G1
EC leaders back UN conf 6-22, 476G1
Malaysia turns back Viets 6-25, 6-27, 474B1
Thais delay Cambodian ousters, await UN conf 6-25, 474F1
Malaysia asks US to set up camps, threatns to expel 6-26, 474D1
US, Japan discuss 6-26, 494A2, 495E2
US to double admissn quota 6-28, 473D2
Tokyo summit asks UN conf 6-28, 473E2
ASEAN meets, natns bar more admissns 6-28–6-30, 495A2
China weighs Viet aid, seeks coordinated US positn 6-28, 495A3
2,600 Viets land in Hong Kong 6-29, 495B3
Viets bar W Ger sea rescue 6-30, 495C3
Waldheim calls intl conf 6-30, 549A1
Thais rptdly halt Cambodian expulsns 6-30, temporary asylum OKd 7-10, 550F1
ASEAN asylum sought by US, Japan vows more UN refugee aid 7-2, 495E2
Malaysia bars 1,050 Viets, admits 623 7-2; 1,000 force landing 7-4, 495D3
US seeks Australia Viet quota hike 7-4, 501C1
Malaysians score US policy 7-6, 550B2
Indonesian island setlmts rptd 7-7–7-8, temporary stay OKd 7-14, 550C1
Japan admissns cut seen, total rptd 7-10; aid set 7-13, 549E2
Japan rptdly delays Viet trade pact 7-11, ships shun Viet waters 7-15, 550A1-C1
Canada to take 50,000 by '80 7-18, 549D2
Canada admissns plan scored by Trudeau 7-19, 563D2
Geneva intl conf vows aid, Viet to halt flow 7-20–7-21, 549A1
Viet scores China re Cambodia refugees 7-20, 575B3
US Navy rescue ordrd 7-21, 19 saved 7-23, 549E1
85 Viets rptd shot 7-22, 550A2
US, Viet agree on visa processing 7-23, 549C2
Italy navy rescues Viets 7-25, 575B2
US Navy rescues 74 Viets 7-27, 7-30; Viet, Malaysia vs missns 7-28, 7-30, 575G1, C2
Viet exodus rptd spurred by US rescue missn 7-28, 575C2
2 boats rptd sunk 7-31, 8-8, 626F1
Italian ships pick up 700 7-31, 626A2
Commonwealth conf topic 8-2, 8-7, 590D2
Viet protests US Navy role 8-2, 626A1
Merchant ship aid rptd 8-2, 626G1
UN scores asylum denials 8-3, 626B1
US resettlemt plagued by disease, ethnic conflicts 8-3–8-25, 659D3-660F1
Decline rptd by US Navy 8-4, UN 8-22; 1st 1/2 June-Aug data 625E3
US reps tour camps 8-4–8-7, visit Hanoi 8-8–8-9; link Viet ties, refugee aid 8-11, 607G1
Viet refugee origin shift rptd 8-5, 626C1
US Navy rescues total 163 8-9, 626B2
Hong Kong sentences Viet boat smugglers 8-9, 626C2
Viets deny US visa processing agrmt 8-11, 607E2
US KKK clash re boat people 8-19, 866B2
532 arrive in Hong Kong 8-20; US patrols sight 7 boats 8-25–8-28, warship rescues 154 9-3, 659G2
Carter defends Viet policy 8-22, 622A3
Thailand, Laos rpt pact 8-25, 659B3
Mondale in Hong Kong, meets ambs of 5 states 9-1–9-2, 660A3

1980

Cambodians return from Laos, Viet, Thai 11-13, 951G3
More Viets flee to Singapore, Malaysia, Indonesia 11-19, 952D1

1976

INDOCHINA War—*See VIETNAM War*
INDONESIA—*See also ADB, ASEAN, NONALIGNED Nations Movement, OPEC*
Listed as 'partially free' 1-19, 20C3
'75 oil output drops 2-11, 144A3
At intl econ conf 2-11—2-20, 148B1
UN Palestine com member 2-26, 162C1
Pertamina revamped 3-4, 176F3
Australia wheat deal rptd 3-11, 187D3
Australia aid set 4-14, 309F2
WHO com rpts Israel W Bank, Gaza health data 5-10, 338F2
WHO vs rpt on Israel 5-17, 355A2
2 quakes hit 6-26—6-28, 7-14, 544G2
US GOP platform text cites 8-18, 609A3
Anti-Suharto plot aired 9-22, 735A1
Earthquake hits New Guinea 10-29, 931E3
'75-76 US bank loans cited 11-10, 915F1
'65 coup prisoners freed 12-1, 949E2
Portuguese Timor Relations—*See TIMOR*
South Moluccan Issue
Dutch rpt on '75 terrorism issued 1-16, 102D2
Dutch cabt meets with S Moluccans 1-17, 102E2
Trials held for '75 train hijack, emb seige; 7 convictd 3-10—3-25, 255A1
Emb terrorists sentenced 4-8, 366E1
Timor Relations—*See TIMOR*

INDRA, Alois
On Czech Presidium 4-16, 289A2
INDRIANJAFY, Georges Thomas
Named justice min 8-20, 926B1
INDUSTRIAL National Corp.
Rptd on FRB 'problem' list 1-22, 111B2
INDUSTRY—*See BUSINESS & Industry*
INDUSTRY Indemnity Co.—*See under CRUM & Foster Insurance Cos.*
INEX-Adria Airlines (Yugoslavia)
Brit Airways collisn 9-10, 696C3
INFANTILE Paralysis—*See 'Diseases' under MEDICINE*
INFLATION—*See under ECONOMY*
INFLUENZA—*See 'Diseases' under MEDICINE*
INGALLS Shipbuilding Corp.—*See under LITTON*
INGERSOLL, Robert S.
Rpts US to free Lockheed data 3-5, 191D1 ★
Details payoff disclosure plans 3-5, 199F3 ★
Replaced as State dep secy 4-7, 262E3
INGERSOLL, Adm. Royal E.
Dies 5-20, 404A2
INGERSOLL-Rand Co.
SEC rpts no paymts 5-12, 728A2

1977

INDOCHINA War—*See VIETNAM War*
INDONESIA—*See also ASEAN, NONALIGNED Nations Movement, OPEC*
UN Assemb member 4B1
Ups crude oil price 1-1, 12A2
Gen Dynamics wins US loan guarantee 1-19, 55E1
Intl rubber buffer-stock plan rejctd 1-23, 169G2
Hughes Aircraft payoffs chrgd 1-25, govt probes 2-4, 2-14, 182G2
W Ger arms sales set 2-2, 139E2
'76 econ growth rptd 2-16, 147C2, F2
'76 forgn investmts rptd down; inflatn, reserves, debt svc cited 4-18, 392F2-C3
Gokar wins electns 5-2, fraud chrgd 5-5, 392C3
Viet refugees barred 6-19, 497F1
US arms aid signed 8-4, 668C1
Fretelin given amnesty 8-16, 658G2
Quake strikes 8-19, 747A3
Malaysia takes Indochina refugees 8-31, 685F2
Amnesty Intl lists jailed lawmakers 9-5, 753A2
Sutowo cleared of chrgs, held 9-23, 747F1
Amnesty Intl chrgs prisoners held, vows campaign 10-18, 805E3
Exxon admits paymts 10-25, 818A2
Amnesty Intl lists jailed med workers 11-28, 956G2
Hosts copper talks 12-7, 975B1
Bauxite base price OKd by 10 natns 12-7, 975F1
Amnesty Intl chrgs 50,000-100,000 pol prisoners 12-8, 956D2
Govt frees 10,000 prisoners, Amnesty Intl doubts 12-20, 984A3
Pertamina (& developments)
Govt-shipping firm ct fight 1-18, 2-7, 2-24, 304E3
US chrgs shakedown 2-2, 93G1
Sutowo on Pertamina debts 2-14, 304D3
Sutowo, aides face probe on Pertamina, other chrgs 3-29; arrests rptd 4-9, 304F2
'76 forgn investmts rptd down 4-18, 392F2-C3
Pertamina settles US chrgs 6-1, 540C2
Foreign debt settled 8-11, 637B3
South Moluccan Issue
Dutch hostages seized 5-23, terrorist deadline passes 5-25, 411D3-412A1
Terrorists free Dutch children 5-27, Army attack frees remaining hostages 6-11, 467D3
Terrorists funeral draws 5000 6-14, 468A1
Dutch train-hijacking trial 9-6—9-9; violence erupts; police raid Moluccan homes, search trains 9-7—9-12, 707C1
Dutch sentence hijackers 9-22, 729E2

INDONESIAN Enterprises Inc.
US chrgs shakedown 2-2, 93C2
Settles US chrgs 6-1, 540C2
Ramayana Restaurant (N.Y.)
US chrgs Pertamina shakedown 2-2, 93C2
Settles US chrgs 6-1, 540C2
INDUSTRIAL Production Index—*See BUSINESS—Statistics*
INDUSTRY—*See BUSINESS & Industry*
INFORMATION, Freedom of—*See PRIVACY Issue*
INGALLS Shipbuilding Division—*See LITTON Industries*
INFLATION—*See under ECONOMY*
INFLUENZA—*See MEDICINE—Diseases*

1978

INDOCHINA War—*See VIETNAM War*
INDONESIA—*See also ASEAN, GATT, NONALIGNED Nations Movement, OPEC*
Dissident students rptdly sought Suharto mtg 1-12, 55F2
7 papers banned, student unrest cited 1-20—1-23, 55E2
Student dissent suppressed 1-21, 1-26, press ban protested 1-24, 1-25, 71F3
ASEAN head ousted for student support 1-23, 72E1
'77 quake deaths rptd 1-29, 480A2
Detainee toll, press curbs eased 2-5, 122C3
'77 pol prisoner releases cited 2-9, 102E1
Student unrest in Java 2-16, 122A3
Moslem party challenges govt 3-19, 246A2
Suharto reelected pres 3-22, sworn 3-23, forms new Cabt 3-29, 246E1
Student unrest, 131 jailed students rptd freed 3-30, 246B2
Pol prisoners to be freed 4-11, 288C3
Timor, W Irian fighting rptd 4-15, 318B3
Suharto critic arrested 5-1, 632B1
1,324 prisoners freed 9-27, 774C3
Sri Lanka jet crash kills 183 11-15, 908G1
Foreign Relations (misc.)—*See also 'Monetary, Trade, Aid & Investment' below*
Australia recognizes '76 Timor takeover 1-20, 72F1
PNG holds 2 West New Guinea rebels 2-27, 192D3
Brunei independence backed 6-30, 533D3
UN Assemb member 713F3
French seamen end strike 11-4, 882D1
Monetary, Trade, Aid & Investment
Viet trade missn ended 21B3
Islamic bank poor-natn aid rise rptd 4-9, 257F2
Australia port strike setld 4-9—4-10, 350B1
US dvpt loan signed 5-6, 360G3
Dutch Shell drops coal pact 7-24, 631G3
UK cancels debts 7-31, 592E1
South Moluccan Issue
Moluccan exile ldr shot 1-29, 90D3
Militants seize Assen govt bldg 3-13, Dutch assault frees hostages 3-14, 191D3
Dutch, Moluccan ldrs in talks 3-16, 192D1
'75 Dutch train hijacker kills self 6-10, 454E3
1,000 mark '77 Dutch train hijacking 6-11, 454E3
Dutch jail 3 in Assen death 6-30, 574F3-575A1
U.S. Relations
US concerned re student detentns 2-8, 122B3
US issues rights rpt 2-9, 101D3, 102D1
Ford Philco bribe rptd probed 4-25, stockholder sues 5-16, 390C3, F3
Mondale visits; lauds prisoner releases, signs dvpt loan 5-6, 360G3
Katy paymts violatns chrgd, suit setld 8-30, 737C1
ITT paymts chrgd 11-2, 876C1

INDUSTRIAL Production Index—*See BUSINESS—Statistics*
INDUSTRY—*See BUSINESS & Industry*
INEZ, Juana (deceased)
Price of Genius opens 6-26, 887E2
INFANTILE Paralysis (poliomyletis)—*See MEDICINE—Diseases*
INFERTILITY—*See CHILDBIRTH*
INFLATION—*See under ECONOMY*
INFORMATION Security Oversight Office—*See U.S. GOVERNMENT—GENERAL Services Administration*
INFORMATION Services
CBS seeks IMS purchase 2-15, rejctd 2-22, 185B1
IN Front of a Mirror (painting)
Stolen from W Ger museum 7-30, 1029B1
INGLIS, Billy
Hired as Sabres interim coach 12-6, 991D1

1979

US Navy, others save 500 Viets 9-3–10-9, 763F3
Cambodians mass at Thai border 9-9, 684E2
US religious group aid rptd 9-21, 755C3
Thais to accept Cambodians 9-26, Sept exit sets record 10-3, 764A1
70,000 Cambodians flee to Thailand 10-10–10-20, camps shelled 10-12, 10-14, 811B3
Sihanouk seeks US aid on Thai ousters 10-11, 811F2
Thais to take Cambodians, Laotians, Viets 10-19, 811G2
US reps urge US-USSR airlift 11-1, 863A3
Meo refugees rpt gas attacks 11-3, 12-12, 979B1
Cambodia opens Kompong Som, Mekong R routes 11-5, 863G2
Mrs Carter visits Thai camps 11-8–11-10, 863G1
Thais shell Cambodian camp 11-8, 863C2
China gets UN resetlmt grant 11-11, 863D3
US congresswomen in Pnompenh 11-12, 863F2
Cambodia relief rpts conflict 11-25–12-3; Thais block border aid 12-3, 917G1-G2
Thais declare 2 Cambodia camps 'safe havens' 11-29, 917G2

INDOCHINA War—*See VIETNAM War*
INDONESIA—*See also ASEAN, DISARMAMENT–Geneva Committee, GATT, NONALIGNED Nations Movement, OPEC*
Oil prices raised 1-1, 52F1
Java hit by volcanic eruptn 2-21, 140A3
W Java, E Kalimantan floods rptd 5-26, 6-13, 472B3
N Sumatra airline crash kills 61 7-11, 639F1
Lomblem I tidal wave kills 539 7-22, 638F3
Quake, tidal waves kill 100 9-13, 800E2
2,000 prisoners freed 10-10, 796C3
E Timor famine rptd 10-30, 838C2; detailed 11-3, 11-6, 11-8, 856A1
Oil price hike set 11-14, 864A2
E Timor populatn cut by war, starvatn 12-4, 12-15, 994F3-995B1
Amnesty Intl lauds prisoner release 12-9, 980A2
Oil price per barrel rptd 12-21, hike set 12-28, 977B2, C2
Foreign Relations (misc.)—*See also 'Monetary' and 'UN' below*
UN Viet refugee plan OKd 3-30, 299G1
Waldheim in refugee talks 5-9, 379D2
Viet refugee conf held, island offered for processing 5-15–5-16, 379E1, B2
Viet refugee arrivals rptd 5-19, 379C2
W Bank, Gaza health probe set 5-23, 398F2
More Viet refugee admissns barred 6-30; US, Japan seek aid 7-2, 495A2
Viet refugees rptd on Anambas, Riouw 7-7–7-8, temporary stay OKd 7-14, 550C1
N Korea note to US relayed 7-10, 537A2
Monetary, Trade, Aid & Investment
Australia wheat deal rptd 1-22, 56F3
US OKs LNG imports 8-14, 9-27, 769C2
UN Policy & Developments
Viet refugee plan OKd 3-30, 299G1
Membership listed 695E2
U.S. Relations
US issues rights rpt 2-10, 107D3
Ford stockholders suit barred 3-8, 202B3
US asks Indochina refugee asylum 7-2, 495D2
N Korea note relayed 7-10, 537A2
US reps visit Viet refugee camps 8-7, 607G1
US OKs LNG imports 8-14, 9-27, 769C2
Mondale in refugee talks 9-1, 660A3
E Timor starvatn probed 12-4, 995A1

INDUSTRIAL Production Index—*See BUSINESS–Statistics*
INDUSTRY—*See BUSINESS*
INFANTILE Paralysis (poliomyelitis)—*See MEDICINE–Diseases*
INFERTILITY—*See CHILDBIRTH*
INFLATION—*See under ECONOMY*
INFORMATION for Industry Inc.
1st 1/2 mergers rptd 7-2, 500F3
INFORMATION Services
White House conf held 11-15–11-19, 901B1-A2
INGALLS Shipbuilding Division—*See LITTON Industries*
INGE, William
Dark at the Top opens 11-29, 956G2
INGERSOLL, Andrew
On Jupiter's atmosphere 3-8, 216D1

1980

INDOCHINA War—*See VIETNAM War*
INDONESIA—*See also ADB, ASEAN, GATT, GENEVA Committee, NONALIGNED Nations, OPEC*
Jakarta purchasing power rptd low 2-12, 125E3
Defns-GNP ratio rptd 2-19, 132G1
E Timor revolt seen over 6-10; rebels rptd active 7-23, 604B2
Foreign Relations (misc.)—*See also 'Monetary' below*
Pacific orgn studied 1-20, 78C2
Viet refugee boat seizures chrgd 2-25, 141G1
Surinam coup fails, mercenaries seized 5-1—5-2, 410A3
Pl drops claim to Malaysian Sabah State 10-31, 902D3
Australia bans book on E Timor policy 11-9, 885E1; upheld by High Ct 12-1, 99F2
Anti-Chinese rioting 11-14—11-26, 943B1
More Viet refugees arrive 11-19, 952E1
Australian newsprs publish banned articles 12-2, 991G2
Suharto ask Iran-Iraq peace 12-15, 951D2
Monetary, Trade, Aid & Investment
US co trust suit review declined 2-25, 188B1
Ford paymts probe rptd dropped 3-13, 224D3
World Bank '80 loans rptd 9-22, 720E1
Brazil oil sales rptd 10-2, 759A2
E Timor intl relief barred 12-9, 943D1
U.S. Relations
US co trust suit review declined 2-25, 188B1
Ford paymts probe rptd dropped 3-13, 224D3
E Timor revolt seen over 6-10, 604D2
CIA ex-agent indicted on espionage 10-24, pleads guilty 10-29, 856B1
E Timor relief barred 12-9, 943D1

INDUSTRIAL Investment Development Corp.
Mitsui trust case declined by Sup Ct 2-25, 188B1
INDUSTRIAL Production Index—*See BUSINESS & Industry*
INDUSTRY—*See BUSINESS*
INFANTILE Paralysis (poliomyelitis)—*See MEDICINE*
INFERTILITY—*See CHILDBIRTH*
INFLATION—*See ECONOMY--Inflation & Recession*
INFLATION, Committee to Fight
Policy statemt issued 6-21, 481D1
INFLUENZA—*See MEDICINE--Diseases*
INGELFINGER, Dr. Franz J.
Dies 3-26, 279E3
IN God We Trust (film)
Released 9-26, 836C3
Top-grossing film 10-1, 796G3

1976

INGRAO, Pietro
Elected Chamber speaker 7-5, 497E1
INLAND Steel Co.
Withdraws price hike plan 8-30, 646C3
Hikes prices 6% 11-26, 897E2
INNAUER, Toni
Wins Olympic medal 2-15, 159E1
INNIS, Roy
Recruits for Angola 2-10; US blacks score 2-14, 2-19, 163A3
INNOCENTS, The (play)
Opens 10-21, 1014F3
INOH, Shigejiro
Chrgs Kishi Lockheed role 3-9, 191A2
INOUYE, Sen. Daniel K. (D, Hawaii)
Named to intelligence com 5-20, 377D1
Wild acquitted 7-27, 566A1
Rues Bush CIA resignatn 11-24, 917D2
INOUYE, Hank
Loses election 11-2, 825C1
INSECTS
Australia rpts plagues 12-30, 997D3
INSTITUTE for Policy Studies (Washington, D.C.)
Letelier, Moffitt killed 9-21, Chile DINA chrgd 9-21—9-23, 710C2
Rpts FBI Venez probe re Letelier; chrgs Cuba exile-DINA link 10-18, 844F2
INSTITUTE for Strategic Studies, International (IISS) (London)
Alistair Buchan dies 2-4, 124D3
Kissinger addresses 6-25, 466D1
Warns re NATO superiority 9-3, 760A3
INSTITUTE for World Order
Arms spending study released 2-29, 182G3

INSURANCE
Calif co indicted 1-14, unit chrgd 2-2, 160A1
Feb CPI rptd up 3-19, 215B2
CIA co ownership rptd 4-26, 299D2
Ford urges regulatory reform 5-13, 347A1
Dem platform text 6-15, 471E2
GOP platform text 8-18, 603E1, 605G3
Automobile Insurance—*See 'Insurance' under AUTOMOBILES*
Medical & Malpractice Insurance—*See 'Insurance' under MEDICINE*
INSURANCE Commissioners, National Association of
'75-76 MD malpractice data rptd 7-28, 1016D3

1977

INGRAHAM, Hubert
Govt seeks forgn capital 8-19, 710F1
INGRAHAM v. Wright
Spankings upheld 4-19, 342E1
INK, Printing
Inmont bought by Carrier 8-11, 629A3
INLAND Steel Co.
Contract OKd 4-9, 273G2
Japan technology edge rptd 8-13, 776A1
USW strike ended 12-16, 977C3
INMAN, William P.
Scores saccharin ban 3-9, 176E3
INMONT Corp.
Carrier buys 8-11, 629A3
INOUYE, Sen. Daniel K. (D, Hawaii)
Elected Dem conf secy 1-4, 6E1
CIA paymts stand cited 2-23, 123G3
Intell com surveillnc rptd 2-26, 150A3
On rpts of Panama Canal talks bugging, blackmail 9-19, 716D2
Backs CIA bar vs press, clergy contacts 12-1, 941A2
INSECTS
World food loss rptd 2-22, 183E3
Medal of Sci won by Wilson 11-22, 952C1
INSPIRATION Consolidated Copper Co.
Copper prices raised 3-18, 209C2
Strike begins 7-1, 558G1
Jacob on price cut 7-20, 577F2
INSTITUTE for Advanced Studies (Princeton, N.J.)
Whitney gets Medal of Sci 11-22, 952C1
INSTITUTE for Policy Studies (Washington, D.C.)
Raskin scores Chile econ policies 6-5, 448E3
INSTITUTE for Strategic Studies, International (IISS) (London)
On Israel arms sales to Latin Amer 1-15, 28F3
Carter policies scored 4-28, 401D1
US-Sovt strategic weapons compared 751C3
'77-78 E-W mil balance rpt issued 9-2, 686D1
INSULATION—*See HOUSING*
INSULIN—*See MEDICINE—Drugs*

INSURANCE
NYC debt repaymt plan OKd 3-10, 193D2
Pritchards indicted 3-10, 203F3
Richmond OKs Continental bid 4-12, 274C3
Reinsurance agreemts backed 4-26, 382D3
Norin '76 sales rise rptd 340C1
Equity Funding lawsuit setld 5-11, 408G3
Pension mgt concentratn chrgd 6-28, 578D2
Privacy panel rpts abuses 7-12, 632B1
Tenneco buys Phila Life 8-25, 650F3
White House backs phone ad curbs 10-21, 921C1
Airline employe liability case review refused 10-31, 835C3
Teamster deal probed by Sen panel 10-31—11-2, 837E1
'76 fraud costs rptd 11-17, 919D1
Natl Women's Conf urges bias end 11-19—11-21, 917D3
Automobile Insurance—*See AUTOMOBILES—Insurance Issues*
Medical & Malpractice Insurance—*See MEDICINE—Insurance*
Unemployment Insurance—*See LABOR—Employment & Unemployment*

1978

INGOLDSBY, John
Flood influence-selling chrgs detailed 1-27, 240F2
INGRAM, John R.
Faces US Sen primary runoff in NC 5-2, 342B3
Beats Hodges in runoff 5-30, 426C2
Carter attends NC rally 8-5, 605F3
Loses electn 11-7, 852F3
Electn spending disparity rptd 11-15, 898B1
INLAND Container Corp.
Indicted for price fixing 1-25, 67D2
Time Inc plans purchase, '77 profits cited 5-19, 403G2-C3
INMONT Corp.
'77 Carrier takeover cited 9-25, 896G1
INNES, Michael
Candleshoe released 8-4, 969F3
INNIS, Roy
Elected CORE chrmn, dir 9-8—9-10; ex-ldrs score 9-18, 810C1
INNOCENTI, Umberto Degli
Shot 5-4, 393A2
INOUYE, Sen. Daniel K. (D, Hawaii)
Lauds Carter intell reorganizatn 1-24, 49A2
US bars shipping rebate probe delay 2-3, 184E3
Votes for Panama Canal neutrality pact 3-16, 177D2
Votes for 2d Canal pact 4-18, 273B1
IN Search of Enemies: A CIA Story (book)
Published 5-8, 367A2
IN Search of History: A Personal Adventure (book)
On best-seller list 9-4, 708C1; 10-9, 800B3; 11-6, 888A1
INSECTICIDES—*See PESTICIDES*
INSECTS—*See also PESTICIDES*
Locusts plague Africa Horn; aid asked, India sighting rptd 6-6—6-14, 465C2
Grasshoppers invade west US 7-12—7-31, 654A3
Mosquito insecticide immunity rptd 8-6, 635F3
Earthworm rumor hurts fast-food chains 11-16, 942G1
INSPECTOR General, The (play)
Opens 9-21, 1031A2
INSTITUTE for Advanced Study (Princeton, N.J.)
Kurt Godel dies 1-14, 196A3
INSTITUTE for Policy Studies (Washington, D.C.)
US seeks 2 in Moffitt murder 2-21, 146A2; **for subsequent developments, see CHILE—Letelier Murder Probe**
Chile bank loans rptd undercutting US rights policy 4-11, 312A2
INSTITUTE for Strategic Studies, International (IISS) (London)
NATO, Warsaw Pact forces compared 2-20, 162D3
US Africa policy scored 5-24, 488C1
E-W mil balance assessed 9-1, 676A3
INSULATION—*See HOUSING*
INSURANCE
OPIC loses new-policy writing power 1-1, trade protectionism cited 1-3, 67A1
John MacArthur dies 1-6, 96G2
NYC fscl recovery plan issued 1-20, 87B2
Bank holding co sales denied review 2-27, 143B2
'64-78 spending pattern chngs reflected in new CPIs 222D2
Great Southn, Equitable Gen merger planned 4-17, 283G1
OPIC extension signed 4-24, 323C2
Sex-based pensn plans barred by Sup Ct 4-25, 322D3
Pornographer's arson damages cited 971E2
Skokie anti-Nazi ordinances struck down 5-23, 447A3
Aetna vows exec pay curbs 6-1, Admin steps up campaign 6-6, 428A1
US study finds arson rise 6-4, 440C2
US chrgs USSR ship insurance bias 6-9, 499D3
4 indicted in union scheme 6-15, 560G2-D3
Chicago anti-Nazi ordinance waived 6-20, 6-29, 529B2
Equitable Gen sets new merger 6-26, 553D2
Policy holder trust suits backed by Sup Ct 6-29, 567C3
Ostrer indicted 7-18, 599D1
John Hancock agents strike 7-21—8-17, 680C3
NYC $2.55 bln loan agreed 7-27, 609B1
LNG fed liability fund urged 7-31, 610D1
SEC censures Dirks, 4 cos re Equity Funding 9-4, 681G1
Teamster fund trustees sued 10-16, 792E1-A3; US set back 11-1, 11-7, 899C1
Borg-Warner, Firestone to merge 11-28, 935E1
Carter eases fringe benefit-test for wage rule 12-13, 957F1, E2
Toxic-waste plan mandates 12-14, 982D3
Automobile Insurance—*See AUTOMOBILES—Insurance Issues*
Medical & Malpractice Insurance—*See under MEDICINE*
Unemployment Insurance—*See LABOR—Employment & Unemployment*
INSURANCE Administration, Federal—*See U.S. GOVERNMENT—GENERAL Services Administration—Federal Insurance Administration*
INSURANCE Workers International Union (AFL-CIO)
John Hancock struck 7-21—8-17, 680D3

1979

INGRAM, John W.
Rock Island RR firing rptd 10-5, 830D3
INGRAM, Michael
Savara opens 2-11, 292F2
INLAND Container Corp.—*See TIME Inc.*
IN-Laws, The (film)
Released 6-15, 820D1
Top-grossing film 8-1, 620G3; 9-26, 800G3
INMAN, Henry (1801-1846)
Peabody to sell portraits 2-9, 173G2
INMAN, Joe
2d in Atlanta Classic 6-10, 587B3
INMAR Associates Inc.
US sues re NJ pollutn 2-7, 130B1
INNOCENT, The (film)
Released 1-11, 174G2
INOUYE, Sen. Daniel K. (D, Hawaii)
Sen Dem Conf secy 71A2
Votes vs Talmadge denunciatn 10-10, 769F1
IN Praise of Older Women (film)
Released 2-8, 174G2
IN re Winship
Case cited by Sup Ct 6-28, 558G2
INS—*See U.S. GOVERNMENT-JUSTICE-Immigration & Naturalization Service*
INSECTICIDES—*See PESTICIDES*
INSIDERS, The (book)
On best-seller list 2-4, 120C3; 3-4, 173F3
INSTITUTE for Policy Studies (Washington, D.C.)
PLO offcl addresses mtg 4-11, 319G2
FBI to end spying 10-4, 787G1
INSTITUTE for Strategic Studies, International (IISS) (London)
US, USSR strategic weapons compared 338G3
'79-80 world mil balance assessed 9-4, 825A2-C3
Sovt E Eur troop deploymt rptd 761G2
INSTRUMENT Landing (race horse)
Wins Wood Memorial 4-21, 448C3

INSURANCE
House subcom scores life insurance sales practices 1-2, 15D3
HEW to step up anti-smoking drive 1-11, 23D1
'Debit' insurnc scored by FTC staff 1-28, 91D2
Price rules disputed 2-24, guidelines revised 3-16, 264G2-A3
3 Mile I A-accident compensatn vowed 3-31, 244B2
Carter urges privacy bill 4-2, 264F3
3 Mile I paymts detailed 4-5, 250F2-A3
Iowa clergy malpractice coverage OKd 4-9, 376D1
Stone confrmd CFTC chrmn 4-11, 681D2
Armored car losses cited 4-17, 316A2
Iran cos natlzd 6-25, 486E2
Nicaragua cos to be kept pvt 7-25, 574C1
Press freedom plan set 9-27, 859E2
Justice Dept cites '77 Sup Ct tax case errors 10-8, 848A2
Pensn safeguards urged 11-26, 905B1
Automobile Insurance—*See AUTOMOBILES-Insurance Issues*
Medical & Malpractice Insurance—*See under MEDICINE*
Mergers & Acquisitions
NLT acquires Great Southn 1-17, 88G3
Amer Brands acquires FDS 2-14, 132B2
Dutch co seeks Life Insurnc Co of Ga 3-23, 942D2
Southn Pacific to buy Ticor 3-28, 283D1
Allianz-Versicherungs to buy N Amer Life 5-11, Fidelity Union 6-25, 942C2
Transamerica wins Interway bidding 5-29, 560C2
Gelco to buy Reliance Group unit 7-16, 560D2
CIT ends Integon merger talks 8-24, 682E2
Congoleum-Fibic merger OKd 9-21, 942A2
ERC Corp spurns Conn Gen 10-18, Charter Co to make offer 12-21, 986C3
Tenneco to acquire Southwestn Life 12-11, 986A3

1980

INGRAM Jr., Samuel Alden
Hijacks jet to Cuba 1-25, 617A3
INGRAM, Judge William
Convicts Bonnano, nephew 9-2, 712F3
INK Spots Quartet (musical group)
Bernard Mackey dies 3-5, 280B1
INKSTER, Juli Simpson
Wins US Women's Amateur golf title 8-17, 714E3
INLAND Steel Co.
USW contract settled 4-15, 289B2
Prices cut 7-10, 575F2
INMAR Associates Inc.
NJ dump suit partly setld 1-30, 93G3
IN Memory of a Summer Day (recording)
Del Tredici wins Pulitzer 4-14, 296F2
INNAUER, Anton
Wins Olympic medal 2-17, 155D3
INNAURATO, Albert
Happy Birthday Gemini released 5-2, 416A3
Passione opens 5-22, 756F3
INNIS, Thomas J.
Police interrogatn defined by Sup Ct, case remanded 5-12, 386C2
INNOCENT Blood (book)
On best-seller list 7-13, 568B3
INOUYE, Sen. Daniel K. (D, Hawaii)
Wins renominatn 9-20, 745E1
Reelected 11-4, 840E1, 845A3, 846F3, 852C2
Reelected Sen Dem conf secy 12-4, 936G2
INS (Immigration & Naturalization Service)—*See under U.S. GOVERNMENT--JUSTICE*
IN Search of Enemies: A CIA Story (book)
US suit vs Stockwell opens 3-3, 268A3
Stockwell settles suit 6-25, 516E3
INSECTICIDES—*See PESTICIDES*
INSECTS
Mt St Helens damage assessed 5-24—7-4, 503E3
INSIDE Moves (film)
Released 12-19, 1003A2
INSIDE Sports (magazine)
Garvey article reprint OKd despite libel suit 8-14, 637E2
INSTITUTE for Strategic Studies, International (IISS) (London)
Sovt '78 defense budget estimate cited 1-28, 70A3
Sovt ICBMs rptd accurate, said US threat 9-18, 730E2
INSTITUTE of World Socialist Economics
Sovts pledge COMECON energy export rise 10-1, 753B3

INSURANCE
State ct jurisdictn narrowed by Sup Ct 1-21, 93D2
FBI Brilab probe rptd 2-8—2-9, 111G2, B3
Bond investmt drop cited 2-21, 126G3
FTC funding blocked 3-15—4-30, shuts down 5-1, reopens 5-2, 348C1
Mutual fund fraud case refused by Sup Ct 3-24, 265E1
N Sea oil platform accident losses rptd 3-27, 256C2
Lloyd's NBC Olympic coverage rptd 3-28, 259E1
NY exchng opens; Lloyd's financial losses, liability cited 3-31, 265G3
'79 forgn investmt in US rptd 4-8, 329C1
NBC hints revised Olympic coverage 4-14, 283G2
NBC drops Olympic telecast, estimates loss 5-6, 379E3
Pre-ERISA insured pensn benefits backed by Sup Ct 5-12, 426B3
Baseball contract dispute setld 5-23, 402B2
FTC probe power curbed 5-28, 702G3
Ford electn to Tiger Intl bd rptd 6-25, 600A3
Lloyd's study issued, reforms urged 6-26, 509C3
Canadian crop insurance depleted 6-27, 520F2
Iran assets seizure damages backed 7-10, 546E1
Bush addresses independent agents conf 9-29, 781G1
Itel rpts huge '79 loss; liability claims, premiums rptd 10-16, 784F1, C2
Lloyd's OKs reforms 11-4, 855C3
Boston bond rating lowered 12-2, 939F3
Mich asks Chrysler paymt 12-26, 984G2
Medical & Malpractice Insurance—*See MEDICINE--Insurance*
Mergers & Acquisitions
Charter Media buys Phila Bulletin 4-10, 376G3
Marsh & McLennan to buy Bowring 4-14, 386B1
ERC OKs Getty offer 6-5, 557F2
Capital Holding, Natl Liberty agree 6-13, 746E1
Engelhard OKs NN Corp acquisitn 6-24, 557D3

1976

INTELLIGENCE Issues—*See SECURITY, Internal; also specific related subjects (e.g., WIRETAPPING); also U.S. GOVERNMENT, subheads CENTRAL Intelligence Agency and FEDERAL Bureau of Investigation*

INTER-American Development Bank (IDB) (Argentina, Barbados, Bolivia, Brazil, Canada, Chile, Colombia, Costa Rica, Dominican Republic, Ecuador, El Salvador, Guatemala, Haiti, Honduras, Mexico, Nicaragua, Panama, Paraguay, Peru, Trinidad & Tobago, U.S., Uruguay, Venezuela)
Guatemala hydro loan rptd 1-9, 55A2
OKs Peru loans 1-23, 1-30, 142E2
Chile '75 copper losses rptd 1-29, 99A3
Bolivia loan rptd 4-13, 416D1
Annual mtg rpts record '75 loans, 3 Andean natns score; 12 new members set 5-17—5-19, 465E2-G3
US Cong clears fund authorzn 5-20, 392A3
Ford signs fund bill 5-31, 982E1
OKs Bolivia elec loan 6-18, 456B3
OKs 3 Mexico loans 6-18, 694F3
OKs Chile loans 8-13, 9-2, 10-22, 871C1
OKs Argentina gas pipe loan 8-27, 649C3
'77 US funds signed 10-1, 806E3
Guatemala dvpt loans rptd 10-13, 1005E1
INTER-American Foundation
Paraguay accused 4-5, 403F2
INTER-American Press Association (IAPA)
Meets 7-12—7-13, scores UNESCO press conf 7-23, 619G3
Asks Brazil 'terrorism' end 11-17, 916A2
INTERCONTINENTAL Air Freight Inc.
Boycott rpt released 10-18, 10-20, 786B1, A2
INTERCONTINENTAL Ballastic Missile (ICBM)—*See 'Missiles' under ARMAMENTS*
INTERCONTINENTAL Diversified Corp.
SEC lists forgn paymts 5-12, 728A2
INTER-Continental Hotels
US Jews cancel Brazil tours 1-15, 27G2
INTERHARVEST Inc.
Chavez contract signed 1-31, 153B2
INTERNAL Security—*See SECURITY, Internal*
INTERNATIONAL—*For organizations not listed below, see key words*
INTERNATIONAL Business Machines Corp.
On '75 Fortune 500 list 437B1, D1
US OKs Sovt sale 9-2, 752C2
Backus gets Science Medal 10-18, 858C3
INTERNATIONAL Chess Federation
USSR asks Korchnoi bar 9-4, 857C1
INTERNATIONAL City Bank & Trust Co.—*See ICB Corp.*
INTERNATIONAL Commission of Jurists (ICJ)
Scores Chile prisoners' rights decree 2-2, 100G1
Siracusa vs Uruguay torture rpt 4-21, 383A1
Rpt chrgs Iran prisoner torture 5-28, 418B2
Angola mercenary appeal rptd 7-5, 519E3
Rpts on Uruguay torture 7-16, 542A2
Kennedy: Cuba denies prison access 8-28, 791A2
Chrgs contd Chile abuses 8-31, 711B1
US bans aid to Uruguay 10-1, 814F2
Scores Angola trial 12-21, 995E3
INTERNATIONAL Controls Corp. Investors Overseas Services, Ltd. (IOS) (defunct)
Vesco, 6 others indicted 1-14, 78C2
CR repeals 'Vesco Law' 11-2, 1000F2
INTERNATIONAL Criminal Police Organization—*See INTERPOL*

1977

INTEGRATION—*See under EDUCATION*
INTELLIGENCE Issues—*See SECURITY, Internal; also specific related subjects (e.g., WIRETAPPING); also U.S. GOVERNMENT, subheads CENTRAL Intelligence Agency and FEDERAL Bureau of Investigation*
INTELLIGENCE Oversight Board—*See under U.S. GOVERNMENT*
INTELLIGENCE & Research, Bureau of—*See under U.S. GOVERNMENT—STATE*
INTER-American Commission on Human Rights—*See under ORGANIZATION of American States*

INTER-American Development Bank (IDB) (Argentina, Austria, Barbados, Belgium, Bolivia, Brazil, Canada, Chile, Colombia, Costa Rica, Denmark, Dominican Republic, Ecuador, El Salvador, France, Great Britain, Guatemala, Haiti, Honduras, Israel, Japan, Mexico, Netherlands, Nicaragua, Panama, Paraguay, Peru, Spain, Sweden, Trinidad & Tobago, U.S., Uruguay, West Germany, Yugoslavia, Venezuela)
'76 Chile loan total rptd 3-18, 449E1
Carter asks US pledges met 4-14, 296B1
Kidnap mars annual mtg; '73-76 lending rptd, rights debated 5-29—6-1; table 438G1-349E1
'76 Latin growth rptd; '61-75 GDP variation table 5-30, 439A1, E1
Panama $98-mln hydro loan OKd 9-2, 786F1
US '78 funds cleared 10-19, 815F2; signed 11-1, 834D1
Mex $1 bln credit OKd 11-22, 967D1
INTER-American Press Association (IAPA)
Young scored re press curbs 8-16, 647G1
INTERCOLLEGIATE Association of Amateur Athletes of America (IC4A)—*See specific sport (e.g., TRACK & Field)*
INTERCONTINENTAL Ballistic Missile (ICBM)—*See ARMAMENTS—Missiles*
INTEREST Rates—*See under BANKS*
INTERGOVERNMENTAL Committee for European Migration—*See EUROPEAN Migration, etc.*
INTERGOVERNMENTAL Relations, Advisory Commission on—*See under U.S. GOVERNMENT*
INTERIOR, Department of the—*See under U.S. GOVERNMENT*
INTER-Maritime Management S.A. (Geneva)
Pertamina debt settled 8-11, 637C3
INTERNAL Revenue Service—*See under U.S. GOVERNMENT*
INTERNATIONAL—*For organizations not listed below, see key words*
INTERNATIONAL Association of Bridge, Structural and Ornamental Iron Workers v. Linbeck Construction Corp.
Lawyer fees case refused 11-14, 878E3
INTERNATIONAL Atomic Energy Agency—*See under UNITED Nations*
INTERNATIONAL Bank for Economic Cooperation—*See under COMECON*
INTERNATIONAL Bank for Reconstruction and Development—*See under WORLD Bank Group*
INTERNATIONAL Business Machines Corp. (IBM)
Hills elected bd dir 2-22, 140G2
Stock repurchased 2-22—3-9, 409G1
Cabt holdings rptd 2-25, 147F3, G3, 148A1
To promote S Africa equality 3-1, 160B3
On '76 Fortune 500 list 340E1, C3
B Graham fund holdings rptd 6-26, 732A1
Xerox wins Canada patent suit 7-5, 525B3
Canada unit appeals Xerox ruling 8-17, IBM seeks Xerox license 8-31, 705A3
Xerox OKs patent use 9-23, 764D1
To halt India operatns 11-15, 984E2
INTERNATIONAL Commission of Jurists (ICJ)
Asks Uganda death probe 2-17, 139C1
Blames Amin re killings, scores UN inaction 5-17, 429G1
Rpt Lule denied killings 7-2, 600E3
Pl torture chrgd 7-31, 618B3
INTERNATIONAL Committee of Support for Charter 77
Bellow joins 1-21, 82G2
INTERNATIONAL Controls Corp.
Sup Ct bars Vesco case review 2-22, 150F1
Lawyers, auditors scored re Vesco, suit vs urged 11-29, 980A3
Settles IOS Vesco claims 12-7, 980G2
INTERNATIONAL Court of Justice—*See under UNITED Nations*
INTERNATIONAL Criminal Police Organization—*See INTERPOL*
INTERNATIONAL Currency Review (magazine)
Secret US-Saudi pact rptd 6-27, 474D1

1978

INTELLECT
Child dvpt study rptd 7-8, 1023D2
INTELLIGENCE Agency, Defense—*See U.S. GOVERNMENT—DEFENSE Intelligence Agency*
INTELLIGENCE Issues—*See specific related subjects (e.g., ESPIONAGE, WIRETAPPING); also U.S. GOVERNMENT subheads CENTRAL Intelligence Agency, FEDERAL Bureau of Investigation and INTELLIGENCE Agencies*
INTERAGENCY Task Force on Workplace Safety and Health—*See under U.S. GOVERNMENT*
INTER-American Commission on Human Rights—*See under ORGANIZATION of American States*
INTER-American Court of Human Rights—*See HUMAN Rights, Inter-American Court of*
INTER-American Defense Board—*See under OAS*

INTER-American Development Bank (IDB) (Argentina, Austria, Barbados, Belgium, Bolivia, Brazil, Canada, Chile, Colombia, Costa Rica, Denmark, Dominican Republic, Ecuador, El Salvador, France, Great Britain, Guatemala, Haiti, Honduras, Israel, Japan, Mexico, Netherlands, Nicaragua, Panama, Paraguay, Peru, Spain, Sweden, Trinidad & Tobago, U.S., Uruguay, West Germany, Yugoslavia, Venezuela)
Nicaragua offices bombed 2-21, 150C2
El Salvador rights situatn rptd worse 8-5, 723A3 ★
Latin '77 econ rated poor 9-10, 828D2-A3
INTER-American Press Association (IAPA)
Argentina abuses scored 10-9, 792C3
34th assemb backs press freedom 10-13, 829D1-F2
INTER-American Regional Labor Organization—*See ICFTU*
INTERCO Inc.
FTC chrgs setld 7-14, 768E3
American Can outbids for Fingerhut 8-14, 718D1
INTERCOLLEGIATE Athletics, National Association of (NAIA)—*See specific sport (e.g., BASKETBALL)*
INTERCOLLEGIATE Athletics for Women, Association for (AIAW)—*See also specific sport (e.g., BASKETBALL)*
Conv; Mushier elected pres 1-7—1-11, 40F2
INTERCONTINENTAL Ballistic Missile (ICBM)—*See ARMAMENTS—Missiles*
INTERCONTINENTAL Hotels Corp.—*See under PAN American World Airways*
INTEREST Rates—*See under BANKS*
INTERFERON (anti-viral protein)—*See BIOLOGY*
INTERIOR, Department of the—*See under U.S. GOVERNMENT*
INTERIOR Decoration
Ford sued re kickbacks 4-25, 391A1
INTERIORS (film)
Released 8-2, 970F1
Top-grossing film 10-4, 800G3
INTERNAL Revenue Service—*See under U.S. GOVERNMENT*
INTERNATIONAL—*For organizations not listed below, see key words*
INTERNATIONAL Amateur Athletic Federation—*See TRACK & Field*
INTERNATIONAL Atomic Energy Agency—*See under UNITED Nations*
INTERNATIONAL Bank for Reconstruction and Development (World Bank)—*See under WORLD Bank Group*
INTERNATIONAL Business Machines Corp. (IBM)
Greyhound trust case review denied 1-16, 33E2
Xerox patent suit filed 2-23, 510B2
Heir convicted in murder plot 4-26, 380F2
US rests trust case 4-26, 510C2
On '77 Fortune 500 list 5-8, 325E1, A2
India operatn halted, employes take over 6-1, 415B3
Nigeria operatns closed 6-26, 798G2
Memorex case mistrial 7-5, 510F2
Xerox patent dispute setld 8-1, 664E2
Pfeiffer named NBC chrmn, RCA dir 9-13, 759C3
Top-ranked cash-rich US co 9-18, 716D3
Nigeria joint venture rptd 11-6, 906B3
Shroud of Turin studied 11-7, 926A1
4-for-1 stock split set 12-19, 1003F3
INTERNATIONAL Cambodia Hearing
Cambodian atrocities chrgd 4-21—4-23, 301C2
INTERNATIONAL Civil Aviation Organization (ICAO)—*See under UNITED Nations*
INTERNATIONAL Commission of Jurists (ICJ)
Says Chile rights abuse continues 1-4, 17C2
El Salvador rights abuse chrgd 9-20, 823B3; prisoner torture 10-13, 881G2
INTERNATIONAL Controls Corp.
Vesco case review barred 1-9, 13A2
INTERNATIONAL Court of Justice (World Court)—*See under UNITED Nations*
INTERNATIONAL Criminal Police Organization—*See INTERPOL*
INTERNATIONAL Cycling Union—*See BICYCLING & Bicycles*

1979

IN Tam
Sihanouk exile group formatn disclosed 10-4, 811C2
INTEGON Corp.
CIT ends merger talks, cites RCA deal 8-24, 682E2
INTEGRITY (Episcopalian gay group)
Church bans gay ordinatn 9-17, 755D2
INTELLECT
Racial poll rptd 2-20, 307A1
INTELLECTUAL Life in the Colonial South (book)
Wins Natl Book Award 4-23, 356B2
INTELLIGENCE Agency, Defense—*See U.S. GOVERNMENT-Defense Intelligence Agency*
INTELLIGENCE Issues—*See specific related subjects (e.g., ESPIONAGE, WIRETAPPING); also U.S. GOVERNMENT subheads CENTRAL Intelligence Agency, FEDERAL Bureau of Investigation and INTELLIGENCE Agencies*
INTER-American Commission on Human Rights—*See under ORGANIZATION of American States*
INTER-American Development Bank (IDB) (Argentina, Austria, Barbados, Belgium, Bolivia, Brazil, Canada, Chile, Colombia, Costa Rica, Denmark, Dominican Republic, Ecuador, El Salvador, Finland, France, Great Britain, Guatemala, Guyana, Haiti, Honduras, Israel, Italy, Jamaica, Japan, Mexico, Netherlands, Nicaragua, Panama, Paraguay, Peru, Spain, Sweden, Switzerland, Trinidad & Tobago, U.S., Uruguay, Venezuela, West Germany, Yugoslavia)
Nicaragua aid rptd 8-2, 8-4, 603D1-G1
INTER-American Press Association (IAPA)
Meets in Trinidad; Peru journalist hunger strike backed 3-21, 255G3
INTER-American Regional Labor Organization (ORIT)—*See TRADE Unions, International Confederation of F ree*
INTERCO Inc.
FTC data disclosure to states OKd 3-28, 308D2
Ethan Allen merger deal set 8-13, 664B1
INTERCOLLEGIATE Athletics for Women, Association for (AIWA)—*See also specific sport (e.g., BASKETBALL)*
LA conv refines divisn reorg, honors Meyers, elects Grant pres 1-8—1-10, 103G1
Mushier backs Title IX guidelines 12-4, 1000B3
INTERCONTINENTAL Ballistic Missile (ICBM)—*See ARMAMENTS-Missiles*
INTERIOR, Department of the—*See under U.S. GOVERNMENT*
INTERNAL Revenue Service—*See under U.S. GOVERNMENT*
INTERNATIONAL—*For organizations not listed below, see key words*
INTERNATIONAL Association of Machinists v. Anderson
Case declined by Sup Ct 6-4, 439A2
INTERNATIONAL Atomic Energy Agency—*See under UNITED Nations*
INTERNATIONAL Bank for Economic Cooperation—*See under COMECON*
INTERNATIONAL Bank for Reconstruction and Development (World Bank)—*See under WORLD Bank Group*
INTERNATIONAL Business Machines Corp. (IBM)
Trust case marks 10th yr 1-17, 88D3
Iran office occupied by rebels 2-24, 144B3, D3
Carey on regulatory costs 3-14, 230B3
On '78 Fortune 500 list 5-7, 304E1
Dow Jones index adds to roster 6-28, 481F2
Trust case judge's ouster asked 7-19, 610E2
Watson confrmd USSR amb 8-1, 794D3
MCA joint video disk venture set 9-5, 756E1
Bond sale set 10-4; price drops on FRB credit move, loss rptd 10-11, 765D1
Transamerica trust suit won 10-18, 851F2
USSR mil computer use chrgd 11-8, 857A1
Telex lawyer fee case declined by Sup Ct 12-3, 964C2
Saudis buy notes 12-27, 986F1
INTERNATIONAL Commission of Jurists (ICJ)
Iran press curbs scored 8-14, 615B1
Masie Nguema trial said fair 9-24—9-29, 742A2
INTERNATIONAL Court of Justice—*See under UNITED Nations*
INTERNATIONAL Criminal Police Organization—*See INTERPOL*

1980

INTELSAT—*See INTERNATIONAL Telecommunications Satellite Consortium*
INTENGAN, Rev. Romeo
Sought in Pl bombing 10-31, 874B2

INTER-American Development Bank (IDB) (Argentina, Austria, Barbados, Belgium, Bolivia, Brazil, Canada, Chile, Colombia, Costa Rica, Denmark, Dominican Republic, Ecuador, El Salvador, Finland, France, Great Britain, Guatemala, Guyana, Haiti, Honduras, Israel, Italy, Jamaica, Japan, Mexico, Netherlands, Nicaragua, Panama, Paraguay, Peru, Spain, Sweden, Switzerland, Trinidad & Tobago, Uruguay, U.S., Venezuela, West Germany, Yugoslavia)
Jamaica debt accord set 4-15, 314E2
El Salvador aid rptd blocked re rights repressn 10-15, 829E1
Ortiz reelected pres; finance data, Nicaragua aid rptd 11-1, 864E3
El Salvador gets $45.4 mln loan 12-18, 993G1
INTER-American Press Association (IAPA)
Haiti law stifles press criticism 4-11, 294F2
INTERCOLLEGIATE Athletics for Women, Association for (AIAW)
Conventn: NCAA women's title tourn move scored 1-6—1-10, 103D3-104D1
INTERCONTINENTAL Ballistic Missile (ICBM)—*See ARMAMENTS--Missiles*
INTERESTED Neighborhood Action Inc.
Hayes indicted 5-13, 414F3
INTERFAITH Center on Corporate Responsibility (ICCR)
Guatemala Coca-Cola plant unrest protested 4-16—5-1, 463C3
INTERFERON
Lab productn rptd 1-16, 62G2
Productn rptd increasing 3-5, 317B3
Some cancer success rptd 5-28, 526B2
Genentech stock offer success rptd 10-14, 806A1
INTERIOR, Department of the—*See under U.S. GOVERNMENT*
INTERNAL Revenue Service—*See under U.S. GOVERNMENT*
INTERNATIONAL—*For organizations not listed below, see key words*
INTERNATIONAL Atomic Energy Agency—*See under UNITED Nations*
INTERNATIONAL Bank (Washington, D.C.)
Bahamas bank looting suit rptd 3-3, 229A1
INTERNATIONAL Bank for Reconstruction and Development—*See under WORLD Bank Group*
INTERNATIONAL Bank of West Africa
Citibank funds frozen 1-16, 48D1
INTERNATIONAL Business Council (Chicago, Ill.)
Reagan addresses 9-9, 699C2
INTERNATIONAL Business Machines Corp. (IBM)
In Dow Jones indl avg 76F1
CBS, RCA sign video disk pact 1-10, 120G1
Trust case judge's ouster rejected 2-25, 266C2
Opel elected chief exec officer 3-25, 224E3
Lloyd's computer leasing insurnc losses cited 3-31, 266F1
Phone industry deregulatn set by FCC 4-7, 370D2
On '79 Fortune 500 list 5-5, 290E1
EEOC sues vs Md job bias 6-3, 485G1
Cary named to Synfuels Corp bd 9-13, withdraws 9-24, 725F2
Itel rpts huge '79 loss 10-16, 784G1
Memorex trust suit win rptd upheld 11-20, 917E3
Opel named chief exec 12-21, 986F2
INTERNATIONAL Court of Justice—*See UNITED Nations--World Court*
INTERNATIONAL Development Association—*See under WORLD Bank Group*

1976

INTERNATIONAL Development Association—*See under WORLD Bank Group*

INTERNATIONAL Energy Agency (IEA) (Austria, Belgium, Canada, Denmark, Great Britain, Ireland, Italy, Japan, Luxembourg, Netherlands, New Zealand, Norway, Spain, Sweden, Switzerland, Turkey, U.S., West Germany)
Mtg OKs energy plan 1-30—1-31, 108D1
N Sea oil Euroloans rptd 2-5, 173F3
OKs atomic, oil plans 5-20—5-21, 372F3 *
US GOP platform text cites 8-18, 611B2
Sees OPEC consumer drop 12-20, 975D3

INTERNATIONAL Fund for Animal Welfare
Cancels Canada seal-hunt protest 3-17, 250E3

INTERNATIONAL Herald Tribune (newspaper)
USSR to make more Westn dailies available 1-21, 76A3
Faces Thai censorship 10-11, 775E3

INTERNATIONAL Ladies Garment Workers Union (AFL-CIO)
Chaikin backs Jackson 1-6, 22B3
Chaikin endorses Carter 7-22, 551F1

INTERNATIONAL League for Human Rights (formerly International League for the Rights of Man)
Accuses Paraguay, urges US end aid 4-5, 403E2

INTERNATIONAL Minerals & Chemicals Corp.
Indicted 6-29, 748F1

INTERNATIONAL Monetary Fund (IMF)
Mauritius links rupee to SDR 1-5, 104G2
Jamaica violence 1-6—1-9, 50F3, 51A1
Rpts oil-facility purchases 1-7—4-1, 339F3, 340A2
Jamaica accord on monetary reform 1-8; US, other comments 1-8, 1-9, 13A1-14G2, B3; text excerpts 1-9, 15A1
S Africa standby loan OKd 1-21, 76E2
Italy seeks $500 mln loan 1-22, terms rptd 1-27, 74A2, E2
CAR SDR purchase OKd 2-2, 204C2
Finland import deposit phase-out rptd 2-4, 155D2
Argentina econ plan protested 3-5—3-13, 212C2
Zaire SDR buy, standby loan OKd 3-23, 270D2
Eases oil-facility drawing rules 3-24, 339E3
OKs Uruguay SDR purchase 3-29, 383A1
Turkey SDR purchase OKd 4-1, 315F1
Oil-facility program ends, data rptd 4-1, 339G2, 340A2
OKs Argentina loan 4-2, 264C3
OKs Morocco, Cyprus SDR purchases 4-6, 4-29, 457F1, 458G2
Uganda SDR purchase OKd 4-6, 502A3
OKs Rumania SDR purchase 4-27, 420D3
Wage protest staged 4-28, 340D1
Johan Beyen dies 4-29, 368E2
Gold sales set 5-5; 1st auction 6-2; bidders, buyers rptd 6-3, 6-9, 430G1
Rpts '75 Latin paymts deficit up 5-10, 465G3
Yugo loans OKd 5-24, 5-27, 6-1, 543E3
Spain credit OKd 6-15—6-16, 501F2
7-natn aid to Italy seen 6-27—6-28, 462G1
Cameroon loan rptd 6-30, 910F2
Australia buys SDRs 7-2, 496C2
2d gold auctn 7-14, 530F1
Argentina loan, debt renegotiatn rptd 7-23, 7-25, 553G3, 554B1
NZ OKs SDR purchase loans to: Kenya 7-29, 1012A3; Zambia 8-2, 949G3; Sierra Leone 9-20, 1013C2; S Africa 11-12, 1011A1; 11-29, 1013A2
OKs Uruguay standby credit 8-4, 755D1
Argentina standby credit OKd 8-6, 649A3
S Africa gets loan 8-6, 655B1
Sets new gold auctn procedures 8-24, 624B3
OKs Greek loan 9-9, 854A2
Vietnam joins 9-15, 721D3
3d gold auctn, buyers listed 9-15, 739C3
Gold price rise, auctn linked 9-16, 9-17, 739G3
UK to seek $3.9 bln loan 9-29, 721B1
Group of 24 drops debt moratorium demand 10-2, 778F1
Pl protest march thwarted 10-3, 752A1
Joint World Bank mtgs in Manila 10-4—10-8; analysis 10-10, 10-18, 777A1
Lending funds rptd low; '76, '75 loan totals cited 10-26, 915B1
4th gold auction 10-27; buyers rptd 10-29, 832B2
Rpt banks OK Zaire paymt plan 11-8, 890E2
France backs UK loan 11-12, 880B2 *
Queries US-Portugal aid scheme 11-25, 966C3
5th gold auction, reserves restitutn set 12-8, 915A3
Andreotti ends US visit 12-8, 947D1
British Loan Issue
Group of 10 in UK loan offer 6-7; UK long-term request seen 6-8, 407A2, F2
UK hikes lending rate 10-11, 773C1

1977

INTERNATIONAL Development Association—*See under WORLD Bank Group*

INTERNATIONAL Development Issues, Independent Commission on
Meets 12-9—12-11, 977F3

INTERNATIONAL Economic Policy, Council on—*See under U.S. GOVERNMENT*

INTERNATIONAL Energy Agency (IEA) (Austria, Belgium, Canada, Denmark, Great Britain, Ireland, Italy, Japan, Luxembourg, Netherlands, New Zealand, Norway, Spain, Sweden, Switzerland, Turkey, U.S., West Germany)
Carter energy plan reactn 4-21, 320D3
Oil '85 consumptn lid OKd 10-5—10-6, 793E3-794C1

INTERNATIONAL Finance Corp.—*See under WORLD Bank Group*

INTERNATIONAL Harvester Co.
To promote S Africa equality 3-1, 160B3

INTERNATIONAL Herald Tribune S.A. (newspaper)
Trib NY files trust suit 9-13, 723E1

INTERNATIONAL Joint Commission (IJC)
Rpt scores US Garrison projct 1-7, 60C3
US halts Garrison projct 2-18, 133A1
Scores Garrison projct 9-19, 725G3

INTERNATIONAL Labor Organization—*See under UNITED Nations*

INTERNATIONAL Ladies Garment Workers Union (ILGWU)
Chaikin sees Carter, workers protest imports 4-13, 271E2, A3
Louis Stulberg dies 12-14, 1024D3

INTERNATIONAL League for Human Rights (formerly International League for the Rights of Man)
Kurd deportatns chrgd 1-16, 257B1

INTERNATIONAL Longshoremen's Association v. NLRB
Sup Ct refuses review 1-10, 57G1

INTERNATIONAL Minerals & Chemical Corp.
Price-fixing chrgs dismissed 6-10, 483D3, F3

INTERNATIONAL Monetary Fund (IMF)
Vietnam gets loan 1-11, 23G2
SDR defined 87G2
'76 lending sets record 3-7, 208F3
Carter addresses UN 3-17, 185B2
Paymts debt managing role rptd 3-28, com backs lending facility 4-29, Saudis rpt role 5-3, 5-4, 362A3
Arab fund created 4-18, 317G3
7-natn summit backs paymts fund 5-7—5-8, 357A2
Intl consortium OKs Egypt aid 5-11—5-12, 390B3
Bankers conf on 3d World debt 5-22—5-25, 437C3, G3
Rpts '74-77 banks forgn lending 6-5, 438B1
Group of 10 membership cited 438F1
Trade protectionism seen rising 7-31, 586A3
'76 world trade rptd up 7-31, 586C3
Witteveen paymts fund agreed 8-6, 754B2
World econ survey issued 9-11, 700C2
Turkey devalues lira 9-21, 730F3
Witteveen to retire 9-21, 754E2
Commonwealth finance mins discuss loan terms 9-21—9-24, 936D2
Joint World Bank mtgs in DC 9-26—9-30, Witteveen speaks 9-26, 9-30, 753C2
Loans rptd down Jan-Aug 9-26—9-30, 754D2
African Developments
Tanzania loan OKd 1-26, 102B3
Congo loan OKd 2-2, 203F1
Gambia loan OKd 3-16, 394B3
Guinea-Bissau joins 3-24, 309C2
Zaire loans OKd 4-26, 394B2
Gambia standby loan OKd 5-18, 710G2
Malawi loan OKd 5-20, 710D3
Mauritania standby loan OKd 5-25, 710E3
Sao Tome e Principe admitted 9-30, 754D2
S Africa ex-dir killed 11-23, 934E3
British Loan Issue
UK loan set 1-3, 7C3
UK sterling accord set 1-12, 20B3
UK sets indl, sterling policies 1-12, 44F2
Gold Issues
Gold auction 1-26, trust loans set 2-4, 87F1-G2
Gold auctions, new schedule set 3-2, 4-6, 5-4, 145D3, 335G3
London gold price, auctions linked 3-18, 336C1
Gold sale proceeds rptd 10-5, 792F3
Gold auctns held 11-2, 12-7, total proceeds rptd 12-7, 933E3
Italy Loan Issue
Loan endangered by labor dispute 1-6, 8F2
Bonn backs loan 1-18, 64F3
Italy acts to meet terms 1-26 2-4, 116E2, A3
Loan OKd 4-25, 527C2
Latin American Developments
'76 Chile loan total rptd 3-18, 449E1
Peru loan terms stir controversy 4-13—5-17, 427D2
Mex $1.2 bln loan rptd 5-6, 527D3
Peru sets austerity program 6-10, 488F1, C2
Peru econ min, bank execs quit 7-6, 7-11; new min contacts IMF 7-12, 563E2-B3
Jamaica loan granted 7-12; terms detailed, radicals score 10-7, 884G2, D3
Peru rejects more devaluatns 7-20, 618E2

1978

INTERNATIONAL Development Association (IDA)—*See under WORLD Bank Group*

INTERNATIONAL Dunes Hotel (Salt Lake City, Utah)
Widow, 6 children die in plunge 8-3, 685C3

INTERNATIONAL Energy Agency (IEA) (Austria, Belgium, Canada, Denmark, Great Britain, Greece, Ireland, Italy, Japan, Luxembourg, Netherlands, New Zealand, Norway, Spain, Sweden, Switzerland, Turkey, U.S., West Germany)
Oil shortage by '85 warned; import curbs lag; US, Canada inactn scored 6-5, 449E3 *, 450B1

INTERNATIONAL Energy Associates Ltd.
Study backs breeder dvpt 5-10, 346C3

INTERNATIONAL Finance Corp.—*See under WORLD Bank Group*

INTERNATIONAL Harvester Co.
In Dow Jones indl avg 66E2
McCardell heads '77 top-paid execs list 5-15, 364E3, 365B1
USSR seizes Crawford 6-12, 476C2; Carter scores 6-26, 491E1
Crawford released 6-26, 506G1
Suspends USSR deals 7-16, 575D3
Crawford sentence suspended 9-7, leaves USSR 9-8; sales resume 9-11, 742B3

INTERNATIONAL Investment Bank
US banks shun Comecon loan 8-17, 660D3

INTERNATIONAL Labor Organization (ILO)—*See under UNITED Nations*

INTERNATIONAL Ladies Garment Workers Union
Chaikin in Chile, says labor repressn continues 5-23, 452C3

INTERNATIONAL League for Human Rights (formerly International League for the Rights of Man)
Rpts Paraguay rights 'crisis' 1-10, 113B2
Iran rights improvemt seen 11-23, 954F1

INTERNATIONAL Monetary Fund (IMF)
SDR defined 148A3
Spain $295 mln credit OKd 2-7, 395B1
Turkey devalues currency 23% 3-1, 170A3
US sells SDRs to W Ger 3-13, 234C3
Turkey $450 mln loan granted 3-24, 291G3
Burns urges $ defns measures 3-31, 235C2
Offcl gold price abolished 4-1, 300G3
SDR valuatn revised 4-3, 300A3
UK proposes loan repaymt 4-11, 267F2
UK tax votes threaten budget limit 5-8, 5-10, 415B2
EC monetary zone, reserve fund proposed 7-6—7-7, 545D2
US Cong OKs Witteveen fund contributn 9-22, 731E2, 732B1 *
Interim com backs quota hike, SDR issue 9-24, 731E3
Joint World Bank mtg marked by optimism, growth rate convergence stressed 9-25—9-28, 731B2
US Cong clears Witteven fund contributn 10-13, Carter signs 10-18, 862F2
US Cong aid actn cited 10-15, 784G3
US loan to aid $ rptd, denied 10-30—10-31, 825G2
UK repays $1 bln 10-30, 838D3
US sets $ rescue plan 11-1, 825B2
Turkey rejcts austerity demands 11-4, 905A3
US borrows marks, yen 11-7, 998C3
African Developments
Zambia mission 2-14—3-7, loans OKd 4-26, 333D2
Mauritius standby purchase OKd 2-27, 333D3
Gabon loan OKd 6-1, 596B2
Zaire emergency aid OKd 6-13—6-14, 478A1, D1
Sudan loans set 6-29, 595E1
Zambia loan cited 6-29, 617A2
Sen OKs Uganda trade ban amendmt to funds bill 7-28, 616E2
Sudan loan rptd 9-21, 925E3
Zambia reopens Rhodesia RR 10-10, 783A3
Senegal SDR purchase rptd 10-30, 885C3
Zaire aid OKd by creditors 11-10, 1021B2
Kenya loan OKd 11-14, 968A2
Latin American Developments
Jamaica devalues $ 1-20, 94G3
Peru aid barred 3-10, talks rptd 5-11, 353E1
Argentina '78 budget deficit rptd 3-24, 310G2
Peru sets price hikes 5-15, warns IMF 5-20; offcls see intl bankers 5-23—5-24, 394A1, G1, C2
Jamaica $245 mln loan OKd, govt sets austerity 6-12, 777A2
New Peru pact reached 8-7, 669D1
Guyana OKs loan terms 8-8, 688A3
Peru miners strike broken 9-8, 775A3
Peru $311 mln loans cleared 9-19, 776D1
Nicaragua loan postponed 11-1, 883G2
Portugal Loan Issue
Portugal austerity pact 1-19, Soares vows talks renewal 1-30, 91G3, 92B1
US grants $300 mln loan 3-2, 229A2
Talks resume 3-29, austerity measures agreed 4-3, 4-5; Assemb OKs budget 4-13, 331B2
GNP growth target rptd 3% 4-14, 331F2
Da Costa govt backs austerity pact 9-7; govt falls 9-14, 758B1

1979

INTERNATIONAL Energy Agency (IEA) (Austria, Belgium, Canada, Denmark, Great Britain, Greece, Ireland, Italy, Japan, Luxembourg, Netherlands, New Zealand, Norway, Spain, Sweden, Switzerland, Turkey, U.S., West Germany)
Exxon defends Canada oil shipmt cuts 2-15, 153E2
5% oil demand cut agreed, OPEC welcomes 3-2, 161F3-162C1
Australia joins 3-2, 162C1
France OKs EC oil import cut 3-13, 180G1
US ends domestic oil price controls 4-5, 250G2
Belgium sets oil consumption curbs 4-12, 396E3
Japan asks Sunday gas statn closings 5-21, 389C2
Oil cutback vow renewed 5-22, 380E1
US oil import subsidy scored 6-1, 417A2
Sweden oil aid rptd 6-4, 396E2
Tokyo summit sets energy tech group 6-29, 493F2
Canada rptd top gas user 7-11, 542B3

INTERNATIONAL Harvester Co.
In Dow Jones indl avg 72F1
McCardell on '78 top-paid execs list 5-14, 347E3
UAW strikes 10-31, 987G1

INTERNATIONAL Home Video Club Inc.
Times gets Peoples Temple tape copy 3-15, 219G2

INTERNATIONAL Ladies Garment Workers Union (ILGWU) (AFL-CIO)
Chaikin urges Meany emeritus role, less Carter criticism 2-20, 149C1
NE workers pact set 5-30, 402E1
Chaikin backs Carter reelectn 7-30, 593C3

INTERNATIONAL Monetary Fund (IMF)
Conf held in DC, EMS rptd set 3-7, 160E3
Gold sale cutback set, profits rptd 5-14, 435D3
Annual rpt sees '80 stagflatn, cites OPEC increases 9-16, 719F3-720E1
Joint World Bank mtgs in Belgrade marked by $, inflatn woes 10-2—10-5; de Larosiere speaks 10-2, 10-5, 779F2-F3
'70s gold trading role cited 12-31, 978D2
African Developments
Ghana standby loan OKd 1-10, 172G3
Zaire anti-corruptn drive rptd 2-11, 215E1, A2
Senegal loan OKd 3-30, 411G2
Zaire loan set 8-28, 999B1
European Developments
Poland econ to be monitored by Westn banks 1-11, 60A1
UK rpts early loan repaymt 4-3, 268G1
Rumania loan OKd 4-6, 374B3
Latin American Developments
Jamaica gas price riots 1-8—1-10, 21E2
Peru strike fails 1-10, 39B2
St Lucia dvpt aid rptd 2-21, 181F2
Nicaragua devalues currency, seeks standby loan 4-6, 270A1*, 372F3
Nicaragua standby loan protested 4-25, 332E1; 5-10, 373A1; OKd 5-14, 372B3
Jamaica $350 mln loan OKd 6-13, 566B2
Guyana strikes threaten loan 7-23—8-28, 687F2
Nicaragua loan probe rptd urged 8-6, 603G1
Jamaica austerity plan fails 10-9, loan to be rescheduled 12-15; Cabt resigns 12-17, 995G3-996B2
Peru debt prepaymt agreed 11-26, 951F2
Nicaragua loan misuse rptd 11-27, 909F3
Bolivia peso devaluatn backed, loan set 12-3, 926D1, G1
Middle East Developments
Saudi money reserves rptd less 12-12, 968C3
Portugal Loan Issue
Portugal meets current acct deficit limit 1-30, 212A3
Talks resume, no pact reached 2-7—3-6, 212B3
Intl banks lend Portugal $300 mln 5-25, 409F2
Turkey Loan Issue
Aid demand dispute cited 2-7, 116F3
Econ rescue plan announced 3-16, devaluatn barred 3-21, 214F1-C2
Currency devalued 4-10, 333A2
Aid, negotiatns linked 5-30, 397F1, B2
USSR econ deal, negotiatns linked 6-5, 488B3
Devaluatn, other austerity steps set 6-12, 447C1
Accord announced 6-13, 447E1

1980

INTERNATIONAL Development Research Center
Rpt calls 3d World aid matter of survival 8-27, 669E1

INTERNATIONAL Energy Agency (IEA) (Australia, Austria, Belgium, Canada, Denmark, Great Britain, Greece, Ireland, Italy, Japan, Luxembourg, Netherlands, New Zealand, Norway, Spain, Sweden, Switzerland, Turkey, U.S., West Germany)
'80 oil import cuts, '81 quotas delayed; '79 moves rptd 2-19, 142B1
Venice summit endorses goals 6-23, 473D2
Paris emergency mtg: oil stock depletn pledged; reserves estimated 10-1, 759A2
OPEC stockpiling data disputed, '80 supplies estimated 11-23, 895A3
'81 oil buying curb set 12-9, 932A1

INTERNATIONAL Federation of the Rights of Man
Sovt poison gas use in Afghan rptd 3-5, 205G2-A3

INTERNATIONAL Harvester Co.
In Dow Jones indl avg 76F1
UAW strike ends 4-20, 308E2
Arab boycott data released 10-20, 801B1

INTERNATIONAL Labor Organization—*See under UNITED Nations*

INTERNATIONAL Ladies Garment Workers Union (ILGWU) (AFL-CIO)
Backs Carter-Mondale ticket 1-15, 32A3
Chaiken seconds Carter renominatn 8-13, 611C3
Polish worker aid rptd 9-4, 659C3
Carter addresses conv 9-29, 738G3
Bobbie Brooks '77 bias case setld 12-21, 988C1

INTERNATIONAL Monetary Fund (IMF)
Gold sale nets record price 1-2, 30B2
UN dvpt aid fund disputed 2-9, 124C2
N-S study urges aid plan 2-12, 124D3
Interest rates on SDRs lifted 3-27, 302A2
$ support plan shelved, 1st 1/4 loans rptd 4-24, 301F3
Venice summit backs 3d World credit reforms 6-23, 474C1
World econ forecast rptd 6-24, 477D2
Muskie, Rao address UN aid talks 8-25, 642C3, E3
Group of 10 studies oil debt role 9-15, US House OKs fund quota-hike authorizatn 9-18, 720A1
SDR valuatn method chngd, currency 'basket' cut to 5 9-17, 695C1
US fund quota hike clears Sen 9-23, signed 10-7; funding rider clears Cong 12-15, signed 12-16, 981D3, 982C1
Joint World Bank mtg in DC 9-30—10-3, Carter cites 'political' threat 9-30, 761A2, G3, 766A3
OPEC postpones 3d World aid mtg 10-6, 759D1
50% quota increase OKd, US share delayed; Jan-Oct lending rptd 12-1, 913F3
African Developments
Zaire fails to meet loan terms, new conditns set 4-24, 356B2
Morocco $1.1 bln loan rptd OKd 10-17, 778E1
Asian Developments
China admitted, Taiwan removed 4-17, 302C2
SDR valuatn revised, yen gains in currency 'basket' 9-17, 695E1
Pak loan OKd, Sovts protest 11-25, 904D3
European Developments
SDR valuatn revised; mark, franc, pound gain in currency 'basket' 9-17, 695E1
Latin American Developments
Jamaican prime min sees Larosiere, loan talks fail 1-15; '79 forgn debt cited 1-17, 99E1
CR '79 austerity pkg, standby credit rptd 2-1, 117F1
Jamaica bars new talks 3-25; intl banks rejct loan request, urge IMF compromise 4-7, 276A1
Jamaica, forgn banks reach debt agrmt 4-15, 314C2
Jamaica debt refinancing plan advances 6-4, 465C1
Guyana loan OKd 7-25, 791C2
Bolivia debt paymts postponed 9-3, 686B3
Manley sets Oct 30 electns 10-5, 791F3
El Salvador aid rptd blocked re rights repressn 10-15, 829E1
Seaga wins Jamaica electn 10-30, new talks seen 11-1, 854D2
Haiti aid OKd 12-5, 943A1
Brazil seeks trade surplus 12-17, 991F3
Middle East Developments
Saudis, Kuwait freeze loans to World Bank over PLO issue 8-2, 592A2
PLO statue disputed; US, Arabs threaten funding cutoff 9-4—9-22; dirs bar observer role 9-18, 719D3-720A1
Turkey Loan Issue
Lira devalued 1-24, 61A1, C1
New econ steps rptd 1-25, 80B1
Turkey loan OKd 2-21, 135D3
OECD aid pkg deferred 3-26, 236E2
IMF econ proposals rptd 5-6, 446C1
$1.6 bln loan OKd 6-18, 468D1

1976

UK £ fall linked to loan requiremt rumors 10-25, 809D3, 810A1
UK £ at record low 10-28, loan seen 11-11, 853C2, F2
UK seeks loan link to sterling balances plan, US vs 11-16—11-17, 880C3
UK sets budget cuts, rpts loan support 12-15; OECD panel OKs 12-21, 1003A3-G3
Group of 10 OKs loan 12-21, 1004A1

INTERNATIONAL Nickel Co.
No Guatemala quake damage rptd 2-24, 155F3

INTERNATIONAL Olympic Committee (IOC)—*See SPORTS—Olympic Games*

INTERNATIONAL Paper Co.
Trust suit dvpts 2-18—10-5, 886D1, F2

INTERNATIONAL Telephone & Telegraph Corp. (ITT)
Spanish unit struck 1-12, 54D2
House intellignc com rpt leaked 1-26, 93G1
Belgian phone head sentncd 2-23, 220A3
Forgn payoffs rptd 3-12, 4-16, 5-12; limited disclosures ordrd 5-5, 360F3-361F1
Fortune rpts '75 work force drop 437F2
SEC lists paymts 5-12, 728B2
Hendrix chrgd re Chile probe 11-5, 869E2
Sheraton Corp. of America
US Jews cancel Brazil tours 1-15, 27G2
Privacy comm probe testimony 2-13, 151E2, G2
Corp, units indicted 11-17, 989F2

INTERPOL (International Criminal Police Organization)
Argentina asks Lopez Rega arrest 10-25, 997F1

INTERSTATE Folding Box Co.
Trust suit dvpts 2-18—10-5, 886D1, E2; Bergstein sentncd 11-30, 921G2

INTEXT Inc.
US files consent decree 7-27, 989A2

IN The Beginning (book)
On best seller list 1-25, 80B3; 2-29, 208E3; 12-5, 972G2

IN the Shadows of the Angels (film)
Israel protests at Cannes 5-14—5-28, 460A2

INTRAUTERINE Device (IUD)—*See BIRTH Control & Family Planning*

INVESTIGATIVE Reporters and Editors Inc. (IRE)
Probes Ariz crime 10-2, 849B2

INVESTORS Diversified Services Inc.
Carter defends Mondale tax bill 7-20, 532C2

INVESTORS Overseas Services, Ltd. (IOS)—*See under INTERNATIONAL Controls Corp.*

IOANNIDES, Brig. Gen. Demetrios (ret.)
Sentenced on 2 more chrgs 1-10, 73E1
Sentncd re '75 conspiracy 3-16, 221C3

IOC (International Olympic Committee)—*See SPORTS—Olympic Games*

IONIAN Sea
US, Sovt ships collide 8-28, 941B3

IONITA, Gen. Ion
Replaced 6-15, 440B2

IOWA
Carter wins Dem vote, Ford edges Reagan 1-19, 40G3
Des Moines on US jobless list 5-5, 347E2
Indian ldr shot, 4 seized 5-5, 384E2
Mrs Ford, Reagan in Des Moines 6-18, 451B1
GOP conv results 6-19, 450F2, 451A1
Dem conv women delegates, table 508B2
Dem conv pres vote, table 7-14, 507C2
GOP pre-conv delegate count 8-14, 583B3
Reagan seeks conv delegates 8-17, 601B3
GOP conv pres, vp vote tables 8-18—8-19, 8-19, 599C1, C3
Carter in Des Moines 8-24—8-25, 631G2, G3
Dole in Des Moines 8-26, 632B2, E2
Fscl '75 per capita income, tax burden rptd 9-15, 10-12, 959C2
Mondale campaigns 10-6, 763D3
Dole in Waterloo 10-17, 804E1
Dole stumps 11-1, 827B3
Election results 11-2: pres 818B1, G1, E2, 819A2; cong 820D2, 823C2, 829C3

1977

Peru, IMF offcls meet 8-22—8-23, 9-26—9-30; loan agreemt reached 9-30, sol floated 10-10, 784F2, 785A2
Argentina $137 mln loan OKd 9-19, 981F2
Colombia '77 inflatn rptd 11-14, 1011E1
Mex loan terms spurs Cabt crisis 11-17, Portillo backs IMF 12-2, 966C3
Peru gets 90 mln SDRs line 11-18, 1015C2
Mex austerity progrm success rptd, loan ceiling hike seen 12-1, 967A1, D1
Mex '78 budget announced 12-15, 985G1
US lauds Peru pact 12-17, 1015C2
Portugal Loan Issue
Portugal-US loan talks 4-20—4-22, Eanes wary 4-25, 330A3
Portugal CP score austerity measures 8-26, govt rejcts loan terms 11-15, 886F1, C2
Portugal premr defends talks 12-6, 947E2

INTERNATIONAL Olympic Committee (IOC)—*See SPORTS—Olympic Games*

INTERNATIONAL Rescue Committee
Viet refugees arrive US 9-20, 739G3

INTERNATIONAL Telephone & Telegraph Corp. (ITT)
Carbon takeover cited in table 880G1
Indonesia Fed Elec contract rptd 1-25, 182C3
Hamilton named chief exec 2-9, 140C2
Hartford age-bias suit rptd 2-9, 279B1
Merger cited 2-18, 274A3
Hartford suits setld 3-4, 194B3
Land-fraud setlmt rptd 3-11, 203D3
On '76 Fortune 500 list 340E1
Sheraton Hawaii unit fined 5-11, 504D2
French left seeks natlizatn 5-17, 543B1
Sues AT&T 6-10, 520C2
Norton Simon buys Avis control 6-27, 519A2
SEC trust chrgs re Hartford settled 10-13, 980B3
Westn Union Hawaii svc case review declined 10-17, 798A1
'71 Hartford divestiture setlmt cited 11-14, 880A1

INTERNATIONAL Wool Secretariat
Australian productn drop forecast 8-19, 652E3

INTERPOL (International Criminal Police Organization)
Bonn denies Daoud warrant role 1-10, 9A2
Confirms Roschmann death 8-13, 670E3

INTER Press Service (news agency)
M'Bumba interview 4-8, 266B1

INTERSTATE Commerce Commission—*See under U.S. GOVERNMENT*

INTERSTATE United Corp.
Rebates, pol paymts rptd 3-16, 215F2

IN the Region of Ice (film)
Wins Oscar 3-28, 264D1

INTRAUTERINE Device (IUD)—*See BIRTH Control*

INUIT (Eskimos)—*See also CANADA—Indians & Inuit*
Intl conf held 6-13—6-17, 619C2
Greenland, Denmark accord rptd 7-13, 672A2
Sirica vs whaling ban 10-21; ruling reversed, Burger backs ban 10-24, 835A2
Whaling ban lifted, quota scored 12-7, 936A3, D3

INVENTORIES—*See BUSINESS—Statistics; ECONOMY—GNP*

INVESTIGATIVE Reporters and Editors Inc. (IRE)
Ariz Mafia ties probed 3-13—4-20, 568F1
Ariz drug rings rptd 4-3, 332G3
2 guilty in Ariz rptr's death 11-6, 871E2

INVESTORS Diversified Services Inc.
SEC sues, settles 7-19, 612A3

INVESTORS Overseas Services Ltd. (IOS) (defunct)
CR suit vs Vesco rptd 6-9, 506G1
CR ordrs Vesco fraud trial 9-12, 767D1
ICC settles Vesco claims 12-7, 980G2

IOC (International Olympic Committee)—*See SPORTS—Olympic Games*

IONA (Mich.) State Hospital
CIA mind-control tests revealed 8-1—8-9, 611E1

IONESCU, Constantin
Rptd ousted 11-23, 948A2

IOWA
Legislature schedule rptd 6D2
US Sup Ct sidesteps Miranda rule review 3-23, 275B3
Fed spending inequities chrgd 4-6, 423D3
'76 per-capita income table 5-10, 387D2
Des Moines econ data table 5-16, 384F2
Smith obscenity convictn upheld 5-23, 444C2
Drought damage to corn crop rptd, fed aid OKd 8-24, 660A1
'76 per capita income, tax burden table 9-13, 10-18, 821C2
Carter in Des Moines 10-21—10-22, 817B1
Farm strike backing rptd 12-22, 1003D1

1978

INTERNATIONAL Olympic Committee (IOC)—*See SPORTS—Olympic Games*

INTERNATIONAL Paper Co.
In Dow Jones indl avg 66F2
Indicted for price fixing 1-25, 67B2
Settles '76, '78 trust suits 8-25, 10-1, 768D3
Fined 10-13, 1005G2
Atlanta & St. Andrews Bay Railroad
Fla derailmt kills 8 2-26, US rpts sabotage 3-3, 196F1

INTERNATIONAL Stores Holdings Ltd.—*See under B.A.T. Industries*

INTERNATIONAL Stud (play)
Opens 5-22, 887A2

INTERNATIONAL Telephone & Telegraph Corp. (ITT)
GTE trust suit won 3-1, 510A3
Gerrity, Berrellez chrgd for '73 Chile testimony; Geneen suit declined 3-20; CIA cover-up hinted 3-21, 206C3
On '77 Fortune 500 list 5-8, 325E1
Geneen on '77 top-paid execs list 5-15, 364F3
Hartford merger case cited 7-28, 767F1
US drops 3 chrgs vs Gerrity 8-18, 643B3
Sup Ct denies stay on sealed SEC data 10-30, 832C2
SEC sues, chrgs forgn paymts 11-2, 876B1-B3

INTERNATIONAL Velvet (film)
Released 7-19, 970G1

INTERPOL (International Criminal Police Organization)
Honduras offcl seized in drug scandal 4-24, 614E3
Scientologists indicted 8-15, 644D3

INTERSTATE Brands Corp.—*See DPF Inc.*

INTERSTATE Commerce Commission (ICC)—*See under U.S. GOVERNMENT*

IN the Deserts of This Earth (book)
Translatn wins Natl Book Award 4-10, 315A3

IN the Recovery Lounge (play)
Opens 12-7, 1031B2

INTOURIST (Soviet tourist agency)
NY office bombed 7-10, 542A3

INUIT (Eskimos)—*See also CANADA—Indians & Inuit*
Maria Kuhne dies 4-16, 356A3
Covered in US minority business contracts ruling 9-23, 811E2

INVADERS, The (black group)
King death role denied 11-17, 938D2

INVASION of the Body Snatchers (film)
Released 12-21, 1030A3

INVENTIONS & Inventors—*See also PATENTS*
Columbia U gets Armstrong papers 5-21, 844C2
Roberts wins Sears patent suit 10-2, 844B2
Obituaries
Bray, John R 10-10, 888E2
Hasselblad, Victor 8-6, 708A3
Lear, William Powell 5-14, 440B3
Poulter, Thomas C 6-14, 540E3

INVESTIGATION, The (book)
On best-seller list 6-4, 460D3

INVESTORS Diversified Services Inc.
Kirby-Murchison '60 proxy fight cited 3-24, 402A3

INVESTORS Overseas Services Ltd. (IOS) (defunct)
Vesco ICC case review barred 1-9, 13A2
Vesco indicted in CR 3-16, 269C3
Vesco chrgs dismissed 4-30, 354F2
Vesco 'pol fix' chrg denied by Admin 9-10; Anderson revises column 9-11, 719G3

INVOLUNTARY Servitude—*See CRIME—Kidnaping*

IOANNIDES, George
Named Cyprus min to the pres 3-8, 189A2

IOC (International Olympic Committee)—*See SPORTS—Olympic Games*

IOS—*See INVESTORS Overseas Services*

IOWA
Legislature schedule rptd 14E3
'67, '77 sales-tax rates rptd 1-5, 15D3
Cowles Communicatns to liquidate 1-6, 75G3
State govt tax revenue table 1-9, 84C2
Press info order case review refused by Sup Ct 5-15, 388A1
Primary results 6-6, 448E1
Dems pres nominatn rules 6-9, 448G2
Business tax formula backed by US Sup Ct 6-15, 468E2
A-plant moratorium cited 8-17, 665F2
Election results 11-7: cong 845D1, 846B1, A3, 848F1, 850C4, 854B2, D2; state 847C1, 853E2, 854C2, 897B3
Palo A-plant rating rptd 11-25, 940D3
Rape law revisn cited 12-27, 1028D3

1979

INTERNATIONAL Olympic Committee (IOC)—*See SPORTS—Olympic Games*

INTERNATIONAL Paper Co.
In Dow Jones indl avg 72F1
Bodcaw purchase set; Weyerhaeuser, Mobil outbid 3-8, 350A1
Mobil bid to acquire Gen Crude OKd 3-28, 282G3
1st 1/4 merger rise rptd 4-10, 349B3
Gee on '78 top-paid exec list 5-14, 347F3
Bodcaw purchased 8-9, Placid to buy oil interests 8-10, 664F1

INTERNATIONAL Society for Krishna Consciousness v. Bowen
Case refused by Sup Ct 11-26, 919G2

INTERNATIONAL Systems and Controls Corp. (ISC)
SEC chrgs forgn paymts 7-9, 541E3

INTERNATIONAL Telephone & Telegraph Corp. (ITT)
Long-distance phone svc OKd 1-4, 15A2
US drops Berrellez perjury chrgs 2-8, 88C1
Rayonier paper workers strike ends 2-13, 345G2
US drops Gerrity perjury chrgs 3-7, 188G1
Continental bread fiber chrg setld 3-25, 308C3
Long-distance phone svc offered 4-23, 350F3
On '78 Fortune 500 list 5-7, 304E1
Hamilton quits as chief exec, Araskog succeeds 7-11, 517A2
SEC paymt chrgs setld 8-8, 648D1

INTERPOL (International Criminal Police Organization)
Stolen film probe rptd 1-10, 102E2

INTERSTATE Commerce Commission—*See under U.S. GOVERNMENT*

INTERWAY Corp.
Transamerica to acquire 5-29, 560B2

IN Through the Out Door (recording)
On best-seller list 9-5, 672F3; 10-3, 800F3

INUIT (Eskimos)—*See CANADA-Indians & Inuit*

INVASION of the Body Snatchers (film)
Top-grossing film 1-10, 80G3

INVENTIONS & Inventors—*See also PATENTS*
Exxon unveils alternating current synthesizer 5-18, 404G1
Sears ordrd to pay Roberts 5-31, 466C2
Borg-Warner develops alternating current inverter 10-2, 770E2
Obituaries
Blodgett, Katharine 10-12, 860B2
Gabor, Dennis 2-8, 176A3

INVESTORS Overseas Services Ltd. (IOS) (defunct)
Vesco jury foreman quits, claims cover-up 8-29, 647F2
Cornfeld acquitted 10-15, 817F3

IOC (International Olympic Committee)—*See SPORTS—Olympic Games*

IONA (British Island)
Rptd for sale 3-23, 268C2
Purchased by Scottish millionaire 5-24, 407E1

IOWA
Blizzards hit 1-12–1-14, 1-24–1-27, 120F1
Criminal confessn case declined by US Sup Ct 1-22, 54G1
Clergy malpractice insurnc OKd 4-9, 376D1
Legal drinking age cited 4-16, 309E3
Diesel fuel shortage rptd 5-18, 361A3
State age bias filings required by US Sup Ct, time limit barred 5-21, 400D2
Marijuana med use rptd OKd 6-1, 492B3
Amish polio outbreak rptd 6-5, 472F1
Clark '78 labor gifts rptd 6-13, 595D1
Indian land case laws backed by Sup Ct 6-20, 516A2
Burger assails Sup Ct bar admissn 6-25, 541B2
'78 per capita income rptd 9-16, 746D2
Cnty employees papal holiday suit filed 9-24, 760D3
Pope visits country parish, farm museum 10-4, 759B1-A2; cost estimated 761A2
Milwaukee Rd embargoes track 11-1–11-5, 867G2
Politics & Government
Legislature schedule rptd 5D3
Dole speaks in Des Moines 2-16, 124E1
Carter in Des Moines 5-4, 346C3-347A1
Draft-Kennedy activity rptd 5-23, 384E2
Carter backers fear pres caucus defeat 8-2, 593B1
Carter addresses crowds 8-19, holds Burlington town mtg 8-22, 622D2, G2, 662D2
Carter wins straw vote 11-3, 866G2-B3
Kennedy campaigns 11-12, 11-29, 962D1, E1
Brown invited into debate 12-4, 962A3
Connally urges Reagan join GOP forum 12-12, 982E3
Carter to skip debate 12-28; reactn 12-28–12-31, 983E2

1980

INTERNATIONAL Paper Co.
In Dow Jones indl avg 76F1
Fine paper trust suit acquittal rptd 12-3, 917A2

INTERNATIONAL Rescue Committee
Cambodia blocks aid convoy 2-6, 108B2

INTERNATIONAL Research and Exchanges Board
US-USSR exchngs said continuing 2-22, 135G1

INTERNATIONAL Shoe Co. v. Washington
Case cited by Sup Ct 1-21, 93G1

INTERNATIONAL Telecommunications Satellite Consortium (Intelsat)
CBS barred from Cuba broadcast 5-22, 397F1
CBS Cuba broadcasts cleared 6-1, 420G2

INTERNATIONAL Telephone & Telegraph Corp. (ITT)
AT&T trust chrgs setld 2-27, 240B1
On '79 Fortune 500 list 5-5, 290E1
Austria offcl rptd arrested in hosp scandal 8-27, 667G2

INTERNATIONAL Telecommunications Satellite Consortium (Intelsat)
US asks Iran bar 4-17, 281E1

INTERSTATE Commerce Commission (ICC)—*See under U.S. GOVERNMENT*

INTERSTATE Paving Co.
Offcls bid-rigging guilty pleas rptd 7-5, 655A2

INTERVIEW, The (play)
Opens 4-24, 392C3

INUIT (Eskimos)—*See also CANADA--Indians*
USSR '79 census rptd 2-9, 152E3
Govt constructn grants upheld by Sup Ct 7-2, 510C1
Alaska offshore oil lease curbs lifted 7-3, 7-8, 552G3

INVENTIONS & Inventors
G&W claims elec car dvpt 6-5, 541E3
Patent law revisn clears Cong 11-21, 915E3; signed 12-12, 982B1
Obituaries
Drew, Richard G 12-7, 1004D1
Gifford, William 3-9, 279B3
Kennedy, George C 3-18, 279F3
Laker, Edwin Francis 3-1, 279G3
Mauchly, John W 1-8, 104B3
Sisler, Frederick D 3-2, 280B2

INVESTMENT Company Institute
FRB money mkt funds reserve rule contested 3-20, 223E2, 224A1
FRB rejcts money mkt reserve rule plea 5-22, 400G1

ION, Corneliu
Wins Olympic medal 7-25, 623D2

I Ought to be in Pictures (play)
Opens 4-3, 392D3
Manoff wins Tony 6-8, 692C3

IOWA
Des Moines Register privacy case refused by Sup Ct 2-25, 188A1
Stockport grain elevator scandal rptd 2-25, consumer suit filed 3-12, 237F3
Milwaukee Rd svc cut set 2-25, 346B1
Ia City firefighter wins breast-feeding case 3-20, 441G3
Farm cancer study rptd 4-15, 357A3
Alcan gas pipe eastn leg OKd 4-24, 331A1
DES in cattle rptd 4-24, 358F1
Stockport grain fraud probe rptd 5-14, 414E2
Schools buy White House uniforms 5-16, 460A3
'Pyramid' money schemes rptd 5-17, 655A3
Politics & Government—*See also other appropriate subheads in this section*
Legislature schedule rptd 18D1
Election results 11-4: cong 837D2, 840F1, 842C4, 845A2, 851A1; state 845E2, 847G2, B3
'80 census rptd 12-31, 983E1
Presidential Election (& Transition)
Pres campaign dvpts 1-4—1-10, 10E1, 12F2-13F1, A2, G2-D3
GOP pres debate in Des Moines 1-5, 4C2
Kennedy campaigns 1-11, 1-14, 32B3, E3
Reagan, Carter lead in polls 1-11, 33D1-A2
Mondale debates Kennedy, Brown 1-12, 32D2
GOP platform hearing set 1-14, 32A1
State of State message 1-15, 269A2
Pre-caucus campaign ends 1-16—1-20, 50F2-C3
Carter, Bush win caucuses 1-21, 50D1
Kennedy reaffirms candidacy 1-28, 74E2
Primary results 6-3, 439D3
Mondale in Des Moines 9-3, 780F1
Bush visits Des Moines 9-10, 780E3
Reagan at farm rally 9-30, 738A3
Election results 11-4, 838B1, 839A2, E3

1976

IOWA State University (Ames)
Ford addresses 10-15, 784F1

1977

IOWA State University (Ames)
Loses Peach Bowl 12-31, 1020D2
IRA (Irish Republican Army)—*See NORTHERN Ireland—Unrest*

1978

IOWA, University of (Iowa City)
Wrestling rank rptd 3-13, wins NCAA title 3-18, 379F2-A3
IOWA Beef Processors Inc.
Pacific Holding acquisitn plan rptd 11-6, 1005B2
IOWA State University (Ames)
Wrestling rank rptd 3-13, Iowa wins NCAA title 3-18, 379F2-A3
Loses Hall of Fame Bowl 12-20, 1025C2
IRA (Irish Republican Army)—*See NORTHERN Ireland—Unrest*

1979

IOWA, University of (Iowa City)
Grant elected AIAW pres 1-10, 103C2
Wins NCAA wrestling title 3-10, 507D3
Barry in basketball HOF 4-30, 526F3
Kennedy visits 11-29, 962F1
IOWA State University (Ames)
Bruce named Ohio State coach 1-12, 175D3
2d in NCAA wrestling 3-10, 507D3
NCAA basketball tourn results 3-26, 238B3
IOWA v. Omaha Indian Tribe
Case remanded by Sup Ct 6-20, 516A2
IPEKCI, Abdi
Killed 2-1, 117A1*
Murderer arrested 6-24, 568D2
IRA (Irish Republican Army)—*See NORTHERN Ireland-Unrest*

1980

IOWA, University of (Iowa City)
NCAA basketball tourn results 3-24, 240E1
Farm cancer study rptd 4-15, 357A3
Alcoholism, genetics link rptd 6-7, 715G1
Lester in NBA draft 6-10, 447C1, F2
IRA (Irish Republican Army)—*See NORTHERN Ireland-Unrest*
IRAKERE (recording)
Irakere wins Grammy 2-27, 296G3
IRAKERE (singing group)
Wins Grammy 2-27, 296G3

IRAN

1976

IRAN—*See also DISARMAMENT—Geneva Committee, OPEC*
Listed as 'not free' nation 1-19, 20D3
9 guerrillas executed 1-24, 78G1
Oil revenue drop rptd, budget deficit seen 2-3, 101F3
2 trade mins ousted in sugar deal 2-10, 156C3
Oil price cut 2-16, 126C2
Navy men sentncd re corruptn 2-24, 156B3
Terrorists slain 4-20—5-18, 365D2
'75 oil output down 4-25, 298B3
Jet crash in Spain 5-9, 404B3
Alleged slayers of Islamic ldr rptd seized 5-17, 365B3
Police, terrorist clash toll rptd 5-20, 418G2
WHO cancer studies rptd 6-3, 484B3
14 guerrillas slain 6-23, 6-29; amnesty offered 7-5, 497B1
2 terrorists executed 8-30, 652B2
3 terrorists slain 9-2, 9-3, 679F1
3 gunmen slain, 7 taken 11-16, 910F2
Turkish quake hits 14 villages 11-24, 896F3
8 guerrillas slain 12-23, 1012F3

1977

IRAN—*See also CENTO, DISARMAMENT—Geneva Committee, OPEC*
'77-78 budget, defns outlays cut 2-20, 201G1
Earthquakes hit 3-22—3-23, 4-6, 312C2
'Terrorist' trial opens 4-11; 11 sentncd 4-12, terms cut 5-11, 527G1
Intl A-energy conf ends 4-13, 334E2
Pak chrgs mil threat 5-11, 378A2
Intl consortium OKs Egypt aid 5-11—5-12, 390C3
2 slain in raid vs Jewish agency 5-12, 527B2
Energy crisis rptd 6-16, 527E1
Hoveida quits 8-6; Amouzegar replaces, econ measures ordrd 8-7, 618E1
Prisoners freed, press curbs eased 8-17, 8-18, 655C3
Indl expansn plans cut 8-18, 655G2-C3
Shah's sister escapes assassinatn 9-13, 745F2
Cholera outbreak rptd 9-26, 748A1
Gen Moqarrebi convctd as spy 12-6, executed 12-25, 1019F1
Earthquake hits 12-20, 1023C1

1978

IRAN—*See also DISARMAMENT—Geneva Committee, OPEC*
A-bomb seen unlikely before '84 1-26, 61C2
'77 quake deaths rptd 1-29, 480A2
Locust plague threat seen 6-12, 465E2
Heat wave kills 10 6-12, 479E3
9 die in rebel raid 9-16, 740F1
Quake kills 25,000 9-16, 9-26, 758D3
Nuclear cutback planned 10-22, 816A3

1979

IRAN—*See also DISARMAMENT-Geneva Committee, NONALIGNED Nations Movement, OPEC*
Quake hits 1-16, '78 deaths cited 1-25, 140D2, G2
Quake kills 248 11-14, 918B1
Muharram observed 11-30–11-31, 895D2
Azerbaijan Developments
Truce ends clashes 4-26, 321B2
Violent clashes erupt 7-15, 544A3
Charter vote boycott 12-2–12-3; violence erupts, Tabriz seized 12-5–12-6, 915F2
Shariat asks autonomy 12-7, 935F3
Tabriz pro-Shariat rally 12-7, gov barred from state house 12-8, 935G3
Rebel, pro-Khomeini forces clash 12-9–12-10; Bani-Sadr peace missn arrives in Tabriz 12-10, 936A1
Radical Party ldr escapes, 6 arrested 12-8, 936D2
Shariat, Khomeini clash on policy 12-10–12-11, 935E3, 936E1-C2
Charter protested by 700,000 in Tabriz 12-13, 936C2
9 guards taken hostage 12-27, rally backs 12-30; release vowed 12-31, 975E3
Economy & Labor—*See also 'Oil' below*
Leftists seek worker control of industry 2-23, 145B1
Slowdown rptd 5-12, 358G1
Banks natlzd 6-7, govt explains 6-8; banks closed, compensatn vowed 6-9–6-10, reopened 6-11, 469E1-C2
Draft charter unveiled, some natlzn OKd 6-18, 486B2
Insurnc cos natlzd 6-25, 486E2
Key industries nationalized 7-5, 503F2
Worker morale called good; jobless, inflatn rates high 12-6, 915B2
'79 GNP down 12%, mfg off 40-70%; '80 agri expansn seen 12-17, 976B1

1980

IRAN—*See also GENEVA Committee, NONALIGNED Nations, OPEC*
Jet crash kills 128 1-21, 80F3
Azerbaijan Developments
Tabriz fighting rages 1-4—1-6, 4A1
Shariat denies Moslem People's Party tie 1-5, 4C1
Tabriz clashes continue 1-7—1-9; Shariat visitors barred 1-8, curfew imposed 1-10, 20A2
Tabriz death toll rptd 1-11, 30C1
11 Tabriz rebels executed; riots erupt, 4 die 1-12, 30A1
2 rebel ldrs executed 5-22, 419E3

1976

Foreign Relations (misc.)
Recalls ambs from 7 Persian Gulf states 1-7, 12F3
Japan oil pact signed 1-7, 141G1
Oman troop aid rptd 1-9, 52A2
Austria rptd in W Ger-USSR gas pact 1-19, 97E3
In W Ger univ deal 1-20, 102G1
'75 Swiss arms sales data 1-22, 104D1
UNESCO literacy drive fails 2-4, 85C2
At intl econ conf 2-11—2-20, 148B1
India fears arms to Pak 3-31, 278B3
Total IMF oil loan rptd 4-1, 340F2
At Pak, Turk econ summit 4-21—4-22, 298A2
'75 Sovt trade rptd 5-5, 341A1
Slain rebels linked to Cuba, other natns 5-10, 5-19, 365E2, D3
French pres visits US 5-17—5-22, 372A2
Libya tied to terrorists 5-22, 418G2
Seeks US arms relay to Morocco via Jordan 5-22, 458C2
Intl jurists chrg torture 5-28, 418B2
At Timor Assemb meeting 5-31, 423A1
Japan to aid petrochem plant 8-27, 643E1
Swiss expel Mahdair 8-30, Gyger recalled 8-31, 735E1
Sovt pilot defects, asks US asylum 9-23; USSR protests 9-26, 773D2
Rpt Greece OKs bank 9-29, 854G1
French A-pact signed 10-6, 773E2
France to honor A-sales 10-11, 772C3
Buys Krupp interest 10-19, 782C2
Sovt defector returned 10-25; protested 10-28, 11-1, 854B2
UN refugee comr vs Sovt defector return 11-1, 854D2
Keykavoussi shot in Paris 11-2, 1002F2-A3
UN Assemb condemns apartheid 11-9, 842G2
UK oil-arms deal signed 11-18, 906F1
Czech pipeline pact rptd 11-22, 946A2
Buys shares in 2 Krupp cos 11-23, 949E1
S Yemen downs jet 11-24; chrgs spying, bans overflights 11-25—11-29, 913F2-914C1
Amnesty Intl chrgs torture 11-28, 925G2
French A-plant deal set 12-16, 1002E3
Vs Saudis on oil price hike 12-20, 975B3

1977

Foreign Relations (misc.)—*See also 'Oil' below*
UN Assemb member 4B1
Forgn aid cuts set 1-11, 11E3
Concorde purchases cited 2-1, 99E1
Dutch boycott threat dropped 2-3, 250F1
Pak, Turkey pact signed, RCD revitalized 3-12, 190B2
UN ECOSOC admits PLO 7-22, 572G2
Tito visits 9-8, 710C1
Somalia arms aid rptd 10-22, 830B1
Lufthansa hijackers identified 10-25, 10-27, 868G2
Sadat ends visit 11-3, 850A2
W Ger A-plant deal signed 11-10, 926C2
UN S Africa oil ban abstentn 12-16, 1016A2

1978

Foreign Relations (misc.)—*See also 'Monetary, Trade, Aid & Investment' and 'UN' below*
Ethiopia warned vs Somalia invasn 1-2, 43G3
Shah meets Sadat, backs Mideast peace moves 1-9; briefs Saudis 1-10, 26C2
OAU warns vs Ethiopia role 1-20, 100G1
Harassmt of students in UK denied 1-30, 190E2
Ethiopia protests Somalia role 2-1, 100D1
France, W Ger OK ESA rocket launcher 2-6—2-7, 122B1
Kenya ties cut re Horn of Africa 2-18, 137F2
Students storm emb in E Berlin 2-27, 152E3
Students besiege E Ger mission in Bonn 2-28, 190C2
Amnesty Intl chrgs rights breach 2-28, 190D2
E Ger amb to be recalled 3-2, trade ties cut 3-5, 190B2
Sovt spy ring rptd smashed 3-27, 4-16, 288G3
Afghan ties pledged 5-6, 349F2, A3
Shah postpones Eur trip 5-11, 352F3
Afghan pro-Sovt stance, Pak unrest feared 5-19, 391D1
Pak warned vs Bhutto executn 5-19, 391G1
Pak amb named 6-6, 427D3
Spain king visits 6-14—6-15, 576A2
Sovts down 2 army copters 6-21; Iran, Sovt rpts 7-17, 7-18, 573F3
USSR scores China premr Hua on visit 8-5, 8-21, 8-27, 675D3
Hua visits 8-29—9-1, culture pact signed 8-31, 674G2, 675B3
Shah tied to missing Leb Moslem ldr 8-31, 713E2
Iraq frees Khomeini, goes to Paris 10-6, 774F3
UK assures shah on backing 10-22, 827G3
US to renew Pak econ aid 10-24, 840B1
UK emb burned 11-5, 857F2
Forgn workers leave 11-10, 869C1
Empress Farah in Iraq 11-18—11-19, 893G2
Shah vs aid to prevent ouster 11-18, 894A1
USSR warns US vs interfernc, US rebuts 11-19, 893D3
Rights groups chrg torture 11-23, 12-11, 954E1
Intl rights league sees improvemt 11-23, 954F1

1979

Foreign Relations (misc.)—*See also 'Monetary', 'Oil' and 'UN' below*
Westn-natn Guadeloupe summit topic 1-5–1-6, Turkey aid offer linked 1-12, 12G2, 40E2
Shah in Egypt 1-16, 25A1; ends visit, in Morocco 1-22; vacatn plan rptd 1-23, 49B3, G3
CENTO exit planned 2-6, 81C2
USSR F-14 access feared by US 2-12, 106D1
Pak, USSR set Khomeini ties 2-12, 106A2
UK queen tours Arab states 2-12–3-2, 190A1
USSR broadcasts prompt US protests 2-14–2-16, 125D3
PLO ldr visits; gets Khomeini aid vow, Israeli legatn bldg 2-17–2-19, 126A1
Israel ties cut 2-18, Dayan regrets 2-19, 126A1
USSR warned vs interference 2-20, 123B3; 2-24, 145D1
PLO: Jerusalem 'liberatn' backed 2-26, 144F1
Egypt Moslems vs Sadat for backing shah 161F3
S Africa ties cut 3-4, 161A3
Pak forgn min ends visit 3-11, 181C3
Afghan chrgs border incursn; USSR chrgs rebel aid 3-18, 209A2, D2
Afghan war refugees enter 3-22, rebel aid denied 3-23, 232F3, G3
Afghan aide ousted 3-22, 233A1
Egypt Emb stormed 3-25, 222D2
USSR naval activity cited 4-12, 313G3
Intl rights group scores executns 4-13, 276E3
Afghan rebel aid chrgd 4-22, 4-27, 360C2
PLO denies link to Arab natls 4-26, 321F2
Egypt ties severed 4-30, 408A2
Israel scores Jew's executn 5-9, 353D2
World Zionist ldr warns vs Jewish mistreatmt, sees Israel action 5-9, 357B2
Begin, USSR scored by protesters 5-24, 407A3
Sadat may offer shah asylum 5-24, 408G1
Bahamians seek shah removal 5-30, 408E1
PLO group, Kuwait, Iraq tied to Khuzistan unrest 6-3, 6-6, 446D1
Iraq jets hit Kurdistan 6-4, mistake seen 6-5; Teheran warns 6-14, 446F1
Shah in Mex, Teheran threat scored 6-10, 445E3

1980

Foreign Relations (misc.)—*See also 'Monetary', 'Oil & Gas', 'Soviet-Afghan Issue', 'U.S. Hostage Issue', 'UN Policy' below*
Turkey-US base pact curbed 1-9, 22C3
NZ closes emb 2-7, 122C3
UK rptrs chrgd re gifts from shah 2-9, 122B3
Canada aid to US diplomats detailed 2-12, 106E1
Shah in Panama hosp 3-11—3-14, operatn delayed 3-16, 204F1
Jewish immigratn since Khomeini takeover estimated 3-14, 178G1
EC, Greece may cut ties 3-20, 204C1
Shah leaves panama 3-23; in Egypt, gets permanent asylum 3-24, 217A1
Arabs vs stand on gulf states, islands 261B1
Shah's extraditn from Panama filed 3-24, 217B1
Egypt warned vs shah's asylum, Sadat discounts 3-25, 217B2, D2
Iraq border attacks 3-29, 4-7; army alerted, Iraq ousts 7,000 Iranians 4-7, 260G3-261A1, E1
Forgn travel curbed 4-8, 258A2
Leb Moslem factns clash, Iranair office bombed 4-15—4-17; Iraqi Shiite ldr's executn chrgd 4-22, 300G1-C2
Iran Arabs seize London Emb 4-30; Ghotbzadeh denounces Iraq 4-30, 5-1; deadlines pass 5-2, 324E2-C3
Iran Arabs slay 2 London Emb hostages; UK commandos storm emb; 19 rescued, 5 killed 5-5, 337A1
Emb guards in Paris attacked 5-14, 463G1, A2
China, Japan discuss 5-27—6-1, 422B1
Leb Moslem factns clash 5-28, 465A2
Emb in Kuwait attacked 6-4, 451G2
Yugo backs independnc 6-25, 474C3
Sovt emb aide expelled as spy 6-30, Sovt staff cuts ordrd 7-2, 491B1
Canada pavillion rental to Egypt scored 7-3, 520G3-521B1
Sovts fear emb takeover, Ghotbzadeh reassures 7-7, 507C2
Bakhtiar, forgn states chrgd in coup plot 7-11, 7-16, 539C2
Bakhtiar eludes death try in Paris; 5 seized, PLO linked 7-18; Iran warned, denies role 7-18—7-19, 545A1
Ghotbzadeh cancels Nicaragua visit 7-18, 545E1
3 UK rptrs flee to Italy 7-25, 572B1
Leb Moslem factns clash 7-28, 579A3
Swiss deliver US hostage plea to parlt 7-29, 571E3

1976

1977

1978

France warns Khomeini on activities 12-4, 929A2
Amnesty Intl rpts torture 12-11, 954E1
Khomeini warns vs shah support 12-13, anti-Israel stand cited 953A3
USSR, US trade interventn chrgs 12-28, 994F1
Libya, PLO rptdly aid shah foes 12-29, 993E2
El Al office attacked 12-31, 993E2

Government & Politics—*See 'Unrest' below*

1979

USSR scored re Khuzistan unrest, Afghan role 6-12, 445G3-446D1
Iraq jets, troops raid border 6-14, 469D1
SALT II summit topic 6-15–6-18, 449D1
Shah assassin squad sent 6-16, Mex denies attack rpt 6-27, 486G2
Egypt offers shah asylum 6-23, 486A3
Iraq Baathist's ouster linked 7-16, 544F3
Press curbs rptd 7-23, 565G3
Bakhtiar appears in Paris 7-31, 582F2
Afghan links to army revolt 8-5, 599E2
Israel linked to seized newspr 8-7, 602C2
Press curbs widened 8-13, IJC protests 8-14, 614F3
6 forgn newsmen ousted 8-21, 635A2
Sovts chrg press distortn re Afghan role 8-22, 666G2
UK newsman ousted 9-1, 670D2
New rules on rptrs set 9-3, 670C2
Nonaligned movemt joined 9-3, 675E1
UK newsman ousted 9-5, 708B3
Leb Moslem hijackers surrender 9-8, 677B3
USSR scores Khomeini rule 9-8, 688C1
Israel cites potential mil threat 9-12, 693E2
Kuwait deports Khomeini envoy 9-26; UAE, Bahrain ousters cited; clergy score 9-27, 752G2
Ex-defense min goes to France 9-28, 752C2
Bahrain annexatn threat spurs Egypt aid offer 9-28, Bahrain rejects 10-2, 752C3
Persian Gulf security conf meets 10-14–10-16, 804A2
W Ger exec slain, UK Emb alerts natls 10-14, 814C3
Afghan links coup try 10-16, 810F3
UK Emb occupied 11-5, 841G1
Sovt mil pact cancelled 11-5, 841G1
5 Asian natls detained in US Emb 11-5, 841E1; freed 11-22, 895A3
PLO seeks US Emb hostage mediatn 11-7–11-11; papal nuncio, 4 other forgn envoys visit hostages 11-9–11-10; Khomeini scores intl pressure 11-10, 862G1-D2
Sadat offers shah asylum, scores Khomeini 11-9, 862B3
W Eur heroin supply role cited 11-11, 972E3
Mex closes emb 11-12, 862C3
World reactn to US Emb takeover 11-20–11-27, 895B3
Israeli role in Mecca mosque takeover chrgd 11-21, 893C1; 11-24, 895B2
Arab League bars Tehran delegatn; Arafat, Assad, Leb ldr see 11-21, 916D2
Pak raid on US Emb lauded 11-22, 894E1
Mex bars shah's reentry 11-29, 897C1
Pope seeks Christian-Moslem ties 11-29, 930E3
Egypt renews shah's asylum offer 11-30, 914D1
Mex denies US pressure to readmit shah 12-3, 914F1
Leb volunteer force planned 12-5, 12-8; Beirut bars, Syria, PLO silent 12-10, 937E2
Shah's nephew slain in Paris, Khalkhali takes credit 12-7; secret police role seen 12-8, 935B1
Mideast, Eur envoys convey US hostage plan 12-8, 934B1
Egypt fears US Mideast setlmt attentn diverted 12-8, 938B1
Amnesty Intl scores shah, Islamic govt 12-9, 980D2
US thanks NATO re support 12-12; 959C2
Iraq invasn rptd, denied 12-14; Iraq assails rpt 12-15, 958B3
Shah quits US for Panama 12-15, thanks Panama 12-16; Panamians protest 12-18, 957A1, G1
UK backs Carter re crisis 12-17, 968G1
Volunteers in Syria 12-18–12-20; Leb vs entry 12-18, Syria reassures Leb 12-20, 979G3
Panama curbs anti-shah protests 12-19–12-21, 975B3
Intl tribunal role barred by ex-CIA agent 12-23, 991E2
Sovt Afghan invasn opposed 12-28, 974C2

Government & Politics—*See also other appropriate subheads in this section*

Ayatollahs listed 297F2-B3
Freedom House lists as partly free 12G3
Khomeini photo 82A1
Bakhtiar gets prelim parlt OK, issues policy statemt 1-3; named premr 1-4, 2C2
Natl Front scores Bakhtiar, cancels protests 1-4, 2G2
Shah vacatns 1-4–1-5, 2A3; **for complete list of shah developments, see PAHLEVI, Shah Mohammed Riza**
Shah names Gharabaghi mil staff chief, Oveissi quits 1-4, 2B3
Bakhtiar installed; Moslems, Natl Front oppose 1-6, 11D2
Bakhtiar appointees listed 1-6, 1-11; presents Cabt to lower house, outlines policy 1-11, 11F2, B3
Bakhtiar ends censorship, eases martial law 1-6, 11A3
Shah asks kin to cede assets 1-9, 12B1

1980

Moslems demonstrate in Rome, Beirut, Manila, London 8-4—8-8; Khomeini backs protests 8-6, 635F1
3 UK missionaries arrested 8-8, 8-9, 671C3
Sovt border breach, Kurdish rebel aid chrgd 8-12, 644D3
UK closes embassy 8-17, 634D1
Sovts bar Iran Emb shift, forced to close prov consulate 8-19, 644C3
Sovt interventn to counter US moves seen 8-25, 644A2
France sets visa requirement 9-3, 670D1
UK detentn of Iranians scored 9-4, 671A3
4 remaining UK aides leave, UK deports arrested Iranians 9-9, 689C1
Leb missing Moslem ldr rptd jailed in Libya 9-9, 709E1
Khomeini scores US-Egypt link 9-12, 693E1
Egypt recognizes govt 11-1, 859A3
Khomeini factns clash in W Ger 11-2, 969C2

Government & Politics—*See also other appropriate subheads in this section*

Red Cross rpts on shah's jails issued 1-9, 47B2
Shah extraditn from Panama asked 1-12, 47B1; for complete list of shah developments, see PAHLEVI, Shah Mohammed Riza
Shah denies massacres 1-17, 47G1
Khomeini hospitalized 1-23, 47F2
Bani-Sadr elected pres 1-25; final results 1-28, 66C3
Bani-Sadr inaugurated pres 2-4, 88G1
Bani-Sadr consolidates Rev Cncl power 2-5, 2-7; scores militants, curbs media access 2-6, 105G1
Info min seized by militants 2-6, Cncl forces release 2-7; militants score 2-9, 105D2
Revolutn anniv marked 2-11, 106A1
Bani-Sadr heads armed forces 2-19, 122D2
Khomeini names charter protectn group 2-19, 122F2
Pres urges people's army 2-25, 137E2
Khomeini released from hosp 3-2, 164D2

1976

1977

1978

1979

Regency cncl for shah formed, 3 refuse to serve 1-13, 25F1
Khomeini sees Islamic state 1-12; forms Revolutn Cncl, vows new govt 1-13, 25G1-C2
Parlt OKs Bakhtiar govt 1-15, 1-16, 25D2
Shah leaves Iran, permanent exile seen; in Egypt 1-16, 25A1
Khomeini hails shah's exit, vows new govt 1-16; urges contd resistance 1-17, 25E2, G2
Justice min resigns re Hoveida trial plans 1-17, 25D2
Bakhtiar defies Khomeini on successn 1-18, 26B1
Regency cncl head in France 1-18; meets Khomeini, quits cncl 1-22, 49F2
Khomeini: shah 'dethroned' 1-19, 49G1-B2
Bakhtiar vows to keep office 1-19, 49B2
Khomeini to return 1-20; airports closed 1-24, return delayed 1-25, 49B1-G1
Army vows to back Bakhtiar 1-22, 49E2
Khomeini vs Bakhtiar electn plan 1-24, 49C1
Bakhtiar meets Khomeini aide 1-24, 49E1
Bakhtiar offers Khomeini mtg in France 1-27, Khomeini rejects 1-28, 67D1
Khomeini return OKd 1-29, airports reopened 1-30, returns, asks Bakhtiar quit, threatens arrest; Bakhtiar rebuts 2-1, 66C3-67C1
Bakhtiar OKs Khomeini backers in govt, Khomeini vs 2-2, 81F1
Khomeini says new const drawn 2-3, 81D1
Khomeini power transfer detailed; Bakhtiar warns vs force, mil gov OKs marches 2-4, 81G1
Bakhtiar sees Bazargan 2-4, 82G1
Khomeini names Bazargan to head provisional govt 2-5, Bakhtiar bars resignatn 2-5, 2-6, 81A1
Bakhtiar aide rpts govt stalled 2-7, 81E2
Bakhtiar backs vote on new govt, const chngs 2-8, 81G2
Bakhtiar overthrown 2-11, 105A1, E1
Khomeini wins CP backing 2-13, faces challenge from leftists 2-14–2-18, 124F3
Cabt mins named 2-19, 125D1, F2*
Leftists seek govt role 2-23, 2-24, 145A1
80 gens rptd retired 2-25, 144D3
Bakhtiar flight rptd, Khomeini asks info 2-25, 144G3
Bazargan scores Khomeini cncl, threatens resignatn 2-28, 144G2
Khomeini returns to Qom, scores West 3-1, 161A2
Shah bars abdicatn 3-5, to be tried in absentia 3-6, 161G1
'63 family protectn law abolished 179C2
Khomeini curbs women's garb 3-7, qualifies order 3-8, 179B2
Khomeini calls Bazargan govt 'weak' 3-7; Bazargan offers resignatn, Khomeini bars 3-8, asks support for Bazargan 3-9, 179B3
2 new parties formed 3-7, 180A1
Women exempted from mil svc 3-8, 179D2
Moslem ldr vs referendum plan 3-11, 179E3
Bazargan scores trials, executns 3-14; Khomeini suspends, Hoveida trial halted 3-16, 199C1, G1
Bakhtiar tape scores Khomeini 3-24, 229C1
Turkomans ask referendum boycott 3-26, 247F2
Madani urges mil cuts, seeks new arms sources 3-27, 228G3
Armed Forces chief replaced 3-27, defns min resigns 3-30, 247D2
Islamic repub voted; Kurds, Turkomans boycott 3-30–3-31; Khomeni proclaims new govt 4-1, 247B2
Shah leaves Morocco for Bahamas 3-30, 247B3
Bakhtiar rptd in France 3-30, 247C3
Hoveida trial reopens 4-4, found guilty, shot 4-7; other ex-offcls executed; reactn 4-9–4-13, 276E2-G3
Teleghani quits politics 4-12, Sanjabi quits Cabt 4-15; Khomeini rule protested 4-14–4-17, 276G3
Bazargan vs komitehs, secret trials, executns 4-12, 4-24, 297F1, E2
Taleghani backs Khomeini, komitehs 4-18–4-19, 297B2
Yazdi named forgn min; Bani Assadi, dep premr 4-24, 297B2
Khomeini forms new militia 5-5, 353F2
Khomeini vs secular critics 5-24, 407E3
Bar Assn asks draft const publicatn 5-28, 425F3
Bazargan, Nazih vs Khomeini policies 5-28, 407B3
Khomeini rule scored by Natl Front, Taleghani, Natl Oil dirs 6-2, 425B3
Shah aides, kin assets seized 6-7, 469F1
Shah in Mexico 6-10, 445E3
Charter critics scored, draft unveiled 6-18; rally urges new const 6-22, 486F1
Islamic militia curbs denied 7-1, 503B3
Khomeini declares gen amnesty 7-9, 524D3
Mil police cmdr defies dismissal order 7-9, Khomeini backs 7-10, 525F1
Bazargan, Khomeini to share power 7-19, 565D2
New mil chief replaced 7-21, 565G2

1980

General amnesty issued 3-18, 204A2
1st-round parlt electn fraud chrgd 3-14; 2d-round delayed 3-26, 218D1; 1st-round results 3-14, 2d-round results pending 5-9, 373G1
Bani-Sadr asks premr selectn 5-6, Khomeini OKs 5-9; Rev Cncl blocks 5-12, 373F1
Bani-Sadr strips Khalkhali of power 5-13, 373C2
Parlt convenes 5-28, 394F1-D2
Oveissi sees Khomeini overthrow 6-11, 433F2
Anti-Khomeini plot rptd 6-12, 464G3
Guard cmdr quits 6-17, broadcast head 6-19; mil cmnd shifted 6-19, 464B2
Plot vs Bani-Sadr rptd 6-19, 464E2
Khomeini scores Bani-Sadr, Rev Cncl 6-27; Bani-Sadr responds 6-29, 490D1, A2
Bojnourdi named Rev Guard cmdr 6-29, 490C2
Mil coup plot fails 7-10, confessns rptd 7-13, 539B2
2 Bakhtiar cousins arrested in anti-Khomeini plot 7-17, 545G1
Cncl of Guardians chosen 7-17, 571B3
Parlt swears Bani-Sadr 7-22, picks speaker 7-29, 571A3
Mir-Salim nominated premr 7-26; parlt takes no actn, adjourns 7-27, 571E2
Shah dies; reactn 7-27, 571B1, C2
Bakhtiar plans coup, denounces Khomeini rule 8-8, 644E2
Mir-Salim rejctd as premr, Rajai named 8-9; parlt OKs 8-11, 619G3-620A1
Jew in parlt ousted 8-17, 644G2
New Cabt named, Bani-Sadr vs 8-31; parlt delays OK 9-2, 671B2
Khomeini asks Bani-Sadr OK partial Cabt 9-5; accepts 14 mins 9-7, parlt approves 9-10; Rev Cncl disbands 9-11, 688G3*-689C1
Bakhtiar plans exile govt 9-26, 769D1
Shah's son claims title 10-31, 859F2
Ghotbzadeh arrested 11-7, freed 11-10, 862C1
Khalkhali chrgd, quits as drug prosecutor 12-7, 943F1
Human rights record scored 12-10, 978B3

Iraqi Relations

Iraq border attacks 3-29, 260G3-261A1; for subsequent developments, see 'Iraqi' subheads below
Iraq dep premr death try fails 4-1; Iranians, Iraqi students clash in Baghdad 4-5, 261C1
Iran, Iraq oust diplomats 4-5, 4-6, 261D1
Iraq linked to US 'imperialism' 4-7, 261F1
Iraqi coup threatened, Hussein defies 4-8, 299G3
Iraqi air clash 4-9; plot chrgs, warnings exchngd 4-9, 4-11; 5,700 natls deported 4-10, 300C1
Ghotbzadeh blames Iraq for London Emb seizure 5-1, 324A3
Iraq Emb in Rome attacked 6-4, 451E2
Iraq mil bases rptd 6-11, 434B1
Iraqi Vienna bomb plot fails 7-30, diplomats expelled 7-30, 7-31, 604G2
Sovt arms to Iraq chrgd, amb recall threatened 8-8, 644E3
Iraq border clashes 9-6—9-11, 689F1
Khomeini ties US to unrest 9-12, 693E1
Iraq border clashes 9-13, 9-17, 9-18, 694F2
Iraq cancels '75 border pact, Iran admits ignored pact 9-17; Baghdad move scored 9-18, 694G1-E2

Iraqi War (military developments)

Border clashes increase, Iran calls up reservists 9-20; Iraq jets strike 9-21—9-22, 717B1
War widens; jets hit cities, oilfields, airports; Iraqis invade Iran 9-22—9-24; oil exports stopped; Abadan, Khurramshahr under siege 9-24, 717E1
War zone map 718D1
Iraq says Khurramshahr taken 9-25, admits 'premature' 9-26, Hussein claims capture 9-28, 734G1, D2*
Iraq hits oil cntrs 9-26, 734F1
Iraq: goals 'achieved' 9-27, 734C2
Battle for Ahwaz, Dizful, Khurramshahr 9-28—9-29, 10-1, 734E2
Iran warns Gulf states on haven for Iraq ships, UAE shelter chrgd 9-29, 735G1
Iran jets bomb Iraq A-center 9-30, Iraq bombs Banda Khomeini plant 10-1, 734F2, G2
Iraq to halt combat for 4 days 10-1, 734D1
Iraq: main goals attained 10-2, 758A2
Oman war role rptd blocked by US, UK, others 10-3, 758F1
Iraq sets cease-fire, Iran rejects 10-5, 758B2
Iraq jets hit Teheran 10-6; Iran forces attack forgn ships at Khurramshahr 10-7, planes hit Baghdad 10-8, 758B1
Dizful, Andimeshk hit by surface-to-surface missiles, 110 civlns die 10-8, 10-9; Iraq, Iran oil fields, Kharg I bombed 10-8, 10-10, 10-13, 773F1-B2
Iraqis launch Abadan drive 10-10, within 1 mi 10-16, 773A1
Waldheim asks limited truce to free merchant ships 10-10; Iran replies, Iraq ignores 10-13, 774F1
Khomeini cedes war powers 10-12, 773D2
Dizful area battle 10-14, Ilam 10-15; Baghdad, Irbil, Tabriz attacked 10-15, 773B2
Battle for Abadan, Khurramshahr 10-18—10-22, 799E2
Iran sets total mobilizatn 10-19, 799A3

1976

1977

1978

1979

Khomeini bans radio, TV music 7-23; bar qualified, defied 7-24, 565A3
Bakhtiar electn role seen 7-30, scores Khomeini 7-31, 582F2
Natl Dem Front vs assemb electns 8-2, 615D1
Charter assemb electn 8-3, clergy win majority 8-11, 615B1
Arms for illegal groups banned 8-20, 635B2
Bazargan offers resignatn 8-31, 670E1
Taleghani dies 9-10, 687G3-688C1
Charter shift to give Khomeini top power 9-12, 708G2
Cabt chngs; Nazih ousted from oil post, Khomeini threatns treason trial 9-28, 752B2
Khomeini orders executns halt 10-18, 814A3
Shah in NY hosp 10-22, 843B1; protest staged 11-4, 841A1-C2; for subsequent developments, see 'U.S. Embassy Takeover' below
Bazargan, govt resign; Revolutn Cncl takes over 11-6, 841C1, 842G1
Bani-Sadr becomes forgn min 11-10, 862G1
Shah's wealth assessed, figures in dispute 11-22–11-26, 897B3-898B1
Shah's assets probed 11-26, $56.5 bln damage suit filed 11-28, 897A2-B3
Charter OKd, Khomeini rules for life; minorities boycott 12-2–12-3, 915F2, G3
Shah accused of embezzlemt 12-11, 935G1
Shah quits US for Panama 12-15, 957A1

1980

Iraq: oil field capture 'ultimate aim' 10-21, 799D2
Air raids vs Kirkuk, Baghdad 10-21—10-22; Iraqi jets hit Bandar Khomeini 10-22, 799G2
Iraq says Khuzistan cut off 10-22, 799C2
Iraq jets hit Khuzistan oil depots 10-23; Iraqis claim Khurramshahr capture 10-24; Ahwaz attacked 10-25, Dizful 10-26, 10-29, Abadan 10-27—10-29, 820D1
Iran rpts Khuzistan losses 10-23, 820F1
Iraq jets hit Kirkuk, Baghdad area 10-29, 820D1
Khurramshar forces stalled 10-30, 854F3
Iran oil min, aides captured 10-31; Iran demands release 11-2, Iraq rejects 11-3, min rptd wounded 11-6, 854B3
Iraq drive vs Abadan 10-31—11-6, 854E3
Abadan fighting continues 11-1—11-12, 879B2
Iran jets hit Kuwait 11-12, 11-16, 879B2
Susangird battle 11-14—11-18, 879F1
Jets hit Iraqi dam, Iraqi missiles hit Gilan 11-21, 913F1
Iranians fail to break Abadan siege 11-25, 913G1
Iran jets hit Kirkuk area oil fields, 2 downed 11-26, 913A2
Persian Gulf air, sea clash 11-28—11-30, 913B2
Iran starts new war phase, Iraq denies 12-3, 913C1
Oil centers bombed 12-4, 12-5, 12-7, 931C3
Iraq claims Shatt al-Arab control 12-8, 931F3
Iran demands oil min release 12-15—12-16, 951E2
Jets hit Iraq oil fields 12-19, 978E1
Iraq invades Kurdistan 12-25, 977E3
68 Iranians, 20 Iraqis rptd killed 12-25, 978D1
UN truce to free forgn ships in Shatt al-Arab stalled by flag feud 12-29, 978E1

Iraqi War (nonmilitary developments)

US record oil inventories rptd 9-5, Admin assured vs shortfall 10-3, 785E3
Sovts meet Iraqis; vow neutrality, rptdly deny arms request 9-21—9-22, 719D1
Khomeini calls for Pres Hussein ouster 9-22, 717C2
UN Cncl asks end to war 9-23, 718D3
US, USSR vow neutrality 9-23, 9-25, 718G3-719C2
Hormuz Strait oil glut end seen, Iran threatns blockade 9-24, 718B1
Iraq ups pipeline pumping 9-24, seeks Leb pipeline use 9-25, 718A2
US seeks contd oil flow 9-24, 718B2
King Hussein, other Arabs back Iraq 9-24, 719C2
Arafat, Arab League mediatn effort cited 9-24, 719F2
Reagan blames US policies 9-24, 723A1
Iraq sets peace terms 9-25, 718A3
US bars engine exports to Iraq 9-25, 719B1
Islamic Conf sets mediatn, Iran vs 9-26; Zia missn 9-27—9-30, rpts failure 10-1, 734C1
Saudis ask US air defns aid, fear Iran raid 9-26; US sends 4 AWACS 9-30, assures Iran 10-1, 734A3
Iraq halts oil exports 9-26, rpts some shipmts 9-27, 734E3
US urges free oil passage, hints at intl force; Bonn, Japan oppose 9-26, 735C2
Iraq rpts Syria pipeline in use, Syria contradicts 9-27, 735E1
Iraq proposes truce 9-28; Iran vs 9-29, 9-30, 733C1
UN Cncl asks truce, mediatn 9-28; Iraq backs 9-29, Iran vs 10-1, 733F1, D2-734B1
US warns Iraq vs Iran oil seizure 9-28, 735B2
Iran blames US 9-29, 733F1
US-Iraqi talks, limited war stressed 9-30, 733G1
Sovts urge setlmt, blame US 9-30, 758G2
Iran vows to keep Hormuz Strait open; scores US, UAE backing for Iraq 10-1, 735F1
Iraqi Kurds renew autonomy fight 10-1, 735F2
IEA emergency mtg 10-1, 759A2
US backs Iraqi truce bid 10-2, 733G1
Brazil oil scramble rptd 10-2—10-3, 759E1-A2
Iraq ousts 3 forgn newsmen 10-2, expands order 10-10, 774D3
King Hussein in Baghdad 10-4—10-5; Jordan OKs supplies, forgn ships access to Iraq 10-6, 757A1
Rajai sees Sovt amb 10-4, arms bid rptd rejected 10-5, 758B3
US sends more air defns gear to Saudis 10-5, offers aid to other Gulf states 10-7, 758A1
Saudi, Kuwait, UAE oil export boosts rptd set 10-5—10-6, 758D3
Sovt forgn arms stockpiles rptdly sent to Iraq; Iraqi planes stationed in Kuwait, N Yemen, Oman 10-6, 757D1
OPEC mtgs postponed 10-6, 10-8, 759B1
US: Turkey cuts airlifts 10-6; Syria aid to Iran blocked, China airspace for N Korea airlift OKd 10-8, 774E2
Iran, US, Israel fear Jordan role 10-7; Israel complains to US 10-8; Israel, Egypt urged US active Gulf role 757E1-A2
Syria blames Iraq for war, denies troops in Iran 10-7, 757B2

1976

1977

1978

Monetary, Trade, Aid & Investment—*See also 'Oil Developments' and 'U.S. Relations' below*
Denmark, Italy trade ban lifted 1-11, 55F2
Somalia arms sources rptd 1-24, 44C1

1979

Kurdish Dispute
Autonomy demands intensify 2-22–3-1, 145D2
Kurds revolt 3-18, 100 die 3-21; truce ineffective, Khomeini sends missn 3-20, 198B3
Autonomy set, gov gen named 3-25; prisoners freed 3-26, 228D3
Islamic repub vote boycotted 3-30–3-31, 247C2
Turkish-Kurdish clashes 4-21, army halts 4-23, 297C3
Kurds chrg army attacks 4-25, truce ends Azerbaijan clashes 4-26, 321B2
Iraq jets hit Kurdistan 6-4, error seen 6-5; Teheran warns 6-14, 446F1
10 die in Kurdistan clashes 6-26, 503D3
Kurds battle govt troops 7-26, 16 captives freed 7-31, 582D3
Kurds rebel in Paveh 8-14–8-18, Mehabad 8-20–8-21, 634F3
Gen mobilization ordrd, Kurdish party outlawed 8-19, 635B1
Khomeini offers rebels money to end revolt 8-22, blames 'democrats' 8-25, 653B2
Saqqiz clashes 8-23, truce ends fighting 8-28, 653G1-D2
US urges restraint 8-24, 653G2
Rebels warn 'all-out war' 8-25, 653D2
Iraq gets complaint on escaping rebels 8-25, 653F2
Kurd executn toll 45 8-27, 20 more executed 8-28, 653E2
Khomeini rejects truce 8-28, 670B1
USSR, Iraq, Israel aid to Kurds chrgd 8-31, 9-1, 670C1
Mehabad retaken by govt 9-4, 670A1, D1
Rebel ldrs flee to Iraq 9-4; last stronghold falls, arms surrender asked 9-6, 688F1
USSR denies rebel aid 9-4, 688B2
USSR scores Khomeini rule 9-8, 688E1
Rebels renew attacks 9-24, 10-3, 10-7, 773D3
Mehabad retaken in Kurd advance 10-10–10-22, 814E2
Charter vote boycott 12-2–12-3; truce fails, violence erupts 12-6, 915F2, E3
Monetary, Trade, Aid & Investment—*See also 'Oil' below*
US affirms arms pacts 1-17, 26A2
Forgn contracts to be reviewed 2-4, 82C2
Sovt F-14 acquisitn concerns US 2-12, 106D1; 8-10, 634F3

1980

Iran seeks world arms purchase 10-7; US rpts N Korea sale 10-8, 757F2
US cites Sovt restraint 10-7, 758E1
King Hussein on troop aid 10-8, 757A2
US AWACS surveillance rptd 10-8; US deploys cruiser to Persian Gulf, planes to Saudi 10-11, 773E2, G2
Sovts deny arms offer to Iran 10-8, 774F2
China airspace for N Korea-Iran airlift rptd 10-8, 774F2
Libya backs Iran, appeals to Saudis, other Gulf states; Iraq cuts Libya, Syria, N Korea ties 10-10, 774A2
Libya-Iran airlift rptdly uses Sovt, Greek, Bulgaria airspace 10-10, 774D2
Syria denies arms to Iran, scores Iraq invasn 10-11, 774D2
King Hussein in Riyadh, asks backing for Iraq 10-11—10-12; rpt Saudis vs direct mil aid 10-13, 774G2
Iran ends UN Cncl boycott, Rajai to appear; Iraq defends invasn 10-15, 774C1
UN Cncl hears Rajai score truce, US AWACS to Saudis, Iraq; Iraq defends '75 pact chrg 10-17, 798D2
Iraq chrgs US, Israel, Iran plot; says Rajai seeks US spare parts 10-18, 799A2
Turkey trade rptd sought 10-18, 821G1
Iran rejects Islamic mediatn 10-19, 10-20, 799B3
Libya-Saudi exchng on US AWACS 10-19, 10-22; Saudis cut ties 10-28, 820C3
UN Cncl gets US peace plan 10-22—10-23, US cites Iraq threat 10-23, 799B1
Iran vows to keep Hormuz Strait open 10-22, 799F1
Iraq to free 12 Iranians 10-22, 799G1
Palestinian curbs rptd tightened 10-22, 821B2
Carter lauds Iraq jet success 10-24, 816A3
Iraq warns US vs arms to Iran 10-25, 10-26; King Hussein warns US 10-29, 820F2, B3
King Hussein visits Iraq, renews backing 10-27—10-28, 820F3
Abadan refinery loss impact on world oil supply cited 10-27, 822A2
Carter, Reagan TV debate 10-28, 814D2
France sets Hormuz mine-sweeping force 10-28, 821D2
Khomeini blames Carter 10-29, 820C1
Sadat calls Iraq aggressor 11-1, 859B3
Iraq threatens increased peace demands 11-4, Khomeini rejects truce bid 11-5, 854G3-855C1
UK vs arms to Iran, Iraq 11-4, 879B3
UN Cncl asks peace missn 11-5; Palme named envoy 11-11, missn to Teheran, Baghdad ends 11-24, rpts to Waldheim 11-25, 894G2
OPEC pledges Africa exports 11-9, 864E2
Iraq vows 'holy war' 11-9, renews truce bid 11-10, 879D2
Iran sets austerity measures 11-9, 879C3
Iraq seeks more Sovt arms; sends missns to UK, France, Czech, Bulgaria 11-11—11-12, 879G2
Cuba mediatn effort 11-11—11-14, 894D3
Iran ends forgn press ban 11-15, 879E3
US 'concerned' re Iran raid on Kuwait, Gulf states pledge to Kuwait cited 11-17, 879C2
OPEC warns stockpilers 11-17, 895F2
Iraq resumes oil pumping 11-20, 894A2
Saudi ports open for Iraq supplies 11-20, 894D2
Kharg I oil terminal use resumed 11-21, 894C2
OPEC Sept output at 5-yr low; Iran, Iraq export cuts rptd 11-23, 895C2
UN rpts agrmt on trapped forgn ships 11-26, 913C2
Arab League urges truce, Hussein scores Syrian role 11-27, 911F1, G1
Iran seeks more war funds 12-3, 913E1
Iran: one mln left homeless 12-4, 931E3
King Hussein: Iraq slows drive 12-8, 931E3
Iraq awards Jordan 30 captured US tanks for war backing 12-9, 12-10, 931F3
Brezhnev offers Persian Gulf peace plan 12-10; US rejects 12-11, 930D1
Iraq rations fuel 12-13, halts pipeline deliveries 12-29, 978G1
Indonesia asks peace 12-15, 951D2
Hussein urges Iran accept demands 12-25, 977F3
Kurdish Dispute
Truce ends clashes 1-2, pact announced 1-3, 4D1
Govt troops quit Sanandaj 1-29, 89D1
Rebel-govt clashes 1-30—2-2, rebels yield Kamyaran 2-2, 89B1
Firing squad photo wins Pulitzer 4-14, 317E2
Sanandaj clashes 4-17—5-8; truce broken 4-29; govt peace missn fails 4-30, 373D2
Rebel-govt clashes 4-19—4-22, 299F3
2 rebels executed 5-24, 419G3
Iraq mil bases rptd 6-11, 434B1
US anti-Khomeini broadcasts rptd 6-29, 490A3
Sovt rebel aid chrgd 8-12, 644D3
Kurds subdued in 2-day battle 10-14, 774C3
Monetary, Trade, Aid & Investment
See also 'Oil & Gas' below
Eur bank assets rptd moved 1-2, 29D2
Gold prices soar 1-2—1-18, 30B3
US embargo urged by Dole 1-3, 5F1; for sanctions, see 'U.S. Hostage Issue' below

1976

1977

Obituaries
Eghbal, Manouchehr 11-25, 952C2
Oil Developments—*See also OPEC*
'76 oil price rise in effect 1-1, export drop cited 1-11, 11F3
NIOC warns cos on commitmts 1-5, 12A1
Oil barter, forgn aid cuts set 1-11, 11D3
Jan exports rptd down, Saudi comments 2-9, 107E3, 108A1
'77 sales forecast, revenue reliance cut 2-20, 201G1
Feb exports rptd up 3-2, purchase agrmts honored 3-8, 227A3
Mex reserves compared 3-18, 240D3
Venez pres visits 4-27—4-30, 362A1
Backs N-S 'oil dialogue' 6-3, 437D2
USSR '76 exports rptd 6-11, 513G1
Brazil trade pact signed 6-23, 524F1
Shah sees Carter, backs '78 price freeze 11-16, 897B1, B2
UN S Africa ban abstentn 12-16, 1016A2

1978

Ethiopia protests Somalia aid 2-1, 2-14, 100C1, D1
E Ger trade ties cut 3-5, 190B2
Rial added to new SDR basket 4-3, 300E3, F3
Zaire emergency aid rejected 6-13—6-14, 478A1, B1
Spain king in trade talks 6-14—6-15, export data rptd 6-16, 576A2
Krupp purchase paymts completed 7-27, 617B1
A-plant curbs set 10-22, 816C3
Air strikers demand rial freed vs US $ 11-1, 827F2
Khomeini calls shah business deals invalid 11-9, 858A2
USSR, US clash on arms sales, talks stalled 12-5—12-15, 996A3
Forgn exchn mkt reactn to unrest 12-29, 998C2

Oil Developments—*See also OPEC*
OAU vs S Africa sales 1-20, 100G1; 7-22, 561F1
Jan output rptd down 2-22, 158E2
US imports cited re shah backing 9-10, 693F2
Refinery workers stage job actn 10-1, setlmt rptd 10-3, 774G3, 775A1
40,000 workers strike; output, exports cut; troops dispatched 10-31; some workers return 11-1, 827F1
US monitors strike 10-31, 827D2
Shah warns vs econ paralysis 11-6, 857F3
Shortage grows, exports drop 11-6—11-7; Japan impact rptd 11-7, 858C2
Riots 11-11, striking workers ordrd back 11-12; many return, output rises 11-13—11-14, 869A1
Strikes cut output 12-4, govt workers face pay loss 12-6, 929A1
Striking workers stay out, productn drops 12-12, 953F2
Khomeini warns buyers 12-13, anti-Israel stand cited 953A3
OPEC price hike linked to turmoil 12-17, 977C3
Workers stage gen strike 12-18; exports stop 12-26, ratning starts 12-28; output at record low 12-31, 993G2
US, Iran oil co execs slain 12-23, 993B2
'78 productn rptd down 12-26, 1000B3, D3

1979

Swiss asked to freeze shah assets 2-23, 144G3
Iran Air cuts back US, Eur svc; cancels Airbus, Boeing, Concorde contracts 2-25, 144E3
Forgn assets, debts rptd 2-25, 144F3
Swiss bar blocking shah's assets, Iranian '78 assets rptd 3-5, 161E1
F-14 return to US hinted, US arms policy scored 3-27, 228G3
Exchng rate rptd altered 5-7, 358B2
US, other forgn banks natlzd 6-7; compensatn vowed 6-10, 469E1-C2
US, other forgn insurnc cos natlzd 6-25, 486E2
Afghans chrg rebel aid 8-9, 666F2
W Ger co cancels A-plant deal 7-31, 586F2; compensatn demanded 8-10, 634E3
US arms deals canceled 8-10, 634D3
USSR, Iraq, Israel aid to Kurds chrgd 8-31, 9-1, 670C1
USSR denies Kurdish rebel aid 9-4, 688B2
US resumes arms spare parts shipmts 10-5, 773B3
France freezes Eurodif share 10-24, 976E2
US freezes assets 11-14, 861F1; order confrmd, banks attach assets; risks detailed 11-15–11-18, total estimate hiked 11-19, 879C3-880G1
US bank declares Iran default 11-21, 896D2
Forgn debts repudiated 11-23, 896B2
Pahlevi family fund transfers documented 11-26, 897D2, E3
US bank attaches W Ger assets 11-28, 896E2
Japan bank rpts loan repaymt 11-28, 896G2
US banks sued for UK, French assets freeze 11-30, 12-5, 915A2
UK upholds US assets freeze 12-5, 915F1
W Ger curbs credit guarantees, arms exports 12-7, 934A1
Japan dominated syndicate retains 2 loans 12-7, 976F1
US seeks W Eur, Japan econ sanctns 12-10–12-11, 933B2
France upholds US assets freeze 12-12, 12-21, 976B2
US oil drilling co suit filed 12-13, 976D2
US Eximbank declares loans in default 12-21, 976E1
US embargo seen by Dole 12-26, 983B2
UN sanctns exempt food, med purchases 12-31, 974A3

Oil & Gas Developments
Bakhtiar vs oil to Israel, S Africa 1-3, 2D2
US chrgs Sun Co with pricing abuses 1-3, 17E1
Strikes end 1-5, 2C3
Gas productn resumed; southn oil pipe reopens 1-5, heating oil reaches Teheran 1-6, 12A1
S Africa plans vs cutoff rptd 1-9, 22A1
Israel, S Africa shipmts barred 1-11, 11C3
Carter confident re US independnc 1-17, 26C2
USSR gas cutoff rptd 1-23, 50B2
US to send fuel, gas 1-24, 50G1-A2
Japan imports drop in '78 1-24, 98D2
Saudi output rise seen 1-30, 69G3
Khomeini scores shah US sales 2-1, 67A1
Oil firms rpt sales cutbacks 2-6, 2-8, 83A1, B1
Schlesinger terms crisis serious 2-7, Blumenthal challenges 2-8, 82F2-B3
Shutdown affects gold price, US $ 2-7–2-8, 83C1-C2
Saudi denies productn cutback 2-7; 3 OPEC states raise prices 2-15, 2-21, mtg set 2-19, 126D1-A2
Carter urges US conservatn 2-12, 109C3
Canada prov OKs output rise 2-12, 153B3
Cutoff impact on US, world assessed 2-13–2-21, 126A2-C3
US cuts Canada deliveries 2-15, 153B2
Strikers return to work, leftist sympathers remain out 2-17, 2-19, 125B2
Bazargan seeks export resumptn, names state co chrmn 2-19, 125D2
USSR gas deals scored 2-24, 145E1
Exports urged, forgn debt cited 2-25, 144F3
Kuwait, Venezuela hike prices 2-26; Saudi, Iraq bar 1st 1/4 hike 2-27, 145F2
US plans conservatn 2-26, 2-27, 145B3
Crude export resumptn set 2-27, Westn consortium sale barred 2-28, 145F3
US firms curb sales 3-1–3-13, 183A3
Indl natns OK 5% demand cut 3-2, 161G3, 162B1
Exports resume, output cut 3-5, 161B3
Price rise effect on US econ warned 3-7, 182D2
S Africa Mideast imports rptd 3-26, 270G2
Canada oppositn ldr scores Exxon 3-27, 266E3
US Feb imports rptd down, cutoff cited 3-28, 252F2
US ends domestic price controls 4-5, 250C2
USSR gas deliveries resumed 4-5, 279G1
Oil productn rise rptd 4-13, price hiked 13% 4-15, 279E1

1980

France freezes Citibank funds 1-16, 48B1
UK trade reductn cited 1-16, 59F1
Sovt, Rumania, E Ger trade deals set 4-23, 298G1
Eurodif status unresolved 5-2, 409E1
Eur gold deposits returned 6-17, 464A3
Eur drug co units taken over 7-9, 546A2
US ct backs seized assets damages 7-10, Iran appeals 7-11, 546D1
US assets freeze, other econ measures scored 7-29, 571G3
W Ger shipping line insolvency rptd, trade reductn linked 8-18, 674F1
IMF revises SDR valuatn method, rial dropped from currency 'basket' 9-17, 695C2
Algeria quake aid rptd 10-11, 776E1

Oil & Gas Developments—*See also 'Iraqi War' above*
US threat backed by Connally 1-3, 5F1
Turkey oil deal rptd 1-10, 22C3
Econ sanctns warning issued, oil cutoff threatened 1-11, 29C2
US '79 consumptn drop, oil cutoff rptd linked 1-17, 90C2
USSR sales cited 3-2, 166B1
Khuzistan oil fields bombed 3-6—3-8; daily output cited 3-9, 178A2
Japan talks fail 4-17, price hike scored 4-19, trade threatened 4-20, 298D3
Japan oil supply substitutes rptd found 4-25; US offers aid 5-1, 341F1
Khuzistan pipe saboteurs executed 5-22, 5-23, 419F3*
US absolves oil cos in '79 shortage 7-17, 552C1
Crude oil price cut $1 7-17, 628B2
OPEC pricing agrmt lauded 9-18, 694A3
Iraq, Iran jets hit oilfields, exports stopped 9-21—9-24, 717E1; for subsequent developments, see 'Iraqi War' above

1976

Sports
Olympic results 7-18—7-31, 573E3, 576D2, D3

1977

1978

Sports
World Cup soccer finals, sidelights 6-1—6-25, 519F3
UN Policy & Developments
Leb peace force (Unifil) formed 3-19, 197D2; **for peacekeeping developments, see MIDDLE EAST—LEBANON**
Unifil expansn voted 5-3, 340F1
UNDOF mandate renewed 5-31, 400B2
FAO fears locust plague 6-12, 465E2
Assemb member 713F3
Unrest
Moslem riot quelled 1-9, 22C2
Pol prisoners estimated 2-9, 102C2
Tabriz anti-govt riots 2-18—2-19; death toll rpts 2-20, 2-21, 133A1
Govt troops quit Tabriz 2-23, police chief ousted 3-1, 152D3
Antigovt riots 3-26—4-2, 288F3
Govt counterviolence hinted 4-8, 4-12, 4-18, 352G3
Antigovt riots continue 5-8—5-11, 352D3
Teheran protest vs govt 5-15; Univ riots 5-30—5-31, 6-1, dorms shut 6-3, 437E3-438A1
Rights group vs repressn 5-16, 438C1
Shah warns vs Tudeh takeover 5-31, 438A1
Security chief dismissed 6-6, replacemt named 6-7, 437C3
Ex-Savak head out as amb to Pak 827B3
Moslems in anti-govt rallies 6-17, 573G3
Moslems to demand electns 7-12, 574A1
Antigovt riots 7-23—7-25, 8-10—8-13, 639F3
Movie house fires 8-18, 8-20; 430 die in Abadan fire, 10 arrested; Moslem fanatics blamed, ldr denies tie 8-20, 639C3
Abadan riots 8-22—8-23, 8-25; govt probe rpt 8-24, 668B1
Emami replaces Premr Amouzegar, appeases Moslems 8-27, 667E3
13 die in riots 8-31, 9-2, 693E1
Teheran anti-govt unrest 9-6—9-7; martial law imposed, rioters slain 9-8; violence continues 9-9—9-11, 693A1
Parlt protests vs martial law 9-10, 9-12, 693A2
Shah ties intl subversn to riots 9-11, 693G1
Dissidents seized, corruptn curbed 9-12, 693F1
Moslem ldrs ask passive resistance 9-13, 9-14, 740E1
Emami govt OKd; policies outlined, CP plot chrgd 9-16, 740A1
Parlt debates martial law 9-17, 740D1
Anti-govt riot in Golayegan 9-23, 740G1
Shah curbs royal family dealings 9-26, 740A2
Labor unrest 9-30, 10-1; bank, oil strikes end 10-3, 774G3
Iraq arrest of exiled activist protested 10-1; Khomeini freed, goes to Paris 10-6, 774F3
Exiled activists amnestied 10-2, 775A1
Shah vows contd reforms 10-6, 775B1
Strikes, riots continue 10-8, 10-11, 797F2
Press gives Khomeini coverage 10-10, 797D2
Press ban imposed 10-11; newsprs strike 10-11, 10-12; govt lifts ban 10-13, some newsprs return 10-16, 797B2

1979

Oil prices hiked again 5-10, 360F2
US oil firm-shortage link seen 5-15, 361F2
Japan exports cut 15% 5-18, 389C2
Oil prices hiked again 5-31, 396B2
Natl co dirs quit re attacks on Nazih 6-2, 425F3
Shell Group interests natlzd 7-5, 503A3
Abadan pipelines bombed 7-7–7-10, mil protectn asked 7-11, 524F3
USSR gas exports cut, pipe plans dropped; US co shipmts ended 7-28, 582G3
US Feb-May oil shortage detailed 8-6, 628F3
US sale announced 8-21, Carter defends 8-22, 622C3
Productn drop, gold rise linked 8-22, 645B3
Productn shortfall denied 8-24, 645B2
'79 1st 1/2 world oil output rptd 8-28, 645F1
US kerosene deal jeopardized 9-2, 708C3
Productn rptd down 9-5, 708E3
US '79 shortage studied 9-13, 702A3
State oil chrmn assailed, backers strike 9-24; ousted 9-28, 752B2
Oil prices hiked above OPEC ceiling 10-15, 781C1
Khuzistan pipelines blown up 10-17, 814G2
Forgn delivery 5% cut confrmd 11-8, 843F1
US bans oil imports, impact rptd 11-12, 861A1-862A1
Sales to US cos ended, US rpts allies' support 11-15; $ paymt shift hinted 11-19, 11-20, 879E2-C3
Daily revenue rptd $70 mln 11-20, 897B1
US $ paymts barred 11-23, hostile natns boycott ordrd 11-25, '80 productn cut set 11-26, 896D3
Pahlevi family '73-78 revenue skimming rptd 11-26, 897F2, F3
Carter scores US dependnc 11-28, 894D3
Japan dominated syndicate retains loan 12-7, 976G1
Japan defends oil purchases 12-11, 933E2
'79 revenues, output rptd; '80 1st 1/4 forecast 12-17, 976D1
Price per barrel rptd 12-21, 977B2
UN sanctns exempt oil sales 12-31, 974A3
UN Policy & Developments
Membership listed 695E2
US Emb hostage aid vowed 11-6, 841C2; **for subsequent developments, see 'U.S. Embassy Takeover' below**
Unrest—*See also 'Azerbaijan' and 'Kurdish Dispute' above, 'U.S. Embassy Takeover' below*
Teheran airport strike 1-1; mil takeover, foreigners leave 1-2, 2D3
Anti-govt riots, labor stoppages ease 1-2, 1-4, 1-5, 2F2, C3
Southn pipe reopens 1-5, heating oil reaches Teheran 1-6, 12A1
Rallies oppose Bakhtiar, shah 1-6–1-11, 11D3
Pol prisoners freed 1-9, 1-11, 11C3
Rail strike, tanker trains delayed 1-10, 12A1
Bakhtiar warning vs mil coup publshd 1-10, 12A2
8 slain in Shiraz 1-11, 26E1
Westn-natn aid offer to Turkey linked 1-12, 40E2
Teheran U rally 1-13, 26F1
6 soldiers slain in army clash 1-14, American slain 1-15, 26D1
US, UN emb workers strike 1-16, 26F2
Ahwaz, Dizful clashes 1-17, 1-18, 26F1
Pro-Khomeini rallies 1-19, 49G1-B2
Rezaiyeh riots, 8 die 1-22, 49F2
Govt to ban pub rallies 1-25, 49C2
Pro-Bakhtiar rally 1-25, 49D2
Troops fire at protesters in Teheran, Tabriz, Resht 1-26–1-28, 67E1
US mil aide shot 1-28; emb protest staged, consul beaten 1-29, 67D2
Army shows force, 4 killed in Teheran 2-1, 67B1
AF shows Bakhtiar support, anti-govt march held 2-6, 81D2
Khomeini backers take over 3 cities 2-7, 81E2
Anti-govt marches, 9 die in Gurgan 2-8, 81F2
Army factns clash, Khomeini forces join 2-9–2-10; army withdraws, **Bakhtlar overthrown 2-11**; clashes continue 2-12–2-13, 105A1-E2
US issues rights rpt 2-10, 107D3
3 top gens seized 2-11, 3 slain 2-11, 2-12, 105G1-A2, D2
Teheran riot, prisoners freed 2-11, 125F3
Gunmen asked to cede arms 2-12–2-13, 105B2
People's Fedayan issue demands 2-14, 125C1
US Emb attacked, marine kidnaped 2-14; freed 2-21, 125E2-B2
Savak head, mil ldrs executed 2-16, 2-20, 125D1
Imperial Guard dissolved 2-17, army discipline rptd restored 2-20, 125A2
Oil strikers, others return to work; leftist sympathizers remain out 2-17, 2-19, 125B2
Bakhtiar rptd in hiding 2-18, 125G1
Khomeini appeals to vigilantes 2-18, 125G1

1980

Shah of Iran—*See PAHLEVI, Shah Mohammed Riza*
Soviet-Afghan Issue
Afghan exiles protest Sovt interventn 1-1, 1-3, 1-6, 2A3-3B1
Sovt troops in Afghan near border 1-10, 1-16, 26C1, E1
Sovt role seen by Connally 1-11, 91F3
Shah extraditn from Panama asked 1-12; Panama arrest rptd 1-23, 1-24; Panama denies arrest 1-23, 47B1
Afghan rebels backed 1-14, 1-17, 27E2
Baluchi aid to Afghan rebels rptd 1-15, 26B2
Afghan asures on Sovt invasn, Bani Sadr vs Sovt move 1-16, 27B2
Sovt Afghan troops mass, border bolstered 1-19; Ghotbzadeh concerned 1-19, 1-22, 44D1
US rpt on Sovt invasn deterrent issued 2-1, 84B1, A2
Sovt Afghan invasn scored by Khomeini 2-4, 88A2; 2-11, 106A1
Sovt role opposed by US 2-5, 83B2
US says Sovts mass 2-8; Iran confirms 2-9, Sovts deny 2-10, 123E2
Moscow Olympic boycott set 4-11, 325D3
USSR links Afghan exit 4-24—4-25, 351G3
Afghan asks talks on Sovt troop exit 5-14, 361E2, F2
US rpts Afghan refugee total 5-17, 387G2
Islamic Conf 5-17—5-22, USSR scored 5-19, talks proposed 5-22, 395F2, D3
Afghans in Teheran anti-Sovt protests 12-27; USSR scores attack on emb 12-28, 990G3
Sports
Moscow Olympic boycott set 4-11, 325D3
IOC bans from Moscow Olympics 5-27, 420D3
UN Policy & Developments—*See also 'U.S. Hostage Issue' above*
Cncl meets on US emb takeover 1-11—1-12; votes sanctns, Sovts veto 1-13; reactn 1-11—1-14, 28G3-29C2
Waldheim presses for hostage release 1-20, 2-4, 88G2-A3
Kennedy urges probe 1-28, 74C3
Comm to probe shah formed, members listed 2-17, 122A1; see 'U.S. Hostage Issue' below
Women's conf in Denmark 7-14—7-30, 587B2
UN silence on US jailing of Iranians scored 8-2, Waldheim role urged 8-4, 587A1, D1
Cncl asks Iraqi truce, mediatn 9-23, 718D3; for subsequent developments, see 'Iraqi War' above
UN bars flag display by trapped ships 12-29, 978F1
Unrest—*See also 'Azerbaijan Developments', 'Iraqi War', 'Kurdish Dispute' above*
9 hostages freed in Tabriz 1-2, 4D1
Shiite, Sunni clashes 1-4—1-6, 4A1
Forghan ldr rptd arrested for Mofateh, other assassinatns 1-10, 20C2
US newsmen ousted 1-14, 29G2
Tabriz plot arrests rptd 1-19, 89D1
Israel sees no Palestinian-crisis link 1-20, 48F2
Militants attack newspr, newspr closes 2-3, 88D2
US issues rights rpt 2-5, 87F2
Airmen end 5-day sit-in protest 2-19, 122E2
7 in Forghan executed after trial 3-3, 164A3
Khuzistan oil fields bombed 3-6—3-8; Moinfar warns 3-9, 178A2
Labor unrest, student rallies curbed 4-8, 258G1
Leftist students, Moslems clash; Bani-Sadr, Khomeini score 4-18—4-22, 299F2
Ex-Min Parsa executed 5-8, 373E1
Executions resume 5-21—5-26, 419C3
Jew executed for 'spying' 6-5, 644B3
Khomeini warns of internal 'chaos' 6-10, 433C2
Drug dealers, others executed 6-10, 7-3, 7-8, 507A2
Exile base in Iraq rptd 6-11, 433G2-434A1
Leftists, Khomeini backers clash 6-12, 464C3
Khomeini backs schl takeover 6-14, 464F3
MD executed 6-29; MDs strike in protest 7-2, 507A1
Water workers strike 7-1—7-2, 507A1
Women protest Islamic clothing rule 7-5, 131 fired 7-8, 507C1
Sovts fear emb takeover; Ghotbzadeh reassures 7-7, 507C2
Mil coup plot fails 7-10; Bakhtiar, forgn states chrgd 7-11, 7-16; 2 confessns rptd 7-13, 539B2
41 executed 7-14, 7-20—7-21, 545F1
11 plotters executed, total at 36 7-31, 571C3
28 more plotters executed, total at 64 8-7, 8-15, 644D2
Bakhtiar plans govt overthrow 8-8, 644E2
Amnesty Intl scores executns 8-28, 671E2
More plotters shot, toll 92 8-28, 8-30, 671G2
'78 arsonists executed 9-4, 689F1
Iranians battle Kurdish rebels 12-5—12-30, 978B1
Riots in Caspian Sea towns 12-30, 978C1

1976

1977

1978

Nationwide strike honors Teheran dead 10-16, 797G2
Antigovt riots, 58 die; Oct toll 70 10-22—11-1, 827F2
Pol prisoners freed 10-23, 10-25; total release set 11-1, 827C3
34 Savak offcls ousted 10-29, 827B3
2 Cabt mins replaced 10-30, 827E3
Oil strike, exports cut; Premr Emami scores, wins confidence vote 10-31; some workers return 11-1, 827F1
Natl airline strike 11-1, 827E2
Moslem ldr wants govt on reforms 11-1, 827F3
Shah foes shun coalitn efforts 857E3
Teheran U riots, 3 die 11-4; 2 mins quit in protest, UK emb burned 11-5, 857F2
Emami, Cabt quit, mil takes over media 11-5; **mil rule imposed, Azhari heads 11-6, 857D2**
Shah vows anti-corruptn drive, free electns 11-6, 857D3
Parlt opening delayed 11-6, 857G3
Natl Front scores new govt 11-6, 858D1
Khomeini warns of civil war 11-6, says shah business deals invalid 11-9, 858E1
Ex-govt offcls, businessmen arrested 11-7, 11-8, 857G3
Coms formed to probe riots, shah family finances 11-9, 869E1
Oppositn urges contd strikes, protests 11-9, 869G1
6 killed in oil city riots 11-11, 869D1
Natl Front ldr arrested, further govt crackdown seen 11-11, 869C2
Anti-govt riots 11-11—11-14, 869E2
Striking oil workers ordrd back 11-12; some return, output rises 11-13—11-14, 869A1
Air strike ends, teachers strike 11-12, 869E1
8 more civilns in Cabt 11-16, 893G2
Kurds join protests 11-16, 893C3
Police launch corruptn search 11-17, 893A3
Meshed anti-govt riots 11-17, 893B3
Premr vows to restore order 11-18, 893A3
210 pol prisoners freed 11-19, 893F2
Shah renews free electn vow 11-19, 893F2
Forgn rights groups chrg torture 11-23, 12-11, 954E1
Anti-govt riots in Teheran 12-1—12-2, Tudeh Party blamed 12-3, 929C1
Khomeini asks soldiers desert 12-3, France scores 12-4, 929A2
Strikes cut oil output 12-4, govt workers face pay loss 12-6, 929A1
Teheran police statn raided 12-4, 929F1
Azhari blames 'atheists, saboteurs' 12-5, 929G1
Natl Front ldrs released 12-6, 929C2
Ashura march ban lifted 12-8, marches held 12-10—12-11, 953F1, C2
Grumman hq bombed 12-8, 954D1
US firms charter planes to evacuate dependents 12-8, 954D1
40-50 die in Isfahan riots 12-11—12-12; pro-govt counterrallies 12-13, 953E1
Striking oil workers stay out, productn drops 12-12, 953F2
Anti-govt riots, 100s die 12-14—12-31, 993A2
Oil strike, OPEC price rise linked 12-17, 977C3
Shah names Sadiqi to form govt 12-17; fails, Natl Front disavows 12-21, 993E1
Oil workers stage gen strike 12-18, 993G2
Sanjabi demands shah ouster 12-25, 993G1
'78 oil productn rptd down 12-26, 1000B3, D3
Shah names Bakhtiar to form civiln govt, foes oppose 12-29; Natl Front ousts Bakhtiar 12-30, 993A1
Shah departure plans denied 12-29, 993D1
Libya, PLO rptdly aid shah foes 12-29, 993E2
Forgn exchng mkt reactn 12-29, 998C2
Bakhtiar on new Cabt, shah status 12-30, 993D1

1979

Officer executed 2-23, 144B3
People's Fedayeen stage rally 2-23, Mujahedeen back 2-24, 145A1
IBM office occupied by rebels 2-24, 144B3, D3
Women protest curbs 3-8–3-12; US feminist backs protest 3-10, scores Khomeini 3-11, 179B2-A3
Rapist, ex-offcls executed 3-9, 3-13, 179F3; 13 others 3-14, 199E1
Turkomans revolt 3-26, issue demands 3-27; truce set 4-2, 247E2
Hoveida, others executed; reactn 4-7–4-13, 276E2-G3
Khomeini excesses spur Sanjabi, Teleghani departures 4-12–4-17, 276G3
12 executed 4-20, 4-23, 297B3
Qaraneh slain 4-23; funeral, Bazargan murder try rptd 4-24, 297C1
Komiteh purge launched 4-25, 321A3
Iran Arabs ask autonomy, PLO denies link 4-26, 4-27, 321D2-A3
Ayatollah Motahari slain 5-1; Khomeini scores, 1000's protest 5-2, 321D1
Executn toll at 200, 2 civilns included 5-7–5-9, 353G1-F2
Newspr closes after Khomeini attack 5-12, 357G2
Khomeini limits executns to murderers 5-13, denies amnesty 5-16, 357A1
Shah, kin, ex-offcls condemned 5-13, 357A1, E1-A2
Khomeini assures Jews 5-15, 357D2
Islamic workers force newspr strike 5-15, Khomeini lauds 5-15, 5-16, 358D1
213th execution 5-18, 389C1
Masjid-i-Sulaiman riot 5-18, Teheran protest vs press censorship 5-19, 389D1
Khalkhali Islamic ct ldrshp denied 5-21; Khalkhali rebuts 5-22, quits ct post 5-23, 389A1
Anti-US protests 5-24–5-25, 407F2
Ayatollah Rafsanjani shot 5-25, Khomeini blames US 5-26, 407D2
Khomeini meets Khuzistan ldr on Arab unrest 5-27, 408C1
Govt battles Khuzistan Arabs 5-30–5-31, 407G3
Khuzistan clashes 6-1; Khorramshahr autonomy rally 6-2, emergency lifted 6-4, 446A2
Khuzistan ldr chrgs govt bias 6-1, 446C2
Outsiders tied to Khuzistan unrest 6-3, 6-6, 446D1
Khomeini scores secular critics 6-5, 426A1
3 ex-aides executed 6-17, 6-24, 10 others on vice chrgs 7-12–7-13, 544B3
Arab ldr insulted, riots ensue 6-21–6-22, 525D1
Abadan pipelines bombed 7-7–7-10, Khuzistan clash rptd 7-11, 524F3, 525C1*
Khomeini supporter slain 7-8, 525E1
Khuzistan Arabs boycott natl holiday 7-10, 525C1
Khuzistan Arab violence 7-15, 5 executed 7-15–7-16, 544E2
Khomeini aide shot 7-15, 544A3
Moslem figure slain 7-21, 565D3
5 executed, toll at 350 7-21, 565E3
US 4-man TV crew ousted 8-6, 602D2
Leading newspr shut, staff arrested 8-7; 2 others get warning 8-8, 602G1
Khomeini foes, backers clash over new press rules 8-12–8-14; rallies curbed 8-14, 614A3
Rival guards clash at US Emb 8-12, 614C3
Gen mil mobilizatn ordrd 8-19, 635B1
26 newsprs closed 8-20, 8-21; Tudeh Party, Natl Dem Front hq seized 8-20, 635F1
2 Khomeini backers slain 8-26, 653A3
2 ex-MPs, shah's MD executed 9-24, 814B3
Khuzistan Arab attacks 9-30, 10-5, 10-7; 8 executed 10-4, 773D3
W Ger exec slain, Moslem guerrillas take credit 10-14, 814C3
Khuzistan pipelines blown up 10-17, 814G2
Executns halt ordrd 10-18, 814A3
Pope seeks Christian-Moslem ties 11-29, 930E3
Khomeini ally slain; US blamed, denies 12-18, 958F2
Baluchistan clashes, 12 die 12-20–12-22, 975E2-B3

U.S. Embassy Takeover

Carter pres campaign muted 10-24–12-13, 961G1
Bazargan meets US aide in Algiers 11-1, clergy vs mtg 11-4, 842B2
Iran guards block anti-US rally near emb 11-2, 862F2
Emb seized by students; hostages held, shah's return demanded 11-4, 841A1
Iranians freed; US, other natls held; 2 empty US consulates seized 11-5, 841E1, G1
Iran cancels mil pact 11-5, 841G1
US bars shah's return, asks intl help 11-5, 11-6; Waldheim vows aid 11-6, 841B2
Bazargan assures hostage release aid, quits govt 11-6, 841C1, 842G1
PLO seeks mediatn 11-6; US welcomes move, Iran rebuffs 11-8, 842B1
2 more Americans seized 11-7, 841F1
2 US mediators barred, scored by students 11-7, 841D2
US Cong reactn 11-7, 11-8, 842C3-843B1

1980

U.S. Hostage Issue

Waldheim in Iran on hostage missn 1-1—1-3; doubts release 1-4; briefs Carter 1-6, Cncl 1-7, 3F2
GOP reactn 1-1—1-5, 4E3, 5A1, E1
Nuclear 'doomsday clock' moved up 1-1, 12D3
Hostages a US pres campaign topic 1-4—1-7, 12F2, 13B2, B3
Emb militants demand Laingen 1-4; Khomeini ruling asked 1-5, rejctn hinted 1-8, 29E3
Viet war crimes trial for US hostage hinted 1-4, 29G3
Egypt offers bases to US to help free hostages 1-7, 11F1
Sadat, Begin discuss crisis 1-7—1-10, 12F1
CBS-TV barred 29A3
US, Egypt joint air games rptd 1-8, 11C1
US sees no break in crisis 1-8, 1-9, 29B3
Turkey-US bases pact curbed 1-9, 22C3
Carter poll status slips 1-10, 32G2

1976	1977	1978	1979	1980

1979

PLO reps in talks 11-7–11-11, 862G1
US studied shah's entry in July 11-8, 841G2
Carter cancels Canada trip, Vance urges calm; US protests staged 11-8, 842E2-C3
Papal nuncio asks hostage safety 11-8, visits 11-10, 862C2
Carter scores terrorism 11-8, 874B2
Emb seizure described, US rptd warned 11-9, 862D2
Egypt offers shah asylum 11-9, 862B3
Anti-Iran protests in US 11-9–11-11; ships, planes face US boycott 11-9, 863A1, D2
Carter asks US calm, meets hostage kin 11-9, 863A1
Bani-Sadr backs takeover 11-10, 862F1
4 forgn envoys visit hostages 11-10, 862A2
Hostages ask shah's return 11-10, 862B2
World reactn mixed 11-10–11-16, 878A3-D3
Khomeini scores Carter, Pope, intl pressure 11-11, 862B2
US Emb in Beirut seized 11-11, 862A3
US bans oil imports 11-12, freezes assets; reactn 11-14, 861A1-862A1
Mex closes emb 11-12, 862C3
Iran seeks UN Cncl debate, offers new terms 11-13; US blocks Cncl mtg 11-14, 861B1, 862A1
US orders status review for Iranians 11-13, 863F1
US shipping boycott spreads 11-13, 879C1
US freezes assets 11-14, 861F1
Mediator Clark recalled to US 11-14, 862G2
US scores threats 11-15, 877E2, 885E1
Armed Iranian seized in US 11-15, 879F1
Natl Iranian Oil ends sales to US cos 11-15, 879E2
US confrms, clarifies assets freeze 11-15, banks attach assets 11-16, 11-18; forgn reactn 11-15–11-18, 879C3-880G1
Students warn on shah's removal from US 11-16, 877D2
Anti-Iranian feeling in US high, restraint urged; deportatns, other measures rptd 11-16–11-27, 879D1, 898C1-E2
Khomeini orders blacks, women released; students balk 11-17; 13 describe ordeal; freed, flown to W Ger 11-18, 11-20, 878A1-D2
Carter rptd calm in crisis 11-17, 887C1
Hostages called 'CIA agents', 'spies'; trial threatnd 11-18–11-20, 877F1
US saw danger in shah's entry 11-18, 879F1
US demands all hostages freed 11-19, 877G2-878A1
US asks UN Cncl oppose hostage trial 11-19; Cncl refuses; Waldheim, Assemb pres issue pleas 11-19–11-20, 878D2
US White House rally ban upheld 11-19, 878D3
US threatens mil actn, reinforces naval presence 11-20, 877A1
Hansen in Iran, sees hostages 11-20–11-28; reps score visit 11-26, 895E2
World reactn backs US 11-20–11-27, 895B3
Khomeini: captors uncontrollable 11-21; US scores treatmt, warns of mil retaliatn 11-21–11-23, 894C2
Freed US hostages read captors plea 11-21, 894F2
Arab League bars Iran emissaries 11-21, 916D2
US denunciatns mount 11-22–11-26, 895A2
Forgn natls freed, 2 stay on 11-22, 895A3
US's Miller in Persian Gulf, rpts mil actn feared 11-23–11-28, 896A3
US $ oil paymts barred 11-23, other econ actns threatened 11-25, 11-26, 896D3
Waldheim asks UN Cncl debate; US, Iran agree 11-25; Bani-Sadr seeks delay, Cncl OKs 11-27, 896A1
Evacuatns, travel curbs ordrd 11-26, 894A2
Shariat Madari vs takeover 11-26, 895F3
US indicts Iranian arms smugglers 11-26, 898F2
Emb rptd mined 11-27, 895G1
Khomeini vs UN Cncl debate 11-27, fires Bani-Sadr 11-28, 896E1
Carter stresses firmness; defends shah's entry, denies Kissinger role 11-28, 894G2
US exec taken hostage 11-29, 895G2
US files World Ct suit 11-29, 896G1
Muharram mourning, const vote escalates rift 11-30–11-31, 895C2
Iran refuses to attend UN Cncl mtg 11-30, 913F1
Egypt renews asylum offer to shah 11-30, oppositn ldr scores 12-4, 914D1
Hostage status disputed 11-30–12-1; spy trial threatened 12-1, 12-4, chrgs bolstered 12-6, 914G1-A3
Anti-US protests in Mideast, Asia 11-30, 12-2, 914B3, 915C1
US banks sued for UK, French assets freeze 11-30, 12-5, 915A2
UN Cncl meets 12-1–12-2, asks hostages freed 12-4; Waldheim contacts Iran 12-5, 913A1, G1
US seeks haven for shah 12-1, 12-3; Egypt, S Africa, 2 Latin natns ruled out 12-5, 914B1

1980

UN Cncl meets on emb takeover 1-11—1-12; votes sanctns, Sovts veto 1-13; US scores, USSR defends 1-14, 28G3-29A2
Iran warns vs sanctns 1-11—1-14, 29A2
US pres candidates note 1-11—2-7, 91C2, E2, A3, F3
Mondale boosts Carter 1-12, 32E2
US newsmen ousted; UK, W Ger rptrs warned 1-14; Teheran defends move 1-15, 29D2-A3
Wounded Khomeini aide treated in US 1-17, 30C1
Hostages letters publshd 1-18—1-20, 47A3
Waldheim presses for hostage release 1-20, 2-4, 88G2-A3
Carter State of Union topic 1-21, 1-23, 41E1, 42B1, D1, 43G3
US naval force deploymt scored 1-22, 44F1
US press aide called spy 1-22, 47G3
Shah-Panama hostage deal opposed 1-24, 47F1
Bani-Sadr on hostages, captors dispute 1-26—1-28, 67B1
Canada aids 6 US diplomats escape, closes emb 1-28; pol motive denied 1-29; Iran warning dismissed 1-30, 66C1-B3
Bani-Sadr electn response 1-28, 67E1
Kennedy scores Carter, urges UN comm probe 1-28, 74C3
Islamic conf vs US hostage holding 1-29, 67G1
US thanks Canada for rescue 1-31; details rptd 2-1, 88B3
Militants say govt ignores US spy charges 2-1, 2-2, 88C2
Canada describes US envoy rescue 2-1, 88F3
Militants plan mass rally 2-2; cancel 2-3, 88B2
Iran newpsr ed linked to US press attache visit; newspr closes 2-3, 88D2
Revolutionary Cncl OKs intl comm 2-3; Bani-Sadr sets hostage release terms 2-11—2-13, rpts secret plan OKd 2-13, 105D1
Rev Cncl OKs intl comm 2-3, Bani-Sadr sets hostage release terms 2-11—2-13, rpts secret plan OKd 2-13, 105D1
125 Iran envoys 'missing' in US roundup 2-4, 122G2
Bani-Sadr denounces US Emb militants 2-6—2-7; militants claim Khomeini mandate 2-9, 105A2
US DJ fired, '79-80 'captivity' cited 2-6, 199D3
US delays sanctions 2-7, 88E2
Melkite cleric visits hostages 2-8, 106D1
Newsmen chrgd re gifts from shah 2-9, 122B3
US group sees emb militants 2-10, 106B1
Carter pol ads cited 2-10, 109E1
PLO observes Iran anniv rites 2-11, 106B1
US Emb escapee airs more details 2-12, 106E1
Kennedy, US Admin exchng chrgs re intl probe comm; other issues 2-12—2-13, 109B2-C3, E3, 110G1-D2
Carter backs intl comm plan, sees 'positive signs' for hostage release 2-13, 105A1, 109C2, C3
Reagan vs US apology, defends shah 2-14, 128D3
UN comm to probe shah set 2-17, Iran OKs, bars hostage role 2-18, 2-19; comm member hints linkage 2-20, 122D1
Kennedy vs US complicity with shah 2-18, 130B2
Khomeini renews demand for shah return, backs militants 2-20; militants link shah return to hostage freedom 2-21, 122A2
US policy scored by GOP pres candidate 2-20, 129D3
Comm arrives 2-23; meets pres, forgn min 2-24, hears testimony 2-26, visits victims' cemetery 2-27, seeks hostage mtg 2-28, 137A1, F2
Delay in hostage release hinted 2-23, 2-27; Carter warns vs 'pessimism' 2-24, 137C1, E1, C2
US stresses UN comm hostage release role, cites Waldheim statemt 2-23, 2-27, 137F1-C2
Bani-Sadr denies US moderate claim; at anti-US rally 2-25, 137D2
US newsmen reentry OKd 2-26; AP invited 2-27; 2 US newsmen turned back 2-28, 138E1-A2
Reagan 'basic speech' scores Carter 2-29, 207D3
Prosecutor seeks hostage re Forghan link 3-2; Ghotbzadeh replies 3-4, 164G2
'60 Minutes' airs Iran segmt 3-2, US govt pressure rptd 3-6, 239B1
Hostage kin score US policy 3-4, 164D2
Militants set conditns for comm hostage visit 3-5, 164C2
Comm delays Iran departure 3-6, 164D1
Militants to yield hostages to govt 3-6, 164E1, B2
Ghotbzadeh, captors clash on release 3-7—3-9, 177B2
Newsmen readmitted 3-7, 178C2
Connally cites in 'basic speech' 3-7, 184E3, 185E1
Carter vs apology on US actions 3-8, 177F2
Khomeini backs captors, sets release terms, links comm rpt to hostage visit 3-10; comm quits Iran, Ghotbzadeh sees return 3-11, 177A1
US rejects terms, says Iran breaks comm pact 3-10, weighs action 3-11, 177F1-A2

1976

1977

1978

1979

Mex denies US pressure to readmit shah 12-3, 914F1
Kennedy anti-shah remarks draw fire in US 12-3, 918D3
US plans econ pressure vs Iran 12-4, 12-5, 913B2
Carter reelectn announcemt subdued 12-4, 918F2, 919C1
USSR chrgs US mil 'blackmail', US scores 12-5, 913E2
UK upholds US assets freeze 12-5, 915F1
Carter poll gain linked; R Carter, Mondale heckled in NY 12-5, 918E2, A3
Iran affirms hostage trial 12-5, 12-7, 934F1
US seeks sanctns in W Ger 12-6; Bonn curbs credit guarantees, arms exports 12-7, 934A1
SALT Sen debate delay linked 12-6, 938E3
Carter, aides brief hostage kin 12-7, 934D1
US hostage plan conveyed by Mideast, Eur envoys 12-8, 934B1
Intl tribunal to probe US 'crimes' 12-8, 12-11; US protests 12-10, 934C2
Laingen linked to Azerbaijan rebel ldr 12-8, 936E2
Egypt fears US Mideast setlmt attentn diverted 12-8, 938B1
Iran vs World Ct hostage role 12-9, US files plea 12-10, 933D1
US sees intl pressure 12-9, 933F2
UN assured on hostage safety 12-9, 934F2
US pres candidate reactn 12-10–12-26, 982A2-983C2
Vance in Eur; seeks econ sanctns, scores Japan 12-10–12-11, 933B2
NBC interviews hostage 12-10; networks, Admin score 12-11, 934A3
Carter poll leads linked 12-11, 962E3
US check of student visas ruled illegal 12-11, 935F2
US ousts Iran diplomats 12-12, 933A1
US thanks NATO for support 12-12, 959D2
Khomeini OKs intl tribunal, clergy visit 958A2, B2
Carter rptd hopeful 12-14, 958E2
Japan cuts oil imports 12-14, backs US pressure vs Iran 12-17–12-18, 958D3-959C1
Shah leaves for Panama 12-15, Iran calls departure 'victory' 12-16, 957A1
World Ct rules Iran must free hostages 12-15, 957C2
Forgn min, students on hostage trial, release for Xmas 12-15–12-18, 958D1-A2
US blamed for shah 'crimes', escape' to Panama 12-16, 958C1
UN outlaws hostage-taking 12-17, 957F2-958A1
Khomeini backs students on hostages, denies policy power, scores Carter on shah's exit to Panama, explains UN Cncl mtg boycott 12-17, 958A1
UK backs Carter 12-17, 968G1
US hints at punitive moves 12-18, 958B2
Iranian amb to Sweden seized, US ties cited 12-19, 975G3
US seeks UN econ sanctns 12-21, warns USSR vs veto 12-22; Cncl OKs US-sponsored res 12-31, 974F2
Khomeini OKs Christmas svcs 12-21; US, French clergy see hostages 12-24–12-25, Iran forgn min 12-27; captive total disputed 12-25–12-28, 975B1-B2
Ex-CIA agent barred tribunal role 12-23, Iran rejctd CIA files-hostage exchng plan 12-27, 991E2
Iran broadcasts anti-shah statemts by 2 hostages 12-25, 975E1
US check on student visas upheld; deportatns, other data rptd 12-27, 975B2
Carter bars Ia debate 12-28, 983E2
Iran cool to Waldheim missn 12-30; Waldheim, 2 aides depart 12-31, 974D3

1980

Bani-Sadr vs militant, Rev Cncl stand 3-11, 177D1
Waldheim lauds govt role on hostages 3-11; meets Vance 3-12, 178B1
UN comm rpts mtg with 3 US aides in Iran Forgn Ministry 3-12, 178C1
Immigratn data since emb takeover rptd 3-12, 178F1
US confirms 50 hostages 3-13, 178D1
Carter defends immigration policy 3-14, 209G1
US appeals to World Ct 3-18—3-20, 203C3
EC, Greece may cut Iran ties 3-20, 204C1
Ghotbzadeh chrgs US plot vs shah's extraditn 3-22, 217G1
US calls shah's Egypt asylum set back 3-23; discounts hostage trial 3-24, bars mil move 3-26, 217G2
Ghotbzadeh warns on shah's asylum, Sadat discounts threat 3-25, 217B2, D2
US 'apology' notes rptd; US denies, admits 3-25, 4-1, 241G1,C2
Hostage trial asked by Islamic ldr 3-26, 217F2
US, Turkey sign base pact 3-29, 255D3
EC ldrs ask hostages release 3-31, 242C1
Iranian student deportatn ban denied by US Sup Ct 3-31, 291G2
Carter defers sanctns, cites hostage transfer pledge 4-1, 241A1
Carter sees breakthrough 4-1, 246F2
Carter bars apology 4-1, 247B1
Intl mediatn group formed, mission fails 4-5, 258D1
Rev Cncl shifts hostage decisn to Khomeini 4-6, Khomeini upholds militants' control 4-7, 257B1, 258B1
US clerics visit hostages 4-6, 258C2
Carter cuts ties, ousts Iran aides, imposes sanctns; statemt text 4-7; aides leave US; students, others exempt 4-8, 257A1-C2
Bush, Reagan score Admin 4-7, 4-8, 264E2, A3
US asks allied support vs Iran 4-8, 4-9, 257D2
Khomeini hails end of ties 4-8; militants threatn to kill hostages 4-9, 258E1
Italy cancels copter deliveries 4-8, 282D1
Hostages on TV, chrg US spying; US denies 4-9, 258B2
Hostage spy confessns claimed 4-9, 4-10, 282A3
Carter defends policy 4-10, 264G1
EC scores Iran, withholds sanctns 4-10, Cncl of Europe, Japan endorse; US disappointed 4-10, 4-11, 281G2
3 US TV networks vs hostage film purchase 4-10, 282C3
Forgn natns neutrality on US policy asked 4-11, 4-12, 282F1
EC, Japan plead for hostages, recall ambs 4-12, 282E1
Khomeini gets papal plea on US ties 4-12, replies 4-15, 282A2
US vs Iranian visa extensns 4-12, US ouster orders challenged 4-17, 282D3
Carter presses allies to back sanctns, hints mil moves 4-13, 281C2
Red Cross aides visit hostages 4-14, rpt; US reactn 4-14, 4-15, 282B2
Bani-Sadr: US blocked accord on shah 4-16; US denies 4-17, 283C1
US threatens mil actn, widens sanctns 4-17, 281A1
Portugal bans trade 4-17, 281F2
US warned vs more sanctns 4-18, 298C2
Timms in Teheran 4-19, see son 4-21, 299E1-B2
Schmidt sympathizes with US 4-20, 303E1
Anderson, Bush score Carter 4-20, 328D1, B2
US methodists voice sympathy for Iran 4-21; delegation sees Carter, Farhang 4-23, 324C3
US aides see mil moves 4-22, Carter decisn disavowed 4-23, Sen seeks role 4-24, 297C2, 298F2-A3
EC votes econ, diplomatic sanctns 4-22, US lauds 4-23, 298C1
Canada, Japan set sanctns 4-23, 4-24, 298B3
Hostage kin seek W Eur support 4-23, 299C2
US newsmen ousted 4-23, 378E2
US rescue try fails, 8 die 4-24; US statemt, text 4-25, 297A1
Egypt, Oman, Israel rescue role debated 4-24, 297A2
Iran warns US vs port mining 4-24, 298A3
Map of rescue mission 322A1
USSR scores rescue try 4-24—4-25, 352A1
Iran lauds rescue failure 4-25, 297B2
US details rescue missn 4-25, 4-27—4-29, Col Beckwith rpts 5-1, 321A1-322G2
Khomeini, Ghotbzadeh, Bani-Sadr score US rescue try 4-25, 4-26, 322A3, B3, 323B1
Foreign reactn to rescue attempt 4-25—4-27, 324B1
Hostages moved out of US Emb 4-26, 322D3
Mrs Timm scores rescue mission 4-26, returns to US 4-28, 323B1
Iran shows film of rescue site 4-26, 323C1
Iran displays dead US raiders 4-27, Carter scores 4-28; Red Cross, papal reps to repatriate bodies 4-28, 323D1
Vance resigns re rescue oppositn 4-28, 323A2, E2

1976	1977	1978	1979	1980

Carter defends rescue missn 4-29, 323D3
Capucci arranges repatriatn of dead US raiders 4-29; bodies returned via Switz, Carter declares offcl mourning 5-6, 337A2
US condemns Iran Emb seizure in UK 4-30, 324C3
Carter ends campaigning ban 4-30, 328F1, A2
Japan urges US moderatn 5-1, 341E1
Iran Emb rescue in UK lauded 5-6, 337D1
Hostage dispersal completed, militants retain control 5-6, 337E2
Carter leads in ABC poll 5-6, 342G1
US free-lance rptr arrested 5-6, 434B1
US Defense Dept issues rescue missn rpt, Sen com's probe 5-7, 337G2
Muskie for incentives-sanctns pkg 5-7, 343D1
Carter skips Tito funeral 5-8, 338D3
'79 terrorism deaths rptd 5-11, 365E3
UN comm role renewed 5-17; Waldheim briefs rep 5-22; Westn diplomats oppose missn 5-23; comm rep in Iran 5-26, 393C2
EC imposes limited sanctns, US lauds 5-18; UK modifies stand 5-19; Bonn, US deplore 5-20, 5-21; Bonn, Paris implement move 5-21, 378F1-E2
W Ger leftists back US Emb takeover 5-18, 500E3
Student immigratn case refused by US Sup Ct 5-19, 440B2
Turkey bars sanctns 5-22, 393B2
Islamic Conf opposes sanctns, rescue move 5-22, 395B3
World Ct demands hostages freed, US lauds ruling 5-24, 393A1
3 Eur Socialists visit 5-25—5-26; Kreisky warns vs new sanctns 5-27, 394C1
Parlt meets 5-28, 394G1-B2
UK modifies sanctns further 5-29, 393E1
Carter cites 'terrorism' 5-29, 423F3
US warns citizens vs travel ban violatn 5-30, 419A1
Canada forgn min vs US mil moves 6-1, 429A2
Clark group defies US travel ban, attends anti-US conf 6-2—6-5; US post-shah plot aired 6-2, 418E2, 419A1
Clark group members listed 6-2, 419C1
Clark sees Bani-Sadr, OKs US probe comm; group hears Khomeini score Carter 6-4, 418C3
2 US clerics meet militants at US Emb 6-4, 418E3
US Sen com study faults rescue missn 6-5, 419E1
Iran discloses rescue missn details 6-5, 419E2
Clark scored by anti-US conf, Teheran radio; Ghotbzadeh defends 6-6, 433A1
3 US group members leave 6-6, 433C2
Clark, 5 others meet militants 6-7, leave Iran 6-8, 433A2
US seeks Clark trip probe 6-7, Muskie seen lenient 6-8, Carter for prosecutn 6-10, 6-16; Clark reacts 6-11, 6-15, 459A3
Bani-Sadr vs hostage trial 6-9, 433G1
US-Oveissi aides mtg rptd 6-11, 434A1
Carter bars mil steps 6-12, 506F3
UN comm rep ends visit, Iran vs return 6-16; missn failure confrmd 6-19, 464E1
Eur gold deposits returned 6-17, 464B3
US Sen vs pvt citizen negotiatns 6-18, 460A1
Plot vs Bani-Sadr rptd 6-19, 464G2
Yugo, US urge release 6-25, 474C3
Iran indepndnc backed 6-25, 474C3
Portugal vows US support 6-26, 475C1
NATO condemns terrorism 6-26, 490B1
UPI admits error in Clark story 6-27, 507D2
Bani-Sadr crisis 'insoluble' 6-28, 490D2
US denies anti-Khomeini broadcasts 6-29, 490F2
Carter scores Iran govt 7-4, 505E2
Hostages moved again 7-6, 506D3
Queen hospitalized 7-7; release ordered 7-10, freed 7-11, arrives US 7-18, 539E1
Carter thanks Japan for sanctns support 7-8, 506E1
US ct backs seized asset damages 7-10, Iran appeals 7-11, 546D1
Reagan pres nominatn acceptance speech 7-17, 533B1, 534G3
Queen sees Carter 7-19, details captivity 7-21, 545G2
US anti-Khomeini protests canceled 7-22, 545E2
B Carter role rptd 7-22—7-24, 549B1
Mock executn of hostages rptd 7-24, 572A1
Last 2 US newsmen, 3 UK rptrs flee 7-25, 572B1
US walks out on Iranian UN speech 7-25, 572D2
Canadians honored for escape role 7-25, 578A1
Shah's death no effect on hostages 7-27, 571C2
US Cong sends parlt hostage plea via Swiss 7-29, 571D3
Hostage debate delayed 8-4, 587C1
Carter rpts on brother's role 8-4, 592D3, 593B2, B3
US Sen opens B Carter probe 8-4, 595A3
US pro-Khomeini marches 8-7, 8-8, Iranian funding denied 8-9, 635F1, C2
Hostage kin conf 8-8—8-9; letter to Rafsanjani asks talks 9-8; letter aired 9-15, backed by US 9-16, 693F2
Parlt ldr gets Westn natns hostage plea 8-16; rebuffs Westn diplomats appeal 8-17, 634C3

1976

U.S. Relations
Helms named terrorist target 365G2
US colonels' slayers executed 1-24, 78G1
CIA Kurd aid request rptd 1-26, 93B1
Mrs Javits quits post 1-27, 160A2
Iran arms purchase drop seen 2-4, 102C1
F-14 jet order canceled, F-16s sought, commissn disputed 2-17, 140B1
Northrop repays agent fee, denies Iran seeks Page penalty deductn 2-23, 156F2
Kurd ldr scores Kissinger 2-25, 146D1
US sen rpts on visit 2-28, 161B1
AWACS plane offer cited 3-2, 183F2
US Navy secy censured re gratuity 3-16, 200C3

1977

U.S. Relations
US issues rights abuse rpt, contd arms sales urged 1-1, 51C1
Boeing rpts consultant 1-5, ct backs secrecy 2-25, 215C3
US SEC rpts GTE paymts 1-27, 79C2
Zahedi mediates Hanafi surrender 3-11, 192A3
Terrorist sentnc cut link to US rights policy denied 4-11, 527A2
Carter plans AWACS sale 7-7, drops deal 7-28, 8-2, 611D2
Carter visit scheduled 9-23, 738F1
Carter visit deferred 11-7, 854A1; rescheduled 11-29, 914B2
7 US AWACS, 16 F-16s purchased 11-8, 905A3

1978

U.S. Relations
US troop presence rptd 1-2, 5E2
US ct OKs drug trust suit 1-11, 33D3
Textron paymts queried 1-24—2-28; CIA, Defns info on Khatemi rptd 1-25, 2-17, 161F1-G2
CIA sees no A-bomb before '84 1-26, 61C2
US sets arms sales ceiling 2-1, 106B3
US issues rights rpt 2-9, 101D3, 102B2
Textron bribe evidence rptd destroyed 5-8, 449B1
A-fuel export license deferral rptd 5-20, 408B2
Arms sales cutback urged 7-16, 564A2
Boeing chrgd re payoffs 7-28, 642G3
Parsons payoff cited 8-4, 643C2 ★, D2

1979

U.S. Relations—*See also 'Monetary', 'Oil' and 'U.S. Embassy Takeover' above*
Anti-shah riot in Calif 1-2, US govt warns 1-4, 3E1
US cancels naval task force move 1-2, 3E1
US advises shah on departure 1-3, vows Bakhtiar cooperatn 1-4, 3B1
Iran army cmdr seeks US refuge 1-4, 2C3
Grumman paymts chrgd 1-4, 16A2
Bakhtiar backs US ties 1-5, 3D1
Guadeloupe summit topic 1-5–1-6, 12G2
US gen contacted mil ldrs 1-8, 12G1
US jets to visit Saudi 1-10, 12B2
US consulate flag burned 1-11, 11G3

1980

US invasn plan rptd, denied 8-16, 635A1
US issues final rpt on rescue missn 8-23, 644B1
US discounts invasn plan, Sovt interventn feared 8-25, 644G1
Militants move hostages, warn US vs mil actn 8-25, 644B2
Amnesty Intl cites hostage pleas 8-28, 671F2
Muskie asks hostage release 8-31, US denies new initiative 9-1, 671E1
Parlt panel drafts hostage release plan 9-1, 671G1
Rajai scores Muskie plea, Muskie letter aired 9-9, 688C3
Khomeini sets release terms; omits trial, apology 9-12, statemt text aired 9-15; US reactn 9-12, 9-15, 693A1-A2
Reagan urges hostage release concessns 9-13, 699G3
Parlt com urges debate 9-14, debate delayed 9-16, 693E2
Parlt speaker demands US apology, scores Khomeini terms 9-15, 693C2
Carter admits hostage release prospects bleak 9-15—9-18, 699E1
US-Bani-Sadr exchng aired 9-17, 693A2
Carter cites talks 9-18, 698C3
US briefs Western leaders 9-19, 719B3
US renews hostage plea, parlt head restates demands 9-22, 719G2
Parlt members visit US Emb 9-22, 719A3
Parlt sets study comm 9-30; 7 named, US talks barred 10-2, 769B1
Relief act clears Cong 9-30, signed 10-14, 981B2
US Sen issues B Carter rpt 10-2, 763E3
Carter, Muskie seek Rajai mtg in NYC 10-16, 799G3
US denies spare parts-hostage trade 10-16, 800B1
Rajai: US uses Iraqi war re hostage release 10-17; US denies 10-18, 798A3, 799A1
Iraq sees hostage, spare parts deal 10-18, 799C2
US to unfreeze assets for hostages 10-20, Iran rejcts 10-22, 799G3
Reagan hits issue 10-20—10-22, 802D1
Carter ridicules Reagan stance 10-21, 10-22, 802C3
Parlt member sees early release 10-22, 799D3
Rajai: US set to meet terms 10-22, 799E3
Parlt debates terms 10-26—10-27, 10-29; adjourns for lack of quorum 10-30, 819F2
Carter, Reagan TV debate 10-28, 813D1, 814D2-B3, 820B3
Reagan avoids issue 11-2, 840A2
Carter interrupts campaign windup 11-2, 841A1
Parlt sets release terms, text 11-2; govt takes hostage custody, comm named 11-3, 853A1, F2
Carter, Muskie hopeful re Parlt move 11-2, 11-3, 853A1, F2
Algeria named intermediary, delivers terms 11-3, US vs quick reply 11-4, 853F2, B3
Iraq links oil min capture 11-3, 854D3
Carter sees electn influence 11-4, 837E1, 848G1, E2, E3
EC vows trade ban end on hostage freedom 11-4, 879C3
Reagan cautns vs delays 11-6, 839D1
Ghotbzadeh arrest linked 11-7, 862G1
US offcls in Algeria 11-10—11-11; Algeria delivers US response 11-12, Iran com sets study 11-13, 861A1
Laingen interview broadcast in US 11-11, 862B1
Carter on US response to terms 11-12, 861F1, 865D3
US assets freeze backed by ct 11-13, 861D2-862A1
Hostage release demands rptd OKd 'in principle' by US 11-20; Iran vs response 11-22, 912C3-913A1
US-Algerian talks in US 11-26—11-27, Algiers 12-2—12-3; US rpts 12-4, 912E3-913A1
Militants, govt rpts on hostage control conflict 11-27, 12-1; US seeks info 12-2, 913A1
Iran asks $24 bln for hostage return 12-19; text released, US rejects 12-21; Iran revises demands 12-27, 973A1, A2
Iran warns of trials 12-22, 12-31, 973G2
US concerned re treatmt 12-22; Iran prelate, Algerian aide visit, allay fears 12-25—12-26, 974E1
Reagan assails Iran 12-24, 12-28; Rafsanjani replies 12-29, 974B1
Film clips broadcast in US 12-25-12-26, 974E1, F2
US airs secret earlier plan, calls it 'basic' offers new plan 12-30, 973B2
US offers new plan on hostages 12-30, Algeria takes plan to Iran 12-31, 973E2

U.S. Relations—*See also 'Iraqi War', 'Soviet-Afghan Issue', 'U.S. Hostage Issue' above*
US for stable govt 2-5, 83B2
US issues rights rpt 2-5, 87F2
Iran coup plot fails 7-10, 539D2, F2
US GOP platform text 7-15, 536B3
Tabatabai slain in US 7-22; 2 suspects seized, 3d sought 7-23, 545B1, B2
Iranian protesters in US arrested 7-27, freed 8-5; Iran backing chrgd 8-7, 586D1, C3
Iran protests US arrests 8-2—8-5, 586D3
Khomeini scores US 8-6, 635G1
Tabatabai 3d suspect flees US 8-6, 671D3
Moslems in DC pro-Khomeini marches 8-7, 8-8, 635F1

1976

US air cos in oil barter talks 5-9, 5-11, US asks oil price freeze 5-9, 340A1
French pres visits US 5-17—5-22, 372A2
Iran seeks arms relay to Morocco 5-22, 458C2
Police denies torture, CIA anti-terrorist aid 5-26, 418F2
Occidental deal set 6-20, 6-21, 450B2
US Sen rpts on arms sales 8-1, shah rebuts 8-6, 581C2
Kissinger meets shah 8-6; arms, trade pact signed 8-7, 581A2
Drops Occidental deal 8-27, 643D1
F-14 sale, Nixon donatn linked 8-27; sale probed 9-15—9-26, 979D3-G3
3 Amers slain 8-28; US, West tighten security 8-29, 8-30, 652F1
Ford defends arms sales 9-9, 665C2
Rpt Iran seeks 300 F-16s 9-10, 773A3
Civln force for F-16 jets set, US offcls ask Sen OK 9-16, 773F2
Sovt defector asks asylum 9-23, 773D2
Ford, Carter debate 10-6, 742A1
Carter arms sales data disputed 10-8, 764A1
US Gen Brown remarks rptd 10-17—10-18, clarified 10-18, 787D1, B2, G2
USAF training pact rptd 11-24, 925E2

1977

Shah in US; sees Carter on rights, A-power, arms sales 11-15—11-16; pro, anti-shah demonstratns, 100 hurt 11-15, 897A1-D2
Navy ex-officers acquitted on contract fraud 11-24, 942E2
'76 New Orleans investmt rptd 12-5, 997C3
Grumman F-14 comm settlemt rptd 12-15, 978B1
Carter visits 12-31, 1000E3, G3

1978

US reaffirms shah support; oil, arms sales cited 9-10, 693E2
Moslem ldr scores Carter 9-13, 740F2
US again supports shah 10-10, 797A3
US A-work faces curbs 10-22, 816C3
US monitors oil strike 10-31, 827D2
Carter assures shah of support 10-31, 827G3
Air strikers demand rial freed vs US $ 11-1, 827F2
ITT paymts chrgd 11-2, 876C1
US backs mil rule 11-6, 858B2
US workmen, kin leave 11-10, 869C1
Nixon backs shah 11-11, 900A3
Shah vs aid to prevent ouster 11-18, 894A1
USSR warns US vs interventn, US rebuts 11-19, 893D3
Carter backs shah, shuns interventn 11-30, 936E2
US sets long-range crisis study 12-4, 929E2
US, USSR clash on arms sales, talks stalled 12-5—12-15; US rift rptd 12-19, 996A3
US kin flee, no evacuatn planned 12-6, 929C2
US to pay for kin exodus 12-6, departures increase 12-9, 12-11, 954A1
Carter unsure of shah survival, US denies confidence loss 12-7, 953E3
Grumman hq bombed 12-8, 954D1
Carter vs Khomeini role, reaffirms shah support 12-12, 953C3
Khomeini warns on oil 12-13, 953B3
US emb staff bolstered 12-13, 953G3
US intelligence failure feud rptd 12-20, 994C2
US oil exec slain 12-23, 993C2
Rally at US emb 12-24, 993E2
US, Sovts trade interventn chrgs 12-28, 994F1
US alerts PI naval force 12-29, 993C1, 994D1
US rpts Libya, PLO anti-shah role 12-29, 993F2
US asks dependents quit 12-31, 994B2

1979

US backs shah vacatn, Bakhtiar 1-11, 12E1
CIA UFO probe detailed 1-12, 93D1
Students protest in Ga 1-14, 31A3
Berkowitz slain 1-15, 26D1
Shah leaves for visit 1-16, 25C1
Carter backs Bakhtiar, defends intell rpts 1-17, 26G1
Khomeini vs US cooperatn plea 1-18, 26A1
US airmen quit Dizful base 1-18, 26F1
CIA monitor rptd dismantled 1-18, 26E2
Ford: shah scored US policy shift 1-21, 50A1
Carter State of Union Message cites crisis 1-23, 48F1
Shah delays visit, US policy shift blamed; US: invitatn stands 1-23, 49B3, 50A1
US jets leave Saudi 1-23, 50F1
US House panel blames Admin for intell failure 1-24, 67D2
US mil aide shot 1-28, 67D2
Iran troops protest at US Emb, consul beaten 1-29, 67D2
US surveys forgn students, plans visa probe 1-29, 93F2
US ordrs kin evacuated 1-30, 1,350 leave 1-31, 67A2 2-5, 84C3
Zahedi out as amb to US 2-6, 81D2
US renews Bakhtiar backing 2-6, 82D2
Teng vs US stand 2-7, 84B1
Young lauds Khomeini 2-7; sees reps, assured re minorities 2-10, 106F1
US newsman slain 2-10, 105B2, 176D3
US issues rights rpt 2-10, 107D3
US defns secy reassures 4 Mideast natns 2-10–2-18, 142B2, E2, C3
Prison riot frees 2 US natls 2-11, businessman claims credit 2-19, 125F3
Carter seeks Khomeini ties 2-12, 106A1
US evacuatn alert set 2-12, 106C1
US concerned re F-14 safety, intell post protectn rptd 2-12, 106D1
Emb attacked, Marine kidnaped 2-14, freed 2-21, 125E2-B3
USSR broadcasts prompt US protests 2-14–2-16, 125D3
Bazargan govt recognized 2-16, 125B3
1,700 US natls evacuated 2-17–2-18, 125C3
Carter bars interventn, warns USSR 2-20, 123E2, A3
3 consulates closed 2-20, 125D3
Intell posts banned 2-21; US personnel flee, secrets safety disputed 2-24–2-28, 145F1
Carter vs simplistic criticism 2-22, 124D1
IBM office held by rebels 2-24, 144B3, D3
Iran Air cuts NY flights, cancels Boeing contract 2-25, 144E3
Iran takes over US listening post 3-1, US fears secret data lost 3-2, 161C2, F2
2 US activists ousted 3-5, 3-19, 199B2
US sets student visa crackdown 3-8; enrollmt chart rptd 167D2, A3
Millet backs women protesters 3-10, scores Khomeini 3-11, 179F2
CIA tap of Khomeini aide rptd barred 3-11, 180B1
Hoveida trial halted 3-16, 199G1
US offers shah residency 3-29, 247C3
U-2 use for SALT verificatn seen 4-3, 258E2
Intell posts loss cited re SALT verificatn 4-11, 295D1
US denounces executns 4-12, 276E3
Khomeini: US foments disunity 4-17, 277B2
Shah asked to stay out of US 4-19, US denies ban 4-20, 297E3
US in Turkey base talks 5-7, 5-8, 397A3
US scores executions 5-9, 353E2
US concerned re executns, minority treatmt 5-15, 357D2
US Sen res vs executns 5-17; US, Sen Javits, wife scored, amb arrival delayed 5-20; Javits defends res, wife chrgd again, US concerned 5-21, 388B3
Iran softens attacks 5-21, 388G3
Javits safety pledged 5-23, 408G2
US executns res, Carter scored 5-24–5-25, 407F2
Young compares US, Iran executns 5-25; reactn 5-26, 400E1
Khomeini blames US for aide shooting 5-26, 407E2
Mrs Javits lobby effort rptd 5-30, 408B2
Iran bars new amb 6-4; US role in Africa, Zaire cited 6-5, 425F2
SALT II summit topic 6-15–6-18, 449D1
LA Times rptr expelled 7-1, 525D2
ISC paymts alleged 7-9, 541F3
Arms role rift rptd 7-9, 525A2
Nixon visits shah in Mex 7-13, 544C2
NYT rptr ousted 7-22; US regrets ouster, press curbs 7-23, 565F3
Textron discloses overseas payoffs 7-26, 923D2
NBC 4-man TV crew ousted 8-6, 602D2
CIA linked to seized newspr 8-7, 602C2
US denies spy aid 8-9, 664C2
Newsweek writer arrives 8-15, ousted 8-16, 670D2
US asks Iran, Kurd restraint 8-24, 653G2
AP office ordered closed 9-4, 670G1
S Korean cites US policy 9-16, 710B3
Israel says US 'lost' 9-18, 694B1
Wall St Journal rptr expelled 9-26, 814B3
New US envoy named 10-2, 752F2
Shah enters NY hosp 10-22, Iranians stage protests 11-4, 843B1

1980

Iran denies funding US protests 8-9, 635C2
Savama head's secret visit rptd 8-14, 671E3
US ex-amb scores Brzezinski '79 policy 9-6, 694B1
Khomeini: US, Iran 'at war' 9-12, 693D1
US tied to Iraq attacks 9-13, 9-17, 693E1, 694E2
Carter seeks contd oil flow 9-24, 718B2
US vs Pahlevi title claim 10-31, 859G2
Reagan electn reactn 11-5, 11-6, 853F3

1976 | 1977 | 1978 | 1979 | 1980

1979

'53 coup book rptd recalled 11-10, 886E3
US role in Mecca mosque takeover chrgd 11-21, 893C1; 11-24, 895B2
Pak raid on US Emb lauded 11-22, 894E1
US halts flight training 11-23, 898G1
Shah, wife sued in US 11-28, 897A2-B3
Shah leaves hosp for US AF base 12-2, 913G2
Kennedy scores shah 12-2, draws fire 12-3, 918F2, B3
Reagan urges US asylum for shah 12-10, Connally scores 12-12, 982B2, F3
Bogus Kennedy letter aired 12-12, 935C3
4 US natls killed in Turkey 12-14, 998D1
US blamed for slaying cleric 12-18, 958F2
Dole comments on crisis 12-26, 983B2

1976

IRAN Air
Mrs Javits quits post 1-27, 160A2
IRANI, C. R.
Loses passport 1-24, seeks return 2-16, 139C3

1977

IRAN Air
CAB acts on NY-London budget fare 9-9, 9-15, Carter overrules 9-26, 860E2

1978

IRAN Air
Workers strike 11-1, 827E2
Strike ends 11-2, 859E1

1979

IRAN Air
Mrs Javits lobby effort rptd 5-30, 408B2
Leb volunteer force stranded 12-10, 937B3
IRAN-American Society
Koob detained in US Emb 11-19, 878D2
IRAN Oil Participants Ltd.
Iran bars exports 2-27, 145G3
IRAN: The Illusion of Power (book)
Cited in suit vs shah, wife 11-28, 897G2

1980

IRANAIR
Leb office bombed 4-16, 300B2
IRANIAN Freedom Foundation
Tabatabai slain 7-22, 545E2
DC protesters arrested 7-27, freed 8-5, 586F1
IRANIAN Students, Confederation of
Deportatn ban denied by Sup Ct 3-31, 291G2
DC protesters arrested 7-27, freed 8-5, 586F1
IRANIAN Students Association
DC protesters arrested 7-27, freed 8-5, 586F1

1976

IRAQ—*See also ARAB League, NONALIGNED Nations Movement, OPEC*
Listed as 'not free' nation 1-19, 20D3
Hussein seeks Sahara setlmt 1-29, 58C2
Sahara diplomatic efforts continue 2-1—2-6, 107A3
At intl econ conf 2-11—2-20, 148B1
Natl sentenced in CAR 2-14, 204C2
Australia Labor electn fund alleged 2-25—3-2, 172B2
US sen rpts on visit 2-28, 161B1
Australia electn fund dvpts 3-5—3-9, 187F1; 3-17, 203C3
Australia fund probe rpt 3-25, 237C1
'75 oil output up 4-25, 298B3
'75 Sovt trade rptd 5-5, 341A1
French pres visits US 5-17—5-22, 372A2
Kosygin visits 5-29—5-31, 385C2
Bomb kills ex-Iraqi aide in Syria 7-10, Iraq blamed 7-11, 679A3
'75 OPEC raid role rptd 7-15, 531F1
Olympic withdrawal rptd 7-21, 528B3
Syria arrests bomb plotters 8-22, 679G2
Vs Saudis on oil price hike 12-18, 975A3
Iran Relations—*See also 'Kurdish Dispute' below*
Iran recalls amb 1-7, 12G3
Kurdish Dispute
Iran CIA aid request rptd 1-26, 93B1
Kurds vow new struggle, score US, Iran 2-25, 146A1
Kurds plan new drive 3-24; fighting rptd 7-26, 7-27, 547D2, A3
Iraq halts Kurd deportatns 7-5, 547F2
Middle East Conflict—*See MIDDLE EAST*
UN Policy & Developments
Scores Israel at Assemb 10-5, 760B1
Shuns Assemb Geneva conf vote 12-9, 914D1

1977

IRAQ—*See also ARAB League, NONALIGNED Nations Movement, OPEC*
UN Assemb member 4B1
France arrests Daoud 1-7, 9D2
$1 bln Japan aid pact signed 1-21, 65D2
Israel boycott curbs retained 2-18, 167D2
Venez pres visits 4-30—5-3, 362A1
US ties to intl terror groups 5-8, 380D1
US to challenge USSR role 6-10, 460D2
Syria executes 2 agents 6-13, 457B3
Blamed for Damascus bombings 7-14, 7-10, 534F1
Somalia arms aid rptd 9-1, 684A3
Cmnd Council expanded 9-4, 695E2
Cholera outbreak suspected 9-26, 748A1
Somalia arms aid rptd 10-22, 830B1
Syria blames for UAE attack 10-25, 10-26, 811E3
Abstains on UN Assemb Israel occupatn vote 11-25, 910D2
Egypt recalls amb 12-4, cuts ties 12-5, 929A1, C2
Arab-Israeli Conflict—*See MIDDLE EAST*
Kurdish Dispute
Iraq presses mil drive 1-16, Kurds free 7 forgn hostages 3-28, 256F3
Kurd deportatns chrgd 1-16, 257B1
Oil Developments—*See also OPEC*
Demand for oil rptd down 1-26, 107G3
USSR oil cartel plan rptd rejected 1-29, 108G1
'76 oil output drop rptd 3-21, 227G3
Oil field protectn rptd 5-31, 440F2
Vs N-S 'oil dialogue' 6-3, 437D2
Turkey pipeline opened 6-11, 565B2
Price hikes rescinded 7-5, 535E2, G2

1978

IRAQ—*See also ARAB League, NONALIGNED Nations Movement, OPEC*
14 CP members executed; Baathists, CP policy dispute cited 5-26, 415G3
21 CP members executed 6-7, 439C3
Ex-Premr Naif shot 7-9, dies 7-10, 522E2
Arab-Israeli Conflict—*See MIDDLE EAST*
Foreign Relations (misc.)
Cambodia visit ended by amb 1-21, 43D2
Syria cancels talks 1-29, 78C3
US OKs Saudi jet sale, Iraq buildup cited 2-14, 97E1
USSR rift re Israel policy cited 416B1
Arab fund poor-natn aid rise rptd 4-9, 257D2, F2
Saudis stress defense needs 5-13, 358E2
USSR warned vs Eritrea rebel aid, Baghdad emb relocated 5-25, 416D1
Poland accused of backing Israel 416F1
Egypt recalls journalists 5-26, 414F3
At ILO conf 6-7—6-28, $1 mln pledge rptd 6-14, 524A1
UK holds Naif murder suspects 7-12, 582A3
Egypt athletes to boycott 7-24, 573C1
UK ousts missn, terror chrgd; UK missn ousted 7-27, 582F2
Arab fund loan to Sudan rptd 8-17, 925F3
UN Assemb member 713G3
Iran religious ldr freed 10-6, 774F3
Syria reopens frontier 10-22, 803B2
To join forces with Syria 10-24—10-26, 803E1
Iranian queen visits 11-18—11-19, 893G2
W Ger terrorist haven suspected 11-18, 906B2
Kurdish Dispute
14 CP members executed 5-26, 416D1
Palestinian Dispute—*See MIDDLE EAST—PALESTINIAN Developments—Iraq Dispute*

1979

IRAQ—*See also ARAB League, NONALIGNED Nations Movement, OPEC*
Bakr quits; Hussein replaces, shifts Cabt 7-16, 544D3, E3*
Plotters seized 7-28, executns rptd 7-31, 583C1, E1*
Plotters sentncd 8-7, 21 executed 8-8, 602E2
Arab-Israeli Conflict—*See MIDDLE EAST*
Foreign Relations (misc.)—*See also 'Kurdish Dispute', 'Oil' and 'UN' below*
Khomeini lectures excerpted 50B1
In Syrian talks, unity delayed 1-28–1-30, 69F2
Sovt MiG-23 buildup rptd 2-13, 143A3
A-reactor sought from France sabotaged, forgn agents suspected 4-6, 276D1
Islamic conf suspends Egypt 5-9, 360D1
France vows A-reactor replacemt 5-9, 371F2
7 Cubans fail to gain Venez asylum 5-25, 411C2
Amin presence rptd 5-27, 429F1
Iran ties to unrest 6-3, 6-6, 446F1
Iran border raided 6-14, 469D1
In Syrian talks 6-17–6-18, joint pol cmnd set 6-19, 462D1
Canada warned vs Israel Emb move 6-27, 502B2
UK business embargo lifted, to review Briton's life sentnc 7-5, 583A2
France A-reactor agrmt rptd 7-11, 564C1
Iran-linked Baathist ousted 7-16, 544F3
Syria linked to plotters 7-30, 583G1; Assad accused 8-5, denies 8-6, 602A3
Libya fete shunned 9-1, 688D3
Poor natn aid vowed 9-4, 675G1
Canada envoy tours Mideast 9-9–10-20, 833D2
Israel cites mil threat 9-12, 693D2
Saudi denies Egypt chrgs, Sudan unrest role 10-10, 801G2-802A1
Persian Gulf security conf shunned 10-14–10-16, 804B2-A3
Canada lumber deal loss rptd 10-22, 833G2
Iran rpts invasn 12-14; Iraq scores rpt 12-15, 958B3
Kurdish Dispute
Kurds press Iran autonomy demands 2-22–3-1, 145E2
Iran Kurdistan bombed 6-4, error seen 6-5; Teheran warns 6-14, 446F1
Kurdish rebels gain 6-5, 446G1
Iran protests Kurd rebel refuge 8-25, 653F2
Iran chrgs Kurd aid 9-1, 670C1
Iran Kurdish ldrs seek refuge 9-4, 688A2
Obituaries
Barzani, Mustafa al- 3-1, 272B2
Oil & Gas Developments
1st 1/4 price hike barred 2-27, 145A3
Moderate stance reversed, crude oil price hike rptd 3-5, 162E1
Sudan oil shipmts halted 4-10, 278A2
Turkey imports cited 6-5, 488A3
France export hike vowed 7-11, 564C1
Poor natn importers vowed aid 9-4, 675G1
Oil prices hiked 10% 10-18, 781E1
Price per barrel rptd 12-21, hike set 12-28, 12-21, 977B2, C2
UN Policy & Developments
Membership listed 695E2
U.S. Relations
US co fined re boycott violatn 8-27, 648A3
US sets evacuatns, travel curbs 11-26, 894A2

1980

IRAQ—*See also ARAB League, NONALIGNED Nations, OPEC*
Freedom House lists as not free 87E3
Hussein foes in Syria vow ouster, demands listed 11-13, 895B1
Human rights record scored 12-10, 978B3
Foreign Relations (misc.)—*See also 'Oil & Gas' below*
USSR Afghan invasn scored 1-6, 10C3
Saudis execute mosque raider 1-9, 22B1
France OKs enriched A-fuel, reactor shipmt 2-27, 192D3
Italy A-aid seen; US concern noted 3-17, disputed 3-18, 3-17, 220G2
Iran border attacks 3-29, 260G3-261A1; for subsequent developments, see 'Iraqi' subheads under IRAN
PLO gunman dies in Israel raid 4-7, 260E2
Leb Moslem factns clash 4-15—4-17, Iran chrgs Shiite ldr executed 4-22, 300G1-C2
Leb Moslem factns clash 5-28, 465A2
Emb in Rome attacked, Iran role debated 6-4, 451D2
W Ger drug arrest rptd 6-13, 517G1
Hussein disclaims A-weapon plans 7-20—7-21; Israel vs French A-deal 7-28, 573A3
Leb Moslem factns clash 7-28, 579A3
Vienna anti-Iran bomb plot fails 7-30, 604G2
W Berlin arrests 2 diplomats in bomb plot 8-1, 604E2
Saudi urges holy war vs Israel 8-14, 627A3
Syria diplomats ousted 8-18, Syria expells amb 8-23, 652F2-A3
W Berlin OKs diplomats release 9-15, 712A2
Bakhtiar rpts visits 9-26, 769E1
Israel '65-75 Kurdish mil aid rptd 9-29, 735A3
OPEC postpones Baghdad mtg 10-8, 759B1
Libya, Syria, N Korea ties cut 10-10, 774C2
Jamaica loan rptd 10-30, 854C2
Sovt '79 arms sales rptd 12-10, 933A3
Iran—*See IRAN--Iraqi Relations*
Kurdish Dispute
Kurds bomb Iraq pipeline in Turkey 9-26, Iraq rpts repair work 9-27, 735D1
Israel '65-75 mil aid rptd 9-29, 735A3
Kurds renew autonomy fight 10-1, 735F2
Oil & Gas Developments
Brazil accord signed 1-9, 95F2
US links Italy A-aid, oil exports 3-17, 220D3
Jamaica loan rptd 6-4, 465E1
Oil price hike set 6-11, 435G2
June productn drop rptd 8-17, 662D2
Iran, Iraq jets hit oilfields, exports stopped 9-21—9-24, end to oil glut seen 9-24; pipeline pumping increased 9-24, Leb pipe use sought 9-25, 717E1, 718B1
UN Policy & Developments
Anti-Sovt Afghan res abstentn 2-14, 123E3
Cncl asks Iran truce, mediatn 9-28, 733D2; for subsequent developments, see IRAN—Iraqi War
Hamadi defends '75 Iran pact stand 10-17, 798A3
A-reactor inspectn barred 11-7, 864B2
U.S. Relations
Carter Persian Gulf defns pledge scored 1-25, 65D1
Pentagon rpt backs improved ties 2-1, 84B2
US issues rights rpt 2-5, 87E2
US scores France fuel shipmt OK 2-27, 192G3
US offcls see Italy A-aid; concern noted 3-17, disputed 3-18, 220G2
US 'resigned' to France A-deal 7-28, 573D3
US bars commercial jet sale 8-29, 662C3

1976

IRELAND, Republic of (Eire)—*See also EUROPEAN Community, IEA, OECD; for Northern Ireland dispute, see NORTHERN Ireland*
Armada ships found 1-11, 124C3
Herrema kidnaper in ct exchng 1-13, 157A1
Listed as 'free' nation 1-19, 20C3
North Sea oil finds rptd 2-1, 157B1
Govt bars '2-tier' mgt bds 2-10, 156F3
O'Connell freed 4-9, 278E1
WHO cancer studies rptd 6-3, 484B3
'75 unemploymt rptd up 7-28, 589C2
Bank strike ends 8-24, 735C1
Parlt declares state of emergency 9-1, opens debate on IRA curbs 9-2, 676F1 ★
O'Connell sentenced 10-13, 855C1
Emergency bill signed 10-16, IRA broadcast curbs expanded 10-18, 838A1
Emergency bill review scored 10-18—10-21, O Dalaigh resigns 10-22, 837D3
Hillery named pres-elect 11-9, 873E1
Facts on Hillery 873G1
Econ problems rptd 11-29, 1006A2
Donegan shifted to lands min 12-2, 1006C2
British Relations—*See 'Anglo-Irish Relations' under NORTHERN Ireland*
Foreign Relations (misc.)
Oct '75 trade surplus rptd 1-12, 156E3
Angola MPLA recognized 2-18, 163B1
Vs WHO anti-Israel stand 5-19, 355D2
Canada sets tariff rise 5-25, 400E3
EC entry pattern cited 7-27, 853E3
Argentina tortures, expels priest 10-11—12-3, 996B1
Rpt Greece fears EC entry block 11-3, 853G3
OECD: econ critical 11-29, 1006A2
Obituaries
Costello, John 1-5, 56B3

IRELAND, Andrew P.
Elected 11-2, 829B2
IRIBARREN Borges, Ignacio
Ford asks OPEC restraint 12-1, 934D3
IRISH Sea
BP well rptd dry 8-13, 638A2
IRON—*See STEEL & Iron*
IRON and Steel Institute, American
Seeks coke oven emissn curb review 10-20, 848B1
IRON Workers, International Association of Bridge, Structural and Ornamental (AFL-CIO)
Lyons quits Ford com 1-8, 4C1
IROQUOIS (Canadian warship)
In Intl Naval Review 7-4, 488C3
IRREGULAR Route Carriers
Accepts Teamsters pact 4-2, 248D3
IRVING, Clifford
Leventhal dies 1-6, 56F3
Howard Hughes dies 4-5, 336E1
IRVING Trust Co. (N.Y.)
Del Farmers Bank aid rptd 2-23, 6-10, 437E3

1977

IRELAND, Republic of (Eire)—*See also EC, IEA, OECD*
Portlaoise hunger strike ends 4-22, 487A3
Sen rejcts birth control reform 5-5, 567B1
O'Fiaich named Cath Primate 8-22, 728E3
Police brutality chrgd 9-28, govt probe set 10-7, 782C3
Militant killed in Dublin 10-5, 782E3
British Relations—*See also NORTHERN Ireland, subheads 'Anglo-Irish' and 'Unrest'*
UK Rockall oil rights disputed 2-3, arbitratn set 2-17, 329B2
Economy & Labor (domestic)
Inflatn, jobless rate rptd 1-20, 64C2 ★
Natl wage agreemt reached 1-21, 64F2
'77 budget presented 1-26, 64C2
Dec '75-76 inflatn rate rptd 2-7, 87C2
Fishing vessel curbs set 2-15, 146B3
Inflatn, jobless rate rptd 6-16, 475B2
Union ldr rejcts pay plan 6-29, 599C1
New econ ministry formed 7-5, 598E3
Aug jobless rate rptd 9-26, 771A2
Foreign Relations (misc.)—*See also 'Monetary, Trade & Aid' below*
UN Assemb member 4B1
'76 Eur Cncl pact vs terror cited 9G2
In 14-natn sulphur-dioxide pact 1-19, 109B3
Rhodesia rebels slay clerics 2-6, 85A1
Eur Cncl to study Turkey rights abuses in Cyprus 9-8, 764G1-A2; rpt shelved, Greece protests 11-3, 946E3
Abstains on UN Assemb Israel occupatn vote 11-25, 910D2
Government & Politics—*See also other appropriate subheads in this section*
Cosgrave govt loses electn 6-16, 475G1-A3
Parties choose new ldrs 7-1, 530F2
Lynch takes office; names Cabt, forms new ministry 7-5, 598E3
Fianna Fail wins Sen edge 8-27, 728D3 ★
O'Brien speech spurs parlt party resignatn 9-20, 782A3
Dail opens, Lynch addresses 10-12, 782F2
Helsinki Agreement—*See EUROPE—Security and Cooperation*
Monetary, Trade & Aid Issues (including all foreign economic developments)
'76 paymts deficit rises 1-20, 64A2
Fishing vessel curbs set 2-15, 146B3
Contraceptive imports barred 5-5, 567B1
Fishing vessel curbs ordrd lifted 7-13, 771A3
'77 paymts deficit forecast 7-31, 586D2
Sweden quits 'snake' 8-29, 708G3
Northern Ireland—*See under 'N'*
Obituaries
Conway, Cardinal 4-17, 356G2
Sports
US wins Walker Cup 8-27, Ryder Cup 9-27, 951F1, A2
U.S. Relations
Fitzgerald visits 3-16—3-19, lauds US anti-IRA stand 3-19, 329D1
NY gov visits 4-22, 329G1
Shannon confrmd US amb 6-21, 626E3
Ulster peace aid pledge reactn 9-1, 729G3
ESA satellite launching aborted 9-13, 735G3
IRENES Challenger (Greek tanker)
Splits off Midway I 1-17, 214G2
IRENEY, Metropolitan
Succeeded by Theodosius 10-25. 906F3
IREY Jr. Inc., Frank
Sup Ct backs OSHA penalties 3-23, 276F1
IRISH Americans
US aid halt to IRA asked 3-17, 222D3
Irish min lauds anti-IRA stand 3-19, 329D1
IRISH Republican Army (IRA)—*See 'Unrest' under NORTHERN Ireland*
IRON—*See STEEL & Iron*
IRON Constitution (race horse)
Seattle Slew wins Triple Crown 6-11, 491C1
IRON & Steel Institute, American
Productn, utilizatn rate rptd 5-7, 385F2
IRRIGATION—*See AGRICULTURE*
IRS—*See U.S. GOVERNMENT—INTERNAL Revenue Service*
IRVINE Foundation, James
Irvine Co.
Land co takeover battle rptd 3-3, 274E3
Takeover battle rptd 3-3, 274E3
1-family housing boom, speculatn rptd 5-2, 554E3
Taubman group wins takeover 5-22, 519C1
IRVING, Frederick
Named amb to Jamaica 5-19, confrmd 5-25, 499F3
IRWIN, Hale
Wins Atlanta Classic 5-29, HOF tourn 8-28, 675D3, 676E1
2d in World Series of Golf 9-5, 950C3
Wins Texas Open 10-16, 950E3
PGA top money winner 10-30, 950G3
ISAAC, Bobby
Dies 8-14, 696G2

1978

IRELAND, Republic of (Eire)—*See also COUNCIL of Europe, EC, GATT, IEA, OECD*
Bishops ease stand vs contraceptive sales 4-5, 289A2
Dublin Financial Times office vandalized 5-5, 373G2
A-plant protest rptd 8-20, 671E3
British Relations—*See NORTHERN Ireland, subheads 'Anglo-Irish Relations' and 'Unrest'*
Economy & Labor (domestic)
Employers meet on wage talks collapse 1-30, 72B3
'78 budget presented 2-1, union reactn rptd 2-2, 72D2
'77 GNP growth rate rptd 2-1, 72C3
Unions OK wage pact 3-22, 289G1
Telecommunicatns strike ends 5-4, business losses rptd 5-4; Lynch urges reforms 5-10, 392F3
Aer Lingus strike ends 5-5, 393B1
Foreign Relations (misc.)—*See also 'Monetary, Trade, Aid & Investment' and 'UN' below*
ESA communicatns satellite launched 5-12, 384D3
Italy abortn reform enacted 5-18, 375G1
W Eur natns join A-plant protest 8-20, 671E3
Government & Politics—*See also other appropriate subheads in this section*
Lynch interview causes furor 1-8—1-10, 18B3
Police chief fired 1-19, scandals cited 1-21, 1-24, 72A2
Helsinki Agreement—*See EUROPE—Security and Cooperation*
Monetary, Trade, Aid & Investment
US '77 thoroughbred import ban cited 539E2
At Brussels monetary summit 12-4—12-5, EMS entry deferred 12-5, 951B3, F3, 952B1
EMS entry announced 12-15, 979D1
Northern Ireland—*NORTHERN Ireland*
Obituaries
O Dalaigh, Cearbhall 3-21, 252B3
Sports
US battles equine VD 3-15—7-13, 539E2
UN Policy & Developments
Leb peace force (Unifil) formed 3-19, 197D2; **for peacekeeping developments, see MIDDLE EAST—LEBANON**
Unifil expansn voted 5-3, 340F1
Sea Law Conf talks continue 5-23—7-15, 8-21—9-16, 732E3
Racism conf censures, 12 Westn natns quit 8-14—8-26, 676G1-C2
Racism conf boycotted 8-26, 676B2
Assemb member 713G3
U.S. Relations
Lynch urges Ulster aid cutoff 2-18, scores US rep on IRA 2-22, 289C1
US launches ESA satellite 5-12, 384D3
US seabed mining bill debated at UN conf 8-21—9-16, 732E3

IRELAND, Rep. Andrew Poysell (D, Fla.)
Reelected 11-7, 850F2
IREY, Mary
This Room opens 6-15, 760E3
IRISH Affairs, Ad Hoc Committee for
Lynch scores IRA support 2-22, 289E1
IRISH Americans
Lynch asks Ulster aid cutoff 2-18, scores Biaggi IRA link 2-22, 289C1
IRISH National Caucus
Lynch urges aid cutoff 2-18, scores IRA support 2-22, 289C1
IRISH Northern Aid Committee
Lynch urges aid cutoff 2-18, 289F1
IRISH Republican Army (IRA)—*See NORTHERN Ireland—Unrest*
IRON—*See STEEL & Iron*
IRON & Steel Institute, American
'77 record US steel imports rptd 2-14, 158D1
11-mo steel imports rptd up 12-28, 1005E3
IRON Workers, International Association of Bridge, Structural and Ornamental (AFL-CIO)
'Prehire' picketing curbed 1-17, 33G3
IRRIGATION—*See AGRICULTURE*
IRS—*See U.S. GOVERNMENT—INTERNAL Revenue Service*
IRVING, George S.
Once in a Lifetime opens 6-15, 887C2
IRVIS, Leroy K.
On DC voting rep amendmt defeat 11-14, 878A2
IRWIN, Hale
2d in Heritage Classic 3-26, 355F3
Ties for 3d in US Open 6-18, 580B2
Ties for 2d in HOF Classic 8-27, 672G3
PGA top money winner 10-31, 990B3
Wins Australian PGA 11-12, 990D2

1979

IRBY, Dean
Plays From Africa opens 1-14, 292D2
IRELAND, Republic of (Eire)—*See also COUNCIL of Europe, EC, GATT, IEA, OECD*
French oil tanker explodes 1-8, 201C1
O'Fiaich installed cardinal 6-30, 640D2
Irish Sea storm, 18 yachtsmen drown 8-14, 799G3; rpt issued 12-10, 955D1
British Relations—*See NORTHERN Ireland, subheads 'Anglo-Irish Relations' and 'Unrest'*
Economy & Labor
'78 inflatn rptd 8% 1-8, 13C1
Bus drivers strike 1-15–1-21, postal workers 2-18, 155B1
PO attacks rptd 1-22, 97B1
'78 living standards ranked 2-2, 109B2
'79 budget presented, '78 growth rate noted 2-7, 154E3
Fianna Fail backs wage curbs 2-23–2-25, 155D1
Tax protest idles industry 3-20, 211D3
Wage, tax accord detailed 4-24, 371D3-372B1
Dublin tax protest 5-1, 372B1
Postal, telecommunicatns workers accept pay offer 6-25, 486B3
Econ growth slowdown seen 8-28, 688C2
Energy
Govt assumes oil distributn powers 4-12, lowers speed limit 5-15, 396B3
Gas price at $1.69 per gal 5-19, hiked to $2 5-20, 397A1
Econ slowdown seen 8-28, 688D2
Foreign Relations (misc.)—*See also 'Monetary' below*
Papal visit planned 8-29, 642B1
UN membership listed 695F2
Pope visits; sees bishops, addresses youth 9-29–10-1, 760D1-A3
France sentncs Breton separatist 10-20, 835E2
Government & Politics—*See also other appropriate subheads in this section*
Fianna Fail conf held 2-23–2-25, 155D1
Eur Parlt electns 6-7, 433A1, 434B2
Lynch resigns 12-5, 950A2
Haughey elected prime min 12-7, 950E1
Helsinki Agreement—*See EUROPE-Security and Cooperation*
Monetary, Trade, Aid & Investment
'78 trade deficit at £150 2-7, 155A1
EMS forces UK £ parity end 3-30, 268E3-269A1
EMS currencies realigned 6-24, 719A1
Current-acct deficit rise seen 8-28, 688D2
EC draft budget cuts aid 9-12, 719E1
EC poorest natns ranked 9-17, 719B2
Northern Ireland—*See NORTHERN Ireland*
Sports
US wins Walker Cup 5-31, 587A3
US wins Ryder Cup 9-16, 969E3
U.S. Relations
US House speaker visits 4-19, 312E2
Serbian hijacker extradited 6-21, 491E2, A3
Lynch visits US 11-8, 11-9, 874A2

I Remember Mama (play)
Opens 5-31, 711G3
IRICK, Samuel I.
Sentenced in GSA scandal 6-1, 964E3
IRISH Americans
US offcls fault UK re N Ireland, MPs score 4-19–4-24, 312E2
IRISH Republican Army (IRA)—*See NORTHERN Ireland–Unrest*
IRISH Sea
Storm, 18 yachtsmen drown 8-14, 799G3; rpt issued 12-10, 955D1
IRON Workers, International Association of Bridge, Structural and Ornamental (AFL-CIO)
Lyons on Pay Advisory Com 10-16, 829A3
IRS—*See U.S. GOVERNMENT–INTERNAL Revenue Service*
IRVINE, William
Zimbabwe agri min 5-30, 393F1
IRVING, Amy
Voices released 3-13, 528F3
IRVING, George S.
I Remember Mama opens 5-31, 711G3
IRVING, John
Natl Book Awards rptd 4-23, 356G1
World According to Garp on best-seller list 5-6, 356E2; 6-3, 432C2; 7-1, 548C3; 8-5, 620D3
IRWIN, Bill
NASL goalkeeping ldr 8-12, 654G3
IRWIN, Hale
3d in Inverray Classic 3-11, 220B3
Wins US Open 6-17, 587A1
US wins golf World Cup 11-11, 970C2
IRWIN II, John
Backs IBM case judge's ouster 7-19, 610B3
IRWIN, Dr. Robert
Chrgs Belfast police brutality 3-11, 190D1, B2

1980

US ties to Iraq attacks 9-12, 9-17, 693E1, 694E2
US bars turbine engines export 9-25, 719B1
Reagan electn scored 11-6, 841C3
IRELAND, Rep. Andrew P. (D, Fla.)
Small business aid signed 9-19, 784C2
Reelected 11-4, 842F2
IRELAND, Republic of(Eire)—*See also COUNCIL of Europe, CSCE, EC, GATT, IEA, MBFR, OECD*
Economy & Labor
Tax system protested 1-22, 98A3
'79 inflatn rptd up by OECD 2-13, 125C3
'80 budget presented 2-27, 150F3-151C1
Labor costs rptd 8-12, 698E1
Wage pact set 9-18, 751D1
Foreign Relations (misc.)—*See also 'Monetary', 'UN Policy' below*
Palestinian rights backed 2-10, 284C1
Olympic com rejcts Moscow boycott 3-22, 259C3
USSR May Day parade shunned 5-1, 354G2
Olympic com OKs Moscow participatn 5-20, 379A3
ESA rocket test fails 5-23, 397G2
ESA plans comet probe 7-15, 548A1
Westn labor costs compared 8-12, 698E1
Monetary, Trade, Aid & Investment
Current acct deficit cut planned 2-27, 150G3, 151B1, C1
Northern Ireland—*See NORTHERN Ireland--Irish Republic Relations*
Obituaries
Barry, Tom 7-2, 608C1
Sports
Olympic com rejcts Moscow boycott 3-22, 259C3
Olympic com OKs Moscow participatn 5-20, 379A3
US wins Curtis Cup 6-7, 715A1
Moscow Olympic results 7-20—8-3, 588C3, 622E1, 624F3
UN Policy & Developments
Leb Christns, UNIFIL troops clash 4-7; captured troops freed 4-9, 260F1
UNIFIL pro-PLO bias in Leb chrgd 4-11, 284C1
UNIFIL soldiers slain in Leb 4-18; Leb exit barred 4-20, Christn enclave area quit 4-22, 300F2
Assemb Palestinian state res abstentn 7-29, 572F1
Cncl seat won 11-13, 896E1
U.S. Relations
US groups aiding IRA attacked 7-27, 604B3

IRISH National Caucus (Washington, D.C.)
IRA link hinted 7-27, 604C3
IRISH Republican Army (IRA)—*See NORTHERN Ireland--Unrest*
IRON & Steel Institute, American
Foy warns vs dumping 2-28, 204G2
IRS (Internal Revenue Service)—*See under U.S. GOVERNMENT*
IRS v. Long
Case refused by Sup Ct 4-28, 369F1
IRURZIN, Hugo Alfredo
Slain 9-18, 697C3, D3
IRVING, Amy
Competition released 12-3, 972D3
IRVING, John
World According to Garp wins Amer Book Award 5-1, 692A2
IRVING Bank Corp.
Irving Trust Co.
Prime rate cut to 17.5% 5-7, 367D3
IRWIN, Hale
2d in Western Open 7-6, 715C1

1976

ISAACS, Kendal
Replaced as oppositn ldr 1-12, 104A2
ISELIN, Philip
Dies 12-28, 1015F1
ISHIBASHI, Masashi
Chrgs Miki Lockheed coverup 3-24, 286D1
ISHIHARA, Shintaro
Japan envronmt min 12-24, 1006B3
IS It Something I Said? (record album)
Wins Grammy 2-28, 460C3
ISKANDER, Ahmed
Denies PLA in Leb 1-19, 34B2
Says Syria vs exit from Leb 6-13, 429G1
On Syrian troops for Leb 10-27, 798F1

ISLAM—*See also country names*
Christian-Moslem conf 2-1—2-6, 272E2

ISLAMIC Conference, Organization of the
Annual mtg in Turkey 5-12—5-15, 373B1
Comoro Islands join 5-12, 373B2
Aids PI-rebel pact 12-15—12-23, 1008E3
ISMAIL, Abdul Samad Bin
Arrested 6-22, 497G3
ISMAIL, Ahmed Abu
Replaced in housing post 11-10, 852F1

ISRAEL—*For Arab-Israeli dispute, see appropriate subheads under MIDDLE EAST*
Strike vs mine closure 1-5—1-6, 31E1
Cabt OKs censorship plan 1-18, defers 1-20, 34B3
Listed as 'free' nation 1-19, 20C3
Rabin wins confidence vote 2-9, 106E2
Pound devalued 2-11, 157E1
Avineri in forgn min post 2-15, 125G2
'76-77 budget raises taxes, cuts svcs 2-24, 157C1
Meir joins Labor Party ldrship, Zarmi withdraws resignatn 3-5, 253A3
A-bomb strength estimated 3-11, 216F2
Prices raised, pound devalued again 3-14, 253D3
Sharon quits as Rabin adviser 3-21, 253C3
Rabin scores CPs, wins confidence vote 3-31, 227A2
Devalues pound 4-18, 335A2
Defense budget reduced 6-20, 459G3
Value-added tax 7-1; delayed in W Bank 487C2
Currency ties broadened, pound devalued 7-18, 538D3
Pound devalued 8-25, 9-29, 854A3
Yadlin bank appointmt delayed 10-17; arrested 10-18, 810D3
Yadlin bank nominatn dropped, 10-24, Gafny sworn 10-31, 854E2
Govt no-confidence vote loses 10-26, 854F2
Food, fuel prices up 11-4, 854G2
Yadin forms new party 11-22, 949G2
Rabin wins no-confidence vote 12-14; ousts NRP from coalitn 12-19; quits, sets new electns 12-20, 964B3
Arab Economic Boycott—*See under BUSINESS*
Foreign Relations (misc.)—*See also 'UN Policy' below*
French Mirage purchase cited 1-16, 36C2
Forgn censorship plan deferred 1-20, 34C3
Rabbis seek Vatican ties 2-8, 272G2
Maritime Fruit default threatens UK deals 2-9, 173G3

1977

ISAACS, Allen
Loses Cabt post 1-4, 46A1
ISAACS, William
Jamaica labor min 1-4, 46C1
ISBELL, Dr. Harris
CIA mind-control tests revealed 8-1—8-9, 611F1
ISHAM, Heyward
Replaced as amb to Haiti 8-3, 626E2
ISHKOV, Alexander A.
Vs Japan fishing claims 4-12, 319B2
Signs Japan fishing pact 5-27, 458A3
ISKANDAR, Ahmed
Says Syria, Egypt back Sudan 2-28, 143B3
Sees Mideast war 8-28, 663B2
Rules out Geneva conf 11-25, 909B2
ISLAM—*See also country names*
Hanafis take 134 hostage 3-9—3-11, gunmen chrgd 3-14, 192F2
Saudis, UAE mediate Pak feud 4-28—4-29, 348D3
Kenya editor quits re Aga Khan 5-3, 393E1
Hanafis indicted 5-3, 396A1
Hanafis convctd 7-23, sentncd 9-6, 711D1
Cholera threat to pilgrimage cited 9-26, 748B1
'73 Hanafi massacre figure cleared 11-5, 871G2
ISLAM, Moinul
Sentenced in absentia 2-26, 183D1
ISLAMIC Center (Washington, D.C.)
Hanafis seize 3-9—3-11, 192F2
Hanafis indicted 5-3, 396A1
Hanafis sentncd 9-6, 711A2
ISLAMIC Conference, Organization of the
PI-rebel agrmt disclosed 3-20, 241E3
ISLAM in the West, World Community of (formerly Black Muslims)
Hanafis take 134 hostage 3-9—3-11, 192A3
Griffin cleared in '73 Hanafi slayings 11-5, 871G2
ISMAIL, Maj. Gen. Mohammed Nabawi
Egypt interior min 10-25, 824C1
ISOKRARI, D.
Nigeria soc dvpt comr 3-15, 393D2

ISRAEL—*See also IDB*
Hosp drug deaths rptd 2-28, 224E2
Bar-Ilan Univ pres elected 3-2, 354B2
Atty curbed for PLO ties 3-31, 246B2
Mil copter crash kills 54 5-10, sabotage discounted 5-11, 396E2
Cholera outbreak rptd 9-26, 748A1
Capucci freed after Pope plea 11-6, 850G2-C3
Dead Sea scroll analyzed 11-21, 1022F3
Arab Boycott—*See under BUSINESS*
Arab-Israeli Conflict—*See MIDDLE EAST*
Corruption
Rabin studies Ofer corruptn probe, bars role 1-1—1-3; Ofer kills self 1-3, 8E1
Yadlin admits bribery 2-14, sentenced 2-22, 435G1
Rabin, wife tied to illicit US bank fund 3-15, 3-20, 4-8; Rabin admits lie, quits electn race 4-8, 266E3
Cabt drops Ofer probe 4-9; press, oppositn protest 1-10, 21D1
Rabin fined 4-11, 267A2
Rabin's wife fined 4-17, 329F2
Eban faces currency probe 4-23, 4-24, 329A3
Economy & Labor (domestic)
Pound devalued 1-18, 99E2
'77 econ forecast cited 99D2
'77-78 budget submitted 1-24, 99C2
Pound devalued 3-2, 3-21, 257E1
Dock strike 3-22—3-24; govt OKs wage talks 3-28, 257C1
Austerity plan set, prices up, pound devalued 7-17; Histadrut scores 7-18, 562F2
Free econ set, £ devalued, subsidies cut 10-28; protest strikes 10-31—11-1; £ value drops 10-28, 842C3
Suez oil find 11-25, 955E1
Foreign Relations (misc.)—*See also 'Monetary, Trade & Aid' and 'UN Policy' below*
Protests French release of Daoud 1-11—1-12, 9F2; 1-13, 27F2
Canada bars UDI probe 2-1, 114G1
Rabin sees Ivory Coast pres 2-4, rpts 2-5, 86B3

1978

ISA, Guiliano
Protests jail conditns 5-28, 453A3
ISA Conde, Narciso
Named DR CP pres candidate 1-27, 94C2
ISAKSSON, Ulla
Summer Paradise released 3-11, 620A1
ISGUZAR, Hilmi
Named Turkey soc sec min 1-5, 21G2
ISIK, Hasan Esat
Named Turkey defense min 1-5, 21E2
Greek waters violatn chrgd 11-1, 905D3
ISKANDER, Ahmed
Vows force vs Christns 7-9, 522B1
In Arab summit delegatn to Cairo 11-4, 859D2
ISLAM—*See also country names*
Christians ask Israel conversn study 2-1, 294B2
French survey rptd 3-24, 352G2
Islamic League asks Burma protest 5-8, 412B3
Comoro coup ends repressn 5-13, 371B2
'Test-tube baby' reactn rptd 7-25, 597E1
Black Muslim ldr quits 9-10, 810A2
ISLAMIC Development Bank (Afghanistan, Algeria, Bahrain, Bangladesh, Cameroon, Egypt, Guinea, Indonesia, Jordan, Kuwait, Libya, Malaysia, Mauritania, Morocco, Nigeria, Oman, Pakistan, Qatar, Saudi Arabia, Somalia, Tunisia, Turkey, United Arab Emirates, Yemen Arab Republic)
Poor-natn aid rise rptd 4-9, 257F2
ISLAMIC League, World
Burma expulsns scored 5-8, 412B3
ISLAMIC Conference, Organization of the
PI-Moslem rebel talks asked 650G1
ISLAM in the West, World Community of al- (formerly Black Muslims)
Rap Brown rpts conversn name chng 6-15, 844D2
W Muhammad quits as ldr, 16-member cncl to replace 9-10, 810A2
ISLAND, The (book)
Record movie price rptd 9-1, 759D2
ISLAND Creek Coal Co.
Barker credited with coal pact progress 3-14, 182A1
ISLE of Man (British dependency)
Eur ct hears birching chrg 1-17, 36G3
ISMAIL, Abdel Fattah
Rubaya executed 6-26, takes power in S Yemen 6-27, 499C1, D1
Purges ruling group 6-28, 522D2
Elected S Yemen pres 12-27, 1022E1

ISRAEL—*See also GATT, IDB*
'74 A-weapons possessn rptd 1-26, Israel reactn 1-27, 61F1

Arab Boycott—*See under BUSINESS*
Arab-Israeli Conflict—*See MIDDLE EAST*

Economy & Labor (domestic)
June '77-78 world inflatn rates ranked 10-18, 914E1

Foreign Relations (misc.)—*See also 'Monetary, Trade, Aid & Investment' and 'UN' below*
Dayan meets Pope 1-12, 10G2
Begin in Geneva, sees Jewish ldrs 2-8, 78D1
Ethiopia ousts natls 2-18, 138B1
Consul in Ecuador shot at 2-22, 194B2
Dutch mark Israel anniv 5-11, 454E3

1979

ISCOVE, Rob
Peter Pan opens 9-6, 956F3
ISHERWOOD, Christopher
Mtg By the River opens 3-28, 712D1
ISIK, Hasan Esat
Quits as Turk defns min 1-14, 40F2
ISKANDER, Ahmed
Links Moslem extremists, US 6-27, 505A3
ISKERSKY, Erick
Loses NCAA singles tennis title, wins doubles title 5-28, 570A2

ISLAM—*See also country names*
Khomeini views publshd 50B1
Mozambique adherents rptd 215C3
UK queen tours Arab natns 2-12—3-2, 190B1
Richard Ettinghausen dies 4-2, 356D3
US sets evacuatns, travel curbs 11-26, 894F1
Carter denies 'cold war' 11-28, 895E1
Pope urges Christian ties 11-29, 930D3
Muharram observed in Iran 11-30—11-31, 895D2
Anti-US protests in Mideast, Asia 11-30, 12-2, 914B3, 915C1
Mecca Mosque Takeover—*See under SAUDI Arabia*
ISLAMIC Government (book)
Excerpts rptd 50B1

ISLAMIC Conference, Organization of the
Egypt urges E Jerusalem 'liberatn' 5-3, 360F1
Mtg opens, Egypt barred 5-8; Egypt suspended 5-9, 360D1
Mtg ends, Jerusalem declared Palestine capital 5-12, 394G1
ISLAM of the West, World Community of (formerly Black Muslims)
NYC harrassmt rpt 11-24, 898B2
ISLAND, The (book)
On best-seller list 7-1, 548B3; 8-5, 620B3
ISMAEL, Gerard
Last Romantic Lover released 10-5, 1007G3
ISMAIL, Abdel Fattah (South Yemen president)
Signs Yemen unification plan 3-29, 250C1
In USSR 10-24, signs friendship pact 10-25, 802B1
ISMAIL, Mohammed Nabawi
Chrgs Syria terror plot 4-24, 296F1
Plotters arrested 8-17, 633E1

ISRAEL—*See also GATT, IDB*
Vegetarian diet study rptd 2-22, 140A2
Dead Sea Scroll contents told 3-2, 217A3
Talmudic study completed 7-14, 640A2
Abortn curb defeated 11-12, law tightened 12-17, 12-25, 995B1

Arab Boycott—*See under BUSINESS*
Arab-Israeli Conflict—*See MIDDLE EAST*

Economy & Labor
25% defns budget cut planned 2-13, 143F2
Inflatn, £ drop linked 4-20, 389G1
Gas price rptd at $2.01 per gal 5-19, 397A1
Food subsidies kept, oil prices hiked 7-19, 566C1
Begin wins confidence vote 7-30, 583D2
Price rise protest staged 8-13, 638A3
Begin survives no-confidence vote 10-23, 801A2
'80 energy cost forecast 11-25, 916G2
Foreign Relations (misc.)—*See also 'Monetary' and 'UN' below*
Iran airport strikers ask El Al ban 1-1, 3A1
Canada chrgs Quebec terrorist in '70 envoy kidnap plot 1-6, 19A2; gets bail 1-11, 37B2
El Salvador honorary consul kidnaped 1-17, killed 3-21, 234B3

1980

ISACCS, Carl
Extortn scheme chrgd 11-8, 927C1
ISACHENKO, Boris
Wins Olympic medal 8-2, 622C1
ISA Conde, Narciso
Arrested 5-31, 462C2
ISHIHARA, Takashi
Nissan seeks US truck plant 4-17, 288E1
ISHKOV, Alexander Akimovich
Resignatn rptd 4-15, 354D3

ISLAM—*See also country names*
US GOP chrmn urges Moslem natn aid offer vs USSR 1-1, 5C1
Carter State of Union address 1-23, 42C2, D3
Sovt Moslem birth rate rptd up 2-9, 152F3
UK film on Saudi princes strains ties 4-10, 294B1; 4-22—4-25, 313C2-B3
Australia bars Saudi film telecast 4-15, 309F3
US broadcast of Saudi film protested 5-8, aired 5-12; cts rule on dispute 5-9, 5-12, 375F2-376A1
W Ger sees Sovt Afghan invasn impact 6-30, 489G1
Saudi urges holy war vs Israel 8-14, 627F2
ISLAMIC and Arab Peoples, League of
Meets in Cairo 11-10, 895A2
ISLAMIC Conference, Organization of the
Mtg proposed 1-7; held: Sovt Afghan invasn, Israel-Egypt pact opposed; Olympic boycott backed; Afghan dropped 1-27—1-29, 67F1
Sovt Afghan troop exit plan proposed 5-15, 362A1, C1
Conf proposes Afghan talks; backs PLO, vs US, Israel 5-17—5-22, 395F2
UN Cncl res scores Israel Jerusalem moves 6-30, 491B2
3-day conf ends, Israel UN ouster sought 9-20, 736C2
Iran-Iraq war mediatn set 9-26; Zia in talks 9-27—9-30, rpts failure 10-1, 734C1
Israel UN ouster plan dropped 10-9, 775F1
Iran rejcts Iraq war mediatn 10-19, 10-20, 799B3
Econ conf held 11-4—11-6, 865B1
ISLAM of the West, World Community of (formerly Black Muslims)
Iran ex-aide slain 7-22, assassin sought 7-23, 545C2
ISLAND, The (book)
On best-seller list 4-6, 280D3
ISMAIL, Abdel Fattah (South Yemeni president; resigned Apr. 23)
At hard-line Arab summit 4-14—4-15, 284G2
Resigns, power struggle hinted 4-23, 315D3
N Yemen guerrilla war escalatn rptd 6-1, 468E2
ISMAIL, Mohammed Nabawi
Assures Copts re Moslem attacks 3-31, 273F3
ISMAN, Fabio
Convicted 5-24, journalists strike 5-26, 408C3
ISOGAMI, Shuichi
Lujan TKOs 4-2, 320C3
ISRAEL—*See also GATT, IDB*
Reform rabbi ordained, Goren calls invalid 2-19, 134A1

Arab Boycott—*See under BUSINESS*
Arab-Israeli Conflict—*See MIDDLE EAST*
Atomic Energy & Safeguards
'79 A-blast mystery unresolved 1-23, 49A3
'79 A-blast laid to S Africa A-test 2-21, 141E3
'79 A-blast dispute continues 7-14, 548A3
Mideast A-ban proposed 11-13, 864A2

Economy & Labor
'79 inflatn at 111.4%, austerity efforts cited 1-15, 59A2
Austerity measures defended 1-23; vital svcs strike 1-27, 133A3
'80 budget OKd by Cabt, Med Assn protests cuts 2-10, 133C3
Inflatn spurs shekel intro 2-22—2-24, 151D1
Begin survives no-confidence vote; fscl '80 COL rise, other econ data cited 11-19, 880D1

Foreign Relations (misc.)—*See also 'Monetary', 'UN Policy' below*
Turkey El Al rep killed 1-2, suspects arrested 2-13, 135G3, 136A1
Syria blames for Paris Emb bombing 1-29, 89C3
Greek terrorist plot vs emb chrgd 2-15, 150D3
Canada Emb issue cited 2-18, 121G1

1976

Total IMF oil loan rptd 4-1, 340D2
S Africa premr visits; econ pact signed 4-8—4-12, 275D3
Protests Cannes film 5-14—5-28, 460A2
Ethiopia mil aid rptd 5-18, 364G2
US Cong backs IDB entry 5-20, 392B3
US Jews ask Spain ties 6-3, 459A3
IDB entry set 6-3, 465D3
Uganda chrgs air threat 7-7, 516C2
Uganda chrgs mercenaries in Kenya 7-17, 548B2
Pound linked to US $, 4 W Eur currencies 7-18, 538D3
Portugal to seek full ties 7-19, 558E1
SWAPO scores 8-22, 654A3
Lauds Egypt hijack action 8-24, 629C3
Pound devalued 8-25, 9-29, 854A3
Amin returns private jet 9-6, 663A3
S African coal deal rptd 10-31, 928A1
Rodriquez Fabregat dies 11-21, 970B3
E Ger OKs US Jews reparatn 11-22, 889A2
Rpt UDI gets Canada-S Korea A-sale fee 11-22, 11-24, 904E1; Canada confrms 11-29, probe opens 11-30, 923C3
Rumania ties cited 11-22, 907B2
Rabin addresses Soclst Intl 11-27, 935C3
Canada probe continues 12-2—12-9, 962C3
Canada sets UDI audit 12-21, 998D1

1977

Sudan coup role chrgd 2-6, 117E2
French ties reconciled 2-8, 87B1 ★
Uganda chrgs Amin plot 2-16, 138E3
'64-68 Africa CIA funds rptd 2-22, 124B2
Soclst Intl at Labor Party conv 2-22, 135E1
Kreisky addresses Labor conv 2-23, 425G1
Uganda claims invasn threat 3-2, 141C2
Amin chrgs aggression 3-8, 170D2
Red Sea conf scores 3-22—3-23, 208E2
Egypt assesses Rabin resignatn 4-9, 267G2
'69 French gunboat seizure cited 5-30, 416E3
66 Viet refugees rescued 6-8, granted asylum 6-21, 6-26, 497G1
USSR: US Jews influence policy 7-22, 589A2
Ethiopia mil team rptd 7-26, 588B1
W Ger scored re Kappler extraditn bar 8-19, 638F1
Begin visits Rumania 8-25—8-29, 663C2
Dayan sees NATO cmdr 9-15; in Paris 9-16; briefs Begin 9-17, 713G2
Torrijos visits 9-27—9-30, 755E3
W Ger hijack rescue lauded, commando training rptd 10-18, 790E1
Sadat visit discussed 11-9—11-15, set 11-17, 873A1; **for subsequent developments, see MIDDLE EAST—EGYPT-Israel Peace Moves**

1978

Nazi extraditn from Brazil rptd sought 6-8, 477C2
Import co in W Ger bombed 6-22, 500G1
Cypriot sentncd for PLO link 7-7, 547G1
Shcharansky trial scored 7-10, 543A1
OAU scores 7-12, 561G2
S Africa play performance rptd scored 7-19, 633C3
'64 papal visit cited 8-6, 601A2
USSR sci conf boycott rptd 8-16, 670E2
W Ger terrorist rptd in hiding 8-17, 651D3
Syria-imposed Qantas curbs probed by Australia 10-18, 836E1
Sadat sends Meir condolences 12-8, 1032G1
Rumania ties cited 12-9, 965F3
El Al office in Iran attacked 12-31, 993E2

1979

Viet refugees accepted 1-7, 1-8; 100 arrive 1-24, 51G2-A3
Canada oppositn ldr visits 1-14–1-17, 57F2
Iran cuts ties 2-18, Dayan regrets 2-19, 126A1
Iran IBM office occupied by rebels 2-24, 144D3
Italy anti-Semitic protest staged 3-7, 212E1
Iraq A-reactor sabotage in France linked 4-6, 276G1; probe cited 5-9, 371G2
Iran Jews protectn seen 5-12, 357B2
Dutch order Menten retrial 5-22, 409E1
Iran protesters score Begin 5-24, 407A3
Entebbe hijack victim's body found 5-30, 429D1
Canada promises Emb in Jerusalem 6-5, 424B1
Canada Emb move plans scored by Arabs 6-7, 6-19, 467B3
Nazi's extradtn denied by Brazil 6-20, 483A3
Indochina refugee admissns hiked 6-21, 474B2
Canada delays Emb move 6-23, 502F1
Syria links to Moslem extremists 6-28, 505A3
Austria scored re Arafat visit 7-8, Kreisky rejcts chrg 7-9, 511B3, E3
Turkey student admits consul murder plan 7-11, 568E2
Canada Emb move scored by Trudeau 7-19, 563D2
Swedish envoy '45 USSR disappearance case reopened 8-4, 690C2
Iran seized newspr linked 8-7, 602C2
Nazi fugitive loses Paraguay citizenship 8-8, bounty offered 8-10, 616E3
USSR allows reps at pol sci mtg 8-12–8-18, 637B1
China, USSR chrg Young resignatn role 8-15, denial issued 8-16, 606D2
Syria tank arsenal compared 8-28, 643C2
Young urges Africa restore ties 9-5–9-20, discounts S Africa links 9-7, 720A3, 721F1
Canada envoy visits 9-9–10-20, warns vs emb chng 10-20; move dropped 10-29, 833B2
Dayan in W Ger 9-10, 677B1
2 W Gers sentncd for '76 jet plot 9-11, 677C2
Spanish non-recognitn explained 9-14, 695C1
Argentine editor gets visa 9-25, 728A1
Lisbon Emb attacked, Eldar hurt 11-13, 882B1
Iran chrgs Mecca mosque takeover role 11-21, 893C1; 11-24, 895B2

1980

'79 blast laid to S Africa-aided A-test; denied 2-21, 141E3
Colombia amb seized in DR Emb raid 2-27, 141B1
Canada envoy backs ties 2-29, 230D3
Austria status for PLO aide protested 3-14, 206B1
Syria blames for antigovt unrest 3-17, 213A1
Iran hostage rescue role denied, try backed 4-25, 297A2, 324E1
Colombia DR Emb siege ends, amb freed 4-27, 335F1
Olympic com OKs boycott 5-22, 421E1
Iran executes 'spy' 6-5, parlt ousts Jewish member 8-17, 644A3
Iran chrgs coup plot role 7-11, 539D2
Iraq disclaims A-weapon plans 7-20—7-21; French-Iraq A-deal protested 7-28, 573A3
Egypt amb at shah's funeral 7-29, 571G1
Qaddafi: 'Arab unity' move opposes 9-8, 697F1
Begin: Syria unrest prompts Libya merger 9-9, 697D2
Nazi kills self in Brazil 10-3, 810E1
Jordan war aid to Iraq feared 10-7, 10-8, 757F1, A2
EC scored re terrorist violence 10-7, 767B3
France anti-Semitism scored 10-13, 790A1
Iraq ties to US, Iran plot vs Baghdad 10-18, 799A2
Redgrave backs Israel destructn 11-2, 908F3
W Ger Jews ask papal support 11-17, 905C2
Syria-Jordan feud interventn threatnd 11-26, 911E3
CSCE Madrid mtg hears rep 11-27, 950E2
Turkey cuts ties 12-2, 912A1

1977

Government & Politics—*See also other appropriate subheads in this section*

Rabin gets new govt mandate 1-4; parlt dissolves, new electns set 1-5, 8B2
Peres seeks premiership 1-11, 48B2
Eban to run for premier 1-24, withdraws 2-3, 135G1
Abortion law OKd 1-31, 135D2
Rabin renominated for premr 2-23, 135C1
Rabin quits electn race 4-8, 266E3
Peres denies hawk views, seeks Mapam aid 4-8; Mapam stays in coalitn 4-11, 267C2
Allon defers premr bid 4-9, Labor picks Peres 4-10, 267B2 ★
Rabin takes leave, Peres assumes powers 4-22, 329E2
Kahane parlt bid cited 5-1, 335G2
Likud ousts Labor in parlt electns, party lineup 5-17, 377A1, C1 ★; **for reactn, see appropriate headings under MIDDLE EAST**
Peres bars unity govt 5-19, 377F1
Begin hospitalized 5-23, 401D2
Likud seeks DMC coalitn 5-24, 401B2
Dayan OKs Begin Cabt bid 5-25, 401E2
DMC-Likud talks collapse 5-26, resume 6-7, 450A2, D2
Dayan quits Labor Party 5-27, Begin delays apptmt 5-29, 450F1
Begin asked to form govt, renews Labor plea 6-7, 450C2
Final parlt lineup 450D2
Begin offers Agudat Israel concessns 6-9, 474A3
DMC bars Likud Cabt role 6-13; NRP, Agudat Israel join coalitn 6-19, 474A2, C2
9th Knesset opens, Shamir elected speaker 6-13, 474F2
Begin presents Cabt 6-20; parlt OKs, Begin becomes premr 6-21, 474G1
Cabt list 474D2
Labor wins Histadrut vote 6-21, 547F3
Begin hospitalized 9-30, heart ailmt rptd 10-3, 749F1
DMC joins govt 10-20, 801A3; 4 join Cabt 10-24, 827A2

Lebanon Civil Strife—*See LEBANON*

Monetary, Trade & Aid Issues (including all foreign economic developments)—*See also 'U.S. Relations' below*

Forgn arms sales rptd 1-6, 1-8, 1-15; US consults 1-8, 1-14, Honduran deal OKd 1-17, 28G2
'76, '77 arms shipmts estimated 1-14, 28F3
EEC trade pact set 1-18, 73F3
Ecuador jet sale barred 1-24, 87A3
EEC pact signed, terms protested 2-8, 146C1
'66-75 Latin arms sales rptd 4-8, 415C3
USSR chrgs Zaire aid 4-18, 317D2

1978

Government & Politics—*See also other appropriate subheads in this section*

Christians ask conversn study 2-1, '77 law repeal 3-1, 294G1
'48 war film banned 2-6, ban lifted 2-13, 112E3
Weizman urges coalitn govt 3-24, 214C2
Begin ouster plan denied 3-26; Cabt, Knesset back 3-29, 214D1
Anti-Begin protests 4-1, 4-26, 235E1, 300D1; counterdemonstratn 4-15, 300G1
Eitan rplcs Gur as staff chief 4-16, Cabt backs policy statemt 5-14, 359B1
Navon elected pres 4-19, sworn 5-29, 418C2
30th anniv of indepndnc 4-30—5-7, 339G1
Weizman denies resignatn plan re Begin, Dayan W Bank policy dispute 6-23; Cabt discusses feud 6-25, 489E1
Labor Party questns Begin health 7-20; MD calls Begin fit 7-21; Begin, Cabt score Labor 7-23, 563C2
Mil exempts religious women 7-20, 592F1
DMC splits, 6 quit coalitn 8-23, 668F1
Transport min resigns 9-13, 798F3
DMC rebels form new party 9-14, 798F3
Hurvitz quits Cabt 9-28, 729C1
Begin wins Nobel Peace Prize 10-27, 886D1
Golda Meir dies 12-8, funeral 12-12, 1032D1
Begin accepts Nobel 12-10, 950B3-951A1

Lebanon Conflict—*See LEBANON—Civil Strife, MIDDLE EAST—LEBANON*

Monetary, Trade, Aid & Investment—*See also MIDDLE EAST—ARMAMENTS*

W Ger, Dutch orange exports poisoned 2-1, 60F3-61A1
Ethiopia arms sales revealed 2-6, 100A1; Israeli expulsns rptd 2-18, 138B1
US A-export controls clear Sen 2-7, 82B3
Diamond speculatn, weak £ rptd 3-17, 319E1
US OKs jet sale to Taiwan 7-2, 7-4; Taiwan rejects 7-6, 524D2
Rhodesia arms source rptd 7-23, 616C2
US econ aid authorzn signed 9-26, 734E1

1979

Government & Politics—*See also other appropriate subheads in this section*

Begin reelected Herut chrmn 6-6, 436G2
Dayan hospitalized 6-23, cancer rptd 6-28, 527G2
Confidence vote won on Arab slayer leniency 7-4, 496D2
Ehrlich resignatn asked 7-18, 566D1
Begin in hosp 7-19; brain artery rptd blocked 7-23, recovery seen 7-30, 583G2
Begin wins confidence vote 7-30, 583D2
Begin leaves hospital 8-4, 591D2
Dayan offer resignatn 10-2, quits over Palestinian issue 10-21, leaves office 10-23, 801A1
Rabin book censored 10-22, Allon denies '48 Arab evictn 10-24, 823F1
Begin wins no-confidence votes 10-23, 801G1
Ehrlich replaced, gets domestic affairs post; Yadin rejects forgn min post 10-29, 856B2

Lebanon Conflict—*See MIDDLE EAST–LEBANON*

Monetary, Trade, Aid & Investment—*See also 'U.S.' below*

Iran premr vs oil sale 1-3, 2D2; shipmts barred 1-11, 11C3
Rhodesia chrgd re illegal US copters 1-5, 7F3
Egypt pact tied to Sinai oil access 1-5, 51B2
Iran oil cutoff impact assessed 2-20, 126A3
£ drops in Mar, Apr 4-20, 389F1-A2
Forgn debt per capita rank cited 5-21, 369G3
Uganda aid rptd 5-28, 429C2
Nicaragua junta vs debt paymt 7-25, 574C1

1980

Government & Politics—*See also other appropriate subheads in this section*

Allon dies 2-29, 175D3
Shamir named forgn min 3-9, confirmed 3-10, 179A3
Defns Min Weizman quits, mil budget freeze cited 5-25; Weizman, Begin letters trade chrgs 5-27, 429A3
Begin proposes Shamir, Modai apptmts, Cabt opposes 5-27; Begin, Zipori interim defns posts set 6-1, 429E3
Extremists attack peace group, Shelli Party 6-7, 6-8; party forms 'militia' 6-11, 434A3
Begin suffers heart attack 6-30, 498G2-B3
Tamir quits Justice post 7-31, Nissim replaces 8-13, 653E3
Arens rejcts defense min post 9-1, 712D2
Parlt defeats Begin no-confidence motion 11-19, 880D1
Weizman threatns to form new party 11-22; Herut ousts, govt loses parlt majority 11-23, 901F3
Religious affairs min indicted 12-1; police chief admits rights abuses 12-30, ousted 12-30, 994D3
Human rights record scored 12-10, 978G2
Labor Party conv held; Peres reelected chrmn, to run vs Begin in '81 12-17—12-18, 966E1
Defense budget cut OKd by Cabt 12-21, 994C3

Monetary, Trade, Aid & Investment—*See also 'U.S. Relations' below*

Jewish '79 aid cited 1-15, 59C2
'79 trade deficit rptd 1-15, 59E2
Mex '80 oil imports seen 1-15, 60B2
Shekel introduced 2-22—2-24, 151D1
US protests UN rejctn of Israeli constructn bid 6-19, 476B2
Medit-Dead Sea canal, hydro plan set; Jordan role asked 8-24, 643F2
Jordan Dead Sea canal, hydro plan rptd 8-30, 661G1
'65-75 Iraq Kurdish mil aid rptd 9-29, 735A3
US Cong clears '81 aid authrzn 12-3, signed 12-16, 981C3

1976

Obituaries
Elazar, David 4-15, 315G3
Lavon, Pinhas 1-24, 80E3
Unterman, Issar Yehuda 1-26, 124G3
Soviet Jews Emigration Issue—*See 'Emigration Developments' under USSR*
UN Policy & Developments—*See also UN DEVELOPMENTS under MIDDLE EAST*
OKs Medit pollutn pact 2-16, 126C3
Scored at ECOSOC racism debate 4-27—4-30, 320F2, C3
Scored at UNCTAD conf 5-5, 320D2
S Africa ties cited 9-8, 682D2
IAEA dir cites 9-21, 760F3
Asked to bar aid to S Africa 11-5, 842B3

U.S. Relations—*See also 'United States' under MIDDLE EAST—INTERNATIONAL Developments; for Arab economic boycott, see under BUSINESS*
US Sen OKs arms aid 2-18, 151D3, 152A1; House OKs 3-3, 181A2
CIA estimates A-bomb strength 3-11, 216F2
Moynihan lauds A-bomb rpt 3-25, 243B2
US, Israel dispute aid 4-7—4-9, 258E1
US oil deal signed 5-4, Israel OKs 5-6, 338A3
Ford vetoes aid 5-7, 344C3; signs new bills 6-30, 532E2, 533C2
US Cong backs IDB entry 5-20, 392B3
US Jews ask Spain ties 6-3, 459A3
Carter urges greater unity 6-23, 451F2
US arms aid authorizatn, funds signed 6-30, 532E3, 533C2
Ship in US Bicentennial event 7-4, 488C3
Israel broadens currency link 7-18, 538D3
Pound devalued 8-25, 9-29, 854A3
Ford, Dole defend arms sales 9-9, 665C2, 666B1
Bank Leumi buys US bank 9-16, 940D1
Carter trip disclosed 9-29, 723D2
'77 econ, arms aid signed 10-1, 806C3
Ford, Carter debate 10-6, 741F3, 742A1
Ford lifts arms sale ban 10-11, 759G1
Ford defends arms sale 10-14, 788A1
US delays agri deal 10-16; Bar-Lev cancels flight 10-19, 810G3
US Gen Brown remarks rptd 10-17—10-18, explained 10-18; Admin backs, others score 10-18—10-20, 787C1
Reactn to Carter electn 11-3—11-4, 826A2
Sen visit to A-plant denied 11-8, 878F1
Israel rptd vs Sovt Jews emigratn to US 11-10, 12-12, 966F3
US F-15 jets arrive 12-10, 964E3
Mil aid grant cited 12-22, 958E1

ISSA, Ali Mshangama
Appeals, chrgs torture 10-19, 1013C3
ISSA, Salah
Hijackers seek release 8-23, 629A3
ISSAEV, Khassan
Wins Olympic medal 7-31, 576C3

1977

'68 uranium hijack role denied 4-29, 335G1-A2
'68 uranium purchase plot rptd 5-30, 416F2
Ecuador scores jet sale bar 6-2, 454C3
Barbados seizes Guatemala arms shipmt 6-25; arms sale to Guatemala rptd 7-6, 553E2
US affirms jet sale bar to Ecuador 7-6, 511C1
USSR chargs S Africa A-bomb aid 8-9, 657A1
Publishers at USSR book fair 9-6—9-14, 765E3
S Africa steel sales rptd 10-10, 887D3
S Africa boat, missile purchases cited 851E2
Rumania trade expansn rptd, '77, '78 forecast 12-10, 987B3
Obituaries
Yafeh, Yossi 2-28, 164G3
Weisgal, Meyer 9-29, 788A3
Soviet Jews Emigration Issue—*See USSR—Human Rights*
UN Policy & Developments
Assemb member 4B1
Herzog sees Sovt rep 2-3, 86D3
Waldheim visits 2-10, 86F2; 2-11, 107D1
Rights comm scores occupation 2-15, 107E2
Israel vs Leb troop use 2-27, 143E2
Rights comm chrgs cited 3-11, 207A2
ILO drops inquiry 3-21, 227D2
Herzog denounces Jordan, Egypt Cncl proposals 3-25, 3-28, 226G3
ECOSOC admits PLO 7-22, 572G2
Desert conf held 8-30, 770D1
UNESCO '74 ban to end 8-31, 663F2-A3
Herzog chrgs Fahmy blocks peace progress 9-28, 734E1
Pollutn conf ends, Medit pact reached 10-21, 876B2
French evacuatn of Mayotte opposed 10-26, 869A1
Israel explains Leb raid 11-11, 874C3
Assemb condemns occupatn 11-25, 910D2
Herzog meets Egypt envoy 11-27, 909E2
Waldheim pre-Geneva conf proposal rejctd 11-30, 910B2
S Africa ties scored 12-14, 1016C2
S Africa oil ban abstentn 12-16, 1016A2
U.S. Relations—*For Arab-Israeli conflict, see LEBANON—Civil Strife; also MIDDLE EAST, subheads EGYPT-Israel Peace Moves and U.S. DEVELOPMENTS*
Forgn arms sales talks 1-8, 1-14, 28F2
Long-term US aid cited 1-24, 99D2
US bars jet sale to Ecuador 2-7, 87A3
Carter '77 aid hike request cited 2-7, 87A3
US to review bomb sale 2-8, 88A3
US vs Suez oil drilling 2-14, 107B2
Vance visits 2-15—2-17; US cancels bomb sale 2-17, govt comment 2-19, 121A1
'64-68 CIA paymts rptd 2-22, 124B2
Rabin meets Carter, F-16 jets promised 3-7—3-8, 165A1-A2
Likud wants debate on US peace plan 3-10, 166C1
Rabin illicit US bank fund admitted 3-15, 3-20, 4-8, 266F3
Rabin resignatn assessed 4-8, 267E2
Tank shell firing problems rptd 4-10, 343D2
Egypt returns 2 Israeli spies hanged in '55 4-14, 297B2
Lewis confrmd amb 4-25, 418F1
US A-export curbs proposed 4-27, 334F1
Kahane parlt bid cited 5-1, 335G2
US briefs on Assad talks, assures on ties 5-11, 5-12; Israel pleased 5-12, 360G3, 361D1
Carter sets arms-sales policy 5-19, 380G2
Ecuador scores US jet sale bar 6-2, 454C3
Begin asks strong ties 6-21, 474D2
US vs communicatns system co-dvpt 6-22, 511E1
Carter seeks arms sale 6-25; Begin thanks 6-26, 511G1
US affirms jet sale bar to Ecuador 7-6, 511C1
Begin in US, sees Carter 7-19—7-20, 549A1
US OKs mil aid package 7-22, 570B3
USSR: Jews influence US policy 7-22, 589A2
Security funds signed, mil balance backed 8-4, 668D1, E1
Vance visits 8-9—8-10, 605F1
Ford, Coca-Cola, AMC vow contd trade 863C2
US Palestine group accuses Israel in '67 Liberty attack 9-18, 715A1
Dayan in US 9-19—9-27, 713G1, 714A1, 733D2
Dayan for Haifa base 9-20, US vs 9-22, 714B1
Vance meets Dayan 9-26, 733F2
Dayan in US, sees Carter 10-4—10-5, 749C1, A2
US '78 security aid funds cleared 10-19, 815G2; signed 11-1, 834D1
US denies F-16 co-productn 11-8, 850D3
Vance meets Begin 12-10—12-11, 954A1
Begin arrives 12-14, 955A1

ISSEL, Dan
Scores 15,000th point 12-3, 991B1
ISSUES & Answers—*See AMERICAN Broadcasting Cos.*
ISTHMIAN Canal Convention (1903)
Panama Canal Treaty supercedes 9-7, 679E2

1978

US econ aid funds signed 10-18, 862D2
Iranian oil workers strike 10-31, 827D2
US OKs more Kfirs to Taiwan 11-6, 872A3
US churchmen ask Nicaragua arms trade halt 11-8, 883F3
Iran Moslem ldr oil shipmt oppositn cited 12-13, 953B3
Mex '79 oil price hike set 12-20, 978F2
Obituaries
Lourie, Arthur 10-4, 888B3
Meir, Golda 12-8, 1032D1
Rosen, Pinhas 5-3, 440D3
Occupation Policies—*See MIDDLE EAST subheads, ARAB-Israeli Developments—Israeli Occupation Policies and EGYPT-Israel Peace Moves*
Soviet Jews Emigration Issue—*See USSR—Human Rights*
UN Policy & Developments—*See also MIDDLE EAST—UN*
ILO defeats anti-Israel res 6-27, 523D3
Assemb member 713G3
Assemb asks arms ban 11-27, 931A3
UNESCO scores Jerusalem digs 11-29, 931F1
U.S. Relations—*For Arab-Israeli conflict, see MIDDLE EAST, subheads ARMAMENTS, EGYPT-Israel Peace Moves, LEBANON and U.S. ROLE—Israel*
US woman sentncd as spy 1-9, 10B3
CIA issues '74 rpt on A-weapons 1-26, reactn 1-27, 61F1
US A-export controls clear Sen 2-7, 82B3
US issues rights rpt 2-9, 102D2
Dayan arrives in US 4-25, 307F1
Begin in US, sees Carter 4-30—5-8, 339G1
US Arab convicted of PLO ties 6-6, sentncd 6-12, 489B2
Mondale, Jewish ldrs visit 6-30—7-3, 501B2
US OKs jet sale to Taiwan 7-2, 7-4; Taiwan rejcts 7-6, 524D2
Air svc pact reached 7-15, 640B2
Carter signs econ aid authorzn 9-26, 734E1
Zim shipping fined for rebates 10-1, 752G3
US Arab paroled 10-18, expelled 10-20, 783C2
Carter signs econ aid funds 10-18, 862D2
US OKs more Kfir jets to Taiwan 11-6, 872A3
Kissinger eulogizes Meir 12-8, 1032A2

ISSUES & Answers—*See under AMERICAN Broadcasting Cos.*

1979

UK tank use cited 8-28, 643C2
Iran chrgs Kurd aid 9-1, 670C1
USSR publishers entry bar scored 9-4, 690A2
S Africa arms embargo compliance cited 9-7, 720D3
Mex oil imports rptd 11-23, 909B3
Obituaries
Rabinowitz, Yehoshua 8-12, 671E3
Occupation Policies—*See MIDDLE EAST-ARAB-Israeli Developments-Israeli Occupation Policies and EGYPT-Israel headings*
Soviet Jews Emigration Issue—*See USSR-Human Rights*
Sports
Italy basketball game protested 3-7, 212E1
UN Policy & Developments—*See also MIDDLE EAST-U.N.*
WHO ouster move blocked 5-23, 398E2
S Africa arms embargo compliance cited 9-7, 720D3
Membership listed 695F2
U.S. Relations—*For Arab-Israeli conflict, see MIDDLE EAST, EGYPT-Israel and LEBANON headings*
US mil ex-ldrs urge Carter support 1-12, 15C1
Ex-Pres Ford visits 1-21, 50A1
US issues rights rpt 2-10, 107B2, F3-108D2
Defns Secy Brown visits, jet shipmt speedup asked 2-13-2-15, 143F2-B3
Separate aid agrmts signed 3-26, texts released 3-28, 221B1, G2, 227A1-F2
US trade group visits 4-18, 296C1
Entebbe hijack case declined by Sup Ct 4-30, 364F3
US House com hearing on aid 5-8, 341B2
US threatens to quit WHO re Arab moves 5-12, 398B3
Carter addresses Cong on SALT II 6-18, 459E2
Fleener paroled 6-29, deported 6-30, 496F1
Jordan tank sale noted in US talks 7-27, 574A3
US M-48 tank use cited 8-28, 643C2
US assn scores USSR publishers entry bar 9-4, 690A2
Young urges Africa restore ties 9-5-9-20, 720A3, 721F1
Evron sees Vance, asks more US aid 9-11, 677A2
US SCLC visit opposed 9-20, 694E2
Jesse Jackson visits, Begin shuns 9-25, 762G3
Carter vows support 9-25, 723E2
Black groups visit, back govt 10-14-10-17, 780C3
US oil supply treaty effected 11-25, 916G2

ISRAEL, Agudat
Abortn law tightened 12-25, 995C1
ISSUES & Answers—*See under AMERICAN Broadcasting Cos.*
ISUZU Motors Ltd.
GM interest cited 9-7, 745E3

1980

Obituaries
Allon, Yigal 2-29, 175D3
Benedictos I 12-10, 1004A1
Joseph, Bernard (Dov) 1-6, 104A3
Neumann, Emanuel 10-26, 876G2
Talmon, Jacob L 6-16, 528F3
Sports
Moscow Olympics stand rptd 1-21, 45B3
Olympic com OKs boycott 5-22, 421E1
UN Policy & Developments
UNEP rejctn of Nairobi hq bid protested 6-19, 476B2
Women's conf attended 7-14—7-30; US racism motion withdrawn 7-28, 5-yr plan opposed 7-30, 587G1-A3
UNESCO conf oppositn cited 9-23—10-28; Arafat address boycotted 10-27, 821E3
US scores move to oust Israel 9-29, 739A1
Moslems drop ouster plan 10-9, 775F1
A-ban in Mideast proposed 11-13, 864F1
U.S. Relations—*See also MIDDLE EAST*
Bases offered to US 1-4; US refuses 1-9, 11E1-G1
Israel aid request cited 1-15, 59C2
'79 A-blast mystery unresolved 1-23, 49A3
US issues rights rpt 2-5, 87C2
'79 A-test claimed 2-21; Israel denies, cancels US rptr's credentials 2-24, 141E3
US assures on arms to Egypt 2-25, 140E2
Israel to build own jet fighter, asks US aid 2-25; 100 F-16 purchase dropped 2-29, 180E1
Begin scores on Sovt Jewish emigres 4-2, 262C3
Iran hostage rescue role denied, try backed 4-25, 297A2, 324E1
US mil base constructn lags 6-12, 498B3
Vs extra gear for Saudi F-15s 6-17, 450C2
UN rejctn of Israeli constructn bid protested 6-19, 476B2
Anderson visits 7-8—7-11, 549F3
US sens vs F-15 gear to Saudis 7-9, 538G2
'79 A-blast dispute continues 7-14, 548A3
GOP platform adopted 7-15, 536G1-537A1
Carter pres renominatn acceptance speech 8-14, 613E1
$3 bln aid sought 8-20, 662F3
Anderson platform offered 8-30, 665A2
Pres candidates vow Israel support 9-3—9-4, 681A3
Carter scores UN ouster move 9-29, 739A1
Reagan vows UN support 10-1, 738B2
Oil agrmt set 10-15, signed 10-17, 775E3
Carter vs some Saudi F-15 gear 10-24, 821A1
Weizman on Carter campaign jet 10-27, 816C3
Weizman scored for electn tour with Carter 10-28, 830D2
US OKs jet sale to Mex, Venez, Colombia 10-31, 865A2
Reagan electn approved, Begin sends message 11-5, 841D2
Begin arrives US 11-9, meets Carter 11-13; cuts visit for govt confidence vote 11-19, 880D2
US Cong clears '81 aid authrzn 12-3, signed 12-16, 981C3
Haig apptmt praised 12-17, 955E2
Liberty '67 attack case settled 12-18, 966A2

ISSEL, Dan
NBA scoring ldr 3-30, 278C3
ISSUES & Answers—*See AMERICAN Broadcasting Cos.*
ISTOMIN, Eugene
Wife gets Kennedy Cntr post 2-26, 199C2
ISTOMIN, Marta Casals
Kennedy Center artistic dir 2-26, 199C2

1976

ITALIAN American Foundation Inc.
Reps meet Carter 8-12, 616G3

ITALIAN Americans
Carter meets group reps 8-12, 616G3
Carter in NY 8-31, 645D2
Ford tours Phila 9-24, 724A1
Carter cites Butz '74 slur 10-2, 744G1

ITALY—*See also ADB, DISARMAMENT—Geneva Committee, EUROPEAN Community, IEA, NATO, OECD*
Renaissance frescoes found 1-2, 104D3
5 Red Brigades members seized 2-18, 141B1
Alpine cable car crash 3-9, 384E1
Justice Min bombed 4-7, 297G1
Bombings, arson rptd 4-19—4-23, 297F1
Oil exec shot 4-21, 297D1
Rightist assassinated, 3 held in leftist stabbings 4-29, 333A3
Quake hits, relief granted 5-6—5-11, 352F2
US wins world bridge title 5-8, 352G3
CP youth slain 5-28, neo-fascist rallies banned 5-29, 403B1
Leftists, rightists clash in Rome 6-4, 418C3
Genoa prosecutor slain 6-8, 418A3
Gunmen kidnap Rome shopowners 6-16, 446B1
Seveso chem plant blast 7-10, evacuatns 7-26—7-28, 560A3
Getty kidnapers sentncd 7-29, 816B3
Seveso chem blast antidote, abortion dvpts 8-11—10-11, 840B3
'69 Milan bombers freed 8-28, 676B3
Tremors hit Friuli region 9-11—9-16, 756E1
Givaudan pays blast damages 12-2, 932A1

Abortion Issue
Pope vs legalizatn 1-4, 32D3
Vatican stand protested 1-17, Pope scores 1-21, 124C2
Parlt curbs abortns 4-1; Soclsts ask referendum 4-2, women protest 4-3, 254A1
Referendum set 4-16, 333B3
Abortions rptd re Milan chem blast; church scores 8-13—8-25, 840D3

Economy & Labor (domestic)
A-plant plans rptd OKd 1-5, 74B3
List of failing firms rptd 1-6, 29D3
Nationwide strike 1-8, 29D3
'75 oil data rptd 1-12, 74B3
Econ rpt issued 1-26, 74A3
'75 auto productn rptd down 1-29, 74C3
Singer layoffs rptd 1-30, 141D1
Banks tighten credit, curb speculatn 2-2, 2-11, 140F2
Austerity plan proposed 2-4, 140C2
Innocenti layoffs completed 2-4, 141C1
Econ plan revisns pledged 2-13, 140A2
Moro govt quits 4-30, 296F2, A3
CP electn goals rptd 5-16, 402A3
CP urges austerity progrm 6-13, 445B2, G2
Econ turmoil cited 6-27—6-28, 462E1
Andreotti sees oppositn on budget curbs 7-22—7-23, 557A1
Austerity program offered 8-4, 573A2
June price rise rptd slowed 8-11, 676E3
July CPI, 12-mo inflatn rptd up 9-1, 696C2
Rail workers strike 9-13, 732C1
Austerity measures set 10-1; CP, labor reactn 10-2, 10-4, 751E2
Turin auto workers strike 10-8, 10-12, 10-13, 838D2
New austerity measures set; CP, labor reactn 10-15, 10-18, 838D1, B2
Austerity measures OKd 11-12, 947F1
Salary freeze barred 11-23, 947B2
Workers strike, wage freeze legis withdrawn 11-23, 947B2
Strike data rptd 11-29, 896D2
Oct '75-76 inflatn rate rptd 12-6, 976B1

European Force Reduction Issues—*See under EUROPE*

Foreign Economic Developments—*See also 'Political Payments' below*
Run on lira 1-1—1-20, currency exchng closed 1-21; franc bolstered 1-21—1-22, 74D1, G1
French wine growers protest exports 1-7—2-5, agri mins conf 1-30, 138B3-129A1
SDR rate rptd 1-15, 14A3
US, Bonn, IMF loans sought 1-22, 74A2, E2

1977

ITAKA, Boris
Named as defector 8-10, rptd in US 8-11, 606F2

ITALIAN-American Foundation
Sup Ct hears Bakke case arguments 10-12, 834D3

ITALY—*See also DISARMAMENT—Geneva Committee, EC, ESA, IEA, NATO, OECD*
Seveso chem blast contaminatn rptd, Lombardy govt acts 2-7—2-18, 135E2-136B1
Hosp drug deaths rptd 2-28, 224E2
Rumania quake felt 3-4, 204F1
Spain jet hijacked 3-14—3-16, 224A3
Adriatic poison cargo recovery begun 4-4, 284B3
Mt Etna eruptions rptd 8-29, 747D2
Heroin addictn rptd up 10-17—10-21, 971E3
Genoa, northn regions flooded 11-5—11-10, 888E3

Atomic Energy & Safeguards
Canada A-sale agent tied to pol paymts 1-7, 43B1
Canada warned vs A-sale disclosure 1-25, 114D1
Suppliers conf scores Carter plans 4-28—4-29, 403F1-A2
7-natn summit debates A-sales, sets study 5-7—5-8, 357D2, E2
French 'Super Phoenix' OKd 7-5, environmentalists protest 7-31, 597C2, C3
Carter sees Andreotti, backs A-dvpt 7-25—7-27, 581B2
Suppliers conf OKs safeguards 9-21, 717D1
Canada uranium price policy suit rptd 12-13, 982B3
Canada cooperatn pact rptd signed 12-15, 982G2

Economy & Labor (domestic)
Unions offer cost curbs 1-5; rejct govt plan 1-6, CP backs 1-7, 8D2
20% inflatn rate rptd 1-6, 8E2
Nov, 12-mo consumer price rise rptd 1-7, 29C3
Aircraft union S Africa boycott fails 1-21, 67B3
Nov '75-76 COL rptd up 1-25, 65B1
Wage accord reached 1-26, scored 1-28, 116B2
'76 factory wages rptd 1-28, 158C3
New taxes set 2-4, 116E2
'76 indl output rptd up 2-6, 136B1
Dec '75-76 inflatn rate rptd 2-7, 87C2
Police form union 2-14, 135C3
'76 econ growth rptd 2-22, 146C2
Ferrari to resign 3-19, 396G2
Wage accord finalized 3-30, Sen OKs 3-31, 527E2
Egam dissolved 4-7, 284F2
Inflatn actn vowed 5-7—5-8, 357D1
Christian Dem-CP pact 6-29, 544F2
Aug jobless rates rptd 8-9, 9-26, 771A2, C2
Daily American closes 8-23, 729C2
Workers protest in Rome 12-2, meet govt offcls 12-10, 1015A1

1978

ITALIAN-American Civil Rights League
Colombo dies 5-22, 440D2

ITALY—*See also COUNCIL of Europe, DISARMAMENT—Geneva Committee, EC, GATT, IEA, NATO, OECD*
Trains collide near Bologna 4-15, 460B2
Pitti Palace art theft 4-21, paintings recovered 4-23, 355A2
Adriatic poison cargo recovery completed 4-25, 330E3
Opera dirs arrested in corruptn probe 5-30, 6-1, 15 freed 6-5, 454B1
Energy conservatn progress rated 6-5, 449E3 ★, 450F1
Pompeiian statues stolen 6-8, 579E2
Trento lead factory blast 7-15, 689A2
Seveso firm condemned for '76 blast by parlt comm 7-27, 689E1 ★
8,000 convicts amnestied 8-4, 724B3
'78 high chic fashion rptd 8-4—8-11, 10-27—11-3, 1029C2
Alpine flooding kills 23 8-8, 655B1
Shroud of Turin exhibited 8-26—10-8, studied 10-4—11-14; photo 926A1-C3
Genoa chem plant accident 9-19, 724G2
Pisa U coronary study rptd 12-7, 992A3
108 die in Alitalia crash off Sicily 12-23, 1031G3

African Relations
Algeria pres in Malta 1-3, 39C2
Somalia asks arms aid 1-16, 43A3
At Ogaden conf in US 1-21, 43E2
Ethiopia protests Somalia aid 2-1, 100D1
Somalia makes 2d aid bid 2-4, 99G3
Somalia visited by CP rep 2-20—2-22, 137G2
Zaire emergency aid OKd 6-13—6-14, 478A1
Rhodesia arms source rptd 7-23, 616D2

Atomic Energy & Safeguards
'77 A-export safeguard pact detailed 1-11, 11B2
US alerts to Sovt A-satellite fall 57E1
Australia joins A-supplier group 2-24, 129C2
US study backs breeder dvpt 5-10, 346G3

Economy & Labor (domestic)
Fiat workers in Turin strike 1-4, 19B2
Bank offcl held in Sindona case 1-11, 19G2
Police union accord reached 3-7, 191B3
Govt econ plans rptd 3-10, 191B1
Banco di Roma dir resigns 3-10, 454C2
CP labor group break with federatn 3-14, 191A3
Unions call protest strike over Moro kidnaping 3-16, 199C3
Montedison rpts $595 mln loss in '77 3-21, 330F2
Govt to aid 16 firms 3-27, 330B2
36 indicted in Montedison fraud 4-3, 330C3
Sindona bankruptcy plea rejctd 4-3, US orders extraditn 5-19, 454F1
Workers protest unemploymt 4-5, 258F2
Italsider '77 losses rptd 4-5, 330E2
Gen strike, rally protest Moro death 5-9, 5-10, 337G1
Alfa Romeo pres, 3 execs sentncd 5-29, 454E2
Messina bridge planned 7-13, 689E3
Growth target of 1.5% set 7-17, 544B2
Business rescue bill enacted; Liquichimica, Societa Italiana Resine setbacks cited 8-1, 724E1
Inflatn rate rptd 12-13% 8-31, 724G2
'79-81 econ plan presented, unions dispute 9-1, 724C2
Chem indus rescue plan 10-26, 817B2
Hosp workers strike, Parlt backs Andreotti wage policy 10-31, 882G3
Calabrians demonstrate for aid 10-31, 883F1
Sindona extraditn upheld by US ct 11-15, 906A3

1979

ITA (International Track Association) (defunct)—*See TRACK & Field*

ITALIAN Americans
DiLeo reverse bias case declined by Sup Ct 4-23, 346D2

ITALY—*See also COUNCIL of Europe, DISARMAMENT—Geneva Committee, EC, GATT, IDB, IEA, NATO, OECD*
Loren acquitted of currency-smuggling, Ponti convicted 1-23, 79B1
La Spezia church robbery 2-1, 119G1
Virus kills 65 babies 2-15, 138E3
'Last Supper' restoratn rptd 2-27, 173B3
Seveso '76 chem blast cited 3-1, 167G1
Cruise ship burns, sinks 3-30, 316B3
'79 fashion roundup rptd 1006F1
Venice sinkage rptd ended 5-18, 437C3
Flemish art stolen from Rome convent 6-3, 656F1
Mt Etna erupts 8-4, 8-6, 639C1
Octuplets born in Naples 8-16, 656C2*
Mt Etna erupts, kills 9 9-12, 800B2
Da Vinci mural believed found 11-1, 892E1
Shroud of Turin age test awaited 11-21, 931E2

Atomic Energy & Safeguards
A-energy group head nominated 1-8, 21C1
US A-accident sparks protest 4-1, 246A2

Economy & Labor
'78 inflatn rptd 11.5% 1-8, 13C1
State co heads nominated 1-8, controversy sparked 1-8, 1-18, 20F3, 38D3
'79-81 econ plan revealed 1-15, 38C2
Stockbrokers strike 1-17, 38D3
CP ends govt support 1-26, 76C2
'78 living standards ranked 2-2, 109B2
Chem group rescue planned 2-8, 97B3
'78 indl productn up 2-8, 169F3
Central bank offcls chrgd 3-24, 3-26; protests sparked, employees strike 3-24—3-27, 237G1-D2
Credit ceilings revised 4-9, 269G1-A2
Wage moderatn urged 4-10, 269B2
Central bank offcl suspended 4-17, 313D2
7-natn indicators index rptd 6-11, 513A3
'78 deficit rptd at 15% GDP, '79 rise seen; black mkt, pub employees scored 6-26, 486D3
Metalworkers' pact set 7-16, 566E1-A2
Chem pact set; textile, constructn pacts cited 7-24, 584C1
Public workers strike 9-13, transport workers 9-17, 709C1
Alfa Romeo offers survival plan 9-13, 709E1
Westn wage rates compared 9-19, 697D3
Cabt OKs draft '80 budget, union oppositn noted 9-29—9-30, 752E3-753C1
Central bank gov replaced, employees strike 10-5, 793E1
Fiat fires 61 10-10, 793B1
Central bank offcl indicated by ct 11-14, 909D2
61 Fiat plant dismissals cited 12-14, 995D2

Energy—*See also 'Atomic' above*
Gas shortages seen 5-15, 396G2
Gas price rptd at $2.23 per gal 5-19, 397A1
OPEC price hike impact seen 5-28, 473C2
Diesel, heating oil prices hiked 6-26, 486G3
Tokyo summit 6-28—6-29, 493B1-F2

1980

ITALIAN-Americans
Reagan tells ethnic joke 2-16, apologizes 2-18, 128B2
Reagan addresses DC fete 9-13, 699E3

ITALY—*See also ADB, COUNCIL of Europe, CSCE, EC, GATT, GENEVA Committee, IDB, IEA, MBFR, NATO, OECD*

Accidents & Disasters
Seveso '76 blast damages agrmt rptd 3-26, 233B1
Jet crash kills 81 6-28, 769A3
Quake hits, map 11-23; death toll, devastatn rptd 11-24—11-28, 893A1-C2
Quake relief stirs controversy; death toll disputed, rescue efforts detailed 11-26—12-11, 943B2-944E1
New Seveso damage accord set 12-19, 995F1

Arts & Sciences
Loren art collectn claim rptd denied 2-9, 200B2
Titian forgeries chrgd 2-26, 472B3
Monument preservatn planned 5-20, 409A1
'Last Supper' crack rptd 6-16, 472F3
'80 fashion roundup rptd 998D1

Atomic Energy & Safeguards
Govt panel backs A-dvpt 1-9, 20D3
USSR buys equipmt 1-10, 28A1
EC OKs A-fusion funds 2-5, 125B2
French breeder reactor role cited 2-26, 149F2
Iraq A-aid seen; US concern noted 3-17, disputed 3-18, 220G2
Eurodif share cut 5-2, 409D1
7-natn Venice summit backs 6-23, 473F2
Trudeau, Cossiga to press reactor sale 6-24, 486F1

Crime & Civil Disorders—*See also 'Terrorism & Unrest' below*
Caltagirone bros flee, evade arrest 2-11, 151E2
Loan fraud chrgd, 38 held 3-4, 173F1
44 suspected in Italcasse 'black funds' scandal, govt scored 3-7, 212G2
Caltagirone tax debt estimated 3-12, 255G1
Alleged tax evaders listed 3-19, 233E1
Sindona convicted in US, extradition sought 3-27, 237D1
10 Italcasse suspects freed 4-1, new bank fraud chrgs rptd 4-2, 254G3
Calabria rpt publshd 6-30; constructn co bars Mafia paymts 7-11, 564B3
Loren sets return in tax case 9-10, 908B1
Oil tax scandal arrests, chrgs rptd 10-24—11-5; govt probe rptd set 11-5—11-6, 873D2-C3
Mafia quake relief theft rptd 12-11, 943G3

Economy & Labor
Chem group aid OKd by Cabt 1-11, 20F3
Alien worker curbs set 1-12, 59C3
1-day gen strike held 1-15, 59G2
'79 inflatn up 1-21, 59D3; 2-13, 125C3
Venice aid re Adriatic floods vowed 3-8—3-9, 194C2
Air controllers stage job actn 3-12, 194A2
Chem firm ends losses 3-20, 233D2
Cossiga stresses inflatn 4-20, 314D1
Fiat layoff plans rptd 5-20, 408D3
Rptrs hold protest strike 5-26, 408C3
Scala mobile revisn barred 7-1, 523G3, 524B1
Indl workers strike 7-1, 524B1
Anti-inflatn pkg OKd 7-2, PCI union split spurred 7-8, 7-10, 523D3-524C1
Steel cutback plan rptd opposed 7-29, 628F3
Labor costs rptd 8-12, 698E1
Anti-inflatn pkg wins confidence vote 8-27, 671G3-672B1
Fiat sets Peugeot project 9-15; seeks investmt, research capital 9-23, 751E3
Alfa Romeo, Nissan project OKd 9-20, 751B3
Govt loses econ plan vote, resigns; Fiat cancels layoffs 9-27; discount rate hiked 9-28, 751F1
Fiat tentative labor pact set 10-15, 791F2

Energy—*See also 'Atomic Energy' above*
US links Iraq oil exports, Italy A-aid 3-17, 220D3
Eur auto makers agree on research 4-14, 303B3
Grandi named ENI head 5-6, 408F3
7-natn Venice summit 6-22-6-23, 473A1-474E1
Gas price hike OKd 7-2, 523E3
Libya disputes Malta offshore oil project 8-21, 709F1
Iraq oil shipmts set 11-20, 894C2

1976

Lira stabilizes on Eur, US exchngs 1-23—1-26, 74D2
Mauritania compensates iron co 1-28, 104F2
Poland suspends cattle shipmts 1-29, 74G2
US Singer layoffs rptd 1-30, 141D1
Lira drop hits W Ger farmers 2-10, decline continues 2-12, 140D2
Jan trade surplus rptd 2-13, 254A1
'75 trade deficit rptd down 2-17, 140F3
France wine talks 2-24, 163D3
6-natn export credit pact rptd 2-25, 164C2
French protest wine exports 3-1—3-4, 204A3
Currency exchng reopens 3-1, lira drops 3-1—4-5, 253E3
US in monetary talks 3-7—3-10, 253F3
To join A-safeguards group 3-13, 243G2
Total IMF oil loan rptd 4-1, 340A2
France OKs fast-breeder reactor 4-15, 372C3
US bars shoe import curbs 4-16, 322C1
US ends car dumping probe 5-4, 321D1
'75 Sovt trade rptd 5-5, 340F3
Import controls set, lira drop continues 5-5, 365E3
US quake aid OKd 5-11, 352B3
US lira acquisitns rptd 5-17, 396G3
7-natn summit set 6-1, 6-3, 388G3
IDB entry planned 6-3, 465D3
CP asks oil, meat import curbs 6-13, 446B1
Export credit terms tightened 6-15, 529F3
Paris Club defers Zaire debt 6-17, 488A2
Carter urges intl aid 6-23, 451E3
7-natn econ summit held, aid pledged 6-27—6-28, 461G2, 462A2
US, W Eur loan ban disclosed 7-16, scored 7-19, 530D3
CP chrgs govt agreed to loan ban 7-20, 557A1
Forgn investmt law extended 8-12, 624F1
Sovt steel sale OK rptd 8-20, 752D2
July paymts surplus rptd 8-23, 676C3
July trade balance surplus rptd 9-13, 732B1
Lira drops vs $ 9-30, 721C2
Lira protectn measures set 10-1, 751E2
IMF takes no actn on gold sales 10-8, 778E2
Lira falls vs $ 10-18, 838G1
Lira drops vs $, mark 10-20, 782E1
IMF lending funds rptd low 10-26, 915D1
Rpt Greece fears EC entry block 11-3, 853G3
US stock price fall linked to Italy finances 847C1; 12-14, 12-15, 962A3
Venez signs econ pact 11-21, 929C3
Canada A-sale to Argentina probed 11-22, 11-24, 904D1
Libya buys into Fiat 12-1, Sovt benefits denied 12-10, 964F3-965E1
Rumania trade credit rptd 12-1, 1010F1
Giscard asks 3d summit 12-2, 964E1
IMF, US aid sought 12-8, 947D1
US study rpts CP paymts 12-20, 985F2
Not in IMF UK loan 12-21, 1004B1
Canada-Argentina pact delay rptd 12-22, 998G1

Foreign Relations (misc.)—*See also 'UN Policy' below*
Granelli asks Chile democracy restored 1-3, 47D2
Russell ct meets 1-10—1-17, 61B2, E2
Europn soclsts meet 1-18—1-19, 48F2, C3
USSR to make more dailies available 1-21, 76G2
Rpt Chile ousted 2 priests in '75 1-23, 100C2
PI deports 2 priests 103C2
Southn socialists meet, de Martino absent 1-24—1-25, 120B1, D1
2 Australia consulates cut back 2-4, 97A2
Angola MPLA recognized 2-18, 163B1
Berlinguer addresses Sovt CP Cong 2-27, sees Brezhnev 3-1, 195E3
Libyan saboteurs seized 3-6, 205B2
Europn socialists meet 3-13—3-14, 222F3
Eur liberals meet 3-26—3-27, 260C3
Sadat visits 4-5—4-8, 275G1
Reps at Czech CP Cong 4-12—4-16, 289G1
W Ger head cites CP 4-15, 503D1
Eur CPs meet, cong set 5-4—5-6, 341F1
Meinhof death protested 5-10, 383C2
France assures US re CP 5-18, 372B2
Soclsts score Chile 'fascism' 5-25, 449C3
CP discounts Sovt threat 6-15, 446D1
US evacuates 10 from Leb 6-20, 448C1
Berlinguer at Eur CP conf, backs pluralism 6-29—6-30, 461E1
'70 Sovt hijackers arrive from Turkey 7-11, 543G3
CP asks clemency for Polish food rioters 7-20, 543D3
Angola mercenary corpse shipped 7-26, 559C3
Spain CP holds Rome mtg 7-28—7-31, 753F1
E Ger rues border shooting 8-6, 589B3
Dutch royal couple curbs visit 8-23, 626A3
Yugo sentncs Slovenes 9-16, 10-15, 910D1
Czech student defects 9-27, 852C1
Syrian emb raided 10-11, 759C1
Canada immigratn rptd 11-3, 851E1
Venez pres visits 11-17—11-21, 929C3
France bars joint Eur defns 11-30, 905A3
Andreotti visits Giscard 12-2, 964E1
CP scores USSR re pol prisoners 12-22, 955E3

1977

Foreign Relations (misc.)—*See also 'Atomic Energy' above, 'Monetary, Trade & Aid' and 'UN Policy' below*
Andreotti in Bonn 1-17—1-18, 65A1
In 14-natn sulphur-dioxide pact 1-19, 109B3
Rpt Saudi fears CP role 1-24, 50B2
Malta scores security talks delay 2-10, 136A3
Spain seizes rightists 2-22, 307B2
Bulgaria exiles ask CP support 2-23, 314C2
Berlinguer sees France, Spain CP ldrs 3-2—3-3, 242E3
Banker kidnaped in Colombia 3-13, 255G1
Communist disputes party on NATO 4-2; reactn 4-9, 284A2
'75 Trieste pact exchanged 4-2, 309D2
Eritrea consulate closed 4-23, 327F2
Spain-USSR Eurocommunism dispute 6-23—6-27; CP avoids stand 6-28, 507G1, A3
Foreign students banned 6-28, 527B3
USSR renews Carrillo attack 7-6, 545D3
Observers at USSR mil exercises 7-11, 551C1
Andreotti sees Giscard, Barre 7-19, 581E2
Somali history cited 587F3
Nazi escapes, W Ger mtg put off 8-15; extraditn asked 8-17, 637E3
Nazi escape causes Italy pol crisis 8-18—9-18, 728G3-729E1
Brandt warns of Nazi revival, other reactn 8-19—8-26, 658A2
Nazi escape detailed 8-19, 9-15, 729F1
Govt asks Nazi confinemt 8-26, W Ger rejcts extraditn 9-21, 729G1
USSR bars publicatns entry 9-6, 766A1
Eur Cncl to study Turkey rights abuses in Cyprus 9-8, 764G1-A2; rptd shelved, Greece protests 11-3, 946E3
Panama ldr visits re Canal, sees Pope 10-4—10-6, 792C2
W Ger jet hijackers refuel 10-13, 789D1
W Eur heroin conf 10-17—10-21, 971E3
W Ger terrorists suicides spur protests 10-19, 791C1
Berlinguer addresses Sovt Central Com, parlts 11-3, 865G3
Malta premr threatens Libya defns pact 11-23, 925A3
Polish ldr visits 11-28—12-1, 987B1
Schmidt meets Andreotti in Verona 12-1, 1014G3
Terrorists linked to Baader-Meinhof gang hunted 12-28, 1014E2

1978

European Force Reduction Talks—*See under EUROPE*
Foreign Relations (misc.)—*See also 'Atomic Energy' above, 'Monetary, Trade, Aid & Investment' and 'UN' below*
At Westn natns Ogaden conf 1-21, 43E2
Yugo Tito foe chrgs kidnap 1-24, 292A2
France, W Ger OK ESA rocket launcher 2-6—2-7, 122B1
Kappler dies in W Ger 2-9, 114C3
Spain joint mil exercise rptd, UK '74 bomb incident cited 2-11, 133F2
Sadat visits, seeks Mideast peace moves backing 2-13, 98B3
CP labor group breaks Moscow ties 3-14, 191A3
W Ger terrorism linked, police join Moro search 3-20, 200B1
Red Brigades claim policy info 3-29, 246D3
Swiss host 4-natn terrorism mtg, 'hot line' set 4-8—4-9, 438B2
Pope pleas for Moro release 4-23, 313F3
Eur conservative group formed, Christian Dems rejct affiliatn 4-24, 424D3
Egypt terror group linked to Red Brigades 4-26, 300D2
W Ger co exec shot 5-4, 393A2
USSR chrgs US interventn 5-7, 349B3
Moro mourned by world ldrs 5-9, 337G2
ESA communicatns satellite launched 5-12, 384D3
USSR dissident sentence scored by CP 5-24, 401B2
W Ger terrorist linked to Red Brigades 5-30, 439A1
Club Medit '77 robbery cited 6-11, 473F3
Shcharansky, Ginzburg trials scored 7-11, 7-12, 543A1
Hijacking pact signed 7-17, 544G2
San Marino CP coaltn played down 7-19, 575B2
W Ger '76 papal kidnap plot rptd 8-6, 689A3
Leb Moslem ldr fails to arrive 8-31, 713D2
Argentine pres in Rome, leftists protest 9-5, 689D3, 793C1

1979

Conservatn steps announced 9-14, 708G3
ENI payoffs scandal spurs Saudi oil cutoff 12-5; Mazzanti ousted as head pending probe 12-7, 995B3

European Force Reduction Talks—*See under EUROPE*
Foreign Relations (misc.)—*See also 'Monetary' and 'UN' below*
USSR forgn min visits 1-22–1-26, 60E2
W Ger terrorist arrested 1-27–1-28, 98F1
Spain Basques protest French deportatns 2-5, 192B1
China Viet invasn scored by CP 2-19, 122G2
Israel team protest target 3-7, 212E1
Australia jet hijack foiled 4-4, 266F2
Bhutto executn scored 4-4, 247A2
Paris Red Brigades base chrgd 4-24, 331F2
Chile refugee relocatn rptd 5-7, 369B3
Zimbabwe soldiers kill missionary 7-6, 546G3
200 Viet refugees rescued 7-25, 575B2
More Viet refugees rescued 7-31, 626A2
Libyans occupy Rome Emb 9-3, 688F2
Leb Moslems seize Alitalia jet 9-7, surrender in Iran 9-8, 677B3
Argentine expelled editor flies to Rome 9-25, 728A1
Czech dissident trial scored 10-23, 802D2
China premr arrives 11-3, pacts OKd 11-6, 853E3, 854C2
Australian's '77 death linked to secret group 11-6, 870F2

1980

Foreign Relations (misc.)—*See also 'Atomic Energy' above, 'Monetary', 'Soviet-Afghan Issue', 'UN Policy' below*
Forgn, Italy terrorist links chrgd 1-2, 20F2
Controls on aliens set 1-12, 59B3
Sakharov exile condemned by CP 1-22, 1-23, 46C3, 86A1
USSR dancer defectn rptd 1-23, 88F1
Leb Emb guard killed 2-6, 99D1
Colombia amb seized in DR Emb raid 2-27, 141B1
Turkey airline office bombed 3-10, amb to Vatican attacked 4-17, 316G1-A2
Air controllers stage job actn 3-12, 194A2
French seize Moro suspects 3-28, 255D1
PCI rejects Paris CP parley 4-2, 254C3
Berlinguer visits China 4-14—4-22; renews PCI ties 4-15, bars anti-Sovt front 4-22, 314F1
2 Libya execs killed 4-19, 5-10, 373D3
Iran hostage kin seek support 4-23, 299D2
Iran hostage rescue missn scored 4-25, 324B2
Europn CPs meet 4-28—4-29, 327C2, C3
Tito funeral held 5-8, 339B1, C1
Brigadists warn Westn ldrs 5-17, 408G2
ESA rocket test fails 5-23, 397G2
Iraq Emb attacked 6-4, 451D2
Libyan exile killed, 2d wounded 6-11, 451A3
W Ger drug arrests rptd 6-13, 517E1, G1
7-natn Venice summit 6-22—6-23, 473A1-474E1
France arrests terrorist suspects 7-7—7-8, 523G2
ESA plans comet probe 7-15, 548A1
Sovt Olympic press crackdown rptd 7-21, 590F1
3 UK rptrs flee from Iran 7-25, 572B1
Iranians demonstrate at Vatican 8-8, 635A2
Westn labor costs compared 8-12, 698E1
Iran parlt ldr rebuffs hostage appeal 8-17, 634D3
Brazil expels RC priest 10-30, 870G3

1976

Government & Politics—*See also other appropriate subheads*
Moro govt fails 1-7, 10F1
Socialists quit, govt falls; interim rule set 1-7, 10F1
Christian Dems, Socialist overtures 1-9—1-13, CP reacts 1-11, 29B2
La Malfa bars govt role 1-9, 29F2
Moro to form new govt, bars CP 1-13, 29G1
CP bares '75 finances 1-16, 74D3
Listed as 'free' nation 1-19, 20C3
Moro coalitn govt bid fails 1-24—1-25, 74C1
Socialists, Radicals to abstain in vote 2-5; Moro forms minority govt 2-11, 140E1
Parlt Mafia comm rpts issued 2-5, 141C1
Party congs held by Soclsts 3-3—3-7, Soc Dems 3-12—3-16, Christian Dems 3-18—3-24, 254F1
Socialists demand CP role 4-7, 254B1
Christian Dems, CP overtures 4-7—4-16, 296D3
Soclsts back gen electns 4-9, 4-15, 296C3
Christian Dems elect Fanfani chrmn 4-14, 297G1
CP shuns defense, forgn portfolios 4-18, 297C1
Moro govt falls, interim rule set 4-30, 296E2
Parlt dissolved 5-1, electns set 5-3, 333G2
Naples CP mayor quits 5-8, 366B1
CP urges post-electn coalitn 5-13, 352D1
CP electn campaign opens, Christian Dems scored 5-16, 402F2-A3
Independents rptd on CP ticket 5-17, 5-30, 402C3
Berlinguer bars premr bid 5-28, 402B3
CP, Christian Dems exchng chrgs 6-11—6-17, 445B2
CP gains in electns, 6-20—6-21, 445A1 ★; table 446A1
Socialist ldr resigns 6-21, 445C1
CP bars oppositn role 6-30, 497B2
Communist elected Chamber speaker, Fanfani heads Sen 7-5, 497E1
Moro quits 7-9, Andreotti succeeds 7-13, 538G3
Rome prosecutor killed 7-10, neo-fascist probe cited 7-12, 539B1
Soclst head quits 7-13, replaced 7-16, 539A1
CP drops Cabt demands 7-22, formatn role seen 7-24—7-27, 556C3
Andreotti, oppositn parties confer 7-22—7-23, 556G3
CP wins 4 Chamber seats, Sen bid rptd 7-26, 556A3
Andreotti meets CP Cabt demand 7-29, 573C1
New Cabt sworn 7-30, 573B1
Andreotti offers austerity program 8-4, 573A2
Rev Franzoni defrocked 8-4, 951B2
Sen votes confidence 8-6, 589E2
Sen, Chamber OK Andreotti govt, CP abstains 8-6, 8-11, 624C1
Leftist coalition wins in Rome 8-7, CP mayor named 8-8, 589G2
Moro heads Christian Dems 10-14, 890C3

Obituaries
Lercaro, Giacomo Cardinal 10-18, 970B2
Piccioni, Attilio 3-10, 240F3
Visconti, Luchino 3-30, 240G3

Political Payments Issues
Gulf paymts detailed 133G3, 134A1
CIA aid to centrists rptd 1-7, 10E2
CP scores CIA aid chrgs 1-8, 29G2
Colby denies aid 1-9, 29B3
CIA agents rptd 1-16, 50C1
CP denies Sovt aid 1-16, 74D3
Christian Dems urge CIA disclosures 1-26, 74C3
US House com rpt leaked 1-26, 92E1, F3
CIA aid recipients named 1-31, 140A3
Andreotti for CIA aid disclosures 2-2, 140E3
Lockheed payoffs rptd 2-4, 2-6, 130E2, 131A1
Lockheed recipients named, Interior min quits 2-11—2-12, 132G1
Lockheed chrgs probed, 2 sought 2-17—2-18, 132C2
Arrests, chrgs rptd 2-20—3-24, 298D1
Northrop admits paymts 2-20, 362B3
Turkey Lockheed probe rptd 3-5, 192C2
Social Dems oust Tanassi 3-16, 254A2
Tanassi, Gui probes rptd 3-26, 4-2, 298E1

1977

Government & Politics—*See also other appropriate subheads in this section*
Socialists score Rome mayor 1-6, 8A3
Liberal abortn bill defeated 6-7, 527F2
Christian Dem-CP pact 6-29, 544B2
Nazi escape causes pol crisis; guards disciplined, Lattanzio demoted 8-18—9-18, 728G3-729E1
Friuli quake relief scandal, Zamberletti resigns 8-27—9-8, 783B1

Helsinki Agreement—*See EUROPE—Security and Cooperation*

Monetary, Trade & Aid Issues (including all foreign economic developments)—*See also 'Atomic Energy' above*
Labor dispute endangers IMF loan 1-6, 8F2
Sovt trade talks 1-10—1-13, '76 data rptd 1-12, 64A3
'76 Eur Cncl pact vs terror cited 9G2
'76 trade deficit rptd 1-13, 64D3
Andreotti-Schmidt talks 1-17—1-18, 64F3
Swiss '76 currency interventn rptd 1-18, 84A2
ICFTU S Africa boycott fails 1-21, 67B3
IMF loan term moves 1-26, 2-4, 116E2, A3
2 ex-mins indicted in Lockheed scandal 1-29, 116A3
IMF SDR defined 87G2
'76 forgn exchng mkt tensions rptd 3-2, 188D3
Ex-mins claim innocence 3-8, Lockheed trial set 3-10, 284B1
IMF paymts debt managing role rptd, loan cited 3-28, 362F3, 363D1
US bars shoe import curbs 4-1, 248E2, B3
EEC OKs loan 4-15, IMF 4-25, 527C2
Gabes oil rig withdrawn 497F2
At 7-natn econ summit 5-7—5-8, 357A1-358B2
Intl consortium OKs Egypt aid 5-11—5-12, 390C3
'68 Israeli uranium purchase rptd 5-30, 416C3
Group of 10 membership cited 438F1
In 11-natn Portugal loan 6-22, 530B3
Zaire debt rescheduled 7-7, 583E1
Carter seeks arms sales curbs 7-28, 574B3
Somali OKs US, UK arms aid 7-28, 608A2
'77 paymts deficit forecast 7-31, 586D2
Sweden quits 'snake' 8-29, 708G3
W Ger '74 loan repaymt begun 9-6, 729B2
IMF-World Bank mtgs see econ recovery effort 9-26—9-30, 753D3
Govt steel subsidy impact minimized 10-7, 776D2
'76 car exports cited 10-11, 853A3
US co chrgs steel dumping 10-20, 836E3
Exxon settles paymts chrgs 10-25, 818E1
Malta premr presses for econ, mil aid 11-23, 925B3
$ drops 12-30, 997F2

Obituaries
Mardersteig, Giovanni 12-27, 1024D2
Rossellini, Roberto 6-3, 532F3

1978

Government & Politics—*See also 'Terrorism' and other appropriate subheads in this section*
CP demands govt role 1-4, Christian Dems bar 1-11, 19B1
Andreotti govt resigns 1-16, 37F3
2 jailed in Friuli quake-relief scandal 1-23, 103F3
CP, 3 small parties back Andreotti 3-8; Christian Dem rift rptd 3-9, new Cabt formed 3-11, 190G2, 191C1 ★
Parlt adjourns after Moro kidnaping, Andreotti calls emergency Cabt sessn 3-16, 199F2
Andreotti wins confidence vote 3-17, CP backs anti-terrorism bills 3-20, 200B1
Parlt OKs abortn reform bill 4-14, 5-18, 375C1
Parlt pays tribute to Moro 5-10, 338A1
Interior min resigns 5-10, 338F2
Local electns set; CP, Christian Dem accord rptd in jeopardy 5-11, 338C1
Andreotti takes over Interior post 5-11, 393F2
Christian Dems gain in local electns 5-16, 375A2
Andreotti wins confidence vote 5-17, 453D1
Christian Dems, Soclsts gain in Sicily local electns; CP slips 5-30, 453E3, F3 ★
Natl referendum backs pol party pub funding law 6-11—6-12, 453G1, C2
Rognoni named Interior min 6-13, sworn 6-14, 558B2
Leone resigns over Lockheed scandal chrgs, Fanfani assumes pres 6-15, 516F2
Pertini elected pres 7-8, sworn 7-9, 558A1

Helsinki Agreement—*See EUROPE—Security and Cooperation*

Monetary, Trade, Aid & Investment—*See also 'Atomic Energy' above*
Algeria pres visits Malta 1-3, 39C2
US $ swap pact cited 1-4, 27B2
Swiss Credit chrmn probed in lawsuit 1-10, secrecy breach denied 1-11, 151C1
Iran lifts trade ban 1-11, 55F2
'77 paymts surplus rptd 1-13, 38A1
Somalia asks arms aid 1-16, 43A3
'77 $ drop rptd 1-23, 27D2
Ethiopia protests Somalia aid 2-1, 100D1
Somalia makes 2d aid bid 2-4, 99G3
UK prime min urges Bonn summit plan 3-14, sees Carter 3-23, 226D3
Red Brigades claim multinatl info 3-29, 246D3
Lira in new SDR basket 4-3, 300F3
Zaire aid OKd 6-13—6-14, 478A1
French customs job slowdown 6-28, 532F3
Malta Arab aid threat rptd discounted 7-4, 592G2
At 7-natn Bonn econ summit 7-16—7-17, 543C3, 544B2, G2
Swiss unit scored for Seveso '76 blast 7-27, 689E1 ★
Libya seizes 2 Sicilian fishermen 7-30, 689G3
USSR warns vs China arms sales 10-26, 814C1
EC Comm orders fiber cartel modificatn 11-9, 871F3
At Brussels monetary summit 12-4—12-5, EMS entry deferred 12-5, 951B3, F3, 952B1
EMS entry backed despite CP oppositn 12-12—12-13, 952D1
Ireland to join EMS 12-15, 979G1, B2
OPEC price hike adverse impact seen 12-18, 978F1
Greek EC entry terms set, agri curbs noted 12-21, 1017C3, E3
US probes steel dumping chrgs 12-28, 1006B1
France delays EMS start 12-29, 999E1

Obituaries
De Chirico, Giorgio 11-20, 972A3
Gronchi, Giovanni 10-17, 888B3
Jacoppuci, Angelo 7-21, 600B2
John Paul I, Pope 9-28, 746B3
Nobile, Umberto 7-29, 620C3
Paul VI, Pope 8-6, 601A1

1979

Government & Politics—*See also other appropriate subheads in this section*
Parlt controversy sparked re state co nominatns 1-8, 1-18, 20F3, 38C3
CP demands more influence 1-18, 38A3
CP withdraws support 1-26, Andreotti resigns govt 1-31, 76E1-C2
La Malfa asked to form Cabt 2-22, 155F1
La Malfa gives up Cabt bid 3-2, Andreotti asked again 3-7, 169B3
Andreotti announces new Cabt 3-20, sworn 3-21, 212A1
La Malfa dies 3-26, 254A3
Andreotti loses confidence vote 3-31, parlt dissolved 4-2, 254E2
Electns held; Christian Dems retain plurality, CP set back 6-3, 6-4, 426C1-D2
Eur Parlt electns 6-10, 433A1, G2, 434A1
Andreotti fails to form govt 7-2—7-7, Socialists asked 7-9, 525F2-E3
CP reorganizes, Berlinguer gains power 7-10, 525E3
Craxi fails in Cabt bid 7-24, Pandolfi to try 7-27, 583G2
Cossiga govt sworn 8-5, 602C3
Cossiga wins confidence votes 8-11, 8-12, 615E1
Berlinguer seeks talks with Soclsts 8-11, 615G1

Helsinki Agreement—*See EUROPE—Security and Cooperation*

Monetary, Trade, Aid & Investment
Israel asks equal basis in Sinai oil access 1-5, 51C2
Portugal sets farm seizure compensatn 1-11, 212E3
EMS rptd opposed by CP 1-18, 38C3
'78 paymts surplus rptd 1-18, 38F3
USSR trade talks 1-22—1-26, 60A3
3 convicted in Sindona US bank case 1-23, 205B3
Carter Westn econ summit warning to Japan rptd 2-10, rpt disputed 2-15, 160F1
Iran oil cutoff impact assessed 2-20, 126G2
EMS set 3-7, 160F3
US indicts Sindona, Bordoni 3-19, 205C2
W Ger ranks exporter labor costs 5-1, 374C2
Fiat-Poland deal signed 6-18, 487F1-A2
EMS currencies realigned 6-24, 719A1
Iran insurnc cos natlzd 6-25, 486E2
Large '78 deficit rptd 6-26, 486D3
OPEC price hike impact seen 6-28, 473C2
Oil import targets set at Tokyo summit 6-28—6-29, 493B1
Fiat Argentine mkt share rptd 7-20, 562A2
French knitwear import curbs protested 8-20, 668D3
Fiat announces investmt plan 9-12, 709B2
EC draft budget cuts aid 9-12, 719E1
Alfa Romeo plans joint ventures 9-13, 709E1
EC contributns rptd 9-17, 719B2, C2
Brazil strike hits Olivetti unit 10-29, 833B2
China pacts OKd 11-6, 854D2
Saudis cut off oil re ENI payoffs scandal 12-5, 995B3
US seeks econ sanctns vs Iran 12-11, 933C2

Obituaries
DiJorio, Alberto 9-5, 756B2
La Malfa, Ugo 3-26, 254A3
Mussolini, Rachele 10-30, 860G2-A3
Natta, Giulio 5-2, 432C3
Nervi, Pier Luigi 1-9, 104E3
Ottaviani, Alfredo 8-3, 671C3

1980

Government & Politics—*See also other appropriate subheads in this section*
Soclsts end govt support 1-18, 59F2
Christian Dems bar CP Cabt posts 2-21, 134C1
Evangelisti quits post in scandal 3-4, 173A2
Piccoli chosen Christian Dem party secy 3-6, 194E2
44 suspected in Italcasse 'black funds' scandal, govt scored 3-7, 212G2
Cossiga Cabt resigns 3-19, 212D2
Cossiga forms new govt, Cabt sworn 4-4, 275A3
CP split with Soclsts intensifies, chrgs vs Formica rptd 4-17, 314D1
Cossiga govt wins confidence vote 4-20, 314C1
Parlt comm probes terrorist tipoff; Cossiga cleared, Donat-Cattin resigns 5-29—5-31; CP, coalitn split 6-2, 6-3, 430B1-D2
Local electns back Cossiga 6-8—6-9, 445D2
Naples retains Communist rule, neo-fascists advance 7-22, 579D1
Parlt upholds Cossiga in terrorist probe 7-27, 578G3
Cossiga wins confidence vote 7-31, 605A2
Cossiga loses econ vote, govt resigns 9-27; Forlani agrees to form govt 10-2, 751F1-A3
Forlani sworn, forms govt 10-18, 808F3
Govt wins confidence votes 10-25, 10-29; Craxi attack on Pope strain coalitn 10-25, 873G1
Pertini scores quake rescue efforts 11-26, Interior Min submits resignatn 11-27; CP asks govt ouster 11-28, Forlani defends 12-2, debate continues 12-4, 943C2, E2

Monetary, Trade, Aid & Investment
USSR A-equipmt purchase rptd 1-10, 28A1
Supertanker bound for Genoa sinks 1-17; S Africa oil sale suspected, Kuwait warns 2-7, 108A3, B3
CP funds from E Eur trade deals chrgd 3-7, 212C3
Iraq A-aid seen; US concern noted 3-17, disputed 3-18, 220G2
US Steel files dumping complaint 3-21, 225D1
EC summit postponed 3-24, 242G1
US fiber import suspensn ordrd 4-4, 294B3
Iran copter deliveries canceled 4-8, 282D1
US sets steel import probe 4-10, 367F3
Fiat in Europn auto research effort 4-14, 303B3
Turkey aid OKd 4-15, 295A3
US finds steel import damage 5-1, 456C1
Albania trade increase rptd 5-2, 356F2
Eurodif share cut 5-2, 409D1
Fiat layoff plans rptd 5-20, 408E3
Sovt trade blitz rptd 5-22, 430G3-431A1
US cruise missile shipmt set for '83 6-3, 450A3
Fiat balks at SEAT acquisitn 6-4, 467A3
7-natn Venice summit 6-22—6-23, 473A1-474E1
Trudeau, Cossiga to press A-sale 6-24, 486F1
Lire, paymts deficit steps OKd 7-2, 523E3
Libya disputes Malta offshore oil project 8-21, 709F1
Fiat, Peugeot project set 9-15, 751F3
Alfa Romeo, Nissan project OKd 9-20, 751B3
Hormones in cattle feed banned 10-1, 737C3
Iraq oil shipmts set 11-20, 894C2

Obituaries
Amendola, Giorgio 6-5, 528A1
Brosio, Manlio Giovanni 3-14, 279F1
Longo, Luigi 10-16, 876D2
Marini, Marino 8-6, 676B2
Nenni, Pietro 1-1, 104C3
Pignedoli, Sergio 6-15, 528C3

Soviet-Afghan Issue
Sovt invasn scored by CP 1-5, 1-6, 2F2, 57A3, B3
France bars US-Eur mtg 2-8, 106E2
CP scores USSR, US 2-17; CP govt role barred 2-21, 134D1, E1
Vance seeks backing vs USSR 2-21, 139B2
Olympic com rejcts Moscow boycott 3-22, 259C3
USSR May Day parade shunned 5-1, 354G2
Athletes warned vs Moscow Olympics 5-19, com defies 5-20, 379A3
Sovt trade blitz rptd 5-22, 430G3
US, Italy score Sovts 6-20, 474B2
7-natn Venice summit seeks total Sovt exit 6-22, 473B1

1976

US Lockheed data pact 3-30, 286A1
Turkey mil trial starts 4-7, 298F1
BP, Shell admit bribes 4-13, 267F1
3 ex-premrs deny link to Lockheed 4-22, 298A1
Turkey gens cleared 4-30, 322A3
CP asks Rumor resign 6-11, 445C2
US clears Leone 6-15, 445D2
US disclosure bill proposed 8-3, 668B2
Andreotti denies Lockheed payoffs 8-31, letters publshd 9-1, 684B3
Andreotti probe dropped 10-13, 858A2

Sports

Winter Olympics results 2-4—2-15, 158D3-159B2
Italian Open results 5-30, 656C2
Summer Olympic results 7-18—7-31, 573D3, G3, 574C2-G3, 575A2, D3, 576G1, C2

1977

Sports

Italian Open results 5-22, 430A3
Australia wins Davis Cup 12-4, 970F1

Terrorism & Unrest (domestic)

Prisoners escape 1-2, 1-5, security scored 1-5, 65B1
Kidnapers arrested 1-6, 1-25, Jan record set 2-2, 116D3
Students riot, Rome U occupied 2-1—2-17, 135F2
Bologna police, students clash; ultra-left ldr killed 3-11; students protest 3-12, 1014F1
Rome policeman killed in student clash, demonstratns banned 4-21, 1014G1
Curcio trial in Turin postponed 5-3, sentncd in Milan 6-23, 1014A2
Anti-police protests in 6 cities 5-13—5-15, 1014A2
Miceli treason trial opens 5-30, 1014G3
Rome Univ dean shot 6-21, 1014A3
Riots follow anti-terrorism agrmt 6-30, 1014B2
Palermo anti-Mafia police chief killed 8-21, 1014C3
Andreotti testifies at '69 Milan bombing trial 9-15, 1014D3
Rossi death protests 9-30, 1014C2
Mafia activity rptd up 10-4, 1014B3
'77 kidnapings rptd 11-9, 1014C3
De Laurentis escapes jail 11-10, 1014C2
Police battle students in Rome, 4 other cities 11-12, 1014D2
La Stampa ed dies after shooting, other attacks rptd 11-29, 1014F2
Communist stabbed, Bari riots 12-1—12-2, 1014E2
450 terrorist attacks rptd, violence up 12-2, 1014B1
Rome workers stage march 12-2, 1015A1
Communist Frontline hunted 12-28, 1014E2
Pistolesi killed 12-28, 1014E2

1978

Sports

Milan WCT results 4-2, 419B1
Messner climbs Everest without oxygen 5-8, 480C2
3d in Nations Cup 5-15, 419D1
Italian Open results 5-28, 418E2
World Cup soccer finals, sidelights 6-1—6-25, 519F3, 520F1
Eur middlewgt bout 7-19, Jacoppuci dies 7-21, 600B2
Italian Grand Prix site switched 10-27, 968E3

Terrorism & Unrest (domestic)—*For labor unrest, see 'Economy & Labor' above*

Fires set in CP, Christian Dem offices 1-2, 19C2
Fiat exec in Turin slain, workers strike 1-4, 19A2
Rome paper, book publisher bombed 1-4, 19C2
Rome bldg exec kidnaped 1-4, 19D2
2 right-wing youths killed in Rome 1-7; riots, firebombings rptd 1-8—1-9, City Cncl meets 1-9, 19D2
Andreotti testifies at Miceli trial 1-9, 19G1
15 sentenced for '77 de Martino kidnap 1-10, 133G2-A3
13 arrested in kidnap fund laundering 1-20, 133C3
Milan magistrate resigns in Belloli kidnap controversy 1-22, 133A3
Telephone co exec wounded in Milan 1-24, 133G1
Rome ct acquits 113 of fascism 1-24, 133A2
Red Brigades '77 shootings rptd 1-25, 133E1
Concutelli trial opens in Florence 1-30, 133B2
Rome leftists, police clash 1-30, 133B2
Naples jobless protesters, police clash 2-1, 133C2
Rome firebombs injure 7 policemen 2-4, 133D2
Rome judge killed 2-14; Red Brigades claim credit, Turin trial cited 2-14—2-15, 133D1, F1
Alfa Romeo exec wounded in Milan 2-16, 133D2
Ammon ransomed 2-17, 133E3
Varese police shoot neo-fascist 2-19, 133D2
Rome banker shot 2-24, 133E2
Student violence in Rome, other cities 2-25—2-26, 3-7, 191F2, A3
Leftists bomb MSI Rome office 3-3, 191G2
Turin bomb blasts 3-4—3-5, 191E2
Rome leftists, police clash 3-6, 247F2
Turin trial jury set 3-9, police offcl slain 3-10, 191G1
Turin trial halted 3-10, new defns atty appointed 3-13, 191C1, C2
Moro kidnaped, 5 guards killed 3-16; labor, pol, religious ldrs protest 3-16—3-19, 199C2
Moro search pressed by police 3-16—3-20; photos released 3-17, suspect detained 3-19, 199D3
Moro kidnapers release photo; plan trial, play down Turin 'farce' 3-18, 200D1
Sossi '77 kidnap cited 3-18, 200G1
2 Milan youths killed 3-18, violence erupts 3-19, 247G2
Moro kidnaping linked to W Ger terrorism, W Ger police join search 3-20, 200B1
Turin defendants disrupt trial 3-20, 200A2
CP backs anti-terrorism bills, other pol ldrs urge strong actn 3-20, 200C2
Moro kidnap cars returned, 2 suspects freed 3-20; police search scored 3-24, 247F1
Emergency crime measures OKd 3-21, 246D2
Ex-mayor of Turin wounded 3-24, 247D2
Rome leftist firebombings 3-24, 247G2
Crime ldrs threaten Red Brigades 3-28, 247B2
Moro letters received, 'trial' rptd 3-29, 4-4; Christian Dems bar secret talks, prisoner exchng 3-30—4-5, 246A3
Press debates terrorist coverage 4-2, 247D1
100 leftists detained 4-4, 247C2
Bombings in Rome, Turin, Bologna; rally ban blamed 4-6, 330D1
Genoese businessman shot 4-7, 330C1
More Moro letters received; release asked, prisoner exchng debated 4-8—4-25; Christian Dem rift rptd 4-21, 313F2-314A1

1979

Sports

Boxing title bouts 2-4, 4-18, 412D3, G3
Israel basketball game protested 3-7, 212E1
Milan WCT results 4-1, 391B3
Italian Open golf results 5-6, 587F2
Nations Cup bid lost 5-14, Italian Open tennis results 5-14, 5-27, 570C2
Pinto swims Strait of Otranto 7-14, 656F3
Scheckter wins Italian Gr Prix 9-9, 1005D1
Bologna Grand Prix tennis results 11-25, 1003G3
US wins Davis Cup 12-16, 1003G2

Terrorism & Unrest

'78 kidnappings down 1-2, 21C1
Calabrian Mafia trial closes, 28 sentncd; suspected ldr killed 1-4, 21E1
Leftist radio statn attacked 1-9, rightist killed in retaliatn 1-11, 21A2
Turin prison offcl killed 1-19, 2 cops wounded 1-20, 98D1, E1
Cagliari Coronas police statn bombed 1-19, 98E1
Genoese CP labor offcl killed 1-24, 98C1
CP ends govt support 1-26, 76A2
6 Moro kidnap suspects arrested 1-27-1-28, 98F1
Milan prosecutor killed 1-29, 98B1
Christian Dem, Vatican link to Moro kidnap chrgd 2-7; CP asks parlt probe 2-8, 97D3-98A1
Moro parlt probe OKd 2-9, 136B1
US offcl expelled re critical intelligne rpt 2-14, 136F1
Curcio Milan trial opens 2-15, 212A2
Bologna radiologist attacked 2-19, 2 die in Turin shootout 2-28, 212G1
Anti-Semitic protest, 10 indicted 3-7, 212E1
CD offcl kidnaped 3-8, freed 3-11, 212F1
Turin Fiat exec wounded 3-14, 212D1
Rptr's homes firebombed 3-14, 269E1
Exec injured by car bomb 3-21, 269E1
Rome police station bombed 3-28, 269F1
Christian Dem ldr rptd killed, ed's son shot 3-30, 269F1
Leftists held as terrorists 4-7, 4-8, 269A1
Rome, Florence, Padua violence 4-12, 331G2
Moro probe implicates 12 4-16, 313E2
Anti-terrorist cop killed 4-19, 331B3
Palace of Sens bombed 4-20, 313F1-C2
Neofascist party offices bombed, police station attacked 4-23, 331B3
Red Brigades Paris base chrgd 4-24, 331F2
Journalist, Christn Dem shot 4-24, 331C3
Rome Christn Dem hq attacked, electns linked 5-3, 331F1
Bombings in Naples, Genoa 5-4, Rome, Perugia 5-18, 426G2-A3
Army joins anti-terror effort 5-9, 372B1
Moro death anniv marked 5-9, 372E1
St Francis Inst bombed 5-21, 426A3
Genoa cnclwoman attacked 5-23, car bombed 6-1, 426C3
Forgn Min offices bombed 5-24, 426D3
Front Line suspects arrested 5-27, 5-28, 426F2
Christian Dem candidate, professor shot 5-29, 5-31, 426E3
Moro suspects arrested, linked to Christn Dem hq attack 5-30, 426E2
3 more Moro suspects seized 6-6, murder weapon rptd found 6-19, 487B1
Red Brigades wound Fiat watchman 6-8, 487D1
Councilman shot in Sicily 6-14, 487E1
Rome PCI office bombed 6-16, Genoa govt bldg 6-18, 487E1
Rome cop killed 7-13, 584A1
Red Brigades split revealed 7-25, 7-28, 583D3
Red Brigades ldrship letter scores dissidents 8-10, 635C2
French arrest 2 Moro suspects 8-18, 9-14, 709D2
Anti-kidnaping measures barred 9-12, 709E2
Kidnapings total rptd 9-13, 709G2
Turin Fiat exec murdered 9-21, 793B2
Moro suspect captured 9-24, 793A2
Sicilian judge murdered 9-25, 793C2
Fiat unrest, 61 fired 10-10, 793B1
Red Brigade ldrs sentncd 10-17, 793D2
Terrorist activity rptd up 11-15, 882A2
Genoa Carabinieri, Rome police officers killed 11-21, 11-27, 12-7, 995E2
Naples jail raided 11-30, 995A3
Rome bomb blast injures 9 12-9, 995F2
Turin Univ business schl invaded, 10 kneecapped 12-11, 995B2

1980

Sports

Lake Placid Olympic results 2-12—2-24, 154F2, 155F2-156D1
Soccer scandal rptd 3-6, 194F2
Antuofermo loses world middlewgt title 3-16, 320E2
Olympics com rejcts Moscow boycott 3-22, 259C3
Milan WCT tennis results 3-30, Women's Italian Open 5-11, Florence Grand Prix 5-18, Italian Open 5-25, 607A3, C3, D3
Argentina wins Nations Cup 5-12, 607A2
Milan soccer team demoted 5-18, 409B1
Athletes warned vs Moscow Olympic 5-19, com defies 5-20, 379A3
Eur Soccer Championship results, soccer scandal impact seen 6-22, 771C2
US OKs paid amateur meets 6-28, 891E3
Moscow Olympic results 7-20—8-3, 588A3, D3, 622D1-624G3
Czechs win Davis Cup finals 12-7, 946C3
Soccer players rptd acquitted 12-22, 12-24, 995E1

Terrorism & Unrest

Prosecutor's rpt accuses 21 re Moro affair, backs separate probe of intellectuals 1-2, 20E2-A3
Sicilian ldr murdered 1-6, 20B3
3 Milan cops slain 1-8, 20C3
Sens accuse Rome magistrates 1-11, 59F3
New anti-terrorist actn urged 1-11, 59G3
Controls on aliens set 1-12, 59C3
Police barracks bombed 1-19, 59E3
Leftist radio statn raided 1-22, 59F3
Genoa Carabinieri cmdr killed 1-25, 99A1
Rome targets bombed 1-26, 99B1
Montedison exec slain 1-29, 99C1
Fiat watchman killed 2-1, 99C1
Parlt OKs security rules 2-2, 98C3
Chem exec slain 2-5, 99C1
Leb Emb guard killed 2-6, 99D1
Front Line kills trial witness 2-7, 151C2
Turin CP offcl wounded 2-9, 151D2
Milan businessman wounded 2-10, 151D2
Rome Univ law prof killed 2-12, 151A2
Suspected guerrillas captured in Parma 2-15, 151E2
2 Moro suspects arrested 2-20, 194E3
Student murdered 2-22, protest held 2-23, 151A3
Italcantieri exec attacked 2-29, 194D3
Rome offices, bldgs bombed 3-8, 3-9, 194C3
Turkey airline office bombed 3-10, amb to Vatican attacked 4-17, 316G1-A2
More Padua arrests ordrd 3-12, 194B3
3 magistrates killed 3-16—3-19, magistrates strike 3-21, 3-22, 233F1-D2
3 police killed outside Turin, Genoa U prof hurt 3-24, 255E1
Sindona kidnap chrgs cited 3-27, 237G1
4 Red Brigadists slain in police raid 3-28, 255B1
French seize Moro suspects 3-28, 255D1
Milan banks attacked 3-28—3-29, 255G1
Christian Dem workers wounded in Milan 4-1, 294G3
Rome police station bombed 4-4, 294G3
Law enforcemt urged 4-14, 314C1
Turin, Milan, Biella arrests rptd 4-15, 294D3
Libyan execs killed 4-19, 5-10, 373D3
Lawyer suspect kills self 4-19, another arrested 4-20, 408G1-A2
Red Brigades, Front Line seen hampered by arrests 4-27, 353D1
Alunni, others escape jail; recaptured 4-28, 353B1
Rome, Milan attacks wound 4 5-6, 5-7, 408E1
CIA rpts '79 reductn 5-11, 365F3
Venice police offcl slain 5-12, death described 408C1, A3
Christn Dem vp's son sought 5-13, 408C1
Westn ldrs threatened 5-17, 408G2
Christn Dem wounded in Rome 5-17, 408B3
Christn Dem slain in Naples, 4 Brigadists captured 5-19, 408E2
Prosecutor's aide arrested 5-20, 523A3
Rptr convicted 5-24, journalists strike 5-26, 408C3
Neo-Fascists burn Rome movie houses 5-25, attack police 5-28, 408C2
Milan reporter slain 5-28, 408A2
Parlt comm probes terrorist tipoff; Cossiga cleared, Donat-Cattin resigns 5-29—5-31; CP, coalitn split 6-2, 6-3, 430B1-D2
Milan police bldg bombed 6-3, 523B3
Iraq Emb attacked 6-4, 451D2
2 Argentines arrested 6-5, 523C3
Libyan exile killed, 2d wounded 6-11, 451A3
Alunni, 25 others sentncd 6-22, 523C3
Rome magistrate slain 6-23, 564G2
Rome Red Brigadists seen 3/4 eliminated 7-3, 523G2
Turin, Paris arrests rptd 7-5—7-8, 523F2
Parlt upholds Cossiga in terrorist probe 7-27, 578G3
Milan city hall bombed 7-30, 605F1
Red Brigadist rptd dead in cell 8-1, 605G1
Bologna blast kills 76, neo-fascists suspected 8-2, 604E3

1976

1977

1978

Swiss host 4-natn mtg, 'hot line' set 4-8—4-9, 438B2
Turin cop killed, Red Brigades gunman captured 4-11, alleged interview rptd 4-28, 329C3
Moro executn rptd, lake searched 4-18; Brigades claim hoax, renew exchng offer 4-20, 4-23, 313C2, G3
Alfa Romeo showrooms bombed 4-22, 4-30, 330E1, G1
Red Brigades tied to Egypt terror group 4-26, 300D2
Rome Christian Dem shot 4-26, 330E1
Fiat labor mgr shot 4-27, 330F1
Police search Genoa for Moro 4-28, 330G1
Moro family plea published 5-3, 337E2
Fiat autos bombed in Milan; other bombings rptd in Turin, Pisa, Bologna, Catania 5-4, 393G1
Exec for W Ger co shot 5-4, worker's car firebombed 5-8, 393A2, C2
Italsider exec shot in Genoa 5-4, 393B2
Moro executn announced 5-5, farewell message received 5-7, 337E1
Bomb defused at Rome trial of 119 neo-fascists 5-5, 393A2
Leftists rptd arrested 5-7, CP warns 5-11, 338A2
Novara prison MD shot 5-7, 393B2
Natl health offcl shot 5-8, 393B2
Red Brigades tactics rptd 5-8, 393C2
Moro found murdered in Rome 5-9; gen strike, rallies called; security forces rptd mobilized 5-9, 5-11, 337A1, G1
Moro mourned by world ldrs 5-9, parlt pays tribute 5-10, 337G2, 338A1
Berlinguer lauds Moro; urges CP, Christian Dem rift healed 5-9, 338D1
Moro pvt funeral svc held 5-10, state ceremony scheduled 5-13, 337B2, F2
Turin trial ejects Curcio, associate 5-10, 338B2; sentenced for ct comments 5-18, 393B3
Interior min resigns, police failure in Moro death cited 5-10, 338F2
Montedison dir shot 5-10, 393D2
Milan chem bank mgr shot 5-11, 393D2
Red Brigades ask terrorist unity 5-12, 393E2
Milan Christian Dem secy shot 5-12, 393F2
Bomb explodes in Rome; other violence rptd in Turin, Milan, Cosenza 5-12, 393F2
Turin Red Brigades gunman's apartmt searched 5-12, 393A3 ★
Moro state funeral held 5-13, 689D2
Turin cop shot by Front Line 5-17, 393A3 ★
Anti-terrorism laws passed 5-17, 453D1
2 Red Brigades hideouts found in Rome 5-18, 5-19, 393C1
Moro blackmail revelatns feared 5-20, 393C3
Moretti sought in Moro case 5-20, 393C3
Red Brigades release message, Il Messaggero prints 5-20; govt to prosecute editor 5-22, 393D3
Rome, Milan bombings rptd 5-22, 393F3
Ostia terrorist hide out found 5-23, 393G3
Andreotti denies negligence in Moro death 5-23, Moro's widow denounces 5-25, 689F2
Terrorist shooting 'lull' rptd 5-28, 6-7, 453G2
3 Turin defendants protest jail conditns 5-28, 453A3
2 Turin judges rptdly threatened 5-29, 453A3
Turin prosecutn asks prison terms 5-29, 453B3
Rome army computer cntr bombing fails 5-29, 453C3
W Ger terrorist linked to Red Brigades 5-30, 439A1
3 Rome Christian Dem offices bombed 6-1, 453D3
Milan power lines bombed; Rome, Ostia Vicenza blasts rptd 6-2, 453D3
Moretti, 8 others chrgd in Moro case 6-5, 6-6; Marini warrant issued 6-26, 689B2, C2 ★
Undine prison warden killed 6-6, 453D2
Natl referendum backs widened police powers law 6-11—6-12, 453F1-D2
Club Medit '77 robbery cited 6-11, 473F3
Rome power statn bombed 6-14, 517G1
Red Brigades kill Genoa police offcl 6-21, 517E1
Bombs explode in Turin, Milan, Bologna, Rome, 6-21, 517A2
Alfasud exec shot in Naples 6-22, 517A2
Red Brigades Turin trial ends, 29 sentncd 6-23, 516E3-517D1
Pirelli exec shot in Milan 7-5, 517B2
Turin businessman shot 7-6, 517B2
Red Brigades wound Gasparino in Genoa 7-7, 574E1
Policeman wounded in Milan 7-10, 574E1
CP offcl wounded in Naples 7-10, 574E1
Fiat showroom in Turin bombed, press assn in Rome 7-10, 574F1
Rome Univ firebombed 7-13, 574F1
Rightists sentncd in coup plot 7-14, 574B2
Turin computer cntr arson 7-15, 574G1
Front Line raids police statn near Rome 7-15, 574G1
Hijacking pact signed 7-17, 544G2
Front Line wounds Russo in Turin 7-19, 574A2
Rome regional-govt bldg bombed 7-19, 574A2
Random terrorism rptd 7-26, 574C1
3 gunmen raid Montano Lucino town offices 7-27, 689G2

1979

Turin Fiat plants attacked 12-14, 995D2
Anti-terrorist measures effected, Dalla Chiesa cited as Milan Carabinieri head 12-17, 995E1
Rome youth killed 12-17, 995F2
Guerrilla cache seized in Sardinia 12-19, 995G2
4 kneecapped in Rome, Milan, Turin 12-21, 995A3

1980

Bologna blast suspect arrested 8-6; death toll reaches 79 8-7, 620B1; more suspects rptd arrested 8-27, 8-31, 672B1
Bologna bombing suspects arrest mount 9-22—9-23, 752A1
Front Line suspects arrested 10-6, 10-13, 791A3
Red Brigade suspects arrested 10-28, 923A1
Red Brigades kill 2 Milan execs 11-12, 11-28, 922E3
Dolo office attacked 11-18—11-19, 922G3
Rome prison MD slain 12-1, 944G1
Front Line ldr, suspects arrested 12-4, 944E1
Pagani mayor slain 12-11, 943G3-944A1
2 Red Brigade suspects killed 12-11, 966C3
Red Brigades kidnap magistrate 12-12; manifesto issued, negotiatns studied 12-14—12·15, 966D2
Donat-Cattin arrested in Paris 12-18, 995E1
Asinara prison closure set 12-26, 995C1
Trani prison revolt quelled 12-29, 994F3
Carabinieri gen killed 12-31, 995D1

1976

UN Policy & Developments
Cncl member 62F2; 720C1
Abstains on Cncl PLO seating 1-12, 18B1
Abstains on pro-Palestine resolutn 1-26, 59G2
Abstains on rights comm resolutn vs Israel 2-13, 125E2
OKs Medit pollutn pact 2-16, 126C3
Abstains on Cncl S Africa censure 3-31, 228B2
Abstains on 2 WHO anti-Israel resolutns 5-17, 5-19, 355G1, D2
Abstains on Israel Arab land exit 6-29, 464C1
Backs anti-terror resolutn 7-14, 515F3
Asks Greek-Turk talks on Aegean 8-25, 643F2
Abstains on S Africa arms ban 10-19, 781D3
Abstains on PLO in Cncl debate 11-1, 842F1
Vs anti-S Africa aid stand 11-5, 842C3
ILO rpts strike data 11-29, 896D2
U.S. Relations—*See also 'Foreign Economic Developments' and 'Political Payments Issues' above*
Paper links 8 to CIA 1-16, 50C1
Pope Paul '42-50 intellignc ties alleged 1-31, 140D3
Vatican CIA infiltratn rptd 2-14, 140E3
Kissinger warns vs CP govt role 4-13, 296G3
CP scores Kissinger 4-18, 277B2
France assures US re CP 5-18, 372B2
Kissinger remarks scored 5-19, 357D3
Kissinger warns again vs CP role 5-20, 354B1
US evacuates 10 from Leb 6-20, 448C1
Kissinger repeats CP warning 6-22, 446C2
US quake aid authorized 6-30, 532G3
Ship in US Bicentennial event 7-4, 488A3, C3
Ford vs CP govt role 7-19, 532E1
US comments on CP policy 7-22, 556D3
Angola mercenary corpse shipped 7-26, 559C3
Ford, Carter debate 10-6, 741B1
Dole, Mondale debate 10-15, 783G3
Reactn to Carter electn 11-3—11-4, 826E1
Andreotti ends US visit 12-8, 947D1
United Brands revises paymts estimate 12-10, 985G3
Vatican Relations—*See also ROMAN Catholic Church*
Pope urges defense of unborn 1-4, 32D3
Feminists protest abortn stand 1-17, Pope scores 1-21, 124C2
Pope Paul '42-50 US intellignc ties alleged 1-31, 140D3
CIA, SID infiltratn rptd 2-14, 140D3
Vatican urges vote vs CP 5-11—5-25, reactn 5-24, 6-1, 402D3
Poletti scores Franzoni CP support 6-17, 446D1

ITOH, Hiroshi
Quits Marubeni, testifies on Lockheed payoffs 2-17, 132F1, 191B1
Rptdly rejoins Marubeni 2-20, 191C1
Diet subpoenas 2-26, testifies again 3-1, 190C3
Arrested 7-2, 497E2
Indicted for bribery 7-16, 624B2
2 others arrested 7-19, 557B2
Indicted for perjury 7-23, 557C2
ITOH & Co., C.
Ataka 'affiliatn' rptd 2-17, 221F2
IVANISSEVICH, Oscar
Dies 6-5, 524G2
IVANOV, Alexander
Wins Olympic medal 7-31, 576C3
IVANOV, Stoyan
Wins Olympic medal 7-24, 576B3

1977

UN Policy & Developments
UN Assemb member 4B1
Abstains on Israel occupatn abuse res 2-15, 107E2
UNESCO press parley held 4-18—4-20, 319F2
Pollutn conf ends, Medit pact reached 10-21, 876B2
Abstains on Assemb Israel occupatn vote 11-25, 910D2
S Africa oil ban abstentn 12-16, 1016A2

U.S. Relations
Gardner named US amb 1-7, 14D2
US rejects air fare rise 1-10, 324B3
Mondale visits 1-26, 69C1
2 ex-mins indicted in Lockheed scandal 1-29, 116A3
US speeds Sovt Jews' visas 1-30, 117A2
US-ESA flight set 2-16, 170C3
Lockheed trial set 3-10, 284B1
Carter bars shoe import curbs 4-1, 248E2, B3
Suppliers conf scores Carter plans 4-28—4-29, 430F1-A2
Carter summit diplomacy hailed 5-11, 359A2
US students banned 6-28, 527B3
CP press plans US office 7-20, 581F2-A3
Andreotti in US, sees Carter 7-25—7-27, 581A2
Carter seeks arms sale curbs 7-28, 574B3
ESA satellite launching aborted 9-13, 735G3
US panel minimizes govt subsidy impact 10-7, 776D2
US co chrgs steel dumping 10-20, 836E3
Exxon settles paymts chrgs 10-25, 818E1

Vatican Relations
Socialists score Rome mayor 1-6, 8A3
Benelli named Florence archbp 6-2, 768G2
Lefebvre scores RC modernism 6-6, 470E3

IT Didn't Start with Watergate (book)
On best-seller list 8-14, 643A2
ITO, Yoshio
Seizes hostages 3-3—3-4, 201A3
ITOH, Hiroshi
Lockheed bribe trial starts 1-27, 83D2
ITT—*See INTERNATIONAL Telephone & Telegraph*
IUD (intrauterine device)—*See BIRTH Control*
IVAC Corp.
Lilly buys 7-20, 650E3

1978

Papal appeal for Moro cited 8-6, 601F2
W Ger '76 papal kidnap plot rptd 8-6, 689A3
Rome anti-fascist war meml blast 8-30, 689C3
Rome buses firebombed 9-1, 689C3
Florence-Bologna rail line bombed 9-5, 689D3
Rome leftists protest Argentina policies 9-5, 689D3
Curcio prison transfer rptd 9-7, 724D1
Red Brigades ldr arrested 9-13, sentncd 9-20, 723F3
Turin, Rome firebombings, sniper fire 9-13, 724D1, E1
John Paul I told of violence 9-28, 747A1
Red Brigades shoot Lancia, Alfa Romeo execs 9-29; justice offcl killed 10-10; Naples, Verona incidents 10-11, 10-24, 816E3-817C1
Red Brigade suspects arrested in Milan, Moro 'trial' documts found 10-1, 817C1
Milan '69 bomb trial suspect rptd missing 10-4, 817A2
6 Red Brigades sentncd 10-28, 1018G1
Bergamo boutiques bombed by women's group 11-1, 1018C2
Milan drug dealer killed 11-7, 1018A2
Prosecutor, aides killed by leftists 11-8, 1018E1
Bomb blasts in Rome, Naples, Milan, Bologna 11-10, 1018B2
San Vittore ex-offcl shot 11-13, 1018B2
UN Policy & Developments
Waldheim pleas for Moro release 4-25, 314A1
Sea Law Conf talks continue 5-23—7-16, 8-21—9-16, 732E3
Racism conf boycotted 8-26, 676B2
Assemb member 713G3

U.S. Relations—*See also 'Atomic Energy', and 'Monetary, Trade, Aid & Investment' above*
US troop presence rptd 1-2, 5C2
Carter warns vs CP govt role 1-12, 19E1
US alerts to Sovt satellite fall 57E1
At Ogaden conf in US 1-21, 43E2
US jet bombs Sardinia in joint mil exercise 2-11, 133E2
CIA, business paymts linked 2-17, 161F2
CP labor union OKs AFL-CIO ties 3-14, 191B3
USSR chrgs US interventn 5-7, 349B3
Milan Chem Bank mgr shot 5-11, 393D2
US launches ESA satellite 5-12, 384D3
Honeywell warehouse fire 5-12, 393G2
US orders Sindona extradited 5-19, 454F1
Alien deportatn trial backed by US Sup Ct 6-6, 447F2
Leone resigns over Lockheed scandal chrgs 6-15, 516F2
Sindona named US bank co-conspirator 7-13, 681F1
US seabed mining bill debated at UN conf 8-21—9-16, 732E3
Auto firebombed at Turin emb 9-13, 724D1
ITT paymts chrgd 11-2, 876C1, G2
Sindona extraditn upheld by US Ct 11-15, 906A3
Vatican Relations—*See also ROMAN Catholic Church*
Pope Paul pleas for Moro release 4-23, 313F3
Pope Paul dies 8-6, 601A1; buried 8-12, 658D2
'76 papal kidnap plot rptd 8-6, 689A3
Venice cardinal elected Pope 8-26, 657A1-658F1
Pope John Paul I dies 9-28, buried 10-4, 746B3
Polish cardinal elected Pope 10-16, conclave disunity rptd 10-16, 10-19, 781A1, 782B1

ITF (International Tennis Federation)—*See TENNIS*
IT'S a Heartache (recording)
On best-seller list 6-7, 460F3
IT'S in the Air (race horse)
Named top 2-yr old filly 12-12, 1028C1
ITT—*See INTERNATIONAL Telephone & Telegraph*
IVANCHENKOV, Alexander
Docks with Salyut 6-17, 505F3
Remains aboard Salyut 7-5, sets space record 8-2, 622D3
Has visitors 8-27, breaks endurance mark 9-20, 714A1-D1
Returns to Earth 11-2, 861A1
IVIE, Mike
NL batting ldr 10-2, 928E2
Carew rejcts Giants trade 12-7, 1026A1

1979

UN Policy & Developments
Indochina refugee conf asked 6-28, 473E2
Membership listed 695F2

U.S. Relations—*See also 'Monetary' above*
Art theft symposium held 2-12-2-14, 119B2
US offcl expelled re critical intellignc rpt 2-14, 136D1-A2
Lockheed discloses bribes 2-16, 306A2
6 convicted re Lockheed 3-1, 155B2
Lockheed scandal assessmt rptd 8-6, 603B1
Sindona rptd missing in NY 8-6, 635A3
Sindona reappears in NY, enters hosp 10-16, 793E2
Terrorist activity rptd up 11-15, 882A2
Vance in Rome, seeks sanctns vs Iran 12-11, 933C2, G2

Vatican Relations
USSR forgn min visits 1-24, 60E2
Moro kidnap link chrgd 2-7, 97E3
Cardinals installed 6-30, 640C2

ITF (International Tennis Federation)—*See TENNIS*
ITOYA, Hisao
My Love released 1-4, 174B3
ITT—*See INTERNATIONAL Telephone & Telegraph*
IVANCHENKOV, Alexander
Soyuz 32 launched 2-25, 163G1
IVANOV, Maj. Georgi
In Soyuz 33 flight 4-10—4-12, 279B2
IVANOW, Mike
NASL goalkeeping ldr 8-12, 654G3
IVERSON, Yale H.
Burger assails Sup Ct bar admissn 6-25, 541B1
IVERY, Eddie Lee
In NFL draft 5-3, 335F1
IVORY, Horace
NFL '78 touchdown ldr 1-6, 80B1

1980

UN Policy & Developments
Assemb Palestinian state res abstentn 7-29, 572F1

U.S. Relations—*See also 'Soviet-Afghan Issue' above*
Terrorist links to US leftists seen 1-2, 20F2
CP scores Sovt Afghan invasn retaliatn 1-6, 2G2
Sindona convicted in NY, extraditn sought 3-27, 237A2
US fiber import suspensn ordrd 4-4, 294B3
US sets steel import probe 4-10, 367F3
CP vs anti-Sovt front 4-22, 314B2
Iran hostage kin seek support 4-23, 299D2
Sindona aide sentenced in NY, return seen 4-23, 415D1
Iran hostage rescue missn scored 4-25, 324B2
CIA rpts '79 terrorism 5-11, 365F3
US cruise missile shipmt set for '83 6-3, 450A3
Carter visits Rome, sees ldrs 6-19—6-21, 474A2
2 US newsmen flee from Iran 7-25, 572B1
Iran parlt ldr rebuffs hostage appeal 8-17, 634D3

Vatican Relations
Lefebvre holds outlawed mass 4-7, oppositn rptd 4-26, 364A1
Craxi scores Pope abortn stand 10-25, 873B2

ITEL Corp.
Settles Lloyd's claim, SEC probe cited 1-16, 131C3
'79 loss rptd $443.3 mln 10-16, 784D1
IT Goes Like It Goes (song)
Wins Oscar 4-14, 296G1
ITHACA (N.Y.) College
Loses NCAA Div III football title game 12-6, 999G2
ITO, Masayoshi
Japan acting premier 6-12, 434D3
Japan forgn min 7-17, 539B3
In Canada auto talks 8-2—8-11, 618G1
In Pak; signs aid pkg, pledges refugee funds 9-1, 686F1
Meets Sovt forgn min in NY 9-24, 752D1
Warns vs Kim Dae Jung executn 11-28, 944B3
IT'S Still Rock and Roll to Me (recording)
On best-seller list 7-9, 568E3; 8-13, 640A3
ITT—*See INTERNATIONAL Telephone & Telegraph Corp.*
ITURBE Abasolo, Domingo (alias Txomin)
Identified as ETA mil wing head 7-7, 367E1
ITURBI, Jose
Dies 6-28, 528B2
IVCHENKO, Yevgeny
Wins Olympic medal 7-30, 624C1
IVES, David O.
On Mobil PBS funding 5-8, 375D3

1976

IVORY Coast—*See also AFRICAN Development Bank, NONALIGNED Nations Movement, OAU*
US ups econ aid re UN vote 1-9, 2B1
IMF oil loan rptd 1-13, 4-1, 339G3, 340D2
Listed as 'not free' nation 1-19, 20D3
Cabinet shuffled 3-4, 594D2
At Zambia mtg on Rhodesia 3-24—3-25, 240D2
At France-Africa summit 5-10—5-11, 355G2
EC aid set 7-8, 529A3
Canada sugar loan rptd 8-12, 1012G3
Stearns confrmd US amb 9-30, 808D1
ECOWAS rptd ratified 11-6, 974E2
Kenya sets probe 12-3, 947E2
World Bank OKs loans 12-16, 1012G3
I WRITE The Songs (song)
On best-selling list 1-28, 104G3
IYAD, Abu—*See KHALEF, Saleh*

1977

IVORY Coast—*See also NONALIGNED Nations Movement, OAU*
UN Assemb member 4B1
IFC textile loan rptd 1-5, 24A2
US coffee boycott urged 1-11, 74A3
Houphouet meets PLO reps 1-25, briefs Rabin 2-4, 86B3
Hijacked Iberia jet lands 3-14, 224B3
Film wins US Oscar 3-28, 264D1
At France-Africa summit 4-20—4-21, 316F3
US ambs confer 5-9—5-12, Young sees Houphouet 5-12, 398A3, C3
Vorster sees Houphouet 5-22, 398F1
Nightclub blaze kills 41, 6-9, 604G1
Ghana smuggling rptd 7-1, 598E2
Cabt shifted, increased 7-30, 772B1
In Brazil-Colombia coffee pact 11-9, 876D3
Kenya bans game skin sales 12-12, 976E1
IVY, Dr. Andrew C.
Amphetamine-morphine painkiller rptd 3-31, 288D1
IWC—*See WHALING Commission, International*
IYAD, Abu—*See KHALEF, Saleh*

1978

IVORY Coast—*See also GATT, NONALIGNED Nations Movement, OAU*
Giscard visits; shipping, oil pacts set 1-11—1-15, 71A1
UN Chile rights abuse res abstentn 3-6, 210F1
At W African mtg; backs ECOWAS, upgrades ties 3-18; USSR scores 3-20, 237D1
Page paymt to Ahoua chrgd 4-13, 449C2
Houphouet backs France mil aid 5-23, 382G2
S Africa econ pressure rptd asked 6-2, 633B2
Zaire pan-Africa force rptd backed 6-8, 442D1
Zaire peace troops rptd 6-19, 478A2
UN Assemb member 713G3
IVY, Dr. Andrew
Dies 2-7, 196B3
I Wanna Hold Your Hand (film)
Released 4-21, 619E2
IYAD, Abu—*See KHALEF, Saleh*
IZAGUIRRE, Alejandro
Accused of buying AD post 5-5, 395A2
IZHAR, S.
'48 war film banned 2-6, ban lifted 2-13, 112F3
IZVESTIA (Soviet government newspaper)
US reviews rptrs status 6-30, 7-5, 518F2

1979

IVORY Coast—*See also GATT, NONALIGNED Nations Movement, OAU*
Abidjan train derailmt kills 15 6-17, 639A2
Ghana executns rptd scored 6-30, 524D2
US chrgs ISC paymts 7-9, 541F3
CAE student massacre probe rptd 8-6, 601A3
Zaire troop exit rptd 8-14, 733G3
Young, US trade delegatn visit; pvt investmt data rptd 9-8–9-11, 720A3, F3
UN membership listed 695F2
Bokassa finds asylum 9-24, 720D2
IVRI, Maj. Gen. David
On Israeli-Syrian air clash 9-24, 740D2
On downed Israel spy plane 10-7, 763F3
I Will Survive (recording)
On best-seller list 2-14, 120E3; 3-7, 174D1; 4-4, 271C2
IWO Jima (U.S. aircraft carrier)
Navy fire probe rptd 7-5, 519G3
IYAD, Abu—*See KHALEF, Saleh*

1980

IVORY Coast—*See also GATT, NONALIGNED Nations, OAU*
Liberia ex-vp arrives 4-27, 353G2
Pope visits 5-10—5-12, 363E3-364A1
Liberia arrests Tolbert's son 6-14, 499E1
Gurandou-N'Diaye elected IOC vp 7-16, 590E3
Bokassa confirms Giscard gifts 9-17, 729A1
I Want to Hold Your Hand (recording)
Lennon slain 12-8, 934C3
I Will Survive (recording)
Gaynor wins Grammy 2-27, 296B3

J

1976

JABARI, Sheik Mohammed Ali
Resigns 3-20, stays 3-22, 210G2
Loses reelection 4-12, 458A3
JABER, Fayez
Killed 7-3; named as hijacker, key PFLP man 7-5, 485C1, F2
JABER al-Ahmed al-Sabah, Crown Prince (Kuwait)
Resigns 8-29, 642F1
Forms new Cabinet 9-6, 679G1
JABLONSKI, Henryk
Oppositn to charter chngs rptd 3-19, 268A2
Renamed State Cncl chrmn 3-25, 268C2
JABRE, Antoine
Vs Sovt on Syria Leb role 8-31, 642D1
JACKSON, Miss.—*See MISSISSIPPI*
JACKSON, George (d. 1971)
San Quentin 6 verdict 8-12, 656D1
JACKSON, Gordon
Wins Emmy 5-17, 460B2
JACKSON, Grant
In World Series 10-16—10-21, 815D3
JACKSON, Sen. Henry M(artin) (D, Wash.)
Gets US campaign subsidy 1-2, 22E3
Opens '76 pres effort 1-6, 22A3
Common Cause rpts campaign code backing 1-9, 23A1
Trails in Iowa precinct vote 1-19, 41B1
Stresses health care issue 1-22, 41A3
CIA contacts rptd 1-26, 1-28, 92E1, 93F1
Meany lauds labor record 2-16, 149A1
Wins Mass primary 3-2, comments 3-3, 164G2, 165E1
In Dem campaign exchngs 3-3—3-4, 166F1
Fed fund total listed 3-4, 180C3
3d in Fla primary 3-9, 179D1-B3
Scores Kissinger role 3-11, 198C1
Gallup poll results 3-15, 197E1
Ends NC campaign, loses primary 3-23, 214B1
Urges Leb interventn 3-30, USSR scores 4-8, 241G2, 245B3
Humphrey upstages in NY 4-1, 233D2
Sovt criticism cited 4-5, 260C1
Wins NY primary 4-6, 244E2
4th in Wis primary 4-6, 245D1
On Carter's 'ethnic' remark 4-8, 260G3
2d in delegate count 4-9, 261A1
Carter offers health plan 4-16, 281G3
Loses Sup Ct funds plea 4-23, 306C1
Loses Pa primary 4-27, 304E3, G3, 305C1
Rockefeller apologizes 4-27, 305D3
Ends 'active' candidacy 5-1, 324F2
Note to black Dem caucus 5-2, 343B3
Ind primary results 5-4, 323F1
Neb, Conn vote results 5-11, 342E2, F3
Mich, Md primary results 5-18, 356G2, 357G1
Gets more FEC funds 5-21, 391E3
Primary results 5-25, 374B2-E3; 6-1, 390B2-E2; 6-8, 409B1
Primary delegates totaled 6-8, 409A3
To release delegates 6-9, 409F1
Dem platform supported 6-15, 432A3
Endorses Carter 6-16, 432D1
FEC denies fed funds 6-23, total rptd 7-1, 490F3, 491A1
Carter vp mtg set 7-8, 489F3
Sees Carter on vp spot 7-10, 506A2
Dem conv pres vote, table 7-14, 507E2
Cited in Dole biog sketch 614D3
Wins primary 9-21, 804D3
Reelected 11-2, 820D1, 825E1, 828D3
US-USSR offcls, trade cncl vs amendmt 12-1, 947C3, E3
FEC certificatn total rptd 12-31, 979G2
JACKSON, Rev. Jesse L.
Platform com testimony 5-20, 357E3
Meets Carter 7-12, 513A2
Sees Kissinger on S Africa 8-23, 654E2
JACKSON, Mayor Maynard (Atlanta, Ga.)
Absent from Carter rally 4-13, 261D2
Meets Carter 7-12, 513C2
JACKSON, Rashleigh Esmond
Leb emb discusses crisis 6-9, 406A3
JACKSON, Reggie
Traded to Orioles 4-2, 444B3
AL batting ldr 10-4, 796C1
Signs with Yankees 11-29, 951B3

1977

JABER al-Ahmed al-Sabah, Crown Prince (Kuwait)
Becomes Kuwait ruler 12-31, 1019A2
JABLON v. Califano
Old-age benefits test voided 3-21, 230E1
JACKLIN, Tony
Loses Crosby Pro-Am 1-23, 104A1
JACKSON, Allen A.
Sup Ct remands tank injury suit 11-14, 878A3
JACKSON, Dr. Edith B.
Dies 6-5, 532B3
JACKSON, Sen. Henry M(artin) (D, Wash.)
'76 spec interest gifts rptd 1-15, 128F3, 129F1
Questns Warnke nominatn 2-2, 89B1
Fights vs Warnke nominatn 2-22—3-9, 172A1-G2
On arms talks 4-5, 247D2
Sees Carter on arms talks 5-18, 401B1
Vs fed rules on utility rates 9-14, 757D2
SALT extensn opposed 751D1
Vs US-Sovt Geneva plan 10-2, 750E1
Energy tax amendment fails 10-27; bill clears Sen 10-31, 832C2
SALT leaks chrgd 11-7, denied 11-8, 996G2-B3
JACKSON Jr., James E.
Murder chrg dropped 12-19, 991F2
JACKSON, Rev. Jesse L.
Blacks meet re govt 'neglect' 8-29, 702D1
Shapp defends black's ouster 9-28, 800E2
JACKSON, Johnny B.
Murder chrg dropped 12-19, 991F2
JACKSON, Marjorie V.
Slain, robbed 5-7, 492F1
JACKSON, Mayor Maynard (Atlanta, Ga.)
Reelected 10-4, 879E1
JACKSON, Reggie
Dispute with Martin 6-18, 644B3
AL batting ldr 10-2, 926G3
In AL playoff, Martin benches 10-5—10-9, 807G1
In World Series; sets records, named MVP 10-11—10-18, 806D1-807C1
Assault case dismissed 11-1, 927C2

1978

JABLON, Seymour
Questns cancer-radiatn link at Hanford facility 2-17, 164F2
JABOUILLE, Jean-Pierre
4th in LeMans, sets speed record 6-11, 538A3
JACK, Hubert O.
On Burnham const plan 7-10, 688G2
JACKSON, Anne
Diary of Anne Frank revived 12-18, 1031D1
JACKSON, Harold
NFL '77 pass receiving ldr 1-1, 56F2
Traded to Patriots 8-16, 1024F3
JACKSON, Sen. Henry M(artin) (D, Wash.)
On Sadat arms plea 2-7, 78B1
On US jet sale to Saudis 3-14, 177B1
Votes for Panama Canal neutrality pact 3-16, 177D2
Scores Cong energy confs 3-22, 219F3
Sees gas price compromise veto unlikely 4-12, 304B2
Votes for 2d Canal pact 4-18, 273B1
Scores Carter re neutron bomb 6-11, 469B3
Coal conversn bill clears Sen 7-18, 550A1
Vs USSR oil equipmt sale 9-6, 743D1
Gas bill consumer impact estimate rptd 9-28, 733G1
Attacks SALT 11-27, 995C2
USSR scores '74 Trade Act amendmt 12-4, 966G1
JACKSON, Rev. Jesse L.
Addresses GOP Natl Com 1-20, 568D2
Protests Spinks-Ali rematch plan 3-8, 212G1
Scores media racism 4-8, 419E3
Outlines black vote issues 4-10, 568F2-B3
Scores Sup Ct Bakke ruling 6-28, 482E2
Character witness for Diggs convicted 10-7, 791F3
JACKSON, Larry
4th in Idaho primary for gov 8-8, 625E3
JACKSON, Mahalia (1911-72)
Mahalia opens 6-5, 887A2
JACKSON, Michael
Wiz released 12-25, 970F3
JACKSON, Monte
Traded to Raiders 8-21, 1024E3
JACKSON, Phil
Traded to Nets 6-8, 457D2
JACKSON, Reggie
Reggie candy bar debuts 4-13, 779F3
Misses All-Star Game 7-11, 559G2
Suspended 7-17; Martin scores 7-23, quits 7-24; rehired 7-29, 618A1
Yankees win AL pennant 10-7, 778F3
In World Series 10-10—10-17, breaks Gehrig HR record 10-10, 799C3

1979

JABARA, Paul
Wins Grammy 2-16, 336F3
Wins Oscar 4-9, 336B2
JABLONSKI, Henryk (Polish president)
Greets Pope 6-2, 413D1
JACK, Del
Richard Pryor Live released 2-15, 174E3
JACKER, Corinne
Later opens 1-15, 292F1
JACKSON, Anne
Bell Jar released 3-20, 528D1
JACKSON, Bernard
NFL '78 interceptn ldr 1-6, 80C1
JACKSON, Everett
PR prisoner trade denied 9-6, 666A2
Released 9-17, 706F3, 707A1
JACKSON, Glenda
Class of Miss MacMichael released 1-26, 528A2
Lost & Found released 7-13, 820F1
JACKSON, Grant
Pirates win NL pennant 10-5, 797C2
In World Series 10-10–10-17, 816C1
JACKSON, Sen. Henry Martin (D, Wash.)
Energy Com chrmn 1-23, 71D2
GAO warns on higher oil prices 3-7, 182E2
Scores Calif-Tex pipe cancelatn 3-13, 183E1
USSR '74 Trade Act amendmt cited 4-21, 314G1
Chrgs 'appeasemt' re SALT II 6-12, 6-17, 449G2, 459F2-G3
Scores Carter re Cabt, staff shake-up 7-18, 531A1
Sees Kennedy '80 pres bid 7-24, Carter responds 7-25, 556B2-D2
Byrd defends Carter reelectn bid 7-28, 593F3
For arms hike link to SALT 8-2, 591B1
On China oil find 8-24, 664F3
Bars SALT re Sovt troops in Cuba 9-6, 9-11, 674F1
On Carter energy plan concessns 9-11, 702F2
On Carter defense spending plan 12-13, 963C2
JACKSON, James A.
Criminal evidence standard eased by Sup Ct 6-28, 558D2
JACKSON, Rev. Jesse L.
US revokes Knoetze visa 1-9; judge enjoins 1-11, scores 1-12, 1-13, 79F2
St Louis teacher strike ends 3-12, 187C3
Ends S Africa visit, controversy spurred 8-1, 617D1-C2
Deplores Young UN resignatn, asks black-Jewish mtg 8-15, 606F1
Vs Jews on black cooperatn 8-19, 624C2
Jerusalem mayor welcomes visit 9-19, Israeli officials oppose 9-20, 694E2
In Mideast; Israeli offcls snub; sees Arafat 9-25–10-5; PFLP scores 10-6; briefs US offcls 10-8, 762F3
2 US Jewish ldrs quit tour 9-26, 763B2
US Arab group gives PUSH $10,000 10-13, 780G3
Jordan vs black support for PLO 10-14, 780E2
Meets Jordan, 'unity' reaffirmed 10-17, 780B3
JACKSON, Jimmy
USSR wins World Cup wrestling 4-1, 507G3
JACKSON, Michael
Don't Stop on best-seller list 10-3, 800E3
JACKSON, Nagle
Utter Glory opens 5-13, 712C3
JACKSON, Reggie
Martin returns as Yankees mgr 6-19, 619A2

1980

JABARI, Mohammed Ali
Dies 5-29, 448G1
JABER, Adnan
Admits Sovt mil training 10-31, 912G2
JABER, Khalid
Arrested in W Berlin 8-1, 604F2
W Berlin release set 9-15, 712B2
JABLONSKI, Henryk (Polish president)
At Gdansk memorial rite 12-16, 976D2
JABOTINSKY, Vladimir (1880-1940)
Anniv marked 11-9, 880D2
JACKASS Flats—*See NEVADA*
JACKLIN, Philip D.
Dismissed re sex harassmt 1-9, 77E3
JACKSON, Earl Lloyd
Calif ct upholds death sentnc 10-23, 868F3-869A1
JACKSON, Eddie
Dies 7-16, 608B2
JACKSON, George (d. 1971)
Stender dies 5-21, 448G2
JACKSON, Glenda
Hopscotch released 9-26, 836B3
JACKSON, Sen. Henry Martin (D, Wash.)
Open conv move forms 7-25—7-31, discounts pres bid 7-28, 570D3
Alaska lands bill passes 8-19, 631E2, A3
Campaigns with Carter 10-13, 778F3
Named Reagan forgn policy advisor 11-6, 839G2
JACKSON, Rev. Jesse L.
Scores pres candidates 2-29, 190E2
Mediates Chicago strike 3-6, 187B3
Urges Chattanooga 'peace patrols' 7-25, 576A1
Reagan confers 8-5, 597B3
Econ plank compromise fails 8-12, 610A3
Meets Carter, scores antibusing 'extremists' 12-4, 954C1
Meets with Reagan 12-11, 956F2
JACKSON, Leroy
Named NAIA basketball tourn MVP 3-15, 240D3
JACKSON, Mayor Maynard (Atlanta, Ga.)
Backs Carter in conv rules fight 8-11, 610A1
FBI agents assigned in child slaying probe 11-5, 927G3
JACKSON, Michael
Rock With You on best-seller list 1-2, 40F3; 2-6, 120F3
Off the Wall on best-seller list 2-6, 120G3; 3-5, 200F3; 4-2, 280F3; 4-30, 360A1
Wins Grammy 2-27, 296C3
JACKSON, Reggie
Hits 400th homer 8-11, 636A3
AL batting ldr 10-6, 926E3
2d in AL MVP vote 11-18, 925D3

1976

JACKSON (Mich.) Citizen Patriot, The (newspaper)
Newhouse buys Booth chain 11-8, 901B3
JACKSONVILLE, Fla.—*See FLORIDA*
JACOBS Jr., Rep. Andrew (D, Ill.)
Wife reelected 11-2, 825D2
Reelected 11-2, 829C3
JACOBS, Harold M.
At Othodox Jewish group mtg 11-25—11-28, 912B1
JACOBSEN, Jake
Sup Ct bars plea-bargaining review 5-19, 393D3
Gets 2 yrs probatn 8-20, 1016A1
JACOVELLA, Tulio
Asks Peron quit 2-19, 154B2
JAE-Sup Jeon
Wins Olympic medal 7-31, 576C3
JAFFAR, Prince Said Mohamed (Comorro Islands)
Term expires 1-2, 119A1
JAGAN, Cheddi
Backs PNC govt 2-21, 252F3
JAGIELSKI, Mieczyslaw
Polish deputy premr 3-27, 268F2
JAGODA, Barry
US-Cuba baseball series vetoed 1-7, 23E1
JAHIDIN, Hussein
Arrested 6-22, 498B1
JAI Alai
Bailey cleared in Conn scandal 1-12, 271D1
JAIDEH, Ali
Named OPEC secy gen 12-17, 934C3
JAKES, John
Furies on best seller list 1-25, 80D3; 2-29, 208F3
JALLOUD, Abdel Salam
Denies Tunisia plot chrg 3-22, 239E2
Tries Leb mediatn 5-17—5-18, 355B1
Seeks 'rejectn front' 5-20, 369C2
Mediates Leb crisis 6-11—6-16, 429F2
Works out Leb peace plan 6-20, holds implement talks 6-22—6-23, 448C2, G2
Vs Arab Leb force lag 6-21, 448F2
Pro-Syrian gen released 6-23, 448F2
Christians ignore protest on camp attacks, leaves Leb 6-29, 463D3
Syria vows Saida exit 7-12, 514A2
Syrians end Saida siege 7-13—7-14, 527D2
Syrians-PLO meet 7-21—7-22, 528C1
Mediates Syria, PLO pact 7-29, 546D3
Arafat disavows Syria pact 7-30, 578A1
Denies border area annexatn 696F2

1977

JACKSON, Tom
Denver wins in playoffs 12-24, 1019F3
JACKSON, Robert
In NFL draft 5-3, 353B2
JACOB, J. Myles
On copper price cut 7-20, 577F2
JACOB and the Liar (screenplay)
Author visits West 12-19, 984A2
JACOBS, Rep. Andy (D, Ind.)
Stimulus tax bill cleared 5-16, 381F3
JACOBS, Herbert
Sentenced 10-21, 991E3
JACOBSEN, William
S Africa detains 6-10, 469A2
JACOVIELLO, Alberto
To open US office 7-20, 581F2-A3
JACQUIN & Cie. Inc., Charles
Settles SEC rebate chrgs 10-17, 860E1
JAFFE, Frederick S.
On abortn alternatives 7-19, 786E3
JAFFE, Saul
Dies 11-1, 952E2
JAGAN, Cheddi
Burnham rejects coalitn plan 9-9, 767C2
JAGGER, Mick
Mrs Trudeau denies link 3-28, 281E3
At Pele tribute 10-1, 827D2
JAHN & Son Inc., Henry R.
Chrgd re Arab boycott 1-7, 167A2
JAIDAH, Ali Mohammed
Says OPEC price split ended 7-3, 535F2
On OPEC price freeze 12-21, 973C1
JAI Hyon Lee
Testifies on Korea lobbying 10-19—10-21, 816F2
JAIN, Dr. Anrudh K.
Smoking-birth pill study rptd 3-29, 287E3
JAIN, Shanti Prasad
Dies 10-27, 872D2
JAKES, John
Warriors on best-seller list 5-1, 356D2; 6-4, 452B2
JAKOBSEN, Svend
Danish fisheries min 2-25, 373E1
JALIS, Ibrahim
Death rptd 12-5, 967F3
JALLOUD, Maj. Abdel Salam
Sees Algeria, French ldrs on Sahara kidnap 11-2—11-3, 852C2

1978

JACKSON, Tom
Scores pay, price statemt rejectn 11-15, 903D2
JACKSON County, Kan.—*See KANSAS*
JACKSON (Miss.) State University
Short in NBA draft 6-9, 457F3
JACKSONVILLE, Fla.—*See FLORIDA*
JACOBI, Lou
Cheaters opens 1-15, 760F1
JACOBS Jr., Rep. Andrew (D, Ind.)
Vs S Korea food aid cutoff 6-22, 467E2
Reelected 11-7, 850C4
JACOBS, Franklin
Sets indoor high jump record 1-27, 76A3
JACOBS Jr., Harry A.
$ rescue steps, Dow recovery linked 11-2, 827A1
JACOBS, Helen
US Open results 9-10, 707F1
JACOBS, Jerry Wayne
Ala death penalty upheld 5-19, 388G3
JACOBS, Jim
Grease released 6-16, 619C2
JACOBS, Melvan M.
Sued re Katy bribe 8-30, 737B1
JACOBS, Michael
Cheaters opens 1-15, 760F1
JACOBS, Paul
Dies 1-3, 96D2
JACOBSEN, Svend
Danish fishermen protest 5-5, 371E2
JACOBSON, Alf
Loses Sen primary in NH 9-12, 736E1
JACOPUCCI, Angelo
Minter KOs 7-19, dies 7-21, 600B2
JAECKEL, Barry
Wins Tallahassee Open 4-16, 356A1
JAEHN, Lt. Col. Sigmund
Docks with Salyut 8-27, returns 9-3, 714A1
JAEN, Albertina de
Leads hunger strike 4-4—4-27, son leaves solitary 4-19, 375B3, F3, 376B1
JAEN, Marcio
Mother leads hunger strike 4-4—4-27, leaves solitary 4-19, 375B3, F3, 376B1
JAFFE, Herb
Who'll Stop Rain released 8-25, 1030G3
JAFFE, Leo
Columbia Pictures reorganizatn rptd 7-21, 599C2
JAGAN, Cheddi
Vs constitutnl reform bill 4-10, 378B3
JAGGER, Bianca
Files for divorce 5-15, 420C3
JAGGER, Mick
NASL Phila club ownership cited 1-5, 23C1
Wife files for divorce 5-15, 420C3
OKs Rolling Stones benefit 10-26, 842F1
JAGUAR (Anglo-French jet)—*See ARMAMENTS—Aircraft*
JAHN, Renate
E Ger sentences for spying 1-26, 61F3
JAI Alai
NJ gambling proposal loses 11-7, 847G1, 849D1
JAIDAH, Ali Mohammed
On OPEC parley on $5-7, 341D3
Asks OPEC oil-refining role 10-9, 871C1
JAKES, John
Lawless on best-seller list 4-30, 356A2; 6-4, 460D3; 7-2, 579D3
JAKOBSEN, Svend
Fishermen ask resignatn 5-10, 436C3
Named Danish fisheries min 8-30, 688A1
JALLOUD, Abdel Salam
In Sovt-Syrian talks 2-21—2-22, 139E2
Visits China 8-4—8-10, 691G2

1979

JACKSON, Ron
AL batting ldr 9-30, 955F3
JACKSON, Terry
NFL '78 interceptn ldr 1-6, 80G1
JACKSON, Tom
TUC conf: govt scored 9-3–9-7, 707E2
JACKSON Manufacturing Co., W. L.
No-contest plea cited 10-22, 986E1
JACKSONS (singing group)
Shake Your Body on best-seller list 5-30, 448E3
JACKSONVILLE, Fla.—*See FLORIDA*
JACKSON v. Virginia
Case decided by Sup Ct 6-28, 558D2
Case cited by Sup Ct 10-9, 784C1
JACOBOWSKY and the Colonel (play)
Grand Tour opens 1-11, 292E1
JACOBS, Lawrence-Hilton
I Love My Wife opens 5-15, 711F3
JACOBY, Joseph
Great Bank Hoax released 3-22, 528C2
JACOBY, Neil H.
Dies 5-31, 432A3
JADE, Claude
Love On The Run released 4-5, 528A3
JAECKIN, Just
Last Romantic Lover released 10-5, 1007G3
JAFARI, Lt. Gen. Fazollah
Executed 4-20, 297C3
JAFARIAN, Gen. Bjorkat
Slain 2-11, 105G1
JAFFE, Leo
Wins Oscar 4-9, 336C2
JAFFE, Rona
Class Reunion on best-seller list 9-2, 672B3
JAFFE, Sam
FBI chrgs Sovt spy role 8-11, 611E1
JAFFE, Stanley R.
Kramer vs Kramer released 12-19, 1007F3
JAFFEE, Stanley
Loses A-test radiatn liability case, notificatn suit OKd 2-9, 112D2
A-test radiatn liability case refused by Sup Ct 5-21, 400A3*
JAFFEE v. U.S.
Case refused by Sup Ct 5-21, 400A3*
JAGAN, Cheddi
Burnham postpones electns 10-22, 814C1
JAGGER, Bianca
Divorced 11-2, 1006C1
JAGGER, Mick
Divorced 11-2, 1006C1
JAGO, Gordon
Whitecaps win NASL title 9-8, 755G2
JAHANBANI, Nader
Executed 3-13, 179G3
JAIDAH, Ali Mohammed
'76 oil bribe alleged 4-9, 305F3
JAILBIRD (book)
On best-seller list 10-14, 800A3; 11-4, 892A3
JAKOBSEN, Svend
Named Danish finance min 10-26, 855A1
JALIL, Ghanem Abdul
Arrested as plotter 7-28, 583E1
Sentenced 8-7, executed 8-8, 602F2

1980

JACKSON, Tom
Cautns re labor reform 2-3, 98D1
JACKSON Laboratory (Bar Harbor, Me.)
Snell wins Nobel 10-10, 889F3
JACKSONVILLE (Fla.) University
Ray in NBA draft 6-10, 447F2
JACOB, John E.
On Jordan shooting 5-29, 401C3
Leads Urban League conv 8-3—8-6, gives keynote address 8-3, 597B1, E2
JACOBS, Seaman
Oh, God! II released 10-3, 836C3
JACOBS Jr., Rep. Andrew (D, Ind.)
Reelected 11-4, 842C4
JACOBS Jr., Harry A.
On Hunt debt, Bache shake-up 3-31, 245A3
On Carter econ renewal plan 8-28, 663D3
Hunts liquidate Bache holdings 10-21, 867F3
JACOBS, John Gregory
Weatherman fugitive surrenders 7-8, 576E3
JACOBSEN, Peter
Wins Buick Open 8-25, 2d in BC Open 8-31, 972F1, G1
JACOBSON, Howard (Buddy)
Flees jail 5-31, sentenced for murder 6-3; DeRosa indicted 6-4, 502A2
Recaptured 7-9, 997D2
JACOBSON, Michael
Scores alcohol ingredient labeling order 6-10, 485C3
Scores FDA caffeine warning 9-4, 726E2
JAEGER, Andrea
Wimbledon results 7-4—7-6, 606E2
Loses US Clay Cts 8-9, Volvo Cup 8-24, US Open semifinal 9-5, 691E2, B3, D3
Wins Riviera Women's Classic 9-21, Fla Fed 11-16, 947G1, E2
US wins Wightman Cup 11-1, 946G3
JAFFE, Rona
Class Reunion on best-seller list 7-13, 568D3
JAGAN, Cheddi B.
Loses Guyana electns 12-15, 994A3
JAGER, Lena
Labor Party conf chrmn 9-29—10-3, 768E1
JAGGER, Mick
French manor house buy rptd 9-18, 908A3
JAGIELSKI, Mieczyslaw
Heads Polish strike probe comm 7-18, named labor negotiator 8-21, 625G2, 626E1
In Polish strike talks 8-23, 8-26, 641C1, E2
Reaches prelim strike accord 8-30, formalized 8-31, 657C2, 658A1
Reaffirms Sovt ties 9-4, 658C3
Named Polish 1st dep 9-6, 678C3
Sees Sovt ldrs, aid hike pledged 9-10—9-11, 679D1
Sees trade union ldrs 9-24, 720C2
Warns unions on new strike 10-1, 761B1
Meets union ldrs on arrests 11-25, 909D1
At '70 riot memorial 12-17, 976G2
Visits Moscow 12-29, 976C3
JAHL, Evelin
Wins Olympic medal 8-1, 624C2
JAILBIRD (book)
On best-seller list 1-13, 40A3; 2-10, 120C3
JAKES, John
Americans on best-seller list 3-9, 200C3; 4-6, 280D3
JAKLIN Klugman (racehorse)
3d in Ky Derby 5-3, 447B2

1976

JAMAICA—*See also CARIBCOM, COMMONWEALTH of Nations, NONALIGNED Nations Movement, OAS, SELA*
Gun crimes penalty bill offered 1-5; '74, '75 rulings cited 50G3, 51A1
Kingston violence flares; martial law set 1-6—1-9, 50F3-51F1
High jobless rate cited 1-11, 51E1
Listed as 'free' nation 1-19, 20C3
Kingston violence continues; PLP, other plots chrgd 5-10—6-29; emergency declared, 300 seized 6-19, 522B1
Cited in Barbados campaign 8-28, 673C1
Jobless, bauxite output rptd 10-1, 965E2
Press self-censorshp rptd 10-12, 965C3
Clarke: $200 mln left Jamaica illegally in '75-76 11-12, 965G2
Marley wounded 12-3; other campaign violence 12-13, 965A3
Press censored 12-12; pol mtgs, rallies banned 12-14, 965E3
Manley, PNP win electns 12-15, 965F1
Govt claims less violence under emergency, 470 rptd held 12-17, 965B3
Foreign Relations (misc.)
UN rights covenant '75 ratificatn rptd 1-4, 36D3
N Viet ties set 1-6, 51B2
IMF conf accord 1-8, 13A1
At intl econ conf 2-11—2-20, 148B1
Total IMF oil loan rptd 4-1, 340D2
Peru amb slain 6-15, 522C2
Scores Chile rights abuse 6-18, 464D2
Haiti assassins arrive 8-27, 1005F3
Rpt US execs visit Cuba 9-27, 791C2
Bauxite, alumina exports rptd down 10-1, 965F2
Castro chrgs CIA re July bombing 10-15, 780A2
Evidnc vs Cuba exile rptd 10-31, 844D1
Canada immigratn rptd 11-3, 851E1
Jan-Sept tourism down 11-15, 965F2
Manley-Castro ties cited 12-15; Cuba hails PNP win 12-16, 965A2, D2, F3

1977

JAMAICA—*See also COMMONWEALTH of Nations, NONALIGNED Nations Movement, OAS*
New Cabt named, pay cut set 1-4, 46A1
Churchill kin raped, robbed 1-6, suspects held 1-10, 258D1
Sovt, COMECON ties planned 1-19, 1-28, 257E2
Kingston violence flares, unemploymt cited 2-2, 258C1
Feb tourism rptd down 2-22, 258D1
PNP sweeps local electns 3-8, Seaga replacemt seen 3-25, 258A1
Water rationing rptd 4-12, 312F2
'61-75 GDP variatns table 5-30, 439B1
Alex Bustamante dies 8-6, 696D2
PNP conflict grows 9-16; mobilizatn min, 'radicals' quits 9-18, 9-30, 884D2-A3
High unemployment rptd 9-27, 884C3
Foreign Relations (misc.)—*See also 'Monetary, Trade & Aid' below*
UN Assemb member 4B1
Emergency econ plan set 1-19, 257G1
Sovt ties planned 1-19, 257E2
Canada '76 emigratn rptd 4-13, 389D2
Belizean ties cited 5-19, 414D3
Belize independnce backed 6-16, 494G2
Belize oppositn fears Price ties 553D2
Illegal emigratn to Bahamas cited 7-19, 579E1
Manley sees Torrijos, regional ldrs 8-5—8-6; new Panama Canal pact backed 8-6, 606B3, 608B2
Nyerere visits 8-11—8-12, 624D1
Castro visits 10-16—10-21; reactn 10-16, 10-23, 883E3-884E1

1978

JAMAICA—*See also CARIBBEAN Community, COMMONWEALTH of Nations, GATT, NONALIGNED Nations Movement, OAS*
Freedom House lists as free, notes rights decline 44A2
Tourism revives as crime drops 1-19, 94G3-95A1
Sugar workers end 2-wk strike 3-3, 194D2
JLP sens quit re Green Bay killings 7-7, 777B2
4 leftists slain by security forces, JLP asks probe 9-7, 885A3
Press freedom rptd by IAPA 10-13, 829A2
Foreign Relations (misc.)—*See also 'Monetary, Trade, Aid & Investment' below*
IMF OKs $245 mln loan, austerity set 6-12, 777A2
Manley at Panama Canal pact instrumts exchng 6-16, 463F2, 464A1
Uruguay, Paraguay, Chile rights abuse scored 6-23, 489E3
UN Assemb member 713G3

1979

JAMAICA—*See also CARIBBEAN Community, COMMONWEALTH of Nations, GATT, IDB, NONALIGNED Nations Movement, OAS*
Montego Bay flood drowns 32 6-24, 638E3
Manley marks reelectn 12-15, 996G1
Cabt resigns 12-17, 996A2
Economy & Labor
Gas price raised 1-8; 7 killed in riots, tourism disrupted 1-8–1-10, 21C2
Professionals rptd leaving; '75-78 data, '79 forecast 9-30, 996E1
'74-79 GDP decline rptd; bauxite output down, tax halved 10-9, 996A1, D1
Econ crisis spurs Cabt resignatn 12-17, 996A2
Foreign Relations (misc.)
IATA conf opens 1-31, 112A1
Grenada coup 3-13, 190C3
Grenada rebel regime recognized 3-21, 236A3
Mex-CR missn on Nicaragua dispatched 5-21, 409B1
IMF OKd $350 mln loan 6-13, 566B2
Nicaragua interventn opposed 6-21, 461A1
UN membership listed 695F2
IMF austerity plan fails; oil import costs, export sag forecast 10-9, 995G3-996D1
IMF loan to be rescheduled 12-15, 996G1

1980

JAMAICA—*See also COMMONWEALTH of Nations, GATT, IDB, NONALIGNED Nations, OAS*
Nursing home fire kills 157 5-20, 391B3
Hurricane Allen hits 8-6, 621C2
Economy & Labor
Manley rejcts budget cut, layoffs 1-17, 99F1
Econ crisis worsens; inflatn, jobless rates soar 4-7, 287E1
Econ recovery seen, bauxite expansn set 6-4, 465F1
Manley econ failure chrgs cited 10-5, 791F3
Seaga sworn, campaign vows cited; econ data rptd 11-1, 854B2-G2
Foreign Relations (misc.)
Colombian consul released from DR Emb 4-6, 293B3
Castro-Manley link spurs electn issue 10-5, 791G3
UN Cncl seat replacemt set 11-13, 896D1
Cuba ex-offcl asks UN probe prison hunger strike 12-4, 965D2
Guyana electn observed 12-15, declared 'fraudulent' 12-19, 994A3
Government & Politics—*See also other appropriate subheads in this section*
Manley asks early electns 2-3, 99A2
Finance min quits 3-26, 287B1
Manley sets Oct 30 electns 10-5, 791F3-792A1
Seaga, JLP defeat Manley 10-30, Seaga sworn 11-1, 854B1

1976

Sports
Olympic results 7-18—7-31, 573D3, 575F3, G3

U.S. Relations
US consul guard killed, emb stoned 1-7, 51B1
US drug sales rptd 1-8, 51F1
Revere unit sues vs bauxite tax 1-13, 51G1
US 'destabilizatn' campaign chrgd; bauxite dispute, Cuba ties cited 5-14, 5-25, 6-20, 522F1
Reynolds, Kaiser admit pol paymts 6-2, 6-10, 690D2
'70-72 Aloca paymts rptd, de Roulet linked 7-16, 7-19, 690E1-D2
Alcoa bauxite ownership talks rptd 7-16, 690C2
Rpt US execs visit Cuba 9-27, 791C2
Castro chrgs CIA re July bombing 10-15, 780A2
CIA agents identified 11-18, 946B3
PNP vows better US ties 12-15, 965C2

JAMES, Charles A.
Niger amb 9-2; confrmd 9-23, 808A1
JAMES, Lee
Wins Olympic medal 7-26, 576E2
JAMESON, Pfc. Bernard Lowell
Arrested 9-17, 792B2
JAMES River
EPA urges toxic chem law 2-26, 171C3
Allied Chem indicted 5-7, 349A1
Allied Chem fined 10-5, 767D3
JAMIESON, Donald C.
Sworn external affairs secy 9-15, 692D1
Sees Kissinger, backs Rhodesia fund 10-15, 843D2
Signs Spain tax pact 11-23, 962G3
A-export rules tightened, Pak tie cut 12-22, 998B1
JAMIL, Air Vice Marshal Naji
Mediates Leb pact 1-21—1-22, 33F1
Warns of Leb mil drive 9-11, 720E2
In truce talks 9-17, 9-19; scores Arafat 9-19, 698F2, A3
Defends Leb newspaper seizures 12-20, 953F2
JANE'S Fighting Ships (book)
Editor hits NATO waste 8-31, 760G2
JANSEN, Alfred
Rptd bugged in '58 1-9, 48D3
JANSEN, Punt
Replaced in Bantu post 1-22, 76E1
JANSSEN, Peter
Scores Tunisia 9-6, 662C3
JAO Shu-shih
Cited in Mao death announcemt 659C2
JAOYYOUSHI, Mutasem
In Damascus raid 9-26, executed 9-27, 720C3, 721A1

1977

Monetary Trade & Aid Issues (including all foreign economic developments)
COMECON ties planned 1-19, 1-28, 257E2
Kaiser, Reynolds control acquired 2-2, 3-31; other deals planned 2-10, 257F2
'75-76 trade, paymts table 3-11, 189A2 ★, C2
Barclays Bank natlizatn set 3-23, 257D2
IMF grants loan 7-12, terms detailed 10-7, 884D3
Regional coffee fund set 8-6, 608B2
US vows more aid 8-7, 646B2
Venez to buy aluminum 9-2, 884E3
US aid resumed 9-12, 11-9, 884C2
Jan-June trade gap narrowed 9-27, 884B3
Venez, Hungary loans rptd 9-27, 884E3
Castro vows aid 10-16—10-21, 884C1
Bauxite base price OKd 12-7, 975E1

U.S. Relations
US amb confrmd 5-25, 499F3
Mrs Carter visits; econ, Cuba ties discussed 5-30—5-31, 454E1, B2
Young visits, more US aid vowed 8-5—8-7, 646E1, A2
US aid resumed 9-12, 11-9, 884C2
CIA death plots vs Manley rptd 11-2, 884E1
Manley in US, sees Carter on Cuba, Panama Canal pacts 12-16, 1019G1

JAMAL, Amir
Shifted to Tanzania transport post 2-13, 161B2
JAMES, Joseph
NY ct voids death penalty 11-15, 919C3
JAMES River
Kepone clean-up fund set up 1-28, 95C1
Ship hits Hopewell bridge 2-24, 204F3
JAMIESON, Donald C.
Asks Brazil sign NPT 1-28, 190F1
Denies Warren dispute 2-17, 132E3
US-Canada trust com rptd set 6-18, 525G2
Scores Smirnov activity 7-20, 579G3
Sees China forgn min 10-4—10-7, 801E1
On US nickel dumping 10-24, 924B1
Bars Arab boycott list disclosure 12-16, 1010B2
Rpts S Africa econ ties cut 12-19, 1016D2
JAMIL, Maj. Gen. Naji
Plans drive vs Christns 4-3, 246E1
JANE'S All the World's Aircraft (book)
US B-1 cancellatn scored 12-7, 942B1
JANE'S Fighting Ships (book)
'77-78 editn ranks subs 8-25, 686E2
JANIS, Jay
Named HUD undersecy 3-4, confrmd 3-23, 272B3
JANISH, Joseph
Indicted re Torres 10-20, 821A1
JANKOWSKI, Gene F.
Named CBS broadcast pres 10-17, 846G1
JANN, Horst
Sentenced in E Berlin for spying 11-23, 968E2
JANUARY, Don
2d in Australian Open 11-20, 950F3

1978

Monetary, Trade, Aid & Investment
Venez aluminum deal, Mex shipping pact; Trinidad Jan-Oct '77 imports rptd 1-13, 100F2, C3
Trade, paymts deficits cited 1-13, 100G2
Dollar devalued at IMF behest 1-20, 94G3
US, Canada banks curb operatns 2-3, 95A1
Hungary alumina refinery aid rptd; Mex, Venez sales planned 2-28, 194E2
Belize defns aid agreed 3-10, 211C2

Sports
WCT Challenge Cup results 12-17, 1027D2

U.S. Relations
US banks curb operations 2-3, 95A1
Manley at Canal pact instrumts exchng 6-16, 463F2, 464A1

JAMES, Bill
Loses US House electn 11-7, 849D3
JAMES, Charles
Dies 9-23, 778D1
JAMES Jr., Gen. Daniel (Chappie) (ret.)
Dies 2-25, 196C3
JAMES Jr., Forrest (Fob)
Faces Ala primary runoff for gov 9-5, 699A2 ★
Wins nomination 9-26, 769E1
Elected 11-7, 849F2, 853D2
JAMES, John
NFL '77 punting ldr 1-1, 56F3
JAMES, Naomi
Sails solo around world 6-8, 653C2
JAMES Cleveland Live at Carnegie Hall (recording)
Wins Grammy 2-24, 316A1
JAMIESON, Donald C.
In China, sees Viet forgn min 2-1, 80G1
Chrgs USSR spy ring, cancels trip 2-9, 110D3
At Namibia mtg 2-11—2-12, sees progress 2-13, 113G3
Plans USSR satellite search paymt claim 2-13, 103E1
On US fish dispute 6-2, 435F1
JAMIL, Maj. Gen. Naji
Replaced as Syrian AF head 3-27, 269G3
JANHU, Abdul-nur
Killed 2-8, 99F1
JANISH, Joseph
Sentncd in Torres case 3-28, appeal rptd 12-14, 991C3
JANKINS, Carol Mayo
Zinnia opens 3-22, 760G3
JANKLOW, William J.
On Banks extraditn bar 4-19, 327G1
Wins SD primary for gov 6-6, 448G1
Elected 11-7, 853E3, 855B1
JANKOWSKI, Gene F.
Wussler quits CBS Sports 3-15, 252B2
JANROT, Pierre
L'Aurore editor quits 11-26, 1017A1
JANSEN, Karl-Heinz
Chrgs Nazi prosecutn lag 2-22, 477E2
JANSON, Punt
S Africa black educ min 11-14, 904B3
JANUARY, Don
2d in Mexico Cup tourn 12-10, 990E2

1979

U.S. Relations
Rose fired re US kickbacks, flees 1-29; govt probes 2-4, 101B2
'75-78 emigratn rptd, '79 forecast 9-30, 996F2
US banks rejctd standby loan 10-9, 996B1
Calif pot output up 10-29, 972G1

JAMES Jr., Gov. Forrest (Fob) (D, Ala)
Named ct agent for prison receivership 2-2, 112B3
JAMES, Robert
Scores Blunt 11-21, 908F3
JAMES A. Fitzpatrick Nuclear Power Plant—*See NEW York State–Atomic Energy*
JAMIESON, Donald C.
US fishing talks effort asked 1-5, 37B1
USSR billed for satellite search 1-23, 96D1
Quits Parlt for Newfoundland premr bid 5-27, 424C1
Wins Newfoundland legis seat 6-18, 468B1
Parlt resignatn cited 10-9, 788A3
Liberals retain seat 11-19, 907E3
JANELLE, Richard
Joins PCs 9-19, 729B1
JANISH, Joseph
Wins Torres case appeal 2-6, 156C2
Resentenced 10-30, 839B3
JANNI, Joseph
Yanks released 9-19, 820G3
JANOFSKY, Leonard S.
Installed ABA pres 8-15, 769B1
JANUARY, Don
Ties for 2d in Colonial Natl 5-20, 587F2

1980

Monetary, Trade, Aid & Investment
Manley sees IMF dir, loan talks fail 1-15; '79 forgn debt cited 1-17, 99E1
Manley breaks with IMF 3-25; intl banks rejct loan request, urge IMF compromise 4-7, 276A1
Jan forgn debt rptd 4-7, 276E1
Forgn bank debt accord reached at IDB mtg, default averted 4-15, 314C2
Debt refinancing plan advances; intl loan, bauxite deal rptd 6-4, 465B1
Mex, Venez sign oil supply guarantee 8-3, 605D3
Manley IMF loan failure cited 10-5, 791F3
Seaga rpts forgn exchng status, Iraqi loan; IMF talks resumptn seen; forgn debt, trade, reserve problems cited 11-1, 854B2-G2

Sports
Moscow Olympic results 7-20—8-3, 588B3, 622E2, 624B2

Unrest
Manley shot at 4-14, oppositn party fund-raisers slain 4-20, 336C1
Soldiers seized in coup attempt 6-22, JLP denies role 6-23, 498E3
Kingston curfew imposed; June, July deaths rptd 7-18, 579F1
Security offcl, aide killed; '80 death toll over 450 10-14, 791D3
Seaga attacked on electn day, Oct deaths rptd 10-30, 854F1

U.S. Relations
US grain shippers sued for fraud 2-4, 99B2
Finance min seeks loan in NY 4-7, 287C1
Manley in NY 6-4, 465D1
US Emb aide named as CIA operative 7-2, Kingston home machine gunned 7-4, 564E3-565A1
Seaga win hailed 10-30, US aid cited 10-30, 854F1, E2
US '81 aid hike, Seaga electn rptd linked 12-20, 981B3

JAMAL, Amir
Vows PLO role at World Bank-IMF mtg 9-19, 719F3
Addresses World Bank-IMF mtg 9-30, 762D1
JAMES Jr., Gov. Forrest (Fob) (D, Ala)
Hines '78 rape convictn overturned 3-18, 215G2
Assails Reagan Klan remark, Reagan clarifies 9-2, 664A1, D1
JAMES, P. D.
Innocent Blood on best-seller list 7-13, 568B3
JAMES, Roland
In NFL draft 4-29, 336F2
JAMES Herriot's Yorkshire (book)
On best-seller list 1-3, 40C3; 2-10, 120D3
JAMESON, Jerry
Raise the Titanic released 8-1, 675D3
JAMES River
NRC clears Va A-plant 8-5, 649C1
JAMES River Corp.
Gulf & Western forest unit purchase agreed 2-1, 3-27, 385E3
JAMIESON, James
Brigadoon opens 10-16, 892A3
JANCEK, Steve
Loses US House electn 11-4, 851B3
JANI, Robert F.
Manhattan Showboat opens 7-1, 756E3
JANIS, Jay
Money mkt funds testimony rptd 3-21, 223E3
On S&L loan plan 7-31, 600C1
Resigns FHLBB chrmnship 12-15, named Calif Fed pres 12-18, 959G1
JANKOWSKI, Gene F.
CBS resignatn hoax 5-23, 501A2
JANNEY, Leon
Dies 10-28, 876B2
JANNOTTI, Harry P.
Indicted in Abscam probe 5-22, 402A3
Convicted 9-16, 740B2
Conviction dismissed 11-26, 919A2
JANOFSKY, Leonard S.
Smith succeeds as ABA pres 8-6, 744A2
JANSEN, Wim
Traded to Diplomats 3-6, 770B3
JANSSEN, David
Dies 2-13, 176F1
JANTAR, Anna
Killed in Polish jet crash 3-14, 214B1
JANUARY, Don
2d in Los Angeles Open 2-24, Legends of Golf 4-27, 412E2, E3

JAPAN

1976

JAPAN—*See also ADB, DISARMAMENT—Geneva Committee, IEA, OECD*
Pan Am sets world mark 5-3, 912G3
Izu Penninsula flooded 7-11, 796C2
Newsman's '74 acquittal reversed 7-20, 539D1
Typhoon Fran hits 9-8—9-13, 796B2
Lumber ship sinks off Hawaii 11-11, 892D1

1977

JAPAN—*See also DISARMAMENT—Geneva Committee, IDB, IEA, OECD*
'74 Turkish jet crash setld 4-14, 312C1
25 coal miners killed 5-11, 808D1
Mt Usu erupts 8-7—8-10, 747B2
Plane crashes in Malaysia 9-27, 808B1
Hijacked Malaysian jet crashes 12-4, 992B2

1978

JAPAN—*See also DISARMAMENT—Geneva Committee, GATT, IDB, IEA, OECD*
Quakes hit Izu, Sendai, other cities 1-13—6-12, 479E3
Drug damages awarded 3-1, 232B1
Heart death increase rptd 3-20, 598C1
Narita airport riots 3-26—3-27, govt stays opening 3-28, 227E3
Uemura reaches North Pole 5-1, 420A2
Waste combustn energy rptd 5-11, 367C1
Narita airport opens 5-21, 416F1

1979

JAPAN—*See also DISARMAMENT-Geneva Committee, GATT, IDB, IEA, OECD*
Cancer drug research rptd 1-28, 139D1
Tokyo on '78 world's busiest airport list 6-1, 421C1
Kyushu floods kill 22 6-26—6-30, 639A3
Satowaki installed cardinal 6-30, 640D2
Quake hits Tokyo 8-12, 619G3

1980

JAPAN—*See also ADB, GATT, GENEVA Committee, IDB, IEA, OECD*
Avg height increase rptd 4-6, 314G3
DNA repair, lifespan link questioned 8-28, 716F1

1976

Chinese Relations—*See 'Japanese Relations' under CHINA*

Economy & Labor (domestic)

'76 mil, econ budgets OKd 1-1, 1-2, 30D1, F1
Xmas '75 bonuses rptd down 1-10, 51F3
'75 bankruptcies up 1-13, 141G1
Union spring plans rptd 1-14, 1-17, 51D3
Jobless total rptd 1-20, 51F3
Unions seek pay boost 1-21, 2-9, 141E1
4 steel firms OK merger 1-28, 208D3
Dec '75, Jan jobless rptd 2-6, 3-9, 191D2
Ataka-Itok 'affiliatn' rptd 2-17, 221F2
'75 indl output rptd down 2-23, 6-mo profits forecast 3-6, 191D2
'75 GNP rptd up 3-4, 191C2
'75 joblessness rptd up 3-13, 297E3
Govt-union wage talks fail 3-29; transport, dockworkers strike 3-30—4-20, 290G2, D3
Stopgap budget OKd 3-29, 290E3
Lower house OKs '76 budget 4-9, 313E2
3 specialty steel firms merge 4-26, 419C1
Econ growth cited 6-27—6-28, 462E1
Stock mkt down 11-4, 826E2
RR fares, phone costs hiked 11-4, 889G3
Oct '75-76 inflatn rate rptd 12-6, 976B1

Foreign Economic Developments—*See also 'Lockheed Bribe Scandal' below*

'76 budget OKs Eximbank credits rise 1-2, 30D1
Iranian oil pact signed 1-7, 141G1
Arms export ban end urged 1-9—2-1, 157F1-A2
Datsun tops US '75 imports 1-11, 280G1
SDR rate rptd 1-15, 14A3
Joint US, Dutch oil consortium rptd 1-16, 208C3
Australia coal plan OKd 1-20, 46G1
Steel exports to EEC curbed 1-20, 85B1
'75 exports down 1-20; Jan imports, paymts balance up 2-10, 2-19, 141B2
China oil import rise set 1-22, 208C3
China fertilizer deal rptd 1-26, 100F3
In 7-natn A-safeguards agrmt 1-27, 84A1
Finnish electronic deal rptd 1-27, 104E2
US Sen OKs 200-mi fishing zone 1-28, 94F1
12-mi waters limit sought 2-2, 141A2
US fishing talks sought 2-2, 141B2
Australia talks 2-4—2-15, 137C3
Venez oil purchase, mktg deals rptd 2-6, 2-11, 208B3
China outbids Indonesia on oil 144A3
At intl econ conf 2-11—2-20, 148B1
Nissan buys Australia VW plant 2-12, 137E3
Canada refinery bankruptcy dvpts, US Ataka unit role rptd 2-13—3-12, 221D2
US bank files bankruptcy 2-20, 167C1
Australia steel project deferred 2-24, 154D3
Jan-Sept '75 EC auto exports rptd 2-24, Feb exports 3-2, 191E2
6-natn export credit pact rptd 2-25, 164C2
Jan paymts balance revised 2-27, Feb reserves up 3-3, 191E2
IDA fund hike opposed 3-2, 191A3
US rules on stainless steel imports 3-2, 213B3
Poor natns eased import curbs opposed 3-3, 191G2
US threatens steel quotas 3-16, 212G3
Firms off Arab blacklist 3-24—4-3, 242C1
US, USSR gas pact reached 3-31, 655C3
Fscl '75 trade surplus, paymts deficit rptd 4-16, 291B1
Paraguay paper cellulose investmt set 4-30, 403B3
US ends car dumping probe 5-4, 321D2
'75 Sovt trade rptd 5-5, 340B3, D3
US Cong backs IDB entry 5-20, 392B3
UNCTAD OKs commodity fund 5-30, 388G2

1977

Atomic Energy & Safeguards

Australia uranium deals cited 1-26, 81F2
US A-talks 3-21—3-22, 209F2
Australia cancels uranium contracts 3-24, 218D1
US OKs spent A-fuel export 3-28, 235D1
US A-proposals scored 3-30, 4-2, 329C3
Carter proposes US plutonium ban 4-7, 268B1, G1
Intl A-energy conf ends, US plutonium ban scored 4-13, modificatn sought 4-21, 334F2, 335D1
US A-fuel export delay rptd 4-14, 268C2
1st breeder operational 4-24, 335B1
Carter proposes US A-export curbs 4-27; Japan fuel reliance noted 4-28, 334D2
Supplier natns score Carter plans 4-28—4-29, 403F1-A2
Carter OKs uranium shipmt 5-6, 403D2
7-natn summit debates A-sales, sets study 5-7—5-8, 357D2, E2
Curbs vs A-treaty non-signers asked 8-11, 686B3
US reprocessing pact signed 9-12, 812B3
Suppliers conf OKs safeguards 9-21, 717D1
US, Canada OK uranium export 11-15, 913D1
USSR A-pact rptd 11-21, 988G1

Bribery Scandals

Lockheed probe end; Osano, Kodama indicted 1-21, 83F2
Tanaka, other Lockheed trials start 1-27, 1-31, 83B2
Boeing kickback chrgd 2-14, '72 deal probed 2-15, 136D1
Sony settles rebate chrgs 8-19, 651B1
Exxon admits paymts 10-25, 818A2

Economy & Labor (domestic)

'74-75 recessn job data rptd 1-3, 29E3
Nov, 12-mo consumer price rise rptd 1-7, 29C3
Dec '76 WPI up 1-11, 65G1
Local govts reduce hiring 1-13, 65E2
Cabt OKs budget increase 1-20, 65E1
'76 factory wages rptd 1-28, 158B3
Dec '75-76 inflatn rate rptd 2-7, 87B2
'76 econ growth rptd 2-16, 147B2
Econ slowdown rptd 3-12, 201D2
Bank discount rate cut 3-12, 4-18, 329G3
Mar business bankruptcies up 4-10, 330A1
'77 growth goal set 5-7—5-8, 357C1
'76 GNP rptd up 6-2, 467E1
Steel tech advance rptd 8-13; steel output 9-19, 775F3, 776D1
Govt spending rise set, supplementary budget issued 10-3, 783A2
Aug jobless sets record 10-9, 885B1
Yen curbs set 11-17, effected 11-21, 932G2
Econ situatn grave 11-26; new Cabt installed 11-28, task force formed 11-29, 932F1-F2
Inflatn-adjusted growth forecast 11-29, 932F2
3d ¼ growth rate rptd 12-9, 6.7% projectn doubted 12-19, 974B2, 985A1
'78 econ growth, deficit spending rise planned 12-15, 973G2-974A2
15-mo stimulus budget planned 12-19, 984G3
Sept-Nov motor vehicle output rptd 12-20, 1015F1
Cabt OKs '78 7% growth-rate goal 12-21, 1015F1
Cabt OKs '78 budget, plans bond issues 12-26, 1015D1

1978

Atomic Energy & Safeguards

'77 A-export safeguard pact detailed 1-11, 11B2
US alerts to Sovt A-satellite fall 57E1
US trade missn planned 1-13, 27A1
US split on A-bomb plans 1-26, 61C2
Canada uranium pact initialed 1-26, 88E3
Australia joins A-supplier group 2-24, 129C2
Australia seeks treaty 3-20, 208B3
US fusion-research fund rptd discussed 5-4, 341B3
US study urges joint breeder dvpt effort 5-10, 346B3, G3
UK A-reprocessing contracts rptd signed 5-25, 437A3
Breeder research pact with France, W Ger rptd 6-23, 548E3
Canada uranium pact signed 8-22, 667B1
Uranium import fund set 9-3, 694D1
US joint energy research planned 9-6, 695B3

Bribery Scandals

6 more tied to Lockheed deal 1-30, 72C3
CIA, business paymts linked 2-17, 161F2
Nakasone cited in ct depositn by Lockheed ex-offcl, denies link 10-26, 838E3-839A1
McDonnell Douglas paymts rptd 12-15, 982G2

Economy & Labor (domestic)

7% fscl '78 growth target set 1-13, 26B3
Tokyo issues munic bonds, averts bankruptcy 2-15, 150D1-A2
Eidai declares bankruptcy 2-20, 150A1
Unions lower wage goals 3-20, 695G2
Fscl '77, Mar record bankruptcies rptd 4-10, 314A2
7% fscl '79 growth sought 5-3, 341A3
Econ stagnatn scored as energy solutn 6-13, 450F2
Growth target of 1.5% affirmed 7-17, 544G1
'77 per capita GNP ranked 17th 7-18, 624D1
'77 jobless rise rptd 7-28, 677D1
$13 bln growth plan proposed, 2d ¼ lag rptd 9-3, 693G2
'78 growth target imperiled by export drop 9-8, 694G1
Growth rate hike backed 9-25, 9-26, 731B3
June '77-78 world inflatn rates ranked 10-18, 914F1
Jobless highest since '59 10-31, 839B1
Ohira scores 7% growth rate 11-27, 912E3
'78 growth target dropped 12-8; lower rate seen 12-11, 12-12, 988G1
Sperm whale quotas rptd cut 12-25, 1001A3
Tokyo stock mkt gains rptd; graph 12-28, 1001C1, E3

1979

Atomic Energy & Safeguards

US A-accident sparks protests, govt affirms A-policy 4-1, 4-2, 246B2, F2
A-plants shut after US safety warnings 4-14, 323D2
Japan, US OK safety efforts 5-2, 320F2

Bribery Scandals

Grumman payoff scandal probed 1-9, Nissho exec kills self 2-1, 98E2
Grumman denies paymts 2-8, 305C3
Lockheed ex-aides' probe dropped by US 2-15, bribes disclosed 2-16, 306E1, A2
S Africa pol bribes chrgd 3-21, 213F1
4 indicted in Nissho scandal 4-5, 5-15, 389D2
Lockheed pleads guilty, fined 6-1, 422F2

Economy & Labor

Fscl '79 budget passed 2-3, 286G1
Discount rate hike set 4-16, 615D3
7-natn indicators index rptd 6-11, 513A3
Banks dominate world '78 top 300 6-19, 476G1
Econ slowdown seen 7-19, 554G2
7-yr plan adopted 8-11—8-12, 615B2
Oil price impact noted 8-13, 615A3
Westn wage rates compared 9-19, 697D3
Discount rate hiked; consumer, wholesale prices cited 11-1, 836D2, 838G1

Energy—*See also 'Atomic' above*

Iran oil cutoff impact assessed 2-15, 126D2
5% oil demand cut agreed 3-2, 162A1
Australia coal prices cut 3-13, 233B2
US research pact signed 5-2, 320E2
Iran cuts oil exports 15% 5-18, 389C2
Gas price rptd at $1.98 per gal 5-19, 397A1
Sunday gas statn closings asked, '78 imports cited 5-21, 389B2
US coal exports hike set 6-2, 416E2
Ohira, Carter confer 6-26, 494A2
Tokyo summit 6-28—6-29, 493A1-F2
Carter energy plan assessed 7-16, 534E3, 535A1
Oil spot mkt agrmt rptd 7-16, 494F2
Econ plan links growth rate drop, urges conservatn 8-11—8-12, 615B2, G2
Oil price impact noted 8-13, 615A3
Oil price hikes, paymts deficit linked 10-30, 836A3
Iran export cut confirmed 11-8, 843F1
Iran oil use data rptd 11-12, 861E2
Iran excess oil import curb seen 11-15, Ohira warns cos 11-16, 879G2-A3
Iran bars US $ oil paymts 11-23, 896D3
Oil import costs, current acct deficit linked 11-27, 996F2
China oil dvpt pact signed 12-6, 939E3
Okita at conf in Paris 12-10, 933C2
Ohira defends Iran oil buys 12-11, 933E2

1980

Atomic Energy & Safeguards

Australia pact discussed 1-16, 78B2
7-natn Venice summit backs 6-23, 473F2
Suzuki urges dvpt 8-18, 635A3

Bribery Scandals

3 get suspended sentnc in Nissho case 7-24, 605B2

Economy & Labor

Stock exchng hits record high average 1-14, 100C1
Tokyo purchasing power rptd low 2-12, 125E3
'79 inflatn rptd down by OECD 2-13, 125C3
Space industry research rptd 2-16, 160G2, B3
Jan wholesale prices up 2.1%, rampant inflatn feared 2-18, 151F3
Defns-GNP ratio rptd 2-19, 132G1
Naval maneuvers protested 2-22, 2-24, 2-26, 151D3
Inflatn rate cited 3-7, 182D2
Anti-infltatn plan announced, Feb wholesale prices cited 3-19, 276C2
Defns spending plans cited 3-20, 219G2
Arms spending hike urged 7-2, 539D3
1st 1/2 auto productn rptd 7-7, 541E3
Cabt backs defns budget hike 7-29, 579C2
Weapons dvpt urged 8-5, 635B3
Labor costs rptd 8-12, 698E1, F1
Suzuki outlines admin goals 8-18, 635F2

Energy—*See also 'Atomic Energy' above*

Mex '80 oil imports seen 1-15, 60B2
Australia talks note 1-16, 78F1
'79 oil import costs rptd 1-25, 100B1
Trade deficit linked 4-15, 314F3
Iran oil talks fail 4-17, price hike barred 4-19; imports threatened, alternative supplies seen 4-20, 298D3
Iran oil supply substitutes rptd found 4-25; US offers aid 5-1, 341F1
Mex oil talks 5-2—5-4, 341G1
US coal purchases rptd 5-7, 350C2
OPEC sets pricing plan 5-7—5-8, 364C3
Mex oil pact signed 5-28, 409C2*
7-natn Venice summit 6-22—6-23, 473A1-474E1
US-W Ger synfuel pact signed 7-31, 666D2
Suzuki urges alternate sources 8-18, 635F2, A3
Canada oil co loan set 8-23, 651C1
US record oil inventories rptd 9-5, Admin assured on shortfall 10-3, 785E3
US plan for intl force to protect Gulf oil opposed 9-26, 735E2
Oil costs spark trade gap rise 11-18, 902B1
Iraq oil shipmts set 11-20, 894C2
Panama Canal clogged by Venez imports 11-24, 895D3

1976

7-natn summit set 6-1, 6-3, 388G3
IDB entry set 6-3, 465D3
Loan to prop UK £ OKd 6-7, 407C2
US steel quota pact OKd 6-9, 430F3, 431B1
Australia OKs auto projects 6-10, 438B3
Export credit terms tightened 6-15, 529F3, 530A1
Australia trade reaffirmed 6-16, 481B1
Paris Club defers Zaire debt 6-17, 488A2
7-natn econ summit held; warned re trade surplus, yen 6-27—6-28, 461G2, 462E2
Australia-UK coal-mining projct set 7-7, 496A2
7-natn A-waste conf opens 7-12, 739G1
China cancels shipping talks 7-16, 555E2
Italy loan ban disclosed 7-17, 531A1
USSR ends shipping rate war 7-19, 558E3
Argentina bank loan rptd 7-23, 554B1
Australia scores curbs 8-12, 623A2
Nissan, Australia deal set 8-15, 650F1
1st ½ US deficit rptd 8-26, 668D1
To aid Iran petrochem plant 8-27, 643E1
Nixon bid for Grumman donatn rptd 9-13; denied 9-15, 9-16, 979G1-D3
US rates auto fuel-econ 9-22, 766A2-769D1
Australia iron deal rptd 9-23, 770E3
UK to seek IMF loan 9-29, 721D1
Vs World Bank funds rise 10-5, 778D1
IMF take no actn on floating rate watch 10-8, 778E2
Trudeau visits 10-20—10-26, pact signed 10-21; Canada trade cited 836G2
Mitsubishi bank sets Chile loan 10-20, 871D1
N Korean debt cited 10-22, 799E3
Cited re US-Korea mil contracts 10-27, 982A3
Oct US car sales rptd 11-3, 885A3
Reactn to US electn 11-4, 826E2
Australia sees USSR oil threat 11-4, 850C2
US hits Sovt machinery sales 11-4, 880B1
Fishing talks impasse 11-8—11-12, 863B3
Australia uranium ban lifted 11-11, 888C1
'75 COMECON trade gap rptd 11-18, 977D1
Marubeni rptd Canada A-sales agent 11-29, 923G3
Giscard asks 3d 7-natn summit 12-2, 964D1
Oil imports down 12-6, 936B1, A2
Fishing conf impasse 12-13—12-17, 1006C3
In IMF UK loan 12-21, 1004B1

Foreign Relations (misc.)—*See also 'UN Policy' below*

Miki acts re A-pact ratificatn 1-9, forgn motives rptd 1-19, 51C2
Returns stolen painting to France 1-29, 104C3
Australian consulate cutback 2-4, 97B2
S Korea party delegatn visits 2-6, 122B1
Angola MPLA recognized 2-19, 163D1
Amb to Australia arrives 3-9, 187E3 ★
Yugo sentences Belgrade atty 3-10, 223G3
Australia pact set 5-6, 349D3
Ratifies A-pact 5-24, documents deposited 6-9, 418E3
Australia lauds ties 6-1, 438G2
Fraser signs treaty 6-16, ends visit 6-20, 481A1
Japan warns vs Taiwan, Sovt policy chngs 7-12, 555E2
Thai gen exiled 794G3
Seoul ldr kidnap protested 10-13, 838E3
Zaire names amb 10-18, 949G3

1977

Foreign Relations (misc.)—*See also 'Monetary, Trade & Aid' and 'UN Policy' below*

Australia mins mtg 1-17—1-18, 60B2
US S Korea pullout concern cited 1-18, 60C2
French transport min visits 1-21, 73C3
Ethiopian amb seeks asylum 3-11, 238G2
US reaffirms S Korea defns commitmt 3-22, 209F2
More Viet refugees flee 3-25, 243F3
Viet refugee arrivals cited 5-3, 470G1
Viet refugees barred 6-8, 497A2
Australia friendship treaty ratified 7-21, 596A1
US briefs on ROK troop exit plan 7-27, 572A2
N Korea sea limits opposed 8-2, 591C1
Indochina refugee pleas studied 8-25, 685G2
Malaysia takes Indochina refugees 8-31, 685E2
Jet hijacked to Bangladesh 9-28, surrendered in Algiers 10-3; Algeria bars extraditn 10-5, 756G2, A3 ★
W Ger hijacking reaction 10-19, 790B2

1978

Foreign Relations (misc.)—*See also 'Atomic Energy' and 'Bribery' above, 'Monetary, Trade, Aid & Investment' below*

Sovt peace talks deadlocked 1-9—1-10, 28C3
China-Japan pact feared 1-9—1-10, 28E3
Red Army terrorists rptd in Colombia 2-18, 147D3
French CP ldr calls 'backward' 2-20, Japan amb protests 2-23, 167C2
Sovt peace bid rejected 2-22, draft publshd 2-23; Cabt ignores 2-24, 121D3
PLO Israel raiders sought Okamoto release 3-11, 175G2
Israel: terrorists train in Leb 4-7, 256D3
LDP ldrs rptd vs China talks 4-7, 278B2
China boats anchor off Senkakus 4-12; Japan protests 4-14, China denies chrg 4-15; boats rptd out 4-16, 278C1
USSR release of Korean jet passengers mediated 4-20—4-23, 302F1
El Salvador guerrillas kidnap exec 5-17; presumed dead 7-7, 722E1
China for peace talks 5-23, 384B3
'74 demonstratns, KCIA linked 6-6, 433D1
Sovt Kurile maneuvers protested 6-7, 585B3
Trilateral Comm study faults energy policy 6-13, 450B2, F2
China peace talks to resume 6-14, start 7-21; pact signed 8-12, 637A1
Sovts vs China-Japan pact 6-19, 8-12, 637G1
Algeria: Japan Red Army hijackers expelled 7-3, 524D3
Kosygin compares Sovt indus growth 7-5, 518D3
Solomons gain independnc 7-7, 549E1
Hijacking pact signed 7-17, 544G2
Defense white paper chrgs Sovt threat in Asia 7-28, 585C2
China rptdly drops Senkaku claim, Taiwan reaffirms claim 8-12, 637E1, E2
El Salvador guerrilla manifesto published 8-25, 722B2, 723F2 ★
China warns vs Sovt Asia role 9-6, 696D1
Forgn activists curbed 10-4, 764F3
Exec found dead in El Salvador 10-13, 881C3
Diet OKs China pact 10-16, 10-18, 802A1
China's Teng starts visit 10-22, peace pact implemented 10-23; text 801A1-802A1
Mex pres visits 10-30—11-4, 903B3
'71 Korea campaign gifts rptd 11-1, 862D3
USSR Pacific buildup rptd 11-9, 914A2
Teng interviewed 11-26, 950B1
Ohira backs W Eur ties 11-28, 912E3
El Salvador exec kidnaped 12-7, release talks rptd 12-21, 986D3
China-US tie rptd lauded 12-16, 977D1
IWC rptdly cuts whale quotas 12-25, 1001A3

1979

Foreign Relations (misc.)—*See also 'Atomic' and 'Bribery' above, 'Monetary' and 'UN' below*

Canada oppositn ldr visits 1-7–1-11, 57F2
Sovt A-test protested 1-19, 52D1
Taiwan oppositn ldr arrested 1-21, 116F1
USSR mil buildup in Kuriles chrgd 2-5, test fire rptd 2-6, 85A3
Teng visits 2-6–2-7, 84B1
China Viet invasn concern voiced 2-18, 123G1
USSR recon over Viet-China battle zone rptd 2-21, 122B1
El Salvador FARN seek ransom 3-19, 234C3
500 Viet refugees accepted 4-3, 299A2
S Korea noted in US talks 5-2, 320D2
China-US direct mail svc set 5-25, 406B1
More Viet refugees to be accepted 6-18, 460C3
Ohira, Carter discuss refugees 6-26, 494A2, 495E2
Viet refugee admissns cut seen, total rptd 7-10; aid set 7-13, 549E2
PEN Club asks Korea dissidents freed 7-21, 554A1
UK's Mountbatten funeral excludes 9-5, 669E1
174 Viets rescued at sea 9-21, 763G3
China backs closer ties 9-22, 751C2
USSR Kuriles buildup rptd 9-26, 9-27, protested 10-2, 742B1
USSR vs US defns secy's visit 10-16; talks note Kuriles 10-20, 803C3
USSR newsman leaves after defectn 10-24, 856D3
Ohira in China; Indochina, Korea discussed 12-5–12-7, 939C3
Okita at energy conf in Paris 12-10, 933C2
US backed on pressure vs Iran 12-17–12-18, 958D3-959C1 1003C1

1980

Foreign Relations (misc.)—*See also 'Atomic Energy' above, 'Monetary', 'Soviet-Afghan Issue', 'UN Policy' below*

Ohira in Australia, sees prime min 1-16; Pacific orgn studied 1-20, 78E1
McCartney arrested on drug chrgs 1-16, deported 1-26, 200E2
3 arrested as Sovt spies 1-18, 60A1
Sovt spy case prompts mil resignatns 1-28, 2-3, 99C3
USSR dancers defect to US 2-6, 88D1
Navy joins 4-natn Pacific maneuvers 2-26, 151C3
Westn natn mil spending compared 3-20, 219A3
PI arrests natls in Chile pres death plot 3-23, 231E3
Panama pres visits, sees Ohira 3-25, 234B3
China defns support cited 4-7, 314E3
EC votes Iran hostage plea 4-11, 281G2, 282C1
Iran asks neutrality on US hostages 4-11, 282G1
Iran gets US hostage plea, amb recalled 4-12, 282E1
Italy CP vs anti-Sovt front 4-22, 314B2
US moderatn in Iran urged 5-1, 341F1
Ohira in Mex 5-2—5-4, 341G1, 409C2*
Tito funeral held 5-8, 339B1
Chinese Premr Hua visits 5-27—6-1, 421G3
7-natn Venice summit 6-22—6-23, 473A1-474E1
USSR chrgs Japan, US, China 'axis' 7-8, 7-10, 506F1
Ohira rites attended 7-9, 506B1, D1
India launches satellite 7-18, 547E3
Sovt mil buildup spurs defns hike 7-29, 579D2
Westn labor costs compared 8-12, 698E1, F1
Iran parlt ldr rebuffs hostage plea 8-17, 643D3
Sovt A-sub crippled off Okinawa 8-20, territorial waters entered 8-22, no A-leak rptd 8-24, 8-20, 653B1
Ito in Pak 9-1, 686F1
China-US pact sets flight stopovers 9-17, 707C1
Ito meets Sovt forgn min 9-24; mil power chrg denied 9-25, 752D1
US plan for intl force to protect Gulf oil opposed 9-26, 735E2
Kim Dae Jung death sentnc opposed 11-4, 11-28, 11-29, 12-7; S Korea scores 11-26, 944B3
USSR offers Persian Gulf peace plan 12-10, 930E1
USSR Backfire bomber coastal deploymt rptd 12-11, 953C1

1976

Government & Politics—*See also other appropriate subheads in this section*
JCP vs 'permissive' society 1-8—1-9, 1-14, 52A1
Party stance on A-nonproliferatn pact rptd 1-9, 1-19, 51D2
LDP reveals '76 program 1-18, 51A3
Listed as 'free' nation 1-19, 20C3
Elections postponed 2-7, 131B3
Opposition Diet boycott rptd 3-10, 191A2
Electn system ruled invalid 4-14, 290B2
Miki ouster sought 5-13; Miki defends policy 5-26, 458G1-C2
LDP faction seeks new party 6-14, 458E1 ★
LDP factn forms new party 6-25, 497A3
Miki resignatn sought 8-23, 8-24, Miki vs 8-24, 626C3
Miki offers Cabt, party chngs 8-30, LDP members ask resignatn 9-7, 676F3
Ono quits broadcast post 9-4, 838E3
Miki shuffles Cabt, LDP 9-15; special Diet session held 9-16, 694D1
Utsonomiya quits parlt, LDP 10-13, 838D3
Fukuda heads anit-Miki factn 10-20, 838G3
Miki foes ask resignatn 10-21, 839A1
LDP conventn cancld 10-29, 838F3
Fukada quits Cabt to challenge Miki, Noda replaces 11-5, 889F3
Hirohito marks 50-yr reign 11-10, 890A1
LDP suffers electn set back 12-5, retains majority 12-6; Miki takes blame 12-7, 925C3
Miki quits as premr, LDP head 12-17; Fukuda heads LDP 12-23; elected premr, names Cabt 12-24, 1006D2
New house composition listed 1006B3
Lockheed Bribe Scandal
Lockheed payoffs rptd 2-4, 2-6, 130E1-E2, D3
Lockheed payoff chrgs probed; arms deal canceled, Marubeni cuts ties 2-5—2-17, 131B3
All Nippon, Marubeni execs deny wrongdoing 2-5, 2-16, 131F3, 132F1
Miki vows Diet probe 2-6, 131B3, G3
Diet hearings 2-16—1-17, 132F1
Lockheed probes pressed; deals threatened, workers protest, Diet boycott rptd 2-19—3-10; US to free data 3-5, 190A2-191B2 ★
Diet probe reopens, 9 subpoenaed 2-26, 190F2
US offers secret Lockheed data 3-11, Japan accepts 3-12, 199E3
Diet boycott continues 3-12, suspended 3-25; DSP ends 4-5, 286C1, 290F3
Kodama indicted 3-13, assets seized 3-15; assassinatn fails 3-23, 286F1
US data pact signed 3-23; anti-govt protests 3-24, 3-27, prosecutors get info 4-16, 286A1
Tanaka denies payoff rumors, '72 Nixon deal 4-2, 286B2
Rpt CIA had '50s Lockheed data 4-2, 286C2
Workers vs Lockheed probe 4-14, 290B3
Diet boycott ends, Miki pledges Lockheed probe 4-22, 313F2
New charges vs Kodama filed 5-10, 6-1, 450D3
Witness Fukuda dies 6-10, 450E3
Marubeni dir, 3 All Nippon execs arrested 6-22, 450A3
5 more seized in Lockheed case 7-2, 7-7, 7-8, 497D2
All Nippon vp arrested 7-9, 557A2
Ex-Marubeni head, 3 All Nippon execs indicted 7-13, 557B2
Marubeni exec, aide arrested 7-19; Itoh indicted 7-23, 557B2
Tanaka arrested 7-27, quits LDP; Miki vows full probe 7-28, 557D1 ★
More All Nippon indictmts 7-28, 624D2
Tanaka chauffeur found dead 8-2, 624F2
US disclosure bill proposed 8-3, 668B2
Tanaka, secy, 2 Marubeni execs indicted 8-9, 8-16, freed on bail 8-17, 624G1
Sato, Hashimoto arrested 8-20, 8-21, 628C2
Miki resignatn sought 8-23, Miki vs 8-24, 626C3
Parlt com vs Tanaka, Nakasone testifying 8-26, 677B1, D1 ★
Miki offers Cabt, party chngs 8-30, 676F3
Broadcast head quits 9-4, 838E3
Sato, Hashimoto indicted 9-10, 740B2
Miki shuffles Cabt, LDP 9-15, 694D1
Miki sees probe delay 9-24, 740A3
Kodama, Tachikawa trials delayed 9-30, 838C3
Utsonomiya quits parlt 10-13, 838D3
Interim probe rpt issued 10-15, 838E2

1977

Government & Politics—*See also other appropriate subheads in this section*
Upper house electns 7-10, 544G2
Justice, Transport mins resign 10-4, 756D3
New Cabt formed 11-28, econ task force 11-29, 932F1-F2

Monetary, Trade & Aid Issues (including all foreign economic developments)—*See also 'Atomic Energy' above*
UK '76 car imports rptd up 1-8, 45D1
In UK sterling balances pact 1-10, 20C2
Dec '76 exports to US, W Eur drop 1-10, 65B2
'76 Taiwan trade data rptd 1-12, 139F3
Australia trade mtg; beef, fishing pacts set 1-17—1-18, 60A2
Cited re Danish shipyd decline 1-17, 62B1
EC shipbldg plan rejctd 1-17, trade talks rptd stalled 1-18; comm study issued 1-24, 73F2
Australia shipping dispute 1-17—2-21, ANL pact set 2-16, 253E1-D2
Gen Dynamics wins US loan guarantee; Burmah LNG contract, Japan Lines dispute cited 1-19, 55E1, B2, E2
Iraq to get $1 bln aid 1-21, 65D2
France issues shipbldg plea 1-21, 73C3
'76 trade surplus rptd 1-24, 65A2
Australia '76 coal imports rptd 1-25, 81B3
Swiss watch exports rptd down 1-27, 138D1
US links GNP hike, world trade, aid 1-28 92D2
Mondale vows cooperatn 1-31, 69D1, G1, A2
'76 EC trade deficit rptd 1-31, 74C1
China poster compares econ 2-1, 98F1
IMF SDR defined 87G2
EC fines for ball-bearing dumping 2-7, 109D1
US fishing pact signed, Japan '76 fish catch estimated 2-10, 136G1
'75-76 China trade drop rptd 2-15, 180C1
Rpts Asia '76 growth 2-16, 147B2
Brazil raw material orders rptd 2-21, 253B2
W Ger leads West in '76 currency reserves 2-22, 260B3
ASEAN talks urged 2-24, 145B3
Sovt Kurile fishing curb protested 2-26, rejected 3-8, 250C1
Sovt 200-mi limit agrmt rptd 3-1, 147E1
US fishing pact approved 3-3, 173D3
US rules TV imports injury 3-8, asks tariff hike 3-14, 208D3
Bank discount rate cut 3-12, 3-16, 201C2
Sovt fishing talks at impasse 3-15—3-31, 249G3
Australia dock bldg set 3-15, 253D2
US trade talks 3-21—3-22, 209F2
US color TV probe voted 3-23, 318C3
US Feb TV imports rptd 3-23, 318D3
TV, auto mfrs study US investmt rise 3-28; Mitsubishi Calif plans rptd 4-14, 318F3
Fishing limit extensn planned 3-29, 250C1
Japan bars ships from Sovt zone 3-31, 250A1
US asks Portugal aid 4-1, 330C3
US ups TV bond requiremt 4-7, 318G2-B3
US TV export talks end 4-8, 318E3
US states seek investmt 4-11, 385B3
US rpts Mar fishing violatns 270C2
Electronics import duties ordrd by US ct 4-12; protested 4-13, 4-14, 318G1
Sovts score fishing demands 4-12, 319B2
Sovt fishing talks impasse continues 4-13—4-14, Kurile dispute unresolved 4-13, 4-16, 319F1-E2
'76 electronics imports to US rptd 318E2
US CIA oil import rise forecast 4-18, 294E1
Euro-yen bond issue rptd 4-19, 318C1
US House OKs oil export ban 4-20, 323E3
Territorial waters extended, Sovt talks cited 4-28, 5-2, 411B2
At 7-natn econ summit, paymts deficit move OKd 5-7—5-8, 357A1-358B2
Saudi oil pipe fire reactn 5-11—5-12, 362D2
Israel gets US arms preference 5-12, 361E1
US sets arms-sales policy 5-19, 380G2
US TV export limit OKd 5-20, Apr exports rptd 5-30, 415E3, 416E1
US electronics duty order probed by GATT 5-23, 416B2
Turkey delays import paymts 5-24, 565E2
US asks paymts deficit move 5-25, 437D3
Sovt fishing pact signed 5-27, ratified 6-10, 458F2-A3

1978

Government & Politics—*See also other appropriate subheads in this section*
Joint Staff chief ousted, replacemt rptd 7-25, 574C2
Fukuda loses party electn to Ohira; Ohira premrshp assured 11-27, 912D2
Revised electn system described 11-27, 912F2
Ohira vs mil strengthening 11-27, 912E3
Facts on Ohira 913A1
LDP feud delays Ohira confirmatn 12-6; Diet confirms, Cabt formed 12-7, 945D2

Monetary, Trade, Aid & Investment—*See also 'Atomic Energy' and 'Bribery' above*
US steel trigger prices issued 1-3, reactn 1-4, 3C2-B3
'77 forgn aid at record high 1-3, 28E2
Steel trigger plan scored in US rpt 1-7, 80A3
US '77 steel dumping ruling revised 1-9, 80C2
Canada '75 investmt rptd 1-10, 70C3
'77 US futures trading, $ drop linked 1-12, 84B1
Dai-Ichi Kangyo Bank syndicates Venez loan 1-12, 332F1
US trade pact set 1-13, reactn 1-13, 1-16, 26E2-27E1
'77 trade surplus record set 1-20, 44A3
'77 $ drop rptd 1-23, 27D2
US $ strategy rptd 1-23, 27F2
EC imposes steel dumping levies 1-23, 80B2
NZ fishing, trade ties disputed 1-25—5-23; 200-mi limit in effect 4-1, accord reached 5-23, 497G3
US arms sales ceiling exempts 2-1, 106E2
China-EC 5-yr trade pact initialed 2-3, 102G2
US $ policy analyzed 2-6—3-6, 119A1, F1
US OKs computer sale to China 2-8, 111D2
UK auto export curbs barred; '77, Jan sales rptd 2-8, 112E2
US bars nuts, bolts import curbs, $ drop cited 2-10, 181A3
US steel trigger plan scored by Bethlehem 2-12, 158D1
'77 US steel imports rptd 2-14, 158E1
China pact signed 2-16, 103C3
Australian coal pacts rptd 2-20, 145E1
US steel-import minimum price ordrd 2-23, Carter overrrules 4-24, 444B1
US-Taiwan textile pact rptd 2-27, 140C3
US Steel drops dumping suit 3-1, 158B1
Australia coal pact price cut rptd 3-1, 165D2
EC seeks steel export agrmt 3-2, 158C2
Japan to curb UK car exports 3-3, 168A1
Fraser scores trade curbs 3-7, 265F2
Bank of Tokyo bars Peru loan refinancing 3-10, 353F1, B2
Trade surplus moves 3-11, 235A2
UK prime min urges Bonn summit plan 3-14, sees Carter 3-23, 226D3
Yen curbs announced 3-15, bank discount rate cut 3-16, 235E1
Australia iron, coal curbs barred 3-20, 208A3
$1 bln purchased 3-28; US aid halted, $ hits new low 4-3; total purchases rptd 4-2, 234F1, D3
US hikes CB radio tariffs, 3-28, 443E3
USSR '77 trade cited 3-29, 230A1
Yen in new SDR basket 4-3, 300F3
Bank of Tokyo in Chile loan 4-7, 312E1
Toyota hikes US car prices, $ drop cited 4-14, 283F2
Australia wool imports rptd down 4-14, 411A2
Fscl '77, Mar record trade, paymts surpluses rptd 4-15; surplus curbs set 4-17, 4-21, 314A1, E1
Australia trade talks rptd, commodity fund planned 4-23, 391C2
Fukuda in US, vows trade surplus cut, other commitmts 5-1—5-5, 341E2-C3
US '78 arms sales forecast 5-19, 387B1
Australian iron imports set 5-25, 411D1
US vs oil exports 5-26, 408F1
Zaire emergency aid OKd 6-13—6-14, 478A1
US residual fuel oil exports set 6-15, 470F3-471B1
US trade deficit poses pol problems for Fukuda 6-19, 695E1
US rebuffs Zenith on import duty 6-21, 491G2
US weighs oil import fee 6-22, 511A3
Greece halts imports 6-23, 631A2
Australia eased import curbs asked 6-27, iron contract revisns 7-4, 514G1
US bars stainless steel utensil tariff hike 7-2, 805G1
Australia coal strike halts exports 7-13, 555E1
US $ up vs yen 7-14, 523F2, B3
At 7-natn Bonn summit; export curbs, aid hikes vowed 7-16—7-17, 543C3, 544G1, F2, G2
US export curb pledge rptd 7-17, 544A2
Taiwan moves to cut trade surplus 7-17, 574E3
US car import prices hiked, drop cited 7-17, 665E1

1979

Government & Politics—*See also other appropriate subheads in this section*
LDP wins local electns 4-8, 324B1
House dissolved, electns set 9-7; LDP wins, margin reduced 10-7, 762B2
Ohira resigns formally 10-30; challenged by Fukuda 11-2, reelected 11-6, 844B3
Ohira names new Cabt 11-8, 874F2

Monetary, Trade, Aid & Investment—*See also 'Bribery' above*
Peru bank debt renegotiated 1-2, 22C3
'78 color-TV operatns in US up, exports down 1-9, 1-17, 160B2, F2
Taiwan trade rise cited 1-15, 27C3
Australia wheat deal rptd 1-22, 56F3
'78 record trade surplus rptd; US, EC deficit rise cited 1-24, 98G1-D2
US '78 trade gap rptd 1-30, 71E3
US $ value vs yen rptd 2-2, 2-8, 83C2
Carter warning re trade, Westn econ summit link rptd 2-10, rpt disputed 2-15; Ohira notes surplus cut 2-22, 160E1
Canada sets loan 2-14, 153E1
Iran oil cutoff impact assessed 2-15, 126D2
Fscl '78 trade surplus, US data rptd 2-18, 286E1
China cancels plant equipmt deals 2-26, 181D3
US Jan trade gap rptd 2-28, 159B2
El Salvador trade missn relocates in Panama 3-1, businessmen exit 3-9, 235E1
5% oil demand cut agreed 3-2, 162A1
US trade talks held, Blumenthal warns re imbalance; surplus data cited 3-4—3-5, 159F3-160D1
USSR '78 trade rptd 3-6, 172A2
Australia iron ore price rise set 3-6, 188E2
US $ defense rptd 3-7, 159D3
Australia coal prices cut 3-13, 233B2
UNCTAD commodity fund set 3-20, 200E2
US Feb trade gap rptd 3-28, 252A3
US halts trade talks 3-29, 229D3
Hungary loans cited 3-30, 279C3
Australia sets whaling ban 4-4, 284C2
Australia trade accord signed 4-6, 266A2
GATT pact signed ending Tokyo round, tariff cuts seen 4-12, 273A1, F1, B2, 274D1
US demands TV dumping paymt 4-13, Yamashita scores 4-26, 298F2
US lauds discount rate hike 4-16, 615E3
US Mar trade gap rptd 4-27, 325D2
Calif cargo container taxes voided by US 4-30, 364B3
W Ger ranks exporter labor costs 5-1, 374C2
Carter, Ohira meet re trade goals, NT&T dispute cited 5-2; US warned vs protectionism 5-3, 320F1, F2
Mitsubishi acquires Chrysler Australia share 5-14, 368F2
Eximbank gives China credit 5-15, 484G3
Honda-BL productn planned 5-17, 388B2
Iran cuts oil exports 15% 5-18, '78 imports cited 5-21, 389C2
US Apr trade gap rptd 5-30, 403B1
US sales pact signed 6-2, 416B1
Iran banks natlzd 6-7, compensatn vowed 6-10, 469A2
Mex steel, pipeline projct proposed; bank loan rptd 6-8, 487E3
China revives contracts 6-12, 484E3
Banks dominate world '78 top 300, yen rise cited 6-19, 476G1-C2
EC seeks imports rise 6-22, 476F1
US May trade gap rptd 6-27, 480G3
Oil import targets set at Tokyo summit 6-28—6-29, 493B1
Viet trade pact rptdly delayed 7-11; refugee aid set 7-13, waters shunned 7-15, 549F2
Whaling banned, Indian O sanctuary set 7-11, 554D2
Oil spot mkt agrmt rptd 7-16, 494F2
OECD sees paymts deficit 7-19, 554E3
US June trade gap rptd 7-29, 577B3
Australia iron strike ends 8-3, 666E3
Current acct drop seen, oil import cut urged 8-11—8-13, 615E2-B3
Gold rise, oil cutoff fears linked 8-22, 645B3
US steel co loan rptd 8-28, 682E1
US July trade gap rptd 8-28, 646C3
US car co deal set 9-7, 745D3
Mitsubishi to buy remaining Chrysler share 9-15, 699A2
IMF sees less paymts surplus 9-16, 720D1
EC ball bearing dumping probe opened 9-20, 719E2
US Aug trade gap rptd 9-27, 745E2
US Sept trade gap rptd 10-30, 828B2
1st 1/2 fscl '79 record paymts deficit rptd 10-30, 836G2
Australia 200-mi fishing zone effected 11-1, 832A2

1980

Government & Politics—*See also other appropriate subheads in this section*
Ex-gen, 2 offcrs arrested as spies 1-18, 60A1
Army chief quits in Sovt spy scandal, 10 penalized 1-28; Defns Agency barred intell data 1-31, defense head replaced 99C3
Parlt defense panel formed 4-7, 314C3
Ohira loses confidence vote 5-16; Diet dissolved, electns set 5-19, 380F3-381C1
Ohira in hosp 5-31, dies 6-12; Ito becomes acting premr 6-12, 434C3
LDP wins parlt electns 6-22, 499A1
Ohira mem'l svcs held 7-9, 506B1, D1
Suzuki elected LDP head 7-15, elected premr, names Cabt 7-17, 539F2-D3
Suzuki outlines admin goals 8-18, 635E2
Health min quits in scandal, Sonoda named 9-19, 752E1
Suzuki vs major defns buildup 9-25, 752B1
Monetary, Trade, Aid & Investment
World Bank capital increase OKd 1-4, 49G3-50A1
US Honda car plant set 1-11, 35F2
US asks Toyota, Nissan plants 1-13, 35C2
US asks Japan F-plane purchase 1-14, 31B2
Mex '80 oil imports seen 1-15, 60B2
Australia talks note resources, air fare cuts 1-16, Pacific orgn 1-20, 78E1-D2
Australia stocks make gains 1-18, 56C1
'79 record trade, paymts deficit rptd; US surplus at $9 bln; exports, imports, other data cited 1-23, 1-25, 1-29, 99E3-100B1
Sovt strategic sales curbed 1-25, 67D3
US '79 trade gap rptd 1-29, 77D2
Canada '79 exports up 2-2, 96B2
Nissan, Toyota US sales rptd up 2-5, 127B3
'79 US mfg investmt rptd 2-6, 92D3
Australia alumina plant consortium formed 2-8, 95G1
US car plants asked by UAW pres 2-11—2-14; govt urges action 2-12, Nissan, Toyota respond 2-18, 127B1
Mitsubishi to finance Chrysler imports 2-12, 127F2
Yen falls vs $; discount, reserve rates raised 2-18, 151E3
US $-yen exchng rate chart 2-18—3-20, 202A2, D2
USSR OKs steel deal delay 2-19, 235F3
US co trust suit vs Mitsui review declined 2-25, 188B1
US co indicted on TV rebates 2-26, 251G3
US Jan trade gap rptd 2-28, 167F3
Yen 5-pt rescue plan set; US, Swiss, W Ger role rptd 3-2, 173C2
Yen rebounds in heavy trading 3-3, 173B3
US' Connally 'basic speech' excerpts 3-7, 184B2
Australia wool needs cited 3-11, 191B1
US $ soars vs yen, central bank intervenes 3-17; profit-taking slows surge 3-19—3-20, 202E3
Discount rate hiked, controls tightened 3-18—3-19, Swiss swap currency 4-1; yen continues $ slide 4-8, 276A2
Australia wool strike setld 3-21, 229G2
Panama canal feasibility study agreed 3-25, 234B3
'79 USSR debt down 3-26, 235D3
US Feb trade gap rptd 3-27, 247D3
IMF hikes SDR interest rate 3-27, 302B2
Swiss currency swap effected 4-1, yen $ slide continues 4-8, 276A2
Mitsubishi to continue Chrysler import financing 4-1, 287C1
US group files unfair-trade complaint 4-4; rice accord set 4-12, 314G2
US asks Iran export ban 4-13, 281D2
Turkey aid OKd 4-15, 295A3
Fscl '79-80 trade deficit rptd 4-15, 314F3
Australia bars coal projct bid 4-15, 334F1
Iran oil talks fail 4-17, price hike barred 4-19; imports threatened, alternative supplies seen 4-20, 298D3
W Europn auto cos plan research 4-22, 303A3, C3
US sets typewriter duties 4-22, 368B1
Zaire debt rescheduled 4-23, 356G1
Iran sanctns imposed 4-24, 298B3
Iran oil supply substitutes rptd found 4-25; US offers aid 5-1, 341F1
US TV dumping case setld 4-28, US ct blocks 5-9, 368C1
US Mar trade gap rptd 4-29, 329A1
Mitsubishi buys Chrysler Australia unit 4-30, 350E1
Central banks rptd active in forgn exchng mkts 4-30, 436B3
Mex oil talks 5-2—5-4, 341G1
EC dumping chrgs cited 5-6, 412B1
Australia labor dispute spurs US coal purchases 5-7, 350C2
OPEC sets pricing plan 5-7—5-8, 364C3
US OKs TV import curbs end 5-13, 368A2
US concerned re auto imports 5-14, 384G1
US auto parts tariff to end 5-15, 482B1
US raises truck import duty 5-20, 384A2
Fiat layoff plans linked to competitn 5-20, 408E3
Toyota raises US car prices 2.8% 5-27, 482A1
US Apr trade gap rptd 5-28, 401D1
Mex oil-credit pact signed 5-28, 409C2*
US OKs yen futures trading 5-28, 481C2
SEAT investmt talks rptd 6-4, 467C3

1976

1977

Turkey exports barred 6-2, 451B2
Group of 10 membership cited 438F1
S Korea oil pact effected 6-8, 467G1
Jan-Mar exports rptd up 6-9, 467F1
US OKs exports 6-12, 460D1
1st ¼, June color TV exports rptd 6-14, 7-28, 587G1-B2
Australia trade data rptd 6-22, 504F2
In 11-natn Portugal loan 6-22, 530B3
IWC cuts whaling quotas 6-24, 496E3
US drops Alaska oil transport plan 6-24, 498A2, D2
ASEAN backs ties 6-27—6-29, 537E1
Rhodesia chrome imports chrgd 6-28, denied 6-29, 512C2
'76 trade surplus up 6-28, 586D1
Fukuda plans forgn reserves cut; cites imports, paymts study 6-29, 544D3
Australia sugar pact dispute 6-30—7-27, 578B3
UK natlizes shipbldg 7-1, 526D2
Yen value at 4-yr high 7-5, 544B3
Sumitomo buys US bank branches 7-6, 578E1; purchase challenged 8-9, 669B3 OKd 10-19, 97902
Zaire debt rescheduled 7-7, 583E1
US bars Alaska oil trade 7-10, 538B1
Australia imposes car import quotas 7-12, 560F3
US ends color TV probe, OKs consent pact 7-14, 587E1
GATT warns US re duties order 7-16, 587C1
Jan-June record trade surplus 7-19, 586C1
$ drops, US backs depreciatn 7-21, 552A1-G1
NZ scores farm import curbs 7-21, 638D2
Argentina cuts trade deficit 7-25, 614A3
EC drops ball-bearing duty 7-27, 624B3
$ drops 10% vs yen 7-28, 585E2
US warning on trade imbalance rptd 7-28, 586E1
US electronics import order reversed 7-28, 586D3
6-mo paymts surplus rptd 7-31, 586B2
US pact vs Rhodesia chrome rptd; '76 US imports cited 8-3, 662E1
Australia sugar talks fail again 8-4, 615C2
Fukuda sees ASEAN ldrs 8-6—8-7, 607A2
US trade deficit-reducing strategy rptd challenged 8-8, 585G1-586B1
Australia coal pact signed 8-8, 615E2
'76 China trade drops 8-11, 635F3
US press rpts steel tech superiority 8-13, govt aid, export growth 9-19, 775G3
Australia lifts uranium ban 8-25, 693B2
'75 EC steel trade curb pact cited 9-19, 775A2
'76 US steel export gain cited 9-19, 775C2
Australia warns on trade disputes 9-23, more beef imports agreed 10-28, 862A1
Econ growth policies, '76 poor natn aid level scored at IMF-World Bank mtg by US, IMF 9-26, 753F2-F3, 754G1
Australia beef import plan rejctd 9-26, 800C3
Japan indl ldrs score Canada econ, prefer US 9-27, 780F2
Zenith to buy stereo equipmt 9-27, 974D2
Australia state files sugar suit 9-28, 800E2
US Steel files dumping chrgs 9-30; Gilmore chrgs upheld 10-3, 774B3, 775A1
Forgn trade pressures noted 10-3, 783B2
US steel mktg pact terms set 10-4, EC asks talks 10-11, 775D1
US wage-price panel on competitive edge 10-7, 776B2, D2
EC min vs US steel trade curbs 10-11, 775F1
'76 car export lead, rising US mkt share rptd 10-11, 853G2
Sakhalin oil find announced 10-12, 853E3
Sept, Oct trade surplus rptd up 10-17, 11-15, 884F3
$ falls vs yen 10-17, 11-15, 884G3, 885B1
$ drops 10-18; US bars support, trade impact cited 10-19, 792D2
Canada chrgs steel dumping 10-18, 862G3
US Steel, Armco dumping chrgs probed 10-19, 11-22, 933F2, B3
1st ½ fscl export rise rptd, US '75-77 trade deficit up 10-20, 792B3
Australia sugar pact set 10-26, 839G2-B3
Oct forgn reserves rptd up 11-1, 885C1
1st in China forgn trade 11-7, 882D3
US trade talks 11-17—11-21, press scores US demands 11-23; Ushiba comments 12-8, 931A2
Yen curbs set 11-17, effected 11-21, 932G2
Toyota, Honda hike US prices 11-24, 932F3
'76 oil-use rise rptd 11-24, 999C1
New Cabt installed 11-28; econ task force formed, US setlmt sought 11-29, 932F1-D2
'78 trade surplus drop forecast, oil imports cited 11-29, 932E2
GATT assured on trade surplus, US lauds 11-29, 933C2
'77 yen rise vs $ rptd 11-30, 932E3
Chrysler unveils front-drive cars 12-5—12-9, 962C1
US offers trigger price plan for steel imports 12-6, 931B3
Whale kill quotas raised 12-6, 12-7, 936B3

1978

Jan-June record trade surplus 7-19; countermeasures urged 7-21, 574F2
$ falls below 200 yen 7-24, drops further 8-15, 622D1
US June, 6-mo trade deficit rptd 7-26, 607C1
USSR rptd leading Far East shipper 8-1, 670D3
China peace pact signed, econ exchngs urged 8-12, 637B1
Comecon loan rptd 8-17, 660E3
UK co sets joint plant 8-23, 667C3
US fiscal policies scored 8-28, 695B2
US July, 7-mo trade deficit rptd 8-29, 680E1
Yen rise, 2d ¼ growth lag linked 9-3, 694A1
Import stimulus measures proposed 9-3, 694C1
US imports sought, missn to Japan set 9-4, 694E2
US trade talks fail; beef, citrus quotas at issue 9-5—9-7, '77 data cited 694D3
China trade ties pressed 9-6, 695C2
Export boom rptd slowing, Apr-June data cited; yen revaluatn linked 9-8, 694G1
US vs Alaska oil exports 9-12, 702D1
Aug auto, ship exports drop 9-13, 694D2
Import markups rptd high 9-18, 694A3
IMF asks growth rate hike 9-25, US backs 9-26, 731B3
US sets '79 arms sales lid 9-26, 734A2, E2
Trade % of GNP rptd 9-26, 804D2
US Aug trade gap rptd 9-27, 752A2
Australia iron ore imports rptd down 9-29, 754E2
9-mo US $ loss vs yen rptd 10-2, 732F1
US trade missn starts 10-2, partial success seen 10-15, 797C3-798C1
June '77-78 US $ drop rptd 10-4, 790F1
USSR color TV deal rptd 10-5, 820F3
Toyota, Datsun US prices hiked, $ drop linked 10-8, 10-29; Nov sales rptd down 12-6, 935F3
8 forgn trade missns visit, S Korea group arrives 10-15, 798C1
China pact implemented 10-23, 801B1, D2
Mitsubishi to buy Australia Chrysler share 10-25, 836B2
Brazil steel loan set 10-25, 837A1
US Sept trade gap rptd 10-26, 804D3
Mex pres in oil loan, tourism pacts 10-30—11-4; Mex oil shipmt arrives 11-5, 903D3
US $ hits record low 10-31; rescue set 11-1, $ recovers 11-2, 825B1, G1, E2, 826A1
Iran oil strike cuts exports 10-31, 827D2; shortage rptd 11-7, 858D2
US shipping malpractice bill vetoed 11-4, 897G2
IMF lends US yen 11-7, 998C3
Australia reserves rptd up, loans cited 11-21, 944E1
Sovt-bloc debt rptd 11-21, 999G1
Australia issues bonds 11-24, 944F1
Ohira backs regional econ expansn 11-28, 912E3
China, Japan business offices set 11-28—11-29, 986F2
US Oct trade gap rptd less 11-29, 918D3
China steel mill set 12-5, 986D2
US citrus, beef pact signed 12-5, 988D2
Australia-US coal deal rptd 12-11, 963D2
West vs lower growth rate target 12-11, 988B2
Australia investmts rise seen 12-13, 985B2
OPEC $ use seen as aid 12-17, 977F3
OPEC price hike long-term impact seen 12-18, 978G3-A2
GATT accord with US 12-18, 998B1
US trade deficit rptd 12-18, 1003A3
Mex '79 oil price hike set 12-20, 978F2
US $ closes down vs yen 12-29, 998E2

1979

Yen drop, fscl '79 6-mo trade deficit spur discount rate hike 11-1, 836E2
Swiss hike lending fees 11-2, 875F3
Iran oil export cut confrmd 11-8, 843G1
Iran oil use data rptd 11-12, 861E2
Iran excess oil import curb seen 11-15, Ohira warns 11-16, 879G2-A3
US hikes steel trigger price, yen drop linked 11-20, 965G3
Iran bars US $ oil paymts 11-23, 896D3
US $ hits high vs yen 11-27, closes down 12-31, 978E3
Forgn exchng controls adopted 11-27, 12-3, 12-5; yen value rises vs $ 12-28, 996B2
Oil import costs, current acct deficit linked 11-27, 996F2
Iran loan repaymt rptd 11-28, 896G2
US Oct trade gap rptd 11-29, 922C1
Zaire emergency aid OKd 11-29, 999D1
Taiwan Jan–Oct trade rptd 12-4, 952F3
Ohira visits China, pacts signed 12-5–12-7, 939C3
US Steel aid rptd 12-5, 941C3
US seeks econ sanctns vs Iran 12-10, Ohira defends oil buys 12-11, 933C2
'79 auto productn record seen 12-12, 963E3
Auto exports rptd up 12-12, 963E3
2 Iranian loans retained, oil dependnc cited 12-12, 976G1-A2
Iran oil imports to be cut 12-14, 958D3
USSR steel pact signed by Nippon, US co, Eximbank funding cited 12-17, 997C2
BL-Honda accord signed 12-27, 994E1
US Nov trade gap rptd 12-28, 984G3

1980

US auto union asks import curbs, '75-79 exports to US, Eur cited 6-12, 457G2, A3
7-natn Venice summit 6-22—6-23, 473A1-474E1
US May trade gap rptd 6-27, 492A3
US lifts TV import curbs 6-30, 515C3
US unions, Ford ask auto import curbs 7-1, 8-4; Carter seeks ruling 7-8, 505B1, 599C1
Nissan fears US productn tariff rise 7-1, 7-29, 599G1, B2
US rptd surpassed as top auto maker 7-7, 541E3
Carter rptd grateful for Iran sanctns support 7-8, 506E1
Ford-Toyota productn talks revealed 7-9; Ford rejectn rptd 7-14, 556G2-A3
Reagan seeks US car co aid 7-12, 535D1
US blocks auto import probe speedup 7-18, 556G1-B2, 599F1
US June trade gap rptd 7-29, 574A3
US-W Ger synfuel pact signed 7-31, 666D2
Canada auto, trade talks held; US role cited 8-2—8-11, 618G1
US July auto sales rptd 8-5, 599A1
Discount rate cut 8-19, 672C1
Canada oil co loan set 8-23, 651C1
US July trade gap rptd 8-27, 666B2
Pak aid pkg signed, refugee funds pledged 9-1, 686F1
Reagan vows auto import curbs 9-2, 664F2
Australia coal strike ends 9-4, 705C2
Nicaragua debt rescheduled 9-5, 689G2-A3
US record oil inventories rptd 9-5, Admin assured vs shortfall 10-3, 785E3
IMF revises SDR valuatn method, yen gains in currency 'basket' 9-17, 695E1
UN protests Franco-Sovt steel deal 9-19, 728D3
Alfa Romeo, Nissan project OKd 9-20, 751B3
World Bank '80 loans rptd 9-22, 720F1
US Aug trade gap rptd 9-26, 741A2
Suzuki backs liberalized trade 9-26, 967A1
Carter unveils steel indus aid plan 9-30, 740C3
Canada Aug imports rptd down 10-4, 788A2
US tightens work visas 10-6, 870A2
SEAT-Toyota talks rptd 10-8, 793A3*
US auto import hearings held 10-8—10-10, 823E1
Forgn currency lending limit eased 10-16, 967A1
US trade talks resume 10-19, 864A3
US Sept trade gap rptd 10-29, 824G1
Grain imports dependence cited 10-29, 855G1
US $ drops vs yen with Reagan pres electn, bank lending rate cut cited 11-5, 845B1
ITC bars US auto import curbs 11-10, 866D3
US steel-import trigger price hiked 11-18, 884A3
Oct trade gap widens on oil costs, Sept data rptd 11-18, 902B1
Iraq oil shipmts set 11-20, 894C2
US tobacco tariffs eased 11-21, 902E1
Panama Canal clogged by oil, grain, coal imports 11-24, 895D3
US Oct trade gap rptd 11-28, 916A2
Taiwan trade talks fail, '81 missn set 11-28, 967C1
Forgn investmt, currency holding rules eased 12-1, 966D3
VW, Nissan project planned 12-3, 924D3
US auto import curb res dies in Cong 12-4, 982B3
US $ gains on yen 12-10, 932F1
Swiss bank buys W Ger dept store interest 12-12, 969F1
Telecommunicatns equipmt pact signed 12-19, 995B2
US Nov trade gap rptd 12-30, 984A2
Yen up 15% vs US in '80 12-31, 983F2

1976

Obituaries
Fuchida, Mitsuo 5-30, 524E2
Fukuda, Taro 6-10, 450D3
Shimada, Shigetaro 6-7, 524E3

Soviet Relations
Peace talks stalled re Kurile 1-10—1-13, 29F3
USSR frees 23 fishermen 1-19, 52C1
Brezhnev stresses ties 2-24, 194C1
Sovt CP Cong boycotted 2-24—3-5, 195B3
Polyansky named amb 4-17, 314B1
'75 Sovt trade rptd 5-5, 340B3, D3
Sovt rptr chrgd as spy on US fleet, US aids probe 5-12—5-14, 356E1
Alleged spy freed, USSR warned 5-22, 373B2
Japan ratifies A-pact 5-24, deposits documents 6-9, 419C1
USSR ends shipping rate war 7-19, 558E3
MiG-25 pilot defects, asks US asylum 9-6; USSR chrgs US-Japan plot 9-14, 695D3-696D1
Chrgs traded in MiG-25 incident 9-9, 9-20, 10-5; talks begin 10-12, USSR scores 10-25, 839F2
Australia see Sovt oil threat 11-4, 850B2
USSR sales stir NATO concern 11-4, 880B1
Japan returns MiG-25 11-12, USSR frees 7 fishermen 11-18, 908D1

Sports
Olympic results 7-18—7-31, 573C3, 574B3-575B1, 576C2-D3

UN Policy & Developments
Cncl member 62F2; 720C1
Asks broad Mideast resolutn 1-14, 18C2
OKs pro-Palestine resolutn 1-26, 59G2
ILO rpts jobless up 3-13, 297E3
Abstains on Cncl S Africa censure 3-31, 228B2
Abstains on Timor resolutn 4-22, 334F3
Vs WHO rejectn of Israel rpt 5-17, 355F1
UNCTAD OKs commodity fund 5-30, 388G2
OKs Israel Arab land exit 6-29, 464C1
Backs anti-terror resolutn 7-14, 515G3
Abstains on S Africa arms ban 10-19, 781D3

U.S. Relations—*See also 'Foreign Economic Developments' and 'Lockheed Bribe Scandal'*
Norwegian freighter search suspended 1-16, 79E3
LDP to revise constitutn 1-18, 51C3
Ford State of Union message 1-19, 38A3
Joint defns com planned 1-19, 51F2
Kissinger backs Sovt confrontatn 1-29, 88F3
US aids Sovt spy probe 5-12—5-14, 356B2
Alleged Sovt spy freed 5-22, 373B2
Japan ratifies A-pact 5-24, deposits documents 6-9, 419C1
Dem platform text cites ties 6-15, 477B1, 478B1, C2, D2
Carter urges partnership, lauds achievements 6-23, 451F2, A3, D3
Ship in US Bicentennial event 7-4, 488A3-D3
Japan warns vs China concessns 7-12, 555E2
Japan newsman's '74 acquittal reversed 7-20, 539F1
GOP platform text cites ties 8-18, 609C2, 611B3
Ford conv acceptance speech cites 8-19, 612B1
Sovt MiG-25 pilot defects, asks US asylum 9-6; USSR chrgs Japan-US plot 9-14, 695D3-696D1
Ford, Carter debate 10-6, 740D3, 741E3
Dole queried on WWII 10-25, 804C2
Tokyo Rose seeks US pardon 11-17, 892C2

1977

Hitachi-GE TV venture rptd 12-7, 974B2
$ closes up vs yen 12-8, 933D1
US TV plant planned by Toshiba 12-14, 974A2
US trade talks end, Japan backs higher econ growth, deficit financing, tariff cuts 12-15; US reactn 12-15, 12-16, 973G2-974A2
Trade, paymts surpluses cited; US scores re paymts 12-15, 974E1-A2
$ at record low 12-15, rallies 12-30, 997F2
Nov trade surplus $1.03 bln, US exports up 12-16, 985D1
Surplus cut vowed 12-19, 984E3

Obituaries
Eda, Saburo 5-22, 452G2
Kido, Kiochi 4-6, 356C3
Maeda, Seison 10-27, 872E2
Murayama, Nagataka 8-7, 696D3

Sports
Oh breaks HR record 9-3, awarded Medal of Honor 9-5, 748E2
US Cosmos beat all-star soccer team, attendance record set 9-14, 827G2

Terrorism & Unrest
Rightists seize hostages 3-3—3-4, 201F2
Tokyo airport riot 5-7—5-8, 411E2
Facts on Red Army 756F3
Red Army gunmen hijack jet to Bangladesh 9-28; demands met 10-1, surrender in Algiers 10-3; 2 Cabt mins quit 10-4; Algeria bars extraditn 10-5, 756G2, A3 ★
Govt plans anti-terrorism measures 10-4, bars air piracy ransom 10-8, 801E3-G3
Red Army outlines aims 10-4, 902A3
Police raid leftist hq, seize documts 10-12, 801G3

UN Policy & Developments
UN Assemb member; Oda on World Ct 4B1, G1
US backs permanent Cncl seat 3-21, 209C3
UN plea on Indochina refugees studied 8-25, 685G2

U.S. Relations—*See also 'Atomic Energy', 'Bribery Scandals' and 'Monetary Trade & Aid' above*
Mondale visit announced 1-8, 14E2
Concern re US Korea pullout cited 1-18, 60C2
Ford pardons Tokyo Rose 1-19, 36B2
Mondale visits 1-31, 69D1-70B1
Rightists protest US security treaty 3-3—3-4, 201A3
US plans S Korea pullout 3-9, 202E3
Fukuda sees Carter, communique issued 3-21—3-22, 209E2
Carter energy plan 4-18, 294E3; reactn 4-21, 320F3
Mansfield confrmd amb 4-21, 418G1
Carter sees Fukuda 5-7, 358F1
US plot vs Hussein chrgd 5-8, 360C3
US Okinawa land rights extended 5-18, 411G1-B2
S Korea troop exit rptd set 6-5, 440F3
US briefs on ROK troop exit plan 7-27, 572A2
US stresses US-Taiwan ties 8-19, 645D2
US plea on Indochina refugees studied 8-25, 685G2
Vance briefs on China trip 8-26, 664E2
US Cosmos beat all-star soccer team 9-14, 827G2
Red Army vs US 'imperialism' 10-4, 802C1

1978

Obituaries
Hamada, Shoji 1-5, 96C2
Hoshino, Naoki 5-29, 440G2
Katayama, Tetsu 5-30, 440A3

Sports
Suntory Cup results 4-23, 418B3
Oh hits 800th homer 8-30, 780A1
Pacific Club Masters results 10-8, Dunlop Phoenix 11-26, 990A2, D2
World Gym Championships 10-23—10-29, 928B3
Tokyo Intl tourn results 11-5, 1027C2

UN Policy & Developments
Sea Law Conf talks continue 5-23—7-15, 8-21—9-16, 732E3
At ILO conf 6-7—6-28, $1 mln pledge rptd 6-14, 524A1
ILO rpts '77 jobless rise 7-27, 677D1
Assemb member 713G3

U.S. Relations—*See also 'Atomic Energy', 'Bribery' and 'Monetary, Trade, Aid & Investment' above*
US troop presence rptd 1-2, 5D2
US '77 rpt warns vs extensive troop cuts 1-6, 5E3
US alerts to Sovt satellite fall 57E1
US, Japan mediate release of Korean jet passengers in USSR 4-20—4-23, 302F1
Mitsubishi unit indicted 5-9, 404B2
Brzezinski visits, briefs on China talks 5-23—5-24, 384B3
US links '74 demonstratns, KCIA 6-6, 433D1
China-Japan pact lauded 8-12, 637F2
Seabed mining bill debated at UN conf 8-21—9-16, 732E3
WWII secret documts issued 9-10—9-18, 744D2-G3
US activist visa denial backed by ct 10-4, 764F3
China lauds US-Japan treaty 10-23, 802A1
Defns Secy Brown arrives 11-8, Japan to pay more for US forces 11-9, 872D3
Shippers settle US rebate chrgs 11-8, 961F3
USSR Pacific buildup rptd 11-9, 914G1
Ohira backs US ties 11-28, 912E3
US sen questns US-China tie 12-15, 976B1
Ohira rptd informed re US-China tie 12-16, 977D1

1979

Obituaries
Tomonaga, Shinichero 7-8, 588E3

Sports
WBA featherwgt title bout 1-9, 79C3
East wins Japan Bowl 1-14, 63C2
Boxing title bouts 1-29, 3-14, 4-18, 412C3-F3
World Cup wrestling results 4-1, 507G3
Oh hits 814th home run 5-20
World Invitatn tennis results 5-20, 570C2
Toray Sillock tennis results 9-16, 734E2
World Gym Championships results 10-5—10-9, 1005C2
Hiroshima wins baseball title 11-4, 1002G1
Tokyo World Tennis Singles results 11-4, 1003F3
Wins US-Japan golf team title 11-11, 970B2

UN Policy & Developments
UNCTAD commodity fund set 3-20, 200E2
Indochina refugee conf asked 6-28, 473E2
Refugee High Comr aid hike OKd 7-2, 495E2
Membership listed 695F2
Cambodia relief aid pledged 11-5, 863C3

U.S. Relations—*See also 'Atomic', 'Bribery' and 'Monetary' above*
US sees Asia stability re China tie 1-15, 27C2
WWII secret files released 2-3, 2-6, 93F1
Student enrollmt in US rptd 167D2
Blumenthal visits 3-4—3-5, 159F3-160D1
Ohira in US 5-2—5-3; energy research pact signed 5-2, 320F1-B3
Asian Society, NYC museum get Japan gifts 5-4, 375A2
US-China direct mail svc set 5-25, 406B1
Carter addresses Cong on SALT II 6-18, 459E2
Carter visits, sees Ohira 6-24—6-27, 494D1
Carter energy plan assessed 7-16, 534E3, 535A1
Mondale briefs Ohira on China talks 9-3, 660B3
Nixon sees closer China ties 9-22, 751C1
US rpts Sovt Kurile buildup 9-26, 742C1
USSR vs US defns secy's visit 10-16, 803E3
US defns secy visits, Sovt moves in Kuriles discussed 10-20, 803C3
USSR newsman flies to US after defectn 10-24, 856D3
US asks calm in S Korea crisis 10-27, 822F1
Vance sees Okita, seeks sanctns vs Iran 12-10, 933C2
US assured on pressure vs Iran 12-17—12-18, 958D3-959C1

1980

Soviet-Afghan Issue
Afghan invasn opposed 1-5, 2E2
Sovt strategic sales curbed 1-25, 67D3
Persian Gulf defense steps seen 1-29, 65B1
Olympic boycott movemt joined 2-1, 84G3
USSR OKs steel deal delay 2-19, 235F3
US urges sanctions vs Sovts 3-12, 205E1
Parlt defense panel formed 4-7, 314C3
Olympic boycott stand reaffirmed 4-15, 283B3
Moscow May Day parade shunned 5-1, 354G2
Olympic com OKs boycott, absence effect seen 5-24, 421A1, D1
7-natn Venice summit seeks total Sovt exit 6-22, 473B1
Carter rptd grateful for Olympic boycott 7-8, 506E1
Moscow Olympics boycotted 7-19—8-3, 587F3, 588E2

Sports
West wins Japan Bowl 1-13, 62C2
Moscow Olympic boycott movt joined 2-1, 2-1, 84G3
Lake Placid Olympic results 2-12—2-24, 154F2, 155F2-156D1
Tokyo Invitatnl tennis results 4-13, 607B3
Olympic boycott stand reaffirmed 4-15, 283B3
Olympic com OKs boycott, absence effect seen 5-24, 421A1, D1
Harimoto gets 3000th hit 5-31, 637D1
Carter rptd grateful for Moscow Olympic boycott 7-8, 506E1
Moscow Olympics boycotted 7-19—8-3, 587F3, 588E2
US-Japan, other golf tourn results 9-7, 11-2, 11-9, 972G1, F2
Nakajima loses WBC jr flywgt challenge 9-17, 1001A1

UN Policy & Developments
Cncl seat won 11-13, 896E1

U.S. Relations—*See also 'Monetary', 'Soviet-Afghan Issue' above*
Brown sees Ohira, urges defns spending hike 1-14, 31F1
USSR defector linked to Japan spy arrests 1-18, 60C1
2 USSR dancers defect to US 2-6, 88D1
Japan joins Pacific naval games 2-26, 151C3
Japanese cars fail US crash tests 2-28, 225E2
Carter anti-inflatn plan praised 3-15, 202F2
Mil talks held in DC 3-20, 3-21, Ohira seeks more US troop support 3-24, 219F2
Iran crisis support asked 4-8, 257D2
US support on Iran withheld 4-11, 281G2, 282C1
Iran asks neutrality on US hostages 4-11; amb sees Bani-Sadr, pleads for release 4-12, 282E1
US asks Iran pol sanctns 4-13, 281D2
Iranian oil stance lauded 4-17, 299A1
Ohira in DC, meets Carter; sci pact signed, Iran crisis noted 5-1, 341B1
Army cuts overseas duty time 6-6, 458A3
Japan panel urges arms spending hike 7-2, 539D3
Carter at Ohira rites 7-9, 506B1, D1
US calls defns hike too small 8-1, 579E2
Iran parlt ldr rebuffs hostage plea 8-17, 634D3
Suzuki pledges bigger defense effort 8-18, 635F2
Bush in Tokyo, sees Suzuki 8-19, 646A1
'Shogun' aired in US 9-15—9-19, top ratings rptd 9-24, 835F2
US plan for intl force to protect Gulf oil opposed 9-26, 735E2
US tightens work visas 10-6, 870C1-B2
US scientific literacy lag rptd 10-22, 990C1
Reagan aide quits post 10-30, 817G3
Defns Secy Brown visits; asks defns outlay hike, cites Sovt threat 12-11—12-12, 952G3-953C1
Haig apptmt praised 12-17, 955E2

1976

JAPANESE-American Citizens League
Tokyo Rose seeks pardon 11-17, 892C2
JARMAN, Rep. John (R, Okla.)
Edwards wins seat 11-2, 822G2
JAROSZEWICZ, Piotr
Renamed State Cncl pres 3-25, 268C2
Drops food price hikes 6-25; CP rallies back 6-26—6-28, 482B2, A3
In UK, signs econ pact 12-15—12-17, 966D1
JARRIN, Col. Bolivar
Ecuador Govt min 6-12, 693C1
JARROT, Andre
Dropped from French govt 1-12, 49E2
JARUZELSKI, Wojciech
Polish defense min 3-27, 268A3
JASCALEVICH, Dr. Mario E.
Indicted for murder 5-19, 384A3
JASINOWSKI, Jerry
Carter transition aide 11-23, 881B3
JAVED, Dr. Arshad
On Quinlan treatmt 6-3, 423E2
JAVITS, Sen. Jacob Koppel (R, N.Y.)
Panama visit rptd 1-11, 52F2
In Mex talks 1-26, 75F1
Wife quits Iran Air post 1-27, 160G1
Asks cruise missile test halt 2-25, 183D1
Releases desegregatn data 6-19, 992C3
Urges wider gene research rules 7-19, 860C3
Aide killed in hijack try 8-11, 578B3
GOP conv speech disrupted 8-18, 598E1
Asks Butz dismissal 10-1, 744E1
Scores Carter tactics 10-11, 763F2
JAVITS, Marion (Mrs. Jacob Koppel)
Quits Iran Air post 1-27, 160G1
JAWORSKI, Leon
Dem conv pres vote, table 7-14, 507E2, E3
Right & Power on best-seller list 12-5, 972B2
JAWS (film)
'75 top rental film 1-7, 32F3
Score wins Grammy 2-28, 460A3
Williams wins Oscar 3-29, 240A3
JAYCEES (Junior Chamber of Commerce of the U.S.)
Ford addresses at White House 9-17, 704C1
JEAKI Cho
Wins Olympic medal 7-31, 575B1
JEANMAIRE, Jean-Louis
Arrested for spying 8-16, 640A1
Accused as Sovt spy 11-10, 1011B3
JEBRIL, Ahmed
Barred from PLO meeting 11-26, 894B1
JEFFERSON, Thomas (1743-1826)
Quoted at Dem conv 7-12, 508G1
JEFFERSON Mortgage Corp.
Sued 4-15, 285G1
JEFFORDS, Rep. James M. (R, Vt.)
Reelected 11-2, 821E3, 830F4
JEFFREY, Mildred
Asks delegate selectn study 5-27, 413G3
JEFFREY Associates, Alan
Statistics Canada probe cites 11-3, 870B3-D3
JEHOVAH'S Witnesses
WCC chrgs Malawi persecutn 6-14, 497E3
JENKINS, Clive
TUC ldrs back pay curbs 6-16, 439E3
JENKINS, Edgar L.
Elected 11-2, 822E1, 829D2
JENKINS, Roy
Bids for prime min 3-17, withdraws 3-25, 239G1
Retains Cabt post 4-8, 266D3
Meets Southall ldrs on racism 6-8, 482D1
Riot probe asked 8-31, 651E2
Quits Cabt for Eur Comm 9-10, 693C3
Meets Europn Comm 12-22—12-23, 977E1
JENKINS, Thomas J.
FBI probe rptd 3-21, 248G1
Retirement announced 8-11, 634B1
JENKINSON, Noel
Dies in UK jail 10-9, 774A1
JENNER, Bruce
Wins Olympic medal 7-30, 576C1

1977

JAPAN, Sea of
USSR sets 200-mi limit 3-1, 147E1
JAPAN Air Lines
Boeing kickback chrgd 2-14, probed 2-15, 136D1
Plane crashes in Malaysia 9-27, 808B1
Jet hijacked 9-28, surrendered 10-3, 756G2
JAPANESE Americans
Calif bank branch bias chrgd 8-9, 669B3
Sumitomo affirmative actn OKd 10-19, 979D2
JAPAN Lines Inc.
Burmah paymts to Park cited 1-19, 55B2
JARA, Enrique
Arrested 4-14, freed 4-23, 345B3
JAROSLAWICZ, Pinchos
Body found 9-28, 871B3
JAROSZEWICZ, Piotr (Polish premier)
Ousts dep premr, 2 mins 12-17, 987F1
JARRIER, Jean-Pierre
2d in Le Mans 6-12, 531B2
JARRIN, Col. Bolivar
Resignatn asked in striker deaths 10-25, 823B3
JATTI, Basappa Danappa (Indian president; replaced July 21)
Named India pres 2-11, 116A1
Reads Desai Parlt speech 3-28, 240C1
9 state assembs dissolved 4-30, 348F1 ★
CDP joins Janata Party 5-1, 348D2 ★
Reddy succeeds as India pres 7-21, 637A3
JAUSOVEC, Mima
To be in Va Slims tourn 3-27, 431D1
Wins French Open 6-5, 548B2
JAVITS, Sen. Jacob Koppel (R, N.Y.)
On Sovt mil aims estimate 1-18, 40A1
Backs pot decriminalizatn 3-14, 332B2
Lauds tax rebate plan withdrawal 4-14, 270E3
On Nixon Watergate interview 5-5, 367E3
US reply on anti-terror moves rptd 5-8, 380D1
Carter authrzd to halt shipmts to Cuba 5-11, 389E3
Vs US Mideast peace plan 6-27, 495B3, E3
In Israel, sees Begin 509E1
Queries Lance 9-17, 718G2
Energy tax bill clears Sen 10-31, 832E2
Warns Baker vs Canal pact divsn 11-13, 912F1
Seeks Shcharansky release 11-17, 955B2
JAWORSKI, Leon A.
On Nixon-Frost interview 5-16, 367C3
Law firm on 5 largest list 5-16, 383A2
House Korea probe role OKd 7-20, 7-21, 556E1, G1, F2
Opens House Korea probe 10-19, 816B2
House asks Korea aid probe 10-31, 915D1
Park immunity oppositn rptd 11-5, 915F2
Scores Park testimony deal 12-30, 1002C3
JAWS (film)
Star Wars tops rental mark 11-19, 1021B3
JAY, Peter
US amb apptmt scored 5-11, 391F3
JAYEWARDENE, Junius Richard (Sri Lankan president)
Party wins electns 7-21, sworn prime min 7-23, 571C3
Asks Tamils drop secession 8-18, 658A1
Says riots 'under control' 8-23, 657D3
In peace plea 8-29, 674D1
Pres system set 10-5, 10-20, 843D3
JAZZ—*See MUSIC*
JEANMAIRE, Gen. Jean-Louis
Admits spying 6-14, sentncd 6-17, 489C2
Panel reviews case 10-27, 904B3
JEANMAIRE, Marie-Louise
Acquitted 6-17, 489D2
JEBRIL, Capt. Ahmed
Factions clash 2-10—2-11, 106F2
Rival groups clash 4-13, 266C3
JEHOVAH'S Witnesses
Nathan Knorr dies 6-15, 532C3
JENAN, Maj. Ali
Assassinatn rptd 10-14, 824F1
JENKINS, Ferguson
Traded to Rangers 12-14, 990G1
JENKINS, Roy
Eur Comm posts set 1-7, 74G1
Mondale visits 1-24, 70C1
Wins no-confidence vote 3-23, 269E1-A2
Conservative wins seat 3-31, 239A3
7-natn summit role disputed 5-7—5-8, 358F1
Scores Chile rights abuse 9-7, 743B2
Sees Spain oppositn ldr 9-23, premr 11-4, 867A2, B2

1978

JAPAN Air Lines
Nakasone cited in Lockheed case 10-26, 838G3
JARAMILLO Salazar, Alfonso
Named Colombia health min 8-7, 629D3
JAROSLAWICZ, Pinchos (d. 1977)
Killers convicted 10-6, 824E2
JARREAU, Al
Wins Grammy 2-24, 315F3
JARRIN, Gen. Bolivar
Ecuador junta dismisses 12-20, 1021B3
JARVIS, Howard A.
Property-tax-cut amendmt OKd 6-6; reactn 6-7—6-8, 425A1-426F1
Spearheads natl tax-cut movemt 8-17, new group formed 8-21, TV message aired 9-26, 735A3
Vs public works bill 10-5, 765C1
JARVIS-Gann Amendment (Proposition 13)—*See TAXES—Reform & Tax Cut Proposals*
JASCALEVICH, Dr. Mario E.
Curare murder case press freedom controversy 6-30—8-30, 678D2
Acquitted in curare murder case 10-24, 841F1-B2
Farber wins release, NY Times fine ended 10-24, 841C2
NY Times press freedom case declined by Sup Ct 11-27, 937F1
JAUSOVEC, Mima
Wins German championship 5-21, 419D1
Loses French Open 6-11, 540E1
JAUSSAUD, Jean-Pierre
Wins LeMans 6-11, 538G2
JAVITS, Sen. Jacob Koppel (R, N.Y.)
Scores Sen Banking Com rpt on NYC 2-9, 87D1
Votes for Panama Canal neutrality pact 3-16, 177E2
Votes for 2d Canal pact 4-18, 273B1
Introduces NYC aid bill 4-25, 608A3
Vs Mideast jet package 5-15, 357E1
Backs CIA evidence on Cuba role in Zaire 6-9, 442E2
Vs Israel W Bank, Gaza stand; scores Sadat 6-21, 461C2
Upholds legislative vetoes 6-21, 466B2
Sen votes conditnl end to Rhodesia sanctns 7-26, 588F1
Visits USSR 11-11—11-18, 905A2
On new China policy 12-15, 976B1
JAWORSKI, Leon
US House incumbents seen implicated in Korean scandal 1-20, 63A2
Asks House res on Korea probe cooperatn 1-20, 64B1
Seeks testimony from Koreans 3-9, 203F3
Disputes Park, Dore testimony 4-3, 4-5, 239F2, D3
Vs House com res on Korea 5-24, 406C2
Quits Korea probe 8-2, evaluates results 8-7, 604D3
JAWS 2 (book)
On best-seller list 6-4, 460C3; 7-2, 579D3; 8-6, 620C2
Record movie price for Benchley book rptd 9-1, 759E2
JAWS 2 (film)
Released 6-16, 619E2
Top-grossing film 7-6, 579F3; 7-26, 620E1
Star Wars world rental mark rptd 8-2, 672B1
Record movie price for Benchley book rptd 9-1, 759E2
JAYEWARDENE, Junius Richard (Sri Lankan president)
Becomes pres 2-3, 92E3
Renames mins 2-6, 116C1
Bans strikes 10-2, 758C2
JEAN d'Aire (sculpture)
Stolen 2-20, 335C1
JEBRIL, Ahmed
PLO rivalry chrgd, denied 8-14, 638A1
JEFFERSON, John
In NFL draft 5-2, 336F2
JEFFORDS, Rep. James M. (R, Vt.)
Unopposed in Vt primary 9-12, 716E2
Reelected 11-7, 848A1, 852C3
JEFFRIES, Jim
Wins US House seat 11-7, 850D4, 854F2
JEHOVAH'S Witnesses
15 rptd arrested in Argentina 2-19, 208D1
Argentina arrests 90 3-21, 3-29, 286D1
Malawi pres backs ouster 6-30, 534G3
JEIDY, Ron
Iowa wins NCAA wrestling title 3-18, 379G2
JEMISON, Greg
Traded to Yankees 11-10, 1026C1
JENKINS, Rep. Edgar Lanier (D, Ga.)
Reelected 11-7, 850B3
JENKINS, Louis (Woody)
Loses Sen primary in La 9-16, 736E3
JENKINS, Roy
Sees Caramanlis on EC entry 1-26, 149C2
On EC econ policy shift 4-7—4-8, 257C3
Visits Spain, sees king 4-27—4-28, 395D1
Hails EC monetary proposal, '77 plan cited 7-7, 545G1, F3
At 7-natn Bonn econ summit 7-16—7-17, 543D3
JENKINS, William L.
Quits TVA 5-5, 390A2, D2, E2
JENN-Air Corp.
Carrier plans acquisitn 10-4, 896G2
JENNER, Bruce
2d in Sullivan Award vote 2-7, 780F2
JENNEWEIN, Carl Paul
Dies 2-22, 196C3

1979

JAPAN Air Lines
US issues '77 Alaska crash rpt 2-13, 412F1
DC-10 safety flaws rptd 5-31, 412D1
JAPAN Line Ltd. v. County of Los Angeles
Case decided by Sup Ct 4-30, 364C3
JAROUDI, Mohsen
Arrested in PLO aide slaying 8-20, 625D2
JARREAU, Al
Wins Grammy 2-16, 336E3
JARRIN, Gen. Bolivar
Linked to Calderon murder 1-12, 62E2
To be tried in mil ct 3-12, 256F3
JARVIS, Howard A.
New ballot initiative sought 7-2, 499A3
JARVIS, William
Canada fed-prov relatns min 6-4, 423F3
Loto Canada sale OKd 8-21, 651D2
JARVIS-Gann Amendment (Proposition 13)—*See TAXES–Reform*
JASCALEVICH, Dr. Mario E.
Trial costs ordrd paid by NY Times 8-14, 656E2
JASPIN, Elliot G.
Wins Pulitzer 4-16, 336E2, A3
JATTI, Basappa D.
Replaced as India vp 8-9, 634C3
JAVITS, Sen. Jacob Koppel (R, N.Y.)
Sen votes res vs Iran executns 5-17; Iran scores 5-20; wife chrgd again, US vows protectn 5-21, 388C3
Finances disclosed 5-18, 383E2
Iran envoy pledges safety 5-23, 408G2
Wife rptdly aided Iran lobby 5-30, 408B2
Clashes with Kennedy on Brown confirmatn 9-25, 901E3
Navy chngs Hispanic recruiting policy 10-15, 850A3
JAVITS, Marion (Mrs. Jacob Koppel)
Iran scores 5-20, chrgs shah ties 388D3
Iran envoy pledges safety 5-23, 408G2
Iran lobby role bared; reactn 5-30, 408B2
JAWORSKI, Ron
NFL '78 passing ldr 1-6, 80E1
JAWS (film)
Viewed on TV by 80 mln 11-4, 1006F3
JAY, Fla.—*See FLORIDA*
JAY Norris Inc.
FTC ad case refused by Sup Ct 12-3, 964D2
JAY Norris Inc. v. FTC
Case refused by Sup Ct 12-3, 964D2
JEFFERSON, John
NFL '78 touchdown, receiving ldr 1-6, 80B1, C1
JEFFERSON, Thomas (1743-1826)
Stuart portrait goes to Natl Gallery 4-10, 375A1
JEFFREY, Mildred
Loses NWPC pres electn 7-15, 578D3
JEHOVAH'S Witnesses
Paraguay bans 1-4, 22B3
JENKIN, Len
New Jerusalem opens 2-15, 712G1
JENKIN, Patrick
UK social svcs secy 5-5, 338G1
Health offcls' revolt squelched 8-1, 582C2
JENKINS, Clive
UK smallpox rpt released 1-3, 7D2
JENKINS, Ferguson
AL pitching ldr 9-30, 955G3
JENKINS, Roy
Greek EC entry treaty signed 5-28, 407C2
Urges center coalitn 11-22, 950A1
JENKINS, Thomas E.
Sentenced in GSA scandal 5-31, 964D3

1980

JAPANESE Americans
US electn results 11-4, 846B2, F3
JARA, Jose Eduardo
Kidnaped 7-26; freed, dies 8-2, 603F2
Right-wing terrorists arrested 8-12, 618C3
JARDIN du Poete Arles, Le (The Garden of a Poet in Arles) (painting)
Sold for record sum 5-13, 472E1
JARMAN, Walton Maxey
Dies 9-9, 755D3
JAROSZEWICZ, Piotr
Ousted as Poland premier 2-15, 152C2
JARRELL, David A.
Escapes prison 7-28, recaptured 7-30, 654F1
JARRETT, Jacqueline
Child custody case refused by Sup Ct 10-20, 807B1
JARRETT, Walter
Child custody case refused by Sup Ct 10-20, 807B1
JARRETT v. Jarrett
Case refused by Sup Ct 10-20, 807A1
JARVIS, Howard
Calif rejects income tax cut 6-3, 439C2
JARVIS Inc.
AT&T trust suit settled 8-18, 917C2
JASCHKE, Martina
Wins Olympic medal 7-26, 623F3
JASPER, Zina
My Mother, My Father opens 1-9, 136D3
JAURON, Dick
NFL '79 interceptn ldr 1-5, 8D2
JAUSOVEC, Mima
Loses US Open quarterfinal 9-3, 691E2
JAUSSAUD, Jean-Pierre
Wins LeMans 6-15, 637A3
JAVITS, Sen. Jacob Koppel (R, N.Y.)
At GOP platform hearings, urges NATO oil route protectn role 1-14, 32B1
Sen com asks consultatn on Iran 4-24, 297D2
Backs Reagan tax-cut plan 6-25, 480D2
Loses NY Sen primary 9-9, 682D1
Mental health authrzn clears Cong 9-24, 9-30, signed 10-7, 804B1
Loses reelectn 11-4, 845G1, 846A1, 848A3
JAWORSKI, Leon
Bush denies '70 campaign gift coverup 2-7, 129A1
Announces Dems for Reagan 9-29, 738F2
JAWORSKI, Ron
NFL '79 passing ldr 1-5, 8E2
JAWS (film)
Williams named Boston Pops conductor 1-10, 199F2
JAYEWARDENE, Harry W.
On UN comm to probe shah 2-17, 122B1
JAYEWARDENE, Junius Richard
Brother on UN comm to probe shah 2-17, 122B1
JAZZ Singer, The (film)
Released 12-19, 1003B2
JEFFERSON, Michael E.
Indicted 5-9, 459A2
JEFFERSON, Thomas (1743-1826)
Kennedy conv speech 8-12, 613D2
Libertarian pres candidate cites 10—28, 828F2
JEFFERSONS, The (TV series)
'79-80 Nielsen rating rptd 4-22, 376C1
JEFFERSON Starship (singing group)
NY record co indicted 2-28, 237D3
JEFFORDS, Rep. James M. (R, Vt.)
Reelected 11-4, 844C3, 849D1
JEFFRIES, Rep. Jim (R, Kan.)
Reelected 11-4, 842D4
JEHOVAH'S Witnesses
Chicago teacher firing case declined by Sup Ct 1-7, 15E3
Poland OKs alternative mil svc 1-23, 88C1
JEM (book)
Wins Amer Book Award 5-1, 692F2
JEN Jong
Tibet CP ldrshp loss rptd 5-29, 462D1
JENKINS, Dennis
Pre-arrest silence testimony backed by Sup Ct, murder convictn upheld 6-10, 512C1
JENKINS, Rep. Edgar L. (D, Ga.)
Reelected 11-4, 842B3
JENKINS, Ferguson
Gets 100th AL win 5-3, 636C3
JENKINS, Ray H.
Dies 12-26, 1004B2
JENKINS, Roy
Center party rpts cited 1-23, 79E2
Carter note on US Steel suits rptd 3-27, 243C1
Liberals woo Labor dissidents 9-12, 708A2
JENKINS v. Anderson
Case decided by Sup Ct 6-10, 512C1

1976

JENRETTE Jr., Rep. John W. (D, S.C.)
Reelected 11-2, 830A4
JENSEN, Erling
Named Danish labor min 9-9, 712F1
JENSEN Inc., Norman G.
Boycott rpt released 10-18, 10-19, 786A1, D1
JERSEY Journal (Jersey City, N.J. newspaper)
Carter endorsement rptd 10-30, 831G2
JERUSALEM—*See ISRAELI Policies under MIDDLE EAST*
JESUITS (Society of Jesus)
Paraguay priest expelled 4-19; schl closing, arrests rptd 5-8, 403C2
Arrupe on rice for Bangladesh 8-2, 596D2
Brazil priest killed, reactn 10-12—10-16, 836B1
Brazil bishops score violence 11-16, 903D2
JETHMALANI, Ram
Gets US asylum 8-24, 676B1
JET Power Inc.
Cargo jet crash in Bolivia 10-13, 876G2
JET Propulsion Laboratory (JPL) (Pasadena, Calif.)
Viking 1 lands on Mars, sends data 7-20—7-22, 525E2 ★, 526E1—527A1
Viking soil tests begin 7-28, 549C1
JEWELRY
Louis Arpels dies 3-20, 240D3
JEWISH Armed Resistance
Claims credit for anti-Sovt incidents in NY 2-27, 3-25, 229D2, B3; 4-2, 259F3
JEWISH Defense League (JDL)
Bombs found near UN hq 1-12, Iraq missn 1-13, 18E2
Belgium deports Kahane 2-19, 206C3
Lauds Sovt UN missn attack 4-2, 259G3
Sup Ct bars wiretap review 4-19, 331F1
Kahane leads anti-Arab riot 5-19, 354D2
Kahane arrested in Hebron 8-25, 699F3
20 plan move to W Bank town 10-17, 799C1
Sup Ct refuses Kelner convictn 12-13, 960E3

JEWS & Judaism—*See also ISRAEL, MIDDLE EAST; group and personal names*
'75 US synagogue attendance rptd 1-3, 32A3
Argentina rightists vow exectns 1-26, 96C1
Orthodox cncl backs Papal stand on sex 1-26, 124C2
Miami club exclusn upheld 4-15, 307G3
US rabbinical ldr sworn 5-26, 932E2
Spain queen at Madrid rite 5-28, 459A3
Spain king in US mtg 6-3, 459G2-B3
Carter reassures Jews 6-6, 410F3
Argentina Nazi publicatns scored, rightists bombings rptd 8-15—8-30, 672A2
Carter seeks support 8-30, 8-31, 645A2, D2
Anti-Semitism chrgd in Ariz Sen primary 687A3
Argentina bans anti-Semitic publicatns 9-14, 996G3
Mondale sees Phila ldrs 9-30, 725D1
Sup Ct bars review of Fla club bias case 10-4, 766A1
Brown '74 slur cited 787D1
Brown dismissal rptd sought 10-20, 787D1, C3
Carter support cited 11-11, 845D2
Spain neo-fascist attacks rptd 11-12, 909E2
E Ger sets reparatns 11-22, 889G1
E Ger reparatns rejected 11-23, 949D2
US, Canada Orthodox mtg 11-25—11-28, 912A1 ★
US-USSR linguist exchng canceled 12-7, 1011G1
Argentina admits bias vs Gelbard 12-10, 997G1
Bell US apptmt controversy 12-20—12-22, 956E3
Rpt Syria ends ban 12-28, 974F1
Arab Boycott—*See under BUSINESS*

1977

JENNINGS, Dr. John
On FDA laetrile hearings 5-2, 376B1
JENSEN, Arthur
AAAS honors protested 2-23, 183C3
JENSEN, Egon
Danish interior min 2-25, 373D1
JENSEN, Erling
Danish labor min 2-25, 373D1
Named Denmark justice min 10-1, 882F3
JENSEN, Max
Gilmore executed 1-17, 40F1
JEREZ, Rev. Cesar
Rejcts rightists' death threat 7-17, 580D1
JEROME, James
Vows probe of MP tap 10-31, 841G2
JERUSALEM—*See MIDDLE EAST, subheads ARAB-Israeli Developments—Israel Occupation and EGYPT-Israel Peace Moves*
JERUSALEM Post, The (newspaper)
Geneva plan leak rptd 10-13, 769F1
JESUITS (Society of Jesus)—*See ROMAN Catholic Church*
JESUS Christ
Sadat visits alleged burial site 11-20, 889E1
JESUS of Nazareth (TV film)
To be shown annually 5-16, 395F2
JETER, Gary
In NFL draft 5-3, 353A2
JETHMALANI, Ram
Seeks to return to India 2-1, 71F2
Returns to India, seeks Gokhale seat 2-10, 160B1
Wins Parlt seat 3-16—3-20, 205C2
JET Propulsion Laboratory (JPL) (Pasadena, Calif.)
Voyager II launched 8-20, 664B1
JEWELRY
Swiss watch exports rptd down 1-27, 138C1
Vereshchagin death rptd 2-23, 164F3
Arpels fined 4-20, 312G2-A3
'77 fashion wrap-up rptd 6-6, 1022G1
Diamond dealer murders probed 7-28—10-19, 871B3-G3
Jules Glaenzer dies 8-16, 696G2
Mafia figure, NYC jeweler sentncd 10-21, 991D3
JEWISH Defense League (JDL)
Kahane sparks W Bank riots 4-17, 4-26, barred; parlt bid noted 5-1, 335G2
JEWISH Documentation Center (Vienna)
Mengele rptd in Paraguay 8-17, 803C2
JEWISH Organizations, Conference of Presidents of Major American
US assures on Mideast views 3-9, 166A1
Schindler on Carter Israel stance 6-11, 6-13, 474B1
Schindler vs US-Sovt Geneva plan 10-2, 750F1
Hears Vance, vs US Mideast policy 10-26, 831C1
JEWISH Organizations of Williamsburg Inc., United
Sup Ct backs racial voter redistricting 3-1, 174F3—175D1
JEWISH Publishers' Association, American
At USSR book fair 9-6—9-14, 765F3
JEWS for Jesus
Caths, Jews score proselytism; evaluate appeal 3-28—5-13, 492D2

JEWS & Judaism—*See also ISRAEL, MIDDLE EAST, NAZIS; group and personal names*
Argentina attacks resume 1-7, 1-14, 42D1; 2-26, 3-3, 198G1, D1
Bell US apptmt controversy continues 1-11—1-18, 34G1
Daoud release protested 1-14, 1-18, 28D1
Rumania visa denials rptd 2-20, 315B1
Sup Ct backs racial voter redistricting 3-1, 174F3-175D1
Spain anti-Semitic groups rptd 3-2, 307G2
Afro-Arab summit vs Zionism 3-7—3-9, 170E1
New Reform prayer book issued 3-7, 471A3
Rabin addresses US ldrs 3-9, 165E2
Proselytism scored, cult trends evaluated 3-28—5-13, 492C2
Davidson Coll tenure policy chngd 5-6, 471F3
Carter meets US ldrs 7-6, 509F2
Argentina anti-Semitism debate rptd 7-7, 614F3
Messianic Jews at charismatic conf 7-20—7-24, 620E3
Begin asks UN aid on Syrians 7-22, 571A1
USSR: US Jews influence forgn policy 7-22, 589G1
Argentine youth kidnaped 7-28, rescued 8-3, Nazi insignia rptd found 8-26, 670A3
Diamond dealer murders probed 7-28—10-19, 871D3
Argentina kidnapings, arrests 8-27—11-12; Vance sees ldrs 11-21, 912G2, 922D2
Torrijos in Israel rptdly re US Jews Canal pact support 9-27—9-30, 755E3
Sup Ct hears Bakke case arguments 10-12, 834E3
Dead Sea scroll analyzed 11-12, 1022F3
New RC catechism repudiates anti-Semitism, cites common heritage 11-17, 906B2
Arab Boycott—*See under BUSINESS*

1978

JENNINGS, Dave
NFL '77 punting ldr 1-1, 56F3
JENNINGS, Doug
Chrgs Lynch, Holding corruptn; denials issued, judicial probe barred 9-14, 771D1
JENNINGS, Peter
ABC news show chngs set 4-19, 419B3
JENRETTE Jr., Rep. John W. (D, S.C.)
Reelected 11-7, 852B2
JENSEN, Dwight
Wins Idaho US Sen primary 8-8, 625F3
Loses electn 11-7, 856C1
JENSEN, Egon
Named Danish relign min 8-30, 688A1
JENSEN, Erling
Named Danish social min 8-30, 688A1
JENSEN, Robert
Defends FBI King probe 11-22, 938F2
JEPSEN, Roger
Wins Iowa US Sen primary 6-6, 448F1
Elected 11-7, 846B1, 848F1, 854B2
JEROME, James
Chrgs Rooney influence peddling 1-31, 88B2
2 chrgd in '77 MP tap 4-3, 244A2
Ejects LaSalle from Parlt 5-16, 391B3
JERSEY City, N.J.—*See NEW Jersey*
JERUSALEM—*See MIDDLE EAST, subheads ARAB-Israeli Developments—Israeli Occupation Policies and EGYPT-Israel Peace Moves*
JESSIE, Ron
Rams win in playoffs 12-31, 1024G1
JESUITS (Society of Jesus)—*See ROMAN Catholic Church*
JESUS Christ
Oberammergau vs revised Passion Play 1-12, 95F2
Shroud of Turin exhibited 8-26—10-8, studied 10-4—11-14; photo 926A1-C3
JET Propulsion Laboratory (JPL) (Pasadena, Calif.)
Volcanos rptd on Venus 1-26, 293F2
Shroud of Turin studied 10-4, 926E1
JEWELRY
Nigeria import ban rptd 4-4, 248C1
Apr finished-goods rise rptd 5-4, 344D3
Stolen diamond recovered in autopsy 5-4, 380E1
'78 high chic fashion rptd 8-4—8-11, 10-27—11-3, 1029A3
Harry Winston dies 12-8, 1032G3
JEWISH Agency
USSR emigratn rise, 10-yr total rptd 9-28, 947B1
JEWISH Armed Resistance
Claims NY Sovt office bombing 7-10, 542A3
JEWISH Committee, American—*See AMERICAN Jewish Committee*
JEWISH Organizations, Conference of Presidents of Major American
Sadat invitation declined 2-1, 77G2
Schindler vs Carter, Brzezinski Mideast stand 3-9, 176G2
Concerned re US Mideast role 12-19, 978G3
JEWISON, Norman
F.I.S.T. released 4-26, 619A2

JEWS & Judaism—*See also ISRAEL, MIDDLE EAST, NAZIS; group and personal names*
Bench jokes upset audience 1-7, 195B1
Oberammergau vs revised Passion Play 1-12, 95E2
Begin chrgs Egypt anti-Semitism 1-21—1-23; Egypt press denies 1-24, 41E1, A2, G2-42D1
Sadat plea to US Jews 1-29, ADL reply refused 2-1, 60B3
'53, '78 cong membership compared 1-30, 107F2
Christians ask conversn study 2-1, Israel '77 law repeal 3-1, 294G1
Argentina orders non-Catholics register 2-14, 208E1
Eur fascist mtg protested 3-4—3-5, 238D3
French survey rptd 3-24, 352G2
'Holocaust' aired in US 4-16—4-19, 120 mln viewers rptd 4-20, 316A2
Argentina ex-publisher leaves jail 4-17, 286A1
US Sen OKs Mideast jet pkg 5-15; reactn 5-15—5-18, 357E1, 358C1, D2
Bell Canada bias chrgd 5-15, ordrd ended 9-11, 772F3
Rabbinical ldr vs gay rights 5-18, 410B1
French anti-Semitism rptd increasing 6-14, 474C1
Israel: Shcharansky trial an example of anti-Semitism 7-10, 543A1
'Test-tube baby' reactn rptd 7-25, 597E1
Nonaligned score Zionism 7-30, 583D3
'64 papal guidelines cited 8-6, 601A2
Singer wins Nobel 10-5, 886F1-A2
Syria-imposed Qantas curb probed 10-18, 836E1; Syria drops demand 10-20, 900E3

1979

JENNINGS, Dave
NFL '78 punting ldr 1-6, 80F2
JENNINGS, Waylon
Wins Grammy 2-16, 336F3
JENRETTE Jr., Rep. John W. (D, S.C.)
Denies drug role probe 8-8, 650B1
JENSON, Jerry N.
Cocaine trade growth rptd 9-5, 972E2
JEPSEN, Sen. Roger (R, Iowa)
S Africa '78 campaign contributn chrgd 3-21, 213C1
Scores SALT treaty 4-5, 258G1
JERK, The (film)
Released 12-14, 1007E3
JEROME, James
Named Canada House speaker 10-9, 788G2
JERSEY Central Power and Light Co.—*See under GENERAL Public Utilities Corp.*
JERSEY City, N.J.—*See NEW Jersey*
JERUSALEM—*See under MIDDLE EAST*
JERVIS, Verne
On forgn student survey 1-29, 93G2
JESUITS (Society of Jesus)—*See ROMAN Catholic Church*
JESUS, An Experiment in Christology (book)
Theologian faces Vatican heresey chrgs 12-18, 999B3
JET Propulsion Laboratory (JPL) (Pasadena, Calif.)
Mars surface water rptd 8-9, 692C3
JEWELRY
Tiffany OKs Avon bid 1-18, 89E1
'79 fashion roundup rptd 1006G2
USSR hikes prices 7-2, 504D2
Demand, gold price rise linked 8-30, 645C3
Robert Hocq dies 12-8, 1008C3
JEWISH Chronicle (London weekly)
Sadat interviewed 5-24, 408A2
JEWISH Community Relations Advisory Council, National
Nazi resurgence rptd top '78 concern 1-19, 102B1
Lauds black-Jewish cooperatn 8-19, 624B2
Black criticism rejctd 8-23, 661E3
JEWISH Organizations, Conference of Presidents of Major American
US stand on PLO opposed 1-17, 69G1
Israel torture rpt scored 2-7, 108B2
Connally Mideast peace plan scored 10-11, 783C2
JEWISON, Norman
And Justice for All released 10-19, 1007G2

JEWS & Judaism—*See also group, personal names*
Khomeini views publshd 50B1
B Carter's rptd anti-Semitic remarks stir controversy 1-9—1-13, 31C2
'78 mixed marriage data rptd 1-15, 101C3
Nazi resurgence rptd top '78 concern 1-19, 102A1
RC abortn stand protested by NY rabbis 1-22, 63B3
Orthodox rabbis oppose ERA, hold sexes equal 1-26, 101G3
Conservative Assemb OKs women rabbis 1-30, 101F3
1st US woman rabbi resigns NY post 2-2, 176F1
Khomeini reps assure Young re rights 2-10, 106A2
Syrian abuse chrgd 2-22, denied 2-23, 148G1, A3
US releases Auschwitz photos 2-22, 193D1
Carter on brother's remarks 2-27, 149E2
Dead Sea Temple Scroll contents told 3-2, 217G2
Italy anti-Semitic protest 3-7, 212E1
Le Monde bombing linked 4-29, 330E2
1st Iranian executed 5-9, 353C2
Zionists warn Iran 5-12, Jews assured by Khomeini 5-15, 357B2
Ala inmate rights case refused by Sup Ct 6-4, 439F1
Pope cites Nazi victims 6-7, 414D1
Weber case Sup Ct ruling opposed 6-27, 477E2
Sen rejcts direct pres vote 7-10, 515C1
Talmudic study completed 7-14, 640G1
Veil voted EC Parlt pres 7-17, 537A3
US religious tolerance gains rptd 8-4, 639C3
Rabbis denounce Life of Brian 8-27, 859G1
Satmar Hasidim appoint ldr 9-10, 931E3
French writer slain 9-20, 772F2
Syria emigratn curbs chrgd 10-24, 857B3
Black Relations
Jews, blacks score Carter Palestinian-civil rights analogy 8-1, 575G1
Black-Jewish mtg urged following Young resignatn 8-15, 8-16, 606E1-B2
Jews, blacks seek to heal rift 8-19, 8-22, 624F1

1980

JENNINGS, Dave
NFL '79 punting ldr 1-5, 8F3
JENNINGS, Peter
Iran chrgs shah gave gifts 2-9, 122B3
JENRETTE Jr., Rep. John W. (D, S.C.)
Facts on 81E2
Linked to bribery in Abscam probe 2-2, 2-3, 81A2, 82F1
Indicted in Abscam probe, scores Justice Dept 6-13, 454C1
Wins runoff electn 6-24, 496F1
Abscam trial opens 9-5, convicted 10-7, 782D3
Abstains on Myers House expulsn 10-2, 740A2
Ethnics com begins expulsn hearings 10-7, 783C1
Loses reelectn 11-4, 846A2, 850E1
Resigns from House 12-10, 962E1
JENRETTE, Rita (Mrs. John W.)
Testifies in husband's defense 9-22, 783A1
JENSEN, Bjoerg Eva
Wins Olympic medal 2-20, 156B1
JERBO, Maj. William
Rptd killed in escape try 5-15, 381F3
JERIOVA, Kveta
Wins Olympic medal 2-15, 155C3
JERK, The (film)
Top-grossing film 1-9, 40G3; 1-30, 120A3
JEROME, Denis
Organic superconductor rptd 4-5, 415C3
JEROME, James
Named to Federal Ct 1-4, 38C2
Replaced as House speaker 2-29, 171D2
JERSEY City—*See NEW Jersey*
JERUSALEM—*See under ARAB-Israeli Developments*
JERUSALEM Post (Israeli newspaper)
Egypt sale begins 1-16, 48C3
JESSIE, Ron
Steelers win Super Bowl; injury cited 1-20, 61A3-62C1
JET (magazine)
Reagan sees editors 8-5, 597B3
JET Propulsion Laboratory (JPL) (Pasedena, Calif.)
15th Jovian moon rptd discovered 5-6, 416C1
Solar radiatn drop rptd 8-6, 716D1
JEWELRY
June producer price rise rptd 7-8, 513D3
'80 fashion roundup rptd 998C2
JEWISH Agency
Begin vs Sovt Jews in US 4-2, 262D3
JEWISH Organizations, Conference of Presidents of Major American
3 ex-chrmn back W Bank compromise 7-1, 509D1
JEWISH Publication Society
Grayzel dies 8-12, 676E1
JEWISH Women, National Council of
UN women's conf racism motion withdrawn 7-28, 587F2

JEWS & Judaism
'79 synagogue attendance rptd 1-4, 8C1
Redgrave TV role protested 1-13, 120C2
Israeli reform rabbi ordained, called invalid by chief rabbi 2-19, 134A1
Carter sees ldrs 3-4, 164D1
Iranians rptd entering US 3-12, Jewish immigratn estimated 3-14, 178G1
Iran 'spy' executed 6-5, parlt member ousted 8-17, 644G2
Calif shopping cntr petitn access backed by Sup Ct 6-9, 512B2
US withdraws racism motion at UN women's conf 7-28, conf OKs 5-yr plan 7-30, 587F2, A3
Carter rpts on brother's case 8-4, 592F3
Wiesenthal honored by Carter 8-5, 638G1
Canada E Eur immigratn records rptd found 8-20, 651A2
Baptist ldr disparages prayers 8-22; Tannenbaum, others denounce 9-18, 9-19, 811A1
Gravel loses Alaska primary 8-26, 683B2
France bans right-wing extremist group 9-3, 670E3
W Berlin immigratn curb set 9-24, 833D1
French targets attacked 9-26, 9-28, 750A1
Redgrave TV film aired by CBS, protests rptd 9-30, 835C3
France synagogue blast kills 4 10-3, protests ensue 10-4, 10-7, militants retaliate 10-8; Giscard sets measures 10-8, 767A2-768A1
TV evangelist reverses prayer stance 10-11, 811F1
French rightists attacked by Jewish group 10-12; Begin scores France anti-Semitism 10-13, 789F3-790C1
Redgrave links fascist Ger, Israel 11-2, 908F3
Sioux Falls (SD) schls case refused by Sup Ct 11-10, 868B2
2 killed in Paris attack 11-13, 921C3
Pope meets W Ger ldrs 11-17, 905A2
Israeli, W Eur reps at Madrid CSCE 11-27, 12-5, 950D2, E2

1976

Obituaries
Beber, Sam 8-25, 656E3
Franklin, Sidney 4-26, 368F2
Unterman, Issar Yehuda 1-26, 124G3
Soviet Issues—*See 'Jews' under USSR*
Zionism
Mex forgn min replacemt 'unconnected' 1-8, 75G2
US Jews cancel Brazil tours 1-15, 27G2
UNESCO conf postponed 1-15, 36E2
US delegatn in Mex 1-26, 75E1
Christian-Moslem text denounces 2-6, Vatican rejects text 2-11, 272E2
Moscow rabbi scores Zionists 2-16, 206C3
Arab League-OAU mtg scores 4-22, 356B1
UN ECOSOC debate 4-27—4-30, 320F2
US Dem platform cites UN res 6-15, 478B1
UN res cited re Mex forgn min resignatn 7-8, 620C2
US GOP platform text cites UN res 8-18, 610D3
Amer Indep Party scores 8-26, 666F1
US, West rptd vs Echeverria UN bid 10-5, 906E3
US, Canada Orthodox mtg 11-25—11-28, 912A1 ★
Grenada UN vote cited 12-7, 925F1
JIFFY International Ltd.
Chrgd re Arab boycott 10-19, 10-20, 786E1
JIMENEZ de Arechaga, Justino
Scores OAS re Chile rights abuse 3-5, 310F1
JIMENEZ Sarmiento, David
Killed 8-11, 677D1-F1 ★
JIROUS, Ivan
Sentenced 9-23, 851E3
JIRYIS, Sabri Elias
US expels 11-23, 878G1
JOANA, Lt. Col. Mampila
Named defns min 8-20, 926B1
JOHANSSON, Bernt
Wins Olympic medal 7-26, 574C2
JOHANSSON, Olof
Names to Swedish Cabt 10-8, 794C2

JOHN XXIII, Pope (Angelo Giuseppe Roncalli) (1881-1963)—*See Vol. 23, p. 204B2-E3 for biog. data*
Vatican CIA, SID infiltratn rptd 2-14, 140E3

JOHN Birch Society
Sen intelligence com cites as target 4-28, 330F1
Grady wins Fla Sen primary 9-7, 687C3
JOHNCOCK, Gordon
3d in Indy 500 5-30, 424G2

1977

Obituaries
Ben-Ami, Jacob 7-22, 604E2
Feldman, Abraham 7-21, 604B3
Mark, Julius 9-7, 788F1
Robinson, Jacob 10-24, 872G2
Szold, Robert 11-9, 952E3
Weisgal, Meyer 9-29, 788A3
Soviet Issues—*See USSR—Human Rights*

JEZEK, Linda
Sets swim record 8-18—8-21, 828F3
JEZRAWI, Taha Yassin
Quits anti-Sadat mtg sessn 12-5, 929E1
JICK, Dr. Hershel
Drug death study rptd 2-28, 224F2
Smoking, early menopause linked 6-25, 620D1
JIMINEZ, Carlos Maria
Cervantes TKOs 6-27, 828A1
JIMENEZ de Arechaga, Eduardo
World Ct pres 4F1
JIMENEZ de Parga, Manuel
Spain labor min 7-5, 545C2
JIMENEZ Gallo, Gen. Guillermo
Quits Cabt in oil dispute 10-11, 902A1
Anti-Banzer plot foiled 12-9, 1009D3
JIMENEZ Ruiz, Gen. Eliseo
Named interim Oaxaca gov 3-3, 240G1
Fires rector 12-7, scores 12-14, 985F2
JOB Corps—*See U.S. GOVERNMENT—LABOR—Manpower Administration*
JOBERT, Michel
Party gains in electns 3-13, 3-20, 221C2
JOBS—*See LABOR, subheads 'Employment' and 'Job Bias'*
JOBST, John A.
Disability benefits loss upheld 11-8, 857B1
JOEST, Reinhold
Daytona endurance 2-6, 531E2
JOHN, Patrick (Dominica prime minister)
Rpts independnc talks completed 6-5, 567B1
Asks govt workers end strike 10-11, 949C2
JOHN, Tommy
NL pitching ldr 10-2, 926E3
In NL playoff 10-4—10-8, 807F1
In World Series 10-11—10-18, 806F2
Carlton wins NL Cy Young Award 11-2, 927F1

JOHN Birch Society
Assassinatn plot jury deadlocks 3-10, 261G2
Laetrile smugglers sentncd 5-16, 508G2
Bunker dies 10-10, 872B1
Rally vs women's conf 11-19, 918A1
JOHN Hancock Mutual Life Insurance Co.
Employer records case rejctd 5-16, 419E1
JOHN Hell (book)
Decoin wins Prix Goncourt 11-21, 927F2

1978

Obituaries
Halprin, Rose 1-8, 96B2
Pollak, Emile 1-6, 96C3
Soviet Issues—*See USSR—Human Rights*

JEZEK, Linda
Sets 200-m backstroke mark 8-24, 780C1, B2
JI, Maharaj—*See MAHARAJ Ji, Guru*
JIMENEZ, Joe
Wins PGA Senior title 2-5, 355A3
JINDAL, Siresh
Chess Players released 5-17, 619A1
JOB Corps—*See U.S. GOVERNMENT—LABOR—Manpower Administration*
JOBS—*See LABOR, subheads 'Employment' and 'Job Bias'*
JOEL, Billy
Just the Way You Are on best-seller list 3-8, 196B1
Stranger on best-seller list 3-8, 196B1; 4-5, 272G3
52nd St on best-seller list 11-8, 888D1; 12-6, 971E1
JOFFE, Charles H.
'Annie Hall' wins Oscars 4-3, 315B3
Interiors released 8-2, 970F1
JOGGING
Smog regulatn eased 6-16, 512G2
JOHANNES, Axel
Detained 4-8, 269F2
JOHANNESSON, Eve Helen
Killed 6-27, 519E1
JOHANNESSON, Henry
Dies 7-3, 519E1
JOHANNESSON, Olafur (Icelandic premier)
Currency transactns halted 8-28, krona devalued 15% 9-4, 689C1
Forms Icelandic coalitn govt 8-31, 688B3

JOHN XXIII, Pope (Angelo Giuseppe Roncalli) (1881-1963)—*See 1963, p. 204B2-E3 for biog. data*
Successor dies 8-6, 601E1
Pope Paul buried 8-12, 658A3
New Pope elected, takes name 8-26; Venice patriarchy, '63 papal electn cited 657F2, 658F1, C2
JOHN, Emilio
Named ASL top rookie 9-5, 707G3
JOHN, Patrick R. (Dominica prime minister)
Dominica becomes independent, socialist state vowed 11-2, 861A3
DeGazon elected pres 12-21, 1021G2
JOHN, Tommy
Dodgers win NL pennant 10-7, 779A1
In World Series 10-10—10-17, 799G2
Signs with Yankees 11-22, 1025F3
Kuhn vs free-agent system 12-5, 1026D2
JOHNCOCK, Gordon
3d in Indy 500 5-29, 538D2
3d in Calif 500 9-3, 968G3
JOHN Hancock Mutual Life Insurance Co.
Dist agents strike 7-21—8-17, 680C3
JOHN Paul I, Pope (Albino Luciani)
Elected Pope 8-26, States goals 8-27; photo, biog data 657A1-658F1
Reappoints Vatican aides 8-28, 658F1
Argentina pres at installatn 9-5, 689D3, 793C1
Nikodim dies during audience 9-5, 778G1
Dies 9-28, funeral 10-4, 746B3
Foul play linked to death 10-6, Vatican denounces 10-12, 782E1
Successor elected, takes name 10-16, 781C1-782D1
JOHN Paul II, Pope (Karol Wojtyla)
Elected Pope 10-16, addresses cardinals 10-18; photo, biog data 781A1-782A1, C1
Shuns inaugural pomp 10-18, leaves Vatican posts open 10-19, 782A1
Asks more Beagle Channel talks, Chile: Argentina talks fail 12-12, 979D2; mediator role set 12-23, envoy arrives Argentina 12-26, 999A3
Poland rptdly censors Xmas message 12-21, 1019D2

1979

SCLC meets PLO, Israeli, Jewish ldrs; backs PLO 8-21, 623F3
Jewish groups reject criticism 8-23, 661B3
Harris seeks black-Jewish reconciliatn 8-29, 661G2
Carter urges black-Jewish amity, denies Young tap 8-30, 661B2
McHenry named UN amb 8-31, 661A1
NAACP backs US-PLO talks, Israel existence; seeks closer black-Jewish ties 677E1, G1
Ga SCLC honors Qaddafi 9-16, 694B3
SCLC ldrs in Leb 9-18—9-20; Israel rebuffs visit 9-20, 694F1, E2
SCLC ends Leb visit 9-21, 763C2
Young: black PLO support 'natural' 9-22, 721B2
Carter denies Jewish pressure to oust Young 9-23, 763E2
Young: Dayan aired Terzi mtg 9-24; Young meets Dayan, absolves 9-26, 763G2
Jesse Jackson in Mideast, Israeli offcls snub; meets Arafat 9-25—10-5; PFLP scores 10-6; briefs Strauss, Saunders 10-8, 762F3
2 US Jewish ldrs quit Jackson tour 9-26, 763B2
Jordan, Hooks vs PLO support 10-11, 10-14; Baptist Conv scores criticism 10-14, 780C2-A3
SCLC drops invitatn to Arafat 10-11, 780F3
US Arab group gives PUSH $10,000 10-13, 780G3
NAACP, Urban League, others in Israel; back govt, Palestinians; oppose black support of PLO 10-14—10-17, 780C3
Hooks, 3 other black ldrs ask halt to debate; Jordan, Jackson 'reaffirm unity' 10-17, 780B3
US rep rebuts Young on Terzi mtg 10-28, 823D2
Middle East Issues—*See MIDDLE EAST*
Nazis Issues—*See NAZIS*
Obituaries
Brodie, Israel 2-13, 176F2
Levison, Stanley 9-12, 756G2
Schultz, Henry E 5-5, 432F3
Teitelbaum, Joel 8-19, 671F3
Soviet Issues—*See USSR-Human Rights*
JIMENEZ, Clotildo
Nazi fugitive loses Paraguay citizenship 8-8, 616A3
JIMENEZ, Gloria
Scores price guidelines, Admin rebuts 2-24, 264A3
JIMENEZ, Ramon Emilio
Orfila elected OAS secy gen 10-24, 824D2
JIMENEZ-Leal, Orlando
El Super released 4-28, 528B2
JIMENEZ Rodriguez, Manuel
Army plot foiled 9-25—9-26, 752A1
JIMINEZ, Nestor (Baba)
Gomez KOs 3-9, 412D3
JIMINEZ, Rosie (1951-78)
Abortion fund set 1-21, 63G2
JOBERT, Marlene
Your Turn, My Turn released 1-27, 175A1
JOBS—*See LABOR, subheads 'Employment' and 'Job Bias'*
JOEL, Billy
My Life on best-seller list 1-10, 80E3
52nd St on best-seller list 1-10, 80F3; 2-14, 120F3; 4-4, 271E2
Wins 2 Grammys 2-16, 336C3
Performs in Cuba 3-1—3-4, 238E2
JOFFE, Charles H.
Manhattan released 4-24, 528A3
JOHANSON, Donald
Claims new hominid species 1-18, Leakey disputes 2-17, 137F3-138D1
JOHN, Elton
In USSR 5-21—5-30, 410C2
Unions demand resignatn 5-30, 424A3
JOHN, Patrick R. (Dominican prime minister; replaced June 29)
Dissolves Parlt, calls new electns 6-15; Cabt resigns amid unrest 6-16—6-18, 468D2
Replaced as prime min, govt probe vowed 6-29, 502C3
US sets Carib policy 11-29, 960E3
JOHN, Robert
Sad Eyes on best-seller list 10-3, 800E3
JOHN, Tommy
AL pitching ldr 9-30, 2d in Cy Young vote 10-30, 955C2, F3, G3
JOHN F. Kennedy (U.S. aircraft carrier)
Fires rptd 4-9, 6-5, Navy probes 7-5, 519G3
JOHN Paul II, Pope (Karol Wojtyla)
Beagle Channel mediatn agreed 1-8, envoy returns to Vatican 1-9, 51B3
Poland visit rptd set 60G2
Sees Gromyko 1-24, 60E2
In DR, Mex 1-25—1-31; opens CELAM mtg 1-27, plays down church pol role 1-28, 67A3
Attack on 'liberatn theology' denied by Latins 2-1, 2-3, 108B3, F3
CELAM asks Latin repressn end 2-13, 108E2, B3
Pak pres scorns Bhutto clemency plea 2-14, 116B2
Presents 1st encyclical 3-15, 216E3
Upholds free choice 4-22, 376C1
Names state secy, finance dir 4-30, 376E1
Names Capucci Melkite inspector, reassures Israel 5-7, 376B3*
Poland prepares for visit 5-25—6-4, 414G1

1980

Nazis Issues—*See NAZIS*
Obituaries
Frank, Otto 8-19, 676D1
Grayzel, Solomon 8-12, 676E1
Grunwald, Levi Y 4-12, 360A2
Kaminska, Ida 5-21, 448B2
Neumann, Emanuel 10-26, 876G2
Soviet Issues—*See UNION of Soviet Socialist Republics--Human Rights*
U.S. Presidential Election (& Transition)
Kennedy wins Fla primary voters 3-11, 189D3
Kennedy wins NY primary 3-25, 221C2
Reagan upholds prayer 10-3, 763A3
Carter warns vs Reagan win 10-6, 762E3
Reagan deplores Carter 'hysteria' 10-7, 763D2
Carter drops Reagan attack 10-9, 778D2
Carter heckled in NYC 10-13, 778E3
Bush scores Carter 'flipflop' 10-16, 10-19, 817C3
Mondale: Carter 'delivered' 10-26, 816E3
Carter, Reagan TV debate 10-28, 814E2
Reagan wins vote 11-4, 837D1, 838A3

JIANG Qing (Chiang Ching)
Trial set 9-27, confessn bar delays 11-1, 859A1
Zhao Dan dies 10-10, 876G3
Kang Xie purged 10-31, 859F1
Indictmt aired 11-15—11-18, trial starts 11-20, 877C1, D2
Testifies 11-26, 12-3; ct outbursts 12-12, 12-23, 12-27; case summatn 12-23; pleads innocent 12-24; death sentnc asked 12-29, 974G2-975B2
Mao Cultural Revolutn role scored by press 12-22, 975F2
JIANG Tengjiao
Admits plot role to kill Mao 11-25, 975C2
JI Dengku
Ousted from Politburo 2-29, 171F3
Resigns as dep premr 4-16, 351F1
JIMENEZ Villalba, Camilo
Meets DR emb captors 3-2—3-13, 180C2
JIMENEZ, Leocadio
Sentenced for '77 murders 3-4, 196C2
JIMENEZ, Ricardo (Dickie)
Arrested 4-4, 308G3
Convicted 7-30, 601D1
Indicted 12-10, 963F3
JINNAH, Mohammed Ali (1876-1948)
Nehru, Mountbatten affair alleged 8-27, 890B3
JOBIM, Antonio Carlos
'Ipanema' lyricist dies 7-9, 608F1
JOEL, Billy
Wins 2 Grammys 2-27, 296A3
NY record co indicted 2-28, 237D3
Glass Houses on best-seller list 4-2, 280F3; 4-30, 448F3; 7-9, 568E3; 8-13, 640C3
It's Still Rock and Roll to Me on best-seller list 7-9, 568E3; 8-13, 640A3
JOFFREY Ballet
Reagan's son makes NY debut 10-10, 908A3
JOHANNESON, Kent
Wins ND US Sen primary 9-2, 683D1
Loses US Sen electn 11-4, 851B2
JOHANSON, Louis C.
Indicted in Abscam probe 5-22, 5-27, 5-28, 402E2, F2, A3
Convicted in Abscam trial 8-31, 684B2
Schwartz, Jannotti convicted 9-16, 740C2
Appeals ct backs Abscam tapes broadcast 10-1; Sup Ct refuses stay, tapes aired 10-14, 781D2
JOHANSON, Robert
Canterbury Tales opens 2-12, 136A3
JOHANSSON, Per
Wins Olympic medal 7-27, 623G2
JOHANSSON, Sven
Wins Olympic medal 7-23, 623D2
JOHN, Patrick
Loses reelectn bid 7-21, 636A1
JOHN, Tommy
NL wins All-Star Game 7-8, 636E1, G1, A2
AL pitching ldr 10-6, 926G3
Royals win AL pennant 10-10, 796A1
JOHNCOCK, Gordon
CART membership cited 6-30, 1002A2
JOHN F. Kennedy (U.S. aircraft carrier)
Trible says unfit, scores deploymt 6-30, 517F3
JOHN Gabriel Borkman (play)
Opens 12-18, 1003C3

JOHN Paul II, Pope (Karol Wojtyla)
At Dutch bishops synod 1-14—1-31, 156A3
Names US archbp to Vatican educ post 1-15, 199C2
W Ger theologian's ouster backed, Vatican controversy detailed 2-5, 157C1
Latin mass support rptd 3-21, 364E1
Names Ukrainian church ldr 3-27, 413E3
Violence mars Romero funeral 3-30, 253C3
Lauds Romero 4-3, 341D3
US intercommunion poll rptd 4-4, 413A3
W Ger theologian setlmt reached 4-10, 364A2
Sends Iran plea on US ties 4-12, Khomeini replies 4-15, 282A2
Iran to turn over dead US raiders 4-28, 323G1

1976

JOHNS, John S.
Withdraws USW pres bid 8-29, 669D3
JOHNS Hopkins University (Baltimore, Md.)
Receives Pratt grant 1-9, 80C2
Rpts high cancer areas 2-16, 224E3
New cancer operation 5-3, 384C2
Charles Haines dies 5-25, 524F2
JOHNSON, Albert
On Hearst 'mute' stand 5-12, 367E3; 5-28, 423G1
Hearst sentenced 9-24, 735D2
On Hearst prison safety 11-11, 891A3
JOHNSON, Rep. Albert (R, Pa.)
Scored by environmt group 3-25, 220A1
JOHNSON, Bill
Named Bengals coach 1-1, 31C2
JOHNSON, David
Found guilty 8-12, 656C1
JOHNSON, Donald M.
Quits as Aetna dir 1-8, 80E2
JOHNSON, Jr., Judge Frank M.
Orders Ala prison reform 1-13, 25G2
JOHNSON, Lt. Cmdr. Guy David
Rptd killed in Viet 9-6, 678B3
JOHNSON, Rep. Harold T. (Bizz) (D, Calif.)
Reelected 11-2, 828G3
JOHNSON, Rep. James P. (R, Colo.)
Reelected 11-2, 824E1, 829F1
JOHNSON, Lyndon Baines (1908-73)—*See 1973, p. 53D2-B3 for biog. data*
Blakely dies 1-5, 56A3
House intelligence com rpt leaked 1-26, 93E1
Mansfield to retire 3-4, 181E1
Nixon testimony on Chile issued 3-11, 183C3
Primary precedent cited 231G3
Sen com rpts FBI tap use 5-9, 344E2
Carter on Admin 6-14, 433D1, G1
Cited in Dem platform text 6-15, 469F2
Carter hails rights role 7-15, 510F1
Mondale record cited 512B3
Cited in Ford biog sketch 613F3-614A1
Cited in Dole biog sketch 614F2
Carter Playboy interview cites 9-20, Carter regrets 9-22, 704C2
Lady Bird rues Carter remarks 9-23, Carter admits 'mistake' 9-24, 724E2
Paul Douglas dies 9-24, 970F1
'68 SIU donatn cited 9-25, 723A1
Ford cites re Arab boycott 10-20, 784B3
Daughter campaigns with Carter 10-31, 827B2
Carter aides named 12-16, 936A3; 12-23, 956F2; 12-31, 978E3
JOHNSON, Mrs. Lyndon Baines (Claudia Alta Taylor) (Lady Bird)
Carter rues references to LBJ 9-22, 704E2
Issues statemt on Carter references to LBJ, sees Mrs Carter 9-23, 724B3
JOHNSON, Malcolm
Dies 6-18, 524G2
JOHNSON, Mordecai Wyatt
Dies 9-11, 716C3
JOHNSON, R. Tenny
CAB member 2-2; confrmd 3-22, 232E1
JOHNSON, Robert
Defeated 11-2, 822C1

1977

JOHNS, Thomas L.
Califano hiring defended 3-24, 3-25, 236B1, G1
JOHNS-Manville Corp.
Stocks fall 1-26, Quebec investmt delayed 1-28, 82D1
To resume Quebec investmt 3-7, 254F2
JOHNSON, Albert W.
Scores US TV influence 6-14, 485G2
Rebuts CRTC bias chrg 7-21, 579G2
JOHNSON, Barrie
Loses electn 6-8, 466E3
JOHNSON, Ezra
In NFL draft 5-3, 353C2
JOHNSON Jr., Judge Frank M.
Named FBI dir 8-17, 626A2
Facts on 626A2
Withdraws as FBI nominee 11-29, 914C2
JOHNSON, Rep. Harold T. (Bizz) (D, Calif.)
'76 spec interest gifts rptd 2-4, 128G3, 129B2
JOHNSON, Harry G.
Dies 5-8, 452C3
JOHNSON Jr., Judge J. B.
Orders mine violence ended 8-17, 937A3
JOHNSON, Lester D.
Dies 4-17, 356B3
JOHNSON, Lyndon Baines (1908-73)—*See 1973, p. 53D2-B3 for biog. data*
Vance confrmatn hearing 1-11, 34C3
Ex-aides named to US posts 1-18, 1-19, 52D3, F3
Warnke named to US post 2-2, 88G3
Carter asks Job Corps funds 3-9, 173G1
Carter bars shoe import curbs 4-1, 248D3
Latin neglect chrgd 4-17, 296C1
Nixon TV interview 5-19, 405G3-406B1
S Korea gifts chrgd 6-5, 442D1
'48 Sen primary fraud chrgd 7-30; denied 8-1, 8-3, 631G1
Archbp Lucey dies 8-1, 696B3
'41 Sen bid fraud seen 8-6, 631F2
Panama Canal treaties signed 9-7, 677E1
Foundatn award presented 10-26, 870B1
Robb elected Va lt gov 11-8, 855G1
Anti-sex bias order cited 11-17, 914E2
JOHNSON, Mrs. Lyndon Baines (Claudia Alta Taylor) (Lady Bird)
At Panama Canal pact signing 9-7, 677E1
At Natl Women's Conf 11-19, 917E3
JOHNSON, Marques
In NBA draft 6-10, 584A2
JOHNSON, Nathaniel R.
Indicted 8-2, 631B3
JOHNSON, Nunnally
Dies 3-25, 264B3

1978

JOHNS, Brig. Gen. John H.
On Army drug use survey 5-24, 433D2
JOHNS Hopkins University (Baltimore, Md.)
Lightning linked to cosmic rays 1-12, 293E2
Wins NCAA lacrosse title 5-27, 540A2
Teen contraceptive-use rptd 6-7, 598B2
Nathans, Smith win Nobel 11-12, 886E2
US emb study discounts Sovt microwave harm 11-20, 924E3
JOHNS-Manville Corp.
In Dow Jones indl avg 66F2
Olinkraft bidding won 10-27, Morgan Stanley sued 11-8, 896A3, F3
JOHNSON, Beverly
Climbs El Capitan alone 10-26, 843A3
JOHNSON, Billy (White Shoes)
NFL '77 punt, kick return ldr 1-1, 56C3, D3
Fired as Bengals coach 10-2, 1024A3
JOHNSON, Butch
NFL '77 kick return ldr 1-1, 56G3
Cowboys win Super Bowl 1-15, 39F2
JOHNSON, Charles
Bullets win NBA title 6-7, 457E1, G1
JOHNSON, Dennis
Bullets win NBA title 6-7, 457D1
JOHNSON Jr., Judge Frank M.
Rules Ala State U white bias 5-1, 348A3
JOHNSON, George
In NBA draft 6-9, 457G2
JOHNSON, George T.
NBA shot blocking ldr 4-9, 271G1
JOHNSON, Rep. Harold T. (Bizz) (D, Calif.)
Reelected 11-7, 850D1
Asks ICC deregulatn halt 12-7, O'Neal rejct, 12-21, 1007C2
PAC contributns rptd 12-24, 1008D1
JOHNSON, Haynes
Scoops Haldeman book excerpts 2-16, 124F2
JOHNSON, Rep. James P. (R, Colo.)
Reelected 11-7, 850C2
JOHNSON, John
Traded to A's 3-15, 195A1
JOHNSON, Lamont
Somebody Killed Her Husband released 9-29, 970C3
JOHNSON, Lonnie
Postal pact revised 9-15, 766B2
JOHNSON, Lyndon Baines (1908-73)—*See 1973, p. 53D2-B3 for biog. data*
Cong support rating cited 1-7, 12A3
Finney dies 1-30, 96G1
Meany compares Carter 2-23, 142D1
Ex-press aide's son kills teacher 5-18, 396B2
Blamed for '60s inflatn 5-22, 427B2
Moyers interviews Carter 11-13, 914C2
Brother dies 12-11, 1032A3
JOHNSON, Phil
Fired as Kings coach 1-8, 272F2
JOHNSON, Pierre-Marc
Sees Munro re Quebec labor law 7-20, 571D3
JOHNSON, Ron
In NFL draft 5-2, 336G2
JOHNSON, Sam Houston
Dies 12-11, 1032A3
JOHNSON & Johnson McNeil Laboratories
Anacin ads re Tylenol enjoined 5-2, 347G3
JOHNSON Outboards—*See OUTBOARD Marine Corp.*
JOHNSTON Jr., Sen. J. Bennett (D, La.)
Votes vs Panama Canal neutrality pact 3-16, 177F2
Votes vs 2d Canal pact 4-18, 273B1
Wins primary 9-16, 736C3
Reelected 11-7, 855B2, 858C2

1979

In Poland 6-2–6-7, 413A1-414D1; 6-8–6-10, 435E1
Installs 14 new cardinals 6-30, 640A2, B2*
Chinese bishop rejctd 8-17; ties sought, recognitn disputed 8-19–8-21, 639E2, B3
Visit to N Ireland barred 8-29, 642B1
Church-state issues challenged in US 9-13–10-3, 760A3
In Ireland 9-29–10-1; US, affirms traditionalism; addresses UN 10-1–10-7; photos 757A1-760A3, E3-761A2
Carter lauds visit 10-9, 767F1
Thatcher vows Ulster peace role 10-12, 792A1
Carter quotes in KC speech 10-15, 807G2
Chicago mass crowd figures disputed 10-21, 931C2
US asks aid in freeing hostages in Iran 11-6, 841C2
Asks safety of US hostages in Iran 11-8; Khomeini scores 11-11, 862C2, D2
Vatican rpts deficit 11-9, 931D1, G1
Pauline Fathers US crime probe rptd 11-9, 906A1
US, womens ordinatn poll rptd 11-11, 930F2
US Bishops reject prayer chng 11-14, 930F1
In Turkey; seeks RC-Eastn Orthodox reunificatn, Islam ties 11-28–11-30, sees Dimitrios I 11-29, 11-30, 930A3
US priest silenced, female ordinatn issue cited 12-1, 1000A1
Jesuits ordrd to curb liberal theology 12-7, 999C3
Vatican censures liberal theologian 12-18, 999C2, G2
JOHNS Hopkins University (Baltimore, Md.)
Estrogen, uterine cancer link rptd 1-4, 23F1-A2
Enlarged heart detectn method rptd 1-13, 64A3
Eisenhower letter rptd 1-28, 79E1
Wins NCAA Lacrosse title 5-26, 507F2-C3
JOHNS-Manville Corp.
In Dow Jones indl avg 72F1
JOHNS-Manville Federal Credit Union
Broker sentncd 3-13, 239C3
JOHNSON, Alexandra U.
Chrgs Israel torture 2-8; US rights rpt, UN envoy deny claim 2-10; 2-11, 107G3, 108C1, D2
JOHNSON, Butch
Steelers win Super Bowl 1-21, 63G1
JOHNSON, Dennis
Sonics win NBA title, named playoff MVP 6-1, 506E3, 507A1, B1 *
JOHNSON, Duane (1964-78)
Harper sentncd to death 11-7, 891A1
JOHNSON, Earvin (Magic)
Mich State wins NCAA basketball title, named MVP 3-26, 238A3, D3
Renounces coll eligibility 5-11; in NBA draft, signs with Lakers 6-25, 507A2, C2
JOHNSON Jr., Judge Frank M.
Puts Ala prisons in receivership, names gov agent 2-2, 112A3
JOHNSON, Rep. Harold T. (D, Calif.)
Softens trucking deregulatn stand 1-9, 111E3
Public Works Com chrmn 1-24, 71E1
JOHNSON, Howard B.
Backs sale to Imperial Group 9-10, 942C3
JOHNSON, John
Sonics win NBA title 6-1, 506G3
JOHNSON, Lady Bird (Claudia Alta Taylor) (Mrs. Lyndon Baines)
At Rockefeller funeral 2-2, 104E2
JOHNSON, Lee
In NBA draft 6-25, 507B2
JOHNSON, Louis
Miss Truth opens 7-22, 712E1
JOHNSON, Lyndon Baines (1908-73)—*See 1973, p. 53D2-B3 for biog. data*
Luci files for divorce 1-19, 79B2
Connally announces pres bid 1-24, 70F2
Rockefeller dies 1-26, 104B1
Contract-denial use cited 2-5, 127D3
CIA '63 Castro death plot rptd confrmd 5-2, 367G3
Furness on Carter mtg 6-1, 418G1
Cited in Carter SALT address 6-18, 458G2
CIA spying on antiwar activists rptd 7-16, 561D2
Mayoral Cabt apptmt cited 7-27, 577E1
Luci divorced 8-31, 859B3
JFK backed McNamara pres bid 9-23, 748B3
White House tapes alleged 10-29, 869C1
Coffin compares Viet bombing, Iran sanctns 12-23, 975C1
JOHNSON, Lynn-Holly
Ice Castles released 2-22, 174F2
JOHNSON, Marques
NBA scoring ldr 4-8, 290D2
On NBA all-league team 6-6, 526B2
JOHNSON, Marvin
Franklin KOs for WBC light heavywgt title 4-22, 412G3
KOs Galindez for WBA light heavywgt title 11-30, 1004D3
JOHNSON, Mary Lea
Sweeney Todd opens 3-1, 292C3
JOHNSON, Monica
Real Life released 3-1, 174E3
JOHNSON, Ruth Carter
Named Natl Gallery trustee 5-3, 375F1
JOHNSON, Sandy
Harper sentncd to death 11-7, 891D1

1980

In 6-natn African tour 5-2—5-10; Zaire mass violence, bars priests from politics 5-4, 341B2, 363B1-364A1
In France 5-30—6-2, meets Giscard 5-31, affirms traditionalism 6-1, 476F2-477B1
Sees Carter, urges Mideast peace 6-21, 474D2
In Brazil; defends human rights, urges reforms 6-30—7-11, 537A2-538F2
Scored re jailed Iranians in US 8-3, 587A1, C1
Iranians demonstrate at Vatican 8-8, 635A2
Supports Polish strikers 8-20, 626B3
Anti-abortionists lose US primary 9-16, 724E2
Opens bishops family life conf, affirms traditionalism 9-26, 810C2
Scores wedded lust 10-8, controversy ensues 10-11, 10-22, 810C3
Sets dispensatn guidelines 10-14, issues social justice encyclical 12-2, 969F3-970E1
Italy Soclst scores abortn stand 10-25, 873B2
In W Ger; seeks ecumenical ties, affirms traditionalism 11-15—11-19; youth ldrs denounce 11-19, 904F3-905A3
Visits Italian quake area 11-25, 893B2
Offers Beagle Channel solutn 12-12, 978C3-979A1
JOHNS Jr., Walter
Wins Polk award 2-25, 692E3
JOHNS Hopkins University (Baltimore, Md.)
Maternity smoking risks rptd 1-4, 23E3
TB vaccine study rptd 1-20, 63G1
'79 endowmt earnings rptd 3-24, 319C2
Wins NCAA lacrosse title 5-31, 638B1
X chromosome fragmts rptd cloned 8-30, 716A2
JOHNS-Manville Corp.
In Dow Jones indl avg 76F1
JOHNSON, Ben
Terror Train released 10-3, 836G3
JOHNSON, Brian
Wins Oscar 4-14, 296A2
JOHNSON, Darrell
Fired as Mariners mgr 8-4, 926A2
JOHNSON, Sgt. Dewey L.
Killed in Iran rescue mission 4-24, 321E2
JOHNSON, Diane
Shining released 5-23, 675D3
JOHNSON, Douglas
My Mother, My Father opens 1-9, 136D3
JOHNSON, Earvin (Magic)
Lakers win NBA title; named playoff MVP 5-16, 432C1, A2
2d in NBA top rookie vote 5-29, 656C3
JOHNSON, Eddie
Chrgd with cocaine possessn 7-13, 656B2
JOHNSON, Gerald W.
Dies 3-23, 279F3
JOHNSON, H. Charles
Arrested in Jamaica coup try 6-22, 498F3
JOHNSON, Rep. Harold T. (Bizz) (D, Calif.)
Loses reelectn 11-4, 837E1, 846E1, 852A2
JOHNSON, Haynes
Abscam probe criticism aired 2-6, 82E2
JOHNSON, J. J.
Bull Pen opens 6-12, 756C3
JOHNSON, James
Deplores NC KKK acquittals 11-18, 898C3
JOHNSON, Johnnie
In NFL draft 4-29, 336F2
JOHNSON, Johnnie L.
Escapes prison 7-28, recaptured 7-30, 654F1
JOHNSON, Lady Bird (Claudia Alta Taylor) (Mrs. Lyndon Baines)
Carpenter gets Educ Dept post 1-9, 18C2
JOHNSON, Lyndon Baines (1908-73)—*See 1973, p.53D2-B3 for biog. data*
Ford cites '64 race 3-2, 167D1
Lowenstein slain 3-14, 214G2
Okun dies 3-23, 280D1
Gerassi defies US travel ban to Iran 5-30, 6-2, 419E1
Hill dies 6-15, 528A2
'64 press endorsemts cited 11-1, 841F3
Shoumatoff dies 11-30, 928D3
JOHNSON, Mark
US Olympic hockey team beats Sovts 2-22, wins gold medal 2-24, 155B2
JOHNSON, Marvin
Gregory TKOs for WBA light-heavywgt title 3-31, 320E1
JOHNSON, Mary Lea
Goodbye Fidel opens 4-23, 392G2
JOHNSON, Pete
NFL '79 touchdown ldr 1-5, 8B2
JOHNSON, Reggie
In NBA draft 6-10, 447F1

1976

JOHNSON & Johnson
Rpts foreign payoffs 3-9, 361F3
SEC lists forgn paymts 5-12, 728B2
Exec jet crashes in Va 9-26, 840G2
Mexico City offices bombed 11-29, 907B1
Ortho Pharmaceutical Corp.
Sequentials withdrawn 2-25, 224B3
JOHNSON Matthew Bankers Ltd. (London)
Buys IMF gold 9-15, 739D3
JOHNSTONE, Jay
NL batting ldr 10-4, 795F3, G3
JOKSOVIC, Gen. Branko
On Yugo mil threat 1-11, 55E1
JOLIET, Ill.—*See ILLINOIS*
JONES, Rep. Ed (D, Tenn.)
Reelected 11-2, 830B4
JONES, Jack
Asks worker incentive plans 6-16, 439G3
Denies longshoreman strike rpt 11-11, 853F2
Warns vs spending cuts 11-20, 889A3
Scores UK spending cuts 12-15, 1003E3
JONES, Rep. James R. (D, Okla.)
Pleads guilty on campaign chrg 1-29, 134D1
Guilty plea cited 7-27, 566G1
Reelected 11-2, 830C3
JONES, Kirby
Rptd escorting US execs to Cuba 9-27, 791D2
JONES, Randy
NL wins All-Star game 7-13, 544A2
Gets Cy Young award 11-2, 952D1
JONES, Rep. Robert E. (D, Ala.)
Travel expense probe ends 10-27, 981G3
Flippo wins seat 11-2, 821F3
JONES, Thomas V.
Renamed Northrop chrmn 2-18, 133C1
JONES, Timothy
Operation replaces bone 5-3, 384D2
JONES, Rep. Walter B. (D, N.C.)
Reelected 11-2, 830D2
JONES, Judge William B.
Hammer pleads guilty again 3-4, 180F3
JONES & Laughlin Steel Corp.
Hikes prices 6% 11-24, Carter mtg urged 11-30, 897E2, E3

1977

JOHNSON, William (Skinny)
Joins basketball HOF 5-2, 490F3
JOHNSON Foundation, Lyndon Baines
Garfield gets award 10-26, 870B1
JOHNSON Publishing Co.
2d largest black-owned firm 6-1, 519F3
JOHNSTON, J. Bruce
USW talks open 2-14, 130F3
On steel pact cost 4-9, 273G3
JOHNSTON, Velma (Wild Horse Annie)
Dies 6-27, 532B3
JOHNSTOWN, Pa.—*See PENNSYLVANIA*
JOHORE, Strait of—*See STRAIT of Johore*
JOINET, Louis
Chrgs Brazil tortures minors 2-13, 168D1
JOINT Center for Political Studies
Williams at black ldrs mtg 8-29, 702F1
JOINT Chiefs of Staff—*See under U.S. GOVERNMENT*
JOINT European Torus (JET)
EC defers site decisn 6-29—6-30, Callaghan concerned 7-1, 624G2-A3
W Ger, UK set EC vote 10-18; UK site chosen 10-25, 852G3
JONES, Brenda—*See HOUGHTON, Brenda*
JONES, Bert
NFL officiating scored 12-18, 1020F1
JONES, Gen. David C.
Sees unionizatn threat 4-5, 342G3
On AF computer project 5-3, 5-10, 421D3
JONES Jr., J. Walter
Pleads guilty 3-10, sentenced 4-4, 312C3
JONES, Jack
Asks increased worker effort 1-5, 44C3
On S Africa boycott 1-13, 29B2
Evans elected TGWU head 4-21, 392F1
JONES, James
Dies 5-9, 452C3
JONES, Rep. James R. (D, Okla.)
Campaign fund guilty plea cited 2-16, 111G3
JONES, Maurice
Returns to UK, arrested 7-24, 617G2
Fined 9-28, 864F1
JONES, Peter
S Africa police arrest 8-18, 735A3
JONES, Reginald H.
Carter rpts anti-inflatn role 4-15, 298G3
On Miller selection 12-28, 1000B3
JONES, William B.
Named amb to Haiti 7-26, confrmd 8-3, 626E2
JONES, Winston
Jamaica soc security min 1-4, 46C1
JONES Construction Co., J. A.
Rpts forgn payoffs 5-16, 503F1
JONES & Laughlin Steel Corp.—*See LTV Corp.*
JONESVILLE, N.C.—*See NORTH Carolina*
JONES v. General Mills Inc.
Double-jeopardy bar upheld 3-28, 276F3
JONES v. Rath Packing Co.
Double-jeopardy bar upheld 3-28, 276F3

1978

JOHNSTON, Willie
Suspended from Scottish soccer 6-5, 520B3
JOHNSTONE, Jay
Traded to Yankees 6-14, 779B3
JOHNSTOWN, Pa.—*See PENNSYLVANIA*
JOINT Center for Political Studies
Blacks in state posts rptd 11-28, 915C3
JOINT Chiefs of Staff—*See under U.S. GOVERNMENT*
JONES, Barbara S.
Wins Provenzano case 3-25, 232E2
JONES, Barry
Asks wartime hangings probed 5-8, 350C1
JONES, Bert
NFL '77 passing ldr 1-1, 56A2
JONES, Blanche Calloway
Dies 12-16, 1032A3
JONES, Bobby
NBA field-goal ldr 4-9, 271F1, E2
Traded to 76ers 8-16, 655G3
JONES, Clarence B.
Clothing workers set NY Life bd bid 9-11, 699A3
JONES, Gen. David C.
Named Joint Chiefs Chrmn 4-5, 281F1
Turkish arms embargo end urged 4-6, 276F2
Sees Sovt buildup, urges defns budget hike 10-30, 833A3
Urges draft registratn 11-21, 895A1
JONES, Rep. Ed (D, Tenn.)
Reelected 11-7, 852D2
JONES, Grier
2d in Inverrary Classic 2-26, 355D3
JONES, James (1921-77)
Whistle on best-seller list 4-2, 272B3
JONES, James Earl
Paul Robeson opens 1-19, 760A3
JONES, Rep. James R. (D, Okla.)
Carter vs tax proposal 6-26, 491D2
House com OKs tax cut 7-27, 586A3
Reelected 11-7, 851G3
JONES, James T.
Loses Idaho US Sen primary 8-8, 625F3
JONES, Rev. Jim (James Warren)—*For Jonestown mass suicide-murder details, see PEOPLES Temple*
Photo 890A1
Guyana cult defector files affidavit detailing Jonestown abuses 6-15, 891C3
US probe team arrives Guyana 11-15; dies in Jonestown mass suicide 11-18; reactn, other dvpts 11-18—11-24, 889A1-892A2
Guyana govt releases US refs 11-20, Mrs Carter denies remembering 11-21, 891D1
San Fran pol posts, New West Aug article cited 11-21, 892C2
Guyana govt silent on ties, oppositn scores 11-24, 909G2
US defends pre-suicide probes 11-24, 910B1
Sexual tyranny rptd, '73 lewdness arrest confrmd 11-24, 911F1, C2
Body identified in US 11-27, autopsy planned 11-29, 910E1, G1
Moscone slain 11-27, 920D2
Aides held in murder probes; detail instructns, Sovt ties 11-28, 910F2, B3, 911A1
Son held 11-28, 911B1
Tape of death ritual rptd found 12-8, 954E3
Guyana ambush order denied by Layton, confrmd by witnesses 12-13, 955C2
'Hit list' feared by survivors 12-14, 955E2
Guyana jury calls murderer, murder victim 12-22, 999E3
JONES, Johnny (Lam)
Texas wins Sun Bowl 12-23, 1025D2
JONES, Larry
Traded to 49ers 4-14, 336F1
JONES, Maj. Gen. Lawrence
W Ger union scores job plan 1-11, 55B2
JONES, Marceline (Mrs. Jim Jones)
Mass suicide protest heard in tape 12-8, 955A1
JONES, Reginald L.
Sees Carter, backs inflatn plan 4-20, 361G3
Backs Carter anti-inflatn plan 10-25, 806C3
JONES, Robert C.
Coming Home released 2-15, 619B1
JONES, Stephan
Held in Guyana murder probe 11-28, 911B1
Confesses 12-18, Guyana indicts 12-19, 1000A1
JONES, Timothy
Limits testimony re Guyana murders 12-27, 1000G1
JONES, Tommy Lee
Eyes of Laura Mars released 8-4, 970C1
JONES, Rep. Walter B. (D, N.C.)
Reelected 11-7, 851B3
JONES & Laughlin Steel Corp.—*See LTV Corp.*
JONES v. U.S.
Police auto search power broadened by Sup Ct 12-5, 959E2

1979

JOHNSON, Sonia
Tried by Mormon ct 12-1, excommunicated 12-5, 929B3
JOHNSON, Vinnie
In NBA draft 6-25, 507A2
JOHNSON, Virginia E.
Rpts on homosexual therapy 4-16, book published 4-23, 315E3-316D1
JOHNSON, Wallace D.
Wins Chicago mayoral primary 2-27, 150A1; loses electn 4-3, 251G3
JOHNSON Matthey & Co. Ltd.
London gold price role described 2-7, 83C1, G1
JOHNSON v. Ryder Truck Lines
Case declined by Sup Ct 4-2, 281D2
JOHNSON v. U.S.
Case declined by Sup Ct 4-16, 303B1
JOHNSTON Jr., Sen. J. Bennett (D, La.)
Scores NRC A-plant closing order 3-13, 186B2
JOHNSTONE, Eddie
Signs to coach Black Hawks 6-9, 470D3
JOINER, Judge Charles W.
Orders Ann Arbor standard English teaching plan 7-12, 597B1
Ann Arbor OKs 'Black English' teacher progrm 8-15, 650A3
JOINT Chiefs of Staff—*See under U.S. GOVERNMENT*
JOLIET, Ill.—*See ILLINOIS*
JONATHAN, Stan
Bruins, fans brawl in NYC 12-24, 1004D1
JONES, Alan
3d in Grand Prix standings 9-9, 1005D1
JONES, Anthony
American Game released 4-28, 528C1
JONES, Charles
Iran captivity confrmd 12-25, 975F1
JONES, Gen. David C.
Warns of Sovt threat 1-25, 52C2
In missn to Saudi, Jordan 3-17–3-18, 198B1
Cited in SALT II communique, Carter Cong address 6-18, 457C1, 458E3
Backs SALT, mil spending hike 7-11, 510F2; 7-24, 643D3
JONES, Ed (Too Tall)
Steelers win Super Bowl 1-21, 62G3-63A2
JONES, Elinor
A Voice of My Own opens 5-2, 712C3
JONES, Grier
2d in Inverrary Classic 3-11, 220B3
JONES, Rep. James R. (D, Okla.)
Wins Budget com seat 1-23, 70G3
House OKs oil profits tax 6-28, 541D2
JONES, Rev. Jim (James Warren) (d. 1978)
IRS probes cult pol activities 1-13, 117F3
Estate sued by Jonestown kin 1-28, 117D2
Jonestown radio message transcripts rptd 1-29, 118D1
'78 cremation cited 2-1, 117G2
Son retracts 'confessn' 2-2, 117G3
Swiss banks block funds 3-12, 250E1
Temple property auctioned 3-14, 220A2
Jonestown tape copy rptd 3-15, 219G2
State Dept rpt finds cult probe neglect 5-3, 335D3
Temple funds transfer from Switz rptd 8-2, 592B3
JONES, Judge Ligon L.
Surry A-plant saboteurs convicted 10-16, 807E1
Sentences Surry A-plants saboteurs 11-27, 925B2
JONES, Peter
On civil svc cost review 6-11, 469A1
JONES, Preston
Dies 9-19, 756E2
JONES, Randall
Sues Daly estate 3-16, 289F1
JONES, Rickie Lee
Rickie Lee Jones on best-seller list 5-30, 448F3
JONES, Robert C.
Wins Oscar 4-9, 336A2
JONES, Ruppert
Traded to Yankees 11-1, 1002C3
JONES, Stephan
Jonestown radio message transcripts rptd 1-29, 118E1
Retracts murder 'confessn' 2-2, 117G3
JONES, Terry
Life of Brian released 8-17, 820A2
JONES, Thad
Wins Grammy 2-16, 336E3
JONES, Walton
1940's Radio Hour opens 10-7, 956E3
JONES, Willie
North wins Sr Bowl, named MVP 1-13, 63B2
JONES & Laughlin Steel Corp.—*See LTV Corp.*
JONES v. Wolf
Case remanded by Sup Ct 7-2, 559C1

1980

JOHNSON, Sonia
Mormon ldrs uphold excommunicatn 7-1, 638A2
JOHNSON, Tom (Sarge)
Killed in Polish jet crash 3-14, 214A1
JOHNSON, Willie
Dies 5-3, 448G1
JOHNSON v. Board of Education
Case dismissed by Sup Ct 10-20, 807C2
JOHNSON v. Hampton
Case declined by Sup Ct 6-2, 513C1
JOHNSON v. J.O.L.
Case accepted by Sup Ct 10-6, 782B3
Case remanded by Sup Ct 11-17, 882G1
JOHNSTON, David
On Mt St Helens eruptn 3-26, 252A2
JOHNSTON, Dick
On Canada separatism poll 11-24, 941C1
JOHNSTON, Donald
Canada treas bd pres 3-3, 171C2
Statistics Canada cleared 4-1, 272F3, 273A1
Rejcts PSAC contract demands 9-23, warns strikers 10-5, 808A1, D1
JOHNSTON, Eugene
Elected to US House 11-4, 843B4, 849G3
JOHNSTON, J. J.
Saudi completes Aramco takeover, retains bd seat 9-4, 662A2
JOHNSTON County—*See CALIFORNIA*
JOINER, Charlie
NFL '79 receiving ldr 1-5, 8C2
JOINT Chiefs of Staff—*See under U.S. GOVERNMENT*
JOINT Effort, The (underground newspaper)
Schl censorship power upheld 6-13, 583A1
JOLIET—*See ILLINOIS*
JOLLEY, LeRoy
Genuine Risk wins Ky Derby 5-3, 447B2
JOLSON, Al (Asa Yoelson) (1883-1950)
Jazz Singer released 12-19, 1003B2
JOLYOT, Paskal
Wins Olympic medal 7-23, 622A3
JONES, Alan
Wins Argentine Gr Prix 1-13, Spanish Gr Prix 6-1, French Gr Prix 6-29, British Gr Prix 7-13, Canadian Gr Prix, world title 9-28, US Gr Prix 10-5, 1001F3
JONES, Caldwell
NBA rebound ldr 3-30, 278E3
Lakers win NBA title 5-16, 432D1
JONES, Cyril
Wife, son kidnaped 1-5, 19E3
JONES, David (Deacon)
Enters Pro Football HOF 8-2, 999A2
JONES, Gen. David C.
Warns of Sovt aggressn 1-29, 65E1, C2
Scores Carter defns budget 5-29, 424E2
JONES, Ed (Too Tall)
Arrested for rape 1-31, complaint dropped 2-1, 320D3
JONES, Eddie
Act of Kindness opens 9-11, 756B3
JONES, Rep. Ed (D, Tenn.)
Reelected 11-4, 844D2
JONES, Howard Mumford
Dies 5-11, 448A2
JONES, J. D. F.
Negotiates Spooner release in Bolivia 8-12, 668F1
JONES, James Earl
Lesson From Aloes opens 11-17, 1003D3
JONES, Rep. James R. (D, Okla.)
Reelected 11-4, 843G4
JONES, Jeff
Weatherman fugitive surrenders 7-8, 576E3
JONES, Jennifer (Mrs. Norton Simon)
Bouts painting bought for record sum 4-16, 472G2
JONES, Rev. Jim (James Warren) (d. 1978)
2 Temple defectors, daughter slain 2-26, 190D3
Layton wins trial delay 4-1, Beikman sentenced for murder attempt 4-8, 313B3
'Guyana Tragedy' aired 4-15, 4-16, ratings rptd 4-22, 376D1
JONES, Johnny (Lam)
In NFL draft 4-29, 336E2, D3
JONES, Dr. Kenneth
Alcoholism, mental retardatn link rptd 1-4, 23G3
JONES, Lawrence (Biff)
Dies 2-12, 176G1
JONES, Leroy
Holmes TKOs 3-31, 320F1
JONES, Owen
Kidnaped 1-5, ransom demand rptd 1-7, 19D3
Freed 8-10, 707D2
JONES, Reginald H.
Welch to replace as GE chrmn, chief exec 12-19, 986G2
JONES, Richard M.
Named Sears vice chrmn 10-7, 959F2
JONES, Sam J.
Flash Gordon released 12-5, 972E3
JONES, Stephanie
Attacker sentenced 4-8, 313C3
JONES, Telery
Kidnaped 1-5, ransom demand rptd 1-7, 19D3
Freed 8-10, 707D2
JONES, Tommy Lee
True West opens 12-23, 1003F3
JONES, Rep. Walter B. (D, N.C.)
Reelected 11-4, 843B4
JONES & Laughlin Steel Corp.—*See also LTV Corp.*
JONES v. U.S.
Case cited by Sup Ct 6-25, 541B1
JONG, Erica
Fanny on best-seller list 716B3; 10-12, 9-14, 796D3

1976

JOPLIN, Scott (1868-1917)
Wins Pulitzer 5-3, 352F3

JORDAN, Hashemite Kingdom of—*See also ARAB League, NONALIGNED Nations Movement*
Listed as 'not free' nation 1-19, 20E3
EC trade talks rptd 2-2, 64B3
Hussein visits Australia 3-2—3-9, 204B1
Hussein in Moscow 6-17—6-28, 464F1; visit cited 7-31, 561A2
Rifai quits, Badran succeeds 7-13; Badran quits 11-27, 949A3
Middle East Conflict—*See MIDDLE EAST*
UN Policy & Developments—*See also UN DEVELOPMENTS under MIDDLE EAST*
Backs anti-Zionism stand 4-28, 320B3
U.S. Relations—*See also 'Jordan' under MIDDLE EAST—ARAB Policies*
Hussein visits 3-30—4-4, 242E1
Hawk deal cancelatn denied 4-14, 4-15, 274A3
Arms relay to Morocco sought 5-22, 458C2
US arms aid authorizatn, '76 funds signed 6-30, 532E3, 533C2
To get US air defense system 7-31, 561F1
US '77 aid funds signed 10-1, 806D3

JORDAN, Rep. Barbara C. (D, Tex.)
Dem conv keynoter 7-12, 505E1, 508B1
Dem conv pres vote, table 7-14, 507E2
Reelected 11-2, 830E4
JORDAN, Edward G.
Conrail offcls named 3-3, 235B3
On Conrail 1st ¼ loss 8-12, 648F1
On Conrail losses 11-11, 887B2
JORDAN, Hamilton
Delegate prediction 5-5, 322D3
Carter outlines campaign strategy 7-16, 532A3
Carter campaign chrmn 7-20, 7-24, 565F3
Heads personnel selectn 11-15, 864C1
Carter personnel advisor 11-23, 881F2
JORDAN, Vernon
Carter rues 'ethnic' remark 4-8, 261D1
Carter personnel advisor 11-19, 881D3
Declined Carter post 12-16, 937A2
JORDEN, William
Gets Panama protest 9-17, chrgs denied 9-21, 792F1, E2
Torrijos vs chrgs re blasts 11-29, 1008A3

1977

JONG, Erica
How to Save Your Own Life on best-seller list 5-1, 356C2

JORDAN, Hashemite Kingdom of—*See also ARAB League, NONALIGNED Nations Movement*
EC trade pact signed 1-18, 73E3
Queen Aliya, health min die in air crash 2-9, 87D1
Arab monetary fund created 4-18, 318C1
Cholera outbreak rptd 9-26, 747G3-748C1
Hussein meets Sadat re PLO 12-8—12-9, 953G1
Arab-Israeli Conflict—*See MIDDLE EAST*
Cairo Conference—*See MIDDLE EAST—EGYPT-Israel Peace Moves*
UN Policy & Developments
UN Assemb member 4B1
Waldheim visits 2-8—2-9, 86F2
Israel scores occupatn monitoring request 3-25, 226G3
U.S. Relations—*For Arab-Israeli conflict, see MIDDLE EAST—U.S. DEVELOPMENTS*
Vance visits 2-18—2-19, Hussein reactn to Sadat plan for PLO link rptd 2-19, 121D2
CIA paymts rptd, Jordan assails; US, PLO statemts 2-18—2-23, 123A3, 124C2
US, Hussein defend CIA paymts; Post mtg rptd 2-24—2-28, 151E1, G2
Carter plans visit 3-8, 165A2
Hussein in US, sees Carter 4-25—4-26, 315G3-316B1
Arms aid signed 8-4, 668C1, D1
Vance meets Hussein 8-5—8-7; briefs on Israeli talks 8-11, 605B1, G2
Carter meets Sharaf 9-28, 734B1
US '78 security aid funds cleared 10-19, 815G2; signed 11-1, 834D1
Vance meets Hussein, asks Sadat peace backing 12-12, 954C1

JORDAN, Rep. Barbara C. (D, Tex.)
At Natl Women's Conf 11-19, 917E3
Bars 4th term 12-10, 1005B3
JORDAN, Edward G.
Conrail '76-77 losses rptd 3-31, 325C2
On Conrail 2d ¼ loss 8-4, 612F3
Conrail 3d ¼ loss rptd 11-9, 899G3
JORDAN, Hamilton
Named Carter asst 1-14, 35F2
To lead Canal treaty ratificatn fight 8-15, 622C1
On Lance banking probe 8-18, 626C1
Canal pact ratificatn drive under way 9-7, 678G3
Saw FBI rpt on Lance 9-12, 701E3
JORDAN, Hugh Lowe (Jimmy)
Kidd, Gilbreth acquitted 5-20, 424E1
JORDAN Jr., Vernon E.
Bell confrmatn hearings 1-11—1-18, 34B2
Scores Carter energy plan 4-21, 320F2
Scores Carter 7-24; Carter rebuts, meets privately 7-25, 7-28, 573C1, F2
Black Caucus backs 7-29, 592G3
Blacks meet re govt 'neglect' 8-29, 702D1
Sees Carter 12-14, 960E1
JORDAN River
Israel seeks diversn bar 10-10, 769B2

1978

JONGBLOED, Jan
Argentina wins World Cup, photo 6-25, 520E1, B2, F2

JORDAN, Hashemite Kingdom of—*See also ARAB League, NONALIGNED Nations Movement*
Islamic, Arab poor-natn aid rise rptd 4-9, 257F2
Egypt terror group rptd smashed 4-26, 300D2
Hussein announces engagemt 5-15, 420A3
Hussein names successors 6-8, 580C1
Hussein marries, wife proclaimed queen 6-15, 580B1
Arab fund loan to Sudan rptd 8-17, 925F3
June '77-78 world inflatn rates ranked 10-18, 914F1
Arab-Israeli Conflict—*See MIDDLE EAST*
UN Policy & Developments
Chile rights abuse res abstentn 3-6, 210F1
Assemb member 713G3
UNESCO scores Israel 11-29, 931F1
U.S. Relations—*For Arab-Israeli conflict, see MIDDLE EAST—EGYPT-Israel Peace Moves*
Carter in talks with Hussein 1-1—1-2, 2A2, E2
Carter signs econ aid authorzn 9-26, 734F1
US econ aid funds signed 10-18, 862D2

JORDAN, Rep. Barbara C. (D, Tex.)
Not standing for reelectn 5-6, 363A1
Leland wins runoff 6-3, 426G2
Leland wins seat 11-7, 855D3
JORDAN, Edward G.
Seeks more aid for Conrail 2-15, 224B3
Disputes Conrail safety rpt 3-15, 225A1
JORDAN, Hamilton
Legal separation rptd 1-9, 96B1
Coal strike talks open in White House 2-15, 105C1
Barroom incident rptd 2-19, White House defends 2-20, 3-2, 141G1-B2
Schindler vs US Mideast stand 3-9, 176A3
Firmer Cabt control rptd planned 4-29, 306E3
Denies anti-Israel lobby remark 5-16, 358E1
Denies 'pol fix' chrg 9-10, Anderson revises article 9-11, 719E3, 720B1
Stresses tight budget 11-14, 875E1
JORDAN, Nancy (Mrs. Hamilton)
Legal separation rptd 1-9, 96B1
JORDAN Jr., Vernon E.
On youth jobless, scores Carter 3-15, 811B2
On Carter urban-aid plan 3-27, 217F3
Outlines black vote issues 4-10, 568G2-A3
On Sup Ct Bakke ruling 6-28, 482D2
At Urban League conf 8-6—8-8, 811A1-B1
Speaks to HEW workers 9-21, 811C1
Meets Carter, scores budget plans 12-4, 936A3
JORDEN, William
In Nicaragua, Somoza OKs US 'cooperatn' in crisis 9-25, intl mediatn 9-30, 757A3
JORGE, Paulo
Sees US Sen McGovern 12-13, 985B1

1979

JOOS, Kurt
Dies 5-22, 432A3
JOPLIN, Janis (1943-70)
Rose released 11-17, 1008C1
JORDAN, Hashemite Kingdom of—*See also ARAB League*
Jet crashes in Qatar 3-14, 240C3
Pol unrest rptd 4-15, 278G2
Arab-Israeli Conflict—*See MIDDLE EAST*
Foreign Relations (misc.)—*See also 'UN' below*
Canada oppositn ldr visits 1-14–1-17, 57F2
Saudis seek aid to N Yemen 3-6, 157G2
Egypt amb withdrawn, Cairo recalls aides 3-29, 248B3
Libya fete attended by Hussein 9-1, 688C3
Canada envoy tours Mideast 9-9–10-20, 833D2
Hussein in France 9-10, 676B3
Israel cites mil threat 9-12, 693C2
Obituaries
Jumaa, Saad 8-19, 671E2
UN Policy & Developments
UN sets West Bank probe 3-22, 198E2, A3
Membership listed 695F2
U.S. Relations
US issues rights rpt 2-10, 107A3
US defense secy visits 2-12, 143B2, D2
Saudis ask US aid in Yemen war 3-6, 157G2
US missn seeks Egypt-Israel pact support 3-18; Hussein chrgs 'arm-twisting' 3-20, 197F2, 198B1
US to sell M-60 tanks 7-26, deal delayed 7-31, 574A3
Mideast policy cited re Libya ties 9-1, 688C3
Jesse Jackson visits 9-27, 763C1

JORDAN, Hamilton
Dismisses Abzug 1-12, 30G2
Scores '78 4th ¼ profit rise 3-20, 201B2
Cited in SALT II summit communique 6-18, 457C1
Named Carter staff chief 7-17; Cabt, staff shake-up, reactn 7-18–7-20, 529A1, C2, 531C1, A3
Issues staff evaluatn forms 7-17, 529G1, 530C2
Meets with O'Neill 7-17, Adams 7-19, 530G1, A3, 531A2
Cited re Califano firing 7-20, 556D1
Carter defends appointmt 7-25, 555D3
Donovan apptd Carter adviser 7-25, 556F1
Announces Carter staff shuffle 8-10, 608C2
Denies cocaine chrg 8-24; aides back 8-25, Landau disputes 8-28, 647D1-E2
Vesco jury foreman resigns, claims cover-up 8-29, 647F2
Vesco emissary money offer cited 8-30, 725A3
Cocaine probe continues 8-31–9-28, FBI expands 9-13, 767B2
Carter on cocaine probe 10-9, 767B2
Alleged cocaine supplier indicted 10-23, 891D3; pleads guilty 12-18, 1000E1
Disco owners plead guilty to tax chrgs 11-2, 891C3
Cocaine probe spec prosecutor named 11-29, 900C3
Arranges shah departure to Panama 12-11–12-13, 957C1
JORDAN, Joseph
Orders schl violence probe 10-19, 850B2
JORDAN, Kathy
Loses Richmond Intl 8-19, 734C2
JORDAN, Richard
Old Boyfriends released 3-21, 528C3
JORDAN Jr., Vernon E.
Urban League rpt details black econ plight 1-17, 35D1-C2
Keynotes Urban League conf 7-22, 560D1
Vs black support for PLO, Baptist Conv scores 10-14; meets Jackson, 'unity' reaffirmed 10-17, 780D2, A3, B3
JORDAN, William H.
Sentncd in GSA kickback scandal 3-20, 367A3

1980

JONNA Dan (Liberian freighter)
Rams Fla bridge 3-8, 391G1
JOPLING, Judge Wallace
Sentences Bundy to death 2-12, 136D2
JORDAN (Hashemite Kingdom of Jordan)—*See also ARAB League, NONALIGNED Nations*
Prime Min Sharaf dies 7-3, 608C3
Rimawi named prime min 7-3; quits, Badran named 8-28, 698G1
Human rights record scored 12-10, 978B3
Foreign Relations (misc.)—*See also 'Iran', 'UN' below*
Persian Gulf defns role cited by US 2-1, 84C2
French pres visits, backs PLO role in talks 3-9, 180C1
Iran hostage rescue missn scored 4-27, 324C2
Olympic boycott stand reversed 5-25, 421G1
Israel sets Medit-Dead Sea canal, hydro plan; map 8-24, 643D3
Red Sea-Dead Sea canal plan rptd 8-30, 661G1
Troops mass vs Syrian move 11-26; Syria chrgs aid to Moslem Bro'hood, Hussein defies 11-29, 11-30, 911A2
Israel warns interventn if Syria invades 11-26, 911E3
Saudis mediate Syria feud 11-30; Syrian terms rejected 12-3, 911F2-A3
Hussein: Sovts prod Syria vs Jordan 12-1, 911D3
Hussein to attend Syria feud talks 12-5, border troops withdraw 12-10—12-11, 931F2
Iran-Iraq War
Iraq backed 9-23, 719C2
Hussein in Baghdad 10-4—10-5, Iraq aid ordrd 10-6, troop presence denied 10-8, 757A1, A2
Iran, US, Israel score Iraq aid 10-7, 157E1, A2
Hussein in Riyadh, asks backing for Iraq 10-11—10-12; rpt Saudis vs direct mil aid 10-13, 774G2
Hussein cancels Sovt visit 10-11, 774B3
Iran calls 'prime supplier' of Iraq 10-17; US comments 10-18, 798F2, D3
US assures Iran on aid to Iraq 10-18, 798D3
Iraq sees US, Israel, Iran plot 10-18, 799B2
Hussein visits Iraq, vows support 10-27—10-28, 820F3
Hussein warns US vs arms to Iran 10-29, 820B3
Saudi ports open for Iraq war supplies 11-20, 894F2
Hussein scores Syria support to Iran 11-27, 911G1
Hussein: Iraq slows drive 12-8, 931E3
Iraq awards 30 captured US tanks for war backing 12-9, 12-10, 931F3
Obituaries
Sharaf, Abdul Hamid 7-3, 608C3
UN Policy & Developments
Nusseibah scores Israel 12-8, Israel chrgs anti-Semitism 12-10, 952A3
U.S. Relations—*See also 'Iran' above*
Pentagon rpt on Persian Gulf defns issued 2-1, 84C2
Debakey visits 3-29, 242F1
Iran hostage rescue missn scored 4-27, 324C2
Carter meets Hussein on Palestinian autonomy 6-17—6-18; US pledges tanks 6-19, 450A1, E1
Reagan electn reactn 11-5, 841C2
Hussein seeks arms speedup 12-1, 911B3
JORDAN, Barbara
Wins Australian Open 1-1, 213E1
JORDAN, Edward G.
Named Cornell business schl dean 5-21, 456F2
Resigns from Conrail, named Cornell dean 9-29, 959D2
JORDAN, Hamilton
Studio 54 owners sentenced 1-18, 64D3
In Panama, asks shah to stay 3-21; missn fails 3-23, 217C1
Vesco grand jury ends 4-1, 251E3
Denies Carter OKd mil actn vs Iran 4-23, 298F2
Cleared re cocaine chrgs 5-28, 402C3
Named campaign com dep chrmn 6-11, 439A1
NY drug dealer sentenced 6-30, 503A2
Carter cites chrgs 8-4, 594D2
Econ plank compromise fails 8-12, 610A3
Kraft cocaine probe rptd 9-14, 700C1
JORDAN, Kathy
US wins Federatn Cup 5-25, 607C1
Wins French Open women's doubles 6-6, Wimbledon 7-5, 606A3, E3
US wins Wightman Cup 11-1, 947A1
JORDAN, Ralph (Shug)
Dies 7-28, 608C2
JORDAN, Richard
Raise the Titanic released 8-1, 675D3
JORDAN Jr., Vernon E.
Urban League rpt doubts '70s progress 1-22, 94C2
Wounded in Ft Wayne 5-29, 401D2
Carter visits 6-1; moved to NY hosp 6-12, 442G1
Pres candidates visit 8-4, 8-6, 597D2
On electn results 11-4, 847A1
Meets with Reagan 12-11, 956F2
JORDAN, Wilbur
Dies 6-3, 528C2
JORDAN-Simer Inc.
FTC chrgs misleading birth control ads, complaint setld 2-28, 358F2

1976

JORGENSEN, Anker
Kissinger visits 1-20, 62A1
On Spanish socialist aid 1-24, 120G1
Rpts Viet orphans to stay 3-16, 252D1
At intl soc dems mtg 5-23—5-25, 449B3
Lauds Israel Uganda raid 7-4, 486G1
Austerity plan adopted 8-19, 637A3
Scores Argentina violence 8-26, 672D2
Shuffles Cabt 9-9, 712F1
Greenland mineral rights kept 11-8, 949B2
JORON, Guy
Named energy min 11-26, 903A3
JOSEPH, Richard
Dies 9-30, 970B2
JOSEPH Co., I. S.
'75 Cuba visit rptd 9-27, 791E2
JOSPIN, Lionel
Scores new CP line 119G2
JOURNALISM—*See PRESS*
JOY, Greg
Wins Olympic medal 7-31, 576D1
JOYAL, Serge
Air pact talks cited 7-1, 496A3
To represent Quebec air union 8-3, 587A3
J R (book)
Wins Natl Book Award 4-19, 292C3

JUAN Carlos I, King (Spain) (formerly Prince Juan Carlos de Borbon)
Amnesty petitions rptd 1-3, 12E1
Elections postponed 1-15, 54A3
Confirms electn postponemt 1-27, 77D1
Visits Catalonia 2-16—2-18, 144B2
Warns cncl re reforms 3-4, Cabt OKs penal reform 3-18, 269E1
Names 2 key mil cmdrs 3-28, 314B3
Legis process speeded 4-24; govt struggle rptd 4-27, 314A2
New legislature proposed 5-7, 422C1
Holidays changed 5-19, 422G1
Queen attends Jewish service 5-28, 459A3
With queen in DR 5-31—6-1, US 6-1—6-5, 459A2-C3, D3
Pol torture rptdly continues 501D2
Popular Soclst ldr scores govt 6-6, 459B1
US warned vs legalizing CP 6-8, 6-19, 459C3
Father urges Spain backing 6-14, 459E1
Intl bank loan rptd sought 6-23, 501A3
Fires Arias 7-1, names Suarez premr 7-3, 500A3
Rpt reformers refuse Cabt posts 7-6, score Suarez 7-8, 523B2
Cabt sworn 7-8, addresses 7-9, 523G1, F2
Renounces bishop veto power 7-16, 541E1
Cabt to ask pol amnesty 7-17, 540F3
Archbp asks broad amnesty 7-25, 753B3
Vatican Concordat revised 7-28, 753D3
US assurance on CP ban rptd 7-30, 753C1
'77 electn plan unveiled 9-10, 752B3
Adviser assassinated 10-4, 774G2
Opens Ford plant 10-25, 929A2
OKs Cambio 16 rpts on Lockheed 10-28, 909D2
Pol reform bill passed 11-18, 908C2
At meml mass for Franco 11-20, 909A1
Venez pres visits 11-28, 930A1
JUAN Sebastian de Elcano (Spanish sailing ship)
In Operation Sail 7-4, 488A3
JUANTORENA, Alberto
Wins Olympic medals 7-25, 7-29, 575F3, 576B1
JUDD, Frank
Named overseas dvpt min 12-21, 1004F1
JUDD, Neil M.
Dies 12-26, 1015F1
JUDGE, Lance Cpl. Darwin L.
S Viet returns body 2-22, 157A2
JUDGE, Gov. Thomas L. (D, Mont.)
Unopposed in primary 6-1, 411G1
Reelected 11-2, 820B3, 824B2, 831F1
JUDGES—*See COURTS; JUDICIARY under U.S. GOVERNMENT*
JUDO
Olympic results 7-28—7-31, 574G3, 575A1
JUDY, Nancy
Defeated 11-2, 822G3
JULIANA, Queen (Juliana Louise Emma Marie Wilhelmina) (Netherlands)
Lockheed payoff cited 2-6, 130F3
Cabt confrms Bernhard bribe 2-8, probe opens 2-11, 131F2
Sees Den Uyl on Bernhard probe, bars abdicatn 8-23, 626G2
Parlt vs Bernhard prosecutn 8-30, 642D2
On '77 budget proposals 9-21, 732A2, C2

1977

JORGENSEN, Anker
Parlt dissolved, electn set 1-22, 61D3
Asks newspr strike delay 1-31, 115E2
Soc Dems in electn gains 2-15, 115D1
Names Cabt 2-25, 372G3
On election results 3-1, 373D1
Govt asks tax increase 8-22, 672F2
Announces Cabt chngs 10-1, 10-3, 882E3
JORLING, Thomas C.
Named EPA asst admin 6-1, confrmd 6-21, 626F2
JORON, Guy
Home insulatn plan rejected 7-28, 597B1
JOSEPH, Sir Keith
Scores union practices 10-11, 863F3
JOURNALISM—*See PRESS*
JOURNAL of the American Medical Association—*See AMERICAN Medical Association*
JOVA, Joseph P.
Replaced as amb to Mex 5-25, 499G3
JOVANIC, Gen. Djoko
Tito's wife accused 10-25, 844B2
JOVOVIC, Bogdan
Rptd seized 12-17, 1018B3
JOZAMI, Lila Pastoriza de
Rptd kidnaped 7-15, 595F2

JUAN Carlos I, King (Spain) (formerly Prince Juan Carlos de Borbon)
Rightists score 1-29, 102B1
Sees Pope 2-10, 242D3
Mex ties renewed 3-28, 242B3
Natl Movemt dissolved 4-1, 286D1
Army scores CP legalizatn 4-14, 307A1
Suarez to run for lower house 4-25, 331B1
Names 41 sens, parlt pres 6-15, 453D1
Asks Suarez to form new govt 6-17, 506C3
Sees Catalan Socialists, vows more autonomy 6-21, 507B1
Gonzalez rpts mtg 6-23, 507A1
Swears in new Cabt 7-5, 545E1-C2
Addresses Cortes, asks new const 7-22, 582B1
Bomb plot foiled 8-17, leftist groups blamed 8-20, 826G2
In Venez, Central Amer 9-8—9-17, 804F3
Restores Catalonia Generalitat 9-29, 843A1
New amnesty bill OKd 10-14, 826D1

JUBANY, Archbishop Narciso Cardinal
Asks full pol amnesty 1-1, 21F3
JUBILEE (book)
Haley, Doubleday sued re Roots 4-22, reissue set 4-25, 356E1
JUDGE Horton and the Scottsboro Boys (TV film)
Libel suit vs NBC dismissed 7-12, 643B1
JUDGES—*See COURTS; U.S. GOVERNMENT—JUDICIARY*
JUDICIARY, U.S.—*See under U.S. GOVERNMENT*

JULIANA, Queen (Juliana Louise Emma Marie Wilhelmina) (Netherlands)
Den Uyl to form govt 3-22, 221B3
Den Uyl fails to form govt 5-25—8-25, 656C1
Abortn rift healed 9-2; names den Uyl mediator 9-5, 729F2
Soc Dems ask monarchy end 10-13—10-15, poll repudiates 10-17, 986B2
Asks van Agt to form govt 12-8, swears Cabt 12-19, 985A3

1978

JORGENSEN, Anker (Danish premier)
Sees parlt ldrs re free city suit 2-2, 89E3
French electn comment spurs dispute 2-23—3-1, 167G1
On US energy policy 4-7—4-8, 257G3
Danish fishermen protest 5-5, 371E2
Assumes forgn mins duties, weighs broader coalitn 6-2, 596E1
Coalitn govt formed, retains premrship 8-30, 687G2, 688A1
Sets 6-mo freeze, VAT tax 8-30, 687C3
Opens parlt, outlines legis goals; workers protest 10-3, 774A1
JOSEFSSON, Ludvik
Fails to form govt 8-16—8-24, bars progesssive coalitn role 8-31, 688G3-689B1
JOSEPH, Burton L.
Denied reply to Sadat peace plea 2-1, 60D3
JOSEPH, Helen
Appeal rptd lost 1-23, 114F1
JOSEPH, John
Film wins Oscar 4-3, 315D3
JOSEPH Andrews (film)
Released 4-13, 619F2
JOSS, Adrian (Addie) (1880-1911)
Inducted into Baseball HOF 8-8, 617D3
JOUBERT, Lucian
Referees Ali-Spinks bout 9-15, 726G1
JOURDAN, Louis
13 Rue De L'Amour opens 3-16, 760D3
JOURNALISM—*See PRESS*
JOURNALISM Education, Institute for
Maynard scores media racism 4-7, 419F3
JOY, Greg
Sets indoor high jump record 1-13, Jacobs breaks 1-27, 76F2, A3
JOYCE, James (1882-1941)
Mr Joyce opens 4-23, 760F2
JOYCE, William D.
'76 earnings rptd 2-20, 365B2
JOYFUL Company (painting)
Vandalized 4-11, 335A2
JOYVIES, Billy Keith (d. 1975)
2 Houston ex-cops chrgd in cover-up 12-14, 991D2
J. P. STEVENS v. N.L.R.B.
Contempt challenge refused 2-21, 125F3
JUAN Carlos I, King (Spain)
In Libya re Canaries 1-21, OAU com backs separatists 2-21, 136G1
Sees EC Comm pres 4-28—4-28, 395D1
Visits Iran, China 6-14—6-19, 576A2
Giscard visits 6-28—7-1, 649E1
Contraceptive law rptd signed 10-12, 822B2
Anti-govt plot by security offcrs rptd 11-16—11-21, 967E2
Visits Mexico, Peru, Argentina 11-17—11-30, 967G2
Carter lauds const referendum 12-7, 967B1
Signs new Constitutn 12-27, 1022G1

JUBILEE (book)
'Roots' plagiarism suit dismissed 9-21, 759A3
JUDAISM—*See JEWS*
JUDGE, Gov. Thomas (D, Mont.)
Names Hatfield to Metcalf Sen seat 1-22, 52B3
JUDGES—*See COURTS; U.S. GOVERNMENT—JUDICIARY; personal names*
JUDICIAL Conference of the U.S.—*See under U.S. GOVERNMENT—JUDICIARY*
JUDICIARY—*See COURTS; U.S. GOVERNMENT—JUDICIARY*
JUELFS, Stanley R.
Loses primary for Neb gov 5-9, 363E1
JUILLIARD Quartet
Wins Grammy 2-24, 316C1
JULIA (film)
Wins Oscars 4-3, 315C3
JULIEN, Pauline
Wins '70 arrest suit 9-12, 755D2

1979

JORGENSEN, Anker (Danish premier)
Urges gasoline conservatn 5-22, 396C3
Plans A-power referendum 8-22, 668E1
Resigns, calls electns 9-28, 751A3
Soc Dems gain in electns 10-23, 812A3
Forms new govt 10-26, 855A1
Sets wage-price freeze 11-4, 855C1
Outlines legis progrm 11-6, 855F1-A2
JORY, Jon
Getting Out opens 5-15, 711B3
JOSEPH, Judith
Loudspeaker opens 4-30, 712C1
JOSEPH, Sir Keith
UK industry secy 5-5, 338E1
Steel plant closings planned 7-12, 543G1
Rpts depressed area aid cut 7-17, 543A2
On Post Office reform 9-12, 687D1
Names new NEB members 11-21, 949F3
Vows BL aid 12-20, 994C1
JOSHUA, Larry
Kid Champion opens 8-27, 712A1
JOUHANDEAU, Marcel
Dies 4-7, 356E3
JOURDAIN, Roger
Red Lake violence flares 5-20, 465D1
JOURNALISM—*See PRESS*
JOYCE, James (1882-1941)
Portrait of the Artist released 4-21, 528C3

JUAN Carlos I, King (Spain)
Scores army unrest 1-6, 61A1
At requiem mass for slain gen 3-6, 191F3
Marks Armed Forces Day 5-27, 428G2
Meets Arafat 9-13—9-15, 694D3

JUANTORENA, Alberto
Pan Am Game results 7-1—7-15, 798C3
Coe breaks 800-m run mark 7-5, 911E1*
JUAYAMAN
Mecca mosque takeover role rptd 11-30, 899G1; 12-16, 997B1
JUDAISM—*See JEWS*
JUDICIARY—*See COURTS, U.S. GOVERNMENT—JUDICIARY*
JUHL, Jerry
Muppet Movie released 6-22, 820C2
JULIA, Raul
Othello opens 8-8, 712A2

1980

JORGENSEN, Anker (Danish premier)
Proposes armed forces cut 1-21, 96F3
Austerity plan rptd 4-10, 273F2
Sets new econ plan 5-5, 351A2
JOSEPH, Bernard (Dov)
Dies 1-6, 104A3
JOSEPH, Sir Keith
New Brit Steel chrmn named 5-1, 352E1
Telecommunicatn monopolies to be curbed 7-16, 7-21, 564B1
On Brit Steel aid hike 9-26, 750F2
JOSEPH, Lafontant
Arrested 11-29, 922B3
JOSEPHSON, Erland
To Forget Venice released 1-28, 216F3
JOST, Reinhold
Wins Daytona endurance 2-3, 637F3
JOURNALISM—*See PRESS*
JOURNIAC, Rene
Dies 2-8, 176A2
JOUSTS (recording)
Peterson wins Grammy 2-27, 296E3

JUAN Carlos I, King (Spain)
Madrid gen dismissed, '79 speech cited 1-25, 101C2
'78 coup plotters sentenced 5-7, 355A2

JUDAISM—*See JEWS & Judaism*
JUDGE, Gov. Thomas L. (D, Mont.)
Defeated in primary 6-3, 439G2
Schwinden wins seat 11-4, 847E1, 851G3
JUDICIARY—*See under U.S. GOVERNMENT*
JUDO
Moscow Olympic results 7-25—8-2, 623B1
JUDY, Steven
Murder convictn appeal discharge OKd 10-28, 869E1
JUHL, Donald F.
Hired as D Kennedy drug therapist 1-22, 199F3
JULIA Child and More Company (book)
Wins Amer Book Award 5-1, 692D2
JULIAN, Joseph
Act of Kindness opens 9-11, 756A3

JULIANA, Queen Mother (Juliana Louise Emma Marie Wilhelmina) (Netherlands)
Sets abdicatn 1-31, 100D1
Andriessen quits Cabt 2-21, 173D3
Abdicates, daughter invested 4-30, 353C3

1976

JUMBLAT, Kamal
Forces fight in Chuf area 1-13, 17F3
Sees 'decisive battle' 1-15, 17E3
Opposes Leb reforms 125G1
Backs new accord 1-22, 33F1
Says both sides rearm 1-31, 83B2
Vs Christian pres 2-11, 107B2
2 US aides freed 2-25, 145C2
Meets Khaddam, vs war renewal 2-25, 162E2
Meets Khaddam 3-10, 209E1
Syria presses for truce 3-23; rejcts truce, asks Franjieh quit 3-24, 210E1, F1
Balks at truce, chrgs Syria pressure 3-26, 3-29—3-30; softens stand 3-31, OKs 4-1, 225D1, D2
US backs moderates 3-30, 226A2
Meets US envoy 4-1—4-2, 241E2
Chrgs Syria port seizure, protests to Karami 4-4, 241E1
Saiqa, Moslem left feud rptd 4-5, 241C2
Meets US mediator 4-8, 4-12, 258E1
Shuns parlt meeting 4-10, 257C2
Vs Syrian troops in Leb 4-11, protests to Arab League 4-12, 257E1
OKs truce extension 4-11, 257D2
Assad airs Damascus talks 4-12, 257F1
Says Syria blocks food to Leb 4-15, 273D2
Meets Arafat, backs Leb peace plan 4-16, 273E1
Plans leftist admin 4-24, 296D1
Vs electn date 4-27, 296A1
Chrgs Syrian interference 4-28, 296B1
Baathists vs electn stand 4-29, 296D1
Moslems vs Sarkis as pres, back Edde 4-30, 319B1
Chrgs Syria plot 5-3, asks Syria troop exit 5-4, 319C1
Calls for general strike 5-7, 337C1
Offers Sarkis cooperatn 5-10, 5-11, 337A2
Meets Iraq mediator 5-17, 355D1
Meets Sarkis on truce moves 5-20, 369B2
Vs French peace force 5-22, 369E1
Sister killed 5-27, 385D2
Scores Syria invasn, blames Karami, Franjieh 6-1; sees Sarkis, B Gemayel 6-2, 385D1
Force joins united command 6-5, 405G1
Syria chrgs plot vs peace 6-13, 429A2
Scored for opposing Syrian troops 6-15, 429C2
Warns vs refugee camp attacks 6-29, 463C3
Asks Arab aid vs Syria 7-11, 514A3
USSR seeks to bar defeat 7-13, 514D3
Assad defends mil role in Leb 7-20, 528A2
Rpts Moslems form civil govt 7-22, 527G3
Syria, PLO talks rptd 7-27, 546F1
Plans 'popular army' 8-13, 617G2
Sees long war 8-23, 628G3
Shuns Sarkis inaugural 9-23, 699F1
Meets Sarkis on truce 9-26, 720G2
Sees Sadat in Cairo 9-28, 720D2
Orders mobilizatn 10-6, 758C3
Israel denies ship attacked 759D3
Opposes truce agrmt 10-9, 758C2
Bomb blast near home 12-5, 913E1
JUNG-Mo Yang
Wins Olympic medal 7-31, 576C3
JUNIOR, Alfredo dos Santos
Release from prison rptd 1-23, 53A2
JUOLA, Arvo E.
Grade averages drop rptd 9-7, 993B3
JUPITER (planet)—*See ASTRONOMY*
JURIES—*See COURTS*
JURISTS, International Commission of—*See INTERNATIONAL Commission of Jurists*
JUSTINIANO, Adm. Horacio
'75 plot vs Pinochet rptd 1-9, 47F1
JUVENILE Delinquency—*See YOUTH*

1977

JULME, Jean
Haiti frees, exiles 10-14, 905G2
JULTAK, Ira
Berkowitz found fit for trial, insanity plea planned 10-21, 848E3
JULY 26 Movement
FBI Cointelpro papers released 11-21, 940E3
JUMBLAT, Kamal
Slain 3-16; reprisals 3-16—3-17, 188C1
Son heads Druse clan 3-17, 208D2
Revenge slayings end 3-18, 208G1
JUMBLAT, Walid
Heads father's Druse clan 3-17, asks restraint 3-20, 208D2
JUMPER, Hershel
Boteler convicted 1-8, 60E1
JUNGERS, Frank
Says Saudis to up oil output, gives Aramco figures 5-11, 362G1
JUNOT, Philippe
Engagement announced 8-25, 808B3
JUNSCHKE, Klaus
Sentenced to life 6-2, 601F3
JUPITER (planet)—*See ASTRONAUTICS—Interplanetary Projects*
JUREK, Jerry Lane
Executn filming protested 1-3, Sup Ct stays 1-17, 40B3
JURIES—*See COURTS*
JURIS Doctor (magazine)
Largest US law firms rptd 5-16, 383B2
JURISTS, International Commission of—*See INTERNATIONAL Commission of Jurists*
JUSTICE, Department of—*See under U.S. GOVERNMENT*
JUVENILE Delinquency—*See YOUTH—Crime*

1978

JUNOT, Philippe
Wedding plans announced 4-24, 420G2
Married 6-28, 6-29, 580D1
JUPITER (planet)
'Germane' rptd part of atmosphere 1-7, 293C2
JURGENSON, Sonny
Tarkenton breaks pass completn record 12-3, 1024C1
JURIES—*See COURTS*
JURISTS, International Commission of—*See INTERNATIONAL Commission of Jurists*
JUSTICE, Department of—*See under U.S. GOVERNMENT*
JUSTICE, International Court of—*See UNITED Nations—International Court of Justice*
JUSTICE, Milton
Patio/Porch opens 4-13, 887D2
JUST the Way You Are (recording)
On best-seller list 3-8, 196B1
JUVENILE Delinquency—*See YOUTH—Crime*
J. W. BATESON Co. v. U.S.
Contractor paymt bond coverage curbed 2-22, 126A3

1979

JUMAA, Saad
Dies 8-19, 671E2
JUPITER (planet)
Carter budgets research 1-22, 46G1
Voyager I photos 2-13, 3-4, 162D2
Voyager I makes close approach 3-5, findings detailed 3-5–3-17, 215E3-216D3
Voyager I hot cloud detectn rptd 6-9, 692G1
Voyager II flies by, findings detailed 7-9, 552B3-553E1
Pioneer 11 flies by Saturn; findings listed 9-1, 696G1
14th moon rptd discovered 10-17, 1000D2
JURGENS, Curt
Goldengirl released 6-15, 820C1
JURIES—*See COURTS*
JURIETTI, Charles
Sanchez decisns 10-7, 839D1
JURISTS, International Commission of—*See INTERNATIONAL Commission of Jurists*
JUST a Little Less Than Normal (play)
Opens 5-20, 711G3
JUSTICE, Department of—*See under U.S. GOVERNMENT*
JUSTICE, Jimmy
Sancocho opens 3-28, 712C2
JUST Like At Home (film)
Released 4-19, 528F2
JUST the Way You Are (recording)
Wins Grammys 2-16, 336C3
JUST You and Me, Kid (film)
Released 7-27, 820D1
JUVENILE Delinquency—*See YOUTH*
JUVENILE Disease Foundation
Virus found to cause diabetes 5-23, 471F3

1980

JUMBAZ, Hisham
Slain near Damascus 8-16, 673B3
JUMBE, Aboud
Reelected Tanzania vp, Zanzibar cncl chrmn 10-26, 888E1
JUMP, Stewart
Arrows win MISL title 3-23, 771B2
JUNOT, Philippe
Divorced 10-9, 890D3
JUPITER (planet)
15th moon rptd discovered 5-6, 416C1
16th moon rptd discovered 9-6, 716C2
Voyager 1 flies by Saturn 11-12, 932B3
JUSTE, Gen. Jose
Named to Madrid post 1-24, 101A2
JUSTICE, Donald R.
Wins Pulitzer 4-14, 296E2
JUST Tell Me What You Want (film)
Released 2-8, 216A3
JUVENILE Delinquency—*See YOUTH--Crime*

K

1976

KABORE, Alfred
Upper Volta forgn min 2-9, 269D3
KACAR, Tadija
Wins Olympic medal 7-31, 574C1
KACZMAREK, Zbigniew
Wins Olympic medal 7-21, 576D2
KADAR, Janos
Pullai replaced 10-27, 947B1
KADDOUMI, Farouk
Addresses UN Cncl 1-2, 18D1
Chrgs Fatah-Leb links 5-10, 337F1
Asks Islamic Conf aid 5-13, 373A2
KAGELMANN, Uwe
Wins Olympic medal 2-7, 159B1
KAHANE, Rabbi Meir
Belgium deports 2-19, 206C3
Leads anti-Arab riot 5-19, 354D2
Arrested in Hebron 8-25, 699G3
Plans move to Qiryat Arba 10-17, 799C1

1977

KABORE, Alfred
Replaced as forgn min 1-14, 183A2
KABSI, Capt. Zaid al-
Fails in Ghashmi death try, executed 10-19, 824E1
KACOWICZ, Naum
Home bombed 1-7, 42E1
KADAR, Janos
Sees Pope Paul 6-9, 492B2
Lefebvre scores mtg with Pope 6-29, 620D2
Scores Eurocommunism 7-3, 590D3
KADI, Hamdi
Slain by PLO 12-26, 995E2
KADUMA, Ibrahim
Replaced in Tanzania Cabt 2-13, 161B2
KAHANE, Rabbi Meir
Sparks W Bank riots 4-17, 4-26; barred; parlt bid noted 5-1, 335G2
KAHLIG-Scheffler, Dagmar
Arrested for spying 5-4, 602G1
KAHN, Alfred E.
Vs airline cigar, pipe smoking ban 11-22, 900G1

1978

K2—*See Mt. GOODWIN Austen*
KADAR, Janos
Rumania envoy visits 2-16—2-19, 180E2
Nemeth promoted 4-20, 534A2
NY Times interview rptd 6-10, 534E2
In France, stresses detente 11-15—11-17, 894E2
KADDOUR, Nasser
Protests Israeli invasn 3-15, 174D3
KADIR, Hatem Abdul
Held in PLO deaths 8-3, 582B3
Admits Iraqi ties 8-4, 602A3
Chrgd with PLO deaths 8-5, 602G2
KAGAN, Jeremy Paul
Big Fix released 10-6, 969C3
KAGAN, Saul
Indicted 4-12, 326A2
KAGERA River
Bridge destroyed in Tanzania-Uganda border conflict 11-3; map 860F1
KAHLIG-Scheffler, Dagmar
Sentenced for spying 10-5, 776D3
KAHN, Alfred
Named anti-inflatn chief 10-25, 806C2
Vs mandatory wage-price controls 10-25, 806B3
At St Louis wage-price forum 11-1, 863B3
On Meany wage-price criticism, sees '79 strikes 11-5, 863F2
Sees depressn if Carter plan fails 11-15, Carter comments 11-16, 11-30, 917B3
Hails RR rate hike 11-24, 1007A3

1979

KACZENDER, George
In Praise of Older Women released 2-8, 174A3
KADAR, Jan
Dies 6-1, 508B3
KADAR, Janos
Meets Brezhnev 5-30–6-1, 416F3
KAHN, Albert E.
Dies 9-15, 756E2
KAHN, Alfred E.
Natl trust comm rpt issued 1-16, 88G2
Rpts 207 big cos vow compliance 2-6, 127F3
Scores business on prices 3-13, 182A1
Threatens trucking deregulatn 3-15, 251G1
Scores '78 4th ¼ profit rise 3-20, 201B2
Carter backs 4-10, 263E3
Teamster pact lauded 4-11, 262A2
Sees rubber industry chiefs 4-20, urges wage-guide compliance 5-4, 344G3, 345A2
On Mar CPI rise 4-26, 325A1
Ct bars wage-guide contract denial 5-31, 399C2, A3
Carter econ team rptd revamped 6-4, 463E1
Carter orders timber sales 6-11, 441B1
On June CPI rise, energy prices 7-26, 556E3
Praises UAW-GM settlemt 9-15, 698D2
Unhappy with GM-UAW pact 9-30, 744G1
Calls '79 inflatn goal unattainable 10-26, 828B1

1980

KA-BOOM! (play)
Opens 11-20, 1003C3
KACAR, Slobodan
Wins Olympic medal 8-2, 622A2
KACHUSITE, Lina
Wins Olympic medal 7-23, 623C3
KADAR, Janos
12th CP cong meets, Politburo shuffled 3-24—3-28, 274D3, 275A1
At Moscow summit on Poland 12-5, 929E1
KADUNGURE, E. R.
Zimbabwe transport min 3-11, 198D1
KAGAN, Marilyn
Foxes released 2-29, 216E2
KAHANE, Rabbi Meir
Seized as anti-Arab plotter 5-13, 362B3
Sentenced 9-15, 902A1
KAHN, Alfred E.
On '79 CPI increase 1-25, 75A3, D3
Vs wage-price controls 3-2, 168F1
Fraser scores 3-7, 225A3
New pay guidelines OKd 3-13, 182A3
Sees continued inflatn 5-23, 400A3
On May CPI 6-24, 481A1

1976

KAHN, Ben
Dies 2-5, 124E3
KAIFI, Toshiki
Japan educatn min 12-24, 1006B3
KAIM, Franciszek
Polish deputy premier 3-27, 268E2
KAISER, Marvin L.
FBI purchasing irregularities rptd 1-1, 6B1
KAISER Industries Corp.
Exec's daughter killed in Argentina 10-20, 996A2
KAISER Aluminum & Chemical Corp.
Admits Jamaica paymts 6-10, 690D2
National Steel & Shipbuilding Co.—*See separate listing*
KAISSOUNI, Abdel Moneim
Egyptian dep premier 11-10, 852E1
KAJIYAMA, Hiroshi
Wins Olympic medal 7-23, 574C3
KALAMAZOO (U.S. warship)
In Intl Naval Review 7-4, 488E3
KALAMAZOO (Mich.) Gazette, The (newspaper)
Newhouse buys Booth chain 11-8, 901B3
KALLINGER, Joseph
Sentenced to life 10-14, 972E1
KALLINGER, Michael
In Pa detentn center 10-14, 972G1
KALLIOMAKI, Antti
Wins Olympic medal 7-26, 576A1
KALMOKO, Capt. Leonard
Upper Volta planning min 2-9, 269C3
KALVEX Inc.
SEC lists paymts 5-12, 726B1, 728B2
KAMENSKE, Bernard H.
Vs VOA ban on PLO contacts 10-8, 759F3
KAMIL, Abdallah Mohammed
Named Afars & Issas pres 7-29, 696C2 ★
KAMING, Joseph S.
Indicted 5-26, 442A3
KAMOL Dechatungka, Air Chief Marshal
Named supreme commander 775A3
Heads Thai armed forces 10-6, 754C1 ★
Heads natl security 10-8, 775A3
KAMPMANN, Viggo
Dies 6-3, 524A3
KANAWHA County, W. Va.—*See WEST Virginia*
KANGAS, Orvokki
Sworn Finnish 2d soc affairs min 9-29, 750D3
KANI, John
Expelled 10-24, 813B2
KANINIAS, Spyros
Welch death probe ends 5-21, 402D2

KANSAS
Reagan, Ford win GOP delegates 5-11, 343A1
Reagan visits Topeka 5-22, 374E1
Dem conv women delegates, table 508B2

1977

KAHN, Jack E.
Scores funeral industry 8-16, 651E3
KAISER, Henry J.
HMO unit certified 10-26, 870B1
KAISER, Philip M.
Named amb to Hungary 6-22, confrmd 6-30, 626F2
KAISER Aluminum & Chemical Corp.—*See KAISER Industries*
KAISER Industries Corp.
Jamaica buys bauxite unit assets 2-2, 257F2
Kaiser Aluminum shuts 2 potlines 2-20, 244E3
New Kaiser Alum-USW pact reached 5-24, 422E1
Kaiser Alum ups prices 6-14, 577F1
Kaiser-Permanente HMO certified; Garfield honored 10-26, 869G3
CPSC sues Kaiser Aluminum 10-27, 900E3
KAISSOUNI, Abdel Moneim
Quits, resignatn rejctd 1-19, 43E3
Gulf group aid rptd 3-25, 390C3
Gets planning min post 10-25, 824B1
KAKIS, Kyriacos
UK base in Cyprus bombed 11-31, 946F3
KALDERON, David
Tied to Yadlin kickback chrg 2-14, 135C2
KALE, Kogale
Post-electn fighting in Kamtai 6-22, 7-13, 639B2
KALIX, Christian
Sentenced in E Berlin for spying 11-23, 968E2
KALMOGO, Capt. Leonare
Upper Volta finance min 1-14, 183A2
KAMEL, Mohammed Ibrahim
Named Egypt foreign min 993E1
Heads pol com in Israel talks 12-26, 993E1
Airs Egypt peace plan 12-31, 995A1
KAMEN, Milt
Dies 2-24, 164B3
KAMIL, Abdallah Mohammed
Named Djibouti forgn min 7-15, 583C2
KAMINSKAYA, Dina
Expelled from USSR 12-4, 956B1
KAMINSTEIN, Abraham L.
Dies 9-10, 788C1
KAMISEASE, Mara (Fiji prime minister)
Dissolves Fiji parlt 6-1, 547E3
KAMPMANN, Jens
Danish tax min 2-25, 373C1, E1
KANAMORI, Hiroo
Richter scale revised 2-14, 161B3
KANAPA, Jean
Giscard scores US talks 4-2, 255D2
KANAWHA River
FMC plant shut 3-9, reopened 3-15, 196B3, D3
KANE, Robert J.
Elected USOC pres 4-29, 491A3
KANE, Thomas
Boyle convictn upset 1-28, 95E3
KANON, Denis Bra
Ivory Coast agri min 7-30, 772C1

KANSAS
Legislature schedule rptd 6D2
'75 interstate gas sales cited 1-28, 76C3
Snowstorm kills 2 3-10—3-12, 204A3
'76 per-capita income table 5-10, 387E2
Topeka econ data table 5-16, 384F2

1978

On Oct CPI rise 11-28, 918G1
Paper union sues Admin re wage plan 12-1, 934D2
Asks state pay hike rollbacks 12-4, 935B1
Rpts gas shortage probe, studies rationing 12-6, 962E3
Carter vs consumer boycotts 12-12, 957C1
On wage-price rule revisns 12-13, 957F1, G2, B3
Chicago offcls OK pay hike cut 12-13, 957D3
Scores OPEC price hike 12-17, 978B1
KAHN, Madeline
On 20th Century opens 2-19, 887D2
KAHN, Sarilee
Gay Divorce opens 3-9, 760C2
KAID, Ahmed
Dies 3-5, 252A3
KAISER, Georg
Approaching Zero opens 11-30, 1030G3
KAISER Aluminum & Chemical Corp.—*See KAISER Industries*
KAISER Aluminum & Chemical Corp. v. Consumer Product Safety Commission
Case refused by Sup Ct 10-2, 751E1
KAISER Aluminum & Chemical Corp. v. Weber
Case accepted by Sup Ct 12-11, 980F2
KAISER Cement & Gypsum Corp.
Medusa merger agreed 3-16, 283D1
Medusa takeover canceled 8-22, 700C3
KAISER Industries Corp.
Kaiser Alum NW productn resumed 1-10, 24F1
Aluminum wire dispute refused by Sup Ct 10-2, 751F1
Weber reverse job-bias case accepted by Sup Ct 12-11, 980A3
KAISSOUNI, Abdel Moneim
Ousted as Egypt econ min 5-7, 392G2
KALAK, Ezzedine
Assassinated 8-3, 582B3
Death tied to Iraqi agents 8-4, 602A3
Funeral held, revenge vowed 8-5, 602G2
KALCHEIM, Lee
Winning Isn't Everything opens 12-3, 1031C3
KALMBACH, Herbert W.
Reinstated by Calif bar, joins ex-gov's law firm 7-11, 844B1
KALYUBI, Ibrahim al-
Rpts terror group smashed 4-26, 300C2
KAMEL, Mohammed Ibrahim
Arrives Jerusalem, states Sadat demands 1-15; Begin scores 1-17, 25C1
In Israel pol talks 1-17—1-18, recalled to Cairo 1-18, 25B1
Meets Begin, denies talks breakdown 1-18, 25G1
Israel Cabt scores pol talks role 1-18, 25B2
Meets US aide on peace moves 1-30—2-1, 60D1
Meets Vance 2-4, 77B2
Vs Israel Leb invasn 3-15, 174F3
US reassures on Carter Palestine statemt 5-1, 339G2
Lauds US Sen jet pkg OK 5-16, 358B2 ★
Vs Israel W Bank, Gaza stand 6-19, 461F2
On plan for W Bank, Gaza 6-24; Israel rejcts 6-25, deplores actn 6-26, 488E3
To attend London peace conf 7-2, 502A1
Meets Israel forgn min in UK 7-18—7-19, 546C1
Calls Israel talks waste 7-26, 562A3
Quits to protest summit pacts 9-18, 710F3, 712C1
Salem: Sadat gets full support on summit pact 9-19, 730B2
Successor sought 10-5, 774B3
KAMEMARU, Shin
On Joint Staff chief ouster 7-25, 574E2
KAMM, Henry
Wins Pulitzer Prize 4-17, 315A2
KAMM, Robert B.
Unopposed in Okla Sen primary 8-22, 683B1
Loses electn 11-7, 855G2
KAMPILES, William P.
Arrested on spy chrg 8-17, 645D2 ★
Spy chrg raises CIA security issues 10-2—11-9, 940C2-F2
Trial opens 11-6, convicted 11-18, 940F1
Sentenced 12-22, 1011C3
KAMPUCHEA, Democratic—*See CAMBODIA*
KAN, Dr. Yuet Wai
Sickle cell anemia test rptd 11-4, 948D1
KANAGA, Consuelo
Dies 2-28, 196C3
KANE, Shaikh Saad Bouh
Ousted as Mauritania justice min 1-26, 95D1
KANEKO, Ippei
Japan finance min 12-7, 945E2
KANG Sheng (d. 1975)
Poster criticizes 11-23, 949A2
KANG Shih-en
Named China dep premr 2-26—3-5, 153E1
KANI, Ali Naqi
Named Iran relig endowmts min 8-27, 668A1
KANSAS
Legislature schedule rptd 14E3
'67, '77 sales-tax rates rptd 1-5, 15D3
State govt tax revenue table 1-9, 84C2
Postal competitn convictn refused by US Sup Ct 3-27, 241E2

1979

KAHN, Gus
Whoopee opens 2-14, 292F3
KAHN, Michael
Month in the Country opens 12-11, 1007D2
KAHNWEILER, Daniel-Henry
Dies 1-11, 104B3
KAIFU, Hachiro
Signed Grumman contract in Japan 1-9, 98G2
Indicted 5-15, 389E2
KAISER Aetna Co.
Pub access to waterways curbed by Sup Ct 12-4, 988A1
KAISER Aetna v. U.S.
Case decided by Sup Ct 12-4, 988A1
KAISER Aluminum & Chemical Corp.—*See KAISER Industries*
KAISER Aluminum & Chemical Corp. v. Weber
Case argued in Sup Ct 3-28, 262C3
Case decided by Sup Ct 6-27, 477B1
KAISER Industries Corp.
Weber reverse job-bias case argued in Sup Ct 3-28, 262D3
Weber affirmative actn challenge rejctd by Sup Ct, reactn; majority opinion excerpts 6-27, 477B1-478E1
KAISER Steel Corp.
Hamersley shares sale to Conzinc planned 6-4, 562B3
KALAMAZOO, Mich.—*See MICHIGAN*
KALFIN, Robert
Strider opens 5-31, 712F2
KALODNER, Philip
On Gulf overchrg allegatn 6-12, 580B3
KALP, Malcolm
Hostage status disputed 11-30—12-1, spy trial threatened 12-1, 12-4, 914A2
KAMOUGUE, Wadal Abdelkadar
Named Chad vice pres 8-21, 638E2
KAMPILES, William P.
US spy satellite data rptd compromised 4-28, 318D3
KAMPVILLE, Ill.—*See ILLINOIS*
KANE, Carol
When A Stranger Calls released 10-12, 1008A2
KANE, Sister Mary Theresa
Challenges Pope on female ordinatn 10-7, 759E3
KANE, Robert G.
Villain released 820E3
KANEE, Stephen
Teibele and Her Demon opens 12-16, 1007F2
KANEKO, Ippeo
Blumenthal sees re trade imbalance 3-4, 160A1
KANGAROOS—*See WILDLIFE*
KANG Shih-en
Heads trade missn to Brazil 5-21, signs maritime pact, 5-22 443B3
KANIA, Eugene B.
Indicted for REA funds misuse 3-8, 239F3
KANNEL, Judge Samuel
OKs NH A-plant constructn cost pass-on 1-26, 186A3

KANSAS
Legislature schedule rptd 5D3
Blizzards hit 1-12—1-14, 1-24—1-27, 120F1
Wichita TV rptr contempt review refused by US Sup Ct 2-21, 128C3

1980

KAHN, Madeline
Simon released 2-29, 216E3
Happy Birthday Gemini released 5-2, 416A3
First Family released 12-25, 1003G1
KAIFU, Hachiro
Gets suspended sentnc 7-24, 605D2
KAISER Jr., Edgar F.
Replaced as Kaiser chief exec 9-5, 702B1
KAISER Industries Corp.
USW pact settled 5-30, 482F2
KAISER Steel Corp.
Kjelland named pres, chief exec 9-5, 702B1
KAITCHER, Leonard
Found dead 2-9, 194G1
KALAMAZOO—*See MICHIGAN*
KALB, Marvin
Rpts Ghotbzadeh slur vs Khomeini, Iran bars CBS-TV 29A3
Gets NBC post 6-18, 638G2
KALINE, Al (Albert Williams)
Elected to Baseball HOF 8-3, 796B2
KALININA, Irina
Wins Olympic medal 7-21, 623F3
KALIVIANAKIS, Nicholas
Indicted re A-plant 3-26, 249E1
Acquitted 8-8, 649E1
KALKIN, Robert
Hijinks! opens 12-18, 1003B3
KALLUR, Anders
NHL scoring ldr 4-6, 296E1
KALP, Malcolm
Fellow hostage calls spy 4-9, 282C3
KAMEN, Michael
Reggae opens 3-27, 392F3
KAMINSKA, Ida
Dies 5-21, 448B2
KAMINSKY, Sherman
Letelier murder trial testimony ruled inadmissible 9-15, 703F3
KAMM, Henry
Arrested in Malaysia 9-6, ousted 9-7, 810A2
KAMM, Tom
Glass Menagerie opens 11-4, 892D3
KAMOUGUE, Wadal Abdelkadar
Joins Oueddei's forces 4-10, 311F1
KAMPELMAN, Max M.
Warns Sovts on Polish invasn 12-19, 950F1
KAMPUCHEA, Democratic—*See CAMBODIA (Democratic Kampuchea)*
KANAWHA River (West Virginia)
FMC pleads guilty re pollutn 11-10, 869A2
KANDINSKY, Nina
Slain 9-3, 755E3
KANDINSKY, Wassily (d. 1944)
Wife slain 9-3, 755E3
KANE, Carol
Sunday Runners opens 5-4, 392G3
KANE, Michael
Smokey & the Bandit II released 8-15, 675E3
Foolin' Around released 10-17, 836G2
KANE, Phil
2d in Penn Relays mile 4-25, 892D2
KANE, Robert
Carter urges shift of Moscow Olympics 1-20, 45C2
KANE & Abel (book)
On best-seller list 8-17, 640E3
KANE-Miller Corp.
On '79 Fortune 500 list 5-5, 291C1
KANGAI, K. M.
Zimbabwe labor min 3-11, 198D1
KANGEROOS—*See WILDLIFE*
KANG Sheng (d. 1975)
Ousted from CP 10-31, 859E1
Cited in Gang of 4 indictmt 11-15, 11-16, 877C1, A2
Gang of 4 trial defendant 11-20—12-29, 975E2
KANG Shien
Censured re '79 oil rig accident 8-25, 651C3
KANIA, Stanislaw (Polish Communist Party first secretary)
Named Polish party chief, USSR lauds 9-6, 678E2-A3
Vows labor agrmt implementatn 9-6; visits Gdansk 9-8, Silesia 9-9, 678A3-679A1
Addresses CP Central Com: scores Gierek, sees continued crisis 10-4, 10-6, 760B3
Meets Warsaw Pact forgn mins 10-19—10-20, 800D2
In USSR, affirms ties 10-30, 859G3
Meets Walesa 11-14, 878B1
Reveals Sovt aid, scores unionists 12-1, 910B1
Moczar reelected to Politburo 12-2, 910A1
Pledges Polish loyalty at Moscow summit 12-5, 929C1
KANNENSOHN, Michael
Mandatory sentnc study rptd 3-29, 359G1
KANSAS
Legislature schedule rptd 18D1
State of State message 1-7, 403F2
Pres primary results 4-1, 246E1-A3
Tornado hits 4-7—4-8, 391A3

1976

Dem conv pres vote, table 7-14, 507C2
GOP pre-conv delegate count 8-14, 583B3
GOP conv pres, vp vote tables 8-18—8-19, 8-19, 599B1, B3
Reagan seeks conv delegates 8-18, 601C3
Ford in Russell 8-20, 631B2
Dole in Wichita 10-16, 804F1
Election results 11-2: pres 818B1, 819B1; cong 820D2, 823D2, 825D2, 829D3
Dole Vice-Presidential Campaign—See DOLE, Robert
KANSAS City, Mo.—*See MISSOURI*
KANSAS City Star, The (newspaper)
Ariz crime probed 10-2, 849D2
KAO Kang (902-54)
Cited in Mao death announcemt 659C2
KAOUANE, Noel Mouloud
France denies spy chrg 1-9, 45D2, C3
KAPEK, Antonin
Czech Presidium member 4-16, 289A2
KAPITONOV, Ivan V.
CP Secretariat member 3-5, 195F2
KAPPEL, Frederick Russell
Replaced as Postal Svc gov 8-8, 808A1
KARAGEORGEVICH, Prince Paul (Yugoslavia)
Dies 9-14, 932E3
KARAMI, Rashid
Asks election delay 1-5, 1E2
AF assault scored 1-16, 33D2, F2
Sets new truce 1-17, resigns 1-18, 33B1, G2
Sees Moslem ldrs, Khaddam; withdraws resignatn 1-24, 58D3, 59D1
Assures Christians on sovereignty 1-25, 59G1
Mil group pullback OKd 1-25, 59A2
On Leb-Syria pol talks 2-11, 107A2
CP Secretariat member 3-5, 195F2
Cabt meets on army crisis 3-8, 3-10, 209E1
Ahdab demands resignatn 3-11, 209A2
Syria-bound plane attacked 3-19, 210C1
In Damascus, meets Assad 3-20, 210C1
US backs mediation 3-30, 226G1
Jumblat protests Syria ports seizure 4-4, 241E1
Meets French, US mediators 4-10, 258D1
Meets with truce group 4-19, 273F2
Higher Mil Com meets 5-3, 319A2
Meets US mediator 5-4, 319E1
New truce call 5-14, 354D3
Vs French peace force 5-23, 369G1
Jumblat chrgs OKd Syrian invasn 6-1, 385D1
In Natl Union Front 7-11, 514D3
Moslems form civil govt 7-22, 528C1
Meets on Tel Zaatar fall 8-12, 577E1
Loses power in Cabt shift 9-15, 682F2
In Cairo talks 9-18, 698C3
Shuns Sarkis inaugural 9-23, 699F1
Cabt resigns 12-9, 913C2
KARASEK, Svatopluk
Sentenced 9-23, 851F3
KARASINSKI, Andrzej Jaroslaw
Hijacks plane, surrenders 11-4, 907A2
KARIM, Tayeh Abdel
On Yamani walkout at OPEC mtg 12-16, 934B3
KARITHII, Geoffrey
90 Minutes at Entebbe publshd 7-26, 547B2
KARJALINEN, Ahti
Sworn Finnish v premr 9-29, 750D3
KARKER, Edward
Weds Makarova 2-22, 271E3
KARKOSZKA, Alojzy
Polish deputy premier 3-27, 268F2
Named to Secretariat 12-2, 926D3
KARLOV, Vladimir A.
Named to Central Com 10-26, 839E2
KARNICK, Nick
Loses Cong primary 6-8, 409D3
KARPPINEN, Pertti
Wins Olympic medal 7-25, 575D1
KARTH, Rep. Joseph E. (D, Minn.)
Vento elected 11-2, 823G2
KARUME, Sheik Abeid Amani
Plotters appeal 10-18, 1013C3
KARUNANIDHI, Muthuvel
Ousted from state post 1-31, 101F2
KASAHARA, Masanori
Quizzed on Lockheed 7-31, 8-1, found dead 8-2, 624F2
KASHLEV, Yuri B.
Vs West on press plan 11-25, 895G3
KASIMIER, Helmut
Loses Lower Saxony electn 1-15, 77A2
CDU wins Lower Saxony revote 2-6, 157G2
KASIS, Father Charbel
Assured on Leb sovereignty 1-25, 59G1
KASPUTYS, Joseph E.
Commerce asst admin 1-27; confrmd 2-26, 186A2
KASSA, Lt. Bewookatu
Rptd executed 8-12, 674C2
KASSIS, Rev. Charbel
Backs Syrian invasion 6-6, 406B2
KASTEN Jr., Rep. Robert W. (R, Wis.)
Reelected 11-2, 831A4
KASTENMEIER, Rep. Robert W. (D, Wis.)
On copyright revisn 2-20, 152E2
Reelected 11-2, 831A3
KATAYAMA, Shig
Home searched 2-24, Diet subpoenas 2-26, 190F2, G2
KATO, Sawao
Wins Olympic medals 7-21, 7-23, 574B3, C3
KATORI (Japanese warship)
In Intl Naval Review 7-4, 488D3
KATS, William A.
Dole denies fund chrg 9-6, 665F3
KATTAH, Brig. Alphonse Kojo
Awoonor rptd freed 10-24, 858A2

1977

KC seeks interstate integratn 5-26, 446E1
3 steel firms indicted 6-6, 504D1
KC LEAA office to close 6-20, 630E2
Wheat farmers income drop rptd 8-8, 612B1
KC integratn plan challenged 8-15, 631D1
State oil trust suits merged 9-12, 691G3
'76 per capita income, tax burden table 9-13, 10-18, 821C2
Gas royalties dispute review refused 10-3, 760G1
Boeing Wichita struck 10-4—11-17, 1005A2
Ft Riley tank injury suit remanded 11-14, 878A3
Farmers protest in Plains 11-25, 916E1
Farm strike backing rptd 12-22, 1003D1
KANSAS, University of (Lawrence)
Butler in NFL draft 5-3, 353B3
KANSAS City, Kan.—*See KANSAS*
KANSAS City, Mo.—*See MISSOURI*
KANSAS City Star Co.
Capital Cities buys 2-15, 216F1
KANSAS State University (Manhattan)
Bark on drought effects 2-21, 183G2
KANTOR, MacKinlay
Dies 10-11, 872D2
KAPITONOV, Ivan V.
Arrives Czechoslovakia 2-8, 115B1
KAPOOR, Yashpal
Arrested 8-15, 637D2
KAPPLER, Anneliese
Smuggles husband to W Ger 8-15, 637E3
On husband's jail escape 8-19, 9-15, 729E1
KAPPLER, Herbert
Escapes Italy jail 8-15, extraditn asked 8-17, 637E3
W Ger asylum arouses concern 8-19—8-26, 658A2
Wife details escape 8-19, 9-15, 729F1
Italy asks W Ger confinemt 8-26, W Ger rejcts extraditn 9-21, 729G1
Schmidt meets Andreotti 12-1, 1015A1
KARASINSKI, Andrzej
Jailed in Austria 2-15, 425A2
KARATE
Carter call-in topic 3-5, 171F1
Intl book fair held 9-6—9-14, 765E3
KARDELJ, Edvard
Visits US 9-28—10-4, 785D3
KARGOUGOU, Moussa
Upper Volta forgn min 1-14, 183A2
KARPOV, Yevgeny P.
Named in Sovt spy complaint 1-7, 41B3
KASEMEHAS, Nicholas
Young cleared in Thevis aid chrg, allegatns cited 10-19, 861E3
KASENGA, Mpinga (Zaire prime minister)
Named prime min 7-6, 583B1
KASURI, Ahmed Raza
Bhutto tied to murder plot 9-5, 707C2
Bhutto formally chrgd 10-11, 803C1
KASURI, Mahmoud Ali
Named to PNA post 5-3; arrested 5-5, 348F3
KATAGIRI, Hisao
On Kurile claim 4-16, 319A2
KATALI, Capt. Xavier
Named interior min 4-5, 282F2
KATES, Robert W.
Sci Acad sets forgn dissident probe 4-27, 315C2
KATO, Takenori
Named Japan home affairs min 11-28, 932B2

1978

Wichita gay rights vote set 4-25, 327B2; law repealed 5-9, 409D3
18 die in tornadoes 6-17, 479B3
Wichita makes bad-air list 7-5, 513D1
Grasshopper invasn rptd, EPA aid asked 7-13—7-31, 654B3
Bad-air list corrected 7-19, 644B2
Primary results 8-1, 606D1
Wichita firemen, police strike 9-11—9-20, 753D1
Election results 11-7: cong 845F1, 846F1, F2, A3, 848G1, 850D4, 854E2, F2; state 845G1, 847A1, 853F2, 854E2, G2, 897C3
KANSAS, University of (Lawrence)
Hadl named asst coach 2-9, 171F3
KANSAS City, Mo.—*See MISSOURI*
KANSAS State University (Manhattan)
Evans in NBA draft 6-9, 457G3
KAPETANOVIC, Dragan
Resigns as Metros coach 6-13, 707C3
KAPITSA, Pyotr L(eonidovich)
Wins Nobel Prize 10-17, 886C2
KAPLAN Award, Lou—*See HOCKEY—Awards*
KAPPLER, Herbert
Dies 2-9, 114C3
Geiss fined for Nazi salute 7-24, 652B1
KAPUUO, Chief Clemens
Dies 3-27, 229C2
Funeral held, tribes clash 4-8—4-9, 269C2
Steyn gets emergency powers 4-8, 299B2
KAPWEPWE, Simon
Sets Zambia pres candidacy 8-1, 617E1
Kaunda elected, UNIP rule change cited 12-12, 989G2
KARAASLAN, Ahmet
Named Turkey housing min 1-5, 21F2
KARAMESSINES, Thomas H.
Dies 9-4, 778D1
KARAMAL, Babrak
Named Afghan vice pres 5-2, 349E2 ★
Loses Cabt post, reassigned 7-10, 538A1
KARASAVINA, Tamara
Dies 5-26, 440G2
KARGOUGOU, Moussa
Named Upper Volta defns min 7-18, 596C3
KARINA, Anna
Bread & Chocolate released 7-14, 969E3
KARPONOSOV, Gennadji
Wins world figure-skating title 3-11, 316E3
KARPOV, Anatoly
Retains world chess title 7-18—10-17, USSR award rptd 10-28, 843A1, C2
KARR Preventative Medical Products Inc.
Boone held liable for acne ads 5-11, 702F2-A3
FTC injunctn halts acne ads 10-10, 942B1
KARUME, Sheik Abeid Amani (d. 1972)
Babu freed 4-26, 479D2
KASAKOFF, E. G.
Thread of Scarlet opens 12-8, 1031B3
KASSEBAUM, Nancy Landon
Wins Kan US Sen primary 8-1, 606E1
Elected 11-7, 845F1, 846F1, 848G1, 854E2
KASTEN Jr., Rep. Robert W. (R, Wis.)
Loses primary for gov 9-12, 736G1
KASTENMEIER, Rep. Robert William (D, Wis.)
Reelected 11-7, 852C4
KASTNER, Elliott
Little Night Music released 3-7, 619A3
KASURI, Ahmed Raza
Bhutto gets death sentnc 3-18, 228F3
KATAYAMA, Tetsu
Dies 5-30, 440A3
KATO, Mutsuki
Tied to Lockheed scandal 1-30, 72E3
KATS, Boris
Leaves USSR 11-30, 946C3
KATS, Jessica
Leaves USSR, illness exaggerated 11-30, 946C3
KATS, Natalya
Leaves USSR 11-30, 946C3
KATSARIS, Anthony
Wounded in Guyana cult ambush, sister dies in mass suicide 11-18, 890G2
KATSARIS, Maria
Dies in Guyana cult mass suicide 11-18, 890G2
Jonestown survivors say aided escape, sent money to Sovts 11-28, 910B3
Autopsy planned in US 11-29, 910G1
Death ruled suicide in Guyana 12-22, 999E3
KATSELLIS, Stellos
Named Cyprus state secy 3-8, 189A2
KATT, William
Big Wednesday released 7-27, 969D3

1979

Sen Kassebaum divorced 3-17, 271F3
Dole announces pres bid 5-14, 363B3
Diesel fuel shortage rptd 5-18, 361A3
Carlin scores rail decontrol bill 6-6, 579G2
Wichita schl busing rptd set 9-2, 679E3
'78 per capita income rptd 9-16, 746D2
Amtrak derailmt kills 2 10-2, 800A2
2 in FBI rptd removed for theft 10-17, 787C2; ex-agent pleads guilty 11-15, 906G1*
KANSAS, University of (Lawrence)
Bell speaks on presidency 1-25, 110A2
KANSAS City, Mo.—*See MISSOURI*
KANSAS City Southern Industries Inc.
RR takeover of Rock Island ordered 9-26, 722C3
KANSAS City Star, The (newspaper)
'63 death threat vs Oswald revealed 2-18, 166E2
Lauds Carter energy speech 7-16, 534E3
KANSAS City Terminal Railway Co.
Rock I takeover ordered 9-26, 722F3
Rock I resumes svc, mgt chngs rptd 10-5, 830C1
Rock I takeover order extended 11-28, 989C2
KANTER, Jay
Quits Fox Film 6-7, plans Warner unit assn 7-4, 587G3
KAPLAN, Gabriel
Fast Break released 3-1, 174E2
KAPLAN Award, Lou—*See HOCKEY–Awards*
KAPLAN Educational Centers Ltd., Stanley H.
FTC study issued 5-29, 785C2
KAPLER, Aleksei Y.
Death rptd 9-15, 756F2
KAPLIN, Marc
Fast Break released 3-1, 174E2
KAPP, Joe
Trust damages case declined by Sup Ct 4-16, 302G3
KAPP v. National Football League
Case declined by Sup Ct 4-16, 302G3
KARAALSAN, Ahmet
Quits as Turkey housing min 9-29, 775C2
KARAT Inc.—*See ALKATH Corp.*
KARDELJ, Edvard
Dies 2-10, 176B3
KARINA, Anna
Just Like At Home released 4-19, 528F2
KARMAL, Babrak (Afghan president)
Takes over in Afghan coup 12-27, names Cabt 12-28; Brezhnev lauds 12-28, 973C1, C2
KARPIS, Alvin (Old Creepy)
Dies 8-26, 671E2
KARPONOSOV, Gennadi
Wins world figure-skating title 3-15, 392A1
KARPOV, V. P.
Cited in SALT II summit communique 6-18, 457D1
KARR Preventive Medical Products Inc.
Acne ad refunds set 7-2, 596D2
KASPUTIN, Sergei
Sovts win Challenge Cup 2-11, 118F2, B3
KASSAB, Alfred
MacDonald gets life for '70 slayings 8-29, 817E3
KASSEBAUM, Sen. Nancy Landon (R, Kan.)
Divorced 3-17, 271F3
Finances disclosed 5-18, 383E2
KASSEBAUM, Philip
Divorced 3-17, 271F3
KATCHEFF, Ted
North Dallas Forty released 8-1, 820D2
KATSELAS, Milton
When You Comin' Back released 2-8, 174F3
KATSH, Abraham I.
Talmudic study completed 7-14, 640G1
KATT, William
Butch & Sundance released 6-15, 819G3

1980

Wichita blacks in rampage 4-22, 333F1
DES in cattle rptd 4-24, 358F1
Drought, heat wave hits; livestock losses rptd 6-23—8-15; Carter declares disaster area 7-16, 616D1, G1-B2
US Sen primary results 8-5, 682E3
Wichita busing, housing integratn study rptd 11-16, 899E3
'80 census rptd 12-31, 983E1
KANSAS, University of (Lawrence)
Forer sees US Emb militants in Teheran 2-10, 106C1
Wiley NCAA aid limit case declined by Sup Ct 5-12, 426B3
KANSAS City—*See MISSOURI*
KANSAS City Star, The (newspaper)
Mondale hails centennial 9-18, 780B2
Carter pres endorsemt rptd 11-1, 841G3
KANSAS City Terminal Railway Co.
Rock I svc extended 2-22, 147G3
KANSAS State University (Manhattan)
NCAA basketball tourn results 3-24, 240F1
KANYGIN, Igor
Wins Olympic medal 7-22, 624B3
KAO Chun-ming
Sentenced 6-5, 468B1
KAPELMAN, Judge William
Sentenced Jacobson 6-3, 502B2
KAPITANCHUK, Viktor
Sentence suspended 10-9, 863C2
KAPLAN, Jacob
Jewish targets attacked 9-26, 9-28, 750D1
KAPLAN, Nelly
Charles & Lucie released 5-9, 675B2
KAPLAN, Robert
Canada solicitor gen 3-3, 171B2
KAPLAN, Steve
Incomparable Max opens 6-15, 756D3
Front Page opens 12-22, 1003B3
KAPNICK, Harvey
Ousted in First Chicago shakeup 4-28, 456A2
KARABIN, Dan
Wins Olympic medal 7-30, 624D3
KARAKAS, Cahit
Pres electn deferred 3-22, 236D1
KARBI, Ras
Reggae opens 3-27, 392F3
KARDELJ, Edvard (1910-79)
Tito successn concern cited 1-20, 49E2
KARJALAINEN, Jouko
Wins Olympic medal 2-19, 155B3
KARKOSZKA, Alojzy
Quits as Polish CP ldr 11-18, 878C2
Ousted from Polish Politburo 12-2, 909G2
KARMAL, Babrak (Afghan president)
Asks support in 1st pub appearance 1-2, 3D2
On power takeover 1-10, 27C3
Assures Iran on Sovt invasn 1-16, 27B2
US issues rights rpt 2-5, 87A1
Says Sovts invaded 10 days before '79 coup 2-7, 85E2
Ouster denied 2-16, 123G2
USSR vs UK neutrality plan 3-11, 205A1
Bars role in peace talks 4-5, 271F1
Protester leaflets denounce 5-15, 387F2
3 ex-mins executed 6-16, 475C2
Asks purge 7-13, consolidates power 7-20, 561A1
In Moscow, Sovts vow contd aid 10-16; communique 10-19, 827C1
KARMEL, Roberta S.
Resigns from SEC 2-1, 224G3
KAROLYI, Bela
Vs Olympic women's gymnastics scoring 7-24, 589E2
KARPONOSOV, Gennadi
Wins Olympic medal 2-17, 155F3
KARPPINEN, Pertti
Wins Olympic medal 7-27, 623G1
KARSKI, Ryszard
COMECON to keep fixed prices for Sovt commodities 5-29, 451F1
KARUGU, James
Protests US sailor's murder sentence 10-20, 859F3
KASDAN, Lawrence
Empire Strikes Back released 5-21, 675D2
KASHII, Eiichi
Arrested as spy 1-18, 60B1
KASSEBAUM, Sen. Nancy Landon (R, Kan.)
Female draft registratn amendmt defeated 6-10, 478G1
Addresses GOP conv 7-14, 531C3
2d woman elected to US Sen 11-4, 846A3
KASSEM, Abdul-Rauf (Syrian premier)
Syrian premier 1-16, 102G1
Sees unrest widespread; blames Israel, US 3-17, 212G3-213A1
Admits anti-govt unrest 3-31, 295B2
KAST, Miguel
Chile econ recovery detailed 1-14, 19C3
KASTEN Jr., Robert W.
Wins Sen primary 9-9, 700C3
Elected to US Sen 11-4, 840F3, 845A2, 851G2
KASTNER, Detlef
Wins Olympic medal 8-2, 622A2
KASTNER, Elliott
Saturn 3 released 2-15, 216D3
Ffolkes released 4-18, 416F2

1976

KATUSHEV, Konstantin
CP Secretariat member 3-5, 195F2
In Rumania re Eur CP mtg 5-28, 420B3
KATZ, Julius L.
State asst secy 9-3; confrmd 9-23, 808A1
KAUFFMANN, Howard C.
Vs House boycott legis 9-19, 746D3
KAUFMAN, Gerald
Testifies for Concorde 1-5, 5F2
KAUFMAN, Henry
Asks bank regulatory reform 1-12, 111F2
KAUFMAN, Judge Irving R.
ABA forms Rosenberg unit 1-8, 70F2
KAUFMAN, Stephen B.
Indicted 6-7, 442A3
KAUL, M. G.
In US econ talks 3-25—3-26, 253A3
Sees Schaufele 9-9, 681G1
In Kissinger talks 9-16, 681F1
Backs gen Namibia conf 9-17, 698C1

KAUNDA, Kenneth D. (Zambian president)
Scores OAU Angola summit 1-13, 16C1
Invokes emergency powers 1-28, 77D3
Warns of Rhodesia war 2-15, lauds Mozambique sanctns 3-3, 175D3
Chrgs Angola copper seizure 2-20, 163E2
Sees Rhodesia war, asks UK force 3-19, 3-29, 240B2
Meets black ldrs on Rhodesia 3-24—3-25, 240D2
Chitepo murder rpt issued 4-9, 428B2
Kissinger visits 4-26—4-27, 293B1, C2, 295F1
Sees Machel re Rhodesia 4-26, 295E1
OKs guerrilla raids on Rhodesia 5-28, 427D2
Accuses Salisbury re Lusaka bombing 6-13, 427A3
Chrgs S Africa border attack 7-16, 539G3
S African plot chrgd 7-27, 653G2
Greets new Sovt amb 8-10, 950B1
Urges S Africa, Rhodesia black arms aid 8-19, 622A1
Sees Neto, 8-21; ties, joint com OKd 9-22, 862F2 ★
At conf re ANC rift 9-6—9-7, 661D3
Sees Kissinger 9-20, 717G2
Scores Rhodesia plan 9-26, 718C1
Natlst accord at conf rptd urged by US 10-26, 797F2, 798A1
Sees Reinhardt 11-5, 843G1
KAUPER, Thomas E.
Trust bill backing cited 3-18, 247B1
Replaced as asst atty gen 8-6, 807E3
KAWASMA, Fahad
Elected Hebron mayor 4-12, 458A3
KAWASMEH, Fahad
Blames Jews for Hebron riot 10-3, 737E2
KAY, Jean
Tindemans reshuffles Cabt 12-8, 1012E2
KAYEX Corp.
Hamex chrgd re Arab boycott 10-19, 786E1
KAYIBIGI, Maj. Philibert
Named agri min 11-13, 1012G2
KAYO Oil Co.—*See CONTINENTAL Oil*
KAYSER-Roth—*See GULF & Western*
KAYSONE Phoumvihan (Laotian premier)
In N Viet talks 2-11, 121F1
Cabt meets on unrest 3-12, 222E1
China aid pact signed 3-18, 222A2
KAZANKINA, Tatyana
Wins Olympic medals 7-26, 7-30, 576F1, A2
KAZEN Jr., Rep. Abraham (D, Tex.)
Reelected 11-2, 830E4
KEANE, David
GOP conv vp vote table 8-19, 599F3
KEARNS, Carroll D.
Dies 6-11, 484E3
KEARNS, Doris
Lyndon Johnson on best-seller list 12-5, 972C2
KEARNS, Henry
Sued re stock sale 8-9, 709B3
KEASER, Lloyd
Wins Olympic medal 7-31, 576D3

1977

KATUSHEV, Konstantin F.
Named Mins Cncl vp, COMECON rep 3-16, 306D3
Central Com ousts 5-24, 412C2
KATZ, Julius L.
Keeps State Dept post 1-21, 53E1
KATZ, Shmuel
In US to promote Begin stand 6-2, 440C2
Says US policy misconceived 9-13, 697G1
State-owned radio rejcts W Bank terminology 10-10, 793D2
KATZ, Yisrael
Israeli labor min 10-24, 827B2
KATZIR, Ephraim (Israeli president)
Mandates new Rabin govt 1-4, 8C2
Names Begin to form govt 6-7, 450C2
Begin presents Cabt 6-20, 474G1
Pope asks Capucci release 10-30, freed 11-6, 850G2-C3
Sees Sadat 11-19, 11-21, 889B1, D2
KAUFFMAN, Bob
Pistons interim coach 12-15, 991E1
KAUFMAN, Judge Frank A.
Sentences ex-CIA employe 6-1, 462G2
KAUFMAN, Gerald
On Leyland strike 2-28, 201D1
KAUFMAN, Judge Irving R.
Backs JFK Concorde ban 6-14, 463F1
Backs NY Concorde ruling 9-29, 738E3
Backs protectn of journalists' thoughts 11-7, 920C3

KAUNDA, Kenneth D. (Zambian president)
Sees Richard 12-30-76, 3A2; 1-10, 11F1
Backs Patriotic Front 1-9, 11C1
Scores Richard 1-29, 72A3
Sees Young re Rhodesia 2-5, 105D1, C2
Lauds USSR 3-25, sees Podgorny 3-26, 247E3
Owen sees re Rhodesia 4-15, 296A3
Reshuffles Cabt 4-24, 490F1
Declares war on Rhodesia 5-16, 413A1
Sees Young, asks Rhodesia oil ban 5-23, 400A1
Scores Rhodesia regime 6-9, 487C1
OKs Cuba, Somalia aid 7-8, 536F1
Ousts Mudenda, Chona replaces 7-20, 583F1
Milner ousted 8-2, 674E3
At UN apartheid conf, asks guerrilla aid 8-22, Young rebuts 8-25, 661G2
Chrgs Rhodesia napalm raid 9-11, 811A1
On UK-US Rhodesia plan 9-24, 734C3
Sees Smith 9-25, mtg detailed 10-26, 810F1
Backs Patriotic Front rule 10-21, 810E2
Patriotic Front frictn re Smith mtg rptd 10-30, 875C3
Sees UK, UN reps 11-7—11-8; Rhodesia electns barred 11-8, 875F3
Bars UK-US Rhodesia setlmt, backs Patriotic Front 12-6; Nyerere quarrel rptd 12-18, 1015B3
Muzorewa aide ousted 12-10, 1016E1

KAUSHIK, Purushottam
Indian tourism min 3-26, 240B1
KAWASAKI Steel Corp.
US dumping chrgs upheld 10-3, 774D3
KAWASMEH, Fahad
On West Bank Arab rights 8-15, 623B2
KAWAWA, Rashidi
Shifted to Tanzania defns post 2-13, 161B2
KAY, Jean
Dassault cleared 4-21, 598B1
KAYO Oil Co.—*See CONTINENTAL Oil*
KAYSONE Phoumvihan (Laotian premier)
In Viet talks 7-15—7-18, 553A1
KEABLE, Jean
Opens Quebec RCMP probe 10-3, 800F3
'72 raid authorizatn disputed 10-25—10-26, 841F1
RCMP names probe overseer 10-25, 841C2
On '72 RCMP raid disclosures 10-28, 841F1
RCMP probe hearings 11-1, scope widened 11-3, 902B3
Asks '73 PQ break-in documts 11-2, Fox limits 11-11, 903A1
RCMP '72 raid authorizatn chrgd 11-2—11-11, 903D1
Ottawa fails to halt RCMP probe 11-23, 11-25, 923A3
3d bid to halt RCMP probe foiled 12-11, 965A1
Probe adjourns 12-12, 982F2
4th bid to halt probe foiled 12-16, 982E2
KEAN, Thomas H.
Loses primary for gov 6-7, 446D3
KEARNEY, John J.
Indicted 4-7, pleads not guilty; Kelley lauds 4-14, 275F1-G2
FBI probe attys, Bell clash 12-7, 940C1
Bell drops oppositn to more indictmts 12-13, 979D3
KEARNEY, Patrick Wayne
Surrenders 7-1, indicted 7-13, 603F2
Pleads guilty, sentncd 12-21, 991A3
KEARNS, Doris
Hints '41 fraud cost LBJ Sen bid 8-6, 631F2
KEAST, James D.
Replaced as Agri gen counsel 8-4, 626F3

1978

KATZ, David
Allergy suppressant study rptd 3-11, 334D2
KATZ, Miguel
Chile planning min 12-26, 1014D2
KATZIR, Ephraim
Navon succeeds as Israel pres 5-29, 418C2
KATZKA, Gabriel
Rubber Gun released 4-24, 619E3
Who'll Stop Rain released 8-25, 1030G3
KAUFFMAN, Bob
Resigns as Pistons gen mgr 7-14, 656B1
KAUFFMAN, Howard
Scores Carter 'export consequences' order 10-10, 804B3
KAUFFMANN, John (deceased)
King murder plot alleged 7-26, 589B3
King murder bounty alleged 11-29, 938A2
KAUFMAN, George S. (1889-1961)
Once in a Lifetime opens 6-15, 887C2
KAUFMAN, Philip
Invasn of Body Snatchers released 12-21, 1030A3
KAUFMAN & Broad Inc.
FTC complaint rptd setld 7-7, 702C2

KAUNDA, Kenneth D. (Zambian president)
Sets consumer subsidy end 1-1, 55D3
Rhodesia role cited 59D2
Muzorewa scores 3-19, 210G2
Sees Young 3-22—3-24, 248D3
In UK, US; seeks econ aid, Rhodesia solutn 5-15—5-23, 395C2
Schmidt in Zambia, EC copper actn vowed 6-28—6-30, 584D1
Kapwepwe, Nkumbula set candidacy 8-1, 617D1
At Smith-Nkomo mtg 8-14, backs talks 9-2, 740G2, E3
Regrets Kenyatta death 8-22, 639B3
Scores UK on Rhodesia sanctns-breaking 9-18, meets Callaghan 9-22, 756F2-B3
Sets Rhodesia RR rte reopening 10-6, 783E2, C3
Scores US on Smith visit, rejcts talks resumptn 10-23, 819G1
Denounces attacks vs whites 11-13, 893E2
Sets arms spending rise 11-20, 912B1
Doubts new UK Rhodesia missn 11-24, 911F3
Scores white farmers threats 11-26, 912E1
Reelected, UNIP rule change cited 12-12, 989D2

KAUSOV, Sergei
Marries Christina Onassis 8-1, 844E3
KAVANAGH, Brian
Indicted 6-15, 560G2
KAVNER, Julie
Wins Emmy 9-17, 1030F1
KAWAGUCHI, Matsutaro
Geisha released 6-1, 619B2
KAWASAKI Steel Corp.
US '77 dumping ruling revised 1-9, 80E2
Australia iron imports set 5-30, 411F1
KAYE, John
Amer Hot Wax released 3-16, 618A3
KAYE, M. M.
Far Pavilions on best-seller list 10-9, 800A3; 12-3, 971A1
KAYSONE Phoumvihan
Backs Viet in China feud 7-22, 603F1-A2
KAZAKHSTAN Republic—*See USSR—Republics*
KAZAN, Nicholas
Safe House opens 4-13, 760C3
KAZARIAN, Dennis S.
Loses US House electn 11-7, 856F3
KAZEN Jr., Rep. Abraham (D, Tex.)
Reelected 11-7, 852B3
KAZMIERSKI, Joyce
2d in Mayflower Classic 7-3, 672C3
KEABLE, Jean
Fox bares fake FLQ communique, informant recruiting tactics; reaffirms documt control 1-9, 35C1
'73 PQ break-in aims detailed 1-19—1-26, 88F2, A3
Quebec ct halts RCMP probe 2-21, 129E2
Quebec probe status decisn stayed by ct 5-26, probe ended 5-31, 451F2
Sup Ct limits probe 10-31, 879C3
KEAN, Norman
Broadway Musical opens 12-21, 1031B1
KEARNEY, John
Indictment dismissed 4-10, 262C1
KEARNEY, Patrick Wayne
Pleads guilty to more trash bag murders 2-21, 232B3
KEARNEY (Neb.) State College
Loses NAIA basketball title game 3-18, 272B2
KEARNY, N.J.—*See NEW Jersey*

1979

KATY Industries Inc.
Mo-Kan-Tex RR takeover of Rock Island ordered 9-26, 722C3
KATZ, Dr. Arthur
Rpts A-war survivors face grim future 3-23, 232A3
KATZ, Gloria
More Amer Graffiti released 8-17, 820B2
French Postcards released 10-19, 1007D3
KATZ, Shmuel
Begin defeats for Herut post 6-6, 436G2
KATZKA, Gabriel
Butch & Sundance released 6-15, 819F3
KAUFFMAN, Rear Adm. Draper L.
Dies 8-18, 671F2
KAUFFMAN, Howard C.
Unveils Exxon energy-saving device, rpts Reliance merger talks 3-18, 404B2
KAUFFMAN, Jeannie
Beggars Soap Opera opens 7-23, 711E1
KAUFMAN, Judge Ira G.
Bars Ford heir from contesting will 7-16, 631E1
KAUFMAN, Judge Irving R.
Marshall decries 'state of mind', pretrial detentn rulings 5-27, 422E1
Reverses Berkey trust award 6-25, 517E2-A3
KAUFMAN, Michael
Warriors opens 5-22, 712D3
KAUFMAN, Philip
Wanderers released 7-13, 820F3
KAUFMAN, Robert
Love At First Bite released 4-12, 528G2
KAUFMAN, Rose
Wanderers released 7-13, 820F3

KAUNDA, Kenneth D. (Zambian president)
Rhodesian air attack toll rptd 4-12, 294D1
Chipanga freed 5-6, 374C3
Lauds Zimbabwe plan 8-7, 589C1
Defies Zimbabwe corn ban 11-6, 844A3
In London re Zimbabwe transitn plan 11-8—11-10, Patriotic Front OKs 11-15, 881E1
Orders war alert re Zimbabwe raids; Thatcher, Muzorewa react 11-20, 899C2, E2
Backs UK High Comm attack 11-23, 899A3

KAVA, Caroline
Nature and Purpose opens 2-23, 292C2
KAVAJA, Nikola
Hijacks jet 6-20, surrenders 6-21; sentncd in '75 Chicago bombings 6-22, 491E2
KAVANAGH, Michael
Provenzano, Konigsberg '78 murder convictns upset 6-7, 491G3
KAWASMEH, Fahad
Vs Israel-Egypt pact 3-14, 178B1
KAYE, Clarissa
Faith Healer opens 4-4, 711G2
KAYE, M. M.
Far Pavilions on best-seller list 1-7, 80B3; 9-2 672C3; 10-14, 800D3
KAYSONE Phoumvihan (Laotian premier)
Signs Thai peace pact 4-4, 298D2
KAZAKHSTAN Republic—*See USSR—Republics*
KAZANILAN, Howard
More Amer Graffiti released 8-17, 820B2
KAZIN, Alfred
Book awards protest rptd 8-9, 755F3
KAZMIERSKI, Joyce
2d in Europn Open 8-5, 970A1
KEABLE, Jean
RCMP inquiry reopens 2-13, 189E2
KEADY, Judge William
Upholds Tenn-Tombigbee projct 3-13, 188A3
KEARTON, Lord
N Sea oil assets sale barred 9-14, 707B2

1980

KATY Industries Inc.
BN-Frisco merger stayed by Powell 11-21; appeals ct OKs link 11-24, Sup Ct lifts stay 11-25, 937A3
KATZ, George
Indicted in Abscam probe 10-30, 824E2
KAUFHOF A.G.
Swiss bank buys shares 12-12, 969E1
KAUFMAN, Boris
Dies 6-23, 528C2
KAUFMAN, Henry
Asks wage-price controls 2-21, 144E3
Predicts prime rate drop, bond mkt rallies 4-16, 286E2-A3
KAUFMAN, Robert
Nothing Personal released 4-18, 416D3
How to Beat the High Cost of Living released 7-11, 675A3
KAUFMAN, Walter
Dies 9-4, 755E3

KAUNDA, Kenneth D. (Zambian president)
Lauds Mugabe victory 3-4, 162D1
Asks econ indepndnc from S Africa 4-1, 243F1
Orders curfew 10-23; chrgs S Africa backed coup, denied 10-27, 833F2-B3
Shuffles Cabt 12-4; lifts curfew 12-8, 969E2, A3

KAWASMEH, Fahad
Israel scored for UN visit bar 3-1, 162G3
UN Israel res text cites 3-1, 179C2
Vs Hebron setlmt plan OK 3-24, 3-26, 219B1
Israel deports 5-3; W Bank protests; US, UN scores 5-3—5-8; Arafat visits 5-7, 340B2, D3
W Bank return barred 5-11, 362D2
UN censures Israel, Sup Ct orders ouster probed 5-20, 381D1
Successor chosen 5-25, 417F2
Israel ct backs ouster 8-19, 627B3
Meets 2 Israeli CP parlt members 9-25, 736F3
Returns to appeal ouster 10-14; hearing 10-15—10-16, ouster upheld 10-20, Sup Ct delays 10-23, 822E2
Begin vs Gaza, Bethlehem mayors pleas 10-21, 822A3
Redeported 12-5, vows UN appeal 12-6; W Bank riots 12-6—12-9, 931A2
UN asks Israel readmit; stages sit-in, hunger strike 12-19, 952B2
Israel vs UN backing 12-22; ends hunger strike 12-24, 976E3
KAY, Richard
Gets 1% of NH vote 2-26, 142E2
KAYE, Nora
Nijinsky released 3-20, 216D3
KAYLOR, Phoebe
Carny released 6-13, 675B2
KAYLOR, Robert
Carny released 6-13, 675B2
KAZAMA, Kiyoshi
Serrano TKOs 4-3, 320D3
KAZANKINA, Tatyana
Wins Olympic medal 8-1, 624B2
KAZEL, Dorothy
Found slain in El Salvador 12-4, 921B1
KAZEN Jr., Rep. Abraham (D, Tex.)
Reelected 11-4, 844B3
KBCI-TV (Boise, Ida. TV station)
Raided by police, prison riot tapes seized 7-26, 582B2
Loy defends rights 7-29, statn sues prosecutor over prison tapes raid 8-1, 732A3
KC-Plane Series—*See ARMAMENTS—Aircraft*
KEACH, Stacy
Twinkle, Twinkle Killer Kane released 8-8, 675E3
KEAN, Robert Winthrop
Dies 9-21, 755F3
KEANE, Christopher
Hunter released 8-1, 675A3

1976

KEATING, Justin
Rpts Ireland oil finds 2-1, 157B1
KEATING, Paul
In Australia shadow cabt 1-29, 116E1
Shadow cabt reshuffled 3-25, 237B1
KEBEDE Worku, Gen.
Slain 2-15, 173A1
KEDYAROV, Alexander
Wins Olympic medal 7-23, 575B2
KEECH, Everett T.
AF asst secy 8-31; confrmd 9-10, 808B1
KEELER, William W.
Tax fraud chrgd 9-2, 725G2
KEENAN, John
Quits 6-7, 416E3 *
Canada air strike 6-20—6-28, 481A2
KEENAN, John F.
Named NYS prosecutor 6-25, 1016E1
KEFAUVER, (Carey) Estes (1903-63)
Primary precedent cited 231G3
KEHL, Edward
Testifies on Army meat fraud 5-10, 395C2
KEITH, Hastings
Chrgs mil recruitmt bias cover-up 6-8, 454A2
KEJA, Wim
Dutch Dassault bribe case opens 2-10, 141G2

KEKKONEN, Urho Kaleiva (Finnish president)
Govt resigns 5-13, 350G2
Bars Cabt resignatn 5-13, coalitn restored 5-18, 364A3
Miettunen Cabt resigns 9-17, 731E2
Swears in new Cabt 9-29, 750B3
KELLENBERG, Most Rev. Walter P.
Retires 6-3, 424D1
KELLER, Robert F.
Blames Navy on overruns 6-1, 454C1
KELLEY, Clarence M.
ACLU sues for Harrises 1-5, 70A2
Denies FBI aided terrorists 1-11, 42A1
Rosenberg papers contempt denied 1-13, 70D2
Addabbo, Leggett payoffs probed 2-19, 171E1
Probe of aides rptd 3-21, 248G1
Denies forgn intellignc penetratn 4-5, 248F2
Apologizes for FBI abuses 5-8, 344G2
On letter bombs 6-15, 504B1
Admits '70s burglaries 6-30, 569G1
Testifies on SD '75 FBI deaths 7-7, 640F2 *
Refers Ford funds chrg to Levi 7-13, 761F1
Fires Callahan 7-16, names Held 7-20, 634C1
Chrgs break-in deceptn, vows disciplinary actn 8-8, 634F1
Rpts FBI reforms, Jenkins retiremt 8-11; clarifies SWP classificatn 8-16, 633A2-634E3
Mondale, Carter score 8-12, 8-13, 617B1
Admits favors, gifts 8-31; Justice rpt, Ford back Kelley 9-4, 666C2
Marriage plans announced 9-4, 680F2
Carter gives views 9-7, 9-9; Ford rebuts 9-8, 664D2, E3, 665D1
Ford funds probe rptd 10-1, 723G2
KELLEY, Ruby Dyeantha Pickett (Mrs. Clarence M.) (d. 1975)
Justice Dept cites illness 9-4, 666D3
Kelley to wed Dyckes 9-4, 680F2
Carter cites illness 9-9, 664F3
KELLY, James J.
Defeated 11-2, 822A1
KELLY, Joseph F.
7 seized in gun plot 5-15—5-17, 401G1-C2
KELLY, Rep. Richard (R, Fla.)
Reelected 11-2, 829B2
KELNER, Russel
On bombs near UN hq, Iraqi missn 1-13, 18E2
Sup Ct bars convictn review 12-13, 960E3 *
KEMOS, Theodore
Convicted 12-23, 988F1
KEMP, Geoffrey
Evaluates US mil capabilities in Pacific, Indian O 1-25, 68F2
KEMP, Rep. Jack F. (R, N.Y.)
Reelected 11-2, 830D2
KEMPE, Rudolf
Dies 5-11, 524A3
KEMPNY, Josef
On Czech Presidium, Secretariat 4-16, 289B2
KENDAL, Dr. Alan P.
Missing flu vaccine enzyme rptd 10-17, 795E2
KENDRICK, John
On Aug indicator drop 9-28, 768D1
On 3d ¼ GNP, inflatn rpt 10-19, 805G1-B2
KENMOTSU, Eizo
Wins Olympic medals 7-23, 574C3, D3
KENNECOTT Copper Corp.
Bars boycott compliance 3-18, 747B2
Haiti pact signed 3-24, copper find rptd 3-25, 267A3
'75 poles drop rptd 437E1
To sell Peabody Coal 12-14, 985C1

KENNEDY, Sen. Edward M(oore) (D, Mass.)
Meany lauds 2-16, 148G3
Asks cruise missile test halt 2-25, 183D1
Scores US-Brazil pact 2-26, 177D1
Shriver ends pres bid 3-22, 214D2
US ends pocket-veto stand 4-13, 284F1
Carter offers health plan 4-16, 281G3

1977

KEATING, Justin
Elected to Irish Sen 8-27, 728E3
KEBEDE Gabre
Greece grants asylum 3-10, 238G2
KEBEDE Gebre Michael
Killed 12-3, 998F2
KEEGAN Jr., Maj. Gen. George J.
Sovt aims, power rpt stirs controversy 12-26-30—1-18, 39A3
Retires 1-1, 39B3
Joint Chiefs deny Sovt mil edge 1-30, 70F2
KEFALOGIANNIS, Emmanuel
Named Greek shipping min 11-28, 925B2
KEITA, Modibo
Dies 5-16, 452D3

KEKKONEN, Urho Kaleiva (Finnish president)
Asks electn 2-1, 182C1
Kosygin in trade talks 5-22—5-26, 391C2

KELLEHER, Judge Robert
US spy gets life sentnc 7-18, 576F3
Sentences Boyce 9-12, 732F3
KELLEN, Robert M.
Scores saccharin ban 3-9, 176G3
KELLER, Greta
Dies 11-4, 952F2
KELLER, Rev. James G.
Dies 2-7, 164C3
KELLEY, Clarence
Vs prosecution of Kearney 4-14, 275E2
Successor at FBI named 8-17, 626A2
KELLY Barnes Dam (Toccoa, Ga.)
Bursts 11-6, 888F2 *; seepage blamed 12-21, 1023E3
KELLY, Rev. Clarence
Tex church consecrated 7-10, 620A3
KELLY, Grace—*See GRACE, Princess*
KELLY, John B.
Elected USOC 1st vp 4-29, 491A3
KELLY, Bishop Thomas C.
On excommunicatn for remarrieds 11-10, 906E3
KELSO, Louis
AT&T sets employes stock plan 5-6, 409F1
KEMP, Rep. Jack F. (R, N.Y.)
Rebuts Carter energy plan 6-2, 443G1
KENG Piao
Stresses Sovt threat 1-26, 61G2
In Politburo 8-21, 645G2
KENNA, E. Douglas
Scores Carter econ plan 1-10, 14E1
KENNECOTT Copper Corp.
Peabody Mont coal lease revoked 1-13, 59A1
Copper prices raised 3-22, 209C2
Peabody sold 6-30, 520F1
Struck, settles 7-1, 558B1
Cuts prices 7-2, 7-20, 577D2
FTC divestiture order cited 520F1
3d ¼, 9-mo loss rptd 10-30; Peabody sale, strike setlmt linked to indus woes 10-31, 859D1
Carborundum purchase backed by bd 11-16; merger table cited 880A1, F1
Carborundum purchase cited 12-11, 1004E2
KENNEDY, Dr. Donald
Defends saccharin ban 4-14, 280F1
Orders fluorocarbon warning 4-26, 323B2
FDA laetrile ban continues 5-6, 375B3
On saccharin ban proposal 6-27, 530G3
On animal feed drug curbs 9-23, 847B3
On liquid protein deaths 11-9, 992C3

KENNEDY, Sen. Edward M(oore) (D, Mass.)
King named Carter spec asst 1-14, 35B3
Sorensen withdraws CIA nominatn 1-17, 35F1
Lauds Viet pardon action 1-21, 51G2
Backs cong electn funds bill 3-7, 232D3

1978

KEATING, Paul
Lauds mineral export plan 10-24, 836D1
KEATON, Diane
Wins Oscar 4-3, 315B3
Interiors released 8-2, 970F1
KEEFFE, Barrie
Gimme Shelter opens 12-10, 1031G1
KEELAN, Kevin
NASL goalkeeping ldr 8-6, 655D2
On NASL All-Star team 8-20, 707A3
KEELER, William H. (Wee Willie) (1872-1923)
Rose ties game hit record 7-31, 618F2
KEENE (N.H.) State College
Sex-bias ruling voided by Sup Ct 11-13, 874F1-C2
KEITEL, Harvey
Duellists released 1-14, 619F1
Blue Collar released 2-9, 618D3
Fingers released 3-2, 619G1

KEKKONEN, Urho Kaleua (Finnish president)
Reelected 1-16, 36D2

KELAVA, Bozo
Convicted 12-1, 933B3
KELDYSH, Mstislav Vsevolodovich
Dies 6-24, 540A3
KELLER, Sheldon
Movie, Movie released 11-22, 970C2
KELLEY, Clarence M.
Past FBI abuses rptd 1-10, 15B2
Webster named FBI dir 1-19, 32D1
KELLOGG Co.
Tropicana merger talks cited 3-5, 184G3
KELLY, George
Show-off opens 5-18, 760C3
KELLY, Martine
Let's Face It released 7-14, 970G1
KELLY, Pat
Fired as Rockies coach 11-23, 991C1
KELLY, Rep. Richard (R, Fla.)
Reelected 11-7, 850F2
KELLY, Roberto
Chile econ min 12-26, 1014D2
KELLY Jr., Thomas
Unopposed in Ark US Sen primary 5-30, 426B2
Loses electn 11-7, 855A2
Outspent by opponent 11-15, 898D1
KELSO (race horse)
Forego retired from racing 6-10, 539D3
KELSO, James L.
Dies 6-28, 540A3
KEMBER, Jane
Indicted 8-15, 644G3, 645A1
KEMP, Rep. Jack F. (R, N.Y.)
House rejcts tax cut amendmt 8-10, 604G1
GOP stages cross-country blitz for tax-cut bill 9-20—9-22, 734D3-735B1
Admin tax cut bill cleared 10-15, 785B2
Reelected 11-7, 851A4
KEMPES, Mario
Argentina wins World Cup, photo 6-25, 520E1, A2-B3
KEMP-Roth Bill—*See TAXES—Reform & Tax Cut Proposals*
KENDALL, Fred
Traded to Red Sox 3-30, 779C3
KENDALL, Oscar E.
Sentenced 5-5, 380B2
KENDALLS, The (singing group)
Win Grammy 2-24, 316A1
KENG Piao
Named China dep premr 2-26—3-5, 153E1
Denies Senkaku intrusn plan 4-15, 278A2
KENILOREA, Peter (Solomon Islands prime minister)
Sworn Solomons prime min 7-7, 549E1
KENN, Mike
In NFL draft 5-2, 336F2
KENNECOTT Copper Corp.
Curtiss-Wright seeks takeover; suit filed, denunciatns exchngd; prelim tally fails 3-13—5-24, 402A1-403D1
NYSE closing price 4-5, 402C3
'77 profits, assets cited 5-24, 402D1
Curtiss-Wright wins vote challenge, new electns ordrd 9-28, 752D2
Morgan Stanley sued re Olinkraft merger 11-8, 896E3
Curtiss-Wright feud setld 12-15, 1004G3
Carborundum Corp.
Curtis-Wright proposes sale 5-23, 402C3
'77 takeover, profits cited 5-24, 402D1, A2
KENNEDY, Donald
Backs generic drugs 9-13, 727C2

KENNEDY, Sen. Edward M(oore) (D, Mass.)
Backs criminal code revisn 1-30, 64G1
Onassis joins Doubleday 2-13, 172C2
Votes for Panama Canal neutrality pact 3-16, 177D2
Scores Ulster violence 3-16, 373B3

1979

KEATING Jr., Charles H.
Connally campaign post cited 12-19, 983B1
KEATING, Paul
Roxby Downs mining OKd 10-9, 811B1
KEATON, Diane
Manhattan released 4-24, 528B3
KEEFE, Jim
Aborigine health study rptd 11-28, 906F3
KEEGAN, Maj. Gen. George (ret.)
Sovt beam-weapon threat discounted 1-10, 52G3
Criticizes SALT 4-11, 295D1
KEELAN, Kevin
NASL to probe suggested goal fix 8-17, 776A2
KEELEY, Steve
Loses natl paddleball 3-18, 527B2
KEENE, David
Shift from Reagan to Bush campaign cited 11-14, 982E2
KEENE, Judge William
Sentences 'Hillside Strangler' 10-22, 818A3
KEITH, Kenneth
NEB members resign over Rolls-Royce transfer 11-20, 949C3
KEIZNACH, Ingeborg
Arrested 1-27—1-28, 98F1
KEKKONEN, Urho Kaleva (Finnish president)
Koivisto sworn premr 5-26—5-27, 406G3
KELLER, Helen (1880-1968)
Miracle Worker opens 1-6, 292B2
KELLER, Judge John W.
Bars Wilson Coll closing 5-26, 482C1
KELLER, Marthe
Fedora released 4-14, 528C2
KELLEY, DeForest
Star Trek released 12-8, 1008F1
KELLEY, Fred
Heart transplant aid rptd 10-10, 1005D3
KELLEY, Maj. Gen. Paul X.
Marines to join 'quick-strike' force 12-5, 923E3
KELLEY, Rich
NBA rebound ldr 4-8, 290F2
KELLIE, Florence (d. 1975)
Simants acquitted in retrial 10-17, 890G3
KELLIE, Henry (d. 1975)
Simants acquitted in retrial 10-17, 890E3
KELLIN, Mike
On The Yard released 1-18, 174C3
KELLOGG, Marjorie
Bell Jar released 3-20, 528C1
KELLOGG Co.
S Africa unit recognizes black union 8-29, 732G2
FTC trust suit environmt statemt sought 10-9, 810A1
KELLY, Emmett
Dies 3-28, 272G2
KELLY, Frank
Lauds Hooker dump suit setlmt 10-24, 808F3
KELLY, James Lawrence
Brass Ring opens 7-2, 711F1
KELLY, Pat
Orioles win AL pennant 10-6, 797G2
KELLY, Patsy
N Amer Irregulars released 4-12, 528B3
KELLY 3rd, Thomas J.
Wins Pulitzer 4-16, 336B3
KELSER, Greg
Mich State wins NCAA basketball title 3-26, 238B3, D3
In NBA draft 6-25, 507A2, F2
KEMENY, John
Ice Castles released 2-22, 174F2
KEMENY, John G.
Named to 3 Mile I probe 4-11, 275C1
3 Mile I comm gets subpoena power 5-17, 5-21, 417G2, F3
Gives Carter 3 Mile I comm final rpt; scores NRC, Met Ed 10-30, 825D2-826C1
Lauds Carter response to 3 Mile I rpt 12-7, 940D2
KEMP, Rep. Jack F. (R, N.Y.)
Talks to Midwest GOPs, offcls rate 3-10, 186A1, D1
Named Reagan campaign policy dvpt head 11-14, 982C2
KEMP, Steve
AL batting ldr 9-30, 955E3
KENCO Chemical Co.
Jacksonville plant fire injures 15 6-7, 572B3
KENDALL, Henry
Scores A-plants pipe leaks 5-2, 322D3
KENG Piao
Warns Viet vs border raids 7-26, 575B3
KENG Yutian
Accuser's trial halted 10-29, 854A3
KENNECOTT Copper Corp.
Fortune rpts '78 rank, cites Carborundum acquisitn 5-7, 305C1
Chile expropriatn cited 5-10, 369C3
KENNEDY, David
Testifies on Sindona loan 1-9, 205D3
Hospitalized, NYC drug-related robbery cited 9-12, 859F3
KENNEDY, Donald
Backs food-safety rules, saccharin ban 3-2, 195E1
Nader group suits curbed 3-14, 308A2
Leaves FDA for Stanford 4-17, 310G2-A3; 6-16 527F3

KENNEDY, Sen. Edward Moore (D, Mass.)
Introduces trucking deregulatn bill 1-22, clashes with Cannon 2-7, 111G2
Judiciary Com chrmn 1-23, 71E2
Ends Cannon trucking dispute 3-21, 308G3

1980

KEATHLEY, George
Heartbreak House opens 4-29, 392B3
KEATING, Barbara
Scores 'Big Business Day' 4-17, 308D2
KEATING Jr., Charles H.
Heads Connally campaign 1-25, 91G3
KECKES, Stjepan
On Medit pollutn pact 5-17, 381A3
KEDIR, Mohammed
Wins Olympic medal 7-27, 624B1
KEDROVA, Lila
Tell Me a Riddle released 12-17, 1003E2
KEELEY, Robert
Opens Zimbabwe Embassy 4-18, 301F2
KEENAN, Brian
Convicted re '79 bombings 6-25, 619B3
KEENEY, Barnaby C.
Dies 6-18, 528C2
KEETON, William
Dies 8-17, 676G1
KEHRL, Howard H.
Named GM vice chrmn 9-9, 701G3
KEITEL, Harvey
Saturn 3 released 2-15, 216E3
KELBERER, John J.
Saudi completes Aramco takeover, retains bd seat 9-4, 662A2
KELLER, George M.
Saudi completes Aramco takeover, retains bd seat 9-4, 662A2
Named SOCAL chrmn, chief exec 9-24, 959A3
KELLERMAN, Sally
Foxes released 2-29, 216F2
KELLNER, Irwin L.
On Carter econ renewal plan 8-28, 663C3
KELLOGG Co.
US job bias chrgs setld 2-6, 115A3
KELLOGG Co. v. FTC
Case refused by Sup Ct 6-16, 511E3
KELLY, Brian
Edmonton wins Grey Cup 11-23, 999C2
KELLY, Capt. James
On Navy women at sea 6-28, 517D2
KELLY, Rep. Richard (R, Fla.)
Facts on 81G2
Linked to bribery in Abscam probe 2-2, 2-3; explains role 2-6, 81A2, 82F1
Quits House GOP conf 2-21, 143B3
Indicted in Abscam probe 7-15, 554F1
Loses primary 9-9, 700A2
Votes vs Myers House expulsn 10-2, 740A2
McCollum wins seat 11-4, 849D2
KEMP, Frederick John
Freed in Kabul 6-22, 486B2
KEMP, Rep. Jack F. (R, N.Y.)
At GOP platform hearings, on tax cut goals 1-14, 32F1
Reagan unveils tax-cut plan 6-25, 480C2
Addresses GOP conv 7-15, gets votes as vp nominee 7-17, 529G1, 531A3
GOP platform adopted 7-15, 536B1
Carter cites tax plan 8-14, 613A2
Reelected 11-4, 843A4
Budget cuts urged 11-23, 897A2
Heads House GOP caucus 12-8, 936C2
Reagan studies budget cuts 12-17, 956D1
KENDRICK, Pearl L.
Dies 10-8, 876B2
KENEMY, John G.
3 Mile I study cited 7-2, 550F3
KENG, Peao
US OKs mil equipmt sale 5-29, 397E3, G3
KENLEY, Dr. James B.
OKs Va 'test-tube baby' clinic 1-8, 24F1
KENNARD, Byron
At Earth Day fete 4-22, 307F3
KENNECOTT Copper Corp.
Prices raised to record high 1-17, 30F3
USW strike settled 8-27, 805D2
KENNEDY, Adam
Raise the Titanic released 8-1, 675D3
KENNEDY, David
MD found guilty on drug chrgs 1-18, drug therapist rptd hired 1-22, 199E3-G3
Calif drunken driving arrest 7-27, 639C2
KENNEDY, Donald
Named Stanford pres 6-13, 638D2

KENNEDY, Sen. Edward Moore (D, Mass.)
Antitrust & Merger Issues
Would tame monopolies 1-28, 75A1
Urges trust enforcemt 2-6, 91B1

1976

Gets 4% vote in Neb 5-11, 342G1
Platform com testimony 5-18, 357B3
Denies pres ticket bid 5-20, 357D2
Scores Argentina pol murders 5-21, 399C2
Scores rpt on FDA rpt 5-23, 392G1
Primary results 5-25, 374E3
Move to cut missile funds loses 5-26, 411C2
Joins move behind Carter 6-9, 409A2
Dem conv pres vote, table 7-14, 507E2
Urges wider gene research rules 7-19, 9-22, 860C3, D3
US natls to leave Viet 7-21, 593B2
Sees Australia prime min 7-26, 554G1
Scores Cuba re prison access 8-28, 791G1
Carter visits 8-31, 645B2
Wins renomination 9-14, 705A1
Asks Letelier murder probe 9-21, 710D2
Campaigns with Carter 9-30, 742E3
Uruguay pres scores 10-8, 814F1
Reelected 11-2, 820C1, 828G1
Prescriptn drug panel formed 11-30, 931G2
AMA vs health insurnc bill 12-7, 931D2
Sees flu progrm end 12-17, 950A2
At Daley funeral service 12-22, 969D3

1977

Assassinatn com dispute resolved 3-8, 3-29, com extended 3-30; Trafficante subpoenaed 3-16, 228A2, F2
WW II germ warfare rptd 3-9, 195A3
Asks halt to US IRA aid 3-17, 222E3
De Mohrenschildt found dead 3-29, 228B3
On Carter energy plan 4-20, 293G2
'76 campaign surplus rptd 5-4, 482G1
Sees health-care reform endangered 5-16, 381F2
On wiretap curb proposal 5-18, 386C3
Rebuts AHA re hosp costs testimony 5-24, 479G1
Backs Carter Mideast moves 6-29, 496C1
Coal, uranium, acquisitn curbs defeated 9-8, 702F3
CIA drug-tests probed 9-20, 9-21, 721E2, D3
Modifies DNA bill 9-27; safety debate cited 10-6, 10-8, 846F2, B3, F3
M-X arms control impact feared 10-7, 777E1
J Onassis quits Viking 10-13, 927B3

1978

DeConcini reservatn critique in Torrijos UN note 4-7, 255F2
Votes for 2d Canal pact 4-18, 273B1
Leads Carter in poll 5-7, Carter discounts 5-25, 404B3, D3
Oil lobbyist's link to Energy Dept scored 5-15, 408B3
Personal finances rptd 5-19, 385D3
Sees Chile exiles in Geneva 6-1, 452F2
Exxon scores oil pipe divestiture plan 6-21, 471G1
LEAA revision proposed 7-10, 525D1
Backs F-18 authorzn 7-11, 526A3
White discounts challenge 7-26, 682B3
Sees Carter, scores health plan; Califano defends 7-28, 585G3, 586E2
Probe group in Viet 7-31—8-7, 603D2
Carter expects support 8-11, 682E2
At Pope Paul's funeral 8-12, 658B3
Tops Dem pres poll 8-13, 682E2
DC voting amendmt clears Cong 8-22, 661C1, A2
Addresses govs conf, urges natl health plan 8-28, 681D3, G3
In USSR 9-4—9-10; confident re dissident exits 9-11, Pravda scores 9-15, 742G3
Airline deregulatn compromise clears conf com 10-6, 765E2
Asks Nicaragua econ, mil ties cut 10-12, 823D3
Gets low rating from conservatives 10-24, 865C3
On Carter anti-inflatn plan 10-25, 806G3
In Lynn with Carter 10-28, 831C2
Challenges Bell re Lykes-LTV merger, asks FTC probe 11-9; Bell rptd angry 11-16, FTC rejcts probe 11-21; shareholders OK merger 12-5, 935D2
Levich emigratn role cited 11-30, 946G2
At Dem midterm conf 12-8—12-10, scores Carter budget 12-9, 956E1
Asks Chile disappearances probe 12-8, 1014C1
Backs Chile trade boycott 12-8, 1014B2
Carter downplays dissent 12-12, 956D3
Backs full China ties 12-16, 976A1
Gets high ADA rating 12-17, 981E2

1979

Boston library sale of Stuart portraits halted 4-14, 374G3
Clashes with Javits on Brown confirmatn 9-25, 901E3

Antitrust & Merger Issues
Natl trust comm rpt issued 1-16, 88G2
Offers consumer trust bill 1-31, 308B2
Introduces merger-limit bill 3-8, 202D2
Merger curbs rptd backed 5-7, 349F2

Economy
Attacks Carter budget 1-13, 70D1
Lauds free enterprise 9-27, vs Carter on agri 11-12, 11-29, 962A1, D1, E1
Declines comment on FRB moves 10-6, 766B1
Vs Carter on inflatn 11-7, 847F1

Energy
Asks oil co pipe ownership curb 1-4, 55E2
Scores NRC on 3 Mile I A-accident 4-4, 260G1
Asks A-plant constructn stay 5-7, 344B1
3 Mile I comm gets subpoena power 5-17, 417F3
On Carter energy speech 7-16, 534B3
Addresses Urban League 7-23, 560C1, E1
Offers energy plan 7-25, 557B3
Canada vs common mkt 7-26, 581B2
Scores Carter, stresses coal 11-2-12-13, 962B1, E1, A2
Vs Carter on oil decontrol 11-7, 847E1
Calls Carter 'anti-coal' 12-13, 987D1
Scores oil-price policy 12-20-12-21, 983G2

Foreign Issues
Carter warns re Taiwan legis 1-26, 66B3
Lauds slain Guatemala sen 1-26, 97F1
Backs SALT treaty 2-20, 258D1
Canada vs common energy mkt 7-26, 581B2
Seeks Chile loan disclosures 10-1, 750D2
Scores shah 12-2, draws fire 12-3, 918F2, B3
Denies Khomeini letter 12-12, 935C3
Vs Admin re OPEC price hikes 12-20-12-21, 983A3
Coffin backs comment on shah 12-23, 975C1

Intelligence Issues
Introduces FBI charter 7-31, 599A3
FBI audit shows compliance with informant rules 8-9, 747F2

Labor & Employment
Carter attacks positns at AFL-CIO conv 11-15; attends 11-19, 885E1, F1
Addresses UMW 12-13, 987D1

Medicine & Health
Carter restores some '80 health budget cuts 1-4, 3D3

1980

Cities
Dem conv speech 8-12, 610B1, 613F3, 614B1

Defense & Armed Forces
Draft registratn funding signed 6-12, 478D2

Economy
Vs Sovt grain embargo 1-5—1-9, 12G2, 13B1; 1-12, 32F2
Warns vs decline 1-14, 32C3
Cites inflatn, interest rates 1-20, 50D2; 3-4, 167A1
Urges wage-price controls, scores Carter; GOP rebuts 1-28, 74E2, F3, 75G1
Issues policy paper 2-6, 90F3-91C1
Brookings economists back controls 2-6, 2-7, 126A3
Addresses consumers, stages mock debate with Carter 2-7, 91F1, C2
Wage-price proposal cited 2-15, 126E2
Calls Carter policy intolerable 3-9, 206E3
'Basic speech' excerpts 3-10, 183B1, 184A2
Scores Carter inflation plan 3-14, 201D2
Stressed in NY 3-25, 221C2
Likens Carter, Reagan 4-10, 264B3
Pa campaign intensifies 4-18—4-23, 304F1, A2
Deplores Carter policies 5-21, 383F1
Cites public anguish 6-5, 423F1
Urges actn vs recessn 6-10, 438E3
On Dem goals 6-14, 480F1
Trucking decontrol bill OKd 6-19, 6-20, 479C1; comments 7-1, 494D1
Dem platform drafted 6-24, 479G2
Plans conv econ planks speech 8-6, 596D2
Dem conv speech reaffirms commitmt 8-12; 609D1, 610D1; text excerpts 613D2-614C3
Wins platform planks 8-12; Carter accepts intent, conv OKs 8-13, 609D1, 610E2, 611F1-612A2; text excerpts 614C2
Sees Carter on econ progrm 8-25, 646A3
On Carter econ renewal plan 8-28, 663G2

Energy
Proposes gas rationing, scores Carter re Persian Gulf defns 1-28, 74E2, F2, E3
GOP vs gas rationing 1-28, 75G1
Issues position papers 2-2, 2-6, stages mock debate 2-7, 91B1, C1
Attacks Carter A-policies 2-20, 130C2
'Basic speech' excerpts 3-10, 183C1, C2, E2
Dem platform drafted 6-24, 479G2
Dem conv speech asks 'safe energy' 8-12, 610E2, 614F1
Dem platform plank voted 8-13, 611F2

Environment & Pollution
Dem conv speech 8-12, 610B2, D2, 613F1, 614C1

Foreign Issues
Attacks Sovt grain embargo 1-5—1-9, Powell, Mondale score 1-8, 1-10; rebuts 1-10, 12G2, 13B1
Seeks Mideast mil presence 1-11, 32E3
Scores Carter, Sovt grain embargo 1-12, 32E2
Says forgn policy 'adrift,' seeks firm stand re USSR 1-14, 32B3
US policy 'out of control' 1-20, 50E2
Scores Carter re Persian Gulf defns, Afghan, Iran 1-28, 74D2, F2-E3
In Admin exchng on Iran intl comm, other issues 2-12—2-13, 109B2-110C1, F1-D2
Vs US complicity with shah 2-18, 130B2
Scores Carter on arms race 2-20, 130D2
Reagan 'basic speech' scores re Cuba 2-29, 207B3
Scores Israeli setlmt vote at UN 3-4, 164C1; 3-10, 183D3
'Basic speech' excerpts 3-10, 184E1, C2, F2
Helps Cuban poet immigrate to US 3-16, 231C3
Scores Carter UN gaffe 206F3
Visits Mex 4-28, 327F2
Sees Reagan, backs SALT pact 11-19, 881D1

Labor & Employment
UAW's Fraser endorses 1-15, 33C1
Urges wage-price controls, GOP scores 1-28, 74E2, F3, 75G1; 2-15, 126E2
Pushes wage controls 2-6, 90F3
Releases 'guest worker' rpt 2-13, 147C2
'Basic speech' excerpts 3-10, 183F1, B2, E2
Carter attacks controls 4-1, 247C1
AFSCME endorses 4-2, 247G1
Addresses AFSCME, urges jobs progrm 6-10, 438B3
Dem platform drafted 6-24, 479G2
Addresses Svc Employees Union, vows platform fight 6-25, 480B1
Addresses Urban League, vows jobs 8-4, 597D1
Dem conv speech asks jobs 8-12, 610G1, C2, 613F2, 614B1, G1
Wins jobs plank 8-12; Carter accepts intent, conv adopts 8-13, 609D1, 610E2, 611F1, A2, D2; text excerpts 614F2, F3, 615A1
Addresses AFT conv 8-21, 629B3
Sees Carter on jobs plan 8-25, 646G2
Scores Reagan farm worker record 10-22, 817D1
Sees Reagan, urges jobs progrms 11-19, 881D1

Medicine & Health
Cites natl plan 1-28, 75A1
'Basic speech' excerpts 3-10, 183D1-F1, G2, 184A2

1976 1977 1978 1979 1980

1979

Backs Mrs Carter mental health funds plea 2-7, 112D1
At hosp cost bill ceremony 3-6, 163C2
Backs hosp cost-control bill 3-9, 194F3
Introduces natl health plan 5-14, 362C1
Sponsors mental health bill 5-15, 365G1
Carter unveils natl health plan 6-12, 438A2, F2
Scores Valium abuse 9-10, 734C3
Vs 'peacemeal' health care approach 10-26, 11-8, 962B1, C1

Personal

Denies Mrs Trudeau liaison 3-20, 271D3
Finances disclosed 5-18, 383D2
Says Chappaquiddick no bar to presidency 7-17, 539F1-D2
Financial disclosure statemt studied 9-1, 702A1
Med, financial rpts issued 11-7, 847G1
Secret Svc agents subdue woman with knife 11-28, 962D2

Politics—*See also other appropriate subheads in this section*

Leads Carter in poll 4-26, 384F2
Pres draft move launched 5-23, 384B2
Carter confident vs '80 bid 6-12, 440D1
ADA backs '80 pres bid 6-24, 482C2
Hooks sees black support 6-24, 559D3
Califano fired, ties cited 7-18, 529G2
Jackson sees '80 bid 7-24, Carter responds 7-25, 556B2-D2
McGovern backs '80 pres bid 7-26, 556A2
Labor ldrs neutral re '80 bid 7-30, 593E3
Carter primary tension rptd 8-2, Mass legis bars date chng 8-6, 592G3-593E1
Clements discounts '80 run 8-19, 627D3
Mondale '80 pres race suggested 9-5, 662C1
Considers '80 pres race 9-6–9-11, 679E3-680A2
Gets Secret Svc protectn 9-20, 723G3
Carter on ldrship 9-25, gets Carter letter 9-26, 723B3-F3
Stumps country 9-27–12-14, 961E3-962B2
Straus resigns as VOA head 10-1, 771E1
Carter com challenges pres funding 10-4, 783A3
Carter on '80 race 10-9, 767B1
Fla pres caucuses 10-13, Carter win rptd 10-19, 783B1
Seeks support of Chicago mayor 10-15; with Carter at JFK library dedicatn 10-20, rivalry intensifies 10-22, 807C3-808C1, 905D1
FALN bomb defused at Chicago hq 10-18, 786C2
McGovern, Brennan endorse bid 10-19, Chicago mayor, others 10-30, 847B2-D2
Campaign finance dir named 10-24, 847G1
Mondale on pres bid 10-30, 961B3
Carter wins Ia straw poll 11-3; '80 debate set 11-6, 866G2-A3
Leads Carter in poll 11-4, 847D2
Announces pres candidacy in Boston, scores Carter 11-7, 847B1
Dem Natl Com bias protested 11-8, 961C2
Byrne represents at Dem Natl Com mtg 11-9, 961D2
Loses Fla straw vote 11-18, 887C1
Mobil exec joins campaign 11-19, 962C2
Goldschmidt warns Chicago aid loss 11-20; scores 11-28, 11-28, 983G3, 984A1, C1
Strauss sees Carter gains 12-4, 918D2
Brown invited into Ia debate 12-4, 962A3
New Dem Coalitn backs 12-9, 962B2
Drops in polls 12-11, 962C3, D3, E3
Udall endorses 12-18, 962B2
Crangle gets campaign post 12-20, 983C3
Vs Carter Ia debate bar 12-28, 983F2

1980

Dem platform drafted 6-24; vows floor fight 6-25, 479G2-480D1
Dem conv speech asks natl plan, loses platform fight 8-12, 610E2, D3, 614E1
Mental health authrzn signed 10-7, 804B1, C1

Personal

Chappaquiddick questned by 2 publicatns, rebutted 1-14, 1-15, 32F3-33C1
Wife defends re Chappaquiddick 1-18, 50A3
Chappaquiddick plea aired 1-28, 75A1
Chappaquiddick phone record queried 3-12, 184C1
Powell seeks financial data disclosure 4-15, 305E1
Chappaquiddick linked to negative poll rating 4-18, 305B1
Releases tax returns 4-19, 305E1
Visits V Jordan in hosp 5-29, 401B3

Politics—*See also other appropriate subheads in this section*

FEC OKs matching funds 1-4, 5B2, C2
Trails Carter in poll 1-8, 13F1
Carter nominates Ala black US judges 1-10, 744E2
Carter leads in Ia poll 1-11, 33A2
Debates Mondale, Brown in Ia 1-12, 32D2
UAW's Fraser endorses 1-15, 33C1
In Iowa, wife defends re Chappaquiddick 1-18, 50A3
Gets zero rating from ACU 1-18, 53D3
Carter beats in Iowa caucus 1-21, 50D1
Renews candidacy in major speech, Carter com rebuts 1-28, 74D2-75C1
Stages mock debate with Carter 2-7, 91E1, A2
2d in Me caucus vote 2-10, 109C1, D1, E1
Scores Carter debate bar 2-12, Carter defends 2-13, 109G3, 110C2
Campaigns in NH, Mass 2-14—2-20; assails Carter media use 2-14, 130G1
Slips in Times/CBS poll 2-20, 130D2
Carter wins NH primary 2-26, 142E2, F2, F3
Ford on campaign strategy 3-2, 167G1
Wins Mass primary, loses Vt; NY, Ill campaigns said troubled 3-4, 166B2-167C1
'Basic speech' excerpts 3-10, 183A1, 184A2
Fares poorly in Fla, Ga, Ala primaries 3-11, 183A3
Claims Alaska caucus vote 3-11, 209B1
Loses PR primary 3-16, 208B2
Loses Ill primary, delegate count cited 3-18, stresses NY vote 3-19, 206B2, F3, 207B1
Wins NY, Conn primaries 3-25, 221A2, C3
Trails Carter in poll 3-31, 247A1
2d in Wis, Kan primaries 4-1, 246E1-G2
AFSCME endorses 4-2, 247G1
Carter wins La primary 4-5, 264F3, 265A1
Bush agrees re Carter 4-7, 264D2
Addresses editors 4-10, 264B3
Poll rating negative 4-18, 305A1
Anderson prefers to Reagan 4-20, 328C1
Urges 'no more Carter' 4-21, 304F1
Wins Pa primary 4-22, 303G3-304A2
Strauss notes concern 4-23, 304B2
Edges Carter in Mich caucuses 4-26, 327D2
Supporters' petitn rejctd by Sup Ct 4-28, 369A2
Carter drops campaigning ban 4-30, 328G1
Loses Tex primary 5-3, on delegate selectn 5-4, 342B2, B3
Carey asks open conventn 5-5, 342E3
Dem Party head scored 5-5, 366E3-367A1
Loses Tenn, Ind, NC primaries; wins DC 5-6, 341G2-342A2
Carter leads in ABC poll 5-6, 342G1
Byrd urges Carter debate 5-10, 367B1
Loses Md, Neb primaries 5-13, 366F2-E3
Presses for debate 5-15, 383A2
Carter on incumbency 5-19, 399C3
Loses Ore primary 5-20, 383D1
Loses Ark, Ky, Nev, Ida primaries 5-27, 399B1-A2, C2-E2
Says Carter a Reagan 'clone' 5-30, bars platform offer 6-1, 422G3
Carter makes overtures 5-31—6-4, mtg set 6-4, 422G2
Carter poll lead 2 to 1 6-1, 452E2
Wins 5 primaries; Carter gains delegate majority 6-3, 422D2, 423B2-G2, 424B1
Polls rpt voter discontent 6-3, 423C1
Pres delegate count, primary vote total 6-4, 596A2
Meets Carter, continues race 6-5, 423D1
Carter addresses Mayors Conf; speech date switch denied 6-10, 438C3
Addresses ADA, vows to stay in race 6-14, 480D1
Dem platform drafted 6-24; vows floor fight 6-25, 479G2-480D1
Addresses NAACP 7-2, 515E2, F2
Connally cites at GOP conv 7-15, 531E3
Quits B Carter probe 7-23, 549E1
Open conv move forms 7-25—7-31; sees Anderson, holds news conf 7-31, 570E1-D3
Byrd joins open conv move 8-2, 596F2
Dem govs neutral on open conv 8-3—8-5, 595F3
Addresses Urban League, visits Jordan 8-4, 597D1, D2

1976

KENNEDY, Jane
'76 Nobel nominatn rptd 3-4, 272D1
KENNEDY, John F. (U.S. aircraft carrier)
F-14 sinks 9-14, recovered 11-11, 941E1
KENNEDY, John Fitzgerald (1917-63)—*See 1960, p. 244F2-D3 for biog. data*
Exner sells story 1-13, 80G2
Nixon cites Chile role 3-11, 183C3
CIA memos on Oswald-Cuba link rptd 3-20, 3-21, 217A2
Sugar lobby wiretaps rptd 5-9, 344G2
Carter on Admin 6-14, 433D1
Cited in Dem platform text 6-15, 469F2
Carter, Mondale quote 7-15, 506D3, 510B1, F1, 511E2
Cited in Ford biog sketch 613F3
Carter draws parallel 9-6, 664C2
House sets assassinatn probe 9-17, 728G3
Diefenbaker accuses 10-4, 837C1
Ford motorcade in Dallas 10-9, 763C2
Ford on Arab boycott 10-20, 784B3
Carter aides named 12-14, 936F1-E3; 12-23, 956F2
Warren Commission—*See under U.S. GOVERNMENT*
KENNEDY, Robert F(rancis) (1925-68)—*See 1960, p. 457G1 for biog. data*
FBI oppostn to Rev King rptd 5-5, 344B1
United Brands linked to '61 Cuba raid 10-21, 844E3

1977

KENNEDY, John Edward
Convicted 9-20, sentncd 9-30, 848D2
KENNEDY, John Fitzgerald (1917-63)—*See 1960, p. 244F2-D3 for biog. data*
Korry: started forgn pol paymts 1-9, 18E2
Sorensen withdraws CIA nominatn 1-17, 35D1, E1
Alexander named Army secy 1-18, 52F3
House assassinatn com revived 2-2, 77D1
Assassinatn com dispute rptd 2-10—2-21, 126F3; Gonzalez quits 3-2, 149A1
Carter bars shoe import curbs 4-1, 248D3
Latin Amer neglect chrgd 4-17, 296C1
House com funds OKd 4-28, 339B2
Nixon interview 5-19, 405G3-406B1
Kenneth O'Donnell dies 9-9, 788B2
Young compares Biko death 9-13, 708C1
FBI assassinatn files released 12-1, 12-7, 943C1
KENNEDY, Robert Francis (1925-68)—*See 1960, p. 457G1 for biog. data*
Korry: started forgn pol paymts 1-9, 18E2
Kenneth O'Donnell dies 9-9, 788B2
FBI releases JFK assassinatn files 12-7, 943C2
KENNEDY, Walter
Dies 6-26, 532B3

1978

KENNEDY, Florynce
Scores House com on Ray plot 11-30, 938E1
KENNEDY, Joan (Mrs. Edward M.)
Details alcoholism 7-20, 844F2
KENNEDY, John Fitzgerald (1917-63)—*See 1960, p. 244F2-D3 for biog. data*
CIA bid to discredit Warren Comm critics chrgd 1-4, 14C3
Cong support rating cited 1-7, 12A3
More FBI assassinatn files released 1-18, 109E3
Finney dies 1-30, 96G1
House assassinatn com funds OKd 3-13, 183A1
Dutton named Saudi lobbyist 237B1
Gen Clay dies 4-16, 356D2
Garrison affirms death conspiracy 6-15, 844A1
'63 Berlin remark recalled 7-15, 544E3
Cuba ex-consul cites Oswald emb visit 8-2, 831D1
House assassinatn com hearings 9-6—9-11, 697D3-698C2
House com ends hearings 9-28, 749A2
Hunt denies murder role 11-3, 11-4, 898D3
Murder film assessed, House panel reactn 11-26, 916E1-E2
House com finds murder plot likely, acoustics testimony cited 12-30, 1002A1-E2
KENNEDY, Robert Francis (1925-68)—*See 1960, p. 457G1 for biog. data*
Cited at JFK death hearing 9-27, 750F1
KENNEDY, William J.
Named in US Teamster fund suit 2-1, 83F1

1979

KENNEDY Jr., Edward Moore
With father in Iowa 11-12, 962D1
KENNEDY, Ethel (Mrs. Robert F.)
Oldest son marries 2-3, 176B1
KENNEDY, George
Concorde Airport '79 released 8-3, 820A1
KENNEDY, Harold J.
Candida opens 3-6, 711A2
Manny opens 4-18, 712C1
KENNEDY, Jimmy
Spokesong opens 3-15, 712F2
KENNEDY, Joan (Mrs. Edward Moore)
OKs husband's pres bid 9-6, 679F3
Husband enters pres race 11-7, 847E1
KENNEDY, John Fitzgerald (1917-63)—*See 1960, p. 244F2-D3 for biog. data*
Justice review of murder plots asked 1-1, delayed 1-2; Ruby crime link rptd probed 1-3, 4A1
House com cong mandate expires 1-3, 4F1
House com acoustic evidence disputed 1-4–1-5, 4F1-G2
Author files Oswald exhumatn suit 1-9, wins med data access 2-23 166A3
Oswald 'look-alike' dies 1-14, 93C2
Connally announces pres bid 1-24, 70F2
3 House com members challenge findings 1-26, 91F1
Mental health policy cited 2-7, 112D1
New '63 murder film rptd 2-8, 166C1
'63 death threat vs Oswald revealed 2-18, 166E2
House com draft rpt released: Hoffa, organized crime death role suspected; acoustics experts firm on 2d gunman 3-16–3-17, 204C3, G3
CIA agent rptd ousted re rifled House com files 6-17, 6-18, 466A3
Cited in Carter SALT address 6-18, 458G2
Autopsy photo forgery denied 7-9, 520G2
House com final rpt: death plot likely, Oswald crime links cited; findings scored 7-17, 537F2-538D2
Mayoral Cabt apptmt cited 7-27, 577E1
Salinger arrested, freed in Belfast 9-4, 669G3
Family OKs Ted pres bid 9-6, 679G3
Backed McNamara pres bid 9-23, 748A3
Library dedicated 10-20, 807D3, 905D1
Oswald exhumatn sought; substitutn theory discounted 10-22, 905A3
White House tapes alleged 10-29, 869C1
KENNEDY 2d, Joseph P.
Marries 2-3, 176B1*
Speaks at JFK library dedicatn 10-20, 807F3
KENNEDY, Richard T.
3 Mile I NRC transcripts released 4-12, 275D3
Scores oil-pricing policy, Carter rebuts 4-30, 324A2, E2
Absent from Met Ed license vote 10-26, 826B2
KENNEDY, Robert Francis (1925-68)—*See 1960, p. 457G1 for biog. data*
Oldest son marries 2-3, 176B1
Cited in House com draft rpt on JFK 3-16, 24C3
CIA '63 Castro death plot rptd confrmd 5-2, 368A1
Family OKs Ted pres bid 9-6, 679G3
Son David hospitalized, robbery in NYC cited 9-12, 859F3
JFK backed McNamara pres bid 9-23, 748A3
Son Joseph speaks at JFK library dedicatn 10-20, 807F3
Sirhan parole hearing denied 11-7, 953B3
KENNEDY, Rose (Mrs. Joseph Patrick)
OKs son's pres bid 9-6, 679F3
With son in Iowa 11-12, 962D1
KENNEDY, William H.
Backs Carter bank law reform 5-22, 403A2

1980

Carter post-conv unity pledged; platform, rules debate agreed 8-5, 596E1
Plans conv econ planks speech 8-6, 596D2
Williams asks delegates freed 8-6, 596E2
Ends pres bid after open conv move fails 8-11, 609C1, E1
Udall Dem conv keynote speech 8-11, 612A2*, B2
Wins econ, other platform planks 8-12, 609D1, 610F2-611C1
Speech stirs conv 8-12, 609D1, 610D1; text excerpts 613D2-614B3
Carter issues platform statemt; wins endorsemt, conv adopts 8-13, 609D1, 611C1; text excerpts 614C2-615C3
Photo with Carter 8-14, 609A1
Carter renominated 8-14, 609C1, 611G2-C3
Carter acceptance speech 8-14, 612G1, E2
Greets Carter warmly, urges reelectn 8-21, 629A3, B3
To 'campaign actively' for Carter 8-25, 646A3
Lucey joins Anderson ticket 8-25, 646D3
FEC issues campaign rules 9-5, Admin sets Cabt guidelines 9-8, 681G2
Campaigns with Carter in Mass, NJ 10-15, 778F3; NY 10-20, 803B1
Stumps Tex for Carter 10-22, 817C1
Loses Judiciary com chrmnship 11-4, 837E1
Sees Reagan, vows cooperatn 11-19, 881C1
On Haig apptmt 12-16, 955B2
Social Services
Carter pres renominatn acceptance speech 8-12, 610B2, 613F3
Sees Reagan, urges 'sensitive' cuts 11-19, 881D1
Fair-housing legis debated 12-4—12-9, dropped 12-9, 954B2
Women
Dem conv speech backs rights 8-12, 610E2, 614B2
KENNEDY, George
Death Ship released 4-25, 416F2
KENNEDY, George C.
Dies 3-18, 279F3
KENNEDY, Joan (Mrs. Edward M.)
Defends Chappaquiddick story 1-18, 50A3
KENNEDY, John Fitzgerald (1917-63)—*See 1960, p. 244F2-D3 for biog. data*
Justice to reopen murder probe 1-4, 17E1
Snepp novel rptd submitted for CIA OK 6-13, 517C1
Carter pres renominatn acceptance speech 8-14, 613A3
Reagan invokes name 10-1, 738G1
Reagan hits Carter record 10-29, 817A2
KENNEDY, Joseph Patrick (1888-1969)
Son releases tax returns 4-19, 305G1
Swanson affair alleged 10-13, 907E3
KENNEDY, Louisa (Mrs. Morehead)
Sees Giscard 4-23, 299C2
KENNEDY, Morehead
Wife sees Giscard 4-23, 299C2
KENNEDY, Richard T.
Scores NRC membership 7-1, 551C3
KENNEDY, Robert Francis (1925-68)—*See 1960, p.457G1 for biog. data*
Son David rptd in drug therapy program 1-22, 199F3
Son David arrested on drunken driving chrgs 7-27, 639C2

1976

KENNEDY International Airport (Queens, N.Y.)
Concorde landing hearing 1-5, 5C2
Concorde test OKd 2-4, oppositn continues 2-4—2-5, 94D2, D3
Concorde flights barred 3-11, 378A3
'75 Eastern crash rpt issued 5-1, 736D2
Concorde flights to US begin 5-24, 378F2, C3
Sup Ct bars Concorde landing review 11-15, 882B2
KENNON, Robert
Endorses Ford 9-26, 723C3
KENNY, Robert W.
Dies 7-20, 716D3
KENT (O.) State University
Sup Ct lets stand flag-burning convictns 4-26, 359C2
KENT County, Mich.—*See MICHIGAN*
KENTRON—*See RODHELM Reiss*

KENTUCKY
Primary date set 22B2
Byrd weighs primary bid 1-9, 21F3
House votes ERA rescissn 2-18, 172F1
Scotia Oven Fork mine blasts 3-9—3-11; Sen OKs safety bill 3-18, 256A3
Louisville police libel suit denied 3-23, 218C3
Reagan campaigns 5-12, 343B1
Primary results 5-25, 373F1-B3, 374B1
Louisville busing hearings 6-14—6-16, 453E1
Dry Ridge bank closed 6-25, 495F1, A2
Dem conv women delegates, table 508B2
Dem conv pres vote, table 7-14, 507C2
Miners' strike spreads 7-27, 553B2
GOP pre-conv delegate count 8-14, 583C3
GOP conv pres, vp vote tables 8-18—8-19, 8-19, 599C1, C3
Dole campaigns 9-13, 687A1
Louisville integratn incident noted 9-14, 992G3
Fscl '75 per capita income, tax burden rptd 9-15, 10-12, 959D2
Coal mines to hire women 10-21, 943A1
Election results 11-2: pres 818B1, 819B2; cong 822F1, 829E3
Scotia miners bodies removed 11-19, 892B1
Louisville teachers strike 11-30—12-13, 991F1
US Sup Ct refuses maiden name case 12-13, 960B3

KENTUCKY, University of (Lexington)
Dole visits 9-13, 687B1
Wins Peach Bowl 12-31, 1014G2

KENYA—*See also AFRICA Development Bank, COMMONWEALTH of Nations, NON-ALIGNED Nations Movement, OAU*
Listed as 'partially free' 1-19, 20C3
UN Cncl opens Angola mtg 3-26, 228C2
Total IMF oil loan rptd 4-1, 340D2
Oil to Rwanda blocked 4-7, 502G2
India nationals vs curbs 4-24, 313F1

1977

KENNEDY Center for the Performing Arts (Washington, D.C.)
Show business tribute to Carter 1-19, 26F2
KENNEDY International Airport (Queens, N.Y.)
Copter tips over in NYC 5-16, 412B3
Bus hijacked, 2 slain 7-4, 568D3
Blackout closes down 7-13—7-14, 537F2
Laker 'Skytrain' svc begins 9-26, 860C2
Concorde Issue
Carter backs trial flights 2-16, 131G2; 3-9, 212E3
Ruling delayed 3-7, runway plan reviewed 3-9, 212E2, E3
Noise study rptd 4-9, FAA endorses 4-14, 368E2
Giscard on landing rights 5-9, 358E2
Judge lifts ban; reactn 5-11, 368B1-D2
Community protest 5-22, 463B2
House anti-Concorde amendmt fails 6-8, 463B2
Appeals ct backs ban 6-14, 463D1
Judge overturns ban; reactn 8-17, 627D1-B2
US backs expanded landing rights 9-23, 738C2
Appeals Ct upholds NY ruling 9-29, 738D3
Landing delay barred by Appeals Ct 10-6; Marshall issues stay 10-7, Sup Ct lifts 10-17, 797A3
Port Auth offers noise optns 10-8, opponents protest 10-9, 10-17, 819F3
Operatns begin, noise data cited 10-19, 10-20, 819A3
Anti-Concorde protests 11-20, 11-22, 900E1
Passenger svc begins 11-22, 900D1
KENNEDY-Minott, Rodney O.
Named amb to Sweden 7-26, confrmd 8-3, 626G2
KENSIL, Jim
Quits as NFL exec dir, joins Jets 6-6, 659B2
KENTRIDGE, Sydney W.
Questns Biko death rpts 11-15, 887D2
Biko inquest clears police 12-2, 933G3
KENT (O.) State University
Gym protesters arrested, constructn delayed 7-12, 560E1
Protests continue 7-29—10-25, 820E2-A3
'75 damage suit retrial ordrd 9-12, 820B3

KENTUCKY
Legislature not scheduled 6D2
FPC OKs gas purchase 1-19, schl closings re shortage cited 53G3, 54C2
Sup Ct bars Louisville busing review 1-25, 80D1
Gas, weather layoffs rptd 2-7, 91F2
Louisville-Jefferson busing success cited 2-15, 112G1
Retroactive porno prosecutn barred 3-1, 175F1
Storms, floods hit 4-3—4-6, disaster areas declared 4-7, 311F2-A3
Coal co exec dies in air crash 4-5, 286E3
'76 per-capita income table 5-10, 387E2
Louisville econ data table 5-16, 384E2
Beverly Hills nightclub fire 5-28, 429D2
Beverly Hills nightclub fire rpt 6-10; damage suits rptd 7-29, 740A1, C1
'76 Scotia mine blasts laid to spark 6-13, 8-10; widows' suit dismissed 9-12, 900F3, 901A1
UMW wildcat strikes 6-18—9-6, 690F2, D3
TVA sued on air pollutn 6-22, 521B3
Lexington hosp mind-control tests rptd 8-1—8-9, 611E1
Louisville schls open calmly 8-30, anti-busing rally held 9-5, 838B1
'76 per capita income, tax burden table 9-13, 10-18, 821D2
Stearns mine strike violence 10-17, 937F2-B3
Louisville busing review declined 10-31, 835A3
Secretariat's missing mare rptd found 12-9, 971B2

KENTUCKY, University of (Lexington)
2 in NFL draft 5-3, 353A3, C3
Adolph Rupp dies 12-10, 1024B3
KENTUCKY Fried Movie (film)
Top-grossing film 8-31, 712G3
KENTUCKY River
Floods rptd 4-3—4-6, 311A3

KENYA—*See also COMMONWEALTH of Nations, EAST Africa Community, NON-ALIGNED Nations Movement, OAU*
Smallpox outbreak rptd 2-5, 224B1
Party electns canceled 4-2; parlt re-opens 4-5, 393D1
Githii quits paper 5-3, 393E1
Anyona arrested 5-4, 393C1

1978

KENNEDY International Airport (Queens, N.Y.)
Lufthansa cargo terminal robbed 12-11, 1028G2
KENNEY, Douglas
Animal House released 7-27, 970D2
KENNY, Bill
Dies 3-23, 252B3
KENON, Larry
East wins NBA All-Star game 2-5, 271D3
KENOSHA, Wis.—*See WISCONSIN*
KENTON, Lance
Chrgd in rattlesnake attack 10-17, 841F2
KENTON, Stan
Son chrgd in rattlesnake attack 10-17, 841B3

KENTUCKY
Legislature schedule rptd 14E3
'67, '77 sales-tax rates rptd 1-5, 15E3
State govt tax revenue table 1-9, 84C2
Vance in Louisville re Canal pacts 1-12, 58B2
'Prehire' union picketing curbed 1-17, 33G3
Prosecutors' plea-bargaining power expanded 1-18, 64E3
Blizzard hits 1-25—1-26, 105G2
Coal shortage rptd 2-11, Carter sees gov 2-16, 104D1, D2
Carter sees Carroll on coal strike 2-23, 122E3
Bowling Green suit vs Col Sanders dismissed 3-12, 420E3
Equine VD disrupts breeding 3-15—7-13, 539D2
ERA rescinded by legis 3-16; lt-gov vetoes 3-20, ct challenge planned 4-1, 494D2
Miners return to work delayed 3-28, 217F1
Pulitzer awarded for Beverly Hills nightclub '77 fire coverage 4-17, 315A2
Coal strike utility billing probe set 5-10, 366F3
Primary results 5-23, 406D2
Covington chlorine leak sickens swimmers 6-28, 636E3
Nixon honored in Hyden 7-2, 513A2
Louisville makes bad-air list 7-5, 513D1
Louisville firemen end strike 7-18, 565D2
Bad-air list corrected 7-19, 644B2
'77 Beverly Hills nightclub fire indictmts barred 8-2, 972C1
ERA rescissn amendmt rejected by US House 8-15, 661G2
Jefferson Cnty curbs abortns 8-22, 743G2
Self-abortn trial ends in acquittal 8-30, 743B2
N&W strike ends 9-30, 809E2
ERA rescissn amendmts rejctd by US Sen 10-3, 788C1
Pornographer's arson trial cited 10-25, 971E2
US bond tax case refused by Sup Ct 10-30, 832A3
Election results 11-7: cong 846A2, A3, 848G1, 850E4, 853B3
Earthworm rumor hurts fast-food chains 11-16, 942G1
Ft Campbell C-130 crash kills 5 12-10, 984F2

KENTUCKY, University of (Lexington)
'77 football rank rptd 1-3, 8A3
Wins NCAA basketball title 3-27, 272A1
Hagan in basketball HOF 5-1, 457E3
Still in NFL draft 5-2, 336E3
2 in NBA draft 6-9, 457F3, G3
KENTUCKY Fried Chicken Inc.
Col Sanders libel suit dismissed 3-14, 420E3

KENYA—*See also COMMONWEALTH OF Nations, GATT, NONALIGNED Nations Movement, OAU*
Author's arrest confirmed 1-12, 75D1
Cholera rptd 3-22, slums evacuated 4-5, 270E1
Ex-agri min dies in plane crash 5-24; Uganda chrgd 5-26, denies 5-27, 479B1

1979

KENNEDY Center for the Performing Arts (Washington, D.C.)
Feinstein to resign 9-17, 892E2
KENNEDY International Airport (Queens, N.Y.)
Lufthansa cargo terminal theft arrests 2-17, 2-20, 155C3
FAA updates radar improvemt 3-12, 206A2
US swaps Sovt spies, dissidents 4-27, 317C1
'78 world's busiest airports listed 6-1, 421C1
Delta jet hijacked to Cuba 6-11, 442B1
Sovt dancer detained 8-24, released 8-27, 8-24, 644G3
Jet parked for shah of Iran 11-28, 897D1
KENNEDY Library, John F. (Boston, Mass.)
JFK tape on pres successor rptd 9-23, 748B3
Dedicatn held 10-20, 807D3, 905D1
KENNY, Finbar B.
Fined for Cook I '78 electn fraud role 8-2, 648B2
KENNY International Corp.
Fined for Cook I '78 electn fraud role 8-2, 648G1
KENOSHA, Wis.—*See WISCONSIN*
KENTON, Stan
Dies 8-25, 671F2
KENT (O.) State University
'75 damage suit settled 1-4, 5C2

KENTUCKY
Pub schl cost share rptd 3-5, 282E3
Louisville baptism rites mtg ends 3-31, 375F2
Sex bias case refused by US Sup Ct 4-23, 346A3
EPA upheld re Ohio coal use 5-7, 351D1
Bishop Hosea vs church seccessn 5-12, 375D3
Gubernatorial primary results 5-29, 420C1
Louisville hosts NAACP conv 6-25—6-30, 559B3
Govs Assn meets in Louisville 7-8—7-10, 517B3
Ex-Rep Breckinridge dies 7-29, 588D2
Carter visits Bardstown 7-31, 592E2
'78 per capita income rptd 9-16, 746E2
Scotia mine widows suit declined by Sup Ct 10-1, 768F1
Amtrak Boston-Catlettsburg train ends svc 10-1, 868B1
Manslaughter convictn vacated by Sup Ct 10-9, 784C1
Brown elected gov 11-6, 846G1, C2
Midwest quake threat rptd 11-15, 954C1

KENTUCKY, University of (Lexington)
Macy in NBA draft 6-25, 507B3
KENTUCKY Fried Chicken Inc.
Brown wins primary for gov 5-29, 420C1
KENTUCKY v. Whorton
Case decided by Sup Ct 5-21, 400E3

KENYA—*See also COMMONWEALTH of Nations, DISARMAMENT-Geneva Committee, GATT, NONALIGNED Nations Movement, OAU*
Leakey disputes new hominid species claim 2-17, 138D1
Electns held, Moi reconfrmd pres 11-8, 874A3

1980

KENNEDY Center for the Performing Arts (Washington, D.C.)
Istomin named artistic dir 2-26, 199D2
KENNEDY Galleries, The (N.Y., N.Y.)
Fleischman buys Homer oil 10-17, 998A1
KENNEDY International Airport (Queens, N.Y.)
Aeroflot boycotted 1-11, 55C2; 1-18, 45E1
US Customs corruptn probed 1-11, 359A3
Aeroflot radar tampering probed 1-31; USSR to end flights 2-4, 114F3
Abscam bribe paymt site 8-5: Williams, 3 others indicted 10-30, 824C3
KENNEY, Douglas
Death rptd 9-1, 755F3
KENNY (recording)
On best-seller list 1-2, 40F3
KENNY, Anthony
Czechs oust 4-13, 326D3
KENTON, Lance
Convicted in rattler attack 7-15, 655F3
Psychiatric evaluatn ordered 9-3, 860F2

KENTUCKY
Ohio boundary placemt upheld by Sup Ct 1-21, 93F2
GM plans Bowling Green plant 1-31, 287B2
Ashland plans advanced refinery 3-31, 251F1
Harvester strike ends 4-20, 308G2
DES in cattle rptd 4-24, 358F1
Hunts' bailout loan collateral listed 5-28, 425D3, 426B1
Yatesville Dam funds bill clears Cong 6-25, 9-10, Carter signs 10-1, 803D2
10 Commandmts schl law upset by Sup Ct 11-17, 881B3
Herbert Agar dies 11-24, 928G1
EPA halts aid funds 12-11, 963B1
Accidents & Disasters
Blizzards hit, 1 killed 3-1—3-2, 292B2
Tornado hits 4-7—4-8, 391A3
Forest fires destroy 40,000 acres 10-31—11-13, 971A1
Crime & Civil Disorders
Firearms convictn case remanded by Sup Ct 1-14, 37G1
Illegal search protectn narrowed by Sup Ct 6-25, 541F1
Road builders bid-rigging probe rptd 7-5, 655G1
Politics & Government—*See also other appropriate subheads in this section*
Legislature schedule rptd 18D1
Primary results 5-27, 399B1-E2
Carter in Henderson 7-21, 549E3
Anderson battle for ballot access rptd 9-27, 818B2
Reagan in Louisville 10-20, 802B1, D1
Election results 11-4: pres 838B1, 839B2, E3; cong 840G1, 842E4, 845A3, 846B3, 849A3; state 845E2
'80 census rptd 12-31, 983E1

KENTUCKY Fried Chicken, Inc.
Col Sanders dies 12-16, 1004C3
KENTUCKY v. Rawlings
Case decided by Sup Ct 6-25, 541A1

KENYA—*See also COMMONWEALTH of Nations, GATT, GENEVA Committee, OAU*
Adamson found dead 1-3, 104D1; slaying suspect chrgd 2-2, 238B3
'30 Rift Valley Fever epidemic cited 3-2, 318B3

1976

Notes Sovt arms aid to Somali 4-25, 295A1
Commerce min demoted 320G1
UNCTAD conf opens, Kenyatta boycotts 5-5, 320F1
IBRD suspends EAC loans; Uganda scored 5-11, 371F3
UNCTAD conf ends 5-30, 388E2
Hijackers demand prisoners freed 6-29, 463C1; **for subsequent developments, see 'Entebbe' under MIDDLE EAST—AVIATION Incidents**
Olympic withdrawal rptd 7-21, 528B3
IMF OKs loan 7-21, 1013B1
Ethiopian hotel attacked 8-4, 581B1
EAC ry hq closed 8-4, projct near collapse 9-12, 974A3
Mombasa cncl dissolved; Nairobi electns canceled 8-11, 1013A1
Successn chng urged 9-25—9-26, 10-3; subject forbidden 10-6, 947B2
UNESCO starts mtg 10-26, 842A2
Express train crashes 11-29, 912G1
UNESCO conf convenes 11-30, 895E3
Wildlife abuse probe set 12-3, Somali killings rptd 12-14, 947E2
Tanzania feud re EAC 12-7, 974E2-A3
EAC airline paymts OKd 12-14—12-16, 974A3

Rhodesian Relations—*See RHODESIA*
Ugandan Relations—*See under UGANDA*

U.S. Relations
Kissinger visits 4-24—4-25, 295A1
Kissinger Lusaka speech lauded 4-27, 293C2
Kissinger visits 5-5, addresses UNCTAD 5-6, 317A1, 318G2, C3
Rumsfeld visits, sets arms credits, F-5 sales 6-15—6-17, 466F3
US jets, ship visits 7-10, 7-12, 7-13, 516E3
Kissinger sees Kenyatta 9-23, 718A1

KENYATTA, Jomo (Kenyan president)
Kissinger visits 4-25, 295A1
Demotes commerce min 320A2
Boycotts UNCTAD conf 5-5, 320E1
Hijackers seek prisoners freed 7-4, 485D2
90 Minutes at Entebbe publshd 7-26, 547B2
Amin says 'not African' 7-28, 548B3
Signs Uganda accord 8-7, 580E3
Sees Kissinger 9-23, 718A1
Successn chng urged 9-25—9-26, 10-3; subject forbidden 10-6, 947C2
KENYATTA, Margaret
Electns canceled 8-11, 1013B1
KEPA, Jozef
Named deputy min 12-2, 926C3
KEPFORD, Vern A.
Not guilty plea cited 11-30, 921D3
KEPONE—*See PESTICIDES*
KERBY, Philip P.
Wins Pulitzer Prize 5-3, 352E3
KEREKOU, Lt. Col. Mathieu
Benin, Togo reopen border 3-27, 372C1
KERENSKY, Alexander (1881-1970)
Frei scored 1-21, 99D3
KERMER, Romy
Wins Olympic medal 2-7, 159B1
KERN, Harold G.
Dies 2-19, 192E3
KERNER, Otto
Dies 5-9, 368F2
KEROES, Martin
Sentenced 3-9, 271C2
KERR, Sir John
Whitlam chrgs deceit in '75 ouster 2-9, 116E1
Booed at Parlt opening 2-17, 137B3
Ellicott chrgs Whitlam libeled 3-4, 187D2
Flees student protest 8-23, 650B1
KERR Glass Co.
Bias action vs rptd 9-11, 943G3
KERR-McGee Corp.
Scotland oil find rptd 8-19, 675A3
KETCHEM, Rep. William M. (R, Calif.)
Reelected 11-2, 829B1
KETH Reth, Col.
Cambodia asks Thais return 9-4, 734F3

1977

Hunting banned 5-19, 470D2
Ethiopia gets aid offer 9-9, 715G2
Wildlife game skin sales banned 12-12, 976E1

Foreign Relations (misc.)—*See also 'UN Policy' below*
IMF loan set 2-4, 87E2
Tanzania closes border 2-4; tourists, workers airlifted 2-6—2-11, 106C1
Afro-Arab policy statemt scored 3-3—3-5, 170B2
Djibouti independnc set 3-19, 221G2
UK rptr ousted 4-13, 393E1
Tanzania shuts border permanently 4-18, 392E3
Somalia raid chrgd 6-30, 512E2
Quits EAC 6-30, 573B1
Sudan ties improve, pro-Arab shift rptd 7-6, 588E1
Somali border pact set 7-20, 588C1
Somali land claims cited 587F3
Ethiopia royal family escapes to Sweden 8-5, 649E1
French min cuts short Africa tour 8-18, 662F2
Amnesty Intl lists jailed lawmakers 9-5, 753B2
US-Somalia land claims deal rptd 9-19, 715F3
Tanzania ousters rptd 10-5; air links cut 11-1, 913E1
Somali Ogaden recruitmt chrgd, ties worsen 10-15—10-20; facts on border 830A2
Sweden cancels debts 11-8, 904A1
Ethiopia port use OKd 11-30, 998B2
Rhodesian Relations—*See RHODESIA*
Uganda Relations
Anti-Amin plot chrgd 2-16, 138E3
Uganda refugees detail purge 2-25, 3-2, 141G2
Uganda claims invasn threats 2-27, 3-2, 141C2, E2
Amin chrgs aggression 3-8, 170D2
Uganda refugee spying rptd 3-9, 308A2
Uganda coffee smuggling rptd 3-16, 11 arrested 4-13, 308D3
Amin assassinatn plot rptd 6-23—6-24, 507E3-508A1
Uganda executns rptd 8-6, 8-17, 641A2
Amin foes rptd uniting 8-8, 641F1
Commercial vehicles barred 10-4, 805C2
Amin chrgs EAC assets 'grabbed' 10-9, 805B2
Arab hostility re '76 Entebbe raid cited 10-20, 790D2
UN Policy & Developments
UN Assemb member 4B1
Desert conf held 8-29—9-9, 770C1
U.S. Relations
US airlifts Tanzania tourists 2-6, 106E1
Young in Nairobi 2-7, 105C1
CIA paymts to Kenyatta rptd 2-19, 124F1
US Navy ends good-will visit 2-23, 141E2
US natls arrive from Uganda 3-1, 3-2, 141B2
LeMelle confrmd amb 5-9, 418E1
US-Somalia land claims deal rptd 9-19, 715F3
KENYA Airlines
Formed 2-3, 88F1, 106C1
KENYATTA, Jomo (Kenyan president)
CIA payments rptd 2-19, 124F1
Bans game skin sales 12-12, 976E1

KENZO (Kenzo Takada)
'77 fall fashions rptd 7-29, 1022C1
KEPLINGER, Othmar
Arrested 11-23, 991G1
KEPONE—*See PESTICIDES*
KEREKOU, Lt. Col. Mathieu (Benin president)
Coup attempt detailed 2-1, 2-4, 96C3
OAU mtgs boycotted 6-23—7-5, 512B1
Amin on death plot 7-4, 512A2
KERKYRA (formerly Scheersberg A) (Israeli steamer)
Israeli uranium plot rptd 5-30, 416E3
KERR, Clark
Coll curriculum reform urged 12-15, 1009F1
KERR, George
Sets water radiatn treatmt 1-5, 43G2
Tightens Ontario pollutn rules 9-28, 763F3
KERR, Sir John
UK monarchy ties protested 3-7—3-13, 199E1
CIA connectn chrgd 5-4, 372D1
Quits as gov gen 7-14, 541C1
Gov-gen term ends 12-7, successor sworn 12-8, 963F3
KERR, Richard
Prov aid study cited 4-16, 327C1
KERR Glass Manufacturing Corp.
Strike ends 10-14, 818F3
KERRIGAN, Joe
Traded to Orioles 12-7, 990D1
KERR-McGee Nuclear Corp.
Filmmaker gets 1st Amendmt protectn 9-23, 921E2
KERSHAW, Jack
Vs Ray prison transfer 6-14, 459F2
KETCHUM, Rep. William (R, Calif.)
House lifts Soc Sec earnings limit 10-27, 814D3

1978

Locust threat seen 6-6, 465E2
Kenyatta dies 8-22; facts on, photo 639D1
Moi sworn interim pres 8-22, 639A3
Kenyatta buried 8-31, 784D3
Moi elected pres 10-10; names Cabt 10-11, sworn 10-14, 784A3
KANU electns held, Odinga barred 10-28, 885F2
Anti-corruptn effort set 10-31, police chief quits 11-1, 885A3
Pol prisoners freed 12-12, 968G1
Foreign Relations (misc.)
Somalia guerrilla raid rptd 1-26, 137G2
Uganda pardons coffee smugglers 1-31, 95C2
Uganda seeks improved ties, rail shipmt halt cited 2-8, 3-8—3-10, 289C2
Egypt air dispute 2-13—2-16, Somalia-bound plane intercepted 2-15, 137D2
Iran breaks ties 2-18, 137F2
Somali ex-amb rpts Barre plot 2-28, 269G1
Ethiopia demands Somalia renounce all forgn land claims 3-10, 178B3
Moi ends Westn quest for arms 3-11, 289F2
Tanzania border closed 3-22, Somalia bans food imports 3-24, 270E1
Tana R dam contracts rptd 4-9, 478D1
51 Viets get asylum 4-17, 341B2
S Africa arms embargo compliance lags 4-28, 377B2
Seychelles chrgs plot aid 5-8, 378D3
Somalia invasn plan rptd foiled 5-8, 758B2
Uganda chrgd in plane crash 5-26, chrg denied 5-27, 479B1
Somali troops rptd in Ogaden 6-7, 584G3
Sudan oppositn disbands 7-3, 595C1
UK cancels debts 7-31, 592E1
UK, Zambia regret Kenyatta death 8-22, 639B3
UN Assemb member 713G3
Uganda-Tanzania mediatn offered 11-5, 860A2
IMF OKs loan 11-14, 968A2
Sports
World Amateur Boxing tourn results 5-6—5-20, 600D2

U.S. Relations
Moi gets arms aid assurance 3-2, 289F2
US planes delivered 3-31, 289E2
Carter eulogizes Kenyatta 8-22, 639B3
McDonnell Douglas paymts rptd 12-15, 982F2

KENYATTA, Jomo (Kenyan president)
Dies 8-22; facts on, photo 639D1
Moi sworn interim pres 8-22, 639A3
Buried 8-31, 784D3
Moi elected pres 10-10, 784A3

KENZO (Kenzo Takada)
'78 high chic fashion rptd 8-4—8-11, 10-27—11-3, 1029B2, D2
KEON, Dave
Named WHA top sportsman 7-6, 656D3
KEPROS, Nicholas
Othello opens 1-30, 887D2
KERBY, Bill
Hooper released 8-4, 970F1
KERN, Jim
Traded to Rangers 10-3, 779A3
KERR, Donald
A-arms test backing rptd 11-3, 877A2
KERR, George
Phones atty 8-14, Munro scandal spurs resignatn 9-9; replaced 9-12, 721C3
KERR, Sir John
Resigns UNESCO post 3-2, 165E1-A2
Whitlam quits politics 7-14, 555B2
KERR, Walter
Wins Pulitzer Prize 4-17, 315B2
KERSHNER, Irvin
Eyes of Laura Mars released 8-4, 970C1
KERTESZ, Akos
Rain & Shine released 12-21, 1030D3
KERTTULA, Jalmar M.
Loses Alaska primary for gov 8-22, 682F3
KESSINGER, Don
Hired as White Sox mgr 10-19, 1026A2
KETCHUM, Rep. William M. (R, Calif.)
Dies 6-24, 540B3
KETELSEN, James L.
Named Tenneco chrmn, chief exec 6-30, 809C1
KETRON, Larry
Rib Cage opens 5-28, 887G2

1979

Moi shuffles Cabt 11-28, 969A2

Foreign Relations (misc.)
Import controls, Jan-June '78 trade deficit rptd 1-5, 22F2
Uganda rebel group claims bombings 2-5, 101B3
OAU mtg opens 2-21, 147A1
Westn rptrs believed killed in Uganda 4-9, 257E2
Uganda senior offcl rptd arrested 4-18, 288E1
Uganda trade rptd 5-28, 429C2
Astles returned to Uganda 6-8, 488G3
Uganda refugee policy cited 6-8, 489C1
Israel sentncs 2 W Gers for '76 jet plot 9-11, 677C2
Young leads US trade missn, regrets Angola policy 9-16—9-17, 720A3, 721B1
UN membership listed 695F2
US to seek bases for moves vs Iran 12-18, 958D2
In Zimbabwe peacekeeping force 12-23, 976E3

KENYATTA, Jomo (d. 1978)
Moi wins pres electn 11-8, 874A3

KENYON & Eckhardt
Chrysler contract rptd 3-1, 188C1
KEO Chanda
Cambodian info min 1-8, 10B1
KERBY, Bill
Rose released 11-17, 1008C1
KERKORIAN, Kirk
Trust case dismissed 8-14, 756D1
KERN, Harry F.
Signed Grumman contract in Japan 1-9, 98G2
Grumman denies Japan bribes 2-8, 305C3
KERN, Jim
NL wins All-Star Game 7-17, 569C1, D1
KEROSENE—*See PETROLEUM*
KERR, Clark
HS system scored in rpt 11-27, 925E1
KERR, James
Fed judge in Tex slain 5-29, 431A3
Resigns as asst US atty 8-15, 819B1
KERR-McGee Corp.
Oil-price refund agreed 2-8, 112G3
Gas allocatns announced 3-4, 183B3
Loses Silkwood A-damages suit 5-18, 381D1
Silkwood damages award upheld 8-20, 629G3
KESHTMAND, Soltan Ali
Death sentence commuted 10-8, 787F2
KESSINGER, Don
Resigns as White Sox mgr 8-2, 619C2
KESSLER, Beto
Convicted 3-1, 155A3
KESSLER, Judge Gladys
Reinstates DC teachers' contract 3-28, 262A3
KETRON, Larry
Frequency opens 4-25, 711B3

1980

Foreign Relations (misc.)
Ex-EAC leaders meet 1-2, 90E1
Moscow Olympic boycott movemt joined 2-2, 2-2, 85C1
IOC boycott list rptd 3-28, 259F3
S Africa trade cited 4-1, 243B2
Pope visits 5-6—5-8, 363F2
UN rejctn of Israeli constructn bid protested 6-19, 476D2
Moscow Olympics boycotted 7-19—8-3, 587F3
Moi visits China 9-14, 706G3
Somali land claims end asked, arms shipmt ban urged 12-4, 933E1

U.S. Relations
US to seek mil bases 1-9, 11G1, A2
Moi in US, Carter to seek aid hike, bases rptd discussed 2-20—2-22, 142A2
US mil base pact set 4-21, 303A1
UN rejctn of Israeli constructn bid protested 6-19, 476D2
US sailor convicted of murder 9-30, sentence rptd scored 10-13, 10-20, 859C3

KEOUGH, Matt
AL pitching ldr 10-6, 926F3
KERKORIAN, Kirk
MGM Filmco stock control sought 5-30, 501A3
Sues Columbia 9-30, Columbia countersues 10-2, 10-20, 906D2
KERLOC'H, Jean-Marie
Joins A-protest 1-31, 149A3
KERN, Ronni
Change of Seasons released 12-17, 1003G1
KEROUAC, Jack (Jean-Louis Lefris de Kerouac) (1922-69)
Heart Beat released 4-25, 416A3
KERR, Clark
On coll enrollmt decline 1-22, 319A3
KERR, Jean
Lunch Hour opens 11-12, 892D3
KERR Jr., Robert S.
In Okla US Sen primary; runoff set 8-26, 683B1
Loses runoff 9-16, 724B3
KERR-McGee Corp.
3 Mile I gas venting danger seen 6-18, 550D3
KERRY, Mark
Wins Olympic medal 7-26, 623E2
KERSHNER, Irvin
Empire Strikes Back released 5-21, 675D2
KERSTEN, Peter
Wins Olympic medal 7-27, 623G1
KESHTMAND, Sultan Ali
Wounded in shootout 2-7, 123A3
KESSLER, Herbert
Vorarlberg vote backs autonomy 6-15, 520A2

1976

KEUCH, Robert L.
Named dep asst atty gen 1-14, 78G3
KEYKAVOUSSI, Homayoun
Wounded in Paris 11-2, 1002F2-A3
KEYS, J. D.
Scores bilingualism 8-17, 637A2
KEYS, Rep. Martha E. (D, Kan.)
Reelected 11-2, 825D2, 829D3
KHADDAM, Abdel Halim
Warns vs Leb partition 1-7, 1B2
Mediates Leb pact 1-21—1-22, 33F1
Karami drops resignatn 1-24, 59D1
Assures Christians on sovereignty 1-25, 59G1
Returns to Damascus, escort ambushed 1-27, 59B2
Reaffirms Leb sovereignty vow 1-29, 83F1, G1
On Beirut press raid 2-1, 83C1
Seeks Leb reform backing 2-14—2-18, 125E1
Jumblat meets, vs war renewal 2-25, 162E2
Defers Leb mediation 2-26, 162D2
In Leb mediation 3-10—3-11, phones Franjieh 3-16, 209E1, 210B1
Riad sees on Arab force 6-12, 429F2
PLO talks rptd 7-27, pact signed 7-29, 546A2, D3
Syria OKs Leb summit 8-24, 628A3
OKs Saudi Golan exit 10-3, 738B2
Asks Leb arms surrender 11-29, 893F2
Wounded in attack 12-1, 894C3
KHADDOUMI, Farouk
US thanks for Leb evacuatn 6-21, 448E1
Syria talks rptd 7-27, pact signed 7-29, 546A2, D3
In truce talks 8-31, 663A1
On PLO DC office 11-23, 878C2
KHALAF, Karim
Resigns 3-15, 210B3
KHALALI, Abu Khalidai
Killed 7-3, named as hijacker 7-5, 485C1, F2
KHALATBARI, Abbas Ali
Vs renaming Persian Gulf 1-7, 12G3
KHALED, Hassan
Arafat pressed truce 3-31, 225E2
KHALED, Leila
Finds Wahab body 12-24, 973G2
KHALEF, Saleh (Abu Iyad)
Bars Israel recognition 2-15, 126C1
Denies secret Leb pact 4-20, 274A1
Vs French peace force 5-24, 369A2
Chrgs Syrian attacks 6-29, 463C3
Warns vs refugee camp fall 7-3, 487A1
Sees long war in Leb 8-15, 618D1
Syria warns of mil drive 9-11, 720E2
Denies PLO role in Syria emb raids 10-11, 759F1
KHALID ibn Abdul Aziz, King (Saudi Arabia)
Sends aid to Palestinian camps 1-15, 17D2
Meets Sadat, vows aid 2-21—2-26, 162E1
In Leb crisis talks 6-21, 448F3
Joins Sudan, Egypt in pact vs Libya 7-18—7-19, 531B3
At Riyadh peace conf 10-17—10-18, 778A3
Sees Yamani re OPEC mtg 12-16, 934B3
KHALIFA, Emir Sheik Isa bin Sulman al-
Visits France 3-2, 204F3
KHAMA, Seretse (Botswanan president)
At conf re ANC rift 9-6—9-7, 661D3
KHAMSING Srinawk
Arrested 10-15, 794E2
KHAN—*Asian names bearing this title are indexed by surname (e.g., WALI Khan, Khan Abdul)*
KHANNA, H. R.
Vs political jailings 4-28, 313C2

1977

KEWANEE Industries Inc.
FTC asks Gulf purchase delay 8-3, Gulf buys 8-9, 612E2
Gulf merger cited in table 880F1
KEYS, Rep. Martha E. (D, Kans.)
Spec interest gifts rptd 3-7, 232C3
KEYSTONE Consolidated Industries Inc.
'76 Fortune 500 list drops 341D1
Canada steel dumping chrgd 11-3, 836F3 *
KEY West, Fla.—*See FLORIDA*
KHAALIS, Hamaas Abdul
Leads Hanafi DC seige 3-9—3-11, chrgd 3-14, 192F2
Jailed 3-31, indicted 5-3, 396A1
Convicted 7-23, sentncd 9-6, 711E1
Griffin cleared in '73 slayings 11-5, 871A3
KHADDAM, Abdel Halim
Visits Sadat 2-3, 87B1
Vows '69 Cairo pact enforcmt 6-8, 440A1
Asks UN suspend Israel, Arabs sanctn 9-4, 685D1
Meets Carter 9-28, 734A1
For PLO at Geneva conf 10-10, 793F1
Escapes assassinatn, blames Iraq 10-25, 811C3
In USSR, Gromyko bars Cairo conf 11-29, 910E1
KHADDOUMI, Farouk
Denies Israel-PLO contacts 1-3, 10F2
For Israel eliminatn 3-14, 166C2
Israel curbs Langer 3-31, 246D2
On PLO at Geneva conf 5-1, 360E3
Warns re Likud electn win, scores US 5-19, 401B3
Vs Israel peace plan 10-11, 769C2
Vs Carter Palestine stand 12-15, 995C1
KHALAF, Karim
Bars Geneva role, backs PLO 12-5, 930C3
KHALATBARI, Abbas Ali
Signs Treaty of Izmir 3-12, 190C2
Remains in Iran Cabt 8-7, 618F1
KHALEF, Saleh (Abu Iyad)
Scores Saleh slaying 1-9, 9D2
In truce talks 7-21, 7-25, 571C1
KHALID, Mansour
Named Sudan forgn min 2-11, 117F2
Backs Zaire vs rebels 4-7, 265E2
Dismissed from Cabt 9-10, 844A1
KHALID, Nasser Muhammed Ali Abu
Hijacks jet 6-5, seized 6-6, 497D3
Release rptd 8-29, 736B2
KHALID, Salah Mohammed
Executed 11-16, 949B3
KHALID ibn Abdul Aziz, King (Saudi Arabia)
Meets Giscard 1-22—1-25, 50F1-D2
Vows econ aid to Egypt 1-22, 62F2
In UK for treatment 4-25—4-27, 362B1
Meets Sadat, Assad re Israel electn 5-19, 401E3
W Ger ldr asks hijack aid 789E2
Meets Assad on Cairo conf 12-8—12-9, 954F2
Meets Vance 12-14, 954C2
Carter: PLO 'negative' 12-15, 954D3
KHALIFA, Sheik Isa bin Sulman al-
Meets Assad on Cairo conf 12-10, 954B3
KHAMA, Seretse (Botswanan president)
Sees Richard 1-5, 3D2
Rhodesia kidnaped students stay in Botswana 2-6, 85G1
Owen sees 4-14, 296F2
Sees UK, UN reps 11-6, 875F3
KHAN—*Asian names bearing this title are indexed by surname (e.g., NASRULLAH Khan, Nawabzada)*
KHANNA, H. R.
Passed over as chief justice 1-29, 71B3
To probe corruptn 4-18, 304A2

1978

KEY, Alexander
Return From Witch Mt released 7-14, 970G2
KEY, Ted
Cat From Outer Space released 6-30, 618F3
KEYS, Rep. Martha (D, Kan.)
Loses reelectn 11-7, 846F2, 854F2
KEY West, Fla.—*See FLORIDA*
KFIR Planes—*See ARMAMENTS—Aircraft*
KHACHATURIAN, Aram
Dies 5-1, 440A3
KHADDAM, Abdel Halim
Sets Leb peace agrmt 2-11—2-12, 99A1
Backs Leb army in south, vows stand vs Israel 8-3, 583F1
Vs Camp David summit, rallies hardliners 9-7, 673D2
Warns vs Christn-Israel ties 10-16, 783B1
KHADDOUMI, Farouk
Iran revolt role rptd 12-29, 993F2
KHADIR, Col. Abdul
Led Afghan coup 5-2, 349E2
Arrested as coup leader 8-17, 671F1
KHAIBIR, Mir Akbar
Killed 4-17, 317E1
KHALATBARI, Abbas Ali
Replaced as Iran forgn min 8-27, 668B1
KHALEF, Saleh (Abu Iyad)
On Leb truce 3-28, 3-29, 213C1, E1
Affirms Israel shelling freeze, bars PLO Leb exit 5-28, 400G3
Seeks PLO-Christn accord 10-30, 11-13, 870B1
KHALIDI, Walid
Seeks PLO-Christn accord 11-13, 870B1
KHALID ibn Abdul Aziz, King (Saudi Arabia)
Meets Carter 1-3, differences cited 1-4, 1C1, 2A3
Vs Israeli invasn of Leb 3-15, 175A1
On need for US F-15s 5-13, 358E2
US asks peace talks renewal 5-19, 424D2
Vance summit pact missn set 9-18, 709E2
Vance sees on summit pact 9-21, 713A1
Egypt seeks aid for summit pact 9-24, 730A3
KHALIL, Mustafa
Defends dissident crackdown 6-29, 573B2
Named Egypt premier 10-2, 746C2
Sees Carter, Vance on Israel pact impasse 12-1—12-2, 930F2
Meets Vance, Dayan; pact talk revival fails 12-24, 997E3
KHAMA, Seretse (Botswanan president)
Rhodesia role cited 59D2
UK, UN reps see re Rhodesia talks 1-6—1-9, 59G1
Clears slain UK student 5-17, 596A1
Soldier cleared in UK student's death 11-13, 906F2
KHAMBULE, Tamasanga Wilkie
Denied S African passport 6-9, 536C3
KHAN—*Asian names bearing this title are indexed by surname (e.g., WALI Khan, Khan Abdul)*
KHAN, Aslam
Foiled in Pak hijack attempt 1-21, 212F2
KHAN, Nur
Wounded in Pak hijack attempt 1-21, 212E2

1979

KEUSCH, Erwin
I Am My Film released 4-19, 528F2
KEYES, Bert
But Never Jam Today opens 7-31, 711G1
KEYES v. School District No. 1
Case cited by Sup Ct 7-2, 539F2
KEY v. Penn Central Corp.
Case refused by Sup Ct 10-1, 768E1
KEY West, Fla.—*See FLORIDA*
KHACHIAN, L.G.
Major algorithm rptd 10-6, 1000D2
KHADIR, Col. Abdul
Death sentence commuted 10-8, 787F2
KHAJENOURI, Mohsen
Executed 9-24, 814B3
KHALATBARI, Abbas Ali
Executed 4-11, 276C3
KHALEF, Saleh (Abu Iyad)
Asks alliance vs US, Israel, Egypt 3-25, 222A2
KHALI, Lt. Gen. Abdel Magid Hamid
Named Sudan vp 8-13, 618A1
KHALID ibn Abdul Aziz, King (Saudi Arabia)
Carter offers security talks 2-11, 143C2
Greets UK queen 2-17, 190C1
Carter plea re Egypt feud rptd 5-21, 378D3
Sadat fears Libyan link 10-10, 801F2
KHALIL, Dr. Mahmoud Shihadi
Death rptd 9-1, 710G3
KHALIL, Mustafa
Meets US aide on Israel deadlock 1-26—1-27, 69D1
In Vance, Dayan prelim pact talks 2-22—2-25; Israeli Cabt, parlt briefed 2-26—2-28, 142F2, A3, C3
Sadat balks at high-level US, Israel talks 2-25, 142F2
Israeli Cabt bars Begin talks 2-27, Begin defends refusal 2-28, 142F2, A3, 143C1
Gives Vance plan for Israel pact 3-8, 157E1
Says Israel pact means land return 3-17; Begin vows no Palestine state 3-20, 197F1
Vs separate US-Israel pact 3-28, 222C1
Bars Arab League hq shift 4-7, 278F1
On Syria war backing 4-9, Israel protests 4-10, 295E3
Meets Dayan, travel agrmt set 6-6, 415E2
New Cabt sworn 6-21, 468G2
On Emb raid in Turkey 7-15, 536G2
Seeks Res 242 chng at Palestinian autonomy talks 8-6, 8-7, 591C3
Meets US envoy on autonomy talks 9-10, 676G2
Autonomy talks held 9-26—9-27, 740B3
Hints at need for summit 10-18, 823C1
Autonomy talks held, lauds Linowitz 12-12, 938D1
KHALKHALI, Ayatollah Sadegh
Urges assassinatn of shah, kin, ex-offcls 5-13, 357A1, E1-A2
Yazdi denies ct role 5-21; rebuts 5-22, resigns 5-23, 389A1
Sent squad to assassinate shah 6-16, 486A3
Insults spur Arab protests 6-21—6-22, 525D1
Claims credit for death of shah's nephew 12-7, 935D1
KHAMA, Seretse (Botswanan president)
Reelected 10-20, 815A3
KHAN, Sharif
Wins N Amer squash tourn 1-14, 527A2
KHANDEKAR, Dr. Janardan D.
Rpts Laetrile lethal to rats 7-13, 571C1
KHANI, Ayatollah Mahdavi
Komiteh purge launched 4-25, 321B3
Named dep interior min 7-19, 565F2

1980

KEUCH, Robert L.
On new JFK murder probe 1-4, 17G1
Testifies at B Carter probe 8-6, 595C3
KEYES, Daniel
Charlie & Algernon 9-14, 892B3
KEY to Rebecca, The (book)
On best-seller list 10-12, 796C3; 12-7, 948D3
KEY West—*See FLORIDA*
KEZY-AM-FM (Calif. radio station)
T Leary rptd fired 11-1, 890D2
KHABARELI, Shota
Wins Olympic medal 7-29, 623C1
KHADDAM, Abdel Halim
Paris emb bombed on arrival 1-29, 89C3
Says Israel plans Leb attack 2-5, 89A3; 2-23, 140B3
Seeks Syria-Libya merger support 9-10, 697G1
Asks for delay of Arab League summit 11-22, 911C1
KHADDOUMI, Farouk
Scores Camp David pact at UN 7-22, 572C2
KHALED, Leila
Scores Israel at UN women's conf 7-14, 587A2
KHALEF, Karim
Bomb maims 6-2; blames Israel 6-3, 417B1
US offers med aid, Israel scores 6-10, 434G2
US treatment rptd 7-9, 547B2
Returns to Ramallah 12-25, 977E1
KHALID ibn Abdul Aziz, King (Saudi Arabia)
Shifts armed forces ldrship 1-1, 22D1
Sees French pres 3-10, 180D1
UK visit rptd canceled 4-23, 313A3
Qaddafi urges Iran support, US radar planes removal 10-10, 774A2
King Hussein visits, asks support for Iraq 10-11—10-12; direct aid barred 10-13, 774G2
Vs Qaddafi stand on US AWACS 10-22, 820E3
To mediate Syria-Jordan border feud 12-5, 931A3
KHALIL, Mustafa (Egyptian premier)
To oust Sovt experts from Egypt 1-28, 69F1
Autonomy talks progress 1-31—2-1, 89F1
Resigns 5-12, 389G1
Rpt briefed PLO on autonomy talks 6-7, 434B2
KHALKHALI, Ayatollah Sadegh
Displays dead US raiders 4-27, 323E1
Loses title, power 5-13, 373C2
Orders drug dealers executed 5-21, 419C3
Scores parlt boycotters 10-30, 820B1
Chrgd, quits as drug prosecutor 12-7, 943F1
KHAMA, Seretse (Botswanan president; replaced July 18)
Dies 7-13, 562A1

1976

KHARLAMOV, Mikhail
Defends Sovt Angola aid, scores China 3-30, 228F2
KHARLAMOV, Valery
Flyers beat Sovt team 1-11, 56G1
KHASHOGGI, Adnan M.
Gen Tire payoff chrgd 5-10, 360F1
KHATIB, Lt. Ahmed al-
Forms rebel army 1-21, vs amnesty 3-10, 209C1, F1
Ahdab backs 3-11, 209G1
Jumblat vs truce 3-26, 225F1
Moslems back army role 5-11, 337B2
Sees Sarkis 5-27, 385D2
Army reps meets Israelis 8-4, 578A2
Vs Gemayel-Salam talks 8-8, 578B1
KHEFACHA, Hedi
Dies 5-25, 503C3
KHEISH, Antoine
Arafat pressed truce 3-31, 225E2
KHIEU Samphan
Heads State Presidium 4-14, 265D1
KHLEIFAWI, Maj. Gen. Abdel Rahman
Syria premr 8-1, Cabt set 8-8, 594F2
Damascus raiders crushed 9-26, 720G3
KHOLY, Hassan Sabry el-
Leb truce effort fails 6-29, 486B3
Arranges Leb truce 7-24, seeks implementatn 7-26, 546E1, B2
Tel Zataar shelling rptd 7-24, Christians disavow truce 7-26, 546C2, F2
Syria, PLO talks rptd 7-27, 546F1
Tel Zaatar to evacuate wounded 8-2, 561B1
On Tel Zaatar losses, Syria-Christian collusn rptd 8-12, 577B1, D1
Leb peace moves pressed 8-25, 628G2
Meets Christns on peace plan 8-26—8-27; rpts to Syrians 8-29, 662E3
Meets PLO offcl on truce 8-31, 663A1
In truce talks 9-17, 9-19, 698G2
In Leb truce talks 10-4, 737F1
Rpts Leb truce agrmt 10-9, 10-11, 758F1, A2

1977

KHAR, Ghulam Mustafa
Bhutto tied to Ahmed death 9-5, 707E2
KHATIB, Sheik Riyadh al-
Meets Pak prisoners 4-28, 348D3
KHATIB, Zahir
Detained 3-18, 208B2
KHATIM, El-Sharif el-
Named Sudan finance min 2-11, 117F2
KHATTAK, Yusuf
Resigns 1-13, 66G2-A3
KHELIL, Ismael
On EEC-Arab ties 2-10, 146A2
KHIERALLAH, Gen. Kamal
Gets interior min post 2-1, 83G1
KHIEU Samphan (Cambodia president)
Pol Pot in China 9-28, 741B3
KHMER Republic—*See CAMBODIA*
KHODOROVICH, Sergei
To direct dissident fund 11-6, 956C1
KHODOROVICH, Tatyana
Leaves USSR 11-6, 956C1
KHOLY, Col. Mohammed al-
Chrgs arms collectn stalling 1-13, 28E1
Asks Christns cut Israel ties 4-9, 266C2

1978

KHATEMI, Gen. Mohammed (d. 1975)
Textron payoff chrgd, denied 1-24—2-28, 161A2-A3
KHATIB, Col. Sami el-
Syria aids Leb vs Israel air raids 3-16, 173G1
KHEEL, Theodore W.
NY newspaper strike ends 11-6, 865D1
KHIEU Samphan (Cambodian president)
Met Scandinavian ambs 1-22, 43D2
Chrgs Viet aggressn 4-16, 277G3
KHLEIFAWI, Abdel Rahman (Syrian premier; replaced Mar. 27)
Quits as premier 3-27, 269F3
KHOMEINI, Ayatollah Ruhollah
Protesters ask return 9-7, govt statemt issued 9-12, 693C1
Asks anti-govt resistance 9-13, 9-14, 740E1
Backers riot 10-1, 774F3
Shah amnesties 10-2, 775A1
Iraq frees, goes to Paris 10-6, 774F3
Gets Iran press coverage 10-10, 797D2
Rioters ask exile end 10-11, 797G2
Issues strike call 10-16, 797A3
Vs shah coalitn govt plea 857E3
Warns of civil war 11-6, says shah business deals invalid 11-9, 858D1
Vows contd anti-shah stand 11-9, 869A2
Sanjabi arrested 11-11, 869C2
Disputes Meshed death rpt 11-17, 893B3
Anti-govt riots 12-1—12-2, Azhari discounts ldrshp 12-5, 929E1, G1
Asks troop desertn 12-3, France warns 12-4, 929A2
Strike plea heeded 12-4, 929B1
Warns oil buyers 12-13, anti-Israel stand cited 953A3
Sanjabi bars shah govt role 12-17, 993E1
Libya arms bid rptd 12-29, 993F2

1979

KHAQANI, Ayatollah Mohammed Taher
Iran Arabs demonstrate 4-27, 321A3
Meets Khomeini, Khuzistan ldr on Arab unrest 5-27, 5-30, 408C1
Chrgs govt bias 6-1, 446C2
Insulted, riots ensue 6-21–6-22, 525D1
Escapes shooting 7-15, 544G2
KHASHOGGI, Adnan
Churchill admits affair with ex-wife 12-15, 994A3
KHASRODAD, Gen. Manucher
Arrested 2-11, 105D2
KHATIB, Lt. Ahmed
Chrgs assassinatn attempt 10-27, 823B3
KHIBA, Michael
Sentenced 5-11, 373F1
KHIEU Samphan (Cambodian president, premier)
Asks UN aid vs Viet invasn 1-2, 1E1
Urges forces to rally 5-14, 360E2
In Cuba, barred from nonaligned summit 8-30, 674C3, 675D1
Named premr 12-27, 977E2
KHNOKH, Leib
Release cited 4-29, 317D2
KHO'I, Ayatollah Haj Seyyed Abluqassam
Listed in Moslem hierarchy 297A3
KHOMEINI, Hojatolislam Ahmad
Bogus Kennedy letter aired 12-12, 935D3
KHOMEINI, Ayatollah Ruhollah
Photo 82A1
Political views publshd 50B1
Asks followers oppose Bakhtiar govt 1-6, 11F2
Bakhtiari tribe backs 1-10, 11G3
Sees Islamic state 1-12; forms Revolutn Cncl, vows new govt 1-13, 25G1-C2
Bazargan vs regency cncl apptmt 1-13, 25G1
Hails shah's departure 1-16, urges contd resistance 1-17, 25E2
Carter: give Bakhtiar 'chance' 1-17, 26G1
Vs Carter plea, Bakhtiar defies govt successn plan 1-18, 26A1
Regency cncl head in France 1-18; meets, quits cncl 1-22, 49F2
Massive rallies back, says shah 'dethroned' 1-19, 49G1-B2
Bakhtiar vows to keep office 1-19, 49B2
Plans Iran return 1-20, airport closure delays 1-25, 49B1, G1
Bakhtiar meets aide 1-23, 49E1
Shah vs US backing 1-23, 49D3
Rejects Bakhtiar electn plan 1-24, 49C1
Rally backs Bakhtiar 1-25, 49D2
Iran return set 1-29, govt OKs 1-30, 67C1
Returns; asks Bakhtiar quit, threatens arrest 2-1, 66C3
Vs Bakhtiar bid for backers in govt 2-2, 81F1
Says new const drawn 2-3, 81D1
Offers power transfer 2-4, 81G1
Bakhtiar warns followers 2-4, 81B2
Iran to review forgn contracts 2-4, 82C2
Names Bazargan to head provisional govt 2-5, 81A1
Backers take over 3 cities 2-7, 81E2
Young lauds 2-7, reps assure re minorities 2-10, 106F1
Forces clash with army 2-9–2-11, overthrow Bakhtiar 2-11, fighting continues 2-12–2-13, 105A1-D2
Warns of holy war 2-10, asks backers to cede arms 2-12–2-13, 105E1, B2
Carter seeks ties 2-12, 106A1
Pak, USSR set ties 2-12, 106A2
Wins CP backing 2-13, faces leftist challenge 2-14–2-21, 124F3
US emb attacked, Marine kidnaped 2-14, freed 2-21, 125E2-B3
Oil strikers, others return to work; leftist sympathizers remain out 2-17, 2-19, 125B2, D2
Arafat visits, gets aid vow 2-17–2-19, 126A1
Asks vigilante restraint 2-18, 125G1
Cncl executn order rptd 2-20, 125F1
Kurds intensify autonomy demands 2-22–3-1, 145D2
Leftists stage rally 2-23, 145A1
Warns USSR, scores gas deals 2-24, 145D1
Rpts Bakhtiar flight, asks info 2-25, 144G3
Denounces forgn colonialism 2-27, 146B1
Bazargan scores cncl, threatens resignatn 2-28, 144G2
Returns to Qom, scores West 3-1, 161A2
Bazargan rivalry cited 161E2
Calls Bazargan govt 'weak' 3-7, vs resignatn 3-8, asks backing 3-9, 179B3
Curbs women's garb 3-7, qualifies order 3-8; women protest 3-8–3-12, US feminist denounces 3-12, 179C2
Shariat vs referendum plan 3-11, 179E3
US tap of aide rptd barred 3-11, 180C1
Pahlevi ex-offcls executed 3-13, 179G3
Suspends trials, executns 3-16, 199C1
Kurds revolt 3-18, acts 3-20, 198C3, 199A1, C1
Bakhtiar scores govt 3-24, 229C1
Kurds granted autonomy 3-25, 228E3
Proclaims Islamic repub 4-1, 247B2
Bazargan rptdly vs komitehs 4-12, 297E2
Sanjabi quits Cabt, komitehs scored 4-15–4-17; US blamed 4-17, 277A1, A2
Taleghani backs on komitehs 4-18–4-19, reaffirms komiteh power 4-19, 297B2

1980

KHATIB, Ruhi al-
Meets US aide on autonomy talks 1-30, 89C2
KHIEU Samphan (Cambodian president, premier)
Refutes Pol Pot excesses 2-28, 181F1
In China, Peking vows aid 3-9; asks intl backing 3-11, 181E1
Ieng Sary on Pol Pot ouster 11-29, 913F2
KHJ-TV (Los Angeles, Calif. TV station)
FCC lifts RKO Gen license 1-24, 119F2
KHOEINY, Hojatolislam Asghar Mousavi
On com to probe hostage case 10-2, 769B1
Sees early release of hostages 10-22, 799D3
Sees Reagan electn delaying hostage release 11-5, 853F3
KHOF-TV (San Bernadino, Calif. station)
FCC revokes Faith Center license 10-10, 907D1
KHOLOV, Makhmadula
Claims 'bandits' delay Sovt Afghan exit 8-18, 650A2
KHOMEINI, Hojatolislam Ahmad
Father vs Sovt Afghan invasn 2-4, 88B2
Visits hostages 2-8, 106D1
Reads father's message to parlt 5-28, 394A2
Scores militants' attack 6-14, 464E3
KHOMEINI, Ayatollah Ruhollah
Bars Waldheim mtg 1-2, 3G2, E3
Connally urges deadline 1-3, 5G1
Backers clash in Qom, Tabriz 1-4—1-6, 4A1
Asked for ruling on US envoy 1-5, rejctn hinted 1-8, 29G3
Azerbaijani unrest continues 1-7—1-9, curfew imposed 1-10, 20B2
CBS rpts Ghotbzadeh slur 29A3
Carter sees no break in crisis 1-8, 29C3
Tabriz executns protested 1-12, 30B1
Afghan pres assures on Sovt invasn 1-16, 27B2
Wounded aide treated in US 1-17, 30C1
Hospitalized 1-23, 47F2
Bani-Sadr elected pres 1-25, 67A1
Militants say govt ignores US spy chrgs 2-1, 88C2
Vs Sovt Afghan invasn 2-4, 88A2
Installs Bani-Sadr 2-4, 88A2
Backs Bani-Sadr as Cncl head 2-7, 105A2
Militants claim mandate 2-9, 105G2
Marks revolutn anniv; scores US, USSR 2-11, 105G2
OKs secret plan for hostage release 2-13, 105D1
Names Bani-Sadr to head armed forces 2-19, 122D2
Airmen end 5-day protest 2-19, 122F2
Names charter protectn body 2-19, 122F2
Renews demand for shah return, backs militants 2-20, 122A2
Hints delay in US hostage release 2-23, Carter comments 2-24, 137C1, G1, C2
Bani-Sadr urges militia 2-25, 137E2
Released from hosp 3-2, 164D2
Pub prosecutor's request for hostages stalled 3-4, 164B3
Militants set conditn for UN comm hostage visit 3-5, 164C2
Militants to yield hostages to govt 3-6, 164B2
Sets hostage release terms, UN comm balks 3-10, 177A1
Jewish immigratn estimated 3-14, 178G1
US accuses in World Ct plea 3-18—3-20, 203E3, 204A1
Issues general amnesty 3-18, 204A2
Brother chrgs vote fraud 3-18, 218G1
Clerics score Ghotbzadeh, Bani-Sadr 3-25, 217F2
2d-round parlt electns delayed 3-26, 218E1
Carter 'apology' rptd received 3-29, 241D2
Scores US re shah's move to Egypt 4-1, 241E1
US Methodists voice sympathy for Iran 4-2, 324C3
Govt asks hostage decisn 4-6, vs hostage transfer 4-7, 257B1, 258B1
Carter cuts Iran ties 4-7; hails 4-8, 257B1, F1, 258E1
Urges Iraqi coup 4-8, linked to plotters 4-9, 300A1, D1
Gets papal plea on US ties 4-12, replies 4-15, 282A2
Shiite ldr's executn rptd 4-15, accuses Iraq 4-22, 300A2, C2
Timms seek audience 4-19, 299F1
Vs leftist university role 4-21, 299D3
Scores US rescue mission 4-25, 322A3
PLO scores US rescue missn 4-27, 324D2
Carter ends campaigning ban 4-30, 328A2
US raiders bodies returned to US 5-6, 337A2
Bani-Sadr asks premr selectn 5-6; OKd 5-9, Rev Cncl bars move 5-12, 373G1
2 Azerbaijan ldrs executed 5-22, 419E3
Message read to new parlt 5-28, 394A2
Anti-US conf in Iran 6-2—6-5; scores Carter 6-4, 418E2, D3
Iraq Emb in Rome attacked 6-4, 451E2
Iran radio scores Clark 6-6, 433E1
Warns of Iran 'chaos' 6-10, 433C2
Oveissi sees overthrow 6-11, 433F2
Leftists, backers clash 6-12, 464C3
Backs schl takeover 6-14, 464F3
Scores Bani-Sadr, Rev Cncl 6-27; Bani-Sadr responds 6-29, 490D1, A2
Orders US hostage freed 7-10, 539F1

1976

KHOMEINI, Mohammed
Alleged Shamsabadi slayers seized 5-17, 365C3
KHORANA, Dr. Har Gobind
Synthetic bacterial gene rptd 8-28, 735C3
KHOREISH, Patriarch Antonious
Meeqs Al Fatah official 9-4, 663C1
KHOULY, Col. Mohammed al-
At Leb truce group meeting 4-19, 273F2
KHRISTOV, Valentin
Wins Olympic medal 7-26, 576F2
KHRUSHCHEV, Nikita S. (1894-1971)
Neizvestny emigrates 3-10, 206E3
'60 rocket accident cited 11-6, 948G3
Satyukov, Lysenko die 11-17, 11-20, 970D2, C3
KHUE, Most Rev. Joseph Marie Trinh Nhu
Named cardinal 5-24, 423G3
KHUNYING Lursakdi Sampatisri
Communicatns min 10-22, 813F2
KIANO, Julius
Set Marcos visit to UNCTAD conf, Kenyatta demotes 320G1
KICKBACKS—*See 'Bribery' under CRIME, 'Political Payments' under BUSINESS*
KIDD Jr., Adm. Issac C.
On F-14 salvage 11-11, 941F1
Scores Eur navies 11-15, 879B3

1977

KHORAM, Avi Ahmed
Slain 11-16, suspect seized 11-17, 969E2
KHOURY, Col. Victor
Heads Leb army 3-28, 227C1
KHRUSHCHEV, Nikita S. (1894-1971)
Nixon reminisces 5-12, 385F3, 386D1
Brezhnev elected pres 6-16, 469E2
Albania scores Tito, China dispute cited 9-2, 710D1
KHVOSTANTSEV, Lev G.
Deported 2-24, 159E1
KIBIRA, Bishop Josiah M.
Lutheran World Fed head 6-24, 732E1
KICKBACKS—*See BUSINESS—Payments Issues; CRIME—Bribery*
KIDD, Culver
Acquitted 5-20, 424D1

1978

KHRUSHCHEV, Nikita S. (1894-1971)
Pervukhin death rptd 7-25, 620D3
US sentences 2 Sovt spies 10-30, 835B2
Lacey dies 12-11, 1032B3 ★
KIBAKI, Mwai
Kenya vice pres 10-11, 784C3
KICKBACKS—*See BUSINESS—Payments Issues; CRIME—Bribery; POLITICS—Corruption*
KIDD, Culver
Acquitted 4-21, 309E3

1979

Orders Egypt ties cut 4-30, 408A2
Scores Motahari death 5-2, 321A2
Forms new militia 5-5, 353F2
Insulters executed 5-7, 5-8, 353B2
Scores newspr articles 5-10, paper closes 5-12; lauds Islamic press blockage 5-15, 5-16, 357G2-358G1
Limits executns 5-13, denies amnesty 5-16, 357A1
Assures Jews 5-15, 357D2
Protesters ask press freedom 5-19, 389E1
Scores US Sen res, Javits 5-20; asks Bakhtiar, Emami executns 5-22, 388C3, 389B1
Vs secular critics 5-24, 407E3
Young compares US, Iran executns 5-25; reactn 5-26, 400D1
Aide shot 5-25, blames US 5-26, 407D2
Meets Arab ldr on Khuzistan unrest 5-27, 408C1
Bazargan, Nazih vs policies 5-28, 407B3
Natl Front calls dictator, Natl Oil Co dirs resign 6-2, 425B3, F3
Scores secular critics 6-5, 426A1
Scores Sovts re Khuzistan role, aid to Afghan govt 6-12, 445G3-446D1
Scores charter critics 6-18, 486C2
Islamic militia curbs denied 7-1, 503C3
US rptr ousted 7-1, 525E2
Declares gen amnesty 7-9, 524D3
Backs mil police cmdr 7-10, 525A2
Aide shot 7-15, 544A3
Iraq Baathist's ouster linked 7-15, 544F3
Bazargan to share power 7-19, 565D2
Bans music 7-23; bar qualified, defied 7-24, 565A3
Bakhtiar vs Islamic rule 7-31, 582A3
Foes, backers clash over press rules 8-12–8-14, 614A3
Says govt, mil lack zeal 8-17; ordrs drive vs Kurdish rebels 8-18; ordrs gen mobilizatn, outlaws Kurdish party 8-20, 635A1
Offers Kurds money to end revolt 8-22, blames 'democrats' for unrest 8-25, 653B2
2 backers slain 8-26, 653A3
Bazargan offers resignatn 8-31, 670E1
Rejects Kurd truce 9-1, 670B1
USSR scores rule 9-8, 688C1
Taleghani dies 9-10, 688A1
Charter shift would give top power 9-12, 708G2
Loses confidence in Nazih 9-24, threatens treason trial 9-28, 752E2
Kuwait ousts envoy 9-26; UAE, Bahrain expulns cited 752G2
Orders executns halt 10-18, 814A3
Scores shah's US entry, asks actn 11-1, 879C2
US emb seized 11-4, bars US mediators 11-7, 841D1, D2
Says UK harbors Bakhtiar; UK emb seized, freed 11-5, 841A2
Bazargan quits; takes over country 11-6, 841C1, 842G1
US Cong urges hostages freed 11-7, 842C3
Sadat calls 'lunatic' 11-9, 862B3
Iranian rally in US backs 11-9, 863C1
Scores Carter, Pope, intl pressure re US hostages 11-11, 862B2
US mediator recalled 11-14, 862G2
Orders US black, women hostages freed 11-17, 878B1
Calls US hostages spies, threatens trial 11-18–11-20; US threatens mil move 11-20, 877B1-D2
Hints US, Israel role in Mecca mosque takeover 11-21, 893C1
Calls US Emb captors uncontrollable 11-21, 894C2
Lauds Pak raid on US Emb 11-22, 894E1
Denunciatns of US mount 11-22–11-26, Mecca mosque chrgs repeated 11-24, 895A2
Shariat Madari vs US Emb takeover 11-26, 895F3
Vs UN Cncl debate 11-27, fires Bani-Sadr 11-28, 896E1
Charter OKd, named ruler for life 12-2–12-3, 915F2
Connally vs Kennedy anti-shah remarks 12-3, 918F3
Shariat Madari vs charter, meets on Qom riots 12-6, 915A3
Students bar orders from Ghotbzadeh 12-7, 934A2
Shariat Madari defies, backs Azerbaijan autonomy 12-7; supporters, rebels clash 12-7–12-13, 935E3
Bogus Kennedy letter aired 12-12, 935C3
OKs intl tribunal 12-13, 958A2
Backs students on hostages, deny they set policy 12-17, 958A1
Mofateh slain 12-18, 958F2
Baluchistan unrest 12-20–12-22, 975A3
OKs clergy svcs for hostages 12-21, 975D1
Scorns Waldheim hostage missn 12-30, 975A1
KHOMEINI, Sayed Ahmed
Calls US Emb hostages 'CIA agents' 11-20, 877C2
KHORRAM, Rahim Ali
Executed 5-9, 353D2
KHOSRODAD, Gen. Manucher
Executed 2-16, 125E1
KHRUSHCHEV, Nikita S. (1894-1971)
Cyrus Eaton dies 5-9, 432E2*
KID Champion (play)
Opens 8-27, 712A1
KIDD, Adm. Isaac C.
Backs SALT 7-17, 536A2

1980

Coup plot fails 7-10, chrgs forgn role 7-11, 539B2
2 Bakhtiar cousins arrested in alleged plot 7-17, 545F1
Guardians Cncl completed 7-17, 571B3
Ex-hostage on captivity 7-21, 545C1
Tabatabai slain in US 7-22, 545E2
Iranian protesters in US arrested 7-27, freed 8-5, 586D1
Blames Pope re jailed Iranians in US 8-3, 587A1
Carter rpts on brother's Libyan role 8-4, 593C3-F3
Scores US, urges intl protests 8-6, 635F1
Bakhtiar plans coup, denounces rule 8-8, 644G2
Fardust secret visit to US rptd 8-14, 671F3
Militants warn US vs hostage rescue 8-25, 644C2
Asks Bani-Sadr OK partial Cabt 9-5, 689C1
US ex-amb scores Brzezinski '79 Iran policy 9-6, 694C1
Leb missing Moslem ldr rptd jailed in Libya 9-9, 709E1
Sets hostage release terms, omits trial, apology demand 9-12, statemt text aired 9-15; US, Iran reactn 9-12, 9-15, 693A1-A2, C2
Reagan urges hostage release concessns 9-13, 699G3
Bani-Sadr backs hostage terms 9-17, 693B2
Iraq ends border pact 9-17, 694B2
Calls for Iraq pres overthrow 9-22, 717C2
Iran restates hostage demands 9-22, 719A3
Bakhtiar: 'End is near' 9-26, 769E1
Vs Iraq truce bid 9-30, 733E1
Cedes war powers to Defns Cncl 10-12, 773D2
Iraq says exports revolutn 10-15, 774E1
Urges total mobilizatn vs Iraq 10-19, 799A3
Rejects Islamic war mediatn 10-19, 10-20, 799B3
Rajai says US set to meet hostage terms 10-22, 799E3
Palestinian curbs rptd tightened 10-22, 821D2
Blames Carter for Iraq invasn 10-29, 820B1
Iran parlt sets hostage release terms, govt gets hostage custody 11-2, 853B1, E2
Factns clash in W Ger 11-2, 969C2
Vs new Iraq peace offer 11-5, 855B1
Ghotbzadeh arrested 11-7, freed 11-10, 862D1, A2
KHRISTOV, Pavel
Wins Olympic medal 7-22, 624G2
KHRUSCHEV, Nikita S. (1894-1971)
Kosygin resigns 10-23, 797C1
KHUBULURI, Tengiz
Wins Olympic medal 7-27, 623D1
KHYAZHEV, Dr. Marat
Examines Tito 1-5, 49D2
KID, Kenneth K.
Rpts stuttering, genetics link 1-5, 63C3
KIDD, Michael
Music Man opens 6-6, 756F3

1976

KIDDER Peabody & Co.
Denies Egypt payoff 2-19, 138G2
KIDNAPINGS—*See CRIME; country names*
KIDNEY—*See MEDICINE & Health*
KIDRON, Mordecai
Vs anti-Israel Habitat conf resolutns 6-11, 431C3
KIEFFER, Jarold A.
Replaced as AID asst admin 4-1, 262D3
KIENDL, Frederick W.
Indicted 11-4, 886F3
KIET, Vo Van
Heads Saigon city govt 1-21, 54D1
KIFLE Wodajo
Sees US amb re Eritrea 6-9, 457D2
KIHKA, Mansur Rashid
On UN Viet membership vote delay 9-14, 682C1
Vs Leb attack on Palestinians 10-14, 759B1
KILDEE, Dale E.
Elected 11-2, 823E2, 829D4
KILIC, Selahattin
In USSR, gets loan 12-21, 1011B2
KILJAE Gyong
Expelled from Sweden 10-22, 799D2
KILLANIN, Lord
On Taiwan withdrawal 7-11, 528G3
Closes Montreal Olympics 8-1, 562D1
KILLEN, James
A-ship safety demanded 1-22, 46D1
Rpts rocket range closing, US arms deal 2-18, 154C3
New radar set for air force 5-12, 380B2
On '76-80 defns budget 5-25, 399E3
Denies '70 Viet massacre 8-3, 571E3
Details defense plan 11-4, 850G1, B2
Orders Darwin cyclone aid probe 11-18, 902D2
Fire destroys 7 navy planes 12-5, 922F3
KILLER Elite (film)
Dec '75 top-grossing film 32G3
KILLILEA, James
Nominates McCormack at conv 7-14, 506E1
KIM, Nelli
Wins Olympic medals 7-19—7-22, 563B1, 574D3-E3
KIMANI, Kihika
Succession change urged 10-3, 947C2
KIMBALL, Spencer W.
Carter visits 10-7, 762D1
KIMBALL, Thomas
Sees Carter 12-16, 937C2
KIM Dae Jung
Signs anti-Park statemt 3-1, 176F2
Arrested, wife freed 3-10, 223B1
Sentenced 8-28, 655D1
Japan ldr vs kidnaping 10-13, 838E3
Sentence reduced 12-29, 1013G2
KIM Dong Jo
On US electn results 11-3—11-4, 826A2
Waldie campaign gift rptd 11-4, 900F1
KIM Duk Yong
Sentenced 4-22, 334C2
KIMELMAN, Henry
'72 campaign gift listed 4-25, 688D1
KIM Hong Chul
Expelled from Denmark 10-15, 799B3
KIM Il
Resigns 4-30, 335B2

KIM Il Sung (North Korean president)
Asks N-S cong 7-22, 557F2
Regrets US deaths 8-21; US rejcts 8-22, eases stand 8-23, 625B2

KIM Jae Kyun
Named KCIA dir 12-4, 928G2
KIM Ok Son
Denied passport 2-6, 122A1
Convicted 12-7, 928A3
KIM Sang Keun
S Korea probe role, asylum bid rptd 12-1, 900B1
KCIA head ousted 12-4, 928F2
KIM Seong Jin
Lauds DMZ tree-felling 8-21, 625F1
KIM Sung Joo
Rpts on arrests 9-19, 734C1

1977

KIDDE & Co. Inc., Walter
US Lines settles SEC chrgs 6-6, 651B1
Ex-US Rep Garmatz indicted 8-1, 603E3
KIDNAPINGS—*See CRIME; country names*
KIDNEYS—*See MEDICINE & Health*
KIDO, Kiochi
Dies 4-6, 356C3
KID Pambele—*See CERVANTES, Antonio*
KIESINGER, Kurt Georg
'68 Israeli uranium purchase rptd 5-30, 416A3
KIEV (USSR aircraft carrier)
In submarine exercise 7-28, 591A2
KIKADIDI, Capt. Barthelemy
Ngouabi slain 3-18, 220A2
Sentenced in absentia 3-25, 282B3
KILDEE, Rep. Dale E. (D, Mich.)
Child abuse bill cited 5-23, 432F3
KILLEN, James
Rpts Nov '76 troop strength 1-10, 96A2
Plans UK radar equipmt deal 2-1, 96A2
Named Australia defns min 12-19, 982A2
KILLGORE, Andrew I.
Named amb to Qatar 7-26, confrmd 8-3, 626G2
KIM, Alexander
Named KCIA agent 6-5, 442B1
KIM, Charles C.
KIM, Hancho C. (Kim Han Cho)
Named Korea lobbyist 6-5, 6-8, 441F3, 442C2
$200,000 in gifts chrgd 7-26, 688G2
Indicted 9-27, 773B3
Pleads not guilty 10-6, 816C3
US House outlines lobbying role 10-19—10-21, 816D2
Ford mtg bid, rejctn rptd 11-11, 915A2
Named KCIA agent 6-5, 442B1
SEC accuses, consent filed 9-28, 774C1
KIMBALL, Spencer W.
Ex-Mormon loses suit 3-10, 310B2
KIM Dae Jung
Sentence upheld 3-22, 306D1
KIM Dong Jo
US House votes Korea lobbying probe 6-8, 442C2
US House outlines lobbying role 10-19—10-21, 816B2, E2, F2
KIM Hyung Wook
Details Korea lobbying effort 6-5—6-7, 441A3
On Korean scheme 6-22, Park threat 7-2, 556F3
Claims Kim Han Cho gave $200,000 7-26, 688F2
Named Park co-conspirator 9-6, 687F2
Named in Hanna indictmt 10-14, 816C1
Bid to block testimony chrgd 11-30, 914F3

KIM Il Sung (North Korean president)
Tito visits 8-24—8-29, 709F3
Forms new Cabt, sets 6-yr econ plan 12-15, 986D3

KIM Kwan Suk, Rev.
Scores US amb 4-20, 306A1
Sees US offcl on troop exit 5-25, 441B1
KIMOMBWA, Samson
Sets 10,000-mtr run mark 6-30, 603D1
KIMPTON, Lawrence A.
Dies 11-1, 952F2
KIM Sang Keun
US House votes Korea lobbying probe 6-8, 442C2
Park order to curb lobbying rptd 6-20, 556E3
Kim Han Cho indicted 9-27, 774A1
Testifies at US House lobbying probe 10-19—10-21, 816D2 ★

1978

KIDDE & Co. Inc., Walter
Garmatz indictmt dropped 1-9, 16A1
US Lines fined 9-18, 752F3
KIDNAPINGS—*See CRIME; county names*
KIDNEYS—*See MEDICINE—Diseases*
KIDWAI, Mohsina
Wins Uttar Pradesh by-electn 5-9, 374G3
KIENDL, Frederick W.
Sentenced 9-21, 768B3
KIERNAN, Walter
Dies 1-8, 96D2
KIESL, Erich
Wins Munich mayoral bid 3-5, 211E1
KILDEE, Rep. Dale E. (D, Mich.)
Reelected 11-7, 851E1
KILIC, Mustafa
Named Turkey state min 1-5, 21E2
KILI Island (U.S. trust)
Bikini residents relocated 8-31, 685A2
KILLEN, James
Confrms Maralinga A-waste mass 10-5, 771C3
A-waste monitoring centralized 11-9, 900D2
KILLIAN, Lt. Gov. Robert K. (D, Conn.)
Loses primary for gov 9-12, 716E2
KIM, Hancho C. (Kim Han Cho)
Convicted 4-8, 279A3
Sentenced 5-19, 406A2
KIMBALL, Spencer W.
Ends Mormon ban on black priests 6-9, 480G2
Discourages interracial marriage 7-15, 907C2
Opens prayer rites to women 10-7, 907G1
Calls for doubling missionary force 10-13, 907B2
KIM Chang Kyu
USSR frees 4-29, 318D1
KIM Chong Pil
Unificatn Church-KCIA link probed 3-15—3-22, 203E1
KIM Dae Jung
Quits New Dem Party 3-29, 269E3
'71 Park campaign gifts rptd 11-1, 862D3
Freed from jail 12-27, 1022D1
KIM Dong Jo
US House testimony sought 1-23, barred 1-31, 64D1
House coms seek testimony 2-22, 3-9; held 'bigger fish' than Park 2-28, 203G3-204A1, C1
Cited in Hanna guilty plea 3-17, 202G3
Cited in Passman indictmt 3-31, 239E1
US access rptd possible 3-31, 239D3
House probers rpt Cong paymts 5-22—5-25, 432B3
House com res links access, Korean aid 5-24, 406B2
House votes aid warning 5-31, 432G1
US House votes food aid cutoff 6-22, 467C2-A3
Resigns S Korea post, cites lobbying scandal 6-23, 527E2
Jaworski quits Korea probe 8-2, 604D3
US House ethics com OKs written testimony 8-3, 605D1
KIM Hyung Wook
Cited in Hanna guilty plea 3-17, 203B1

KIM Il Sung (North Korean president)
Cambodia asks aid vs Viet 1-3, 4F1
'77 plot vs son rptd 2-5, 115E3
Meets China Premr Hua 5-5—5-10, S Korea scores 5-11, 340D2
Warns nonaligned movemt vs splits 7-25, 583E2
China backs on Korea reunificatn 10-25, 802D1
KIM Jung Il
'77 assassinatn try rptd 2-5, 115E3
KIM Kwang
Mitchell: '71 FBI memo linked KCIA 3-21, 203E2
KIMOMBWA, Samson
10000-mtr run mark broken 6-11, 600G2
KIM Sang Keun
Hancho Kim convicted 4-8, 279D3
KIM Sudoc
Denies lobbying chrgs, Unificatn Church link 11-1, 862F3

1979

KIDDER, Margot
Amityville Horror released 7-27, 819D3
KIDNAPINGS—*See CRIME; country names*
KIDNEYS—*See MEDICINE—Diseases*
KIDS Are Alright, The (film)
Released 6-15, 820E1
KIEWIT, Peter
Dies 11-2, 932B3
KILLE, Leonard
MDs cleared in psychosurgery suit 2-9, 139E3
KILLEN, Denis
On defense upgrading 8-23, 683G2
KILLER Fish (film)
Released 12-7, 1007E3
KILROY, Frank (Bucko)
Named Patriots gen mgr 4-6, 335A3
KIM, Billy
Carter discloses Park conversn effort 8-5, 639B2
KIM, Charles
Chrgd in Moon church fraud case, '77 complaint cited 5-1, 376A3
KIM, Hancho C. (Kim Han Cho)
Loses appeal 3-12, 209E1
Indicted in Korean scandal 4-10, 283C2
Indictmt dismissed 6-15, 521A2
KIM, Nelli
Shaposhnikova wins Spartakaide gymnastics title 7-26, 799E1
Wins world gym title 10-5—10-9, 1005E2
KIMBALL, Spencer W.
Rpts black progress in Mormon Church 6-8, 508A1
KIM Chi Ha
PEN seeks release 7-21, 554A1
KIM Chi Yol
Rptr arrests defended 8-24, 654C1
KIM Dae Jung
Scores Park 1-2, police questn 2-10, 116A3
Asks Carter cancel S Korea visit 5-15, 389G3
Links Carter visit, dissident curbs 6-21, 470B1
Visits rptd barred 9-16, 710C3
Chung vs pres bid 11-28, 928G2
Freed 12-8, 952C1
KIM Han Cho—*See KIM, Hancho C.*
KIM Hyung Wook
Rptd missing 10-25, 810C3

KIM Il Sung (North Korean president)
Waldheim confs on S Korea feud 5-3, 341G3

KIM Jae Kyu
Slays Park, arrested 10-26; plot chrgd 10-28, 821A1-G2
Foes continue Assemb boycott 11-5, 844B1
Park coup plot detailed 11-6, 843D2-D3
Trial suspended 12-4, 928A2
Chung arrested 12-12, 959D3
Gets death for Park slaying 12-20, 997D1
KIM Jong Pil
Named S Korea ruling party ldr 11-12, 875E2
Meets oppositn ldr 11-17, 952A1
On Choi pres term 12-6, 951F3
KIM Kae Won
Implicated in Park death 11-6, 843G2-D3
Gets death for Park slaying 12-20, 997D1
KIM Kwan Suk, Rev.
Vows rights drive 5-12, 389F3
Says aides detained re Carter visit 6-28; meets Carter 7-1, 495C1
Dissident ldr beaten 11-27, 928E2
KIM Kyong Sook
Funeral held 8-28, 653G3
KIM Seong Jin
Seeks N Korea talks renewal 3-26, 341D3
Rpts on Park slaying 10-26, 821G1
KIM Sung-Jun
Decisns Giussipi 6-3, Carupo 7-28; KOs Yokai 10-4, 838G3-839C1

1980

KIDDER, Peabody & Co.
DeNunzio named Securities Indus Assn chrmn 11-6, 959B2
KIDEE, Rep. Dale E. (D, Mich.)
Reelected 11-4, 843E1
KID Gavilan (Gerardo Gonzalez)
Rptd broke 4-1, 320E3
KIDNAPING—*See under CRIME*
KIELAN, Urszula
Wins Olympic medal 7-26, 624A2
KIFNER, John
Wins Polk award 2-25, 692E3
KIGHT, Morris
Scores Navy lesbian probe 6-13, 517E3
KIL Chon Sik
Arrested re corruptn 7-19, 566E2
KILLANIN, Lord Michael John
Scores Moscow Olympic boycott plan 1-6, 3C1
Vs Olympic shift 1-14, 28D3; Carter stand 1-20, 45E2
IOC backs Moscow Olympics, rejcts US proposal 2-12, 107D1
On IOC anti-boycott moves; asks Carter, Brezhnev mtg 4-23, 325C2
Meets with Brezhnev 5-7, Carter 5-15, 379E1
Rejects IOC reelectn bid 5-19, 379A2
Moscow invitatn deadline extended 5-26, 420C3
IOC elects successor 7-16; rips boycott 7-18, pleads for intl peace 8-3, 590D3
KILLEN, James
Orders Agent Orange rpt 3-26, 252F2
US B-52 base talks set; defense dvpt plans rptd 9-9, 705D1
KILLINGS on the Last Line (play)
Opens 6-5, 756E3
KILLION, Wilbert
Named UMW vp 2-13, 147C1
KIM, Dr. John
Arrested, freed by S Korea 6-28, 499F3
KIM, Nelli
Wins Olympic medal 7-25, 589A3, 623A1
KIMBALL, Rev. Charles
Sees Iran militants 6-4, 419A1
KIMBERLY-Clark Corp.
Fine paper trust suit rptd setld 9-29; acquittal rptd in 2d suit 12-3, 917B2, C2
KIM Chi Ha
Released 12-11, 968E1
KIM Chong Hwan
Placates S Korean students 5-15, 380D3
Remains defense min 5-21, 395C1
KIM Chong Il
Party conf elevates 10-10—10-14, 792A3
KIM Dae Jung
Amnestied 2-29, 195D3
Scores NDP leader 3-1, 195E3
Arrested 5-18, 380F2
Rioters ask release 5-21, 394A3
Chrgd as plotter 5-22, 395E1
Linked to Kwangju rebellion 5-31, 430D3
Indicted 8-1, 620D3
Sedition trial 8-14—9-13; gets death sentnc, 23 backers jailed 9-17, 711C1
US leniency pleas rejected 8-15, 711B2
US questns seditn trial chrgs 8-28, 673A2
Backers' trial ends 9-8; 25 sentncd 9-11, 711A2
Son, brother sentenced 9-11, 711A2
N Korea pres scores arrest 9-25, 737B1
Mil ct upholds death sentnc 11-3, appeals to Sup Ct 11-8; US, Japan vs death 11-4—12-7; S Korea scores Japan 11-26, 944F2-E3
Affected by purge order 11-12, 874A3
8 pol prisoners freed 12-11, 968A2
US pleas for leniency 12-13, 953C1
KIM Dong Whie
On N Korea DMZ loudspeaker speeches 9-6, 945F1
US amb warns vs Kim Dae Jung executn 12-6, 944B3
KIM Il Sung (North Korean president)
Pays Sihanouk air trip to US 2-22, 141F2
Sees US rep, drops demand for S Korea CP law repeal 7-18, 547A1, D1
Cancels talks with S Korea 9-25, 737A1
Party conf elevates son 10-10—10-14; on S Korea unity, 10-10, asks US troop exit 10-12, 792A3
S Korea denounces unity plan 10-15, 809F3
KIM Jae Kyu
Col Pak executed 3-6, Chung sentncd 3-13, 195F3, G3
Chon succeeds as KCIA head 4-14, 295C1
Executed 5-24, 395F1
KIM Jong Pil
Arrested 5-18, 380F2
Chgd with corruptn, to quit politics 6-18, 499F2
Pol activies curbed 11-12, 874A3
KIM Jwah Kyum
S Korea min without portfolio 5-21, 395D1
KIM Kae Won
Death sentnc commuted 1-30, life sentnc upheld 5-19, 395G1
KIM Kyong Wan
Named to S Korea pres staff 8-27, 645A2
KIM Pyong Hun
Named to S Korea pres staff 8-27, 645A2
KIM Sung-Jun
Mamby KOs for WBC super lightwgt title 2-23, 320B3
KIM Tae Hyon
Sentenced 9-11, 711A2
KIM Tae-Shik
KOs Ibarra for WBA flywgt title 2-17, 320B3
Decisns Arrozal 6-29, 1000G3
Mathebula decisns for WBA flywgt title 12-13, 1001B1

1976

KIM Yong Ju
- Sentenced 4-22, 334C2

KIM Yong Kyu
- Lands S Korea, kills guards 9-19; surrenders 9-20, 910B3

KIM Young Sam
- Kim Duk Yong sentncd 4-22, 334C2
- Party split 5-25, reelectn ruled invalid 6-10, quits 6-11, 440E2

KINDNESS, Rep. Thomas N. (R, O.)
- Reelected 11-2, 830G2

KINDUELLU, Kapelia
- Named Japan amb 10-22, 949G3

KING, Billy Jean
- Wins Federatn Cup, US Open mixed doubles 8-29, 9-12, 716D1, A2

KING, Rev. Clennon
- Barred from Plains church 10-31, 826E3
- Plains church ends ban 11-14, 864F2
- Attends Carter church 11-21, 881F3

KING, Coretta Scott (Mrs. Martin Luther King Jr.)
- FBI opposition rptd 5-5, 344D1
- Dem conv speaker 7-13, 509E3
- With Carter in Calif 11-1, 827C1

KING Jr., Martin Luther (1928-68)—*See 1968, p. 140E1 for biog. data*
- Cited re KKK informer 2-26, 316A3
- Sen intellignc rpt cites as target 4-28, 330E1, A2, C2
- Levi orders probe 4-29, 344E1
- Sen Com staff details FBI harrassmt 5-5, 343G3
- Ray appeal denied 5-10, 384F2
- Dem platform text cites 6-15, 472G1
- Cited in Carter biog sketch 512B2
- Ray changes prisons 8-13, 640D3
- House sets assassinatn probe 9-17, 728G3
- Hooks to head NAACP 11-6, 892B2
- Sup Ct bars review of Ray plea withdrawal 12-13, 960D2
- Young named UN amb 12-16, 936C2

KING Sr., Rev. Martin Luther
- Renews Carter support 4-13, 261G1

KING, William Lyon Mackenzie
- '44, '45 diaries publshd 1-1, 8C1

KING Features Syndicate
- On Brown interview publicatn 10-22, 787D2

KINGMAN, Dave
- NL batting ldr 10-4, 795G3

KINGSLAND Jr., Louis
- On Viking seismometer failure 7-22, 527A1

KINOSHITA, W. T.
- Guadeloupe volcano erupts 8-30, 643E3

KIPPING, Vernon L.
- Hearst trial testimony 2-5, 114E1

1977

KINENE, Khalid Younis
- On Luwum death probe 2-24, 142C1

KINFLICKS (book)
- On best-seller list 4-3, 264A2; 5-1, 356D2

KING, Bernard
- In NBA draft 6-10, 584A2

KING, Billie Jean
- Va Slims contract dispute 3-18, 431D1
- Loses Family Circle Cup 4-3; wins Port Washn Lionel Cup 4-17, 430C3, E3
- Apples win WTT title 8-27, 787E3, F3
- US Open results 9-11, 787G1

KING, Carleton
- Dies 11-19, 952G2

KING, Rev. Clennon
- Plains church bars membership 1-9, 53C2

KING, Coretta Scott (Mrs. Martin Luther King Jr.)
- Pickets Stevens 3-1, 153G3
- Blacks meet re govt 'neglect' 8-29, 702G1
- Natl Women's Conf OKs minority res 11-19—11-21, 917C3
- Sees Carter 12-14, 960B1

KING, Don
- Boxing scandal rpt issued 9-3, 828C1-D2
- WBC softens threat vs Ali 12-1, 970B2

KING, James
- Named Carter personnel asst 1-14, 35B3

KING, Jonathan
- DNA safety concern rptd 10-6, 846D3

KING Jr., Martin Luther (1928-68)—*See 1968, p. 140E1 for biog. data*
- Suit vs FBI dismissed, tapes ordered sealed 1-31, 77C2
- House assassinatn com revived 2-2, 77D1
- Justice Dept rpts Ray acted alone 2-2, 77A2
- Assassinatn com dispute rptd 2-10—2-21, 127C1; open hearing proposed 3-3, 149D1
- Justice Dept study issued 2-18, 149F1-E2
- Assassinatn com dispute resolved 3-8, 3-29, com extended 3-30; new ballistic tests ordrd 3-17, Ray questnd 3-22, 228A2, G2
- Young for S Africa sanctns 4-5, 272E2
- Assassinatn com funds OKd 4-28, 339B2
- Ray escapes jail 6-10, recaptured 6-13; conspiracy discounted 6-14, 459A1
- Young compares Biko death 9-13, 708C1
- Ray sentenced for escape 10-27, 848C1

KING, Mary E.
- Named ACTION dep dir 2-24, confrmd 3-4, 211E1

KING, Richard
- Settles Citicorp dispute 6-26, new pact set 9-21, 871C1

KING, Stephen
- Carrie on best-seller list 2-6, 120G3

KING, Steve
- SC loses coll baseball title 6-18, 568B1

KING Alphonse—*See LIZANETZ, Alex*

KING Associates, Mary
- King confrmd ACTION dep dir 3-4, 211E1

KING Jr. Center for Social Change, Martin Luther—*See MARTIN Luther King Jr., etc.*

KING Kong (film)
- Top-grossing film 2-2, 120D3

KINGMAN, Dave
- Traded to Padres 6-15, 644F2
- Signs with Cubs 11-30, 989F3

KINNEY, Lewis
- Indicted re Torres 10-20, 821A1

KINOY, Ernest
- Wins Emmy 9-11, 1021G3

KINTU, Dan
- Death rptd 8-17, 641A2

1978

KIM Yong Shik
- Sees O'Neill on House probe 1-18; OKs Park testimony, affirms Kim immunity 1-31, 64D1

KIM Young Sam
- S Korea pres bid thwarted 4-17, 377G3

KINDNESS, Rep. Thomas N. (R, O.)
- Reelected 11-7, 851E3
- Loses GOP chrmn bid 12-4, 958A2

KING, Bernard
- NBA scoring ldr 4-9, 271E2

KING, Betsy
- 2d in Borden Classic 7-16, 672D3

KING, Billie Jean
- Loses Houston Va Slims 1-22, KC Va Slims 3-5, Phila Va Slims 3-26, 419F1-A2
- Wimbledon results 7-7, 540A1
- Wins US Open doubles title 9-9, loses mixed doubles 9-10, 707G1, A2
- US wins Federatn Cup 12-3, 1026G3

KING, Bruce
- Wins primary for NM gov 6-6, 448B2
- Elected 11-7, 853G2, 855C2, E2

KING, Charles
- Loses primary for Ariz gov 9-12, 736B2

KING, Coretta Scott
- Diggs convicted 10-7, 791F3
- Hails Humphrey-Hawkins bill OK 10-15, 808G1

KING, Gov. Cyril Emanuel (D, Virgin Islands)
- Dies 1-2, 96E2
- Luis elected successor 11-7, 915E3

KING, Dick
- USAC sets new rules 12-28, 1028A2

KING, Don
- Holmes wins WBC heavywgt title 6-9, 600B1

KING, Edward F.
- Loses primary for Mass gov 9-19, 736A3

KING, Edward J.
- Wins primary for Mass gov 9-19, 736G2
- Elected 11-7, 847C2, 853F2

KING, Gordon
- In NFL draft 5-2, 336F2

KING, Larry L.
- Best Little Whorehouse opens 4-17, 760D1

KING Jr., Martin Luther (1928-68)—*See 1968, p. 140E1 for biog. data*
- Carter: 'spiritual son' to Gandhi 1-2, 1C2
- House assassinatn com funds OKd 3-13, 183A1
- Black ldr cited in FBI '64 conspiracy memo 5-29; sources name Wilkins; SCLC, others dispute 5-29—5-31, 410F2
- Murder plot alleged 7-26, 589G2
- House com hearings 8-14—8-18; Ray chrgs 'Raoul' frame-up, denies following King 8-16—8-18, 641A1-B3
- Ray confessn alleged by UK ex-cop, atty scores 8-18, 641C3
- Ray alibi retracted 8-18, 642B1
- Preyer says conspiracy evidence 9-24, 898E1
- James Earl Ray wed 10-13, 844D3
- House com hearings resume: Ray testimony declined; conspiracy theory, FBI link discounted 11-9—11-17, 898D1-D3
- House com hearings end: Ray family plot, bounty offer alleged; FBI role denied, probes scored 11-17—12-1, 937G3-938F2
- Carter commemorates 12-9, 956C3
- Ray seeks FBI tapes 12-12, 1002A3
- Tenn gov's aides arrested 12-15, 1011A2
- House com finds murder plot likely, Justice review sought 12-30, 1002A1, E2

KING, Perry
- Different Story released 6-13, 619E1

KING, Stephen
- Shining on best-seller list 2-5, 116D3; 3-5, 195F3

KING, Susan B.
- Named CPSC chairwoman 6-29, 589A2

KING Jr., Woodie
- Do Lord Remember Me opens 4-4, Run'ers' 5-3, 887F1, A3

KINGFISHER, The (play)
- Opens 12-6, 1031B2

KINGMAN, Dave
- NL batting ldr 10-2, 928E2

KING of Hearts, The (play)
- Opens 11-22, 1031B2

KING of the Gypsies, The (film)
- Released 12-19, 1030B3

KING Range National Conservation Area (Calif.)
- '79-82 authorization signed 8-20, 697D2

KING'S Department Stores Inc.
- Grace plans purchase 1-23, 66C2

KINGSLEY, Sidney
- Dead End opens 5-4, 760G1

KING Tut (recording)
- On best-seller list 7-5, 579G3

KIPNESS, Joseph
- King of Hearts opens 11-22, 1031C2

KIPNIS, Alexander
- Dies 5-14, 440A3

1979

KIM Wount-Gie
- Retained as S Korea finance min 12-14, 997G1

KIM Young Sam
- Chrgs govt raids electn hq 5-27, elected NDP head 5-30; scores govt actions vs dissidents 6-11, 6-18, 469F3
- Meets Carter 7-1, 495C1
- Park resignatn call rptd 7-30, paper seized 7-31, 617F3
- Scores party hq raid 8-11, 617D3
- Seeks Seoul cop chief ouster 8-28, 653G3
- Ousted as NDP ldr 9-8; scores US in interview 9-16, 710F2
- Assemb ousts 10-4, US recalls amb 10-5, 762F2
- Oppositn Assemb members quit 10-13, 794A3
- US amb returns to Seoul 10-17, 803A3
- Deplores Park slaying 10-28, 822B1
- At Park funeral 11-3, 843E3
- Asks charter revision 11-4, 844B1
- Party continues Assemb boycott 11-5, 844B1
- Vs govt election plans 11-10, 875D2
- Sees ruling party head 11-17, 952A1

KING, Bernard
- Fined for drunk driving 2-16, 291D1

KING, Betsy
- 2d in Wheeling Classic 10-7, 970F1

KING, Billie Jean
- US wins Federatn Cup 5-6, 391E2
- Wins Wimbledon doubles, sets victory record 7-7, 570B1
- Loses US Open doubles title 9-8, other results 9-9; wins Toray Sillock 9-16, 734F1, G1, E2
- Wins Women's Stockholm Open 11-6, 1003F3

KING, Gov. Bruce (D, N.M.)
- Signs death penalty bill 4-1, 400B2

KING, Coretta Scott
- At Teng luncheon in Atlanta 2-1, 83F2

KING, Gov. Edward J. (D, Mass.)
- Reaffirms A-power support 4-4, 262A1
- Signs anti-abortn law 6-12, 547G2
- Signs death penalty bill 8-14, 989G1
- Gets reassurance on heating fuel supply 8-28, 703C2
- Signs arts cncl lottery bill 11-15, 892G2
- Takes over Boston transit line 12-18, 989B3

KING, Adm. Ernest J. (1878-1956)
- Eisenhower WWII secret diary rptd 9-16, 9-17, 748D1

KING Jr., Eugene Thomas
- Arrested in NYC bank robbery 8-8, 656D1

KING, Jeff
- Sunnyside released 6-1, 820D3

KING Jr., Martin Luther (1928-68)—*See 1968, p. 140E1 for biog. data*
- House com murder plot findings review delayed 1-2, 4A1
- House com Cong mandate expires 1-3, 4F1
- Carter seeks natl holiday 1-14, 31G2
- Ray parole deal rptd too costly 1-18, escape convictn upheld 2-21, 156D2
- House com findings challenged 1-26, 91G1
- SCLC feuding rptd 4-10, 283F1
- House com final rpt: death plot said likely 7-17, 537F2, 538C1-F1
- Kennedy backs birthday as holiday 7-23, 560D1
- KKK marchers arrested in Ala 8-12, 631C1
- Levison dies 9-12, 756G2
- Ray jail break fails 11-5, 891E2
- Natl holiday bill withdrawn 12-5, 945B2

KING, Reggie
- In NBA draft 6-25, 507B2

KING, Stephen
- Dead Zone on best-seller list 10-14, 800A3; 11-4, 892B3

KING, William Lyon Mackenzie
- '48 diaries released 1-1, 19A2

KING Jr., Woodie
- Take It From The Top opens 1-19, 292D3
- Glorious Monster opens 7-10, 711D3

KINGMAN, Dave
- NL batting ldr 9-30, 955E2

KING of Schnorrers (play)
- Opens 11-28, 956B3

KING Ranch Inc.
- Kleberg dies 5-8, 432B3

KINGSLEY, Sidney
- Men in White opens 7-11, 712D1

KINGSLEY, Susan
- Getting Out opens 5-15, 711B3

KINSETH, Bruce
- Iowa wins NCAA wrestling title 3-10, 507E3

KINSKI, Klaus
- Woyzeck released 8-24, 820G3

KINSKI, Nastassia
- Stay As You Are released 12-21, 1008G1

KIPNESS, Joseph
- Goodbye People opens 4-30, 711D3
- I Love My Wife opens 5-15, 711F3
- Teibele and Her Demon opens 12-16, 1007F2

1980

KIM Woun-Gie
- On S Korea trade balance 1-12, 101E1
- Revises S Korea deficit estimate 7-1, 499C3

KIM Yong Hyu
- On govt purge 7-15, 566B2
- Retained as S Korea state admin 9-2, 673B1*

KIM Yong Il
- Sentenced 9-11, 711A2

KIM Young Sam
- NDP leadership challenged 3-1, 195E3
- Arrested 5-18, 380F2
- Pol activities curbed 11-12, 874A3

KIM Young Tae
- Arrested re corruptn 7-19, 566E2

KIN-Buc Inc.
- Agrees to cap Edison dump 1-30, 93D3

KINCANNON, Jack F.
- Retires at Sears 10-7, 959F2

KINCH, Chad
- In NBA draft 6-10, 447G1

KINCSES, Tibor
- Wins Olympic medal 8-1, 623B1

KINDNESS, Rep. Thomas N. (R, Ohio)
- Reelected 11-4, 843E4

KING, Adrienne
- Friday the 13th released 5-10, 675F2

KING, Alan
- Just Tell Me What You Want released 2-8, 216B3

KING 3rd, Alvin Lee
- Charged in Tex church murders 6-22, 568E2

KING, Bernard
- Arrested for sex abuse, drug possessn 1-2; sentncd 6-4, 656A1

KING, Billie Jean
- Wins Avon tourn 2-24, 607D2
- Wins US Open women's doubles 9-6, 691F2

KING, Gov. Bruce (D, N.M.)
- State of State message 1-25, 269E3

KING, Charles
- Executed 4-22, 353A2

KING, Coretta Scott
- Seconds Carter renominatn 8-13, 611C3
- Meets with Reagan 12-11, 956F2

KING, David
- Loses US House electn 11-4, 852C1

KING, Gov. Edward J. (D, Mass.)
- State of State message 1-14, 483B3
- Takes over Boston transit system 11-18; ct bars move 11-28, system shuts down 12-6; signs funding bill 12-7, 939A2

KING, Judge James L.
- Upholds Haitian refugee rights, halts deportatns 7-2, 514E1

KING, Kim
- On US Emb aides escape 1-29, 66D2

KING Jr., Martin Luther (1928-68)
- Justice to review murder probe 1-4, 17C2
- Peace Prize award rptd 1-28, 200B1
- Widow seconds Carter renominatn 8-13, 611C3
- Gray withdraws as US judge nominee 9-17, 744D2
- Reagan meets black ldrs 12-9, 956B2

KING, Perry
- Trouble with Europe opens 1-28, 136F3

KING Jr., Richard
- Dies 3-30, 279G3

KING, Stephen
- Stand on best-seller list 2-10, 120E3; 3-9, 200C3
- Shining released 5-23, 675D3
- Dead Zone on best-seller list 8-17, 640G3; 9-14, 716C3
- Firestarter on best-seller list 9-14, 716B3; 10-12, 796C3; 12-7, 948D3

KINGMAN, Dave
- Quits as sportswriter 7-2, 637B2

KING Ranch Inc.
- Richard King Jr dies 3-30, 279G3

KINHOFER, Christa
- Wins Olympic medal 2-23, 155A3

KINNEY, E. Robert
- Retires as Gen Mills chief exec 12-16, 959E1

KINSKI, Nastassia
- Tess released 12-12, 1003E2

KINSMAN, N. Richard
- Named as CIA operative 7-2, Kingston home machine gunned 7-4, 564F3-565A1

KINTNER, Robert E.
- Dies 12-20, 1004C2

KIOI-FM (San Francisco, Calif. radio station)
- Charter Co acquires 11-6, 907A2

1976

KIRBO, Charles
Helps Carter on vp list 6-17—7-8, 489C3
KIRCHWEY, Freda
Dies 1-3, 56E3
KIRILENKO, Andrei P.
At French CP cong 2-4—2-7, 119C2
Named to Politburo, Secretariat 3-5, 195C2★, F2
Backs Husak at Czech CP Cong 4-12—4-16, 289E2
KIRKHAM, Peter
Ordrs Statistics Canada probe 11-4, 870E3
Stats Canada testimony set 11-15, 888G2
KIRKLAND, Lane
Carter personnel advisor 11-19, 881D3
KIRKPATRICK, Rev. Frederick Douglass
Named pres candidate 6-18, 490D3
KIRKPATRICK, Jeane
Denied USSR visa 10-31, 907F3
KIRKSEY, Henry Jay
Runs for Senate 6-1, 411A2
KIRKWOOD, James
Chorus Line wins Pulitzer 5-3, 352C3
KIROS, Maj. Alemayehu
Rptd suicide 8-26, 674C2
KISCH, Michael
US oil deal OKd 5-6, 338D3
KISHI, Nobusuke
Lockheed payoff probes 2-5—2-17, 131C3, D3
Lockheed role chrgd 3-9, 191B2
KISIEL, Henryk
Polish finance min 3-27, 268G2
KISIELEWSKI, Stefan
Polish charter chng protest cited 268E1
KISLYAK, Ivan
Rptd USSR spy in Paris 1-19, 50A1
UN Medit pollutn pact signed 2-16, 126D3
KISSINGER, Henry Alfred
Ties US econ aid to UN votes 1-9, 2A1
Moynihan chrgs US aid 'blackmail' 1-23; backing reaffirmed 1-28, 67E2
Urges pub, Cong support 2-3, 88A2
Ford orders business paymts probe 2-10, 134D2
Rejects cruise missile test halt 2-25, 183E1
US offers Japan Lockheed data 3-11, 200C1
Sees Australia forgn min 3-17, 204B1
Named to business probe panel 3-21, 262E2
Morton sees '76 resignatn 4-4, clarified 4-5, 4-7, 245D2
Ford reaffirms support 4-7, 245C2
Asks new intl sea law 4-8, 342B2
Addresses UNCTAD conf 5-6, 317A1-318G1
Vs UNCTAD proposal rejectn 6-1, 388E2, B3
Asks 4-power conf on Korea 7-22, 557C2
Addresses Urban League 8-2, 580C3
Admits India A-blast aid 8-2, 581D3
State Dept black personnel policy disputed 8-2—8-3, 922G1
In Pak talks on French A-plant 8-8—8-9, 581G2
Urges UN seabed agrmt 8-13, offers funds 9-1, 700G1
Addresses UN Assemb 9-30, 719B1
Rptd vs Arab boycott tax penalties 10-7, 787B1
Meets Canada state secy 10-15, 843D2
Rpts Pl base pact agrmt 12-1, Pl denies 12-5, 12-6, 926E2
Donates papers to US 12-20, press com plans access suit 12-28, 980F2
Africa
Diggs scores Angola policy 1-11, 16A2
Sets Moscow trip despite Angola 1-14, 17A1
Sees ambs on Angola, sets visit 1-15, 16B2
Briefs NATO on Angola fighting 1-15, 16D2
FNLA denies collapse in northn Angola 1-16, 35G2
In Moscow, rpts Angola issue unresolved 1-21—1-23, 61F3
Testifies on open Angola aid, Sovt confrontatn 1-29—1-30, 88B3
Sees Moroccan envoy 1-29, 107G2
USSR scores Angola statemts 2-1, 2-4, 82B3
Scores Cong aid bar 2-3, 88C2
Scores Cuba role in Angola 2-5, 138C1
Sees Latin ldrs on Angola issue 2-16—2-23, 177F2, 178B1, E1
Warns USSR re Angola 3-11, 197D3
Castro dismisses warning 3-14, 251D3
Warns Cuba again 3-22, 3-23, 214C3
Tours 4 natns 4-24—4-29; policy speech stresses Rhodesia, Namibia 4-27; text excerpts 293A1-295A2
Rhodesia scores 4-27, 293D2
Rhodesia mediatn proposal 4-28, 293E2
In Liberia, seeks Cuba exit from Angola 4-30, 318A2
Rebuts Reagan attack on Rhodesia policy 4-30, 323C3
Sees 4 forgn mins in Nairobi 5-5, tour ends 5-6, 317A1, 318C3
France for dvpt aid 5-10—5-11, 355D3
Cuba troops to quit Angola 5-24, comments 5-25, 370C3, 371A1
Vorster sees Smith 6-13—6-14, 427G1
Vorster mtg plan confrmd 6-15, 6-17, 6-18, 426C1, 427D1★; meets Vorster 6-23—6-24, 446E1-447A1
Cites Nairobi UNCTAD mtg 6-21, 450G1
S Africa bars Rhodesia sanctns 6-22, 446G2
Rhodesia ANC asks govt talks 6-27, 522C3
Schaufele begins 6-natn tour 7-7, 523A1
Scores Angola mercenary death 7-10, 519D3

1977

KIRANGSAK Chamanand, Gen.
Drug link hinted, leaves country 4-21, 331F2
KIRBO, Charles
On US-Cuba trade 3-4, 181B1
KIRBY, Richard
Leaves S Africa 11-4, 852D1
KIRBY, Robert E.
Vs US breeder research curb 4-27, 334B3
KIRBY Lumber Corp.—*See SANTA Fe Industries*
KIRILENKO, Andrei Pavlovich
Revolutn anniv fete photo 11-7, 865D2
KIRITSIS, Anthony G. (Tony)
Kidnaps exec 2-8, arrested 2-11, 162G1
KIRKLAND, Lane
Scores Carter shoe import ruling 4-5, 248C2
Salary increased 12-12, 961A2
Vs FEC suit vs AFL-CIO 12-20, 980B1
KIRKS, Rowland F.
Dies 11-2, 952G2
KIRSCH, Sarah
Leaves E Germany 8-29, 684D1
KIRVES, Lauri
Protests devaluatn 9-1, 764E3
KIRYCZENKO, Wiktor
Denmark ousts 1-10, 62B1
KISSINGER, Henry Alfred
Forgn rights abuse rpts released 1-1, 50F2
Sells memoirs 2-7, NBC-TV contract rptd 2-17, 131F1
To head non-govt energy panel 2-12, 110E3
Assassinatn plot rptd 2-23, 261A3
Named to Chase bank com 3-21, 396D3
Micronesia surveillnc detailed 5-3, 386G3
Nixon reminisces 5-12, 385F3, 386E1
Spying suits vs US rptd 5-22, 422D3
Nixon on praying scene 5-25, 420E2
Georgetown U teaching job set 6-2, 532B2
At Pele tribute 10-1, 827D2
Loses ruling on transcripts 12-8, 962D2
Africa
Sahel aid plan budgeted 1-17, 31A2
Vorster, Smith compromise on Rhodesia seen 1-20, 29A1
Smith rejects new UK plan 1-24, 49C1, F1
Vorster bars Smith pressure 1-28, 73B1
Botha named S Africa forgn min 2-11, 160E3
Young on UK-Rhodesia role 2-12, Carter clarifies 2-13, 105E2
Scores USSR re Zaire invasn 4-5, 261E1
IISS lauds setlmt role 4-28, 401A2
Nigeria ldr visits US 10-11—10-12, 797C2

1978

KIRALY, Karoly
Chrg of Hungarian bias rptd 1-24, rpts exile 3-1, 180A2
KIRBO, Charles
At Carter strategy sessn 4-15—4-16, 306A3
To monitor GSA probe 9-7, 715D1
Denies 'pol fix' chrg 9-10, Anderson revises article 9-11, 719E3, 720B1
KIRBY 2nd, Fred M.
On Kennecott bd rival slate; Alleghany '60 proxy fight cited 3-24, 3-27, 402A3
KIRCHER, Dudley P.
Loses US House electn 11-7, 854E1
KIRITSIS, Anthony G. (Tony)
Pulitzer awarded for '77 kidnap photo 4-17, 314G3
KIRKHAM, Willi
Contessa of Mulberry St opens 1-4, 887E1
KIRKLAND, Lane
'77, '78 salary rptd 5-15, 365C2
KIRKLAND & Ellis
Dual-rep case refused by Sup Ct 11-6, 873G3
KIRKWOOD, Gene
Comes A Horseman released 11-1, 969G3
KIRKWOOD, James
PS Your Cat is Dead opens 3-22, 887F2
KISELYOV, Ludmilla
Sentenced 9-7, 742B3
KISELYOV, Vladimir
Sentenced 9-7, 742B3
KISMET (play)
Timbuktu opens 3-1, 760E3
KISSINGER, Henry Alfred
Haldeman book chrgs tap role, other allegatns rptd 2-16—2-17; denial issued 2-16, 124B2, 125B1, D1
Rhodesia majority-rule pact set 2-20, 119G2
Korea lobbying knowledge probed 3-21, 203C2, C3
Weicker quits ethics com 4-14, 279F3
Testifies on Korea scandal 4-20, 280A1
At 26th Bilderberg Conf 4-21—4-23, 302D3
Snepp book ruling scored 7-7, 527C3
Albania scores China re '71 visit 7-30, 635E1
Named NASL bd chrmn 10-4, 969C2
Rhodesia interim govt support rptd 10-15, 819B1
Eulogizes Meir 12-8, 1032A2
Backs full China ties 12-15, 976C1

1979

KIRBO, Charles H.
Buys land from Carter's brother 3-1, 'hush money' hinted 3-22, 203A2
Denies Carter peanut loan scheme 3-11, 184G1-A2
Carter peanut business documts rptd subpoenaed 5-27, 5-28, 401A2
Carter reclassifies trust 5-30, releases financial data 5-31, 420F1, C2
On B Carter business share option 6-19, 500F2
Vesco jury foreman resigns, claims cover-up 8-29, 647F2
KIRCHSCHLAGER, Rudolf (Austrian president)
Greets Carter, Brezhnev 6-15, 449F1
KIRGIZ Soviet Socialist Republic—*See UNION of Soviet Socialist Republics--Republics*
KIRIBATI (formerly Gilbert Islands)
Independence from UK attained 7-12, 526B1
KIRKLAND, Lane
At Carter-Meany mtg 1-12, 13C3
On AFL-CIO pol endorsemt 2-21, 149F1
Rpts Meany AFL-CIO retiremt 9-28, 744D1
On Pay Advisory Com 10-16, 829F2
Elected AFL-CIO pres, bids all unions to join 11-19, 884G3, 885G1, B2
KISON, Bruce
In World Series 10-10—10-17, 816A1
Signs with Angels 11-16, 1001F3
KISSINGER, Henry Alfred
Elliott dies 1-9, 104A3
At Teng dinner in DC 1-29, 66G1
Phone records case accepted by Sup Ct 4-16, 302B3
Shah asked to stay out of US 4-19, 297G3, 298A1
Aids shah entry to Mex, mtg rptd 6-11, 445F3
Ruled liable in tap suits 7-12, 611E2
Backs SALT, arms budget link 7-31, 8-2, 590G2
Defense budget hike request cited 9-11, 678G1
Secret Svc protectn cited 9-20, 724B1
Carter on Sovt troops in Cuba 10-1, 737B2
'50s FBI link rptd 11-3, 870B2
Iran blames for shah's US entry 11-14, 861C2
Role in shah's US entry detailed 11-18, 879G1
Carter denies role in shah's US entry 11-28, 895A1

1980

KIRBO, Charles H.
Vesco grand jury ends 4-1, 251E3
Carter news conf cites 8-4, 594G1
KIRBY, Lou
London newspr merger set 10-1, 750E3
KIRCHSCHLAGER, Rudolph (Austrian president)
Reelected pres 5-18, 388F1
KIRGIZ Soviet Socialist Republic—*See UNION of Soviet Socialist Republics--Republics*
KIRIBATI (formerly Gilbert Islands)—*See also ADB, COMMONWEALTH of Nations*
Island trade pact rptd 7-24, 576G2
KIRILLIN, Vladimir Alexeyevich
Resignatn rptd 1-22, 46E3
KIRK Jr., Paul G.
Assails Dem Party head 5-5, 366F3
KIRKHAM, Peter
Quits Statistics Canada 3-31, 273B1
KIRKLAND, Lane
AFL-CIO exec cncl meets 2-18—2-25; scores Admin 2-18, on inter-union talks 2-19, 146D3, 147C1
Warns of wage-price guidelines breakdown 2-22, 144E2
Scores Carter revised budget, econ policies 3-31, 244E1, 247A2
Meets Mondale, asks new job programs 5-2, 344B3
Says US guidelines no curb, scores Admin on natl accord 5-6, 385E1
OKs Carter platform statemt 8-13, 611A2
Urges Polish strike support 8-21, 627B1
Woman named to AFL-CIO exec cncl 8-21, 647C3
Named Econ Revitalizatn Bd co chrmn 8-28, 663C2
Praises Polish workers 8-31, 659C3
Defends Polish worker fund 9-4, 679A2
Carter names to Synfuels Corp bd 9-13, Sen panel OKs 9-25, 725F2
Carter names to interim Synfuels Corp bd 10-5, 786F2
US Percy support of Palestine state rptd 12-5, 938F3
On Donovan apptmt 12-16, 955A3
KIRKPATRICK, Jeane J.
Named US rep to UN 12-22, 979F2
KIRKUS, Virginia
Dies 9-10, 755G3
KIRKWOOD, Gene
Idolmaker released 11-14, 972F3
KIROV, Nikolai
Wins Olympic medal 7-26, 624A1
KIRST, Jutta
Wins Olympic medal 7-26, 624A2
KISELEV, Tikhon
Named alternate Politburo member 10-21, 798E1
KISELYOV, Vladimir
Wins Olympic medal 7-30, 624D1
KISIEL, Henryk
Rpts Sovt aid, pledges Westn debt paymts 9-8, 679E1
KISS (singing group)
NY record co indicted 2-28, 237D3
KISSINGER, Henry Alfred
White House Years on best-seller list 1-13, 40C3
Phone records access blocked by Sup Ct 3-3, 209C3
On Ford draft 3-8, 207F1
Iran chrgs plot vs shah's extraditn 3-22, 217G1
Addresses newspr editors 4-10, 264A1
Iran says helped shah to Egypt 4-16, 283D1
White House Years wins Amer Book Award 5-1, 692E2
Taps case accepted by Sup Ct 5-19, 440D1
USSR-Trigon spy controversy rptd 7-14—10-4, 754B1
Meets with Reagan, addresses GOP conv 7-15, 533A3, 534B3
Meets Reagan reps re Ford vp spot 7-16, 530B1
Campaigns with Reagan 8-20, 802C1
Reagan backs 'linkage', names advisor 11-6, 839D2, F2
Taps case argued in Sup Ct 12-8, 937C2

1976 | 1977 | 1978 | 1979 | 1980

1976

Backs UK Rhodesia plan 8-2, 580D3
S Africa min backs race policy reforms 8-13, 653B2
US blacks ask action vs S Africa 8-23, 654E2
Hits white rule 8-31, Vorster rebuts 9-1, 660A3
US blacks hit Vorster mtg 9-2, 660C3
Waldheim sees 9-2, lauds efforts 9-16, 681A2
Meets Vorster in Zurich 9-4—9-6, 660B2
African, intl reactn to missn 9-8, 9-9, 681G1
Sees Tanzania, Zambia ldrs 9-15—9-16, 681A1
In Pretoria talks with Vorster, Smith, others 9-17—9-20, 697A1
Sees 4 ldrs re Vorster, Smith talks 9-20—9-23, 717G2-718B1
Smith accepts proposal 9-24, Vorster talks role cited 9-25, 9-27, 717A1, F1
Sees UK forgn min re Rhodesia 9-24, 717C2
Denies rptd US Rhodesia policy chng 9-24, 781A2
USSR scores Rhodesia talks 9-25, 718B3
Rhodesia chrgs misled Smith 9-28, 718F2
Sees Rhodesia progress 9-28, 718A3
Gromyko scores missn 9-28, rebuts 9-30, 719B1
Nujoma sees 9-29, 793G3
Scores Sovt-Cuba Angola role 9-30, 719E1
Canada backs Rhodesia fund 10-15, 843D2
US vetoes S Africa arms ban in UN 10-19, 781E3
ANC ldrs score Rhodesia plan 10-22, 10-24, 10-26, 797D1
Says Rhodesia plan negotiable 10-24, 797D2
Smith asks Rhodesia conf role 10-25, 797C2
Rpt ordered Schaufele to Geneva 10-27, 797F2
Schaufele in Geneva 10-30, 831G3
Smith vs natlst demands 11-1, 831E3
Smith leaves Geneva conf 11-3, backs Kissinger plan 11-5, 842D3, 843A1
Denies Rhodesia mil guarantee 11-20, 879C2
Rhodesia natlists rejct interim govt plan 11-30, 893E1
Sees Crosland re UK Rhodesia role 12-10—12-11, 935E1
Richard sees 12-21, 974C2

China

Chou En-lai dies 1-8, 9C2
Pays last respects to Chou En-lai 1-15, 48F1
Reagan scores China policy 2-10, 109D2
Nixon rpts on trip 3-22, 215B1
Asks 4-power talks on Korea 7-22, 557C2
Sees rep on Korea killings, repeats conf call 8-19, 619A1
Regrets Mao death 9-9, 658C1
Stresses mutual interests 9-30, 719C2
Meets foreign min 10-9, 858B1
Computer sale confrmd 10-28, 832A3

Europe

CIA aid to Italy centrists rptd 1-7, 10F2
Briefs NATO on Angola fighting 1-15, 16D2
Sees Danish premr in Copenhagen 1-20, 62A1
Briefs NATO on Sovt SALT talks 1-23, 61G3
In Madrid, signs defns pact 1-24, 62A1, 76E3
Italy CIA aid recipients named 1-31, 140B3
Anti-CP lobbying rptd 2-5, 120B2
Scores RFE Olympics coverage bar 2-13, 158C3
Scores policy critics 3-11, 197G3
Sonnenfeldt statemts on US E Eur policy rptd 3-22; Reagan quotes 3-29; chrgs denied 3-29, 4-1, 232E2, G2, C3, 233B1; Ford defends 4-2, 4-7, 245B2
Signs Turkey base pact 3-26, defends at House com hearing 3-29, 244F1, B2
Warns vs CP govts 4-7, 4-13, 259A3, 296G3
Sovt, E Eur, Italy press score 4-9—4-18, 276G3-277C2
Initials Greece base pact, letters exchng on Cyprus released 4-15, 259D1, A2
Sees Giscard re Africa 5-7, 318A3
Scored on Italy CP remarks 5-19, 357D3
Reassures NATO allies, warns on CP role in Italy 5-20, 353D2-354B1
In Sweden 5-24, 370C3
Hosts Spain king, forgn min 6-3, 459F2
Sees Spain finance min 6-15—6-16, 501G2
Warned Spain king vs legalizing CP 6-19, 459D3
At OECD conf, backs multinatl code 6-21—6-22, 446C2, 450C1-B2
Repeats Italy CP warning 6-22, 446C2
Meets Vorster in W Ger 6-23—6-24, protest staged 6-23, 446E1-D3
In London, on W Eur unity, E-W ties 6-25, 466D1
On 7-natn aid to Italy 6-28, 462B2
Sees Bonn forgn min 7-15, 530F2
Italy loan ban disclosed 7-18, 530E3
Yugo frees jailed American 7-23, 559E2
Spain CP ban backing rptd 7-30, 753C1
Backs Rhodesia plan 8-2; in London talks 8-5, 580C2
In Pak talks on French A-plant 8-8—8-9, 581G2
Mediates Aegean dispute 8-14, 622A3
Sees ldrs re Vorster mtg 9-6, 9-7, 660E2
Giscard mtg re UN Viet membership rptd 9-14, 682D1

1977

China

Nixon vowed normal US-China ties 4-10, 298F2
Teng: vowed Taiwan break 9-6, 686E3
China reaffirms anti-Taiwan stand 10-4, 781B1

Europe

W Eur CP policy cited 4-2, 255E2
At 25th Bilderberg conf 4-21—4-24, 359C3
Concerned about W Eur 6-9, 458B3

1976

Sees UK forgn min re Rhodesia 9-24, 717C2
Asks UN talks, Turkish troop reductn 9-30, 719E2
Limits Helsinki pact fact-finders 11-1, 880A2
Andreotti visits 12-6, 947E1
At NATO mtg, gives Carter pledge 12-9—12-10, 933B2

Indochina
N Viet claims Nixon aid vow 2-1, 103C1
On proposed Hanoi talks 3-26, 255B2
Vs Hanoi aid demand 4-14, 291E1
Cites Hanoi Asian threat 7-22, 557E2
Giscard mtg re UN Viet membership rptd 9-14, 682D1
Scores GAO Mayaguez study 10-6, 749G2

Intelligence Issues
CIA aid to Italy centrists rptd 1-7, 10F2
Tap depositn filed 1-12, Nixon depositn released 3-10, 184A1
Italy CIA aid recipients named 1-31, 140B3
Pike scores House com rpt curbs 2-2, 150D2
Scores leaks, probes 2-4, 89A1
Scores House rpt leak 2-12, 151E1
Scores critics 3-11, 197E3
Censures aides on leaks 3-12, 198B2
Editor files tap suit 5-10, 349F2
Cleared re Halperin tap 12-16, 981A1

Korea
Asks 4-power conf 7-22, 557C2
Chairs NSC mtg 8-18—8-19; sees China rep, repeats conf call 8-19, 618G3
DMZ tree felling OKd 8-20, North chrgs mil buildup 8-20, 625E1
Asks 'amends' for US deaths 8-20, 625A2
US vs rpt on mil buildup 9-1, 641A2
Asks 'phased' talks 9-30, 719E2
S Korea backs talks 10-1, 858C2

Latin America
Says Cuba 'exports revolutn' 2-5, 138C1
Tours 6 natns 2-16—2-24, briefs Ford 2-25, 177A1
Kennedy scores Brazil pact 2-26, 177D1
Castro dismisses warning 3-14, 251D3
Warns Cuba vs mil roles 3-22, 3-23, 214C3
Seeks Cuba exit from Angola 4-30, 318A2
Cuba troops to quit Angola 5-24, comments 5-25, 370C3, 371A1
On Latin tour; addresses OAS 6-6—6-13, 465A2
Role in Letelier '74 release cited 9-21, 710C3
Panama asks relocate Canal Zone employes 9-22, 792G2
Scores Sovt-Cuba Angola role 9-30, 719E1
Sees Boyd, Panama Canal talks set 10-7, 792E3
On Cuba jet crash, hijack pact end 10-15, 780B1
Plea for Chile aid cited 10-20, 871C1
FBI Cuba exile contacts confrmd 10-25, 844B2
Suit vs Panama Canal talks filed 10-26, thrown out 12-18, 1008F2
Torrijos scores chrgs re Canal Zone blasts 11-29, 1008A3
At Mex inaugural 12-1, lauds Lopez 12-3, 906G2
Sees Panama forgn min 12-3, 1008D2

Middle East
Meets Allon on UN strategy, vows veto vs PLO 1-7—1-9, 18E2, A3
Sees Rabin 1-27—1-29, 60D1-A2
Kurdish leader scores 2-25, 146D1
Sadat: step-by-step diplomacy over 2-27, 162A2
Scores aides on info leaks 3-12, 198B2, F2
Warns vs Leb interventn 3-22, text issued 3-30, 226D3
Israel protests Scranton remarks 3-24, 211C2
In Ford-Hussein talks on Leb 3-30, 226C3
Rabin on Ford aid veto threat 4-8, 258C2
Says 1,000 Syria troops in Leb 4-9; warns vs Israel interventn 4-14, 257D1, F2
Egypt C-130 deal OKd 4-14, 275B2
USSR vs shuttle diplomacy 4-28, 296C2
Leb mediator reports 319D1
France offers Leb peace force 5-21, reaction 5-22, 369D1
Sees Israel amb re Leb 6-14, 430B1
At emergency mtg on Leb 6-16, 425C2
On US Leb policy 6-17, 425D2
Bodies of 2 slain US Leb envoys flown to US 6-19, 448F1
Thanks PLO for Leb evacuatn aid 6-21, 448E1
Meets 4 US ambs on Leb crisis 6-22, 448A2
In Iran 8-6; signs arms, trade pact 8-7, 581A2
Scores Sovt role, asks renewed Geneva talks 9-30, 719A2, D2
Israel scores US UN vote 11-12, 863B1
Sees Dinitz, urges Leb border restraint 11-23, 877B2
US ousts PLO aide 11-23, 878B2

Presidential Election (& transition developments)
Reagan scores 3-4, 165F3-166C1
Scores critics 3-11; Reagan, Carter reply 3-11, 3-13, 3-15, 197G2-198D1
Ford defends policy 3-12, 198G1
Reagan attacks 3-31; rebuttals 3-31, 4-1, 232E2, 233B1
Reagan FEC protest rptd 5-14, cancels Calif speeches 5-18, 359D1
Prefers to leave office 5-16, 359B1
Scored at Dem platform hearing 5-19, 357C3

1977

Korea
Korea scandal coverup chrgd 7-7, 557B1
Nixon cites 'hard line' 9-3, 693A1
Scandal cover-up rptd confrmd 9-5, 688F1

Latin America
Rights abuse rpts released 1-1, 50F2
Cuba '74-75 secret talks disclosed 3-28, 283D2
Jamaica seeks closer US ties 5-30—5-31, 454E2
Backs Canal accord 8-16, 8-17, 622D1; Carter cites 8-23, 649B3
At Canal pact signing, backing cited 9-7, 677E1, 678A1
Testifies on Canal treaties 9-14, 716A3
CIA plots vs Jamaica ldr rptd 11-2, 884G1

Middle East
Vs Daoud release 1-11, 10B1
Vs Palestine state 11-3, 831B1
PLO ties to Carter policy 12-15, 995D1

1978

1979

1980

1976

Ford intends to retain 5-25, 374C1
Carter scores technique 6-23, 451E2
Urges nonpartisan forgn policy 7-6, 535C3
Strauss deplores GOP admin 7-12, 508G3
Not at GOP platform com hearing 8-9, 583G1
GOP conv platform plank scores 8-17—8-18, comments 8-18; at conv 8-19, 600D3-G3, 601C1
Ford, Carter debate 10-6, 740D2, D3, 741G1, C2
On Ford E Eur remark 10-7, 762D3
Carter: Ford dependent 10-8, 762F1
Dole, Mondale debate 10-15, 783B3
Forgn reaction to electn 11-3—11-4, 826D1-D2
To meet with Carter 11-16, 864B2
Briefs Carter 11-20, 881D1
Carter names Vance 12-3; Vance meets 12-6, 916D2
USSR—*See also 'Africa' above*
Sets SALT trip 1-14, 17A1
In SALT talks, rpts progress 1-21—1-23, 61A3
Bars trade curb end 1-30, 88C3
Seeks support for detente 2-3, 2-4, 88A2, G3
Reagan scores policies 2-10, 109D2
Assails policy critics 3-11, 197B3
Sonnenfeldt statemts on US policy re Sovt-E Eur ties rptd 3-22; Reagan quotes 3-29; chrgs denied 3-29, 4-1, 232E2, G2, C3; Ford defends 4-2, 4-7, 245B2
Lauds A-test curb draft 4-9, 242A3
Pravda, E Eur press score 4-9—4-14, 276G3-277B2
Proposes Sahel aid program 5-1, 318F2
Hardens anti-Sovt line 5-20, 353F2
On E-W ties, strength 6-25, 466G1, D2
Cites Asian threat 7-22, 557E2
Sees Gromyko in NY 9-29, 10-1, 719E3
KISTNER, Dr. Robert W.
Changes view on pill 1-10, 32A2
KITSON, Penelope Ann
Named in Getty will 6-8, 444B2
KITTANNING, Pa.—*See PENNSYLVANIA*
KLAAR, Norbert
Wins Olympic medal 7-23, 575A2
KLAMMER, Franz
Wins Olympic medal 2-5, 158D3
KLAPEZYNSKI, Ulrike
Wins Olympic medal 7-30, 576A2
KLARSFELD, Beate
Husband gets suspended sentnc 2-9, 158D1
KLARSFELD, Serge
Gets suspended sentnc 2-9, 158D1
KLEBAN, Edward
Chorus Line wins Pulitzer 5-3, 352C3
KLEIN Jr., Guillermo Walter
Argentina econ coordinatn secy 3-29, 236F2
KLEIN, Harold P.
On Viking I data 8-10, 594C3
KLEIN, Lawrence R.
Heads Carter econ panel 4-23, 305E2
Briefs Carter on econ 7-27, 551B1
On US oil imports, trade deficit 10-28, 833E2
At NE govs mtg 11-13—11-14, 864C3
Carter econ adviser 12-1, 898F2
KLEIN, Tommy
On Ky pres ballot 5-25, 374B2
KLEINE, Piet
Wins Olympic medals 2-11, 2-14, 158F3, G3
KLENERT, Lt. William Blue
Vietnam rpts killed 9-6, 678B3
KLEPPE, Per
Norway finance min 1-12, 30A2 ★
KLEPPE, Thomas S.
Replaced as SBA admin 2-6, 110B2
OKs New River as scenic unit 3-12, 219C3
Utah power project dropped 4-14, 284F2
Strip-mine rules adopted 5-11, 359A3
Scores Alaska pipeline inspectn system, fears leaks 8-12, 691B1
Carter disavows 'dumping' memo 8-13, 616F3
OKs Colo oil shale lease suspensns, reviews request re Utah 8-23, 648G3, 649C1
Pocantico landmark dedicated 11-21, 887A3
KLIMKE, Reiner
Wins Olympic medal 7-30, 574E2
KLINEMAN, Kent
Trial venue chng rptd 12-22, 1016F2
KLING, Lee
Renamed to Dem post 7-16, 532B3
KLIPPER, Miriam
Relaxatn Response on best-seller list 12-5, 972B2
KLIX, Maj. Gen. Jose Maria
Argentina defense min 3-29, 236C1 ★
KLM Royal Dutch Airlines
Bernhard resigns post 8-26, 626G1
Jet hijacked 9-4, returned 9-5, 662D2
KLOCHEK, Vasily
Rpts '75 trade data 5-5, 340C3
KLOPPERS, Andrew
Lauds Namibia plan 8-20, 654D1
Scores const conf 10-22, 832B2
KLOSS, Ilana
Wins US Open doubles 9-12, 716D1
KLOTZ, Florence
Wins Tony 4-18, 460E2
KLUG, Alexander
Wins Cannes film award 5-28, 460G1
KLUNDT, Marvin E.
Contaminated in A-accident 8-30, 670E3
KNAPE, Ulrika
Wins Olympic medal 7-26, 575E3
KNAPP, Judge Dennis
Miners defy back-to-work injunctn 7-16, 7-23, 553A2, B2
Would drop UMW action 7-27, 669G3

1977

USSR
Assesses arms talks, human rights stand; scores Sovts re Zaire invasn 4-5, 247A2, 261E1 ★
IISS lauds policies 4-28, 401G1
USSR wiretap stand cited 7-10, 551A2
Spy's release from USSR rptd blocked 7-14, 564E2
Vietnam
Vs US aid to Vietnam 5-4, 333G1
Lies re peace talks chrgd 5-14, 403B3
US evacuatn scored in Snepp book 11-18, 898B1
KISUMO, Peter Abdullah
Resigns 1-23, 161D2
KITE, Tom
Ties 3d in Masters 4-10, 311E1
KIWANIS International
Charter withdrawal case review refused 10-3, 760D3
KKK—*See KU Klux Klan*
KLAGSBRUN, Dr. Samuel C.
At FDA laetrile hearings 5-2, 376C1
KLAMATH National Forest (Calif.)
Hog Fire burns 8-10—8-23, 660E2
KLASSMAN, Marcos
Loses pol rights 2-16, 186F2
KLEBANOV, Vladimir A.
Rpts worker protests 12-20, 988B2
Rptd arrested 12-20, 1017C2
KLEIN, Calvin
'77 fall fashions rptd 6-6, 1022D1
KLEIN, Hans-Joachim
Traube cleared 3-16, 259C3
KLEIN, Jose
Dies in Geneva 10-4, 922A3
KLEINBERG, Howard
Denies false IRS coverage 1-7, 16C1
KLEINDIENST, Richard G.
Voting rights power upheld 6-20, 517B1
Teamsters insurnc deal probed 10-31—11-2, 837E1, A2
KLEINSCHMIDT, Edward E.
Dies 8-9, 696A3
KLEINSCHMIDT, Ilona
Sentenced re Mandela trial 9-7, 825G3
KLEPIKOVA, Yelena
USSR exit rptd 6-9, 512E3
KLEPPE, Per
Presents '78 budget 10-13, 967F1
KLEPPE, Thomas S.
Revokes Mont coal leases 1-13, 58F3
Cited in Park indictmt 9-6, 688E1
Coal-leasing plan barred 9-27, 1007D2
KLIX, Gen. Jose Maria
Rejects US mil credits 3-1, 142C2
KLM Royal Dutch Airlines
Canary I Pan Am collisn 3-27, 244C1
Canary I suits filed 3-31—4-6; probe rpts 4-9, 4-11, 311B3
KLOCK, Donald M.
Sentenced 1-26, 103B2
KLONICA, Leon
Named Poland agri min 12-17, 987F1
K mart Corp. (formerly S. S. Kresge Co.)
Presley book order sets record 8-20, 696E1
Fyrol FR-2 warning rptd 9-29, 820C2
KNAPP, Chris
Traded to Angels 12-5, 990C1
KNAPP, Judge Dennis R.
OKs NIOSH data access 12-22, 1008F2

1978

KISS You All Over (recording)
On best-seller list 9-6, 708F1; 10-11, 800E3; 11-8, 888C1
KITAHARA, Hidea
Protests remarks by French CP ldr 2-23, 167C2
KITE, Tom
Ties for 2d in British Open 7-15, 580D2
Ties for 2d in HOF Classic 8-27, 672G3
Wins BC Open 9-4, 990G1
KITT, Eartha
Timbuktu opens 3-1, 760E3
KITT Peak National Observatory (Ariz.)
Sighting of young star rptd 1-6, 11E2
Planets in galaxy estimated 4-21, 294B1
KIYOMURA, Ann
Strings win WTT title 9-21, 1027F1
KKK—*See KU Klux Klan*
KLANE, Robert
Thank God It's Fri released 5-19, 620B1
KLAR, Christian
Eludes police 8-21, 724G3
KLEBANOV, Vladimir A.
Rptd freed 1-3, 21A1
Announces union creatn 1-26; arrested 2-7, 180B1
KLEE, Paul (1879-1940)
Paintings destroyed in Brazil museum fire 7-8, 579A2
KLEIBER, Wilburt L.
Indicted 3-23, 243F1
KLEIN, Hans-Joachim
Reveals '76 papal kidnap plot 8-6, 689A3
Rptd in Israel 8-17, 651D3
KLEINDIENST, Richard
4 indicted on union insurnc scheme 6-15, 560D3
KLEINSCHMIDT, Ilona
Appeal rptd lost 1-23, 114F1
KLEISER, Randal
Grease released 6-16, 619C2
KLEPPE, Per
Presents '79 austerity budget 10-5, 775C1, 883G3
KLIMUK, Col. Pyotr
Docks with Salyut 6-28, 506A1
Ends Soyuz 30 flight 7-5, 623C3
KLINE, Allen
Greek Tycoon released 5-12, 619C2
KLINE, Ernest P.
Loses primary for Pa gov 5-16, 389B3
KLINE, Kevin
On 20th Century opens 2-19, 887D2
Wins Tony 6-4, 579A3
KLING Partnership, The
Hartford arena roof collapses 1-18, 95D3
KLM Royal Dutch Airlines
US air svc accord 3-10, 206A3
Canary I '77 crash rpt issued 10-18, Dutch score 10-23, 888A2
KLOPFLEISCH, Erich
Convicted as E Ger spy 2-13, 115D1
KLOSE, Hans-Ulrich
On W Ger dockers strike setlmt 1-30, 94A1
KLUTZNICK, Philip
Sadat asks peace backing 2-6, 77G2

1979

KISSINGER v. Reporters Committee for Freedom of the Press
Case accepted by Sup Ct 4-16, 302E3
KITAMURA, Haruo
Oil conservatn remark rptd 8-8, 615A3
KITCHNER, Barry
Whitecaps win NASL title 9-8, 775A3, B3
KLARWEIN, Eleanore
Peppermint Soda released 7-15, 820G2
KLEBERG Jr., Richard M.
Dies 5-8, 432B3
KLEIBER, Wilburt L.
Convicted 8-16, 704F1
Fined, put on probatn 12-10, 947B1
KLEIN, Allen
Convicted on tax fraud 4-26, 392F3
Sentenced 7-10, 656E2
KLEIN, Guillermo Walter
Home bombed 9-27, 748G3
KLEIN, Norman E.
Indicted 8-2, 744D3
KLEIN, Paul
Quits as NBC-TV program chief 3-5, 334G3
KLEIN, Robert
They're Playing Our Song opens 2-11, 292E3
KLEINSCHMIDT, Ilona
Jailed 12-13, 969F1
KLEPPE, Per
Norway planning min 10-5, 774E1
KLEPSCH, Egon
Seeks strong EC Parlt 12-13, 960G2
KLIBI, Chedli
Named Arab League head 6-28, 475E2
KLINE, Kevin
Loose Ends opens 6-6, 712C1
KLINGER, Tony
Kids Are Alright released 6-15, 820E1
KLIVECA, Ray
Named Cosmos interim coach 6-1, 655B2
KLM Royal Dutch Airlines
Dutch probe Canary I '77 crash 5-29, 412C2
DC-10 grounded indefinitely 6-6, 421B1
KLOSTER, Knut
'France' sails to W Ger 8-19, 633F3
KLOUSE, Monte
Arrested 1-8, 102E2
KLUTZNICK, Philip
Named Commerce secy 11-16, 883C3
K MART Corp.
Scholl dispute refused by Sup Ct 1-15, 32B1
KNACK (singing group)
My Sharona on best-seller list 8-1, 620E3; 9-5, 672E3; 10-3, 800E3
Get the Knack on best-seller list 8-1, 620F3; 9-5, 672E3; 10-3, 800F3P
KNAPP, Chris
Angels lose AL pennant 10-6, 797G2

1980

KISSINGER v. Halperin
Case accepted by Sup Ct 5-19, 440D1
Case argued in Sup Ct 12-8, 937B2
KISSINGER v. Reporters Committee for Freedom of the Press
Case decided by Sup Ct 3-3, 210B1
KITE, Tom
2d in Phila Classic 8-3, Pensacola Open 10-12, 972E1, D2
KITTIS, Constantinos
Named Cyprus commerce min 9-9, 749G2
KITTY Hawk (balloon)
2 Amers cross N Amer 5-12—5-15, 470F3
KIWANIS International
Bush addresses Mich club 9-18, 781A1
KIZIM, Leonid
Launched into space 11-27, 914A2
Ends flight 12-10, 933B1
KJELLAND, Roland A.
Kaiser Steel pres, chief exec 9-5, 702B1
KLAMMER, Franz
Injured 3-3, 470A1
KLARSFELD, Serge
3 sentncd for WW2 crimes 2-11, 118G1
KLASA, Josef
Warns vs Polish strike 11-7, 862G2
KLEBER, Ina
Wins Olympic medal 7-23, 623B3
KLEIN, Chuck (Charles Herbert) (1904-58)
Elected to Baseball HOF 8-3, 796D2
KLEIN, Dr. Harvey
Rpts new blood disease treatmt 1-23, 159E3
KLEIN, Lawrence R.
Wins Nobel Prize 10-15, 890A1
KLEIN, Norman E.
Sentence rptd 2-19, 237A3
KLEINE, Piet
Wins Olympic medal 2-23, 156A1
KLEISER, Randal
Blue Lagoon released 6-20, 675G1
KLIBI, Chedli
Backs Iraq in Iran war 9-23, 719E2
KLIER, Johanna
Wins Olympic medal 7-28, 624A2
KLINE, Steve
Borderline released 10-31, 972D3
KLOPPER, Gerald
Sentenced 10-13, 833C1
KLUGER, Bruce
Ka-Boom! opens 11-20, 1003C3
KLUTZNICK, Philip M.
USSR export licenses rejected 1-11, 28C2
Bars USSR computer exports 1-21, 45F1
On USSR phosphate ban 2-25, 139F3
Moscow Olympic product ban ordrd 3-28, 259C1
On steel import probe 4-10, 367G3
On May housing figures 6-17, 455C2
On June indicators 7-30, 574G1
Vs steel indus tax breaks 8-1, 575C3
On July indicators 8-29, 666C1
On Aug housing starts 9-17, 701E3
ON 3d 1/4 paymts surplus 12-18, 984C2
Lauds '80 census 12-31, 983A2
KLUTZNICK v. Shapiro
Stay extended by Sup Ct 12-15, 957D2
KNACKE, Christiane
Wins Olympic medal 7-24, 623C3

1976

KNAPP, J. G.
AF asst secy 1-20; confrmd 3-10, 232F1
KNEBEL, John A.
Named Agri acting secy 10-4, 744E3
Ford ups grain-support rates 10-13, 787D3
Israel agri deal delayed 10-16; reason cited 10-18, 810G3
KNEIP, Gov. Richard F. (D, S.D.)
SD primary results 6-1, 390B1
KNIGHT, Archbishop Alan
On Guyana schl takeover 10-1, 1005G2
KNIGHT, John S.
Retires 4-30, 504C2
KNIGHT 3d, John S. (d. 1975)
2 convicted 5-20, 6-14, 503G3
KNIGHT, Shirley
Wins Tony 4-18, 460E2
KNIGHT, Ted
Wins Emmy 5-17, 460B2
KNIGHT-Ridder Newspapers
J S Knight retires 4-30, 504C2
Heir's killers convicted 5-20, 6-14, 503G3
KNOCK, Knock (play)
Opens 2-24, 6-6, 1014B3
KNOX, James Cardinal
At Intl Eucharistic Cong 8-1—8-8, 596B3
KNOXVILLE, Tenn.—*See TENNESSEE*
KNOXVILLE News-Sentinel
Ford endorsement rptd 10-30, 831F2
KNUD, Prince (Denmark)
Dies 6-14, 484E3
KNUFELMAN, Manfred
Arrested as spy 8-16, 640B2
KNULL, Lt. Kenneth M.
Convicted 6-22, 941G2
KOBAYASHI, Masami
In new party 6-25, 497B3
KOBELINSKI, Mitchell
SBA admin 12-9-75; confrmd 2-6, 110B2
KOCH, Bill
Wins Olympic medal 2-5, 158G2, 159C1
KOCH, Rep. Edward I. (D, N.Y.)
Probes privacy invasion 2-11, 151C2
Chrgs Uruguay torture 4-21, 382F3
House panel vs Uruguay mil aid 6-5, 441F1
Testimony re Uruguay aid rptd 9-20; Uruguay press scores 10-15, 814C2, E2
Reelected 11-2, 830B2
KODAMA, Yoshio
Lockheed payoffs probed 2-4—2-17, 130G1, E3, 131D3, 132G1
Diet subpoenas 2-26, questnd 3-4, 190A3, G3
Indicted 3-13, assets seized 3-15; assassinatn fails 3-23, 286F1
New charges filed 5-10, 6-1, 450C3
Tachikawa arrested 7-2, 497D2
Nakasone-Lockheed link rptd 677D1 ★
Tied to Osana payment 838C3
Lockheed probe delay seen 9-24, 740A3
Trial delayed 9-30, 838C3
KODDOUS, Ihsan Abdel
Loses newspaper post 3-28, 333F1
KOELLIKER Frers, Arturo
Rptd missing 12-30, 996E3
KOENIG, Yisroel
Rpt on Galilee Arab curbs aired 9-8, 683G1
Galilee Arabs vs rpt 9-22, strike 9-28, 738C1
KOEPPLER, Heinrich
On CDU-CSU split 11-23, 930D3
KOH, T. T. B.
Sets UN seabed treaty terms 8-27, 700B2
KOHL, Helmut
On CDU Lower Saxony win 2-6, 157B3
On Boex spy chrg 5-17, 383E1
Urges E Ger trade curbs 8-8, 630E3
Defeated in electns 10-3; asks FDP alliance, sees Scheel 10-4, 754C2-D3
Resigns as prime min; to lead oppositn 10-7, 857B3
Scores Leber on gens dismissal 11-8, 930F3
Scores CSU split 11-20, 930D2
On CDU electn platform 11-21, 930A3
CDU, CSU reunite 12-12, 968G2
KOHLER, Christa
Wins Olympic medal 7-20, 575E3
KOHLER Jr., Walter J.
Dies 3-21, 316A1
KOHN, Rev. Dr. William
New Lutheran denominatn pres 12-4, 932B2
KOHNSTAMM & Co., Inc., H.
Red #2 ban in effect 2-12, challenge continues 2-13, 137D1
KOHOUT, Pavel
CIA-RFE link chrgd 3-10, 289G2
KOINANGE, Mbyo
Reads Kenyatta UNCTAD conf speech 5-5, 320G1
KOIVISTO, Arto
Wins Olympic medal 2-8, 159C1
KOLAKOWSKI, Leszek
Polish charter chng protest cited 268F1
KOLBE, Peter
Wins Olympic medal 7-25, 575D1
KOLCHINSKI, Alexander
Wins Olympic medal 7-24, 576B3
KOLEILAT, Ibrahim
Jumblat vs truce 3-26, 225F1
KOLEKA, Spiro
Replaced as dep premr 10-14, 949G1; named Presidium chrmn 12-30, 1012B2
KOLESNIKOV, Nikolai
Wins Olympic medal 7-19, 576D2
KOLEV, Ivan
Wins Olympic medal 7-24, 576A3
KOLEV, Vladimir
Wins Olympic medal 7-31, 574C1

1977

KNEBEL, John A.
Replaced as Agri dep secy 3-15, 211G1
KNEE Jr., Robert
US sues union fund 4-4, 280C2
KNIGHT, Billy
Traded to Braves 9-1, 991A1
KNIGHT-Ridder Newspapers Inc.
On most reliable govt news source list 12-10, 1009B1
KNOCHE, E. Henry
Resignatn announced 7-13, 576B2
Carlucci gets CIA post 12-22, 1001F3
KNOLL, Andrew
Oldest fossils of life found 10-15, 908G1
KNORR, Nathan H.
Dies 6-15, 532C3
KNOWLTON, Winthrop
At USSR book fair 9-6—9-14; hosts dissidents 9-8, 766B1
On USSR book pact 12-7, 955D2
KNOX, James Cardinal
Scores Bishop Dozier 3-25, 375D2
KNOX, Judge William W.
Fines Gulf Oil 11-22, 944A1
KNYRKOV, Maj. Gen. Alexander V.
At NATO war games 9-13, 700B1
KOBE Steel Ltd.
US dumping chrgs upheld 10-3, 774D3
KOBEH Gonzalez, Roberto
Butler payoff rptd 5-17, 503B1
KOCH, Rep. Edward I. (D, N.Y.)
Nicaragua aid cutoff plea rptd 3-4, 168F2
Backs pot decriminalizatn 3-14, 332B2
Anti-Concorde amendmt fails 6-8, 463C2
Cites Nicaragua rights abuse chrgs 6-14, 475E3
Chrgs Long deceptn on Nicaragua mil aid 7-1, 656C3
NY mayoral primary 9-8; wins runoff 9-19, 723G1
Carter snubs after Mideast protest 10-4, 761B1
Elected NYC mayor 11-8, 855F1, E2
On Moody's NYC note rating 11-10, 881F1
KOCH, Gary
Wins Fla Citrus Open 3-6, 311D2
KOCHER Coal Co.
Anthracite mine flood 3-1, 204C3
KODAMA, Yoshio
Indicted 1-21, 83F2
KOENIG, Linda
Negotiated Peru-IMF pact 9-30, 785A2
KOGLER, Rudi
Killed 8-6, 624D2
KOHL, Helmut
Sees Schmidt re Baader trial, buggings 3-18, 260A2
On Baader gang suicides 10-20, 791B1
Chrgs spy scandal cover-up, asks Leber resignatn 12-15, 968C2
KOHL, Michael
Recalled 1-24, 62E1
Gaus chrgs NKVD betrayal 2-8, 102A2
KOHOUT, Pavel
Detained 1-7, 20C1
Austria offers asylum 1-25, refuses 1-28, 82B3, D3
KO Ko, U
Quits Cabt post 3-29, 243C3

1978

KNEALE, George
A-plant radiatn linked to cancer 2-17, 164C2
KNEE Jr., Robert
To return $560,000 1-3, 4E2
KNEIP, Gov. Richard F. (D, S.D.)
Singapore amb appt rptd 6-6, 448G1
KNEPPER, Bob
NL pitching ldr 10-2, 928G2
KNIGHT, Billy
Traded to Celtics 7-7, 655A3
KNIGHT, Bobby
Disciplines Indiana players 12-12, 1028A1
KNIGHT-Ridder Newspapers Inc.
Gannett circulatn compared 5-8, 345A3
KNOCHE, E. Henry
Vs excessive intell agency curbs 4-5, 306C2
KNOLL, Michael
Wounded, captured 9-24; dies 10-7, 884G3
KNOPF Inc., Alfred A.
Shevchenko '75 book contract cited 4-26, 302B3
KNOX, Chuck
Resigns as Rams coach, joins Bills 1-12, 171D2
KNOX, Roger
Charged by SEC 10-5, 770C3
KNOXVILLE, Tenn.—*See TENNESSEE*
KOBE Steel Ltd.
US '77 dumping ruling revised 1-9, 80E2
Australia iron imports set 5-30, 411F1
KOCAS, Said
Questns UK rptr's '71 death 7-24, 631A3
KOCH, Mayor Edward I. (N.Y., N.Y.)
Green wins US House seat 2-14, 108F1
Financial Crisis
Role in NYC fscl crisis 86A2, C2
Backs more fed aid for NYC 1-9, 87F2
Unveils NYC recovery plan 1-20, 87E1
Meets with Carter 2-2, 87B1
Agrees on state aid for NYC 2-6, 87C2
Sen Bank Com rpt issued; fed aid renewal, recovery plan opposed 2-9, 86G2
Reactn to Sen com rpt 2-9, 87B1
On Carter urban-aid plan 3-27, 218A1
Gets US aid pledge for S Bronx 4-12, 285F1
Carter signs NYC aid bill 8-8, 608E1, D2, F2
KOCH, John
Dies 4-19, 356A3
KOCH, Marita
Sets 400-mtr dash mark 7-2, 692G3
KOCO-TV (Okla. TV station)
FCC OKs WJLA-TV exchng 1-12, 109B3
WJLA-TV swap OKd again 3-9, Allbritton halts deal 3-24, 270A3
KODAMA, Yoshio
Named Nakasone contact in Lockheed case 10-26, 838F3
KODJO, Edem
Elected OAU secy gen 7-22, 561D2
KODZOMAN, Mile
Convicted 12-1, 933B3
KOFOED, Niels Anker
Named Danish agri min 8-30, 688A1
KOGOVSEK, Ray P.
Wins US House seat 11-7, 850C2, 855G3
KOHL, Helmut
Barred Berlin entry 1-15, 36E1
2 more CDU reps denied Berlin entry 1-16, 61F3
Mil svc objectors law altered 4-13, 354F1
KOHL, Herbert
Wins Natl Book Award 4-10, 315A3
KOHL, Judith
Wins Natl Book Award 4-10, 315A3
KOHOUT, Pavel
Leaves for Austria 10-28, 885E2
KOINANGE, Mbiyu
Kenya resources min 10-11, 784C3
KOJAK (TV series)
Silverman to head NBC 1-20, 75F2
KOLE, Tom
Pleads guilty 1-16, sentncd 3-31, 310C1
KOLLEK, Teddy
On Jerusalem bomb blast 6-2, 424A3
Meets Mondale 6-30, 501D2

1979

KNATCHBULL, Nicholas
Killed by IRA 8-27, 641B1
KNATCHBULL, Timothy
Injured by IRA 8-27, 641B1
KNIGHT, Arthur
Named new NEB head 11-21, 949F3
KNIGHT, Billy
Traded to Pacers 1-16, 526D2
KNIGHT, Bobby
Arrested in Pan Am assault 7-8, convctd 8-22, resignatn rejctd 8-24, sentncd 9-10, 798B3, D3
KNIGHT, Darrin
Wins Oscar 4-9, 336B2
KNIGHT, Harold
Bank reserve requiremt raised 1-16, 57B1
KNIGHT, Jean
US protests Sovt abuse chrg 4-20, 390F1-A2
KNIGHT, Larry
In NBA draft 6-25, 507B2
KNIGHT, Ray
NL batting ldr 9-30, 955D2
KNIGHT, Robin
US protests Sovt abuse chrg 4-20, 390F1-A2
KNIGHT, Shirley
Lovely Sunday opens 1-21, 292A2
Losing Time opens 9-30, 956C3
KNIGHT-Ridder Newspapers Inc.
Gannett claims circulatn lead 12-12, 1007E1
KNOCK on Wood (recording)
On best-seller list 5-2, 356A3
KNOCKOUT (play)
Opens 5-6, 712A1
KNOETZE, Kallie
US revokes visa 1-9, judge enjoins 1-11; KOs Sharkey, fight protested 1-13, 79C2
KNOIZEN, Rear Adm. Arthur K.
Disperses PR protesters 5-19, 385C3
KNOLL, Erwin
Scores H-bomb article censorship 3-14, 193F3; publicatn barred 3-26, 230C1
Lauds H-bomb article censorship end 9-17, 713G1
KNOTTS, Don
Apple Dumpling sequel released 8-31, 819E3
KNOWLES, Dr. John H.
Dies 3-6, 272A3
KNOX College (Galesburg, Ill.)
Barry in basketball HOF 4-30, 526F3
KOBAYASHI, Royal
Pedroza TKOs 1-9, 79C3
KOCH, David
Named '80 Libertarian vp candidate 9-8, 680G2
KOCH, Mayor Edward I. (N.Y., N.Y.)
Signs offcls' pay hike bill 7-27, 580G1
On NYC bank robberies 8-22, 656C1
Reviews prostitutn rpt 10-9, 'John Hour' debuts 10-23, 887E1
Attends Carter dinner 10-24, 961F2
Doubts NYC long-term borrowing 11-8, 920D2
KOCH Industries Inc.
Abko buys Chrysler unit 8-22, 663D2
KOENING, Laird
Bloodline released 6-28, 819E3
KOH, T. T. B.
Scores Viet SE Asia policy 1-13, 28G1
KOHEN, Arnold
On E Timor famine 11-3, 856F1, A2
KOHL, Helmut
CDU wins in Schleswig-Holstein 4-29, 333C3
CDU-CSU alliance faces split 5-24, 5-28, 489E1
Strauss wins CDU support 7-2, 506A1
KOHLBERG, Andy
Loses NCAA doubles title 5-28, 570B2
KOHLBERG, Kravis, Roberts & Co.
Heads Houdaille takeover 4-2, 283B1
Foremost-McKesson bid rptd 10-17, 986B3
KOHN, John
Goldengirl released 6-15, 820C1
KOHOUT, Pavel
Citizenship revoked 10-8, 838G1
KOIRALA, Bisheswar Prasad
Detained 4-27, freed 5-9, 389B3
KOIVISTO, Mauno (Manu) (Finnish premier)
Sworn Finnish premier, outlines govt progrms 5-26–5-27, 406F3, 407C1
KOK, Wim
On Rotterdam strike 8-29, 653E3
KOLBE, Rev. Maximilian
Pope honors, beatificatn cited 6-7, 414A1
KOLLEK, Teddy
Arranges Jesse Jackson seminar 9-25, 763B1*

1980

KNEIP, Richard F.
Political gaffes rptd 1-30, 200C2
KNIFE in the Head (film)
Released 4-23, 416B3
KNIGHT, Patrick
Arrested 11-7, freed 11-10, 888B3
KNIGHT, Ray
NL wins All-Star Game 7-8, 636G1, A2
NL batting ldr 10-6, 926F2
KNOWLES, James
Convicted for '79 Fla drownings 4-18, 336B1
KNOWLES, Dr. John H. (d. 1979)
Lyman named Rockefeller Foundatn pres 1-26, 200E1
KNOX, Robert
Hired as Ariz State athletic dir 1-3, 175F2
KNOX, William
On anti-abortn bill defeat 5-30, 428F2
KNUDSEN, Semon E.
Replaced as White Motor chrmn 4-23, 456D2
KOBOTA, Enji
Ousted as Japan defense head 2-3, 99C3
KOCH, Mayor Edward I. (N.Y., N.Y.)
On pres primary vote 3-25, 221A3
On transit strike 4-2, 268G1
Scores transit setlmt 4-11, 289C2, F2
MD sentncd in egg assault 6-6, 639G2
On labor setlmt impact 7-3, 518C1
At NYFE opening 8-7, 616E3
Revises fscl recovery plan 8-11, sees Miller on fed loan guarantees 9-10, 743C1
Accompanies Mondale 9-15, 780B2
Greets Carter 9-29, 739C1
Reagan praises 10-1, 738C1
KOCH Jr., Howard W.
Idolmaker released 11-14, 972F3
KOCH, Marita
Wins Olympic medal 7-28, 624A2
KOCIOLEK, Stanislaw
Replaces Warsaw CP ldr 11-18, 878C2
KOCMAN, Vladimir
Wins Olympic medal 7-27, 623D1
KOCSIS, Ferenc
Wins Olympic medal 7-23, 624B3
KOGOVSEK, Rep. Ray (D, Colo.)
Reelected 11-4, 842D2, 851D3
KOH, Tommy T. B.
Backs Pol Pot govt UN seat 10-13, 775C2
KOHL, Michael
Signs W Ger transport pact 4-30, 355D3
KOHLBERG Kravis Roberts & Co.
Foremost-McKesson rejects takeover 2-6, 386B1
KOHLER, Gundolf
Allegedly killed in Munich blast 9-28, 754F3
KOIRALA, Bisheswar Prasad
On Nepal electn results 5-14, 409F3
KOISOVA, Vera
Wins Olympic medal 7-28, 624A2
KOJIMOTO, Keith
Seized for assault on US, Sovt aides at UN 4-30, 325B2
KOKOMO—*See INDIANA*
KOKOSCHKA, Oskar
Dies 2-22, 176A2
KOKSALOGLU, Abdurrahman
Murdered 7-15, 544F3
KOLCHINSKY, Aleksandr
Wins Olympic medal 7-24, 624C3
KOLCZONAY, Erno
Wins Olympic medal 7-28, 622B3
KOLEV, Nedeltcho
Wins Olympic medal 7-24, 624F2
KOLISEVSKI, Lazar
Named Yugo interim pres 5-4, 338D2
Mijatovic installed 5-15, 381G3
KOLLEK, Teddy
Urges Begin act vs vandals 1-21, 133F3*
Vs Jerusalem land seizure 3-10, US condemnatn 3-13, 178F2, C3
Vs Jerusalem sovereignty law 8-23, 643D2

1976

KOLMAN, Arnosht
Resigns from CP 10-6, 857D1
KOLOSKOV, Vyacheslav
Flyers beat Sovt team 1-11, 56A2
KOLSTAD, Lt. Cmdr. Thomas C.
Vietnam rpts killed 9-6, 678B3 *
KOMOTO, Toshio
Urges arms export ban end 1-29, 157G1
KONDAKOV, Juriy
Wins Olympic medal 2-13, 158F3
KONDER, Rodolfo
Details Brazil torture 1-26, 98E1
KONIGSBERG, Harold (Kayo)
Indicted 6-23, 460B1
KONO, Ichiro
Kishi Lockheed role chrgd 3-9, 191B2
KONO, Yohei
LDP faction seeks Miki ouster 6-14, 458F1
Heads new party 6-25, 497B3
KONOPACKI, Henryk
Named chem min 12-2, 926D3
KONSTANTINOV, Vitaly
Wins Olympic medal 7-24, 576G2
KOORNHOF, Pieter
S Africa cabt shifted 1-22, 76F1 *
OKs multiracial sports 9-23, 793E3
KOORY Jr., Fred
Loses US House race 11-2, 824C1
KOOSMAN, Jerry
NL pitching ldr 10-4, 796A1
KOPECHNE, Mary Jo (d. 1969)
Uruguay pres scores Kennedys 10-8, 814G1
KOPOLOW, Dr. Louis E.
Rpts mental illness, econ link 1-26, 159B3
KOPPERS Co. Inc.
SEC lists forgn paymts 5-12, 728B2
KOPROWSKI, Dr. Hilary
Rpts new rabies vaccine 9-4, 972F3
KORBUT, Olga
Wins Olympic medals 7-19—7-22, 563D1, 574D3
KORCAK, Josef
Czech Presidium member 4-16, 289B2
KORCHAK, Alexander
In CSCE monitor group 5-13, 408B2
KORCHNOI, Viktor
Defects 7-27, 558F3
USSR strips of honors 9-4, 857C1
KORDA, Michael
Power on best-seller list 12-5, 972D2
KOREA (North), People's Republic of—*See also NONALIGNED Nations Movement*
Gulf Oil paymts rptd 134A1
China pipeline links rptd 1-8, 78B1
S Korea discovers oil 1-15, 54C1
Listed as 'not free' nation 1-19, 20E3
Aide visits bombed Cambodian town 3-2—3-4, 238B2
S Korea sentences spies 4-30, 334B2
Premr Kim quits, Chul replaces 4-30, 335B2
Rejects South visit plan 6-9, 440B3
US Dem platform text cites 6-15, 478E2
South asks pol talks resumptn 7-4, 557G2
At COMECON summit 7-7—7-9, 722D2
Rpt Libya trains terrorists 7-15, 531B2
US urges 4-power talks, Kim asks N-S cong 7-22; UN aide rejcts US plan 7-23, 557C2
US, S Korea war plan chrgd 8-5, 625E2
Pak warns vs US presence in South 8-17, nonaligned natns back 8-20, 621B3, F3
US GOP platform text cites 8-18, 609D2
US repeats 4-power talks call 8-19, 619A1
China delegatn views Mao body 9-13, 711F3
Choi Yong Kun dies 9-20, 970B2
US asks 'phased' talks 9-30, 719E2
S Korea for US talk plan 10-1, 858C2
China scores US role 10-5, 760A1
US vs N Korea talks 10-9, 858B2
Scandinavia expels diplomats re illegal sales 10-15—10-22, forgn debt cited 10-22, 799D2
S Korea rpts spy surrenders, 12 seized 10-30, 910B3
USSR ousts envoys, illegal sales cited 12-8, 967D1
Armistice Violations (& developments)
DMZ clashes 6-19, 8-5, 619E1
N Koreans slay 2 US Army officers in DMZ tree trimming 8-18; US, S Korea condemn; troops alerted 8-18—8-20, 618B3
US protests slayings 8-19, 8-20; Kim regrets 8-21, US, S Korea react 8-22—8-24, 625A2
Slayings cited re US stock prices 8-19—8-20, 846F3
US displays mil force, fells tree 8-21; N Korea deplores 8-21, 8-22, 625A1
US mil buildup continues 8-23, 8-24, 626D1
N Korea chrgs US naval movemts 8-24, 641C2
N Korea asks DMZ partitn 8-25, 626A1
Armistice Comm meets 8-28, 8-31, 9-1, 641A1
N Korea seizes ROK fishing boat 8-30; N-S communicatns cut 9-1, 641C2
US ends B-52 runs 8-31, to resume 9-1, 641B2
US details tree-cutting move 9-1, 641D1
Armistice Comm mtgs 9-2—9-4, partitn OKd; US, S Korea hail 9-6, US ends extra alert 9-7; map of partitn area 559G2
DMZ partition implemented 9-16, 722D2
Sports
Olympic results 7-18—7-31, 573E3, 574A1, B1

1977

KOLTON, Paul
Retiremt announced 7-15, Levitt to succeed 11-10, 859D3
KOMAR, Vitaly
Melamid exit rptd 10-31, 956E1
Joins Malamid in Israel 12-20, 1017D2
KOMAREK, Karel
Austria offers dissidents asylum 1-25, 82B3, D3
KOMOTO, Toshio
Named Japan intl trade min 11-28, 932A2
KOMPFNER, Rudolf
Dies 12-3, 1024C2
KONE, Abdoulaye
Ivory Coast finance min 7-30, 772C1
KONTOGIOGIS, George
Greek min for EC talks 11-28, 925G1, B2
KOORNHOF, Pieter
Asks nonwhite govt role 5-24, 428B3

KOREA (North), People's Republic of—*See also COMECON, NONALIGNED Nations Movement*
US to lift travel ban 3-9, 172F3, 173D1
US plans S Korea troop exit 3-9, 202F3
S Korea-Japan oil pact scored 6-8, 467B2
US assures S Korea 7-25, seeks 4-party talks 7-27, 572A2, C2
200-mi econ, 50-mi mil zones 8-1; US, Japan, ROK, UN vs 8-2, 590F3
Tito visits 8-24—8-29, 709D3, F3
Ne Win visit cited 779F2
Rpt S Korea sought to block US ties 11-29, 914A3
New Cabt formed, 6-yr econ plan set; '71-76 forgn debt cited 12-15, 986C3
Armistice Violations (& developments)
S Korea soldier dies in ambush 5-4; US protests, N Korea denies 5-9, 411G2
N-S sea clash rptd 5-14, North denies abductn 5-15, 411B3
US copter downed, 3 die 7-13; US rpts 7-14; men returned 7-16, 552F2-G3
Post-truce incidents, death toll data 552G3

1978

KOMARKOVA, Vera
Climbs Annapurna in Nepal 10-15, 843G2
KOMER, Robert
Haig frictn rptd 4-25, 298G2
KOMOTO, Toshio
On yen appreciation 3-15, 235A2
US urges trade policy chng 10-3, 797G3
Ohira wins LPD electn 11-27, 912A3
KONDRASHIN, Kirill Petrovich
Defects 12-4, 946E3
KONE, Lt. Col. Missa
Named Mali health min 1-7, 75F1
KONIGSBERG, Harold (Boom Boom)
Convicted 6-14, sentenced 6-21, 480B2
KONUK, Necat (Turkish Cypriot premier; resigned Mar. 24)
Resigns despite Denktash plea; price hikes, party oppositn cited 3-24, 226C2
Replaced as Turk premr 4-22, 329A1
KOORNHOF, Pieter G. J. (Piet)
S Africa plural relations min 11-14, 904A3
Tours Cape Town shantytown 11-21; delays destructn 11-30, 989G1
KOOSMAN, Jerry
Traded to Twins 12-8, 1026C1
KOPPERS Corp.
Cutler move vs Tyco cited 7-7, 553A2, C2
KOPRULULER, Teoman
Named Turkey trade min 1-5, 21E2
KORBUT, Olga
Marries 1-7, 95G3
KORCHNOI, Viktor
Loses world chess championship 7-18—10-17, 843B1

KOREA (North), People's Republic of—*See also COMECON, NONALIGNED Nations Movement*
'77 plot vs Kim's son rptd 2-5, 115E3
GNP, forgn debt, other econ data rptd 2-27, 340C3
Armistice Violations (& developments)
UN chrgs North dug DMZ tunnel 10-27, 860D3
Foreign Relations (misc.)
Cambodia asks aid vs Viet 1-3, 4F1
S Korea econ compared 2-27, 340B3
S Korea oppositn to talks with North, US rptd 4-5, 4-19, 277A3
Israel: terrorists train in Leb 4-7, 256D3
S Korea claims spy boat sunk 4-28, 340F3
China Premr Hua visits; backs Kim on reunificatn, US mil presence 5-5—5-10; S Korea scores 5-11, 340D2
S Korea fears US troop exit 5-29, 399D2
USSR '50 war role chrgd by US 6-7, 423C3
S Korea trade bid barred; US talks sought, slow troop exit scored 6-23, 497D2
Kim warns nonaligned vs splits 7-25, 583E2
US, S Korea see as threat 7-27, 594G3
Afghan cuts S Korea ties 9-18, 738D2
Japan ties China pact to reunificatn 10-18, 802B1
China backs Kim on reunificatn 10-25, 802D1
UN chrgs armistice violatn 10-27, 860D3
US-S Korea joint cmnd set 11-7, protested 11-8, 872B3
U.S. Relations
US affirms Asia commitmt 2-20, 126D3
CIA compares N, S Korea econ 2-27, 340B3
S Korea oppositn to talks with North, US rptd 4-5, 4-19, 277A3
China Premr Hua backs Kim on US mil presence 5-5—5-10; S Korea scores 5-11, 340E2
S Korea fears US troop exit 5-29, 399D2
Carter chrgs USSR role in '50 war 6-7, 423D3
Vance pledges A-arms restraint 6-12, 445A2
US lauds S Korea trade bid; North bars, seeks US talks, vs slow troop exit 6-23, 497F2
US, S Korea see as threat 7-27, 594G3
US-S Korea joint cmnd set 11-7, protested 11-8, 872B3
US backs interest paymt on frozen forgn assets 11-14, 977G1

1979

KOMPLEKTOV, V. G.
Cited in SALT II summit communique 6-18, 457D1
KONIGSBERG, Harold (Boom Boom)
'78 murder convictn upset 6-7, 491F3
KONTOGEORGIS, George
Greek EMS entry vowed 4-4, 268D3
KOOB, Kathryn L.
Detained in US Emb 11-19, 878D2
KOORNHOF, Pieter G. J. (Piet)
Vows homes to crossroads squatters 4-5, 270D3
In Soweto with Botha 8-31, 732D3
KOOSMAN, Jerry
AL pitching ldr 9-30, 955G3
KOPECHNE, Mary Jo (1941-69)
Kennedy: Chappaquiddick no bar to presidency 7-17, 539F1-D2
Carter denies Chappaquiddick comments 9-25–9-26, 723D3-F3
KOPIT, Arthur
Wings opens 1-28, 292G3
KOPP, Quentin
Loses vote for San Fran mayor 12-11, 946E3
KOPPE, Johannes
Evades espionage arrest 1-23, 61C3
KOPRULULER, Teoman
On trade policy 8-21, 637E2
KORCHNOI, Bela (Mrs. Viktor)
Despairs of reunion 11-17, 980B3
KORCHNOI, Igor Viktorevich
Sentncd for draft evasn 12-19, 980B3
KORCHNOI, Viktor
Swiss grant asylum 9-24, 721E3
Son sentncd for draft evasn 12-19, 980B3
KORDY, Ildiko
Just Like At Home released 4-19, 528F2

KOREA (North), People's Republic of
Armistice Violations (& Developments)
S Korea sinks spy ship 7-21, 567C3
DMZ tunnel discovered 9-1, 709E3
Foreign Relations (misc.)
Aides in Cambodia escape to Thailand 1-8, 10A1
South exchng on peace talks 1-19, 1-25, 1-26, 69A3
New panel in S Korea talks sought 2-5; talks renewed 2-17, fail 3-7, 180C2
South talks deadlocked 3-14; renewal fails 3-26, 4-1, 4-10, 341C3
UN head visits, seeks mediatn 5-2–5-5, 341F3-342B1
Reunificatn talks asked 7-1, backed 7-4, 494B3-495F1
3-way talks re South opposed 7-10, 537E1
S Korea talks, US troop exit halt linked 7-20, 567A3
S Korea to up defns spending 8-20, 654D1
S Korea teacher arrests linked 8-26, 654A1
US, China discuss 8-28, 644E2
Cambodia exile group formatn disclosed 10-4, 811C2
ROK warns vs moves after Park slaying 10-27, 10-28, 822A1
ROK chrgs WCC bias 11-28, 928F2
China, Japan in pol talks 12-5–12-7, 939F3
Sports
Table tennis championship results 4-10, 527F1
U.S. Relations
US ups army strength estimate 1-3, 38G3
US rights report omits 2-10, 107A2
US maneuvers protested 3-7, 180F2
US confirms mil buildup 6-11, 6-21, 495F1
Carter, S Korea back reunificatn talks 7-1; North vs US role, Carter S Korea visit 7-4, 494B3-495F1
North vs 3-way talks 7-10, US hopeful 7-16, 537E1
US halts S Korea troop exit 7-20, 567A3
S Korea to up defns spending 8-8, 654D1
US, China discuss 8-28, 644E2
DMZ tunnel discovered 9-1, 709E3
US alerts forces in South, warns North 10-26, sees no threat 10-27; US carrier, AWAC planes sent 10-28, 821C1, 822C1

1980

KOLPAKOVA, Tatiana
Wins Olympic medal 7-31, 624B2
KOMOTO, Toshio
Party factn in Cabt, gets minor post 7-17, 539A3, C3
KONAKBAEV, Serik
Wins Olympic medal 8-2, 622F1
KONDRATYEVA, Lyudmilla
Wins Olympic medal 7-26, 624G1
KONECKY, Isobel Robins
Charlie & Algernon opens 9-14, 892B3
KONOMIS, Nicolaos
Named Cyprus educ min 9-9, 749G2
KONUTCHE, Senyi (Niger president)
Ends visit to Syria 6-26, 525G3
KOOL-TV (Phoenix, Ariz. station)
Firebombed 9-30, 835D3
KOOPMANS, Rudi
Mustafa Muhammad TKOs 11-30, 1001B1
KOORNHOF, Pieter G. J. (Piet)
Black visit limits rptd eased 2-7, 195G1
Rpts homelands need forgn aid 2-8, 134E2
Blacks protest Soweto citizenship 10-15, 793E1
Proposes apartheid chngs 10-30, 887C2
KOO Tae Hwoe
Arrested re corruptn 7-19, 566E2
KOPEC, Aleksander
Reaches accord with miners 9-2, 658B2
On econ problems 11-12, 878A3
KOPECHNE, Mary Jo (1941-69)
Kennedy phone record queried 3-12, 184C1
KOPELEV, Lev
Vs Sakharov exile 1-29; Pravda scores 2-3 86C1
Wife censured re Sakharov 3-12, 3-15, 181C3
Sovts expel 11-12, 863G1, A2
KOPELSON, Arnold
Foolin' Around released 10-17, 836G2
KOPITUK, Dorthy
Sentenced 1-11, 64A2
KOPITUK, Raymond
Sentenced 1-11, 64A2
KOPLIAKOV, Sergei
Wins Olympic medal 7-21, 623G2
KOPPLER, Heinrich
SPD win linked to death 5-11, 390E3
KORBAN, Gennady
Wins Olympic medal 7-24, 624B3
KOREA, People's Republic of (North Korea)—*See also NONALIGNED Nations Movement*
Armistice Violations (& Developments)
S Koreans kill 3 infiltrators 3-23, sink spy boat 3-25, 220E2
2 die in DMZ clash, US warns North 3-27; UN blames North 3-28, 365F2
S Korea KCIA head named 4-14, 295A1
ROK force spots N Korean boat 6-20, sinks 6-21, 499A3
S Korea chrgs mil moves 6-30, 525B2
Kim denies tunneling, infiltratn 7-18, 547C1
N Korea resumes DMZ loudspeaker speeches 9-4, S Korea vs retaliatn 9-6, 945E1
S Korea accused of raids 9-25, 737C1
S Korea kills 3 infiltrators 11-4, 903A2
S Korea kills infiltrators, sinks boat 12-2, 12-6, 945D1
Foreign Relations (misc.)
In S Korea talks; premr conf, hot-line reopening agreed 2-6, 89E3
USSR Afghan support barred 2-6—2-7, 109A2
S Korea talks on premr conf held, progress seen 2-19, 3-4, 181D3
Kim pays Sihanouk fare to US 2-22, 141F2
USSR-US detente scored in US pres hopeful's 'basic speech' 2-29, 207A3
S Korean talks 3-18, 4-1, 365G2
S Korea says foments riots 5-18, 380G2
China doubts attack on South, Japan warns vs attack 5-27, 422A1
S Korea talks delayed 6-24, 547F1
S Korea CP law repeal demand dropped 7-18; reactn 7-21, 547A1, D1
S Korea talks canceled, Chun scored 9-25, 736G3
US rpts arms sales to Iran 10-8, 757F2
China airspace for Iran airlift rptd 10-8, 774F2
Kim gives reunificatn terms 10-10, 10-12, 792C3
S Korea denounces unity plan 10-15, 809F3
S Korea sees invasn threat 12-13, 953D1
Government & Politics—*See also other appropriate subheads in this section*
Party cong elevates Kim Chong Il 10-10—10-14, 792A3
Sports
Moscow Olympic results 7-20—8-3, 588B3, 622E1, 624D2, C3, D3
U.S. Relations
US amb's pol gaffes rptd 1-30, 200C2
US issues rights rpt 2-5, 87C2
Reagan 'basic speech' scores Sovt-US detente 2-29, 207A3
US warns vs South intervention 5-19, 380F3; 5-22, 394C3-395A1
US rep visits 7-18, sees more ties 7-20, 547A1
US rpts arms sales to Iran 10-8, 757F2
US S Korea troop exit, US pact asked 10-12, 792D3
US, S Korea discuss invasn threat 12-13, 953D1

1976

KOREA (South), Republic of—*See also ADB*
Oil discovered near Pohang 1-15, 54B1
Listed as 'partly free' 1-19, 20D3
Canada A-reactor agrmt 1-26, 103C3
French A-plant purchase canceled, US pressure cited 1-29, 1-31, 103G2
Ex-Dep Kim denied passport 2-6, 122A1
2 reporters jailed 2-8, 121G3
Payoffs to 2 US reps probed 2-19, 171D1
Anti-Park statemt signed 3-1; 17 dissidents detained 3-4, 176E2
11 dissidents arrested 3-10; freed 3-11, 223B1
400 univ profs ousted 3-12, 223F1
Choi elected premier 3-12, 223A2
More crackdowns warned 3-16, 223G1
Australia trade talks rptd 3-23, 237A2
Total IMF oil loan rptd 4-1, 340D2
US bars shoe import curb 4-16, 322C1
Plotters, dissidents sentncd 4-22, 4-30, 5-3, 334B2
Giscard on A-sale cancelatn 5-20, 372E2
New Dem Party split 5-25, Kim reelectn ruled invalid 6-10, quits 6-11, 440E2
North vs visit plan 6-9, 440B3
US Dem platform text cites 6-15, 478D2
Carter on troops, repressn 6-23, 451D3
Churchmen deny Red links 6-26, 540G1 ★
US arms aid authorizatn signed 6-30, 533D1
Asks N-S pol talks resumptn 7-4, 557G2
Detained clergymen freed 7-6, 7-8, 540E1
US urges 4-power talks, Kim asks N-S cong 7-22, 557C2
China urges US pullout 8-15, 619F1
US GOP platform text cites 8-18, 609D2, 610A2
US repeats 4-power talks call 8-19, 619A1
Nonaligned conf vs US presence 8-20, 621A3; US scores 8-25, 626D1
18 dissidents sentncd 8-28, 655C1
US' Carter for more rights 9-8, 664B3
US ends '50 emergency 9-14, 689B2
Rev Moon ends US ministry, 9-18, 970E3
Social controls imposed 9-19, 734A1
Limb dies 9-21, 1015G1
US asks 'phased' talks 9-30, 719E2
US arms credits signed 10-1, 806F3
China scores US role 10-5, 760A1
Ford, Carter debate 10-6, 741E2
Japan ldr vs Kim kidnaping 10-13, 838E3
US influence peddling, KCIA harrassmt probes rptd 10-24—12-1, 898D3-900B2; 981F1; 12-7, 919A2
Ford vs troop pullout 10-26, 803B1
Bid-rigging of US mil contracts chrgd 10-27, 982A2-A3
KCIA rpts N Korea spy surrenders, 12 seized 10-30, 910B3
Kim reactn to US electns 11-3—11-4, 826A2
Canada A-sales irregularities rptd 11-22, 904C1; probe opens 11-30, 923B3
Canada probe continues 12-2—12-9, 962C3
Cabt shift, KCIA head ousted 12-4, 928F2
Kim Ok Son convicted 12-7, 928A3
2 trade unionists jailed 12-15, 1013G2
Canada to audit A-sale agent 12-22, 998D1, F1
Flying Tiger gifts rptd 12-29, 986F1
18 dissident convctns upheld 12-29, 1013F2

Armistice Violations—*See under KOREA (North)*

1977

KOREA (South), Republic of
Park foes ask end to curbs 1-14, 1-26, 116G3 ★
Capital shift planned 2-10, 116E3
'76 econ growth rptd 2-16, 147C2, E2
Dissident jail terms upheld, antigovt charter aired 3-22, 306B1
Govt anticorruptn drive 4-2, 306F1
Police raid vs dissidents 4-12, govt on raid 4-19, 305F3
RC declaratn scores govt 4-18, 306E1
Assemb asks end to emergency law 7-6, 551E3
14 dissidents freed 7-17, Park foes questn move 7-19, 551C3
2,123 prisoners freed 8-15, 711B1
Textile growth curb ordrd 10-5, 804D3
Univ students demonstrate 10-7, 804C3
Freight train explodes 11-11, 928B3
Park reshuffles Cabt 12-20, 1017C1

Armistice Violations—*See under KOREA (North)*

Foreign Relations (misc.)—*See also 'Monetary, Trade & Aid' below*
Japan concerned re US pullout 1-18, 60C2
Japan reassured on US pullout 3-22, 209F2
Amb to Canada named KCIA agent 6-5, 442A1
Canada A-agency head fired 7-7, 541E3
Tito, Kim ask troop pullout 8-29, 709G3
Amnesty Intl lists jailed lawmakers 9-5, 753C2
EC textile pact reached 12-2, 998C1

1978

KOREA (South), Republic of—*See also GATT*
A-bomb seen unlikely before '84 1-26, 61C2
Dissidents score Park rule 2-24, 135E2
GNP, other econ data rptd 2-27, 340B3, D3
Kim quits New Dem Party 3-29, 269E3
NDP bars natl conv 4-17, 377F3
Electoral panel protests, arrests 5-8—5-9; 18 rptd released 5-10, 377E3
Pres electors chosen, Park assured reelectn 5-18, 377D3
Opposition ldrs detained 7-5, 538B2
Park reelected 7-6, 538A2
5 seized in housing scandal, others probed 7-14, 594D3
A-arms effort rptd 11-1, 862D3
Kim Dae Jung, others freed 12-27, 1022D1
Park inaugurated 12-27, 1022D1

Armistice Violations—*See under KOREA (North)*

Foreign Relations (misc.)—*See also 'Monetary, Trade, Aid & Investment' below*
PI rebels free natl 2-2, 248C2
Laos, Viet bar from air lane 2-11, 140B1
N Korea econ compared 2-27, 340E3
N Korea, US talks rptd opposed 4-5, 4-19, 277A3
Japan LDP ldrs rptd vs China talks 4-7, 278C2
Jet downed over USSR, 2 die 4-20; Sovt, passenger versns differ 4-21; passengers returned to Tokyo, Seoul, 2 crewmen detained 4-22—4-24, 301G3
N Korea spy boat rptd sunk 4-28, 340F3
USSR frees crewmen 4-29, 318D1
China backs N Korea on merger, US mil presence 5-5—5-10; S Korea scores 5-11, 340D2
USSR chrgs US puppet regime 5-7, 349B3
USSR role in '50 war chrgd by US 6-7, 423D3
N Korea ties effort scored; North seeks US talks, vs slow mil exit 6-23, 497E2
Japan warns vs US exit, cites Sovt threat 7-28, 585A3
Afghan cuts ties 9-18, 738D2
Japan ties China pact to reunificatn 10-18, 802B1

1979

KOREA (South), Republic of—*See also GATT*
Kim scores Park 1-2, police questn 2-10, 116A3
16 dissidents freed 5-12, 389E3
Dissidents chrg more govt curbs 5-27–6-21, 469F3-470B1
Kim Young Sam elected NDP head 5-30, 469F3
Independents join governing party 6-7, 470B1
Anti-govt rally blocked 6-18, 469E3
63 dissidents detained 6-28, 495C1
86 dissidents freed 7-17, 567B3
PEN asks 2 dissidents' freed 7-21, 554A1
New Dem Party paper seized, ed jailed 7-31; hq raided, 198 arrested 8-11, 617C3
Christian teachers chrg torture 8-6–8-10, 654A1
10 rptrs sentenced 8-24, 654B1
NDP sit-in ends, Seoul police chief ouster sought 8-28, 653F3
NDP ousts Kim 9-8; students protest 9-11; Kim scores US 9-16, 710F2
Yulsan Group pres sentncd 9-14, 710D3
Kim Dae Jung contacts barred 9-16, 710C3
Assemb ousts Kim Young Sam 10-4, 762F2
Assemb oppositn members quit 10-13, 794A3
Pusan anti-govt riots, 10-16–10-17, martial law imposed 10-17, 794F2
Masan, Changwan unrest erupts 10-18–10-19; troops move in 10-20, calm prevails 10-21, 803B2
Seoul seminary shut 10-20, 803D2
Unrest injuries, arrests tolled 10-21, 803E2
Park, 6 bodyguards slain; Kim, 5 KCIA aides seized 10-26; death rpts differ 10-26, 10-28; martial law set 10-27, eased 10-30, 821A1-G2
Choi named acting pres 10-26, appeals for unity 10-27, 821B1, 822A1
Kim Young Sam deplores Park death 10-28, 822A1
Park funeral held 11-3, 843D3
Ex-Pres Yun on Park funeral com 11-3, freed from house detentn 11-6, 843E3, 844D1
NDP ldr asks charter chng 11-4, 844B1
Assemb meets, oppositn continues boycott 11-5, 843G3
Park slaying rpt issued, Kim plot chrgd 11-6, 843D2
Electn plans set, govt foes score 11-10, 875B2
Ruling party picks leader 11-12, 875E2
DRP, NDP form charter com 11-17, 951G3
Anti-govt unrest; dissidents seized, martial law ldr denounces 11-24–11-28, 928A2
Park assassinatn trial suspended 12-4, 928F1
Choi elected pres 12-6; dissident decree lifted 12-7, 68 freed 12-8, 951E3-952D1
Choi names premr 12-10, Cabt 12-14; inaugurated 12-21, 997E1
Army rebels seize martial law head, 16 officers re Park murder 12-12; cmnd shift rptd 12-13, 959A3
7 get death for Park slaying 12-20, 997C1
Gen Chung formally detained 12-24, 997E1

Armistice Violations—*See under KOREA (North)*

Atomic Energy & Safeguards
A-power progrm to continue 4-6, 323C2
Westinghouse reactor deal set 8-3, 742A2

Bank Issues
4 bank chiefs ousted in bankruptcy scandal 4-13, 287A2
10 bank dirs replaced 4-29, 324E1
Banks rptd among '78 world's top 300 6-19, 476C2

Economy & Labor—*See also 'Bank Issues' above*
Defense outlay increase OKd 8-8, 654C1
GNP '79 growth drops 12-5, 997A2

Foreign Relations (misc.)
North exchng on peace talks 1-19, 1-25, 1-26, 69A3
North for new panel in talks 2-5; talks renewed 2-17, fail 3-7, 180C2
North talks deadlocked 3-14, renewal fails 3-26, 4-1, 4-10, 341B3
Forgn currency diversn scandal 4-13, 287B2
Japan seeks reduced US role 5-2, 320D2
UN head visits, seeks mediatn 5-2–5-5, 341F3-342B1
Reunificatn talks asked 7-1, N Korea backs 7-4, 494B3-495F1
N Korea vs 3-way talks 7-10, 537E1
N Korea talks, US troop exit halt linked 7-20, 567A3
USSR allows reps at pol sci mtg 8-12–8-18, 637B1
US, China discuss 8-28, 644E2
N Korean DMZ tunnel discovered 9-1, 709E3
USSR publisher entry bar scored 9-4, 690A2
Australia trade accord rptd 10-16, 788C1
ROK warns North vs moves after Park slaying 10-27, 10-28, 822A1
Iran holds natl in US Emb 11-5, 841E1; frees 11-22, 895A3

1980

KOREA, Republic of (South Korea)—*See also ADB, GATT*

Armistice Violations—*See KOREA, People's Republic of--Armistice Violations*

Atomic Energy & Safeguards
Canada prov sets uranium ban 2-27, 148E2

Economy & Labor
Won devalued, interest rates raised 1-12, 101E1
Defns-GNP ratio rptd 2-19, 132G1
Won float set, $ value rptd 2-27, 196A1
Labor unrest rptd 4-30, 374E3
Shin sees 'econ bankruptcy' re unrest 5-15, 380C3
Strikes banned 5-18, 380F2
Govt purge continues 7-19, 566D2
New business policy unveiled 9-29, 809C3
Econ stimulus moves rptd 11-12, 944G3-945D1

Foreign Relations (misc.)
'79 trade rptd, '80 estimated 1-12, 101E1
'80 acct deficit estimated 1-12, 101F1
In N Korea talks; premr conf, hot-line reopening agreed 2-6, 89E3
N Korea talks on premr conf held, progress seen 2-19, 3-4, 181D3
Canada prov sets uranium ban 2-27, 148E2
N Korean talks 3-18, 4-1, 365G2
N Korea cited re KCIA apptmt 4-14, 295B1
Tito funeral held 5-8, 339B1
N Korea riot role chrgd 5-18, 380G2
China doubts North attack, Japan warns vs attack 5-27, 422A1
N Korea delays talks, chrgs Kwangju atrocities 6-24, 547F1
Deficit estimate revised up 7-1, 499C3
N Korea drops demand for CP law repeal 7-18; reactn 7-21, 547A1, D1
World Bank '80 loans rptd 9-22, 720E1
N Korea cancels talks, scores China 9-25, 736G3
N Korea gives unity terms 10-10, 10-12, 792C3
N Korea unity plan denounced 10-15, 809F3
Japan vs Kim Dae Jung death sentnc 11-4, 11-28, 11-29, 12-7; Japan scored 11-26, 944B3

1976

Sports
Olympic results 7-18—7-31, 573D3, 574G3, 575A1, 576C2, C3

1977

Monetary, Trade & Aid Issues (including all foreign economic developments)—*See also 'U.S.' subheads below*
Danish shipyd decline rptd 1-17, 62B1
Canada bars UDI books in A-sale probe 2-1, 114G1
Airbus use cited 4-28, 441F2
Japan oil pact effected 6-8, 467G1
Import curbs eased 6-14, 470G2
UK natlizes shipbldg 7-1, 526D2
Japan briefed on US pullout plan 7-27, 572A2
N Korea sea zones opposed 8-2, 591B1
Eur textile import curbs seen 10-5, 804D3

U.S.-Korean Political Payments
US probes Burmah paymts to Park 1-19, 55A2
Mondale visit declined 1-28, contd aid vowed 2-1, 69G2
US House lobbying probes OKd 2-3, 2-9; ethics com info access agreed 6-8, 442F1
CIA paymts to Rhee rptd 2-19, 124F1
US House adopts ethics code 3-2, 173C2
E-Systems paymts rptd 3-10, 233B3
Ex-KCIA head details lobbying effort 6-5—6-7, 441A3
US subpoenas 2 Amers in Korea 6-18, 556B3
Pres mansion tap rptd 6-19, 556C3
Park order to end scheme rptd 6-20, 556E3
Kim Hyung Wook testifies in US 6-22, rpts Park threat 7-2, 556F3
Assemb asks US act vs unfair bribery chrgs 7-7, 551F3
Thomson denies KCIA link chrg 7-7, 556G3
Caputo to seek Nixon tapes 7-7, 557A1
Ethics com survey rptd 7-11, 557B1
House ethics com probe dispute rptd 7-12, counsel quits 7-15, replaced 7-20, 7-21, 556E1
US spec prosecutor sought 7-16, Carter bars 7-18, 556C2
$200,000 gifts chrgd 7-26, 688F2
US info sharing agreed 8-3, 688C2
US Sen lobbying role seen 8-8, 688D2
CIA denies Park taps 8-9, 688E2
Ethics com questns Thomson 8-17, 8-25, Park interview rptd foiled 8-20, 688G1, C2
Park denies KCIA agent chrg 8-24, 687C3
Kissinger, Haig cover-up rptd 9-5, 688F1
Park indicted, 3 others named co-conspirators; campaign gift recipients listed 9-6, 687D2, 688C1
US seeks Park extraditn, S Korea hedges 9-6, 9-8, 687E3
Ties rptd strained, close House aid vote cited 9-8, 774A2
KCIA NY head defects 9-16, 774C2
Carter immunity offer to Park rptd 9-17, refusal seen 9-21, 774G1
Kim Han Cho indicted; FEC chrmn, US rep cited 9-27, 773B3, F3 ★
SEC accuses Park, others, Diplomat bank 9-28, 774B1
Sen questionnaires sent 10-5, response rptd 11-19, 915B3
Kim Han Cho pleads not guilty 10-6, 816C3
O'Neill rent records subpoenaed 10-7, 816D3
'70 Pentagon knowledge rptd 10-12, 816E3
Hanna indicted; Price, Patten, 2 ex-KCIA heads named 10-14, 815F3
US fails in Park interrogatn bid 10-16—10-20, 816D1
US House ethics com hearings 10-19—10-21, 816A2, D2 ★

1978

China backs Kim on reunificatn 10-25, 802D1
Japan '71 Park paymts rptd 11-1, 862D3
North protests joint cmnd 11-8, 872C3
USSR Pacific buildup rptd 11-9, 914G1
China-US tie reactn 12-15, 977E1

Monetary, Trade, Aid & Investment—*See also 'U.S.' subheads below*
EC imposes steel dumping levies 1-23, 80B2
Canada A-sale probe com rpts 2-27, 166A3
EC seeks steel export agrmt 3-2, 158C2
NZ fishing accord signed, steel deal rptd 3-13, 498F1
Jan-Apr trade deficit, acct deficit up 5-10, 378A1
N Korea vs trade bid 6-23, 497D2
Trade group arrives Japan 10-15, 798C1
USSR, US clash on arms sales, talks stalled 12-5—12-15, 996A3

U.S.-Korea Political Payments
US House seeks Korea cooperatn 1-4—1-23; Park testimony OKd, Kim Dong Jo immunity affirmed 1-31, 63G3
Justice Dept, Korea sign Park testimony deal 1-10, 1-11; terms rptd 1-13, 63G2-B3
Park testifies in Korea 1-13—2-1, total paymts rptd 1-14; House incumbents seen implicated 1-20, 1-26, 63A2, F2, C3
Kim Dong Jo testimony sought 2-22, 3-9; rptd 'bigger fish' than Park 2-28, 203G3, 204A1, C1
US Cong presses Korea cooperatn, warns aid blocks; Brown opposes 2-22, 204B1
Dissidents accuse Park govt 2-24, 135E2
House ethics com hears Park Tong Sun 2-28—3-9, 203C3
Park testimony to Justice Dept re KCIA links rptd 3-1, 203E3
US House Intl Relatns subcom hearings 3-15—3-22, 203C1-C3
Pres Park implicated 3-15, 3-21; role denied 3-17, 203D1-A2
Unificatn Church, KCIA link probed by US House com 3-15—3-22, 203D1
Ex-rep Hanna pleads guilty, Park Tong Sun, Kim roles cited 3-17, 202E3
Dem, GOP contributns claimed 3-21, 3-22; Dems deny 3-21, 203A2
FBI memos to Nixon offcls probed, Mitchell testifies; NSA probe curb disputed 3-21, 3-22, 203C2
Ex-rep Passman indicted 3-31, 239B1
Kim Dong Jo access rptd possible 3-31, 239D3
Park testifies at House ethics com open session, denies Korean agent 4-3—4-4; testimony disputed 4-4, 4-5, 239G1-D3
Hancho Kim convicted 4-8, 279A3
Weicker quits Sen ethics com in jurisdictn dispute, Stevenson defends probes 4-14, 279E3
Kissinger testifies 4-20, 280A1
Hanna sentenced, calls Justice probe 'overzealous' 4-24, 323F3-324A1
Passman indicted on tax chrgs 4-28, 324B1
Hancho Kim sentenced 5-19, 406A2
Kim Dong Jo paymts to US reps rptd 5-22—5-25, 432B3
US House com res links aid, Kim Dong Jo access 5-24, 406B2
US rice dealer chrgd 5-26, 432E3
US House votes aid warning, Kim access 5-31; US, Korea reactn 5-31—6-1, 432F1
Justice Dept sees probe indictmts end 6-1, 432G2
Nixon ex-aide testifies 6-1, 433A1
Moon subpoenaed by US House subcom, departure rptd 6-6, 433C1
US Sen ethics com rpts McClellan gift from Park, 3 others dispute chrgs 6-19, 527D2

1979

N Korea WCC bias chrgd 11-28, 928F2
Jan-Nov trade up, record deficit seen 12-5, 997B2
China, Japan in pol talks 12-5—12-7, 939F3

Sports
WBC flywgt title bout 3-18, 412E3

U.S.-Korea Political Payments
US Justice closes Bayh perjury probe 1-5, 4A3
Hancho Kim loses appeal 3-12, 209E1
Passman acquitted 4-1, 265B3
Galifianakis, Hancho Kim indicted 4-10, 283C2
Connell prosecution dropped 4-16, 283D2
Hancho Kim indictmt dismissed 6-15, 521A2
Galifianakis chrg dismissed 8-3, 630A2
Park indictmt dropped 8-16, 630D1-A2
KCIA ex-chief rptd missing 10-25, 810C3
McDonnell Douglas paymts alleged 11-9, 886G1, D2

1980

N Korea invasn threat seen 12-13, 953D1

Government & Politics—*See also other appropriate subheads in this section*
Park aide's death sentnc commuted 1-30, life sentnc upheld 5-19, 395G1
Kim Dae Jung challenges Kim Young Sam NDP role 3-1, 195E3
Park plotter executed 3-6, 195E3
Chon heads KCIA 4-14, 295A1
Charter draft com meets 5-19, Assemb loses charter role 6-2, 430G2
Premr Shin's govt resigns 5-20, 380D2
New Cabt formed, Park Choong Hoon named premr 5-21, 395C1
Kim Dae Jung chrgd as plotter 5-22, 395E1
Park slayer, 4 others executed 5-24, 395F1
Pres Choi visits Kwangju 5-25, 394B3
Security com formed, Chon heads 5-31, quits KCIA post 6-2, 430E2
Chon extends power, overshadows Cabt 6-4; govt denies mil power rules 6-16, 466G3-467C1
10 chgd with corruptn, to quit politics 6-18, 499F2
KCIA purged 6-20, 499E2
232 high govt offcls purged, others probed 7-9, 525G1-A2
Gen Yu named KCIA head 7-14, takes office 7-18, 566A2
Govt purge continues 7-15, 7-19, 17 arrested 7-19, 566B2
Journalists, educators purged 7-24—8-1; Kim Dae Jung indicted 8-1, 17 sentenced, purge ends 8-2, 620A3
Chun promoted to full gen 8-6, sees mil ldrship 8-8, 620F2
Kim Dae Jung trial 8-14—9-13; gets death sentnc, 23 others jailed 9-17, 711C1
Choi resigns as pres 8-16, Chun nominated 8-18, 628B1, 645B2
Chun quits mil 8-22; elected pres, names 2 civilns to key posts 8-27, 645G1
Chun sworn pres, vows martial law end 9-1; names Cabt 9-2, 673A1, C1
Kim Dae Jung backers trial ends 9-8; 25 sentncd 9-11, 711A2
Voters back new charter 10-22, results rptd 10-23, 809A3
Kim Dae Jung death sentnc upheld by mil ct 11-3, appeals to Sup Ct 11-8; US, Japan vs death 11-4—12-7, 944F2-B3
811 politicans purged 11-12, 874G2
Media regrouping ordered 11-14, 888A1
Party ban eased 11-21, 903G1

Sports
Park loses WBC flywgt title 5-18, 1000F3

Unrest
'79 protesters sentncd 1-25, 2 spared 1-29, 101C1
687 dissidents amnestied 2-29, 195B3
Student unrest 3-19—5-10, 375A1
Seoul riots 5-12—5-15, 380B3
Govt urges calm, vows reforms 5-15; students call off rallies 5-16, 380C3
Total martial law imposed, govt foes seized 5-18; Kwangju riots 5-19—5-20, 380D2-B3
Rebels seize Kwangju 5-21; govt troops retake 5-27, 394E2
Kwangju rebels rptd sought 5-28; rebellion rpt links Kim Dae Jung 5-31, 430D3
9,000 detainees freed 8-30, universities reopened 9-1, 673B2
Korea Univ closed after riots 10-17, 809G3
Pol prisoners guaranteed human rights 10-22, 809B3
Kwangju rioters sentncd 10-24, 944F3
8 pol prisoners freed in unity bid 12-11, 968E1

1976

KOREAN Cultural and Freedom Foundation (Washington, D.C.)
Influence peddling probed, NY to seek fund-raising bar 10-30—11-2, 899C2
KOREAN War (1950-53)
US CIA arms purchases cited 4-26, 299G3
Reagan vs limited war 5-21, 374G1
Veneris US visit OKd 6-29, 484F2
Mondale, Dole debate 10-15, 782A3
Ford, Carter debate 10-22, 800F2
KORHONEN, Keiko
Sworn Finnish forgn min 9-29, 750D3
KORMANN, Peter
Wins Olympic medal 7-23, 574B3
KOROL, Piotr
Wins Olympic medal 7-21, 576E2
KORRY, Edward M.
On Anaconda anti-Allende move 12-23, 999B2
KORSHUNOVA, Tatyana
Wins Olympic medal 7-30, 574A2
KORSMO, Lisbeth
Wins Olympic medal 2-8, 159A1

1977

Derwinski probed re KCIA defector 10-28, 816F3
House asks Korea aid ethics probe, Park testimony bid 10-31, 915C1
Passman gift of $190,000 rptd, denied 11-2, 915C2
Carter on Park immunity offer, scores Korea 11-5, State Dept negotiatns continue 11-30, 915E2
Ford-Kim Han Cho mtg bid, rejctn rptd 11-11, 915A2
'76 influence plan documt disclosed 11-29, 914G2
Park diary rptd sought by IRS 11-29, 915A3
E-Systems vp, Korean Resrch Inst probed 11-29, 915D3
KCIA bid to block Kim Hyung Wook testimony chrgd 11-30, 914F3
Passman records subpoenaed 11-30, 915E2
Albert, record subpoenas rptd 12-1, 915F1
Park testimony deal OKd, Jaworski scores 12-30, 1002A3

U.S. Relations—*See also other 'U.S.' subheads in this section*
Shoe-import injury ruled 1-6; Carter bars curbs, talks underway 4-1, 248D1, D2-B3
US notes rights abuses 2-23, 126E2; bars aid cutoff 2-24, 142F1
US bars aid cut despite rights abuses 2-24, 142F1
US adopts fishing agrmt 3-3, 173D3
TV import injury ruled 3-8, tariff hike asked 3-14, 208D3
US issues rights rpt 3-12, 187B1
Mar fishing violatns rptd 270C2
US cong group visits; meets Park, dissidents 4-12, 305E3
US concerned over rights 4-13, 305E3
Moon denied NYC tax exemptn 4-14, 310F1
US clerics asks Carter aid govt foes 4-19, 305C3
US amb scored 4-20, 306A1
US shoe export pact draft OKd 5-16, 416C2, F2
Shoe export pact signed 6-21, 587E2
US dvpt policy bill signed 8-17, 667A3
US briefs on Vance China missn 8-27, 664E2
US aid cut amendmt defeated 9-8, 774A2
NY KCIA head defects 9-16, 774B2
Witteveen scores shoe pact 9-26, 753F3

U.S. Troop Pullout
Japan concerned re US exit 1-18, 60C2
NDP warns vs US pullout 3-7, 203A1
US plans exit, stresses rights 3-9; NDP, govt protests 3-12, 3-16, 202D3, 203B1
US reassures Japan on exit 3-22, 209F2
US missile pullout starts 4-14, 306A2
US House vs troop cuts 4-25, 324E1
US Gen Singlaub removed for policy criticism 5-19—5-25, 403G2-404G1; Carter defends ouster 5-26, 417A2
US sets exit 5-24—5-26, timing detailed 6-5; Park foes protest 5-26, 440E3
Sen backs exit policy compromise 6-16, 477D3
US careful procedure urged 7-6, 551F3
Park-Brown talks 7-25—7-26; US to keep bulk until '82 7-26, 572D1-C2
US policy dvpt bill signed 8-17, 667B3
Tito, Kim urge quick exit 8-29, 709G3

KOREAN War (1950-53)
Melvin Vorhees dies 2-6, 164F3
US-China finance talks rptd 5-1, 333C2
KORRY, Edward M.
Rpts CIA, multinatls anti-Allende drive 1-9, 1-11, 16B2
Frei rpts regrets 2-21, 219C2
KORUTURK, Fahri (Turkey president)
On May Day violence 5-3, 351B1
Asks Demirel to form govt 7-4, 530D2
KOSCIUSKO-Morizet, Jacques
Gets US protests on Daoud 1-13, 1-14, 28B1
KOSNER, Edward
Disputes CIA link 9-12, 720G3

1978

US House votes food aid cutoff 6-22, 467B2-A3
Kim Dong Jo resigns 6-23, 527E2
US House ethics com cites 4 reps for misconduct, clears O'Neill 7-13, 527A1-C2
Boeing chrgd re payoffs 7-28, 642G3
Jaworski quits US House ethics probe 8-2, evaluates results 8-7, 604D3-605D1
US House ethics com OKs Kim written testimony 8-3, 605D1
US House reprimands 3 reps 10-13, 831D3-832A1
US Sen probe ends 10-16, 832C1
US House Intl Relatns subcom details lobbying, asks Unificatn Church probe; reactn 11-1, 862A3, F3
McFall loses US House seat; Patten Roybal, Wilson reelected 11-7, 849C1, 856B3
Wilson, Roybal exempted from US House ethics rule chng 12-6, 958D2

U.S. Relations—*See also other 'U.S.' subheads in this section*
CIA sees no A-bomb before '84 1-26, 61C2
US issues rights rpt 2-9, 101D3; dissidents score 2-17, arrests rptd 2-17, 2-21, 135B2
US to bolster air power 2-18, 135G2
US affirms Asia commitmt 2-20, 126D3
Eximbank loan, mil aid linked to lobbying probe cooperatn 2-22, 204B1, D1
US-Taiwan textile pact rptd 2-27, 140C3
CIA compares N, S Korea econ 2-27, 340B3
S Korea oppositn to talks with North, US rptd 4-5, 4-19, 277A3
US, Japan mediate USSR release of Korean jet passengers 4-20—4-23, 302F1
USSR chrgs puppet regime 5-7, 349B3
Brzezinski visits 5-24—5-25, 399C2
Carter chrgs USSR '50 war role 6-7, 423D3
US lauds trade bid to N Korea; North bars, seeks US talks 6-23, 497F2
US bars stainless steel utensil tariff hike 7-2, 805G1
Mil talks, North threat seen 7-26—7-27, 594G3
US vows 'support' vs North attack 7-27, 595A1
US defns equipmt transfers authorized 9-26, 734F2
US defns equipmt transfers authorized 9-26, 734F2
Defns Secy Brown visits 11-6—11-8; joint cmnd set 11-7, protested 11-8, 872B3, D3
USSR Pacific buildup rptd 11-9, 914G1
US, USSR clash on arms sales, talks stalled 12-5—12-15; US rift rptd 12-19, 996A3
US sen questns US-China tie 12-15, 976B1
US-China tie reactn 12-15, 977E1
McDonnell Douglas paymts rptd 12-15, 982F2

U.S. Troop Pullout
US troop presence rptd 1-2, 5D2
US '77 rpt warns vs cuts 1-6, 5E3
Brown warns vs aid bar 2-22, 204E1
US to slow exit 4-21; S Korea lauds, USSR scores 4-22, 301C3
China backs N Korea on US mil exit 5-5—5-10; S Korea scores 5-11, 340E2
US House fails to block exit 5-24, 406G3
Brzezinski visit fails to calm fears 5-29, 399D2
US gen scores troop exit 6-2, 433B2
N Korea vs slow exit 6-23, 497F2
Japan warns vs exit 7-28, 585A3
US defns equipmnt transfers authorized 9-26, 734F2
US defns equipmt transfers authorized 9-26, 734F2
China urges exit 10-25, 802C1
House subcom links A-arms effort, lobbying cover-up 11-1, 862D3, F3

KOREAN Air Lines
Plane downed over USSR 4-20, 2 crewmen detained 4-24, 301G3
USSR frees crewmen 4-29, 318G1
KOREAN War (1950-53)
US gives ex-PW honorable dischrg 8-31, 843F3
KOREY, William
Vs UN pro-Palestinian drive 10-7, 762C3
KORGURE, Michiyo
Geisha released 6-1, 619B2
KOROM, Mihaly
Named Hungary SWP Central Com secy 4-20, 534C2
KORRY, Edward M.
Cover-up chrg vs US re ITT, CIA Chile role rptd 3-21, 206E3

1979

U.S. Relations—*See also other 'U.S.' subheads in this section*
N Korea armed strength compared 1-3, 39B1
US color-TV export limit OKd, '78 data cited 1-17, 160A2
War debt to US rptd past due 2-5, 84B3
US issues rights rpt 2-10, 107E3
Student enrollmt in US rptd 167E2
Dissidents get US note on rights 3-7, 389G3
US airlift exercise 3-8—3-10, 180F2
Japan seeks reduced role 5-2, 320D2
Dissident releases tied to Carter visit 5-12, Kim Dae Jung vs visit 5-15, 389E3
Dissidents seek to air grievances 6-11; Carter visit, dissident curbs linked 6-21, 470A1
Dissidents detained re Carter visit, US scores 6-28, 495C1
Carter visits, meets Park, dissidents; joint communique 6-29—7-1, 494B3-495C1
N Korea vs US role in reunificatn talks 7-4, 495E1
N Korea vs 3-way talks 7-10, 537E1
86 dissidents freed 7-17, 567B3
Westinghouse reactor deal set 8-3, 742A2
Carter discloses Park conversn effort 8-5, 639B2
ROK to increase defns outlay 8-8, 654D1
US deplores oppositn party hq raid 8-14, 617E3
US, China discuss 8-28, 644E2
US assn scores USSR publisher entry bar 9-4, 690A2
Kim scores Carter visit, US policy 9-16, 710B3
US vs Assemb ouster of Kim Young Sam 10-4, recalls amb 10-5, 762F2
US newsman barred 10-13, entry OKd 10-14, 803B3
Mil conf held; US to weigh intl dvpt loans 10-17—10-19, 803E2
US amb returns 10-17, 803A3
Park gets Carter note on dissidents 10-18, 803F2
US alerts forces; warns Korea 10-26, sees no threat 10-27; US carrier, AWAC planes sent 10-28, 821C1, 822C1
Carter lauds Park 10-27, 822G1
US asks orderly transitn 10-30, 822F1
Vance, Chip Carter at Park funeral; Vance meets offcls 11-3, 843F3
Army revolt spurs US concern 12-12, protest over joint cmnd troop use 12-15, 959D3, F3

U.S. Troop Pullout
US House panel vs pullout 1-3, 39C1
Japan seeks reduced US role 5-2, 320D2
N Korea vs 3-way talks 7-10, 537G1
US halts exit 7-20, move hailed 7-21, 567F2-B3
N Korean DMZ tunnel discovered 9-1, 709G3

KOREAN Airlines
Owners named in McDonnell Douglas paymts chrg 11-9, 886D2
KOREAN Evangelical Church
Peoples Temple bldg bought 3-14, 220G1
KOREAN War (1950-53)
Forgn debt to US rptd past due 2-5, 84B3
KORIR, Amos
Shares 6000-m relay mark 4-28, 911A3
KORNIYENKO, G. M.
Cited in SALT II summit communique 6-18, 457D1

1980

U.S. Relations—*See also 'U.S. Troop Pullout' below*
Carter cites US policy 1-23, 42G1
US amb's pol gaffes rptd 1-30, 200C2
US issues rights rpt 2-5, 87A2
Won float set, $ value rptd 2-27, 196A1
US seeks TV import curbs extensn 5-13, 368A2
US deplores crackdown, warns North 5-19, 380E3; 5-22, 5-27, 394C3-395C1
US sends air, naval reinforcemts 5-22, 395A1
Kwangju rebels ask US set truce 5-26, 394C3
US wary of mil's power 5-28, 6-2, 430B3
US retaliates vs Chon power extensn 6-12, 461D1
2 US MDs arrested, freed 6-28, 499F3
TV import curbs eased 6-30, 515C3
US rep visits N Korea 7-18; reactn 7-21, 547A1, D1
Chun pres support denied 8-8, 620A3; 8-11—8-16, 645B2
Kim Dae Jung leniency pleas rejected 8-15; sentncd to death 9-17, 711G1, B2
Chun support qualified, govt reforms asked 8-28, 673F1
US amb at Chun inauguratn 9-1, 673E1
Reagan electn welcome 11-5, 841E2
Kim Dae Jung death sentnc opposed 11-18, 11-19, 12-6, 944G2-B3
Defns Secy Brown sees Chun; pleas for Kim, discusses N Korea threat 12-13, 953D1

U.S. Troop Pullout
China concerned re US presence 1-8, 11E2
Connally cites in 'basic speech' 3-7, 184G3
US Army sgts recalled 9-5; combat divisn drain cited 9-8, 683D3
N Korea urges 10-12, 792D3

KORF Industries Inc.
Steel trigger price return suit dismissed 5-16, 455E3-456A1
KORF-Stahl, A.G.
Kuwait 25% interest rptd 6-25, 562E1
KORIR, Amos
Wins Penn Relays 6,000-m medley 4-25; IC4A outdoor 3,000, 10,000-m runs 5-24—5-25, 892B2, C2
KORMAN, Harvey
Herbie Goes Bananas released 9-12, 836B3
KORNILAEV, Sergei
Wins Olympic medal 7-29, 624C3
KOROLKOV, Nikolai
Wins Olympic medal 8-3, 622G2
KORUTURK, Fahri (Turkish president)
Mil warns pol ldrs, urges unity 1-2, 7A2
Gens seek united parties 1-2, 22E3
Pres electn deferred 3-22, 236E1, G1
Pres term ends 4-6, 278B2
KORVETTES Inc.—*See AGACHE-Willot*
KOSCIELNIAK, Zdzislaw
Union registratn conditns scored 10-24, 830D3
KOSEDOWSKI, Krzystof
Wins Olympic medal 8-2, 622F1
KOSEKI, Kip
Wins Drake Relays 5,000, 10,000-m runs 4-25—4-26, 892F2
KOSHKIN, Alexander
Wins Olympic medal 8-2, 622A2
KOSTELANETZ, Andre
Dies 1-13, 104A3

1976

KORUTURK, Fahri
Signs Iran, Pak econ pact 4-22, 298A2
US offers quake aid 11-25, 897D1
KOSAKA, Zentaro
Japan forgn min 9-15, 694E1
KOSCIUSKO-Morizet, Jacques
Offers US bicentennial gifts 1-12, 80A3
KOSEDOWSKI, Peszik
Wins Olympic medal 7-31, 574B1
KOSENKOV, Alexander
Wins Olympic medal 7-22, 575D3
KOSHEVAIA, Marina
Wins Olympic medals 7-21, 7-24, 575A3
KOSHEVOI, Marshal Pyotr
Dies 8-30, 892A3
KOSIC, Karel
CIA-RFE link chrgd 3-10, 289G2
KOSLO, William J.
Indicted 2-18, stiffer penalties asked 10-5, 886E1; sentncd 11-30, 921G2
KOSTANTINOV, Lev
USSR chrgs Austria internmt 2-4, 122C2
KOSTELANETZ, Andre
Lily Pons dies 2-13, 160G3
KOSTMAYER, Peter H.
Elected 11-2, 830E3
KOSTOV, Dimo
Wins Olympic medal 7-31, 576E3
KOSYGIN, Alexei
Rpts to CP cong on economy 3-1, 194B3
Politburo named 3-5, 195C2
In Iraq 5-29—5-31, Syria 6-1—6-4, 385B2, 406F2
Rptd ill 8-30; aide named 9-2; appears in public 10-18, 857A2
At Warsaw Pact summit 11-25—11-26, 896E3
KOSZEGI, Gyorgy
Wins Olympic medal 7-18, 576D2
KOTAIDA, Manubhai
Backs coalition break 3-22, 222D1
KOTCHIAN, A. Carl
Testifies re Lockheed payoffs 2-6, 130D3; Japan exec denies chrgs 2-16, 132F1
Sees Japan Soclst delegatn 2-12—2-13, 132E1, 190B3
Quits Lockheed post 2-13, 131D1
Subpoenaed by Japan Diet 2-26, 190F2
Settles SEC suit 4-13, 285G2
Cited in Bernhard probe rpt 8-26, 627F3
Rptdly ties Nakasone to Lockheed 677C1
Andreotti denies payoffs 8-31, letters publshd 9-1, 684C3
On Kodama-Osano link 838B3
KOTEI, Brig. Robert
Acting army cmdr 11-14, 1003F2
KOULIDIATI, Capt. Jean-Luc
Killed 9-14, 949F3
KOUNTCHE, Lt. Col. Seyni
Cabt shuffled 2-21, 205A3
Coup plot foiled 3-15, 205F2
Niger, Algeria, Libya set closer ties 4-8, 372A1
At France-Africa summit 5-10—5-11, 355G2
KOUROUKLIS, Gen. George
Forms new party 11-27, 1004F2
KOVALEV, Vladimir
Wins Olympic medal 2-11, 159B1
KOVENS, Irvin
Mistrial declared in Mandel case 12-7, 922C3
KOVIC, Ron
Speaks at Dem conv 7-15, 506C3 ★
KOVPAN, Valentina
Wins Olympic medal 7-30, 573F3
KOWALIK, Adam
Named trade min 12-2, 926D3
KOYAMBA, Alphonse
Named treas min 9-5, 924F2
KOZNIEWSKA, Halina
State Cncl member 3-25, 268D2
KOZOL, Dr. Harry
Hearst questioning disputed 1-7—1-23, 69D3
Testifies vs Hearst 3-15, 202B2, C2
KRABBE, Hanna
Trial opens 5-6, 503F1
KRAFT, Joseph
FBI files to be destroyed 3-30, 235C1
Pres debate panelist 10-22, 800A1, E1, 801D2
KRAFTCO Inc.
SEC lists paymts 5-12, 728C2
KRAISELBURD, David
Kidnaped 9-1, 996F3
KRAISELBURD, Raul
Son kidnaped 9-1, 996F3
KRANISH, Arthur
On CIA AIAA briefing 3-15, resignatn request rptd 3-19, 216A3
KRASKO, Wincenty
State Cncl member 3-25, 268D2
KRATOCHWILL, Richard F.
SEC sues, settles 6-29, 984B2
KRATSCHMER, Guido
Wins Olympic medal 7-30, 576C1
KRATZER, Myron B.
Says S Korea cancels French A-plant 1-29, 103G2
Backs S Africa A-deal 5-27, 388E1
KRAUSE, Barbara
Sets world swim marks 6-1—6-5, 424G3
KRAUSE, R. F.
Sentenced 11-30, 921G2

1977

KOSTMAYER, Rep. Peter H. (D, Pa.)
Asks Korea probe spec prosecutor 7-16, 556C2
Asks FBI probe inquiry 12-8, 979F3
KOSTOV, Vladimir Borisov
France grants asylum 7-7, 606G2
KOSYGIN, Alexei Nikolaevich
Sees Castro 4-4—4-6, 249F3
In Finland re trade, A-plant 5-22—5-26, 391A2
Revolutn anniv fete photo 11-7, 865D2
Sadat says sought '71 Meir mtg 12-6, 929F2
KOTCHIAN, A. Carl
Lockheed payoffs rpt accuses 5-26, 502A3
KOTESWAR, Silla
Stabbed 11-28, 966G2
KOUFAX, Sandy
Seaver betters strikeout mark 6-7, 644C2
KOULIDIATI, Capt. Jean-Luc (d. 1976)
Replaced as posts min 1-14, 183B2
KOUMBA, Lt. Brahim Abakar
Named Chad coup ldr 4-6, 490D2
KOVADLOFF, Jacobo
Flees Argentina 6-28, 7-8, 615C1
KOVALEV, Sergei A.
US science acad seeks info 4-27, 315A2
KOVALYONOK, Lt. Col. Vladimir
On Soyuz 25 missn 10-9—10-11, 771C3
KOVENS, Irvin
Convicted 8-23, 652F1, A2
Sentenced 10-7, 807D2
KOWAL, Charles
Rpts 'mini-planet' discovery 11-8, 908C2
KOWALSKI, Robert J.
State police meal stipends taxable 11-20, 919F1
KOYANA, Digby
Scores S Africa shantytown demolitn 8-9, 640D1
KRABBE, Friedrike
Sought in Schleyer kidnaping 10-21, 868C2
KRABBE, Hanna-Elise
Sister sought in Schleyer case 10-21, 868D2
KRAFT, Joseph
Nixon China stand rptd 4-10, 298F2
KRAFT, Tim
Named Carter apptmts asst 1-14, 35B3
KRAFT Inc. (formerly Kraftco Corp.)
Rpts milk discounts 5-22, 503D2
Metro Containers
Strike ends 10-14, 818G3 ★
KRAMBLES, George
Blames motorman in CTA crash 3-16, 412F3
KRAMER, Tommy
In NFL draft 5-3, 353C2
KRASNOFF, Sanford
Loses Cong election 8-27, 693C1
KRATTER, Marvin
Drops Gerovital FDA approval bid 6-2, 508C3
KRATZER, Walter
Czechs detain 2-6, 2-14, 114C3
KRATZERT, Bill
Wins Hartford Open 8-7, 676B2
PGA top money winner 10-30, 950G3
KRAUSE, Dr. Richard
Antiviral drug rptd 8-10, 675E2

1978

KORTY, John
Film wins Oscar 4-3, 315D3
Oliver's Story released 12-14, 1030C3
KORUTURK, Fahri (Turkish president)
Ecevit names new Cabt 1-5, 21C2
KOSCHNICK, Hans
SPD to ease pub employe hiring 10-16, 823G1
KOSTAVA, Merab
Sentenced 5-19, 401D2
KOSTMAYER, Rep. Peter H. (D, Pa.)
Reelected 11-7, 852C1
KOSTOV, Vladimir Borisov
Rpts attack 9-14, 748E3
KOSYGIN, Alexei Nikolaevich
In Japanese peace talks 1-10, 28D3
On USSR downing of S Korean plane 4-21, 302B1
Urges Comecon integratn 6-27, 504G3
Asks US-Sovt trade hike 7-5, 518C3
Offers Dominica ties 11-2, 861E3
Signs Viet pact 11-3, 859E2
Sees record grain crop 11-4, 884C3
Sees US sens, denies Cuba MiG threat 11-16, 905C1, E1
KOTCHEFF, Ted
Great Chefs of Eur released 10-6, 970D3
KOTCHIAN, A. Carl
Files Lockheed bribe case depositn, links Nakasone 10-26, 838E3-839A1
KOTEI, David
Lopez TKOs 2-15, 379B2
KOTEI, Maj. Gen. Robert E. A.
Named Ghana dep ldr 7-6, 515E2
KOUNTCHE, Lt. Col. Seyni
Chad peace plan OKd 2-24, 130B2
KOUSSEVITZKY, Olga
Dies 1-5, 96E2
KOUSSEVITZKY, Serge (1874-1951)
Widow dies 1-5, 96E2
KOVALYONOK, Col. Vladimir
Docks with Salyut 6-17, 505F3
Remains aboard Salyut 7-5, sets space record 8-2, 622D3
Has visitors 8-27, breaks endurance record 9-20, 714A1-D1
Returns to Earth 11-2, 861A1
KOVANKO, Liliga
Near & Far Away released 3-24, 619B3
KQED-TV (San Francisco TV station)
Press prison-data access curbed by Sup Ct 6-26, 566A3
KRABBE, Friedrike
Rptd in Colombia 2-18, 147C3
KRAFT Jr., Christopher
New astronauts named 1-16, 157G3-158A3
KRAFT, Joseph
Rpts US aware of Israel setlmt plan 2-7, 78G1
Haldeman book rpts Nixon tap order 2-16—2-17, 125B1
KRAFT, Tim
Named pol group liaison 4-27, 306G3
KRAG, Jens Otto
Dies 6-22, 540B3
KRALL, Dung
2 convicted on spy chrgs 5-19, 389G3-390A1
KRAMER, Ken
Wins US House seat 11-7, 850D2, 855G3
KRAMER, Terry Allen
Crucifer of Blood opens 9-28, 1031C1
KRANTZ, Judith
Scruples on best-seller list 4-2, 272B3; 4-30, 356G1; 6-4, 460B3; 7-2, 579B3; 8-6, 620A2; 9-4, 708B1
KRASTEV, Gancho
Dismissed as Bulgaria agri min 4-29, 530F3
KRATZERT, Bill
2d in Hawaiian Open 2-5, 355B3
3d in Houston Open 4-23, 355A3
2d in Memorial Tourn 5-21, 580E3
Ties for 2d in Greater Hartford Open 7-30, 672D3
PGA top money winner 10-31, 990B3
KRAUSE, Barbara
Wins 100-m freestyle title 8-28, 780B2
KRAUSE, Charles
Arrives Guyana 11-15, visits cult commune with US delegatn 11-17; survives cult ambush 11-18, rescued 11-19, 889G1-A2
KRAUSE, Petra
'77 Italy extraditn cited 4-12, 438E2

1979

KORUTURK, Fahri (Turkish president)
Chrgs re Kurdish unrest rptd 8-24, 795F3
Demirel govt formed 11-12, 876D1
Meets Pope 11-28, 930C3*
KORVETTES Inc.—*See AGACHE-Willot*
KORYAKIN, Yuri
A-safety article rptd publshd 10-14, 815C2
KOSYGIN, Alexei Nikolaevich
Congratulates Cambodia rebels 1-9, 11G1
Iran govt recognized 2-12, 106A2
Vows aid to Viets vs China 3-1, 159B1
In India 3-9—3-15, signs aid agrmts 3-14, 200A2
Reelected 4-18, 314B1
Sees US reps, backs SALT 4-20, 314A2
India A-plant bid rejctd 5-2, 323F2
In Czech, urges Sovt bloc energy conservatn 5-24, 397B1
Asks India Afghan role 6-14, 443F1
Denies Comecon oil shortage 6-29, 497C2
Gives US sens Backfire pledge 8-30, 657E2
Skips revolutn anniv parade, illness cited 11-7, 856F2
Tikhonov named full Politburo member 11-27, 929C1
Heart attack confrmd 11-28, 929D1
KOTCHIAN, A. Carl
US drops paymts probe 2-15, 306D1
Lockheed pleads guilty, fined 6-1, 422B3
KOTELLY, John
US drops case vs ITT exec 2-8, 88E1
KOTLER, Milton
Vs urban displacemt rpt 2-14, 132C3
KOVALEV, Vladimir
Wins world figure-skating title 3-15, 391E3
KOVALEVA, Elena
Banned from track 10-26, 912A1
KOVALYONOK, Col. Vladimir
Soyuz 32 launched 2-25, 163G1
KOVIN, Vladimir
Sovts win Challenge Cup 2-11, 118E3
KOZAK, Roberto
Rpts Chile refugee relocatn 5-7, 369A3
KOZLOFF, Philip
Rpts condominium trend 6-23, 482G2, B3
KOZLOV, Leonid
Defects to US 9-16, 697C2
KOZLOV, Valentina
Defects to US 9-16, 697C2
KRAAY, Hans
Fired as Drillers coach 7-23, 1004E2
KRABBE, Jeroen
Soldier of Orange released 8-16, 820D3
KRAFT, Tim
Named Carter campaign com dir 8-10, 608F2
Backs Jordan cocaine denial 8-25, 647A2
Challenges Kennedy pres funding 10-4, 783B3
Strauss named Carter campaign com head 11-6, 961B2
KRAMER, Stanley
Runner Stumbles released 11-16, 1008D1
KRAMER, Terry Allen
A Meeting By the River opens 3-28, 712D1
I Love My Wife opens 5-15, 711F3
KRAMER vs. Kramer (film)
Released 12-19, 1007F3
KRANTZ, Judith
Scruples on best-seller list 6-3, 432C2; 7-1 548C3; 8-5, 620D3
Paperback rights sold for record sum 9-12, 755D3
KRATZERT, Bill
Ties for 2d in San Diego Open 1-28, 220D3
2d in Pensacola Open 10-21, 970A2
KRAUS, Sgt. Kenneth
Kidnaped 2-14, freed 2-21, 125A3
KRAUSS, Barry
In NFL draft 5-3, 335F1
KRAUSS, Marvin A.
Teibele and Her Demon opens 12-16, 1007F2

1980

KOSTIC, Petar
Yugo financial controls tightened 9-18, 833G1
KOSTMAYER, Rep. Peter H. (D, Pa.)
Loses reelectn 11-4, 848G3
KOSYGIN, Alexei Nikolaevich (Soviet premier; resigned Oct. 23)
Reappears after illness, scores US 2-21, 153A1
Resigns as Sovt premr, ill health cited 10-23, 797A1
Brezhnev lauds, press ignores resignatn 10-24, 831E3, G3
Death rptd 12-19, 951B1
Death confirmed 12-20, 996G1-B2
KOTELAWALA, John
Dies 10-2, 876C2
KOURIS, George
Sentncd re Caramanlis article 12-30, 996E3
KOURIS, Makis
Sentncd re Caramanlis article 12-30, 996F3
KOVACS, Istvan
Wins Olympic medal 7-31, 624E3
KOVENS, Irvin
Appeal refused by Sup Ct 4-14, 307B1
KOVSHOV, Yuri
Wins Olympic medal 8-1, 622A3
KOWALCYK, Stanislaw
Ousted from Polish Politburo 12-2, 909F2
KOWALCZYK, Jan
Wins Olympic medal 8-3, 622G2
KOZAKIEWICZ, Wladyslaw
Wins Olympic medal, sets pole vault mark 7-30, 589C1, 624C1
KPIX-TV (San Francisco, Calif., TV station)
FCC backs license 1-30, 119C3
KRACHEVSKAYA, Svetlana
Wins Olympic medal 7-24, 624G1
KRAFT, Tim
Vs Carey open conventn proposal 5-5, 342G3
Asks Kennedy quit race 5-6, 342F1
Jordan joins campaign com 6-11, 439A1
Cocain probe rptd, steps down as campaign mgr 9-14, 700B1
Probe suspended 12-12, 989G2
KRAFT Inc.
Dart merger set 6-5, 557D1
Dart pres quits 7-23, 600B3
KRAKER, Steffi
Wins Olympic medals 7-25, 623A1
KRAMER, Rep. Ken (R, Colo.)
Reelected 11-4, 842D2, 851D3
KRAMER vs. Kramer (film)
Top-grossing film 1-9, 40G3; 1-30, 120A3; 2-27, 200G3; 3-26, 280G3; 4-23, 360B3
Wins Oscars 4-14, 296F1
KRAMORENKO, Boris
Wins Olympic medal 7-22, 624A3
KRANTZ, Judith
Princess Daisy on best-seller list 2-10, 120B3; 3-9, 200A3; 4-6, 280A3; 5-4, 359C3; 6-8, 448B3
KRASILNIKOV, Anatoly
Leaves Spain re spy chrg 2-16, 141A3
KRATOCHVIL, Lilada
Defects 3-17, 262E2
KRATOCHVIL, Peter
Defects 3-17, 262E2
KRATOCHVILOVA, Jarmina
Wins Olympic medal 7-28, 624A2
KRATZERT, Bill
Wins Greater Milwaukee Open 7-13, 715D1
Ties for 2d in Buick Open 8-25, 972F1
KRAUSE, Barbara
Wins Olympic medals, sets 100-m freestyle mark 7-21, 7-24, 588G3, 623C3, D3
KRAUSE, Charles A.
Bolivia detains, frees 6-9, 443F2
KRAYNAK v. Marshall
Case declined by Sup Ct 1-7, 15G3

1976

KRDJIC, Gen. Milan
On Yugo mil threat 1-11, 55E1
KREBS, Rep. John (D, Calif.)
Reelected 11-2, 829B1
KREIBOHM, Bernhard
Scores CDU Lower Saxony victory 1-15, 77D2
KREINER, Kathy
Wins Olympic medal 2-13, 158E3
KREISKY, Bruno (Austrian chancellor)
Rpt Wiesenthal ends Nazi hunt 1-9, 97D3
At Europn socialist confs 1-18—1-19, 48A3; 3-13—3-14, 222F3
Visits Prague 2-17—2-19, 289D2
Soclst cong, reelected chrmn 3-11—3-13, 380D2
Sadat visits 4-10—4-12, 275E2
At intl soc dems mtg 5-23—5-25, 449B3
Minority rights bill approved 7-7, 554B3
Scores Argentina violence 8-26, 672D2
KREMERS-Urban International Corp.
Boycott rpt released 10-18, 786B1
KRENWINKEL, Patricia
Denied new trial 8-13, 640C3
KREPS, Juanita Morris
Carter econ adviser 12-1, 898G2
Named Commerce secy; disputes Carter on female apptmts 12-20, 956F1, 957A1
Photo 956C1
Biographical sketch 957B3
KRESS, Stan
Loses US House race 11-2, 824G1
KRIANGSAK Chamanand, Gen.
Denies mil witch-hunt 10-25, 813C3
KRIEGER, Gabriella Teldman
Hint Uganda hijacker 7-5, 485G2
KRIEGSMAN, Alan M.
Wins Pulitzer 5-3, 352E3
KRIEL, Gen. David
Sees worse unrest 11-3, 856B1
KRIMSKY, George
Sovt press chrgs CIA link 5-25, 5-26, 371B3, E3
KRIS Sivara, Gen.
Dies 4-23, 315E1
KRISTOFFERSON, Kris
Wins Grammy 2-28, 460C3
KROC, Ray
'72 campaign gift listed 4-25, 688B1
KROLIKOWSKI, Herman
Rues border shooting 8-6, 589B3
KROLIKOWSKI, Werner
E Ger Politburo enlarged 5-22, 381E2
KRONGARD, Robert R.
Slain 8-28, 652G1
KRONK, Paul
Runner-up in US Open doubles 9-12, 716D1
KRONMARK, Eric
Named to Swedish Cabt 10-8, 794C2
KROVOPUSKOV, Vikor
Wins Olympic medal 7-22, 574E2
KRUCZEK, Wladyslaw
State Cncl member 3-25, 268C2
KRUEGER, Rep. Robert C. (D, Tex.)
Loses gas deregulatn fight 2-5, 108G2-109A1
Reelected 11-2, 830E4 ★
KRUGER, James T.
On guerrilla recruiter arrests 4-26, 428G3
Police chrgd in Mduli death 6-11, 428E3
On township violence 6-17, 426D1, E2; 6-19—6-21, 447F1, C2
On riot death, arrest toll, says riots organized 6-25, 500G1, C2, F2
Denies riot victims mass funeral 6-30, 500E2
Sets security measures 7-15, 539F2
On rioting 8-4, 8-8, 8-12, 579C2, 580F1
Scores black-power ideology 8-19, 639E3
On Soweto death toll 8-27, 652G3
Extends ban on mtgs 9-2, 662C1
Rpts detainee total 10-19, 794E1
Sees unrest manageable 11-5, 856B1
Offers student refugees amnesty 11-15, 927E1
On Johannesburg bombing 12-8, 927B1
Rpts prison inspectn, schl reopenings 12-8, 927C1
Detainees freed 12-20—12-28, 1010D2
KRUGER, Marise
Wins Tennis Week Open 8-29, 716A2
KRUGLOV, Nikolai
Wins Olympic medal 2-6, 159F1
KRUMM, Philip
US vs Taiwan ruling 7-12, 7-17, 529B1, D1
KRUPINSKI, Lt. Gen. Walter
Dismissed 11-1, 930E3

1977

KRECH, David
Dies 7-14, 604C3
KREDIETBANK S.A. Luxembourgeoise
1st ¼ Eurobond trading rptd 4-13, 318E1
KREISKY, Bruno (Austrian chancellor)
Warns vs Czech dissidents deportatn 1-27, 1-31, 82C3
Sees PLO moderatn 2-13, 107G1
Sees Clifford 2-16, 122A2
In Tel Aviv 2-23, 425G1
In US talks 3-14, 425E1
Defense chief resigns 5-30, 424E3-425A1
Tax protesters petitn 9-13, 763A2
Denies shilling devaluatn 9-28, 10-3, 763D1
Presents austerity plan 10-3, 762E3
Czech trade talks open 11-22, 936G2
KREPS, Juanita Morris
Confrmatn hearing 1-10; confrmatn recommended 1-19; confrmd 1-20, 34B1, A3
On public works aid 2-3, 89E2
Rpts personal finances 2-25, 148B1
Sees USSR '77 import cut 6-10, 530E1
Addresses govs conf 9-8, 719B2
KRESGE Co., S. S.—*See K mart Corp.*
KRESHOWER, Merylee
Krishna indictmts dropped 3-17, 287A2
KREVER, Horace
RCMP probe set 12-1, 945B2
KRIANGSAK Chamanand, Gen. (Thai premier)
Says Pol Pot named CP head 8-19, 741F2
Joins mil coup 10-20, 827A1
Named premr 11-11, forms Cabt 11-13, 904D3
Warns Cambodia re clashes 12-22, 999C3
KRIEGEL, Frantisek
Austria offers asylum 1-25, refuses 1-28, 82C3, D3
KRIMSKY, George
USSR asks removal 1-24, ousts 2-4, 101C1
LA Times rptr held 6-11—6-15, 474D3
KRIPILANI, J. B.
Picks Desai as prime min 3-24, 205D1
KRISHNA Consciousness, International Society for
Indictmts dismissed 3-17, 287F1
Patrick sentncd for deprogramming 3-28, 287E1
Jewish trend evaluated 4-18, 492F2
Bhaktivendanta dies 11-4, 952C2
KROC, Ray
Bavasi quits Padres 9-20, 768E2
KROCHER, Norbert
12 plotters indicted 7-25, 709G1
KROCHER-Tiedemann, Gabriele
Swiss arrest 12-20, 1017E3
KRUEGER, Judge Moria Mackert
Elected judge 9-7, 712D1
KRUGER, James T.
On detainee deaths 1-26, 1-27, 100F3; 2-23, 160F2
On Johannesburg unrest 6-13, 469B1
On Biko death 9-14, 707G3
Biko death disputed 9-14—9-17; ouster asked 9-19, 735C2
Disputes Biko death press rpts 10-7—10-12, 804D2-B3
Explains black ban, foes denounce 10-19, 804A1
Blames US for unrest 10-21, 825E1
Rpts prelim Biko autopsy 10-21, 825F1
Reaffirms black ban, detentns; eases press curbs 10-23, 825G1
Confrms Biko autopsy rpts 11-9, 887B2
Rptr gets damages for false arrest 11-18, 935F1
KRUISINGA, Roelof
Named Dutch defns min 12-19, 986A1
KRUMM, William
Replaced as USOC pres 4-29, 491A3

1978

KREISKY, Bruno (Austrian chancellor)
Visits USSR, sees Brezhnev 2-6—2-8, 110C2
Sees Sadat, arranges Peres mtg 2-11, 98G2
Bars UN troop role in Leb 3-29, 214C1
Arranges Sadat-Peres talks, gives peace plan 7-9; plan made public 7-10, 521B2
On A-plant vote 10-23; voters rejct 11-5, 878G3-879D1
KRENTZMAN, Judge Ben
Gurney trial press-curb review declined by Sup Ct 4-17, 308D2
KREPS, Rep. John (D, Calif.)
Loses reelectn 11-7, 856C3
KREPS, Juanita
Heads export expansn study group 4-11, 260G1-A2
On 1st ¼ real GNP drop 4-19, 303B3
Wis U computer research secrecy order lifted, probe vowed 6-12, 514C1
Warns on Propositn 13 6-21, 526D1
Export promotn plan set 9-26, 804C2
US trade missn to Japan arrives 10-2, lauds trade curb removals 10-3, sees Fukuda 10-5, 797D3, 798A1
In US-USSR trade talks 12-4—12-7, 966B1
KRESS, Stan
Wins Idaho US Sen primary 8-8, 625F3
KRIANGSAK Chamanand, Gen. (Thai premier)
Cambodia mil role disputed 2-10, 2-16, 121B2
Sees Mondale 5-4, 360F3
Shifts Cabt, takes defns post 8-13, 691B2
Viet premr visits; econ, refugee agrmts reached 9-6—9-10, 696E1-A3
Lauds US-China tie, Taiwan link 12-16, 977D1
KRIM, Arthur B.
Resigns from United Artists 1-13, 75A3
KRISHNA Consciousness, International Society for
· Argentina '76 ban cited 208E1
KRISTOFFERSON, Kris
Convoy released 6-28, 619C1
KRIVACS, Jim
Texas wins NIT, named co-MVP 3-21, 272A2
KROC, Ray
Vs Kuhn bar on Blue sale 3-3, 194F3
KROCHER-Tiedemann, Gabriele
Cited in death of Swiss cop 4-12, 438G2
Swiss trial opens 4-25, 353E3
Swiss jail 6-30, 558F2
KROLL, Fred J.
Pullman porters join BRAC 2-28, 185D2
On new pact, Norfolk & Westn rail strike 7-14, 565F1
KRON-TV (San Francisco, Calif.)
Sex abuse suit OKd by Sup Ct 4-24, 322B2
Sex abuse suit vs NBC dismissed 8-8, 635C2-A3
KRUEGER, Rep. Robert (D, Tex.)
Wins US Sen primary 5-6, 362F3
Loses electn 11-7, 846B2, 855C3, D3
KRUGER, James T.
Qoboza, others freed 3-10, 193E2
Rpts '77 detainee deaths 4-24, 377G2
Admits Biko probe errors, closes case; '77 deaths cited 5-17, 455F3
Sets detainee death probe 7-11, 535F3
KRUGER, Marise
Wimbledon results 7-7, 540A1
KRUISINGA, Roelof
Vs neutron bomb 2-23, 140A3; 2-24, resigns 3-4; Parlt OKs anti-bomb resolutn 3-8, 169D1, B2
KRUMMHEUER, Eckert
Finds bomb in car 5-31, 439F2

1979

KREBS, Eric
King of Schnorrers opens 11-28, 956C3
KREISKY, Bruno (Austrian chancellor)
Wins 4th term 5-6, 352B1
Sees Arafat, scores Israel setlmts 7-6—7-8, 511A3
Details US amb-PLO mtg 8-22, 625B1
KREPS Jr., Clifton H.
Suicide fails 6-29, 527G2
Wife leaves Cabt post 10-4, 829C2
KREPS, Juanita
On Taiwan, China, US trade ties 1-15, 27B3
On 1st ¼ GNP rpt 4-19, 280B2
Arrives Peking 5-5, 352G3
Opens trade talks, pacts initialed 5-7—5-14, 369G3-370F1
Husband's suicide fails 6-29, 527G2
China trade pact signed 7-7, 523C2
Resigns as Commerce secy 10-4, 829B2
Klutznick named successor 11-16, 883C3
KREVER, Horace
Health plan probe continues 3-9, 189B3
KRIANGSAK Chamanand, Gen. (Thai premier)
In US, meets Carter; arms aid vowed 2-6—2-7, 84A2
Signs Laos peace pact 4-4, 298D2
Electns held, power seen unabated 4-22, 314D2
New Cabt rptd named 5-25, 428F3
Asks Pol Pot halt refugee flow, China accept Cambodians 6-12, 436B1
Cambodia refugee ousters delayed 6-25, 474F1
Cambodian refugee vow rptd 6-30, 550G1
Sees war, famine threat to Cambodians 8-30, 684C2
To accept Cambodian, Laotian, Viet refugees 10-19, 811G2
Meets Viet aide on border feud 10-19—10-20, 811D3
Mrs Carter visits refugee camps 11-8—11-10, 863G1
KRIEK, Johan
US Open results 9-9, 734D1
Loses Swiss Indoor 10-21, 1003E3
KRISHNA Consciousness, International Society for
LA sues re solicitatns 1-25, 102F1
Ind solicitatn rights case refused by Sup Ct 11-26, 919F2
KRISTEL, Sylvia
5th Musketeer released 9-7, 820B1
KRISTOFFERSON, Kris
Performs in Cuba 3-1—3-4, 238D2
KROC, Ray
Rpts record baseball fine; to give up Padres operatn 8-24, 1003A1
KROGER Co.
Ads ruled deceptive by FTC 6-21, 596C2
KROGH, Egil
Adams cites Nixon appointmt 7-20, 530B3
KROLL, Fred J.
39-mo pact reached 1-13, 87G1
KRONES, Kip Richard
Festival opens 5-7, 711A3
KRUEGER, Robert
Named Mex amb-at-large 6-22, Lucey resigns 10-8, 793D3
On Mex oil blowout cleanup cost 8-23, 689B1
KRUEGER, Steve
Arkansas 2d in NCAA baseball final 6-8, 569B3
KRUGER, James T.
Censors scandal rpt 3-12, 191E1
Named Sen pres 6-14, 469G2
KRUMHOLZ, Normal
Scores neighborhoods panel rpt 3-15, 208A3

1980

KREISKY, Bruno (Austrian chancellor)
PLO aide given special status 3-13, Arafat lauds 3-15, 205G3-206B1
Kirschschlager reelected pres 5-18, 388F1
In Iran hostage missn 5-25—5-26, warns vs new sanctns 5-27, 394C1
Hosp scandal spurs reforms proposal 9-3, reforms OKd, Androsch to comply 9-9, 705D2
Androsch wins confidence vote 10-8, 870F3
Androsch sets resignatn 12-11, 964C2
KREISSER, Jurgen
Arrested as spy 11-10, 925G2
KREMBER, Jane
Sentenced 12-19, 997C3
KREMER, Elena
Seeks W Ger asylum 8-19, 908E1
KREMER, Gidon
Seeks W Ger asylum 8-19, 908E1
KRESS & Co., S. H.—*See GENESCO Inc.*
KRIANGSAK Chamanand, Gen. (Thai premier; replaced Mar. 3)
Shifts Cabinet 2-11, 196F3
Quits as premr 2-19, replaced 3-3, 196D3
KRIEK, Johan
Loses Frankfurt WCT tourn 3-23, 607A3
Loses Stowe Grand Prix 8-17, US Open semi-finals 9-6, 691B2, C3
KRISTEL, Sylvia
Nude Bomb released 5-9, 675B3
KRISTOFFERSON, Kris
Heaven's Gate withdrawn from theaters 11-19, 906B1
KROESON, Gen. Frederick J.
Orders sex harassmt crackdown 4-23, 347E3
KROL, John Cardinal
Meets with Reagan 9-8, 699B3
KROLL, Fred
Abstains on Carter endorsemt 8-20, 647A3
KRONE, Gerald S.
Home opens 5-7, 392C3
KRONENBERGER, Louis
Dies 4-30, 360C2
KRONSBERG, Jeremy Joe
Any Which Way You Can released 12-17, 1003F1
KROVOPUSKOV, Viktor
Wins Olympic medal 7-25, 622B3
KROWN, Kevin
Indicted in offshore bank fraud 10-20, 860B3
KROWN, Dr. Susan
On interferon study 5-28, 526E2
KRUCZEK, Wladyslaw
Ousted from Polish Politburo 12-2, 909F2
KRUGER, Karl-Heinz
Wins Olympic medal 8-2, 622G1
KRUGLOV, Pvt. Aleksandr
Flees to US Emb in Kabul 9-15, 704G2; leaves 9-21, 727A2

1976

KRUPP GmbH. Fried.
China chem plant deal rptd 1-6, 78B1
Iran buys interest 10-19, 782C2
Iran buys into 2 Brazil cos 11-23, 949E1
KRUPSAK, Mary Anne
Supports Carter 6-14, 432C1
Speaks at Dem conv 7-12, 509D1
KRUZENSHTERN (USSR sailing ship)
In Operation Sail 7-4, 488A3
KUBADINSKI, Pencho
On Bulgaria Politburo 4-2, 250C1
KUBEL, Alfred
Retires, Christian Dem succeeds 1-15, 77G1
KUBITSCHECK, Juscelino
Dies 8-23, 836F2
KUDO, Akira
Wins Olympic medal 7-31, 576C3
KUHLMAN, Kathryn
Dies 2-20, 192E3
KUHN, Bowie
US-Cuba baseball series barred 1-7, 23E1
Voids Blue, Rudi, Fingers sale 6-18, 444C3
Yankees walkie-talkies stir Series dispute 10-16—10-17, 815E2
KUHN, Hildegard
Named in Getty will 6-8, 444D2
KUHNE & Nagel Inc.
Boycott rpt released 10-20, 786B2
KU Klux Klan (KKK)
3 freed in '57 slaying 4-15, 316D2
Sen rpt cites FBI informer 4-28, 327A3, 330G2
Assault by black marines probed 11-13—12-6, 983C1
Carter church ends black ban 11-14, 864G2
KUKRIT Pramoj
Asks rice price rise 1-1; protested 1-5, plan withdrawn 1-6, 30G3
Expands coalition 1-6, shifts cabt 1-8, 30E3
Resigns 1-12, 30C3
In ASEAN-Australia talks 1-16—1-17, 46D1
Signs ASEAN pact 2-24, 148D2
Socialist leader slain 2-28, 176E3
On collapse of US base talks 3-20, for smooth US exit 3-22, 223D2
Loses electns, Seni to replace 4-4, 255C3 ★
Seni sworn 4-22, 315D1
KULAGIN, Boris
On Sovt hockey 1-5, 56C2
KULAKOV, Fyodor D.
Politburo, Secretariat named 3-5, 195C2, F2
At Bulgaria CP Cong 3-29—4-2, 250E1
KULAKOVA, Galina
Olympics penalize re drug use 2-7, 158A3
Wins Olympic medals 2-7, 2-10, 159D1
KULCSAR, Gyozo
Wins Olympic medal 7-23, 574F2
KULIKOV, Gen. Viktor G.
Ustinov named defense min 4-29, 334A3
KULIKOV, Yevgeny
Wins Olympic medal 2-10, 158E3
KULSKI, Julian S.
Dies 8-18, 656F3
KUNAYEV, Dinmukhamed A.
Politburo named 3-5, 195C2
KUNSTLER, William M.
Williams freed 1-16, 79D1
2 cleared in SD '75 FBI deaths 7-16, 640F2
KUON Samelith, Lt.
Rpts executions 5-7, 350D1
KUO Yu-hsin
Taiwan electn fraud rptd chrgd 1-2, 123F1
KUPCHAN, Morris S.
Dies 10-19, 892B3
KUPFERMAN, Justice Theodore R.
Nixon disbarred in NY 7-8, 493F3
KURAMOTO, Koji
Wins Olympic medal 7-29, 574G3
KURILE Islands
USSR, Japan talks fail 1-10—1-13, 30B1
KURON, Jacek
Italy CP asks clemency for food rioters 7-20, 543D3

KUWAIT—*See also ARAB League, NONALIGNED Nations Movement, OPEC*
Iran recalls amb 1-7, 12G3
French Mirage purchase cited 1-16, 36C2
Listed as 'partly free' 1-19, 20C3
Sahara plea rptd 1-29, 58D2
Rpt 30,000 Pak residents 2-8, 121A2
Angola MPLA recognized 2-23, 163E2
Total IMF oil loan rptd 4-1, 340F2
'75 oil output down 4-25, 298A3
Maestrone confrmd US amb 4-28, 412F1
'75 Uruguay trade rpt 7-9, 542G1
Libya min of state visits 7-18, 548C2 ★

1977

KTIMATIAS, Ioannis
Sentncd in Davies murder 6-21, 530E2
Sentncd for '74 riot role 6-21, 764E2
KUBISH, Jack B.
Replaced as amb to Greece 7-13, 626E3
KUCINICH, Mayor Dennis J. (Cleveland)
Elected Cleveland mayor 11-8, 855F1, F2
Police dispute ends 12-16, 1005F1
KUHN, Bowie
Clashes with Finley over player sales 2-18—4-7, Finley loses suit 3-17, 310A3
On Cuba games 3-8, 181C1
OKs Cuba exhibitn games 4-11, 283B2
Vs Turner mgr role 5-13, suspensn power upheld 5-19, 567C3
Sets HOF selectn review 8-7, 644C1
Baseball owners fail to agree on DC team 8-17, 768B1
'No-litigatn' clause upheld 8-30, 768E1
On Oh HR record 9-5, 748A3
Alters HOF entrance rule, expands selectn com 10-3, 768G1-A2
House subcom probes TV sports 11-2, 949F3
Lifts Turner suspensn 12-8, 990D2
Says Blue trade questnable 12-9, 990A1
KUHN, Heinz
On N Rhine A-plant ban 1-13, 117A3
KUHN Loeb & Co.
Plans Lehman Bros merger 11-28, 1004F2-A3
KUHRMEIER, Ernst
Arrested 4-24, 350G2
KUJAWA, Leonard J.
Vs 2d Panama canal 7-25, 589G3
KUKLARNI, Sumitra
Quits Congress Party 3-2, 205G2
KU Klux Klan (KKK)
Byrd elected majority ldr 1-4, 6B1
Ga rally upset by car crash 7-2, 540A1
Ohio rally disrupted 7-4, 540D1
Ohio anti-busing rally 9-5, 838C1
Chambliss convicted 11-18, 907G2
FBI Cointelpro papers released 11-21, 940B3
KULIKOV, Marshal Viktor G.
Named Warsaw Pact cmdr 1-9, 47B3
Named marshal 1-14, 88G1
KUNNERT, Kevin
LA player injures rival 12-9, fined $10,000 12-12, 990B3
KUNZE, Reiner
Emigrates 4-14, 314D3
KUO Wei-cheng
Heads Chengchow rail post 1-3, 1D1
KUPCHAK, Mitch
Named to NBA all-rookie team 5-16, 584F3
KURDS—*See IRAQ—Kurdish Dispute*
KURILE Islands
Japan protests Sovt fishing curb 2-26, USSR rejcts 3-8; talks at impasse 3-31, 250B1
Sovt-Japan impasse continues 4-13—4-14, 4-16, 319F1-E2
Japan extends territorial waters 4-28, 5-2, 411E2
KURON, Jacek
Rpts dissident journal seized 12-20, 987C2

KUWAIT—*See also ARAB League, NONALIGNED Nations Movement, OPEC*
UN Assemb member 4C1
Black Africa funds vowed 3-7, 170A2
Gulf group aids Egypt 3-25, 390D3
Sovt mil aid pact signed 4-13, 394D3
Venez pres visits 4-23—4-25, 362A1
Intl consortium OKs Egypt aid 5-11—5-12, 390C3
Middle East jet hijacker seized 6-6, 497C3; freed 8-29, 736B2
Palestinians hijack jet 7-8—7-10, 535B1
Mediates Egypt-Libya feud 7-24—7-25, 570A1

1978

KRUPP G.m.b.H. Fried.
Iran completes purchase paymts 7-27, 617B1
KRUPSAK, Lt. Gov. Mary Anne (D, N.Y.)
Rpts Radio City Music Hall rescue plan 4-13, 293D1
Loses primary for gov 9-12, 716A2
KRYSKOW, Dave
Winnipeg wins WHA title 5-22, 458C2
KSTP-TV (Minneapolis TV station)
NBC drops fall TV lineup 11-29, 1030D1
KTOQ (Rapid City, S.D. radio station)
SBA loan guarantee to TV host rptd 11-16, 919D3
KUCINICH, Mayor Dennis J. (Cleveland, O.)
Fires police strikers 7-13, 565D2
Wins recall vote 8-13, 663A2
City default dvpts 12-12—12-28, 1008B3
City defaults, Muny Light issue cited 12-16, 1008G1-A2, G2-A3
Brother arrested 12-18, 1008G3
Clashes with Forbes 12-28, 1008B2
KUCINICH, Perry
Arrested 12-18, 1008G3
KUDO, Masashi
Decisns Gazo 8-9, 969D1
KUHN, Bowie
Cancels Blue sale to Reds 1-30, 20 owners back 3-3, 194G2
Bars role in Blue trade to Giants 3-16, 194G3
Calls off A's sale 3-27, 354G3
Upheld again on player sales 4-7, 355F1
Women rptrs gain locker room access 9-25, 1026C3
Authority challenge refused by Sup Ct 10-2, 751A2
Urban League seeks Griffith punishmt 10-2, 779F2
Scores free-agent system 12-5, 3-div plan to be pursued 12-7, 1026B2, C2
KUHN, Heinz
Replaced as N Rhine-Westphalia premr 9-19, 725G3 ★
KUHNE, Marie Peary
Dies 4-16, 356A3
KUHNEN, Michael
Arrested 7-24, 652B1
Arrested again 8-4, 652D1
KUHUWAEL, Theo
Shot 1-29, 90D3
KU Klux Klan (KKK)
Reusch loses Ohio primary 6-6, 448D1
100 parade in Fla 7-8, 529C2
FBI informant rptd agent-provocateur 7-9, 7-11; Justice probes violence, cover-up 7-12, 527E3-528B2
King murder link rptd probed 11-22, 938F2
KULAKOV, Fyodor Davidovich
Dies 7-16, 620G2
Politburo apptmts rptd 11-27, 924E3
KULIKOV, Evgeny
Heiden breaks 1000-mtr speed-skating mark 3-12, 316C3
KULKO v. Superior Court
Calif jurisdictn in child-support case denied by Sup Ct 5-15, 387G3
KUMALO, Dumisani Shadrack
US asylum request rptd 4-20, 314B3
KUMP, Peter
Modigliani opens 5-17, 760E2
KUNERALP, Nekla
Slain 6-2, 476D3
KUNERALP, Zehi
Wife slain 6-2, 476D3
KUNNERT, Kevin
Traded to Clippers 7-7, 655A3
KUO Mo-jo
Dies 6-12, 540B3
KUO Wei-cheng
Chinese rail min 10-26, 837G3
KUPCHAK, Mitch
Bullets win NBA title 6-7, 457A2
KURDS—*See also IRAQ—Kurdish Dispute*
In anti-shah protests 11-16, 993C3
KURENS, Philip
Denies GSA kickbacks 9-19, 714F3
KURFESS, Charles F.
Loses primary for Ohio gov 6-6, 448C1
KURILE Islands
Japan-Sovt talks deadlocked 1-9—1-10, 28C3
Japan rejcts Sovt peace bid 2-22, 121G3
Japan protests Sovt maneuvers 6-7, 585B3
KURISU, Gen. Hiroomi
Loses mil post 7-25, 574C2
KUROSAWA, Akira
Dersu Uzala released 1-13, 619E1
KURSCH, Donald
Ousted by USSR 1-19, 39F1
KURTZ, Swoosie
History of Amer Film opens 3-30, 760D2

KUWAIT—*See also ARAB League, GATT, NONALIGNED Nations Movement, OPEC*
Freedom House lists as partly free 44F1
Kuwait city expenses rated 1-14, 28B3
Heavy crude oil price discount, OPEC OK rptd 2-2, 158A3
Cyprus jet hijackers denied landing 2-18, 117A2
Econ dvpt plans rptd slowed 2-20, 122E1, G1
Islamic, Arab poor-natn aid rise rptd 4-9, 257C2, F2
PLO aide slain 6-15, 489A2
Leb Pres Sarkis asked to stay on 7-9, 522C1

1979

KRUPP G.m.b.H. Fried.
USSR steel deal rptd 3-26, 237D3
US bank attaches Iran assets 11-28, 896F2
KUBACH Trucking Co.—*See under F.C.S. Industries*
KUBOTA, Enji
Japan defense min 11-8, 874G2
KUBRICK, William
VA malpractice award reversed by Sup Ct 11-28, 944C3
KUCINICH, Mayor Dennis J. (Cleveland, O.)
Voters OK tax rise, Muny Light retentn 2-27, 150B1
Seeks state purchase of city notes, vs control bd 2-28, 150F1
Cleveland Trust cleared 3-14, 204E2
Repaymt plan agreed 6-9, 519E3
City default tied to recall moves 7-17, 579A3
Forbes acquitted 7-18, 580F1
Muny Light rpts '78 profit 7-29, 580D1
Cleveland defaults again 8-31, 920G2, A3
Survives primary vote 10-2, 829C1
Loses reelectn 11-6, 846G1, F2
KUDO, Masashi
Decisns Gonzalez 3-14, 412E3
KOs Gonzalez 6-20, 839A1
KUEHNEN, Michael
Sentncd re neo-Nazi activity 9-13, 733E3
KUHN, Bowie
Carew traded to Angels 2-3, discloses $ deal ban 2-4, 619F1
At All-Star Game 7-17, 568F3
Mays to cut baseball ties 10-29, 1002G3
Warns Martin 11-29, 1002D1
Warns owners on free agents 12-3, 1002D2
KUHN, Maggie
Joins Citizens Party 8-1, 594F3
KUHNS, William G.
On GPU dividend, salary cuts 4-26, 322C2
KUHRMEIER, Ernst
Chrgd re Chiasso scandal 2-15, 137D1
Sentenced 7-3, 505C2
KU Klux Klan (KKK)
FBI informant's extraditn OKd 2-7, 120C1
Membership growth, renewed activity rptd 3-15, 7-22, 11-11, 865A1
Parades, black clashes in Ala 5-26, 6-9, Ga 8-18; Calif 8-19, 865E3-866B2
Calif klansman sentncd for '78 murder 6-19, 492G1
FBI sued over '65 Liuzzo death 7-5, 521D1
Military activity rptd 7-23, 561C3
200 marchers arrested in Ala 8-12, 631A1
Navy orders anti-racist policy 8-29, 664F2
NC Communists clash 7-8, 5 slain in anti-KKK rally, 14 chrgd 11-3; Carter orders probe 11-6, 864C2-865D3
West Pt hazing scandal rptd 11-9, 868A3
22 arrested in NJ 11-24, 991C3
14 indicted in NC anti-KKK rally deaths 12-13, 991E3
KULUKUNDIS, Eddie
Once A Catholic opens 10-10, 956F3
KUNG, Rev. Hans
Censured, scores Vatican actn 12-18, 999B2
KUNNERT, Kevin
Walton compensatn set 9-18, 1003D2
KURAISHI, Tadao
Japan justice min 11-8, 874G2
KURDISTAN (British tanker)
Splits off Nova Scotia 3-15, 201D1
Oil loss rptd 8-15, 608F1
KURDS—*See also IRAN—Kurdish Dispute*
Turkey Cabt rift linked 4-17, 287E3
Turkey extends martial law 4-25, 333F1
Turkish unrest probed 8-21—8-24, 795E3-796A1
KURDYAVTSEVA, Nadezhda
Banned from track 10-26, 912A1
KURILE Islands
Japan chrgs Sovt buildup 2-5, USSR test fire rptd 2-6, 85A3
Sovt buildup rptd 9-26, 9-27, Japan protests 10-2, 742B1
USSR vs US defns secy's visit to Japan 10-16, talks note Sovt moves 10-20, 803C3
KURON, Jacek
Arrested 4-18, 374G2
Freed 5-25, 414D2
KURYS, Diane
Peppermint Soda released 7-15, 820G2
KUSH, Frank
Fired 10-13, sues univ 11-9, 1001C3
KUSUMAATMADJA, Mochtar
On Viet refugee setlmts 7-14, 550E1

KUWAIT—*See also ARAB League, GATT, NONALIGNED Nations Movement, OPEC*
'78 per capita GNP ranked 2d 7-24, 575D3
Foreign Relations (misc.)—*See also 'UN' below*
UK queen tours Arab states 2-12—3-2, 190C1
Egypt emb stormed 3-25, 222D2
Yemen unificatn plan agreed 3-29, 250C1
Egypt recalls envoy 4-7, 278D1
Egypt ties cut 4-22, Egypt retaliates 4-23, 296D1

1980

KRUPP G.m.b.H. Fried
'79 profits rptd 6-11, 446B3
KRYLOV, Alexander Petrovich
Oil dvpt methods scored 2-13, 235C3
KRYLOV, Andrei
Wins Olympic medals 7-21, 7-24, 623G2
KUBASOV, Valery
Launched into space 5-26, 397C3
Returns 6-3, 477C1
KUBRICK, Stanley
Shining released 5-23, 675D3
KUHN, Bowie
Aaron boycotts awards ceremony, chrgs racism 1-28, 637G1
Fines Mets for ad campaign 5-1, 637C1
KUHN Loeb & Co.
'79 univ endowmt earnings compared to bond index 3-24, 319E1
KUHRTZ, Steven
On Cleveland utility air rule 6-17, 494G3
KUHT-TV (Houston TV station)
Cts rule on Saudi film telecast 5-9, 5-12, 375F3
KUIPER, Hennie
2d in Tour de France 7-20, 835E1
KUKK, Yuri
Arrested 3-18, 262E1
KU Klux Klan (KKK)
'63 Ala church bombing prosecutn rptd blocked, FBI informant probe cited 2-18, 227D2
Blacks seek US probe 2-29—3-2, 190D2
Rallies, violence in Tenn, Calif, Ind, NC 3-15—4-26, 333E1-A2
Hines '78 rape convictn overturned 3-18, 215A3
Metzger wins Calif US House primary 6-3, 439B2
Canada hq opened 6-26, 497C1
2 acquitted in Chattanooga shooting 7-22, racial disorders erupt 7-22—7-26, 575F3
Reagan gets endorsemts 7-30, 9-2, 664E1
Carlson wins Mich US House primary 8-5, 682D3
Carter in Tuscumbia, Reagan notes Klan 'birthplace' 9-1; remark stirs furor, Reagan clarifies 9-2, 663D2
Mondale scores Reagan gaffe 9-3, 780F1
Rallies in Conn 9-13, Miss 10-4, 884C3-E3
Carter deplores Reagan racism 9-16, clarifies 9-18, 698B2
Black convicted of assault 10-2, 884F3
Buffalo area black slayings prompt probe 10-13, 997G1
Rights group files suit 11-4, 884G3-885A1
6 acquitted in NC slayings 11-17; US vows review, other reactn 11-17—11-18, 898D2-C3
KULA, Dainis
Wins Olympic medal 7-27, 624B1
KULIK, Buzz
Hunter released 8-1, 675A3
KULIKOV, Yevgeny
Wins Olympic medal 2-15, 155G3
KULONGOSKI, Ted
Wins US Sen primary in Ore 5-20, 404D3
Loses US Sen electn 11-4, 852E2
KUNAR, Ghulam Sakhi
Rpts Sovt Afghan drive 10-2, 766C1
KUNG, Rev. Hans
Ouster backed by 7 colleagues, Vatican controversy detailed 2-5, 157A1
Setlmt reached in Vatican controversy 4-10, 364A2
Papal petitn rptd 11-15, 905B1
KUNZ, Joachim
Wins Olympic medal 7-23, 624E2
KURAGINA, Olga
Wins Olympic medal 7-24, 624F1
KURBEGOVIC, Muharem (alias Isaac Rasim)
Convicted 10-16, sentncd 11-24, 927A2
KURDS—*See appropriate subheads under IRAN, IRAQ, TURKEY*
KURKJIAN, Stephen A.
Wins Pulitzer 4-14, 296F2
KURON, Jacek
Arrested 8-20, 625D2, 658F1
Released 9-1, 658A2, F2
Czechs, E Gers score 11-5, 860A2
Scores RC warning to Polish dissidents 12-20, 976D1
KURTZ, Gary
Empire Strikes Back released 5-21, 675D2
KURTZ, Jerome
Plans curbs on commodities trading tax straddles 5-22, 481F1
KUSA, Musa
Threatens exiles 6-12, UK expels 6-13, 463F2
KUSH, Frank
Settles with Ariz State 1-29, 175D2
KUTSENKO, Yuri
Wins Olympic medal 7-26, 624A1

KUWAIT—*See also ARAB League, GATT, OPEC*
Foreign Relations (misc.)—*See also 'Oil & Gas' below*
UN Cncl replacemts seated 1-1, 12C2
Saudis execute 3 mosque raiders 1-9, 22B1
French pres visits; backs Palestinian rights, indl cooperatn 3-3, 180A1
Iran hostage rescue try scored 4-27, 324C2
Iran Emb attacked 6-4, 451G2
Brazil VW stake acquired 6-25, other W Ger investmts rptd 6-25, 7-15, 542E3, 562C1

1976

Confrms Egypt troop mass 7-25, 547D3
Joins Egypt aid fund 8-21, 630A1
Egypt plans French missile resale 8-27, 675B1
Govt quits 8-29; Palestinian populatn cited 8-31, 642E1
New Cabinet formed 9-6, 679G1
Investmt co joins Venez co 9-17, 875E1
Forgn paymts rptd accepted 12-20, 985A3
Listed as not free 12-22, 977B3
Middle East Conflict—*See MIDDLE EAST*

1977

Cholera outbreak rptd 9-26, 748A1
Hijacked Japan jet refuels 10-3, 756C3
W Ger hijackers refused landing 10-13, 789F1
UN Cncl elects member 10-24, 852F3
Assad visits re Cairo conf 12-9, 954G2
Sabah dies, Jaber named ruler 12-31, 1019A2
Arab-Israeli Conflict—*See MIDDLE EAST*
Lebanon Civil Strife—*See LEBANON*
Oil Developments
To cut crude oil output 1-3, 12B1
Major oil buyers seek purchase cuts 1-20; Jan oil output rptd down 1-26; Saudi comments 2-9, 107F3, 108A1
Tanker breaks up off Taipei 3-3, 214C3
Mex reserves compared 3-18, 240D3
Feb oil output rptd up 3-24, 227B3
US oil co natlized 9-19, 805G3

1978

Tops '77 per capita GNP list 7-18, 624C1
Arab fund loan to Sudan rptd 8-17, 925F3
UN Assemb member, named to Cncl 9-19, 713A3, G3
Arab-Israeli Conflict—*See MIDDLE EAST*
U.S. Relations
US co, SEC sue al-Fulaij 2-17, 3-18, SEC suit settled 3-19, 204B2, B3
Boeing chrgd re payoffs 7-28, 642G3

1979

Egypt aid group disbanded 4-27, 319D2
Iran ties to Khuzistan unrest 6-3, 446E1
Libya fete attended by Arab ldrs 9-1, 688C3
Khomeini envoy deported 9-26, Iran clergy score 9-27, 752G2
At Persian Gulf security conf 10-14–10-16, 804A2
Saudis capture mosque raiders 12-4, 916B1
Oil Developments—*See also OPEC*
Crude oil prices hiked 2-26, 145G2
Prices hiked again 5-20, 396C2
Prices hiked 10% 10-9, 781B1
Price per barrel rptd 12-21, hike set 12-30, 12-21, 977B2, E2
UN Policy & Developments
Membership listed 695F2
Unifil troops Leb exit cited 5-7, 341A2
Iran sanctns res abstentn 12-31, 974G2
U.S. Relations
US UN Amb Young, PLO rep meet; Res 242 proposal discussed 7-26, 605F1
US freeze of Iran assets scored 11-18, 880D1
Miller tours Persian Gulf, discusses Iran crisis 11-23–11-28, 896A3
US sets evacuatns, travel curbs 11-26, 894G1
Anti-US protest held 11-30, 915C1

1980

Forgn assets exceed $40 mln 7-15, 542E3
World Bank loans frozen over PLO issue 8-2, 592A2
PLO status in World Bank, IMF disputed, funding cutoff threatened 9-4—9-22; dirs bar observer role 9-18, 719F3
Syria seeks backing for Libya merger 9-10, 697G1
Yugo loan rptd 9-20, 833C2
Iraq war use of Oman rptd blocked 10-3, 758G1
Iraqi planes rptd stationed 10-6, 757D1
Palestinian curbs rptd tightened 10-22, 821D2
Iranian jets bomb border post 11-12, 11-16; Gulf states pledge cited 879B2
Obituaries
Sayegh, Fayez A 12-9, 1004D3
Oil & Gas Developments
Liberian supertanker sinks off Senegal 1-17; S Africa sale suspected, Shell sues 2-7, 108G2, B3
25% productn cut set 2-20, 165G3
French oil supply agrmt reached 3-3, 180B0
Oil price hike set 6-11, 435G2
Getty Oil 15% interest sought 7-14, 542A3; bid rejctd 7-18, 556G3
UN oil focus warning rptd 8-27, 642A1
IMF oil debt role studied 9-15, 695F2
Gulf war prompts halt to 10% cut plan 9-26, 735C1
Export hike rptd set 10-5—10-6, 758D3
Oil price rise hinted 10-15, 775D1
$5 premium on extra productn sought 10-28, 822D2
U.S. Relations
Carter Persian Gulf defns pledge scored 1-25, 65C1
Iran hostage rescue try scored 4-27, 324D2
Getty Oil 15% interest sought 7-14, 542A3; bid rejctd 7-18, 556G3
Financial Gen deal set 7-25, 600E3
US debates forgn bank takeovers 8-28, 9-17, 806A3
Carter scores 'politics' at IMF-World Bank mtg 9-30, 762A1
US offers air defense aid 10-7, 758D1
US 'concerned' re Iran raid 11-17, 879D2

1976

KUWANA, Mr. & Mrs. Elisha
Killed 12-14, 1009C2
KUZNIAK, Valerian
Arrested as spy 8-16, 640B2
KWIECINSKI, Czeslaw
Wins Olympic medal 7-24, 576B3
KY, Nguyen Cao
Sach plot cited 176B3

1977

KUZNETSOV, Vasily Vasilyevich
Named to Politburo 10-3, 785C3
Named USSR 1st vp 10-7, 785B3
KYEMBA, Henry
Disclosures on Amin published 6-8, 487A1
Defectn cited 7-2, 600E3
KYLE, Richard W.
ICC suspends 6-8, 500C3
ICC fires Oswald 12-8, 1007G3
KYPRIANOU, Achilleas
Abducted 12-14, freed 12-18, 982F3-984B1

KYPRIANOU, Spyros (Cypriot president)
Cyprus acting pres 8-3, 616C1; named interim pres 8-13, 636B2, C2 ★
Sworn 8-31; rptd ill 9-21, 764B2
Chrgs Turks ignore UN 11-19, 946C3
Son abducted 12-14, 12-17, freed 12-18, 983F3-984B1
Clerides drops pres bid 12-16, 984C1

1978

KUWAIT Fund for Arab Economic Development
Poor-natn aid rise rptd 4-9, 257F2
KUZMIN, Mikhail
Scores US re trade 12-4, 966F1
KWAK Hu Sop
Seized in housing scandal 7-14, 594E3
KWANG PI
Rpts Cambodian purges 8-8, 659F3
KY, Nguyen Cao
Protests Calif welfare cuts 8-2, 844E2
KYAZIMOV, Saladin
Killed 6-29, 519A1
KYLE, Aaron
Cowboys win Super Bowl 1-15, 39A3
KYLE, Richard W.
Resigns ICC 6-5; withdraws resignatn, fired 6-7, 570F1
KYPRIANOU, Achilleas
Anti-govt plotters arrested 4-11, 288B1
KYPRIANOU, Spyros (Cypriot president)
Wins pres term unopposed 1-26, 74G3
Scores US rights rpt 2-5, 148C1
EOKA-B rptd disbanded, '77 kidnap role cited 2-10, 147F3
Visits Greece 2-14, 148B1
In Palestinian hijack negotiatns 2-18, disputes Egypt on commando raid 2-21, 2-22, 117G1, 118A2, F2
Egypt rebuffs, cuts ties 2-22, 118A2
Fires dep police chief 2-22, 138D2
Urges Sadat to renew ties 2-23, 138F2
US denies taking sides in Egypt feud 2-26, 138A3
Takes office, seeks Egypt rift end 3-1, 148A1
Names new Cabt 3-8, 189E1
Scores US on Turkey arms embargo end 4-5, 277G1
Rejects Turkish plan 4-19, 4-27, 328F3
Scores US on Turkey arms embargo end 8-2, 588A1
Pavlides leads prison siege 9-15—9-19, 894D3
Spares Sebai slayers 11-14, 870F1
KYRIAKAKOS, George
Elected Piraeus mayor 10-22, 816F2

1979

KUYKENDALL, William E.
Chrgd in Va A-plant sabotage 6-18, 466F1
Convicted 10-16, 807D1
Sentenced 11-27, 925B2
KUZNETSOV, Anatoly V.
Dies 6-13, 508C3
KUZNETSOV, Eduard S.
Freed in spy swap 4-27; honored in NY, leaves for Israel 4-29; facts on 4-27, 317B1, B2, G2
KY, Nguyen Cao
'75 coup try rptd stopped by US 1-7, 29E1, G1
KYLE, Richard W.
ICC dismissal backed 3-5, 309D1

KYPRIANOU, Spyros (Cypriot president)
New intercommunal talks set 5-19, 387D2

1980

KUYKENDALL, William E.
NRC clears Va A-plant 8-5, 649A1
KUZNETSOV, Vasily V.
Sovt-Syrian pact implemented 12-2, 911F3
KUZNETSOV, Victor
Wins Olympic medal 7-21, 623E2

KYPRIANOU, Spyros (Cypriot president)
Sets unity bid 1-14, 96B3
UN-sponsored talks resume 8-9, 633E2
Shuffles Cabt 9-9, 749E2
KYTE, Mary
Tintypes opens 10-23, 892F3

L

1976

LAABS, Herbert
Secy seized as spy 6-2, 442A1
LABADY, Mahmoud
Says US amb slayers arrested 6-17, 425D1
LABEYRE, Vincent
Loses by-electn 5-9, 350C3

1977

LAABS, Herbert
W Ger Defns Min spy scandal rptd 12-12, probe set 12-13, 968E1
LABADY, Mahmoud
Hints PLO shift on UN Res 242 8-8, 605C1
Scores Israeli air raid 11-10, 849B2
LABAKI, Kesrouan
EEC pact initialed 2-16, 269C3
LABELING—*See CONTAINERS & Packaging*
LaBERGE, Walter B.
Named Army undersecy 6-27, confrmed 7-21, 626A3
LaBIANCA, Leno and Rosemary (d. 1969)
Manson convictn review denied 4-25, 342G2
Van Houten mistrial declared 8-6, 3d trial planned 9-1, 711D2

1978

LABADY, Mahmoud
Vs Carter Palestine stand 1-4, 3E1 ★
LABBE, Claude
On Gaullist econ plan 10-4, 815F2
LABELING—*See CONTAINERS & Packaging*
La BERCEUSE (The Lullaby) (painting)
Slashed 4-5, 335F1
LaBIANCA, Leno and Rosemary (d. 1969)
Van Houten sentncd 8-11, 824F2
LABOR (non-U.S.)—*See also country, group names*
EC urges shorter hours, overtime curbs 2-16, 258E2
EC Jan, Feb jobless rate rptd 3-22, 258G2
Eur workers protest unemploymt 4-5, 258F2
EC youth jobs program rptd 4-7, 258D2
ILO denies USSR dissidents recognitn 4-14, 275F2
ILO rpts '77 jobless rates 7-28, 677D1
Latin '77 jobless rated high by IDB 9-10, 828D2-A3

1979

LABELING—*See CONTAINERS*
LABOR (non-U.S.)—*See also country, group names*
EC '78 jobless rptd 1-22, 85C2
WHO rpts alcohol-related absenteeism up 3-9, 218B3
EC urges jobs actn 3-13, 180A2
Westn natn costs ranked 5-1, 374A2
OECD sees jobless hike 7-18, 554C3
Westn wage rates compared 9-19, 697B3

1980

LABADY, Mahmoud
Denies PLO plan to destroy Israel 6-5, 434E2
LABAREE, Leonard W.
Dies 5-5, 448B2
LABELING—*See CONTAINERS & Packaging*
LABOR (non-U.S.)—*See also country, group names*
Westn costs compared 8-12, 698C1
World Bank '80 econ forecast grim 8-17, 628B3
Islamic econ conf 11-4—11-6, 865C1
World illiteracy study rptd 12-4, 953A3
Free trade unions scored 12-26, 976B3

LABOR

1976

LABOR—*See also LABOR, Department of under U.S. GOVERNMENT; also union names; specific countries, organizations*
1st ¼ productivity rptd 4-26, 376F1
2d ¼ productivity, labor costs rptd, 1st ¼ revised 7-26, 567D2
Productivity slowdown analyzed 8-2, 647A2
3d ¼ productivity, labor costs; 2d ¼ revised 10-27, 918D1

1977

LABOR—*See also U.S. GOVERNMENT—LABOR, Department of; also union names; countries, organizations*
Sen Human Resources Com proposed 2-4, 90F1, D3, 91D1
AT&T sets employe stock plan, other ESOP cos cited 5-6, 409E1
Ohio KKK rally disrupted 7-4, 540E1

1978

LABOR (U.S.)—*See also U.S. GOVERNMENT—LABOR, Department of; also union names*

1979

LABOR (U.S.)—*See also U.S. GOVERNMENT—LABOR, Department of; also union names*

1980

LABOR (U.S.)

AFL-CIO

1976: **AFL-CIO**—*See AMERICAN Federation of Labor and Congress of Industrial Organizations*
1977: **AFL-CIO**—*See AMERICAN Federation of Labor and Congress of Industrial Organizations*
1978: **AFL-CIO**—*See AMERICAN Federation of Labor and Congress of Industrial Organizations*
1979: **AFL-CIO**—*See AMERICAN Federation of Labor and Congress of Industrial Organizations*
1980: **AFL-CIO**—*See AMERICAN Federation of Labor*

Black Americans

1976: **Black Americans**—*See 'Employment' under BLACK Americans*
1977: **Black Americans**—*See under 'B'*
1978: **Black Americans**—*See BLACK Americans—Employment*
1979: **Black Americans**—*See BLACK Americans–Employment*
1980: **Black Americans**—*See BLACK Americans--Employment*

Contract Negotiations & Settlements

1976: **Contract Negotiations & Settlements**—*See also 'Strikes & Settlements' and 'Wages & Hours' below*
IUE, UEW OK GE pact 6-27, 536G3
Auto talks 7-19, 7-20, 570E1
Can co contracts extended 8-18, 670A1
UAW picks Ford as target co 8-24, rejects 1st offer 8-31, 669B2
GM cites UAW talks 8-25, 647B1
URW, Mansfield Tire accord 10-10, 867B1
Oct jobless rate rptd 11-5, 846D1
Burns warns vs stimulating econ for jobs 11-11, 865F1
NE govs urge plan 11-14, 865A1

1977: **Contract Negotiations & Settlements**—*See also 'Strikes & Settlements' below*
Steel talks open 2-14, 130E3
NFL pact signed 3-1, 163A2-B3
Arbitratn under expired contracts backed 3-7, 211B3
NFLPA labor pact OKd 3-25, 263F3
Steelworkers OK contract 4-9, 273D2
NFL labor pact challenged 4-25, 491E2
USW aluminum pacts set 5-24, 421F3
Steel pact worth estimated 6-1, 481G2
Clothing workers get pact 6-9, 481B3
UMW plans talks 6-14, 462D3
Steel price hike, contract linked 7-21, 577E1
AT&T, CWA settle 8-6, 613F2
3d ¼ wage, benefit hikes rptd 10-28, 836C1
Steelworkers OK can pacts 10-31, 837A1
Stevens 'bad-faith' bargaining chrgd 12-21, 1005C1

1978: **Contract Negotiations & Settlements**—*See also 'Strikes & Settlements' below*
'77 wage, benefit gains rptd 1-27, 128D2
New CPIs described, link to settlmts cited 222F2
Maritime Comm jurisdictn enlarged 3-1, 143C3-144C1
A-plant constructn accord reached, Carter hails 4-18, 281A3
1st ¼ wage, benefit gains; '77 revised 4-27, 389C2
UMW ratifies anthracite pact 4-30, 324E2
Southn constructn pact OKd 5-22, 429A3
Postal pact reached 7-21, reactn 7-21—7-23, 564D2-565A1
RR pact set with 4 unions 7-21, 565B1
Meany, Admin trade chrgs; collective bargaining com set, postal pact disputed 8-7—8-11, 624A2-G3
Govt role in Teamster talks seen 8-22, 8-23, 680F2-C3
Conrail OKs crew-size pact 9-14, 700C1
Postal pact revised 9-15; Meany backs 9-22, 2 unions OK 10-10, 10-11, 765F3, E2
NHL compensatn clause ruled illegal 9-18, 990E3
AMC signs 2-yr pact 9-25, 737G2-C3
Carter inflatn plan sets voluntary guidelines 10-24, Fitzsimmons comments 10-25, 806G1, E3

1979: **Contract Negotiations & Settlements**—*See also 'Strikes' below*
Washn Star pacts set 1-1, 5E1-C2
Gulf oil workers settle within US wage guides 1-11, 87B1; Carter cites 2-12, 109E3
Railway clerks settle 1-13, 87F1-A2
NYSE workers settle 2-21, 131C1
Teamsters issue demands 3-6, Kahn warns 3-15, 251D1
Teamster talks spur Admin concern 3-13, 182C1
Rail clerks, Conrail set pact 3-23, 262F2
UAW bars US role 4-17, 280A1
Carter averts rail dispatchers strike 5-8, accord reached 5-31, 598E2
Collective bargaining on food issues backed by Sup Ct 5-14, 383B2
NHL reserve clause upheld 5-22, 448E1
ILGWU gets 25%, 3-yr pact 5-30, 402E1
GE, Westinghouse IUE talks cited 5-31, 391C3
UAW warns Admin 6-30; Big 3 talks begin 7-16, Chrysler gets no-strike pledge 7-18, 598A1
GE contract ratified by 2 unions 7-11, 598C2
UPS-Teamster pact ratificatn rptd 7-26, wage cncl OKs 7-27, 744E2
1st 1/2 wage gains rptd 7-29, 578B1
UAW bars Chrysler wage freeze plea 8-3, 662B3
UAW targets GM 8-30, 9-10; accord reached 9-14, signed 9-19, 698A1
UAW-GM pact provisn disclosed 9-18; contract rptd ratified, Kahn vs 9-30, 744F1
UAW, Ford contract ratified 10-22, 805G3
UAW, Chrysler reach accord 10-25, 805E2
UFW field talk case refused by Sup Ct 11-5, 884B3
Baseball owners meet 12-3—12-7, 1002A2

1980: **Contract Negotiations & Settlements**—*See also 'Strikes' below*
UAW, Chrysler set contract revisns 1-5, UAW council OKs pact 1-8, 14C1
NYC contract talks open 1-31, 186D3
UAW OKs Chrysler concessns 2-1, 127C2
NBA pact OKd 2-4, 119G1
Sutter baseball contract arbitrated 2-25, 637A1
Phila fire pact cited 3-1, 187D1
Va shipyd, USW pact signed 3-31, 251B2
Baseball strike voted 4-1, 637C2
Chicago teachers pact renegotiatn dispute seen 4-2, 292E1
USW basic pact set 4-15, 288G3
1st 1/4 wage gains rptd 4-25, 329G1
NFL free agent rule upheld by arbitrator 5-16, 998F2
Baseball strike averted; free agent dispute deferred, other issues setld 5-23, 401G3-402C2
ILA dock pact setld 5-27, 482F1-C2
USW-aluminum pact setld 5-30, 482D2*
NYC unions settle 6-19, 7-3, 518A1
Container pact ban refusal affirmed by Sup Ct 6-20, 555E2
AT&T reaches pacts with CWA, 2 other unions 8-9, 648B1
USW reaches Kennecott, Phelps Dodge copper settlmt 8-27, 10-8, 805D2
NFL rookie contracts set $ mark; Sims pact cited 8-27, 998G2
AMC-UAW pact set 9-17, 725B1
ILA OKs contract, 3 ports holdout 9-18, Phila OKs 10-2, 826F2-D3
Stoughton declared NHL free agent 10-3, 1000F2-A3
NASL NLRB order refused by Sup Ct 10-14, labor pact set 12-5; owners, player reps ratify 12-12, 12-18, 1001D2
JP Stevens setlmt announced 10-19, 805B1-D2
TV, film actors pact set 10-23, 805B3
Met Opera pact set 10-25, 883E3
Winfield signs record pact with Yankees 12-15, 999F3-1000B1
UAW OKs Chrysler renegotiatn 12-22, 984D2

Corruption

1976: **Corruption**—*See 'Unions' below*
1977: **Corruption**—*See 'Unions' below*

1978: **Corruption**
Ohio Teamster fund bd revised, aide returns $560,000 1-3, 4E2
US sues to regain Teamster funds 2-1, 83B1
Boyle convicted again 2-18, 129A1
Provenzano convicted for kickbacks 3-25, 232B2
USW sues 9 foundatns over Sadlowski funding 4-19, 309G3
Teamster chief's son, others acquitted 4-28, 324C2
22 indicted on port corruptn 6-7, 480D2
AFL-CIO fined for campaign gift abuses 6-12, 509C3
Provenzano convicted of Castellito murder 6-14, sentncd to life 6-21, 480B2
4 indicted on insurnc scheme 6-15, 560G2-D3
Provenzano sentncd for kickbacks 7-11, 560D2
Insurance promoter indicted for Teamster embezzlemt 7-18, 599D1
Paperworkers' chief Tonelli indicted 7-19, 598D3
Parsons sued re union payoffs 8-4, 643C2★, E2
Teamster pensn funds scored 8-14, 625C1
5 NJ Teamsters indicted 10-5, 770F3
US sues Teamster fund trustees 10-16, 792D1-A3
US set back in Teamster fund suit 11-1, 11-7, 899C1

1979: **Corruption**
Johnny Dio dies 1-12, 176F2
ILA's Scotto indicted 1-17, 87G2-C3
5 Teamsters indicted in NJ 2-22, 155F3
ILA, other waterfront indictmts continue 3-6, 220A2
Tenneco fined in La bribe case 3-17, 239C3
S Africa bribes re '77 trade boycott chrgd 3-21, 213F1
Dock indictmts mount 4-9, 292B1
NJ indicts 8 in Genovese 'family' 5-23, 508G1
Provanzano, Konigsberg '78 murder convictns upset 6-7, 491F3
Curran told to repay NMU benefits 7-27, 744G2
Teamster chief's son indicted 8-2, 744C3
ILA's Scotto convicted 11-15, 890A1

1980: **Corruption**
7 ILA ldrs sentenced 1-11, 64E1-C2
ILA's Scotto, Anastasio sentenced 1-22, 1-23, 64G2
FBI Brilab probe rptd 2-8—2-13, 111D2-112C1; for subsequent developments, see U.S. GOVERNMENT—FEDERAL Bureau of Investigation—Brilab Probe
Teamster chief's son, 2 others rptd sentenced 2-19, 237F2
Waterfront racketeer convicted 5-2; 7 sentncd 5-20, 927F2
NY Deliverers Union head convicted 5-15, 370E3; sentncd 6-26, 656D1
W Coast Teamster offcl sentenced 5-23, 482G2
GAO scores Teamster pension fund probe 8-25, 704C3
Presser's Reagan transitn role queried, backed 12-15, 12-18, 955E3

Employment & Unemployment

1976: **Employment & Unemployment**—*See also 'Government Employment' 'Job Bias' and 'Presidential Election' below; also MINORITIES*
Jobless index described 21C1
Shift from unemploymt to welfare benefits rptd 1-7, 128G2
Dec, '75 jobless rate rptd 1-9, 20F2-21C1
'46-75 GNP revised 1-16, 90E1
Ford State of Union message 1-19, 37B2-B3, 39F1
Muskie rebuts Ford 1-21, 40E1-D2
'77 budget proposals 1-21, 62C3-63C3, 65E2, F3
Ford Econ Rpt 1-26, 66A3; excerpts 67A1
Mental illness, jobless rate linked 1-26, 159B3
House OKs pub works-urban aid, Ford vows veto 1-29, 93C3
Ford vs public jobs programs 1-31, 87F3
Jan jobless rate rptd, '75 revised 2-5, 152A3

1977: **Employment & Unemployment**—*See also 'Government Employment' and 'Job Bias' below; for transfer payments, see INCOMES*
BLS jobless index described 37F3-38E1
US shoe-import injury ruled 1-6, 248G2
Carter plans major jobs efforts 1-7, 5D1
AFL-CIO urges $30 bln US prgrms 1-10, 14E1
Ford State of Union message 1-12, 13C1, F2, G2
Dec '76 jobless rate rptd 1-12, revised 1-18, 37E2, F3
Jobless benefits cited in CBO poverty rpt 1-13, 80C3
Ford '78 budget proposals 1-17, 30B1, B2, 32F2, A3, 33C2
Gas shortage forces layoffs 1-17, 37C2
CEA redefines 'full employmt', projcts '77 jobless rate, cites Carter plans 1-18, 36D1
Layoffs re gas shortages estimated 1-19, 1-22, 53C3, 54B2, C2; 1-30, 75F3
Gen Dynamics loan guarantee saves jobs in Mass, SC 1-19, 55F2

1978: **Employment & Unemployment**—*See also 'Government Employment' and 'Job Bias' below; for transfer payments, see INCOMES*
Jobless index described 50G3
OPIC loses new-policy writing power 1-1, 67B1
Econ indicator index described 128A1
Dec '77 jobless rate, Aug-Nov revised 1-11, 12B2, 50F2
Carter State of Union Message 1-19, 29B1-D2, F3, 30A2-C2, A3, 31G3
Carter Econ Message 1-20, 48A3, C3
Carter budget proposals 1-23, 44E2, D3, 46E2, 47G3; tables 45E2, F2, 46B2
Jobless benefits rptd cut 1-26, 51B2
GOP rebuts Carter proposals 1-26, 63F1
Carter urges proposals kept intact 1-30, 62B3
Jan jobless rate 2-3, 127C3
Student aid progrm unveiled 2-8, 85A1
Redwood Park expansn clears Cong 2-9, 85F2; 3-21, Carter signs 3-27, 218F1

1979: **Employment & Unemployment**—*See also 'Government Employment' and 'Job Bias' below; for transfer payments, see INCOMES*
Jobless index described 34G1
Carter to resubmit countercyclical aid program 1-2, 3E3
Carter aide warns Dems on 'new realities' 1-4, 3E2
Dec '78 jobless rate rptd 1-14, 34B1
'77, '78 job gains rptd 1-14, 34D1
Carter on '80 budget funds 1-17, 29F2
Anti-pollutn job gains seen 1-19, 129C3
Carter budget proposals 1-22, 41G1, 44A1, B1; tables 42C2, E2, 43B2
O'Neill vs Carter budget 1-22, 70E1
Carter State of Union Message 1-23, 46F2, D3, 47D1, E1, G1, C2
'79 jobless rate forecast, '78 cited; Rivlin disputes 1-25, 48D3, 49A2
Humphrey-Hawkins bill goals, '79 growth rate linked 1-25, 48D3
Food Fair closes 123 supermkts 1-27, 131G2

1980: **Employment & Unemployment**—*See also 'Job Bias' below*
Jobless index described 33A3-34A2
State of State messages 1-2, 2-6, 270E1, B3; 1-9—1-15, 483A1, D3, 484D1, C2; 1-10, 1-15, 403A3, D3
Ford, GM set layoffs 1-3, 1-10, 35F1-B2
Carter asks youth training progrm 1-10, 16G1-F2
Dec '79 jobless rate rptd 1-11, 33D2
'78, '79 job gains rptd 1-11, 33F2
UAW pres links auto layoffs, imports 1-13, 35D2
MIT '69-76 new job data rptd 1-18, 455E3
Carter cites gains 1-20, 50D2
Carter State of Union proposals 1-21, 1-23, 41G2, 43A1, C2, D3
Uniroyal plants to close 1-22, 52G2
White-black '70s jobless hike compared 1-22, 94E2
Carter budget proposals 1-28, 69C2, E2, D3, 72D1; tables 70D1, E1, 71B2, C2, 72D3

1976

Ford hails jobless drop 2-6, 109B1
House OKs pub svc jobs bill 2-10, 134F2
Ford vetoes pub works bill 2-13, 127E3; comments 2-17, 129B3; Sen sustains 2-19, 135C2
AFL-CIO urges full employmt program 2-16, 2-21, 149C1
State curbs on aliens upheld 2-25, 169F1
Ford: on 'crusade' vs 2-28, 165B3
Auto, steel workers win Trade Act aid 3-1—4-26, 348E2-B3
Feb jobless rate rptd, Meany disputes 3-5, 198B3, 199A1
Prisoner training rpt issued 3-9, 271D2
Cong panels score Ford 3-10, 3-15, 230E2, E3
Jobless total rptd up 3-13, 297E3
'75 steel jobless rate rptd 3-17, 213C1
House Budget Com proposals; Cong reactn 3-23, 231F1, G2, B3
Fiscal '77 Ford, House com budgets table 231B1
March jobless rate rptd 4-2, 263A1
Sen OKs pub works bill 4-13, 283C1
Pub svc jobs bill enacted 4-15, 282C2
Ford scores jobs bill 4-26, 307B3
Fortune rpts '75 data 437E2
Regional jobless area list revised 5-5, 347D2
Apr jobless rate steady 5-7, 347F1-D2
Trade Act aid to shrimp workers urged 5-11; mushroom growers win aid 5-17, 431F1, C2
Cong OKs '77 budget target 5-12, 5-13; Ford OMB, Cong budgets table 358F1, G1, C2
AFL-CIO warns re jobless 5-19, 391C1
May jobless rate rptd 6-4, 412C2
Ford workers get Trade Act aid, total rptd 6-7, 431A2
Auto industry layoffs rptd 6-10—11-16, 885A2
Mayors for jobs, pub works bills 7-1, 493E1
June jobless rate rptd 7-2, 494A1
Govs OK welfare plan 7-6, 492B3
Ford vetoes pub works bill 7-6, 518B2, D2
'76 jobless forecast revised 7-16, 535G3
Pub works veto overridden 7-22, 533E2
July jobless up, labor force at peak 8-6, 586F2
Aug jobless rptd up, Admin revises '76 forecast 9-3, 667C2
Pa VW pact signed 9-15, 988A1
Cong sets '77 budget levels, table 9-16, 706C2
Cong clears pub works, svc bills 9-22, 727F3; signed 10-1, 982F1
Aug layoff, hiring rate rptd 9-28, 768B1
Cong OKs countercyclical aid 9-29, 765F1, A2; signed 10-12, 982G1
'77 manpower funds veto overridden 9-30, 727B3
Full employmt, youth jobs bills not cleared 10-2, 883B1, G3, 884B1
Sup Ct bars review of strikers benefits rule 10-4, 807E2
Sept jobless rate rptd 10-8, 768E1
Jobless benefits revision signed 10-20, 788C1-A2
Mayors seek jobs aid 11-8, 845C3
Burns warns vs stimulating econ 11-11, 865F1
AMC workers get Trade Act aid 11-17, 855D2
Lance on jobless rate 12-5, 917A1
Nov jobless rate rptd, Meany on 'realistic' rate 12-5, 917D3

1977

Carter inaugural 1-20, 27A2
Carter revises econ plan 1-27, 52B1-A2; submits to Cong 1-31, 75A2
Jobs plan for vets set 1-27, 52A2
Carter econ plan debated 1-27—2-4, 89A2
Econ indicators index described 1-28, 92C3; **for data, see 'Statistics' under BUSINESS**
6 states get US fund offer 2-1, 75G3
Carter defends econ plan 2-2, 75A2
Jan jobless rate drops 2-4, 110G3
Some gas layoffs ease; total layoffs rptd 2-7, 91E2
Carter on econ plan formula chng 2-8, 88D3
CBO questns Carter goals 2-15, 126F1
Feb state jobless claims up 2-16, 176C2
Gas crisis abates, 1 mln workers return 2-18, 152E2
Carter budget revisns 2-22, 124F3, 126D1
AFL-CIO urges $30 bln program 2-24, 153A3
House, Sen OK stimulus bills 2-24, 3-10, 174A2
Cong sets new '77 budget levels 3-3, 174D1
Feb jobless rate up 3-4, 176E1-B2
Carter call-in topic 3-5, 171C1-E1, G2
HUD grant program detailed 3-7, 178D1
Calif drought losses estimated 3-8, 244F2
Carter proposes youth progrms 3-9, 173D1
Saccharin worker layoffs set 3-10, 177B1
TV imports linked to US jobs loss 3-14, 208C3
Feb worker recalls rptd 3-17, 194D1
Carter trade policy dilemma seen, Strauss role outlined 3-22—3-31, 248F3-249E1
Giaimo proposes '78 budget 3-23, 228F3, 229A1
NH A-plant constructn halted 3-31, 344E3
Carter bars shoe-import curbs 4-1, reactn 4-1—4-5, 248F1
Mar jobless rate rptd 4-1, 252C1
Meany, others see Carter on import curbs 4-6, 4-13; workers protest Admin policy 4-13, 271D2
Calif drought losses scaled down 4-9, 376E3
Auto layoffs 4-11—4-15, 6-2, 463C3
Jobless benefits extended 4-12, 272E3
Carter outlines anti-inflatn plan 4-15, 298G3
Meany cites jobs problem 4-15, 299D2
Carter energy plan 4-18, 4-20, 289B2, 295C1; fact sheet 291B1, 292B1
Redwood Pk expansn asked 4-19, 323B1
Carter energy plan opposed 4-21, 4-23, 320C2
Carter defends energy plan 4-22, 321F2
Admin revises '77 jobless forecast 4-22, 408B1
Inmate rights rpt issued 4-26, 383E2
Carter gets illegal alien plan 4-27, 370A2
Carter outlines welfare reform goals 5-2, 337C3-338A1
Public works jobs bill clears Cong 5-3, 365E1; Carter signs 5-13, 380D3
Ohio benefits law upheld 5-3, 461C3
Stimulus, other funds clear Cong 5-5, 365E2; Carter signs 5-13, 380D3
April jobless rate down 5-6, 383D3
Carter at 7-natn econ summit 5-7—5-8, 357A1
Soc Security tax hike asked 5-9, 363G3
Carter scores liberals' criticism 5-12, McGovern responds 5-13, 380F3, 381D2
Countercyclical aid extensn OKd 5-16, 382D1
Urban business confidence rptd, econ data table 5-16, 384B2, D2
Employe record disclosure case refused 5-16, 419C1
Sup Ct '69-76 cases rptd 5-17, 419A3
Carter environmt message 5-23, 404B2
NY jobless aid for strikers upset 5-24, 463A1
May jobless rate down 6-3, 444F3
NYS jobless benefits case refused 6-6, 478G3
Chicago summer youth jobs set 6-7, 464D3
Capital-spending rise, jobless drop linked 6-7, 518D3
NBA owners set 11-man rosters 6-15, arbitrator upholds 11-4, 870C1
HEW jobless-benefits standards law upheld 6-20, 516D3-517A1
Jobless index to be released earlier 6-28, 554D2
US revises jobless forecast 7-1, 518F3
June jobless rate up 7-8, 554B1
Cargo preference debated 7-11—9-9, 720F1
Carter: too many jobless 7-21, 575D1
Carter rebuts criticism re urban poor 7-25, 7-28, 573E1, A3
Drought-related job loss rptd 7-28, 659E3
Carter proposes illegal alien plan, Meany scores 8-4, 592B1, E1
Youth jobs bill enacted 8-5, 609A2
July jobless rate drops 8-5, 611G2
Carter welfare program proposed 8-6, 608C2-609E1
Job dissatisfactn rise found 8-9, 632G1
Poll rpts top family concern 8-10, 632C2
Steel layoffs rptd 8-18—10-12, 775B3
3 youth job corps cntrs open, youth-adult program begun 8-31, 692E2 ★
Aug jobless rate up 9-2, 692E1
Carter sees Black Caucus, vows job actn; Humphrey-Hawkins full employmt bill problems rptd 9-7, 702A1

1978

AFL-CIO offers stimulus plan 2-20, Meany scores Carter 2-20, 2-23, 141F3, 142B1
CETA extensn, chngs proposed 2-22, 124D1
Vance talk vs protectionism 2-27, 145C1
New CPIs described 222B2
Coal strike-related jobless rptd 3-4, 3-6, 160A2, C2
Feb jobless rate 3-10, 221F3-222B1
Humphrey-Hawkins full employmt bill OKd in House 3-16, 182F2
Coal strike layoffs cited 3-25, 217B1
Carter unveils urban-aid plan 3-27, reactn 3-27—3-30, 217F2-218D1
Mar jobless rate rptd 4-7, 262B2
Carter cites jobless rate drop 4-11, 260A2
S Bronx offered US aid 4-12, 285G1
Youth job progrms excluded from Educ Dept proposal 4-14, 279E1
Firestone jobless benefits challenge declined by Sup Ct 4-17, 308B3
OPIC extensn protects job loss 4-24, 323D2, G2
Carter renews jobless vow 4-25, 307C3
Apr jobless rate rptd 5-5, 345C1
Carter scales down tax-cut plan 5-12, 361B1
Cong '79 budget targets cleared 5-17, 385F1, A2, A3
Purchasing control exemptns set 5-18, 405G1
Pvt Sector Initiative Progrm set, CETA operatn cited 5-23, 405A1
'77 4th ¼, '78 1st ¼ costs rptd up 5-30, 429D1
Employmt cost index described 429G1
May jobless rate rptd 6-2, 429C2
Carter links jobless rise, tax cuts 6-14, 446D3
Alaska oil job preference law voided by Sup Ct 6-22, 508F3
Oil import fee seen as job threat 6-29, 512B1
Kemp on tax-cut benefits 7-3, 735B1, F1
'78, '79 forecast revised 7-6, 506F2
Cong Budget Office rpts on Propositn 13 impact 7-6, 525G2
June jobless rate rptd 7-7, 552E2
Extended jobless aid rptd in 9 states, PR 7-10, 552A3
Hooks urges jobs legis 7-21, 568B2
'70-78 2-income families rptd 7-24, 679F3
Jobless benefits tax, business credits OKd by House com 7-27, 587B1, E1
Productivity, jobs gain linked 7-27, 606C3
'77 jobless drop rptd 7-28, 677D1
July jobless rate rptd 8-4, 607G2-D3
Extended jobless aid rptd in 4 states, PR 8-4, 607C3
Defns purchasing for jobless areas rejctd by House 8-8, 604E2
Meany links jobless rate, inflatn 8-8, 624A3
Poll finds pessimism growing 8-13, 679F2
Admin switch on credit policy, inflatn worries linked 8-18, 679A2
Aug jobless rate rptd 9-1, 679C3
Energy Dept coal strike performance faulted 9-11, 701A3
Meany cites progress 9-18, 715E2
NHL compensatn clause ruled illegal 9-18, 990D3
Airline deregulatn compromise clears conf com 10-6, 765B3
Women's labor-force rate passes 50% mark 10-6, 790F2
Sept jobless rate rptd 10-6, 790F2-B3
Carter rpts on Viet vets, reactn 10-10, 878B1-G1
CETA extensn clears Cong 10-14, 807C1; Carter signs 10-27, 873A2
Humphrey-Hawkins bill cleared 10-15, reactn 10-21, 784F3, 808A1, G1; Carter signs 10-27, 873A2
Jobs tax credit, benefits clear Cong 10-15, 785C3, 786G1
Oct jobless rate rptd 11-3, 864A3
Mo right-to-work law loses, NM debate cited 11-7, 847F1, 854E3, 855F2
Carter cites jobless commitmt 11-27, 914C3
3d ¼ employmt costs rptd up 11-30, 1003D2
Southn job opportunities, migratn halt linked 12-3, 943D1
Nov jobless rate rptd 12-8, 958C1
Carter job spending cuts scored 12-9, 956G1, G2
Solar energy study rptd 12-12, 983C1
Vocational schl job ad rules issued 12-13, 963B1
Carter '80 budget problems seen 12-14, 980D1
Carter hikes CETA '80 budget funds 12-22, 1002D3

1979

Illegal alien issue detailed 1-29, 127D1
Job gains, coll enrollmt decline linked 1-29, 367D2
Boston Navy Yd renovatn set 2-1, 94A1
Jan jobless rate rptd 2-2, 110B3
'77-79 women workers, 2-income family rise rptd 2-2, 110D3
'77 cigaret mfr rise rptd 2-11, 211E2
Drug abuse job costs rptd 2-12, 140C2
Adams outlines urban-aid policy 2-13, 129A2
AFL-CIO vs job-training aid cuts 2-26, 149A1
Carter submits countercyclical aid plan 3-6, 164A2
Feb jobless rate rptd 3-8, 182A3
Admin revises budget forecast 3-15, 183E3
Neighborhoods panel urges full-employmt policy 3-15, 208C3
Jobless pay for strikers upheld by Sup Ct 3-21, 231D1
US no longer top DC area employer 3-24, 232G1
Carter urges privacy bill 4-2, 264G3
Coll 'malaise' linked 4-2, 282A3
Auto workers idled by Teamsters strike 4-5, 251D2
Mar jobless rate rptd 4-6, 280F2
GM layoffs re Teamster strike cited 4-10, 262D2
Layoffs seen from GATT pact 4-12, 274E1
1st 1/4 productivity drop, job rise linked 4-30, 362A3
Fla fed training funds challenge refused by Sup Ct 4-30, 365A1
Apr jobless rate rptd 5-4, 362B3
Carter vows Mex aliens protectn 5-5, 347B1
May jobless rate rptd 6-1, 422C2
Milwaukee Rd svc cut denied 6-1, 465B2
Ohio utility air rule ease lauded 6-6, 423A1
Waste cleanup legis provisn scored 6-13, 441B2
Unemploymt, inflatn fight linked 6-13, 463B2
Carter sees jobless rise re OPEC price hike 7-1, 494D2
June jobless rate rptd 7-6, 516C3
Carter links trade bill, jobs 7-26, 646E3
Citizens Party platform backs job guarantees 8-1, 595A1
July jobless rate rptd 8-3, 621E2
Record industry staff cutbacks rptd 8-10, 618D1
Aug jobless rate rptd 9-7, 680E3
Job training, literacy progrm link urged 9-8, 786C1
Calif lawyer survey rptd 9-17, 787D1
AFL-CIO plans Mex oil spill suit 9-18, 718C3
Carter defends record 9-25, 723F2
Ford sets layoffs 9-27, 10-22, 806F1
Sept jobless rate rptd 10-5, 766G1
Carter sees affirmative action success 10-9, 767F1
Battle Creek seeks trust suit impact statemt 10-9, 810A1
Carter constructn job pledge 10-11, 807F2
Milwaukee Rd embargoes track, furloughs workers 11-1; Carter signs aid bill 11-4, 867E2-C3
Oct jobless rate rptd 11-2, 866C3
Ind pregnancy jobless pay case refused by Sup Ct 11-13, 902A2
US Steel, Jones & Laughlin set layoffs 11-27, 11-28; US aid pledged 12-3, 941C2, E3
Carter notes jobs issue 12-4, 918B3
R Carter, Mondale heckled in NY 12-5, 918A3
Nov jobless rate rptd 12-7, 941D1
Auto industry layoffs mount 12-12, 963B3
Supplementary jobless benefits OKd in Amer Ballet pact 12-20, 987B2

1980

'80 jobless rate forecast, '79 cited 1-30, 74C2
Jan jobless rate rptd 2-1, 92B2
Chicago teacher layoffs set 2-11, 114B2
'Guest worker' study rptd 2-13, 147C2
Kirkland berates Admin 2-18, 146D3
Job project gains rptd few 2-27, 228E3
Youth jobless rate said higher 2-28, 228A3
US Steel Ohio plant closings blocked 2-28, 266A2
Feb jobless rate rptd 3-7, 182C3
Connally 'basic speech' excerpts 3-7, 184G2, C3
Kennedy 'basic speech' excerpts 3-10, 183F1
Auto layoffs increase 3-27—4-16, 287D1
Carter revised budget proposals; Admin jobs forecast, Kirkland scores 3-31, 243F3, 244B1, E1
Mar jobless rate rptd 4-4, 263D1
'80, '81 jobless aid to auto workers miscalculated 4-9, 330F1
Citizens' Party seeks full employmt 4-13, 288B3, D3
Apr jobless rate rptd 5-2, 344E2
Kirkland meets Mondale, asks new job programs 5-2, 344B3
Reagan scores Carter policies 5-2, 344C3
LaSalle Extensn U ads ruled misleading 5-12, 703A2
Immigratn attitudes polled 5-16—5-18, 396D3
Mt St Helens damage assessed 5-24—7-4, 504A3, C3
Reagan on jobless 5-29, 6-3, 423C3, G3
Rock I RR aid law upset 6-2; Sup Ct bars actn 7-2, 11-10, 868E2
May jobless rate rptd; Miller comments, Reagan scores 6-6, 437B2, G2
Carter stresses jobs program 6-9, 439F1
Carter addresses mayors 6-10, 438F2
Kennedy urges jobs progrm 6-10, 438B3
Steel indus layoffs rptd 6-10, 575B3
Mil recruiters to stress joblessness 6-11, 458C2
Ford sees 800 new jobs 6-12, 465D2
Auto worker layoffs rptd 6-21, 481E3
Carter pledges new jobs 6-22, 646F2
IMF forecasts jobless rise 6-24, 477B3
Dem platform drafted 6-24, Kennedy vows floor fight 6-25, 479E3, 480C1
Reagan scores Carter 6-25, 480B2
Protectionism poll rptd 6-26, 515F3
Cong OKs auto, steel jobless aid bill 7-2, Carter signs 7-8, 515G1
June jobless rate rptd 7-3, 513D2
Carter unveils auto worker aid plan; GOP scores 7-8, 505A1-B2
Reagan scores auto layoffs 7-12, 535G1
Ford, Vander Jagt score Carter 7-14, 7-16, 534A2, E2
Reagan sees unemployed workers 7-15, 534B1
Reagan pres nominatn acceptance speech 7-17, 531B2, G2, 532B3
Admin sees rising unemploymt 7-21, 550D1-A2
US Steel plant closings upheld 7-25, 575G1
Klutznick sees employmt drop 7-30, 574G1
July jobless rate rptd 8-1, 599D2
Urban League issues jobless study 8-2; conv hears pres candidates 8-3—8-6, 597B1, E2
Kennedy Dem conv speech 8-12, 610G1, C2, 613F2, 614B1, G1
Kennedy jobs plank OKd 8-12; Carter accepts intent, conv adopts platform 8-13, 609D1, 610E2, 611F1, A2, D2; text excerpt 614F2, F3, 615A1
Mondale vp renominatn acceptance speech 8-14, 612C1
Carter pres renominatn acceptance speech 8-14, 613C2
Auto worker US jobless aid OKd 8-14, 647E3
Carter pledges massive jobs program 8-15, 629E3
Kennedy sees Carter on jobs plan 8-25, 646G2
Lucey joins Anderson ticket 8-25, 646D3
Carter offers econ renewal plan 8-28, 663E1
Anderson platform offered 8-30, 665F1
Bush stresses jobs issue 8-30—9-18, 780B3, E3, 781B1
Reagan vows jobs for NJ 9-1, 664C2
Aug jobless rate rptd 9-5, 683E1-684A1
Jobless benefits extended 9-8, 684A1
Detroit budget woes, layoffs rptd; July jobless rate 18.5% 9-8, 743F2
Reagan proposes 5-yr plan 9-9, 699B2
Carter pledges jobs, vs 'quick-fix' approach 9-18, 698C3, G3
Immigratn econ impact rptd 9-22, 826E3
Mondale cites Phila shipyd jobs 9-30, 780C2
Reagan hits jobs issue 10-1—10-2, 738A1
Carter vows aid to auto workers 10-1, 739G1-C2
Sept jobless rate rptd 10-3, 783C2
Carter warns vs Reagan win 10-6, 762D3
Japan visas tightened 10-6, 870C1-B2
Carter scores Reagan on jobless benefits 10-10, 778D2
Carter sees 'full employmt' 10-12, 10-14, 779D1, E1
UAW gets US jobless aid 10-14, 823G2
Bush vows pvt minority hiring 10-16, 817A3
Carter sees expanding jobs 10-20, 803A1
Kennedy scores Reagan record 10-22, 817D1
Reagan hits Carter record, cites 'misery index' 10-24, 10-29, 817G1-B2

1976

Government Employment—*See also 'Strikes' below; also EDUCATION—Teachers, PUBLIC Works; CIVIL Service and other appropriate headings under U.S. GOVERNMENT; state, city names*
Dec, '75 payrolls rptd 1-19, 91D2
'77 budget proposals 1-21, 63F3, 66D2
Feb payrolls rptd 3-17, 215G3
'77 budgets compared 231B1
Hatch Act repeal clears Cong 3-31, 234A2
Ford to veto Hatch Act repeal 4-3, 245G1; vetoes 4-12, 284D1; veto sustained 4-29, 346E1
Carter offers jobs plan 4-23, 305D2
Cong clears fed wage hike funds 5-19, 411D3; signed 6-1, 982F1
Job bias suit rights extended 6-1, 414E2-G2
Cong OKs countercyclical aid 6-23, Ford vetoes 7-6, 518D2; Cong overrides 7-22, 533G2
Sup Ct bars patronage ousters 6-28, 468A3
Carter backs pub svc jobs 6-29, 468E1
Mil constructn bill vetoed 7-2, 518B1
Dem conv OKs Hatch Act plank revisn 7-13, 509C2
GOP platform text 8-18, 606B1
New mil constructn bill clears Cong 9-16, 745D2
Cong clears pub svc extensn, 9-22, 727F3; signed 10-1, 982F1
Carter, Ford debate 9-23, 702C1, B3
Ford orders 4.8% pay rise 9-29, 742B3
Financial disclosure bill not cleared 10-2, 884D1
Jobless benefits revision signed 10-20, 788D1-A2
Sup Ct backs union contract debate right 12-8, 960E1-C2
Sup Ct bars review of EEOC rptg rule 12-13, 960C3
Mayors urge pub svc jobs 12-14, 937A3

Health & Safety Issues
Chrysler police file use chrgd 1-18, 45A2
Muskie rebuts Ford 1-21, 40A2
Sup Ct upholds coal mine penalty procedure 1-26, 87B3
House expands black-lung program 3-2, 181F3
Black-lung law upheld 7-1, 568E3
Sen OKs sick pay tax credit 8-6, 586C1
GOP platform text 8-18, 606C1
Coke oven emissns curb set 10-20, 847E3-848A1
Velsicol worker poisoning probed 12-6, 950B2
'75 injury, illness, deaths down 12-9, 950F2

1977

Amtrak redcap svc end blocked 9-12, 778G2-A3
Cong sets '78 budget levels 9-15, 719F2
Zenith layoffs rptd 9-27, 974E2
NJ jobless benefits case review declined 10-3, 760F2
Sept jobless rate down 10-7, 776A3
Detroit topic for Carter 10-21, 817A1
Carter cites gains 10-27, 813F3
Copper layoffs rptd 10-31, 859F1
Oct jobless rate rptd 11-4, 858D2
NY, Pittsburgh referenda 11-8, 879G1, A3
NY jobless aid for strikers upheld 11-9, 899A2
Carter on econ stimulus effect 11-10, 877E1
Carter backs full employmt bill compromise 11-14, 876E3
Student career guidance aid clears Cong 11-29, 959A2
Nov jobless rate rptd 12-3, 961F2
Idaho student jobless benefits law upheld 12-5, 939C1
Chrysler layoffs set 12-6, 962A1
Admin urban plans stress jobs 12-7, 959C3
Mondale scores protectionism 12-9, 961A1
Business faults Admin 12-14, 962G1
Carter plans tax cut 12-20, 976A3
Miller to succeed Burns 12-28, Carter-Burns dispute examined 12-28, 12-29, 1000D2, C3
Carter sees 4% jobless goal difficult 12-28, 1002B1

Government Employment—*See also PUBLIC Works; CIVIL Service and other appropriate headings under U.S. GOVERNMENT; state, city names*
Carter plans jobs expansn 1-7, 5G1
Sup Ct upholds NYS jobs law 1-10, 57E1
Ford '78 budget proposals 1-17, 33D2, C3
Sup Ct backs Calif tax right 1-25, 80G2
Carter revises econ plan 1-27, 52F1; submits to Cong 1-31, 75A2
Vets job effort planned 1-27, 52C2
Carter econ plan debated 2-3, 89F2, C3
Pay hikes take effect 2-20, 127D2
AFL-CIO seeks coverage, Hatch Act revisn 2-22, 153B2, D2
Sen bars 2d pay hike 3-10, 191E3
Carter asks Hatch Act eased 3-22, 210D2, F2
Gay rights group sees Carter aide 3-26, 278D2
Regional inequities scored 4-6—4-26, 423A3
Pay hike funds signed 5-4, 339F1
Stimulus, other funds clear Cong 5-5, 365E2; Carter signs 5-13, 380D3
Agency shops upheld 5-23, 444C1
Carter welfare plan outlined 5-25, 445E2
House eases Hatch Act 6-7, 442G2
CETA extensn signed 6-15, 500F3
Cong aides pay bias rptd 7-31, 8-4, protectn sought 8-31, 669E3
Mil base closing notificatn signed 8-1, 668E2
GOP offers Soc Sec plan 9-9, 720B2
Sen votes vs mil unionizatn 9-16, 759D3-760C1
Mandatory retiremt curb voted by House 9-23, 737C2
Food stamp 'workfare' projcts set 9-29, 737A2
Brown bars mil strikes, unionizatn 10-6, 777E3
Vets job preferne law backed 10-11, 774D2
Soc Sec extensn rejctd by House 10-26, 814F3
Correctns officer firing case remanded 11-14, 878C3
TVA bias suit case review refused 12-5, 939D1
AFL-CIO urges job programs 12-12, 961C1

Health & Safety Issues
Asbestos workers sue HEW 2-15, 422C2
Sup Ct backs OSHA penalties 3-23, 276F1
GAO scores OSHA, HEW unit 3-23, 280G1-A2
Benzene exposure curbed 4-29, 345D1
Sick pay tax rule delayed 5-16, 382C1
OSHA aims changed 5-19, 422F1
Maritime worker compensatn law affirmed 6-17, 518E2
DBCP exposure curbed 9-8, 723G2
Pregnancy benefits voted by Sen 9-16, 737G3
RR regulatn dispute review refused 10-3, 760E2
OSHA streamlines carcinogen rules 10-3, 778E1
Mine safety rules, agency reorganizatn signed 11-9, 855E3
OSHA to drop 1,100 rules 12-5, 937B3
Coal miners strike 12-6, 937A2
OSHA fines curbed by Cong 12-7, 958D3
US medical data access upheld 12-22, 1008F2
OSHA probes grain explosns 12-28, 1023A2

1978

Government Employment—*See also 'Job Bias' below; also PUBLIC Works; CIVIL Service and other appropriate headings under U.S. GOVERNMENT; state, city names*
AFL-CIO offers stimulus plan 2-20, 141F3
CETA extensn, chngs proposed 2-22, 124B1
Educ aid plan submitted 3-2, 141D3
Fed Reserve chrmn urges pay restraint 3-15, 181C1
Carter unveils urban-aid plan 3-27, 217C3
Double-dipping barred in mil pensn overhaul 4-10, 281C1
Carter asks pay hike limit, reactn 4-11, 259D2, 260G2
Double-dipping rule review declined by Sup Ct 4-17, 308C3
US base closings, cutbacks proposed 4-26, 368D1
CETA operatns cited re new jobs projct 5-23, 405B1
Welfare compromise cuts pub svc jobs 6-7, 446A2
Carter proposes new emergency agency 6-19, 466D2
Carter asks 5.5% pay hike 8-31, 681D2
Pay hike funds signed 9-8, 681F2
Carter urges Viet vet jobs 10-10, 878E1
CETA extensn clears Cong 10-14, 807C1; Carter signs 10-27, 873B2
Carter inflatn plan sets payroll cut, hiring freeze 10-24, 805C3
DC pensn reform vetoed 11-4, 897E2
Miss female bias rule repealed 11-7, 852F3
Carter plans contd hiring freeze 11-9, 874G3
Adultery firing case declined by Sup Ct 12-11, 981A1
Carter hikes CETA '80 budget funds 12-22, 1002D3

Health & Safety Issues
EPA curbed on asbestos rule 1-10, 13F2
4MMPD, tetrachloroethylene curbs urged 1-13, 86A1
Acrylonitrile rule issued 1-16, 85F3
Black lung bills clear Cong 1-24, 2-15, finance measure signed 2-10, 125E1-E2
Benzene exposure rule issued, API scores 2-2, 85G2, C3
Asbestos workers get $20 mln setlmt 2-8, 326C3
UMW bargaining cncl rejcts tentative contract terms 2-12, 104B3
P&M coal pact rejected by miners 2-26, 160A1
Texaco fined for '77 Tex fire 3-2, 212F3
UMW lists strike issues 3-8, 159C3-E3
'77 business costs, HMO plans rptd 3-10, 5-10, 578D1
UMW, operators in new tentative accord 3-14, 182C1, E1, A2
OSHA sets DBCP rule 3-15, 186F2-A3
NM A-worker wins damages for neurosis 3-15, 242F2
Stewardess maternity rule review refused by Sup Ct 3-20, 205G3
Carter vows coal indus study 3-25, 217G1
Anaconda brass plants ratify pact 4-3, 284D3
Asbestos workers warned by HEW 4-26, 326F2
W Va scaffold collapses 4-27, negligence chrgd 6-8, 459F2
Dental insurnc coverage rptd up 5-21, 578C2
OSHA warrantless searches curbed by Sup Ct 5-23, 405B2

1979

Government Employment—*See also 'Job Bias' and 'Strikes' below; also CIVIL Service and other appropriate headings under U.S. GOVERNMENT; state, city names*
Employe free speech backed by Sup Ct 1-9, 14F2
Carter budget proposals 1-22, 44B1; table 42B2
Forgn svc retiremt rule upheld by Sup Ct 2-22, 151A1
Ark grievance policy backed by Sup Ct 4-30, 364D3
Schl staffing rptd up 5-12, 312E2
Carter offers pub-svc jobs plan 5-23, 384C1
Conrail employee fund rptd depleted 5-27, confirmed 5-30, 465B2
Vets' preferne law upheld by Sup Ct; reactn 6-5, 421D1-D2
Carter asks fed pay revisn 6-6, 419C2
Cleveland repaymt plan agreed 6-9, 580A1
Sup Ct workforce data rptd 6-11, 464F1
Cong OKs pay hike funds bill 7-17, 7-20, Carter signs 7-25, 700G1
Carter OKs pol '80 Census hiring 8-9, 631E1
Carter proposes 7% '80 fed pay hike 8-31, 700D2
Alaska workers quit Soc Security 9-10, 726F3-727B1
ACLU sues vs Iowa cnty papal holiday 9-24, 760D3
Chicago-Cook Cnty patronage ruled illegal 9-24, 770C3
Detroit layoffs announced 9-28, 921E1
Carter sees affirmative action success 10-9, 767G1
Cong sets 5.5% fed pay hike limit, Carter signs 10-12, 900F1
Wayne Cnty (Mich) goes broke 10-19, lays off workers 10-23, 921C1
Fed workers smoking case declined by Sup Ct 10-29, 844D2
Newark layoffs set 11-13, 921A2
Newark hiring ordinance vetoed 11-15, override fails 11-20, 992F1
Chicago job reductn rptd 11-16, 921A1
Passaic (NJ) layoff threat rptd, jobless rate cited 11-26, 921G1
N Orleans layoffs planned 11-29, 921F1

Health & Safety Issues
2 unions ask HEW radiatn safety studies 1-30, 90D3
Portsmouth shipyd A-cancer study begins 1-31, 91A1
Alcohol-related absenteeism rptd up 3-9, 218B3
Business rpts OSHA rule compliance costs 3-14, 230A3
3 Mile I radiatn study set 4-4, 260F1
Coal miner pay hike case declined by Sup Ct 4-30, 364C3
Kennedy offers natl health plan 5-14, 362D1
Silkwood estate wins A-suit 5-18, 381D1
MD-managed insurnc plan cuts hosp costs 6-14, 570F3
Dockworker negligence suits backed by Sup Ct 6-27, 558B2
Cocaine use cited 9-5, 972E2, A3
OSHA magistrates warrants case refused by Sup Ct 10-1, 768C1
Ky mine widows suit declined by Sup Ct 10-1, 768F1
UAW OKs Chrysler insurnc cuts 10-25, 805E3
Onshore dockers benefits upheld by Sup Ct 11-27, 919B3

1980

Carter, Reagan TV debate 10-28, 813C1, 814B1, G1, B2, 815G2, D3
Steel indus job losses seen 10-30, 822E1
Special aid re imports rejected 11-5, 870B2
Oct jobless rate rptd 11-7, 876B1
Carter plans to speak out 11-12, 865F2
US Steel plant suit ends 11-14, 917A1
Kennedy urges jobs progrms 11-19, 881D1
Pentagon contract funds clear Cong 12-5, 935B3
Nov jobless rate rptd 12-5, 938B1
Pentagon contract funds signed 12-15, 982B2

Government Employment—*See also 'Job Bias', 'Strikes' below*
State of State messages 1-4—2-6, 269D1, 270A2, G2, B3; 1-9, 1-15, 2-19, 403G2, 404B1, E1; 1-15, 484D1
Saco (Me) workers default rptd 1-7, 54F1; paid 1-10, 187F1
NYC contract talks open 1-31, 186D3
Phila police, fire layoffs set 2-4, take effect 3-1, 187B1
Benton Harbor (Mich) 'payless payday', layoffs cited 2-5, 744B1
Reagan backs fed hiring freeze 2-20, 129C3
Illegitimate child aid backed by Sup Ct 2-26, 188G1
US judges granted 12.9% pay hike 3-24, 250F1
Carter revised budget proposals, Kirkland scores 3-31, 244B1, E1
Political firings barred by Sup Ct 3-31, 291G1-E2
Reagan cites fed hiring freeze vow 4-8, 264G2
NYS resident preference case declined by Sup Ct 4-21, 344C2
San Fran layoffs planned 6-4, 744A1
NYC fscl '81 budget OKd 6-16, 743B1
NYC unions settle 6-19, 7-3, 518A1
US summer jobs progrm rptd 6-30, 495G3
DC fiscal recovery plan proposed 7-19, 742A3, D3
Carter offers econ renewal plan 8-28, 663E1
Carter OKs fed pay hike 8-29, 685C2
Wayne Cnty (Mich) 'payless payday' 9-19, 743C2
Reagan readies hiring freeze 11-6, 837F1, 839B3
Boston transit system shuts down 12-6; funding bill signed 12-7, 939G2
Judicial pay hikes backed by Sup Ct 12-15, 956C3-957D1

Health & Safety Issues
State of State messages 1-9, 483A3, 484B2
Meany backed natl health care 1-10, 14C3, D3
Meal tax case refused by Sup Ct 1-14, 36G3-37A1
Waterway constructn injury case remanded by Sup Ct 1-14, 37F1
OSHA job cancer rules set 1-16, 35G3
Airline ozone measures rptd 2-12, 159A1
Tax liability in RR compensatn backed by Sup Ct 2-19, 131C1
Hazardous work refusals backed by Sup Ct 2-26, 188C1
OSHA chrgs Va shipyd abuses 2-27, 147C3
Carter warns vs anti-labor efforts 4-1, 247F1
Mo workman's compensatn law voided by Sup Ct 4-22, 344A1
UAW cancer probe rptd 4-22, 356G3
Child labor law fines upheld by Sup Ct 4-28, 369A1
Longshoreman fatality damages ruling affirmed by Sup Ct 5-12, 426D3
OSHA chlorine rules partial stay granted by Sup Ct 5-19, 440A3
OSHA eases access to data 5-21, 404E3
Baseball contract dispute setld 5-23, 402B2
Onshore docker state injury benefits backed by Sup Ct 6-23, 555B1
OSHA benzene standard rejected by Sup Ct 7-2, 510D3
Auto plant lead, arsenic curbs to ease 7-8, 505E1
Kennedy Dem conv speech 8-12, 610D2, 614C1

1976

Job Bias & Quota Issues—*See also MINORITIES and group names (e.g., BLACK Americans, WOMEN); also REVERSE Discrimination*
Fed employe bias suit rights extended 6-1, 414E2-G2
Dem platform text 6-15, 469G3-470A1
Sup Ct rules rights laws protect whites 6-25, 479G1
States held liable for bias damages 6-28, 569C1
Conn liability in reverse bias case affirmed 6-28, 569C1
Reagan scores reverse bias 7-6, 490F2
Revenue-sharing progrm scored 8-4, 943E3
NYC constructn union bias barred 9-1, 943F3
New rules for fed contractors proposed 9-15, 884A3
Sup Ct bars review of Washn reverse bias case 10-12, 848G2
New exam rules set 11-17, 884C2
Rpt EEOC cuts backlog 11-19, 922C1
'55-74 male-female earnings gap rptd wider 11-28, 943E1
Sup Ct refuses La reverse bias case 11-29, 900F3
Sup Ct accepts physical job requiremt review 11-29, 901C1
Sup Ct rules re EEOC complaint deadline 12-20, 959F3

Legislation & Legal Actions—*See appropriate subheads in this section; also 'Labor' under U.S. GOVERNMENT—SUPREME Court*
Migrant Workers—*See under AGRICULTURE*

1977

Job Bias & Quotas—*See also BLACK Americans—Employment*
Prudential hiring plan rptd 1-10, 278C3
Seniority layoffs scored 1-18, 278E3
EEOC employe wins '71 bias suit 1-20, 278F3
Exxon age-bias judgmt reversed 1-30, 279A1
Chicago police hiring goals accepted 2-6, impounded funds released 3-25, 279G2
Hartford Fire age-bias suit rptd 2-9, 279B1
NBC sex-bias suit accord rptd 2-13, 279C1
NYC banks sued 2-23, 279G1
NLRB backs union certificatn 2-28, 154A1
Sup Ct rejects NYC compensatn case 2-28, 175C2
Eastn Air attendants wgt standards OKd 3-3, 279F1
Frontier Airlines suit rptd 3-15, 279B2
HEW secy backs quotas 3-17, 217B3
NYC constructn union ruling overturned 3-21, 279D2
Gay rights group sees Carter aide 3-26, 278D2
HEW secy backs down on quotas 3-31, 235B2
Handicapped submit rules 4-5, 301A3
Handicapped rules signed 4-28, 338E3
Coors OKs pact, EEOC drops suit 5-9, 819D1
Employer record access case refused 5-16, 419D1
Pregnant employe dismissal case declined 5-16, 419B2
AMC sued on age bias 5-20, 422A2
Kansas City accuses state 5-26, 446G1
Pre-'64 seniority bias upheld 5-31, 461A2
LA, NYS, NJ sued re police, fire dept bias 6-2, 9-8, 10-4; La cities consent 6-29, 819F1-E2
Miami gay rights law repealed 6-7, 446E2
Employe religious rights limited 6-13, 517C3
House bars HEW quota enforcemt 6-17, 478B1
EEOC time-limit barred 6-20, 517C1
Ala prison employe standards voided 6-27, 538E3
Sen backs HEW affirmative actn 6-28, 515E2, D3
GM back-pay award case refused 6-29, 557C3
EEOC rpts reorgnztn plan 7-20, 669E1
Cong aides pay bias rptd 7-31, 8-4, seek protectn 8-31, 669E3
Japan-controlled Calif bank chrgd 8-9, 669A3
US study scores TV industry 8-15, 642G2
Constructn jobs for women proposed 8-16, 819E2
US acts vs fed contractors 8-25, 669E2
NBC sex-bias suit settled 8-31, 979C2
Carter vows affirmative actn 9-7, 702A1
Pregnancy bias barred by Sen 9-16, 738E1
Mandatory retiremt curb voted by House 9-23, 737C2
Amer Air stewardesses win pregnancy suit 10-3, 819B1
Vets job preferenc law backed 10-11, 774D2
Sup Ct hears Bakke case arguments 10-12, 834D3
Japan-controlled Calif bank acquisitns OKd 10-19, 979E2
Reader's Digest sex-bias suit setld 11-4, 979A2
Carter urges US job opportunities for women 11-17, 914E2
Natl Women's Conf urges bias end 11-19—11-21, 917D3
US reinstates fed contractor 11-23, 979F2
Test pilot age bias case refused 11-28, 919D2
Age bias filing time extended 11-29, 919A2
Career guidance aid clears Cong 11-29, 959B2; signed 12-13, 1001G2
TVA bias suit case review refused 12-5, 939D1
Maternity leave seniority rights upheld 12-6, 938C2
Maternity sick-leave pay rule remanded 12-6, 938A3
Mandatory pensn-plan retiremts backed 12-12, 960G1-D2
Govt job list drops sexist titles, age refs 12-17, 979G2

Legislation & Legal Actions—*See other appropriate subheads in this section; also U.S. GOVERNMENT—SUPREME Court—Labor*
Migrant Workers—*See under AGRICULTURE*

1978

Mine safety inspectn case remanded by Sup Ct 6-5, 431E2
Cotton dust rules issued, suits filed 6-19, 471C3
Carter health plan scored 7-28, 586G1
EPA asks DBCP curbs 9-19, 719C2
Acrylonitrile final rule set 9-29, 753G3
Employer retaliatn case declined by Sup Ct 10-2, 751C1
Benzene exposure rule upset 10-5, 833G3-834C1
OSHA drops 928 rules 10-24, 833C3
Lead exposure rule set, industry challenges 11-13, 899A3, C3
US task force urges chngs 12-8, 984D3

Job Bias & Quotas
EEOC to monitor corp 1-4, 5B1
HEW bias suits rptd setld 1-4, 5C1
Age bias in fed progrms rptd 1-10, 14C1
Handicapped rules issued 1-13, 14G1
Employers curbed on legal fees 1-23, 65A2
Minn name chng bias denied 2-13, 172C3
NJ transsexual wins disability pay 2-16, 327D2
Stewardess pay bias challenge refused 2-21, 125G3
Jury trials in age bias suits backed 2-22, 126F2
Carter proposes EEOC reorgn 2-23, 123D3-124B1
3d party job bias case review denied by Sup Ct 3-6, 162F1
Mandatory retiremt curb signed 4-6, 238F2, E3
Media racism scored 4-7, 4-8, 419E3
Minority press-employmt survey rptd 4-13, 835B3
Black coll bias vs whites ruled 5-1, 348A3
Black-white wage gap rptd less, affirmative actn cited 5-8; disputed 8-8, 810B3, F3, 811G1
Rochester (NY) police hiring challenge case declined by Sup Ct 5-22, 388B2
Coal indus probed, affirmative actn ordrd 5-30, 565A3
Munic legal immunity ended by Sup Ct 6-6, 447D1-A2
Business, educ funds barred by House 6-13, 445G3
GE complaint setld 6-15, 1006B3
WPIX-TV license renewed 6-16, 672D1
Class actn certificatn appeals curbed by Sup Ct 6-21, 509G2
Alaska oil job preference law voided by Sup Ct 6-22, 508F3
Race-based affirmative actn principle backed by Sup Ct 6-28, 482E1
AT&T case declined by Sup Ct 7-3, 55F3
Calif contractors reverse bias case sent back by Sup Ct 7-3, 551B1
Energy Dept '75-77 sex bias admitted 7-14, 1006A3
Black bias found at US Steel Pa plant 8-3, 811B3
Vets preference retained by House 9-11, 696C2
Sen bias-bd vote blocked 9-20, 720A3
Dan River settles black bias suit 9-28, 811C3
NY Times settles sex bias suit 9-28, 835F2
Carter broadens Contract Compliance Office powers 10-6, 811F2
ACLU hails pregnancy benefits law 10-20, 981B3
NLRB backs union right to job data 11-3, 899A1
Miss female bias rule repealed 11-7, 852F2
Seattle gay rights repeal fails 11-7, 857C3
Coll sex-bias ruling voided by Sup Ct 11-13, 874F1-C2
Chicago sex bias suit setld 11-17, 1006G2
UAL NYS maternity leave case refused by US Sup Ct 11-27, 937A2
Weber reverse bias case accepted by Sup Ct 12-11, 980E2-D3
EEOC issues guidelines 12-12, 1006B2
Calif fire dept minority plan overturned 12-26, 1006F2
Coal miners sex bias suit setld 12-26, 1006F2

Legislation & Legal Actions—*See also other appropriate subheads in this section; also U.S. GOVERNMENT—SUPREME Court—Labor*
Freedom of Info in NLRB cases barred 6-15, 468F2
Migrant Workers—*See under AGRICULTURE*

1979

Job Bias & Quotas
AT&T cleared on '73 decree 1-17, 92F1
Cancer patients find job hostility 2-10, 139A3
Sears sues US over conflicting laws 1-24, 92B1
Racial attitudes surveyed 2-20, 307E1
Job-testing data disclosure reversed by Sup Ct 3-5, 184A3
EEOC curb on Burlington data upheld by Sup Ct 2-21, 128F3
Business rpts US rule compliance costs 3-14, 230A3
NYC Transit Auth ex-addict ban backed by Sup Ct 3-21, 231B2
LA fire dept case found moot by Sup Ct 3-27, 263G1
Weber reverse bias case argued in Sup Ct 3-28, 262B3
Retroactive seniority case declined by Sup Ct 4-2, 281C2
Reverse Freedom of Info suits curbed by Sup Ct 4-18, 345F3
Ky factory sex bias case refused by Sup Ct 4-23, 346A3
Sears ends fed contract work, cites suit 4-24, 366A1
Sears suit vs US dismissed 5-15, 365A3
Carter urges black vote 5-20, 384G2
Vets' preferenc law upheld by Sup Ct; reactn 6-5, 421D1-D2
Congressmen ruled liable to suits by Sup Ct 6-5, 463G3-464F1
KKK law use curbed by Sup Ct 6-11, 479A1
Pa jobs-wanted ad case declined by Sup Ct 6-18, 499E1
Union recognitn denial case declined by Sup Ct 6-18, 499E2
Gender-based welfare plan ruled illegal 6-25, 539D3
Merck OKs hiring plan 6-26, 521F1
Weber affirmative actn challenge rejctd by Sup Ct; reactn; majority opinion excerpts 6-27, 477A1-478E1
'78-79 Sup Ct term ends, affirmative actn rulings cited 7-2, 558F1
KKK protesters arrested in Ala 8-12, 631C1
Ex-Rep Passman settles sex bias suit 8-23, 649E3
Carter sees affirmative action success 10-9, 767G1
Sears sued by US 10-22, 885C3
Uniroyal sex bias suit setld 10-23, 885F2
Westn Elec case refused by Sup Ct 10-29, 884C2
Ind pregnancy jobless pay case refused by Sup Ct 11-13, 902A2
NJ bus line fires Iranians 11-22, 898C2
Title IX funds cutoff bar declined by Sup Ct 11-26, 919D2

Migrant Workers—*See MIGRANT Workers*

1980

Carter accepts pres renominatn 8-14, 613A1, C2
Carter worker protectn laws praised 8-20, 647B3
Anaconda to close 2 Montana units 9-30, 825G2
OSHA cotton dust standard case accepted by Sup Ct 10-6, 782C1
Carter, Reagan TV debate 10-28, 815F1-A2
Pittston coal unit fined 12-4, 962G3
EPA airborne lead standards challenge refused by Sup Ct 12-8, 937F1
OSHA lead exposure rule stayed by Sup Ct 12-8, 937G1
Mich asks Chrysler worker insurance 12-26, 984G2

Job Bias & Quotas
Lee Way settles bias suit 1-10, 17C2
US rights comm rpts minority unemployment, lauds Weber ruling 1-14, 36G2, C3, E3
Conn, Wis ERISA cases declined by Sup Ct 1-14, 37B1, C1
Kellogg sex bias chrgs setld 2-6, 115A3
Calif dual seniority system backed by Sup Ct 2-20, 146F2-B3
Affirmative actn plan ordrd for fed cts 3-6, 250B2
Bank uniform case declined by Sup Ct 3-17, 226F1
Ia firefighter wins breast-feeding case 3-20, 441G3
Firestone accused on Tex plant 3-21, 251G2
EEOC bars sex harrasmt, sets regulatns 4-11, 441E2
Purposeful bias cases declined by Sup Ct 4-28, 369A2
EEOC class actn process avoidance backed by Sup Ct 5-12, 426G1
Itinerants registratn upset in La 5-13, 370F2
US female bindery workers win bias suit 5-20, 442C1
Sears Ala suit dropped 5-22, 485D1
San Jose, Santa Clara voters vs gay rights referenda 6-3, 439F2
IBM sued re Md bias 6-3, 485G1
Firestone US contracts voided 7-15, 560B2
Dem platform plank adopted 8-13, 615C1
NY Times settles '74 suit 9-17, 746A3
EEOC suits setld vs CF&I 9-22, Motorola 9-23, Rockwell 9-26, 746D3
La itinerant worker registratn ruling affirmed by Sup Ct 10-20, 807D2
NFL black hiring practices scored 10-27, 998C3
LA settles suit 11-21, 962A3
Ford settles EEOC case 11-25, 899B2
Faculty sex-bias Title IX case accepted by Sup Ct 12-1, 918B2
Boston settles US suit 12-5, 962B3
Schering settles case 12-14, 962D3
Job bias suit filing time limit upheld by Sup Ct 12-15, 957B2
Bobbie Brooks '77 case setld 12-21, 988B1

1976

Obituaries
Feather, Victor 7-28, 716A3
Roche, Josephine 7-29, 716E3

Pensions & Retirement—*See under 'P'*
Politics—*See also 'Presidential Election' and other appropriate subheads in this section*
House OKs FRB reform bill 5-10, 345F1
FEC revisn bill signed 5-11, 346F2
United Brands rpts slush fund, Field indicted 12-10, 985D3
Presidential Election (& transition)
Jackson rpts endorsemts, offers jobs plan 1-6, 22A3
Shriver urges jobs plan 1-7, 22G2
AFL-CIO reviews plans 2-16, 2-18, 148F3, 149B1
Jackson on Mass win 3-3, 165E1
Brown stresses full employmt 3-12, 197G2
Carter for full-employment bill 4-8, 261F1
Carter offers jobs plan 4-23, 305A2, D2
Carter wins in Pa 4-27, 305C1, F1
Jobs a Pa Dem primary issue 4-27, 305E1
Woodcock backs Carter 5-7, 343D2
Reagan sees auto job losses 5-14, 356G3
Carter visits Meany 5-14, 391B1
Jobs top Dem platform item 5-20, 357A3
Dem com OKs platform 6-15, 432A3
Dem platform text 6-15, 469F1-470D3, 473A2, F3, G3, 474B2, C2, 474A3, 475A3-C3, 476C1, A2, 477C2
Dole acceptance speech 6-19, 613A1, C1
Carter on jobs prgrm 6-29, 468E1
Carter visits Meany 6-30, 468E1
Reagan scores reverse bias 7-6, 490F2
Strauss cites joblessness 7-12, 509B1
Dem conv OKs Hatch Act plank revisn 7-13, 509C2
Daley cites jobs as Dem issue 7-13, 509C3
Udall urges jobs bill 7-14, 506D1
Mondale cites joblessness 7-15, 507G2, 511B2, D3
Carter acceptance speech 7-15, 510D2, F2, C3
AFL-CIO bd backs Carter 7-19, 532D2
Shanker, Chaikin, Corbett back Carter 7-22, 551E1
Reagan names Schweiker vp choice 7-26, 549D2
Carter stresses jobs goal 7-28, 551A1
Schweiker gives views 7-30, 8-4, 564E1
Mondale stresses jobs 8-15—8-17, 617B3
Conv delegates' views on jobs rptd 8-17, 616A3
GOP platform text 8-18, 602C2, E2, 603E2, 605A3, G3, 606A1, A2, G2, 611A2
Ford acceptance speech 8-19, 612A1, D2
Ruff probe of union gifts to Ford rptd 8-19—9-25, 722G1-F2, F3
Ford: jobs a top issue 8-27, 645D1
Mondale scores Admin 8-28, 645A3, B3
FEC rules on TV debate financing 8-30, 644E1
Carter sees AFL-CIO bd, Meany vows support 8-31, 645B2, C2
Carter stresses jobs 9-3, 664F1
Carter on welfare option 9-6, 664C2; 9-13, 686E2
Mondale stresses jobs 9-6, 665F2, C3
Carter addresses 2 union convs 9-10, 9-15, 686B2, D3
Ford urges post-HS job-training 9-15, 686D1
Mondale stresses jobs 9-16, 687B2
Dole links Carter, Meany 9-17, 9-23, 724C3
Ford, Carter debate 9-23, 700F3, 701A1-B2, 702C1, A2, C2, A3
Mondale addresses 2 unions 9-23, 9-28, 725B1, C1
Chavez backs Carter 9-25, 724D1
Carter sees Westn AFL-CIO ldrs 9-27, 724C2
Carter stresses jobs 9-30, 742E3
Carter in San Fran, Cleveland 10-7, 10-9, 762B1, C2
Ford scores Carter re defense cuts 10-7, 763A2
Ford cleared re union funds 10-14, 761G1, E2
Mondale, Dole debate 10-15, 782D3, G3, 783B1, E1, A2-B3
Mondale discusses 10-16—10-26, 803B3
Dole scores Dem ties 10-16—10-27, 804C1
Ford, Carter debate 10-22, 800C1-G2, F3, 801E2, E3, 802A1, B1, A3
Rptd major donor 10-22, 938B3
Carter sees NY, NJ ldrs 10-27, at Bklyn rally 10-28, 803E2, G2
Dole scores Calif propositn 10-30, 827G2
Dole on right-to-work laws 10-31, 827A3
Carter elected 11-2, 818G2, B3
Ark, Calif voters reject propositns 11-2, 822A1, 825B1, E3
Stock mkt reactn to electn 11-3—11-4, 826B1
Carter sees tax cut, jobs link 11-4, 819F2
Carter on jobs goals 11-15, 863D2-E3
Carter sets 1½% jobless cut 11-23, 881C2
Carter plans jobs programs 12-9—12-14, 937D2-938A1
Meany lauds Marshall Labor apptmt 12-21, 957F3

1977

Obituaries
Dunn, Robert 1-21, 84G2
Housewright, James 9-19, 788C1
Stulberg, Louis 12-14, 1024D3
Widman, Michael 8-14, 696G3

Pensions & Retirement—*See under 'P'*
Politics
Cong '76 contributns rptd 1-15, 2-4, 2-15, 129D1-129E2; 3-7, 232F2, A3, C3
Reps at White House reception 1-21, 53A2
AFL-CIO seeks Hatch Act revisn 2-22, 153D2
Carter asks Hatch Act eased 3-22, 210D2, F2
'76 pres, cong donatns rptd 4-28, 482D1
Carter energy plan scored 5-18, 443E2
Houses eases Hatch Act 6-7, 442G2
AFL-CIO unit OKs Dem 'hit list' 11-30, 961A2
Carter cites campaign vow 12-28, 1002A1

1978

Obituaries
Robertson, James R 8-1, 708D3

Pensions & Retirement—*See PENSIONS*
Politics
'53, '78 cong membership compared 1-30, 107G2
AFL-CIO backs lobbying bill 4-26, 323C2
Carter plans budget cuts 5-25, 404A3
AFL-CIO fined for campaign gift abuses 6-12, 509C3
'Reverse check-off' gifts barred 7-21, 565F2-A3
Carter, Meany dispute flares 8-7—8-11, 624A2-G3
Corp PACs multiply, 'PAC democracy' feared 9-7, 753C2, F2
Flood indicted for payoffs 10-12, 792C1
Cong legis roundup rptd 10-16, 784E3
Business-labor coalitn vs energy bill rptd 10-16, 786F3
Referenda results 11-7, 847F1, 854E3, 855F2, 857C3
PAC gifts to cong com chrmn rptd 12-24, 1008B1
Right-to-Work—*See 'Unions' below*
Social Security—*See under U.S. GOVERNMENT*

1979

Obituaries
Dioguardi, J (Johnny Dio) 1-12, 176F2
McDonald, David J 8-8, 671G2
Potofsky, Jacob S 8-5, 671D3
Randolph, A Philip 5-16, 432E3
Travis, Robert 11-19, 932F3
Wolchok, Samuel 1-16, 104G3
Pensions & Retirement—*See PENSIONS*
Politics
Carter, Meany mtg 'clears air' 1-12, 13B3
Fitzsimmons asks ICC chrmn firing 1-18, 111G3
DC A-protest draws few 5-6, 343F3
'78 PAC gifts rptd up 5-10, 363G1
Carter addresses Food Workers 6-7, 419E3
Carter sees ldrs at Camp David 7-6—7-11, Admin briefing planned 7-12, 513E2, F2
6 union ldrs back Carter reelectn 7-30, 593B3
Carter thanks Camp David participants 7-30, 608F3-609A1
UAW holds energy job action 8-22, oil industry protested 10-17, 831B2-B3
Carter praises 9-3, 661C1
Chicago-Cook Cnty patronage ruled illegal 9-24, 770C3
Carter announces 'natl accord', sets Pay Advisory Com 9-28; members named 10-16, 829G2-B3
NTEU backs Kennedy 10-30, 847C2
Meany vs Admin policies at AFL-CIO conv, Carter speaks 11-15; Kennedy attends 11-19, 11-15, 877F2, 885A1, C1
Kennedy at UMW conv 12-13, 987D1
Social Security—*See under U.S. GOVERNMENT*

1980

Obituaries
DeLury, John J 2-12, 175G3
Gorman, Patrick E 9-3, 755C3
Hall, Paul 6-22, 528G1
Hollander, Louis 1-3, 104A3
Meany, George L 1-10, 14G2

Pensions & Retirement—*See PENSIONS*
Politics—*See also other appropriate subheads in this section*
Natl ERA support cited 1-13, 54C3
ILGWU backs Carter ticket 1-15, 32A3
UAW's Fraser backs Kennedy 1-15, 33C1
Reagan backs fed hiring freeze 2-20, 129C3; 4-8, 264G2
UFW's Chavez aided Brown campaign 4-1, 246D3
AFSCME backs Kennedy 4-2, 247G1
Citizens' Party seeks full employmt 4-13, 288B3, D3
Reagan weighs trust laws for unions 4-22, 328A1
Lubbers confrmd NLRB cncl 4-22, 333F2
GOP scored at Dem conv 8-12, 8-14, 610B2, 612C1
AFL-CIO cncl backs Carter, scores Reagan 8-20, 647F2-B3
Carter gets AFT endorsemt 8-21; addresses conv, sees clear choice 8-22, 646E2
Reagan addresses Ohio Teamsters, sees 'Carter depressn' 8-27; defends remark 9-1, 664G1-C2
Mondale addresses rallies 9-1—10-9, 780D1, F1, F2
Reagan sees Gleason, other union ldrs 9-11, 699E3
Carter addresses ILGWU 9-29, 738G3
PAC donatns case accepted by Sup Ct 10-6, 782B2
Coalitn sues over oil price setlmts 10-8, 960G1
Reagan proposes ombudsman 11-3, 840B3
Reagan wins blue-collar vote 11-4, 837D2, 838A3
Reagan visits Teamsters hq 11-18, 880D3
AFL-CIO may endorse candidates early 12-5, 938F3
Presser's Reagan transitn role queried, backed 12-15, 955E3
Social Security—*See under U.S. GOVERNMENT*

1976

Strikes & Settlements
Constructn picket bill vetoed 1-2, union ldrs quit Ford com 1-8, 3C3
Natl Airlines strike ends 1-4, 5E1
Dunlop resigns 1-14, 23B1
Pittsburgh teachers end strike 1-26, 95G2
'75 strike data 1-26, 137A2
Newark teachers end strike 2-8, 153G2-A3
Craft unions cross Washn Post picket line 2-16, 2-23, 153E3
Natl Airlines 'no strike' pact 2-19, 153A3
Reagan vs public strikes 2-28, 166D1
NJ bus strike 3-9—3-22, 220G1
Truck strike, Dow avg linked 3-29, 413B2
NY transit strike averted 4-1, 235C3
Teamsters strike 4-1—4-3, 248A3
Rubber workers strike 4-21, 308C3
1st ¼ strike activity down 4-28, 307F1-B2
NY apartment strike 5-3—5-19, 379B1
Teamsters pact ratified 5-10, 348G3
Guild strikes Time 6-2, 398B1
Anheuser-Busch strike ends 6-6, 436A2
Dem platform text 6-15, 470B3
Guild ends Time strike 6-21, 454C2
Mass workers strike 6-21—6-24; OK pact 12-4, 921G1
Sup Ct vs sympathy strike injunctns 7-6, 535D1
NY hospital strike 7-7—7-17, 553E2
Chrysler plant strike ends 7-11, 570C2
Westinghouse strike 7-12—7-20, 536B3
Washn Post pressmen indicted 7-14, 7-21, 553B3
Wildcat mine strike begins 7-19, 553F1
Calif cannery strike ends 7-31, 570C1
2d NY hosp strike 8-4—8-7, 648B1
Wildcat mine strike ends 8-16, 669E3—670A1
GOP platform text 8-18, 606B1
URW ends Goodyear, Firestone strikes 8-28, 8-29, 647A3
URW pacts with Uniroyal, Goodrich set 9-7, 9-8, 866F3
UAW strikes Ford 9-14, 689D2
Parcel svc strike 9-16—12-13, 942F2-D3
Sup Ct vacates product picketing ruling 10-4, 807G1-B2
Sup Ct bars review of benefits for strikers 10-4, 807E2
UAW ratifies Ford contract 10-12, 789B1
Sept indl output, strikes linked 10-15, 806G1; Sept indicator linked 10-29, 833D1
UAW, Chrysler pacts 11-5, 11-7, 847A3
UAW sets GM strike deadline 11-8, 847C3
Deere & Co strike ends 11-9, 847D3
Chrysler pact ratified 11-17, 887G1
GM pact set after 'mini-strike' 11-19, 887C1
Greenwich teachers settle 11-24, 991G1
Louisville teachers strike 11-30—12-13, 991F1
UAW ratifies GM pact 12-8, 991E1
Miami Beach hotel strike 12-25—12-31, 991E2

Unions—*See also other appropriate subheads in this section; also specific union names*
NLRB bars hosp interns unionizatn 3-22, 220E1
NLRB backs journalists rights 4-5, 249C1
Food stamp revisns protested 5-26, 434E3
Clothing, textile unions merge 6-3, 436E1
Sup Ct rules on city withholding of dues 6-7, 435A1
Dem platform text 6-15, 470C3
Provenzano indicted 6-23, 460A1
Teamster pensn fund probe rptd 6-24, 7-1, 492B2
Sup Ct upholds overtime bar 6-25, 552B2
O'Brien of Teamsters arrested 7-7, 570D2
Schoene dies 7-19, 656G3
GOP platform text 8-18, 606C1
Teamsters fund probes linked to bd chng 10-26; loans listed 12-28, 990E3

1977

Strikes & Settlements
Teachers strike in Racine 1-25—3-17; KC 3-21—5-8; Milwaukee 4-7—5-10; Cincinnati 4-13—5-10, 481C2
Sup Ct curbs secondary strikes 2-22, 149D3
AFL-CIO backs constructn picket bill 2-22, 153C2
NYC schl maintenance strike 2-23—2-28, 153C3
Strike fear boosts copper prices 3-18, 3-21, 3-22, 209B2
UMW wildcat case review barred 3-21, 230B3
Construction picket bill fails 3-23, 229C1-D2
Food-stamp chngs sought 4-5, 250E2
Carter scored re constructn picket bill defeat 4-6, 271G2
NBA referees strike 4-10—4-25, 331G3
E Coast dock protest 4-14—4-18, 324D2
NY jobless aid upset 5-24, 463A1
Ohio job benefits law upheld 5-31, 461C3
NYS jobless benefits case refused 6-6, 478G3
UMW wildcat strikes 6-18—9-6, 690E2
Copper strike begins; Kennecott settles 7-1, Magma 558B1
Wis state workers strike 7-3—7-18, 558E2
Detroit city workers strike 7-6, 558G2
NYC teachers union fined 7-20, 558D2
Copper price cut, strike linked 7-20, 577E2
USW strikes ore ranges 8-1, 593E2
Dayton (O) firemen strike 8-8—8-10, 613B3
July indl output down 8-15, 628E3
Strikers' food stamps OKd 9-29, 737A2
ILA strikes selected ports 10-1, 777G3
NJ jobless benefits case review declined 10-3, 760F2
IAM strikes aerospace firms 10-4—12-31, 1005G1
Brown bars mil strikes 10-6, 777E3
Sept indl output gain, strike endings linked 10-14, 798A2
Glass workers end strike 10-14, 818B3
Ky UMW local violence 10-17, 937F2-B3
IFALPA cancels strike 10-21, 11-3, 852C3, 868C3
Kennecott Copper settlemt linked to industry woes 10-31, 859D1
Hawaii sugar strike 11-2—11-22, 899D2
NY jobless aid upheld 11-9, 899B2
Oct exports drop, port strike linked 11-28, 933G1-B2
ILA strike ends 11-29, 915F3
Cleveland teachers strike 11-29—12-8, 939B3
AFL-CIO bldg unit OKs campaign vs on-site picket opponents 11-30, 961A2
Coal miners strike 12-6, 937B1-E2; AFL-CIO pledge support 12-13, 961E1
Farmers strike 12-14—12-22; protest in Plains 12-23, see Carter 12-24, 1002E3
Cleveland police sick call 12-15—12-16, 1005F1
USW ore-range strike ends 12-16, 977C2
Dock strike impact on Nov trade deficit cited 12-28, 1003F1
Coal talks break off 12-30, 1005F2

Unions—*See also other appropriate subheads in this section; also specific union names*
Sup Ct voids steelworker electn rule 1-12, 57E3
Sup Ct upholds poultry drivers bargaining right 1-14, 58A1
Coll faculty oppositn rptd down 1-14, 157E2
Teamster pres son, others indicted 2-4, 102G3-103B1
McBride elected USW pres 2-8, 130B3
AFL-CIO seeks Taft-Hartley repeal 2-22, 153B2
Unionists protest at Stevens mtg 3-1, 153E3
Mental distress suits backed 3-7, 211G2
UFW-Teamsters sign pact 3-10, 177D3
Teamsters to revise pensn posts 3-13, 195C1-C2
Interstate United rpts paymts 3-16, 215G2
Missing Nev ldr found slain 3-17, US sues to protect pensn fund 3-30, 261C3

1978

Strikes & Settlements
Lockheed strike ends 1-2, 4B2
Coal talks resume 1-12, Carter bars interventn 1-30, 62B3; **for subsequent developments, see COAL—Strike**
McDonnell Douglas workers strike 1-13—4-16, pact ratified 4-15—4-16, 284E2
Farmers rally in DC 1-18—1-21; meet Bergland 1-20, hiss Sen testimony 1-24; meet Carter 2-14, 163C2
Farmers block Mex food imports, 200 arrested 3-1, 3-3, 163F1-B2
Farmers in DC protest 3-15, occupy USDA 3-16, Carter OKs farm aid plan 3-29, 219E1
Normal (Ill) firemen strike 3-21—5-15, 565E2
Coal mine constructn workers tentative pact reached 3-28, 217E1
Anaconda brass plants ratify pact 4-3, 284C3
NYC nursing homes struck 4-4—4-7, 284F3-285A1
Coal mine constructn workers ratify pact 4-5, 265E1
Brunswick (O) teachers jailed 4-8—4-14; Toledo schls struck 4-10, 279G2-A3
Northwest pilots strike 4-29—8-15, 680E3
NY Daily News struck 6-13—6-17, 625A2
Unions curbed on supervisor discipline by Sup Ct 6-21, 509E1
Memphis firemen strike 7-1—7-4, 513D2
Munic strikes break out 7-6—7-25, 565G1-E2
Norfolk & Westn Rwy struck 7-10, 565F1
Sanitatn workers strike in Phila 7-14—7-21; New Orleans 7-18—7-21, 565C2
Postal workers walk out in Jersey City 7-21, Richmond (Calif) facility 7-22, 564F3
John Hancock agents strike 7-21—8-17, 680D3
3 NY newspapers struck 8-9, 625E1
Memphis police, firemen strike 8-10—8-18, 644C2
Baseball umpires strike 8-25—8-26, 779F1
Firemen strike in Anderson (Ind) 8-26—9-1, Wichita 9-11—9-20, Butte 9-17, Biloxi 9-18—9-20, 753C1-F1
Schl term marred by strikes 8-30—9-11, 698D2-A3, 699A1
Wichita police strike 9-14—9-20, 753D1
US acts to end expanded N&W Rwy strike 9-26—9-29, strike ends 9-30, 809A2
NY Post resumes publicatn 10-5; Times, News strike ends 11-6, 864E3-865A2
Airline mutual-aid pact compromise clears Cong conf com 10-6, 765B3
VW plant in Pa 10-9—10-15, revised contract ratified 10-21—10-22, 809C3
Cleveland teachers settle 10-16, 1008E3
RR strike, Sept indl output linked 10-17, 790E2
Steel haulers strike 11-11, 1006F1-A2
St louis papers struck 11-20, 1006A2
Rail clerk strike stay renewal refused by Sup Ct 11-27, 937E2
Coast paper mill strike cited 12-1, 934F2

Unions—*See also other appropriate subheads; union names*
'Prehire' picketing curbed 1-17, 33F3
Carter State of Union Message 1-19, 31B1
NYC fscl recovery plan issued 1-20; crisis role cited 86D3, 87A2
UFW ends unionizing boycotts 1-31, 83F1
Top-paid ldrs rptd 2-20, 5-15, 365D1, E1
Stevens contempt challenge refused by Sup Ct 2-21, 125F3
Mgrs overtime pay challenge refused by Sup Ct 2-21, 126A1
Hosp intern unionizatn bar denied review by Sup Ct 2-27, 143B2
Pullman porters join BRAC 2-28, 185B2
Stevens' head forced off bank bd 3-7, 163A1
Avon chrmn quits Stevens bd, cites union pressure 3-21, 205D1
Briguglio murdered 3-21, 232G2
Stevens NC plant bargaining rep ordrd 3-26, 243B2

1979

Strikes & Settlements
N&W Rwy, clerks OK accord 1-8, 87B2
St Louis papers resume publicatn 1-14, 1-15, 87E2
St Louis teachers strike 1-16-3-12, 187A3
Carter warns vs Teamsters strike 1-17, 251D2
Steel haulers end strike 1-18, 87C2
UFW strikes Calif lettuce farms 1-19, natl boycott set 4-26, 327A1
Westn paper strikes end 1-30-5-9, 345D2
New Orleans police strike 2-8-3-4, 165E3-166C1
8 NJ colleges struck 3-20, 207D1
Jobless pay for strikers upheld by Sup Ct 3-21, 231D1
DC teachers end 23-day strike 3-29, 262G2
IAM strikes United 3-31-5-24, 402A2
Teamsters call guidelines strike, industry locks out 4-1, 251B1
Baton Rouge (La) teachers strike ends 4-2, 599D1
Boston U strikes 4-5-4-22, 326D3
Teamsters' pact set 4-10, 262C1
Soccer players strike 4-13-4-18, NLRB orders owners to bargain 5-3, 431B3-432B1
Truck mechanics end strike 4-16, 384E3
Va shipyd strike violence 4-16, 560G3, 561C1
Va shipyd strike suspended 4-22, 306C2
Dissident steel haulers end strike 4-29, 384C3
URW strikes Uniroyal 5-9, 344A3
St Regis Paper strike 5-15-6-23, 598A3
Teamsters ratify pact 5-18, 384A3
Baseball umpires' 3-mo walkout setld, terms rptd 5-18, 569B2
URW links setlmt, wage-guide contract denial bar 5-31, 399D3
Apr indicators drop, strikes linked 5-31, 463F2
Indep truckers strike 6-7-6-15, 462D3-463A1
UFW Calif lettuce strike violence 6-11, strike settled 8-31, 698G2
URW sets pact with Goodrich 6-15, Uniroyal 6-18, 480C1
Truckers' strike, violence persist; impact assessed 6-18-6-28, 479B2-A3
Carter, Admin move on trucker demands; task force formed 6-21-6-27, 479B3
NY tug strike ends 6-27, 500D3
Admin sets 6-point truckers' plan 6-29, strike ebbs 7-7, 7-9, 516D2
Toledo (O) city workers walkout 7-3-7-4, ratify pact 7-5, 599D1
Grain handlers strike 7-6; pact set 9-14, setlmt reached 9-23, ratified 9-25, 722C1, D3
NJ white-collar workers strike 7-10-7-14, accord reached 7-21, 599B1
LA Cnty deputies end 'sickout' 7-12, 599E1
Westinghouse struck 7-16-9-2, 744B2
Chrysler gets no-strike pledge 7-18, 598E1
Hawaiian police end 'sickout' 7-18, 599F1
UAW holds energy job action 8-22, 831B3
UAW stages 'ministrikes' vs GM 8-23-8-27, 698E2
Teachers strike in 14 states 8-27-9-13, 679A1
Rock Island RR struck 8-28, 8-29, Carter orders return 9-20; pay issue resolved 9-26, 722A1-C3
BART svc curtailed 8-31-11-21, 922B3
UAW strikes Caterpillar, Deere setlmt cited 10-1-12-19, 987E1
Rock Island RR svc resumes 10-5, accord reached 10-22, 830C3, G3
San Fran teachers end strike 10-23, 850F1
UAW strikes Intl Harvester 10-31, 987G1
Godunov ABT resigntn rptd 11-21, 1005E3
Grain handlers strike impact seen minimal 11-29, 922C1
Hawaii workers return 12-3, 922G2
Wildcat strike liability limited by Sup Ct 12-10, 988C1
UMW plans strike fund 12-13, 987B1
Chicago transit strike 12-17-12-20, 987C2
Amer Ballet settles 12-20, 987G1-B2

Unions—*See also other appropriate subheads; union names*
Religious rail worker dues case refused by Sup Ct 1-8, 14E3
Carter seeks less recruitmt curbs 1-25, 70D2
Clerks, Meat Cutters to merge 1-26, 130F3
AFL-CIO revises reform legis, scores 'union-busting' 2-23, 148G3
NLRB to probe USW Va shipyd vote 3-2, 187C2
Job-testing data disclosure reversed by Sup Ct 3-5, 184A3
Shoe, clothing unions merge 3-6, 207A1
FAA air-safety crackdown planned 3-16, 206G1
Muffler assn denied tax break by Sup Ct 3-20, 203F3
Church schl interventn barred by Sup Ct 3-21, 231E2
NYC printing contract case refused 4-2, 281F2

1980

Strikes & Settlements
Cleveland teachers end strike 1-3, 5A3
Oil workers strike 1-8; industry offer rejctd 2-28, unions back demands 3-1, 187G1
Meany backed picket line protectn 1-10, 14C3
LIRR pres strike bd rpts; '79 agrmt cited 1-14, 53D1
Phila Journal strike ends 1-25, 115F2
Chicago teachers strike ends 2-11, 111G1
Chicago firemen strike 2-14—3-8, 187E2
W Va miners strike 2-21—3-3, 169G3-170D1
Allis-Chalmers-UAW pact set 3-15, 308A3
KC fire fighters end strike 3-22, 227D3
NYC transit strike starts 4-1, impact rptd 4-1—4-10, unions fined 4-8, 267D3, 268B1-D2
LIRR struck 4-1, 267E3-268B1
NY transit strike ends 4-11, 289C2
LIRR pact reached 4-11, 289C3
Puget Sound ferry strike ends 4-16, 308B3
UAW ends Intl Harvester strike 4-20, 308E2
USW copper strike drags on 7-1—10-24; Kennecott, Phelps Dodge settle 8-27, 10-8, 805D2
NYC transit strike fines hiked 7-2, 518E1
Detroit workers strike 7-2, 518G1; strike ends 7-12, 542G1
Mobile (Ala) munic strike 7-14—7-24, 576D1
TV, film actors strike 7-21, 684A3
San Fran hotel pact ends 27-day strike 8-12, 647G3-648B1
PATH strike ends 9-1, 704D2
Teachers strike in 10 states 9-2—9-8, 723G2
AMC strike 9-16, UAW pact set 9-17, 725B1
Calif winery strike ends 9-22, 747A3*
Met Opera cancels season over musicians' strike 9-29, strike setld 10-25, 883E3
TV, film actors end strike, musicians continue 10-23, 805B3
Sunshine Mining strike ends 11-8, 883D3
USW copper strike ends 11-21, 987E3
LA city pact ratified 12-12, 988A1
Continental Air strike ends 12-20, 988E1

Unions—*See also other appropriate subheads in this section*
Meany backed right to organize 1-10, 14C3
AFL-CIO rpts Teamster reaffiliatn talks 2-19, organizing unit plan 2-23, 147B1
Pvt coll faculty unions curbed by Sup Ct 2-20, 146C1-B2
Carter anti-inflatn plan unveiled to ldrs 3-14, 201A1
USW suit vs foundatn dissident funding refused by Sup Ct 3-31, 291B3
Carter warns vs anti-labor efforts 4-1, 247F1
Hosp limits case declined by Sup Ct 4-14, 307C1
Canada wage hikes compared 5-27, 406C2
AT&T begins reorgn, OKs pensn plan consolidatn 8-20, 648C2
Poland strike aid rptd, Admin cautns 8-31, 9-4, 659G2
AFL-CIO OKs Polish worker fund 9-4; Warsaw protests 9-9—9-10, US disavows 9-11, 679F1-D2

1976

Provenzano fed chrgs dismissed 10-29, 972B1
Ark, Calif defeat worker rights proposals 11-2, 822A1, 825B1, E3
Ex-Teamster fund aide indicted 11-30, 991C1
UAW wins GM vote in South 12-22, 991D1

Wages & Hours
Dec, '75 payrolls rptd 1-19, 91B2
'75, 1st ¼ wage pact gains rptd 1-23, 4-25, 306B3
Ford Econ Rpt 1-26, 66F3
'74, '75 food mktg wages rptd 2-11, 216A2
Feb payrolls rptd 3-17, 215G3
Mar real pay rptd 4-21, 306C2
4th ¼ '75, Jan-Mar real pay, labor costs rptd 4-26, 376B2
Apr real pay rptd 5-21, 375F1
Dem platform text 6-15, 470A3
1st ¼, 6-mo labor costs rptd 6-18, 494F1
Labor cost index described 6-18, 494D2
May real pay rptd 6-22, 453D3
US min wage laws ruled not binding on states, localities 6-24, 468A2
June real pay rptd 7-21, 536E2
2nd ¼ wage gains rptd, 1st ¼ revised 7-23, 567E1
GOP platform text 8-18, 606A1
UAW sees 4-day week 10-12, 789B1, D1
3d ¼ wage setlmts up, 2d ¼ revised 10-22, 805G3
'74 sex, race averages rptd 11-28, 943F1

Women—*See WOMEN*

1977

US sues Ohio Teamster fund 4-4, 280B2
Washn Post pressmen plead guilty 4-14, 345F1-A2
Harry Bridges retires 4-18, 324G2
Teamsters pres, 3 other pensn trustees quit 4-29, fiduciary named 6-17, 558C2
RC-NLRB dispute case refused 5-2, 406D2
Mafia racketeering role rptd 5-16, 568E1
UAW conv 5-18—5-19, 408E1-E2
NYS jobless benefits case refused 6-6, 478G3
UMW reelect Miller 6-14, 462A3; vote certified 7-21, 691A1; reelectn affirmed 10-11, 937E2
Herman replaces Bridges at ILWU 6-23, 481E3
Inmate union curbs upheld 6-23, 539C2
Carter asks labor law reform; reactn 7-18, 555C2-C3
Teamster pensn fund loans to gangsters rptd 7-18, 558A2
Labor law reform a Carter town mtg topic 7-21, 575B1
Visa curbs on communists eased 8-17, 667F2
Stevens found in contempt 8-31, 724F1
Canal pact opponents plan campaign 9-9, 698B3
Sen votes vs mil unionizatn 9-16, 759D3-760C1
UAW shelves AFL-CIO reentry 10-5, 762D1
Brown bars mil unionizatn 10-6, 777E3
Reform Act OKd by House 10-6, 795B2
Stevens labor-law fines set 10-27, 899F1
Teamsters insurnc deal probed 11-1—11-2, 837E1
Stevens sued by union 11-1, 11-10, 899B1
NYC pub note sale canceled 11-10, 881D1
USW vote probe ended 11-11, 899G2
Provenzano kickback chrg dropped 11-11, 928C1
Lawyer fees case refused 11-14, 878D3
AFL-CIO membership data 961D2
ILA's Field sentenced 12-2, 937E3
AFL-CIO conv; Meany reelected 12-8—12-13, 960D3
Provenzano reindicted 12-19, 991B3

Wages, Hours & Productivity—*See also INCOMES*
'76, 4th ¼ productivity rptd; 3d ¼ revised 1-26, 130A1
4th 1/4 '76 compensatn, unit labor costs rptd; 3d 1/4 revised 1-26, 130C1
Econ indicator index described 1-28, 92D3, G3; **for data, see 'Statistics' under BUSINESS**
'76 factory wage study rptd 1-28, 158B3
AFL-CIO sets legis goals 2-22, 153E2
Employment cost index described 154F2
'76, 4th 1/4 employmt costs rptd 3-3, 154C2
Workweek data rptd 3-18, 194G2-A3
Admin asks $2.50 min wage, AFL-CIO scores 3-24, 229D2
Admin min wage plan scored 4-6, 271G2
Feb wages, hours up 4-17, 194C1
Inmate rights rpt issued 4-26, 383E2
1st ¼ productivity rptd; '76, 4th ¼ revised 4-27, 339D3
1st ¼ compensatn, unit labor costs rptd; 4th ¼ '76 revised 4-27, 339F3
Illegal alien plan proposed 4-27, 370D2
Low US costs, forgn US investmt rise linked 5-11, 5-25, 385C3
Urban factory wage table 5-16, 384D3
Fraser sees 4-day workweek 5-19, 408E2
Carter backs $2.65 min 7-12, 533B1, 534A1
2d ¼ productivity, labor costs, real compensatn; 1st ¼ revised 7-29, 704D1
2d ¼ employmt costs, 1st ¼ revised 8-31, 704G1
Min wage hike OKd by House; indexing provisn cut, tip credit retained; small business exemptn expanded 9-18, 758E3
A&P overtime suit filed 9-27, 778C2
Wage-price panel analyzes steel industry 10-7, 776E2
Final min wage bill cleared, tip credit reduced 10-20, 795E2; signed 11-1, 834B1
3d ¼ productivity, unit labor costs rptd; 2d ¼ revised 10-27, 836E1
US ranked 6th in world pay scale 11-6, 853C3
3d ¼ employmt costs rptd 11-30, 941D3

Women—*See WOMEN*

1978

Legal fee liability case review denied by Sup Ct 4-17, 308D3
Stevens settles NLRB suit 4-28, 324E1-C2
Unions held subject to trespass laws by Sup Ct 5-15, 387A2
Law revisn filibuster continues 5-16—6-14, 446C2, E2 ★
Supervisor discipline curbed by Sup Ct 6-21, 509D1
Law revisns returned to Sen com 6-22, 508B2
Pol organizing backed by Sup Ct 6-22, 508A3
Hosp organizing backed by Sup Ct 6-22, 508E3
Fraser quits Admin panel, scores reform bill oppositn 7-19, 611A2
Carter, Meany dispute flares over law revisn defeat 8-7—8-11, 624A2
Bakery, tobacco unions merge 8-16, 700G1-B2
2d ¼ union, nonunion pay hikes compared 8-30, 680C2
Corp PACs multiply, 'PAC democracy' feared 9-7, 753C2, D2
UAW, GM in southn plant agrmt 9-11, 699B3
Stevens loses more directorships, union pressure cited 9-12, 699C2
Carter stresses law reform 9-20, 715G2
USW bans outside electn aid 9-21, 737C2
UAW vs United Tech-Carrier merger 10-30, stay lifted 11-10, 896D2
NLRB backs right to job data 11-3, 898G3
Mo right-to-work law loses, NM debate cited 11-7, 847F1, 854E3, 855F2
AFT to organize nurses 11-29, 961A1

Wage-Price Developments—*See under ECONOMY*
Wages, Hours & Productivity—*See also 'Contract Negotiations' and 'Strikes' above*
Econ indicator index described 128A1
Carter State of Union Message 1-19, 29A2, 30E3
'77 productivity, labor costs rptd 1-26, 128B2
'77 wage, benefit gains rptd 1-27, 128D2
UMW bargaining cncl rejcts tentative contract terms 2-12, 104C3
Dec '77, Jan, Feb real earnings drop rptd 2-27, 3-28, 222G1
New CPIs described, link to wages cited 222G2, A3
Business ldrs back Carter wage-price plan 4-20, 5-11, Admin scores critics 5-8, 361A3, G3
1st ¼ productivity, labor costs rptd; '77, 4th ¼ revised 4-25, 345F1-C2
1st ¼ wage, benefits rise rptd; '77 revised 4-27, 389C2
Carter bars wage-price controls 5-4, 321C2
Black-white wage gap rptd narrowed 5-8, 810G2
Meany, labor ldrs see Carter; rejct wage-restraint plea 5-10; Bosworth backs stand 5-11, 361F2, D3
'77 4th ¼, '78 1st ¼ employmt cost rptd up 5-30, 429D1
1st ¼ union, nonunion pay hikes compared 5-30, 429F1
Carter links wages, budget restraint 6-14, 446C3
'77 indl productivity drop rptd 6-14, 469G3-470B1
Minimum wage hike, inflatn linked 6-19, 427D2
Jan, May purchasing power drop; '72 erosn rptd 6-30, 507B1
2d ¼ productivity, labor costs rptd; '77, 1st ¼ '78 revised 7-27, 606C3
Meany scores Bosworth, Carter sets bargaining panel 8-7, 624B2
Strauss scores deceleratn noncompliance 8-29, 682C1
2d ¼ employmt costs rptd up 8-30, 680A2
Cited re '73-78 food price rise 9-8, 717E2
Wage control a topic at USW conv; Carter, Meany address 9-17—9-20, 715E1-G2
Aug real earnings rptd down 9-26, 752E1
'78 wage hikes, '50-78 productivity decline analyzed by Admin 10-4, 790B1
'67-78 minority-white real earnings gap rptd 10-19, 812G2
Carter inflatn plan sets voluntary guidelines 10-24, 805C2-807B1; **for subsequent developments, see ECONOMY—Carter Anti-Inflation Plan**
Sept real earnings rptd down 10-27, 864F1
3d ¼ productivity, labor costs rptd up; 2d ¼ revised 10-27, 864D2
3d ¼ profits rise, productivity gain linked 10-30, 919E2
Oct purchasing power drop rptd 11-28, 918A3
Nov real earnings rptd up 12-22, 1003B2

Women—*See WOMEN*

1979

Soccer players seek union recognitn 4-13—4-18, NLRB orders owners to bargain 5-3, 431B3-432B1
Ark pub worker grievance policy backed by Sup Ct 4-30, 364D3
NLRB dismisses USW Va shipyd vote fraud chrgs 5-4, orders Newport News bargaining 6-26; appeal set 7-3, 560G3
Punitive damages vs unions barred by Sup Ct 5-29, 421B3
IAM free speech religion cases declined by Sup Ct 6-4, 439F1, G1
Ariz farm labor law restored by Sup Ct 6-5, 464A3
Clerks, Meat Cutters merge 6-6, 419F3
Union recognitn denial case declined by Sup Ct 6-18, 499E2
Hosp organizing curbs backed by Sup Ct 6-20, 516A2
Weber affirmative actn challenge rejctd by Sup Ct, reactn; majority opinion excerpts 6-27, 477A1-478E1
Stevens '77 suits dismissed 7-18, 8-6, 598C3
Textile union sues Stevens, others in Ga 7-18; Grumman, local offcls settle 8-1, 598E3
UAW wins Okla City GM organizing dispute 7-19, 598F1
'76, '78 membership data rptd 8-31, 666B1
Calif gov vetoes anti-UFW bill 9-7, 698E3
UAW wins bargaining powers in GM pact 9-14, 698A2
UFW field talk case refused by Sup Ct 11-5, 884B3
Iran seizure of US hostages protested 11-9, 863D1
Kirkland bids all unions join AFL-CIO, membership data cited 11-19, 885A2, C2
Nonunion coal output growth cited 12-10, 987A1
Wildcat strike liability limited by Sup Ct 12-10, 988C1

Wage-Price Developments—*See under ECONOMY*
Wages, Hours & Productivity—*See also 'Contract Negotiations' and 'Strikes' above*
Carter bars min wage, constructn wage chngs 1-4, 3F3
'78 job gains, productivity drop linked 1-14, 34F1
Productivity decline seen in anti-pollutn rules 1-19, 129E3
Carter budget proposal 1-22, 41D2
Carter wage insurnc tax credit opposed in Cong 1-23, 55C3
Dec '78 real earnings rptd down 1-24, 73C2
'78, 4th 1/4 productivity, labor costs rptd; 3d 1/4 revised 2-9, 110F3
CEA productivity forecast cited; '48-77 data rptd 2-9, 111B1
Amer Cyanamid back pay rule upheld 2-10, 131A1
'78, 4th 1/4, 3d 1/4 employmt cost index rptd 2-28, 183B1
1st 1/4 productivity, labor costs; '78, 4th 1/4 revised 4-30, 362F2
Apr real earnings rptd down 5-25, 402E3
1st ¼ employmt costs rptd 5-31, 463D3
Productivity, wage gain, inflatn fight linked 6-13, 6-19, 463G1-A2
June spendable earnings rptd 7-26, 557B1
2d 1/4 productivity, labor costs; 1st 1/4 revised 7-30, 577B3
July real earnings rptd down 8-25, 646E2
2d 1/4 employmt costs rptd 8-30, 701A2
Westn natns' wage rates compared 9-19, 697D3
Natl Agenda Comm created 10-24, 810A3
Oct real earnings rptd down 11-27, 903A3
3d 1/4 productivity, labor costs rptd; 1st, 2d 1/4 revised 11-28, 940E2
3d 1/4 employmt cost index rptd 11-29, 922E2
Nov real earnings rptd down 12-21, 984G2

Women—*See WOMEN*

1980

Reagan urges union plants 10-2, 738D2
Textile workers, Stevens come to terms 10-19, 805B1-D2
Stevens plants access case refused by Sup Ct 10-20, 807A2
Deering Milliken '56 pay dispute setld 12-3, workers OK 12-14, 962D2

Wage-Price Developments—*See under ECONOMY*
Wages, Hours & Productivity—*See also 'Contract Negotiations', 'Strikes' above*
Meany backed min wage 1-10, 14C3
Pay Advisory Com backs high raises 1-22, 52C1
'79, 4th 1/4 productivity, labor costs rptd 1-28, 77E1
'79, 4th 1/4 employmt costs rptd 2-28, 168C1
Pay Advisory Com recommendatns OKd 3-13, 182G2
Carter warns vs anti-labor efforts 4-1, 247F1
1st 1/4 productivity, labor costs rptd 4-25, 329D1
1st 1/4 employmt costs rptd 5-29, 400D3
Ford scores Carter 7-14, 534E2
2d 1/4 productivity; 1st 1/4 revised 7-28, 574A2
Dem platform plank adopted 8-13, 614D3
Carter cites minimum wage in pres renominatn acceptance speech 8-14, 613C2
Carter praised on min wage role 8-20, 647B3
Anderson platform offered 8-30, 665F1, C2
Carter seeks productivity gains vs 'quick-fix' approach 9-18, 698C3, G3
Aug indicators rptd up 9-30, 740G3
Carter scores Reagan on min wage 10-10, 778D2
Bush cites '76-79 productivity drop 10-16, 817B3
Carter ridicules Reagan 'secret plan' 10-22, 802F3
Carter chrgs Reagan 'flipflop' on min wage 10-27, 816B3
Carter, Reagan TV debate 10-28, 813E1, 814E1, C2
Oct income rptd 11-18, 883D1
2d 1/4, 3d 1/4 employmt costs, compensatn index rptd 11-28, 938E1, A2
Reagan renews youth min wage support 12-11, 956D2
US guidelines ended 12-16, 983A2
Nov income rptd 12-22, 984B1

1976

LABOR Party, U.S.
Final pres vote tally 12-18, 979C2
LACAYO, Hank
Carter personnel advisor 11-19, 881E3
LACKEY, Kenneth
Dies 4-16, 316A1
LACLEDE Steel Co.
Fined 4-10, 988E3
La COSTA Land Co.
Teamsters fund loan rptd 12-29, 991B1
LADDON, I. M.
Dies 1-14, 80E3
LADIES Home Journal (magazine)
Buys Quinlan story rights 6-4, 423A3
LADIES Professional Golf Association (LPGA)—*See GOLF*
LADY (book)
On best seller list 1-25, 80D3
LADY From the Sea, The (play)
Opens 3-18, 1014C3
LaFALCE, Rep. John J. (D, N.Y.)
Reelected 11-2, 830D2
LAFAYETTE, Ind.—*See INDIANA*
LAFAYETTE, La.—*see LOUISIANA*
LAFTA—*See LATIN American Free Trade Association*
LaGACE, Sherry
Death rptd 1-27, 80E3
LAGHI, Msgr. Pio
Asks justice for priest killers 7-14, 571D2
LAGOMARSINO, Rep. Robert J. (R, Calif.)
Reelected 11-2, 829C1
LaGUARDIA Airport (N.Y.)
Croats hijack jet; questned re '75 blast 9-10—9-12, 685D1, C2
LAHA, Gaston
Named culture min 8-20, 926C1
LAIRD, Bruce
Heads Ontario Liberal wing 4-25, 350E2
LAIRD, Melvin
Sen com cites '69 DCI link 4-26, 304G2
LAI Ya-Li
Clashes with USSR on Mideast 1-15, 60A1
LAKE, Nancy
Seconds Ford nominatn 8-18, 598A1
LAKE, W. Anthony
Carter liaison 11-23, 881A3
LAKE Crystal, Minn.—*See MINNESOTA*
LAKE Michigan—*See MICHIGAN, Lake*
LAKE Superior—*See SUPERIOR, Lake*
L'ALLIERS, Jean-Paul
Aids French controllers 9-7, 692F2
LALONDE, Fernand
Chrgs RCMP re Sky Shops info 4-21, 309F3
LALONDE, Marc
Judicial interference chrgd 2-20, denied 3-3, 3-4, 187G3
Seeks end to Liberal split 3-7, 238C3
Cleared in Deschaines rpt 3-12, 220F3
Rpts flu immunizatn shots set 3-30, 238E3
Air pact talks cited 7-1, 496A3
Stays health min 9-14, 692C2
La MALFA, Ugo
Bars govt role 1-9, 29F2
LAMANNA, Giuseppe
Sentenced 7-29, 816C3
LAMBERT, Allen T.
Oppositn asks probe 11-25, 924B2
LAMBERTUS, Walter
Defects 7-28, Canada OKs status 7-31, 562E2
LAMBERZ, Werner
E Ger Politburo enlarged 5-22, 381E2

1977

LABOR, Department of—*See under U.S. GOVERNMENT*
LABOR Relations Board, National—*See U.S. GOVERNMENT—NATIONAL Labor Relations Board*
LACAYO, Carmela
Dem natl vice chrmn 1-21, 53B2
LACERDA, Carlos
Dies 5-21, 452D3
LACHMON, Jaggernath
Coalitn loses electns 10-31, 844F1
LACHS, Manfred
World Ct member 4G1
LACKAWANNA, N.Y.—*See NEW York State*
LACOMBE, Brigitte
Czechoslovakia expels 3-2, 220E3
LACOVARA, Philip
House Korea probe dispute rptd 7-12; quits, Flynt scores 7-15, Jaworski to replace 7-20, 556F1
Watergate probe resignatn cited 556G1
LACY, Lee
In World Series 10-11—10-18, 806A2
LADECO Airlines (Chilean airline)
Jet hijacked to Peru 7-5, 537B2
LADIES Professional Golf Association (LPGA)—*See GOLF*
LAETRILE—*See under MEDICINE*
LAFAYETTE, Ind.—*See INDIANA*
LAFFRANCHI, Claudio
Arrested 4-24, 350G2
LAFLEUR, Guy
NHL season ldr 4-3, 262A3, F3
Montreal wins Stanley Cup, named playoff MVP 5-14, 429F3
Named Canada top male athlete 12-19, 1021E1
LaGARDE, Tom
In NBA draft 6-10, 584A2
LAGUARDIA International Airport (N.Y.)
Croats '76 hijack convictns 5-5, 451G2
NY Airways copter run cited 5-16, 412D3
Blackout shuts down 7-13—7-14, 537F2
LAIRD, Melvin R.
Defns budget reform ordrd 10-26, 857A3
Chrgs USSR ABM pact violatns 11-23, 997C1
LAISE, Carol C.
Keeps Forgn Svc post 1-21, 53E1
LAJARA Burgos, Rear Adm. Luis Homero (ret.)
Sets pres bid, vows multinatl asset seizure 9-11, 767E1
Wessin sets pres bid 9-30, 786F1
LAKE, Judge Neil A.
Orders rpt on Hughes '38 will 1-17, 120B2
LAKE, W. Anthony
Named Policy Planning dir 1-7, 14B2
LAKE Erie—*See ERIE, Lake*
LAKE Michigan—*See MICHIGAN, Lake*
LAKER Airways
US air svc pact set 6-22, 500A2
3 airlines seek lower US-UK fares 7-24, 7-29, 8-1, 593D1
UK OKs svc chngs 9-14, 9-29; 'Skytrain' begins 9-26, profit rptd 10-24, 860B2
LAKEVILLE Miss (race horse)
Named top 2-yr old filly 12-13, 970F3
LAKEWOOD, N.J.—*See NEW Jersey*
LAL, Bansi
Loses Parlt seat 3-16—3-20, 205C2
Faces corruptn probe 4-1, 283B3★
Passport taken, probe set 4-18, 304G1, A2
Arrested 8-23, 655E2
LALIQUE, Marc
Dies 10-26, 872D2
LALONDE, Marc
Arsenic pollutn probe set 1-18, 61A2
Backs abortion clinics 3-4, 237A3
Arsenic pollutn rpt issued 6-6, 448C1
Named Canada prov relatns min 9-16, 725F2
Reassumes women's post 9-23, 763D3
LAMA, Luciano
Speech stirs student riots 2-17, 135G2
LaMARSH, Judy
Rpt scores TV violence 6-15, 485A2
LAMB, Ralph
Pleads not guilty 4-21, 312B3

1978

LABOR, Department of—*See under U.S. GOVERNMENT*
LABORERS' International Union of North America (AFL-CIO)
Fosco, Reed on '77 top-paid labor ldrs list 5-15, 365G1
Union insurnc scheme chrgd 6-15, 560G2, B3
Postal pact reached 7-21, 564F2
Postal pact revised 9-15, 766C2
LABOR Relations Board, National—*See U.S. GOVERNMENT—NATIONAL Labor Relations Board*
LABOR Statistics, Bureau of—*See under U.S. GOVERNMENT—LABOR*
LABOURIER, Dominique
Celine & Julie released 2-24, 618G3, 619A1
LACALLE Herrera, Luis
Sent poisoned wine 9-6, 799F1
LACEY, Judge Frederick B.
Scores Farber book deal 8-11, 678C3
Sentences 2 Sovt spies 10-30, 835A2
LACK, Steve
Rubber Gun released 4-24, 619E3
LACROSSE
Hopkins wins NCAA title 5-27, 540A2
Penn State wins women's title 5-28, 540B2
LACY, Lee
In World Series 10-10—10-17, 799B3
LACY, William S. B.
Dies 12-11, 1032B3
LADDERS
OSHA drops wood rule 10-24, 833E3
LADIES Home Journal (magazine)
McCarthy drug addictn, White House pot use rptd 11-19, 943C2
LADIES Professional Golf Association (LPGA)—*See GOLF*
LADY Byng Memorial Trophy—*See HOCKEY—Awards*
La ESPRIELLA, Ricardo de
Elected Panama vice pres 10-11, 764D3
LAETRILE—*See under MEDICINE*
LaFALCE, Rep. John J. (R, N.Y.)
Reelected 11-7, 851A4
LAFAYETTE, La.—*See LOUISIANA*
LAFAYETTE v. Louisiana Power & Light Co.
La cities trust law liability upheld by Sup Ct 3-29, 280F1
LAFFER, Arthur
Laffer Curve cited re Kemp-Roth bill; diagram 7-3, 735D1
LAFLEUR, Guy
In NHL top paid player list 4-6, 296G3
NHL scoring ldr 4-9, 296D1, D2-E2
Montreal wins Stanley Cup 5-25, 458C1
Named NHL MVP 6-12, 458D2
LaGARDE, Tom
Traded to SuperSonics 6-9, 457E2
LAGHARI, Farook
Subversn chrg denial rptd 4-9, 268D2
LAGOMARSINO, Rep. Robert J. (R, Calif.)
Reelected 11-7, 850F1
LAHTI, Christine
Hooters opens 4-30, 760D2
LAING, John
Rubber Gun released 4-24, 619E3
LAINO, Domingo
Scores govt at OAS, asks US end aid 7-6; arrested 7-7, US amb protests 7-11, 559C1
Released on judge's orders 8-8, 640G3
LAIRD, E. Cody
Football TV contract tax value backed 1-9, 13B2
LAIRD, Melvin
Buzhardt dies 12-16, 1032D2
LAITY, Congress of the—*See CONGRESS of the Laity*
La JOLLA, Calif.—*See CALIFORNIA*
LAKAS, Demetrio (Panamanian president; replaced Oct. 11)
Torrijos pres candidacy seen 8-7, 632G1
Royo replaces as pres 10-11, 764E3
LAKE Havasu City, Ariz.—*See ARIZONA*
LAKE Michigan—*See MICHIGAN, Lake*
LAKER, Freddie
London-Sydney svc barred 10-11, 793C3
LAKER Airways
CAB waives charter rules for stranded travelers 8-4, 640E3
LAKESIDE v. Oregon
Judge's jury instructn on silent defendant backed by Sup Ct 3-22, 221G1
LAKE Superior—*See SUPERIOR, Lake*
LAL, Devi
Ousted as Haryana State chief min 7-4, restored in Janata compromise 7-9, 631C3
LALLI v. Lalli
NYS illegitimate child inheritance law upheld by Sup Ct 12-11, 981B1
LALONDE, Marc
Rpts queen backed const chngs 8-16, 647B2
Scores Levesque on const 11-1, 866G2
Canada justice min 11-24, 921D3
La MALFA, Ugo
Scores terrorists, asks death penalty 3-20, 200E2
Calls for Leone resignatn 6-14, 516C3
LAMB, Peter
Named to S Africa Davis Cup team 2-12, 251C3
LAMBERT, Paul A.
Convicted in computer drug plot 3-10, 380B1
LAMBERZ, Werner
Killed 3-6, 228D1

1979

LABOR, Department of—*See under U.S. GOVERNMENT*
LABOR Party, U.S.
LaRouche '76 pres funds suit cited 12-18, 984B2
LABOR Relations Board, National—*See U.S. GOVERNMENT-NATIONAL Labor Relations Board*
LABOR Statistics, Bureau of—*See under U.S. GOVERNMENT-LABOR*
LABOUISSE, Henry
On blocked Cambodia relief 12-13, 977C3
La BOUTEILLE de Vin (The Bottle of Wine) (painting)
Sold for record sum 7-3, 672C1
LABUS, Thomas
Convicted 2-22, sentncd 3-19, 220F2
LACEY, Judge Frederick B.
Named to wiretap ct 5-18, 442D3
LACHS, Judge Steven M.
Sworn Calif judge 9-17, 748B2-A3
LACKLAND Air Force Base—*See TEXAS*
LACLEDE Steel Co.
Price violatn chrgd 5-17, 385A2
LaCOSS, Mike
Reds lose NL pennant 10-5, 797D2
LACQUA, Joseph A.
Indicted 1-17, 87A3
LACROSSE
Penn State wins WLA title 5-13, 507C3
Hopkins wins NCAA title 5-26, 507F2-C3
LADD Jr., Alan
Quits as Fox Film pres 6-7, plans Warner unit assn 7-4, 587G3
LADD, Pete
Traded to Astros 6-14, 1002A3
LADIES Professional Golf Association—*See GOLF*
LADY Bying Memorial Trophy—*See HOCKEY-Awards*
LAETRILE—*See under MEDICINE*
La FAYE, Julian—*See CARROLL, John*
LAFFRANCHI, Claudio
Chrgd in Chiasso scandal 2-15, 137D1
Sentenced 7-3, 505C2
LAFLEUR, Guy
Sovts win Challenge Cup 2-11, 118C2
NHL scoring ldr 4-8, 355E2
La FRENAIS, Ian
Prisoner of Zenda released 5-25, 820A3
LaFRENIERE, Celine
City on Fire released 9-14, 819G3
LAFTA—*See LATIN American Free Trade Association*
LAGERFELD, Karl
'79 fashion roundup rptd 1006C2, F2
LaGRANGE, Ill.—*See ILLINOIS*
LaGRANGE, Ulysses J.
Defends Exxon 3d 1/4 profits 10-22, 804F2
LaGUARDIA International Airport (Queens, N.Y.)
Aircraft near-collisn 2-11, FAA updates radar improvemt 3-12, 206A2, C2
NYC near-collisn rpt issued 4-9, 412D2
Serbian hijacks jet 6-20, 491G2
LAHEY, Dr. Frank H. (1880-1953)
FDR rptd possible cancer victim 12-2, 925D3
LAHTI, Christine
The Woods opens 4-25, 712G3
LAI, George
Quits re morals chrg 2-12, 109E1
LAINGEN, L(owell) Bruce
Named US envoy to Iran 10-2, 752F2
Told US will admit shah 10-20, 879B2
Detained in Iran 11-4, shah's US entry rptd planned 11-8, 841F1, G2
Iran warning issued 11-9, 862F2
Hostage status disputed 11-30—12-1, spy trial threatened 12-1, 12-4, 914A2, E2
Linked to Azerbaijan rebel ldr 12-8, 936E2
Iranian amb arrested 12-19, 976A1
Sees clergy 12-27, 975A2
LAITIN, Joseph
Food stamp probe rptd 2-2, 93B3
LAKE County Estates v. Tahoe Regional Planning Agency
Bi-state agency immunity curbed by Sup Ct 3-5, 185C1
LAKE Michigan—*See MICHIGAN, Lake*
LAKE Ontario—*See ONTARIO, Lake*
LAKER Airways
US grounds DC-10s, forces shutdown 6-6, 421A1
LAKESIDE, Calif.—*See CALIFORNIA*
LAKEWOOD, Ga.—*See GEORGIA*
LALONDE, Marc
In Trudeau shadow cabt 7-19, 563G2
La MALFA, Ugo
Asked to form govt 2-22, 155F1
Gives up Cabt bid 3-2, 169D3
Named dep premr 3-20, 212C1
Dies 3-26, 254A3
LAMAR University (Beaumont, Tex.)
NCAA basketball tourn results 3-26, 238B3
LAMB, David
Expelled from Iran 7-1, 525D2
Iran sets press curbs 7-23, 566B1
LAMB, Michael
Questions Carter on A-power 8-22, 622D3
LAMBERT, Anne
Picnic At Hanging Rock released 2-22, 174D3
LAMBERT, Louis
Loses electn for La gov 12-8, 946C3
LAMBERTINI, Cardinal Egano Right
Installed cardinal 6-30, 640C2

1980

LABOR, Department of—*See under U.S. GOVERNMENT*
LABOR Party, U.S.
LaRouche wins 2% of NH vote 2-26, 142F2
LaRouche wins 3% of Conn vote 3-25, 221D3
LaRouche wins 13% of Mich vote 5-20, 383G1
LABREQUE, Thomas G.
Named Chase pres 6-25, 600D2
LACEY, Franklin
Music Man opens 6-6, 756F3
LACHANCE, Douglas
Convicted 5-15, 370E3
Sentenced 6-26, 656D1
LACHMON, Jaggernath
Army sergeants stage coup 2-25, 153B2
LACORTE, Frank
Phillies win NL pennant 10-12, 796B1, A2
LACROSSE
Hopkins wins NCAA title 5-31, 638B1
LADD, Cheryl
NY actress to join Charlies Angels 6-17, 638D2
LADIES Home Journal (magazine)
Charter Media dissolved; Charter Co retains ownership 9-30, 836C2
Jos Kennedy, Swanson affair rptd 10-13, 907F3
LADIES Professional Golf Association (LPGA)—*See GOLF*
LADY (recording)
On best-seller list 12-3, 948A3
LADY From Dubuque, The (play)
Opens 1-31, 136C3
LAETRILE—*See under MEDICINE*
LAFALCE, Rep. John J. (D, N.Y.)
Reelected 11-4, 843A4
LAFAYETTE—*See INDIANA*
LAFAYETTE Radio Electronics Corp.
Files for bankruptcy 1-4, 131E3
LAGARDE, Tom
In NBA expansn draft 5-28, 447D1
LAGOMARSINO, Rep. Robert J. (R, Calif.)
Reelected 11-4, 844B1
LAGORCE 2d, John O.
Stepfather adoptn right ruling vacated by Sup Ct 11-17, 882G1
LAGORIO, Lelio
Italy defense min 4-4, 275F3
LA HAYE, Tim
Scores US Families Conf 7-12, 601F2
LAHNSTEIN, Manfred
Sees IMF role in oil debt 9-15, 695E2
LAIDLEY, Leon
Tanker strike accord scored 3-14, 229B3
Fraser vs Arbitratn Comm 3-27, 271F3
LAINGEN, L(owell) Bruce
Emb militants demand 1-4; Khomeini ruling asked 1-5, rejctn hinted 1-8, 29E3-30A1
Pub Prosecutor asks Forghan link probe 3-2, Ghotbzadeh replies 3-4, 164G2
Warning re shah's US asylum cited 3-4, 164F2
UN comm visit rptd 3-12, 178C1
Interview broadcast in US 11-11, 862B1
Prelate visits 12-25, 974A2
LAJEVARDI, Assadollah
Ghotbzadeh arrested 11-7, released 11-10, 862E1
LAKE Jr., I. Beverly
Loses NC gov electn 11-4, 849G3
LAKE, James
Reagan fires as press secy 2-26; scores 2-28, 143G1-C2
LAKE Michigan—*See MICHIGAN, Lake*
LAKE Placid—*See NEW York*
LAKER, Edwin Francis
Dies 3-1, 279G3
LAKER Airways
Miami-London svc OKd 5-15, 516D2
LAKES
Acid rain defined 145B3
Pollutn control benefits seen 4-21, 308C1
LAKE Tahoe—*See TAHOE, Lake*
LAL, Bansi
Congress-I wins electn; gains Parlt seat 1-3, 1-6, 11E3
LALONDE, Marc
Canada energy, environmt min 3-3, 171B2
Sets US gas price pact 3-24, 229G3
Sets oil-sand price cut 3-28, 272D3, E3
Bars US gas sale limits 4-21, 334G3
On offshore oil finds 5-16, 406C2
Sees oil accord, scores price policy 5-30, 428E3
Warns on oil prices 6-16, Leitch talks fail 6-18—6-19, deadline extended 6-19, 486C1
On Alcan pipe costs, revenue 7-17, 562F2
Rpts '79 oil profits up 8-12, 618A1
Urges increased Ottawa energy revenues 10-1, 787G3-788B1
Alberta oil talks fail again 10-2, 787D3
Offers oil sands project aid 11-19, 920F3
BC bars fed gas tax paymt 12-20, 992C1
LA MALFA, Giorgio
Italy budget min 4-4, 275F3
Scores govt defeat 9-27, 751B2
LAMB, Derek
Wins Oscar 4-14, 296A2
LAMBERT, Jack
NFL '79 interceptn ldr 1-5, 8D2
Steelers win Super Bowl 1-20, 61G3-62C1
LAMBERT, Louis
FBI Brilab probe target 2-9, 111F2

1976

LAMBRAKIS, Gregory (d. 1963)
Panagoulis dies 5-1, 351G3
LAMBROU, Vassilios
Arrested 12-16, 1004D2
LAMIZANA, Gen. Sangoule
Vows pay hikes, const rule 1-17; dismisses govt 1-29, names new Cabt, quits justice post 2-9, 269A3
At France-Africa summit 5-10—5-11, 355G2
LAMONT, Ali & Jackie
Acquitted, '74 convictns cited 2-6, 124F1
LAMONT, Bishop Donal
Sentenced 10-1, Pope regrets 10-2, 812D3
Appeal rptd 12-8, 1010C1
LAMONTAGNE, Pierre
Air Canada appeal rejected 9-22, 730D2
LAMOURE County (U.S. warship)
In Intl Naval Review 7-4, 488D3
L'AMOUR Les Yeux Fermes (book)
Henry wins Prix Renaudot 11-15, 911G3
LAMRANI, Karim
Sees Kissinger 1-29, 107G2
LAMURE, Denis
Named soc affairs min 11-26, 903A3
LAMY, Jean Baptiste (1814-88)
Horgan wins Pulitzer 5-3, 352D3
LAMY of Santa Fe (book)
Horgan wins Pulitzer 5-3, 352D3

LANCE, Thomas Bertram
Biog data 916E3
'70 Carter campaign donor 10-17, 805B1
Slated for Carter Cabt 11-23, 898D2 *
Named OMB dir 12-3, 916D1
On econ, reorganizatn plans 12-5, 917A1
On econ aid plan 12-9, 937D3

1977

LAMBROS, Judge Thomas
Bars Kent State gym ban 8-17, 820B3
LAMBS—*See LIVESTOCK*
LAMBSDORFF, Count Otto
Backs Brazil A-pact 4-9, 268D3
Named W Ger econ min 10-7, 969B2
LAMINE, Mohamed
Warns foreigners 5-21, 440D3
LAMIZANA, Gen. Sangoule
Forms new Cabt 1-14, 183A2
LAMO de Espinosa, Emilio
Quits Cortes 4-19, 307C1
LAMONT, Bishop Donal
Sentnc cut 2-24, deported 3-23, 223B3
LAMONTAGNE, Gilles
Wins election 5-24, 410C3
LANC, Erwin
Named Austria interior min 5-31, 425D1
LANCE (missile)—*See ARMAMENTS—Missiles*
LANCE, LaBelle (Mrs. Thomas Bertram)
'74-75 bank overdrafts rptd 8-18, 625D3
Lance loans probed 9-7, 690G1
Sen com staffers cite evidence vs 9-19, 718B3

LANCE, Thomas Bertram (Bert)
Sen com OKs nominatn 1-18, confrmd 1-20, 34B1, 35A1
Sworn in 1-23, 52E2
Econ plan hearings 1-27—2-4, 52A1, 89C2
Rpts personal finances 2-25, 148C1
Carter drops rebate plan 4-14, 270G3, 271E1
On energy plan impact, cost 4-21, 294G1
On econ forecast revisns 4-22, 407G3
On Apr WPI rise 5-5, 383G2
Personal debt rptd 5-23; other estimates 719B1
Scores prime rate hike, FRB 6-1, 6-7, 577E3
Carter agrees to sign HEW-Labor funds 6-15, 459C3
Ga bank rpts 1st ½ loss 7-5, 7-13, 574D2
Sen com rpts Carter request re bank stock sale 7-12; meets with com 7-5, 573F3-574D1
Exec office reorgnzatn asked 7-15, 555E3
Sen com hearing: Lance testifies; com clears, bars probe 7-25, 573C3, 574E1-D2
Heimann probe set 7-25, 574B2
Ga bank stock buyer rptd 7-26, 574C2
Ga bank dividend rptd omitted 8-9, 626F1
Bars comment on Carter plane use 8-11, 626E1
Heimann rpts banking practices 'unsafe & unsound', not illegal; cites '74 race, 2 pending probes 8-18, 625F1-626B1
Carter defends 8-18, 625G1, 626C1-F1
Sen com, other cong probes planned 8-18, 626A1
Comments on Heimann rpt; White House reactn 8-18, 626B1
Carter defends, sees bank reform need 8-23, 649F1
Powell: Carter knew of overdrafts, borrowings 8-23, 649F1, D2
Carter to reimburse Ga bank for plane use 8-24, 649E3
Ribicoff, Percy meet Carter, ask Lance resignatn, spec prosecutor 9-5, 689F3-690A1
Sen com sets probe, House subcom opens hearings 9-6, 690B1
Heimann rpts on correspondent bank loans, overdrafts 9-7, 690E1
SEC probe opened 9-7, 690D2
Heimann: Chicago bank loan 'substandard'; earlier rpt clarified 9-8, 690D2
Sen com hearings 9-9—9-15; testifies, scores critics, cites '74 race probe, plane use 700B3, 701B1, C2
Byrd predicts, Costanza urges resignatn 9-10; bars resignatn 9-13; Carter's mind 'open' 9-15, 701E3
Carter aides saw pre-confrmatn critical FBI rpt 9-12, 701D3
Ribicoff regrets press 'lies', Percy apologizes 9-15, 700C3
Sen com hearings 9-16—9-19, 718C2-G3
Justice Dept sets special panel 9-19, 719A1
Sen com issues affidavit contradicting testimony 9-20, 718G3
Resigns, Carter defends 9-21, 718A1
Regulators defend at Sen Banking Com hearings 9-26—9-27, 761G1
Young cleared re prisoner transfer; campaign gift allegatns cited 10-19, 861F3
Successor at OMB named 12-27, 1001B3
Sells bank shares to Saudi 12-27, 1003E2

1978

LAMBETI, Alfredo
Shot 5-4, 393A2
LAMBRUSCHINI, Vice Adm. Armando
Daughter slain in blast 8-1, 612A1
LAMBSDORFF, Otto
Retains W Ger econ post 2-3, 93A3
Downplays OPEC price hike impact 12-18, 978F1
LAMIZANA, Gen. Sangoule (Upper Volta president)
Elected Upper Volta pres 5-28, 479E2
LAMM, Gov. Richard D. (D, Colo.)
On Carter Colo visit 5-3, 342C2
Lauds natl water plan 6-7, 427C1
Unopposed in primary 9-12, 736D2
Reelected 11-7, 853D2, 855F3
LAMMINPORRAS, Aarno
Hijacks Finnair jet, arrested 9-30—10-1, 927C1
LAMO Espinosa, Jaime
Named Spain agri min 2-24, 394G2
LAMONTAGNE, Gilles
Named to Canada Cabt 1-19, 2-2, 70F1
LAMOS, Mark
City Sugar opens 6-5, 887D1
LANATTA Piaggio, Gabriel
Named Peru industry min 5-15, 394E2
LANCASTER, Bill
Bad News Bears released 7-14, Go Tell Spartans 9-23, 969C3, 970E1
LANCE (missile)—*See ARMAMENTS—Missiles*
LANCE, LaBelle (Mrs. Thomas Bertram)
Bank stock purchase cited 3-18, 204F2

LANCE, Thomas Bertram (Bert)
Carter Friendship Force apptmt rptd 1-17, Eur trip cited 3-9, 204B3
Chicago, Knoxville bank-loan repaymt rptd 1-17, Saudi deal cited 2-13, Abedi role revealed 3-22, 204C3
Becomes ABC-TV commentator 2-6, 172F2
Financial Gen sues 2-17, testimony delayed 3-9, 204B3
SEC sues re Financial Gen takeover bid 3-18, settles 3-19, Carter friendship seen unchngd 3-23, 204F1, F3
Diplomatic passport surrendered, keeps White House pass 3-20, 204F3
Scores press coverage 4-12, 324F3-325A1
Safire wins Pulitzer for banking expose 4-17, 315B2
Chrgd by SEC, comptroller for Ga bank practices; case setld 4-26, 324F2-F3
Carter campaign com, Ga bank fined for '76 plane use 6-26, 509B3
Banking reform bill signed 11-10, 1002G3

1979

LAMBIOTTE, France
Femme de Jean released 1-8, 174E2
LAMBS—*See LIVESTOCK*
LAMBSDORFF, Otto
On 4% '79 growth forecast 1-23, 62A1
OKs BP-Veba deal 3-5, 214F3
Backs bank rate rises 3-29, 334A1
Oil conservatn steps urged 5-16, 373F3
Banking reforms proposed 5-22, 411F1
Mineral stockpile plans rptd 6-21, 489D3
On US credit-tightening 10-8, 765D3
On US freeze of Iran assets 11-18, 880D1
LAMM, Gov. Richard D. (D, Colo.)
Vs Colo U-Fairbanks deal 4-3, 335D2
Abstains in govs vote on Carter '80 support 7-8, 518D1
LAMP, Dennis
Brock gets 3000th hit 8-13, 619D2
LAMPSON, Lawrence
Scores CIA on Paisley death probe 7-8, 520F2
LANCASTER, Pa.—*See PENNSYLVANIA*

LANCE, Thomas Bertram (Bert)
Ga bank audit com details practices, favors to Carter firm 1-17; Carter said unaware, to pay for plane use 1-18, 1-17, 30E3-31B2
Ga bank bars repaymt 1-23, 55D3
Beasly pleads not guilty re '77 loan to Carr 3-28; pleads no contest 5-14, 380E3
'78 oil deal influence attempt alleged 4-9, 305E3-306B1
Grand jury dismissal motn rejctd 4-13, 327F3
Carter testifies on family business loans 5-18, 381A1
Indicted in Ga bank plot 5-23, pleads not guilty 5-24, 380A2
Carter peanut business documts rptd subpoenaed 5-27, 5-28, 401A2
Green plea bargain blocked 6-6, 500A3
Blumenthal probe role cited 7-18, 529F2
Carter peanut business cleared 10-16, 782C3

1980

LAMBROS, Judge Thomas
Blocks US Steel Ohio plant closings 2-28, 266A2
LAMBRUSCHINI, Adm. Armando
Junta delays naming Videla successor, Viola oppositn cited 9-30, 747G2
Viola named Videla successor, junta rift resolved 10-3, 766A2
LAMBSDORFF, Otto
Poland visit cancellatn cited 1-30, 103F1
Lauds Carter anti-inflatn plan 3-15, 202F2
Vs E Eur trade sanctns 4-17, 303C2
Vs UK for Iran sanctions reversal 5-20, 378E2
Sovt trade pact set 5-29, 411C2
On EC steel cutback plan 10-30, 822B1
Sworn W Ger econ min 11-5, 925E1
LAMER, Antonio
Named to Canada Sup Ct 3-28, 273C2
LAMIZANA, Sangoule (Upper Volta president; deposed Nov. 25)
Overthrown by coup 11-25, 924G1
LAMM, Gov. Richard D. (D, Colo.)
State of State message 1-4, 269C1
LAMONICA, Thomas A.
Pleads guilty in bribe case 8-7, 600A2
Sentenced 10-27, says bribes 'condoned', civil suit loss rptd 12-8, 957F3, 958B1
LAMONTAGNE, Gilles
Canada defense min 3-3, 171B2
Sees Brown, OKs F-18 deal 7-8, 544A1
Rpts destroyer upgrade plan 8-8, 618D2
LA MOTTA, Jack
Raging Bull released 11-14, 972G3
L'AMOUR, Louis
Bendigo Shafter wins Amer Book Award 5-1, 692G2
LAMP, Jeff
Virginia wins NIT 3-20, 240F2
LAMPERT, Jerry
Mitchell wins Ontario by-electn 11-20, 900C3
LANCE, LaBelle (Mrs. Thomas Bertram)
Atlanta mansion rptd sold 7-9, 639A2
LANCE, Thomas Bertram (Bert)
Ga bank fraud trial opens 1-14, chrgs reduced 4-9, 291E3
Cleared on fund misuse, mistrial declared on 3 counts 4-30, 332D3
Congratulates Talmadge on US probe end 5-30, 428A1
US case dropped 6-9, 459F2-A3
Atlanta mansion rptd sold 7-9, 639A2
Testifies re B Carter 9-22, 764C1

1976

LANCIA S.p. A.
Turin workers strike 10-8, 10-12, 10-13, 838D2
LAND—*See REAL Estate; RESOURCES, Natural*
LANDAU, Chaim
Vs Rabin statemt on US arms bid 2-9, 106G2
Vs Leb Arab Army talks 8-4, 578B2
LANDER, Aristides
Quits police post 7-27, 592C3
LANDON, Alfred M.
Addresses GOP conv 8-16, 615G1
LANDON Jr., George K.
Indicted 11-4, 886F3
LANDRIEU, Mayor Moon (New Orleans)
Outgoing US Mayors Conf head 7-1, 493C1
LANDRUM, Rep. Phil M. (D, Ga.)
Jenkins wins seat 11-2, 822E1
LANDRY, Bernard
Named econ dvpt min 11-26, 903A3
LANE, George
Meets Leb Pres Sarkis 11-5, 841E2
LANE, Justice Myles J.
Nixon disbarred in NY 7-8, 493F3
LANG, Fritz
Dies 8-2, 816E3
LANG, Otto E.
On Trudeau econ remarks 1-8, 27D3
Presents new rail plan 1-29, 98G3
Air strike ends, probe comm named 6-28, 481F2
Air pact talks cited 7-1, 496G2
Bilingual comm limits air strike pact 7-6, 537F2
Air rules curb French 7-23, 7-27, 572D2
Stays transport min 9-14, 692B2
LANGDON, Steven
Loses electn 10-18, 808D2
LANGLEY Research Center (Hampton, Va.)
Viking 1 lands on Mars 7-20, 525E2
LANGMUIR, Dr. Alexander D.
New Legionnaire disease probe set 9-30, 815E1
LANGUAGE—*See country names*
LANKOANDE, Ali
Upper Volta educatn min 2-9, 269D3
LANUSSE, Lt. Gen. Alejandro Agustin (ret.)
Bomb kills daughter-in-law 2-9, 212B2
Scores prof arrests 8-4; held 8-6—8-11, 672F2-A3
LANUSSE, Maria Caride de
Killed 2-9, 212B2
Pol prisoners escape 4-26, recaptured 4-28, 333D3

LAOS—*See also ADB, NONALIGNED Nations Movement*
Armed forces alerted 1-15, 222G1
Listed as 'not free' nation 1-19, 20E3
ICC disbands 1-21, 55D2
Anti-govt unrest rptd 3-12, 3-14, 222E1
RC church assailed 3-29, 267E3
'Cultural drive' rptd 4-11, 267C3
Birth control banned 9-9, 735F1
Foreign Relations (misc.)
Thais reopen border 1-1, 31F1

1977

LANCET (journal)
Smoking, early menopause linked 6-25, 620D1
LAN-Chile Airlines
Jet hijacked to Argentina 6-21, 537C2
LAND—*See REAL Estate, RESOURCES, Natural*
LAND, Edwin H.
Unveils Polaroid instant movies 4-26, 409A1
LANDAU, George W.
Sees Chile forgn min 11-17, 983E2
LAND Management, Bureau of—*See under U.S. GOVERNMENT—INTERIOR*
LANDO, Barry
Journalists' thoughts protected 11-7, 920B3
LANDSAT (Earth Resources Technology Satellite)—*See ASTRONAUTICS—Satellites, Earth*
LANE, George
Mediates Syria Leb troop moves 1-26, 1-29, 2-1, 72A1
Heads US 'interest office' in Cuba 9-1, 686A1
Sees Leb mins on fighting 9-14—9-17, 714B3
LANE, Stonney
Discounts Ray escape plot 6-14, 459D2
LANG, Dr. Ivor
At Biko inquest 11-21, 934B1
LANG, Otto Emil
French curb upheld 1-12, 17C3
On US wheat-price pact 2-25, 158F2
On air safety enforcemt 11-28, 965F3
LANGAH, Taj Mohammad
Quits Pak ruling party 4-8, 305F2
LANGER, Felicia
Curbed for PLO ties 3-31, 246B2
LANGER, William L.
Dies 12-26, 1024D2
LANGFIELD II, William
SEC sues, settles 7-19, 612B3
LANGLOIS, Henri
Dies 1-12, 84C3
LANIEL, Maurice
On Levesque auto mishap 2-21, 159C1
LANKOANDE, Ali
Replaced as educ min 1-14, 183B2
LANSING, Mich.—*See MICHIGAN*
LANSKY, Meyer
Ariz, Fla Mafia operatns rptd 3-13—3-20, 6-19, 568A2
LANUSSE, Lt. Gen. Alejandro Agustin (ret.)
Scores Sajon arrest 4-4, 345G2
Arrested 5-4, bars testimony 5-5, 371A1
Freed from jail 6-13, 522D3

LAOS—*See also COMECON, NONALIGNED Nations Movement*
UN Assemb member 4C1
Ex-King Savang, kin seized; tied to rebel raids 3-12, 201C3
Poppy crop cited 4-1, 393E3
Thais get protest on rebel aid 4-9, Vientiane alert 4-10, 305C1
Rebel isles retaken, Thai border closed 4-11, 305A1
Postwar rpt published 5-3, 337E1

1978

LANCET (UK journal)
PBB study cited 10-9, 769D2
LANCIA & Co. SpA.
Exec killed 9-28, 816F3
LANCTOT, Jacques
6th Cross kidnaper alleged 11-2, 880C1
LANCTOT, Louise—*See COSSETTE-Trudel, Louise Lanctot*
LAND—*See REAL Estate, RESOURCES, Natural*
LANDAU, George W.
Pressure on Chile to deport Townley rptd 4-9, 266D3
Recalled re Letelier probe snags 6-23, 495E3
Asks 3 extradited in Letelier case 9-20, 755G2
Letelier suspect rptdly sees US evidence 10-13, 795A3
letelier murder suspect cites 10-24, 1014F3
LANDERS, Matt
Working opens 5-14, 887E3
LANDFIELD, Timothy
Crucifer of Blood opens 9-28, 1031C1
LANDIS, John
Animal House released 7-27, 970D2
LAND Management, Bureau of—*See under U.S. GOVERNMENT—INTERIOR*
LANDMARK Communications Inc.
Va judicial inquiry law voided by Sup Ct 5-1, 363A3
LANDMARK Communications v. Virginia
Va judicial inquiry law voided by Sup Ct 5-1, 363A3
LANDON, Alf
Daughter wins Kan US Sen primary 8-1, 606E1
Daughter wins electn 11-7, 845F1, 854E2
LANDOVSKY, Pavel
Held 1-28, 180E2
LANDRY, Greg
NFL '77 passing ldr 1-1, 56E2
LANDRY, Philippe
Named Francophone dir-gen 9-7, 721E3
LANDRY, Tom
Cowboys win Super Bowl 1-15, 39F3
LANDSCAPE After Battle (film)
Released 2-9, 619F2
LANE, Lyle
Sees Castro 5-17, 382A1
US disputes Castro rpt 6-13, 442B3
LANE, Mark
King assassinatn probed by House com 8-14—8-18, 641F1, B3-F3, 642B1
King hearings resume 11-9, 11-17, 898G1, B3, C3
Visits Guyana cult commune with US delegatn 11-17, escapes mass murder-suicide 11-18; Guyana troops rescue 11-19, 889G1-890C3
FBI King plot allegatns scored 11-17, 938C2
Switzerland trip re Peoples Temple funds rptd 12-15; denies 12-16, 1000E1
LANG, Jennings
Nunzio released 5-13, 619C3
LANG, John F.
Sues Ford 4-25, suit amended 5-16, 390A3
LANG, Otto Emil
Sworn Canada justice min 8-9, 647C1
Sup Ct to hear const plan 9-13, 754E3
OKs Cabt papers to McDonald probe 10-27, 837D2
Rpts Air Canada-Nordair merger overruled 11-7, 879E3
Lalonde gets justice post 11-24, 921E3
LANGLEY Air Force Base, Va.—*See VIRGINIA*
LANGLOIS, Yves—*See SEGUIN, Pierre*
LANGTON, Basil
13 Rue De L'Amour opens 3-16, 760D3
LANGUAGE & Linguistics—*See also BILINGUALISM; country names*
Mario Pei dies 3-2, 252C3
Carter signs 'plain English' order 3-23, 218D2
Harvard revises curriculum 5-2, 348D2
LANHAM, Maj. Gen. Charles Trueman (Buck) (ret.)
Dies 7-20, 620A3
LANIER, Bob
NBA scoring ldr 4-9, 271E2
LANIER, Willie
Traded to Colts 4-24, 336G1
Retires 7-20, 1024C3
LANKES, Johann Christian
Ethiopia ousts 1-22, 44A1
LANOUX, Victor
Servant & Mistress released 6-6, 619F3
Replay released 7-10, 970G2

LAOS—*See also NONALIGNED Nations Movement*
Refugee exit data rptd 10-11, 776C2
Refugee flow rptd high 11-10, 870A3
Foreign Relations (misc.)
Viet troops rptd moving toward Cambodia 2-1, 80D1
Aerial shortcut with Viet reopened 2-11, 140B1
Thais force refugees back, UN distressed 2-16; 3 rptd killed 2-24; refugee data rptd 139C3-140B1

1979

LAN-Chile Airlines
Letelier case funds shift probed 10-9, 772D2
LANCTOT, Jacques
Returns to Canada, arrested 1-6, 19F1
Chrgd, bail set 1-11, 37B2
Trial opens 11-7, sentncd 11-8, 872D1
LAND, David
Evita opens 9-25, 956A3
LAND, Public
Alaska land bill clears House com 3-1, 187E1; House 5-16, 366E3
Land grant easemt right curbed by Sup Ct 3-27, 263B2
Carter proposes wilderness bill 4-16, 282E1
West mounts 'Sagebrush revolt' vs fed managemt 7-13, 703E3
Interior Dept seeks to protect 47 areas 9-7, 703B3
LAND, Stewart F.
Grand Tour opens 1-11, 292E1
LANDAU, Barry M.
Disputes Jordan cocaine denial 8-28, 647C2
LANDAU, Chaim
Votes vs Israel-Egypt pact 3-22, 197B1
Balks at Egypt pact, reneges 4-10, 295D3
LANDAU, George W.
Testifies in Letelier trial 2-8; rptdly tied Pinochet to assassins 2-9, 114F3-115B1
Recalled 5-15, 369D2
Returns to Chile 6-7, 506F2
Recalled again 10-2, 750C2
LANDAU, Jack C.
Scores Sup Ct 'state of mind' libel ruling 4-18, 302C2
Scores ctroom press access ruling 7-2, 515D3
LANDAU, Moshe
Suspends Elon Moreh constructn 6-20, 461E3
LANDAU, Richard
Black Hole released 12-21, 1007A3
LANDGRAF, Lt. Col. William
Rescinds Spanish language ban 2-7, 89D2
LANDIS, Sam
King of Schnorrers opens 11-28, 956C3
LAND Management, Bureau of—*See under U.S. GOVERNMENT–INTERIOR*
LANDO, Barry
'State of mind' libel queries backed by Sup Ct, '73 suit cited 4-18, 302A1
LANDREAUX, Ken
Traded to Twins 2-3, 619E1
LANDRIEU, Moon
Named HUD secy 7-27; facts on 577B1, F1, B2
Confirmed 9-12, 700F2
LANE, Burton
Carmelina opens 4-8, 711A2
LANE, Diane
Little Romance released 4-27, 820F1
LANE, Lyle
Walks out on Castro harangue 1-1, 20C1
LANE, Mark
Sued by Jonestown kin 1-28, 117D2
LANG, Edgar
Killed 4-16, funeral 4-18, 332D1
LANG, Jennings
Concorde Airport '79 released 8-3, 820A1
LANG, Otto Emil
Disputes air safety rpt 2-8, 134E1
'72 RCMP tap role noted in Cabt documts 3-28–3-30, 253A3
Australia wheat accord rptd 4-3, 253A1
Loses electn 5-22, 377D2
LANGE, Anders (deceased)
S Africa '73 pol gifts chrgd 3-21, 213E1
LANGE, Ann
Rat's Nest opens 2-2, 292D2
LANGE, Jessica
All That Jazz released 12-20, 1007F2
LANGELLA, Frank
Dracula released 7-13, 820A1
LANGHAM, Michael
Coriolanus opens 3-14, 292C1
LANGLEY, Harry Lee
Sees 'foul play' in Paisley death 6-27, 520C2
LANGUAGE & Linguistics
China sets Pinyin transliteratn 1-1, 75D2
US armed svcs review 'sexist' language 1-19, 89D3
US Army rescinds Spanish ban 2-7, 89D2
US coll test scores rptd down 9-8, 785F2
US comm urges forgn-language study 11-7, 944E1
Obituaries
Partridge, Eric 6-1, 508D3
LANSBURY, Angela
Sweeney Todd opens 3-1, 292C3
LANSFORD, Carney
AL batting ldr 9-30, 955F3
LANSING, John
Sunnyside released 6-1, 820D3
LANSKY, Meyer
Ruby crime links detailed 7-17, 538B2
LANTZ, Walter
Wins Oscar 4-9, 336C2

LAOS—*See also NONALIGNED Nations Movement*
Souvanna rpts ex-aides detained 3-24, 331C3
Gas raids vs Meo rebels rptd 11-3, 12-12, 979A1
Foreign Relations (misc.)—*See also 'UN' below*
Viet, Cambodia sign friendship pact 2-18, 123C2
China assails Viet-Cambodia pact 2-18, bars role 2-27, 141F2, 142B2

1980

LANCI, Thomas
Convicted in FBI bribery plot 7-3, 655E2
LAND, Edwin H.
Retires as Polaroid chief exec 3-7, 225B1
LAND, Public
State of State messages 1-7, 1-8, 403D2, F3; 1-14, 1-15, 268D3, 269A1, B1; 2-12, 484F2
Me Indians OK setlmt 3-15, 210A3
Gulf natl park drilling rights affirmed by Sup Ct 3-31, 291A3
Alaska land bill clears Sen 8-19, 631C2-A3
Gravel loses Alaska primary 8-26, 683A2
Bush hits Carter leasing policy 9-10, 780F3
Alaska lands bill sent to Carter 11-12, 866E2-C3
Gen Tire donates land in Fla 12-19, 987F1
$25 mln gifts for forests, endangered sites rptd 12-20, 987A2
Watt plans 'good neighbor' policy 12-22, 980A1
LANDA, Malva
Exiled internally 3-26, 262A2
LANDAU, Edie
Hopscotch released 9-26, 836B3
LANDAU, Ely
Hopscotch released 9-26, 836B3
LANDAU, Moshe
Backs W Bank ldrs ouster 8-19, 627C3
LANDAU, Saul
Wins Polk award 2-25, 692F3
LANDE, Stephen L.
Japan eases US tobacco tariffs 11-21, 902B2
LANDER, Ann-Marja
On Continental strike setlmt 12-20, 988F1
LANDIS, John
Blues Brothers released 6-20, 675A2
LANDREAUX, Ken
AL batting ldr 10-6, 926E3
LANDRIEU, Moon
On home mortgage rates 4-28, 329G2
On housing shortage 7-2, 518C2
LANDSDOWNE—*See PENNSYLVANIA*
LANG, Czeslaw
Wins Olympic medal 7-28, 622F2
LANG, Erik
In Iran crisis mediatn group 4-5, 258D1
LANG, Dr. Ivor
Biko probe squashed 6-29, 525E1
LANG, Jennings
Nude Bomb released 5-9, 675B3
LANG, Richard
Change of Seasons released 12-17, 1003G1
LANG, Ronald
Scores OSHA job cancer rules 1-16, 36E1
LANGE, Jessica
How to Beat the High Cost of Living released 7-11, 675A3
LANGELLA, Frank
Those Lips released 9-9, 836G3
LANGER, Felicia
Meets Arafat, 3 W Bank mayors 9-25, 736E3
Vs Arab univ closing 11-19, 880B1
LANGER, Lucyna
Wins Olympic medal 7-28, 624A2
LANGUAGE & Linguistics
Algeria plans more Arabic use 1-14, 55F3
Hispanic immigrants in US surveyed 5-11—5-14, 396D2
Obituaries
Farb, Peter 4-8, 360E1
LANSBURY, Angela
Mirror Crack'd released 12-18, 1003C2
LANSING—*See MICHIGAN*
LANSING, Sherry
20th Century-Fox pres 1-1, 199B1
LANTOS, Tom
Elected to US House 11-4, 842E1, 852B2

LAOS—*See also ADB*
Foreign Relations (misc.)
UN res vs Sovt Afghan invasn opposed 1-14, 25G1
Viet takeover cited in US pres hopeful's 'basic speech' 3-3, 208C3
China joins IMF 4-17, 302E2
Thai boat attacked, border closed 6-15; peace talks deadlocked 7-21—7-23, 547A3
Thais vs Viet Cambodia-Thai DMZ plan at forgn min talks 7-18, 591F1

1976

N Viet ties bolstered 2-11, 121D1
Rpt Burma rebels flee to 2-11, 144G2
US Sen votes refugee aid 2-16, 182C1
UN Palestine com member 2-26, 162C1
Pilot defects to Thailand 3-9, 222F1
Soviet emb bombed 3-12, 222G1
China aid pact signed 3-18, 222A2
Refugees land in Australia 3-19, 237B2
Rpt Burma Reds get war arms 3-31, 265C1
Sovt emb bombers sentncd 4-16, 333G3
Thais rpt Sovt radar statn 4-27, 315E1
US refugee aid signed 6-30, 533C2
At COMECON summit 7-7—7-9, 722D2
Thai border, prisoner release pact 8-3, 677G3
US GOP platform text 8-18, 609F2, 610A2
Rpt refugees arrive US 9-16, 696B3
US limits forgn aid use 10-1, 806E3
US tied to Thai coup 10-8, 775F3-776A1
Thai govt-in-exile set 10-12, 794F3
Thai border clash 10-14, 795C1
Thai border clashes 10-17, 10-20, 814A1
Thais chrg Viet invasn plan 12-8, 949D3
Sovt missile silos rptd 12-27, 1013C1

La PASIONARIA—*See IBARRURI, Dolores*
LAPOINTE, Louis
Arraigned 4-22, 309D3
LAPRADE, J. Walter
FBI burglary OKs rptd 8-20, 635D1
LARA, Gen. Timon
Spain Armed Police chief 12-23, 1011G2
LARAKI, Ahmed
Summons forgn ambs re Sahara 1-28, 58B2
LARDINOIS, Pierre
Named French-Italian wine mediator 1-20, 138E3
In France-Italy wine talks 2-24, 163D3
Quits EC post, scores budget curbs 4-9, 276A2
Rpts milk-feed plan revisn 4-14, 276G2
LARDNER-Burke, Desmond W.
Shifted to commerce post 1-13, 53E3
Sees Kissinger 9-19, 697C1
LaROUCHE, Lyndon H.
Final pres vote tally 12-18, 979C2
LAROUSSI, Mahfoud
Rptd killed 6-8, named Polisario ldr 6-21, 466B3
LASATER, Donald E.
Acquittal, appeal rptd 3-1, 181C1
LASER, Christine
Wins Olympic medal 7-26, 576F1
LASERS
US denies Sovt use vs satellite 11-23, 961A2
LASKER Medical Research Awards, Albert
Presented 11-17, 910D3
LASKIN, Bora
Backs inflatn plan ruling 7-12, 554D3
LaSORDA, Tom
Named Dodgers mgr 10-3, 816A1
LASSO, Carmen
Forced to leave Colombia 2-1, 118A3
LASTIRI, Norma Lopez Rega de
Prelim corruptn chrgs filed 5-6, 399G2
Indicted for embezzlemt 10-25, 997E1
LASTIRI, Raul
Peron shuffles cabt 1-15—1-16, 71D2
Prelim corruptn chrgs filed 5-6, 399G2
Rights revoked, arrest ordrd 6-23, 520C1
Indicted for embezzlemt 10-25, 997E1
LAST Meeting of the Knights of the White Magnolia, The (play)
Opens 9-21, 1014E3
LAST Tango in Paris (films)
Brazil offcls see 8-3—8-5, 851C1
LAS Vegas, Nev.—*See NEVADA*

1977

Refugee boat rptd off Singapore 6-12, 497C1
ASEAN backs ties 7-5—7-8, 537C1
Viet group visits 7-15—7-18; pacts signed, ties bolstered 7-18, 552G3
Thais protest Cambodian raid 7-25, 572C1
ASEAN asks ties 8-5, 607E1
Cambodia border clashes rptd 8-6, 607A3
Malaysia eases refugee ban 8-31, 685D2
Cambodia hints at clashes 10-2, 779G3
W Eur heroin conf 10-17—10-21, 972A1
Thais lift trade embargo 10-19, 885D1
New Thai rulers for talks 10-21, 827D1
U.S. Relations
US missn on MIAs visits 3-19—3-20, 206B1, B2
NY Times rpts postwar conditns 5-3, 337E1
US Sen vs loans 6-14, 477C3
US aid bar signed 8-4, 668B2
MIAs listed by US 9-30, 795E1
US stand re intl agency loans set 10-19, 815A2-C2
US heroin flow rptd down 11-7, 972B1
US bars plea on food aid 12-16, 989C1

LAP, Vu
Hints minority resistance 10-1, 989A1
LaPLANTE, Deby
Sets 60-yd hurdle mark 2-25, 602F3
LARA Castro, Carmen de
Credits Carter in prisoner releases 2-23, 167B3
LARAKI, Ahmed
Fears OAU rift re Zaire 4-23, 317A2
On Mauritanian envoy assault 7-7, 543C2
LAROCQUE, Michel
NHL season ldr 4-3, 262B3, G3
LARSON, Judge Earl R.
NFL labor pact signed 3-1, 163B2
OKs NFL suit setlmt 3-29, 263G3
NFL labor pact challenged 4-25, 491E2
OKs NFLPA class-actn suit setlmt 8-1, 658F3
LARSON, Leonard
Death rptd 6-8, 466E3
LASERS
USSR tests, US research rptd 5-2, 5-3, 343D3
Gould awarded patent 10-11; '77 indus growth rptd 10-24, 860A1
ERDA fusion research authorized 11-15, 878C1
USSR T-80 laser sight rptd 12-8, 942A1
Uranium enrichmt advances rptd 12-14, 12-17, 975F1-G2
LASKARIS, Constantine
Named Greek labor min 11-28, 925B2
LASKER, Judge Morris F.
Sentences ILA aide 12-2, 937F3
LASKER Medical Research Awards, Albert
Presented 11-16, 927A3
LASKIN, Bora
US TV ad deletn upheld 11-30, 946A2
LASKY, Victor
It Didn't Start with Watergate on best-seller list 8-14, 643A2
LASORDA, Tom
In World Series 10-11—10-18, 806G1
Named NL top mgr 10-26, 927A2
LASSER, Robson, Rhoads & Dunwoody
Lasser to quit firm 8-22, 650G2
LAST Chance Diet, The (book)
Liquid protein deaths rptd 11-9, 992D3
LASTRA, Cecilio
'77 WBA boxing champion 12-17, 970A2 ★
Decisns Ortega, wins featherweight title 12-17, 970D3 ★
LASTUVKA, Vladimir
Rptd jailed 9-28, 752D2
LAS Vegas, Nev.—*See NEVADA*
LATCHFORD Glass Co.
Strike ends 10-14, 818F3
LATE Show, The (film)
Top-grossing film 4-27, 356E2

1978

Rebel forces battle, Meos flee to Thailand 3-24, 3-28, 237F2
Australian journalist rescues girlfriend 5-27, 420D2
Comecon observer 6-27—6-29, 504G3
French aid to rebels chrgd 6-30; aides ousted 7-3, 548D3
Backs Viet in China feud 7-22, 603F1
Viet pacts anniv marked 7-22, 603B2
France ends ties 8-22, 660C3
UN Assemb member 713G3
China chrgs Viet aggressn 9-19, 748A1
U.S. Relations
US barred from air lane 2-11, 140B1
US distressed by Thai refugee policy 2-16, 140A1
US to provide rice 6-1, 400F1
US cong missn visits, given bodies of 4 US MIAs 8-25; returned to US 8-27, 660B3

LaPENTA, James
Postal pact negotiated 7-21, 564F2
LaPLANTE, Deby
Sets indoor 60-yd high hurdles mark 2-24, 100-mtr hurdles mark 6-8—6-10, 600C3, D3
LAPOINTE, Hugues
Signs Eng version of Bill 101 2-1, 88C3
LAPOINTE, Louis
Giguere cleared; death rptd 6-29, 515A1
LAPORTE, Pierre (d. 1970)
Lortie, Rose paroled 7-16, 7-17, 556D3
LaPRADE, J. Wallace
Bell asks disciplinary actn 4-10, 262A1
Transferred, decries pol influence 4-13, 285B1
Fired by Bell, claims 'scapegoat' 7-6, 507G2
La RAZA, National Council of
House ethics com scored re Roybal discipline 10-12, 832A1
Illegal alien plan scored 12-20, 1010F2
LARCENY—*See CRIME—Robbery*
LARGENT, Steve
NFL '77 touchdown ldr 1-1, 56B2
LARKIN Jr., Frederick G.
To retire as Sec Pacific chrmn 10-17, 809F1
LaROCHELLE, Pierre Drieu
Woman at Her Window released 6-9, 620C1
LAROQUE, Michel
NHL goaltending ldr 4-9, 296E1
LARRAZABAL, Jaime
World Bank oil loan set 10-8, 840C3
LARRIEU, Francie (Mrs. Mark Lutz)
Sets indoor mile run mark 2-24, 600E3
AAU suspends 6-23, 692E2
LARSEN, Allan E.
Wins Idaho primary for gov 8-8, 625E3
Loses electn 11-7, 856B1
LARSON, Jonathan Z.
New Times to halt publicatn 11-15, 1029G3
LaSALLE, Roche
Ejected in Parlt tax debate 5-16, 391G2
LaSALLE National Bank v. U.S.
IRS summons power backed by Sup Ct 6-19, 492F2
LASERS
China dvpt plan outlined 5-28, 436F1
San Andreas Fault shift rptd 6-18, 480C1
US Navy rpts anti-missile use 8-23, 683E3-678A1
LASORDA, Tom
Yankees win World Series 10-17, 800G1
LASSWELL, Harold D.
Dies 12-18, 1032B3
LAST Dance (recording)
On best-seller list 7-5, 579G3; 8-2, 620F1
LASTRA, Cecilio
Pedroza TKOs 4-16, 379D2
LAST Supper, The (film)
Released 5-5, 619G2
LAST Tango in Paris (film)
Canada prov censorship upheld 1-19, 111A2
LAST Waltz, The (film)
Released 4-25, 619G2 ★
LAST Wave, The (film)
Released 12-18, 1030B3
LAS Vegas, Nev.—*See NEVADA*

1979

USSR rpts China troop mass 3-2, 200D1
Chinese incursns chrgd 3-7, 3-14, 3-15, 199G3-200B1
China roadbldg end asked 3-7, China regrets request 3-15, 200B1
Viet troops confirmed 3-22, 229G1
Troops aid Viets in Cambodia, Pol Pot group asks support 3-24, 229E1
250,000 refugees rptd in Thailand 3-24, 331E3
Thai peace pact signed 4-4, 298C2
Refugee data rptd 4-25, 5-19, 379C2, F2
China asks Viet exit 4-26, 298F1
Viets: China seeks aid vs Cambodia 6-1, 474F2
Viet links troop exit, China 'aggressn' end 7-5, 537B1
Thai refugee entries rptd 8-22, 625F3
Thai refugee pact rptd 8-25, 659B3
China chrgs Viet troops mass 9-6, 660B2
Cambodia relief aid rptd 9-30, 741C1
Thais to accept refugees 10-19, 811G2
UN Policy & Developments
Membership listed 695F2
U.S. Relations
Laos chem warfare confrmd 11-3, 12-12, 979B1
Mrs Carter visits Thai refugees 11-8—11-10, 863B2

LAPINE, James
Table Settings opens 3-23, 712G2
LaPLANTE, Deby
Young breaks 60-yd indoor hurdles mark 2-23; sets 100-m hurdles mark 6-17, 911B2, E2
LAPPIN, Judge Francis
Sentncs siblings for incest 7-31, 656B2
LARA Sanchez, Augusto
Colombia detains 1-24, 115A2
LARGAESPADA, Col. Fulgencio
Surrenders Natl Guard 7-19, 535B3
LARGENT, Steve
NFL '78 receiving ldr 1-6, 80C1
NFC wins Pro Bowl 1-29, 79F3
LARIJANI, Gen. Mehdi Rahemi
Named Teheran mil gov 1-6, 11A3
LARIMER, Bob
But Never Jam Today opens 7-31, 711G1
LARIOS, Bernardino
Eur, Latin arms aid missn set 8-31, 689A3
LAROCCA, James
On NY energy plan 8-7, 609G3
LAROQUE, Michel
Montreal wins Stanley Cup 5-21, 447B3
Shares NHL top goalie award 6-12, 470D2
LaROUCHE Jr., Lyndon H.
FEC OKs matching funds 12-18, 984A2
LARRIEU, Francie
AAU reinstatemt cited 11-28, 956F1
LARRY, Heath
Defends '78 4th ¼ profit rise 3-21, 201D2
On Pay Advisory Com 10-16, 829F2
LARRY, Sheldon
Sorrows of Stephen opens 12-11, 1007E2
LARSEN, Kenneth
Rat's Nest opens 2-2, 292E2
LARSEN, Roy E.
Dies 9-10, 756F2
LARSON, Glen A.
Buck Rogers released 3-29, 528E1
Battlestar Galactica released 5-17, 528C1
LaRUSSA, Tony
Hired as White Sox mgr 8-2, 619C2
LaRUSSO 2d, Louis
Knockout opens 5-6, 712A1
LARWILL Costilla Ranches Inc.
Colo land sale refunds set 5-8, 596A1
LARY, Yale
Enters HOF 7-28, 1001C1
LaSALLE, Roche
Canada supply min 6-4, 423F3
LASERS
Solar power satellite danger cited 1-10, 36E1
Fusion advance rptd 6-16, 692B1
LASH, Jonathan
Describes Carter mtg 6-1, 418B2
LASKARIS, Constantine
Defends proposed pay curbs 2-22, 135D3
LASKER, Judge Morris E.
Sentences Alexander's for TV rebates 3-29, 298D3
LASKY, Moses
Telex fee case declined by Sup Ct 12-3, 964B2
LASKY v. U.S.
Case declined by Sup Ct 12-3, 964C2
LASORDA, Tom
NL wins All-Star Game 7-17, 569A2
LAST Dance (recording)
Wins Grammys 2-16, 336E3
Wins Oscar 4-9, 336B2
LAST Embrace (film)
Released 5-3, 528F2
LAST Enchantment, The (book)
On best-seller list 9-2, 672A3; 10-14, 800A3
LAST Romantic Lover (film)
Released 10-5, 1007F3
LAST Supper, The (fresco)
Restoratn rptd 2-27, 173A3
LAS Vegas Sun, The (newspaper)
SEC suit vs Hughes settled 1-19, 88B2
LATE Great Planet Earth, The (film)
Top-grossing film 2-7, 120G3; 2-28, 174B2

1980

Cambodian refugees return home 11-13, 951G3
U.S. Relations
Bush 'basic speech' cites Viet takeover 3-3, 208C3
Chem weapons use chrgd 8-7, 628E3

LAPIERRE, Dominique
Fifth Horseman on best-seller list 10-12, 796D3; 12-7, 948D3
LAPOINTE, Charles
Canada small business min 3-3, 171C2
LAREDO—*See TEXAS*
LARGENT, Steve
NFL '79 receiving ldr 1-5, 8C2
LARIOS, Col. Bernardino
Arrested in alleged coup plot 9-11, 709C3
Sentenced 10-31, 874G1
LAROUCHE Jr., Lyndon H.
FEC OKs Bush, Kennedy funds 1-2, 1-4, 5C2
Wins 2% vote in NH 2-26, 142E2, F2
Conn primary vote 3% 3-25, 221D3
Mich primary vote 13% 5-20, 383G1
LARRIEU, Francie
Decker breaks indoor mile mark 2-16, 891E1
2d in Penn Relays mile 4-25, 892D2
LARRY, Sheldon
Sunday Runners opens 5-4, 392G3
LARSEN, Ray
Morning's at Seven opens 4-10, 392E3
Home opens 5-7, 392C3
LARSON, Reed
In NHL All-Star game 2-5, 198A3
LA Salle (U.S. command ship)
Sailor convicted of Kenya murder 9-30, sentence rptd protested 10-13, 10-20, 859D3
LA SALLE University (Philadelphia, Pa.)
Brooks in NBA draft 6-10, 447F2
LASCELLES, Kendrew
Reggae opens 3-27, 392F3
LASCH, Christopher
Culture of Narcissism wins Amer Book Award 5-1, 692D2
LA SCOLA, Dr. Raymond L.
3 chrgs dropped in insulin-slaying 12-29, 997A2
LASERS
CBS, RCA sign video disk pact 1-10, 120G1
Pioneer to enter US video disk mkt 3-26, 376E3
LASKIN, Bora
Broadens rape case questioning 6-27, 520D3
LASSER, Louise
Marie & Bruce opens 2-3, 136C3
In God We Trust released 9-26, 836C3
LAST Enchantment, The (book)
On best-seller list 1-13, 40B3
LAST Married Couple in America, The (film)
Released 2-8, 216B3
LAST Supper, The (fresco)
Crack rptd 6-16, 472E3
LAS Vegas—*See NEVADA*
LASZLO, Dr. John
Pot cancer aid study rptd 4-15, 358B1

1976

LATHAM, Aaron
House com subpoenas 8-25, testifies 9-15, released from subpoena 9-22, 749A1, G1
LATHAM, Arthur
Vs spending cut, tax hike plan 7-22, 7-26, 556B2
Moderate Laborites assail leftists 11-16, 906F1
LATIN America—*See also specific countries, organizations (e.g., OAS, SELA)*
Regional defns spending rptd 1-2, 60E3
'66 rights covenant effected 1-4, 36E3
'75 WCC rights abuse protest rptd 1-9, 61F2
Russell ct scores 11 govts 1-10—1-17, 61B2
'75 econ decline noted 1-13, 60C3
Freedom House survey rptd 1-19, 20B3
Cuba Angola role scored 1-24, 138G1
40 ACP-natns OKd EC pact 2-3, 164D3
Guatemala quake aid sent 2-10, 120E3
Dutch prince cancels trip 3-4, 254C3
Food output data rptd 5-7, 466C1
'75 paymts deficit up 5-10, 465G3
WHO rejcts Israel rpt 5-17, 355G1
'74, '75 econ growth, foreign debt rptd 5-17—5-19, 465A3
Latin, Eur soc dems meet 5-23—5-25, 449E2-C3
Leftists at Spain Popular Soclst cong 6-5—6-6, 459C1
UNESCO press mtg, regional agency planned 7-12—7-21; IAPA scores 7-23, 619C3
World Bank chart on poverty data 778C1
Rise in repressn rptd 10-31, 975C1
Brazil bishops discuss anti-church violence 11-5, 850A3
Brazil bishops score natl sec ideology 11-16, 903A2
Chile rejects Bolivia seaport plan 11-26, 975G1
Soclst Intl vs dictatorships 11-27, 935F3
U.S. Relations—*See also IDB, OAS*
'70 CIA media manipulatn rptd 1-16, 92C3
Russell ct scores US 1-17, 61B2
Ford State of Union message 1-19, 38B3
In 4-natn drug drive 1-20, 61A1
US corp bribe scandal spreads 2-7—2-23, 147E1
Kissinger visits 6 natns 2-16—2-24; summit cancelled 2-17; briefs Ford 2-25, 177A1
AID labor union aid rptd 3-10, 253F1
US exports up in '75 3-19, 466B1
US stresses Panama Canal talks 4-15, 4-19, 281A2, B2
Kissinger on tour 6-6—6-13, 465A2
US Dem platform text cites 6-15, 478F2, G2
US GOP platform text cites 8-18, 609E3
Ford acceptance speech cites 8-19, 612B1
Castro group terrorism rptd 8-22, 791B1
US panel advises Carter 12-14, 974D3
Forgn paymts rptd accepted 12-20, 985F2

LATIN American Economic System (SELA) (Argentina, Bolivia, Brazil, Chile, Colombia, Costa Rica, Cuba, Dominican Republic, Ecuador, El Salvador, Guatemala, Guyana, Haiti, Honduras, Jamaica, Mexico, Nicaragua, Panama, Paraguay, Peru, Trinidad & Tobago, Uruguay, Venezuela)
1st ministerial mtg held 1-12—1-15, 60D2
Kissinger, Perez discuss 2-16—2-17, 177E2
Venez backs 5-18, 465G3
LATIN American Free Trade Association (LAFTA) (Argentina, Bolivia, Brazil, Chile, Colombia, Ecuador, Mexico, Paraguay, Peru, Uruguay, Venezuela)
Stroessner, Pinochet back 3-24—3-27, 4-21—4-24, 382D3
La TORRE, Gen. Arturo
Peru mines min 1-31, 142A3
LATSIS, Ioannis
Govt chrgs rptd 11-2, 854D1
LATTA, Rep. Delbert L. (R, Ohio)
Warns vs House Arab boycott legis 9-22, 746G2
Reelected 11-2, 830G2
LATTANZIO, Vito
Sworn Italy defense min 7-30, 573E1, F1
LATTER-Day Saints, Church of Jesus Christ (Mormons)
Black's ordinatn voided 4-3; ordainer barred from conf 10-3, 951C2
Hughes alleged will found 4-27, 335D3
Udall ties disputed 5-15, 5-17, 357C1
Hughes will disputed 7-13, 7-16, 596E3
Carter visits Kimball 10-7, 762D1
Hughes will forgery chrgd 12-13, 971B2
LATVIAN Soviet Socialist Republic—*See 'Republics' under USSR*

LAUGERUD Garcia, Gen. Kjell Eugenio (ret.)
Rpts on quake devastatn 2-4, 81E1
Looters executed 2-8, 120G3
Sees Kissinger 2-24, 178F1
Rightists control Cong 7-18, 1005B1

1977

LATIN America—*See also specific countries, organizations*
3,000 prisoners rptd freed 1-1, 2D3
At pan-Africa fete 1-15—2-12, 106B1
Mid-'75 populatn rptd 1-30, 123G2
'75-76 trade, paymts data; table 3-11, 189A1, A2 ★
WHO launches immunizatn drive 4-7, 287C3
'66-75 arms transfers rptd, table 4-8, 415A2, D2
Carib water rationing rptd 4-12, 312F2
'76 regional growth rptd; '61-75 GDP variatns table 5-30, 439A1, E1
6 ldrs meet 8-5—8-6; new Panama Canal pact backed, coffee fund set 8-6, 606A3-607A1, 608B2
Cocaine flow to Eur rptd 8-29, 972F1
Malaria upsurge rptd 9-4, 747D3
Brazil, Paraguay, Argentina in hydro talks 9-22—9-23, 794D3
USSR arms sales rptd 10-13, 949B2
Univ reps at Panama Canal pact vote 10-23, 809D1
Chile-Grenada ties seen threat to Carib 10-26, 869B1
France affirms arms sales 11-22, 1012F3
Amnesty Intl chrgs rights abuses 12-8, 956D2
U.S. Relations
US acts on air fares 1-14, 3-11, 324D3, 325C1
SEC chrgs GTE payoff 1-27, 79E2
US policy vs arms sales cited 2-7, 87B3
Carter notes rights abuses 2-23, 126E2
Castro chrgs totalitarian support 2-26—2-27, 180E3
Carter asked to end Nicaragua aid 3-25, 476B1
'66-75 arms transfers rptd 4-8, 415A2, D2
Carter policy address; A-ban ratificatn, rights stressed 4-14, 295C2-296C1
Todman in 4 natns 5-8—5-17, 414C1
Carter vows cooperatn 5-22, 397F1
Carter signs A-ban pact 5-26, 415D3
Mrs Carter tours 5-30—6-12, 454D1
NSA wiretap criticism cited 7-10, 551C2
US delays police arms sales 7-17, 572E3-573A1
Young tours Carib, pledges econ aid 8-5—8-17, 646E1
Latin ldrs back new Panama Canal pact 8-6, 606A3-607A1
Panama Canal pact reached 8-10, Carter backs 8-12, 621D1, F2
US pvt investmt rptd at $24 bln, 76 trade $34 bln 8-22, 679C1
US cocaine traffic rptd 8-29, 972F1
Carter receptn of dictators protested 9-6—9-7, 678B1
Ldrs at Canal pact signing 9-7, 677F2-678E1
Chile: Alliance for Progress led to Sovt aggressn 9-11, 724F3
Hollings Aug tour cited 9-20, 755C3
Vance visits Argentina, Brazil, Venez 11-20—11-23, Admin policy examined 11-24, 912D2-913C1
Jamaica warns on Canal pacts rejectn threat to Latin ties 12-16, 1019A2

LATIN America, Economic Commission for (ECLA)—*See under UNITED Nations*
LATIN America, Washington Office on
El Salvador vote fraud chrgd 3-9, 206C3
LATIN American Newspapermen, Federation of
Uruguay release of Mex rptr sought 7-15, 601E1
LATTANZIO, Vito
Demoted 9-18, 728G3, 729D1
LATTER-Day Saints, Church of Jesus Christ of (Mormons)
Dummar confesses re Hughes will 1-11, 120D1
Black's ordainer loses suit 3-10, 310G1
Hughes will declared fake 4-15, 354C3
Polygamist sect ldr slain 5-10, 6 chrgd 9-27, 847G3
LAUDA, Niki
Wins Grand Prix 10-1, 870C3, E3

LAUGERUD Garcia, Gen. Kjell Eugenio (Guatemalan president)
'74-76 disappearances, exectns rptd 2-21, 168A3
Warns UK vs Belize independnc 5-17, 415D1
Severs Panama ties 5-19, scores Torrijos, warns re Belize 5-20, 414B3
At IDB mtg 5-30—6-1, 438F2
Scores UK troops in Belize, rightist pressure rptd 8-5, 706E2
At Panama Canal pact signing 9-7, 678D1
Spain king backs 'aspirations' re Belize 9-13, 805D1
LAUGHING Gas (Nitrous Oxide)—*See CHEMICALS*

1978

LATHAM, Arthur
Asks London race riot probe 6-11, 452F3
LATIMER, Don
In NFL draft 5-2, 336G2

LATIN America—*See also country, organization names*
Japan '77 aid sets record 1-3, 28F2
Chile murder suspect implicated in Latin bombing 4-26, 371B1
E Carib tourism set back by air strike 6-2, 559A2
5 ldrs at Canal treaty rite 6-16, 463F2, 464A1
China backs Spain policy 6-18, 576E2
Carter vows rights conv ratificatn effort 6-21, 489D3
Amazon pact signed by 8 natns 7-3, 829B2
Human Rights Conv enacted, ct formed 7-18, 828E3-829C1
'64 papal visit cited 8-6, 601B2
Malaria rptd on rise 8-6, 636A1
China scores Sovt hegemony 8-16, 674E3
Regional export bank founded 9-8, 828C3
IDB: '77 econ growth poor 9-10, 828D2-A3
World Bank loans rptd up 9-15, 828A3
Sovt bloc shipping data rptd 9-17, 820C3
Dominica becomes independent 11-2, 861G2
USSR-US arms sales talks stalled 12-5—12-15, 996C3
U.S. Relations
Carter State of Union Message 1-19, 31G2
US-Carib econ talks rptd 1-22, 100C3
US Sen debates Canal pact 2-8, 120F1
Carter visits Venez, Brazil; rights stand noted 3-28—3-31, 233A1-F2
US Sen ratifies Canal treaty 4-18, 273G1
USSR chrgs puppet regimes 5-7, 349A3
US '77 arms bid rejctns rptd 5-19, 387A1
Carter at Canal treaty rite, stresses inter-Amer cooperatn, Latins back 6-16, 463F2, 464A1
Carter policy address stresses rights 6-21, 489D2
Rights drive lauded by US panel 6-24, 490A1
CIA chrgd re false subversn chrgs 8-1, 831C1
Carter policy scored by GOP pres hopeful 11-29, 938E3
US-USSR arms sales talks stalled 12-5—12-15, 996C3
LATIN America, Washington Office on—*See WASHINGTON Office on Latin America*
LATIN American Council of Churches
Mtg rptd, Nicaragua pres resignatn asked 10-13, 823D3
LATIN American Protestant Churches, Assembly of
Latin Amer Church Cncl mtg rptd, Nicaragua pres resignatn asked 10-13, 823E3
LATTA, Rep. Delbert L. (R, Ohio)
Rebuts Carter budget proposals 1-31, 63D1
Reelected 11-7, 851D3
LATTER-Day Saints, Church of Jesus Christ of (Mormons)
'53, '78 cong membership compared 1-30, 107F2
Hughes will ruled fake 6-8, trial costs rptd 6-12, 458F3, 459A1
Black priest ban ended 6-9, 1st black ordained 6-11, 480G2
Guatemala murder scored 7-21, 722D2 ★
Excommunicated member kills self 8-3, 695D3
LATTER-Day Saints, Reorganized Church of Jesus Christ (Mormons)
Homemaker role for women affirmed 4-1, 907E2
Smith installed as pres 4-5, 294F2
Relief Soc pres opposes ERA 5-5, 907D2
Intermarriage discouraged 7-15, 907C2
Prayer rites opened to women 10-7, 907G1
Kimball calls for doubling missionary force 10-13, 907B2
Ida electn issue cited 11-7, 856B1
Carter accepts award, women's group protests 11-27, 915A1
LATTIMORE, Owen
Judge Youngdahl dies 6-21, 540G3
LATVIAN Soviet Socialist Republic—*See USSR—Republics*
LAUDA, Niki
3d in world driving title 9-10, 968C3
LAUDICINA, Dino
Crane's Way opens 7-12, 760G1
LAUGERUD Garcia, Gen. Kjell Eugenio (Guatemalan president)
Indifference to pol murders chrgd 2-22, 168D3
Hints Belize compromise 2-24, 230C3
Pol move to center cited re govt-MLN split 3-9, 168F2
Lucas named pres-elect by Cong 3-13, 190G1
Blames guerrillas for rural clashes 6-1, 497C1
Lucas replaces as pres, asks 'peaceful' Belize solutn 7-1, 538F1
Lucas keeps 2 Cabt mins 7-21, 722D3 ★
Panama ties resumed 8-29, 798B3

1979

LATER (play)
Opens 1-15, 292F1
LATHAM, Arthur
Urges smallpox precautions 1-4, 7C2
LATHROP, Calif.—*See CALIFORNIA*

LATIN America—*See also DEVELOPING Nations; country, organization names*
Trade boycott of Chile, Nicaragua, Cuba dropped by unions 1-15—1-16, 28C3
Amnesty Intl cites rights violatns 2-1, 85G2
RC bishops ask repressn end 2-13, 108E2-109A1
Baptism rites agrmt reached 3-31, 375F2
Illegal abortns rptd common 4-29, 547D3
Forgn aid to Carib rptd 7-6, 960G3
PEN chrgs 6 natns on rights 7-21, 553G3
Hurricane David hits Carib 8-30—8-31, 690A3
Fiat announces investmt plan 9-12, 709C2
Spain premr delays trip 9-25, 754C2
'78 smoking rise rptd 11-22, 970F2
Amnesty Intl reviews '79 rights 12-9, 980D2
U.S. Relations
Castro: US caused repressn, deaths 1-1, 20B1
AMC, Renault sign sales pact 1-10, 131F2
US defends 'new diplomacy' 5-1, 347D2
US 'globalism' defined 5-10, 416D3
US oil import subsidy set 5-25, 417C2
Carter addresses Cong on SALT II 6-18, 449E2, 459A3
Carib aid rptd 7-6, counter Cuba policy set 11-29, 960B3
Sovt troop presence in Cuba feared by US 8-31, 657E1; **for subsequent developments, see CUBA–Soviet Relations**
NAACP seeks closer ties 9-9, 677A2
US to up mil watch, econ aid 10-1, 737G1, 739A1
Carib naval presence urged 10-16, 781D2
US cigaret exports cited 11-22, 970G2

LATIN American Citizens, The League of United (LULAC)
Bonilla elected pres 6-17, 810E1
Bonilla scores judge in Torres case 10-30, 839F3
LATIN American Episcopal Conference (CELAM)
Pope opens Mex mtg 1-27, plays down church pol role 1-28, 67A3, F3
Mtg ends; reforms, soc justice urged 2-13, 108E2-B3
LATIN American Free Trade Association (LAFTA) (Argentina, Bolivia, Brazil, Chile, Colombia, Ecuador, Mexico, Paraguay, Peru, Uruguay, Venezuela)
Andean Group to strengthen ties 5-26—5-28, 398B2
LATTER-Day Saints, Church of Jesus Christ of (Mormons)
Excommunicated member killed 1-18, 94E1
RC abortion stand protested by NY clerics 1-22, 63E3
Membership rise rptd 5-4, 640A1
Black progress rptd 6-8, 6-15, 508A1
Life of Brian legal action barred 10-26, 859D1
Va feminist tried 12-1, excommunicated 12-5, 929B3
LATTUADA, Alberto
Stay As You Are released 12-21, 1008G1

1980

LATHAM, Aaron
Urban Cowboy released 6-11, 675F3
LATHAM, John R.
Dies 2-21, 176B2
LATHAN, Christina
Wins Olympic medal 7-28, 624A2

LATIN America—*See also country, organization names; also related headings (e.g., DEVELOPING Nations)*
Mex gets Sec Cncl seat 1-7, 12A2
Malaria outbreak rptd 5-31, 478B1
Venice summit notes Carib refugees 6-22, 473D1
Vatican issues clergy reassignmt plan 7-22, 970F1
Mex, Venez sign oil supply guarantee 8-3, 605C3
IDB finance data rptd 11-1, 864G3
U.S. Relations
US issues rights rpt 2-5, 87E1, G2
Italy CP scores US role 2-17, 134E1
Air fare hikes OKd by CAB 3-12, 3-24, 346E2; 5-15, 516E1
Hispanic immigrants surveyed 5-11—5-20, 396A2
Castro scores Reagan 'Big Stick' 7-19, 565C3
Moynihan warns of 'Soviet empire' 8-11, 612D3
US Dem platform plank adopted 8-13, 615C1
'81 refugee quota cut 9-19, 883C3

LATSKEVICH, Alexander
Wins Olympic medal 7-28, 623D1
LATTA, Rep. Delbert L. (R, Ohio)
Reelected 11-4, 843D4
Budget reconciliatn signed 12-5, 936F1
LATTER-Day Saints, Church of Jesus Christ of (Mormons)
Va feminist excommunicatn upheld 7-1, 638A2
LAU, Ha Van
Vs Pol Pot govt UN seat 10-13, 775D2
Vs UN Cambodia res 10-22, 801E1
LAUCK, Chester A. (Lum)
Dies 2-21, 176B2

1976

LAURENT, Jean
Anderson arrested 1-8, 45B3
LAURENTIN, Lt. Col. J. M.
Lockheed Disney bribe rptd 2-7, 147F3
LAURIN, Camille
Named cultural dvpt min 11-26, 903A3
LAURIN, Fernand
Haiti works, transport min 4-1, 267E2
LAURIOL, Marc
Cites 'franglais' abuses 1-4, 50C2
LAUTENBERG, Frank
'72 campaign gift listed 4-25, 688D1
La VALLE, Raniero
Rptd on CP ticket 5-17, 5-30, 402C3
Scores Vatican CP attacks 6-1, 403A1
La VERA Velarde, Gen. Luis
Replaced 7-16, 590F2
LAVERY, James
Arraigned 4-22, 309D3
LAVI, Houshang
Accuses Iran gen 2-17, 140D1
LAVILLA, Landelino
Justice min 7-8, 523D2
LAVON, Pinhas
Dies 1-24, 80E3
Obituaries
Armstrong, Barbara 1-18, 56G2
Ernst, Morris 5-21, 404F1
Kenny, Robert W 7-20, 716D3
Miller, William 4-12, 316B1
Morgan, Gerald 6-15, 484F3
LAW & Lawyers—*See COURTS & Legal Profession*
LAWLOR, John
Angola sentences 6-28, 480B2
LAWTON, Okla.—*See OKLAHOMA*
LAWTON, Mary C.
On FBI guidelines 3-10, 217D3
LAXALT, Sen. Paul (R, Nev.)
On Reagan delegate count 8-16, 601E3
Nominates Reagan 8-18, 598A1
Backs Dole as vp 8-19, 598C3
GOP conv vp vote table 8-19, 599F3
LAZAR, Edward (d. 1975)
Murder cited 484C1
LAZARSFELD, Paul
Dies 8-30, 680F3
LEACH, Daniel E.
EEOC member 2-10; confrmd 3-3, 186A2
LEACH, James A. S.
Elected 11-2, 823C2, 829C3
LEAD
Sen OKs paint poison bill 2-19, 170F3
EPA gas curb upheld 3-19, 219D2
Cong clears paint poison bill 6-7, 434F2; signed 6-23, 982F1
Car gas deadlines eased 9-24, 767B3
LEAF, Munro
Dies 12-21, 1015G1
LEAGUE of Women Voters Of The United States
Wins FEC stay 2-27, 169F3
Study scores revenue sharing 3-2, 187B1
Presidential Campaign Debates—
For details, see under POLITICS
Pres TV debate talks open 8-26, 632D3
FEC OKs debates 8-30, 644D1
Debate ground rules set 9-1, 644C1
More debate rules rptd 9-8; 2d, 3d debates set 700F3, 703A2
Mondale cites rating 10-15, 783A3
LEAHY, Sen. Patrick J. (D, Vt.)
On US, Sovt naval strength 4-13, 394A2

1977

LAUREL, Rich
In NBA draft 6-10, 584B2
LAUREN, Ralph
'77 fall fashions rptd 6-6, 1022D1
LAURENCE, William L.
Dies 3-19, 264B3
LAURIA Lesseur, Carmelo
Venez industries min 1-7, 23F2
Secy gen of presidency 7-15, 566B1
LAURIN, Camille
White paper vs bilingualism 4-1, 254C2
On French-speaking hiring stand 5-17, 425A3
LAUSECKER, Karl
Named Austria transport min 5-31, 425D1
LAVER, Rod
'Heavywt championship' fee probe rptd 7-8, 548E2
LAVILLA, Landelino
Retains Justice post 7-5, 545F1
LAVIN Farina, Lt. Col. Jaime
US ends visit 1-28, Chile denies torture chrg 2-2, 219D2
LAVOIE, Jacques
Quits PC 6-14, 505C2
LAVON, Pinhas
Egypt returns 2 hanged spies 4-19, 297B2
LAW Enforcement Assistance Administration—*See under U.S. GOVERNMENT—JUSTICE*
LAW Institute, American—*See AMERICAN Law Institute*
LAW & Lawyers—*See COURTS & Legal Profession*
LAW of the Sea, UN Conference on the—*See under UNITED Nations*
LAWRENCE, Judge Alexander A.
Rules on '71 Ga chem blast 6-23, 604B1
LAWRENCE, Allan
Polysar rebates scored 7-7, 542A1
LAWRENCE, Harding L.
Braniff-Concorde pact rptd 2-11, 213D1
LAWRENCE, T(homas) E(dward) (1888-1935)
Biography wins Pulitzer 4-18, 355D2
LAWYERS Guild, National
Spying suit vs US rptd 3-2, 423F1
LAXALT, Sen. Paul (R, Nev.)
Vs Sen ethics code 4-1, 251F3
Announces 'truth squad' campaign vs Canal pacts 9-9, 698A3
On TV vs Canal pacts 10-29, 912C1
LAYCRAFT, James
Probe bares minor corruptn 12-6, 12-8, 965B2
LAZARD Freres & Co.
ITT suits settled 3-4, 194D3
SEC chrgs re ITT settled 10-13, 980B3
LAZAR Inc., H.L.
Penney official sentncd 8-5, 848C2
LEAA—*See 'Law Enforcement Assistance Administration' under U.S. GOVERNMENT—JUSTICE*
LEAD
McDonald's halts glass promotn 7-8, 7-17, sues Mass agency 7-12, 560A1
Air-pollutn curb proposed 12-12, 1007G2
LEAGUE of Nations
Begin cites in Knesset speech 11-20, 894B1
LEAGUE of Women Voters of the United States
Benson named to State Dept 1-7, 14G1
Waterman electd Common Cause chrmn 4-23, 396C3
LEAHY, Justice John J.
Drops Krishna indictmts 3-17, 287F1

1978

LAUNDRIES & Laundering
OSHA drops 'nuisance' rules 10-24, 833D3
LAURE, Carol
Get Out Handkerchiefs released 12-17, 1030A3
LAUREN, Ralph
'78 high chic fashion rptd 8-4—8-11, 10-27—11-3, 1029C2
LAURIN, Camille
Scores language suit fund 3-10, 188E2
LAVALLEE, David
Gray Lady Down released 3-10, 619C2
LAVENDER, Kenneth D.
Pardons voided 12-20, 1011B2
LAVERNE and Shirley (TV series)
Silverman to head NBC 1-20, 75F2
LAW Enforcement Assistance Administration (LEAA)—*See under U.S. GOVERNMENT—JUSTICE*
LAW Institute, American—*See AMERICAN Law Institute*
LAW & Lawyers—*See COURTS & Legal Profession*
LAWLESS, The (book)
On best-seller list 4-30, 356A2; 6-4, 460D3; 7-2, 579D3
LAW of the Sea, UN Conference on the—*See under UNITED Nations*
LAWRENCE, D(avid) H(erbert) (1885-1930)
'Chatterley' judge dies 4-17, 356C2
Fight for Barbara opens 11-27, 1031F1
LAWRENCE, George
On natural gas supplies 11-2, 900A1
LAWRENCE, Jerome
1st Monday in Oct opens 10-3, 1031F1
LAWRENCE, Josephine
Dies 2-22, 196D3
LAWRENCE, Rolland
NFL '77 interceptn ldr 1-1, 56G2
LAWRENCE, Rear Adm. William P.
Assumes Naval Acad cmnd 8-16, 843D3
LAWRENCE Aviation Industries Inc.
Indicted on price fixing 9-28, 768D2
LAWRENCE Township, N.J.—*See NEW Jersey*
LAWTHER, Derrick
Named ASL top coach 9-10, 707G3
LAXALT, Sen. Paul (R, Nev.)
Leads Panama Canal 'truth squad' tour 1-17—1-19, 58B2
Says Canal pacts invite Sovt, Cuba interventn 2-8, 120F1
Votes vs Panama Canal neutrality pact 3-16, 177G2
Votes vs 2d Canal pact 4-18, 273B1
Visits USSR 11-11—11-18, 905A2
LAYCRAFT, James H.
RCMP probe rpts 7-25, 590D2
LAY Down Sally (recording)
On best-seller list 4-5, 272F3
LAYTON, Joe
Platinum opens 11-12, 1031F2
LAYTON, Larry
Shoots US visitors after Guyana cult probe 11-18, arrest rptd 11-20, 899D2, 890A2, C2, C3
Chrgd in Guyana airstrip deaths 11-22, cultists held as witnesses 11-28, 910C2
Indicted for Ryan murder 12-8, takes 'full responsibility' 12-13, 955B2
LAZAROS, Peter N.
Diamond recovered in autopsy 5-4, 380E1
LAZARUS, Paul N.
Capricorn One released 6-2, 618E3
LAZO, Carlos
Jail term commuted to exile 3-27, flies to France 4-1, 267F1
LEAA—*See U.S. GOVERNMENT—JUSTICE—Law Enforcement Assistance Administration*
LEACH, Claude (Buddy)
Faces La US House runoff 9-16, 736E3
Elected 11-7, 850F4, 855C2
LEACH, Rep. James A. S. (R, Iowa)
Reelected 11-7, 850C4
LEACH, Rick
3d in Heisman vote 11-28, 1025A2
LEACH, Wilford
All's Well That Ends Well opens 7-5, 760B1
LEACH v. Sawicki
Ohio gag-order case review barred 1-9, 13E1
LEAD
McDonald's glasses rptd safe 1-31, 348B1
Italy factory blast 7-15, 689A2
Air-pollutn curb issued 9-29, 754C1
Price upturn cited 10-20, 805D1
OSHA sets exposure rule, industry challenges 11-13, 899A3, C3
LEAD Industries Association
Challenges OSHA standard 11-13, 899D3
LEAGUE of Women Voters of the United States
DC voting amendmt ratificatn drive backed 8-22, 661C2
LEAHY, Judge John J.
Drops chrgs vs Amer Chicle 2-15, 212D3
LEAHY, Sen. Patrick J. (D, Vt.)
Backs Panama Canal pacts 2-1, 58E1
Votes for Panama Canal neutrality pact 3-16, 177D2
Votes for 2d Canal pact 4-18, 273B1

1979

LAU, Ha Van
Vs Cambodia plea at UN 1-11, 10C2
Challenges Pol Pot govt UN seat 9-18, 695B2
LAUB, Kenneth D.
Break a Leg opens 4-29, 711G1
LAUCK, Gary
6 neo-Nazis sentncd 9-13, 733C3
LAUGHING Gas (nitrous oxide)—*See CHEMICALS*
LAUREN Bacall By Myself (book)
On best-seller list 2-4, 120B3; 3-4, 173D3; 4-8 271A2; 5-6, 356D2
LAUX, Gar
Chrysler positn cited 9-20, 700C1
LAVER, Rod
Loses Tennis Legends tourn 4-22, 391C3
LAVINSKY, Larry M.
Vs Weber case Sup Ct ruling 6-27, 477E2
LAW Enforcement Assistance Administration—*See under U.S. GOVERNMENT-JUSTICE*
LAW & Lawyers—*See COURTS & Legal Profession*
LAWLESS, Sue
Tip Toes opens 3-26, 712A3
LAW of the Sea, UN Conference on the—*See under UNITED Nations*
LAWRENCE, Allan
Canada solicitor gen 6-4, 423F3
To probe discarded govt papers 6-4, 444B3
On RCMP emb bugging plan 7-5, 522A3
LAWRENCE, John
Murdoch press takeover bid dropped 11-22, 906B3
LAWRENCE, Marjorie
Dies 1-13, 104C3
LAWSON, John Howard
Loudspeaker opens 4-30, 712C1
LAWTON, Okla.—*See OKLAHOMA*
LAWYERS' Committee for Civil Rights Under Law
Activist leaves S Africa 8-10, 617E2
LAXALT, Sen. Paul (R, Nev.)
Votes vs Talmadge denunciatn 10-10, 769G1
LAYTON, Larry
Guyana dismisses chrgs 3-7, 220E1
LAZARD, Freres & Co.
Andre Meyer dies 9-9, 756B3
LAZARUS, Paul N.
Hanover Street released 5-17, 528D2
LAZARUS, Tom
Just You & Me Kid released 7-27, 820D1
LEAA—*See U.S. GOVERNMENT-JUSTICE-Law Enforcement Assistance Administration*
LEACH, Bernard
Dies 5-6, 432B3
LEACH, Rep. Claude (Buddy) (D, La.)
Pleads not guilty to vote buying 7-24, 561D1
Acquitted 11-3, 900E2
LEACH, Kimberly (d. 1978)
Bundy gets death penalty 7-31, 604A3
LEACH, Wilford
Coriolanus opens 6-28, 711C2
LEACHMAN, Cloris
N Amer Irregulars released 4-12, 528B3
Scavenger Hunt released 12-25, 1008E1
LEAD
Cyanamid sterilizatn suit threatnd 1-4, 56B3
Acad impact study rptd 3-29, 266E1
FDA drive vs canned food contaminatn rptd 8-30, 736G3
LEAGUE of Women Voters of the United States
Anna Strauss dies 2-23, 176F3
LEAHY, Pat
NFL '78 kicking ldr 1-6, 80B1

1980

LAUREL, Salvador
Quits Pl ruling party 2-11, 152F2
LAUREN, Ralph
'80 fashion roundup rptd 998G1
LAUREN Bacall By Myself (book)
On best-seller list 2-10, 120D3
LAURENTS, Arthur
West Side Story opens 2-14, 136G3
LAUSELL Hernandez, Luis
Loses PR gov electn 11-4, 852E3
Romero declared winner in recount 12-18, 988B2
LAUTERBACK, Steven
Hostages' letters publshd 1-18—1-20, 47D3
LAVALLEE, Calixa (deceased)
O Canada proclaimed natl anthem 7-1, 496E3
LAVASANI, Abbas
Killed 5-5, 337F1
LAVENDER, Joe
NFL '79 interceptn ldr 1-5, 8G2
LAVER, Rod
Connors matches WCT singles title mark 5-4, 607A1
Borg breaks Wimbledon match win mark 7-6, 606D2
LA VERNE (Calif.) College
Dean makes appearance 4-23, 333E3
LAWE, John E.
Fined 4-8, 268E1
Transit strike ends 4-11, 289A3
LAW & Lawyers—*See COURTS*
LAW of the Sea, UN Conference on—*See under UNITED Nations*
LAWRENCE, Amos (Famous Amos)
NC wins Bluebonnet Bowl 12-31, 999E3
LAWRENCE, Harding L.
Resigns as Braniff chrmn, chief exec 12-31, 986A3
LAWRENCE, Jerome
Incomparable Max opens 6-15, 756D3
LAWRENCE, Rolland
NFL '79 interceptn ldr 1-5, 8G2
LAWSON, Leigh
Tess released 12-12, 1003E2
LAWZI, Selim al-
Kidnaped 2-26; found slain 3-4, 179F3
LAXALT, Sen. Paul (R, Nev.)
Asks Miller-Textron spec prosecutor 2-11, 145B2
Reagan retains Brock 6-13, 452A3
Nominates Reagan at conv 7-16, 529F1, 534C1
Lauds choice of Bush, announces Reagan com appointmts 7-22, 549G2
Wins primary 9-9, 700E2
Reelected 11-4, 840E2, 845B3, 852A1
LAYDEN, Frank
NBA cocaine use rptd 8-19, 656F1
LAYE, Camara
Dies 2-4, 176C2
LAYTON, Joe
Barnum opens 4-30, 392D2
LAYTON, Larry
Wins trial delay 4-1, 313D3
Acquitted of attempted murder, other chrgs pending 5-22, 407F3-408B1
LAZARD, Freres & Co.
MacGregor to leave for Brit Steel, UK compensatn set 5-1, 352F1
LAZARUS, Frank
Day in Hollywood opens 5-1, 392F2
LAZARUS, Ralph
Retires as Federated chief exec 12-8, 959A1
LEACH, Rep. Claude (Buddy) (D, La.)
Faces runoff 9-13, 724G2
Loses US Sen electn 11-4, 849D3
LEACH, Rep. James A. S. (R, Iowa)
Reelected 11-4, 842C4
LEACH, Kimberly (d. 1978)
Bundy gets 3d death sentence 2-12, 136D2
LEACH, Reggie
Wales Conf wins NHL All-Star game; named MVP 2-5, 198G2, A3
NHL scoring ldr 4-6, 296E1
LEACH, Cpl. Stewart
Wounded in IRA attack 3-1, 194C1
LEACH, Wilford
Marie & Bruce opens 2-3, 136C3
Mother Courage opens 5-13, 392E3
LEACHMAN, Cloris
Herbie Goes Bananas released 9-12, 836B3
LEAD
USSR buying noted 2-5, 85E1
Va shipyd health abuses chrgd 2-27, 147E3
Auto plant curbs to ease 7-8, 505E1
Gulf Coast toxic waste suit filed 10-9, 825D1
EPA airborne standards challenge refused by Sup Ct 12-8, 937F1
OSHA exposure rule stayed by Sup Ct 12-8, 937G1
Chem clean-up bill signed 12-11, 936B1, C1
LEAD Industries Association v. EPA
Case refused by Sup Ct 12-8, 937F1
LEAGUE of Women Voters of the United States
Carter rejcts 3-way debate 9-9, controversy ensues 9-9—9-10, 680D2
Sponsors Reagan, Anderson TV debate 9-21, 721D2-722E2
Reagan declines 2d debate 9-25, 739F3
Vice pres debate canceled 9-29, 739G3
Carter, Reagan debate set 10-21, 801F3
Sponsors Carter, Reagan TV debate 10-28, 813F1
LEAHY, Sen. Patrick J. (D, Vt.)
B Carter probe opens 8-4, 595B3
Chastises B Carter re Libya 8-22, 647G1-A2
Unopposed in primary 9-9, 700B3
On B Carter probe 9-17, 701A2, D2
Reelected 11-4, 840E3, 845A3, 849B1

1976

LEARNED, Stanley
Tax fraud chrgd 9-2, 725G2
LEARY, Dr. Timothy F.
Denied paroie 3-1, 272D1
Voted parole 4-20, released 6-7, 424G1
LEAVENWORTH, Kan.—*See KANSAS*
LEAVITT, Brenton
On FRB 'problem' list 1-22, 2-3, 112G2-D3
LEAVITT, Dixie L.
Loses Utah primary for gov 9-14, 705F1

LEBANON—*See also ARAB League, NON-ALIGNED Nations Movement*
15 killed in Saudi air crash 1-1, 79G3
French Mirage purchase cited 1-16, 36C2
Listed as 'partially free' 1-19, 20C3
Canada emb siege 2-23, 145G2
Dependents quit China quake area 8-1, 561E2
Hoss named premr 12-8, forms Cabt 12-9, 913C2
Parlt OKs decree rule 12-24, 974B1

Civil War—*See under MIDDLE EAST—ARAB Policies*
Middle East Conflict—*See MIDDLE EAST*

1977

LEAMING, Cletus
Miranda rule review sidestepped 3-23, 275E3
LEARNED Societies, American Council of
China bars US exchngs 6-28, 505G3
LEASURE, Althea (Mrs. Larry Flynt)
Acquitted 2-8, 118E2

LEBANON—*See also ARAB League, NONALIGNED Nations Movement*
Banks reopen 1-10, 28C2
Not in EC trade pact 1-18, 73F3
Forgn press curbs end 1-25, 72C2
EEC pact initialed 2-16, 269B3
Press curbs eased 3-12, reimposed 3-13, 188C2
Turkish hijackers arrested 3-19, 224F3
Canada '76 immigratn rptd 4-13, 389D2
Hijacker diverts jet to Kuwait 6-6, 497C3
'76 Turk emb aide death cited 6-9, 565A2
Press curbs reimposed 6-30, protested 7-4, 511A1
Govt decree powers extended 8-4, 648A2
Kuwait frees hijacker 8-29, 736B2
Cholera outbreak rptd 9-26, 747G3-748C1
Makhlouf proclaimed saint 10-9, 845F3
Hijackers denied landing 10-13, 789F1
Christns stage gen strike 12-12, 954G1
Arab-Israeli Conflict—*See MIDDLE EAST; for civil strife, see below*
Cairo Conference—*See MIDDLE EAST—EGYPT-Israel Peace Moves*
Civil Strife (& developments)
4 die in Palestinian-leftist exchng 1-1, 2F1
Press curbs set 1-1, imposed 1-3, 2G1
Christian hq blast, 40 die 1-3; protest strike, ldrs meet 1-4, 2B1, E1
Casualties listed 1-3, 28F2
4 Christians slain in Durah 1-4, 2C1
Arms collectn, PLA exit set 1-7; arms roundup completed 1-12, Syria chrgs stalling 1-3, 28D1
Postwar reconstructn moves 1-8, 28E2
Franjieh vs Palestinian arms guarding 1-10, 28A2
PLA troops quit 1-10—1-13, 28B2
League widens Beirut control 1-23, 1-26; Christians strike 1-24, 72E1
Christian-Palestinian clash 1-24, 72G1
Syrian League troops move near Israeli line 1-25; Israel warns 1-25, 1-28, 1-31, 71E3
US mediates Syria troop moves 1-26, 1-29, 2-1, 72A1
League troops take all ports 1-28, 71G3
Israel objectns to Syrian moves scored 1-28, 72D1
League troops block Saida blast 1-29, 72A2
Syria coordinatn pact 2-2, 72B2
US gets Israel complaint on Syrian troops 2-6, Syria quits border 2-13—2-15, 106G1
Palestinian factns clash, Syria intervenes 2-10—2-11; arrests rptd 2-12, 106D2
League sets Palestinian curbs 2-12, 106G2
Syrians ease camp siege 2-15, 106C3
Arafat sees Syria ldrs 2-15, Fatah blames Palestinians for clashes 2-16, 106D3, 107A1
Christns seize Moslem town in south 2-18, fighting spreads 2-21, 2-28, 143C1
Palestinians OK south exit 2-23, agrmt ratified 2-25; Israelis doubt 2-27, 143A2, E2
UN troop use weighed, Israel vs 2-27; USSR, US, France advised, crisis seen 3-1, 143C2
Christns cross into Israel, seek aid vs Palestinians 3-2, 143F1
Palestinian rivals clash 3-6—3-7, 166D2
League force term extended 6 mos 3-9, 188B2
Leb police deployed in south 3-12, 188A2
Christians raid Kafr Kila, 12 die 3-14, 188A2
Jumblat slain 3-16; 66 die in reprisals, Syrian troops dispatched 3-16—3-17, 188C1
Cabt meets, urges restraint; Arafat vows reprisals 3-16, 188F1
Jumblat son heads Druse clan 3-17, asks restraint 3-20, 208D2
Jumblat revenge slayings ebb, 200 die; Syrian troops reinforced 3-18, 208G1
Chamoun heads Leb Front 3-18, 208C2
Christians ask protectn 3-18, 3-19, 208C2
Palestinians protest Syria role 3-20, 208E1
League force formally extended 6 mos 3-27, 227B2
New army head named, Christians strike 3-28, 227C1
Christians-Palestinians clash in south; Israel, Syria aid rptd 3-31—4-5, 245E2
Christns vs Syria demand to end Israel aid 246F1
Syria blames Israel for clashes 4-4, 246E1
Christns admit Taibe fall, take wounded to Israel 4-6, 266F2

1978

LEAKE, Dr. Chauncey D.
Dies 1-11, 96E2
LEAKE v. Gordon
Case refused by Sup Ct 11-13, 874C3
LEAKEY, Mary D.
Hominid track discovery rptd 3-4, 334B2
LEAR, William Powell
Dies 5-14, 440B3
LEARSY, Raymond J.
Elected Trib chrmn 1-17, 75D3
LEATH, Marvin
Wins US House seat 11-7, 852A3, 855D3
LEAVIS, Frank Raymond
Dies 4-14, 356B3

LEBANON—*See also ARAB League, NONALIGNED Nations Movement*
Hoss govt quits 4-19, 299D3
Hoss renamed to form Cabt 4-28; rpts failure, Cabt reinstated 5-15, 359D1

Arab-Israeli Conflict—*See MIDDLE EAST—LEBANON; for civil strife, see below*
Civil Strife—*For Israeli invasion of Lebanon and subsequent developments, see MIDDLE EAST—LEBANON*
Christn-PLO clashes, Israelis back Christns 1-3—1-4, 10D3
PLO-Christns clash in south 1-17—2-5; Chamoun chrgs Tyre arms shipmts 1-25, 79D2
PLO-Syria secret base agrmt rptd 2-1, 2-5, 78G2
Terror incidents 2-1, 2-7, 79C2
PLO quits Saida, other sites 2-2, 2-3, 79F2
Leb army units, Syrians clash in Beirut 2-7—2-9; truce talks 2-8, 78D3-79G1
Leb, Syria agree to end violence 2-11—2-12; casualties rptd 2-13; Parlt OKs joint mil ct 2-14, 98C3-99D1
New fighting erupts in south 2-13, 99E1
Arab League peace force extended 3-28, 215C1
Beirut clashes, 102 dies; PLO, Israel blamed 4-9—4-13, 256C1
Hoss govt quits 4-19; militia, Palestinian curbs proposed 4-23, PLO scores 4-25, Parlt OKs 4-27, 299C3-300A1
12 die in Christian, PLO-Leb leftist clash 5-30, 401B1
Foreign Relations (misc.)—*See also 'Civil Strife' above, 'UN' below*
Belgium rptdly seizes Ulster arms shipmt 1-6, 7F3
Arab fund poor-natn aid rise rptd 4-9, 257F2
Egypt recalls Beirut newsmen 5-26, 414F3
Eritrea rebels meet 6-29, 584F2
UK holds suspect in Iraq amb death try 8-2, 582F2
Iraq amb escapes death try 8-2, 582D3
Arab fund loan to Sudan rptd 8-17, 925F3
Moslem ldr in Libya 8-25, rptd missing 8-31; Beirut strike protest 9-15, 713B2

1979

LEAKEY, Louis S. B. (1903-72)
Son wins Kenya electn 11-8, 874C3
LEAKEY, Mary D.
Rpts hominid footprints 3-21, 691B2
Son wins Kenya electn 11-8, 874C3
LEAKEY, Philip
Wins Kenya parlt electn 11-8, 874C3
Kenya asst environmt min 11-28, 969B2
LEAKEY, Richard
Disputes new hominid species claim 2-17, 138B1
LEAR, Peter
Goldengirl released 6-15, 820C1
LEATHER
GATT pact signed, tariff cuts seen 4-12, 273G1
LEAUD, Jean-Pierre
Love On The Run released 4-5, 528A3
LEAVE It to Beaver Is Dead (play)
Opens 4-3, 712B1
LEBANON—*See also ARAB League, NONALIGNED Nations Movement*
MDs stage 24-hr strike 2-7, 126D3
Premr Hoss, Cabt resign 5-16, 378F2
Hoss asked to form new govt 7-2, announces Cabt 7-16, 671D1
Michelangelo icon believed found 10-20, 892G1-A2

Arab-Israeli Conflict—*See MIDDLE EAST—LEBANON*
Civil Strife—*See MIDDLE EAST—LEBANON*

Foreign Relations (misc.)—*See also 'UN Policy' below*
Ghana econ exploitatn chrgd 5-28, 425B2
3 Moslems hijack Alitalia jet, protest Sadr disappearance in Libya 9-7; surrender in Iran 9-8, 677B3
Canada envoy tours Mideast 9-9—10-20, 833D2
Iranians seize US Emb 11-11, 862A3
Arab League pledges reconstructn aid 11-20—11-22, 916G1

1980

LEAR, Norman
Stapleton to quit TV series 4-2, 471B3
LEARY, Timothy
Calif radio statn firing rptd 11-1, 890D2
LEAVIN, Paul
We Won't Pay! opens 12-17, 1003G3

LEBANON—*See also ARAB League*
Parlt member kidnaped 2-13; freed 3-9, 179E3
Editor kidnaped 2-26; found slain 3-4, 179F3
Premr Hoss quits 6-7; resignatn accepted, Solh named 7-20, 579C3
Wazan named premr 10-22, forms Cabt 10-25, 874A1

Foreign Relations (misc.)—*See also 'Military' below*
Rome Emb guard killed 2-6, 99D1
Chad fighting resumes 3-22, natls evacuated 3-24, 221F1
Israel deports W Bank ldrs 5-3, Arafat visits 5-7, 340B2, F2
Israel bars W Bank ldrs return 5-11, 362D2
Egypt scores W Bank ldrs ouster 5-15, 362B2
Sovt Armenian immigratn estimated 5-24, 467F2
Iraq Emb in Rome attacked 6-4, 451E2
Pope urges just attentn 6-21, 474D2
France seizes 2 in Bakhtiar death try 7-18, 545C1
W Ger pol asylum rules rptd tightened 7-31, 581E2
Iranians demonstrate in Beirut 8-8, 635A2
Israel ct backs W Bank ldrs ouster 8-19, 627B3
Libya assails Israel, seeks Syria merger 9-1, 660D3
Imam Sadr rptd jailed in Libya 9-9, 709B1
Iraq seeks pipeline use 9-25, 718B2
Supply ships for Iraq rptd at Jordan port 10-6, 757C1
UNICEF plan for S Leb dvpt signed 10-14, 775E2
Military Developments
Syrian troop mandate extended 1-23, 89G2
Israel crossing, shelling claimed 1-28, 1-29, 89B3
Syria to pull out Beirut troops 2-4; defers 2-5, 89E2
Syria fears Israeli attack 2-5, 89A3
Israel vows aid to Christns vs Syrian attack 2-7, forces alerted 2-8, 107C3
Beirut, southn Leb clashes, artillery exchng 2-10—2-12, 107A3
Israel says PLO gets Sovt tanks 2-12, 107E3
Syrian-Christn clashes, 60 die 2-12—2-17, 125D2
Palestinian-Christn clash in south, UNIFIL fears spread 2-13, 125F2
Leb urges Syria keep troops in Beirut 2-13, 125G2
Rival Christns clash 2-14, 125E2
Syria says Israel plans attack 2-23, delays Beirut exit 2-24; PLO calls up reserves 2-25, 140G2

1976

1977

1978

1979

1980

1977

Map of battle zone 266A2
Christn plea to halt clashes 4-7, 266D2
Palestinians capture Khiam 4-7, Israelis shell 4-8, 266G2
Saiqa offcl home bombed 4-8, 266E3
Syria warns Christns vs Israel ties 4-9, 266C2
Syria curbs support fire 4-9, asks halt to fighting 4-10, 266E2
Arafat meets Assad 4-9, Palestinians ignore truce order 4-10, 266B3
Fighting intensifies at Merj 'Uyun 4-11, 266B3
Security cmnd shifts 4-11, 297A3
Fighting subsides 4-12, US rpts mediatn effort role 4-13, 266D1
Israel warns vs Palestinian force near border 4-12, 266F1
Rival guerrilla groups clash 4-13, 266C3
Rival Palestinians clash 4-16, 297G2
Palestinian entry barred 4-17, 297B3
Christns chrg Palestinian atrocities 4-18, 297E2
Leb seeks PLO curbs 4-19, 316F2
2 Syrians killed 4-22; Syrians clash with Moslems 4-23—4-26, 316B2
Damur Palestinian shift ordrd 4-22, 316A3
US mil aid asked 4-25, 316B3
Syrians, Christns clash 5-14—5-15, 402E1
Palestinian rivals clash 5-20—5-21, 402A2
Arafat warns re Israel-Palestinian clash 5-24, 401E3
Syrian slayers executed 5-24, 402B2
Israeli artillery fire, raids rptd 5-24—6-7, 439G1
Palestinian buildup rptd 5-26, Israelis alerted 6-2, 439F2, C3
League peace com mandate ends 5-26, 440A1
Palestinians, Christns clash 5-27, 6-1, 439E2, B3
Christns renounce '69 Cairo pact, call Palestinian presence illegal 5-27, 439F3
PLO creates new army 5-31, 6-1, 439C3
Palestinians deny buildup, Israeli raid 6-6, 439D3
Syria vows Cairo pact enforcmt 6-8, 440A1
PFLP-Saiqa clashes; 25 casualties 6-9—6-12; 6-27—6-28, 510G1
PFLP cmdr slain 6-12, 510F1
US gets Leb plea on Israel shelling 6-16, 510C2
PLO asked to quit Israel border area 6-16, 510C2
Leb army rebuilding slowed 6-24, 510D3
US sen vs Carter peace plan 6-27, 496A1
Israel aid to Christns rptd 6-27, 510D2
Gunman hijacks UK plane 6-29, 535B2
US weighs funds for Leb force 6-30, 7-2, 510C3
Rival Christn groups clash 7-1, 510B2
Israel rptdly warns interventn 7-1, 7-2; Leb, US deny threat 7-2, 510E2
Christns seize, lose Yarin 7-2; fighting continues 7-4, 510G2
Syria paper scores enemies 7-4, 534F2
Israel mil plans chrgd 7-5, 510B3
Christian-PLO clashes 7-6, 7-7, 571A2
Palestinian rivals clash 7-14; Iraq vows rejectnst aid 7-16, 571D2
Truce pacts violated 7-21, 7-22, 571D1
New truce announced 7-25, 571A1
Truce violated 7-26—7-27, 589B1
Troops guard refugee camps, other truce pact details 7-30; Christn newspr scores pact 7-31, 588E3
Christn-Palestinian combat intensifies 8-4—8-24, 648A1
Christn cmdr chrgs Syrian pro-Palestinian moves 8-5, 648B1
Israel admits mil aid to Christians 8-8, 605A2
Palestinians chrg Israeli shelling, gunboat moves 8-10, 648C1
Moslem-Christn clash in Chuf area, 18 die 8-21—8-22; chrgs traded 8-21—8-23, 647B3
Syria troops move into Chuf area 8-22—8-23, 647E3
US admits Israel uses US arms, denies law breach 8-22, 648C1
Israel heavy mil role rptd 8-22, 648D1
Christn-Moslem peace com formed 8-23, 647A3
Beirut blast kills 3, Druse ldr slain 8-25, 647F3
Christns meet on Chuf unrest, chrg Palestinians arm 8-25, 647G3
PLO cncl warns Israel 8-26, 663B1
Assad chrgs Israel exploitatn 8-26, 663G1
Christns warn Palestinians re violence 8-27, 697A2
Israeli raids, shelling rptd 9-2, 9-5, 697D2
UN truce forces attacked 9-4, PLO escorts denied 9-11, 698A1
Israel warns Druse ldrs 9-9, 697G3
US seeks to end fighting 9-14—9-20, Israel restraint urged 9-19, 714A3
Israelis aid Christn drive vs Palestinians; Leb chrgs troop incursns, PLO sends reinforcemts 9-16—9-22, 714G1
Israeli towns shelled 9-21, 9-23—9-24, 9-26, 733F1
Egypt chrgs Israel 'naked aggression' 9-22, 714F1
Sarkis seeks to end fighting 9-22, 714C3
Khiam shelled 9-23—9-24, 733G1
US arranges truce, Israeli troops pull out 9-26, 733A1
PLO conditns troop exit from south 9-26, 733D1
Truce violated 10-5—10-14, 793E2, D3
PLO pullout rptd 10-8, Christns deny 10-10, 793C3

1980

Beirut bomb blast kills 8 2-23, 140E3
Syrian troops start Beirut pullout 3-7, 179D3
Christian militia-UNIFIL clash 4-7; 9 captured UNIFIL men freed 4-8, 260E1
Israelis cross border re kibbutz raid 4-9; reinforce, UNIFIL protest 4-10; map 260C1, A2
Haddad chrgs Irish UNIFIL pro-PLO bias 4-11; 284B1
UNIFIL-Christn clash, 2 die; UNIFIL base shelled 4-12; Waldheim rpts 4-16, 284D1
2 Christn civilns slain 4-12; Christns retaliate, kill 2 Irish UNIFIL soldiers 4-18; Irish bar exit 4-20, quit Christn enclave area 4-22, 302F2
Israelis pull out 4-13, 4-14, 283G3
Iraqi-backed PLO unit, Moslem Shiites clash 4-15—4-17, 300G1-B2
Moslem factns clash, death toll high 4-15—4-17, 300G1-B2; 5-28, 465G1
Christns oust 4 UNTSO soldiers from Heen 4-17, 302D3
Israelis raid PLO base 4-18, 302F2
UN Cncl scores Israel incursn; US, USSR, E Ger abstain 4-24, 302E3
Haddad injured by mine 4-29, blames UNIFIL 4-30, 363A1
UNIFIL asks Israel end Christn militia backing 5-2, 362D3
Israeli raids kill 4 PLO 5-8, 340F3-341A1
Christian factns clash, 12 die 5-12, 381A2
Israelis kill 11 in coast raids 5-15, 381G1
Christns kill 6 in Nabatiyeh 5-17, 381A2
Moslem factns clash 5-28, leftist militia raid mil convoy in south 6-3, 465G1
Israelis raid PLO base 6-4, block PLO coastal raid 6-16, 449E2
Phalangists defeat NLP 7-7—7-8; Christn militia merger rptd 7-9; Palestinians warned 7-10, 524D1-A2
D Chamoun quits as NLP cmdr 7-9, 524F1
Press head slain 7-23; gunmen clash at funeral, 14 die 7-26, 579F2
Baath ldr slain; Shiites, pro-Iraq group clash 7-28, 579A3
Israel raid kills 40 PLO, Hoss scores 8-19, 627D3
PLO orders full alert 8-19; Israel clashes 8-20—8-21, Syrian jet downed 8-24, 643E1
US amb condemns Israel raid, State Dept disavows 8-21, 644A1
US reassures on peace efforts 8-28, 643G3
Waldheim: Israel blocks UNIFIL role 9-12, 775A2
Israel raids PLO bases 9-17, 10-9, 10-16; US cautns, Begin discounts 10-17, 800F2-B3
Israel continues to hit PLO bases 10-17, 10-22, 11-7, 863E3
Phalangists drive rivals out of E Beirut 10-29; E, W Beirut violence continues 11-5, 11-10, 873D3
2 PLO infiltrators killed 11-13, 912E2
Israeli seaborne force hits PLO near Beirut 12-3, 912B2
Village raided, Israel denies role 12-18; Israelis raid PLO base, kill 10 PLO, 3 Syrians 12-19; Syrians shell 2 Christn sites in retaliatn 12-20, 977D2
Christn rivals clash; Syrians intervene, 5 slain 12-19; Syrians battle Phalangists 12-21—12-26, 977G1
S Leb protesters raid 2 UN offices in Beirut 12-23, 977B3
Israelis slay 5 PLO raiders 12-25, 977G2
UN head asked to end Syrian siege 12-26, 977C2
UNIFIL: Christns dynamite home 12-26, 977A3
Israeli jets raid PLO bases, down 3 Syrian MiGs; Syria claims 2 Israeli jets 12-31, 977A3

Sports

Moscow Olympic results 7-20—8-3, 588C3, 624C3

1976

UN Policy & Developments—*See also UN DEVELOPMENTS under MIDDLE EAST*
OKs Medit pollutn pact 2-16, 126C3

U.S. Relations—*See also 'Lebanon' under MIDDLE EAST—ARAB Policies*
Meloy confrmd amb 4-28, 412G1
US relief aid authorized 6-30, 532G3

LEBEDEVA, Natalia
Wins Olympic medal 7-29, 576A2
LEBER, George
Asks NATO oust Close 3-19, 297F2
Cites aid to Portugal 6-11, 449D2
Dismisses 2 gens 11-1, CDU scores 11-8, 930D3
Hospitalized 11-11, 930G3
LeBLANC, Norman
Indicted 1-14, 78B2
LeBLANC, Romeo
Canada Interim environmt min 7-12, 555E1
Sworn fisheries, environmt min 9-15, 692G1
Le BRETON, David F. B.
Anguilla self-govt in effect 2-10, 270B3
LECANUET, Jean
French justice, state min 1-12, 49D2
Army union probe documts bared 1-15, 119F3
New party pres 5-23, 418B1
Chirac scores coalitn foes 6-6, 418A1
Named planning min 8-27, 650D3, F3
LE Chung Hwan
Heads S Korea party 6-11, 440F2
LEDERER, Raymond F.
Elected 11-2, 821B3, 830D3
LEDERLE Laboratories—*See AMERICAN Cyanamid*
LEDERMAN, Leon
New atomic particle observed 2-8, 124B1
LEDESMA, Juan Eliseo
ERP seeks release 5-5, 399B1
LEDNEV, Pavel
Wins Olympic medal 7-22, 575B1
LEE, Blair
Greets Brown 4-28, 343A2
LEE, Rex D.
On fed handgun study 2-17, 170C2
LEE Bu Yong
Jailed 2-8, 122A1
LEE Chul Seung
Leads anti-Kim faction 5-25, 440A3
LEE Hae Dong, Rev.
Sentence suspended 12-29, 1013G2
LEEK, Eric C.
Wins NJ lottery 1-27, 160G2

1977

Premr ties troop deploymt to Israel combat halt 10-12, 793A3
US: pressing peace 10-12, 793A3
Israel bars Leb army truce talks 10-13, US intervenes 10-14, 793E2
Leb army cmdr takes Saida post 10-13, 793B3
PLO chrgs Israel, Christns break truce 10-14, 793B3
Israel renews truce talks 10-25, 850D1
Sarkis meets Assad on peace moves 11-5, 850C1
PLO shells Israel town, 3 die 11-6, 11-8; Israelis retaliate 11-6—11-8; **1st Israel air bombings in 2 yrs 11-9**, Leb, Israel statemts 11-9, 11-10, 849A1; Israel explains to UN 11-11, 874B3
Map of north Israel, south Leb battle zone 849D1
PLO vs pullout from south 11-6, 849D2
Israel sets new peace terms 850B1
Syria asks PLO pullback 11-10, PLO admits 11-11; bars exit 11-12, 874E2
Israel bombs Lebanon again, claims Israel town shelled 11-11, 874D2
Natl Movemt chrgs Israel truce breach 11-12, 874A3
Arab League scores Israel raids, asks PLO exit 11-14, 874G1
Christns stage gen strike 12-12, 954G1
UN Policy & Developments
Assemb member 4C1
Waldheim visits 2-6—2-7, 86F2
UN troop use weighed 2-27, 143C2
Truce forces attacked 9-4, PLO escorts denied 9-11, 698A1
Pollutn conf ends, Medit pact reached 10-21, 876B2
Israel explains Nov 9 raid 11-11, 874C3
Chile rights abuse res opposed 12-16, 983F1
U.S. Relations—*See also 'Civil Strife' above*
Parker confirmed US amb 2-10, 148F3
Vance visits, Leb seeks Geneva conf role 2-18, 121F2
Vance visits 8-3, 588D3
US security aid OKd 8-4, 668D1
Israel OKs Geneva working paper 10-11, 769C1
Vance visits, seeks Sadat peace backing 12-13, 954F1
LeBARON, Ervil M.
Charged with Allred murder 9-27, 848A1
LEBER, George
Suspends Laabs 12-13, Kohl calls for resignatn 12-15, 968G1
LeBLANC, Romeo
Retains fisheries post 9-16, 725B3
LEBON (race horse)
Vet indicted in horse-switch scandal 12-2, 971B1
Le BRETON, David
Names Gumbs chief min 2-2, 190D2
LECANUET, Jean
Ousted from Cabinet 3-30, 239D1
Le CARRE, John
Schoolboy on best-seller list 11-6, 872C3; 12-4, 1021G2
LECHIN Oquendo, Juan
Bolivia amnesty excludes 12-21, 1009G3
LECLERC & Co. (Geneva, Switzerland)
Ordered closed 5-9, 489B3
LEDERER, Jiri
Rptd arrested 1-17; Austria offers asylum 1-25, 82B3, E3
Czech ct sentences 10-18, 812C1
LEDESMA, Genaro
Kidnaped 2-10, 241G2
LeDOUX, Scott
Chrgs tourn irregularity 2-13, 828D1
LEE, Andrew Daulton
Arrested 1-6, arraignmt rptd 1-18, 41E2-A3
Trial opens, Boyce convicted 4-28, 344C2
Convicted 5-15, 409B3
Gets life sentence 7-18, 576E3
Cited re Australia-US talks 8-4, 633A1
Boyce sentenced 9-12, 732G3
LEE, Bernard
King suit dismissed 1-31, 77D2
LEE, Lt. Gov. Blair (D, Md.)
Mandel transfers powers 6-4, to stay actg gov 8-25, 625D1 ★
LEE, Bob
Raiders win Super Bowl 1-9, 24G3
Vikings win in playoffs 12-26, 1020A1
LEE, Butch
Marquette wins NCAA title, named MVP 3-28, 262A2, C2
LEE, H. Rex
Amer Samoa elects gov 11-22, 943G3
LEE, Myrra Leonore
Teacher of the year 3-22, 354A2
LEE, Rex E.
Replaced as asst atty gen 3-4, 211D1
LEE, Ron
Named to NBA all-rookie team 5-16, 584F3
LEE, Stan
2d in New Orleans Open 4-24, 676B1
LEE Chul Seung
Asks end to curbs 1-26, 116G3 ★
Vs US troop exit 3-7, 203A1
LEE Hu Rak
Named Park co-conspirator 9-6, 687F2
Hanna indictmt names 10-14, 816C1

1978

UN Policy & Developments—*See also MIDDLE EAST, subheads LEBANON and UN—UNIFIL*
Assemb member 713G3

U.S. Relations—*For Arab-Israeli conflict, see MIDDLE EAST—LEBANON*
US cuts emb staff 7-27, 581C2
Boeing chrgd re payoffs 7-28, 642G3

LEBANON, United Nations Interim Force in (UNIFIL)—*See MIDDLE EAST, subheads LEBANON and UN—UNIFIL*
LEBER, George
Linked to new tap scandal 1-24, offers resignatn 2-1, 74F2-C3
Hails US tank gun choice 1-31, 82B1
Resigns 2-3, 93B2
Austria protests W Ger secret svc surveillnc 2-14, 110B3
Schmidt testifies at spy probe 2-24, 210G3
Maihofer resigns 6-6, 456E3
LeBLANC, Romeo
Bars Canada ban on US sport fishing 6-5, 435G1
LEBON (race horse)
Vet sentncd in '77 horse switch 11-3, 1028A2
LEBRECHT, Hans
Cleared of PLO link 7-7, 547A2
LECAL, Jean-Phillipe
Named French culture, communicatns min 4-5, 245G2
Le CARRE, John
Honourable Schoolboy on best-seller list 1-8, 24D3; 2-5, 116B3; 3-5, 195D3
LECHIN Oquendo, Juan
Receives amnesty 1-18; labor unions regain rights 1-25, 411B3
Rejcts pres bid, seeks labor reorganizatn 5-5, 411B3
Chrgs govt harassmt 5-5, 411F3
LeCLERC, Robert
Arrested in Switzerland 1-19, 95A2
LeCOMPTE, Elizabeth
Nayatt School opens 5-12, 887B2
LEDERBERG, Joshua
Named Rockefeller U pres 1-18, 172A2
LEDERER, Rep. Raymond F. (D, Pa.)
Reelected 11-7, 852C1
LEDESMA, Gerardo
Rpts death threats 9-3, gang assault 9-15, 776A1
LEE 3rd, Acting Gov. Blair (D, Md.)
Signs death penalty bill 3-10, 388F3
Loses primary for Md gov 9-12, 716E1
LEE, Butch
Named coll basketball player of yr 3-13, 272D2
In NBA draft 6-9, 457F2
LEE, Christopher
Return From Witch Mt released 7-14, 970G2
LEE, Gary A.
Wins US House seat 11-7, 849B2, 851G3
LEE, Irving Allen
Broadway Musical opens 12-21, 1031B1
LEE, James E.
On '77 top-paid execs list 5-15, 364F3
LEE, John
Condemns Saudi whippings 6-15, 516B1
LEE, Kalulani
Safe House opens 4-13, 760C3
LEE, Robert E.
1st Monday in Oct opens 10-3, 1031F1
LEE, Ron
NBA stealing ldr 4-9, 271G1
LEE IV, W. Spencer
Vesco dealings rptd 9-1, 9-14, 9-15, 720B1
LEE Chul Seung
Bars NDP natl conv 4-17, 377G3
LEEDS & Northrup Co.
Gen Signal buys Cutler holdings 6-22; merger planned, Tyco loses takeover bid 7-7, 553D1

1979

UN Policy & Developments
Membership listed 695F2

U.S. Relations
CIA alleged agent named 1-4, 17C3
SCLC ldrs visit, see Sarkis 9-18–9-20, 694F1
SCLC ends visit 9-21, 763C2
Jesse Jackson visits, sees Hoss 9-28–9-30, 10-3–10-5, 763C1, E1
Iranians seize US Emb 11-11, 862A3
US sets evacuations, travel curbs 11-26, 894A2

LEBANON, United Nations Interim Force in (UNIFIL)—*See MIDDLE EAST, subheads LEBANON and U.N.–UNIFIL*
LeBARON, Ervil Morel
Sought in Allred murder 3-20, 240C2
LEBOWSKY, Stanley
1940's Radio Hour opens 10-7, 956E3
LEBRON, Lolita
Sentence commuted 9-6, 666E1
Freed 9-10; returns to PR, affirms commitmt 9-12, 682G3
LECANUET, Jean
Attacks Gaullists 2-17–2-18, 135F1
LECHIN Oquendo, Juan
Rejcts pres bid; asks police, mil cuts 3-12, 233G2
Gueiler replaces Natusch 11-16, 888F2
LECKETT, Henry
Gets fetal liver transplant 8-20, 736B3
LED Zeppelin (singing group)
In Through the Out Door on best-seller list 9-5, 672F3; 10-3, 800F3; 11-7, 892F3
LEE, Alan
Faeries on best-seller list 1-7, 80C3
LEE, Andrew Daulton
US spy satellite data rptd compromised 4-28, 318G2
LEE 3rd, Acting Gov. Blair (D, Md.)
Mandel reclaims office 1-15, 56D1
LEE, Butch
Traded to Cavaliers 1-30, 526E2
LEE, Kyung Soo
Ousted as bank pres 287C2
LEE, Ron
Traded to Jazz 1-12, 526C2
LEE, William S.
On Oconee A-plant closings 4-27, 322D1
LEE 4th, W. Spencer
Harden '77 mtg rptd 8-30, 725A3
Carter to videotape Vesco testimony 12-5, 943E2
LEE Chul Seung
Kim says govt favors 5-27, loses NDP post 5-30, 469F3, 470A1
Kim ousted as NDP ldr 9-8, 710A3
LEE Hi Song, Gen.
Named martial law head 12-13, 959D3
LEE Hu Rak
Joins S Korea governing party 6-7, 470C1

1980

UN Policy & Developments—*See 'Military' above*

U.S. Relations
US issues rights rpt 2-5, 87E2
Iranians demonstrate at US Emb 8-8, 635A2
Dean sees Butros, escapes death try 8-28, 643F3
Carter quotes Reagan '76 troop proposal 9-23, 722D3

LEBANON, UN Interim Force in—*See UNITED Nations--UNIFIL*
LEBANOV, Ivan
Wins Olympic medal 2-14, 155A3
LEBARON, Ervil Morel
Convicted of murder 5-28, sentenced 6-2, 502A3
LEBARON, Verlan
Brother convicted of murder 5-28, sentenced 6-2, 502A3
LEBAS, Alain
Wins Olympic medal 8-2, 622C2
LEBLANC, Romeo
Canada fisheries min 3-3, 171B2
Ups Atlantic fish quota 6-12, 461A2
LEBOUTILLIER, John
Elected to US House 11-4, 843D3
LE CARRE, John
Smiley's People on best-seller list 1-13, 40A3; 2-10, 120B3; 3-9, 200B3; 4-6, 280B3
LECHIN Oquendo, Juan
Arrested 7-17, feared dead 8-1, 602C3
LEDBETTER, Stewart
Wins Sen primary 9-9, 700B3
Loses US Sen electn 11-4, 849B1
LEDERER, Jiri
Prison release rptd 1-13, 40B1
Expelled by Czechs, arrives W Ger 9-2, 680F1
LEDERER, Rep. Raymond F. (D, Pa.)
Linked to bribery in Abscam probe 2-2, 2-3, 81A2, 82F1
Facts on 81E2
Indicted in Abscam probe 5-28, 402E2
Abscam judge quits case 8-7, 599E3
Votes vs Myers House expulsn 10-2, 740A2
Reelected 11-4, 844B1, 846A2, 848F3
LEDNEV, Pavel
Wins Olympic medal 7-24, 623E1
LEDOUX, Scott
Holmes TKOs 7-7, 1000D3
LED Zeppelin (singing group)
John Bonham dies 9-25, 755C2
LEE, Andrew Daulton
Boyce prison escape rptd 1-22, 55A2
LEE, Christopher
Wicker Man released 3-26, 416G3
LEE, Lt. Col. David
Memphis area illness probed 4-2, 331A3, B3
LEE, Rep. Gary A. (R, N.Y.)
Reelected 11-4, 843G3
LEE, Jack
Nazi draws NC GOP vote 5-6, 405A2
LEE, Johnny
Lookin' for Love on best-seller list 10-8, 796B3
LEE, Robert
Arrested in Afghan 2-22, 138E2
Afghans call spy 3-19; on TV, scores CIA 3-26; accuses West, China 4-3, 271F2
Release rptd 5-16, 443D1
LEE, Robert E.
Incomparable Max opens 6-15, 756D3
LEE 4th, W. Spencer
Vesco grand jury ends 4-1, 251C3
LEE Chul Seung
Pol activities curbed 11-12, 874B3
LEEFLANG, Franklin
Gets Surinam civiln post 2-28, 174F3
LEE Hi Song, Gen.
Martial law powers widened 5-18, 380E2
Eases party ban 11-21, 903G1
LEE Hu Rak
Chrgd with corruptn, to quit politics 6-18, 499A3

1976

LEE Kuan Yew
In ASEAN-Australia talks 1-17—1-18, 46D1
Signs ASEAN pact 2-24, 148D2
Sees Mao in China 5-12, 439D2
Party wins electns 12-23, 1013D2
LEE Pu Yong
Sentenced 5-3, 334D2
LEE Sun Jung, Gen.
S Korea justice min 12-4, 928A3
LEE Yong Hee
S Korea unificatn min 12-4, 928A3
LeFANTE, Joseph A.
Elected 11-2, 821C2, 830E1
LEFEBVRE, Antonio
Arrested 3-22, indictmt rptd 3-27, 298D1 ★
LEFEBVRE, Most Rev. Marcel
Pope scores 5-24, 424B1
Ordains priests in Switz 6-29, suspended 7-24, defies papal ban 8-29, 655D3
Australia priests hold banned Masses 8-31, 691F3
Continues to defy papal ban 9-5—11-14; sees Pope 9-11, Vatican issues plea 11-30, 932F2
LEFEBVRE, Ovidio
Sought in Lockheed probe 2-17, 132C2
Indictmt rptd 3-24, 298D1
LEFFERDINK, Allen J.
Sentenced 4-26, 384G2
LEFKOWITZ, Louis J.
Dismisses Nadjari 6-25, 1016D1
Holds gene research hearing 10-21, 860E3
LeFLORE, Ron
AL batting ldr 10-4, 796B1-D1
LEGAL Aid—*See LAW & Lawyers*
LEGAL Services Corp.
'77 funds signed 7-14, 534D2
Carter disavows Cook dumping memo 8-13, 616F3
LEGARETA, Agustin
In US talks 1-26, 75F1
LEGER, Jules
Reads govt policy speech 10-12, 771E2
LEGER, Marcel
Named environmt min 11-26, 903A3
LEGGETT, Rep. Robert L. (D, Calif.)
S Korea payoffs probed 2-19, 171D1
S Korea probe rptd 10-30, 11-13, 900G1
Reelected 11-2, 820B2, 829A1
LEGRAND, Michel
Wins Grammy 2-28, 460B3
LEHIGH & Hudson River Railway Co.
Conrail begins operation 4-1, 235E1
LEHIGH Navigation-Dodson Co.
Indicted 11-19, 989E2
LEHIGH Valley Coal Sales Co. Inc.
Indicted 11-19, 989E2
LEHIGH Valley Railroad Co.
Conrail begins operation 4-1, 235E1
LEHMAN, August McCormick
Chrgs Pl torture 6-26, 500E1
LEHMAN, Rep. William (D, Fla.)
Reelected 11-2, 829C2
LEHMANN, Lotte
Dies 8-26, 892B3
LEIGH Guzman, Gen. Gustavo
Denies rpts of discontent 1-7, 47D1
Backs Pinochet 1-28, 99F3
LEIGHTON, Margaret
Dies 1-13, 56E3
LEILA, Abou
Rpts PLA in Leb 1-21, 34C2
LEKAI, Laszlo Cardinal
Named archbp of Esztergom 2-12, cardinal 4-27, 336C2, D2
Lauds state ties 9-18, 947B1
LEMON, Bob
Named to Hall of Fame 8-9, 816B1
Le MONDE (French newspaper)
Launches Portugal edition 2-8, 143E2
LENART, Jozef
On Czech Presidium; Secretariat drops 4-16, 289B2
LENNON, John
Gets US residency 7-27, 640F3
LENT, Rep. Norman F. (R, N.Y.)
Reelected 11-2, 830G1
LENTZ, Roger Lyle
Killed in Denver 4-19, 383E3
LENZLINGER, Hans
E Ger operatns detailed 1-26, 85G1
LEO, Joseph
Cuba exile link chrgd 10-17, confirmd 10-25, 844A2
LEON, Eduardo A.
On Philip Morris DR paymts 12-28, 1001C2
LEON, Imeldo Barreto
Rescued 1-18, 79E3
LEON, Luis
Asks Peron quit 2-10, 154E2

1977

LEE Kuan Yew (Singapore prime minister)
Teng sentenced 1-8, 223F3
Sees W Ger min on rights 4-28, 394F3
At Commonwealth conf 6-8—6-15, 487D1
At ASEAN summit 8-4—8-5, 607A2
LEE Way Motor Freight, Inc.—*See under PEPSICO*
LEFEBVRE, Archbishop Marcel
Preaches vs modernism 5-22—6-6, 470D3
Ordains traditionalist priests 6-26, 6-29, 620C2
Consecrates Tex church 7-10, 620F2
In Latin Amer 7-12—7-26, 620F1
LEFKOWITZ v. CDR Enterprises Ltd.
NYS pub work job ruling affirmed 1-10, 57E1
LEFKOWITZ v. Cunningham
Forced immunity waiver ruled illegal 6-13, 57B2
LeFLORE, Ron
AL batting ldr 10-2, 926F3-927A1
LEFTIS, Neptolemos
Sentenced for '74 riot role 6-21, 764E2
LEGAL Services Corporation (LSC)—*See under U.S. GOVERNMENT*
LEGESSE, Solomon
Killed 11-13, 998F2
LEGION Fever—*See MEDICINE—Diseases*
LEGISLATION, U.S.—*See under U.S. GOVERNMENT—CONGRESS*
LEGROS, Hubert
Rptd held in Haiti 9-30, 805E3
LEHIGH Navigation-Dodson Co.
Fined 3-21, 520B3
LEHIGH Valley Coal Sales Co. Inc.
Fined 3-21, exec indicted 6-2, 520A3
LEHMAN, August McCormick
Sentenced 2-10, 100B1
LEHMAN Brothers Inc.
Kuhn Loeb merger planned 11-28, 1004F2-A3
LEIDESDORF, S. D.
SEC accuses 2-16, 156C2
LEIGHTON, Judge George N.
Appraisers OK anti-bias rule 11-11, 898B3
LEIJON, Anne-Greta
Target of terrorist plot 4-1, 428G3
12 plotters indicted 7-25, 709G1
LEIS Jr., Simon L.
Hustler publisher sentncd 2-8, 118F2
LEISURE (film)
Wins Oscar 3-28, 264D1
LEIZAOLA, Jesus Maria de
Cortes Basques recognize 6-19, 507D1
LEKAI, Laszlo Cardinal
Pope Paul audience rptd 5-2, 492B2
LeMAIRE, Jacques
Montreal wins Stanley Cup 5-14, 429F3
LeMAISTRE, George
Testifies on Lance banking abilities; backs stiffer loan, overdraft policies 9-26, 761A2
LEMBO, Claudio
Scores Geisel pol reforms 4-29, 523B3
LeMELLE, Wilbert John
Named amb to Kenya, Seychelles 4-7; confrmd 5-9, 418F1
LEMON, Chet
AL batting ldr 10-2, 926G3
LEMON, Denis
Fined for blasphemy 7-12, 617E3
Le MONDE (newspaper)
Carter summit diplomacy hailed 5-11, 359F1
Scores W Ger re terrorism 10-19, 790G1
LENIN, Vladimir Ilyich Ulyanov (1870-1924)
USSR issues draft const 6-4, 433G2, 434C2
USSR scores Eurocommunism 6-23, 507B2
USSR natl anthem revised 9-1, 766D2
LENOX Hill Hospital (New York City)
USTA rejcts Richards sex test 4-12, 354E1
LENZER, Terry F.
Alaska pipe waste chrgd 8-7, 627A3
LEONARD, Dennis
AL pitching ldr 10-2, 927A1

1978

LEE Kuan Yew (Singapore prime minister)
Commonwealth conf meets 2-13—2-16; scores Australia trade barriers 2-15, urges Indochina refugee aid 2-17, 121F2, G2
LEE Kun Shik
USSR frees 4-29, 318D1
LEEMANS, Alphonse (Tuffy)
Enters Pro Football HOF 7-29, 1025D1
LEE Mun Yong
Arrested 2-17, 2-21, 135E2
LeFANTE, Rep. Joseph A. (D, N.J.)
Guarini wins seat 11-7, 849C1
LEFEBRE, Antonio
Leone resigns over Lockheed chrgs 6-15, 516F2
LEFEBRE, Ovidio
Leone resigns over Lockheed chrgs 6-15, 516F2
LeFLORE, Ron
AL batting, stolen base ldr 10-2, 928E3-F3
LE Freak (recording)
On best-seller list 12-6, 971D1
LEGAL Aid—*See COURTS & Legal Profession*
LEGAL Services of Nashville and Middle Tennessee Inc.
Tenn prison bldg ordrd closed 1-30, 440F1
LEGGETT, Rep. Robert L. (D, Calif.)
Aquaculture bill vetoed 10-19, 807F3
Fazio wins seat 11-7, 856D3
LEGIONELLA Pneumophila (Legionnaires' Disease)—*See MEDICINE—Diseases*
LEGIONNAIRES' Disease (Legionella Pneumophila)—*See MEDICINE—Diseases*
LEGISLATION, U.S.—*See under U.S. GOVERNMENT—CONGRESS*
LEHMAN, Robert
Crane's Way opens 7-12, 760G1
LEHMAN, Susan
Price of Genius opens 6-26, 887F2
LEHMAN, Rep. William (D, Fla.)
Reelected 11-7, 850G2
LEHMAN Brothers, Kuhn, Loeb Inc.
Clay dies 4-16, 356D2
LEIGH, Richard
Song wins Grammy 2-24, 316A1
LEIGH Guzman, Gen. Gustavo
Oppositn to plebiscite rptd 1-5, 16C3, D3 ★
Scores Pinochet, asks civiln rule 3-26; Pinochet plays down rift 3-29, 267A2
On Pinochet Cabt shuffle, denies rift 4-14; Pinochet agrees 4-21, 351B1
Offers civiln rule plan 7-18, Pinochet backers score 7-20, 7-21; junta fires 7-24, 572D2
AF gens replaced 7-25; drops appeal 7-26, 591F1-C2
Dismissal opposed 8-24, 796D1
LEIGHTON, Bernardo
Chile OKs return 5-13, 452B3
LEIGHTON, Richard
Modigliani opens 5-17, 760E2
LEIJON, Anne-Greta
5 jailed in '77 kidnap plot 1-31, 93A1
Kidnap plotters jail terms extended 6-29, 691E1
LEK Neaomali
Named Thai interior min 8-13, 691C2
LELAND, Mickey
Wins Tex US House Primary runoff 6-3, 426G2
Elected 11-7, 852B3, 855D3
LELOUCH, Claude
Cat & Mouse released 5-6, 618F3
Le MESURIER, John
Arrested in murder plot 8-4, 614C2
Newton testifies 11-27, 945E2
Murder-conspiracy trial ordrd 12-13, 987E3
LEMMON, Jack
Tribute opens 6-1, 887D3
LEMON, Bob
Resigns as White Sox mgr 6-30, 560E1
Named Yankee mgr 7-24, '80 gen mgr 7-29, 618C2
Yankees win AL East playoff 10-2, 778D2
Yankees win World Series 10-17, 799G3
Named AL top mgr 10-24, 928B2
LEMON, Chet
NL wins All-Star Game 7-11, 559E3
AL batting ldr 10-2, 928D3
LENARDUZZI, Bob
Named top NASL N Amer player 8-25, 707A3
LENIN, Vladimir Ilyich Ulyanov (1870-1924)
Spain CP drops 'Leninist' label 4-19—4-23, PSOE drops 'Marxist' 5-22, 821D3
Mikoyan dies 10-22, 888D3
LENNON, John
Sgt Pepper's released 7-21, 970B3
LENNOX (Chilean island)—*See BEAGLE Channel*
LENT, Rep. Norman F. (R, N.Y.)
Reelected 11-7, 851C3
LEO XI, Pope (d. 1605)
Pope John Paul I dies 9-28, 747D1
LEO Burnett Co., Inc.
Black, white female consumers compared 4-12, 811G3-812D1
LEON, Arturo
Arguello decisns 11-10, 969D1
LEON, Sonny
At nonwhite united front mtg 1-11, 20C3
LEONARD, Dennis
AL pitching ldr 10-2, 928G3
Royals lose AL pennant 10-7, 778G3
779C1

1979

LEE Kuan Yew (Singapore prime minister)
Meets Waldheim on refugees 5-11—5-12, 379D2
LEEMANS, Alphonse (Tuffy)
Dies 1-19, 104C3
LEESE, Paul
On 3 Mile I A-accident evacuatn 4-1, 245A1
LEE Sun Ku
Ouster demanded 8-28, 653G3
LeFLORE, Ron
AL stolen base ldr 9-30, 955F3
Traded to Expos 12-7, 1002F2
LE Freak (recording)
On best-seller list 1-10, 80E3; 2-14, 120E3; 3-7, 174D1
LEGACY, The (film)
Released 9-28, 820E1
LEGISLATION, U.S.—*See under U.S. GOVERNMENT—CONGRESS; also CARTER—LEGISLATION*
LEGRAND, Michel
Umbrellas Of Cherbourg opens 2-1, 292E3
Le GRANGE, Louis
Named S Africa police min 6-14, 469A3
LEHAR, Franz (1870-1948)
Merry Widow wins Grammy 2-16, 336G3
LEHIGH University (Bethlehem, Pa.)
3d in NCAA wrestling 3-10, 507F3
Loses NCAA Div 1-AA football title game 12-15, 1001F2
LEHMAN, John F.
Scores Carter defns policy 3-1, 165B3
LEIB, Hans Joachim
Slain in Iran 10-14, 814C3
LEIGH, Carolyn
Peter Pan opens 9-6, 956F3
LEIGH, Janet
Boardwalk released 11-14, 1007A3
LEIGH, Mitch
Sarava opens 2-11, 292F2
LEIGHTON, Bernardo
Townley testimony on murder plot curbed 1-23, 75C1
LEIS v. Flynt
Lawyers' interstate rights limited by Sup Ct 1-15, 31B3
Le JEUNE Marin (The Young Sailor) (painting)
Sold for record sum 7-3, 672A1
LEKACHMAN, Robert
On '80s econ forecast 11-1, 827E1
LELAND, Rep. Mickey (D, Tex.)
Sees Castro 10-13, 779E1
LEMAIRE, Jacques
Montreal wins Stanley Cup 5-21, 447E3
Le MARMOT (race horse)
3d in Arc de Triomphe 10-7, 876C3
LeMAT, Paul
More Amer Graffiti released 8-17, 820B2
LEMBO, Claudio
Scores Brazil pol party reform 11-9, 926C3
Le MESURIER, John
Acquitted 6-22, 485E3
LEMMON, Jack
China Syndrome released 3-16, A-accident impact rptd 3-29, 4-1, 246D3, G3, 528G1*
LEMON, Bob
Fired as Yankees mgr 6-18, 619G1
NL wins All-Star Game 7-17, 569A2
LEMON, Chet
NL wins All-Star Game 7-17, 569A1, B1
AL batting ldr 9-30, 955E3, F3
Le MONDE (Paris newspaper)
Offices bombed 4-29, 330E2
LENGANE, Jefferson
Sentenced 5-11, 373F1
LENIHAN, Brian
Vs EC Parlt budget veto 12-13, 960A3
LENIN, Vladimir Ilyich Ulyanov (1870-1924)
Kapler death rptd 9-15, 756F2
LENNON, Peter
Good Lads opens 3-27, 711E3
LENTERIC, Bernard
Last Romantic Lover released 10-5, 1007G3

1980

LEE Kwang Pyo
Chrgs North mil moves 6-30, 525B2
LEE Se Hon
Chrgd with corruptn, to quit politics 6-18, 499A3
LEE Way Motor Freight Inc.—*See under PEPSICO Inc.*
LEFEBVRE, Archbishop Marcel
Holds outlawed mass 4-7, oppositn rptd 4-26, 364A1
LEFLORE, Ron
NL batting, stolen base ldr 10-6, 926E2, F2
LEFT-Handed Woman, The (film)
Released 4-2, 416B3
LEFTWICH, James T.
Dies 7-6, 608C2
LEGATOR, Marvin
On office machine cancer risks 4-11, 357B2
LEGER, Jules
Dies 11-22, 928F2
LEGIONNAIRES Disease—*See MEDICINE—Diseases*
LEGISLATION, U.S.—*See under U.S. GOVERNMENT, CARTER*
LE GRANGE, Louis
Warns vs more terrorism 1-25, 100F3
On '79 hangings 2-7, 134C3
LEHMAN, John F.
At GOP platform hearings, seeks defense spending hike 1-15, 32B2
LEHMAN, Rep. William (D, Fla.)
Reelected 11-4, 842G2
LEHMANN, Karl-Heinz
Wins Olympic medal 7-25, 623C1
LEHR, Lewis W.
Named 3M chrmn 5-13, 456E2
LEIBMAN, Ron
I Ought to be in Pictures opens 4-3, 392D3
Up the Academy released 6-6, 675F3
LEIDER, Jerry
Jazz Singer released 12-19, 1003B2
LEIGH, Janet
Fog released 2-29, 216E2
LEIGH Guzman, Gen. Gustavo
Scores Pinochet rule, plebiscite vote 9-2, 669E2
LEIGHTON, Ted
Hunter released 8-1, 675A3
LEINSTER, Colin
Outsider released 6-3, 675C3
LEISER, Ernest
On CBS electn projectns lag 11-5, 866B1
LEITCH, Mervin
Seeks oil price hike 5-6, 428G3
Oil price talks with Lalonde fail 6-18—6-19, deadline extended 6-19, 486C1
Ottawa oil talks fail again 10-2, 787E3
LELAND, Rep. Mickey (D, Tex.)
Reelected 11-4, 844B3
LEMMON, Jack
Tribute released 12-13, 1003F2
LE MOIGNAN, Michel
Named Canada UN party ldr 3-3, 230E1
LE MONDE (Paris newspaper)
Bani-Sadr interviewed 2-11, 105E1; 3-11, 177E1
Editors chrgd re ct system articles 11-7, 872C1
Diamond affair figure released 11-29, 921G2
LEMOUNIER, Jean-Francois
Iraq expels 10-2, 775A1
LENDL, Ivan
Loses Austrian Grand Prix 7-27, US Open quarterfinals 9-4; wins Canadian Open 8-17, 691A2, A3, B3
Wins Spanish Grand Prix 10-12, Swiss Indoor 10-19, Taipei Grand Prix 11-16, 947A2, B2, E2
Czechs win Davis Cup 12-7, 946E3
LENG, Gen. Peter
Praises US mil exercise performance 10-11, 777F1
L'ENGLE, Madeline
Swiftly Tilting Planet wins Amer Book Award 5-1, 692D2
LENIHAN, Brian
Backs Palestinian rights 2-10, 284C1
LENIN, Vladimir Ilyich Ulyanov (1870-1924)
China orders portraits removed 8-16, 651F2
Free trade union oppositn cited 9-25, 753A1
LENNON, John
Slain in NYC, ex-mental patient chrgd 12-8; reactn 12-9; background, photos 933D2-934F3
LENT, Rep. Norman F. (R, N.Y.)
Reelected 11-4, 843D3
LEO, Sue
US wins Federatn Cup 5-25, 607C1
LEONARD, Bob
Fired as Pacers coach, gen mgr 6-2, 656F3
LEONARD, Dennis
AL pitching ldr 10-6, 926G3
Royals win AL pennant 10-10, 795G3
In World Series 10-14—10-21, 811F2, 812A2

1976

LEONARD, Jacques
Named planning min 11-26, 903A3
LEONARD, Maj. James E.
Angola mercenary role denied 2-2, 82E1
LEONARD, Ray
Wins Olympic medal 7-31, 574C1
LEONARD Jr., Will E.
Asks shoe tariff hike 2-21, 213E2
LEONARDOS, George
On Panagoulis death 7-9, 538C1
Accepts Moro resignatn 7-9, names Andreotti premr 7-13, 539A1
US, W Eur loan ban rptd 7-16, 531C1
LEONE, Giovanni
Moro resigns 1-7, 10G1
Soclsts ask Parlt dissolutn 4-15, 296D3
Sets abortn referendum 4-16, 333B3
Denies link to Lockheed 4-22, 298A1
Moro resigns 4-30, 296G2
Dissolves Parlt 5-1, 333G2
Cleared in Lockheed probe 6-15, 445D2
Swears in new gov 7-30, 573B1
Sees Venez pres 11-17, 929C3
LEONIDAS, Col. Armando
El Salvador mil chief 5-22, 401F1
LEONTIEF, Wassily
World econ rpt issued 10-13, 760E1
LEOPARD (German tank)—*See 'Tanks' under ARMAMENTS*
LEOPIZZI, Judge Bruno L.
Carter, Artis retrial opens 10-19, 860D1
Carter, Artis convicted 12-21; sets sentencing 12-23, 1015D3, G3
LEORO Franco, Gen. Luis
On mil junta 1-11, 28E1
LEPAGE, Octavio
Scores student deaths 2-16, vows riot curbs 2-27, 208D1, A2
On US exec kidnap arrests 7-27, 592C3
Le PEN, Jean-Marie
Object of bomb attack 11-2, 1002E2
LEPTOPHOS—*See PESTICIDES & Herbicides*
Le QUESNE, Sir Martin
Implicated in Nigeria coup 2-17, 2-18, recalled 3-4, 191D3
LERCARO, Giacomo Cardinal
Dies 10-18, 970B2
LEROY, Mervyn
Wins Oscar 3-29, 240B3
LESLIE, Edgar
Dies 1-22, 80E3
LESOTHO—*See also AFRICAN Development Bank, COMMONWEALTH of Nations, NONALIGNED Nations Movement, OAU*
Listed as 'partly free' 1-19, 20D3
Angola MPLA recognized 2-17, 163E2
Transkei border closing rptd 11-13, 927E3
UN chrgs S Africa pressure re Transkei recognitn 12-22, 954B3
LESSARD, Lucien
Named transpt, pub works min 11-26, 903A3
LESSARD, Marc
Stays regional econ expansn min 9-14, 692C2
LESTER, Larry
Mormon ordinatn voided 4-3, 951C2
LESURE, Annie
Dropped from French govt 1-12, 49E2
LETELIER, Isabel
Chile rights com rally 9-10, 710G3
LETELIER, Orlando
Loses Chile citizenship 9-10, 710C3, G3
Killed in US 9-21; DINA accused 9-21—9-23, 710C2
US mass held 9-26, buried in Venez 9-29, 780F3
US widens murder probe 10-9; Cuban exiles linked 10-12, 10-19, 779B3, 780F2
FBI Venez probe rptd; exile-DINA link chrgd 10-18; exile murder role denied 10-20—10-21, 844E2
LET My People Come (play)
Opens 8-11, 1014D3
LETTER Bombs—*See 'Bombings' under CRIME*
LETTIRE, Robert
Adamson chrgd in Bolles murder 6-21, 483A3, D3
LETTUCE—*See FRUITS & Vegetables*
LEUPIN, Eric
Rpt Colombia blocks ransom 6-17, 731B2
LEVEILLE, Remillot
Haiti agri min 4-1, 267E2
LEVENSON, Harold G.
Carter, Artis convicted 12-21, 1015E3
LEVENTHAL, Albert Rice
Dies 1-6, 56E3
LEVER, Harold
Retains Cabt post 9-10, 694A1
In US sterling balance talks 11-16—11-17, 880D3
LEVESQUE, Rene
Facts on 870F2
Elected 11-15; on econ dvpt, separation 11-16, 870G1
Sworn 11-25, names Cabt 11-26, 903E2
Scores fed-prov tax plan 12-14, 962D2, F2
On Olympic debt, scores govt 12-22, 998F3

1977

LEONARD Jr., Will E.
For shoe-import tariff hike 1-6, 248B3
LEONE, Giovanni (Italian president)
2 ex-mins face Lockheed trial 3-10, 284D1
LEOPARD (German tank)—*See ARMAMENTS—Tanks*
LEOPIZZI, Judge Bruno L.
Sentences Carter, Artis 2-9, 140D1
LEPAGE, Octavio
Venez interior min 1-7, 23E2
Minimizes guerrilla threat 9-27, 867D3
LERNER, Louis A.
Named amb to Norway 7-1, confrmd 7-13, 626A3
LERNER Newspapers
Lerner confrmd amb to Norway 7-13, 626A3
LeROUX, Edward (Buddy)
Ct OKs Red Sox sale 12-6, AL owners veto 12-8, 989F2
LERUDE, Warren L.
Wins Pulitzer Prize 4-18, 355F2
LESBIANS—*See HOMOSEXUALITY*
LESHER, Richard L.
Scores energy tax proposals 5-18, 443C2
Scores Carter labor bill 7-18, 555B3
LESOTHO—*See also COMMONWEALTH of Nations, NONALIGNED Nations Movement, OAU*
UN Assemb member 4C1
'77-78 budget rptd 4-9, 490E1
Norland confrmd US amb 6-23, 626B3
US regional aid authorizatn OKd 8-4, 668D1
LESSARD, Marc
On Quebec cos exodus 4-28, 346D2
LETELIER, Orlando (d. 1976)
Murder probe implicates DINA, Cuban exiles 9-7—9-10, 743D2
LETOURNEAU, Jean-Paul
Scores language bill 7-13, 561E2
LEUKEMIA—*See MEDICINE—Cancer*
LEVENSON, Milton
Says breeder reactor safe 3-26, 235A1
LEVENTHAL, Judge Harold
Backs FCC obscenity order 3-16, 216A1
LEVENTHAL, Paul
Rpts '68 high seas uranium loss 4-29, 335E1
LEVESQUE, Rene
In NY, asks US investmt 1-21—1-25, 81D3
Seeks early separatism vote 1-27, 113C3
Montreal police slowdown 1-31—2-3, 97E2
In car mishap 2-6, 113D3; cleared 2-21, 2-25, 159C1
Hits Trudeau US speech 2-23, 132D3
Opens Quebec Assembly 3-8, 179F1
Disputes Quebec cos exodus 4-29, 346E2
Chirac backs separatism 4-29, 346A3
New language bill introduced 7-12, 561E1
Offers provs language deal 7-22, reactn 7-27—7-29, 596D3
Provs rejct language deal 8-19, 653A1
Scores language bill opponents 8-26, 671A2
OKs Inuit mtg 8-30, retracts 9-1, 694B1
Rejcts language amendmt 9-9, 741F3
Queen Eliz visits 10-15, 10-16, 822C2
In France, gets Legion of Honor 10-23—11-4; Ottawa scores 11-4, 862B2, B3
On RCMP PQ raid 11-2, 841E1
Confrms PQ info-gathering network 12-9, 965A2
France clarified Quebec ties 12-9, 965A3

1978

LEONARD, Hugh
Da opens 3-13, 887E1
Play Wins Tony 6-4, 579F2
LEONARD Jr., James F.
Defends ouster of Viet UN amb 2-9, 103B3
Lauds UN disarmamt sessn 6-30, 523B1
LEONARD, Peter
Convicted of murder, '77 convictn reversal cited 9-7, 824G2
LEONARD, William A.
Vs children's TV ad curbs 2-28, 347C2
To head CBS News 7-14, 599A3
LEONE, Giovanni (Italian president; resigns June 15)
Andreotti govt resigns 1-16, 37F3
At Moro state funeral 5-13, 689E2
Swears in Rognoni as Interior min 6-14, 558B2
Resigns over Lockheed chrgs 6-15, 516F2
LEONE, Richard C.
Loses Sen primary in NJ 6-6, 448A1
LEOPOLD, John R.
Wins Hawaii primary for gov 10-7, 791C3
Loses electn 11-7, 857C1
LEPICIER, Eugene
Violette released 10-9, 1030F3
LER, Leopold
Sets 3-yr econ experimt 2-14, 189B2
LESAR, James
On Ray's brother's role in King plot 11-30, 938E1
LESHER, Richard L.
Lauds consumer agency defeat 2-8, 82A2
On labor law revisn 6-22, 508G2
LESINSKIS, Imant
Granted US asylum 9-18, 946G3
LESLIE, Diane
Coolest Cat opens 6-23, 760F1
LESOTHO—*See also COMMONWEALTH of Nations, NONALIGNED Nations Movement, OAU*
S Africa editor in Botswana 1-3, 8F1
US bars Peace Corps from S Africa hospitals 5-15, 633A1
UK cancels debts 7-31, 592E1
UN Assemb member 713B3
LESSAC, Michael
Moliere opens 3-12, 887B2
Zinnia opens 3-22, 760G3
Ballroom in St Patrick opens 12-1, 1031A1
LESSARD, Marcel
On Canada Econ Dvpt Bd member 11-24, 921B3
LESTER, Mark
Crossed Swords released 3-2, 619D1
LETELIER, Isabel (Mrs. Orlando)
Study on US bank loans to Chile released 4-11, 312A2
Sues Chile re husband's death 8-8, 647G3
LETELIER, Orlando (d. 1976)—*See under CHILE*
Le THEULE, Joel
Named French transport min 4-5, 245G2
UK role in Airbus OKd 10-24, 902A3
LET'S Face It (film)
Released 7-14, 970G1
LET'S Get Small (recording)
Wins Grammy 2-24, 316B1
LETTER Carriers of the United States of America, National Association of (AFL-CIO)
New contract negotiated 7-21, 564G2
Meany scores contract 8-10, 624B3
Contract revised 9-15, OKd 10-10; Vacca ousted, Sombrotto named pres 10-10, 766A1, D2
LEUKEMIA—*See MEDICINE—Cancer*
LEUTWILER, Fritz
Scores US $ policy, says franc overvalued 9-27; $ soars 9-28, 732E1
LEVEE, Michael
Slow Dancing released 11-8, 970B3
LEVENTHAL, Marvin
Antimatter rptd in Earth galaxy cntr 5-6, 653E3
LEVESQUE, Rene
Trudeau threatens force vs Quebec separatn 1-1, 7A1
FLQ exiles ask amnesty 1-3, 7E1
Scores Sun Life relocatn 1-12, 35G3
Eng versn of Bill 101 signed 2-1, 88D3
Scores Trudeau on econ, bars joint communique 2-13, 111E1
At premiers language conf 2-23, 166D3
Scores federal '78-79 budget 4-11, 266C1
Scores fed electn delay 5-14, 370D1
On new Quebec currency plan 5-18, 412E3
Divorced 9-8, 844G3
Clarifies separatism 10-10, Ryan scores 10-11, 837C1
In const talks 10-31—11-1, 866F2
PQ backs separatism plan 12-3, 963E3-964A1
On Cossette-Trudel sentencing 12-13, 964B2

1979

LEONARD Jr., James F.
Abstains on anti-Israel UN res 3-22, 198G2
Named to Mideast post 5-12, 379B1
LEONARD, Jeff
2d in NL top rookie vote 11-28, 956A1
LEONARD, Ray (Sugar Ray)
TKOs Benitez for WBC welterwgt title 11-30, 1004B3
LEONARD, William A.
Scores Sup Ct 'state of mind' libel ruling 4-18, 302B2
LEONARDO Da Vinci—*See Da VINCI, Leonardo*
LEONE, Giovanni
6 convicted re Lockheed 3-1, 155F2
LEONETTI, Tommy
Dies 9-15, 756F2
LEONTIEF, Wassily
On '29 Depression, '80s econ forecast 11-1, 827F1
LEO Sheep Co. v. U.S.
US land grant easemt right curbed by Sup Ct 3-27, 263C2
LERNER, Alan Jay
Carmelina opens 4-8, 711A2
LERNER, Alexander
Barred from pol sci conf 8-12—8-18, 637C1
LEROY, Roland
Ousted from CP post 5-14, 371E2
LEROY v. Great Western United Corp.
Case decided by Sup Ct 6-26, 540G3
LESKO, John
Utter Glory opens 5-13, 712C3
LESOTHO—*See also COMMONWEALTH of Nations, NONALIGNED Nations Movement, OAU*
UN membership listed 695F2
S Africa unions bar natls 9-25, 732E2
LESSING, Gottfried
Rptd killed in Uganda 6-1, 429B2
LESTER, Mark L.
Roller Boogie released 12-19, 1008C1
LESTER, Richard
Butch & Sundance released 6-15, 819F3
Cuba released 12-21, 1007B3
LETELIER, Isabel (Mrs. Orlando)
Lauds verdict vs husband's assassins 2-14, 114A3
LETELIER, Orlando (d. 1976)
Murder Case—*See CHILE–Letelier Case*
LETERRIER, Francois
Your Turn, My Turn released 1-27, 174G3
Le THEULE, Joel
On rail strike costs 8-22, 634A1
LETTUCE—*See FRUITS & Vegetables*
LEUKEMIA—*See MEDICINE–Cancer*
LEVENSON, Keith
City Suite opens 4-2, 711B2
LEVENTHAL, Judge Harold H.
Dissents on Diggs convictn appeal 11-14, 900B3
LEVESQUE, Rene
In US; reassures on defens ties, investmt 1-25, 74E3
Vs Unity Task Force rpt 1-25, 74E3
Vs const chng re TV control 2-5—2-6, 113D3
Seeks Barre 'Vivre Quebec' statemt 2-13, 133F3
Remarries 4-12, 392D2
PQ candidate loses by-electn 4-30, 329D1
Backs Asbestos Corp takeover 5-4, 352A3
Cabt min quits 5-17, 378C1
Details sovereignty plan 6-1, PQ backs 6-3, 424E1
Sets '80 referendum 6-21, 483D3
Prov premrs rejct autonomy plan 8-17, 632C2
Shuffles Cabt, Tremblay quits 9-21, 750B1
Starts James Bay generator 10-27, 833D3
Presents PQ white paper 11-1, 853D1
PQ loses 3 by-electns 11-14, 889B2
Vs Sup Ct Bill 101 decisn 12-13, 948F3; 12-14, 967C2
Referendum bill presented 12-20, 992F2

1980

LEONARD, Hugh
A Life opens 11-3, 892G2
LEONARD, Ray (Sugar Ray)
KOs Green 3-31, 320E2
Duran decisns for WBC welterwgt title 6-20, 772D2
Hart KOs Denny 6-20, Denny dies 7-7, 907C3
TKOs Duran for WBC welterwgt title 11-25, 907B2
Duran fined 11-26, Duran rejcts retiremt 11-28, 1000A3
LEONARD, Silvio
Wins Olympic medal 7-25, 623G3
LEONARD, William A.
Govt pressure vs '60 Minutes' Iran segmt rptd 3-6, 239D1
LEONEILI, Mr.
Separatists take captive 1-6, surrender 1-11, 58C1
LEOPARD (German tank)—*See ARMAMENTS--Tanks*
LE PEN, Jean-Marie
Chrgd re bias 1-4, 20C1
LEPEU, Jean-Marc
Named AMC vp 9-29, 959E2
LERNER, Alan Jay
Brigadoon opens 10-16, 892A3
LERRO, Capt. John
Tanker rams Fla bridge 5-9; safety record rptd 5-10, 391G1
LERTXXUNDI, Roberto
ETA kidnaps, releases 12-10, 968D2
LESAGE, Jean
Dies 12-11, 1004D2
LESOTHO—*See also COMMONWEALTH of Nations, OAU*
At regional econ unity mtg, S Africa dependnc cited 4-1, 243D1, B2
S African activist flees 5-6, 374A3
LESOVAYA, Tatyana
Wins Olympic medal 8-1, 624C2
LESSARD, Jacques
Olympics contractor chrgd 5-9, 406F2
LESSER, Sol
Dies 9-19, 755G3
LESSON From Aloes, A (play)
Opens 11-17, 1003D3
LESSOV, Petar
Wins Olympic medal 8-2, 622E1
LESTER, Cy
Named CBS video divisn pres 1-31, 239E3
LESTER, Ronnie
In NBA draft; traded to Bulls 6-10, 447C1, F1
LETELIER, Orlando (d. 1976)—*See CHILE--Letelier Case*
LE THEULE, Joel
Saudi naval aid set 10-14, 790D1
LEUE, Eckhard
Wins Olympic medal 8-2, 622C2
LEVAI, Istvan
Wins Olympic medal 8-2, 622B2
LEVENE, Sam
Horowitz & Mrs Washn opens 4-2, 392C3
Dies 12-28, 1004D2
LEVENSON, Sam
Dies 8-27, 676G1
LEVER, Lord
Steel strike settled 4-1, 254B2
LEVER Brothers Co.
'79 top TV advertiser 4-4, 376B2
On '79 Fortune 500 list 5-5, 291E1
FTC ends detergent indus probe 5-12, 703B2
LEVESQUE, Rene
Sets referendum date 4-15, 293F1
Trudeau campaigns vs referendum, scores 5-2, 350D2-E2
Referendum defeated 5-20, 377A1-F1
Agrees to const negotiatns 6-9, 443D3
Vs Canada const 'patriatn' 9-8, 706A1

1976

LEVI, Edward H.
FBI probe request rptd 1-1, 6B1
'75 Mexico visit rptd 1-19, 61F1
Ford seeks law vs security leaks 2-18, 137D3
Ordrd Addabbo, Leggett payoffs probed 2-19, 171E1
FBI guidelines issued 3-10, 217B3
FBI probe ordrd renewed 3-21, 248G1, A2
Named to business probe panel 3-21, 262F2
FBI to destroy '69 files on Kraft 3-30, 235C1
Forms panel to study FBI targets 4-1, 235A1
Pocket-veto use limited 4-13, 284E1
Sen intellignc com rpt cites 4-28, 329F1
New Rev King probe set 4-29, 344E1
Ford orders challenge to FEC revisn 5-11, 346B2
Ford seeks busing ruling review 5-18, 5-19, 377E2-D3
Ford defends view vs busing 5-26, 391E1
Drops Boston busing review 5-29; Ford, other reactn 5-29—6-2, 391E1
On Mex opium poppy fields 6-8, 419E3
Carter vs checks on vp list 6-17, 452D1
Refers Ford funds chrg to Ruff 7-16, 761F1
Ford offers Watergate bill 7-19, 532A1
Ford backs Kelley re favors, gifts 9-4, 666D2-A3
Carter urges Kelley probe 9-7, 664F2
Ford asks emergency powers curb challenge 9-14, 689A2
Ford funds probe rptd 10-1, 723E2
Bars Ford coverup probe 10-20, 784F3
LEVI, Eli
SEC suit settled 5-11, 360B3
LEVICH, Benjamin
Scores Ford rights stand 6-25, 540A3
LEVIN, Ira
Boys From Brazil on best-seller list 12-5, 972F2
LEVIN Jr., Joseph J.
Carter transition aide 11-23, 881A3
LEVIN, Jules
Final pres vote tally 12-18, 979C2
LEVIN, Marlin
Time rpts Israel '73 A-bombs, Israel denies 4-5, 243G1
LEVINE, Abner
'72 campaign gift listed 4-25, 688D1
LEVINE, Richard B.
On potato futures default 5-25—5-27, 397C1-A2
LEVINGER, Rabbi Moshe
Chrgd re Hebron role 10-26, 895G1
LEVINSON, Charles
Rubber boycott backed 4-26, 309B1
LEVINSON, Jerome J.
Says shah drops oil-jet barter deal 9-10, 773B3
LEVI Strauss & Co.
FTC chrgs price-fixing 5-7, 989D3
SEC lists forgn paymts 5-12, 728C2
LEVITAS, Rep. Elliott, H. (D, Ga.)
Reelected 11-2, 829D2
LEVOYER, Col. Richelieu
Ecuador interior min 1-14, vows partial amnesty 1-16, 49B1
Govt, pol parties hold talks 2-3—3-16, 363E2
Rptd replaced 6-12, 693B1
LEVY, Gustave L.
Dies 11-3, 970C2
LEVY, Pierre
Donates art works to Troyes 1-31, 124F2
LEWINE, Francis
Elected to Gridiron Club 3-5, 272A1
LEWIS, Arthur D.
On Conrail's 1st ¼ 8-12, 648F1
On Conrail 2d ¼ loss 11-11, 887B2
LEWIS, Diana
'72 campaign gift listed 4-25, 688D1
LEWIS, John
'72 campaign gift listed 4-25, 688D1
LEWIS, Richard Warrington Baldwin
Wins Pulitzer 5-3, 352C3
LEWIS, Salim
'72 campaign gift listed 4-25, 688D1
LEWIS, Thomas
Replaced as New S Wales premr 1-20, 46F1
LEWISTON, Me.—*See MAINE*
LEXINGTON, Ky.—*See KENTUCKY*
LHEVINNE, Rosina
Dies 11-9, 970C2
LIAO Chih-kao
Fukien arrests rptd 11-23, 904G3
LIBEL—*See under CRIME*

1977

LEVI, Edward H.
FBI informer guidelines set 1-5, 15B3
King probe rpt cited 2-2, 77B2
Voting rights power upheld 6-20, 517A1
LEVICH, Benjamin
Oxford conf scores treatmt 7-13, 551D2
Questnd re Shcharansky 7-20, 551G2
USSR scores 8-24, rebuts 8-29, 683F3
LEVIN, Judge Dov
Fines Rabin's wife 4-17, 329G2
LEVIN, Ira
Boys from Brazil on best-seller list 4-3, 264A2
LEVITT Jr., Arthur
Named Amex chrmn 11-10, 859C3
LEVY, David
Israel immigrant min 6-20, 474E2
LEVY, Dr. David M.
Dies 3-1, 264B3
LEVY, George Morton
Dies 7-19, 604C3
LEVY, Marv
Named Chiefs coach 12-20, 1020A2
LEWIS, Arthur D.
Conrail '76-77 losses rptd 3-31, 325D2
LEWIS, David S.
'76 top salary rptd 5-23, 408D3
LEWIS, John R.
Wins US House runoff spot 3-15, 191G3
Loses runoff election 4-5, 252B1
Named ACTION assoc dir 7-13, confrmd 8-4, 626A3
LEWIS, Ross
Dies 8-6, 696A3
LEWIS, Samuel W.
Named amb to Israel 4-7; confrmd 4-25, 418F1
Sees Allon on Carter policy 5-31, 440A2
Carter vs new W Bank setlmts 8-18, 623A1
Asks Israel resume Leb truce talks 10-14, 793F2
Sadat gets Israel invitatn 11-15, 873F1
LEWIS, Sinclair (1885-1951)
Mark Schorer dies 8-11, 696F3
LEWISTON (Ida.) Morning Tribune (newspaper)
Secret news source review refused 10-31, 835F2
LEXINGTON, Ky.—*See KENTUCKY*
LEYLAND—*See BRITISH Leyland*
LIAISSINE, Mohamed
Algeria heavy indus min 4-23, 470B2
LIAS, Thomas L.
Replaced as HEW asst secy 3-29, 272D3
LIBBEY-Owens-Ford Co.
Buys own gas field 1-27, 76A2

LIBEL (& Slander)
Sup Ct bars Buckley case review 1-17, 58B1
Alioto wins Cowles damages 5-3, 532A2
Wyo jurisdictn review refused 6-20, 517C1
'Scottsboro' suit vs NBC dismissed 7-12, 643B1
Atkinson loses NFL suit, Blount suit cited 7-22, 659C1, E1
Vesco wins suit vs CR investor 9-12, 767D1
Sup Ct rulings scored 10-31, 879B1
Fla bldg inspector case refused 11-7, 857C2
Journalists' thoughts protected 11-7, 920F2
Rinaldi, Glover, Fadell cases refused 11-28, 919A3
NY Times-Audubon case review declined 12-12, 960E2

1978

LEVICH, Benjamin
Kennedy confident re exit 9-11, 743B1
Emigrates 11-30, 946F2
LEVIN, Carl
Wins Mich US Sen primary 8-8, 625G3
Elected 11-7, 846D1, 853C3, 858C2
LEVIN, Ira
Death Trap opens 2-26, 760A2
Boys From Brazil released 10-5, 969D3
LEVIN, Irving
Heinsohn fired as Celtic coach 1-3, 40G3
NBA OKs Celtics-Braves ownership swap 7-7, 655F2
LEVINE, Joseph E.
Magic released 11-18, 970A2
LEVINE, Richard P.
Magic released 11-18, 970A2
LEVI Strauss & Co.
Hungary opens jean factory 8-8, 882D3
E Ger begins unrestricted sales 11-29, 1021A3
LEVITAS, Rep. Elliott Harris (D, Ga.)
House votes quota curb 6-13, 445G3
Reelected 11-7, 850A3
LEVITON Manufacturing Co.
Stiff trust case sentnc imposed 2-3, 142E2
LEVITT, Arthur
Role in NYC fiscal crisis 86C2
Sen Banking Com rpt vs future NYC aid 2-9, 86G2
LEVYNE, H. David
Pleads guilty to GSA corruptn 10-4, 753E3
LEWIS, Arthur
Brass Target released 12-21, 1030E2
LEWIS, David
On Navy A-sub contract dispute setlmt 6-9, 469D1, G1
LEWIS, Jerry
Wins US House seat 11-7, 850B2, 856F3
LEWIS, John
Mahalia opens 6-5, 887B2
LEWIS, Marvin E.
Sex abuse suit vs NBC dismissed 8-8, 635C2-A3
LEWIS, Judge Oren R.
Finds Snepp broke secrecy pledge, grants US book profits 7-7, 527G2
LEWIS, Samuel
Gets Begin setlmt views 2-1, 60E2
Israel frees US Arab 10-18, 783D2
LEWIS, Rev. W. T.
Scores CORE conv, Innis 9-18, 810D1
LEWITT, H. N.
Beasts opens 2-8, 760C1
L'EXPRESS (French magazine)
Goldsmith buys control 4-27, 352A3
LEY, Rick
Winnipeg wins WHA title 5-22, 458C2
LEYLAND—*See BL Ltd.*
LHA (amphibious assault ship)—*See ARMAMENTS—Ships*
L'HEUREUX, Louise (Mrs. Rene Levesque)
Divorced 9-8, 844G3
LHIW Inc.—*See SUN Oil Co.*
LIAO Cheng-chih
Forgn trip curbs eased 1-4, 17G2
On Chinese fleeing Vietnam 5-1, 341C1
LIBEDINSKY, Marcos
Quits Letelier murder probe 3-21, 209D3

LIBEL (& Slander)
Col Sanders suit dismissed 3-14, 420E3
Govt Printing Office immunity challng refused by Sup Ct 4-17, 308A3
NM press info order review refused by Sup Ct 5-15, 388B1
Synanon threats vs Time ed probed 10-15, 842A1
'71-77 state discipline vs MDs rptd up 12-1, 992F3

1979

LEVI, Edward H.
Supports FBI charter 7-31, 599A2, A3
LEVI, Wayne
Ties for 2d in San Diego Open 1-28, 220D3
Wins Houston Open 5-6, 587E2
LEVICH, Benjamin G.
Named Einstein prof at City Coll 3-2, ousted by Sovt Acad 4-5, 272E1
LEVIN, Sen. Carl (D, Mich.)
Labor '78 campaign gifts rptd 6-13, 595D1
In USSR re SALT 8-28–8-30, 658D1
LEVIN, Ira
Break a Leg opens 4-29, 711G1
LEVINE, Joseph E.
Wyeth paintings rptd sold 3-22, 375B2
LEVINSON, Barry
And Justice for All released 10-19, 1007G2
LEVISON, Stanley
Dies 9-12, 756G2
LEVITTOWN, Pa.—*See PENNSYLVANIA*
LEVITCHENKO, Stanislav
Flies to US after Japan defectn 10-24, 856D3
LEVY, Franklin R.
Festival opens 5-7, 711A3
LEVY, Jeremy
Rich Kids released 8-17, 820B3
LEVY, Lisa (1957-78)
Bundy gets death penalty for '78 slaying 7-31, 604D2
LEVY, Dr. Robert I.
Rpts strokes decline in US 2-23, 195G1, G2
LEVYNE, H. David
Sentenced in GSA scandal 5-29, 964C3
LEWIN v. N.J.
Case declined by Sup Ct 10-9, 784D1
LEWIS, Sir Arthur
Wins Nobel Prize 10-17, 858G1-B2
LEWIS, Carolyn
3 Mile I probe comm gets subpoena power 5-17, 5-21, 417G2
Scores NRC licensing decision 8-23, 665C1
LEWIS, Col. Charles
Rpts gas raids vs Laos rebels 12-12, 979C1
LEWIS, David P.
City on Fire released 9-14, 819G3
LEWIS, Floyd W.
On 3 Mile I comm final rpt 10-30, 826D1
LEWIS, H. W.
'75 A-safety rpt called unreliable 1-19, 54C2
LEWIS, Harry
Sues Woolworth re Brascan bid 4-12, 304A2
Investor suits vs advisers curbed by Sup Ct 11-13, 902A1
LEWIS, Jim
Traded to Yankees 11-1, 1002C3
LEWIS, John
Songs From the City Streets opens 4-9, 712E2
LEWIS, Mel
Wins Grammy 2-16, 336E3
LEWIS, Judge Oren R.
Upholds Va religious schl expulsn 8-23, 650G1
Sentences Head for bribery 10-24, 906D1
LEWIS, Randy
Iowa wins NCAA wrestling title 3-10, 507E3
LEWIS, Samuel
Israel OKs 2 new W Bank setlmts 4-23, 296B2
Mediates Israel-Egypt pact feud 4-25, 295G2
Gives Begin note on Leb raid, Syria clash 6-27, 496A2
LEWIS Jr., Sherman R.
Loeb Rhoades, Shearson to merge 5-14, 366C3
LEWISBURG, Pa.—*See PENNSYLVANIA*
LEWIS Galindo, Gabriel
Panama Canal Comm member 12-6, 939D1
L'EXPRESS (French magazine)
Iran ousts newsman 8-21, 635A2
LEY, Rick
Named WHA top defenseman 5-16, 470F2
In NHL expansion draft 6-13, 470B2
LEYDEN, John
Scores air traffic computer safety 11-20, 988G3
LEZCANO, Sixto
AL batting ldr 9-30, wins Golden Glove Award 11-20, 955D3, 956C1
L'HEYREUX, Louise
Ex-husband remarries 4-12, 392D2
LIAI Mo-sha
Followers rehabilitated 8-3, 651B3
LIBEL (& Slander)
Amer Express sues McGraw-Hill 1-18, 53F2
'State of mind' queries backed by Sup Ct 4-18, reactn 4-18, 4-23, 301F3, 302B2
Calif newspr loses case 4-18, plaintiffs awarded $4.56 mln 4-19, 334B2
Sup Ct worker fired re news leaks 4-20, 302A3
Buian damage case declined by Sup Ct 4-23, 346A3
Marshall decries 'state of mind' ruling 5-27, 422D1
Right to sue broadened by Sup Ct 6-26, 540D2
Rathjens denies H-bomb letter chrgs, threatens suit 9-17, 714C2
Brennan criticizes press 10-17, 848E1
Arnheiter cases declined by Sup Ct 10-29, 884G1

1980

LEVI, Wayne
Wins Pleasant Valley Classic 9-7, 972G1
LEVIN, Sen. Carl (D, Mich.)
Scores year-end spending waste 7-20, 598E2, A3
Scores Percy Palestine stance 12-9, 936F1
LEVINE, Philip
Ashes wins Amer Book Award 5-1, 692F2
LEVINSON, Barry
Inside Moves released 12-19, 1003A2
LEVINSON, Fred
Perfectly Frank opens 11-30, 1003E3
LEVI Strauss & Co.
Haas buys Oakland A's 8-23, 795B3
Wrangler trademark suit win rptd 11-19, 917B3
Retail price fixing suits rptd setld 12-2, 917G2
LEVITAS, Rep. Elliot (D, Ga.)
Revenue sharing amendmt OKd 12-12, 955A1
LEVITCHENKO, Stanislav
Japan arrests 3 as spies 1-18, 60C1
LEVITT, Arthur
Dies 5-6, 448C2
LEVITT, Steven
Those Lips released 9-9, 836G3
LEVY, Dana
Anatomy Illustrated wins Amer Book Award 5-1, 692C2
LEVY, George
Indicted 2-28, 237D3
LEVY, Harold
Scores $1.8 bln MCI award 6-13, 456G3
LEVY, Capt. Howard B.
Mil petitn limits upheld by Sup Ct 1-21, 93E1
LEVY, Lisa (1957-78)
Bundy gets 3d death sentence 2-12, 136E2
LEVY, Dr. Robert
Scores cholesterol rpt 6-1, 432B3
LEVY, Robert L.
Smokey & the Bandit II released 8-15, 675E3
LEW Byung Huyn, Gen.
US warns vs Kim Dae Jung executn 11-19, 944A3
LEWIS, Alfred
Dies 10-30, 876C2
LEWIS Jr., Andrew L. (Drew)
Named GOP com dep chrmn 6-13, 452B3
Named Transport secy 12-11, 935D1
LEWIS Jr., Bob
2d in US Amateur golf championship 8-31, 714D3
LEWIS, Fred
On Hughes flying boat 5-22, 560A3
LEWIS, George
Iran chrgs shah gave gifts 2-9, 122B3
LEWIS, Capt. Harold
Killed in Iran rescue mission 4-24, 321E2
LEWIS, Jerry
Wife files divorce suit 9-5, 908F1
LEWIS, Rep. Jerry A. (R, Conn.)
Reelected 11-4, 842B2
LEWIS, Jerry Lee
MD indicted 5-16, 414B2
Lennon slain 12-8, 934B3
LEWIS, Martyn
Afghan Olympic wrestler denies defectn plan 7-21, 590B2
LEWIS, Patti (Mrs. Jerry)
Files divorce suit 9-5, 908F1
LEWIS, Robert
Harold & Maude opens 2-7, 136B3
LEWIS, Roger
Night Games released 4-11, 416D3
LEWIS, Samuel
Begin defends Jerusalem land seizure 3-13, 178C3
Queries Begin on E Jerusalem office move 6-25, 476A2
Israel vs US UN vote on Jerusalem 8-21, 643C2
LEWIS, Trey
Wins AIAW doubles tennis title 6-11, 607E1
LEWISBURG—*See PENNSYLVANIA*
LEWIS v. BT Investment Managers
Case decided by Sup Ct 6-9, 512F2
LEWIS v. McGraw-Hill
Case declined by Sup Ct 11-3, 856A2
LEWIS v. U.S.
Case decided by Sup Ct 2-27, 188F2
L'EXPRESS (French magazine)
Marchais defends war record 3-8, 193E1-A2
LIBBY, Willard F.
Dies 9-8, 756A1

LIBEL (& Slander)
Hellman sues McCarthy, Cavett 2-15, 199D2
Nader case declined by Sup Ct 2-19, 131E1
Penthouse publisher wins case 3-1, 239B2; award cut 4-17, 405A3
Crane sues W Ger mag 7-16, 890C2
Flynn biographer sued 8-1, 639F1
Garvey article reprint OKd 8-14, 637D2
Calif 'pub figures' case refused by Sup Ct 10-6, 782E2
Del Law Schl case declined by Sup Ct 11-10, 868B3
McCarthy TV film case refused by Sup Ct 12-1, 918D2

1976

LIBERAL Party
Carter at NY dinner 10-14, 827E1
Alex Rose dies 12-28, 1015E2

LIBERIA—*See also AFRICAN Development Bank, NONALIGNED Nations Movement, OAU*
Listed as 'partly free' 1-19, 20D3
Angola MPLA recognized 2-13, 163E2
Carter confrmd US amb 4-1, 262C3
Kissinger visits 4-30—5-1, 318A2, B3
ECOWAS rptd ratified 11-6, 974E2
Tanker spills off Nantucket, fisherman file suit 12-15—12-22, 968D3

LIBEROFF, Miguel
Kidnaped in Argentina 5-19, 399D2
LIBERTAD (Argentine sailing ship)
In Operation Sail 7-4, 488A3
LIBERTARIAN Party
Final pres vote tally 12-18, 979B2
LIBERTY (magazine)
Carter interview cited 10-2, 743C2
LIBERTY National Corp.
Rptd on FRB 'problem' list 1-22, 111C3
LIBRARIES—*See also LIBRARY of Congress under U.S. GOVERNMENT*
House votes aid extensn 2-17, 170D3
Ford asks educ aid plan 3-1, 166E3
Dem platform text 6-15, 472D3
Mrs Carter tours LBJ library 9-23, 724B3
Cong clears copyright revisns 9-30, 765G3; signed 10-19, 982G1
Ford library planned 12-14, 980E2

LIBYA—*See also AFRICAN Development Bank, ARAB League, NONALIGNED Nations Movement, OAU, OPEC*
Univ protesters slain 1-4—1-5, students demonstrate 1-8—1-12, 205C2
5-yr econ plan presented 1-15, 205E2
Listed as 'not free' nation 1-19, 20E3
Christian-Moslem conf 2-1—2-6, 272F2
Meheishi ousted from RCC, Cabt 3-15; denounces Quaddafi 4-22, 334D1
Amnesty for 15 ex-offcls rptd 5-4, 334D1
Hijacker surrenders 7-6, 539G1, A2 ★
Egyptian Relations—*See 'Libyan Relations' under EGYPT; also 'Libya' under MIDDLE EAST—ARAB Policies*
Foreign Relations (misc.)—*See also 'UN Policy' below*
Students occupy embs in Egypt, UK 1-8—1-12, 205C2
French Mirage purchase cited 1-16, 36C2
Plotters seized in Italy, Egypt; Libya retaliates 3-6—3-11, 205G1-C2
Tunisia rpts expulsns 3-21, 239F2
Tunisia arrests commandos, recalls amb; Libya denies plot 3-22, 239C2
French premr ends visit, pacts signed 3-22, 239B3
Closer Algeria, Niger ties set 4-8, 372A1
Pl hijacked jet arrives 4-13, hostages freed 4-14, 260B2
Bars hijackers asylum 4-15, hostages return to Pl 4-16, 313B3
Tunis rpts Qaddafi assassinatn try 4-19, 334F1
Tunis sentncs 1 in death plot, Quaddafi scored 4-19—4-23, 335B1
Bangladesh bars exile return 4-20—4-30, 332A2
Tunis rpts expulsns 5-3, 335D1
Giscard visits US 5-17—5-22, 372A2
Iran ties to terrorists 5-22, 418G2
Sovt mil presence rptd 6-13, 467C1
Tied to Sudan coup try; ties severed 7-6, denies coup role 501D3, F3
France vs Mirage transfer to Uganda 7-8; 30 rptd sent 7-9, 516A3
World terrorist network rptd 7-15, US confrms 7-19, 531D1, 532F1

1977

LIBERIA—*See also NONALIGNED Nations Movement, OAU*
UN Assemb member 4C1
IMF loan set 2-4, 87E2
Oil tanker incidents rptd 2-7, 2-24, 214C3, D3
China ties set 2-22, Taiwan cuts ties 2-23, 243D3
Africa silence re Luwum murder scored 3-18, 308B3
UNCTAD shipping study rptd 4-17, 337E2
Young visits 5-13, 399A1
Ship safety rules set 7-19, 736A2
Canada metric conversn rptd 9-6, 705F2
Southwestn Bell loses slander suit, AT&T acquitted 9-12, 724B2
Saudis boycott ships 12-10, 955D1

LIBERTY, U.S.S. (electronics ship)
Israel accused re '67 attack 9-19, 715A1
LIBERTY Bowl—*See FOOTBALL—Collegiate*
LIBERTY Glass Co.
Strike ends 10-14, 818F3
LIBERTY Trucking
ICC sues 11-3, 861D1
LIBRA Bank Ltd.
Brazil steel loan granted 6-20, 524E2
LIBRARIES
Coll curriculum reform urged 12-15, 1009D1
LIBRARY of Congress (Washington, D.C.)
Fuel-bill study issued 2-2, 76A1
Kissinger loses transcripts ruling 12-8, 962E2

LIBYA (People's Socialist Libyan Arab Public)—*See also ARAB League, NONALIGNED Nations, OAU, OPEC*
People's cong meets 2-28—3-2; govt, country names chngd 3-3, 348E2
Civilian sentences altered 3-24, executns rptd 4-12, 348A3
'75 coup plotters executed 4-2, 348A3
56 Moslems die in jet crash 12-2, 992E2
Arab-Israeli Conflict—*See MIDDLE EAST*
Egyptian Relations—*See EGYPT—Libyan Relations*
Foreign Relations (misc.)—*See also 'UN Policy' below*
France arrests Daoud 1-7, 9D2
Chad rebels free Claustres 1-30, Qaddafi thanked 2-1, 84C2
Pl-Moslem talks 2-5—3-3; Qaddafi tied to revolt 3-10, 202D2
Malta scores security talks delay 2-10, 136A3
Uganda rpts invasn aid set 2-24, 141D2
Sudan joins Egypt-Syrian cmnd 2-28, 143A3
Castro visits, signs pact 3-1—3-10, 249F1, A2
Ethiopia coup backed 3-11, 238A3
Pl-Moslem pact reached 3-20, 241C3
Egypt seeks US arms re Sovt threat 4-5, 245C1
Pl-Moslem mediatn fails 4-30, 468F2
Pak feud mediatn 5-4, 348E3
Sudan scores Sovt role 5-17, 450E1
Chad chrgs frontier seizure 7-2—7-5, 512E1
Chad interventn chrgd 7-14, denied 7-15, 597A2
Ethiopia mil aid rptd 7-26, 588B1
USSR restraint re Egypt conflict noted 7-28, 574B3
Pl rebel aid denied 10-17, 824F2
Sudan frees natls 10-17, 843F3
W Ger asks more Tripoli airport security 10-23, 868D3
Sahara kidnap mediatn offered 11-2, French aid plea rptd 11-3, 852C2

1978

LIBERIA—*See also NONALIGNED Nations Movement, OAU*
Oil tanker spill fouls French coast 3-17, 201C3; 3-23—3-29, 238B1
At W African mtg, backs ECOWAS 3-18; USSR scores 3-20, 237E1
Carter visits, oil tanker safety rules urged 4-3, 233B1, 234C1
S Africa econ pressure rptd asked 6-2, 633B2
French sen comm rpts on supertanker spill costs; probe bd ends hearings 7-1, 524C1
France sues Amoco on tanker spill 9-13, 749C1
UN Assemb member 713B3

LIBERMAN, Alberto
Rptd freed 9-1, 793G1
LIBERTARIAN Party
Calif gov electn results 11-7, 856D2
LIBERTY Bowl—*See FOOTBALL—Collegiate*
LIBERTY House Inc.—*See AMFAC*
LIBERTY National Life Insurance Co.
Equitable Gen bid ended 6-21, 553E2
LIBRARIES
Miss female bias rule repealed 11-7, 852F3
LIBRARY Of Congress—*See under U.S. GOVERNMENT*

LIBYA (People's Socialist Libyan Arab Public)—*See also ARAB League, NONALIGNED Nations Movement, OAU, OPEC*
Copter crash kills 11 3-6, anti-Qaddafi plot hinted 3-28, arrests rptd 3-29, 228D1
Arab-Israeli Conflict—*See MIDDLE EAST*
Egyptian Relations—*See EGYPT—Libyan Relations*
Foreign Relations (misc.)—*See also 'UN' below*
Algeria pres visits Malta 1-3, 39C2
Spain king visits 1-21, 136G1
Chad cuts ties; chrgs rebel aid, land seizure 2-6, 89E1
Qaddafi in Tunisia, Libya agitatn chrgd 2-6, 170C1
Malta '77 aid rptd 2-17, 228B3
Cyprus jet hijackers denied landing 2-19, 117B2
Chad truce announced 2-20, peace plan OKd 2-24, 130A2
In Syrian-Sovt talks 2-21—2-24, 139E2
E Ger offcls killed in copter crash 3-6, 228D1
Bhutto death sentnc reversal plea rptd 3-22, 229B1
Islamic, Arab poor-natn aid rise rptd 4-9, 257D2, F2
Zaire chrgs Shaba rebel aid 5-14, 359A2
Qaddafi in Algeria 5-31—6-6, shifts stance on Polisario 6-3, 562D2
Canada Westinghouse contract boycott clause scored 6-1, 435F2
Zaire pan-Africa force rptd opposed 6-8, 442D1
Chad chrgs invasn 6-22, troops estimated 7-5, 572B2
Chad peace talks fail 7-3—7-6, 572B2
Qaddafi in Malta; mil aid, oil price cuts agreed 7-3—7-4, 592E2
Zaire clashes re French role in Africa 7-7, 561E2

1979

Novelist case refused by Sup Ct 12-3, 964F1
NM newspapers case refused by Sup Ct 12-3, 964A2

LIBERIA—*See also NONALIGNED Nations Movement, OAU*
Oil tanker '78 spill rpt issued 3-8, 163A1
US' Gov Brown in Monrovia 4-7, 271E3
Riots re price hikes 4-14—4-15, Guinean troops arrive 4-17, 279F3
Tolbert rejcts price hikes 4-18; closes univs 4-21, gets emergency powers 4-27, 314F3
Habeas corpus suspended 5-2, 374G2
Tanker collides off Tobago 7-19, 553A3
CAE student massacre probe rptd 8-6, 601A3
Tanker fleet safety record rptd 8-15, 608E1
Young, US trade missn visit; Israel ties urged 9-6, 9-7, 720A3, B3, E3
UN membership listed 695F2
Freighter, tanker collide off Tex 11-1, 954F3

LIBRARIES
Coll theft studied 4-18, 282C2
Boston U strike ends 4-22, 326F3
JFK library dedicatn held 10-20, 807D3, 905D1
White House Conf held 11-15—11-19, Carter stresses 11-16, 901B1-A2
LIBRARY and Information Services, White House Conference on
Held 11-15—11-19, 901B1
LIBRARY of Congress—*See under U.S. GOVERNMENT*

LIBYA (People's Socialist Libyan Arab Public)—*See also ARAB League, NONALIGNED Nations Movement, OAU, OPEC*
Qaddafi coup anniv marked 9-1, 688A3
Arab-Israeli Conflict—*See MIDDLE EAST*
Foreign Relations (misc.)—*See also 'Oil' below*
Chad rebelln thwarted 2-14, 114A2
Freed Palestinians flown to Tripoli 3-14, 178G2
Uganda troop role rptd 3-31—4-4, withdrawn 4-7, 257E1-B2
Qaddafi at Malta fete re UK troop exit 3-31, 269D2
Pak denies A-bomb chrg 4-8, 277F2
'71, '75 A-bomb bids rptd 4-14, 299C3
Chad invasn falters 4-20, 329A3
Islamic conf suspends Egypt 5-9, 360D1
Amin presence rptd 5-27, 429F1
Amin residence confirmed 6-13, 489A1
Egypt ties Qaddafi to Emb raid in Turkey 7-16, 536A3
8 Arab ldrs at Qaddafi anniv fete 9-1, 688B3
Embs abroad occupied by Libyans 9-3, 688F2
Qaddafi tied to missing Leb Moslem ldr 9-8, 677E3
Israel cites mil threat 9-12, 693D2
UN membership listed 695F2
CAR arrests 37 soldiers 9-22, 720C2
Sadat fears Saudi link 10-10, 801F2
Canada deal losses rptd 10-22, 833A3
Iran urged to free US Emb hostages 11-20, 895C3
Uganda returns prisoners 11-28, 998D2
PLO hq under seige 12-6, offcls protest 12-9; Qaddafi scores disunity 12-10, 937B23

1980

LIBERAL Party
Carey vows Carter reelectn support 8-28, 663F2
Anderson wins endorsemt 9-6, 681D1
Javits seeks nominatn 9-9, 682F1
LIBERATORE, Anthony D.
Convicted in FBI bribery plot 7-3, 655E2
LIBERIA—*See also NONALIGNED Nations, OAU*
Freedom House lists as partly free 87E3
Supertanker sinks off Senegal 1-17, 108F2
13 cleared re ritual murder 1-17, 154G1
Bahamas bank looting case rptd 3-3, 229A1
Oppositn ldr asks Tolbert ouster 3-7, arrested 3-9, 278C2
Tolbert killed in coup; Doe replaces, frees oppositn ldr 4-12, names Cabt, vows 'new society' 4-13, 284A3
NY consulate, UN missn occupied by students 4-12, 284E3
Dennis US asylum bid rptd 4-12, US denies 4-29, 353D2
Revolt rptd foiled 4-14, 353F2
Shipping registratn business to continue 4-15, 284C3
Tolbert buried 4-15; facts on 284D3, F3
4 looters shot in Monrovia 4-17, calm rptd 4-18, 353E2
13 ex-govt offcls executed 4-22, intl outcry halts deaths 4-29, 353F1
Const suspended; junta assumes full exec, legis power 4-25, 353FL, D2
Ex-vp seeks guerrilla army 4-28; Methodists fearful, plan exit 4-30, 353F2
Ex-vp bars overthrow plan 5-2, 381F3
Tanker rams Fla bridge 5-9, 391C1, A2
Countercoup rptd foiled 5-14; oppositn major rptd killed 5-15, 381F3
Doe barred from CEAO mtg 5-28, 469G1-A3
Tolbert's son seized at French Emb 6-14, France protests 6-15, 499C1
Oil tanker runs aground in Gulf Coast hurricane 8-9, 621A3
US job bias suit filing time limit upheld by Sup Ct 12-15, 957B2
LIBERTARIAN Party
Clark urges Anderson quit pres race 8-20, 682B1
Clark on 50 state ballots; ideology cited 10-28, 818E2
Clark press endorsemts rptd 11-1, 841E3
LIBERTY, U.S.S. (intelligence ship)
US, Israel settle '67 case 12-18, 966A2
LIBERTY Baptist College (Lynchburg, Va.)
Falwell profiled 9-15, 819C3
Reagan visits 10-3, 763F2
LIBESKIND, Dr. Bernard
Visits US hostages in Iran 4-14, rpts 4-14, 4-15, 282B2
LIBIN, Paul
Major Barbara opens 2-26, 392D3
LIBIO Tiburcio, Tito
Released from DR Emb, held as suspect 4-6, 293C3
LIBRARIES
Amer Book Award presented 5-1, 692F1
Higher educ authrzn clears Cong 9-18, 9-25, signed 10-3, 803D3
Maurice Tauber dies 9-21, 756F2
Amer Book Awards revamped 10-19, 906C2
LIBRARY Court
Evangelical Christian pol actn profiled 7-11—9-15, 819F1
LIBYA (People's Socialist Libyan Arab Public)—*See also ARAB League, NONALIGNED Nations, OAU, OPEC*
Dissident crackdown seen 4-26, 353B3
Dissidents warned 6-7, 451B3
Tobruk mutiny rpt denied 8-18, 652A3
Human rights record scored 12-10, 978B3
Foreign Relations (misc.)—*See also 'Oil' and 'UN' below*
Al Fatah ties severed 1-5, 107F3
CAR breaks ties 1-22, 336C2
Tunisia blames re Gafsa attack 1-28, 90A1
French emb, consulate wrecked 2-4, France withdraws staff, expels Libyans 2-5, 90D1
Syria says Israel plans attack 2-23, 140C3
Arab League mtg re Gafsa attack ends 2-28, comm named in Tunisia dispute 2-29, 197B1
Chad factn support cited 3-31, 331G1
Anti-Sadat front backed 4-2, 273C3
Exiles shot in UK 4-11, 4-15, Qaddafi dissident crackdown seen 4-26, 353A3
Arab hardliners meet 4-14—4-15, 284E2
2 execs killed in Rome 4-19, 5-10, 373D3
Iran hostage rescue missn scored 4-27, 324D2
France missn bombed 5-6, 373D3
Embs in Eur, Asia occupied by Libyans 5-10, 373A3
UK ousts 4, arrests 3 in dissident murders 5-12, 373C3
Jamaica loan rptd 6-4, 465D1
Exile murdered, 2d wounded in Italy 6-11, 451A3
Qadafi rptdly backs anti-Sadat move 6-11, Arab mtg set 6-22; Egypt reimposes martial law at border 6-16, 451C3

1976

Sudan ties to coup 7-15, 531C3
Sudan, Egypt, Saudis join forces 7-18—7-19, 531B2
Confrms Mirage transfer to Uganda 7-18, 548C2 ★
Olympic withdrawal rptd 7-21, 528B3
Egypt chrgs Sudan coup role 7-22, 547A3
Recalls Saudi amb 7-25, 547D3
BBC denies use of news sources re Sudan 8-6, 857D2
Sudan protests BBC news sources 8-6, 857D2
Egypt masses troops, chrgs Libya infiltratn plan 8-13; Arab League mtg asked 8-15, 629E3
Egypt chrgs Chad, Sudan, Tunisia plot 8-13, 629G3
Sovt arms in parade 9-2, 682D3
Jalloud denies border area seizure 696F2
New maps rptdly take in Algeria, Chad, Niger areas 9-9, 696E2
Indian jet seized 9-10, 685E3
Malta forgn policy cited 9-20, 713F1
Buys into Fiat 12-1, Qaddafi in USSR 12-9, Sovt benefits denied 12-10, 964G3-965E1
Qaddafi, Brezhnev signs pacts 12-6—12-9, 949B1
In Pl-rebel talks 12-15—12-23, 1008G3
French binocular fraud rptd 12-25—12-30, 1006D3
Middle East Conflict—*See MIDDLE EAST*

UN Policy & Developments—*See also UN DEVELOPMENTS under MIDDLE EAST*
Cncl member 62F2
Shuns pollutn pact signing 2-16, 126B3
OKs Israel Arab land exit 6-29, 464C1
Cncl gets Sudan protest 7-5, 501E3
Anti-Israel res withdrawn 7-14, 515F3
Shuns vote on anti-terror 7-14, 515G3
S Africa arms ban vetoed 10-19, 781D3
Bars vote on UNEF 10-22, 799B2
Shuns UNDOF vote 11-30, 895B2
Shuns Assemb Geneva conf vote 12-9, 914D1

LIBYAN Arab Airlines
Hijacker surrenders 7-6, 539G1
LIDDY, G. Gordon
Calif break-in convictn upheld 5-17, 379D1
LIEBER, Dr. Charles S.
New alcoholism test rptd 12-3, 950C3
LIEBLING, Herman
On Apr indl output rise 5-14, 375C2

LIECHTENSTEIN
Listed as 'partly free' 1-19, 20D3
Jobless total rptd 2-4, 123D1 ★
Winter Olympics results 2-4—2-15, 158D3, E3, 159B2
US suit vs Gen Tire setld 5-10, 360D1, B2
Amer Hosp sued 12-29, 986A2

LIENDO, Brig. Gen. Horacio
Argentina labor min 3-29, 236C1 ★
LIEVANO Aguirre, Indalecio
Sees Kissinger 2-22—2-23, 178D1
LIFE Science Products Co.
Kepone poisoning probed 2-26, 171A3
Indicted 5-7, 349C1
Fined $3.8 mln 10-5, 767E3
LIFTON, Dr. Robert J.
Hearst trial testimony planned 2-4, 114C1
Testifies for Hearst 2-25—2-27, 202B1

1977

Sudan ties to be renewed 11-13, 874C2
Cuba mil aides cited 11-17, 896G1
Malta threatens defns pact 11-23, 925A3

Oil Developments—*See also OPEC*
US firms awarded damages 3-2, 488E1
'76 oil output rise rptd 3-21, 227G3
Differs from OPEC on oil price 6-29, 535E2, G2
US Sup Ct declines Hunt suit case review 12-5, 938E3

UN Policy & Developments
Assemb, Cncl member 4C1, E1
World Ct awards US cos damages 3-2, 488E1
World Ct to hear Tunisia Gabes dispute 6-10, 497E2
Shuns vote on UNEF extensn 10-21, 812A1
Shuns Medit pollutn mtg 10-21, 876B2
Cncl electns held 10-24, 852F3
S Africa econ, permanent arms sanctns vetoed; apartheid res OKd 10-31, 851G2
Envoys burn flag 11-19, 890A3
U.S. Relations
Boeing rpts consultant 1-5, ct backs secrecy 2-25, 215C3
US firms awarded damages 3-2, 488E1
Egypt seeks US arms 4-5, 245C1
US ties to intl terror groups 5-8, 380D1, G1
Sudan asks US arms 5-24, 400C1
Qaddafi urges closer ties 6-12, US sets terms 6-13, 488B1
Carter on Egypt conflict restraint 7-28, 574B3
US firms damages set 9-26, 772C2

LIDDY, G. Gordon
Carter commutes term 4-12, 325C3
Nixon-Frost interview 5-4, 366B2
Freed from prison 9-7, 725A1
Carter rpts no contact 10-27, 814D1

LIECHTENSTEIN
'76 jobless, GNP data rptd 4-4, 309E2
Women vote 4-17, 567C1
3 Swiss Credit Bank officers arrested 4-24, 350A3
Chiasso scandal spreads 4-26—6-20, new bank rules signed 6-27, 564D3, 565A1
Death sentence issued 11-26, 949F2
Helsinki Agreement—*See EUROPE—Security and Cooperation*

LIENDO, Brig. Gen. Horacio
Office bombed 10-26, 921C3
Scores econ min policies 11-6, 981C2
LIETZKE, Bruce
Wins Tucson, Hawaiian 1-16, 2-6, 104D1, E1
2d in Hope Desert Classic 2-13, 311C2
2d in Tourn of Champs 4-17, 676A1
PGA top money winner 10-30, 950G3
LIFE After Life (book)
On best-seller list 2-6, 120G3; 3-6, 184G3
LIFE Science Products Co.
Allied fine cut to $5 mln 2-1, 95C1

1978

OAU asks Chad border solutn 7-22, 561E1
2 Italian fishermen seized 7-30, 689G3
Jalloud in China 8-4—8-10; ties set, Taiwan links retained 8-9, 691F2
Iraq emb aide slain 8-16, 674D1
Arab fund loan to Sudan rptd 8-17, 925F3
Leb Moslem ldr arrives 8-25; rptd missing, Qaddafi link suspected 8-31; Beirut strike protest 9-15, 713B2
Castro visits, sees Qaddafi 9-19, 776G3
USSR A-power deal rptd 10-4, 821A1
Uganda-Tanzania mediatn offered 11-5, 860A2
W Ger terrorist suspects refuge seen 11-18, 906B2
Iran revolt support rptd 12-29, 993F2
Sports
Athletes attack Egypt players in Algiers 7-22; Egypt to boycott 7-24, 573C1

UN Policy & Developments
Cncl actn vs Israeli Leb invasn asked 197C2
ILO anti-Israel res defeat scored 6-27, 523E3
Assemb member 713B3

U.S. Relations
US revokes oil co tax credits 1-16, 69D1
Egypt seeks US arms 2-7, 78B1; US OKs F-5 jets 2-14, 97E1
US blocks plane sales 2-21, 139C2
Westinghouse Canada contract scored 6-1, 435F2

LI Chiang
On China-EC trade pact 4-3, 302E3
Visits Australia, gets favored trade status 10-11, 836A2
Signs China-France trade deal 12-4, 986A2
LICHTBLAU, John H.
Sees oil demand drop 6-5, 449F3
LICK Observatory (Calif.)
Galaxy surrounding BL Lacertae rptd 1-15, 293D2
LIEBERSON, Will
Dead End opens 5-4, 760G1
LIEBOWITZ, Samuel S.
Dies 1-11, 96F2

LIECHTENSTEIN—*See also COUNCIL of Europe*
Brunhart elected premier 2-3, 95B1
Swiss Credit plans Texon holdings sale 2-10, illegal deposits total rptd 3-1, 151G1-A2
Hosp Corp paymts conduit named 10-26, 876F3, 877B1
Eur Cncl OKs entry 10-29, 777D2
ITT paymts chrgd 11-2, 876B3
Helsinki Agreement—*See EUROPE—Security and Cooperation*
Sports
Wentzel wins world skiing title 2-5, 316G2
LIENDO, Gen. Horacio
Cabt replacemt seen 11-6, 865E2
LIETZKE, Bruce
2d in Tallahassee Open 4-16, 356A1
Wins Canadian Open 6-25, 580G3
LIEVANO Aguirre, Indalecio
Named Colombia forgn min 8-7, 629C3
Elected UN Assemb pres 9-19, 713F2
Uribe replaces as forgn min 9-22, 815A1
LIFE, Regge
Do Lord Remember Me opens 4-4, 887F1
LIGGETT Group Inc.
Philip Morris buys forgn operatns; US mkt share drop cited 7-26, 718C1
Servomation control won by GDV 8-31, 700A3
To buy SC Pepsi bottler 11-16, 1005C2
LIGHTNING—*See STORMS & Floods*

1979

Qaddafi scores Arafat 12-11; PLO offices closed 12-16, ties cut 12-22, 980C1

Oil & Gas Developments
Oil prices raised 2-21, 126D1-A2
Oil prices, surchrg hiked 3-27, 227C3
Oil prices hiked 5-16, 360A3; 5-29, 396D2
Turkey oil imports cited 6-5, 488A3
Oil prices hiked again 6-28, 473F1
Oil export halt threat rptd, clarified 6-29—6-30, 496B1
Spain oil imports rptd 7-4, gas imports forecast 7-10, 546F1, B2
Oil prices hiked above OPEC ceiling 10-15, 781C1
Algeria hikes prices 10-24, 864G1
US declines Hunt-Coastal States suit review 12-10, 988G1
Price per barrel rptd 12-21, hike set 12-28, 12-21, 977B2, C2

U.S. Relations
B Carter hosts group in US 1-9, alleged anti-Semitic remarks spur controversy 1-11—1-13, 31D2
US OKs plane sales 3-2, 250G1
B Carter confrms '78 trip funding 4-15, 310C1
US to challenge coastal sea claims 8-10, 646A3
US Mideast policy scored at Qaddafi fete; B Carter attends 9-1, 688B3, D3
DC Emb occupied 9-3, 688F2
US black group honors Qaddafi 9-16, 694B3
Iran US Emb hostage release aid offered 11-16, 878D3
Iran urged to free US Emb hostages, US warned vs mil actn 11-20, 895C3
US sets evacuatns, travel curbs 11-26, 894A2
US Emb attacked 12-2; protests lodged 12-2—12-3, diplomatic activity suspended 12-5, 914A3-915B1
US declines Hunt-Coastal States suit review 12-10, 988G1

LI Chiang
Announces econ cutback 5-6, 352E3
Initials US trade pact 5-14, 370A1
US trade pact signed 7-7, 523E2
LIEBERMAN, Nancy
Old Dominion wins AIAW basketball title 3-25, 239A1
Named top woman coll basketball player 3-29, 290F3
LIEBERSON, Will
Light Shines opens 1-11, 292G1
Men in White opens 7-11, 712E1
LIEBES, Ernesto
Kidnaped 1-17, killed 3-21, 234B3
LIEBMAN, Ron
Wins Emmy 9-9, 858D2
LIEBMAN, Steve
Big Bad Burlesque opens 8-14, 711E1
LIECHTENSTEIN—*See COUNCIL of Europe*
Helsinki Agreement—*See EUROPE—Security and Cooperation*
LIEKOSKI, Timo
Named NASL top coach 8-25, 776C1
Quits as Hurricane coach 9-17, hired by Drillers 9-19, 1004E2
LIEM, Dinh Nho
Offers China peace pact 6-28, Cambodia, Laos troop exit 7-5; rpts China talks failure 7-18, 536G3, 537B1
LIETZKE, Bruce
Wins Tucson Open 2-18, 220E3
Ties for 2d in Tourn of Champs 4-22, 587C2
PGA top money winner 11-30, 969F2
LIFE Insurance, American Council of
Sales practices defended 1-2, 15E3
LIFE Insurance Co. of Georgia
Dutch firm seeks 3-23, 942D2
LIFE of Lorena Hickok, The (book)
Reviewed 11-5, 860C1
LIGGETT Group Inc.
Ordrd to obey FTC subpoena 1-25, 91E3
C&O to buy US cigaret business 1-26, 283E1
C&O talks end 6-14, 517G1
LIGHT Airborne Multipurpose System (LAMPS)—*See ARMAMENTS—Aircraft*
LIGHT Shines in Darkness (play)
Opens 1-11, 292G1

1980

Exiles threatened in UK 6-12, envoy expelled 6-13, 463F2
Malta-Italy offshore oil project disputed 8-21; Malta expels mil advisers 8-28, 709E1-A2
Qaddafi proposes Syria merger 9-1, Syria OKs 9-2, 660C3
Syria merger talks 9-8—9-9, unity OKd 9-10; Arab backing sought 9-10, 697C1-C2
Begin: Syria unrest prompts merger move 9-9, 697D2
Leb missing Moslem ldr rptd jailed 9-9, 709B1
Map of Syria merger 9-10, 697A1
W Ger neo-Nazis links chrgd 9-30, 755D1
Syria denies troops fight Iraqis 10-7, 757E2
Iran backed vs Iraq, asks Saudi aid; Iraq cuts ties 10-10, 774A2
Saudis scored for US AWACS 10-19, cut ties 10-28, 820C3
Egypt chrgs Arab world split 11-1, 859B3
Sovt '79 arms sales rptd 12-10, 933A3
Chad capital occupied by troops 12-16, 965D1
Syria merger delayed 12-16—12-18, 978B2
OAU split on Chad war role 12-23—12-24, 979B1
Oil & Gas Developments
Oil min rptd ousted 1-8, 40D1
US, UK oil cutoff warned 5-9, 373A3
US oil co employes expelled 5-12, detained 5-13, 373F3
Oil price hike set 6-22, 435A3
Malta-Italy offshore project disputed 8-21, 709F1
Africa exports vowed 11-9, 864D2
UN Policy & Developments
Sovt Afghan res shunned 1-14, 25F2
Hq relocatn urged 4-27, 324D2

U.S. Relations
US closes emb 2-7, 198D2
US ousts 2 envoys 4-18, 353B3
Iran hostage rescue missn scored 4-27, 324D2
4 natls occupy DC Emb 5-2, leave US 5-11, 373F2
US shuts Tripoli Emb 5-5, 373F3
25 US natls expelled 5-12, 2 detained as spies 5-13, 373E3
B Carter registers as agent 7-14, 542A2; US Sen probe set 7-24, 548F2; for subsequent developments, see CARTER, Billy
Carter hits Reagan on A-arms 10-29, 816C2

LICAVOLI, James T.
Acquitted in FBI bribery case 7-3, 655D2
LI Ching-yung
Sentenced 5-15, 375D2
LICHTENSTEIN, Roy
Painting sold for record sum 5-15, 472A2
LIDDY, G. Gordon
Book excerpts reveal Anderson, Hunt death plots 4-21; Dean discounts 4-23, 333G2, E3
Will on best-seller list 6-8, 448C3
LIEB, Fred
Dies 6-3, 528D2
LIEBERMAN, Joseph I.
Loses US House electn 11-4, 848D1
LIEBERMAN, Nancy
Named top '79 female coll athlete 1-8, 104D1
Old Dominion wins AIAW basketball title 3-23, 240B3
Named top coll basketball player 3-26, 240G3
LIECHTENSTEIN—*See also COUNCIL of Europe, CSCE*
Sports
Lake Placid Olympic results 2-12—2-24, 154F2, 155F2-156D1
Wenzels win world skiing titles 3-2, 3-11, 469F3
Moscow Olympic stamp issue canceled 5-2, 379D2
IOC issues Olympic acceptance list 5-27, 420E3
LIEM, Dinh Nho
Quits China talks 2-8, 124E1
LIENEMANN, George
Viets capture 6-25, release 6-29, 508F2
LIETZKE, Bruce
Ties for 2d in Inverrary Classic 3-9, wins Colonial Natl 5-18, 412G2, G3
LIFE, A (play)
Opens 11-3, 892G3
LIFT Up The Name of Jesus (recording)
Blackwood Brothers win Grammy 2-27, 296E3
LIGGETT Group Inc.
Grand Met raises merger bid, Standard Brands quits 5-14; bid accepted 5-16, 557A3

1976

LI Hsien-nien
Chou En-lai dies 1-8, 8E3
Hua named 'acting' premr 2-7, 117C2
May Day CP unity rptd 5-2, 332E3
Cited as possible Mao successor 9-9—9-10, 658G1
Listed in China ldrshp 9-10, 712A1
At Hua rally 10-24; ranked as China ldr 10-25, 809F1
Scores Sovts 11-2, 11-15, 871C3
On Chiao's ouster 12-3, 904E2
LILIENTHAL, David E.
Urges A-materials export ban 1-19, 115B3
LI Lisan
Cited in Mao death announcemt 659B2
LILLEY, Robert D.
Announces AT&T retiremt 1-21, 160D2
LILLEY 3rd, William
Steel price rise study dropped 8-30, 646G3
On steel price hike 11-24, 12-2, 897G2, 898C1
LILLY, David M.
FRB member 4-26; confrmd 5-28, 412F1
LILOV, Alexander
On Bulgaria Politburo 4-2, 250D1
LIMA, Salvatore
Mafia ties alleged 2-5, 141C1
LIMB, Ben C. (Lim Pyong Jik)
Dies 9-21, 1015G1
LIM Pyong Jik—*See LIMB, Ben C.*
LINARES, Gen. Hugo
Bordaberry, 5 others get back pol rights 10-7, 814B3
LINCOLN, Ill.—*See ILLINOIS*
LINCOLN, Abraham (1809-65)
Ford State of Union message cites 1-19, 39A3
Quoted at Dem conv 7-12, 508F2
LINCOLN, Capt. Arthur
On Cadet immunity plea 8-27, 670C3
LINCOLN Bank (Philadelphia)
Buys Centennial Bank 10-21, 940G1
LINCOLN (Neb.) Journal (newspaper)
Ford endorsement rptd 10-30 831F2
LIND, Joan
Wins Olympic medal 7-24, 575F1
LIND, Ulrich
Wins Olympic medal 7-19, 575G1
LINDER, Staffan Burenstam
Named to Swedish Cabt 10-8, 794C2
LINDHOLM, William L.
Named AT&T pres 1-21, 160D2
LINDSAY, John V(liet)
Former aide slain 6-6, 442D3
Ex-aide buys The Nation 11-28, 901D3
LINDSTROM, Fred
Named to Hall of Fame 8-9, 816C1
LINH, Nguyen Van
On Populatn shift 12-15, 968B1
LINK, Gov. Arthur A. (R, N.D.)
Unopposed in primary 9-7, 687F3
Reelected 11-2, 820E3, 823E3, 831G1
LINOWITZ, Sol M.
Gives Vance Latin policy rpt 12-14; Brzezinski mtg rptd 12-19, 975B1
LIN Piao (1907-71)
'Deviationists' scored 2-6, 2-8, 117B2, G2
Cited in Mao biog, death announcemt 659E1, C2
Cited in Hua biog 758B1
LIN Yutang
Dies 3-26, 316D1
LIPIEN, Kazimier
Wins Olympic medal 7-24, 576G2
LIPINSKI, Edward
Polish charter chng protest cited 268E1
LIPPINCOTT, Joseph W.
Dies 10-22, 970C2
LIPPISCH, Alexander
Dies 2-11, 160E3
LIPSCOMB Jr., William Nunn
Wins Nobel Prize 10-18, 840E1
Criticizes Ford 10-26, 840B2
LIPSHUTZ, Robert J.
Carter campaign treas 7-20, 7-24, 565F3
'70 Carter campaign donor 10-17, 805A1
Rpts Carter campaign cost 11-17, 938F1-A3

1977

LI Hsien-nien
US congressmen in China 4-9—4-17, 298C2 ★
Asks industrial speedup 4-20, 449C2
Vows force vs Taiwan 7-4, 514B1
In Politburo post 8-21, 645F2
Vs US Taiwan stand 8-29, 664A3
Reaffirms anti-Taiwan stand 10-4, 780G3
LI Jong-ok
Name N Korea premier 12-15, 986C3
LIKHACHEV, Viktor Ivanovich
Urges A-test ban 2-15, 147D1
LILLIS, Harry—*See CROSBY, Bing*
LILLY, Eli
Dies 1-24, 84C3
LILLY & Co., Eli
Eli Lilly dies 1-24, 84C3
DNA patent order lifted 2-24, 184C2
DES Chicago suit filed 4-25, 431A3, E3
Endowmt funds Inuit conf 6-13—6-17, 619G2
Buys Ivac 7-20, 650E3
Pneumonia vaccine success rptd 10-26, 907E1
Nicholas Noyes dies 12-25, 1024E2
LILLY Endowment Inc.—*See LILLY & Co.*
LIMAYE, Madhu
Freed 2-7, 116A2
LINBECK Construction Corp.
Lawyer fees case refused 11-14, 878E3
LINCOLN, Abraham (1809-65)
Carter on cong ties 2-8, 88E3
Carter cites 5-22, 397F2
LINCOLN Conspiracy, The (book)
On best-seller list 11-6, 872F3
LINDBLAD, Paul
Sold 2-19, deal OKd 3-3, 310C3
LINDEN, Ronald
Davidson tenure policy chngd 5-6, 472A1
LINDINGER Ivory (Danish cargo ship)
Pirates raid 11-21, 986E2
LINDSAY, John V(liet)
NYC clean-air case review declined 10-17, 797D3
LINEHAN, John A.
Named amb to Sierra Leone 5-23, confrmd 6-23, 626A3
LINHARES, Marcelino
Scores govt re '78 pres vote 10-12, 840C1
LIN Li-Ming
Dies 8-19, 696A3
LINN, Dr. Robert
Liquid protein deaths rptd 11-9, 992D3
LINOWES, David F.
Privacy comm submits rpt 7-12, 632B1
LINOWITZ, Sol
Joins Panama Canal talks 2-8; opposed 2-21, suit vs rptd 3-16, quits bank bd 3-19, 379B1
Rpts Canal accord 8-10, begins ratificatn campaign 8-16, 621D1, 622C1
House com scores Canal pact 8-17, 622A2
Sees Reagan, Canal pacts scored 8-25, 678G2
Canal pact ratificatn campaign under way 9-7, 678G3
Testifies on Panama rights record 699E1
Lauds Torrijos on rights probes 9-13, 699A2
Testifies re Canal talks tap rpt 9-19, 716D2
Testifies at Sen Canal pact hearings 9-26, 754F2, B3
LIN Piao (1907-1971)
Plot vs Mao detailed 9-8, 694E2
LIPATI, Valentin
Addresses Helsinki review conf 10-4, 752B2
LIPPINCOTT, J. B.
Harper & Row purchase OKd 12-23, 1004D3
LIPSET, Seymour Martin
Surveys Carter Mideast policy 10-31, 831G1
LIPSHUTZ, Robert J.
Named Carter counsel 1-14, 35E2
On spec prosecutor bill 5-3, 338G1
Saw FBI rpt on Lance 9-12, 701E3
LIPSKI, Jan Jozef
Freed 6-8, 513D1

1978

LI Hsien-nien
Heads Congress meeting 2-25, 154D2
LI Huan
Kuomintang Party reshuffled 1-6, 38B2
LIKHACHEV, Viktor Ivanovich
Scores French disarmamt plan 1-31, 61C3
LILIENFELD, Dr. Abraham
Discounts Sovt emb microwave harm 11-20, 924G3, 925B1
LILIENTHAL, David E.
Eisenhower '47 oppositn to Nev A-test site rptd 12-18, 1012C1
LILIENTHAL, Peter
Calm Prevails released 4-6, 618E3
LILLIS Jr., Joseph H.
Coolest Cat opens 6-23, 760F1
LILLY, David
Vs discount rate hike 1-6, 28F1
LIMA, Manuel Ferreira
Sworn Portugal transport min 1-30, 91C3
LIME
EPA sets mfg plant rules 3-22, 263F2, A3
LIMJOCO, Antonio
Seized by PI rebels 1-20, 248C2
LINCOLN, Abraham (1809-65)
Carter State of Union Message 1-19, 30C1, 31C1
Letter given to U of Rochester 4-15, 335G2
LINCOLN Center for the Performing Arts (N.Y., N.Y.)
Rockefeller 3d dies 7-10, 620D3
LIND, Nathalie
Named Danish justice min 8-30, 688A1
LINDAHL, Hedda
Swedish dep soc welfare min 10-18, 822A3
LINDBERG, Lt. Cmdr. Arthur F.
2 Sovt spies sentncd 10-30, 835B2
LINDBERGH, Charles Augustus (Lucky) (1902-74)
3 Amer balloonists cross Atlantic 8-11—8-17, 652F3
LINDBLAD, Paul
Kuhn cancels Blue sale to Reds 1-30, 194C3
In World Series 10-10—10-17, 799C3
LINDBLOM, Gunnel
Summer Paradise released 3-11, 620A1
LINDER, Richard
Dies 4-16, 356B3
LINDO, Dean
Vows non-pol independnc talks 6-2, 478D2
LINDSTROM, Willy
Winnipeg wins WHA title 5-22, 458B2
LINEHAN, Kim
Sets 400-m freestyle mark 8-2, 780C1, E2
LINGOLD, Buford
Acquitted 4-21, 309E3
LINHART, Tony
NFL '77 kicking ldr 1-1, 56B2
NFC wins Pro Bowl 1-23, 56E1
LIN Hu-chia
Becomes Peking mayor 10-10, 773F3
LINICHUK, Natalia
Wins world figure-skating title 3-11, 316E3
LINK, Peter
Mighty Gents opens 4-16, 760E2
King of Hearts opens 11-22, 1031C2
LINK, Ron
Neon Woman opens 4-16, 760G2
LIN Piao (1907-71)
Cited for freedom lack 7-3, 532C2
Poster links to Mao 11-23, 949F1
LINSON, Art
Amer Hot Wax released 3-16, 618A3
LINTRAMI, Arialdo
Protests jail conditns, 5-28, 453A3
LIONS Club (Waseca, Minn.)
Griffith remarks cause furor 9-28—10-2, 779B2
LIONS International
Flood wins Pa club award 3-16, 240A3
LIPATI, Valentin
Scores Helsinki review conf 3-9, 179D2
LIPAVSKY, Sanya L.
CIA link rptd 3-6, 179D3
Slepak sentenced 6-21, 503G3
LIPPMANN, Walter
Carter cites in anti-inflatn plan 4-11, 260D2
LIPSHUTZ, Robert J.
Schindler vs US Mideast stand 3-9, 176A3
Rejects ABA legal aid plan 8-7, 626B2
LIPTON, James
Mighty Gents opens 4-16, 760E2
LIPTON Inc., Thomas J.
NASL Boston club awarded 1-5, 23C1

1979

LI Hsien-nien (Li Yiannian)
In Pak 1-20, vows aid vs 'aggressn' 1-22, 59C3
Hints at China Viet exit 3-1, 158G2
Speech on econ problems rptd 6-14, 444C3
Hua admits econ errors 6-18, 484F2
LI I-che
Rehabilitated 2-6, 134B3
LIMA, Mario Augusto Castro
Brazil health min designate 1-19, 95E1
LIMANN, Hilla (Ghanaian president)
Ghana pres runoff vote set 6-22, 485A3
Elected pres 7-10, vows anti-corruptn fight 7-11, 524F1
Inaugurated 9-24, 721C2
LIMON, Rafael (Bazooka)
Arguello TKOs 7-8, 839B1
LINDEN, Hal
When You Comin' Back released 2-8, 174F3
LINDNER, Carl H.
Settles SEC chrgs, repaymt set 7-2, 746A1
LINDO, Dean Russell
UDP Dec '78 munic electn win rptd 1-19, 78C1
Loses parlt seat 11-21, 907B1
LINDSAY, Maj. James
Ill papal mass crowd estimated 10-21, 931E2
LINDSAY, Joan
Picnic At Hanging Rock released 2-22, 174D3
LINDSAY, John Vliet
Scotto indicted 11-15, 890B2
LINDSAY-Hogg, Michael
Whose Life opens 4-17, 712E3
LINDSTROM, Willy
Winnipeg wins WHA title 5-20, 448B1, D1
LINICHUK, Natalia
Wins world figure-skating title 3-15, 392A1
LINIHAN, Rosaleen
Portrait of the Artist released 4-21, 528D3
LINOWITZ, Sol. M.
Visits Egypt, Israel as new Mideast envoy 12-8—12-12, 938A1
LIN Piao (d. 1971)
Blamed for attacks on business class 1-22, 75B2
Mao critics rehabilitated 8-3, 651D3
LIONELLO, Alberto
Till Marriage Do Us Part released 7-20, 820E3
LIPPE-Weissenfeld, Prince Alfred zur
Antiquities seized 9-14, resigns UN post 9-15 751E2
LIPSHUTZ, Robert J.
Resigns as pres counsel 8-10, 608C2
Cutler replaces 8-17, 623E1

1980

LI Honglin
Vs Hua '76 promotn 9-28, 788A3
LI Hsien-nien (Li Yiannian)
Visits Australia 5-7—5-11, 387F3
LIJEK, Cora A. (Mrs. Mark J.)
Escapes Iran 1-28, 66E2
LIJEK, Mark J.
Escapes Iran 1-28, 66E2
LILLY, Bob
Enters Pro Football HOF 8-2, 999A2
LILLY & Co., Eli
Nader coalitn attacks 4-17, 308B2
LIMA, Guillermo
Fails in hijack try 9-12, 704G1
LIMA, Jose A.
Kidnaped 6-17, ransom demand rptd 6-20, 487F2
Freed 9-10, 731B3
LIMANN, Hilla (Ghanaian president)
Meets Pope 5-8, 363B3
LIMAYE, Madhu
Vs new security decree 9-22, 729F2
LIMON, Rafael (Bazooka)
KOs Bethlemi for WBC super featherwgt title 12-11, 1001B1
LIN Biao (Piao) (d. 1971)
Gang of 4 trial set 9-27, delayed 11-1, 859B1
Kang, Xie purged 10-31, 859F1
Cited in Gang of 4 indictmt 11-15, 11-17, 877C1, D1, B2
Gang of 4 trial defendant 11-20—12-29; plot to kill Mao admitted 11-25, 975B2, E2
LINCOLN, Abraham (1809-65)
Reagan pres nominatn acceptance speech 7-17, 531D2, F2
Carter pres renominatn acceptance speech 8-14, 613A3
LINCOLN Center for the Performing Arts (N.Y., N.Y.)
Violinist found slain at the Met 7-24, 654A1; stagehand indicted 9-7, 713B1
Sills gives final performance 10-27, 908F2
LINCOLN Land Community College (Springfield, Ill.)
Carter speaks on energy 9-22, 722G2
LINDANE—*See PESTICIDES*
LINDEN, Allen
Convicts Hoffmann-La Roche 2-6, 116F2-C3
LINDSAY, John Vliet
Loses NY US Sen primary 9-9, 682C2
LINEHAN, Kim
Wins US Swimming titles 7-29—8-2, 834D3
LINGE, Heinz
Dies 3-17, 280A1
LINI, Walter (New Hebrides prime minister)
On New Hebrides separatist revolt 5-28, 422B3
New Hebrides declares independnc, named prime min 7-30, 580F3
LINICHUK, Natalia
Wins Olympic medal 2-17, 155F3
LINK, Gov. Arthur A. (D, N.D.)
Grain price support increase ordered 7-28, 575F1
Unopposed in primary 9-2, 683D1
Loses reelectn 11-4, 847C1, 851B2
LINK, Constance
Complete Critical Prose wins Amer Book Award 5-1, 692G2
LIN Liguo
Rpt plotted vs Mao 11-17, 877B2
Gang of 4 trial defendant 11-20—12-29; admits role in plot vs Mao 11-25, 975C2, E2
Wu regrets AF apptmt 11-23, 975D1
LINO, Edward
Indicted 3-3, 215E1
LINOWITZ, Sol M.
Sees Hussein re Palestinian autonomy 1-26, Sadat 1-29, W Bank notables 1-30, 89A2
Maps advance in autonomy talks 1-31—2-1; briefs Saudis 2-2, Moroccan king 2-4, 89F1-D2
Israel amb warns vs US anti-Israel vote at UN 3-1, 163A3
Burg misses Hebron setlmt vote 3-24, 218C3
Sees Begin, setlmt freeze, security talks opposed 3-25, 219G1-A2
Discounts deadline for autonomy talks 3-27, 219E1
Sees Sadat on autonomy talks delay 5-8, 362E1
Autonomy talks renewal OKd 7-2—7-3, 539C1
In Israel, Egypt; seeks autonomy talks renewal 9-1—9-3; Israel, Egypt OK 9-3, 660C2
Rpts progress in autonomy talks 10-15, 775A3
Says Reagan backs Camp David process, rpts on autonomy progress 12-7, 930B3
Begin, Sadat reaffirm Camp David process 12-18; lists differences 12-19, 952C3
LIN Zuopeng
Admits Lin Biao plot to kill Mao 11-25, 975C2
LIOPART, Jorge
Wins Olympic medal 7-30, 624C1
LIPIEN, Jozef
Wins Olympic medal 7-24, 624A3
LIPKIN, Semyon
Resignatn rptd 1-12, 47A1
LIPPOLD, Eberhard
Arrested as spy 11-10, 925G2
LIPPS, Inc. (singing group)
Funkytown on best-seller list 6-4, 448E3; 7-9, 568E3

1976

LISAGOR, Peter
Dies 12-10, 1015A2
LISCHKA, Kurt
Klarsfeld gets suspended sentnc 2-9, 158D1
LISMONT, Karel
Wins Olympic medal 7-31, 576E1
LI Ta-chang
Dies 5-3, 368G2
LI Teh-sheng
Listed in China ldrshp 9-10, 712B1

1977

LIQUEFIED Natural Gas (LNG)—*See GAS, Natural*
LIQUID Protein—*See FOOD*
LIQUOR—*See ALCOHOLIC Beverages*
LIST, Robert
Hughes Mormon will declared fake 4-15, 354B3
LISTER, Allen
On Bermuda riots 12-1—12-3, 935A3
LISTER, John
2d in Phila Classic 7-31, 676B2
LISTERINE—*See COSMETICS & Toiletries*
LI Teh-sheng
Liaoning unrest rptd 3-14, 220D1
In Politburo 8-21, 645G2

1978

LIQUEFIED Natural Gas (LNG)—*See GAS, Natural*
LIQUID Protein
Diet hazards rptd 6-26, 727G2
LIQUOR—*See ALCOHOLIC Beverages*
LISCHKA, Kurt
Chrgd for war crimes 7-24, 652C1
LISKA, Regina B. de—*See REGINA XI*
LISNER, Audrey
Screen Gems embezzlmt role cited 7-14, 599G2
LIST, Lt. Gov. Robert (D., Nev.)
Wins primary for gov 9-12, 736E2
Elected 11-7, 853G2, 857D1
LISTERINE—*See COSMETICS & Toiletries*
LISTON, Sonny (Charles) (1932-71)
Spinks decisns Ali 2-15, 171B2
Ali decisns Spinks for 3d heavywgt title 9-15, 726D1

1979

LIQUEFIED Natural Gas (LNG)—*See GAS, Natural*
LIRA, Johnny
Espana TKOs 8-4, 839C1
LIST, Gov. Robert (D, Nev.)
Orders A-dump closed 7-2, 519A2
Reopens A-dump 7-24, 561G2
Closes Beatty A-dump 10-22, 806A3, 885G3*-886A1

1980

LI Qiang
Signs US-China grain pact 10-22, 801A2
LIQUEFIED Natural Gas (LNG)—*See GAS, Natural*
LIRA, Raul
Escapes Colombia Emb attack 4-14, 294A1
LISCHKA, Kurt
Sentncd for WW2 crimes 2-11, 118F1
LISKER, Joel
Questions B Carter veracity, cites Libya cables 7-30—7-31; discounts Vesco role 7-30, 569D2, F2, 570C1, D1
Civiletti withheld B Carter info 8-6, 595B2
Testifies in B Carter probe 9-4, 700E3
LISNYANSKAYA, Inna
Resignatn rptd 1-12, 47A1

LITERATURE

1976

LITERATURE—*See also PUBLISHING*
Mackenzie King diaries publshd 1-1, 8C1
Exner sells serializatn 1-13, 80G2
Totalitarian Temptatn publicatn rptd 1-20, 119A3
Alger Hiss book review publshd 3-17, 218E1
Brooks admitted to Natl Arts Inst 5-19, 504C3
90 Minutes at Entebbe publshd 7-26, 547F1
Cong clears copyright revisns 9-30, 765E2; signed 10-19, 982G1
Giscard book published 10-11, 852C3
Furious Days publshd 11-4, 902E2
Agee chrgs UK on ouster 11-17, 946B3

Awards
Natl Book Awards presented 4-19, 292C3
Pulitzer Prizes 5-3, 352C3
Arts & Letters awards 5-19, 504C3
Bellow wins Nobel 10-21, 840D1
Prix Goncourt, Renaudot presented 11-15, 911G3

Best Sellers (fiction)
Agent in Place, MacInnes 12-5, 972E2
Boys From Brazil, Levin 12-5, 972F2
Choirboys, Wambaugh 1-25, 80B3; 2-29, 208E3; 12-5, 972E2
Crowned Heads, Tryon 12-5, 972F2
Curtain, Christie 1-25, 80B3; 2-29, 208E3; 12-5, 972F2
Deep, Benchley 12-5, 972E2
Dolores, Susann 12-5, 972E2
Eagle Has Landed, Higgins 12-5, 972G2
1876, Vidal 12-5, 972E2
Gemini Contenders, Ludlum 12-5, 972F2
Greek Treasure, Stone 1-25, 80B3; 12-5, 972F2
In The Beginning, Potok 1-25, 80B3; 2-29, 208E3; 12-5, 972G2
Nightwork, Shaw 12-5, 972G2
Ordinary People, Guest 12-5, 972F2
R Document, Wallace 12-5, 972G2
Ragtime, Doctorow 1-25, 80B3; 2-29, 208E3; 12-5, 972F2
Saving the Queen, Buckley 2-29, 208E3; 12-5, 972F2
Slapstick, Vonnegut 12-5, 972G2
Sleeping Murder, Christie 12-5, 972G2
Storm Warning, Higgins 12-5, 972A3
Stranger in the Mirror, Sheldon 12-5, 972E2
Touch Not the Cat, Stewart 12-5, 972F2
Trinity, Uris 12-5, 972E2
West End Horror, Meyer 12-5, 972A3

Best Sellers (general)
Adams Chronicles, Shepherd 12-5, 972D2
Adolf Hitler, Toland 12-5, 972D2
Angels, Graham 1-25, 80C3; 2-29, 208F3; 12-5, 972B2
Bring on Empty Horses, Niven 1-25, 80C3; 2-29, 208E3
Doris Day, Hotchner 2-29, 208F3; 12-5, 972B2
Final Days, Woodward & Bernstein 12-5, 972B2

1977

LITERATURE
US authors back Czech dissidents 1-19, 1-21, 82G2-A3
Kissinger sells memoirs 2-7, 131F1
Ford, wife plan memoirs 3-9, 236C3
Roots sources doubted 4-10, 4-22, 356B1
Biology text barred in Ind 4-14, 471E3
Mao's 5th volume publshd 4-15, 347B1
Child porno rptd 5-15—5-23, Chicago bookstore crackdown 5-20, 432D2, C3
Haley sued 5-24, 643D1
USSR scores Carrillo book 6-23, 507G1
Time to buy Book-of-the-Month 7-5, 519D2
E Ger arrests Bahro 8-23, ousts Ruchs 8-29, 684E1
USSR hosts intl book fair 9-6—9-14, 765C3
Berger's Govt by Judiciary published 10-31, 878E3

Awards
Natl Book Awards 4-11, 355G1
Pulitzer Prizes 4-18, 355C2
Aleixandre wins Nobel 10-6, 951F2
Prix Goncourt 11-21, 927F2

Best Sellers (fiction)
Beggarman, Thief, Shaw 12-4, 1021G2
Condominium, MacDonald 7-3, 548D3
Crash of '79, Erdman 2-6, 120E3; 3-6, 356C2; 4-3, 264F1; 5-1, 356C2; 6-4, 452G1; 7-3, 548D3; 8-14, 643F1; 9-4, 712C3
Daniel Martin, Fowles 11-6, 872D3; 12-4, 1021G2
Delta of Venus, Nin 8-14, 643F1; 9-4, 712D3; 10-2, 808D3
Dynasty, Elegant 10-2, 808D3
Falconer, Cheever 4-3, 264G1; 5-1, 356B2; 6-4, 452G1; 7-3, 583D3; 9-14, 643F1
Full Disclosure, Safire 9-4, 712D3
Honourable Schoolboy, le Carre 11-6, 872D3; 12-4, 1021G2
How to Save Your Own Life, Jong 5-1, 356C2
Illusions, Bach 8-14, 643F1; 9-4, 712C3; 10-2, 808D3
Immigrants, Fast 11-6, 872D2
Oliver's Story, Segal 4-3, 264F1; 5-1, 356B2; 6-4, 452G1; 7-3, 548D3
Raise the Titanic, Cussler 2-6, 120E3; 3-6, 184E3; 4-3, 264G1
Silmarillion, Tolkien 10-2, 808C3; 11-6, 872C3; 12-4, 1021F2
Sleeping Murder, Christie 2-6, 120E3; 3-6, 184E3
Storm Warning, Higgins 2-6, 120F3
Thorn Birds, McCullough 6-4, 452A2; 7-3, 548D3; 8-14, 643F1; 9-4, 712C3; 10-2, 808C3; 11-6, 872C3; 12-4, 1021F2
Trinity, Uris 2-6, 120E3; 3-6, 184E3; 4-3, 264F1; 5-1, 356C2; 6-4, 452A2
Users, Haber 3-6, 184E3

Best Sellers (general)
All Things Wise, Herriot 10-2, 808D3; 11-6, 872D3; 12-4, 1021G2
Blind Ambition, Dean 2-6, 120F3
Book of Lists, Wallechinsky, Wallace & Wallace 7-3, 548E3; 8-14, 643G1; 9-4, 712D3; 10-2, 808E3; 11-6, 872D3; 12-4, 1021G2
Camera Never Blinks, Rather & Herskowitz 9-4, 712E3
Changing, Ullman 4-3, 264A2; 6-4, 452A2

1978

LITERATURE—*See also POETRY*
Goebbels diary on W Ger best-seller list 1-2, 22C1
US sues CIA ex-analyst Snepp 2-15, 129C1
Haldeman book publicatn plans upset by Post scoop; installmts highlighted 2-16—2-17, 124G1-125E1
Gutenberg Bibles sold 3-10, 4-7, 295D2
Forsyth episode in 'Dogs' rptd staged 4-16, 335A3
'Holocaust' sales figures rptd 316D2
Garbo chrgs biog hoax 4-21, 335B3
Md obscenity rule review declined by Sup Ct 4-24, 322F2
Shevchenko '75 Knopf contract cited 4-26, 302B3
Nixon memoir excerpts publshd 4-30, 5-1, 319D2-320A2
Harvard revises curriculum 5-2, 348D2
CIA ex-agent's book publshd 5-8, 367A2-368C1
Honorable Men published in US 5-22, France 11-19, 917F1-C2
CIA ex-analyst Snepp to lose book profits 7-7, 527F2
Papal reforms cited 8-6, 601D2
Haldeman legal fees to exceed book profits 8-17, 844C1
Hauser book links CIA, American's death in Chile 9-12, 795D3
Alexander plagiarism suit vs Haley dismissed, Courlander suit cited 9-21, 759A3
Kenya writer freed 12-12, 968A2
Courlander suit vs Haley setld 12-14, 1029E3

Awards
Arts Institute honors 3 2-7, 316E1
Natl Book Awards 4-10, 315C2
Pulitzer Prizes 4-17, 315B1, C1
Singer wins Nobel 10-5, 886C1, F1-A2

Best Sellers (fiction)
Black Marble, Wambaugh 2-5, 116B3; 3-5, 195D3
Bloodline, Sheldon 3-5, 195D3; 4-2, 272A3; 4-30, 356F1; 6-4, 460B3; 7-2, 579B3; 8-6, 620A2; 9-4, 708B1
Chesapeake, Michener 8-6, 620A2; 9-4, 708B1; 10-9, 800A3; 11-6, 887F3; 12-3, 971A1
Daniel Martin, Fowles 1-8, 24D3
Evergreen, Plain 9-4, 708B1; 10-9, 800A3; 11-6, 887F3; 12-3, 971A1
Eye of the Needle, Follett 9-4, 708B1
Far Pavilions, Kaye 10-9, 800A3; 12-3, 971A1
Fools Die, Puzo 10-9, 800A3; 11-6, 887F3; 12-3, 971A1
Holcroft Covenant, Ludlum 4-30, 356F1; 6-4, 460B3; 7-2, 579C3; 8-6, 620A2
Honourable Schoolboy, le Carre 1-8, 24D3; 2-5, 116B3; 3-5, 195D3
Human Factor, Greene 4-30, 356G1; 6-4, 460B3
Illusions, Bach 1-8, 24D3; 2-5, 116B3
Scruples, Krantz 4-2, 272B3; 4-30, 356G1; 6-4, 460B3; 7-2, 579B3; 8-6, 620A2; 9-4, 708B1
Second Generation, Fast 10-9, 800A3; 11-6, 887F3
Silmarillion, Tolkien 1-8, 24C3; 2-5, 116A3; 3-5, 195D3; 4-2, 272B3
Stained Glass, Buckley 7-2, 579C3
Thorn Birds, McCullough 1-8, 24D3; 2-5, 116B3; 3-5, 195D3, 4-2, 272A3; 4-30, 356F1; 6-4, 460A3
War & Remembrance, Wouk 11-6, 887F3; 12-3, 971A1
Whistle, Jones 4-2, 272B3
Women's Room, French 7-2, 579C3; 8-6, 620A2

Best Sellers (general)
Adrien Arpel's 3-Week Crash Makeover, Arpel, Ebenstein 4-30, 356A2
All Things Wise, Herriot 1-8, 24D3; 2-5, 116B3; 3-5, 195E3; 4-2, 272C3
Amer Caesar, Manchester 10-9, 800B3; 11-6, 887G3; 12-3, 971B1
Amityville Horror, Anson 1-8, 24E3★; 2-5, 116C3; 3-5, 195E3
Book of Lists, Wallechinsky, Wallace & Wallace 1-8, 24E3; 3-5, 195E3
Coming into the Country, McPhee 2-5, 116C3

1979

LITERATURE
USSR authors issue censored works 1-18, 100B2
Bible availability in Sovt bloc rptd 3-13, 238E1
USSR authors rptd banned 4-6, 317A2
Masters & Johnson homosexual study publshd 4-23, 315F3-316D1
E Ger writer prosecutn rptd 4-25, 370C3; fined 5-22 406D2
Blake book sold for record sum 6-13, 672E1
Sullivan memoirs publicatn rptd set 6-24, 521B1
Talmudic study completed 7-14, 640G1
PEN Club cong ends 7-21, 553G3
USSR hosts 2d intl fair, 44 US books seized 9-4—9-10, 689E3-690C2
Harcourt Brace sues Goldwater 9-14, 859G3
S Africa censor ousted 10-5, 774A3
Yugo dissident fined 10-15, 838D2
Israel deletes Rabin book excerpt 10-22, 823F1
UK spy ring explored in Boyle book 10-28, 10-29, 873F3; 4th spy named 11-15, 908D2
Lorena Hickok biog rptd 11-5, 860C1
Iran '50s coup book recalled for 'correctns' 11-10, 886E3
'Brethren' publicatn stirs controversy 12-2, 988A2
USSR authors reinstatemt rejctd 12-17, Aksyonov hints union resignatn 12-19, 12-17, 980E2-A3

Awards & Honors
Tuchman Arts Inst pres 2-27, 176G1
Natl Book Awards 4-23, 356F1
Natl Book Award chngs set 6-27; writers protest, dirs defend 8-8, 8-9, 755F3-756C1
Elytis wins Nobel 10-18, 857G3
Pulitzer Prizes Awarded 4-16, 336C2
PEN Club joins book awards protest 11-25, 1007A2

Best Sellers (fiction)
Chesapeake, Michener 1-7, 80A3; 2-4, 120A3; 3-4, 173C3; 4-8, 271G1; 5-6, 356C2
Class Reunion, Jaffe 9-2, 672B3
Coup, Updike 2-4, 120B3
Dead Zone, King 10-14, 800A3; 11-4, 892B3
Dress Gray, Truscott 3-4, 173D3
Establishment, Fast 11-4, 892A3
Far Pavilions, Kaye 1-7, 80B3
Good as Gold, Heller 4-8, 271A2; 5-6, 356C2; 6-3, 432G1
Hanta Yo, Hill 6-3, 432A2
Island, Benchley 7-1, 548B3; 8-5, 620B3
Jailbird, Vonnegut 10-14, 800A3; 11-4, 892A3
Last Enchantment, Stewart 9-2, 672A3; 10-14, 800A3; 11-4, 892B3
Matarese Circle, Ludlum 4-8, 271G1; 5-6, 356C2; 6-3, 432G1; 7-1, 548A3; 8-5, 620A3; 9-2, 672A3
Overload, Hailey 2-4, 120B3; 3-4, 173D3; 4-8 271G1
Second Generation, Fast 1-7, 80A3
Shibumi, Trevanian 7-1, 548A3; 8-5, 620B3
Silmarillion, Tolkien 1-7, 80B3
Sophie's Choice, Styron 7-1, 548A3; 8-5, 620B3; 9-2, 672A3; 10-14, 800B3
SS—GB, Deighton 5-6, 356C2
Stories of John Cheever, Cheever 2-4, 120B3; 3-4, 173D3
Third World War: Aug 1985, Hackett 6-3, 432A2; 7-1, 548B3; 8-5, 620B3; 9-2, 672B3
Triple, Follett 10-14, 800B3; 11-4, 892B3
War & Remembrance, Wouk 1-7, 80A3; 2-4, 120A3; 3-4, 173C3; 4-8 271G1; 5-6, 356C2; 6-3, 432A2

Best Sellers (general)
American Caesar, Manchester 1-7, 80C3; 2-4, 120C3; 3-4, 173E3
Aunt Erma's Cope Book, Bombeck 11-4, 892C3
Broca's Brain, Sagan 9-2, 672C3
Bronx Zoo, Lyle, Golenbock 7-1, 548C3; 8-5, 620D3; 5-6, 356D2; 6-3, 432B2
Cruel Shoes, Martin 6-3, 432B2; 7-1, 548B3; 8-5, 620C3; 9-2, 672B3; 10-14, 800C3
Distant Mirror, Tuchman 1-7, 80B3; 2-4, 120C3; 3-4, 173E3

1980

LITERATURE
E Ger author rptd arrested 1-4, 57C2
2 poets quit Sovt Writers Union re Metropole controversy 1-12, 46G3
Hellman sues McCarthy 2-15, 199E2
Snepp CIA disclosure limits upheld by Sup Ct 2-19, 130C3
CIA ex-agent Stockwell sued re Angola book 3-3, 268A3
'Scarsdale Diet' MD slain 3-10, 214E3
Cuban dissident poet emigrates to US 3-16, 231A3
Justice Dept suit vs Agee OKd 4-1, 268E2
Snepp rehearing denied by Sup Ct 4-14, 307F1
Sovt authors plan emigratn 4-16, 4-17, 326B3
Agnew notes book 4-20, 333D3, E3
Liddy book excerpts publshd 4-21, 333G2, E3
Snepp novel rptd submitted for CIA OK 6-13, 517A1
Donated porno warrants required by Sup Ct 6-20, 555G2
Stockwell settles suit 6-25, 516D3-517A1
Aksyonov leaves Moscow for US 7-22, 566E3
Hoffman autobiog publshd 9-2, 713E2
Agee profits denial refused by ct 10-2, 990G2
Inventory tax ruling impact rptd 10-5, 836B1
Australia bans book on US ties 11-9, 885D1; High Ct upholds 12-1, 919E2
Da Vinci ms sold for $5.28 mln 12-12, 997E3

Awards & Honors
Yourcenar elected to French Acad 3-6, 471G2
Pulitzer Prizes 4-14, 296B2
Amer Book Awards 5-1, 692E1
Milosz wins Nobel 10-9, 889D2
Amer Book Awards revamped 10-19, 906A2
Malamud elected to Arts Inst 12-5, 998C1

Best Sellers (fiction)
Bourne Identity, Ludlum 3-9, 200A3; 5-4, 359C3; 6-8, 448B3; 7-13, 568B3; 8-17, 640E3
Come Pour the Wine, Freeman 12-7, 948D3
Covenant, Michener 12-7, 948D3
Devil's Alternative, Forsyth 2-10, 120B3; 3-9, 200A3; 4-6, 280B3; 5-4, 359C3; 6-8, 448B3
Executioner's Song, Mailer 1-13, 40B3
Fanny, Jong 9-14, 716B3; 10-12, 796D3
Fifth Horseman, Collins, Lapierre 10-12, 796D3; 12-7, 948D3
Firestarter, King 9-14, 716B3; 10-12, 796C3; 12-7, 948D3
Innocent Blood, James 7-13, 568B3
Jailbird, Vonnegut 1-13, 40A3; 2-10, 120C3
Kane & Abel, Archer 8-17, 640E3
Key to Rebecca, Follett 10-12, 796C3; 12-7, 948D3
Last Enchantment, Stewart 1-13, 40B3
No Lost Love, Van Slyke 5-4, 359C3; 6-8, 448B3
Portraits, Freeman 3-9, 200B3; 4-6, 280B3; 5-4, 359C3
Princess Daisy, Krantz 2-10, 120B3; 3-9, 200A3; 4-6, 280A3, 5-4, 359C3, 6-8, 448B3
Rage of Angels, Sheldon 7-13, 568A3; 8-17, 640E3; 9-14, 716A3; 10-12, 796D3
Random Winds, Plain 6-8, 448B3; 7-13, 568B3; 8-17, 640E3; 9-14, 716B3
Smiley's People, Le Carre 1-13, 40A3; 2-10, 120B3; 3-9, 200B3; 4-6, 280B3
Spike, De Borchgrave, Moss 7-13, 568B3; 8-17, 640E3; 9-14, 716B3
Triple, Follet 1-13, 40B3; 2-10, 120C3

Best Sellers (general)
All You Need to Know About the IRS, Strassels, Wool 4-6, 280C3; 5-4, 359E3
Anatomy of an Illness, Cousins 2-10, 120C3; 3-9, 200C3; 5-4, 359E3
Aunt Erma's Cope Book, Bombeck 1-13, 40B3; 2-10, 120C3; 3-9, 200C3
Brethren, Woodward, Armstrong 1-13, 40B3; 2-10, 120C3; 3-9, 200B3; 4-6, 280C3
Cosmos, Sagan 12-7, 948E3
Crisis Investing, Casey 9-14, 716B3; 10-12, 796D3; 12-7, 948E3

1976

Fire and Ice, Tobias 12-5, 972D2
Loretta Lynn, Lynn 12-5, 972D2
Lyndon Johnson, Kearns 12-5, 972C2
Man Called Intrepid, Stevenson 12-5, 972A2
Memoirs, Williams 12-5, 972D2
Passages, Sheehy 12-5, 972B2
Power, Korda 12-5, 972D2
Relaxation Response, Benson 1-25, 80C3; 2-29, 208F3; 12-5, 972C2
Right & the Power, Jaworski 12-5, 972D2
Rockefellers, Collier & Horowitz 12-5, 972C2
Roots, Haley 12-5, 972D2
Russians, Smith 12-5, 972B2
Scoundrel Time, Hellman 12-5, 972B2
Spandau, Speer 12-5, 972C2
Sylvia Porter's Money Book, Porter 1-25, 80C3; 12-5, 972D2
Winning Through Intimidation, Ringer 1-25, 80C3; 2-29, 208F3; 12-5, 972C2
World of Our Fathers, Howe 12-5, 972A2
Year of Beauty, Sassoon 12-5, 972B2
Your Erroneous Zones, Dyer 12-5, 972C2

Best Sellers (mass market paperback)
Aspen, Hirschfeld 2-29, 208F3
Centennial, Michener 1-25, 80D3; 2-29, 208F3
Furies, Jakes 1-25, 80D3; 2-29, 208F3
Helter Skelter, Bugliosi, Gentry 1-25, 80C3; 2-29, 208F3
Lady, Tryon 1-25, 80D3
Moneychangers, Hailey 2-29, 208F3
Total Woman, Morgan 1-25, 80D3

Foreign Censorship—*See country names*
Obituaries
Bjoerneboe, Jens 5-9, 404F1
Bosco, Henri 5-4, 368E2
Christie, Agatha 1-12, 56B3
Dennis, Patrick 11-6, 970E1
Gallico, Paul 7-15, 716B3
Hopper, Vincent 1-19, 56D3
Hughes, Richard 4-28, 368F2
Joseph, Richard 9-30, 970B2
Leaf, Munro 12-21, 1015G1
Lin Yutang 3-26, 316D1
Lippincott, Joseph 10-22, 970C2
MacInnes, Colin 4-22, 524A3
Malraux, Andre 11-23, 970D2
Millet, Fred 1-1, 56F3
Morand, Paul 7-23, 970F2
Morison, Samuel 5-15, 368G2
Rascovich, Mark 12-10, 1015D2
Roy, Mike 6-26, 524E3
Sansom, William 4-20, 524E3
Schoonmaker, Frank 1-11, 56F3
Smith, H Allen 2-23, 192G3
Stern, Susan 7-31, 892F3
Streeter, Edward 3-7, 484G3
Tolstoy, Mary 11-21, 970C3
Villegas, Daniel 3-10, 240G3
Weingarten, Violet 7-17, 716G3

1977

Complete Book Of Running, Fixx 12-4, 1021A3
Dragons of Eden, Sagan 7-3, 548E3; 8-14, 643G1; 9-4, 712E3; 10-2, 808E3; 11-6, 872E3
Gamesman, Maccoby 4-3, 264A2; 5-1, 356C2
Gnomes, Huygen 12-4, 1021A3
Grass is Always Greener, Bombeck 3-6, 184F3
Haywire, Haywood 5-1, 356D2; 6-4, 452A2; 7-3, 548E3
Hite Report, Hite 2-6, 120F3; 3-6, 184F3
It Didn't Start with Watergate, Lasky 8-14, 643A2
Looking Out for Number One, Ringer 8-14, 643A2; 9-4, 712E3; 10-2, 808E3; 11-6, 872D3; 12-4, 1021A3
Passages, Sheehy 2-6, 120F3; 3-6, 184F3; 4-3, 264A2; 5-1, 356C2; 6-4, 452A2; 7-3, 548E3
Roots, Haley 2-6, 120F3; 2-20, 118E3; 3-6, 184F3; 4-3, 264G1; 5-1, 356C2; 6-4, 452A2
Six Men, Cooke 11-6, 872E3
Your Erroneous Zones, Dyer 2-6, 120E3; 3-6, 356C2; 6-4, 452A2; 4-3, 264G1; 5-1, 356C2; 7-3, 548E3; 8-14, 643G1; 10-2, 808E3

Best Sellers (mass market paperback)
Auctioneer, Samson 3-6, 184G3
Audrey Rose, DeFelitta 2-6, 120G3
Boys from Brazil, Levin 4-3, 264A2
Carrie, King 2-6, 120G3
Ceremony of Innocent, Caldwell 11-6, 872F3
Crash of '79, Erdman 12-4, 1021A3
Deep, Benchley 6-4, 452B2; 7-3, 548F3
Dolores, Susann 6-4, 452B2; 7-3, 548F3
Elvis, Dunleavy 10-2, 808F3
Final Days, Woodward & Bernstein 2-6, 120G3; 3-6, 184G3
Golden Gate, MacLean 7-3, 548F3
Grass is Always Greener, Bombeck 10-2, 808F3
Hite Report, Hite 5-1, 356D2; 6-4, 452B2; 7-3, 548F3
Kinflicks, Alther 4-3, 264A2; 5-1, 356D2
Life after Life, Moody 2-6, 120G3; 3-6, 184G3
Lincoln Conspiracy, Balsiger & Sellier 11-6, 872F3
Lonely Lady, Robbins 4-3, 264A2; 5-1, 356D2; 6-4, 452B2
Mavreen, Lorrimer 3-6, 184G3
Moonstruck Madness, McBain 3-6, 184G3; 4-3, 264B2
Once an Eagle, Myrer 2-6, 120G3
Ordinary People, Guest 9-4, 712F3
Other Side of Midnight, Sheldon 8-14, 643A2; 9-4, 712F3
Passages, Sheehy 7-3, 548F3; 8-14, 643A2; 9-4, 712E3; 10-2, 808F3; 11-6, 872F3; 12-4, 1021A3
Pride of the Peacock, Holt 8-14, 643A2
Raise the Titanic, Cussler 11-6, 872E3; 12-4, 1021A3
Roots, Haley 12-4, 1021A3
Star Wars, Lucas 8-14, 643A2; 10-2, 808F3
Stranger in the Mirror, Sheldon 4-3, 264A2; 5-1, 356D2
Touch Not the Cat, Stewart 9-4, 712F3
Trinity, Uris 10-2, 808E3
Users, Haber 8-14, 643A2
Warriors, Jakes 5-1, 356D2; 6-4, 452B2
Your Erroneous Zones, Dyer 11-6, 872E3; 12-4, 1021A3

Obituaries
Bissell, Richard 5-4, 452D2
Cain, James 10-27, 872C1
Carr, John Dickson 2-27, 164D2
Dahlberg, Edward 2-27, 164E2
DuBois, Shirley Graham 3-27, 356A3
Eiseley, Loren 7-9, 604A3
Fedin, Konstantin 7-15, 604A3
Foley, Martha 9-5, 788A1
Habe, Hans 9-30, 788C1
Hellman, Geoffrey 9-26, 788C1
Herberg, Will 3-27, 264G2
Holloway, Emory 7-30, 604B3
Jones, James 5-9, 452C3
Kantor, MacKinlay 10-11, 872D2
Nabokov, Vladimir 7-2, 604E3
Nin, Anais 1-14, 84D3
Rostand, Jean 9-3, 788D2
Sandburg, Lillian 2-18, 164E3 ★
Schorer, Mark 8-11, 696F3
Schumacher, E F 9-4, 788D2
Shipton, Eric 3-28, 264F3
Untermeyer, Louis 12-18, 1024E3
Vorhees, Melvin 2-6, 164F3 ★
Wheatley, Dennis 11-11, 952G3
White, Katherine 7-20, 604G3
Winslow, Ola Elizabeth 9-27, 788B3
Woodham-Smith, Cecil 3-16, 264G3

1978

Complete Book of Running, Fixx 1-8, 24E3; 2-5, 116D3; 3-5, 195E3; 4-2, 272B3; 4-30, 356G1; 6-4, 460C3; 7-2, 579C3; 8-6, 602B2; 9-4, 708C1; 10-9, 800B3; 11-6, 888A1
Distant Mirror, Tuchman 10-9, 800C3; 11-6, 887G3; 12-3, 971B1
Ends of Power, Haldeman, DiMona 4-2, 272B3
Gnomes, Huygen, Poortvliet 1-8, 24E3; 3-5, 195E3; 4-2, 272C3; 4-30, 356A2; 12-3, 971B1
If Life Is a Bowl of Cherries, Bombeck 4-30, 356G1; 6-4, 460B3; 7-2, 579C3; 8-6, 620A2; 9-4, 708B1; 10-9, 800C3; 11-6, 887G3; 12-3, 971B1
In Search of History, White 9-4, 708C1; 10-9, 800B3; 11-6, 888A1
Mommie Dearest, Crawford 12-3, 971A1
My Mother/My Self, Friday 4-2, 272C3; 4-30, 356A2; 6-4, 460C3; 7-2, 579D3; 8-6, 620B2; 9-4, 708C1
Pulling Your Own Strings, Dyer 6-4, 460C3; 8-6, 620B2; 9-4, 708C1
RN: Memoirs of Richard Nixon, Nixon 6-4, 460C3; 7-2, 579D3; 8-6, 620B2
Running and Being, Sheehan 7-2, 579D3
Second Ring of Power, Castaneda 2-5, 116C3; 3-5, 195E3

Best Sellers (mass market paperback)
All Things Wise, Herriot 10-9, 800C3; 12-3, 971C1
Amityville Horror, Anson 9-4, 708D1; 10-9, 800D3
Attachments, Rossner 9-4, 708D1
Beggarman, Thief, Shaw 9-4, 708D1
Book of Lists, Wallechinsky, Wallace & Wallace 4-2, 272C3
Centennial, Michener 11-6, 888B1; 12-3, 971C1
Close Encounters, Spielberg 1-8, 24F3; 2-5, 116D3; 3-5, 195F3
Coma, Cook 1-8, 24F3; 2-5, 116C3; 3-5, 195F3; 4-2, 272C3; 4-30, 356B2
Crash of '79, Erdman 1-8, 24F3
Dare to Love, Wilde 4-2, 272D3; 4-30, 356B2
Dragons of Eden, Sagen 6-4, 460D3
Dreams Die First, Robbins 9-4, 708D1
Dynasty, Elegant 10-9, 800D3
Full Disclosure, Safire 8-6, 620C2
Ghost of Flight 401, Fuller 4-2, 272D3
Hobbit, Tolkien 2-5, 116D3
Immigrants, Fast 11-6, 8888B1
Investigation, Uhnak 6-4, 460D3
Jaws 2, Searls 6-4, 460C3; 7-2, 579D3; 8-6, 620C2
Lawless, Jakes 4-30, 356A2; 6-4, 460D3; 7-2, 579D3
Looking Out For Number #1, Ringer 7-2, 579E3; 8-6, 620C2
My Mother/My Self, Friday 11-6, 888A1; 12-3, 971C1
Oliver's Story, Segal 4-30, 356B2
Passages, Sheehy 1-8, 24F3
Promise, Steel 6-4, 460D3
Seawitch, Maclean 8-6, 620C2
Shining, King 2-5, 116D3; 3-5, 195F3
Thorn Birds, McCullough 7-2, 579D3; 8-6, 620B2; 9-4, 708D1; 10-9, 800C3; 11-6, 888B1; 12-3, 971C1
Twins, Wood & Geasland 7-2, 579E3
Women's Room, French 11-6, 888A1; 12-3, 971C1
Your Erroneous Zones, Dyer 1-8, 24F3; 2-5, 116C3; 3-5, 195F3; 4-2, 372D3; 4-30, 356B2

Obituaries
Baldwin, Faith 3-19, 252C2
Bieber, Margarete 2-25, 196C2
Borland, Hal 2-22, 196C2
Busic, Bruno 10-16, 805A2
Catton, Bruce 8-28, 708C2
Chase, Ilka 2-15, 196E2
Cozzens, James Gould 8-9, 708D2
De Madariaga, Salvador 12-14, 1032E2
Evans, Bergen 2-4, 196G2
Flanner, Janet 11-7, 972A3
Highet, Gilbert 1-20, 96C2
Kuo Mo-jo 6-12, 504B3
Lawrence, Josephine 2-22, 196D3
Leavis, Frank Raymond 4-14, 356B3
Martinson, Harry E 2-11, 196D3
Mason, F van Wyck 8-28, 708B3
Scott, Paul 3-1, 252E3
Shaw, Robert 8-28, 708D3
Utely, Freda 1-21, 96F3
Williams, Jay 7-12, 620G3
Wilson, Michael 4-9, 356G3

1979

Faeries, Froud, Lee 1-7, 80C3
Gnomes, Huygen, Poortvliet 1-7, 80B3*; 2-4, 120C3
How To Prosper, Ruff 4-8, 271A2; 5-6, 356D2; 8-5, 620C3; 9-2, 672C3; 10-14, 800B3; 11-4, 892C3
Lauren Bacall By Myself, Bacall 2-4, 120B3; 3-4, 173D3; 4-8 271A2; 5-6, 356D2
Mommie Dearest, Crawford 1-7, 80B3; 2-4, 120B3; 3-4, 173E3; 4-8 271B2
Powers That Be, Halberstam 6-3, 432B2; 7-1, 548C2
Pritikin Program, Pritikin, McGrady 6-3, 432B2; 7-1, 548C3; 8-5, 620C3; 9-2, 672C3; 10-14, 800C3
Restoring American Dream, Ringer 10-14, 800C3; 11-4, 892C3
Right Stuff, Wolfe 11-4, 892C3
Scarsdale Diet, Tarnower, Baker 3-4, 173E3; 4-8, 271A2; 5-6, 356C2; 6-3, 432A2; 7-1, 548B3; 8-5, 620C3; 9-2, 672C3; 10-14, 800B3; 11-4, 892B3
Sophia, Hotchner 4-8, 271A2; 5-6, 356D2

Best Sellers (mass market paperback)
Alien, Foster 7-1, 548D3
Amityville Horror, Anson 1-7, 80D3; 2-4, 120D3; 9-2, 672D3
Bloodline, Sheldon 3-4, 173F3; 4-8, 271B2; 5-6, 356E2; 7-1, 548D3
Centennial, Michener 1-7, 80D3
Chesapeake, Michener 10-14, 800C3; 11-4, 892D3
Evergreen, Plain 8-5, 620D3; 9-2, 672D3; 10-14, 800D3
Eye of the Needle, Follett 8-5, 620D3
Far Pavilions, Kaye 9-2, 672C3; 10-14, 800D3
Final Payments, Gordon 2-4, 120D3
Fools Die, Puzo 11-4, 892C3
Holcroft Covenant, Ludlum 3-4, 173F3; 4-8 271C2
Human Factor, Greene 3-4, 173F3
If Life is a Bowl of Cherries, Bombeck 4-8, 271B2; 5-6, 356E2; 6-3, 432C2
Immigrants, Fast 1-7, 80D3
Insiders, Rogers 2-4, 120C3; 3-4, 173F3
Mortal Friends, Carroll 7-1, 548D3
My Mother/My Self, Friday 1-7, 80C3; 2-4, 120C3; 4-8 271B2; 6-3, 432C2
Nurse, Anderson 11-4, 892D3
Pulling Your Own Strings, Dyer 10-14, 800D3; 11-4, 892D3
Scruples, Krantz 6-3, 432C2; 7-1, 548C3; 8-5, 620D3
Second Generation, Fast 10-14, 800C3; 11-4, 892D3
Silmarillion, Tolkien 4-8, 271C2
Sisters & Strangers, Van Slyke 9-2, 672D3
Tears of Gold, McBain 5-6, 356E2; 6-3, 432C2
Wifey, Blume 8-5, 620D3; 9-2, 672D3
Women's Room, French 1-7, 80C3; 2-4, 120D3; 3-4, 173F3; 5-6 356E2
World According to Garp, Irving 5-6, 356E2; 6-3, 432C2; 7-1, 548C2; 8-5, 620D3

Obituaries
Ardizzone, Edward Jeffrey 11-8, 932B2
Bishop, Elizabeth 10-6, 860B2
Farrell, James T 8-22, 671C2
Goldman, Pierre 9-20, 772E2
Hayward, Max 3-18, 272F2
Jouhandeau, Marcel 4-7, 356E3
Kahn, Albert E 9-15, 756E2
Kuznetsov, Anatoly V 6-13, 508C3
Marques, Rene 3-22, 272B3
Monsarrat, Nicholas 8-7, 671A3
Perelman, S J 10-17, 860C3
Rhys, Jean 5-14, 432E3
Richards, I A 9-7, 756D3
Simonov, Konstantin 8-28, 671E3
Skinner, Cornelia Otis 7-9, 588D3
Stafford, Jean 3-26, 272F3
Tate, Allen 2-9, 176G3
Tolstoy, Alexandra 9-26, 756E3
Van Slyke, Helen 7-3, 588F3
Velikovsky, Immanuel 11-17, 932F3
Waltari, Mika 8-26, 671G3
Williams, T Harry 7-6, 588G3

1980

Cruel Shoes, Martin 1-13, 40C3
Donahue, Donahue 3-9, 200C3; 4-6, 280C3; 5-4, 359D3
Free to Choose, Friedman 3-9, 200B3; 4-6, 280B3; 5-4, 359D3; 6-8, 448C3; 7-13, 568C3; 8-17, 640F3; 9-14, 716C3; 10-12, 796E3
Gourmet Diet, Clairborne, Franey 10-12, 796E3
James Herriot's Yorkshire, Herriot 1-13, 40C3; 2-10, 120D3
Little Gloria, Goldsmith 8-17, 640F3; 9-14, 716C3
Men in Love, Friday 6-8, 448C3; 7-13, 568C3; 8-17, 640F3
Music for Chameleons, Capote 9-14, 716C3; 10-12, 796E3
Peter the Great, Massie 12-7, 948E3
Pritikin Program, Pritikin, McGrady 2-10, 120D3; 4-6, 280C3
Real War, Nixon 7-13, 568C3
Shelley, Winters 8-17, 640F3; 9-14, 716B3; 10-12, 796E3
Side Effects, Allen 12-7, 948E3
Sky's the Limit, Dyer 12-7, 948E3
Third Wave, Toffler 5-4, 359D3; 6-8, 448C3; 7-13, 568C3
Thy Neighbor's Wife, Talese 6-8, 448C3; 7-13, 568B3; 8-17, 640F3
White House Years, Kissinger 1-13, 40C3
Will, Liddy 6-8, 448C3

Best Sellers (mass market paperbacks)
Americans, Jakes 3-9, 200C3; 4-6, 280D3
Bright Flows the River, Caldwell 1-13, 40D3
Chesapeake, Michener 1-13, 40D3
Class Reunion, Jaffe 7-13, 568D3
Dead Zone, King 8-17, 640G3; 9-14, 716C3
Empire Strikes Back, Glut 7-13, 568D3
Establishment, Fast 10-12, 796F3; 12-7, 948F3
Fools Die, Puzo 1-13, 40D3
Ghost Story, Straub 5-4, 359E3; 6-8, 448D3
Green Ripper, MacDonald 6-8, 448D3
How To Prosper, Ruff 2-10, 120E3; 3-9, 200D3
Island, Benchley 4-6, 280D3
Lauren Bacall By Myself, Bacall 2-10, 120D3
Lost Love, Last Love, Rogers 12-7, 948F3
Matarese Circle, Ludlum 3-9, 200G3; 4-6, 280D3
Memories of Another Day, Robbins 9-14, 716D3; 10-12, 796F3
Mommie Dearest, Crawford 1-13, 40C3
Necessary Woman, Van Slyke 5-4, 359E3
Oregon, Ross 5-4, 359F3
Overload, Hailey 2-10, 120D3
Petals on the Wind, Andrews 7-13, 568C3; 8-17, 640G3; 9-14, 716D3
Portraits, Freeman 12-7, 948F3
Scarsdale Diet, Tarnower, Baker 2-10, 120D3; 3-9, 200C3; 4-6, 280D3; 5-4, 359E3; 6-8, 448D3
Shibumi, Trevanian 7-13, 568D3; 8-17, 640G3
Shogun, Clavell 10-12, 796E3
Sophie's Choice, Styron 8-77, 640G3; 9-14, 716D3; 10-12, 796F3
Spring of the Tiger, Holt 6-8, 448D3
SS-GB, Deighton 4-6, 280D3
Stand, King 2-10, 120E3; 3-9, 200C3
Star Trek, Roddenberry 1-13, 40C3
Third World War: Aug 1985, Hackett 5-4, 359F3
Triple, Follett 12-7, 948F3
Unholy Child, Breslin 12-7, 948F3
War & Remembrance, Wouk 6-8, 448D3
Woman of Substance, Bradford 7-13, 568D3; 8-17, 640G3; 9-14, 716C3; 10-12, 796F3

Obituaries
Adamson, Joy 1-3, 104D1
Agar, Herbert 11-24, 928F1
Alsop, Mary 10-14, 876A1
Andersch, Alfred 2-21, 279C1
Anson, Jay 3-12, 279C1
Ardrey, Robert 1-14, 104E1
Arnold, Elliot 5-13, 448B1
Barthes, Roland 3-25, 279D1
Beaton, Cecil 1-18, 104F1
Bernays, Doris 7-11, 608D1
Braly, Malcom 4-7, 360C1
Brand, Millen 3-19, 279F1
Cane, Melville H 3-10, 279G1
Collier, John 4-6, 360D1
Farago, Ladislas 10-15, 876D1
Fromm, Erich 3-18, 279G2
Gary, Romain 12-2, 1004G1
Griffin, John Howard 9-9, 755C3
Grubb, David Alexander 7-24, 608A2
Gunning, Robert 2-29, 279C3
Johnson, Gerald W 3-23, 279F3
Jones, Howard Mumford 5-11, 448A2
Kronenberger, Louis 4-30, 360C2
Laye, Camara 2-4, 176C2
Levenson, Sam 8-27, 676G1
Mandelstam, Nadezhda 12-29, 1004E2
McLuhan, Marshall 12-31, 1004F2
Miller, Henry 6-7, 528F2
Patterson, William L 3-5, 280F1
Porter, Katherine Anne 9-18, 756G1
Randall Jr, John H 12-1, 1004B3
Sartre, Jean-Paul 4-15, 360C3
Snow, C P 7-1, 608D3
Stewart, George R 8-22, 676C3
Tarnower, Herman 3-10, 214E3
Teale, Edwin Way 10-18, 876D3
Trask, Willard R 8-10, 676D3
Travers, Ben 12-18, 1004D3
Tynan, Kenneth 7-26, 608E3
Wright, James 3-25, 280G2

1976

LITTLE Prince, The (record album)
Wins Grammy 2-28, 460C3
LITTLE Rock, Ark.—*See ARKANSAS*
LITTLE Rock Gazette (newspaper)
Carter endorsement rptd 10-30, 831G2
LITTON, Rep. Jerry L. (D, Mo.)
Wins Sen primary, dies with family in plane crash 8-3, 565C2
Hearnes named nominee 8-21, 633E1
Coleman, wins seat 11-2, 823B3
LITTON Industries, Inc.
'75 arms sales listed 2-6, 147C3
US files publishing unit consent decree 7-27, 989A2
Top '76 defns contractor 12-21, 961B3
Ingalls Shipbuilding Division
Defns Dept to pay Navy debt 4-8, 309B2
Navy paymt talks stalled 6-10, 453F3
LIU Ping
Rptdly repents errors 3-25, 266A1
LIU Shao-chi (d. 1969)
'Deviationists' scored 2-6, 2-8, 117B2, F2
Teng revisionism scored 2-28, 189C2
Cited in Mao biog, death announcemt 659E1, C2
LIU Wen-hui
Dies 6-24, 524G3
LIVELY, John
Elocutionist wins Preakness 5-15, 368G3

1977

LITHUANIAN Soviet Socialist Republic—*See USSR—Republics*
LITT, Nahum
FPC splits on Alaska gas pipe route 5-2, 369E3
LITTELL, Franklin H.
Sup Ct bars Buckley libel case review 1-17, 58B1
LITTELL, Mark
Traded to Cardinals 12-8, 990F1
LITTLE, Joan
Escapes 10-15, captured 12-7, 992A1
Paul '75 convictn case review declined 10-17, 797G3
LITTLE, Brown & Co.—*See TIME, Inc.*
LITTLE, Sally
2d in Colgate Winners Circle 4-3, 951B1
LPGA top money winner 11-27, 951F1
LITTLE Happiness (race horse)
Cauthen sets earnings mark 12-10, 970F2
LITTLER, Gene
Loses Tucson Open 1-16, 104D1
Wins Houston Open 5-1, 676B1
2d in PGA Championship 8-14, 659E2
LITTLE Spokane River (Washington)
Flow rptd 80% below normal 5-4, 376C3
LITTLE Tennessee River
Fish halts Tellico Dam 1-31, 95G2-C3
LITTON Industries Inc.
Ingalls Shipbuilding Division
Indicted 4-6, 343G3
LITVINOV, Ivy
Dies 4-28, 356C3
LIU Chen, Gen.
Becomes Sinkiang army chief 8-3, 616E3
LIU Chuan-hsin
Tied to '76 Peking riots 1-10, 61E2
LIU Chung-Yang
Tied to academy bugging 3-9, 180E1
LIU Hsi-yao
China educatn min 1-29, 98B2
LIU Ping
Rehabilitatn rptd 3-9, 180G1
LIU Po-cheng
In Politburo 8-21, 645F2
Plot vs Mao detailed 9-8, 694A3
LIU Yin-nung
Scored at rally 6-29, 562A1
LIVERS, Ron
Nears triple jump mark 7-1—7-2, 602E2

1978

LITHGOW, John
Once in a Lifetime opens 6-15, 887C2
LITHUANIAN Soviet Socialist Republic—*See USSR—Republics*
LITTLE, Joan
Carey orders extraditn 2-23, NYS ct backs 5-9; Marshall delays 5-30, Sup Ct declines appeal 6-5, 431G1-B2
Extradited to NC 6-9; indicted 6-18, sentenced 7-12, 560E3
LITTLE, Sally
Wins Crosby Classic 3-19, 355F3
2d in US Women's Open, sets round record 7-23, 2d in Eur LPGA 8-6, 672G2, A3, E3
LPGA top money winner 11-20, 990C3
LITTLE, Steve
In NFL draft 5-2, 336F2
LITTLE Night Music, A (film)
Released 3-7, 619A3
Wins Oscar 4-3, 315C3
LITTLE Night Music, A (song)
Wins Oscar 4-3, 315C3
LITTLER, Gene
2d in San Diego Open 1-29, 76E1
LITTLE Tennessee River
Rare fish halt of Tellico constructn upheld by Sup Ct 6-15, 468A2
LITTMAN, Mark S.
Black urban populatn study rptd 11-30, 943F1
LITTON Industries Inc.
A-sub billing indictmt dismissal reversed 4-5, 368F1
LHA, detroyer contract dispute with Navy settled 6-20, 469A2
Proxmire scores Navy contract setlmt 7-6, 528B3
A-sub billing indictmt case refused by Sup Ct 10-2, 751A2
Navy contract setlmt funded 10-20, 833A2
LITTON Systems Inc. v. U.S.
Litton fraud indictmt refused by Sup Ct 10-2, 751A2
LIU Chien-hsun
Replaced in Honan post 10-23, 814F1
LIU Shao-chi (d. 1969)
Presidency not revived 2-26—3-5, 153D1
LIUZZO, Viola (d. 1965)
FBI informant probed 7-12, 527G3
FBI informant indicted 9-20, 720D2
LIVE and More (recording)
On best-seller list 11-8, 888D1; 12-6, 971F1

1979

LITHGOW, John
Spokesong opens 3-15, 712F2
LITHIUM
H-bomb letter, diagram cites 9-16, 9-18, 714D3-716B2
LITHUANIAN Soviet Socialist Republic—*See UNION of Soviet Socialist Republics–Republics*
LITTLE, Maj. Cynthia
On female AF pilot training 9-10, 725A1
LITTLE, Joan
Paroled 6-9, 527D3
LITTLE, Russell J.
Murder convictn reversed 2-27, 156C1
LITTLE, Sally
Wins Bent Tree Classic 3-5, 220G3
Ties for 2d in Lady Keystone Open 6-24, Greater Baltimore 7-22, 587C3, F3
Wins Barth Classic 8-20, Columbia Savings Classic 9-9, 970B1, D1
LPGA top money winner 11-30, 969G2
LITTLE Eyolf (play)
Opens 6-29, 712B1
LITTLER, Gene
Ties for 2d in Colonial Natl 5-20, 587F2
LITTLE Romance, A (film)
Released 4-27, 820F1
LITTON Industries Inc.
FTC chrgs deceptive ads 2-1, 91F3
6th in '78 defns contracts 8-1, 609C1
Ingalls shipyds damaged by hurricane 9-12, 691F1
LIU Ching
On dissident trial halt 10-29, 854A3
LIU Hsi-yao
Replaced as China educ min 2-6, 134A3
LIU Shao-chi (d. 1969)
Govt confirms death 1-18, 75E1
Widow rptd tortured 5-6, 353F1
Cultural Revolutn deplored 9-29, 750G2
LIUT, Mike
WHA goaltending ldr 4-18, 355G2
LIUZZO, Viola G. (d. 1965)
FBI informant's extraditn OKd 2-7, 120D1
FBI sued over murder 7-5, 521D1
LIVE in Munich (recording)
Jones, Lewis win Grammy 2-16, 336E3
LIVER—*See MEDICINE—Diseases*

1980

LITHGOW, John
Salt Lake City opens 1-23, 136E3
Division St opens 10-8, 892B3
LITHUANIAN Soviet Socialist Republic—*See UNION of Soviet Socialist Republics--Republics*
LITTLE, Sally
Wins LPGA Championship 6-8, WUI 7-27; 2d in Mayflower 7-6, 714B3, 715C1, E1
LPGA top money winner 10-12, 971F3
LITTLE Darlings (film)
Top-grossing film 3-26, 280G3; 4-23, 360B3
Released in NY 3-28, 416C3
LITTLE Gloria...Happy At Last (book)
On best-seller list 8-17, 640F3
LITTLE Jeannie (recording)
On best-seller list 7-9, 568E3
LITTLE Miss Marker (film)
Released 3-21, 216B3
LITTLER, Gene
Wins World Seniors Invitatnl 9-28, 972C2
LITTLE Rascals, The (film series)
Allen Hoskins dies 7-26, 608B2
LITTLE Richard (Richard Penniman)
Lennon slain 12-8, 934B3
LITTLE Romance, A (film)
Delerue wins Oscar 4-14, 296G1
LITVINOV, Sergei
Wins Olympic medal 7-31, 624D1
LITWACK, Leon
Wins Pulitzer 4-14, 296E2
LIUNGBECK, Benni
Wins Olympic medal 7-24, 624A3
LIU Shaoqi (Liu Shao-chi) (d. 1969)
Rehabilitated 2-29, 171C3
Memorialized 5-17, 388F3
Cited in Gang of 4 indictmt A 11-15, 877D1, E1
Chen Boda admits persecutn 11-28, Jiang admits 12-3, 975D1, G1
LIUT, Mike
NHL goaltending ldr 4-6, 296E1
LIUZZO, Viola Gregg (d. 1965)
FBI informant probe cited 2-18, 227B3
LIVE From Studio 8H: A Tribute to Toscanini (TV special)
Wins Emmy 9-7, 692E1
LIVERMORE (Calif.) Laboratory, Lawrence
Quakes force evacuatn 1-24—1-27, 80G2
Skin cancer cases rptd 4-22, 356E3

1976

LIVESTOCK & Poultry—*See also MEAT*
Dec '75 WPI down 1-9, 21C2
FDA asks DES ban in feed 1-9, 25E3
Dec, '75 CPI 1-21, 90A2
West Coast drought ends 2-5, 271C3
March WPI rptd 4-1, 262G3
Cong OKs Beef Bd 5-3, 5-12, 358E3-359A1
Pacific exchng closes, US sues 5-10, 348C2
Ford urges regulatory reform 5-13, 346G3
Agri Dept asks retail price cut 8-30, 667G3
Aug CPI rptd 9-21, 708E2
Aug export rptd up 9-27, 770D1
Land-use bill signed 10-21, 834D1, E1
US ups brandy duties, EC poultry war cited 11-26, 976G2-C3
Coyote-poison ban kept 12-23, 980B2
Nov trade rptd 12-28, 983A3
International Developments
Poland halts Italy shipmts 1-29, 74G2
Paraguay gets World Bank loan 2-27, 205C3
EC sets milk-feed plan 3-6, OKs revisn 4-14, 276F2
Finnish foodworkers strike ends 4-8, 266E1
Argentina cattle stock up 4-9, 264D3
EEC farmers seek drought aid 6-19, 7-19, 548D1, F1
Iran, Occidental deal 6-20, 450C2
Eur drought effect on feed crops rptd 12-31, 977D3

1977

LIVESTOCK—*See also MEAT, POULTRY*
CIA linked to Cuba '71 swine fever 1-9, 19E2
NZ sets UK lamb trading 2-22, 253E1
Price rise, soybean trading linked 4-18, 301B2
'76 SD cattle loss rptd 4-18, 376F3
DES cancer risk rptd less 5-3, 432F1
Drought-related price cut rptd 6-23, Calif losses projctd 8-9, 659F3, 660C1
Feed prices rptd down in June 7-8, 554A2
Carter asks feed grain reserve 8-2, 666E2
Antibiotic curbs in feed grain proposed 8-30, 10-21; House com hearing 9-23, 847F2
Farm bill signed, feed grain reserves set 9-29, 736D2, F3
Disaster aid ceiling lifted by Cong 10-25, 833B3; signed 11-8, 1001E2
Sheep disease hits Australia 11-14, 881D3
Carter cuts '78 feed grain acreage, record stock seen 11-15, 916C2
US, 5 other govts ban Australia imports 11-23, 922F3
Australia drops plan to kill diseased cattle 11-28, 945E1
Mid-Nov feed grain prices rptd 11-30, 916F2
Farm strike impact on trading rptd small 12-21, Calif backing lags 12-22, 1003C1

1978

LIVERS, Ron
Sets triple jump mark 6-1—6-4, 600G3
LIVESTOCK—*See also MEAT*
Grazing-fee-increase moratorium backed by Bergland 1-9—1-13, 34A2
Australia drought losses rptd 1-11, 16B1
Belgium bank fails 1-24, 94E1
McKerrow dies 1-27, 96A3
Anti-tick virus rptd 2-23, 334F1
Cattle shortage linked to Feb index 3-9, 222D3
Australia port strike starts 4-11, 349F3-350A1
Cattle herd cutbacks, beef price rise linked 6-8, 428F2
Embryo transplants cited 7-25, 597E1
PBBs contaminate Mich feed 10-9, 769C2; suit dismissed 10-27, 834C1
Grazing land laws revisn cleared 10-11, 807D2
'78 cattle futures vol rptd up 1004B3
Feed Grain—*See GRAIN*
LIVING At Home (play)
Opens 12-11, 1031C2
LIVING in the U.S.A. (recording)
On best-seller list 10-11, 800F3; 11-8, 888D1
LIVINGSTON, Rep. Robert L. (R, La.)
Reelected 11-7, 850F4
LI Yong Mu
Tied to assassinatn plot 2-5, 115F3
LJUBICIC, Gen. Nikola
Visits US 9-24—9-29, jet engine sale rptd 9-28, 758D1
LLAPUR, Santiago
Last Supper released 5-5, 619G2
LLERAS Camargo, Alberto
Concerned re Valencia pres bid 5-28, 413A3
LLERAS Restrepo, Carlos
Lopez pro-Turbay bias chrged 2-20, Liberal following rptd 2-27, 2-28, 147A2
Loses Liberal pres nominatn 2-26, campaign name-calling rptd 2-28, 147C1
Turbay scores Betancur 5-28, 413B2
LLERENA Amadeo, Juan
Argentina educ min 11-6, 865D2
LLOREDA Caicedo, Rodrigo
Named Colombia educ min 8-7, 629C3
LLOYD, David
US wins Davis Cup 12-10, 1026F3
LLOYD, Euan
Wild Geese released 11-11, 970E3
LLOYD, Rep. James F. (Jim) (D, Calif.)
Reelected 11-7, 850B2
LLOYD, John
Loses Australian Open 12-31-77, 22G3
US wins Davis Cup 12-10, 1026E3
LLOYD, Rep. Marilyn (D, Tenn.)
Reelected 11-7, 852C2
LLOYD, Selwyn—*See SELWYN-Lloyd, Lord of Wirral (John Selwyn Brooke Lloyd)*

1979

LIVESTOCK
US wilderness proposal scored 1-4, 16D2
Utah sheep '53 A-deaths rptd 2-14, 112F1-A2
UK '78 aid to Portugal rptd 2-20, 212F3
Jan CPI rise rptd 2-23, 151B2
Mar farm price rptd up 3-30, 280C3
Mich PBB cover-up indictmt 4-26, 597E3
King Ranch bd chrmn dies 5-8, 432B3
Pa cattle deaths near 3 Mile I rptd 5-20, 382E1
Antibiotics in feed rptd risky 6-25, 734G3
DES banned in animal feed 6-28, 571F2
Latin fish-meal output drop rptd 7-3, 555D1
EC sheep import curbs cited 8-21, 632A1
PCB feed grain contaminatn rptd 9-17, 704A3
French-UK lamb dispute progress rptd 11-14, 873B1
Feed Grains—*See GRAIN*

1980

LIVESTOCK
Grain futures trading suspended 1-6, 2C1
DES controversy cited 1-25, 63B3
US dietary guidelines scored 2-4, 157E3
King Ranch heir dies 3-20, 279G3
US Mar farm price drop rptd 3-31, 263F3
Iowa farm cancer study rptd 4-15, 357E3
DES violators warned 4-15, widespread use rptd 4-24, 358D1
Mt St Helens eruptn impact rptd 5-22, 382E2
Hunts' bailout loan collateral listed 5-28, 426D1
Midwest, South hit by drought, damage rptd 6-23—8-15, 616C1, G1-B2
June farm prices rptd 6-30, 492D2
Lindane use curbs sought 7-3, 519D3
July farm prices rptd 7-31, 575D1
Midwest, South drought damage final rpt 9-7, 857B2
Beef pricing trust case refused by Sup Ct 10-14, 781G3
Oct farm prices rptd 10-31, 883C1
US '80 futures price down 12-31, 984G3
Feed Grain—*See GRAIN*
Foreign Developments (including U.S. international news)
Africa Rift Valley Fever epidemic rptd 3-2, 318F2-D3
Australia drought threat rptd 4-7, 272A1
Mex cattle threatened by drought 6-13, 524B2
Canadian drought forces herd sell-offs 6-27, 520C2
USSR 1st 1/2 farm productn rptd down 7-16, 711G2
EC bans cattle hormone use 10-1, 737B3

1976

LIVING for the City (recording)
Wins Grammy 2-28, 460A3
LIVINGSTON, James
Air controller strike averted 5-31, 416D3
Approves new air rules 7-26, 572C2
LIVINGSTON, Robert E.
Defeated 11-2, 822A2
LIVINGSTON Jr., William Kyle
Indicted 3-5, freed 4-14, 316E2
LIVONIA, Mich.—*See MICHIGAN*
LIZARDS—*See REPTILES*
LJUBEK, Matija
Wins Olympic medals 7-30, 7-31, 574E1, F1
LLERAS Restrepo, Carlos
Lopez rejects reelectn move 1-7, 31C1
Electn results 4-18, 310G3
LLOPIS, Rodolfo
Returns to Spain 1-22, 77F1
LLOYD, David
Wins Emmy 5-17, 460B2
LLOYD, Rep. Jim (D, Calif.)
Reelected 11-2, 829E1
LLOYD, Rep. Marilyn (D, Tenn.)
Reelected 11-2, 830B4

1977

LIVINGSTON, James
Vs Parlt back-to-work order 8-10, 616B2
LIVINGSTON Jr., Robert L.
Wins Cong primary 6-25, 501F1
Elected 8-27, 693B1
LIZANETZ, Alex (King Alphonse)
Murder plot rptd 1-15, 162B1
Alleged murder plot cited 11-6, 871C2
LJUBICIC, Nikola
US mil cooperatn set 10-13, 785G3
LLADO y Fernandez Urrutia, Jose
Spain transport, communicatns min 7-5, 545C2
LLERAS Restrepo, Carlos
OKs '78 pres primary 3-21, 255A2
Reaffirms '78 primary plan 8-17, 727D2
LLOYD, John Henry (Pop) (d. 1965)
Inducted into baseball HOF 8-8, 644B1
LLOYD, Peter
Confirms '73 death sentncs 5-2, 374D2

1979

LIVING History Farms (Iowa museum)
Pope visits 10-4, 759C1
LIVINGSTON, Harold
Star Trek released 12-8, 1008F1
LLOYD, Chris Evert (Mrs. John)
Loses Oakland Avon tourn 1-15, 391C2
'78 top ranking by ITF rptd 1-18, 103G2
Marries John Lloyd 4-17, 392A2
US wins Federatn Cup 5-6, 391D2
Wins Vienna Open 5-20, French Open 6-9, Eastbourne Intl 6-23; loses Wimbledon 7-6, 569D3, 570E1, C2
Wins US Clay Cts 8-12, Volvo Cup 8-26; loses US Open 9-9, 734F1, C2, D2
Loses Phoenix Open 10-14, Eng Women's Grand Prix 11-25, 1003E3, 1004A1
US wins Wightman Cup 11-4, 1003C3
LLOYD, John
Marries Chris Evert 4-17, 392A2
LLOYD, Sherman P.
Dies 12-15, 1008C3

1980

LIVINGSTON, Sgt. David
Killed in Ark A-missile silo blast 9-19, 765C2
LIVINGSTON, Robert H.
Turns opens 6-16, 756G3
LIVINGSTON, Rep. Robert L. (R, La.)
Wins primary 9-13, 724G2
Reelected 11-4, 842F4
LLERAS Restrepo, Carlos
Leftists ask Panama mtg 4-19, 311G2
LLOYD, Chris Evert—*See EVERT Lloyd, Chris*
LLOYD, Danny
Shining released 5-23, 675D3
LLOYD, Rep. Jim (D, Calif.)
Loses reelectn 11-4, 852A2

1976

LLOYD'S Bank, Ltd.
Norwegian freighter lost at sea 1-19, 79D3
Lloyds Calif reopens failed bank 5-23, 438B1
L & M EXPORT Co.
Chrgd re Arab boycott 10-8, 785C3
LOBBYING & Lobbyists—*See under U.S. GOVERNMENT—CONGRESS*
LOCAL Governments—*See CITIES, Suburbs & Localities*
LO Chang-lung (1901-49)
Cited in Mao death announcemt 659B2
LOCKHEED Aircraft Corp.
'75 arms sales listed 2-6, 147C2
Canada purchase deadline extended 4-1, 250D2
3 in downed Saudi plane 4-12, 259B1
Canada contract signed 4-30, 332F2
Fortune rpts '75 stock mkt return 437D2
Canada deal collapses 5-18, 363G1
Canada Cabt repercussns 6-1—6-8, 416A2
Australia sale rptd 7-1, 481E1
Canada deal revised 7-21, 554G3
Australia budgets P3C buys 8-17, 636F3
Brit Airways orders 12 jets 8-18, 675D3
'74, '75 zero tax paymt rptd 10-2, 847F1, G1
Iran AF training pact rptd 11-24, 925F2
Top '76 defns contractor 12-21, 961A3
Political Payments
Japan, Turkey, Europe payoffs rptd 2-4; Kotchian, testifies 2-6, 130E1-131D1
Probe panel formed 2-5, 131C2
Japan probes payoff chrgs, cancels arms deal; Marubeni cuts ties 2-5—2-17, 131B3
Latin paymts probed 2-7—2-16, 147E1, E3
Dutch confrm Bernhard bribe 2-8, probe opens 2-11, 131D2
W Ger chrgs rptd 2-8, 2-11, 132D2
Japan presses probes; deals threatened, workers protest 2-9—3-10; US to free data 3-5, 190A2-191B2
Turkey probe rptd 2-9—3-12, 192A2
Italy recipients named 2-11—2-12, chrgs probed 2-17—2-18, 132G1
Hong Kong airways dir quits 2-11, 132G2
Haughton, Kotchian quit, Haack named chrmn 2-13, 131D1
Italy arrests, indictmts rptd; probes underway 2-20—4-2, 298D1
Dutch probe advances 2-25—3-5; US data rptd 2-27, 254G2
AF payoffs chrgd 2-29, 3-1, Pentagon sets probe 3-2, 200D2
Belgium sets probe 3-9, 220B3
W Ger probe closed 3-10, 200A2
US offers Japan data 3-11, 199E3
Bonn sets probe 3-15, 270C1
Italy Social Dems oust recipient 3-16, 254A2
Swiss Parlt bars probe 3-16, 314F3
US in data pacts with Japan 3-23, Italy, Dutch 3-30, Nigeria 4-20, 286A1, E1
Tanaka denies '72 Nixon deal 4-2, 286B2
Rpt CIA had '50s Japan data 4-2, 286C2
Turkey mil officers on trial 4-7, 298F1; cleared 4-30, 322A3
Settles SEC suit, probe com set 4-13, 285F2
US releases info to Dutch govt 4-14, 322B2
Dutch press rpts Bernhard link 4-21, 322C2
3 Italy ex-premrs deny link 4-22, 298A1
Australia payoff chrgd 4-29, 322F1-A2
Japan files new chrgs vs Kodama 5-10, 6-1, arrests 4 6-22, 450A3
SEC lists forgn paymts 5-12, 726B1, 728C2
Greek pact sets data exchng 5-20, 402C2
Italy CP scores Christian Dems 6-11, US clears Leone 6-15, 445C2
Cited in Nigeria gun plot arrest rpt 6-19, 498E2, G2
Colombia gets data 6-22; ct scores delays, takes over probe 9-1, 740F1
5 arrested in Japan 7-2, 7-7, 7-8, 497D2
More Japan arrests, indictmts 7-9—7-27; full probe vowed 7-28, 557D1
Japan ex-premr, others indicted 7-28—8-16, 624G1
Ford submits disclosure legis 8-3, 668B2
More Japan arrests, premr urged to quit 8-20—8-24, 626C3
Dutch probe rpt detailed, Bernhard resigns posts 8-26, 626F1; text excerpts 627A1, D2
Japan parlt com bars Tanaka, Nakasone testimony 8-26, 677B1
Dutch parlt vs Bernhard prosecutn 8-30, 642C2
Ex-UK min rptd bribed 8-30, 642F2-A3
Miki offers Cabt, party chngs 8-30, 676F3
Andreotti denies payoffs 8-31, letters publshd 9-1, 684B3
Dutch legislators rptd approached 9-1, 684B2
Bernhard role in '71 W Ger buy rptd 9-2, 684F2
Japan broadcast head quits 9-4, 838E3
Japan indicts 2 9-10, probe delay seen 9-24, 740B2
Japan Cabt, LDP shuffled 9-15, 694D1
Strauss letter termed forgery 9-22, W Ger files rptd missing 9-17, 740B1
W Ger campaign issue 9-29, 10-1, 754C3
Kodama, asst trials in Japan delayed 9-30, 838C3
Japan parlt member quits 10-13, 838D3
Andreotti probe dropped 10-13, 858A2
Japan interim probe rpt issued 10-15, 838E2
Spain rpts paymts to AF offcls, others 10-15—11-8, 909D1

1977

LLOYD'S Bank, Ltd.
Calif bank takeover cited 3-1, 155C2
Lugano branch to close 8-24, 658E1
Co-finances Argentina loan 11-10, 981G2
Mex gets $1.2 bln intl loan 11-18, 967C1
LNG (Liquefied Natural Gas)—*See GAS, Natural*
LOAN Sharking—*See CRIME—Bribery, Fraud & Extortion*
LOBBYING & Lobbyists—*See under U.S. GOVERNMENT—CONGRESS*
LOCKE, Bobby
Inducted into golf HOF 8-23, 675E3
LOCKHEED Aircraft Corp.
'71 US loan guarantee cited 1-19, 55F1
Carter for noise standards 3-5, 171C3
Navy overbilling chrgd 6-13, denied 6-14, 482G2
Canada to buy Orion anti-sub aircraft 7-13, 579E3
Navy overbilling chrg error admitted 8-22, 649G3
US backs Egypt jet repairs 9-15, 698D1
Bernhard's return to pub life rptd 9-28, 986B2
Anderson succeeds Haack, co named changed 9-29, 858D3
IAM strikes 10-10—12-31, 1005C2
Haack: US made money on loan guarantee; guarantee ended 10-12, 858C3
Political Payments
Paymts total cited 1-21, 79F1
Japan ends probe, indicts 2 1-21, 83F2
Japan trials of Tanaka, others open 1-27, 1-31, 83B2
2 Italy ex-mins indicted 1-29, 116A3
Italy trial set 3-10, 284B1
Rpts grand jury, IRS probes 4-8, 502F3
GAO: overseas sales unharmed 4-28, 502E3
Rpts '70-75 total to SEC 5-26, 502E2-D3
W Ger clears in paymts probe 6-22, 602E1

1978

LLOYD Carr & Co.
Offcls arrested 1-10, Abrahams flees, alias revealed 1-14, apprehended 1-24; co receiver named 1-19, '77 revenues rptd 1-24, 83B2-E3
Abrahams sentenced on probatn violatn 4-20, 283C1
Abrahams, others indicted 8-3, 665C2
LLOYDS Bank Ltd.
El Salvador execs kidnaped 12-1, release talks rptd 12-21, 986C3
LLUBERES Montas, Maj. Gen. Salvador
Replcd as DR AF staff chief 8-16, 648E2
LNG (Liquefied Natural Gas)—*See GAS, Natural*
LOBBYING & Lobbyists—*See under U.S. GOVERNMENT—CONGRESS*
LOCKE, Bobby
Player wins 3 consecutive tourns 4-9, 4-16, 4-23, 355E2
LOCKETT v. Ohio
Ohio death penalty law voided by Sup Ct 7-3, 552D1-A2
LOCKHART, Warren L.
Film wins Oscar 4-3, 315D3
LOCKHEED Aircraft Corp.
IAM strike ends 1-2, 4B2
2d in '77 defense contracts 3-28, 224F2
Pan Am buys L-1011 jets 4-4, 264D2
Canada govt employe wins libel suit 4-13, 287A1
GAO clears on overbilling chrg 6-22, 493B3
Navy settles '71 claims 7-28, 665E3
AF grounds C-130 fleet after crash 12-11, 984E2
Political Payments
W Ger scandal linked 1-13—1-17, 74C2
6 in Japan tied to bribe 1-30, 72C3
Italian pres resigns over chrgs 6-15, 516F2
FTC chrgs setld 8-18, 643C1
Kotchian files Japan ct depositn, links Nakasone to bribe case; Nakasone denies 10-26, 838E3-839A1

1979

LLOYD Carr & Co. (defunct)
5 offcls convicted 2-22, sentncd 3-19, 220E2
CFTC bars options trading resumptn 9-5, 681G3
LLOYD-Jones, Donald J.
Disputes DC-10 crash findings 7-12, 539D1
On Chicago DC-10 crash rpt 12-21, 988B3
LLOYDS Bank Ltd.
El Salvador execs ransomed 7-2, 547G1
On tanker collisn off Tobago 7-21, 553B3; 8-2, 592B3
LLUBERES Montas, Maj. Gen. Salvador
Named DR mil attache in UK 1-12, 62D2
LNG (Liquefied Natural Gas)—*See GAS, Natural*
LOBBYING & Lobbyists—*See under U.S. GOVERNMENT—CONGRESS*
LOCKHEED Aircraft Corp.
DC-10s grounded 6-6, 421A1
4th in '78 defns contracts 8-1, 609C1
Political Payments
US drops Japan probe of Kotchian, Haughton 2-15, 306C1
Overseas paymts disclosed 2-16, 306F1-A2
6 convicted in Italy 3-1, 155B2
Japan payoffs guilty plea, fined 6-1, 422F2
Italian ct statemt rptd 8-6, 603B1
Turkey chrgs cover-up 9-20, 775F1

1980

LLOYD Carr & Co. (defunct)
Founder sentenced 6-20, 503C1
LLOYDS Bank Ltd.
Nicaragua debt rescheduled 9-5, 689A3
LLOYD'S of London
Itel settles claim 1-16, 131C3
Shell files cargo claim 2-7, '79 ship losses rptd 2-18, 108B3, E3
RCA satellite claims cited 2-20, 160D3
N Sea oil platform accident losses rptd 3-27, 256C2
NBC Olympic coverage rptd 3-28, 259E1
NY Insurnc Exchng opens; financial losses, liability cited 3-31, 266A1
NBC drops Olympic telecast, estimates loss 5-6, 379E3
2-year study issued, reforms urged 6-26, 509C3
Itel rpts huge '79 loss 10-16, 784A2
Reforms OKd 11-4, 855C3
LNG (Liquefied Natural Gas)—*See GAS, Natural*
LOBANOV, Vladimir
Wins Olympic medal 2-19, 156A1
LOBBYING & Lobbyists—*See under U.S. GOVERNMENT--CONGRESS*
LOBELL, Michael
Windows released 1-18, 216G3
LOCKE, Sondra
Bronco Billy released 6-11, 675A2
Any Which Way You Can released 12-17, 1003F1
LOCKERIDGE, Rocky
Pedroza decisns 10-4, 1001A1
LOCKHART, Calvin
Reggae opens 3-27, 392F3
LOCKHEED Aircraft Corp.
5th in '79 defns contracts 5-28, 403F1
UK Trident acquisitns set 7-15, 544D2
'Stealth' aircraft said to evade radar 8-20, 630C2; disclosure scored 9-4, 665D3

1976

Greece rptdly clears 11-2, 854A1
Marubeni rptd Canada A-sales agent 11-29, 923G3
Cited re Philip Morris DR payoffs 12-28, 1001D2
LOEB, William H.
Not at Ford press meeting 1-22, 41A2
LOENING, Grover C.
Dies 2-29, 192E3
LOEWE, Lothar
E Germany ousts 12-22, 1001D3
LOFTUS, John
Dies 3-23, 484F3
LOGAN International Airport (Boston, Mass.)
Bomb blast 7-2, 796B3
LOIJEN, Lambertus
Sentenced for war crimes 12-14, 1007D2
LOIKANEN, Jouko
Sworn Finnish 2d finance min 9-29, 750D3
LOKTEV, Konstantin
Flyers beat Sovt team 1-11, 56B2
LONBORG, Jim
NL pitching ldr 10-4, 796A1
Reds win pennant 10-12, 796F1
LONDON (British warship)
In Intl Naval Review 7-4, 488C3
LONDON Daily Mail (newspaper)
Bessell interview rptd 5-11, 351C1
LONDON Metal Exchange
Metals gain 3-3, 175B3
LONDON Stock Exchange
S Africa stocks fall 3-3, 175B3
LONELY Lady, The (book)
On best-seller list 12-5, 972E2
LONE Pine, Calif—*See CALIFORNIA*
LONG, Rep. Clarence D. (D, Md.)
Reelected 11-2, 829A4
LONG, Gerald
On developing natns press pool 7-19, 619B3
LONG, Rep. Gillis W. (D, La.)
Reelected 11-2, 822B2, 829G3
LONG, Herman H.
Dies 8-8, 816F3
LONG, Huey P. (1893-1935)
Gerald L K Smith dies 4-15, 316C1
LONG, Sen. Russell B. (D, La.)
For revenue sharing 2-23, 149D3
Sugar industry lobbying cited 9-21, 721C3
Carter meets cong ldrs 11-17, 864A2
LONG Beach (Calif.) State College
Stones sets high jump mark 6-5, 444G3
LONGHORN Machine Works
Chrgd re Arab boycott 10-8, 785C3
LONG Island, N.Y.—*See NEW York State*
LONG Island Press (newspaper)
Carter endorsement rptd 10-30, 831G2
LONG Island University (Brooklyn, N.Y.)
Sidney Rolfe dies 3-10, 240F3
LONGLEY, Gov. James B. (Ind., Me)
Gov election results 11-2, 820F2
At NE govs mtg 11-13—11-14, 864C3 ★
LONGSHOREMEN'S Association, International (AFL-CIO)
Gleason backs Jackson 1-6, 22B3
New Orleans grain extortn chrgd 8-3, 990C3
Field indicted 12-10, 986A1

1977

LOCKHEED Shipbuilding and Construction Co.—*See LOCKHEED Aircraft Corp.*
LOEB Rhoades & Co.
Plans Hornblower merger 10-27, 1004A3
LOEFF, Josephus
On Australia farm import demands 10-30, 862D1
LOEN, Vernon
Ford, Kim Han Cho mtg bid rptd 11-11, 915A2
LOESCHNAK, Franz
Named Austria state secy 5-31, 425D1
LOEWS Corp.
Lorillard forgn paymts, pol gifts rptd 2-14, 233A3
LOGAN Township, N.J.—*See NEW Jersey*
LOISEAU, Luis Gustavo ('Caloi')
Presumed kidnaped 8-8, 670F2
LO Jui-ching
Central Com member 8-20—8-23, 646A1
Promoted; at Mao rites 9-9, 706B1
LOKOLOKO, Tore
Elected PNG gov-gen 2-18, 203B2
LOLLAR, Sherman
Dies 9-24, 788D1
LOMBARDI, Ernie (Schnoz)
Dies 9-26, 788D1
LOMBARDO, Guy
Dies 11-5, 952G2
LOMPOC, Calif.—*See CALIFORNIA*
LOME Convention
PNG membership rptd 3-30, 309A3
LONDON Economic Summit—*See ECONOMY (non-U.S.)*
LONDON Metal Exchange
Tin price hits record high 3-4, 169E1
LONDON Sugar Association
Australia sues Japan refiners 9-28, 800F2
LONELY Lady, The (book)
On best-seller list 4-3, 264A2; 5-1, 356D2; 6-4, 452B2
LONETREE Reservoir (N.D.)—*See DAMS & Reservoirs*
LONG, Rep. Clarence (D, Md.)
Nicaragua mil aid cutoff deceptn chrgd 6-21—8-6, 656B3
LONG, Rep. Gillis W. (D, Tex.)
'76 campaign surplus rptd 5-3, 482A2
LONG, Adm. Robert L. J.
Defends Panama Canal pacts 9-27, 755C2
LONG, Sen. Russell B. (D, La.)
'76 spec interest gifts rptd 1-15, 128F3, 129F1
Backs business tax credit 3-8, 174G2
On rebate plan end 4-14, 270F3
Carter backs waterway 4-18, 299D3
On Carter energy plan 4-20, 290D3, 293F1
AT&T adopts employe stock plan 5-6, 409F1
Sen filibusters vs gas deregulatn 9-22—10-3, 757G3
Carter on energy plan effort 10-13, 772D3
Energy tax bill passes Sen 10-31, 832G1-E2, E3
Schlesinger scored re energy bill comments 11-22, 916F3
Carter denies energy deal 11-30, 914C1
Energy conf com adjourns without bill 12-22, 1002B2
LONG, Steve
Hartwick wins NCAA soccer title 12-4, 1020F3
LONG Beach, Calif.—*See CALIFORNIA*
LONGET, Claudine
Convicted 1-14, sentenced 1-31, 102E3
LONG Island Lighting Co.
NH A-power backers rally 6-26, 498D3
LONGLEY, Gov. James B. (Ind., Maine)
On Indian land claims 2-28, 197A1
Vs Carter welfare plan 9-9, 719A2
LONGSHOREMEN'S Association, International (ILA) (AFL-CIO)
Sup Ct bars loading case review 1-10, 57F1
Dock protest 4-14—4-18, 324D2
Containerships struck 10-1, 777G3
Strike ends 11-29, 915F3
Field sentncd 12-2, 937E3
LONGSHOREMEN'S and Warehousemen's Union, International (ILWU) (unaffiliated)
USSR reps denied visas 4-16, 306G2
Bridges retires 4-18, 324G2
Herman elected pres 6-23, 481E3
Hawaii sugar strike 11-2—11-22, 899F2
LONG Transportation
ICC sues 11-3, 861C1
LON Nol
Rpts Cambodia death toll over 2½ mln 9-12, 710G1
Cambodia vs paying UN dues 9-20, 713C1
LONRHO Ltd.
Sues Rhodesia sanctn breakers 5-31, 413C2
Zambia sues Rhodesia sanctn breakers 8-22, 662E1
Smith-Kaunda mtg set 9-25, 810E2
LOOK (defunct magazine)—*See COWLES Communications*
LOOKING for Mr. Goodbar (film)
Top grossing film 12-7, 1021B3
LOOKING Out for Number One (book)
On best-seller list 8-14, 643A2; 9-4, 712E3; 10-2, 808E3; 11-6, 872D3; 12-4, 1021A3

1978

LOCKHEED Shipbuilding & Construction Co.—*See LOCKHEED Aircraft Corp.*
LOCUSTS—*See INSECTS*
LODGE, Lily
Choices opens 12-10, 1031C1
LOEFFLER, Thomas G.
Wins US House seat 11-7, 852B3, 855D3
LOEWS Corp.
3 NYC hotels purchased 5-31, 404G1
LOFTHOUSE, Geoffrey
Wins UK by-electn 10-26, 867E1
LOFTIS Jr., John
Scores offshore lease sale delay 1-31, 108A3
LOFTLEIDIR Inc.—*See ICELANDIC Airlines*
LOFTON, James
In NFL draft 5-2, 336E2
LOGAN, Robert
Sea Gypsies released 4-26, 619E3
LOGAN International Airport (Boston, Mass.)
Blizzard closes 2-5—2-10, 105D2
Port Auth to aid stranded Amsterdam travelers 7-16, 640D3
LOIACONO, Anthony
Indicted 7-19, 598F3
LO Juiching
Dies 8-3, 708A3
LONDEN, Jack
Loses primary for Ariz gov 9-12, 736B2
LONDON Philharmonic Orchestra
Record wins Grammy 2-24, 316C1
LONDON Symphony Orchestra
Record wins Grammy 2-24, 315G3
LONDON Town (recording)
On best-seller list 5-3, 356E1; 6-7, 460G3
LONELY Star Shipping Corp.
ITT paymts chrgd 11-2, 876F2
LONG, Rep. Clarence D. (D, Md.)
Queries Westinghouse Pl A-plant contract 2-8, 134D3
Vs US jets to Egypt, Saudi, Israel 2-24, 139E1
Scores Rumania visa curbs 4-11, 291G1-A2
Reelected 11-7, 851B1
LONG, Rep. Gillis W. (D, La.)
Reelected 11-7, 851A1
LONG, Larry H.
Populatn trend chngs rptd 11-30, 12-3, 943C1, F1
LONG, Sen. Russell B. (D, La.)
Sees crude oil tax unlikely 3-7, 220E1
Canal pact vote sought 3-9, pact OKd 3-16, 177F1, D2
Vs Soc Sec funding from Treas 4-5, 241A1
Votes for 2d Canal pact 4-18, 273B1
Personal finances rptd 5-19, 385D3
Gulf illegal paymt rptd 6-2, 449E1
'76 tax nonpaymt by rich rptd down 7-8, 554B2
Criticism of compromise gas bill rptd 9-28, 733B2
Proposes value-added tax 11-30; Schultze, Ullman comment 12-3, 12-6, 962A2
LONG Beach, Calif.—*See CALIFORNIA*
LONG Beach Naval Hospital
Mrs Ford hospitalized 4-10—5-5, 420A1
LONGEST Walk—*See INDIANS, American*
LONG and Happy Life, A (book)
Early Dark opens 4-25, 760B2
LONG Island Sound
Oil spills rptd 1-10, 3-16, 524F1, A2
LONG Island Sports
Nets sale agreed 8-28, 1027E3
LONGLEY, Gov. James B. (Indep, Mo.)
Not standing for reelectn 6-13, 467A1
LONGO, Bruce—*See DAVID, Immanuel*
LONGSHOREMEN'S Association, International (ILA) (AFL-CIO)
Gleason in Chile, says labor repressn continues 5-23, 452C3
Offcls indicted on port corruptn 6-7, 480E2
Chile trade boycott backed 11-24, 1014F1
LONGSHOREMEN'S and Warehousemen's Union, International (ILWU) (unaffiliated)
Maritime Comm contract jurisdictn enlarged 3-1, 143C3-144C1
James Robertson dies 8-1, 708D3
LONG v. U.S.
Port of entry porno case declined by Sup Ct 5-30, 430B3
LON Nol
Ex-aides purged 8-8, 8-10, 659G3-660B1
Says Cambodia killed 3 mln, asks 'free Khmers' in UN 9-21, 748A2
LONRHO Ltd.
Tanzania expels re Rhodesia 6-2, 479B2
Tanzania sets '67 compensatn 7-3; natlizatn setlmt talks begin 7-25, 635G1
Tanzania talks fail, holdings seized 9-16; Rhodesian support chrgd 9-26, 905D2
Rhodesia paper banned 10-2, 781F1
LOOK (defunct magazine)—*See COWLES Communications*
LOOK Homeward, Angel (book)
Angel opens 5-10, 760C1
LOOKING Out For Number #1 (book)
On best-seller list 7-2, 579E3; 8-6, 620C2

1979

LOCKWOOD, Skip
Signs with Red Sox 11-27, 1002A1
LOEB Sr., John L.
Shearson, Loeb Rhoades to merge 5-14, 366B3
LOEB, William
Crane scores sex allegatns 6-8, 594G1
Settles pensn fund suit 7-9, 640E3
LOEB Rhoades, Hornblower & Co.
Shearson merger set 5-14, 366A3
LOESSER, Frank
Dancing in Dark opens 1-21, 292D1
Most Happy Fella opens 10-11, 956D3
LOEWENHEIM, Francis L.
Eisenhower secret diary rptd 9-16, 9-17, 748A1
Eisenhower tapes revealed 10-21, 868G3-869C1
LOEWS Corp.
Lorillard ordrd to obey FTC subpoena 1-25, 91E3
LOFF, Deborah
Seized by El Salvador leftists 12-13, 968D1; freed 12-21, 993E2
LOGAN International Airport (Boston, Mass.)
Air Canada DC-9 emergency landing 9-17, 830D2
LOGICAL Song, The (recording)
On best-seller list 7-4, 548E3
LO-JI Sales v. New York
Case decided by Sup Ct 6-11, 478A3
LOMBARDI Award, Vince—*See FOOTBALL—Collegiate*
LOME Convention
EC talks collapse 5-26, 398E3
Accord reached 6-27, 512D3
Extensn signed 10-31, 845E1
LONDON Daily Telegraph (newspaper)
Iran ousts newsman 9-11, 670D2
LONE Star Industries Inc.
Boise Cascade to buy unit 4-11, 440E3
LONG, Barry
Winnipeg wins WHA title 5-20, 448D1
LONG, Rep. Clarence D. (D, Md.)
Nicaragua aid pkg OKd 9-11, 731G2
LONG, Huey P. (1893-1935)
Williams dies 7-6, 588G3
LONG, Oliver
On GATT pact 4-12, 273C1
LONG, Sen. Russell B. (D, La.)
Finance Com chrmn 1-23, 71D2
Says tax cut unlikely 4-30, 327C2
Asks catastrophic health insurnc 5-14, 362A2
Finances disclosed 5-18, 383D2
On Carter health plan 6-12, 438A3
On Miller Textron ties 8-2, 627C2
Financial disclosure statemt studied 9-1, 701D3
Votes vs Talmadge denunciatn 10-10, 769G1
LONG Beach (Calif.) Naval Hospital
Sen Talmadge rpts alcohol treatmt 2-26, 176E1
Billy Carter hospitalized 3-7, 271A3
Pursch details Valium abuse 9-10, 734G2
LONG Island, N.Y.—*See NEW York State*
LONG Island Lighting Co. (LILCO)
New Haven reactors rejected 10-12, 807C1
LONGO, Antonio
Nominated Italy state insurance co head 1-8, 21C1
LONG Run, The (recording)
On best-seller list 11-7, 892F3
LONGSHOREMEN'S Association, International (AFL-CIO)
Scotto, others indicted 1-17, 87G2-C3
3 more offcls indicted 3-6, 220B2
Gardner indicted 4-9, 292B1
88-day tug strike ends 6-27, 500D3
Iran US Emb seizure protested 11-9, 863D1
Scotto, Anastasio convicted 11-15, 890A1
LONGSHOREMEN'S and Warehousemen's Union, International (ILWU) (unaffiliated)
Iranian cargo boycott spreads 11-13, 879C1
LONGVIEW Fibre Co.
Western paper strikes end 1-30—5-9, 345F2
LONREIRO Dos Santos, Joao
Remains Portugal defense min 7-30, 603E3
LONSDALE, Michael
Moonraker released 6-29, 820B2
LOOK (magazine)
Rolling Stone partial merger completed 5-7, 430E3
Rolling Stone tie ended, Wenner fired 7-3, 640B3

1980

LODEN, Barbara
Death rptd 9-22, 756B1
LOEFFLER, Rep. Thomas (R, Tex.)
Reelected 11-4, 844B3
LOESSER, Frank
Perfectly Frank opens 11-30, 1003D3
LOEWE, Frederick
Brigadoon opens 10-16, 892A3
LOEWS Corp.
Film productn OKd by Dist Ct 2-27, 229D1
LOGAN, Joshua
Horowitz & Mrs Washn opens 4-2, 392C3
LOH Shon Young
Named S Korea forgn min 9-2, 673C1
LOLICH, Mickey
Carlton breaks southpaw strikeout mark 7-6, 636D3
LOMBARDI, Vince
Steelers win Super Bowl 1-20, 61G2-62C1
LONDON, Carl Jerry
Convicted in absentia 2-4, 270E3
LONDON Observer, The (newspaper)
Kenneth Tynan dies 7-26, 608E3
LONDON University (England)
Blunt controversy rptd 8-24, 652F1
LONE Ranger, The (TV show)
'Tonto' dies 3-5, 280A2
LONG, Rep. Clarence D. (D, Md.)
Vs Somali mil sales 9-18; Pentagon briefs, subcom OKs pact 9-30, 735E3, F3
Reelected 11-4, 843B1
LONG, Rep. Gillis W. (D, La.)
Wins primary 9-13, 724A3
Reelected 11-4, 843A1
Heads House Dem caucus 12-8, 936E2
LONG, Sen. Russell B. (D, La.)
Wins primary 9-13, 724E2
Reelected 11-4, 840G1, 845A3, 849C3
LONGER (recording)
On best-seller list 3-5, 200E3
LONG Island Lighting Co. (Lilco)
Shoreham (NY) A-plant protest 9-29, 961D3
LONG Island Rail Road (LIRR)
Pres strike bd rpts; '79 agrmt cited 1-14, 53D1
Struck 4-1, 267E3-268B1
Setlmt reached 4-11, 289C3
LONG Island University (Brooklyn, N.Y.)
Polk awards presented 2-25, 692D3
LONGLEY, James B.
Dies 8-16, 676A2
LONGO, Luigi
Dies 10-16, 876D2
LONG Run, The (recording)
On best-seller list 1-2, 40F3
LONGSHOREMEN'S and Warehousemen's Union, International (ILWU) (unaffiliated)
Shuns Sovt ship boycott 1-8, 9E1
LONGSHOREMEN'S Association, International (AFL-CIO)
Boycotts Sovt ships 1-8, 9D1
7 offcls sentenced 1-11, 64E1-A2
US to buy corn in ports 1-19, 45C1
Scotto, Anastasio sentenced 1-22, 1-23, 64D2
Sovt boycott end asked 1-28, cts back, ships loaded 1-29, 2-1, 169B1
3 offcls sentenced 5-20, 927F2
Master pact setld early 5-27, 482F1-C2
Container pact ban refusal affirmed by Sup Ct 6-20, 555E2
Polish cargo boycott cited 8-21, 627B1
Reagan breakfasts with Gleason 9-11, 699E3
Contract OKd, 3 ports hold out 9-18, Phila OKs 10-2, 826F2-D3
LONGWORTH, Alice Roosevelt
Dies 2-20, 176C2
LONGWORTH, Nicholas (1869-1931)
Widow dies 2-20, 176C2
LOOKIN' for Love (recording)
On best-seller list 10-8, 796B3

1976

LOOP Inc.
Coleman to OK superport 12-17, 992E1
LOPES, Dave
NL batting ldr 10-4, 795G3
LOPES Cardoso, Antonio
Rpts land reform curbed 1-9, 75D3
Farmers score 1-11, 75F3
Farmers continue protests 1-30—2-1; compromises 2-10, 143E1, A2
Rpt Soares rejected pres bid 5-2, 366F3
Portugal agri min 7-23, 558G1
On agri reform, land return; Soares backs 9-22, 811G2-A3
LOPES de Cruz, Francisco Xavier
Reports Fretelin defeat 2-14, 192F1
LOPES de Souza, Ney
Loses pol rights 8-4, 850F3
LOPEZ, Epifanio Pedrom
Rescued 1-18, 79E3
LOPEZ, Luis Alfonso
Elected Cong pres 6-25, 1005D1
LOPEZ Aranguren, Jose Luis
Univ chair restored 8-7, 753B3
LOPEZ Arrelano, Gen. Oswaldo (Ret.)
United Brands details '74 bribe 12-10, 985E3
LOPEZ Bravo, Gregorio
Suarez named premier 7-3, 500E3, 501C1
LOPEZ Leyton, Col. Raul (ret.)
Deported to Chile 2-22, 238D1

LOPEZ Michelsen, Alfonso
Posada asks reelectn move 1-4; rejcts 1-7, 31C1
Vows siege end 1-16, recants 1-29, 118C1
Sees Kissinger 2-22, 2-23, 178D1
Issues new security measures 3-18, 251B2
Electn results 4-18, 310G3, 311A1
On Mercado murder 4-19, 311E1
Intervenes in MD strike 9-13, 731B1
Reimposes state of siege 10-7, 924G2
Cabt quits 10-13, new govt named 10-19, 924F3

LOPEZ Portillo, Jose
CP names Campa pres candidate 1-9, 75D2
Sets terms for Spain ties 1-10, 75E2
Vows econ, govt chng 6-27, 498G1-D2
Elected pres 7-4, 498C1
Election confirmed 7-14, 677D2
Sister attacked 8-11, 677E1 ★
Govt devalues peso 8-31—9-12, 694C2
Mexico City bombings 11-29, 907B1
Hosts Mrs Carter 11-30—12-2, 906A3
Inaugurated pres 12-1, swears Cabt 12-2, 906C2

LOPEZ Portillo, Margarita
Attacked 8-11, 677E1 ★
LOPEZ Raimundo, Gregorio
Arrested 10-21, 909D1
LOPEZ Rega, Jose
Peron cabt shift scored 1-17, 1-18, 71D2, A3
Rptd AAA organizer 2-4, 212B1
New Argentina cabt asked 2-20, 154C2
Extraditn sought 3-8, 211G3
Prelim corruptn chrgs filed 5-6, 399G2
Rights revoked, arrest ordrd 6-23, 520C1
Goods frozen 7-1, 520A2
Argentina indicts, seeks extraditn 10-25, 997E1
LOPEZ Salinas, Armando
Lauds Cabt policy statemt 7-18, 541D1
LOPEZ Trujillo, Msgr. Alfonso
Scores Ecuador re bishops expulsn 8-16, 692E3
LORBER, Richard P.
Wins RI Sen primary 9-14, 704E3
Loses electn 11-2, 821C3
LORD, Judge Miles W.
Removed in pollutn case 1-6, 25C2
Declares '69 drug trust suit mistrial 8-17, 988A3
LORDSTOWN, O.—*See OHIO*
LORENTZEN, Annemarie
Norway consumers min 1-12, 30A2
LORETTA Lynn. Coal Miner's Daughter (book)
On best-seller list 12-5, 972D2
LORSCHEIDER, Aloisio Cardinal
Named cardinal 4-27, 336C2

1977

LOOMIS, Glen H.
On drought impact 7-28, 659D3
LOOP—*See LOUISIANA Offshore Oil Port Inc.*
LOPES, Dave
In World Series 10-11—10-18, 806F1
LOPES, Henri
Named finance min 4-5, 282F2
LOPEZ, Al
Inducted into baseball HOF 8-8, 644A1
LOPEZ, Alex
Says Cuba ready for US tourists 2-8, 181E1
LOPEZ, Danny
'77 boxing champion 12-17, 970A3
LOPEZ Jr., Eugenio
Trial delayed 2-7, 100A1
Escapes to US 10-1, 10-2, 803A3
LOPEZ, Hector
Arrested 1-2, 140A2
LOPEZ, Nancy
2d in US Womens Open 7-24, LI Charity Classic 8-14, Mixed Team tourn 12-4, 950C3, 951A1, D1
LOPEZ Guevara, Carlos
Scores Canal talks tap rpt 9-16, 716F2
Disputes US treaty interpretatns 9-30, controversy ensues 10-4—10-5, 754D3

LOPEZ Michelsen, Alfonso (Colombia president)
Blamed for growing violence 1-12—3-18, 255A2
Backs Panamanian Canal demands 1-18, 46G1
Oil workers OK arbitratn 3-9, 254E3
US envoy visits 5-8—5-10, 414E1
Mrs Carter visits 6-10, 455C2
CP ldr chrgs 500 'executed' 7-5, 636C1
Pres candidates score 7-16—9-16, 727B2
Sees Torrijos, regional ldrs 8-5—8-6; new Panama Canal pact backed, Intl Coffee Fund set 8-6, 606B3, 608A3
Liberal pres hopefuls reaffirm '78 primary plan 8-17, 727E2
Party member kidnaped 8-19, freed 9-16, 727C1
Union talks fail 9-1, warns vs strike 9-12, 727A1
Sees Carter 9-6; at Panama Canal pact signing 9-7, 678A1
Scores strikers 9-14—9-15, new strike threatened 9-19, 726C2

LOPEZ Portillo, Jose (Mexican president)
Cts to resolve land disputes 1-3, 65F2
Backs Panamanian Canal demands 1-18, 46F1
Visits US 2-14—2-17, 110D1, 127D3, 136B3
Rptdly speeds oil exploitatn 2-18, 240F3
Sees Oaxaca gov 3-1, 240E2
Spain exile govt ties broken 3-18, 242B3
Diaz Ordaz amb apptmt stirs controversy 4-7—5-11, 529G1
US prisoner abuses rptd down 4-16, 529F1
Backs '76 land seizures, offers compensatn 5-4, 528F1
Names Echeverria roving amb 5-16, 529A3; UNESCO envoy 7-8, 563A1
Sees Torrijos, regional ldrs 8-5—8-6; new Panama Canal pact backed, Intl Coffee Fund set 8-6, 606C3, 608A3
Sees US amb Young 8-7—8-8, 646C2
Adviser scores US alien plan 8-28, 746A2, C2
Canal pact oppositn rptd 9-9, 716F3
Replaces top econ mins 11-17, backs IMF policies 12-2, 966B3
'78 budget eases austerity program 12-15, 985G1

LOQUASTO, Santo
Wins Tony 6-5, 452E1
LORENZ, Peter
Sweden deports '75 kidnapers 4-3, 429A1
Baader, others sentncd 4-28, 352D3
Krocher-Tiedemann captured 12-20, 1017F3
LORILLARD International Sales Corp.—*See LOEWS Corp.*
LORRIMER, Claire
Mavreen on best-seller list 3-6, 184G3
LORUSSO, Pierfrancesco
Killed 3-11, students protest 3-12, 1014F1
LOS Alamos, N.M.—*See NEW Mexico*
LOS Angeles (magazine)
Felker assn barred 1-7, 48G3
LOS Angeles (U.S. nuclear submarine)
Carter takes ride 5-27, 417C3

1978

LOOK to the Rainbow (recording)
Jarreau wins Grammy 2-24, 315F3
LOOMIS, Henry
Fleming named CPB pres 9-14, 759E3
LOPES, Dave
NL wins All-Star Game 7-11, 559E3
NL stolen base ldr 10-2, wins Golden Glove Award 11-21, 928F2, A3
In World Series 10-10—10-17, 799B3
LOPES, Jose da Silva
Sworn Portugal finance min 8-29, 671G3
LOPETEGUI, Gen. Javier
Named Chile AF staff chief 7-25, 591G1
LOPEZ, Alvaro (Yaqui)
Galindez decisns 5-6, 379E2
Decisns Burnett 7-3, 600G1
LOPEZ, Danny
TKOs Kotei 2-15, 379B2
KOs Malverez 9-15, 726C2
TKOs Clemente 10-21, 969E1
LOPEZ, Rev. Hermogenes
Murdered 6-30, 722C2 ★
LOPEZ, Nancy
Wins Bent Tree Classic 2-26, Sunstar tourn 3-12, 355D3, E3
2d in Crosby Classic 3-19, 355F3
Sets LPGA win record, rookie earnings mark 5-14—6-18, 580D2, C3
Wins Greater Baltimore Classic 5-14, 580E2
Wins LPGA Classic 5-21, 580F2
Wins Kent Golden Lights 5-29, 580F2
Wins LPGA Championship 6-11, 580G2
Wins Bankers Trust Classic 6-18, 580B3
16th in Lady Keystone Open 6-25, 580G3
Wins Eur LPGA 8-6, 672E3
Wins Far East Open 11-12, 990D2
LPGA top money winner 11-20, top player, rookie 12-11, 990F2, C3
LOPEZ Leyton, Col. Raul
Bolivia interior min 11-24, 913D1

LOPEZ Michelsen, Alfonso (Colombian president)
Electoral ct collapses 2-20, pro-Turbay bias chrgd 2-20, 2-28, 147E1, A2
Carter consults on DR electn 5-19, 414C3
Betancur scores Turbay 5-28, 413D2
At Panama Canal pact instrumts exchng 6-16, 463F2, 464A1
Turbay, Cabt sworn in 8-7, 629B3
Turbay all-male Cabt scored 8-9, 629E3
Pardo Buelvas assassinated 9-12, 814B3

LOPEZ Portillo, Jose (Mexican president)
Aide arrested for corruptn 3-21, 289B3
At Panama Canal pact instrumts exchng, shuns fetes 6-16, 463F2, 464A1
Rpts proven oil, gas reserves up 9-1, 690B1
Scores Margain slaying, sets dissident amnesty bill 9-1, 690D2
Amnesty bill enacted 9-28, 817E2
Vows actn on Oaxaca land claims 10-20, 817B3
Visits China 10-24—10-30, Japan 10-30—11-4, PI 11-4—11-5, 903B3
Rejcts Mex OPEC entry 11-2, 903G3
Sees Spain king 11-17—11-22, 967C3

LOPEZ Raimundo, Gregorio
Book hints Trotsky murder secrets 2-24, 136D2
LOPRESSOR (metoprolol)—*See MEDICINE—Drugs*
LOPUKHOV, I.
Named as Sovt spy 3-30, 247F3
LORA, Francisco Augusto
Accepts DR pres nominatn 2-10, 136C3
Wessin, Fernandez back 3-3, 292E2
Oppositn coalitn talks fail 5-6, 354A3
LORD Of the Rings, The (film)
Released 11-15, 970A2
Top-grossing film 11-29, 970G3
LOREN, Sophia
Brass Target released 12-21, 1030E2
LORENZ, Peter
Trial of '72 kidnapers opens 4-11, 353B3
Meyer escapes W Berlin prison 5-27, 438B3
Kidnap suspect arrested in Bulgaria 6-22, 500B1
UK arrests terrorist suspect 9-15, 725B2
LORILLARD v. Poons
Jury trial in age bias suit backed 2-22, 126F2
LORIOT, Noelle
No Time For Breakfast released 9-15, 970D2
LORTIE, Bernard
Paroled 7-16, 556E3
LOS Alamos (N.M.) Scientific Laboratory
Worker wins mental health damages 3-15, 242F3

1979

LOOMIS, Henry
Nixon Admin pub TV moves disclosed 2-24, 194D2
LOOSE Ends (play)
Opens 6-6, 712B1
LOPES, Dave
NL wins All-Star Game 7-17, 568D3, G3
NL batting, stolen base ldr 9-30, 955F2
LOPEZ, Alfonso
Gushiken KOs 4-8, 412F3
LOPEZ, Cynthia
Beggars Soap Opera opens 7-23, 711E1
LOPEZ, Danny (Little Red)
KOs Castanon 3-10, 412E3
KOs Ayala 6-17, Caba 9-26, 839C1
LOPEZ, Edgardo
5 indicted in arms plot 5-14, 386D3
LOPEZ, Jose
Arrest protested 5-4, 371A1
LOPEZ Jr., Sgt. Joseph
Marines suspend 6-27, beating incident probed 7-7, 520B1
LOPEZ, Nancy
Bent Tree, Sunstar results 3-5, 3-11, 220G3
Wins Sahara Natl Pro-Am 3-25, 3d in Women's Kemper 4-1, 2d in Winners Circle 4-8, 587A2-C2
Wins Women's Intl 5-6, Coca Cola 5-20, Golden Lights 6-3, Lady Keystone 6-24; 2d in Peter Jackson 7-29, 587E2-F3
Wins Europn Open 8-5, LPGA Team tourn 9-16, Mary Kay Classic 9-30, 970A1, E1, F1
LPGA top money winner 11-30, 969G2
Named LPGA top player 12-12, 970C2
LOPEZ Angulta, Maria del Carmen
Arrested 7-27, 585C3
LOPEZ Guevara, Carlos
On canal treaties violatn 12-6, 939A1

LOPEZ Portillo, Jose (Mexican president)
Greets Pope 1-26, 67C3
Hosts Carter; discusses oil, gas, alien issues; cooperatn pact signed 2-14—2-16, 124F1, 127A1
Rejcts phone strike demands 5-1, 372A3
10-yr dvpt plan rptd 5-4, 353D3, F3
Reyes, 2 other Cabt mins ousted 5-16, 408B3, G3
Sees Castro 5-17, 372D2
Cuts Nicaragua ties 5-20, 409A1
OKs Japan steel, pipeline projcts 6-8, 487F3
Shah admitted, Kissinger mtg cited 6-10, 445G3
PRI wins cong electns 7-1, 545B1
Brown mtg set 7-30, 593G1
Bars oil blowout damages, US pressure 8-24, 688E3
State of union address notes energy prospects, inflatn threat 9-1, 689D1
Visits US; addresses UN, sees Carter 9-27—9-29, 753C1
Marks Canal treaty implementatn, lauds Carter 10-1, 754A1, C1
US amb to Mex resigns 10-8, 793C3
Denies US pressure to readmit shah 12-3, 914F1

LORAIN, O.—*See OHIO*
LORDI, Joseph P.
OKs Resorts Intl casino license 2-26, 152A1
LOREN, Sophia
Acquitted of currency-smuggling 1-23, 79B1
Sophia on best seller list 4-8, 271A2; 5-6, 356D2
LORENZEN, Ursel
Defects to E Ger 3-5, 180E3
LORING Air Force Base, Me.—*See MAINE*
LORIO, Philip
On A-waste storage shortage 10-23, 806C3
LORSCHEITER, Bishop Jose Ivo
Backs Nicaragua, El Salvador prelates 2-12, 108F3
LORTEL, Lucille
Getting Out opens 5-15, 711B3
LOS Alamos (N.M.) Scientific Laboratory
Justice Dept admits H-bomb documt security error 6-8, 713E1; Hansen letter cites 715F2
Shroud of Turin age test awaited 11-21, 931G2

1980

LOOMIS, Carol
Panelist in pres TV debate 9-21, 721C3
LOPEZ, Danny (Little Red)
Sanchez TKOs for WBC featherwgt title 2-2, 320F2
Sanchez TKOs 6-21, 1000G3
LOPEZ, David
Wins Olympic medal 7-23, 623F2
LOPEZ Sr., Eugenio (deceased)
Marcos murder plot chrgd 8-5, 672F3
LOPEZ, Priscilla
Day in Hollywood opens 5-1, 392F2
Wins Tony 6-8, 692C3
LOPEZ Gonzales, Roberto
Arrested 1-25, 94B1
LOPEZ-Melton, Nancy
2d in Vegas Natl Pro-Am 3-23, wins Women's Kemper Open 3-30, 412B3
2d in Golden Lights 6-1, Greater Baltimore 7-20; wins Sarah Coventry 6-29, 715A1
2d in Women's World Series 9-7, United Va Bank Classic 9-14, Dallas Classic 9-29; wins Mixed Team tourn 12-14, 972A1, D1, B2, C2
LPGA top money winner 10-12, 971F3
Alcott wins Vare Trophy 12-9, 971D3

LOPEZ Michelson, Alfonso
Leftists ask Panama mtg 4-19, 311G2

LOPEZ Portillo, Jose (Mexican president)
Bars GATT entry 3-18, 234A1
Announces '80 oil productn hike 3-18, 234G1
Pemex caps blown-out well 3-24, 233E3
In US energy talks 4-2—4-3, 315G1
Kennedy visits 4-28, 327G2
Japan oil talks 5-2—5-4, 341G1; pact signed 5-28, 409C2
In France, W Ger, Sweden, Canada 5-16—5-28, 409G1, C2
Visits Brazil, Cuba, CR; signs trade agrmts 7-27—8-3, 605F2-D3
Delivers State of Natn address 9-1, 729G2-730F1
Warns Reagan vs interventn 11-5, 841G2
Fuel conservatn concern cited 11-20, 902A3
Attends Santa Marta conf 12-17, 992A3

LOPEZ Rivera, Oscar
Sought as FALN suspect 4-4, 309C1
Indicted 12-10, 963G3
LORAL Corp.
Schwartz scores Carter anti-inflatn plan 3-15, 202F1
LORCA, Federico Garcia
Dona Rosita opens 3-20, 392F2
LORD, James
Heartaches of a Pussycat opens 3-19, 392A3
LORD, Judge Joseph
Blocks draft registratn 7-18, 597G3
LORDI, Joseph P.
OKs FBI Abscam interview, denies Ritz link 2-5, 111B1, C1
LORELCO—*See MEDICINE--Drugs & Health-Care Products*
LOREN, Sophia
Art collectn claim rptd denied 2-9, 200B2
Blood Feud released 2-22, 216C2
Sets Italy return in tax evasn case 9-10, 908B1
LORENTZSEN, Norman
Bressler replaces 5-19, 456F2
LORENZ, Arthur Lloyd
Convicted 4-23, 372B1
Sentenced 6-16, 486F1
LORENZ, Dietmar
Wins Olympic medals 7-27, 8-2, 623D1
LORENZ, Peter
Kidnapers sentenced 10-13, 833A1
LORENZONI, Marcel
Separatist unrest 1-6—1-11, surrenders to police 1-11, 58C1-E1
LOSABERIDZE, Keto
Wins Olympic medal 8-2, 622D1

1976

LOS Angeles, Calif.—*See CALIFORNIA*
LOS Angeles, Professional Educators of—*See PROFESSIONAL Educators, etc.*
LOS Angeles Herald-Examiner (newspaper)
Ford endorsement rptd 10-30, 827F3
Farr wins ct test 12-21, 995C1
LOS Angeles Press Club
Ford at breakfast 5-25, 374C1
LOS Angeles Times (newspaper)
MD slowdown survey cited 2-5, 144C3
Kerby wins Pulitzer 5-3, 352E3
Angola ousts Geyer 6-15, 480C3
Prints Croat hijacker demands 9-11, 685E1
Sup Ct bars Hartley review libel suit 10-4, 807D2
Nelson on pres debate panel 10-22, 800A1, 801A1
Barred pres endorsement 10-30, 827D3
LOSCH, Helmut
Wins Olympic medal 7-27, 576F2
LOTT, Rep. Trent (R, Miss.)
Endorses Ford 7-30, 563F3
Reelected 11-2, 830A1
LOTTERIES—*See GAMBLING*
LOUGANIS, Greg
Wins Olympic medal 7-27, 563B1, 575D3
LOUGHEED, Peter
On fed-prov tax plan 12-15, 962E2
LOUIS Jr., John J.
Soc Sec withdrawals rptd 3-23, 994G1
'72 campaign gift listed 4-25, 688B1
MD malpractice bill signed 7-2, hosp slowdown ends 7-3, 1016E3
Fscl '75 per capita income, tax burden rptd 9-15, 10-12, 959D2
Monroe defaults 9-17, gets fed aid 9-18, 994G1 ★
Ex-Gov Noe dies 10-18, 970F2
New Orleans bank fails 12-3, sold 12-5, 939E3-940A1
Oil stockpile plan proposed 12-15, 991D3
Grand Isle superport to be OKd 12-17, 992E1
UAW wins Monroe GM plant vote 12-22, 991D1
N Orleans transatlantic air route rejctd 12-28, 992E2

LOUISIANA
Wildlife Federatn rpt issued 1-18, 45E1
Sup Ct sets death sentnc review 1-22, 87G2
Sup Ct backs 1-member dists 3-3, 219D1
Reagan campaigns 5-6, ups delegate lead 5-11, 342G3
French pres visits US 5-17—5-22, in New Orleans, Lafayette 372F1
Brown seeks delegates, Edwards endorses 6-10, 432F1
Rotary conv in New Orleans 6-14, 484D2
New Orleans street vendor curb upheld 6-25, 552F1
US Sup Ct voids death penalty law 7-2, 491G1
Dem conv women delegates, table 508C2
Dem conv pres vote, table 7-14, 507C2
Treen, 2 other delegates switch to Ford 7-29, 550E2
Oil refinery blast 8-12, 816A2
GOP pre-conv delegate count 8-14, 583C3
Passman beaten, runoff set for Hebert seat 8-14, 633A1
Reagan seeks conv delegates 8-17, 601B3
GOP conv pres, vp vote tables 8-18—8-19, 8-19, 599C1, C3
'74 offshore lease sale cited 8-25, 648F3
Ford campaigns 9-25—9-26, 723A3
Tanker, Miss ferry collide 10-20, 976G1
H Rap Brown '68 arms chrg dropped 10-21, 912C3
Edwards admits Park gifts 10-25, 900D1
Carter in New Orleans 10-30, 827E1, G1
Carter for Atlantic offshore oil search 10-30, 827G1
Dole visits Baton Rouge 10-31, 827A3
Election results 11-2: pres 818B1, 819B2; cong 822G1-B2, 829F3
US Sup Ct sets mandatory death sentence review 11-29, 900F2
US Sup Ct refuses HS reverse bias case 11-29, 900F3
Grain Export Probe—*See 'Export Probe' under GRAIN*

1977

LOS Angeles, Calif.—*See under CALIFORNIA*
LOS Angeles County-University of Southern California Medical Center
Burn patient death choice rptd 8-11, 712D2
LOS Angeles Times (newspaper)
USSR detains Toth 6-11—6-15, 474C3
Wyo libel jurisdictn review refused 6-20, 517C1
USSR chrgs Toth as spy 7-12, 564F1
FTC challenges ad policy 8-17, 658C3
On most reliable govt news source list 12-10, 1009B1
LOS Padres National Forest (Calif.)
Marble Cone Fire 8-1—8-19, 660D2
LOTTERIES—*See GAMBLING*
LOUBET, Nat
On boxing scandal rpt 9-3, 828D2
LOUDON, Dorothy
Wins Tony 6-5, 452C1
LOUDON, John H.
Kissinger to succeed on bank com 3-21, 396E3

LOUISIANA
Shreveport record low temperatures rptd 1-14, 37B2
US plans oil storage 1-17, 31D2
FPC OKs emergency gas sale 1-20, 54C1
'75 interstate gas sales cited 1-28, 76C3
Sovt boxing match in Shreveport 2-3, 263B2
Falstaff, Dixie bribery chrgd 2-16, 215D2
New Orleans shipyd job-bias accord rptd 3-21, 279C2
19 chrgd with sex crimes 4-11, 432F2
Carter backs Red R waterway 4-18, 299D3
Carter energy plan reactn 4-20, 320D2
FPC OKs LNG terminal 4-29, 370C1
'76 per-capita income table 5-10, 387E2
Mandatory death sentncs curbed 6-6, 478D2
Legalizes laetrile 6-23, 508E1
Cities OK police, fire fighter quotas 6-29, 819F1-A2
Tex superport project threatnd 7-12, 559C2, G2
FPC-Texaco gas dispute resolved 7-14, 559A3
Carter in New Orleans 7-22, 575G1
Superport license signed 8-1, 724B3
'76 per capita income, tax burden table 9-13, 10-18, 821D2
ILA dock strike begins 10-1, 778C1
Anti-abortn amendmt rptd sought 10-6, 786B3
Econ boycott by ERA forces rptd 11-14, 918D1
ILA dock strike ends 12-1, 916C1
Iran '76 New Orleans investmt rptd 12-5, 997D3
Oil rig copter crashes 12-8, 1023F2
N Orleans 'gateway' air svc OKd 12-21, 1006C2
Westwego grain elevator blast 12-22, 1023E1
Grain Export Probe—*See 'Export Probe' under GRAIN*
Politics & Government
Legislature schedule rptd 6D2
Tonry resigns 5-4, indicted 5-12, 418A3
Local officeholder rule voided 5-16, 419B2
Tonry loses primary 6-25, 501E1
Tonry gets 1-yr sentence 7-28, 603A3
GOP wins Tonry seat 8-27, 693B1
Judicial conduct code review refused 11-7, 857D2
New Orleans elects black mayor 11-12, 879C1

1978

LOS Angeles, Calif.—*See under CALIFORNIA*
LOS Angeles County Bar Association—*See AMERICAN Bar Association*
LOS Angeles County v. Associated General Contractors
Reverse bias case sent back by Sup Ct 7-3, 552B1
LOS Angeles Times (newspaper)
Shaw wins Pulitzer 4-17, 315A2
Toth denies Shcharansky link 7-11, 541D1
LOS Angeles v. Manhart
Sex-based pensn plans barred by Sup Ct 4-25, 322A3
LOTT, Rep. Trent (R, Miss.)
Reelected 11-7, 851C2
LOTTERIES—*See GAMBLING*
LOUGHEED, Peter
Sees Mondale re gas sales 1-18, 53D3
Lafayette, Plaquemine trust law liability upheld by US Sup Ct 3-29, 280F1-E2
In oil-price talks 11-27, 944F2

LOUISIANA
Legislature schedule rptd 14E3
'67, '77 sales-tax rates rptd 1-5, 15E3
State govt tax revenue table 1-9, 84C2
Vance in N Orleans re Canal pacts 1-12, 58B2
Korean gifts to Edwards rptd 1-14, 63D3
Oil spill into Gulf rptd 1-31, 524G1
McDermott pleads guilty, fined 2-22, 142F2-B3
New Orleans clean-air rating rptd 2-23, 144E3
Spinks-Ali N Orleans rematch contract signed 4-11, 378E3
Tornadoes hit 4-17—4-18, 479A3
Westwego '77 grain blast violatns rptd 5-16, 636F2
'76 tanker, Miss ferry collisn rpt issued 5-17, 460B1
Construction pact signed 5-22, 429D3
Garrison sworn appeals ct judge 6-15, 843G3
Creole interstate gas sales probed 6-22, 471B2
N Orleans garbage strike 7-18—7-21, 565C2
Burger urges judgeship bill OK 7-23, 626F3
New Iberia oil storage site scored 8-16, 701C3
N Orleans teachers strike 8-30—9-11, 698G2
Abortn law delayed 9-7, 743D3
New Orleans hosts Ali-Spinks title bout, 3 others 9-15, 726B1-E2
Primary results, cong runoff set 9-16, 736C3
Hackberry oil reserve fire 9-21—9-26, 738E1
'Head & master' case declined by US Sup Ct 10-10, 789D3
Cholera, outbreak rptd 10-11, 927G2
Election results 11-7: cong 846A2, 848G1, 850F4-851A1, 855B2; state 915F2
Nixon at Shreveport airport 11-10, 900B3
WTT Nets operatns end rptd 11-10, 1027B1
Natural gas price controls suit filed 11-20, 900B1
Bossier City, Heflin hit by tornado 12-3, 972G1-B2
New Orleans populatn ranked 12-6, 942G3
Kaiser Gramercy plant reverse job-bias case accepted by US Sup Ct 12-11, 980A3

1979

LOS Angeles, Calif.—*See CALIFORNIA*
LOS Angeles Herald-Examiner (newspaper)
Chamberlain interview rptd 3-21, 291C1
LOS Angeles Times (newspaper)
Morris slain in Iran 2-10, 105B2, 176D3
China OKs office 5-30, 406B2
Daily, Sunday circulatn listed 6-6, 431C1
Condominium trend rptd 6-23, 482F2-A3
Lamb expelled from Iran 7-1, 525D2
Iran sets press curbs 7-23, 566B1
Film industry ad condemns 'McCartyism' 8-8, 593B3
Israel atrocity article rptd 9-13, 802F1
FBI admits '70 Seberg slander 9-14, 705C1
Calif Sup Ct inquiry ends 11-5, 869A2
LOS Angeles Valley State College (Van Nuys, Calif.)
U of New Mex basketball scandal detailed 12-13—12-21, 1003A2
LOS Angeles v. Davis
LA fire dept bias case found moot by Sup Ct 3-27, 263B2
LOSEY, Gavrik
Agatha released 2-8, 174C2
LOSING Time (play)
Opens 9-30, 956C3
LOST and Found (film)
Released 7-13, 820F1
LOTTERIES—*See GAMBLING*
LOUDSPEAKER (play)
Opens 4-30, 712C1
LOUGHEED, Peter
Offers fed loan for oil price hike, OKs Quebec loan 9-13, 728F3
Threatns oil cutoff 10-29, 853E2
Backs oil price rise 11-12, 889B1
LOUGHERY, Kevin
NBA tech fouls ldr 4-8, 290B3
LOU Grant (TV series)
Wins Emmy 9-9, 858D2
LOUISA, Va.—*See VIRGINIA*

LOUISIANA
Med malpractice arbitratn rptd 1-28, 139E3
N Orleans police strike, Mardi Gras fete marred 2-8—3-4, 165E3-166C1
Amer Cyanamid Westwego employes to get back pay 2-10, 131B1
Juvenile trial jury ban refused by US Sup Ct 2-21, 128B3
Floods unfix N Orleans barges, shut port 3-15; threaten levees 4-18, 288F3
KKK operatn rptd 3-15, 7-22, 865E2
Kaiser Gramercy plant reverse job-bias case argued in Sup Ct 3-28, 262D3
Woolworth takeover stayed 4-20, 304C2
Kaiser Gramercy plant affirmative actn challenge rejctd by Sup Ct, reactn; majority opinion excerpts 6-27, 477C1-478E1
'78 cholera cases rptd 7-6, 620F2
Hurricane Bob kills 1 7-11, 639A3
Tropical storm floods coast 7-24—7-28, 638D3
Fetal liver transplant in N Orleans 8-20, 736B3
Miss R barge blast kills 3 8-30, 800D1
State workers Soc Security non-participatn cited 9-10, 727B1
'78 per capita income rptd 9-16, 746F1, E2
Life of Brian furor rptd 10-30, 859C2
New Orleans real estate investmt by shah rptd 11-26, 897G3
Travel Act bribery convictn upheld by Sup Ct 11-27, 919F3
N Orleans layoffs planned 11-29, 921F1
Shell '70 accident liability case refused by Sup Ct 12-3, 964E2
Pub access to bayous curbed by Sup Ct 12-4, 988A1
Energy
Ashland unit offshore holdings sold 2-4, 560F3
Tenneco fined in St Bernard Parish bribe case 3-17, 239B3
N Orleans gas shortage rptd 6-23, 479C1
Tenneco fined re gas shipmt 7-27, 629A2
Gulf of Mex oil, gas lease bids placed 7-31, accepted 8-28, 664E3
US strategic oil reserve storage cited 9-26, 781B2
Tex supertanker port OKd 10-15, 769F3
Gulf of Mex oil, gas lease bids placed 11-27, 943A1
Gulf of Mex lease bids accepted 12-10, 990C2
Politics & Government—*See also other appropriate subheads in this section*
Legislature schedule rptd 5D3

1980

LOS Angeles—*See CALIFORNIA*
LOS Angeles County Museum of Art
Hammer to donate Da Vinci ms 12-12, 997F3
LOS Angeles Herald Examiner (newspaper)
Garvey article reprint OKd 8-14, 637D2
LOS Angeles International Airport
Nuisance award case refused by Sup Ct 10-6, 782A3
'Alphabet bomber' sentncd 11-24, 927A2
LOS Angeles Press Club
Kennedy addresses 5-15, 383B2
LOS Angeles Times (newspaper)
FBI Seberg probe rptd extensive 1-9, 55C1
Bush denies '70 campaign gift coverup 2-7, 128E3, G3, 129C1
Iran readmits newsmen 3-7, 178C2
Quotes Jordan denial on Iran mil action 4-23, 298F2, G2
ADA head interviewed 6-15, 480G1
McManus flees Iran 7-24, 572C1
Chun interview rptd 8-8, US disputes 8-11, 620G1, 645D2
NBA cocaine use rptd widespread 8-19, 656E1
May in pres TV debate 9-21, 721C3
LOS Angeles v. Blake
Case declined by Sup Ct 4-28, 369B2
LOS Angeles v. Greater Westchester
Case refused by Sup Ct 10-6, 782B3
LOS Padres National Park (Calif.)
Gulf Oil drilling rights affirmed by Sup Ct 3-31, 291A3
LOST in Love (recording)
On best-seller list 4-30, 360A1; 6-4, 448F3
LOST Love, Last Love, (book)
On best-seller list 12-7, 948F3
LOTT, Rep. Trent (R, Miss.)
Named House GOP whip 12-8, 936C2
LOTTERIES
Fed oil leasing suspended, scandal hinted 2-29; resumptn ordrd 4-7, 330B2
Pa fraud chrgs rptd 9-19, 786B3
LOUANNE
Oh, God! II released 10-3, 836D3
LOUGHEED, Peter
Trudeau oil price mtg set 6-19, 486D1
Ottawa oil talks fail 7-25, Alberta hikes price 7-31, 577A2, A3
Vs Canada bill of rights 9-18, 728A2
Vows Alberta oil productn cutback 10-30, Ottawa offers price negotiatns 10-31, 858G2
Rpts econ plans re oil project delay 11-19, 920E3
Westn separatism polls rptd 11-24, 11-25, 941B1, D1
LOUGHRAN, Thomas J.
Named CFTC div chief 7-22, 558F3
LOU Grant (TV series)
Wins Emmy 9-7, 692C1
LOUIS, Francois
Discovered on Cayo Lobos 11-22, 920D1
LOUIS, Joe
Holmes breaks heavywgt KO mark 10-2, 772E1
LOUIS, Victor
Rpts Afghan peace force hint 2-27, 165F1
LOUISIANA
N Orleans real estate brokers ruled subject to trust 1-8, 16C1
N Orleans port congestn rptd 1-19, 45C1
Byrd dies 1-30, 104A2
New Orleans-London air svc agreed 3-5, 172B3, E3
Gonorrhea epidemic rptd 4-9, 584E3
Hunts' bailout loan collateral listed 5-28, 425F3
US chem-dump suit filed 7-15, 558F3
Accidents & Disasters
Drought, heat wave hit 6-23—8-15; Carter declares disaster area 7-16, 616D1, G1
Lake Peigneur 'swallowed' in salt-mine collapse; illus 11-20, 970C2, E2
Crime & Civil Disorders
'Miranda rights' waiver proof backed 1-21, 93B3
FBI Brilab probe rptd 2-8—2-9, 111F2, C3; indictmts 6-17, 454D3
FBI 'Miporn' probe rptd 2-14, 136A2
Kraft cocaine probe rptd 9-14, 700C1
Energy
Carter outlines A-waste storage plan 2-12, 127F3
Davis named gas tax case fact-finder by Sup Ct 3-3, 210G1
Oil reserve stockpiling stalled 3-5, 165E3
Oil leasing rights denied by Sup Ct 4-28, 369C1
US intrastate gas sale power affirmed 6-6, 552B3
'79 oil stockpiling cited 6-16, 552B2
13 oil workers die in hurricane evacuatn 8-9, 621F2
Gulf coast leasing bids set records 9-30, 785G1
PPG accused of fuel-switching 11-25, 899D3
Oil reserve stockpiling hike clears Cong 12-1, 954F2; signed 12-12, 982B1
Labor & Employment
ILA loads Sovt cargo 1-29, 169B1
Itinerants registratn voided 5-13, 370F2
N Orleans not in dock pact 5-27, 482A2
Itinerant worker registratn ruling affirmed by Sup Ct 10-20, 807D2
Politics & Government—*See also other appropriate subheads in this section*
Legislature schedule rptd 18E1
Pres primary results 4-5, 264F3
Tauzin elected to cong 5-17, 404D3

1976

LOUISVILLE, Ky.—*See KENTUCKY*
LOUISVILLE Courier-Journal and Times (newspaper)
Wins Pulitzer 5-3, 352E3
LOURENCO, Brig. Gen. Vasco
Keeps mil post, cncl seat 8-12, 733E2
Scores 'reactionary forces' 10-22, 812C1
LOVE Rollercoaster (song)
On best-selling list 1-28, 104G3
LOVER Please (recording)
Wins Grammy 2-28, 460C3
LOVE Will Keep Us Together (recording)
Wins Grammy 2-28, 460G2
LOW, George M.
Quits NASA post 3-19, 232A2
LOW, Stephen
Zambia amb 7-14; confrmd 8-4, 808B1
LOWDER, Carroll
Williams freed 1-16, 79B1
LOWELL, Mass.—*See MASSACHUSETTS*
LOWELL, Dr. Francis C.
On cold drugs 9-8, 680D2
LOWESTOFT (British warship)
In Intl Naval Review 7-4, 488C3
LOWRY, John
Kunstler to ask chrgs dropped 1-17, 79D1
LOWRY, Judith
Dies 11-29, 932E3
LOWRY, Laurence S.
Dies 2-23, 192E3
LOY, William
Acquitted 5-5, 342E3
LOZANO, Domingo
Killed 10-10, 996F1
LOZANO Jr., Ignacio Jr.
El Salvador amb 7-21; confrmd 8-4, 808B1
LSD—*See NARCOTICS & Dangerous Drugs*
LTV Corp.
LTV Aerospace Corp.
'75 arms sales listed 2-6, 147A3
Vought Corp.
Navy stops cruise missile dvpt 3-8, 183C1
LU Ann Hampton Laverty Oberlander (play)
Opens 9-22, 1014E3
LUBIENSKI, Konstanty
Polish State Cncl member 3-25, 268D2

1977

LOUISIANA Land and Exploration Co.
'76 sales return rise rptd 340B2, 341B1
LOUISIANA Offshore Oil Port Inc. (LOOP)
Tex superport projct threatnd, Loop backers rptd firm 7-12, 559C2, G2
License signed 8-1, 724B3
LOUISIANA-Pacific Corp.
Redwood Pk expansion asked 4-19, 323A1
LOUISIANA State University (Baton Rouge)
Duhe in NFL draft 5-3, 353B3
Morial elected mayor 11-12, 879C1
Loses Sun Bowl 12-31, 1020D2
LOUISVILLE, Ky.—*See KENTUCKY*
LOUISVILLE, University of
Cox in NBA draft 6-10, 584B3
LOUISVILLE Courier-Journal and Times (newspaper)
CIA links charged 9-12, 720B3
LO-Vaca Gathering Co.—*See COASTAL States Gas Co.*
LOVE, Philip H.
Dies 8-17, 696B3
LOW, Stephen
Tours Southn Africa 5-17—6-1, 457C1 ★
In Zambia, Rhodesia 7-5—7-10, 536A1
LOWE, Victor
FBI domestic intell cutback rptd 11-9, 861A3, C3
LOWELL, Robert
Dies 9-12, 788E1
LOWENSTEIN, Allard
Backs S Africa isolatn 2-28, 145A2
On UN comm bloc votes 3-5, 207G1
Drops Sovt rights probe bid 3-7, 207E1
Visits Chile 8-8, 635B2
LOWENSTEIN, James G.
Named amb to Luxembourg 5-13, confrmd 5-25, 499G3
LOWERY, Rev. Joseph
Scores Carter 8-18, 702A2
Blacks meet re govt 'neglect' 8-29, 702E1
LOWMAN, Dr. Charles LeRoy
Dies 4-17, 356D3
LOZA, Elijah Nkwekwe
Death rptd 8-1, 640G1
LOZANO, Ignacio
On US-El Salvador ties 3-26, 373F3
Scores US on El Salvador rights 7-21, 580B2
LSD (Lysergic Acid Diethylmide)—*See NARCOTICS & Dangerous Drugs*
LTV Corp., The
Jones & Laughlin contract OKd 4-9, 273G2
Jones & Laughlin hikes price 5-12, 385C2
3d ¼ loss; Jones & Laughlin, Wilson, Vought earnings rptd 10-28, 943C3
Lykes merger planned 11-4, 943F2-D3
LUBBOCK (Tex.) Avalanche-Gazette (newspaper)
Striking farmers delay delivery 12-21, 1003B1
LUCAN, Earl of
Goldsmith drops Pvt Eye suit 5-16, 527C1
LUCAS, Frank
Indicted 2-24, 155F2
LUCAS, George
Star Wars on best-seller list 8-14, 643A2; 9-4, 712E3; 10-2, 808F3
Star Wars sets rental mark 11-19, 1021B3
LUCAS, John
Named to NBA all-rookie team 5-16, 584F3
LUCAS, Judge Malcolm M.
US to return seized Scientology papers 7-20, 628D2
LUCAS, Maurice
Fined for NBA playoff brawl 5-27, 490C3

LUCAS Garcia, Gen. Romeo
Guatemala pres candidate 10-16, 869D1

1978

LOUISIANA Land & Exploration Co.
'77 top sales return rptd 5-8, 325B3
LOUISIANA State University (Baton Rouge)
Loses Liberty Bowl 12-23, 1025E2
LOUISVILLE, Ky.—*See KENTUCKY*
LOUISVILLE Courier-Journal (newspaper)
Whitt wins Pulitzer 4-17, 315A2
LOUISVILLE & Nashville Railroad Co.—*See under SEABOARD Coast Line Industries*
LOURIE, Arthur
Dies 10-4, 888B3
LOVE, Nicholas
Killed 3-27; Botswana clears of chrgs 5-17, 596A1
Soldier cleared in death 11-13, 906D2
LOVE Canal (Niagara Falls, N.Y.)
Disaster area declared 8-7, 703A1
EPA issues dump site rpt, cites cleanup costs 11-21, 899E2, G2
LOVE Is Thicker than Water (recording)
On best-seller list 2-4, 116F3; 3-8, 196B1
LOVERA, Waldino
Arrested in Paraguay 11-17, 989F3
LOVE Story (film)
Sequel released 12-14, 1030C3
LOW, Stephen
Joins UK Rhodesia envoy 11-28, 912A1
LOW-Beer, Dr. Gerald
Rpts USSR dissidents sane 4-20, 360D1
LOWE, A. Lynn
Unopposed in Ark gov primary 5-30, 426C2
Loses electn 11-7, 855G1
LOWERY, Joseph
Disputes FBI '64 memo on King conspiracy 5-29, 410D3
Sees Carter, scores budget plans 12-4, 936D3
LOWRY, Gordon
Dancin' opens 3-27, 887F1
LOWRY, Mike
Wins US House seat 11-7, 852B4
LOY, Frank E.
Elected Penn Central pres 10-24, 876A1
LPGA (Ladies Professional Golf Association)—*See GOLF*
LTV Corp.
'76 tax nonpaymt rptd 1-27, 65G2
Bell backs Lykes merger 6-21, 492C3
Lykes merger probe by FTC asked by Kennedy 11-9, rejctd 11-21; shareholders OK merger 12-5, 935C2
LUAHINE, Iolani
Dies 12-11, 1032C3
LUBIN, Isador
Dies 7-6, 620A3
LUBMAN, Leonid
Rptd sentenced 4-10, 416A3
LUCAS, John
NBA assist ldr 4-9, 271G2
Warriors OK Barry compensatn award 9-5, 1027D3
LUCAS, Judge Malcolm
Upholds FBI '77 Scientology raids 7-6, 554E1

LUCAS Garcia, Gen. Romeo (Guatemalan president)
Violence, fraud chrgs delay pres vote count 3-5—3-9, 168G1
Electn results disputed 3-10—3-11, offcl figures rptd 3-14, 190F1
Named pres-elect by Cong 3-13, 190D1
Backers win most cong seats 4-28, 354C3
Rural land ownership cited re peasant clashes 6-9, 497F1
Inaugurated as pres; asks 'peaceful' solutn to Belize issue 7-1, 538E1
Civilns dominate Cabt 7-21, 722B3 ★
Panama ties resumed 8-29, 798B3

1979

N Orleans loses GOP conv bid 1-23, 70E3
Ex-Rep Passman acquitted on Korean paymts 4-1, 265B3
Regulatory bds rptd segregated 4-9, 307A2
Leach pleads not guilty to vote buying 7-24, 561D1
Landrieu named HUD secy 7-27, 577B1, F1; confirmed 9-12, 700F2
Leach acquitted 11-3, 900E2
Treen elected gov 12-8, 946C3
Ex-rep Hebert dies 12-29, 1008B3
School Issues
E Baton Rouge segregatn case refused by US Sup Ct 1-15, 32E1
Baton Rouge teachers strike ends 4-2, 599D1
New Orleans suburb hit by teachers strike 8-27, 679B1, E1
Shreveport busing rptd set 9-2, 679E3
Sports
NBA OKs N Orleans team move, oppositn rptd 6-8, 527B1
N Orleans gets WBL team 6-12, 526G2
LOUISIANA Land & Exploration Co.
Record copper price posted 10-2, 740A2
LOUISIANA-Pacific Corp.
Fortune rpts '78 sales gain 5-7, 305G1
Portland Timbers purchase OKd 10-15, 1004C2
LOUISIANA State University (Baton Rouge)
Forgn student enrollmt listed 167E3
Scales suspended from basketball 3-5, 291B1
NCAA basketball tourn results 3-26, 238B3
Alexander in NFL draft 5-3, 335F2
Williams dies 7-6, 588G3
Wins Tangerine Bowl 12-22, 1001A3
LOUISIANA Technical University (Ruston)
Loses AIAW basketball title 3-25, 239A1
LOUISVILLE, Ky.—*See KENTUCKY*
LOUISVILLE & Nashville Railroad Co.—*See SEABOARD Coast Line Industries*
LOUISY, Allan (St. Lucian prime minister)
Party wins electns, named prime min 7-2, 545C3
LOURDES, Shrine of Our Lady of (Lourdes, France)
'Cross of Lourdes' refunds set 1-19, 91C3
LOVE At First Bite (film)
Released 4-12, 528G2
Top-grossing film 5-2, 356F2; 5-23, 448G3
LOVE Canal (Niagara Falls, N.Y.)
Chem dump hearings, Hooker held aware of seepage in '58 4-10, 4-11, 281B3
Carter cites re legis 6-13, 441F1
Chem dump probe rptd 6-18, 597A2
US sues Occidental 12-20, 990E1
LOVELL, Dyson
Champ released 4-3, 528F1
LOVELY Sunday For Creve Coeur, A (play)
Opens 1-21, 292A2
LOVE On The Run (film)
Released 4-5, 528A3
LOW, George
To head air safety panel 12-19, 988F3
LOW, Stephen
'78 Africa fact finding missn rpt issued 1-17, 39F3
LOWE, Douglas
On Labor win in Tasmania 7-29, 612F1
LOWELL, Susan
Explains teachers' strikes 9-4, 679D1
LOWENSTEIN, John
Orioles win AL pennant 10-6, 797D2
In World Series 10-10—10-17, 816B1
LOWERY, Rev. Joseph E.
Williams' dismissal upheld 4-10, 283G1
Leads Ala protest marches 6-9, 7-20, 865F3, 869D3
On Young UN resignation 8-15, asks Black-Jewish mtg 8-16, 606G1, A2
Meets PLO, Israeli, Jewish ldrs; backs PLO 8-21, 623G3
With SCLC group in Lebanon 9-18—9-20, deplores Israeli rebuff 9-20, 694G1, E2
Ends Leb visit, Arafat rejects nonviolence plea 9-21, 763D2
LOWRY, Pat
Vs BL strike 2-5, 115E3
LOYOLA University (Chicago, Ill.)
Knight in NBA draft 6-25, 507B3
LSD (lysergic acid diethyamide)—*See NARCOTICS*
LTV Corp.
Ohio Jones & Laughlin Steel to close; Pa plants US aid cited 11-28, 941E3
LUBIN, Moshe
Laser fusion advance rptd 6-16, 692B1
LUCAS, George
More Amer Graffiti released 8-17, 820B2
LUCAS, John
NBA assist ldr 4-8, 290G2
LUCAS Garcia, Gen. Romeo (Guatemalan president)
Army staff chief slain 6-10, 445C3
Nephew kidnaped 10-7, 792C3
Family buys ads for nephew's kidnapers 10-26, 813E3

1980

Leach faces runoff; Long, other incumbents reelected 9-13, 724E2
Bush speaks in N Orleans 9-29, 781G1
5th judicial circuit split 10-14, 918A3
Reagan in Shreveport 10-22, 802G1
Reagan in New Orleans 10-30, 840A1, B1
Election results 11-4: pres 838B1, 839B2, E3; cong 840G1, 842F4-843A1, 845A3, 849C3; state 845F2
'80 census rptd 12-31, 983E1
Sports
N Orleans hosts WBC welterwgt bout 11-25, 907C2
Athletic Comm fines Duran 11-26, 1000A3
LOUISIANA Land & Exploration Co.
Hunts sell shares to meet margin calls on silver, NYSE halts trading 3-27, 223C2
On '79 Fortune 500 list 5-5, 291E1
LOUISIANA State University (Baton Rouge)
Rein presumed dead 1-11, Stovall replaces as football coach 1-12, 175A3
NCAA basketball tourn results 3-24, 240F1
Ervin addresses 10-22, 908A2
LOUISVILLE—*See KENTUCKY*
LOUISVILLE, University of
Wins NCAA basketball title, Griffith named tourn MVP 3-24, 240D1-D2
Wilson in NFL draft 4-29, 336F3
Griffith in NBA draft 6-10, 447C1, E2
LOUISVILLE Courier-Journal (newspaper)
Adams, Detjen win Polk awards 2-25, 692F3
Brinkley, Mather win Pulitzers 4-14, 296G2
LOUVRE, The (Paris museum)
Titian forgeries chrgd 2-26, 472C3
LOVE Canal (Niagara Falls, N.Y.)
NY sues Occidental, Hooker 4-28, 331C3
Health defects rptd 5-16; homeowners demand evacuatn 5-19, US OKs, Carey reacts 5-21, 386D3-387E1
LOVELY, Victor Burns
Held in PI bombing 10-31, 874B2
LOVE Me Do (recording)
Lennon slain 12-8, 934C3
LOVERA, Virgilio
Seized in Colombia DR Emb raid, suffers heart attack 2-27, 141C1
Suffers 2d heart attack 3-17, 211A3
Emb siege ends, freed in Cuba 4-27, 335G1
LOW, George M.
Asks FAA overhaul 6-26, 519A1
LOWENSTEIN, Allard
Slain 3-14, suspect chrgd 3-18, 214C2
LOWERY, Bill
Elected to US House 11-4, 842C2
LOWERY, Rev. Joseph E.
At Wrightsville (Ga) rally 4-12, 333C1
Endorses Carter 10-23, 803C1
Meets with Reagan 12-11, 956F2
LOY, Bob
Defends rights 7-29, KBCI-TV sues Idaho prosecutor over tapes raid 8-1, 732C3
LOZANO, Manuel
Released 4-4, 293B3
LPGA (Ladies Professional Golfers' Association)—*See GOLF*
LTV Corp.
Standard Oil (Ind) to buy coal properties 3-25, 385C3
Jones & Laughlin-USW pact set 4-15, 289B2; prices cut 7-10, 575G2
Pneumo merger set 8-28, 746B1
LUBACHIVSKI, Most Rev. Myroslav Ivan
Named Ukrainian RC ldr 3-27, 413E3
LUBBERS, William
Confrmd as NLRB counsel 4-23, 333E2
Deering Milliken '56 labor dispute setlmt rptd 12-3, 962G2
LUBENOV, Lubomir
Wins Olympic medals 8-1, 8-2, 622B2, C2
LUBIN, Leonard
Birthday of Infanta wins Amer Book Award 5-1, 692B2
LUBISHI, Johnson
Sentenced to death 11-26, 968B1
LUCAS, George
Empire Strikes Back released 5-21, 675D2
LUCAS, John
NBA assist ldr 3-30, 278E3
LUCAS Jr., Dr. Virgil S.
Pot cancer aid study rptd 4-15, 358B1

LUCAS Garcia, Gen. Romeo (Guatemalan president)
VP resigns in rights protest 9-2, 670F3
Bomb kills 7 in Palace plaza 9-5, 708E3

1976

LUCE, Charles F.
Defends A-plant safety 2-10, 115A2
LUCEY, Gov. Patrick J. (D, Wis.)
Protestors taunt Wallace 3-30, 245F3
LUCUMBERRI-Martinez, Javier
Arrested 1-8, France accuses 1-11, 45C2-B3, D3; sentncd 3-3, 454F3-455A1
LUDER, Italo
Peron shuffles cabt 1-15—1-16, 71B2
Rejcts Peron impeachmt 3-4, 211F3
LUDLUM, Robert
Gemini on best-seller list 12-5, 972F2
LUELLEN, Charles J.
Indicted 6-1, 412E3
LUFTHANSA-German Airlines
Lockheed payoffs rptd 2-4, 130D3
LUGAR, Richard Green
Wins Sen primary 5-4, 323B2
Elected 11-2, 819D3, 823B2, 828E1
LUGE
Winter Olympic results 2-7, 2-10, 159G1
LUGO, Freddy
Arrested 10-7, 779C3
FBI agent contact denied 10-25, 844C2
Trinidad deports 10-26, indicted 11-2, 843F2, 844A1
LUJAN Jr., Rep. Manuel (R, N.M.)
Reelected 11-2, 823F3, 830F1
LUKEN, Thomas A.
Elected 11-2, 823F3, 830F2
LUKONIN, Mikhail K.
Dies 8-5, 892C3

LUMBER (& Lumber Products)
Canada '75 trade deficit rptd 1-30, 116B3
CAR '75 exports rptd 2-2, 204D2
France proposes price stabilizatn fund 5-10—5-11, 355E3
Ford urges regulatory reform 5-13, 347A1
GOP platform text cites 8-18, 608B1
Fiirms effective tax rate cited 10-14, 847C2
Land-use bill signed 10-21, 834D1
Clear-cutting bill signed 10-22, 833F3
Sup Ct rules vs Foster in tax case 11-2, 867E1
Oct WPI rptd 11-4, 846C2

LUMMIS, Annette Gano
At Hughes burial 4-7, named Tex executor 4-14, 335C3, 336B1
On Hughes will, legal residence 7-13, son named Summa bd chrmn 8-4, 596C3
Hughes relatives file pact 8-27, 971F2
LUMMIS, William R(ice)
Named Hughes Tex executor 4-14, Summa admin 5-5, 335C3
Summa bd chrmn 8-4, 596C3
Hughes relatives file pact 8-27, 971F2
Hughes will forgery chrgd 12-13, 971B2
LUND, Robina
Named in Getty will 6-8, 444D2
LUNDINE, Stanley
Elected to Congress 3-2, 166D2
Reelected 11-2, 830D2
LUNETA, Jose
Arrested 638A3
LUNGS—*See 'Heart & Lungs' under MEDICINE*
LUNKOV, Nikolai M.
Protests UK Tory ldr's attack 1-22, 101F1
Sees Callaghan on Africa 3-15—3-19, 229A1
LUNS, Joseph M. A. H.
In Iceland, UK fishing talks 1-14—1-15, 1-19, 50D3
Iceland-UK mediatn fails 2-12, 156C1
On NATO mins mtg 5-21, 353C2
Caramanlis bars Cyprus mediatn 11-12, 897B3
On Sovt missile threat 11-18, 879D2
Lauds Carter NATO pledge 12-9, 933C2

1977

LUCAS Industries Ltd.
Strike threatens Leyland productn 7-4, 695B1
LUCCHESI, Frank
Slugged by player 3-28, 310E3 ★
Fired as Texas mgr 6-22, Randle fined for attack 7-28, 644G2, B3
Sues Randle 9-21, 768D2
LUCE, Don
Chrgs PI suppression 8-25, 664G3
LUCEY, Patrick J.
Named amb to Mex 5-19, confrmd 5-25, 499G3
Replaced as Wis gov 7-7, 560B3
LUCEY, Archbishop Robert E.
Dies 8-1, 696B3
LUERS, William H.
Signs US-Cuba pact 5-30, 455E3
LUETGENDORF, Karl
On arms shipmt to Syria 1-26; resigns 5-30; replaced 5-31, 424D3-425A1
LUFKIN (Tex.) News, The
Wins Pulitzer Prize 4-18, 355E2
LUFTHANSA-German Airlines
Indicted for rate-fixing 2-3, 93F2
Jet hijacked 10-13, raid frees 10-18, 789A1-790D2
Airport security tightened 10-23—10-24, Algeria flight canceled 11-8, 868C3-E3
Hijackers identified 10-25, 10-27, 868E2
Terrorists threaten jets 11-5, 868G2
Passenger bookings fall 11-29, 969D2
LUGAR, Sen. Richard Green (R, Ind.)
'76 spec interest gifts rptd 2-15, 128E2
LUGHOD, Ibrahim Abu
Denies Geneva invitatn 11-15, 873E2
LUGO, Freddy
Tried in mil ct re '76 crash 10-10, 868C1
LU Jui-kin
Replaced as Kweichow head 3-6, 179E3
LULE, Godfrey
Defectn rptd 7-2, 600D3
LULEJIAN & Associates, Inc.
3 acquitted on Iran contract fraud 11-24, 942F2

LUMBER (& Lumber Products)
Asia '76 econ growth rptd 2-16, 147C2
US modifies duty-free list 2-28, 189E3
Minn natl forest case review barred 3-7, 211A3
Redwood Pk expansn asked 4-19, 323A1
Eastn forest expansn urged 4-28, 323D1
'76 sales rise rptd 340B1
Pacific NW output, job rise rptd 5-16, 385C1
S Korea eases import curbs 6-14, 470A3
Guyana-USSR dvpt pact rptd 7-11, 710C3
July WPI rptd 8-11, 629B1
Forest fire losses rptd 8-23, futures prices up 8-29, 660A2, A3
Aug WPI rptd 9-1, 692C1
Canada co expansn bid cited 764A1
US Sept WPI rise rptd 10-6, 776G3
'69-Sept '77 CPI rise rptd 10-21, 817F3
Champion Intl convictn review declined 11-7, 857B2

LUMIANSKY, Robert M.
China vs scholar exchngs 6-28, 505F3
LUMMIS, William R.
Ousts Davis 5-28, sued 6-8, 472G2
LUNDSFORD, Devin
Taiwan wins Little League title 8-27, 768C2
LUNGS—*See MEDICINE—Heart & Lungs*
L'UNITA (Italy CP newspaper)
US office OKd 7-20, 581F2-A3
LUNS, Joseph M. A. H.
Mondale visits 1-24, 70C1
On Cyprus threat to NATO 5-9, 359D1
Rpts USSR SS-20 deploymt 6-9, 530G1
Scores UK '78-79 defns cuts 9-16, 957C1

1978

LUCCHESI, Frank
Settles suit vs Randle 12-8, 1026F2
LUCEY, Patrick J.
Wis primary results 9-12, 736A2
Schreiber loses relectn 11-7, 854A2
LUCHINI, Fabrice
Perceval released 10-6, 1030D3
LUCIANI, Albino—*See JOHN Paul I, Pope*
LUCILLE (recording)
Rogers wins Grammy 2-24, 316A1
LUCKINBILL, Laurence
Prayer For My Daughter opens 1-17, 760B3
LUDLAM, Charles
Utopic Inc opens 12-4, 1031C3
LUDTKE, mellissa
Gains locker room access 9-25, 1026C3
LUDLUM, Robert
Holcroft Covenant on best-seller list 4-30, 356F1; 6-4, 460B3; 7-2, 579C3; 8-6, 620A2
LUDWIG, Daniel K.
Paymts to Brazil offcls rptd 1-13, 165G3
LUDWIG, Harvey A.
Indicted 3-8, pleads guilty 3-16, 184B3
SEC rebate setlmt cited 10-23, 876C3
LUEKING, Herman A.
Named in US Teamster fund suit 2-1, 83F1
LUFTHANSA-German Airlines
Colombia office bombed 2-17, W Ger terrorists take credit 2-18, 147B3
'77 hijacker sentncd in Somalia 4-25, 353F3
Terrorist threats cut '77 profits 5-18, 417C2
US, W Ger air svc accord 10-25, 831F1
NYC cargo terminal robbed 12-11, 1028G2
LUFTIG, Paul
Indicted 7-13, 681B1
LUGAR, Sen. Richard Green (R, Ind.)
Votes vs Panama Canal neutrality pact 3-16, 177F2
Votes vs 2d Canal pact 4-18, 273B1
Says labor law revisn killed 6-22, 508E2
Backs Gartner resignatn 6-28, 513C3
LUIS, Acting Gov. Juan (Independent, Virgin Islands)
Elected to full term 11-7, 915E3
LUJAN, Jorge
TKOs Ruvaldino 3-18, 379C2
Decisns Davila 9-15, 726D2
LUJAN Jr., Rep. Manuel (R, N.M.)
Reelected 11-7 851C3, 855D2
LUKEN, Rep. Thomas A. (D, O.)
Reelected 11-7, 851D3
LUKENS Steel Co.
Eur steel dumping chrgs probed 12-28, 1005G3, 1006A1
LUKOWICH, Morris
Nordiques win WHA All-Star game 1-17, 76F3
LUKYANENKO, Lev
Sentenced 7-20, 634B2
LULU (play)
Opens 2-17, 760D2

LUMBER (& Lumber Products)
Indus reps assured on roadless forest lands study 1-9—1-13, 34C2
Japan plans US trade missn 1-13, 27A1
'77 environmental gain rptd 85A2
US forest sales sealed-bid repeal clears Cong 2-6, 107C3; signed 2-20, 218A2
Redwood Park expansn clears Cong 2-9, 85F2; 3-21, Carter signs 3-27, 218E1
Paraguay '77 exports cut by Argentina curbs 2-17, 292F3
Japan firm declares bankruptcy 2-20, 150A1
More govt harvesting backed by Fed Reserve chrmn 3-15, 181F1
USSR in Nigeria deal 3-21, 248F1
Carter asks timber harvest hike 4-11, 260A1
Carter policy scored by Colo sen 5-2, 342B2
Carter clarifies timber harvest plans 5-4, 320G3, 321B1
Time Inc to buy Inland Container 5-19, 403B3
Japan, NZ trade accord rptd 5-23, 498A1
Gabon productn drop cited 6-1, 596B2
Carter bars clothespin import quota 10-2, 805E1
Brazil, France in port pact 10-8, 772B3
US land purchase registratn signed 10-14, 897C2
Norway, Sweden sign econ pact 12-8, 965A3
Chilea indus rptd affected by forgn trade boycott 12-15, 1014A2

LUMET, Sidney
Wiz released 10-25, 970E3
LUNDINE, Rep. Stanley N. (D, N.Y.)
Reelected 11-7, 851A4
LUNG Association, American
Lung damage rptd in chronic marijuana users 5-15, 728G2
LUNGREN, Daniel E.
Wins US House seat 11-7, 850B2, 856C3
LUNGS—*See MEDICINE—Heart & Lungs*
LUNS, Joseph M. A. H.
Sees Caramanlis 1-26, 149C2
On Carter neutron bomb deferral 4-7, 254B2
Haig resignatn threat rptd 4-25, 298F2
Rpts AWACS approval near 5-19, 398E1
Vs NATO concern with Africa 5-31, 397A2

1979

LUCEY, Patrick J.
Resigns 10-8, 793A3
LUCIER, James
Zimbabwe conf role rptd 9-19; UK denies protest 9-20, 718G1
LUDLAM, Charles
Enchanted Pig opens 4-23, 711F2
LUDLOW Corp.
Tyco seeks takeover 2-9, bid dropped 5-3, 560C3
LUDLUM, Robert
Holcroft Covenant on best-seller list 3-4, 173F3; 4-8, 271C2
Matarese Circle on best-seller list 4-8, 271G1; 5-6, 356C2; 6-3, 432G1; 7-1, 548A3; 8-5, 620A3; 9-2, 672A3
LUDWIG, Daniel K.
Brazil sets Jari projct probe 6-8, 443G2
Brazil to takeover Jari projct 7-12, 542B2
LUDWIG, Karen
Nasty Rumors opens 4-12, 712F1
LUDWIG, Klaus
Wins LeMans 6-10, 490D3
LUFTHANSA-German Airlines
NYC cargo terminal theft arrests 2-17, 2-20, 155B3
LUFTIG, Paul A.
Convicted 1-23, 205A3
Sentncd 3-27, 291E3
LUGAR, Sen. Richard Green (R, Ind.)
In USSR re SALT 8-28—8-30, 658D1
On Baker campaign goals 11-1, 828G3
Baker campaign chngs noted 12-3, 983A2
Chrysler aid compromise set 12-19, 981B3
LUGGAGE
GATT pact signed, tariff cuts seen 4-12, 273G1
LUGOSI, Bela (d. 1956)
Heirs publicity right denied 12-3, 1005E2
LUJAN, Jorge
KOs Garcia 4-8, 412F3
LUKASH, Dr. William
Carter drops out of foot race 9-15, calls fit 9-16, 700E3-701A1
LUKENS Steel Co.
Phoenix Steel fed aid rptd blocked 8-28, 682G1
LUKOWICH, Morris
Winnipeg wins WHA title 5-20, 448B1, C1
LULE, Yusufu Kironde (Ugandan president; replaced June 20)
Names Cabt 4-11, 257D2
Sworn pres 4-13; vows atrocity probe 4-14, 288A1, F1
Ousted 6-20, leaves Uganda 6-22; protests back 6-21, 6-25, 488D3
Tanzania frees; flies to UK 7-8, 3 backers arrested 8-19, 637G2
Binaisa shuffles Cabt 11-19, 998A2
LULU (opera)
Complete versn debuts in Paris 2-25, 173G3-174C1
LULY, Lt. Col. Mohammed Mahmoud Ould (Mauritanian head of state)
Replaces Salek 6-4, 417E1
LUMBARD, Judge J. Edward
Named to special prosecutor panel 1-12, 56G1
LUMBER (& Lumber Products)
US wilderness proposal scored 1-4, 16D2
Canada prov sets stock giveaway 1-11, 37A3
US budgets less timber sales 1-22, 46D1
Norway-Sweden pact imperiled 1-26, 77C2
Stone Container rejcts Boise Cascade bid 1-30, Boise to buy Lone Star unit 4-11, 440E3
House com OKs Alaska lands bill 3-1, 187E1
Intl Paper to buy Bodcaw 3-8, 350B1
Rumania sets price hikes 3-12, 279E3
ITT bread fiber chrg setld 3-25, 308C3
GATT pact signed, tariff cuts seen 4-12, 273G1
Wilderness dvpt proposed 4-16, 282G1
La-Pacific '78 sales gain rptd 5-7, 305G1
US timber sales ordrd hiked 6-11, 441A1
Formaldehyde-cancer link rptd 10-18, 971E1
Canada-Iraq deal rptd lost 10-22, 833G2

LUNDBERG Letter, The (magazine)
Retail gas price rise rptd 5-26, 395E3
LUNGS—*See MEDICINE—Heart & Lungs*
LUNS, Joseph M. A. H.
Denies Nazi tie 3-2; NATO employe defectn linked 3-5, 181A1

1980

LUCEY, Patrick J.
Replaced as Mex amb 4-3, 315E1
Named Anderson running mate 8-25, 646B3
Garth named campaign mgr 8-28, 665C3
Anderson platform issued 8-30, 664F3
TV debate canceled 9-29, 740A1
LUCKINBILL, Laurence
Past Tense opens 4-24, 392F3
LUDLUM, Robert
Matarese Circle on best-sellers list 3-9, 200C3; 4-6, 280D3
Bourne Identity on best-seller list 3-9, 200A3; 4-2, 280A3; 5-4, 359C3; 6-8, 448B3; 7-13, 568B3; 8-17, 640E3
LUDMAN, Anna Maria
Slain 3-28, 255C1
LUDWIG, Daniel K.
Threatns Jari project halt 8-5, 787D2
LUETHY, Jacques
Wins Olympic medal 2-22, 155G2
LUFTIG, Paul A.
Fraud appeal refused by Sup Ct 2-19, 131A1
LUFTIG v. U.S.
Case refused by Sup Ct 2-19, 131A1
LUGAR, Sen. Richard Green (R, Ind.)
Addresses GOP conv 7-14, 530B3
B Carter probe opens 8-4, 595B3
LUGE
Winter Olympic results 2-16—2-19, 156B1
LUGNINI, Giovanni
Accused re Moro affair 1-2, 20G2
LUGO, Freddy
Acquitted in '76 Cuba jet bombing 9-26, 794A3
LUI, Giancarlo
Caligula released 2-2, 216C2
LUIS Cabaco, Jose
Mozambique informatn min 4-3, 278E2
LUJAN, Jorge
TKOs Isogami 4-2, 320C3
LUJAN, Rep. Manuel (R, N.M.)
Reelected 11-4, 843C3, 852B1
LUKAS, Wayne
Codex wins Preakness 5-17, 447D2
LUKASZEWICZ, Jerzy
Ousted 8-24, 641F1
LUKEN, Rep. Thomas A. (D, Ohio)
Reelected 11-4, 843D4
LULE, Yusufu
Obote scores 5-27, 446A2

LULY, Lt. Col. Mohammed Mahmoud Ould (Mauritanian president; deposed Jan. 4)
Deposed, Haidala replaces 1-4, 20G3

LUMBER (& Lumber Products)
Indl Investmt trust suit vs Mitsui declined by Sup Ct 2-25, 188B1
Indian land managemt fed liability limited by Sup Ct 4-15, 306G1
Mt St Helens damage assessed 5-21, 382B2; 5-24—7-4, 503E3, G3
Lindane use curbs sought 7-3, 519D3
Canada forest fire losses rptd 8-2, 633B2
Reagan vows more productn 10-2, 738E2
Alaska lands bill clears House 11-12, 866A3
Alaska lands bill signed 12-2, 916A1
Fuel bill clears Cong 12-8, 953E2; signed 12-19, 982C1

LUMET, Sydney
Just Tell Me released 2-8, 216A3
LUM 'n' Abner (radio series)
Lauck dies 2-21, 176B2
LUNCH Hour (play)
Opens 11-12, 892D3
LUNDBERG Letter, The (magazine)
Exxon opted '79 top US gas seller 1-2, 90D3
LUNDINE, Rep. Stanley N. (D, N.Y.)
Reelected 11-4, 843A4
LUNDQUIST, Dale
Wins Boston Five Classic 6-15, 715B1
LUNDQUIST, Steve
Sets 100-m breaststroke mark 4-12, 7-29, 834C3, 835A1
LUNDVALL, Bjoern
Death rptd 9-22, 756C1
LUNGREN, Rep. Daniel E. (R, Calif.)
Reelected 11-4, 842B2
LUNGS—*See MEDICINE—Heart & Lungs*
LUNS, Joseph
Scores US hostage rescue try 4-25, 324C2

1976

LUPIANO, Justice Vincent A.
Nixon disbarred in NY 7-8, 493F3
LURIE, Ranan R.
Interviews Brown 4-12, remarks rptd 10-17, 10-18, 787F1, B2
LUSHCHIKOV, Gennady
Wins Olympic medal 7-19, 575G1
LUTHERANS
4 in Mo synod ousted 4-2, plan breakaway church 9-30, 776B3
Neunaber resigns as Southn dist pres 8-31, 776G3
Carter in Phila church 9-7, 663G3-664A1, E2
ALC meets, denies partisanship 10-10—10-11, 932C2
Mo synod dissidents found new church 12-3—12-4, 932A2
LUTZ, Bob
Runner-up in Rotterdam WCT tourn 2-29, 716D2
LUTZE, Lothar
Seized on spy chrgs 6-2, 441G3
LUTZE, Renate
Seized on spy chrgs 6-2, 441G3
LUVUALU, Pascal
Defends Sovt, Cuban aid 3-26, 228E2

LUXEMBOURG—*See also EUROPEAN Community, IEA, NATO, OECD*
Listed as 'free' nation 1-19, 20C3
Angola MPLA recognized 2-20, 163B1
Eur liberals meet, Gaston elected federatn pres 3-26—3-27, 260C3
Farkas quits as US amb 5-4, Ginn confirmed 5-20, 412E1, B2
France vs joint Eurpn steel firm 7-6, 521G1
W Ger mark revalued 10-17, 782B1
Rhine pollutn pacts signed 12-4, 977A2
European Force Reduction Issues—*See under EUROPE*
UN Policy & Developments
Vs WHO Anti-Israel stand 5-19, 355D2
Thorn replaced as Assemb pres 9-21, 719A1
Vs anti-S Africa aid stand 11-5, 842C3
Vs black Namibia support 12-20, 955C1

LUZINSKI, Greg
NL batting ldr 10-4, 795F3
LYDICK, Judge Lawrence T.
Sentences Hammer 3-23, 442B2
LYIN' Eyes (recording)
Wins Grammy 2-28, 460A3
LYLE, Albert (Sparky)
In World Series 10-16—10-21, 815E2
LY Lim Kuan, Lt.
Defects to Thailand 4-30, asks asylum 5-2, 335E1
LYME, Conn.—*See CONNECTICUT*
LYNCH, Mel Patrick
Acquitted of Bronfman kidnap, found guilty of extortion 12-10, 952A3
LYNCH, Phillip
Denies devaluation rpts 1-5, 7B3
Heads new cabt com 1-14, 26A3
Chairs new econ panel 1-20, 46A2
Details econ, tax measures 1-26, 97D1
Rpts W Ger loan 3-4, 172A3
Outlines investmt policy 4-1, 249A3
Govt spending curbs announced 4-19, 309A3
On forgn ownership of mines 5-2, 350A1
Parlt gets tax plan 5-6, 362D3
On new tax plan, spending cuts 5-20, 380C1
Announces US loan 5-21, 400A1
Sets suplmtl funds for states 7-14, 554C2
Introduces budget 8-17, 636D3
Names econ advisory bd 9-14, 730E1
On US bond issue 11-4, 850F1
Monetary curbs set 11-7, 850C1
Govt borrowing policy cited 11-9, 869D3
Rpts forgn reserves down 11-26; devalues currency, sets new exchng system 11-28, 896A2
On revaluatn 12-6, capital inflow 12-8, 923B1
Pub spending cut set 12-16, 961E3
LYNCHBURG, Va.—*See VIRGINIA*
LYNDON Johnson and The American Dream (book)
On best-seller list 12-5, 972C2

1977

LUNT, Alfred
Dies 8-3, 696B3
LUPESCU, Magda (Princess Elena)
Dies 6-29, 532C3
LUPU, Petre
Dismissed 1-25, 100F1
LURIA, Aleksandr R.
Dies 8-16, 696C3
LURIE, Ranan R.
Gen Brown article rptd 3-27, 231G3
LUSINCHI, Jamie
Pinerua wins AD pres nominatn 7-17, 566C1
LUSNEY, Norm
Wins electn 6-8, 466E3
LUTALI, A. P.
Loses electn for gov 11-22, 943E3
LUTHERAN Immigration and Refugee Service
Viet refugees arrive in US 9-20, 739G3
LUTHERANS
400 taken from Rhodesian schl 1-30, 73C1
Bolivia rights panel formed 5-14, 414F2
Charismatic conf held 7-20—7-24, 620D3
World Lutheran Federation
Ethiopia natlizes radio 3-12, 238C3
Black African elected pres 6-24, 732E1
LUTZ, Bob
Loses Ocean City Intl 2-20, Volvo Classic 3-20, 430C3, 431B1
S Africa Davis Cup match protests 4-15—4-17, 353G2
LUTZ, Francie Larrieu
Wins mi run, sets 2-mi run mark 2-25, 602D3
LUTZE, Lothar Erwin
Named in W Ger Defns Min spy scandal 12-12, 968E1
LUTZE, Renate
Named in W Ger Defns Min spy scandal 12-12, 968E1
LUVUALU, Pascal
Backs Patriotic Front 1-9, 11C1
LUWUM, Archbishop Janani
Killed 2-16, intl protests 2-17—2-21, 138B3, 139A1
Waldheim asks death probe 2-24, 142B1
Amin letter cited 3-5, 308C3
AACC scores African silence 3-18, 308B3
Wani replaces 3-19, 308F2
Amin ex-min rpts death ordrd 6-8, 487A1
Amin arms smuggling chrg rptd 7-15, 600B3

LUXEMBOURG—*See also EC, IEA, NATO, OECD*
UN Assemb member 4C1
Sodetex probe rptd 1-5, 44A2
'76 Eur Cncl pact vs terror cited 9G2
Dec '75-76 inflatn rate rptd 2-7, 87A2
Kredietbank '77 Eurobond data cited 4-13, 318E1
US amb confrmd 5-25, 499G3
Birthrate decline worries govt 7-21, tax benefits weighed 8-31, 745A3
Sweden quits 'snake' 8-29, 709A1
Eur Cncl to study Turkey rights abuses in Cyprus 9-8, 764G1-A2; rpt shelved, Greece protests 11-3, 946E3
Chretien replaces 9-16, 725G2 ★
UN Assemb condemns Israel occupatn 11-25, 910D2
UN S Africa oil ban abstentn 12-16, 1016A2
Helsinki Agreement—*See EUROPE—Security and Cooperation*
LUZINSKI, Greg
NL wins All-Star Game 7-19, 567C2
NL batting ldr 10-2, 926C3
Foster named NL MVP 11-8, 927C1
LVOV, Valery
US tour results 1-29—2-5, 263G1
LWIN, U
Quits as deputy premier 3-29, 243C3
Rptd Central Exec Com head 10-8, 779D3
LYING-In Hospital (Chicago, Ill.)
DES experiment suit filed 4-25, 431A3
LYKES Corp.
Youngstown contract OKd 4-9, 273G2
Youngstown hikes steel price 5-6, rolls back 5-10, 385F1
Youngstown operatns cut back 9-19, 775E3
LTV merger planned 11-4, 943F2-D3
3d ¼ loss, Youngstown writeoff rptd 11-4, 943B3
LYLE, Sparky
NL wins All-Star Game 7-19, 567E2
In World Series 10-11—10-18, 806F1
Wins AL Cy Young Award 10-25, 927D1

LYNCH, Jack (John Mary) (Irish prime minister; resigned Dec. 5)
Facts on 475G2
Party wins electn 6-16, 475G1-G2
Takes office; names Cabt, forms new ministry 7-5, 598E3
Asks united Ireland, UK exit 7-6, 599A1
SDLP policy paper issued 9-21, 783A3
Meets Callaghan on Ulster power-sharing 9-28, 782A2
Drops detentn law 10-6, 782D3
Opens Dail, asks UK back reunificatn 10-12, 782E2
LYNCH, Mel Patrick
Sentenced 1-6, 103C1
LYNCH, Philip
Presents '77-78 budget 8-16, 670E3
Hospitalized 11-10, 901E2
Land-deal scandal chrgd 11-15—11-21, resigns 11-18, 901C2
Govt reelected 12-10, 963F2
Named indus, commerce min; elected Liberal Party dep ldr 12-19, 982E1-A2

1978

LUNT, Lawrence
Prisoner swap rptd discussed 4-24, 318F2
LUQUE, Leopoldo
Argentina wins World Cup 6-25, 520B2
LURIE, Art
Spinks decisns Ali 2-15, 171C1
LURIE, Bob
A's sale fails 3-27, 355A1
LUTER, Edward
Backs USSR oil equipmt sale 9-6, 743F1
LUTFI, Ali
Egypt finance min 10-5, 774B3
LUTHERAN Church in America—*See under LUTHERANS*
LUTHERANS
Swedish church-state separatn backed 1-19, 93C1
Israel tour bus blast kills 2 W Gers 4-26, 300G2
American Lutheran Church
Female clergy survey rptd 3-23, 295B2
Lutheran Church in America
Female clergy survey rptd 3-23, 295B2
LUTZ, Bob
Loses WCT doubles title 5-7, 418A3
Wins US Open doubles title 9-9, 707G1
US wins Davis Cup 12-10, 1026F3
LUTZ, Charles
Cromwell opens 7-12, 887E1
LUTZ, Francie Larrieu—*See LARRIEU, Francie*

LUXEMBOURG—*See also COUNCIL of Europe, EC, GATT, IEA, NATO, OECD*
US alerts to Sovt satellite fall 57E1
Brazil-Paraguay hydro loan rptd 3-30, 311C2
Graiver bank ties cited 4-12, 326B2
Eur conservative party union shunned 4-24, 424D3
UN Sea Law Conf talks continue 5-23—7-15, 8-21—9-16, 732E3
French workers block traffic 6-23, 6-27, 532C3
UN racism conf boycotted 8-26, 676B2
UN Assemb member 713B3
W Ger mark revalued up 10-16, 798C2
Hungary devalues forint 11-11, 906G2
At Brussels monetary summit, EMS entry backed 12-4—12-5, 952C2
European Force Reduction Talks—*See under EUROPE*
Helsinki Agreement—*See EUROPE—Security and Cooperation*
LUYT, Louis
Named in press scandal 11-2, 868B2
LUZINSKI, Greg
NL wins All-Star Game 7-11, 559C3
NL batting ldr 10-2, 928E2
LVOV, Valery
Wins World Amateur Boxing tourn 5-6—5-20, 600E2
LYKES Corp.
Ind plant shutdown warned 5-24, 492G3
Bell backs LTV merger; '77, 1st ¼ losses cited 6-21, 492C3
LTV merger probe by FTC asked by Kennedy 11-9, rejctd 11-21; shareholders OK merger 12-5, 935C2
LYLE, George
Winnipeg wins WHA title 5-22, 458C2
LYLE, Ron
Chrgd in shooting death 1-6, 56C1
Acquitted 12-16, 1028D2
LYLE, Sparky
Traded to Rangers 11-10, 1026B1
LYMPHOMA—*See MEDICINE—Cancer*
LYNCH, Jack (Irish prime minister)
Reunificatn remarks cause furor 1-8—1-10, Ulster interparty talks collapse 1-9, 18A2, 18B3
Fiaich urges UK end Ulster rule 1-16, 37C2
Garvey fired, explanatn asked 1-19, 72D2
Bids US cut Ulster aid 2-18, scores Biaggi-IRA link 2-22, 289C1
Unions OK wage pact 3-22, 289A2
Urges telecommunicatn reforms 5-10, 393A1
Scores EMS entry terms 12-5, 952B1
Ireland to join EMS 12-15, 979D1
LYNCH, Phillip
Sets steel import limits 7-10, 530G1
Pol corruptn, land deal chrgd; denials issued, probe barred 9-14, 771D1
Rpts mfg subsidy cut 11-13, 944D1
LYNCH, William
Heads GSA probe 9-20, 753F3
LYNDON Baines Johnson Library (Austin, Tex.)
Viet documt possessn by ex-amb rptd probed 9-13, 720B2

1979

LUNT, Lawrence K.
PR prisoner trade denied 9-6, 666G1
Released 9-17, 706D3
Lu PONE, Patti
Evita opens 9-25, 956A3
LURIE, Paul M.
Chicago patronage ruled illegal 9-24, 770F3
LUTHERAN Church in America—*See under LUTHERANS*
LUTHERANS
USSR emigratn rptd backed in US 2-26, 172F2
Baptism rites agrmt reached 3-31, 375G2
Empie dies 9-1, 756C2
Lutheran Church in America
Fair-mkt property acquisitn backed by Sup Ct 5-14, 383B3
LU Ting-yi
Promotion rptd 9-28, 750E3
LUTZ, Bob
Loses US Open doubles title 9-8, 734G1
US wins Davis Cup 12-16, 1003A3
LUTZE, Lothar & Renate
Sentncd on spy chrgs 6-18, 489E3

LUXEMBOURG—*See also COUNCIL of Europe, EC, GATT, IEA, NATO, OECD*
'78 living standards ranked 2-2, 109A2
Uniroyal operatns sale set 4-17, 560G3
Eur Parlt electns 6-10, 433A1, 434C2
Ruling coalitn loses electn 6-10, Thorn resigns govt 6-11, 469C2
EC green currencies revised 6-21, 513G1
Remerschen A-plant plans dropped 6-27, 506A3
Soc Christn coalitn govt sworn 7-19, 568A3
UN membership listed 695G2
EMS currencies realigned 9-24, 719A1
European Force Reduction Talks—*See under EUROPE*
Helsinki Agreement—*See EUROPE—Security and Cooperation*

LYAKHOV, Vladimir
Soyuz 32 launched 2-25, 163F1
Soyuz 33 linkup fails 4-10—4-12, 279B2
Space endurance record set 7-15, 553E1
Ends record flight 8-19, 626D2
LYKES Corp.
China-Lykes Bros pact rptd 2-23, 146G2
LYLE, Sandy
Wins Europn Championship 9-9; 2d in Lancome Trophy tourn 10-28, 970C1, B2
LYLE, Sparky
Bronx Zoo on best-seller list 5-6, 356D2; 6-3, 432B2; 7-1, 548C3; 8-5, 620C3
LYMAN, Dorothy
Later opens 1-15, 292G1

LYNCH, Jack (John Mary) (Irish prime minister; resigned Dec. 5)
Wage restraint backed 2-23—2-25, 155E1
Blaney wins Eur Parlt seat 6-7, 434C2
Bars trans-border suspect pursuit, extraditn 9-2; sees Thatcher 9-5, 669G2, E3
Greets Pope 9-29, 760E1
N Ireland security accord set 10-5, 792F3
In US, sees Carter 11-8; urges Ireland reunificatn 11-9, 874A2
UK contributn cut to EC rejctd 11-29—11-30, 917D3
Resigns 12-5, 950A2
Haughey elected successor 12-7, 950E1
LYNCH, Phillip
Cabt operatns streamlined 2-4, 113D2
On Labor win in Tasmania 7-29, 612B2
Tariff cut put off 8-24, 650B2
Vs NSW auto pollutn curbs 10-31, 888A1
LYNDE, Paul
Villain released 7-20, 820E3
LYNEN, Feodor
Dies 8-8, 671G2

1980

LUPONE, Patti
Wins Tony 6-8, 692A3
LURASCHI, Tony
Outsider released 6-3, 675C3
LURIE, Dan
Ferrigno wins privacy-invasn suit 11-3, 890F2
LURZ, Dagmar
Wins Olympic medal 2-23, 155F3
LUSKIN, Bert
Upholds NFL free agent rule 5-16, 998F2
LUSSA, Raymond
Music Man opens 6-6, 756F3
LUSSIER, Robert
5th of July opens 11-6, 892C3
LUTHER, Martin (1483-1546)
Pope visits W Ger 11-15—11-19, 905A1, B2
LUTHERANS
USSR detains US min 4-18, 431A2
LUTZ, Bob
Loses Wimbledon men's doubles 7-5, 606G2
Wins Stowe Intl 8-17, US Open men's doubles 9-6, 691F2, C3
Wins Cologne Cup 11-2, 947C2

LUXEMBOURG—*See also COUNCIL of Europe, CSCE, EC, GATT, IEA, MBFR, NATO, OECD*
OECD sees Belgium joint current acct deficit 1-17, 56C2
Bahamas bank looting case rptd 3-3, 229B1
USSR May Day parade shunned 5-1, 354G2
Dutch to probe S Africa sanctns 6-27, 499A2
Wine scandal suspected 11-3, 11-18, 925E2
UN Policy & Developments
Assemb Palestinian state res abstentn 7-29, 572F1
U.S. Relations
US Steel files dumping complaint 3-21, 225D1
US sets steel import probe 4-10, 367F3
US finds steel import damage 5-1, 456C1
Reagan US electn reactn 11-5, 841B3

LUZINSKI, Greg
Phillies win NL pennant 10-12, 796B1
LYE, Len
Dies 5-15, 448C2
LYE, Mark
2d in Tallahassee Open 4-21, 714F3
Ties for 2d in Buick Open 8-25, 972F1
LYLE, Sandy
2d in World Match Play tourn 10-14, 972E2
LYMAN, Richard W.
Named Rockefeller Foundatn pres 1-26, 200D1
Kennedy named Stanford pres 6-13, 638D2
LYNCH, David
Elephant Man released 10-3, 836E2
LYNCH, Mark
Argues Nixon taps case in Sup Ct 12-8, 937B2
LYNCH, Michael
At ITC auto import hearings 10-8, 823G1
LYNCH, Paul
Prom Night released 8-15, 675C3
LYNCH, Phillip
Vs 35-hour week 7-16, 602B2
Fed job freeze, probe set 11-18, 900F1
LYNCHBURG—*See VIRGINIA*
LYNCHBURG (Va.) Training School & Hospital
Sterilizatn progrm rptd 2-23, 158F3
LYNE, Adrian
Foxes released 2-29, 216E2

1976

LYNN, Fred
'75 top male athlete 1-13, 31F3
NL wins All-Star game 7-13, 544B2
AL batting ldr 10-4, 796B1
LYNN, James T.
On 'padding' memo 2-4, 115G3
Named to business probe panel 3-21, 262F2
Scores Adams proposals 3-23, 231A3
Briefs Carter 11-22, 881D1
LYNN, Laurence
Carter econ adviser 12-1, 898G2
LYNN, Loretta
Book on best-seller list 12-5, 972D2
LYNN, Judge Seybourn H.
Awards black RR workers 1-9, 25D3
LYONS, John
TUC ldrs back pay curbs 6-16, 439F3
LYONS, John H.
Quits Ford panel 1-8, 4C1
LYONS, Leonard
Dies 10-5, 970C2
LYONS, Lt. Thomas
On US-based Cuban terrorism 8-22, 791C1
LYSENKO, Trofim D.
Dies 11-20, 970D2

1977

LYNN, Fred
NL wins All-Star Game 7-19, 567D2
LYNYRD Skynyrd (rock music group)
3 die in charter plane crash 10-20, 888G3
LYON, Sterling
Wins Manitoba electn 10-11, 823D1
LYSERGIC Acid Diethylmide (LSD)—*See NARCOTICS & Dangerous Drugs*
LYSYK, Kenneth
Asks gas pipe delay 8-2, 596A3
LYTTELTON, Charles John—*See COBHAM, Viscount*

1978

LYNG, John
Dies 1-18, 96F2
LYNN, Mass.—*See MASSACHUSETTS*
LYNN, Rev. Barry
Vs lobbying bill 4-26, 323B2
LYNN, Carroll M.
Convicted of extortion 12-14, 991A2
LYNN, Donald
On Shroud of Turin study 10-4, 926E1
LYNN, Fred
AL batting ldr 10-2, wins Golden Glove Award 11-21, 928A3, D3
LYNX (helicopter)—*See ARMAMENTS—Aircraft*
LYON, Rev. Don
Loses House GOP primary 3-21, 207E1
LYON, Milton
Pins & Needles opens 7-6, 760B3
LYONS, Ivan
Great Chefs of Eur released 10-6, 970E3
LYSINGER, Pat
Shay opens 3-7, 887B3
LYTLE, Rob
Broncos win conf title 1-1, 8G3
Cowboys win Super Bowl 1-15, 39D3

1979

LYNN, Barry
Scores draft registratn 11-13, 868G2
LYNN, Carroll M.
Sentenced 1-29, 79C1
LYNN, Fred
NL wins All-Star Game 7-17, 568F3
AL batting ldr 9-30, wins Golden Glove Award 11-20, 955D3-F3, 956C1
LYON, Ben
Dies 3-22, 272A3
LYON, James K.
Rpts Brecht '43-56 FBI surveillnc 3-29, 367C3
LYON, Dr. Joseph
Utah '50s leukemia study rptd 2-14, 112A2
LYONS, John
On Pay Advisory Com 10-16, 829A3
LYONS, Marty
In NFL draft 5-3, 335F1

1980

LYNN, Barry
Asks amnesty for draft evaders 8-4, 597F3
Disputes draft registratn figures 9-4, 683E2
LYNN, Fred
NL wins All-Star Game 7-8, 636E1
Wins Golden Glove Award 12-6, 926D1
LYON, Rachel
Tell Me a Riddle released 12-17, 1003E2
LYON, Sterling
Vs Canada bill of rights 9-18, 728A2
LYONS, Patti
3d in Boston Marathon 4-21, 527C2
LYTLE, Alev
Tell Me a Riddle released 12-17, 1003E2

M

1976

M-60 Tank—*See 'Tanks' under ARMAMENTS*
MABONI, Rev. Florentino
Arrested 10-31, 903D2
MABROUK, Ezzedin al-
Announces oil price rise, asks Saudi OPEC ouster 6-8, 407E3
MACAO (Portuguese colony)
Portugal sets autonomy 1-10, 53A3
MACAPAGAL, Diosdado
Vs Marcos rule, US denies asylum 4-1, 255C2
MacBRIDE, Roger
Final pres vote tally 12-18, 979B2
MacBRIDE, Sean
Warns re Cuba, USSR Namibia role 8-30, 660F3
Chrgs S Africa sets Angola attack 12-10, 995G3
MacDONALD, Daniel J.
Stays veteran affairs min 9-14, 692B2
MACDONALD, David Robert
On Eur, Canada car price hikes 8-16, 988C1
Named Navy undersecy 9-8, 808C1
MACDONALD, Donald S.
Rpts '75 monetary reserves down 1-5, 28D1
Ontario OKs inflatn progrm 1-13, 46F3
Wage, price controls extended 3-8, 204F1
Federal-province finance talks open 4-1, 265G1
Backs Ontario Liberal split 4-25, 350E2
Presents '76 budget 5-25, 400F1
Proposes forgn bank operatns 8-23, 637C2
Corp profit limit eased 9-7, 730G2
Stays finance min 9-14, 692B2
On A-sale paymts 11-29, 12-2, 923D3
On Polysar rebates 11-29, 924B1
On reserve drop 12-2, 945F2
Meets prov mins re taxes 12-6—12-7, 945B1
MacDONALD, Flora
Loses PC ldrship bid 2-23, 188F2
MACDONALD, Rep. Torbert Hart (D, Mass.)
Dies 5-21, 404A2
MACDONELL, J. J.
Scores govt acctg method 11-22, 903F3
A-sale agent audit OKd 12-21, 998D1 ★
MacEACHEN, Allan Joseph
Pak A-talks suspended 3-2, 174G3
India bars A-sales 5-18, 363A2
Sets 200-mi offshore limit 6-4, 417D1
Signs EEC pact 7-6, 496E3
On Taiwan Olympics ouster 7-16, 529E1
N-S conf deadlocked 7-17, 530F1
Sworn Privy Cncl pres 9-15, 692C1
MacGIOLLA, Tomas
Scores Provisional IRA 1-18, 146A2
MACHA, Vitezslav
Wins Olympic medal 7-24, 576A3
MACHEKHIN, Alexander
Japan chrgs espionage 5-12—5-14, 356E1

1977

M-60 Tank—*See ARMAMENTS—Tanks*
MABAWA, Marco
Resigns 1-23, 161D2
MABROUK, Ezzedin al-
Sees short OPEC price freeze 12-21, 973D1
MacAFFEE, Ken
Loses in Heisman voting, wins Downtown AC Trophy 12-8, 950A2
MacARTHUR, Gen. Douglas (1880-1964)
Laurence Bunker dies 10-10, 872B1
MacBRIDE, Sean
Dec '76 retiremt rptd 109D3
UK sets Agee ouster 2-16, 134C2
MACCOBY, Michael
Gamesman on best-seller list 4-3, 264A2; 5-1, 356C2
MacDONALD, Gen. A. L.
Named defns staff chief 4-20, 302F3
MacDONALD, David Robert
Replaced as Navy undersecy 3-4, 211A2
MACDONALD, Donald Stovel
Bars Argentine A-deal cancelatn 2-3, 114F1
Presents budget 3-31, 253F3-254B2
On uranium cartel, scores US 6-16, 6-17, 480C2 ★
Asks actn vs Polysar 7-8, 542D1
Inflatn forecast cited 7-27, 597E1
Resigns 9-6, 694B2
Replaced 9-16, 725G2 ★
MacDONALD, John
Orlov defense asked 4-20, 314E1
USSR denies visa 5-4, 436G2
Holds mock Orlov trial 6-13, 512D3
MacDONALD, John D.
Condominium on best-seller list 7-3, 548D3
MacDONALD, Peter
Indicted 2-9, 162E3
Acquitted 5-17, 492A1
MACDONELL, James J.
Bars UDI records review 2-1, 114G1
Parlt gets audit rpt 12-1, 946A1
MacEACHEN, Allan Joseph
In US gas pipe talks 9-1—9-2, 687C1
Named Canada dep prime min 9-16, 725E2
Signs Canada pipeline pact 9-20, 725D3
MacFARLAND, Bill
Replaced as WHA pres 8-22, 1021E1
MacGUIGAN, Mark
Prison rpt issued 6-7, 466E2 ★
MACHACEK, Ales
Rptd jailed 9-28, 752D2
MA Chao-chun
Dies 9-19, 788F1

1978

M60 (machine gun)—*See ARMAMENTS—Firearms*
M-60 Tank—*See ARMAMENTS—Tanks*
M-X Missile—*See ARMAMENTS—Missiles*
MABASA, Lybon
Forms AZAPO 4-30, arrested 5-4, 377D2
MABROUK, Ezzedin al-
Backs $ as oil price base 5-7, 341F3
On OPEC price freeze 6-19, 465G1
Calls OPEC price rise pitiful 12-17, 977C3
MAC (Municipal Assistance Corp.)—*See NEW York City—Finances*
MacAFEE, Ken
In NFL draft 5-2, 336F2
MACAO (Portuguese colony)
Chinese urged to visit China 17B3
MACAPAGAL, Diosdado
Meets Mondale 5-3, 360E3
MacARTHUR, Charles
On 20th Century opens 2-19, 887C2
MacARTHUR, Gen. Douglas (1880-1964)
John Fine dies 5-21, 440F2
Amer Caesar on best seller list 10-9, 800B3
MacARTHUR, John D.
Dies 1-6, 96G2
MacARTHUR Park (recording)
On best-seller list 11-8, 888C1; 12-6, 971D1
MacCALLUM, C. J.
Antimatter believed in galaxy center 5-6, 653E3
MACCARI, Auggero
Viva Italia released 7-9, 970C3
MacDIARMID, Alan
Polymer with elec conductivity rptd 5-18, 654D1
MacDONALD, John
Holds mock Orlov trial 5-15, 360A1
MacDONALD, Margo
Loses Hamilton by-electn 6-1, decline seen 6-1—6-2, 437F1, B2, D2
MACDONELL, James J.
1st comptroller-gen named 2-20, 145E3
Rpts contd mismanagemt 11-23, 921F3
MacENULTY, David
Fight for Barbara opens 11-27, 1031F1
MacGRAW, Ali
Convoy released 6-28, 619C1
MACHADO, Vitor Sa
Sworn Portugal forgn min 1-30, 91C3

1979

M (singing group)
Pop Muzik on best-seller list 10-3, 800E3; 11-7, 892E3
M-60 Tank—*See ARMAMENTS-Tanks*
MACAO (Portuguese colony)
China-Portugal ties set 2-8, 134C3
Viet refugee asylum rptd 5-11, 379D2
MACAPAGAL, Diosdado
Sedition probe set 9-7; suspended 9-12, 710A1
Scores Carter re Marcos support 9-15, 815F1
Probe resumes 9-19, 815E1
MacARTHUR, Gen. Douglas (1880-1964)
Amer Caesar on best-seller list 1-7, 80C3; 2-4, 120C3
Eisenhower WWII secret diary rptd 9-16, 9-17, 748C1
MACAULAY, Eunice
Wins Oscar 4-9, 336B2
MACBETH (play)
Umbatha opens 4-9, 712B3
MacBRIDE, Judge Thomas Jamison
Named to wiretap ct 5-18, 442D3
MacCLEHOSE, Murray (Hong Kong governor)
Reapptd gov 9-25, 730C2
MacDERMOT, Galt
Hair released 3-13, 528D2
MacDONALD, Colette (d. 1970)
Husband gets life for slaying 8-29, 817A3
MacDONALD, David
Canada communicatns min 6-4, 423F3
MacDONALD, Flora
Canada external affairs secy 6-4, 423E3
Arabs warn vs Israel emb move 6-7, 467C3
Indochina refugee admissns hiked 7-18, 549E2
Rights speech linked to Argentina A-sale loss 10-2, denies 10-3, 788D3
MacDONALD, Dr. Jeffrey R.
Murder trial challenge declined by Sup Ct 3-19, 203G2-A3
Gets life for '70 slayings 8-29, 817F2
MacDONALD, Margo
On devolution vote 3-2, 169C1
MacDONALD, Michell
Queen Victoria secret marriage rptd 5-22, 388F2
MacDONALD, Robert David
Chinchilla opens 6-4, 711B2
MacDONALD v. U.S.
Case declined by Sup Ct 3-19, 203A3
MACEDO, Murilo
Brazil labor min designate 1-19, 95D1★
Metalworkers strike 3-13–3-27, 328D3
Ends metalworker interventn, reinstates union ldr 5-15, 399G1
Proposes automatic wage hikes 8-3, 612E2
MACEY, Louis
Loses Houston mayoral vote 11-20, 904E3
MACHADO, Luis Alberto
Venez intelligence dvpt min 3-10, 192D3
MACHARSKI, Cardinal Franciszek
Consecrated Krakow archbp 60G2
Installed cardinal 6-30, 640B2

1980

MAANINKA, Kaarlo
Wins Olympic medals 7-27, 8-1, 624B1, E1
MABROUK, Ezzedin al-
Ouster rptd 1-8, 40D1
MACAO (Portugese colony)
Viet refugee flow continues 6-10, 476E1
MACARTHUR, Charles
Front Page opens 12-22, 1003B3
MACARTHUR, Gen. Douglas (1898-1964)
WWII 'gift' dispute rptd 1-30, 1-31, 115E1
William Sebald dies 8-10, 676G2
MACARTHUR, John D. (1898-1978)
Foundatn buys Harper's 7-9, 582B3
MACARTHUR Foundation, John D. and Catherine T.
Harper's purchased 7-9, 582B3
MACARTHUR Memorial Foundation (Norfolk, Va.)
MacArthur WWII 'gift' confrmd 1-30, 115B2
MACAUSLAND, Earle
Dies 6-4, 528D2
MACDONALD, Daniel
Canada veterans min 3-3, 171A2
MACDONALD, Flora
Backs US on Sovt grain ban 1-7, 9C2*
Rpts 3 Sovts ousted for spying 1-21, 56F2
On escape of 6 US diplomats from Iran 1-29, 1-30, 66E1, B3
On Sovt envoy ouster 2-7, 95F3
Warns future US draft dodgers 2-7, 95G3
MACDONALD, Dr. Jeffrey R.
Murder convictn voided 7-30, 654F3
MACDONALD, John D.
Green Ripper wins Amer Book Award 5-1, 692E2
Green Ripper on best-seller list 6-8, 448D3
MACDONALD, Kenneth N.
Linked to bribery in Abscam probe 2-2, 2-3, 81B2
Quits NJ casino comm re Abscam 2-5, 111C1
MACDONALD, Walter E.
Saudi completes Aramco takeover, retains bd seat 9-4, 662A2
MACDONELL, James J.
Proposes civil svc cuts 4-16, 334A3
MACEACHEN, Allan Joseph
Canada dep prime min, finance min 3-3, 171A2
Outlines tax changes 4-21, 310D2
On 1st 1/4 GNP decline 6-17, 461E3
Signs US tax treaty 9-26, 748B2
Scores Canada forgn aid record 10-1, 766A3
Introduces energy plan, '81 budget 10-28, 857G3
Backs Canada tight money policy, scores US 12-19, 992E2
MACEDO, Murilo
Threatens metalworkers' strike interventn 4-1, 272F2
MACFADDEN Group Inc.
Us magazine purchase rptd 3-7, 239A2
MACFIELD Texturing Inc.
EC exempts from polyester duties 9-1, 662F2
MACGRAW, Ali
Just Tell Me released 2-8, 216B3
MACGREGOR, Ian
Named new Brit Steel chrmn 5-1, 352E1
On British Steel record loss 7-30, 578D2
Outlines Brit Steel recovery plan 12-10; seeks wage curbs 12-11, layoffs 12-12, 965E2
MACGUIGAN, Mark
Canada external affairs min 3-3, 171B2
Canada backs Olympic boycott 4-22, 325A3
Scores US policies 6-1, 429A2
Scores US overfishing 6-12, 461C2
Addresses UN aid talks 8-26, 669B1
Addresses UN Assemb: scores Sovts, S Africa 9-22, 749E3-749B1
Scores Sovts at Madrid CSCE conf 11-12, 863C1
MACHADO, Mario
Named ASL com 12-17, 1001B3
MACHARSKI, Archbishop Franciszek
At Gdansk memorial rite 12-16, 976E2

1976

MACHEL, Samora (Mozambican president)
Natlizes pvt homes, renames capital 2-3, 123D1
Scores Rhodesia Pafuri attack, shuts border 3-3, 175D1, 176A1
'75 UK aid offer rptd 3-4, 175G2
At Zambia mtg on Rhodesia 3-24—3-25, 240E2
Sees Kaunda re Rhodesia 4-26, 295E1
In USSR 5-17—5-23, 403C1
Rhodesia bombs base 6-10, 427B2
Rhodesia accuses re raid 8-24, 661F2
At conf re ANC rift 9-6—9-7, 661D3
Vows Rhodesia rebel war 9-19, 739A1
Sees US, UK reps 10-2, 738D3
MACHETE, Rui
Portugal social affairs min 1-2, 11A2
MACHINERY (& Machine Tools)
'77 budget tax proposal 1-21, 63D2
'75 4th ¼ farm equipment profits rptd 2-3, 215A3
E Ger gets Euro$ loan 6-4, 417C2
1st ¼ labor costs rptd 6-18, 494G1
Deere & Co strike ends 11-9, 847D3
MACHINISTS and Aerospace Workers, International Association of (AFL-CIO)
Overtime bar in Wis case upheld 6-25, 552C2
Backs Canada inflatn protest 8-15, 623F3
Carter addresses conv 9-10, 686C2
Braniff bias setlemt OKd 11-23, 943A3
MACIEL, Lysaneas
Scores govt, fired 4-1, 287E3
MACIEREWICZ, Antonin
Detained 11-15, 966F1
MacINNES, Colin
Dies 4-22, 524A3
MacINNES, Helen
'Agent' on best-seller list 12-5, 972E2
MACK, David
Meets Leb Christn ldrs 8-22—8-24, 628E3
MACK, James
Conv vote bribe bid chrgd, denied 8-17, 616G1
MACK, Dr. Thomas M.
Cancer-estrogen links rptd 6-3, 460G3
MACKASEY, Bryce S.
Resigns 9-14, 692E1
MACKAY, Kenneth
Ouellet ruled in contempt 1-23, 72E1
Chrgs 3 mins interfere 2-20, 187G3
Deschaines rpt presented, Lalonde '70 incident cited 3-12, 220E3, G3
Ct rules on Ouellet appeal 10-20, 851F2
MacKELLAR, Michael
Rpts illegal immigrants amnesty 1-25, 71F3
Immigrant quotas raised 5-20, 400E1
Australia admits Viet refugees 12-18, 997C3
MacKINNON, Judge George E.
Watergate case dissent 10-12, 770C2
Dissents re Nixon tapes 10-26, 849D3
MacLEAN, Angus
Wins by-election 11-8, 888D2
MacMILLAN, H. R.
Dies 2-9, 160E3
MACMILLAN, John F.
Loses CLC pres bid 5-20, 401D1
MACMILLAN Inc.
US files consent decree 7-27, 989A2
MACOMBER Jr., William
Sovt hijackers refused US asylum 6-24, 544B1
MACON, Ga.—*See GEORGIA*
MACPHEE, Ian
Australia productivity min 11-8, 870A1
MADAGASCAR—*See MALAGASY*
MADANI, Col. Ali Al-
Syria-bound jet attacked 3-19, 210C1
At Leb truce mtg 4-19, 273F2
Sees Sarkis 5-28, 385E2
Christian collusn chrgd 8-12, 577D1
MADDEN, Rep. Ray J. (D, Ind.)
Loses primary 5-4, 323A2
Travel expense probe ends 10-27, 981F3
Benjamin elected 11-2, 823B2
MADDOX, Garry
NL batting ldr 10-4, 795F3, G3
MADDOX, Lester G.
Cited in Carter biog sketch 512E1-B2
Amer Indep Party pres nominee 8-27, 666D1
Threatens suit re debates 9-2, 644F1
FCC rejects pres debate bid 9-20, 703F2
Dole scores Carter 10-16, 804F1
Loses pres electn 11-2, 818E2
Final pres vote tally 12-18, 979B2
MADEIRA (Portuguese Island)
PPD wins local electns 6-27; Ramalho warns secessionists 6-28, 482E3
Assembly opens 10-23, 812C2
MADEKUROZWA, Edgar (d. 1975)
Chigowe sentncd to die 4-14, 428C2
MADIGAN, Rep. Edward R. (R, Ill.)
Reelected 11-2, 829A3
MADISON, Wis.—*See WISCONSIN*
MADISON, James A. (1751-1836)
House funds library bldg 2-24, 171B1
MADISON Capital Times (newspaper)
Carter endorsement rptd 10-30, 831B3
MADLOCK, Bill
NL batting ldr 10-4, 795E3

1977

MACHEL, Samora Moses (Mozambican president)
Richard sees 1-6, 3D2
Backs Patriotic Front 1-9, 11C1
At Frelimo cong, reelected party ldr 2-3—2-7, 137A1, C1
Castro visits 3-21, 249A3
Owen sees re Rhodesia conf 4-12, 296B2
Lauds West re Rhodesia, Namibia 5-16; sees Young 5-17, 399D1
Portuguese natls rptd ousted 6-1, 467A3
MACHINES (& Machine Tools)
EC fines Japan for ball-bearing dumping 2-7, 109D1
'75-76 Japan-China trade rptd down 2-15, 180D1
Cincinnati Milacron rpts payoffs 4-11, 503E1
1st, 2d ¼ profit drop rptd 4-28, 7-28, 668B3, F3
EC drops Japan ball-bearing duty 7-27, 624B3
US-USSR 1st ½ trade rptd 9-12, 766B2
E Ger-PI trade pact set 12-7, 1000C2
MACHINISTS and Aerospace Workers, International Association of (IAM) (AFL-CIO)
Aerospace firms struck 10-4—12-31, 1005G1
Winpisinger joins AFL-CIO exec cncl 12-12, 961F1
MACK, John E.
Wins Pulitzer Prize 4-18, 355D2
MacKAY, Andrew
Wins by-electn 3-31, 239B3
MacKAY, Barry
Italian Open results 5-22, 430A3
MacKAY, Donald
Missing 7-15, 578A3
MacKAY, Elmer
Chrgs RCMP destroyed files 6-20, 541C3
Finds tap in office 10-31, 841E2
Fox denies RCMP tap role 11-1, 902E2
MacKELLAR, Michael
Australia immigratn min 12-19, 982A2
MACKENZIE, Courtlandt
Issues arsenic pollutn rpt 6-6, 447F3
MacKENZIE, Judge John A.
Rules on shipbldg claims 3-8, 232C2
MACKENZIE, Louis-Robert
Chrgd in Mehu murder 7-3, held 7-12, 583D2
MacKENZIE, Ronald C.
Convicted 2-25, sentenced 3-23; resigns 3-31, 252G3
MACKEY International Airlines
Miami office bombed, drops Cuba svc plan 5-25, 456E2
MacLEAN, Alistair
Golden Gate on best-seller list 7-3, 548F3
MacLEAN, Angus
Wood wins seat 5-24, 410C3
MacLEHOSE, Murray
Grants police limited amnesty 11-5, 936B1
MACMILLAN Co.
Hagstrom Map Co.
Hagstrom dies 10-8, 872B2
MacMILLAN Ring-Free Oil Co.
US trust suit setld 8-31, 691D3
MacMILLEN, Mary Rule
CIA damages backed 5-12, 423C1
MacNEIL-Lehrer Report—*See PUBLIC Broadcasting Service*
MACOMBER Jr., William B.
Replaced as amb to Turkey 5-25, 500B1
MACOMB Reservation State Forest (N.Y.)
Mohawks granted state parkland 5-13, 632D2
MACOMB State Park (N.Y.)
Mohawks granted land 5-13, 632E2
MacPHEE, Ian
Australia productivity min 12-19, 982B2
MACTAS, Mario
Kidnaped 3-1, freed 3-7, 198C1
MACY & Co., R. H.
CPSC sues 8-19, Tris clothing sale halted 8-20, 651F3
MADAGASCAR—*See MALAGASY*
MADDALONI, Michael
On assassinatn plot 2-23, 261A3
MADDOX, Elliot
Signs with Mets 11-30, 989F3
MADEIRA Islands
Swiss charter jet crashes 12-18, 1023E2
MADISON, Wis.—*See WISCONSIN*
MADISON Square Garden Corp.
Gulf + Westn plans takeover bid 3-7, 275D1
NY Nets move to NJ set 7-26, 584D2
House subcom probes TV coverage 11-2, 949G3
Gilbert takes PR post 12-6, 1021E1

1978

MACHEL, Samora (Mozambican president)
Rhodesia role cited 59D2
UK, UN reps see re Rhodesia talks 1-6—1-9, 59F1, G1
Cabt shuffled 4-22, 331C1
OKs Portuguese natls return 7-2, 596G2
Backs USSR, Cuba, Africa role 7-18, 561B2
Vs Nkomo-Smith mtg 9-2, 740E3
Sees Kaunda on RR reopening 10-7, 783E3
MACHIN, Jose Maria
Says terrorism no excuse for rights abuse 6-23, 490A1
MACHINES (& Machine Tools)
China '77 trade rptd 1-16, 89D2
Australia threatens EC boycott 1-25, 69B3
Nigeria in USSR deal 3-21, 248E1
Chain saw industry to set safety rules 3-31, 348E1
USSR, Turkey sign trade pact 4-5, 477D1
E Ger-Brazil deal rptd 7-13, 649D1
Sears loses patent suit 10-2, 844B2
OSHA drops 'nuisance' rules 10-24, 833D3
MACHINISTS and Aerospace Workers, International Association of (IAM) (AFL-CIO)
Lockheed strike ended 1-2, 4B2
Anaconda strike ends 4-3, 284E3
Air Canada suspends svc in contract dispute 8-25—9-5, 686B2
Winpisinger rptd vs Carter wage curb 11-21, 917B3
MacINNES, Helen
Husband dies 1-20, 96C2
MACKASEY, Brice Stuart
Scowen wins seat 7-5, 514B3
MacKAY, Elmer
Bares '75 Allmand, MP tap 2-22, 166G1
2 chrgd in '77 office tap 4-3, 244G1
MACKAY, Kenneth
Fines sugar refineries 10-6, 794F3
MacKELLAR, Michael
OKs Indochina refugee entry 3-15, 187E2
Australia to admit 9,000 Indochinese 5-17, 369A3
Sets new immigratn policy 6-7, 451A1
MacLAUGHLIN, Patrick
Named Ireland police chief 1-20, 72D2
MACLEAN, Alistar
Seawitch on best-seller list 8-6, 620C2
Force 10 released 12-21, 1030G2
MacLEHOSE, Murray (Hong Kong governor)
Term extended 3-23, 259B3
MacMILLEN, Mary Rule
CIA mail-opening damages upheld 11-9, 940D1
MacNAUGHTON, Donald S.
Retires as Prudential chrmn 2-15, named Amer Hosp Corp chrmn 6-28, 808G3
MacNELLY, Jeffrey K.
Wins Pulitzer Prize 4-17, 315B2
MACOMBER, William B.
Named Met Museum pres 4-18, 335C3
MacPHAIL, Lee
A's sale fails 3-27, 355A1
Father inducted into Baseball HOF 8-8, 617E3
McPHAIL, Leland S. (Larry) (1890-1975)
Inducted into Baseball HOF 8-8, 617D3
MacPHERSON, M. A.
Upholds Saskatchewan potash tax 11-17, 922D1
MADAGASCAR—*See MALAGASY*
MADAME Cezanne in a Yellow Armchair (painting)
Stolen from Chicago museum 12-27, 1028F3
MADAME Rosa (film)
Released 3-19, 619A3
Wins Oscar 4-3, 315D3
MADAN, Arun
Details solar cell advance 11-30, 983F1
MADDOX, Garry
Phillies lose NL pennant 10-7, 779D1
Wins Golden Glove Award 11-21, 928B3
MADDOX, Dr. Tom
Rpts Ky equine VD data 7-13, 539A3
MADDY, Ken
3d in primary for Calif gov 6-6, 447D3
MADIGAN, Rep. Edward R. (R, Ill.)
Reelected 11-7, 850F3
MADISON Square Garden Corp.
Werblin assumes presidency 1-1, 95F3
NASL Diplomats purchase rptd 10-5, 969G2
MADLOCK, Bill
NL batting ldr 10-2, 928D2

1979

MACHEL, Samora (Mozambican president)
Admits Zimbabwe troop role 12-26, 976B1
MACHINES (& Machine Tools)
Cooper acquires Gardner-Denver 1-22, 89B1
Lawn mower safety rules adopted by CPSC 1-25, 91E3
China cancels Japan deals 2-26, 181D3
Houdaille Industries sold 4-2, 283B1
GATT pact signed, tariff cuts seen 4-12, 273A2
Sears ordrd to pay Roberts 5-31, 466C2
Turkey imports set 7-31, 637E1
EC ball bearing dumping probe opened 9-20, 719E2
Caterpillar struck 10-1–12-19, 987E1
E Ger, USSR sign pact 10-5, 761C2
Intl Harvester struck 10-31, 987G1
US Mannesmann unit withdraws Harnischfeger bid 11-4, 942G2
USSR mil aided by '74 US ball bearing sales 11-8, 857B1
Bendix wins Warner & Swasey 12-17, 986F2
MACHINISTS and Aerospace Workers, International Association of (IAM) (AFL-CIO)
HEW radiatn safety studies asked 1-30, 90E3
United Airlines strike 3-31–5-24, 402A2
Truck mechanics end strike 4-16, 384F3
St Regis Paper struck 5-15, pact ratified 6-23, 598B3
Free speech, religion cases declined by Sup Ct 6-4, 439F1, G1
OPEC trust suit dropped 8-23, 647C3
Winpisinger backs oil industry protest 10-17, 831C2
MACHIORO v. Chaney
Case decided by Sup Ct 6-4, 439D1
MACKAY, Donald (d. 1977)
Secret group blamed for death 11-6, 870F2
MacKAY, Elmer
Canada econ expansn min 6-4, 423F3
MacKELLAR, Michael
In Malaysia, Indochina refugees OKd 5-7, 379F2
MacKENZIE, Julia
Little Eyolf opens 6-29, 712B1
MACKEY v. Montrym
Case decided by Sup Ct 6-25, 540A2
MacKINNON, Judge George E.
Named to wiretap ct 5-18, 442C3
Vs wage-guide contract denial 6-22, 480F2*
Dissents on Taiwan defns treaty suit 11-30, 919E1
MACK Trucks Inc.—*See SIGNAL Cos.*
MACLEAN, Donald
Spy ring scandal reopened 10-28, 10-29, 873G3
Blunt named 4th spy 11-15, 908D2-909B3
MacLEAN, J. Angus
Elected PEI premr 4-23, 311F1
MacMILLAN, Bob
Named NHL best sportsman 6-12, 470D2
MACMILLAN, Harold
Thatcher wins UK electn 5-3, 338E2
MacMILLAN, John H.
Blames Met Ed for 3 Mile I accident 6-5, 518B3
MACMILLAN Inc.
Mattel bid accepted 8-30; spurned, ABC offer accepted 10-16; talks end 11-22, 942A3
MacNEIL, Robert
Nixon Admin pub TV moves disclosed 2-24, 194C1, G1
MacPHAIL, Lee
Umpires' strike setld 5-18, 569D2, E2
Warns Martin 12-13, 1002E1
MACPHEE, Ian
On industry task force 5-16, 423A3
MacSHANE, Anita
But Never Jam Todays opens 7-31, 711A2
MACY, Kyle
In NBA draft 6-25, 507B2
Injured in Pan Am Games 7-10, 798B3
MADAGASCAR—*See MALAGASY*
MADANI, Adm. Ahmad
Urges mil cuts; OKs US personnel return, F-14 repurchase 3-27, 228G3
Qaraneh replaced 3-27, 247E2
Resigns as Iran defns min 3-30, 247D2
Meets Arab ldr on Khuzistan clashes 5-30, 408C1
Blames outsiders for Khuzistan unrest 6-3, chrgs Iraq arms shipmnts 6-6, 446D1
MADDEN, John
Resigns as Raiders coach 1-5, 175E2
MADDEN, John (director)
Wings opens 1-28, 292G3
MADDEN, Peter
One Man released 7-27, 820E2
MADDOX, Garry
Wins Golden Glove Award 11-20, 956D1
MADDOX, Rev. R. L.
To join Carter staff 4-15, 300E3
MADISON, Wis.—*See WISCONSIN*
MADISON, James (1751-1836)
Stuart portrait goes to Natl Gallery 4-10, 375B1
MADISON (Wis.) Press Connection (newspaper)
H-bomb letter published 9-16, 713B1, B2; text of letter, diagram 714D1-717E3
MADISON Square Garden Corp.
Dems pick for '80 conv 6-28, 518E1
MADLOCK, Bill
Traded to Pirates 6-28, 1002A3
In World Series 10-10–10-17, 816F1

1980

MACHEL, Samora Moses (Mozambican president)
Shifts econ priorities, backs pvt enterprise 3-18; shuffles Cabt 3-21, 234C2
Shuffles Cabt again 4-3, 278D2
Zimbabwe security vows rptd 5-30, 469C1
Currency exchng implemented 6-16—6-18, 582A1
Scores Morocco war vs Polisario 7-1—7-4, 509E1
Army occupies rebel base 7-10, 565A2
Visits Zimbabwe 8-4—8-9, 674C3
MACHINES (& Machine Tools)
Tech exports to USSR suspended 1-9, 9F1
African dependence on S Africa cited 4-1, 243A2
Harvester strike ends 4-20, 308E2
PCB rules publshd 5-9, 387A2
Bendix, Warner & Swasey trust chrgs rptd setld 7-14, 917E2
White Motor files for bankruptcy 9-4, 985E3
El Salvador gets IDB loan 12-18, 993A2
MACHINISTS and Aerospace Workers, International Association of (IAM) (AFL-CIO)
Lee Way settles job bias suit 1-10, 17E2
Winpisinger vs Carter endorsemt 8-20, 647A3
MACHT, Dr. Lee
Found guilty on drug chrgs 1-18, 199G3
MACKAY, Elmer
2 guilty in '77 office bugging fraud 4-28, 335A1
MACKELLAR, Michael
On costly computer error 4-4, 292G2
MACKEY, Bernard
Dies 3-5, 280B1
MACKINNON, Judge George
Overturns Letelier murder convictns 9-15, 703F3
MACLAINE, Shirley
Change of Seasons released 12-17, 1003G1
MACLAURY, Bruce K.
Urges wage-price controls, gas rationing 2-7, 126G2
MACLEAN, Donald
USSR honors Philby 7-15, 566A3
MACLEHOSE, Murray
Hong Kong sets new immigrant policy 10-23, 855D2-C3
MACLEOD, Michael
Garth replaces as Anderson campaign mgr 8-28, 665C3
MACMILLAN, Dr. Robert
Scores MD billing ban proposal 9-3, 687E2
MACMILLAN Inc. (of ABC)
Evans replaces Hagel as bd chrmn 2-11, 224G3-225A1
LaSalle Extension University
FTC judge rules ads misleading 5-12, 703G1
MACMILLAN Press Ltd., The
St Martin's Liddy book excerpts publshd 4-21, 333A3
MACON, Maj. Gen. Robert Chauney (ret.)
Dies 10-27, 876E2
MACPHAIL, Lee
On White Sox sale 8-23, 795B3
MACPHEE, Ian
Ethnic broadcast unit planned 1-24, 116C1
Immigratn rules set 6-19, 485D2
Rpts immigratn rise 11-18, 900G1
MACRO Communications Inc.
Financial World buys Saturday Review 5-20, 582D3
MACVICAR, Robert
Praises Pac-10 transcript scandal penalties 8-11, 875A2
MADANI, Adm. Ahmad
Loses Iran electn 1-28, 66C3
MADDOX, Diana
Changeling released 3-28, 416E2
MADDOX, Garry
Phillies win NL pennant 10-12, 796D1-F1, A2
In World Series 10-14—10-21, 811A3-812B3
Wins Golden Glove Award 12-6, 926E1
MADDOX, Lester G.
Ga pension bill fails 2-27, 200A1
MADEIRA School (Greenway, Va.)
Headmistress chrgd in 'Scarsdale Diet' MD slaying 3-11, 214E3
MADIGAN, Rep. Edward R. (R, Ill.)
Reelected 11-4, 842F3
MADISON Square Garden Corp. (of Gulf & Western)
NASL puts Diplomats on notice 11-24, terminates 12-8, 1001D1
MADIYEH, Mohammed al-
Becomes Halhul mayor 5-25, 417F2

1976

MADUT Ring, Bona Malwal
In Sudan Cabt 2-10, 502D1
MAEDA, Masao
Loses House seat 12-5, 925E3
MAENO, Mitsuyasu
Fails in Kodama assassinatn 3-23, 286B2
MAESTRONE, Frank
Amb to Kuwait 3-16; confrmd 4-28, 412F1
MAFENI, Bernard
On Equatorial Guinea worker evacuatn 1-26, 62D1
MAFIA—*See 'Organized Crime' under CRIME*
MAGALHAES da Silveira, Alexandre
Arrest confirmed 3-9, 288B1
MAGAZINES—*See PRESS, PUBLISHING; specific names*
MAGIC Show, The (play)
Long runs listed 12-31, 1015A1
MAGINNIS, Mary
Named in Getty will 6-8, 444C2
MAGORO, Lt. Col. M.
Nigeria transport min 3-15, 222A3
MAGUBANE, Peter
Home firebombed 8-4, 579E2
Rptd detained 8-27, 653F1
Freed 12-28, 1010E2
MAGUIRE, Rep. Andrew (D, N.J.)
Reelected 11-2, 830D1
MAGYAR, Zoltan
Wins Olympic medal 7-23, 574D3
MAHDI, Sadik al-
Role in Sudan coup cited 7-2, 502A1
Admits Sudan plot role, warns vs executns 8-4, 592E2
Sentenced to die 9-30, 857C2
MAHEU, Robert A.
Howard Hughes dies 4-5, 336E1
MAHGOUB, Mohammed
On boycott vs Israel 4-3, 242C1
Warns vs Sinai drilling 7-24, 561C2
MAHJUB, Mohammed
Scores Syria on Leb 5-12, 337D2
MAHLER, Dr. Halfdan T.
Accepts Lasker award 11-17, 910G3
Rpts on African fever outbreak 11-21, 931C3
MAHLER: Kindertotenlieder (record album)
Wins Grammy 2-28, 460E3
MAHMUD, Azin
Arrested 6-22, 498B1
MAHON, Rep. George H. (D, Tex.)
On defns budget 'padding' 2-4, 116C1 *
Reelected 11-2, 830E4
Carter meets cong ldrs 11-17, 864B2
MAHROUG, Ismail
Presents '76 budget 1-2, 45F3
MAIDOU, Henri
Named educ min 9-5, 924E2
MAIHOFER, Werner
A-plant permit announcemt rptd 11-11, 931F1
MAIL—*See POSTAL Service under U.S. GOVERNMENT*
MAILER, Norman
Dole cites Carter interviews 10-6, 763F3
MAINBOCHER (Main Rousseau Bocher)
Dies 12-27, 1015A2

MAINE
Speculators default on potato futures 5-25, 397C1-398B1
Dem conv women delegates, table 508C2

1977

MAEDA, Seison
Dies 10-27, 872E2
MAES, Nicolaus (1632-1693)
Painting defaced 10-7, man arrested 10-8, 848F2
MAESSE Roca, Rear Adm. Santiago
Loses Cabt post 10-13, 902C1
MAFIA—*See 'Organized Crime' under CRIME*
MAGALHAES Pinto, Jose de
Lauds Todman visit 5-14, 414C2
Sets '78 pres bid 7-26, 615D3
Gains ARENA, pub support 9-24, 740G3-741A1 *
On pres candidacy 9-30, 840F1
2d in execs pres poll 11-7, 964A2
MAGAZINE Publishers Association
Carter interview 6-10, 460C2
MAGDOUB, Maj. Gen. Taha el-
At Cairo conf 12-14—12-15, 953G1
MAGMA Copper Co.—*See NEWMONT Mining Corp.*
MAGNUSON, Sen. Warren (D, Wash.)
'76 spec interest gifts rptd 1-15, 128F3, 129A1, G1
MAGRUDER, William M.
Dies 9-10, 788F1
MAGSAYSAY, Ramon (1907-57)
CIA payments rptd 2-19, 124F1
MAGUBANE, Peter
Wins journalism award 2-22, 160G3-161A1
MAHDI, Sadik al-
Nimeiry reconciliatn rptd 7-18, 602C2
Pardoned 8-13, 711B1
Returns 9-27, Nimeiry greets 9-28, 843E3
MAHER v. Buckner
Review declined 10-17, 797F3
MAHER v. Roe
Abortn funding curb upheld 6-20, 516F2
MAHESH Yogi, Maharishi
TM banned from NJ schls 10-20, 845D3
MAHEU, Robert A.
Summa ordrd to pay Greenspun 6-3, 472E2
MAHGOUB, Mohammed
Warns US on boycott laws 6-8, 511F3
Masons boycotted 6-9, 511F3
Vows contd Ford boycott 11-3, 863C2
MAHMOUD, Captain—*See ASASHA, Zuhair Yousof*
MAHMUD, Masud
Removal as Pak force chief rptd 545C1
Sentenced 9-5, 707F2
MAHON, Rep. George H. (D, Tex.)
'76 spec interest gifts rptd 2-4, 128G3, 129E2, F2
Backs B-1 funds bar 10-20, 796F1
MAHONEY, John R.
Sued re sugar lobby gifts 7-20, 614C1
MAHONING River (Ohio)
Steel cos OK clean-up pacts 6-30, 521C3
MAIDANA, Antonio
Freed 1-27, 'house arrest' chrgd 2-16, 167D3
MAIER-Witt, Silke
Sought in Ponto slaying 7-30, 601C3
MAIHOFER, Werner
Traube taps rptd 2-27; defends 3-1; bars resignatn 3-8; Traube cleared 3-16, 259B3
Baader trial adjourned 3-17; denies taps role 3-18, 260G1, C2
On E Ger spying 6-27, 602B2 *
On Baader gang deaths 10-18, 791A1
MAIL—*See U.S. GOVERNMENT—POSTAL Service*
MAIL Surveillance
FBI informer guidelines set 1-5, 15G2
CIA prosecutn barred 1-14, 41D3
Brown backs surveillnc 3-27, 231F3, 232B1
Ex-FBI official indicted 4-7, 275F1-G2
CIA damages re letters to USSR backed 5-12, 423B1
Customs Svc openings backed 6-15, 478E3
FBI domestic spying rptd curbed 11-9, 861E2
FBI probe attys clash with Bell 12-7, 940B1
Canada—*See CANADA—RCMP*
MAIN Bank (Houston, Tex.)
Pharaon, Connally ownership cited 12-27, 1003G2

MAINE
Legislature schedule rptd 6D2
Indian land dispute setlmt urged 1-11—1-21, 59C1-A2
Bonds sold 2-25, 197B1

1978

MAFIA—*See CRIME—Organized Crime*
MAGALHAES Pinto, Jose de
Gomes backs for pres 1-20, 165C3
Scores Figueiredo, asks direct electns 2-15, 165B3
Leads Figueiredo oppositn, seeks MDB support 5-29—7-9, 555F3-556A1
Drops pres bid 8-8, 646E2
MAGAZINE Editors, American Society of
Carter interview 8-11, 682F2
MAGAZINES—*See PRESS, specific names*
MAGELLAN, Strait of
Argentina-Chile Beagle Channel talks fail 5-22—11-2, 860E2
MAGIC (film)
Released 11-18, 970A2
Top-grossing film 11-29, 970F3
MAGIC Of Lassie, The (film)
Released 8-3, 970A2
MAGNUSON, Sen. Warren G. (D, Wash.)
Votes for Panama Canal neutrality pact 3-16, 177D2
Disaster funds signed 4-4, 261D3
Votes for 2d Canal pact 4-18, 273B1
Carter visits Spokane 5-5, 342A2
Vs defeat of Sen office bldg funds 8-17, 681A3
MAGUIRE, Rep. Andrew (D, N.J.)
Consumer group lauds 3-4, 183D1
Reelected 11-7, 851A3
Shell trust probe rptd, 11-28, 939D3
House ethics proposal defeated 12-6, 958F2
MAGUIRE, Brian
Kills self 5-10, 373F2
MAGUIRE, James
Death protested, police reveal IRA link 5-11, 474F2
MAHAFFEY, John
Wins PGA Championship 8-6; Pleasant Valley, sets tourn mark 8-13, 672E2, E3
US wins golf World Cup 12-3, 990E2
MAHALIA (play)
Opens 6-5, 887A2
MAHAN, Simon
Vs Fiaich call for UK Ulster rule end 1-16, 37D2
MAHARAJ JI, Guru
Argentina arrests 87 followers 2-15, 208C1
MAHDI, Sadik al-
Nimeiry, Natl Front sign pact 4-12, 293C1
MAHDI al-Tajir, Mohammed
Boeing cites re paymts 7-28, 643B1
MAHLER, Gustav (1860-1911)
Symphony No 9 wins Grammy 2-24, 316C1
MAHMOOD, Taha
Slain in Iraq consulate raid 8-2, 582D3
MAHMOUD, Abou-Naama
Held in Iraq amb death try 8-2, 582F2
MAHMUD, Abdul Taib bin
Named Malaysia defns min 7-27, 592E2
MAHMUD, Musa
Kills self 6-28, 543A2
MAHN Ngwe Aung
Gets death sentence 2-23, 145C2
MAHON, Rep. George H. (D, Tex.)
Not standing for reelectn 5-6, 363B1
Carter defense veto upheld 9-7, 677F2
Hance wins seat 11-7, 855E3
MAHONING River (Ohio)
Steel cos cleanup deadline cited 1-3, 4B3
MAHONING River Ecumenical Coalition
Youngstown steel rescue backed 4-10, LTV merger OKd 6-21, 493D1
MAIDMENT, Nigel
Saudis whip 5-15, return to UK 6-15, 515G3
MAIDOU, Henri (Central African Empire premier)
Named CAE premr 7-14, 596C1
MAIER, Sepp
Sets World Cup goal-tending record 6-21, 520E3
MAIHOFER, Werner
Retains W Ger interior post 2-3, 93A3
On Schleyer hunt error 3-7, 332E2
Neo-Nazism rptd on rise 4-29—4-30, 477G2
MPs protest leftist border checks 5-19, 439B2
Schleyer rpt issued, police effort scored 6-3—6-4; resigns 6-6, 456A3
Free Dems lose 2 state electns 6-4, 456F2
Baum named interior min 6-6, 456C3
Baumann resigns 7-3, 651E2
MAIL—*See U.S. GOVERNMENT—POSTAL Service*
MAIL Fraud—*See U.S. GOVERNMENT—POSTAL Service*
MAILMAN, Bruce
Neon Woman opens 4-16, 760A3
MAIL Surveillance
Carter orders intell agency curbs 1-24, 49A3
Bell asks disciplinary probes of 68 FBI agents, rpts '77 chrgs vs ex-offcl dropped 4-10, 262B1
Poll finds Canadians back 8-30, 686C3
'Mail cover' case declined by Sup Ct 11-6, 874C1
CIA damages upheld 11-9, 940C1
SWP scrutiny held unconst, 'mail cover' curbed 11-29, 949G3
FBI penalizes 4 12-5, 939F2

MAINE
Legislature schedule rptd 14E3
'67, '77 sales-tax rates rptd 1-5, 15E3
State govt tax revenue table 1-9, 84C2
Blizzard hits 2-5—2-7, 105E2

1979

MADMAN and the Nun, The (play)
Opens 1-18, 292A2
MADRID, Roberto de la
Tijuana newspaper stormed 11-1, 875B1
MADRID Hurtado, Miguel de la
Named Mex planning secy 5-17, 408C3
Econ policy choices rptd 6-1, 487C3
MADSEN, Petty Officer 3rd Class Lee Eugene
Chrgd re US secrets sales 8-14, 611D1
Pleads guilty to espionage 9-25, 747E3
Sentenced 10-26, 831F3
MAESANO, Libero
Seized in Moro probe 6-6, 487C1
MAFIA—*See CRIME—Organized Crime*
MAGAZINES—*See PRESS; specific names*
MAGELLAN Petroleum Australia Ltd.
Aborigine land rights probed 1-24, 94B3
MAGICIAN of Lublin (film)
Released 11-9, 1007G3
MAGILL, Arthur
Gives Wyeth paintings to SC museum 3-22, 375B2
MAGNUSON, Sen. Warren G. (D, Wash.)
Sen pres pro tempore 71A2
Appropriations Com chrmn 1-23, 71C2
MAGRUDER, Jeb Stuart
Starts mktg exec job in Pa 8-8, 656G2
MAGUIRE, Rep. Andrew (D, N.J.)
Scores White House shake-up, Jordan appointmt 7-18, 531C1
MAHAFFEY, John
Wins Hope Desert Classic 1-14, 220C3
US wins golf World Cup 11-11, 970C2
MAHAN, Marvin H.
US files pollutn suit 2-7, 130B1
MAHAR, William Ross
Dies 8-20, 818B2
MAHATHIR, Mohammad bin
Threatens Viet refugees in Malaysia 6-15, 460E1
MAHDJAN, Hussein
Wounded 8-26, 653A3
MAHE Jr., Eddie
Shifts campaign strategy 12-15, 982A3
MAHER, T. J.
Wins Eur Parlt seat 6-7, 434C2
MAHEU, Robert A.
SEC suit vs Hughes settled 1-19, 88B2
MAHJUB, Mohammed
Arrested as plotter 7-28, 583E1
Sentenced 8-7, executed 8-8, 602F2
MAHLANGU, Solomon
Hanged for '77 Johannesburg attack 4-6, 270B3
MAHONEY, David
Heads '78 top-paid execs list 5-14, 347E3
MAHONEY, Raymond
Loeb settles pensn suit 7-9, 640E3
MAIBAUM, Norman
Knockout opens 5-6, 712A1
MAIL—*See also U.S. GOVERNMENT–POSTAL Service*
US-China direct svc set 5-25, 406A1

MAINE
Legislature schedule rptd 5D3
Med malpractice arbitratn rptd 1-28, 139E3

1980

MAD Love (recording)
On best-seller list 3-5, 200F3; 4-2, 280F3
MAD Magazine
Mingo dies 5-8, 448D2
MADRUGA, Ivanna
Loses French Open women's doubles 6-6, 606E3
MAFIA—*See CRIME--Organized Crime*
MAFOKO, Fanie
Buried 2-9, 134B3
MAGAZINES—*See PRESS*
MAGER, Manuela
Wins Olympic medal 2-17, 155F3
MAGIC (recording)
On best-seller list 8-13, 640A3; 9-10, 716E3
MAGICIANS of the Silver Screen (film)
Released 12-26, 1003B2
MAGNAVOX Co.—*See under NORTH American Philips*
MAGNUSON, Sen. Warren G. (D, Wash.)
Gets Carter rpt on Iran rescue mission 4-27, 321D1
Wins renomination 9-16, 724B2
Loses reelectn 11-4, 837D1, 845A2, 852G2
MAGUIRE, Rep. Andrew (D, N.J.)
On Somali refugee problem 4-6, 274C1
Loses reelectn 11-4, 848F2
MAGUIRE, Anne
Commits suicide 1-21, 59D1
MAGYAR, Zoltan
Wins Olympic medal 7-25, 622E3
MAHAFFEY, John
Wins Kemper Open 6-1, 714G3
MAHAN, Marvin H.
Pollutn suit partly setld 1-30, 93G3
MAHANTA, P. K.
Vs Assam crackdown 4-19, 352D3
MAHDI, Sheik Abdullah
Aviatn post resignatn cited 1-1, 22E1
MAHE Jr., Eddie
Replaced as Connally campaign mgr 1-25, 91G3
MAHER v. Gagne
Case decided by Sup Ct 6-25, 541A1
MAHFOUZ, Sheik Khaled Bin
Connally bank connectns, '78-79 fund transfers rptd 2-11, 129C2
MAHMOUD, Hay Ali
Arrested in W Berlin bomb plot 8-1, 604F2
W Berlin release set 9-15, 712B2
MAHONEY, John
On LIRR strike 4-2, 267F3
MAHRE, Phil
Wins Olympic medal 2-22, 154D3, 155G2
MAHWAH—*See NEW Jersey*
MAIER, Mayor Henry W. (Milwaukee, Wis.)
Reelected to 6th term 4-1, 247B2
MAILER, Norman
Executioner's Song on best-seller list 1-13, 40B3
Wins Pulitzer 4-14, 296C2, E2
Boycotts Amer Book Awards 5-1, 692G1

MAINE
Influenza outbreak rptd 2-15, 158C3
Slot machines banned by voters 3-11, 185C1, A2
Indians OK land setlmt 3-15, 210A3

1976

Dem conv pres vote, table 7-14, 507C2
4 bombing suspects indicted 7-14; sentncd 10-8, 796B3
GOP pre-conv delegate count 8-14, 583C3
GOP conv pres, vp vote tables 8-18—8-19, 8-19, 599C1, C3
Fscl '75 per capita income, tax burden rptd 9-15, 10-2, 959A2
Mondale in Lewiston 9-20, 704B1
Carter in Portland 9-30, 723D1; Biddeford 10-1, 743A1
Dole campaigns 10-2, 743C2
Dole in Presque Isle 10-25, 804A2
Election results 11-2: pres 818B1, G1, E2, 819A2; cong 820C1, 821C1, 828F1, 829G3; state 821D1, 825B3
New potato futures contract OKd 11-2, 990B1

MAIZE—*See CORN*
MAJIDI, Abdol Majid
Submits econ rpt 2-3, 101G3
MAJOR League Baseball Players Association—*See BASEBALL Players Association, Major League*

MAKARIOS, Archbishop (Michael Mouskos) (Cypriot president)
US coup role rptd scored 1-20, 93F2
Sampson faces plot chrg 2-3, 155D1
Secret pact rptd 2-27, Clerides replaced as negotiator 4-8, 311C2
Sampson arrested 3-16; sentncd 8-31, 858E1
Vs compromise 7-20, 772B2
Backers win electn 9-5, 772E1
3 held in plot 11-10, 963D3

MAKAROVA, Natalia
Weds Karker 2-22, 271E3
MAKHATSKWA, Rev. Mangaliso
Arrested 8-13, 624A3
MAKHAYA, T. J.
Home firebombed 8-4, 579E2

MALAGASY Democratic Republic (formerly Madagascar)—*See also NON-ALIGNED Nations Movement, OAU*
Pre-'75 pol amnesty set 1-1, 55E2
Ratsiraka sworn pres 1-4, names Rakotomalala premr 1-11, 55F2
Listed as 'partly free' 1-19, 20D3
Unesco literacy drive fails 2-4, 85C2
UN Palestine com member 2-26, 162C1
Recognizes Sahara republic 3-5, 178G2
Total IMF oil loan rptd 4-1, 340D2
Razarimahatratra named cardinal 4-27, 336C2
Olympic withdrawal rptd 7-21, 528B3
Prime Min, Cabt named 8-20, 926A1
Capital name chng rptd 9-18, 926C1
Ousts 2 US emb workers 9-23; US ousts envoy 10-29, 925G3
Comoro-Malagasy workers clash 12-20, Comoro forgn min in talks 12-23—12-26, 1013C1
Listed as not free 12-22, 977B3
MALAWI—*See also AFRICAN Development Bank, COMMONWEALTH of Nations, NON-ALIGNED Nations Movement, OAU*
US ups econ aid re UN vote 1-9, 2B1
Listed as 'not free' nation 1-19, 20E3
Angola MPLA recognized 2-17, 163E2
Total IMF oil loan rptd 4-1, 340D2
EC aid set 4-6, 276C2
Expelled Goans arrive UK 5-16; UK warns Malawi 5-18, 382B2
More expelled Goans arrive UK 5-23, Banda scores 5-29, 497C3
New Cabt cut, Banda takes justice post 5-31, 497D3

1977

Justice Dept backs Indian claims 2-28, 196E3
Pot law impact rptd 3-31, 332A3
Fed spending inequities chrged 4-6, 423D3
'76 per-capita income table 5-10, 387C2
Baxter State Park burns 7-17—8-2, 660C3
Defense job loss rptd 8-10, 629E2
'76 per capita income, tax burden table 9-13, 10-18, 821G1, B2
Schl tax law repealed 12-5, 939F3
Pot law detailed 12-11, 972D3

MAINTENANCE Employes
NYC schls struck 2-23—2-28, 153B3
MAISON International Ltd.
Chrgd re Arab boycott 1-7, 167A2
MAIZAR, Abdul Mohsen abu
Briefs Arab League on Leb 11-14, 874A2
MAJIDI, Abdol Majid
On oil barter, foreign aid 1-11, 11D3
On oil, gas sales 2-20, 201G1
MAJORS, Johnny
Pittsburgh ranked 1st 1-2, 1-3, 8D3

MAKARIOS, Archbishop (Michael Christodouros Mouskos) (Cypriot president; succeeded Aug. 31)
Meets Denktash, talks set 1-27, 2-12; press conf 2-13, 108B3
Plans to resign 2-16, 147B1
CIA payments rptd 2-19, 124F1
Clifford visits 2-23—2-26, 147A1
Davies murder trial ends 6-3, 467B1
At Commonwealth conf 6-8—6-15, 487D1
Scores Denktash on Famagusta 7-22, 764B2
Dies, successors named 8-3; reactn 8-4—8-12; funeral 8-8, 616G3-617B2
Facts on 617F1
Kyprianou named interim pres 8-13, 636B2
Successor sworn 8-31, 764B2
Successor formally elected 11-12, ordained 11-13, 924C1
MAKEBA, Miriam
At pan-Africa festival 1-15—2-12, 106B1
MAKHLOUF, Sharbel
Canonized 10-9, 845F3
MAKOWSKI, Mayor Stanley M. (Buffalo, N.Y.)
Declares emergency 1-27, 75A3
MALAGASY Democratic Republic (formerly Madagascar)—*See also NON-ALIGNED Nations Movement, OAU*
UN Assemb member 4C1
Mayotte islanders asks repatriatn; Majunga fighting rptd 1-7, 24B2
Holds S Africa plane 1-19, 29A3
New Cabt named 8-8, 772D1
Cuba mil aides rptd 11-17, 896G1

MALARIA—*See MEDICINE—Diseases*
MALAVIYA, K. D.
Arrested 10-3, 765C1

MALAWI—*See also COMMONWEALTH of Nations, NONALIGNED Nations Movement, OAU*
UN Assemb member 4C1
2 offcls sentncd re plot 2-14, 309E2
IMF loan OKd 5-20, 710D3
Cabt dismissed 7-7, replaced 7-8, 772C1
Abstains on UN anti-Israel res 10-28, 830G2

1978

Portland harbor oil spill 2-6, 524G1
Carter visits, backs Hathaway reelectn 2-17, 123D1, F2-A3
Portsmouth Shipyd radiatn-cancer link probed 2-19—2-28, 164D1, B3
Sun Day celebrated 5-3, 321G3
Porno film distributor sentncd 5-19, 396G3
Income-tax cut rptd 5-25, 425D1
Canada fishing dispute rptd 6-2—6-5, 435B2
Primary results 6-13, 466G3
Ex-sen Payne dies 6-15, 540D3
Extended jobless aid rptd 7-10, 552A3; ends 8-4, 607D3
3 balloonists depart from Presque Isle 8-11, 652G3
A-plant moratorium cited 8-17, 665F2
Pan Am to end Boston-Portland svc 9-7, 701A2
Carter at Portland rally 10-28, 831C2
Election results 11-7: cong 845D1, 846B1-F1, F2, 847C2, F2, 848C2, 850A1; state 845G1, 847B1, E2, 853F2, 897D3, 915E2

MAINTENANCE Employes
New Orleans schls struck 9-1, 698G2
MAINZ, Rolf
Sentenced 1-6, 36C2
MAIRESSE, Valerie
Faces of Love released 7-7, 970C1
MAIZE—*See CORN*
MAJLUTA, Jacobo
Rptd shot at during campaign 5-12, 372G1
Sworn DR vice pres 8-16, 648C2
MAJOR Indoor Soccer League (MISL)—*See SOCCER*
MAJOR League Umpires Association—*See UMPIRES Association, Major League*
MAJOR Superiors of Men
McCoy asks US oust Somoza 11-8, 883E3

MAKARIOS, Archbishop (Michael Christodouros Mouskos) (1913-77)
EOKA-B rptd disbanded, '74 coup role cited 2-10, 147F3
Kyprianou names new Cabt 3-8, 189E1

MAKAROV, Oleg
Soyuz 27 docks with Salyut 1-11, 11C2
Returns to Earth 1-16, 157A3

MALAGASY Democratic Republic (formerly Madagascar)—*See also GATT, NONALIGNED Nations Movement, OAU*
Freedom House lists as partly free 44F1
54 sentenced for '76 riots 2-4, 115A3
3 sentncd re '77 plane landing 3-22, 230G3
Philibert Tsiranana dies 4-16, 356E3
Students, gangs riot 5-29—5-30, 479D1
UN Assemb member 713B3
Polisario recognitn cited 11-10, 999G2

MALARIA—*See MEDICINE—Diseases*
MALATHION—*See PESTICIDES*
MALAVASI, Ray
Hired as Rams coach 8-13, 1024F2

MALAWI—*See also COMMONWEALTH of Nations, GATT, NONALIGNED Nations Movement, OAU*
US, UK reps visit re Rhodesia 6-2—7-18, 615B2
Bophuthatswana passport barred 6-10, 536E3
Natl Assemb electns 6-29, 534D3
Zambia aid re RR set 6-29, 617G1
Banda sees forgn rptrs; defends ousters, S Africa ties 6-30, 534E3
Asian forced migratn to cities rptd 7-1, 535A1

1979

Portland 2d opinion surgery plan evaluated 1-29, 140A1
Viking artifact identified 2-7, 138E1
Potato futures trading halted 3-9; farmers, gov protest 5-9, 348C1
Pub mtg smoking ban vetoed 3-13, 218F2
Loring AF base to be revamped 3-29, 265E3
Legal drinking age cited 4-16, 309E3, G3
Wood fuel use rptd 5-20, 419G1
Downeast plane crash kills 17 5-30, 412E2
Hathaway '78 labor gifts rptd 6-13, 595D1
Truckers stage protest 6-28, 479C2
Winter heating fuel supply promised 8-28, 703C2
State workers Soc Security non-participatn cited 9-10, 727B1
'78 per capita income rptd 9-16, 746C2
Bush wins GOP straw poll 11-3, 866B3
Returnable-bottle law, 3 bond issues OKd 11-6, 846B2, F3, 847B1
Kennedy opens campaign 11-7, 847F1
Portland '79 living costs ranked 12-28, 991A1
Atomic Energy
Portsmouth shipyd A-cancer study begins 1-31, 91A1
Maine Yankee (Wiscasset) A-plant ordrd shut 3-13, 186F1
Maine Yankee A-plant '78 operatn record rptd 4-15; pipe leaks 5-2, 322F2, B3
Maine Yankee A-plant unhurt by quake 4-17, 323E1

MAIN Event, The (film)
Released 6-21, 820G1
Top-grossing film 6-27, 548G3
MAIN Event/Fight, The (recording)
On best-seller list 9-5, 672E3*
MAINE Yankee Atomic Power Plant—*See MAINE-Atomic Energy*
MAINTENANCE Employes
Hawaii strike shuts schls 10-26–11-16, 922B3
BART job dispute ends 11-21, 922C3
MAIRE, Edmond
CGT joint progrm set 9-19, 729B3
MAJANO, Col. Adolfo Arnoldo
Leads El Salvador coup 10-15, 790B2
Vows pol prisoner probe 10-18, 813D1
MAJOR League Umpires Association—*See UMPIRES Association, Major League*
MAJORS, Lee
Killer Fish released 12-7, 1007F3

MAKARIOS, Archbishop (Michael Christodouros Mouskos) (1913-77)
New intercommunal talks set 5-19, 387E2

MAKAROV, Sergei
Sovts win Challenge Cup 2-11, 118E3
MAKEYEV, Yevgeny N.
On Bolshoi dancer's detentn 8-27, 645E1
MAKEYEVA, Marina
Sets 400-m hurdles record 7-27, 799E1

MALAGASY Democratic Republic (formerly Madagascar)—*See also GATT, NONALIGNED Nations Movement, OAU*
UN membership listed 695G2

MALAWI—*See also COMMONWEALTH of Nations, GATT, NONALIGNED Nations Movement, OAU*
Freedom House lists as not free 13A1
UN membership listed 695G2
Zimbabwe cuts Zambia road link 11-18–11-19, 899D2

1980

Farmers ask Canada potato import ban 3-27, 368D2
ILA dock pact setld 5-27, 482B2
Right to sue states broadened by Sup Ct 6-25, 540C3
Dickey-Lincoln Dam funds clear Cong 6-25, 9-10, Carter signs 10-1, 803E2
Atomic Energy & Safeguards
Maine Yankee (Wiscasset) A-plant shut down defeated 9-23, 723C2
Politics & Government—*See also other appropriate subheads in this section*
Legislature schedule rptd 18E1
State of State message 1-2, 269C2
Saco '79 default rptd 1-7, 54E1; workers paid 1-10, 187F1
Kennedy scores Carter 1-30, 2-7, 91A2-D2
Mondale speaks in Saco 2-5, 91E2
Dem pres caucus results 2-10, 109B1
Saco voters repeal property tax ceiling 4-29, 744A1
Mitchell gets Muskie seat 5-8, 367B2
Ex-Gov Longley dies 8-16, 676A2
Anderson battle for ballot access rptd 9-27, 818B2
Election results 11-4: pres 838B1, 839A2, E3; cong 840G1, B2, 843A2, 848G1, B2; state 845F2
'80 census rptd 12-31, 983E1

MAINE Nuclear Referendum Committee
Maine votes to keep A-plant 9-23, 723F2
MAINE v. Thiboutot
Case decided by Sup Ct 6-25, 540C3
MAINE Yankee Atomic Power Plant—*See MAINE--Atomic Energy & Safeguards*
MAIRE, Edmond
Lauds Polish workers, CGT-CFDT rift widens 9-4, 688E1
MAJANO, Col. Adolfo Arnoldo
3 civilns join junta 1-9, 20A1
Announces econ reforms 2-11, 117E2; land reforms 3-6, 172C1
Rightist coup attempt, resignatn demands linked 5-2; ousted as mil chief 5-12, 372F2*, D3*
Scores leftist strike 6-24, 497G2
Rift with Gutierrez threatens junta 8-31, 669A3
Escapes assassinatn 11-3, 871F3
Removed from junta 12-7, 941B3
Duarte sworn pres 12-22, 993E1
MAJERUS, Raymond E.
Named UAW secy-treas 6-4, 457A2
MAJLUTA Azar, Jacobo
Demoted 6-6, 462E2
MAJOR Barbara (play)
Opens 2-26, 392D3
MAKARIOS, Archbishop (Michael Christodouros Mouskos) (1913-77)
Armenian support cited 3-1, 197E2

MAKAROV, Oleg
In new Soyuz missn 11-27, 914A2
Ends flight 12-10, 933B1
MAKEPEACE, Chris
My Bodyguard released 8-1, 675B3
MAKHINA, Antonina
Wins Olympic medal 7-26, 623B2
MAKOVSKI, Claude
Charles & Lucie released 5-9, 675B2
MAKWABA, Petrus
White soldiers held in death 11-7, 887C3

MALAGASY Democratic Republic—*See GATT, NONALIGNED Nations*

MALAGASY Republic—*See OAU*
MALAMUD, Bernard
Helps Cuban poet immigrate to US 3-16, 231B3
Elected to Arts Inst 12-5, 998C1
MALAN, Gen. Magnus
Named S Africa defense min 8-26, 689G3
MALARIA—*See MEDICINE--Diseases*

MALAWI—*See also COMMONWEALTH of Nations, GATT, NONALIGNED Nations, OAU*
Foreign Relations (misc.)
IOC rpts Olympic boycott 3-28, 259F3
At regional econ unity mtg 4-1, 243D1

1976

WCC chrgs Jehovah's Witness persecutn 6-14, 497E3
UN Assemb condemns apartheid 11-9, 842G2
Abstains on UN Gaza resetlmt res 11-23, 878F2

MALAYSIA—*See also ADB, COMMONWEALTH of Nations, NONALIGNED Nations Movements*
Razak dies 1-14, Hussein sworn premr 1-15, 55F2
Australia in SE Asia talks 1-16—1-17, 46C1
Listed as 'partly free' 1-19, 20D3
UN Palestine com member 2-26, 162C1
Australia names High Comr 3-23, 237B2
PI jet hijackers denied asylum 4-8, 260A3
Guerrilla attacks 4-22, 4-25, 4-26, 334G1-B2
Thais vs force presence 5-17, 403D3
At Timor Assemb meeting 5-31, 423A1
4 Sabah mins die in air crash, Saleh sworn chief min 6-6, 419D1
Thais ask to quit border area 6-6, replaced 6-17, 502A2
2 newsmen seized as plotters, Singapore arrests 2 6-22, 497F3
US GOP platform text cites 8-18, 609A3

MALDIVES
Listed as 'partly free' 1-19, 20D3
Reed confrmd US amb 5-26, 412A2

MALEK, Maj. Fouad
On Tel Zaatar losses 8-12, 577C1

MALEK, Gustavo
Rptd sought, Lanusse defends 8-4; denies chrgs in Uruguay 8-5, 672G2-A3
Rptd acquitted of subversn 9-12, 996D1

MALEK Mahdavi, Ahmad
Switzerland expels as spy 8-3, 735E1

MALENO, Steven
Convicted in Knight murder 6-14, chrgd with 2d death 503G3

MALFATTI, Franco
Sworn Italy educ min 7-30, 573F1

MALFONADO, Orlando
Wins Olympic medal 7-31, 574A1

MALI—*See also AFRICAN Development Bank, NONALIGNED Nations Movement, OAU*
Listed as 'not free' nation 1-19, 20E3
UNESCO literacy drive fails 2-4, 85C2
Total IMF oil loan rptd 4-1, 339F3, 340D2
Algeria, Libya, Niger ask cooperatn 4-8, 372B1
US proposes Sahel aid 5-1, 318D2
At France-Africa summit 5-10—5-11, 355G2
Sovt mil presence rptd 6-13, 467C1
Mercenary role in Sudan coup chrgd 7-6, 501E3
Olympic withdrawal rptd 7-21, 528B3
Byrne confrmd US amb 9-15, 807E3
Single party formed 9-21, 1013D1
ECOWAS rptd ratified 11-6, 974E2
IDA credit OKd 12-16, 1013E1

MALIANGA, Morton
Arrested 4-4, 295E3

MALIBU, Calif.—*See CALIFORNIA*

MALIK, Adam
Rpts Timor troop exit 4-17, 335A1

MALIK, Yakov A.
Clashes with China on Mideast 1-15, 60A1
Injured in NY car crash 3-15, 260A1
USSR protests UN missn shooting 4-2, 259G3
UN removal confirmed 11-23, 908F1
Returns USSR 12-13; replaced at UN 12-14, 967C1

MALINOWSKI, Bronislaw
Wins Olympic medal 7-28, 576B1

MALLEGG Inc., O. O.
Chrgd re Arab boycott 11-17, 986C3

MALLIOS, Evanghelos
Dies 12-15; Welch killers linked 12-18, 1004A2

MALLORY, Mae
Kunstler to ask chrgs dropped 1-17, 79E1

MALLOUM, Brig. Gen. Felix
Assassinatn try fails 4-13, 270E3

MALONE, John F.
Baxtrum role in SWP burglaries rptd 7-29, 570A1

MALONEY, Mayor Thomas C. (Wilmington, Del.)
Loses electn 11-2, 821A1

MALRAUX, Andre
Dies 11-23, 970D2

MALTA—*See also COMMONWEALTH of Nations, NONALIGNED Nations Movement*
Listed as 'free' nation 1-19, 20C3
Joins Group of 77 108C1
OKs UN Medit pollutn pact 2-16, 126C3
Angola MPLA recognized 2-17, 163E2
UN Palestine com member 2-26, 162C1
Electns 9-17—9-18; Labor win rptd, Mintoff policies cited 9-20, 713B1-A2

1977

MALAYSIA—*See also ASEAN, COMMONWEALTH of Nations, NONALIGNED Nations Movement*
UN Assemb member 4C1
Bolivia tin pact bar rptd 1-10, 169G1
Joins Thai drive vs rebels 1-14—1-17, base rptd seized 1-29, 87F3
Intl rubber buffer stock plan rejctd 1-23, 169G2
'76 econ growth rptd 2-16, 147C2
Thai border pact signed 3-4, 203C1
More Viets seek refuge 3-25, 243F3
US amb confrmd 5-25, 500A1
Rejects Viet refugees 6-19, 497F1
PI drops claim to Sabah 8-4, 607G1
Thai drive vs rebels aided 8-7, 607F3
Indochina refugee ban eased 8-31, 685D2
Amnesty Intl lists jailed lawmakers 9-5, 753B2
Japan Air jet crashes 9-27, 808B1
Exxon admits paymts 10-25, 818A2
Kelantan riots, emergency set; 4 Cabt mins quit in protest 11-8; fed rule set 11-9, 885F1-B2
Hijacked jet crashes 12-4, 992B2

MALAYSIAN Airlines System
Hijacked jet crashes 12-4, 992B2

MALAZA, Bonaventura Sipho
Death rptd 11-18, 935B1

MALCOLM X (Malcolm Little) (1926-65)
Hanafis take 134 hostage 3-9—3-11, 192D3

MALDIVES
UN Assemb member 4C1
Sovt base bid opposed 10-2, 844G3

MALDONADO, Jose
Dissolves Spain exile govt 6-21, 507F1

MALDONADO, Col. Osiris
Assassinated 7-6, 636A1

MALDONADO Gonelha, Antonio
Portugal labor min 3-25, 330F2

MALEK, Redha
Algeria info min 4-23, 470C2

MALFATTI, Franco
Students protest reforms 2-10, 135A3

MALE, John
Death rptd 8-17, 641A2

MA LI
Named Kewichow head 3-6, 179D3

MALI—*See also NONALIGNED Nations Movement, OAU*
UN Assemb member 4D1
Afro-Arab summit shunned 3-7—3-9, 170E1
At France-Africa summit 4-20—4-21, 316F3
Sahel dvpt plan OKd 6-1, 458E3
New Sahel famine seen 9-19, 770A2
Solar energy obstacles cited 12-11, 975E3
Obituaries
Keita, Modibo 5-16, 452D3

MALIANGA, Moton
Muzorewa group defectn rptd 8-8, 662D2

MALIK, Yakov
Troyanovsky in UN post 4B2

MALLET, Jacques
Sees Amalrik 2-24, 143B1 ⋆

MALLEY, George
Sets 3000-mtr steeplechase mark 6-9—6-11, 602B3

MALLIOS, Evanghelos (d. 1976)
Stamatis attack foiled 1-18, 182E2

MALLOUM, Brig. Gen. Felix
Claustres freed 1-30, 84D2
'76 plotters sentncd 3-26, 4 executed 4-4, 309B2
Coup attempt rptd crushed 4-1, 309B2
9 plotters executed 4-6, 490D2
Chrgs Libya annexatn aim 7-14, 597A2

MALONE, Maurice
Language requiremt voided 10-6, 780B2

MALONE, Moses
NBA final standings 4-10, 325D3

MALPICA Abaunza, Felipe
Says execs oppose Somoza 10-19, 864F2

MALPRACTICE, Medical—*See MEDICINE—Physicians*

MALTA—*See also COMMONWEALTH of Nations, NONALIGNED Nations Movement*
UN Assemb member 4D1
'76 Europe Cncl pact vs terror cited 9G2
New oppositn ldr elected 1-16, 136C2
Budget presented 1-31, 136E2
Bakers strike ends 2-8, 136F2
Livestock subsidy cuts protested 2-8, 2-14, 136G2
France, Italy security talks delay scored 2-10, 136A3
Cuba ties rptd 4-11, 309G2
Labor unrest, workers suspended 7-4—7-11; striking MDs fired 7-21, 655E3
Eur Cncl to study Turkey rights abuses in Cyprus 9-8, 764G1-A2

1978

UK cancels debts 7-31, 592E1
Forgn rptrs banned 8-14, 677G1
UN Assemb member 713B3

MALAYSIA—*See also ASEAN, COMMONWEALTH of Nations, GATT, NONALIGNED Nations Movement*
Fed rule ends in Kelantan 2-12, electns set 2-13, 115B3
Govt party wins Kelantan electns 3-12, 250E3
Ruling party wins electns 7-8, 592A2
New Cabt formed 7-27, 592C2
'77 hijacked jet crash rpt issued 9-7, 888F1
Cholera outbreak rptd 10-27, 927F2
Foreign Relations (misc.)—*See also 'Monetary, Trade, Aid & Investment' below*
Brunei independence backed 6-30, 533D3
UN Assemb member 713C3
China dep premr visits 11-9—11-12, Hussein scores CP support 11-10, 894D1
Indochina Refugee Issue—*See INDOCHINA—Refugees*
Monetary, Trade, Aid & Investment
Viet trade missn ended 21B3
Australia sugar talks ended 1-11, 34C3
Australia sugar pact setld 2-13, 110A2
Islamic bank poor-natn aid rise rptd 4-9, 257F2
US A-fuel export license deferral rptd 5-20, 408B2
Australia tariff proposals scored 8-17, 646B2
Sports
Far East Open results 11-12, 990D2
U.S. Relations
Page paymt to Salleh chrgd 4-13, 449B2
US A-fuel export license deferral rptd 5-20, 408B2
AF capt sentncd for Northrop kickback 6-6, 439D3
Viet refugee boat gets supplies 11-14, 871B1

MALDIVES—*See also NONALIGNED Nations Movement*
UN Assemb member 713C3

MALDONADO, Col. Abundio
Declared Guatemala City mayor-elect 4-28, 354D3

MALECELA, John
Asks locust plague aid 6-6, 465C2

MALFATTI, Franco Maria
Named Italy finance min 3-11, 191B1

MALI—*See also NONALIGNED Nations Movement, OAU*
Drought danger rptd 1-3, 24A2
Cabt shuffled 1-7, 75E1
4 mins arrested for treason 2-28, 3-9, 250F3
6 W African natns back ECOWAS 3-18, USSR scores 3-20, 237E1
UN Assemb member 713C3

MALICK, Terrence
Days of Heaven released 9-13, 970A1

MA Lien-pao
Ousted in test scandal 2-20, 130E2

MALIK, Adam
Gets protest on press ban 1-25, 72D1
Elected Indonesia vp 3-22, 246E1

MALIS, Claire
PS Your Cat is Dead opens 3-22, 887F2

MALISZEWSKI, Ray
Sees elec shortages in '80s 9-11, 702A1

MALLE, Louis
Pretty Baby released 4-5, 619C3

MALLORQUIN, Mario
Arrested in Paraguay 11-17, 989F3

MALLORY & Co., P. R.
Dart bid OKd 11-17, 1005C2

MALLOUM, Brig. Gen. Felix (Chadian president)
4 natns OK peace plan, rebel mtg set 2-24, 130B2
Asks French aid vs rebels 4-15, 572G1
Chrgs Libya invades 6-22, 572B2
Habre named premier 8-29, 732G3

MALLOWAN, Max
Dies 8-19, 708B3

MALMIERCA Peoli, Isidoro Octavio
Says Cuba backs Eritrea negotiatns 6-26, 584C3
Defends Cuba Africa role 7-28, 583G2

MALONE, Moses
NBA rebound ldr 4-9, 271F2

MALONE v. White Motor Corp.
Minn pensn funds law backed by Sup Ct 4-3, 308E3

MALPRACTICE, Medical—*See under MEDICINE*

MALTA—*See also COMMONWEALTH of Nations, COUNCIL of Europe, GATT, NONALIGNED Nations Movement*
Freedom House lists as free, rights decline noted 44A2
Bombings, pol violence rptd 1-8, 2-19, 228G1-C2
'77 GDP rptd 2-15, 228A3
'78 budget presented 2-17, 228G2
Univ to be dismantled 3-21, 228D2
Teachers strike 5-15—5-16, effect disputed 5-17, 416A2
Mintoff party merges with union 5-23, 416D2
Educatn adviser resigns, scores govt bill 6-6, 592D3

1979

MALAYSIA—*See also ASEAN, COMMONWEALTH of Nations, GATT, NONALIGNED Nations Movement*
Foreign Relations (misc.)—*See also 'Indochina Refugees' below*
PI civil war refugees flee to Sabah 3-5, 193C1
Pol Pot Cambodia forces backed 8-30, 674D3
UN membership listed 695G2
UNCTAD rubber pact reached 10-5, 781B3
Indochina Refugees
Viet refugees barred 1-5, 51A3
104 drown 3-31, UN protests 4-2, 299D1
Data rptd 4-25, 5-7, 5-19, 379B2-F2
Refugee expulsn, shooting set 6-15; US concerned 6-16; shooting threat dropped after intl pleas 6-18, 460D1
UN issues plea 6-16; denies access 6-19, threatns expulsns 6-26, 474C1
500-800 land 6-17, ousted 6-18, 460F2
Expuln data 6-25, 6-27, US camps asked 6-26, 474B1, D1
More admissns barred 6-30; US, Japan seek aid 7-2, 495B2
1,050 barred, 623 admitted 7-2; 1,000 force landing 7-4, 495D3
Refugee plan submitted at intl conf 7-20, 549B2
US policy scored 7-6, 550B2; US, other rescue missns scored 7-30, 575D2
UN vs asylum bar 8-3, 626C1
US reps visit camps 8-7, 607G1
Mondale in talks 9-1, 660A3
U.S. Relations—*See also 'Indochina Refugees' above*
Grumman admits paymts 1-3, 16F1

MALCOLM X (Malcolm Little) (1926-65)
FBI neutralizatn plan rptd 11-5, 886A3

MALDEN, Karl
Beyond the Poseidon Adventure released 5-24, 528E1
Meteor released 10-19, 1008A1

MALDIVES—*See also NONALIGNED Nations Movement*
UN membership listed 695G2

MALEK Ukil, Abdul
Fails to win parlt seat 2-18, 172F3

MALI—*See also NONALIGNED Nations Movement, OAU*
France debt relief vow rptd 5-4, 371C3
UN membership listed 695G2

MALIK, Brig. Gen. Manucher
Executed 2-20, 125F1

MALINDI, Kesiwe
Hails US Sen vote to end sanctns 5-16, 359D2

MALLOUM, Brig. Gen. Felix (Chadian president; deposed March 23)
Habre rebelln thwarted 2-14, 114G1-A2
Nigerian mediatn rptd OKd 3-1, 153F3
Signs peace pact 3-20, 211F1
Leaves for Nigeria 3-23, 329C3

MALLOY, Jim
SIU-Edwardsville wins NCAA soccer title 12-9, 1004A2

MALNUTRITION—*See FOOD–Diet*

MALONE, Moses
NBA scoring, rebound ldr 4-8, 290D2, F2, A3
Named NBA MVP, rebound record cited 5-23, 526F1
On NBA all-league team 6-6, 526B2

MALONE v. White Motor Corp.
Case decided by Sup Ct 10-15, 847F3

MALONEY, Dave
Montreal wins Stanley Cup 5-21, 447D3

MALONEY, James
Slays FBI agents, self 8-9, 727F3

MALOOF, Naji P.
Scores CIA on Paisley death probe 7-8, 520F2

MALPRACTICE, Medical—*See under MEDICINE*

MALTA—*See also COMMONWEALTH of Nations, COUNCIL of Europe, GATT, NONALIGNED Nations Movement*
UK withdraws last troops, Qaddafi attends fetes 3-31, 4-1, 269C2
Libyans occupy Valetta Emb 9-3, 688F2
UN membership listed 695G2
Mintoff's office shot up, assailant seized 10-15, 782G1*

1980

MALAYSIA—*See also ADB, ASEAN, COMMONWEALTH of Nations, GATT, NONALIGNED Nations*
Defns-GNP ratio rptd 2-19, 132G1
Foreign Relations (misc.)
US to take Indochina refugees 1-12, 49G1
Pacific orgn studied 1-20, 78C2
Viet refugee total declines, immigratn data rptd 8-10, 645D1
US rptr, son arrested 9-6; ousted 9-7, 810G1
PI drops claim to Sabah State 10-31, 902D3
Islamic League meets 11-10, 895B2
More Viet refugees arrive 11-19, 952E1

MALDIVES—*See ADB, NONALIGNED Nations*

MALI—*See NONALIGNED Nations, OAU*

MALIK, Redha
Delivers Iran terms on US hostages 11-3, 853B3

MALIK, Yakov Aleksandrovich
Dies 2-11, 176D2

MALINOWSKI, Bronislaw
Wins Olympic medal 7-31, 624D1

MALKEN, Joy
Ford paternity suit settled 2-28, 199A2

MALLE, Louis
Marries Candice Bergen 9-27, 908F1

MALLEY, Simon
France expels 10-3, 790B2

MALLINSON, James
Wins Grammy 2-27, 296F3

MALLON, Seamus
Lauds Haughey speech 2-17, 133B2

MALLORY, Walter H.
Dies 6-17, 528E2

MALMED, Judge Edwin S.
Convicts Phila radicals in '78 murder 5-8, 414B1

MALMIERCA Peoli, Isidoro Otavio
Seeks to mediate Afghan-Pak feud 3-25—3-27, 271C2
Bars UN refugee involvmt 6-5, 435A2
Tries to mediate Iran-Iraq war 11-11—11-14, 894D3-895B1

MALNIK, Alvin I.
Caesars gets NJ gambling license 10-25, 988B3

MALONE, Mark
In NFL draft 4-29, 336G2

MALONE, Mike
Reggae opens 3-27, 392F3

MALONE, Moses
In NBA All-Star Game 2-3, 279B1
NBA scoring, rebound ldr 3-30, 278C3, E3

MALONEY, Jim
Fiendish Plot of Dr Fu Manchu released 8-8, 675E2

MALOON, James H.
Rpts Itel huge '79 loss 10-16, 784E1

MALOUF, Albert
Drapeau blamed for '76 Olympic debt 6-5, 444D1

MALPRACTICE, Medical—*See MEDICINE--Malpractice*

MALTA—*See also COMMONWEALTH of Nations, COUNCIL of Europe, CSCE, GATT, NONALIGNED Nations*
Libya disputes offshore oil rights 8-21, Libya mil advisers expelled 8-28, 709E1-A2
Olivier dies 10-29, 876A3
Sports
Chess Olympiad results 12-7, 972A3

1976

MALTBIE, Roger
Loses Phoenix open 1-18, 123E2
MALTSEV, Aleksandr
Flyers beat Sovt team 1-11, 56C2
MALUF, Chafic
Dies 12-27, 1015A2
MAMIAKA, Gen. Raphael
Named min of state 10-19, 1003A2
MAMMOGRAPHY—*See X-RAYS*
MANAFORT, Paul
Bailey cleared in Conn scandal 1-12, 271G1
MAN Called Intrepid, A (book)
On best-seller list 12-5, 972A2
MANCHAM, James
Seychelles independnc set 1-22, 271A1
At France-Africa summit 5-10—5-11, 355A3
Seychelles pres 6-28, 483E2
MANCHESTER, N.H.—*See NEW Hampshire*
MANCHESTER Union Leader (newspaper)
Editor not at Ford press mtg 1-22, 41A2
Ford endorsement rptd 10-30, 831F2
MANCUSO, Antonio
Sentenced 7-29, 816C3
MANDEL, Gov. Marvin (D, Md.)
Greets Brown 4-28, 343B2
Brown wins pres primary 5-18, 357C2
Pallotine loan cited 6-18, 951A1
Dem govs back Carter 7-6, 492C3
Mistrial declared 12-7, 922E2
2 indicted re mistrial 12-28, 1016G2
MANDELA, Nelson
Forced use of Afrikaans dropped 7-6, 500B2
Home firebombed 8-4, 579D2
Wife arrested 8-13, 624G2
Wife freed, banned 12-28, 1010E2
MANDELA, Winnie
On Soweto riots 6-16, 426G1
On forced Afrikaans use end 7-6, 500B2
Home firebombed 8-4, 579D2
Arrested 8-13, 624G2
Home ransacked 10-20, 794D1
Freed, banned 12-28, 1010E2
MANDUNGU Bula Nyati
Zaire natl guidance min 2-4, 270C2
MANFULL, Melvin L.
Replaced as amb to Liberia 4-1, 262C3
MANGANESE
Australia ocean find rptd 2-26, 154F3
MANGWENDE, Tafirenyika
Named to Rhodesia Cabt 4-27, 295C2
MANHATTAN Center (N.Y.)
Unificatn Church buys 9-8, 971D1
MANILOW, Barry
Songs on best-selling list 1-28, 104G3
MANKIEWICZ, Frank
Loses Cong primary 5-18, 357A2
Cited in Dole biog sketch 614D3
MANLEY, Henry A. (d. 1973)
Carson, 5 others acquitted; '74 convictns cited 2-6, 124G1

MANLEY, Michael (Jamaican prime minister)
Scores Kingston violence 1-9, 50G3, 51C1
'Destabilizatn' campaign seen 5-25, 6-20, JLP plot chrgd 6-29, 522D1, F1
Party admits Alcoa donatn 7-19, 690A2
PNP wins electns 12-15; asks unity 12-16, 965F1

MANN, Rep. James Robert (D, S.C.)
Reelected 11-2, 830A4
MANN, John
For Tokyo Rose pardon 11-17, 892C2
MANNHARDT, Karin
Named in Getty will 6-8, 444D2

1977

World Medical Assemb backs MDs 9-9, 925B3
UN pollutn conf ends, Medit pact reached 10-21, 876B2
Mintoff provokes Sovt, E Eur walkout in Peking 11-3, 925E2
Mintoff announces Chinese aid 11-16, 925A3
Mintoff presses for France, Italy aid; threatens Libya defns pact 11-23, 925A3
Helsinki Agreement—*See EUROPE—Security and Cooperation*

MALTSEV, Nikolai A.
Named USSR oil min 4-5, 306C3
MALVINAS—*See FALKLAND Islands*
MAMMOGRAPHY—*See X-RAYS*
MAMONE, Russell B.
Chrgs FPC gas testimony reprisal 3-10, 196B1
MANAGEMENT & Budget, Office of—*See U.S. GOVERNMENT—BUDGET*
MANASCO, Carter
Scores strip-mine bill 7-23, 575F2
MANCHAM, James
Outlines dvpt plan 1-1, 24G2
Ousted, blames USSR 6-5, 450F3
Not at Commonwealth conf 6-8—6-15, 487F1
Denies countercoup plot 6-9, 489D1
US, UK recognize Rene govt 6-13, 489B1
MANCHESTER, N.H.—*See NEW Hampshire*
MANDEL, Gov. Marvin (D, Md.)
Asks US aid fishermen 1-20, 54D2
Vetoes death penalty 5-26, 594A2
Transfers powers to Blair 6-4, 652D1
Convicted 8-23, 652A1-A2
Sentenced to 4 yrs 10-7, 807D2
Prosecutor joins FBI probe 12-13, 979C3
MANDELA, Nelson
Wife freed on bail 7-28, 600B1
MANDELA, Winnie
Banished 5-19, 399G3
Freed on bail 7-28, 600A1
2 sentncd re info refusal 9-7, 825G3
MANGANESE
UN Sea Law Conf adjourns 7-15, US scores rpt 7-20, 572B3
S Africa deal rptd barred, productn data cited 8-16, 657B2
MANGOPE, Lucas
Bophuthatswana independnc declared 12-5, 935C2
MANHARDT, Meryl
Wis judge recalled 9-7, 712B1
MANILOW, Barry
Wins Tony 6-5, 452E1
MANLEY, Beverly (Mrs. Michael)
Scores PNP youth 9-16, 884F2
MANLEY, Douglas
Jamaica health min 1-4, 46C1

MANLEY, Michael (Jamaican prime minister)
Names new Cabt 1-4, 46A1
Outlines emergency econ plan 1-19, 257G1
Hails Kaiser, Reynolds purchases 2-10, 3-31, 257C3, G3
Sees Mrs Carter 5-30—5-31, 454B2
Sees Torrijos, regional ldrs 8-5—8-6; new Panama Canal pact backed, Intl Coffee Fund set 8-6, 606B3, 608A3
Sees US amb Young 8-6—8-7, 646A2
PNP conflict grows 9-16—10-7; assumes mobilizatn post 9-18, 884D2-A3
Castro visits, pledges aid 10-16—10-21, 883E3-884E1
CIA death plots rptd 11-2, 884E1
In US talks re Cuba, Panama Canal pact 12-16, 1019G1

MANN, Erroll
Raiders win Super Bowl 1-9, 24D3, F3
MANNE, A. S.
At Salzburg A-conf 5-2—5-13, 402G3

1978

Mintoff addresses House of Reps 7-10, 592B3
Foreign Relations (misc.)
UK RAF group 203 disbanded 1-2, 39C2
Algeria pres visits 1-3, 39B2
Envoy recalled from Australia, aid bar cited 1-24, 228B3
Rhodesia mtg opens 1-30, 59D1
'77 paymts surplus rptd; UK base revenue, Libya, China and cited 2-15, 228B3
Libyan ldr visits; mil aid, oil price cuts agreed 7-3—7-4, 592E2
France, Italy rptd cool to Arab aid threats 7-4, 592G2
Mintoff's daughter disrupts UK Parlt 7-6, 533C3
UK rptrs banned 7-9, radio statn closed 7-16; retaliatn denied 7-10, 592A3
UN Assemb member 713C3
Helsinki Agreement—*See EUROPE—Security and Cooperation*

MALTBY Jr., Richard
Ain't Misbehavin' opens 5-9, 760A1 ★
Wins Tony 6-4, 579A3
MALUF, Paulo Salim
Wins Sao Paulo gov race 6-5, 556C1
MALVEREZ, Juan
Lopez KOs 9-15, 726D2
MALVINAS—*See FALKLAND Islands*
MAMET, David
Water Engine opens 1-5, 760G3
MAMMALS—*See also mammal names*
Early mammals rptd nocturnal, cool-blooded 3-23, 334D3
Gene transfer rptd 10-28, 1023B3
MANCA, Gavino
Shot in Milan 7-5, 517B2
MANCHAM, James
Accused in plot 4-29, Kenya aid chrgd 5-8, 378C3
MANCHESTER, N.H.—*See NEW Hampshire*
MANCHESTER, William
Amer Caesar on best-seller list 10-9, 800B3; 11-6, 887G3; 12-3, 971B1
MANCUSO, Thomas
A-plant radiatn linked to cancer 2-17, 164C2
MANDEL, Alan
Goin' South released 10-6, 970D1
MANDEL, Marvin
Pallottine priest indicted 1-6, 24B3
Ordrd to pay back alimony 2-15, 172B3
Primary results 9-12, 716F1
Hughes elected Md gov 11-7, 848A3
MANDEL, Mel
My Old Friends opens 12-2, 1031E2
MANDELA, Nelson
6 sentenced in terrorism trial 4-7, 269B2
MANDELA, Winnie
Gets suspended sentences 2-9, 114D1
MANFREDI, Nino
Bread & Chocolate released 7-14, 969E3
MANGANESE
US House OKs seabed mining bill 7-26, 588F3
MANGENA, Alfred Nikita
Assassinatn attempt denied 4-24, 455G2
Killed 6-28, 594A3
MANGIONE, Chuck
Feels So Good on best-seller list 5-3, 356E1; 6-7, 460G3
MANGURIAN, Harry
NBA OKs Celtics-Braves ownership swap 7-7, 655F2
MANILOW, Barry
Even Now on best-seller list 3-8, 196C1; 4-5, 272G3
Can't Smile Without You on best-seller list 4-5, 272F3; 5-3, 356D1
MANITOBA (Canadian province)—*See CANADA*
MANKIN, Charles
Sees gas output hike unlikely 4-27, 322E1

MANLEY, Michael (Jamaican prime minister)
At Panama Canal pact instrumts exchng 6-16, 463F2, 464A1

MANN, Daniel
Matilda released 6-22, 619B3
MANN, Errol
NFL '77 kicking ldr 1-1, 56B2
MANN, Rep. James R. (D, S.C.)
Campbell wins seat 11-7, 853C1
MANN, Stanley
Damien released 6-8, 619D1
MANN, Theodore
13 Rue De L'Amour opens 3-16, 760D3
Once in a Lifetime opens 6-15, 887C2
Man & Superman revived 12-17, 1031D2
Concerned re US Mideast role 12-19, 978G3
MANNEKIN Pis (sculpture)
Stolen 4-25, 4-27, 355C2
MANNI, Roberto
Turin bomb blasts 3-4—3-5, 191E2

1979

MALTBY, Barbara
Loses women's intl squash open 1-28, US women's open 2-11, 1-28, 527C2
MAMA Don't Let Your Babies Grow Up To Be Cowboys (recording)
Jennings, Nelson win Grammy 2-16, 336F3
MAMET, David
The Woods opens 4-25, 712F3
Poet & Rent opens 5-9, 712A2
MAMMALS
Cloning advance rptd 7-28, 692E2
MAN, a Woman and a Bank, A (film)
Released 9-28, 820G1
MANCHESTER, William
Amer Caesar on best-seller list 1-7, 80C3; 2-4, 120C3; 3-4, 173E3
MANCHESTER (N.H.) Union Leader (newspaper)
Crane scores Loeb articles 6-8, 594G1
Loeb settles pensn fund suit 7-9, 640E3
MANCUSO, Thomas
2 unions ask HEW radiatn safety studies 1-30, 90E3
MANDEL, Loring
Promises in the Dark released 11-2, 1008B1
MANDEL, Marvin
Conviction upset 1-11, 17G3
Reclaims office 1-15, 56D1
Convictn reinstated 7-20, 604D3
MANDELA, Winnie
White supporters jailed 12-13, 969F1
MANESCU, Manea
Replaced as Rumania premr 3-30, 279D3
MANFREDO, Fernando
Panama chrgs US treaties violatn 12-6, 939E1
MANGIONE, Chuck
Wins Grammy 2-16, 336E3
MANGURIAN, Harry
NBA OKs Celtics purchase 5-7, 527D1
MANHATTAN (film)
Released 4-24, 528A3
Top-grossing film 5-23, 448G3
MANILOW, Barry
Wins Grammy 2-16, 336D3
MAN in the Iron Mask (book)
5th Musketeer released 9-7, 820B1
MANION, Clarence E.
Dies 7-28, 588A3
MANITOBA (Canadian province)—*See CANADA*

MANLEY, Michael (Jamaican prime minister)
Gas price raised 1-8; 7 killed in riots 1-8–1-10; chrgs anti-govt plot 1-10, 21C2
Sees IMF loan rescheduling, marks reelectn 12-15, 996G1
Cabt resigns, econ policies scored 12-17, 996A2

MANN, Stanley
Meteor released 10-19, 1008A1
MANN, Theodore
Vs US stand on PLO 1-17, 69G1
Lauds black-Jewish cooperatn 8-19, 624B2
MANNESMANN A.G.
US unit withdraws Harnischfeger offer 11-4, 942G2

1980

MALYSHEV, Lt. Col. Yuri
In space flight 6-5—6-9, 477B1
MAMET, David
Twelfth Night opens 12-16, 1003F3
MAMONOVA, Tatyana
USSR expels, arrives Austria 7-20, 680C2
MANANA, Napthali
Sentenced to death 11-26, 968B1
MANASSE, George
He Knows You're Alone released 9-26, 836A3
MANCA, Enrico
Italy trade min 4-4, 275G3
MANCHESTER—*See NEW Hampshire*
MANCHESTER v. U.S.
Case declined by Sup Ct 3-24, 265C1
MANCINI, Marlene
Charlotte opens 2-27, 392D2
MANDEL, Jean (Mrs. Marvin)
Sued 1-4, 18D2
MANDEL, Marvin
Sued 1-4, 18D2
Appeal refused by Sup Ct 4-14, 307A1
Begins prison sentence 5-19, 471E2
MANDELA, Nelson
ANC seizes bank, demands release 1-25, 100E3
3 African natlsts sentncd to death 11-26, 968D1
MANDELSTAM, Nadeshda
Dies 12-29, 1004E2
MANDELSTAM, Osip Emilievich (d. 1938)
Complete Critical Prose wins Amer Book Award 5-1, 692G2
Widow dies 12-29, 1004E2
MANDEL v. En Banc Court of Appeals
Case refused by Sup Ct 4-14, 307C1
MANDEL v. New York
Case dismissed by Sup Ct 5-19, 440C2
MANDEL v. U.S.
Case refused by Sup Ct 4-14, 307C1
MANDLIKOVA, Hana
Loses WTA Championship 4-20, French Open semifinals 6-6, 606D3, 607B3
Defaults Austrian Grand Prix 7-27, wins Volvo Cup 8-24, 691A3, D3
Loses US Open 9-6, 691D2
Loses Riviera Women's Classic 9-21; wins Atlanta Classic 9-28, Women's Stockholm Open 11-2, Dutch Indoor 11-16, Australian Open 11-30, 947G1, C2-G2
MANES, Fritz
Any Which Way You Can released 12-17, 1003F1
MANGE, James
ANC rebels demand release 1-25, 100E3
MANGLAPUS, Raul
Arrest warrant issued 10-20, 809G1
Chrgd in PI plot 10-28, US arrest ordrd 11-3, 874D2, E2
MANGOPE, Chief Lucas (Bophuthatswana chief minister)
Hails Mafeking transfer 9-19, 753C2
MANHATTAN Showboat (play)
Opens 7-1, 756E3
MANLEY, Michael (Jamaican prime minister)
Sees IMF dir, loan talks fail 1-15; asks early electns 2-3, 99E1-B2
Breaks with IMF 3-25; banks rejct aid request, urge IMF compromise 4-7, 276A1
Shot at 4-14, 336E1
Forgn bank debt accord reached 4-15, 314C2
Sees econ recovery; rpts intl loans, bauxite dvpt progrm 6-4, 465B1
Soldiers seized in coup plot 6-22, 498E2
Bars ouster of US intell agents 7-4, 565A1
Condemns violence, bars state of siege 7-18, 579A2
Sets Oct 30 electns, Seaga oppositn cited 10-5, 791F3
Security offcl, aide killed 10-14, 791E3
Loses reelectn, retains parlt seat 10-30, 854B1
MANN, Jimmy
NHL penalty minutes ldr 4-6, 296E1
MANN, Katharina (Mrs. Thomas)
Dies 4-18, 360C2
MANN, Marty
Dies 7-22, 608D2
MANN, Theodore
Major Barbara opens 2-26, 392D3
Past Tense opens 4-24, 392F3
MANN, Thomas (1875-1955)
Widow dies 4-18, 360C2
MANNESMAN A.G.
Co-determinatn compromise proposed 11-24, 904D2
Co-determinatn restructuring rptd 12-1, 924G3

1976

MANNING, Herbert C.
McCloy rpt detailed 133F2
Ousted from Gulf post 1-15, 132C3, 133A1
MANOLESCU, Gersce
Rptd killed 7-12, 649F2
MANRIQUE, Javier
Accuses bishops 8-25, 693A1
MANSFIELD, Sen. Michael J(oseph) (Mike) (D, Mont.)
On State of Union proposals 1-19, 40A1
Picks Muskie to rebut Ford 1-21, 40F1
To retire 3-4, 181D1
Scores Magna Carta trip critics 4-5, 283A3
Rockefeller apologizes to Sen 4-27, 305G3
Names intelligence com members 5-20, 377D1
Melcher wins Sen primary 6-1, 411F1
Japan warns vs China concessns 7-12, 555E2, A3
Melcher wins seat 11-2, 820C1, 824A2
Carter meets cong ldrs 11-17, 864F1
MANSFIELD, Judge Walter R.
Upholds NYC clean-air plan 4-26, 308D1
MANSFIELD Tire & Rubber Co.
URW pact OKd 10-10, 867B1
MANSON (film)
Sup Ct bars review of ban 4-19, 331C2
MANSON, Charles M.
Denied new trial 8-13, 640C3
Murphy escapes jail 8-14, 640A3
Farr wins 5-yr ct test 12-21, 995C1
MANTHATHA, Thomas
Arrested 6-29, 500D2
MANTILLA, Carlos
Dies 7-20, 680F3
MANTOVANIA, Nadia
Seized 2-18, 141B1
MANUFACTURERS Hanover Corp.
Rptd on FRB 'problem' list 1-29, 113A1
Hamilton loan rptd 2-20, 167D1
Rpt Spain seeks intl loan 6-23, 501A3
Spain Eurocurrency loan rptd 7-13, 541B3
Citibank sues re Zaire loan 8-9, 621C2
Spain signs intl loan 8-9, 929G1
'75 zero tax paymt rptd 10-2, 847F1
Citibank, Bankers Trust drop suits 10-13, 890G2
MAN Who Skied Down Everest, The (film)
Wins Oscar 3-29, 240B3
MAN Who Would be King, The (film)
Top-grossing film 2-25, 208G3; 3-31, 240C3
MAO Jen-sheng
Cited in Mao biog 658B2
MAO Tse-tung
Facts on 658B2
'65 poems published 1-1, 9D2
Letter from students rptd 1-2, 9G3
Youth relocatn policy rptd 1-6, 48G1, B2
Not at Chou En-lai rite 1-15, 48C1
New edition of poems publshd 1-19, 100E3
Educ policies backed 1-21—1-27, 100G2
A-test rptd inspired by poems 1-25, 83F3
'Deviationists' scored 2-6, 117A2
Hua ties rptd 2-8, 117E2
Campaign vs Teng launched; central com split, Chiang Ching role rptd 2-10—3-9, 188D3-189D2
Sees Nixon 2-23, 189C3
Pro-Chou rallies 4-1—4-4, riot 4-5, govt scores 4-7, 244A1
Teng ousted, Hua named premr 4-7, 243C3
Teng plot rptd 4-10, 4-27—4-28, 333B1
Meets Egypt vp 4-20, 275F2
Pravda article scores 4-28, 341A3
Sees NZ, Singapore, Pak ldrs, health cited 4-30—5-27; to end greetings role 6-15, 439D2
May Day CP unity rptd 5-2, 332E3
Article honors ideology 5-7, 439D1
Chu Teh dies 7-6, 520F3
Wu Teh to head People's Cong 7-24, 555A2
Proposed script introduced 8-1, 588B2
Not at quake relief rally 9-1, 673A3
Dies 9-9, reactn 9-9—9-10, 657A1; announcemt text excerpts 659A2-F3
Mourning period observed 9-11—9-18, 711A3
USSR avoids criticizing 10-1, 752F1
Hua succeeds 10-7, 871E2
Remains to be displayed 10-8, 758D1
Hua appointment announced 10-12, wall posters oppose 10-14, 757A1, D2
Widow, other radicals rptd arrested, will forgery cited 10-12—10-14, 757E1-E2
Cited in Hua biog 757G2, 758A1, D1
Hua acclaimed in rally 10-24, 809E1-D2
Hua selectn, warning re radicals cited 10-24, 10-25, 809G1-D2
Chiang chrgs rptd 10-25, 10-26, 809D2
Brezhnev avoids mentn 10-25, 839C2
Cited in editorial urging Chiang purge restraint 11-28, 904B3
Chrg 'gang of 4' sought power 12-18, 999F3
MAO Yuan-hsin
Rptd arrested 10-12, 10-13, 757B2
MAPHUMULO, Chief Hlabunzima
Zulu pol struggle setld 1-15—1-19, 76C2
MAPS—*See ILLUSTRATIONS*
MARATHON Manufacturing Co.
UK govt wins ship natlzn ruling 5-27, 401G3 ★
MARATHON Oil Co.
In Viet oil talks 4-24, 352B2
MARATHON Shipbuilding Co.-U.K. Ltd.—*See MARATHON Manufacturing Co.*
MARBURG Disease—*See 'Diseases' under MEDICINE*
MARCHAIS, Georges
CP 22d cong, reelected secy gen 2-4—2-7, 119D1
Sovt CP Cong 2-24—3-5, 196A1
Joint '77 electn drive stalled 5-21, 381A3

1977

MANOS, Judge John M.
Bars Bahama tax evidnc 4-28, 395C3
MANPOWER Administration—*See under U.S. GOVERNMENT—LABOR*
MANSFIELD, Michael J(oseph) (Mike)
Byrd elected majority ldr 1-4, 5E3
In missn to Viet, Laos 3-16—3-20; Carter gets rpt 3-23, 206B1
Named amb to Japan 4-7, confrmd 4-21, 418G1
Warning to Japan on trade imbalance rptd 7-28, 586E1
MANSFIELD, Judge Walter R.
Backs JFK Concorde ban 6-14, 463F1
Backs NY Concorde ruling 9-29, 738F3
MANSLAUGHTER—*See CRIME—Murders*
MANSON, Charles M.
Sup Ct refuses convictn review 4-25, 342G2
Van Houten mistrial declared 8-6, 711C2
MANSOUR, Faiz
Slain 6-12, 510F1
MANTILLA, Manuel
Venez Fed District gov 1-7, 23F2
MANUFACTURERS, National Association of (NAM)—*See NATIONAL Association of Manufacturers*
MANUFACTURERS Hanover Corp.
Manufacturers Hanover Trust Co.
Pension managemt cited 6-28, 578C2
Lance cleared in govt probe 8-18, 625B2
SEC rpt chrgs NYC '74-75 financial deceptn 8-26; reactn 8-26—8-27, 665A3, 666A1
MANUFACTURERS Hanover Trust Co. (N.Y.)—*See under MANUFACTURERS Hanover Corp.*
MANZHULO, Alexei
Rpts 9-mo trade deficit cut 11-23, 988D1
MANZO Gonzalez, Jose
Venez labor min 1-7, 23E2
MAO Tse-tung (1893-1976)—*See 1976, p. 658B2 for biog. data*
Greater discipline urged 2-7, 98D1
Hangchow unrest detailed 4-11, 282C2
5th vol published 4-15, 347B1
Econ progress cited 5-4, 449F2
Nixon reminisces 5-12, 385F3, 386C1
No improved China-USSR ties seen 5-14, 5-26, 458D2
Chang tied to Shanghai plot 5-17, 449C3
Wang accused of violence 6-3, 449G2
Nephew scored in Liaoning 6-24, 562C1
3-world theory explained 595D1
Hua cites at CP Cong 8-12—8-18, 646D1
Wang Tung-hsing in Politburo 8-21, 645F2
Tito visits mausoleum 8-31, 710C1
'71 plot detailed 9-8, 694D2
Creed modificatn urged 9-9, 694B3
Mausoleum opened 9-9, 706A1
Govt hints policy shift 9-10, 706C1
Tighter econ controls asked 9-12, 705F3
China tests A-tipped missile 9-12, 706B2
Hsu urges army discipline 9-19, 743F3
Kwangsi dissent hinted 9-22, 744C1
Science policy chng rptd 9-22, 781E1
'75 mtg with Cambodia ldr rptd 10-2, 780A1
Anti-Taiwan stand reaffirmd 10-4, 781B1
Educ policies reversed 10-21, 823C2
Police abuses chrgd 11-28, 983C3
MAO Yuan-hsin
Scored in Liaoning Prov 6-24, 562C1
MAPLE Leaf Mills Ltd.—*See NORIN Corp.*
MAPS—*See CARTOGRAPHY, ILLUSTRATIONS—Maps*
MARA, Ratu Sir Kamisese
New Fiji electn set 4-6, 394A3
Alliance party wins electns 9-25, 767B2
MARARI, Sherbaz
Released 6-3, 450A3
MARATHON Oil Co.
Pan Ocean takeover cited in table 880G1
Loop license signed 8-1, 724E3
MARAVICH, Pete
NBA final standings 4-10, 331B3
Named to NBA all-star team 6-13, 584G3
MARCEAU, Louis
Upholds French ban 1-12, 17B3
MARCELO Curto, Francisco
Replaced as labor min 3-25, 330F2
MARCHAIS, Georges
Scores Czech, Sovt repressn 1-6, 1-25, 63B2
Sees Berlinguer, Carrillo in Spain 3-2—3-3, 242F3
Brezhnev shuns on French trip 6-20—6-22, 495F1
Clashes with Mitterrand on A-policy 8-9, 727B3
Shuns USSR 60th anniv 11-2—11-7, 865G3
Rpts Sahara rebels to free French natls 12-14, 998C3
Gunmen attack home 12-25, 1011F3

1978

MANNING, Archie
NFL '77 passing ldr 1-1, 56E2
MANNING & Napier
SEC censures re Equity Funding 9-4, 681A2
MANOS, Judge John M.
Bars oil co rebates to consumers 1-20, 108F3
MANPOWER Administration—*See under U.S. GOVERNMENT—LABOR*
MANSFIELD, J. Kenneth
Vs energy emergency plans 9-11, 701C2-A3
MANSFIELD, Mike
Sees China oil potential 10-16, 871G2
MANSLAUGHTER—*See CRIME—Murder*
MANSON, Charles M.
Van Houten sentncd 10-11, 824F2
MAN and Superman (play)
Opens 12-17, 1031D2
MANTLE, Mickey
Stargell surpasses strikeout record 8-6, 779D3
MANTOVANI, Nadia
Arrested 10-1, 817E1
MANUFACTURERS Hanover Corp.
Stevens' head forced off bd 3-7, 163A1
S Africa held credit risk 4-23, 377G1-A2
Chrmn Hauge to retire, McGillicuddy named 10-17, 809E1
Manufacturers Hanover Ltd.
Venez $1.2 bln loan rptd 1-12, 332F1
Manufacturers Hanover Trust Co.
Clothing workers force Stevens' head off bd 3-7, 163B1
Peru loan refinancing barred 3-10, Sovt-Peru deal cited 3-14, 353F1, B2
Peru offcls meet intl bankers 5-23—5-24, 394C2
Franklin ex-offcrs indicted 7-13, 681C1
Dropped from world '77 top 10 11-8, 914B1
MANUFACTURERS Hanover Trust Co.—*See under MANUFACTURERS Hanover Corp.*
MANUFACTURERS and Traders Trust Co.
FDIC paymt case declined by Sup Ct 10-16, 789F1
MANUFACTURING—*See BUSINESS & Industry*
MANUSAMA, Johannes
Kuhuwael shot 1-29, 90D3
MANZ, Linda
Days of Heaven released 9-13, 970A1
MAO Tse-tung (1893-1976)—*See 1976, p. 658B2 for biog. data*
French premier in China 1-19—1-24, 71E1
New charter announced 3-5, 154A1
Reevaluatn of ideas rptd urged 6-3, 532E2
Criticized for democracy lack, '62 speech cited 7-3, 532B2
China pragmatic approach cited re Hong Kong bank order 7-6, 532A2
China ends Albania aid 7-13, 549B1
Chinese get 1st cigaret warning 8-28, 727A2
Injustices cited 10-26, 837E3
Posters, press link to 'Gang of 4' 11-15, 11-16, 11-19, 901E2
Posters ask '76 Peking riot probe 11-20; rally suppressn, Teng purge role chrgd 11-23, 11-25, 949A1-C2
Teng: '76 purge 'wrong' 11-26, 950B1
Teng vs critical posters 11-27, 949E2
Chiang Ching attack on Tao Chu chrgd 12-10, 950F1
'79 econ goals set 12-22, 1015D1
MAP (Multiple Aim Point)—*See ARMAMENTS—Missiles*
MAPES v. U.S.
Case refused by Sup Ct 12-11, 981D1
MAPS—*See under ILLUSTRATIONS; also Facts On File Atlas*
MARATHON Oil Co.
Egypt pact signed 2-16, 139B3
MARATHON Swimming—*See SWIMMING*
MARCELLO, Carlos
Cited at JFK death hearing 9-26, 750B1
MARCHAIS, Georges
Breaks left-wing electn accord 1-7, 54F1
Vs Giscard 'interference' 1-27, 70G3
Electn campaign proposals rptd 2-6, 148E3
In TV debate, scores Japan 2-20; amb protests 2-23, 167C2
Affirms left alliance 3-20, 201B2
Confers with Giscard 3-26—3-31, 245E3
Scored by party dissidents 4-27, 351F3-352D1
Kadar sees during visit 11-15—11-17, 894G2

1979

MANNING, Archie
NFL '78 passing ldr 1-6, 80D1
MANNY (play)
Opens 4-18, 712C1
MANOS, Dean
Sweeney Todd opens 3-1, 292C3
MANOS, Judy
Sweeney Todd opens 3-1, 292C3
MANOSALVAS, Martin
Quits Ecuador Cabt 11-29, 967E3
MANOWSKI, Phil
Traded to Mets 10-31, 1002B3
MANSFIELD, O.—*See OHIO*
MANSLAUGHTER—*See CRIME–Murder*
MANSON, Charles M.
NC MD gets life for '70 slayings 8-29, 817A3
Denied parole 11-27, 953D3
MANUFACTURERS, National Association of (NAM)
Larry defends '78 profit rise 3-21, 201D2
Larry on Pay Advisory Com 10-16, 829F2
MANUFACTURERS Hanover Corp.
Manufacturers Hanover Trust Co.
Poland econ monitor plan set 1-11, 59G3
Spain OKs local operatn 1-26, 100F3
Hungary loan plan rptd 3-30, 279C3
GOP credit card plan blocked 6-21, 595A2
Nicaraguan debt paymts in doubt 9-28, 753F2
Money supply error admitted 10-26, 828C2
McGillicuddy cautious re Chrysler loans 10-30, 845C3
Iran assets attached, loans repaid 11-18, 880A1
Peru debt prepaymt agreed 11-26, 951D2
Iran sues UK branch for assets freeze 11-30, 915A2
MANUFACTURERS National Corp.
Manufacturers National Bank of Detroit
Columbia U sells stock 3-23, 271A1
MANUFACTURING—*See BUSINESS*
MANUS, Allen
Arrested re stock fraud 1-10, 37D2
MAO Tse-tung (1893-1976)
Hu gets top China party posts 1-4, 6F3
Cuban calls Sihanouk 'pawn' 1-11, 10E2
Albania CP ldr scores 1-27, 69D3
Anti-govt posters barred 3-31, 259F1
Hunan radio lauds, Teng criticism rptd 5-29, 406C1
Rehabilitated offcls rptd in Tibet 6-13, 445A1
Critics rehabilitated 8-3, 651A3
Bodyguard rptd probe target 8-22, 652A1
Cultural revolutn deplored 9-29, 750G2
Chang Kuo-ta dies 12-4, 1008C2
MAPLES, Ladell
Describes ordeal as hostage 11-18, freed 11-19, 878A1, F1, B2
MAPS—*See under ILLUSTRATIONS; also Facts On File Atlas*
MARA, Tim
Young hired as Giants operatns dir 2-14, 175C2
MARA, Wellington
Young hired as Giants operatns dir 2-14, 175C2
MARAINI, Dacia
Teresa the Thief released 5-5, 528F3
MARAN, Elaine
City Suite opens 4-2, 711B2
MARASESCU, Natalia
Banned from track 10-26, Rumanian protest rptd 11-15, 912A1
MARASHI-Najafi, Ayatollah Haj Seyyed Shahbeddin
Listed in Moslem hierarchy 297A3
MARATHON Manufacturing Co.
Penn Central to purchase 8-10, 664D1
MARATHON Oil Co.
US overchrg claims denied 5-2, 343B2
May gas allocatn rptd unchngd 5-7, 343A1
July gas supplies rptd 6-25, 479E1
Overchrgs alleged 11-14, 905G2-A3; 11-18, 943F1; 12-19, 990E2
MARCELLO, Carlos
House com suspects JFK death link 3-16, 204E3
House com final rpt cites 7-17, 538B1, G1
MARCHAIS, Georges
Leftist censure votes fail 3-16, 235G2
Opens CP cong, reelected secy gen 5-10—5-14, 371G1
Mitterrand seeks left alliance 8-20, 633G1
Weighs Soclst ties 8-22, 652F3
Scores press re Boulin suicide 10-30, 835B1
China premr rptd shunned 11-6, 854F2

1980

MANNING, Archie
NFL '79 passing ldr 1-5, 8E2
MANNING, Gordon
Defends NBC early electn projectns 11-5, 866C1
MANNING, Madeline
Wins natl outdoor 800-yd run 6-15, 892C1
MANNING, Robert
Whitworth named Atlantic Monthly ed 9-22, 908G2
MANOFF, Dinah
I Ought to be in Pictures opens 4-3, 392D3
Wins Tony 6-8, 692C3
MANOS, Judge John M.
Bobbie Brooks case setld 12-21, 988D1
MANPOWER Demonstration Research Corp.
Job project gains rptd few 2-27, 228E3
MANRIQUE, Archbishop Jorge
Denounced by Bolivian mil ldrs 8-17, 9-3, chrgs rights abuses 9-10, 686C3
MANSFIELD, Mike
On Japan mil spending 3-20, 219A3
MANSFIELD Tire & Rubber Co.
Liquidates 9-19, 985F3
MANSLAUGHTER—*See CRIME--Murder*
MANSON, Charles
Atkins denied parole 7-29, 639D2
MANTEK, Frank
Wins Olympic medal 7-27, 624F2
MANTOVANI, Annunzio Paolo
Dies 3-29, 280B1
MANUFACTURERS, National Association of (NAM)
Anti-labor filibuster broken 4-22, 333F2
MANUFACTURERS Bank (Los Angeles, Calif.)
Prime rate cut to 13% 6-4, 438C1
Prime cut to 10.75% 7-24, 574F3
MANUFACTURERS Hanover Corp.
Manufacturers Hanover Trust Co.
Hungary loan rptd 2-18, 142B3
Brazil oil loan rptd 3-5, 191F1
Prime rate cut to 17.5% 5-7, 367D3
Prime cut to 14.5% 5-23, 401G1
Prime cut to 12.75% 6-12, 438D1
Kellner on Carter econ renewal plan 8-28, 663C3
Nicaragua debt rescheduled 9-5, 689A3
Prime hiked to 13.5% 9-12—10-1, 764D2
MANUFACTURING—*See BUSINESS & Industry*
MANUFACTURING Data Systems Inc.
Schlumberger merger set 9-18, 746B1
MAO Tse-tung—*See MAO Zedong*
MAO Zedong (Mao Tse-tung) (1893-1976)
Liu rehabilitated 2-29, 171D3
Policies scored 7-8, 8-10, portraits ordered removed 8-11; USSR denounces 8-17, 651C2
Hua quotes philosophy 9-7, 678B1
'4 Freedoms' abolished 9-10, 677B2
US weighs China police gear request 9-20, 788F2
Hua '76 successn criticized 9-28, 788B3
Canton Grand Prix held 10-19, 947D1
Kang purged 10-31, 859F1
Widows bars confessn, Gang of 4 trial delayed 11-1, 859A1
Gang of 4 indictmts aired, death plot chrgd 11-15—11-18, trial starts 11-20, 877B1, B2
Wu Han death cited 11-16, 877G1
Chinese press vs Cultural Revolutn role 12-22, 975F2
MAPCO, Inc.
Earth Resources merger set 12-5, 985E1
MAPLE, Eddie
Temperence Hill wins Belmont 6-7, 447A3
MAPP, Arthur
Wins Olympic medal 8-2, 623E1
MAPP, John
Loses US House electn 11-4, 850E2
MAPS—*See under ILLUSTRATIONS*
MARAGOS, Jack K.
Chrgd in lottery fraud 9-19, 786D3
MARAGOS, James
Chrgd in lottery fraud 9-19, 786D3
MARAGOS, Jean Ella
Chrgd in lottery fraud 9-19, 786D3
MARAGOS, Peter K.
Chrgd in lottery fraud 9-19, 786D3
MARANGELLO, Nicholas
Indicted 3-3, 215D1
MARANTZ, Paul
Synanon founder, 2 aides convicted in rattler attack 7-15, 655G3
Synanon founder gets probatn 9-3, 860D2
MARASESCU, Natalia
Decker breaks track marks 1-1, 2-8, 891C1
MARATHON Oil Co.
Oil import fee blocked by Dist Ct 5-13, 366B1
Gasoline prices cut 7-9, 553F1
MARCELLINO, Fred
Birdy wins Amer Book Award 5-1, 692E2
MARCELLO, Carlos
FBI Brilab probe target, LA bribe plot rptd 2-8—2-9; organized crime summit rptd canceled 2-13, 111G2, A3, 112A1-C1
Indicted 6-17, 454D3
MARCHAIS, Georges
Meets Italy CP ldr 1-5, goes to USSR 1-7, pro-Sovt stand scored 1-8—1-13, backs Afghan invasn 1-11, 57F2, F3
On CP rights group formatn 2-20, 149B3
Defends war record vs L'Express chrgs 3-8, 193E1-A2
At Tito funeral 5-8, 339C1
At papal receptn 5-30, 476D3
Gets CP pres nominatn 10-12, 790G1

1976

MARCHAND, Jean
Resigns 6-28, 496E2
Replaced 7-12, 555E1
Fisheries min sworn 9-15, 692G1
MARCHAND, Leonard S.
Sworn industry state min 9-15, 692F1
MARCHANT, Kevin J.
Angola sentences 6-28, 480B2, E2
MARCHENKO, Anatoly
In CSCE monitor group 5-13, 408B2
MARCHENKO, Vladimir
Wins Olympic medal 7-23, 574B3
MARCHESE, Judge William J.
Replaced in Carter, Artis case 10-19, 860C1
MARCHOVSKY, Eusebio
Arrested 9-15, 792C2
MARCONA Corp.
Peru natlzatn cited 1-12, 142A2
Peru OKs natlizatn paymts 9-23, 1013A2
MARCORA, Giovanni
Sworn Italy agri min 7-30, 573F1
MARCOS, Ferdinand Edralin
In ASEAN-Australia talks 1-16—1-17, 46D1
Bars electn, keeps powers 1-21, 75A3
UNCTAD fund pledge 108C1
Signs ASEAN pact 2-24, 148D2
Shifts mil command 3-27, 255B3
Macapagal scores rule 4-1, 255C2
Named in torture charge 4-23, 313C3
Kenyatta boycotts UNCTAD 5-5, 320G1
Declares disaster area 5-24, 404E2
In Moscow, ties set 5-31—6-2, 440F1
Decrees Manila capital 5-31, in force 6-24, 500F1
US prisoner chrgs torture 6-26, 500E1
Aquino trial starts 8-3, 695F1
Sets quake emergency 619B2
Says quake toll up 8-22, 638B3
Quizzes captured CP ldr 8-26, 638G2
Continues martial law 8-27, 694G3
Orders punishmt for torturers 9-29, 751C3
Foes vs referendum 9-29, 10-10, 10-13, 839C1
Accuses ousted US newsman 11-6, 855D1
Ousts soldiers for torture 11-8, 855B2
Rejects US base pact 12-4, 926D2
Ends operatns vs rebels 12-24, 1008E3
Plebiscite set on Moslem autonomy 12-27, 1009A1

MARCOS, Imelda
Sets rebel-govt talks 11-17, 1009C1
MARDIAN, Robert C.
Conviction upset 10-12, 770C2
Cleared in wiretap case 12-16, 981A1
MARDIN, Arif
Wins Grammy 2-28, 460B3
MARGARET, Princess (Countess of Snowdon) (Great Britain)
Separates from husband 3-19, 252A3
MARGRETHE, Queen (Alexandrine Thorhildur Ingrid) (Denmark)
Prince Knud dies 6-14, 484E3
Tito cancels visit 9-13, 734G2
MARIANA Islands (U.S. trust territory)
US Sen votes commonwealth status 2-24, 170E2
MARIANI, Felice
Wins Olympic medal 7-30, 574G3
MARIANO, Frank
Dies 8-8, 892C3
MARI Bras, Juan
Chrgs govt wiretapping 8-2; govt obtains tapes 11-10, 994F3
MARIJUANA—*See NARCOTICS & Dangerous Drugs*
MARIN, Edison
Rptdly tortured to death 3-5, 207C3
MARINE, David
Dies 11-26, 970E2
MARINE Engineers' Beneficial Association, National (AFL-CIO)
Ford gifts rptd probed 9-21, 9-25; Calhoun comments 9-21, 722G1, F2, F3
Ford cleared 10-14, 761E2
Calhoun donatn to Carter rptd 10-22, 939C1
MARINE Midland Banks Inc.
Rptd on FRB 'problem' list 1-22, 111B2
Marine Midland-New York
Rptd on FDIC, FRB 'problem' lists 1-23, 1-29, 112C2, 113B1
MARINHO, Boberto
Home bombed 9-23, 835F3
MARION, Ill.—*See ILLINOIS*
MARION International Inc.
Arab boycott rpts released 10-18, 10-19, 786A1, D1
MARITIME Industry—*See SHIPS (& Shipping)*
MARITIME Union of America, National (AFL-CIO)
Com scores USSR re grain shipmts 8-17, 655F2
MARK, Robert
On London fair riot 8-31, 651C2
MARKERT, Louis
Ct rules on immunity 1-5, 7B1, D1
US Sup Ct bars appeal 12-6, 920C3
MARKEWICH, Justice Arthur
Disbars Nixon in NY 7-8, 493F3
MARKEY, Edward J.
Elected 11-2, 829C4

1977

MARCHAND, Leonard Stephen
Named Canada environmt min 9-16, 725B3
MARCHETTI, Victor L.
Chrgs CIA pol party funding 5-4, 372B1
Chrgs CIA-RCMP link 11-24, 923D1
MARCH for Life
Rally vs women's conf 11-19, 918A1
MARCOR Inc.—*See MOBIL Corp.*

MARCOS, Ferdinand Edralin (Philippine president)
Scores US rights rpt, threatens mil ties cut 1-7; eases threat 1-24, 83G2
2 plotters trials delayed 2-7, 4 sentncd 2-10, 100A1
Backs ASEAN talks with US, Japan 2-24, 145B3
Rpts rebel talks off 3-5; vows new try, ties Qaddafi to unrest 3-10, 202D2
On Moslem agrmt 3-26, reassures Christians 3-29, 241C3, F3
Voters vs southn autonomy 4-23, 330G1
Ct-martial for torture suspects ordrd 5-13, 468E2
To end mil courts 6-3, 468B2
Meets Aquino on case 7-6, 619B1
Rights group chrgs troture 7-31 618C3
At ASEAN summit, drops Sabah claim 8-4—8-5, 607G1
Eases martial law 8-22, threatens extensn 8-26, 665C1
In US base talks 9-22—9-23, 824B3
Offers reward for rebels 10-10, 803F2
Gives 5-yr civilian death toll 11-7, 885D3
On Sison capture 11-19, 1019B2
Orders Aquino retrial 11-28, 947A1

MARCOS, Imelda (Mrs. Ferdinand Edralin)
To aid govt-rebel talks 3-10, 202G2
Pl Moslem agrmt reached 3-20, 241D3
MARCUS, Edward S.
Dies 4-4, 356D3
MARDERSTEIG, Giovanni
Dies 12-27, 1024D2
MARDIAN, Robert C.
Reinstated to Sup Ct bar 2-28, 175B2
Claims vs Nixon funds rptd 5-6, 482G2
MAREN, Arthur
Jailed for contempt 7-29, released 9-14, 940D2
MARGARINOS, Ernesto
Kidnaping rptd 2-25, 198B1
MARI Bras, Juan
FBI Cointelpro operatn disclosed 11-21, 941B1
MARIETTA, Ga.—*See GEORGIA*
MARIJUANA—*See NARCOTICS*
MARIJUANA Laws, National Organization for the Reform of (NORML)
Stroup backs decriminalizatn 3-14, 332C2
MARINARO, Ed
Campbell wins Heisman 12-8, 950C2
MARIN County, Calif.—*See CALIFORNIA*
MARINE Corps—*See under U.S. GOVERNMENT*
MARINE Floridian (U.S. tanker)
Hits Va bridge 2-24, 204F3
MARINE Midland Banks Inc.
Marine Midland-New York
Linowitz role in Panama Canal talks scored 2-21, 3-16, quits bd 3-19, 379D1
MARINE Navigation Sulfur Carriers Inc.
Virginia sues 2-25, 204F3
MARINESCU, Mihai
COMECON OKs formal EC talks 9-21, 771D2
MARINE Transport Lines Inc.
Virginia sues 2-25, 204F3
MARINOVICH, Marislav
Arrested 4-23, 314F1
MARION, Charles
Freed 10-27, 871A2
MARITIME Administration—*See under U.S. GOVERNMENT—COMMERCE*
MARITIME Commission, Federal—*See U.S. GOVERNMENT—FEDERAL Maritime Commission*
MARITIME Industry—*See SHIPS (& Shipping)*
MARK, Hans M.
Named AF undersecy 5-23, confrmd 7-21, 626A3
MARK, Rev. Dr. Julius
Dies 9-7, 788F1
MARKEL, Lester
Dies 10-23, 872E2
MARKEY, Rep. Edward J. (D, Mass.)
Scores TV violence report 10-24, 921A2
On TV sports hearings 11-2, 949D3

1978

MARCHAND, Nancy
Wins Emmy 9-17, 1030F1
MARCHETTI, Mario
Shot 11-13, 1018B2
MARCH of Dimes
Genetic disease grants halted 3-8, 744B2
MARCK, Albert C.
Munro phones 8-18, probe rpt prompts resignatn 9-8, 721E2
MARCORA, Giovanni
Named Italy agri min 3-11, 191C1
MARCOR Inc.—*See under MOBIL Corp.*

MARCOS, Ferdinand Edralin (Philippine president, premier)
Purges 86 mayors 1-15, 55B3
Ordrs Herdis group sold, Westinghouse probe 1-16, 38D2
Calls for electn plans 1-17, 268G3
US Cong queries Westinghouse contract 2-8, 134E3
Party wins Assemb electns 4-7, 268G2
Frees seized electn protesters 4-11, 268D3
Vs forgn press electn coverage 4-11, 269C1
Mondale trip debated in US 4-28; Mondale visits 5-2—5-3, 360D3
Names wife to new Cabt post 6-1, 473G2
Orders oppositn ldrs freed 6-3, 455A1
Amnesties 631 detainees 6-10, 475E2
Names new Cabt 6-11, 475F2
Sworn premier, convenes Assemb 6-12, 475C2
Hosts Mex pres 11-4—11-5, 904B1
US mil base pact signed 12-31, 1000B3
MARCOS, Imelda (Mrs. Ferdinand Edralin)
Rpts Sovt A-plant offer 2-14, 134B3
Elected to Pl Assemb 4-7, 268B3
Gets new Cabt post 6-1, 473G2
MARCUS, Miron
Released in 3-way swap 4-23, 318B2
MARDENN, Bennes
Beasts opens 2-8, 760C1
MAREI, Sayed
On Sadat absence from Nobel award rites 12-1; accepts prize for Sadat 12-10, 950B3
MARGAIN, Hugo
Son slain 8-29, suspects seized 9-3, 690C2
MARGAIN Jr., Hugo
Slain 8-29, suspects seized 9-3, 690C2
Leftists seized in murder 9-15, 818D1
MARGARET, Princess (Countess of Snowdon) (Great Britain)
Divorced 5-24, 420D3
At Dominica independnc rites 11-2, 861G2
MARGON, Bruce
'Nearby' quasar discovered 6-8, 654F1
MARGULIS, G. A.
Wins Field Medal 8-15, 1023F2
MARIANI, Gabriella
Red Brigades hideout found 5-19, 393E1
MARI Bras, Juan
Chrgs Soclst youths slain by cops 7-25, 627C2
MARIJUANA—*See NARCOTICS & Dangerous Drugs*
MARIMOW, William K.
Wins Pulitzer Prize 4-17, 315D1
MARIN, Cheech
Up In Smoke released 9-22, 970C3
MARIN Bernal, Rodrigo
Named Colombia labor min 8-7, 629D3
MARINE Corps—*See under U.S. GOVERNMENT*
MARINE Fisheries Service, National—*See U.S. GOVERNMENT—COMMERCE—National Oceanic & Atmospheric Administration*
MARINE Midland Banks Inc.
Hongkong Bank to buy 4-5, 263E1-A2
MARINE Underwriters, American Institute of
USSR discriminatn chrgd 6-9, 499E3
MARINHO, Francisco
Joins Cosmos 11-25, 969C2
MARINI, Antonio
Wife sought in Moro case 6-26, 689D2
MARINI, Barbara
Sought in Moro case 6-26, 689D2
MARINOVICH, Miroslav
Rptd sentenced 3-30, 275B3
MARION, Ill.—*See ILLINOIS*
MARISKOVA, Regina
Wins Italian Open 5-27, 418E2
MARISOL
Elected to Arts Institute 2-7, 316D1
MARITIME Commission, Federal—*See U.S. GOVERNMENT—FEDERAL Maritime Commission*
MARITIME Consultive Organization, Inter-Governmental
US copies safety canon 10-17, 808C3
MARITIME Industry—*See SHIPS (& Shipping)*
MARK, J. Carson
A-arms test oppositn rptd 11-3, 877A2
MARKEY, Rep. Edward J. (D, Mass.)
Reelected 11-7, 851C1
MARKEY, Judge Howard T.
Vs FCC cable-TV access rules 2-24, 195E2, A3

1979

MARCH for Life Inc.
DC protest held, rejects NOW conf 1-22, 63F2
MARCHIBRODA, Ted
Fired as Colts coach 12-26, 1001F1
MARCHIONDO, William C.
NM newspaper libel case refused by Sup Ct 12-3, 964B2

MARCOS, Ferdinand Edralin (Philippine president, premier)
US issues rights rpt 2-10, 107D2
Ford stockholders suit barred 3-8, 202B3
Halts nuclear project 6-15, 487G3
Wife signs China trade pact 7-8, 567B1
Shuffles Cabt, on econ ills 7-23, 566G3
Spratly I annexed by Pl 9-7, 660D3
Rejects martial law end 9-10, 9-14; orders Macapagal probe suspended 9-12, 710A1
Macapagal vs Carter support 9-15, 815F1
Students protest econ problems 9-26, 815G1
Frees 1,602 prisoners 9-27, 815A2

MARCOS, Imelda (Mrs. Ferdinand Edralin)
Signs China trade pact 7-8, 567B1
MARCUSE, Herbert
Dies 7-29, 588B3
MAREDI, Salaelo
Homeland opens 4-16, 711F3
MAREE, Sydney
Shares 6000-m relay mark 4-28, 911A3
MAREMONT Corp.
Swiss firm acquires 7-30, 770G2
MARGARET, Princess (Countess of Snowdon) (Great Britain)
In US, alleged remarks about Irish rptd 10-13, 860B1
MARGARETHE II, Queen (Alexandrine Thorhildur Ingrid) (Denmark)
Jorgensen resigns, electns called 9-28, 751A3
Jorgensen forms new govt 10-26, 855A1
MARGARINE—*See DAIRY Products*
MARGOLIN, Janet
Last Embrace released 5-3, 528G2
MARGOLIN, Stuart
Wins Emmy 9-9, 858D2
Man, Woman & Bank released 9-28, 820G1
MARGOLIS, Jeff
Richard Pryor Live released 2-15, 174E3
MARGOSHES, Steven
Umbrellas Of Cherbourg opens 2-1, 292E3
MARI Bras, Juan
Links Romero, soclsts '78 deaths 4-30, 350B2
MARIE, Dominique
Arrested in Giscard tax case 10-12, 791C2
MARIJUANA—*See NARCOTICS & Dangerous Drugs*
MARIJUANA Laws, National Organization for the Reform of (NORML)
More states OK pot medical use 6-1, 492B3
MARINE Corps—*See under U.S. GOVERNMENT*
MARINE Midland Banks Inc.
FRB OKs Hongkong Bank takeover 3-16, 205C1
MARINO, Vincent E.
Indicted 1-17, 87A3
MARION, Charles
Kidnap suspect acquitted 1-2, 6A2
De Varenne jailed 4-6, 267D1
MARION, Frances
Champ released 4-3, 528F1
MARITIME Consultive Organization, Intergovernmental
Steering gear rule review urged 3-8, 162B3
MARITIME Industry—*See SHIPS (& Shipping)*
MARITIME Union, National (NMU) (AFL-CIO)
Curran, others told to repay benefits 7-27, 744A3
MARK, Robert
Cops suspended in corruptn probe 4-6, 268D2
MARK, Dr. Vernon
Cleared in malpractice suit 2-9, 139E3

1980

MARCHAND, Nancy
Morning's at Seven opens 4-10, 392E3
Wins Emmy 9-7, 692C1
MARCHEI, Mario
2d in Boston Marathon 4-21, 527B2
MARCHIBRODA, Ted
McCormack hired as Colts coach 1-16, 413B1
MARCORA, Giovanni
Italy agri min 4-4, 275F3
MARCOS Jr., Ferdinand E.
Threats to life rptd 11-16, father asks US protectn 11-17, 902A3

MARCOS, Ferdinand Edralin (Philippine president)
Ousts info min 1-17, 100B3
Party wins local electns 1-30, 100A3
Orders electn fraud probe 2-6, admits party fraud role 2-11, 152D2
Warns Moslem terrorists 2-26, asks peace talks 3-18, 235C1
Chile pres cancels 11-day Asian tour 3-22, cuts Pl ties 3-24; assassinatn plot revealed 3-25, 230F3-231E1
Pl to miss Olympics, blames funding 3-28, 259F3
Chile restores ties 4-2, 311D2
Aquino released 5-8, 354E2
Freedom march 7-4, dissenters chrgd 7-5; arrests ordrd 7-20, 566B1
Aquino warns of violence 8-4, 8-20, 672C3
20 chrgd in murder plot 8-5, 672E3
Coalitn seeks to unseat 8-29, 672A3
Manila terrorist bombings 9-12; orders crackdown 9-13, 709G3-710B1
Warns foes vs US role 9-20, 752A3
A-plant building resumes 9-25, 752E3
Sets new terrorist curbs 10-11, 809A2
Escapes Manila bomb blast 10-19; orders arrests 10-20, threatens martial law extensn 10-21, 809D1-A2
Death plot chrgd 10-28, 23 arraigned 11-3, 874D2
Rpts bombing suspect arrested 10-31, 874A2
Rpts son's life threatened 11-16, asks US protectn 11-17, 902A3

MARCUM, Ted
Loses US House electn 11-4, 849B3
MARCUS, Garcia
Arrested 11-28, 922G2
MAREE, Sydney
Wins IC4A indoor 5,000-m run 3-9; 6,000-m Penn relay 4-25, 892C2, D2
MAREI, Mustafa
Vs 'law of shame' 2-15, 149B1
MARGARINE—*See DAIRY Products*
MARGOLIN, Stuart
Wins Emmy 9-7, 692C1
MARIANA Islands (U.S. territory)
Carter sets econ plan 2-14: govs meet, set projcts 2-19—2-22, 495A1
Residents lose US citizenship 3-7, 495F1
Self-rule seen 10-31, 884C1
MARIE and Bruce (play)
Opens 2-3, 136C3
MARIJUANA—*See NARCOTICS*
MARIN, Jose
Escapes prison 6-25, 521A2
MARINE Corps—*See under U.S. GOVERNMENT*
MARINELLO, Vincent A.
Indicted in Brilab probe 6-17, 454E3, 455A1
MARINE Midland Banks Inc.
Marine Midland Bank
Prime cut to 13% 6-4, 438C1
Mello named First Women's pres 6-12, 600G2
MARINHO, Festus
Announces oil price hike 1-4, 4G1
MARINI, Marino
Dies 8-6, 676B2
MARITIME Industry—*See SHIPS*
MARK, Hans
On US combat planes parts shortage 3-30, 267D2
On Matlovich setlmt 11-24, 962C2
MARKEY, Rep. Edward J. (D, Mass.)
Reelected 11-4, 843C1

1976

MARKLEY Jr., Rodney W.
Ford golf trip cited 9-30, 723G1
MARKO, Rita
Replaced 12-30, 1012C2
MARKS, John D.
Colby disputes on CIA book data 3-17, 217G1
MARKS, Marc
Elected 11-2, 821C3, 830F3
MARLENEE, Ron
Elected to US House 11-2, 824A2, 830B1
MARLEY, Bob
Wounded 12-3; at govt rally 12-5, 965B3
MARLEY Sr., Kemper
Linked to Bolles murder, 859B3
MAROIS, Pierre
Named soc dvpt min 11-26, 903G2
MARQUETTE, J. Arthur
United Brands linked to '61 Cuba raid 10-21, 844E3
MARQUEZ, Jose
Identified as Uruguay abductor 7-7, 542A3
MARQUISE d'O, La (film)
Wins Cannes award 5-28, 460G1

MARRIAGES
Sidney Poitier 1-23, 271E3
Natalia Makarova 2-22, 271E3
W Ger OKs reform bill 4-8, 4-9, 270G1
Male-female, black-white marital status data rptd 4-27, 379D3, 380B1
Frank Sinatra 7-11, 640F3
Episc Church OKs rites revisn 9-20, 755F2
Spain adultery law opposed 10-9—11-16, 909F2
US Cath conf for married priests 10-21—10-23, 859C1
Tenn bishop grants absolutn for adultery 12-5, 12-12, 951F1-B2

MARRIOTT, Dan
Wins Utah Cong primary 9-14, 705G1
Elected to US House 11-2, 824A3, 830F4
MARS (planet)—*See 'Interplanetary Projects' under ASTRONAUTICS*
MARSH, John O.
Transitn work under way 11-5, 845D1
MARSHALL, Freddie Ray
Named Labor secy 12-21, 956E2
Photo 956D1
Biographical sketch 957D3
MARSHALL, Judge Prentice
Sets racial quotas for Chicago police 1-5, 6G1
MARSHALL, Rev. Robert J.
Rptdly vs Mo synod ousters 5-29, 776E3

1977

MARKS, Stanley
Sup Ct bars retroactive porno prosecutn 3-1, 175E1
MARLBORO Racetrack (Mass.) (defunct)
Mandel, 5 others convicted 8-23, 652F1
MARLBOROUGH, Duchess of (Gladys Marie Deacon)
Dies 10-13, 872E2
MARLEY Sr., Kemper
Bolles murder suspect pleads guilty 1-15, 162A1, C1
Bolles murder convictns 11-6, 871C2
MARONITE Church—*See under EASTERN Orthodox Churches*
MARQUARDT, Judge Eduardo
Orders Lanusse, ex-aides seized 5-4, 371C1
MARQUETTE University (Milwaukee, Wis.)
Wins NCAA basketball title 3-28, 262E1
Ellis in NBA draft 6-10, 584B3

MARRIAGES
Moreau weds Friedkin 2-8, 140G3
Alice Crimmins 848E1
Polygamists chrgd in rivals death 9-27, 847F3
Spain to reform adultery laws 10-25, 867B1
Sup Ct upholds disability benefits loss 11-8, 875A1
Adultery scored by US bishops 11-16, 906E2
Soc Sec revisns clear Cong 12-15, 958B2

MARS—*See ASTRONAUTICS—Interplanetary Projects*
MARSCHAK, Jacob
Dies 7-27, 604D3
MARSDEN, Brian
On mini-planet discovery 11-8, 908E2
MARSH 3rd, Henry L.
Elected Richmond (Va) mayor 3-8, 252C3
MARSHALL, Anthony D.
Replaced as Kenya, Seychelles amb 5-9, 418F1
MARSHALL, F(reddie) Ray
Confrmatn recommended 1-18, delayed 1-20, 34C1, G3
Confrmd 1-26, sworn 1-27, 52B3
Plans vets job effort 1-27, 52A2
Meany lauds 2-21, 153G2
Personal finances rptd 2-25, 148D1
Teamsters to revise pensn posts 3-13, 195E1
Presents min wage proposal 3-24, 229D2
E Coast dock protest ends 4-18, 324F2
Proposes illegal alien plan 4-27, 370C2
Curbs worker benzene exposure 4-29, 345E1
OSHA refocused 5-19, 422F1
Welfare spending warning rptd 5-27, 445B3
Asks law reform 7-18, 555C2
Testifies on Teamster fund 7-18, 558C2
Acts in UMW wildcat strikes 8-5, 8-17, 8-19, 690A3, B3
Rpts July black youth jobless rate, 3 jobs corps cntrs open 8-31, 692C2
Revises OSHA carcinogen rules 10-3, 778E1
US withdraws from ILO 11-1, 829A1
Sees coal negotiators 12-2, 937E1
At OECD youth mtg 12-15—12-16, 998F3
MARSHALL, Judge Prentice H.
Potash firms acquitted 2-25—6-10, 483E3
Releases Chicago funds 3-25, 279G2
MARSHALL, Brig. Gen. S. L. A. (Slam) (ret.)
Dies 12-17, 1024E2

1978

MARKOV, Georgi Ivanov
Dies 9-11, ruled murder 9-29, 748C3
MARKOWSKI, Paul
Killed 3-6, 228D1
MARKS, Jessica
Patrick deprogramming suit rptd 4-7, 295D3
MARKS, Rep. Marc (R, Pa.)
Reelected 11-7, 852A2
MARKSON, Ralph
Sees sun-Earth weather link 5-11, 654C1
MARKUN, David J.
Sets censures in Equity Funding case 9-4, 681A2, C2
MARLAND Jr., Sidney
Flood influence-selling chrg rptd 2-15, 240D2
MARLENEE Rep. Ron (R, Mont.)
Reelected 11-7, 851E2, 856E1
MARLIN, Barry
Sentenced in swindles 4-10, 380C2
MARLINO, Tommaso
Named Italy budget, econ planning min 3-11, 191B1
MARMORSTEIN, Malcolm
Return From Witch Mt released 7-14, 970G2
MARQUETTE National Bank v. First of Omaha
State interest rates on natl bank credit cards backed by US Sup Ct 12-18, 981C2
MARQUETTE University (Milwaukee, Wis.)
NCAA conventn 1-11—1-13, 40C1
Lee named top coll basketball player 3-13, 272D2
NCAA basketball tourn results 3-27, 272B1
Lee in NBA draft 6-9, 457F3
MARQUEZ de la Plata, Alfonso
Sworn Chile agri min 4-21, 350G3

MARRIAGE—*See also ADULTERY*
Olga Korbut wed 1-7, 95G3
Tax law case review barred 1-9, 13A2
Wis remarriage law voided 1-18, 65B1
Gallagher, Dugdale marry 1-24, 172E2
Duchess of Alba marries 3-16, 420E2
Franklin, Turman wed 4-12, 420F2
Symington, Watson to wed 4-12, 420F2
Princess Caroline to wed 4-24, 420G2
King Hussein to wed 5-15, 420A3
Redlining curbed 5-18, 410E2
Spain ends adultery penalties 5-30, 576B3
King Hussein wed 6-15, 580B1
Princess Caroline wed 6-28, 6-29, 580D1
Prince Michael, baroness wed 6-30, 580F1
Mormons discouraged from intermarriage 7-15, 907C2
Mickey Rooney wed 8th time 7-28, 844D3
Christina Onassis weds Sovt citizen 8-1, 844E3
Papal reforms cited 8-6, 601D2
La 'head & master' case declined by Sup Ct 10-10, 789D3
James Earl Ray wed 10-13, 844D3
Susan Ford engaged 10-17, 844C3
Tax challenge refused by Sup Ct 12-11, 981C1

MARRIOTT, Rep. David Daniel (R, Utah)
Reelected 11-7, 852C3, 856F1
MARROW, Ester
Mahalia opens 6-5, 887B2
MARSH, Graham
2d in Australian PGA 11-12, Dunlop Phoenix tourn 11-26, 990D2
MARSH, Rodney
NASL scoring ldr 8-6, 655D2
On NASL All-Star team 8-20, misses title game 8-27, 707B2, B3
MARSHALL, Alan
Midnight Express released 10-6, 970C2
MARSHALL, E. G.
Interiors released 8-2, 970F1
MARSHALL, F(reddie) Ray
Presses coal strike setlmt; White House talks open, deadlock continues 2-3—2-16, 104D3-105E1
Urges coal pact ratificatn 2-26, 3-1, 159G3, 160A1, D1
Coal industry study planned 3-25, 217A2
Soc Sec rptd sound, hosp insurnc reform urged 5-16, 368C3
Southn constructn pact OKd 5-22, 429A3
Rpts pvt sector youth jobs plan 5-23, 405C1
Welfare compromise prepared 6-7, 446B2
Cotton dust rules issued 6-19, 471D3
Conciliates Meany, curbs Bosworth 8-7; protests postal pact role 8-11, 624C2, D3
Teamster talks role forecast 8-23, 680C3
Addresses USW conv 9-19, 715E2
Calls rail talks to DC 9-27, 809B3
Scores Meany wage-price criticism 10-31, 863D2
MARSHALL, Larry
NFL '77 punt return ldr 1-1, 56F3
MARSHALL, Larry
Broadway Musical opens 12-21, 1031B1
MARSHALL, Mike
AL pitching ldr 10-2, 928F3

1979

MARKOVICH, Terrence
Light Shines opens 1-11, 292G1
MARKOWITZ, Robert
Voices released 3-13, 528F3
MARKS, Jack
Arrest touches off strike 6-12, 443E2
MARKS, John
Loses Australian Open 1-3, 103D2
MARKS, John D.
'71 Canada CIA drug tests rptd 1-29, 96A1
MARKY, Raymond
Scores Young comment on Spenkelink executn 5-26, 400E1
MARLER, David
US wins Can-Am Bowl 1-6, 8C3
MARQUAND, Richard
Legacy released 9-28, 820E1
MARQUARD, William A.
On '78 top-paid execs list 5-14, 347G3
MARQUES, Rene
Dies 3-22, 272B3
MARQUETTE University (Milwaukee, Wis.)
Hickey in basketball HOF 4-30, 526E3
MARQUIS of Keith, The (play)
Opens 3-13, 712D1
MARRE, Albert
A Meeting By the River opens 3-28, 712D1

MARRIAGE
Shevchenko wed in US 1-8, 79D1
Mixed marriages by Reform rabbis rptd up in '78 1-15, 101C3
Joseph Kennedy 2d weds 2-3, 176B1*
Tito rptd wed 2-4, 176C1
Susan Ford weds 2-10, 176B1
Soc Sec chng for women urged 2-15, 132F3
US racial poll rptd 2-20, 307A1
Dead Sea Scroll contents told 3-2, 217C3
Polygamists acquitted in '77 death 3-20, 240B2
Patricia Hearst weds 4-1, 271G2
Carter's nephew rptd wed in jail 4-4, 271B3
Levesque remarries 4-12, 392D2
Chris Evert weds 4-17, 392A2
Marvin ruling cites 4-18, 289E1
Lee Radziwill postpones wedding 5-3, 392B2*
Beneficial Corp credit bias chrgd 5-8, 596F1
Brooke remarries 5-12, 392C2
Queen Victoria secret marriage alleged 5-22, 388F2
T Cullen Davis weds 5-25, 527C3
Siblings marry 5-25, sentnd for incest 7-31, 656B2
Karpov wed 6-1, 527D2
Maria Niarchos marries 6-15, 527E2
Sevareid marries 6-30, 527E2
Vatican criticism of sexual ethics book rptd 8-11, 640F2
Anglican ldr backs remarriage 9-7, 755A3
S Africa racial law chng sought 9-25, 774B2
Pope in US; opposes pre-marital relatns, backs priestly celebacy 10-1—10-5, 757D2, 758C3, 759B2, C2
US mil problems cited 10-9, 809B1
MARS (planet)
Voyager I hot cloud detectn rptd 6-9, 692G1
Surface water rptd 8-9, 692B3
MARSH, Hugh
Blamed for Japan Air '77 Alaska crash 2-13, 412G1
MARSH, Peter
WHA scoring ldr 4-18, 355G2
In NHL expansion draft 6-13, 470A2
MARSH, Rodney
Whitecaps win NASL title, retiremt set 9-8, 775C3
MARSHACK, Megan Ruth
Rockefeller dies 1-26, 104F1
Publicity agent job rptd 11-13, 1005G2
MARSHALL, Judge Arthur K.
Rules in Marvin case 4-18, 289B1
MARSHALL, F(reddie) Ray
Carter, Meany mtg 'clears air' 1-12, 13B3
On '77-78 Admin job gains 1-14, 34D1
At Brazil pres inaugural 3-15, 210E1
On wage-price guidelines 4-3, 251B2
Welfare plan presented 5-23, 384F1
Backs Weber case Sup Ct ruling 6-27, 477A3
Uniroyal suit settled 10-23, 885A3
At AFL-CIO conv, bids labor support Carter 11-15, 885E1
MARSHALL, George Catlett (1880-1959)
Eisenhower letter disclosed 1-28, 79E1
MARSHALL, Jim
Named A's mgr 2-12, 619B2
MARSHALL, Larry
Spell #7 opens 7-15, 712E2
Comin' Uptown opens 12-20, 1007C2
MARSHALL, Mike
Sutter wins Cy Young Award 11-7, 955B3

1980

MARKIN, Viktor
Wins Olympic medal 7-30, 624C1
MARKS Jr., Albert A.
Fires Parks 1-4, 198G3
MARKS, Rep. Marc (R, Pa.)
Reelected 11-4, 844E1
MARLENEE, Rep. Ron (R, Mont.)
Reelected 11-4, 843E2, 852A1
MARLIN (Bahamian patrol boat)
Cuba sinks sister ship 5-10, 371E2
MARLIN Oil Co.
US intrastate gas sale power affirmed 6-6, 552D3
MARMON Group
Trans Union merger set 9-22, 746F1
MAROS, Magda
Wins Olympic medal 7-24, 622C3
MARQUARD, Richard (Rube)
Dies 6-1, 528E2
MARQUETTE University (Milwaukee, Wis.)
Anderson addresses 3-25, 221F3
MARQUEZ v. Carter
Case decided by Sup Ct 11-3, 869C2

MARRIAGE
San Fran mayor weds 1-20, 199E1
Spouse testimony upheld by Sup Ct 2-27, 188A2
Calif schl sniper's father marries cellmate 3-26, 638G3
India dowry murders rptd 4-9, 275D2
Pope in Africa, affirms traditional stance 5-2—5-10, 363F1
S Africa Dutch Reformed Church split rptd 5-10, 374G1
Duvalier marries 5-27, 471F1
US Families Conf opens 6-5, 442C3; asks tax reform 7-12, 601C2
Caron Carter remarries 6-21, 639B1
Angela Davis marries 7-5, 639A1
Racquel Welch weds 7-5, 639B1
Cianfrani, Foreman wed 7-14, 890A2
Carter offers econ renewal plan; 'marriage tax penalty' reductn sought 8-28, 663F1
China enacts new law 9-10, 677B2
Bergen, Malle wed 9-27, 908F1
RC bishops family life conf opens 9-29, annulmts challenged 10-6, 810D2, A3
Pope scores wedded lust 10-8, controversy ensues 10-11, 10-22, 810C3
Pope issues dispensatn guidelines 10-14, 970C1
Pope in W Ger; affirms traditionalism, OKs ecumenical talks 11-15—11-19; youth ldrs assail 11-19, 905D1, B2, F2
Reagan's son weds 11-24, 998B1

MARSH, Earle
Complete TV Directory wins Amer Book Award 5-1, 692E2
MARSH, Graham
2d in Japan Open 9-7, 972G1
MARSH, Henry
Sets 3000-m steeplechase mark in Olympic trials 6-28, 891B2
MARSHALL, Alan
Fame released 5-16, 675D2
MARSHALL, E. G.
John Gabriel Borkman opens 12-18, 1003C3
MARSHALL, F(reddie) Ray
Lauds workplace cancer rules 1-16, 35G3
Voids Firestone US contracts 7-15, 560D2
Addresses AFL-CIO exec cncl 8-20, 647A3
Backs union aid to Polish workers 8-31, 659F3
Jobless benefits extended 9-8, 684A1
Rpts Rockwell job bias setlmt 9-26, 746G3
On UAW jobless aid progrm 10-14, 823G2
MARSHALL, Garry
Roast opens 5-8, 392G3
MARSHALL, Jim
Fired as A's mgr 2-13, 637A2
MARSHALL, Ken
West Side Story opens 2-14, 136G3
MARSHALL, Mike
Released by Twins 6-6, 637C1

1976

MARSHALL, Justice Thurgood—*For Supreme Court developments not listed here, see SUPREME Court under U.S. GOVERNMENT*
Vs IRS emergency procedure 1-13, 23E3
Vs Pa police misconduct rule 1-21, 42F3
Vs warrantless arrests 1-26, 87F2
Rules on campaign law 1-30, 86F3, 87A2
Vs Firestone libel ruling 3-2, 169B3
Backs limited prosecutor immunity 3-2, 169E3
Vs shopping center pickets ruling 3-3, 218G3
Vs jury bias questioning curb 3-3, 219F1
Backs retroactive seniority 3-24, 218E2
Vs mil pol activity curb 3-24, 218A3
For hearing on homosexual case 3-30, 261C3
Vs redistricting review ruling 3-30, 262D1
Backs city-suburb housing plan 4-20, 308A3
For convicts 5th Amendmt rights 4-20, 331F2
Vs govt access to bank records 4-21, 331E1
Vs drug convictn rule 4-27, 349D2
Not in grand jury bias ruling 5-3, 319B2
Vs prisoner's garb ruling 5-3, 359A2
Not in FPC job bias rule 5-19, 393C3
Rules on alien jury duty bar 6-1, 414D2
Not in fed employe job bias suit rule 6-1, 414G2
Dissents re police job tests 6-7, 435E1
Vs NC police firing 6-10, 552F2
Vs trial transcript curb 6-10, 552A3
Upholds oil-import fees 6-17, 452C3
Vs teacher dismissal ruling 6-17, 552D3
Vs some church coll-aid 6-21, 452F3
Vs summary rule on police bargaining 6-21, 553A1
Vs US wage rule re states 6-24, 468E2
Vs sex-show zoning 6-24, 479A1
Vs 'doorway' arrests ruling 6-24, 553D1
Vs defns info-access ruling 6-24, 553E1
Extends rights laws to whites 6-25, 479C2
Vs mandatory retiremt law 6-25, 552D1
For New Orleans vendor curb 6-25, 552G1
Vs prison transfer ruling 6-25, 552B2
For patronage ouster bar 6-28, 468D3
For contd schl rezoning 6-28, 478F3
Vs nonlawyer judge use 6-28, 492F1
Vs rejection of lower ct mining injunctions 6-28, 569B1
Vs business record seizure 6-29, 535D2
Vs illegitimates benefits rule 6-29, 568E3
'72 vote vs death penalty cited, dissents in '76 decisn 7-2, 491A2, G2
Suffers heart attack 7-5, 519D2
Vs fed cts curb on criminal appeals 7-6, 534E3
Vs fed cts illegal evidence curb appeals 7-6, 534E3
Vs alien warrantless interrogatn 7-6, 535A1
Vs tax case evidence rule 7-6, 535B1
Vs car search ruling 7-6, 535C1
Vs sympathy strike ruling 7-6, 535G1
OKs Atlantic offshore lease sale 8-17, 648C3
For review of Fla club, housing bias cases 10-4, 766A1, B1
For arguments on double jeopardy protectn case 10-12, 848E2
For review of Ind auto suit curbs, vs summary decisns 11-8, 883E3
For review of Pa youth curfew 11-15, 882E2
For prisoners med care ruling 11-30, 920E3
Vs Austin busing ruling 12-6, 920F2
For pregnancy benefits 12-7, 920F1
On pub employe contract debate right 12-8, 960B2
Vs Soc Sec for divorced mothers 12-13, 940D3
Vs vacating Gilmore stay 12-13, 952F2
For review of Ky maiden name case 12-13, 960B3
Vs EEOC complaint delay ruling 12-20, 960C1

1977

MARSHALL, Justice Thurgood—*For Supreme Court developments not listed here, see U.S. GOVERNMENT—SUPREME Court*
Byrd opposition cited 1-4, 6A1
Vs Ill restrictive suburban zoning 1-11, 15D1
Bars Gilmore hearing 1-17, 40D2
Sup Ct delays Jurek executn 1-17, 40C3
Vs expanded govt tap use 1-18, 58D2
Vs Miranda rights limitatn 1-25, 80A2
Voids Brunswick trust ruling 1-25, 80E2
Vs secondary strike curb 2-22, 149G3
Vs police informant ruling 2-22, 150C1
Abstains in racial voter redistricting rule 3-1, 175B1
Rules on death sentencing 3-22, 230G3
Sidesteps Miranda rule review 3-23, 276C1
Vs Sioux reservatn land laws 4-4, 342A1
Backs inmate legal aid 4-27, 383D1
Backs 'for sale' sign ban end 5-2, 406A2
Backs US fishing laws 5-23, 444B2
Vs pre-'64 seniority bias 5-31, 461F2
Vs death penalty 6-6, 478E2
Backs pensn credit for mil svc 6-6, 478A3
Backs employe religious rights 6-13, 517G3
Vs 1-man police lineups 6-16, 518E1
Vs Medicaid abortn curbs 6-20, 516B3
Vs curbs on inmate unions 6-23, 539E2
Issues Concorde landing stay 10-7, Sup Ct lifts 10-17, 797B3
Hears Bakke case arguments 10-12, 835C1
Vs mandatory pensn-plan retiremts 12-12, 960C2

MARSHALL Field & Co.
Burnham dies 10-10, 872B1
Carter Hawley bid rejctd 12-14, 1004G1
MARSHALL News Co.
Hustler publisher convicted 2-8, 118G2

1978

MARSHALL, Justice Thurgood—*For Supreme Court developments not listed here, see U.S. GOVERNMENT—SUPREME Court*
AT&T rate rise stay lifted 1-9, 13C2
Not in SC teacher test rule 1-16, 33D2
Vs prosecutors' plea-bargaining power 1-18, 65A1
Vs Wis remarriage law 1-18, 65C1
Vs PR welfare benefits rule 2-27, 143D1
Vs med student ouster rule 3-1, 143A3
Vs Maritime Comm labor contract jurisdictn 3-1, 144B1
Vs curbs on oil tanker regulatn 3-6, 162B1
Backs Indian ct trials of non-Indians 3-6, 162E1
Vs damages for suspended students 3-21, 220D3
Vs testimony thru illegal search 3-21, 221A1
Vs state police alien ban 3-22, 221C1
Vs judge's jury instructn on silent defendant 3-22, 221F1
Vs judicial immunity in sterilizatn case 3-28, 241E3
Backs Nixon tapes to broadcasters 4-18, 308B2
Vs clergy pub office ban 4-19, 309E1
Backs bar on sex-based pensn plans 4-25, 322G3
Vs corp pol free speech 4-26, 343D3
Curbs SEC trading suspensns 5-15, 387F1
Vs trespass laws union rule 5-15, 387D2
Vs fed tap power 5-15, 387G2
Backs Indian tribal authority 5-15, 387C3
Backs tax liability in bankruptcy 5-22, 388D1
Backs exclusn of children from porno rule 5-23, 405E3
Vs Mont hunting fee disparity 5-23, 406A1
Delays Little extraditn 5-30, declines appeal 6-5, 431A2
Vs newsroom searches by police 5-31, 430G1
Backs FCC cross-media ban 6-12, 467F3
Backs '75 double jeopardy doctrine 6-14, 468E3
Rebuffs Zenith on import duty 6-21, 491D3
Backs union supervisor discipline 6-21, 509D2
Not in press prison data access case 6-26, 566D3
Vs Bakke med schl admissn, backs race-based affirmative actn principle; opinion excerpt 6-28, 481C1-F2, 487B1
Backs Minn pensn funds law 6-28, 567E1
Vs juvenile case reviews 6-28, 567A2
Vs FCC 'Filthy Words' ban 7-3, 551E3
Vs Ohio death penalty law 7-3, 552G1, A2
Vs Calif, NM water rights 7-3, 552C2
Voting alignmts shift noted 7-3, 565G3-566C1
Bars Farber sentence stay extensn 8-4, 678B3
Backs coll sex-bias ruling 11-13, 874C2
Vs cities' power over suburbs 11-28, 937D3
Vs Ga schl bd pol rule 11-28, 937F3
Vs broader police auto search power 12-5, 959C3
Backs Calif auto franchise law 12-5, 959F3
Backs FRB bank-holding co power 12-11, 980E3
Backs extraditn probe bar 12-18, 981B2
MARSHALL County, Kan.—*See KANSAS*
MARSHALL Field & Co.
Liberty House purchase set 1-20, Houston store planned 2-7; Carter Hawley drops takeover bid 2-22, 185E1
MARSHALL Islands (U.S. trust)
Bikini '54 A-test radiatn imperils residents, relocatn planned 4-12, 278C2-A3
Bikini residents relocated to Kili 8-31, 685A3
MARSHALL v. Barlow
OSHA warrantless searches curbed by Sup Ct 5-23, 405C2
MARSHALL v. Daniel Construction Co.
Case declined by Sup Ct 10-2, 751C1
MARSHALS Service, U.S.—*See under U.S. GOVERNMENT—JUSTICE*
MARSIKOVA, Regina
French Open results 6-11, 540F1
Wins Canadian Open 8-19, 1027A2
MARSTERS, Joe
Dies 5-15, 440B3
MARSTON, David W.
Dismissal controversy 1-10, 1-12, 12C2; Bell ousts 1-20, 32F1
Carter, Bell cleared by Justice probe 1-24, 62D2
Carter defends removal 1-30, 62D1
Flood, Eilberg influence-selling probe cited 2-8, 240A1, C1
Carter defends delay in naming successor 3-9, 161A1
Vaira named successor 3-23, 243C3
Sen panel finds no probe cover-up, Mathias disputes 4-24, 309A3
Sen rejects cover-up rpt 5-4, Civiletti confrmd 5-9, 342D3, 343A1
Loses primary for Pa gov 5-16, 389C3
Eilberg indicted 10-24, pleads not guilty 11-1, 835E2
MARSTON, Garth
OKs redlining curb 5-18, 410F2
MARSTON, Dr. John H.
Embryo transplant research cited 7-25, 597B1

1979

MARSHALL, Justice Thurgood—*For Supreme Court developments not listed here, see U.S. GOVERNMENT—SUPREME Court*
Vs limited lawyers' interstate rights 1-15, 31F3
Vs corp name curbs 2-21, 128G2
Vs A&P milk price actn 2-22, 150D3
Vs forgn svc retiremt rule 2-22, 151B1
Vs Blue Shield drug plan trust rule 2-27, 165A2
Backs job-testing data disclosure 3-5, 184D3
Vs Ill right-to-counsel rule 3-5, 185C2
Backs jobless pay for strikers 3-21, 231G1
Vs NYC Transit Auth ex-addict ban 3-21, 231C2
Backs church schl labor interventn 3-21, 231G2
Backs Fla death penalty appeal review 3-26, 231A1
Backs cable TV pub-access rule 4-2, 281B2
Vs IRS tap evidence 4-2, 281E2
Vs NYS alien teacher ban 4-17, 325E3
Vs 'state of mind' libel queries 4-18, 302F1
Vs covert US entries for 'bugging' 4-18, 346A2
Vs unwed father damage suit bar 4-24, 364G1
Vs verbal rights waiver 4-24, 364C2
Vs Ark pub worker grievance policy 4-30, 364F3
Vs pretrial detentn curbs 5-14, 383A2
Vs fed ct welfare suits 5-14, 384B1
Discloses finances 5-15, 382D2
Vs innocence instructn refusal 5-21, 400E3
Decries 'state of mind', pretrial detentn rulings 5-27, 422C1
Vs state parole discretn 5-29, 421A3
Bars punitive damages vs unions 5-29, 421D3
Vs co-defendant confessns 5-29, 422B1
Vs NY gun-in-car law 6-4, 438E3
Vs vets' job-prefernc law 6-5, 421A2
Differs on Ariz farm labor law finding 6-5, 464B3
Backs FDA Laetrile ban 6-18, 498G2
Backs broader Cong legal immunity 6-18, 498G3
Backs customer suits vs accountants 6-18, 499D1
Vs child mental commitmt rules 6-20, 516B1
Vs warrantless phone surveillnc 6-20, 516F1
Backs youth probatn officer consultatn right 6-20, 516C2
Vs 'good faith' arrest 6-25, 540E1
Backs Wolston libel suit right 6-26, 540E3
Backs Idaho takeover law challenge 6-26, 540F3
Vs rights violatn proof in false arrest suits 6-26, 541A1
Backs unwed mothers survivors' aid 6-27, 558A2
Backs wage-price case review 7-2, 498D2
Vs ctroom pub access curbs 7-2, 515A3
'78-79 Sup Ct term ends, voting alignmt rptd 7-2, 558A1
Vs Mass abortn-consent law 7-2, 559D2
Backs Bell contempt case review 10-9, 783E3
Backs ICC trucking order reversal 10-15, 848A1
Injured in fall 10-17, 848G2
Backs Bishop executn stay 10-21, 817D2
Vs curb on advisers investor suits 11-13, 902D1
Backs VA malpractice ruling 11-28, 944F3
Backs pub access to waterways 12-4, 988C1
Vs Taiwan treaty case review 12-13, 940C1

MARSHALS Service, U.S.—*See under U.S. GOVERNMENT-JUSTICE*
MARSIKOVA, Regina
Loses Berlin Intl 5-27, 570D2
MARSTELLER Inc.
Young & Rubicam to buy 6-27, 560E2
MARSTON, David W.
Wins Phila mayoral primary 5-15, 363D2
Loses electn 11-6, 846A3
MARSTON, Romona
Sought in '77 polygamist's death 3-20, 240C2
MARSTON, Thomas
Acquitted in polygamist's '77 death 3-20, 240B2

1980

MARSHALL, Justice Thurgood—*For Supreme Court developments not listed here, see U.S. GOVERNMENT--SUPREME Court*
Vs environmental impact ct review limit 1-7, 15D3
Not in real estate antitrust case 1-8, 16F1
Vs citizenship revocatn law 1-15, 51F2
Not in inmate escape justificatn case 1-21, 93A1
Not in mil petitn limits case 1-21, 93F1
Vs narrowed state ct jurisdictn 1-21, 93B2
Stays Medicaid abortn aid order 2-14, Sup Ct reverses, accepts case 2-19, 130A3
Vs CIA disclosure limits 2-19, 130F3
Vs tax liability in RR worker compensatn 2-19, 131C1
Backs pvt coll faculty unions 2-20, 146A2
Vs NYS pvt schl reimbursemt 2-20, 146E2
Vs Calif dual seniority system 2-20, 146A3
Vs IRS handwriting orders 2-20, 170A2
Not in damage suit geographic relevance cases 2-20, 170C3
Backs fed worker illegitimate child aid 2-26, 188G1
Backs fed gun law prior convictn limit 2-27, 188A3
Not in Kissinger records case 3-3, 210B1
Backs fed funded group info access 3-3, 210D1
Backs 'insider' stock trading convictn 3-18, 226F2
Vs Tex habitual-offender law 3-18, 226C3
Not in forgn dividends tax case 3-19, 249D3
Backs Freedom of Info ct order bar 3-19, 250C1
Vs cooperatn standard in sentencing 4-15, 306A2
Vs at-large local electns 4-22, 343A3
Backs child labor law fines 4-28, 369B1
Not in La oil leasing case 4-28, 369D1
Vs police interrogatn rule 5-12, 386B3
Not in Atlanta schl integratn case 5-12, 386C3
Vs atty conflict of interest case result 5-12, 426G2
Vs Ga death penalty 5-19, 440B1
Vs narrowed 'exclusionary rule' 5-27, 453E2
Vs lower PR welfare aid 5-27, 453E3
Vs DEA detainmt procedure 5-27, 454A1
Vs SEC fraud intent proof 6-2, 512E3
Backs Panther shootout trial legal fees award 6-2, 513B1
Vs pre-1920 oil shale mining claims 6-2, 513D1
Backs Wis out-of-state corp earnings tax 6-10, 511G3
Vs defendant pre-arrest silence testimony 6-10, 512E1
Vs GE microbe patent 6-16, 453D1
Backs cts power to suppress evidence 6-23, 554E3
Not in nursing home aid case 6-23, 554G3
Vs magistrates pretrial role 6-23, 555A1
Vs narrowed illegal search protectn 6-25, 541G1
Vs unpatented key ingredient monopolies 6-27, 511D2
Backs govt minority constructn grants 7-2, 510D1, F1
Backs OSHA benzene standard 7-2, 511A1
'79-80 Sup Ct term ends, voting alignmts rptd 7-2, 540C2
Backs unwed couples child custody case review 10-20, 807C1
Backs Calif probe of Ark prisons 12-8, 937E1
Vs lenient sentence appeal 12-9, 936F3
Vs rail pensn revisn 12-9, 937B1
Backs defendants fed ct civil rights suits 12-9, 937C1
Vs job bias suit filing time limit 12-15, 957C2
Dissents in census ruling 12-30, 982F3

MARSHALL Islands (U.S. trust)
Eniwetok Atoll resetld 4-9, 349B3
Self-rule pact signed 10-31, 884C1
MARSHALL v. Jerrico
Case decided by Sup Ct 4-28, 369A1
MARSHALS Service, U.S.—*See under U.S. GOVERNMENT--JUSTICE*
MARSH & McLennan Cos. Inc.
To buy Bowring 4-14, 386B1
MARSIKOVA, Regina
Loses Family Circle tourn 4-13, 607B3
Wins Phoenix Classic 10-12, 947A2

1976

MARTIN, Aubran
Sentencing delayed 9-3, 816B3
MARTIN, Billy
Daughter sentenced 1-21, 160A3
Vs World Series scheduling 10-21, 815A2, F3
MARTIN, Graham
Italy CIA aid recipients named 1-31, 140B3
MARTIN, Rep. James G. (D, N.C.)
Reelected 11-2, 830E2
MARTIN Jr., James S.
On Viking scoop failure 7-22, 527A1
On Viking seismometer malfunctn 7-25, 549C1
MARTIN, Kelly Ann
Sentenced in Colombia 1-21, 160A3
MARTIN, Leo
Named IRA staff chief 2-10, 147D1
MARTIN, William F.
Tax fraud chrgd 9-2, 725G2
MARTINELLI, Giuseppe
Wins Olympic medal 7-26, 574C2
MARTINEZ, Eugenio R.
Calif break-in convictn upset 5-17, 379D1
MARTINEZ, Luis
Wins Olympic medal 7-31, 574D1
MARTINEZ, Samuel R.
Community Svcs Admin dir 3-16; confrmd 4-7, 262D3
MARTINEZ Baca, Alberto
Pol rights revoked, arrest ordrd 6-23, 520C1
MARTINEZ Carro, Santiago
Suarez selectn role rptd 7-6, 501C1
MARTINEZ de Hoz, Jose
Argentina econ min 3-29; econ plan detailed 3-31, 236B1, G1
Describes govt econ plan 4-2, 264D2
Argentina budget deficit set 7-9, 649F3
Rpts forgn debt renegotiated 7-25, 553G3
MARTINEZ Ferrate, Rodolfo
Guatemala dvpt loans rptd 10-13, 1005E1
MARTINEZ Manattou, Emilio
Mexico health min 12-2, 907A1
MARTIN Gamero, Adolfo
Cabt post refusal rptd 7-6, replaced 7-8; censorship cited 7-13, 523B2, C3
MARTIN Marietta Corp.
'75 arms sales listed 2-6, 147B3
MARTINON, Jean
Dies 3-1, 192F3
MARTINS, Joao Filipe
Bars Unita, FNLA coalitn 1-19, 35F3
MARTIN Villa, Rodolfo
Sworn interior min 7-8, 523E2
In Basque region re unrest 9-16—9-20, 775A1
Araluce slain 10-4, 774B3
MARTSCHINK, Sherry Shealy
Seconds Ford nominatn 8-18, 597G2-598A1
MARTINIQUE (French overseas department)
Alleyne seized re Barbados 'plot' 10-25, 962D1
MARTY, Francois Cardinal
Rptd vs French arms sales 1-25, 126F2
MARUBENI Trading Corp.
Named in Lockheed payoff rpt 2-4, 130D2
Denies Lockheed chrgs; cuts ties, offcls resign 2-5—2-17, 131F3-132G1
Offcls rptd rehired 2-20, 3-3, 191C1
Offices raided 2-24, 190E2
Lockheed probes pressed 2-26, 3-1; bd chrmn quits 3-3, contracts suspended 3-4, 3-6, 190C3, 191B1, ★ C1
Okubo arrested 6-22, 450A3
Itoh arrested 7-2, 497F2
Hiyama arrested 7-13, Tanaka linked 7-27, 557D1 ★
Okubo indicted for perjury 7-13, 557A2
Mori, aide arrested 7-19; Itoh indicted for perjury 7-23, 557B2
Hiyama, Okubo, Itoh indicted for bribery 8-16, 624A2
Japan offcls arrested 8-20, 8-21, 628D2
Rptd Canada A-sales agent 11-29, 923G3
MaRV (maneuverable re-entry vehicles)—
See 'Missiles' under ARMAMENTS
MARX, Barbara
Marries Sinatra 7-11, 640F3
MARX, Karl (1818-83)
Soclst Intl meets 11-26—11-28, 935G3
MARX, Werner
Ends China visit 3-2, 190E1
MARX, Zeppo (Herbert)
Ex-wife married 7-11, 640F3

MARYLAND
Primary date set 22B2
Carey pleads guilty, sentncd 1-9, 32F2
High cancer rate rptd 2-16, 224E3
Baltimore violent crime rptd up 3-2, 336D3
HEW cutoff of state, Baltimore schl funds barred 3-8, 203D1
Pentagon officials censured re Rockwell trip 3-16, 200C3
Southern-Delmarva talks fail 3-23, Conrail takes over tracks 4-1, 235E2-A3
Brown, Carter campaign 4-28—5-12, 343G1; 5-15, 5-16, 357B2
SEC suit vs Emersons setld 5-11, 359D3
Carter in Rockville 5-14, 390E3
Primary results 5-18, 356D2, 357E1-A2
7 oil cos, trade assn indicted 6-1, 412F3
Pallotine fund-raising scheme rptd, Mandel linked 6-18, 10-24; pact, probe set 8-24, 950E3
Pvtly insured S&Ls cited 6-20, 495E1
US Sup Ct OKs some church-college aid 6-21, 452D3

1977

MARTIN, Americo
MIR nominates for pres 8-20, 674C2
MARTIN, Billy
Dispute with Jackson 6-18, job rptd saved 6-21, 644C3
Benches Jackson 10-9, 807A2
Yankees win World Series; bonus, job security rptd 10-11—10-18, 806D1-G3
MARTIN, Graham
US evacuatn from Viet scored 11-18, 898B1, F1
MARTIN, Guy Richard
Named Interior asst secy 3-3, confrmd 4-11, 272B3
MARTIN, Leonard
Protests Rumania treatmt of offcl 10-8, 948E1
MARTIN, Lloyd
On TV re child abuse 5-15, 432A2
MARTIN, Rick
Wales Conf wins NHL All-Star 1-25, 104F1
MARTIN, Stephen A.
Blamed for CTA crash 3-16, 412F3
MARTINEZ, Arabella
Named HEW asst secy 1-19, 53B1
MARTINEZ, Eugenio R.
Nixon com to pay $50,000 2-22, 157G2
MARTINEZ, Florentino
Jail beating rptd 9-7, 727A1
MARTINEZ, Jose
Killed by guerrillas 10-26, 921C3
MARTINEZ de Genique, Jose Enrique
Spain agri min 7-5, 545C2
MARTINEZ de Hoz, Jose
Policies scored 10-21, 11-6, 981C2
MARTINEZ Silva, Praxedes
Gets amnesty for Oct plot 12-6, 970C1
MARTINEZ Soriano, Felipe
Resigns 3-3, 240G1
Arrested, beaten; drops Oaxaca rectorship bid 4-24, 528F2
Fired 12-7; students protest, univ occupied 12-14, 985E2
MARTINEZ Verdugo, Arnoldo
On UNAM strike 7-1, 528C2
MARTINIQUE
Haiti exiles ex-interior min 10-14, 905A3
MARTIN Linen Supply Co.
Sup Ct broadens double jeopardy protectn 4-4, 341C3
MARTIN Luther King Jr. Center for Social Change
Mrs King at black ldrs mtg 8-29, 702G1
MARTINS, Ismael
Angola finance min 8-31, 772A1
MARTIN-Trigona, Anthony
FCC reverses pol ad stand 5-6, 376B2
MARTIN Villa, Rodolfo
Bans Basque mayors mtg 1-16; sees reps 1-18, concessns OKd 1-19, 68E1
UCD launched 5-3, 453G1
Named to Spain Senate 6-15, 453E1
Retains Interior post 7-5, 545F1
Scored re police abuse 9-12—9-15, 826F3
MARTIS, Nikolaos
Named Northn Greece min 11-28, 925B2
MARTY, Francois Cardinal
Bans Lefebvre mass 5-22, 471A1
MARUBENI Trading Corp.
Lockheed bribe trials open 1-27, 1-31, 83D2
MARX, Andrew
Grandfather dies 8-20, 696D3
MARX, Arthur
Father dies 8-20, 696D3
MARX, Groucho (Julius)
Dies 8-20, 696C3
MARX, Gummo (Milton)
Dies 4-21, 356D3
MARX, Karl (1818-83)
USSR scores Eurocommunism 6-23, 507B2
MARXISM
Ernst Bloch dies 8-3, 696D2
Angola MPLA sets program 12-4—12-11, 1009B2
MARY Kathleen Uranium Ltd.
Uranium cartel rptd 4-25, 479D2

MARYLAND
Legislature schedule rptd 6E2
FPC OKs emergency gas purchase 1-19, 53G3
Mandel asks US aid fishermen 1-20, 54D2
US offers emergency job funds 2-1, 75G3
US disaster aid rptd granted 2-5, 91A2
Ft Detrick gene lab plans, germ warfare tests rptd 3-8, 184G2, 195F2
James Pollack dies 3-15, 264D3
Conrail line cuts set 3-31, 325F2
Baltimore on '75 10 largest cities list 4-14, 388A1
'76 per-capita income table 5-10, 387D2
Baltimore papers settle trust case 5-26, 504A2
Mandel transfers powers to Blair 6-4, 652D1 ★
HEW jobless-benefits standards law upheld 6-20, 516E3-517A1
Arthur Perdue dies 6-27, 532E3
'76 per capita income, tax burden table 9-13, 10-18, 821B2

1978

MARTIN, Billy (Alfred Manuel)
NL wins All-Star Game 7-11, 559C3
Suspends Jackson 7-17; assails Jackson, Steinbrenner 7-23; quits Yankees 7-24, rehired for '80 7-29, 618A1
Yankees win World Series 10-17, 799A3
In barroom brawl 11-11, chrgd with assault 11-12, 1026D2
MARTIN, Christopher
Henry IV opens 11-27, 1031A2
MARTIN, Graham
Secret document possessn rptd probed 9-13, 720F1
MARTIN, Harvey
Cowboys win Super Bowl, named co-MVP 1-15, 39E3
MARTIN, James D.
Unopposed in Ala US Sen primary 9-5, 699A2
Switches elections 10-2, 769F1
Loses electn 11-7, 849B3
MARTIN, Rep. James G. (R, N.C.)
Reelected 11-7, 851C3
MARTIN, Kathy
2d in Wheeling Classic 7-9, 672C3
MARTIN, Louis E.
Named pres liaison to blacks 8-11, 663G3-664A1
MARTIN, Mary
Somersaults opens 1-9, 760A2
MARTIN, Millicent
King of Hearts opens 11-22, 1031C2
MARTIN, Rick
Wales Conf wins NHL All-Star game 1-24, 76D3
MARTIN, Roger
Loses primary for Oregon gov 5-23, 406G2
MARTIN, Steve
Record wins Grammy 2-24, 316B1
King Tut on best-seller list 7-5, 579G3
Wild & Crazy Guy on best-seller list 11-8, 888D1; 12-6, 971E1
MARTINELLI, Angelo R.
Loses US House electn 11-7, 849A2
MARTINEZ, Mario
Serrano decisns 2-18, 379B2
MARTINEZ, Ramon
Wins award for neurosis 3-15, 242F3
MARTINEZ de Hoz, Jose
Chrgs guerrilla campaign 4-12, 285C3
On Mar inflatn 4-14, 310F1
Videla pres term extended despite objectns 5-2, 611A3
China trade pact signed 6-9, 793A3
Retained in Cabt shuffle 11-6, 865E2
MARTINEZ Montenegro, Roberto
Shot 2-13, dies 2-15, 289F3
Called criminal 4-20, 517G2
MARTIN Marietta Corp.
Bunker, Grunow on Kennecott bd rival slate 3-27, 402G3
Airco purchase offer 4-2, 4-3, bid withdrawn 4-7, 403F3
Titanium unit indicted 9-28, 768D2
MARTINS, Maj. Jose da Costa (ret.)
Angola expels, Portugal arrests 5-31, 594D1
MARTINSON, Harry E.
Dies 2-11, 196D3
MARTIN, Tate, Morrow & Marston
Tate installed ABA pres 8-9, 626C3
MARTIN v. Corpus Christi Parish
Case declined by Sup Ct 10-10, 789D3
MARTIN Villa, Rodolfo
Pledges Basque unrest probe 7-11, 537B2
Mediates in Basque unrest 7-12, scores police 7-13, 576E1
MARUBENI Trading Co.
6 tied to Lockheed scandal 1-30, 72D3
MARVIN, Mel
History of Amer Film opens 3-30, 760C2
MARX, Groucho (Julius Henry) (1895-1977)
Arthur Sheekman dies 1-12, 96E3
MARXISM
Spain CP drops 'Leninist' label 4-19—4-23, PSOE drops 'Marxist' label 5-22, 821D3
Eur conservative group formed 4-24, 424B3

MARYLAND
'67, '77 sales-tax rates rptd 1-5, 15A3, E3
State govt tax revenue table 1-9, 84D2
'77 open-space effort rptd 85C2
Coal shortage rptd 2-11, Carter sees gov 2-16, 104D1, D2
Genetics lab opens in Frederick 3-17, 334E3
Obscenity rule review declined by US Sup Ct 4-24, 322F2
Coal strike utility billing probe set 5-10, 366F3
Refiner-run gas statn ban upheld by US Sup Ct 6-14, 491F3
Baltimore oppositn to postal pact rptd 7-21, 565A1
Annapolis command taken by Lawrence 8-16, 843D3
HEW bias suit refused by Sup Ct 10-2, 751F2
Chesapeake Bay collisn kills 11 10-20, 908C3
Baltimore populatn ranked 12-6, 942E3
Orioles purchase bid rptd 12-21, 1026F2

1979

MARTELL, Ralph
Shelley opens 4-14, 712D2
MARTENS, Wilfried (Belgian premier)
Sworn Belgian premr 4-3, 253B2
Rpts '80 anti-deficit steps 10-2, 832A3
MARTHESHEIMER, Peter
Despair released 2-15, 174D2
MARTIN, Billy (Alfred Manuel)
Settles battery chrg 5-24, returns as Yankees mgr 6-19, 619G1-B2
In fight 10-23, Yankees fire 10-28; Kuhn, MacPhail warn 11-29, 12-13, 1002B1
MARTIN, Christopher
Wild Oates opens 1-8, 292G3
Marquis of Keith opens 3-13, 712D1
MARTIN, Graham
Secret documt possessn prosecutn dropped 3-30, 252F3
MARTIN, Harvey
Steelers win Super Bowl 1-21, 62F3-63A2
MARTIN, John Bartlow
Rpts JFK backed McNamara pres bid 9-23, 748A3
MARTIN Jr., Manuel
Beggars Soap Opera opens 7-23, 711D1
MARTIN, Margaret
Gives birth after hysterectomy 5-16, 392B3
MARTIN, Ralph
Backs commodity options trading resumptn 9-5, 681B2
MARTIN, Randal
Festival opens 5-7, 711A3
MARTIN, Steve
Wild & Crazy Guy on best-seller list 1-10, 80F3
Wins Grammy 2-16, 336F3
Cruel Shoes on best-seller list 6-3, 432B2; 7-1, 548B3; 8-5, 620C3; 9-2, 672A3; 10-14, 800C3
MARTIN, Terry
Sentncd for '78 murder 6-19, 492G1
MARTIN, William
Frequency opens 4-25, 711B3
MARTIN Jr., William McChesney
On '29 mkt crash, '80s econ forecast 11-1, 827B1
MARTINA, Dom (Netherlands Antilles premier)
Takes office 11-13, 882C3
MARTIN-Antajo, Alberto
Dies 9-1, 756A3
MARTINEZ, Dennis
In World Series 10-10—10-17, 816G2
MARTINEZ, Ricardo
Venez planning office chief 3-10, 192C3
MARTINEZ, Tippy
In World Series 10-10—10-17, 816G1
MARTINEZ de Hoz, Jose Alfredo
Aide's home bombed 9-27, 749A1
Aide escapes shooting 11-7, 887F3
MARTINIQUE (French overseas department)
Hurricane David hits 8-30, 690C3
MARTIN Luna, Juan
Escapes Spain jail 12-17, 997E3
MARTINZ, Luis
Arrested in Panama coup plot, denies role 10-24, 836F3
MARVIN, Lee
Unwed couple suits rptd 2-22—4-17, 289D2-A3
Breach of contract suit setld 4-18, 289B1
MARVIN, Michelle Triola
Unwed couple suits rptd 2-22—4-17, 289D2-A3
Breach of contract suit setld 4-18, 289B1
MARX, Karl (1818-83)
China premr visits birthplace 10-23, grave 10-31, 854C1, B2
MARX, Zeppo (Herbert)
Dies 11-30, 932B3

MARYLAND
ITT Baltimore long-distance phone svc OKd 1-4, 15E2
$99 cross-country air fares, Baltimore route OKd 1-12, 35E2
Chesapeake Bay '78 collisn rpts 1-20, 140F3; 2-26, 3-2, 240E3; Cuyahoga cmdr convicted 11-3, 887B3
Blizzard hits Baltimore 2-18—2-19, 176B2
Baltimore radium waste sites alleged 3-5, 187B2
Baltimore bishop named to '80 Rome synod 5-3, 376B1
Nuns set Potomac hq sale 7-2, 640G2
USSR land deal set 7-13, 568B2
Hurricane David hits 9-7, 690B1
'78 per capita income rptd 9-16, 746C2
Baltimore bond ratings listed 9-20, 920F3
Army BZ stockpile rptd 9-24, 727A2
Baltimore longshoremen boycott Iranian cargo 11-13, 879C1

1980

MARTENS, Wilfried (Belgian premier)
Reunites coalitn parties 1-10, 37G2
FDF leaves coalitn 1-16; makes Cabt chngs 1-23, 56F1
Govt spending cuts rptd 3-24, 237B1
Govt resigns 4-3, 4-9, 272B1
Heads new govt 5-18, 388A2
Belgium to accept A-missiles 9-19, 737C2
Submits govt resignatn 10-4, delay asked 10-5; resignatn OKd 10-7, 766F2
Forms new coalitn, sets econ plan 10-16, 787C1
New govt sworn 10-22, 860C2
MARTIN, Billy (Alfred Manuel)
Hired as A's mgr 2-21, 637A2
Named top AL mgr 11-20, 926B1
MARTIN, David
Elected to US House 11-4, 843G3
MARTIN, Doug
In NFL draft 4-29, 336F2
MARTIN, Elliot
Clothes for a Summer Hotel opens 3-26, 392E2
MARTIN, Jean-Michael
3d in LeMans 6-15, 637B3
MARTIN, Jennifer
'Charlie's Angels' fraud probe rptd 5-1, 376G2
LA DA ends 'Charlie's Angels' probe 12-2, 1002E2
MARTIN, Kenneth A.
Indicted 1-10, 216C1
Convicted 12-21, 997A3
MARTIN, Lynn
Elected to US House 11-4, 842F3, 846C2, 850D3
MARTIN, Mardik
Raging Bull released 11-14, 972G3
MARTIN, Philippe
3d in LeMans 6-15, 637B3
MARTIN, Raymond
3d in Tour de France 7-20, 835E1
MARTIN, Renie
In World Series 10-14—10-21, 811A3, 812C1, E3
MARTIN, Robert
Testifies on commodity futures trading curbs 4-15, 290C1, C2
MARTIN, Steve
Cruel Shoes on best-seller list 1-13, 40C3
MARTIN, Strother
Dies 8-1, 676B2
MARTIN, William McChesney
Deplores Carter FRB criticism 10-3, 763G1
MARTIN Jr., William Thorton (Pete)
Dies 10-13, 876F2
MARTINEZ, Armando
Wins Olympic medal 8-2, 622A2
MARTINEZ, Julie
Gives birth to 21st child 1-12, 200F1
MARTINEZ, Maria
Dies 7-20, 608D2
MARTINEZ de Hoz, Jose Alfredo
Major pvt bank closed in Argentina 3-28, 252F2
Argentine banking system shaken by bankruptcies 4-25, 350D1
In Brazil trade talks 5-15—5-17, 405E2
Jet seized, extortn fails 6-30—7-1, 519G2
Sets fiscal reforms 7-11, 561B2
Viola named Videla successor 10-3, 766B2
MARTINEZ Soriano, Felipe
Leads emb seizures 2-18, modifies demands 2-21, 152C1
MARTINEZ v. California
Case decided by Sup Ct 1-15, 51F1
MARTINIQUE (French overseas department)
French-Cuban trade accord rptd, Castro noninterventn pledge linked 4-1, 253B3
MARTINS, Helder Fernando Brigido
Ousted in Mozambique Cabt shuffle 3-21, 234E2
MARTORELL, Fernando Abril
Spain sets energy conservatn 1-8, 22B2
Suarez shuffles Cabt 5-2, 355D1
Removed as Spain dep premr 9-8, 690D2
MARUBENI Ltd.
US unit convicted of racketeering 11-5, 957B3
MARVICH, Mary
Votes 11-4, 890G2*
MARVIN, James I.
Rpts 2 Anaconda units to close 9-30, 825G2
MARVIN, Mel
Tintypes opens 10-23, 892F3
MARX, Karl (1818-83)
China orders portrait removed 8-16, 651F2

MARYLAND
Baltimore port congestn rptd 1-19, 45C1
Schl prayer law cited 2-6, 156A2
Ft Meade sex harassment alleged 2-11, 188F3
Baltimore-London air svc expansn agreed 3-5, 172B3
World Air cuts fares 4-9, 346B3
IBM sued re job bias 6-3, 485G1
Families Conf in Baltimore 6-5, 442A3
Schl censorship power upheld 6-13, 583A1

1976

Dem conv women delegates, table 508C2
Dem conv pres vote, table 7-14, 507C2
Miners strike spreads 7-27, 553B2
Cong tax exemptn vetoed 8-3, 636B3
GOP pre-conv delegate count 8-14, 583C3
GOP conv pres, vp vote tables 8-18—8-19, 8-19, 599C1, C3
Dole campaigns 8-30, 646A1
'74-75 Baltimore SATs rptd 9-13, 993G1
Fscl '75 per capita income, tax burden rptd 9-15, 10-12, 959B2
Pa-Baltimore rail link agreed 9-15, 988A1
Mondale in Baltimore 9-26, 725B1
Carter campaigns 10-2, 743F2
Carter in Chevy Chase 10-2, 762E1
Fallout rptd from China A-test 10-5, 791A1
Richardson vows Arab boycott info 10-20, 786G2
Election results 11-2: pres 818B1, 819B2; cong 819F3, 831D1, 825F2, 828G1, 829A3; state 821F1
Carter primary spending rptd 11-17, 938A3
Anti-boycott law rptd enacted 12-1, 987A2
Mistrial in Mandel case 12-7, 922E2
Flu shot paralysis rptd 12-17, 950E1
Katharine Byron dies 12-28, 1015B1
2 indicted re Mandel mistrial 12-28, 1016G2

MARY Tyler Moore Show, The (TV series)
Wins Emmy awards 5-17, 460B2
MASEKO, Isaac (Isic Sigho)
Injured in bomb attempt 12-7, 927B1
MASH (TV series)
Wins Emmy 5-17, 460B2
MASHABELA, Harry
Arrested 7-29, 592C1
Freed 11-21, 927F2
MASHEROV, Pyotr M.
At Sovt CP Cong 2-24—3-5, 195D3
Politburo alternate member 3-5, 195D2
MASHININI, Tsietse
2d Soweto strike call 9-11—9-12, 695C2

MASIE Nguema Biyogo Ngue Ndong (Equatorial Guinea president)
100,000 natls rptd in exile 1-24, 61A2
Nigeria evacuates Equatorial Guinea workers 1-26, 62F1
US severs ties 3-15, 239A1

MASMOUDI, Mohammed
Egypt detains 3-9, 205A2
MASON, Jim
In World Series 10-16—10-21, 815C3
MASON, Roy
Threatns resignatn re defns cuts 1-14, cuts OKd 1-15, 101E1
Named Northern Ireland min 9-10, 693D3, 694A1
Violence greets in Belfast 9-13, 732E2
MASON, Tony
Defeated 11-2, 824D1

1977

Bethlehem Steel to clean up Sparrows Pt plant 9-22, 762E1
Free abortions contd 10-12, 787A1
ILA Baltimore dock slowdown rptd 12-1, 916C1
Crime
Agnew friend sentenced 4-4, 312C3
Nixon quotes Agnew 5-25, 420B1
Death penalty bill vetoed 5-26, 594A2
Garmatz indicted 8-1, 603C3
Mandel, 5 others convicted 8-23, 652A1-A2
5 indep oil cos convicted 8-30, 691G2; fined 9-16, 918F2
Mandel, 5 others sentenced 10-7, 807D2

MARYLAND, University of (College Park)
Loses Cotton Bowl 1-1; '76 rankings 1-3, 8E3
2d in IC4A indoor track championships 3-7, 603B1
Campbell in NFL draft 5-3, 353A3
Wins IC4A outdoor track championships 5-21, 603C1
Davis in NBA draft 6-10, 584B3
Wins Hall of Fame Bowl 12-23, 1020B2
MARY Tyler Moore Show, The (TV series)
Wins Emmys 9-11, 1022A1
MARZOUK, Moshe (d. 1955)
Body returned to Israel 4-19, 297A2
MASCELLANI, Maria Nilde
Acquitted 6-24, 525C1
MASEEMUDDIN Ahmed, Khandakar
Acquitted 2-26, 183D1

MASIE Nguema Biyogo Ngue Ndong (Equatorial Guinea president)
28 rptd executed 7-11, 658F2

MASIRE, Quet
Backs Patriotic Front 1-9, 11C1
MASON, David
Bars Krimsky removal 1-24, 101F1
MASON, Frederick
Chrgd 2-24, 159B1
MASON, Roy
On Ulster econ aid 8-1, 639A1
Affirms UK direct rule, bars exit 9-10, 730A1
MASONS—*See FREEMASONS*
MASSA, Andrew G.
To quit pension post 3-13, 195E1

1978

Camp David Summit—*See under MIDDLE EAST—EGYPT-Israel Peace Moves*
Crime & Civil Disorders
Pallottine priest indicted 1-6, 24B3
Garmatz indictmt dropped 1-9, 15G3
Mandel ordrd to pay back alimony 2-15, 172B3
Agnew case papers released 3-3, 164E3
Death penalty bill signed 3-10, 388F3
Lawyer competency case declined by US Sup Ct 5-1, 363F3
Pallottine priest sentenced 5-9, 380F1-A2
Juvenile case reviews upheld by US Sup Ct 6-28, 567F1
Prison populatn ordrd cut 8-4, 627A3
CIA ex-offcl found dead 10-1; Sen panel probe rptd 10-5, suicide suspected 10-20, 10-26, 835D3
Inmate suits judicial-aid case refused by Sup Ct 11-13, 874C3
CIA ex-offcl's suicide disputed 11-25, 917C2
Camp David Marines relieved for alleged pot use 12-9, 960B3
Baltimore GSA kickback indictmts 12-16, 1011C1, E1
Politics & Government—*See also other appropriate subheads in this section*
Legislature schedule rptd 14E3
Ex-sen Butler dies 3-16, 252E2
Primary results 9-12, 716E1
Rep Byron dies 10-11, 888G2
Election results 11-7: Cong 846F2, A3, 848C2, A3, 851B1; state 847C1, G1, 848B2, B3, 853F2, 915E2

MARYLAND, University of (College Park)
Nehemiah sets indoor 60-yd high hurdles record 1-27, 76B3
2d in IC4A track titles 3-6, 5-21, 692E3, F3
Iowa wins NCAA wrestling title 3-18, 379F2
Loses AIAW basketball title 3-25, 272C2
Social-actn group case refused by Sup Ct 5-1, 364B1
Loses women's lacrosse title 5-28, 540C2
Loses Sun Bowl 12-23, 1025D2
MARYLAND Public Interest Research v. Elkins
Md U social-actn group case refused by Sup Ct 5-1, 364C1
MARYLAND v. Marzullo
Lawyer competency case declined by Sup Ct 5-1, 363F3
MARYLAND v. Wheeler
Obscenity rule review declined by Sup Ct 4-24, 322F2
MARZULLO, Victor D.
Lawyer competency case declined by Sup Ct 5-1, 363F3
MASCHINO, Dalila
Kidnap rptd 4-24, Canada protests 7-1, 7-4, 531E3
MASCHINO, Denis
Chrgs wife kidnaped 4-24, Canada protests 7-1, 7-4, 531E3
M*A*S*H (TV series)
Silverman to head NBC 1-20, 75F2
MASIE Nguema Biyogo Ngue Ndong (Equatorial Guinea president)
Ousted in coup 8-3, surrender demanded 8-7, 613E3*
Captured 8-18, 638G2*
Trial opens, denies chrgs 9-24; executed 9-29, 742E1
MASIELLO, James
Loses Sen primary in NH 9-12, 736E1
MASMOUDI, Mohammed
Tunisia labor ldr rptd ally 2-5, 170A2
MASON, Clifford
Verandah opens 5-4, 760F3
MASON, F. van Wyck
Dies 8-28, 708B3
MASON, James
Boys From Brazil released 10-5, 969E3
MASON, Jim
Traded to Expos 12-8, 1026D1
MASON, Kenneth
Warns on '78-79 budget 8-15, 628B3
MASON, Marshall W.
5th of July opens 4-27, 760C2
In Recovery Lounge opens 12-7, 1031B2
MASON, Roy
Sees partial UK troop exit 1-4, 7F3
Scores Lynch interview 1-9, 18E3
Sees Callaghan on Belfast bombing, urges calm 2-19; bars death penalty 2-21, 132D2
Fallon scores UK Parachute Regimt recall 4-3, 268A2
Ulster police brutality chrgd 6-1, inquiry set 6-8, 474B2
Refutes Irish RC primate on jail conditns 8-1, 630D1
MASSA, Andrew G.
Named in US Teamster fund suit 2-1, 83F1

1979

Crime & Civil Disorders
Mandel conviction upset 1-11, 17G3
Mandel reclaims office 1-15, 56D1
Paisley death probe urged 1-24, 55A1
Baltimore GSA guilty pleas rptd 1-26, 92F3
Baltimore looting 2-18; curfew imposed 2-19—2-20, arrests rptd 2-22, 176B2
Baltimore nurse freed in mercy deaths 3-29, 291F1-A2
Paisley death probe dropped by Justice Dept 4-18, 283G3; Sen panel to probe 4-30, 368B1
'Catonsville 9' fugitive surrenders 6-19, 492E1
Warrantless phone surveillnc upheld by Sup Ct 6-20, 516D1
Paisley death questioned 6-27, CIA scored on probe 7-8, 520B2-G2
Truckers' strike violence 6-28, 479C2
Mandel convictn reinstated 7-20, 604D3
SBA minority-aid abuse rptd 9-28, 947A3
Armed Iranians seized at airport 11-15, 879F1; indicted 11-26, 898F2
Conrad extraditn fight cited 12-18, 1000G1
Energy
Geothermal drilling starts 5-14, 362A1
US gas allocatn suit filed 6-26, 479G1
Odd-even gas rationing begins 6-21, 462F2
Geothermal drilling results poor 7-14, 787C1
Odd-even gas rules lifted 9-10, 683G1
Politics & Government—*See also other appropriate subheads in this section*
Legislature schedule rptd 5D3
GOP ldrs meet in Easton 2-3—2-4, 86C1
DC voting rep amendmt rejectn rptd 3-19, 204B3
Carter visits Baltimore 8-7, 592E2, E3
Baltimore all-white club judicial membership surveyed 9-19, 901F2
Schaefer reelected Baltimore mayor, other electn results 11-6, 846B2, D3
Sports
Baltimore Orioles sold 8-2, 619A1
MARYLAND, University of (College Park)
Nehemiah sets 5 world hurdle marks 1-20—5-6, 911A1
2d in IC4A track champs 3-4, 5-21, 911F2, A3
2d in NCAA Lacrosse 5-26, 507F2-C3
Spinal replacement surgery rptd 8-31, 736E2
MARY Poppins (film)
FBI seizes stolen copy 1-8, 102E2
MASHAMBANHAKA, Terence
Killed 9-16, 718B2
MASHHADI, Abdel Hussein
Ousted from Baath Party 7-16, 544G3
Ties Assad to Iraqi plot 8-5, 602B3

MASIE Nguema Biyogo Ngue Ndong (Equatorial Guinea president; replaced Aug. 3)
Ousted in coup 8-3, surrender demanded 8-7, 613E3*
Captured 8-18, 638G2*
Trial opens, denies chrgs 9-24; executed 9-29, 742E1
MASON, James
Murder By Decree released 2-8, 174B3
Faith Healer opens 4-4, 711G2
Bloodline released 6-28, 819F3
MASON, John
On NSW police corruptn chrg 6-5, 467D2
MASON, Marsha
Promises in the Dark released 11-2, 1008B1
Chapter Two released 12-14, 1007B3
MASON, Marshall W.
Minnesota Moon opens 1-31, 292B2
Winter Signs opens 3-11, Talley's Folley 5-3, Murder at Howard Johnson's 5-17, 712F1, G2, F3
MASSACESI, Ettore
On Alfa Romeo survival plan 9-13, 709E1

1980

Crime & Civil Disorders
Mandel, wife sued 1-4, 18D2
Real estate convictn appeals declined by Sup Ct 1-21, 93B3
FBI 'Miporn' probe rptd 2-14, 136F1
Mandel, co-defendants appeal refused by Sup Ct 4-14, 307A1
Mandel begins prison sentence 5-19, 471E2
Ct backs death penalty law, voids Tichnell sentence 6-10, 869F1
Bethlehem Steel ex-offcl pleads guilty in bribe case 8-7, 600A2
Politics & Government—*See also other appropriate subheads in this section*
Legislature schedule rptd 18E1
State of State message 1-16, 269E2-A3
DC voting rep amendmt OKd 3-17, 576G1
Ex-Rep Fallon dies 3-21, 279E2
Pres primary results 5-13, 366D2
Hughes heads China delegatn 6-15, 452E3
Agnew papers placed on sale 7-10, 639B2
Baltimore hosts pres TV debate 9-21, 721G2
Anderson ct battle for ballot access rptd 9-27, 818B2
Election results 11-4: pres 838B1, E1, A2, 838E3; cong 840C2, 843B1, 845B3, 846B2, 848B2
'80 census rptd 12-31, 983E1
Sports
Racing comm upholds Codex Preakness victory 6-4, 447D2

MARYLAND, University of (College Park)
Davis named fact-finder by Sup Ct 3-3, 210G1
Wins IC4A outdoor track champ 5-24—5-25, 892A2
Marxist historian denied faculty post 6-12, 638C3
Nehemiah in US Olympic trials; injury, track team resignatn cited 6-24, 891A2
Loses Tangerine Bowl 12-20, 999C3
MARYLAND v. Louisiana
Fact-finder named by Sup Ct 3-3, 210A2
MARYSVILLE—*See OHIO*
MASBACK, Craig
Wins Penn Relays mile 4-25, 892D2
MASHIGO, Petrus
Sentenced to death 11-26, 968B1
MASIKA, George
Chief justice apptmt rptd 12-2, 946G1
MASIRE, Quett (Botswanan president)
Elected Botswana pres 7-18, 562B1
MASON, Anthony
Upholds ban on press articles, book 12-1, 919E2
MASON, Elvis
Defends Hunt bailout loan 5-30, 425D2
MASON, James
Ffolkes released 4-18, 416F2
MASON, Marshall W.
5th of July opens 11-6, 892C3
MASON, Raymond K.
Charter Co acquires Phila Bulletin 11-6, 907A2
MASON, Tony
Indicted for fraud 7-24, 875A3
MASRI, Zafer el-
Vs Israel, Egypt amb exchng 2-26, 140A2

1976

MASSACHUSETTS
Primary date set 22A2
Food stamp ineligibility rate rptd 2-11, denied 2-12, 129B1
Pres primary results 3-2, 164G2-165G1
Medicaid fraud effort set 3-26, 249F1
Lowell GM auto dealer convicted, other suits pending 4-1, 287E1
Suffolk, Newburyport bombings 4-22, 7-2; 4 indicted 7-14, 1 sentncd 10-8, 796B3
US Rep Macdonald dies 5-21, 404A2
State workers strike 6-21—6-24; OK pact 12-4, 921G1
Sup Ct upholds retiremt law 6-25, 552C1
US Sup Ct rules on abortn law 7-1, 518E2, F3
Cambridge halts DNA research 7-7, 736A1
Dem conv women delegates, table 508C2
Dem conv vote, table 7-14, 505F1, 506F1, 507C2
Australia prime min in Cambridge 7-30, 554B2
GOP pre-conv delegate count 8-14, 583C3
GOP conv pres, vp vote tables 8-18—8-19, 8-19, 599C1, C3
Anti-boycott law signed 8-19, 987A2
Sen primary results 9-14, 705A1
Fscl '75 per capita income, tax burden rptd 9-15, 10-12, 959E1, A2
US Sup Ct upholds police, firemen unpaid duty rule 10-12, 848A3
Richardson vows Arab boycott info 10-20, 786G2
Election results 11-2: pres 818B1, E1, 819A2; cong 820C1, 821F1, 828G1, 829B4; state 821G1, 825G2, C3, D3
Nantucket oil spill 12-15, 968D3; hearing 12-28—12-31, suit delayed 12-30, 1013E3
3 convicted in GM warranty-fraud case 12-23, 988F1

Boston
Jackson opens pres bid 1-6, 22A3
Wallace opens pres bid 1-9, 22C2
US Sup Ct declines police questionnaire rule review 1-12, 24F1
Appeals Ct upholds busing plan 1-14, 42D2
Busing plans protested, student violence 1-20, 1-21, 42F2
GSA contract violatns rptd 1-20, 71D1
US budgets DC rail aid 1-21, 66A1
Schl integration study rptd 1-24, 95F2
Cong clears revised RR aid 1-28, 68F3
Busing protest violence 2-15, 202G3
School admin quota set 2-24, 202E3
Schl attendance rptd up 2-25, 203D1
Jackson scores Carter 3-4, 166A2
Conrail bill OKs Boston-DC funds 3-30, 233F2
Amtrak to buy Boston-DC line 4-1, 235B2
Fultz wins Marathon 4-19, 292E3
Asbestos rptd in water 4-30, 349F1
Gen Tire irregularities chrgd 5-10, 360A2
Justice Dept, Ford seek busing rule review 5-14, 5-18; White, Hicks laud 5-15, 377E2-E3
US drops busing review 5-29; Ford, other reactn 5-29—6-2, 391E3
Sup Ct declines busing review 6-14, 452G2 ★
Carter at fund-raiser 6-22, 452E1
Logan Airport bombed 7-2; 4 indicted 7-14, 1 sentncd 10-8, 796C3
Bicentennial marked 7-4, 489D2
Queen Eliz visits 7-11, 489G2
Amtrak Boston-DC plan set 8-29, 648G1
'74-75 SAT average rptd 9-13, 993G1
Integratn incidents cited 9-14, 10-25; ratio rptd 11-13, 992G3, 993A1
New Boston Bank fails 9-15, 984A1
Geo P Gardner dies 9-18, 1015E1
Carter, Kennedy campaign 9-30, 723D1, 742E3
Saxe mistrial delcared 10-13, 816B2
US Sup Ct bars review of rape case 11-1, 867D3
US sues re job bias 11-26, 944E1

1977

MASSACHUSETTS
Legislature schedule rptd 6E2
Oil tanker rptd sunk off Cape Cod 1-11, 104E3, 214D3
Sorensen Chappaquiddick role cited 1-18, 35F1
Gen Dynamics loan guarantee saves Quincy jobs 1-19, 55F2
Cambridge ends DNA research ban 2-7, 103C2
Indian land claims rptd 2-7, 197D1
Saxe sentenced 2-11, 140E1
Cambridge DNA rules scored 2-22, 184F1
Carter talks at Clinton town mtg 3-16, 187D3, 190A3
Cambridge DNA rules cited 3-16, 452A1
2 state sens sentncd 3-23, seats vacated 3-31, 4-4, 252G3; DiCarlo loses reelectn bid 5-24, 446F3
Brook Farm fire 3-27, 396B2
Fed spending inequities chrged 4-6, 423D3
Carter energy plan reactn 4-20, 320E2
Blue laws upheld 4-21, 388F1
'76 per-capita income table 5-10, 387C2
Fed fishing law priority upheld 5-23, 444C2
RC ed's dismissal cited 6-16, 471B2
Health agency orders McDonald's glasses off mkt 7-8, McDonald's sues 7-12, 560A1, C1
Sacco, Vanzetti vindicated re S Braintree '27 murder 7-19; records made pub 8-9, 652E2-A3
Defense job loss rptd 8-10, 629D2
Kenneth O'Donnell dies 9-9, 788B2
'76 per capita income, tax burden table 9-13, 10-18, 821B2
Anti-abortn amendmt rptd sought 10-6, 786B3
Vet job prefernc law backed 10-11, 774E2
Free abortions contd 10-12, 787A1
Execs visit Cuba 10-24—10-28, O'Neill sees US prisoners 10-26, 896C2

Boston
US Sup Ct refuses HS receivership case 1-10, 57D1
Violence closes Hyde Park HS 1-10, 112D3
'68 NYS stock transfer tax amendmts ruled illegal 1-12, 57F2
Schl instructn decline rptd 1-16, 112C3
Rail corridor aid budgeted 1-17, 33C1
Populatn ranking rptd down 4-14, 388D1
S Boston HS clashes, arrests 5-12—5-16, 446A2
Econ data table 5-16, 384D2
LEAA office to close 6-20, 630E2
Stock exchange closed 7-14, 537B3
US bars charters to Jerusalem 8-1, 589C1
Mental hosp mind-control tests rptd 8-1—8-9, 611F1
Schls open peacefully 9-8, 837G3-838A1
Concorde landing rights proposed, offcls score 9-23, 738C2, B3
Election results 11-8, 855D3
Retroactive utility rate rise let stand 11-14, 878C3
Mysterious blasts rptd 12-2—12-22, 1008G3
Red Sox sale vetoed by AL owners 12-8, 989E2

1978

MASSACHUSETTS
Legislature schedule rptd 14F3
'67, '77 sales-tax rates rptd 1-5, 15E3
Wampanoags land claim set back 1-6, 6C1-B2
State govt tax revenue table 1-9, 84D2
FTC cites Ford re auto engine defect 1-13, 67A3
Offshore lease sales delayed 1-30, 108D2
McDonald's glasses rptd safe 1-31, 348B1
Blizzard paralyzes state, Carter declares disaster area 2-5—2-13; business losses rptd 2-27, 105F1, A2
Salem Sound oil spill 2-6, 524A2
4th in US defense contracts 2-21, 127D2
Wampanoag land claim dismissed 3-24, 327A1
Sup Ct justice suspended 4-13, censured 7-8; resigns 8-6, 844A1
Corp pol free speech backed by Sup Ct 4-26, 343E2
NH A-plant site review ordrd 4-28, 347B1
Brooke admits false loan disclosure 5-26 406B1
Canada fishing dispute rptd 6-2—6-5, 435B2
Union insurnc scheme chrgd 6-15, 560B3
Extended jobless aid rptd 7-10, 552A3; ends 8-4, 607D3
New Bedford prison riot rptd 8-8, 627A3
Primary results 9-19, 736F2
Carter at Lynn rally 10-28, 831C2
Election results 11-7: cong 845E1, B2, D2, 846E1, 847F2, C3, 848C2, 851C1; state 845B2, 847B1, E1, A2, C3, D3, 853F2
Drunk rights waiver ruling affirmed by US Sup Ct 12-11, 980G3
Schl inspectn for asbestos danger asked 12-21, 1009B2

Boston
NASL team awarded to Lipton 1-5, 23C1
Lloyd Carr offcls arrested 1-10, 1-24; receiver named 1-24, 83B2-D3
NE rail offcls resign 1-30; more funds allocated 2-11, projct delay rptd 2-24, 225B1
Blizzard closes roads, airport; blackouts, looting rptd 2-5—2-13, 105G1, B2, D2
Cadillac agency closes 3-1, 142F3 ★
UK air-fare dispute setld 3-17, 206D2
Wayne undergoes surgery 4-3, 420B1
Rodgers wins Marathon 4-17, 692G2
'77 living costs rptd 4-26, 349F1
Amtrak route cutbacks proposed 5-8, 366E1
2-carrier London air svc to end 6-9, 570E1
Pan Am offers Amsterdam trial fare 6-15—7-31, Port Auth to aid stranded travelers 7-16, 640C3
Air quality rated bad 7-5, 513D1
Transit strike 7-6, 565A2
Air quality rpt corrected 7-19, 644B2
WGBH-TV license renewed 7-20, 599G1
Natl Govs Assn meets 8-28—8-29, 681D3
Schools open peacefully 9-6, 698F2
Pan Am to end Portland svc 9-7, 701A2
Fox fined for 'block booking' 9-12, 759C2
Seabrook A-plant protesters arrested 10-7, 941C1
US, W Ger air svc pact expanded 10-25, 831F1
WTT Lobsters fold 10-27, 1027B1
Boston Edison rate limit case refused 10-30, 832G2
Tax referendum lobby injunctn lifted by Sup Ct 11-6, 874A1
Anti-busing plan excludes 11-7, 847A2, D3
Populatn ranked 12-6, 942G3

1979

MASSACHUSETTS
ITT Boston long-distance phone svc OKd 1-4, 15E2
Carter budgets NE rail subsidy cut 1-22, 45D1
Boston Navy Yd renovatn set 2-1, 93G3-94A1
Paramount resumes 'Warriors' ads 2-22, 174G1-A2
S Africans banned from Boston Marathon 4-12, Rodgers wins 4-16, 911C3
Boston library sale of Stuart portraits halted 4-14, 374E3 5D3
Legal drinking age raised 4-16, 309E3, F3
US-French air svc pact rptd 5-12, 465C3
Vets' job-prefernc law upheld by Sup Ct; reactn 6-5, 421D1-D2
Driver license suspensn rule upheld by Sup Ct 6-25, 540G1
Boston TV statn license fitness doubted 7-18, 618A2
Puritan site found in Cambridge 8-9, 631B3
Army recruiting fraud probed 8-19, 649G2
State workers Soc Security non-participatn cited 9-10, 727B1
'78 per capita income rptd 9-16, 746G1, C2
Papal mass legal challenge dismissed 9-25, 760C3
Pope in Boston; Commons mass held, traditional values affirmed 10-1, 757D1, F1; cost estimated 761B1
Amtrak Boston-Catlettsburg train ends svc 10-1, 868B1
Jury approval case refused by Sup Ct 10-29, 884A2
Arts cncl lottery set 11-15, 892G2-A3
Boston transit line taken over by gov 12-18, 989B3
J Onassis Martha's Vineyard home rptd planned 12-20, 1005B3
Boston '79 living costs ranked 12-28, 990E3, 991A1

Atomic Energy
Pilgrim (Plymouth) A-plant called unsafe 1-26, 90D3
Seabrook A-protesters arrested 3-9, 186E2
Pilgrim A-plant community studied 3-17, 207E3
Protests held in Plymouth 4-1, Boston 4-1, 4-4; King reaffirms dvpt 4-4, 261F3-262A1
Pilgrim A-plant delay seen 5-9, 382D1
Yankee (Rowe) protest staged 6-2, 416C2
Pilgrim protest staged 6-3, 416D2
A-protesters arrested in Boston bank 8-31, 742F3

Crime & Civil Disorders—*For A-protests, see 'Atomic Energy' above*
Edelin '75 convictn reversal cited 3-15, 272B1
Boston hotel fires 3-29, busboy chrgd 3-30, 316C3
Death penalty bill signed 8-14, 989G1
Man sentncd for rape of wife 9-24, 819F1
Boston schl violence erupts 10-17–10-19, probe ordrd 10-19, 850G1
Iranians protest in Springfield 11-9, 863C1

Energy—*See also 'Atomic' above*
Georges Bank oil-lease ban lifted 2-20, 186F3
'78 per capita gas use rptd 5-27, 395G2
Boston hit by gas shortage 6-23, 479C1
Gasohol sales test set in Boston 8-10, 649G1
Winter heating fuel supply promised 8-28, 703C2
Carter mailing planned, scored 9-17, 703G2
Georges Bank lease sale delayed 11-6, OKd 11-9, 867E1-A2
Georges Bank lease bids placed 12-18, 990A2

Medicine & Health
Laetrile treatmt for 3-yr-old ordrd ended 1-23, 1-30, parents flee 1-25, 139C1
MDs cleared in psychosurgery suit 2-9, 139E3
Cyanide rptd in blood of 3-yr-old 3-7, 196B1
Laetrile shipmt recalled 3-8, 196A1
Edelin '75 convictn reversal cited 3-15, 272B1
Medicaid abortn funds case refused by Sup Ct 5-14, 383D1
Anti-abortn law signed 6-12, 547G2
Abortn-consent law voided by Sup Ct 7-2, 559G1-D2
Framingham man gets heart transplant aid 10-10, 1005D3
3-yr-old leukemia victim dies 10-12, 905A2

Obituaries
Saltonstall, Leverett 6-17, 508E3

Politics & Government—*See also other appropriate subheads in this section*
Legislature schedule rptd 5E3
Referendum spending case refused by US Sup Ct 1-8, 14A3
Legis OKs DC voting rep amendmt 3-19, 204G2
Boston, Worcester fiscal status rptd 3-20, 204F1, G1
Brooke cleared of wrongdoing 3-20, 208F2
Stone confrmd CFTC chrmn 4-11, 681D2

1980

MASSACHUSETTS
Chicopee Falls Uniroyal plant to close 1-22, 52G2
Boston TV statn license lifted, sale blocked 1-24, 119F2, B3
Schl prayer law in effect 2-5, stay denied 2-13, 156D1
Boston home prices rptd high 3-29, 248A1
Natl securities mkt failure scored 9-12, 806F1
Springfield busing, housing integratn study rptd 11-16, 989E3
Boston settles US job bias suit 12-5, 962B3

Crime & Civil Disorders
State of State message 1-14, 483D3
Prof indicted in welfare fraud 5-13, 414D3
Illegal search protectn narrowed by Sup Ct 6-25, 541B1
Boston judge rules 'Caligula' not obscene 8-1, 640A2
Rape trial press exclusn case remanded by Sup Ct 10-14, 782B1
Death penalty law struck down 10-28, 868D3

Energy
Georges Bank lease bids rptd accepted 1-7, 18A1
State of State message 1-14, 483C3

Medicine & Health
State of State message 1-14, 483E3
Life aid ordrd in 'Right-to-Die' case 1-24, 158C2
Influenza outbreak rptd 2-15, 158C3
Boston hay fever study rptd 2-18, 159G3
Boston area toxic fume evacuatn 4-3, 392E1

Politics & Government—*See also other appropriate subheads in this section*
Legislature schedule rptd 18E1
State of State message 1-14, 483B3
ACU '79 voting survey rptd 1-18, 53C3
Drinan drops reelectn bid 5-5, 341D2
Ex-Rep Casey dies 9-2, 755D2
Anti-abortionists lose primary 9-16, 724C2
Detroit census revisn ordrd, Boston undercount claimed 9-25, 741G2
Election results 11-4: cong 840C2, 843C1, 846D1, 848D2; state 847D2, 848D2
Ex-Rep McCormack dies 11-22, 928G2
Boston bond rating lowered 12-2, 939C3
'80 census rptd, reapportmt seen 12-31, 983E1

1976

MASSACHUSETTS Institute of Technology (MIT) (Cambridge)
Rolfe dies 3-10, 240F3
Synthetic bacterial gene rptd 8-28, 735F2
Ting wins Nobel 10-18, 840G1
2 get Science Medals 10-18, 858C3
MASSERA, Adm. Emilio
On high cancer rate areas 2-16, 224E3 *
In mil junta 3-24, 211E2
Junta takes final exec powers 3-25, 236C1
Diaz Bessone tie rptd 10-29, 996D3
MASSEY, Jack
'72 campaign gift listed 4-25, 688B1
MASSIE, Suzanne
Scores Sovt visa denial 7-3, 540B3
MASS Transit—*See under TRANSPORTATION*
MASSUE, Sadi Conrado
Rpt chrgs Peron embezzlemt 6-4, 520E1
MASTBAUM, William E.
Sentenced 11-30, 921F2
MASTERS, Edward E.
Bangladesh amb 9-16; confrmd 9-30, 808C1
MASTER Shipping Agency Inc.
Arab boycott rpt released 10-19, 786D1
MATANIC, Peter
Hijacks TWA jet 9-10, arraigned in US 9-13, 685C2
MATANO, Robert
Mombasa cncl dissolved, Nairobi electns canceled 8-11, 1013A1
MATANOSKI, Dr. Genevieve
Rpts high cancer areas 2-16, 224E3
MATANZIMA, George
Actors arrested 10-11, 813C2
MATANZIMA, Chief Kaiser Daliwonga
Vs Xhosa citizenship bill 6-6, 428C3
Arrests opponents 7-26, 592B2
Party wins electn 9-29, 813G1
Proclaims Transkei independnt 10-26, 813A1

1977

MASSACHUSETTS, University of (Amherst)
Janis confrmd HUD undersecy 3-23, 272B3
MASSACHUSETTS Institute of Technology (MIT) (Cambridge)
Relativity evidence rptd 1-7, 170E3
Urban cntr rpts on house costs 3-3, 178B2
'77-78 costs rptd 3-27, 483G1
Church addresses 5-2, 335A1
King rptd in DNA debate 10-6, 846D3
Cohen gets Medal of Sci 11-22, 951G3
MASSACHUSETTS Mental Health Center (formerly Boston Psychpathic Hospital)
CIA mind-control tests revealed 8-1—8-9, 611F1
MASSACHUSETTS v. Feeney
Sup Ct upholds vets job preferne 10-11, 774E2
MASSAMBA-Debat, Alphonse
Arrested 3-18, 220B2
Linked to cardinal's death 3-23, 220E2
Executed 3-25, 282G2
MASSE, Gilles
On police slowdown 2-1, 2-4, 97F2
MASSENGALE, Rik
Wins Hope Desert Classic 2-13, 311C2
Ties 3d in Masters 4-10, 311C1
MASSERA, Adm. Emilio
Graiver client protectn rptd 4-22, 371E2
Orders Bulgaria boats shelled 10-1, 944C3
Scores econ min policies 11-6, 981C2
Sees Vance 11-21, 912F2
MASSERA, Jose Luis
US science acad seeks info 4-27, 315B2
MASSEY Ferguson Ltd.
Admits overbilling 12-29, 1010G2
MASS Transit—*See under TRANSPORTATION*
MASTERMAN, John
Dies 6-6, 532D3
MASTER Puppeteer, The (book)
Wins Natl Book Award 4-11, 355B2
MASTER Tung's Western Chamber Romance (book)
Wins Natl Book Award 4-11, 355B2
MASTROCOLA Jr., Frank
Wins Mass Dem primary 5-24, 446G3
MATANIC, Peter
Convicted 5-5, 551A3
Sentenced 7-20, 642C2
MATANZIMA, Chief Kaiser Daliwonga
Party cong opens 3-8, 350E2
MATAR, Elias
Scores intell com watch 2-26, 151C1
Gets Leb Christian aid plea 3-2, 143G1

1978

MASSACHUSETTS, University (Amherst)
Loses women's lacrosse title 5-28, 540C2
S Africa stock divestiture rptd 6-18, 633D1
Gravity wave evidence rptd 12-14, 12-16, 1023D3
Loses Pioneer Bowl 12-16, 1025C2
MASSACHUSETTS Institute of Technology (MIT)
Seamans named engineering schl dean 4-26, 420E1
Sun/Earth weather link explored 5-11, 654C1
Nitrite cancer study rptd 8-11, 728A1
Urban Studies cntr rpts on redlining 12-7, 942F2-A3
MASSACHUSETTS v. White
Mass drunk rights waiver ruling affirmed by US Sup Ct 12-11, 980G3
MASSARI, Lea
Faces of Love released 7-7, 970C1
MASSERA, Adm. Emilio (ret.)
Beagle Channel dispute dvpts 1-6—2-10, 101B1, A2
In France, sees Montoneros 4-9, 285E3
Videla pres term extended 5-2, 611A3
Successor's daughter killed in blast 8-1, 612E1
Sees Spain king 11-28, 968A1
MASSEY, Debbie
2d in Sunstar tourn 3-12, 355E3
2d in Bankers Trust Classic 6-18, 580C3
Ties for 2d in LI Classic 8-13, 672F3
MASSIE, Ian
Kidnaped in El Salvador 12-1, negotiatns for release rptd 12-21, 986C3
MASS Transit—*See under TRANSPORTATION*
MASTER and Margarita, The (play)
Opens 11-11, 1031D2
MASTERS, Geoff
Loses Australian Indoor 10-22, 1027B2
MASTERS, John
On natural gas find 6-27, 571G3
MASTERSON, Peter
Best Little Whorehouse opens 4-17, 760D1
MATABELELAND—*See RHODESIA*
MATANZIMA, Chief Kaiser Daliwonga
Breaks S Africa ties re land claim 4-10, 258A3
MATARACI, Tuncay
Named Turkey customs min 1-5, 21E2
MATCHES
CPSC standards cited 2-8, 185A3
MATERNITY—*See CHILDBIRTH*

1979

Brooke remarries 5-12, 392C2
Kennedy: Chappaquiddick no bar to presidency 7-17, 539F1-D2
Pres primary date chng barred 8-6, 593A1
Mrs Carter greets Pope 10-1, 757F1
JFK library dedicatn; Carter, Kennedy speak 10-20, 807D3, 905D1
Boston reelects Mayor White 11-6, 846C3
Kennedy announces pres bid in Boston 11-7, 847B1
Brown in Boston 11-8, 847A3
Reagan speaks in Boston 11-14, 982B1

MASSACHUSETTS, University of
Amherst Campus
2d in women's lacrosse title 5-13, 507C3
Boston Campus
JFK library dedicated 10-20, 905F1
MASSACHUSETTS General Hospital (Boston)
Crib death preventn device rptd 1-15, 64G1
MDs cleared in psychosurgery suit 2-9, 139G3
Robboy rpts DES study 3-6, 196C1
Cancer cocoon discovery rptd 8-20, 735E1
MASSACHUSETTS Institute of Technology (MIT) (Cambridge)
Forgn student enrollmt listed 167E3
Sovt beam-weapon threat discounted 1-10, 52F3
'75 A-safety rpt called unreliable 1-19, 54C2
Illegal alien issue detailed 1-29, 127F1
Study sees grim future for A-war survivors 3-23, 232A3
Magnet-synthesizing bacteria rptd 4-8, 691B2
Kendall scores A-plant pipe leaks 5-2, 322D3
Millon named to Natl Gallery post 5-7, 375G1
Baker energy-saving device unveiled 5-18, 404A2
WCC mtg ends; religion, sci rift eased 7-24, 640D1
Quasar sighting studied 8-23, 691G2
Ting backs quantum chromodynamics 9-2, 692F3
H-bomb letter printed 9-16, 9-18, Rathjens denies chrgs 9-17, 713G2, 714C2; text of letter 714D1-717E3
Wallace on Pay Advisory Com 10-16, 829G2
DNA alternate structure rptd 12-13, 1000E2
MASSEY, Debbie
Ties for 2d in US Women's Open 7-15, 587D1
Wins Wheeling Classic 10-7, 970F1
MASSIE, Ian
Freed in El Salvador 7-2, 547G1
MASSINE, Leonide
Dies 3-16, 272B3
MASS Transit—*See under TRANSPORTATION*
MASTER, Karen
Marries T Cullen Davis 5-25, 527C3
MASTERS, Charles D.
Revises US oil reserves estimate 1-5, 17F1
MASTERS, Edward
On E Timor starvatn 12-4, 995A1
MASTERS, Dr. William H.
Rpts on homosexual therapy 4-16, book published 4-23, 315E3-316D1
MASTROIANNI, Marcello
Wifemistress released 1-6, 174G3
Divine Nymph released 10-12, 1007C3
Stay As You Are released 12-21, 1008G1
MASURSKY, Harold
On Venus findings 5-29, 692A1
MATANZIMA, Chief Kaiser Daliwonga (Transkei president)
Elected Transkei pres 2-19, 215D3
MATARESE Circle, The (book)
On best-seller list 4-8, 271G1; 5-6, 356E2; 6-3, 432G1; 7-1, 548A3; 8-5, 620A3; 9-2, 672A3
MATBUI, Maj. Gen. Iraj
Executed 9-24, 814B3
MATERA, Albert A.
Sentenced in GSA scandal 10-19, 964G3
MATERNITY—*See BIRTHS*

1980

Presidential Election (& Transition)
Kennedy gets matching funds 1-4, 5B2; for complete coverage, see KENNEDY, Edward Moore
Kennedy Chappaquiddick role questnd by 2 publicatns 1-14, 1-15, 32F3-33C1; wife defends 1-18, 50A3
Kennedy Chappaquiddick plea aired 1-28, 75A1; phone record queried 3-12, 184C1
Reagan in Springfield 1-29, 91C3
Kennedy in Boston 1-30, 91D2
Reagan in Worcester, assails Carter forgn policy 2-15, 128B3
Anderson strategy detailed 2-15, 129F2
Kennedy, Bush win primaries 3-4, 166B2
Pres candidates address Amer Legion conv in Boston 8-19—8-21, 629E1, D2, F3
Kennedy greets Carter warmly, urges reelectn 8-21, 629A3
Reagan, Anderson debate abortn 9-21, 722G1
Anderson ballot access challenged 9-27, 818B2, C2
Kennedy at Carter rallies 10-15, 778F3
Election results 11-4, 838B1, 839A2, E3
Sports
Ruiz Boston Marathon win disputed 4-21, Garreau named winner 4-29, 527A2-F2
Transportation
State of State message 1-14, 483D3
Boston-London expanded air svc expansn agreed 3-5, 172B3
Somerville rail accident 4-3, 392E1
World Air Boston-London svc OKd 4-10, 346C2
Amtrak aid bill signed by Carter 5-30, 427G1
Transit system broke, state takes over 11-18; ct bars move 11-28; system shuts down 12-6; funding bill signed 12-7, 939A2
MASSACHUSETTS Institute of Technology (MIT) (Cambridge)
'69-76 new job data rptd 1-18, 455E3
GAO scores cancer-nitrite study 1-31, 159F1
'79 endowmt earnings rptd 3-24, 319B2
Pluto moon theory rptd 4-22, 416D1
Nitrite study cited 8-19, 726E1
MASSACHUSETTS v. Meehan
Case declined by Sup Ct 2-26, 188A2
MASSENGALE, Rik
2d in Phoenix Open 1-20, 412B2
MASSEY, Debbie
2d in Arden Classic 2-10, Sunstar Classic 3-9, Women's Kemper Open 3-30, Coca-Cola Classic 5-18, 412D2, G2, B3, 413A1
MASSEY-FERGUSON Ltd.
Ottawa, Ontario reject aid plea 9-4; 3d 1/4 loss rptd 9-8, 728D2
Equity plan announced 12-13; '80 loss rptd 12-17, 992D1-B2
MASSIE, Robert K.
Peter the Great on best-seller list 12-7, 948E3
MASS Transit—*See under TRANSPORTATION*
MASTROIANNI, Armand
He Knows You're Alone released 9-26, 836A3
MASTROIANNI, Marcello
Blood Feud released 2-22, 216C2
MASURSKY, Harold
Reveals Sovt Venus missions plan 11-23, 933C1
MATALON, Vivian
Morning's at Seven opens 4-10, 392E3
Wins Tony 6-8, 692C3
Brigadoon opens 10-16, 892A3
American Clock opens 11-20, 1003G2
MATARESE Circle, The (book)
On best-seller list 3-9, 200C3; 4-6, 280D3
MATE, Ilya
Wins Olympic medal 7-30, 624E3
MATERNITY—*See CHILDBIRTH*
MATHEBULA, Peter
Decisns Kim for WBA flywgt title 12-13, 1001B1

1976

MATHEMATICS
Muskhelishvili dies 7-15, 716E3
Chern gets Science Medal 10-18, 858D3
MATHERNE, Louis H. C.
Pleads guilty 3-5, 247G2
MATHESON, Scott M.
Wins Utah primary for gov 9-14, 705F1
Elected 11-2, 820C3, 824B3, 831D2
Briefs Carter 11-22, 881D1
MATHEWS, F. David
Admits HEW funds misuse 1-26, 128E1
Ford calls for flu vaccine 3-24, 224C2
Sets Medicaid fraud effort 3-26, 249E1
FDA inquiry criticized 5-23, 392E1
Ford suspends HEW ruling 7-7, 535B3
Defends HEW re Medicaid 8-30, 715C2
MATHIAS Jr., Sen. Charles McCurdy (R, Md.)
Drops CIA disclosure request 2-17, 150E2
Refused Angola visa 7-12, 519E3
Asks Butz dismissal 10-1, 744E1
MATHIS, Rep. Dawson (D, Ga.)
Reelected 11-2, 829D2
MATHY, Francois
Wins Olympic medal 7-27, 547D2
MA Tien-shin
Posters denounce 10-18, 790C3
MATLOVICH, Tech. Sgt. Leonard P.
Court upholds dismissal 7-16, 944F1
MATOS, Huber
Cuba rejects Montes exchg 12-18, 955D3
MATSUNAGA, Rep. Spark M. (D, Hawaii)
Wins Sen primary 10-2, 764D2
Elected to Senate 11-2, 820A1, 825B1, 828D1
MATSUNO, Raizo
Barred as LDP head 9-15, 694E1
MATSUOKA, Katsuhiro
Arrested 7-19, 557B2
MATTALAB, U. A.
Nigeria supply min 3-15, 222B3
MATTEI, Gen. Fernando
Chile health min 3-8, 288F2
MATTER of Gravity A (Play)
Opens 2-3, 1014B3
MATTHES, Roland
Wins Olympic medal 7-19, 575C2
MATTHEWS, Beverley
Rpt on Gulf paymts detailed 133B2
MATTHEWS, Gary
Contract rptd signed 12-5, 951D3
MATTHEWS, Thomas Dean
Cited in Hearst trial 2-4, 2-9, testifies 2-10, 113E3, 114D2, C3
Testifies vs Hearst 2-11, 201F1
Testifies 7-15, Harrises convicted 8-9, 595E3
MATTOX, James Alabon
Elected to US House 11-2, 822F3, 830C4
MATUTE Fernandez, Jose
Torture trial begins 6-28, 501E2
MAUDLING, Reginald
Thatcher changes shadow Cabt 11-19, 1004G1 ★

MAURITANIA—*See also AFRICAN Development Bank, ARAB League, NON-ALIGNED Nations Movements, OAU*
IMF oil loans rptd 1-7, 4-1, 339F3, 340A1, 340D2
Listed as 'not free' nation 1-19, 20E3
Miferma compensatn set 1-28, 104F2
Angola MPLA recognized 2-13, 163E2
Algeria ties cut 3-7, 178A3
US proposes Sahel aid 5-1, 318D2
ECOWAS rptd ratified 11-6, 974E2
Sahara—*See SAHARA*

1977

MATHEMATICS
Richard Brauer dies 4-17, 356G2
NSF '78 authorizatn signed 8-15, 689E1
'63-77 SAT scores drop, test scored 8-23, 8-24, 739D1-C2
Medals of Sci awarded 11-22, 952A1, C1
MATHESON, Gov. Scott M. (D, Utah)
Rejects Gilmore stay 1-14, 40A2
MATHEWS, F. David
Handicapped protest HEW 4-5—4-16, 301E2
HEW handicapped rules signed 4-28, 338A3
HEW sets Medicaid cuts 6-8, 460D3
MATHEWSON, Arthur
Canada defns modernizatn set 7-13, 579E3
MATHIAS Jr., Sen. Charles McCurdy (R, Md.)
Votes vs Bell confrmatn 1-19, 34D1
Backs cong electn funds bill 3-7, 232D3
Estimates Lance debt 719B1
MATHIASON, Carl R.
Sup Ct limits Miranda rights 1-25, 80F1
MATLACK, Jon
Traded to Rangers 12-8, 990B1
MATOS, Huber
Prison mistreatmt cited 9-17, 781G3
MATOSEVICH, Mykola
Arrested 4-23, 314F1
MATSUNAGA, Sen. Spark M. (D, Hawaii)
Cited in Park indictmt 9-6, 688D1
In Panama, backs pacts 11-9—11-12, 911C2, E3
MATSUSHITA Electric Industrial Co. Ltd.
US TV productn cited 3-28, 319A1
US TV operatns cited 12-14, 974B2
MATTEL Inc.
Andersen OKs paymt 4-26, 519E3
MATTHEWS, Gary
Kuhn's power vs Turner backed 5-19, 567D3
MATTHEWS, Herbert L.
Dies 7-30, 604D3
MATTHIASEN, Niels
Danish culture min 2-25, 373E1
MATTHOEFER, Hans
On A-plant protests 1-13, 117B3
MATTI, Rodolfo
Killed by guerrillas 10-26, 921C3
MATTINI, Luis
New ERP ldr 7-20, 595D3
MATTOX, Rep. James Alabon (D, Tex.)
'76 spec interest gifts rptd 2-15, 128E2
MAUDLING, Reginald
Scored re Poulson scandal 7-26, 581G1
MAUGHAN, Justice Richard J.
Vs Utah death penalty law 11-26, 919F3
MAUNG Kha, U
Elected Burma premier 3-29, 243B3

MAURITANIA—*See also ARAB League, NONALIGNED Nations Movement, OAU*
UN Assemb member 4D1
Israel boycott eased 2-18, 167F2
Defense min rptd replaced 3-18, 394E3
Arab monetary fund created 4-18, 318C1
IMF standby loan OKd, worsening paymts deficit seen 5-25, 710E3
Sahel dvpt plan OKd 6-1, 458E3
Envoy shot in Paris 7-7, 543B2
Cabt shuffled 8-4, 772E1
New Sahel famine seen 9-19, 770A2
Sahara—*See SAHARA*

1978

MATHEMATICS
Harvard revises curriculum 5-2, 348D2
Computer program patents curbed by Sup Ct 6-22, 509B1
Field Medals awarded 8-15, 1023F2
SAT scores drop again 9-16, 754A2
Obituaries
Begle, Edward G 3-2, 252D2
Godel, Kurt 1-14, 196A3
Keldysh, Mstislav V 6-24, 540A3
MATHESON, Albert D.
Named in US Teamster fund suit 2-1, 83E1
MATHESON, Gov. Scott (D, Utah)
On Carter water plan 6-6, 427A1
MATHEWS, Edwin L. (Eddie)
Inducted into Baseball HOF 8-8, 617D3
MATHEWS, Jay
PI electn coverage protested 4-11, 269C1
MATHIAS Jr., Sen. Charles McCurdy (R, Md.)
Votes for Panama Canal neutrality pact 3-16, 177F2
Votes for 2d Canal pact 4-18, 273B1
Scores Carter re Marston affair 4-24, 309C3
Seeks Civil Svc reform chngs 8-24, 661E3, G3
MATHIS, Johnny
'Too Much' on best-seller list 5-3, 356D1; 6-7, 460F3
MATHIS, Rep. M. Dawson (D, Ga.)
Reelected 11-7, 850A3
MATILDA (film)
Released 6-22, 619A3
MATISSE, Henri (1869-1954)
Paintings destroyed in Brazil museum fire 7-8, 579A2
MATLACK, Jon
AL pitching ldr 10-2, 928F3
MATLOVICH, Leonard P.
AF dischrg held unfair, review ordrd 12-6, 960B2
MATOBAKO, Jankie Makiomola
Dies 3-19, 6 policemen chrgd 7-20, 633C2
MATOS Gonzalez, Maj. Gen. Ramiro
DR 1st Mil Brigade cmdr 8-16, 648E2
Named army cmdr 10-2, seen 'nonpolitical' 10-16, 881C1
MATSU (Taiwan-held island)
Peking ends shelling 12-31, 995D1
MATSUDA, Hiroo
Message From Space released 11-17, 970B2
MATSUI, Robert T.
Wins US House seat 11-7, 850D1, 856D3
MATSUMOTO, Fujio
El Salvador guerrillas kidnap 5-17, presumed dead 7-7, 722E1
Found dead 10-13, 881C3
Death cited 12-7, 986D3
MATSUNAGA, Sen. Spark M. (D, Hawaii)
Votes for Panama Canal neutrality pact 3-16, 177D2
Votes for 2d Canal pact 4-18, 273B1
MATTA Ballesteros, Ramon
Linked to army chief in land deal 6-9, 615B1
MATTEL Inc.
Handler, 4 others indicted 2-16, 116D2
MATTHAU, Walter
Casey's Shadow released 3-17, 618F3
California Suite released 12-21, 1030E2
MATTHEI, Church
Vows Seabrook A-plant protests 8-7, 609A3
MATTHEI, Gen. Fernando
Named Chile junta member, AF cmdr 7-21, 572E2, E3
AF gens replaced 7-25, 591F1
MATTHEWS, Clay
In NFL draft 5-2, 336F2
MATTHEWS, Edgar (Coots)
Puts out oil reserve fire 9-16, 738G1
MATTHIASEN, Niels
Named Danish culture min 8-30, 688A1
MATTHOEFER, Hans
Named W Ger finance min 2-3, 93E2, A3
'79 budget presented 9-20, 906D1
Mark revalued up vs snake countries 10-16, 798D2
MATTIOLI, Rocky
KOs Obed 3-11, 379C2
KOs Duran 5-14, 379E2
MATTOX, Rep. James Alabon (D, Tex.)
Reelected 11-7, 852E2
MATUSEVICH, Mikola
Rptd sentenced 3-30, 275B3
MATUTE Canizales, Eugenio
Honduras educatn min 8-9, 691D3
MAUGE, Rene
6th in pres electn 7-16, 557A1
MAULL, Hanns W.
Study faults govts on energy policy 6-13, 450G2

MAURITANIA—*See also ARAB League, GATT, NONALIGNED Nations Movement, OAU*
Cabt shuffled, mins cut 1-26, 95C1
Western, Arab banks in iron ore loan 1-27, 95E1
6 W African natns back ECOWAS 3-18, USSR scores 3-20, 237E1
Islamic bank poor-natn aid rise rptd 4-9, 257F2
French mil aid rptd 5-24, 382C3
Ould Daddah deposed 7-10, Cabt formed 7-11, 535B1
Salek OKs civil freedoms 7-14; Ould Daddah transfer, 2 ex-offcls release rptd 7-17, 577G1
UN Assemb member 713C3
Sahara Conflict—*See SAHARA*

1979

MATHEMATICS
US-China pact set 5-13, 370E1
US SAT scores drop 9-8; elementary, HS tests 9-13, 785F1, D2
Sovt algorithm rptd computer programming breakthrough 10-6, 1000D2
MATHESON, Margaret
All Things Bright & Beautiful released 3-8, 528B1
MATHESON, Gov. Scott M. (D, Utah)
Releases '53 A-test documts 2-14, 112F1-A2
MATINE-Daftari, Hedayatollah
New Iran party formed 3-7, 180B1
Khomeini scores 5-24, 407F3
Arrest sought 8-20, 635G1
MATISON, Chris
Australian Open results 1-3, 103E2
MATISSE, Henri (1869-1954)
Painting sold for record sum 7-3, 672A1
MATOS, Brig. Delio Barbosa de
Brazil AF min designate 1-19, 95E1
MATOS, Haroldo
Brazil communicatns min designate 1-19, 95D1
MATOS, Huber
Freed by Cuba 10-21, flies to CR 10-22, 812E2
MATSUNAGA, Sen. Spark (D, Hawaii)
Finances disclosed 5-18, 383G3
MATT, Maj. Gen. Danny
Nablus mayor's expulsn ordrd 11-8, 881E2
Reassigned, post abolished 11-15, 916E3
MATTEL Inc.
To buy Westn Publishing 1-9, 16B1
Recalls space toys 1-11, ACT scores 2-27, 308A3
Macmillan accepts, rejects bid 8-30, 942B3
Ringling Brothers-Barnum & Bailey Combined Shows Inc.—*See separate listing*
MATTEOLI, Jean
Named French labor min 11-8, 872F3
MATTES, Eva
Woyzeck released 8-24, 820G3
MATTHEWS, Gary
NL wins All-Star Game 7-17, 568G3
MATTHIESSEN, Peter
Wins Natl Book Award 4-23, 356A2
MATTHOEFER, Hans
On proposed banking reforms 5-22, 411B2★
On Ger econ expansn plans 5-28, 489C2
US rptd upset re defense spending 9-21, 733C2
MATTICK, Bobby
Hired as Blue Jays mgr 10-18, 1002F1
MATTIN, Steve
Jerk released 12-14, 1007E3
MATTSON, Roger J.
3 Mile I NRC transcripts released 4-12, 275A1
MATTSON, Walter
Named NY Times Co pres 7-23, 640D3
MAUDE, Angus
UK paymaster general 5-5, 338G1
MAUDLING, Reginald
Dies 2-14, 176C3
MAULDIN, Karl
Amer Express travelers check TV ad chngd 8-29, 903C1

MAURITANIA—*See also ARAB League, GATT, NONALIGNED Nations Movement, OAU*
Egypt ties cut 4-24, 296E1
Bouceif in France, seeks aid 5-3, 324A1
Bouceif, 11 others die in plane crash 5-27, 412E1
Salek resigns, Luly replaces 6-4, 417D1
Algeria ties restored 8-14, 626G3
UN membership listed 695G2
Sahara Conflict—*See SAHARA*

1980

MATHEMATICS
Female interest increase rptd 4-15, 559D2
US scientific literacy lag rptd 10-22, 990D1
MATHER, Jay
Wins Pulitzer 4-14, 296G2
MATHER, Lt. Col. Paul
In Viet MIA missn 10-1—10-4, 855C2
MATHESON, Richard
Somewhere in Time released 10-3, 836F3
MATHESON, Gov. Scott M. (D, Utah)
State of State message 1-14, 270G1
Reelected 11-4, 845E3, 847D1, 852E1
MATHEWS, F. David
Named to public educatn post 6-11, 638E2
MATHIAS, Bob
Thompson wins Moscow Olympics decathlon 7-26, 589B1
MATHIAS Jr., Sen. Charles McCurdy (R, Md.)
Gets zero rating from ACU 1-18, 53D3
On B Carter probe 9-17, 701D2
Reelected 11-4, 840C2, 845B3, 848B2
MATHIAS, John
OKs Seabord-Tiger merger 5-8, 516A2
MATHIESSEN, Peter
Snow Leopard wins Amer Book Award 5-1, 692A2
MATHIEU, Gilles
On US gratitude for Iran rescue 2-1, 88C3
MATHIS, Rep. Dawson (D, Ga.)
Hatcher wins seat 11-4, 849A3
MATISSE, Henri (1869-1954)
Painting stolen in Argentina 12-25, 991E1
MATLOVICH, Leonard P.
AF reinstatemt ordered 11-9, setlmt reached 11-24, 962G1
MATOS, Adolfo
Convicted 7-30, 601D1
Indicted 12-10, 963G3
MATOS, Huber
Seeks UN Boniato hunger strike probe 12-4, 965C2
MATSUI, Rep.Robert T. (D, Calif.)
Reelected 11-4, 842D1, 846F3
MATT, Maj. Gen. Danny
On deportatn of Arab ldrs 5-3, 340B2
MATTARELLA, Piersanti
Murdered 1-6, 20B3
MATTEL Inc.
Ringling Bros.-Barnum & Bailey Combined Shows Inc.
Fla tax case refused by Sup Ct 3-24, 265A2
MATTFELD, Jacquelyn A.
Resigns 5-28, 471B1
MATTHAU, Walter
Little Miss Marker released 3-21, 216C3
Hopscotch released 9-26, 836B3
MATTHEWS, David Wayne
Acquitted 11-17, 898G2
MATTHEWS, Gabriel Baccus
Asks Tolbert ouster 3-7, arrested 3-9, 278C2
Tolbert slain in coup, Doe frees 4-12; named Liberian forgn min 4-13, 284B3, 285A1
MATTHEWS, Hale
Lady From Dubuque opens 1-31, 136C3
Happy New Year opens 4-27, 392A3
MATTHEWS, Ira
NFL '79 kick return ldr 1-5, 8C3
MATTHEWS, Wes
In NBA draft 6-10, 447D1, F1
MATTHIAS, Bernd T.
Dies 10-27, 876F2
MATTHOEFER, Hans
In Turkey aid role, reassures Greece 2-16—2-19; IMF OKs loan 2-21, 135B3
Turkey mil aid plans noted 2-25, 153F3
Budget supplement OKd 4-30, 355E3, F3
Sworn W Ger finance min 11-5, 925E1
Compares US, W Ger soldrs 11-6, 904C1
Rpts '81 draft budget OKd 12-17, 968G3
MATTINGLY, Mack
Wins Ga US Sen primary 8-5, 683D2
MATTOX, Rep. James Alabon (D, Tex.)
Reelected 11-4, 844E2
MAUCH, Gene
Quits as Twins mgr 8-24, 926B2
MAUCHLY, John W.
Dies 1-8, 104B3
MAUGHAM, (William) Somerset (1874-1965)
Sutherland dies 2-18, 176F3

MAURITANIA—*See also ARAB League, GATT, NONALIGNED Nations, OAU*
Luly deposed, Haidala named pres 1-4, 20G3

1976

MAURITIUS—*See also AFRICAN Development Bank, COMMONWEALTH of Nations, NONALIGNED Nations Movement, OAU*
Rupee linked to SDR 1-5, 104G2
Listed as 'free' nation 1-19, 20C3
At France-Africa summit 5-10—5-11, 355F2, A3
Govt workers strike 6-7—6-9, 543B3
Olympic withdrawal rptd 7-21, 528B3
Leftists win electns 12-20, 1013F1
MAUZE, Abby Rockefeller
Dies 5-27, 404B2
MAVALANKAR, P. G.
Scores rights curbs 1-5, 28E3
MAVROS, George
Backs US-Turkish pact protest 3-31, 259D2
Chrgs crime in MP death 5-2, 351F3
MAWICKE, David
Indicted 10-29, 886C3
MAXWELL-Hyslop, Robin
Govt wins ship natlzn ruling 5-27, 401G3 ★
MAY, Lee
AL batting ldr 10-4, 796C1, D1
MAYAGUEZ, S.S. (U.S. merchant ship)
GAO faults US '75 action 10-5, 749B2
MAYER, Jean
Named Tufts U pres 7-1, 504D2
MAYNARD, Robert C.
Scores Schorr 2-13, 151B1
Pres debate panelist 10-22, 800A1, B3
MAYORS, U.S.—*See also specific names*
Ford budget briefing 1-20, 40D1
US Conf dir attacks revenue sharing critics 3-2, 187F1
Natl Conf of Dem Mayors meets 4-1, 233C2
US Conf sues vs food stamp revisns 5-26, 434E3
US Conf meets, Carter addresses 6-26—7-1, 468A1, 493B1
US Conf challenges gas rate hike 7-28, wins refund 8-9, 635G2
Ford to poll GOP re vp 7-31, 564B1
Rizzo recall vote barred 9-30, 994D1
US Conf meets, seeks Carter commitmt 11-7—11-8, 845G2
Carter meets group in Atlanta 12-14, 937A3
MAYOTTE—*See COMORO Islands*
MAYS, Dr. Benjamin
Endorses Carter 4-13, 261C2
MAYSON, Cedric
Seized, Archbp of Canterbury asks release 11-25, 927C2
Release rptd 12-12, 1010F2
MAYTAG, Marquita M.
Amb to Nepal 2-21; confrmd 3-3, 186B2
MAZDA—*See TOYO Kogyo Ltd.*
MAZELLA, D. John
Indicted 6-2, 414D3
MAZEWSKI, Aloysius
On Ford remark re E Eur 10-7, 10-8, 762B3
MAZUROV, Kiril T.
Politburo named 3-5, 195C2
2d Kosygin aide named 9-2, 857B2
MAZZOLI, Rep. Romano L. (D, Ky.)
Reelected 11-2, 829E3
MBOKOU, Marie-Christiane
Named finance min 9-5, 924F2
MBOUMOUA, Eteki
Uganda-Kenya mediatn effort set 7-27, 548A3
M'BOW, Amadou-Mahtar
Unesco conf postponed 1-15, 36E2
Defends Latin press parley 7-18, 620B1
UNESCO feud compromise 11-29, 895F3 ★
McAFEE, Jerry
Named Gulf chrmn 1-15, 132B3
MCA Inc.—*See MUSIC Corporation of America*

1977

MAURITIUS—*See also COMMONWEALTH of Nations, NONALIGNED Nations Movement, OAU*
UN Assemb, Cncl member 4D1, E1
At France-Africa summit 4-20—4-21, 316F3
Qantas halts S Africa flights 9-20, 762C3
UN S Africa econ, permanent arms sanctns vetoed; apartheid res OKd 10-31, 851G2
MAURY County, Tenn.—*See TENNESSEE*
MAVREEN (book)
On best-seller list 3-6, 184G3
MAVROS, George
Early Greek electns planned 9-19, 728D2
Electn results 11-20, 11-23, 924E3, 925E1
Resigns as DCU head 11-27, 925C2
MAWICKE, David
Acquitted 11-1, 918A3
MAXWELL, Cedric
In NBA draft 6-10, 584B2
MAXWELL Air Force Base, Ala.—*See ALABAMA*
MAY, Rudy
Traded to Expos 12-7, 990D1
MAY, Scott
Named to NBA all-rookie team 5-16, 584F3
MAYER, Sandy
Apples win WTT title 8-27, 787E3
MAYER-Witt, Silke
Linked to Baader atty 11-18, 969A1
MAY 4th Coalition
Kent State suit dismissed 8-17, 820A3
MAYILA, Louis Gaston
Gabon tourism min 7-13, 772B1
MAYNES, C. William
Named State asst secy 1-21, 53D1
MAYORS, U.S.—*See also specific names*
US Conf scores Carter energy plan 5-18, 443E2
Electn results 11-8, 855F1, E2-E3
Cities League conf debates Admin plans 12-4, 12-7, 959C3
MAYOTTE—*See COMORO Islands*
MAYSER, Luis
Anti-Banzer plot foiled, rpts arrest 12-9, 1009F3
MAYTAG, Marquita M.
Replaced as amb to Nepal 5-25, 499F3
MAZARI, Sherbaz
Arrested 3-18, 223C1
MAZUROV, Kirill Trofimovich
Revolutn anniv fete photo 11-7, 865D2
MBFR—*See EUROPE—Force Reduction Talks*
M'BUMBA, Gen. Nathaniel
Vows Mobutu overthrow 4-8, 266B1
MCA Inc.
Coca-Cola Bottling of LA OKs NW takeover 10-17, 880B2
New Times acquired 11-10, 1004E3
Star Wars tops domestic rentals mark 11-19, 1021C3
McAFEE, Jerry
Denies Gulf withholds gas 2-23, 152G1
On paymts crackdown aftermath 2-28, 233E1
Gulf chrgd re uranium cartel 6-9, 479D3
McAULIFFE, Gen. D. P.
Defends Panama Canal pacts 9-27, 755B2
Sees Dem sens 11-11, 911F2
McAULIFFE, Eugene V.
Replaced as amb to Hungary 6-30, 626F2
McAULIFFE, Bishop Michael
On women in RC church 11-15, 906F2
McBAIN, Laurie
Moonstruck on best-seller list 3-6, 184G3; 4-3, 264B2
McBRIDE, Bake
Traded to Phillies 6-15, 644E2
McBRIDE, Lloyd
Leads union pres vote 2-8, Sadlowski files protest 2-18, 130B3
On steel contract 4-9, 273F2
Backs steel import curbs 10-13, 775A3
US ends union vote probe 11-11, 899A3

1978

MAURITIUS—*See also COMMONWEALTH of Nations, GATT, NONALIGNED Nations Movement, OAU*
IMF standby purchase OKd 2-27, 333D3
Spinks-Ali rematch plan protested, site chngd 3-8, 3-9, 212A2
Spinks-Ali US rematch signed 4-11, 378E3
UN Cncl, Assemb member 713A3, C3
MAURY, Dorius
PNG confrms detentn 2-27, 192D3
MAURY County, Tenn.—*See TENNESSEE*
MAVROS, George
Scores US on Turkey arms embargo end 4-2, 277B1
Quits DCU 4-11, 374A1
MAVROULES, Mayor Nicholas (Peabody, Mass.)
Wins US House primary 9-19, 736B3
Elected 11-7, 847C3, 851C1
MAXACULI, Gregory
Black-mkt uranium sale bid probed 3-19, 242E2, G2
MAXWELL, Neal A.
Affirms homemaker role for women 4-1, 907E2
MAXWELL House—*See GENERAL Foods Corp.*
MAY, Deborah
Once in a Lifetime opens 6-15, 887C2
MAY, Elaine
Heaven Can Wait released 6-27, 619D2
California Suite released 12-21, 1030E2
MAYAGUEZ, S. S. (U.S. merchant ship)
Hanoi cites '75 seizure 4-7, 278B1
MAYER, Jerry
Taudshow opens 3-24, 887D3
MAYER, Sandy
Wins St Louis WCT 2-12, 419A1
Wimbledon results 7-8, 539E3
MAYER, Timothy S.
Tennis Game opens 11-5, 1031A3
MAYER-Witt, Silke
Rptd in Colombia 2-18, 147C3
MAYES, Wendell
Go Tell Spartans released 9-23, 970E1
MAYET, Juby
Arrested 5-29, 456E1
Rptd freed, banned 12-19, 989C2
MAYNARD, Clement
In Bahamas Cabt com on investmt 3-6, 194A2
MAYNARD, Robert
Scores media racism 4-7, 419F3
MAYO Clinic (Rochester, Minn.)
Alvarez dies 6-18, 540D2
MAYORS (U.S.)
Carter unveils urban-aid plan 3-27, reactn 3-27—3-30, 217C2-218D1
US Conf hears Kreps 6-21, 526D1
Election results 11-7, 848A2
Carter addresses Natl League of Cities 11-27, support pledged 11-29, 914F2, F3
Carter sees 8 urban ldrs on budget 12-20, 980C2
MAYRON, Melanie
Girlfriends released 8-16, 970D1
MAYS, Danny H.
Chrgd in '77 Webster death cover-up 6-3, 991G2
MAYTAG, Lewis
Eastern seeks Natl merger 12-11, 1007C3
MAZUROV, Kirill Trofimovich
Quits USSR Politburo 11-27, 924D3
MAZURSKY, Paul
Unmarried Woman released 3-4, 620B1
MAZZOLI, Rep. Romano L. (D, Ky.)
Reelected 11-7, 850E4
MBFR—*See EUROPE—Force Reduction Talks*
MBOUMOUA, William Eteki
Kodjo replaces in OAU post 7-22, 561D2
M'BOW, Amadou Mehta
UNESCO backs free press 11-22, 931D1
MBOYA, Tom (d. 1969)
Kenyatta dies 8-22, 639B2
McADAMS v. McSurely
Cong immunity case refused by Sup Ct 6-26, 566D2
McADOO, Bob
NBA scoring ldr 4-9, 271D2
MCA Inc.
Star Wars world rental mark rptd 8-2, 672B1
New Times—*See separate listing*
McALLISTER, Miller
Killed 4-22; suspect kills self 5-10, 373D2, F2
Police link suspect, IRA 5-11, 474G2
McANUFF, Des
Gimme Shelter opens 12-10, 1031G1
McARTHUR, Duncan R. B.
Canada metric changes set 1-16, 89B1
McAULIFFE, Maj. Gen. Dennis
Sees DR pres-elect 8-15; at inaugural 8-16, 648A2
Presses Somoza on plebiscite 12-21, 1018G2
McBRIDE, Lloyd
Backs LTV Youngstown rescue 4-10, 6-21, 493C1
USW sues 9 foundatns 4-19, 310A1
On wage, inflatn curbs 9-17, 9-20, 715F1
USW bans outside electn aid 9-21, 737F2
McCAGG, David
Sets 400-m freestyle relay mark 8-22, 780C2

1979

MAURITIUS—*See also COMMONWEALTH of Nations, GATT, NONALIGNED Nations Movement, OAU*
Freedom House lists as partly free 12G3
UN membership listed 695G2
MAUTI, Rich
NFL '78 kick return ldr 1-6, 80G2
MAUZE, Abby Rockefeller (1904-76)
Brother dies 1-26, 104A2
MAX, Werner
Secy's E Ger defectn rptd 3-12, 180B3
MAX Havelaar (film)
Released 1-20, 174A3
MAXWELL, Cedric (Cornbread)
NBA field-goal ldr 4-8, 290E2, A3
MAXWELL, Paul
Killed by IRA 8-27, 641B1
MAXWELL Air Force Base, Ala.—*See ALABAMA*
MAY, Georges
Named Yale provost 5-4, 392D2
MAY, Milt
Signs with Giants 12-12, 1002A1
MAY, Rudy
Signs with Yankees 11-8, 1001F3
MAYER, Gene
Loses Houston WCT 4-22, 391C3
Wins Colonge Grand Prix 11-4, loses Stockholm Open 11-13, 1003F3, G3
MAYER, William
Cited in H-bomb letter 9-16, 9-18, 714E1
MAYNARD, Andrew
On shah's presence in Bahamas 5-30, 408F1
MAYO, Paula
Angels win WBL title 5-2, 507D1
MAYO Clinic (Rochester, Minn.)
Stroke study finds decline 2-28, 195C2
Powell urological surgery rptd 8-31, 744G3
MAYORGA Quiroz, Roman
Joins El Salvador junta 10-17, 790F2
Announces junta program 10-18, 813C1
MAYORS (U.S.)
US Conf holds conv, gets new pres; Carter policies backed 6-9—6-13, 439F2-440D1
Carter sees ldrs 7-6—7-11, 513F2
Landrieu, Goldschmidt in Carter Cabt 7-27, 577B1, E1
MAYRAND, Yves
Cossette-Trudels sentenced 8-7, 632C3
Dismisses chrgs vs Campbell, Gordon 10-15, 812D2
Sentncs Lanctot 11-8, 872E1
MAYS, Willie
Inducted into Baseball HOF 8-5, 618C3
Yastrzemski gets 3000th hit 9-12, 1002D3
To cut baseball ties 10-29, 1002G3
MAYS Inc., J. W.
Shulman convctd of IRS bribe 3-26, 239E3
MAY 6 Coalition
DC A-protest draws 65,000 5-6, Carter rejcts plant closings 5-7, 343A3-344C1
MAZANKOWSKI, Donald
Canada transport min 6-4, 423F3
Sets bilingual air control 8-21, 650E3
Vows chem transport legis 11-13, 872B1
MAZDOORYAR, Maj. Sherjan
Out as Afghan frontier min 9-14; move sparks fighting 9-14—9-15; 695D3, 696B1
MAZE, Paul
Dies 9-17, 756G2
MAZIBUKO, Seth
Sentenced 5-11, 373F1
MAZIN, Stan
Festival opens 5-7, 711A3
MAZURSKY, Paul
Man, Woman & Bank released 9-28, 820A2
MAZZANTI, Giorgio
Nominated ENI head 1-8, 21A1
Suspended pending payoffs probe 12-7, 995E3
MAZZEI, Julio
Named Cosmos tech dir 6-5, 655B2
MAZZILLI, Lee
NL wins All-Star Game 7-17, 569C1, A2
NL batting ldr 9-30, 955E2
MBFR—*See EUROPE–Force Reduction Talks*
MBOI, Ben
Rpts tidal wave deaths 7-22, 638F3
MCA Inc.
Sony video recorder copyright trial opens 1-22, 120E2
McADOO, Bob
Traded to Celtics 2-12, 507D2
NBA scoring ldr 4-8, 290D2
McAFEE, Jerry
Meets with Carter 5-31, 418D1
Records unit staff firings cited 8-10, 618E1
IBM joint video disk venture set 9-5, 756E1
Video recorder use upheld 10-2, 858F2
'Jaws' viewed on TV by 80 mln 11-4, 1006F3
Lugosi heirs publicity right denied 12-3, 1005F2

1980

MAURITIUS—*See also COMMONWEALTH of Nations, GATT, NONALIGNED Nations, OAU*
OAU demands return of Diego Garcia 7-1—7-4, 509G1
MAURY-Laribiere, Michel
Kidnaped 6-28, rescued 7-9, 522E1
MAVI, Joseph
Arrested in Johannesburg municipal strike 8-1, 690A2
MAVROS, George
Forms Center Party 11-16, 901E3
MAVROULES, Rep. Nicholas (D, Mass.)
Reelected 11-4, 843C1
MAX Perkins: Editor of Genius (book)
Wins Amer Book Award 5-1, 692C2
MAXWELL, Cedric (Cornbread)
NBA field-goal ldr 3-30, 278C3, F3
MAXWELL, David O.
Named Fannie Mae pres 9-24, 960A1
MAXWELL, Judge Robert
Orders W Va coal miners strike halt 2-26, rules miners in contempt 2-29, 170B1
MAXWELL, Ronald F.
Little Darlings released 3-28, 416C3
MAY, Lee
Panelist in pres TV debate 9-21, 721C3
MAY, Mark
Wins Outland Trophy 11-20, 999G2
MAY, Rudy
AL pitching ldr 10-6, 926F3
Royals win AL pennant 10-10, 796A1
MAY, William F.
To become NYU business school dean 3-18, 224E3
MAYAGUEZ S.S. (U.S. merchant ship)
US mil computer system failure rptd 3-10, 210D2
MAYBANK, Burnet R. (1899-1954)
Addabbo amendmt adopted by House 9-16, 741E3*
MAYEKAWA, Haruo
On yen rescue plan 3-5, 173B3
MAYER, Gene
Wins Denver Grand Prix 2-24, Kramer Open 4-20; loses Rotterdam WCT 3-16, 607F2, G2, B3
Wimbledon results 7-4—7-6, 606A2
Loses US Pro Outdoor 7-20, wins Western Open 8-17, 691G2, C3
Loses London Gen Prix 11-16, 947D2
MAYER, Jerry
You Know Al opens 11-13, 892G3
MAYER, Sandy
Loses Surrey Grass Cts tourn 6-21, 607E3
MAYO, T. Sgt. Joel C.
Killed in Iran rescue mission 4-24, 321F2
MAYO Clinic (Rochester, Minn.)
FDA OKs Laetrile testing 1-3, 23E2
MAYORGA Quiroz, Roman
Resigns 1-3, 6B2
Junta replacemt named 1-9, 19G3
MAYORS (U.S.)
US Conf dir scores Carter revised budget 3-31, 244F1
Conf presses Carter on Haitian refugee plight 5-7, 340C1
NAACP warns re blacks' despair 5-29, 460A2
US Conf visited by Reagan 6-8, Anderson 6-9, Carter 6-10; Kennedy date switch denied 6-10, 438E2-G3
MAZEY, Emil
Replaced as UAW secy-treas 6-4, 457A2
MAZIN, Viktor
Wins Olympic medal 7-22, 624E2
MAZOROV, Judge Platon D.
World Ct demands Iran free US hostages 5-24, 393B1
MAZZANTI, Giorgio
Grandhi named ENI head 5-6, 408G3
MBFR—*See MUTUAL and Balanced Force Reduction*
MCA Inc.
CBS, RCA sign video disk pact 1-10, 120G1
'Bionic' trademark case declined by Sup Ct 3-31, 291D3
In Getty Oil pay-TV film venture 4-22, Justice Dept to probe 4-24, 376E2
Pay-TV film plan draws trust suit 8-4, 639F3
Universal City Studios Inc.
McCarthy TV film libel case refused by Sup Ct 12-1, 918D2

1976

McALESTER (O.) Democrat (newspaper)
Carter endorsement rptd 10-30, 831B3
McALPIN, Clovis
Figueres sued in NY 9-22, 1000B3
McARTHUR, Sir Malcolm
Sovt meat deal set 8-3, 587C2
McAULIFFE, Eugene V.
Defense asst secy 3-4; confrmd 5-3, 412G1
McBRIDE, Bake
NL batting ldr 10-4, 795E3, F3
McBRIDE, Katherine E.
Dies 6-3, 484F3
McBRIDE, Lloyd
Abel backs USW slate 9-1, 669D3
McBRIDE, Mary Margaret (Martha Deane)
Dies 4-7, 272F3
McCALL, C. W.
Convoy on best-selling list 1-28, 104G3
McCANN, Thomas P.
'United Fruit' publshd 10-21, 844E3
McCARTHY, Eugene J(oseph)
Vs Common Cause campaign code 1-9, 22G3
Sup Ct rules on campaign law 1-30, 86F1
Names running mate 2-5, 95B1
Primary precedent cited 231G3
Threatens suit re debates 9-2, 644F1
Pres debate suit rejected 9-17, 703E2
Suit re 3d pres debate cited 765G3
Gallup poll results 10-21, 804B3
NM press endorsemt rptd 10-30, 827E3
Loses pres electn 11-2, 818E2
Final pres vote tally 12-18, 979B2
McCARTHY, Joseph (1908-57)
Millet dies 1-1, 56F3
McCAULL, Phillip
Named in grain fraud 3-11, 247D3 ★
Sentenced 11-17, 990A3
McCHESNEY, Ian
Captured 5-2; freed 10-2, 1002B2
McCLAINE, Mary B.
Defeated 11-2, 823C1
McCLINTOCK, Robert M.
Dies 11-2, 970E2
McCLORY, Rep. Robert (R, Ill.)
Scores House com intelligence rpt 2-3, 150C2
Reelected 11-2, 829G2
McCLOSKEY, Michael
Backs Ford park plan 9-1, 644C3
Sees Carter 12-16, 937C2
McCLOSKEY Jr., Rep. Paul N. (R, Calif.)
On N Viet PW talks 2-1, 103E1
'72 Nixon spending rptd 4-25, 688A2
Reelected 11-2, 829B1
McCLOY, John J.
Gulf Oil paymts rpt detailed 133E1
McCLURE, Sen. James A. (R, Ida.)
GOP conv vp vote table 8-19, 599F3
McCLURE, Pvt. Lynn E.
Dies 3-13; Marines sued 4-11, ct-martials ordrd 4-28, 378F1
Marine probe continues 5-25—6-9, 435F2-C3
Court-martial starts 6-14, 435D3
Bronson acquitted 6-28, 493B2
Walraff convicted 7-19, 586E3
Final charges 8-18, 942B2
New damage suit rptd 10-8, 942E2
McCLUSKEY, Harold
Injured 8-30, 670E3
McCOLLISTER, John Y.
Loses electn 11-2, 823C3
McCORMACK, Ellen
Mass, Vt primary results 3-2, 165B1, A2
Fed fund total listed 3-4, 180C3
Wins one Wis delegate 4-6, 245D1
Pa primary results 4-27, 304F3
Gets 5% of vote in Ind 5-4, 323G1
Neb, Conn vote results 5-11, 342G1, F3
Md primary results 5-18, 357G1
FEC funds released 5-21, 391E3
Ky, Tenn, Ore vote results 5-25, 374C2-E2, E3
SD, RI vote results 6-1, 390B1, C2, D2
Calif, NJ vote results 6-8, 409B1
FEC denies fed funds 6-23, total rptd 7-1, 490F3, 491B1
Nominated at conv, gets 22 votes 7-14, 505G1, 506E1, 507A2
Dem conv pres vote, table 7-14, 507A3
Campaign costs rptd 8-28, 688G3
FEC certificatn total rptd 12-31, 979G2
McCORMACK, Mike
Named as Bengals asst coach 1-1, 31D2
McCORMACK, Rep. Mike (D, Wash.)
Reelected 11-2, 831A2
McCOY, George Braidwood (The Real)
Dies 12-22, 1015A2
McCOY, Jack
Loses electn 11-2, 824F3
McCOY, Van
Wins Grammy 2-28, 460B3

1977

McCAMLEY, Graham
On sheep disease in North 11-15, 881F3
McCARROLL, Marion C. (Beatrice Fairfax)
Dies 8-4, 696D3
McCARTHY, Archbishop Edward A.
Successor installed 3-22, 375G2
McCARTHY, Eugene J(oseph)
Sup Ct declines pres debate suit review 4-4, 341D3
Lawyer fee case declined 12-5, 939B1
McCARTHY, Joseph R(aymond) (1908-57)
William Gropper dies 1-6, 84C3
Cited re attacks vs Sorensen 1-17, 35D2
McCLANAHAN, Brent
Raiders wins Super Bowl 1-9, 24D3
McCLEARY, Joel
Named Dem Party treas 1-21, 53B2
McCLELLAN, Sen. John L(ittle) (D, Ark.)
'76 spec interest gifts rptd 1-15, 128F3
Votes vs Marshall 1-26, 52B3
Dies 11-27, 952A3
Carter pays tribute 11-30, 914A2
Hodges fills Sen seat 12-10, 1005A3
McCLORY, Rep. Robert (R, Ill.)
On Nixon-Frost interview 5-5, 367F3
McCLOSKEY Jr., Rep. Paul N. (R, Calif.)
Porpoise kill limit set 6-11, 442F3
Notes GAO rpt in cargo preference debate 7-29, 720A1
Shipping rebate curb rejctd 10-31, 856C2
McCLURE, Don
Killed 3-27, 328F1
McCLURE, Sen. James A. (R, Idaho)
Sues vs Linowitz in Panama Canal talks 3-16, 379E1
Environmt cncl nominatn deferred 10-17, 800G1
McCOMB, Justice Marshall F.
Forced to retire 5-2, 388B2
McCONE, John A.
Suits vs US spying rptd 5-22, 422C3
McCONN, Jim
Elected Houston mayor 11-22, 900B3
McCORD, Gary
2d in Milwaukee Open 7-3, 676G1
McCOVEY, Willie
Wins Hutch Award; grand-slam homer mark cited 11-14, 990E2
McCREE Jr., Wade Hampton
Cited as US solicitor gen choice 1-11—1-18, 34D2
Named solicitor gen 2-16, confrmd 3-4, 211F1
Argues Bakke case 10-12, Sup Ct orders more briefs 10-17, 834F3, 835A1, F1
McCULLOCH, Robert
Dies 2-25, 164C3
McCULLOCH Oil Corp.
Land developer convicted 2-22, 156F1
Robert McCulloch dies 2-25, 164C3
McCULLOCH Properties, Inc.—*See McCULLOCH Oil Corp.*
McCULLOUGH, Colleen
Paperback record sum rptd 3-1, 356A2
Thorn Birds on best-seller list 6-4, 452A2; 7-3, 548D3; 8-14, 643F1; 9-4, 712C3; 10-2, 808C3; 11-6, 872C3; 12-4, 1021F2
McCULLOUGH, Mike
2d in Tournament Players 3-20, 311D2
McCULLOUGH, William J.
Stirs US Open racial dispute 9-8, 787F2

1978

McCALL, C. W.
Convoy released 6-28, 619C1
McCALL, Larry
Traded to Rangers 11-10, 1026B1
McCALL, Reese
In NFL draft 5-2, 336G2
McCALL, Thomas
Loses primary for Oregon gov 5-23, 406F2
McCALL'S (magazine)
Joan Kennedy interview publshd 7-20, 844F2
McCANN, Dan
Film wins Oscar 4-3, 315D3
McCARDELL, Archie R.
Heads '77 top-paid execs list 5-15, 364E3, 365B1
McCARTHY, Charlie
Edgar Bergen dies 9-30, 777E3
McCARTHY, Joseph R(aymond) (1908-57)
John Butler dies 3-16, 252E2
Judge Youngdahl dies 6-21, 540G3
Called drug addict 11-19, 943C2
McCARTHY, Joseph V. (Marse Joe)
Dies 1-14, 96G2
McCARTNEY, Paul
Sgt Pepper's released 7-21, 970B3
McCAULEY, Don
NFL '77 touchdown, receiving ldr 1-1, 56B2, C2
McCLEAN, Ronald A.
Japan ct backs visa denial 10-4, 764F3
McCLEERY, Donald
Denies RCMP informer in '70 Cross kidnap 11-6, 880E1
McCLELLAN, Irina Astakhova
Detained 5-20, US protests 5-21, 360B1
McCLELLAN, John L(ittle) (1896-1977)
Ark Sen primary results 5-30, 426B2
Park gift rptd by Sen ethics com 6-19, 527D2
Immunity case refused by Sup Ct 6-26, 566E2
McCLELLAND, Robert
On addict treatment law 12-18, 1013C3
McCLORY, Rep. Robert (R, Ill.)
Vs curbs on natl security taps 9-7, 697C1, E1
Reelected 11-7, 850E3
McCLOSKEY Jr., Rep. Paul N. (R, Calif.)
US chrgs Israeli use of cluster bombs in Leb 4-7, 257D1
Rpts Israel agrmt on cluster bombs 5-12, 358G2
Reelected 11-7, 850E1
McCLURE, Sen. James A. (R, Idaho)
Votes vs Panama Canal neutrality pact 3-16, 177G2
Votes vs 2d Canal pact 4-18, 273B1
Unopposed in primary 8-8, 625E3
Gas plan vote, A-breeder vow linked 8-23—8-26, 677G3-678E1
Reelected 11-7, 848F1, 856C1
Gets low ADA rating 12-17, 981E2
McCOLLUM, Schact V.
McDermott payoffs cited 2-22, 142G2-A3
McCOMB (Miss.) Enterprise-Journal
John Emmerich dies 8-17, 708F2
McCORKLE Jr., William C.
1-house veto case review barred 1-9, 13B1
McCORKLE v. U.S.
'73 pay raise veto review barred 1-9, 13A1
McCORMACK, Rep. Mike (D, Wash.)
Vs A-breeder compromise 3-17, 242F1
Reelected 11-7, 852B4
McCORMICK, Brooks
Scores Crawford arrest 6-16, 476E2
McCOURT, Dale
NHL compensatn clause ruled illegal 9-18, 990D3
McCOVEY, Willie
Hits 500th home 6-30, 560A1
McCOY, Rev. Alan
Asks US oust Nicaragua pres 11-8, 883E3
McCOY, Timothy (Tim) John Fitzgerald
Dies 1-29, 96G2
McCRACKEN, Paul
On business spending cautn 9-18, 717B1
McCRAY, Ivey
Run'ers' opens 5-3, 887A3
McCREE, Wade
Carter, Bell cleared on Marston ouster 1-24, 62D2
McCULLEY, Pete
Named 49ers coach 1-11, 171D2
Fired as 49ers coach 10-31, 1024A3
McCULLOUGH, Colleen
Thorn Birds on best-seller list 1-8, 24D3; 2-5, 116B3; 3-5, 195D3; 4-2, 272A3; 4-30, 356F1; 6-4, 460A3; 7-2, 579D3; 8-6, 620B2; 10-9, 800C3; 11-6, 888B1; 12-3, 971C1
McCULLOUGH, David
Wins Natl Book Award 4-10, 315D2
McCULLOUGH, Merrell
Denies black activists role in King plot 11-17, 938E2

1979

McALLISTER, Susie
2d in United Va Bank Classic 10-14, 970F1
McANUFF, Des
Leave It to Beaver opens 4-3, 712B1
Holeville opens 12-4, 956B3
McAULIFFE, Lt. Gen. Dennis P.
Testifies on Panama role in Nicaragua unrest 6-20, 481B2
Assumes Panama Canal Comm post 10-1, 754D1
Panama chrgs US treaties violatn 12-6, 939E1
McAVOY, Edward J.
Blames Munson death on pilot error 9-16, 1002F3
McBAIN, Laurie
Tears of Gold on best-seller list 5-6, 356E2; 6-3, 432C2
McBRAYER, Terry
Loses primary for Ky gov 5-29, 420D1
McBRIDE, Bake
NL batting ldr 9-30, 955F2
McBRIDE, Lloyd
Named to 3 Mile I probe 4-11, 275C1
McCAIN, Frances Lee
Real Life released 3-1, 174E3
McCALL, Nellie
Tellico Dam completed 11-29, 990C1
McCALL, Penelope
Frampton suit dismissed 4-17, 289D2
McCANDLESS (U.S. aircraft carrier)
Navy fire probe rptd 7-5, 519G3
McCARDELL, Archie R.
On '78 top-paid execs list 5-14, 347E3
McCARTHY, Eugene Joseph
Backs draft registration 11-13, 868F2
McCARTHY, Joseph R(aymond) (1908-57)
Ex-Sen Cain dies 3-3, 272B2
Widow dies 12-15, 1008C3
McCAUGHEY, William
Wins Oscar 4-9, 336B2
McCLAIN, Samuel
Sentncd in GSA kickback scandal 3-24, 3-26, 367G2
McCLAUGHRY, John
Vs neighborhoods panel rpt 3-15, 208B3
McCLERNON, James
On VW US plant plans 7-26, 663E3
McCLOSKEY Jr., Rep. Paul N. (R, Calif.)
H-bomb letter published 9-16, 9-18, 713C2; text of letter 714D1-717E3
On '70 Black Panther murder convictn 9-27, 886F2
McCLURE, James
New Jerusalem opens 2-15, 712G1
McCLURE, Sen. James A. (R, Idaho)
Votes vs Talmadge denunciatn 10-10, 769G1
McCLUSKER, Marilyn
Dies 10-2, 860G2
McCOMAS, Walter Donald
Indicted in arms plot 5-14, 386F3
McCOMIE, Valerie
Elected OAS asst secy gen 10-24, 824E2
McCONN, Mayor Jim (Houston, Tex.)
Faces runoff 11-6, 846D3
Reelected 11-20, 904E3
McCONNELL, Maj. Bernd
S Africa ousts as spy 4-12, 286F3
McCONNELL, Lorne
Defends Lake Huron A-plant 5-3, 352D3
McCOURT, Dale
NHL reserve clause upheld 5-22, 448F1
McCOY, Frank
Wins libel case 4-18, shares award 4-19, 334C2
McCOY, Van
Dies 7-6, 588B3
McCOY Elkhorn Coal Corp.—*See under GENERAL Energy Corp.*
McCREADIE, Eddie
Fired as Rogues coach 5-15, 1004D2
McCRORY, Charles David
Testimony in Davis kill-for-hire trial rptd 1-22, 64E3
Davis acquitted 11-9, 890E2
McCULLUM, Judge Donald
Dismisses chrgs in Newton murder case 9-27, 818C3
McCUMBER, Mark
Wins Doral Open 3-18, 587G1

1980

MCATEER, Edward E.
Political role profiled 7-11—9-15, 819G1
MCBRIDE, Bake
NL batting ldr 10-6, 926D2, E2
Phillies win NL pennant 10-12, 796D1, F1
In World Series 10-14—10-21, 811G2-812G3
MCBRIDE, Lloyd
Lauds Va shipyd pact 3-28, 251F2
MCBRIDE, Richard L.
Marubeni, Hitachi units convicted 11-5, 957C3
MCBRIDE v. Rockefeller Family Fund
Case refused by Sup Ct 3-31, 291C3
MCCALLUM, David
Watcher in the Woods released 4-16, 416G3
MCCANN, Elizabeth I.
Morning's at Seven opens 4-10, 392E3
Home opens 5-7, 392C3
MCCARRON, Chris
Splendid Girl sets speed mark 5-14, 447D3
Named top jockey; earnings cited 12-17, 1002C2
MCCARTER, James T.
Sentenced for murder 2-27, 238D3
MCCARTHY, Eugene Joseph
Brown quits pres race 4-1, 246D3
Endorses Reagan 10-23, 802D2
MCCARTHY, John
Vs Anderson fed funding 9-4, 665F2
MCCARTHY, Joseph Raymond (1908-57)
Morris Rubin dies 8-8, 676F2
TV film libel case refused by Sup Ct 12-1, 918D2
Army-McCarthy hearings Sen counsel dies 12-26, 1004C2
MCCARTHY, Mary
Hellman sues 2-15, 199E2
MCCARTHY v. McCarthy
Case accepted by Sup Ct 10-20, 807A3
MCCARTNEY, Paul
Arrested in Japan 1-16, deported 2-26, 200E2
NY record co indicted 2-28, 237D3
Coming Up on best-seller list 6-4, 448E3; 7-9, 568E3
McCartney II on best-seller list 7-9, 568F3
On Lennon slaying 12-9, 934A2, B3
MCCARTNEY II (recording)
On best-seller list 7-9, 568F3
MCCARTY, Mary
Dies 4-5, 360D2
MCCLANAHAN, Rob
US Olympic hockey team beats Sovts 2-22, wins gold medal 2-24, 155B2, C2
MCCLEAN, Robert
Dies 12-5, 1004F2
MCCLELLAND, Robert
Scores budget, energy plan 10-30, 858D3
Bars Canada fed gas tax paymt 12-20, 992A1
MCCLENDON, Charlie
Rein presumed dead 1-11, Stovall replaces as LSU football coach 1-12, 175B3
MCCLORY, Rep. Robert (R, Ill.)
Reelected 11-4, 842E3
McCLOSKEY Jr., Rep. Paul N. (R, Calif.)
Wilson reprimand motn rejctd 6-10, 438A2
Reelected 11-4, 842E1
MCCLOSKEY, Robert
Signs Greek cooperatn pact 4-22, 352F2
McCLURE, Sen. James A. (R, Idaho)
Supports Symms electn 11-4, 851F3
Named Sen GOP conf chrmn 12-2, 915E2
MCCOLLUM, Bill
Fla US Sen primary runoff set 9-9, 700B2
Wins runoff 10-7, 807D3
Elected to US House 11-4, 842F2, 849E2
MCCOLOUGH, C. Peter
Urges mandatory pensns 5-23, 404G1
MCCORMACK, John W.
Dies 11-22, 928G2
MCCORMACK, Mike
Hired as Colts coach 1-16, 413B1
MCCORMACK, Rep. Mike (D, Wash.)
Loses reelectn 11-4, 852C3
MCCORMICK, Harold (Mack)
Loses US House electn 11-4, 851D3
MCCORMICK & Co. Inc.
Sandoz takeover offer rejctd 3-18, 386C1
MCCORQUODALE, Timothy
Escapes prison 7-28, recaptured 7-30, 654F1
MCCOVEY, Willie
Sets retiremt 6-22, 637B1
MCCOY, Andre
Killed in Polish jet crash 3-14, 214A1
MCCOY, Sheila
Marries cellmate's father 3-26, 638G3
MCCREE, Wade H.
Abortn funding cases argued in Sup Ct 4-21, 306D2
Argues Nixon taps case in Sup Ct 12-8, 937C2
MCCRIMMON, Don
Scores Ottawa Indian plan 10-4, 828A2
MCCULLOCH, William Moore
Dies 2-22, 176E2
MCCULLOUGH, James
Convicted 10-28, sentncd 12-11, 990A1
MCCUNE Jr., William J.
Named Polaroid chief exec officer 3-7, 225B1
MCCURDY, Dave
In Okla US House primary; runoff set 8-26, 683B1
Wins runoff 9-16, 724B3
Elected to US House 11-4, 844A1, 850C1

1976

McCUTCHEN, Glyn
Sentencd 7-21, 544D1
McCUTCHEN Jr., Ned
Sentenced 7-21, 544D1
McDADE, Rep. Joseph Michael (R, Pa.)
Reelected 11-2, 830E3
McDEVITT, Ruth
Dies 5-27, 524B3
McDONALD, Henry
Dies 6-12, 524B3
McDONALD, Jack
Loses primary for gov 6-1, 411G1
McDONALD, Rep. Lawrence P. (D, Ga.)
Reelected 11-2, 829D2
McDONNELL, Sam
Defeated 11-2, 822G3
McDONNELL Douglas Corp.
'75 arms sales listed 2-6, 147B2
Japan Lockheed probe cites 3-1, 190D3
Bars boycott compliance 3-18, 747B2
SEC lists paymts 5-12, 728C2
French jet accord set 8-12, 588D3
Japan Lockheed indictmts cite 8-16, 624C2
'74 Iran sale probed 9-26, 979G3
Top '76 defns contractor 12-21, 961G2, A3
McEWEN, Rep. Robert Cameron (R, N.Y.)
Reelected 11-2, 830C2
McFALL, Rep. John J. (D, Calif.)
Reelected 11-2, 829B1
Admits S Korea paymts 11-4, 11-25, 900C1
Loses majority whip post, S Korea gifts cited 12-6, 919B1, A2
Brademas named whip 12-8, 981E1
McGANN, Most Rev. John R.
Named bishop 5-4, 424B1

1977

McDADE, Dr. Joseph E.
Rpts Legion disease bacteria 1-18, 81E1
McDANIEL, Judge Joseph
Rules in Greenspun suit 6-3, 472E2
McDERMOTT & Co., Inc., J. Ray
Rpts payoffs 4-12, 503A3
Wins United Tech bidding war, acquires Babcock 8-25, 666E3
Babcock takeover cited in table 880F1
To buy remaining Babcock shares 12-8, 1004C2
Babcock purchase cited 12-11, 1004E2
McDONALD, David
RCMP abuses rptd 11-9—11-14, 882C1, F1, A2
Plans Army probe 11-13, 882E2
Opens royal comm RCMP probe 12-6, 965C1
McDONALD, Lanny
NHL season ldr 4-3, 262F3
McDONALD'S Corp.
'Glasses to Go' promotn halted 7-8, 7-17; sues Mass agency 7-12, 559F3
McDONNELL Douglas Corp.
Japan Lockheed trial opens 1-27, 83C2
Concorde landings backed 3-10, 213F1
'74 DC-10 crash settlement 4-14, 312C1
Test pilot age bias case refused 11-28, 919D2
McDONOUGH, James
On Chicago train crash 1-5, 104A3
McDONOUGH v. Morgan
Sup Ct bars review 1-10, 57D1
McENROE, John
Borg wins Wimbledon 7-2, 548E1
McEVOY, Peter
US wins Walker Cup 8-27, 951G1
McFADDEN, Mary
'77 fall fashions rptd 6-6, 1022F1
McFALL, Rep. John (D, Calif.)
Cited in Park indictmt 9-6, 688D1

1978

McCUTCHEON, Lawrence
NFL '77 touchdown, rushing ldr 1-1, 56E2, E3
McDADE, Rep. Joseph Michael (R, Pa.)
Reelected 11-7, 852C1
McDANIEL, Paul A.
Tenn clergy pub office ban upset by Sup Ct 4-19, 309D1
McDANIEL v. Paty
Tenn clergy pub office ban upset by Sup Ct 4-19, 309D1
McDERMOTT, Dennis
Elected Canada CLC pres 4-6, 266C2
Postal union scores 4-7, 266C2
Backs Quebec labor law 7-21, 571E3
McDERMOTT & Co., J. Ray
Pleads guilty, fined 2-22, 142E2-G3
United Tech takeover battle for Babcock cited 9-25, 896G1
McDONALD, David
RCMP '74 break-in bared 1-11, 35D2
APLQ '72 raid purpose disputed 1-13, 35E2
Tap cover-ups bared 4-11, warrantless break-ins revealed 4-18, 311F3-312A1
RCMP documts rptd destroyed 4-26, 328E2
RCMP probe asks Cabt papers 10-13, 837G1
McDONALD, Rep. Lawrence P. (D, Ga.)
Faces primary runoff 8-8, 625B3
Wins primary runoff 8-29, 683E1
Reelected 11-7, 850B3
McDONALD'S Corp.
Glasses rptd safe 1-31, 348B1
Earthworm rumor impact rptd 11-16, 942F1
McDONNELL, Mary
Buried Child opens 11-6, 1031B1
McDONNELL, William
Testifies at Korea lobbying hearing 3-21, 203B3
McDONNELL Douglas Corp.
Workers strike 1-13—4-16, 284E2
6 in Japan tied to Lockheed scandal 1-30, 72F3
Top '77 defense contractor 3-28, 224D2
Pan Am buys Lockheed jets 4-4, 264E2
Cited as Saudi F-15 contractor 4-10, 257B2
Data 100 purchase planned 5-18, 404F1
Settles FTC chrgs re paymts 8-18, 643C1
Nakasone cited in Lockheed case 10-26, 838G3
SEC sues re paymts 12-14, suit setld 12-15, 982D2
McELROY, Hal
Last Wave released 12-18, 1030B3
McENROE, John
Wins NCAA tennis title 5-29, 419D2
US Open results 9-10, 707C1
Wins Stockholm Open 11-17, Benson & Hedges tourn 11-19, 1027C2
US wins Davis Cup 12-10, 1026D3
McENTEE, Patrick
Kidnaped, slain 6-25, 630G2
IRA scores RC primate 7-1, 630A2
McEWEN, Rep. Robert Cameron (R, N.Y.)
Reelected 11-7, 851G3
McFADDEN, Mary
'78 high chic fashion rptd 8-4—8-11, 10-27—11-3, 1029F2
McFALL, Byron
KKK informant probed 7-12, 528A2
McFALL, Rep. John J. (D, Calif.)
Cited for misconduct by ethics com re Park gift 7-13, 527B1
Reprimanded in Korean scandal 10-13, 831D3
Loses reelectn 11-7, 846D2, 856B3
McFALL, Robert
Transplant order denied 7-26, 597F2
Dies 8-10, 708B3
McGAHN, Joseph L.
Scores NJ laetrile bill 1-10, 23D3

1979

McDERMOTT, John
Named ASL top rookie 9-11, 776E2
McDERMOTT & Co., J. Ray
Babcock and Wilcox Co.
3 Mile Island A-plant accident 3-28; safety in Rancho Seco, 6 other plants questnd 4-1—4-2, 241D2, 245E1, C3
3 Mile I errors, clean-up detailed; crisis declared over 4-4—4-9; NRC orders other plants inspected 4-5, OKs reactors 4-6, 259G2, 260A1, A3, C3, 261E3
3 Mile I NRC transcripts released 4-12, 275F3
Reactor flaw warning rptd 4-16, 275D1
NRC orders A-plants closed, 3 Mile I reaches shutdown 4-27, 321D3-322B2
Met Ed blamed for 3 Mile I accident 6-5, 518A3
NRC: 3 Mile I preventable 8-2, 609B2
McDONALD Jr., Alonzo L.
On GATT pact 4-12, 273D1
Named Carter asst 8-10, 608G2
McDONALD, David
Documts, ex-RCMP offcrs hold Cabt aware of illegalities 3-28—3-30, 253D2-E3
Allmand admits break-in knowledge 4-3—4-5, 311E2
McIlraith testifies 4-26, 329B2
Dare testifies on emb bugging, '72 APLQ break-in 7-4, 522F2, B3
McDONALD, David J.
Dies 8-8, 671G2
McDONALD, Dennis
Kidnaped 9-21, 729D2
Freed 11-7, 872F2
McDONALD'S Corp.
Kroc rpts record baseball fine, to give Padres operatn 8-24, 1003B1
McDONALD v. Santa Fe Trail Trans. Co.
Weber case ruling cites 6-27, 477D3
McDONNELL, James S.
Denies paymts chrg 11-9, 886B2
McDONNELL 3d, James S.
Indicted on paymts chrg 11-9, 886A2
McDONNELL Douglas Corp.
4 indicted in Japan bribe scandal 4-5, 5-15, 389F2
DC-10s grounded for inspectn 5-29, safety flaws rptd 5-30, 412C1
DC-10s grounded indefinitely, forgn flights banned; stock drops 6-6, 420E2, D3, 421A1
Chicago DC-10 crash rpt issued by FAA 7-10, findings disputed 7-12, 538G3-539E1
DC-10 flight ban lifted 7-13, 538E2
2d in '78 defns contracts 8-1, 609C1
DC-9 inspectns ordrd 9-19, order expanded 10-9, 830C2
Pak Intl Air sues re overchrg 9-25; US indicts re paymts 11-9, 886F1
Chicago DC-10 crash rpt issued by Safety Bd 12-21, 988A3
McDOUGALL, Donald
Heads Petro-Canada breakup study 9-5, 385B1
McELDUFF, Ellen
Southern Exposure opens 2-27, 292B3
McELREATH, Jim
2d in Pocono 500 6-24, 491E1
McELROY, Hal
Picnic At Hanging Rock released 2-22, 174D3
McELROY, James
Picnic At Hanging Rock released 2-22, 174D3
McENROE, John
Wins Grand Prix doubles 1-7, Masters 1-14, 103A3
Grand Prix dispute setld 2-10, 391F1
Wins Milan WCT 4-1, N Orleans Grand Prix 4-25; loses Rotterdam WCT 4-8, 391A3-B3
Wins WCT singles title 5-6, 391D1
Wins Stella Artois tourn 6-18, Wimbledon doubles 7-7, 570D1, D2
Loses Canadian Open 8-20; wins US Open titles 9-8, 9-9, 734A1, D2
Wins Stockholm Open 11-13, London Grand Prix 11-18, 1003G3
US wins Davis Cup 12-16, 1003G2
McENTEER, Ben
On 3 Mile I A-accident impact 4-2, 245B3
McEVEETY, Vincent
Apple Dumpling sequel released 8-31, 819E3
McEVEN, William E.
Jerk released 12-14, 1007E3
McFADDEN, Brian J.
Brass Ring opens 7-2, 711F1
McFADDEN, Lynn
On Calif pro-nuclear rally 10-13, 806E3
McGAFFEY, David
Beaten by Iran mob 1-29, 67D2

1980

MCCUTCHEN, Bill
Hide & Seek opens 5-4, 392B3
MCCUTCHEON, Lawrence
Steelers win Super Bowl 1-20, 61F3-62C1
MCDADE, Rep. Joseph Michael (R, Pa.)
Reelected 11-4, 844C1
MCDERMOTT, Dennis
Mediates PSAC strike 10-6—10-7, 808F1
MCDERMOTT, James A.
Wins Washn primary for gov 9-16, 724A2
Loses Wash gov electn 11-4, 847C1, 852B3
MCDERMOTT, John
Stoners win ASL title; named game offensive MVP 9-18, 771B1, G1
MCDERMOTT, Keith
Harold & Maude opens 2-7, 136C3
MCDERMOTT & Co., J. Ray
On '79 Fortune 500 list 5-5, 291C1
Pullman merger bid offered 6-30, Wheelabrator buys control 9-25, 784G2
Babcock and Wilcox Co.
Crystal River A-plant accident 2-26, NRC orders plant review 3-4, 169A2-F2
GPU sues over 3 Mile I 3-25, 249C1
NRC asks fine re '77 Ohio plant accident 4-10, 332B1
MCDONALD, Alonzo
Watson named staff chief 6-11, 439B1
MCDONALD, David
Clark releases RCMP probe rpt 1-11, 78E2
Rpts RCMP '71 suspect list sent abroad 2-28, 192B1
RCMP '70s sabotage unit rptd 4-20, 350A3
Cabt informer testifies 4-24, 350E3
MCDONALD, F. James
GM pres, chief operating officer 9-9, 701G3
MCDONALD, Judge Gabrielle
Orders Saudi film telecast 5-9, order overturned 5-12, 375G3
MCDONALD, John W.
Vs UN dvpt aid fund 2-9, 124C2, F2
MCDONALD, Lanny
NHL scoring ldr 4-6, 296E1
MCDONALD, Rep. Lawrence P. (D, Ga.)
At Somoza funeral 9-17, 721E1
Reelected 11-4, 842B3
MCDONALD'S Corp.
'79 top TV advertiser 4-4, 376B2
Frankie trust suit acquittal 9-29, 917B3
MCDONNELL Jr., James S.
Dies 8-22, 676C2
MCDONNELL Douglas Corp.
FAA seeks DC-10 safety chngs 1-12; no pylon defects found, civil fine paid 1-23, 53D2-G2
Canada to buy F-18As 4-16, 293C2
FAA ends DC-10 probe, pylon chng ordered 5-16; ct allows crash suits 5-23, 518F3-519A1
2d in '79 defns contracts 5-28, 403E1
Canada offered F-18 discount 7-11, 541A1
FAA orders jet engine inspectns 7-16, 667B1
3 get suspended sentnc in Japan bribe case 7-24, 605D2
Chrmn McDonnell dies 8-22, 676C2
MCDOWELL, Malcolm
Caligula released 2-2, 216C2
MCDUFFIE, Arthur (d. 1979)
4 Miami cops acquitted in death 5-17, riots erupt 5-17—5-17, 382F2-E3
US grand jury probes case 5-21, 401E3
Ex-cop indicted 7-28, 576C1; acquitted 12-17, 989F3
Ex-cop acquitted 12-17, 989F3
MCELDERRY, John
Loses US House electn 11-4, 851D3
MCELFISH, Roberta
Religious deprogrammer convicted 8-29, 727C1; sentenced 9-26, 857B3
MCELWAINE, Robert M.
Testifies on auto imports 10-1, 823F2
MCENROE, John
Wins Grand Masters doubles title 1-12, singles results 1-13, 213A2
Loses US Pro Indoor 1-27, Tokyo Invitatnl 4-13, Tourn of Champs 5-12; wins Richmond Classic 2-3, US Natl Indoor 3-2, Milan WCT 3-30, Queens Club Grass 6-15, 607E2-E3
Argentina wins Davis Cup Amer Zone 3-9, 607F1
Loses WCT singles title 5-4, 607A1
Loses Wimbledon 7-6, 606G1
USTA, pros settle rules dispute 7-16, 691G3
Loses US Open doubles 9-6, wins US Open singles 9-7, 691F1, F2
Wins Pacific champ 10-12, Australian Indoor 10-19, London Grand Prix 11-16; loses Stockholm Open 11-10, 947A2, B2, D2
Declines S Africa match 10-16, 947E1
Wins WCT Challenge Cup 12-14, 1002D2
MCEVEETY, Vincent
Herbie Goes Bananas released 9-12, 836A3
MCEWEN, John
Dies 11-20, 928A3
MCFADDEN, Cyra
Serial released 3-28, 416E3
MCFARLANE, William D.
Dies 2-18, 176E2
MCGAGH, William G.
Resigns as Chrysler up, treas 10-29, 959C3
MCGANN, Roy
Slain 10-14, 791D3

1976

McGARR, Judge Frank J.
Fines Nixon papers' appraiser 1-6, 6C3
McGEE, Sen. Gale W. (D, Wyo.)
Unopposed in primary 9-14, 705C2
Loses reelection 11-2, 819E3, G3, 824C3
McGOVERN, Sen. George S. (D, S.D.)
Wallace compares Carter 214F1
Campaigns for Udall in Wis 4-5, 245A3
'72 electn costs, donors rptd 4-25, 688C1
Udall 2d in SD 6-1, 390B1
Joins Carter camp 6-9, 409A2
Dem conv speaker 7-13, 509G2
Cited in Carter biog sketch 512D2
US natls to leave Viet 7-21, 593B2
Schweiker ADA rating cited 7-26, 549E2
Rpt Jones escorts corp execs to Cuba 9-27, 791D2
McGRAW Edison International Sales Corp.
Arab boycott rpt released 10-18, 786A1
McGRAW-Hill, Inc.
Leventhal dies 1-6, 56E3
US files consent decree 7-27, 989A2
McGUINESS, Martin
Detained 2-8, 146C2
McGUIRE, John A.
Dies 5-28, 524B3
McGUIRE, Ralph J.
Replaced as Mali amb 9-15, 807E3
McHUGH, Rep. Matthew F. (D, N.Y.)
Reelected 11-2, 830C2
McINGVALE, Cynthia
Wins Olympic medal 7-20, 575E3

1977

McGARR, Judge Frank J.
Finley loses suit vs Kuhn 3-17, 310A3
Lifts Hunts soybean trading ban 5-6, backs comm curbs 6-7, 464C1
Upholds baseball 'no-litigatn' clause 8-30, 768E1
Rules Hunt soybean trading illegal 9-28, 858E3
McGEE, Gale
Seeks OAS budget share cut 5-13, 415F1
McGEE, Jerry
2d in Memphis Open 6-12, 676F1
Wins Phila Classic 7-31, 676B2
McGILL University (Montreal, Canada)
CIA mind-control tests revealed 8-1—8-9, 611B1
McGOVERN, Sen. George S(tanley) (D, S.D.)
Scores leaks re Sorensen oppositn 1-17, 35D2
Votes vs Bell 1-25, 52A3
Scores Admin farm plan 3-23, 214D1
Visits Cuba 4-4—4-9, asks US embargo end 4-11, 282C3
Castro sends cigars 4-22, 390F1
On Nixon-Frost interview 5-5, 367E3
Attacks Carter economics 5-7; O'Neill protests 5-8, 364E2, A3
Cuba embargo ease backed by Sen com 5-10, 389D3
Carter rejcts criticism 5-12; replies 5-13, 380G3, 381D2
Carter denies pol threat 5-12, 381C1
McGUCKEN, Archbishop Joseph
Successor installed 4-26, 375A3
McGUIRE, Al
Marquette wins NCAA title 3-28, 262A2
McGUIRE, Frank
In basketball HOF 5-2, 490F3
McHENRY, Donald F.
On Namibia plan 6-10, 457A2
Backs Viet UN membershp 7-19, 572E2
At Biko funeral 9-25, 735D3

1978

McGARRY, Daniel
Chrgd in PC MP tap 4-3, 244A2
McGARRY, John W.
Named to FEC 10-25, Common Cause sues Carter 10-26, 831F2-B3
McGEE, Jerry
2d in Hope Desert Classic 2-13, 355C3
McGEECHAN, Wallace
Prisoner talks role ordrd halted 1-10, 34C3
McGILLICUDDY, John F.
Mfrs Hanover chrmn, chief exec 10-17, 809E1
McGINLEY, Phyllis
Dies 2-22, 196D3
McGINNIS, George
Traded to Nuggets 8-16, 655F3
McGLYNN Jr., Judge Joseph C.
Injunction halts umpires strike 8-25, 779G1
McGOFF, John P.
Denies S Africa role in Wash Star '74 purchase bid 11-1, SAAN bid 11-2, 868D2
McGOVERN, Sen. George S(tanley) (D, S.D.)
Scores Chile plebiscite 1-5, 17B2
Scores Sen mtg on Torrijos drug link 2-21, 120D2
Votes for Panama Canal neutrality pact 3-16, 177D2
Sen votes farm aid 3-21, 218A3
Backs farm bill 4-10, 261F2
Votes for 2d Canal pact 4-18, 273B1
Seeks Cuba Zaire role proof 5-26, 418B2
Doubts CIA proof on Cuba Zaire role 6-9, 442E2
Vs pres conv rule chngs 6-9, 448E2
Scores Propositn 13 6-17, 526B1
Asks intl force to oust Cambodia govt 8-21, US bars 8-22, 659B3
Defense cut amendmt fails 10-5, 833D1
Signs Cambodia rights probe plea; Cambodia denounces 10-12, 794A2
Scores 95th Cong 10-15, 784G2
In Angola 12-13, 985A1
McGOWAN, Pat
2d in Canadian Open 6-25, 580G3
McGRATH, Paul
Dies 4-13, 356B3
McGRAW, Tug
Phillies lose NL pennant 10-7, 779D1
McHARGUE, Darrel
Named top jockey 12-13, 1028C1
Sets earnings record 12-31, 1028E1
McHENRY, Donald F.
Angola visit results rptd 547G2 ★
In Angola 6-21—6-26, 487F3
McHUGH, Rep. Matthew F. (D, N.Y.)
Reelected 11-7, 851F3
Dem caucus OKs ethics rule chng 12-6, 958B2
MCI Communications Corp.
AT&T phone svc case review rejected 1-16, 33A2
AT&T phone svc case stay denied by Sup Ct 5-22, 388A2
AT&T connectns case declined by Sup Ct 11-27, 937A2
McILRAITH, George
Rptd aware of RCMP illegalities 10-24, 837B2
McINALLY, Pat
NFL '77 punting ldr 1-1, 56B3
McINTIRE, Tim
Amer Hot Wax released 3-16, 618A3
McINTYRE, Dennis
Modigliani opens 5-17, 760E2

1979

McGARR, Judge Frank J.
Named to wiretap ct 5-18, 442D3
On Rock Island RR cash positn 9-21, 722E2
Orders Rock I RR reorganizatn plan 10-10, 830E3
Rock I reorganizatn plan filed 12-28, 989D2
McGARRY, John W.
Confrmd to FEC 2-21, 130C3
McGEE, Jerry
Wins Kemper Open 6-3, 587A3
Wins Greater Hartford Open 8-14, 970A1
McGILL, William J.
Urges pub broadcast chngs 1-30, 78C2
Rpts Columbia U stock sale 3-23, 271A1
Columbia U A-reactor start-up halted 4-6, 261C3
Named Natl Agenda Comm chrmn 10-24, 810A3
McGILLICUDDY, John
Cautious re Chrysler loans 10-30, 845C3
McGILL University (Montreal, Canada)
Dryden retires from hockey 7-9, 655B3
McGIRL, Francis
Chrgd re Mountbatten murder 8-30, 669G1
Acquitted 11-23, 909G1-A2, C2
McGOFF, John P.
S Africa role in '74 Washn Star bid chrgd 3-21, 213F1
S Africa tie confirmed 6-4, 427D3
FCC revokes Mich TV licenses 7-12, 618F2
Denies S Africa link 7-18, 567G1
McGOOHAN, Patrick
Escape from Alcatraz released 6-21, 820B1
McGOVERN, Sen. George Stanley (D, S.D.)
Testifies in Letelier case 1-16, 57G3
Scores SALT treaty 3-4, 258A2
Son-in-law loses vote 4-3, 265C2
Backs Kennedy '80 pres bid 7-26, 556A2
Byrd defends Carter reelectn bid 7-28, 593F3
Vs arms hike link to SALT 8-3, 591D1
Conservative PAC plans drive 8-16, 627F3
Votes present on Talmadge denunciatn 10-10, 769G1
Endorses Kennedy 10-19, 847C2
McGRADY Jr., Patrick M.
Pritikin Program on best-seller list 6-3, 432B2; 7-1, 548C3; 8-5, 620C3; 9-2, 672C3; 10-14, 800C3
McGRATH, James
Canada fisheries min 6-4, 423F3
McGRATH, Archbishop Marcos
Backs Nicaragua, El Salvador prelates 2-12, CELAM documt 2-13, 108A3, F3
On US tuna embargo 9-4, 667A2
McGRAW Jr., Donald C.
Drops McGraw-Hill proxy battle 2-23, 151D3
McGRAW Jr., Harold W.
Vs Amer Express bid 1-9, 15G3
Amer Express bid rejctd 1-15; named in suit 1-18, 53D2, G2
McGRAW-Edison Co.
Studebaker-Worthington merger set, '78 income rptd 7-24, 682F2-A3
McGRAW-Hill Inc.
Amer Express seeks to buy 1-9, 15G3
Amer Express bid rejctd 1-15; tender offer filed 1-16; suits 1-18, 1-19, 53B2-A3
Morgan Guaranty role in Amer Express bid scored 1-22, 53A3
Amer Express sweetened bid rejctd 1-31, proxy battle dropped 2-23, offer expires 3-1, 151B3
Woolworth suit compared 4-12, 304B1
Data Resources acquired 8-28, 682F3
Iran '53 coup book rptd recalled 11-10, 886F3
McGREGOR, Scott
Orioles win AL pennant 10-6, 797G2
In World Series 10-10–10-17, 816C2
McGUIRE, E. Patrick
On international terrorism rise 11-15, 882F1
McGUIRE, John R.
Carter orders timber sales 6-11, 441C1
McGUIRE, Robert J.
Orders police protectn for banks 8-22, 656B1
McGUIRE, William Anthony
Whoopee opens 2-14, 292F3
McGURN, Barrett
Sup Ct workforce data rptd 6-11, 464G1
McHENRY, Donald F.
Questns Bolshoi dancer 8-27, 645E1
Named UN amb 8-31; facts on 660F2-661B1
Young in Africa tour 9-5–9-21, 720F2
Sworn 9-23, 763F2
Warns Iran on US hostages 12-1, lauds UN Cncl res 12-4, 913C1
MCI Communications Corp.
AT&T data access case declined by Sup Ct 3-26, 231B1
ITT offers long-distance phone svc 4-23, 350F3
McILRAITH, George
Held aware of RCMP illegalities 3-28, 253C3
Testifies re RCMP 4-26, 329A2
McINALLY, Pat
NFL '78 punting ldr 1-6, 80B2
McINTIRE, Carl
Cape May hotel destroyed 5-11, 572B3
McINTYRE, Dianne
Spell #7 opens 7-15, 712E2

1980

MCGARR, Judge Frank J.
Orders Rock I RR liquidatn 1-25, 131F1
Warns ICC on Rock I paymt 4-1, 345D3
OKs Rock I RR abandonmt, upsets worker aid law 6-2, 868F2
Rules in Pullman merger cases 7-31—9-19, 784B3-F3
MCGARRY, Daniel
Guilty in '77 MP bugging fraud 4-28, 335A1
MCGARRY, John W.
Elected FEC chrmn 12-18, 955E3
MCGAULEY, Pat
USF wins NCAA soccer title 12-14, 1001D3
MCGIFFERT, David E.
Arranges Egypt arms sale; briefs Israel 2-21, 140C2
Israel to build jet fighter 2-25, 180G1
MCGILL, William J.
Sovern named Columbia U pres 1-7, 200D1
MCGINN, Hugh
Slain 12-28, 994E1
MCGIVEN, Arthur
S Africa spying chrg spurs Natl Security Dept reorgn 1-15, 60D3
MCGIVENEY, Michael
Quick Change opens 10-30, 892D3
MCGOFF, John P.
Loses S Africa documt disclosure suit 3-17, 278B1
McGOVERN, Sen. George Stanley (D, S.D.)
Wins primary 6-3, 439B3
Vs anti-Anderson moves 6-24, 493A3
Backs open conv in rules fight 8-11, 610B1
Loses reelectn 11-4, 837D2, 845A2, 851E2
MCGOWAN, William
MCI wins $1.8 bln AT&T suit 6-13, 456G3
MCGRADY Jr., Patrick M.
Pritikin Program on best-seller list 2-10, 210D3; 4-6, 280C3
MCGRATH, Raymond
Elected to US House 11-4, 843D3
MCGRAW, Tug
Phillies win NL pennant 10-12, 796C1, F1, A2
In World Series 10-14—10-21, 811A3-812G3
MCGRAW-Edison Co.
Powers resigns 12-8, 959F3
MCGRAW-Hill Inc.
Photocopy co sued 2-5, 119G3
Photocopy suit rptd setld 3-21, 376D3
Amer Express takeover case declined by Sup Ct 11-3, 856A2
MCGREGOR, Jack
Carter cites visit 8-4, 594G3
Testifies at B Carter probe 8-20, 647D2
MCGREGOR, Scott
AL pitching ldr 10-6, 926G3
MCGRIEVY, Susan
On Navy dismissal of lesbian chrgs 8-21, 899A1
MCHALE, Kevin
Virginia wins NIT 3-20, 240F2
In NBA draft 6-10, 447B1, E1
MCHENRY, Donald F.
Warns on Sovt Afghan invasn 1-6, 2C2; 1-12, 26A1
Scores Iran sanctns veto 1-13, 29A1
Votes vs Israel setlmt policy 3-1, Vance takes blame 3-4; comments, Sen com plans vote probe 3-5, 163B1, E2-B3, 164B1
Shuns Sen com vote probe 3-20, 218F2
Says US contacts Israel in Leb crisis 4-13, 284B1
Vetoes Palestinian state res 4-30, 325F1
Abstains on Cncl vote vs W Bank bombings 6-5, 417C2
On UN hostage mission failure 6-19, 464A2
Abstains on Cncl res vs Israel Jerusalem moves 6-30, 491D2
In Nicaragua, marks Somoza downfall 7-19, 565E2
Denies R Botha Namibia chrgs 9-9, 710F3
Scores NY Turkish cntr bombing 10-12, 794F1
Offers Iran-Iraq peace plan 10-22—10-23, cites Iraq threat to Iran 10-23, 799F1
Debates USSR Afghan move 11-20, 899F3
Backs Cncl res on 2 W Bank mayors 12-19, 952C2
2 deported W Bank mayors end protest 12-24, 976E3
MCHUGH, Rep. Matthew F. (D, N.Y.)
Reelected 11-4, 843G3
Loses as House Dem Caucus chrmn 12-8, 936E2
MCI Inc.
Wins $1.8 bln AT&T suit 6-13, 456B3
MCI Communications Corp.
FCC seeks small cos regulatn end 12-16, 987D3
MCINALLY, Pat
NFL '79 punting ldr 1-5, 8B3
MCINERNEY, Sheila
Loses AIAW doubles tennis title 6-11, 607F1
MCINTOSH, Capt. Lynn D.
Killed in Iran rescue mission 4-24, 321F2

1976

McINTYRE, Malcolm
Angola sentences 6-28, 480B2
McKAY, Rep. K. Gunn (D, Utah)
Reelected 11-2, 824B3, 830F4
McKEE, Tim
Wins Olympic medal 7-25, 575F2
McKELWAY, Benjamin
Dies 8-30, 680G3
McKENNA, Bridget
Shot 10-10, 773E3
McKENZIE, Andrew G.
Sentenced to die 6-28, 480G1, A2
Executed 7-10, 519A3
McKENZIE Bridge (race horse)
2d in Belmont 6-5, 424E3
McKEOUGH, Darcy
Ontario OKs inflatn progrm 1-13, 46F3
Presents Ontario budget 4-6, 265F2
McKINLEY, Chuck
Borg matches Wimbledon record 7-3, 504F1
McKINNEY, Rep. Stewart B. (R, Conn.)
Reelected 11-2, 829G1
McLAUGHLIN, Charles
Dies 2-5, 124E3
McLAUGHLIN, W. Earle
Queries Trudeau econ remarks 1-11, 27G3
McLAUGHLIN, Judge Walter
Declares Saxe mistrial 10-13, 816B2
McLENNAN, Gordon
Addresses Sovt CP Cong 3-1, 196C1
McLEOD, Fred
Dies 5-8, 524B3
McLUCAS, James L.
Aircraft noise rules set 11-18, 868G3
McMAHON Jr., Pvt. Charles
S Viet returns body 2-22, 157A2
McMAHON, William
Wants secrets act 7-16, 537G1
McMANUS, Edward
2 cleared in SD '75 FBI deaths 7-16, 640A3
McMILLAN, Frew
Runner-up in US Open 9-12, 716D1
McMILLAN, Kathy
Wins Olympic medal 7-23, 576E1
McNALLY, Dave
Free agent rule upheld 2-4, 951E3
McNAMARA, John
Rehired 10-4, 816A1
McNAMARA, Robert S(trange)
'75 letter on OPEC aid to poor natns cited 1-12, 15D1
China ICBM projct rptd dropped 2-24, 190D1
Chile loan opposed 3-19, 3-23; defends 4-12, 310E2
Addresses IMF-World Bank mtg on aid re to poor 10-4; Simon vs bank fund rise 10-5, 777B2
Bank policies rptd opposed 11-22, 12-26, 976C1
McRAE, Hal
AL batting ldr 10-4, 796B1, C1

1977

McINTYRE Jr., James T.
Acting budget dir 9-21, 719E1
New dir apptmt deferred 10-2, 761E2
Named OMB director 12-27, 1001B3
McINTYRE, Sen. Thomas J. (D, N.H.)
Fears M-X arms control impact 10-7, 777E1
McKAY, John
Bell in NFL draft 5-3, 353D2
McKEE-Berger-Mansueto Inc.
2 Mass sens sentncd 2-25, 253A1
McKELLAR, Roderick
Ct to cut Parlt size 2-1, 113A2
McKEOUGH, Darcy
Presents Ontario budget 4-19, 303E3
Asks inter-prov trade 10-5—10-6, 780E2
McKINNEY, Robert H.
Redlining curb set 11-9, 898E2
McKNIGHT, Phillip R.
Sued re sugar lobby gifts 7-20, 614C1
McLAUGHLIN, Sister Janice
Rhodesia deports 9-22, 811G1
McLAUGHLIN, Michael
On Pa plane crash 2-24, 204D3
McLEAY, John
Named Australia constructn min 12-19, 982A2
McLUCAS, John L.
Comsat pres electn rptd 4-19, 396F3
McMAHON, J. Alexander
Vs Carter hosp cost plan 4-26, 322G1
McMANN, Harris
Mandatory pensn-plan retiremt backed 12-12, 960A2
McMANUS, Frank
Irish Indepndnc Party formed 10-8, 783D3
McMILLAN, Frew
Wins US Open doubles title 9-9, 787B2
McMILLAN, Judge James
Voids A-plant liability limit 3-31, 277C2
McNAIR, Denise (d. 1963)
'63 bomber convicted 11-18, 907B3
McNAIR, Fred
US beaten in Davis Cup 4-29—5-1, 353C3
McNAMARA, Robert S.
Reapptd World Bank pres 4-24, 532F1
Addresses World Bank mtg 9-26, 753D2, 754E1
World Bank funding clears Cong 10-19, 815B2; Carter signs 11-1, 834D1
Brown orders defns budget process revamped 10-26, 857G2-A3
Brandt intl dvpt comm meets 12-9—12-11, 997G3
McNAUGHTON, Andrew R. L.
Laetrile smugglers sentncd 5-16, 508G2
McNEA, William
Police dispute ends 12-16, 1005F1
McNEIL, Kenneth
Jamaica parlt affairs min 1-4, 46C1
McNICHOL, Kristy
Wins Emmy 9-11, 1021G3
McPHERSON, William
Wins Pulitzer Prize 4-18, 355A3
McRAE, George
Arrested 12-7, 992A1
McRAE, Hal
AL batting ldr 10-2, 926G3-927A1

1978

McINTYRE, James T.
Presents Educ Dept plan 4-14, 279F1 ★
Tax-cut plan scaled back 5-12, 361E1
On civil defns reorganizatn 6-19, 466B3
Natl health plan delay urged 6-26, 491F2
OMB cash flow chngs rptd, Ga progrm cited 8-19, 715G3
'80 defns budget oppositn rptd 11-18, 895D2
McINTYRE, Marilyn
Promise opens 3-8, 760C3
McINTYRE, Sen. Thomas J. (D, N.H.)
Carter backs reelection 2-18, 123E1
Says Navy vs cancer-radiatn probe 2-28, 164D3
Votes for Panama Canal neutrality pact 3-16, 177D2
Votes for 2d Canal pact 4-18, 273B1
Wins renomination 9-12, 736E1
Loses reelectn 11-7, 846B1, 847E3
MCI Telecommunications Corp.—*See under MCI Communications Corp.*
McKAY, Rep. K. Gunn (D, Utah)
Reelected 11-7, 852C3, 856F1
McKELLIPS, Roger D.
Wins primary for SD gov 6-6, 448G1
Loses electn 11-7, 855B1
McKENZIE, Bruce Roy
Dies in plane crash 5-24, 479B1
McKEON, Jack
Hired as A's mgr 5-23, 560D1
McKEOUGH, Darcy
Quebec tax objectns rptd 5-17, 391F3
McKEOWN, Ciaran
To quit peace movemt 4-15, disputes rptd 4-17, 373B1
McKERROW, Gavin W.
Dies 1-27, 96A3
McKINNEY, Robert H.
OKs redlining curb 5-18, 410F2
Variable rate mortgages OKd 7-24, 605D2
House Banking Com testimony 8-7, 605C2
McKINNEY, Rep. Stewart B. (R, Conn.)
Reelected 11-7, 850D2
McKINNON, Neil
Defends racial slurs, MPs demand resignatn 1-6, 18D1
McKINSTRY, Margaret
Loses primary for Wyo gov 9-12, 736B2
McKISSICK, Floyd
Innis ldrship challenge cited 9-18, 810F1
McKITTERICK, Tom
Fathers & Sons opens 11-16, 1031E1
McLAGLEN, Andrew V.
Wild Geese released 11-11, 970E3
McLAREN, Conrad
Porch opens 11-14, 1031G2
McLEAY, John
Australia admin svcs min 11-30, 943G3
McLENDON, Mac
Wins Fla Citrus Open 3-5, 355D3
Wins Pensacola Open 10-30, 990C2
McLEOD, Keith
Wins Mich Cong primary 8-8, 626B1
McMAHON, Thomas A.
Caravans released 11-1, 969F3 ★
McMASTER University (Hamilton, Canada)
Neurotransmitter study described 334B2
McMICHAEL, G. Speights
Past FBI corruptn rptd 1-10, 15E2
McMILLAN, Frew
Wins N Amer Zone Davis Cup match 3-18, 252B1
Wins US Open mixed doubles title 9-10, 707G1
McMILLEN, Judge Thomas H.
Denies US suit vs Teamsters 11-1, 899C1
McMURTRY, Roy
Bars chrgs vs Fox 2-23, 166C2
Chrgs Ottawa re RCMP health file access 2-28, 209G1
Sworn Ontario interim solicitor-gen 9-12, 721E3
McNAGNY Jr., Judge Phil M.
Sentncs CIA ex-aide in spy case 12-22, 1011D3
McNAIR, Fred
Loses N Amer Zone Davis Cup match 3-18, 252B1
McNAIR, Jean (Carol Allen)
Sentncd in '72 hijacking 11-23, 926F3
McNAIR, Melvin
Sentncd in '72 hijacking 11-23, 926F3
McNAMARA, John
Hired as Reds mgr 11-28, 1026F1
McNAMARA, Robert S.
At IMF-World Bank mtg; asks trade curbs end, bank capital hike 9-25, 732F2-B3
McNEILL, James
Warns vs oil imports 4-10, 265D3
McNEIL Laboratories—*See under JOHNSON & Johnson*
McPHEE, John
Coming into the Country on best-seller list 2-5, 116C3
Casey's Shadow released 3-17, 618F3
McPHERSON, James Alan
Wins Pulitzer Prize 4-17, 315C1
McQUEEN, Armelia
Ain't Misbehavin' opens 5-9, 760B1
McRAE, Hal
AL batting ldr 10-2, 928E3-F3
McSHERRY, John
Throws manure in Commons 7-6, freed on bail 7-7, 533B3
McSURELY, Alan
Cong immunity case refused by Sup Ct 6-26, 566E2
McSURELY, Margaret
Cong immunity case refused by Sup Ct 6-26, 566E2

1979

McINTYRE, Cardinal James Francis
Dies 7-16, 588B3
McINTYRE Jr., James T.
Carter econ team rptd revamped 6-4, 463E1
Addresses govs, sees balanced budget threatened by energy plans 7-8, 517F3
Obey scores 7-19, 531A3
McKAY, Anthony
Welfare opens 5-10, 712D3
McKAY, Heather
Wins women's intl squash open 1-28, US women's open 2-11, 527B2
McKENNA, T. P.
Portrait of the Artist released 4-21, 528D3
McKENZIE, Arthur
Rpts oil spill, tanker safety records 8-15, 608A1
McKEON, Jack
Marshall named A's mgr 2-12, 619C2
McKINNEY, Robert H.
Scores bank takeovers by industry 3-7, 205B2
McKINNON, Allan
Canada defense min 6-4, 423F3
McKISSICK, Floyd
HUD withdraws Soul City support 6-28, files suit 8-17, injunctn denied 8-27, 665F1
McKOWN, Ben
Wins NCAA doubles title 5-28, 570B2
McLAIN, H. B.
Disputes JFK acoustics evidence 1-4, 4C2
New JFK murder film rptd 2-8, 166D2
McLAHEN, Lynne
Flying Blind opens 11-15, 956B3
McLAUGHLIN, Joey
Traded to Blue Jays 12-5, 1002E2
McLEAN Securities Inc.
Indicted re price fixing 6-1, 423D2; pleads no contest, fined 6-8, 442B2
McLENDON, John
In basketball HOF 4-30, 526E3
McLERIE, Allyn
Dancing in Dark opens 1-21, 292D1
McMAHON, (John) Alexander
Vs hosp cost-control bill 3-6, 163C3; 3-9, 194G2
McMAHON, Thomas
Chrgd re Mountbatten murder 8-30, 669G1
Sentenced 11-23, 909F1-C2
McMANUS Jr., Charles A.
Heads draft Haig com 9-10, 680C2
McMILLAN, Judge Byron
Calif schl sniper pleads guilty 10-1, 819F2
McMILLAN, Frew
Loses US Natl Indoor doubles 3-4, 391A3
Loses Wimbledon mixed doubles 7-7, 570E1
Loses US Open mixed doubles title 9-9, 734A2
McMILLAN, John L.
Dies 9-2, 756A3
McMILLEN, Judge Thomas R.
OKs Milwaukee Rd borrowing 5-4, denies svc cut 6-1, 465G1
OKs Milwaukee Rd westn embargo 9-26, lifts order 11-5, 867F2, B3
Rules Milwaukee Rd bailout legal 11-25, 989B2
McMULLEN, John J.
Houston Astros purchased 5-11, NL owners OK 5-16, 619D1
McMURTRY, Roy
On Mississauga evacuatn 11-11, 871F3
McNAMARA, Harold
Guilty in dredging fraud 5-5, 352A2
Sentenced 6-11, 468C2
McNAMARA, Robert Strange
JFK backed pres bid 9-23, 748A3
McNEE, Sir David
Cops suspended in corruptn probe 4-6, 268D2
McNEESE State University (Lake Charles, La.)
Loses Independence Bowl 12-15, 1001G2
McNEIL, Al
Hired as Flames coach 6-7, 470C3
McNEIL, Wilfred
Dies 8-30, 671A3
McNICHOL, Kristy
Wins Emmy 9-9, 858D2
McNICHOLS, Mayor Bill (Denver, Colo.)
Reelected 5-15, 363A3
McNICKLE, Artie
Ties for 2d in San Diego Open 1-28, 220D3
McPHEE, John
H-bomb letter cites Taylor interviews 9-16, 9-18, Taylor denies chrgs 9-17, 714B1, B2; text of letter 717G1
McPHERSON, Keith
Scores press takeover bid 11-21, 906A3
McPHERSON, Mary Patterson
Ct rules vs Wilson post 5-26, 482E1

1980

MCINTYRE Jr., James T.
Estimates Cuban refugee resetlmt costs 5-25, 396D1
Rpts midyr budget review 7-21, 550D1
MCKAY, John
Denies USC faulty athletic admissns link 10-15, 875E2
MCKAY, Rep. K. Gunn (D, Utah)
Loses reelectn 11-4, 846F1, 852D1
MCKELLEN, Ian
Amadeus opens 12-17, 1003G2
MCKELWAY, St. Clair
Dies 1-10, 104C3
MCKENNA, Sean
Comatose 12-18, in 'good conditn' 12-24, 993G2
MCKINLEY, John K.
Named Texaco chrmn 6-30, 600B3
MCKINNEY, Jack
Hired as Pacers coach 6-3, 656F3
MCKINNEY, John
Hijinks! opens 12-18, 1003B3
MCKINNEY, Robert
Wins NM paper ownership suit 6-30, 582E2-A3
MCKINNEY, Rep. Stewart B. (R, Conn.)
Reelected 11-4, 842D2, 848C1
MCLAGLEN, Andrew V.
Ffolkes released 4-18, 416F2
MCLAIN, Denny
NL wins All-Star Game 7-8, 636D1
MCLAIN v. Real Estate Board
Case decided by Sup Ct 1-8, 16C1
MCLAUGHLIN, W. Earle
Frazee rptd successor 9-5, 687B1
MCLEAN 3rd, William L.
Sells Phila Bulletin to Charter Media 4-10, 376G3
MCLEAN Hospital (Belmont, Mass.)
New drug rptd effective vs heroin addictn 2-2, 160C2
MCLEAY, John
Ousted from Australia Cabt 11-2, 857F2
MCLEROTH, John
'Exclusionary rule' narrowed by Sup Ct 5-27, 453B2
MCLEROY, Watt
Home for cats rptd purchased 2-9, 200G1
MCLUHAN, Herbert Marshall
Dies 12-31, 1004F2
MCMAHON, Jim
BYU wins Holiday Bowl 12-19, 999B3
MCMANUS, Doyle
Flees Iran 7-24, 572C1
MCMILLAN, Capt. Charles T.
Eliz (NJ) chem dump burns 4-22, 331B2
Killed in Iran rescue mission 4-24, 321F2
MCMILLAN, Frew
Loses US Open mixed doubles 9-7, 691F2
MCMILLAN, Kathy
Loses US Olympic trials long jump; chrgs Anderson steroid use 6-28, 891D2
MCMILLEN, Judge Thomas R.
Upholds Chicago Bd silver trade curbs 2-11, 114F1*
Orders Milwaukee Rd RR svc cut 2-25, 345F3, 346A1
MCMINN, Holt
Agent Orange rpt ordered 3-26, 252B3
MCMONAGLE, Judge George T.
Acquits judge of sex-bartering, convicts on other chrgs 6-13, 503B2
MCMULLEN, Jay
Named mayoral press secy 1-9, 199F1
MCMULLEN, Kathy
3d in US Women's Open 7-13, 714B3
MCNAB, Peter
Suspended over NYC brawl 1-25, suspensn upheld 1-30, 198C3
MCNAMARA, Peter
Wins Wimbledon men's doubles 7-5, 606G2
Loses Melbourne Indoor 10-26, 947C2
McNAMARA, Robert Strange
Visits China 4-11—4-16, 302D2
China admitted to World Bank 5-15, 389E1
To quit World Bank 6-9; addresses joint IMF mtg 9-30, 761A2
Clausen named World Bank pres 10-30, 826A2
MCNAMEE, Paul
Wins Wimbledon men's doubles 7-5, 606G2
Loses Sicilian Grand Prix 9-14, 947F1
MCNARY, Gene
Wins Mo US Sen primary 8-5, 682F3
Loses US Sen electn 11-4, 851F1
MCNAUGHTON, W. Hugh
Chrgd in Bahamas bank looting suit 3-3, 229D1
MCNEAL, Don
In NFL draft 4-29, 336G2
MCNEESE State University (Lake Charles, La.)
Loses Independence Bowl 12-13, 999A3
MCNEIL, Robert A.
To Forget Venice released 1-28, 216F3
MCNICHOL, Kristy
Little Darlings released 3-28, 416C3
MCQUEEN, Butterfly
Sues Greyhound 1-4, 199A3
MCQUEEN, Steve
Hunter released 8-1, 675A3
Dies 11-7, 928B3
MCQUINN, W. Jones
Saudi completes Aramco takeover, retains bd seat 9-4, 662A2
MCRAE, Hal
AL batting ldr 10-6, 926F3
In World Series 10-14—10-21, 811F2-812G2

1976

McVEIGH, Richard L.
Indicted 7-8, 816F2
MDLULI, Joseph
Arrested 3-18, dies 3-19, police chrgd 6-11, 428E3 ⋆
Police acquitted re death 10-28, 927D2
MEAD Corp., The
Trust suit dvpts 2-18—10-5, 886D1, E2
MEAD-Johnson Co.
Sequential pills withdrawn 2-25, 224B3
MEADOWLANDS (NJ sports complex race track)—*See NEW Jersey*
MEADVILLE Corp.
Indicted 6-1, 412D3
MEANS, Russell C.
Shot 5-5, 384E2
Acquitted 8-6, 640D2
MEANY, George
On Dunlop resignation 1-14, 23D1
Garn votes vs Usery 2-4, 110F1
Scores Ford business bias 2-16, 2-17, 148D3
Scores govt jobless data 3-5, 199B1
Rubber boycott backed 4-21, 308E3
Sees Carter 5-14, comments 5-19, 391B1
USSR scores labor delegatn visa denials 5-25—5-28, 408A1
Backs actn vs Stevens at clothing, textile union merger 6-3, 436F1
Carter visits 6-30, 468E1
Exec Cncl backs Carter 7-19, 532E2
Vows aid to Carter 8-31, 645C2
Dole links to Carter 9-17, 9-23, 724B3, D3
Dole, Mondale debate 10-15, 783F2-B3
Ford scores Carter 10-15, 784G1
On 'realistic' Nov jobless rate 12-5, 918C1
Lauds Marshall apptmt 12-21, 957F3
MEARS, Walter
On pres debate panel 10-15, 782B3

MEAT (& Meat Products)—*See also country names*
Blackmun bars beef standards stay 1-9, 24B2
France to press EC on beef prices 1-16, 139B1
FDA bans Red #2 dye 1-19, 44D2
Dec, '75 CPI 1-21, 90A2
Argentina beef exports to Eur down 2-2, 96C3
Australia-Japan talks 2-4—2-15, 137E3
W Ger hit by lira drop 2-10, 140E2
Europn Parlt votes beef policy 2-12, 163F3
New US beef grading rules in effect 2-23, 186D1
Feb CPI up 3-19, 215G1
New grading rules upheld 3-22, 218E2
Hungary-Sovt barter pact rptd 4-1, 543A3
Argentina beef sales to USSR cited 4-9, 264C3
March CPI rptd 4-21, 306B2
Cong OKs Beef Bd 5-3, 5-12, 358E3-359A1
Army beef-purchasing scandal chrgd 5-7—5-12, 395A2
Latin output rptd 5-7, 466C1
Beef Board signed 5-28, 982E1
EEC farmers seek drought aid 6-19, 7-19, 548E3, F3
May CPI rptd 6-22, 453B3
Hungary raises prices 7-5, 925B2
Australia-Sovt deal set 8-3, 587C2
GOP platform text 8-18, 603D1
Agri Dept asks retail price cut 8-30, 667G3
Aug CPI rptd 9-21, 708E2
Ford sets import quota 10-9, 787G3
Canada scores US quota 10-11, 837A1
Rabbit inspection vetoed 10-17, 919E2
Canada sets import quota 10-19, 837B1
Canada '69-73 import data cited 837C1
Sept CPI rptd 10-21, 805G2
US, suppliers OK '77 export limit pact, Canada agrmt disputed 12-15, 976A2

1977

McWHIRTER, Ross (d. 1975)
Slayers sentenced 2-10, 222G2
MEAD, Margaret
At AAAS conf 2-21—2-25, 183B3
MEADE, James
Wins Nobel Prize 10-14, 951E3
MEADOR, Daniel J.
Named asst atty gen 2-14, confrmd 3-18, 211F1
MEADVILLE Corp., The
Convicted 8-30, 691A3
Fined 9-16, 918F2
MEANOR, Judge H. Curtis
Bans TM from NJ schools 10-20, 845D3
MEANS, Rev. Jacqueline
Ordained 1-1, 119B3
MEANY, George
On wage-price proposals 2-21, 2-24, 153E2
Lauds Marshall 2-21, 153G2
On planned legis drive 2-22, 153A2
On Sovt rights abuse 2-25, 142D3
Scores Admin min wage plan 3-24, 229E2
Sees Carter on shoe, textile import curbs 4-6, 4-13; Carter reactn rptd 4-18, 271D2
Carter rpts anti-inflatn role; reactn 4-15, 298G3, 299D2
On Carter hosp cost plan 4-25, 322A2
Scores Carter image-making 5-4, 364B3
Backs KC teachers strike 5-6, 481E2
Lauds Carter Soc Security plan 5-9, 364A2
Carter urges cooperatn 5-12, 381A1
Backs Carter labor law bill 7-18, 555G2
Scores Carter illegal alien plan 8-4, 592E1
Backs Panama Canal pacts 8-29, 679B1
Joins blacks vs Carter 8-30, 702B2
Minimum wage bill signed 11-1, 834C1
Backs suit vs J P Stevens 11-10, 899D1
Backs revised jobs bill 11-14, 877B1
Sakharov gets invitatn 11-30, 955C3
AFL-CIO conv 12-8—12-13, reelected pres 12-12, 960D3-961G1
MEARS, Walter
Wins Pulitzer Prize 4-18, 355F2
MEASLES—*See MEDICINE—Diseases*

MEAT (& Meat Products)
EEC sets Australia levies 1-5, 60C2
CIA linked to '71 Cuba swine fever 1-9, 19D3
Japan to import more Australia beef 1-18, 60B2
Australia limits Canada sales 2-17, 179C1
US modifies duty-free list 2-28, 189E3
State weight-labeling rules curbed 3-29, 277B1
Beef fraud convictn review denied 4-4, 341G3
Mrs Carter in CR, cites US imports study 6-1, 454F2
Australia scores EC protectionism 6-1, 595F3
Uruguay '76 export data rptd 7-8, 601G2
Rhodesia subsidies rptd 8-25, 730E3
Australia denies exported meat diseased 8-29, 725B2
US orders nitrate data 8-31, 10-18, 820A1
Japan bars Australia beef import plan 9-26, 800C3
Japan OKs more beef imports 10-28, 862A1
EC rejcts Australia beef import demands 10-30, 862D1
Rabbit meat inspectn vetoed 11-10, 897B3
Sheep disease hits Australia 11-14, 881D3
Japan assures GATT on beef imports 11-29, 933E2

1978

McTEAR, Houston
Sets indoor 60-yd dash records 1-7, 1-27, 76G2, B3
Bests 60-yd dash record 2-24, 600C3
McVAY, John
Fired as Giants coach 12-18, 1024B3
McVIE, Tommy
Fired as Caps coach 10-9, 991B1
McWILLIAMS, Larry
Stops Rose hitting streak 8-1, 618G2
MEAD, Margaret
Dies 11-15, 972D3
MEAD Corp.
Indicted for price fixing 1-25, 67B2
Occidental seeks takeover 8-11, bid rejected 8-18, 767C2
US sues vs Occidental takeover 10-11; Occidental offers consessns 10-23, US expands suit 10-25, 895A3
Occidental restrained by ct 12-9, ends takeover fight 12-20, 1004C3
MEADOW, Lynne
Catsplay opens 4-16, Rib Cage 5-28, Strawberry Fields 6-4, 887C1, G2, D3; Rear Column 11-19, Nongogo 12-3, 1031F2, A3
MEADOW Brook National Bank—*See C.I.T. Financial Corp.—National Bank of North America*
MEADOWS, Algur Hurtle
Dies 6-10, 540C3
MEAGHER, Tony
Boston U wins NCAA hockey title 3-25, 296C3
MEANOR, Judge Curtis H.
Fines Sea-Land on rebates 4-11, 449E2
MEANS, Delton L.
Contests divorce 4-4, 420B3
MEANS, Rev. Jacqueline
Asks for divorce 4-4, 420B3
MEANY, George L.
Vs wage guidelines 1-20, 48E3
Scores Carter on coal strike, jobs 2-20—2-24; Carter responds 3-2, 141D1, 142B1
Vs food-stamp cut-off to striking miners 3-11, 182D2
Sees Carter; rejcts wage-restraint plea, scores GM 5-10; Bosworth backs 5-11, 361F2, D3
'77, '78 salary rptd 5-15, 365C2
Scores Carter health plan 7-28, 586G1
Scores Bosworth, Admin panel created 8-7, 624B2
Carter dispute flares over labor law reform, postal pact 8-8—8-11, 624A2, E2-G3
Addresses USW on wage curbs 9-18, 715A2
Backs revisd postal setlmt 9-22, 766E2
Scores Carter wage-price, $ defns plans 10-31, 11-1, 11-5; Marshall, Kahn comment 10-31, 11-5, 863G1-G2
Carter defends wage-price plan 11-9, 875B1
Evaluates electn results, Carter bid 11-9, 875C2
Backs Chile trade boycott 12-10, 1014B2
CWA pres scores Carter attacks 12-11, 960F3
Vs revised wage-price rules, asks controls 12-13, 957G1
Denounces China ties 12-20, 975F3
MEASLES—*See MEDICINE—Diseases*
MEAT (& Meat Products)
Striking farmers block Mex imports 3-1, 3-3, 163F1
Feb finished-goods prices rptd up 3-9, 222C3, D3
Mar, 1st ¼ CPI rptd 4-28, 345A1
Nitrate-cured bacon curbed 5-15, 728F1
Hamburger frying, cancer link rptd 5-16, 598G2
Short supplies, food price inflatn linked 5-30, 428C2
Apr CPI rise rptd 5-31, 428C3
Carter hikes import quotas, beef price rise cited 6-8, 428D2
May beef price rise rptd 6-30, 506G3
June beef price rise rptd 7-28, July price drop 8-10, 607F1, D2
EPA to ease water rules 8-10, 644A2
Nitrate additives linked to cancer 8-11, FDA proposes phase-out 8-31, 727G3
Carter vows import limit, bars price controls 8-14, 626F1
July beef prices rptd down 8-29, 679A3
Sept producer price rise rptd 10-5, 790A2
Grazing land laws revisn cleared 10-11, 807E2
Pacific Holding to buy Iowa Beef 11-6, 1005B2
Earthworm rumor hurts fast-food chains 11-16, 942G1
Oct CPI costs rptd 11-28, 918C2

Foreign Developments
Japan sets beef quota hikes 1-13, 27A1
Australia scores EC import curbs; '73, '77 data compared 1-24, 69G2
Paraguay '77 exports cut by EC curbs 2-17, 292E3
Nigeria import ban rptd 4-4, 248C1
Australia port strike starts 4-11, 349F3-350A1
Japan, NZ trade accord rptd 5-23, 498A1
NZ strike halts lamb exports 5-25, 498C2
Poland hikes prices 6-1, 650C2
Australian cattle herds rptd down 6-14, 472F1
Turkey, USSR sign trade pact 6-21—6-23, 595E2
Australia scores Japan beef quotas 6-27, 514B2
Australia seeks EC beef deal 7-13, 530B2

1979

McVAY, John
Perkins hired as Giants coach 2-22, 175E2
McVIE, Tom
Hired as WHA Jets coach 2-28, 470B3
MDLULI, Joseph (d. 1976)
Widow gets damages 3-19, 213D2
MDLULI, Lydia
Gets damages re husband's death 3-19, 213D2
MEAD, Margaret (1901-78)
Park dedicated 9-15, 892D2
MEAD Corp.
Price-fixing acquittal 4-29, 327C3
MEADOW, Lynne
Dancing in Dark opens 1-21, 292D1
Just a Little Less opens 5-20, 712A1
MEADOW Industries Inc.
Textile union files Ga suit 7-18, 598F3
MEAGHER, Robert J.
US files pollutn suit 2-7, 130B1
MEANOR, Judge Curtis H.
Sentncs Provenzano for extortn 7-10, 548E1
MEANY, George L.
Mtg with Carter 'clears air' 1-12, 13B3
Chile trade boycott dropped by ORIT 1-15–1-16, 28D3
At AFL-CIO exec cncl mtg, maps plans 2-19–2-26, 148D2-149F1
Wage-guide suit filed 3-13, 182C2
Scores '78 4th ¼ profit rise 3-21, 201C2
Ct bars wage-guide contract denial 5-31, 399E3
Appeals ct backs wage-guide contract denial, asks Sup Ct review 6-22, 480G2
Backs Weber case Sup Ct ruling 6-27, 477G2
Carter praises labor 9-3, 661D1
To retire as AFL-CIO pres 9-28, 744D1
Bids AFL-CIO farewell at conv, Carter lauds 11-15; Kirkland succeeds 11-19, 884G3-885D1, G1
MEARS, Rick
Wins Indy 500 5-27, 490G2

MEAT (& Meat Products)
Meat Cutters union merger set 1-26, 130F3; effected 6-6, 419F3
Nitrite-safety law revisns urged 3-2, 195D1
Carter proposes regulatory reform 3-25, 230A2
Mar CPI rise rptd 4-26, 324G3
Apr beef price rise rptd 5-25, 402E3
May producer price drop rptd 6-7, 422A2
Truckers strike 6-7–6-15, 462G3-463A1; 6-18–6-28, 479A3
Antibiotics in animal feed rptd risky 6-25, 735B1
PCB contaminated products destroyed 9-17, 704E3
Sept producer price rise rptd 10-4, 766E1
'78 LA-area beef-price suit setld 10-22, 985D3

Foreign Developments
Australia gets US trade concessns 1-8, 36F2
Rumania '78 output rptd short 2-6, 170G3
UK '78 aid to Portugal rptd 2-20, 212F3
Australia-Japan accord 4-6, 266A2
GATT pact signed 4-12, 273F2
Australia-EC accord set 5-29, 404G3, 405A1
Nicaragua beef boycott proposed by US; '78, 1st ¼ exports rptd 6-5, 427G1-B2
Zimbabwe exports rptd 7-8, 547C1
US bans Nicaragua beef 8-6, 616C2
Nicaragua export controls set, '78 trade cited 8-9, 616F1
EC beef import curbs cited 8-21, 632A1
China hikes pork prices 11-1, 854D3
French-UK lamb dispute rptd 11-14, 873B1

1980

MCTAVISH, Craig
Fined over NYC brawl 1-25, 198D3
MCVEIGH, Tom
Australia housing min 11-2, 857F2
MCWILLIAMS, Carey
Dies 6-27, 528F2
MEAD, Margaret (1901-78)
Gregory Bateson dies 7-4, 608D1
MEAD Corp.
Guilty in box price fixing suit 9-15, 917E1
Fine paper trust suit rptd setld 9-29, acquittal rptd in 2d suit 12-3, 917B2, C2
MEADVILLE Theological School (Chicago, Ill.)
Burhoe wins Templeton prize 5-13, 471E2
MEAGHER, Mary T.
Sets 100-m butterfly mark 4-11, 834F3
Sets 200-m butterfly mark 7-30, beats Metschuck Olympic time 8-2, 834G2, B3
MEAGHER, Robert J.
Pollutn suit partly setld 1-30, 93G3
MEANOR, Judge H. Curtis
Clears Helstoski of '76 chrgs 2-27, 228B1
MEANY, George L.
Dies 1-10, 14G2
MEARS, Rick
CART membership cited 6-30, 1002A2

MEAT (& Meat Products)
GAO scores cancer-nitrite study 1-31, 159G1
US dietary guidelines issued 2-4, 157B3, C3
Mar producer prices rptd 4-4, 263C1
Mar CPI rise rptd 4-22, 305C2
Apr farm prices rptd 4-30, 329A3
Cholesterol rpt issued 5-27, 432A3
De Angelis sentncd in pork swindle 7-21, 655B1
July producer prices rptd 8-15, 630B3
Nitrite ban rejected 8-29, 726C1-A2
Sept farm prices rptd 9-30, 741B2
Beef pricing trust case refused by Sup Ct 10-14, 781G3
'80 pork bellies futures trading up 12-31, 984G3

Foreign Developments (including U.S. international news)
French-UK lamb dispute continues 2-14—2-20, 125A1
Connally 'basic speech' excerpts 3-7, 184B2
African dependence on S Africa cited 4-1, 243A2
Australia beef prices down 4-7, 272A1
USSR decline seen 4-9, 316A1
Canada drops fraud chrgs vs 57 stores 4-11, 372E1
Canada plans import curb 4-14, 293A1, C1
USSR-Argentine deal signed, 1st 1/4 trade rptd 4-15, 336F1
Canada convicts 6 in tainted meat sale 4-23, 372A1
French-UK lamb dispute setld 5-29, 421A3
Canada sentncs 6 6-16, 486E1
US chrgs Sovt anthrax cover-up 6-29, 500B1
Poland hikes prices 7-1, sees shortages 7-9, 566E1
Australia-EC sheepmeat talks founder 7-15, 561C3
USSR farm productn rptd down 7-16, 9-7, 711G2, D3
Poland bars price rollback 8-15, 625D1
Egypt bans sale for 1 month 9-1, 691C1
USSR convictns in anthrax outbreak rptd 9-25, 742B2

1976

MEDEIROS Ferreira, Jose
Portugal forgn min 7-23, 558F1
On Portugal EC entry bid 9-20, 812F2
On Cncl of Eur admissn 9-22, 733F2
MEDICAID—*See under MEDICINE*
MEDICAL Assistance Programs, Inc.
Guatemala quake aid rptd 2-10, 120E3
MEDICAL College of Georgia (Augusta)
Ahlquist wins Lasker award 11-17, 910E3
MEDICAL Supplies—*See 'Drugs' under MEDICINE*
MEDICARE—*See under MEDICINE*

1977

MEAT Cutters and Butcher Workmen of North America, Amalgamated (AFL-CIO)
Poole joins AFL-CIO exec cncl 12-12, 951G1
MEDICAID—*See under MEDICINE*
MEDICAL Schools—*See EDUCATION, sub-heads 'Colleges' and 'Federal Aid'*
MEDICARE—*See under MEDICINE*
MEDICH, George (Doc)
Signs with Rangers 11-10, 989F3

1978

Papal reforms cited 8-6, 601D2
US-Japan beef quota talks fail 9-5—9-7, 695A1
Spain: Argentina trade talks 11-26—11-30, 967A3
Japan-US beef pact signed 12-5, 988D2
MECHAM, Evan
Wins primary for Ariz gov 9-12, 736B2
Loses electn 11-7, 855E1
MECHELLI, Girolamo
Wounded 4-26, 330E1
MECOM, John
Fires Stram, becomes Saints gen mgr 1-31; names Nolan coach 2-6, 171A3
MEDAVOY, Mike
Resigns from United Artists 1-16, 75A3
MEDAWAR, Peter
Pregnancy-cancer immunity link rptd 1-19, 334A1
MEDENNIKOV, Anatoly
1000-mtr speed-skating mark rptd 4-16, 316C3
MEDIATION Board, National—*See U.S. GOVERNMENT—NATIONAL Mediation Board*
MEDICAID—*See under MEDICINE*
MEDICAL College of Virginia—*See VIRGINIA Union University*
MEDICAL Schools—*See EDUCATION, sub-heads 'Colleges' and 'Federal Aid'*
MEDICARE—*See under MEDICINE*

1979

MEATBALLS (film)
Released 7-3, 820A2
Top-grossing film 8-1, 620G3
MEAT Cutters and Butcher Workmen of North America, Amalgamated (AFL-CIO)
Clerks union merger set 1-26, 130F3; takes effect 6-6, 419F3
MEAT Packers Inc.
Settles '78 beef-price suit 10-22, 985E3
MECKLENBURG, William G.
Loses Peat Marwick electn 10-10, 851F3
MEDEIROS, Gen. Otavio Aguiar
Brazil intell min designate 1-19, 95E1
MEDIA, Franklin
Till Marriage Do Us Part released 7-20, 820E3
MEDICAID—*See under MEDICINE*
MEDICARE—*See under MEDICINE*

1980

EC sets sheepmeat policy 9-30, 737E2
USSR shortages rptd 10-21, 10-22, 797G2, 798G1
Polish shortage rptd 11-12, rationing set 11-19, 878G2, 879B1
USSR sets 11th 5-yr plan 12-1, 945F2
MEAT Cutters and Butcher Workers of North America, Amalgamated (AFL-CIO)
Gorman dies 9-3, 755C3
MECCA (play)
Opens 2-2, 136D3
MEDAK, Peter
Changeling released 3-28, 416E2
MEDAL of Honor (U.S.)
WW II vet awarded 7-19, 638E1
MEDARED, Dr. Frantz
Haiti interior, defns min 4-26, 336A1
MEDEIROS, Cardinal Humberto
Anti-abortionists lose Mass primary 9-16, 724C2
Reagan, Anderson debate abortn issue 9-21, 721F2, 722G1
MEDFORD, Kay
Dies 4-10, 360E2
MEDIA Change, Community Coalition for
FCC rejects Westinghouse unit license challenge 1-30, 119D3
MEDIATEX Communications Corp.
New West purchase rptd 8-27, 732E3
MEDICAID—*See under MEDICINE*
MEDICARE—*See under MEDICINE*

MEDICINE & HEALTH

1976

MEDICINE & Health—*See also country names*
US health rpt issued 1-12, 31G3-32G1
Dec, '75 costs rptd 1-21, 90E1
'74 death rate rptd 2-3, 123D3
France-Bahrain pact signed 3-2, 204G3
Feb CPI up 3-19, 215A2
Sup Ct bars review of health spa bias 4-5, 262G1
Jan-Mar CPI up 4-21, 306C2
1900-73 female life expectancy data rptd 4-27, 379E3, G3
Apr CPI up 5-21, 375F1
Schweiker backs pvt sector role 8-4, 564E1
July CPI rptd 8-20, 635G1
PHS 5-yr plan issued 9-7, 680E1, F1 ★
Lab standards bill defeated 9-20, 883F3
Aug CPI rptd 9-21, 708E2
Oct '75-76 CPI rise cited 11-19, 885A1
Venez, UK pact signed 11-23, 929D3
'75 job injury, illness, death data rptd 12-9, 950F2
Nov '75-76 CPI costs rptd 12-21, 958A2
Abortion—*See under 'A'*
Alcoholism—*See ALCOHOLIC Beverages*
Birth Control & Family Planning—*See under 'B'*
Blood
Boston U gets hypertensn grant 1-30, 123G3 ★
Sickle cell zinc treatmt rptd 2-24, 159F2
EPA leaded gas curb upheld 3-19, 219E2
Cong OKs sickle cell, Cooley's, other research funds 4-12, 282E2, A3
Olympic 'blood doping' rumored 7-29, 563C2-A3
2 get Lasker 11-17, 910F3
Cancer—*See also 'Smoking-Health Link' under TOBACCO*
Concorde hearing 1-5, 5E2
DES ban in animal feed asked 1-9, 25E3
HEW rpts '75 rise 1-12, 32A1, C1
FDA bans Red #2 dye 1-19, 44A2
'75 death data error noted 1-28, 123B3
'74 death rate rptd 2-3, 123F3
High rate areas rptd 2-8, 2-16, 224D3
Boyse wins Adler prize 2-11, 272C1
Sequential pills withdrawn 2-25, 224C3
EPA urges toxic chem law 2-26, 171B3
US cncl issues pollutn rpt 2-27, 171D2
US environmt agent clearinghouse set 3-29, 384A2
FDA seeks chloroform ban 4-6, 249E2
ACN, vinyl chloride link cited 4-21, 308C2
Johns Hopkins team replaces bone 5-3, 384C2
FDA to keep cyclamate ban 5-11, 414F3
Pittsburgh radiatn subjects recalled 5-12, 384B2
More estrogen links rptd 6-3, 460E3
WHO studies rptd 6-3, 484G2

1977

MEDICINE & Health—*See also country names*
Carter statemt to world 1-20, 26G1, A3
Privacy comm submits rpt 7-12, 632B1
Abortion—*See under 'A'*
Alcoholism—*See ALCOHOLIC Beverages*
Birth Control & Family Planning—*See under 'B'*
Births—*See under 'B'*
Blood
Patient survives surgery without blood supply 6-2, 620A1
'78 authorizatn signed 8-1, 689A3
Lasker Award presented 11-16, 927B3
Cancer—*See also 'Laetrile' below*
Canada arsenic pollutn chrgd 1-16, probe set 1-18, 61G1
US, Canada set saccharin bans 3-9, 176B3, 177E1
GAO scores OSHA, HEW unit 3-23, 280A2
Sleepwear flame retardant banned 4-7, 302E2 ★; **See CHEMICALS—Tris**
US saccharin ban modified 4-14, 280D1, F1
Chicago DES suit filed 4-25, 431A3
Adenosis-DES link rptd 4-25, 431E3
Fluorocarbon aerosol warning ordrd 4-26, 323B2
Handicapped bias rules signed 4-28, 338E3
Benzene worker exposure curbed 4-29, 345D1
NH A-plant protests 4-30—5-3, 344G3
DES risk rptd less 5-3, 432C1
Hysterectomy excesses chrgd 5-9, 732A3
WHO environmental study set 5-10, 431G1

1978

MEDICINE & Health—*See also U.S. GOVERNMENT—HEALTH, Education & Welfare; also country names*
Amer Med Pol Actn Com ranked 4th-top PAC fund-raiser 9-7, 753B2
Nobels to 3 announced 10-12, 886C1, E2
Hughes Med Inst breaks secrecy 12-7, 1010C3-1011A1
Abortion—*See ABORTION*
Birth Control & Family Planning—*See BIRTH Control*
Births—*See CHILDBIRTH*
Blood & Blood Pressure
Neurotransmitter measurability rptd 334B2
Hypertensn treatmt-heart attack reductn link rptd 1-7, 598D1
HEW anti-smoking drive set 1-11, 23E2
Donor labeling ordrd 1-13, 231A3
Benzene exposure rule issued 2-2, 85A3
Sickle cell tests halted by March of Dimes 3-8, 744C2
2 new cholesterol drugs rptd 5-27, 1023G1
New high blood pressure drug OKd 8-7, 727E3
China cigaret warning issued 8-28, 727G1
Blood test pinpoints marijuana use 8-29, 728C3
Sickle cell anemia study publshd 9-28, amniotic fluid test rptd 11-4, 948D1
Muscular distrophy test rptd 10-19, 948B1
Trauma transfusn treatmt rptd 12-6, 960E3
Platelets suspected in artery spasms 12-7, 992B3
Brain—*See also INTELLECT*
Neurotransmitter measurability rptd 334B2
Protein study rptd 2-18, 334E1
Tissue recovery after alcoholism rptd 6-10, 1023C2
Herpes simplex encephalitis drug OKd 10-24, 948G2
Encephalitis virus kills 480 in India 10-29, 992G3
Cancer—*See also 'Laetrile' below*
Vocal cord radiatn therapy cure rate cited 1-9, 13E3
EPA curbed on asbestos rule 1-10, 13A3
HEW anti-smoking crusade set 1-11, 23F2
NJ death rate studied 1-12, 23E3
Acrylonitrile worker exposure curbed 1-16, 85F3
Early pregnancy, breast cancer immunity link rptd 1-19, 334A1
Anti-smoking drive budgeted 1-23, 48E2
EPA asks chem water filtratn 1-25, 86B1
Benzene exposure rule issued 2-2, 85A3
Marijuana use with chemotherapy OKd by NM 2-22, 7-13, 598C3
Fluorocarbon aerosols banned 3-15, 186A2
Asbestos workers warned 4-26, 326A3
CPSC votes benzene curbs 4-27, 348A2
Tris garment exports banned 5-5, 347B3
Colon cancer, herpes virus linked 5-6, 1023A2
Nitrate-cured bacon curbed 5-15, 728F1
Hamburger frying risk rptd 5-16, 598G2

1979

MEDICINE & Health—*See also country names*
Carter urges privacy bill 4-2, 264D3
Waste cleanup legis provisn scored 6-13, 441B2
Nobel to 2 announced 10-12, 858E1
Abortion—*See ABORTION*
Alcoholism—*See ALCOHOLISM*
Birth Control & Family Planning—*See BIRTH Control*
Births—*See CHILDBIRTH*
Blood & Blood Pressure
Strokes rptd down 2-23, 2-28, 195F1
Sleep breathing study rptd 3-9, 196G2-C3
Moderate alcohol use, heart disease preventn linked 3-19, 219D1
Lead levels acad impact rptd 3-29, 266E1
Prenatal hemophilia test rptd 4-26, 315D2
Hypertensn drug linked to cancer 5-1, 354D3
Birth pill-hypertensn study rptd 5-7, 355F1
Hallucinogen tested by Army in '64 9-24, 727F1
Brain—*See also INTELLECT*
Strokes rptd down 2-23, 2-28, 195F1
New shock therapy tested 3-1, 290B1
Animal grafting rptd 5-11, 691G2
Pot use risks rptd 10-14, 972C1
Cancer—*See also 'Laetrile' below*
Estrogen, uterine cancer link rptd 1-4, 23F1-A2; 1-31, 139E1
Breast cancer rptd less with nursing 1-5, 64D2
Leukemia A-test link rptd ignored by PHS, HEW probe ordrd 1-8, 17B2
A-cancer apology asked by Utah offcl 1-13, 91C1
Benzaldehyde treatmt rptd effective 1-28, 139D1
Leukemia, '57 A-test linked 1-29, 2-1, 91E1
HEW radiatn safety studies asked 1-30, 90F3
Portsmouth shipyd A-study begins 1-31, 91A1
Viet vets file Agent Orange suit 2-1, 90A1
A-test funds case appeal lost, notificatn suit OKd 2-9, 112C2
Leukemia study sees less therapy 2-9, 139A2
Patients find job hostility 2-10, 139A3
Cigaret mfr rise rptd 2-11, 218E2

1980

MEDICINE & Health
State of State messages 1-2, 2-6, 269G1, 270F1; 1-15, 483D2
Islamic econ conf 11-4—11-6, 865C1
Abortion—*See ABORTION*
Alcoholism—*See ALCOHOLISM*
Birth Control & Family Planning—*See BIRTH Control*
Births—*See CHILDBIRTH*
Blood & Blood Pressure
New blood transfusn treatmt rptd 1-23, 159B3
Selacryn probe rptd 1-25, 63G3-64C1
US dietary guidelines issued 2-4, 157A3
Exercise, low cholesterol linked 2-14, 158E1
Crib death link rptd 2-28, 358E3
Iowa farm cancer study rptd 4-15, 357B3
Senility, aluminum link rptd 4-19, 415G3
Exercise, clot dissolutn linked 5-1, 674G3
NAS cholesterol rpt discounts health impact 5-27, stirs controvesy 6-1, 432G2
Toxic-shock syndrome cases rptd 6-6, 584B3
Toxic-shock syndrome, tampon use linked 9-17; recall ordered 9-22, 726F2-E3
Brain
Dopamine, schizophrenia link rptd 1-10, 415E1
Brain chem productn rptd 5-10, 715F1
Tex chem workers cancer cases rptd 7-24, 584C2
Cancer—*See also 'Laetrile' below*
Lung cancer among women rptd up 1-14, 40A2
OSHA sets job rules 1-16, 35G3
Interferon rptd produced in lab 1-16, 62G2
Life span changes rptd 1-19, 63B1
New blood transfusn treatmt rptd 1-23, 159C3
DES perils cited 1-25, 63F2, B3
Risks chart 357B1
GAO scores cancer-nitrite study 1-31, 159F1
US dietary guidelines issued 2-4, 157A3
Commercial THC dvpt rptd 2-4, pot found beneficial 3-24, 357F3
Cyclamate ban rptd upheld by FDA 2-7, 317D2
Atromid-S risk rptd 2-17, 159G2
Interferon productn rptd up 3-5, 317B3
Saccharin risk disputed 3-6, 317D1
3 Mile I gas venting proposed 3-12, Middletown (Pa) residents vs 3-20, 248E3

1976

Harvard DNA research halted 7-7, 736B1
Thermography research rptd 7-28, 680B1
'75 death rate rptd 7-31, 911F1
Breast cancer, estrogen link rptd 8-16, 680C1
NCI dir defends breast X-rays 8-22, guidelines issued 8-23, 679E3-680A1
Aerosol curb urged 9-13, 691D2
Tar, nicotine study rptd 9-14, 875F3
Morris Kupchan dies 10-19, 892B3
Coke oven emissns curb set 10-20, 847F3
China A-blast linked to thyroid cancer 12-27, 992F1

Cosmetic Industry—*See COSMETICS*

Death Issues
Quinlan wins right to die 3-31, 292C2
Quinlan off respirator 5-22, moved 6-10, 423D2
GOP platform text 8-18, 605A2
Calif right-to-die bill signed 9-30, 770E2
Sup Ct bars Quinlan case review 11-1, 867F3

Dentistry—*See also under 'Insurance' below*
UAW seeks benefits 3-18, 220D1
Medicaid fraud chrgd 8-30, 715E2

Diseases & Epidemics—*See also 'Blood' and 'Cancer' above, 'Heart' and 'Swine Flu' below*
Brazil '75 meningitis deaths totaled 1-8, 27A3
Angola typhoid threat rptd 1-9, 16D3
HEW rpts '75 arthritis, diabetes up 1-12, 32D1
Ulcers linked to econ 1-26, 159C3
'75 flu epidemic data rptd 1-28, 123B3
'74 stroke deaths rptd 2-3, 123F3
New asthma drug rptd 2-17, 159F2
Virus link to MS rptd 2-28, 224F2
US flu deaths rptd 2-28, 271B3
Cong OKs funds for arthritis, genetic programs 4-12, 282G2
Malaria parasite cultured 6-1, 423A3
Cong clears disease control bill 6-7, 434B2; signed 6-23, 982F1
US Dem platform text 6-15, 471D3
New arthritis strain rptd in Conn 7-18, 911G2
23 Legionnaires die 7-27—8-5, 573C2
'75 stroke deaths rptd 7-31, 911F1
Israel orders Leb polio immunizatn 8-6, 578E2
Rand alcoholism study backed 8-8, 814D3
Legionnaire cases total 179 8-31, 656D2-A3
Gonorrhea strain resists penicillin 9-2, 815A1
VD cited in PHS 5-yr plan 9-7, 680A2
FDA cold, asthma, allergy drugs study issued 9-8, 680A2
Polio vaccine danger rptd 9-23, 776B1
New Legionnaire probe set 9-30, 815D1
'Marburg' disease hits Zaire, Sudan 10-7, 795G2
Nobel won for hepatitis, neurology work 10-14, 840C1
Arthritis, diabetes programs signed 10-19, 834G2

1977

Breast X-rays curbed 5-10, 431C2
Detectn device exempted from fluorocarbon ban 5-11, 387A2
WHO doubts saccharin link 5-13, 531D1
Mich '74 DES suit dimissed 5-16, 431F3-432B1
US panel rpts saccharin risk 6-7, 531A1
Canada study links saccharin, smoking to bladder cancer 6-17, 530D3
Danes block PVC plants 7-7, 672F1
CIA mind-control tests revealed 8-1—8-9, 611A1
'78 authorization signed 8-1, 689A3
Govt orders nitrate data 8-31, 10-18, 820B1
S Africa to build cyclotron 9-15, 825A3
CIA tests on patients denied 9-20, 721D2
Hudson R water found toxic 9-28, 762A2
OSHA revises job rules 10-3, 778E1
Hair dye link rptd 10-17, 12-14, 962D3, 963A1
Saccharin ban delay clears Cong; label warning, additive studies ordrd 11-4, 878D1; signed 12-20, 1001F2
Narcotics study for pain relief urged 11-16; NIH study cited 992E3, G3
FDA bans 6 coloring dyes 12-12, 980G3
Leukemia, '57 A-bomb test link probed 12-13, 1022C3
NIOSH med data access upheld 12-22, 1008G2

Death Issues
Quinlan conditn rptd stable 3-31, 355A1
State right-to-die bills rptd 355D1
Swiss euthanasia directives issued 4-21, Zurich backs law 9-25, 767A1
Burn patients' choice rptd 8-11, 712D2
Canada Anglicans get rpt 8-17, 732G1

Dentistry
ADA chrgd re price-fixing 1-14, 156G2
Novocain cited in Gerovital 5-20, 508B3
Gen Foods sued on cereal ads 6-30, 613D2

Diseases & Epidemics—*See also 'Cancer' above*
Legionnaire bacteria rptd found 1-18, 81E1
Flu outbreak 1-26, shots resumed 2-8, 103F2
CDC dir asked to resign 2-4, 103C3
Smallpox spreads to Kenya 2-5, 224B1
Rocky Mt spotted fever kills 2 in Ga 2-27, 3-1, 288B2
Australia cholera strain identified 3-9, 199G1
Diabetes Assn scores saccharin ban 3-10, 177D1
Reye's syndrome cases rptd 3-11, 224E1
UN Water Conf held 3-14—3-25, 250F1
Australia cholera danger passes 3-16, 280C3
Measles upsurge rptd 3-19, 224C1
Flu damage claims rptd, Guillain-Barre cited 3-21, 224G1-C2
GAO scores OSHA, HEW unit 3-23, 280A2
HEW sets 7-disease immunization drive 4-6, 287E2
WHO launches immunizatn drive 4-7, 287B3
Cambodia malaria, cholera, dysentery rptd 5-2, 337A1
Airlines act on ozone illness 5-6, 369G1
Asthma spray exempted from fluorocarbon ban 5-11, 387G1
Carter forgn policy address 5-22, 397F2
Insulin gene reproductn rptd 5-23, 451E3
Arthritis forces Barnard retiremt 7-11, 619G3
Carter rebuts black criticism 7-25, 573G1
Diabetic drug sales barred 7-25, 603A2
Herpes encephalitis ara-A treatmt rptd 8-10, 675E2
Ulcer drug OKd by FDA 8-23, 748C2

1978

Fluoride-cancer link dismissed 5-18, 598A3
US-Sovt MD exchng delayed 5-26, 401G1
CPSC adopts cancer agent rules 6-1, 702C3
Neutron beam treatmt rptd 6-13, 598E2
Asbestos rule chngd by EPA 6-15, 512E3
Pregnancy x-ray risk seen 7-11, 598G2
Saccharin, cyclamate studies rptd inconclusive 7-19, 7-28, 727B3
Vet wins A-test exposure claim 8-1, 702E3
Indus funded AMA smoking study rpts hazards 8-5, 726G3
Niagara (NY) chem dump site declared disaster area 8-7, 703D1
'Tolerable' cigaret rpt debated 8-9, 8-10, 726F2-D3
Nitrate additives linked to lymphoma 8-11, phase-out proposed 8-31, 727G3
China cigaret warning issued, deaths noted by WHO 8-28, 727G1, A2
DBCP pesticide curbs asked 9-19, 719C2
Acrylonitrile exposure rule issued 9-29, 753G3
Benzene exposure rule upset 10-5, 834A1
Mich PBB contaminatn, liver cancer risk rptd 10-9, 769D2; suit dismissed 10-27, 834D1
Tris compensatn bill pocket vetoed 11-8, 941D3
Carcinogen curbs retained 12-21, 1009C1
Asbestos danger in schls cited 12-21, 1009G1
Nev A-test claims filed 12-21, 1011F3

Childbirth—*See CHILDBIRTH*

Death Issues
Calif 'right-to-die' response few 3-18, 597D3
Quinlan care cost rptd 4-10, still alive 5-14, 597B3
Calif MD mistrial in abortn death 5-5, 369E2

Dentistry
Ultrasonic equipmt exempted from rules 2-17, 231D3
Fluoride-cancer link refuted 5-18, 598A3
Insurnc coverage rptd up 5-21, 578C2
Polident ad complaint rptd setld 8-31, 702E2
Carter econ plan sets fee hike ceiling 12-13, 957B2

Diseases & Epidemics—*See also 'Cancer' and other appropriate subheads in this section*
Blood donor labeling ordrd, hepatitis data cited 1-13, 231B3
VD '77 decline rptd 1-28, 270F1
Glaucoma treatmt with marijuana OKd in NM 2-22, 598D3
Epilepsy drug OKd by FDA 2-28, 231B2
Diarrhea drug damages awarded in Japan 3-1, 232B1
Tay-Sachs tests halted by March of Dimes 3-8, 744C2
Allergy suppressant study rptd 3-11, 334D2
Ky battles equine VD 3-15—7-13, 539D2
Cystitis drug OKd by FDA 3-20, 231E2
Cholera rptd in Tanzania; Kenya, Somalia take precautions 3-22—4-5, 270B1
Anti-viral agent advance rptd 4-16, 334A3
Kidney patients, dialysis costs rptd 4-27, 578F1
Electrode implant paralysis treatmt rptd 5-6, 1023E1
Herpes virus linked to colon cancer 5-6, 1023A2
Glaucoma victim wins marijuana case 5-19, 728F3
Smallpox notificatn asked by WHO 5-26, 2 cases rptd in Eritrea 8-2, 636B1
Legionnaires' deaths rptd 5-28—8-8, bacterium isolated 8-11, 635C3
Kidney Medicare revisns signed 6-13, 466A1
Malaria rptd up in US, world 6-26, 8-6, 635F3
Measles cases rptd down 7-15, 636A1
Dutch polio epidemic declines 7-30, Canadian cases confrmd 8-10, 635A3
Ulcer-smoking link rptd in indus funded AMA study 8-5, 726D3, F3

1979

Utah '50s leukemia study rptd 2-14, 112B2
Blacks' rate rptd up 2-16, 139E2
Herpes warning issued 2-19, 140F1
Filter cigarets rptd less perilous 2-22, 218G1
Diagnosis secrecy study rptd 2-26, 218E1
Low-level radiatn risks seen 2-27, 207G3-208B1
Food-safety law revisns urged, saccharin ban backed 3-2, 195A1
Colo radium waste sites rptd 3-5, 187G1
Death rate rise rptd 3-5, 195A3
DES risk rptd less 3-6, 196C1
Facts on radiatn exposure 244D3
3 Mile I radiatn impact denied 4-4, 260E1
Psoriasis treatmt link rptd 4-12, 315B2
Hair dryer recall re asbestos sought 4-19, 308E2
GAO chrgs Cancer Inst blunders 4-24, 315G2-C3
Mich PBB cover-up indictmt 4-26, 597F3
Blood-pressure drug linked 5-1, 354D3
Low-level, A-power risks reviewed 5-2, 609E2, A3
3 Mile I radiatn estimate hiked 5-3, 344C1
Hair dryer recall praised 5-17, 595F3
Silkwood estate wins A-suit 5-18, 381E2
A-test radiatn liability case refused by Sup Ct 5-21, 400B3
Terminally ill treatmt rptd limited 5-31, 471F2
Ulcer drug OKd by FDA panel 6-1, 471D2
More states OK pot use 6-1, Ore law signed 6-18, 492C3
NC PCB dumping chrgd 6-4—6-13, disposal disputed 6-5, 597A3
Cancer Inst backs less radical breast surgery 6-6, 471B3
Methapyrilene drugs recalled 6-8, 471F1
DES banned in animal feed 6-28, 571G2
Mammal cloning advance rptd 7-28, 692F2
Film stars' deaths tied to '53 A-test 8-4, 630B1
Cancer cocoon discovery rptd 8-20, 735E1
Breast cancer drug rptd effective 9-11, 736C1
Kidney cancer linked to genetic defect 9-13, 735B2
Uterine cancer linked to estrogen use 9-14, 735A3
Cancer agents found in beer, warning urged 9-19, 9-22, 735E3-736B1
Pot use impact rptd 10-14, 972D1, E1
Formaldehyde link rptd 10-18, 971C1
Radioactive research threatned by A-dump closings 10-23, 806C3
Washn A-dump reopens 11-19, 885F3
GIs Agent Orange exposure rptd 11-24, 904D2
FDR rptd possible victim 12-2, 925E2

Childbirth—*See CHILDBIRTH*

Death Issues
Calif ct OKs respirator removal 2-15, 291B2
Md nurse freed in mercy deaths 3-29, 291F1-A2
Terminally ill treatmt rptd limited 5-31, 471E2
Artist carries out suicide plan 6-10, 521B2

Dentistry
Mil shortage rptd 2-16, 130D2
Dental ad accord reached 4-27, 596D1
Teeth replanted in China 5-1, 355B1
Fluoride efficacy doubted 9-1, 1000A2
'Laughing gas' hazard rptd 10-24, 971E2

Diseases & Epidemics—*See also 'Cancer' and other appropriate subheads in this section*
UK smallpox rpt released 1-3, 7A2
MS, heredity linked 1-4, 289E3
Crib death preventive device rptd 1-15, 64G1
Crib death risk increased by smoking 1-16, 64B1
Gonorrhea pill treatment rptd 1-20, 64B3
TB cases feared unrptd 2-9, 138C3
2 MDs cleared in epilepsy misdiagnosis 2-9, 139F3
Acne treatmt rptd 2-14, 138C2
Synctial virus kills 65 Italian babies 2-15, 138E3
3 VDs pose threat 2-19, 140D1
Pseudofolliculitis barbae case declined by Sup Ct 2-21, 128D3
Rickets found in vegetarian children 2-22, 140G1
Swiss animal rabies vaccine experimt rptd 2-28, 196E1
Psoriasis treatmt complicatn rptd 4-12, 315B2
Smallpox virus vials found 4-21, 315C3
Prenatal hemophilia test rptd 4-26, 315D2
Ulcer drug-sperm study rptd 5-3, 354E3
Vitamin C anti-infectn role studied 5-5, 691D2
New Parkinson's treatmt seen 5-11, 691A3
Flu vaccine progrm rptd underutilized, '76 Guillain-Barre link cited 5-18, 471B1
Virus found to cause diabetes 5-23, 471F3
Hepatitis A virus grown 5-31, 691D3
Ulcer drug OKd by FDA panel 6-1, 471C2
More states OK pot use 6-1, Ore law signed 6-18, 492B3

1980

Minn plant ends asbestos waste dumping 3-16, 227C1
Fewer detectn tests urged 3-20, 316B3-317D1
CPSC sued over Tris ban 3-24, 348F2
Breast cancer, enzyme link rptd 3-29, 415B3
Memphis area illness probed 4-2, 331A3
Office machine risks rptd 4-11, 357B1-A3
Iowa farm study rptd 4-15, 357A3
Calif A-lab cases rptd 4-22, 356E3
UAW probe rptd 4-22, 356G3
DES in cattle rptd 4-24, 358D1
'80s deaths rise seen 4-28, 356B3
PCB rules publshd 5-9, 387A2
Niagara chem dump study rptd 5-16, 386E3
Detergent carcinogen OKd 5-27, 526C3
Interferon success rptd 5-28, 526B2
CPSC seeks asbestos use data 5-30, 703F2
Beer carcinogen levels rptd down 6-12, 526D3
3 Mile I gas venting danger seen 6-18, krypton vented 6-28—7-11, 550E2-E3
Tighter chem controls urged; '70-76 rate rptd up 6-29, 494A3
OSHA benzene standard rejected by Sup Ct 7-2, 510D3
Tex chem worker cases rptd 7-24, 584C2
Nitrate ban rejected 8-19, 726C1
EPA toxic waste suits filed 10-7, 10-9, 825C1, F1
Nobel announced 10-10, 889E3
DES liability case refused by Sup Ct 10-14, 781D3

Death Issues
Life aid ordrd in Mass 'Right-to-Die' case 1-24, 158C2
Vatican issues euthanasia statemt 6-26, 970G1-C2

Dentistry
US dietary guidelines issued 2-4, 157A3

Diseases & Epidemics—*See also 'Cancer' above, 'Heart & Lungs' below*
Fetal skin disease test rptd 1-10, 64C1
Interferon rptd produced in lab 1-16, 62G2-E3
Life span changes rptd 1-19, 62F3
TB vaccines rptd ineffective 1-20, 63D1
New blood disease treatmt rptd 1-23, 159B3
Animal, bacteria gene differences rptd 1-23, 160C1
Gout remedy aids heart attack survival 1-31, 159E2
US dietary guidelines issued 2-4, 157A3
VD epidemic rptd, NGU rise blamed 2-5, 157G3
US influenza deaths rptd up 2-15, 158A3
Faster hay fever treatmt rptd 2-18, 159E3
Crib death heredity link rptd 2-28, 358C3
Penthouse publisher wins libel case 3-1, 239D2
Africa Rift Valley Fever epidemic rptd 3-2, 318F2-D3
Fed funded research info access curbed by Sup Ct 3-3, 210C1
Interferon productn rptd up 3-5, 317B3
'79 Sovt anthrax epidemic rptd 3-18, denied 3-20, 3-26, 235B2; cover-up chrgd 6-29, 500A1
Memphis area illness probed 4-2, 331G2
3 Mile I health study rptd 4-2, 332F2
La gonorrhea epidemic rptd 4-9, 584E3
Brazil polio drive stalled 4-16, 310G1-C2
Pollutn control benefits seen 4-21, 308B1, D1
Sneezing record rptd 4-29, 471D1
Cuban refugees rptd ill 5-6, 339G3
PCB rules publshd 5-9, 387A2
Niagara chem dump linked to nerve damage 5-21, 387B1
Malaria outbreak rptd 5-31, 478B1

1976

Pa plant illness identified 11-5, 911G1
UN smallpox progrm gets Lasker 11-17, 910G3
Legionnaires hotel closes 11-18, 911F2
Zaire outbreak contained 11-21, virus named 11-30, 931B3
Legionnaires probe scored 11-23—11-24, 911B2
New rabies vaccine rptd 12-13, 972D3
Guillain-Barre halts flu program 12-16, 950D1

1977

Australia denies salmonella in meat exports 8-29, 725B2
Pneumonia strain rptd resistant to drugs 9-2, 10-21, 847F1
Malaria up in Latin Amer, Asia 9-4, 747D3
Cholera widespread in Mideast; other deaths rptd in Ethiopia, S Pacific, Bangladesh 9-19—9-26, 747G3-748D1
Legion fever cases rptd 9-23, 748D1
Meningitis A vaccine rptd 9-28, 907G1
Gonorrhea strain rptd resistant to penicillin 10-22, 847D2
Diarrhea outbreak linked to DNA recombinatn 10-27, 846G3
Pneumonia vaccine gets FDA OK 11-21, 907A1

1978

Diabetes misdiagnosis rptd common 8-29; drug treatmts studied 9-7, 11-6, 947C3-948B1
New rabies vaccine rptd 9-10, 992F2
Smallpox death in UK 9-11; lab virus destructn asked 10-27, WHO continues countdown 11-7, 927F1-D2
Diabetic food labeling rule set 9-21, 770C1
Measles campaign announced by HEW 10-4, 927D3
Cholera outbreaks rptd in US, 6 other natns 10-8—11-30, 927E2
Muscular distrophy test rptd 10-19, 948B1
Syphilis rptd on rise 10-20, VD epidemic among homosexuals noted 11-6, 992F2
Herpes simplex drug OKd 10-24, 948G2
Infant botulism traced to honey 11-1, 948A2
Fungal keratitis drug OKd 11-1, 948A3
Arthritis drug OKd 11-1, 948B3
Measles, rubella infestatn rptd in military; immunizatn asked 11-10, 927A3
Legionnaires' data rptd 11-10; experts meet 11-13—11-15, scientific name assigned 11-18, 927F3
Rabies epidemic in Ala rptd 11-10, 992E2
Swine flu law challenge refused by Sup Ct 12-4, 959B2
Malaria, trenchfoot treatmt advances rptd 12-6, 960E3
Microwave safety scored 12-11, 962C3

1979

Polio outbreak among Amish rptd 6-5, vaccine sent 6-9, 472D1
PHS team sent to Asia 6-5, refugees strain San Fran health svcs 7-18, 550C2
Guillain-Barre flu shot claims rptd stalled 6-10, 470E3
Antibiotic-resistant bacteria rptd 6-25, 735A1
PCB limits in food cut 6-28, 571D2
Diabetes, virus linked 7-5, 692D2
'78 cholera cases rptd high 7-6, 620E2
Rabies cases rptd up 7-14, 620F2
Narcolepsy treatmt cited 7-16, 571F3
Cholera vaccine advance rptd 8-2, 692A3
Guillain-Barre flu shot claim settled, fatalities cited 8-14, 771E1
Parasites rptd in Viet refugees 8-25, 659D3
Allergies, cocaine use linked 9-5, 972B3
New drug to treat Gonorrhea rptd 9-6, 736C2
Immunizatn progrm rptd effective, childhood diseases down 9-11, 736D3
Pot use impact rptd 10-14, 972C1-E1
'Laughing gas' linked to kidney, liver, nervous diseases 10-24, 971E2
PPA pneumonia strain rptd 11-1, 971A2
Gonorrhea cases leveling off, syphilis rptd up 11-18, 971F1
Nonsurgical gallstone removal rptd 11-26, 897F1
Australia Aborigine health study ordrd 11-28, 906E3

1980

Toxic-shock syndrome cases rptd 6-6, 584A3
Rabies vaccine OKd 6-9, 526A3
Legionnaires disease rptd widespread 6-9, 527B1
Tighter chem controls urged 6-29, 494G2
Toxic-shock syndrome, tampon use linked 9-17; recall ordered 9-22, 726F2-E3
USSR convictns in anthrax outbreak rptd 9-25, 754A2

1976

Doctors—*See 'Physicians' below*
Drugs & Medical Supplies—*See also other appropriate subheads in this section; also NARCOTICS under 'N'*
FDA asks DES animal feed ban 1-9, 25E3
13 drug cos rpt forgn paymts 1-9—4-27, 361G1-362G1
FDA bans Red #2 dye 1-19, 44A2
Jackson urges generic drug use 1-22, 41B3
Red #2 ct challenge 1-27—2-13; FDA ban in effect 2-12, 137C1
'75 4th ¼ profits rptd 2-3, 215A3
Sup Ct rules on drug sales to hosps 3-24, 218A3
Medicaid fraud effort set 3-26, 249F1
FDA seeks chloroform ban 4-6, 249D2
Cong curbs FDA vitamin rules 4-12, 282E2, A3
1st ¼ profits rptd 4-29, 376C3
SEC lists corp paymts 5-12, 726C1
FDA med supply powers voted 5-13, 377E1
NJ MD chrgd re curare 5-19, 384A3
FDA inquiry scored 5-23, 392D1
Sup Ct voids price ad ban 5-24, 393E1
Supply regulatn signed 5-28, 982E1
Dem platform text 6-15, 471F2
Nurses chrgd in '75 Pavulon deaths 6-16, 503F3
Red dye ban upheld 7-6, 571C1
SEC sues Foremost, settles 7-7, 669A2
Olympics disqualify 3 re steroids 7-30, 563A2
'69 trust suit ends in mistrial 8-17, 988A3
Medicaid fraud chrgd 8-30, 715E1, E2
Red #4, carbon black dyes banned 9-22, 729A3
Sup Ct bars review of NC tetracycline antitrust suit 10-4, 807B3
Marijuana use for glaucoma OKd 10-5, 860F3
Sarett gets Science Medal re chemotherapy, cortisone 10-18, 858F3
2 get Lasker 11-17, 910F3
Prescriptn drug panel formed 11-30, 931G2
Forgn paymt studies issued 12-18, 12-20, 985G1, D2
Euthanasia—*See 'Death Issues' above*

1977

Doctors—*See 'Physicians' below*
Drugs & Health-Care Products—*See also 'Laetrile' below; also NARCOTICS under 'N'*
Sterling, Carter-Wallace rpt forgn paymts 1-3, 94B1
Vitamin ads to children barred 2-7, 217C1
Sup Ct voids NY prescriptns rule 2-22, 150F1
DNA patent order lifted 2-24, 184C2
Hospital deaths rptd 2-28, 224D2
New drugs linked to DNA resrch 3-7—3-9, 184E2
Canada sets saccharin ban 3-9, 177F1
Medtronic forgn paymts rptd 3-11, 233C3
Rorer-Amchem sued re payoffs 3-16, 503B2
Sharon Steel ends Foremost takeover bid 4-5, 275E1
Birth pill warning to MDs, druggists ordrd 4-8, 355D1
US-Cuba trade sought 4-11, 283G1
Chicago DES study suit filed 4-25, 431G2
Adenosis-DES link rptd 4-25, 431E3
Fluorocarbon aerosol warning ordrd 4-26, 323E1
DES cancer risk rptd less 5-3, 432C1
Mich '74 DES suit dimissed 5-16, 431F3-432B1
Gerovital mfr OKd in Nev Novocain component cited 5-20, 508A3
Insulin gene reproductn rptd 5-23, 451D3
222 Medicaid violatns rptd 6-18, 643G2
'75 Pavulon death convictns 7-13, 568F2
Hercules buys Warren-Teed 7-19, 650F3
Lilly buys Ivac 7-20, 650E3
Phenformin sales barred 7-25, 603A2
2d ¼ profit drop rptd 7-28, 668B3
CIA mind-control tests revealed 8-1—8-9, 610F3
Listerine corrective ad order upheld 8-2, 613F1-A2
Ara-A advance in herpes encephalitis rptd 8-10, 675E2
Tagamet OKd by FDA 8-23, 748C2
Antibiotic curbs in animal feed asked 8-30, 10-21, 847F2
Antibiotic-resistant pneumonia rptd 9-2, 10-21, 847F1
Propranolol, other beta-blockers rptd successful for heart ailmts 9-22, 907E2
Erythromycin used vs legion fever 9-23, 748G1
Meningitis A vaccine rptd 9-28, 907G1
Lincomycin microbe patent OKd 10-6, 847E1
Miles, Alcon takeovers OKd 10-17, 11-17, 880D1
Penicillin-resistant gonorrhea rptd 10-22, 847D2
Antibiotic-resistant bacteria linked to DNA recombinatn 10-27, 847A1
Pneumonia vaccine gets FDA OK 11-21, 907A1
Religious mental patient case refused 11-28, 919B3
Insulin, hormones from bacteria rptd 12-1, 1022B3

1978

Doctors—*See 'Physicians' below*
Drugs & Health-Care Products—*See also 'Laetrile' below; also NARCOTICS*
Tetracycline trust suit by forgn nations OKd 1-11, 33D3
Sun Oil buys Becton 1-17, Cong probe asked 1-27, 65F3
Carter State of Union Message 1-19, 32B1
FDA sets ultrasonic standards 2-17, 231C3
Valproate OKd for epilepsy 2-28, 231B2
Quinoform damages awarded in Japan 3-1, 232B1
Sun Oil sued re takeover 3-9, 223F1
Vitamin A, D curbs revoked 3-14, 231F3
Respiratory drugs exempted from fluorocarbon ban 3-15, 186B2
Drug law revisn proposed, PMA scores 3-16, 231C1-A2
DMSO OKd for cystitis 3-20, 231E2
FDA benylin seizure case refused by Sup Ct 3-27, 241E1
Listerine corrective ad rule review denied by Sup Ct 4-3, 280C3
Anacin ads enjoined 5-2, 347F3
Boone held liable for acne ads 5-11, 702F2-A3
FTC adopts eyewear ad proposal 5-24, 434C1
Colestipol, nicotinic acid rptd effective vs cholesterol 5-27, 1023G1
NJ curare murder case-press freedom controversy 6-30—8-30, 678D2
Drug-resistant malaria rptd 8-6, 635F3
Metoprolol (Lopressor) OKd for high blood pressure 8-7, 727E3
FDA issued oil of wintergreen (methyl salicylate) warning 8-17, 727F3
Butorphanol tartrate (Stadol) OKd as pain killer 8-30, 727F3
Polident ad complaint rptd setld 8-31, 702E2
Synthetic gene insulin research rptd 9-7, 947D3
House subcom probes mislabeling abuses 9-8, 727E2
FDA backs generic drugs 9-13, 727C2
Expiratn date labeling ordrd 9-13, 727F2
Anacin ads ruled misleading 9-16, 769F3
Dobutamine hydrochloride (Dobutrex) OKd 10-3, 948E2
FTC injunctn halts acne cure ads 10-10, 942B1
Progestin pregnancy risk cited by FDA 10-12, 948D2
Thalidomide victim bears child 10-13, 948F3
NJ MD acquitted in curare murder case 10-24, 841F1-B2
Injectable vidarabine (Vira-A) OKd 10-24, 948G2
'Beta blocker' propranolol (Inderal) withdrawal risk cited 11-1, 948G1
Natamycin OKd for fungal keratitis 11-1, 948A3
Sulindac (Clinoril) OKd 11-1, 948A3
Drug data case refused by Sup Ct 11-6, 873F3
Tolbutamide (Orinase), other diabetes drugs tied to heart attacks 11-6, 948A1
ND, Ark referenda results 11-7, 855A1, B1
Swine flu vaccine liability case refused by Sup Ct 12-4, 959B2
Nitroglycerin, aspirin for artery spasms studied 12-7, 992C3

1979

Doctors—*See 'Physicians' below*
Drugs & Health-Care Products—*See also 'Laetrile' below; also NARCOTICS*
Estrogen, uterine cancer link rptd 1-4, 23F1-A2; 1-31, 139E1
Generic drug drive stepped up, FDA releases list 1-9, 23B2
Childbirth anesthetics, pain-killers effect on babies rptd 1-16, 64C1
Tetracycline rptd effective for gonorrhea 1-20, 64B3
Daylin OKs Grace takeover, drops Narco bid 1-24, 88E3
Benzaldehyde rptd effective vs lung cancer 1-28, 139D1
Vitamin A variant for acne rptd 2-14, 138C2
Darvon (propoxyphene) ban rejected by HEW; FDA hearing, MD warning ordrd 2-15, 138F2
Synctial virus vaccine research rptd 2-15, 138F3
Blue Shield drug plan trust rule upheld by Sup Ct 2-27, 165A1
Hypertensn drugs linked to stroke decline 2-28, 195G2
DES cancer risk rptd less 3-6, 196C1
Hosp cost-control hearings open 3-9, 194G3
Skaggs to take over Amer Stores 3-14, 283C1
Nader group suits curbed 3-14, 308A2
Calif hearing-aid ad case refused by Sup Ct 3-19, 203B3
Carter proposes regulatory reform 3-25, 230G1
Price guidelines tightened 3-29, 264A2
Carter resubmits drug law plan 4-20, 315A2
UK thalidomide article censorship scored 4-26, 331A1
Sleep aid, nose spray ban asked 5-1, 354B3
Reserpine linked to cancer 5-1, 354D3
Cimetidine (Tagamet)-sperm study rptd 5-3, 354E3
Vitamin C anti-infectn role studied 5-5, 691D2
Arminone rptd effective for heart failure 5-8, 472C1
Phenylpropanolamine, benzocaine OKd as diet aids 5-12, 571F3
NJ co ups women's pay 5-13, 482G3
Flu vaccine program underutilized 5-18, 471B1
FTC backs nonprescriptn ad limits 5-22, 596G1
Terminally ill treatmt rptd limited 5-31, 471F2
Hepatitis A vaccine progress seen 5-31, 691D3
Tagamet OKd by FDA panel 6-1, 471C2
Methapyrilene drugs recalled 6-8, 471F1
Polio vaccine for Amish sent 6-9, 472D1
Guillain-Barre flu shot claims rptd stalled 6-10, 470E3
Consumers' right to sue protected by Sup Ct 6-11, 478E2
Long-wear contact lenses OKd by FDA 6-13, 572D1
MD-managed insurnc plan cuts costs 6-14, 570D3
FDA drug approval process scored 6-19, 572B2
Nonprescriptn daytime sedatives banned 6-22, 572G1
Antibiotics in animal feed rptd risky 6-25, 734F3
Merck OKs minority jobs plan 6-26, 521F1
Yellow No 5 labeling ordrd 6-26, 571A2
Merck added to Dow Jones index 6-28, 481F2
DES banned in animal feed 6-28, 571B3
Prescription drug leaflets urged by FDA 6-29, 571E1
Acne ad refunds set 7-2, 596D2
Cholera vaccine advance rptd 8-2, 692A3

1980

Doctors—*See 'Physicians' below*
Drugs & Health-Care Products—*See also 'Laetrile' below; also NARCOTICS*
Molsidomine rptd effective vs angina 1-3, 24B1
Interferon rptd produced in lab 1-16, 62G2
TB vaccines rptd ineffective 1-20, 63D1
DES, problem pregnancies rptd linked 1-25, 63C2
FDA Selacryn probe rptd 1-25, 63G3-64C1
Sulfinpyrazone aids heart attack survival 1-31, 159C2
Buprenorphine rptd effective vs heroin addictn 2-2, 160E1
Foremost-McKesson merger talks end 2-6, 386D1
Lorelco, Atromid-S risks rptd 2-17, 159G2
Faster hay fever treatmt rptd 2-18, 159E3
FTC scores birth control ads, complaint setld 2-28, 358F2
Interferon productn rptd up 3-5, 317B3
McCormick vs Sandoz merger bid 3-18, 386B1
African dependence on S Africa mfg cited 4-1, 243A2
DES violators warned 4-15, widespread cattle use rptd 4-24, 358D1
3 Mile I health study rptd 4-17, 332B3
Darvon (propoxyphene) to be curbed; '78-79 related deaths rptd 4-24, 358A2
Anturane sale blocked 4-25, 526G3
'79 Fortune 500 data rptd 5-5, 291E1
Heart disease curb rptd 5-22, 527F1
Interferon success rptd 5-28, 526B2
Chloroquin resistant malaria cases rptd 5-31, 478B2
Rabies vaccine OKd 6-9, 526A3
Iran takeover of Eur co units rptd 7-9, 546A2
Tranquilizer warnings set 7-11, 584E1
US banned item export curb set 8-2, 599G2
DES liability case refused by Sup Ct 10-14, 781D3
Dow buys Richardson-Merrell unit 11-3, 985E2
New England Nuclear, Du Pont merger set 12-8, 985A2
Schering settles job bias case 12-14, 962D3

1976

Federal Aid—*See also 'Insurance', 'Presidential Election' and other appropriate subheads*
Ford State of Union message 1-19, 36F3, 38A1, F2, 39E2
'77 budget proposals 1-21, 62B3, C3, 63F1, 64E3, 66E2
HEW funds veto overridden 1-27, 1-28, 69A2
Ford notes states' need 2-23, 149A3
Fscl '77 Ford, House com budgets table 231B1
Cong OKs health program funds 4-12, 282D2
Health program funds signed 4-22, 982E1
Cong OKs '77 budget target 5-12, 5-13; Ford, OMB, Cong budgets table 358F1, C2
Cong clears added funds 5-19, 411E3
Cong clears disease control, health promotion funds 6-7, 434B2; signed 6-23, 982F1
Cong '77 budget levels, table 9-16, 706C2
Cong clears Indian aid 9-16, 745D3; signed 9-30, 982G1
Cong OKs HEW inspector gen 9-29, 765G2-C3; signed 10-15, 982G1
'77 HEW funds veto overridden 9-30, 727A3
Cong OKs veterans bill 10-1, 807D1; signed 10-21, 982G1
Block grant bill not cleared 10-2, 883E3
Educ aid signed 10-13, 788E2
Emergency care extensn signed 10-21, 834A3
Transitn ¼ fed spending rptd down 10-27, 866D1
Mayors urge spending 12-14, 937A3

Food Contamination—*See FOOD*

Handicapped
Anchorage anti-bias law passage rptd 1-3, 7D1
'77 budget proposals 1-21, 62B3, 65D1, G1
Cong OKs rehabilitatn act extensn 2-17, 3-2, 182D1
Disability cutoff procedures upheld 2-24, 169B2
Ford asks educ aid plan 3-1, 166D3
Rehabilitatn Act extensn cleared 3-2, 182D1; signed 3-15, 982E1
Soc Sec trustees rpt to Cong 5-24, 398C3
Dem platform text 6-15, 472F3
Carter acceptance speech 7-15, 510G2
Ford signs housing aid 8-3, 566F3
Dole support cited 8-16, 8-19, 599F1
GOP platform text 8-18, 604G3, 605G3
Tax bill exempts sick pay 9-16, 705E3
Vet benefits hiked 9-21, 10-1, 807A1-E1; signed 9-30, 982G1

Heart & Lungs—*See also 'Smoking-Health Link' under TOBACCO*
HEW rpts '75 heart disease down 1-12, 32A1, B1
New artery x-ray tech rptd 1-21, 159C2
Coronary disease, econ linked 1-26, 159C3
Boston U gets hypertensn grant 1-30, 123G3 ★
'74 death rate rptd 2-3, 123F3
New asthma drug rptd 2-17, 159E2
House expands black-lung benefits 3-2, 181F3
Cong OKs research funds 4-12, 282E2, A3
FDA pacemaker powers voted 5-13, 377E1
High-risk flu group identified 6-10, 443C2
Dem platform text cites black lung disease 6-15, 470D3
Black-lung law upheld 7-1, 568E3
'75 death rate rptd 7-31, 911F1
Tar, nicotine study rptd 9-14, 875F3
UMW asks black-lung safeguards 9-23—10-2, 748E2
Coke oven emissns curb set 10-20, 847F3
Swine flu progrm limited 11-15, 911C1
2 get Lasker 11-17, 910F3

1977

Federal Aid
Ford '78 budget proposals 1-17, 32C1, F2
Carter budget revisions 2-22, 125A2, D3
Carter call-in topic 3-5, 171D1
HEW reorganizatn effected 3-9, 175A3
Handicapped protest at HEW, demand rules signed 4-5—4-16, 301D2
Carter energy plan 4-20, 290G1; fact sheet 292C1
Handicapped rules signed 4-28, 338E2
Armed svs schl funds signed 5-4, 339G1
Carter scores liberals' criticism 5-12, 380F3
Cong sets '78 target 5-17, 405A1
'78 health progrms extensn signed 8-1, 689G2
Conn hosp constructn halted 8-25, 669F2
Vet benefits review signed 10-8, 773A2
Forgn aid funds clear Cong 10-19, 815E2; Carter signs 11-1, 834D1
Rural clinic aid, urban study projects clear Cong 11-29, 938F1; signed 12-13, 1001G2
Forgn-trained US student transfer rule eased 12-7, 959C2; signed 12-20, 1001A3

Food Contamination—*See FOOD*

Handicapped
NYC schl discriminatn chrgd 1-18, 112C2
Hearing-aid sale rules set 2-13, 217F1
Protest at HEW 4-5—4-16, 301D2
FAA sets passenger rules 4-7, 325G2
HEW educ office reorganized 4-11, 302A1
HEW rules signed 4-28, 338E2
Carter seeks Soc Security chngs 5-9, 363G2
HEW sued re Southn schls 5-11, 446D2
Tax credit for blind cleared 5-16, 381G3
Carter welfare plan outlined 5-25, 445F2
US plans child adoptn subsidy 7-12, 628F2
Carter welfare proposals 8-6, 608E3, 609A1
Bus riders' 'bill of rights' set 8-8, 627D2
Amtrak redcap svc end blocked 9-12, 778A3
Vets mil disability pensn hike signed 10-3, 877F3
Soc Sec revisns clear House 10-27, 814E3
Vets non-mil disability hike clears Cong 11-3, 877E3
Benefits loss on marriage upheld 11-8, 857A1
Career guidance aid, anti-bias projcts clear Cong 11-29, 959B2; signed 12-13, 1001G2

Heart & Lungs
Asbestos workers sue HEW 2-15, 422C2
Coronary bypass surgery questnd 3-9, 9-22, 907B2
Flu damage claims rptd 3-21, 224G1-C2
Longest heart transplant survivor dies 3-22, 264C2
Birth pill-smoking risk rptd 3-29, 287F3
Handicapped bias rules signed 4-28, 338E3
Asthma spray exempted from fluorocarbon ban 5-11, 387A2
Pregnant women warned vs alcohol 6-1, 472F1
Heart patient survives surgery without blood supply 6-2, 620A1
Baboon heart implant fails 6-20, future chimpanzee transplants seen 6-21, 619B3
Heart disease, smoking linked in post-menopausal women 6-25, 620C1
Barnard rpts early retiremt 7-11, 619G3
'76 heart disease deaths down 7-25, 962B3
'78 authorization signed 8-1, 689A3
Heart surgery hosp designatns proposed 9-26, 869A3
Chimpanzee implant fails 10-17, 847C3
Liquid protein diet deaths rptd 11-9, 992C3
Lasker Award presented 11-16, 927A3
Pneumonia vaccine OKd 11-21, 907A1

1978

Federal Aid—*See also 'Medicaid' and 'Medicare' below*
Carter budget proposals 1-23, 44F2, 47C1, 48G1; table 45E2
Cabt-level Educ Dept proposed 4-14, 279C1
Carter tax proposal rejctd by House com 4-17—4-19, 305G3
Health Planning Act upheld by Sup Ct 4-17, 308A3
Kidney dialysis costs rptd 4-27, 578F1
Cong '79 budget target res cleared 5-17, 385F2
Hosp cost bill OKd by House com 7-18, 550E3
Mondale cites Admin cost-cutting effort 8-7, 811C1
Rural health progrm planned 10-2, 770D1
Viet vets progrm urged 10-10, 878E1
Amateur sports omnibus funds clear Cong 10-15, 842D2
Carter anti-inflatn plan to monitor costs 10-24, 806D1
Inner-city progrm urged 12-20, 1009F1
Carter restores '80 budget funds 12-22, 1002E3

Food Contamination—*See FOOD*
Genetics—*See GENETICS*
Handicapped—*See HANDICAPPED*

Heart & Lungs
Hypertensn treatmt-heart attack reductn link found 1-7, 598D1
HEW anti-smoking drive set 1-11, 23E2
Anti-smoking drive budgeted 1-23, 48E2
Black lung bills clear Cong 1-24, 2-15, finance measure signed 2-10, 125E1-E2; eligibility measure signed 3-1, 218B2
Heart victim hosp study rptd 2-2, 578A2
Asbestos workers get $20 mln setlmt 2-8, 326C3
Paraquat peril in marijuana warned 3-10, rptd exaggerated 8-3, 728B2
Respiratory drugs exempted from fluorocarbon ban 3-15, 186B2
Japan heart death rise rptd 3-20, 598C1
Strenuous work found reducing heart attacks 3-24, 597F3
White lung disease, cancer warning issued asbestos workers 4-26, 326A3
Lung damage rptd in chronic marijuana users 5-15, 728G2
2 new cholesterol drugs rptd 5-27, 1023A2
Women smokers risk rptd 6-8, 727A1
Brown lung preventn rules issued, suits filed 6-19, 471C3
Liquid protein diet risk rptd 6-26, 727A3
Indus funded AMA smoking study rpts hazards 8-5, 726D3
New high blood pressure drug OKd 8-7, 727E3
'Tolerable' cigaret rpt debated 8-9, 8-10, 726F2-D3
China cigaret warning issued 8-28, 727G1
FTC egg ad case declined by Sup Ct 10-2, 751D2

1979

NJ MD curare case costs ordrd paid by NY Times 8-14, 656E2
Guillain-Barre flu shot claim settled 8-14, 771E1
Revlon to buy Technicon 9-6, 664A1
Cefoxitin rptd effective vs gonorrhea 9-6, 736C2
Fed immunizatn progrm rptd effective 9-10, 736D3
Tamoxifen rptd effective vs breast cancer 9-11, 736C1
Estrogen use linked to uterine cancer 9-14, 735A3
Bristol-Myers ads assailed by FTC 10-12, 902F3
'Laughing gas' hazard rptd 10-24, 971E2
Corticosteroid drugs linked to PPA pneumonia 11-1, 971A2

Federal Aid—*See also 'Medicaid' and 'Medicare' below*
Carter aide warns Dems on 'new realities' 1-4, 3E2
Carter restores some '80 budget cuts 1-4, 3D3
Carter budget proposals 1-22, 41E2, 44D2-B3; table 42E2
Flu vaccine progrm rptd underutilized 5-18, 471B1

Food Contamination—*See under FOOD*
Genetics—*See GENETICS*
Handicapped—*See HANDICAPPED*

Heart & Lungs
Enlarged heart detectn method (echocardiology) rptd 1-13, 64G2
Smog rule eased, protests ensue 1-26, 90E1, F1
Benzaldehyde rptd effective vs lung cancer 1-28, 139D1
Cigaret mfr rise rptd 2-11, 218E2
Blacks' lung cancer rate rptd up 2-16, 139G2
Filter cigarets rptd less perilous 2-22, 218G1
Amputatn linked to heart deaths 2-26, 219G1
Lung cancer rise rptd 3-5, 195C3, E3
Female exertn tests rptd inaccurate 3-8, 196D2
Hosp cost-control hearings open 3-9, 194E3
Sleep breathing (apnea) study rptd 3-9, 196F2-C3
Heart disease preventn, alcohol use linked 3-19, 219A1
Coal miner pay hike case declined by Sup Ct 4-30, 364C3
Heart-transplant survivals rptd 5-6, 355C1
Heart failure pill rptd effective 5-8, 472C1
Silkwood estate wins A-suit 5-18, 381E2
Tuberculosis rptd in Viet refugees 8-25, 659D3
Army sued on San Fran '50 germ warfare test 9-16, 727D1
Hallucinogen tested by Army in '64 9-24, 727F1
Mass man heart transplant aid rptd 10-10, 1005D3
Pot use risks rptd 10-14, 972C1-D1

1980

Federal Aid—*See also 'Medicaid', 'Medicare' below*
Carter State of Union proposals 1-23, 43A1, F2
Carter budget proposals 1-28, 69D3, E3; table 70E1
Black Caucus vs Carter budget 2-5, 94G2
Kennedy 'basic speech' excerpts 3-10, 183D1-F1, G2, 184A2
Cuban, Haitian assistance set 6-20, 485A1
US, Canada health care costs compared 7-16, 562C3
Cuban, Haitian refugee funds budgeted 8-13, 617E1
Mental health authrzn clears Cong 9-24, 9-30, signed 10-7, 803E3

Food Contamination—*See FOOD--Contamination Issues*
Genetics—*See GENETICS*
Handicapped—*See HANDICAPPED*

Heart & Lungs
Molsidomine rptd effective vs angina 1-3, 24B1
Lung cancer among women rptd up 1-14, 40A2
Life span changes rptd 1-19, 63B1
TB vaccines rptd ineffective 1-20, 63D1
Heart attack survival aided by gout remedy 1-31, 159C2
US dietary guidelines issued 2-4, 157A3
Pneumonia linked to VD 2-5, 158B1
Airline ozone measures rptd 2-12, 159A1
Exercise, reduced heart attack risk linked 2-14, 158E1
US pneumonia deaths rptd 2-15, 158A3
Anti-cholesterol drug risk rptd 2-17, 159G2
Crib death heredity link rptd 2-28, 358C3
Smoking risk to nonsmokers rptd 3-26, 318F1
Retarded youth surgery case refused by Sup Ct 3-31, 291B3
Anturane sale blocked 4-25, 526G3
Exercise, clot dissolutn linked 5-1, 674F3
Heart disease curb rptd 5-22, 527F1
NAS cholesterol rpt discounts link 5-27, stirs controversy 6-1, 432F2
Exercise study questns disease preventn 7-5, 715D3
OSHA cotton dust standard case accepted by Sup Ct 10-6, 782D1

1976

Hospitals & Nursing Homes—*See also 'Insurance' below*
HEW rpts '75 admittance 1-14, 32G1
8 PHS units face closings 1-21, 65C1
Ill nursing home fires 1-30, 2-4, 271G2
Hollander pleads guilty 2-2; sentncd 5-4, 5-18, 384C3
AFL-CIO plan nursing home drive 2-20, 149E1
NLRB rules vs interns, residents 3-22, 220E1
Sup Ct rules on drug sales 3-24, 218A3
Sup Ct bars review of rule on husband in delivery room 4-5, 262B2
NJ MD indicted re curare deaths 5-19, 384A3
US Dem platform text 6-15, 473B1
Nurses chrgd in '75 VA Hosp deaths 6-16, 503D3
US Sup Ct rules on laws 6-24, 468A2
Calif MD convicted 6-24, 860D2
La pub hosp slowdown ends 7-3, 1016E3
NY strike 7-7—7-17, 553E2
Carter spending record cited 512C2
2d NY strike 8-4—8-7, 648B1
Ill nurse killer denied parole 9-15, 860A2
Pres candidates dispute church taxatn 10-2, 743E2, G2
Amer Hosp sued 12-29, 986G1

Insurance—*See also 'Medicaid', 'Medicare' and 'Presidential Election' below*
HEW rpts '75 coverage 1-12, 32E1
Ford State of Union message 1-19, 38A1, 39F2
Mansfield sees catastrophic coverage 1-19, 40A1
'77 budget proposals 1-21, 62C3, 64E3
Jackson for natl program, malpractice re-insurnc 1-22, 41A3
Calif MD slowdown ends 2-5, 144B3
Disability cutoff procedures upheld 2-24, 169B2
Black Dems draft plank 5-1, 343E3
Ill MD wins malpractice suit 6-1, 1016A3
Carter vs 'instant approach' 6-3, 411D1
Blue Cross studies alcohol coverage 6-9, 443F1
Dem platform goal 6-15, 432B3
Flu vaccine-maker to lose insurance 6-15, 443F1
Sup Ct upholds black-lung law 7-1, 568E3
La MD malpractice bill signed 7-2, 1016E3
'75-76 MD malpractice data rptd 7-28, 1016D3
Cong OKs flu vaccine liability 8-10, 586C2
'69 drug trust suit ends in mistrial 8-17, 988C3
Flu immunizatn plan delayed 9-1, 656D3
Hawaii malpractice law in effect, Argonaut rates hiked 9-1, 1016E3 ★
PHS 5-yr plan issued 9-7, 680E1
Cong eases HMO aid rules 9-23, 765B2; signed 10-8, 982G1
Calif right-to-die bill signed 9-30, 770G2
No cong actn on natl plan 10-2, 883D3
'73-75 MD fees, malpractice rates linked 10-25, 1016F3

1977

Hospitals & Nursing Homes
Ford seeks PHS closings 1-17, 32F1
Carter asks HEW cost study 1-31, 89G3
Carter signs emergency gas bill 2-2, 76D2
Carter budget revisions 2-22, 125D3
Drug-related deaths rptd 2-28, 224D2
Carter for cost curbs; 'creeping controls' scored 4-15, 299C1, E2
Carter energy plan 4-20, 290G1; fact sheet 292C1
Carter for cost control legis 4-25; reactn 4-25—4-26, 322A1, G1
CAT scanner curbs proposed 5-2, 869B3
Califano chrgs hosp fund-wasting; AHA vs Admin costs role 5-24, 479F1
Medicaid cuts for 20 states set 6-8, 460B3
Califano, AMA debate cost control 6-19, 479B1
State abortn curbs upheld 6-20, 516D2
NYS, SD abortn rulings vacated; NJ case refused 6-27, 538G3
NYC blackout affects 7-13—7-14, 537G2
'75 VA Hosp death convictns 7-13, 568F2
CIA mind-control tests revealed 8-1—8-9, 610C3
House OKs Carter energy pkg 8-5, 609B3, 610A1
HMOs hailed for cost control 8-5, 643E2
Califano urges Cong act on costs 8-17, 643A3
US halts Conn constructn 8-25, 669F2
Califano notes cost increases 9-9, proposes cutbacks 9-26, 869D2
Pa hosp oxygen, anesthesia mixup rptd fatal 9-10, 748G1
Gas deregulatn bill cites 10-4, 758B2
Energy tax credits clear Sen 10-31, 832G2
NJ, Va referenda OKd 11-8, 879C2
Rural clinic aid, urban study projcts clear Cong 11-29, 938F1; signed 12-13, 1001G2
VA Hosp convictns overturned 12-19, 991G2

Insurance—*See also 'Medicaid' and 'Medicare' below*
Sup Ct bars Fla malpractice law review 1-10, 57A2
CBO on natl program cost 2-15, 126G1
Carter asks hosp cost controls 4-25, 322E1
CAT scanner curbs urged 5-2, 869D3
Kennedy sees reforms endangered 5-16, Carter vows natl plan 5-17, 381F2
Califano cites goal 6-19, 479E1
'76 Hyde abortn amendmt vacated 6-29, 557B3
Copper cos strike 7-1, 558E1
Carter town mtg topic 7-21, 575B1
Pregnancy, disability benefits voted by Sen 9-16, 738A1
Kaiser-Permanente HMO certified 10-26, 869G3
Natl Women's Conf urges more benefits 11-19—11-21, 917D3
Carter to offer plan in '78 12-28, 1002B1

1978

Dobutrex OKd for heart failure 10-3, 948E2 ★
Progestin birth-defect risk cited 10-12, 948D2
'Beta blocker' withdrawal danger rptd 11-1, 948F1
Diabetes pills tied to attacks 11-6, 947G3
Coronaries linked to artery spasms 12-7, 992A3

Hospitals & Nursing Homes—*See also 'Malpractice' below*
Amer Medicorp OKs Humana bid 1-10, 66A3
Carter State of Union Message 1-19, 32A1
Carter budget proposals 1-23, 46G1, 48A2
Eilberg fund role probe cited 1-24, 62E2
Bergman sentenced 2-2, 232F3
Heart victim hosp study rptd 2-2, 578A2
Hosp interns, residents no-union rule denied review 2-27, 143B2
Surplus beds rptd 3-21, Blue Cross offers plan 6-20, 577E2
NYC nursing homes struck 4-4—4-7, 284F3-285A1
Cath laity pastoral role rptd 4-7, 294G3
Carter asks cost-containmt bill OK, cites higher costs since '50 4-11, 259F3
Cong energy conferees OK insulatn provisn 4-21, 304G3, 305G1
Hosp insurnc fund reform urged 5-16, 368D3
Oral Roberts hosp OKd 5-25, 577A3
LA plans layoffs 6-7, 425B3
Cost containmt trust exemptn denied 6-13, 577C2
Nurses rpt understaffing 6-18, 578B2
Police interrogatns curbed by Sup Ct 6-21, 509E2
AMA asks chrgs curbed 6-21, 578C1
Union organizing backed by Sup Ct 6-22, 508E3
NJ curare murder case press freedom controversy 6-30—8-30, 678C2
Cost control bill OKd by House com, lid rejected 7-18, 550D3
Carter vs House com on cost-containmt 7-20, 549E3
Eilberg chrgd by ethics com 9-13, 697A2
Gas bill OKd by Sen 9-27, 733D3
Viet vets progrm urged 10-10, 878E1
Cost lid bill dies 10-15, 785B1
Energy bill clears Cong 10-15, 787C2
Carter anti-inflatn plan to monitor costs, urges cost-control bill OK 10-24, 806D1
Eilberg indicted 10-24, pleads not guilty 11-1, 835D2
NJ MD acquitted in curare murder case 10-24, 841F1-B2
SEC paymts chrgs vs Hosp Corp setld, Amer Hosp suit cited 10-26, 876D3-877C1
ND cost curb referendum loses 11-7, 855A1
ND, RI referenda results 11-7, 855A1 915E2
NJ curare case-press freedom rule declined by Sup Ct 11-27, 937E1
Cities' power over suburbs backed by Sup Ct 11-28, 937C3
AFT to organize nurses 11-29, 961A1
HEW sets cost guide 12-28, 1012G1

Hypertension—*See 'Blood' above*
Implants—*For embryo implants, see CHILDBIRTH*
Insurance—*See also 'Malpractice' and 'Medicaid' below*
Carter State of Union Message 1-19, 31B1
Carter omits budget proposal 1-23, 44G2
'77 business costs, HMO plans rptd 3-10, 5-10, 578D1
Blacks cite as vote issue 4-10, 568G2
NH mental health challenge denied by Sup Ct 4-17, 308B3
Sex-based pensn plans barred by Sup Ct 4-25, 322D3
Dental coverage rpt up 5-21, 578C2
MD malpractice claims study rptd 6-8, 577E3
Admin readies natl plan 6-26, 491E2
Carter sees Kennedy re natl plan; Kennedy, labor ldrs score, Califano defends 7-28, 585G3
Carter plan outlined, reactn; text 7-29, 585F2, 586A1, E2
Kennedy urges natl plan at govs mtg 8-28, 681G3
Dem midterm conf debates natl plan 12-9, urges enactmt 12-10, 956F1, C3
Wage rule fringe benefit test eased 12-13, 957F1, E2

1979

Hospitals & Health-Care Facilities—*See also 'Malpractice' below*
Breast-feeding in pvt hosps rptd up 1-5, 64B2
Carter budget proposals 1-22, 44D2
Carter State of Union Message 1-23, 46F3, 47A2, 48A1
Cancer diagnosis secrecy study rptd 2-26, 218F1
Blue Cross curbs test paymts 2-6, 138F1-C2
Carter urges cost-curb legis 2-12, 109F3; plan faces Cong hurdles 2-13, 110B1
Eilberg pleads guilty in plea-bargain 2-24, 152C2
Elderly share of '77 costs rptd 2-24, 164A1
Carter sends cost-control bill to Cong 3-5, opens lobbying campaign 3-6, 163A2-C3
MD, nursing schl fund cuts trimmed 3-6, 163D3
'78 cost rise rptd 3-8; Sen hearings open, hosps fight bill 3-9, 194E2
Carter proposes regulatory reform 3-25, 230G1
Price guidelines tightened, HEW monitoring set 3-29, 264G1
Md nurse freed in mercy deaths 3-29, 291F1-A2
3 Mile I A-accident evacuatn rptd 4-2, 245A3
Mental hosp commitmt standard tightened by Sup Ct 4-30, 364D2
Blue Cross asks presurgery tests cut 5-1, 404C3
Kennedy offers natl health plan 5-14, 362D1
Carter scores cost-control bill defeat 5-25, 401B2
Terminally ill treatmt rptd limited 5-31, 471F2
Schls right to bar disabled backed by Sup Ct 6-11, 478F1
Carter unveils natl health plan 6-12, 438B2
MD-managed insurnc plan cuts costs 6-14, 570C3
Primary care MD shortage disproven 6-14, 571A1
Disabled nurse firing case refused by Sup Ct 6-18, 499D2
Union organizing curbs backed by Sup Ct 6-20, 516A2
Merck OKs minority jobs plan 6-26, 521A2
AMA chrgd in NY chiropractors suit 7-5, 570F2
LA Cnty (Calif) 'sickout' 7-12, 599F1
Califano fired, cost bill role cited 7-18, 530A1
NYC hosp closing plan cited 7-27, 580A3
Energy conservatn measure clears House 8-1, 595F2
NJ MD trial costs ordrd paid by NY Times 8-14, 656E2
City hosps decline rptd 9-2, 970E3-971C1
Improvemt projcts, literacy progrm link urged 9-8, 786C1
NJ Medicaid reimbursemt case declined by Sup Ct 11-5, 884C3
Carter cost-control bill rejctd by House 11-15, 883B1
VA malpractice ruling reversed by Sup Ct 11-28, 944C3

Hypertension—*See 'Blood' above*
Insurance—*See also 'Malpractice' and 'Medicaid' below*
Carter budget omits funds 1-22, 44G2
Carter State of Union Message 1-23, 48A1
2d opinion surgery plans evaluated 1-29, 140C1
Blue Cross curbs hosp test paymts 2-6, 138F1-C2
Cancer study finds benefits cut 2-10, 139C3
Califano backs natl plan 2-13, 110E1
Elderly share of '77 costs rptd 2-24, 163G3
Blue Shield drug plan trust rule upheld by Sup Ct 2-27, 165A1
Dole backs catastrophic illness plan 3-10, 186D1
NY Life sets 2d-opinion surgery coverage 3-19, 218E3
Blue Cross asks presurgery tests cut 5-1, 404C3
Kennedy introduces natl health plan, Califano scores 5-14, 362C1
Long proposes catastrophic health plan 5-14, 362A2
Carter unveils natl health plan 6-12, 438G1
Mass anti-abortn law signed 6-12, 547A3
MD-managed plan cuts hosp costs 6-14, 570C3
Califano fired, natl plan role cited 7-18, 529G2-530A1
Carter scores Kennedy health plan record 9-25, 723E3
Kennedy hits health-care issue 10-26, 11-8, 962B1, C1

1980

Hospitals & Health-Care Facilities
Fed heating aid given despite lodging 1-9, 54E2
State of State messages 1-9, 1-10, 483D1, 484E2
Carter budget proposals 1-28, 69E3, 72E2
Lab tests found 14% inaccurate 3-23, 358F3--359C1
Union limits case declined by Sup Ct 4-14, 307C1
NYC labor pact setld 6-19, 518C1
Nursing home aid summary cutoff backed by Sup Ct 6-23, 554F3
Nursing home rights detailed 7-9, 583G3
AMA adopts health plan res 7-24, 583F3
Kennedy Dem conv speech 8-12, 614E1
Mental health authrzn clears Cong 9-24, 9-30, signed 10-7, 803G3
Records privacy bill defeated by House 12-1, 982C2

Insurance—*See also 'Medicaid', 'Medicare' below*
Meany backed natl health care 1-10, 14D3
Carter asks natl health care system 1-21, 43F3
Carter budget proposals 1-28, 72G2
Kennedy cites natl plan 1-28, 75A1
Baseball contract dispute setld 5-23, 402B2
Dem platform drafted 6-24, Kennedy vows floor fight 6-25, 479E3, 480D1
AMA adopts health plan res 7-24, 583F3
Kennedy conv speech asks natl plan, Dem platform plank weak 8-12, 610E2, D3, 614E1, E3
Lucey joins Anderson ticket 8-25, 646D3
Carter backs natl health plan 10-10, 778B3
Carter, Reagan TV debate 10-28, 814C2

1976

Sup Ct vs mandatory pregnancy benefits 12-7, 919G3
AMA backs natl progrm 12-7, 931C2

Medicaid
HEW scored on funds use 1-7, 1-25, 2-16, 128B1, A2
Reagan for state operatn 1-12, 22E1
Ford State of Union message 1-19, 38C1, 39E2
'77 budget proposal 1-21, 65A1
Mo abortn rule review denied 1-26, 87B3
Hollander pleads guilty 2-2, sentncd 5-18, 384C3
HEW sets fraud effort 3-26, 249E1
Carter cites cheating 4-16, 281F3
Sup Ct bars NY stay of order 4-26, 359D2
Dem platform text 6-15, 471B3, 472B1
Sup Ct rules on Mo abortn law 7-1, 518C3, E3
GOP platform text 8-18, 605G1, 606B2
HEW bars MD collectn agent use 8-26, 715B3
Sen rpt cites fraud, abuse 8-30, 714G3-715A3
2 convictd NYC chiropractors blame system 8-31, 715G2
NY bars fee-splitting for leases 9-5, 715B3
Carter cites waste 9-6, 664D2
PHS 5-yr plan issued 9-7, 680F1
Carter scores mismanagemt 9-13, 686D2
Ford, Carter debate 9-23, 702F1
Ga gov scores Ford remark 9-25, 725A2
Cong OKs HEW inspector gen 9-29, 765A3; signed 10-15, 982G1
Abortion fund curb veto overridden 9-30, 726F2, G3
Block grant, cost reform bills not cleared 10-2, 883E3, F3
Mondale, Dole debate 10-15, 783C1
Abortn aid curb voided 10-22; Sup Ct bars stay 11-8, 848F1

Medicare
Chiropractor paymt bar upheld 1-13, 44C3
Soc Security financing plan rejctd 1-19, reform asked 1-24, 59G3
Hollander pleads guilty 2-2, sentncd 5-4, 384C3
'76 budget proposals 2-3, 67B3, 69C3
Treas funding urged, Ford vs 3-7, 162F3
Adams questions Ford budget estimate 3-23, 231F2
Carter proposes reforms 4-16, 281F3
Sup Ct upholds aliens' benefits ban 6-1, 414B2
Dem platform text 6-15, 473A1
Mondale record cited 512B3
Cella, 3 others sentncd 7-20, 860E2
Moss on MD fraud 7-28, 715C3
GOP platform text 8-18, 605G1, 606E2
Ford acceptnc speech cites 8-19, 612C2
PHS 5-yr plan issued 9-7, 680F1
Cong OKs HEW inspector gen 9-29, 765A3; signed 10-15, 982G1
'Catastrophic' coverage, cost reform bills not cleared 10-2, 883E3, F3

Mental Health
'77 budget proposal 1-21, 65A1
Mental illness, econ linked 1-26, 159A3
Cong OKs rehabilitatn act extensn 2-17, 3-2, 182D1
'75 Marine recruit rejctns cited 6-9, 435C3
Dem platform text 6-15, 471F3, 472E3
GOP platform text 8-18, 605G1-A2
Govt panel backs psychosurgery 9-10, 715E3

1977

Labor Issues—*See LABOR—Health & Safety*

Laetrile
Cts grant cancer patients access 1-21, 4-8, 4-17, 376C1
FDA issues warning 4-14; hearings open 5-2, ban reaffirmed, smuggling rptd 5-6, 375B3, 376A1
States challenge FDA ban 4-17, 5-1, 5-2, 375F1
Smugglers sentenced 5-16, 508E2
Nev legalizes 5-20; Del, Okla 6-21; La 6-23; other state data 508E1, B3
Infant dies of overdose 6-11, 508G1
Sloan-Kettering finds useless 6-15, 508A2
AMA rejcts over-counter sale 6-21, 508D2
NCI to test on humans 6-23, 508F1

Medicaid
CBO issues poverty rpt 1-13, 80B3
Ford '78 budget proposals 1-17, 32E1
Calif health facility fraud probe controversy 2-4—3-23, 235B3
Welfare cost rptd 2-19, 176C1
Carter budget revision 2-22, 125G3
HEW reorgnizatn effected 3-9, 175A3
FBI fraud probe aid set 3-20, 236A1
Carter asks hosp cost controls 4-25, 322D1
Carter asks child health progrm 4-25, 322G1
'76 subsidized abortns rptd 6-1, 787B1
Adoption bill OKd by House 6-7, 628C3
HEW sets cuts for 20 states 6-8, 460B3
House bars HEW abortn funds 6-17, 478B2
537 cases of fraud rptd pending legis cited 6-18, 643F2
Sup Ct upholds abortn fund curbs 6-20, 516C2
Child care found lacking 6-22, 643B3
Carter child health plan scored 6-22, 643D3
NYS, SD abortn rulings vacated; NJ case refused 6-27, 538G3
Sen votes abortn fund curb 6-29, 515E2
Carter backs abortn curbs 7-12, 533B1, F2
US adoption subsidy proposed 7-12, 628B3
Sup Ct vacates abortn ban stay 7-27, 557B3
Abortn funding curbs debated 7-27—10-11, stay lifted 8-4, 786G1
State funding of abortns rptd 10-12, 786G3
Conn law re property sales upheld 10-17, 797F3
Fraud, abuse curbs signed 10-25, 814D1
Rural clinic aid clears Cong 11-29, 938F1; signed 12-13, 1001G2

Medicare
CBO issues poverty rpt 1-13, 80B3, F3
Ford '78 budget proposals 1-17, 32D1
Calif health facility fraud probe controversy 2-4—3-23, 235B3
Carter budget revisions 2-22, 125F3
HEW reorgnizatn effected 3-9, 175A3
FBI fraud probe aid set 3-20, 236A1
Carter asks hosp cost controls 4-25, 322D1
Fraud bill rptd pending 6-18, 643G2
Fraud, abuse curbs signed 10-25, 814D1
2d opinions on surgery urged 11-1, 869E3
Rural clinic aid clears Cong 11-29, 938F1; signed 12-13, 1001G2

Mental Health
Carter names special asst 1-14, 35C3
NYC schl bias chrgd 1-18, 112C2
Suits vs unions backed 3-7, 211F2
HEW reorganizatn effected 3-9, 175B3
Calif psychotherapist rule review declined 4-4, 341E3
Mrs Carter maps role 4-18, 4-19, 322C2
2 win Pulitzer for Fairview expose 4-18, 355F2
Child porno effort rptd 5-15, 432E2
Sup Ct refuses Pa youth rights case 5-16, 418G3
'69-76 Sup Ct cases cited 5-17, 419B3
US plans child adoptn subsidy 7-12, 628F2
CIA mind-control tests revealed 8-1—8-9, 610C3
'78 authorization signed 8-1, 689A3
Gay teacher case review refused 10-3, 760E1

1978

Labor Issues—*See LABOR—Health*

Laetrile
NJ legalizes 1-10, 23B3
Risk rptd by Calif U 3-6, 598C3

Malpractice
Vasectomy failure liability ruled in Mich 5-23, 597B2
MD claims study rptd 6-8, 577E3
Embryo implant trial begins in NYC 7-17, 597G1
'71-77 state discipline vs MDs rptd up 12-1, 992D3

Medicaid
Carter budget proposals 1-23, 48A2-C2
Abortion rules issued 1-26, 116F1
'77 errors rptd costly, new rules issued 3-31, 577G3
NYC nursing homes struck 4-4—4-7, 284F3
Quinlan costs estimated 4-10, 597D3
NYS eligibility case refused by Sup Ct 6-12, 468C1
Abortn fund curb OKd by House 6-13, 445C3
17 states, DC continue funding abortns 6-20, 743A3
HEW for paymt error limit 7-10, 684B3
HEW asks legis to cut losses 7-20, 684E3
ABA backs abortn funds 8-9, 626B3
'77 poverty level data rptd 8-12, 684E2

Medicare
Carter budget proposal 1-23, 48B2
GAO scores MD list 3-15, 578B1
Hosp insurnc fund reform urged 5-16, 368D3
Kidney program revisns signed 6-13, 466A1
HEW asks legis to cut losses 7-20, 684E3

Mental Health
Neurotransmitter measurability rptd 334B2
Age bias in fed programs rptd 1-10, 14C1
Brain protein study rptd; retardatn, schizophrenia benefits seen 2-18, 334D1
Mongolism tests halted by March of Dimes 3-8, 744C2
NM A-worker wins damages 3-15, 242F3
Judicial immunity in sterilizatn case backed by Sup Ct 3-28, 241G2
NH insurnc challenge denied by Sup Ct 4-17, 308B3
Aggression linked to spinal fluid 6-3, 1023B2
Niagara (NY) child retardates, chem dump site linked 8-7, 703B1
Cocaine motivatn in monkeys rptd 8-11, 771C1
Viet vets progrm urged 10-10, 878E1, G1
Miss dorm fire kills 15 12-9, 971E3

1979

Laetrile
Mass Ct orders treatmt ended for 3-yr-old 1-23, 1-30, parents flee 1-25, 139C1
Benzaldehyde cancer treatmt rptd effective 1-28, 139D1
Cyanide death rptd 2-1, 138G3
Cyanide rptd in blood of 3-yr-old 3-7, 196B1
FDA orders shipmt recalled 3-8, 196A1
Cancer Inst delays testing 3-13, 195F3
FDA ban upheld by Sup Ct 6-18, 498D2
Rat study finds tumors enlarged, cynide lethal 7-13, 571C1
3-yr-old leukemia victim dies 10-12, autopsy rptd 10-21, 905G1
Calif ban challenge declined by Sup Ct 11-13, 902E1

Malpractice
Va convict gets prison abuse award 1-5, 24B2
Atkins cleared 1-16, 78F3
Tex abortn record access case declined by Sup Ct 1-22, 54A2
Arbitratn in 13 states, PR rptd 1-28, 139C3
Hosp test paymts curbed by Blue Cross 2-6, 138B2
2 cleared in psychosurgery suit 2-9, 139E3
NY plastic surgeon loses "bellybutton" suit 5-3, 392A3
'Belly button' suit award cut 6-4, 527F2
Medicare-Medicaid hosp cost rules modified 7-1, 570A3
VA ruling reversed by Sup Ct 11-28, 944C3
Presley MD chrgs rptd 12-19, 1005C3

Medicaid
Drug paymt curb set by HEW 1-9, 23E2
NJ state abortn paymts ordrd 1-9, 315D1
NARAL scores abortion-fund cuts 1-21, March for Life hails 1-22, 63E2-A3
Carter budget proposals 1-22, 41D2, 44E2
Califano backs natl plan 2-13, 110F1
Carter sends hosp cost bill to Cong 3-5, 163B3
'78 abortn decline rptd 3-8, 315A1
Mass abortn funds case refused by Sup Ct 5-14, 383D1
Carter unveils natl health plan 6-12, 438A2, D2
Mass anti-abortn law signed 6-12, 547A3
Funding cuts set 6-19, 561E1
Malpractice cost rules modified 7-1, 570B3
NJ reimbursemt case declined by Sup Ct 11-5, 884C3
Abortn funding cases accepted by Sup Ct 11-26, 919B2

Medicare
Drug paymt curb set by FDA 1-9, 23E2
Carter budget proposals 1-22, 41E2, 44E2; table 42E2
Califano backs natl plan 2-13, 110F1
Elderly share of '77 costs rptd 2-24, 164A1
Carter sends hosp cost bill to Cong 3-5, 163B3
Terminally ill treatmt rptd limited 5-31, 471E2
Carter unveils natl health plan 6-12, 438A2, D2
Malpractice cost rules modified 7-1, 570B3
Finance chngs urged 12-7, 946D2

Mental Health
Depressn, heredity linked 1-4, 289E3
Va convict antipsychotic drug reactn cited 1-5, 24C2
Carter budget proposals 1-22, 44B3
Ia criminal confessn case declined by Sup Ct 1-22, 54G1
Sears sues US on bias laws 1-24, 92D1
Admin drafting legis 1-25, 70D2
Mrs Carter asks more fed funds 2-7, 112B1
2 MDs cleared in psychosurgery suit 2-9, 139E3
New shock therapy tested 3-1, 290B1
Mental hosp commitmt standard tightened by Sup Ct 4-30, 364D2
Kennedy offers natl health plan 5-14, 362D1
Carter proposes plan 5-15, 365B1
Sears suit vs US dismissed 5-15, 365B3

1980

Laetrile
FDA OKs testing 1-3, 23C2
FDA ban challenge declined by Sup Ct 10-20, 807F1
McQueen treatmt rptd 11-7, 928B3

Malpractice
Presley MD license suspended 1-19, 199C1
Prisoners right to sue broadened by Sup Ct 4-22, 343D3
Presley MD indicted 5-16, 414B2

Medicaid
Utah State of State message 1-14, 270B2
Abortn aid ban voided 1-15, 35A3
Carter budget proposals 1-28, 72D2
Marshall stays abortn aid order 2-14, Sup Ct lifts stay, accepts case 2-19, 130F2-B3
Abortn funding cases argued in Sup Ct 4-21, 306A2
Mass prof indicted in fraud case 5-13, 414G3
Cuban, Haitian refugees get eligibility 6-20, 484F3, 485A1
Nursing home aid summary cutoff backed by Sup Ct 6-23, 554F3
Abortn funding limits upheld by Sup Ct; reactn 6-30, 491E2-492A2
GOP platform draft backs abortn funds bar 7-9, 506D2
Nursing home rights detailed 7-9, 584B1, D1
DC fscl recovery plan proposed 7-19, 742E3
Abortn funding review denied by Sup Ct 9-17, 703A3
Carter assails Reagan stand 10-1, 739A2
Carter vows fed aid to cities 10-20, 803F1
Budget reconciliatn chngs clear Cong 12-3, signed 12-5, 936F1, 981A1

Medicare
Carter budget proposals 1-28, 72F2
Nursing home aid summary cutoff backed by Sup Ct 6-23, 554F3
Nursing home rights detailed 7-9, 584B1, D1
Carter pres renominatn acceptance speech 8-14, 613A1
Carter assails Reagan stand 10-1, 739A2
Carter scores Reagan oppositn 10-10, 778C3, D3
Carter ridicules Reagan 'secret plan' 10-22, 802E3
Carter, Reagan TV debate 10-28, 813B2, 815D2
Budget reconciliatn chngs clear Cong 12-3, signed 12-5, 936F1, 981A1

Mental Health
Infant mental retardatn, alcoholism linked 1-4, 23G3
State of State messages 1-10, 2-19, 403D3, 404C1; 1-14, 1-15, 483B3, 484D1; 2-6, 269G1
Schizophrenia, dopamine link rptd 1-10, 415E1
Life span changes rptd 1-19, 62G3
Carter budget proposals 1-28, 72C3
Va sterilizatn progrm rptd 2-23, 158D3
Ala '78 rape convictn overturned 3-18, 215E2
Prison inmate hearings backed by Sup Ct 3-25, 265D2
3 Mile I health study rptd 4-17, 332A3
'Son of Sam' plea rptd faked 8-4, 639G2
NRC staff backs 3 Mile I cleanup 8-14, 649E2
Authrzn clears Cong 9-24, 9-30, signed 10-7, 803E3

1976

Narcotics & Dangerous Drugs—*See under 'N'*
Noise Abatement—*See under ENVIRONMENT*
Obituaries
Bailey, Pearce 6-23, 524C2
Beecher, Henry 7-25, 680F3
Dam, Henrik 4-17, 368E2
Fishbein, Morris 9-27, 1015D1
Haddow, Alexander 1-21, 80D3
Heidegger, Martin 5-26, 404A2
Marine, David 11-26, 970E2
Mauze, Abby Rockefeller 5-31, 404B2
Monod, Jacques 5-31, 404D2 ★
Nash, Dorothy 3-5, 484F3
Penfield, Wilder 4-5, 316B1
Phillips, Robert 9-20, 1015D2
Rosebury, Theodor 11-25, 1015E2
Scudder, John 12-6, 1015F2
Thomas, James 1-23, 80G3
Whipple, George H 2-1, 124G3
Wiener, Alexander 11-6, 970D3

Physicians—*See also 'Insurance above; personal names*
HEW rpts on health issues 1-12, 32F1
NLRB rules vs interns, residents 3-22, 220E1
Quinlan wins right to die 3-31, 292D2
Cong OKs educ incentives 4-12, 282G2
NJ MD indicted re curare 5-19, 384A3
PHS 5-yr plan issued 9-7, 680G1
Calif right-to-die bill signed 9-30, 770F2
Health educ aid, foreign MD curbs signed 10-13, 788E2
Family MDs get 1st exam 10-29, 972F3
Radiologists bar price-fixing, '75 MD agrmts cited 11-17, 988F3
Prescriptn drug panel formed 11-30, 931G2
EC MD mobility OKd 12-20, 977B2
Poisons & Poisoning—*See substance names*
Presidential Election
Reagan for state operatn 1-12, 22E1
Muskie rebuts Ford 1-21, 40A2, D2
Ford rpts govs back budget plan 1-22, 41C2
Jackson stresses issue 1-22, 41A3
Carter proposes plan 4-16, 281D3
Black Dems draft plant 5-1, 343E3
Carter vs instant approach 6-3, 411D1
Dem platform goal 6-15, 432B3
Dem platform text 6-15, 469C2, E2, 470D3, 471F2-D3, 472B1, E3, F3, 473A1, B1, A2, 474E2, E2, 475A3
GOP platform topic 6-21, 451E1
Carter lauds Europe 6-23, 451A3
Udall urges natl bill 7-14, 506D1
Carter acceptance speech 7-15, 507E1, 510G2, A3
Mondale asserts commitmt 7-15, 511D3
Carter spending record cited 512C2
Mondale record cited 512B3
GOP platform com actn on insurance 8-13, 583D1
Dole support cited 8-16, 8-19, 599F1
GOP conv delegates' views on insurance rptd 8-17, 616G2
GOP platform text 8-18, 603E3, 604G3, 605C1-A2, 606B2, E2
Ford cites as top issue 8-27, 645D1
Mondale scores Admin 8-28, 645B3
Carter cites Medicaid waste 9-6, 664D2
Carter hits Medicaid mismanagemt 9-13, stresses health care 9-14, 686D2, A3
Ford vows health-care prgrm 9-15, 686A1
Ford, Carter debate 9-23, 702F1
Ga gov scores Ford Medicaid remark 9-25, 725A2
Tax on church-owned facilities disputed 10-2, 743E2, G2
Dole, Mondale debate 10-15, 782F2, G3, 783C1, A2
Carter on health care 10-19, 785E1
Ford, Carter debate 10-22, 801C3, D3
Professn rptd major donor 10-22, 938B3
Radiation Hazards—*See under ATOMIC Energy*
Research—*See also other appropriate subheads in this section; also GENETICS*
'77 budget proposal 1-21, 65C1
Cong OKs funds 4-12, 282E2, F2
GOP platform text 8-18, 605A2
2 share Nobel Prize 10-14, 840B1
Davis gets Science Medal 10-18, 858D3
Lasker awards presented 11-17, 910D3

Smoking-Health Link—*See under TOBACCO*
Swine Flu
Swine-type flu rptd 2-19, Ford urges vaccine 3-24, govt tests set 3-25, 224A2-F2
Ford urges flu vaccine 3-24, 224B2
Canada sets flu immunizatn shots 3-30, 238E3

1977

US rejcts Sovt statemt on dissident abuses 10-28, 866A2
Pa Soc Sec benefits seizure dispute declined 11-7, 857C2
Religious patient drug case refused 11-28, 919B3

Narcotics & Dangerous Drugs—*See under 'N'*
Obituaries
Adrian, Edgar Douglas 8-4, 696B2
Bibring, Grete L 8-10, 696C2
Cotzias, George 6-13, 532G2
Fowler, Herbert 1-2, 84A3
Goldblatt, Harry 1-6, 84B3
Jackson, Edith 6-5, 532B3
Levy, David M 3-1, 264B3
Lilly, Eli 1-24, 84C3
Lowman, Charles 4-17, 356D3
Luria, Aleksandr 8-16, 696C3
Miller, Harry 1-1, 84C3
Milstone, Jacob 1-27, 164D3
Murphy, Charles 9-20, 788A2
Muschenheim, Carl 4-27, 356E3
Paul, William 12-19, 1024F2
Peer, Lyndon 10-8, 872F2
Pitts, Robert 6-6, 532E3
Powell, Clilan 9-22, 788C2
Romm, May 10-15, 872G2
Soper, Fred 2-9, 164E3
Physicians
AMA '76 Cong gifts rptd 2-15, 128E1
Podiatrists sued re fee-fixing 2-15, 156B3
Mil malpractice case review barred 3-7, 211E2
Carter asks hosp cost controls 4-25; reactn 4-25—4-26, 322C1, A2
FDA orders IUD labeling 5-6, 431F2
AMA crackdown rptd, hysterectomies disputed 5-9, 732A3
Califano cites fee problem 6-7, 479F1
315 Medicaid violatns rptd 6-18, 643G2
Barnard rpts early retiremt 7-11, 619G3
Garfield gets LBJ award 10-26, 870B1
Amnesty Intl lists pol prisoners 11-28, 956E2
Poisons & Poisoning—*See substance names*

Radiation Hazards—*See under 'R'*
Research—*See also other appropriate subheads in this section; also GENETICS*
Carter energy plan 4-20, 293B2
US-USSR cooperatn pact 5-18, 400A3
CIA mind-control tests revealed 8-1—8-9, 610C3
'78 authorization signed 8-1, 689A3
Nobel shared by 2 10-13, 951C3
Lasker awards presented 11-16, 927A3
Medals of Sci awarded 11-22, 951G3-952C1

Smoking-Health Link—*See under TOBACCO*
Statistics
Nov, Dec '76 cost rptd 1-19, 78B1
Feb CPI rise rptd 3-18, 215D1
March CPI rptd 4-21, 324C2
'60-61, '72-73 family spending compared 5-10, 423E2
Apr CPI rise rptd 5-22, 406B3

1978

Narcotics & Dangerous Drugs—*See NARCOTICS*
National Health Plan—*See 'Insurance' above*
Obituaries
Alvarez, Walter Clement 6-18, 540D2
Atkinson, Walter 1-6, 96C1
Best, Charles H 3-31, 252D2
Ivy, Andrew 2-7, 196C3
Leake, Chauncey 1-11, 96E2
Quick, Armand J 1-26, 96C3
Organ Donation—*See 'Surgery' below*

Physicians—*See also 'Malpractice' above*
Carter budgets Natl Health Svc 1-23, 48D2
'53, '78 cong membership compared 1-30, 107G2
Interns, residents no-union rule denied review 2-27, 143B2
Med student ouster upheld 3-1, 143D2
Amnesty Intl holds torture conf 3-10—3-11, 180B3
Rural shortage rptd 4-6—4-7, forecast bleak despite '85 surplus 7-23, 577C3
Carter cites higher fees since '50 4-11, 259G3
Cabt-level Educ Dept proposed 4-14, 279C1
HEW sends asbestos data 4-26, 326F2
Carter attacks AMA 5-5, 342A1
NYS alien rule review declined by Sup Ct 5-15, 388A1
GAO rpts too many specializing 5-19, 597E2
FTC adopts eyewear ad proposal 5-24, 434D1
AMA asks fee curbs 6-21, 578C1
MD surplus by '90 seen 8-3, 597C2
Rural health progrm planned 10-2, 770E1
'77 black med schl enrollmt down 10-8, 811C2
HEW vs new med schls 10-24, 948C3
Army MD dismissed, recruiters scored 11-4, 877A3
Army MD shortage rptd 11-27, 916D3
Ad ban voided 11-29, AMA to appeal 11-30, 947D2
'71-77 state discipline rptd up 12-1, 992D3
Carter econ plan sets fee hike ceiling 12-13, 957B2
Poisons & Poisoning—*See substance names*

Radiation Hazards—*See also 'Cancer' above*
Microwave safety faulted 12-11, 962B3

Smoking-Health Link—*See under TOBACCO*
Statistics
Vocal cord cancer cure rate data cited 1-9, 13E3
NJ cancer rate data cited 1-12, 23E3
Jan, Feb CPIs 2-27, 3-28, 222E1, F1
Mar CPI 4-28, 345B1
May CPI costs 6-30, 507A1

1979

Carter unveils natl health plan 6-12, 438B2
Mont homicide convictn reversed by Sup Ct 6-18, 499F1
Child commitmt rules backed by Sup Ct 6-20, 515E3
Pot use risks rptd 10-14, 972D1
Library outreach urged 11-15–11-19, 901G1
Novelist libel case refused by Sup Ct 12-3, 964G1
Narcotics & Dangerous Drugs—*See NARCOTICS*
National Health Plan—*See 'Insurance' above*
Obituaries
Chain, Ernst B 8-12, 671A2
Forssmann, Werner 6-1, 508F2
Franzblau, Rose N 9-2, 756D2
Fremont-Smith, Maurice 5-4, 432F2
Knowles, John H 3-6, 272A3
Merritt, H Houston 1-9, 104D3
Murphy, Gardner 3-19, 272D3
Sugiura, Kanematsu 10-21, 860F3

Physicians & Medical Personnel—*See also 'Malpractice' above*
Pa abortn control law voided by US Sup Ct 1-9, 14A1
Carter proposes med schl cuts 1-22, 44F2
Mil shortage rptd 2-16, 130C2
Cancer diagnosis secrecy study rptd 2-26, 218E1
SC abortn prosecutn ban voided by Sup Ct 3-5, 185B1
Med schl fund cuts trimmed 3-6, 163D3
Edelin '75 convictn reversal cited 3-15, 272B1
US no longer top DC area hirer 3-24, 232B2
Top '78 PAC spenders cited 5-10, 363F1
Diet aids approved 5-12, 571G3
Kennedy offers natl health plan 5-14, 362D1
Pvt Title IX suit allowed by Sup Ct 5-14, 382D3
Terminally ill treatmt rptd limited 5-31, 471E2
Carter unveils natl health plan 6-12, 438B2
MD-managed insurnc plan cuts hosp costs 6-14, 570C3
Primary care MD shortage disproven 6-14, 570F3
FDA drug approval process scored 6-19, 572E2
Prescription drug leaflets urged by FDA 6-29, 571F1
AMA chrgd in NY chiropractors suit 7-5, 570E2
Drug profiteering cited 9-5, 972E2
AMA ad ban, other curbs ordrd ended 10-24, 902F2
Boxing suspended in NYS 11-28–12-27, 1004G3

Radiation Hazards—*See also 'Cancer' above*
HEW safety studies asked 1-30, 90D3
Low-level risks seen 2-27, 207G3-208B1
Colo radium waste sites rptd 3-5, 187F1
3 Mile I A-accident 3-28–4-3, 241B1–246A1; for subsequent developments, *see PENNSYLVANIA—Atomic Energy*
Facts on radiatn exposure 244C2
Low-level, A-power risks reviewed 5-2, 609E2, A3
Silkwood estate wins A-suit 5-18, 381D1
Mutatn link disproved in mouse experimts 7-28, 692F2
'50s A-fallout, SAT decline linked 9-17, 747A2
Smoking-Health Link—*See under TOBACCO*
Statistics
Dec '78 CPI rise 1-24, 73A2
Jan CPI costs up 2-23, 151B2
'78 hosp cost rise 3-8, 194G2
Feb CPI costs up 3-25, 252G1
Mar CPI rise 4-26, 324G3
May CPI rise 6-26, 480D3

1980

NJ bond issue OKd 11-4, 847G3
Hines declared unfit for retrial 11-21, 927F1

National Health Plan—*See 'Insurance' above*
Obituaries
Andrews, Gould A 7-1, 608B1
Erickson, Milton H 3-25, 279D2
Gantt, William 2-26, 176B1
Halberstam, Michael J 12-5, 939F3
Ingelfinger, Franz J 3-26, 279E3
Kendrick, Pearl L 10-8, 876B2
Peshkin, M Murray 8-17, 676D2
Rhine, Joseph 2-20, 176B3
Sauer, Louis W 2-10, 176C3
Stein, William 2-2, 176D3
Summerskill, Edith 2-4, 176E3
Tarnower, Herman 3-10, 214E3
Warren, Shields 7-1, 608G3

Physicians & Medical Personnel—*See also 'Malpractice' above*
Nurses win life aid in Mass 'Right-to-Die' case 1-24, 158E2
Wyo State of State message 2-12, 484G2
Utah abortn parental notificatn case accepted by Sup Ct 2-25, 187G3
'Scarsdale Diet' MD slain 3-10, 214E3
MD oversupply rptd 4-17, 318C1
DC tax case declined by Sup Ct 5-27, 454A1
MD sentncd in Koch assault 6-6, 639G2
Tranquilizer warnings set 7-11, 548E1
Mobile (Ala) paramedics strike 7-14—7-24, 576D1
AMA adopts ethics code 7-22, 583F2
Kennedy Dem conv speech 8-12, 614E1
Carter vetoes VA MD pay hike 8-22, Cong overrides 8-26, 649E3
Mental health authrzn clears Cong 9-24, 9-30, signed 10-7, 804B3
PAC donatns case accepted by Sup Ct 10-6, 782A2
Nobel to 3 announced 10-10, 889E3
Newsroom searches curb signed 10-14, 835C2
Nursing schl faculty bias case accepted by Sup Ct 12-1, 918C2
DC MD slain 12-5, 939F3
La Scola insulin-slaying chrgs reduced 12-29, 997G1

Radiation Hazards
3 Mile I health study rptd 4-15, 332F2
Plutonium removing chem dvpt rptd 9-12, 9-13, 716F2

Smoking-Health Link—*See under TOBACCO*
Statistics
Dec, '78 CPI rise 1-25, 75A3
Jan CPI rise 2-22, 144D2
Feb CPI rise 3-25, 222C2
Mar CPI rise 4-22, 305D1
Apr CPI rise 5-23, 400C3

1976

Swine flu bill enacted 4-15, 282G1
Flu vaccine test begins 4-21, 316G1
Swine flu vaccine error rptd 6-2, 423C3
WHO finds no swine flu 6-3, 423E3
NYC gets flu vaccine funds 6-6, 443B2
High-risk flu group identified 6-10, 443C2
Vaccine-maker to lose insurance 6-15, 443F1
Ford vows flu immunizatn 7-19, 532F1
Cong OKs fed flu vaccine liability 8-10, 586C2
Liability bill signed 8-12, 982F1
Flu immunizatn plan delayed 9-1, 656B3
Canada limits program 9-28, 795F2
3 in Pa die after shots 10-11, some prgrms halted 10-12—10-17, 795F1
2½ mln get shots 10-15, 795C2
Missing vaccine enzyme rptd 10-17, 795D2
Youth progrm limited 11-15, adult turnout rptd low 12-2, 911A1
Mo case rptd 11-22, CDC doubts 11-27, 911D1
Legionnaires probe scored 11-23—11-24, 911C2
34.9 mln vaccinated 12-4, 950G1
Paralysis halts program 12-16, 950C1

1977

May CPI rptd 6-22, 482B1
June CPI rptd 7-21, 554D2
'76 life expectancy data 7-25, 12-13, 962B3
July CPI rise rptd 8-19, 651F1
'76 health care revenue data 9-26, 869F2
Surgery—*See also other appropriate subheads in this section; also ABORTION under 'A'*
Hysterectomy excesses chrgd, '75 data cited 5-9, 732E2
2d opinions urged 11-1, 869E3

1978

June CPI costs 7-28, 607G1
Aug CPI costs 9-26, 752D1
'76-77, Jan-Aug CPI costs up 10-4, 790A1
Oct CPI costs up 10-28, 918E2, G2
Nov '77-78 CPI costs up 12-22, 1003A2
Surgery—*See also 'Malpractice' above*
Ultrasonic equipmt exempted from rules 2-17, 231D3
French organ donatn law chngd 4-3, 597A3
Electrode implant paralysis treatmt rptd 5-6, 1023E1
Business health-benefit rules rptd 5-10, 578D1
Spleen regeneratn in children rptd 6-22, 598F1
Pa transplant ordr denied 7-26, 597F2; patient dies 8-10, 708B3
Mrs Ford has cosmetic surgery 9-14, 844B3
Transplants—*See 'Surgery' above*

1979

July CPI rise 8-25, 646E2
Aug CPI rise 9-25, 725E2
Sept CPI rise 10-26, 828A1
Nov CPI rise 12-21, 984E2
Surgery—*See also 'Malpractice' above*
2d opinion plans evaluated 1-29, 140A1
Unneeded surgery crackdown sought, AMA scores 2-5, 3-19, 218D3
Amputatn linked to heart deaths 2-26, 219G1
Hosp cost-control hearings open 3-9, 194G3
Teeth replanted in China 5-1, 355B1
Blue Cross asks presurgery tests cut 5-1, 404C3
Chinese MDs build hand 5-2, 355A1
NY plastic surgeon loses malpractice suit 5-3, 392A3
Heart-transplant survivals rptd 5-6, 355C1
Siamese twins separated 5-30, 527F2; leave hosp 7-17, 656C2
NY malpractice suit award cut 6-4, 527F2
Less radical breast cancer surgery backed 6-6, 471B3
Fetal liver transplanted 8-20, 736B3
Spinal column replaced 8-31, 736E2
Transplants—*See 'Surgery' above*

1980

Surgery
Retarded youth case refused by Sup Ct 3-31, 291B3

1976

MEDINA, O.—*See OHIO*
MEDINA, Jose Ramon
Orders police arrests re torture death 8-6, 874G2
Sup Ct rules in Niehous case 8-12, 874F2
Prisoners on hunger strike 10-1, 875A1
MEDINA Carreira, Henrique
Portugal finance min 7-23, inexperience scored 7-24, 558G1, A2
MEDITERRANEAN Sea
Sovt anchorage sites rptd 1-19, 73A2
UN pollutn conf opens 2-2, pact signed 2-16, 126A3
PLO, USSR warn US on rptd moves 3-30, 4-8, 241F2, 242A1
Egypt ends Sovt fleet svc 4-15, 275C1
NATO mins discuss balance of forces 5-21, 353B2
USSR sends aircraft carrier 7-18, 540F2; 7-22, 558B3
US GOP platform text cites 8-18, 609D1
Turkish ship on oil search 11-12, 897B2
MEDJEBER, Smail (alias Claude-Pascal Rousseaux)
Arrested 1-8, France accuses 1-11, 45C2-E3; sentncd to die 3-3, 454G3
MEDVEDEV, Zhores
On Sovt A-waste, rocket disasters 11-6, 948A3
MEEDS, Rep. Lloyd (D, Wash.)
Reelectn undecided 11-2, 825F1, 831B1
Wins reelection count 11-16, 865D1
MEEKER, Barry
Fined 1-14, 158B1
MEER, Fatima
Gets S Africa banning order 7-24, 592G1
Son arrested 8-12, 624C3
MEER, Rashid
Arrested 8-12, 624C3
MEEROPOL, Michael & Robert (Rosenberg)
Judge to see Rosenberg papers 1-13, 70D2
MEGELEA, Gheorghe
Wins Olympic medal 7-26, 576A1
MEGUID, Ahmed Esmat Abdel
Urges Palestinian rights resolutn 1-13, 18A2
Vs US UN veto 3-26, 227G2
Vs Israeli occupatn policy 5-4, 5-5, 320B1
MEHEISHI, Maj. Omar Abdullah
Egypt seizes Libyan plotters 3-9, 3-11, 205G1
Ousted from RCC, Cabt 3-15; denounces Qaddafi 4-22, 334E1
Libyan sentenced 4-23, 335C1
Hijackers seek plotters released 8-23, 629G2
MEHRIGE Jr., Judge Robert R.
Release of Nixon tapes OKd 10-26, 849D3
MEHROTRA, L. L.
Rpts China amb exchng 4-15, 278E3
MEHTA, Asoka
Released 5-15, 365B2
Addresses anti-govt rally 10-16, 810C3
Scores charger change 11-2, 837G1
MEHTA, Jagat S.
Pakistan ties set 5-12—5-14, 356A3
MEHTA, Om
Reports 7,000 arrests 5-17, 382E1
MEIDNER, Rudolf
Soc Dems defeated 9-20, 714C2
MEINHOF, Ulrike
Trial testimony 1-13, 1-27, 77G2
Found hanged 5-9; protests staged 5-10, 5-15; trial adjourned 5-13, 383G1
Cohorts escape 7-7, 593C3
MEIN Kampf (book)
Circulated in Argentina 8-15—8-30, 672B2 ★
MEINS, Holger (d. 1974)
Cited in Baader-Meinhof trial 1-27, 77B3
MEIR, Golda
Chairs intl Sovt Jews' rights conf 2-17—2-19, 206G2
Joins party leadership 3-5, 253A3
Rpt ordered A-arms activated in '73 war 243E1
MEISSNER, Milton F.
Indicted 1-14, 78B2

1977

MEDINA, William A.
Named HUD asst secy 4-25, confrmd 5-25, 499G3
MEDIOBANCA S.p.A.
ITT suits settled 3-4, 194D3
MEDITERRANEAN Sea
Yugo bars Sovt base use 1-9, 24C1
'76 spec interest gifts rptd 2-15, 128E2
'68 uranium loss rptd Israeli plot 5-30, 416E3
UN pollutn conf ends, pact reached 10-21, 876A2
MEDTRONIC Inc.
Forgn paymts rptd 3-11, 233C3
MEDUSA Corp.
Record trust fine levied on unit 10-5, 918D2
MEER, Antonio M.
SEC sues 1-12, 79B3
MEET the Press—*See RCA Corp.—National Broadcasting Co.*
MEFANE, Emmanuel
Replaced as culture min 7-13, 772B1
MEGUID, Abdel Razzak Abdel
Assumes UN post 10-25, 824B1
MEGUID, Ahmed Esmat Abdel
Asks 'push Israel to peace' 3-25, 226G3
Says US asked for UN Cncl adjournmt 3-29, 227B1
Walks out on Syria speech 11-22, 894G1
Meets Israel UN envoy 11-27, 909E2
At Cairo conf 12-14—12-15, 953C1
MEHAIGNERIE, Pierre
Named agriculture min 3-30, 239G1
MEHTA, Asoka
In Gandhi exchange 1-5, 45D3
MEHU, Delorme
Slain 7-3, aide held 7-12, 583C2
MEIER, Bill
Sets world filibuster record 5-4, 532G1
MEINHOF, Ulrike (d. 1976)
Sweden arrests terrorists 4-1, deports 2 4-3, 428E3
Buback killed 4-7, Baader-Meinhof linked 4-9, 4-13, 286B2, F2
Baader, others sentncd 4-28, 352A3
Baader gang ldrs kill selves 10-18, 790D3
MEINS, Holger (d. 1974)
Baader, others sentncd 4-28, 352B3 ★, C3
Baader gang ldrs kill selves 10-18, 790D3
MEIR, Golda
Peres seeks premiership 1-11, 48B2
Greets Sadat 11-19, 889C1
Sadat: Sovts sought '71 mtg 12-6, 929F2
MEITTUNEN, Martti
Govt resigns 5-11, 391D1
MEJIA Soto, Gen. Alvaro
Gunmen attack home, kill guards 7-1, 635G3
MELAMID, Alexander
Emigratn rptd 10-31, 956D1
Partner joins in Israel 12-20, 1017D2

1978

MEDINA, Elizabeth
Fight for Barbara opens 11-27, 1031F1
MEDITERRANEAN Sea
Helsinki conf sets parley 3-8, 179D1
US moves to lift Turkey arms embargo 4-1—4-6, 276A2
French controller slowdowns affect resorts 7-14—8-21, 640A3
NATO maneuvers begin 9-5, 748C2, D2
MEDOFF, Mark
Halloween Bandit opens 12-18, 1031A2
MEDRANO, Jorge
Panama health min 10-12, 884B2
MEDUSA Corp.
Kaiser merger set; Moore-McCormack, Oglebay bids cited 3-16, 283D1
Kaiser deal canceled 8-22, Crane takeover set 9-1, 700C3
MEDUSA Touch, The (film)
Released 4-14, 619B3
MEEDS, Rep. Lloyd (D, Wash.)
Alaska lands amendmt rejected 5-18, 386A2
Not standing for reelectn 9-19, 736F3
Swift wins seat 11-7, 857B3
MEET The Press—*See RCA—National Broadcasting Co.*
MEGAW, Mike
Anti-tick virus rptd 2-23, 334F1
MEGUID, Abdel Razzak
Named Egypt planning min 5-7, 392G2
MEHAIGNERIE, Pierre
Renamed French agri min 4-5, 245G2
MEIER, John
Ordrd to repay Summa $7.9 mln 3-29, 459E2
MEINHOF, Ulrike (d. 1976)
Andy Warhol's Last Love opens 6-30, 887A1
Dutch jail 3 terrorists 8-21, 725C1
MEIR, Golda
VS Begin stand on Res 242 3-9, 156B3
S Africa play showing rptd scored 7-19, 633C3
Scores Begin outbursts 7-20, 563E2
Dies 12-8, funeral 12-12; facts on 1032D1
MEISNER, Michael
Scientologists indicted 8-15, 644D3, E3, 645B1
MEJIA, Hipolito
DR agri min 8-16, 648D2
MEJIA Duque, German
Guerrillas kill 9-8, 814A3
MELANCIA, Carlos
Sworn Portugal industry min 1-30, 91C3

1979

MEDINA Castillo, Ceferino
Venez cong relatns min 3-10, 192D3
MEDIOLI, Enrico
Innocent released 1-11, 174G2
MEDOFF, Mark
When You Comin' Back released 2-8, 174F3
MEDVEDEV, Roy A.
Sup Sovt candidacy set 2-2, 100E1, G1
MEEHAN, Thomas
I Remember Mama opens 5-31, 711G3
MEEROPOL, Michael & Robert
Seeks FBI files preservation 6-26, 521A1
MEERS, Nelson
On Sydney elec bus plan 11-13, 888E1
MEETING By the River, A (play)
Opens 3-28, 712D1
MEET The Press—*See RCA Corp.-National Broadcasting Co.*
MEGUID, Ahmed Esmat Abdel
Backs UN res on Palestinians 8-23, 642B2
MEHRJUI, Darius
Cycle released 2-12, 174D2
MEJIA Gonzalez, Gen. Federico
Heads Natl Guard 7-17, breaks off rebel talks 7-18, 535A2

1980

MEDINA Munoz, Raul
Eludes Colombia emb raiders 2-27, 141C1
MEDITERRANEAN Sea
US, Turkey sign bases pact 3-29, 255D3
Pollutn pact signed 5-17, 381G2
Israel plans Dead Sea canal; map 8-24, 643F2
Jordan Red Sea-Dead Sea canal plan rptd 8-30, 661G1
MEDOFF, Mark
Children of a Lesser God opens 3-30, 392D2
MEDVEDEV, Zhores
US confirms '57 Sovt A-mishap 2-13, 153C1
MEEHAN, Walter
Indicted re A-plant 3-26, 249E1
Acquitted 8-8, 649E1
MEEK, Marvin
Urges grain loan paymts 1-6, 10C1
MEEKER, Richard C.
Kills self 10-15, 890A2
MEESE 3rd, Edwin
Rpts Reagan campaign themes 7-19, 549B3
Allen quits Reagan post 10-30, 817E3
Gets Reagan transitn post 11-6, 839A3
On planned budget cuts 11-12, 866C2
Named pres counselor 11-14, 881E1
Optimistic on Sovt arms talks 11-30, 914F3
Addresses black conservatives conf 12-14, 956G2
Presser's transitn role queried 12-18, 956B1
Says econ emergency act unlikely 12-28, 980G2
MEET the Press—*See RCA Corp.--National Broadcasting Co.*
MEGENS, John William
Convicted 4-23, 372B1
MEGUID, Ahmed Esmat Abdel
Scores W Bank bombings 6-5, 417D2
MEHAIGNERIE, Pierre
On French lamb curbs 2-18, 125C1
On Spanish produce dispute 6-19, 525D3
MEHDIYAN, Maj. Gen. Sayed
Iran coup plot confessn rptd 7-13, 539E2
Executed 8-15, 644E2
MEIR, Golda (1898-1978)
Carter cites funeral 8-4, 594G2
MEISTER, Robert Jay
Convicted 2-4, 270D3

1976

MELCHER, Rep. John (D, Mont.)
Chrgs grain scandal coverup 1-29, 136D1
Wins Senate primary 6-1, 411F1
Elected to Sen race 11-2, 820A1, 824A2, 828C2
MELCHUK, Igor
Loses post re Sakharov defns 3-26, 314A1
MELEN, Ferit
Lockheed probe quashed 4-30, 322B3
MELENDEZ, Isais (Felix) (d. 1975)
Knight killers chrgd 504B1
MELGAR Castro, Gen. Juan Alberto
Pol parties back const plan 1-6, 55C2
MELIA, Judge Aloysius J.
Dismisses Blumenthal case 4-13, 271B1
MELLISH, Robert
Quits Cabt 4-8, 266G3
MELLON, Andrew W. (1855-1937)
Gulf Oil payoffs detailed 133A2
Family role in Gulf shakeup rptd 1-15, 132D3
MELO Antunes, Maj. Ernesto de
Cuba defies Azores refueling ban 1-10—1-15, 53D2
In Hungary, Czech 1-12—1-16, Brussels 1-28, 143B1
Mil rule proposal offered 1-13, 52E3
Meets UN aide 2-11, 192F1
Sees Spain forgn min 2-12, 143C1
Replaced as forgn min 7-23, 558F1
MELOY Jr., Francis E.
Amb to Leb 4-26; confrmd 4-28, 412G1
Slain 6-16, 425A1-C2
Body returned to US 6-19, 448F1
Americans evacuated from Leb 6-20, 447G1
Seelye replaces in Beirut 6-22, 448G1
PLO protects US aides 7-30, 578F2
Replaced as Guatemala amb 8-26, 807E3
US aide meets Sarkis 11-5, 841E2
MELVILLE, Kerry—*See REID, Kerry Melville*
MEMBERS Of Congress for Peace Through Law (MCPL)—*See 'Membership' under U.S. GOVERNMENT—CONGRESS*
MEMOIRS (book)
On best-seller list 12-5, 972D2
MEMPHIS, Tenn.—*See TENNESSEE*
MENDEZ, Aparicio
Natl Cncl chrmn 6-27, Uruguay pres 7-14, 542A1
Vegh vs pres term length 8-11, 678C2
Sworn, bans pol ldrs rights 9-1, 678D1
Offcl quits re pol ban 9-8; Bordaberry, others get back rights 10-7, 814B3
Scores US Dems, Kennedy 10-8; denies comments 10-10, 814F1
MENDOZA, Gen. Cesar
Backs Pinochet 1-28, 99F3
MENENDEZ, Gen. Benjamin
Hard-line generals retired 12-3, 996B3
MENGISTU Haile Mariam, Maj.
1st natl address 4-20, 311G2
Province unrest rptd 5-7, 364F2
Attacked 9-23, 4 executed 11-2, 1002D1
MENINGITIS—*See 'Diseases' under MEDICINE*
MENOMINEE Indians—*See INDIANS, American*
MENSAROS, Andrew
Australia oil dvpt planned 3-22, 237E2
MENSHIKOV, Mikhail
Dies 7-21, 716D3
MENTAL Health—*See under MEDICINE*
MENTAL Retardation, Institute for Basic Research in (N.Y.)
Virus linked to MS 2-28, 224A3 ★
MENTEN, Pieter
In Swiss custody 12-7, returned 12-22, 1007B2
MENZEL, Donald H.
Dies 12-12, 1015B2
MENZIES, June
Named AIB vice chrmn 8-9, 750B2
MENZIES, Sir Robert
Lockheed payoff chrgd 4-29, 322G1
MERCADO, Jose Raquel
Kidnaped 2-15, 251F1
M-19 kills 4-19, 311C1
MERCANTILE Bancorp Inc.
SEC lists paymts 5-12, 728C2
Mercantile Trust Co. (St. Louis)
'64-70 political costs rptd 2-27; Lasater acquittal appeal rptd 3-1, 181A1

1977

MELGAR Castro, Col. Juan Alberto (Honduras president)
Mil staff shuffled 1-3, 45F1
Backs Panamanian canal demands 1-18, 46F1
At canal pact signing 9-7, 678D1
Oct plotters get amnesty 12-6, 970C1
MELLON, Andrew W. (1855-1937)
David Finley dies 2-1, 164G2
Art prize announced 8-1, 808F2
MELLON Bank (Pittsburgh)
Pensn mgt concentratn chrgd 6-28, 578D2
MELOY Jr., Francis E. (d. 1976)
Replaced as amb to Leb 2-10, 148F3
MELTROL (phenformin)—*See MEDICINE—Drugs*
MELVILLE, Ward
Dies 6-5, 532D3
MELVILLE Corp.
Ward Melville dies 6-5, 532D3
MEMOREX Corp.
'76 stockholder equity rise rptd 340D2, 341B1
MEMPHIS, Tenn.—*See TENNESSEE*
MEMPHIS State University
Rush in NFL draft 5-3, 353C3
MENDELSOHN, Robert H.
Interior apptmt withdrawn, quits as consultant 11-11, 877A2
MENDES-France, Pierre
At Brandt comm mtg 12-9—12-11, 998A1
MENDEZ, Aparicio (Uruguayan president)
Curbs powers of judiciary 7-1, 600F3
Excelsior asks Pascale release 7-6; Waldheim, Orfila pleas rptd 7-15, 601E1
'81 electn plan set 8-9, 905A1
On detained Mex newsman 9-6, 905C2
At Panama Canal pact signing 9-7, 678D1
MENDEZ, Francisco
Arrested 1-11, 140A2
MENGELE, Josef
Rptd in Paraguay 8-17, 803C2
MENGISTU Haile Mariam, Lt. Col. (Ethiopian head of state)
Dergue reorganizatn rptd 1-7, 62G3
Teferi plot chrgd 2-3, 98E2
Asks support, scores Saudi, Sudan 2-4, 98G2
Govt role set 2-6, 98A3
Gains sole power 2-11, 238C2
Pro-Sovt policy seen; backing rptd, ambs received 2-11, 238A3
Cabt named 3-11, 238E2
Sees Castro, backs alliance re Djibouti 3-14—3-16, 249C2
Urges mobilizatn vs Sudan 4-12, 328C2
Asks anti-dissident drive 5-1, 427A2
In USSR 5-4—5-8, 390E3
Warns re encirclemt 6-25, 547D3
At OAU mtg 7-2—7-5, 512D1
USSR concern re govt rptd 8-4, 608A2
Asks mobilizatn vs Ogaden rebels 8-24, forms mil cmnd 8-29, 684C2, E2
Gains in factional strife 9-9, 716B1
Sees extended Ogaden fighting, denies Cuba troop role 9-18, 715D2
Ogaden troop visit rptd 10-13, 875C2
Atnafu executed 11-13, 875D2
Sees 2 US reps 12-13, 998D2
MENINGITIS—*See MEDICINE—Diseases*
MENNONITES
Charismatic conf held 7-20—7-24, 620D3
MENOPAUSE—*See WOMEN—Medicine & Health*
MENOTTI, Gian Carlo
Thomas Schippers dies 12-16, 1024B3
MEN'S International Professional Tennis Council—*See TENNIS*
MENTAL Health—*See under MEDICINE*
MENTAL Health, President's Commission on—*See under U.S. GOVERNMENT*
MENTAL Retardation, President's Committee on—*See under U.S. GOVERNMENT*
MENTEN, Pieter
Anti-Nazi burns home 7-18, 986E1
Sentncd for war crimes 12-14, 986B1
MENZIES, Sir Robert Gordon
Honored by Queen 3-17, 280E2
Vs 2 charter changes 3-29, 447D1
MERAMEC Dam (Missouri)
Cong OKs funds cut 5-3, 365D2
MERCANTILE National Bank (Chicago)
Gleason pleads guilty 6-21, 540B3

1978

MELBOURNE, Ark.—*See ARKANSAS*
MELCHER, Sen. John (D, Mont.)
Votes vs Panama Canal neutrality pact 3-16, 177F2
Votes vs 2d Canal pact 4-18, 273B1
Vs Calif fuel oil exports 6-16, 471B1
MELFI, Leonard
Taxi Tales opens 12-29, 1031A3
MELGAR Castro, Gen. Juan Alberto
Drug scandal breaks 4-24, 614E3
Rightists angered by new pol parties, '75 massacre rpt 4-28, 614D3
Campaign song distributed 7-21, 615C1
Overthrown 8-7, junta vows to continue policies 8-8, 614A3
Junta retains 7 in Cabt 8-9, 691D3
MELLON, Paul
Natl Gallery additn opens 6-1, 578E2
MELLON Bank (Pittsburgh Pa.)
Small business interest rate set 11-14, 918E1
MELLON Bank N.A. v. Southland Mobile Homes of South Carolina
Case refused by Sup Ct 10-10, 789G2
MELLON Foundation, Andrew W.
Natl Gallery additn opens 6-1, 578E2
MELNICK, Daniel
Columbia Pictures film chief 6-1, 599E2
MEMOREX Corp.
IBM case mistrial 7-5, 510F2
MEMORY—*See MEDICINE & Health—Brain*
MEMPHIS, Tenn.—*See TENNESSEE*
MEMPHIS Light, Gas & Water Division v. Craft
Utility customer hearings backed by Sup Ct 5-1, 364B1
MEMPHIS State University
Simpson in NFL draft 5-2, 336F3
MENA, Gen. Odlanier
Scores Christian Dems 7-21, 572C3
MENARD, Kevin
Sentenced 5-19, 396G3
MENDELSOHN, Robert H.
Calif suit setld 4-18, named interior aide 6-10, 446F3
MENDENHALL, Edward J.
Arrested in A-sub plot 10-4, 824F1
Convicted 12-14, 992E1
MENDES, Francisco
Dies 7-7, 620A3
MENDEZ, Aparicio (Uruguayan president)
Alvarez installed as army chief 3-2, 292E1
Amnesty Intl asks torture probe 5-3, 395G3
Poisoned wine sent to 3 ex-congressmen 9-6, 799G1
MENDEZ, Francisco
Sentenced 2-7, 380G3
MENDEZ Docurro, Eugenio
Arrested for corruptn 3-21, repudiates confessn 3-22, 289G2
Freed on bail 4-21, 518A1
MENDON, Kevin
Emporia State wins NAIA baseball title, pitches no-hitter 6-1, 560A2
MENDOZA, Gen. Cesar
Junta fires Gen Leigh 7-24, 572D2
MENDOZA, Valentin
Honduras planning min 8-9, 691E3
MENESES Cantarero, Gen. Edmundo
Killed by Guatemala guerrillas 9-16, 777F1
MENGISTU Haile Mariam, Lt. Col. (Ethiopian head of state)
Warns West vs Somalia aid 2-14, 100C1
Sees US delegatn 2-17—2-18, Somalia invasn vow rptd 2-21, 137G1
Admits Cubans fighting in Ogaden 3-2, 178D3
In Cuba 4-21—4-27, 372B3 ★
Warns Somalia vs rebel support 5-12, 372B3
Offers Eritrea rebel amnesty 6-7, 584G2
Assassinatn tries rptd 6-28, 585D1
Signs USSR pact 11-20, 922D3
MENJOU, Adolphe
Woman of Paris released 4-13, 620D1
MENTAL Health—*See under MEDICINE; also country names*
MENTEN, Pieter
Convictn overturned 5-29, 454G2
Spec ct orders release 12-4, 965B2
MENZA, Alexander J.
3d in NJ Sen primary 6-6, 448A1
MENZIES, Robert Gordon
Dies 5-14, 440B3
MERCADER, Ramon
Dies 10-18, 888B3
MERCEDES-Benz—*See DAIMLER-Benz*

1979

MELCHER, Sen. John (D, Mont.)
Indian Affairs Com chrmn 1-23, 71E2
Votes vs trade bill 7-23, 646G3
Votes vs Talmadge denunciatn 10-10, 769G1
MELEN, Ferit
Lockheed bribe role chrgd 9-20, 775F1
MELENDEZ, Marciano
Arrest protested 5-4, 371A1
MELLAR, Stephan
Suicide In B Flat opens 3-13, 292B3
MELLI, Robert
Indicted 3-6, 220D2
MELLON, Paul
Resigns as Natl Gallery pres, named bd chrmn 5-3, 375E1
MELNIK, Mikhail
Kills self 3-6, 238D1
MEMOIRS of a Thief (book)
Teresa the Thief released 5-5, 523F3
MEMOREX Corp.
Rejects Amdahl, Storage Tech bids 10-28; ends Amdahl talks 11-20, 942D2
MEMPHIS, Tenn.—*See TENNESSEE*
MENA, Jose
Arrest protested 5-4, freed 5-11, 371A1, C1
MENDENHALL, Edward J.
Sentenced 3-15, 240E2
MENDEZ Montenegro, Julio Cesar
Fuentes Mohr assassinated 1-25, 97G1
MENDOZA, Carlos
Gomez TKOs 9-28, 838E3
MENENDEZ, Gen. Luciano Benjamin
Arrested, rebelln crushed 9-29, 748G2-F3
Moderate named Argentine army chief 12-7, 947F2
MENGELE, Josef
Loses Paraguay citizenship 8-8, bounty offered 8-10; past detailed 616A3
MENGISTU Haile Mariam, Lt. Col. (Ethiopian head of state)
Lauds USSR, Cuba, S Yemen mil aid 8-23, 791C1
MEN in White (play)
Opens 7-11, 712D1
MENKEN, Alan
God Bless You Mr Rosewater opens 5-20, 711D3
MENNEA, Pietro
Sets 200-m dash record 9-12, 799A2
MENNINGER Foundation (Topeka, Kan.)
Ex-dir Murphy dies 3-19, 272D3
MENNONITES
Baptism rites agrmt reached 3-31, 375A3
Amish polio outbreak rptd 6-5, vaccine sent 6-9, 472D1
'Shunned' Pa farmer acquitted in abductn case 12-4, 932C1-A2
MENTAL Health—*See under MEDICINE*
MENTEN, Pieter
Retrial ordered 5-22, 409D1
Ruled unfit for trial 9-24, 731D2
MEPERIDINE (Demerol)—*See MEDICINE—Drugs*
MERCADO, Hector Jaime
Sancocho opens 3-28, 712C2
MERCEDES-Benz—*See DAIMLER-Benz*

1980

MELATO, Mariangela
To Forget Venice released 1-28, 216F3
MELENTEV, Aleksandr
Wins Olympic medal 7-20, 623C2
MELIA, Josep
Sworn Spain min for Basques 10-21, 832C2
MELLO, Judy Hendren
Named First Women's pres 6-12, 600G2
MELLON Foundation, Richard King
$15 mln gift for forests rptd 12-20, 987A2
MELNICK, Daniel
First Family released 12-25, 1003G1
MELNIKOVA, Antonina
Wins Olympic medal 8-1, 622E2
MELOY, Francis E. (d. 1976)
US amb to Leb escapes death try 8-28, 644A1
MEMINGER, Dean (The Dream)
Stars win WBL title 4-10, 432C2
MEMOREX Corp.
IBM win in trust suit rptd upheld 11-20, 917E3
MEMORIES of Another Day (book)
On best-seller list 9-14, 716D3; 10-12, 796F3
MEMPHIS—*See TENNESSEE*
MEMPHIS (Tenn.) Press-Scimitar
Memphis area illness probed 4-2, 331A3
MENA, Gen. Odlanier
Removed as Chile security chief 7-24, 603E2
MENDENHALL, Sylvia
DEA detainmt procedure backed by Sup Ct 5-27, 453G1-454A1
MENDES, Bishop Luciano
'79 attack rptd 1-11, 95C3
MENDEZ, Alfredo (Freddie)
Convicted 7-30, 601D1
Indicted 12-10, 963F3
MENDEZ Herbruger, Oswaldo
Wins Olympic medal 8-3, 622G2
MENDEZ Manfredini, Aparicio (Uruguayan president)
New const published 11-2; oppositn ldrs arrested at protest 11-14, 888A3
Const proposal defeated 11-30, 924E2
MENDOZA, Humberto
Kidnaped, slain 11-27, 921F1
MENDOZA Azurdia, Col. Oscar
Elected Guatemala VP 9-2, 670G3
MENGISTU Haile Mariam, Lt. Col. (Ethiopian head of state)
Scores US-Somali mil pact 9-12, 735G3
Urges Somali land claims end, arms shipmt ban 12-4, 933E1
MENIGON, Nathalie
Arrested 9-13, 750F1
MEN in Love (book)
On best-seller list 6-8, 448C3; 7-13, 568C3; 8-17, 640F3
MENNEA, Pietro
Wins Olympic medal 7-28, 624B1
MENTAL Health—*See under MEDICINE*
MENTEN, Pieter
Sentenced 7-9, 509F3
MENZEL, Jiri
Apple Game released 1-16, 216B2
Magicians released 12-26, 1003B2
MERBAN Corp.
Nicaragua debt rescheduled 9-5, 689A3
MERCADO, Alberto
In Moscow for Olympics 6-29, 588B2
MERCANTILE Bank (Bahama Islands)
Looting suit rptd 3-3, 229A1
MERCED—*See CALIFORNIA*

1976

MERCER, Jane R.
IQ test rptd 2-18, 203G1
MERCER, Johnny
Dies 6-25, 524C3
MERCHANT, Livingston
Dies 5-15, 404B2
MERCHANT Shipping, American Institute of
Reynolds scores Panama Canal toll hike 11-24, 1008C3
MERCK & Co. Inc.
Rpts foreign payoffs 3-9, 361G1
SEC lists forgn paymts 5-12, 728C2
Sarett gets Science medal 10-18, 858F3
Merck Sharpe & Dohme
Flu immunizatn plan delayed 9-1, 656C3
MERCORELLA, Anthony J.
Indicted 5-26, 442G2
Madjari chrgs dismissed 12-22, 1016F1
MERCURY
UN Medit pollutn pact signed 2-16, 126D3
EPA bans pesticides 2-18, 137F1
Paint pesticide ban lifted 5-31, 571C1
MERCY Killing—*See 'Death Issues' under MEDICINE*
MEREDITH, Scott
Nixon 'love letters' called 'hoax' 6-4, 438A2

MERGERS & Acquisitions—*See also country names*
US comptroller scored re bank mergers 2-17, 3-1, 185D2, C3
Falstaff-Ballantine merger cited 5-11, 360F2
Clothing, textile workers merge 6-3, 436E1
Dem platform text 6-15, 470E2
Cong clears trust bill 9-16, 728D1 ★; signed 10-1, 982F1
Newhouse buys Booth Newsprs 11-8, Morgan buys The Nation 11-28, 901F2, C3
Murdoch to buy NY Post 11-19, 887D2
GE, Utah Intl merge 12-16, 984G3
Detroit bank acquisitn OKd 12-19, 983F3-984A1
The Nation sale fizzles 12-21, 995E1
New Boston Bank buys Capital Bank 12-31, 984A1

1977

MERCHANT Marine Academy (Kings Point, N.Y.)
Cong authorizes $14.66 mln 11-1, 856F2; Carter signs 11-2, 1001E2
MERCK & Co., Inc.
Merck Sharpe & Dohme Research Laboratories
FDA OKs pneumonia vaccine 11-21, 907B1
MERCK Sharp & Dohme Research Laboratories—*See under MERCK & Co., Inc.*
MERCOURI, Melina
Elected to Greek parlt 11-20, 925E1
MERETRAN—*See NARCOTICS & Dangerous Drugs*

MERGERS & Acquisitions
Murdoch takes control of NY Post 12-30-76, acquires NY Mag 1-7, 48B3
'76, '77 big takeovers table 880F1
Arco buys Anaconda 1-12, 55F2
Far-Mar-Co, Farmland merger set 2-11, 408E3
Milwaukee Rd-BN bid rejected 2-16, 213E2
Racal acquires Milgo 2-17, 275A1
Rise in activity rptd 2-18, 274G1
Newhouse, GE purchases, ITT merger cited 2-18, 274E2-A3
Elec utility rules asked 3-1, 148C2
Cross-media ownership barred 3-1, 216B1
Irvine takeover battle rptd 3-3, 274D3
ITT Hartford suits settled 3-4, 194B3
Gulf + Westn plans Madison Sq Garden takeover bid 3-7, 275C1
FTC vs Tenneco bid for Monroe 3-15, 274G3
Hunts seek Sunshine Mining 3-21, 275C1
WCT, Grand Prix merger set 3-23, 353F3-354C1
United Tech makes Babcock bid 3-29; suit filed 4-4, 274B3
Sharon Steel ends Foremost takeover bid 4-5, 275E1
Richmond OKs Continental bid 4-12, 274C3
Molycorp OKs Union Oil bid 4-14, 274F3
Gannett Okla, Mo purchases OKd 4-14; Speidel merger set 5-10, 395C2
Anderson Clayton seeks Gerber 4-18, ends bid 9-19, 799E1
Fortune 500 rpts '76 mergers 340C1, 341A1, B1
Volvo, Saab plan merger 5-6, 469B3
Cleveland NHL team sale OKd 5-12, 430F1
NYSE-Amex talks fail 5-19, 520F3-521C2
Irvine won by Taubman group 5-20, 519B1
Kennecott divestiture order cited 520F1
Du Pont-Christiana merger OKd 6-16, 518A1
Raytheon to buy Falcon Seaboard 6-22, 519C2
Norton Simon buys Avis control 6-27, 519G1
Cigar makers merger blocked 6-28, 520E3
Beaverbrook newspaper chain sold 6-30, 526F3-527B1
Time to buy Book-of-Month 7-5, 519D2
United Tech's Babcock takeover blocked 7-5, 520D1
Sumitomo, Wells Fargo buy 27 Bank of Calif branches 7-6, 578D1; Sumitomo purchase challenged 8-9, 669B3
Milwaukee road stock purchase OKd 7-15, 593C2
BN purchase of Green Bay OKd 7-15, 613D1
Hercules buys Warren-Teed 7-19, 650F3
Lilly buys Ivac 7-20, 650E3
Gulf buys Kewanee 8-9, 612E2
NHL rejcts WHA merger 8-9, 644D3
Carrier buys Inmont 8-11, 629A3
Great Westn, Anderson Clayton bid-cutting strategy rptd 8-12, 799C1-E1, F2
Touche Ross, Lasser merge 8-22, 650E2
Tenneco buys Phila Life 8-25, 650F3
McDermott wins Babcock bidding war, United Tech withdraws 8-25, 666E3
Esquire sold to Felker group 8-26, 695G2
NYSE brokerage house mergers rptd 8-29, 691C2
Oil, gas firms acquisitn curbs rejctd 9-8, 702F3
Allegheny wins Chemetron control 9-8, 880C2
FRA to buy C&NW stock 9-9, 778B3
Ashland OKs Commonwealth stock purchase 9-22, 723B1
Dean Witter, Reynolds merger set 10-3, 799G2
Great Westn, Sunshine Mining end feud 10-4, 798F3
Donaldson Lufkin buys Pershing, Wood Struthers 10-11, 799G3
ITT, Lazard settle chrgs re Hartford 10-13, 980B3
Miles Lab OKs Bayer takeover 10-17, 880E1
Coca-Cola Bottling of LA OKs NW takeover 10-17, 880A2

1978

MERCER, Marian
Stop the World opens 8-3, 887C3
MERCER County, N.D.—*See NORTH Dakota*
MERCK & Co., Inc.
Clinoril OKd by FDA 11-1, 948A3
MERCURY—*See also FOOD—Contamination Issues*
Olin indicted on dischrgs 3-23, 243E1
MERDES, Edward
Trails in Alaska gov primary 8-22, 682F3
Primary loss official 10-20, 831E2
MEREDITH, Burgess
Magic released 11-18, 970A2

MERGERS & Acquisitions
Budd takeover bid rptd 1-6, Thyssen named suitor 1-12, talks OKd 1-17, 66D1
Amer Medicorp OKs Humana bid, Hilton bid withdrawn 1-10, 66D2
'77 merger activity rptd down 1-11, 65D3
WJLA, KOCO-TV exchng OKd 1-12, Time to buy Washington Star 2-3; FCC scores Allbritton 2-13, 109E2
Sun Oil buys Becton Dickenson shares 1-17; Wms Act violatn chrgd, Cong probe asked 1-27, 65F3
Marshall Field to buy Liberty House stores 1-20, 185F1
Grace plans King's purchase 1-23, 66C2
Dayton Hudson to buy Mervyn's 1-23, 66C2
Gannett buys 2 Wilmington papers 1-30, 109D3
Arts Inst '77 merger cited 2-7, 316F1
Financial Gen sues Lance, others re takeover bid 2-17; SEC sues Lance group 3-18, chrgs setld 3-19, 204F1, B3
CBS seeks IMS purchase rejctd 2-22, 185B1
Carter Hawley drops Marshall Field bid 2-22, Wanamaker merger planned 3-8, 185E1
Guest takeover of Sachs halted 2-23, 211B1
Pullman porters join railway clerks 2-28, 185B2
United Tech to buy Ambac 3-2, 185A1
Beatrice to buy Tropicana; Kellogg talks cited 3-5, 184F3
Atlanta Landmarks buys Fox theater 3-5, 293A2
Plains Monitor, Atlanta Gazette '77 sale cited 187B1
French govt acquires Dessault stock 3-8, 313E1
Sun Oil sued by SEC 3-9, 223E1
WJLA, KOCO-TV swap reaffirmed 3-9, Allbritton rejcts 3-24, 270G2
Kennecott blocks Curtiss-Wright takeover bid 3-13—5-24, 402B1-403D1
Gen Cable plans Automation Indus purchase 3-15, 404F1
Kaiser, Medusa merger set 3-16, 283D1
NZ state-owned airways merge 4-1, 498D2
Forgn bank activity in US rptd up 4-3, 4-12, 263A2
Honkong Bank to buy Marine Midland 4-5, 263E1-A2
Airco OKs BOC purchase, Martin Marietta withdraws 4-7, 403C3
Merrill Lynch to buy White Weld 4-14, 283B2
Great Southern, Equitable Gen to merge 4-17, 283G1
Philip Morris seeks 7-Up takeover 5-1, 5-11; bid accepted 5-15, 364F2-C3
Heinz to buy Weight Watchers, Foodways agrmt cited 5-4, 364D2
NRC OKs paper div sale to BAT Industries 5-5, 345B3
Talcott to sell 2 divisns to Gulf + Western 5-7, 404E1
Gannett plans Combined purchase 5-8, 345E2
NatWest to buy Natl Bank of NA 5-12, 364F1
Dymo sought by Pricel, Esselte, Daylin 5-12—5-24; Esselte bid OKd 5-26, 404B1
Petro-Lewis plans Shenandoah purchase 5-15, 403G3-404A1
McDonnell Douglas to buy Data 100 5-18, 404F1
Time Inc to buy Inland Container 5-19, 403G2-C3
Tenneco offers Albright & Wilson purchase 5-23, 404E1
UK bank to buy Union Bancorp 6-8, 553B1
Petro-Canada, Occidental in Husky Oil bidding war 6-10—7-27; Alberta Gas wins control 6-27, 628E3-629E2
NHL North Stars, Barons merge 6-14, 656F2
Bell backs LTV-Lykes merger 6-21, 492C3
Cutler OKs Eaton takeover 6-26, 553C2
Equitable Gen sets new merger with Gulf United 6-26, 553D2

1979

MERCER, David
Ride A Cock Horse opens 3-18, 292E2
MERCER, Marian
Bosoms and Neglect opens 5-3, 711F1
MERCIER and Camier (play)
Opens 10-25, 956C3
MERCIER Corp.
Erie Coke & Chemical Co.
EPA sues vs Ohio pollutn 2-5, 90G2
MERCK, Albert W.
Questns NJ casino hiring policies 2-26, 152B2
MERCK & Co.
Minority hiring plan OKd 6-26, 521F1
Dow Jones index adds to roster 6-28, 481F2
Iran unit mgr slain 10-14, 814C3
MERCK Institute for Therapeutic Research (West Point, Pa.)
Hepatitis A virus grown 5-31, 691D3
MERCURY
Olin convicted for dumping 8-16, 704E1
NJ Meadowlands cleanup ordrd 8-26, 704A2
Olin fined for dumping 12-10, 947A1
MEREDITH, Burgess
Great Bank Hoax released 3-22, 528C2
MEREDITH, Judge James H.
Refuses St Louis busing order 4-12, 596C3
Named to wiretap ct 5-18, 442D3

MERGERS & Acquisitions—*See also specific industries (e.g. AVIATION, PETROLEUM); country names*
Tender offer, arbitrage defined 72G3
Kennedy introduces merger-limit bill, Justice Dept backs 3-8, 202D2
1st 1/4 merger rise rptd 4-10, 349F2
Fortune cites '78 activity 5-7, 305B1
Merger dangers seen by FTC chrmn 5-7, 349C2
Idaho takeover law challenge rejctd by Sup Ct 6-26, 540E3
1st 1/2 mergers rptd 7-2, 500F3

1980

MERCER, David
Dies 8-8, 676C2
MERCER, Robert E.
Named Goodyear chief exec 12-2, 959B2
MERCHANTS National Bank & Trust Co. (Indianapolis, Ind.)
De Angelis sentncd in pork swindle 7-21, 655D1
MERCK & Co. Inc.
In Dow Jones indl avg 76F1
W Ger pricing chrgs cited 2-12, 154E1
Iran unit takeover rptd 7-9, 546D2
MERCURY
Medit pollutn pact signed 5-17, 381C3
MEREDITH, Judge James H.
Orders St Louis schl desegregatn 5-21, 559B2

MERGERS & Acquisitions
Tender offer, arbitrage defined 76D2, G3
'79 merger rise rptd 1-15, 52E2
'Insider' stock trading convictn voided by Sup Ct 3-18, 226B2
1st 1/4 activity slows 4-8, 386F1-A2
FTC offcl resigns in protest 5-27, 703A1
1st 1/2 activity slows 7-9, 557C1

1976

MERHIGE Jr., Judge Robert R.
OKs Westinghouse uranium pact 2-3, 115E3
Sets Kepone case fines 10-5, 767E3
MERINO, Francisco
Mexico agri min 12-2, 907A1
MERINO Castro, Adm. Jose Toribio
Backs Pinochet 1-28, 99E3
On prisoner release 11-22, 963E1
MERIWETHER, Dr. H. Delano
Flu immunizatn plan delayed 9-1, 656D3
MERRELL National Co.
Flu immunizatn plan delayed 9-1, 656C3
MERRILL Lynch & Co.
Merrill Lynch, Pierce, Fenner & Smith Inc.
Files consent decrees in job bias suits 6-4, 414D1
Bomb injures 4 6-14, 504D1
Rpts USSR gold sales 7-21, 530D2

1977

Loeb Rhoades, Hornblower merger planned 10-27, 1004A3
Kennecott Peabody sale linked to copper industry woes 10-31, 859D1
Lykes, LTV plan merger 11-4, 943F2-D3
MCA acquires New Times 11-10, 1004E3
Takeover pace rptd up, '60s period compared 11-14, 879B3
Kennecott-Cardorundum deal OKd 11-16, 880A1
Alcon OKs Nestle takeover 11-17, 880D1
Brae Corp seeks Green Bay line 11-22; ICC OKs BN bid 11-30, BN drops offer 12-1, 1007B1
Lehman Bros, Kuhn Loeb plan merger 11-28, 1004F2-A3
BN, Frisco OK merger 12-5, 1007D1
McDermott to buy remaining Babcock shares 12-8, 1004C2
US vs Revere sale to Alcan 12-9, 1004E3
Unilever plans Natl Starch takeover 12-11, 1004C2
Marshall Field vs Carter Hawley bid 12-14, 1004G1
Natl Distillers, Emery plan mergers 12-19, 1004B3
Time plans cable-TV purchase 12-22, 1004C3
Lippincott OKs Harper & Row bid 12-23, 1004D3

MERHIGE Jr., Judge Robert R.
Cuts Allied Kepone fine 2-1, 95B1
OKs Eastern weight standards 3-3, 279F1
Urges Westinghouse, utilities setlmt 11-9, 895B2
MERIDIAN Mortgage Co.
Exec kidnaped 2-8—2-10, 162G1
MEROLA, Mario
3 chrgd in '76 Bronx fire 1-2, 1-11, 140A2
MERRILL, James
Wins Pulitzer Prize 4-18, 355D2
MERRILL Lynch & Co.
Merrill Lynch, Pierce, Fenner & Smith Inc.
Hughes estate appraised 3-15, 354F2
SEC rpt chrgs NYC '74-75 financial deceptn; reactn 8-26, 665B3, 666A1
Dean Witter, Reynolds merger set 10-3, 799B3
NYC cancels pub note sale 11-10, Goldin bars new sale 11-13, 881A1, G1

1978

Leeds-Gen Signal merger plans end Tyco, Cutler bidding battle 7-7, 553D1
N Central, Southn airlines to merge 7-13, 684D1
Tex Eastn, Olinkraft to merge 7-17, 700E3
'More' ceases publicatn, merges with Columbia Journalism Review 7-21, 672G1
Philip Morris buys Liggett forgn operatns 7-26, 718C1
Iran completes Krupp paymts 7-27, 617B1
Justice, FTC offcls testify on conglomerate merger growth, cite '71-77 data 7-27, 7-28, 767E1
Allis-Chalmers to buy American Air Filter 7-28, 718F1
ITT-Hartford case cited 7-28, 767F1
Grand Union, Colonial stores to merge 8-1, 718A1
Beatrice-Tropicana trust challenge rejctd 8-2, cos merge 8-7, 767C2, D3
Reynolds seeks Del Monte 8-3, merger OKd 9-25, 752A3
Peugeot to buy Chrysler Eur units 8-10, 623B2
Idaho takeover law ruled unconst 8-10, 700E3
Occidental seeks Mead takeover 8-11, Mead rejcts 8-18, 767C2
American Can outbids Interco for Fingerhut 8-14, 718D1
Bakery, tobacco unions merge 8-16, 700G1-B2
Medusa-Kaiser deal canceled 8-22, Crane merger set 9-1, 700C3
UK, Japan cos set joint plant 8-23, 667C3
Westn, Continental airlines to merge 8-31, 684B1
GDV outbids Liggett for Servomation 8-31, 700A3
Justice asks notificatn, 9-5; 120 bids rptd, challenges studied 10-4, 767B1
Amax bars Socal bid 9-7, NYSE to probe trading 9-11, 700B2
Gen Electric, Utah Intl merger cited 9-7, 700D2
Pan Am, Natl Airlines set merger 9-7, TXI scores 9-12, 700G3
Consolidated Foods to buy Hanes 9-14, 717G3
Business cash holdings, acquisitns linked 9-18, 716F3
Pillsbury to acquire Green Giant 9-18, 752C3
United Tech seeks Carrier merger 9-18; Carrier vs 9-25, US sues 11-13, 896D1
Kennecott victory over Curtiss-Wright voided, new electns ordrd 9-28, 752D2
Abitibi plans Price takeover 9-29, 772C3
Celanese plans Olin takeover 10-3, 767G3
Carrier plans Jenn-Air acquisitn 10-4, 896F2
Milwaukee Rd wins BN merger plea 10-5, 812B2
Airline deregulatn compromise clears Cong conf com 10-6, 765G2
US sues vs Occidental-Mead merger 10-11; Occidental offers concessns 10-23, US expands suit 10-25, 895A3
Simmons OKs Gulf+Westn bid 10-15, 808A2
Allegheny drops planned sale to Bayer unit 10-24, 897E1
Olinkraft OKs Johns-Manville offer, ends Tex Eastn bidding 10-27; Morgan Stanley sued 11-8, 896A3, D3
Diamond Shamrock to buy Falcon Seaboard 11-2, 1005A2
Pacific Holding, Iowa Beef plan rptd 11-6, 1005B2
ICC proposes trucking deregulatn; indus, cong ldrs leery 11-7—12-31, 1007E1
Lykes-LTV probe by FTC asked 11-9, FTC rejcts 11-21; shareholders OK merger 12-5, 935C2
Celanese-Olin merger ended 11-10, 897C1
Petro-Canada buys Phillips unit 11-10, 11-20, 901A2
Chessie, Seaboard set rail merger 11-16, 897A1
Liggett to buy SC Pepsi bottler 11-16, 1005C2
Mallory OKs Dart bid 11-17, 1005C2
Firestone, Borg-Warner to merge 11-28, 935D1
Pacific Power to buy RCA Alaska phone unit 11-30, 935B2
Occidental restrained by ct 12-9, ends Mead takeover fight 12-20, 1004C3
Eastn seeks Natl merger 12-11; Pan Am, TXI bids rptd probed 12-22, 1007B3
Carter questns oil industry acquisitns 12-12, 983E2
Kennecott, Curtiss-Wright settle 12-15, 1004G3
Simpsons drops Simpsons-Sears merger, Hudson's Bay takeover seen 12-18, 986B1
Reliance Elec to buy Fed Pacific Elec 12-18, 1005A2
Dictaphone OKs Pitney-Bowes bid 12-21, 1005E1
Hershey to buy Friendly Ice Cream 12-26, 1005G1-A2
MERINO Castro, Adm. Jose Toribio
Plebiscite oppositn cited 1-5, 16C3, D3 ★
Junta fires Gen Leigh 7-24, 572D2
MERRILL, Jan
Sets 3000-mtr run mark 6-8—6-10, 600C3
MERRILL, Philip L.
Loses Me primary for gov 6-13, 467A1
MERRILL Lynch & Co. Inc.
White Weld purchase planned 4-14, 283B2

1979

MERHIGE, Judge Robert R.
Bagley acquitted 8-1, 578F2
MERIDEN, Conn.—*See CONNECTICUT*
MERIT Student's Encyclopedia
H-bomb letter cites article 9-16, 9-18, 715G2, 717E1
MERIT System Protection Board—*See under U.S. GOVERNMENT*
MERIWEATHER, Joe C.
Traded to Knicks 1-5, 526D2
MERKERSON, S. Epatha
Second Thoughts opens 5-4, 712C2
MERLE, Pierre
Wins libel case 4-18, shares award 4-19, 334C2
MERRILL, James
Wins Natl Book Award 4-23, 356B2
MERRILL Jr., James A.
Chrgd in Va A-plant sabotage 6-18, 466F1
Convicted 10-16, 807D1
Sentenced 11-27, 925B2
MERRILL Lynch & Co. Inc.
NYC note sale successful 1-22, 56C1
Top-ranked size cited 5-14, 366B3

1980

MERILUOTO, Paivi
Wins Olympic medal 8-2, 622D1
MERINO Rabago, Francisco
Blames US for drought 6-19, 524E2
MERL, Volkert
Wins Daytona endurance 2-3, 637F3
MERRICK, David
42d Street opens 8-25, 756D3
MERRICK, John (deceased)
Elephant Man released 10-3, 836E2
MERRILL, James A.
NRC clears Va A-plant 8-5, 649A1
MERRILL, Jan
Wins Penn Relays mile 4-25, 892D2
Decker breaks outdoor 1500-m mark 7-12, 891F1
MERRILL Lynch & Co. Inc.
Metal futures trading halted 1-21, 68C3
Peru silver futures losses rptd 2-15, 152G1
Hunt asks silver margin call delay 3-27, 223D2
Money mkt fund unit listed 3-31, 223F3
Hunt silver debts rptd 5-2, 345C1
Nicaragua debt rescheduled 9-5, 689A3
Birk named chrmn, chief exec 12-17, 959D1
MERRILL Trust Co.
Saco (Me) loan cited 1-10, 187F1

1976

MERRIMACK, H.H.—*See NEW Hampshire*
MERRITT, Dr. John C.
Marijuana use for glaucoma OKd 10-5, 860F3
MERRITT, Kim
Finishes Boston Marathon 4-19, 292F3
MERY, Gen. Guy
Article sparks controversy 6-1—6-3, 417B3
MESA Espinoza, Salom
Seized re US exec kidnap 8-3, 592D3
Sup Ct voids arrest, OKs mil probe 8-25; immunity lifted 8-26, 874D2
MESSERSMITH, Andy
Free agent rule upheld 2-4, 951E3
MESYATS, Valentin K.
Sovt agriculture min 3-16, 206B2
METALS & Metal Products
Canada '75 trade deficit rptd 1-30, 116B3
'75 4th ¼ profits rptd 2-3, 215A3
1st ¼ profits rptd 4-29, 376C3
China-Albania combine opens 4-30, 331E3
'75 top 500 indls ranked 437E1
Price hike study planned 8-30, 646G3
US warns NY Commodity Exchng 9-15, 990D2
METAMORPHOSIS (film)
Wins Cannes award 5-28, 460G1
METCALF, Sen. Lee (D, Mont.)
Chrgs fed advisor job bias 9-17, 944F1
METCALFE, Rep. Ralph H. (D, Ill.)
Beats Daley candidate 3-16, 196F2
Tax probe dropped 4-15, 286D3
Reelected 11-2, 829F2
METELO, Lt. Col. Antonio
Mother, daughter wounded 1-1, 11A1
METELO, Maria Teresa
Wounded 1-1, 11A1
METEORITES—*See ASTRONOMY*
METEOROLOGICAL Organization, World—*See WORLD Meteorological Organization*
METEOROLOGY
NASA Jupiter symposium 5-24, 443C3
Mars weather rptd 7-21, 526C3
Geneva com OKs US, Sovt weather-war pact 9-3, 761B2
METHE Jr., Arthur M.
Arrested 12-15, 952F3
METHE, Edna
Arrested 12-15, 952F3
METHODISTS
United Methodist Church
Moorefield '75 affiliatn rptd 4-9, 755E3
Conv. homosexuals opposed 5-5, 951G2
METROPOLITAN Museum of Art (N.Y.)
Pope-Hennessey apptmt rptd 5-25, 504D2
METROPOLITAN Opera Association (N.Y.)
Elisabeth Rethberg dies 6-6, 444G2
METZ, Maj. James H.
Vietnam rpts killed 9-6, 678B3
METZENBAUM, Howard Morton
'72 campaign gift listed 4-25, 688D1
Wins Senate primary 6-8, 409C3
Elected 11-2, 819A3, 823E3, 828A3
METZGER, Butch
Named rookie of year 11-23, 952F1
MEUSER, Fred C.
Dutch probe interviews end 3-5, 254G2
Bernhard bribe chrg rptd 4-21, 322C2
Cited in Bernhard probe rpt 8-26, 626B2, 627F3
MEXICAN American Legal Defense and Education Fund
Rptd vs Calif U reverse bias appeal 11-11, 882F1
MEXICAN Americans
Sup Ct declines Denver schl integratn rule review 1-12, 24F1
Aliens warrantless interrogatn upheld 7-6, 535A1
Carter in Calif parade 9-26, 724F1
Key support for Carter win 11-2, 818G2
Oppositn to Calif U reverse bias appeal rptd 11-11, 882F1
Sup Ct vacates Austin busing plan 12-6, 920B2
Garza rejected Cabt post 12-16, 937B1

MEXICO—*See also DISARMAMENT—Geneva Committee, IDB, LAFTA, OAS, SELA*
'74 mil forces rptd 1-2, 60G2
CP names pres candidate 1-9, 75D2
Listed as 'partly free' 1-19, 20D3
Jailed leftists escape 1-23, 75C2
Earthquake hits 2-4, 81B1
De la Torre kidnaped 3-8, ransomed 3-16, 419B2
Villegas dies 3-10, 240G3
Sonora peasants disarmed 4-8; Chiapas clashes 5-11—5-12, 419C2

1977

MERSZEI, Zoltan
Top '76 salary rptd 5-23, 408D3
MESKILL, Judge Thomas J.
Vs protectn of journalists' thoughts 11-7, 920D3
Upholds jobless aid for strikers 11-9, 899B2
MESSCHAERT, Nicholaas
Asks pub aid terrorist manhunt 11-11, 888C1
MESSER, John
On Saskatchewan oil royalty cuts 3-22, 237G1
MESSERSMITH, Andy
Traded to Yankees 12-7, 990D1
MESSIANIC Jews—*See JEWS*
MESSING, Shep
Cosmos win NASL title 8-28, 676E2
MESSMER, Pierre
Loses Lorraine electn 1-6, 63A2
MESYATS, Valentin K.
On record '76 harvest, US imports 1-5, 21G3
METALS (& Metal Products)—*See also specific metals (e.g., TIN)*
Sovt bloc chrgd re Rhodesia sanctns 2-10, 123A1
UN rpts '76 prices up 2-14, 146B1
Sovt space tests rptd 2-26, 170G2
'76 stockholder equity rise rptd 340A3
Futures contract trading cited 7-5, 521F2
Medal of Sci awarded 11-22, 951G3
METCALF, Sen. Lee (D, Mont.)
Scores independent auditors 1-17, 78D3
Cong hearings re auditors 4-19—6-13, 519A3
METEORITES—*See ASTRONOMY*
METHADONE—*See NARCOTICS & Dangerous Drugs*
METHANOGENS
Identified as new life form 11-2, 907G3
METHODISTS
Police accused in S Africa unrest 1-25, 100A3
Bolivia rights panel formed 5-14, 414F2
Charismatic conf held 7-20—7-24, 620D3
METRIC Board, U.S.—*See under U.S. GOVERNMENT*
METRIC System
US road sign conversn proposed 4-27, 369D1
US drops road sign plan 6-24, 522G1-A2
Canada changes road signs 9-6, 705D2
US delays weather conversn 10-18, 820D3
METRO Containers—*See KRAFT Inc.*
METROMEX—*See WEATHER*
METROPOLITAN Life Insurance Co.
Sup Ct declines employer records case 5-16, 419E1
METROPOLITAN Meteorological Experiment (METROMEX)—*See WEATHER*
METZENBAUM, Sen. Howard Morton (D, Ohio)
'76 spec interest gifts rptd 2-15, 128C2
Backs Carter on rights 3-25, 226G2
Filibusters vs gas deregulatn 9-22—10-3, 757G2
In Panama, backs pacts 11-9—11-12, 911C2, D3
METZNER, Judge Charles M.
Sentenced Amrep offcls 3-10, 203C3
MEUSEL, Bob
Dies 11-28, 952B3
MEXICAN-American Legal Defense Educational Fund
Carter illegal alien plan scored 8-4, 592E1
MEXICAN-American Political Association
Gen Foods sued on cereal ads, 6-30, 613E2
MEXICAN Americans
Morales death modifies dual prosecutn rule 2-11; Hayes convctd 9-29, 821C1
Intra-group grand jury bias affirmed 3-23, 276C2
Coors boycott ends 4-8; antibias pact OKd, EEOC drops suit 5-9, 819D1
Hudspeth (Tex) prisoner death rptd 821D1
LA police dept sued re job bias 6-2, 819D2
Gen Foods sued on cereal ads 6-30, 613E2
LA schl integratn plan rejctd 7-6, 631B1
Carter illegal alien plan 8-4, 592D1
Tex police brutality alleged re Rodriquez 9-29, 821D1
4 ex-Houston police indicted re Torres 10-20, 820F3

MEXICO—*See also DISARMAMENT—Geneva Committee, IDB, OAS*
Lefebvre denied entry 7-12, 620G1
Drought rptd in farming regions 8-8, 660D1
Hurricane hits Calif 8-15—8-17, 747G2
Independence day observed 9-16, 745F3

1978

MERSZEI, Zoltan
Named Dow chrmn 5-3, 809F1
MERVYN'S Inc.
Dayton Hudson buy planned 1-23, 66F2
MERYL, Cynthia
Gay Divorce opens 3-9, 760C2
MESQUITA Neto, Julio de
Sees Carter in Rio 3-31, 233E2
MESSAGE From Space (film)
Released 11-17, 970B2
MESSEL, Oliver
Dies 7-13, 620B3
MESSERSCHMITT, Willy
Dies 9-15, 778E1
MESSERSMITH, Andy
Injures shoulder 3-16, 195C1
MESSINA, Straits of
Italy plans bridge 7-13, 689E3
MESSING, Shep
Signs with MISL Arrows 11-16, 969E2
MESSNER, Reinhold
Climbs Everest without oxygen 5-8, 420C2
MESYATS, Valentin K.
US agri secy visits 5-9, 499E2
METALS (& Metal Products)—*See also specific metals (e.g., STEEL)*
Hungary hikes prices 1-9, 55D2
'77 4th ¼ nonferrous profits rptd down 2-7, 282E3
Toys sharp-edge tests OKd 3-10, 265A1
1st ¼ '77, '78 profits rptd down 4-27, 403E2
Japan to hike nonferrous stockpile 5-3, 341G2
'77 return on sales, stockholder equity rptd 5-8, 325C3
Turkey, USSR sign trade pact 6-21—6-23, 595E2
EPA to ease water rules 8-10, 644A2
Turkey seeks forgn investmt 10-19, 10-26, 840F2
US 3d ¼ profits rptd up 10-30, 919A3
METCALF, Sen. Lee (D, Mont.)
Dies 1-12, 96A3
Carter State of Union Message 1-19, 31D3
Hatfield named to Sen seat 1-22, 52A3
METCALF, Terry
NFC wins Pro Bowl 1-23, 56F1
Signs with Argonauts 3-6, 171G3
METCALFE, Rep. Ralph H. (D, Ill.)
Dies 10-11, 853B2, 888C3
Stewart wins seat 11-7, 853B2
METHANE—*See GAS, Natural*
METHAQUALONE—*See NARCOTICS*
METHODISTS
Pensn fund fraud suit settled 5-21, 480F3
Transkei bars S Africa church 5-27, 617C3
United Methodist Calif immunity case declined by Sup Ct 10-16, 789E2
WCC rebel aid protested 11-4, 907B1
METHOXYCHLOR—*See PESTICIDES*
METHYL Salicylate (oil of wintergreen)—*See MEDICINE—Drugs*
METIS—*See CANADA—Indians & Inuit*
METOPROLOL (Lopressor)—*See MEDICINE—Drugs*
METRIC System
Canada sets '78 changes 1-16, 89B1
METROPOLITAN Museum of Art (N.Y.)
Macomber named pres, Dillon bd chrmn 4-18, 335C3
Payson pledge ordrd paid 7-11, 579C2
METZENBAUM, Sen. Howard Morton (D, Ohio)
Votes for Panama Canal neutrality pact 3-16, 177D2
Votes for 2d Canal pact 4-18, 273B1
Vs Calif fuel oil exports 6-16, 471B1
Gets Cong Watch top rating 10-28, 665A3
Gets consumer top rating 11-8, 981G2
Gets ADA top rating 12-17, 981E2
METZGER, Eugene J.
Financial Gen sues 2-17, 204B3
SEC accuses 3-18, settles 3-19, 204B2, D2
METZNER, Judge Charles
Sentences Provenzano 7-11, 560D2
MEXICANA de Aviacion (Mexican airline)
Ground workers strike 11-2, get wage hikes 11-4, 904D1
MEXICAN Americans—*See HISPANIC Americans*

MEXICO—*See also DISARMAMENT—Geneva Committee, IDB, OAS*
Latin church cncl mtg rptd 10-13, 823E3
Press curbs rptd by IAPA 10-13, 829B2

1979

MERRITT, Dr. H(iram) Houston
Dies 1-9, 104D3
MERRY Widow, The (recording)
Wins Grammy 2-16, 336G3
MESA Petroleum Co.
Ashland unit holdings sold 2-4, 560E3
MESRINE, Jacques
Slain 11-2, 890A3
MESSING, Shep
Named MISL playoff MVP 3-25, 432C1
Discloses suggested goal fix 8-16, NASL to probe 8-17, 776G1
MESZAROS, Marta
Just Like At Home released 4-19, 528F2
METALS (& Metal Products)—*See also specific metals (e.g., STEEL)*
US sues NJ cos re pollutn 2-7, 130A1
US-Sovt '78 trade rptd 3-6, 172G1
GATT pact signed, tariff cuts seen 4-12, 273G1
'78 Fortune 500 data rptd 5-7, 305E1
METALWORKERS Federation, International
Rebhan hails UK engineers' pact 10-4, 773C1
METCALF, Mark
Head Over Heels released 10-19, 1007E3
METEOR (film)
Released 10-19, 1008A1
METEOROLOGY
US-China pact set 5-13, 370F1
METHADONE—*See NARCOTICS*
METHAPYRILENE—*See CHEMICALS*
METHODISTS
Neto medical scholarship cited 9-10, 705C2
Gay pastor upheld 11-1, 931F3
NJ munic powers case declined by Sup Ct 11-13, 902F1
Legal immunity cases declined by Sup Ct 11-26, 919E2
METHVEN, John
On trucker wage hike impact 1-31, 75E3
Scores TUC-govt accord 2-14, 115A3
Backs lending rate hike 11-15, 889A3
METRIC System
Canada conversn program scored 6-6, 444A2
METRO-Goldwyn Mayer Inc.
Kerkorian trust case dismissed 8-14, 756D1
Begelman named movie div pres 12-18, 1007D1
METROPOLE (book)
Issued in US 1-18, 100B2
Authors rptd banned in USSR 4-6, 317A2
Sovt writers back ousted authors 12-17, 12-19, 980E2-A3
METROPOLITAN Columbus Schools Committee
Schl busing begins peacefully 9-6, 679G2
METROPOLITAN Correctional Center (N.Y., N.Y.)
Restrictns backed by Sup Ct 5-14, 383F1
METROPOLITAN Edison Co.—*See under GENERAL Public Utilities Corp.*
METROPOLITAN Museum of Art (N.Y., N.Y.)
Rockefeller dies 1-26, 104F1
Greek sculpture stolen 2-9, recovered 2-14, 119D1
Rockefeller art bequeathed 2-9, 173F2
Japan gifts presented 5-4, 375A2
Ternbach to restore Poncet sculpture 5-6, 375D1
Tut exhibit benefits rptd 7-30, 672B2
METZENBAUM, Sen. Howard Morton (D, Ohio)
Sen income limit stayed 3-8, 185F2
Backs hosp cost-control bill 3-9, 194B3
Ct upholds clean-air amendmt 5-7, 351D1
On easing of Ohio air rule 6-6, 423C1
Vs arms hike link to SALT 8-3, 591D1
Scores Valium promotn 9-10, 734D3
Addresses oil industry protesters, backs reform 10-17, 831E2
METZGER, Tom
Calif KKK, protestors clash 8-19, 866B2
MEXICANA Airlines
Ground workers strike 11-1, 874E3; setlmt agreed 11-27, 909F2
MEXICAN Americans—*See HISPANIC Americans*

MEXICO—*See also DISARMAMENT-Geneva Committee, IDB, OAS*
'78 quake cited 1-25, 140G2
Mex City rocked by quake 3-14, 316G3
Quake hits Mex City 6-23, 619F3
Mex City archbp installed cardinal 6-30, 640B2
Quake hits Mexicali 10-15, 799A2
Mex City air crash kills 74 10-31, 912B2; rpt blames crew 12-14, 996B3

1980

MERSZEI, Zoltan
Replaced as Occidental pres 8-4, 702A1
MERTLE, Deanna—*See MILLS, Jeanie*
MERTLE, Elmer—*See MILLS, Al*
MESSERER, Mikhail
Defects to US 2-6, 88D1
MESSERER, Sulamith
Defects to US 2-6, 88D1
MESSERSCHMITT-Bokow-Blohm G.m.b.H.
W Europn fighter planned 4-14, 303F1
MESSNER, Tony
Australia veterans min 11-2, 857F2
METAL Bank of America Inc.—*See under UNION Corp.*
METALLGESELLSCHAFT, A.G.
Kuwait 10% interest rptd 6-25, 562E1
METALS (& Metal Products)
Australia '79 stock gains cited 1-18, 56D1
USSR strategic metals buying noted 2-5, 85D1
Canada '79 4th 1/4 corp profits rptd up 2-7, 116B2; 2-22, 211E2
French-Cuba accord rptd 4-1, 253G2
'79 Fortune 500 data rptd 5-5, 290B3
Kuwait investmts in W Ger rptd 7-15, 542E3
Bendix sells back Asarco shares 10-29, 985F2
METAL Workers, International Federation of
Polish worker aid rptd 8-31, 659B3
METCALF, William
On Haitian refugees 4-13, 294D2
METEORITES—*See ASTRONOMY*
METHODISTS
Liberia missnaries plan exit 4-30, 353G2
African Methodist Episcopal Church
Protestant unity mtg ends, common ministry OKd 1-24, 156F2
African Methodist Episcopal Zion Church
Protestant unity mtg ends, common ministry OKd 1-24, 156G2
Christian Methodist Episcopal Church
Protestant unity mtg ends, common ministry OKd 1-24, 156G2
United Methodist Church
Protestant unity mtg ends, common ministry OKd 1-24, 156G2
Khomeini sent message of sympathy 4-21; delegatn sees Carter, Iran UN rep 4-23, 324C3
Natl conv: homosexual stand reaffirmed, TV venture set 4-21, 413B3
Pacific Homes fraud suit setld 12-10, 963C3
METHVEN, John
Scores labor law 2-3, 98B1
METRIC System
Canada conversn rptd 50% complete 3-31, 335C1
METRINKO, Michael J.
Red Cross aides visit 4-14, 282F2
METRO-Goldwyn Mayer Film Co. (MGM Filmco)
Creation approved 5-30, 501F2
METRO-Goldwyn Mayer Inc.
Loews film productn OKd by Dist Ct 2-27, 229F1
Film, hotel unit split voted 5-30, 501F2
Kerkorian sues Columbia 9-30, Columbia countersues 10-2, 10-20, 906E2
Las Vegas hotel-casino fire kills 84 11-21, probe rptd 11-25, 893C2
Penn Central, GK Technologies drop merger 11-25, 985G1
METROPOLITAN Life Insurance Co.
Pan Am NYC bldg bought for record price 7-28, 985B3
Stevens, union come to terms 10-19, 805F1-D2
METROPOLITAN Museum of Art (N.Y., N.Y.)
Titian forgeries chrgd 2-26, 472C3
METROPOLITAN Opera Association (N.Y., N.Y.)
Robinson dies 5-14, 448E2
Violinist found slain 7-24, 654A1; stagehand indicted 9-17, 713B1
Season canceled over musicians' strike 9-29; strike setld 10-25, 883E3
METROPOLITAN School District v. Buckley
Case declined by Sup Ct 10-6, 782A3
METSCHUCK, Caren
Wins Olympic medals 7-21, 7-24, 623C3
METZ, Frank
Anatomy Illustrated wins Amer Book Award 5-1, 692C2
METZENBAUM, Sen. Howard Morton (D, Ohio)
Scores Percy Palestine stance 12-9, 936F1
METZGER, Tom
Wins Calif US House primary 6-3, 439B2
Loses US House electn 11-4, 852B2
METZKER, Max
Wins Olympic medal 7-22, 623A3
MEXICAN American Legal Defense and Educational Fund
Austin busing plan set 1-3, 5C3
MEXICAN Americans—*See HISPANIC Americans*
MEXICO—*See also GENEVA Committee, IDB, OAS*
Hurricane Allen hits Yucatan 8-7, 621G1, E2
Quake hits 10-24, death toll rptd 10-26, 874F3--875B1

1976

Student unrest 4-20—5-4, 419E2
Leftists slay cops 5-6, 6-4, 5 rptd arrested 5-6, 419F1, A2
Communist League existnc questnd 6-6, 8-22, 677F1
Lopez Portillo vows govt chngs 6-27, elected pres 7-4, 498C1
Campaign vs Excelsior chrgd 7-7—7-29; dir, aides ousted, 200 quit 7-8, 620C1
Lopez electn confirmed 7-14; rpt PRI dominates vote 7-16, 677B2
Floods rptd 7-21, 544C3
Alleged League ldr killed in attack on Lopez' sister 8-11; arrests rptd 8-12, 8-20, 677D1, E1 ★
Hurricane Liza cracks dam 10-1, 840D2
Train collisn 10-10, 816G1
Mexico City bombings 11-29, 907A1
Lopez Portillo inaugural 12-1; Cabt sworn 12-2, 906C2

Economy & Labor (domestic)

'74 defns budget rptd 1-2, 60G2
Petrochem plant rptd planned 1-2, 75B1
Proven oil reserves rptd 1-16, 75B1
'75 inflatn rate down 1-18, 74F3
High underemploymt rate rptd 1-21, 74G3
'76 oil output, profits forecast 1-23, 75A1
Phosphoric acid co purchased 1-23, 75C1
Tire cos admit payoffs 5-19, 419B3
Lopez Portillo vows chngs 6-27, 498A2
Rpt Baja Calif oil found 8-20; Pemex to hike Reforma productn 8-31, 694E3
Peso floated 8-31, stabilized 9-12; anti-inflatn moves set, prices rise, pay hikes demanded 9-1—9-14, 694A2
Peasant land deeds signed 11-30, 906D3
Lopez Portillo asks austerity, vows reforms 12-1; peso rises 12-2, 906C2

Foreign Economic Developments

$300 mln forgn bank loan set 1-2, 75D1
Brazil iron projct rptd planned 1-9, 75C1
4th ¼ '75 oil exports rptd 1-23, 75A1
In Canada trade talks 1-24—1-26, 116E2
In US econ cooperatn talks 1-26, 75E1
Pledges Guatemala quake aid 2-4, 81F1
At intl econ conf 2-11—2-20, 148B1
Lockheed AF bribe rptd 2-23, 147F1
US ad firm admits paymts 3-3, 419D3
'75 paymts deficit, US sales rptd 3-19, 5-10, 466B1
Gen Tire paymts chrgd 5-10, 360B1; admitted 5-19, 419D3
US '75 shrimp import data rptd 5-11, 431G1
200-mi offshore limit enacted 6-6, 420A2
Kissinger vows improved ties 6-10—6-13, 465E2
US Dem platform text cites 6-15, 478F2
IDB OKs 3 loans 6-18, 694F3
Lopez Portillo vows chngs 6-27, 498A2
Overall, US Jan-June trade deficit rptd 8-23, 9-8, 694D3
Peso float ends US $ parity 8-31, stabilized 9-12, 694A2
Import, export controls set 9-1, 9-8, scored 9-13, 694E2, B3
Echeverria at MexFair '76 in US 9-7, 694C3
US triples sugar duties 9-21, 721D3
'75-76 US bank loans cited 11-10, 915F1
'76 US Eximbank loan default rptd 11-11, 915A3
US study rpts forgn paymts 12-20, 985G2
'76 intl borrowing rptd 12-22, 976G1
Amer Hosp paymts cited 12-29, 986C2

Foreign Relations (misc.)—*See also 'UN Policy' below*

Alejo '75 Spain overtures rptd, Rabasa resignatn linked 1-8, 75F2
Terms for Spain ties proposed 1-10, 75E2
Canada prime min visits 1-24—1-26, 116E2
Angola MPLA recognized 2-21, 163D1
Press scores US-Brazil pact 2-23, 177D1
Takes Uruguay pol refugees 3-3—3-12, 207G3
Amnesty Intl unit chrgs Uruguay torture 3-5, 207D3
Tito on tour, nonaligned natn membership rejectd 3-9—3-22, 256C2
Emb takes more Uruguay refugees, 52 get safe conduct 3-16—4-9, 382A3
Excelsior scores Orfila re Pinochet 3-18; Orfila replies 3-19, 310G1
Argentina emb refugees leave 4-3, 264G1
Pinochet protest demonstratn staged 4-22, 382E3
114 refugees in Uruguay emb 5-18, 441D2
Campora rptd in Argentina emb 5-20, 399E3
Protests Chile repressn 5-20, 464C2
Belgian amb's daughter kidnaped 5-25, ransomed 5-29, 419G1, A2
Torres body arrives from Argentina 6-7, 415A3
Torres buried 6-9, 456E1, F2
106 Uruguay refugees arrive 6-24—7-2, 542B3
At nonaligned conf 8-16—8-20, 622C1
Uruguayan takes emb asylum 8-21, 678A2
Cuban terrorism rptd 8-22, 791C1
Nicaragua OKs safe conduct for 4 9-10, 926G1
Rpt US execs visit Cuba 9-27, 791C2
Cuba to honor hijack pact 10-15, 780D1
Castro chrgs CIA re July kidnap-death 10-15, 780B2
Evidnc vs Cuba exile rptd 10-31, 844C1
102 dels at Lopez inaugural 12-1, 906A3

1977

Economy & Labor (domestic)

Cts to rule on land seizures 1-3, 65F2
Oil output hike set; new finds cited, reserves revised 1-14, 66D1
'76 factory wage study rptd 1-28, 158C3
Oil exploitatn hike rptd 2-18, reserves estimated 3-18, 240C3
Sicartsa steel expansn delayed 4-1, merger set 5-12, 528B1
'76 land seizures backed, compensatn offered 5-4, 528F1
Inflation abates 5-6, 527C3
$1.2 bln IMF loan rptd 5-6, 527D3
Jobless data rptd; pvt, govt sectors set jobs progrm 5-6, 5-13, 527E3
'61-75 GDP variatns table 5-30, 439B1
1st ¼ indl productn down 6-7, 528A1
Strike closes UNAM 6-20, PRI blames CP 7-1, 528A2
Oil reserves estimate hiked 6-22, 528D1
Police raid UNAM 7-7, 6 indicted 7-9, strike settled 7-10, 562C3
Steel workers end strike 7-12, 562F3
'76 job proposal detailed 9-23, 746A2
Top econ mins replaced in austerity dispute 11-17; Portillo backs IMF demands 12-2, 966B3
'77 growth rate behind populatn rise, undernourishmt rptd in south 11-17, 967C1
Jobless, underemploymt at 53%; wage ceiling protested 11-18, 967B1
Inflatn down, budget deficit at 6.5% 12-1, 967A1
Oil productn, refining progrm rptd 12-1, 967E1
Solar energy obstacles cited 12-11, 975D3
'78 budget eases austerity progrm 12-15, 985G1

Foreign Relations (misc.)—*See also 'Monetary, Trade & Aid' and 'UN Policy' below*

Amnesty Intl on pol prisoners 1-1, 3F1
Honduras shifts mil attache 1-3, 45A2
Peru exile taken 1-8, 46C3
Cuba-Rhodesia spy plan rptd 1-10, 17A3
Uruguay pol refugees arrive 1-16, 352B1
Argentine safe-conduct for Campora, others asked 1-18, 66B2
US-Cuba mediatn role offered 2-15, 110D1, 136F3
Nicaraguans seek pol asylum 3-2, 168G2
Spain ties renewed 3-28, 242A3
Sweden arrests 2 terrorists 4-1, 429B1
Spain amb apptmt stirs controversy 4-7—5-11, 529F1
Belgian's kidnapers seized 4-13—4-14, 528G3
El Salvador rebels seek refuge 4-19, 373C2
Echeverria named roving amb 5-16, 529A3
Panama seeks Guatemala mediatn 5-27, 415A1
Nicaragua pol refugees arrive 6-8, 476D1
Chile exiles protest disappearances 6-14—6-23, 493G1
Uruguay arrests 2 Excelsior rptrs, frees 1 7-4—7-21, 601C1
Guatemala rebels rptd armed by smugglers 7-4, 673F1
Lopez sees Torrijos, regional ldrs; backs new Panama Canal pact 8-5—8-6, 606C3
Canal pact oppositn rptd despite denials 9-3, 678D1; 9-9, 716F3
Uruguay still holds Excelsior rptr 9-6, 905C2
Spain Belize stand explanatn sought 9-17, 805D1
Nicaragua emb harbors guerrillas 10-12—10-26, 865B1
Bolivia exiles score electn plan 11-11, 901F3

1978

Economy & Labor (domestic)

Min wage up 10-15% 1-1, 331A1
Mexico City expenses rated 1-14, 28B3
Food, svc price controls lifted; prices soar 2-17, 331A1
Unemploymt, underemploymt 53% 2-26, 331A1
'77 econ growth 2.8%, populatn growth 3.6% 2-26, 331B1
'77, 1st ¼ inflatn rptd 4-10, 330G3
Matamoros strikes 6-27, 517E2
Strikes by independt unions rptd smashed 7-31, 690A2
Land distributn agrmts rptd signed 9-1, 817D3
Air traffic controllers strike 9-17—9-18, 10-5, 818G1-B2
Jan-June prices up 17.7% 10-6, 818C2
Oaxaca peasants seize land 10-8; Lopez vows reform, peasants withdraw 10-20, 817A3
Air traffic controllers end strike 10-28; Mexicana ground workers strike 11-2, get wage hike 11-4, 904C1
New oil reserves claimed by govt, productn data rptd 11-13, 903E2

Foreign Relations (misc.)—*See also 'Monetary, Trade, Aid & Investment' and 'UN' below*

Uruguay frees Excelsior newsman 1-5, 136F3
Argentine guerrillas chrg murder threat 1-18, 208F1
Nicaragua troops beat rptr 2-1, 91B2
French overseas voting scandal rptd 2-25, 167D1
Nicaragua guerrilla rptd in Managua emb 3-27, 376A2
Graiver '76 death questnd 4-12, 326D1
Vesco leaves CR, visit planned 4-30, 354E2
Club Medit '77 robbery cited 6-11, 473F3
Lopez Portillo at Panama Canal pact instrumts exchng, shuns fetes 6-16, 463F2, 464A1
Amer rights conv enacted 7-18, 829A1
Nicaragua guerrillas seek asylum 8-22, 659A1
Nicaragua oppositn considers as mediator 9-14, 705C3
Air traffic controllers strike 9-17—9-18, 10-5, 818A2
Nicaragua emb harbors 52 refugees 10-13, 7 oppositn ldrs 10-25, 839F1, F2
Lopez Portillo in China 10-24—10-30, Japan 10-30—11-4, PI 11-4—11-5, 903B3
Spain king visits 11-17—11-22, 967G2, B3
Intl rights group founded by Colombia novelist 12-21, 1015B3

Government & Politics—*See also other appropriate subheads in this section*

Police corruptn detailed 4-2, 289D3
Govt aid free on bail 4-21, 518B1
Coffee offcl indicted 4-29, 517E3
CP, 2 other parties registered 5-3; pol reform progrm cited 5-7, 517B3
Portes Gil dies 12-10, 1032D3

1979

Economy & Labor

Proven oil reserves doubled in '78 1-2, 22A3
Telephone strike ends 5-2, 372F2
10-yr dvpt plan rptd 5-4, 353C3
'78, 1st ¼ growth, inflatn rptd 6-1, 487B2
Inflatn, populatn growth forecast 9-1, 689E1
Puebla businessmen strike 10-30, 874F3
Airline ground workers strike 11-1, 874E3; setlmt agreed 11-27, 909F2
Tijuana newspaper stormed 11-1, 875A1
'79 staple crop productn down 18% 12-12, 950C2

Foreign Relations (misc.)—*See also 'Monetary', 'Oil' and 'UN' below*

DR names Reyes mil attache 1-12, 62D2
El Salvador leftists seize emb 1-16, gain Mex asylum 1-18, 59F1
Chilean '75 assassinatn plot cited 1-18, 58E1
Pope visits 1-26–1-31, opens CELAM mtg 1-27, 67A3, C3
Troops aid fight vs Guatemala guerrillas 1-26, 97C2
CELAM mtg ends 2-13, 108E2
French pres visits 4-1–4-4, 372F1
Castro visits 5-17–5-18, 372D2
CR pres visits 5-20, 409B1
Nicaragua ties cut 5-20; Latin missn dispatched, support asked 5-21, 409A1
El Salvador rebels offered asylum 5-31, 424E3
Shah admitted, Iran threat scored 6-10; US aid cited 6-11, 445E3
Nicaragua interventn opposed 6-21, 461A1
Iran shah attack denied 6-27, 486G2
Shah visited by Nixon 7-13, 544C2
Swiss Emb occupied 8-3, retaken 8-10, 671E1
Canal treaty implementatn marked 10-1, 754A1, C1
Shah leaves for US 10-22, 843C1; reentry barred 11-29, 897C1
Brandt, Soares visits scored 10-30, 874G3
Iran Emb closed 11-12, 862C3
Argentina grants Campora safe passage from emb 11-20, 906A2

Government & Politics—*See also other appropriate subheads in this section*

Reyes, 2 other Cabt mins ousted 5-16, 408B3
PRI wins cong electns 7-1, 545A1
Lopez state of union address 9-1, 689D1
Puebla conservatives score govt 10-30, 874F3

1980

Economy & Labor

Value-added tax set 1-6, 21B1
Coca-Cola workers strike 4-24, 463E3
Chiapas land dispute violence erupts 5-31, 465G2
Ford plant jobs seen 6-12, 465D2
Drought threatens cattle, crops in North 6-13; US blamed 6-19, 7-1, 524B2
'80 econ, labor data rptd; salary hike offered 9-1, 729A3-730F1
Inflatn at 30%, oil curbs set 11-19, 902C2, E2

Foreign Relations (misc.)—*See also 'Monetary', 'Oil & Gas', 'UN Policy' below*

Belgian, Danish Embs occupied 2-18, 152A1
Colombia, DR Emb captors talk 3-2—3-13, 180D2; 3-24, 3-26, 231F2
Junta member flees El Salvador 3-4, 172F1
Mex cardinal at El Salvador archbishop's funeral 3-30, 253D2
USSR science conf attended 4-13—4-15, 326F2
Colombia DR Emb siege ends, amb freed 4-27, 335G1
Japan premr visits 5-2—5-4, 409C2
Lopez visits France, W Ger, Sweden, Canada 5-16—5-28, 409G1, C2
El Salvador leftist visits, seeks support 5-26, 444A3
Lopez visits Brazil, Cuba, CR 7-27—8-3, 605F2-D3
El Salvador amb recalled 8-14, leftist ties hinted 8-18, 633B3
Bolivia coup condemned by Santa Marta conf 12-17, 992A3

Government & Politics—*See also other appropriate subheads in this section*

Freedom House lists as partly free 87E3
Lopez delivers State of Natn address 9-1, 729G2-730F1

1976

Narcotics & Drugs
Joint US drug drive rptd launched 1-2, '75 Levi talks rptd 1-19, 61D1
Joint US drug comm rptd agreed 1-20, 61A1
Drug ring with US connectns broken, 3 Colombians seized 3-5, 420D1
14 US prisoners flee 3-12; probe ordrd 3-18, extraditn asked 5-15, 420E1
Gertz, US offcls trade drug drive chrgs 3-15—3-18; friction denied 6-9, 419G3
US guns rptd traded for drugs 4-14, 420D1
Opium poppy fields rptd destroyed 6-8, 419E3

Sports
Olympic results 7-18—7-31, 573E3, 574B1, 575E3

UN Policy & Developments
Forgn min resignatn link disputed 1-8, 75G2
In US pol cooperatn talks 1-26, 75E1
Echeverria chances for secy gen rptd 10-5, sets bid 11-29, 906D3; loses 12-7, 914D2
Assemb condemns apartheid 11-9, 842G2

1977

Monetary, Trade & Aid Issues (including all foreign economic developments)
'76 fruit, veg exports rptd 1-3, 65D3
Oil export hike set, prices rptd 1-14; OPEC entry pressure seen 1-25, 66D1, G1
Rpt Israel prime arms seller 1-15, 28E3
US sues Uniroyal 1-27, 93E3
No '75 gas imports to US rptd 1-28, 76C3
'76-80 share of world oil supply estimated 1-28, 108B2
US OKs gas imports 2-4, 91B3
Amer Airlines rpts paymts 2-9, 112B1
Oil export hike planned 2-18, 240F3
US sets 200-mi fishing limit 3-1, 147G1
'76 forgn exchng mkt tensions rptd 3-2, 188D3
'75-76 trade, paymts data; table 3-11, 189C1, A2 ★
Petrobond issue set, peso rptd down 3-14, 240G3
'66-75 arms transfers table 4-8, 415B2
US CIA oil forecast 4-18, 294G1
Petrobonds oversubscribed 4-18, on sale 4-29, 528C1
Peso stabilized 5-6, 527D3
Amer Airlines slush fund, Butler payoff recipient rptd 5-17, 503A1
IMF, US '76 bank loans rptd 6-5, 438E1, F1
US 1st ¼ trade deficit down 6-13, 528D1
Tourism earnings up 6-17, 528E1
IWC cuts whaling quotas 6-24, 496G3
Lopez, Latin ldrs set Intl Coffee Fund 8-6, 608A3
US trade concessns sought 8-7—8-8, 646D2
US indl dvpt aid plan rptd 9-23, 746E2
Zenith plans TV operatns 9-27, 974E2
Brazil coffee policy backed 10-21, 11-9, 876C3
Top econ mins replaced in IMF austerity dispute 11-17, Portillo backs demands 12-2, 966B3
Intl banks, IDB grant credits 11-18, 11-22; IMF loan ceiling hike seen 12-1, 967C1
Trade gap down, peso stabilized 12-1, 967A1
Oil investmt, export progrm rptd 12-1, 967E1
US commodity pact OKd 12-2, 976G1
IMF austerity dispute compromise 12-15, 985G1
US Eximbank OKs Pemex loans 12-15, 985C2

Obituaries
Pellicer, Carlos 2-16, 164E3

UN Policy & Developments
UN Assemb member 4D1
Echeverria named UNESCO envoy 7-8, 563A1

Unrest (domestic)—*See also 'Economy & Labor' above*
500 pol prisoners rptd 1-1, 3G1
Rebels kill 8 in Mex City 1-16, 1-20; police set drive 1-21, bodyguards rptd up 1-26, 65E3
Oaxaca clashes 2-22—3-2; army occupies, gov quits 3-3, 240F1
Pol prisoner amnesty vowed 3-14, 424 freed 4-11, 528A3

1978

Monetary, Trade, Aid & Investment
Jamaica shipping co pact rptd 1-13, 100F2
Volkswagen 'beetle' productn to continue 1-19, 74F3
'77 oil output rptd up 2-14, 158D3
'77 oil sales up, trade deficit $1.27 bln 2-15, 331B1
Jamaica plans alumina deal 2-28, 194E2
US farmers block food imports 3-1, 3-3, 163F1
Nicaragua rebel aid rptd 3-2, 192G2
Coffee exports to be withheld 3-10, 181B3
Oil competes with Venez in US mkt 4-16, 331G3
Belize '76 oil find rptd 4-21, 354B2
Coffee offcl chrgd for smuggling 4-29, 517E3
US A-fuel export license deferral rptd 5-20, 408B2
Agri loan rptd OKd by forgn banks 8-15, 690G1
Oil wealth sparks US hopes 8-24; oil, gas reserves estimates rise 9-1, 690B1
Jan-June trade gap doubles 8-25, 818C2
Forgn reserves up; peso called 'stable' 9-1, 690F1
World Bank loan rise rptd 9-15, 828B3
Lopez Portillo signs trade, loan pacts in China, Japan 10-24—11-4; discusses oil in Japan 11-2, Pl 11-4—11-5; Japan gets oil shipmt 11-5, 903B3
Lopez Portillo vs OPEC entry 11-2, 903G3
'80 oil export hike seen 11-13, 903B3
Spain king visits, trade discussed 11-17—11-22, 967A3, C3
US rejcts Algerian gas imports 12-18, 983F3
Pemex '79 price hike set 12-20, 978E2
US birth control, job aid proposed 12-20, 1010E2

Obituaries
Chavez, Carlos 8-2, 708C2
Portes Gil, Emilio 12-10, 1032D3

Sports
World Cup soccer finals, sidelights 6-1—6-25, 519F3
Mexico Cup tourn results 12-10, 990E2

UN Policy & Developments
Leb UN force troops vowed 4-1, reneges 4-5, 236E1
US urged to rejoin ILO 6-7, 523F3
Assemb member 713C3

Unrest—*For labor unrest, see 'Economy & Labor' in this section above*
Sinaloa rptr shot 2-13, dies 2-15; newsmen score murder, gov OKs probe 2-14—2-16, 289F3
Culiacan drug activities detailed 3-17, 290C1
Govt aide seized for corruptn 3-21, disavows confessn 3-22; reactn 3-27, 289G2

1979

Monetary, Trade, Aid & Investment—*See also 'Oil' below*
Carter in trade talks, cooperatn pacts signed 2-14–2-16, 124F1
French trade agrmts signed 4-1–4-4, 372F1
10-yr dvpt plan rptd 5-4, 353D3
Cuba trade talks 5-17–5-18, 372F2
1st 1/4 trade, paymts, reserves rptd 6-1, 487F2
Japan steel projct proposed, bank loan rptd 6-8, 487E3
US vegetable growers withdraw dumping chrgs, '78 tomato exports cited 7-19, 553G1, B2
Nicaragua aid team arrives 7-21, 574B2
Mex intl bank debt estimated 7-28, 584B2
US bank loan rptd 7-28, 584E1
US clears vegetable growers re dumping chrgs 10-30, 831F1
'79 grain imports, farm trade surplus rptd; '80 forecast 12-12, 950E2

Obituaries
Diaz Ordaz, Gustavo 7-15, 588F2

Oil & Gas Developments
Proven oil reserves doubled in '78, US imports cited 1-2, 22B3
Carter on prospects 1-17, 30B1
Carter in talks 2-14–2-16, 124F1, B3
Price maintenance planned 2-27, 145A3
French supply assured 4-1–4-4, 372F1-D2
US gas talks rptd 4-5, 250E3
10-yr dvpt plan rptd 5-4, 353D3
Cuba trade talks 5-17–5-18, 372E2
1st ¼ oil productn rptd 6-1, 487C2
Yucatan well blows out 6-3–6-16, 462A2, A3
Japan pipeline projct proposed 6-8, 487E3
US blowout talks agreed 6-28–6-29, 753A2
Natural gas finds rptd 7-4, 522E2
US seeks to buy gas 7-8, 517E3
Canada vs common energy mkt 7-26, 581A2
Pemex $1.5 bln US bank loan rptd 7-28, 584E1
Pemex oil spill hits Tex beaches 8-9, 608G1
Pemex scored, Sedco role noted 8-21, 635E3-636B1
US asks blowout damages, cleanup costs rptd 8-23; Lopez bars liability 8-24, 688E3, 689B1
US gas talks break down 8-31, 688G3
Proven oil reserves up 12.5% 9-1, 689D1
Pemex oil spill suits filed in Tex 9-13–9-18; dir questnd, audit OKd 9-20, 718G2
US gas sales agreed 9-21, 718D2
Intl energy plan proposed 9-27, 753C1
Oil price hiked 10-9, 781B1
Pemex cones blown-out well 10-14, total spill estimated 10-16, 782B1
Permargo oil spill cleanup suit filed by Tex 10-18, 809G2
US consortium buys natural gas 10-18, 814E3
Nov output up 6.9%; US export hike barred; Spain, Israel sales cited 11-23, 909G2
US natural gas imports finalized 12-29, 996G2

Sports
World U Games hosted 9-8–9-13, 799F1

UN Policy & Developments
Membership listed 695G2
Lopez addresses Assemb, proposes energy plan 9-27, 753D1

Unrest
Alleged rights abuses protested 2-15, 124A3
27 occupy Swiss Emb 8-3, police retake bldg 8-10, 671E1
Tijuana newspaper stormed 11-1, 875A1

1980

Monetary, Trade, Aid & Investment
US shrimp fishermen barred 1-1, 21D1
Silver mine trading banned 1-24; 40% tax on silver, gold sales levied 1-25, 68E3
US finds tomatoes toxic 2-20; 3 packing plants closed, border checks stiffened 3-12, 233A3
GATT entry barred, US trade cited 3-18, 234A1
US dismisses vegetable 'dumping' suit 3-24, 233F2
Coca-Cola plant struck 4-24, 463E3
French econ cooperatn agrmt signed 5-18, 409D2
W Ger plastics deal set, tech transfer pacts renewed 5-21, 409F2
Swedish joint projects studied 5-24, 409A3
Canada credit set, joint projcts studied 5-27, 409C3
Japan credit deal signed 5-28, 409C2*
1st 1/4 US trade data, total deficit rptd 6-6, 465F2
Ford plans engine plant 6-12, 465B2
US investmt growth forecast, mfg cited 6-13, 465D2
1st 1/2, May grain imports rptd 6-13, 524C2
US tuna boats seized 7-8, 7-10; US retaliates, bans tuna imports 7-14, 565B1
World Bank OKs $325 mln agri loan 7-10, 605D2
Brazil trade talks 7-27—7-31, 605F2-A3
Cuban trade embargo aid vowed 8-1, 605B3
'80 paymts deficit, forgn debt rptd 9-1, 729G3
US OKs Israeli jet sale 10-31, 865A2
9-month trade deficit rptd 11-19, 902E2
Panama Canal clogged by trade shipmts 11-24, 895E3
US fishing accords ended, waters dispute blamed 12-29, 995A3

Obituaries
Garcia, Sara 11-21, 1004F1

Oil & Gas Developments
Oil prices hiked, US exports cited 1-2, 4F1
Oil profits, value-added tax linked 1-6, 21C1
Pemex spill continues, total loss rptd 1-10, 60D2
US gas sales start 1-15, 60E1
'80 productn, exports, long-term supply rptd 1-15, 60F1-B2
New oil field discovered 1-15, 60B2
GATT entry barred 3-18, 234C1
US gas price hiked, future increases set 3-18, 234E1
'80 productn target lifted, '79 export earnings rptd 3-18, 234G1
Pemex well capped, total spill rptd 3-24, 233C3
Ashland unveils new refining process 3-31, 251A2
US energy talks, cooperatn agreed 4-2—4-3, 315G1
Japan trade growth seen 4-20, 299D1
Japan oil talks 5-2—5-4, 341G1; 3-yr pact signed 5-28, 409C2*
Lopez in France, W Ger, Sweden, Canada; trade agrmts signed 5-16—5-28, 409G1, C2
'80 oil exports, US share rptd 5-28, 409B2
Brazil trade talks 7-27—7-31, 605A3
Latin supply guarantee set with Venez 8-3, 605C3
'80 reserves, productn data rptd 9-1, 729B3
Export limits set, US levels cited 11-19; domestic price hikes studied 11-20, 902C2

Sports
Moscow Olympic results 7-20—8-3, 588B3, 622G2, A3, 623E3

UN Policy & Developments
Cncl seat won 1-7, 12G1
Iran sanctns vote abstentn 1-13, 29A1

Unrest
Belgian, Danish embs occupied; govt rejcts demands 2-18; leftists ease terms 2-21, 152A1
Chiapas land dispute violence 5-31, death toll disputed 6-1, 465G2

1976

U.S. Relations—*See also 'Foreign Economic Developments' and 'Narcotics' above*
US prisoner abuse hearing 1-15, 75G1
In US pol cooperatn talks 1-26, 75E1
Press scores US-Brazil pact 2-23, 177D1
Kissinger visits, vows prisoner review 6-10—6-13, 465E2
Aliens warrantless interrogatn upheld 7-6, 535A1
US GOP platform text 8-18, 609E3
US-based Cuban terrorism rptd 8-22, 791C1
Ryan transfer to border post rptd 9-20, 814E2
Rpt US execs visit Cuba via 9-27, 791C2
US rptd vs Echeverria UN bid 10-5, 906E3
Johnson & Johnson bombed 11-29, 907B1
Mrs Carter, Kissinger at Lopez inaugural 11-30—12-2, 906G2

MEXICO, Gulf of—*See GULF of Mexico*
MEYER Jr., Harry M.
Flu vaccine test begins 4-21, 316G1
MEYER, Nicholas
'Horror' on best-seller list 12-5, 972A3
MEYERHOFF, Robert
'72 campaign gift listed 4-25, 688D1
MEYER Tomatoes
Chavez contract signed 1-31, 153C2
MEYNER, Rep. Helen S. (D, N.J.)
Reelected 11-2, 830E1
MEZUE, Jacques Ovono
Replaced as labor min 10-19, 1003B2
MEZVINSKY, Rep. Edward (D, Ia.)
Loses reelectn 11-2, 823C2
MGUYA, William
Hijackers seek release 9-4, 662G2

1977

Guerrero attys list 257 'disappeared' 3-30, 528D3
Univ crisis rptd 4-13; Oaxaca univ reoccupied 4-24, rightist terror rptd 6-18, 528D2
Guerrillas seized 4-13—4-14, 6-12, 528F3
'68 Tlateloco massacre records rptd missing 5-20, 529F2
Rights group raided 7-7, govt anti-church campaign chrgd 8-4, 746D1
Anti-Communist commandos seized 8-10, 746C1
Police battle Sept 23 guerrillas 8-11, 8-20, 746B1
FRAP guerrillas die in shootout 8-17, bus hijacking 8-21, 745G3
Leftist bombs hit 3 cities 9-14, police alerted 9-15, 745D3
Oaxaca students killed, rector fired 12-7; troops occupy univ 12-14, 985D2

U.S. Relations—*See also 'Monetary, Trade & Aid' above*
Lee arrested 1-6, FBI cites in spy chrg 1-16, 41E2-A3
Mex backs Panamanian canal demands 1-18, 46F1
Rebels kill US exec 1-20, 65G3
Illegal US firearms rptd in use 1-26, 66C1
Lopez Portillo in US 2-14—2-17, 110D1, 136B3; addresses Cong 2-17, 127D3
US Cong speeches opposed 2-17, 127D3
CIA paymts to Echeverria rptd 2-19, 124F1
US rpts rights abuses 3-12; Mex forestalls debate, frees pol prisoners 3-14—4-12, 528C3
Carter on water projct 3-16, 210C1
US drug smuggling rptd 4-3, 4-8, 332D3-G3
US exec's killers seized 4-13—4-14, 528G3
US drug offenders freed, police abuses rptd down 4-16—6-21, 529B1
Drug ring broken 4-20, 711C3
Carter gets illegal alien plan 4-27, 370F1
US laetrile smuggling rptd 5-6, 375C3
US laetrile smugglers sentncd 5-16, 508E2
Lucey named amb 5-25, 499G3
Cuba frees 10 US prisoners 6-12, 456C1
US ratifies prisoner exchng 7-21, transfers estimated 9-22, 746F2
Carter illegal alien plan 8-4, 592D1
Lopez lauds Panama Canal talks 8-6, 606C3
Young visits, illegal alien plan discussed 8-7—8-8, 646A2, C2
US OKs ulcer drug treatmt 8-23, 748E2
US alien plan scored 8-28, 746A2
Canal pact oppositn rptd despite denials 9-3, 678D1; 9-9, 716F3
Leftists bomb US-owned cos 9-14, 745E3
Prisoner exchng bill signed 10-28, 834E1
Illegal entry attempts rptd up 11-17, 967B1
FBI campaign vs communists revealed 11-21, 941B1
1st prisoners exchngd 12-9, 957B2
US air svc agrmt initialed 12-19, 1006A3

MEXICO, Gulf of—*See GULF of Mexico*
MEYER, Ken
Named 49er coach 4-19, 1020A2
MEYER, Perry
Bars language law provisn 10-6, 780A2
MEYER, Robert H.
Personal lobbying halted 9-30, 773D1
Quits Agri post 10-20, 814B2
MEYERS, Gerald C.
Elected AMC chief exec 10-21, 962C1
MEYERS, Pvt. Lawrence
Desertn rptd 1-7, 11C2
MEYNER, Rep. Helen (D, N.J.)
In South Korea 4-12, 305F3
MEZA Cuadra, Antonio
Held for questioning 8-30—8-31, 784D2
MEZA Espinoza, Salom
Message read to MEP conv 9-25, 867A3

1978

Police corruptn detailed 4-2, 289D3
Sinaloa rptr called criminal 4-20, 517G2
Drug offenders rptd tortured 6-17, 818A1
3 die in Matamoros riot 6-26; more violence 6-28, order restored 6-29, 517C2
Amb's son slain 8-29, suspects seized 9-3, 690C2
Amnesty bill set by pres 9-1, 690D2
More suspects seized in death of amb's son 9-15, 818D1
Drug dealers killed in Culiacan 9-19; 6000 rptd arrested 10-3, 817F3
Amnesty bill enacted 9-28, pol prisoners rptd freed 10-1, 10-6, 817E2-A3
Sugar offcl, wife slain 10-6, 818F1
Freed pol prisoners total 157 10-27, 1021G3
Domecq heiress kidnaped 10-30, rescued 11-12, 926C3

U.S. Relations
Carter bars migrant workers 1-30, 62D3
Illegal emigratn to continue 2-26, 331B1
Tex farmers block food imports 3-1, 3-3, 163F1
US prisoner exchng ends 3-6, 290D1
DEA ex-agents convicted in drug plot 3-10, 380C1
Paraquat contaminated pot peril warned 3-10, rptd exaggerated 8-3, 728C3
Culiacan drug traffic rptd 3-17, 290C1
Rios Camarena extraditn cited 3-21, 289B3
Mex coffee smuggling indictmt 4-29, 518A1
Vesco leaves CR, plans visit 4-30, 354E2
A-fuel export license deferral rptd 5-20, 408B2
US urged to rejoin ILO 6-7, 523F3
Lopez Portillo at Canal pact instrumts exchng, shuns fetes 6-16, 463F2, 464A1
Tourism to Mex reopens 6-29, 517G2
Ray alleges smuggling operatn 8-16—8-18, 641A2
US hopeful on Mex oil wealth 8-24, 690C1
Amb's son slain 8-29, suspects seized 9-3, 690C2
Gas price to US unchanged 9-1, 690D1
More suspects seized in death of amb's son 9-15, 818D1
US shipping rebate fine rptd 10-1, 752G3
US drug dealers rptd seized 10-3, 817G3
Border fence planned by US 10-24, 818B1
ITT paymts chrgd 11-2, 876C1
McDonnell Douglas paymts rptd 12-15, 982G2
US rejcts Algerian gas imports 12-18, 983F3
US House com seeks illegal alien curbs, scores Carter plan 12-20, 1010B2-B3

MEXICO, Gulf of
Oil spill off La rptd 1-31, 524G1
Tiger Shoal gas output hike set, reserves rptd overestimated 4-27, 322D1, F1
Offshore leasing chngs clear Cong 8-22, 662F2, E3
New Mex oil reserves claimed 11-13, 903F2
MEYER, Irwin
Working opens 5-14, 887E3
MEYER, Ken
Fired as 49ers coach 1-10, 171D2
MEYER, Till
Escapes W Berlin prison 5-27, 438A3
4 RAF terrorists rptd arrested 5-29, 438F3
Free Dems lose 2 state electn 6-4, 456G2
Arrested in Bulgaria, extradited 6-22, 500A1
Baumann resigns 7-3, 651B2
MEYERS, Ann
Unsigned by WBL 12-9, 1027A3
MEYERS, Rep. Gary A. (R, Pa.)
Atkinson wins seat 11-7, 849F2
MEYERS, Gerald C.
Named AMC chrmn 10-20, 809G3
MEYERS, Pat
2d in Birmingham Classic 4-16, 355G3
Ties for 2d in Lady Stroh's 8-24, 672F3
MEYNER, Robert B.
On Kennecott bd rival slate 3-27, 402G3
MEYNIER, Pascal
Bonjour Amour released 6-11, 618D3
MEZVINSKY, Edward M.
Scores Argentina re rights 3-6, 208A1
MIAGKOV, Gregory
Tied to KGB 7-26, ousted by ILO 7-31, returns to USSR 8-3, 676C1

1979

U.S. Relations—*See also 'Oil' above*
Student enrollmt in US rptd 167D2
Carter on upcoming visit 1-17, 30B1
Mass boy in Laetrile clinic 1-26, 139C1
Illegal alien issue detailed 1-29; '64-78 deportation table 127B1, A2
Carter visit protested 2-7, 2-15, 124A3
UFW striker shot in Calif 2-10, 327E1
US rpts Mex record Jan crossings 2-11; entry policies protested, pol activism seen 2-12, 127D2-A3
Carter visits; oil, gas, alien issues discussed; cooperatn pact signed; comr named 2-14—2-16, 124F1, 127A1
Alien deportatn spurs protests 3-9, 3-10, 308E1
US A-fuel delay cited 4-1—4-4, 372B2
US drops border fence 4-26, 327F2-B3
Carter alleged death plot probed 5-5—5-29, 404F1
Nicaragua ties end urged 5-20, 409A1
FDA Laetrile ban upheld by Sup Ct 6-18, 498F2
Rabies cases rptd up 7-14, 620A3
Fla vegetable growers withdraw chrgs 7-19, 553G1
US bank loan rptd 7-28, 584E1
Brown visit begins 7-30, 593G1
US lifts gay alien curb 8-14, 631A3
Lopez visits US, sees Carter 9-27—9-29, 753C1
Lopez lauds Carter Latin policy 10-1, 754C1
Mass boy dies in Laetrile clinic 10-12, 905G1
Shah in NY 10-22, 843C1; reentry barred, US surprised 11-29, 897D1
Calif pot output up 10-29, 972G1, A2
US clears vegetable growers re dumping chrgs 10-30, 831F1
Reagan urges closer ties 11-13, 866D2
US sets Carib policy 11-29, 960G3
US pressure to readmit shah denied 12-3, 914F1
Amnesty Intl scores US on illegal aliens 12-9, 980B2
'80 illegal alien rise seen 12-12, 950G2

MEXICO, Gulf of
Oil platform collapses 5-10, 472G3
Mex oil well blows out 6-3, 462B2
Lease bids placed 7-31, accepted 8-28, 664E3; 11-27, 942F3; 12-10, 990C2
Mex oil blowout hits Tex beaches 8-9, 608G1; US asks damages 8-23, 688E3, 689B1
Mex oil blowout suits filed 9-13—9-18, 718G2
US, Mex oil blowout talks agreed 9-28—9-29, 753A2
MEYER, Andre
Dies 9-9, 756B3
MEYER, Charlotte
Acquitted re war crimes 4-19, 333E3
MEYER, Cord
On '71, '75 Libyan A-bomb bids 4-14, 299C3
MEYER, Lt. Gen. Edward C.
Named Army staff chief 5-2, 347F2; installed 6-22, 482C3
MEYER, Irwin
Break a Leg opens 4-29, 711G1
MEYER, Ray
In basketball HOF 4-30, 526C3
MEYER, Russ
Beneath the Valley of Ultravixens released 5-11, 528D1
MEYERHOFF, Harry
Spectacular Bid loses Triple Crown 6-9, 448D2
MEYERHOFF, Teresa
Spectacular Bid loses Triple Crown 6-9, 448D2
MEYERHOFF, Tom
Spectacular Bid loses Triple Crown 6-9, 448D2
MEYERS, Ann
Named '78 top female coll athlete 1-10, 103B2
Waived by NBA team 9-9, signs with WBL Gems 11-14, 1003E2
MEYERS, Gerald C.
Backs Chrysler fed aid 9-18, 699G2
MEYERS, Pat
Wins Greater Baltimore Classic 7-22, 587F3
MEYERS, Lt. Gen. Paul
On mil MD shortage 2-16, 130E2
MEZVINSKY, Edward M.
On Israel torture chrgs 2-11, 108D2
MIAGUL Jan Agha
Flees to Pakistan

1980

U.S. Relations—*See also 'Oil & Gas' above*
US shrimp fishermen barred 1-1, 21D1
US citizenship revocatn law backed by US Sup Ct 1-15, 51D2
Silver, gold sales tax scored 1-25, 68G3
US illegal aliens rptd 2-4, 147E1
US 'guest worker' study rptd 2-13, 147D2
Toxic tomatoes detected 2-20; 3 packing plants closed, border checks stiffened 3-12, 233A3
Mex bars GATT entry 3-18, 234B1
US dismisses vegetable 'dumping' suit 3-24, 233F2
Duncan sees Lopez for energy talks 4-2—4-3, 315G1
US amb confrmd 4-3, 315E1
Coca-Cola workers strike 4-24, 463E3
Kennedy visits Mex City 4-28, 327F2
1st 1/4 trade data rptd 6-6, 465F2
Ford plans engine plant 6-12, 465B2
US investmt growth forecast, mfg cited 6-13, 465E2
Drought blamed on US hurricane tests 6-19, 7-1, 424D2
El Salvador aliens rescued in Ariz desert 7-4—7-9, 518E2-C3; 4 held 7-11, 7-19, 560E2
Mex seizes tuna boats 7-8, 7-10; US retaliates, bans tuna imports 7-14, 565B1
Lopez vows Cuba aid vs trade embargo 8-1, 605B3
El Salvador policy conflict hinted 8-18, 633D3
Reagan urges eased immigratn rules 9-16, 699F3
El Salvador alien deportatn proceedings begin 10-18, 2 smugglers convicted 10-20, 825F3, G3
US OKs Israeli jet sale 10-31, 865A2
Reagan warned vs interventn 11-5, 841G2
Panama Canal clogged by trade shipmts 11-24, 895E3
US panel backs amnesty for illegal aliens, higher quotas 12-7, 939G1
Fishing treaties ended, waters dispute blamed 12-29, 995D2
MEXICO, Gulf of
Mex oil spill continues 1-10, 60D2
Mex caps blown-out well, total spill rptd 3-24, 233D3
Storms hit 4-25—4-28, 326D1
Oil, gas leasing speedup OKd 6-17, 552F2
Hurricane Allen hits 8-7, 621G1, D2
MEYER, Gen. Edward C.
Orders Eur, S Korea sgts recalled 9-5, 683D3
MEYER, Dr. Mary B.
Maternity smoking risks cited 1-4, 23E3
MEYER, Ray
Named top coll basketball coach 3-21, 240F3
MEYER, Till
Sentenced 10-13, 833B1
MEYERS, Gerald C.
On Renault loan 7-1, 556B3
On Renault-AMC rescue plan 9-24, 724F3
MGM Grand Hotels Inc.
Creation approved 5-30, 501G2

1976

MIAMI, Fla.—*See FLORIDA*
MIAMI, University of
Onsager dies 10-5, 970G2
MIAMI Beach, Fla.—*See FLORIDA*
MIAMI Herald (newspaper)
Miller wins Pulitzer 5-3, 352D3
Ford endorsement rptd 10-30, 827F3
MIAMI National Bank—*See under DATA Lease Financial Corp.*
MIAMI News (newspaper)
Venez ousts Inclan 10-22, 844F1
Carter endorsement rptd 10-30, 831G2
MICELI, Gen. Vito
Named CIA aid recipient 1-31, 140B3
MICHAELSON, Robert
Arrested 5-15, 401D2
MICHALKE, Ronald
Freed 6-3, 457C3
MICHEL, Rep. Robert H. (R, Ill.)
Scores House reforms 6-1, 551B3
Vs House Arab boycott legis 9-22, 746G2
Reelected 11-2, 829A3
House minority whip 12-8, 981D3
MICHELANGELO Buonarroti (1475-1564)
Renaissance frescoes found 1-2, 104D3
MICHELINI, Margarita
Kidnaping rptd 7-19, 571A3
MICHELINI, Zelmar
Kidnaped 5-18, body found 5-20, 399E1-D2 ★
Mourners seized at funeral 5-25, 441C2
Govt linked to death 5-28, 441B2
Daughter rptd kidnaped 7-19, 571A3
MICHELIN Tire Co.
Ga tax upheld by Sup Ct 1-14, 23B3
MICHENER, James
Centennial on best seller list 1-25, 80D3; 2-29, 208F3

MICHIGAN
Williams freed in NC 1-16, 79C3
Police unit ordered disbanded 1-18, 45E1
To purchase Ann Arbor RR 4-1, 235F1
Fugate paroled 6-8, 442D3
Nurses chrgd in '75 Ann Arbor VA Hosp deaths 6-16, 503E3
US Sup Ct upholds porno zoning 6-24, 478G3
Fruehauf execs sentncd 6-30, 524A1
Sup Ct allows antitrust suit vs elec co 7-6, 569F1
Chrysler Trenton plant strike ends 7-11, 570C2
US A-plant hearing ordrd 7-21, 570C3
Sen rpt chrgs Medicaid fraud 8-30, 715B1
Fscl '75 per capita income, tax burden rptd 9-15, 10-12, 959B2
'70 Hamtramck default cited 9-17, 994A2
Air Force tanker plane crash 9-26, 840G3
Newhouse buys Booth chain 11-8, 901F2
Flu shot paralysis rptd 12-17, 950E1

Detroit—*See also 'Politics' below*
Group seeks police files 1-18, 45G1
Busing starts peacefully 1-26, 95E1
Banks buy downgraded Detroit notes, '76 budget deficit cited 3-24, 994D2
Youth crime dvpts 8-15—9-16, 776F1
Dep Police Chief Blount suspended, DEA probe rptd 8-20; chief replaced 9-28, cmdr found dead 9-29, 776C2
'74-75 SATs rptd 9-13, 993G1
RC conf held in Detroit 10-21—10-23, 859B1
Sup Ct to review Detroit school integratn plan 11-15, 882E2
Leads US heroin use, deaths 12-12, 972A3
Young rejected US post 12-16, 937A2
Bank acquisitn OKd 12-19, 983F3

1977

MIAMI, Fla.—*See FLORIDA*
MIAMI, University of
Edwards in NFL draft 5-3, 353A3
MIAMI International Airport
Cuban '75 bomber sentncd 3-18, 288E3
MIAMI News, The
Scored re '75 IRS rpts 1-6, 16A1
MICELI, Gen. Vito
Treason trial begins 5-30, Andreotti testifies in Milan 9-15, 1014E3, G3

MICHIGAN
Legislature schedule rptd 6E2
NYS stock transfer tax amendmts ruled illegal 1-12, 57F2
FEA orders home heat oil hike 1-24, 54G1
US declares emergency status 2-5, 91B2
'72 schl aid cutoff cited 2-17, 156E3
Carter call-in 3-5, 171C1
US Sup Ct upholds electn rules 3-21, 230C3
Pontiac botulism outbreak 4-2—4-6, 288E1
Fed spending inequities chrgd 4-6, 423D3
Young in Lansing 4-12, 272B1
'76 per-capita income table 5-10, 387D2, A3
Flint econ data rptd 5-16, 384C3
DES '74 suit dismissed 5-16, 431F3-432B1
'75 Ann Arbor VA Hosp death convictns 7-13, 568F2
Seafarer funds authorized 7-14, 576C1
USW strikes ore ranges 8-1, 593E2
Iona hosp mind-control tests rptd 8-1—8-9, 611D1
'76 per capita income, tax burden table 9-13, 10-18, 821C2
Gerber takeover bid dropped 9-19, 799F1
ICC sues trucking firms 11-3, 861A1
Battered wife acquitted 11-3, 928E1
Bridgman A-plant closed 11-18, 917G1
US facilities cited for pollutn 11-25, 944C2
Seafarer site backed by Navy 12-15, local oppositn rptd 12-16, 977D3-978B1
USW ore-range strike ends 12-16, 977A3
VA Hosp convictns overturned 12-19, 991G2

Detroit
Police chrg reverse bias 1-4, 278A3
Canada OKs emergency fuel exports 1-19, 54A1
Young named Dem com v chrmn 1-21, 53B2
US rights comm backs Detroit busing 2-15, 112E1
Detroit on '75 10 largest cities list 4-14, 388A1
Detroit sued on water pollutn 5-6, 422D2
Econ data rptd; table 5-16, 384F2
Detroit teacher agency shop upheld 5-23, 444E1
Remedial educ bias progrms upheld 6-27, 538A3
City workers strike 7-6, 558G2
Natl govs conf held 9-8—9-9, 719G1
Carter in roundtable talk 10-21, 817A1
Zerilli dies 10-30, 872B3
Young reelected mayor 11-8, 855F1, G2
Young debates Admin urban policy 12-7, 959F3
Pharaon bank sale cited 12-27, 1003A3

1978

MIAMI, Fla.—*See FLORIDA*
MIAMI, University of
Latimer in NFL draft 5-2, 336G3
MIAMI Herald, The (newspaper)
Sadat plea to US Jews published 1-29, 60B3
MIAMI Herald Publishing Co.
Gurney trial press-curbs review declined by Sup Ct 4-17, 308D2
MIAMI Herald Publishing Co. v. U.S.
Gurney trial press-curbs review declined by Sup Ct 4-17, 308D2
MIAMI University (Oxford, Ohio)
NCAA basketball tourn results 3-27, 272B1
S Africa divestiture voted 4-30, 377E1
S Africa divestiture canceled 6-3, 633B1
MICA, Dan
Wins US House seat 11-7, 849D3, 850G2
MICELI, Gen. Vito
Andreotti testifies at trial 1-9, 19G1
MICHAEL, Prince (Duke of Kent) (Great Britain)
Married 6-30, 580F1
MICHAELIDES, Petros
Named Cyprus justice min 3-8, 189A2
MICHEALOV, Valerian
Offers PI A-plant 1-5, 134B3
MICHEL, Anna
Convicted in exorcism death 4-21, 379E3
MICHEL, Anneliese (d. 1976)
4 convicted in exorcism death 4-21, 379D3
MICHEL, Josef
Convicted in exorcism death 4-21, 379E3
MICHEL, Mike
Eagles lose in playoffs 12-24, 1024E1
MICHEL, Paul R.
On Park Tong Sun testimony 2-1, 63G3
MICHEL, Rep. Robert H. (R, Ill.)
Mugged in DC 7-21, 843B3
Reelected 11-7, 850F3
Reelected minority whip 12-4, 958G1
MICHELS, Donald G.
Loses Sen primary in W Va 5-9, 363C1
MICHENER, James A.
Chesapeake on best-seller list 8-6, 620A2; 9-4, 708B1; 10-9, 800A3; 11-6, 887F3; 12-3, 971A1
Caravans released 11-1, 969F3 ★
Centennial on best-seller list 11-6, 888B1; 12-3, 971C1

MICHIGAN
'67, '77 sales-tax rates rptd 1-5, 15E3
NASL '77 Detroit franchise cited 1-5, 23B1
EPA curbed on asbestos rule 1-10, 13F2
Lloyd Carr receiver named 1-19, 83B3
Blizzard hits, blackout rptd 1-25—1-26; auto indus losses rptd 2-6, 105G2, C3, E3
Pollutn suit vs Ford Motor filed 2-1, 163C3
GM assessed $2.5 miln in car crash case 2-9, 185E3
Coal shortage rptd 2-11, Carter sees gov 2-16, 104D1, D2
Detroit-London air-fare agreed 3-17, 206D2
Midland A-plant ruling curbed by US Sup Ct 4-3, 280F2
Detroit Anaconda strike ends 4-3, 284E3
Franklin, Turman wed 4-12, 420F2
Firestone jobless benefits challenge declined by US Sup Ct 4-17, 308B3
GM, UAW set plant accord 9-11, 699E3
Firestone suits rptd 9-22, 835F1
PBB contamination rptd widespread 10-9, 769C2; suit dismissed 10-27, 834C1
Chessie, Seaboard set merger 11-16, 897B1
Big Rock Pt, Bridgman A-plant ratings rptd 11-25, 940D3
Detroit populatn ranked 12-5, 942E3
Detroit lays off workers 12-27, 1012F1

Crime & Civil Disorders
'75 VA Hosp death chrgs vs 2 nurses dropped 2-1, 116C2
Actress killed in Highland Pk auditn 4-10, 380F2
Arson probe search warrants backed by Sup Ct 5-31, 431E1
'77 prison populatn rptd up 6-3, 440C1
Extraditn probes barred by US Sup Ct 12-18, 981G1

1979

MIAMI, Fla.—*See FLORIDA*
MIAMI, University of (Coral Gables, Fla.)
Saban named West Pt football coach 1-4, 175B3
Anderson, Smith in NFL draft 5-3, 335F2
MIAMI-Dade Community College (Miami, Fla.)
Forgn student enrollmt listed 167D3
MICHAEL, Lee F.
Price-fixing chrgs dismissed 4-29, 327D3
MICHAELS, Lorne
Gilda Radner Live opens 8-2, 711C3
MICHAELS, Walt
Named top NFL coach 1-14, 175B2
MICHAUX, Andre
Killed, Sykes murder linked 3-22, 228B3
MICHEL, Rep. Robert H. (R, Ill.)
House minority whip 71B1
USSR A-accidents disclosed 4-22, 323F1
Medicaid, welfare cuts set 6-19, 561F1
MICHELANGELO (Michelagniolo Buonarroti) (1475-1564)
Icon found in Lebanon 10-20, 892F1-A2
MICHELIN & Cie
Spain execs kidnaped 2-5—3-1, 192C1
Canada prov OKs labor bill 12-28, 992E3
MICHELSON, Carl
On A-reactor warning 4-16, 275D1
MICHENER, James A.
Chesapeake on best-seller list 1-7, 80A3; 2-4, 120A3; 3-4, 173C3; 4-8, 271G1; 5-6, 356C2; 10-14, 800C3; 11-4, 892D3
Centennial on best-seller list 1-7, 80D3

MICHIGAN
Blizzards hit 1-12—1-14, 1-24—1-27, 120F1
Med malpractice arbitratn rptd 1-28, 139E3
Laetrile shipmt recalled 3-8, 196A1
Ford stockholders suit barred in NY 3-8, 202A3
Detroit emergency air landing 4-4, 412G1
Legal drinking age cited 4-16, 309E3
UAW conv in Detroit 4-17, 280E1
Indian fishing rights upheld 5-8, 368C1
Hamtramck Chrysler plant to shut 5-29, 576G2
No-fault auto insurnc case refused by Sup Ct 6-11, 478G3
FCC revokes Panax TV licenses 7-12, 618E2
Ford heir barred from contesting will 7-16, 631C1
Detroit Cath church membership loss rptd 7-16, 640B1
Willow Run, Flint GM plants struck 8-23—8-27, 698F2
'78 Detroit FRB funds cited 9-6, 840G3
'78 per capita income rptd 9-16, 746D2
Detroit bond ratings listed 9-20, 920E3
Detroit layoffs announced 9-28, 921E2
Kalamazoo Amtrak crash kills 3 10-12, 800A2
Wayne Cnty goes broke 10-19, lays off workers 10-23, govt reorganizatn accord reached; state aid vowed 11-1, 921A1
Milwaukee Rd embargoes track 11-1—11-5, 867G2
Detroit auxilary bishop in Iran 12-24—12-27, 975B1

Atomic Energy
Detroit Ed shareholders defeat A-power delay 4-23, 322G3
Palisades A-plant pipe leaks rptd 5-2, 322B3
DC Cook (Bridgman) A-plant pipe cracks rptd 6-25, 518G3
Consumers Power fined for Palisades A-plant violatn 11-9, 867A1

Crime & Civil Disorders—*See also 'Politics' below*
Detroit '78 Nazi activity rptd 1-19, 102B1
Galante jail release ordrd 2-27, 156F1
4 convicted in Nev racketeering scheme 3-13, 209B1
'78 inmate totals rptd 6-21, 548C2
Detroit 'good faith' arrest backed by Sup Ct 6-25, 540B1

Energy—*See also 'Atomic' above*
'78 per capita gas use rptd 5-27, 395G2
Ann Arbor oil facility fire 6-16, 572C3

Environment & Pollution—*See also 'Atomic' above*
Velsicol indicted for PBB feed grain contaminatn cover-up 4-26, pleads not guilty 5-7, 597E3
Hooker sued for Montague pollutn 6-22, 597C2
PBB contaminatn rpt issued 10-9, Velsicol settles suits 10-23, 808G2-D3

1980

MIAMI—*See FLORIDA*
MIAMI Herald, The (newspaper)
Blais wins Pulitzer 4-14, 296G2
Anderson pres endorsemnt rptd 11-1, 844F1
MIAMI News (newspaper)
Wright wins Pulitzer 4-14, 296G2
MICA, Rep. Dan (D, Fla.)
Reelected 11-4, 842G2
MICALETTO, Rocco
Arrested 2-20, 194E3
MICHAEL, Gene
Hired as Yankee mgr 11-21, 926G1
MICHAELS, Joel B.
Changeling released 3-28, 416E2
Tribute released 12-13, 1003F2
MICHAELS, Lorne
Gilda Live released 3-28, 416G2
MICHAELS, Sidney
Tricks of the Trade opens 11-16, 892F3
MICHEL, Rep. Robert H. (R, Ill.)
Reelected 11-4, 842F3
Named House GOP leader 12-8, 936A2
MICHENER, James A.
Chesapeake on best-seller list 1-13, 40D3
Covenant on best-seller list 12-7, 948D3

MICHIGAN
Tornadoes hit 4-7—4-8, 5-13, 391B2, G2
Lansing contraceptive distributn case declined by Sup Ct 10-6, 782G2

Crime & Civil Disorders
Teamster chief's son rptd sentenced 2-19, 237F2
Defendant pre-arrest silence testimony backed by Sup Ct 6-10, 512C1
Flint print shop police raid cited 7-26, 582D2

Energy
Ct blocks ND synfuels projct 12-8, 962C1

Environment & Pollution
Dow chrgs EPA spying 3-25, 387A3, C3
Gratiot Cnty PBB dump cleanup sought 4-17, 331D2, F2
DES in cattle rptd 4-24, 358F1
Chemcentral-Detroit toxic waste suit filed 10-7, 825G1

Labor & Plant Issues
Chrysler aid OKd 1-9, 14E1
Detroit Uniroyal plant to close 1-22, 52G2
GM to shut Pontiac plant, Lake Orion replacemt site set 1-31, 287B2
Benton Harbor 'payless payday' 2-5, 744B1
Sterling Heights set as VW plant site 2-12, 127B3
Chrysler loan bill rptd OKd 3-7, 287B1
Ford Dearborn foundry shut 4-15, 287F1
Chrysler to keep Lynch River plant open 6-3, 457E1
Detroit workers strike 7-2, 518G1; strike ends 7-12, 542G1
Carter unveils auto industry aid plan 7-8, 505A1
Reagan sees auto execs, workers; vows import curbs, scores fed regulatns 9-2; Admin disputes 9-3, 664E2
Detroit police, teacher layoffs rptd; July jobless rate 18.5% 9-8, 743E2, G2
Bush stresses jobs issue 9-18, 781B1
Wayne Cnty 'payless payday' 9-19, 743D3
Carter visits Wayne auto plant, vows job aid 10-1, 739G1-C2
Chrysler worker insurnc asked 12-26, 984G2

1976

Politics
Primary date set 22B2
Ex-gov Swainson sentenced 1-26, 70A3
Ford sees GOP in Dearborn 1-31, 87D3
Pres campaign dvpts 5-12, 343C1; 5-14—5-17, 356E3
Primary results 5-18, 356D2
Dem conv women delegates, table 508C2
Dem conv pres vote table 7-14, 507C2
US Sen primary results 8-3, 565F2-A3
GOP pre-conv delegate count 8-14, 583C3
GOP conv pres, vp vote tables 8-18—8-19, 8-19, 599C1, C3
Sears recalls defeat 8-18, 615B3
Carter campaigns 9-15—9-16, 686D3
Ford Kent Cnty funds rptd probed 9-21, 9-25, 722F1, F3
Mondale in Flint 9-23, 725B1
Ford cleared re funds 10-14, 761G1, E2
Carter speaks in Detroit 10-15, 785E1
Ford winds up campaign 11-1, 826A3, B3
Carter, Mondale end tour 11-1, 827D1, E2
Election results 11-2: pres 818B1, 819A1; cong 820A1, D2, 823E2, 828G1, 829D4; state (Detroit) 823F2, 825B3, D3
Philip Hart dies 12-6, 1015E1

1978

Politics & Government
Legislature schedule rptd 14F3
State tax revenue data 1-9, 84D2, G3
Carter sees gov 2-16, 104D2
Diggs indicted 3-23, 220C2
Govt spending curbs cited 6-6, 425C1
Dems bar 'open primary' 6-9, 448G2
GOP natl com meets in Detroit 7-21, 568A2
Primary results 8-8, 625G3
GOP tax-cut tour in Detroit 9-21, 734F3
Diggs convicted 10-7, 791D3-792A1; sentncd 11-20, 900A2
Carter at Flint rally 11-2, 862A2
Election results 11-7: cong 845E1, D2, 846E1, E2, A3, 848C2, 851D1, 853C3, 854B1; state 847C1-F1, 853F2, 854A1, C1, 915E2
Black secy of state noted 11-28, 915D3

1979

Battle Creek seeks trust suit environmt statemt 10-9, 809G3
Hooker settles Montague dump suit 10-24, 808E3
Politics & Government—*See also other appropriate subheads in this section*
Legislature schedule rptd 5D3
Detroit chosen '80 GOP conv site 1-23, 70A3
Fscl '78 tax revenue rptd 2-13, 152B2
Diggs expulsion rejctd by House 3-1, 165E2
Levin '78 labor gifts rptd 6-13, 595D1
Detroit loses Dem conv 6-28, 518E1
Diggs admits funds misuse, accepts House censure 6-29, 515D1
Carter in Detroit for energy address 7-16, 532F2, 534F1
Diggs censured by House 7-31, 578D1
HS voter turnout law signed 8-14, 724D2
Diggs sued by US 8-16, 649G3-650B1
Diggs conviction upheld 11-14, 900F2
Ex-Sen Potter dies 11-23, 932D3
Detroit ex-mayor Cavanagh dies 11-27, 932C2
School Issues
Integratn study rpts urban lag 5-9, 650F1
Ann Arbor standard English teaching plan ordrd 7-12, 597B1
Ann Arbor OKs 'Black English' teacher progrm 8-15, 650A3
Teachers strike in Detroit, 24 other districts 9-10, 679B1

1980

Politics & Government—*See also other appropriate subheads in this section*
Legislature schedule rptd 18E1
Benton Harbor fscl crisis 2-5, 744B1
Fscl '79 tax revenue rptd 2-20, 307B3
Diggs convictn review refused by Sup Ct 6-2, Diggs resigns 6-3, 428A1
Diggs enters prison 7-24, Justice Dept drops suit 8-4, 908D3
Detroit bond rating lowered 8-6; tax revenue drop, layoffs rptd 9-8, 743E2-B3
Wayne Cnty 'payless payday' 9-19, 743C2
Detroit census revisn ordrd 9-25, 741D2
Election results 11-4: cong 840C2, 843E1, 846C2, E3, 851C1; state 845F2
Detroit census order stayed 12-24, Sup Ct bars stay 12-30; '80 figures released, reapportnmt seen 12-31, 982G3, 983E1
Presidential Election (& Transition)
Dem caucus results 4-26, 327D2
Bush in Detroit 5-12, 366B3
Pres primary results 5-20, 382E3, 383F1
GOP platform com meets in Detroit 7-7—7-10, 506C2
Carter in Detroit, unveils auto industry aid plan; GOP scores 7-8, 505A1-B2
GOP natl conv in Detroit 7-14—7-17, 529C1-537G1
GOP natl com meets in Detroit 7-18; Reagan, Bush campaign 7-19, 549F2
US House primary results 8-5, 682A3
Carter addresses AFT conv in Detroit 8-22, 646E2
Reagan in Detroit, Klan remark stirs furor 9-1—9-2, 663E3, 664E2
Bush campaigns in Detroit, other cities 9-18—9-24, 781A1, C1
Carter visits Wayne, holds Flint town mtg 10-1, 739G1-C2
Reagan, Bush in Detroit 10-16, 802B2, 817G2
Kennedy visit rptd 10-22, 817E1
Carter in Grand Rapids 10-24, 816F2, A3
Reagan cites Detroit jobless in TV debate 10-28, 814C2
Carter stumps 10-30, 841A1
Reagan tours with Ford 11-1, 840A2
Press endorsemts rptd 11-1, 841F1
Mondale, Carter in Detroit 11-2, 11-3, 841C1, D1
Election results 11-4, 838B1, 839A2, E3
School Issues
Carter addresses AFT in Detroit 8-22, 64E2
Teachers strike in 22 districts 9-8, 723D3
Detroit busing challenge declined by Sup Ct 10-6, 782G2
Saginaw busing, housing integratn study rptd 11-16, 989E3
Sports
Detroit hosts WBA welterwgt bout 8-2, 907F2

1976

MICHIGAN, Lake
US House OKs Ind Dunes park expansn 2-17, 171A1
Ind Dunes expansn signed 10-18, 834B3
Sup Ct bars review of A-plant OK 11-8, 882D3
MICHIGAN, University of (Ann Arbor)
Loses Orange Bowl 1-1, '75 rank rptd 1-2, 31B3
Sickle cell zinc treatmt rptd 2-24, 159G2
Consumer confidence survey rptd 3-26, 230B2
Ford plans kick-off speech 9-3, 664G3
Ford opens campaign 9-15, 685F2, E3
Harris vs Ramses repair 11-8, 912A3
Alex Eckstein dies 12-4, 1015D1
Ford library planned 12-14, 980E2
Mrs Ford honored 12-19, 980D2
MICHIGAN Paper Co.—*See St. REGIS Paper*
MICHIGAN State University
Dip in coll grades rptd 9-7, 993A3
MICHINAGA, Hiroshi
Wins Olympic medal 7-30, 573F3
MICOMBERO, Michel
Ousted 11-1, 857G3
MICRONESIA (U.S. trust)
GOP platform text 8-18, 605E3
MICROWAVES
Sovt taps in US emb rptd 2-6—2-10, 122D2
Sovts tie emb rays to US taps 2-26; US denies med problem 2-29, 196C2
Sovt level in US emb rptd down 7-7, 540C3
US GOP platform text cites Sovt use 8-18, 610B3
Mid-America Dairymen Inc.
US files consent decree 5-28, 989B2
MIDDENDORF 2nd, J(ohn) William
On US, Sovt naval spending 3-10, 394G1
Censured re Rockwell trip 3-16, 200A3

1977

MICHIGAN, Lake
Frozen 1-19, 54G2
US Steel settles EPA case 6-16, 461G1
Milwaukee ordrd to end pollutn 7-29, 595B1
MICHIGAN, University of (Ann Arbor)
Loses Rose Bowl 1-1; '76 rankings 1-2, 1-3, 8E3
Rhodes named Cornell U pres 2-16, 140F2
Ford lecture 4-6, 247F2
Cobb in NFL draft 5-3, 353B3
Green in NBA draft 6-10, 584B3
MICHIGAN State University (Lansing)
Wesley Fishel dies 4-14, 356B3
MICHIGAN Wisconsin Pipe Line Co.—*See under AMERICAN Natural Resources Co.*
MICRONESIA (U.S. trust)
US surveillance detailed 5-3, 386G3
MICROWAVES
US emb discounts Sovt threat 1-4, 22F1; employe tests ordrd 1-19, 1-21, 161G1-A2
US probe rules out harm 6-27, 530D1
MID-Atlantic States—*See also specific state names*
AT&T job loss seen 8-7, 629F2
MIDDENDORF 2nd, J(ohn) William
Replaced as Navy secy 2-11, 148D3

1978

MICHIGAN, Lake
US sues firm on PCB pollutn 3-17, 243B1
MICHIGAN, University of (Ann Arbor)
Loses Rose Bowl 1-2, '77 rank rptd 1-3, 8A3, B3
2 in NFL draft 5-2, 336F3, G3
Fleming named CPB pres 9-14, 759F3
Hayes fired by Ohio State 12-30, 1025A3
MICHIGAN Chemical Co.—*See NORTH-WEST Industries Inc.—Velsico Chemical Corp.*
MICHIGAN State University (East Lansing)
NCAA basketball tourn results 3-27, 272B1
Bethea in NFL draft 5-2, 336G3
MICHIGAN v. Doran
Extraditn probes barred by US Sup Ct 12-18, 981G1
MICHIGAN v. Tyler
Arson probe search warrants backed by Sup Ct 5-31, 431E1
MICOMBERO, Michel
Ndabemeye freed 5-6, 596C1
MICROWAVES
ICAO picks US TRSB landing system 4-19, 319B2
US amb chrgs USSR 'paranoid' 10-14, 821C1
US emb study discounts Sovt harm 11-20, 924E3
GAO faults US agencies on safety 12-11, 962A3
MIDDENDORF 2nd, J(ohn) William
SEC accuses 3-18, settles 3-19, 204D2

1979

MICHIGAN, Lake
Indian fishing rights upheld 5-8, 368C1
PCDF contaminated fish rptd 9-11, 736B2
MICHIGAN, University of (Ann Arbor)
Loses Rose Bowl 1-1, '78 rank rptd 1-2, 1-3, 8C2, G2
East wins Shrine Game, Davis breaks records 1-6, 8C3
Giesler in NFL draft 5-3, 335G2
Hubbard in NBA draft 6-25, 507B3
Loses Gator Bowl 12-28, 1001B3
MICHIGAN State University (East Lansing)
Wins NCAA basketball title 3-26, 238F2
Johnson, Kelser in NBA draft 6-25, 507C2, F2, A3
US mil spending inequities rptd 11-18, 904F1
MICHIGAN v. DeFillippo
Case decided by Sup Ct 6-25, 540B1
MICHNIK, Adam
Arrested 4-18, 374G2
Freed 5-25, 414D2
MICROWAVES
ITT long-distance phone svc OKd 1-4, 15C2
Solar power satellite danger cited 1-10, 36E1
USSR source rptd destroyed 1-22, 60D2
Litton deceptive ads chrgd 2-1, 91F3
USSR beams rptd stopped 5-29, 410A1
USSR beams rptd renewed 7-19, 568C2
MIDAS International Corp.—*See IC Industries*

1980

MICHIGAN, Lake
Ill A-plant '79 dischrg data rptd 4-7, revised 4-27, 441A2
MICHIGAN, University of (Ann Arbor)
Credit card use study rptd 1-30, 92G2
Greer in NFL draft 4-29, 336E3
MICHIGAN State University (East Lansing)
Rogers hired as Ariz State football coach 1-17, 175F2
Young appointmt rptd 1-18, 199A1
MICRONESIA, Federated States of (U.S. trust)
Self-rule pact signed 10-31, 884C1
MICROWAVES
US rejects USSR export licenses 1-11, 28D2
Georg Goubau dies 10-17, 876G1
MIDDENDORF 2nd, J. William
Financial Gen deal set 7-25, *
Auto-Train investmt plan rptd 11-26, 958A3

MIDDLE EAST

1976

ARAB Commandos—*See 'Palestinian Developments' under ARAB Policies below*
ARAB Policies & Actions—*See also SINAI, SUEZ and UN headings in this section below; see also country names in Index*
Aid to Ethiopia rebels rptd 5-18, 364F1
Ford: Arab natns trust US 10-20, 784G2
Algeria
Libya seeks rejection front 5-20, 369C2
Syria proposed joint front vs Israel 6-13, 429B2

1977

ARAB Boycott—*See under BUSINESS under 'B'*
ARAB-Israeli Developments—*See also EGYPT-Israel Peace Moves and other appropriate headings in this section; for Lebanon civil strife, see LEBANON under 'L'*
Israel weighs PLO-Jordan plan 1-2; Sadat renews plan 1-3, 10E1
Egypt wants PLO at Geneva conf 1-4, 10A2

1978

ARAB Boycott—*See under BUSINESS under 'B'*
ARAB-Israeli Developments—*See also EGYPT-Israel Peace Moves and LEBANON in this section below; also LEBANON—Civil Strife under 'L'*
Terror group poisons Israeli oranges in Eur 2-1, 60F3-61A1
Israel lifts '48 war film ban 2-13, 112E3
Sadat scores Syria '73 war pullout 2-25, 139A3

1979

ARAB Boycott—*See under BUSINESS under 'B'*
ARAB-Israeli Developments—*See also other appropriate headings in this section*

1980

ARAB-Israeli Developments
Armaments
Egypt to buy US F-16s, tanks; Israel concerned, US assures 2-25, 140B2
Egypt F-4E problems rptd 7-8, US squadron deployed for joint war games 7-10, 548A2

1976

Gets Arafat, Jumblat pleas vs Syria 7-11, 514G2, A3
Assad defends mil role in Leb 7-20, 528B2
Amb sought in Syria emb raid 10-11, 759F1
Gets Arafat plea vs Syria 10-13, 758D2
Arab League—*See under 'A'; for Lebanon peace role, see 'Lebanon Civil Strife' in this section below*
Bahrain
Sadat visits, gets aid vow 2-27, 162C1
Boycott—*See under BUSINESS under 'B'*
Egypt—*See also SINAI in this section below; also 'Libyan Relations' under EGYPT under 'E'*
Backs Geneva conf renewal, PLO role 1-5, 1-13, 18F3
Warns Israel vs Leb interventn 1-12, 17G3
French Mirage purchase cited 1-16, 36C2
'73 US war info rptd scored 1-20, 93B3
Syria, Leb blamed for war 1-25, 2-3, 83D2
Sadat in Arab oil states; gets aid vow, discusses PLO, Syria feuds 2-21—2-29, 162C1
Israel backs US peace moves 2-22, 145A1
Brezhnev stresses ties 2-24, 194B2
Sadat: US step-by-step moves ended 2-27, 162A2
US Sen Stevenson rpts on visit 2-28, 161B1
US seeks jet sale, Israel vs 3-3, 161D1
US House OKs arms aid, sales 3-3, 181A2
Sadat scores USSR re India MiG parts ban 3-14, 193C1
Sadat lauds US peace effort 3-14, 193D1
Ends 15-yr Sovt pact 3-15, 193A1
India confrms MiG parts ban 3-17, 275C3
US hails Sovt break 3-19, USSR scores 3-22, 227C3, F3
France vows arms aid 3-26, 275E1
Asks Arab force in Leb 3-28, 226D2
Sadat in 6 Eur natns; comments on Sovt break, Leb crisis, Israel A-power 3-29—4-12, 274D3-275E2
Saiqa chrgs Jumblat plot vs Syria 4-5, 241D2
USSR: '73 arms pact honored 4-6, 275C2
Rpt Sovt A-arms shipmt in '73 243F1
US C-130 deal gets tacit OK 4-14, 275A2
Last Sovt warships leave 4-15, 275C1
China lauds Sovt pact end 4-19; signs MiG parts accord, USAF comments 4-21, 275E2, B3
Sadat lauds W Bank electn results 5-1, 319G2
Rpt PLO feud settled 5-5, 319C2
Syria talks canceled 5-19, renewal sought 5-23, 370G1
Press accuses Syria on Leb 5-23, 370D2
Chamoun denies arms purchase 5-24, 369E2
Vs Syrian Leb invasn, anti-Syrian riots 6-3; diplomatic missns recalled 6-5—6-8, 406E1
Sadat: Syria blocks peace 6-4, 406G1
US thanks PLO for Leb evacuatn aid 6-21, 448E1
Sadat in Leb crisis talks 6-21, 448F3
In Syria reconciliatn talks 6-23—6-24, 448G3
Vs Christian drive vs Leb refugee camps 6-25, 6-28, 463F3
PFLP hijackers assail 6-28, 463C1
US arms aid bills signed 6-30, 532E3, 533C2
Scores Israel Uganda raid 7-4, 486D2
Told of Syria threat to Beirut 7-8, 514C3

Gets Arafat, Jumblat pleas vs Syria 7-11, 514G2, A3

Urges tanks to Leb 7-12, 514D2
Rptd Libya terror target 7-15, 531E1
Arafat disavows Syria peace pact, Cairo chrgs coercion 7-30, 577G2
Israel seizes Leb freighter 8-5, 578F1
Vs Syria on Tel Zaatar capture 8-13, Syria rebuts 8-14, 618C1
Ford acceptance speech cites 8-19, 612B1
Jet hijacked 8-23, 629B2; hijackers sentncd 9-18, 700C1
USSR backs Libya, warns Egypt 8-30, 682C3
PLO voted Arab League member 9-6, 663C2
Rpt US sees Libya border buildup aid to Israel 9-12, 683A1
Israel troop exit plan rptd 9-17, 699D2
Blamed for Leb truce impasse 9-19, 9-20, 698G2, B3
Vows aid to Sarkis 9-23, 699C2
Sadat vs Syrian Leb drive 9-28, 720B2
Damascus raid rpt questnd 9-28, 720C2
Asks Arab summit on Leb 9-29, 737B2
Israel orders probe of Amoco contact 9-29, 759A3
Sovts ask Geneva conf 10-1, 738F1
Saudi Golan exit linked to Syria Leb role 738A2

Gets Arafat plea vs Syria 10-13, 758D2

Guerrillas land at Tel Aviv 10-13, 759E2
Sadat at Riyadh conf 10-17—10-18, 778A3
Normal ties with Syria OKd 10-18, 779A1
At summit on Leb war 10-25—10-26, 798D1
Reactn to US electns 11-3—11-4, 826B2
Fahmy, Sovt forgn min meet 11-3—11-4, 841F2
Carter bias to Israel cited 11-4, 841G2
Sadat meets US sens, reps re peace bid; Israel doubts 11-11—11-17, 877G2
Mediates Syria-Iraq border feud 11-24—11-25, 895B1

1977

Egypt warns war if peace try fails 1-11, 10B2
Hussein sees Sadat; PLO peace role, Palestine state backed 1-14—1-15, 50C1
Saudi ties oil prices to setlmt 1-17, 107C3
Israel vs PLO at Geneva 1-19, 50E1
Rpt Egypt troops quit Sinai for riot duty 1-21, 62G2
Egypt for Jordan-PLO link 2-17; US, Israel, Jordan react 2-18, 2-19, 121B1, G1-E2
PLO, Jordan OK link 2-22—2-23, 122C1
Israel reaffirms Geneva conf terms, backs separate Arab setlmts 3-8, 165F1
Arafat, Hussein meet 3-8, 170C2
Palestinians reaffirm Israel policy 3-12—3-20; reactn 3-20—3-21, 207F3, 208E1
PLO offcl backs Israel eliminatn 3-14, 166C2
4 Arab ldrs at Red Sea summit 3-22—3-23, 208E2
Israeli Arabs vs land policies 3-30, 246G1
Jordan for Geneva conf delay 4-2, 245D2
Sadat: Arabs back PLO-Jordan tie 4-3, 245B2
Israel, Egypt swap jailed Arabs for '73 war dead, 2 '55 hanged spies 4-14, 4-19, 297F1
Arabs must ease stand 4-25, 316F1
Hussein on Palestinian homeland, Jordan ties 4-27, 316C1
Israel cautious on Geneva conf 4-27, 316E1
Egypt, Israel Sinai war games rptd 5-4—5-9, 361G1
Assad for demilitarized zones 5-5, 360D2
Libya backs Palestine 'rejectnists' 5-8, 380G1-A2
Arab, PLO Palestine state plan rptd 5-9, 5-10, 360G2
Likud ousts Labor Party in parlt electns 5-17, 377A1, C1 ★
Begin assures Arabs on peace 5-17, Arabs denounce win 5-18, 377B2, F2
PLO warns Israel on Likud win 5-18, 5-19, 401B3
3 Arab ldrs meet 5-19, Sadat sees no chng 5-20, 401D3
Egypt air exercises rptd 5-20—5-22, 401F3
Israel war threat 5-21, Iraq protects oil fields 5-31, 440F2
Begin vs PLO at talks, on Palestine 'homeland' 5-22, 401G2
Syria, PLO warn vs Israel raids in Leb 5-24, 401E3
Dayan oppositn cited 5-29, 450B2
Egypt to ask Israel oil paymt 5-29, 496D1
Iraq seeks eastn front vs Israel 5-31, 440D2
Iraq sees Mideast war 5-31, 440D2
Hussein sees war 5-31, 496E1
Egypt-USSR talks 6-9—6-10, 457A3
Syria bars Israel recogntn 6-15, 496F1
Likud forgn policy plank 6-17, 474F2
Assad, Arafat meet; vow hard line vs Israel 6-20, 496A2
Begin becomes premr, *asks Jordan, Egypt, Syria peace talks 6-21, 474G1, C2*
Begin denies 'ultimatum' 6-23, 495B3
Sadat rptdly sees no Arab-Israel ties 7-2, 509G1
Begin for Oct Geneva talks, Sadat backs 7-4; Begin replies 7-5, 509D1
Bomb blast in Israel kills 1; PDFLP, PLO take credit 7-6, 511A3
Sadat, Hussein back PLO-Jordan tie to assure PLO in Geneva conf 7-9—7-10, 534G2
PFLP scores Egypt, Jordan 7-14, 534G3
Egypt backs Israel pact 7-16, 550F1
Iraq backs Palestinian rejectionist oppositn to Israel peace talks 7-16, 571C2
Israel Labor Party gets Begin peace plan 7-19, oppositn rptd 7-20, 549G2
Egypt returns 19 Israeli bodies 7-19, 550F1-A2
Begin airs Israeli peace plan 7-20; Arab, Israeli reactn rptd 7-20, 7-21, 549A1-550A1
Israel bomb blasts injure 40 7-28—7-29, 589F1
Sadat: would sign Israel peace pact 'tomorrow' with total exit 8-2, 588E2
Israel backs Sadat pre-Geneva conf plan 8-3, 588D3
Sadat reassures Arafat on pre-Geneva conf plan 8-4, 588F2
Israelis smash infiltrators 8-4, 589D1
Sadat notes Sinai pact expiratn 8-11, 606A1
Dayan sees pact with Egypt, Jordan, Leb; Begin doubts Egypt stand 8-11, 623B3
Syria vs 'proximity talks' 8-12, 623D3
Jordan vs separate pact with Israel 8-14, 623E3
Israel bomb blast hurts 9, PLO vows new drive 8-16, Netanya blast 8-25, 648E2
Assad for Israel peace, vs ties 8-26, 663F1
Israel silent on PLO cncl mtg 8-28, 663C1
Syria sees war if peace talks fail 8-28, 663B2
League maps strategy vs Israel 9-3—9-6, 685A1
Israel submits peace plan, US urges pan-Arab Geneva role 9-19, 713G1
Dayan sees peace formula; cites Egypt, Jordan 'attitude' 9-20, 713E2
Rpt Dayan meets Jordan premr 9-20, 713G2
Egypt: Arabs set 'to accept Israel' 9-22, 714E1

1978

Syria chrgs Israel mine kills 12 on Golan Hts, Israel denies 4-2, 236B3
Israel alerted re PLO attack 4-9, hoax hinted 4-10, 257D1
Arafat asks US, Sovt guarantees for Israel, Palestine state 5-1, 339B3
'73 chem warfare evidence rptd 6-5, 433G1
Egypt mil moves rptd 602D1
Tel Aviv blast kills 1, Israeli jets bomb PLO base in Leb 8-3, 583B1
Israel blocks PLO raid on Elath 9-30, details 10-1, 746E2
PLO shells Qiryat Shmona, 1 killed 12-21, 997B3
Algeria hard line cited 12-27, 1012F2
Algiers Summit—*See EGYPT-Israel Peace Moves below*
Haifa-Tel Aviv Raid—*For Israeli invasion of Lebanon, see LEBANON below*
PLO raids Haifa-Tel Aviv area; Israel rpts 35 Israelis, 9 gunmen slain 3-11; raid detailed 3-12, 175C1-A3
PLO rpts 33 Israeli troops die 3-11, aim of raid 3-12, 175A3
Begin warns reprisal 3-12, 3-13, 175E3
Sadat scores PLO raid, Arabs laud 3-13, 3-14, 176B1
US urges Israeli restraint 3-13, 176G1
PLO survivor, Israel on raid 3-19, 3-31, 236G2-B3

1979

1980

Israel asks $1.76 bln US aid 8-20, 662F3
Carter lauds Israeli jet success 10-24, 816A3
Egyptian-Israeli Relations—*See also other appropriate subheads*
Newspapers exchanged 1-16, 48B3
Land route agreemt 1-24, 68B2
Border opened 1-27, 107A3
Egypt ends econ boycott of Israel 2-5, 107G2
Embs opened 2-18, 2-21, ambs exchngd 2-26; Cairo, other protests staged 2-26, 140C1
Direct air flights start 3-3, 3-5, 180A2
US Israel mil base constructn lags 6-12, 498D3
Anderson gives Begin message to Sadat 7-12, 549G3
Egypt sees no break despite Jerusalem feud 8-3, 585E1
Israel pres in Egypt, ties expanded 10-26—10-30, 822C3
Oppositn ldrs visit Egypt 11-7—11-9, 863E2
Egyptian-Israeli Treaty
Carter cites role 1-20, 50G1
Islamic Conf scores 1-29, 67C2; 5-22, 395D3
Carter lauds pact on 1st anniv 3-23, 260C3
Egypt Moslems score Sadat 4-4, 273G3-274A1
Arab hardliners reaffirm oppositn 4-14—4-15, 284E2
PLO scores Camp David pact 7-22, Israel lauds 7-23, 572B2, C2
Begin chrgs Ghali breach 8-8, 585G1
Israel links treaty, US aid request 8-20, 662F3
Syrian-Libya merger opposes 9-10, 697E1
US-Israel oil agrmt set 10-15, signed 10-17, 775E3
Sadat scores Arab oppositn 11-1, 859B3
Sadat fears Reagan policy shift 11-23, 894E1
Reagan backs Camp David process 12-7, 930B3
UN Assemb scores pact 12-15, 952F2
Begin, Sadat reaffirm process 12-18; Linowitz lists obstacles 12-19, 952C3

1976

Asks Geneva conf, vs Israel plan 12-2, 894A3
To seek Leb arms collectn 12-5, 913B1
Leb war refugees fled to 974F1
Sadat meets Assad, Syrian union set 12-18—12-21, 954D2
Backs Jordan-Palestine tie, Israel exit, Leb at Geneva conf 12-29; says Arabs for 'final' peace setlmt, Israel lauds 12-30, 973A1

Iraq

Beirut press offices raided 1-31, 82D3
Leb-Syria talks denounced 2-8, 107C2
US Sen Stevenson rpts on visit 2-28, 161B1
Leb: Syria blocks arms, pressures Fatah 3-30, 225A2
Leb: Syria blocks food relief 4-15, 273D2
Chrgs Syria Leb interventn 5-12, 5-13, 337D2
Libya seeks rejection front 5-20, 369C2
Kosygin visits 5-29—5-31, 385C2
Troops mass near Syria 6-9, 6-12, 6-13; Syria reacts 6-10, 430C1
Syria proposed joint front vs Israel 6-13, 429B2
Syrian pilot defects to 6-15, 430F1
Gets Jumblat plea vs Syria 7-11, 514A3
Leb troop role chrgd 8-5, 8-7, 577B2
Intl airlines bar KLM hijacker flight return 9-6, 662F2
Damascus hotel raided 9-26, 720C3, 721A1
Vs Syrian Leb drive 9-29, 737B2
Gets Arafat plea vs Syria 10-13, 758D2
At summit on Leb war 10-25—10-26, 798E1
Rpt Syria border shut 11-2; Iraq denies 11-3; troop-pullback pact 11-24—11-25, 895B1
Palestinian terror drive plan rptd 12-2, 894D3
Black June blamed for Syrian attack 12-2, 894D3
Airport bomb blast kills 3 12-14; Iraq blames Syria 12-15; rebel Iraqis take credit 12-16, 953G2

Islamic States, Conference of

Backs PLO, bars Leb aid 5-12—5-15, 373C1, A2

Jordan

Secret Israeli talks, Jordan PLO offer rptd 1-12, 19D1
Joint Syrian war games rptd 1-18, 35B1
Electns cancelled 2-4; Parlt reconvened, Israelis see W Bank bid 2-5, 83F2
US-Israel agrmt on peace moves rptd 2-6, 106D3
Denies Israel, PLO rpts on W Bank aims 2-9, 107A1
Rpt PLO uninformed on Parlt mtg 2-10, 107D1
PLO scores US re W Bank policy 2-15, 126D1
Student slays 2 Amer Univ deans 2-17, 12A2
Israel backs US peace moves 2-22, 145A1
Geneva conf boycott plan rptd 2-27, 162C2
Hussein in Australia talks 3-2—3-9, 204C1
Hussein in US, backs Syria role in Leb 3-30—4-1, 225D1, 226F2-C3
Condemns 2 W Bank Arabs 3-31, 227F2
Hussein ends US visit, sees Hawk missile sale delay 4-4, 242E1
PLO backers win in W Bank 4-12, 258D3
US denies Hawk deal canceled 4-14, 4-15, 274A3
Syria proposed joint front vs Israel 6-13, 429B2
Hussein seeks Sovt arms, US warns 6-16, 464A2
Hussein in Moscow 6-17—6-28, 464F1
US arms aid bills signed 6-30, 532E3, 533C2
Rptd Libya terror target 7-15, 531E1
To get US air defense system 7-31, 561F1
W Bank Arabs vs Hussein 9-12, 9-16, 699D3, G3
Egypt acquits alleged hijacker 9-18, 700D1
Damascus raiders executed 9-27, 721A1
Sovts ask Geneva conf 10-1, 738F1
Mediator meets Leb Christns 11-1, 841G1
8 die in Amman raid 11-17, 11-18, 861F1
9th raid victim dies 11-23, 878D2
Hussein, Assad in merger talks 12-7—12-8, 913A2
Raider convicted 12-9, hanged 12-18, 954A3
PLO expansn vote impasse 12-12—12-14, 954B2
Leb war refugees fled to 974F1
Egypt backs Palestine link 12-29, 973A1

Kuwait

Scores raids on Leb camps 1-15, 17D2
Buys UK tanks 2-16, 126B2
Sadat visits, gets aid vow 2-27—2-29, 162C1
Leb: Syria blocks food relief 4-15, 273D2
Syria, Egypt talks dropped 5-19; seeks renewal 5-23, 370A2
Syria, Egypt reconciliatn conf 6-23—6-24, 449D1
Turks thwart Israel jet hijack 8-11, 578C3
Govt shift tied to Palestinian feud 8-29, 8-31, 642E1
Egypt asks summit on Leb 9-29, 737B2
Sabah at Riyadh conf 10-17—10-18, 778A3
At summit on Leb war, peace force set 10-25—10-26, 798D1
To seek Leb arms collectn 12-5, 913B1

1977

Israel OKs US peace plan, sets conditns 9-25; Dayan on Palestine issue 9-27, 733G1
Arabs vs Israel peace conditns 9-25, 9-26, 9-28, 734A1
Syria backs PLO at talks; seeks Iraq, Palestinian alliance 10-10, 793F1
Israel Cabt OKs Geneva conf working paper 10-11; text disclosed 10-13, 769A1
Dayan: US, Israel bar PLO at talks 10-13; US denies 10-14, 793D1
PLO demands peace role 10-16, 793E1
Arafat-Egypt talks 10-18—10-19, 793B1
Egypt asks PLO at Geneva 10-19, 792G3
DMC joins Israel govt 10-20, 801C3
PLO rptdly seeks W Bank, Gaza delegatn 10-24, 831E2
Sadat for pre-Geneva agenda 11-4, Israel rejects 11-6, 850G1-B2
Arab League delays actn 11-12—11-14, 874B2
Sadat rpts Sinai clash averted 11-26, 909D1
PLO bomb kills 2 in Israel 12-29, 995F2

Cairo Conference—*See EGYPT-Israel Peace Moves below*

Israel Occupation Policies—*For foreign statements on Israeli withdrawal, see other appropriate headings in this section; for Sadat-Begin proposals, see EGYPT-Israel Peace Moves below*

Arab PWs in Israel end hunger strike 1-19; protests 1-19, 1-20, 2-1, 72D2
Israelis seize W Bank saboteur suspects 1-30, 72F2
Jerusalem bombers seized 2-6, 87C1
Israel Labor party backs W Bank return to Jordan 2-25, 143B3
Hebron Jewish shrine vandalized 2-25, Arabs accused 2-27, 144A1
W Bank Jewish settlers evicted 2-27, 143G3
W Bank Arabs riot 3-6—3-8, 166F2
Palestinians reaffirm Israel struggle 3-12—3-20, 207G3
W Bank protests 3-30, 246A2
JDL ldr Kahane sparks W Bank riots 4-17, 4-26, Israelis bar 5-1, 335G2
Gush Emunim starts new W Bank setlmt 5-1, 335F2
2 die in W Bank riots 5-4, 335C2
Begin affirms hard-line policy 5-17, Peres rejcts unity bid 5-19, 377F1, C2
Sadat demands Israel exit 5-18, 378A1
Begin asks more W Bank settlmts 5-19, 401F2
Likud eases stand 5-24, 401A2
Labor oppositn to Begin cited 6-7, 450C2
DMC vs joining Likud Cabt 6-13, 474C2
Likud forgn policy plank 6-17, 474G2-A3
Sunday London Times chrgs torture 6-19, Israel denies 7-3; W Bank, Gaza beatings rptd 7-7, 511A2-A3
Dayan bars ceding W Bank 6-22, 495G2
Sadat: 'backbone of peace' 7-2, 509E2
W Bank gen strike 7-5, 511C3
PFLP: Jordan arrests blocked W Bank, Gaza operatns 7-14, 535A1
Begin peace plan bars Palestine state in W Bank 7-20, 549F1
Begin: Rabin violated secret memo 7-25, 570D3
3 W Bank setlmts legalized 7-26; Begin upholds actn, Knesset vs future setlmts bar 7-27, 570A1, D2
Legalized W Bank settlemts map 570A2
US scores setlmt legalizatn 7-27, 7-28, 570C1
Nablus jail terrorism rptd 7-29, 589F1
US-W Bank flights barred 8-1, 589B1
W Bank ldrs see Vance 8-10, 605B2
W Bank, Gaza Arabs to get 'equal rights' 8-14, other reactn 8-14, 8-15, Begin defends move 8-15; 623D1-B2
3 new W Bank setlmts planned 8-17; US, Palestinians protest 8-17, 8-18, 622A3
Egypt scores W Bank setlmts 8-19, 648C2
Dayan rpts W Bank admin sharing plan 8-19, 648D2
Israel defends W Bank setlmts vs US criticisms 8-21, 648B2
PLO scores W Bank, Gaza policies 8-26, 663A1
Jenin area paramil setlmt rptd 8-26, 685B2
Israel OKs UNESCO probe 8-31, 663F2-A3
Major setlmt plan proposed 9-2, 685F1-A2
League OKs anti-Israel setlmt proposal 9-4, 685C1
Hebron area setlmt starts 9-7, 685B2
Israel proposes greater autonomy, contd mil role 9-19, 713A2, D2
2 W Bank setlmts barred 9-25, 9-28, 734D2
2 W Bank setlmts started 10-2, 10-6; 6 more OKd 10-10, 793A2
Israeli newsmen vs govt edict on W Bank rptg 10-10, 793D2
DMC to abstain on W Bank votes 10-20, 801D3
PLO kills pro-Israel Arab 12-26, 995D2

Tripoli Conference—*See EGYPT-Israel Peace Moves below*

1978

Israeli Occupation Policies—*For peace moves and UN Resolution 242 controversy (and reaction), see EGYPT-Israel Peace Moves below*

Israel bars new Sinai setlmts, expands existing ones 1-8, 10F1
4 W Bank settlmts OKd 1-10, 10D2
Dayan meets Pope on Jerusalem status 1-12, 10G2
Carter: occupied setlmts 'illegal' 1-12, 12A2
Gush Emunim plant trees at Shiloh 1-23, 78B2
Israel sets up 4 W Bank setlmts 1-29, 1-31; Carter questns Begin, Shiloh setlmt 1-29, 1-30; Begin sees US amb, clarifies policy 2-1, 60G1
Israel halts new Sinai setlmts 1-31, dvpt of existing setlmts continues 2-12, 98G1
Dayan denies '77 W Bank setlmt pledge to Carter 2-1, 60F2
Israel Labor Party, press score Shiloh setlmt 2-2—2-5, 78C2
US, Israel in setlmt feud 2-3—2-7, 78E1; text of US statemt 79A1
Jerusalem bomb blast kills 2 2-4, 99E1
Sadat: Israeli setlmts major peace obstacle 2-5, 77B2
US restates Israel setlmt oppositn 2-8, 77D1
PLO slays W Bank Arab 2-8, 99F1
Vance reaffirms US setlmt oppositn 2-9; Admin backs, Israel protests 2-12—2-13, 97E2-98G1
Sadat lauds W Ger setlmt oppositn 2-9, 98E2
UN rights comm condemns Israel 2-14, 99G1
Begin clarifies statemt on US setlmt policy 2-15, 97B2
Israel retains setlmt policy 2-20, 2-26, 138B3-139B1
Weizman bars new Sinai setlmt 3-1, 157E1
Weizman bars W Bank setlmts 3-5, to quit if disobeyed 3-6, 3-7; Cabt rift rptd 3-7, 157C1
W Bank Arabs protest Israeli Leb invasn 3-18, 198B3
Israeli troops tear gas W Bank students 3-21, mil govt cmdr rplcd 5-2, 340G1
Sinai air base use by US rptd 3-26, US denies 3-27, 215E1-A2
Israeli Sinai oilfield in operatn 3-26, 215B2
Israel rally vs Begin 4-1, 235E3
Israel rally backs Begin 4-15, 300G1
W Bank settlmt work renewed 4-17, 275E1
Israel groups oppose Begin 4-25, 4-26, 300D1
W Bank bomb blast kills 2 4-26, 300F2
Cairo plan for Jordan, Egypt to get W Bank, Gaza sent to US 5-10, 5-28, 424E2
Israel plans expansn of 6 W Bank setlmts 5-17, Arab oppositn delays 5-25, 400B2
Bethlehem mayor chrgs property takeover plan, Israel denies 5-23, 400E2
Jerusalem bus blast kills 5, PLO takes credit 6-2, 6th dies 6-3, 424G2-B3
Settlers repel PLO W Bank raid 6-12, 503D3
Weizman policy dispute with Begin, Dayan rptd 6-23; Cabt discusses 6-25, 489E1
Carter scores Israel rejectn of Egypt W Bank, Gaza plan 6-26, 491G1
Israel Cabt com OKs 5 W Bank setlmts 6-28; Cabt announces plan 8-13, cancels 8-14; US lauds move 8-14, 638C3
2 die in Jerusalem blast, PLO takes credit 6-29; US condemns Fatah, absolves PLO 6-30, 503F2
Blast kills 2 Arabs in Gaza 8-30, 746G2
Jerusalem blast 9-5, policeman dies 9-9, 746A3
Guerrillas give up near Qiryat Shmona 9-16, 746B3
Israel bars UN film unit 10-7, 762B3
Saunders meets Hussein, W Bank Arab ldrs; talks on setlmts, E Jerusalem anger Israelis 10-17—10-19, 802A2
Israel to expand W Bank, Gaza setlmts 10-25; Begin vows actn, Dayan cites Saunders remarks, US annoyed 10-26, 802F1
Begin reaffirms setlmt plan to Carter 10-29, 858G3-859A1

1979

Israeli Occupation Policies—*For peace moves and post-treaty developments, see EGYPT-Israel headings below; for Resolution 242 controversy, see 'Rights and Recognition Issues' under PALESTINIAN Developments and 'Security Council' under U.N. in this section below*

Troops block W Bank settlers 1-1–1-2, 28B3
Gush Emunim, Arabs clash in W Bank 1-4, 28B3
Israelis rally vs new setlmts 1-13, 28G2
3 new setlmts in Gaza, W Bank planned 1-15, 28F2
PLO raid in Jerusalem, 21 hurt 1-18, 50E2
Dayan: W Bank, Gaza PLO backers face ouster 1-23, 50G3
Israel blows up W Bank homes 1-30, 69D2
Rights abuses chrgd, Israel denies 2-6–2-8, 2-11; US issues rpt 2-10, US UN envoy statemt 2-11, 107B2, F3-108D2
US defns secy in W Bank 2-14, 143A3
UN rights comm condemns Israel 2-21, 148D1
Syria cites Arab prisoner rights abuse by Israel 2-23, 148B3
4 W Bank raiders slain 3-10, 177A2
Riots vs Carter missn, Israel-Egypt pact; 2 die 3-11–3-15, 177A1
UN votes W Bank setlmt probe, Israel to bar 3-22, 198E2-A3
W Bank protest vs Israel-Egypt pact 3-26, 222C2
W Bank, Gaza rule eased 3-27, 222C3
PLO bars W Bank, Gaza plan; warns Israel, Egypt, US 4-5–4-6, 4-8, 278B3
2 new W Bank setlmts OKd 4-22, US objects 4-23, 296A2
Begin reaffirms W Bank, Gaza control 5-2, 320B1
W Bank riot 5-2; 2 US students ordrd deported 5-10, leave 5-14, 360G1
Jordan sees Israel W Bank, Gaza retentn 5-3, 319F3
2 W Bank colls closed 5-3, 360B2
Israel gets Vatican pledge on Capucci 5-7, 376C3
WHO sets W Bank, Gaza health probe 5-23, 398F2
Israel frees 16 Arabs 5-28, 394A1, D3, 395A1
Israel sees more W Bank, Gaza setlmts 5-30, 415B2
Weizman: W Bank, Gaza 'parts of Israel' 5-31, 415D2
Moslem ldr slain in Gaza 6-1; PFLP takes credit 6-2, threatens Gaza mayor 6-3, 414E2
Israel OKs Nablus setlmt 6-3, US objects 6-4, 415E1-B2
Israel raids W Bank terrorist homes 6-4, 415B1
Dayan reaffirms hold on W Bank, Gaza 6-4, 415G2
Dayan: Jerusalem to remain as undivided capital 6-4, 415G2
Begin bars Palestinian state 6-6, 436F2
Elon Moreh project starts 6-7; Peace Now, Arabs protest 6-9–6-10, 436C2
Begin defends setlmts 6-11, 436G1-D2
Elon Moreh setlmt protests 6-16, 6-17; Dayan vs setlmt 6-18, constructn halted 6-20, 461D3, G3
New W Bank setlmt started 6-18, 461F3
EC vs policies 6-18, Israel rejects 6-20, 462C2
US Jews urge Begin chng setlmt policy 6-20, 462A1
W Ger pressure vs setlmts rptd sought by US 7-9, 511B2
Israel ct halts work on 2 setlmts 7-12, 7-24, lifts ban on 3d 7-25, 693G1
UN rpt vs setlmts 7-14, Israel scores 7-18; UN Cncl OKs 7-20, 551B2
Gaza bank bombed 8-26; Al Fatah, other terrorists arrested 9-7, 676E3
Liberia seeks Israel exit 9-7, 720C3
Bethlehem mayor sees US envoy, backs Jordan federatn 9-11, 676D3
Israel lifts W Bank, Gaza land-purchase ban 9-16; Egypt, US object 9-17, 9-18, 693A1
Jesse Jackson in W Bank 9-25–9-26, 763B1
Egypt vs Israeli land-purchase plan 9-26, 740B3

1980

Israeli Occupation Policies—*See also 'Jerusalem', 'Palestinian Autonomy' below*

Settlers quit Elon Moreh 1-17, 48A3
W Bank, Gaza local vote delayed 1-22, 48G2
New W Bank setlmt rptd 1-23, 107E2
Elon Moreh dismantled 1-29, 107F2
Jewish youth slain in Hebron 1-31, kidney transplant arouses controversy 2-8, 107B2
US issues rights rpt 2-5, 87C2
Israel OKs Jewish setlmts in Hebron 2-10, US scores 2-12, 107G1-A2, D2
Parlt funds W Bank outposts 2-13; Arabs propose counter plan 2-17, 178D3-179A1
US asks Hebron setlmt vote delay 2-17, 218D3
W Bank protest vs Israel-Egypt amb exchng 2-26, 140A2
UN Cncl asks Israel raze setlmts 3-1; US backs vote 3-1, disavows 3-3, Vance takes blame 3-4, 162E2, 163D1-B3
UN Cncl res text 3-1, 179C1
Begin scores UN setlmts res, US vote reversal 3-6, 179B1-B2
UN vote vs Israeli setlmts scored by Kennedy 3-10, 183D3
Carter calls UN vote 'honest breakdown', says US policy unchanged 3-14, 209F1
US Cong probes UN setlmt vote, Vance defends Admin stand 3-20, 3-21, 218B2
Israel confrms Hebron setlmt plan 3-24; mayor, others protest 3-24, 3-26, 218B3
Israel vs US plan for setlmt freeze 3-25, 219G1
Israelis vs new setlmts in US poll 3-25, 219B2
Sadat scores setlmts 4-10, 260A3
Settlers raid Arab town 4-23, 340C3
W Bank unrest leads to shooting of Arab youth 5-1, 340A3
6 settlers killed by PLO 5-2, 3 W Bank ldrs deported 5-3; protests erupt, security tightened 5-3—5-5; US, UN scores 5-6, 5-8; Arafat visits 5-7, 340E1, D3
30,000 acres expropriated for new setlmts 5-2, 340C3
Hebron schools' approval blocked 5-6, 340G2
Israeli soldiers seized in arms plot 5-9, 362C3
W Bank ldrs return barred 5-11, strike thwarted 5-12, 362D2-A3
Israeli anti-Arab plotters arrested 5-13, policy on suspects announced 5-14, 362A3
Egypt vs W Bank ldrs ouster 5-15, 362B2
Bethlehem families banished to Jericho 5-16; order canceled 5-21, 417D2
Israel group asks W Bank compromise 5-19, US Jewish ldrs back 7-1, 509B1
UN censures for ousters, Israel ct ordrs explanatn 5-20, 381C1
Hebron, Halhul mayors replaced 5-25, 417E2
2 W Bank mayors maimed in bomb attacks; Begin, US score violence, PLO asks UN Cncl mtg 6-2; Gaza, Bethlehem mayors quit 6-2, 6-3; victims blame Israel 6-3, 417A1
W Bank merchants strike 6-3, Israel thwarts 6-4, 417B1
10 new W Bank setlmts planned, Hussein talks confrmd 6-4; US criticism scored 6-10, 434E1
Jordan treats maimed Nablus mayor 6-5; US offers aid, Israel scores bid 6-10, 434F2
Gaza, Bethlehem mayors withdraw resignatns 6-5, 547C2
EC vs Israel occupatn, setlmts 6-13, 449B1
Hussein stresses Israeli exit stance 6-16, 450B1
Israeli agent slain 6-25, Arab suspect killed in shootout 547C2
W Bank, Gaza mil plan released 6-27, 491F1
OAU scores W Bank setlmts 7-1—7-4, 509A2
Arabs restricted 7-6, 547E2
Nablus mayor returns home 7-9, 547A2
Ramallah mayor rptd in US for treatmt 7-9, 547B2
Arabs die making bombs 7-9, 7-11, 547D2
2 fasting Arabs die in Israeli prison 7-23, 7-24; Arab protests 7-23—7-25, 573D1

1976

Lebanon—*See also 'Lebanon Civil War' below*
Israelis kill 4 infiltrators 1-13, 19B1
French Mirage purchase cited 1-16, 36C2
Turkish emb aide slain 2-16, amb car attacked 2-17, 125A2
2 slain at Amer Univ 2-17, 125G1
2 US aides freed, Israel denies release role 2-25, 145B2
US Sen Stevenson rpts on visit 2-28, 161B1
2 W Bank Arabs deported to 3-27, 227C2
Egypt chrgs Syria plot 5-23, 370D2
Lebanon Civil War (& post-truce developments)
Israel warns Syria vs interventn 1D2
Moslems vs Christian stand 1-2, 1E2
Jail, police station raided 1-3, 1A2
Phalangists blockade 2 Palestinian camps 1-4; clash 1-4—1-7, 1A1
Karami asks election delay 1-5, 1E2
Syria warns vs partitn 1-7, 1C2
US warns Israel, Syria 1-8, 1D2
Palestinians seen as main combatant 1-8, 17A2
Moslem drive fails to lift camp blockade 1-8, 17E2
Beirut hotel area clashes 1-9, 17F2
Palestinian threat to lift camp siege 1-9, 17G2
2 Leb soldiers die in Christian, Phalangist attacks 1-11, 17A3
Dbaiye refugee camp under Christian siege 1-12, seized 1-14, 17B2
Egypt warns Israel vs interventn 1-12, 17G3
Christian village attacked, other clashes 1-13, 17C3
Damur under siege 1-13—1-15, 17C3
War spreads to Chuf area, Jumblat forces lead 1-13, 17F3
Saudi, Kuwait react to refugee camp raids 1-15, 17D2
Jumblat: 'Decisive battle' ahead 1-15, 17E3
Palestinians chrg Damur reinforcemts 1-15, 33D2
Army jets attack 1-16, 33B1, C2
Clash closes Beirut airport, communicatns suspended 1-16, 33E2
Damur siege tightens, Jiyeh captured 1-17, 33F2
Karami sets new truce 1-17, fighting continues; Karami quits 1-18, urged to stay 1-19, 33G3
Christians take Karantina, other clashes 1-18, 34B1
PLA move in from Syria 1-18—1-21; US confrms, Syria denies 1-19, 34F1
US warns vs interventn 1-20, 34G2
Moslems widen control 1-21, 34E1
Israel reinforces border 1-21, 34D2
Rebel army formed, Al Fatah backs, Khatib heads 1-21, 209C1
Syria mediates truce, pol pact 1-22, 33A1
Syria backs Leb unity 1-22, 33G1
Truce takes hold 1-23, Palestinians enforce 1-26, 58C3
Phalangists vs Palestinian Beirut takeover 1-23, 59C1
Israel: Syria warnings saved Christians 1-23, 59E2
Karami sees Moslem ldrs, Khaddam; withdraws resignatn 1-24, 58D3, 59D1
Clashes mar truce 1-24, 1-25, 59C1
Chamoun backs Syria peace move, party seeks assurances 1-24, 59F1
Christians assured on sovereignty 1-25, 1-27, 59G1, C2
Israel welcomes refugees 1-25, 59C2
Israel warns vs interventn, censures Vatican for Christian plight 1-25, 59D2
Sadat blames Leb, Syria for war 1-25, 2-3, 83D2
Mil groups pull back 1-26, 59B2
Khaddam returns to Damascus, escort ambushed 1-27, 59B2
Australia seizes secret rightist army 1-27, 71G3
Khaddam vows sovereignty, meets Palestinians 1-29, 83G1
Guerrillas raid 2 press offices, 7 die 1-31; PLO, Saiqa reps score Saiqa factn 1-31, 2-1, 82D3
Truce group fired on 1-31, 83B1
Christians demand control 1-31, 83A2
Moslems, Christians rearm 1-31, 2-2, 83B2
US-Christian contact rptd 2-2; US denies 2-3, 83E1
Interventn pleas to US, France rptd 2-2, 83F1
Franjieh meets Assad, sovereignty assured 2-7; PLO briefed 2-8; top post sharing retained 2-11, 107F1-B2
Iraq vs Franjieh-Assad talks 2-8, 107C2
Private banks reopen 2-12, 125D2
Cabt OKs reforms, PLO advised 2-14; Moslem-Christian backing sought 2-15—2-18, 125A1
Christians vs Franjieh call for 'Arab' state, cabt reforms 162F2
Salam, Jumblat vs reforms 2-15, 125F1
Rpt 70 abducted, most freed 2-18, 125C2
Civil war losses listed 2-21, 145E2
Jumblat vs war renewal 2-25, 162E2
Syria defers mediation 2-26, 162C2
Rebels seize army garrisons 3-8—3-10, 209D1
Cabt meets 3-8, asks Syria mediatn 3-9; Khaddam holds talks 3-10—3-11, 209E1
Army rebels offered amnesty, cabt meets on army breakup 3-10, 209F1
Ahdab proclaims self mil gov, backs Khatib, asks Franjieh, Karami quit; OKs amnesty offer 3-11, 209G1

1977

1978

Israel: UN rpt backs policy 11-13, 931G1
W Bank mtg ban reimposed 11-17, 893F1
4 die in W Bank bus blast, Al Fatah linked 11-19, 893D1
W Bank demonstration 11-19, 893E1
UNESCO scores re Jerusalem digs 11-29, 931F1
Israelis raze 2 W Bank homes of jailed terrorists 12-4; Egypt protest 12-5; Arabs demonstrate 12-6, 951B2
Israel halts Sinai mil gear pullout 12-20, 979B1

1979

Connally backs Israeli exit 10-11, 783G1
Israel to expand 7 W Bank setlmts 10-14; Israeli, Egypt, US reactn 10-14–10-15, 780C1
Dayan proposes Arab role in W Bank, Gaza 10-18; policies disputed, quits 10-21, 801B1
Israeli ct bars Elon Moreh, W Bank Arabs laud rule 10-22, 801B2
Begin survives no-confidence vote 10-23, 801A2
Nablus mayor tied to terrorism, ordrd deported; ct delays 11-8; W Bank protests 11-11–11-18; W Bank, Gaza mayors quit 11-13–11-14; Israel widens chrgs 11-15, 881C2
Israel backs setlmts, bars pvt land confiscatns 11-11, 882A1
US asks Israel not to expel Nablus mayor 11-15, 881D3
W Bank pol admin reassigned, post abolished 11-15, 916E3
Elon Moreh removal delayed, evictn vowed 11-18, 881F3
Arab League to press Israeli exit 11-22, 916C2
Israeli-Arab W Bank clashes 11-27–12-22, 979C3
Nablus mayor deportatn appeal ordrd 11-22, hearing held 11-29; freed, reinstated 12-5, 916A3
Amnesty Intl chrgs Israel W Bank rights abuses 12-9, 980E2
Elon Moreh move delayed 12-30, 979B3

1980

Waldheim urges Israel quit '67 lands 7-25, UN Assemb demands exit 7-29, 572E1, G2
4 W Bank univs curbed 7-30, 661A1
W Bank Natl Guidance Com curbed 8-7, 660G3-661A1
Sadat, Begin spar on setlmts 8-11, 8-12, 627D1
Sadat says setlmts block autonomy talks 8-15, 627A2
Golan annexatn pressed in Knesset 8-17, 8-26, US opposes 8-25, 661D1
Israel plans Medit-Dead Sea canal; map 8-24, 643D3
W Bank ldrs ouster backed by Israel ct 8-29, 627A3
Jordan Red Sea-Dead Sea canal plan rptd 8-30, 661G1
US seeks Israel 'good-will gesture' 9-2, 660G2
PLO plot thwarted 9-10; Hebron attackers' home razed 9-16, 698A1
Hebron slayers, 6 others seized 9-12, 9-16, 697G3-698B1
Kahane sentncd 9-15, 902A1
W Bank mayor arrested 9-23, 736C3
2 W Bank mayors return to appeal ouster 10-14; plea hearing 10-15—10-16, ouster upheld 10-20, Sup Ct delays 10-23, 822E2
36 Gaza prisoners freed 10-16, 822B3
Begin meets Gaza, Bethlehem mayors on W Bank ousters 10-21, 822G2-A3
Hebron slayer admits Sovt training 10-31, 912F2
Bir Zeit U rites 11-13; univ closed 11-14; riots in Ramallah, Bethlehem protest closing 11-18; others protest 11-19, 879F3
Gaza Arab ldr slain 11-18, 880B1
W Bank riots renewed, spread to E Jerusalem 11-20; Bir Zeit U riot quelled, 24 arrested 11-24, 895E1
Begin vows contd W Bank security control 11-20, 895G1
Arab summit seeks anti-Israel policy, 6 states boycott 11-25—11-27, 911A1
Ramallah riot quelled 11-29, 912A2
Israel bars pro-PLO conf 12-1, 912D1-A2
Bir Zeit acting pres arrested 12-1, 912A2
2 W Bank mayors redeported 12-5, vow UN appeal 12-6; W Bank protests 12-6—12-9, 931A2
UN hears Jordan, Israel exchng chrgs 12-8, 12-10; asks Israeli exit, threatens sanctns 12-15, 952F2
USSR, India vs Israeli occupatn 12-11, 930E2
Israel sets W Bank press curbs 12-14, 977C1
Peres outlines solutn 12-17, 966F1
Begin, Sadat reaffirm peace process 12-18; Linowitz lists obstacles 12-19, 952E3
UN asks 2 deported W Bank mayors readmitted; mayors stage sit-in, hunger strike 12-19, 952B2
Israel protests UN support to deported W Bank mayors 12-22; mayors end hunger strike at UN 12-24, 976E3
Israel Cabt vs Golan takeover 12-22; Knesset upholds 12-24, 976G3-977B1
Ramallah mayor returns home 12-25, 977E1
Jerusalem—*See also 'Palestinian Autonomy' below*
Islamic Conf asks Israel quit E Jerusalem 1-29, 67C2
Christns score vandalism, Begin vows protectn 2-4, 133D3
E Jerusalem protest vs Israel-Egypt amb exchng 2-26, 140A2
UN scores Israeli rule 3-1; US backs vote 3-1, disavows 3-3, 162F3, 163A1, B2-B3
UN Israel res text 3-1, 179E1, F1, F2
Israel seizes 1,000 acres for Jewish housing 3-10; US scores 3-12, Begin defends 3-13, 178D2
US Cong probes UN vote, Vance defends Admin stand 3-20, 3-21, 218D2
Knesset bill calls capital of Israel 5-14; Egypt scores, Israel explains 5-15, 362F1, B2
Islamic Conf vs Israeli annexatn 5-22, 395C3
Begin vs Saudis re division 5-27, 395D2
EC vs Israeli control 6-13; Israel scores 6-15, 449C1, B2
Pope: sees pivotal status 6-21, 474D2
Begin to move office to E Jerusalem 6-22; US queries 6-25, objects 6-26, 476F1-A2
UN Cncl scores Israel moves, US abstains 6-30, 491B2
OAU scores Israeli annexatn 7-1—7-4, 509A2
Burg, Ali see no concessns 7-3, 539D1
Anderson in E Jerusalem 7-11, 549F3
Tamir calls capital of Israel, Ghali disputes 7-13—7-15, 538G3-539C1
Highway, terminal project OKd 7-18, 572G3
Israel parlt reaffirms capital status 7-23, 7-30; Egypt, Jordan oppose 7-30, 7-31, 572B3, E3
Arabs protest death of 2 prisoners 7-23—7-25, 573E1
Waldheim asks Israel quit E Jerusalem 7-25, 572G2
Venez to move emb to Tel Aviv 7-28, 572G3
UN Assemb asks Israel quit E Jerusalem 7-29, 572E1
Map 585A2
Sadat vs Israeli law, seeks autonomy talks delay 8-3; US, Israel reply 8-4, 8-8, 585A1

1976

Ahdab, Parlt urge Franjieh quit 3-11, 3-12; Ahdab asks Parlt replace 3-14, 209C2
Christian group asks Franjieh quit, Syria mediatn 3-14, 209G2
Civil war resumes, Moslems advance, 200 die 3-14—3-23, 210G1
Rebels threaten Franjieh palace, As Saiqa blocks 3-15, 210A1
Syria mediatn 3-16; raid on Karami plane interrupts 3-19; resumed 3-20, 210A1
Ahdab forms cmnd council 3-21, 210B2
Charter change OKs pres electn 3-22; Syria mediatn team arrives 3-23, 210D1
US warns vs interventn 3-22, 3-30, 226D3
Jumblat bars truce, asks Franjieh quit 3-24, 210F1
Moslems advance vs Christians 3-24—4-1, 225F2
Franjieh palace shelled, flees 3-25, 210F1
Waldheim warns on crisis 3-26, 3-30, 225C1, 226A2
Christians flee to Cyprus 3-28, 226D1
Egypt asks Arab force 3-28, 226D2
Moslems vs truce 3-29; Syria renews plea 3-30; Jumblat hints OK 3-31; Syria for Franjieh resignatn 4-1, 225E1
Leb: Syria halts arms, food 3-29, 3-30, 225A2-B2
US plans civilian removal 3-29, 226F1
Hussein asks Syrian troops 3-30—4-1, 225D1, 226F2-C3
US backs mediation moves 3-30, 226G1
Rpt Syria asks US, France, Vatican guarantee vs Israel move 3-30, 226A3
PLO, Sovts warn US on fleet 3-30, 4-8, 241F2, 242B1
US pres campaign issue 3-30, 245B3
US mediator arrives 3-31, 225B1, 226E1
USSR offers mediation 225C1
League vs UN role 3-31, 226D2
10-day truce OKd; Syria, PLO role cited 4-1, 225A1
US envoy sees ldrs 4-1—4-5, 241E2
Truce starts 4-2; fighting rptd 4-2—4-7, 241A1
Rpt Syrians take 3 Moslem ports, block arms 4-4, 241E1
Saiqa takes oil refinery 4-4, 241G1
Sadat urges Franjieh quit, blames Syria for war 4-4, 275D1
Syrians shell UK ship 4-5, 241G1
Saiqa scores Jumblat 4-5, 241C2
French dispatch mediator 4-8, talks open 4-10, 258D1
US mediatn effort continues 4-8, 4-10, 4-12, 258E1
Libya, Algeria, Niger vs interventn 4-8, 372B1
Syria troops move in 4-9—4-13; left, PLO protest 4-11—4-14, 257A1, C1, B2
Kissinger on Syria troop move 4-9, 257D1
Parlt to meet in new site 241C1, C2
Parlt OKs const amendmt on Franjieh successn 4-10, 257C1, C2
10-day truce extended, fighting continues 4-11, 257B1, D2
Syria-Israel consultatns rptd, Israel Cabt briefed 4-11, 258B1
US: Syria incursn 'show of force' 4-11, 258D1
Assad warns vs war, airs Jumblat talks 4-12, 257F1
Israel sets 'red line' on Syria incursn 4-14, 257B1
US warns Syria vs Israel provocatn 4-14, 257F2
Mil clashes 4-14—4-22; new truce fails 4-20, PLA take up Beirut posts 4-21, 273B2
Leb: Syria blocks food trucks 4-15, 273D2
Israel cautions Syria on role 4-15, 4-16, 274C1
Arafat, Assad announce peace plan 4-16, 273A1
Jumblat backs peace plan 4-16; Christians split 4-17, 4-19, 273E1
Revived Higher Mil Com meets 4-19—4-20, 273F2
US lauds Syria, Israel restraint 4-19, 4-20, 274B1
Peace plan 'secret clauses' denied 4-20, 274A1
Moslems demand Franjieh quit, threaten takeover 4-22, 273G1
Franjieh signs charter amendmt 4-24, pres electn set 4-27, 295F3-296F1
Jumblat plans leftist admin, Syria scores 4-24, 296D1
Moslems vs electn date 4-25, 4-27, 4-28, 295G3
Assad sees Syrian pres on electns 4-26, 295G3
Edde nominated pres 4-26, 296B1
Jumblat chrgs Syria electn role 4-28, 296B1
Chamoun asks electn delay 4-28, 296C1
Israel wary of interventn, warns Syria 4-28, 296F1
Baathists vs Jumblat electn stand 4-29, 296C1
75 die in clashes 4-29, 296F1
Major clashes erupt 4-30; subside 5-5, 318D3, 319E1-C2
Pres electns delayed 4-30, 318D3
Syria vs electn delay 4-30, 319C1
US envoy rpts to Ford, Kissinger; returns Beirut 4-30; leftists score 5-2, meets Karami 5-4, 319D1
Moslems back Edde 5-1, 319B1
Moslems OK truce extensn 5-2, 319G1
Jumblat chrgs Syria plot 5-3, asks Syria troop exit 5-4, 319C1
PLA sets up buffer zone 5-5, 319C2
Rpt PLA enters fighting 5-5, 338C1

1977

ARAB Policies & Actions—*See ARAB-Israeli Developments, EGYPT-Israel Peace Moves and other appropriate subheads in this section; also ARAB Countries under 'A'; country and organization names*

ARMAMENTS—*See under 'A'; also country names*

1978

ARAB Policies & Actions—*See ARAB-Israeli Developments, EGYPT-Israel Peace Moves, LEBANON and other headings in this section; also ARAB Countries under 'A'; country and organization names*

ARMAMENTS
Syria-Sovt deal rptd 1-11, 42C2
Egypt, France rptd in Mirage talks 2-13, 98B3
Syria gets more Sovt arms 2-24, Egypt scores 2-25, 139E2, G2
Egypt cites Syria's war tank losses 2-25, 139A3
Egypt said to order French jets 3-1, 139B2
France signs AIO pact, UK deal cited 3-14, 237B1
Israel rpts Sovt arms capture in Leb 4-12, 256D3
Iraq seizes Fatah arms plant, China cargo 7-17, 546C3
Assad in USSR, Syria gets more arms 10-5—10-6, 762C2

1979

Palestinian-Israeli Conflict—*See also 'Israeli Occupation Policies' above; also LEBANON and 'Rights and Recognition Issues' under PALESTINIAN Developments below*
Maalot raid, 3 PLO men slain 1-13, 28C2
Arafat asks more raids vs Israel 1-18, 50E2
PLO shells Israeli towns 1-19–1-20, 1-23, 50B3, E3
6 pro-PLO Arabs ousted from Hebrew U 1-25, 69E2
Bomb kills 2 in Natanya 1-28, 3d victim dies 1-30, 69B2
Israel Arab students back PLO terror 1-29, 69E2
Dayan sees PLO role, policy shift denied 2-13; reactn 2-14, 144C1
Syria cites Arab prisoner rights abuse by Israel 2-23, 148B3
Israeli-guerrilla prisoner swap 3-14, 178E2-A3
Israel bombed re Egypt pact 3-23, 3-27, 222G1, E2
PLO bomb blast in Tel Aviv 4-10, Israel jets retaliate 4-10–4-11, 278C2
4 PLO gunmen slain in Israel, Jordan warned 4-15, 278E2
6 PLO guerrillas slain in Israel 4-16, 278G2
El Al jet raid in Brussels thwarted 4-16, 278A3
Nahariya raid, 3 Israelis die 4-22; Egypt, US deplore raid, reprisal 4-22–4-24, 296D2, F2-B3
Israel sets death penalty for terrorists 4-29, 319C3
Begin asks Arabs solve refugee problem 5-7, 341F1
PLO blasts Tiberias 5-14, Petach Tikva 5-23, 378G1, B2
Israel gunboat sinks terrorist vessel 6-3, 415A1
Israel govt wins confidence vote on Arab slayer leniency 7-4, 496D2
Israel sentncs 2 for '76 jet plot 9-11, 677D2
Israeli slain in Jerusalem 9-16; 2 die in Jerusalem blast 9-19; US black ldr deplores 9-20, 694D2
Israel convicts 2 terrorists 10-23, sentences to life 10-25, 802C1
PLO denies Lisbon ambush role, Israel blames PLO 11-13, 882C1
Israelis block naval raid, kill 2 11-19, 882D1
Jerusalem bus blasts injure 11 11-19, 882E1

ARAB Policies & Actions—*See ARAB-Israeli Developments and other headings in this section; also ARAB Countries; country names*

ARMAMENTS
Iraq, Syria MiG-23 buildup rptd 2-13, 143A3
Libyan '71, '75 A-bomb bids rptd 4-14, 299C3
USSR T-72 shipmt to Syria rptd, Israel arsenal compared 8-28, 643B2

1980

Israel decisn on capital scored by Iran 8-6, 635A2
Egypt bars autonomy talks renewal on law 8-9; Sadat, Begin notes rptd 8-11, 8-12, US calls law 'obstacle' 8-12, 627C1
Saudi urges holy war vs Israel 8-14, 627F2
Sadat says law blocks autonomy talks 8-15, 627A2
UN Cncl scores Israel policies, US abstains; Muskie explains 8-20, 627C2
Israel vs US abstentn on UN res 8-21, 643B2
Mayor Kollek vs parlt law chng 8-23, 643D2
4 Latin natns, Dutch to move embs; Arab threats cited 8-26, 643E2
Begin defends capital status move; scores US stand, Saudi threat 8-28, 660G2
Colombia sets emb shift, Turkey to close consulate 8-28, 660C3
US seeks Israel 'good-will gesture' 9-2, 660G2
Guatemala, DR emb shifts rptd set 9-7, 800E3
Islamic Conf vows holy war 9-20, 736D2
Christian group backs as unified capital 9-22, Israelis, Christians march 9-30, 800C3
E Jerusalem shops vandalized by Arab youths 11-20, 895E1
E Jerusalem riot quelled, 30 Arabs arrested 11-28, 912G1
Arabs ask Madrid CSCE aid 11-28, 950F2
Turkey cuts Israeli ties 12-2, 912A1, C1
UN vs Israeli annexatn 12-15, 952G2
Begin, Sadat reaffirm peace process 12-18; Linowitz lists obstacles 12-19, 952F3

Lebanon—*See LEBANON--Military Developments*

Palestinian Autonomy
Begin, Sadat meet in Egypt; Sadat offers Gaza, W Bank plan 1-7—1-10, 12E1
Egypt vs Israel plan 1-17; Israel sees Egypt 'hardening' 1-20, 48B2
Saudis hopeful re US recognitn 1-26, 65C1
US' Linowitz sees Hussein 1-26, Sadat 1-29, W Bank notables 1-30, rpts progress 1-31—2-1; briefs Saudis 2-2, Moroccan king 2-4, 89F1, D2
Irish forgn min backs 2-10, 284C1
9th round held in Holland 2-27—2-28, 179A3
Canada envoy issues rpt, backs closer ties 2-29, 230C3
French pres backs, urges PLO role in talks; Israel protests 3-3, 3-9, 179G3, 180E1
Talks speedup agreed 3-17, 219F1
Carter invites Begin, Sadat 3-19; meets Sadat on talks impasse 4-8—4-9, 260F2, B3
Sadat demands deadline 3-21; Egypt, Israel discount 3-27, 219D1
Linowitz sees Begin on impasse 3-25, 219G1-A2
US vs French stand 3-31, 260F3
Carter sees Begin 4-15—4-16, Sadat OKs talks speedup 4-16, 284F1, A2
Hussein vs Israel Labor Party plan 4-23, 325C1
Israel Labor Party ldr gives Carter W Bank plan 4-24, 324G3
Begin vs PLO talks 4-28, 418C2
US vetoes Palestinian state at UN 4-30, 325D1
Talks held 5-1—5-7, Egypt suspends 5-8, US asks renewal 5-13; Egypt OKs 5-14, again suspends, Israel reactn 5-15, 362D1, B2
Arafat warns W Eur, France on pro-Israel stand 5-18, 418F1
Islamic Conf backs PLO 5-22, 395C3
Saudis propose peace role 5-25, Begin asks Fahd to address parlt 5-27; Israeli, Fahd reactn 5-28, 395G1
US cautions W Eur vs UN Cncl Res 242 chng, UK request cited 5-31, 417F2, 418B1
French-Vatican talks 5-31, 476D3
Egypt PLO briefing on talks rptd 6-7; Begin vs move 6-8, 434A2
US seeks talk renewal 6-8; Israel, Egypt OK 6-9; US announces 6-11, 434C1-A2
Muskie urges Egypt, Israel effort 6-9; Begin opposes setlmt remark 6-10, 434E1
EC backs PLO peace role 6-13; US, PLO, Israel reactn 6-13—6-15, 449A1
Hussein sees Carter in US, vs joining talks 6-17—6-18, 450A1
Pope urges just attentn 6-21, 474D2
NATO backs 'legitimate rights' 6-26, 490A1
Israel W Bank, Gaza mil plan released 6-27, 491F1
Talks renewal OKd 7-2—7-3; talks held 7-13—7-15, 538E3-539E1
UN Assemb meets 7-22, backs Palestine state, US vs 7-29, 572E1
Waldheim backs Palestine state 7-25, 7-28, Israel rebukes 7-28, 572F2
Jewish youth killed in Antwerp 7-27, Palestinian seized 7-28, 573D2
Egypt scores Jerusalem claim, threatens talks suspensn 7-30, 572E3
EC peace missn aide meets Begin 7-31—8-1, Arafat 8-4; Israel chrgs Arafat 'double talk' 8-5, 585E2-586D1
Saudis, Kuwait freeze loans to World Bank 8-2, 592A2
Sadat seeks delay in talks re Israel Jerusalem stand 8-3; US responds 8-4, Begin 8-8, 585A1, F1

1976

Syria vs pres electn delay 5-6, 337D1
Moslems urge gen strike 5-7, 337C1
Sarkis elected pres 5-8; Franjieh delays resignatn 337A1
Sarkis seeks war end 5-8—5-12, 337C1
Moslems vs Sarkis electn 5-8, 337E1
PLA-Leb clash 5-8, 337F2
22 Saiqa men die in clashes 5-8, 337G2
Fatah-Leb tie charged 5-10, 337F1
Palestinian interventn chrgd 5-10, 337G1
Christian-Syria link chrgd 5-10, 337G1
Sarkis offered Moslem cooperatn 5-10, 5-11, 337A2
Ain Tur battle 5-10, 337G2
Beirut, other clashes 5-10, 5-12—5-13, 338A1
Gemayel for Syrian troops 5-11, 337C2
US envoy ends mission 5-11, 337C2
Iraq chrgs Syria interventn 5-12, raid on Baath aide home 5-13, 337D2
PLO chrgs Syria hit refugee camp 5-12, 354G2
Saiqa takes Tripoli points 5-13, 338C1
Clashes, hundreds die 5-13—5-20, 354E2
PLO asks Islamic Conf aid 5-13, 373A2
PLO asks Syria, PLA end role 5-14, 354F2
PLA quits Beirut buffer zone 5-14, 354C3
Truce set 5-14, ignored 5-15, 354D3
PLA force quits Tripoli 5-15, 354A3
Libya mediation 5-17—5-18, 355B1
French-US talks 5-17—5-18, France offers peace force 5-21; US, Arab reactn 5-21—5-24, 369A1-B2, 372A2
Sarkis talks to Moslems 5-20, 369B2
Clashes, 125 die 5-20—5-24, 369D2
Ahdab quits armed forces 5-21, 369B2
Edde claims Phalangist death plot; rival forces clash, 30 die 5-23, 369F2
Chamoun denies arms purchased in Egypt 5-24, 369E2
Edde wounded in ambush 5-24, 370A1
Saiqa clashes with Fatah, Leb Arab Army 5-25, 370C1
France denies troop offer 5-26, 385E2
Jumblat's sister slain 5-27, 385D2
Sarkis mtg with Jumblat canceled, sees Khatib, Saiqa 5-27; meets PLO, Syrian officers 5-28; urges ceasefire 5-31, 385D2
300 die in escalated fighting 5-29—5-30, 385C2
Syrian troops invade, disarm Bekaa leftists, PLO 5-31—6-2, 385A1
Jumblat scores Syria invasn, blames Karami, Franjieh 6-1, 385D1
US, Israel reactn to Syrian invasn 6-1, 6-2, 385F1
Kosygin in Syria, communique issued 6-1—6-4, 385A2, 406F2
Jumblat meets Sarkis, Gemayel 6-2, 385E1
Egypt vs Syrian invasion 6-3, 406E1
Reagan scores US inactn 6-3, 410G1
Leb leftists, Palestinians form joint command 6-5, 405G1
Syrian air strikes, camps shelled; Saiqa Beirut strongholds taken 6-6—6-7, 405C2
4 Syrian tanks destroyed 6-6—6-7; Beirut airport closed 6-7, 405F2
Christians back Syrian invasn 6-6, 406A2
Saiqa battle 6-7—6-8, Ruessat Sofar 6-8, 405G2
Syria reinforces, 12,000 total 6-8, 406B1
Arafat: Syrian 'massacre' 6-8, 406C1
Truce set 6-9; Arab League OKs peace force, fighting eases 6-10, 405A1
Syrian drive slowed 6-9, 406D1
USSR asks end to forgn role 6-9; Syria denies interventn 6-10, 406E2
Nablus Arabs vs Syrian invasn 6-9, 406B3
Franjieh, Gemayel vs peace force 6-10, 405D1
US backs Arab peace moves, cautious on peace force 6-10, 406C2
Syrians tighten Beirut hold, reinforce troops, push near Israel border 6-10—6-15, 429F1, A3
Christians vs Arab League troops 6-11, 6-15, 429D2
Libya mediates 6-11—6-16, 429F2-A3
Riad discusses Arab peace force 6-12, 6-15, 429E2
Syria bars exit, chrgs plot vs peace 6-13, 429G1-B2
Israel sees no Syrian threat 6-13, 430C1
US, Israel talks on crisis 6-14, 430B1
Syria scores troop foes 6-15, 429C2
Israel vs Syria, PLO control 6-15, 429G3
US amb, aide, driver slain; US reaction 6-16; 3 seized, PLO deplores 6-17, 425A1-E2
US weighs evacuation 6-17, 425C2
Assad meets French pres on crisis 6-17—6-19, 448C3
US emb asks US natls leave 6-18; Navy evacuates US, forgn natls 6-20, 447F3, 448B1, 451B1
US amb, aide bodies taken to Syria 6-18, flown to US 6-19, 448F1
Fighting delays UK evacuatn convoy 6-19—6-21; leaves with 200 6-22, 448A1
Syria vs PLO in peace moves 6-19, 448D3
US thanks PLO for evacuation aid 6-20, 6-21, 448D1
Jalloud ends mediatn 6-20, 1st Arab League peace force arrives 6-21, 448B2
League head sees 1,000-man force, Arab wariness rptd 6-20, 448F2
Jalloud vs Arab peace-force lag 6-21, 448F2
Sadat, Arafat, Khalid meet in Riyadh 6-21, 448F3

1977

1978

Egypt-Israel-Saudi Plane Package
F-plane sales planned 2-14; Israel deplores, other reactn 2-14—2-15, 97A1-E2
Dayan sees Carter, Vance; warns vs jets to Saudi 2-16, 139F1
Israel vs sale to Saudis, US reassures 2-16, 139G1
Carter defends sale 2-17, 123C2
Vance: Saudi jet transfer to Arabs barred 2-21, 139E1
Vance calls sale pkg deal 2-24, 139B1
Egypt said to order French jets 3-1, 139B2
US Jewish aide quits Carter staff 3-9, 176D2
Saudis press F-16 sale, US sen sees no sale 3-14, 176G3
Saudis rptdly hired US pub relatns co 3-31, 236F3-237B1
US assurnc to Israel on F-15s to Saudi rptd 4-10, 257G1
Carter reaffirms pkg deal, bars legis delay 4-25, 307A1, B1
Dayan opposes deal 4-27, 299F2
Carter optimistic re legis 5-4, 321D2
Israel promised more F-15s 5-9, Saudi curbs rptd 5-10, 357D1, A2
US Sen com splits vote on pkg, refers issue to Sen 5-11, 357G2
Saudis vs conditns 5-12, stress need for F-15s 5-13, 358D2
US Sen OKs package; debate detailed, Carter effort rptd 5-15, 357A1
Saudi security needs revealed to Sen 5-15, 357C2
Carter lauds vote 5-15, 358A1
US reassures sale opponents 5-15—5-16, 5-18, 358B1
Israel scores US Sen OK; Egypt, Saudis laud 5-16, 358G1
Saudis deny funds to Egypt 10-19, delivery delayed 10-20, 783B2

U.S. Developments—*See also 'Egypt-Saudi-Israel Plane Package' in this section above*
Sadat seeks arms 1-20, Syria scores 1-22, 41G1, 42E1
Israel A-weapon capability rpt released 1-26, 61F1
Sadat presses US 2-3—2-8, Begin scores 2-8, 77A1, G2-78D1
F-planes sought by Egypt 2-6, 2-7, 78B1
Carter vows sales cut 2-17, 123D2; Admin forgn mil aid cut proposed 2-22, 127F1
Libya plane sale blocked 2-21, 139C2
Israel seeks arms 3-8, 176E3
AIO pact cited 3-14, 237C1 ★
Saudis hire US firm as F-15 lobbyist 3-31, 236F3-237B1
Israel arms agrmt breach hinted 4-5, Israel denies 4-6, 236C2
Israel illegal use of cluster bombs in Leb chrgd 4-6, 4-7; curbs sought 4-12, 256F3
US, Israel talks on cluster bomb use rptd 4-13, 300A2
Israel calls cluster bomb use a mistake 4-20; Gur rpts '76 use vs PLO 4-21, 300G1
Israel agrmt on cluster bomb use rptd 5-12, 358G2
US church group scores Israel on cluster bombs 5-12, 358B3
'77 arms bid rejctns rptd 5-19, 387A1
US OKs Israel Kfir jet fighters sale to Taiwan 7-2, 7-4; Taiwan rejcts 7-6, 524D2
US sales policy assessed 7-16, 564G1, B2
Camp David summit pact sets limits 9-17, 711B2
Carter signs '79 aid authorzn 9-26, 734D1
Carter signs '79 aid funds 10-18, 862D2

1979

Egypt-Israel-Saudi Plane Package
US-Saudi talks on Egypt jet funds rptd 5-8, 341C2
Egypt sees Saudi reneging on jet funds 5-12, 360A1

U.S. Developments—*See also 'Egypt-Israel-Saudi Plane Package' in this section above*
N Yemen, Sudan sales pledged 2-11, 143C2
Israel asks F-16 shipmt speedup 2-13, 143G2
Egypt asks jets, other arms 2-16–2-18, 143C3
US sends warships 3-5, offers F-15s to back Saudis war 3-7, 157E2-158A1
Israel asks arms speedup 3-17, 198C2
Israel F-15 use in Leb cited 6-27, 475G1, A2
Jordan to get M-60 tanks 7-26, deal delayed 7-31, 574A3
Israel '52 pact breach hinted 8-7, 592D1
Israel, Egypt ask more aid 9-11, 677A2
Israel seeks aid vs Arab threat 9-12–9-14, 693B2
Israel use of F-15s vs Syria backed 9-25, 740D2

1980

Moslems in US pro-Palestinian marches 8-7, 8-8, 635F1
Egypt bars early talks renewal 8-9; Begin, Sadat notes rptd 8-11, 8-12, US asks talks resumptn 8-12, 627C1
Sadat asks new 3-way summit 8-15, Begin cool 8-19, 627F1
US seeks talks renewal 9-1—9-3; Israel, Egypt OK; summit conf with US planned 9-3, 660C2
Carter bars PLO ties 9-4, 681F3
2 CP Knesset members meet Arafat, 3 W Bank mayors 9-25, 736E3
Carter scores World Bank-IMF politics 9-30, 762B1
US-Israel prelim talks 10-12—10-13; formal talks, progress rptd 10-14—10-15; Israel denies major concessn 10-14, 775G2
Gulf states tighten Palestinian curbs 10-22, 821B2
Sadat, Navon meet on new approaches to talks 10-26—10-30, 822D3
Arafat addresses UNESCO conf 10-27, 821E3
Sadat: Reagan electn will slow talks 11-5, 841B2
NCC urges PLO role 11-6, 864B1
Israel Labor Party proposes Jordan-Palestine state 11-8; plan scored 11-9, 863B3
Begin, Carter meet, stress talks 11-13, 880E2
Sadat warns Reagan on Arab policy 11-23, 894F1
Arabs ask Madrid CSCE aid 11-28, 950F2
Pro-PLO Israeli Arab conf banned 12-1, 912D1
Talks suspended pending Reagan Admin 12-4, 912B3
US Sen Percy support of Palestinian state rptd 12-5, Reagan aides, others disavow 12-7, 12-9, 931B1
Reagan backs Camp David process; Linowitz gives progress rpt 12-7, 930C3
Peres outlines peace plan 12-17, 966F1
Begin, Sadat reaffirm process 12-18; Linowitz lists disagrmts 12-19, 952F3

1976	1977	1978	1979	1980

Moslem-Christian fighting resumed, 2 refugee camps attacked 6-22—6-23, 448D2, A3
Jalloud seeks to implement pact 6-22—6-23, 448G2
Some Syrian troops leave 6-22—6-23, 448A3
Beirut airport reopened 6-23, 448C2
Pro-Syrian gen freed 6-23, 448F2
Syria, Egypt back peace talks in Arab country 6-24, 449C1
Christians press drive on 2 refugee camps, airport; leftists launch diversionary actns 6-24—6-29, 463B2
Syrians quit Beirut field 6-24, rpt more League troops brought in 6-28, 464A1
Israel gives med aid, food to war victims 6-24, 527F3
Egypt vs Christian drive 6-25, 6-28; asks forgn mins meet 6-29, 463F3
Syrian attacks chrgd 6-28, 6-29, 463B3
Khalef, Jumblat warn vs refugee camp attacks 6-29, 463C3
Jalloud rebuffed on refugee camps, returns Libya 6-29, 463D3
Saudis, Sudan lag on peace force 6-29, 463E3
Jalloud scores Libya, Syria re peace force 6-29, 463E3
Christians take Jisr al-Pasha camp 6-29, leftists rpt Syrian aid 486A3, C3
League truce effort fails 6-29, 486B3
Leftists: Syrians attack Saida 6-29, 486C3
Franjieh vs Libya in peace force 6-30, 487B2
Christians attack Tel Zaatar 7-1, capture rpt denied 7-5, 486D3
Saudis, Sudanese join peace force 7-1, 487G1
League sets truce 7-2, ignored 7-3, 487F1
Khalef warns vs Tel Zaatar capture 7-3, 487A1
Beirut-Damascus road clashes 7-3, 487G1
Libya chrgs Sudan-US collusn 501F3
Red Cross aid in Tel Zaatar prevented 7-5, 487C1
Chekka clashes bar League mediatn 7-5—7-7, 487D1
Sudanese, Libyans clash 7-5, 487A2
Christians take Amioun, Chekka; Syria role chrgd 7-8, 514C1
Arab mediatn fails 7-8, 7-12—7-13, 514C2
PLO chrgs Syria threat vs Beirut 7-8, 514C3
Enfeh under siege 7-9, falls 7-11; Christians in Tripoli suburb 7-12, 514D1
Syrians shell oil tank near Saida 7-9, 514B2
Epidemic warning issued 7-9, 514B3
3-day death toll at 3,866 7-10, 514E1
Syrians shell 2 refugee camps 7-10, 514E1
Arafat, leftists ask Egypt, other Arab aid 7-11, 514F2-A3
Natl Union Front formed vs Syrians, Palestinians 7-11, 514C3
Syria eases Saida siege 7-12, PLO denies 7-13, 514A2
Chamoun bars truce 7-12, 514E2
Phalangist mil head slain at Tel Zaatar 7-13, 514F1
Syrians enter Baalbek 7-13, 514G1
Rpt Sovts seek to bar Moslem defeat 7-13, 514D3
Syrians lift Saida siege 7-13—7-14; pressure Tripoli 7-14—7-15, 527D2
PLO gets Syria peace plan 7-14, 528D1
PLO asks Sovt pressure vs Syria 7-15, 528E1
Rptd Libya terror target 7-15, 531E1
US plans evacuatn 7-16, leftists fear anti-Moslem drive 7-17—7-18; evacuatn delayed 7-19, 527E1
Syrians reinforcemts at Maasna 7-17; clash near Sofar 7-19, 527F2
Tel Zaatar clashes, wounded removal plan fails 7-18—7-21, 527G2
24-hr death toll 158 7-19, 527G2
Rpt Sovts asks Syria pullout 7-19, 528F1
Sudan, Egypt, Saudi back League peace force 7-19, 531B3
Rpt Israel ships arms to Christians 7-20, Israel denies 7-22, 527D3
Syria defends mil presence 7-20, 528G1-B2
Saudi peace troops deployed 7-21, 527C3
PLO-Syria peace talks 7-21—7-22, 528C1
Moslems form civil govt 7-22, 527G3
Red Cross Tel Zaatar evacuatn fails; shelling continues, water supply cut, 500 feared dead 7-23—7-27, 546B2, A3
League sets new truce 7-24; Saudi, Sudan troops fired on 7-25, 546D1, F2
Christians vs troop rplcmt 7-25, 546A2
League presses truce talks 7-26, 546B2
US evacuates 308 forgn natls, thanks PLO 7-27; Israel rues 7-28, 546A1
Syria, PLO talks rptd 7-27, 546E1-A2
6 die in Junieh Christian clash 7-27, 546B3
Syria, PLO sign peace pact 7-29, 546C3-547D1
Israel aids refugees 7-29—8-6, 578C2
Arafat disavows Syria pact, Egypt chrgs coercn 7-30, 577G2
PLO, Leb Arab Army protect US aides 7-30, 8-2, 578F2
Israel presses Leb border patrols 8-2, 578D1
Tel Zaatar wounded removed 8-3, 8-4, 561A1
Truce signed, fails 8-4, 8-5, 577F1

1976	1977	1978	1979	1980

Israel-Leb Arab Army talks 8-4, 578A2
Truce group talks delayed 8-5, 8-7, 577G1
Iraqi troop role chrgd 8-5, 8-7, 577B2
Israel seizes ships 8-5, 8-10, 578E1
90 Tel Zaatar wounded removed, evacuatn suspended 8-6, 577E1
Salam, Gemayel meet 8-7; Khatib scores 8-8, 578C1
Libya jet interventn chrgd 8-9, 577D2
Limited Beirut truce ignored 8-9, 577F2
Final Tel Zaatar drive launched 8-10; 12,000 refugees flee, camp captured 8-11—8-12, 577A1
Left vs truce group 8-10, 577E2
Moslems meet on Tel Zaatar fall 8-12, 577E1
Palestinians meet on Tel Zaatar fall, anti-Syrian force sought 8-13, 617G2
Jumblat plans 'popular army' vs Syria 8-13, 617G2
Tel Zaatar losses, atrocities rptd 8-13, 617G3
Arafat chrgs Tel Zaatar 'massacre' 8-13, 618B1
Phalangists see new drive 8-13, 618B1
Egypt chrgs Syria re Tel Zaatar loss 8-13, Syria rebuts 8-14, 618C1
Syria curbs border traffic, sends in more troops 8-13, 8-16, 618F1
Gemayel: partitn a 'reality' 8-14, 618E1
Leb army units deployed 8-14, 618A2
Khalef sees long war 8-15, 618D1
Christian-Moslem clash in mt 8-15, 618B2
Franjieh truce bid 8-16, left rejects 8-17, 618E2
Israel blockade rptd 8-16, Peres denies 8-17, 618F2
Syrians hit in guerrilla raids 8-17, 618D2
US GOP platform text cites 8-18, 609E1
Pact bars civiln shelling 8-18; violated 8-19, 629A1
7 Syrians die in ambush 8-18; Syrians enter Bednayel 8-19, 629B1
Rpt Syria sets peace deadline 8-19, 628B3
Libya mediates Syria-PLO feud; left vs Syria truce com plan 8-19, 628C3
Arab mt peace plan rejected 8-20, plan pressed 8-25, 629C1
Tripoli area fighting 8-21—8-24, 629E1
2 US aides meet Christn ldrs 8-22—8-24, Jumblat scores missn 8-23, 628D3, 629A1
Jumblat sees long war 8-23, 628G3
Beirut fighting 8-23—8-24; shelling ebbs after pact 8-25, 629G1
Arab League seeks summit 8-24—8-25, 628G2
Karami: Leb to be at summit 8-24, 628A3
2 US oil firms quitting 8-25; Pan Am drops employes 629A2
Arab League peace plan discussed 8-26—8-27; Syria informed 8-29, 662E3
Sovt asks Syria troop exit 8-27, 8-29; Leb amb vs views 8-31, 642B1
PLO orders army draft 8-28, 663B2
Christian-Palestinians clash near Israeli border 8-30, 9-1, 641F2-642A1
Israel tightens security 8-31; rpt vows aid to Christians 9-1, 642A1
Sarkis meets Assad on ties 8-31, plan rptd 9-3, 662G3
League-PLO talks 8-31, 663A1
150 die in Beirut clashes, limited truce at palace bldg 9-3, 663F1
Al Fatah, Christians meet 9-4, 663C1
Mountain clashes, 130 die 9-4, 663G1
Arab peace force fired on 9-4—9-8, 663G1
Phalangist-Syrian talks 9-6, 663B1
Beirut crosspoint closed 9-7—9-8, 663A2
Sovts score leftists 9-8, leftists query policy change 9-9, 663D1
Clashes 9-8—9-20, 698D3-699D1
Syria warns 'mil option' 9-11, 720D2
USSR asks Syria exit 9-11, Assad rejects 10-1, 10-5, 737G1
Franjieh shifts Cabt, Karami loses power, leftists protest 9-15, 682E2
Truce talks deadlock 9-17, 9-19; Egypt, Palestinians blamed 9-19, 9-20, 698F2
Christian rivals clash 9-20, 720A3
Sarkis sworn, Moslems shun rites; Arafat vows truce; Egypt, US comment 9-23, 699E1
Sarkis truce efforts 9-23—9-24, 9-26, 720F2, G2
Sarkis moves into palace 9-24, 720G2
Sarkis accepts Karami resignatn 9-26, 720A3
Syrians, Christians open drive 9-28, 720D1
Arafat asked to back Sarkis, Syria interventn 9-28, 720D1
Arafat asks Arabs block Syrian drive 9-28, 720E1
Sadat vs Syrian drive 9-28, 720B2
Syrians, Christians rout Palestinians 9-29—10-2; truce impasse 9-30, 737A1
Egypt asks summit 9-29, 737B2
Iraq scores Syrian drive 9-29, 737B2
Saudi Golan exit tied to Syria role 738A2
Truce talks resumed 10-4, 737E1
Syrians blame Arafat 10-4, 737F1
Jumblat ordrs mobilizatn 10-6, 758C3
Israel-Christian cooperatn rptd 10-7, 758B3
Chrg Israel aids Christians 10-8, 758A3
Truce talks, agrmt rptd 10-9, 10-11, 758F1
Syrians open drive in south 10-12; Beirut area drive cancels talks 10-13, 758E1, E2

1976	1977	1978	1979	1980

1976

Syria scores Palestinians 10-12, 758C2
Arafat asks Arabs to stop Syria 10-13, 758D2
Arafat asks Saudi aid vs Syria 10-14, 779D1
Syrians take Bhamdun 10-14; fire at Saida 10-15, 779E1
Saudis ask Syrian, Palestinian truce 10-15; truce set 10-16, 779C1
Arab Riyadh conf sets truce, bigger peace force 10-17—10-18, 778A3
Christians take Hannine, Israeli role chrgd 10-17, 779G1
Christians capture Merj 'Uyn barracks 10-18, 779D2
Hundreds die in Beirut shelling 10-18—10-20, 779E2
Christians discuss Riyadh pact 10-20, 779C1
Assad, Arafat meet 10-20, 779E1
Moslems take Aichiyeh 10-20, 779E2
Truce takes effect 10-21, 778G2
Israel confirms aid to Christians 10-21, 779A2
Christian drive vs Palestinians in south 10-22—10-27, civiln exodus rptd 10-25, 798F1, D2
Israeli, Christn officers meet 10-22, 798B2
Christns ask Rabin mtg 10-24; Rabin vs 10-25, 798E2
Arab Cairo summit OKs truce 10-25—10-26; Syria gets lead role in peace force 10-27, 798A1
Israeli Mt Hermon thrust rptd 10-25, 798G2
Christians fear new Palestinian-Syrian ties 10-25, 798C3
Sovt scores West, regrets Syria role 10-25, 839D2
Israel denies troop role 10-26, 798F2
Arafat Trail rptd reopened 10-26, 798A3
Israel vs Syria-Palestinian troop moves 10-27, 798G2
Palestinians move to south 10-27—10-28, 798A3
Post-truce clashes 10-28, 11-10, 841A2
Jordan aide meets Christns 11-1, 841G1
PLO hail Ford defeat 11-3—11-4, 826C2
Hajj heads Arab peace force; Ghoneim missn ends 11-4, 841E1
US aide meets Sarkis 11-5, 841E2
Israel-Palestinian naval clash 11-6, 841B2
Sarkis asks Arab force OK 11-7—11-8; Christns concur, 11-9, 841C1
Christn rally vs Syrians 11-9, 841F1
Syrians enter east Beirut 11-10, 841A1
Palestinians clash 11-11, 861D1
21 die in Beirut shellings, abductns 11-12; 7 more 11-13, 861E1, F1
Syria completes Beirut occupatn 11-15, 861A1
Clashes, Edde escapes assassinatn 11-15, 861C1
Christns, Moslems clash in south; Palestinians fight in Beirut camp 11-18, 877E2
Israel shelled 11-19, 11-21; Palestinians claim reprisal 11-22, 877D1
Tripoli clash 11-20, 877C1
Syrians occupy Tripoli, Saida 11-21, 877A1
Israel warns vs Syria, Palestinian border actn; masses force, eases press curbs 11-21—11-23, 877B1, E1-B2
Sarkis lauds peace force 11-21, 877C1
League weighs peace force move near Israel border; Syria blames Israel for tensn 11-23, 877C2
Southern towns shelled 11-24, 894F1
Drive to clear southern border area 11-24, 894F1
Syria vs Israel border stand 11-24, 894A2
Syria anti-arms drive 11-25, 894E1
PLO chrgs Syria troop bias 11-26, 894A1
PLO bars giving up heavy arms 11-27, Syria demands 11-29, 893E2
Israel renews border warnings 11-28; for Leb army border role 11-28, 11-29, 894C2-A3
Libya troops to quit in protest 11-29, 894B2
Red Cross rpts widespread destitutn 12-2, 913G1
Arafat meets Assad, vows arms surrender 12-3, 913C1
Beirut bomb blast kills 5 12-4, Syria blamed 12-5, 913D1
Sarkis extends arms collectn deadline 12-5, 913A1
35 die in rival Palestinian clash 12-6, 913F1
Interim Cabt formed 12-8—12-9, 913C2
Moslem-Christian truce in south 12-10, 953A1
Edde escapes death try 12-11, complains to Sarkis 12-13, 953C1
Chamoun car ambushed, 2 die in shootout 12-12, 953D1
NLP accuses Phalangists, quits front, reneges 12-12, 953E1
Bomb destroys Phalangist offcl's car 12-14, 953F1
Syrians seize hostile newspapers 12-15—12-20; defend move 12-20, 953C2
Arms roundup snag 12-16, 953B2
Palestinians clash 12-17, 12-21—12-22, 953F1
War refugees return 12-17, 974E1
Syrians attacked in Beirut 12-23, 974D1
PFLP leader slain 12-24; PFLP scores death 12-25, 12-26, 973F2
Parlt OKs decree rule 12-24, 974B1
Christian-Palestinian clashes in south 12-25—12-31, 973G1
Palestinian arms moved into south 12-27, 12-28, 973B2
UAE troops arrive 12-28; Israel doubts Palestinian restraint 12-30, 973E2

1976	1977	1978	1979	1980

Egypt backs at Geneva conf 12-29, 973C1
New Leb force planned 12-29, 973E2
Beirut newspaper suspends 12-30, 974D1

Libya—*See also 'Libyan Relations' under EGYPT*
French Mirage purchase cited 1-16, 36C2
Egypt fears Sovt base, cites arms order 4-4, 275D1
Tries Leb mediation 5-17—5-18, 355B1
Seeks rejection front 5-20, 369C2
Mediates Leb crisis 6-11—6-16, 429F2-A3
Syria proposed joint front vs Israel 6-13, 429B2
Jalloud ends Leb mediatn 6-20; holds implement talks 6-22—6-23, 448C2, G2
Peace force arrives Leb 6-21, 448C2
Hijacked jet refuels 6-27, 462D3
Jalloud rebuffed, ends Leb mediatn 6-29, 463D3
Leb pres vs peace force role 6-30, 487B2
Chrgs Sudan-US collusn vs Leb, Palestinians 501F3
Clashes with Sudan troops in Leb 7-5, 487A2
Gets Arafat, Jumblat, pleas vs Syria 7-11, 514A3
Syrians lift Saida siege 7-13—7-14, 527E2
Terror plan vs Arab states, Israel rptd 7-15, 531E1
Assad defends mil role in Leb 7-20, 528B2
Arafat scores Syria pact role 7-30, 578A1
Jet shipmnt to Leb rptd 8-9, 577D2
Mediates PLO-Syria feud 8-19, 628C3
USSR backs, warns Egypt 8-30, 682C3
Rpt US sees Egypt border buildup aid to Israel 9-12, 683A1
Amb sought in Syria emb raid 10-11, 759F1
At summit on Leb war, peace force set 10-25—10-26, 798C1, E1
Troops to quit Leb 11-29, 894B2

Morocco
Rptd Libya terror target 7-15, 531E1

Palestinian Developments—*See also 'Palestinian-Israeli Developments' below; also country subheads in this section and under INTERNATIONAL Developments below; also AVIATION Incidents and UN DEVELOPMENTS below*
Mohsen sees no Geneva conf 2-27, 162C2
Arafat meets Habash 3-30, 225C2
PLO at nonaligned conf 8-16—8-20, 622C1
PLO becomes Arab League member 9-6, 663C2
US bars VOA contacts with PLO 10-8, 759C3
PLO aide seeks US office 10-19, US ousts 11-23, 878G1
Fatah suspect killed near Hebron 11-7, 895F1
Syria vs guerrilla ldrs at Natl Cncl conf 11-24; PLO scores 11-27, 894C1
PLO exec mtg, warns Syria on rights 11-26, 894A1
Rpt plans terror drive vs Arab moderates 12-2, 894D3
PLO meets 12-12—12-14, 954G1

Palestinian-Israeli Developments—*See also AVIATION Incidents below*
Jerusalem bomb blast 1-9, 19D1
Israel cntr in W Berlin bombed 2-8, 107D1
PLO bars Israel recogntn 2-15, 126B1
Israel suspends Arab paper in Jerusalem 2-19, 161D2
W Bank Arabs back PLO 3-15, 210B3
Arafat meets Habash 3-30, 225C2
PLO backers win in W Bank 4-12, 258F2
Jerusalem blast kills 2 policemen 4-28, 30 others hurt 5-3, 319G3
Tel Aviv blast injures 3 5-11, 354E2
Injured blast victim dies 5-16, 354E2
Israel kills 3 infiltrators 5-17, 354E2
PLO asked to join front vs Israel 6-13, 429B2
PLO becomes Arab League member 9-6, 663C2
5 land at Tel Aviv 9-25, named as Fatah men 10-13, 759C2
PLO for Palestine state 12-14, 954G1

Qatar
Sadat visits, gets aid vow 2-27, 162C1
At summit on Leb war 10-25—10-26, 798D1

Saudi Arabia
Scores raids on Leb camps 1-15, 17D2
French Mirage purchase cited 1-16, 36C2
Sadat visits, gets aid vow 2-21—2-26, 162C1
US Sen Stevenson rpts on visit 2-28, 161B1
Sovt links Egypt break to aid 3-22, 227E3
Hussein sees no funding for US Hawk missile sale 4-4, 242E1
Israelis force down jet 4-12, release 4-13, 258D3
Jordan says US Hawk deal off 4-14, 274B3
Rpt PLO feud settled 5-5, 319C2
Syria, Egypt talks canceled 5-19; seeks renewal 5-23, 370G1
Leb crisis talks held 6-21, 448F3
Egypt, Syria hold talks 6-23—6-24, 448G3
Lags on Leb peace force 6-29, 463E3
Joins Leb peace force 7-1, 487A2
Gets Jumblat plea vs Syria 7-11, 514A3

1976

Peace troops deployed in Leb 7-21, 527C3
Leb peace force fired on 7-25, 546F2
To get US air defense system 7-31, 561F1
US Sen com bars arms sales 9-24, Admin warns 9-27, 746A3
Egypt asks summit on Leb 9-29, 737B2
Carter, Mondale on arms sales 9-30, 725D1, 742F3
Arms sales a US pres campaign issue 9-30, 725D1, 742F3
Troops quit Golan Heights 10-4, 738G1
Gets Arafat plea vs Syria 10-13, 758D2
Arafat asks aid vs Syria 10-14, 779D1
Asks Syria, Palestinian truce 10-15; truce set 10-16, 779C1
Riyadh conf sets Leb truce 10-17—10-18, 778G2
At Arab summit on Leb war, peace force set 10-26, 798C1, D1
To seek Leb arms collectn 12-5, 913B1
Saudi killed in Iraq airport blast 12-15, 954B1
Leb war refugees fled to 974F1

Sudan

Vs hijackers landing 6-27, 462D3
Lags on Leb peace force 6-29, 463E3
Joins Leb peace force 7-1, 487A2
Libya chrgs US collusn vs Leb, Palestinians 501F3
Clashes with Libya troops in Leb 7-5, 487A2
Rptd Libya terror target 7-15, 531E1
Leb peace force fired on 7-25, 546F2
Troops in Leb clashes 9-13, 699B1
Gives PLO aide false visa to US 10-8, 878A2
At summit on Leb war, peace force set 10-25—10-26, 798C1

Syria—*See also 'Lebanon Civil War' above*

Joint Jordan war games rptd 1-18, 35B1
US, Israel reaffirm Geneva PLO bar 1-29, 60B2
Israel backs US peace moves 2-22, 145A1
Geneva conf boycott plan rptd 2-27, 162C2
US Sen Stevenson rpts on visit 2-28, 161B1
UK ship shelled 4-5, 241G1
Israel A-bomb alert in '73 war rptd 243E1
Kosygin visits 6-1—6-4, 385B2, 406F2
Iraqi troops mass 6-9, 6-12, 6-13; Syria plans countermoves 6-10, 430C1
Asked unified front on Israel border 6-13, 429B2
Pilot defects to Iraq 6-15, 430F1
Assad in France 6-17—6-19, 448D3
Egypt reconciliatn talks 6-23—6-24, 448G3
PFLP hijackers assail 6-28, 463C1
Soldier defects to Israel 9-13, 683E1
Golan Druse reunion 9-15, 683C1
Pro-Palestinians raid Damascus hotel, 5 die 9-26; 3 gunmen hanged 9-27, 720B3
Fatah denies raid role 9-26, 720E3
Sadat questns Damascus raid rpt 9-28, 720C2
Sovts ask Geneva conf 10-1, 738F1
Embs raided in Rome, Pak; PLO denies role 10-11, 759C1
Normal ties with Egypt OKd 10-18, 779A1
Iraq border shut 11-2; Iraq denies 11-3; troop-pullback pact 11-24—11-25, 895B1
Italy sentncs 3 emb raiders 11-6, 861E2 ★
Vs Palestine guerrilla ldrs at Natl Cncl conf 11-24; PLO scores 11-27, 894C1
PLO warns on rights 11-26, 894A1
Khaddam wounded 12-1, Black June blamed 12-2, 894C3
Assad, Hussein in merger talks 12-7—12-8, 913A2
PLO expansn vote impasse 12-12—12-14, 954B2
Iraq blames for airport blast 12-15, 954B1
Assad meets Sadat, Egypt union set 12-18—12-21, 954D2
Rpt ends ban on Jews 12-28, 974F1
Sadat: talks backed final peace setlmt 12-30, 973E1

Tunisia

Hijacked KLM jet refuels 9-4; pilot scores re landing 9-6, 662D2, C3

United Arab Emirates

Sadat visits, gets aid vow 2-27, 162C1
At summit on Leb war, peace force set 10-25—10-26, 798C1, D1
Troops arrive Lebanon 12-28, 973E2

Yemen, People's Democratic Republic of (formerly Southern Yemen)

Amb sought in Syria.emb raid 10-11, 759F1
At summit on Leb war, peace force set 10-25—10-26, 798C1

Yemen Arab Republic

At summit on Leb war, peac force set 10-25—10-26, 798C1

AVIATION Incidents

2 die in Tel Aviv airport blast 5-25, 370E2
Israel jet hijack in Turkey blocked, 4 die 8-11; PFLP denies role 8-12, 578A3
Egypt jet hijacked 8-23, 629B2; hijackers sentncd 9-18, 700C1
Sup Ct bars review of TWA liability in '73 case 10-12, 848B3
Turkey sentncs 2 11-16, 861C2

1977

AVIATION Incidents—*See AVIATION—Middle East Incidents*

EGYPT-Israel Peace Moves (& aftermath)

Sadat urges talks, vows visit to Israel parlt 11-9, 850D1
Sadat visit discussed 11-9—11-14; gets formal invitatn 11-15, accepts 11-17, 873A1
US lauds Sadat stand 11-10, 850D2

1978

AVIATION Incidents

Lufthansa '77 hijacker sentenced 4-25, 353F3
French slay 3 guerrillas at Paris airport 5-20, Israel role cited 5-20, 5-21; gunmen identified 5-22, 383E3
El Al crew bus attacked in London, 2 die 8-20, 638B1

Cyprus Airport Attack—*See PALESTINIAN Developments—Cyprus Terrorist Attack in this section below*

EGYPT-Israel Peace Moves (& aftermath)

Carter in talks with Hussein 1-1—1-2, King Khalid 1-3, Sadat 1-4, 1C1, 2G1
PLO vs US positn 1-1, 1-2, 1-4, 3B1
Sadat for US pressure on Israel 1-2; Egypt offcls on Palestinian stand 1-3, 2D2

1979

AVIATION Incidents

El Al jet raid in Brussels thwarted 4-16, 278A3
Entebbe hijack case declined by US Sup Ct 4-30, 364F3
Entebbe victim's body found 5-30, 429E1
Israel sentncs 2 W Gers for '76 plot 9-11, 677D2

EGYPT-Israel Peace Moves—*For post-treaty developments, see EGYPT-Israel Relations below*

Pact Talks (& Developments)—*See also 'Reaction to Treaty' below; for post-treaty developments, see EGYPT-Israel Relations below*

1980

1976

Iraq airport blast kills 3 12-14; Syria blamed 12-15; rebel Iraqis take credit 12-16, 953G2

Air France Jet Hijacking (Entebbe airport)

PFLP hijacks jet after Athens takeoff, refuels in Libya 6-27, lands in Uganda 6-28, 462C3
Israel warns gunmen 6-27, 463G1
Amin, Renard negotiate 6-28, 463A1
Hijackers score US, France, Israel, Egypt, Syria 6-28, 463B1
Hijackers demands announced 6-28, France rejects 6-29, 463C1
Kenya denies holding prisoners 6-29, 463E1
Gunman free 47 hostages 6-30, 101 7-1, 463F1
Israel, others asked to meet demands; Israel asks resistance 6-30, 463F1
Israel OKs hostage talks 7-1, 463A2
Arab League vs hijacking 7-1, 486E2
Rpt France asked Arafat role 486F2
Air France sets non stop flights to Israel 7-2, Israel asks all airlines 7-5, 486A2
Israelis land in Uganda, rescue 103, 31 die in airport clash 7-3; refuel in Kenya, return to Tel Aviv 7-4, 485A1-A2
Amin confirms raid, losses, chrgs Israeli ruse; Israel denies, accuses Uganda 7-4, 485D1-A2
Hostages, French chrg Uganda complicity 7-4; crew head denies 7-5, 485B2
Amin rptdly bars French mediatn role, repeats hijacker demands 7-4, 485C2
Kenya denies tie to raid 7-4, 486E1
Intl reactn to raid 7-4—7-5, 486F1-F2
France plans tighter security 7-4, 486A2
W Gers, Swiss vs prisoner release 7-4, 486B2
Uganda names Arab hijackers 7-5, 485F2
Israel says PFLP lost key men, cites Gers 7-5, 485F2
Amin hints reprisals, chrgs Kenya link 7-5, 486B1
Kenya: Israel violated airspace 7-5, 487C3
UK-Uganda controversy on missing hostage 7-7—7-12; Amin ousts UK aide, warns natls 7-13, 515D2
Ger convict escapes jail 7-7, 593E3
Israel details raid, Kenya stop cited 7-8; Dayan missn vetoed 7-10; Amin impersonated in raid 7-12, 514E3-515G1
Waldheim denies anti-Israel statemt 7-8, 516G1
Rpt Amin lauded raid 7-9, 515G1
Rabin chrgs Amin ties 7-11, 515B2
PFLP denies involvemt 7-11, 515C2
Missing hostage body rptd seen 7-13, 515C3
Israel scores Amin on missing hostage 7-13, 515D3
Mondale lauds Israeli action 7-15, 511C3
Uganda ousts UK envoy 7-17, UK cuts ties 7-28, 547G3, 548D1
Amin releases jet 7-21, arrives Paris 7-22, 547D1
90 Minutes at Entebbe publshd 7-26, 547F1-C2
4 gunmen retaliate in Turkey airport 8-11, 578D3
Egypt links PFLP 8-13, 629G3
GOP platform text 8-18, 604E2
Amin asks Israel compensatn 8-19, 663C3
Uganda photographer arrested 10-14; body rptd found 10-21, 874A2
Uganda issues report 11-16, 861B2

KLM Jet Hijacking

Jet seized over France, refuels in Tunis, lands Cyprus 9-4; Israel bars, gunmen give up in Cyprus 9-5, 662D2
Israelis on gunmen demands 9-5, 662B3
PFLP rptd as hijackers 9-6, 662E2
Pilot scores Tunisians 9-6, 662C3

1977

Sadat asks US Palestinian prof at talks 11-12; 2 deny bid, Israel opposes 11-15, 873D2
Begin to ask Jordan, Syria, Leb ldrs to visit 11-15, 873G1
Israel gen warns vs optimism 11-15, 873B2
US backs Sadat visit 11-15; USSR, Libya, Iraq, radical PLO groups vs 11-15, 873F2
Sadat sees Assad 11-16, 873G1
Rumania go-between role rptd 11-16, 873C2
Egypt forgn min, 2 others resign 11-17, 11-18; defns min backs Sadat 11-19, 890B2
Arab reactn to visit; violence erupts, united front sought 11-17—11-22, 890D2-D3, 894E1
US, Sovt reactn to trip 11-17—11-22, 894E2
Egypt advance party in Israel 11-18, 890A2
Begin thanks Rumania 11-18, 895B1
Sadat arrives Israel 11-19; tours Jerusalem, addresses Knesset 11-20, 889A1
Israel-Egypt phone link in operatn 11-19—11-22, 890A2
Begin, Peres address Knesset 11-20, 889B2
Begin invites Syria, Jordan, Leb ldrs 11-20, 889B2, 893E3
Sadat, Begin speech texts 11-20, 891A1-894D3
Sadat, Begin conf, final communique released 11-21, 889D2-890F1
Egypt hails Sadat return 11-21, 890F1
Syria-Egypt rift grows, Jordan tries mediatn 11-22, 894E1
Egypt envoy walks out on Syria at UN 11-22, 894F1
EC backs trip 11-22, 894G3
Egypt expels 3 PLO offcls 11-23, 909C2
Dayan asks Israel policy review 11-23, 909G2
Syria info min rules out Geneva conf 11-25, 909B2
Sadat asks pre-Geneva Cairo conf, Israel accepts 11-26; Syria rejects, sets Tripoli mtg 11-27, 909A1-A2, D2
PLO bars Cairo conf, backs Tripoli mtg 11-27, 909C2
Jordan bars Cairo, Tripoli confs 11-28, 909C2
Begin on Sadat visit, names Cairo conf envoys 11-28, 909E2
US hesitates, OKs Cairo conf 11-29, names envoy 11-30; US rptdly sought Arab, USSR Cairo acceptnc 12-1, 910B1, 913A2-E3
USSR bars Cairo conf 11-29, 910E1
UN names Cairo envoy, asks 2d pre-Geneva conf 11-29; Israel bars 11-30, 910G1
Egypt amb to Yugo quits 12-1, 930F2
Leb rejcts Cairo conf invitatn 12-1, 930F2-A3
Tripoli mtg forms anti-Egypt front: sets diplomatic 'freeze', econ boycott, Arab League debate 12-2—12-5, 929A1-B2
Begin in UK: backs Egypt pact, regrets Arab rift; urges positive Sovt role; hints W Bank concessns 12-2—12-7, 930C3
Egypt forgn min scores Sadat, cites Libya arms vow 12-3, 930D2
Egypt recalls ambs to Syria, Iraq, Libya, Algeria, S Yemen, USSR 12-4; cuts ties with Arab states 12-5, 929A1, B2
Sovt criticism continues 12-4—12-5; US, USSR confer 12-5—12-6, Vance scores attacks 12-6, 930D1
Iraq asks tough Tripoli stand, quits last sessn; scores Syria 12-5, 929E1
W Bank mayors bar Geneva role, back PLO 12-5, 930A3
Sadat scores Sovt, Arab critics; lauds US 12-6, 929C2
Sadat scores Sovt Tripoli role, Arab econ sanctns 12-6, 929D2, 930B1
Sadat closes Sovt bloc cntrs 12-7, 929B1, 930B1
Hussein sees Assad, Sadat on Arab rift 12-7—12-8, 930B2
Cairo rally backs 12-8, 930A2
Sadat meets Hussein 12-8—12-9, hints Tripoli negated '74 Rabat decisn re PLO 12-10, 953F1
Assad in Saudi, Kuwait, Bahrain, Qatar, UAE; vs Cairo conf 12-8—12-11, 954E2
Vance in Egypt, Israel, Jordan, Leb, Syria, Saudi re Cairo conf support 12-9—12-14; rpts to Carter 12-15, 953E2-954E2
Carter asks Israel respond to Sadat 'courage' 12-9, 954B1
Saudis vs Israel recogntn 12-10, 954G2
Pre-Cairo conf legal feuds setld 12-13, 953G1
Cairo conf opens; Syria, Leb, Jordan, PLO, USSR boycott 12-14—12-15, 953A1
Carter says PLO blocks peace; on Sovt role, Begin missn to US 12-15, 954B3
Begin gives Carter peace plan 12-16; says Carter OKd 12-17, 12-18, 994A3
PLO assails Carter for criticism 12-16, 995D1
W Bank mayors, PLO vs Begin plan 12-18, 12-19, 12-29, 995A3
Israel, Egypt defense mins, Sadat meet 12-20—12-21, 993G1
Cairo conf recesses 12-22, 993B2
Ismailia summit, impasse 12-25—12-26; Begin unveils plan for West Bank, Sinai Gaza, Jerusalem; Knesset OKs; text 12-28, 993A1-994A3
PLO, Libya, Iraq score Sadat-Begin moves 12-25, 12-26, 995B2

1978

Hussein vs talks role re Israel W Bank-Gaza, Jerusalem plan 1-2, 2F2
Begin vs Sadat for US pressure plea, vs Hussein for W Bank stand 1-3; lauds Carter-Sadat talks 1-4, 2B3-3A1
Shah meets Sadat, backs moves 1-9; briefs Saudis 1-10, 26C2
Joint Mil Com meets on Sinai exit 1-11—1-12, 10B1
Weizman meets Sadat 1-11, 10D1
Mil Com talks open 1-11; recess, Sinai understanding rptd 1-13, 26E1
Dayan meets Pope on Jerusalem status 1-12, 10G2
Carter: shares Sadat views 1-12, 12G1-A2
Sadat: 'no hope' for Pol Com talks 1-12, 1-13, 26A2
Egypt forgn min arrives Jerusalem, gives Sadat demands 1-15; in sharp Begin exchng 1-17, 25B1
Pol Com talks delayed, US plan ends agenda impasse 1-15, 26A1
Pol Com talks start 1-17; Sadat suspends, recalls delegatn 1-18, 25A1
Dayan: Pol Com in deadlock 1-17, 25F1
Israel airs 3-pt US proposal 1-17, 25D2
Egypt forgn min sees Begin, denies talks breakdown 1-18, 25G1
Israel Cabt vs Sadat talks suspensn 1-18, Begin rpts progress 1-19, 25B2
UK asks Sadat renew talks 1-18, 25F2
Begin, Vance meet on deadlock 1-19, 25D2
Carter State of Union Message 1-19, 29B1, B3, 31E2
Arab hardliners vs Sadat 1-19, 1-22, moderates score US 1-22, 42D1
Sadat vs Vance plea for talks renewal 1-20, 41C1, G1
Begin on talks breakdown, chrgs Egypt anti-Semitism 1-21—1-23; Egypt press denies slurs 1-24, 41E1, A2-42D1
Sadat on Pol Com talks breakdown, chrgs Israel stalling 1-21, 41F1
Israel vs Mil Com talks resumptn 1-22, 41A2
Begin notes Egypt agrmt on Res 242 1-23, 41E2
Sadat rpts private talks 1-25, 41C1
US rpts talks resumptn near 1-26, 41A1
US aide briefs Hussein 1-27—1-28; in Egypt, ends mediatn effort 1-30—2-1, 60D1
Israel OKs more Mil Com talks 1-29, talks resume 1-31—2-2, 60A1
Sadat plea to US Jews 1-29, ADL says response denied 2-1, 60B3
Sadat seeks Morocco backing 2-2, 60F1
Algiers summit held; anti-Sadat hardliners map strategy, Iraq boycotts 2-2—2-4, 78E2
Iraq seeks Syria rejectn of Res 242, 338 2-2, 78B3
Sadat presses peace drive in US 2-3—2-8; sees Carter, aides at Camp David 2-4—2-5, 77A1, F1
Sadat: Israeli setlmts major obstacle 2-5, 77B2
Sadat chrgs Israel intransigence, seeks US Jewish ldrs aid 2-6, 77C2
Sadat tours 6 Eur natns, seeks peace initiative support 2-9—2-13, 98C2-B3
2 Palestinians slay Egypt editor in Cyprus, hijack jet 2-18, 117A1, E1; **for subsequent developments, see PALESTINIAN Developments—Cyprus Terrorist Attack in this section below**
USSR scores US peace stand 2-21, 139F2
US aide resumes Cairo-Jerusalem mediatn 2-21—3-6; Syria bars visit 2-27; in Amman 3-5, Hussein vs mediatn 3-6, 156D3
Jordan gives terms for talks 2-27, 157A1
Syria bars US aide visit, discounts US missn 2-27, 157C1
Carter backs Res 242, backs Begin-Sadat talks 3-2, 140G2-D3
Begin vs US on Res 242 3-4, Dayan denies conflict 3-6; Carter reaffirms stand 3-7, 3-9; Israel oppositn scores Begin 3-7—3-9, 156G1
Begin: ready to negotiate despite invasn of Leb 3-15, 173E2
Begin in US talks with Carter 3-21—3-22, Carter stresses occupied land issue, Begin restates stance, hopes for Sadat talks renewal 3-22, 199B1
Carter: Begin talks 'halted' diplomatic process 3-23; Begin on Carter demands 3-24, 214F2, C3
Begin in US appeal 3-23, 214B3
Weizman vs US shuttle diplomacy 3-24, 214E2
Israel Cabt, parlt back Begin stand 3-26, 3-29, 214D1
Arab League seeks to end rifts 3-27—3-29, 215A1
Israel seeks new talks 3-28, 3-29; **Weizman sees Sadat 3-30—3-31,** briefs Cabt 3-31, 4-2; Sadat asks Israeli flexibility, lauds US efforts 4-5, 235F2-D3
Israeli rally asks Begin concessns 4-1, 235E3
Heykal: Sadat's moves failed 415C1
Carter, Rumania pres meet, Rumania '77 role lauded, communique asks Israel quit occupied land 4-11—4-12, 290D1
Egypt vs Parlt call for end to talks 4-13, 299B3
Waldheim to seek new formula 4-14; in Israel, Leb 4-17—4-18, 274B2, B3
Israel rally backs Begin 4-15, 300G1
Israel reaffirms Res 242 stand 4-16, 274C3-275E1
US aide in Cairo to seek talks renewal 4-21—4-25, 299A3

1979

Israel ties pact to Sinai oil access 1-5, 51B2
US seeks talks renewal 1-11; US aide in Israel 1-16–1-24, Egypt 1-25, 51E1
Canada oppositn ldr backs peace moves, PLO 57B3
US mediator meets Egypt min 1-26–1-27; sees 'gap' 1-27; mission fails 1-28, 69C1
Sadat bars concessns 2-17, 143D3
Carter urges flexibility 2-20, 123G2
Vance, Khalil, Dayan hold prelim talks 2-22–2-25, 142F2
Saudi ldr cancels US trip 2-24, 143G1
Carter asks high-level mtg, Sadat balks 2-25, 142F2
Begin hints mtg with Carter 2-26, 142A3
Dayan backs Begin, Khalil high-level talks 2-26, 142C3
Dayan rpts on prelim US, Egypt talks 2-26–2-28, 142D3
Israeli Cabt bars Begin talks minus Sadat 2-27, 142F2
Carter: differences minor 2-27, 143C1
Stalemate linked to US Dow drop 2-27, 166C2
Begin: both sides far apart 2-28, 143B1
Begin arrives US; vs 'sham' pact, meets Carter 3-1, 143D1
Begin OKs Carter plan 3-2–3-4, briefs US reps, Israel Cabt OKs 3-5, 157B1, D1
Carter trip to Egypt, Israel set 3-5; in Cairo, sees Sadat 3-8, 157A1
Begin returns, confident 3-8, 157F1
Syria scores US-proposed pact 3-8, 157F1
Carter gets both sides to agree, pact signing near 3-8–3-13; returns US 3-14, 177A1
W Bank, other Arabs protest Carter missn 3-11–3-15, 178A1
PLO, Arab states score Egypt, US, ask sanctns 3-11–3-14, 178C1
Israel Cabt debates, OKs pact 3-12–3-14; Knesset debates 3-12, 177B1, E1
Begin scores US briefings, press coverage 3-13, 177B2
Carter briefs US congressmen on trip 3-14, 177E2
Egypt Cabt OKs pact 3-15, 177C1
Egypt: pact assures Palestine state 3-17, 197F1
US missn seeks Saudi, Jordan support 3-17–3-18, Sadat briefed 3-18; Brzezinski rpts 3-19, 197B2
Hussein, Arafat unite vs treaty 3-17, 198C2
Israel NRP to quit re pact 3-18, 197B1
Israel, Egypt, US talks on Sinai pullback 3-18–3-19, US details aid 3-19, 3-20, 198F1
Pact OKd by Israel Cabt 3-19, Knesset 3-22; Sadat, Carter laud 3-22, 197A1-A2
Begin vows no Palestine state, Egypt deplores remark 3-20, 197D1
Mondale briefs Brazil pres 3-22, 248A1
Arabs protest treaty 3-23–3-27, 222G1
Carter seeks W Bank Palestinian role 3-23, 222G2
Israel, Egypt, US settle Sinai oil issue 3-24–3-25, 221F2
Treaty signed in US 3-26; text of treaty, annexes 3-28, 221A1, 223A1-226G3
Treaty Annex II maps of Sinai 249A1
US-Israel separate agrmt signed 3-26; text 3-28, 221G2, 227A1
Israel Cabt backs pact 4-1, 295D3
Egypt parlt, referendum back pact 4-10, 4-19, 295A3
Mondale briefs Dutch 4-21–4-22, 299D2
Ratificatn papers exchngd, pact in effect 4-25, 295D2-A3
US Cong OKs treaty funds bill 7-17, 7-20, Carter signs 7-25, 700A2

Reaction to Treaty

Arab League penalizes Egypt 3-27–3-31; US, Egypt score 4-1, 4-2, 248B2-D3
Egypt protests separate US-Israel pact, US assures 3-28, 222B1
Carter poll gain rptd 3-29, 231D3
Egypt recalls 7 Arab envoys 4-7, Arab retaliatn vs Egypt continues 4-10–4-18, 278D1-B2
Saudis, 4 others cut Egypt ties 4-22–4-24; Egypt cuts Kuwait, Saudi ties 4-23,
Arab retaliatn vs Egypt intensifies 4-27; Sadat assails Saudis, US disassociates 5-1–5-2, 319E1-E2
Iran severs Egypt ties 4-30, 408A2
US: Saudi ties worse 5-8, 341B2
Islamic States Conf suspends Egypt 5-9, 360C1
Arab People's Cong vows actn vs US; scores Carter, Begin, Sadat 5-10, 341D2
Arab arms plant in Egypt to close 5-14, 359E3
WHO blocks Arab anti-Israel moves 5-22, 398E2
Moslem ldr slain in Gaza, pact support cited 6-1, 414E2
French forgn min vs treaty 6-5, 485D1
Nonaligned mtg condemns pact 6-11, 437E1
PLO aide's murder linked 6-26, 552B1
Arab League defers punitive econ steps vs Egypt 6-28, 475F2
Egypt Emb in Turkey raided 7-13–7-15, 536C2
Arabs protest Sadat OAU speech 7-18, 552F1-A2
Jordan oppositn cited re US tank sale 7-26, 57'B3

1980

1976

1977

Saudis noncommittal on summit 12-25, 995B2
Sovts vs Begin-Sadat summit 12-25, 12-26, 995E3
PLO kills pro-Israel Arab 12-26, 995D2
Israel settlers vs Begin plan 12-27, 995D3
Carter lauds Begin plan 12-28, govt explains stand 12-29, 994B3, F3
Sadat foes plan new summit 12-28, 995F2
Jordan vs Begin plan 12-28, 995G2
Begin lauds Carter stand; Sadat, PLO vs 12-29, 994D3
PLO bomb kills 2 in Israel 12-29, 995F2
Carter on US stance, possible mtg with Sadat 12-30; meets Shah 12-31, 100F3, G3, 1001E1
Egypt airs counterplan 12-31, 994G3
Arafat scores Carter stand 12-31, 995B1

1978

Israel groups vs Begin policies 4-25, 4-26, 300D1
Carter lauds peace progress 4-25, 307G1
Vance, Dayan seek talks renewal 4-26—4-27, 299D2
Egypt: forgn terror group planned to attack Dec talks 4-26, 300C2
Carter backs Begin W Bank self-rule plan 4-30, Egypt reassured 5-1, 339E2
Begin sees talks breakthrough 5-1, 339C2
Cairo plan for Jordan, Egypt to get W Bank, Gaza sent to US 5-10, 5-28, 424E2
Israel staff chief doubts Egypt peace motives, for holding W Bank, Gaza 5-11; Cabt upholds 5-14, 358D3-359C1
US urges talks renewal, awaits Israel reply on W Bank, Gaza 5-19, 424C2
Israel: Egypt proposal to US 'impossible' 5-24, 424E2
Sadat urges Israel compliance 5-30, 6-6; Israel chrgs deadline pressure 5-30, 5-31, 424F1
Sadat threatens war re Israel-held Arab lands, cites Israel separate peace plan 6-7; Israel scorns threat 6-7, 6-8, 461G2
UK lauds Rumania peace role 6-14, 515C3
Israel Cabt backs Begin, defers move on W Bank, Gaza 6-18, parlt OKs 6-19; Egypt, US reactn 6-19—6-22, 461A1-F2
Egypt amb vs Sadat policies 6-19, 473A2
Egypt, Israel contacts rptd 6-21, Israel Cabt OKs 6-25, 489C1
Weizman: Sadat 'sincere' 6-23, 489G1
Egypt plans W Bank, Gaza proposal 6-24, Israel Cabt rejects 6-25; Egypt, US deplore 6-26; Begin vs Carter statemt 6-27, 488D3
Israel vs Egypt plan 6-25, 7-5, 501A2
Carter scores Israel rejectn of Egypt W Bank, Gaza plan 6-26, 491G1
Carter hints at Geneva conf 6-30; Israel, Mondale mission reactn 7-1, 502C1
Begin OKs London conf 7-2, 7-3, 502A1, B1
Egypt gives Mondale W Bank, Gaza plan, OKs London conf 7-3; plan detailed, text 7-5, 501A1, E1
Israel vs Egypt plan, OKs forgn min-Vance mtg 7-9; Sadat 'disappointed' 7-10; Israel explains rejectn 7-11, 521A1-A2
Sadat meets Peres in Austria, OKs Kreisky-Brandt peace plan 7-9; plan detailed 7-10, Dayan vs 7-13, 521A2-E2
Sadat, Weizman meet in Austria; new Egypt plan offered 7-13, 546A2
Sadat: Weizman, Peres talks 'successful' 7-14, 546C2
Israel Cabt defers actn on new Sadat plan; Weizman, Peres mtgs scored 7-16, 546D2
Egypt, Israel mins meet at Leeds Castle (UK), Vance rpts 7-18—7-19, 546C1
Begin, Peres clash on Sadat mtg 7-19, 546B3
Sadat calls Begin 'obstacle' to peace; scores Goldberg, lauds Carter 7-22, 563B1
Israel bars return of El Arish, Mt Sinai 7-23, 563E1
Dayan: offered softened W Bank, Gaza stand 7-24; Egypt rejects 7-25, 563A2
Egypt athletes to boycott 5 rejectionist states 7-24, 573C1
Egypt forgn min calls talks waste 7-26, 526A3
Egypt asks Israel mil mission leave 7-26; mission quits 7-27, 562G2
Begin: Egypt stand hardened, setback not serious 7-26, 562B3
Knesset upholds Begin policy 7-26, 563A1
Atherton meets Begin, Sadat; Saudis chrg Israel 'intransigence' 7-27—7-30, 581E2, 582C1
Sadat bars new talks, vs 'territorial compromise' 7-30; US rebukes, Begin pleased 7-31, 581E2
Fahd meets Sadat 7-30—7-31, 582C1
Nonaligned back Israeli withdrawal 7-30, 583D3
Vance: US to offer no new peace plan; US sens see hard Cairo, Saudi stands 8-1, 582D1
US sens on Egypt, Saudi hard line, urge Vance pressure talks resumptn 8-1, 582E1
Vance chrgs Sadat 'shock tactics' 8-4, 602B2
China, Yugo on dispute solutn 8-25—8-27, 675A3
US troops in W Bank, Gaza hinted 8-30, 8-31; Begin vs 8-31, US denies rpt 9-7, 673F1
Sadat, Begin win Nobel 10-27, 886D1

Camp David Summit—*See also 'Treaty Talks' below*

Carter OKs trilateral talks in US 7-31, Vance plans missn 8-4, 602B1, B2
Vance in Israel 8-6—8-7, Egypt 8-7—8-8; Begin, Sadat accept Carter summit invite, comment 8-8; Syria, PLO score 8-9, 601G2-602C2
Carter, Begin in prelim talks 9-5, 673C1
Talks start; **Carter meets Begin, Sadat 9-6—9-7, 673A1, C1**
Arabs, USSR vs talks 9-6, 9-7, 673D2
Carter defense veto upheld by House 9-7, 677E2
Leb links Syrian raid escalatn 9-10, 713B2

1979

Iraq links plotters, US 7-28, 583F1
Nonaligned natns split re Egypt expulsn 8-28–9-1, 9-3, Egypt stays member 9-9, 674F2, 675A1, E1
Qaddafi scores 'treachery' 9-1, 688A3
Sadat, Begin score Arab hostility 9-5, 658B2
Pope backs Camp David accords 10-2, 758F1
Connally scores treaty 10-11, 783B2
Castro scores treaty 10-12, 778F2
USSR sees Syria stability threatened 10-14, 857F2
UN Assemb rejects treaty 11-29; US, Israel score vote 11-29, 12-2, 979F2
Amnesty Intl scores Egypt on arrest of opponents 12-9, 980E2

EGYPT-Israel Relations

Sadat, Begin meet in Cairo; OK hot-line, other agrmts 4-2–4-3; Begin briefs parlt 4-4, 248E3
Egypt-Israel exchng on Syria war backing 4-9, 4-10, 295D3
Strauss named US mediator 4-24, 295G3-296C1
Egypt wants border opening delayed 5-23, 394D2
Vance meets Sadat in Alexandria 5-24, Israel delegatn head in Jerusalem 5-25, 394C2
Begin meets Vance, says Sadat vowed open border 5-24, 394D2
Border opening announced 5-27, 394B3
Israel frees 16 Arabs, 7 go to El Arish 5-28, 394A1, D3, 395A1
Dayan in Egypt, travel agrmt set 6-4–6-6, 415E2
Israel informs of Leb raid, Syria air clash 6-27, 475B2
Sadat, Begin meet in Haifa; OK joint Sinai patrols, oil sale 9-4–9-6, 658D1
Israel end to Arab land-purchase ban opposed 9-17, 693A1, F1, 695E1
Camp David anniv marked 9-17, 695D1
Israel W Bank setlmt expansn plan opposed 10-15, 780G1

Gaza—*For peace talks, see EGYPT-Israel Peace Moves–Pact in this section above*

Palestinian Autonomy Talks—*See also PALESTINIAN Developments–Rights and Recognition Issues in this section below*

Israel govt plan adopted, Weizman, Dayan vs; Weizman quits delegatn 5-17; Cabt OKs plan; Weizman, Dayan drop oppositn 5-21, 394E2-A3
Talks start in Beersheba, US takes part 5-25, 394E1-395C2
Talks in Egypt, Israel 6-11–6-12, 6-25,-6-26, 474A3
Sharon: US seeks Palestinian state, US denies 6-15, 474D3
Egypt ambs rptdly meet W Bank ldrs 6-16, 475B1
Weizman quits Israel team 6-17, Cabt OKs 6-24, 474C3
Alexandria, mtg, US agenda plan agreed 7-5–7-6, 511D1
Begin, Sadat meet in Alexandria 7-10–7-11; Begin hails mtg 7-12, 511F2
Sadat backs provisional Palestinian govt 7-18, 552G1
Alexandria mtgs continue 7-29–7-31; Israel chrgs US seeks state 8-1, warns 8-2, 574C3
US urges progress 8-1, 575A1
Israel bars PLO talks role 8-5, 591D2
Haifa mtg: electn procedures agreed, Res 242 chng discussed 8-5–8-7, 591G2
Alexandra mtg deadlocked 8-21, 623E3
Young stresses negotiatns 8-24, 642A2
Sadat, Begin meet in Haifa 9-4–9-6, 658D1
Strauss briefed on Haifa mtg, progress rptd 9-9–9-13, 676E2
Sadat: hopeful on Jordan, PLO role 9-9; Hussein bars talks 9-10, 676B3
Hussein vs role 9-24, 741E2
Talks held in Egypt, progress on electn format rptd 9-26–9-27, 740G2-B3
Dayan seeks deadlock end 10-18; disputes Israeli policy, quits 10-21, 10-18, 801B1
Mtgs held in London, breakthru seen 10-18, 10-25,-10-26, 822D3
Talks held in Tel Aviv 11-20, Cairo 12-12, 938C1
Linowitz in Egypt, Israel 12-8–12-12, doubts '80 setlmt deadline 12-9, 938C1
Talks held in Cairo 12-19, 979B3

Sinai—*For peace talks, see EGYPT-Israel Peace Moves in this section above; for post-pact developments, see SINAI below*

Suez—*For peace talks, see EGYPT-Israel Peace Moves in this section above; for post-pact developments, see SUEZ below*

1980

1976 1977 1978 1979 1980

Talks end: Israel, Egypt agree on framework for peace, W Bank-Gaza setlmt; Carter, Begin, Sadat sign; photo 9-17, 709A1
Map on accords 710A2
Texts of agrmts 9-17, 711A1-712C3
Carter gives details to US Cong 9-18, 709E1, E2-710B1
Carter: talks faced collapse, Sadat confrms 9-18, 710D1
Egypt Forgn Min Kamel, amb to US quit in protest 9-18, 710F3, 712C1
USSR denouces pacts, Sadat role 9-18, 712E2
Peres backs pacts; 2 Begin aides doubt 9-18, 712E3
Sadat links 2 agrmts 9-19; for Israel pact in 2 mos 9-20, 710D3
Saudi, Jordan noncommital 9-19, 712D1
PLO, Arab states meet, score pacts 9-19, 9-20, 712E1
Gush Emunim seize W Bank hill in protest 9-19, ousted 9-21, 712G2
Egypt Cabt OKs pact 9-19, Cairo seeks Arab support 9-24, 730A2
Begin: US, Israel disagree on Israeli setlmts; Sadat, Carter yielded on Golan, E Jerusalem 9-20, 710F1-G2
Vance in Jordan, Saudi; seeks pact support 9-20—9-21, 712G3-713A1
Carter stresses US peace role 9-20, 715B3
Sadat briefs Morocco king 9-20—9-23, 730A3
Conferees' letters on Sinai, Jerusalem, W Bank-Gaza released 9-22, 729F1; text 730C2-G3
Arab hardliners seek Hussein support 9-22, 9-26, Hussein fears separate Israel-Egypt pact 9-23, 730C1
Sadat on Syrian role 9-22, 730B3
Vance ends missn to Jordan, Saudi, Syria 9-22—9-24; briefs Carter 9-25, 731B1
Brezhnev scores accords 9-22, 731E1
Carter topic on pol tour; poll status jumps 9-22—9-24, 736B1
Sadat on Jerusalem stand 9-22, 892G3
Israel Cabt OKs pact, separate votes barred 9-24, 729C1
Israel Labor Party OKs pact 9-24, 729E1
Hardliners end conf; sever Egypt ties, seek USSR contact 9-24, 729F2
Israel parlt debates pact, Begin warns 9-25—9-27; pact OKd 9-28, 729A1, D1, E1
Carter prestige gain noted at IMF mtg 9-25, 731F2, 732E2
Carter vs Begin on W Bank setlmt understanding 9-27, 729D2
Assad asks Saudis rejct pact 9-27, 730A2
Carter on Israel setlmt plan 9-27, 859B1
Israel tech team in Cairo 9-28, 729B1
Vance asks Palestinians join talks 9-29, 762E2
Hussein scores separate pact 10-1, 762G1
W Bank Arabs reject pacts, want PLO state 10-1, 762D2
Sadat defends pacts; asks Saudis, Jordan join, scores hardliners 10-2, 746A2
Sadat scores Syria, Palestinian oppositn 10-10, 762E1
Syria, Iraq to fight results 10-24—10-26, 803E1
Dayan denies agrmt to suspend setlmts expansn 10-26, 802E2
Sadat, Begin win Nobel 10-27, 886D1
Carter discusses role on NE tour 10-28, 831C2
Sovts, Arafat score 11-1, 828C1
Arab summit vs, Sadat asked to drop peace moves 11-2—11-5; anti-Sadat moves hinted 11-6, 859D1
Sadat shuns Arab summit delegatn 11-4, 859B2
Carter gives midterm assessmt 11-6, 862B1
Hassan: US made vow on W Bank, E Jerusalem 11-10; US denies 11-12, 892E3-893A1
Arafat warns of effect on Palestinians 11-19, 893C1
Begin, Sadat aide accept Nobel 12-10, 950B3

Treaty Talks (Washington, D.C.)

Carter sees peace treaty despite W Bank, Gaza discord; urges Jordan, Palestinian role 10-10, 766D3
Talks open 10-12; US draft plan OKd 10-13; Carter enters talks, Dayan sees snag 10-17; US denies crisis 10-17, 10-18, 782B2
Carter intervenes, talks adjourned, Israel delegatn recalled 10-21, 802A3
Tentative agrmt announced 10-22, 802G2
Israel Cabt OKs draft, revises; Egypt to seek revisns 10-25, 802F1, B3
Israel setlmt expansn plan seen threat 10-25, US scores plan 10-26, 802F1
Egypt reverses del recall decisn after US plea 10-27, 858G2
Talks resume 10-31, 858E2
Begin meets Carter, Vance in NY 11-2; Vance optimistic 11-3, 858A3
Weizman recalled 11-2; briefs Cabt 11-5—11-6; returns to talks 11-7, 858B3
Sadat demands linkage 11-7, 858C3
Israel vs treaty-W Bank linkage 11-8; Egypt seeks text chng 11-9, 858E2, B3
Carter asks end to linkage feud 11-9, 858E3
Egypt asks W Bank timetable 11-9, demands Gaza Strip 11-14, 892B3
US proposes new plan 11-12; Israel Cabt OKs, vs Egypt timetable; Egypt recalls delegate 11-21, 892D2

1976

GAZA—*See 'Occupation Policies' under ISRAELI Policies below*
INTERNATIONAL Developments—*See also UN DEVELOPMENTS below; for oil issue, see 'Middle East' under PETROLEUM under 'P'*
Nonaligned conf scores 8-20, 621D3
Soclst Intl urges new Geneva conf 11-27, 935D3, E3
Australia
Leb secret army seized 1-27, 71G3
Jordan talks 3-2—3-9, 204C1
Austria
Sadat visits 4-10—4-12, 275E2
2 die in Tel Aviv airport blast 5-25, 370F2
China
Lauds Egypt-Sovt pact end 4-19; signs Egypt MiG parts accord, USAF comments 4-21, 275E2, B3
Cuba
Mil advisers rptd in mideast 1-10, 138F1
Troops rptd in Red Sea area 4-5, 242F1
Cyprus
Leb Christians flee to 3-28, 226D1
Israel arms to Leb rptd 7-20, 527D3
Israel seizes ship 8-5, 578F1
Hijacked KLM jet lands 9-4, 9-5, 662D2
US bars VOA contacts with PLO 10-8, 759D3
Rpt Palestinians flee Leb to Iraq 12-2, 894D3
Denmark
Lauds Israel Uganda raid 7-4, 486G1
Ethiopia
Arab aid to rebels rptd 5-18, 364F1
Europe—*See also specific countries in this section*
Israel welcomes Leb refugees 1-25, 59D2
France
Mirage sales cited 1-16, 36C2
Leb interventn plea rptd 2-2, 83F1
2 diplomats wounded in Beirut emb 3-22, 210C2
Vows Egypt arms aid 3-26, 275E1
Rpt Syria asks assurances vs Israel move in Leb 3-30, 226B3
Bonn assures Egypt on jet deal 3-30, 275B1
Sadat visits 4-3—4-5, 275B1
Mediator sent to Leb 4-8, opens talks 4-10, 258D1
Giscard sees Ford on Leb 5-17—5-18, offers peace force 5-21; US, Arab reactn 5-21—5-24, 369A1, 372A2
Denies Leb mil offer 5-26, 385E2
Sovt chrgs Leb interventn 6-9, 406E2
Assad visits, Leb discussed 6-17—6-19, 448D3
Jet hijacked 6-27, 462C2; **for subsequent developments, see 'Entebbe' under AVIATION Incidents in this section above**
KLM jet hijacked over 9-4, 662D2
Germany (West)
Rabin interview aired 1-11, 18E3
Israel cntr in W Berlin bombed 2-8, 107D1
Sadat visits 3-29—4-2, econ pact signed 3-30, 275A1
'75 exports rptd up 3-31, 270A1
US evacuates 20 from Leb 6-20, 448C1
Hijackers land Uganda 6-28, ask prisoners freed 6-29, 463A1-F1; **for subsequent developments, see 'Entebbe' under AVIATION Incidents in this section above**
Libya '72 Munich raid role rptd 7-15, 531F1
Great Britain
Kuwait buys tanks 2-16, 126B2
Syria shells ship, protests 4-5, 241G1
Leb convoy takes out body of US amb, others 6-18, 448F1
Fighting delays Leb evacuatn convoy 6-19—6-21; leaves 6-22, 448A1
US evacuates 60 from Leb 6-20, 448C1
Israel Uganda raid lauded 7-4, 7-5, 486A2

1977

GAZA—*See ARAB-Israeli Developments—Israel Occupation in this section above; for peace plans, see EGYPT-Israel Peace Moves*
INTERNATIONAL Developments—*See also EGYPT-Israel Peace Moves in this section above*
PLO rep slain in Paris 1-3, 9C1
Saudi urges French peace role 1-24, 50B2
Ivory Coast pres meets reps 1-25, briefs Rabin 2-4, 86B3
EEC bars PLO recognitn 2-10—2-12, 146G1
Austria sees PLO shift 2-13, Israel discounts 2-14, 107G1
USSR admits '67, '73 Egypt aid 2-19, 144D2
Austria backs Palestinians 2-23, 425G1
Afro-Arab summit backs PLO, scores Israel W Bank policy 3-7—3-9, 170F1
Austria-US talks 3-14, 425F1
Palestinian pilots rptd in Uganda 4-2, 308B2
Arafat visits Moscow 4-4—4-8, 297C2
Arab fund created 4-18, 317F3, 318C1
PLO stresses USSR Geneva conf role 5-1, 360E3
Venez-Saudi communique asks Palestine state, Israel W Bank exit 5-6, 362D1
USSR rpt to US: PLO may recognize Israel; US doubts 5-9—5-11, 360F2-C3, 361C1
Nixon on USSR '73 war role 5-12, 386E1
Amin Entebbe raid role rptd 6-8, 487A1
Egypt-USSR talks 6-9—6-10, 457G2
Nicaragua support of Israel cited 6-21, 656A3
EC backs Palestine homeland, Geneva conf role 6-29; Begin scores 6-30, 510C1
Kenya PLO office rptd 7-6, 588G1
USSR study chrgs US Jews role 7-22, 589A2
Rumania backs PLO at Geneva, Israel vs 8-25—8-29, 663C2
Arafat in USSR 8-30—8-31, 663C1
USSR scores US on W Bank setlmts 9-2, 685C2
Dayan in Paris 9-16, rptdly sees Jordan premr 9-20, 713G2
Gromyko meets Vance 9-30, **US-Sovt Geneva plan issued 10-1, 749B2; text 750A1**
US-Sovt plan scored by Israel, in US 10-2—10-3; PLO lauds 10-2, Iraq vs 10-3, 749F2
USSR '76 arms sales cited 10-13, 949B2
US sees better Sovt ties 10-18, 866E1
French-UK summit 12-12—12-13, 1013G1
PLO chrgs US reneges on USSR vow 12-16, 995A2
Daoud Issue
France arrests Daoud 1-7; frees; expels to Algeria 1-11, 9A1
Syria, PLO score arrest 1-9, 9C2
France bars Bonn, Israel extraditn 1-11, 9C1
Israel, US, Bonn score release; PLO lauds 1-11—1-12, 9F2
France defends release 1-13, 1-17, 27B2
US protest rejctd; Bonn, Israel continue criticism 1-13, 27E2
Carter, Giscard talks avoid 1-13; US offcls clarify stand 1-14, 27G2-B3
UK MPs aks protest, govt bars actn 1-13, 28A1
US Cong, Jews protest, back boycotts 1-13, 1-14, 1-18, 28B1
Daoud sees Israel threat 1-14, OKs Bonn trial 1-15, 27E3
Israel vows trial 1-16, 27G3
France, Israel reconcile ties 2-8, 87B1 ★
ISRAELI Policies & Actions—*See ARAB-Israeli Developments, EGYPT-Israel Peace Moves and other appropriate subheads in this section; also ISRAEL under 'I'; LEBANON under 'L'*

1978

Arafat warns of effect on Palestinians 11-19, 893C1
Egypt, Israel, US release treaty text versions 11-20, 11-24, 11-25; US 'surprised' at Egypt, Israel moves 11-23, 11-25, 930G2
Talks deadlocked; Carter deplores 11-30, 12-7, 930G1-E2
US gives Israel new Egypt stand 11-30; Sadat aide in US talks 12-1—12-2, 930F2
Carter: disappointed with setbacks 11-30, 936C2
Egypt denies Sadat protests impasse in shunning Nobel award rites 12-1, 12-2, 950C3
Vance visit to Egypt, Israel set 12-5, 930A2
Vance in Egypt, Israel; drafts new plan with Sadat; Israel vs, Vance recalled 12-10—12-15, 950C2
Carter lauds Sadat 12-13, says pact now up to Israel 12-14, 951A1
Israel Cabt, parlt rejct US-Egypt proposals 12-15, 12-19, Vance scores 12-15, 978G2
Egypt denies pact chng 12-15, 978D3
Vance briefs Carter on shuttle 12-15, 978E3
Dayan on terms for new talks 12-18, 978F3
Vance meets US Jewish ldrs, US pro-Egypt stand chrgd 12-19, 978G3
Israel halts Sinai mil gear pullout 12-20, 979B1
Vance meets Israel, Egypt mins; talk revival fails 12-24, 997E3
Sadat: Arab oppositn aids Begin to block agrmt 12-25, 997F3
Begin: ready for new talks 12-26, 997G3
GAZA—*See ARAB-Israeli Developments—Israeli Occupation Policies in this section above; for peace plans, see EGYPT-Israel Peace Moves above*
GENEVA Peace Conference—*See EGYPT-Israel Peace Moves in this section above*
GOLAN Heights—*See ARAB-Israeli Developments in this section above*
INTERNATIONAL Role—*See country names*
ISRAELI Policies & Actions—*See ARAB-Israeli Developments, EGYPT-Israel Peace Moves, LEBANON and other headings in this section; also ISRAEL under 'I'*
JERUSALEM—*See ARAB-Israeli Developments—Israeli Occupation Policies in this section above; for peace plans, see EGYPT-Israel Peace Moves above*
LEBANON—*See also LEBANON—Civil Strife under 'L'*
Israeli ground forces attack PLO bases in south, planes, boats bomb Tyre, Damur, Saida, Beirut area 3-14; 'security belt' set in south 3-15, 173A1
Leb blames Israel for PLO raid 3-14, 3-15, 174E3
Syria vows air cover for PLO, guns fire at Israeli jets 3-15, 173G1
Israel explains operatn 3-15, 173B2
Map of PLO raid on Israel, Israeli invasn 174B1
Syria, Leb ask world aid vs Israel; PLO plea to Arabs, Leb plea to UN 3-15, 174C3
Leb, Syria discuss crisis; Syria urges US, UK, France, China, USSR act 3-15, 174D3
Egypt scores Israel, appeals to US, UK, France, W Ger 3-15, 3-16; Arab League protests to UN, Saudi to US 3-15, 174F3
USSR links US to Israeli move 3-15, assails Israel 3-16, 175B1
US asks Israeli exit, hints at peace force, Arabs amenable 3-16, 173F2-174A1

1979

GAZA—*See ARAB-Israeli Developments–Israeli Occupation Policies and EGYPT-Israel headings in this section above*
GOLAN Heights—*See ARAB-Israeli Developments in this section above*
INTERNATIONAL Role—*See also country, organization names*
Westn-natn Guadeloupe summit topic 1-5–1-6, 12G2
SALT II summit topic 6-15–6-18, 449D1; communique text 458A2
W Eur oppositn to Israel setlmt policy rptd 10-14, 780E1
ISRAELI Policies & Actions—*See ARAB-Israeli Developments and other headings in this section; also ISRAEL under 'I'*
JERUSALEM
Iran backs 'liberatn' 2-26, 144F1
Egypt asks Islamic states consider 'liberatn' 5-3, 360F1
Islamic conf calls Palestine capital 5-12, 394G1
Egypt demands East returned to Arab rule 5-25, 394F1
Canada Emb move from Tel Aviv planned 6-5, 424B1; Arabs protest 6-7, 6-19, 467B3
Canada Emb move delayed 6-23; Arabs warn 6-27, 6-29, 502F1
Israel govt wins confidence vote on Arab slayer leniency 7-4, 496E2
UN rpt asks Israel setlmt halt 7-14, 551C2
Canada Emb move scored by Trudeau 7-19, 563D2
Israel scores US autonomy talks proposals 8-1, 574D3; bars Arab talks 8-6, 591B3
UN unit scores Israel 'occupatn' 8-21, 642E2
Canada warned vs emb move 9-9–10-20; Arab deal cancelled 10-18, 10-22, Canada drops plan 10-29, 833B2
Israeli slain 9-16; 2 die in blast 9-19, 694D2
Dayan for Moslem, Christn religious role 10-18, 801G1
2 buses bombed, 11 hurt 11-19, 882E1
JORDAN-Israel Relations—*See also ARAB-Israeli Developments–Israeli Occupation in this section above*
Begin in peace bid 5-18, rejctd 5-19, 379B1
Israel concerned re Jordan-US tank deal 7-27, 574A3
Israeli min: Palestinians preferable to Jordan in peace talks 9-7, 677A1
Hussein bars autonomy talks role 9-10, 676B3
Hussein vs peace talks role 9-24, 741E2
LEBANON
Israelis shell Palestinian bases near Tyre 1-3, 28E2
Syria shells Beirut, 18 die 1-13, 85A1
Israelis shell PLO base 1-16, 28C2
UN chrgs Christn harassmt 1-16, 51D1
Israelis hit PLO bases 1-19, artillery fire traded 1-19–1-23, 50D2
Unifil mandate extended 1-19, 51C1
Israel warns civiln retaliatn 1-23, 50F3
UN gets protest on Israeli shelling 1-23, 50F3
Shelling halted; US, UN truce roles cited 1-24, 69A2
PLO names Salameh killing suspect 1-24, 69D2
2 suspects in Salameh killing held 1-26, identified 1-27, 69C2
2 UAE soldiers killed in Beirut 1-30, 85C1
Christn-Syrian clashes 2-2, 85C1
6 Unifil troops die in PLO clash 2-3, 84D3
MDs protest unrest 2-7, 126D3
Israel arrests Unifil offcr, tie to PLO cited 2-18; Israel bars Unifil border crossing 2-19, 157G1

1980

1976

UK-Uganda controversy on missing hostage 7-7—7-12; Amin ousts UK aide, warns natls 7-13, 515D2
Uganda ousts UK envoy 7-17, UK cuts ties 7-28, 547G3, 548D1
90 Minutes at Entebbe publshd 7-26, 547B2

Greece
US evacuates 10 from Leb 6-20, 448C1
Leb evacuees arrive in Athens 6-29, 546A1

India
Sadat cites MiG parts ban 3-14, 193C1
Confrms Egypt MiG parts ban 3-17, 275C3

Iran
US Sen Stevenson rpts on visit 2-28, 161B1
Guerrilla tied to FFLP 365F2
Ford, Carter debate arms sales 10-6, 742A1

Italy
Sadat visits, backs Palestinian rights 4-5—4-8, 275G1
US evacuates 10 from Leb 6-20, 448C1
Libya '73 Rome airport raid role rptd 7-15, 531A2
Syrian emb attacked 10-11, 759C1
3 Syrian emb raiders sentncd 11-6, 861E2 ★

Japan
Natl killed in hijack try 8-11, 578B3

Kenya
Palestinians rptdly seized in Israel plane raid 1-28, 463E1
Hijackers ask prisoners freed, denies holding 6-29, 463C1; **for subsequent developments, see 'Entebbe' under AVIATION Incidents in this section above**

NATO
Israel arms to Leb rptd 7-20, 527D3

Netherlands
Tourist suspect in Israeli airport blast 5-25, 370G2
Jet hijacked 9-4, gunmen surrender in Cyprus 9-5; pilot scores Tunisia 9-6, 662B3

OAU
Amin vs Israel Uganda raid 7-5, 486C1
Resolutn scores Israel Uganda raid 7-5, 487C3

Pakistan
Syrian emb attacked 10-11, 759C1

Switzerland
Hijackers ask prisoner freed 6-29, Amin plea 6-30, 463C1, G1

Turkey
Emb aide slain in Leb 2-16, amb car attacked 2-17, 125A2
OKs PLO office 5-12, 373B2
Israel seizes freighter 8-10, 578G1
Thwarts Israel jet hijack 8-11, 578A3
Guerrillas land from ship at Tel Aviv 9-25, 10-13, 759E2
Sentncs 2 jet raiders 11-16, 861C2

Uganda
Hijacked jet lands 6-28, 462C3; **for subsequent developments, see 'Entebbe' under AVIATION Incidents in this section above**

United States—*See also SINAI in this section below; also ISRAEL under 'I'; for Arab boycott, see BUSINESS under 'B'*
Kissinger meets Allon 1-7—1-9, 18E2
Warns Syria, Israel vs Leb interventn 1-8, 1D2
Ford Golan setlmt protest rptd leaked 34D3
Confrms PLA forces in Leb 1-19, 34A2
Ford State of Union message 1-19, 38B3
Warns vs Leb interventn 1-20, 34G2
'73 war info rptd scored 1-20, 93B3
Israel welcomes Leb refugees 1-25, 59D2
Rabin in US; sees Ford, Kissinger, presses for contd aid 1-27—1-29, 60B1-B2
Leb Christian contacts rptd 2-2; denied 2-3, 83E1
Leb interventn plea rptd 2-2, 83F1
Marine Corps reorganizatn urged 2-2, 95C3
Rabin back from US trip, rpts agrmt 2-6; US arms bid feud 2-9, 106E2
PLO scores re Jordan-W Bank merger plan 2-15, 126D1
US Sen OKs arms aid 2-18, 151D3, G3
Israel backs peace moves with Egypt, Jordan, Syria 2-22, 145A1
2 USIA aides freed in Leb 2-25, 145B2
Sadat: step-by-step moves ended 2-27, 162A2
Sen Stevenson rpts on visit, Arafat peace plan 2-28, 161B1
US seeks Egypt jet sales, Israel objects 3-3, 161D1
House OKs Egypt, Israeli aid 3-3, 181A2
Reagan scores Admin Sovt policy 3-4, 166B1
Kissinger censures aides on info leak 3-12, Ford refutes info 3-17, 198B2-A3
Sadat lauds peace effort 3-14, 193D1
Hails Egypt-Sovt break 3-19, 227F3
Warns vs Leb mil role 3-22, 3-30, 226D3
Israel protests criticism of occupatn policies, US assures on PLO talks stance 3-24, 211C2
US civilian removal from Leb planned 3-29, 226F1
Backs Leb mediation 3-30, 226G1
Hussein in US 3-30—4-1, 226F2-C3
Rpt Syria asks assurances vs Israel move in Leb 3-30, 226A3
Arafat, Sovts warn on Leb fleet move 3-30, 4-8, 241F2, 242B1
US pres campaign statemts 3-30, 4-6, 245A1, B3
Brown arrives Leb 3-31; 226E1; mediates 4-1—4-5, 241E2

1977

JERUSALEM—*See ARAB-Israeli Developments—Israel Occupation Policies in this section above; for peace plans, see EGYPT-Israel Peace Moves above*
LEBANON Civil Strife—*See LEBANON under 'L'*

1978

Sec Cncl meets on Israel invasn 3-17, 197B2
Israelis break out of 6-mi security belt 3-17, 3-18; claim all of south to Litani R, take 2 bridges 3-19; bar Tyre capture 3-20, 198A1-C2
Syria opens borders for aid to PLO 3-18; Iraq, Syria send in arms 3-20—3-21, 198D2
Refugees flee north 3-18, 3-19, 198G2
W Bank, Jordan protests vs Israel 3-18, 3-20—3-21, 198B3
Sec Cncl votes Israeli exit, forms Unifil; res text 3-19, 197A1-C2
Unifil compositn, Erskine cmnd cited 197D2
Arab hardliners vow arms for PLO 3-19—3-20, 198E2
Israel, UN meet on Unifil deploymt 3-21, refugees return 3-22, 197E2
Israel declares truce, PLO noncommital 3-21, 197G2-198C1
Casualty reports 3-21, 198C1
Unifil advance units move to Litani line 3-22, 197C2
Israel-PLO shooting continues 3-22—3-29, 213A1
More UN troops arrive 3-23; French set up Tyre hq 3-24, 213E2
Syria, Leb bar mil aid to PLO 3-24, 213G1-B2
200 Iraq troops for PLO rptdly arrive, Libyans on way; Christn ldr protests 3-24, 213B2
PLO claims gains near Litani R 3-25, 3-27, 213G2
Sweden UN troops in crossfire 3-26, 1 killed 3-29, 213C2
Christns rptdly slay Moslem civilns at Khiam 3-26, 214A1
Israel hints truce break 3-27, 213F1
PLO blocks UN at Litani R span 3-27, 213F2
PLO unclear on truce observance 3-28—3-29, 213B1
Arab League sets summit, extends force 3-28, 215C1
Habash scorns truce 3-30, 236B2
Arafat vows truce 3-31, 236G1
Mex vows Unifil troops 4-1, reversal rptd 4-5, 236E1
Hoss cites Israeli exit, refugee return problems 4-1, 236A2
Israel rpts forces 'thinned out' 4-3, 235G3
Leb asks Israeli, PLO pullback, more Unifil troops 4-4, 236B1
More Unifil troops arrive, total cited 4-4, 236D1
PLO ambushes Israeli unit near Tyre; 3 die, 2 missing 4-5; Israel rpts acct 4-6, 236E1
US hints arms breach by Israel 4-5, Israel denies 4-6, 236C2
Israel tells UN of 2-phase pullback plan 4-6, 235F3
US chrgs Israel illegal use of cluster bombs 4-6, 4-7; US seeks curbs 4-12, 256F3
Waldheim, Leb vs Israel pullback plan 4-7, 4-8, 4-12, 256D2
Israel cmnd rpts PLO losses 4-7, Sovt arms capture 4-12, 256B3
PLO attacks Unifil unit 4-7, 256E3
Israel starts pullback, Unifil moves in 4-11, 256A2
Refugees returning to south 4-11, 256B2
Unifil force at 1,800 4-11; more arrive 4-12, 256E2
Leb, PLO dispute Unifil missn 256G2
Begin briefs Cabt on invasn 4-11, 256A3
Israelis end 2d-phase exit 4-14, 274B3
Waldheim sees Leb ldrs, Arafat, Begin on Unifil, exit plan 4-17—4-18, 274A2
Israelis OK more pullbacks 4-18, 274F2
Israel: cluster bomb use a mistake 4-20; Gur rpts bomb '76 use vs PLO 4-21, 300G1
'Natl accord' seeks Leb control in south 4-23, PLO vs 4-25, 299F3-300A1
Arafat rptdly ordrd Fatah suicide squad arrest; clashes, 3 die 4-24, 300A1
French Unifil troops kill 2 Leb leftists 4-30, 3 French soldiers slain 5-2; PLO seizes Leb suspects in Tyre 5-4, 339F3
Israeli troops pull back 4-30, 340E1
4 Senegalese Unifil troops killed 5-1, 5-5, death toll at 10 339F3
Unifil to be expanded 5-3, 340F1
Arafat vows truce cooperatn 5-5, 340C1
Unifil moves hq to Israel zone 5-8, 340D1
Arafat: PLO vs truce, Unifil creatn 5-11, 383A3
US-Israel agrmt on cluster bomb use rptd 5-12, 358A3
US church group vs Israel cluster bomb use 5-12, 358B3
Unifil spots PFLP unit 5-13; pullout agrmt rptd, more infiltrators seen 5-15, 383C3
Unifil renews Tyre patrols 5-14, 383D3
Unifil cmdr meets Arafat, warns vs PLO presence 5-16, 383G2-A3
Unifil-PLO clash 5-17, 383D3
UN aide meets Sarkis 5-20—5-21, 383D2
French slay 3 guerrillas at Paris airport 5-20, Israel role cited 5-20, 5-21; gunmen identified 5-22, 383E3
Israel vows total exit 5-21; Unifil assures vs PLO infiltratn 5-22, 383C2
Christns accept Israel exit decisn 5-21, 383E2
Israel rpts PLO infiltratn 5-22, 383B3
PLO-Leb pact sets exit 5-24; PLO dissidents vs 5-26, 5-28, 400G2, F3
PLO for 'Palestinian army', 5 dissident groups reject plan 5-24, 400C3
PLO freezes Israel shelling 5-26, 400E3
Unifil: infiltrators barred 5-29, 401A1

1979

Saudis recall troop 2-28, 144B2
PLO, Druse towns shelled, Israelis chrgd 3-5, 157C2
4 die in Beirut clashes 3-6, 157D2
UAE troops to leave 4-9, 341A2
Israel jets bomb PLO in south 4-10—4-11, 278C2
Christns bar govt troops in South 4-15; Israel OKs, briefs Haddad 4-17, 277D3, F3
Leb troops join Unifil; Christns set 'free Leb' in south 4-18, govt scores 4-19, 277C3
Christns raid Unifil positns 4-18—4-19, Israel denies role 4-19, 277G3
Christns reverse plan to lift Unifil base siege, UN Cncl rpt cited 4-21; base gets supplies 4-22, 296C3
US backs govt vs Christn attacks 4-21, 296E3
Haddad gets Christn backing 4-21, 296F3
Christn rivals clash, 11 die 4-21, 296G3
Israelis attack PLO bases 4-22—4-25; Unifil truce halts attacks 4-26, 296C2
Egypt scores Israeli reprisal attacks 4-24, 296B3
UN lauds govt for troop dispatch 4-26, 297A1
Israeli air, naval raids vs PLO in south 5-6—5-8; Israeli troops pursue 3 PLO guerrillas, Unifil bars chase; US scores both sides 5-9, 340C3
Begin vows contd strikes vs PLO 5-7, Arafat rebuts 5-8, 341C1
Leb rejects Israel peace bid 5-7, 341E1
Israel: Syrian army must leave; Saudi, Kuwait exit cited 5-7, 341G1
Christn, Moslem, Palestinian clashes 5-12—5-20, 378D2
Sarkis, Assad meet re unrest 5-14—5-15; Hoss, Cabt resign 5-16, 378G2
Phalangists, Natl Liberals merge 5-16, 378E2
Israel jets raid Insariye 5-18, Damur 5-23, 378G1, B2
Israel-PLO clashes 5-24—5-30, Leb asks UN mtg 5-30; UN truce ends fighting 5-31, 414C3
PLO quitting Tyre hq, southn villages; Arafat vow not to raid Israel cited 6-6, 415C1
Israeli jets hit PLO targets 6-8, 436F3
Unifil-Christn militia clash 6-9, 436E3
Unifil mandate extended 6-14, 436A3
Israel arrests Unifil offcr 6-15, PLO arms smuggling admitted 6-22; Israel chrgs Unifil aids PLO 7-19,
Civiln return to south rptd 6-15, 462F1
Leb troops end Christn Beirut clashes 6-18, 462E1
Israel jets raid Tyre 6-18, 462G1
Tel Aviv bombed, 2 Arabs die; Israel jets raid 7 villages 6-24, 475B2
Israel shells PLO bases; Begin sets preemptive strikes 6-25, 475D2
Israel, Syria jets clash, 5 Syria jets downed 6-27, 475E1
US deplores Israel raid, Syria jet clash 6-27; Begin vows contd raids 6-28, Cabt backs 7-1, 496G1
Arab League force extended 6 mos 6-28, 475F2
Israel jets, troops raid 7-6—7-24; US protests 7-23, 551F2-A3
Kreisky, Brandt, Arafat score fighting 7-8, 511E3
Syria Arab League troops reinforced re PLO aide's murder 7-26, 552C1
Haddad says Unifil lax, vows to hit PLO; UN denies 7-27, 592B1
Israelis raid PLO post, Unifil denies complicity 8-2, 591G3
US hints Israel arms pact breach in raids 8-7, 592D1
Dayan: US OKs raids on PLO 8-13, 625C2
Israel ground, naval, air strikes vs PLO forces 8-14—8-21, 625F1-B2
Unifil troops attacked 8-22—8-24; PLO, Leb leftists infiltrate UN zone 8-26, 643B1
Israelis hit PLO 8-23—8-25; UN sets truce, broken 8-26, 642A3-643B1
Leb asks Arab, US aid vs clashes 8-24, 8-26, 643D1
Israel vows to continue strikes 8-26, 8-27, 642B3, 643A2
US asks halt to clashes 8-29; Waldheim asks truce observance 8-30, 658D2
Begin vs US criticism 8-30, 658A3
Christn militia ldr warns PLO 8-30, 658B3
UN comm condemns Israel 9-5, 659G2
Leb Christians, leftists clash 9-7; PLO rpts Israeli thrust repelled, Israel rebuts 9-21, 740E2
US envoy lauds Israel truce observance 9-12, 676C3
Israel ends censorship re '78 civilian murders 9-14, 802E1
Israel assures US on arms use 9-17, 694B1
US disputes Israel on bombings 9-18, 693E2
US SCLC tours battle zone, meets Leb, PLO offcls, scores Israeli raids 9-18—9-20, 694F1
Senegal pres scores Israel Unifil offcr arrest 9-20, 721G1
SCLC ends visit 9-21, 763C2
Israel jets down 4 Syrian MiGs; Syria claims 2 Israeli jets 9-24; US reactn 9-24, 9-25; Syria vows contd challenge 9-25, 740B2
US urges peace in UN speech 9-24, 741C2

1980

1976

Hussein ends US visit, sees Hawk missile sale delay 4-4, 242E1
Saiqa chrgs Jumblat plot vs Syria 4-5, 241D2
US, Israel dispute aid 4-7—4-9, 258E1
Brown continues Leb mediatn 4-8, 4-10, 4-12, 258E1
Egypt to seek more arms 4-8, C-130 deal gets tacit Cong OK 4-14, 275A2
Kissinger on Syria troops in Leb 4-9, 257D1
Rpt Syria briefed Israel on Leb troop role 4-11, 258C1
Calls Syria troops in Leb 'show of force' 4-11, 258D1
Rpt detected Israel A-arms, '73 war alert cited 243F1
Israel forces down Saudi plane 4-12, 259B1
Warns Syria vs Israel provocatn in Leb 4-14, 257F2
Denies Jordan Hawk deal off 4-14, 4-15, 274A3
Leb proposes new peace plan 4-16, 273D1
Lauds Syria, Israel restraint in Leb 4-19, 4-20, 274B1
Egypt-China MiG parts pact evaluated 4-21, 275B3
USSR asks new Geneva talks 4-28, 296A2
Brown rpts to Ford, Kissinger; returns Beirut 4-30; leftists score 5-2, meets Karami 5-4, 319D1
'73 airlift problems cited 5-3, 345E3
Ford vetoes aid bill 5-7, 344C3
Brown ends Leb mission 5-11, 337C2
Giscard sees Ford 5-17—5-18, offers Leb peace force 5-21; reactn 5-21—5-22, 369D1, 372A2
Feud on Israeli setlmts denied 5-27, 407B1
Syrian invasn of Leb backed 6-1, 385F1
Reagan scores Leb role 6-3, 410G1
Carter outlines views 6-6, 411A1
Sovt chrgs Leb interference 6-9, 406E2
Backs Arab peace moves in Leb 6-10, 406C2
US, Israel discuss Leb crisis 6-14, 430B1
Dem platform text cites 6-15, 477B1, E2, 478F1, F2
Leb Amb Meloy, aide slain; Ford deplores 6-16; evacuation weighed 6-17, 425A1-D2
Warns Jordan on Sovt arms 6-16, 464A2
Kissinger rpts on Leb policy 6-17, 425D2
Leb emb asks US natls quit 6-18; Navy evacuates US, other natls 6-20, 447F3, 448B1, 451B1
Meloy, aide bodies returned from Leb; Ford greets plane 6-19, 448F1
US thanks PLO for Leb evacuation aid 6-20, 6-21, 448D1
Seeyle named amb to Leb, joins US amb meeting on Leb 6-22, 448G1
Carter vows contd Israel aid 6-24, 490C2
Kissinger on detente 6-25, 466D2
Ford signs aid bills 6-30, 532E3, 533C2
Libya chrgs US-Sudan collusn vs Leb, Palestinians 501F3
Ford lauds Israel Uganda raid 7-4, 486F1
Mondale hails Israeli Uganda raid 7-15, 511C3
Plans Leb evacuatn 7-16, delays 7-19, 527D1
US Leb evacuatn 7-27, Israel rues PLO contact 7-28, 546A1
PLO, Leb Arab Army protect aides in Beirut 7-30, 8-2, 578F2
To arm Saudis, Jordan 7-31, 561F1
Javits aide killed in hijack try 8-11, 578B3
FBI OK of '72 Arab cntr break-in rptd 8-17, 634A2
GOP platform text cites 8-18, 610A1, 611B3
Ford acceptance speech cites 8-19, 612A1, B1, A3
2 aides meet Leb Christn ldrs 8-22—8-24, Jumblat scores missn 8-23, 628D3, 629A1
Israel blocks Amoco drilling in Suez gulf 8-31, 9-4, 9-6; US protest 9-6, 663D2
Egypt-Libya border buildup seen aid to Israel 9-12, 683A1
On Sarkis inaugural 9-23, 699C2
Kissinger scores Sovt role, asks renewed Geneva talks 9-30, 719A2, D2
Carter, Mondale on Saudi arms sales 9-30, 725D1, 742F3
Sovts ask Geneva conf 10-1, 738F1
Ford, Carter debate 10-6, 741A1, B2, D2
US bars VOA contacts with PLO 10-8, 759C3
US to lift arms ban to Israel 10-11, 759G1
Ford on Israeli arms sale 10-14, 788A1
Gen Brown remarks rptd 10-17, 10-18, 787G1
PLO aide seeks DC office 10-19; US ousts, PLO rep explains 11-23, 878G1
Ford: Arabs, Israel trust US 10-20, 784G2
Ford scores Carter 10-26, 803B1
Arab, Israel reactn to Carter electn 11-3—11-4, 826A2
Egypt cites Carter bias to Israel 11-4, 841G2
Charge meets Leb pres 11-5, 841E2
Sens, reps get Sadat peace bid, Israel doubts 11-11—11-17, 877G2
Israel scores UN vote 11-12, 863A1
Israel fears Leb border moves 11-23, 877B2
Egypt asks Geneva conf 12-2, 894A3
Vance optimistic 12-3, 916C2
PLO for Palestinian state 12-14, 954A2
Carter favors mtg with ldrs 12-29, 978C3

1977

1978

Unifil rpts Christian, PLO-Leb Leftist clash 5-30, 401B1
Syria, Leb OK troop role in south 5-31—6-1; Moslems, Christns vs 6-4, 6-5, 462C3
Israelis raid PLO base 6-9, 463A1
Israel tells UN of Christn role in exit plan 6-11, 6-12, 462E1
Israelis complete pullout; Christns, not Unifil, get major posts 6-13; UN, Israel dispute actn 6-13, 6-14, 462B1-D2
Unifil head says Christn cmdr has Leb govt OK 6-13, Leb denies 6-14, 462D2
Christn factns clash, T Franjieh among 45 slain 6-13; phalangists deny attack OK, Franjieh vows revenge 6-14, 463G1
Christn factns clash 6-15; cmdrs arrested 6-16, 6-19; Unifil role challenged 6-16, 6-17, 462F2
Leb seizes PLO arms boat 6-18, Israelis recapture 6-19, 463E1
Unifil takes more posts 6-23, 503E2
36 die in Christn clash 6-28, Syria warns 6-30, 7-2, 502B2
Map of Beirut 503C1
Syrians attack Christns in Beirut, 200 die 7-1—7-6, 502A2
Christn death toll at 450 522A1
Chamoun in intl plea to end Syrian 'genocide' 7-2, scores Arab League force 7-4, 502G2
Israel chrgs PLO infiltratn, Unifil tacit agrmt; UN denies 7-4, 503B2
Sarkis threatens to quit over Syria demands; US, Saudi, UK assuage 7-6, 502B3
Israeli jets fly over Beirut, Syria warned to halt attacks; death toll at 400 7-6, 503A1
US asks end to fighting 7-6, 503G1
Christn-Syrian truce agrmt in Beirut 7-6; fighting ebbs 7-7, 521E2
Syrian jets fly over Tripoli 7-6, 521F2
Israel, Syria reinforce troops at borders 7-7, 521F2
Israel warns Syria again 7-7, 521G2
Sovts rptdly vow aid to Syria vs Israel attack 7-8, 522A1
Syria vows to crush Christns 7-9, 522B1
Sarkis meets Kuwait forgn min, vows to resign 7-9; Chamoun vs decisn 7-12, 522B1
Speaker meets Syrian pres 7-11; Sarkis questnd on resignatn 7-12, to stay on 7-15, 547A1
Chamoun asks Syrians leave 7-12, 522E1
Guerrillas detain 40 Unifil troops 7-12; free 7-12—7-13; Fatah, PLF clash over detentns 7-13—7-14, 547D1
Beirut combat halts 7-16, 547C1
Syrian-Christn clash in Beirut 7-22—7-29, 581A2
US, Canada cut emb staffs 7-27, 581C2
Leb plans to move army south 7-28; Israel warns Leb 7-30, US conveys warning 7-31; army moves in, Christns block 7-31, shell 7-31—8-1, 581A1
2 Christn cmdrs ordrd back to Beirut 7-31; Haddad refuses 8-1, 581D1
Leb army, Unifil troops fired at 8-2, 8-7, 638F2-G2
Israeli jets raid PLO base 8-3, 583B1
Syria backs Leb army in south, vows stand vs Israel 8-3, 583F1
Christns ordrd to halt fire 8-3, 638G2
Christn mil ldr vs Leb army in south 8-4, 638G2
Syrians, Christns clash in Beirut 8-5—8-11; Israeli jets warn Syria 8-8, 638G1-C2
Israel: US rptdly restrains to save Christns 8-7, 638C2
Unifil asks Israel act vs Christn firing, cites intl moves to urge Christns OK Leb army in south 8-8, 638B3
Leb army rptdly begins quitting south 8-11, 638E2
Beirut bldg blast, 150-200 die 8-13; PLO rivalry cited, denied 8-14; US, Israel blamed 8-17, 637F2
Israeli jets bomb 2 PLO bases, retaliate for London bus attack 8-21, 638B1
Israel, Syria swap warnings on interventn; US, other aid asked 8-28, 8-29, 8-31, 674E1-C2
Syria seizes Christn area north of Beirut 8-29, 674C2
US aide gets Israel plea on crisis 8-30, 674D2
Christns OK Unifil deploymt 8-30, 713E1
Syria set for Israel attack 8-31, 9-1, 9-4, 674D2
Christns list Syria death toll 8-31, 674E2
Christns fire at Norwegian Unifil troops 8-31, 9-7, 713D1
Israel jets fly over Beirut 9-6, 9-10, 713A2
Syrian-Christn clashes, 8 killed 9-7—9-10, 713G1
Syrian raid escalatn linked to Camp David summit 9-10, 713B2
Christn gen strike protests Syrian shelling, troop presence 9-13, 713F1
Waldheim asks Unifil extensn 9-14, 4-mo mandate OKd 9-18, 713B1
Carter asks end of conflict 9-18, 710C1
Syrian-Christn fighting mounts, losses high 9-24—10-4, 745E2
US asks intl conf to end war 9-28, 9-30; cites Israel, France, Arab 'interest' Chamoun backs 9-29, 745A1, D1, D2
Syria vs US, French pleas 9-30, 10-3, 745B2
US, French peace pleas 10-2, 10-3, 745B1, A2
French peace plan detailed, asks Arab League force exit 10-2, 745F1

1979

Jesse Jackson visits, tours refugee camps 9-28–9-30, 10-3-,10-5, 763C1, E1
Syrians down Israel spy plane 10-7, 763D3
Rival Christn abductns 10-8, 8 die in clash 10-10, 763A3
Syria dissident kidnaps chrgd 10-24, 857B3
Beirut Moslem sectn bombed 10-27, 823A3
Arab League backs PLO presence; scores US, Israel 11-22, 916F1
Iran plans volunteer force 12-5, 12-8; Leb bars, Syria, PLO silent 12-10, 937E2
Iran volunteers arrive Syria 12-18–12-20; Leb vs entry 12-18, Syria reassures 12-20, 979G3
Israel sentncs, expels Unifil offer 12-24, 980B1

1980

1976 1977 1978 1979 1980

1976

U.S.-Israeli Relations—*See 'United States' in this section above*

USSR
US, Israel reaffirm Geneva PLO bar 1-29, 60B2
Brezhnev urges Geneva Conf, cites Egypt ties 2-24, 194B2
US seeks to end Egypt mil dependnc 3-3, 161E1
Reagan scores US policy 3-4, 166B1
Egypt ends 15-yr pact 3-15, 193A1
India confrms Egypt MiG part ban 3-17, 275C3
US hails Egypt break 3-19, 227F3
Scores Egypt on break 3-22, 227C3
Offers Leb mediation 225C1
Egypt rpts navy rights canceled 4-4, warships leave 4-15, 275C1
Egypt fears base in Libya, cites arms order 4-4, 275D1
Cuba troops rptd in Red Sea area 4-5, 242F1
Says Egypt arms pact honored 4-6, Egypt disputes 4-8, 275C2
Warns US on fleet off Leb 4-8, 241F2
Rpt A-arms shipmt in '73 war 243F1
Vs Vorster trip to Israel 275F3
Jordan says US Hawk deal off 4-14, 274C3
China lauds Egypt pact end 4-19, 275A3
Asks new Geneva talks, stresses Palestinian role, scores US 4-28, 296A2
Vs Israel A-arms 4-28, 296E2
Kosygin in Iraq 5-29—5-31, Syria 6-1—6-4, 385A2, 406F2
Australia scores Sovt role 6-1, 438D2
Chrgs forgn role in Leb 6-9; Syria says ties unchanged 6-10, 406E2
Dem platform text cites mil pressure 6-15, 477E2
Hussein visits, seeks arms 6-17—6-28, 464F1
Seeks to bar Leb Moslem defeat 7-13, 514E3
PLO asks pressure vs Syria 7-15, 528E1
Rpt vs Syria Leb policy 7-19, 528F1
Asks Syrians quit Leb 8-27, 8-29; Leb amb vs views 8-31, 642B1
Backs Libya, warns Egypt 8-30, 682C3
Vs Leb leftists 9-8, Leb-PLO reps query policy chng 9-9, 663D1
Asks Syria quit Leb 9-11, Assad rejects 10-1, 10-5, 737G1
Urges Geneva conf renewal 10-1, 738E1
Gets Arafat plea vs Syria 10-13, 758E2
Terms Leb war Westn 'plot', regrets Syria role 10-25, 839D2
Egyptian talks held 11-3—11-4, 841F2
Egypt urges ties restored 11-4, 826C2
Egypt asks Geneva conf 12-2, 894A3

Vatican
Israel censures for Leb Christian plight 1-25, 59E2
US rabbis seek Israel ties 2-8, 272G2
Christian-Moslem text rejcted 2-11, 272E2
Rpt Syria asks assurances vs Israel move in Leb 3-30, 226B3

Yugoslavia
Sadat visits 4-8—4-9, 275D2

Zambia
Secret Israel talks rptd leaked 35A1

ISRAELI Policies & Actions—*See also SINAI, SUEZ and UN headings in this section below; also ISRAEL under 'I'*
Censorship plan deferred 1-20, 34D3
Cabt OKs Galilee land takeover, Arabs protest 2-29, 174E3
Haifa Arabs vs strike 3-25, W Bank Arabs back 3-30, 227D1, A2
Arabs riot in Galilee, 6 die; suspects arrested 3-29—3-31, 227A1
Rabin ties CP to riots, wins confidence vote 3-31, 227F1
Galilee police actn defended 4-4, 258C2
300 Galilee suspects freed 4-4, 258E2
Rpt Israel had 13 A-bombs in '73; denied 4-5, 243D1
Govt to weigh Arab grievances 5-23, 370D1
Rabin meets Arab ldrs, vs Galilee demands 5-24, 370F1
Galilee Arab rpt stirs controversy 9-8, Allon scores 9-13, 683F1
Galilee Arabs vs Koenig rpt 9-22, strike 9-28, 738B1
Asks Helsinki-type Geneva conf 11-27, Egypt scores 12-2, 894F2, A3

Arab Relations—*See appropriate subheads under ARAB Policies in this section above*

Foreign Relations (misc.)—*See appropriate subheads under INTERNATIONAL Developments in this section above*

Jerusalem—*See 'Occupation Policies' in this section below; also 'Palestine-Israel Issue' under ARAB Policies above*

Occupation Policies & Developments—*See also 'Palestinian-Israel' under ARAB Policies above; for UN debate, see appropriate subheads under UN DEVELOPMENTS below*
W Bank Arabs vs Jewish setlmt 1-3, 1F2
Israelis open new Golan setlmt 1-9, 35G1
W Bank Arabs protest occupatn 1-12, Peres denies chrgs 1-13, 35D1
Christian-Moslem conf backs Arabs 2-1—2-6, 272F2
Israel sees Jordan W Bank bid 2-5, 83C3
Nablus demonstrations 126D1
Jordan denies W Bank plans 2-9, 107A1
Israel patrol ambushed in Gaza, Nablus bus attacks 2-9, 126E1
Arabs vs Temple Mt prayer rule 2-13, 126F1-A2
W Bank Arabs protest 2-17, 2-19, 161B2

1978

Sarkis meets Arab ldrs on peace plan 10-2, 10-12, 783B1, F1
US intl plea for truce, French contacts cited 10-5; UN res calls for truce, Waldheim role 10-6; Syria declares unilateral truce 10-7; sporadic clashes 10-7—10-11, 761A1
Leb govt vs French peace plan 10-5, French shocked 10-7, 761B2
Israeli gunboats shell west Beirut 10-5; Israel says raid thwarted PLO attack 10-6, 10-8, 761G2-762D1
US emb shelled 10-6, 761G2
Syria, Sovts score Israeli role 10-6, 762C3
Sarkis-Assad peace talks 10-7—10-9; Sarkis in Saudi 10-9—10-10, UAE 10-10, 761E1-A2
Syrians surround Beirut 10-7, 761C2
Begin vows aid to Christns 10-8, 762D1
PLA force enters from Syria 10-8, 10-11, 783F1
Chamoun scores Sarkis for Assad talks 10-9, 761A2
Beirut Moslems strike vs Sarkis plan 10-10, 761A2
Sadat scores Syrian role 10-10, 762F1
Unifil soldier slain 10-10, 783A2
Leb army deployed in Beirut 10-13, 783E1
7 Arab states meet on crisis, Syrians to quit key posts in Beirut 10-15—10-17; Christns scoff at conf 10-17, 782B3, 783C1
Syria warns vs Israel-Christn ties 10-16, 783B1
France blames Chamoun for clashes 10-16; Chamoun denies, blames Syria 10-17, 783C1
Sudan reaffirms decisn to withdraw troops 10-18, 10-19, 803B1
Saudis replace Syrians in east Beirut 10-20, 802D3
Leb army to try 2 renegade offcrs 10-22, 803D1
PLO moves curbed by govt 10-25, 828F1
Arab force mandate extended 10-26, 803E1
Christn milita attacks Unifil troops, Unifil post vacated 10-26, 828C2
PLO seeks Christn accord 10-30, 11-13, 870A1
Rebel Leb army group hq raided 11-1, 828B2
Forgn min ambush thwarted 11-2, 828B2
Christn-Syrian clashes in Beirut 11-7, 11-11, 11-14, 870D1
Cease-fire plan impasse 11-15, 870E1
Unifil head says missn lags 11-19; UN says Israel, Christns impede Beirut troop role; Waldheim plea cited 11-25, 951D1
5 Syrians, others die in Alekh car blast 11-21, 951A2
US to admit more refugees 11-28, 934F1
Christns to build airport, seaport 12-2, 951A2
US vows refugee aid 12-6, 934E1
Israel jets, artillery bomb PLO bases 12-20, 12-21; US scores Israel 12-20, Begin rebuts 12-21, 997G2

Haifa-Tel Aviv Raid—*See under ARAB-Israeli Developments in this section above*

1976 | 1977 | 1978 | 1979 | 1980

1976

Arab paper suspended 2-19, 161D2
W Bank Arabs riot; mayors, councils quit in protest 3-7—3-23, 210D2
Temple Mt prayer ban upheld 3-21, 211C1
3d W Bank riot victim dies 3-25, 227B2
2 W Bank Arabs deported 3-27, 227C2
50 E Jerusalem students detained 3-28, 227E2
W Bank Arabs back Galilee rioters 3-30, 227D1
Jordan backs W Bank Arab death sentence 3-31, 227F2
W Bank electns 4-12; Peres, others comment 4-13, 258F2
W Bank march; riots resume, 2 die 4-17—4-21, 274E1
Rabin in W Bank, assures Israeli setlmts; more planned 4-20, 274F2
W Bank riots 5-1—5-5, 319A1
Newsmen barred from Ramallah 5-3, 319E3
US newsman detained in W Bank 5-7, 338G2
Rally vs Kadum 5-8, 338B2
Newsmen's riot link probed 5-8, newsmen deny 5-9, 338F2
Kadum settlers ordered moved 5-9, residents score 5-10, 338D1, A2
W Bank settlemts set 5-10, 338F1
WHO health report 5-10, 338C2; rptd rejctd 5-17, 355F1
W Bank, Jerusalem Arabs riot, 3 die 5-15—5-19, 354B1
Anti-riot measures weighed 5-18, 354D2
E Jerusalem riots 5-20, 407E1
Tear gas used in Tulkarm riot 5-20, 407E1
Nablus curfew lifted 5-21; reimposed after rioting 6-5, 407C1
Nablus protests vs Syrian Leb invasn 6-9, 406B3
US Dem platform text cites Jerusalem 6-15, 478C2
Jerusalem prayer ruling voided 6-30, 528B2
W Bank sales tax protests, levy postponed 7-1—7-3, 487C2
Soldier killed near Nablus 7-25, 579C1
Sales tax imposed 8-1, Arab W Bank protest strike 8-8, 579D1
Israeli settlers blocked near Jericho 8-2, 579E1
Israeli bus attacked in Hebron 8-7, 579E1
Israel curbs W Bank-Jordan trade 8-11, 699F3
Nablus shops end sales tax strike 8-21, 699E3
Jewish militants riot in Hebron 8-25, 699F3
W Bank town posters score Hussein 9-12, 699G3
Syrian soldier defects to Israeli Golan 9-13, 683E1
Bireh offcls in sit-down 9-13, 700A1
Israel, Syria aid Golan Druse reunion 9-15, 683C1
Nablus, Hebron unrest vs Israeli settlemts, Hussein 9-16, 699C3
Allon troop exit plan rptd 9-17, Cabt vs debate 9-21, 699D2
Arab dies in Old Jerusalem riot 9-17, 699C3
Arabs stone Hebron Jews 9-21, 700B1
W Bank, Gaza Arabs back Galilee strike 9-28, 738C1
Rabin bars Ezion Bloc transfer 9-29, 738A1
Arabs, Jews feud at Hebron shrine; curfew imposed 10-1—10-4, 737C2
Hebron funeral for desecrated scrolls 10-6, 799B1
Cabt meets on Hebron unrest 10-10, 799A1
Gaza terror suspects taken 10-11, 759F2
Hebron rally blocked 10-12, 799C1
JDL families plan move to Qiryat Arba 10-17, 799C1
Soldier jailed in Arab death, demoted 10-17, 799D1
Hebron shrine reopened 10-20, 798D3
Hebron Arab desecrators, Jews chrgd 10-22, 10-26, 895G1
Nablus Arabs protest 11-22—11-24, 895D1
Terror suspects seized 11-24, 895E1
UNESCO vs Jerusalem digs 11-26, 896B1
3 die in Hebron bomb blast 12-4, 954F1
Tawil detention ended 12-10, 954F1
W Bank riots 12-12, 12-13, 954E1
W Bank one-day strike 12-15, 954C1

Palestinian Issue—*See under ARAB Policies in this section above*

U.S. Relations—*See under INTERNATIONAL Developments above*

JERUSALEM—*See 'Occupation' under ISRAELI Policies in this section above*

PALESTINIAN Developments—*See under ARAB Policies in this section above*

1977

PALESTINIAN Developments—*See also ARAB-Israeli Developments, EGYPT-Israel Peace Moves and other headings in this section; also LEBANON under 'L'*
PLO rep in Paris slain 1-3, 9C1
Syria executes PLO terrorist 1-6, 2C2
PFLP may quit PLO over peace moves 3-6, 166G1-B2
Natl Cncl conf opens 3-12, Arafat addresses 3-17, 187D2, 188A1
Natl Cncl conf ends; 15-pt declaratn adopted, ldrship reelected 3-20, 207F3
Arafat mediates Egypt-Libya feud 7-24—7-25, 569E2
PLO cncl meets 8-25—8-26, 662B3
UAE state min slain, Syrian forgn min escapes, Black June takes credit 10-25, 811B3

Plane Hijackings—*See AVIATION—Middle East Incidents under 'A'*

1978

PALESTINIAN Developments—*See also ARAB-Israeli Developments, EGYPT-Israel Peace Moves and LEBANON in this section above; also LEBANON—Civil Strife under 'L'*
Hammami slain in London 1-4, US, Zionists blamed 1-4—1-5; splinter group claims credit 1-5, 3E1
W Ger, Dutch oranges from Israel rptd poisoned 2-1, 60F3-61A1
PLO to reopen Syria bases 2-1, 2-5, 78F2
Jordan freed 1,000 prisoners 3-3, 157A2, B2
Abu Sayed assassinated 3-8, 157C2
PFLP co-founder dies 3-28, 252G2
Arab fund poor-natn aid rise rptd 4-9, 257F2
Arafat rptdly averted Al Fatah breakup 4-24, 300A1
Egypt terror group rptd smashed 4-26, 300D2

1979

PALESTINIAN Developments
Fatah ldr, 9 others slain in Beirut blast, Israel blamed 1-22; Israel press hails death 1-23, 51A1
Arafat in Iran; gets aid vow, Israel legatn bldg 2-17–2-19, 126A1
PLO scores China Viet invasn 2-20, 123A2
Iran ties stressed 2-26, 144F1
Uganda aid rptd 3-13, 257F1; 5-28, 429C2
PLO to open Amman office 3-17, 198D2
PLO asks Syria, Algeria, Libya, Iraq, USSR alliance vs US, Israel, Egypt 3-25, scores pact supporters 3-25, 3-26, 222A2
PLO disavows attack on French Jews 3-27, 222F2
PLO bars W Bank, Gaza plan 4-5–4-6, 4-8, 278B3

1980

Palestinian-Israeli Conflict
Misgav Am attacked, 3 Israelis killed 4-7; intl PLO unit claims credit 4-8; Israelis raid Leb 4-9, 260G1
Israelis kill 4 PLO in Leb 5-8, 340F3-341B1
Israel kills 3 PLO infiltrators 5-14, 381F1
Fatah conf 5-22—6-1; Israeli downfall vowed, Arafat reelected 6-1, 418A2
Israelis raid PLO base in Leb 6-4, block PLO coastal raid, kill 3 6-16, 449E2
PLO rep denies plan to destroy Israel 6-5, 434D2
Israelis slay 2 raiders in Jordan 6-7; Fatah takes credit, seeks Jordan base 6-9, 434C2
Hussein bars PLO Jordan base vs Israel 6-17—6-18, 450C1
Israel kills 40 PLO in Leb; US to probe weapons use 8-19, 627D3
Arafat visits Leb front, orders alert 8-19, 643B2

1976

1977

1978

Info office opened in Washington 5-1, 340C2
Israel convicts US Arab 6-6, sentncs 6-12, 489B2
Yasin slain in Kuwait 6-15, Iraq linked 6-15, 6-16, 489A2
Israel sentncs Cypriot for PLO link 7-7, 547G1
OAU backs PLO 7-12, 561F2
Israel to get Iraq, S Yemen terrorist training info 8-17, 651E3
Arab fund loan to Sudan rptd 8-17, 925F3
El Al crew bus attacked in London, 2 die 8-20; UK laxity chrgd 8-21, 638B1
UN publicity drive starts 10-7, 762G2-C3
Israel paroles US Arab 10-18, expels 10-20, 783C2
Arafat in Moscow, Camp David pact scored 10-29—11-1, 828C1
Arafat for UN peace force in Palestine state 11-19, 893C1
UN marks Solidarity Day; US, West, Israel boycott 11-29, 951E2
PLO backing of Iran revolt rptd 12-29, 993E2

Cyprus Terrorist Attack (& developments)

2 Palestinians slay Egypt editor Sebai, take hostages 2-18, 117A1, C1
Palestinians hijack jet, leave Cyprus 2-18; Arab, African natns, Greece bar landing; Djibouti OKs refueling 2-18—2-19; jet returns to Nicosia 2-19, 117A1, G1
PLO joins hijack negotiatns 2-18, 117G1
Egypt commandos land, attack jet; Cyprus guards intervene, kill 15 2-19, 117C2
Cairo funeral for Sebai, dead commandos; anti-Palestinian, anti-Cyprus demonstratns 2-19, 2-22, 118B2
Cyprus, Egypt dispute raid events 2-20—2-22, 117D2
Egypt recalls aides from Cyprus 2-20, cuts ties 2-22, 118G1
PLO role in clash hinted 2-21, 118D1
Cyprus police chief suspended 2-22, 138E2
Cyprus chrgs UK newsman 2-22, drops case 2-24, 138F2
Cyprus urges Egypt tie renewal 2-23, 138F2
Carter lauds Sadat raid actn 2-23, Vance assures Cyprus of neutrality 2-26, 138G2
PLO scores Egypt 2-24, 2-28, Egypt curbs Palestinians 2-27, 138C1, B2
Egypt scores Cyprus handling 2-27, probes PLO role 138G1, A2
Cyprus seeks Egypt rift end 3-1, 148A1
Sebai slayers trial starts 3-9, get death sentence 4-4, 236E3
Iraq, Nidal tied to Sebai death 7-13, 546G3
Sebai slayers spared 11-14, 870F1

Iraq Dispute

Fatah links to Yasin murder 6-15, 6-16, 489B2
PLO asks Iraq return Nidal for trial 7-4, 546F3
Iraq, Nidal tied to Hammami, Yasin deaths 7-13, 7-17, 546D3, F3
Fatah chrgs arms plant, supplies seizure, hints Iraq tie to Naif murder 7-17, 546C3
Iraq amb in London escapes death try 7-28; 2 suspects held 8-2, 582G1, D2
Iraq emb in Paris raided, 2 die 7-31; PLO blamed 8-1, 3 emb aides ousted 8-2, 582F1-D2
Pakistan blocks Arab attack on Iraqi consulate 8-2, 582C3
Iraq amb in Beirut escapes death try 8-2, PLO accused 8-3, 582D3-583A1
2 PLO men slain in Paris, Iraq blamed 8-3, 582B3
French police protest emb death 8-3, 649D3
PLO slayers rptdly admit tie to Iraq 8-4, 602A3
PLO ties Iraq to Kalak, Adnan deaths 8-4, 602B3
4 die in raid on Pak PLO office, Iraq blamed 8-5, 602D2
Revenge vowed for 2 PLO men slain in Paris, 2 suspects chrgd 8-5, 602G2
Iraq warns vs raids on missns 8-6, 602F2
PLO factns end feud, Algeria mediates 8-9—8-11, 8-23, 674A2
Iraq emb aide slain in Libya 8-16, 674D1
PLO: Iraq killed Haddad 8-24, 674C1
Iraq ousts Syrian counselor 8-24, 674E1

1979

Egypt quoted on support 4-9, 295E3
Libyan '75 A-bomb effort rptd 4-14, 299D3
Jordan rapproachmt rift rptd 4-15, 278F2
PLO denies link to Iran Arabs 4-26, 321F2
Moslem ldr slain in Gaza 6-1; PFLP takes credit 6-2, threatens Gaza mayor 6-3, 414E2
PLO group tied to Iran unrest 6-3, 446D1
Tunisia intercepts Nicaragua arms 7-11, 512E2
Egypt Emb in Turkey raided, PLO denies role 7-13; rebels surrender, free hostages 7-15; Egypt chrgs Arab ldrs 7-16, 536D2
PLO's Mohsen shot in France 7-25, dies; Israel, Egypt blamed 7-26, 551G3
Syrian replaces Mohsen in PLO post 8-3, 625D2
Swiss arrest Mohsen slayer suspect 8-20, 625D2
UN previews Palestinian film 8-28, 643D2
Arafat visits Spain 9-13–9-15, 694C3
PLO accepts '80 Olympics invite, IOC 'astonished' 10-2, 798G1
Arafat in E Ger 10-7, 761E2
Castro scores Israel genocide 10-12, 778F2
PLO reps in Iran re US Emb hostages 11-7–11-11, rebuffed 11-8, 842B1, 862G1
Libya hq under siege 12-6, offcls protest 12-9; Qaddafi scores disunity 12-10, 937B3
Qaddafi scores Arafat 12-11; PLO offices closed 12-16, ties cut 12-22, 980C1
2 PLO aides slain in Cyprus 12-15, 980F1

Autonomy Talks—*See under EGYPT-Israel Relations in this section above*

Israeli Conflict—*See ARAB-Israeli Developments and LEBANON in this section above*

Lebanon Role—*See LEBANON in this section above*

Rights and Recognition Issues—*See also 'Palestinian Autonomy Talks' under EGYPT-Israel Relations above*

US UN Amb for new approach 1-16, Jews protest 1-17, 69E1
UN rights comm backs Palestinian state 2-21, 148F1
Carter wants ties 3-23, 222G2
Hout in US 4-1–4-21, US House scores 4-24, 319E2; Begin protests 5-2, 320B1
Carter, Schmidt back talks 6-6, 430A1
Begin bars state 6-6, 436F2
Arafat sees Austria, W Ger ldrs 7-6–7-8; Israel recalls Austria amb 7-8, 511A3
Commonwealth ldrs back rights 8-7, 590F2, 625E2
Carter vs state 8-10, 606G2
PLO cncl meets 8-11–8-12, insists on state 8-12, 606E3
Arafat warns US vs blocking state 8-20, 659A2
US SCLC meets PLO, Israeli, US Jewish reps; backs PLO 8-21, 623F3
Dayan meets PLO backer 8-29, earlier mtgs rptd 9-5; talks defended by Dayan 8-30, 9-4, US 9-5, 658C3
Carter: Arabs vs independnt state 8-30, 659C1
Rumania offers Israel mediatn 8-31, Israel rejects 9-2, 659B2
Sadat, Begin disagree on autonomy 9-5, 658E1, A2
UN asks Israel to meet PLO 9-5, 659F2
Dayan '78 mtgs with PLO backers disclosed 9-6, 676G3
Young vs US PLO stance 9-6; Liberia, Senegal on Israel ties request 9-7, 9-20, 720C3, 721A2
Israeli min: Palestinians preferable to Jordan in peace talks 9-7, 677A1
Israel-W Ger talks 9-10; Dayan scores rights stand, Bonn denies tilt 9-11, 677B1
Bethlehem mayor backs Jordan federatn 9-11, 676D3
Spain backs ties 9-15, 694D3
SCLC in Leb 9-18–9-20, meets Arafat 9-20, 694G1, C2
UN Gen Assemb pres calls PLO 'pivotal' 9-18, 695A2
Young scores Israel, calls US black PLO support 'natural' 9-22, 721B2
Carter denies Jewish pressure to oust Young 9-23, 763E2
Young: Dayan aired Terzi mtg 9-24; Young meets Dayan; absolves Dayan, Israel 9-26, 763G2
Jesse Jackson in Mideast, Israeli offcls snub; meets Arafat 9-25–10-5; PFLP scores 10-6; US aides briefed 10-8, 762F3
Turkey gives PLO full status 9-27, 740C3
Pope urges 'just setlmt' 10-2, 758F1
US NAACP warns vs black support 10-11; in Israel with other black groups: PLO support, black criticism scored, Palestinians backed 10-14–10-17; 'unity' reaffirmed 10-17, 780C2-E3
SCLC drops invitatn to Arafat 10-11, 780F3
Connally backs state 10-11, 783A2
US Arab group gives PUSH $10,000 10-13, 780G3

1980

Israeli-PLO clashes in Leb 8-20—8-21, 643G1
US amb to Leb condemns Israel raid, State Dept disavows 8-21, 644A1
Israelis down Syrian jet 8-24, 643E1
US assures Leb on peace efforts 8-28, 643G3
Libya assails Israel 9-1, 660D3
Israel-PLO clash in Leb 9-17, 10-9, 800B3
Israel hits PLO base in Leb 10-16; US cautns, Begin discounts 10-17, 800F2
Israel hits PLO Leb bases 10-17, 10-22, 863F3
PLO blasts injure 16 Israelis 10-26, 864A1
Redgrave backs Israel destructn, pledges Palestinian support 11-2, 908F3
Qiryat Shmona hit 11-6; Israel retaliates in Leb 11-7, 863E3
2 PLO infiltrators killed 11-13, 912E2
Israeli seaborne force hits PLO near Beirut 12-3, 912B2
Leb village raided, Israelis deny role 12-18; Israelis raid PLO base, kill 10 PLO, 3 Syrians 12-19, Syrians shell 2 Christn sites in retaliatn 12-20, 977D2
S Leb protesters raid UN offices in Beirut 12-23, 977B3
Israelis slay 5 PLO raiders in Leb 12-25, 977G2
UN says Christns dynamite Leb home 12-26, 977A3
Israeli jets raid PLO Leb bases, down 2 Syrian MiGs; Syria claims 2 Israaeli jets 12-31, 977A3

1976

SINAI Peninsula
US starts observer site constructn 1-22, 60C2
Egypt takes over UN zone 1-26, 60C2
Peres visits, hails pact 2-19, 145G1
Troop pullbacks completed, pact implemented 2-20—2-22, 145D1
US observer posts operational 2-21, 145F1
Israel sees no pact breach on Suez blacklisting 2-21, 145B2
Sadat rpts 'secret' US agrmt on PLO, Syria 2-29; US comments 3-2, 162E1-A2
Arabs warn vs oil drilling 7-24, 561B2
Arafat disavows Syria pact 7-30, 577G2
Ford, Carter debate 10-6, 741B2
UNEF extended, Waldheim rpts 10-22, 799B2

SUEZ Canal Zone Area
Israeli shipping blacklisted, US ship denied servicing, Israel sees no Sinai pact violatn 2-21, 145G1
Rptd target of Sovt, Cuba mil buildup 4-5, 242B2
US Dem platform text cites 6-15, 478A2
Israel bars Amoco drilling 8-31, 9-4, 9-6; US protest 9-6, 663D2
Israel, US meet on oil feud 9-8, 9-13, 759G2
Israel newspr leaks Amoco rpt document 9-28, Israel probes leak 9-29, 759A3

UN DEVELOPMENTS
Waldheim backs Palestinian rights 1-9, 19A1
Bomb threat vs UN 1-12, Iraq missn 1-13, 18C2
Waldheim meets Leb amb 1-17, urges end to strife 1-18, 34A3
Rights comm chrgs Israel 'war crimes' in Arab areas, US dissents 2-13, 125D2
US Sen Stevenson rpts Arafat peace plan 2-28, 161A1
Waldheim gets W Bank protest 5-16, 354E1
Waldheim in Syria; US, Israel vs 5-25—5-27, 386A1
Israel, Leb vs inactn on crisis 6-9, 406G2-A3
Waldheim vs Israel Uganda raid, aides qualify remark 7-5, 486F2
Waldheim denies anti-Israel statemt on Uganda raid 7-8, 516G1
Egypt missn vs Israel troop exit plan 9-21, 699C3

ECOSOC (Economic & Social Council)
Anti-Zionist resolutn debated 4-27—4-30, 320F2
PLO chrgs Israel-S Africa tie 4-29, 320D3

General Assembly—*For Zionism vote reaction, see country names*
UNESCO Zionism resolutn debate postponed 1-15, 36A2
ECOSOC debates anti-Zionist resolutn 4-27—4-30, 320F2
US Dem platform cites Zionism resolutn 6-15, 478B1
Gromyko, Kissinger address 9-28, 9-30, 719A2, D2, B3, C3
31st sessn debates 10-5—10-7; Israel backs Geneva conf 10-7, 760B1
Leb scores Palestinians, Libya rebuts 10-14, 758D3
Vs Israel Gaza resettlmts 11-23, 878E2
Calls for Palestine state, Israel scores 11-24, 895E2
US, Canada Jews score Gaza res 11-25, 912A1 ★
Egypt asks Geneva conf, Palestinian role 12-2; Israel submits counter plan 12-6; Egypt resolutns OKd 12-9, 914C1
Scranton vows peace role 12-22, 955B1

ILO (International Labor Organization)
PLO seated at job conf 6-4; US, Israel boycott Mizer speech 6-8, 450A1

Palestinian People, UN Committee on the Exercise of the Inalienable Rights of the
Talks open, Israel boycotts 2-26; PLO, Syria in feud 3-4, 161F2
Backs Palestinian return 5-19, 407F1
Cncl upholds Palestinian return, US vetoes res 6-29, 464C1
US scores W bank, Gaza rpt 11-23, 878B3
Assemb backs report 11-24, 895F2

1977

SINAI—See also ARAB-Israeli Developments and EGYPT-Israel Peace Moves in this section above; for UNEF, see under UN DEVELOPMENTS below
Sadat: Sovts tried to falsify '75 Israeli pact 12-6, 929E2

SUEZ—See also EGYPT-Israel Peace Moves in this section above
Dayan lists in 4-pt peace plan 10-10, 769B2
Israel gen chrgs Egypt buildup 11-15, 873B2
Sadat visits Ismailia 11-18, 890A2
Egypt returns 3 Israeli bodies 12-8, 931G1

UN DEVELOPMENTS
Waldheim sees war 1-30; tours 5 Arab states, Israel; queries PLO role 2-2—2-10, 86C2
Israel, Sovt reps meet on PLO peace role 2-3, 86D3
Israel prefers US peace role 2-6, 86A3
Waldheim ends missn in Israel, Egypt 2-11—2-12; sees PLO moderatn 2-16, 107C1
US cites buffer zone safety 6-17, 473F2
Begin asks Waldheim aid on Syrian Jews 7-22, 570G3
Waldheim vs new W Bank setlmts 8-18, 623C1
Waldheim sees contd deadlock 9-19, 713F1
US-Sovt Geneva plan cites 10-1, 750A2
Sadat cites Charter in Knesset speech 11-20, 892D3
Israel, Egypt envoys meet 11-27, 909D2
Cairo conf envoy named, Waldheim asks 2d pre-Geneva conf 11-29; Israel bars 11-30, 910G1
US effort vs Waldheim conf rptd 12-1, 910D1
Tripoli anti-Sadat mtg; Iraq vs res 242, 338 12-2—12-5, 929C1, E1
Vs UN chrmn at Cairo conf 12-13, 953C2
Observer at Cairo conf 12-14—12-15, 953B1, E1
Begin airs peace plan 12-28, 994G1

ECOSOC (Economic & Social Council)
PLO admitted 7-22, 572F2

General Assembly
Carter addresses 3-17, 186D1
Palestinians back natl rights resolutn 3-20, 208B1
US cites '47, '48 Palestine resolutns 5-26, 440D1, E1
League OKs anti-Israel setlmt proposal 9-4, 685C1
Egypt vs Israel peace stand 9-28, 734E1
Carter addresses 10-4, 749A2, 751D3
Dayan submits peace plan 10-10, PLO opposes 10-11, 769A2
Israeli W Bank setlmts 'deplored' 10-28, 830F2
Egypt envoy walks out on Syria 11-22, 894F1
Israel W Bank occupatn scored 11-25, 910C2
Palestine 'rights' publicity OKd 12-2, 931E1

Human Rights, Commission on
Israel occupatn rule scored 2-15, 107E2

ILO (International Labor Organization)
Israel occupied areas probe dropped 3-21, 227D2

Security Council
Waldheim rpts on mission 2-28, 144B1
Palestinians rejct refugee resolutn 3-20, 208B1

1978

SINAI—*See ARAB-Israeli Developments—Israeli Occupation Policies in this section above; for peace plans, see EGYPT-Israel Peace Moves above*

SUEZ—*For peace plans, see EGYPT-Israel Peace Moves above*

U.N. ROLE
Israel cites peace plan setlmt-zone provisn 2-12, 98C1
Arab League asks actn vs Israel Leb invasn 3-15, 174G3
Pro-Palestinian drive starts 10-7, 762G2-C3
Arafat for peace force in Palestine state 11-19, 893C1
Palestinian Solidarity Day marked, Sadat sends message; Israel scores rite 11-29, 951E2

General Assembly
33d sessn opens, issue on agenda 9-19, 713G2
Vance urges Palestinians join Egypt-Israel talks 9-29, 762E2
Pro-Palestinian drive starts 10-7, 762A3

Human Rights, Commission on
3 resolutns condemn Israel; back Palestinian state, PLO 2-14, 99G1

Peacekeeping Missions in the Middle East—*See also 'UNDOF' and 'UNIFIL' in this section below*
Weizman sees Siilasvuo on Leb refugees return 3-22, 197E2
Siilasvuo gets Israeli Leb pullback plan 4-6, 235F3, 236A1
Eitan, Siilasvuo agree on contd Leb exit 4-18, 274F2
Siilasvuo at Leb govt mtg 6-14, 462D2
Israel vs Geneva conf role 7-1, 502G1
Egypt details W Bank, Gaza plan; text 7-5, 501C1, G1, G2

Security Council—*For Resolution 242 controversy, see EGYPT-Israel Peace Moves in this section above*
Leb protests Israel invasn 3-15, 174C3
Meets on Israel invasn of Leb 3-17; res asks Israeli exit, forms peace force; text 3-19, 197A1-C2
Carter: Begin talks failed 3-24, 214G2
Waldheim rpts on Leb, Israel missn 4-20, 274B2
Unifil expansn voted; USSR, Czech, China abstain 5-3, 340F1
Arafat: PLO vs truce, peace force formatn 5-11, 383A3
UNDOF mandate renewed 5-31, 400A2
Leb tells permanent members of army shift to south 7-28, 581E1
Waldheim asks Unifil extensn 9-14, 4-mo mandate OKd 9-18, 713B1
Res urges Leb truce, Waldheim role 10-6, 761C1

UNDOF (United Nations Disengagement Observer Force)
Syria chrgs Israeli violatn of '74 troop pullback pact 4-2, 236D3
Mandate renewed for 6 mos 5-31, 400A2

UNEF (United Nations Emergency Force)
Sadat warns re expiratn date 5-30, 424A2

1979

Canada envoy rpts mtg, denies recognitn 10-20, 833E2
Dayan quits Israeli Cabt in policy dispute 10-21, 801F1
Rabin book censored by Israel 10-22, 823F1
Arab League to press PLO cause 11-22, 916C2
UN Assemb rejcts Israel-Egypt pact 11-29; US, Israel score vote 11-29, 12-2, 979F2
UN marks solidarity day 11-29, 979G2

U.S. Policies—*See 'Palestinian Issues' under U.S. ROLE below*

SINAI—*See also EGYPT-Israel Peace Moves—Pact in this section above*
Israel pullout set 3-26, starts 3-27, 221B2, 223E1, F2, 226G3
Israel exit plan maps 249A1
Israel exit talks start 4-25—4-27, 4-29, 320C1
Israel settlers resist El Arish farmland ouster 5-24, 394D1
Israel starts exit, gives Egypt El Arish 5-25; Sadat visits 5-26, 393G2
Egypt bars Israel settlers in El Arish 5-28, 395C1
Israel reaffirms oilfield return to Egypt 7-12, 511A3
UN rpt asks Israel setlmt halt 7-14, 551C2
UNEF mandate expires, UNTSO replaces; Israel vs, Egypt OKs 7-24; US disputes Israel 7-25, 551A1
Israel returns more land 7-25, 550D3
Vance sees Israel amb re UNTSO 7-27; Egypt, Israel talks asked 7-29, 574F2
UNTSO units take over; US, Sovt offcr departures rptd 8-1, 574D2
US, Israel conf on UNTSO 8-8, 591A2
Israel, Egypt OK joint patrols 9-5, 658D1
US, Egypt, Israel OK pact observance 9-19, 694C1
Israel returns more land 9-25, 740C3
Israel Cabt OKs monitor plan 10-7, 823D1
Israel returns Mt Sinai to Egypt 11-15, Sadat visits 11-19, 881D3
Israel returns Alma oilfield to Egypt 11-25, 916E2

SUEZ—*See also EGYPT-Israel Peace Moves—Pact in this section above*
Israel cargo ship transits canal 4-30, 320E1
Israel warships transit canal 5-29, 395D1
Sadat urges tunnel to channel water to Sinai, Negev 9-5, 658C2
Israel returns Alma oilfield to Egypt 11-25, 916E2

U.N. ROLE
Young for new approach to PLO 1-16, Jewish group protests 1-17, 69E1
Israel Sinai exit maps, schedule 249A1
Young quits after PLO contact 8-15; US, forgn reactn 8-15, 8-16, 605A1, 606E1-F2

General Assembly
Com OKs res on Palestinian rights 8-21, Cncl delays vote 8-24, 642D1, E2
Palestinian film previewed 8-28, 643D2
Vance urges Leb peace, Hussein proposes UN conf 9-24, 741C2
Pope addresses 10-2, 758F1
Castro address scores US, Israel 10-12, 778F2
Israel-Egypt peace pact rejctd 11-29; US, Israel score vote 11-29, 12-2, 979F2
Palestinian Solidarity Day marked 11-29, 979G2

Human Rights, Commission on
Resolutns condemn Israel, back Palestinian state 2-21, 148D1
US delegate backs anti-Israel res 9-5, US govt dissociates 9-6, 659E2

Peacekeeping Missions in the Middle East—*See also other appropriate subheads in this section*
Israel-Egypt pact gives role 3-26, 223C2-226G3
Leb fighting interventn 8-25, truce effected 8-26, 642A3

Security Council
Leb protests Israeli shelling 1-23, 50F3
W Bank setlmt probe voted, Israel to bar 3-22, 198E2-A3
Israel-Egypt treaty signed, Res 242, 338 cited 3-26, 223B1
Leb scores Israel air strike 4-11, 278E2
Waldheim vs Israel, Christn, PLO role in Leb 4-21, 296D3
Leb lauded for sending troops to south 4-26, 297A1
UNDOF mandate renewed for 6 mos 5-30, 395E1
Leb asks mtg on Israel-PLO clashes 5-30, truce set 5-31, 414D3
Waldheim asks Unifil renewal 6-11–6-12, mandate extended 6 mos 6-14, 436A3
Israel setlmts opposed in rpt 7-14, Israel scores 7-18; res seeks halt, US abstains 7-20, 551A2
UNEF mandate expires, UNTSO replaces 7-24, 551A1
Res 242 debate delayed 7-30, 591E3
UNTSO units take over 8-1, 574E2
PLO demands Res 242 chng 8-12, 606E3-607B1
US denies Res 242 chng sought 8-13, 606B3
Young on PLO contacts as Cncl pres 8-7, 624F3; 8-16, 606E1

1980

Sinai
US bases backed by Reagan 1-9, 13E2
Egypt, Israel OK buffer zone policing 1-24, 68B2
Israel ends pullout phase 1-25, 68G1
US airfields backed by Connally 2-20, 129F3

UN Policy & Developments
Cncl res demands Israel raze setlmts, scores E Jerusalem rule 3-1; US backs vote 3-1, disavows 3-3, Vance takes blame 3-4; Israel, intl, US reactn 3-4—3-5, 162E2-164E1
Israel res text 3-1, 179C1
Begin scores Cncl setlmts res, Carter vote reversal 3-6, 179B1-B2
US curbs Israeli setlmt vote info 3-12; Cong coms open probes, Vance defends US stand 3-20, 3-21, 218B2
Carter calls Cncl vote 'honest breakdown', says US policy unchngd 3-14, 209F1
Cncl setlmts res a NY primary issue 3-25, 221C2, B3
Bush scores US 'fiasco' 4-7, 264D2
US vetoes Cncl res for Palestinian state; US, Sovt aides assaulted at mtg 4-30, 325D1, G1
Cncl censures Israel W Bank ousters 5-20, 381C1
Cncl scores Israel for W Bank bombings 6-5, 417A2
US protests Israeli constructn bid rejctn 6-19, 476B2
Cncl res scores Israel Jerusalem moves, US abstains 6-30, 491B2
Assemb meets 7-22; backs Palestine state, asks Israel quit '67 lands, US votes vs 7-29, 572E1
Cncl res scores Israel Jerusalem policies, US abstains 8-20, 627C2
Israel scores US Jerusalem abstentn 8-23, 643B2; 8-28, 660A3
Islamic conf, Syria asks Israel ouster 9-20, 9-30, 736B2
Reagan vows Israel support 10-1, 738B2
Moslems drop Israel ouster plan 10-9, 775F1
Arafat addresses UNESCO conf 10-27, 821E3
2 W Bank mayors to appeal deportatn 12-6, 931E2
Assemb hears Jordan, Israel exchng chrgs 12-8, 12-10; asks Israel quit Arab lands; scores Camp David pact, E Jerusalem annexatn 12-15, 952F2
UNIFIL mandate extended 6 mos 12-17, 977D3
Cncl asks Israel readmit 2 W Bank mayors; mayors stage sit-in, hunger strike 12-19, 952B2
Israel protests Arab mayors support 12-22; mayors end hunger strike 12-24, 976E3
S Leb protesters raid 2 offices in Beirut 12-23, 977B3

U.S. Presidential Election (& Transition)
Reagan backs Sinai bases 1-9, 13E2
Kennedy seeks mil force 1-11, 32E3
Connally backs mil presence, regional alliances 2-20, 129F3

1976

Refugees, Office of the High Commissioner for
Rpts Leb civil war losses 2-21, 145E2
Security Council
Arabs, Israel briefed on US stand 18F2
Israel warns vs peace role 1-4, 1-11, 18C3
US vows veto on PLO resolutns 1-7—1-9, Israel confirms 1-9, 18E2
Israel opens new Golan setlmt 1-9, 35A2
Israel boycotts debate, scores Arab stand 1-12, 18B1, E1
Mideast debate opens, PLO seated; US vs; UK, France, Italy abstain 1-12, 18B1
W Bank Arabs back PLO 1-12, 35E1
Egypt, Syria, Jordan assail Israel 1-13, France, Sweden, Japan urge restraint 1-14, 18G1
China, USSR clash in Palestine debate 1-25, 60A1
US vetoes pro-Palestine resolutn, UK amendmt rejctd; Syria, Jordan, Egypt score 1-26, 59G2-G3
Libya, Pak ask session 3-22, 211E1
Israel ends boycott re PLO 3-22; US statemts on Israeli occupation 3-23, 3-24, vetoes resolutn 3-25, 211E1
Egypt, PLO score US veto 3-26, 227F2
Israel vs Scranton speech 3-26, 227A3
Waldheim warns on Leb 3-30; US, UK back talks 3-30, Arabs vs 3-31, 226A2
Egypt asks mtg on W Bank 5-3; 319F2; debate starts, US vs PLO seating status, Egypt urges anti-Israel vote 5-4, Israel scores Egypt 5-5, 320A1
Israel: Arabs paid for W Bank riots 5-7, 338G2
Israeli setlmts scored, US vs statemt text 5-26, 406B3
Extends UNDOF 6 months 5-28, 385F2
Israel exit asked; US vetoes, Israel scores res 6-29, 464B1
Leb pres vs Libya in peace force 6-30, 487C2
Amin vs Israel Uganda raid 7-5, 486C1
Meets on Israel Uganda raid 7-9; Uganda, Kenya, Israel, US statemts 7-9—7-13; deadlock 7-14, 515D3
Extends UNEF one-yr 10-22, 799B2
Nixon tapes release OKd 10-26, 849A3
Egypt-requested debate on Israel occupatn starts, PLO gets debate role 11-1; Israel condemnd, US joins stand 11-11, 842A1, F1
Extends UNDOF 6 mos; Syrian PLO move blocked by Israel, West 11-30, 895B2
Assemb asks Waldheim Geneva conf rpt 12-9, 914E1
UNCTAD (UN Conference on Trade & Development)
PLO joins 1-27, 85A2
UNDOF (UN Disengagement Observer Force)
Extended 6 months 5-28, 385F2
Extended 6 months 11-30, 895B2
UNEF (UN Emergency Force)
Troops withdraw from Sinai area 1-26, 60C2
Sinai pullback completed 2-22, 145D1
Extended, Waldheim rpts 10-22, 799B2
UNESCO (Educational, Scientific & Cultural Organization)
Racism parley postponed 1-15, 36E2
Sets '77 occupied area probe 11-18, 879B1
Restores Israel membership; scores occupied area policies 11-22, 878D3
UNRWA (Relief & Works Agency for Palestinian Refugees in the Near East)
Assemb vs Israel Gaza resettlmts 11-23, 878G2
UNTSO (UN Truce Supervision Organization)
Supervises Israel, Leb Arab Army talks 8-4, 578A2
WHO (World Health Organization)
Medical rpt on W Bank, Gaza 5-10, 338C2
Rejcts Israel med rpt 5-17; OKs anti-Israel resolutn 5-19, 355F1

1977

Cncl debates, bars PLO Geneva conf role 3-25, 3-28—3-29, 226F3
US expands '73 resolutns 5-26, Israel protests 5-28, 440C1, G1
PLO hints shift on Res 242 8-8, 605C1
PLO vs Res 242 8-26, 662B3
US seeks Res 242, 338 compliance 9-12, PLO response 9-13, 697C1, F1
Israel scores US-Sovt Geneva plan re Res 242, 338 10-1, 750D1
Israel-US Geneva plan backs 242, 338 10-5, 749D1; Israel Cabt OKs 10-11, 769D1
Sadat, Begin cite res in Knesset addresses 11-20, 891B3, 894A3
Begin airs peace plan 12-28, 994G1
UNEF (UN Emergency Force)
Sovts bar funds 12-30-76; renew stand 1-6; US scores 1-7, 4G1
Israel, Egypt swap jailed Arabs for '73 war dead, 2 '55 hanged spies 4-14, 4-19, 297F1
Extended for 1-yr 10-21, 812A1
UNESCO
Israel to lift '74 ban 8-31, 663F2-A3
UNRWA (UN Relief & Works Agency)
US vows more refugee aid 7-12, 550D2

U.S. DEVELOPMENTS—*See also EGYPT-Israel Peace Moves in this section above; also LEBANON under 'L'*
Daoud release scored 1-11—1-12, 9F2; 1-13—1-18, 27E2-B3, 28B1
Vance plans tour; Carter sees '77 conf, PLO role 1-24, 51G3
Israel favors peace role 2-6, 86A3
Israel Suez oil drilling scored 2-14, 107B2
Vance in Israel, 5 Arab states; seeks views on PLO, Geneva conf 2-15—2-21, 121A1-122C1
Vance lauds Sadat PLO-Jordan link plan 2-18, 121C2
CIA paymts to Jordan rptd; Carter, PLO reactn 2-18, 123D3, 124E2; 2-25, 151A3
Carter plans to meet ldrs 2-23, 126F2
Carter meets Rabin; peace plan offered, F-16s promised 3-7—3-8, 165A1-A2
Carter outlines setlmt views; Arabs, Israelis reassured 3-9, 165B1, B2
Egypt scores Carter views 3-10, 166D1
PLO assails Carter plan 3-10, 187B3
Sadat vs Carter on Israeli borders 3-12, 187C2
Vance meets Arab ambs 3-12, 187C3
Rabin vs Carter on Israeli exit, denies total pullout asked 3-13, 187E2
Rabin denies Carter plan same as Rogers 3-14, backs Carter on overall setlmt 3-15, 187G2
Austria-US talks 3-14, 425F1
Carter backs Palestine 'homeland' 3-16; Israel, PLO reactn 3-17, 187D3
Carter addresses UN, greets PLO rep 3-17, 185G1, 186D1
US scores Palestine Natl Cncl policy 3-21, 208E1
Carter defends speaking out 3-24, 230D1
Carter meets Sadat; US aid, Egypt peace plan discussed 4-4—4-5; Sadat rpts differences 4-6, 245A1
Carter sees Hussein, Geneva conf delay backed 4-25—4-26, 315G3-316B1
Israel sees US differences 4-25, 316G1
PLO stresses Geneva conf role, vs Carter 'homeland' ref 5-1, 360E3
PLO chrgs US plot vs Hussein 5-8, 360C3
Carter meets Assad, backs Palestine 'homeland' 5-9, 360G1
USSR rpts: PLO may recognize Israel; US doubts 5-9—5-11, 360F2-C3, 361C1
Vance briefs Allon on Carter-Assad talks, assures Israel 5-11; Carter assures, Israel pleased 5-12, 360G3
Nixon on '73 war 5-12, 385E3, 386E1

1978

UNIFIL (United Nations Interim Force in Lebanon)—*For military developments, see LEBANON in this section above*
Sec Cncl res forms; text 3-19, 197A1-A2
Erskine heads; compositn cited 197D2
Israel, UN meet on deploymt 3-21, 197E2
Austria bars role 3-29, 214C1
Mex vows troops 4-1, reversal rptd 4-5, 236E1
Leb asks more troops 4-4, 236D1
Force at 1,800 4-11, more arrive 4-12, 256E2
Expansn voted; Iran, Fiji, Ireland to give troops 5-3, 340F1
Hq moved to Israel zone 5-8, 340D1
Arafat: PLO vs formatn 5-11, 383B3
PLO vows cooperatn 5-24, 400B3
Waldheim asks extensn 9-14, 4-mo mandate voted 9-18, 713B1
United Nations Disengagement Observer Force—*See 'UNDOF' above*
United Nations Emergency Force—*See 'UNEF' above*
United Nations Interim Force in Lebanon—*See 'UNIFIL' above*
United Nations Relief & Works Agency—*See 'UNRWA' in this section below*
UNRWA (United Nations Relief & Works Agency)
Leb refugees flee Israeli invasn 3-18, 3-19, 198A2

U.S. ROLE—*See also ARAB-Israeli Developments—Israeli Occupation Policies, ARMAMENTS, EGYPT-Israel Peace Moves and LEBANON in this section above*
Palestinian vote backed, separate state opposed 1-6, 10E2
Carter defines real peace 1-30, 62E2
Carter links problems, poll drop 3-2, 141F1
Carter backs Palestinian solutn 3-7—3-9, 194B1
Carter vs indep Palestinan state 4-30, Egypt reassured 5-1, 339E2
Arafat asks guarantees for Palestine state 5-1, 339B3
Carter vows peace committmt 6-26, 491F1
Carter signs '79 aid authorzn 9-26, 734F1
Carter signs '79 aid funds 10-18, 862C2
Camp David Summit—*See under EGYPT-Israel Peace Moves in this section above*
Israel
Carter mtgs with Jewish ldrs disclosed 2-9, 98A1
UN comm res vs Israel opposed 2-14, 99A2
Begin, Weizman to visit 2-15, 97A2
Weizman arrives for talks 3-7, 157F1
Carter aide quits staff, vs US stand 3-8, 3-9, 176C2
Brzezinski rebuts Jewish critics 3-8, 176B3
US Jewish ldr on aide resignatn; scores US policy, Brzezinski 3-9, 176G2
Begin postpones visit 3-11, 175E3, 176B2
Ribicoff vs pro-Israel lobby 3-13, 176C3
Begin in US, Carter talks deadlocked 3-20—3-21; cong coms questn Begin 3-21, 199B1
Carter: Begin talks failed, US bars statemt 3-23, 214F2
Begin asks US pub backing 3-23; returns Israel, calls Carter talks 'difficult' 3-24, 214B3
Israel Cabt reviews Begin-Carter talks, backs Begin 3-26; Knesset backs Begin 3-29, 214D1, G1
Israel, US deny US plan to oust Begin 3-26, 214F1
Begin meets Carter, US aid reaffirmed 5-1; Begin tours US 5-2—5-8, returns Israel 5-9, 339G1
Arafat asks US guarantees 5-1, 339B3
Mondale visits 6-30—7-3, 501B1, B2
US vows to help build 2 air bases 9-28, 9-29, 746E1

1979

Egypt, Israel vs US plan for new res 8-17—8-19, 623A2-B3
Assemb unit OKs Palestinian rights res; text 8-21; debate opens 8-23, vote delayed 8-24, 642D1-A3
US asks halt to clashes 8-29, Waldheim urges truce observance 8-30, 658D2
Arab League to submit peace formula 11-22, 916C2
UNCTAD (United Nations Conference on Trade and Development)
Cuban res urging pro-Palestinian role dropped 6-3, 417B3
UNDOF (United Nations Disengagement Observer Force)
Mandate renewed for 6 mos 5-30, 395E1
UNEF (United Nations Emergency Force)
Mandate expires, UNTSO to replace; Israel vs, Egypt OKs 7-24; US disputes Israel 7-25, 551A1
UNTSO takeover starts 8-1, 574D2
Israel, Egypt, US in Sinai observer pact 9-19, 694C1
UNIFIL (United Nations Interim Force in Lebanon)—*See also ARAB-Israeli Developments–Palestinian-Israeli Conflict and LEBANON in this section above*
Dutch to replace French unit 1-12, troops balk 2-1, 84G3
Christian harassmt chrgd 1-16, 51D1
Mandate extended 5 mos 1-19, 51C1
Israel arrests Senegal offcr 2-18, 157A2; sentncs 5-10, 341A3
Waldheim asks renewal 6-11—6-12; mandate extended 6 mos 6-14, 436A3
Israel arrests Nigeria officer 6-15, PLO arms smuggling admitted 6-22, 551F3
Senegal pres scores Israel offcr arrest 9-20, 721G1
Israel sentncs, expels Nigeria offcr 12-24, 980B1
United Nations Disengagement Observer Force—*See 'UNDOF' above*
United Nations Emergency Force—*See 'UNEF' above*
United Nations Interim Force in Lebanon—*See 'UNIFIL' above*
United Nations Relief & Works Agency—*See 'UNRWA' in this section below*
UNTSO (United Nations Truce Supervision Organization)
Israel Sinai exit monitoring set; Israel vs, Egypt OKs 7-24; US disputes Israel 7-25, 551A1-A2
Vance sees Israel amb re oppositn 7-27; Egypt, Israel talks asked 7-29, 574F2
Sinai units take over; US, Sovt offcr departures rptd 8-1, 574D2
US, Israel confer 8-8, 591A2
Israel, Egypt, US in Sinai observer pact 9-19, 694F1
WHO (World Health Organization)
Arab anti-Israel moves blocked 5-22; W Bank, Gaza health probe set 5-23, 398E2

U.S. ROLE—*See also ARAB-Israel Developments—Israeli Occupation Policies, ARMAMENTS and EGYPT-Israel headings in this section above*
Guadeloupe summit topic 1-5—1-6, 12G2
Israel stops Leb shelling 1-24, 69A2
Brown urges US response to Sovt surrogates 2-8, 89D2
Brown, Schlesinger see US defns of oil interests 2-25; remarks clarified 2-26, 2-27, 143D3-144B1
Strauss named 'superamb' 4-24, 295G3-296C1
Leonard named Strauss dep 5-12, 379B1
Strauss to start job early 5-18, 378D3-379A1
US sen scores Sovt policy 6-12, 459F2
UN rep scores Unifil res 6-14, 436B3
SALT II summit topic 6-15—6-18, 449D1; communique text 458A2
UN Israel setlmts halt res abstentn 7-20, 551B2
UNTSO to replace UNEF 7-24, 551A1
Vance sees Israel amb re UNTSO 7-27; Egypt, Israel talks asked 7-29; US offcr departures rptd 8-1, 574E2
Israel sees US policy shift re Arab oil need 8-7; Carter-Evron conf, policy shift denied 8-8, 591F1, E2
Israel assures US re arms use vs Leb 9-17, 694B1
Israel end to Arab land-purchase ban opposed 9-18, 693A1, E1
US, Israel dispute Leb bombing 9-18, 693E2
Israeli-Syria air clash deplored, Leb peace urged 9-24, 740D2
Carter, Pope issue statemt 10-6, 759D3
Connally outlines peace plan 10-11, 783F1
Castro scores policies 10-12, 778F2
Strauss quits as amb, Linowitz named 11-6, 938A1, 961B2
Palestinian Issues—*See also 'Palestinian Autonomy Talks' under EGYPT-Israel Relations above*
Israel, PLO Leb violence deplored; Israel F-15 use cited 6-27, 475G1
Young meets PLO rep 7-26, informs State Dept 8-11; State gives acct 8-13; Young scored by Vance, Israel 8-14, quits UN post 8-15, 605A1-606A1
Israel assured on PLO 7-27, 575B1

1980

Kennedy scores Israeli setlmt vote at UN 3-4, 164C1; 3-10, 183D3; Carter gaffe 3-18, 206F3
UN Cncl vote a NY primary issue 3-25, 221C2, B3
Bush scores UN 'fiasco' 4-7, 264D2
Anderson in E Jerusalem 7-11, 549F3
Reagan accepts nominatn 7-17, 533A1, E1
Dem platform planks adopted 8-13, 615A3
Mondale accepts renominatn 8-14, 612C1
Carter accepts renominatn 8-14, 613D1
Anderson platform offered 8-30, 665A2
Pres candidates vow Israel support 9-3—9-4, 681A3
Carter cites peace efforts 9-18, 698B3
Carter scores UN move to oust Israel 9-29, 739A1
Reagan vows Israel UN support 10-1, 738B2
Bush scores Carter 'flipflop' 10-16, 10-19, 817C3
Carter lauds Israeli jet success 10-24, 816A3
Mondale hails Carter record, discounts Reagan 10-26, 816E3
Carter, Reagan TV debate 10-28, 813G2, 814E2
Carter hits Reagan on A-arms 10-29, 816C2

U.S. Relations—*See also specific subheads in this section*
Turkey-US bases pact set 1-9, 22C3
Carter calls peace treaty achievemt 1-20, 50G1; 1-23, 42G1, B3
US for peaceful solutn 2-5, 83B2
Arab hardliners reaffirm oppositn 4-14—4-15, 284E2
US evangelicals back Israel 7-11—9-15, 819B1
Carter vows Israel support 9-4, 681E3
Arafat UNESCO address boycotted 10-27, 821E3
Arab summit seeks anti-Israel policy, 6 states boycott 11-27, 911F1

1976

1977

Begin assures US on peace, Carter blamed for electn win 5-17; US reactn 5-18, 377B2, 378B1
PLO scores re Israel electn 5-19, 401B3
Carter stresses peace chance 5-22, 397B1
Begin vs Carter proposals 5-22, 401G2
Carter meets Saudi Prince Fahd; oil embargo barred 5-24—5-25, 401F3
Carter sees Begin moderatn 5-26, 417G1
Carter for Palestine homeland, compensatn; statemt clarified 5-26; Israel protests 5-28—5-31, 440B1
Hussein backs Carter efforts 5-31, 496E1
Begin aide in US 6-2, 440C2
Rpt Carter urged Israel keep Golan, holy shrines 6-11, 6-13, 474B1
US sets terms for Libya ties 6-13, 488D1
Carter assures Israel 6-15, 474A1
US denies vs Palestine state 6-16, 496G1
Mondale ties Israel exit to peace, asks Palestine 'homeland' 6-17; Israel sees no change 6-19, 473B2
Syria blames for Israel hard line 6-17, 496F1
Begin asks strong ties 6-21, 474D2
US presses Israel exit 6-27; Israel denies territory talks oppositn; Rabin chrgs US reneged 6-28, 495C2
Sen Javits vs US peace plan 6-27, 495B3, E3
9 US sens back Carter efforts 6-29, 496B1
Carter sets moratorium on US statemts; stresses US Israel support 6-30, 510A1, C1
Sadat told Carter Israel ties impossible 7-2, 509G1
Carter assures US Jewish ldrs on Israel support; for Arab Israel recognitn 7-6, 509E2
Carter lauds Sadat peace moves, Hussein mtg 7-12, 533E2
More refugee aid vowed 7-12, 550D2
PFLP vs Egypt re US support 7-14, 535A1
Begin meets Carter 7-19—7-20; airs Israeli peace plan 7-20; cites US-Israel differences 7-21, 549A1-B2
US confirms Scranton-PLO mtg, denies US mission role 7-19, 550C2
Vance to visit Mideast 7-20, 549B2
US-PLO contacts rptd 7-20, 550A2
USSR study chrgs US Jews role 7-22, 589A2
Begin, Rabin clash re US confrontatns 7-23, 7-25, 7-27, 570G2, D3-G3
US scores W Bank setlmt legalizatn 7-27, 7-28; Begin rejcts criticism, wins confidence vote on US visit 7-27, 570C1-F2
Vance meets Sadat, backs Arab-Israel pre-Geneva conf plan 8-1—8-2; meets Assad, plan opposed 8-4, 588G1, G2
US-W Bank flights barred 8-1, 589B1
Israel backs Egypt-US conf plan 8-3, 588D3
'78 arms, security aid signed 8-4, 668A1, E1
Vance in Jordan 8-5—8-7, Saudi 8-7—8-9, Israel 8-9—8-10; briefs Syria, Jordan, Egypt ldrs 8-11, 605A1
PLO hints UN Res 242 shift, Carter lauds 8-8, 605C1
Israel, Arab reactn to Vance trip 8-11, 8-12, 8-14, 623B2
US vs new rights for W Bank, Gaza Arabs 8-14, 623B1
Vance briefs Carter on missn, Carter renews Israel peace plea 8-14; US: next move PLO's 8-16, 623B2
US vs new W Bank setlmts 8-17, 8-18, 622C3
Israel rejcts W Bank policy protests 8-18, 623B1
Israel vs W Bank stand 8-21, 648B2
Carter scores W Bank setlmts 8-23, 649D3
PLO vs peace moves 8-26, 662B3
Arafat assails US aims 8-30, 663C1
USSR scores US on W Bank setlmts 9-2, 685C2
US asks Palestinian peace role 9-12; Israel, Arab reactn 9-13, 697A1
Palestinians accuse Israel re '67 Liberty attack 9-18, 715A1
Dayan sees Carter, other US offcls; gives US peace plan, US presses compromise 9-19, 713G1
Dayan at US House com hearing, backs Haifa base 9-20, US rules out 9-22, 714A1
Carter, Vance see Egypt forgn min 9-21, 714D1
Israel OKs US plan, sets terms 9-25; Vance, Dayan on PLO issue 9-26, 9-27, 733G1
Brookings study sees need for US buildup 9-26, 858B1
Carter meets Syria, Jordan reps 9-28, 734A1
Carter for PLO peace role 9-29, 734F1
Gromyko meets Vance 9-30; **US-Sovt Geneva plan issued 10-1, 749B2; text 750A1**
US-Sovt plan scored by Israel, in US 10-2—10-3; PLO lauds 10-2, Iraq vs 10-3, 749F2
Israel, US OK Geneva plan 10-4—10-5; Israel welcomes, Dayan urges Cabt OK 10-5, 749A1-A2
Carter reaffirms Israeli commitmt, backs Palestinian rights 10-4, 749A2, 751D3
Carter sees Fahmy 10-4, 749A2
Libya vs US efforts, asks drive vs Israel 10-8, 793G1
Dayan gives 4-pt plan 10-10, PLO vs 10-11, 769A2
Brzezinski sees better USSR ties 10-18, 866E1

1978

1979

Carter likens Palestinian claims to US civil rights drive, bars Palestinian state 7-31; US Jews, blacks, Israel protest 8-1, 8-2, 575C1
Israel assured re Res 242 7-31, 8-8, 591G1, F3
Carter vs Palestinian state 8-10, 606G2
PLO minimizes contacts 8-11, 607A1
Dayan: US OKs Israel raids on Leb 8-13, 625C2
Strauss repeats Res 242 stance 8-13, 606B3
US amb to Austria met PLO rep 8-15, 605E1; Kreisky details 8-22, 625B1
US, PLO, other forgn reactn to Young resignatn 8-15, 8-16, 606E1-F2
Israel sees policy shift in Young-PLO mtg 8-15, 8-16, 606D2-E2
Young warns Israel of pro-PLO backlash 8-16, 606A1
US, Israel deny Young-PLO talks bugged 8-16, 606D1
Young on PLO contacts as Sec Cncl pres 8-16, 606E1; 8-17, 624F3
NY Times clarifies Carter rights remark 8-17, 607C1
Arafat warns vs blocking state 8-20, 659A2
US Jewish groups reject black PLO support 8-23, 661B3
UN delays vote on res 8-24, 642E1
Young scores US policy, Blum rebuts 8-24, 642F1-B2
Harris seeks black-Jewish reconciliatn 8-29, 661A3
Carter: Arabs vs independent state 8-30, 659C1
Carter urges black-Jewish amity, denied Young tap 8-30, 661B2
Dayan mtgs with PLO backers lauded 9-5, 659C1
Young vs US PLO stance 9-6 seeks Africa Israel ties 9-20, 720C3, 721A2
Strauss reassures Israel on PLO overtures, lauds Leb truce observance 9-11–9-12, 676B3
NAACP backs US-PLO talks, Israel existence 9-11, 677D1
SCLC visits Leb 9-18–9-20, 694F1
SCLC ends Leb visit 9-21, 763C2
Young scores Israel, calls US black PLO support 'natural' 9-22, 721B2
Carter denies US Jewish pressure to oust Young 9-23, 763E2
Young: Dayan aired Terzi mtg 9-24; Young meets Dayan; absolves Dayan, Israel 9-26, 763G2
Jesse Jackson in Mideast, meets Arafat 9-25–10-5; briefs Strauss, Saunders 10-8, 762F3
2 US Jewish ldrs quit Jackson tour 9-26, 763B2
NAACP warns vs black support of PLO 10-11, 780F2
Connally backs state 10-11, 783A2
US Arab group gives PUSH $10,000 10-13, 780G3
NAACP, Urban League, AFL rights dir in Israel: score black support of PLO, back Palestinians, Israel govt 10-14–10-17, 780C2, C3
Baptist Conf scores criticism of blacks 10-14; NAACP, other blacks vs split; Jackson, Jordan 'reaffirm unity' 10-17, 780D2, A3
US rep rebuts Young re PLO mtg rpt, denies Israel, US bugging 10-28, 823D2
PLO reps in Iran re US Emb hostages 11-7–11-11; Iran rebuffs, Clark contacts rep in Turkey 11-8, 841B1, 842B1, F1, 862G1
UN Assemb vote on Egypt-Israel pact scored 11-29, 979G2

1980

1976

WEST Bank—*See 'Occupation Policies' under ISRAELI Policies in this section above*

MIDDLE Eastern Airlines
82 die in Saudi crash 1-1, 79G3
MIDDLETOWN, O.—*See OHIO*
MIDDLETOWN, Pa.—*See PENNSYLVANIA*
MIDLAND, Tex.—*See TEXAS*
MIDWESTERN Grain Co.—*See GARNAC Grain*
MIELKE, Erich
Named to E Ger Politburo 5-22, 381D2
MIELZINER, Jo
Dies 3-15, 240E3
MIETTUNEN, Martti J.
Rpts CP support, Sovt bloc trade moves 2-2, 155A2
'76 legis progrm announced 3-9, 289G3
Submits resignatn, Kekkonen bars 5-13; coalitn restored 5-18, 350F2, 364A3
MIETTUNEN, Martti
Resigns 9-17, 731E2
Sworn Finland premier 9-29, 750B3, C3
MIGHTY Mouse (comic books)
Peru bans 2-3, 142F3
MIGRANT Workers—*See under AGRICULTURE*
MIGUEL, Lorenzo
Negotiates wage hike 1-22, 96D2
Backs Peron cabt shift 1-23, 71E2
Econ plan protested 3-8—3-13, 212F2
Arrested 3-24, 211G2
Pol rights revoked, arrest ordrd 6-23, 520D1
MIHAILOV, Ivan
On Bulgarian Politburo 4-2, 250D1
MIHAJLOV, Mihajlo
Ends hunger strike 3-21, 256D2
Transferred to hospital 4-20, 542G3
MIHARA, Asao
Japan defense min 12-24, 1006B3
MIKADO, The (play)
Opens 5-5, 1014C3
MIKARDO, Ian
Labor opposes EC parlt vote 9-29, 791A3
MIKI, Takeo
Seeks A-pact ratificatn 1-9, 51C2
Urged to end arms export ban 1-9—2-1, 157F1-A2
OKs China peace treaty, rebuffs USSR 1-13, 29F3
Seeks 12-mi waters limit, US fishing talks 2-2, 141A2
Backs Lockheed payoffs probe 2-6, 131A3
In Australia talks 2-12, 137E3
Presses Lockheed payoffs probe 2-19, 190A2
Ford offers secret Lockheed data 3-11, 199E3
Accepts Lockheed data offer 3-12, 286D1
Vows Lockheed probe cooperatn 4-22, 313G2
Ouster sought 5-13; defends policy 5-26, 458G1-C2
Diet ratifies A-pact 5-24, 419B1
Party rebels seek new party 6-14, 458E1
Signs Australia pact 6-16, 481B1
At 7-natn econ summit 6-27—6-28, 461G2, 462E1
Vows full Lockheed probe 7-28, 557E1
Asked to quit re Lockheed 8-23, 8-24, refuses 8-24, 626C3
Offers Cabt, party chngs 8-30, LDP members ask resignatn 9-7, 676F3
Regrets Mao death 9-9, 657D2
Shuffles Cabt, LDP 9-15, special Diet mtg held 9-16, 694D1
Sees Lockheed probe delay 9-24, 740A3
Utsonomiya quits parlt, LDP 10-13, 838D3
Signs Canada pact 10-21, 836G2
Foes ask resignatn 10-21, 839A1
LDP conventn canceled 10-29, 838F3
Fukuda quits Cabt 11-5, 889F3
LDP suffers electn loss 12-5, takes blame 12-7, 925C3, F3
Quits as premr, LDP head 12-17; Fukuda succeeds 12-23, 12-24, 1006D2
MIKLAVCIC, Franc
Arrested 5-17; sentncd 10-15, 910D1
MIKULSKI, Barbara Ann
Elected 11-2, 821E1, 825F2 ⋆, 829A4
MIKVA, Rep. Abner J. (D, Ill.)
Reelectn undecided 11-2, 823A2, 829G2
Declared winner 11-19, 882A1
MILCZAREK, Maria
Named admin, econ min 12-2, 926D3
MILFORD, Rep. Dale (D, Tex.)
Scores House com intellignc rpt 2-3, 150C2
Reelected 11-2, 830F4
MILITARY Academy, U.S.—*See under U.S. GOVERNMENT—ARMY*
MILITOSYAN, Vartan
Wins Olympic medal 7-22, 576E2
MILK—*See DAIRY Products*
MILK Producers Inc., Associated
Jacobsen gets 2 yrs probatn 8-20, 1016A1
MILLAN, Bruce
Scotland secy of state 4-8, 266F3
Named min for Scotland 9-10, 694A1

1977

Syria, PLO vs US-Israeli plan 10-21, 831A2
Vance, Carter assure US Jews on policies 10-26, 11-2; Kissinger vs Palestine state 11-3, 830A3-831F1
Carter on US efforts 10-27, 813G2
Carter pol prospects polled 10-31, 831F1
US proposes W Bank plan 11-5, Israel vs 11-6, 850B2
Egypt bares '75 pacts 11-26, 909E1

WEST Bank—*See ARAB-Israeli Developments—Israel Occupation in this section above; for peace plans, see EGYPT-Israel Peace Moves*

MIDDLE East Airlines
Jet hijacked to Kuwait 6-5, 497D3
Kuwait frees hijacker 8-29, 736C2
MIDWAY Islands (U.S. territory)
Greek oil tanker spill 1-17, 214G2
MIDWEST Stock Exchange
Options trading expanded 3-4, 521E1
SEC limits optns trading, begins probe 10-18, 859C3
MIGRANT Workers—*See under AGRICULTURE*
MIGUEL, Lorenzo
Graiver probe protectn rptd 4-22, 371E2
MIHAI, Florenta
Loses French Open 6-5, 548B2
MIHAJLOV, Mihajlo
Freed in gen amnesty 11-24, Carter lauds 11-25, 956F1, A2
MIHARA, Asao
US to seek 4-power Korea talks 7-27, 572B2
MIJARES Saldivar, Vincente
DeJesus KOs 6-27, 828B1
MIKI, Takeo
Australia friendship treaty ratified 7-21, 596A1
MIKULSKI, Rep. Barbara A. (D, Md.)
Scores TV violence report 10-24, 921A2
MIKVA, Rep. Abner (D, Ill.)
Spec interest gifts rptd 3-7, 232C3
MILES, Chief Warrant Officer Joseph A.
Killed 7-13, body returned 7-16, 552F2, F3
MILES Laboratories Inc.
Bayer takeover OKd 10-17, 880E1
MILFORD, Rep. Dale (D, Tex.)
Backs SST research funds 3-17, 213A2
MILGO Electronics Corp.
Racal acquires 2-17, 275A1
MILITARY Academy, U.S.—*See under U.S. GOVERNMENT—ARMY*
MILITARY Bases—*See U.S. GOVERNMENT—DEFENSE; also country names*
MILITARY Review (magazine)
Brazil cancels US aid pact 3-11, 186E2
MILITIA Association of New York
Hart addresses 9-10, 700D1
MILK—*See DAIRY Products*
MILK, Harvey
Elected San Fran supervisor 11-8, 855D3
MILK Producers Inc., Associated
'76 Cong gifts rptd 2-15, 128F1

1978

WEST Bank—*See ARAB-Israeli Developments—Israeli Occupation Policies in this section above; for peace plans, see EGYPT-Israel Peace Moves above*

MIDDLEGROUND (race horse)
'50 Kentucky Derby victory cited 5-6, 539D1
MIDDLE South Utilities Inc.
La cities trust law liability upheld by Sup Ct 3-29, 280F1
MIDLAND, Mich.—*See MICHIGAN*
MIDLAND Bank Ltd.
Nigeria loan set 11-30, 934A2
MIDNIGHT Express (film)
Released 10-6, 970B2
On top-grossing list 11-1, 888E1; 11-29, 970F3
MIDWAY Islands (U.S. territory)
US troop presence rptd 1-2, 5D2
MIDWEST—*See also state names*
Blizzard paralyzes 6 states, econ losses estimated 1-25—2-11, 105E2, D3
Drought declared over, reservoirs rptd refilling 3-5, 207B2
Carter on coal shortages, jobless 3-6, 160A2
Carter presents urban-aid plan 3-27 217D2
Lead-free gas shortage rptd 11-21, 939F1
City populatn losses rptd 12-6, 942C3
MIDWEST Video Corp.
FCC cable-TV access rules voided 2-24, 195G2
MIGHTY Gents, The (play)
Opens 4-16, 760E2
MIGRANT Workers—*See under AGRICULTURE*
MIGs (Soviet warplane series)—*See ARMAMENTS—Aircraft*
MIGUEL, Benjamin
Scores electn 7-13, asks annulmt 7-15, 571D1
MIGUEL, Col. Mario Firmino
Sworn Portugal defense min 1-30, 91C3
MIHAJLOV, Mihajlo
In US 6-6, 504G2
MIKELLIDES, Andreas
Named Cyprus health min 3-8, 189A2
MIKHALKOV, Nikita
Slave of Love released 8-14, 1030D3
MIKHALKOV-Konchalovsky, Andrie
Slave of Love released 8-14, 1030D3
MIKI, Takeo
Supports Ohira vs Fukuda 11-27, 912C3
Electn reforms described 11-27, 912G3
Backers in Ohira Cabt 12-7, 945E2
MIKOYAN, Anastas Ivanovich
Dies 10-22, 888C3
MIKULSKI, Rep. Barbara Ann (D, Md.)
Reelected 11-7, 851B1
MIKVA, Rep. Abner J. (D, Ill.)
Scores House com tax cut bill 7-27, 586F3
Reelected 11-7, 850E3
MILFORD, Rep. Dale (D, Tex.)
Loses primary 5-6, 362G3
Frost wins seat 11-7, 855E3
MILHOLLAND, Bruce
On 20th Century opens 2-19, 887C2
MILITARY Academy, U.S.—*See under U.S. GOVERNMENT—ARMY*
MILITARY Bases—*See U.S. GOVERNMENT—DEFENSE; country, territory names*
MILITARY Compensation, Presidential Commission on—*See under U.S. GOVERNMENT*
MILITARY Surgeons, Association of
Army MD shortage rptd 11-27, 916D3
MILIUS, John
Big Wednesday released 7-27, 969D3
MILK—*See DAIRY Products*
MILK, Harvey
Slain 11-27, ex-supervisor chrgd 11-29, 920G1-D3
MILK Producers Committee for Thorough Agricultural Political Education, Associated
9th-leading PAC fund-raiser 9-7, 753C2
MILKIS, Edward K.
Foul Play released 7-19, 970D1
MILLAN, Bruce
Cancels seal kill off Scotland 10-16, 816A2

1979

WEST Bank—*See ARAB-Israeli Developments-Israeli Occupation Policies and EGYPT-Israel headings in this section above*

MIDDLE East (magazine)
Iran expels newsman 9-5, 708C3
MIDDLETON, Terdell
NFL '78 touchdown, rushing ldr 1-6, 80E1, E2
MIDDLETOWN, Pa.—*See PENNSYLVANIA*
MIDDLETOWN, O.—*See OHIO*
MIDLAND Bank Ltd.
Walter Heller Corp purchase set 7-6, 682B3
MIDLER, Bette
Rose released 11-17, 1008D1
MIDNIGHT Express (film)
Stone, Moroder win Oscars 4-9, 336A2, B2
MIDNIGHT Magic (recording)
On best-seller list 10-3, 800F3
MIDWAY Airlines
Svc begins 11-1, 989E1
MIDWAY Airport (Chicago, Ill.)
Midway Airlines begins svc 11-1, 989E1
MIDWEST Stock Exchange
SEC asks optns trading overhaul, scores surveillnc 2-15; freeze end seen 2-22, 348B3, C3
MIDWEST Video Corp.
Cable TV pub-access rule upset by Sup Ct 281A2
MIGRANT Workers
Chavez union strikes Calif lettuce farms 1-19, boycott set 4-26, 327A1
Ariz farm labor law restored by Sup Ct 6-5, 464B3
MIJATOVIC, Nick
Named NASL top defensive player 8-25, 776C1
MIKARDO, Ian
On Callaghan devolutn optns 3-2, 169F1
MIKHAILOV, Boris
Soviets win Challenge Cup 2-11, 118D2, B3, D3
MILBURN, Rod
AAU clears for US meets 11-29, 956G1
MILGROM, Jacob
On Dead Sea Temple Scroll 3-2, 217G2
MILHOUSE v. District Court
Case declined by Sup Ct 11-26, 919F2
MILITARY Bases—*See U.S. GOVERNMENT—DEFENSE; country, territory names*
MILIUS, John
1941 released 12-14, 1008B1
MILK—*See DAIRY Products*
MILK, Harvey (1930-78)
Slayer convicted, gays protest 5-22, 386A1
Slayer sentenced 7-3, 547F3

1980

MIDDLETOWN—*See PENNSYLVANIA*
MIDLAND—*See TEXAS*
MIDLAND Bank Ltd.
Crocker takeover set 7-15, 557G1
Forgn bank takeovers debated 8-28, 9-17, 806A3
MIDLER, Bette
Rose on best-seller lists 7-9, 568E3, F3
Divine Madness released 9-25, 836E2
MIDWAY (U.S. aircraft carrier)
Collides with Panamanian freighter, 2 killed 7-29, 675E1
MIDWAY Islands (U.S. territory)
US A-waste plan questioned 5-21, 405G2
MIDWEST Stock Exchange
SEC ends optns trading ban 3-26, 224B2
MIETO, Juha
Wins Olympic medals 2-17, 2-23, 155B3
MIFUNE, Toshiro
'Shogun' aired by NBC 9-15—9-19, top ratings rptd 9-24, 835F2
MIGHTY Clouds of Joy (singing group)
Win Grammy 2-27, 296E3
MIGIAKIS, Stilianos
Wins Olympic medal 7-22, 624A3
MIGNINI, Carolyn
Tintypes opens 10-23, 892F3
MIJATOVIC, Cvijetin (Yugoslav president)
Rotating Yugo ldrship set 5-4, 338D2
Installed pres 5-15, 381G3
Carter sees, backs Yugo indepndnc 6-24, 474E2
MIJNALS, Sgt. Chas
Ousted from mil cncl 8-18, 653G2
MIKI, Takeo
Shuns Ohira confidence vote 5-16, 381B1
MIKITA, Stan
Retires 4-14, 488G2-A3
Gretzky wins NHL honors 6-6, 488B1
MIKOYAN, Anastas Ivanovich (1895-1978)
Kosygin resigns 10-23, 797F1
MIKULSKI, Rep. Barbara Ann (D, Md.)
Reelected 11-4, 843B1
MIKVA, Abner J.
GOP wins cong seat 1-22, 50D3
NRA endorses Reagan 11-1, 844G1
MILBURN, Rod
US Olympic trials ban voided 6-25, 891A3
MILBURY, Mike
Suspended over NYC brawl 1-25, suspensn upheld 1-30, 198C3
MILCZAREK, Maria
Ousted from Polish Cabt 11-21, 909D2
MILESTONE, Lewis
Dies 9-25, 756C1
MILEY, Gregory Matthew
Chrgd in 'freeway murders' 8-22, 727F1
MILHEM, Mohammed
Israel deports 5-3; W Bank protests; US, UN score 5-3—5-8; Arafat visits 5-7, 340B2, D3
W Bank return barred 5-11, 362D2
UN censures Israel, Israel ct ordrs ouster explanatn 5-20, 381C1
Successor chosen 5-25, 417F2
Israel ct backs ouster 8-19, 627B3
Meets 2 Israeli CP parlt members 9-25, 736F3
Returns to appeal ouster 10-14; hearing 10-15—10-16, ouster upheld 10-20; Sup Ct delays 10-23, 822E2
Begin vs Gaza, Bethlehem mayors pleas 10-21, 822A3
Redeported 12-5, vows UN appeal 12-6; W Bank riots 12-6—12-9, 931A2
UN asks Israel readmit; stages sit-in, hunger strike 12-19, 952B2
Israel vs UN backing 12-22; ends hunger strike 12-24, 976E3
MILITARY Balance, The (book)
Sovt '78 defense budget estimate cited 1-28, 70B3
MILK—*See DAIRY Products*

1976

MILLAR, J. Donald
On post-vaccine deaths 10-13, 795A2
MILLAR, Richard W.
Jones named Northrop chrmn 2-18, 133D1
MILLAS, Jorge
Protests Chile U purge 1-8, 47E3
MILLER, Alexander
Indicted 7-8, 816G2
MILLER, Arnold R.
US clears on fund handling 5-18, 379A1
On wildcat strike 7-23, 7-27, 553C2
Suffers setbacks at UMW conv 9-23—10-2, 748F1
MILLER, Arthur
McLaughlin dies 2-5, 124E3
MILLER, Rep. Clarence E. (R, O.)
Reelected 11-2, 830A3
MILLER, D. J.
On fund-raising chrgs 10-30, 899E2
MILLER, Edward S.
On FBI '70s burglaries 8-18, 633F2, 634D2-B3
MILLER, Gene
Wins Pulitzer Prize 5-3, 352D3
MILLER III, Rep. George (D, Calif.)
In Chile 3-11—3-15; chrgs rights abuse 3-17, 310C2
Reelected 11-2, 829A1
MILLER, Herbert J.
Nixon tapes release OKd 10-26, 849A3
MILLER, Hugo
Dies 5-25, 370G2
MILLER, Johnny
Wins Tucson open 1-11, 123D2
Wins British Open 7-10, 716E2
Runner-up in Kaiser Intl golf 9-26, 756B3
MILLER, Lloyd J.
Replaced as amb to Trinidad 2-4, 110B2
MILLER, Marvin
At Kuhn hearing 6-17, 444E3
MILLER, Ruby
Dies 4-2, 524C3
MILLER, Judge William E.
Dies 4-12, 316B1
MILLET, Fred
Dies 1-1, 56F3
MILLHOUSE, Robin
S Australia party formed 5-7, 349C3
MILLIKEN, Gov. William G. (R, Mich.)
Attacks Reagan 5-12, 343D1
Nominates Ford 8-18, 597F2
Cited in Dole biog sketch 614A3
MILLNS, Jim
Wins Olympic medal 2-9, 159B1
MILLS, D. Quinn
Union ldrs quit Pres com 1-8, 3G3
MILLS, Rep. Wilbur D. (D, Ark.)
Tucker wins seat 11-2, 822A1
MILLS College (Oakland, Calif)
White pres apptmt rptd 3-10, 272B1

1977

MILLARD, Judge Richard W.
Nazi tape order upheld 12-21, 1008C2
MILLER, Andrew P.
Loses primary for gov 6-14, 465B1
MILLER, Arnold R.
Reelected UMW pres 6-14, 462A3
Wildcat strikes 6-18—9-6, 690G2, A3, F3-691A1
Election certified 7-21, 691A1
Scored by Dist 17 leaders 8-26, 691B1
Reelectn affirmed 10-11, 937E2
Strike begins 12-6, 937D1-D2
MILLER, Eddie
Traded to Braves 12-8, 990B1
MILLER, Edward Alan
Replaced as Army asst secy 5-9, 418G1
MILLER, Sir Eric
Kills self 9-22, 788G1
MILLER, G. William
Named Fed chrmn 12-28; $ drops, other reactn 12-28—12-29, 997B3, 1000D1
MILLER, Dr. Harry Willis
Dies 1-1, 84C3
MILLER, Henry
Anais Nin dies 1-14, 84D3
MILLER, Herbert S.
Inmate rights rpt issued 4-26, 383E2
MILLER, Jack
Cited in Park indictmt 9-6, 688E1
MILLER, Johnny
2d in Western Open 6-26, 676F1
2d in Southern Open 10-23, 950E3
MILLER, Paul
Successor named 1-18, 140E2
MILLER, Randy
Traded to Expos 12-7, 990D1
MILLER, Robert H.
Named amb to Malaysia 5-13, confrmd 5-25, 500A1
MILLER, Saul
Presents Manitoba budget 4-22, 327G1
MILLER, Terry
Loses in Heisman voting 12-8, 950B2
MILLER, Walter C.
U of Pa radio station loses license 4-4, 395A3
MILLETTE, Claude
Liberal Party records returned 12-11, 965D2
MILLHOUSE, Robin
Wins S Australia electn 9-17, 740B2
MILLIKEN, Gov. William G. (R, Mich.)
Named Natl Govs Assn chrmn 9-9, 719C2
Govs' panel visits DC 11-29, 960A1
Seafarer site oppositn cited 12-15, 977E3

1978

MILLER, Andrew P.
Wins US Sen nominatn in Va 6-10, 467B2
Loses electn 11-7, 846D1, 853E1
MILLER, Anita
OKs redlining curb 5-18, 410F2
MILLER, Arnold R.
Coal strike setlmt pressed; White House talks open, deadlock continues 2-3—2-16, 104D3-105E1
Announces tentative contract 2-6, bargaining cncl rejcts 2-12; setlmt detailed 104D2-C3
Boyle convicted again 2-18, 129C1
Hopeful re ratification 2-26, 160C1
Contract talks resume 3-10, announces new setlmt 3-14, 181G3, 182B1
Recall barred by UMW bd 7-26, 624G3
MILLER, Arthur
At pro-Shcharansky, Ginzburg rally 7-10, 542B3
MILLER, Chris
Animal House released 7-27, 970D2
MILLER, Rep. Clarence E. (R, O.)
Reelected 11-7, 851E3
MILLER, Edward S.
Indicted 4-10, 261F3-262A1
Dismissal motn denied 11-30, 939E3
MILLER, F. E.
Eubie opens 9-20, 1031E1
MILLER, G. William
Carter on interest rates 1-12, 12C1
Sen Banking Com confirmatn hearings probe Textron paymts 1-24—2-28, back nominatn 3-2; confrmd fed reserve chrmn 3-3, sworn 3-8, 161E1-B3
Burns resigns from fed reserve 1-31, 161C3
Backs oil import curbs, anti-inflatn drive 3-15, 181C1-A2
Oil import fee backing by Blumenthal rptd 3-24, 220B2
Backs Carter inflatn plan 4-12, 260G2
Carter vs tax-cut delay 4-25, 307C2
Textron bribe evidence rptd destroyed 5-8, 449A1
Admin scores tight $ policy 5-9, 361E2
Backs Carter tax-cut plan cuts 5-11—5-13, 361E1
Pledges $ defense in Zurich 6-13, 523F2
Vs discount rate hike 6-30, backs rate boost 8-18, 679F1-A2
Carter asks $ aid; Fed hikes fed funds rate, sells D marks 8-16, 622G1
Forgn bank regulatn clears Cong 8-17, 663B1
On OPEC price hike impact 12-18, 978D1
MILLER, Rep. George (D, Calif.)
Reelected 11-7, 850E1
MILLER, Harlet
Forever Yours opens 6-21, 887G1
MILLER, Irene
Climbs Annapurna in Nepal 10-15, 843G2
MILLER, Izetta Jewel
Dies 11-15, 972D3
MILLER, Jack
Sen ethics com rpts Park gift disputed 6-19, 527E2
Sen ethics com asks perjury probe 10-16, 832D1
MILLER, Louis
Scores WCC re Rhodesia rebel aid 8-10, 650B3
MILLER, Millie
Ilford by-electn fills seat 3-2, 167F2
MILLER, Nathan
Loses Sen nominatn in Va 6-3, 467A2
MILLER, Rick
Wins Golden Glove Award 11-21, 928A3
MILLER, Robert (Red)
Cowboys win Super Bowl 1-15, 39D3
Named NFL top coach 1-23, 171E3
MILLER, Robert F.
Loses US House electn 11-7, 849F2
MILLER, Ron
Cat From Outer Space released 6-30, 618F3
Return From Witch Mt released 7-14, 970G2
Candleshoe released 8-4, 969F3
MILLER, Sharon
2d in Rail Charity Classic 9-4, 990G1
MILLER, Terry
In NFL draft 5-2, 336E2
MILLER, Thomas L.
Foul Play released 7-19, 970D1
MILLER, Warren
Nordiques win WHA All-Star game 1-17, 76G3
MILLER Brewing Co.—*See under PHILIP Morris*
MILLER Brewing Co. v. G. Heileman Brewing Co.
Miller 'Lite' trademark review barred 1-9, 13D1
MILLIKEN, Frank R.
Sees Berner on Curtiss-Wright takeover 3-15; denunciatns exchngd 4-6—5-2, Kennecott blocks bid 5-24, 402E1, D2, D3, 403A1
Retiremt rptd 12-15, 1005A1
MILLIKEN, Gov. William G. (R, Mich.)
Unopposed in primary 8-8, 625G3
Reelected 11-7, 853F2, 854A1
Urges minorites, urban committmt at GOP govs mtg 11-27, 916A1
MILLIKEN & Co. v. FTC
Case refused by Sup Ct 11-6, 873D3
MILLS, Al
On Rev Jones sexual tyranny 11-24, 911B2

1979

MILLEDGEVILLE, Ga.—*See GEORGIA*
MILLER, Arnold R.
Resigns as UMW pres 11-15, 885D2
UMW conv held 12-10—12-20, 986E3
MILLER, Arthur
The Price opens 4-19, 712B2
MILLER, Christine
Jonestown tape copy rptd 3-15, 219D3
MILLER, Dave
Nev A-waste storage studied 1-5, 54E3
MILLER, Don C.
Dies 7-28, 588C3
MILLER, Edison
Orange Cnty appt causes furor 7-13—8-8, 593B2
MILLER, F. Don
Says 'Olympathon' to net $3 mln 4-29, 798F1
Rpts Burger King Olympic donatn 5-15, 798E1
MILLER, G. William
Testifies on Admin '79 inflatn, budget deficit forecast 1-25, 48E3
Textron vows wage-price compliance 2-6, 128B1
Vs hostile forgn bank takeovers 3-13, 205F1-A2
On 1st 1/4 GNP rpt 4-19, 280C2
Textron pleads guilty to currency violatns 7-10, overseas payoffs admitted 7-26; Proxmire asks study 10-31, 923B2
Named Treas secy 7-19, 529D1
Confrmd 8-2; sworn, named chief econ spokesman 8-6, 627B2-E2
IMF Nicaragua loan probe urged 8-6, 603A2
On Chrysler aid request, bars natlzn 8-9, 662E1
On recessn 9-14, 701E2
Rejcts Chrysler aid appeal 9-15, demand re outside aid rptd 9-17, 699A1
Gets Cong letter vs Anthony coin 9-25, 727B2
Meets Schmidt re $, mark rates 9-29, 779E3
Vows inflatn fight at IMF-World Bank mtg 10-3, 779B3, D3
Galbraith scores 10-29, 826F3
On Chrysler rescue plan 11-1, 845C2, D3
On Oct jobless rate 11-2, 866D3
On Iran assets in US 11-14, 861B2
On US freeze of Iran assets 11-16, 880F1
Tours Persian Gulf, discusses Iran crisis 11-23—11-28, 896A3
Kennedy vs oil policy 12-20, 983A3
MILLER, Gary
Yeoman pleads guilty to espionage 9-25, 747G3
MILLER, Geoff
Agri outlook warning rptd 3-29, 253G1
MILLER, Judge James R.
Acquits Fairchild on tax chrgs 2-7, 88A1
MILLER, John
Cited in H-bomb letter 9-16, 9-18, 717B2
MILLER, Johnny
2d in Hall of Fame Classic 8-26; wins Lancome Trophy tourn 10-28, 970B1, B2
MILLER, Marilyn Suzanne
Gilda Radner Live opens 8-2, 711C3
MILLER, Robert
Gets Malaysian protest re refugees 7-6, 550B2
MILLER, Ron
N Amer Irregulars released 4-12, 528B3
Apple Dumpling sequel released 8-31, 819E3
Black Hole released 12-21, 1007A3
MILLER, Susan
Nasty Rumors opens 4-12, 712F1
MILLER, Terry
NFL '78 rushing ldr 1-6, 80B2
MILLER, William
In Turkey, Iran bars US hostage release role 11-7, 841D2, F2
MILLER v. Youakim
Foster care benefits backed by Sup Ct 2-22, 151C1
MILLET, Kate
In Iran women's protest march 3-10; scores Khomeini 3-11, 179F2
Iran arrests 3-17, ousts 3-19, 199B2
MILLIKEN, Gov. William G. (R, Mich.)
Signs HS voter turnout law 8-14, 724E2
Wayne Cnty govt reorgnztn accord reached; state aid pledged 11-1, 921A1, D1, F1
MILLION Mile Reflections (recording)
On best-seller list 9-5, 672F3*
MILLON, Henry Armand
Named to Natl Gallery post 5-7, 375G1
MILLS, Frank
Music Box Dancer on best-seller list 4-4, 271D2; 5-2, 356A3
MILLS, Rodney
On Voyager II mission 7-9, 552C3

1980

MILLAR, Dr. Donald
On life span, disease control changes 1-19, 62F3, 63B3, D3
MILLER, Arthur
'Playing for Time' aired by CBS 9-30, 835D3
American Clock opens 11-20, 1003G2
MILLER, Barry
My Mother, My Father opens 1-9, 136D3
MILLER, Rep. Clarence E. (R, Ohio)
Reelected 11-4, 843E4
MILLER, Don
Reveals Ill A-plant '79 dischrg data 4-7, NRC revises 4-27, 441B2
MILLER, Edison
Loses Orange Cnty supervisor vote 6-3, 439E2
MILLER, Edward S.
Convicted 11-6, 884A2
Sentenced 12-15, 963F2
MILLER, F. Don
Vs USSR Olympics boycott 1-14, 28E3
Scores Sears funding-boycott link 4-3, 260B1
MILLER, Frank
Massey-Ferguson aid plea rejected 9-4, 728G2
Scores budget, energy plan 10-30, 858D3
Proposes Ontario tax curbs, scores Ottawa budget 11-14, 885D2
MILLER, Fred
Fired as Ariz State athletic dir 1-3, 175E2
MILLER, G. William
Hints US gold sale suspensn 1-15, 30E2
Textron payoffs knowledge alleged 1-31, denies 2-1; Carter, Civiletti back 2-2, 2-5, 92D1-B2
Testifies re Textron payoffs 2-8, sens ask spec prosecutor 2-8—2-11, 145F1-B2
Vs wage-price controls 3-2, 168F1
Textron spec prosecutor rejctd 3-11, 185C2
Sees IMF $ support delay 3-11, heads Hamburg delegatn 4-24, 302A1
Sees mild recessn 4-15, 286C3
At Tito funeral 5-8, 338B3
Rpts Chrysler loan guarantees OKd 5-10, 383C2
On May jobless rate 6-6, 437G2
Sees House Dems re taxes 6-26, 480C3
On '81 tax cut 6-29, 492G3-493A1
In Detroit re auto aid 7-7, 505A2
On Chrysler loan guarantees 7-15, 541B2
On Chrysler record loss 7-31, 573F3
Sees NYC mayor on loan guarantees 9-10, 743D1
Signs Canada tax treaty 9-26, 748B2
On interest rate rise, money supply curbs 10-2, 763A1
Says N Korea sells arms to Iran 10-8, 757F2
Asks new debt ceiling 12-2, 916D2
MILLER, Rep. George (D, Calif.)
Reelected 11-4, 842E1
MILLER, Henry
Dies 6-7, 528F2
MILLER, Johnny
Wins Inverrary Classic 3-9, 412F2
Ties for 2d in Southern Open 10-5, 972D2
MILLER, Joyce
Named to AFL-CIO exec cncl 8-21, 647C3
MILLER, Junior
In NFL draft 4-29, 336E2
MILLER, Les
Loses US House electn 11-4, 851C3
MILLER, Marilyn Suzanne
Gilda Live released 3-28, 416G2
MILLER, Marvin
Baseball strike averted 5-23, 402A1
MILLER, Melissa
Oh, God! II released 10-3, 836D3
MILLER, Robert
On '79 tobacco consumptn 4-7, 318E2
MILLER, Ron
Watcher in the Woods released 4-16, 416G3
Herbie Goes Bananas released 9-12, 836B3
MILLER, Scott
Fired, '79-80 'captivity' cited 2-6, 199D3
MILLER, Victor
Friday the 13th released 5-10, 675F2
MILLER, Lt. Gov. Zell (D, Ga.)
In Ga US Sen primary 8-5, loses runoff 8-26, 683B2
MILLER Brewing Co.—*See under PHILIP Morris Inc.*
MILLER Brewing Co. v. Jos. Schlitz Brewing
Case refused by Sup Ct 2-19, 131B1
MILLER v. California
Case cited by Boston ct 8-1, 640C2
MILLER v. Zbaraz
Case argued in Sup Ct 4-21, 306B2
Case decided by Sup Ct 6-30, 491F2
MILLIKEN, Gov. William G. (R, Mich.)
Chrysler aid set 1-9, 14E1
Seeks chem dump cleanup 4-17, 331D2
Declares Kalamazoo disaster area 5-13, 391D2
Bush wins Mich primary 5-20, 383C1
Addresses GOP conv 7-14, 531C3
MILLIKEN v. Bradley
Case declined by Sup Ct 10-6, 782A3
MILLS, Al (alias Elmer Mertle)
Slain 2-26, 190A3
MILLS, Daphene
Shot 2-26, dies 2-27 190A3
MILLS, Eddie
Parents slain 2-26, 190A3
MILLS, Hawthorne
Sovt soldier leaves US Emb in Kabul 9-21, 727B2
MILLS, Jeannie (alias Deanna Mertle)
Slain 2-26, 190A3
MILLS, John
39 Steps released 5-2, 416F3

1976

- **MILNER, Aaron**
  - Zambia arrest rptd 2-14, expelled 3-27, 503E2
  - Rpts Zambia-S Africa clash 8-11, 653A3
  - Zambia ousts UNITA 12-27, 995D3
- **MILSTEIN, Nathan**
  - Wins Grammy 2-28, 460E3
- **MILWAUKEE, Wis.**—*See WISCONSIN*
- **MILWAUKEE Journal, The (newspaper)**
  - Ariz crime probed 10-2, 849D2
  - Carter endorsement rptd 10-30, 831B3
- **MILWAUKEE Sentinel (newspaper)**
  - Udall loses early lead 4-6, 245B1
- **MINAREK, Capt. Pavel**
  - Chrgs Dubcek-CIA link 3-10, 289F2
- **MINDSZENTY, Jozsef Cardinal (d. 1975)**
  - Successor named 2-12, 336D2
- **MINENOV, Andrey**
  - Wins Olympic medal 2-9, 159B1
- **MINEO, Sal**
  - Slain 2-12, 160F3
- **MINER, Tom**
  - On Unification Church paper 12-14, 971A2
- **MINERALS**—*See also specific minerals (e.g., COAL)*
  - Bolivians vs Chile land deal 1-3, 27E1
  - '75 environmental loss rptd 1-18, 45B1
  - Group of 77 sets trade guidelines 2-10, 108C1
  - US proposes poor natns' aid 5-6, 317D1
  - Dem platform text 6-15, 475A2
  - UN Sea Law Conf deadlocked 8-2—9-17, 700F1
  - Australia bars Fraser I mining 11-11, 888A2
- **MINES & Mining**—*See also 'Mines' under ACCIDENTS; also specific minerals (e.g., COAL)*
  - '75 4th ¼ corp profits rptd 2-3, 215A3
  - Sen OKs end to natl park mining 2-4, 134G1
  - Sup Ct bars review of Hopi Indian suit 3-29, 261F3
  - Peru sets strike emergency 4-9, 499F2
  - '75 top 500 indls ranked 437C2
  - Forgn ownership in Australia rptd 5-2, 350A1
  - Ford urges regulatory reform 5-13, 346G3
  - Australia investmt policy revised 6-2, 415E1
  - Dem platform text 6-15, 475B1, C1
  - Bolivia gets intl bank loan 6-18, 456B3
  - French-UK talks end 6-24, 481E3
  - US-Australian deal rptd 7-28, 571G3-572B1
  - Dole legis reccrd cited 614F2
  - Peru OKs natlzatn paymts 9-23, 1013A2
  - Natl parks bill signed 9-28, 834B2
  - Strip-mining bill not cleared 10-2, 883A1, F2
  - Land-use bill signed 10-21, 834D1, E1
  - Ford, Carter debate 10-22, 810D2-E2, A3
  - Australia devaluatn welcomed 11-28, 896F1, D2
  - '75 illness, injury rptd up 12-9, 950B3
- **MINETA, Rep. Norman Y. (D, Calif.)**
  - Reelected 11-2, 829B1
- **MINGAS, Maj. Saidi Vieira Dias**
  - Angola finance min 11-27, 995C3
- **MINISH, Rep. Joseph George (D, N.J.)**
  - Reelected 11-2, 830E1
- **MINK, Rep. Patsy T. (D, Hawaii)**
  - Loses Sen primary 10-2, 764D2
  - Akaka wins seat 11-2, 820D2, 825C1
- **MINNEAPOLIS, Minn.**—*See MINNESOTA*
- **MINNEAPOLIS Star (newspaper)**
  - Carter endorsement rptd 10-30, 831G2
- **MINNESOTA**
  - Judge removed in Silver Bay ore plant pollutn case 1-6, 25D2
  - Silver Bay ore plant fined 5-4, 379C2
  - Ford delegates counted 5-11, 343A1
  - Stassen seeks delegate support 6-25, 467E3
  - Ford wins 17 delegates 6-26, 467F2, A3
  - Silver Bay plant deadline set 7-7, 570D3

1977

- **MILNER, Aaron**
  - Ousted 8-2, 674E3
- **MILNER, John**
  - Traded to Rangers, Pirates 12-8, 990C1
- **MILSTONE, Dr. Jacob Haskell**
  - Dies 1-27, 164C3
- **MILWAUKEE, Wis.**—*See WISCONSIN*
- **MILWAUKEE Journal, The (newspaper)**
  - Houston wins Pulitzer 4-18, 355E2
  - Ross Lewis dies 8-6, 696A3
- **MILWAUKEE Road**—*See CHICAGO, Milwaukee, St. Paul & Pacific Railroad*
- **MIN Byung Kwon**
  - Bid to block Kim testimony chrgd 11-30, 915A1
- **MINCHEW, Daniel**
  - On sugar import injury, quota cut 3-3, 3-14, 189E1
- **MIND CONTROL**—*For religious cult deprogramming issues, see RELIGIOUS Cults*
  - CIA tests revealed 8-1—8-9, 610C3
- **MINERALS**—*See also specific minerals (e.g., COAL)*
  - US plans space photos 1-17, 31F1
  - Canada, provs in offshore pact 2-1, 133B3
  - US Sen com created 2-4, 91C1
  - S Korea eases import curbs 6-14, 470A3
  - Guyana-USSR dvpt pact rptd 7-11, 710C3
  - US-USSR 1st ½ trade rptd 9-12, 766B2
  - E Ger-Pl trade pact set 12-7, 1000C2
- **MINES, Bureau of**—*See under U.S. GOVERNMENT—INTERIOR*
- **MINE Safety & Health Administration**—*See under U.S. GOVERNMENT—LABOR*
- **MINE Safety & Health Review Commission**—*See under U.S. GOVERNMENT*
- **MINES & Mining**—*See also ACCIDENTS-Mines; also specific minerals (e.g., COAL)*
  - Ford vs strip mine curbs 1-7, 14D3
  - Dec '76 indl output rptd 1-17, 92G3; **for subsequent data, see 'Statistics' under BUSINESS**
  - Andrus backs strip-mine curbs 1-18, 35A1
  - Carter plans strip-mining bill 2-2, 75E1
  - Jan output drop rptd 2-15, 129D3
  - Labor seeks strip-mine rules 2-22, 153D2
  - UMW wildcat strike case review denied 3-21, 230B3
  - Carter energy plan 4-18, 4-20, 293B3, 295A1; reactn 4-21, 4-24, 319G3-320A1, B3
  - 1st ¼ profit rise rptd 4-28, 668F3
  - '76 sales return rise rptd 340B2
  - Safety device exempted from fluorocarbon ban 5-11, 387A2
  - Carter environmt message 5-23, 404B2
  - Mine safety rules, agency reorganizatn signed 11-9, 855E3
- **MINEU, Ion**
  - Ousted re miners strike 10-21, 948B1
- **MINGAS, Maj. Saidi Vieira Dias**
  - Rptd killed 5-29, 424A2
  - Martins replaces 8-31, 772B1
- **MINIC, Milos**
  - Warns Helsinki reps re detente foes 6-15, 473B1
- **MINING Enforcement & Safety Administration**—*See under U.S. GOVERNMENT—INTERIOR*
- **MINISH, Rep. Joseph (D, N.J.)**
  - '76 campaign surplus rptd 5-3, 482B2
- **MINK, Patsy**
  - Files DES suit 4-25, 431C3
- **MINNEAPOLIS, Minn.**—*See MINNESOTA*
- **MINNEAPOLIS Star & Tribune Co.**
  - Fadell libel case refused 11-28, 919A3
- **MINNESOTA**
  - Legislature schedule rptd 6E2
  - Weather emergency declared 1-18, 54F2
  - FEA orders home heat oil hike 1-24, 54G1
  - Natl Guard mobilized after storm 1-28—1-29, 75F2
  - Ore plant wins dump site 1-31, 95E2
  - Swine flu case cited 2-8, 103C3

1978

- **MILWAUKEE, Wis.**—*See WISCONSIN*
- **MINCEY, Rufus J.**
  - Murder scene search warrant backed, hosp interrogatn curbed by Sup Ct 6-21, 509D2
- **MINCEY v. Arizona**
  - Murder scene search warrant backed, hosp interrogatn curbed by Sup Ct 6-21, 509E2
- **MINCHEW, Daniel**
  - Talmadge denies expense claim knowledge 8-18, 644C1
  - Talmadge chrgd by Sen panel 12-19, 981F3
- **MIND Control**
  - Calif woman wins Synanon suit 9-19, 841D3
- **MINDSZENTY, Jozef Cardinal**
  - '74 papal dismissal cited 8-6, 601D2
- **MINERALS**—*See also kinds (e.g., COAL)*
  - '77 environmental loss rptd 85A2
  - Indians protest in DC 7-15—7-23, 568E3
  - Turkey seeks forgn investmt 10-19, 10-26, 840G2
  - Australia export plan set 10-24, 836A1
  - Japan investmt in Australia rptd 12-13, 985D2
  - Environmtlists urge natl policy 12-20, 1009E1
- **MINES & Mining**—*See also mineral names (e.g., COAL)*
  - US '75 investmt in Canada rptd 1-10, 70C3
  - Carter budgets rules, reclamatn 1-23, 47F2
  - '77 environmental loss rptd 85C2
  - '77 4th ¼ profits rptd down 2-7, 282E3
  - 1st ¼ '77, '78 profits rptd down 4-27, 403E2
  - '77 indus sales return rptd 5-8, 325B3
  - UN Sea Conf talks continue 5-23—7-15, US seabed bill debated 8-21—9-16, 732C3
  - Water-based land claims barred by Sup Ct 5-31, 431F1
  - '77 productivity drop rptd 6-14, 470A1
  - Seabed mining bill clears House 7-26, 588E3
  - Mining impact loan rates revised 8-20, 697E2
  - Japan import fund set 9-3, 694D1
  - Productivity decline cited 10-4, 790D1
  - Seabed mining bill dies 10-15, 785C1
  - Johns-Manville wins Olinkraft bidding 10-27, 896B3
  - 3d ¼ profits rptd up 10-30, 919A3
  - Japan investmt in Australia rptd 12-13, 985C2
- **MINETA, Rep. Norman Yoshio (d, Calif.)**
  - Reelected 11-7, 850F1
- **MINISH, Rep. Joseph George (d, N.J.)**
  - Reelected 11-7, 851B3
- **MINKIN, Ina Meibach**
  - Neon Woman opens 4-16, 760A3
- **MINNEAPOLIS, Minn.**—*See MINNESOTA*
- **MINNEAPOLIS Tribune (newspaper)**
  - Griffith remarks cause furor 9-28—10-2, 779B2
- **MINNELLI, Liza**
  - Haley files for divorce 4-19, 420C3
  - Wins Tony 6-4, 579G2
- **MINNESOTA**
  - Legislature schedule rptd 14F3
  - '67, '77 sales-tax rates rptd 1-5, 15E3
  - State govt tax revenue table 1-9, 84D2
  - Humphrey dies 1-13, 32E2
  - FTC cites Ford re auto engine defect 1-13, 67A3
  - Mrs Humphrey named to husband's Sen seat 1-25, 52F2

1979

- **MILLSTONE Nuclear Power Station**—*See CONNECTICUT-Atomic Energy*
- **MILLUS, John**
  - Apocalypse Now released 8-15, 819D3
- **MILNER, John**
  - In World Series 10-10—10-17, 816F1
- **MILTON, Frank**
  - Bedroom Farce opens 3-29, 711D1
- **MILWAUKEE, Wis.**—*See WISCONSIN*
- **MILWAUKEE Road (Chicago, Milwaukee, St. Paul & Pacific Railroad) /See CHICAGO Milwaukee Corp.**
- **MIMOSA (Liberian freighter)**
  - Collides, explodes off Texas 11-1, 954G3
- **MINCHEW, Daniel**
  - Pleads guilty to fraud 7-30, Sen com votes to denounce Talmadge 9-14, 702G1, B2
  - Sentenced 10-10, 769A2
- **MINEO, Sal (1939-76)**
  - Killer convicted 2-13, 119E2; sentenced 3-15 240D2
- **MINERALS**—*See also specific kinds (e.g., COAL)*
  - Australia backs pre-export processing 3-26, dvpt needs noted 3-27, 233F1-A2
  - GATT pact signed, tariff cuts seen 4-12, 273A2
  - Australia sets export compromise 4-23, 328A1
  - Lome pact talks collapse 5-26, 398G3
  - China, W Ger sign pact 6-19, 637G3
  - W Ger stockpile plans rptd 6-21, 489C3
  - Lome pact extension set 6-27, 513A1
- **MINES (& Mining)**
  - US wilderness proposal scored 1-4, 16D2
  - UV Industries to liquidate 1-18, 131G3
  - Carter budget proposals 1-22, 45E3
  - Australia aborigine rights probed 1-24, 94F2
  - '78 4th ¼ profit rise rptd 2-7, 201B3
  - House com OKs Alaska lands bill 3-1, 187E1
  - Seabed mining noted at UN Sea Law Conf 3-19—4-27, 360D3
  - Cyprus Mines sale set 4-11, 560B3
  - US wilderness dvpt proposed 4-16, 282G1
  - 1st ¼ profits rptd up 4-27, 385D1
  - '78 Fortune 500 data rptd 5-7, 305E1
  - Nicaragua to nationalize 7-25, 574C1
  - 2d 1/4 profits rptd up 8-17, 628A3
  - S Australia dvpt seen 9-16—9-17, 749C2; projct OKd 10-9, 810G3
  - Amax seeks Rosario Resources 10-22, 986D3
  - Lome pact extensn signed 10-31, 845F1
  - 3d 1/4 profits rptd up 10-31, 923C1
  - Wildcat strike liability limited by Sup Ct 12-10, 988D1
- **MINETTI, Jean Kerr**
  - Dies 12-15, 1008C3
- **MINGUS, Charles**
  - Dies 1-5, 104D3
- **MINH, Duong Van (Big Minh)**
  - S Viet '75 Mekong resistance plan rptd 1-7, 29A2
- **MINI, Adel**
  - Slain 4-11, 488F1
- **MINK, Patsy T.**
  - Vs Carter firing of Abzug 1-13, 30B3
- **MINNEAPOLIS, Minn.**—*See MINNESOTA*
- **MINNEAPOLIS Star (newspaper)**
  - Prostitutn expose publshd 10-18, 887G1-B2
- **MINNESOTA**
  - Legislature schedule rptd 5D3
  - Minneapolis-St Paul loses GOP conv bid 1-23, 70E3
  - Planned Parenthood funds ban upset 2-23, 310D2
  - Legis OKs DC voting rep amendmt 3-19, 204G2
  - Duluth fiscal status rptd 3-20, 204G1

1980

- **MILNE, Frank W.**
  - Named to Aramco bd 7-8, 662F1
- **MILOSZ, Czeslaw**
  - Wins Nobel Prize 10-9, 889D2
- **MILTON, Frank**
  - Harold & Maude opens 2-7, 136B3
- **MILWAUKEE**—*See WISCONSIN*
- **MINACHI, Nasser**
  - Seized by militants 2-6; Cncl forces release 2-7, militants score 2-9, 105D2
- **MINCHEW, Daniel**
  - Talmadge finances probe dropped 5-30, 427G3
- **MINENKOV, Andrei**
  - Wins Olympic medal 2-17, 155F3
- **MINERAL**—*See VIRGINIA*
- **MINERALS**
  - Japan, Australia discuss 1-16, 78G1
  - Australia '79 stock gains cited 1-18, 56D1
  - French-Cuba accord rptd 4-1, 253G2
  - BP plans Selectn Trust takeover 7-7, 523A2
  - UN Sea Law Conf yields draft accord 7-29—8-28, 660E1
  - Alaska lands bill clears US Sen 8-19, 631C2
  - USSR-US 1st 1/2 trade drop rptd 8-20, 711D2
  - Alaska lands bill signed 12-2, 916A1
  - Mapco, Earth Resources merger set 12-5, 985E1
  - Beagle Channel accord proposed 12-12, 978E3
- **MINERVINI, Giroloma**
  - Slain 3-18, 233G1
- **MINES (& Mining)**
  - Ct rules vs strip-mine law 1-3, 5D2
  - Pa inspectn case declined by Sup Ct 1-7, 15F3
  - State of State messages 1-9, 2-12, 484B2, F2
  - Hudson Bay seeks Rosario 1-10; Amax to buy Rosario 2-4, 385D3
  - Alaska land protectn extended 2-12, 131F2
  - Connally 'basic speech' excerpts 3-7, 184G2
  - Strip-mining rule stayed by Sup Ct 3-17, 226G1
  - '79 Fortune 500 data rptd 5-5, 290A3, 291D1, F1
  - Amax to buy Borden phosphate unit 5-16, 746E1
  - Pre-1920 oil shale claims upheld by Sup Ct 6-2, 513D1
  - BP plans Selectn Trust takeover 7-7, 523A2
  - Alaska lands bill clears Sen 8-19, 631C2; House 11-12, 866A3; signed 12-12, 916A1
  - Barber Oil liquidates 10-2, 986A1
  - Strip mining cases accepted by Sup Ct 10-6, 782D1
  - Silver miners end strike 11-8, 883D3
  - La lake 'swallowed' in salt-mine collapse 11-20, 970C2
  - EPA clean water enforcemt backed by Sup Ct 12-2, 918C1
  - Pittston coal unit fined $100,000 12-4, 962G3
  - Utah project set 12-16, 987B2
  - Calif desert plan issued 12-22, 987B1
  - UNC Resources seeks Westn Air merger 12-24, 985C1
  - **Foreign Developments (including U.S. international news)**
    - Australia stocks make gains 1-18, 56C1
    - Mex taxes silver, gold sales; US, Canada cos critical 1-25, 68F3
    - Canada '79 profits rptd up 2-7, 116B2
    - Bahamas bank looting case rptd 3-3, 229B1
    - S Africa accident kills 31 3-27, 256E3
    - Australia Aborigines protest 5-8, 371A1
    - Canada cave-in kills 8 5-20, 603G1
    - Mex in Swedish, Canadian agrmts 5-24, 5-27, 409A3, C3
    - UN Sea Law Conf yields draft accord, mining authority set 7-28—8-28, 660C1
    - Australia Aborigines protest sacred site drilling 8-11, 617G2; drilling starts 8-29; Aborigines appeal to UN 9-3, bar talks 9-5, 686G1
    - Poland strike 8-29—9-3, 657A1, G1, 658B1, E2
- **MINETA, Rep. Norman Y. (D, Calif.)**
  - Reelected 11-4, 842E1, 846F3
- **MINEYEVA, Olga**
  - Wins Olympic medal 7-27, 624A2
- **MINGO, Norman**
  - Dies 5-8, 448D2
- **MINISH, Rep. Joseph George (D, N.J.)**
  - Reelected 11-4, 843B3
- **MINK, Patsy**
  - In 'Big Business Day' protest 4-17, 308C2
- **MIN Kwan Shik**
  - Unaffected by purge 11-12, 874B3
- **MINNEAPOLIS**—*See MINNESOTA*
- **MINNEAPOLIS Star and Tribune Co.**
  - Harper's to cease publicatn 6-17, 501A1
  - Harper's sold to philanthropies 7-9, 582A3
- **MINNESOTA**
  - Carter OKs Alaska pipe route 1-17, 56C3
  - Minneapolis-St Paul-London air svc set 1-24, 347A2
  - Acid rain lake peril rptd 2-2, 145B3
  - Influenza outbreak rptd 2-15, 158C3
  - Ore plant ends Lake Superior dumping 3-16, 227B1
  - Name chng case dismissed by US Sup Ct 5-19, 440D2

1976

Dem conv women delegates, table 508C2
Dem conv pres vote, table 7-14, 507C2
Challenges FPC gas rate hike 7-28, wins refund 8-9, 635G2
FBI Cointelpro activities rptd 7-30, 634C1
GOP pre-conv delegate count 8-14, 583C3
Ford, Reagan seek conv delegates 8-16, 8-18, 601A3, C3
GOP conv pres, vp vote tables 8-18—8-19, 8-19, 599C1, C3
Minneapolis co admits shipping rebates 8-23, 690A1
'74-75 Minneapolis SATs rptd 9-13, 993A2
Humphrey to face Brekke 9-14, 705B1
Carter campaign 9-15, 686B3, D3
Fscl '75 per capita income, tax burden rptd 9-15, 10-12, 959C2
Dole in Lake Crystal 9-17, 724B3
Andreas, Dahlberg pol donatns rptd 10-22, 938F3
Election results 11-2; pres 818B1, E1, A3, 819A2; cong 820D1, 823G2, 829F4, 828B2
Anderson opts for Mondale seat 11-10, 865B1
Flu shot paralysis rptd 12-17, 950E1
Minneapolis-St Paul transatlantic air route rejctd 12-28, 992E2
Perpich becomes gov 12-29, Anderson goes to Sen 12-30, 994C1
Mondale Vice-Presidential Campaign—*See MONDALE, Walter*

MINNESOTA Mining & Manufacturing Co.—*See 3M Co.*
MINOR, Gregory C.
Resigns GE A-post 2-3, 115C1

MINORITIES—*See also specific groups (e.g., BLACK Americans, INDIANS, JEWS, WOMEN)*
Anchorage anti-bias law passage rptd 1-3, 7D1
Racial quotas set for Chicago police 1-5, 6G1
US health rpt issued 1-12, 32B1, C1
Revenue sharing bias chrgd 3-2, 187D1
Sup Ct curbs jury bias questioning 3-3, 219E1
Sup Ct backs retroactive seniority 3-24, 218A2
Humphrey scores anti-DC talk 3-24, 233E1
Ford sees ldrs in Wis 4-2, 245B2
Carter 'ethnic purity' incident 4-4—4-13, 260D2-261F2
Sup Ct bars review of health spa bias 4-5, 262G1
Jackson sought help in NY 4-6, 244G3
US files home-loan bias suits 4-15, 4-16, 285G1
Carter addresses med students 4-16, 281D3
Cross-district housing upheld 4-20, 308D2
Multilingual electns ordered 4-21, 307D3
4 US agencies sued on housing bias 4-26, Sen com issues rpt 5-31, 413E2-C3
Sup Ct rules on FPC bias powers 5-19, 393F2
Dem, GOP delegate selectn bias chrgd 5-27, 413F3
VCU affirmative actn plan voided 5-28, 414B1
Merrill Lynch settles job bias suits 6-4, 414D1
Marine Corps probed 6-4, 435A3
Sup Ct upholds DC police test 6-7, 435A1
Carter stresses commitmt 6-14, 433C1
Dem platform text 6-15, 469C2, 470A2, 471F1, 473B3, 477B2
Bias a GOP platform topic 6-21, 451E1
Sup Ct extends rights laws 6-25, 479G1
Treas anti-bias actn scored 7-1, 943E3
Counter-Bicentennial protest in Phila 7-4, 489D1
Ford lauds US diversity 7-5, 488G3
Reagan seeks white ethnic vote 7-6, 490F2
Dem conv rpt on role 7-13, 509G1
Carter seeks end to bias 7-15, 507E1, 510A3
Carter record cited 512F1, A2
Mondale record cited 512G2, C3, D3
Gulf bias settlemt rptd 7-16, 943C3
State Dept hiring plan rptd 8-3, 922B2
Job bias action vs Uniroyal rptd 8-6, 944C2
GOP platform text 8-18, 605B2-F3, 606C1, E3
MCA to aid businesses 8-20, 944B1
Mondale sees ethnic editors 8-25, 645F2
NYC constructn union quota ordrd 9-1, 943F3
Contractor job-bias rule chngs proposed 9-15, 884E3
Panama Canal Zone racism chrgd 9-22, denied 9-23, 792F2
Ford, Carter debate 9-23, 701C1
Revenue sharing bill bars bias 9-30, 764D3
Carter campaigns 10-2, 743A1
Ford sees GOP ethnic ldrs 10-2, 743E2
Sup Ct bars review of housing bias ruling 10-4, 766B1
Sup Ct bars review of housing bias case 10-4, 807G2
Ford, Carter debate 10-6, 740F2, 741D3
Ethnic groups score Ford E Eur remark 10-7, 10-8; admits error 10-12, 762A3, 763D1, E1
Carter sees Chicago group, scores Ford E Eur remark 10-10, 762F2

1977

Stangeland wins US House seat 2-22, 128A1 ★
Bergland rpts net worth 2-25, 147D3
Natl forest logging case review denied 3-7, 211A3
Pot law impact rptd 3-31, 332A3
Herbst confrmd to US Interior post 4-1, 272A3
Fed spending inequities chrgd 4-6, 423D3
Minneapolis populatn rank rptd down 4-14, 388D1
Businessmen visit Cuba 4-18—4-22, 390D1
Carter energy plan reactn 4-21, 4-24, 319G3-320A1, B3
Army dredging case review declined 4-25, 342E3
'76 per-capita income table 5-10, 387E2
USW strikes ore ranges 8-1, 593E2
US proposes wilderness area 9-13, 724D1
'76 per capita income, tax burden table 9-13, 10-18, 821C2
Graham assn files financial rpt 10-21, gift fund OKd 10-26, 845C1
Carter in Minneapolis for Humphrey return to DC 10-23, 817E1
Minneapolis mayoral results 11-8, 855F1, A3
Pot laws detailed 12-11, 972D3
USW ore-range strike ends 12-16, 977A3
Minneapolis/St Paul 'gateway' air svc OKd 12-21, 1006C2

MINNESOTA, University of (Duluth)
Loses Hall of Fame Bowl 12-23, 1020B2
MINNESOTA, University of (Minneapolis)
Williams in NBA draft 6-10, 584A3
MINNESOTA Mining & Manufacturing Co.—*See 3M Co.*
MINO, General Enrico
Disciplines Kappler guard officers 9-3, 729E1

MINORITIES—*See also specific groups (e.g., BLACK Americans, INDIANS, JEWS, WOMEN)*
Prudential hiring plan rptd 1-10, 278C3
Ill restrictive suburban zoning upheld 1-11, 14G3
Seniority-based layoffs scored 1-18, 278E3 ★
Viet pardon actn scored 1-21, 51F2
Regulatory agency apptmts scored 2-9, 131D3
NLRB backs union certificatn 2-28, 153G3
Carter call-in on jobs 3-5, 171E1
HUD grant program detailed 3-7, 178D1
Califano backs jobs, other quotas 3-17, 217B3
NYC constructn union hiring rule overturned 3-21, 279D2
US drive vs home-mortgage bias rptd 3-24, 279E2
Califano backs down on quotas 3-31, 235B2
Carter poll standing 4-4, 251G1
'For sale' sign ban lifted 5-2, 406C1
Intercity bus fare hiked 5-15, 423C2
Burger cites '69-76 cases 5-17, 419G2-A3
Atty Gen voting rights powers upheld 6-20, 517A1
SBA program scored 7-6—7-8, halted 7-8, 577G2
US plans child adoptn subsidy 7-12, 628F2
EEOC rpts reorgnztn plan 7-20, 669E1
Carter on quotas issue 7-28, 574G3
Youth jobs bill enacted 8-5, 609B2
Calif forgn bank bias chrgd 8-9, 669A3
US study chrgs TV bias 8-15, 642A3
SAT tests scored 8-24, 739C2
US acts vs job bias 8-25, 669E2
Cong employes seek equality 8-31, 669F3
Justice Dept files Bakke brief 9-19; Sup Ct hears arguments 10-12, orders more briefs 10-17, 834F2-835G1
Mandatory retiremt curb voted by House 9-23, 737G2
Voluntary mil rptd success 9-25, 777E2
E Ger chrgs US rights violatns 9-28, 752B3
Constructn quota provisn of pub works bill challenged 10-31, 978F3-979C1
SBA lifts aid moratorium 11-4, 859F3
Amnesty Intl probes US 11-5, 942G3-943A1; cites possible rights abuses 12-8, 956D2
Redlining curb set 11-9, 898C2
Real estate appraisers OKs anti-bias rule 11-11, 898B3
2 white concrete cos win minority contract 12-13, 979C1
School Issues (including busing)—*See EDUCATION, subheads 'Federal Aid', 'School Integration' and 'Teachers'*

1978

Dengler denied name chng 2-13, 172C3
Pensn funds law backed by US Sup Ct 4-3, 308D3
St Paul repeals gay rights law 4-25, 327A2
Income tax relief rptd 5-25, 425D1
Bloomington NHL team merges with Barons, shifts divisn 6-14, 656F2
Judge Youngdahl dies 6-21, 540G3
Gartner bank loans rptd 6-27, bars resignatn 6-28, 513E3
Pensn funds law voided by US Sup Ct 6-28, 567B1
Tornadoes 7-5, flash floods 7-6, 654G3
Ore plant to continue mining, pollutn controls agreed 7-7, 553E2
Primary results 9-12, 715G3
Fox fined for 'block booking' in Minneapolis 9-12, 759C2
GOP tax-cut tour in Minneapolis-St Paul 9-21, 734F3, 735A1
Twins owner causes furor with remarks on blacks, players 9-28—10-2, 779B2
Carter visits Duluth 11-3, 862B2
Election results 11-7: cong 845D1, C2, E2, 846B1, Fl, 848D2, 851A2, 854G2, D3; state 845F1, C2, D3, 853F2, 854G2, B3, 897D3, E3
State interest rates on natl bank credit cards backed by US Sup Ct 12-18, 981C2

MINNESOTA, University of (Minneapolis)
Thompson 4th in coll basketball 3-13, 272E2
Thompson in NBA draft 6-9, 457B2, F3
MINNESOTA Mining & Manufacturing Co.—*See 3M Co.*
MINOBE, Ryokochi
Tokyo issues munic bonds, averts bankruptcy 2-15, 150E1

MINORITIES—*See also specific groups (e.g., BLACK Americans, INDIANS, JEWS, WOMEN)*
Suits vs HEW rptd settled 1-4, 5C1
Segregatn, local govt housing policies linked 1-8, 13F3
HEW anti-smoking drive set 1-11, 23G2
FCC OKs WJLA, KOCO-TV swap 1-12, 109C3
Astronauts for space shuttle named 1-16, 157E3
Carter State of Union Message 1-19, 29C2, 30A3
Broadcasting ownership aid proposed 1-31, 195A2
WJLA-TV swap challenged in ct 3-9, 270C3
ERA boycott scored 3-20, 494A3
Media racism scored, press job data cited 4-7—4-8, 419G3
Press employmt survey rptd 4-13, 835B3
Carter to recruit judges 5-4, 320B3
Redlining curb adopted 5-18, 410E2
Coal indus bias probed, affirmative actn ordrd 5-30, 565B3
Carter job apptmt data rptd 6-15, 811E1
GE complaint setld 6-15, 1006B3
Proposition 13 scored by McGovern 6-17, 526C1
Job bias proof qualified by Sup Ct 6-29, 567D3
AT&T bias case declined by Sup Ct 7-3, 551G3
Calif contractors reverse bias case sent back by Sup Ct 7-3, 552C1
Vet Civil Svc job preference voted by Sen 8-24, 662B1
Vets job preference retained by House 9-11, 696E2
Sen job-bias bd blocked 9-20, House abuses chrgd 9-21, 9-22, 720A3
Pub works business quotas upheld by NY ct 9-23, 811E2
Carter broadens Contract Compliance Office powers 10-6, 811F2
ACLU hails affirmative actn fund curb defeat 10-20, 981C3
NLRB backs union right to job data 11-3, 899A1
SBA aid abuse detailed 11-21, 919A3
GOP govs urge committmt 11-27—11-28, 915G3
Carter cites repressn 12-6, 934C1
NY redlining study finds bias 12-7, 942E2-A3
EEOC issues guidelines 12-12, 1006B2
Calif fire dept ratio plan overturned 12-26, 1006F2
School Issues (including busing)—*See also EDUCATION—School Integration*
Bakke med schl admissn ordrd, race-based affirmative actn principle upheld by Sup Ct; reactn, opinion excerpts 6-28, 481A1-483A1, E1-487C2
HEW vs new med schls 10-24, 948F3

1979

Legal drinking age cited 4-16, 309E3
Red River floods, E Grand Forks evacuatn ordrd 4-26—4-30, 472A2
Chippewa Red Lake reservatn violence flares 5-20, 465D1
Marijuana med use rptd OKd 6-1, 492B3
Anderson '78 labor gifts rptd 6-13, 595D1
Minneapolis rptd hit by gas shortage 6-23, 479C1
Emergency declared re truckers' strike 6-28, 479C2
Grain handlers strike, setlmt reached 7-6—9-25, 722D1, D3-723A1
Chippewas sentncd for Red Lake reservatn violence 7-22, 630G3
Carter in St Paul, Wabasha 8-17, 8-18, 622F1, B2
'78 per capita income rptd 9-16, 746E2
Pensn funds law voided by Sup Ct 10-15, 847E3
Minneapolis prostitutn expose 10-18, 887G1-B2
Fraser elected Minneapolis mayor 11-6, 846C3
Minneapolis '79 living costs ranked 12-28, 991A1
Atomic Energy
Prairie (Red Wing) A-plant leak 10-2, cold shutdown reached 10-3; probe 10-7—10-9, 786C3
MINNESOTA, University of (Minneapolis)
Forgn student enrollmt listed 167E3
Heart disease preventn study rptd 3-19, 219D1
Wins NCAA hockey title 3-24, 356E1
Cuba student, teacher exchng rptd 3-27, 238C2
MINNESOTA Moon (play)
Opens 1-31, 292B2
MINOR, Audax—*See RYALL, George*

MINORITIES—*See also specific groups (e.g., BLACK Americans, INDIANS, JEWS, WOMEN)*
AT&T cleared on job-bias decree 1-17, 92F1
Sears sues US on bias laws 1-24, 92C1
Carter seeks property bias curbs 1-25, 70C2
LBJ contract-denial use cited 2-5, 127D3
Carter proposes Educ Dept 2-8, 110A3
Bell reassures ABA on judicial apptmts 2-12, 130F1
Adams outlines urban-aid policy 2-13, 129A3
Business rpts US job rule compliance costs 3-14, 230A3
Sears ends fed contract work, cites suit retaliatn 4-24, 366A1
DC A-protest draws few 5-6, 343F3
Carter proposes mental health plan 5-15, 365E1
Sears suit vs US dismissed 5-15, 365A3
Govt constructn grant case accepted by Sup Ct 5-21, 400F3
Prop 13 jobs impact rptd 6-5, 500D1
DC rpts business contract law ignored 6-13, 442E3
Merck OKs hiring plan 6-26, 521F1
Weber affirmative actn challenge rejctd by Sup Ct, reactn; majority opinion excerpts 6-27, 477A1-478E1
'78-79 Sup Ct term ends, voting alignmts rptd 7-2, 558C1
Commonwealth conf scores bias 8-7, 590F2
KKK protesters arrested in Ala 8-12, 631C1
Calif lawyer survey rptd 9-17, 787G1
SBA aid abuse rptd 9-28, 947B2-B3
Carter sees affirmative action success 10-9, 767F1
Natl Agenda Comm created 10-24, 810A1
US Helsinki com scores bias 11-7, 981B1
Library outreach urged 11-15—11-19, 901G1
Connally vs affirmative actn 11-15, NAACP scores 11-26, 11-15, 982G3-983A1
Govt constructn grants case argued in Sup Ct 11-27, 944F3
Amnesty Intl scores US 12-9, 980B2
School Issues (including busing)—*See also EDUCATION—School Integration*
Coll 'malaise' seen 4-2, 282A3
NYC schl aid denial upheld by Sup Ct 11-28, 944A2

1980

Families Conf meets in Minneapolis 6-19—6-21, 601G1
Crime & Civil Disorders
FBI 'Miporn' probe rptd 2-14, 136F1
DC slaying suspects' Duluth residence rptd 12-7, 940C1
Labor & Employment
Allis-Chalmers pact set 3-15, 308A3
Harvester strike ends 4-20, 308G2
Politics & Government—*See also other appropriate subheads in this section*
Legislature schedule rptd 18E1
State ct jurisdictn narrowed by Sup Ct 1-21, 93C2
State of State message 1-24, 269A3
St Paul cancels bond issue 2-26, 186F1
Reagan gains delegates 5-3, 342D3
Mondale kicks off campaign in St Paul 8-28, 780E1
Election results 11-4: pres 838B1, E1, 839A2, E3; cong 840C2, 843A2, 851E1; state 845F2
'80 census rptd 12-31, 983E1

MINNESOTA, University of (Minneapolis)
Brooks coaches, McClanahan on US Olympic hockey team 2-24, 155F1, C2
Loses NIT 3-20, 240E2
Heart disease curb rptd 5-22, 527F1
McHale in NBA draft 6-10, 447B1, E2
MINNESOTA Mining & Manufacturing Co.
See 3M Co.

MINORITIES—*See also specific groups (e.g., BLACK Americans)*
Carter asks youth training progrm 1-10, 16F2
Lee Way settles job bias suit 1-10, 17F2
US rights comm sees 'drift' in '79 1-14, 36A3
AFL-CIO reserves cncl seat 2-21, 147A1
Chicago firemen OK pact 3-8, 187D3
Firestone cited for job bias 3-21, 251A3
At-large local electns upheld by Sup Ct 4-22, 343A2
New AM statn preference rptd 5-29, 519C2
Govt constructn grants upheld by Sup Ct 7-2, 510A1
Firestone fed contracts voided 7-15, 560B2
FCC proposes UHF TV statn expansn 9-9, 731G3
NY Times settles '74 job bias suit 9-17, 746B3
EEOC suits setld vs CF&I 9-22, Motorola 9-23, Rockwell 9-26, 746D3
US census revisn ordrd for Detroit, other cities claim undercount 9-25, 741C2
Mass death penalty law struck down 10-28, 868E3
LA settles job bias suit 11-21, 962A3
Ford settles job-bias case 11-25, 899B2
NSF authrzn clears Cong 12-2, 953G2; signed 12-12, 982B1
US census revisn ordrd for NY 12-23, Sup Ct overrules 12-30; '80 figures released, reapportmt seen 12-31, 982G3
Presidential Election (& Transition)
Kennedy 'basic speech' excerpts 3-10, 184A2
Dem platform drafted 6-24, 480A1
Reagan Calif record noted 7-16, 534E1
Reagan acceptance speech 7-17, 532C1, F3
Dem conv keynote speech 8-11, 612A2*, A3
Dem platform planks adopted 8-13, 614D2, F2
Mondale acceptance speech 8-14, 612C1
Reagan 'antipathy' scored by AFL-CIO 8-20, 647B3
Anderson platform offered 8-30, 665B2
Bush seeks GOP support 10-1, 781A2
Mondale campaigns 10-3, 10-26, 816G3-817B1
Bush vows pvt jobs aid 10-16, 817A3
Carter hits Reagan debate remark 10-29, 816D2
Reagan wins ethnic vote 11-4, 837D2, 838A3
Carter plans to speak out 11-12, 865F2
Reagan vows rights defense 12-11, 956D2
School Issues—*See also EDUCATION—School Integration*
Aptitude test study disputed 1-14, 36A2
Coll freshmen survey rptd 1-20, 319G3
ABA tables law schl affirmative actn proposal 2-5, 114E3
ABA backs law schl 'opportunities' 8-6, 744D1

1976

Ford meets ethnic ldrs 10-12, 763E2
Sup Ct bars review of reverse-bias case 10-12, 848G2
Biased soc clubs lose tax exemptn 10-20, 835F1
Ford, Carter debate 10-22, 799G3, 801G3
Mondale in NYC rallies 10-31, 827E2
Sup Ct stays Calif U reverse bias ruling 11-15, 882C1
New job exam-bias rules set 11-17, 884C2
EEOC case backlog rptd cut 11-19, 922C1
Calif U to appeal bias ruling 11-19, 995F2
Braniff bias settlemt OKd 11-23, 943G2
Sup Ct declines to review homeowner tax bias rule 11-29, 900G3
Dole urges GOP seek vote 11-30, 917B3
Sup Ct bars review of EEOC racial, ethnic rptg rule 12-13, 960C3*
Carter on Cabt posts 12-16, 937B1
Busing & Other School Issues—*See EDUCATION*

MINTOFF, Dominic
Labor electn win rptd 9-20, 713B1-A2

MINUTEMAN III—*See 'Missiles' under ARMAMENTS*
MINYARD, Frank
On tanker, ferry collisn 10-27, 876C2
MIRA, Benjamin
On '75 Chile copper losses 1-29, 99A3
MIRANDA, Jorge
Scores mil rule proposal 1-18, 53A1
MIRARCHI, Charles P.
Knight murderer convicted 6-14, 504A1
MIRCEA (Rumanian sailing ship)
In Operation Sail 7-4, 488A3
Officer seeks US asylum 8-7, 907B3
MIREX—*See CHEMICALS*
MIRONOV, Evgeni
Wins Olympic medal 7-24, 575F3
MIRV (multiple independently targetable re-entry vehicle)—*See 'Missiles' under ARMAMENTS*
MISAURI, Muraladji
Signs peace pact 12-23, 1008G3
MISKA, Pali
Named deputy premier 10-14, 949G1
MISSILES—*See under ARMAMENTS*
MISSING In Action—*See ARMED Forces under U.S. GOVERNMENT*
MISSING In Action, National League of Families of
Viet return of MIAs doubted 7-23, 593C2

MISSISSIPPI
Wallace wins in caucuses 1-24, 94F3
Savings & loan crisis rptd 5-7—6-8, 438E1
Primary results 6-1, 411G1
Legis closes S&Ls 6-20; run halted 7-8, 494F3-495E1
Dem conv women delegates, table 508C2
Dem conv pres vote, table 7-14, 507C2
GOP delegates reaffirm unit rule 7-25, Reed endorses Ford 7-28, 550B2
Ford, Reagan visit 7-30, 8-4, 563E3, 564C1
Pickering named GOP platform subcom chrmn 8-9, 583B1
NAACP loses Port Gibson boycott suit 8-9, 671C2
Reed warns Ford vs liberal vp choice 8-12, 582E1
Ford delegate gains rptd 8-13, 583C2, F2
GOP pre-conv delegate count 8-14, 583C3
Reagan, Ford seek conv delegates 8-16, 8-17, 601G2, A3, B3
Delegates back Ford on 16-C 8-17, 600E1; Sears reactn 8-18, 615C3
GOP conv pres, vp vote tables 8-18—8-19, 8-19, 599C1, C3

1977

MINTAREDJA, H. M. S.
Chrgs electn fraud 5-5, 392D3

MINTOFF, Dom (Maltese premier)
Scores France, Italy security talks delay 1-10, 136A3
Bakers strike ends 2-8, 136F2
Labor unrest 7-4—7-21, fires MDs 7-21, 655E3
Replys to World Medical Assemb 9-9, 925D3
Provokes Sovt, E Eur walkout in Peking 11-3, 925E2
Announces Chinese aid 11-16, 925A3
Presses for France, Italy aid, threatens to sign Libya defns pact 11-23, 925A3

MINUTEMAN Intercontinental Ballistic Missile—*See ARMAMENTS—Missiles*
MIRANDA, Francisco de (1754-1816)
Statue dedicated in Phila 7-1, 546C2
MIRANDA Pinto, Rolando
Chrgs Lavin torture 1-30, Chile denies 2-2, 219F2
MIRV (multiple independently-targetable reentry vehicle)—*See ARMAMENTS—Missiles*
MISETICH, Antonio
US science acad seeks info 4-27, 315B2
MISHIMA, Yukio (d. 1970)
2 followers in hostage raid 3-3—3-4, 201A3
MISPIRETA, Dr. Luis
Patient survives surgery without blood supply 6-2, 620A1
MISRA, S. N.
Released 1-5, 45D3
MISS America
Perkins wins title 9-10, 808A3
MISSILES—*See under ARMAMENTS*
MISSING In Action—*See under U.S. GOVERNMENT—ARMED Forces*
MISSING In Action, National League of Families of
Carter meets officers 2-11, 110B2
MISSION Corp.
Getty takeover cited in table 880G1

MISSISSIPPI
Legislature schedule rptd 6E2
Ex-road dir convicted 1-8, 60D1
NAACP rpts '76 budget surplus 1-10, 59A3
Layoffs re gas shortage rptd 1-22, 54C2
SEC chrgs GTE payoffs 1-27, 79E2
US Sup Ct broadens corp tax power 3-7, 192D2
Fannie Lou Hamer dies 3-14, 264F2
'76 per-capita income table 5-10, 387E2, A3
Reapportnmt plan rejected 5-31, 461B3
Black RC bishop installed 6-6, 471B2
'77 death row populatn rptd 6-7, 594C1
Executn for rape barred 6-29, 557F2
Carter visits Yazoo City 7-21, 575A1, 589E3
'76 per capita income, tax burden table 9-13, 10-18, 821E1, D2
Rock band charter plane crashes 10-20, 888G3
ERA econ boycott rptd 11-14, 918E1
Hinds Cnty voter apportnmt case refused 11-28, 919F2
Pot laws detailed 12-11, 972D3
Tupelo grain plant explosn 12-22, 1023A2

1978

MINORITIES and the News, National Conference on
Media racism scored 4-7—4-8, 419E3
MINOW, Newton
Named PBS chrmn 2-5, 335F2
MINSHALL, William
Park gift testimony rptd 1-14, 63D3
MINSKOFF, Jerome
King of Hearts opens 11-22, 1031C2
MINTER, Alan
KOs Jacopucci for Eur middlewgt title 7-19, Jacopucci dies 7-21, 600B2
MINTOFF, Dom (Maltese premier)
Algeria pres visits 1-3, 39B2
Malta bombings, pol unrest rptd 1-8, 2-19, 228G1-C2
Envoy recalled from Australia 1-24, 228C3
'78 budget presented 2-17, 228G2
Plans to dismantle univ 3-21, 228D2
Teachers strike 5-15—5-16, effect disputed 5-17, 416B2
Party merges with union 5-23, 416D2
Dahrendorf resigns 6-6, 592D3
Sees Qaddafi; mil aid, oil price cuts agreed 7-3—7-4, 592E2
France, Italy rptd cool to Arab aid threats 7-4, 592G2
Daughter disrupts UK Parlt 7-6, 533C3
Bans UK rptrs 7-9, closes radio statn 7-16; denies retaliatn 7-10, 592A3
MINTOFF, Vana
Throws manure in Commons 7-6, freed on bail 7-7, 533B3
MINUTEMAN Intercontinental Ballistic Missile—*See ARMAMENTS—Missiles*
MIRABELLA, Paul
Traded to Yankees 11-10, 1026B1
MIRAGE Jet—*See ARMAMENTS—Air craft*
MIRALLES, Ramon
Rptd freed 9-1, 793G1
MIRANDINHA (Sebastiao Miranda da Silva Filho)
Cosmos win NASL title 8-27, 707D2
MIRISCH, Walter
Gray Lady Down released 3-10, 619C2
Same Time, Next Yr released 11-22, 970A3
MIRO, Joan
Natl Gallery commissn rptd 6-1, 578C3
Paintings destroyed in Brazil museum fire 7-8, 579A2
MIRO Quesada, Alejandro
Scores govt newspr sale plan 7-22, 692A1
MIRV (multiple independently-targetable reentry vehicle)—*See ARMAMENTS—Missiles*
MISAURI, Muraladji
Leadership challenged 650A2
MISCARRIAGES—*See CHILDBIRTH*
MISHA Abdul Aziz, Princess (Saudi Arabia)
Execution confirmed 2-1, 172G3
MISHRA, Shyam Nandan
Quits over Singh ouster 7-6, 631E3
MISL (Major Indoor Soccer League)—*See SOCCER*
MISSILES—*See under ARMAMENTS*

MISSISSIPPI
Legislature schedule rptd 14F3
'67, '77 sales-tax rates rptd 1-5, 15E3
State govt tax revenue table 1-9, 84D2
Tornadoes hit 4-17—4-18, 479G2
Construction pact signed 5-22, 429D3
Income tax relief rptd 5-25, 425D1
Primary results, Sen runoff set 6-6, 448A1
Dantin wins Sen runoff 6-27, 510C1
FBI informants rptd in '68 Dem conv delegatn 7-3, 507E3
Biloxi firemen strike 8-18—9-20, 753F1
Jefferson Davis US citizenship restored 10-17, 843C3
Election results 11-7: cong 845D1, E1, 846D1, 848D2, 851B2, 852F2; state 852F3
Nixon in Biloxi 11-11, 900A3
Clarksdale hit by tornado 12-3, 972G1, A2
Ellisville dorm fire kills 15 12-9, 971E3

1979

MINOW, Newton A.
On AMA ad ban end 10-24, 902B3

MINTOFF, Dom (Maltese premier)
UK withdraws last troops 4-1, 269C2
Office shot up, assailant seized 10-15, 782G1*

MINUTE by Minute (recording)
On best-seller list 3-7, 174E1; 4-4 271D2; 5-2, 356A3
MINUTEMAN Intercontinental Ballistic Missile—*See ARMAMENTS—Missiles*
MIRABELLA, Paul
Traded to Blue Jays 11-1, 1002C3
MIRABELL: Book of Numbers (book)
Wins Natl Book Award 4-23, 356B2
MIRACLE Worker, The (play)
Opens 1-6, 292B2
MIRAGE Jet—*See ARMAMENTS—Aircraft*
MIRFENDERESKI, Ahmed
Named Iran forgn min 1-6, 11G2
Iran plans CENTO exit, Zahedi out as amb to US 2-6, 81C2
MIRISCH, Walter
Prisoner of Zenda released 5-25, 820A3
Dracula released 7-13, 820A1
MIRV (multiple independently-targetable reentry vehicle)—*See ARMAMENTS—Missiles*
MISHAWAKA, Ind.—*See INDIANA*
MISHKIND, Andrew
Poet & Rent opens 5-9, 712A2
MISHLER, Judge Jacob
Orders Suffolk Cnty, Brentwood bilingual programs 7-18, 7-20, 597C1, D1
MISHRA, Shyam Nandan
Named India forgn min 7-28, 573D1
MISSERI, Federico
Arrested 5-28, 426F2
MISSHO-Iwai Co.
Shimada commits suicide 2-1, 98E2
MISSILE Experimental (MX)—*See ARMAMENTS—Missiles*
MISSILES—*See under ARMAMENTS*

MISSISSIPPI
Legislature schedule rptd 1-1, 5D3
Tenn R projct upheld 3-13, 188B3
Legis redistricting ordrd by US Sup Ct 3-26, 231C1
Regulatory bds rptd segregated 4-9, 307A2
Steens hit by tornado 4-11, 288B3
Pearl R flood hits 4-17, 288D3
Evers '78 labor gifts rptd 6-13, 595C1
Gulf of Mex oil, gas lease bids placed 7-31, accepted 8-28, 664E3
Gubernatorial primary results 8-7, 8-28, 680E2
Hurricane Frederic hits Pascagoula 9-12, disaster aid OKd 9-14, 691C1
'78 per capita income rptd 9-16, 746D1-F1, E2
Hurricane Frederic loss rptd 10-5, 954G2
Pascagoula refinery rptd reopened 10-26, 805C1
Winter elected gov, 17 blacks voted to state legis 11-6, 846G1, E2
Okolona KKK activity cited 865B1
Finch declares pres bid 12-24, 984E1

1980

MINTER, Alan
Decisns Antuofermo for world middlewgt title, victory disputed 3-16, 320B2
Hagler TKOs for world middlewgt title 9-27, 772A2
MINTIKS, Jan
Wife found slain 7-24, 654E1

MINTOFF, Dom (Maltese premier)
Expels Libyan mil advisers 8-28, 709F1

MINUTE by Minute (recording)
Doobie Brothers win Grammy 2-27, 296A3
MINVER, Charles
Judges middlewgt title bout 3-16, 320D2
MIRABITO, Paul S.
Burroughs retiremt set 9-25, 958G3
MIRACAPILLO, Vito
Vs Brazil mass 9-7, ordrd expelled 10-30, 870G3-871E1
MIRAGE Jet—*See ARMAMENTS--Aircraft*
MIRAGLIA, Mario
Wounded 2-10, 151D2
MIRANDA v. Arizona
Case cited by Sup Ct 5-12, 386C2
MIROSHNICHENKO, Viktor
Wins Olympic medal 8-2, 622E1
MIRREN, Helen
Fiendish Plot of Dr Fu Manchu released 8-8, 675E2
MIRROR Crack'd, The (film)
Released 12-18, 1003B2
MIR-Salim, Mostafa
Nominated Iran premr 7-26, 571E2
Nominatn rejctd by parlt 8-9, 620A1
MISHA Abdul Aziz (Mishaal), Princess (Saudi Arabia) (d. 1977)
UK TV film strains Saudi ties 4-10, 4-11, 294B1; 4-22—4-25, 313C2-B3
Australia vs film broadcast 4-15, 309E3
US film telecast protested 5-8, PBS airs 5-12; cts rule 5-9, 5-12, 375E2-376A1
UK regrets film 5-22, 407B3
MISHLER, Judge Jacob
Rules on LIRR labor dispute 3-4, 289E3
Quits Abscam cases 8-7, 599E3
MISHRA, Brajesh Chandra
Backs Sovt Afghan invasn 1-11, 25G2
MISKAROV, Arsen
Wins Olympic medals 7-22, 7-26, 623F2
MISS America (beauty contest)
Parks dropped as emcee 1-4, Ely named replacemt 3-5, 198G3
MISSILES—*See under ARMAMENTS*
MISSISSIPPI
'77 abortn data rptd 1-9, 23A3
Pascagoula port congestn rptd 1-19, 45C1
Schl prayer law cited 2-6, 156A2
Carter outlines A-waste storage plan 2-12, 127F3
Hunts bailout loan collateral listed 5-28, 425F3, 426E1
Gulf coast oil leasing bids set records 9-30, 785A2
NAACP held liable in boycott 12-10, 963C2
Accidents & Disasters
Sledge train derailmt, gas blasts 2-13, 309C2
Tornadoes hit 4-7—4-8, 391A3
Woman survives parachute failure 5-11, 471E1
Crime & Civil Disorders
Road builders bid-rigging scandal rptd 7-5, 655F1
KKK rally in Jackson 10-4, 884E3
Politics & Government—*See also other appropriate subheads in this section*
Legislature schedule rptd 18E1
Reagan wins primary 6-3, 424C1

1976

Reagan vs vp draft move 8-19, 598D2
Fscl '75 per capita income, tax burden rptd 9-15, 10-12, 959B1, D2
Carter campaigns with Eastland, Stennis 9-17, 704E1, G2
Ford campaigns 9-26, 723B3
Dole in Jackson 10-20, 804D1
Election results 11-2: pres 818B1-G1, 819B2; cong 820D1, 822C2, 828B2, 829G4-830A1
US Sup Ct refuses hwy constructn case 11-29, 901C1
Flu shot paralysis rptd 12-17, 950E1

MISSISSIPPI Action for Progress, Inc. (MAP)
Loses boycott suit 8-9, 671C2
MISSISSIPPI River
Polish grain cargo inspected 1-17—1-19, 44A1
Sup Ct bars review of oil-spill liability case 10-4, 807D3
Tanker, ferry collide 10-20, 876G1
MISSISSIPPI River Grain Corp.
Grain abuse plan cited 3-16, 248C1
MISSISSIPPI River Grain Elevator Inc.
Execs named in grain fraud 3-11, 247D3 ★
Fined 5-6, exec indicted 7-13, 990B3

MISSOURI
Sup Ct bars Medicaid abortn rule review 1-26, 87B3
Mercantile bank, Hearnes probes rptd 2-27, 3-1, 181A1
St Louis violent crime up 3-2, 336D3
Clay St Louis travel bills questnd 3-23, 247E1
EPA checks KC water supply 4-30, 349G1
Ford in Independence 5-8, 342A3
Ford delegates counted 5-11, 343A1
Carter support slipping 5-25, 373E3
Anheuser-Busch St Louis strike ends 6-6, 436B2
Reagan sweeps conv vote 6-12, 432B2
Sup Ct upholds police bargaining law 6-21, 553A1
US Sup Ct rules on '74 abortn law 7-1, 518E2
Dem conv women delegates, table 508C2
Dem conv pres vote, table 7-14, 507C2
Litton dies after Sen primary win 8-3, 565C2
GOP pre-conv delegate count 8-14, 583C3
GOP Natl Conv in KC 8-16—8-19, 597A1
GOP conv pres, vp vote tables 8-18—8-19, 8-19, 599C1, C3
Reagan seeks conv delegates 8-18, 601C3
Hearnes named Sen nominee 8-21, 633D1
Mondale, Dole campaign 9-2—9-8, 665A3, G3
Fscl '75 per capita income, tax burden rptd 9-15, 10-12, 959C2
Carter in Kansas City 9-19, 703E3
Ford in St Louis 10-29, 826C3
Carter rally in St Louis 10-29, 827E1
Dole stumps 11-1, 827B3
Election results 11-2: pres 818C1, 819B2; cong 820B1, D2, 823A3, 828B2, 830A1, 831F1; state 820F2, G2, 823C3
Morgan Moulder dies 11-12, 1015B2
Swine flu case unconfrmd 11-27, 911D1
US Sup Ct refuses tuition aid case 12-13, 960A3
St Louis SW Bell tap data cited 12-17, 995A2
St Louis, KC transatlantic air routes rejctd 12-28, 992E2

MISSOURI, University of
Mondale speaks at KC law schl 10-5, 743B3
MISSOURI Public Service Co.
SEC lists pol paymts 5-12, 726B1, 728D2
MITCHELL, Clarence
Scores GOP, Dem platforms 8-24, 8-25, 666G1
MITCHELL, Rep. Donald J. (R, N.Y.)
Reelected 11-2, 830C2
MITCHELL, George
Replaced as FRB v chrmn 1-29, 110B2

1977

MISSISSIPPI, University of (University)
'64 heart transplant cited 6-20, 619C3
MISSISSIPPI Freedom Democratic Party
Fannie Lou Hamer dies 3-14, 264F2
MISSISSIPPI River
Ice blockage rptd 1-14, 37B2
Flow decline rptd 3-8, 244A3
MISSISSIPPI State University (State College)
Sup Ct refuses gay ad case review 4-25, 342C3

MISSOURI
Legislature schedule rptd 6E2
Mississippi R ice blockage rptd 1-14, 37B2
St Louis atmospheric impact rptd 2-24, 184B1
ERA set back 3-15, 279D3
KC teachers strike 3-21—5-8, 481D2
Conway elected St Louis mayor 4-5, 252E3
St Louis populatn rank rptd down 4-14, 388D1
Meramec Dam funds cut cleared 5-3, 365D2
'76 per-capita income table 5-10, 387E2
US Sup Ct backs police deadly force law 5-16, 419F1
KC seeks cross-state integratn 5-26, 446E1
3 steel firms indicted 6-6, 504D1
St Louis abortn fund curb upheld 6-20, 516D2
KC gay rights march 6-26, 560F2
Hazelwood teacher job-bias suit sent back 6-27, 538F3
St Louis Mafia operatns rptd 7-3, 568C2
Charismatic conf held in KC 7-20—7-24, 620A3
Wm Hull Jr dies 8-15, 696G2
House ex-speaker Rabbitt sentncd 8-16, 712A2
KC schl busing starts calmly 9-7, 838A1
KC flooded 9-12—9-13, disaster area declared 9-14, 768C3
'76 per capita income, tax burden table 9-13, 10-18, 821C2
Anti-abortn amendmt rptd sought 10-6, 786B3
ERA econ boycott rptd 11-14, 918E1
Donald Thorman dies 11-30, 952E3
St Lous, KC 'gateway' air svc OKd 12-21, 1006C2

MISSOURI, University of (Columbia)
Towns, Pisarkiewicz in NFL draft 5-3, 353B3
MISSOURI River
ND irrigatn projct scored 1-7, 60C3
ND project halted 2-18, 133A1
Carter proposes ND projct $ cut 2-22, 126E1
Flow decline rptd 3-8, 244A3
ND irrigatn projct scored 9-19, 726E1
MISS Universe
Commissiong crowned 7-16, 808G2
MITCHELL, Austin
Wins Grimsby by-electn 4-28, 374B1
MITCHELL, Bridger M.
On electricity pricing 3-11, 277G3
MITCHELL Jr., Clarence M.
Scores Bell nominatn 1-10, 59C3
Carter energy plan reactn rptd 4-23, 320G2
MITCHELL, David
Wins Tony 6-5, 452D1

1978

MISSISSIPPI, University of (University)
Notre Dame ranked 1st 1-3, 8F2
'76 tanker, ferry collisn rpt issued 5-17, 460B1
MISSISSIPPI River
House votes parks bill 7-12, 526G3
MISSISSIPPI Surveillance Project
FBI informants rptd at '68 Dem conv 7-3, 507E3

MISSOURI
Legislature schedule rptd 14F3
'67, '77 sales-tax rates rptd 1-5, 15A3, E3
NASL '77 St Louis club move cited 1-5, 23B1
State govt tax revenue table 1-9, 84D2
Panama Canal 'truth squad' in St Louis 1-18, 58C2
St Louis museum sculptures stolen 1-21, 2-20, 335C1; Byers rptd implicated 6-26, 589G3
KC hotel fire kills 16 1-28, 212B3
Carter sees gov on coal strike 2-16, 104D2
Gay Lib univ status challenge refused 2-21, 125C3
5th in US defense contracts 2-21, 127D2
St Louis clean-air rating rptd 2-23, 144E3
ERA boycott injunctn sought 2-28, 494F2
Spinks arrested in St Louis 3-19, 4-21; avoids indictmt, pays fine 5-18, 379A1
NRC to probe A-worker firing, GAO review sought 3-29, 242F1
Disaster fund supplemt signed, KC '77 flood cited 4-4, 261D3
Morman ldr installed in Independence 4-5, 294G2
Symington to remarry 4-12, 420F2
Coal strike utility billing probe set 5-10, 367A1
AMA conv in St Louis 6-21, 578C1
St Louis makes bad-air list 7-5, 513D1
Bad-air list corrected 7-19, 644B2
St Louis man alleges King murder plot 7-26, 589G2
Primary results 8-8, 626B1
Carter visits Columbia 8-14, 626C1
Abortn law ruled unconstitutnl 9-13, 744A1
Trade missn rptd in Japan 10-18, 798D1
St Louis forum on Carter wage-price plan 11-1, 863G2
Election results 11-7: cong 848D2, 851C2, 854D3; state 847F1, 854E3
Carter in KC 11-9, 873C1, 874E3, 875B2
St Louis papers struck 11-20, 1006A2
US mayors meet in St Louis 11-27, 914F2
Ray family plot, King death bounty alleged 11-27, 938B1, G1
Ray's brother arrested for burglary 11-27, 938F1
St Louis populatn ranked 12-6, 942B3
2 convicted in A-sub plot wire fraud 12-14, 12-19, 992F2

MISSOURI, University of (Columbia)
Gay Lib status challenge refused 2-21, 125C3
Med student ouster upheld 3-1, 143D2
Wins Liberty Bowl 12-23, 1025E2
MISS You (recording)
On best-seller list 8-2, 620F1; 9-6, 708E1
MR. Joyce Is Leaving Paris (play)
Opens 4-23, 760E2
MITCHELL, Cameron
November People opens 1-14, 760A3
MITCHELL, Clarence
On Carter budget mtg 12-11, 980B2
MITCHELL, David W.
To leave Manufacturers Hanover bd 3-7, 163C1
Quits Stevens bd, cites union pressure 3-21, 205D1
MITCHELL, Rep. Donald J. (R, N.Y.)
Reelected 11-7, 851G3
MITCHELL, Gerard
Loses Liberal ldrshp bid 12-9, 964G1

1979

MISSISSIPPI River
Floods threaten N Orleans 4-18, 288F3
Tank barge blast kills 3 8-30, 800D1
Midwest quake threat rptd, 1811 quake cited 11-15, 954E1
MISSISSIPPI River Grain Elevator Inc.
Cook indemnified, countersuit cited 9-26, 727A3
MISSISSIPPI State University (State College)
US wins Can-Am Bowl 1-6, 8C3
Cal State wins NCAA baseball title 6-8, 569B3
Peck in NBA draft 6-25, 507B3
MISS New York State (beauty contest)
Contest losers to be reimbursed 3-27, 308E3
MISSOURI
Legislature schedule rptd 5E3
Women jury exclusn law voided by US Sup Ct 1-9, 14G2
Blizzards hit 1-12–1-14, 1-24–1-27, 120F1
St Louis papers resume publicatn 1-14, 1-15, 87E2
St Louis teachers strike 1-16–3-12, 187A3
KC, St Louis '78 Nazi activity rptd 1-19, 102B1
KC loses GOP conv bid 1-23, 70E3
St Louis bad air quality cited 1-25, 90C2
ERA conv boycott upheld, impact cited 2-21, 128F1
Nonpatent royalties upheld by Sup Ct 2-28, 165B2
Abortn curb end backed by Sup Ct 3-5, 185A1
Laetrile shipmt recalled 3-8, 196A1
2 sentncd in A-sub plot wire fraud 3-15, 3-20, 240E2
GOP mayor electd in KC 3-27, 231A3
Farmington fire 4-2, 316G2
Tornado injures 16 4-11, 288B3
St Louis busing order denied 4-12, 596C3
Carter declares disaster area 4-21, 472D2
St Louis hit by gas shortage 6-23, 479C1
Carter in KC energy address 7-16, 532B1, F2, 534F1
Carter in Hannibal 8-23, St Louis 8-24, 622G1, 623A1
Amtrak NYC-KC train ordrd cut 8-29, 868B1
'78 per capita income rptd 9-16, 746D2
St Louis all-white club judicial membership surveyed 9-19, 901F2
Carter in KC 10-15, 807G2
Ex-FBI agent pleads guilty of conspiracy 10-15, 906G1
Bond issues approved 11-6, 847A1
Midwest quake threat rptd, 1811 New Madrid quake cited 11-15, 954C1, D1
Ex-Rep Short dies 11-19, 932E3
Sports
St Louis gets WBL team 6-12, 526G2

MISSOURI, University of (Columbia)
Young for new approach to PLO 1-16, Jewish group protests 1-17, 69E1
UN Palestinian state res opposed 2-21, 148F1
Carter wants Palestinian ties 3-23, 222G2
PLO offcl visits 4-1–4-21, US House scores 4-24, 319E2; Begin protests 5-2, 320B1
Winslow in NFL draft 5-3, 335F2
Wins Hall of Fame Bowl 12-29, 1001B3
MISSOURI Pacific Corp.
RR takeover of Rock Island ordered 9-26, 722C3
MISS Truth (play)
Opens 7-22, 712E1
MISTRALI-Guidotti, Luisa
Killed 7-6, 546G3
MITANG, Iris
Elected NWPC pres 7-15, 578C3
MITCHELL, Charlie
Hired as Roughnecks coach 8-31, 1004E2
MITCHELL, Donn
Vs Episcopalian gay ordinatn ban 9-17, 755D2
MITCHELL, Gwen Davis
Novelist libel case refused by Sup Ct 12-3, 964F1

1980

Reagan at Phila fair 8-3, 597B3
Ex-Rep Colmer dies 9-9, 755F2
5th judicial circuit split 10-14, 918A3
Carter repudiates Young racial remark 10-15, 803D1
Evers, ex-Gov Williams back Reagan 10-22, 802C2
Election results 11-4: pres 838B1, 839B2, E3; cong 840D2, 843C2, 849E3; state 845F2
'80 census rptd 12-31, 983E1

MISSISSIPPI State University (State College)
Brown in NBA draft 6-10, 447F2
Loses Sun Bowl 12-27, 999D3
MISSISSIPPI Valley State University (Itta Benna)
Williams in Black Coll All-Star Game 1-5, 62B2

MISSOURI
St Louis hay fever study rptd 2-18, 159G3
Black Jack low income housing case refused by Sup Ct 2-25, 188A1
DES in cattle rptd 4-24, 358F1
Accidents & Disasters
Blizzards hit, 2 killed 3-1—3-2, 292B2
Tornadoes hit 4 cities 4-7—4-8, 391G2
Tornado hits Sedalia, other cities 5-12, 391E2
Drought, heat wave hit, death toll rptd 6-23—8-15; Carter declares disaster area 7-16, 616D1-G1, B2
Drought, heat wave death toll final rpt 9-7, 857A2
Crime & Civil Disorders
'Pyramid' money schemes rptd 5-17, 655A3
Eagleton niece, atty convicted of extortn 10-24, 890C1
Labor & Employment
GM to shut St Louis plant, St Charles county replacmt site set 1-31, 287B2
KC fire fighters end strike 3-22, 227D3
Workman's compensatn law voided by Sup Ct 4-22, 344A1
Politics & Government—*See also other appropriate subheads in this section*
Legislature schedule rptd 18E1
GOP platform hearing set in St Louis 1-14, 32A1
Ex-Sen Donnell dies 3-3, 279B2
'Good faith' municipal immunity ended by Sup Ct 4-16, 328F2
Reagan gains delegates 5-3, 342B3
Primary results 8-5, 682E3
Carter in Independence 9-2, 664A3
Mondale in KC, St Louis 9-18, 780B2, D2
Bush in St Louis 10-3, 781B2
NOW boycott case refused by Sup Ct 10-6, 782F1-A2
Carter in St Louis 10-30, 841B1
Newspaper pres endorsemts rptd 11-1, 841G3
Carter in Springfield 11-3, 841D1
Election results 11-4: pres 838B1, 839B2, E3; cong 840D2, 843C2, 845A3, 851F1; state 845G2, 847C1, F2, G2, C3, 851G1
'80 census rptd, reapportmt seen 12-31, 983E1
School Issues
St Louis schl desegregatn ordered 5-21, 559A2
St Louis busing begins peacefully 9-3, 724G3
Transportation
Union Pacific, MoPac set merger 1-8, 52C3
St Louis-London air svc agreed 3-5, 172B3, D3
McDonnell Douglas ruled open to suit in DC-10 crash 5-23, 519A1
N&W, Southn RR merger sought 6-2, 427E2
ICC OKs Rock I RR segment sale 6-10, 598E3
MISSOURI, University of (Columbia)
Drew in NBA draft 6-10, 447G2
Loses Liberty Bowl 12-27, 999D3
MISSOURI Pacific Corp. (MoPac)
Union Pacific merger set 1-8, 52B3
Union Pacific sets Westn Pacific merger 1-21, 131C2
3-way merger set 9-15, 745G1
MISSOURI Pipe Fittings Co.
Eagleton niece, atty convicted of extortn 10-24, 890E1
MISSOURI v. National Organization for Women
Case refused by Sup Ct 10-6, 782F1
MITCHELL, Cameron
Silent Scream released 2-2, 216E3
MITCHELL, Dan
On Leary firing 11-1, 890E2
MITCHELL, Darryl
Virginia wins NIT 3-20, 240G2
MITCHELL, David
Wins Tony 6-8, 692C3
MITCHELL, Rep. Donald J. (R, N.Y.)
Reelected 11-4, 843G3
MITCHELL, Sen. George J. (D, Me.)
Named to Muskie Sen seat 5-8, 367B2
On toxic waste clean-up legis 11-24, 898E1

1976

MITCHELL, John N.
Sup Ct bars review of JDL wiretap case 4-19, 331F1
Named in wiretap suit 5-10, 349A3
Wife dies 5-31, 404C2
Anti-black strategy chrgd 8-12, 671F2
Watergate convictn upheld 10-12, 770E1-C2
Ford denies pardon rumor 10-20, 784E3
Held liable re wiretap 12-16, 980B3-981B1
MITCHELL, Martha (Mrs. John N.)
Dies 5-31, 404C2
MITCHELL, Rep. Parren J. (D, Md.)
On Adams' budget proposals 3-23, 231B3
Reelected 11-2, 829A4
On Carter meeting 12-16, 937B2
MITHOEFER Jr., William C.
Equatorial Guinea ties cut 3-15, 239A1
MITKOV, Yordan
Wins Olympic medal 7-22, 576E2
MITRE Corp.
Violent crime date rptd 3-2, 336C3
MITRIONE, Daniel (d. 1970)
AID cover cited 10-8, 814E1
MITSCHERLISH, Andrea
Wins Olympic medal 2-8, 159A1
MITSUBISHI International Corp.
Australian coal plan OKd 1-20, 46G1
US ends car dumping probe 5-4, 321D2
Australia coal project set 7-7, 496A2
MITSUI & Co. Ltd.
US sues Kearns, Bostwick 8-9, 709D3
MITTAG, Gunter
E Ger Politburo enlarged 5-22, 381E2
MITTERMAIER, Rosi
Wins Olympic medals 2-8, 2-11, 2-13, 158A3, D3-E3
Quits ski competitn 5-31, 424G1
MITTERRAND, Francois
At Europn socialist mtgs 1-19, 48C3; 1-24—1-25, 120B1, E1; 3-13—3-14, 222F3
Socialists plan econ program 1-27—1-29, 119B3
Scores new CP line 2-6, 119E2
Visits Algeria, scored by govt 2-25—2-27, 204G3
Chirac, Giscard score 3-27, 4-1, 312D3
Joint '77 electn drive stalled 5-21, 381A3
Scores Argentina violence 8-26, 672E2
Spain OKs Socialist conf 11-27, 908E3
MIYAKE, Shoichi
Named dep house speaker 12-24, 1006A3
MIYAZAWA, Kiichi
Japan min without portfolio 12-24, 1006B3
MIYAZAWA, Kiichi
In Sovt treaty talks 1-10, 30B1
Warns US vs China concessns 7-12; China protests 7-16, 7-19, 555E2, A3
Replaced 9-15, 694E1
MIZELL Sr., Wilmer D.
Replaced as Commerce asst secy 8-3, 807F3
Defeated 11-2, 822F2
MIZER, Muhsim Abu
US, Israel boycott ILO speech 6-8, 450A1
MIZUTANI, Bunichi
Arrested 497F2
MLONZI, Lennox
On end to forced Afrikaans use 7-6, 500B2
MLYNAR, Zdenek
CIA-RFE link chrgd 3-10, 289G2
MLYNCZAK, Tadeusz
Polish State Cncl member 3-25, 268C2
MOAKLEY, Rep. John Joseph (D, Mass.)
Reelected 11-2, 829C4
MOBILE (Ala.) Press (newspaper)
Ford endorsement rptd 10-30, 827F3
MOBIL Corp.
Container Corp trust suit dvpts 2-18—10-5, 886B1, F2; execs sentncd 11-30, 921E2-A3
NY dismisses '74 trust case 3-10; 2d case rptd pending 3-11, 413C1
In Viet oil talks 4-24, 352B2
On '75 Fortune list 437A1
Rhodesia sanctn violatns chrgd 6-21, 621D1
Quitting Leb 629A2
Denies chrgs re Rhodesia; SEC notified 8-27, 698C2
Vs House Arab boycott legis 9-12, 746C3
'75 US tax paymt rptd 10-2, 847A2
Sup Ct bars price hike review 10-4, 807A3
No Rhodesia violatns seen 10-17, 855E3

1977

MITCHELL, Jeff
3d in Hall of Fame tourn 8-28, 675E3
MITCHELL, John N.
Liddy's term commuted 4-12, 325E3
Sup Ct appeal decisn leaked 4-21, defense motion denied 5-2, 382C2; appeal denied 5-23, 406D1
Suits vs US spying rptd 5-22, 422D3
Jail delay refused 5-31, 461F3
Enters prison 6-22, 483F2
Sup Ct denies 2d appeal 6-27, 538F3
Halperin awarded $5 in tap suit 8-5, 652B2
Nixon-Frost TV interview 9-3, 692F3
Sentence cut after apology 10-4, 762A1
Sup Ct disbars 10-31, 835A3
MITCHELL, Martha (Mrs. John N.) (d. 1976)
Nixon-Frost TV interview 9-3, 692F3
MITCHELL, Martha M.
Named Carter special asst 1-14, 35C3
MITCHELL, Maurice B.
Succeeds Hutchins 11-21, 927F2
MITCHELL, Rep. Parren J. (D, Md.)
Blacks meet re govt 'neglect' 8-29, 702C1
Carter sees Black Caucus 9-7, 702B1
Seeks Wilmington 10 pardon 12-4, 943B1
MITCHELL, Judge Roy
Fines Ontario lumber co 9-29, 763F3
MITCHELL, Thomas
Lance cleared re finances 7-25, 573G3
MITRE Corp.
A-power study issued 3-21, disputed 3-26, 234A3, G3
MITSOTAKIS, Constantine
Electn results 11-20, 11-23, 925A1
MITSUBISHI Electric Corp.
US TV productn rptd 4-14, 319A1
Calif TV plant cited 12-14, 974B2
MITSUBISHI Heavy Industries Ltd.
Australia ship deal set 2-16, 253G1
MITSUI Mining Co.
25 miners killed 5-11, 808D1
MITTERRAND, Francois
Scores govt on de Broglie case 1-6, 44F1
Assemb passes econ plan 4-28, 328C3
Barre TV debate 5-12, 542G3
At Soclst Party cong 6-17—6-19, 542C3
Clashes with Marchaise on A-policy 8-9, 727B3
Carter barred mtg, US trip canceled 9-16, 883D3
Sees CP-conservative alliance 10-31, CP deny chrg 11-9, 924E2, C3
Sahara rebels set French natls release 12-13, 998C3
MIYAZAWA, Kiichi
Heads Econ Planning Agency 11-28, task force 11-29, 932G1, D2
MIYAZAWA, Yasushi
Affirms Kurile claim 4-13, 319D2
MIZE, Chester
Cited in Park indictmt 9-6, 688D1
MJB Co.
Coffee prices raised 3-16, 209G1
MKAPA, Benjamin
Named Tanzania forgn min 2-13, 161B2
MKHTSHWA, Rev. Smangaliso
Arrested 10-19, 803G3
MLAWAH, Abdel Karim
Jordan arrest rptd 7-14, 535B1
MLYNAR, Zdenek
Austria offers asylum 1-25, rejected 1-28, 82C3 ★
Spain interviewer held 4-2—4-3, 314B3
Dismissal upheld 4-25, 314B2
In Vienna 6-13, news conf 6-16, 513A1
MNYUKH, Yuri
Asks dissident funds 1-10, 22B2
Emigratn rptd 8-8, 606G2
MOBIL Alaska Pipeline Co. v. U.S.
Sup Ct upholds Alaska pipe rate order 11-14, 878E2
MOBIL Corp.
Ads vs Irvine takeover rptd 5-6, loses bid 5-20, 519C1, F1
Washington sues 8-16, 691E3
Zambia sues re Rhodesia sanctns 8-22, 662D1
Schmidt scores Carter attack 10-13, 772G3
Mobil Oil Corp.
To build Saudi pipeline 2-8, 108C2
To mkt extra Saudi oil 2-16, 108C1, D1
Container Corp sentncs cut 2-17, 504E1
To promote S Africa equality 3-1, 160B3
Irvine takeover battle rptd 3-3, 274E3
On '76 Fortune 500 list, Marcor acquisitn cited 340D1, 341A1
US Treas ends Rhodesia probe 5-16, 413E2
Saudi fire forces sale cut 5-19, 402C2
Lonrho sues vs Rhodesia sales 5-31, 413C2
Canada unit to halt Mackenzie drilling 6-4, 466B3
FTC info order review rejctd 6-13, 517G1
Defends Alaska pipeline rate proposal 6-16, 477B2; ICC sets rates 6-28, 498C1, F1
Alaska pipeline opens 6-20, 476B3
Superport projct imperiled 7-12, 559B2
FALN bombs NYC hq 8-3, 613E3
Gas royalties dispute review refused 10-3, 760A2
Sup Ct OKs Alaska pipe interim rate rise 10-20, upholds order 11-14, 878E2
Hunt suit case declined 12-5, 938G3
Montgomery Ward & Co., Inc.
CPSC sues 10-16, 820B2
MOBIL Oil Corp. v. Lightcap
Sup Ct bars royalty case review 10-3, 760A2
MOBUTO, Marie Antoinette (Mama)
Dies 10-22, 872F2

1978

MITCHELL, John N.
Korean lobbying cover-up probed 1-26, 63E2
Testifies on Korea lobbying info 3-21, 203D2
Kissinger cites in Korea testimony 4-20, 280D1
Ehrlichman freed 4-27, 320D2
Nixon memoir excerpts cite Watergate role 4-30, 319E3
Haldeman leaves prison 12-20, 1011A3
MITCHELL, Lydell
Traded to Chargers 8-23, 1024B3
MITCHELL, Mike
In NBA draft 6-9, 457G2
MITCHELL, Rep. Parren J. (D, Md.)
Scores Sup Ct Bakke ruling 6-28, 482F2
Harris cancels testimony 8-7, 605G1
Reelected 11-7, 851B1
MITCHELL, Peter
Wins Nobel Prize 10-17, 886C2
MITCHELL, Tom
Traded to Redskins 4-14, 336F1
MITCHELL, Lydell
NFL '77 receiving, rushing ldr 1-1, 56C2, B3
MITCHUM, Robert
Amsterdam Kill released 3-30, 618B3
MITSOTAKIS, Constantine
Named Greek coordinatn min 5-10, 373D3
Announces econ measures 6-18, 631D1
MITSUBISHI Corp.
US unit indicted 5-9, 404B2
Chrysler Australia investmt plans cited 8-10, 623D3
Chrysler Australia purchase agreed 10-25, 836B2
MITTERRAND, Francois
CP rejcts alliance renewal offer 1-5, 54D1
Confers with Carter 1-6, 2F1
Carter mtg scored 1-6—1-10, 54D1
CP breaks electn accord 1-7, 54A2
Vs Giscard on leftist bar 1-27, 70G3
Rules out CP electn deal 2-8, 148G3
Scores govt on franc decline 2-8, 167E1
Scored in Chirac speech 2-11, 149A1
Danish premr spurs electn dispute 2-23—3-1, 167A2
Overseas voting scandal rptd 2-25, 167A1
Blames CP for electn defeat 3-20, 201G1
Confers with Giscard 3-26—3-31, 245E3
Scores CP 5-1, 352D1
Censure motion fails 10-4, 815D2
Kadar sees during visit 11-15—11-17, 894G2
MITTON, Bernie
Loses N Amer Zone Davis Cup matches 3-17, 3-19, 252B1
MIYAZAKI, Hiromichi
US, Japan, plan joint energy research 9-6, 695C3
MIYAZAKI, Isamu
On econ stimulus plan 9-3, 694E1
MIZOGUCHI, Kenji
Geisha released 6-1, 619B2
MIZRAHI, Moishe
Madame Rosa released 3-19, 619A3
MKHABELA, Ishmael
Forms AZAPO 4-30, arrested 5-4, 377D2
MLADENOV, Yordan
Named Bulgaria supply min 4-29, 530G3
MNOUCHKINE, Alexandre
Dear Detective released 4-24, 619D1
MOAKLEY, Rep. John Joseph (D, Mass.)
Reelected 11-7, 851D1
MOATS v. Landrum
Case refused by Sup Ct 10-16, 789C2
MOBIL Alaska Pipeline Co. v. U.S.
ICC pipe rates backed by Sup Ct 6-6, 447B2
MOBIL Corp.
Low '76 tax paymt rptd 1-27, 65A3
On '77 Fortune 500 list 5-8, 325E1
7th-ranked cash-rich US co 9-18, 716E3
Container Corp indicted 1-25, 67B2
Marcor Inc.
'77 sales rptd up 5-8, 325A2
Mobil Oil Corp.
Rebates to consumers barred 1-20, 109A1
ICC Alaska pipe rates backed by Sup Ct 6-6, 447B2
NJ offshore well rptd dry 12-27, 1010B1, D1
Montgomery Ward & Co.
FTC chrgs warrenty violatn 10-11, 942B1
MOBILE Homes—*See HOUSING*
MOBILE River (Ala.)
Coal carrier rams oil dock 5-26, 524C2

1979

MITCHELL, James
Defeated in electn 12-5, 951D3
MITCHELL, John N.
Paroled 1-19, 176D1
Ruled liable in tap suits 7-12, 611D2
MITCHELL, Lydell
NFL '78 receiving ldr 1-6, 80C1
MITCHELL, Thomas M.
Indicted 5-23, pleads not guilty 5-24, 380D2
MITCHELL v. Bindrim
Case refused by Sup Ct 12-3, 964A2
MITCHELL v. Mid-Continent Spring Co.
Case refused by Sup Ct 4-23, 346C3
MITO, Mitsuko
My Love released 1-4, 174B3
MITSOTAKIS, Constantine
Pay hike curb proposed 2-22, 135B3
Notes pay hike refusals, growth rate expectatns 2-23, 154C3
Defends govt bank strike actns 7-11, 544C1
MITSUBISHI Corp.
Chrysler Australia 1/3 share acquired 5-14, 368F2
Chrysler import deal cited 7-31, 576B2
Chrysler interest cited 9-7, 745E3
Chrysler to sell remaining Australia share 9-15, 699A2
MITSUI & Co. Ltd.
Cook '78 operatns purchase cited 9-26, 727C3
MITTERRAND, Francois
Urges A-plant moratorium 4-3, 246F1
Soclst cong held; keeps top post 4-6—4-8, 267D2
Marchais scores 5-10, 371C2
Quits Eur Parlt in protest 6-20, 485A2
Seeks left alliance 8-20, 633F1
Marchais weighs Soclst ties 8-22, 652G3
Chrgd re pirate broadcasts 8-24, 653B1
MIX, Ron
Enters HOF 7-28, 1001D1
MIZOGUCHI, Kenji
My Love released 1-4, 174B3
MNGOMEZULU, Reginal
Sentenced 5-11, 373G1
MOAYYED, Tariq al-
Rejects Egypt mil aid offer 10-2, 752D3
MOBASHERI, Assadollah
Named Iran justice min 2-19, 125D1
Chrgs Mrs Javits 5-21, 388E3
MOBIL Corp.
Bodcaw takeover bid fails 3-8, 350C1
1st 1/4 merger rise rptd 4-10, 349B3
1st 1/4 oil profits rptd 4-27, 301G1, B2
Container Corp trust setlmt revealed 5-1, 327E3
On '78 Fortune 500 list 5-7, 304E1
Italian unit plans gas cuts 5-15, 396G2
Standby gas rationing plan asked 6-21, 462G2
'79 heating oil price freeze seen 9-16, 703D1
Overchrg refund agreed 9-18, 849F3
3d 1/4 oil profits rptd up 10-25, 804D2, C3
US overchrgs alleged 11-6, 849G2
Belridge suit lost 12-7; Shell acquires 12-10, sues 12-11, 942E1
Mobil Oil Corp.
US files overchrg suit 1-5, 17B1
Gasoline allocatns announced 2-27, 146B1
Gen Crude merger bid accepted 3-28, 282G3
May gas allocatn rptd cut 5-7, 343B1
2d NJ offshore well rptd dry 5-16, 361F3
Carter scores re decontrol 6-1, 418A2
US files new overchrg suit 6-22, 518F1
July gas supplies rptd 6-26, 479F1
Tankers collide, oil spills in Caribbean 7-19, 553D3
Natural gas refunds OKd 11-5, 943B2
Exec joins Kennedy campaign 11-19, 962C2
Gulf of Mex lease bid offered 11-27, 942G3
Overchrg action said improper 12-4, 990B3
Overchrgs alleged 12-13, 990G2
Montgomery Ward & Co.
Ex-chrmn dies 1-16, 104E2
FTC credit abuses setld 5-29, 596A2
MOBILE, Ala.—*See ALABAMA*
MOBILE Homes—*See HOUSING*

1980

MITCHELL, Jeff
Wins Phoenix Open 1-20, 412B2
MITCHELL, John N.
Taps case accepted by Sup Ct 5-19, 440D1
Taps case argued in Sup Ct 12-8, 937C2
MITCHELL, Mike
NBA scoring ldr 3-30, 278C3
MITCHELL, Rep. Parren J. (D, Md.)
Reelected 11-4, 843B1
MITCHELL, Richard
Wins Olympic medal 7-30, 624C1
MITCHELL, Robert
Wins Ontario prov by-electn 11-20, 900C3
MITCHELL, Thomas M.
Fraud chrgs reduced 4-9, 292A1
Acquitted 4-30, 332F3
MITIC, Ilija
Chinaglia breaks NASL scoring mark 5-9, 769G3
MITSOTAKIS, Constantine
Signs US cooperatn pact 4-22, 352F2
US bases, NATO mil re-entry linked 8-20, 652C2
On Turkey coup 9-12, 696G3
MITSUBISHI Corp.
Chrysler import financing set 2-12, 127F2
Chrysler import financing continued 4-1, 287C1
MITSUI & Co. Ltd.
Indl Investmt trust case declined by Sup Ct 2-25, 188B1
MITSUI v. Industrial Investment Development Corp.
Case declined by Sup Ct 2-25, 188C1
MITTAG, Gunter
In W Ger, trade expansn set 4-17, 303B2
MITTELLAND Canal
E, W Ger pact signed 4-30, 355D3
MITTERRAND, Francois
Socists meet 1-12—1-13, 57G3, 58A1
Supports Turkish workers 3-1, 193D1
Berlinguer mtg cited 4-2, 254F3
At papal receptn 5-30, 476D3
Soclst split noted 6-30, 522E1
Scores govt re right-wing terrorism 10-8, 768A1
Sets pres bid, Rocard withdraws 11-8, 886A2
MITTO, Jackie
Reggae opens 3-27, 392F3
MIYANAGA, Gen. Yukihisa (ret.)
Arrested as spy 1-18, 60A1
MIYAZKI, Hiromichi
Disputes OPEC stockpiling data 11-23, 895A3
MLADENOV, Mladen
Wins Olympic medal 7-23, 624A3
MNOUCHKINE, Alexandre
Incorrigible released 3-3, 416A3
MOAKLEY, Rep. John Joseph (D, Mass.)
Reelected 11-4, 843D1
MOBIL Corp.
'79 profit rptd 1-23, 90F2, B3
TV ad rejectn rptd 1-31, 120D1
Newfoundland oil finds rptd 'promising' 2-20, 2-21, 148F1; subsequent rpts less encouraging 3-10, 191E3
Belridge litigatn dropped 3-6, 385C3
1st 1/4 profit rptd 4-25, 331D1, E1
On '79 Fortune 500 list 5-5, 290E1, 291B1
Saudi film telecast protested 5-8, 375F2, B3
Saudi hikes prices 8% 5-14, 365B1
UK OKs North Sea gas pipe 6-19, 463E2
Newfoundland offshore wells rptd productive 7-10, 7-11, 544B1-D1
Nigeria disputes oil-take 8-8, reply 8-11, 620F1, B2
Newfoundland Ben Nevis drilling halted 8-22, 668D3
Saudi completes Aramco takeover, bd members listed 9-4, 662B1, A2
OPEC pricing agrmt impact seen 9-18, 695B1
Saudi exec named to bd 10-31, joins 12-1, 960D3
Mobil Oil Corp.
'79 price violatns chrgd 2-25, 189D3
Vt tax on Aramco dividends backed by Sup Ct 3-19, 249F2
Carter scores pricing, seeks punitive measures 3-28, 4-1, 248F1-E2
Price case settled 4-24, 309E1
Gasoline price case refused by Sup Ct 5-12, 426D2
TransOcean Oil merger set 8-26, 745E2
Montgomery Ward & Co.
Credit restrictions rptd 3-27, 222G2
Japan TV dumping case setld 4-28, ct blocks 5-9, 368D1
MOBILE—*See ALABAMA*
MOBILE v. Bolden
Case decided by Sup Ct 4-22, 343A2
MOBIL Oil Corp. v. Commissioner of Taxes of Vermont
Case decided by Sup Ct 3-19, 249F2

1976

MOBUTU Sese Seko (Zairian president)
Warns Ethiopia vs MPLA ties 1-13, 16A1
Angola MPLA drive rptd 1-15, 16E2
Scores USSR on Angola 1-19, 36A1
Bars Angola mercenary transit 2-3, 82B1
Shuffles Cabt, party bureau 2-4, 270B2
Meets Neto, Zaire recognizes MPLA 2-28, 163G1
In Kissinger talks 4-28—4-29, 295F1; 4-30, 318A3
Sees Kissinger on Rhodesia 9-22, 718A1

MOCATTA Metals Corp.
Buys IMF gold 9-15, 739E3
MOCKEY, Jean-Baptiste
Ivory Coast health min 3-4, 594E2
MOCTEZUMA Cid, Julio Rodolfo
Mexico finance min 12-2, 906G3
MOCZAR, Mieczyslaw
Dropped from State Cncl 3-25, 268D2
MODY, Piloo
Freed 10-6, 751C2
MOELLER, Orla
Confirms '58 bugging of CP dep 1-9, 48D3
MOERTOPO, Gen. Ali
Timor assemb OKs joining Indonesia 5-31, 423A1
MOFFETT, Rep. Anthony J. (Toby) (D, Conn.)
In Chile 3-11—3-15; chrgs rights abuse 3-17, 310C2
Asks Letelier murder probe 9-21, 710E2
Reelected 11-2, 829A2 *
MOFFITT, Michael
Wife killed in bomb blast 9-21, 710C2
MOFFITT, Ronni Karpen
Killed in bomb blast 9-21, 710C2
Death blamed on junta 9-26, 781B1
MOGAARD, Britt
Named to Swedish Cabt 10-8, 794C2
MOGHRABI, Zoheir
Slain 6-16, 425A1-C2
MOHAMMED, Abdallah
Comoro premr 1-6, names cabt 1-10, 119B1
MOHAMMED, Lt. Col. Muktar
Nigeria housing min 3-15, 222A3
MOHAMMED, Gen. Murtala Ramat
Anti-US campaign launched 1-7, 2C3
Promotn rptd 1-9, 102G3
New capital, more states set 2-3, 102B3
Slain 2-13, buried 2-14, 141C3
Coup probe ordered 2-15, 191D3
UK envoy recalled 3-4, 191E3
Assassins executed 5-16, 366F1
MOHAMMED, Capt. Sidi
Niger coup try fails 3-15, 205G2
Executed 4-21, 483D2
MOHAPI, Mapetla
Dies in prison 8-5, 591G3
Black ldrs arrested 8-5, 624C3
MOHLOMI, Godwin
Freed 12-8, 927E2
MOHR, John P.
FBI purchasing probe rptd renewed 3-20—3-23, 248E1
MOHSEN, Zahir
Sees no Geneva conf 2-27, 162C2
Says forces shell rightist towns 4-14, 273D2
New Leb peace plan proposed 4-16, 273E1
Barred from PLO meeting 11-26, 894B1

MOI, Daniel Arap
Denies Israel Uganda raid tie 7-4, 486E1
Denies Uganda blockade 7-18, 548C2
Successn debate banned 10-3, 947D2

MOISEEVA, Irena
Wins Olympic medal 2-9, 159B1
MOJUNTIN, Peter
Killed 6-6, 419E1
MOKWENA, Dan
Arrested 8-13, 624A3
MOLAPO, Charles Dube
On Transkei border closing 11-12, 927F3
Chrgs S Africa pressure 12-22, 954B3
MOLDAVIAN Soviet Socialist Republic—*See 'Republics' under USSR*
MOLINA, Col. Arturo Armando
Scores oppositn 3-8, 289D3

1977

MOBUTU Sese Seko (Zairian president)
Visits Belgium 1-17—1-24, 199G3
CIA payments rptd 2-19, 124F1 *
Visits Kolwezi 3-19, 207F2
Denies Mutshatsha fall 3-24, 260C3
Meets Garba 3-31, 261B1
Rally draws weak support 4-3, 261B1
Asks Morocco troop aid 4-7, 265B1
M'Bumba vows overthrow 4-8, 266B1
Chrgs Sovt-Cuba invasn role, army plot 4-9, 265C2
Rpts Egypt mil team visit 4-9, 265F2
Scores US re Zaire aid 4-11, 265C2
Ends Sovt exchng progrm, chrgs Zambia raid 4-20, 317F1
Amin arrives, pledges aid 4-22, 317B2
On Coca-Cola aid request 4-22, 317C3
Army retakes Mutshatsha 4-25, 317A1
Amin arrives 4-28, 394D1
Egypt sends pilots 5-2, 394B1
Shaba towns retaken 5-20—5-26, 490C1
Thanks Giscard for Shaba aid 6-9—6-10, 490E1
Dismisses Cabt, vows electns 7-1, 583A1
Names Kasenga premr 7-6, 583B1
Retires 28 army officers 7-11, 583B1
Rpts Saudi invasn aid 7-19, 583C1
Ousts natl bank gov 8-11, 641F2
Orders forgn min, tribal chief held 8-13, 641C2
Spares forgn min 9-15, 731C1
Wife dies 10-22, 872F2
Reelected 12-2, 1019F2

MOCTEZUMA Cid, Julio
Replaced in Cabt 11-17, 966B3
'78 budget eases austerity program 12-15, 985A2
MODAI, Yitzhak
Israel energy resources min 6-20, 474E2
On Israel oil strike 11-25, 955E1
MODELS & Modeling
Child porno effort rptd 5-15, 432E2
John Powers dies 7-19, 604F3
Bettina Davis dies 10-9, 872E1
MODELLER, Christian
Captured by Swiss 12-20, 1017E3
MOELLER, Irmgard
W Ger frees hijacked jet 10-18, 789A1
Attempts suicide 10-18, 790F2
Schleyer slain 10-18, 791F1
Denies Baader gang suicide pact 10-26, 868A2
MOELLER, Orla
Danish justice min 2-25, 373E1
Orders secret service probe 7-8, 672G1
Resigns 10-1, 882F3
MOFFET, Rep. Toby (D, Conn.)
Scores Schlesinger energy comments, doubts reassurncs 11-22—11-23, 916F3, 917C1
MOFFETT, James E.
House machine-gunned 3-29, 259F2
MOHAMED, Abdulahi Hassan
Rejects Ogaden truce 9-24, 756F2
MOHAMMAD, Messenger of God (film)
Showings suspended 3-9—3-11, 192C3
Hanafis convicted 7-23, sentncd 9-6, 711A2
MOHAMMED (569?-632)
Sadat visits alleged ascensn site 11-20, 889E1
MOHAMMEDEN Babbah
Mauritania industry min 8-4, 772E1
MOHAWK Indians—*See INDIANS, American*
MOHIEDDIN, Khaled
Denies party link to riots 1-30, 83F1
MOHNHAUPT, Brigitte
Escapes Dutch capture 9-22, 888D1
MOHSEN, Zahir
Plans drive vs Christns 4-3, 246D1
Sees Sarkis on Palestinian shift 4-22, 316A3
Chrgs US plot vs Hussein 5-8, 360C3

MOI, Daniel Arap
Somali border pact set 7-20, 588C1
Curbs Kenyans in Somalia 10-15, 830A2
MOJSOV, Lazar
Elected UN Assemb pres 9-20, 713B1
MOKTAR, Col. M'Barek Ould Mohammed Bonna
Mauritania defns post rptd 3-18, 394E3
Confirms Polisario kidnapings 10-26, 831G2
MOLINA, Col. Arturo Armando
Backs Panamanian canal demands 1-18, 46G1
Protests follow electn 2-20—3-3, siege imposed 2-28, 181F2, C3
'72 electn fraud chrg, coup attempt cited 181G3
Rejects Borgonovo abductors' demands 4-22, 4-29, 373C2
MOLINA, Mario del Rosario
FBI JFK assassinatn files released 12-7, 943C2
MOLINA Canas, Raul
Killed in kidnap attempt 11-12, 969G3
MOLINA Orantes, Adolfo
Scores US rights stand 3-12, 187B2
On Guatemala demands re Belize 7-8, 553A2
Rpt rightists, army asked ouster 8-5, 706F2
Scores UK re Belize 9-23, 767C1
Scores Belize ldr 11-18, 969A3

1978

MOBUTU Sese Seko (Zairian president)
13 executed in plot 3-17, 230G2-B3
CIA '75 Angola funds rptd kept 5-8, 367C2
Shaba prov invaded; accuses USSR, seeks US aid 5-14, 359A2
Shaba rescue operatn 5-18—5-23; scores Belgium delay 5-21, 381C1 382A1
Shaba rebels seek overthrow 5-23, 382F2
At Franco-African summit, seeks mil aid 5-23, 382A3, 417E3
Sees Giscard, Tindemans; Zaire force backed 5-23—5-25, 417D3
In Morocco, seeks Zaire force support 5-29, 417G3
Claims hostages killed 5-30, 417A3
China pledges support 6-7, 441D2
Sets Shaba defense force 6-9, 441F1
Presents Zaire aid plan 6-13, 478C1
Defends Zaire vs corruptn chrgs 6-21, 652D2
Claims Cuban prisoners 6-22, 652G1
Amnesties exiles 6-24, rejctd 6-26, 652C2
Nguza freed 7-14, 652E2
US releases aid 8-16, 652F2
Neto visits 8-19—8-21, 646A1

MOCK, Julio
Panama public works min 10-12, 884B2
MODAI, Yitzhak
Says Israel starts Sinai oil operatn 3-29, 215B2
MODELS & Modeling
Avedon imposter sentenced 5-5, 380B2
MODIGLIANI (play)
Opens 5-17, 760E2
MODIGLIANI, Amedeo (1884-1920)
Modigliani opens 5-17, 760E2
MOELLER, Christian
Cited in death of Swiss cop 4-12, 438G2
Swiss trial opens 4-25, 353E3
Swiss jail 6-30, 558F2
MOELLER, Irmgard
Denies Baader suicide pact 1-16, 115C1
Lawyers protest trial searches 3-6, 250D3
MOFFAT, Lyle
Winnipeg wins WHA title 5-22, 458C2
MOFFET, Rep. Toby (D, Conn.)
Scores pvt energy conf mtgs 4-13, 4-20, 304E2, B3
MOFFETT, Rep. Toby J. (D, Conn.)
Reelected 11-7, 850D2
Shell trust probe rptd 11-28, 939D3
MOFFITT, Michael
Study on US bank loans to Chile released 4-11, 312A2
Sues Chile re wife's death 8-8, 648A1
MOFFITT, Ronni Karpen (d. 1976)
US seeks 2 Chileans in murder probe 2-21, 146A2; **for subsequent developments, see CHILE—Letelier Murder Probe**
MOFOKENG, Zacharia
Arrested 5-5, 377E2
MOGHADAM, Gen. Nasser
Named Iran secret police chief 6-7, 437D3
MOGHRABI, Khouloud
Held in Iraq amb death try 8-2, 582F2
MOHAMMED, Ali
Coup plot trial asked 1-22, 94B2
MOHATAR, Mimoun
Palomino KOs 3-18, 379C2
MOHAWK, Richard
Acquitted 5-24, 396B2
MOHNHAUPT, Brigitte
Arrested in Yugo 5-11, linked to Red Brigades 5-30; extraditn unresolved 5-11—5-31, 438F3, 439A1
Yugo bars extraditn 11-17, release rptd 11-18, 906G1
MOHR, John
Past FBI corruptn rptd 1-10, 15A2, C2
MOHSEN, Zahir
Freezes Israel shelling, bars PLO Leb exit 5-26, 400E3

MOI, Daniel T. Arap (Kenyan President; sworn Oct. 14)
Ends Westn quest for arms 3-11, 289F2
Sworn Kenya interim pres 8-22, 639A3
Elected Kenya pres 10-10; names Cabt 10-11, sworn 10-14, 784A3
Backers win KANU electns 10-28, 885F2
Frees pol prisoners 12-12, 968G1

MOJSOV, Lazar
Scores UN disarmamt sessn 6-30, 523B1
MOKTAR, Col. M'Barek Ould Mohammed Bonna
Ousted as Mauritania defns min 1-26, 95D1
MOLIERE In Spite Of Himself (play)
Opens 3-12, 887B2
MOLINA Orantes, Adolfo
On Belize indep terms 5-18, 478E2

1979

MOBUTU Sese Seko (Zairian president)
US support end urged 3-5, 215E1
Reinstates Nguza 3-6, 215C2

MOCATTA & Goldsmid Ltd.
London gold price role described 2-7, 83C1, G1
MODAI, Yitzhak
Ties Egypt pact to Sinai oil access 1-5, 51B2
Prefers Palestinians to Jordan in peace talks 9-7, 677A1
Israel returns oilfield to Egypt 11-25, 916G2
MOE, Richard
Offers resignatn 7-17, 529B2
MOELLER v. Connecticut
Case refused by Sup Ct 11-13, 902A2
MOFATEH, Mohammed
Slain 12-18, 958F2
MOFFAT, Lyle
Winnipeg wins WHA title 5-20, 448C1 514F2
MOFFETT, Rep. Toby J. (D, Conn.)
Wins Govt Operatns subcom chair 1-31, 86G3
Doubts heating oil supply claims 6-29
Addresses oil industry protesters, backs reform 10-17, 831E2
Questns Hendrie on A-plant sites 11-5, 849D1
MOFFITT, Michael
Testifies in Letelier case 1-15–1-16, 57D3
MOFFITT, Phillip
Esquire purchase rptd 5-1, 334D2
MOFFITT, Ronni Karpen (d. 1976)
Murder Case—*See CHILE–Letelier Case*
MOGAMI, Kennedy
Sentenced 5-11, 373G1
MOGHADAM, Gen. Nasser
Executed 4-11, 276D3
MOGHADM-Maragheil, Rahmatollah
Escapes arrest 12-8, 936D2
MOGULL, Arthur
Break a Leg opens 4-29, 711G1
MOHAN, Rama Chandra
Iran expels 9-26, 814B3
MOHSEN, Zahir
Shot 7-25, dies; Israel, Egypt blamed 7-26, 551G3, 625E2
Replaced in PLO posts 8-3, murder suspect arrested 8-20, 625C2

MOI, Daniel T. Arap (Kenyan president)
Wins pres electn 11-8, 874A3
Shuffles Cabt 11-28, 969A2

MOINFAR, Ali Akbar
On natlzd banks' compensatn 6-10, 469B2
Named Iran petro min 9-28, 752C2
Denies oil export cutoff 11-7, 843C2
Orders hostile natns oil boycott 11-25, cuts '80 productn 11-26, 896G3
Oil price arguments with Yamani rptd 12-21, 977F1
MOJADDIDI, Sibghatullah
On Afghan-rebel clashes 3-22, 232F2
MOK Sakun
Cambodian econ min 1-8, 10B1

1980

MOBUTU Sese Seko (Zairian president)
Warns students vs boycott 4-15, 356D2
Meets Pope 5-4, 363D2

MOCZAR, Gen. Mieczyslaw
Scores Gierek; to head corruptn probe 10-6, 760A3
Reelected to Polish Politburo 12-2, 909F2
MOCZULKI, Leszek
Walesa seeks chrgs dropped 12-22, 976E1
MODAI, Yitzhak
Cabt vs shift to forgn post 5-27, 429E3
MODELL, Art
Brown fined for autobiography chrgs 1-22, 175C3
MODELS & Modeling
Wilhemina dies 3-1, 280F2
Sun Maid model dies 10-14, 876F3
MODIGLIANI, Amedeo (1884-1920)
Painting sold for record sum 5-13, 472G1
MODZELEWSKI, Bishop Jerzy
Broadcasts RC Sunday mass 9-21, 720G2
MOE, Doug
Fired as Spurs coach 3-1, 656G3
MOFATEH, Mohammed (d. 1979)
Forghan ldr rptd arrested 1-10, 20D2
MOFFAT, Donald
On the Nickel released 5-4, 416D3
MOFFETT, Rep. (Anthony) Toby (D, Conn.)
Joins open-conv move 7-25, 570F1
Reelected 11-4, 842E2, 848D1
MOFFITT, Ronni (d. 1976)
Kin awarded damage paymt 11-5, 869F3
MOHAGHEGHI, Gen. Ahmad
Iran coup plot confessn rptd 7-13, 539E2
MOHAMMED, Faiz
Rptd slain 9-14, 727G2, A3
MOHAMMED, Nazar
Rptd slain 9-14, 727G2

MOI, Daniel T. Arap (Kenyan president)
In US, sees Carter 2-20—2-22, 142A2
Visits China 9-14, 706G3
Urges Somali land claims end, arms shipmt ban 12-4, 933E1

MOINFAR, Ali Akbar
Threatens oil cutoff 1-11, 29A2
US newsmen ousted; warns UK, W Ger rptrs 1-14, 29E2
Warns re oil field attacks 3-9, 178B2
Threatens Japan oil embargo 4-20, 299B1
Successor named 8-31, 671D2
Lauds OPEC pricing agrmt 9-18, 694D3
MOISEEVA, Irina
Wins Olympic medal 2-17, 155F3
MOJSOV, Lazar
Elected Yugo CP chief 10-20, 810C1
MOKRI, Mohammed
Asks Sovts bar arms to Iraq 9-23, 719C1
MOLINA, Gen. Arturo Armando
Duarte joins junta 3-9, 192F2
MOLINA Orantes, Adolfo
Dies in fire at Spanish emb 1-31, 98C2

1976

MOLINE, Ill.—*See ILLINOIS*
MOLLEN, Judge Milton
Sentences Hollander 5-18, 384F3
MOLLER, Irmgard
Sentenced 3-16, 503F1
MOLLOHAN, Rep. Robert H. (D, W. Va.)
Reelected 11-2, 831A2
MOMIS, John
Arranges Bougainville truce 1-28, 123B2
Ends secession try 3-26, 256G2

MONACO
Listed as 'partly free' 1-19, 20D3
OKs UN Medit pollutn pact 2-16, 126C3
Olympics disqualify trapshooter 7-19, 563B2

MONARCH Nugrape Co.
Red #2 dye ban in effect 2-12, ct challenge continues 2-13, 137D1
MONCORGE, Jean-Alexis—*See GABIN, Jean*

MONDALE, Sen. Walter F(rederick) (Fritz) (D, Minn.)
Intellignc com issues rpt 4-26, 304D3
Visits Carter as vp prospect 7-8, 489E3
Named vp nominee 7-15, 505D2, 506E2
Acceptance speech 7-15, 507F2-508B1; text 511B1
Photo with Carter after nominatn 7-15, 505A1
Biographical sketch 512E2 ★
Ford scores ticket 7-17, 531F2
AFL-CIO exec cncl backs ticket 7-19, 532D2
Carter on Nixon pardon 7-20, 532B2
Carter defends special tax bill 7-20, 532C2
Fed electn funds OKd 7-20, 565B3
Names campaign chrmn, treas 7-20, 565F3
At briefing sessns 7-27—7-29, 551B1, C1
Farm policy speech 7-31, 565C1
With Carter in DC 8-4, 564D3
Sees Bush in Plains 8-12, 616D3
Meets Ital-Amer group, greets Brown 8-12, 616G3
Scores Kelley 8-12, 617C1
Sees labor, teacher groups 8-15—8-17, 617A3
Willing to debate 8-20, 632F3
Campaigns cross-country, scores Ford priorities, arms sales, jobs plan 8-25—9-2, 9-6—9-8, 645E2, 665E2
TV debate with Dole set 9-1, 644B1
At Carter Ga news conf 9-3, 664E1
Dole attacks 9-10, 686G3; 9-11, 687A1
Scores Admin on foreign policy 9-10; econ, aged 9-13, 9-16, 687C1, B2
On Sup Ct law enforcemt rulings 9-14, 687F1
With Carter in Minn 9-15, 686C3, 687A2
In NYC 9-19, 704D3
Scores GOP re tax relief 9-20, 704B1
'Whistlestop' tour 9-20—9-21, 704C3
Stresses forgn policy, jobs, taxes 9-22—9-30, 724F3
Scores Butz, asks dismissal 10-2, 744G1
Hits GOP ticket on Watergate 10-5, 743A3
In Ia, Ill 10-6, 763D3
Dole scores 10-6, 763E3
On Ford E Eur remark 10-7, 762F3
Stresses econ, Ford E Eur remark 10-10—10-11, 763A3
Debates Dole 10-15, 782E1-784E1
Campaign dvpts 10-16—10-26, 803A3
Criticism of Gen Brown rptd 10-20, 787C3
Ford, Carter debate 10-22, 801A2, C2
Dole attacks 10-25, 804A2, C2
Carter lauds 10-28, 803A3
Ends campaign; stresses Watergate, jobs, inflatn 10-29—11-1, 827D1, B2
Dole attacks 11-1, 827B3
Elected 11-2, 817F1, 818A3, 819E1
Carter stresses vp role 11-4, 819A3
Anderson to seek Sen seat 11-10, 865B1
Carter outlines work 11-15, 864B1
Carter meets cong ldrs 11-17, 864E1
At briefings 11-19, 11-20, 881F1
On steel price hike 12-1, 897F3
Meets Andreotti 12-7, 947F1
Electoral Coll votes 12-13; final tally rptd 12-18, 979B1, C1
At Cabt mtgs; Carter on staff role 12-27—12-29, 978B1, E2
Carter concerned re isolatn 12-30, 978D3
Resigns Sen seat 12-30, 994C1
MONDAY, Rick
NL batting ldr 10-4, 795F3, G3
MONDAY Night Football (TV series)
Wins Emmy 5-17, 460C2
MONDELLI, Emilio
Argentina econ min 2-3, 154G2
Announces 'emergency' plan 3-5, plan scored 3-6—3-13, 212C2
Sought for arrest 3-26, 236E3

1977

MOLINA Pallochia, Gen. Oscar
To be premier in '78 10-4, 784B2
MOLINA Vidales, Virgilio
Kidnaped 5-2, 347E2
MOLLOHAN, Rep. Robert H. (D, W. Va.)
Asks tin reserve release 3-16, 298G1
MOLOKWANA, Nicholas
Killed in S Africa shootout 9-26, 825C3
MOLUCCAS (formerly Spice Islands)—*See INDONESIA—South Moluccan Issue*
MOLYCORP Inc.
Union Oil takeover OKd 4-14, 274F3

MONACO
UN pollutn conf ends, Medit pact reached 10-21, 876B2
Helsinki Agreement—*See EUROPE—Security & Cooperation*

MONDALE, Vice President Walter Frederick (Fritz)
Cong declares VP winner 1-6, 14F2
To visit Europe, Japan 1-8, 14E2
CBO issues poverty rpt 1-13, 80D3
Sworn Vice Pres 1-20, 25F1
Gets Nunn rpt on Warsaw Pact 1-22, 70E2
Visits Eur, Japan, 1-23—2-1; press conf 2-2, 69A1
O'Neill vs forgn speakers 2-17, 127E3
Sullivan loses Cong seat 2-22, 128B1
Inouye rpts intell com watch 2-22, 150F3
Sees Bukovsky 3-1, 142G2
Vs criminal penalties for leaks 3-4, 212G1
Spec interest gifts rptd 3-7, 232A3
Election-law changes urged 3-22, 210D2
Addresses state party heads 3-31, 251B1
Chides Ford for criticism, rpts Nixon aid offer 4-19, 321D3
Carter urges NATO collective deterrence 5-10, 358C3
Tours Eur 5-14—5-23; sees Young 5-15, Vorster 5-18—5-20, 397G2, 398G1, A3
On child adoptn subsidy plan 7-12, 628F2
To head 'priorities' unit 7-15, 555G3
Turner given new powers 8-4, 610G2, B3
Addresses ABA conv 8-8, 630B1
Kardelj visits US 9-28—10-4, 785E3
Aids Sen filibuster end 10-3, defends actn 10-5, 757G2, 758B1
Sees Young on S Africa sanctns 10-24, 851D3
Redlining curb announced 11-9, 898F2
Reaffirms rights commitmt 11-20, 955F1
At AFL-CIO conv 12-9, 961A1
Says Admin overloaded Cong 12-13, 977A1
Rptd vs Burns 12-28, 1000D2
Latin America
Humphrey effort vs Allende chrgd 1-9, 18F2
On Cuba trade ban end 3-4, 181B1
Castro sends cigars 4-22, 390F1
Sees Frei 5-25, 493D1
On Cubans in Ethiopia 5-26, 417A3
Greets Venez pres 6-28, 546E1
Sees Panama Canal negotiators 7-29, 589D2
Middle East
Speaks on Mideast 6-17; Israel sees no policy change 6-19, 473F2
US to sell arms to Israel 6-25, 511G1
Javits scores Mideast speech 6-27, 495F3
In Carter conf with US Jews 7-6, 510A1
Meets Dayan 9-19, 713B2

MONDINI, Giuseppe
Kidnaped 3-13, 255G1
MONETARY Conference, International
Tokyo mtg 5-22—5-25, 437C3

1978

MOLINA Pallochia, Gen. Oscar (Peruvian prime minister)
Named Peru prime min, war min, army chief 1-31, 134G2
MOLITOR, Paul
2d in AL top rookie poll 11-21, 928B2
MOLLO, John
Wins Oscar 4-3, 315C3
MOLLOHAN, Rep. Robert H. (D, W. Va.)
Reelected 11-7, 852B4
MOLNAR, Vladislav
Hijacks jet to W Ger, gets asylum 2-6, 212D2
Sentenced 10-4, 776E3
MOLSON Breweries of Canada Ltd.
NHL Canadiens purchased 8-3, 656A3
MOLYNEAUX, James
Scores Protestant factnl strife 7-12, 630G2
MOMMIE Dearest (book)
On best-seller list 12-3, 971A1
MOMENT by Moment (film)
Released 12-21, 1030C3
MONACO
Natl Dems sweep electns 1-16, 75F1
Princess Caroline to wed 4-24, 420G2
Princess Caroline wed 6-28, 6-29, 580D1
Helsinki Agreement—*See EUROPE—Security and Cooperation*
Sports
Monte Carlo WCT results 4-16, 419C1
MONAHAN, Col. John
Rpts Camp David Marines relieved for alleged pot use 12-9, 960C3
MONDALE, Joan (Mrs. Walter Frederick)
Named honorary Arts cncl dir 2-28, 335E2
MONDALE, Vice President Walter Frederick (Fritz)
Tours Western states 1-9—1-13, 34C1
Humphrey eulogy 1-15, 32A3, C3
In Canada 1-17—1-18, 53F2
Warns re farm-aid veto 3-29, 219D1
At Carter strategy sessn 4-15—4-16, 306A3
Admin debate re Asian trip rptd 4-28, 360C3
Visits Pl, Thailand, Indonesia, Australia, NZ 5-2—5-9, 360B3, D3
Reassures Mideast jet sale opponents 5-15—5-16, 5-18, 358B1
Addresses UN disarmamt sessn 5-24, 421C1
Gulf '66 illegal paymt rptd 6-2, 449D1
Gartner bars resignatn 6-28, 513B3
In Israel 6-30—7-3; in Egypt, Sadat gives peace plan 7-3; text issued 7-5, 501B1, E1, D2
Carter hints at Geneva conf 6-30, reactn 7-1, 502F1
US OKs Israel jet sale to Taiwan 7-2, 524B3
Sees Indian ldrs 7-18, 569A1
At ASEAN econ talks 8-3—8-4, 603C3
Finds GSA aide new post 8-3, 605A3
Addresses Urban League, defends Admin 8-7, 811B1
In Camp David summit talks 9-7, 673E1
Announces rural health program 10-2, 770D1
ERA extensn cleared by Sen 10-6, 788D1
Boschwitz wins seat 11-7, 854A3
Guyana releases letter to Rev Jones 11-20, 891D1
At Dem midterm conf 12-8—12-10, defends Admin 12-10, 956A3

MONDAY, Rick
In World Series 10-10—10-17, 799B3
MONEDERO, Armando
Kidnaped 8-10, guerrillas issue demands 8-24, 722G1
MONELL v. Department of Social Services
Munic legal immunity ended by Sup Ct 6-6, 447C1-A2

1979

MOLINA Pallochia, Gen. Oscar
Retires 2-2, 101G2
MOLINARO, Edouard
Cage aux Folles released 5-12, 528F1
MOLITOR, Paul
AL batting ldr 9-30, 955D3-F3
MOLTHEN, Jack
Peter Pan opens 9-6, 956G3
MOLYNEAUX, James
Opposes home rule talks 10-25, 835D3
MOMMIE Dearest (book)
On best-seller list 1-7, 80B3; 2-4, 120B3; 3-4, 173E3; 4-8 271B2

MONACO
Antique auctn records rptd 6-27, 672F1
Helsinki Agreement—*See EUROPE—Security and Cooperation*
Sports
Monte Carlo WCT results 4-15, 391B3

MONCRIEF, Sidney
In NBA draft 6-25, 507A2
MONDALE, Joan (Mrs. Walter Frederick)
At Brazil pres inaugural 3-15, 210E1
Campaigns in NH 11-29, 961E3

MONDALE, Vice Pres. Walter Frederick (Fritz)
Lauds US-China ties 1-1, 2E1
At Carter-Meany mtg 1-12, 13C3
Rockefeller dies 1-26, at funeral 2-2, 103G3, 104D2
Greets Teng 1-28, 66B2
Educ Dept proposed 2-8, 110A3
Wife at Brazil pres inaugural 3-15, 210E1
Visits Brazil, Venez 3-21—3-24, 247D3-A2
Privacy bill urged 4-2, 264C3
Visits 6 Europn states 4-11—4-22, 299B2
Hatcher wins Gary primary 5-8, 363A3
Carter econ team rptd revamped 6-4, 463E1
Addresses Mayors Conf 6-13, 439A3
Gets cool NAACP receptn 6-26, 559E3
Urges truck strike end 6-27, 479G3
Carter consults re energy 7-5, 497D3
Addresses govs, previews energy policy 7-8, 513G3, 517B3
Moe offers resignatn 7-17, 529B2
At Indochina refugee conf 7-21, 549E1
Strauss rpts on Mideast missn 8-21, 623G2
Offers more mass-transit aid 8-22, 726B1
Arrives China 8-25, meets Teng, Hua 8-27—8-28, pacts signed 8-28, 644B2
Ends China visit 8-31; in Hong Kong 9-1—9-2; briefs Ohira on China talks 9-3; rpts to Carter 9-4, 660D2
'80 pres race suggested 9-5, 662B1
Sees Nicaragua junta ldrs 9-24, 731D3
ICC orders Rock I RR takeover 9-26, 722A1
Marks Canal treaty implementatn 10-1, 754A1, B1
Carter sees as '80 vp 10-9, 767B1
Campaigns for Carter 10-30, 11-28, 12-6, 961A2, B3
Carter urges renominatn 12-4, 918D2
Subs for Carter in NY 12-5, 918G2

1980

MOLINARI, Guy
Elected to US House 11-4, 843E3
MOLINE—*See ILLINOIS*
MOLLAZADEH, Mawlavi Abdol-Aziz
Aids Afghan rebels 1-15, 26B2
MOLLOHAN, Rep. Robert H. (D, W. Va.)
Reelected 11-4, 844B4
MOLNAR, Ferenc
Guardsman opens 1-3, 136B3
MOLOTOV, Vyacheslav
Kosygin resigns 10-23, 797F1
MOLSIDOMINE—*See MEDICINE--Drugs & Health-Care Products*
MOLYNEAUX, James
Boycotts home rule talks 1-7, 39A2
On home rule plan 7-2, 523C1
MOMMIE Dearest (book)
On best-seller list 1-13, 40C3

MONACO—*See also CSCE*
IOC issues Olympic acceptance list 5-27, 420E3
Princess Caroline divorced 10-9, 890D3

MONACO, Lourival do
Outlines alcohol fuel program 4-20, 461C1

MONDALE, Vice President Walter Frederick (Fritz)
In Iowa, scores Kennedy grain embargo stance 1-4, 1-10, Kennedy rebuts 1-10, 12E2
Admin to buy Sovt grain contracts 1-7, 9F2
Vs Olympics in USSR 1-10, 28F2
Debates Kennedy, Brown in Ia; defends Carter on Iran, grain embargo 1-12, 32C2
ILGWU backs ticket 1-15, 32A3
Ends Iowa tour 1-19, 50F2-A3
Speaks in Saco (Me) 2-5, 91D2
Warned by Israel amb vs UN anti-Israel vote 3-1; defends Carter position 3-5, 163A3, 164B1
China power pact signed 3-15, 231B2
Carter wins Ill primary 3-18, 206F3
USOC backs Olympic boycott 4-12, 283G1
Meets Kirkland 5-2, 344C3
Carey asks open conventn 5-5, 342G3
Leads Tito funeral delegatn 5-8, 338B3
Kennedy debate rejected 5-15, 383A2
In Detroit re auto aid 7-7, 505G1
Cabt campaign role set 7-15, 549C3
In Africa 7-17—7-23, signs Nigeria trade pact 7-23, 620C2
Open conv move forms, pres prospects noted 7-25—7-31, 570C3
Wins renominatn, makes acceptance speech 8-14, 612A1
Attacks Reagan record, other campaign highlights 9-1—10-9, 780D1-G2
Hits Reagan policies, defends Carter in coast-to coast campaign 10-3—10-26; sees close Carter win 10-26, 816C3-817C1
On US-Israel oil agrmt 10-15, 775E3
NJ water pipeline set 10-19, 947D3
Pinch hits for Carter 11-2, joins in Ohio 11-3, 841C1, D1
Loses reelectn, Carter lauds 11-4, 837C1, 838D3
Electoral College votes 12-15, 956F1
Settles '67 Liberty attack case 12-18, 966C2

MONDAY Morning (magazine)
Redgrave interview 11-2, 908F3
MONELL v. Department of Social Services
Case cited by Sup Ct 4-16, 328D2

1976 1977 1978 1979 1980

MONETARY DEVELOPMENTS

1976

MONETARY Developments, International—*See also BALANCE of Payments, BANKS, GOLD, IMF; country names*
Mauritius links rupee to SDR 1-5, 104G2
IMF Jamaica accord on currency reform; proposals detailed 1-8, US cites Bretton Woods system 1-9; reactn 1-8; 13A1-14G2, C3; text excerpts 1-9, 15A1
Official SDR rate rptd 1-15, 14G2
Ford State of Union message 1-19, 38B3
Canada $ tops US parity 1-26, 99D1
Group of 77 charter urges reform 2-10, 108B1
Intl econ conf 2-11—2-20, 148B1
Israel pound devalued 2-11, 157E1
Rolfe dies 3-10, 240F3
Zaire devalues currency, pegs to SDR 3-12, 270G2-A3
Israel pound devalued 3-14, 253D3; 4-18, 335A2
Arab fund set 4-26—4-27, 341B1
UNCTAD conf opens 5-5, 320F1; ends 5-30, 388E2
1st ¼ US capital flow rptd 5-17, 396A3-397A1
7-natn summit set 6-1, 6-3, 389B1
US Dem platform text 6-15, 476C2, 478B1
Carter urges system renovatn 6-23, 451G2
7-natn econ summit held, Japan warned re yen 6-27—6-28, 462A1, C1, D2
Intl econ conf deadlocked 7-8—7-10, 7-12—7-17, 530D1
Zambia devalues kwacha 7-9, 950A1
Israel devalues pound 7-18, 538F3
Algeria sets $ issue 7-27, 902B2
US GOP platform text 8-18, 611A2
S Africa rand devaluatn feared 8-18, 654D3
Egypt gets Arab fund aid 8-21, 630A1
Botswana replaces rand 8-23, 857E3
Israeli £ devalued 8-25, 9-29, 854A3
Yen rate cited re US trade deficit 8-26, 668E1
US ends '71 emergency 9-14, 689C2
Group of 24 drops debt moratorium demand 10-2, 778F1
Annual mtg in Manila, 10-4—10-8; analysis 10-10, 10-18, 777A1
Birr replaces Ethiopian $ 10-14, 1002B2
Australia sets curbs 11-7, 850C1
Carter pledges 11-22, 11-23, 881B1, A2
Australia currency devalued, new exchng system set 11-28, 896C1
Canada $ falls below US parity 11-26, 904B2
NZ, PNG devalue currencies 11-29, 896D1, G2
Canada $ at record low 11-30, recovers 12-3, 945E2
3d 7-natn summit urged 12-2, 964D1
Australia revalues 12-6, 922G3; 12-13, 944F2
NZ $ revalued up 12-20, 1013G1

1977

MONETARY Developments, International—*See also BALANCE of Payments, BANKS, GOLD, IMF; country names*
'76 forgn exchng mkt tensns, central bank interventn rptd 3-2, 188C3
US $ gains on tax rebate plan end 4-14, 271C2
7-natn London summit 5-7—5-8, 357A2
North-South talks end 6-3, 437F1
BIS warns US on paymts gap 6-12; Weil cites $ strength despite deficits 6-21, 502C1, D1
Burns vs $ drop 7-26, run on $ halts 7-27; $ falls vs mark, Swiss franc, yen 7-28, 585D2
Blumenthal backs strong $ 7-28; US trade deficit-reducing strategy rptd challenged 8-8, 585B2-E2
PNG revalues currency 8-5, 639C2
Joint IMF-World Bank mtgs 9-26—9-30, 753C2
Blumenthal on US capital inflow, $ strength 9-27, 753F3
Trade gap, weakening of $ feared by Morgan Guaranty 9-29, 754C1
$ drop, forgn investmt in US linked 11-14, 879C3
$ rallies on Carter statemt 12-21, drops on Miller apptmt 12-28, 997G2-B3

African Developments
Uganda bars currency exchng 3-21, 308E3
Zambia suspends Rhodesia paymts 5-24, 413C1
Ghana cedi exchng rate rptd 7-1, 598D2
Nigeria Euroloan rptd 9-1, 746C3
Rhodesia $ devalued 10-13, 824F3

Australian Developments
Australia lifts loan curbs 7-7, 523A1
Australian $ devalued 1.5% 8-3, 615G2
Australian reserves revalued 8-11, 725C2

Canadian Developments
C$ nears US parity 1-5, 17E3
C$ falls 1-26, 82D1
C$ at 7-yr low 3-9, 179E2
C$ up 4-14, 303G3
7-natn London summit 5-7—5-8, 357A2
Canada $ drops 6-1, 448D1
C$ falls 7-27, 597D1
C$ at 8-yr low 8-12, 634D3
C$ at 10-yr low 10-6, 780E3
C$ hits new low 10-17, 792D3
C$ at 40-yr low 10-18-10-24; credit deal set 10-27, $ rallies 10-28, 841A3
'77 C$ drop vs US$ rptd 11-30, 932E3
C$ closes up vs US$ 12-8, 933C1

1978

MONETARY Developments, International—*See also BALANCE of Payments, BANKS, GOLD; country names*
Forgn exchng reserves defined 148G2
US $ defense via swap network set 1-4, reactn 1-9, 27F1, C2
Carter pledges strong $ 1-6, 1E1
US discount rate hiked, $ drop cited 1-6, reactn rptd 1-23; fed funds rate hiked 1-9, 28A1, B2
US $ fears cause Dow drop 1-6—1-11, 28G1
PNG revalues currency 1-9, 192C3
Carter pleas for energy bill 1-12, 12A1
OPEC move from $ as price base seen 1-13, 158A3
Carter State of Union Message 1-19, 29C3, 31A1, G2
Burns links $ drop, inflatn, energy plan 1-30, 161D3
Solomon on US policy 2-6, 2-16; reaction 2-21, 118A3
Carter explains $ defense policy 3-2, 140F3
US $ drop continues, Admin fears rptd 3-7, 234F1-C2
Carter sees strong $ 3-9, 161B1
Unctad poor-natn debt relief talks; '77 debt estimates cited 3-11, 301A1
US $ drop, '77 world trade rise rptd 3-13, 443F2
Miller urges oil import curbs, inflatn progrm 3-15, 181D1
'77 US forgn assets rise rptd, $ drop cited 3-22, 221E3
Blumenthal rptdly backs oil import fees re $ fall 3-24, 220B2
Burns urges gold sale, other $ defns measures 3-31, 235B2
US $ drop, Feb trade deficit linked 3-31, 262A2
US $ drop, forgn bank takeovers linked 4-3, 4-12, 263B2
IMF revises SDR valuation 4-3, 300A3
Carter sets anti-inflatn plan, $ drops 4-11, 260E1, F2
Carter links $, energy actn 4-11, 304G1
Stock mkt gains, $ strength linked 4-19, 303G1, A2
US moves to boost $, weakness persists 4-19—7-14, 523D1
Diamond speculatn, weak $, Israeli £ linked 4-27, 319E1
US $ drop cited re US import car sales drop 5-4—8-4, 664F3
US weighs oil import fee 6-22, 511B3
US bars $ interventn at Bonn summit, $ closes up 7-17, 544D2
US '77 $ drop, per capita GNP rank linked 7-18, 624E1
US $ drop, export surge linked 7-26, 607B1
US $ drops; gold, diamond prices soar 7-28—8-16; Carter concerned 8-16, 622C1, D2
US hikes discount, fed funds rate to aid $ 8-18, 679A1-B2
US $ boost, gas compromise OK linked 9-27, 733E1
Carter stresses anti-inflatn plan 10-10, 766G2
US hikes discount rate, $ weakness cited 10-13, 791A2
Carter energy bill clears Cong, US $ aid disputed 10-15, 786A3
US $ weakness, base metals price upturn linked 10-20, 805D1
US $ down on Carter anti-inflatn plan 10-25, 806A3
US $ drops to new lows 10-30, 825B1
Carter acts to halt $ decline, $ rebounds 11-1, 825A1-B2, G2
Meany scores $ rescue steps 11-1, 863E2
4 US banks dropped from '77 world top 10 list, $ fall linked 11-8, 913F3-914C1
Firestone woes, $ drop linked 11-28, 935B2
US $ drop seen in 3d ¼ paymts gap 12-19, 982E1
US sells gold to aid $ 12-19, 998D2

Africa
Zambia devalues kwacha 10% 3-17, 333F2
Rhodesia devalues $ 4-2, 249E1
Sudan devalues pound 6-8, 479G1
Rhodesia Euromkt loan rptd 7-20, 616D1
Ghana cedi devalued 8-28, 841A1

Asia—*See also 'Japan' below*
Viet currency unified 5-3, 341D1
India revalues rupee 5-24, 415C3
Unificatn Church abuses chrgd by US 11-1 862C3

Australia
Foreign reserve total rptd 3-10, 187E3
OECD warns vs exchng rate adjustmts 4-27, 328B1

Canada
C$ falls below 90¢ 2-1—2-20, 129F3
Forgn loan to boost C$ planned 2-21, 129D3
US bond sales, other credits rptd 2-27—3-13; C$ sinks 3-8, recovers 3-11, 188B1
C$ falls below 88¢ 4-3, 244E1
C$ hits 45-yr low 4-4, 235D1
C$ falls below 87¢ 4-13; rallies 4-25—5-1, 328B1
C$ above 90¢ 5-15, 370E2
Quebec hints new currency 5-16, C$ falls below 90¢ 5-17—5-23, 412C3

1979

MONETARY Developments, International
'78 trade rise, $ drop linked 2-8, 161A1
$ gains analyzed 3-5, 320B3
US Nov '78-Jan '79 record $ defense rptd 3-7, 159A3
US $ seen strengthened by oil price decontrol 4-5, 250G2
US $ defense success cited re gold sale cutback 4-18, 435C3
US oil profits, $ strength linked 4-27, 301A2
US '78 profits, $ drop linked by Fortune 5-7, 305E1
Gold rises vs major currencies 5-27-6-11, 435E2
US $ defense, 1st ¼ paymts surplus linked 6-21, 463C2
NZ$ devalued 6-21, 566G2
NYSE asks currency futures trading OK 6-21, 681D3
Carter Cabt shake-up affects US $ 7-18, 7-19, 530C1, 531C3
Carter links $ aid, trade bill 7-23, 646E3
'78 US $ drop, per capita GNP rank linked 7-24, 575D3
US $ rallies on Volcker nominatn 7-25, 555C2
US $ defense hints, gold drop linked 10-2, 739G3
IMF-World Bank mtgs 10-2–10-5, 779F2-F3
FRB tightens credit to curb inflatn, aid $, end gold speculatn 10-6; $, gold mkt reactn 10-8–10-11, 764C1-765F3
US $ gains on FRB moves 10-22, tumbles 11-14, 11-19, 978B3
Economists on '80s forecast 10-29, 11-1, 826D3-827D2
US $ closes '79 down 12-27, 12-31, 978F3

Africa
S Africa rand floated 1-24, 99F1
S Africa rand revalued 2-8, central bank float set 2-27, 171C3
Ghana sets currency exchng 3-13, 324F1
Zaire devalued 8-28, 999C1
Uganda currency exchange held 10-21–10-28, 998C2
UK retains Zimbabwe exchng controls 10-23, 813B3

Asia—*See also 'Japan' below*
Taiwan $ floated 2-1, 98B3

Australia
Currency futures market set 2-1, 74C1

Canada
C$ below 84 US ¢ 1-31, 95A2
Japan loan to boost C$ set 2-14, Swiss loan sought 2-28, 153E1-A2
'78 C$ value vs US $, 10 other currencies rptd 2-27, 168F2
C$ above US 85¢ 3-12–3-16, 210F2
C$ tops 87¢, Ottawa sells $s 4-9, 284D3
C$ drops re Quebec asbestos plan 5-2, 352D2
C$ strength cited in econ rpt 5-24, 405G1

1980

MONETARY Developments, International
FRB sets new monetary supply terms 2-7, 113C3
Carter anti-inflatn plan reactn 3-15, 3-17, 202F2-203C3
IMF $ support plan shelved 4-24, 301F3
Central banks rptd active in forgn exchng mkts 4-30, 436B3
Venice summit backs reforms 6-23, 474B1
IMF rpts world econ outlook 6-24, 477D2
US GOP platform text 7-15, 535G3
Reagan pres nominatn acceptance speech 7-17, 533E2
Reagan for 'stable' policy 9-9, 699E2
IMF revises SDR valuatn, $ falls in currency 'basket' 9-17, 695C1
World Bank-IMF mtg 9-30—10-3, Carter addresses 9-30, 761A2, G3
Reagan offers 8-pt econ plan 10-24, 817D2
Reagan electn welcomed by traders 11-5, 845A1
IMF OKs 50% quota increase 12-1, 913F3
US $ gains on higher interest rates 12-10, 932E1
US '80 $ gains rptd 12-31, 983D2

Africa
S Africa rand rptd up 1-21, 100G3, 101B1
Zaire devalued 2-22, 356B2
S Africa eases exchng controls 3-26, 277F3
Zimbabwe rpts forgn exchng reserves 4-11, 301E2
Mozambique currency exchngd 6-16—6-18, 582A1

Asia
S Korea won devalued 1-12, 101E1
S Korea won float set, $ value rptd 2-27, 196A1
China black mkt rptd 3-1, 132E2
China sets parallel exchng rates 12-15, 975F3

Canada
C$ over 87 cents 2-21, 148G1
C$ below 86 cents 3-10, 191F3
C$ nears 84 cents 3-24, 253D1
C$ nears 83 cents 4-2, 334E2
C$ over 86 cents 5-21, 377A2
US OKs C$ futures trading 5-28, 481C2
Venice summit backs reforms 6-23, 474B1
US futures exchng opens, C$s traded 8-7, 616E1, 617A1
C$ above 85 cents 10-3, 767E1
C$ below 85 cents 11-3, 871C2

1976

European Developments
Lira run 1-1—1-20, currency exchng closed 1-21; franc bolstered 1-21—1-22, 74D1, G1
EC pacts with Tunisia, Morocco 1-13; Algeria 1-21, 84E2, A3
Lira stabilizes on Eur, US exchngs 1-23—1-26, 74D2
French-W Ger currency accords 2-9, 2-12—2-13, 229D1
Spain revalues peseta 2-9, 422B3
Lira drop hits W Ger 2-10, decline continues 2-12, 140D2
£ drops, franc run rptd 2-14—3-12; France quits snake float 3-15, 229C1
Italy currency exchng reopens 3-1, lira drops 3-1—4-5, 253E3
Belgium, Danes hold snake limit 3-15—3-22; Bonn intervenes; £, franc stabilize 3-25, 229A2
Belgium bolsters franc snake role 3-17, 7-23, 572F1
W Ger, Dutch reject French snake reform 4-1—4-2, 276A1, D1
£ drops vs $ 4-4—4-22, 313C1
£ gains 4-6, hits new low 4-9, 266C3
Lardinois quits EC agri post 4-9, 276B2
EC links currency fluctuatns, expenditures 4-14, 276B2
Italy CP backs EEC policy 4-18, 297C1
Italy exchng controls OKd, lira drops 5-5, 365E3
£ drop continues 5-14—5-17, 365E1
US lira acquisitns rptd 5-17, 396G3
UK £ at record lows 5-21, 5-28, 383F2
US sets 7-natn summit 6-1, 6-3, 389B1
UK £ dips lower 6-3—6-4, loan props £ 6-7, 407A2-B3
UK charts sterling drop, stresses OPEC links 6-16, 457C3
Hungary revalues vs Swiss franc, devalues vs £ 7-6, 925C2
Schilling freed to float 7-13, gains on US $, W Ger mark 7-13—8-4, 572C1
France acts to halt franc slide 7-15—7-27, 555E3
Israel links pound to 4 W Eur currencies 7-18, 538D3
Bonn mark gain pressures float 7-29, 594A1
UK £ drops lower 8-25, 630F2
UK to seek IMF loan 9-29, £ gains after record low 9-30, 721B1
Lira, franc drop vs $; mark, Swiss franc gain 9-30, 721C2
Italy acts to protect lira 10-1, 751E2
Bonn bars mark devaluatn 10-4, 754G2
£ boosted 10-7, 773G1
W Ger mark revalued 10-17; float protectn cited, 7 natns stress joint effort 10-18, 782A1
Lira falls vs $ 10-18, 838G1
£ falls to new low 10-28, 809C3
Franc, mark, guilder react to US electns 11-3, 826F2
£ edges up 11-7, fluctuates 11-8—11-11, 853C2
France backs UK IMF loan, sterling balances plan 11-12, US vs sterling plan 11-16—11-17, 880B2★, C3
£ value rptd 11-12, 880A3; 11-22, 11-23, 905F3, 906B1
Italy sets currency purchase tax 11-12, 947A2
French trade deficit rises 11-18, 964E2
UK pound falls 12-14, 946E3; 12-15, 1003F3
Hungary revaluatn rptd 12-14, 1012E3
COMECON to ease currency exchng 12-17, 977A1

Latin Developments
Chile devalues peso 1-7, 48A1
Brazil '75 devaluatns total 21.9% 1-9, 98E2
Argentina devalues peso 1-12, 26A2
Uruguay devalues peso 1-14, 2-9, 383D1
Chile devalues peso 1-16, 1-28, 99A3
CR exchng rates scored 1-20, 123C1

1977

European Developments
'76 Swiss franc loans rptd 1-4, 48E2
UK £ gains 1-5, 7C3
Belgium snake fund loans repaymt cited 1-5, 24G1
BIS sets UK sterling balances pact; £ up 1-10, 20B2-D3
UK buys $s 1-17, £ rises 1-18, 44G2
Swiss '76 interventn, franc rise rptd 1-18, 84F1
Belgium rejcts franc devaluatn 2-3, 199D3
UK £ falls 2-11, 2-14, 134G2
Sovt-bloc Westn debt rptd 2-13—4-14, 335B3
W Ger leads West in currency reserves 2-22, 260A3
Portugal devalues escudo 2-25, 330C2
Turkey devalues lira 3-2, 259A3
Portugal currency reserves depleted 4-2, 330E3
Eurobond defined, history 318E1
1st ¼ Eurobond trading rptd 4-13, 318E1
Euro-yen bond issue rptd 4-19, 318C1
7-natn London summit 5-7—5-8, 357A2
Turkey forgn exchng reserves depleted 6-2, 451B2
Spain devalues peseta 7-12, 545F2
$ falls vs mark, Swiss franc 7-21, 551G3; 7-28, 585E2
Portugal sets escudo downward float 8-25—9-14, 886D1, A2
Spain reserves up 8-26, 867F1
Sweden devalues krona 10%, quits 'snake' 8-29, 708C3
Denmark, Norway devalue krona 8-29, Iceland 8-30, Finland 8-31, 709B1
Euroloan to Nigeria rptd 9-1, 746C3
Finland devaluatn protested 9-1, 764D3
Italy starts W Ger '74 loan repaymt 9-6, 729B2
Turkey devalues lira 10% 9-21, 730F3
Austria shilling devaluatn denied 9-28, 10-3, 763D1
$ rptd down vs mark, Swiss franc 10-24, 792F2
UK £ floated 10-31, $ drop linked 11-1; Oct forgn fund inflow rptd up 11-2, 829G1
'77 mark, franc, £ rise vs $ rptd 11-30, 932E3
Schmidt scores $ drop, cites EC $ purchases in '77 12-6, 932C3
Bonn: mark overvalued 12-6, 12-8, 933A1
VW asks currency, exchng rates stability; cites export harm in US mkt 12-7, 932D3
Mark rise econ threat seen 12-7, 932G3
$ rate vs mark, franc, £ rptd 12-8, 933C1
VW ups US prices, cites $ drop 12-14, 962D1
$ drops 12-30, 997E2

Japanese Developments
Euro-yen bond issue rptd 4-19, 318C1
Tokyo conf mtg 5-22—5-25, 437B3
Currency reserve cut set 6-29, 544D3
Yen at 4-yr high 7-5, 544C3
$ falls vs yen 7-21, 551G3; 7-28, 585E2
$ falls vs yen in Sept, Oct 10-17, 11-15, 884G3, 885B1
$ down vs yen 10-18, US bars support 10-19, 792D2
$ at new low 11-1, 829D2
Yen curbs set 11-17, effected 11-21, 932G2
Toyota, Honda hike US prices, yen rise cited 11-24, 932F3
'77 yen rise vs $ rptd 11-30, 932E3
$ drop, investmt rise in US linked 12-7, 974C2
$ up vs yen 12-8, 933C1
Slow econ growth blamed on yen rise 12-15, 974C1
$ drops 12-15, 12-30, 997F2

Latin Developments
Uruguay devaluatns 1-10—3-8, 352D1
Jamaica tightens forgn exchng controls 1-19, 257G1, B2
Chile revalues peso up 3-4, 449G1
Brazil devalues cruzeiro 3-8, 209F1
Mex peso rptd down vs $, 'petrobond' issue set 3-14, 240G3

1978

C$ speculatn by MPs chrgd 5-20, retracted 5-24, 412F3
C$ rises vs US$ 7-14, 523C3
C$ rises vs US$ 8-15, 622F1
C$ Aug defense costs rptd 9-5, 703D3
C$ hits 45-yr low 9-11, rises 9-12, 703D3
C$ drop continues 9-26, 10-2; govt moves rptd 10-3, credit deals renegotiated 10-12, bonds offered 10-18, 813E2
June '77-78 US $ rise 6% 10-4, 790F1
C$ closes down vs US$ 12-29, 998E2

Europe
Poland lowers exchng rate for US retirees 1-1, 20E1
US $ drop, recovery rptd 1-4, 27E3
Thyssen takeover bid, $ drop linked 1-12, 66F2
'77 US futures trading rise, $ drop linked 1-12, 84B1
'77 $ drop cited 1-23, 27D2
US $ strategy re Bonn rptd 1-23, 27F2
Poland exchng rate equalized 2-1, 95G1
Franc falls 2-1—2-6; Giscard vows support 2-7, Mitterrand scores 2-8, 167E1
US policy analyzed, '77 depreciatn 2-6—3-6; $ drops vs francs, mark, £ 2-23, 118D2-119A2
Iceland devalues krona 13% 2-8, 94F3
Norwegian krone devalued 8% 2-10, 133F3
Turkey currency devalued 23% 3-1, 170A3
W Ger eases US $ crisis tensns 3-9; joint aid plan proposed 3-13, reactn 3-14, 234F1, D2
Franc value rises 3-10—3-20, 201D2
Denmark '77 forgn loans rptd 3-14, 189D3
UK prime min urges Bonn summit plan 3-14, sees Carter 3-23, 226B3
US $ drops vs mark, francs, £ 4-3, 235C1
Portugal '78 escudo devaluatn set 4-3, 331C2
Poland zloty float rptd 4-5, 535G2
EC plans stabilizatn measures, US $ drop cited 4-7—4-8, 257A3
Bonn rpts '77, 1st ¼ $ defns costs 4-13, 523E2
UK bank to buy US bank, $ mkt cited 5-12, 364C2
Giscard, Schmidt agree on EC zone 6-23; present plan at Bremen summit 7-6—7-7; UK, US, others wary 7-7—7-18, 545D1-546B1
US $ drops vs franc 7-13; up vs mark, Swiss franc, down vs £ 7-14, 523B3
Bonn summit debates EC plan 7-16—7-17, 544D2
US $ drops vs mark, francs, £ 8-15, 622E1
Iceland devalues krona 15% 9-4, 689B1
Swiss score US $ policy, says franc overvalued 9-27; $ soars 9-28, 732E1
US $ 9-mo losses vs Swiss franc, W Ger mark rptd 10-2, 732F1
June '77-78 US $ drop 6.6% 10-4, 790F1
W Ger mark revalued up vs 'snake' countries 10-16, 798C2
US $ drops to new lows 10-30, rebounds after US emergency steps 11-1, 825B2
IMF lends US marks to aid $ 11-7, 998C3
Hungary devalues forint 11-11, 906G2
EC ldrs OK monetary system (EMS) at Brussels summit, set currency unit (ECU) 12-4—12-5, 951A3
UK bars EMS entry; Italy, Ireland defer 12-5; French vs eased terms 12-7, 951B3, F3
US backs EMS 12-7, 952F2
Norway bars EMS entry 12-11, quits snake 12-12, 952B2
Italy backs EMS entry despite CP oppositn 12-12—12-13, 952D1
US sells mark notes 12-13, 998G2
Ireland to join EMS 12-15, 979D1
US $ closes down vs Swiss, French francs, mark, £ 12-29, 998D2
French delay EMS start 12-29, 999B1

Japan
US $ drop, recovery rptd 1-4; '77 drop cited 1-23, 27D2, F3
'77 US futures trading rise, $ drop linked 1-12, 84B1
Forgn exchng review set 1-13, 26C3
US $ strategy rptd 1-23, 27F2
US $ policy analyzed, offcls link econ health 2-6—3-6, 119A1, F1
US bars nut, bolt import curbs; $ drop cited 2-10, 181A3
Yen curbs announced 3-15, 235E1
$1 bln purchased 3-28; US aid halted, $ hits new low 4-3; total purchases rptd 4-4, 234F3, D3
Fukuda asks US stabilize $ 5-3, 341B3
US $ up vs yen 7-14, 523F2, B3
US $ drop cited re US car import price hike 7-17, 665E1
US $ below 200 yen 7-24, falls further 8-6, 622D1
Yen rise, 2d ¼ growth lag linked 9-3, 694A1
Yen revaluatn, export drop linked 9-8, 794A2
US $ 9-mo loss vs yen rptd 10-2, 732F1
June '77-78 US $ drop 21.6% 10-4, 790F1
Toyota, Datsun US prices, $ drop linked 10-8, 10-29, 935F3
IMF lends US yen 11-7, 998C3
US $ closes down vs yen 12-29, 998E2

Latin America
Jamaica devalues $ 1-20, 94G3
Ecuador '77 exchng reserves rptd 2-3, 148G2
Chile '78 peso devaluatn set 2-17, 312F2
Peru devalues sol 5-11, 253D1
Uruguay devalues peso 6-1, 6-14, 6-26, 537F3; 7-10, 577B2

1979

C$ below 85¢, recovers 6-4, 444B1
US $ down on Cabt shake-up 7-18, rebounds 7-19, 531D3
C$ above 86¢ 9-11, 684B3; 9-13, 676D2
C$ below 86¢ 10-9, 771C3
C$ recovers 10-25, 811G3
US $ closes down 12-31, 978F3

Europe
US sells Swiss notes to aid $ 1-17, 84G2
W Ger central bank acts to curb money growth 1-18, 62E1
Swiss ease forgn capital bars 1-24, 78D1
EMS, EC farm proposals linked 1-31, 85D1
US $ rises vs mark, francs, £ 2-8, 83B2
Swiss franc loan sought by Canada 2-28, 153A2
W Ger, Swiss US $ defense rptd 3-7, 159D3, E3
France drops EMS oppositn 3-7, 160A3
EMS begins 3-13, 180E1
Turkey bars lira devaluatn, acts vs forgn currency shortage 3-21, 215G1, C2
Ireland ends UK £ parity re EMS 3-30, 268F3
France backs Mex EC bond float 4-1—4-4, 372C2
Greece vows EMS entry 4-4, 268D3
Turkey devalues lira vs $ 4-10, 333F1
E Ger curbs W Ger mark circulatn 4-16, 285F1
US $ up vs mark, francs, £ 5-1, 321B1
UK Tories weigh EMS role 5-15, 358A3
Portugal '78 reserve rise rptd 5-25, 409A3
Finland revaluatn hinted 5-27, 407D1
UK eases forgn exchng controls 6-12, 445A3
Turkey devalues lira vs $ 6-12, 447B1
US $ drop, '78 bank rankings linked 6-19, 476C2
EC hikes farm prices, revises green currencies; chngs listed 6-21, 513F1
UK £ above US $2.20 7-3, 503C1
US $ down on Carter Cabt shake-up 7-18, rebounds 7-19, 531D3
Swiss top '78 per capita GNP list, franc rise cited 7-24, 575C3
Turkey resumes hard currency use 7-31, 637D1
Rumania rejects Sovt-bloc ruble system 8-1, 645D3
Hungary free exchng rate sought 9-3, 741A3
UK strength, exports linked 9-10, 686G2
US $ down vs mark, francs, £ 9-13, 676D2
EMS currencies realigned, US $ drop vs mark seen 9-24, 718G3
W Ger, US offcls meet re $, mark 9-29, 779E3
UK ends forgn exchng controls, £ drops 10-23, 813A3
W Ger fears US $ decline 10-31, 838F1
Hungary exchng controls, E-W bank linked 11-9, 882B3
UK extends growth curbs 11-15, 889E2
US $ closes down 12-27, 12-31, 978F3

Japan
Yen rise, US color-TV operatns linked 1-9, 160G2
US $ gains 2-2, falls 2-8, 83B2
Yen loan to Canada set 2-14, 153E1
US $ defense rptd 3-7, 159D3, E3
US $ closes up vs yen; oil, trade dvpts cited 3-27-5-1, 320G3-321A1
US $ drop, '78 bank rankings linked 6-19, 476C2
US $ down on Carter Cabt shake-up 7-18, rebounds 7-19, 531D3
US $ down vs yen 9-13, 676D2
Yen drop vs $ cited 11-1, 836E2
Yen drop, US steel trigger price hike linked 11-20, 965G3
US $ hits peak 11-27, closes down 12-31, 978E3 996B2

Latin America
Brazil devalues cruzeiro 2-2, 210A2
Mex EC bond float backed by France 4-1-4-4, 372C2
Nicaragua devalues cordoba 4-6, 270A1*
Nicaragua '78 reserve loss rptd 5-14, 372E3

1980

C$ at 47-yr low 12-11, 964F3
C$ below 83 cents 12-16, near 84 cents 12-31, 992F2

Europe
Turkey devalues lira 1-24, 61A1
Turkey sets debt plan 1-28, 80E1
US $-mark exchng rate chart 2-18—3-20, 202D1, A2
Swiss, W Ger yen rescue role rptd 3-2, 173D2
US $ soars vs mark, franc; central banks intervene 3-17; profit-taking slows surge 3-19—3-20, 202E3
W Ger mark note sale to Saudis rptd 3-24, 236F2-A3
Hunt group sets silver-backed bond issue 3-26, 223C3
Swiss, Japan swap currencies 4-1; yen continues $ slide 4-8, 276A2
Portugal revalues gold reserves 4-2, 277A3
Central banks rptd active in forgn exchng mkts 4-30, 436C3
IMF seeks Turkey devaluatn 5-6, 446D1
US OKs pound, mark, Swiss franc futures trading 5-28, 481C2
OECD backs restraints 6-3—6-4, 422D1
Yugo devalues dinar 6-6, 833A2
Turkey devalues lira again 6-10, 445E3
Iran forgn exchng holdings ordrd returned to UK 6-17, 464B3
IMF OKs Turkey loan 6-18, 468G1
Venice summit backs reforms 6-23, 474B1
US futures exchng opens; pounds, marks, Swiss francs traded 8-7, 616E1, 617A1
Swiss end forgn currency deposit curbs 8-27, 673B3
IMF revises SDR valuatn; mark, franc, pound gain in currency 'basket' 9-17, 695E1
World Bank '80 loans rptd 9-22, 720F1
US $ gains vs mark, francs; drops vs pound 11-5, 845B1; 12-10, 932E1
US $ '80 gains rptd 12-31, 983D2

Japan
'79 forgn reserves, yen decline rptd 1-25, 100A1
Yen falls vs US $ 2-18, 152A1
US $-yen exchng rate chart 2-18—3-20, 202A2, D2
Yen 5-pt rescue plan set 3-2, US $ value rebounds 3-3, 173C2
US $ soars vs yen, central bank intervenes 3-17; profit-taking slows surge 3-19—3-20, 202E3
Swiss currency swap effected 4-1, yen continues US $ slide 4-8, 276A2
Central banks rptd active in forgn exchng mkts 4-30, 436C3
US OKs yen futures trading 5-28, 481C2
Venice summit backs reforms 6-23, 474B1
US futures exchng opens, yens traded 8-7, 616E1, 617A1
IMF revises SDR valuatn, yen gains in currency 'basket' 9-17, 695E1
World Bank '80 loans rptd 9-22, 720F1
US $ drops vs yen with Reagan electn 11-5, 845B1
New forgn exchng rules set 12-1, 966D3
US $ gains vs yen 12-10, 932F1
Yen gains vs US $ in '80 12-31, 983F3

Latin America
Brazil devalues cruzeiro 3.2% 1-8, 191B2
Brazil devalues cruzeiro again, '80 total at 19.56% 5-28, 406C1

1976

Argentina devalues peso 1-26, 96G2
Argentina devalues peso 2-23, 3-5, 212E2
Argentina plans 30% devaluatn 4-2, 264G2
Uruguay devalues peso 5-4, 441F2
Peru devalues sol 6-28, 499G1
Chile revalues peso upward 6-30; sets new devaluatn 11-4, 871G1
Uruguay devalues peso 7-22, 755F1
Mexico peso floated 8-31, stabilized 9-12, 694A2
Uruguay devalues peso 10-8, 814C3
Mexico peso rises 12-2, 906G2
E Carib $ rptd down 12-7, 925G1

Petrodollar Issue—*See 'Arab Boycott' under BUSINESS; also OPEC and OPEC country names*

MONEY (magazine)
Guild begins strike 6-2, 398C1
Guild ends strike 6-21, 454C2
MONEYCHANGERS, The (book)
On best seller list 2-29, 208F3

MONGOLIAN People's Republic (Outer Mongolia)—*See also COMECON, DISARMAMENT—Geneva Committee*
Listed as 'not free' nation 1-19, 20E3
Shuns China fete for Egypt vp 4-19, 275G2
Role in Sovt space program set 9-14, 684D1
USSR pact signed 10-19, 949B3
Sports
Olympic results 7-18—7-31, 573E3, 576D3

MONKS, Robert A. G.
Loses electn 11-2, 821C1
MONNINGTON, Thomas
Dies 1-7, 56F3
MONOD, Jacques
Pleads for Sovt dissident 3-24, 421A3
Dies 5-31, 404D2 ★
MONOPOLIES—*See ANTITRUST Actions*
MONROE, La.—*See LOUISIANA*
MONSOONS—*See STORMS*
MONTAGU & Co. Ltd., Samuel (London)
Buys IMF gold 9-15, 739E3
MONTALE, Eugenio
Pleads for Sovt dissident 3-24, 421A3

MONTANA
Primary date set 22B2
US Sup Ct to hear coal mining environmt impact case 1-12, 23G3
Babcock sentnc upheld 2-10, 144G3
Sup Ct backs Cheyenne mineral rights 5-19, 394A1
Primary results 6-1, 389E2, 390C1, A2, 411F1
Babcock jail term set aside 6-4, 442D2
Reagan gets more delegates 6-26, 467F2
Strip-mining stay reversed 6-28, 569A1
Dem conv women delegates, table 508C2
Dem conv pres vote, table 7-14, 507C2
GOP pre-conv delegate count 8-14, 583C3
GOP conv pres, vp vote tables 8-18—8-19, 8-19, 599C1, C3
Fscl '75 per capita income, tax burden rptd 9-15, 10-12, 959E2
Election results 11-2: pres 818C1, 819A1; cong 820A1, D2, 824A2, 828C2, 830B1, 831F1; state 820B3, 824B2, 825A3

MONTANEZ, Col. Pedro (ret.)
Arrest rptd 2-9, 207E3
MONTANEZ, Willie
NL batting ldr 10-4, 795F3
MONTANO, Galo
Ecuador industry min 1-14, 49A1

1977

US eases Cuba currency curbs 3-25, 283E2
Mex petrobonds oversubscribed 4-18, 1st issue on sale 4-29, 528C1
Brazil devalues cruzeiro 5-1, 524G2
Mexico peso stabilized 5-6, 527D3
Peru sol devalued 5-26, 427E2
Peru sets new devaluatn 6-11, 488A2
Uruguay devalues peso 7-4, 7-8, 7-28, 601F2
Argentina monthly devaluatns rptd 7-8, 614D2
Peru ends 'minidevaluatns' 7-20, 618F2
Peru exchng reserves drained 7-28, 618D2
Peru forgn exchng reserve rptd 8-31, floats sol 10-10, 784D3, 785A2
Peru to devalue sol 9-30, 784B3
Brazil devalues cruzeiro 11-14, 12-6; total '77 devaluatn 27.9% 12-6, 964E3
Uruguay devalues peso for 23d time 11-25, 970E1
Mexican peso stabilized 12-1, 967A1
Middle East Developments
Israel devalues £ 1-18, 99E2
Israel pound devalued 3-2, 3-21, 257E1
Arab fund created 4-18, 317F3
Dinar SDR link, $ value rptd 4-18, 318G1
Egypt exchng rate adjustmt urged 5-11—5-12, 390G2
Israeli pound devalued 10-28, 842C3
UAE asks OPEC $/dinar as US $ replacemt 12-6, 933E1
Petrodollar Issue—*See OPEC and OPEC country names*

MONETARY Developments, U.S.—*See under ECONOMY (U.S.)*
MONGE, Luis Alberto
Named PLN '78 pres candidate 3-13, 506C2
Figueres chrgs CIA press funding 4-23, 506D2
'78 pres race under way 9-2, 710A2
MONGOLIAN People's Republic (Outer Mongolia)—*See also COMECON, DISARMAMENT—Geneva Committee*
UN Assemb member 4D1
Malta premr provokes walkout in Peking 11-3, 925F2

MONOPOLIES—*See ANTITRUST Actions*
MONORY, Rene
Named industry min 3-30, 239G1
MONROE, Col. James L.
CIA mind-control tests revealed 8-1—8-9, 611A1
MONROE Auto Equipment Co.
FTC vs Tenneco takeover 3-15, 274G3
MONROE (Conn.) Bank & Trust Co.
Fails 3-28, 578C1
MONROY, Rene
Retained as industry min 9-26, 744G2
MONSANTO Co.
EPA bars PCB discharges 1-19, 95F1
Sup Ct backs EPA authority 2-23, 150A3
MONTALVO Martin, Protasio
Ends 38 yrs of hiding 7-17, 582F3

MONTANA
Legislature schedule rptd 6E2
Crow coal leases revoked 1-13, 58F3
Drought continues, conservatn urged 2-15, 152E3
Columbia Falls aluminum productn cut 2-16, 244E3
'76 per-capita income table 5-10, 387F2, B3
Rain saves wheat crop 6-16, 492A3
Pattee Canyon fire 7-16—7-20, 660B3
'76 per capita income, tax burden table 9-13, 10-18, 821E2
Butte challenge of pub works bill minority quota provisn cited 10-31, 979C1

MONTANEZ, Willie
Traded to Rangers, Mets 12-8, 990B1

1978

Uruguay devalues peso 1.1% 8-4, 692E1
Mex pres: peso 'stable' 9-1, 690F1
Peru forgn exchng losses rptd 9-15, 775B3
Uruguay devalues peso 19th time 10-11, 1022D2
Brazil devalues cruzeiro 2%, '78 total 22% 10-25, 837A1
Nicaragua near bankruptcy 11-1, 883B3
Brazil cruzeiro devalued 12-6, 12-21, 1021F2
Argentine peso falls to 1,000 vs US$ 12-7, 1021F2

Petrodollar and OPEC Issues—*See OPEC and OPEC Nations*

MONEY Supply, U.S.—*See ECONOMY (U.S.)—Monetary Policy & Developments*
MONGE, Luis Alberto
Loses CR pres electn 2-5, 89E2

MONGOLIAN People's Republic (Outer Mongolia)—*See also COMECON, DISARMAMENT—Geneva Committee*
UN Assemb member 713C3

MONGOLISM—*See MEDICINE—Mental Health*
MONICELLI, Mario
Viva Italia released 7-9, 970C3
MONICO, Michael
Defends ex-CIA aide 11-18, 940A2
On Kampiles sentence 12-22, 1011E3
MONKEYS
Cocaine preference study rptd 8-11, 771C1
MONONGAHELA Power Co.—*See ALLEGHENY Power System, Inc.*
MONOPOLIES—*See ANTITRUST Actions*
MONORY, Rene
Named French econ affairs min 4-5, 245F2
Assemb OKs steel rescue plan 10-11, 815D3
MonPERE, Carol
Mouse & His Child released 7-7, 970C2
MONSANTO Co.
EC Comm orders fiber cartel modificatn 11-9, 871F3
MONSOONS—*See STORMS & Floods*

MONTANA
No state sales taxes rptd 1-5, 15C3
Mondale tours Westn states 1-9—1-13, 34E1
State govt tax revenue table 1-9, 84D2
Sen Metcalf dies 1-12, 96A3
Hatfield named to Metcalf Sen seat 1-22, 52A3
Wilderness area clears Cong 2-9, 109D2; signed 2-24, 218A2
USSR inquiry re radar statn rptd 2-28, 298E1
Hunting fee disparity backed by US Sup Ct 5-23, 405F3
Primary results 6-6, 448A2
Dems bar 'open primary' 6-9, 448G2
Double jeopardy protectn lengthened by US Sup Ct 6-14, 468G3
House votes parks bill 7-12, 527A1
Butte firemen strike 9-17, 753F1
Natl parks authorzn cleared 10-13, 834C3; signed 11-10, 879A2
Election results 11-7: cong 846G1, 848D2, 851D2, 856D1; state 847G1, 856E1
MONTANA, University of (Missoula)
Richardson in NBA draft 6-9, 457F3
MONTANARO, Sabino Augusto
Rpts prisoners freed in Dec '77 1-3, 113D2
MONTAUZIER, Patrick
Arrested for Versailles bombing 6-30, chrgd 7-4, 533F2

1979

Venez to maintain bolivar value 5-28, 429D3
Brazil devalues cruzeiro 5-30, 430E1
Mex 1st 1/4 reserves rptd 6-1, 487G2
Nicaragua currency recalled 8-25—8-26, cordoba rate fixed 9-3, 689F1, E2
Castro seeks new intl monetary system 10-12, 778C3
Brazil devalues cruzeiro 2.4% 10-31, 871D1; 30% 12-7, 948E2
Bolivia devalues peso 12-3, 926D1

Middle East
US $ drops on Iran oil fears 2-7, rebounds 2-8, 83C1-C2
Arab Monetary Fund suspends Egypt 4-18, 278B2
Israel £ drops 4-20, 389F1-A2
Iran exchng rate rptd altered 5-7, 358B2
Saudis, OPEC warn West vs US $ drop 6-28, 473D1
Brown seeks US strong $ committmt to OPEC 11-9, 962E2
US freezes Iran assets 11-14, 861F1; order confrmd, risks detailed 11-15—11-18; estimate hiked 11-19, 879C3-880G1
Iran hints oil $ paymt shift 11-19, 11-20, 879B3; bars $ paymts 11-23, 896D3
Saudi reserves rptd down 12-12, 968B3

MONEY, Eric
Traded to 76ers 2-7, 526F2

MONGOLIAN Peoples Republic (Outer Mongolia)
UN membership listed 695G2
China request for USSR border troop exit rejctd 11-30, 918A1
MONKEYS
Training for handicapped rptd 3-19, 219C2
MONNET, Jean
Dies 3-16, 272C3
MONOCO
Sports
Scheckter wins Gr Prix 5-27, 1005E1
MONONGAHELA River
US Steel pollutn suit settled 7-23, 704F2
MONOPOLIES—*See ANTITRUST Actions*
MONORY, Rene
Price decontrol to continue 1-12, 96C2
On oil price hike impact 8-2, 614C1
On EMS currency revaluatn 9-24, 719B1
MONROE, James (1758-1831)
Stuart portrait goes to Natl Gallery 4-10, 375B1
MONSANTO Co.
Agent Orange suit filed 2-1, 90C1
2d Agent Orange suit filed 11-26, 904A3
MONSARRAT, Nicholas
Dies 8-7, 671A3
MONTAGU & Co. Ltd., Samuel
London gold price role described 2-7, 83C1, G1
MONTAGUE, Mich.—*See MICHIGAN*
MONTAGUE, John
Angels lose AL pennant 10-6, 797E2
MONTALVAN, Wilfredo
Forms Soc Dem Party 9-7, 732B1
MONTANA
Legislature schedule rptd 5E3
Green River Basin oil find cited 1-5, 17G1
ERA rejctd by state Sen 2-13, 128C2
Gross-receipts tax upheld by US Sup Ct 2-22, 151C1
Legal drinking age cited 4-16, 309E3
'Deliberate homicide' convictn reversed by Sup Ct 6-18, 499F1
Forest fires rptd 8-12, 620D1
'78 per capita income rptd 9-16, 746F2
PCBs contaminate food 9-17, 704A3, C3
Milwaukee Rd embargoes track 11-1—11-5, 867G2

MONTANA, Claude
'79 fashion roundup rptd 1006C2
MONTANA, Joe
Notre Dame wins Cotton Bowl 1-1, 8A3
MONTANA v. U.S.
Mont gross-receipts tax upheld by Sup Ct 2-22, 151C1
MONTANEZ, Willie
Traded to Rangers 8-12, 1002B3
MONTAZERI, Hojatolislam Mohammed
Plans volunteers for Leb 12-5, 12-8, Beirut bars 12-10, 937F2
MONTAZERI, Ayatollah Husseinali
Son seeks volunteers for Leb 12-5, 12-8, 937F2

1980

Middle East
Gold prices soar 1-2—1-18, 30A2, B3
OPEC links prices, currency values 2-22, 142F1
Israel introduces shekel 2-22—2-24, 151D1
Saudi mark note purchase, US $ sale agreed 3-24, 236G2, A3
IMF $ support plan shelved 4-24, 301G3, 302E1
OPEC sets pricing plan 5-7—5-8, 364C3
Iran forgn exchng holdings ordrd returned to UK 6-17, 464B3
Islamic econ conf 11-4—11-6, 865C1
Saudi '80 yen, mark buying rptd 12-19, 983G2

MONGOLIAN People's Republic (Outer Mongolia)—*See also COMECON, GENEVA Committee*
UN Afghan res opposed 2-14, 123E3
Sports
Moscow Olympic results 7-20—8-3, 588B3, 623C1, 624D3

MONK, Art
In NFL draft 4-29, 336F2
MONKEYS
Proxmire settles libel suit 3-24, 470D3
Kin recognitn study rptd 6-19, 715C2
MONORY, Rene
Rpts '79 inflatn 1-22, 97E2
MONRONEY, A(lmer) S(tillwell) Mike
Dies 2-13, 176F2
MONSANTO Co.
EC textile duties rptd 5-6, 412A1
MONSON, Arthur L.
Loses US House electn 11-4, 852D1
MONTAGU, Helen
Filumena opens 2-10, 392G2
MONTAGUE, Nicholas Charles
Convicted 4-23, 372B1
MONTALBAN, Oscar Leonardo
Ousted as radio commentator 2-2, 118C1

MONTANA
ICC orders Burlington coal shipping refund 1-4, Sup Ct refuses stay 1-14, 37A3
Influenza outbreak rptd 2-15, 158C3
Milwaukee Rd RR svc cut set 2-25, 346B1
BN, Frisco RR merger OKd 4-17, 345F2
Hunt coal property transfers rptd 5-2, 345A1
US sets PCB rules 5-9, 387B2
Mt St Helens erupts 5-18, 382E1; damage assessed 5-24—7-4, 503E3
Hunts bailout loan collateral listed 5-28, 426D1
Drought damage rptd 6-23—8-15, 616B2
Anaconda to close 2 units 9-30, 825F2
Election results 11-4: pres 838C1, 839A1, E3; cong 840D2, 845B2, 851G3; state 845G2, 847D1, G2
Anaconda Butte workers end strike 11-21, 988A1
'80 census rptd 12-31, 983F1

Five-Year Index —MOORHEAD 625

1976

MONTCLAIR, N. J.—*See NEW Jersey*
MONTEALEGRE, Hernan
Arrested 5-12, 465G1
Church rejects chrgs vs 7-16, 711D2
MONTECINO, Lillian
On Letelier death threats 9-22, 710E3
MONTEFUSCO, John
Pitches no-hitter 9-29, 756G2
NL pitching ldr 10-4, 796A1
MONTERO, Oscar
Sees Castro 3-14, 251C3
On missing US pilots 9-6, 678A3
MONTERO Sanchez, Simon
Detained 11-28, 909C1
MONTES, Jorge
Cuba rejects Matos exchg 12-18, 955D3, 963C1
MONTGOMERY, Rep. Gillespie V. (D, Miss.)
Says Viets renege on agrmt 7-21, 593C2
Sees no hope for MIAs 7-23, 593C2
Reelected 11-2, 830A1
MONTGOMERY, Jim
Wins Olympic medals 7-19, 7-25, 575E2
MONTGOMERY (Ala.) Advertiser (newspaper)
Carter endorsement rptd 10-30, 831G2
MONTGOMERY County, Pa.—*See PENNSYLVANIA*
MONTGOMERY of Alemein, Field Marshal Viscount Bernard Law
Dies 3-24, 240E3
MONTICELLO, Va.—*See VIRGINIA*
MONTORO, Franco
On MDB munic vote loss 11-20, 902G3
MONTOYA, Sen. Joseph M. (D, N.M.)
IRS tax audit rptd 3-24, 247B1
IRS audit irregularities rptd 4-12, 283E3
Wins primary 6-1, 411E1
AFL-CIO donatn rptd 10-22, 938D3
Loses reelection 11-2, 819D3, G3, 824E2
MONTOYA Escobar, Jairo
Seized in cocaine raid 1-24, 118F2
MONTOYA Montoya, Oscar
Colombia labor min 10-19, 925B1
MONTSERRAT—*See CARIBCOM*
MONTY Python Live! (play)
Opens 4-15, 1014C3
MOON—*See 'Moon Exploration' under ASTRONAUTICS*
MOON, Rev. Sun Myung
IRS probe rptd 6-1, property assessed 6-2, 971B1
Yankee Stadium rally 6-1, 971B1
Ends US ministry 9-18, 970E3
Pak US influence peddling rptd 10-24—11-14; rally vs Nixon impeachmt cited 11-7, 899B1, A2-B3
NYC newspaper set 12-14, 971F1
MOONEY, Charles
Wins Olympic medal 7-31, 574A1
MOON Ik Hwan, Rev.
Sentence reduced 12-29, 1013G2
MOORE Jr., Gov. Arch A. (R, W. Va.)
Acquitted 5-5, 342E3
Primary results 5-11, 342D3
Ford to get 20 delegates 6-19, 450F3
Ford hosts W Va delegates 6-25, 467D3
Rockefeller elected 11-2, 823E1
MOORE, Frank
Carter Cong liaison 11-23, 881G2
MOORE, Homer
'70 Carter campaign donor 10-17, 805B1
MOORE, Capt. John E.
Hits NATO waste 8-31, 760G2
MOORE, Manuel
Convicted 3-13, sentncd 3-29, 292F3
MOORE, Mary Tyler
Emmys presented 5-17, 460B2
MOORE, Sara Jane
Gets life term 1-15, 23F1-D2
MOORE 3rd, Rep. W. Henson (R, La.)
Reelected 11-2, 829F3
MOORE, William P.
Indicted 5-7, 349D1
Sentenced 10-5, 767F3
MOOREFIELD, Rev. Marie
'75 Episc Church resignatn rptd 4-9, 755E3
MOORES, Frank
Sees investor confidnc low 12-9, 945D3
MOORHEAD, Rep. Carlos J. (R, Calif.)
Reelected 11-2, 829C1
MOORHEAD, Rep. William S. (D, Pa.)
Reelected 11-2, 830E3
Sets steel-price study 12-2, 898A2

1977

MONTEREY Peninsula—*See CALIFORNIA*
MONTERROSO Miranda, Gen. Doroteo
Chrgs Torrijos Belize investmts 5-24, 415A1
MONTES, Cesar
Rptd Guatemala rebel ldr 7-4, 673D1
MONTES, Jorge
Chile exchngs for 11 E Gers 6-18, 476E1
MONTES, Vice Adm. Oscar
On rights abuse, terrorism 6-14, 494B2
Says no leads on Hidalgo kidnap 8-1, 595D2
Sees Vance 11-21, 912E2
MONTGOMERY, Rep. Gillespie V. (D, Miss.)
In missn to Viet, Laos 3-16—3-20; Carter gets rpt 3-23, 206B1
MONTGOMERY Ward & Co., Inc.—*See under MOBILE Corp.*
MONTORO, Franco
Scores mil govt 6-27, 523E2
MONTOYA, Joseph
Cited in Park indictmt 9-6, 688E1
MONTOYA Montoya, Oscar
Labor unions ask dismissal 11-18, 1011C1
MONTSITSI, Sechaba
Arrested 6-10, 469D1
MONZON, Carlos
Decisns Valdes, sets retiremt 7-30, 827G3
Valdes wins middleweight title 11-5, 970B3
MOODY Jr., Raymond A.
Life After Life on best-seller list 2-6, 120G3; 3-6, 184G3
MOODY'S Investor's Service Inc.
SEC rpt chrgs NYC '74-75 financial deceptn; reactn 8-26, 665C3, 666B1
NYC gets lowest rating; sale canceled, Beame scores 11-10, 881A1, E1
MOON—*See under ASTRONAUTICS*
MOONSTRUCK Madness (book)
On best-seller list 3-6, 184G3; 4-3, 264B2
MOON Sun Myung, Rev.
Disciples in parental custody 3-24, 286F3
Parents lose disciple custody 4-11, 310B1
Denied NYC property tax exemptn 4-14, 310D1
Named KCIA agent 6-5, 441G3
Pak Bo Hi chrgd by SEC 9-28, 774C1
MOORE, Acel
Wins Pulitzer 4-18, 355F2
MOORE, C. Robert
Replaced as amb to Cameroon 5-9, 418A2
MOORE, Cory C.
Frees hostages, talks to Carter 3-9, 178B3
MOORE 2d, Edwin G.
Arrested 12-22-76, 41A2
Convicted 5-5, 409D2
Sentenced 6-1, 462G2
MOORE, Frank
Named Carter cong liaison 1-14, 35A3
MOORE, James R.
Rape convictn reversed 12-12, 960G2
MOORE, Sir John
Rejects govt wage proposals 8-22, 725A2
MOORE, John D.
Replaced as amb to Ireland 6-21, 626E3
MOORE, Capt. John E.
Cites USSR sub superiority 8-25, 686E2
MOORE, Jr., Bishop Paul
Ordains lesbian 1-10; bishops table rebuke 10-3, 845C2
MOORE, Ray
US Open results 9-11, 787E1
MOORE, William
Indicted with Navajo ldr 2-9, 162E3
Acquitted 5-17, 492A1
MOORE McCormack Lines—*See MOORE McCormack Resources Inc.*
MOORE McCormack Resources Inc.
Ex-rep Garmatz indicted 8-1, 603E3

1978

MONTEDISON S.p.A.
$595 mln loss in '77 rptd 3-21, 330F2
Govt aid rptd set 3-27, 330C2
36 indicted in co fraud 4-3, 330C3
Giocomazzi shot in Milan 5-10, 393D2
MONTEFUSCO, John
NL pitching ldr 10-2, 928G2
MONTEGNA, Joe
Bleacher Bums opens 4-24, 760E1
MONTEIRO, Warren
Cromwell opens 7-12, 887E1
MONTERO, Col. Enrique
In US, vows Letelier death probe aid 3-9—3-10, 189B1
MONTES, Vice Adm. Oscar
Quits as Argentina forgn min 10-27, 840G2
MONTGOMERY, Barbara
Nevis Mountain Dew opens 12-7, 1031E2
MONTGOMERY, Rep. Gillespie V. (D, Miss.)
In Viet, Laos missn 8-21—8-25; brings back bodies of 15 US MIAs 8-27, 660G2
Reelected 11-7, 851B2
MONTGOMERY, James
Sets 400-m freestyle relay mark 8-22, 780C2
MONTGOMERY, Wilbert
NFL '77 kick return ldr 1-1, 56G3
MONTGOMERY Ward & Co.—*See under MOBIL Corp.*
MONTINI, Giovanni Batista—*See PAUL VI, Pope*
MONTORO, Franco
Asks direct electns 6-23, 555D3
MONTOYA, Joseph M.
Dies 6-5, 540C3
MONTSERRAT—*See CARIBBEAN Community*
MOODY, Keith
NFL '77 punt return ldr 1-1, 56C3
MOODY, Mayor Tom (Colombus, Ohio)
Pledges Carter support 11-27, 914F3
MOODY'S Investors Service Inc.
Calif bond ratings suspended 4-13, 426F1
Cleveland credit ratings dropped 663A3
Cleveland rating lowered 12-15, 1008D2
MOON, Keith
Dies 9-7, 778F1
MOON, Warren
Washington wins Rose Bowl 1-2, 8B3
MOONJEAN, Hank
End released 5-10, 619G1
Hooper released 8-4, 970F1
MOON Sun Myung, Rev.
NY seminary charter denied; '77 solicitatns bar, deportatns cited 2-22, 295G2
Unificatn Church-KCIA link probed 3-15, 3-22, 203D1
Deprogramming suit rptd 4-16, 295F3
Subpoenaed by House subcom, US departure rptd 6-6, 433C1
US House subcom chrgs abuses, asks interagency probe 11-1, 862C3, G3
Weiss loses deprogramming suit 12-29, 1012A2
MOOR, Bill
Water Engine opens 1-5, 760G3
MOORE, Anne Elizabeth
Guyana jury rules death suicide 12-22, 999E3
MOORE, Arch A.
Wins US Sen primary in W Va 5-9, 363B1
Loses electn 11-7, 846B2, 854F1
MOORE, Frank B.
Griffin firing angers O'Neill 7-28—8-7, 605B3
MOORE, George S.
On Kennecott bd rival state 3-27, 402E3
MOORE, Henry
Natl Gallery commissn rptd 6-1, 578C3
MOORE, Adm. Henry (ret.)
Dies 3-12, 252B3
MOORE Jr., John L.
On PI A-plant safety 2-8, 134D3
MOORE, Marianne (1887-1972)
Zukofsky dies 5-12, 440G3
MOORE, Melba
Timbuktu opens 3-1, 760E3
MOORE, Nat
NFL '77 touchdown, receiving ldr 1-1, 56B2, C2
MOORE, Ray
Loses Ocean City Intl 2-26, 419A1
Quits S Africa Davis Cup team 2-28, 251D3
MOORE, Robert
Death Trap opens 2-26, 760A2
Cheap Detective released 6-22, 619A1
MOORE, Roger
Wild Geese released 11-11, 970E3
MOORE, Tom
Once in a Lifetime opens 6-15, 887C2
MOORE 3rd, Rep. W. Henson (R, La.)
McDermott admits paymts 2-22, 142A3
Vs E Coast oil aid 6-16, 471B1 ★
Reelected 11-7, 851A1
MOORE McCormack Lines—*See MOORE McCormack Resources Inc.*
MOORE McCormack Resources Inc.
Garmatz indictmt dropped 1-9, 16A1
Medusa merger bid cited 3-16, 283F1
MOORES, Frank
In US, defends seal hunt 1-9, 35F2
MOORHEAD, Rep. Carlos J. (R, Calif.)
Reelected 11-7, 850G1
MOORHEAD, Rep. William S. (D, Pa.)
Backs US aid to NYC 2-14, 608D2
Reelected 11-7, 852D1

1979

MONTCLAIR (N.J.) State University
Colasurdo in WBL draft 6-12, 526A3
MONTELLA Jr., William
Scotto convicted 11-15, 890D1
MONTERO, Col. Enrique
Letelier case data curbed by '78 US-Chile pact 1-23, 75A1
MONTES de Oca, Rafael Andres
Venez interior min 3-10, 192C3
MONTESERRAT—*See CARIBBEAN Community*
MONTGOMERY, Ala.—*See ALABAMA*
MONTGOMERY, Barbara
Season to Unravel opens 1-25, 292G2
MONTGOMERY, Rep. Gillespie V. (D, Miss.)
Canal treaty implementatn bill clears House 6-21, 481G1-A2
Draft registratn amendment defeated 9-12, 724A3
MONTGOMERY, Wilbert
NFL '78 touchdown, rushing ldr 1-6, 80E1, E2
NFC wins Pro Bowl 1-29, 79E3
MONTGOMERY Ward & Co.—*See under MOBIL Corp.*
MONTH in the Country, A (play)
Opens 12-11, 1007C2
MONTILLA, Miguel
Cervantes decisns 1-18, 79D3
MONTREUX '77-Oscar Peterson (recording)
Peterson wins Grammy 2-16, 336E3
MONTS, Susan Kay
Men in White opens 7-11, 712E1
MONTSITSI, Daniel Sechaba
Sentenced 5-11, 373F1
MONTY Python's Flying Circus (comedy team)
Religious groups denounce Life of Brian, Warner Bros defends 8-27, other dvpts 10-24—10-30, 859E1-E2
MONTY Python's Life of Brian (film)
Released 8-17, 820A2
Religious groups denounce, Warner Bros defends 8-27, other dvpts 10-24—10-30, 859D1-E2
Top-grossing film 9-26, 800G3*
MOODY, Keith
NFL '78 punt return ldr 1-6, 80C2
MOODY'S Investors Service Inc.
NYC note rating upgraded 1-16, sale successful 1-22, 56A1
Chrysler debt rating lowered 4-12, 7-31, 576C2
Municipal bond ratings listed 9-20, 920E3
Chicago schl bd rating drops 11-13, 943D3
MOON, Keith
Kids Are Alright released 6-15, 820E1
MOON, Warren
Edmonton wins Grey Cup 11-25, 1001G1
MOONEY, Frank
Fined re casino skimming 8-23, 851C1
MOONRAKER (film)
Released 6-29, 820B2
Top-grossing film 8-1, 620G3
MOON Sun Myung, Rev.
UCI bank fraud chrgd 5-1, 376D2; setld 6-6, 547E2
MOONVES, Leslie
Festival opens 5-7, 711A3
MOORE, Charlotte
Lovely Sunday opens 1-21, 292A2
MOORE, Clayton
Defies ct order in Lone Ranger case 8-30, 859D3
Hired by Rangers baseball team 11-15, 1002E3
MOORE Jr., Donald W.
Named FBI exec asst 8-8, 611C1
MOORE, Dudley
10 released 10-5, 1008A2
MOORE, Frank
Cited re Califano firing 7-20, 556D1
MOORE, John
On inflatn pay raise, indexatn 6-27, 483E1
Arbitratn panel chngs OKd 10-18, 852E2
MOORE Jr., John L.
Rpts on Ivory Coast investmts 9-8, 720F3
MOORE, Robert
They're Playing Our Song opens 2-11, 292E3
Chapter Two released 12-14, 1007A3
MOORE, Roger
Moonraker released 6-29, 820B2
MOORE, Sarah Jane
Jail escape try fails 2-5, 156A2
Gets 3 yrs for jail break 6-12, 492E1
MOORE, Adm. Thomas H.
Scores SALT 7-17, 536G1
MOORE, Thomas W.
Nixon Admin pub TV moves disclosed 2-24, 194D2
MOORE 3rd, Rep. W. Henson (R, La.)
House OKs oil profits tax 6-28, 541D2
MOOREHEAD, Agnes
Death tied to '53 A-test 8-4, 630B1

1980

MONTE Carlo
Sports
Monte Carlo Grand Prix tennis results 4-6, 607A3
MONTELEONE, Justice John A.
Fines transit unions 4-8, 268D1, F1
Hikes transit union fines 7-2, 518F1
MONTGOMERY, Rep. Gillespie V. (D, Miss.)
On female draft registratn rejectn 3-6, 188C3
Reelected 11-4, 843C2
MONTGOMERY, Mark
Idaho prosecutor sued over TV tapes raid 8-1, 732C3
MONTGOMERY, Wilbert
NFL '79 touchdown, rushing ldr 1-5, 8E2, E3
MONTOYA, Carrion
Resignatn rptd 4-22, 315D2
MOODY, George F.
Named Security Pacific pres, chief exec 12-16, 959F1
MOODY, John
Sovts detain 7-21, 590F1
MOODY'S Investors Service Inc.
Chicago bond rating lowered 1-31, 186A2
Milwaukee city, cnty bond ratings lowered 6-13, 743G3
NYC pub bond sale moves rptd 9-10, 743A2
Standard & Poor's lowers Boston bond rating 12-2, 939F3
MOON, Warren
Edmonton wins Grey Cup; named game MVP 11-23, 999C2
MOONIE, Clyde
On Engelhard-Hunt silver setlmt 3-31, 245C1
MOONLEAN, Hank
Smokey & the Bandit II released 8-15, 675E3
MOON Toh Sang
Govt probes 7-9, 525A2
MOOR, Terry
Loses Atlanta Open tennis 8-24, 691C3
MOORE, Arch A.
Loses W Va gov electn 11-4, 850G2
MOORE, John
Australia business min 11-2, 857F2
MOORE Jr., John L.
Eximbank loan to Australia co, mtg with Murdoch sparks probe 2-19, 989F1
Defends loan OK to Ansett 5-12, 989E1
Funding legis signed, budget limit warning cited 8-29, 989B1
Eximbank skips dividend, '82 loss seen 12-16, 988G3
MOORE, L. G.
Indicted in Brilab probe 6-12, 454E2
Clayton, 2 others acquitted 10-23, 971C2
MOORE, Marshall
Elected officials drop rptd 1-2, 5D3
MOORE, Mary Tyler
Wins Tony 6-8, 692D3
Ordinary People released 9-19, 836D3
Son kills self 10-15, 890A2
MOORE, Pearl
Stars win WBL title 4-10, 432B2
MOORE, Roger
Ffolkes released 4-18, 416F2
MOORE, Sara Jane
Hijacker's release demand foiled 8-18, 667A3
MOORE, Tom
Division St opens 10-8, 892B3
MOORE, Rep. W. Henson (R, La.)
Wins primary 9-13, 724A3
Reelected 11-4, 843A1
MOORHEAD, Rep. Carlos J. (R, Calif.)
Reelected 11-4, 842G1

1976

MOORER, Adm. Thomas H. (ret.)
Named as Rockwell guest 3-17, 200G3
MOORES, Frank
Newfoundland by-electns 6-30, 520C3
MOOT, Robert C.
Ford campaign com treas 8-24, 688B3
MORAES Neto, Prudente de
AAB bombs press assn hq 8-19, 835D3
MORAIS Penido, Archbishop Geraldo Maria de
Geisel mtg re priest murder rptd 11-5, 850B3
MORALES, Miguel
Forced to leave Colombia 2-1, 118A3
MORALES Bermudez, Gen. Francisco (Peruvian president)
Names Fernandez prime min 1-2, 55B3
Belaude lauds 1-5, 55B3
Shuffles cabt 1-31, 2-3, 142F2
Sees Kissinger 2-18, 177G2
Scores Velasco re press 4-30, 500A1
Mil rebellion fails 7-9, 590D3, 591A1
Cabt revised 7-16, sworn 7-17, 590E2
Roncagliolo arrest ordrd 8-25, 652E2
MORALES Navarrete, Ricardo
Cited re Bosch arrest, US rptrs expulsn 10-24, 11-1, 844F1
MORAND, Donald
Toronto police brutality rptd 7-28, 587G3
MORAND, Paul
Dies 7-23, 970E2
MORCOV, Stelica
Wins Olympic medal 7-31, 576E3
MOREAU, James A.
Wins House runoff spot 8-14, 633D1
Primary loss cited; Tonry elected 11-2, 822A2
MOREIRA, Joaquim Antonio Maria
Bomb blast rptd 1-7, 11F1
MOREIRA Baptista, Cesar
Freed from prison 1-21, 53G1
MORELON, Daniel
Wins Olympic medal 7-24, 574C2
MORGAN Jr., Charles
ACLU resignatn cited, replacemt rptd 9-4, 680F2 ★
MORGAN, Gerald D.
Dies 6-15, 484F3
MORGAN, Joe
NL wins All-Star game 7-13, 544B2
NL batting ldr 10-4, 795F3
In World Series 10-16—10-21, 815C2
Gets MVP 11-24, 952D1
MORGAN, Marabel
Total Woman on best seller list 1-25, 80D3
MORGAN, Sen. Robert B. (D, N.C.)
Named to intelligence com 5-20, 377E1
MORGAN, Thomas B.
The Nation purchase rptd 11-28, 901B3
Nation sale called off 12-21, 995E1
MORGAN, Rep. Thomas E. (D, Pa.)
Deplores foreign aid veto 5-7, 345C1
MORGAN & Co., J. P.
Morgan Guaranty Trust Co.—*See separate listing*
MORGAN Guaranty Trust Co. (N.Y.)
On forgn bank deposit disclosures 1-18, 44C3
Dutch bank deal rptd 1-23, 102C2
Quebec loan planned 6-30, 529G1
In Venez intl bank loan 9-15, 875E1
Lowers prime rate 9-24, 846F2
Cuts prime rate 11-19, 12-10, 939A3
Rpts '76 intl borrowing peak 12-22, 976F1
MORGAN Stanley & Co. Inc.
Australia loan OKd 5-20, 400A1
MORGENTALER, Dr. Henry
Freed from jail 1-26, 72G1
Acquittal upheld 3-15, 537B3
3d acquittal 9-18, chrgs dropped 12-10, 946C1
MORGENTHAU (U.S. warship)
In Intl Naval Review 7-4, 488D3
MORGUN, Fyodor T.
Named to Central Com 10-26, 839E2
MORI, Hidekazu
Arrested 7-19, 557B2
MORIN, Claude
Named intergovt affairs min 11-26, 903G2
MORIN, Jacques-Yvan
Named v premr, educ min 11-26, 903G2

1977

MOORER, Adm. Thomas H. (ret.)
Testifies vs Warnke 2-28, 172B3
Testifies on Panama Canal pacts 10-10, 792C2
MOOSE, Richard M.
Named State dep undersecy 1-7, 14A2
Replaced as State undersecy 8-3, 626D3
Somalia chrgs US deceptn 9-19, 715D3
MOQARREBI, Maj. Gen. Ahmed
Convctd 12-6, executed 12-25, 1019F1
MORA, Andres
Orioles forfeit vital game 9-14, 748C3
MORA, Antonio
Temporary Nicaragua govt head 8-18, 656E3
MORALES, Jerry
NL wins All-Star Game 7-19, 567E2
Traded to Cardinals 12-8, 990E1
MORALES, Richard
US modifies dual prosecutn rule 2-11; Hayes convicted re death 9-29, 821C1
MORALES Bermudez, Gen. Francisco (Peruvian president)
On Sovt arms purchases, denies plan vs Chile 1-1, 2C3
Sees civilian rule 1-1, 21B2
Soc property comments cited 1-7, 46F3
Ex-Velasco aides expelled 1-8, 46D3
Magazines score ban 1-14, 47C1
Pol, econ plan issued 2-6, 241C1
Videla visits, signs A-pact 3-3—3-6, 259E1
To stay pres after army retiremt 4-22; Apra backs, asks 'open dialogue' 5-7, 488C3
Rejcts Central Bank resignatns, names Piazza econ min 5-13, 427B3
Sees Mrs Carter 6-3, lauds talks 6-4, 455B1
Econ min quits, names Saenz 7-6, 563B3
Econ policies oppositn rptd 7-15, 563A3
Lima strike scored 7-19, 563G1
Vows civilian rule for '80 7-28, 618B2
Asks debate on '78 vote plan 8-7, lifts state of emergency 8-28, 673G1
Sees Carter 9-6; at Panama Canal pact signing 9-7, 678A1
In US econ talks 9-7—9-8, 785G1
Chrgs IMF bias vs 3d World 9-8, 785E1
MORALES Ehrlich, Antonio
In vote-fraud protest 2-26, gets CR emb asylum 2-28, 181G2-A3
MORALES v. Turman
1-judge prison ruling upheld 3-21, 230A3
MORAN, Lord (of Manton) (Charles McMoran Wilson)
Dies 4-12, 356E3
MORAN International
North Sea oil well capped 4-30, 336F1
MOREAU, James A.
Tonry resigns 5-4, indicted 5-12, 418C3
Switches to GOP 5-19, 418F3
Loses primary 6-25, 501F1
MOREAU, Jeanne
Weds Friedkin 2-8, 140G3
MOREHOUSE, Clifford
Dies 2-17, 164D3
MOREL, Gen. Enrique
Rpts rights abuses, DINA probe 11-11, 983G1-B2
MORENO, Omar
NL batting ldr 10-2, 926D3
MORFLOT America Shipping Inc.
Soviet ownership cited 10-31, 949A2
MORGAN, Jack B.
Vet indicted in horse-switch scandal 12-2, 971C1
MORGAN, Joe
NL wins All-Star Game 7-19, 567B2
NL batting ldr 10-2, 926D3
MORGAN, Stanley
In NFL draft 5-3, 353C2
MORGAN & Co., J. P.
Morgan Guaranty Trust Co.—*See separate listing*
MORGAN Grenfell & Co.
Brazil steel loan granted 6-20, 524E2
MORGAN Guaranty Trust Co. (N.Y.)
OPEC surplus, demand data rptd 1-28, 108G1
Eurobond definitn cited 318E1
Lowers prime 6-13, 578A1
Pension management cited 6-28, 578C2
Hikes prime 8-1, 704A1
SEC rpt chrgs NYC '74-75 financial deceptn 8-26; reactn 8-26—8-27, 665A3, 666A1
Nigeria loan rptd 9-1, 746D3
Trade gap, weakening of $ feared 9-29, 754B1
NCC urges S Africa ties cut 11-10, 934D3
Mex gets $1.2 bln intl loan 11-18, 967C1
MORGENSTERN, Oskar
Dies 7-26, 604D3
MORIAL, Ernest N.
Elected New Orleans mayor 11-12, 879C1
MORIN, Claude
Ends Paris visit, Chirac backs separatism 4-29, 346A3
Trudeau cites French visit 5-13, 389C2
MORIN, Jacques-Yvan
Warns Prot schls re language law 9-2, 694F1

1978

MOORMAN Mfg. Co v. Bair
Iowa business tax formula backed by Sup Ct 6-15, 468F2
MOOS, Malcolm
Loses Sen primary in Minn 9-12, 716B1
MOOSE, Richard
In Somalia re closer ties 3-18—3-23, 215D2
MORAIS, Marcio Jose de
Blames govt in journalist's death 10-28, 879E1
MORALES, Richard (d. 1975)
Tex marshal sentenced 2-18, 991E3
MORALES Bermudez, Gen. Francisco (Peruvian president)
Says army to retain power after electns 134E2
Ecuador seeks border strife setlmt 1-18, 216B2
Heads off planned gen strike 1-22, 134B2
Retires from army, retains presidency 1-30, 134F2
Scores gen strike, vows civiln govt; warns IMF 5-20, 394G1
Rodriguez seeks audience 6-15, 475F1
Vows cooperatn with Constituent Assemb 7-28, 668B3
MORALITY in Media
FCC renews WGBH license 7-20, 599G1
MORANTZ, Paul
Wins Synanon suit 9-19; attacked by rattler 10-10, 2 members chrgd 10-17, 841G2, D3
Synanon founder chrgd in rattler attack 12-3, 971F1
MORE (magazine)
Ceases publicatn, merges with Columbia Journalism Review 7-21, 672G1
MORE, Sir Thomas (1478-1535)
Westminister mass protested 7-6, 557G3
MOREAU, Ron
Arrested in Chile May Day rally, freed 5-1; rpts jail abuse 5-15, 351D3
MOREELL, Adm. Ben (ret.)
Dies 7-30, 620B3
MOREHOUSE, Edward
Price of Genius opens 6-26, 887F2
MORENO, Gianfranco
Detained in Moro case 3-19, 200A1
Released in Moro case 3-20, 247B2
MORENO, Maj. Gen. Marcos Jorge
Replaced as DR army staff chief 8-16, 648E2
MORENO, Omar
NL batting, stolen base ldr 10-2, 928F2
MORENZIE, Leon
Twilight Dinner opens 4-18, 760F3
MORETTI, Mario
Sought in Moro case 5-20, 393C3
Chrgd in Moro case, police hunt continues 6-5, 689C2 ★
MOREYRA, Manuel
Signs new IMF pact 8-7, 669E1
MORGAN, Andre
Boys In Company C released 1-31, 618D3
Amsterdam Kill released 3-30, 618B3
MORGAN, Gil
Wins LA Open 2-19, 355C3
2d in Phila Classic 7-23, ties for 2d in Pleasant Valley 8-13, 672D3, E3
Wins World Series of Golf 10-1, Pacific Club Masters 10-8; 2d in Europn Open 10-22, 990B1, A2, B2
PGA top money winner 10-31, 990B3
MORGAN, Joe
NL wins All-Star Game 7-11, 559C3
MORGAN, Joseph W.
Named in US Teamster fund suit 2-1, 83E1
MORGAN, Michele
Cat & Mouse released 5-6, 618F3
MORGAN, Sen. Robert B. (D, N.C.)
Votes for Panama Canal neutrality pact 3-16, 177D2
Votes for 2d Canal pact 4-18, 273B1
MORGAN, Stanley
NFL '77 punt return ldr 1-1, 56C3
MORGAN & Co., J.P.
Morgan Guaranty Trust Co.—*See separate listing*
MORGAN Guaranty Trust Co. (N.Y.)
Brazil-Paraguay hydro loan rptd 3-30, 311C2
Chile loan role rptd 4-7, 312E1
Chile loans rptd undercutting US rights policy 4-11, Reuss scores 4-12, 312G1
Kennecott proxy votes misplaced 5-2, 403C1
Dropped from '77 world top 10 11-8, 914B1
Nigeria loan cited 11-30, 934A2
Oct, Dec $ loss from '73 rptd 12-29, 998D2
MORGAN Stanley & Co.
Sued re Olinkraft merger 11-8, 896D3
MORGENTHAU, Robert M.
Rpts Graiver indictmt, questns death 4-12, 326D1
MORIARTY, Michael
Wins Emmy 9-17, 1030G1
MORIGUCHI, Yuko
Wins World Ladies title 4-16, 355G3
MORIN, Claude
On Trudeau warning vs Quebec separatn 1-2, 7B1
Backs Quebec re const talks 11-1, 866A3

1979

MOORES, Frank
Replaced as Newfoundland premr 3-17, 233F3
MOORE v. Sims
Case decided by Sup Ct 6-11, 478F3
MOORMAN, James W.
Testifies re Hooker Chems 4-11, 281E3
MORAIS, Jorge
On Texaco oil pact 9-4, 705B3
MORALES, Jerry
Traded to Mets 10-31, 1002C3
MORALES, William
Convicted on explosives chrgs 3-9, sentncd 4-20; escapes 5-21, 431E1
MORALES Sanchez, Julio
PR soclsts '78 deaths disputed 4-30—5-3, probe ordrd 5-2, 350F1, C2
MORALITY in Media
Life of Brian denounced 8-27, 859B2
MORDOVETS, Alexander
Ousted from CR 8-19, 667C3
MORDOVETS, Olga
Ousted from CR 8-19, 667C3
MORE American Graffiti (film)
Released 8-17, 820B2
Top-grossing film 8-29, 672G3
MOREHEAD (Ky.) State University
Simms in NFL draft 5-3, 335F2
MORELAND v. Sprecher
Case denied by Sup Ct 7-2, 559B1
MORENO, Omar
NL batting, stolen base ldr 9-30, 955F2
In World Series 10-10—10-17, 816C2
MORENZIE, Leon
Plays From Africa opens 1-14, 292D2
MOREYRA Loredo, Manuel
Renegotiates Peru debt paymt 11-26, 951C2
MOR-Flo Industries Inc.
No-contest plea cited 10-22, 986E1
MORFOGENE, George
Biography: A Game opens 4-5, 711E1
MORGAN, Gil
Wins Memphis Classic 7-1, 587C3
MORGAN, Joe
Kroc rpts record fine 8-24, 1003B1
MORGAN, Karl Z.
Scores 3 Mile I A-accident 4-7, 261C1
MORGAN, Kay Summersby (1909-75)
Eisenhower letter disclosed, marriage rumor debunked 1-28, 79F1
MORGAN, Judge Lewis Render
Named to spec prosecutor panel 1-12, 56G1
MORGAN, Mike
Yastrzemski hits 400th homer 7-24, 619F2
MORGAN, Sen. Robert B. (D, N.C.)
Sen Ethics Com membership cited 10-31, 945C3
On Army recruiting abuses 11-19, 904A1
MORGAN & Co., J. P.
Yale stock sale rptd 5-3, 332G3
MORGAN Guaranty Trust Co. (N.Y., N.Y.)
Woolworth suit compared 4-12, 304C1
McGraw-Hill scores Amer Express takeover role 1-22, 53A3
Spain OKs local operatn 1-26, 100F3
Iran W Ger assets attached 11-28, 896E2
MORIAL, Mayor Ernest (New Orleans, La.)
Police strike 2-8—3-4, 166A1, B1
MORIARITY, Joseph Vincent (Newsboy)
Dies 2-24, 176D3
MORIARTY, Michael
GR Point opens 4-16, 711E3

1980

MOOSE, Richard M.
Somali mil pact testimony rptd 8-28, 661F3
MORALES, Oscar
Sentenced 1-11, 64A2
MORALES Bermudez, Gen. Francisco (Peruvian president; replaced May 18)
Belaunde wins pres electn 5-18, 390A2
MORALES Carbonell, Carlos Ernesto
Captured 6-19, 497D3
MORALES Ehrlich, Jose Antonio
Joins El Salvador junta 1-9, 19G3-20A1
Duarte joins junta 3-9, 192F2*
Rightist coup attempt, resignatn demands linked 5-2, 372F2*
Coup ldr's release spurs junta rift 5-13—5-14, 389A3*
Son captured as rebel 6-19, 497D3
MORAL Majority Inc., The
Political actn profiled 7-11—9-15, 819A1, B1, B3
Smith wins Ala US House primary 9-2, 682E2
Nickles wins runoff 9-16, 724B3
Falwell reverses Jewish prayer stance 10-11, 811F1
Alabama candidates win electn 11-4, 849E1, G1
Reagan open to advice 11-6, 839A3
MORAN, Thomas (1837-1926)
Hunts bailout loan collateral listed 5-28, 426B1
MORA Rodriguez, Sgt. Maj. Audell
Attacked in PR 3-12, 190D1
MORELAND, Keith
In World Series 10-14—10-21, 811D3
MORELLI, Gerry
Arrows win MISL title 3-23, 771B2
MORENO, Omar
NL batting, stolen base ldr 10-6, 926E2, F2
MORENO, Rita
Happy Birthday Gemini released 5-2, 416A3
MORETTI, Giancarlo
Shot 3-24, 255F1
MORGAN, Andre
Night Games released 4-11, 416D3
MORGAN, Gil
3d in PGA Championship 8-10, 714C2
2d in Pleasant Valley Classic 9-7, 972G1
MORGAN, Harry
Wins Emmy 9-7, 692C1
MORGAN, Helen (d. 1941)
Froelich dies 2-5, 176B1
MORGAN, Joe
Phillies win NL pennant 10-12, 796C1
MORGAN, Lawrence Gene
Acquitted 11-17, 898G2
MORGAN, Sen. Robert B. (D, N.C.)
Winberry rejctd for US judgeship 3-4, 250F2
Loses reelectn 11-4, 845A2, 849F3
MORGAN, Stanley
NFL '79 touchdown, punt return ldr 1-5, 8B2, C3
MORGAN, Dr. Stephen
Marries 6-21, 639B1
MORGAN Guaranty Trust Co. (N.Y.,N.Y.)
Prime rate cut to 19.5% 4-18, 305E3
Prime rate cut to 18.5% 4-28, 329A2
Hunt silver bailout set 5-2, 344G3
Prime rate cut to 17.5% 5-5, 16.5% 5-12, 367B3
Prime rate cut to 16% 5-19, 14% 5-27, 401E1, C2
Hunt bailout loan defended 5-30, 425D2
Prime rate cut to 13% 6-4, 438C1
Prime rate cut to 11.5% 6-23, 514A1
Prime rate cut to 11% 7-21, 574E3
Prime rate hiked to 13.5% 9-19—10-1, 764E2
Prime rate hiked to 14.5% 10-29, 867G1
Prime rate hiked to 21% 12-16, 983A3
MORGAN Stanley & Co.
Kuwait seeks 15% of Getty Oil 7-14, 542C3; bid rejctd 7-18, 557B1
MORGANTOWN—*See WEST Virginia*
MORGENTHAU, Hans J(oachim)
Dies 7-19, 608E2
MORGENTHAU, Robert M.
NY businesswoman, 2 partners indicted 1-10, 216D1
Galante slaying probe figures indicted 3-3, 215G1
'70 Weatherman fugitive surrenders 7-8, plea bargain rptd 7-18, 576B3*
Graivers win '76 jet crash damages 10-15, 826G3
MORIN, Claude
On prelim const talks 7-25, 603D1

1976

MORISON, Samuel Eliot
Dies 5-15, 368G2
MORITT, Fred G.
Indictmt transferred 8-12, 1016A2
MORLEY, Mike
Loses Bing Crosby tourn 1-25, 123E2
MORLINO, Tummaso
Sworn Italy budget min 7-30, 573F1
MORMONS—*See LATTER-Day Saints*

MORO, Aldo
Govt falls, resigns 1-7, 10F1
Coalitn govt bid fails 1-24—1-25, 74C1
Offers econ austerity plan 2-4, 140C2
Forms minority govt 2-11, 140E1
Econ plan revisns pledged 2-13, 140A2
Christian Dem cong 3-3—3-7, 254G1
Meets Sadat 4-5—4-8, 275G1
Abortn dispute threatens govt 4-7, 254B1
Denies link to Lockheed 4-22, 298A1
Govt falls, interim rule set 4-30, 296E2
Parlt dissolved 5-1, electns set 5-3, 333G2
At 7-nation econ summit 6-27—6-28, 461G2, 462E1
Resigns 7-9, 538G3
On US, W Eur loan ban rpt 7-19, 531B1
New govt excludes 7-30, 573D1
Elected Christian Dem head 10-14, 890C3

MOROCCO—*See also AFRICAN Development Bank, ARAB League, DISARMAMENT—Geneva Committee, NONALIGNED Nations Movement, OAU*
EC pact rptd 1-13, 84E2
French Mirage order rptd 1-15, 1-16, 36A2
Osman in France, sets Hassan visit 1-16—1-18, 36G1
Listed as 'partly free' 1-19, 20D3
EC pact 'bias' protested 2-3, signing delayed 2-4, 164F2 ★
Spain sells phosphate stake 2-9, 107C3
Angola MPLA recognized 2-13, 163E2
OKs UN Medit pollutn pact 2-16, 126C3
Algeria ties cut 3-7, 178A3
IMF oil loans rptd 4-1, 339F3, 340D2
IMF OKs SDR purchases, phosphate exports cited 4-6, 458G2
Officers promoted 4-26, 342A1
Iran seeks to relay US arms via Jordan 5-22, 458C2
Rpt '73 plotters tried 7-8, 6 sentenced 7-20, 559F3
Rptd Libya terror target 7-15, 531E1
Moulay dies 7-17, 716E3
Olympic withdrawal rptd 7-21, 528B3
Independents win electns 11-12, 1007D1
Middle East Conflict—*See MIDDLE EAST*
Sahara—*See SAHARA*
U.S. Relations
US arms shipmt rptd 1-7, 36D2
Anderson confrmd US amb 1-28, 110A2
Lamrani sees Kissinger 1-29, more mil aid pledged 1-30, 107G2
F-5E deal rptd 2-21, 458F2
Gen Tire antitrust, payoffs chrgd 4-27, 5-10, 360B1-C2
Iran seeks US arms relay 5-22, 458C2

1977

MORITA, Tadaaki
Seizes hostages 3-3—3-4, 201B3
MORLEY, Mike
2d in Milwaukee Open 7-3, 676G1
MORMONS—*See LATTER-Day Saints*

MORO, Aldo
2 ex-mins to face Lockheed trial 3-10, 284E1

MOROCCO—*See also ARAB League, DISARMAMENT—Geneva Committee, NONALIGNED Nations Movement, OAU*
UN Assemb member 4D1
'76 EC trade pact cited 1-18, 73E3
Benin coup attempt detailed 2-1, 96F1
IMF loan set 2-4, 87F2
Plotters sentenced 2-15, 160E1
Israel boycott eased 2-18, 167F2
OAU ties broken, Benin chrgs cited 2-25, 160D1
UN issues Benin coup probe rpt 3-8, 243B3
Press curbs lifted 3-8, 467E2
Zaire asks aid 4-7, France airlifts troops 4-9; US reactn 4-8, 4-11, 265A1, F1
Troops join Zaire offensive 4-16, 317B1
Hassan chrgs Cuban role in Zaire 4-18, 317G1
Zaire casualties rptd 5-3, 393G3
Zaire rebels lose 2 towns 5-7, 5-11, 393F3
Troops leave Zaire 5-22, 490D1
'68 Israeli uranium purchase rptd 5-30, 416C3
Electns back king 6-3, SUPF ldr quits Cabt 6-6, 467B2
Castro confrms Angola pullout halted 6-9, 456G1
Cabt dismissed 10-5, replaced 10-10, 772E1
Parlt opens 10-14, pres elected 10-17, 869A2
France drops plan to bar immigratn families 10-30, 1013D1
Amnesty Intl chrgs torture 10-31, 869B2
Sadat Israel trip backed 11-19, 890B3
Sahara—*See SAHARA*

1978

MORISON, Gary
Lauds Sup Ct Bakke ruling 6-28, 482B2
MORLAN International Inc.
Australian Land Title Ltd.
FTC ends Australia land sale 5-1, 327A3
MORLEY, Robert
Great Chefs of Eur released 10-6, 970E3
MORMONS—*See LATTER-Day Saints*

MORO, Aldo
Kidnaped, 5 guards killed 3-16; Parlt adjourns; labor, other groups protest 3-16—3-19, 199C2
Police press search 3-16—3-20; issue photos 3-17, detain suspect 3-19, 199D3
Andreotti wins confidence vote 3-17, 200C2
Kidnapers release photo; plan trial, play down Turin 'farce' 3-18, 200D1
Kidnaping, W Ger terrorism linked; W Ger police join search 3-20, 200B1
Kidnap cars returned, 2 suspects freed 3-20; police search scored 3-24, 247F1
Crime ldrs threaten Red Brigades 3-28, 247B2
Letters received by govt, trial rptd 3-29, 4-4; Christian Dems bar secret talks, prisoner exchng 3-30—4-5, 246A3
Press debates terrorist coverage 4-2, 247D1
Rome leftist protests rptd 4-6, 330E1
More letters received; release asked, prisoner exchng debated 4-8—4-25; Christian Dem rift rptd 4-21, 313F2-314A1
Red Brigades gunman captured 4-11, alleged interview rptd 4-28, 329F3, 330A1
Executn rptd, lake searched 4-18; Brigades claim hoax, renew exchng offer 4-20, 4-23, 313C2, G3
Police search Genoa 4-28, 330G1
Family plea published 5-3, 337E2
Executn announced 5-5, farewell message received 5-7, 337E1
Red Brigades tactics rptd 5-8, 393C2
Found murdered in Rome 5-9, 337A2
World ldrs mourn 5-9, Parlt pays tribute 5-10, 337G2, 338A1
Berlinguer praises 5-9, 338D1
Pvt funeral held 5-10, state ceremony scheduled 5-13, 337B2, F2
Schleyer case compared 5-10, 337E2
Curcio, associate ejected from Turin trial 5-10, 338B2; sentenced 5-18, 393B3
State funeral held 5-13, 689D2
Christian Dems gain in local electns 5-16, 375A2
2 Red Brigades hideouts found in Rome 5-18, 5-19, 393D1
Govt fears blackmail revelatns 5-20, 393C3
Moretti sought in kidnaping 5-20, 393C3
Red Brigades justify death 5-20, 393D3
Govt denies negligence in death 5-23, widow denounces 5-25, 689F2
Terrorist shooting 'lull' rptd 5-28, 6-7, 453F2
W Ger terrorist linked to kidnapers 5-30, 439A1
Christian Dems gain in local Sicily electns 5-30, 453G3
Moretti, 8 others chrgd in death 6-5, 6-6, Marini warrant issued 6-26, 689B2, C2 ★
Rognoni named Interior min 6-13, 558C2
Red Brigades Turin trial ends 6-23, 517A1, C1
Papal requiem mass cited 8-6, 601F2
Pope Paul laid to rest 8-12, 658A3
Red Bridgades ldr sentcnd 9-20, 723F3
Red Brigade suspects arrested, 'trial' documts found 10-1, 817D1, E1

MOROCCO—*See also ARAB League, DISARMAMENT—Geneva Committee, NONALIGNED Nations Movement, OAU*
Freedom House lists as partly free 44A2
Child labor rptd 5-29, 596F2
Locust plague threat seen 6-12, 465E2
Foreign Relations (misc.)
US troop presence rptd 1-2, 5E2
USSR phosphate dvpt loan rptd 1-31, 95E1
Sadat in Rabat, seeks Hassan peace backing 2-1, 60F1
Angola troop raid chrg rptd 2-1, 87G3
Hostage seized in Cyprus 2-18, 117G1
Spain gets fishing pact warning 2-20, 278D3
Islamic, Arab poor-natn aid rise rptd 4-9, 257F2
Zaire pres seeks Shaba force support 5-29, 417G3
Hassan vows Zaire aid 6-2, US airlifts peace force 6-4, 441A1
US details Zaire rescue role 6-5, 441D1
FAO fears locust plague 6-12, 465E2
France ends Zaire exit 6-16, 478A2
Arab fund loan to Sudan rptd 8-17, 925F3
UN Assemb member 713C3
Iran shah bars aid to prevent ouster 11-18, 894A1
Sahara Conflict—*See SAHARA*

1979

MORLAND, Howard
Judge blocks H-bomb article 3-9, 193B3-194A1; 3-26, 230C1
Justice Dept admits documt security error 6-8, judge continues to block article 6-15, 713C1, E1
Sup Ct declines H-bomb article hearing 7-2, 559A1
Hansen H-bomb letter published 9-16, 9-18, 713G2; text 714E1-717E3
Justice Dept ends effort to halt H-bomb article publicatn 9-17, 713A1, D1, F1
MORLEY, Roger H.
McGraw-Hill vs Amer Express bid 1-15, suits filed 1-18, 1-19, 53E2, G2, A3
MORMONS—*See LATTER-Day Saints, Church of Jesus Christ of*
MORO, Aldo (1916-78)
CP ends govt support 1-26, 76A2
Kidnap suspects arrested 1-29–1-28, 98F1
Christian Dem, Vatican link to kidnap chrgd 2-7; CP asks parlt probe 2-8, 97D3-98A1
Parlt probe OKd 2-9, 136B1
Leftist arrests, death probe linked 4-7, 4-8, 269B1
Probe advances claimed 4-16, 313E2
Christn Dem hq attacked 5-3, 331G1
Death anniv marked 5-9, 372E1
More suspects arrested 5-30, 426D2
3 more suspects seized 6-6, murder weapon rptd found 6-19, 487B1
Red Brigades split revealed 7-25, 583G3
Cossiga sworn premier 8-5, 602G3
Suspect arrested 9-24, 793A2
MOROBE, Matison
Sentenced 5-11, 373F1

MOROCCO—*See also ARAB League, DISARMAMENT–Geneva Committee, NONALIGNED Nations Movement, OAU*
Osman resigns as premr, Bouabid named 3-23, 271E1
Foreign Relations (misc.)
Shah visits 1-23, meets newsmen 1-24, 49B3-G3
Shah leaves for Bahamas 3-30, 247B3
Egypt recalls envoy 4-7, 278D1
Egypt ties cut 4-27, 319C2
Hassan got Sadat plea re Jerusalem 5-3, 360G1
Islamic conf, Egypt suspended 5-8–5-9, 360D1
Spanish plane hijackers barred 8-4, 603G3
Zaire troop exit rptd 8-14, 733G3
UN membership listed 695G2
Iran scored for US Emb seizure 11-24, 895D3
Saudis capture mosque raiders 12-4, 916B1
Sahara Conflict—*See SAHARA*
U.S. Relations
US aircraft co admits paymts 1-3, 16F1
Shah asked to stay out of US 4-19, 297E3
US weighs arms aid for Sahara war 8-2, 592B2
Iran US Emb seizure scored 11-24, 895D3

1980

MORLINO, Tommaso
Italy justice min 4-4, 275F3
Cossiga wins confidence vote 7-31, 605A2
MORMONS—*See LATTER-Day Saints*
MORMONS for ERA
Va ERA rally rptd 1-13, 54C3
MORNING'S at Seven (play)
Opens 4-10, 392E3
Wins Tony 6-8, 692C3

MORO, Aldo (1916-78)
21 accused re kidnap-murder 1-2, 20E2
Mattarella slain 1-6, 20B3
Bachelet slain 2-12, 151C2
2 suspects arrested 2-20, 194E3
Freato linked to bank scandal 3-7, 212B3
More Padua arrests ordrd 3-12, 194B3
French seize more suspects 3-28, 255C1
Peci '78 kidnap role rptd 4-15, 294F3
Front Line suspects arrested 10-13, 791B3
Magistrate kidnaped 12-12, 966E2

MOROCCO—*See also ARAB League, GENEVA Committee, NONALIGNED Nations, OAU*
Human rights record scored 12-10, 978B3
Foreign Relations (misc.)
Sihanouk seeks support, cites Hassan advice 2-22, 141D2
Sovt phosphate purchases seen 2-25, 139F3
Cuba ties severed over Polisario 4-23, 2 tankers attacked off Africa 7-12, 563C2
Algeria blames for Berber unrest 4-24, 334D1
Sahara dispute condemned by OAU, Polisario entry shelved 7-1—7-4, 509E1
Cabt min at shah's funeral 7-29, 571G1
Libya mutiny rpt denied 8-18, 652A3
Islamic conf asks Israel UN ouster 9-20, 736C2
Hassan backs Iraq in Iran war 9-23, 719E2
IMF $1.1 bln loan rptd OKd 10-17, 778E1
Iran calls 'prime supplier' of Iraq 10-17, 798F2
Palestinian rights Israel exit from Jerusalem urged 11-28, 950F2
Spain recognizes Polisario 12-17, 995E3
U.S. Relations
US envoy briefs Hassan on Israel-Egypt talks 2-4, 89D2
US issues rights rpt 2-5, 87E2
Carter aides rptdly took oath re leaks 7-16—7-17, 549A2

1976

MORODO, Raul
Seized 3-29; freed, scores govt 3-30, 269A1
Scores govt reform plan 6-6, 459A1
MOROKHOV, Igor D.
Underground A-test pact drafted 4-9, 242C3
Initials underground A-pact 5-12, 371G2
MOROZ, Vanentin
Rptd in mental hosp 5-18, 421F2
MOROZOVA, Olga
Runner-up in US Open doubles 9-12, 716D1
MORRIS Jr., George B.
UAW contract talks open 7-19, 570F1, G1
MORRIS, John
Named min for Wales 9-10, 694A1
MORRIS, Joseph
Scores Trudeau econ remarks 1-11, 27G3
Rejects inflatn progrm 3-22, 238F2
CLC Cong. reelected pres 5-16—5-21, 401A1
On labor protest 8-12, 623B3
MORRIS, Robert
Loses Indep Party bid 8-27, 666D1
MORRISON-Knudsen Co. Inc.
Unit fined re boycott 4-19, 747F1
National Steel & Shipbuilding Co.—*See separate listing*
MORRIS (N.J.) View Nursing Home
Quinlan moved 6-10, 423G2
MORSE, Dr. Robert
On Quinlan treatmt 6-3, 423E2
MORSE Jr., Judge Thomas E.
Mass workers end strike 6-24, 921C2
MORTGAGE Bankers Association of America
Sued for home-loan bias 4-16, 285D2
MORTGAGES—*See HOUSING*
MORTON, Louis
Dies 2-12, 160F3
MORTON, Rogers C(lark) B.
Named Ford aide 1-13, pol role scored 1-14, 21F2-D3
Curtis placated on pol role 1-19, Strauss objcts 1-22, 41C2, F2
Bids Reagan withdraw 3-16, 196G3
Named Ford campaign chrmn 3-30, 233B1
Discounts Reagan TV speech 3-31, 233A1
Sees '76 Kissinger resignatn 4-4, remark clarified 4-5, 4-7, 245D2
Crossover vote 'a problem' 5-5, 322E3
Stresses Mich win 5-11, 343C1
Projects Ford win 6-22, 450G3
Strauss deplores GOP admin 7-12, 508G3
Scores Reagan delegate count 7-19, 531D3
Sees no 'lockup' on nominatn prior to conv 8-3, 563F2
See Connally campaign role 8-9, 584C2
GOP conv Watergate refs 8-16, 615A1
Campaign com chrmn 8-24, 688B3
Campaign duties reassigned 8-25, 631B1
MORTON Grove, Ill.—*See ILLINOIS*
MOSALA, Bernadette
Detained 11-25; released 12-8, 927C2
MOSALA, Leonard
At Soweto meeting 8-1, 579F2
Detained 11-25; released 12-8, 927C2
MOSBACHER, Robert
Ford campaign donatn rptd 10-22, 939A1
MOSCA, Giovanni
Resigns 6-21, 445C1
MOSCONE, Mayor George (San Francisco, Calif.)
39-day strike ends 5-8, 348F3
MOSCOW Idahonian (newspaper)
Ford endorsement rptd 10-30, 827G3
MOSES, Edwin
Wins Olympic medal 7-25, 575F3
MOSKOW, Michael H.
Labor undersecy 5-4; confrmd 5-12, 412G1
MOSLEMS—*See ISLAM*
MOSS, Sen. Frank E. (D, Utah)
On no-fault bill defeat 3-31, 234D2
On Ford, Cong budgets 5-12, 358G1
On Howe sex charge 6-14, 434B2
On Medicare fraud 7-28, 715C3
Sen rpts Medicaid fraud; backs legis 8-30, 715B1, C2
Unopposed in primary 9-14, 705G1
Us FPC gas rate hike 10-30, 868E2
Loses reelection 11-2, 819D3, 824G2
MOSS, Glen
Acquitted 12-2, 927A2
MOSS, Rep. John E. (D, Calif.)
GAO audit of HEW rptd 1-7, subcom rpts 1-25, 128C1
GAO scores FDA on stocks 1-19, 44D3
Vs Ford regulatory plan 5-13, 347B1
Warns FPC comrs impeachmt 9-1, 868A3
On Arab boycott compliance 9-7, 747B1
Vs FPC gas rate hike 10-30, 868E2
Reelected 11-2, 829A1
Scores air bag decision 12-6, 921E1
MOSS Jr., Rev. Robert V.
Dies 10-25, 970E2
MOTA Amaral, Joao
Leads Azores assemb 9-4, 812G1
MOTE, Rev. James O.
On parish secessn 11-28, bishop warns 11-29, 932F1
MOTION Picture Arts & Sciences, Academy of
Oscars presented 3-29, 240F2

1977

MOROSI, Junie
Wins libel suit 4-22, 326A2
MOROZOV, Platon D.
World Ct member 4G1
MORPHINE—*See NARCOTICS*
MORRIS, Joan
Canada union bars permit 8-31, 742F2
MORRIS, Dr. John
Chrgs unneeded hysterectomies 5-9, 732G2
MORRIS, Joseph
Vs wage-price curbs 8-17, 634F2
MORRIS Brown University (Atlanta, Ga.)
Johnson in NFL draft 5-3, 353C3
MORRISON, Dr. Alan S.
Smoking linked to early menopause 6-25, 620D1
MORRISON, Peter A.
Rpts US population shift 2-24, 184A1
MORRISSEY, Judge William J.
Sentences Hustler publisher 2-8, 118A2
MORRIS v. Gressette
Atty gen voting rights power upheld 6-20, 516B1
MORTGAGE Bankers Association of America
Anti-bias suit remains 11-11, 898C3
MORTGAGES—*See HOUSING, REAL Estate*
MORTON, Azie T.
Named US treasurer 6-7, confrmd 8-2, 626B3
MORTON, William Hastings
Killed 3-10, 238E3
MOSCOW, Michael
Replaced as wage price cncl dir 7-22, 626D2
MOSER, Col. Norbert
Sentenced in W Ger for spying 12-6, 969F2
MOSES, Edwin
Sets 400-mtr hurdle mark 6-11, 602A3
MOSKOWITZ, Stacy
Killed by Son of Sam 7-31, 641D3
Berkowitz to stand trial 10-21, 848D3
MOSLEMS—*See ISLAM; country names*
MOSLER, Hermann
World Ct member 4G1
MOSLEY, Glenn
In NBA draft 6-10, 584B2
MOSS, Frank E.
'76 spec interest gifts rptd 2-15, 128C2
MOSS, Rep. John E. (D, Calif.)
AF computer project scored 4-27, 421E2
HEW sets Medicaid cuts 6-8, 460E3
Gulf uranium cartel role probed 6-9, 480A1
Vs natl crime data svc 6-16, 480C3, G3
MOSS, Robert
Angola war rpt published 1-31, 86A1
MOSS, Rev. Robert V. (d. 1976)
Church of Christ pres elected 7-4, 642G2
MOSTEL, Zero (Samuel Joel)
Dies 9-8, 788G1
MOST-Favored Nation Status—*See FOREIGN Trade (U.S.)*
MOTA Pinto, Carlos
Portugal commerce min 3-25, 330E2
MOTE, Rev. James O.
LA priests deposed 8-5, 731A3
MOTELS—*See HOTELS & Motels*
MOTION Picture Arts & Sciences, Academy of
Oscars presented 3-28, 264B1

1978

MORPHETT, Tony
Last Wave released 12-18, 1030B3
MORPHINE—*See NARCOTICS*
MORRIS, Ill.—*See ILLINOIS*
MORRIS, Joseph
Retires as CLC pres 4-6, 266C2
MORRIS, Wayne
NFL '77 touchdown ldr 1-1, 56E2
MORRIS (the cat)
Dies 7-7, 620B3
MORRISON, Bret
Dies 9-25, 778F1
MORRISON, Daniel
Arrested 9-9, 723B1
MORRISON, David
On OPEC price hike, Eur impact 12-18, 978D1
MORROW, Rev. Edward
Ousted from Namibia 7-14, 547B3
MORROW, Vic
Message From Space released 11-17, 970B2
MORTENSEN, Kjeld
On Pnompenh conditions 1-22, 43B2
MORTGAGES—*See HOUSING*
MORTIMER, Charles G.
Dies 12-25, 1032C3
MORTON, Craig
NFL '77 passing ldr 1-1, 56A2
Cowboys win Super Bowl 1-15, 39F2
MORTON, Larry
Record wins Grammy 2-24, 316B1
MOSANTO, Steven
Sentenced 1-19, 95F3
MOSCATELLI, Capt. John
On Guyana cult death toll 11-24, 909F1
MOSCONE, George
Jim Jones pol ties cited 11-21, 891C2
Slain 11-27, ex-supervisor chrgd 11-29, 920G1-D3
MOSCOW Narodny (Soviet bank)
Rptd '77 world's largest bank 11-8, 914D1
MOSELEY, Mark
NFL '77 kicking ldr 1-1, 56F2
MOSER, Annemarie Proell
Wins world skiing titles 2-1, 2-5, 316D2
MOSLEMS—*See ISLAM; country names*
MOSQUE Inc.
Atlanta theater rescued 3-5, 293A2
MOSS, Dave
Loses primary for Ariz gov 9-12, 736B2
MOSS, Rep. John E. (D, Calif.)
Asks Sun Oil Becton purchase probe 1-27, 66B1
Matsui wins seat 11-7, 856D3
Shell trust probe rptd 11-28, 939D3
MOSS, Laurence
Coal Policy Project rpt issued 2-9, 184B2
MOSS, Les
Named Tigers mgr 9-21, 1026G1
MOSSADEGH, Mohammed
Sadiqi asked to form govt 12-17, 993F1
MOSTERT, Anton
Releases probe data 11-2, dismissed 11-7, 868G1
Info Dept probe papers confiscated 11-9—11-10, 904F3
MOTA Pinto, Carlos Alberto da (Portuguese premier)
Named Portugal premier 10-25, 830B2
Names Cabt 11-18, govt program OKd 12-13, 1022B1
MOTHERWELL, Robert
Natl Gallery commissn rptd 6-1, 578C3
MOTION Picture Arts & Sciences, Academy of
Oscars presented 4-3, 315A3
MOTION Picture Association of America
Valenti denies film industry probes 3-2, 251G2

1979

MORODER, Giogio
Wins Oscar 4-9, 336B2
MOROTONI, Yoshitake
Protests Sovt A-test 1-19, 52D1
MOROZ, Valentin
Freed in spy swap 4-27, Harvard U offer rptd 4-29; facts on 4-27, 317B1, G2
MORRIS, Butch
Spell #7 opens 7-15, 712E2
MORRIS, Frank E.
On FRB reserve requiremt cost 4-9, 303G1
MORRIS Jr., George B.
UAW reaches accord with GM 9-14, 698D2
MORRIS, Horace
Vs Carter Palestinian-US civil rights analogy 8-1, 575E1
MORRIS, Jack
AL pitching ldr 9-30, 955G3
MORRIS Jr., Joe Alex
Slain in Iran 2-10, 105B2, 176D3
MORRIS-Knudsen Co.
Teton dam defects rptd 11-28, 954C3
MORRISON, Bill
Flying Blind opens 11-15, 956B3
MORRISON, Philip
Cited in H-bomb letter 9-16, 9-18, 717E2
MORRIS v. Texas
Case declined by Sup Ct 1-22, 54E1
MORROS, Boris (d. 1963)
US drops Sterns '57 spy chrgs 3-22, 232E1
MORSE, Richard
What the Devil opens 4-16, 712E3
MORSE Jr., Judge Thomas R.
Sentences Mass man in rape case 9-24, 819G1
MORTAL Friends (book)
On best-seller list 7-1, 548D3
MORTENSON, R. Stan
Nixon tapes release OKd 7-24, 561F2
MORTGAGES—*See HOUSING*
MORTGAGE Trust of America
Investors suits vs advisers curbed by Sup Ct 11-13, 902A1
MORTON, Craig
NFL '78 passing ldr 1-6, 80A1
MORTON, Rogers C. B.
Dies 4-19, 356E3
MORUCCI, Valerio
Arrested 5-30, 426E2
Red Brigades split revealed 7-25, 7-28, 583E3
Threatened in Curcio letter 8-10, 635F2
MOSCONE, George (1929-78)
Peoples Temple pol activities probed by IRS 1-13, 117G3
Carter attends benefit 5-4, 347A1
Slayer convicted, gays protest 5-22, 386A1
Slayer sentenced 7-3, 547F3
Feinstein elected mayor 12-11, 946E3
MOSCOW, O.—*See OHIO*
MOSCOW State Symphony
US tour canceled 9-27, 774G3
MOSELEY, Mark
NFL '78 kicking ldr 1-6, 80F1
MOSELEY, Thomas E.
FBI ex-agent's statemt in SWP trial sought 1-16, 92D2
MOSER, Tom
Tellico Dam completed 11-29, 990C1
MOSES, Edwin
Expense paymts probe rptd 11-12, 956B2
MOSHED, Hassan
Sovt gas exports cut 7-28, 583B1
MOSK, Judge Stanley
Calif Sup Ct hearing ends 7-17, 869D2
MOSLEMS—*See ISLAM; country names*
MOSS Jr., Ambler M.
Panama chrgs treaties violatn 12-6, delay explained 12-7, 939D1
MOSS, Les
Fired as Tigers mgr 6-12, 619C2
MOSSADEGH, Mohammed (1881-1967)
Bazargan heads provisional govt 2-5, 81C1
New Iran party formed 3-7, 180B1
'53 coup book rptd recalled in US 11-10, 886F3
MOSTEK Corp.
United Tech buys 21% 9-17, 986A3
MOST Happy Fella, The (play)
Opens 10-11, 956D3
MOTAHARI, Ayatollah Morteza
Slain 5-1; Khomeini scores, 1000s protest 5-2, 321D1
Khomeini forms new militia 5-5, 353B3
Khomeini vs newspr article 5-10, 358B1
MOTA Pinto, Carlos Alberto da (Portuguese premier; resigned June 7)
At Brazil pres inaugural 3-15, 210E1
Resigns, govt falls 6-7; caretaker premr named 7-19, 427C2, 545F2
MOTEMADI, Brig. Gen. Nematollah
Executed 2-20, 125F1
MOTHOPENG, Zephania
Sentenced 6-26, 476E3
MOTION Picture Export Association
FTC opens probe 5-23, 430C3

1980

MORONY, Judge Jean
Sentences 2 Calif killers 2-27, 238D3
MORRIS—*See ILLINOIS*
MORRIS, Edmund
Wins Pulitzer 4-14, 296E2
Rise of TR wins Amer Book Award 5-1, 692C2
MORRISON, Dr. Alan S.
On saccharin cancer risk 3-6, 317A2
MORRISON, Bob
Wins Grammy 2-27, 296D3
MORRISON, Hobe
Wins Theater '80 award 6-8, 692D3
MORRISON, Jim
AL batting ldr 10-6, 926F3
MORRISON, Sid
Elected to US House 11-4, 844B3, 852C3
MORSEBURG v. Balyon
Case declined by Sup Ct 11-10, 868C2
MORTADA, Saad
Takes up amb post in Israel 2-26, 140E1
MORTON, Jelly Roll (1885-1941)
Elected to Recording Arts HOF 2-27, 296C3
MOSELEY, Mark
NFL '79 kicking ldr 1-5, 8F2
MOSER, Annemarie Proell
Wins Olympic medal 2-17, 155G2
Retires 3-16, 470A1
MOSER, Sir Claus
Statistics Canada rpt issued 3-14; cleared 4-1, 272G3, 273A1
MOSES, Mayor Winfield (Fort Wayne, Ind.)
On Jordan shooting 5-29, 401E2
Jordan case stymied 6-1—6-12, 442C2
MOSLEMS—*See ISLAM*
MOSLEM Students Association
DC protesters arrested 7-27, freed 8-5, 586F1; Iranian aid denied 8-9, 635D2
MOSLEY, Oswald
Dies 12-2, 1004A3
MOSS, Cruse W.
Named White Motor chrmn 4-23, 456D2
MOSS, Robert
Spike on best-seller list 7-13, 568B3; 8-17, 640E3; 9-14, 716B3
MOTELS—*See HOTELS & Motels*
MOTHER Courage (play)
Opens 5-13, 392E3
MOTHER Jones (magazine)
Reagan aide criticized 10-28, quits post 10-30, 817F3
MOTHER'S Day (film)
Top-grossing film 10-1, 796G3
MOTION Picture Association of America
'79 US revenues rptd 1-31, 120E2
'Cruising' opens, draws gay protests; Gen Cinema contract dispute cited 2-15, 239A3
Valenti praises copyright royalty fee divisn 7-29, 640G2

MOTION PICTURES

1976

MOTION Pictures
Dec '75 top-grossing films listed 32G3; '75 top rentals listed 1-7, 32F3
Peru cuts imports 1-12, 142B2
Cable TV curbs scored by House unit 1-26, Justice Dept 2-5, 135B3, D3
Top-grossing films listed 1-28, 104E3; 2-25, 208G3 3-31, 240B3
Bergman hospitalized 2-3, tax chrgs dropped 3-24, 271C3 ★
Sup Ct bars review of Manson film ban 4-19, 331C2
Bergman, Andersson to leave Sweden 4-22, 368D3
'75 top 500 indls rptd 437D2
US Dem platform text 6-15, 470D2
Sup Ct upholds anti-porno zoning 6-24, 478G3
Turkey sentences dir 7-13, 873G3
Carter sees execs, stars 8-22, 631E2, G2
Nigeria natlizes distributn 10-29, 1007C3
Sup Ct bars review of Calif pornography ruling 11-1, 868A1

Awards
Oscars presented 3-29, 240F2
Cannes festival 5-28, 460F1

1977

MOTION Pictures
Moreau weds Friedkin 2-8, 140G3
Gone With Wind in TV top 10 2-9, 119C1
Sup Ct bars retroactive porno prosecutns 3-1, 175F1
Argentina bans Emanuelle 3-1, 198C1
Polanski indicted for rape 3-24, 262D1
FCC pay-TV rules voided 3-25, Sup Ct appeal OKd 4-14, 376F2, A3
Polaroid instant movies unveiled 4-26, 409A1
Child porno films rptd 4-26, 5-15, 432D2, B3
'76 stockholder equity rptd 340A3
Christ TV film to be shown annually 5-16, 395E2
Canada rpt scores violence 6-15, 485G1
Polanski pleads guilty 8-8, 732C3
Canada union bars forgn stars 9-12, 742D2
Filmmakers given 1st Amendmt protectn 9-23, 921D2
Viacom-RCA satellite pact rptd 10-25, 921E1
20th Century Fox rpts Jan-Sept record profit 11-1, 1021D3
Washn OKs porno curbs 11-8, 879G2
Star Wars tops Jaws in domestic rentals 11-19, 1021B3
UN OKs Palestine film 12-2, 931E1
E Ger author visits West 12-19, 984A2

Awards
AFI honors Davis 3-1, 354G1
Oscars presented 3-28, 264B1

1978

MOTION Pictures
Top United Artists execs quit 1-13, 1-16, Albeck named UA pres 1-17, 75G2-B3
Canada prov censorship upheld 1-19, 111A2
Polanski flees US on morals chrg 2-1, 116A2
Film industry probes rptd 2-4, 2-11, 2-13, Valenti denies 3-2, 251D2
Columbia pres quits in embezzlemt scandal 2-9, indicted 3-31; film contract rptd 3-13, 251C1
Israel lifts TV war film ban 2-13, 112E3
Crawford estate auctioned 2-16, 172D2
Atlanta theater rescued 3-5, 293B2
Columbia stockholder suits filed 4-1, 251C2
Radio City Music Hall saved 4-13, 293F1
Sex abuse suit vs NBC OKd by Sup Ct 4-24, 322D2
Md obscenity rule review declined by Sup Ct 4-24, 322F2
'77 Fortune 500 data rptd 5-8, 325B2, C3, 326A1
Porno distributor sentenced 5-19, 396G3
Columbia names film chief 6-1, ousts pres 7-20, other chngs 7-21, 599C2
Solzhenitsyn scores 'moral violence' 6-8, 444E2, B3
Begelman fined in theft case 6-28, 599A2
New film indus probe set; Screen Gems, Deluxe Gen cases cited 7-14, 599F2-A3
Star Wars grosses $10.1 mln 7-21—7-23, world rental mark rptd 8-2, 672B1
Benchley book record price rptd 9-1, 759D2
Fox fined for 'block booking' 9-12, 759B2
Colson's memoirs premiere in DC 9-24, 844D1

Awards
Oscars presented 4-3, 315A3

N.Y. Releases
American Hot Wax 3-16, 618A3
Amsterdam Kill 3-30, 618B3
Autumn Sonata 10-8, 969B3
Avalanche 8-28, 969B3
Bad News Bears Go To Japan 7-14, 969B3
Barocco 4-7, 618B3
Battle of Chile 1-12, 618C3
Betsy 2-9, 618C3
Big Fix 10-6, 969C3
Big Wednesday 7-27, 969C3
Bloodbrothers 9-27, 969D3
Blue Collar 2-9, 618D3
Bonjour Amour 6-11, 618D3
Boys From Brazil 10-5, 969D3
Boys in Company C 1-31, 618D3
Brass Target 12-21, 1030E2
Bread & Chocolate 7-14, 969E3
Buddy Holly Story 7-21, 969E3
California Suite 12-21, 1030E2
Calm Prevails Over the Country 4-6, 618E3
Candleshoe 8-4, 969F3
Capricorn One 6-2, 618E3
Caravans 11-1, 969F3 ★
Casey's Shadow 3-17, 618E3
Cat from Outer Space 6-30, 618F3
Cat & Mouse 5-6, 618F3
Ceddo 2-16, 618G3
Celine & Julie 2-24, 618G3
Cheap Detective 6-22, 619A1
Chess Players 5-17, 619A1
Chuquiago 4-18, 619A1
Coma 2-1, 619B1
Comes A Horseman 11-1, 969G3
Coming Home 2-15, 619B1
Confessions of Winifred Wagner 3-23, 619C1
Convoy 6-28, 619C1
Corvette Summer 8-4, 969G3
Crossed Swords 3-2, 619C1
Damien-Omen II 6-8, 619D1
Days of Heaven 9-13, 970A1
Dear Detective 4-24, 619D1
Death On the Nile 9-29, 970A1
Deer Hunter 12-14, 1030F2
Dersu Uzala 1-13, 619E1
Different Story 6-13, 619E1
Dona Flor 2-26, 619F1
Dossier 51 12-12, 1030F2
Driver 7-28, 970B1
Duellists 1-14, 619F1
End 5-10, 619G1
Eyes of Laura Mars 8-4, 970B1
Faces of Love 7-7, 970C1
Fingers 3-2, 619G1
First Time 3-28, 619A2
F.I.S.T. 4-26, 619A2
FM 4-28, 619A2
Force 10 from Navarone 12-21, 1030G2
Foul Play 7-19, 970C1
Geisha 6-1, 619B2
Gentleman Tramp 4-26, 619B2
Get Out Your Handkerchiefs 12-17, 1030A3

1979

MOTION Pictures
FBI seizes stolen films in Ohio 1-8, intl probe rptd 1-10, 102D2
Sony video recorder copyright trial opens 1-22, 120E2
Buckley, Sitco partners settle SEC chrg 2-7, 132C1
Mineo killer convicted 2-13, 119E2; sentenced 3-15 240D2
Paramount resumes 'Warriors' ads 2-22, 174F1-A2
China Syndrome impact seen 3-13–4-1, 246D3
Daly companion sues estate 3-16, 289F2
Allied Artists files bankruptcy 4-4, 430G3
Marvin suit setld 4-18, 289B1
'78 Fortune 500 data rptd 5-7, 305D1, G1
FTC opens industry probe 5-23, 430C3
Wayne's will filed 6-20, 527C3
20th Century Fox pres, aides quit 6-27; plan Warner unit assn 7-4, 587G3
Steiger pre-nuptial agrmt upheld 7-5, 527D3
Fonda arts cncl appt defeat causes furor 7-20–8-8, 593D2-B3
Wayne, other film stars' deaths tied to '53 A-test 8-4, 630B1
Kerkorian trust case dismissed 8-14, 756D1
Life of Brian scored by religious groups, Warner Bros defends 8-27, other dvpts 10-24–10-30, 859D1-E2
UN previews Palestinian film 8-28, 643D2
Cocaine use cited 9-5, 972G2
L Blair pleads guilty to drug chrgs 9-6, 859C3
Paramount-EMI deal called off 9-12, 942F2
FBI admits '70 Seberg slander 9-14, 704G3
Bardot on sex in films 9-28, 860A1
Pope's US visit gets record coverage 10-1–10-7, 760E3
Neb porno case jury challenge refused by Sup Ct 10-1, 768F1
Video recorder use upheld 10-2, 858G2
'Jaws' viewed on TV by 80 mln 11-4, 1006F3
Malcolm X neutralizatn plan by FBI rptd 11-5, 886B3
Lugosi heirs publicity right denied 12-3, 1005E2
Begelman named MGM movie pres 12-18, 1007D1

Awards & Honors
Oscars presented 4-9, 336F1

N.Y. Releases
Agatha 2-8, 174C2
Alien 5-24, 527G3
All-Round Reduced Personality 4-23, 528A1
All That Jazz 12-20, 1007F2
All Things Bright & Beautiful 3-8, 528A1
Almost Perfect Affair 4-26, 528B1
American Game 4-28, 528B1
Amityville Horror 7-27, 819D3
And Justice for All 10-19, 1007G2
Apocalypse Now 8-15, 819D3
Apple Dumpling Gang Rides Again 8-31, 819E3
Battlestar Galactica 5-17, 528C1
Bell Jar 3-20, 528C1
Beneath the Valley of Ultravixens 5-11, 528D1
Beyond Poseidon Adventure 5-24, 528D1
Billy in Lowlands 1-31, 174C2
Black Hole 12-21, 1007G2
Bloodline 6-28, 819E3
Boardwalk 11-14, 1007A3
Boulevard Nights 3-22, 528E1
Breaking Away 7-17, 819F3
Buck Rogers 3-29, 528E1
Butch & Sundance 6-15, 819F3
Cage aux Folles 5-12, 528F1
Champ 4-3, 528F1
Chapter Two 12-14, 1007A3
China Syndrome 3-16, 246D3, 528G1*
City on Fire 9-14, 819G3
Class of Miss MacMichael 1-26, 528A2
Colonel Delmiro Gouveia 4-30, 528A2
Concorde Airport '79 8-3, 819G3-820A1
Cuba 12-21, 1007B3
Cycle 2-12, 174C2
Dawn of the Dead 4-19, 528A2
Despair 2-15, 174D2
Divine Nymph 10-12, 1007B3
Dracula 7-13, 820A1
Electric Horseman 12-21, 1007C3
El Super 4-28, 528B2
Escape From Alcatraz 6-21, 820A1
Fast Break 3-1, 174D2
Fedora 4-14, 528B2
Femme de Jean 1-8, 174E2
5th Musketeer 9-7, 820B1
French Detective 3-10, 528C2
French Postcards 10-19, 1007C3
Frisco Kid 7-6, 820C1
Going in Style 12-25, 1007D3
Goldengirl 6-15, 820C1
Great Bank Hoax 3-22, 528C2
Great Train Robbery 2-1, 174E2*
Hair 3-13, 528C2
Hanover Street 5-17, 528D2, E2*
Hardcore 2-8, 174F2
Head Over Heels 10-19, 1007D3
Hurricane 4-11, 528E2
I Am My Films 4-19, 528E2
Ice Castles 2-22, 174F2
In-Laws 6-15, 820D1
Innocent 1-11, 174G2
In Praise of Older Women 2-8, 174G2

1980

MOTION Pictures
20th Century-Fox names woman pres 1-1, 199B1
'79 US revenues rptd 1-31, top domestic rental films listed 2-6, 120E2
FBI 'Miporn' probe rptd 2-14, 136C1, B2
'Cruising' opens, draws gay protests; Gen Cinema contract dispute cited 2-15, 239F2
Loews film productn OKd by Dist Ct 2-27, 229D1
Tex porno film restraints voided by Sup Ct 3-18, 226E3
4 studios in Getty Oil pay-TV venture 4-22, Justice Dept to probe 4-24, 376D2
'79 Fortune 500 data rptd 5-5, 291F1
MGM to split film, hotel units 5-30, 501F2
Pryor burned in blast 6-9, released from hosp 7-25, 638C1
Donated porno warrants required by Sup Ct 6-20, 555G2
Racquel Welch marries 7-5, 639B1
Actors strike; home video mkt, minimum wages at issue 7-21, 684A3
Cable-TV distant signal, syndicatn limits lifted 7-22, 583A2
Copyright royalty fees divided 7-29, 640E2-A3
Evans pleads guilty to cocaine chrgs 7-31, 639B3
Flynn biographer sued 8-1, 639E1
'Caligula' ruled not obscene in Boston 8-1, 640B2
Getty Oil pay-TV plan draws trust suit 8-4, 639D3
Spain to ease censorship 9-8, 690B3
US boxoffice slump rptd 9-10, 732B2
Candice Bergen weds Louis Malle 9-27, 908F1
Columbia sued by Kerkorian 9-30; shareholders 10-7; dirs countersue 10-2, 10-20, 906D2
Evans gets probatn 10-7, 890E1
Actors end strike 10-23, 805B3
Heaven's Gate withdrawn by UA 11-19, 906A1
Warner, Franklin Mint merger set 12-24, 985B1

Awards & Honors
Oscars presented 4-14, 296F1, 376D1

N.Y. Releases
Airplane 7-2, 675G1
American Gigolo 2-1, 216A2
Angi Vera 1-9, 216B2
Any Which Way You Can 12-17, 1003F1
Apple Game 1-16, 216B2
Awakening 10-31, 972C3
Bad Timing/A Sensual Obsession 9-21, 836D2
Blood Feud 2-22, 216B2
Blue Lagoon 6-20, 675G1
Blues Brothers 6-20, 675G1
Borderline 10-31, 972C3
Bronco Billy 6-11, 675A2
Caligula 2-2, 216C2
Carny 6-13, 675B2
Changeling 3-28, 416E2
Change of Seasons 12-17, 1003F1
Charles and Lucie 5-9, 675B2
Coast to Coast 10-3, 836D2
Competition 12-3, 972D3
Coup De Tete (Hothead) 1-21, 216D2
Cruising 2-15, 216D2, 239F2
Death Ship 4-25, 416F2
Die Laughing 5-23, 675B2
Divine Madness 9-25, 836E2
Don't Answer the Phone 8-9, 675C2
Elephant Man 10-3, 836E2
Empire Strikes Back 5-21, 675D2
Fade to Black 10-17, 836F2
Falling in Love Again 11-21, 972D3
Fame 5-16, 675D2
Fatso 2-1, 216D2
Ffolkes 4-18, 416F2
Fiendish Plot of Dr Fu Manchu 8-8, 675D2
Final Countdown 8-1, 675E2
First Deadly Sin 10-24, 836F2
First Family 12-25, 1003G1
Flash Gordon 12-5, 972E3
Fog 2-29, 216E2
Foolin' Around 10-17, 836G2
Formula 12-19, 1003A2
Foxes 2-29, 216E2
Friday the 13th 5-10, 675F2
From the Life of the Marionettes 11-7, 972E2
Getting of Wisdom 8-5, 675F2
Gilda Live 3-28, 416G2
Gloria 10-1, 836A3
Guyana, Cult of the Damned 1-25, 216F2
Happy Birthday Gemini 5-2, 416G2-A3
Hearse 6-7, 675G2
Heart Beat 4-25, 416A3
Heaven's Gate 11-19, 906A1
He Knows You're Alone 9-26, 836A3
Herbie Goes Bananas 9-12, 836A3
Hero at Large 2-8, 216F2
Hide in Plain Sight 3-21, 216G2
Hopscotch 9-26, 836B3
How to Beat the High Cost of Living 7-11, 675A3
Human Factor 2-8, 216G2
Hunter 8-1, 675A3
Idolmaker 11-14, 972F3

1976

Obituaries

Arlen, Richard 3-28, 240C3
Bellah, James Warner 9-22, 1015B1
Berkeley, Busby 3-14, 240D3
Cambridge, Godfrey 11-29, 932D3
Cassidy, Jack 12-12, 1015C1
Cobb, Lee J 2-11, 160C3
Gabin, Jean 11-15, 970F1
Halop, Billy 11-9, 970A2
Henabery, Joseph 2-18, 192D3
Hornblow, Arthur 7-17, 716B3
Howe, James Wong 7-12, 716C3
Lang, Fritz 8-2, 816E3
Leighton, Margaret 1-13, 56E3
Mineo, Sal 2-12, 160F3
Nichols, Barbara 10-5, 970F2
Redfield, William 8-17, 892D3
Reed, Carol 4-25, 368A3
Richter, Hans 2-1, 124F3
Russell, Rosalind 11-28, 932F3
Servais, Jean 2-17, 192F3
Sim, Alastair 8-20, 892F3
Strand, Paul 3-31, 272G3
Trumbo, Dalton 9-10, 1015G2
Visconti, Luchino 3-30, 240G3
Zukor, Adolph 6-10, 444A3

1977

Obituaries

Astor, Gertrude 11-9, 952B2
Barrett, Edith 2-22, 164B2
Beale, Edith Bouvier 2-5, 164C2
Boyd, Stephen 6-2, 532E2
Brooks, Geraldine 6-19, 532F2
Cabot, Sebastian 8-23, 696E2
Castle, William 5-31, 452E2
Chaplin, Charlie 12-25, 1024B1
Clouzot, Henri-Georges 1-12, 84F2
Cortez, Ricardo 4-28, 356A3
Crawford, Joan 5-10, 452F2
Crosby, Bing 10-14, 872D1
Daves, Delmer 8-17, 696F2
Devine, Andy 2-18, 164E2
Finch, Peter 1-14, 84A3
Finklehoff, Fred 10-5, 872F1
Foy, Bryan 4-20, 356B3
Garnett, Tay 10-4, 872G1
Hawks, Howard 12-26, 1024B2
Hubley, John 2-21, 164B3
Hull, Henry 3-8, 264A3
Hyams, Leila 12-4, 1024C2
Johnson, Nunnally 3-25, 264B3
Langlois, Henri 1-12, 84C3
Marx, Groucho 8-20, 696C3
Marx, Gummo (Milton) 4-21, 356D3
Mostel, Zero 9-8, 788A2
Presley, Elvis 8-16, 695G3
Prevert, Jacques 4-11, 356E3
Rattigan, Terence 11-30, 952B3
Ritchard, Cyril 10-18, 1024G2
Rossellini, Roberto 6-3, 532F3
Tetzel, Joan 10-31, 872A3
Tourneur, Jacques 12-19, 1024E3
Vidor, Florence 11-3, 952F3
Waters, Ethel 9-1, 788A3
Wilcox, Herbert 5-15, 452F3

1978

Girlfriends 8-16, 970D1
Go Tell the Spartans 9-23, 970E1
Goin' South 10-6, 970D1
Gray Lady Down 3-10, 619B2
Grease 6-16, 619C2
Greek Tycoon 5-12, 619C2
Halloween 10-15, 970E1
Heaven Can Wait 6-27, 619D2
Hooper 8-4, 970F1
If Ever I See You Again 5-24, 619D2
Interiors 8-2, 970F1
International Velvet 7-19, 970F1
Invasion of Body Snatchers 12-21, 1030A3
I Wanna Hold Your Hand 4-21, 619E2
Jaws 2 6-16, 619E2
Joseph Andrews 4-13, 619F2
King of Gypsies 12-19, 1030B3
Landscape After Battle 2-9, 619F2
Last Supper 5-5, 619G2
Last Waltz 4-25, 619G2 ★
Last Wave 12-18, 1030B3
Let's Face It 7-14, 970G1
Little Night Music 3-7, 619A3
Lord of the Rings 11-15, 970A2
Madame Rosa 3-19, 619A3
Magic 11-18, 970A2
Magic of Lassie 8-3, 970A2
Matilda 6-22, 619A3
Medusa Touch 4-14, 619B3
Message From Space 11-17, 970B2
Midnight Express 10-6, 970B2
Moment by Moment 12-21, 1030B3
Mouse & His Child 7-7, 970C2
Movie, Movie 11-22, 970C2
National Lampoon's Animal House 7-27, 970D2
Near & Far Away 3-24, 619B3
No Time For Breakfast 9-15, 970D2
Nunzio 5-13, 619C3
Oliver's Story 12-14, 1030C3
Once In Paris 10-9, 970E2
Opium War 8-14, 970E2
Other Side of Mountain 3-24, 619C3
Paradise Alley 11-10, 970E2
Perceval 10-6, 1030C3
Piranha 8-4, 970F2
Pretty Baby 4-5, 619C3
Rabbit Test 4-8, 619D3
Rain & Shine 12-21, 1030D3
Renaldo and Clara 1-25, 619E3
Replay 7-10, 970F2
Return From Witch Mountain 7-14, 970G2
Revenge of Pink Panther 7-19, 970A3
Rubber Gun 4-24, 619E3
Same Time, Next Year 11-22, 970A3
Sea Gypsies 4-26, 619E3
Sept 30 1955 3-31, 619E3
Serpent's Egg 1-27, 619F3
Servant & Mistress 6-6, 619F3
Sgt Pepper's Lonely Hearts Club Band 7-21, 970A3
Silver Bears 4-20, 619G3
Slave of Love 8-14, 1030D3
Slow Dancing 11-8, 970B3
Somebody Killed Her Husband 9-29, 970C3
Straight Time 3-18, 619G3
Summer Paradise 3-11, 620A1
Superman 12-14, 1030E3
Teacher 5-13, 620A1
Thank God It's Friday 5-19, 620B1 ★
Unmarried Woman 3-4, 620B1
Up In Smoke 9-22, 970C3
Violette 10-9, 1030E3
Viva Italia 7-9, 970D3
Watership Down 11-3, 1030F3
Wedding 9-29, 970D3
We Will All Meet In Paradise 5-22, 620B1
Who Is Killing the Great Chefs of Eur 10-6, 970D3
Who'll Stop the Rain 8-25, 1030F3
Wild Geese 11-11, 970E3
Wiz 10-25, 970E3
Woman at Her Window 6-9, 620C1
Woman of Paris 4-13, 620C1

Obituaries

Acker, Jean 8-16, 708A2
Ahn, Philip 2-28, 196B2
Bakunas, A J 9-22, 777E3
Baldwin, Faith 3-19, 252C2
Barrie, Wendy 2-2, 196B2
Bergen, Edgar 9-30, 777E3
Betz, Carl 1-18, 96C1
Boyer, Charles 8-26, 708B2
Bray, John R 10-10, 888E2
Brel, Jacques 10-9, 888E2
Brown, Zara Cully 2-28, 196D2
Cazale, John 3-12, 252E2
Chase, Ilka 2-15, 196E2
Compton, Fay 12-12, 1032D2
Crane, Bob 6-29, 540E2
Dailey, Dan 10-16, 888A3
Daly, James 7-3, 620F2
Dauphin, Claude 11-17, 972G2
De Rochemont, Louis 12-23, 1032E2
Eames, Charles 8-21, 708E2
Eiler, Sally 1-5, 96F1
Estabrook, Howard 7-16, 620G2
Etting, Ruth 9-24, 778B1
Geer, Will 4-22, 356F2
Genn, Leo 1-26, 96B2
Greenwood, Charlotte 1-18, 196A3
Homolka, Oscar 1-27, 96E2
McCoy, Tim 1-29, 96A3
McGrath, Paul 4-13, 356B3
Messel, Oliver 7-13, 620B3
Oakie, Jack 1-23, 96B3
Robson, Mark 6-20, 540F3
Shaw, Robert 8-28, 708D3
Sheekman, Arthur 1-12, 96E3
Warner, Jack L 9-9, 778B2
Wills, Chill 12-15, 1032G3
Wilson, Michael 4-9, 356G3
Wood, Peggy 3-18, 252F3
Young, Gig 10-19, 888G3

1979

Jerk 12-14, 1007E3
Just Like At Home 4-19, 528F2
Just You & Me, Kid 7-27, 820D1
Kids Are Alright 6-15, 820E1
Killer Fish 12-7, 1007E3
Kramer vs. Kramer 12-19, 1007F3
Last Embrace 5-3, 528F2
Last Romantic Lover 10-5, 1007F3
Legacy 9-28, 820E1
Little Romance 4-27, 820F1
Lost & Found 7-13, 820F1
Love At First Bite 4-12, 528G2
Love On The Run 4-5, 528A3
Magician of Lublin 11-9, 1007G3
Main Event 6-22, 820G1
Manhattan 4-24, 528A3
Man, Woman & Bank 9-28, 820G1
Max Havelaar 1-20, 174A3
Meatballs 7-3, 820A2
Meteor 10-19, 1008A1
Monty Python's Life of Brian 8-17, 820A2
Moonraker 6-29, 820B2
More American Graffiti 8-17, 820B2
Muppet Movie 6-22, 820C2
Murder By Decree 2-8, 174B3
My Love Has Been Burning 1-4, 174B3
Nest of Vipers 9-7, 820C2
Newsfront 5-30, 820D2
1941 12-14, 1008A1
Norma Rae 3-1, 174C3
North American Irregulars 4-12, 528B3
North Dallas Forty 8-1, 820D2
Old Boyfriends 3-21, 528B3
One Man 7-27, 820E2
Onion Field 9-19, 820E2
On The Yard 1-18, 174C3
Orchestra Rehearsal 8-17, 820F2
Patrick 9-7, 820F2
Peppermint Soda 7-15, 820F2
Perfect Couple 4-5, 528C3
Phantasm 6-1, 820G2
Picnic At Hanging Rock 2-22, 174D3
Portrait of the Artist as a Young Man 4-21, 528D3
Prisoner of Zenda 5-25, 820G2
Promise 3-7, 528D3
Promises in the Dark 11-2, 1008B1
Prophecy 6-15, 820A2
Quadrophenia 11-2, 1008B1
Quintet 2-8, 174D3
Rape of Love 9-23, 820A3
Real Life 3-1, 174E3
Richard Pryor Live in Concert 2-15, 174E3
Rich Kids 8-17, 820B2
Rocky II 6-15, 820B3
Roller Boogie 12-19, 1008C1
Rose 11-17, 1008C1
Runner Stumbles 11-16, 1008D1
Running 11-2, 1008D1
Saint Jack 4-26, 528E3
Scavenger Hunt 12-25, 1008E1
Seduction of Joe Tynan 8-17, 820C3
Shame of the Jungle 9-14, 820C3
Shout 11-9, 1008E1
Silent Partner 5-10, 528E3
Soldier of Orange 8-16, 820D3
Something Short of Paradise 10-5, 1008E1
Star Trek 12-8, 1008F1
Stay As You Are 12-21, 1008G1
Sunnyside 6-1, 820D3
10 10-5, 1008G1
Teresa the Thief 5-5, 528F3
Till Marriage Do Us Part 7-20, 820D3
Villain 7-20, 820E3
Voices 3-13, 528F3
Walk Proud 6-15, 820F3
Wanderers 7-13, 820F3
Warriors 2-9, 174F3
When A Stranger Calls 10-12, 1008A2
When You Comin' Back, Red Ryder 2-8, 174F3
Wifemistress 1-6, 174G3
Winter Kills 5-17, 528G3
Woyzeck 8-24, 820F3
Yanks 9-19, 820G3
Your Turn, My Turn 1-27, 174G3

Obituaries

Allbritton, Louise 2-16, 176E2
Arzner, Doris 10-1, 860G1
Blondell, Joan 12-26, 1008B2
Brent, George 5-26, 432D2
Buchanan, Edgar 4-4, 356C3
Carroll, John 4-24, 356C3
Costello, Dolores 3-1, 272C2
Cousteau, Philippe 6-28, 508D2
Dvorak, Ann 12-10, 1008E2
Fleischer, Dave 6-25, 508E2
Foran, Dick 8-10, 671C2
Gargan, William 2-16, 176A3
Grenfell, Joyce 11-30, 932G2
Griffith, Corinne 7-13, 588A3
Haley Sr, Jack 6-6, 508G2
Hall, Jon 12-13, 1008A3
Kadar, Jan 6-1, 508B3
Kapler, Aleksei Y (rptd) 9-15, 756F2
Lyon, Ben 3-22, 272A3
Marx, Zeppo 11-30, 932B3
Massine, Leonide 3-16, 272B3
Muse, Clarence 10-13, 860G2
Oberon, Merle 11-22, 932C3
Parks Jr, Gordon 4-3, 356F3
Perelman, S J 10-17, 860C3
Pickford, Mary 5-29, 432D3
Ray, Nicholas 6-1, 508D3
Renoir, Jean 2-13, 176D3
Saville, Victor 5-8, 432F3
Seaton, George 7-28, 588D3
Seberg, Jean (rptd) 9-8, 704G3
Tiomkin, Dimitri 11-11, 932F3
Vance, Vivian 8-17, 671F3
Wayne, John 6-11, 508F3
Zanuck, Darryl F 12-22, 1008G3

1980

Immortal Bachelor 2-22, 216A3
Incorrigible 3-3, 416A3
In God We Trust 9-26, 836C3
Inside Moves 12-19, 1003A2
Jazz Singer 12-19, 1003B2
Just Tell Me What You Want 2-8, 216A3
Knife in the Head 4-23, 416B3
Last Married Couple in America 2-8, 216B3
Left-Handed Woman 4-2, 416B3
Little Darlings 3-28, 416C3
Little Miss Marker 3-21, 216B3
Magicians of the Silver Screen 12-26, 1003B2
Mirror Crack'd 12-18, 1003B2
My Bodyguard 8-1, 675B3
My Brilliant Career 2-1, 216C3
Night Games 4-11, 416C3
Nijinsky 3-20, 216C3
Nine to Five 12-19, 1003C2
Nothing Personal 4-18, 416D3
Nude Bomb 5-9, 675B3
Oh, God! Book II 10-3, 836C3
One-Trick Pony 10-3, 836D3
On the Nickel 5-4, 416D3
Ordinary People 9-19, 836D3
Outsider 6-3, 675C3
Popeye 12-12, 972F3
Prom Night 8-15, 675C3
Raging Bull 11-14, 972G3
Raise the Titanic 8-1, 675D3
Return of the Secaucus Seven 9-14, 836E3
Sam Marlowe, Private Eye 10-3, 836E3
Saturn 3 2-15, 216D3
Seems Like Old Times 12-19, 1003D2
Serial 3-28, 416E3
Shining 5-23, 675D3
Silent Scream 2-2, 216E3
Simon 2-29, 216E3
Small Circle of Friends 3-9, 216F3
Smokey and the Bandit, II 8-15, 675E3
Somewhere in Time 10-3, 836F3
Soupcon 3-26, 416E3
Stardust Memories 9-26, 836F3
Stir Crazy 12-12, 1003D2
Tell Me a Riddle 12-17, 1003E2
Terror Train 10-3, 836G3
Tess 12-12, 1003E2
39 Steps 5-2, 416F3
Those Lips, Those Eyes 9-9, 836G3
Tin Drum 4-11, 416F3
To Forget Venice 1-28, 216F3
Tribute released 12-13, 1003F2
Up the Academy 6-6, 675F3
Urban Cowboy 6-11, 675F3
Watcher in the Woods 4-16, 416G3
Wicker Man 3-26, 416G3
Windows 1-18, 216G3
Wrong Move 1-25, 216G3

Obituaries

Adamson, Harold 8-17, 675G3
Arnold, Elliot 5-13, 448B1
Barry, Donald 7-17, 608C1
Beaton, Cecil 1-18, 104F1
Brand, Millen 3-19, 279F1
Britton, Barbara 1-17, 104G1
Chekhova, Olga 3-29, 279A2
Collier, John 4-6, 360D1
Deutsch, Adolph 1-1, 104C2
Durante, Jimmy 1-29, 104C2
Edouart, Alexander F 3-17, 279C2
Emery, Katherine 2-8, 176A1
Farago, Ladislas 10-15, 876D1
Fielding, Jerry 2-17, 176A1
Froman, Jane 4-23, 360F1
Fuller, Frances 12-18, 1004F1
Garcia, Sara 11-21, 1004F1
Gardiner, Reginald 7-7, 608F1
Gear, Luella 4-3, 360G1
Griffith, Hugh 5-14, 448F1
Heindorf, Ray 2-2, 176F1
Hitchcock, Alfred 4-29, 360A2
Hoskins, Allen 7-26, 608B2
Iturbi, Jose 6-28, 528B2
Janssen, David 2-13, 176F1
Kaufman, Boris 6-23, 528C2
Kenney, Douglas 9-1, 755F3
Lesser, Sol 9-19, 755G3
Levene, Sam 12-28, 1004D2
Loden, Barbara 9-22, 756B1
Lye, Len 5-15, 448C2
Martin, Strother 8-1, 676B2
McCarty, Mary 4-5, 360D2
McQueen, Steve 11-7, 928B3
Medford, Kay 4-10, 360E2
Milestone, Lewis 9-25, 756C1
Nugent, Elliott 8-9, 676D2
O'Neil, Barbara 9-3, 756D1
Pal, George 5-2, 448D2

1976

MOTLANA, Nthato
Arrested 8-13, 624A3
MOTOR Carriers Labor Advisory Council
Teamsters pact agreed 4-2, 248D3
MOTT, Stewart R.
'72 campaign gift listed 4-25, 688C1
MOTT Haven Truck Parts Inc.
2 arrested 5-15, 5-17, 401B2, D2
MOTTL, Rep. Ronald M. (D, Ohio)
Reelected 11-2, 830B3
MOUDOUR, Ahmed
Niger coup try fails 3-15, 205G2
Executed 4-21, 483D2
MOULAY Mohammed Ben Arafa, Sidi
Dies 7-17, 716E3
MOULDER, Morgan Moore
Dies 11-12, 1015B2
MOUNTAINEERING
2 Americans climb Everest 10-8, 876B3
MOUNTAIN View, Calif.—*See CALIFORNIA*
Mt. EVEREST
2 Americans climb 10-8, 876B3

1977

Top Grossing Films
Airport 77 4-6, 264E1; 4-27, 356E2
Annie Hall 4-27, 356F2; 6-1, 452C2
Bad News Bears 8-3, 643B2; 8-31, 712G3
Black Sunday 4-27, 356E2
Bridge Too Far 7-6, 548G3
Deep 7-6, 548G3
Domino Principle 4-6, 264E1
Eagle Has Landed 4-6, 264E1
Exorcist II 7-6, 548G3
First Nudie Musical 9-28, 808G3
Fun With Dick and Jane 3-9, 184D3
Greatest 6-1, 452C2
Happy Hooker Goes to Washington 9-28, 808G3
Heroes 12-7, 1021B3
Kentucky Fried Movie 8-31, 712G3
King Kong 2-2, 120D3
Late Show 4-27, 356F2
Looking for Mr Goodbar 12-7, 1021B3
Network 3-9, 184D3; 4-6, 264E1
Oh, God! 10-19, 872G3; 12-7, 1021B3
One on One 8-31, 712G3
Orca-Killer Whale 8-3, 643B2
Other Side of Midnight 7-6, 548G3
Piece of the Action 10-19, 872G3; 12-7, 1021B3
Pink Panther Strikes Again 2-2, 120D3
Rocky 2-2, 120D3; 3-9, 184D3; 4-6, 264E1; 4-27, 356E2; 6-1, 452C2
Rolling Thunder 10-19, 872G3
Search for Noah's Ark 2-2, 120D3
Silver Streak 2-2, 120D3; 3-9, 184D3
Smokey and the Bandit 8-3, 643B2
Spy Who Loved Me 8-3, 643B2; 8-31, 712G3; 9-28, 808G3; 10-19, 872G3
Star is Born 3-9, 184D3
Star Wars 7-6, 548G3; 8-3, 643B2; 8-31, 712G3; 6-1, 452C2; 9-28, 808G3; 10-19, 872G3; 12-7, 1021B3
Sting 6-1, 452C2
You Light Up My Life 9-28, 808G3

MOTLANA, Nthato
Scores power-sharing plan 8-19, 657F1
Arrested 10-19, 803G3
MOTONO, Moriuki
Doubts 6.7% growth rate 985C1
MOTOR Carrier Safety, Bureau of—*See U.S. GOVERNMENT—TRANSPORTATION—Federal Highway Administration*
MOTORCYCLES
Carter environmt message 5-23, 404F2
Honda to build Ohio plant 10-11, 859E2
MOTOR Oil—*See PETROLEUM*
MOTOROLA Inc.
Forgn paymts rptd 3-23, 233G2
MOTOWN Industries
Leading black-owned firm 6-1, 519F3
MOTT, Sir Nevill F.
Wins Nobel Prize 10-11, 951G2
MOTTIN, Jean
Rpts newspaper mediatn fails 2-23, 159B3
MOTTL, Rep. Ronald M. (D, Ohio)
House votes busing curbs 6-16, 478D1
MOUNTAIN Bell—*See AMERICAN Telephone & Telegraph*
MOUNTAINEERING
Eric Shipton dies 3-28, 264F3
MOUNT Diablo State Park (Calif.)
Fire destroys 5,000 acres 8-2—8-7, 660G2
Mt. EVEREST
Eric Shipton dies 3-28, 264F3

1978

Top-Grossing Films
American Graffiti 5-31, 460E3
American Hot Wax 3-29, 272E3
Annie Hall 4-26, 356C1
Betsy 3-1, 196A1
Cheap Detective 7-5, 579F3
Close Encounters of 3d Kind 1-4, 24G3; 2-1, 116E3; 3-1, 195G3; 3-29, 272E3
Coma 3-1, 196A1
Convoy 7-5, 579F3
Death On the Nile 10-4, 800G3
End 5-31, 460E3
Fury 3-29, 272E3
Gauntlet 1-4, 24G3
Goodbye Girl 2-1, 116E3; 3-1, 196A1; 3-29, 272E3; 4-26, 356C1
Grease 7-5, 579F3; 7-26, 620D1; 8-30, 708A2
Greek Tycoon 5-31, 460E3
Harper Valley PTA 5-31, 460E3
Heaven Can Wait 7-5, 579F3; 7-26, 620D1; 8-30, 708
House Calls 4-26, 356C1
Interiors 10-4, 800G3
Jaws 2 7-5, 579F3; 7-26, 620E1
Lord of the Rings 11-29, 970G3
Magic 11-29, 970F3
Midnight Express 11-1, 888E1; 11-29, 970F3
Natl Lampoon's Animal House 8-30, 708G1; 10-4, 800G3; 11-1, 888E1; 11-29, 970F3
Pete's Dragon 1-4, 24G3
Piranha 8-30, 708A2
Rabbit Test 4-26, 356C1
Revenge of the Pink Panther 7-26, 620D1; 8-30, 708G1
Saturday Night Fever 1-4, 24G3; 2-1, 116E3; 3-1, 195G3; 3-29, 272E3; 4-26, 356C1
Semi-Tough 1-4, 24G3; 2-1, 116E3
Somebody Killed Her Husband 10-4, 800G3
Star Wars 7-26, 620D1
Thank God It's Friday 5-31, 460E3
Turning Point 2-1, 116E3
Up In Smoke 10-4, 800G3; 11-1, 888G1
Wedding 11-1, 888E1
Wiz 11-1, 888E1; 11-29, 970G3

MOTLANA, Nthato
Freed 3-23, 229C3
Denied S African passport 6-9, 536C3
Marks Soweto '76 riot 6-16, warned by police 6-19, 535B3, E3
Rpts Viljoen mtg 8-17, 669A3
Banned 9-6, 742D2
MOTLEY, Judge Constance Baker
Women rptrs gain locker room access 9-25, 1026B3
MOTORCYCLES
W Ger '77 sales rptd 1-20, 94B1
EPA proposes noise curbs 3-15, 186D2
Venez bans consumer imports 4-6, 332C1
US '77 deaths rptd 6-29, 636A2
MOTOR Vehicles—*See kinds (e.g., AUTOMOBILES, BUSES, TRUCKS)*
MOTTA, Dick
Bullets win NBA title 6-7, 457F1
MOTTL, Rep. Ronald M. (D, O.)
Reelected 11-7, 851G3
MOTTRAM, Buster
US wins Davis Cup 12-10, 1026D3, F3
MOUGLALIS, Albert
Convicted 5-3, 396B1
MOUNDIS, Nikos
Retrial rejctd 7-10; CIA implicated 7-24, convictn questnd 7-31, 631G2
MOUNTAINEERING
2 climb Mt Everest without oxygen 5-8, 420C2
4 Amers climb K2 in Pak 9-6—9-7, 843E2
1st Amer women climb Annapurna 10-15, 2 killed 10-17, 843G2
1st woman climbs El Capitan alone 10-26, 843A3
Mt. EVEREST (Katmandu, Nepal)
2 climb without oxygen 5-8, 420C2
Mt. GOODWIN Austen (K2) (Pakistan)
4 Amers climb without oxygen 9-6—9-7, 843E2
Mt. HOOD Community College (Gresham, Ore.)
Carter visits 11-3, 862B2

1979

Top-Grossing Films
Alien 6-27, 548G3
Amityville Horror 8-1, 620G3; 8-29, 672G3
And Justice For All 10-31, 892G3
Apocalypse Now 10-31, 892G3
Battlestar Galactica 5-23, 448G3
Breaking Away 9-26, 800G3
California Suite 1-10, 80G3; 2-7, 120G3
Champ 5-2, 356F2; 5-23, 448G3
China Syndrome 4-4, 271F2; 5-2, 356F2
Dawn of the Dead 5-2, 356F2
Deer Hunter 5-2, 356F2
Dirt 8-29, 672G3
Dracula 8-1, 620G3
Escape From Alcatraz 6-27, 548G3
Every Which Way But Loose 1-10, 80G3; 2-7, 120G3
Fast Break 4-4, 271F2
Good Guys Wear Black 4-4, 271F2
Grease 5-23, 448G3
Halloween 10-31, 892G3
Hardcore 2-28, 174B2
Ice Castles 2-7, 120G3; 2-28, 174B2
In-Laws 8-1, 620G3; 9-26, 800G3
Invasion of the Body Snatchers 1-10, 80G3
Late Great Planet Earth 2-7, 120G3; 2-28, 174B2
Love at First Bite 5-2, 356F2; 5-23, 448G3
Main Event 6-27, 548G3
Manhattan 5-23, 448G3
Meatballs 8-1, 620G3
Monty Python's Life of Brian 9-26, 800G3*
Moonraker 8-1, 620G3
More American Graffiti 8-29, 672G3
Muppet Movie 8-29, 672G3
Norma Rae 4-4, 271F2
North Dallas Forty 9-26, 800G3
Prophecy 6-27, 548G3
Rocky II 6-27, 548G3
Seduction of Joe Tynan 9-26, 800G3
Star Wars 8-29, 672G3
Superman 1-10, 80G3; 2-7, 120G3; 2-28, 174B2; 4-4 271F2
10 10-31, 892G3
Warriors 2-28, 174B2
When A Stranger Calls 10-31, 892G3
Wiz 1-10, 80G3

MOTLANA, Nthato
Meets with US' Jackson, domestic black ldrs 7-30, 617B2
MOTORCYCLES
'78 deaths rptd 4-20, 309B2
Calif odd-even gas rationing exemptn 5-9, 342F2
MOTOR Vehicles—*See kinds (e.g., AUTOMOBILES, BUSES, TRUCKS)*
MOTSEPE, Veronica
Sentence suspended 9-28, 774E2
MOTTL, Rep. Ronald M. (D, O.)
On anti-busing amendmt defeat 7-24, 559G2
MOUNTAINEERING
Unsoeld killed in Rainier avalanche 3-4, 272F3
2 climb Annapurna 5-8, 392G2
2 climb Gauri Sankar 5-12, 392F2
2 Yugoslavs climb Everest 5-13, 392A3
MOUNTAIN West Research Inc.
3 Mile I evacuation size, costs rptd 9-23, 743C3
MOUNTBATTEN of Burma, Earl (Louis Francis Albert Victor Nicholas Mountbatten)
IRA kills; UK, Ireland deplore 8-27; facts on 641A1
Ireland chrgs murder suspects, IRA statemt scores UK 8-30, 669F1, B2
Buried with honors 9-5, 669A1
Thatcher sees Lynch 9-5, 669A3
Pope's Armagh visit canceled 760A2
N Ireland security accord set 10-5, 792F3
Murder suspect convicted 11-23, 909F1-C2
Mt. EREBUS (Antarctica)
NZ DC-10 crash kills 257 11-28, 912C1
Mt. ETNA (Italy)
Erupts 8-4, 8-6, 639B1
Erupts, kills 9 9-12, 800B2
Mt. EVEREST (Katmandu, Nepal)
Unsoeld killed 3-4, 272F3
2 Yugoslavs climb 5-13, 392A3
Mt. GAURI Sankar (Nepal)
2 climb 5-12, 392G2

1980

Patrick, Gail 7-6, 608F2
Poe, James 1-24, 176A3
Raft, George 11-24, 928C3
Randolph, Lillian 9-12, 756A2
Renaldo, Duncan 9-3, 756B2
Robbins, Gale 2-18, 176B3
Roberts, Rachel 11-26, 928D3
Roth, Lillian 5-12, 448F2
Sandrini, Luis 7-5, 608G2
Schary, Dore 7-7, 608A3
Sellers, Peter 7-24, 608B3
Silverheels, Jay 3-5, 280A2
Stewart, Donald Ogden 8-2, 676B3
Stoloff, Morris 4-16, 360E3
Stone, Milburn 6-12, 528E3
Stratten, Dorothy 8-15, 713D3
Strong, Michael 9-17, 756E2
Temple Sr, George Francis 9-30, 756F2
Thomas, Billy 10-11, 876E3
Tobias, George 2-27, 176F3
Van, Bobby 7-31, 608F3
West, Mae 11-22, 928F3
Yravers, Ben 12-18, 1004D3
Zhao Dan 10-10, 876G3

Top-Grossing Films
Airplane 8-6, 640C3; 9-10, 716G3
All That Jazz 2-27, 200G3; 4-23, 360B1
American Gigolo 2-27, 200G3
Being There 4-23, 360B1
Black Hole 1-9, 40G3
Black Stallion 4-23, 360B1
Blues Brothers 7-2, 568G3
Brubaker 7-2, 568G3
Caddyshack 8-6, 640D3
Chapter Two 2-27, 200G3
Coal Miner's Daughter 3-26, 280G3
Cruising 2-27, 200G3
Divine Madness 10-1, 796G3
Dressed to Kill 8-6, 640C3
Electric Horseman 1-9, 40G3; 1-30, 120A3
Empire Strikes Back 5-28, 448G3; 7-2, 568G3; 8-6, 640D3; 9-10, 716G3
Fifth Floor 3-26, 280G3
Final Countdown 8-6, 640D3
Fog 3-26, 280G3
Friday the 13th 5-28, 448G3
Going In Style 1-30, 120A3
Gong Show Movie 5-28, 448G3
Hollywood Knights 5-28, 448G3
Hopscotch, 10-1, 796G3; 12-3, 948G3
In God We Trust 10-1, 796G3
In Search of Historic Jesus 1-30, 120A3
Jerk 1-9, 40G3; 1-30, 120A3
Kramer vs Kramer 1-9, 40G3; 1-30, 120A3; 2-27, 200G3; 3-26, 280G3; 4-23, 360B3
Little Darlings 3-26, 280G3; 4-23, 360B3
Mother's Day 10-1, 796G3
My Bodyguard 9-3, 716G3
Ordinary People 10-1, 796G3; 12-3, 948G3
Private Benjamin 12-3, 948G3
Shining 5-28, 448G3; 7-2, 568G3
Shogun Assassin 12-3, 948G3
Smokey and the Bandit, II 9-3, 716G3
Song of the South 12-3, 948G3
Star Trek 1-9, 40G3
Urban Cowboy 7-2, 568G3
Xanadu 9-3, 716G3

MOTORCYCLES
Noise rules set 12-24, 987D2
MOTOROLA Inc.
Job bias suit settled 9-23, 746D3
MOTTA, Dick
Fired as Bullets coach 5-27, hired as Mavericks coach 7-18, 656E3, G3
MOTTL, Rep. Ronald M. (D, Ohio)
Reelected 11-4, 843F4
MOUNTAINEERING
2 climb Statue of Liberty in protest 5-11, 668D1
MOUNTAIN States Legal Foundation
Watt named Interior secy 12-22, 979G2
MOUNTBATTEN, Lady Edwina (1901-60)
Nehru affair alleged 8-27, 890A3
MOUNTBATTEN: Hero of Our Times (book)
Nehru, Mountbatten love affair alleged 8-27, 890A3
MOUNTBATTEN of Burma, Earl (Louis Francis Albert Nicholas Mountbatten) (1900-79)
Wife, Nehru affair alleged 8-27, 890A3

1976

MOUNT McKinley National Park (Alaska)
Sen votes mining halt 2-4, 135A2
Mining curbs signed 9-28, 834B2, C2
MOUNT Sinai Medical Center (N.Y.)
Chalmers scores rpt on FDA 5-23, 392G1
New test for alcoholism rptd 12-3, 950D3
MOUNT Vernon, Va.—*See VIRGINIA*
MOUNT Vernon (Calif.) Memorial Park
Baron indicted 11-30, 991D1
MOUNT Whitney (U.S. warship)
In Intl Naval Review 7-4, 488B3
MOUNT Zion Baptist District Association (Oakland, Calif.)
Funds returned to Carter 8-10, 585C3
MOUNT Zion Deposit Bank (Dry Ridge, Ky.)
Closed 6-25, 495A2
MOUSSA, Maj. Bayere
Niger coup try fails 3-15, 205G2
Executed 4-21, 483D2
MOUSTAFA, Shoukry Ahmed
Rptdly sought as plot leader 8-6, 588A3
MOUZAWOIR Abdallah
In Malagasy 12-23—12-26, 1013C1
MOYNIHAN, Daniel Patrick
Votes vs PLO Cncl seating 1-12, 18C1
Seeks aid 'blackmail' 1-23; Ford, Kissinger reaffirm support 1-28, 67G1-68A1
Vetoes pro-Palestine resolutn 1-26, 59D3
Resigns UN post 2-2, 89B1
Ford upholds policy 2-10, 109E3
Successor named to UN post 2-25, 150C1
Endorses Jackson 3-1, 165D1
Campaigns for Jackson 3-6, 179B3
Lauds Israel A-bomb rpt 3-25, 243A2
Wins Sen primary 9-14; Abzug supports 9-15, 687C2
Campaigns with Carter 9-30, 742E3
AFL-CIO donatn rptd 10-22, 938D3
Elected 11-2, 817E2, 819F3, 821F2, 828D2

MOZAMBIQUE, People's Republic of—*See also NONALIGNED Nations Movement, OAU*
Portugal scores treatmt of natls 1-13, 52F1
Portugal suspends air links 1-14, 52D1
Listed as 'not free' nation 1-19, 20E3
Pvt homes natlized, capital renamed 2-3, 123D1
DePree confrmd US amb 2-4, 110A2
Portugal asks talks 2-7, 143D1
Machel mtg with Botswana, Tanzania, Zambia ldrs rptd 3-4, 175F1
'75 UK aid offer rptd 3-4, 175G2
Montero sees Castro 3-14, 251C3
Reeducatn ordrd in purges 3-16, 4-9, 403E1
S Africa guerrilla network chrgd 4-26, 428G3
US offers aid 4-27, 293E1, C2, 294A2, D2
US cites recognitn 4-30, in talks 5-5, 318B2, C3
Machel in USSR 5-17—5-23, 403C1
Portugal Friendship Assn bombed 6-5, 483C1
Sovt rockets fired on Rhodesia 6-10, 427B2
Sovt mil presence rptd 6-13, 467C1
Portugal to seek closer ties 7-19, 558F1
US Rhodesia, Namibia rebel aid asked 9-14, 681C1
Machel sees UK rep 10-2, 738D3
Rpt rebel training offered S Africa studnts 11-24, 927G1
Rhodesian Relations—*See 'African Relations' under RHODESIA*
MOZART: Cosi Fan Tutte (record album)
Wins Grammy 2-28, 460D3
MRS. Warren's Profession (play)
Opens 2-18, 1014B3
MSIKA, Joseph
Bars more ANC-govt talks 7-12, 522D3
Rhodesia conf delegate 10-14, 781E2
MUBARAK, Lt. Gen. Husni
In China 4-18—4-21, 275F2
Mediates Syria-Iraq border feud 11-24—11-25, 895B1
MUDDY Waters Woodstock Album, The (record album)
Wins Grammy 2-28, 460C3
MUDGE, Dirk
For Namibia independence 8-19, 654E1
Asks troops stay in Namibia 8-27, 660G3
Favors SWAPO role 9-14, 698A1
Adjourns const conf 10-19, 832A2
MUECKENBERGER, Erich
Ger Politburo enlarged 5-22, 381E2
MUELLER, Frederick H.
Dies 8-31, 680G3
MUELLER, Jiri
Freed 12-10, 1012B3
MUELLER, Peter
Wins Olympic medal 2-12, 158F3
MUGABE, Robert
Vs Sithole 9-10, 733C3
Sees ZAPU reps 9-27, 738A3
Invited to Rhodesia conf 10-12, conf set 10-16, 781C1, C2
Arrives Geneva 10-24, warns conf boycott 10-27, 797C1
Independnc bid fails 11-2, 831D3
Rejects intl fund 11-4, 843C2
Meets Richard 11-10, 843E1

1977

MOUNT Hood National Forest (Oregon)
Fire rptd 8-4, 660G2
MOUNT Victory Coal Co.
Guterma dies in plane crash 4-5, 286E3
MOUSKOS, Michael Christodouros—*See MAKARIOS*
MOVIES—*See MOTION Pictures*
MOVING Industry
ICC to curb 5-23, 423E3
MOWRER, Edgar Ansel
Dies 3-2, 264C3
MOYNIHAN, Sen. Daniel P(atrick) (D, N.Y.)
'76 spec interest gifts rptd 2-15, 128C2
Assassinatn plot rptd 2-23, 261A3
Asks halt to US IRA aid 3-17, 222E3
On intelligence com rpt 5-18, 386F3
Chrgs USSR wiretapping 7-10, 551E1
Vs US-Sovt Geneva plan 10-3, 750G1
Seeks Shcharansky release 11-17, 955B2
MOYO, Jason
Killed 1-22, 49D2
MOYO, Nassor
Named Tanzania home affairs min 2-13, 161E2
Kenya border shut 4-18, 392E3

MOZAMBIQUE, People's Republic of—*See also NONALIGNED Nations Movement, OAU*
UN Assemb member 4D1
Sweden to give aid 1-10, 23B1
Borders closed, Frelimo cong cited 1-15, 48C2
Frelimo cong held 2-3—2-7, econ program rptd 2-8, 136G3
Castro visits 3-21—3-23, 249F1, A3
Podgorny visits, signs pact 3-29—4-1, 247G2, 248A1
Young at UN conf, sees Machel 5-16—5-21, 399B1
UK-US team visits 5-30, 457D1
Portuguese natls rptd ousted 6-1, 467F2
Frelimo scored 6-9, 456C3
UN asks defense aid 6-30, 536E1
Coal mine blast 8-2, '76 explosn cited 768E3
US bars arms aid 8-4, 668B1
French min cuts short Africa tour 8-18, 662F2
US aid funds curbed 10-19, 815A2-C2; 11-1, 834D1
Refugees arrive in Portugal despite ban 11-6, 886G3-887B1
Cuba aides rptd 11-17, 896G1
Namibia contact group tours 11-21—12-7, 1016E3
US refugee food aid set 12-2; '77 UN, Sweden, aid cited 12-13, 1000B1
Rhodesian Relations—*See RHODESIA*

MTEI, Edwin
Named Tanzania finance min 2-13, 161C2
MUBARAK, Husni
Rioters sack home 43E3
MUDENDA, Elijah H. K. (Zambian prime minister; ousted July 20)
Named Zambia natl dvpt chrmn 4-24, 49CA2
Ousted 7-20, 583F1
MUDGE, Dirk
Forms new Namibia party 9-28, 770A3
MUELLER, Erwin W(ilhelm) (1911-77)
Awarded Medal of Sci 11-22, 952B1
MUFTI Mahmud, Maulana
Detained 3-14, 202G1
Bars Bhutto talks 3-20, 223E1
Detained 3-23, 259D1
Meets Libya forgn min 5-4, 348E3
Sees Bhutto on demands 5-11, rejcts referendum 5-13, 378E1, A2
Released 6-2, 450A3
Meets Zia, vote vowed 10-13, 803A1

MUGABE, Robert
Rpt ZAPU forms new front 1-6, 3F2
Front-line states back 1-9, 10D3
Sees Richard 1-10, 11E1
London ZANU backs Sithole, CIA link chrgd 1-14, 29D1
Smith rejects UK plan 1-24, 49E1
Banana arrested 1-25, 50B1
Vorster bars Smith pressure 1-28, 73B1
Bars Richard mtg 1-30, 72A3

1978

MOUNT Hood Stages Inc.
Greyhound trust award curbed by Sup Ct 6-19, 492A3
MOUNT Hood Stages Inc. v. Greyhound Corp.
Mt Hood trust award curbed by Sup Ct 6-19, 492B3
Mt. SINAI School of Medicine—*See NEW York, City University of*
MOUREU, Henri
Death rptd 7-20, 620C3
MOUSE and His Child, The (film)
Released 7-7, 970C2
MOUSSA, Ahmed
Overturns newspr seizure 7-12, 573F1
MOUTHWASHES—*See COSMETICS & Toiletries*
MOVE (radical group)
Phila blockades 3-8, 18 surrender 5-7, 410D1-C2
Warrants issued 8-2; police rout; cop killed, 12 chrgd 8-8, 645D1
MOVERS Conference, American
ICC rebuts defamatn chrg 6-30, 589F2
MOVIE, Movie (film)
Released 11-22, 970C2
MOVIES—*See MOTION Pictures*
MOVING Industry
ICC issues reweighing order 5-31; defamatn chrgs rebutted 6-30, 2 firms sued 7-6, 7-25, 589B2
MOYERS, Bill
Interviews Carter 11-13, 914C2
MOYLE, Allan
Rubber Gun released 4-24, 619E3
MOYNIHAN, Sen. Daniel Patrick (D, N.Y.)
Scores Sen Banking Com rpt on NYC 2-9, 87D1
Vs jets to Saudis 2-14, 97E2
Votes for Panama Canal neutrality pact 3-16, 177D2
Scores Ulster violence 3-16, 373B3
NYC ends teacher assignmt by race 4-7, 264E1
Threatens vote vs Canal pact 4-13, 256A1
Votes for 2d Canal pact 4-18, 273B1
Introduces NYC aid bill 4-25, 608A3
Vs Mideast jet pkg 5-15, 357E2
Backs USSR trade halt 7-12, 542A2
Sen votes conditnl end to Rhodesia sanctns 7-26, 588F1

MOZAMBIQUE, People's Republic of—*See also NONALIGNED Nations Movement, OAU*
Bank natlzatn decree rptd 1-4, 22D2
Limited port capacity cited 3-8, 170B1
Westn indep plan for Namibia backed 3-26, 248G2
Mar floods rptd 4-10, 331F1
Cabt shuffled, econ problems cited 4-22, 331C1
Israeli released in 3-way swap 4-23, 318B2
Namibia rebels OK talks 6-11, 475D3
Portuguese natls return OKd 7-2, 596G2
Westn indep plan for Namibia OKd 7-12, 547F2
UN Assemb member 713C3
Zambia rail link with Rhodesia opposed 10-7, reopens 10-10, 783F2, A3, E3
Polisario recognitn cited 11-10, 999G2
Rhodesian Relations—*See RHODESIA*
U.S. Relations
US econ aid authorzn signed 9-26, 734G1
US econ aid funds signed 10-18, 862E2

MSALA, Letsatsi
Arrested 5-4, 377D2
MUCHNICK, Hal
Dead End opens 5-4, 760A2
MUELLER, Arndt
Smuggled guns to jailed Baader gang 1-12, 22A1
MUEZZINOGLU, Ziya
Named Turkey finance min 1-5, 21E2

MUGABE, Robert
Facts on 59C1
Sees US, UK reps in Malta 1-30, 59E1, G1
Malta mtg ends 2-1, 120A1
Addresses UN Sec Cncl on pact 3-9, 192G3
Sees US, UK reps 3-11—3-14; rejects internal pact talks 3-14, 193B1
Claims civiln area control 3-20, 210A3

1979

Mt. RAINIER (Wash.)
Unsoeld dies in avalanche 3-4, 272F3
Mt. SOUFRIERE (St. Vincent)
Erupts 4-13—4-18, 399C1
MOVASSAGHI, Kamran
Assesses shah's wealth 11-25, 897C3
MOVIES—*See MOTION Pictures*
MOVILE Offshore Inc.
Shell accident liability case refused by Sup Ct 12-3, 964E2
MOVING Industry
ICC fines 45 firms 1-15, 92A1
ICC motor carrier damage case refused by Sup Ct 5-29, 421G3
O'Neal to leave ICC post 10-4, 831B1
MOWRER, Elizabeth Hadley
Dies 1-22, 104D3
MOWRER, Paul Scott (1887-1971)
Wife dies 1-22, 104E3
MOXLEY 3rd, Dr. John H.
Backs less radical breast cancer surgery 6-6, 471D3
Rpts Defnse drug abuse progrm lag 11-11, 972E3*
MOYLAN, Mary
Surrenders 6-19, 492E1
MOYNIHAN, Sen. Daniel Patrick (D, N.Y.)
Sen income limit delayed 3-8, 185F2
Kennedy discussn re '80 pres bid rptd 9-8, 680B1

MOZAMBIQUE, People's Republic of—*See also NONALIGNED Nations Movement, OAU*
Church-state tensns rptd 2-8, 215A3
Populatn, relig data rptd 215C3
Uganda govt recognized 4-12, 288C2
E Ger mil aid rptd 5-23, 406A3
UN membership listed 695A3
S Africa unions bar natls 9-25, 732E2
Zambia road link cut by Zimbabwe 11-18—11-19, 899D2
Cuba rptd training children 12-4, 12-10, 981B2
Zimbabwe Rhodesian Relations—*See ZIMBABWE*

MOZART, Wolfgang Amadeus (1756-1791)
NYC library buys Haffner manuscript 7-16, 672G2
MPHEPHU, Chief Patrick (Venda president)
Venda declared independent 9-13, 732B2
MSOMI, Ervomr
Umbatha opens 4-9, 712B3
MSOMI, Lawrence
Umbatha opens 4-9, 712B3
MSOMI, Phillip
Umbatha opens 4-9, 712B3
MSOMI, Welcome
Umbatha opens 4-9, 712B3
MTHEMBU, Susan
Sentenced 5-11, 373F1
MTHIMKHULU, Walter
Rhodesia dep parlt speaker 5-8, 354E1
MUBARAK, Husni
Sees Vance, US aid discussed 9-11, 677B2
Cites Iran threat to Bahrain, offers mil aid 9-28; Bahrain rejects 10-2, 752C3
MUELLENBERG, Kurt W.
Named GSA inspector gen 1-30, 92D3
Confirmed 4-10, 965A3
MUELLER, Gerd (Der Bomber)
Signs with Cosmos 3-6, 655E1
NASL scoring ldr 8-12, 654F3
MUELLER, Lavonne
Warriors opens 5-22, 712D3
MUEZZINOGLU, Ziya
Sees difficult IMF talks 5-30, 397B2

MUGABE, Robert
Rhodesian dispute role described 170C2
Lauds Carter re US trade ban 6-8, 434C3
Muzorewa repeats amnesty offer 7-10, 546A3
Vs Commonwealth Zimbabwe plan 8-7, 589G2, 590C1
To attend UK setlmt conf 8-20, 638E1
London conf opens 9-10, 675F2, F3

1980

MOUNT Hood Stages Inc.
Greyhound trust case declined by Sup Ct 10-6, 782C2
MT. LASSEN (Calif.)
'17 eruptn cited 3-26, 252D1
MT. St. HELENS (Wash.)
Erupts, evacuatn ordrd 3-26, 252D1
Erupts 5-18, death toll, devastatn rptd 5-18—5-23; Washn declared disaster area 5-21, 382A1
Damage assessed 5-24—7-4, eruptns continue 5-25, 6-12; photos 503B3
Cong OKs victim aid bill 7-2, Carter signs 7-8, 515F1
Reagan pollutn remark disputed 10-7, 10-8, 779C2, F2
MT. WILSON Observatory (Calif.)
Sunspots, gas motions rptd linked 8-7, 716A1
MOUSSAVI, Hussein
Named Iran forgn min 8-31, 671D2
MOUSTAFOV, Ismail
Wins Olympic medal 8-2, 622E1
MOVE (radical group)
9 convicted in '78 murder 5-8, 414A1
MOVIES—*See MOTION Pictures*
MOVING Industry
Household moving bill clears Cong 9-25, 9-30; Carter signs 10-15, 915G2
MOYE Jr., Judge Charles A.
Reduces chrgs vs Lance, 3 others 4-9, 291E3, G3
Closes Lance case 6-9, 459F2
MOYERS, Bill
Moderates pres TV debate 9-21, 721C3
MOYNIHAN, Sen. Daniel Patrick (D, N.Y.)
Intell oversight bill voted by Sen 6-3, 458E3
Warns of 'Soviet empire' 8-11, 612C3
Hoffman testimony cited 9-4, 713B2
Seeks Trigon probe 9-10, 754G1
Carter aide cleared in spy leak 12-5, 940B3

MOZAMBIQUE, People's Republic of—*See also NONALIGNED Nations, OAU*
Machel shifts econ priorities, backs pvt enterprise 3-18; shuffles Cabt 3-21, 234C2
Cabt shuffled again 4-3, 278D2
Currency exchngd, borders closed 6-16—6-18, 582A1
Army occupies rebel base, seizes S Africa arms 7-10, 565F1
Foreign Relations (misc.)
UN res vs Sovt Afghan invasn opposed 1-14, 25G1
ZANU dissidents freed 1-28, 80B2
S Africa arms smuggling seen 2-16, 195C2
At regional econ unity mtg, S Africa dependnc cited 4-1, 243D1, B2
IOC bans from Moscow Olympics 5-27, 420D3
Zimbabwe security vows rptd 5-30, 469B1
Morocco war vs Polisario scored 7-1—7-4, 509E1
S Africa rebel arms seized 7-10, 565F1
Machel in Zimbabwe 8-4—8-9, 674C3
UN Namibia talks scheduled 11-24—11-25, 967B2, C2
MOZART, Wolfgang Amadeus (1756-1791)
Amadeus opens 12-17, 1003G2
MR&R Trucking Corp.—*See under SMITH Transfer Corp.*
MSIKA, J. W.
Zimbabwe resources min 3-11, 198C1
MSUYA, Cleopa David (Tanzanian prime minister)
Named Tanzania prime min 11-7, 888F1
M-60 Tank—*See ARMAMENTS--Tanks*
MUBAKO, S.
Zimbabwe justice min 3-11, 198D1
MUBARAK, Hosni
Israel oppositn ldrs in Egypt 11-7—11-9, 863F2
MUCHACHI, C. M.
Zimbabwe public works min 3-11, 198C1
MUDD, Roger
Gets NBC post 7-1, 638F2
MUDDY 'Mississippi' Waters Live (recording)
Waters wins Grammy 2-27, 296G3
MUELLER, Gerd (Der Bomber)
Cosmos win NASL title 9-21, 770G1, C2
MUELLER, Herman J. (d. 1967)
Calif sperm bank donatns rptd 2-28, 990F2
MUELLER, Lavonne
Killings opens 6-5, 756E3
MUELLER, Leah
Wins Olympic medals 2-14, 2-17, 156B1
MUELLER, Merrill (Red)
Dies 12-1, 1004B3
MUGABE, Robert
Vs rebel assemb deadline 1-2, 7B3
Scores Soames 1-8, 31B3
Nkomo returns to Zimbabwe 1-13, 31D2
ZAPU registered as Patriotic Front, party symbol rejected 1-14, 49C1, D1
Truce violatns chrgd 1-15, 1-22, 48F3, 49A1
Returns from exile; scores UK admin, Muzorewa 1-27; ZANU dissidents freed 1-28, 80G1-C2

1976

Conf resumptn delayed 11-13, 862D1
Intra-ZANU clashes rptd 11-15—11-27, 1009B3
Vs new indepndnc date plan 11-16, Muzorewa denounces 11-17, 861G2
Sees Angola, Mozambique reps 11-19, 879A2
OKs independnc date 11-26; asks new interim govt plan 11-30, 893B1, F1
Muzorewa scores on electns 12-4, 914B3
Muzorewa-Smith pact seen, Muzorewa scores 12-14, 935G1, B2
ZANU chrgd in tea massacre 12-20, 1009A2

MUGANGA, Albert
Named forgn affairs min 11-13, 1012G2
MUIR, Dr. Calum S.
Rpts WHO cancer studies 6-3, 484A3
MUJIBUR Rahman, Sheik (d. 1975)
Bangladesh bars exile return 332B2
Electns postponed 11-21, 923G2
MUJICA Montoya, Emilio
Mex communicatns min 12-2, 907A1
MUKHERJEE, Samar
Scores rights curbs 1-5, 28F3
MULCAHY, Edward W.
Amb to Tunisia 2-17; confrmd 3-3, 186B2
MULCAHY, John A.
'72 campaign gift listed 4-25, 688A1
MULDER, Cornelius P. (Connie)
Threatens press restraints 8-14, 639F3

MULDOON, Robert D.
At S Pacific Forum 3-8—3-9, 179C2
In Australia talks 3-8—3-11, 187C3
Visits France 4-16, 372E3
Sees Mao in China 4-30, 439E2
Offers austerity budget 7-29, 589E3
On curbs vs S Africa sports 10-16, 910G2
On Australia devaluatn 11-28, 896G2
Dollar revalued up 12-20, 1013G1

MULLER, Amaury
Scores govt 3-20, fired 3-29, 287D3
MULLER, Charles J.
On Fruehauf sentences 6-30, 524B1
MULLER, Gerhard
Sentenced 3-16, 503F1
MULLER, Hilgard
S Africa recalls Brazil amb 1-2, 11C3
Sees W Ger forgn min 6-22, 447B3
At Kissinger-Vorster mtg 6-23—6-24, 446C3
Backs race policy reform 8-13, 653B2, 661C1
Vows no pressure vs Rhodesia 9-14, 681G2
MULLER & Phillips Export
Arab boycott rpt released cited 10-18, 786B1
MULLEY, Fred
UK defense secy 9-10, 693D3, 694A1
MULLOY, Walton F.
Sentenced 1-9, 43E3
MULRONEY, Brian
Loses PC ldrship bid 2-23, 188F2
MULTINATIONALS—*See under BUSINESS*
MULTIPLE Sclerosis—*See 'Diseases' under MEDICINE*
MULVEY, Judge Harold M.
Clears Bailey in Conn scandal 1-12, 271D1
MUNARIZ, Rev. Jose Miguel
Arrested 4-11, ousted 4-19, 403C2
MUNDEBO, Ingemar
Named to Swedish Cabt 10-8, 794C2

1977

ZAPU kidnaps 400 students 1-30, 73D1
Muller asks pact 2-2, 122A3
At Frelimo cong 2-3—2-7, 137E1
OAU backs Patriotic Front 2-4, 122B3
ZANU chrgd in cleric killings 2-7, 85C1
ZAPU urges Geneva talks resumed 2-22, 145A1
Owen vs Muzorewa, Sithole conf bar 4-11, 296G1
At front-line mtg 4-17—4-18, 296D3
Scores US conf role 5-16, 399F1
Rhodesia raids Mozambique 5-29—6-2, 413A2
Sees UK rep 5-30, 457D1
Muzorewa scores 7-17, 563G3
Civil war fears cited 7-25, 581F3
De Guiringaud cuts short Africa tour 8-18, 662G2
Owen, Young seek new plan support 8-28, 661B2
Vs UK-US plan 9-14, 735B1
Smith sees Kaunda 9-25, 810B2
Patriotic Front unity talks delayed 10-3, 810A3
Sees UK, UN reps 10-21, 875B3
Frictn re Smith-Kaunda mtg rptd 10-30, 875C3
Mozambique hq raid confrmd 11-28, 911C1

MUHAMMED, Elijah (d. 1975)
Hanafis take 134 hostage 3-9—3-11, 192G3
MUHAMMED, Vernell
Joan Little arrested 12-7, 992B1
MUJICA, Hector
Venez CP pres candidate 9-4, 867F2
MULDER, Cornelius P. (Connie)
Scores Young statemts 5-23, 399G3

MULDOON, Robert (New Zealand prime minister)
OKs N Ireland detainee immigratn 2-21, 258D2
Scores gen wage hike 3-2, 222D2
Holyoake named gov-gen 3-7, 222A2
In UK; affirms S Africa policy, scores Amin 3-31, 258A2
At Commonwealth conf 6-8—6-15, 487E1
Presents '77-78 budget 7-21, attacked re tax rise 7-22, 638G1, E2
Meets with ASEAN ldrs 8-6—8-7, 607B2
200-mi fishing zone declared 9-7, 729A3
Asks tap powers 9-8, 729D3
In US, sees Carter 11-9—11-10, 925E3
Scores anti-tap protest 11-14, 925A1

MULENGA, Sefelino
Out as Zambia lands min 4-24, 490B2
MULHOLLAND, Robert E.
Named NBC-TV pres 8-22, 658B3
Testifies on NBC Olympic deal 10-4, 950C1
MULLER, Hilgard
Vs Smith setlmt plan 2-2, 122A3
Replaced as forgn min 2-11, 160D3
MULLEY, Fred
Rejects AWACS 3-31, 360D1
US joint mil info exchng OKd 5-16, 379G3
MULTINATIONALS—*See under BUSINESS*
MULTIPLE Independently-targetable Reentry Vehicle (MIRV)—*See ARMAMENTS—Missiles*
MULUGETTA Alemu, Lt. Col.
Assassinated 8-3, 649C1
MUMPHREY, John W.
Indicted 5-12, pleads not guilty 5-18, 418B3
MUMPS—*See 'Diseases' under MEDICINE*
MUNDHEIM, Robert H.
Named Treas gen counsel 6-15, confrmd 8-2, 626B3
MUNICIPAL Assistance Corp. (MAC)—*See NEW York City—Finances*

1978

Sees Young 3-22—3-24, 248D3
Rhodesian interim govt frees supporters 4-13, 290G3
Sees Vance, Owen; asks Anglo-Amer plan chngs 4-14—4-15, 290E2
Asks Patriotic Front power, rejcts multi-party state 4-15, 290B3
ZANU plot denied 4-23, 455B3
ZANU legalized 5-2, 317F2
Blames security forces re missn deaths 6-25, 594B3
OAU speech, backs Namibia 7-18, 561B2
Backs US-UK conf, scores Nkomo mil effort 9-11, 740C3
Scores US re Smith visit 10-8, ZANU asks US exclusn from talks 10-12, 819B2
Martial law extended 11-10, 893D2
Claims oil depot attack 12-11, 955C3

MUGGERIDGE, Malcolm
Addresses laity conf 2-19, 294E3
MUGHRABI, Dalal
Leads raid on Israel, slain 3-11, 175C3
MUHAMMAD, Elijah (1897-1975)
Son quits as Muslim ldr 9-10, 810B2, F2
MUHAMMAD, Wallace D.
Quits as Black Muslim ldr, record cited 9-10, 810B2
MUJIA, Mario
Murdered 7-22; exec blamed 7-23, death protested 7-22—7-23, 8-4, 722B2 * 723E2-F2
MUKHERJEE, Subash
'Test-tube baby' delivered 10-3, 824E3
MUKHERJEE, Sunit
'Test-tube baby' delivered 10-3, 824E3
MUKHINA, Elena
At World Gym Championships 10-23—10-29, 928C3
MULDER, Cornelius P. (Connie)
In S Africa Cabt shuffle 1-25, 55C1
Sets Soweto by-electns 2-18, 134G3
Soweto cncl sworn 4-18, 314B3
Fails in bid for prime min, Info Dept scandal cited 9-28, 742D1
Named in Info Dept scandal 11-2, resigns from Cabt 11-7, 868D1, A2
Resigns party post 11-11, 905B1
Koornhof replaces 11-14, 904A3
Replaced as Transvaal ldr 11-25, 946D2
Info Dept probers score 12-5, 946F1
Botha blames for Info Dept scandal 12-7, 989D1

MULDOON, Robert (New Zealand prime minister)
Commonwealth ldrs hotel bombed 2-12, 110E1 *, A2
Commonwealth conf meets 2-13—2-16, scores regional shift 2-15, 121F2
Scores Japan trade policies 2-22, 498E1
Rpts Japan trade accord 5-23, 497G3
Presents '78-79 budget 6-1, 497G2
Wins parlt electns 11-25, 924F2
MULHAUSER, Karen
Scores mil abortn fund curb 8-9, 604G2
MULLANE, Ed
Iacocca support rptd 7-17, 642A2
MULLANEY, Joe
To coach Brown U 4-3, 272F2
MULLER, Edward
Fined in Rhodesia arms scandal 7-23, 616A2
MULLER, Robert
Cleveland ratings suspended 7-10, 663B3
MULLER, Robert O.
Scores Carter vets proposals 10-10, 878F1
MULLEY, Fred
On Aldermaston safety study 11-21, 964G3
MULLIGAN, Robert
Bloodbrothers released 9-27, 969D3
Same Time, Next Yr released 11-22, 970A3
MULLIN, Willard
Dies 12-21, 1032C3
MULTINATIONALS—*See under BUSINESS*
MULTIPLE Aim Point (MAP)—*See ARMAMENTS—Missiles*
MUNANGATIRE, Herbert
Newspaper banned 10-2, 784E1
MUNCHAK Corp.
Caldwell pensn upheld by NC ct 7-19, 656G1
MUNCIE, Chuck
NFL '77 rushing ldr 1-1, 56E3
MUNDEBO, Ingemar
Swedish budget, econ min 10-18, 822G2
MUNGUAMBE, Salomao
Named Mozambique external trade min 4-22, 331D1
MUNICIPAL Assistance Corp. (MAC)—*See NEW York City—Finances*
MUNICIPALITIES—*See CITIES, Suburbs & Towns*
MUNICIPAL Museum (Amsterdam)
Van Gogh painting slashed 4-5, 335E1

1979

London talks deadlocked 9-13; OKs white const role 9-24, 717F3
Chimoio camp destroyed 9-27—10-1, 778A2
Vs new UK const proposal 10-8—10-11, unilateral talks begin 10-16, 777B2
OKs UK const plan 10-18, transitn plan deadlocked 10-19—11-2, 844E1
Transitn talks continue 11-9—11-14, OKs UK plan 11-15, 881A1, B1
UK offers cease-fire plan 11-16, accepts gen terms 12-5, 936G3-937F1
Initials cease-fire 12-17, 960A1, D1
Signs cease-fire, other pacts 12-21, 976A3
Salisbury home attacked 12-22, 976B1
Tongogara killed 12-29, 976A1
ZANU separate electn role hinted 12-30, 976C1

MUGICA, Enrique
Injured in Basque riot 12-2, 929B2
MUIR, Malcolm
Dies 1-30, 104E3
MUJIB ur-Rahman, Gen.
Martial law lifted 4-7, 328G2
Deplores US Emb raid 11-24, 893G2-894A1
MUKHINA, Elena
Shaposhnikova wins Spartakaid gymnastics title 7-26, 799F1
MUKOME, David
Zimbabwe forgn min 5-30, 393E1
MULCAHY, Robert E.
Indicted on kickbacks 4-17, 985B3
MULDER, Cornelius P. (Connie)
Quits Parlt re scandal 1-24, 99B2
Rhoodie scandal chrgs rptd 3-10, 191D1
Erasmus comm clears Vorster 4-2, 270D1
Natl Party expels 4-6, 270F1
Forms new party 6-29, contempt chrg rptd 7-3, 567A2
Cleared of contempt 8-30, 732F3

MULDOON, Robert (New Zealand prime minister)
NZ$ devalued 6-21, budget speech rptd 6-22, 566A3
Australia trade union explored 8-21, 631G3

MULHAUSER, Karen
Accepts NOW abortion conf 1-22, 63G2
MULLEN, Jay
CIA-disputed article publshd 4-19, 309B3
MULLER, Louwrens
Quits S Africa Cabt 6-14, 469B3
MULLER, Robert O.
Scores VA 9-25, 725A2
MULLINS, H. Jackson
Indicted 5-23, pleads not guilty 5-24, 380D2
MULTINATIONALS—*See under BUSINESS*
MULTIPLE Independently-Targetable Reentry Vehicle (MIRV)—*See ARMAMENTS—Missiles*
MULTIPLE Sclerosis—*See MEDICINE—Diseases*
MUMPHREY, Jerry
Traded to Indians 12-7, 1002F2
MUNDAWARARA, Silas
Zimbabwe info min, dep prime min 5-30, 393E1
MUNDEBO, Ingemar
Presents '79-80 budget 1-9, 77C1
MUNETIC, Getruda
Tito marriage rptd 2-4, 176C1

1980

Smith favors Nkomo 1-31, 118E3
UN warns UK on fair electns 2-2, UK chrgs voter intimidatn 2-6, 118D2
Escapes assassinatn 2-6, 2-10, 118B3
Nkala barred from campaigning 2-10, 118B3
Soames warns re ZANU vote exclusn 2-12; meets 2-26, 162A3
Pre-electn violence 2-13—2-27, 162B2
Sees Walls, reassured on army coup 2-25, 162G1
Electns held 2-27—2-29, called fair 3-2; urges calm 3-3; win rptd; reactn 3-4, 161A1-162C3
Photo; facts on 161C1, 162A1
ZANU starts army integratn 3-5, 198C2
Sworn, names Cabt 3-11; vows fast changes 3-13, 198A1, E1
Black worker strikes rptd 3-21, 301A3
At regional econ unity mtg 4-1, 243D1
Freedom House scores electn intimidatn 4-11, 301D3
Walls named army head 4-15, 301C3
Zimbabwe indepndnc proclaimed; sworn 4-18, 301C1-G1
Pol clashes continue 4-18, 301F2
Asks more UK mil trainers 5-9, 5-30, 468G3-469B1
Mozambique security vows rptd 5-30, 469D1
Chrgs ZIPRA rebelln 6-27; excludes Nkomo from Matabele mtg, rift rptd 7-26, 581A3
Scores Morocco war vs Polisario 7-1—7-4, 509E1
Walls resigns army post 7-17, 568D1
Tekere chrgd with murder, no party interference pledged 8-6, 621A1, E1
Walls reveals electn void request 8-11, denies coup plot knowledge 8-17; asks Walls leave Zimbabwe 8-29, rpts formal dismissal 9-17, 731D2
In US visit 8-22—8-29; asks business investmt 8-26, meets Carter, Muskie re aid 8-27, 674D2
Zimbabwe joins UN 8-25, 643D1
Guerrilla violence kills 4 9-13—9-27; pledges anti-violence fight 9-25, 795F1
Urges vs Walls return 9-25, bar set 9-26, 755F1
Scores US Somali bases 10-9, 795C1
Rival guerrillas clash 11-10—11-11; considers disarming guerrillas 11-15, 888E3, 889B1
Nkomo supporters arrested 11-21, 946E2
Munic electns early returns rptd 11-23, 946B3
MUGABI, John
Wins Olympic medal 8-2, 622G1
MUGICA Garmendia, Francisco (alias Patxi)
Identified as ETA hit man 7-7, 367E1
MUHLELSEN, Markus
Left-Handed Woman released 4-2, 416C3
MUHLENBERG, Frederick A.
Dies 1-19, 104C3
MUHLER, Marie Sheehan
Loses US House electn 11-4, 848A3
MUIR & Co., John
Rubin to join firm 7-30, 638A3
MULDOON, Robert (New Zealand prime minister)
On Sovt amb ouster 1-24, 100B2
Visits China 9-11, 706D3
Overcomes party challenge 10-23, 830B3

MULHOLLAND, Robert E.
NBC managemt realigned 6-3, 501E2
MULL, Martin
Serial released 3-28, 416E3
MULLANEY, Thomas P.
Quits Dart post 7-23, 600B3
MULLER, Robert
Criticizes Carter 7-1, 496E1
MULLIGAN, Richard
Wins Emmy 9-7, 692C1
MULLINS, Billy
USC transcript scandal rptd 3-18, 469B3
MULLINS, H. Jackson
Fraud chrgs reduced 4-9, 292A1
Cleared on 3 counts, mistrial declared on 1 4-30, 332F3
US case dropped 6-9, 459A3
MULTINATIONALS—*See BUSINESS*
MULTON, Alycia
Loses AIAW singles tennis title 6-11, 607E1
MUNANGA, Paolo
Greets Obote on return 5-27, 446F1*
MUNANGAGWA, E.
Zimbabwe min of state 3-11, 198D1
MUNCIE, Chuck
NFL '79 touchdown, rushing ldr 1-5, 8E2, E3
NFC wins Pro Bowl; named game MVP 1-27, 175C1

1976

MUNN, Keble
On Kingston violence 1-6, 51C1
MUNOZ Ledo, Porfirio
Mexico educ min 12-2, 907A1
MUNOZ Marin, Luis
On statehood proposal 12-31, 994D3
MUNOZ Vega, Archbishop Pablo Cardinal
Scores Ecuador re bishops expulsn 8-16, 692F3
MUNRO, John C.
CLC quits 2 govt bodies 3-23, 238E2
CLC-govt mtg set 5-20, 401B1
Stays labor min 9-14, 692B2
MUNSON, Thurman
NL wins All-Star game 7-13, 544G1
AL batting ldr 10-4, 796B1, C1
In World Series 10-16—10-21, 815B2
Gets MVP 11-16, 952D1
MURATOV, Valery
Wins Olympic medals 2-10, 2-12, 158F3
MURDER on the Orient Express (film)
'75 top rental film 1-7, 32F3
MURDERS—*See under CRIME*
MURDOCH, Daniel
Arrested 5-25, 441C2
MURDOCH, Guillermo
Arrested 5-25, 441C2
MURDOCH, Omar
Seized 5-25, freed 5-29, 441C2
MURDOCK, Margaret
Wins Olympic medal 7-21, 575A2
MURDOCH, Rupert
To buy NY Post 11-19, 887E2
MURPHY, Austin J.
Elected 11-2, 830F3
MURPHY, Caryle
Angola expels 8-15, 649G2
MURPHY, J. Reginald
Abductor sentenced 9-17, 796E3
MURPHY, Jeannette
Banned 11-18, 927C3
MURPHY, Rep. John M. (D, N.Y.)
S Korea probe rptd 10-30, 11-13, 900G1
Reelected 11-2, 830A2
Scores Legion disease probe 11-23—11-24, 911C2 ★
MURPHY Jr., Rep. Morgan F. (D, Ill.)
Reelected 11-2, 829F2
MURPHY, Richard W.
In talks on Leb crisis 6-22, 448B2
MURPHY, Robert D.
Named to intelligence bd 2-17, 127D1
MURPHY, Susan
Escapes jail 8-14, 640A3
MURPHY, Thomas A.
On GM price hike 8-25, 647B1
MURRAY, Len
TUC OKs spending, tax pkg 7-28, 572D3
On unemploymt 8-24, 651B3
Scores UK IMF loan plan 9-29, 721A2
MURRAY, Lionel
Sees Healey on budget, rebuts Thatcher 4-7, 266B3
Vs spending cut, tax hike 7-22, 556B2
MURTAGH, Judge John M.
Dies 1-13, 56F3 ★
Successor named 1-16, 79A1
MURTAUGH, Danny
Dies 12-2, 932F3
MURTHA, Rep. John P. (D, Pa.)
Reelected 11-2, 830E3
MURTINHO, Helber
Police held in Death Squad murders 10-11, 850D2
MUSA, Omari
Loses election 11-2, 824F3
MUSARURWA, Willy
On Rhodesia violence 6-28, 487F3
Rhodesia conf delegate 10-14, 781E2
MUSEUMS—*See specific museums*
MUSHIMBA, Aaron
Sentenced 5-12, 386C2

1977

MUNIZ, Javier
Duran decisions 5-16, 395D1
MUNIZ Barreto, Diego
Kidnaped 2-16, 198A1
MUNN, Keble
Jamaica natl security min 1-4, 46C1
MUNNIK, L. A.
On pvt schl desegregatn 1-24, 67A2
MUNOZ Reyes, Fadrique
Bolivia transport min 10-13, 902D1
MUNRO, John Carr
On labor mins mtg 2-22, 158E3
Vs Japan econ criticism 9-29, 780C3
MUNRO, Ross
China expels 11-27, 946C2
MUNSON, Thurman
In World Series, demands trade 10-11—10-18, 806F1, E2
MUNYALA, James
Sets 3000-mtr steeplechase mark 6-9—6-11, 602B3
MURAYAMA, Nagataka
Dies 8-7, 696D3
MURAYAMA, Tatsuo
Named Japan finance min 11-28, 932A2
MURDERS—*See under CRIME*
MURDOCH, Don
Arrested on drug charge 8-18, 1021E1
MURDOCH, Rupert
Takes over NY Post 12-30-76, acquires NY Mag 1-7; names editors 1-8, 48B3
Morosi wins libel suit 4-22, 326A2
Beaverbrook chain purchased 6-30, 527B1
Felker group buys Esquire 8-26, 695A3
MURPHEYORES Inc.
Dillington rejcts Australia compensatn offer 9-22, 762D2
MURPHY, Angus
Indictmt dropped 3-17, 287G1
MURPHY, Charles B. G.
Dies 9-20, 788A2
MURPHY, Rep. John M. (D, N.Y.)
Child abuse bill cited 5-23, 432F3
Porpoise kill limit set 6-11, 442G3
Fights Nicaragua mil aid ban 6-21, 656A3
US tanker cargo preference backed by Admin 7-11, 538C2
Scores Panama Canal pact 8-17, 622A2
Cargo preference backing, GAO rpt scored 8-27; rebuts 8-29, 719E3
Cited in Park indictmt 9-6, 688D1
Cargo preference defeated 10-19, 815F1, G1
Scores TV violence report 10-24, 921A2
MURPHY Jr. Rep. Morgan F. (D, Ill.)
Offshore leasing bill blocked by Rules Com 10-25, 833G2
MURPHY, Thomas A.
Vs Admin auto emission stand 4-18, 322C3
Vs Carter energy plan 4-21, 320E1
'76 pay rptd 5-23, 408E3
MURPHY Oil Corp.
Loop license signed 8-1, 724E3
MURRAY, Eddie
Named AL top rookie 11-22, 927F1
MURRAY 2nd, Russell
Named Defense asst secy 4-1, confrmd 4-25, 418F1
MURTINHO, Helber
Rpts police on Rio 'death squad' 8-9, 633A3
MUSCHENHEIM, Dr. Carl
Dies 4-27, 356E3
MUSEUMS
'76 business gifts rptd 5-12, 409C2
MUSHIMBA, Aaron
Freed 3-17, 349A3

1978

MUNOZ Marin, Luis
Campaigns vs statehood 7-17, 627A2
House shot at, Soclsts seized 7-27, 627D2
MUNRO, Hector Hugh—*See SAKI*
MUNRO, John Carr
Meets Quebec, Ontario labor mins re constructn worker law 7-12, 7-20, 571D3
Phones judge 8-18, probe rpt prompts resignatn 9-8, 721C2
Aids Air Canada pilots setlmt 8-24, intervenes in IAM dispute 9-1, 686C2, A3
Scandal spurs rsignatn of Ontario solicitor-gen 9-9, 721D3
O'Connell replaces 11-24, 921E3
MUNSON, Thurman
Misses All-Star Game 7-11, 559G2
AL batting ldr 10-2, 928F3
Yankees win AL pennant 10-7, 779B1
In World Series 10-10—10-17, 799E3
MUNZZUK, Maxim
Dersu Uzala released 1-13, 619E1
MUQBIL, Abdul Salam
Executed 11-15, 885C3
MURAD, Helmy
Opposes pol curbs 6-1, 436F3
MURATOV
Named Geidarov assassin 7-4, 519A1
MURCHISON, Clint W.
Kirby '60 Alleghany proxy fight cited 3-24, 402A3
MURCHISON, John D.
Kirby '60 Alleghany proxy fight cited 3-24, 402A3
MURDANI, Gen. Benny
Pol prisoners to be freed 4-11, 288D3
MURDER—*See under CRIME*
MURDOCH, Don
Fined on '77 drug chrg 4-24, suspended by NHL 7-24, 656D3
MURDOCH, Rupert
Plans new NY tabloid 10-18, 865F1
Times, News strike ends 11-6, 865A2
MURDOCK, David H.
Pacific Holding plan to buy Iowa Beef rptd 11-6, 1005B2
MURINDAGOMO, Bishop Patrick
Administers Rhodesia oath 3-21, 210B2
MURPHY, Rep. Austin J. (D, Pa.)
Reelected 11-7, 852E1
MURPHY, Bob
3d in Houston Open 4-23, 355A3
Ties for 2d in Atlanta Classic 5-28, 580E3
MURPHY, Brian
Dismissal for FBI break-ins seen 12-5, 939A3
MURPHY, Calvin
NBA scoring, free-throw ldr 4-9, 271E2, F2
MURPHY, Rev. Hugh
Kidnaped, freed 6-18, 474E2
MURPHY, J. Reginald (Reg)
Asks Hearst release 10-8, 824C1
MURPHY, Rep. John M. (D, N.Y.)
Cleared by ethics com re Park gift 7-13, 527A2
Reelected 11-7, 851E3
PAC contributions rptd 12-24, 1008D1
MURPHY Jr., Rep. Morgan F. (D, Ill.)
Reelected 11-7, 850D3
MURPHY, Robert D.
Dies 1-9, 96A3
MURPHY, Rosemary
Cheaters opens 1-15, 760F1
MURPHY, Thomas A.
Sees Carter, backs inflatn plan 4-20, 361A3
GM price hike pledge rptd 4-28, 362E2
On '77 top-paid execs list 5-15, 364G3
Vows GM exec pay curb 5-19, 427C3
UAW Southn plant pact set 9-11, 699F3, 700A1
Scores Carter 'export consequences' order 10-10, 804B3
Vows GM price compliance 12-1, 934F3
MURPHY, William
Dies 1-29, 96B3
MURPHY Trophy, Dennis A.—*See HOCKEY—Awards*
MURRAY, Anne
You Needed Me on best-seller list 10-11, 800E3; 11-8, 888C1
MURRAY, Brian
Da opens 3-13, 887E1
MURRAY, Len
Scores 5% pay-hike policy 9-6, 763E2
MURRAY, Robert
Hosts Carter in Me 2-17, 123E1
MURTAUGH, Arthur
Testifies at House com King hearings 11-17, 898C3
MURTHA, Rep. John P. (D, Pa.)
Reelected 11-7, 852D1
MURTOPO, Gen. Ali
Rpts Timor, W Irian clashes 4-15, 318B3
MURUROA Atoll
French neutron bomb test rptd 4-17, govt denies 4-24, 312G3
French underground A-test 7-19, 649D2
MUSCIO, Joseph A.
Chrgd in rattler attack 10-17, 841F2
MUSCULAR Dystrophy—*See MEDICINE—Diseases*
MUSEUM of Modern Art (Rio de Janeiro, Brazil)
Fire destroys 100 paintings 7-8, 579A2
MUSEUMS—*See museum names*
MUSGROVE, Malcolm
Fired as Sting coach 6-16, 707D3
MUSHIER, Carole
Elected AIAW pres 1-11, 40C3

1979

MUNIZ, Carlos
Slain in PR 4-18, 350G2
MUNOZ Vazquez, Gen. Agustin
Murdered 3-5, 191E3
Assassins arrested 7-27, 585D3
MUN Pa Shik
Jailed 7-31, 617F3
MUNRO, John Carr
In Trudeau shadow cabt 7-19, 563F2
MUNROE, F. Craig
Rules on BC libel suit 1-17, 57D2
MUNSON, Judge Howard
OKs United Tech-Carrier takeover 1-31, 349G3
MUNSON, Thurman
Killed in jet crash 8-2, 671A3
Death blamed on pilot error 9-16, 1002F3
MUPPET Movie, The (film)
Released 6-22, 820C2
Top-grossing film 8-29, 672G3
MUPPETS (puppets)
Win Grammy 2-16, 336F3
MUPPET Show, The (recording)
Wins Grammy 2-16, 336F3
MURCER, Bobby
Traded to Yankees 6-26, 1002A3
MURCHISON, Clint
Brother dies 6-14, 508C3
MURCHISON, John D.
Dies 6-14, 508C3
MURDER—*See under CRIME*
MURDER at the Howard Johnson's (play)
Opens 5-17, 712E1
MURDER By Decree (film)
Released 2-8, 174B3
MURDOCH, Rupert
Australia pol rptg scored 9-15, 749C2
Drops Australia press takeover bid 11-22, 906G2
Scores Fairfax-Herald link 11-26, 966B3
Named Ansett chief exec 12-18, 966E3
MURDOCK, Abe
Dies 9-15, 756C3
MURENBERG, Lory
Dark at the Top opens 11-29, 956A3
MURPHY, Brian
FBI retiremt rptd 1-26, 92A3
MURPHY, Calvin
NBA free-throw ldr 4-8, 290F2
MURPHY, Frank (1890-1949)
FDR Cabt role cited 7-27, 577E1
MURPHY, Gardner
Dies 3-19, 272D3
MURPHY, J. Reginald
Abductor parole rptd set 12-18, 1005E3
MURPHY, Judge James M.
Sentncs Harper to death 11-7, 891A1
MURPHY, Jeanette
'76 ban lifted 9-17, 732F2
MURPHY, Rep. John M. (D, N.Y.)
Merchant Marine Com chrmn 1-24, 71E1
Loses Commerce oversight subcom chair 1-30, 86F3
Canal treaty implementatn bill clears House 6-21, 481D1
MURPHY, Leslie
Quits NEB 11-20, 949E3
MURPHY, Michael
Class of Miss MacMichael released 1-26, 528A2
Rat's Nest opens 2-2, 292D2
Manhattan released 4-24, 528B3
MURPHY, Morna
Shelley opens 4-14, 712D2
MURPHY, Thomas A.
Vs Chrysler aid, asks fed regulatn reform 8-2, 576G3
MURPHY Trophy, Dennis A.—*See HOCKEY—Awards*
MURRAY, Anne
Wins Grammy 2-16, 336D3
MURRAY, Bill
Meatballs released 7-3, 820A2
MURRAY, Judge Brenda
Clears Seaboard of trust chrgs 2-22, 205G3
MURRAY, David
Spell #7 opens 7-15, 712E2
MURRAY, Eddie
In World Series 10-10—10-17, 816B1
MURRAY, Len
Sees Thatcher 6-25, govt scored 6-27, 502F3
Scores proposed union curbs 7-9, 524G2
Scores trade union reforms 12-7, 949D2
MURRAY, Peg
Lovely Sunday opens 1-21, 292A2
MURRELL, John Paul (Speedy)
Indicted 3-15, 309D2
MURRET, Charles
Oswald crime links detailed 7-17, 538A2
MUSA, Said
Wins parlt seat 11-21, 907B1
MUSE, Clarence
Dies 10-13, 860G2
MUSEUM of Modern Art (N.Y., N.Y.)
Rockefeller dies 1-26, 104F1
Rockefeller art bequeathed 2-9, 173E2
Steichen works to go to Rochester museum 3-24, 375E2
Film dept wins Oscar 4-9, 336C2
MUSEUM of Natural History (Cleveland, O.)
New hominid species claimed 1-18, 137F3
MUSEUM of Primitive Art (N.Y., N.Y.)
Rockefeller dies 1-26, 104G1
MUSEUMS—*See also museum names*
US grants $7.4 mln 9-5, 892A2
MUSEVENI, Yoweri
Removed from Cabt post 11-19, 998G1
MUSHIER, Carole
Backs Title IX sports guidelines 12-4, 1000B3

1980

MUNKELT, Thomas
Wins Olympic medal 7-27, 624A1
MUNOZ, Anthony
In NFL draft 4-29, 336E2
MUNOZ Marin, Luis
Dies 4-30, 360E2
MUNRO, J. Richard
Named Time pres 5-15, 456E2
MUNRO, James
4th chrgd in 'freeway murders' 8-22, 727G1
MUNRO, John Carr
Canada Indian affairs min 3-3, 171A2
MUNSON, Thurman (1947-79)
Family files wrongful-death suit 2-27, 637E1
MUNSTER, George
Book banned 11-9, 885D1
Book ban upheld by High Ct 12-1, 919E2
MUPPET Movie, The (recording)
Henson, Williams win Grammy 2-27, 296G3
MURCH, Walter
Wins Oscar 4-14, 296A2
MURCHISON Jr., Clint W.
Heads Allegheny Ludlum Steel purchase 11-12, 985D2
MURDER—*See CRIME—Murder*
MURDOCH, Rupert
Eximbank loan offer to Ansett, mtg with Carter sparks probe 2-19, 989D1, E1
Cue NY purchase agrmt rptd 3-4, 239G1
New West sale rptd 8-27, 732F3
Melbourne TV, Ansett deal rptd vetoed 9-29, 747G3
MURKOWSKI, Frank H.
Wins Alaska US Sen primary 8-26, 683F1
Elected to US Sen 11-4, 840C1, 846A1, 852F1
MURMANSK Shipping Co.
Sovt freighter rptd seized in Canada debt dispute 10-22, 828F2
MURPHY, Rep. Austin J. (D, Pa.)
Reelected 11-4, 844E1
MURPHY, Betty Southard
Donovan named Labor secy 12-16, 955B3
MURPHY, Calvin
NBA free-throw ldr 3-30, 278D3
MURPHY, Dale
NL batting ldr 10-6, 926E2, F2
MURPHY, Dwayne
Wins Golden Glove Award 12-6, 926D1
MURPHY, Elvin
Chrgd in kidnaping 3-2, 238E2
MURPHY, Rep. John M. (D, N.Y.)
Facts on 81F1
Linked to bribery in Abscam probe 2-2, 2-3, 81C1, 82F1
Votes for Abscam evidence request res 2-27, 143G2
Indicted in Abscam probe 6-18, 454F1-D2
Abscam judge quits case 8-7, 599E3*
Wins NY primary 9-9, 682D2
At Somoza funeral 9-17, 721E1
Loses reelectn 11-4, 846A2, 848C3
Convicted in Abscam case 12-3, 919D1
MURPHY, Richard W.
Escapes Manila bomb blast 10-19, 809E1
MURPHY, Thomas A.
GM retiremt, replacemt set 9-9, 701G3
MURPHY Oil Corp.
'79 price violatns chrgd 3-25, 248E2
MURRA, Prokop
Rptd Albania industry min 5-2, 356E2
MURRAY, Eddie
AL batting ldr 10-6, 926E3
MURRAY, John
Ritz NJ casino project, Abscam linked 2-5, 111A1
MURRAY, Len
Steelworkers strike 1-2, 6F3
'Day of Actn' strike fails 5-14, 373C1
TUC rejects wage restraint 9-3, 688C2
Govt rejects TUC econ plan 10-14, 790E3
Scores new govt econ measures 11-24, 901B3
MURRAY, Lowell
On Clark leadership 2-18, 121G1
MURRAY, Adm. Stuart S. (ret)
Dies 9-19, 756D1
MURRAY, William J.
Apolgizes in schl prayer dispute 5-9, 471F2
MURTHA, Rep. John P. (D, Pa.)
Facts on 81F1
Linked to bribery in Abscam probe 2-2, 2-3, 81A2, 82F1
Named in Abscam probe indictmt 6-18, 454G1
Reelected 11-4, 844C1, 848F3
Testifies at Abscam trial 11-21; Murphy, Thompson convicted 12-3, 919F1
MUSCARE, Frank
Jailed 2-21—3-13, 187G2
MUSCLE Training Illustrated (magazine)
Ferrigno wins suit 11-13, 890F2
MUSEUMS
Titian forgeries chrgd 2-26, 472B3

1976

MUSHROOMS—*See FRUITS & Vegetables*
MUSHTAQUE Ahmed, Khandakar
Arrested 11-29, 923E2

MUSIC
US orchestras get grants 1-12, 32E3
Top-selling records listed 1-28, 104F3
Denmark bars Taiwan opera 8-21, 712G1
Czech rock stars sentncd 9-3, 9-23, 851E3
Cong clears copyright revisn bill 9-30, 764E3; signed 10-19, 982G1
'60-75 consumer spending on records rptd 11-23, 959G2

Awards
Grammy, Hall of Fame 2-28, 460F2, E3
Rubinstein gets Freedom Medal 4-1, 504B3
Rorem, Joplin win Pulitzers 5-3, 352D3, F3
Barber gets Arts Inst medal 5-19, 504C3

1977

MUSHTAQUE Ahmed, Khandakar
Sentenced 2-26, 183C1
Acquitted of 2d chrg 3-10, 309G1
MUSIAL, Joe
Dies 6-6, 532D3
MUSIC
Barshai emigrates to Israel 1-30, 117G1
'76 business gifts rptd 5-12, 409C2
Jazz musicians leave for Cuba tour 5-15, 390G1; give concert 5-18, 456E2
Australia picks natl song 5-21, 447G1
Presley records sold out 8-18, 696C1
E Ger ousts rock performers 8-29, 684E1
Canada union bars US star 9-7, 742F2
E Ger concert riot 10-8, 782A1

Awards
Pulitzer presented 4-18, 355E2

1978

MUSHIOKI, Stephen
Wins World Amateur Boxing tourn 5-6—5-20, 600E2

MUSIC
USSR revokes Rostropoviches' citizenships 3-15, 179B3
Rodgers gives Arts Inst $1 mln endowmt 5-1, 335E3 ★
'77 indus profit rptd 5-8, 325A3
Italy opera dirs arrested in corruptn probe 5-30, 454B1
Solzhenitsyn scores West 6-8, 444B3
Presley fans mark death anniv 8-16, 644A3
Punk rock star accused of murder 10-12, 842D1
Rolling Stone's heroin sentnc suspended 10-24, band OKs benefit 10-26, 842E1
TV licenses challenged 11-27, 1030A1
Kondrashin defects 12-4, 946E3

Awards
Arts Institute honors 2 2-7, 316E1
Grammys presented 2-24, 315D3-316D1
Colgrass wins Pulitzer 4-17, 315C1
2 Amers win Tchaikovsky competitn 7-4, 7-5, 844A2
Marian Anderson honored 10-17, 844F1
Best Sellers (albums)
All 'N' All, Earth, Wind & Fire 2-4, 116G3
City to City, Rafferty 6-7, 460G3; 7-5, 580A1
Darkness On Edge of Town, Springsteen 7-5, 580A1
Don't Look Back, Boston 9-6, 708F1; 10-11, 800F3
Double Vision, Foreigner 8-2, 620F1; 9-6, 708F1; 12-6, 971F1
Even Now, Manilow 3-8, 196C1; 4-5, 272G3
Feels So Good, Mangione 5-3, 356E1; 6-7, 460G3
52nd Street, Joel 11-8, 888D1; 12-6, 971E1
Foot Loose & Fancy Free, Stewart 2-4, 116G3
Grease Soundtrack 7-5, 580A1; 8-2, 620F1; 9-6, 708F1; 10-11, 800F3
Greatest Hits, Streisand 12-6, 971E1
Live & More, Summer 11-8, 888D1; 12-6, 971F1
Living In the USA, Ronstadt 10-11, 800F3; 11-8, 888D1
London Town, Wings 5-3, 356E1; 6-7, 460G3
Natural High, Commodores 8-2, 620G1
News of the World, Queen 2-4, 116G3
Out of the Blue, Electric Light Orchestra 2-4, 116G3
Running On Empty, Browne 3-8, 196C1; 4-5, 272G3; 5-3, 356E1
Saturday Night Fever Soundtrack 2-4, 116G3; 3-8, 196B1; 4-5, 272G3; 5-3, 356E1; 6-7, 460G3
Shadow Dancing, Gibb 7-5, 580A1
Slowhand, Clapton 3-8, 196B1; 4-5, 272G3; 5-3, 356E1
Some Girls, Rolling Stones 7-5, 580A1; 8-2, 620F1; 9-6, 708F1; 10-11, 800F3; 11-8, 888D1
Stranger, Joel 3-8, 196B1; 4-5, 272G3
Stranger In Town, Seger, Silver Bullet Band 6-7, 460G3; 8-2, 620G1
Who Are You, Who 9-6, 708F1; 10-11, 800F3
Wild & Crazy Guy, Martin 11-8, 888D1; 12-6, 971E1
Best Sellers (singles)
Baby Come Back, Player 2-4, 116F3
Baker Street, Rafferty 6-7, 460F3; 7-5, 579G3
Boogie Oogie Oogie, Taste of Honey 9-6, 708E1; 10-11, 800E3
Can't Smile Without You, Manilow 4-5, 272F3; 5-3, 356D1
Emotion, Sang 3-8, 196A1; 4-5, 272F3
Get Off, Foxy 10-11, 800E3
Grease, Valli 8-2, 620E1; 9-6, 708E1
Hot Child In the City, Gilder 10-11, 800E3; 11-8, 888C1
It's a Heartache, Tyler 6-7, 460F3
Just the Way You Are, Joel 3-8, 196B1
King Tut, Martin 7-5, 579G3
Kiss You All Over, Exile 9-6, 708F1; 10-11, 800E3; 11-8, 888C1
Last Dance, Summer 7-5, 579G3; 8-2, 620F1
Lay Down Sally, Clapton 4-5, 272F3
Le Freak, Chic 12-6, 971D1
Love Is Thicker than Water, Gibb 2-4, 116F3; 3-8, 196B1
MacArthur Park, Summer 11-8, 888C1; 12-6, 971D1
Miss You, Rolling Stones 8-2, 620F1; 9-6, 708E1
Night Fever, Bee Gees 3-8, 196B1; 4-5, 272F3; 5-3, 356D1
Shadow Dancing, Gibb 6-7, 460F3; 7-5, 579G3

1979

MUSIAL, Stan
Yastrzemski gets 3000th hit 9-12, 1002D3

MUSIC
Punk rock star freed on bail, ODs 2-2, 156B3
Presley poster dispute refused by Sup Ct 2-21, 128E3
Complete 'Lulu' debuts in Paris 2-25, 173G3-174C1
US performers in Cuba 3-1–3-4, 238D2
Presley estate probated 3-24, 272G1
Fiedler conducts Boston Symphony 3-25, 272F1
Ormandy announces retiremt 4-3, 272F1
Frampton 'live-in-partner' suit dismissed 4-17, 289D1
Broadcast license fee case remanded by Sup Ct 4-17, 325G3-326A1
Beatles ex-mgr convicted on tax fraud 4-26, 392F3
Fiedler opens Boston Pops 50th season 5-1, 392A2
Elton John in USSR 5-21–5-30, 410C2
Berry pleads guilty to '73 tax evasn 6-12, 527A3; sentncd 7-10, 656D2
Beatles ex-mgr sentenced 7-10, 656E2
NYC library buys Mozart manuscript 7-16, 672G2
Iran bans radio, TV music 7-23, 565A3
Record industry slump rptd 8-8, 618D1
EMI-Paramount deal called off 9-12, 942F2
US violinist wins Kreisler contest 9-19, 892F2
Moscow State Symphony cancels US tour, defectns cited 9-27, 774G3
Jagger divorce final 11-2, 1006C2
Cincinati rock concert stampede 12-3, 954G1
Hanson in Arts Institute 12-7, 1005A3
Presley MD drug chrgs rptd 12-19, 1005C3
Awards
Grammys presented 2-16, 336C3
Schwantner wins Pulitzer 4-16, 336G2
Best Sellers (albums)
At Budokan, Cheap Trick 5-2, 356B3; 5-30, 448F3; 7-4, 548F3; 8-1, 620F3
Bad Girls, Summer 5-30, 448F3; 7-4, 548F3; 8-1, 620E3
Best of Earth, Wind & Fire, Earth, Wind & Fire 1-10, 80F3
Blondes Have More Fun, Stewart 2-14, 120F3; 3-7, 174E1; 4-4, 271E2
Breakfast in Amer, Supertramp 5-2, 356A3; 5-30, 448F3; 7-4, 548E3; 8-1, 620E3; 9-5, 672F3; 10-3, 800F3
Briefcase Full of Blues, Blues Brothers 1-10, 80F3; 2-14, 120F3; 3-7, 174E1
Candy-O, Cars 7-4, 548F3; 8-1, 620E3; 9-5, 672F3; 10-3, 800F3
Cornerstone, Styx 11-7, 892F3
Cruisin', Village People 2-14, 120F3
Dire Straits, Dire Straits 3-7, 174E1; 4-4 271E2
52nd Street, Joel 1-10, 80F3; 2-7, 120F3; 4-4, 271E2
Get the Knack, Knack 8-1, 620F1; 9-5, 672E3; 10-3, 800F3
Greatest Hits, Streisand 1-10, 80F3
I Am, Earth, Wind & Fire 7-4, 548F3
In Through the Out Door, Zeppelin 9-5, 672F3; 10-3, 800F3; 11-7, 892F3
Long Run, Eagles 11-7, 892F3
Midnight Magic, Commodores 10-3, 800F3; 11-7, 892F3
Million Mile Reflectns, Charlie Daniels Band 9-5, 672F3*
Minute by Minute, Doobie Brothers 3-7, 174E1; 4-4, 271D2; 5-2, 356A3
Rickie Lee Jones, Rickie Lee Jones 5-30, 448F3
Spirits Having Flown, Bee Gees 2-14, 120F3; 3-7, 174E1; 4-4, 271E2
Tusk, Fleetwood Mac 11-7, 892F3
2 Hot, Peaches & Herb 5-2, 356A3
Van Halen 11, Van Halen 5-2, 356B3; 5-30, 448F3
Wild & Crazy Guy, Martin 1-10, 80F3
Best Sellers (singles)
Babe, Styx 11-7, 892E3
Bad Girls, Summer 7-4, 548E3; 8-1, 620E3
Da Ya Think I'm Sexy, Stewart 2-14, 120E3; 3-7, 174D1; 4-4 271D2
Devil Went Down to Georgia, Charlie Daniels Band 9-5, 672E3
Don't Stop 'Til You Get Enough, Jackson 10-3, 800E3
Good Times, Chic 8-1, 620E3; 9-5, 672E3
Heartache Tonight, Eagles 11-7, 892E3
Heart of Glass, Blondie 5-2, 356G2; 5-30, 448E3
Hot Stuff, Summer 5-30, 448E3; 7-4, 548E3; 8-1, 620E3
I'll Never Love This Way Again, Warwick 9-5, 672E3
I Will Survive, Gaynor 2-14, 120E3; 3-7, 174D1; 4-4 271C2
Knock on Wood, Stewart 5-2, 356A3
Le Freak, Chic 1-10, 80E3; 2-14, 120E3; 3-7, 174D1
Logical Song, Supertramp 7-4, 548E3
Main Event/Fight, Streisand 9-5, 672E3*
Music Box Dancer, Mills 4-4, 271D2; 5-2, 356A3
My Life, Joel 1-10, 80E3
My Sharona, Knack 8-1, 620E3; 9-5, 672E3; 10-3, 800E3

1980

MUSIC
USSR cancels Gilels W Ger tour 1-9, 10A3
Williams named Boston Pops conductor 1-10, 199F2
Summer said born-again 1-25, 199G2
McCartney deported from Japan 1-26, 200E2
Decca merger set 2-14, 132D3
Ia high school bands buy White House uniforms 5-16, 460A3
Sinatra offers Chrysler aid 6-11, 457F1
NYC violinist found slain 7-24, 654A1; stagehand indicted 9-7, 713B1
Copyright royalty fees divided 7-29, 640F2-A3
Sovt violinist seeks W Ger asylum 8-19, 908E1
Ormandy gives final concert 8-23, 908D1
Kate Smith estate feud setld 9-4, 908C2
Met Opera season canceled over musicians' strike 9-29, strike setld 10-25, 883E3
Westinghouse to acquire Teleprompter 10-15, 836F1
Actors settle 95-day strike, musicians' stay out 10-23, 805E3
Sills gives final performance 10-27, 908E2
ABC, CBS in cable-TV deals 12-2, 12-10, 1003A1
Lennon slain in NYC, ex-mental patient chrgd 12-8; reactn 12-9; background, photos 933D2-943F3

Awards & Honors
Grammys presented 2-27, 296A3
Del Tredici wins Pulitzer 4-14, 296F2
Schuller elected to Arts Inst 12-5, 998C1
Best Sellers (albums)
Against the Wind, Seger & Silver Bullet Band 4-2, 280E3; 4-30, 360A1; 6-4, 448F3; 7-9, 568F3
Back in Black, AC/DC 12-3, 948C3
Christopher Cross, Cross 8-13, 640C3; 9-10, 716F3
Cornerstone, Styx 1-2, 40F3
Crime of Passion, Benatar 10-8, 796C3; 12-3, 948C3
Damn The Torpedoes, Tom Petty & Heartbreakers 2-6, 120G3; 3-5, 200F3
Emotional Rescue, Rolling Stones 8-13, 640B3; 9-10, 716F3
Game, Queen 9-10, 716F3; 10-8, 796B3
Glass Houses, Joel 4-2, 280F3; 4-30, 360A1; 6-4, 448F3; 7-9, 568F3; 8-13, 640B3
Greatest Hits, Rogers 12-3, 948B3
Greatest Hits on the Radio, Summer 1-2, 40F3; 2-6, 120G3
Guilty, Streisand 10-8, 796B3; 12-3, 948B3
Hold Out, Browne 8-13, 640C3
Kenny, Rogers 1-18, 40F3
Long Run, Eagles 1-2, 40F3
Mad Love, Ronstadt 3-5, 200F3; 4-2, 280F3
McCartney II, McCartney 7-9, 568F3
Off The Wall, Jackson 2-6, 120G3; 3-5, 200F3; 4-2, 280F3; 4-30, 360A1
One Step Closer, Doobie Brothers 10-8, 796B3
Phoenix, Fogelberg 2-6, 120G3; 3-5, 200F3
Pretenders, Pretenders 6-4, 448F3
River, Springsteen 12-3, 948C3
Rose (soundtrack) 7-9, 568F3
Urban Cowboy 7-9, 568F3; 8-13, 640C3
Wall, Pink Floyd 1-2, 40F3; 2-6, 120G3; 3-5, 200F3; 4-2, 280F3; 4-30, 360A1; 6-4, 448F3
Women & Children First, Van Halen 4-30, 360A1; 6-4, 448F3
Xanadu 9-10, 716F3; 10-8, 796B3
Best Sellers (singles)
All Out of Love, Air Supply 9-10, 716E3; 10-8, 796B3
Another Brick in the Wall, Pink Floyd 3-5, 200E3; 4-2, 280E3; 4-30, 359G3
Another One Bites the Dust, Queen 9-10, 716E3; 10-8, 796A3; 12-3, 948B3
Babe, Styx 1-2, 40E3
Call Me, Blondie 3-5, 200E3; 4-2, 280E3; 4-30, 359G3; 6-4, 448E3
Cars, Numan 6-4, 448E3
Coming Up, McCartney 6-4, 448E3; 7-9, 568E3
Crazy Little Thing Called Love, Queen 2-6, 120F3; 3-5, 200E3; 4-2, 280E3
Do That To Me One More Time, Captain & Tennille 2-6, 120F3
Emotional Rescue, Rolling Stones 8-13, 640B3
Escape, Holmes 1-2, 40E3; 2-6, 120F3
Funkytown, Lipps 6-4, 448E3; 7-9, 568E3
Guilty, Streisand 12-3, 948B3
It's Still Rock and Roll to Me, Joel 7-9, 568E3; 8-13, 640A3
Lady, Rogers 12-3, 948A3
Little Jeannie, John 7-9, 568E3
Longer, Fogelberg 3-5, 200E3
Lookin' for Love, Lee 10-8, 796B3
Lost In Love, Air Supply 4-30, 360A1; 6-4, 448F3
Magic, Newton John 8-13, 640A3; 9-10, 716E3

1976

Obituaries
Anda, Geza 6-13, 524C2
August, Jan 1-17, 56A3
Bachauer dies 8-2, 892F2
Bachauer, Gina 8-2, 892F2
Ballard, Florence 2-22, 192C3
Boswell, Connee 10-11, 816E3
Brailowsky, Alexander 4-25, 524C2
Britten, Benjamin 12-4, 970C1
Burnett, Chester 1-13, 56B3
Davis, Meyer 4-5, 272F3
Dowling, Eddie 2-18, 160D3
Faith, Percy 2-9, 160D3
Hackett, Bobby 6-7, 524F2
Harris, Walter 8-8, 816E3
Hull, Lytle 12-11, 1015E1
Kempe, Rudolf 5-11, 524A3
Lehmann, Lotte 8-26, 892B3
Leslie, Edgar 1-22, 80E3
Lhevinne, Rosina 11-9, 970C2
Martinon, Jean 3-1, 192F3
Mercer, Johnny 6-25, 524C3
Neuman, Herman 5-4, 524C3
Ochs, Phil 4-9, 272G3
Peterson, Charles 8-4, 892D3
Piatigorsky, Gregor 8-6, 892D3
Piston, Walter 11-12, 970A3
Pons, Lily 2-13, 160G3
Rethberg, Elisabeth 6-6, 444G2
Robeson, Paul 1-24, 80F3
Sanjuan, Pedro 10-18, 970B3
Washington, Ned 12-20, 1015A3

MUSIC Corporation of America
New Ventures to aid minorities, women 8-20, 944B1
MUSIC Is (play)
Opens 12-20, 1014F3
MUSKEGON (Mich.) Chronicle, The (newspaper)
Newhouse buys Booth chain 11-8, 901B3
MUSKHELISHVILI, Nikolai Ivanovich
Dies 7-15, 716E3
MUSKIE, Sen. Edmund S(ixtus) (D, Me.)
Rebuts State of Union message 1-21, 40E1
Milk price veto upheld 2-4, 88G1
Seeks Sen majority post 3-5, 181F1
On expanded pub works bill 4-13, 283E1
'72 electn costs rptd 4-25, 688F1
Platform com testimony 5-20, 357E3
Visits Carter re vp choice 7-4, comments 7-6, 489C3, D3
Dem conv speaker 7-13, 509A3
Mondale gets vp nod 7-15, 506B2
Scores tax bill 8-5, 586A2
Lauds Cong budget system 9-15, 706G2
Reelected 11-2, 820C1, 821C1, 828F1
Carter meets cong ldrs 11-17, 864A2

1977

Obituaries
Addinsell, Richard 11-15, 952A2
Barnes, George 9-4, 787F3
Biggs, E Power 3-10, 264D2
Bolan, Marc 9-16, 787G3
Buckner, Milt 7-27, 604F2
Callas, Maria 9-16, 787G3
Callimahos, Lambros 10-28, 872D1
Crosby, Bing 10-14, 872D1
Desmond, Paul 5-30, 452G2
Ford, Mary 9-30, 788B1
Gaines, Cassie 10-20, 888G3
Gaines, Steve 10-20, 888G3
Galich, Alexander 12-15, 1024F1
Garber, Jan 10-5, 872G1
Garner, Erroll 1-2, 84B3
Godfrey, Isidore 9-12, 872A2
Goldmark, Peter 12-7, 1024A2
Keller, Greta 11-4, 952F2
Lombardo, Guy 11-5, 952G2
Presley, Elvis 8-16, 695C3
Schippers, Thomas 12-16, 1024B3
Schoeffler, Paul 11-21, 952C3
Stokowski, Leopold 9-13, 788G2
Van Zant, Ronnie 10-20, 888G3
Waters, Ethel 9-1, 788A3
Wolf, Steve 11-21, 952G3

MUSIKAVANHU, Chief Edgar
Rpt US bars entry 9-25, 811A3
MUSKIE, Sen. Edmund S(ixtus) (D, Me.)
'76 spec interest gifts rptd 1-15, 128F3, 129C1
Ethics code amendmt rejctd 3-22, 251B2
Vs tax rebate plan withdrawal 4-14, 270E3
Vs '77 farm disaster aid bill 10-25, 833F3
Backs clean water rules revisn 12-16, 959G1

1978

Short People, Newman 2-4, 116F3
Stayin' Alive, Bee Gees 2-4, 116F3; 3-8, 196A1; 4-5, 272F3; 5-3, 356D1
Three Times a Lady, Commodores 8-2, 620E1; 9-6, 708E1
Too Much Too Little Too Late, Mathis & Williams 5-3, 356D1; 6-7, 460F3
We Are the Champions, Queen 2-4, 117F3
With a Little Luck, Wings 5-3, 356D1
YMCA, Village People 12-6, 971E1
You Don't Bring Me Flowers, Streisand & Diamond 11-8, 888D1; 12-6, 971D1
You Needed Me, Murray 10-11, 800E3; 11-3, 888C1; 12-6, 971E1
You're the One, Travolta, Newton-John 6-7, 579G3; 8-2, 620F1; 7-5, 579G3

Obituaries
Bradford, Alex 2-15, 196D2
Brel, Jacques 10-9, 888E2
Carter, (Mother) Maybelle 10-23, 888G2
Chavez, Carlos 8-2, 708C2
Davis, Hal 1-11, 96F1
Denny, Sandy 4-21, 356E2
Etting, Ruth 9-24, 778B1
Francois, Claude 3-11, 252F2
Jones, Blanche Calloway 12-16, 1032A3
Kenny, Bill 3-23, 252B3
Khachaturian, Aram 5-1, 440A3
Kipnis, Alexander 5-14, 440A3
Moon, Keith 9-7, 778F1
Nabokov, Nicholas 4-6, 356C3
Noble, Ray 4-3, 356C3
Prima, Louis 8-24, 708C3
Serly, Tibor 10-8, 888E3
Shay, Dorothy 10-22, 888E3
Steinberg, William 5-16, 440E3
Still, William 12-3, 1032F3
Swanson, Howard 11-12, 972E3
Sylvester, Victor 8-14, 708E3
Venuti, Joe 8-14, 708F3

MUSICIANS, American Federation of (AFL-CIO)
Hal Davis dies 1-11, 96F1
MUSIOL, Bogdon
Wins 4-man bobsled championship 2-12, 316G3
MUSKIE, Sen. Edmund S(ixtus) (D, Maine)
Votes for Panama Canal neutrality pact 3-16, 177D2
Scores farm bill 3-21, 218D3
Scores farm bill cost 4-10, 261F2
Votes for 2d Canal pact 4-18, 273B1
On tax cut starting date 4-26, 305F2
Payne dies 6-15, 540D3
Budget deficit level rptd lauded 9-21, 733F3, 734B1
On Carter budget plans 12-14, 979G3, 980B1

1979

No More Tears (Enough is Enough), Streisand, Summer 11-7, 892E3
Pop Muzik, M 10-3, 800E3; 11-7, 892E3
Reunited, Peaches & Herb 5-2, 356G2; 5-30, 448E3
Ring My Bell, Ward 7-4, 548E3; 8-1, 620E3
Rise, Alpert 10-3, 800E3; 11-7, 892E3
Sad Eyes, John 10-3, 800E3
Shake Your Body, Jacksons 5-30, 448E3
Too Much Heaven, Bee Gees 1-10, 80E3; 2-14, 120E3
Tragedy, Bee Gees 3-7, 174D1; 4-4 271D2
We Are Family, Sister Sledge 5-30, 448E3; 7-4, 548E3
What a Fool Believes, Doobie Brothers 4-4, 271D2; 5-2, 356A3
YMCA, Village People 1-10, 80E3; 2-14, 120E3; 3-7, 174D1
You Don't Bring Me Flowers, Streisand, Diamond 1-10, 80E3

Obituaries
Ager, Milton 5-6, 432D2
Bernac, Pierre 10-17, 860A2
Bolton, Guy R 9-5, 756A2
Boulanger, Nadia 10-22, 860C2
Davis, Benny 12-20, 1008D2
Fiedler, Arthur 7-15, 588F2
Fields, Gracie 9-27, 756D2
Flatt, Lester 5-11, 432E2
Harper, Ethel 3-31, 272E2
Harris, Roy 10-1, 860F2
Hunt, Walter 6-28, 508B3
Kenton, Stan 8-25, 671F2
Lawrence, Marjorie 1-13, 104C3
Leonetti, Tommy 9-15, 756F2
McCoy, Van 7-6, 588B3
Mingus, Charles 1-5, 104D3
Novaes, Guiomar 3-7, 272D3
Paray, Paul 10-10, 860B3
Riperton, Minnie 7-12, 588C3
Rodgers, Richard 12-30, 1008D3
Seeger, Charles L 2-7, 176F3
Solovyev-Sedov, Vasily 12-2, 1008F3
Tiomkin, Dimitri 11-11, 932F3
Vicious, Sid 2-2, 156B3

MUSICAL Artists, American Guild of (AGMA)
Amer Ballet OKs pact 12-20, 987A2
MUSIC Box Dancer (recording)
On best-seller list 4-4, 271D2; 5-2, 356A3
MUSIC City Media Inc.
Nashville Banner purchased 7-5, 618C3
MUSICIANS United for Safe Energy (MUSE)
NYC A-protest draws 200,000 9-23, 742A3
MUSKIE, Sen. Edmund Sixtus (D, Maine)
Issues GAO rpt on EPA 1-9, 16G2
Budget Com chrmn 1-23, 71C2
Crane scores Loeb articles 6-8, 594B2

1980

No More Tears, Streisand, Summer 1-2, 40E3
Rapper's Delight, Sugar Hill Gang 1-2, 40E3; 2-6, 120F3
Ride Like the Wind, Cross 4-30, 359G3
Rock With You, Jackson 1-2, 40F3; 2-6, 120F3
Rose, Midler 7-9, 568E3
Sailing, Cross 8-13, 640B3; 9-10, 716E3
Take Your Time, SOS Band 7-9, 568E3; 8-13, 640B3
Upside Down, Ross 9-10, 716E3; 10-8, 796A3
Whip It, Devo 12-3, 948B3
With You I'm Born Again, Billy Preston & Syreeta 4-2, 280E3; 4-30, 359G3
Woman In Love, Streisand 10-8, 796B3; 12-3, 948B3
Working My Way Back to You, Spinners 4-2, 280E3

Obituaries
Alter, Louis 11-3, 928G1
Bignard, Leon A 6-27, 528B1
Bonelli, Richard 6-7, 528C1
Bonham, John 9-25, 755C2
Byrd, Henry 1-30, 104A2
De Moraes, Vinicius 7-9, 608F1
Deutsch, Adolph 1-1, 104C2
Dragonette, Jessica 3-18, 279C2
Evans, Bill 9-15, 755G2
Farr, Thomas Hugh 3-17, 279F2
Fielding, Jerry 2-17, 176A1
Froman, Jane 4-23, 360F1
Goldman, Richard F 1-19, 104F2
Hardin, Tim 12-29, 1004B2
Haymes, Dick 3-28, 279C3
Heindorf, Ray 2-2, 176F1
Iturbi, Jose 6-28, 528B2
Jackson, Eddie 7-16, 608B2
Jantar, Anna 3-14, 214B1
Johnson, Willie 5-3, 448G1
Kostelanetz, Andre 1-13, 104A3
Lennon, John 12-8, 933D2
Mackey, Bernard 3-5, 280B1
Mantovani, Annunzio Paolo 3-29, 280B1
Niles, John Jacob 3-1, 280D1
Nolan, Bob 6-16, 528A3
Robbins, Gale 2-18, 176B3
Robinson, Francis 5-14, 448E2
Roth, Lillian 5-12, 448F2
Sebastian, John 8-18, 676A3
Selvin, Benjamin B 7-28, 608C3
Stoloff, Morris 4-16, 360E3
Vysotsky, Vladimir 7-24, 580C2
Walters, Albert 10-20, 876F3
Wilder, Alec 12-24, 1004G3

MUSIC for Chameleons (book)
On best-seller list 9-14, 716C3; 10-12, 796E3
MUSICIANS, American Federation of (AFM) (AFL-CIO)
Actors settle 95-day strike, musicians' stay out 10-23, 805E3
Met Opera strike settled 10-25, 883E3
MUSIC MAN (play)
Revival opens 6-6, 756F3
MUSICO, Joseph A.
Convicted in rattler attack 7-15, 655F3
Psychiatric evaluatn ordered 9-3, 860F2
MUSIEL, Bishop Francis
Backs vote boycott 3-20, 262G3
MUSKIE, Edmund Sixtus
On Carter anti-inflatn plan 3-14, 201E2
Named secy of state; facts on 4-29, 323A2-C3
Confrmd secy of state 5-7, sworn 5-8, 343A1
Mitchell named to Sen seat 5-8, 367B2
Carter sees 'stronger' role 5-9, 367D1
Addresses State employes 5-9, 367A2
Doubts Sovt Afghan troop exit plan 5-15, 362B1
Sees Gromyko, French forgn min 5-16; scores Franco-Sovt summit 5-20; reactn 5-19, 5-21, 378D3, 379A1
Holds talks on S Korea mil 5-28, 430B3
Meets French forgn min, vs EC mideast peace move 5-30, 418B1
Asks Viet Thai raid halt, Moscow aid 6-25, 508B2
Vows Thailand arms aid 6-27, 491C3
On Schmidt USSR trip 7-2, 489D1
Open conv move forms, pres prospects noted 7-25—7-31, 570C3
Signs Canada acid rain pact 8-5, 603E1
Unaware of A-strategy shift 8-8; reactn 8-10, 8-11, 615C2
Regrets A-strategy ommissn, sees enhanced role 8-13, 630E2
Greece links US bases, NATO mil re-entry 8-20, 652D2
Addresses UN aid talks 8-25, 642G2
AFL-CIO OKs Polish worker fund 9-4; Warsaw protests 9-9—9-10, Sovt forewarning rptd 9-11, 679A2, C2
Indicates US ready for arms talks, hints SALT ratificatn 9-7, 679D3-680B1
Praises SALT, scores Reagan 9-18, 10-16, 776G1
Cong fails to bar India uranium sale 9-24, 723E1
Warns of Reagan's 'endless' wars 10-11, 776G2-C3
Proposes Polish grain credit hike 11-13, 879B1
Says USSR seeks better ties 11-23, 915A2
Lauds NATO warning to Sovts on Poland invasn 12-12, 949C1
Africa
Mugabe meets, seeks aid 8-27, 674F2
House subcom scores Somali mil pact 8-28, 661C3
House subcom vs Somali arms sales 9-18; sales backed 9-30, 735C3

1976

MUSSA, Maj. Abu
Cautions followers on raids 9-1, 642B1
MUSSER, Tharon
Wins Tony 4-18, 460E2
MUSSET, Bernard H.
Sees Kissinger 9-19, 697D1
MUSTAFIN, Farhat
Wins Olympic medal 7-24, 576G2
MUTCH, Thomas A.
Says Martian sky orange-pink 7-26, 549B2

MUZOREWA, Bishop Abel
Backer killed in Gwelo riot 1-12, 54A1
Smith scores guerrillas 2-6, 176G1
Mozambique shuts Rhodesia border 3-3 175E1
At Zambia mtg 3-24—3-25, 240E2
Followers held in Rhodesia 4-4, 295E3
Calls for armed struggle 8-19, 661F3
At conf re ANC rift 9-6—9-7, 661E3 ★
Sithole claims ZANU ldrshp 9-9, 733B3
Sees Nkomo 10-1; returns to Rhodesia 10-3, 738A3
Sees US, UK reps 10-4, 738F2
Asked to Rhodesia conf 10-12, names delegatn 10-15, 781C2, E2
Backers rptd killed 10-15, 10-17, 812C3
Delegates released 10-19, 797G1
In Geneva 10-25, sees Richard 10-26, 797F1
Chrgs Rhodesia torture 10-29, 831F3
Meets Richard 11-10, 843E1
OKs flexible indepndnc date 11-15, scores Nkomo, Mugabe 11-17, 862A1
Independnc date set 11-26; natlsts ask new interim govt plan 11-29, 893C1, F1
Scores Mugabe, Nkomo re interim govt 12-4; asks whites join ANC 12-5, 914B3
Scores Smith, Nkomo, Mugabe 12-12; Smith pact rumored 12-14, 935F1-B2
Chrgs govt in Kuwana killing 12-15, 1009C2
Zambia cuts ties 12-19, 1009C3

1977

MUSLIMS—*See ISLAM*
MUSSOLINI, Benito (1883-1945)
USSR photo censorship rptd 8-18, 657C3
MUSTAFA, Shukri Ahmed
Arrested 7-8, 542A2
Anti-Egypt stand cited 8-11, 636G2
MUTUAL and Balanced Force Reduction Talks—*See EUROPE—Force Reduction Talks*
MUZIKIR, Abdul (Marquette A. Hall)
Convictd 7-23, sentenced 9-6, 711F1

MUZOREWA, Bishop Abel
Front-line states back Patriotic Front 1-9, van der Byl reactn 1-12, 11B1
Scores ANC hangings 1-17, 29E1
OAU backs Patriotic Front 2-4, 122C3
ZAPU urges Geneva talks resumed 2-22, 145A1
Scores protected villages 4-2, 297D1
Owen rejects conf bar 4-11, 296F1
Ends forgn tour, scores Patriotic Front 7-17, 563F3
Scores Smith settlemt plan 7-19, 563F3
Sets '78 majority rule plan 7-24, 581C3
Blames ZAPU for Salisbury blast 8-7, 624B2
Backers quit UANC 8-8—8-21, 662C2
Backs UK-US plan 9-2, 699A3
Kaunda backs Patriotic Front 10-21, 810F2
Sees UK, UN reps 11-4, 875D3
OKs Smith majority-rule talks 11-26, 910C3
Scores Mozambique raid 11-29, 911E1
Boycotts Smith talks 12-2, joins 12-9—12-29, 1015F2
Nyandoro returns 12-10, 1016E1

1978

MUSLIMS—*See ISLAM*
MUSSOLINI, Benito (1883-1945)
Student dies 7-1, 620F3
MUSTAFA, Shukri Ahmed
Executed 3-19, 211E2
MUSTAPHA, Ishem
Held in PLO deaths 8-3, 582C3
Assad chrgd in PLO deaths 8-5, 602G2
MUTINDA, Daniel M.
Kenya informatn min 10-11, 784C3
MUTRUX, Floyd
Amer Hot Wax released 3-16, 618A3
MUTUAL and Balanced Force Reductions Talks (MBFR)—*See EUROPE—Force Reduction Talks*

MUZOREWA, Bishop Abel Tendekayi
Facts on 59A2
Rptd vs Malta mtg 1-16, 59E2
Boycotts internal talks 1-27, to return 1-31, 59F2
OKs majority-rule pact 2-15, asks war preparatn 2-19, 119B2-B3, F3
Signs internal pact, seeks US, UK backing 3-3; lauds Owen mtg 3-6, 154A3, 155G1
UN speech bid rptd abandoned 3-11, 192G3
Salisbury rally hails; on forgn reactn to internal pact 3-19, 210D2
Sworn state cncl member 3-21, 210A2
Patriotic Front discounts rally 3-21, 210G2
Scores front-line mtg, Young 3-26, 248A3
Reveals pol detainees freed 4-6, 290F3
Council of mins sworn 4-14, 291B1
Sees Vance, Owen 4-17, 290D3
Black min ousted 4-28; threatens govt split, probe set 4-28—5-2, 317G1
Boycotts pro-govt rally 5-10, 377A1
Govt split averted 5-14, 376D3-377A1
Backers score Sithole rally 5-20, 455E3
Scores army re civln deaths 5-23, statemt censored 6-12, 455F1, G1
Supporters found dead 7-7, 594E2
In US re sanctns end 7-17, 561D1
UANC rebuts Smith chrgs 7-19, 615E3
Ends US, UK tour, gets no support 8-5, 615F2
WCC OKs Patriotic Front aid 8-10, 650A3
Wins UANC confidence vote 8-13, 650B3
Rebel photos scored 8-13, defended 8-16, 650D3
In US 10-15—10-20, 818D3
WCC grants cited 10-25, 906G3
UANC members score draft 10-27, 830C1
Armed backers rptd 10-28, scored 11-7, 867C3

1979

MUSSOLINI, Benito (1883-1945)
Widow dies 10-30, 860G2-A3
MUSSOLINI, Rachele Guidi
Dies 10-30, 860G2
MUTI, Ornella
Nest of Vipers released 9-7, 820C2
MUTITI, Aaron
Black draft increased 8-10, 638G1
MUTUAL Atomic Energy Liability Underwriters
3 Mile I A-accident compensatn vowed 3-31, 244B2
MUTUAL and Balanced Forced Reductions Talks (MBFR)—*See EUROPE–Force Reduction Talks*
MUTUAL Insurance Co.
Press freedom plan set 9-27, 859F2
MUTUAL Life Insurance Co. of N.Y.
North American Life & Casualty Co.
W Ger firm to buy 5-11, 942C2

MUZOREWA, Bishop Abel Tendekayi (Zimbabwe Rhodesian prime minister)
Rhodesian dispute role described 170A3
Whites OK draft const 1-30, 77B1
Wins electn, Sithole disputes 4-24, 293A1
Backers hold parade 4-25, 332E2
Asks US sanctns end, defends govt 4-29, 332B2
Young chrgs vote fraud 5-3, 354E1
Parlt speaker, dep elected 5-8, 354D1
Blocks Chikerema ouster 5-13, 359F2
Sworn 5-29, names Cabt 5-30, **govt installed 5-31**, 393C1
Scores Carter re trade ban 6-8, 434A3
Oppositn party formed 6-20, 490G1
S Africa trip rptd 6-20, 490D2
Visits US 7-9–7-11, UK 7-12–7-14, 546B2, C3
Offers new rebel amnesty 7-22, 638A2
ZANU ends boycott, vows support 7-31, 586C3
Vs Commonwealth Zimbabwe plan 8-6, Mugabe scores 8-7, 589C2, 590C1
Increases black draft 8-10, 638F1
To attend UK setlmt conf, scores const chngs 8-15, 638A1, E1
On govt-auxiliary clash 8-17, 638B2
London conf opens 9-10; const chng, agenda debated 9-11, 9-12, 675F2, B3, F3
London talks deadlocked 9-13; Smith rift revealed 9-15–9-16; OKs UK const proposal 9-21, 717F3-718F1
OKs new UK const proposal 10-5, unilateral talks begin 10-16, 777B2
UK Tories endorse Thatcher policy 10-10, 791A3
Transitn talks deadlocked 10-19, OKs UK offer 10-27; plan outlined 11-2, 844F1, C2
UK lets sanctn law lapse 11-14, 881G1
Patriotic Front OKs UK transitn plan 11-15, lauds 11-18, 881A1, D1

1980

Iran—*See also 'Iran-Iraq War' below*
Cautions Waldheim on UN comm 5-17, 393E2
Hints leniency re Clark trip 6-8, 459E3
Asks hostages freed 8-31, new initiative denied 9-1, 671E1
Iran hostage plea scored, letter aired 9-9, 688C3
Sees little hope in Khomeini hostage release terms 9-15, 693F1-A2
Says hostage release prospects bleak 9-15, Carter agrees 9-16, 699F1
Renews hostage plea 9-22, 719F2
Seeks Rajai mtg in NYC 10-16, 799G3
Denies spare parts-hostage deal 10-16, 800B1
Hopeful on hostage release terms 11-3, 853A3
Rejects Iran hostage demand 12-21, 973F1
Iran-Iraq War
Meets Waldheim 9-23, Gromyko 9-25, 718E3, 719A2
Meets Iraq forgn min, limited war stressed 9-30, 733G1
Assures Iran on 4 AWACS to Saudis 10-1, 734D3
Backs Iraqi truce bid 10-2, 733G1
Assures Iran on AWACS to Saudis, Jordan aid to Iraq 10-18, 10-19, 798C3
Proposes peace plan 10-20, UN hears plan 10-22—10-23, 799D1
Iraq warns vs arms to Iran 10-25, 10-26, 820G2-A3
Latin America
Carter orders criminal refugees expelled 6-7, 435G1
Announces Bolivia aid cutoff 7-25, 577E1
Lauds Cuban hijack warning 9-16, 704E1
Middle East—*See also 'Iran' above*
Urges Israel, Egypt effort re Palestinians 6-9; Begin vs setlmt remark 6-10, 434E1
Responds to EC stand on PLO 6-13, 449D2
Vs UN vote backing Palestine state 7-30, 572F2
Scores Israel Jerusalem move 8-20, 627E2
Israel vs abstentn on UN Jerusalem res 8-21, 643C2
Begin vs Jerusalem stand 8-28, 660B3
MUSKIE v. Agee
Case accepted by Sup Ct 10-6, 782C3
MUSSELMAN, Bill
Hired as Cavaliers coach 6-11, 656G3
MUSSOLINI, Benito (1883-1945)
Amendola dies 6-5, 528A1
MUSTAFA Muhammad, Eddie (Eddie Gregory)
TKOs Koopmans 11-30, 1001B1
MUSTO, Rep. Raphael (D, Pa.)
Loses reelectn 11-4, 848G3
MUTUAL and Balanced Force Reduction (MBFR) (Belgium, Bulgaria, Canada, Czechoslovakia, Denmark, East Germany, France, Great Britain, Greece, Hungary, Ireland, Italy, Luxembourg, Netherlands, Norway, Poland, Portugal, Rumania, Turkey, USSR, U.S., West Germany)
Talks resume 1-31, 124D1
21st, 22d rounds end 7-24, 12-19, 979E1
NATO studies Sovt talks curb 12-12, 949F1
MUTUAL Broadcasting Co.
Ex-pres Hurleigh dies 8-10, 676F1
MUTUMBUKA, D.
Zimbabwe educ min 3-11, 198D1
MUWANGA, Paulo
Ousted 2-10, 125F3
Forms junta 5-11, 375E1
Obote party ousts Cabt rivals 9-17, 731B1
Electns held, bans results publicatn 12-10—12-11, 945F3-946E1
Reverses electn decisn 12-12, 968F2
MUZOREWA, Bishop Abel Tendekayi (Zimbabwe Rhodesian prime minister; replaced Mar. 11)
Auxiliaries transitn tole OKd 1-6, Mugabe scores 1-8, 31C3
Truce violatns chrgd 1-22, 48F3
Mugabe calls 'coward' 1-27, 80A2
Scores Smith remark re Nkomo 1-31, 118F3
Backs wider Soames powers 2-5, 118A3
Electns held 2-27—2-29, Mugabe win rptd 3-4; fraud chrgd 3-4, 161C1, D2
Mugabe praises Carter actions 8-27, 674F2

1976

MWALE, Siteke G.
Accuses S Africa on raid 7-27, 653F2
MWANANSHIKU, Luke
Presents budget 1-30, 503C2
MWARAIRI Mitima Tanemo
Zaire econ min 2-4, 270C2
MYERS, Rep. Gary A. (R, Pa.)
Reelected 11-2, 830G3
MYERS, Rep. John Thomas (R, Ind.)
Reelected 11-7, 850B4, 853A3
MYERS, Michael
Elected 11-2, 830D3
MY Fair Lady (play)
Opens 3-25, 1014C3
MYFTIU, Manush
Named deputy prime min 10-13, 850B1
MYRDAL, Gunnar
Pleads for Sovt dissident 3-24, 421A3
MYRTLE Grove, La.—*See LOUISIANA*
MZALI, Mohamed
Tunisia educatn min 5-31, 503C3

1977

MUZZAVI, Mussa
Conf OKs rights proposal 8-23, 664F3
MWALE, Siteke G.
Asks revolt vs Smith 1-25, 49D2
MWANT Yav, Chief
Treason chrgd 8-13, 641D2
MWINYI, Ali Hassan
Resigns 1-23, replaced 2-13, 161D2, E2
MX (missile experimental)—*See ARMAMENTS–Missiles*
Seattle Slew wins Triple Crown 6-11, 491A1
MYERS, Rep. John T(homas) (R, Ind.)
Wife testifies on Korea lobbying 10-19—10-21, 816F2
MYERS, Mrs. John T(homas)
Testifies on Korea lobbying 10-19—10-21, 816F2
MYERSCOUGH, Rev. Dunstan
On cleric massacre 2-7, 85B1
MYLER, Lava
Dismissal from Summa rptd 5-28, 472A3
MYRER, Anton
Once an Eagle on best-seller list 2-6, 120G3
MYSTICISM
US data rptd 4-26—4-29, 470D3

1978

Scores electn delay 10-29, 867F2
Sees Botha 11-15, vote delay warning rptd 11-23, 912B2
Agrees to vote delay 11-16, 893B2
Aide quits re Cabt role for whites 12-1, 945E3

MWANAKATWE, John
Sets wage controls 3-9, 333B3
MX (missile experimental)—*See ARMAMENTS--Missiles*
MY Astonishing Self (play)
Opens 1-18, 760F2
MY Cup Runneth Over (play)
Opens 6-22, 760F2
MYERS, Rep. Gary A. (R, Pa.)
Not standing for reelectn 5-16, 389E3
MYERS, Rep. John Thomas (R, Ind.)
Reelected 11-7, 850B4, 853A3
MYERS, Rep. Michael (D, Pa.)
Reelected 11-7, 852B1
MYERS, Mike
Taiwan wins Little League title 8-26, 779G2
MYERSON, Morris (d.1951)
Ex-wife dies 12-8, 1032E1
MY Mother/My Self (book)
On best-seller list 4-2, 272C3; 4-30, 356A2; 6-4, 460C3; 7-2, 579D3; 8-6, 620B2; 11-6, 888A1; 12-3, 971C1
MY Old Friends (play)
Opens 12-2, 1031E2
MYSLIVSEV, Pytor
20-kilo walk mark rptd 5-12, 692F3
MZIZI, Bayempini
'77 death ruled suicide 2-7, 92A2

1979

UK offers cease-fire plan 11-16, accepts 11-26, 937A1, B1
Scores Zambia war alert 11-20, 899E2
Decrees amnesty 11-22, 937D2
Govt dissolves, '65 indepndnc act repealed 12-11, 937A2
OKs cease-fire terms 12-13, initials 12-15; delays signing 12-18, 959G3, 960D1
Signs cease-fire, other pacts 12-21, 976A3

MX (missile experimental)—*See ARMAMENTS–Missiles*
MYEROWITZ, Dr. Richard L.
PPA pneumonia strain rptd 11-1, 971D2, E2
MYINT Maung
Burma quits nonaligned movemt 9-28, 742C2
MY Life (recording)
On best-seller list 1-10, 80E3
MY Love Has Been Burning (film)
Released 1-4, 174B3
MY Mother/My Self (book)
On best-seller list 1-7, 80C3; 2-4, 120C3; 4-8, 271C2; 6-3, 432C2
MY Sharona (recording)
On best-seller list 8-1, 620E3; 9-5, 672B3; 10-3, 800E3
MYSHKIN, Vladimir
Sovts win Challenge Cup 2-11, 118C3, E3

1980

MWALE, Lotte
Saad Muhammad KOs 11-29, 1001B1
MX (missile experimental)—*See ARMAMENTS--Missiles*
MY Bodyguard (film)
Released 8-1, 675B3
Top-grossing film 9-3, 716G3
MY Brilliant Career (film)
Released 2-1, 216C3
MYERS, David
Famous Potatoes wins Amer Book Award 5-1, 692D2
MYERS, et al v. NBC, et al
Stay refused by Sup Ct 10-14, 781D2
MYERS, Eugene Arter
Convicted 2-4, 270D3
MYERS, Rep. John Thomas (R, Ind.)
Reelected 11-4, 842B4
MYERS, Rep. Michael J. (Ozzie) (D, Pa.)
Facts on 81D2*
Linked to bribery in Abscam probe 2-2, 2-3, 81A2*, 82F1
Indicted in Abscam probe 5-27, 402C2*
Abscam judge quits case 8-7, 599E3*
Loses Abscam entrapmt plea 8-8, convicted 8-31, 684B2*, G2
Appeals ct backs Abscam tapes broadcast 10-1; Sup Ct refuses stay, tapes aired 10-14, 781D2
Expelled from House 10-2, 740B1
Abscam entrapmt plea refused by Sup Ct 11-3, 856G1
Loses reelectn 11-4, 846A2, D2, 848F2
Jenrette resigns from House 12-10, 962F1
MYERS, Tom
NFL '79 interceptn ldr 1-5, 8G2
MYERSON, Bess
Loses NY US Sen primary 9-9, 682C2
MYERS v. U.S.
Case refused by Sup Ct 11-3, 856G1
MY Mother, My Father and Me (play)
Opens 1-9, 136D3
MY Secret War (book)
USSR honors Philby 7-15, 566A3
MYSHKIN, Vladimir
Sovt Olympic hockey team loses to US 2-22, 155A2
MZALI, Mohamed (Tunisian premier)
Tunisia interim premr 3-1, 197A1
Confrmd premr, party ldr 4-23, 316A3
MZENDA, Simon V.
Zimbabwe dep prime min, forgn min 3-11, 198D1

N

1976

NAACP—*See NATIONAL Association for the Advancement of Colored People*
NAACP Legal Defense and Education Fund, Inc.
Vs death sentence 3-30, 3-31, 262B1
Asks Sup Ct death rule review 7-16, Powell stays executns 7-22, 568F2
Vs new job-exam bias rules 11-5, 884F2
Vs Calif U reverse bias appeal 11-11, 882F1
NABER, John
Wins Olympic medals 7-19—7-24, 562C3, 575B2-E2
NADER, Ralph
Group testifies vs Concorde 1-5, 5C3
Car safety report 2-23, 186E2-A3
Cockpit smoking ban sought 4-20, 308G1
Unit backs Reagan protest 5-14, 359E1
Wins airline 'bumping' suit 6-7, 435B2
Rpt scores bank diversificatn 7-5, 495B2-A3
Sees Carter 8-7—8-8, 585F1
Carter addresses forum 8-9, 585F1
Connally scores Carter 8-27, 645B1
A-waste cntrs called hazard 9-7, 671B1
FDA cold drugs rpt scored 9-8, 680E2
Lobbying disclosure bill not cleared 10-2, 883D1
Ford scores Carter 10-15, 784F1
'Raider' helps Carter 11-23, 881A3
Scores air bag decision 12-6, 921E1

1977

NAACP—*See NATIONAL Association for the Advancement of Colored People*
NAACP Legal Defense and Educational Fund, Inc.
Integratn rules ordrd for 6 state colls 1-17, 112C2
Cities Svc bias accord rptd 3-2, 279E1
Days confrmd asst atty gen 3-4, 211E1
Sues HEW Southn schl effort 5-11, 446D2
Coll integratn plan issued 7-5, 630G2
Chambers at black ldrs mtg 8-29, 702F1
NABOKOV, Vladimir
Dies 7-2, 604E3 ★
NABR—*See BASKETBALL Referees, National Association of*
NADER, Ralph
Dixon slurs 1-17, apologizes 2-2, 95G3
A-plant accident liability limit voided 3-31, 277D2
Health group files DES suit 4-25, 431B3
Hails air bag order 6-30, 522D1
Phenformin sales banned 7-25, 603D2
DBCP curbed, health group plea cited 9-8, 723B3
Group to aid sports fans 9-27, 820F1
Consumer agency bill shelved 11-1, 856B3
Scores ex-colleague, asks hwy safety admin resignatn 11-30, 1008A1
NADON, Maurice
Denies RCMP probed MPs 8-18, 653D2
Retires, Simmonds replaces 9-1, 742B2
Contradicted on MP probe 9-20, 742B2
NAGARWALA, H. M.
Sanjay Gandhi faces probe 4-1, 283B3
NAIA—*See NATIONAL Association of Intercollegiate Athletics*
NAIRAC, Robert
IRA rpts executn 5-16, 5 chrgd 5-28, 487F2

1978

NAACP—*See NATIONAL Association for the Advancement of Colored People*
NABER, John
Wins Sullivan Award 2-7, 780F2
NABISCO v. Korzen
Northwestn U tax dispute review refused by Sup Ct 5-1, 364E1
NABOKOV, Nicholas
Dies 4-6, 356C3
NADER, Ralph
'73 'bumping' case award cut 1-10, 67F3-68A1
Health group scores HEW anti-smoking plan 1-11, 23G2
Aviatn group scores CAB 1-31, 68A1
Scores consumer agency defeat 2-8, 82A2
Energy Projct scores spent A-fuel storage rpt 3-15, 184A1
Energy Project scores A-plant licensing bill 3-17, 205A3
Oil lobbyist's energy policy role questnd 5-15, 408E2
Scores Pinto recall pact 8-22, Vega safety 8-30; Ford rebuts 8-26, 719D1
Brandon criticism of tax cut bill rptd 10-16, 785E2
Tax group scores reform bill 10-16, 785E2
Cong Watch rates 95th sessn 10-28, 865B2-A3
Cong Watch rpts big spenders win Sen races 11-15, 898B1
NAGEL, Ken
2d in Legends of Golf tourn 4-30, 356B1
NAGUIB, Gamal
On Sadat boycott of Nobel award rites 12-2, 950C3
NAHURY, Elias
Kills self 6-10, 454E3
NAHYAN, Sheik Sultan bin Zaid al
Financial Gen sues 2-17, 204B3
SEC chrgs 3-18, settles 3-19, 204A2
NAIA—*See NATIONAL Association of Intercollegiate Athletics*
NAIF, Abdul Razak al-
Shot 7-9, dies 7-10, 522E2
2 suspects held 7-12, 582A3
Fatah ties Iraq to death 7-17, 546E3
NAIRAC, Capt. Robin (d. 1977)
Murder trial postponed 2-20, 132F3
NAJAFI, Hossein
Iran justice min 10-30, 827E3
Shah for special ct to try accused 11-8, 858C1

1979

NAACP Legal Defense and Educational Fund
NAACP votes to withdraw name 6-25, 559F3
NABISCO Inc.
Williams settles PVM chrg 3-6, 308B3
NABOKOV, Vladimir (1899-1977)
Despair released 2-15, 174D2
NACOGDOCHES, Tex.—*See TEXAS*
NADER, Ralph
Consumer group suits curbed 3-14, 308G1
Urges 3 Mile Island probe 4-5, 260B3
At Diablo Canyon A-protest 4-7, 262A1
Scores Carter A-policy at DC protest 5-6, 343D3
Lauds Citizens Party platform 8-1, 594F3
Vs Cutler apptmt as Carter counsel 8-17, 623F1
Vs radio deregulatn 9-11, 859C1
At NYC A-protest 9-23, 742F2, A3
Backs oil industry protest 10-17, 831D2
Clashes with Garn in Sen hearing 11-20, 1005F3
NADLER, Arch
But Never Jam Today opens 7-31, 711A2
NADON, Maurice
Dare testifies on '72 APLQ break-in 7-4, 522C3
NAEYE, Dr. Richard L.
Sex seen as pregnancy risk 11-29, 971C3-D3, E3
NAFTALIN, Neil T.
Securities fraud convictn upheld by Sup Ct 5-21, 400D3
NAGELSEN, Betsy
Loses Australian Open 1-3, 103D2
NAGY, Ferenc
Dies 6-12, 508D3
NAIA—*See NATIONAL Association of Intercollegiate Athletics*
NAIF Ibn Abd al Aziz, Prince (Saudi Arabia)
On mosque siege end 12-4, 916A1

1980

NAACP—*See NATIONAL Association for the Advancement of Colored People*
NAACP Legal Defense and Educational Fund Inc.
Davis dies 7-12, 608E1
NABAVI, Behzad
US hostage response study com set 11-13, 861D2
Urges US accept demands on hostage issue 12-19, 973D1
NACCACHE, Anis
Seized in Bakhtiar death try 7-18, 545C1
NACHMAN Corp. v. Pension Benefit Guaranty Corp.
Case decided by Sup Ct 5-12, 426C3
NADER, Ralph
Cong Watch ratings issued 1-12, 53A3
Aptitude test study disputed 1-14, 36G1, E2
Scores Abscam probe leaks 2-8, 82C3
Libel case declined by Sup Ct 2-19, 131E1
Cited in Connally 'basic speech' 3-7, 184B3
Ct limits children's work 3-20, 227F1
'Big Business Day' held 4-17, 308G1
'78 Allegheny 'bumping' award overturned 5-16, 703B2
Scores Carter consumer programs 6-9, 703C1
CAB sued on domestic airfare hike OK 6-18, 516C1
'79 A-plant mishaps rptd 7-14, 551D2
Arab boycott data released 10-20, 801B1
NADIG, Marie-Therese
Wins Olympic medal 2-17, 155A3
NAFA, Mahmoud
Killed 4-25, 353A3
NAHAS, Naji
In Hunt silver-backed bond group 3-26, 223B1
NAH-Tipoteh, Togba
Backs private enterprise 4-25, 353D2
NAIK, Naiz A.
Moslems drop Israel UN ouster plan 10-9, 775F1
NAIMI, Ali I.
Named to Aramco bd 7-8, 662F1
NAIRN, Allan
Scores aptitude tests 1-14, 36A2

1976

NADJARI, Maurice H.
Murtagh dies 1-13, 56F3 ★
Sandler replaces Murtagh 1-16, 79A1
Glowa indicted 1-27, 144E3
DeSapio pleads not guilty 5-24, 442B3
Cunningham indicted 5-26, 6-7, 442F2
Jurisdictn limited 6-3, indictmts dismissed 8-12—12-22, 1016F1
Dismissed 6-25, 1016D1
NAGANO, Shigeo
Urges arms export ban end 1-9, 157F1
NAGATSUKI (Japanese warship)
In Intl Naval Review 7-4, 488D3
NAGR, Josef
Named agri min 9-15, 750G2
NAHOLO, Festus
Scores Namibia plan 8-19, 654F1
Asks Angola aid 11-11, 862E2
NAJEIMY, Robert
Slain 2-17, 125G1
NAJEM, Najem
Kills 2 Amer Univ deans 2-17, 125A2
NAKASONE, Yasuhiro
In Miki A-pact talks 1-9, 51D2
Backed Miki 6-14, 458A2 ★
Lockheed link rptd, Parlt com bars testimony 8-26, 677B1
Cabt, party chngs proposed 8-30, 677A1
Miki shuffles Cabt, LDP 9-15, 694F1
NALBANDYAN, Suren
Wins Olympic medal 7-24, 576A3
NALCO Chemical Co.—*See CALGON Corp.*
NAMIBIA (South-West Africa)—*See under SOUTH Africa*
NAMMOCK, John
Angola sentences 6-28, 480B2
NANDI, Sharon
Loses passport 7-18, 538B2
NANTUCKET Island—*See MASSACHUSETTS*
NAPOLITANO, Giorgio
Socres Socialists 1-11, 29F2
Abandons coalitn, asks austerity progrm 6-13, 445G2
NARANJO, David
Daughter kidnaped 3-24, 251D2
NARANJO, Francia
Kidnaped 3-24, 251D2
Ransomed 6-16, 731C2
NARAYAN, Jayaprakash
Indian Express revamped 1-3, 74A1
Assails emergency rule 2-13, 139G3
Aids party merger 3-26, 253F2
Heads civil rights group 10-17, 810A3
NARAYAN, K. R.
Named amb to China 4-15, 278E3
Takes amb post in Peking 7-7, 538C2
NARCISO, Filipina B.
Chrgd with murder 6-16, out on bond 6-30, 503D3

1977

NAMATH, Joe
Waived by Jets 4-1, debuts as Ram 8-6, 659C2
NAMIBIA (South-West Africa)—*See under SOUTH Africa*
NAMIBIA, UN Council on—*See under UNITED Nations*
NANGOLO, Filemon
Hanged 5-30, 457E2
NAOR, Aryeh
W Bank, Gaza Arabs to get rights 8-14, 623F1
NAPALM—*See CHEMICAL & Biological Warfare*
NAPOLITAN, Joseph
On Panama deal 3-24, 379B2
NAPOLITANO, Art
Hartwick wins NCAA soccer title 12-4, 1020F3
NARAIN, Raj
Listed as prisoner 2-1, 71F2
Freed, to seek Gandhi seat 2-7, 116A2
Defeats Gandhi for Parlt seat 3-16—3-20, 205B2
Indian health min 3-26, 240C1
Birth curb program eased 4-2, 283F3
NARAYAN, Jayaprakash
Returns New Delhi 1-22; vs govt rule 1-23, 63E3
Picks Desai as prime min 3-24, 205D1
NARCISO, Filipina B.
Convicted 7-13, 568F2
New trial ordrd 12-19, 991G2

1978

NAJAR, Amiel
Cites UNESCO rpt on Israeli occupatn 11-13, 931G1
NAJARIAN, Thomas
Finds high cancer rate at Portsmouth Shipyd 2-19, 164B3
NAKASONE, Kasuhiro
Backers in Ohira Cabt 12-7, 945E2
NAKAWAGA, Ichiro
In US trade talks 9-5—9-7, 695C1
Signs US citrus, beef pact 12-5, 988D2
Chrgs Tanaka vote fraud 12-6, 945G2
NAKSONE, Yasuhiro
To run for premier 839B1
Cited in Lockheed case, denies link 10-26, 838D3
Ohira wins LDP electn 11-27, 912A3
NAMATH, Joe
Retires from football 1-24, 172C1
Ewbank enters Pro Football HoF 7-29, 1025C1
NAMIBIA (South-West Africa)—*See under SOUTH Africa*
NANNINGA, Dirk
Argentina wins World Cup 6-25, 520E2
NAON, Alberto
Belgian bank chrgs cited 4-12, 326B2
NAOR, Aryeh
Israel reaffirms Res 242 stand 4-16, 275A1
NAPLEY, Sir David
Thorpe trial ordrd 12-13, 987F3
NAPOLITAN, Joseph
Hired by Venez pol party 5-5, 395G1
Candidate loses Venez pres electn 12-3, 953A1
NAPURI, Ricardo
Rpts newspr bombed 9-3, gang assault 9-15, 775G3, 776A1
NARAIN, Raj
Vs govt handling of Gandhi case 6-28; Cabt ask resignatn 6-29, quits 6-30, 516F1
Janata Party averts split 7-9, 631C3
NARAYAN, Jayaprakash
Singh quits Janata posts, party split seen 4-29, 374D3
NARCISO, Filipina B.
Chrgs dropped 2-1, 116D2

1979

NAJARIAN, Dr. Thomas
Portsmouth shipyd A-cancer study begins 1-31, 91B1
NAKANO, Desmond
Boulevard Nights released 3-22, 528E1
NAM—*See MANUFACTURERS, National Association of*
NAMIBIA (South-West Africa)—*See under SOUTH Africa*
NAPOLI Sr., James V.
Priest-pentinent case declined by Sup Ct 10-1, 767G3
NARAIN, Raj
Ray sworn health min 1-24, 97A3
Quits Janata party, scores Desai 6-26, 503B2, 544G1
NARAYAN, Jayaprakash
Dies 10-8, 860A3
NARCOLEPSY—*See MEDICINE–Diseases*
NARCO Scientific Inc.
Daylin drops bid 1-24, 88F3
NARCOTIC Drugs, Commission on—*See UNITED Nations–Economic & Social Council*

1980

NAKAGAWA, Ichiro
In Japanese Cabt 7-17, 539C3
NAKAJIMA, Shigeo
Zapata decisns for WBC junior flywgt title 3-24, 320C3
Zapata TKOs 9-17, 1000G3
NAKANA, Shigeto
Quits as Japan army staff chief 1-28, 99D3
NAKASONE, Yasuhiro
Party factn in Cabt, gets minor post 7-17, 539A3, C3
NAMIBIA—*See SOUTH Africa--Namibia*
NAN Duck Woo (South Korean premier)
Named S Korea premier 9-2, 673A1
NANZ, Robert H.
Scores oil leasing schedule 6-17, 552A3
NAPIER, John
Elected to US House 11-4, 844B2, 850F1
NAPIER, Oliver
Home rule talks begin 1-7, 39A2

NARCOTICS & DANGEROUS DRUGS

NARCOTICS & Dangerous Drugs (1976)
CIA files on '53 LSD death made public 1-10, 24F3
Pot seized in NC, 9 arrested 1-11, 160D1
Ford State of Union message 1-19, 38D2, 39C3
Ford seeks human drug test ban 2-18, 127A3
Leary denied parole 3-1, 272D1
US office, fed funding signed 3-19, 233D3-234A1
Ford seeks minimum sentnc law 4-9, 280G3
Sen com rpts on CIA, other US testing 4-26, 299F2, 303D2-G2
Ford presents program 4-27, 307B2
Sup Ct backs convictn rule 4-27, 349A2
Black Dems draft plank 5-1, 343E3
Leary released 6-7, 424G1
Dems reject pot plank 6-15, 432F3
Dem platform text 6-15, 471D3, 472E3, 474B1
Warrantless 'doorway' arrests affirmed 6-24, 553C1
Ford signs authorizatn bill 6-30, 532F3
Auto traffic violatn searches affirmed 7-6, 535C1
Valium, alcohol head NIDA most abused list 7-9, 524E1-B2
GOP platform text 8-18, 604G1, A2, 605A2, 610E3
Ford acceptance speech 8-19, 611E3
Detroit police dep rptd probed 8-20, 776D2
Howe campaign chrmn arrested 8-24, 636A3
Ford, Carter debate 9-23, 702G1
Pot possessn crime rating lowered 10-4, 796F3
Marijuana use for glaucoma OKd 10-5, 860F3
Mondale, Dole debate 10-15, 782E3
Wis votes pot legalizatn 11-2, 824B1
HS student '76 pot use up 11-23, 931D3
'75 heroin use deaths rptd 12-12, 972A3

NARCOTICS & Dangerous Drugs (1977)
Carter names special asst 1-14, 35C3
Campus views study released 1-14, 157B2
Inaugural protest on marijuana penalties 1-20, 26E2
Homegrown pot decriminalizatn urged 2-4, 332E2
NY prescriptn ruling voided 2-22, 150F1
Chemical Bank indicted 2-24, 155E2
Chem Bank, 2 ex-offcls plead guilty 3-3, 4-14, 540A3
Carter call-in topic 3-5, 171E1
Carter for pot decriminalizatn, sets cocaine review 3-14, 332G1
Chicago motorman denies chrg 3-17, 412F3
Amphetamine-morphine painkiller rptd 3-31, 288B1
Pot decriminalizatn study rptd 3-31, 332G2
Gallup finds pot use up, decriminalizatn backed 4-1—4-4, 972F2-A3
Ariz drug rings rptd 4-3, 332G3
U of Pa radio station loses license 4-4, 395B3
Handicapped rules disputed 4-5, 301C3
Army pot use rptd up 4-6, 343B2
Handicapped rules signed 4-28, 338B3
Okla, Tex OK executn by drugs 5-10, 5-11, 594F1, G1
Ga state sen acquitted 5-20, 424E1
Justice Dept warrantless searches curbed 6-21, 539A1
Cocaine use detailed by NIDA 7-6, 972G1
French Connectn dealer slain 7-26, 642B1
CIA mind-control tests revealed 8-1—8-9, 610F3
Carter urges pot decriminalizatn, drug abuse studies 8-2, 609E1-A2
2 NFL Dolphins sentenced 8-10, 659A2
Ranger player arrested 8-18, 1021E1
CIA mind-control tests probed 9-2—9-21, 721D1
Polanski case cited 9-19, 732D3
A's player arrested 10-28, 927B2
NJ police harassmt case review refused 10-31, 835D2
Ida secret news source case review refused 10-31, 835F2
'Angel dust' health risk rptd 11-1, 972B2
Heroin abuse rptd down 11-7, 972A1
Pot decrminalizatn backed by AMA, ABA 11-13, 972A3
Pain relief study urged 11-16, 992E3
Barbiturate deaths rptd 11-27, 972E3
Major NYC dealer convicted 12-2, 972D1
Pot decriminalizatn statutes rptd 12-11, 972C3

NARCOTICS & Dangerous Drugs (1978)
NYC dealer gets life 1-19, 95E3
Marijuana penalties eased in US crime code revisn 1-30, 64A3
DEA ex-agents convicted 3-10, 380B1
Paraquat peril in marijuana warned 3-10, rptd exaggerated 8-3, 728B2
Sanderson makes NHL comeback 3-15, 296E3
3 Hughes ex-aides indicted 3-16, 6-6, 459F1
'French Connectn' prisoner slain in Ga jail 4-10, 396G2
Spinks arrested 4-21, avoids indictmt 5-18, 379A1
NHL player fined 4-24, suspended 7-24, 656D3
Armed forces abuse rptd up, random tests backed by White House 4-25, 4-27, Pentagon opposes 4-28, 368B2-A3
Fed tap power broadened by Sup Ct 5-15, 387F2
Lung damage rptd in chronic marijuana users 5-15, 728G2
Marijuana OKd for glaucoma victim 5-19, 728F3
US Army drug use studied 5-24, 6-1, 433D2-B3
State soc svc claims setlmt signed 6-12, 465F3
Double jeopardy doctrine reversed by Sup Ct 6-14, 468B3
Cepeda sentenced for pot smuggling 6-14, 1026F2
Murder scene search warrants backed by Sup Ct 6-21, 509D2
Carter unveils pub housing plan 7-10, 525A2
Marijuana treatmt OKd by NM 2-22, 598C3
Ala ex-sheriff arrested re marijuana 7-14, 844G2; sentncd 12-1, 992G1
Bourne quits in methaqualone scandal 7-20, 549G2
Carter staff use rptd, Carter warns 7-20—7-24, 568B1
Cocaine preference by monkeys rptd 8-11, 771C1
Blood test pinpoints marijuana use 8-29, 728C3
Victimless crime study issued 9-11, 842B2
2 Ga prison officers chrgd 9-14, 771B1
Hughes ex-aide cleared 9-21, 1011A1
Carter urges Viet vets progrm 10-10, 878E1
Punk rock star accused of murder 10-12, 842C1
Synanon incidents 9-19—10-17; Calif probes 10-15, forms task force 10-17, 841G3-842B1
Rolling Stone's heroin sentnc suspended 10-24, 842E1

NARCOTICS & Dangerous Drugs (1979)
NY cocaine case challenge declined by Sup Ct 1-8, 14C3
Carter budget proposals 1-22, 44B3
Ford heir arrested 1-23, 202E3
Heroin overdose kills punk-rock star 2-2, 156B3
CBOE raid nabs 10 cocaine traders 2-7, 119C3
NIDA rpts drug abuse costs, pot use 2-12, 140C2
Darvon warning ordrd 2-15, 138A3
Airport luggage search case declined by Sup Ct 2-26, 164G3
Ill prison search nets drugs 3-3, 196G3
Hayes pleads guilty 3-14, sentncd 3-22, 335B3
NYC Transit Auth ex-addict ban backed by Sup Ct 3-21, 231B2
Random car checks by police barred by Sup Ct 3-27, 263D1
Fla pot ring rptd broken 5-1, 492D3
Pres panel rpts pot use up 5-21, 492G2
Drug dealers blamed in Tex judge's death 5-29, 431E2
More states OK pot medical use 6-1, Ore law signed 6-18, 492B3
Califano backs pot controls 6-6, Civiletti urges reforms 6-9, 492A2, D2
Hell's Angels arrested 6-14, 492B1
'Good faith' arrest backed by Sup Ct 6-25, 540C1
Prescriptn drug leaflets urged 6-29, 571F1
Amphetamine curbs urged, abuse detailed 7-16, 571C3
Rep Jenrette denies drug role probe 8-8, 650B1
Yeoman chrgd re US drug secrets sales 8-14, 611E1
Drug dealer convicted in Tex 8-15, 818F3
Jordan denies cocaine use 8-24, aides back 8-25, Landau disputes 8-28, 647D1-E2
Tax loss on illegal income estimated 8-31, 665A3
Jordan cocaine probe continues 8-31—9-28, FBI expands 9-13, 767B2
Cocaine trade growth rptd, use data cited 9-5, 972D2
Army settles LSD suit 9-6, 705F1
Fla '78 FRB deposit growth, drug traffic linked 9-6, 840E3
L Blair pleads guilty 9-6, 859C3
Naval Academy expels 13 9-10, 725B1
Valium abuse detailed in Sen 9-10, 734F2
13 Marines moved on pot suspicion 9-12, 809A2
D Kennedy robbed in NYC 9-12, 859G3
Calif judge arrested 9-20, 748F1

NARCOTICS & Dangerous Drugs (1980)
NBA players chrgd with cocaine possessn 1-2, 7-13; teammate killed in car crash 5-23, 656B2
Prosecution disparities rptd 1-6, 24B3
State of State messages 1-7, 404E2; 1-15, 268E3
Naval Academy expels 2 1-17, 94G3
23 AF guards disciplined in drug probe 1-17, 115F3
D Kennedy MD found guilty on drug chrgs 1-18, 199G3
Presley MD license suspended 1-19, 199C1
D Kennedy drug therapy program rptd 1-22, 199E3
12 AF cadets resign re pot use 1-24, 115E3
Heroin addictn drug treatmt rptd 2-2, 160E1
8 convicted in Fla 'Black Tuna' pot ring 2-4, 270C3
Commercial THC dvpt rptd 2-4, pot cancer use found 3-24, 357F3
Hayes paroled 2-6, released from prison 2-27, 175F2
Spouse testimony upheld by Sup Ct 2-27, 188C2
Addict job project gains rptd 2-27, 228E3
Galante slaying probe figures indicted 3-3, 215C1
KC Royals catcher rpts treatmt 3-14, 637F1
Mandatory sentncs rptd up 3-29, 359E1
Va 40-yr pot case remanded by Sup Ct 3-31, 291F2
Cooperatn standard in sentencing backed by Sup Ct 4-15, 306A2
Barnes convictn review refused by Sup Ct 4-21, 344G1
Darvon to be curbed; '78-79 related deaths rptd 4-24, 358A2
Calif judge resigns, sentenced 5-5, 414F1
Presley MD indicted 5-16, 414B2
'Exclusionary rule' narrowed by Sup Ct 5-27, 453B2
DEA detainmt procedure backed by Sup Ct 5-27, 453G3-454A1
Jordan cleared re cocaine chrgs 5-28, 402C3
Fla bank rules tightened 6-3, drug money linked 6-5, 502A1-A2
Pryor burned in blast 6-9, released from hosp 7-25, 638D1
NY drug dealer sentenced 6-12, 503F1-A2
Schl newspaper censorship power upheld 6-13, 583A1
Illegal search protectn narrowed by Sup Ct 6-25, 541F1
DEA detainmt procedure curbed by Sup Ct 6-30, 511G1

1976

International Developments
US-Mex drug drive rptd launched 1-2; '75 Levi talks rptd 1-19, 61D1
Rpt Jamaicans sell pot, cocaine in US 1-8, 51F1
Ecuador ousts Dutch newsman 1-13, 28F2
US, 4 Latin natns set drug drive 1-20, 61A1
Colombia sentncs US baseball mgr's daughter 1-21, 160A3
Colombia seizes cocaine 1-24, 1-27, 118F2
US convicts Colombia pushers 1-26, 61A2
Danish crackdown rptd 1-26, 101A1
Colombia cultivatn rptd, US airfields uncovered 1-28, 118G2
US, Venez see closer cooperatn 2-17, 177F2
Ford seeks curbs on CIA spying 2-18, 127C3
Chile-US cocaine flow cut 3-1, 288F3-289A1
Mex breaks US-tied ring 3-5, 420D1
US convicts flee jail 3-12, 420E1
US, Mex chrgs rptd 3-15—3-17, 6-9, 419G3
US-Canada extraditn treaty 3-22, 238D3
Canada law review urged 3-25, 250D3
Rpt US guns traded for Mex drugs 4-14, 420E1
Ford seeks cooperatn 4-27, 307G2
Mex rpts on opium poppy fields 6-8, 419E3
US Dem platform text cites 6-15, 477B1
W Ger, France conf on offenses 7-6, 521F1
Australia smuggling ring rptd 7-8, 537E1
Olympics disqualify Cerutti 7-19, 563B2
USSR chrgs China role 7-24, intensive drug drive rptd 8-25, 655A2
US natls rptd held in Yugo 7-27, 559A3
Getty kidnap suspects jailed 7-29, 816C3
USSR cuts UK natl's sentnc 7-30, 655B2
3 US natls sentncd in USSR 8-27, 655E1-A2
USSR sentncs Swiss 9-3, 2 UK natls 9-9, 857F1
Dutch police seize hashish 9-26, 732D2
Police held in Brazil murders 10-11, 850E2
Scandinavia expels N Korea envoys 10-15—10-22, 799E2
US natls lose Sovt ct appeal 10-26, 857F1
USSR ousts N Korean envoys 12-8, 967D1
Latin 'Triangle' convictns 12-9, 971F2-C3
Brazil death squads linked 12-26, 997G3
Yugo drug use rise, Turk smuggling rptd 12-29, 1012G1

1977

Foreign Developments (including U.S. international news)
French Connectn dealer sentncd 1-21, 103B1
Algeria grants UK natl clemency 1-25, 139E3
US-Mex heroin, arms exchng rptd 1-26, 66C1
Thai poppy planting, Golden Triangle output rptd 4-1, 393D3
US-Mex airborne smuggling rptd 4-8, 332D3
US-Far Asia conf opens 4-14, 331G2
Mex frees US offenders 4-16—6-21, 529B1
Mex-US connection broken 4-20, 711C3
US-Bolivia talks 5-16, 414G2
Mrs Carter sees Colombia pres 6-10, 455C2
Australia drug abuses, smuggling rptd widespread; Sen panel backs pot decriminalizatn 7-22—11-18, 944D3-945A1
Australia opens drug trade probe 7-27, 578G2
Cuba to free US pot smugglers 8-11, 653D3
US-Latin cocaine flow estimates revised 8-29, 972E1
Australia probe set 10-5, 779B2
Burma opium crackdown cited 10-6, 779G2
Panama ldr rptd in drug trade 10-13; US clears, implicates brother 10-13, 10-15, 792D1
W Eur heroin conf rpts use up 10-17—10-21, 971B3
US-Golden Triangle heroin trade rptd down 11-7, 972B1 ★
Panama angered by US chrgs 11-13; Dole to get file on Torrijos' brother 11-16, 912C2
Canada raids 11-17—12-8, arrests rptd 12-15, 1010A3
US, Mex prisoners exchngd 12-9, 957G2
Bolivia, US set prisoner pact 12-20, 1010C3

1978

Pattison loses US House seat 11-7, 849G1
McCarthy morphine addictn, White House pot use rptd 11-19, 943C2
'71-77 state discipline vs MDs rptd up 12-1, 992D3
Synanon founder arrested 12-2, 971G1
12 Marines rptd relieved of duties for suspected pot use 12-9, 960B3
Indiana players disciplined for pot use 12-12, 1028B1

Foreign Developments (including U.S. international news)
US Sen probes Panama ldr 2-10, 2-21—2-22; brother's indictmt unsealed 2-21, chrgs denied 2-22, 120B2
W Ger '77 deaths rptd 2-12, 211A2
Mex rptr slain after expose, probe vowed 2-13—2-16, drug traffic detailed 3-17, 289F3
Commonwealth regional mtg sets study 2-16, 121D2
Colombia drug trade, pol ldrs linked 2-28, 147F1, C2
US, Mex end prisoner exchng 3-6, 290F1
US, Venez OK drug trade cooperatn 3-28, 233E1
Canada RCMP break-ins linked 4-18, 311G3
Honduras mil ldrs linked to drug trade; Inter pol chief, rptrs seized 4-24—7-10, 614E3
E-W Ger heroin smuggling, US mil use linked 6-1, 433G2
Scottish soccer player suspended 6-5, 520B3
Mex rptd torturing offenders 6-17, 10-3, 817G3, 818A1
Colombia pres chrgs slander 6-23, 630A1
Australia increases coast patrols 7-9, 530B2
US-Colombia marijuana trade arrests 7-14, 844A3
Belgian cyclist suspended, fined 7-16, 692D2
Colombia marijuana crop triples 9-2; US signs anti-drug pact 9-29, 815B1
Mex drug dealers killed 9-19; 6000 seized over 18 mos 10-3, 817F3
Narcotics control cited in '79 US forgn aid bill 9-26, 734E1
Cuba frees 2 US offenders 10-3, 777A1
Nicaragua pres scores Colombia 10-14, 839C3
Bolivia pres presses anti-smuggling drive 11-15, ousted in coup 11-24, 913G1
Canada prov sets treatmt law 12-18, 1013B3

1979

BZ tested by Army in '64, stockpile rptd 9-24, 727F1
Viet vet abuse revealed 9-25, 725D1
$100, $50 bill use, crime linked 9-25, 727F2
NYU prof indicted 10-4, 839G3
Hell's Angels trial opens 10-4, 840E1
Carter on Jordan cocaine probe 10-9, 767B2
Cocaine seized in Fla, 3 arrested 10-12, 10-14, 819B3
Pot potency spurs health concern 10-14, 971F3
Papa slayers convicted 10-23, 840A2
Jordan alleged cocaine supplier indicted 10-23, 891D3
Calif pot farm growth rptd 10-29, 972F1
NYS trial closure case declined by Sup Ct 11-5, 884E3
Mil heroin use rptd 11-11, 972C3, E3
Cepeda hired by White Sox 11-20, 1002F2
Viet vet dischrgs ordrd upgraded 11-28, 992D1
Boxing suspended in NYS 11-28–12-27, 1005A1
Extended searches curbed by Sup Ct 11-28, 944F2
Jordan cocaine probe spec prosecutor named 11-29, 900C3
Jordan supplier pleads guilty 12-18, 1000E1
Presley MD rptd chrgd 12-19, 1005C3

Foreign Developments (including U.S. international news)
Canada '71 CIA LSD abuse rptd 1-29, 95F3-96B1
US lauds Thai curbs 2-7, 84C2
Canada air safety abuses rptd 2-8–2-14, 134D1
UN comm gets US cost rpt 2-12, 140C3
Australia surveillance bill proposed 3-8, 209C3
Iran halts trial of ex-premr 3-16, 199G1
Venez pres, Mondale discuss 3-23–3-24, 2248E1
UK soccer teams cleared 3-28, 655D2
USSR frees UK smugglers 5-6, 390B2
Australia cop corruptn chrgd 6-5, 467C2, E2
Australia drug bur probe rptd 6-20, 467F2
'Colombia Connection' dealer convicted 8-15, 818F3
Peru, Bolivia cited re US cocaine trade growth 9-5, 972A3
USSR crime fight rptd 9-11, 857C2
E Ger swimmer cites drug use 9-19, 721F3
Pope warns vs drug use 10-1, 757D2
Canada prov law overturned 10-11, 853D2
Colombian arrested in US seizure 10-14, 819C3
7 E Eur women banned from track 10-26, 911F3
Mex, Colombia, Jamaica pot cited re Calif output growth 10-29, 972G1, A2
Australia drug traffic rpt issued, police unit set 11-6, 870D2
W Eur heroin use rptd up; US mil use, seizures noted 11-11, 972C3
Colombia drug smuggling via Bahamas rptd 12-7, 948B2

1980

Hell's Angels mistrial declared 7-2, 568G1
Tranquilizer warnings set 7-11, 584E1
Synanon founder convicted in murder attempt 7-15, 655E3
NYU prof convicted 7-16, 607F3-608A1
Film producer pleads guilty to cocaine chrgs 7-31, 639B3
Hell's Angels sentenced 8-18, 714B1
NBA cocaine use rptd widespread 8-19; league warns players, assn vows fight 8-20, 656E1, G2
2 B Carter associates rptd under investigatn 8-21, 647A2
Synanon founder gets probatn 9-3, 860D2
Hoffman surrenders in NY 9-4, 713G1
Kraft cocaine probe rptd, steps down as Carter campaign mgr 9-14, 700B1
Film producer gets probatn 10-7, 890E1
Libertarian pres candidate cites stance 10-28, 818A3
NYU prof gets 5 yrs 11-13, 997D3
Army LSD setlmt clears Cong 12-5, signed 12-18, 981F3
Kraft probe suspended 12-12, 989F2
Calif MD insulin-slaying chrgs reduced 12-29, 997C2

Foreign Developments (including U.S. international news)
McCartney arrested in Japan 1-16, deported 1-26, 1-16, 200E2
Canada convicts Valium producer, Librium acquittal cited 2-6, 116E2-C3
W Ger ct OKs Hoffmann-La Roche Valium, Librium pricing 2-12, 154C1
Peru launches cocaine crackdown 3-28, 277E1
Iran drug dealers executed 5-21, 419D3
Colombia drug money linked to Fla banks 6-5, 502E1
US Army cuts overseas duty time 6-6, 458B3
GI arrest in W Ger rptd 6-13, '79 total 6-23; heroin use rptd down 6-18, 517D1, B2
Iran drug dealers executed 7-3, 7-8, 507A2; 7-14, 7-20—7-21, 545G2
No Olympic drug use found 8-3, 590G2-B3
US halts Bolivia enforcemt aid 8-13, junta trafficking rptd 8-15, 667E3
RC bishops family life conf opens 9-26, 810C3
Cuba to free US prisoners 10-13, 789A1
Pope in W Ger, warns vs abuses 11-15—11-19, 905G2
Iran drug prosecutor chrgd, quits 12-7, 943F1

1976

NARITA, Tomomi
Loses premiership electn 12-24, 1006F2
NASCIMENTO, Lopo Fortunato Ferreira do
Urges West support MPLA 1-30, 82C2 ★
Confirms Cuban troop pullout 5-25, 370D3 ★
Visits USSR, mil aid vow rptd 5-31, 480F3 ★
Neto named head of state 10-29, 995C3
Named prime min 11-27, 995C3
NASH, Dr. Dorothy Klenke
Dies 3-5, 484F3
NASHUA, N.H.—*See NEW Hampshire*
NASHVILLE, Tenn.—*See TENNESSEE*
NASHVILLE (film)
Song wins Oscar 3-29, 240A3
NASHVILLE (U.S. warship)
In Intl Naval Review 7-4, 488C3
NASHVILLE Banner (newspaper)
Ford endorsement rptd 10-30, 831F2
NASHVILLE Tennesseean (newspaper)
Carter endorsement rptd 10-30, 831B3

1977

NARONG Kittikachorn
Returns to Thailand 7-10, 641A3
NASA—*See U.S. GOVERNMENT—NATIONAL Aeronautics & Space Administration*
NASCIMENTO, Edson Arantes do—*See PELE*
NASCAR (National Association for Stock Car Auto Racing)—*See AUTOMOBILES*
NASDAQ (National Association of Securities Dealers Automated Quotations)
'77 index closing rptd 12-30, 1003G3
NASH, John
Dies 9-23, 788B2
NASHVILLE, Tenn.—*See TENNESSEE*
NASHVILLE Gas Co. v. Satty
Maternity leave seniority rights upheld 12-6, 938D2

1978

NARCOTICS & Dangerous Drugs, Bureau of—*See under U.S. GOVERNMENT—JUSTICE*
NARIA, Giuliano
Genoan police offcl killed 6-21, 517F1
NARRAGANSETT Indians—*See INDIANS, American*
NAS—*See NATIONAL Academy of Sciences*
NASA—*See U.S. GOVERNMENT—NATIONAL Aeronautics & Space Administration*
NASCIMENTO, Edson Arantes do—*See PELE*
NASCIMENTO, Lopo Fortunato Ferreira do
Ousted 12-9, 985D1
NASD—*See National Association of SECURITIES Dealers*
NASDAQ (National Association of Securities Dealers Automated Quotations)
'77 index gain cited 1-1, 66G3
NASHVILLE, Tenn.—*See TENNESSEE*

1979

NARDINI, Tom
Rat's Nest opens 2-2, 292E2
NARIZZANO, Silvio
Class of Miss MacMichael released 1-26, 528A2
NARRON, Jerry
Traded to Mariners 11-1, 1002C3
NARUSAWA, Koei
Australia warned on exports 3-9, 188F2
NAS—*See NATIONAL Academy of Sciences*
NASA—*See U.S. GOVERNMENT–NATIONAL Aeronautics & Space Administration*
NASCIMENTO, Christopher (Kit)
On Peoples Temple assets 1-23, 117B3
NASD—*See SECURITIES Dealers, National Association of*
NASH (U.S. frigate)
Guantanamo maneuvers begin 10-17, 781G2
NASH, Graham
Performs at NYC A-protest 9-23, 742G2
NASH, Murray
Cited in H-bomb letter 9-16, 9-18, 717C1
NASH, N. Richard
Sarava opens 2-11, 292F2
NASHVILLE, Tenn.—*See TENNESSEE*
NASHVILLE Banner, The (Tenn. newspaper)
Gannett Co sells 7-5, 618C3

1980

NARIMISA, Dr. Ismail
Executed 6-29, MDs strike in protest 507B1
NAROZNIAK, Jan
Poles arrest 11-21, free 11-27, 909C1, F1
NAS—*See NATIONAL Academy of Sciences*
NASA (National Aeronautics & Space Administration)—*See under U.S. GOVERNMENT*
NASCAR (National Association for Stock Car Auto Racing)—*See AUTOMOBILE Racing*
NASCIMIENTO e Silva, Geraldo
Shot in Colombia DR emb raid 2-27, injury rptd 3-10, 180B3
Emb siege ends, freed in Cuba 4-27, 335G1
NASH, Charles
Watt TKOs 3-15, 320B3
NASHUA (race horse)
Hunts bailout loan collateral listed 5-28, 426C1
NASHUA Telegraph (newspaper)
GOP debate dispute sparked 2-23, 143D1

1976

NASSAU County, N.Y.—*See NEW York State*
NASSER, Gamal Abdel (1918-70)—*See 1970, p. 960E1 for biog. data*
Cleared of '67 theft chrg 2-4, 119B1
Guerrillas hijack jet 8-23, 629E2
NASSIRI, Mohammad
Wins Olympic medal 7-18, 576D2
NASTAC, Alec
Wins Olympic medal 7-31, 574D1
NASTASE, Ilie
Loses Baltimore intl indoor 1-25, 123G2
Runner-up in Players Assn tourn 3-14, 716C2
Loses Wimbledon 7-3, 504E1
Wins Tennis Week Open 8-29, 716G1
US Open results 9-12, 716B1
NATALI, Lorenzo
European Comm meets 12-22—12-23, 977F1
NATCHER, Rep. William H. (D, Ky.)
Reelected 11-2, 829E3
NATHAN, Gilbert
Loses MD malpractice suit 6-1, 1016C3
NATHAN, Harriet
Loses MD malpractice suit 6-1, 1016A3
NATION, The (magazine)
Kirchwey dies 1-3, 56E3
Purchase announced 11-28, 901C3
Sale to Morgan fizzles 12-21, 995E1
NATIONAL—*For organizations not listed below, see key words*
NATIONAL Academy of Sciences
Panel urges aerosol curb 9-13, 691C2
Handler urges DNA rules 11-1, 891E3
NATIONAL Airlines
Strike ends 1-4, 5E1
ALEA pact 2-19, 153A3
Ford rejcts CAB transatlantic plan 12-28, 992D2

NATIONAL Association for the Advancement of Colored People (NAACP)
Loses Cleveland school constructn plea 1-6, 6C2
Wilkins resigns 1-12, 80B2
Shriver Miss backing rptd 1-24, 95A1
Appeals Detroit schl plan 1-26, 95A2
Sen intellignc com cites as target 4-28, 330E1, G1
Sup Ct rules on FPC job bias powers 5-19, 393A3
Admin seeks busing rule review 5-20, 377C3
Wilkins vs anti-busing bills 6-24, 452D2
Sup Ct declines Chattanooga desegregatn review 6-30, 552A3 ★
Stays Wilkins retiremt actn 7-2, 504G2
Loses Miss boycott suit 8-9, plans appeal 8-12, 671C2
GOP, Dems busing planks scored 8-24, 8-25, 666G1
'Scottsboro Boy' pardoned 10-25, 860A1
Hooks to succeed Wilkins 11-6, 892A2
Scores Bell apptmt 12-20, 956G2

NATIONAL Bank of Georgia
Lance slated for Cabt 11-23, 898D2; named OMB dir 12-3, 916E1

1977

NASIR, Datuk Mohammed
Out as Kelantan chief min 885A2
NASIR, Ibrahim (Maldives president)
Vs Sovt based bid 10-2, 844F3
NASL (North American Soccer League)—*See SOCCER*
NASRULLAH Khan, Nawabzada
Vows contd defiance 3-26, 258F3
Vs Bhutto peace bid 4-15, 305C2
Arrested 4-24, 313B2
Released 6-2, 450A3
NASSER, Gamal Abdel (1918-70)—*See 1970, p. 960E1 for biog. data*
Hussein ousted from Assemb 2-14, 115G3
Sovt scores Sadat 2-27, 144C2
NASTASE, Ilie
WCT tourn results 2-13, 3-27, 4-10; Va Beach 4-23, 430E2-G2, F3
Loses 'heavyweight championship' 3-6; fee disclosure 5-7, FCC rpts probe 7-8, 548E2
Borg wins Wimbledon 7-2, 548E1
Barred from '78 Davis Cup 10-3, 1020A3
NATALI, Lorenzo
Gets Eur Comm post 1-7, 74C2
NATHANSON, Melvyn B.
Denied visa by USSR 10-3, 766G2
NATION, The (magazine)
Sold 12-22, 1004F3
NATIONAL—*For organizations not listed below, see key words*
NATIONAL Academy of Sciences (NAS)
DNA research forum 3-7—3-9, 184D2
Rpt scores EPA 3-21, 252B2
FDA orders fluorocarbon warning 4-26, 323A2
Rights com rptd formed 4-27, 315G1
Institute rpts on CAT scanner 5-2, 869B3
Ruled free from disclosures 5-23, 444B3
US exchng scholar denied Sovt visa 10-3, 766A3
Seafarer studies cited in Navy rpt 12-15, 977F3
NATIONAL Aeronautics & Space Administration—*See under U.S. GOVERNMENT*
NATIONAL Airlines Inc.
Paris, Amsterdam, Frankfurt routes OKd 12-21, 1006D2
NATIONAL Airport (Washington, D. C.)
Germ warfare tests rptd 3-8, 195E2
NATIONAL Archives & Records Service—*See under U.S. GOVERNMENT—GENERAL Services Administration*

NATIONAL Association for the Advancement of Colored People (NAACP)
Mtg rpts '76 budget surplus, opposes Bell as atty gen 1-8—1-10, 59G2
Vs Bell confrmatn 1-11—1-18, 34E1
Carter energy plan reactn rptd 4-23, 320G2
Carter scored at conv 6-27—6-28, 702A2
Vance addresses conv 7-1, 535B3
Hooks to become exec dir 7-27, 583G2-A3
Hooks at black ldrs mtg 8-29, 702E1
Cong anti-busing curbs challenged 12-9, 978E3
Hooks addresses AFL-CIO 12-13, 961E1
NATIONAL Association of Intercollegiate Athletics (NAIA)—*See specific sport (e.g., BASKETBALL)*
NATIONAL Association of Manufacturers (NAM)
Scores Carter econ plan 1-10, 14E1
Mandatory retiremt curb voted by House 9-23, 737G2
Consumer agency bill shelved 11-1, 856B3
NATIONAL Bank of Denver
NBA aids Nuggets 6-15, 584A1
NATIONAL Bank of Georgia (Atlanta)
Bell, Lance rpt holdings 2-25, 147D3, 148C1
Rpts 1st ½ loss 7-5, 7-13, 574D2
Lance cleared on finances, Chicago loan probe set 7-12—7-25; Ga bank stock buyer rptd 7-26, 573C3-574D2
Dividend rptd omitted 8-9, 626F1
Lance cleared in govt probe 8-18, 625F1-626F1
Carter defends Lance, sees regulatns reform need 8-23, 649F1
Carter to reimburse for plane use 8-24, 649E3
Lance practices rptd 9-6, 9-7, 690D1, F1
Lance testifies 9-15, 701D2, F2
Percy cites Lance planes use 9-17, 718D3
Lance sells shares to Saudi 12-27, 1003E2

1978

NASIR, Datuk Mohammed
Fed rule ends 2-12, electns set 2-13, 115B3
NASL (North American Soccer League)—*See SOCCER*
NASSER, Ahmed
USSR visit rptd 6-22, 584F2
NASSER, Gamal Abdel (1918-70)—*See 1970, p. 960E1 for biog. data*
Sadat oppositn curbs endorsed 5-23, 392F2; cracks down on critics 5-26, 5-28, 414F3, G3, 415B1
NASSIRI, Gen. Nematollah
Ousted as security chief, named Pak amb 6-6, 437C3
Oil strikers ask trial 10-31, 827A2
Quits as amb to Pak 827B3
Arrested 11-7, 858A1
NASTASE, Ilie
USTA ranks 10th 1-5, 22E3
Loses Houston WCT 4-23, 419C1
Loses Forest Hills Invitatn 7-16; wins Frankfurt Cup 12-10, WCT Challenge Cup 12-17, 1027G1, D2
Strings win WTT title 9-21, 1027F1
NASTU, Phil
Carew rejcts Giants trade 12-7, 1026A1
NASUR, Lt. Col.
Rptd ousted 4-30, 331E3
NASUTION, Adnan Buyung
Protests press ban 1-25, 72E1
NAT, Marie-Jose
Replay released 7-10, 970G2
NATALI, Lorenzo
Sees '80-81 Greek EC entry 1-26, 149C2
NATAMYCIN—*See MEDICINE—Drugs*
NATEL, Laudo
Loses Sao Paulo gov race 6-5, 556C1
NATER, Swen
NBA rebound ldr 4-9, 271F2
NATCHER, Rep. William H. (D, Ky.)
Reelected 11-7, 850E4
NATHANS, Daniel
Wins Nobel Prize 10-12, 886E2
NATHANSON, Paul
Backs Abitibi takeover of Price 9-29, 772E3
NATIONAL—*For organizations not listed below, see key words*
NATIONAL Academy of Sciences (NAS)
Research Cncl questns cancer-radiatn link at Hanford A-facility 2-17, 164F2
Oil cos cleared of '76-77 gas withholding 4-27, 322D1
19 physicists score Orlov trial, boycott Sovt conf 5-20, 401E1
USSR rights stand warning issued 8-22, 670E2
Range-land herd study set 10-11, 807A3
NATIONAL Aeronautics & Space Administration (NASA)—*See under U.S. GOVERNMENT*
NATIONAL Airlines Inc.
CAB '76 rule review barred 1-23, 65C2
Jet crashes in Fla bay 5-8, 460C2
Fla bay crash pilots fired 6-16, 636E3
TXI, Pan Am stock purchase OKd 8-17, 8-28; Pan Am merger set 9-7, 700G3
Pan Am to end svc to Moscow, 9 other Eur cities 9-7, 701A2
Fla bay crash rpt blames flight crew 11-9, 908F2 ★
Eastn seeks merger 12-11; Pan Am, TXI bids rptd probed 12-22, 1007B3
NATIONAL Airways Corp.
Air New Zealand merged 4-1, 498D2
NATIONAL Archives & Records Service—*See under U.S. GOVERNMENT—GENERAL Services Administration*
NATIONAL Association for the Advancement of Colored People (NAACP)
Carter energy plan scored 1-11, discord rptd 1-14, 68C1
S Africa business boycott asked 1-16, 38E3
Spinks-Ali rematch plan protested 3-8, site chngd 3-9, 212G1
US-S Africa Davis Cup protests 3-17—3-19, 251B1
Turner dies 4-21, 356E3
Dallas busing plan upset 4-24, 309D2
NYC schl ordrd desegregated 5-16, 369B2
Wilkins link to FBI anti-King effort, denial rptd 5-31, 410E3
Hooks on Bakke ruling 6-28, 482D2
S Africa sanctns sought 7-6, 632D3
Hooks addresses GOP Natl Com 7-21, 568B2
Carter sees ldrs on budget plans 12-11, 980A2

NATIONAL Association of Broadcasters v. FCC
FCC cross-media ban backed by Sup Ct 6-12, 467C3
NATIONAL Association of Intercollegiate Athletics (NAIA)—*See specific sport (e.g., BASKETBALL)*
NATIONAL Association of Securities Dealers Automated Quotations—*See NASDAQ*
NATIONAL Automobile Dealers Assn. v. Board of Governors of the Federal Reserve
Case declined by Sup Ct 10-2, 751B2
NATIONAL Bank of Chicago
Jamaica operatn cutback set 2-3, 95B1
NATIONAL Bank of Georgia (Atlanta)
Abedi role in Lance sale rptd 2-13, 204D3
SEC, comptroller file chrgs; case setld 4-26, 324G2-B3
Carter campaign com, bank fined for '76 plane use 6-26, 509A3

1979

NASLPA (North American Soccer League Players Association)—*See SOCCER*
NASSAU (U.S. amphibious assault ship)
Guantanamo maneuvers begin 10-17, 781F2
NASSERY, Zia Khan
On Sovt war role 12-10, 966A1
NASSIRI, Gen. Nematollah
Executed 2-16, 125D1
NASTASE, Ilie
Loses Grand Prix doubles 1-7, 103D3
Loses Cleveland Grand Prix 8-20, US Open results 9-9, 734C1, D2
NASTY Rumors and Final Remarks (play)
Opens 4-12, 712F1
NATER, Swen
NBA field-goal ldr 4-8, 290E2
NATHAN, Michael
Slain in NC 11-6, 864D3
NATIONAL—*For organizations not listed below, see key words; for U.S. departments and agencies, see under U.S. GOVERNMENT*
NATIONAL Academy of Sciences (NAS)
Amputatn linked to heart deaths 2-26, 219A2
Food-safety law revisns urged 3-2, 194G3
Einstein monumt unveiled 4-22, 392E2
Carter addresses 4-23, 300B2
Low-level, A-power radiatn risks reviewed 5-2, 609E2, A3
Army seeks chem test subjects 11-2, 850G2
Research Cncl ozone level risk study rptd 11-17, 1000E2
Air safety panel formed 12-19, 988F3
NATIONAL Airlines Inc.
Fuel shortage forces flight cuts 3-7, 162B2
CAB OKs Pan Am, TXI merger bids 7-10; TXI drops bid 7-28, Pan Am buys TXI holdings 8-2, 578D3
TXI eyes TWA merger 9-13, 830D1
CAB rejects Eastn merger bid 9-27; Pan Am rpts stock acquisitns 10-18, CAB OKs 10-25, Carter approval sought 10-29, 830A1
Carter OKs Pan Am merger 12-22, 989C1

NATIONAL Association for the Advancement of Colored People (NAACP)
Colored People
Bonilla elected LULAC pres 6-17, 810F1
Hooks sees Kennedy win, grudging Dem support 6-24, 559D3
Annual conv maps pol activism, other reforms; gives Mondale cool receptn 6-25—6-30, 559B3, E3
Weber case Sup Ct ruling lauded 6-27, 477G2
Mich HS voter turnout law signed 8-14, 724E2
Anti-KKK march in Columbus 8-18, 866F1
Dirs meet, affirm intl role 9-8—9-9; back US-PLO talks, Israel existence 9-11, 677D1
Hooks cautions blacks on PLO support 10-11, urges debate end 10-17, 780F2, B3
Sues vs Calif anti-busing measure 11-14, 991A2
Vs Connally on affirmative actn 11-26, 983A1
NATIONAL Association of Intercollegiate Athletics (NAIA)—*See specific sport (e.g., BASTKETBALL)*
NATIONAL Association of Regulatory Utility Commissioners v. Brookhaven Cable
Case declined by Sup Ct 4-16, 303A1
NATIONAL Bank of Georgia (Atlanta)
Lance banking practices, Carter favors detailed 1-17; Carter said unaware, to pay for plane use 1-18, 30E3-31B2
Lance, Carter repaymt barred 1-23, 55D3
Carter peanut loan scheme alleged 3-11—3-13, spec prosecutor sought 3-13, 183F3-184B2
Carter peaut probe spec counsel named, GOP scores limits 3-20, 203B1
Carter probe spec counsel gains more power 3-23, 301G2-B3

1980

NASIR, Maj. Gen. Nasir al-Din
Syrian interior min 1-16, 102G1
NASL (North American Soccer League)
See SOCCER
NASSER, Amin el-
Arrested 9-23, 736C3
NASSER, Gamal Abdel (1918-70)
Backers target of 'law of shame' 2-21, 148G3
Arab Socialist Union abolished 5-22, 406G3
Libya warns dissidents 6-7, 451B3
NASSERY, Zia Khan
Claims 'Free Islamic Repub' set 1-25, 67A3
NASTASE, Ilie
Fined at WCT doubles tourn 1-6, 213C2
Loses Dubai Golden 11-23, 947F2
NATCHER, Rep. William H. (D, Ky.)
Reelected 11-4, 842E4
NATER, Swen
NBA rebound ldr 3-30, 278E3, G3
NATHAN, Tony
NFL '79 punt return, kick return ldr 1-5, 8C3
NATION, The (magazine)
McWilliams dies 6-27, 528F2
NATIONAL—*For organizations not listed below, see key words; for U.S. departments and agencies, see under U.S. GOVERNMENT*
NATIONAL Academy of Sciences (NAS)
Energy rpt issued: A-power, coal use backed 1-14, 53D3
USSR mtgs barred re Sakharov 2-24, 181F2
Nutritn panel cholesterol rpt issued 5-27, scored 6-1, 432E2
Research Cncl asks FAA overhaul 6-26, 519A1
NATIONAL Aeronautics & Space Administration (NASA)—*See under U.S. GOVERNMENT*
NATIONAL Airlines Inc.
Pan Am merger completed 1-7, 346F2 •
Pan Am revives discount coupons 3-10, 346D3
Laker Miami-London svc OKd 5-15, 516D2
Jet hijacked to Cuba 8-14, 631B3

NATIONAL Association for the Advancement of Colored People (NAACP)
Austin busing plan set 1-3, 5C3
Hooks warns re despair 5-29, 460F1-A2
Conv held; pres candidates address 6-30—7-4, 515D2
Hooks addresses GOP conv 7-15, 533F3, 535A1
Ruby Hurley dies 8-10, 676F1
Hooks addresses Dem conv 8-13, 611E3
Gray withdraws as US judge nominee 9-17, 744D2
5th judicial circuit split, oppositn cited 10-14, 918D3
Alfred Lewis dies 10-30, 876C2
Electn results called setback 11-4, 846G3
NC KKK acquittals deplored 11-18, 898B3
Miss boycott liability held 12-10, 963C2

NATIONAL Bank of Canada
Loss rptd 9-5, 687A1
NATIONAL Bank of Georgia (Atlanta)
Lance cleared on fund misuse 4-30, 332D3

1976

NATIONAL Book Awards
Presented 4-19, 292C3
NATIONAL Broadcasting Co.—*See under RCA*
NATIONAL Can Corp.
USW contracts extended 8-18, 670C1
NATIONAL Car Rental System Inc.—*See under HOUSEHOLD Finance Corp.*
NATIONAL Central Bank (Lancaster, Penn.)
Arab boycott rpt released 10-20, 786A2
NATIONAL Collegiate Athletic Association (NCAA)—*See specific sport (e.g., TRACK)*
NATIONAL Conference of Christians and Jews
Ford addresses 6-6, 410C3
NATIONAL Council of Churches
Moss dies 10-25, 970E2
NATIONAL Education Association (NEA)
AFSCME quits AFL-CIO unit 2-15, 154B1
Carter sees Utah unit 10-7, 762C1
Wis unit hears Mondale, Ford 10-29, 826C2, D3
NATIONAL Enquirer (newspaper)
Buys Exner story on JFK 1-13, 80G2
NATIONAL Football League (NFL)—*See FOOTBALL*
NATIONAL Guard Association of the United States
Ford addresses 9-1, 645F1

1977

NATIONAL Bank of Washington (D.C.)
Rabin admits illicit account 4-8, 267A1
NATIONAL Basketball Association—*See BASKETBALL*
NATIONAL Broadcasting Co.—*See under RCA*
NATIONAL Cable Television Association
FCC obscenity rule ordrd suspended 9-1, 846C2
NATIONAL Cancer Institute—*See U.S. GOVERNMENT—PUBLIC Health Service—National Institutes of Health*
NATIONAL Can Corp.
Steelworkers OK new pact 10-31, 837E1
Forester Forbes Glass Co.
Strike ends 10-14, 818F3
NATIONAL Catholic Reporter, The (newspaper)
Thorman dies 11-30, 952F3
NATIONAL Collegiate Athletic Association (NCAA)—*See also specific sport (e.g., BASKETBALL)*
Annual conv 1-10—1-12, 104G1
NATIONAL Council of Churches (NCC)
Chilean asked to end US visit 1-28, 219E2
Trifa suspended from bd 2-4, 119F3
TV violence outcry rptd 2-9—2-18, 157E3
Lauds Carter plutonium ban 4-7, 268F1
Seoul office raided 4-12, 305F3
Carter gets protest on S Korea govt foes 4-19, 305D3
Kim meets US offcl 5-25, 441B1
Backs Panama Canal treaties 9-14, 716D3
S Africa investor boycott urged 11-10, 934C3
NATIONAL Distillers and Chemical Corp.
Kickbacks, pol paymts rptd 1-28, 215G1
Emery merger planned 12-19, 1004B3
NATIONAL Education Association (NEA)
'76 cong gifts rptd 2-15, 128G1
Scores SAT study 8-24, 739B2
ERA econ boycott rptd 11-14, 918C1
NATIONAL Endowment for the Arts—*See U.S. GOVERNMENT—NATIONAL Foundation—Arts, National Endowment for the*
NATIONAL Football League (NFL)—*See FOOTBALL*
NATIONAL Football League Players Association (NFLPA)—*See FOOTBALL—Professional*
NATIONAL Foundation on the Arts & the Humanities—*See under U.S. GOVERNMENT*
NATIONAL Gallery of Art (Washington, D.C.)
David Bruce dies 12-4, 1024A1
NATIONAL Geographic Society
Calif mail-order operatns tax upheld 4-4, 341E3
NATIONAL Guard—*See under U.S. GOVERNMENT*
NATIONAL Health Services Corps—*See U.S. GOVERNMENT—PUBLIC Health Service—Health Services Administration*

1978

NATIONAL Bank of North America—*See under C.I.T.*
NATIONAL Basketball Association (NBA)—*See BASKETBALL—Professional*
NATIONAL Basketball Players Association (NBPA)—*See BASKETBALL—Professional*
NATIONAL Book Awards—*See LITERATURE—Awards*
NATIONAL Broadcasting Co. (NBC)—*See under RCA*
NATIONAL Broiler Marketing Association
Trust immunity denied by Sup Ct 6-12, 468A1
NATIONAL Broiler Marketing Association v. U.S.
Poultry group trust immunity denied by Sup Ct 6-12, 468C1
NATIONAL Cancer Institute—*See U.S. GOVERNMENT—PUBLIC Health Service—National Institutes of Health*
NATIONAL Center for Toxicological Research—*See U.S. GOVERNMENT—FOOD & Drug Administration*
NATIONAL Citizens Com. for Broadcasting v. American Newspaper Publishers Assn.
FCC cross-media ban backed by Sup Ct 6-12, 467B3
NATIONAL Citizens Com. for Broadcasting v. Channel Two Television Co.
FCC cross-media ban backed by Sup Ct 6-12, 467B3
NATIONAL Citizens Com. for Broadcasting v. FCC
FCC cross-media ban backed by Sup Ct 6-12, 467C3
NATIONAL Citizens Com. for Broadcasting v. Illinois Broadcasting Co.
FCC cross-media ban backed by Sup Ct 6-12, 467C3
NATIONAL Citizens Committee v. FCC
'Fairness doctrine' case refused by Sup Ct 5-30, 430E3
NATIONAL College of Business (Rapid City, S.D.)
VA educ curbs backed by Sup Ct 3-20, 205E3
NATIONAL Collegiate Athletic Association (NCAA)—*See also specific sport (e.g., BASKETBALL)*
Conv 1-11—1-13, 40D1-C2
USOC rejoined 4-15, 842C3
Amateur sports bill clears Cong 10-15, 842E2-C3; Carter signs 11-8, 1003B1
NATIONAL Commission on Egg Nutrition v. FTC
Case declined by Sup Ct 10-2, 751D2
NATIONAL Commission on Working Women—*See under U.S. GOVERNMENT*
NATIONAL Council of Churches (National Council of the Churches of Christ in the U.S.A.) (NCC)
Roy Ross dies 1-8, 96D3
Korea unit scores US rights rpt 2-17, 135D2
'76 church contributns, membership rptd 3-3, 6-12, 907B3, C3
Female ordinatn study issued 3-23, 295F1-B2
Israel cluster-bomb use scored 5-12, 358B3
Viet receives US wheat 6-1, 400G1
Ware NY Life bd bid rptd 9-11, 699B3
Continental funds withdrawn re S Africa loans 9-21, 742F2
Howard elected pres 11-4, 907E1
Epps asks US oust Nicaragua pres 11-8, 883E3
Paraguay dissident seized 11-17, 989G3
NATIONAL Distillers and Chemical Corp.
Bierwirth dies 4-3, 356B2
RMI indicted on price fixing 9-28, 768D2
NATIONAL Education Association (NEA)
Cabt-level Educ Dept backed 4-14, 279G1
Propositn 13 topic at conv 7-5, 525G3
'Reverse check-off' barred 7-21, 565A3
Strike data rptd 9-8, 698E2
Schl inspectn for asbestos danger asked 12-21, 1009G1
NATIONAL Enquirer (newspaper)
Alibi for Ray retracted 8-18, 642B1
NATIONAL Fire Prevention & Control Administration—*See under U.S. GOVERNMENT—COMMERCE*
NATIONAL Football League (NFL)—*See FOOTBALL*
NATIONAL Football League Players Association (NFLPA)—*See FOOTBALL—Professional*
NATIONAL Gallery (London)
Poussin painting slashed 4-3, 335D1
NATIONAL Gallery of Art (of Smithsonian Institution) (Washington, D.C.)
East Bldg opens, Dresden art featured 6-1, 578D2
NATIONAL Geographic Society
Hominid tracks in Tanzania rptd 3-4, 334B2
Violent behavior in chimps rptd 4-19, 335A1
NATIONAL Governors' Association—*See GOVERNORS, U.S.*
NATIONAL Guard—*See under U.S. GOVERNMENT*
NATIONAL Gypsum Co.
Price fixing ruling upheld by Sup Ct 6-29, 567G2
NATIONAL Health Insurance, Committee for
Carter health plan scored 7-28, 586D2
NATIONAL Health Plan, U.S.—*See MEDICINE—Insurance*
NATIONAL Health Services Corps—*See U.S. GOVERNMENT—PUBLIC Health Service—Health Services Administration*

1979

Lance '78 oil deal influence attempt alleged 4-9, 306A1
B Carter, Guyton deny peanut loan, '76 campaign link; false bank rpts 4-11, 4-12, 301C3
B Carter testifies on family business loans 5-18, 381A1
Lance, 3 others indicted 5-23, plead not guilty 5-24, 380B2
Carter peanut business documts rptd subpoenaed 5-27, 5-28, 401A2
Lance witness plea bargain blocked 6-6, 500C3
Carter peanut business cleared 10-16, 782A3
NATIONAL Bank of North America—*See under C.I.T.*
NATIONAL Basketball Association (NBA)—*See BASKETBALL–Professional*
NATIONAL Broadcasting Co. (NBC)—*See under RCA*
NATIONAL City Bank of Minneapolis
Hungary branch rptd 11-15, 882B3
NATIONAL Collegiate Athletic Association (NCAA)—*See also specific sport (e.g., BASKETBALL)*
West Pt recruiting abuses probed 1-4, 175B3
Cncl, conv delegates rejct House subcom reform proposals, vow Title IX fight 1-8–1-10, 102B3-103G1
Byers vs Title IX guidelines 12-4, 1000C3
U of New Mex basketball scandal detailed 12-13–12-21, 1003A2
NATIONAL Committee Against Repressive Legislation
FBI files preservatn sought 6-26, 521A1
NATIONAL Conference of Christians and Jews
Racial attitudes surveyed 2-20, 306D3
NATIONAL Council of Churches (National Council of the Churches of Christ in the U.S.A.) (NCC)
Church membership rise rptd 5-4, 639F3
Howard in Iran 12-24–12-27, 975B1
NATIONAL Council of U.S.-China Trade
At mtg re US-China tie 1-15, 27A3
NATIONAL Education Association (NEA)
Schl aid by states up 3-5, 282F3
Teacher 'burn-out' rptd 7-5, 786E1
Educ Dept bill backed, amendmt bar seen 7-11, 514F3
119 teacher strikes rptd 9-13, 679G1
Carter endorsed for primaries 9-28, Educ Dept bill signed 10-17, 782A2, E2
Kirkland bids all unions join AFL-CIO 11-19, 885D2
NATIONAL Emergency Civil Liberties Committee
Iranian students fight US visa probe 11-21, 898E1
Iranian student probes ruled illegal 12-11, 935F2
NATIONALE-Nederlanden N.V.
Seeks Life Insurance of Ga 3-23, 942D2
NATIONAL Enquirer (newspaper)
Carter nephew paroled 12-24, 1006B1
NATIONAL Football League (NFL)—*See FOOTBALL–Professional*
NATIONAL Gallery of Art (of Smithsonian Institute) (Washington D.C.)
Stuart pres portrait set acquired 4-10, 375A1
Mellon resigns as pres, named bd chrmn; Stevenson succeeds 5-3, 375E1
1st woman trustee named 5-3, 375F1
Millon named Visual Arts Cntr dir 5-7, 375G1
Time, Control Data to sponsor art shows 7-19, 672D2, E2
NATIONAL Governor's Association—*See GOVERNORS (U.S.)*
NATIONAL Gypsum Co.
Price-fixing case refused by Sup Ct 10-1, 768F2

1980

NATIONAL Bank of Washington (D.C.)
Hodges elected bd chrmn, chief exec 11-15, 959C3
NATIONAL Broiler Council
Poultry drought damage rptd 7-21, 616A2
NATIONAL Chamber Alliance for Politics v. Federal Election Commission
Case refused by Sup Ct 11-3, 856E2
NATIONAL Coalition for Public Education and Religious Liberty v. Hufstedler
Case refused by Sup Ct 10-6, 782G2
NATIONAL Collegiate Athletic Association (NCAA)
Conventn: Div I, II women's title tourns OKd 1-7—1-8; AIAW scores 1-8, 103B3-104C1
Transcript scandal spreads, probe rptd 1-23—5-23, 469B2-D3
Title IX appeal won 4-19, 469D3
Aid limit case declined by Sup Ct 5-12, 426B3
UCLA basketball team 'rewards' probe 7-27, 875C3
Pac-10 punishes 5 schls in transcript scandal 8-11, 875F1, B2
USF vacates '78 NCAA title 11-18, 1001F3
NATIONAL Council of Churches (National Council of the Churches of Christ in the U.S.A.) (NCC)
Citibank ties cut re S Africa loans 3-24, 277G3
Evangelical Christian pol role profiled 7-11—9-15, 819A3
PLO Mideast peace role urged 11-6, 864B1
NATIONAL Council of Community Churches
Protestant unity mtg ends, common ministry OKd 1-24, 156G2
NATIONAL Detroit Corp.
National Bank of Detroit
Prime rate cut to 16.5% 5-7, 367E3
Prime rate cut to 14% 5-28, 438B1
NATIONAL Education Association (NEA)
Carter addresses conv 7-3, endorsemt renewed 7-4, 505C2
Teacher strikes in 10 states rptd 9-4, 723A3
NATIONAL Guard—*See under U.S. GOVERNMENT*
NATIONAL Gypsum Co.
Price fixing case settled 3-3, 557F3

1976

NATIONAL Hockey League (NHL)—*See HOCKEY, Ice*
NATIONAL Potash Co.—*See FREEPORT Minerals Co.*
NATIONAL Presbyterian Church (D.C.)
Ford, Cong attend svc 1-19, 40D1
NATIONAL Press Club (Washington, D.C.)
Train addresses 2-26, 171F2
Shriver news conf 3-22, 214D2
Giscard d'Estaing addresses 5-20, 372D2
Schmidt addresses 7-15, 530F2
Fraser addresses 7-29, 554A2
NATIONAL Public Radio
Frederick moderates pres debates 10-6, 740F2
NATIONAL Railroad Passenger Corp.—*See AMTRAK*
NATIONAL Socialist White People's Party—*See AMERICAN Nazi Party*
NATIONAL Steel Corp.
'75 zero tax paymt rptd 10-2, 847F1
NATIONAL Steel & Shipbuilding
Navy paymt talks stalled 6-10, 453G3
Hikes prices 6% 11-24, 897D2

1977

NATIONAL Highway Traffic Safety Administration—*See under U.S. GOVERNMENT—TRANSPORTATION*
NATIONAL Hockey League (NHL)—*See HOCKEY, Ice*
NATIONAL Institute of Occupational Safety & Health—*See U.S. GOVERNMENT—PUBLIC Health Service—Disease Control, Center for*
NATIONAL Institutes of Health—*See under U.S. GOVERNMENT—PUBLIC Health Service*
NATIONAL Intelligence Tasking Center—*See under U.S. GOVERNMENT*
NATIONAL Jet Service, Inc.
Ind team dies in crash 12-13, 1023C2
NATIONAL Labor Relations Board—*See under U.S. GOVERNMENT*
NATIONAL Land for People Inc.
Western land holding breakup upheld 8-18, 703A2
NATIONAL Oceanic & Atmospheric Administration—*See under U.S. GOVERNMENT—COMMERCE*
NATIONAL Potash Co.—*See FREEPORT Minerals*
NATIONAL Press Club (Washington, D.C.)
Lopez Portillo addresses 2-15, 136C3
Blumenthal backs tax rebates 4-13, 271A1
S Africa curbs scored 10-21, 825C2
NATIONAL Public Radio
Sup Ct Watergate appeals decisn rptd 4-21, 382A2; rpt confirmed 5-23, 406E1
Carter seeks more funds 10-6, 846B1
NATIONAL Railroad Passenger Corp.—*See AMTRAK*
NATIONAL Reconnaissance Office—*See under U.S. GOVERNMENT—DEFENSE*
NATIONAL Right to Work Committee
AFL-CIO sued by FEC 12-16, 980D1
NATIONAL Science Foundation—*See under U.S. GOVERNMENT*
NATIONAL Security Agency—*See under U.S. GOVERNMENT—DEFENSE*
NATIONAL Security Council—*See under U.S. GOVERNMENT*
NATIONAL Semiconductor Corp.
Amex to trade options 2-17, 521F1
NATIONAL Socialist Party of America
Ill rally ban upset 6-13, 517G2
Ill rule review ordrd 6-23, swastika display barred 7-12, 560A2
NC sniper kills 2, self 9-5, 848A3
NATIONAL Starch and Chemical Corp.
On '76 Fortune 500 list 341C1
NATIONAL States Rights Party
NY man kills 5, self 2-14, 162A3
Stoner indicted 9-26, 907D3
NATIONAL Steel Corp.
Steelworkers OK contract 4-9, 273G2
Prices hiked 5-10, 385B2
Chrgs Eur mfrs re steel dumping 10-20, 836E3
LTV, Lykes to merge 11-4, 943G2
Prices hiked 12-22, 1003C2

1978

NATIONAL Heart, Lung & Blood Institute—*See U.S. GOVERNMENT—PUBLIC Health Service—National Institutes of Health*
NATIONAL Highway Traffic Safety Administration—*See under U.S. GOVERNMENT—TRANSPORTATION*
NATIONAL Hockey League (NHL)—*See HOCKEY, Ice*
NATIONAL Institute of Mental Health—*See U.S. GOVERNMENT—PUBLIC Health Service—Alcohol, Drug Abuse & Mental Health Administration*
NATIONAL Institute of Occupational Safety & Health (NIOSH)—*See U.S. GOVERNMENT—PUBLIC Health Service—Disease Control, Center for*
NATIONAL Institute on Drug Abuse (NIDA)—*See U.S. GOVERNMENT—PUBLIC Health Service—Alcohol, Drug Abuse & Mental Health Administration*
NATIONAL Institutes of Health—*See under U.S. GOVERNMENT—PUBLIC Health Service*
NATIONAL Intelligence Tasking Center—*See under U.S. GOVERNMENT*
NATIONAL Invitation Tournament (NIT)—*See BASKETBALL—Collegiate*
NATIONALIST China—*See CHINA, Republic of*
NATIONAL Labor Relations Board—*See under U.S. GOVERNMENT*
NATIONAL Labor Relations Board v. Local Union 103
'Prehire' union picketing curbed 1-17, 34B1
NATIONAL Labor Relations Board v. Robbins Tire & Rubber Co.
Freedom of Info in NLRB cases barred by Sup Ct 6-15, 468G2
NATIONAL Lampoon's Animal House (film)
Released 7-27, 970D2
Top-grossing film 8-30, 708G1; 10-11, 800G3; 11-1, 888E1; 11-29, 970F3
NATIONAL League (NL)—*See BASEBALL*
NATIONAL Marine Fisheries Service—*See U.S. GOVERNMENT—COMMERCE—National Oceanic & Atmospheric Administration*
NATIONAL Mediation Board—*See under U.S. GOVERNMENT*
NATIONAL Oceanic & Atmospheric Administration—*See under U.S. GOVERNMENT—COMMERCE*
NATIONAL Opinion Research Center (Chicago, Ill.)
'72-77 abortn survey rptd 8-9, 744G1
NATIONAL Park Service—*See under U.S. GOVERNMENT—INTERIOR*
NATIONAL Press Club (Washington, D.C.)
Bell addresses 1-10, 12G2
Sadat addresses 2-6, 77C2
Adams issues transport policy statemt 2-8, 109C1
Danish premr addresses 2-23, 167A2
Carter holds news conf 3-2, 140D2, 141C2
Begin addresses 3-23, 214B3
Eizenstat addresses 11-14, 875F1
NATIONAL PTA (National Congress of Parents and Teachers)
Sears sets TV advisory cncl 5-12, 599E3
Schl inspectn for asbestos danger asked 12-21, 1009A2
NATIONAL Public Radio
Sen Panama Canal debate aired 2-8—2-22, 120E1
NATIONAL Railroad Passenger Corp.—*See AMTRAK*
NATIONAL Reconnaissance Office—*See under U.S. GOVERNMENT—DEFENSE*
NATIONAL Register of Historic Places—*See U.S. GOVERNMENT—INTERIOR—National Park Service*
NATIONAL Research Council—*See NATIONAL Academy of Sciences*
NATIONAL Science Foundation—*See under U.S. GOVERNMENT*
NATIONAL Security—*See SECURITY, National*
NATIONAL Security Agency—*See under U.S. GOVERNMENT—DEFENSE*
NATIONAL Security Council—*See under U.S. GOVERNMENT*
NATIONAL Security Studies, Center for—*See CENTER For National Security Studies*
NATIONAL Socialist Party of America
Skokie rally swastika display OKd 1-27, 68F3-69A1
ACLU split on Skokie defns roll 1-27, 69B1
Carter deplores Skokie march, bars interventn 1-30, 62E1, D3
Skokie rally ordinances struck down 5-23; rally delay sought 6-9, Sup Ct denies stay 6-12, 447G2
Skokie march canceled, Chicago rally OKd 6-20—7-7; rally, conter-demonstratns held 7-9, 529E1
Skokie ordinances case refused by Sup Ct 10-16, 789B2
NATIONAL Society of Professional Engineers v. U.S.
Engineers' fee code ruled illegal by Sup Ct 4-25, 323D1
NATIONAL Steel Corp.
'76 tax nonpaymt rptd 1-27, 65G2
Carter sees Stinson on coal strike 2-24, 122F3
Price hike undercuts US Steel, wage cncl lauds 3-30, 263A1

1979

NATIONAL Hockey League (NHL)—*See HOCKEY, Ice*
NATIONAL Institute of Occupational Safety & Health (NIOSH)—*See U.S. GOVERNMENT—PUBLIC Health Service—Disease Control, Center for*
NATIONAL Invitation Tournament (NIT)—*See BASKETBALL-Collegiate*
NATIONALIST China—*See CHINA, Republic of*
NATIONAL Kinney Corp.
Aladdin casino purchase set 12-21, 992A2
NATIONAL Labor Relations Board v. Catholic Bishop of Chicago
Church schl labor interventn barred by Sup Ct 3-21, 231D2
NATIONAL Media Group
Acne ad refunds set 7-2, 596D2
NATIONAL Motor Freight v. ICC
Case refused by Sup Ct 5-29, 422A1
NATIONAL Muffler Dealers Association Inc.
Tax break denied by Sup Ct 3-20, 203D3
NATIONAL Muffler Dealers Association v. U.S.
Muffler assn denied tax break by Sup Ct 3-20, 203C3
NATIONAL Naval Medical Institute (Bethesda, Md.)
Virus found to cause diabetes 5-23, 471G3
NATIONAL Portrait Gallery (of Smithsonian Institution) (Washington, D.C.)
Stuart portraits purchase halted 4-14, 374E3
NATIONAL Press Club (Washington, D.C.)
Graham addresses 1-17, 102E1
Connally announces pres bid 1-24, 70G2
Quebec premr addresses 1-25, 74F3
Brown opens pres campaign 11-8, 847A3
Irish prime min addresses 11-9, 874D2
NATIONAL Railroad Passenger Corp.—*See AMTRAK*
NATIONAL Research Council—*See NATIONAL Academy of Sciences*
NATIONAL Review (magazine)
Buckley settles SEC chrg 2-7, 132E1
NATIONAL Rifle Association (NRA)
Army gun resale suit lost 9-4, 747F1
NATIONAL Security Studies, Center for
CIA spying on antiwar activists rptd 7-16, 561A2
NATIONAL Steel Corp.
United Financial purchase planned 3-6, 205A2

1980

NATIONAL Institutes of Health (NIH)—*See under U.S. GOVERNMENT--PUBLIC Health Service*
NATIONALIST China—*See CHINA, Republic of*
NATIONAL Italian-American Foundation
Reagan addresses dinner 9-13, 699E3
NATIONAL Labor Relations Board v. Yeshiva University
Case decided by Sup Ct 2-20, 146D1-B2
NATIONAL Lampoon (magazine)
Kenney dies 9-1, 755F3
NATIONAL Law Journal
IRS prosecutn guidelines rptd 8-2, 601A3
NATIONAL League—*See BASEBALL*
NATIONAL Liberty Corp.
Capital Holding merger set 6-13, 746E1
NATIONAL Organization for Women (NOW)
Va ERA rally held 1-13, 54B3
Chicagoan indicted in ERA bribe probe 6-5, chrgs denied 6-6, 441C3
Navy lesbian probe scored 6-15, 517D3
ERA rejected by Ill house 6-18, 482E3
Mo boycott case refused by Sup Ct 10-6, 782F1-A2
Cong election results 11-4, 846F2
ERA advocate fined in Ill bribe case 11-7, 997A3
NATIONAL Press Club (Washington, D.C.)
Volcker addresses 1-2, 52D2
Civiletti announces Abscam leaks prosecutor 2-11, 111E1
Ex-Reagan aides hold news conf 2-28, 143A2
Brzezinski addresses 3-12, 205D1
Sadat addresses 4-10, 260A3
Aquino addresses 8-20, 672D3
Carter addresses 10-14, 779E1
Eizenstat addresses 12-4, 938B3
NATIONAL Pro-Family Coalition
Delegates walk out of White House Conf 6-21, 601B2
NATIONAL Public Radio
Frederick rptd honored 7-7, 638F2
NATIONAL Railroad Passenger Corp.—*See AMTRAK*
NATIONAL Republican Senatorial Committee v. Democratic Senatorial Campaign Committee
Stay continued by Sup Ct 10-17, 856F1
NATIONAL Rifle Association (NRA)
Reagan endorsed 11-1, 844F1
NATIONAL Shoes Inc.
Bankruptcy filed 12-11, 985F3
NATIONAL Socialist Party of America
Collin arrested 1-10, 55D3
2 acquitted in '79 NC slayings 11-17; reactn 11-17—11-18, 898D2-C3
NATIONAL States Rights Party
Stoner extradited 1-11, 55A3
NATIONAL Steel Corp.
USW contract settled 4-15, 289B2
US finds steel import damage 5-1, 456F1
Prices cut 7-10, 575F2

1976

NATIONAL Super Spuds Inc.
Sues re potato futures default 5-27, 397D3
NATIONAL Symphony Orchestra
Gets grant 1-12, 32E3
NATIONAL Urban Coalition (Washington, D.C.)
Study scores revenue sharing 3-2, 187B1
NATO—*See NORTH Atlantic Treaty Organization*
NATSHI, Ahmad Hamzi
Deported 3-27, 227C2
NATURAL Gas—*See GAS, Natural*
NATURAL Nydegger Transport Corp.
Arab boycott rpt released 10-19, 786D1
NATURAL Resources—*See RESOURCES, Natural*
NATURAL Resources Defense Council
Tighter A-materials security urged 2-2, 115A3
Sues vs plastic beverage bottle 4-21, 308A2
NYC clean air plan upheld 4-26, 308F1
Ct curbs plutonium use 5-26, 398A2
NRC suit vs S Africa A-deal rptd 5-30, 388F1
Vs Atlantic offshore lease sale 8-13—8-17, 648A3
Urges DNA research curbs 11-11, 891G3
NAUMANN, Konrad
Named to E Ger Politburo 5-22, 381D2
NAURU—*See also COMMONWEALTH of Nations*
Listed as 'free' nation 1-19, 20C3
S Pacific Forum meets 3-8—3-9, 179B2
Commonwealth gets UN observer status 10-18, 799D2
NAVAL Academy, U.S.—*See NAVY under U.S. GOVERNMENT*
NAVARRO, Antonio
Denies payoff collectn 5-19, 419C3
NAVRATILOVA, Martina
Wins Houston Va Slims 1-18, 123A3
NAYAR, Kuldip
Loses press certificatn 2-14, 139C3
NAYEL, Mohammed Ali
Tried 4-19—4-22, sentncd 4-23, 335B1
NAZI Party, American—*See AMERICAN Nazi Party*
NAZIS
Rpt Wiesenthal ends hunt 1-9, 97C3
Klarsfeld gets suspended sentnc 2-9, 158D1
Austrian exec chrgd 3-10, 380E2
Wick withdraws Rotary candidacy 3-19, 484D2
Bolivian envoy slain 5-11, 350F3
Martin Heidegger dies 5-26, 404A2
Drabant sentncd in E Ger 8-9, 772E2
Argentina publicatns scored 8-15, 8-28, 672A2
Rpt US, UK, France return Polish gold 9-28, 907F1
Dole, Mondale debate 10-15, 782A3
Rudel at pilots mtg 10-23, 930D3
Dole queried re WWII 10-25, 804C2
E Ger sets reparatns for Jews 11-22, 889G1
Jews reject reparatns offer 11-23, 949D2
Loijen sentenced 12-14, 1007D2
Menten returned to Holland 12-22, 1007B2

1977

NATIONAL Student Marketing Corp.
Law firm settles suit 5-2, 520A1
NATIONAL Transportation Safety Board—*See under U.S. GOVERNMENT*
NATIONAL War College—*See under U.S. GOVERNMENT—DEFENSE*
NATIONAL Weather Service—*See U.S. GOVERNMENT—COMMERCE—National Oceanic & Atmospheric Administration*
NATION Enterprises Ltd.
Buys Nation magazine 12-22, 1004F3
NATO—*See NORTH Atlantic Treaty Organization*
NATOMAS Co.
On '76 Fortune 500 list 341C1
NATURAL Gas—*See GAS, NATURAL*
NATURAL Gas Pipeline Co. of America—*See under PEOPLES Gas Co.*
NATURAL Gas Supply Committee
Says producers await deregulatn 2-3, 152C2
Carter energy plan reactn 4-21, 319F3
NATURAL Resources—*See RESOURCES, Natural*
NATURAL Resources Defense Council (Washington, D.C.)
Speth confrmd to environmt cncl 4-4, 272C3
TVA sued on air pollutn 6-22, 521C3
Wins coal-leasing rule 9-27, 1007D2
Vs A-fuel storage by govt 794E2
NAUDE, Beyers
S Africa bans 10-19, 803F3
NAURU—*See also COMMONWEALTH of Nations*
NZ to set 200-mi fishing zone 9-7, 729B3
NAVAJO Indians—*See INDIANS, American*
NAVAL Academy, U.S.—*See under U.S. GOVERNMENT—NAVY*
NAVAL Research, Office of—*See under U.S. GOVERNMENT—NAVY*
NAVARRO Oviedo, Rev. Alfonso
Rightists attack 5-11, 373C3
NAVASKY, Victor S.
Group buys Nation mag 12-22, 1004F3
NAVASSA Island (U.S. territory)
CIA tied to '71 Cuba swine fever 1-9, 19A3
NAVRATILOVA, Martina
Wins Va Slims 1-9, 1-30, 103G3, 104A1
Va Slims results 2-6, 2-20, 2-27; Bridgestone 4-10; World Series 4-17, 430D3, E3, 431E1
Wade wins Wimbledon 7-1, 548A2
Wins US Open doubles title 9-11, 787A2
NAVY, Department of the—*See under U.S. GOVERNMENT*
NAVY League of the United States
Holloway addresses conv 4-19, 342F3 ★
NAZAR, Juan
Rptd kidnaped 7-21, 595F2
NAZIS
Ex-US intell agent rpts Czech spy role 1-7, 20A1
Czechs try Topiarz in absentia 1-10, 82G3
Trifa suspended from NCC 2-4, 119F3
NY man kills 5, self 2-14, 162F2, B3
Hess attempts suicide 2-21, 298B3
Spanish organizatns rptd 3-2, 307G2
Alleged US sympathizer vindicated 5-3, 532C2
Ill rally ban upset 6-13, 517G2
Ill rule review ordrd 6-23, swastika display barred 7-12, 560A2
Argentina OKs Roschmann extraditn to W Ger 7-4, 614C3
Roschmann rptd dead in Paraguay 8-11, 670D3
Kappler escapes to W Ger 8-15, Italy asks extraditn asylum 8-17, 637E3
Auschwitz MD rptd in Paraguay 8-17, 803B2
Kappler escape causes Italy pol crisis 8-18—9-18, 728G3-729E1
Kappler extraditn bar arouses concern, Brandt issues warning 8-19—8-26, 658G1
Kappler escape detailed 8-19, 729F1
Argentine Jew kidnaped 8-26, 670A3
Italy asks Kappler confinemt 8-26, W Ger bars extraditn 9-21, 729G1
NC sniper kills 2, self 9-5, 848A3
Franz Boehm dies 9-26, 872A1
USSR accuses US UNESCO envoy 10-19—10-29, chrg denied 10-30, 866E2, A3
J Robinson dies 10-24, 872G2
Sadat visits Yad Vashem 11-20, 889E1, 894D1
Menten sentenced for war crimes 12-14, 986B1
Amer Party tape restraining order upheld 12-21, 1008A2
Carters visit Polish memorials 12-30, 1001C2

1978

Price hike held to 3%, future price lid pledge hedged 6-13, 470F2
Eur dumping chrgs withdrawn 12-28, 1006B1
NATIONAL Tax Limitation Committee
Friedman sets natl plan 7-26, 735F3
NATIONAL Transportation Safety Board—*See under U.S. GOVERNMENT*
NATIONAL Utility Service Inc.
Dec. '76-Mar '78 rate hikes rptd 5-15, 367B1
NATIONAL Van Lines
ICC sues 7-25, 589C2
NATIONAL Velvet (book)
Intl Velvet released 7-19, 970G1
NATIONAL Weather Service—*See U.S. GOVERNMENT—COMMERCE—National Oceanic & Atmospheric Administration*
NATIONAL Westminster Bank Ltd. (Nat-West) (London bank)
US bank purchase planned 5-12, 364F1
Not on '77 top 10 bank list 11-8, 914C1
Nigeria loan set 11-30, 934G1
NATIVE Son (play)
Opens 3-27, 760G2
NATKIN, Rick
Boys In Company C released 1-31, 618D3
NATO—*See NORTH Atlantic Treaty Organization*
NATURAL Gas—*See GAS, Natural*
NATURAL High (recording)
On best-seller list 8-2, 620G1
NATURAL Resources—*See RESOURCES, Natural*
NATURAL Resources Defense Council (Washington, D.C.)
CIA issues '74 rpt on A-weapon spread 1-26, 61B2
Scores Admin A-plant licensing plan 3-17, 205A3 ★
Ct A-plant rulings curbed 4-3, 280F2
NATURE (Scientific journal)
Solar cell advance rptd 11-30, 983F1
NATURE Conservancy
Okefenokee Refuge expanded 3-14, 186B3
NATWEST—*See NATIONAL Westminister Bank Ltd.*
NAURU—*See also COMMONWEALTH of Nations, SOUTH Pacific Islands*
De Roburt becomes pres 5-15, econ dispute cited 5-16, 439F3
NAVAJO Indians—*See INDIANS, American*
NAVAL Academy, U.S.—*See under U.S. GOVERNMENT—NAVY*
NAVON, Yitzhak (Israeli president)
Elected Israel pres 4-19, sworn 5-29, 418C2
NAVRATILOVA, Martina
Sets Va Slims win record 1-8—3-5, wins title 4-2, 419E1
Wins Eastbourne Intl 6-24, Wimbledon 7-7, 539E3, 540A1, D1
Wins US Open doubles title 9-9, loses women's singles 9-10, 707E1, F1
Lobsters lose WTT title 9-21, 1027F1
Loses Atlanta Women's Classic 10-2, Series Championship 11-18, 1027B2, C2
NAVY, Department of—*See under U.S. GOVERNMENT*
NAVY Claims Settlement Board—*See U.S. GOVERNMENT—NAVY*
NAWAZ Khan, Shah
Purged 2-7, 113D1
NAYATT School (play)
Opens 5-12, 887B2
NAZAR, Juan
Freed by kidnapers 8-26, 792E3
NAZARYAN, Robert
Sentence rptd 12-5, 947E1
NAZIS
Goebbels diary on W Ger best-seller list 1-2, 22A1
W Ger anti-Semitic incidents rptd 1-17—2-5; local curbs asked 2-4, 114A2
Ill rally swastika display OKd 1-27, 68F3-69A1
ACLU split on Ill defns role 1-27, 69B1
Carter deplores Ill march, bars interventn 1-30, 62E1, D3
W Ger war crimes trial criticism rptd 1-30, 114B3
Kappler dies 2-9, 114C3
USSR collaborator rptd sentncd 2-21, 151E3
W Ger denies prosecutn lag 2-22, 477D2
Scheel asks Nazis studies 3-5, 477E2
Ukrainian collaborators rptd executed 3-8, 416B3
Puvogel resigns over '36 thesis 3-23, 477F2
Gypsies ask reparatns 4-11, 318A3
'Holocaust' aired in US 4-16—4-19, NBC rpts 120 mln viewers 4-20, 316A2
W Ger neo-Nazism rptd on rise 4-29—4-30, 477G2
W Ger asks USSR propaganda end 5-4, 417G1
CIA, FBI links to war criminals rptd 5-16, 410G3
Skokie rally ordinances struck down 5-23; rally delay sought 6-9, Sup Ct denies stay 6-12, 447F2
Filbinger links harm career 5-28, 477B3
Menten convictn overturned by Dutch 5-29, 454G2
Wagner arrested in Brazil 5-30; W Ger, 3 other natns ask extraditn 5-31, 6-8, 477G1
W Ger protest injures 70 6-3, 477D3
USSR collaborators rptd sentncd 6-7, 499C3
W Ger plea to free Hess rptd rejctd by USSR 6-11, 477E3

1979

NATIONAL Westminster Bank Ltd. (Nat-West) (London bank)
Poland econ monitor set 1-11, 59G3
US OKs bank purchase 3-16, CIT sees hitch 3-19, 205D1
NATO—*See NORTH Atlantic Treaty Organization*
NATT, Calvin
In NBA draft 6-25, 507A2
NATTA, Giulio
Dies 5-2, 432C3
NATURAL Gas—*See GAS, Natural*
NATURAL Resources Defense Council (Washington, D.C.)
Environmt impact rpts on US forgn projects ordrd 1-5, 16F3
EPA coal-use rule opposed 5-25, 404A1
Lash on Carter mtg 6-1, 418B2
US timber sales hike opposed 6-11, 441E1
Va oil refinery opposed 10-4, 770E1
NATURE and Purpose Of The Universe, The (play)
Opens 2-23, 292C2
NATUSCH Busch, Col. Alberto (Bolivian president; replaced Nov. 16)
Heads mil coup, assumes presidency 11-1, 832F3
Dissolves Cong 11-2; declares martial law, sees Gueiler 11-3; lifts martial law 11-7, 852D3
Closes banks, mil officers ask resignatn 11-14, resigns, Gueiler replaces 11-16, 888A2
Army chief rebels, Gueiler relents 11-23-11-25, 907F1*
NATWEST—*See NATIONAL Westminster Bank Ltd.*
NAURU—*See COMMONWEALTH of Nations*
NAVAL Academy, U.S.—*See under U.S. GOVERNMENT-NAVY*
NAVAL Observatory, U.S.—*See under U.S. GOVERNMENT-NAVY*
NAVRATILOVA, Jana
Daughter wins Wimbledon 7-6, 7-7, 570B1
NAVRATILOVA, Martina
Avon tourn results 1-7, 1-15, 2-4, wins title 3-25, 391C2
Wins World Invitatn 5-20, Wimbledon singles, doubles titles 7-6, 7-7; loses Eastbourne Intl 6-23, 569C3, 570B1, C2, E2
Wins Richmond Intl 8-19; loses US Open doubles 9-8, other results 9-9, 734E1, G1, C2
Wins Phoenix Open 10-14, Eng Women's Grand Prix 11-25, 1003E3, 1004A1
NAVY, Department of the—*See under U.S. GOVERNMENT*
NAZEMI, Brig. Gen. Fazollah
Executed 5-7, 353A2
NAZIH, Hassan
Named Iran oil co chrmn 2-19, 125D2*
Sets oil export resumptn 2-27, bars Westn consortium sale 2-28, 145F3
Iran resumes oil exports 3-5, 161C3
Scores Khomeini 5-28, Natl Oil Co dirs quit 6-2, 407C3, D3, 425F3
Islamic offcl chrgs treason, rebuts 6-2, 425G3-426A1
Asks mil protectn for oil fields 7-11, 525A1
Denies oil productn shortfall 8-24, 645B2
Says US kerosene deal jeopardized 9-2, 708D3
Khomeini oppositn rptd, backers strike 9-24; ousted 9-28, 752B2
NAZIH, Gen. Riza
Executed 2-16, 125E1
NAZIS
US Jews' top '78 concern 1-19, 102A1
W Ger broadcasts 'Holocaust' 1-22-1-26, impact noted 1-29, 137B2
W Ger cops raid neo-Nazis 1-29-2-1, 101E1
US WWII secret files released 2-3, 2-6, 93F1
W Ger arrests more neo-Nazis 2-10-2-11, 137B2
US releases Auschwitz photos 2-22, 193D1
Luns denies tie 3-2, NATO employe defectn linked 3-5, 181A1
USSR exiles Crimean Tatar 3-6, 172A3
Schmidt backs contd prosecutn 3-8, 214D3
ESP experimts cited in '50s CIA files 3-11, 208F2
4 W Ger camp guards acquitted 4-19, 333C3
Menten retrial ordrd by Dutch 5-22, 409D1
Carstens elected W Ger pres 5-23, 410C3
Pope visits Auschwitz 6-7, 414A1, B2
Heim convicted of Austria crimes 6-13, 490B1
Wagner extradtn denied by Brazil 6-20, 483A3
W Ger Bundestag OKs limitatns statute end 7-3, 506C2
Mengele loses Paraguay citizenship 8-8, bounty offered 8-10; past detailed 616A3
Wagner detentn rptd; Bohne, Stangl extraditns cited 8-8, 617B1
USSR seizes US books 9-4, 690D1
W Ger sentncs 6 neo-Nazis 9-13, 733C3
Menten ruled unfit for trial by Dutch 9-24, 731D2
Breton separatists linked 10-20, 835F2
SS col arrested in Munich 11-14, 876C2
Amer Party members arrested in NJ 11-24, 991C3

1980

NATIONAL Student Marketing Corp.
Liquidates 9-10, 985F3
NATO—*See NORTH Atlantic Treaty Organization*
NATSHA, Mustafa Abdulnabi al-
Becomes Hebron mayor 5-25, 417F2
NATURAL Gas—*See GAS, Natural*
NATURAL Resources Defense Council
Offshore leasing speedup scored 6-17, 552A3
NATURE Conservancy
Rpts $25 mln gifts for forests, endangered sites 12-20, 987A2
NATUSCH Busch, Col. Alberto
Electns held 6-29, Siles leads 7-3, 508E3
NAURU—*See also COMMONWEALTH of Nations*
Island trade pact rptd 7-24, 576G2
NAVA, Julian
Confrmd Mex amb 4-3, 315E1
NAVAL Academy, U.S.—*See under U.S. GOVERNMENT--NAVY*
NAVARRO Savings Association v. Lee
Case decided by Sup Ct 5-19, 440E2
NAVARRO Savings & Loan Association
Fed unincorporated business trust suits backed by Sup Ct 5-19, 440E2
NAVON, Yitzhak (Israeli president)
Egypt amb presents credentials 2-26, 140E1
In Egypt, meets Sadat, ties expanded 10-26—10-30, 822D3
NAVRATILOVA, Martina
Wins Colgate championship 1-7, WTA Championship 4-20, Sunbird Cup 5-4; loses Clairol Championship 3-30, 607E2, A3-C3
Wins Avon tourns 1-20, 1-27, 2-10, loses title 3-23, 607B2
Named top '79 player by ITF 1-21, 213D2
Wimbledon results 7-4—7-6, 606D2
Wins Players Challenge 7-20, Richmond Intl 7-27, US Open women's doubles 9-6, 691F2, G2, A3
Loses English Women's Grand Prix 10-26, wins Lions Cup 11-23, 947C2, F2
NAVY, Department of the—*See under U.S. GOVERNMENT*
NAZIS
US neo-Nazi ex-ldr arrested 1-10, 55D3
Redgrave TV role protested 1-13, 120B2
US search deadline rptd set 1-16, 226D2
W Ger bans group 1-30, 103G1
3 sentenced for WW II crimes 2-11, 118E1
Gypsies begin hunger strike in W Ger 4-4, 316E2
Johnston Cnty (NC) rally held 4-19, 333G1
Covington draws NC GOP vote 5-6, 405G1
Burger loses Austria pres electn 5-18, 338G1
W Ger arrests ex-Nazi for WW II crimes 6-25, 500B3
W Ger neo-Nazis chrgd re '77, '78 bombings 6-25, 500C3
France arrests extremists 7-1, 522B2
Menten sentncd by Dutch 7-9, 509F3
Flynn biographer sued 8-1, 639E1
Wiesenthal honored by Carter 8-5, 638G1
France bans extremist group 9-3, 670F1
W Ger neo-Nazi allegedly Munich bomber 9-28; PLO, Qaddafi linked 9-30, 754F3, 755C1
Wagner kills self in Brazil 10-3, 810E1
Ill rally cut short 10-19, 884E3
2 acquitted in '79 US deaths 11-17; reactn 11-17—11-18, 898D2-C3
Reichstag '33 fire verdict canceled 12-15, 996C3
Obituaries
Doenitz, Karl 12-24, 1004D1
Mosley, Oswald 12-2, 1004A3
Wagner, Gustov 10-30, 810E1

1976

NAZLYMOV, Vladimir
Wins Olympic medal 7-22, 574F2
NBC—*See 'National Broadcasting Co. under RCA*
NCNB Corp.
Rptd on FRB 'problem' list 1-22, 111C2
North Carolina National Bank (Charlotte)
Rptd on comptroller's 'problem' list 1-26, 113E1
NCOKAZI, Hector
Arrested 7-26, 592B2
NCR Corp.
SEC lists forgn paymts 5-12, 728D2
NDABEMEYE, Lt. Col. Thomas
Ousted 11-1, 858A1
NDIWENI, Kayisa
Named to Rhodesia Cabt 4-27, 295C2
Quits Cabt, forms party 12-29, 1009G3
NDOU, Sampson
Arrested 8-13, 624A3
NEAL, Rep. Stephen L. (D, N.C.)
Reelected 11-2, 822F2, 830E2
NEAVE, Airey
Backs Ulster troop increase 1-7, 19D3

NEBRASKA
Primary date set 22B2
Fremont hotel blast kills 18 1-10, 80F1
Simants gets death 1-29, 492C1
Utility buys N Sea gas 4-7, 521E3
Hijacker killed in Denver 4-19, 383F3
Omaha schl integratn plan OKd 4-27, 453D2
Church, Carter remarks 5-6, 5-12, 343G1
Primary results 5-11, 342D1
Starkweather companion paroled 6-8, 442D3
US Sup Ct voids press gag order in Simants murder case 6-30, 491D3-492C1
Dem conv women delegates, table 508C2
Dem conv pres vote, table 7-14, 507C2
GOP pre-conv delegate count 8-14, 583C3
GOP conv pres, vp vote tables 8-18—8-19, 8-19, 599C1, C3
Omaha integratn praised 9-14, 993A1
Fscl '75 per capita income, tax burden rptd 9-15, 10-12, 959C2
Dole in Trumbull 9-23, 724D3
Dole stumps 11-1, 827B3
Election results 11-2: pres 818C1, 819B1; cong 820B1, D2, 823C3, 828C2, 830C1
Flu shot paralysis rptd 12-17, 950E1

NEBRASKA, University of (Lincoln)
'75 football rankings 1-2, 31C3
Ford gives address 5-8, 342G2
Wins Astro-Bluebonnet Bowl 12-31, 1014A3
NEBRASKA Press Association
Sup Ct voids gag order 6-30, 491D3-492C1
NEDELIN, Air Marshal Mitrofan I. (1902-1960)
Medvedev on death 11-6, 949A1
NEDZI, Rep. Lucien N. (D, Mich.)
Reelected 11-2, 829E4
NEEDHAM, James J.
To quit NYSE 4-27, 347E3-348F1

1977

NBA (National Basketball Association)—*See BASKETBALL*
NBC—*See RCA—National Broadcasting Co.*
NCA (National Coal Association)—*See COAL Association, National*
NCAA—*See NATIONAL Collegiate Athletic Association*
NCC—*See NATIONAL Council of Churches*
NCOKAZI, Hector
Freed 2-25, 160C3
NCUBE, Albert
Escapes 1-9, 11G2
NDJOBA, Cornelius
Rpts Angolans seek refuge 2-21, 145C2
NDONG, Marc Mba
Named Gabon culture min 7-13, 772B1
NDUKA, W. K.
Quits Muzorewa group 8-10, 662D2
NEAKOK, Billy
Scores bowhead whale quota 12-7, 936D3

NEBRASKA
Legislature schedule rptd 6E2
Indiana OKs ERA 1-18, 59C2
Death penalty upheld 2-2, 3 executns set 3-18, 594C1
Snowstorm kills 4 3-10—3-12, 204A3
'76 per-capita income table 5-10, 387E2, B3
Omaha busing order vacated 6-29, 557G2
FRA to buy C&NW stock 9-9, 776B3
'76 per capita income, tax burden table 9-13, 10-18, 821F1, C2
Anti-abortn amendmt rptd sought 10-6, 786B3
Jet hijacked 10-20, 807G3
Carter visits Omaha, SAC 10-22, 817D1
ERA rescission cited 11-14, 918E1

NEBRASKA, University of (Lincoln)
'76 football rankings 1-2, 8E3
Clough Antarctic projct completed 12-9, 971G2
Wins Liberty Bowl 12-19, 1020B2
NEESE, Judge Charles G.
Dismisses libel suit vs NBC 7-12, 643B1
NEFF, Francine
Replaced as US treasurer 8-2, 626B3
NEGEV (desert)
UN desert conf protest 8-30, 770D1

1978

Skokie march canceled, Chicago rally OKd 6-20—7-7; rally, counter-demonstratns held 7-9, 529E1
Israel compares Shcharansky trial 7-10, 543A1
W Ger police battle neo-Nazis in Lentfoehrden 7-22, ldr arrested 7-24, 652A1
W German fined for Nazi salute 7-24, 652B1
Paris Gestapo chiefs chrgd 7-24, 652C1
W Ger sees neo-Nazi terror 7-25, 652D1
W Ger neo-Nazi ldr arrested again 8-4, 652D1
Filbinger quits W Ger post 8-7, 616C3; successor named 8-16, 725E3
Strauss asks Nazi-era amnesty 8-14, 651E3
Italy war meml blast 8-30, 689C3
WWII secret documts issued by US 9-10—9-18, 744D2-G3
Skokie rally ordinances case refused by Sup Ct 10-16, 789B2
W Ger ldrs urge statute of limitatns end 10-28, 11-10, 11-13, 872B2
US deportatn bill signed 10-30, 872C2
W Ger parlt speaker, Scheel confirm past membership 11-1, 11-10, 872E1, G1
Dutch MP quits re SS link 11-7, 871G3
Menten release ordrd by Dutch 12-4, 965B2

NBA (National Basketball Association)—*See BASKETBALL—Professional*
NBC—*See RCA—National Broadcasting Co.*
NBC v. Niemi
Sex abuse suit vs NBC OKd by Sup Ct 4-24, 322B2
NBPA (National Basketball Players Association)—*See BASKETBALL—Professional*
NCAA—*See NATIONAL Collegiate Athletic Association*
NCC—*See NATIONAL Council of Churches*
NCR Corp.
Paper div sale to BAT Industries OKd 5-5, 345B3
NDABEMEYE, Lt. Col. Thomas
Freed 5-6, 596B1
NDIWENI, Chief Kayisa
Quits, asks Nkomo return 11-8, 884E2-A3
NEA—*See NATIONAL Education Association*
NEAL, Rep. Stephen L. (D, N.C.)
Reelected 11-7, 851B3
NEALE, Harry
Quits as WHA Whalers coach, joins NHL Canucks 5-26, 656F3
NEAR and Far Away (film)
Released 3-24, 619B3
NEAVE, Airey
Scores Lynch interview 1-9, 18E3
Says IRA has 12 M60s 2-1, 132C3
Scores Irish RC primate 8-1, 630F1
N.E.A. v. South Carolina
SC teacher tests backed 1-16, 33E2
NEBEL, Long John
Dies 4-10, 356C3
NEBRASKA
Legislature schedule rptd 14F3
'67, '77 sales-tax rates rptd 1-5, 15A3, E3
State govt tax revenue table 1-9, 84D2
Amtrak Omaha route cutback proposed 5-8, 366E1
Primary results 5-9, 363D1
'77 prison populatn rptd down 6-3, 440D1
ERA '77 rescisn cited 494D2
Omaha makes bad-air list 7-5, 513D1
Grasshopper invasn rptd, EPA aid asked 7-13—7-31, 654A3
Bad-air list corrected 7-19, 644B2
ERA rescissn amendmt rejected by US House 8-15, 661G2
ERA rescissn amendmts rejected by US Sen 10-3, 788C1
Police 'deadly force' case refused by US Sup Ct 10-16, 789C2
Electn results 11-7: cong 845E1, 846F1, 848D2, 851E2, 854F3; state 845G1, 846D3, 847B3, 853G2, 854F3, 897F3
State interest rates on natl bank credit cards backed by US Sup Ct 12-18, 981C2

NEBRASKA, University of (Lincoln)
'77 football rank rptd 1-3, 8A3
NEDERLANDER, James M.
Hello Dolly opens 3-5, Stop the World 8-3, 887A2, C3
NEDERLANDER, Joseph
Stop the World opens 8-3, 887C3
NEDZI, Rep. Lucien Norbert (D, Mich.)
Reelected 11-7, 851F1
NEEDHAM, Hal
Hooper released 8-4, 970F1
NEELD, Gregory P.
AHL ban lifted 2-2, 296F3
NEGEDE Gozeze
Cuba backing rptd 5-30, 584F3
NEGM, Ahmed Fuad
Egypt probes, exit barred 5-28, 415A1
NEGOTIABLE Orders of Withdrawal (NOW)—*See BANKS*

1979

NBA (National Basketball Association)—*See BASKETBALL-Professional*
NBC—*See RCA-National Broadcasting Co.*
NCAA—*See NATIONAL Collegiate Athletic Association*
NCR Corp.
Comten purchase OKd 1-21, 89F1
NDABENI, Ernest
Sentenced 5-11, 373G1
NDIWENI, Chief Kayisa
In Rhodesian electn 4-17—4-21, 293D1
In Zimbabwe Cabt 5-30, 393D1
NEAL, Larry
Glorious Monster opens 7-10, 711C3
NEAME, Ronald
Meteor released 10-19, 1008A1
NEAVE, Airey
Slain, IRA suspected 3-30, 254E1
Death penalty ban upheld 7-19, 543F2

NEBRASKA
Legislature schedule rptd 5E3
Blizzards hit 1-12—1-14, 1-24—1-27, 120F1
Abortn law passed 3-19, suspended 4-20, 315C1
Rape bail denial upheld 4-4, 310A2
US Sup Ct worker fired re news leaks 4-20, 302A3
Diesel fuel shortage rptd 5-18, 361A3
States given parole discretn by Sup Ct 5-29, 421E2-B3
Indian land case laws backed by Sup Ct 6-20, 516A2
Nazi ldr cited re W Ger arrests 9-13, 733C3
'78 per capita income rptd 9-16, 746E2
Porno case jury challenge refused by Sup Ct 10-1, 768F1
'Cancer' murderer convicted 10-5, gets death penalty 11-7, 891A1
Rape bail case refused by Sup Ct 10-15, 847E3
Simants acquitted in retrial 10-17, 890E3
Peter Kiewit dies 11-2, 932B3
NEBRASKA, University of (Lincoln)
Loses Orange Bowl 1-1, '78 rank rptd 1-2, 1-3, 8E2, B3
Andrews, Clark in NFL draft 5-3, 335G2
NEDERLANDER, James M.
Grand Tour opens 1-11, 292E1
Whose Life opens 4-17, 712E3
Peter Pan opens 9-6, 956G3
Night & Day opens 11-27, 956E3
Oklahoma opens 12-13, 1007D2
NEEDHAM, Hal
Villain released 7-20, 820E3
NEEDLEMAN, Dr. Herbert
Lead levels study rptd 3-29, 266G1
NEESEMAN, Wolfgang
Heim convicted of war crimes 6-13, 490C1
NEESKENS, Johan
Signs with Cosmos 6-11, 655E1
Named to NASL All-Star team 8-27, 776E1
NEGOTIABLE Orders of Withdrawal (NOW)—*See BANKS*
NEGRI, Antonio
Arrested re terrorism 4-8, 269C1
Threatnd in Curcio letter 8-10, 635F2
NEGRIN, Eulalio Jose
Slain 11-25, FBI probe rptd 11-28, 906B1-D1
NEGRO, Mary-Joan
Wings opens 1-28, 292G3

1980

NBA (National Basketball Association)—*See BASKETBALL*
NBC—*See RCA Corp.--National Broadcasting Co. (NBC)*
NCAA—*See NATIONAL Collegiate Athletic Association*
NEA—*See NATIONAL Education Association*
NEAL, David Franklin
Executed 4-22, 353G1
NEAL, James F.
Ford acquitted in Pinto trial 3-13, 185D3, 186A1
Declines B Carter probe role 8-7, 595E3
NEAL, Rep. Stephen L. (D, N.C.)
Reelected 11-4, 843B4
NEAME, Ronald
Hopscotch released 9-26, 836B3

NEBRASKA
Kellogg settles Omaha site bias chrgs 2-6, 115A3
Influenza outbreak rptd 2-15, 158C3
DES in cattle rptd 4-24, 358F1
Tornadoes hit Grand I 6-3, disaster declared 6-4, 527A3
Oglala Sioux Black Hills compensatn suit dismissed 9-11, 704C2
Politics & Government—*See also other appropriate subheads in this section*
Legislature schedule rptd 18E1
State of State message 1-10, 403B1
DC voting rep amendmt rejctd 2-11, 147B3
Reagan campaigns 4-9, 288E2, F2
Pres primary results 5-13, 366D2
Carter visits Grand I 6-10, 439D1
Election results 11-4: pres 838C1, 839B1, E3; cong 840D2, 843E2, 851A2; state 845G2
'80 census rptd 12-31, 983F1
Transportation
Union Pacific, MoPac set merger 1-8, 52C3
N&W, Southn RR merger sought 6-2, 427E2
NEBRASKA, University of (Lincoln)
Loses Cotton Bowl 1-1, '79 rank rptd 1-2, 23C1, E1
Dana Bible dies 1-19, 104F1
Ottey sets indoor 220-yd dash mark 2-29, 892E1
Miller in NFL draft 4-29, 336E3
Wins Sun Bowl 12-27, 999D3
NECESSARY Woman, A (book)
On best-seller list 5-4, 359E3
NEDERLANDER, James M.
West Side Story opens 2-14, 136G3
Music Man opens 6-6, 756F3
NEDKOV, Ilian
Wins Olympic medal 7-31, 623C1
NEDLOG Technology Group Inc.
Sierra Leone rejects chem waste dump plan 2-20, 154B2
NEEDE, Sgt. Laurens Edward
Arrested 1-30, leads coup 2-25, 153D2
NEEDHAM, Hal
Smokey & the Bandit II released 8-15, 675E3
NEESKENS, Johan
Cosmos suspend 9-11, 770A2
NEGRETTI, Jose Francisco
Arrested in hijacking 12-6, 968F3
NEGRI, Antonio
More extensive probe urged 1-2, 20A3

1976

NEGROES—*See BLACK Americans*
NEISWENDER, Charles E.
Mandel case mistrial declared 12-7, 922A3, D3
Indicted 12-28, 1016G2
NEITA, Ferdie
Wounded 12-13, 965A3
NEIZVESTNY, Ernst
Emigrates to Israel 3-10, 206E3
NELSON, Cindy
Wins Olympic medal 2-8, 158E3
NELSON, Sen. Gaylord (D, Wis.)
Carter meets cong ldrs 11-17, 864A2
NELSON, Jack
Pres debate panelist 10-22, 800A1, 801A1
NELSON, William
Quits as CIA dep dir 4-27, 412B2
NELSON, Willie
Wins Grammy award 2-28, 460A3
NEMETH, Miklos
Wins Olympic medal 7-26, 576A1
NEMTSANOV, Sergei
Defects to Canada 7-29, kidnaping chrgd 7-30—7-31, 562D2, G2
To return to USSR 8-17, 655C2
NEO-Fascism—*See FASCISM*

NEPAL—*See also ADB, NONALIGNED Nations Movement*
Listed as 'not free' nation 1-19, 20E3
Maytag confrmd US amb 3-3, 186B2
NESSEN, Ron
Ford scores CIA Italy aid leaks 1-7, 10D3
Morton named Ford aide 1-13, 21F2
Rpts speechwriters shifted 1-21, 40C3
Ford orders business payoff probe 2-10, 134B2
On Nixon China trip 2-23, 189F3
On NH primary vote 2-25, 148E2
On Ford primary wins 3-2, 165B2
On Feb WPI 3-4, 199D1
On Nixon China trip rpt 3-22, 215A1
Ford 'disappointed' at vote 3-23, 214F1
On Kissinger tenure 4-7, 245D2
On Ford Panama Canal policy 4-14, 4-15, 281F1, 291C3
Lauds Syrian Leb moves 4-19, 274B1
On March CPI 4-21, 306G1
Corrects Ford busing remark 5-27, 391G1
On 7-natn econ summit plan 6-1, 389A1
On busing legislatn 6-2, 392B1
On June jobless rate 7-2, 494B1
Wyo delegate deal denied 7-2, 518G1
Rpts Alaska pipe audit, on-site inspectn 7-6, 690D3
HEW schl ruling suspended 7-7, 535F2
On revised econ forecast 7-16, 535G3
US offers China quake aid 7-29, 545B2
On vp straw poll 7-30, 564A1
Ford OKs DMZ tree felling 8-20, 625F1
On Kim US death regrets 8-23, 625F2
Ford Yellowstone trip paid by GOP 8-29, 644E3
Campaign start delayed 9-3, 665A1
On Viet MIA identificatn 9-6, 678G2
On Carter tax remark 9-18, 9-20, 703D3
On Ford golfing gifts 9-21, 9-28, 722G2-E3
US to back UK IMF loan request 9-29, 721F1
On Butz reprimand 10-1, 744C1
Says Brown matter closed 10-18, 787B3
On 3d ¼ GNP, inflatn rpt 10-19, 805G1; Sept indicators 10-29, 833B1
Powell visits White House 11-16, 864D1
NETHANYAHU, Lt. Col. Yehonathan
Killed in Uganda raid 7-3, 485C1
NETHERLANDS—*See also ADB, DISARMAMENT—Geneva Committee, EUROPEAN Community, IEA, NATO, OECD*
Anti-terrorist moves rptd 1-16, 102C2
Listed as 'free' nation 1-19, 20C3
Rpt conscript wins CO status 2-15, 141B3
Train collisn kills 23 5-4, 560E3
2 held 9-24, hashish seized 9-26, 732D2
Climber joins Everest team 10-8, 876B3
Loijen sentenced 12-14, 1007D2

1977

NEGROES—*See BLACK Americans*
NEGRO Women, National Council of
Height at black ldrs mtg 8-29, 702E1
NEGUSSIE Negassa, Second Lt.
Slaying rptd 4-10, 328D1
NEIER, Aryeh
On religious deprogramming 2-5, 287E1
NEIGHBORHOODS, National Commission on—*See under U.S. GOVERNMENT*
NEIMAN-Marcus—*See CARTER Hawley Hale Stores*
NEJELSKI, Paul A.
Study urges LEAA reorganizatn 6-30, 630C2
NEKRASOV, Paul Y.
FBI arrests Sovt spy 1-7, 41C3
NEL, Jon
Botha wins Parlt seat 5-11, 428D3
NELSON, Sen. Gaylord (D, Wis.)
Heads ethics panel 1-18, 77F2
Votes vs Bell 1-25, 52A3
NELSON, Larry
Loses San Diego Open 1-30, 104C1
Ties 2d in Greensboro Open 4-3, 311F1
NELSON, Robert L.
Named Army asst secy 5-19, confrmd 5-27, 500A1
NEMIKEN, Raisa
Jailed 3-1, 261D2
NEOHESPERIDINE Dihydrochalcone—*See SWEETENERS, Artificial*
NEOPTOLEMOS, Leftis
Sentenced in Davies murder 6-21, 530E2

NEPAL—*See also NONALIGNED Nations Movement*
UN Assemb member 4D1
IMF loan set 2-4, 87F2
US amb confrmd 5-25, 499F3
Amnesty Intl lists lawmakers held 9-5, 753B2
NEPPEL, Peg
Sets 10,000-mtr run mark 6-9—6-11, 602C3
NEPTUNE Worldwide Moving Co.
Employe kills 5, self 2-14, 162E2
NEREY (Soviet trawler)
Argentina seizes 9-21, 944F2; frees 11-9, 982D1
NERVE Gas—*See CHEMICAL & Biological Warfare*
NESTLE Alimentana S.A.
Alcon OKs purchase 11-17; merger table 880D1, G1

NETHERLANDS, The—*See also DISARMAMENT—Geneva Committee, EC, ESA, IDB, IEA, NATO, OECD*
Jet crash on Canary Island 3-27, 244C1
Canary I crash suits filed in US 3-31—4-6; probe begun 4-4, 311B3-312C1
Saccharin curbs set 5-9, 531E1
Amsterdam hotel fire 5-9, 604B2
Amsterdam gay rights march 6-25, 560F2
Anti-Nazi burns Menten home 7-18, 986E1
Abortn issue halts coalitn talks 8-25, 656B1
Heroin addictn rptd up 10-17—10-21, 971C3
Caransa kidnaped 10-28, freed 11-2, 871D1
Menten sentenced for war crimes 12-14, 986B1

1978

NEGROES—*See BLACK Americans*
NEHEMIAH, Reynaldo
Sets indoor 60-yd high hurdle mark 1-27, 76B3
Sets 110-mtr hurdles mark 6-8—6-10, 600B3
NEHMER, Meinhard
2d in 2-man bobsled championship 2-5, 316F3
NEIL, Harold G.
Rules for TWU in fuel dispute 11-20, 921B1
NELSON, Avi
Loses Sen primary in Mass 9-19, 736F2
NELSON, Bill
Wins US House seat 11-7, 849E3, 850F2
NELSON, Donovan D.
Loses primary for Iowa gov 6-6, 448E1
NELSON, Sen. Gaylord (D, Wis.)
Votes for Panama Canal neutrality pact 3-16, 177D2
Votes for 2d Canal pact 4-18, 273B1
Endangered Species Act revised 7-19, 551E2
Scores SBA minority-aid abuse 11-21, 919B3
NELSON, Novella
Run'ers' opens 5-3, 887A3
NELSON, Simon Peter
Convicted 5-22, 396D3
NEMEROV, Howard
Wins Natl Book Award 4-10, 315A3
Wins Pulitzer Prize 4-17, 315C1
NEMETH, Karly
Named Hungary admin secy 4-20, 534G1
NENE, David
Quits re corruptn probe 10-31, 885A3
NEON Woman, The (play)
Opens 4-16, 760G2

NEPAL—*See also NONALIGNED Nations Movement*
Freedom House lists as partly free 44F1
China dep premr visits 2-3—2-5, 111F2
Leb peace force (Unifil) formed 3-19, 197D2; **for peacekeeping developments, see MIDDLE EAST—LEBANON**
2 climb Everest without oxygen 5-8, 420C2
US' Boeing chrgd re payoffs 7-28, 642G3
UK cancels debts 7-31, 592E1
UN Assemb member 713C3
Amer women climb Annapurna 10-15, 2 killed 10-17, 843G2
NEREE, Rev. Luc
Ex-Tontons sentncd re '77 assault 3-21, 292C3
NERVE Gas—*See CHEMICAL & Biological Warfare*
NESSEN, Ron
KCIA recruitmt effort rptd 11-1, 862E3
NESTLE Alimentana S.A.
Nestle sets Uganda coffee ban 5-17, 416E3
NESTLE Co.—*See NESTLE Alimentana S.A.*

NETHERLANDS—*See also COUNCIL of Europe, DISARMAMENT—Geneva Committee, EC, GATT, IDB, IEA, NATO, OECD*
Van Gogh paintings slashed 4-5, 4-25, 335E1, F1
Bomb defused at Hague 5-11, 454E3
Menten convictn overturned 5-29, 454G2
Energy conservatn progress seen 6-5, 449E3★, 450E1
Polio epidemic declines 7-30, 635A3
Canary I '77 jet crash rpt issued 10-18, govt scores 10-23, 888A2
Abortn bill OKd by Cabt 11-16, 965F1-A2
Menten release ordered 12-4, 965B2

Atomic Energy & Safeguards

'77 A-export safeguard pact detailed 1-11, 11B2
US alerts to USSR satellite fall 57E1
Van Agt delays A-plants 1-16, 90A3
Brazil uranium sales, Urenco plant expansn OKd 2-1, Almelo protest 3-4, 162C2, F2
Neutron bomb opposed 2-23, 140A3
Australia joins A-supplier group 2-24, 129C2
Defnse min vs neutron bomb 2-24, resigns 3-4; Parlt OKs anti-bomb resolutn 3-8, 169D1-B2

1979

NEGROES—*See BLACK Americans*
NEHEMIAH, Renaldo (Skeets)
Sets 5 world hurdle marks 1-20–5-6, 911A1, B1
NEHMER, Meinhard
W Gers win world 4-man bobsled title 2-25, 392F1
NEIGHBORHOODS, National Association of
Vs urban displacemt rpt 2-14, 132C3
NEIGHBORHOODS, National Commission on
Rpt issued 3-15, 208G2
NEILSON, Roger
Hired as Sabres coach 6-20, 470A3
NEKIPELOV, Viktor
Arrested 12-7, 939F1
NELL, Nathalie
Rape of Love released 9-23, 820A3
NELSON, Gary
Black Hole released 12-21, 1007A3
NELSON, Sen. Gaylord (D, Wis.)
Small Business Com chrmn 1-23, 71E2
Votes vs trade bill 7-23, 646G3
NELSON, Larry
Wins Inverrary Classic 3-11, 220A3
2d in Memphis Classic 7-1, wins Westn Open 7-8, 587C3, D3
2d in World Series of Golf 9-30, 969B3
PGA top money winner 11-30, 969F2
NELSON, Willie
Wins 2 Grammys 2-16, 336F3
NEMCOVA, Dana
Arrested 5-29, sentncd 10-23, 802B2

NEPAL—*See also NONALIGNED Nations Movement*
Student unrest, 30 die 4-5, 389C3
Dissident ldrs seized 4-27, freed 5-9, 389B3
2 climb Annapurna 5-8, 392G2
2 climb Gauri Sankar 5-12, 392G2
UN membership listed 695A3
NEPOROZHNY, Pyotr S.
USSR A-accidents disclosed 4-22, 323F1
Denies Comecon oil shortage, hints E-W cable link 6-27, 497B2
NERI Mago, Nerio
Venez Eastn relatns min 3-10, 192D3
NERVI, Pier Luigi
Dies 1-9, 104E3
NEST of Vipers (film)
Released 9-7, 820C2

NETHERLANDS—*See also COUNCIL of Europe, DISARMAMENT-Geneva Committee, EC, GATT, IDB, IEA, NATO, OECD*
Menten retrial ordered 5-22, 409D1
Canary I '77 jet crash probed 5-29, 412B2
Fluoride dental value doubted 9-1, 1000A2
Menten ruled unfit for trial 9-24, 731D2

Atomic Energy & Safeguards

Urenco plans contd cooperatn, W Ger A-enrichmt plant 2-7, 101D1
Gasselte A-protest staged 6-2, 416E2
Energy progrm announced 9-19, 731B1
A-protesters blockade Urenco plant 10-15, 782A1

1980

NEGROES—*See BLACK Americans*
NEHEMIAH, Renaldo (Skeets)
In US Olympic trials; injury, track team resignatn cited 6-24, 891A2
NEHRU, Jawaharlal (1889-1964)
Mountbatten affair alleged 8-27, Gandhi denies 8-29, 890A3
NEIL, Dr. Marguerite A.
On tampon, toxic-shock syndrome link 9-22, 726C3
NEILL, Sam
My Brilliant Career released 2-1, 216C3
NEISH, Brig. Gen. Robert
Soldiers seized in coup try 6-22, 498F3
Jamaica moves to quell violence 7-18, 579G1
NEKIPELOV, Viktor
Sentenced 6-13, 680B3
NELFORD, Jim
Canada wins World Cup 12-14, 972A3
NELLIGAN, James L.
Elected to US House 11-4, 844C1, 848G3
NELSON, Rep. Bill (D, Fla.)
Reelected 11-4, 842G2
NELSON, Judge David S.
OKs Boston job bias suit setlmt 12-5, 962C3
NELSON, Sen. Gaylord (D, Wis.)
Unopposed in primary 9-9, 700D3
Loses reelectn 11-4, 837D2, 845A2, 851F2
NELSON, James
Borderline released 10-31, 972D3
NELSON, Jeffrey
Return of the Secaucus 7 released 9-14, 836E3
NELSON, Larry
Wins Atlanta Classic 6-8, 715A1
NELSON-Hall Publishers Inc.
Photocopy co sued 2-5, 119G3
Photocopy suit rptd setld 3-21, 376D3
NEMAPARA, Peter
Zimbabwe min freed in murder case 12-8, 946C2
NEMETO, Spider
Pedroza decisns 1-22, 320A3
NENG-Ping Yao
On G&W elec car dvpt 6-9, 541D3
NENNI, Pietro
Dies 1-1, 104C3
NEPAL—*See also ADB, NONALIGNED Nations*
Voters back partyless govt 5-2, final results 5-14, 409E3
NESTANDE, Bruce
Wins Orange Cnty supervisor post 6-3, 439F2
NESTLE Alimentana S.A.
Guatemala exec kidnaped 6-17, ransom demand rptd 6-20, 487F2
Guatemala exec freed 9-10, 731B3
11 execs killed in NY hotel fire 12-4, 948C2

NETHERLANDS—*See also ADB, COUNCIL of Europe, CSCE, EC, GATT, GENEVA Committee, IDB, IEA, MBFR, NATO, OECD*
Molsidomine use rptd 1-3, 24D1
Menten sentncd 7-9, 509F3
470 flee ocean liner fire off Alaska 10-4, 769B2
Liberal abortn law OKd 12-20, 996F3

Atomic Energy & Safeguards

A-plants backed in rpt 7-17, 565A2
Protesters blockade A-plant 10-19-10-20, 830G2

1976

Economy & Labor (domestic)
'75 indl productn drop rptd 1-6, 102G2
'75 COL rptd up 1-20, 102A2
Jobless rise rptd slowing 1-28, 84F3
Bank cuts discount rate 2-2, 102A3
'76 econ forecast rptd 3-26, 255F1
Prime rate hiked 7-30, 594C1
Drought measures studied 8-24, 630F1
'77 budget submitted 9-21, 732A2
'74 tax rate rptd 11-18, 905G1
Price freeze imposed 12-7, 1007E2
Feed crop loss from drought rptd 12-31, 977D3
European Force Reduction Issues—*See under EUROPE*
Foreign Economic Developments—*See also 'Political Payments' below*
'75 exports rptd down 1-6, 102A3
Rptd vs liberalized IMF credit 1-8, 14C2
SDR rate rptd 1-15, 14B3
Brazil bauxite operatn begun 1-16, 98G2
In Japan-US oil consortium 1-16, 208C3
US bank deal rptd 1-23, 102C2
Oil traces found off Brittany 1-31, 139G2
Potato exports curbed 2-12, 2-16, 141A3
Australia steel projct deferred 2-24, 154D3
1st Auk oil shipmt rptd 2-25, 173D3
To join A-safeguards group 3-13, 243F2
Firms taken off Arab blacklist 3-24—4-3, 242C1
Govt increases N Sea role 3-25, 255E1
French snake reform proposal rejected 4-1—4-2, 276A1, D1
Total IMF oil loan rptd 4-1, 340F2
World Bank OKs bank loan 4-2, 366D1
Australia oil dvpt projct set 4-29, 332C1
N Viet vows oil cooperatn 5-7, 367A3
Paris group wins S Africa A-deal 5-28, 387A2, G3, 388B2
UNCTAD OKs commodity fund 5-30, 388A3
IDB entry planned 6-3, 465D3
Loan to prop UK £ OKd 6-7, 407C2
Paris Club defers Zaire debt 6-17, 488A2
France vs joint Eurpn steel firm 7-6, 521G1
Israel links currency 7-18, 538D3
Backs World Bank funds rise 10-5, 778D1
W Ger mark revalued 10-17, 782B1
Jan-June trade balance rptd 11-2, 1007F2
Guilder reactn to US electn 11-3, 826F2
DISC program ruled illegal 11-5, 976E3
Rhine pollutn pacts signed 12-4, 977A2
In IMF UK loan 12-21, 1004B1
Foreign Relations (misc.)—*See also 'UN Policy' below*
Ecuador ousts newsman 1-13, 28F2
Herrema kidnaper in ct exchng 1-13, 157A1
Europn soclsts meet 1-18—1-19, 48A3; 3-13—3-14, 222F3
7 named as CIA agents 1-21, 50D1
Chile barred priests' return 1-23, 100D2
Angola mercenary aid set 2-2, 82A1
Angola MPLA recognized 2-18, 163B1
Bernhard cancels Latin trip 3-4, US Bilderberg Conf 3-5, 254C3
Yugo sentences Belgrade lawyer 3-10, 223G3
Ex-Nazi nominatn to Rotary protested 3-11, 380B3
Eur liberals meet 3-26—3-27, 260C3
Tourist suspect in Israeli airport blast 5-25, 370G2
Backs US Gertroop plan 6-10—6-11, 449G1
Rpt Colombia blocks consul's ransom 6-17, 731B2
Ship in US Bicentennial event 7-4, 488B3
Amalrik, wife immigrate 7-15, 540G2
Spain emb bomb blast 7-20, 541D2
Sovt chess player defects 7-27, 558F3
Sea limit compromise with UK 7-27, 563C3
Royal couple cuts short Italy visit 8-23, 626A3
Angola ties set 8-30, 862F2
KLM jet hijacked 9-4, gunmen surrender in Cyprus 9-5, 662D2
UK ship rescue aid 9-20, 713A1
Bangladesh sentncs natl 9-20, deports 9-23, 734C3
S African gets asylum 11-12, 927F3
France bars jt Eur defns 11-30, 905A3
Menten in Swiss custody 12-7, returned 12-22, 1007B2

1977

Economy & Labor (domestic)
'74-75 recessn job data rptd 1-3, 29E3
Bank discount rate cut 1-6, 24D2
'76 factory wage study rptd 1-28, 158B3
Dec '75-76 inflatn rate rptd 2-7, 87A2
Strikes end, Rotterdam port opened 2-25, 221D3-222G1
'76 gas reserves drop rptd 3-28, 412E1
Unemploymt, prices estimated 4-1, 412B1
Budget deficit projected 4-4, 412A1
Coalitn profit-sharing agrmt reached 7-27, econ pkg OKd 8-9; criticism rptd 8-15, 656D1
Army union protests NATO discipline 8-18, parades banned 10-26, 986C2
Foreign Relations (misc.)—*See also 'Monetary, Trade & Aid' below*
UN Assemb member 4A1
'76 Eur Cncl pact vs terror cited 9G2
In 14-natn sulphur-dioxide pact 1-19, 109B3
Van Boven named UN comm dir 1-28, 140G3
Socialist rep at Israel Labor Party conventn 2-22, 135F1
Van der Stoel in Czech 2-28—3-2; sees dissident 3-1, 220G2
21 Poles seek asylum 3-26, 315A1
Bilderberg conf 4-21—4-24, 359B3
Eur Cncl to study Turkey rights abuses in Cyprus 9-8, 764G1-A2; rpt shelved, Greece protests 11-3, 946E3
W Ger terrorist shootout 9-22, manhunt aid asked 9-24, 11-11; 4 arrested 10-17, 888D1
Folkerts extraditn barred 9-23, sentncd 12-20, 986G1
Schleyer search rptd 9-27, W Ger asks slayer manhunt aid 10-20, 791B2, A3
W Eur heroin conf 10-17—10-21, 971B3
S Africa amb recall rptd 10-25, 825C1
Lufthansa hijackers identified 10-25, 10-27, 868G2
2 W Ger terrorist suspects captured 11-10, 887E3
UN Israel occupatn res abstentn 11-25, 910D2
Government & Politics—*See also other appropriate subheads in this section*
Govt resigns re land dispute 3-22, 221A3
Terrorism halts campaign 5-23—5-25, Labor Party gains in electns 5-25, 412A1, C1
Den Uyl fails to form govt 5-25—8-25, resignatn accepted 8-25, 656B1
Parties heal rift over abortn 9-2; Queen names den Uyl mediator 9-5, 729F2
Bernhard return to pub life rptd 9-28, 986B2
Soc Dem conf asks monarchy end 10-13—10-15, poll repudiates 10-17, 986A2
CDA, VVD coalitn talks 11-22—12-14; Cabt named 12-15, sworn 12-19, 985A3
Helsinki Agreement—*See EUROPE—Security and Cooperation*
Monetary, Trade & Aid Issues (including all foreign economic developments)
Boeing denies Bernhard consultant 1-5, 215C3
In UK sterling balances pact 1-10, 20C2
IDB member 1-10, 438E3
US F-16 sale review set 1-17, 70D3
ICFTU S Africa boycott fails 1-21, 67B3
Iran drops boycott threat 2-3, 250F1
Irish ban large fishing vessels 2-15, 146C3
Brazil A-plant safeguards asked 3-11, 190F1
Import rise estimated 4-1, 412C1
A-supplier natns score Carter plans 4-28—4-29, 403F1-A2
US F-16 pact set 5-5, 441A2
Carter OKs uranium shipmt 5-6, 403D2
Central Bank lowers discount rate 5-6, 412G1
Intl consortium OKs Egypt aid 5-11—5-15, 390C3
US co to lease Airbus 5-24, 441D2

1978

Neutron bomb forum, protest rally 3-18—3-19, 255C1
US study backs breeder dvpt 5-10, 346G3
Van Agt bars more Brazil talks 6-28, parlt backs uranium sale 6-30, govt crisis averted 7-1, 575A1
Economy & Labor (domestic)
Van Agt policy statemt 1-16, 90E2
Jan jobless rate rptd 1-17, 90G2
Metalworkers setlmt rptd, other union agrmts seen 4-14, 454F3
Waste combustn plant rptd 5-11, 367F1
'79 budget presented; record deficit, growth curbs asked 9-19, 965B1
June '77-78 world inflatn rates ranked 10-18, 914F1
Ford productn problems cited re UK strike 11-22, 923D2
European Force Reduction Talks—*See under EUROPE*
Foreign Relations (misc.)—*See also 'Atomic Energy' above; 'Monetary, Trade, Aid & Investment' and 'UN' below*
W Ger arrests spy couple 1-4, 21E3
At USSR mil maneuvers 2-6—2-10, 103B2
France, W Ger OK ESA rocket launcher 2-6—2-7, 122B1
Eur fascists meet 3-4—3-5, 238D3
W Ger Baader-Meinhof backers stage protest 3-14, 192F1
3 Sovts named as spies 3-30, 247E3
S African church cuts ties 4-4, 269G2
Eur conservative party union shunned 4-24, 424D3
W Ger arrest 5 for arms theft 4-29, 477B3
3 terrorists arrested in W Ger plot 5-5, jailed 8-21, 725C1
Ct rules on extraditn of Folkerts, 2 other W Ger terrorists 5-8, 354C1, 454C3
Hague fete for Israel 5-11, 454E3
ESA communicatns satellite launched 5-12, 384D3
Shcharansky support vowed 7-11, 543C1
Ct broadens Folkerts extraditn rule 9-7, 725E1
Amnesty Intl protest staged re W Ger terrorist treatmt 10-9; 3 terrorists extradited 10-13, 10-17, 885B1, E1
Guard killed at W Ger border 11-1, 885A2
Philips exec kidnaped in El Salvador 11-24, demands met 12-21, 986B3; freed 12-30, 1021E3
USSR conductor defects 12-4, 946E3
Government & Politics—*See also other appropriate subheads in this section*
Van Agt policy statemt 1-16, 90E2-C3
Christian Dems gain in local electns 3-29, 247A3
Christian Dems gain in local electns 5-31, 454A3
'79 budget presented to parlt 9-19, 965B1
Aantjes quits parlt re SS link 11-7, 871G3
Cabt OKs liberalized abortn bill 11-16, 965F1-A2
Helsinki Agreement—*See EUROPE—Security and Cooperation*
Monetary, Trade, Aid & Investment—*See also 'Atomic Energy' above*
Volvo unit rescued by govt 1-5, 93G1
Van Agt vs protectnism, plans poor natn aid 1-16, 90A3
Israeli oranges found poisoned 2-1, 60F3-61A1
'77 gas export drop rptd 2-10, 169D3
W Ger '77 trade rptd 2-14, 169C3
'77 paymts surplus estimated 2-15, 169B3
'77 trade deficit rptd 2-28, 169G2
Guilder in new SDR basket 4-3, 300F3
US backs F-16 review 4-24, 407E2
Philips Brazil strike 5-17—5-23, 412C1
Zaire emergency aid OKd 6-13—6-14, 478A1
4 natns' debts cancelled 7-10, 575E1
UK cancels 17 natns' debts 7-31, 592E1
Rhodesia rebel aid OKd by WCC 8-10, 650A3
W Ger mark revalued up 10-16, 798C2
Trade missn rptd in Japan 10-18, 798D1

1979

Economy & Labor—*See also 'Atomic' above, 'Energy' below*
Barge strike ends 1-10, 136B2
'78 living standards ranked 2-2, 109A2
Printers OK contract 2-6, 136D2
Govt spending cuts protested 6-19, 566D2
'78 per capita GNP ranked 9th 7-24, 575E3
Rotterdam port struck 8-23, 653B3
'80 budget presented, detailed 9-18; scored 9-20, 730G2-731A1
Westn wage rates compared 9-19, 697D3
Rotterdam port strike ends 9-24, 731E1
Tugboat strike ends 10-13, 815A1
Bank lending fee raised 10-31, 838F1
Energy—*See also 'Atomic' above*
Rotterdam oil spot mkt dvpts rptd 7-16, 494F1
Conservatn progrms planned 9-18, 9-19, 730B3, 731B1
Shell refinery hit by strike 9-24, reopening announced 9-27, 731C2
Shell refinery strike ends 9-28, 815C1
European Force Reduction Talks—*See under EUROPE*
Foreign Relations (misc.)—*See also 'Atomic' and 'Energy' above, 'Monetary' and 'UN' below*
UK amb killed, IRA linked 3-22, 228E2-D3
El Salvador Philips exec '78 ransom rptd 3-23, 235G1
W Ger sentncs neo-Nazis 9-13, 733D3
Sovt chess player gets Swiss asylum 9-24, 721E3
UK, W Ger, Belgium unions vowed Shell strikers support 9-24, 731C2
USSR vs A-missiles 10-13—10-16, 880G2
MPs rejct A-missile plan 12-6, 938C2
Theologian faces Vatican heresey chrgs 12-18, 999A3
Government & Politics—*See also other appropriate subheads in this section*
Luns denies Nazi link 3-2, 181A1
Eur Parlt electns 6-7, 433A1, 434B1
Van Agt no-confidence vote threatened 12-6, 938C2
Govt survives confidence vote re NATO missiles 12-20, 959E2
Helsinki Agreement—*See EUROPE-Security and Cooperation*
Monetary, Trade, Aid & Investment
Barge strike ends 1-10, 136B2
Nationale-Nederlanden seeks US co 3-23, 942D2
'78 paymts deficit rptd 3-28, 288D2
W Ger ranks exporter labor costs 5-1, 374B2
EC green currencies revised 6-21, 513G1
EMS currencies realigned 6-24, 719A1
Denmark files Unilever trust chrgs 7-2, 563G3
'80 trade data, current acct surplus predicted 9-18, 730E3
Tobacco export gains rptd 11-22, 970A3

1980

Economy & Labor
Voluntary wage freeze urged 1-7, rejected by FNV, CNV 1-9, 21E1-A2
Pay freeze ordered 1-10, 60G2-B3
Bank workers strike 1-17, 98E1
Govt spending ban ordrd 2-1, 100F1; Andriessen quits Cabt 2-21, 173E3
Amsterdam squatters, cops clash 2-29, 3-3, 276F3-277C1; 4-30, 353E3; 9-8—9-9, 737F3; 12-2, 969B3
GNP 1% growth seen by OECD 3-3, 173F3-174A1
Wage controls protested 3-4, 174B1
House OKs wage freeze bill, pub spending cuts 3-5, 276G2
Unions strike vs wage curbs 3-20, 276B3
Borrowing rptd at new high 3-25, 276D3
Wage pacts rptd set 6-17, 465B3
3 multinatl wage pacts set 6-17, 465B3
Labor costs rptd 8-12, 698C1, F1
Textile aid program rptd 8-22, 672E1
'81 budget proposed 9-16, 709B2
Indl aid measures rptd 9-18—9-19, 792A1
Teachers strike 10-1, 792D1
Energy—*See also 'Atomic Energy' above*
Gasoline prices cut 8-12, 628A2
Algeria LNG deal canceled 9-11, 827A3
Oil stocks termed 'adequate', IEA sets '81 buying curb 12-9, 932D1
Foreign Relations (misc.)—*See also 'Monetary', 'UN Policy' below*
USSR Olympics boycott support cited 1-14, 28C3
Dutch bishops hold Vatican synod 1-14—1-31; traditionalism affirmed, doctrinal disputes cited 1-31, 156G2
Sakharov exile condemned 1-22, 46C3
IRA claims credit for UK amb's '79 death 2-19, 194B1
English Channel tunnel plan rptd 3-4, 193G3
Chad fighting resumes 3-22, natls evacuated 3-24, 221F1
Saudi princess film broadcast cited 4-23, 313F2
Beatrix urges more 3d World ties 4-30, 353E3
USSR May Day parade shunned 5-1, 354G2
Surinam coup attempt fails, mercenary ldr executed 5-1—5-2, 410F2
Olympic com rejects Moscow boycott 5-20, 379A3
ESA rocket test fails 5-23, 397G2
Israel assured no EC peace move 6-4, 418E1
New Hebrides rebels, Phoenix Foundatn linked 6-8, 436C2
W Ger backs NATO A-missiles 7-15, 540C1
ESA plans comet probe 7-15, 548A1
Jewish youth killed in Belgium blast 7-27, Palestinian seized 7-28, 573D2
Westn labor costs compared 8-12, 698C1, F1
Iran parlt ldr rebuffs hostage appeal 8-17, 634D3
Israel Emb move set, Arab threats cited 8-26, 643E2
Iraq expels newsman 10-2, 775A1
W Ger, Swiss natls flee ocean liner fire 10-4, 769A3
France blast injures natl 10-5, 768B1
Sovts scored at CSCE conf 11-12, 863C1
Government & Politics—*See also other appropriate subheads in this section*
Queen Juliana sets abdication 1-31, 100D1
Andriessen resigns 2-20, govt continues 2-21, 173C3
Van der Stee named finance min 3-4, 276E3
Beatrix invested as Queen 4-30, 353C3
Censure vote fails 6-27, 499F1
Monetary, Trade, Aid & Investment
Current acct deficit linked to pay freeze 1-10, 60A3
'79 US mfg investmt rptd 2-6, 92D3
French wine fraud disclosed 3-6, 193B2
US Steel files dumping complaint 3-21, 225D1
'79 current acct deficit up 4-2, 277C1
'79 US investmt rptd 4-8, 329C1
US sets steel import probe 4-10, 367F3
US finds steel import damage 5-1, 456C1
Jamaica loan rptd 6-4, 465D1
S Africa oil embargo barred, econ sanctns probed 6-27, 499F1
Textile aid program rptd 8-22, 672E1
Arab boycott threats force Israel Emb move 8-26, 643F2
Algeria LNG deal canceled 9-11, 827A3

1976

Political Payments
3 admit Gulf Oil paymts 1-11, 134G1
Lockheed bribe to Bernhard confrmd 2-8, probe set 2-9, opens 2-11, 131G2
Swiss lawyer denies payoff role 2-10, 131A3
Dassault bribe case opens 2-10, 141D2; acquittal 2-25, 158E2
Swiss OK Dutch probe 2-25, comm rpts interviews 3-5, 254G2
US data documts Bernhard bribe 2-27, 254B3
Bernhard cancels Latin, US trips 3-4, 3-5, 254C3
US Sen subcom affirms Bernhard bribe 3-10, 200D2
'51 Argentine bribes rptd 3-12, den Uyl confirms 3-18, 254D3
US Lockheed data pact 3-30, 286A1
Shell admits Italy bribes 4-13, 267F1
Probe rptd widened 4-13, US releases Lockheed data 322B2
Dutch press rpts Lockheed, Bernhard link 4-21, 322C2
US disclosure bill proposed 8-3, 668B2
Juliana sees Den Uyl on probe comm rpt, bars abdicatn 8-23, 626G2
Den Uyl details probe comm rpt to Parlt, Bernhard quits posts 8-26, 626F1; text excerpts 627A1, D2
Parlt vs Bernhard prosecutn 8-30, 642C2
3 legislators rptd approached by Lockheed 9-1, 684B2
Bernhard role in '71 W Ger jet buy rptd 9-2, 684F2
W Ger campaign issue 9-29, 10-1, 754C3
South Molucca—*See under INDONESIA*
Sports
Winter Olympics results 2-4—2-15, 158B3-159B2
Rotterdam WCT results 2-29, 716D2
Summer Olympic results 7-18—7-31, 573E3, 574B2, 576B2, B3
2d in Chess Olympiad 11-10, 969A3
UN Policy & Developments
Vs WHO anti-Israel stand 5-19, 355D2
UNCTAD OKs commodity fund 5-30, 388A3
Vs anti-S Africa aid stand 11-5, 842C3
NETO, Agostinho
Cuba vows contd MPLA aid 1-11, 16F3
Scores US, China; for Zaire ties 2-2, 82E2
OAU recognizes MPLA 2-11, 105D2
Meets Mobutu, Zaire recognizes MPLA 2-28, 163A2
Namibia aid offer clarified 2-28—3-6, 206F1
Sees Castro, Cabral, Sekou Toure 3-15—3-16, 251E3
Gulf Cabinda operatns to resume 4-5, 287E2
Angola cuts Portugal ties 5-19, 371E1
Rescinds mil plan 5-21, 455G2
Stresses nonalignmt, socialism 5-23, 455B3
Cuba confirms Angola troop exit 5-26, 371D3
4 mercenaries get death 6-28, 480F1; confrms 7-9, 519A3
Ends Cuba visit 7-29, 649E2
Named commander-in-chief 7-31, 862G2
Sees Kaunda 8-21; ties, joint comm set 9-22, 862F2 ★
At Conf on ANC rift 9-6—9-7, 661D3
In USSR 10-7—10-13; signs treaty 10-8; statemt issued 10-14, 856C3
Named head of state 10-29; Cabt OKd 11-27, 995B3
Chrgs S Africa attacks 11-11, 862D2
SWAPO asks aid 11-11, 862D2
NETTLES, Graig
AL batting ldr 10-4, 796C1
In World Series 10-16—10-21, 815D2
NEUMAN, Herman
Dies 5-4, 524C3
NEUMANN, Alfred
E Ger Politburo enlarged 5-22, 381E2
NEUMANN, Robert G.
Replaced as amb to Morocco 1-28, 110A2
NEUNABER, Rev. Herman F.
Quits as dist pres 8-31, 776G3
NEUREUTHER, Guenther
Wins Olympic medal 7-26, 575A1

1977

US asks move to paymts deficit 5-25, 437D3
Group of 10 membership cited 438F1
'76 Turk Cypriot trade rptd 6-15, 467D1
In 11 natns Portugal loan 6-22, 530B3
French 'Super Phoenix' OKd 7-5, 597C3
Zaire debt rescheduled 7-7, 583E1
'77 paymts surplus forecast 7-31, 586E2
US scores trust probe-blocking laws 8-8, 630A1
Sweden quits 'snake' 8-29, 709A1
S Africa investmt bar backed 9-20, 771B1
A-suppliers conf OKs export safeguards 9-21, 717D1
IMF-World Bank mtgs see econ recovery effort 9-26—9-30, 753D3
US co chrgs steel dumping 10-20, 836E3
Cuba oil products reach US 10-20, 896B3
Nigeria arms purchases cited 11-23, 986A3
Unilever plans Natl Startch takeover 12-11, 1004C2
$ drops 12-30, 997F2
Netherlands Antilles—*See separate listing*
Obituaries
Beel, Louis, 2-11, 164C2
Schermerhorn, Willem 3-12, 264E3
South Moluccan Issue—*See under INDONESIA*
U.S. Relations—*See also 'Monetary, Trade & Aid' above*
US-ESA flight set 2-16, 170C3
ESA satellite launching aborted 9-13, 735G3
Agee asked to leave 12-2, 986E2
Carter expands air svc 12-21, 1006D2
NETHERLANDS Antilles (Aruba, Bonaire, Curacao, Saba, St. Eustatius, St. Maarten)
Aruba independence vote 4-29, 374B2
Elections held 6-17, 566D1
Aruba strikers end blackout 8-17, labor ldr freed 8-18, 675G1
Venez backs independence 8-19, 949G2
NETO, Agostino (Angolan president)
Cuba role in Angola detailed 1-9, 19B1
Sees Young 2-8, 105E1
US rep on Cuban troop cut 2-15, 110A2
Castro visits 3-23—3-31, jt communique backs liberatn movemts 4-2, 249C3
Scores Zaire forgn aid 4-11, 265F2
Sees Owen 4-17, 296C3
At front-line mtg 4-17—4-18, 296D3
Rpts rebellion arrests 5-31, 424A2
Rebellion detailed 6-20, 484A2
Amin on rebelln 7-4, 512A2
Names finance min 8-31, 772A1
In USSR 9-28, 830D1
NETTLES, Graig
AL batting ldr 10-2, 926G3
In World Series, desires trade 10-11—10-18, 806E2
NETWORK (film)
Top-grossing film 3-9, 184D3; 4-6, 264E1
Wins Oscars 3-28, 264B1
Cited re Arledge ABC News apptmt 5-2, 395B2
NEUBAUER, Kurt
Resigns 4-27, Schutz resigns 4-29, 352E3
NEUMANN, John Nepomucene (1811-60)
Sainthood proclaimed 6-19, 731B3
NEUTRON Bomb—*See ARMAMENTS—Atomic Weapons*

1978

Hungary devalues forint 11-11, 906G2
Ford productn problems cited re UK strike 11-22, 923D2
At Brussels monetary summit, EMS entry backed 12-4—12-5, 952C2
Rhodesia chrome cargo impoundmt rptd 12-13, 965D2
Ireland to join EMS 12-15, 979F1
South Moluccan Issue—*See under INDONESIA*
Sports
Rotterdam WCT results 4-9, 419B1
World Cup soccer finals, sidelights 6-1—6-25, 519D3-520G3
Hinault wins Tour de France 7-23, 692B2
UN Policy & Developments
Leb peace force (Unifil) formed 3-19, 197D2; **for peacekeeping developments, see MIDDLE EAST—LEBANON**
Sea Law Conf talks continue 5-23—7-15, 8-21—9-16, 732E3
In ECOSOC debate on poor natns' debts 7-10, 575E1
Racism conf boycotted 8-26, 676B2
Assemb member 713C3
U.S. Relations—*See also 'Atomic Energy' and 'Monetary, Trade, Aid & Investment' above*
US troop presence rptd 1-2, 5C2
US alerts to USSR satellite fall 57E1
Agee residency extensn rejctd 1-25, 90E3
Air svc agreemt reached 3-10, 206F2
US launches ESA satellite 5-12, 384D3
Pan Am fare experiment 6-15—7-31, Boston aids stranded travelers 7-16, 640B3
US seabed mining bill debated at UN conf 8-21—9-16, 732E3
Pan Am to end Amsterdam svc 9-7, 701G1
Seatrain fined re rebates scheme 10-23, 876C3
McDonnell Douglas paymts rptd 12-15, 982G2
NETO, Agostinho (Angolan president)
Rhodesia role cited 59D2
MPLA party purge rptd 1-30, 87C3
Martins expelled re plot 5-31, 594D1
Denies Zaire role 6-10, 441A2
Away during US envoy visit 6-21—6-26, 487G3
Carter unaware of rebel aid 6-26, 491A2
Ends Eanes mtg, OKs Angola cooperatn 6-26, 562A2
Asks US recognitn 7-21, US bars 7-22, 562F1
Agrmt on refugees in Portugal rptd 8-10, 645F3
In Zaire 8-19—8-21, 645G3
Backs Nkomo-Smith mtg 9-2, 740E3
Frees pol prisoners 9-15, 925A3
Chrgs S Africa 'undeclared war' 11-11, 906C2
Ousts Nascimento, Rocha 12-9; stresses independence 12-10, 985D1
Sees US Sen McGovern 12-13, 985A1
NETRNOI (Shorty) Vorasingh
Decisns Castillo 5-6, 379E2
TKOs Estaba 7-29, 600A2
NETTLES, Graig
Yankees win AL pennant 10-7, 779C1
In World Series 10-10—10-17, 800A1
Wins Golden Glove Award 11-21, 928A3
NEUMANN, Jonathan
Wins Pulitzer Prize 4-17, 315D1
NEUSTAT, Betty
Price of Genius opens 6-26, 887F2
NEUTRON Bomb—*See under ARMAMENTS*

1979

Netherlands Antilles—*See separate listing*
Sports
World speed-skating champs 2-4, 392C1
3 sign with NASL teams 4-3—6-11, 655B1, E1
Rotterdam WCT results 4-8, 391B3
UN Policy & Developments
Unifil troops agreed 1-12, svc questnd 2-1, 84G3
Membership listed 695A3
U.S. Relations
UK airline '72 crash case refused by US Sup Ct 1-15, 32D1
Lockheed discloses bribes, Bernhard gift alleged 2-16, 306F1
Nationale-Nederlanden seeks US insurance co 3-23, 942D2
Mondale visits Eur 4-11—4-22, 299D2
Carter sees van Agt, seeks A-missile plan support 12-7, 938E1
NETHERLANDS Antilles (Aruba, Bonaire, Curacao, Saba, St. Eustatius, St. Maarten)
Electns held 7-6; govt installed, indepndnc terms cited 11-13, 882C3
NETO, Agostino (Angolan president; replaced Sept. 20)
Dies 9-10; facts on 705A2
Young regrets death 9-16, 721C1
Dos Santos named offcl pres 9-20, 796F2
Namibia talks reopen 11-12, 889D3
NETTLES, Graig
NL wins All-Star Game 7-17, 569D1
Kroc rpts record fine 8-24, 1003B1
NEUFELD, Mace
Frisco Kid released 7-6, 820C1
NEUFELD, Peter
Evita opens 9-25, 956A3
NEUHARTH, Allen H.
Scores Sup Ct 'state of mind' libel ruling 4-23, 302C2
Scores ctroom press access ruling 7-2, 515C3
Rpts press freedom insurnc plan 9-27, 859E2
NEUMANN, Frederick
Mercier & Camier opens 10-25, 956D3

1980

Sports
USSR Olympics boycott support cited 1-14, 28C3
Lake Placid Olympic results 2-12—2-24, 154F2, 155F2-156D1
World speed skating championship 3-2, 470C1
Rotterdam WCT results 3-16, 607G2
Olympic com rejects Moscow boycott 5-20, 379A3
Moscow Olympic results 7-20—8-3, 588B3, 623D1, E3, 624E1
Zoetemelk wins Tour de France 7-20, 835D1
UN Policy & Developments
Assemb Palestinian state res abstentn 7-29, 572F1
U.S. Relations
'79 mfg investmt rptd 2-6, 92D3
US Steel files dumping complaint 3-21, 225D1
'79 US investmt rptd 4-8, 329C1
US sets steel import probe 4-10, 367F3
US finds steel import damage 5-1, 456C1
Iran parlt ldr rebuffs hostage plea 8-17, 634D3
US scores mil spending 10-3, 737D1
US natls flee ocean liner fire 10-4, 769A3
NETHERLANDS Antilles (Aruba, Bonaire, Curacao, Saba, St. Eustatius, St. Maarten)
Financial Gen deal set 7-25, 600G3
NEUBIG, Thomas S.
Credit card use study rptd 1-30, 92A3
NEUHARTH, Allen H.
Assails NM paper ownership ruling 6-30, 582A3
NEUHAUS, Rev. Richard John
Scores evangelical Christian pol movemt 9-15, 819E2
NEUMANN, Emanuel
Dies 10-26, 876G2
NEUPER, Hubert
Wins Olympic medal 2-23, 155D3
NEUPERT, Uwe
Wins Olympic medal 7-29, 624E3

1976

NEVADA
Primary date set 22B2
Howard Hughes dies 4-5, executors named 4-14, 5-4, 335C3
Ford, Reagan visit 5-19—5-24, 373G3, 374E1
Primary results 5-25, 373F1, G1, 374B3
Emprise convictn re Las Vegas casino cited 483D3
Sup Ct acts to save pupfish 6-7, 435D2
Teamsters conv at Las Vegas 6-13—6-16, 435F3
Dem conv women delegates, table 508C2
Hughes legal residnc disputed 7-13, 596E3
Dem conv pres vote, table 7-14, 507C2
GOP pre-conv delegate count 8-14, 583C3
GOP conv pres, vp vote tables 8-18—8-19, 8-19, 599C1, C3
Hughes relatives file pact 8-27, 971E2
USW conf in Las Vegas 8-30—9-3, 665B3, 669A3
Primary results 9-14, 705C1
Fscl '75 per capita income, tax burden rptd 9-15, 10-12, 959G1, E2
Election results 11-2: pres 818C1, 819B2; cong 820D1, 824C2, 828C2, 830C1
Atomic Tests—*See ATOMIC Energy*

NEVERS, Ernie
Dies 5-3, 368A3
NEVSOROV, Vladimir
Wins Olympic medal 7-29, 574G3
NEWARK, N.J.—*See NEW Jersey*
NEW Boston Bank Trust Co.
Fails, sold 9-15, 984A1
NEWBURYPORT, Mass.—*See MASSACHUSETTS*
NEWCOMBE, John
Loses Australian Open 1-4, 31E3
NEW England Journal of Medicine (magazine)
More cancer, estrogen links rptd 6-3, 460F3
Breast cancer, estrogen link rptd 8-19, 680C1
NEW England Petroleum Co.
St Lawrence oil spill 6-23, 859D2
NEW Guinea, Trust Territory of—*See PAPUA New Guinea*

NEW Hampshire
Nashua credit bur abuses rptd 2-12, 151A3
Merrimack Anheuser-Busch strike ends 6-6, 436B2
4 Seabrook bombing suspects indicted 7-14, 1 sentenced 10-8, 796B3
Fscl '75 per capita income, tax burden rptd 9-15, 10-12, 959A2
Sup Ct bars Granite case review 10-18, 867A3
US Sup Ct refuses EEOC rptg rule appeal 12-13, 960C3
Flu shot paralysis rptd 12-17, 950E1
Politics
Primary date set 22A2
Reagan campaigns 1-5—1-7, 4B3-5C1; 1-15, 22G1; 1-16, 41E1
Ford sees press 1-22, 41A2
Ford in Concord, Nashua 2-7—2-8, 109B1
Thomson campaigns for Reagan 2-11, 109F2
Ford confident 2-17, 129F2
Reagan camp scores Ford 2-18, 130B1
Ford, Reagan end campaigns 2-20, 148G2
Primary results 2-24, 148E1
Ford cites 'momentum' 3-2, 165B2
'72 Nixon spending rptd 4-25, 688G1
Dem conv women delegates, table 508C2
Dem conv pres vote, table 7-14, 507C2

1977

NEVADA
Legislature schedule rptd 6E2
Hughes 'heir' admits lying 1-11, 1-25—1-27; '38 will sought 1-12, 120F1, D2
Sovt boxing match in Las Vegas 1-29, 263A2
Snowfall rptd below normal 2-1, 76G3
ERA fails 2-11, 112F3
Mafia operatns rptd 3-13—3-20, 568A2
Hughes estate appraised 3-15, land assessmt rptd 4-14, 354G2, A3
Missing unionist found slain 3-17, 261C3
Clark cnty sheriff indicted 4-13, 312B3
'76 per-capita income table 5-10, 387G2
Shapp fund repaymt ordrd 5-12, 482C2
Laetrile, gerovital legalized 5-20, 508E1, A3
Hughes co to pay Greenspun 6-3, 472C2
Teamster loan to Las Vegas hotel rptd 7-18, 558B2
Oil cos settle fed suit 8-31, 691C3
'76 per capita income, tax burden table 9-13, 10-18, 821F2
Episc diocese formed 9-14—9-16, 731E2
Bomb test of reactor product rptd 9-14, 812E2
GM cuts '78 Chevette price 9-15, 722F3
ERA econ boycott rptd 11-14, 918D1
'57 A-bomb test, cancer link probed 12-13, 1022C3

NEVADA, University of (Las Vegas)
NCAA basketball tourn results 3-26, 3-28, 262F1
NCAA places on probatn 8-25; coach fired 9-9, reinstated 9-30, 870D2
NEVADA State Journal (newspaper)
3 win Pulitzers 4-18, 355G2
NEVIN, John J.
Backs Japan TV export limit 5-20, 416B1
NEWARK, N.J.—*See NEW Jersey*
NEWARK International Airport
NY Airways copter run cited 5-16, 412D3
Byrne vetoes Port Auth noise rule 12-27, 1006G3
NEWBERRY, Janet
Wins Italian Open 5-22, 430A3
NEW Caledonia (French territory)
Vote favors French ties 9-11, 744A3
NEW Castle, N.Y.—*See NEW York State*
NEWCOMBE, John
'Heavyweight championship' fee probe rptd 7-8, 548E2
NEWELL, Dr.Guy
On NCI laetrile tests 6-23, 508F1
NEW England
'76 per capita income table 5-10, 387C2
Job losses seen 8-7, 8-10, 629D2
'76 per capita income data revised, table 9-13, 10-18, 821A2
NEW England Journal of Medicine
Amphetamine-morphine painkiller rptd 3-31, 288B1
NEW England Telephone & Telegraph Co.—*See AMERICAN Telephone & Telegraph Co.*

NEW Hampshire
Legislature schedule rptd 6E2
Seabrook A-plant constructn halted 3-31, foes protest 4-30—5-3, 344G2
Fed spending effects chrgd 4-6, 423D3
License-plate slogans curbed 4-20, 342E2
Seabrook A-plant foes tried, freed 5-4—5-13; LEAA bars funds 5-19, 409D3
'76 per-capita income table 5-10, 387C2
Manchester business confidence rptd; econ data table 5-16, 384D2, A3
EPA OKs Seabrook A-plant 6-17, 498D2
A-power backers rally 6-26, 498D3
NRC OKs Seabrook A-plant constructn 7-26, 702B2
Seabrook A-plant protest 8-6, 702E2
'76 per capita income, tax burden table 9-13, 10-18, 821B2

1978

NEVADA
'67, '77 sales-tax rates rptd 1-5, 15E3
NASL '77 Las Vegas club move cited 1-5, 23A1
Mondale tours Westn states 1-9—1-13, 34E1
State govt tax revenue table 1-9, 84D2
Hughes domicile dispute rptd 2-13, 3-29, 459E1
'45-62 A-test exposure rptd 2-15, 164G1
ERA boycott injunctn sought 3-3, 494F2
Athletic Comm suspends Spinks 3-9, 212B1
'Right-to-die' law rptd 3-18, 597F3
'77 prison populatn rptd up 6-3, 440D1
Hughes Mormon will ruled fake 6-8, 458E3
AFSCME meets in Las Vegas 6-26, 6-28, 526C1
Wm Harrah dies 6-30, 540G2
Vet wins '57 A-test cancer claim 8-1, 702F3
Bakery union meets in Las Vegas 8-16, 700A2
Primary results 9-12, 736E2
Electn results 11-7: cong 845G1, 848E2, 851E2, 857G1; state 847A1, E1, B2, 853G2, 857D1
A-test site '47 debate rptd 12-18, 1012B1
A-test claims filed 12-21, 1011G3

NEVADA, University of (Las Vegas)
House subcom sports probe cited 1-11—1-13, 40B2
Hughes Mormon will ruled fake 6-8, 458G3
Theus in NBA draft 6-9, 457F3
NEVIS Mountain Dew (play)
Opens 12-7, 1031E2
NEW Albany, Ind.—*See INDIANA*
NEW American Library, Inc.—*See under TIMES Mirror Co.*
NEWARK, N.J.—*See NEW Jersey*
NEW Bedford, Mass.—*See MASSACHUSETTS*
NEW Brunswick (Canadian province)—*See CANADA*
NEW Coalition
Welfare compromise prepared 6-7, 446B2
NEWCOMBE, John
Loses Va WCT 2-5, 418G3
US wins World Cup 3-9—3-12, 252C1
NEW England—*See NORTHEAST; state names*
NEW England Broadcasting Association
FCC rejcts censorship role 7-21, 599F1
NEW England Coalition on Nuclear Pollution
NH A-plant site review ordrd 4-28, 347B1
NEW England Journal of Medicine
Hughes Med Inst described 12-7, 1010C3-1011A1
NEWFOUNDLAND (Canadian province)—*See CANADA*

NEW Hampshire
No state sales taxes rptd 1-5, 15C3
State govt tax revenue table 1-9, 84D2
Blizzard hits 2-5—2-7, 105E2
Carter visits, backs McIntyre reelectn 2-18, 123D1, B3
Thomson issues flag-lowering proclamatn 3-21, US Sup Ct stays 3-24, 221G1; stay extensn denied 4-24, 322G2
Mental health insurance challenge denied by US Sup Ct 4-17, 308B3
'77 prison populatn rptd down 6-3, 440D1
Rape law case refused by Sup Ct 6-5, 431B2
Dems chng pres primary rules 6-9, 448G2
Primary results 9-12, 736E1
Electn results 11-7: cong 845D1, C2, 846B1, 847E3, F3, 848E2, 851F2; state 845G1, C2, 847A1, E3, 853G2, 897C3

1979

NEVADA
Legislature schedule rptd 5E3
ERA rejctd by state Sen 1-16, 128B2
Real estate ad rule affirmed by Sup Ct 3-5, 184G3
Calif joint planning agency immunity curbed by US Sup Ct 3-5, 185C1
State ct immunity curbed by US Sup Ct 3-5, 185D1
Aladdin casino taken over 3-16, 209B1
NJ indictmt details Mafia 5-23, 508A2
No-fault car insurnc repealed 5-29, 466E2-A3
Aladdin casino sale set 6-12; gambling licenses revoked 6-15, bid dropped 6-27, 520F1
'Sagebrush Revolt' mounted 7-13–9-7, 703E3
Holiday Inns to buy Harrah's 9-4, 682C3
MX 'racetrack' deployment sites considered 9-7, 677G3
State workers Soc Security non-participatn cited 9-10, 727B1
'78 per capita income rptd 9-16, 746D1, G2
Bishop executn stay denied 10-21, dies in gas chamber 10-22, 817G1-F2
Argent sale completed 12-10, buyer organized crime probe rptd 12-12, 965B1
Aladdin casino deal rejected 12-15, 965D1
Aladdin casino purchase set 12-21, 992A2
Atomic Energy
A-waste storage studied 1-5, 54D3
A-test cancer link rptd ignored by US 1-8, 17B2
Yucca Flat A-test rptd 1-24, 52E1
'53 A-test radiatn liability appeal lost, notificatn suit OKd 2-9, 112C2
Utah sheep A-deaths, child cancer rates rptd 2-14, 112F1-C2
More A-test claims filed 2-23, 208C1
'53 A-test radiatn liability case refused by US Sup Ct 5-21, 400B3
Beatty A-dump ordered closed 7-2, 519A2; reopened 7-24 561G2
Film stars' deaths tied to '53 A-test 8-4, 630C1
'50s A-fallout, SAT decline linked 9-17, 747B2
Beatty A-dump closed again 10-22, cancer research threatened 10-23, 806A3, 885G3*-886A1
NEVADA State Maximum Security Prison (Carson City)
Bishop executed 10-22, 817G1
NEVADA v. Hall
State ct immunity curbed by Sup Ct 3-5, 185C1
NEVELSON, Louise
Elected to Arts Institute 12-7, 1005A3
NEVES, Tancredo
Heads Brazilian PSD 11-30, 926B3
NEVINS 3rd, Edward
Sues Army on '50 germ warfare test 9-16
NEVINS, James
Scores Army germ warfare test 9-16, 727E1 727B1
NEW American Library Inc.—*See under TIMES Mirror Co.*
NEWARK, Del.—*See DELAWARE*
NEWARK, N.J.—*See NEW Jersey*
NEWARK (N.J.) International Airport
FAA updates radar improvemt 3-12, 206A2
NEW Brunswick (Canadian province)—*See CANADA*
NEWBURGH, N.Y.—*See NEW York State*
NEW Criticism (journal)
Allen Tate dies 2-9, 176G3
NEW Democratic Coalition
Endorses Kennedy 12-9, 962B2
NEWELL, Pete
In basketball HOF 4-30, 526D3
NEW England Journal of Medicine
Acne treatmt rptd 2-14, 138D2
PPA pneumonia strain rptd 11-1, 971D2
Sex-pregnancy risk study rptd 11-29, 971C3
NEWFIELDS, O.—*See OHIO*
NEWFOUNDLAND (Canadian province)—*See CANADA*
NEW Hampshire
Legislature schedule rptd 5E3
Legis rejcts DC voting rep amendmt 4-26, 367D1
Wood fuel use rptd 5-20, 419G1
Winter heating fuel supply promised 8-28, 703C2
'78 per capita income rptd 9-16, 746A2, C2
Carter energy mailing planned, scored 9-17, 703G2
Portsmouth kidnaping spurred by Iran crisis 11-23–11-24, 898D2
Presidential Campaign
Carter visits 4-25, 300A1
Draft-Kennedy activity rptd 5-23, 384E2
Crane scores Loeb articles 6-8, 594G1
Udall told to repay '76 electn funds 6-18, 595E1
Carter backers fear primary defeat 8-2, 593B1
Dem picnic held 9-8, 680C1
Draft Ford movement starts 9-20, 783F2
Thomson announces pres bid 10-31, 829D1
Kennedy opens campaign 11-7, 847E1
Kennedy campaigns 11-21, 962E1
Carter kin campaign 11-29, 961D3
Dole staff resignatns rptd 12-6, 983C2
Baker in Concord 12-19, 983C1
Kennedy campaigns 12-20–12-21, 983G2

1980

NEVADA
Westn Pacific RR sale set 1-24, 131C2
Schl prayer law cited 2-6, 156A2
DES in cattle rptd 4-24, 358F1
MX deploymt rptd chngd 5-6, 369E2
Quakes hit 5-25, 5-27, 527D3
Land developer linked to New Hebrides rebels 6-8, 436E2
'Stealth' aircraft rptd tested at Nellis AF Base 8-20, 630B2
Webb Corp paymts probe cited 11-1, 988D3
Boat racer dies in Lake Tahoe run 11-13, 1002A2
MX sites chosen 11-18, 897A1
Las Vegas hotel fire kills 84 11-21, probe rptd 11-25, 893C2
Las Vegas fscl '80 casino revenue rptd 12-12, 988E3
Atomic Energy & Safeguards
Carter outlines A-waste storage plan, Jackass Flats site studied 2-12, 127F3
Crime & Civil Disorders
FBI 'Miporn' probe rptd 2-14, 136A2
Nurse cleared in murder case 5-30, 656A1
Lake Tahoe casino bombed 8-27, 833F3
Politics & Government—*See also other appropriate subheads in this section*
Bush stops over 5-13, 366B3
Primary results 5-27, 399B1-F2
Sen primary results 9-9, 700E2
Reagan favored in Vegas 11-3, 844G2
Election results 11-4: pres 838C1, 839A1, F3; cong 840E2, 843F2, 845B3, 846B3, 852A1; state 845G2, 847G2, D3
'80 census rptd, reapportmt seen 12-31, 983F1
NEVADA, University of (Las Vegas)
NIT results 3-20, 240E2
NEVILLE Island—*See PENNSYLVANIA*
NEVIN, John J.
Named Firestone chief exec 9-1, 702C1
NEVINS, Deborah
Architect's Eye wins Amer Book Award 5-1, 692C2
NEWARK—*See NEW Jersey*
NEWARK (N.J.) International Airport
US Customs corruptn probed 2-13, 359G2
NEWBERNE, Paul
GAO scores cancer-nitrite study 1-31, 159G1
NEW Brunswick (Canadian province)—*See CANADA*
NEW Caledonia (French territory)
New Hebrides gets French troops 6-11, 436F1
Vanuatu refugees rptd 8-31, 674D1
Vanuatu rebel sentncd 11-21, 903E3
NEW Castle—*See DELAWARE*
NEWCOMBE, Peter
Statistics Canada cleared 4-1, 272G3, 273B1
NEWCOMER, Judge Clarence C.
Topps baseball card trust violatn rptd 7-2, 917E3
NEWELL, Charles
Dies from boxing injury 1-17, 907E3
NEWELL, Mike
Awakening released 10-31, 972C3
NEW England Journal of Medicine
Ex-editor Ingelfinger dies 3-26, 279E3
NEW England Nuclear Corp.
Du Pont merger set 12-8, 985A2
NEW England Rare Coins Galleries (Boston, Mass.)
Gold coin set purchased for record sum 4-10, 472F2
NEW England Telephone and Telegraph Co.
Kennedy phone record queried 3-12, 184D1
NEW England Television Corp.
FCC blocks WNAC-TV purchase 1-24, 119B3
NEWFIELD, Jack
Wins Polk award 2-25, 692F3
NEWFOUNDLAND (Canadian province)—*See CANADA*
NEW Guinea
New malaria outbreak rptd 5-31, 478A3
Australia bans critical book 11-9, 885E1

NEW Hampshire
Schl prayer law cited 2-6, 156A2
Influenza outbreak rptd 2-15, 158C3
Drought rptd 12-1, 947F3
Atomic Energy & Safeguards
Seabrook A-protesters repulsed 5-24—5-26, 441E1
Politics & Government—*See also other appropriate subheads in this section*
Primary results 9-9, 700F2
Election results 11-4: cong 837D2, 840E2, 843F2, 845A2, 848E2, F2; state 845G2, 847C1, 848E2
'80 census rptd 12-31, 983F1
Presidential Election (& Transition)
Reagan campaigns 1-8, 13C3
Kennedy scores Carter 1-30, 2-7, 91A2-D2
Reagan campaigns hard 2-5, 91F2
Reagan in Franklin, assails Bush 2-5, 128F2
Kennedy hits Iran issue 2-13, 109D2
Kennedy campaigns in Exeter, Concord; assails Carter policies 2-14, 2-20, 130B2, C2
Anderson publicity problem rptd, strategy detailed 2-15, 129E2
Reagan tells ethnic joke 2-16, apologizes 2-18, 128A2
Reagan age seen as factor 2-17, 128E2

1976

Thomson withdraws Reagan endorsemt 7-27, 550C1
Carter visits Manchester 8-3, 564D2
GOP pre-conv delegate count 8-14, 583C3
GOP conv pres, vp vote tables 8-18—8-19, 8-19, 599C1, C3
Sears recalls defeat 8-18, 615B3
Primary results 9-14, 705D1
Mondale in Manchester 10-2, 744A2
Election results 11-2: pres 818C1, 819A2; cong 830C1, 831F1; state 820F3
Carter primary spending rptd 11-17, 938A3

NEW Hampshire, University of (Durham)
Ford visits 2-8, 109F1

NEWHART, Bob
TV show debuts in S Africa 1-5, 11B3

NEW Haven, Conn.—*See CONNECTICUT*

NEW Haven Register (newspaper)
Ford endorsement rptd 10-30, 827F3

NEWHOUSE, Fred
Wins Olympic medal 7-29, 576B1

NEWHOUSE, Samuel I.
Buys Booth chain 11-8, 901F2

NE Win
Plotters arrested 7-2, 543D2

NEW Jersey
Bloomfield bank fails 1-10, sold 1-11, 167B2
Record lottery prize 1-27, 160G2
Newark teachers strike 2-3—2-8, 153G2-A3
High cancer rate rptd 2-8, 224D3
Flu rptd at Ft Dix 2-19, 224C2, D2
Suit seeks bar to TM in schools 2-25, 203C2
Bus strike 3-9—3-22, 220G1
Quinlan wins right to die 3-31, 292C2
NRC OKs offshore A-plant 4-9, 284G1-B2
US files home-loan bias suit 4-15, 285G1
Sup Ct voids Oradell canvassers curb 5-19, 393C3
Quinlan off respirator 5-22, moved 6-10, 423D2
Passaic Falls dedicated as natl site 6-6, 410B3
Newark Anheuser-Busch strike ends 6-6, 436B2
Hudson Cnty bank closed 6-14; reopened 6-15, 495F1
Schls ordrd shut 7-1, income tax bill signed 7-8, 995B2
EPA bars ocean sewage-dumping 7-23, 570G3
Hurricane Belle damage rptd 8-9—8-11, 595C2
Offshore lease sale bids accepted 8-25, 648D3
Meadowlands race track opens 9-1, 680C3
'74-75 Newark SATs rptd 9-13, 993A2
Fscl '75 per capita income, tax burden rptd 9-15, 10-12, 959G1, B2
China A-test fallout rptd 10-5, 790G3
US Sup Ct bars review of transsexual teacher, Quinlan cases 10-18, 11-1, 867B3, F3
Sup Ct bars hiring quotas in Montclair case 11-30, 943C2
Flu shot paralysis rptd 12-17, 950E1
Del R oil spill 12-29, 1014F1

Crime
Newark violent crime up 3-2, 336D3
Carter, Artis get new trial 3-17; post bail 3-19, 256D3
MD indicted re curare 5-19, 384A3
7 oil cos, trade assn indicted 6-1, 412F3
Helstoski indicted 6-2, 414C3
Provenzano indicted 6-23, 460A1
US Sen com rpts Medicaid fraud 8-30, 715B1
Carter, Artis retrial opens 10-12—11-11, 860B1
Kallinger gets life 10-14, 972E1
Provenzano fed chrgs dismissed 10-29, 972B1

1977

NEW Haven, Conn.—*See CONNECTICUT*

NEWHOUSE, Samuel I.
Booth purchase cited 2-18, 274E2

NEWHOUSE News Service
On most reliable govt news source list 12-10, 1009B1

NE Win (Burma President)
China, N Korea visits cited; rebel aid end asked 779F2
Plotters arrested 9-3, 779D2
Govt shakeup rptd 10-8, 779B3

NEW Jersey
US Sup Ct bars child custody review 1-25, 80G2
Quinlan conditn stable 3-31, 355A1
Newark populatn ranking drops 4-14, 388D1
Gibson on Carter energy plan 4-15, 320F2
'76 blue laws ruling cited 4-21, 388A2
Willingboro 'for sale' sign ban lifted 5-2, 406A2
'76 per-capita income table 5-10, 387D2
Atlantic City low-income housing effort rptd set 5-27, 424C1
Atlantic City casino gambling signed 6-2, 423G3
Camden RC newspr ed replaced 6-16, 471E1
US Sup Ct refuses abortn case 6-27, 539A1
Forest fires kill 4 7-23—7-25, 660E3
Offshore lease sale OKd by ct 8-25, 650B1
Bayonne schl busing starts calmly 9-7, 838B1
'76 per capita income, tax burden table 9-13, 10-18, 821B2
Paramus gay teacher case review refused 10-3, 760E1
Jobless welfare benefits case review declined 10-3, 760F2
US sues re police job bias 10-4, 819B2
Anti-abortn amendmt rptd sought 10-6, 786B3
TM banned from schools 10-20, 845D3
State police meal allowances ruled taxable 11-20, 919F1
Logan Twp chem plant plast 12-8, 1023D3
Income tax made permanent 12-15, 1008D3

Crime
Sovt spy seized in Lakewood 1-7, 41B3
Carter, Artis sentenced 2-9, 140C1
'70-76 pol indictmts rptd 2-10, 162D3
Pritchards indicted 3-10, 203E3
Rockefeller assassinatn plot mistrial 3-10, 261G2
Chesimard convicted, sentncd 3-25, 288C3
Laetrile smugglers sentenced 5-16, 508A3
Mafia migratn rptd 6-13, 568F1
Arson suspected in forest fires 7-23—7-25, 660E3
Bordentown Reformatory mind-control tests rptd 8-1—8-9, 611D1
Hackettstown sniper kills 6 8-26, 807A3
5 indep oil cos convicted 8-30, 691A3; 9-16, 918F2
Cuban exiles queried re Letelier murder 9-7—9-10, 743E2
Police harassmt case review refused 10-31, 835C2
Provenzano US kickback chrg dropped 11-11, 928E1
Provenzano reindicted 12-19, 991C3

Fuel-Weather Crisis
FPC OKs emergency gas purchase; state of emergency declared 1-19, 53G3, 54A2
Full state of emergency 1-27; layoffs rptd 1-30, US offers job funds 2-1, 75B3-G3
US declares emergency status 2-5, 91B2
Layoff total rptd 2-7, 91F2

1978

Seabrook A-Plant Dispute
NRC gives final OK 1-7, EPA to reopen hearings 3-22, 242A3
NRC orders site review 4-28, constructn workers protest 5-10, 347A1
Protesters mark anniv 4-29, 347C1
Protest 6-24—6-26, Manchester counter rally 6-25, 494A1
Constructn halt ordrd 6-30, 529F2
Cooling plan OKd 8-4, constructn to resume 8-10, foes vow actn 8-7, 8-10, 609G1-A3
Constructn resumes 8-14; protests continue 8-14—12-7, ct appeal fails 8-22, 941A1-E1
Shutdown cost rptd at $1½ bln 10-10, 941F1
'77 protests ruled illegal 12-6, 1009B3
$400 mln bond guarantee rejcted, shutdown seen 12-8, 1009G2

NEW Hebrides (French-British territory)
Primitive art collectn auctnd 6-29, 579E1

NEWHOUSE, Robert
Cowboys win Super Bowl 1-15, 39D3

NEW Iberia, La.—*See LOUISIANA*

NE Win (Burmese president)
Reelected 1-15, 145D2

NEW Jersey
'67, '77 sales-tax rates rptd 1-5, 15E3
State govt tax revenue table 1-9, 84D2
Laetrile legalized 1-10, 23B3
NIH cancer study rptd 1-12, 23E3
Transsexual wins disability pay 2-16, 327E2
10th in US defense contracts 2-21, 127D2
Lawrence hosts Bilderberg Conf 4-21—4-23, 302B3
Quinlan still alive 5-14, 597B3
Patten cited for misconduct 7-13, 527C1
CORE conv in Pittstown 9-8—9-10, 810C1
FCC orders NYC, Phila TV statn studios in state 11-9, 1030D2
Chessie, Seaboard set merger 11-16, 897B1

Atlantic City Gambling
Atlantic City casino opens 5-26, 1st 6 days take rptd 6-5, 434B2
Atlantic City casino profits rptd 10-4, gambling violatns chrgd 10-6, 920B1, E1
Gambling stock trading linked to Atlantic City opening 11-1, 826A3
Crime rate rptd up 25%, casinos blamed 11-10, 920F1
'78 stock speculatn rptd 12-29, 1004C2

Crime
Lloyd Carr fugitive rptd Trenton prison escapee 1-14, 83D2, E2
Byrne pocket vetoes death penalty bill 3-3, 388E3
Provenzano convicted for kickbacks 3-25, 232C2
3 top FBI ex-aides indicted 4-10, 261G3-262A1
IBM heir convicted in murder plot 4-26, 380F2
Cuban exiles sought in Letelier murder case, Novo arrested 5-4, 370D3; Ross moved to DC 6-2, 451F3
Provenzano convicted of murder 6-14, sentncd 6-21, 480B2
Jascalevich curare case-press freedom controversy 6-30—8-28, jailed NY Times rptr freed 8-30, 678C2
Provenzano sentncd for kickbacks 7-11, 560F2
Parsons sued re union payoffs 8-4, 643C2★, D2
Curare controversy continues 8-30—10-6; Jascalevich acquitted, Times rptr freed 10-24, 841F1-F2
5 Teamsters indicted 10-5, 770F3
Times rptr's jailing scored by IAPA 10-13, 829F1
2 Sovt spies sentncd in Newark 10-30, 835A2
Atlantic City rate up 25%, casino blamed 11-10, 920F1
Times press freedom case declined by US Sup Ct 11-27, 937E1
FBI mail scrutiny held unconst 11-29, 940A1
Murder sentencing system upheld by US Sup Ct 12-11, 981C1
Rape law revisn cited 12-27, 1028D3

1979

Seabrook A-Plant Dispute
Police arrest 183 protesters 3-9, 186E2
'77 chrgs vs 709 dropped 7-3, 519C1
4,000 at weekend rally 7-21, 7-22, 743B1
Protesters arrested in Boston bank 8-31, 742F3
Occupatn prevented 10-6—10-8, 806F3

NEW Hampshire, University of (Durham)
Loses NCAA hockey match 3-24, 356E1
Magnet-synthesizing bacteria rptd 4-8, 691C2
3d in women's lacrosse title 5-13, 507C3

NEW Haven, N.Y.—*See NEW York State*

NEWHOUSE, Robert
NFL '78 touchdown ldr 1-6, 80E1

NEWHOUSE, Samuel I.
Dies 8-29, 671B3

NEW Jersey
ITT Newark long-distance phone svc OKd 1-4, 15E2
Medicaid abortn paymts ordrd 1-9, 315D1
$99 cross-country air fares, Newark routes OKd 1-12, 35F2
Jim Jones, followers '78 Clarksboro cremation cited 2-1, 117G2
Newark airport radar improvemt updated 3-12, 206A2
Ft Dix training cntr to close 3-29, 265E3
'78 wiretaps rptd 4-28, 386G3
Cape May hotel fire 5-11, 572B3
Sovt-bloc arms shipmt confrmd 8-1, 627A1
Hurricane David hits 9-7, 690B1
'78 per capita income rptd 9-16, 746A2, C2
Ft Dix training cntr to stay open 10-10, 809D1
Medicaid reimbursemt case declined by Sup Ct 11-5, 884C3
Ocean Grove Methodist munic powers case declined by Sup Ct 11-13, 902F1
Iranians ordrd to leave 11-16, 879E1
Ft Dix sex scandal rptd 12-3, 924A1
UK prime min at Exxon plant 12-18, 968C2

Atlantic City Gambling
Resorts Intl fined 1-3, 'card-counters' barred 2-1, 152D1, F1
Compulsive gambling bill introduced 1-30, 152E1
Resorts Intl granted permanent license, 8 others pending 2-26, 151F3
Caesars World casino opens 6-26, 520D1
Holiday Inns-Harrah's merger set 9-4, 682D3
Tax rates hiked 9-18, 851F1
Card counters OKd 10-24, 851A2; barred, revenue loss cited 12-13, 947C1
Mays to cut baseball ties 10-29, 1002G3

Atomic Energy
Radium waste sites alleged 3-5, 187B2
Oyster Creek (Toms River) A-plant community studied 3-17, 207E3
Pa suspends Met Ed rate hike 4-19, 275B1
Salem reactor licensing delayed 5-21, 381G3
Oyster Creek A-plant reopening set 5-30, 610A1
Salem protest rptd 8-5, 743A1
Salem reactor licensing delay extended 11-5, 849C1

Crime & Civil Disorders
Hoboken, Jersey City arson 1-20, 1-22, 209F1
Provenzano, others indicted 2-22, 155F3
Waterfront figures indicted 3-6, 220C2
Credit union broker sentncd 3-13, 239C3
Grant of immunity broadened by Sup Ct 3-20, 204A1
Dock indictmts mount 4-9, 292B1
Covert 'bugging' entry upheld by US Sup Ct 4-18, 346C1
Mafia detailed in Genovese 'family' indictmt 5-23, 508E1
Addonizio, 2 other ex-offcls subject to rejailing by Sup Ct 6-4, 438G3
Provenzano, 3 others sentenced 7-10, 548E1
Paterson bank exec's wife kidnaped 7-20—7-22; suspects seized, ransom recovered 7-22, 7-26, 604F3
Princeton gallery ordrd to return stolen paintings 7-27, 656F1
HFA kickback scandal rptd, Carter aide quits 8-9, 747C3
Jascalevich trial costs ordrd paid by NY Times 8-14, 656E2
Ex-Mafia informant sues US 9-26, 840F2
Addonizio paroled 10-2, 891F1
Coppolino paroled 10-16, 839G2
Chesimard escapes 11-2, 953C2
Barnegat KKK activity cited 865B1
Newark police hiring ordinance vetoed 11-15, override fails 11-20, 992G1
22 KKK, Nazis arrested in Vineland; anti-Klan rally held 11-24, 991C3
Cuban refugee ldr slain in Union City 11-25, FBI probe rptd 11-28, 906B1-D1

1980

Gun control forum in Concord 2-18, GOP pres debate in Manchester 2-20, 129G2, G3
Nashua limited GOP debate dispute sparked 2-23, 143C1
Primary results 2-26, 142D2
Thomson ends run 4-14, 288F3
Bush in Nashua 9-26, 781F1
Election results 11-4, 838C1, 839A2, F3

NEW Hampshire, University of (Durham)
Acid rain rptd centuries old 9-18, 716E2

NEWHART, Bob
Little Miss Marker released 3-21, 216C3
First Family released 12-25, 1003G1

NEW Hebrides—*See VANUATU*

NEWHOUSE Publications
Random House purchase set 2-6, 386D1

NEW Jersey
Idaho Asarco tax case remanded by Sup Ct 3-24, 265B2
NOW bank accounts OKd nationwide 3-31, 246A1
World Air cuts fares 4-9, 346B3
Cuban immigrants surveyed 5-11—5-14, 396A3
Bradley Beach hotel fire kills 23 7-26, 621B3
FCC proposes VHF TV statn expansn 9-18, 732A1
FCC backs NYC TV statn move 11-6, 906E1

Atlantic City Gambling
State of State message 1-8, 403F3, G3
Abscam probe revealed 2-2, 2-3, 82D1; Casino Control Comm linked 2-4, 2-5, Comm reform proposed 2-11, 110G3
Mafia ldr slain 3-21, 237E2
Caesars, Bally granted permanent licenses, organized crime links rptd severed 10-25, 12-29; Harrah's gets temp license 11-1, 988G2-D3
Williams, 3 others indicted in Abscam probe 10-30, 824A3
6th casino opened by Golden Nugget, '80 revenues forecast 12-12, 988F2, E3

Atomic Energy & Safeguards
Parsipanny demonstratns mark 3 Mile I mishap 3-28, 249A1
Salem A-plant gets start-up license 4-16, 332F1

Crime & Civil Disorders
Scott convictn appeal refused 1-14, 320F3
Abscam probe revealed; Williams, Thompson, Camden mayor, others linked 2-2, 2-3, 81C1-B2
US Customs offcl pleads guilty in corruptn probe 2-13, 359C2
Helstoski cleared of '76 chrgs 2-27, 228B1
Mafia ldr slain 3-21, 237B2
Newark prison riot 3-25—3-26, 370G3
Jersey City FALN apartmt raid uncovers exec hit list, bomb factory 4-8, 309C1
Waterfront racketeer convicted 5-2; 7 sentncd 5-20, 927E2
Camden mayor indicted in Abscam probe 5-27, 5-28, 402E2, F2
Thompson, Silvestri indicted in Abscam probe 6-18, 454F1-D2
Abscam judge quits Thompson, Errichetti cases 8-7, 599E3
2 Cuban refugees seized in hijack plot 8-17, 631E3
Mafia, pizza indus ties probed 8-24, 714D1
Camden mayor convicted in Abscam trial 8-31, 684B2
Eastn hijack attempt thwarted 9-12, 704G1
Appeals ct backs Abscam tapes broadcast 10-1; Sup Ct refuses stay, tapes aired 10-14, 781D2
Williams, 3 others indicted in Abscam probe 10-30, 824C2
Prison bldg bond issue OKd 11-4, 847G3
Thompson convicted in Abscam case 12-3, 919D1
Reagan transitn aide's mob ties alleged 12-15, 955F3

1976

Politics
Primary date set 22C2
Carter campaigns 4-27, Byrne endorses 4-29, 324A1
Humphrey rules out campaign 4-29, 305A3
Carter in E Brunswick 5-6, 343G1
Brown in Elizabeth 5-18, 390D3
Carter campaigns 5-26, 390A3
Uncommitted Dems back Humphrey, Brown 5-27, 390C3
Humphrey, Brown visit 6-2—6-3, 6-7, 409G3
Rep Helstoski indicted 6-2, 414C3
Ford campaigns 6-6, 410C2, B3
Carter visits 6-6, 6-7, 410F3, 411C1
Primary results 6-8, 408F2, 409C1, E3-410B1
Carter meets delegates 6-30, 468F1
Dem conv women delegates, table 508C2
Dem conv pres vote, table 7-14, 507C2
Reagan seeks delegates 7-14, 531G2
Reagan, Schweiker in Elizabeth 8-5, 564C2
Ford, Reagan claim delegate gains 8-7, 8-10, 583A2, E2
GOP pre-conv delegate count 8-14, 583C3
Reagan, Ford seek conv delegates 8-17, 8-18, 601B3, C3
GOP conv pres, vp vote tables 8-18—8-19, 8-19, 599C1,.C3
Reagan scores oppositn 8-19, 615F2
Mondale visits 9-11, 687E1
Carter 'whistlestops' 9-20, 704B3
Ford Clementon golf outings rptd 9-21, 9-23, 722G2, B3
Helstoski renominated 9-21, 725B2
Mondale, Dole in Newark 10-10, 763C3, 764A1
Ford campaigns in suburbs 10-13, 763G2
Carter in N Bergen 10-23, 803B2
Mondale visits 10-25, 803G3
Ford in Atlantic City 10-27, 803D1
Carter for offshore oil search 10-30, 827G1
Election results 11-2: pres 818C1, G1, 819A2; cong 820D1, D2, 821B2, 828D2, 830D1; state (Atlantic City) 821C2, D2 *, 825C3
Carter primary spending rptd 11-17, 938A3

NEW London (Conn.) Day (newspaper)
Carter endorsement rptd 10-30, 831G2
NEWMAN, Cecil E.
Dies 2-7, 160G3
NEWMAN, Constance E.
HUD asst secy 1-27; confrmd 2-24, 186B2
NEWMAN, Edwin
Pres debate moderator 9-23, 700G2
NEWMAN, Kevin
Named environmt min 7-4, 520F2
On uranium export ban end 11-11, 888C1, F1
NEWMAN, Ralph G.
Fined 1-6, 6C3
NEW Mexico
Sen primary results 6-1, 411E1 *
Cong clears Roswell saline water funds 6-7, 434A3; signed 6-22, 982F1
Sup Ct upholds wild horse, burro protectn 6-17, 552G3
Reagan sweeps GOP delegates 6-26, 467F2
Potash producers indicted 6-29, 748E1

1977

Politics & Government
Legislature schedule rptd 6E2
Campbell wins Dem chrmn post 3-31, 251B1
Fed spending inequities chrgd 4-6, 423D3
Gibbs confrmd US Army asst secy 4-25, 418D1
Primary results 6-7, 446C3
Carter stumps for Byrne 9-10, 761C1
Byrne reelected gov 11-8, 855E1, A2
Bond referenda OKd 11-8, 879C2
Bradley sets US Sen bid 11-14, 991A1
Sports
NFL Jets to remain at Shea 2-18, 163E3
Jets-Mets dispute settled 5-26, 491D2
NY Nets move set 7-26, 584F1
Meadowlands arena OKd 10-13, 870C2
Transportation
Byrne Concorde stand rptd 3-9, 212D3
Conrail line cuts set 3-31, 325E2
Port Auth mass transit aid curbed 4-27, 382G3
Concorde landing rights backed 9-23, 738C2
Byrne vetoes Port Auth aircraft noise rule 12-27, 1006E3

NEWLIN, Richard F.
Indicted 6-6, 504C1
NEWMAN, Kevin
Named Australia natl dvpt min 12-19, 982A2
NEW Melones Dam
US water rights upheld 4-4, 253C1
NEW Mexico
Legislature schedule rptd 6E2
Rio Rancho, Amrep convictns 1-24, 156A2; 4 sentncd 3-10, 203A3
Great Westn settles Cochiti land-fraud case 1-26, 156D1
'75 interstate gas sales cited 1-28, 76C3
Mex pot smuggling rptd 4-8, 332D3
'76 per-capita income table 5-10, 387F2

1978

Energy
Offshore drilling challenge refused 2-21, 125E2-B3
Coal strike utility billing probe set 5-10, 366F3
1st offshore oil well rptd dry 6-2, 6-5, 449C3
Texaco offshore gas find rptd 8-14, 8-18, 665C3
Shell gas sale monopoly suit filed 11-30, 939D3
3 more offshore oil wells rptd dry 12-6, 12-11, 12-27, 1010B1
Offshore A-plant contract canceled 12-19, 1009D3
Environment & Pollution
Offshore drilling challenge refused 2-21, 125E2-B3
Waste dumping law voided by US Sup Ct 6-23, 566B2
NY area on bad-air list 7-5, 513C1
House votes parks bill 7-12, 526E3, F3
Bad-air list corrected 7-19, 644B2
Labor
Provenzano convicted for kickbacks 3-25, 232C2
Provenzano convicted for murder 6-14, sentenced 6-21, 480B2
Extended jobless aid rptd 7-10, 552A3; 8-4, 607D3
Provenzano sentenced for kickbacks 7-11, 560F2
Jersey City postal walkout 7-21, Kearny 7-23, 564F3, 565A1
Parsons sued re union payoffs 8-4, 643C2 *, D2
Teamster funds scored 8-14, 625E1
USW conv in Atlantic City 9-17—9-20, 715F1; 9-21, 737D2
Newark layoffs scheduled 12-11, 1012D1
Politics & Government
Legislature schedule rptd 14F3
Gibson reelected in Newark 5-9, 363G1
Primary results 6-6, 425B1, 447F3
Govt spending curb cited 6-6, 425C1
Vance in Atlantic City 6-20, 4[illegible]7D1-B3, 490G2
Legislature OKs DC voting rep amendmt 9-11, 878A3
Electn results 11-7: cong 845E1, 846E1, F2, A3, 848E2, 849A1, 851F2; state 847G1, 849D1, 915C2
Sports
Sports Auth chrmn joins Garden Corp 1-1, 95F3
Cosmos set attendance records 6-21, 655G1
Nets sale agreed 8-28, 1027E3
Jai alai referendum loses 11-7, 847G1

NEWLEY, Anthony
Stop the World opens 8-3, 887C3
NEWLIN, Mike
NBA free-throw ldr 4-9, 271F2
NEW London, Conn.—*See CONNECTICUT*
NEWMAN, David
Superman released 12-14, 1030E3
NEWMAN, Herb
Son crosses Atlantic by balloon 8-11—8-17, 652F3
NEWMAN, Judge Jon O.
SCM-Xerox verdict reversed 7-11, 664C3, D3
Sets aside SCM trust award 12-29, 1005D2
NEWMAN, Sir Kenneth
Denies Ulster police brutality 6-9, 474A2
NEWMAN, Kevin
On plan to cut liquid fuel consumptn 9-7, joint W Ger coal conversn effort set 10-10, 793D3, F3
Australia centralizes A-waste monitoring 11-9, 900D2
Australia planning min 11-30, 944A1
NEWMAN, Larry
Crosses Atlantic by balloon 8-11—8-17, 652E3
NEWMAN, Leslie
Superman released 12-14, 1030E3
NEWMAN, Nanette
Intl Velvet released 7-19, 970G1
NEWMAN, Randy
'Short People' on best-seller list 2-4, 116F3
NEWMAN, Walter
Bloodbrothers released 9-27, 969D3
NEW Melones Dam (Calif.)
Calif water rights backed by Sup Ct 7-3, 552C2
NEW Mexico
Legislature schedule rptd 14F3
'67, '77 sales-tax rates rptd 1-5, 15E3
Mondale tours Westn states 1-9—1-13, 34E1, E2
State govt tax revenue table 1-9, 84D2
Wilderness area clears Cong 2-9, 109D2; signed 2-24, 218A2
Marijuana treatmt OKd 2-22, 7-13,

1979

Energy—*See also 'Atomic' above*
Offshore oil wells rptd dry 1-10, 17A2; 2-14, 186E3; 3-13–5-16, 361D3
Offshore gas find rptd 1-17, 55C2; 5-23, 442F3
'78 per capita gas use rptd 5-27, 395G2
Offshore oil find rptd 6-5, new well dry 7-6, 518D2
Jersey Central rate hike rptd granted 6-19, 519B1
Odd-even gas rationing begins 6-21, 462F2
July gas supply use rptd 6-23, 479G1
3 Mile I reactor kept shut 8-9, 629F3
Winter heating fuel supply promised 8-28, 703C2
Odd-even gas rules lifted 9-6, 683F1
More offshore gas finds rptd 10-22, 11-12, 867A2-C2; 11-23, 943B1
Environment & Pollution
US sues 8 cos re Edison landfill wastes 2-7, 129G3-130B1
Radium Waste sites alleged 3-5, 187B2
Hackensack Meadowlands cleanup ordrd 8-26, 704A2
Labor & Employment
Provenzano, others indicted 2-22, 155F3
Waterfront figures indicted 3-6, 220C2
8 state colleges struck 3-20, 207D1
Dock indictmts mount 4-9, 292B1
Nutley co ups women's pay 5-13, 482G3
Rahway drug co OKs anti-bias plan 6-26, 521G1
Provenzano, 3 others sentncd 7-10, 548E1
State white-collar workers strike 7-10–7-14, accord reached 7-21, 599B1
Woodbridge striking teachers arrested 9-12, 679E1
Newark layoffs set 11-13, 921A2
Newark hiring ordinance vetoed 11-15, override fails 11-20, 992F1
Iranian bus drivers fired 11-22, 898C2
Passaic layoff threat rptd, jobless rate cited 11-26, 921G1
Politics & Government—*See also other appropriate subheads in this section*
Legislature schedule rptd 5E3
Trenton fiscal status rptd 3-20, 204B2
Mondale addresses Hoboken offcls 8-22, 726C1
Carter visits 10-25, 808C1
Electn results 11-6, 846A2, B2, 847A1
Newark budget gap cited 11-13, 921A2
Passaic budget shortfall rptd 11-26, 921G1
School Issues
Pvt schl tax break ban affirmed by Sup Ct 5-29, 421F3
Woodbridge striking teachers arrested 9-12, 679E1

NEW Jersey v. Monmouth Medical Center
Case declined by Sup Ct 11-5, 884D3
NEW Jersey v. Portash
Grant of immunity broadened by Sup Ct 3-20, 204A1
NEW Jerusalem (play)
Opens 2-15, 712F1
NEW London, Conn.—*See CONNECTICUT*
NEW Madrid, Mo.—*See MADRID*
NEWMAN, Barry
City on Fire released 9-14, 819G3
NEWMAN, Kevin E.
On Australia oil imports 11-28, 926B1
NEWMAN, Paul
Quintet released 2-8, 174D3
2d in LeMans 6-10, 490D3
NEWMAN, Walter
Champ released 4-3, 528F1
NEW Mexico
Legislature schedule rptd 5E3
Pub schl cost share rptd 3-5, 282E3
DC voting rep amendment rejectn rptd 3-19, 204B3
Death penalty bill signed 4-1, 400B2
2 AF jets lost 4-12, crewmen feared dead 5-5, 404A3
Elec tax voided by US Sup Ct 4-18, 346B2

1980

Environment & Pollution
US rpts waste suit partially setld, Edison dump to be covered 1-30, 93D3
Eliz chem dump burns 4-22, 331B2
Byrne sets water ratning 9-12, 9-22, Carter declares emergency 10-19; comm issues warning 12-1, 947A3, C3
Natural resources bond issue OKd 11-4, 848A1
Labor & Employment
Ford Mahwah plant shut 4-15, 287E1
Waterfront racketeer convicted 5-2; 7 sentncd 5-20, 927E2
PATH strike ends 9-1, 704D2-C3
Schering settles job bias case 12-14, 962D3
Medicine & Health
Influenza outbreak rptd 2-15, 158C3
Mental health bond issue OKd 11-4, 847G3
Politics & Government—*See also other appropriate subheads in this section*
Legislature schedule rptd 18E1
State of State message 1-8, 403E3
ACU '79 voting survey rptd 1-18, 53C3
Ex-Rep Sundstrom dies 5-23, 448A3
Primary results 6-3, 439A3
Ex-Rep Kean dies 9-21, 755F3
Detroit census revisn ordrd, Newark suit cited 9-25, 741F2
Election results 11-4: cong 843F2-B3, 846A2, C2, 848F2; state 847D3, E3, 848A3
Essex Cnty census data stay extended by Sup Ct 12-15, 957C2
'80 census rptd, reapportmt seen 12-31, 983F1
Presidential Election (& Transition)
Reagan in West Orange 1-29, 91D3
Kennedy counting on win 5-28, 399D1
Primary results 6-3, 422E2, 423C2, 424C1
Poll rpts voter discontent 6-3, 423B1
Bush in Somerset 8-30, 780B3
Reagan in Jersey City; defends 'Carter depressn' remark, praises Polish strikers 9-1, 664C2
Reagan in Paterson 10-1, 738E1
Reagan in Cherry Hill 10-6, 763A3
Kennedy stumps with Carter 10-15, 778G3
Kennedy visit rptd 10-22, 817E1
Carter in Gloucester City 10-24, Newark 10-29, 816D2, A3
Carter in Newark 10-29, 841A1
Reagan winds up campaign 10-30, 840A1
Election results 11-4, 838C1, 839A2, F3
School Issues
Schl prayer law cited 2-6, 156A2
Newark teachers strike 9-3, 723C3
Reagan backs parochial-schl tax credits 10-1, 738F1

NEWLIN, Mike
NBA free-throw ldr 3-30, 278D3
NEWMAN, Judge Jon O.
Vs Myers Abscam entrapmt plea 8-8, 684G2
Backs Abscam tapes broadcast 10-1, 781A3
NEWMAN, Paul
Daytona endurance results 2-3, 637F3
NEWMAN, Stephen D.
Mecca opens 2-2, 136D3
NEW Mexico
DES in cattle rptd 4-24, 358F1
Hunts bailout loan collateral listed 5-28, 426D1
ICC OKs Rock I RR segment sale 6-10, 598E3
Silver mining venture rptd 6-24, 685D3
Gannett purchase of Santa Fe paper rescinded 6-30, 582D2-A3
MX sites chosen 11-18, 897A1

1976

Dem conv women delegates, table 508C2
Dem conv pres vote, table 7-14, 507C2
GOP pre-conv delegate count 8-14, 583D3
GOP conv pres, vp vote tables 8-18—8-19, 599D1, D3
Mondale in Albuquerque 9-7, 665G2
Fscl '75 per capita income, tax burden rptd 9-15, 10-12, 959D2
Sup Ct bars review of benefits for strikers 10-4, 807E2
Carter in Albuquerque 10-8, 762E1
Dole in Albuquerque 10-27, 804A3
Election results 11-2: pres 817C1, 819B1, D3★, 824E2, 828D2, 830F1; state 824F2

NEWMONT Mining Corp.
Peabody Holding Co.—*See separate listing*
NEW Orleans, La.—*See LOUISIANA*
NEW Orleans Bancshares Inc.
Bank buys Intl City 12-5, 939F3
NEWPORT, R.I.—*See RHODE Island*
NEWPORT News Shipbuilding & Dry Dock Co.—*See under TENNECO*
NEW River
OKd for US scenic system 3-12, dam project 3-24, 219A3
Dam bar signed 9-11, 689D1
NEWSDAY (newspaper)
Greene leads Ariz crime probe 10-2, 849B2, E2
Rpts higher S Africa riot toll 12-11, 1010B2
NEWSPAPER Editors, American Society of
Kissinger at annual mtg 4-13, 259C3
Ford news conf 4-13, 261F2
NEWSPAPER Guild, The (AFL-CIO)
Exec bd drops chrgs vs Washn Post dissidents 1-29, 153F3
NLRB rules on ethics code 4-8, 272E2
Strikes Time 6-2, 398B1
Ends Time strike 6-21, 454C2
Wins Washn Post vote 7-22, 553D3
Rpt Steinke scores S Africa detentns 12-9, 927E2
NEWSPAPERS—*See PRESS*
NEWSPRINT—*See PAPER & Paper Products*
NEW Stanton, Pa.—*See PENNSYLVANIA*
NEWSWEEK (magazine)
Rpts Lockheed, Northrop Latin bribes 2-23, 147G1
Denies Sovt spy chrg 5-25, 371A3
Friendly sues Sovt press 6-25, 559B1
Elliott quits as chrmn, Campell named 10-5, 892G1
Faces Thai censorship 10-11, 775E3
Bruno on pres debate panel 10-15, 782B3
S Africa bars editor 10-26, 927G2
Sovt laser use rpt denied 11-23, 961A2
Syrians close Beirut office 12-19, reopen 12-20, 953E2
NEWS World, The (newspaper)
Unificatn Church to publish 12-4, 971G1
NEW Times (magazine)
Rpts Butz racist remark 10-15, 743G3
NEWTON, Huey P.
FBI role in split with Cleaver rptd 5-6, 344D2
NEW World Liberation Front
Claims Hearst estate bombings 2-12, 3-11, 201B3
NEW York (magazine)
Schorr House com rpt leak detailed 2-12, 2-26, 150G3, 151C1
Jerome Synder dies 5-2, 524F3
2 editors subpoenaed in Schorr probe 8-25; probe dropped 9-22, 748G3
NEW York, City University of (CUNY)
Carter at Bklyn Coll 7-7, 664D2
Mt. Sinai School of Medicine
new alcoholism test rptd 12-3, 950D3
NEW York, State University of—*See STATE University of New York*
NEW York Board of Rabbis—*See RABBIS, New York Board of*

1977

Albuquerque business confidence rptd; econ data table 5-16, 384F2, 385B1
Santa Fe Natl Forest burns 6-16—6-22, Los Alamos lab threatened 6-18, 660F3
US asks farm holdings breakup 8-22, 703G2
'76 per capita income, tax burden table 9-13, 10-18, 821E2
United Nuclear, Gulf trial opens 10-31, 895C2
Laser enrichmt of uranium rptd 12-17, 975F2

NEW Mexico University (Albuquerque)
Cole in NFL draft 5-3, 353B3
NEWMONT Mining Corp.
Magma ups copper price 3-21, 209C2
Peabody purchased 6-30, 520G1
Magma struck 7-1, settles 558C1
Peabody Holding Co.—*See separate listing*
NEW Orleans, La.—*See LOUISIANA*
NEWPORT News Shipbuilding & Dry Dock Co.—*See under TENNECO*
NEW Republic, The (magazine)
Rpts CR pol financing scandal 4-23, 506B1
Bruce Bliven dies 5-27, 452E2
NEW Rochelle, N.Y.—*NEW York State*
NEWS American (Baltimore, Md. newspaper)
Trust suit setld 5-26, 504A2
NEW Scientist (magazine)
Rpts on US weather crisis 1-27, 77A1
DNA articles rptd 10-6, 10-27, 846C3 F3
NEWSDAY (newspaper)
On most reliable govt news source list 12-10, 1009C1
NEWSPAPER Editors, American Society of
S Africa curbs scored 10-10, 825D2
NEWSPAPER Publishers Association, American
Fla libel case review refused 11-7, 857D2
NEWSPAPERS—*See PRESS*
NEWSWEEK (magazine)
USSR renews Friendly attack 2-2, 101E1, F1
Khaddoumi interview 3-14, 166C2
Califano backs hiring quotas 3-17, 217B3
Mobutu interview 4-11, 265C2
Carter energy plan poll 4-20—4-21, 320A3
Gallup poll, Jaworski, Buchanan articles on Nixon-Frost interview 5-9, 367C3, G3
Carter summit diplomacy hailed 5-16, 359F1
Rpts secret US-Saudi pact 6-27, 474C1
Giscard interview 7-25, 551A1
CIA links chrgd, denied 9-12, 720C3, G3
Somalia chrgs vs US rptd 9-19, 715D3
On most reliable govt news source list 12-10, 1009B1
NEW Times (magazine)
MCA acquires 11-10, 1004E3
NEWTON, Andrew
Chrgs Scott murder plot 10-19, Thorpe denies link 10-27, 883A2
NEWTON, Huey P.
Leaves Cuba to face '74 Calif chrgs 6-24, in Canada custody 6-25—6-29, 531G3
NEW West (magazine)
Murdoch acquires control 1-7, 48D3
NEW York (magazine)
Staff walks out 1-6, Murdoch gains control 1-7, Brady replaces Felker 1-8, 48B3
Ehrlichman article cited 5-16, 368A1
Felker group buys Esquire 8-26, 695G2
Hellman dies 9-26, 788C1
NEW York, Association for a Better
Concorde ruling backed 5-11, 368D2
NEW York, City University of (CUNY)
Califano addresses City Coll 6-5, 445F3
Brooklyn College
Robert Wolff dies 12-29, 1024G3
NEW York, State University of—*See STATE University of New York*
NEW York Airways Helicopter Service
Copter tips over 5-16, landing rights revoked 5-17, 412A3
NEW York Amsterdam News, The (newspaper)
Cilian Powell dies 9-22, 788C2

1978

598C3
United Nuclear wins Gen Atomic uranium suit 3-2, 144C1, D2
Rain floods drought areas 3-3—3-5, 207D2
A-waste storage test site proposed 3-15, 183C3
Los Alamos A-worker wins neurosis damages 3-15, 242F3
'Right-to-die' law rptd 3-18, 597F3
Gen Atomic denied damage determinatn stay by US Sup Ct 3-20, 206D1
Gen Atomic reveals new evidnc 4-20, 346F2-A3
Gen Atomic documts case declined by Sup Ct 5-15, 387E3
Press info order review refused by Sup Ct 5-15, 388B1
United Nuclear awarded damages 5-16, 366G2
Income-tax relief rptd 5-25, 425D1
Gen Atomic trial judge interference ruled by Sup Ct 5-30, 430G2
'77 prison populatn rptd up 6-3, 440D1
Ex-sen Montoya dies 6-5, 540C3
Primary results 6-6, 448B2
Cruise missile tested at White Sands 6-21, 493A2
Nicaragua pres studies A-plants 6-22, 593B2
Water rights backed by US Sup Ct 7-3, 552C2
Albuquerque on bad-air list 7-5, 513C1
Bad-air list corrected 7-19, 644B2
Taos Pueblo ldr dies 7-30, 620E3
Albuquerque balloonists cross Atlantic 8-11—8-17, 652E3
US parks bill cleared 10-13, 834C3
Electn results 11-7: cong 846A2, 847C1, 848E2, 851B3, 855C2, D2; state 853G2, 855C2, E2
Carlsbad A-waste burial planned 11-15, 961D2

NEW Motor Vehicle Board v. Fox
Auto franchise law upheld 12-5, 959D3
NEW Orleans, La.—*See LOUISIANA*
NEWPORT News, Va.—*See VIRGINIA*
NEWPORT News Shipbuilding and Dry Dock Co.—*See TENNECO Inc.*
NEW Republic, The (magazine)
Strout wins Pulitzer citation 4-17, 315A1
Osborne rpts on Carter strategy sessn 4-29, 306E3
NEW Seabury Corp.
Mass Indian land claim set back 1-6, 6A2
NEWS-Journal Co.—*See under Du PONT de Nemours*
NEWS of the World (recording)
On best-seller list 2-4, 116G3
NEWSOM, David
US to admit more refugees 11-28, 933B1; at UN conf 12-12, 956B2
NEWSOME, Ozzie
In NFL draft 5-2, 336G2
NEWSPAPER Editors, American Society of
CIA press operatns scored 1-5, 15B1
Carter unveils anti-inflatn plan 4-11, 259E2, 260C3-261C1
Lance scores press coverage 4-12, 324F3-325A1
Minority employmt survey rptd 4-13, 835B3
NEWSPAPER Guild, The (AFL-CIO)
NY Daily News struck 6-13—6-17, 625A2
3 NY papers stuck 8-9, 625E1
NY newspaper strike ends 11-6, 865C1
NEWSPAPERS—*See PRESS; specific names*
NEW Stanton, Pa.—*See PENNSYLVANIA*
NEWSWEEK (magazine)
Time to buy Washn Star 2-3, 109A3
Haldeman book syndicatn upset by Post scoop 2-16, 124D2, E2
Moreau arrested in Chile, freed 5-1; rpts jail abuse 5-15, 351D3
NEW Testament Baptist Church (Fla.)
Schl integratn challenge refused 2-21, 126D1
NEW Times (magazine)
To halt publicatn 11-15, 1029G3
NEWTON, Andrew
Thorpe arrested in murder plot 8-4, 614B2
Testifies at Thorpe hearing 11-27, 945C1, F1
NEWTON, Huey P.
Arrested in barroom brawl 5-11; convicted on gun chrg 9-28, sentncd 11-3, 971F2
NEWTON, Jack
Wins Buick Open 6-18, 580F3
NEWTON-John, Olivia
You're The One on best-seller list 6-7, 460F3; 7-5, 579G3; 8-2, 620F1
Grease released 6-16, 619C2
NEW West (magazine)
'77 Peoples Temple rpt cited 11-21, 891C2
NEW York (magazine)
Times, News strike ends 11-6, 865A2
NEW York, City University of (CUNY)
Edelstein scores Bakke ruling 6-28, 482G2
Mt. Sinai School of Medicine
Silikoff PBB study rptd 10-9, 769B3
Queens College
2 acoustics experts assess JFK murder 12-29, 1002F1
NEW York Central Railroad—*See PENN Central Co.*

1979

Sante Fe archbp named to '80 Rome synod 5-3, 376B1
'78 inmate totals rptd 6-21, 548C2
Rabies cases rptd up 7-14, 620G2
MX 'racetrack' deployment sites considered 9-7, 677G3
Interior Dept seeks to protect primitive areas 9-7, 703C3
'78 per capita income rptd 9-16, 746F2
Horizon land sales scored by FTC 10-3, 903F1
Elec suit vs Tex refused by Sup Ct 10-9, 784D1
Carter in Albuquerque 10-10, 807D2
Albuquerque newspapers libel case refused by Sup Ct 12-3, 964B2
Atomic Energy
Nev A-waste storage studied 1-5, 54F3
Carter seeks A-arms disposal site 1-22, 45E2
A-protest rptd 4-28—4-29, 322F3
Church Rock waste spill 7-16, cleanup continues 9-5, 744A1
Gen Atomic arbitratn rule declined by Sup Ct 10-9, 784E1

NEW Mexico, University of (Albuquerque)
Basketball scandal detailed 12-13—12-21, 1003E1
NEW Mexico State University (Las Cruces)
Antimatter detectn rptd 10-15, 1000B2
NEW Mexico v. Texas
Case refused by Sup Ct 10-9, 784E1
NEW Orleans, La.—*See LOUISIANA*
NEW Orleans Insurance Information Institute
Hurricane Frederic loss rptd 10-5, 954G2
NEWPORT News, Va.—*See VIRGINIA*
NEWPORT News Shipbuilding and Dry Dock Co.—*See under TENNECO*
NEW Republic, The (magazine)
Julius Rosenberg article publshd 6-16, 466B1
E Timor famine, casualties rptd 11-3, 856F1
NEWSDAY (Long Island, N.Y. newspaper)
'Son of Sam' interviewed 2-22, 156A3
Daily circulatn listed 6-6, 431C1
NEWSFRONT (film)
Released 5-30, 820D2
NEWS Ltd.
Herald & Weekly Times takeover bid dropped 11-22, 906A3
Fairfax acquires Herald interest 11-26, 966A3
Ansett Transport control gained 12-18, 966E3
NEWSOM, David
Briefs Iran hostage kin 12-7, 934E1
NEWSPAPER Editors, American Society of
Kennedy addresses 4-30, 324A2
Brzezinski addresses 5-1, 347C2
NEWSPAPER Publishers Association, American
Conv; Neuharth scores Sup Ct 'state of mind' libel ruling, 1st Amendmt legal fund set 4-23, 302D2
Carter addresses 4-25, 294A2
Neuharth scores ctroom press access ruling 7-2, 515C3
Neuharth rpts press freedom insurnc plan 9-27, 859E2
NEWSPAPERS—*See PRESS; specific names*
NEW Stanton, Pa.—*See PENNSYLVANIA*
NEWSWEEK (magazine)
Coll enrollmt decline noted 1-29, 367C2
Muir dies 1-30, 104E3
IEA-Sweden oil aid rptd 6-4, 396E2
Giscard interview publshd 6-28—7-2, 493G2
Young-PLO contact tip rptd 8-10, 605G1
Writer arrives in Iran 8-15, ousted 8-16, 670D2
NEWTON, Andrew
Thorpe acquitted 6-22, 485F3
NEWTON, Huey P.
Mistrial ends murder case 3-24, 239C1
2d mistrial ends murder case, chrgs dropped 9-27, 818B3
NEWTON, Jack
Wins Australian Open 11-28, 970C2
NEW York, Association for a Better
Brown addresses 11-20, 962G2
NEW York, City University of (CUNY)
City College
Levich named Einstein prof 3-2, 272E1
Kennedy addresses editors 4-30, 324B2
Queens College
Carter at town mtg 9-25, 723C2
NEW York, State University of (SUNY)
Potsdam Campus
Loses NCAA Div III basketball title 3-17, 239B1
NEW York Building and Construction Industry Board
Govt minority constructn grants case argued in Sup Ct 11-27, 945A1

1980

Atomic Energy & Safeguards
State of State message 1-25, 269F3
Mil waste disposal projct not budgeted 1-28, 71G3
Carter outlines A-waste storage plan, Carlsbad site studied 2-12, 127E3
Crime & Civil Disorders
Santa Fe prison riot 2-2—2-3, 33 rptd dead 2-10, 112B2
'Pyramid' money schemes rptd 5-17, 655A3
U of NM coach, 2 others indicted 5-23, 469C3
U of NM coach acquitted of US chrgs 6-20, 875E3
Politics & Government—*See also other appropriate subheads in this section*
Legislature schedule rptd 18E1
ACU '79 voting survey rptd 1-18, 53C3
State of State message 1-25, 269E3
Kennedy in Albuquerque 5-13, 366B3
Pres primary results 6-3, 423D2, 424C1
Rep Runnels dies 8-5, 676F2
Anderson ct battle for ballot access rptd 9-27, 818B2
Bush in Albuquerque 9-30, 781A2
Election results 11-4: pres 838C1, 839B3; cong 840F2, 843C3, 852B1; state 845C3
'80 census rptd, reapportmt seen 12-31, 983F1

NEW Mexico, University of (Albuquerque)
Transcript scandal spreads 1-23—5-23; Ellenberger, 2 others indicted 5-23, 469C2, B3
Ellenberger acquitted 6-20, 875E3
NEW Milwaukee Lines
Milwaukee Rd westn track purchase rejected in '79 1-7, 53B1
ICC spurns Milwaukee Rd reorganizatn plan 3-19, 346D1
NEWMONT Mining Corp.
USW copper strike drags on 10-24, 805B3
NEW Orleans—*See LOUISIANA*
NEW Orleans Steamship Association
ILA Sovt ship boycott end asked 1-28; ct backs, ship loaded 1-29, 169C1
NEW Orleans Times-Picayune (newspaper)
George Healy Jr dies 11-2, 928F2
NEWPORT News—*See VIRGINIA*
NEWPORT News Shipbuilding and Dry Dock Co.—*See under TENNECO Inc.*
NEWSCO Investments Ltd.
Bids for FP Publicatns 1-9, 1-11, Thomson wins 1-11, 38A2
NEWSDAY (Long Island, N.Y. newspaper)
Abscam probe revealed 2-2, 81B1
3 win Polk awards 2-25, 692E3
NEWS Group Publications Inc.
Cue NY purchase agrmt rptd 3-4, 239G1
NEWS & Observer (Raleigh, N.C.)
Carter pres endorsemt rptd 11-1, 841G3
NEWSOM, David D.
Testifies at B Carter probe 8-4, 595F2
Sees Dobrynin, protests A-test 9-15, 730B2
NEWSPAPER
LaChance sentncd 6-26, 656D1
NEWSPAPER and Mail Deliverers Union of New York and Vicinity (unaffiliated)
LaChance convicted 5-15, 370E3
NEWSPAPER Editors, American Society of
Carter, other pres candidates at conv 4-7—4-10, 264A1-E3
Reagan defends Olympics stand 4-10, 288C2
CIA Dir Turner addresses 4-10, 459A1
Pretrial data secrecy rule opposition rptd 6-19, 632C1
NEWSPAPERS—*See PRESS*
NEWSWEEK (magazine)
Sovt role in Afghan coup rptd 1-21, 44B2
'79 Afghan massacre rptd 2-11, 85B2
Harper expelled from Iran 2-28, 138A2
Iran readmits newsmen 3-7, 178D2
Reagan scores press 4-10, 288B2
Pres poll rptd 6-23, 452G1
Quinn in pres TV debate 9-21, 721C3
Pres poll standings tighten, toss-up seen 10-26, 816G1
NEWSWEEK Inc.
Garvey article reprint OKd despite libel suit 8-14, 637E2
NEW Time Films
Willis, Landau win Polk awards 2-25, 692F3
NEWTON, Huey P.
Stender dies 5-21, 448G2
Awarded PhD 6-15, 638F3
NEWTON, Jack
Ties for 2d in Masters 4-13, 412A2
NEWTON-John, Olivia
NY record co indicted 2-28, 237D3
Magic on best-seller list 8-13, 640A3; 9-10, 716E3
NEWTON-Smith, William
Czechs deport 3-9, 262D2
NEW West (magazine)
Purchased by Tex Monthly 8-27, 732E3
NEW York (magazine)
Cue NY sale agrmt rptd 3-4, 239A2
NEW York, City University of (CUNY)
Queens College (Flushing, N.Y.)
Commoner to accept teaching post 3-17, 471C3

1976

NEW York City
Concorde landing hearing 1-5, 5C2
Ticor indicted 1-14, 160B1
Race quotas for principals voided 1-19, 42G1-C2
Filing fees for state Sup Ct upheld 1-19, 43B1
Colombia drug pushers convctd 1-26, 61A2
Concorde test OKd, Carey scores 2-4, 94C2, D3
Carson, 5 others acquitted 2-6, 124E1
US sues on taxi emissions 2-20, 154C1
Jewish group claims credit for anti-Sovt incidents 2-27, 3-25, 229C2
Mail delivery cutbacks noted 3-8, 186E3
State dismisses '74 oil trust case 3-10, 413C1
'78 Soc Sec withdrawal planned 3-22, 994E1
Transit strike averted 4-1, 235C3
Sovt Aeroflot office, UN mission incidents 4-2, 259E3
Ct upholds clean air plan 4-26, 308B1
EPA checks water supply 4-30, 349G1
Apartment strike 5-3—5-19, 379B1
Rev Moon property rptd 5-12, 6-2, 9-8; church newspr set 12-14, 971C1, G1
Rev Moon holds rally 6-1, 971B1
Guild strikes Time Inc 6-2, 398B1
Spain king, queen visit 6-4—6-5, 459B3
Gets flu vaccine funds 6-6, 443B2
Guild ends Time strike 6-21, 454C2
Sewage closes NY beaches 6-23, 454A3
India emergency rule protested 6-26, 496G3
Ships, naval review mark Bicentennial; photo 7-4, 488C1, 489B1, F1
Voluntary hospital strike 7-7—7-17, 553E2
Ocean sewage-dumping curbed 7-23, 570F3
Australia prime min visits 7-29—7-30, 554B2
Munic hosp strike 8-4—8-7, 648B1
US Sen com rpts Medicaid fraud 8-30, 715F2
Constructn union bias barred 9-1, 943F3
Croat terrorists hijack TWA jet 9-10; cop killed 9-11, hijackers arraigned 9-13, 685B1
Chile rights com rally 9-10, 710G3
'74-75 SAT average rptd 9-13, 993G1
Police stage protests 9-26, 4 arrested 10-6, 991D2
Spain marriage annulmts rptd 10-15, 909D3
Medicaid abortn curb voided 10-22, Sup Ct bars stay 11-8, 848G1
Brit econ problems compared 10-24, 809F3
Bronx social club fire 10-24, 876E2
Intl drug dealers convicted, sentenced in Bklyn 11-5—12-17, 971F2-B3
Schl job bias chrgd 11-9, 921D3
Australian to buy Post 11-19, 887D2
Debt moratorium ruled unconst 11-19, 887B3
Queens gum factory blast 11-21, 969A2
10% get swine flu shots 12-2, 911B1
Bronfman case verdict 12-10, 952A3
Heroin use, deaths rptd 12-12, 972C3
Police win '75 raise 12-22, 991A2

1977

NEW York City
HEW chrgs school bias 1-18, 112C2
Low temp cited 2-6, 91D2
US rights comm backs city-suburb busing 2-15, 112E1
US Sup Ct backs racial voter redistricting 3-1, 174D3-175D1
Sup Ct voids widower benefits rule 3-2, 192D1
Germ warfare tests rptd 3-8, 195E2
Ford speech 3-23, 236F2
Moon denied property tax exemptn 4-14, 310D1
On '75 10 largest cities list 4-14, 388A1, C1
Coffee consumptn rptd down 4-26, 319D1
Amb Young on Queens racism 5-25, 417F2
Everard bathhouse fire 5-25, 429G2-A3
Willig climbs World Trade tower 5-26, 532A2
Australia urges envoy cuts 6-2, 484E3
'77 fashion wrap-up rptd 6-6, 1022C1
Gays march for rights 6-26, 560E2
Venez pres visits 6-30—7-1, 546B2
HEW withholds spec schl aid 7-5, 631E1
Blackout, probes ordrd 7-13—7-14, 537D2
CIA mind-control tests revealed 8-1—8-9, 611C1
Coffin elected Riverside Church min 8-14, 808B2
CIA mind-control tests probed 9-2—9-21, 721E2
Med writers hear Kennedy 9-27, 846G2
Schl desegregatn plan ordrd 10-6, 838C1
Clean-air case review declined 10-17, 797C3

Air Transport—*See also AVIATION—SST/Concorde*
CAB OKs 'Super-Saver' fares 3-15, 325D1
Pvt plane crashes in Pelham Pk 4-5, 286E3
NY Airways copter tips over 5-16, 412A3
Fla Airbus route rptd 5-24, 441C2
Laker 'skytrain' svc OKd 6-13, 500F2
UK air svc pact set 6-22, 500G1, E2
Pan Am, TWA, Brit Airways seek lower US-UK fares 7-24, 7-29, 8-1, 593D1
US bars charters to Jerusalem 8-1, 589C1
CAB acts on London budget fares 9-9, 9-15, Carter overrules 9-26, 860E2
Laker 'skytrain' svc begins 9-26, 860C2

Business & Economy—*See also 'Finances' below*
Murdoch takes over Post 12-30-76, acquires NY Mag 1-7, 48B3
SEC chrgs GTE payoffs 1-27, 79F2
Law business boom rptd 5-16, 383G1-C2
Business confidence signs rptd; econ data table 5-16, 384B2, D2
ICC trucking probe rptd 6-3, 500D3
'77 fashion wrap-up rptd 6-6, 1022C1

Crime
3 arrested re '76 Bronx club fire 1-2, 1-11, 140A2
SEC chrgs GTE payoffs 1-27, 79F2
'70-76 pol indictmts rptd 2-10, 162D3
Coffee thefts rptd 3-6, 169A1
Hare Krishna indictmts dropped 3-17, 287F1
FALN bombs FBI hq, Bronx printing plant 3-21, 261A2
Ex-FBI offcl indicted 4-7, 275F1-G2
Armstrong to probe ABC boxing 4-19, 828F1
Child porno filmmakers arrested 4-26, 432B3
Mafia ldrship struggle rptd 5-16, 568D1
ICC trucking probe rptd 6-3, 500D3
Croats invade UN mission 6-14, 497B2
LEAA office to close 6-20, 630E2
Son of Sam sought 6-26, 532C1; **for subsequent developments, see BERKOWITZ, David R.**
Bus hijacked, 2 slain at JFK 7-4, 568E3
Death-penalty bill vetoed 7-12, 594F2
Blackout violence, arrests 7-13—7-14, 537G2
Vincent Papa slain 7-26, 642C1
Diamond dealer murders probed 7-28—10-19, 871B3-G3
FALN bombs 2 office bldgs 8-3, dud found 8-8, 613D3, G3
Crimmins paroled 9-7, 848D1
Cuban exiles queried re Letelier murder 9-10, 743G2
Rudd surrenders 9-14, dischrgd 10-13, 839C1
'84 Olympics bid lost 9-25, 828C3
Mafia figure, NYC jeweler sentncd re extortn 10-21, 991D3
NL pres robbed, beaten 11-30, 990F2
Drug dealer convicted 12-2, 972D1
Phone surveillnc ct order backed 12-7, 939F1
Joan Little arrested 12-7, 992A1
Salerno mistrial declared 12-15, 992G1

1978

NEW York City
Dayan visits 2-12, 98E1
Radio City Music Hall saved 4-13, 293D1
Met museum names pres, bd chrmn 4-18, 335C3
ABC news show chngs set 4-19, 419A3
Begin visits 5-4—5-8, 339E2
Quebec premier visits 5-18, 412F3
Methodist church conf 5-21, 480F3
Con Ed blamed in '77 blackout 7-6, 529F3
Anti-USSR rallies 7-10, 542A3
Payson museum pledge ordrd paid 7-11, 579C2
Embryo implant trial opens 7-17, 597G1
'73 embryo implant trial opens 7-17, 597G1; damages awarded 8-18, 770G1
Asia Soc gets Rockefeller art 7-20, 628E1
ABA conv 8-3—8-10, 626A2-C3
'65 papal visit cited 8-6, 601B2
Sovt '68 Czech invasn marked 8-21, 691A3
CORE Arab-financed housing dvpt plan cited 9-18, 810G1
Begin addresses Jewish group 9-20, 719F2
VD epidemic among homosexuals rptd 11-6, 992A3
FCC orders TV statn studios in NJ 11-9, 1030D2
NRC A-plant safety progrm scored 11-25, 940F3
Populatn ranked 12-6, 942D3
Redlining study finds race bias 12-7, 942F2-A3

Business & Economy—*See also 'Finances' and other appropriate subheads in this section*
Trib debuts 1-9, Learsy elected chrmn 1-17, 75C3
Expenses rated 1-14, 28G2
Trib ceases publicatn 4-5, 270A2
'77 living costs rptd 4-26, 349G1
'70-77 Fortune 500 hq shift rptd 5-8, 326C1
Loews buys 3 hotels 5-31, 404G1
Grand Central office complex barred by Sup Ct 6-26, 566G3
'78 high chic fashion rptd 8-4—8-11, 10-27—11-3, 1029B2, F2
Firestone suits rptd 9-22, 835G1
Murdoch plans new tabloid 10-18, 865E1

Crime
Harlem drug dealer gets life 1-19, 95E3
Bergman sentenced 2-2, 232F3
'76 Bronx soc club arsonist sentenced 2-7, 380G3
Queens gum factory '76 blast chrgs dismissed 2-15, 212D3
Torrijos drug indictmt unsealed 2-21, 120E2
Carey orders Little extraditn 2-23, appeals ct backs 5-9; Marshall delays 5-30, Sup Ct declines appeal 6-5, 431A2
Provenzano trigger man killed 3-21, Provenzano convicted 3-25, 232C2, F2
2 policemen slain, Attica ex-inmate arrested 4-5, 388C3
FBI ex-offcls indicted, disciplinary actn vs LaPrade sought, '77 chrgs vs Kearney dropped 4-10, 261G3-262D1
Graiver indicted for embezzlmt 4-12, 326C1
LaPrade chrgs pol influence 4-13, 285B1
'77 blackout rpt issued 4-23, 396F1
Bulgari diamond recovered in autopsy 5-4, 380E1
'Son of Sam' pleads guilty 5-8, sentenced 6-13, 500G2
Brooklyn rabbi admits bribery, tax chrgs 5-11, 363C2
5 youths sentenced in '76 racial assault 5-12, 380D3
Port corruptn probe rptd 6-7, 480F2
Little extradited to NC 6-9, 560E3
Welfare fraud crackdown rptd successful 7-3, 684G3
LaPrade fired 7-6, 507A3
Intourist office bombed 7-10, 542A3
Ostrer indicted re union funds, taxes 7-18, 599D1
Tonelli, 4 others indicted re union funds 7-19, 598E3
Croat bombs defused at UN, Grand Central 8-14, 706D3
Cuba UN mission bombed 9-9, 777B1
FBI agent indicted 9-15, 11-6; resigns, pleads guilty 11-9, 886C3
ICC ex-offcl indicted 9-22, 770F2
Diamond dealer '77 killers convicted 10-6, 824D2
Punk rock star accused of murder 10-12, 842C1

1979

NEW York City
ITT long-distance phone svc OKd 1-4, 15E2
Rockefeller dies 1-26, 103E3
1st woman rabbi quits post 2-2, 176F1
Paramount resumes 'Warriors' ads 2-22, 174F1-A2
Occupancy tax collectn curbed by US Sup Ct 3-5, 185E1
Ft Wadsworth to close 3-29, 265F3
Forgn policy groups hear Secy Brown 4-5, 257G2
'79 fashion roundup rptd 1006F1
Dymshits, Kuznetsov honored at rally 4-29, 317B2
Brzezinski addresses news editors 5-1, 347C2
Co-op apartmt growth rptd 6-23, 482G2-A3
Nixon buys apartment 8-11, 656A3
Bolshoi dancer defects 8-23; wife detained 8-24, released 8-27, 644D3-645F1
Hurricane David hits 9-7, 691B1
Brooklyn Viet vet study released 9-25, 725A2
Pope visits; addresses UN, holds mass 10-2-10-3, 757D1, E2-758A3; cost estimated 760G3, 761A2
Press corps papal coverage rptd 10-2-10-3, 760G3
Nixon buys town house 10-5, 860E1
Castro visits amid tight security 10-11-10-14, 778B2-779F1
Shah enters hospital 10-22, Iranians stage protest 11-4, 843B1, E1; medical treatmt completed 11-29, 897E1
Methodists uphold gay pastor 11-1, 931G3
Pahlevi family real estate holdings rptd 11-26, 898B1
Iran sues shah, wife 11-28, 897A2-B3
Shah leaves hosp 12-2, 913G2
Iran consulate staff ordrd cut 12-12, 933C1
Riverside Church pastor in Iran 12-24-12-27, 975B1
'79 living costs ranked 12-28, 990F3, 991A1

Arts & Culture
Met museum sculpture stolen 2-9, recovered 2-14, 119D1
Vandels smash Poncet sculpture 5-6, 375C1
O'Keefe stolen paintings ordrd returned 7-27, 656F1
2 museums get Rockefeller art 2-9, 173E2
Pierpont library buys Mozart manuscript 7-16, 672G2
Tut exhibit benefits rptd 7-30, 672A2
Poncet sculpture rededicated 9-15, 892G2
'78-79 Broadway season rptd successful 11-4, 956D2
Richard Rodgers dies 12-30, 1008D3

Atomic Energy
Radium waste sites alleged 3-5, 187B2
Columbia U A-reactor start-up halted 4-6, 261C3
NRC studies site rules, Indian Pt danger cited 9-17, 743A2
A-protest draws 200,000 9-23, 742G1
Wall St protesters arrested 10-29, 827D2

Crime & Civil Disorders—*For A-protests, see 'Atomic Energy' above*
ILA's Scotto indicted 1-17, 87G2-C3
FBI ex-agent sentenced 1-17, 92B3
Punk rock star freed on bail, ODs 2-2, 156B3
Met museum sculpture stolen 2-9, recovered 2-14, 119D1
Lufthansa cargo terminal theft arrests 2-17, 2-20, 155B3
'Son of Sam' pre-arrest evidence rptd 2-26, 156F2
Waterfront indictmts continue 3-6, 220B2
Morales convicted 3-9, sentncd 4-20; escapes 5-21, 431E1
Holzer convicted of grand larceny 3-15, 239E2
Sindona, Bordoni indicted 3-19, 205C2
Dock indictmts mount 4-9, 292B1
Holzer sentenced 5-3, 431A3
Vandals smash Poncet sculpture 5-6, 375C1; sculpture rededicated 9-15, 892G2
NJ indicts 8 in Genovese 'family' 5-23, 508E1
Marshall decries pretrial detentn rule 5-27, 422D1
Pretrial detectn curbs backed by Sup Ct 5-14, 383F1
Delta jet hijacked to Cuba 6-11, 442B1
Galante slain 7-12, 548A1
Subway receipts rptd stolen 7-23, 656E1
O'Keefe stolen paintings ordrd returned 7-27, 656F1
Bankers Trust robbed of $2 mln 8-3, 2 suspects arrested 8-8, 8-9, 656C1
Sindona rptd kidnaped 8-6, 635A3
13 banks robbed, 2 suspects arrested 8-21–8-22; police protectn ordrd 8-22, 656A1
D Kennedy robbed 9-12, 859G3
Priest-penitent case declined by Sup Ct 10-1, 767F3
Prostitutn rpt reviewed 10-9, 'John Hour' debuts 10-23, 887E1
Author buzzes bldgs in airplane 10-11, 860F1
Sindona reappears, enters hosp 10-16, 793E2

1980

NEW York City
US bars Sovt consulate 1-8, 9B1
Nixon becomes resident 2-14, 199C3
'Cruising' opens, draws gay protests 2-15, 239F2
Idaho Asarco tax case remanded by Sup Ct 3-24, 265B2
Insurance Exchng opens 3-31, 265G3
Hispanic immigrant survey rptd 5-11—5-14, 396D2
Vanderbilt drops River House suit 6-12, 639G1
Pan Am sells bldg for record price 7-28, 985B3
Futures Exchange opens 8-7, 616D3
Mother Teresa visits S Bronx 8-7, 638F1
Mugabe visits Harlem 8-24, 674D2, B3
Black media gets NSC Africa memo 9-16, Admin calls forgery 9-17, 726E3-727B1
Korvettes clearance begins 9-26, closings set 10-9, 985C3

Arts & Culture
Titian forgery at Met Museum chrgd 2-26, 473C3
Poncet sculpture smashed again 3-24, 472D3
British Guiana stamp sold for record sum 4-5, 472D2
Gold coin set sold for record sum 4-10, 472F2
Record art auctns held 5-12—5-16, 471G3-472A2
Met Opera cancels season over musicians' strike 9-29, strike setld 10-25, 883E3
Homer oil sold for $1.7 mln 10-17, 997G3-998A1
Sills gives final performance 10-27, 908E2
Heaven's Gate withdrawn by UA 11-19, 906A1
'80 fashion roundup rptd 998D1

Crime & Civil Disorders
NY businesswoman, 2 partners indicted 1-10, 216B1
US Customs corruptn probed 1-11, 359A3
Sovt airline office bombed 1-13, 55A2
Studio 54 owners sentenced 1-18, 64B3
ILA's Scotto, Anastasio sentenced 1-22, 64G2
FBI 'Miporn' probe rptd 2-14, 136F1
Titian forgery at Met Museum chrgd 2-26, 473C3
Sam Goody, 2 offcls indicted 2-28, 237D3
8 Galante slaying probe figures indicted 3-3, 215C1
Ex-Rep Lowenstein slain 3-14, suspect chrgd 3-18, 214C2
'Insider' stock trading convictn voided by Sup Ct 3-18, 226B2
Poncet sculpture smashed again 3-24, 472D3
Fraunces Tavern '75 bombing suspect seized 4-4, 308G3
Transit strike violence cited 4-9, 268C2
Liberia students occupy consulate, UN missn 4-12, 284E3
Cuban UN missn protest 4-19, 300A3
Barnes convictn review refused by Sup Ct 4-21, 344G1
Waterfront racketeer convicted 5-2; 7 sentncd 5-20, 927E2
2 climb Statue of Liberty in protest 5-11, 667D1
Hispanic immigrant survey rptd 5-12, 396F3
Deliverers Union head convicted 5-15, 370E3; sentncd 6-26, 656D1
Jacobson flees jail 5-31, sentenced for murder 6-3; DeRosa indicted 6-4, 502A2
'Son of Sam' Soc Sec benefits rptd 6-5; insanity plea faked 8-4, 639E2
Koch egg assailant sentncd 6-6, 639G2
Studio 54 drug figure sentenced 6-12, 503F1-A2
Mafia boss indicted 6-30, 502E3
'70 Weatherman fugitive surrenders 7-8, plea bargain rptd 7-18, 576A3
Jacobson recaptured 7-9, 997D2
NYU prof convicted in drug case 7-16, 607F3-608A1

1976

Politics & Government
State primary date set 22A2
Jackson begins pres bid 1-6, 22A3
Murtagh dies 1-13, 56F3 ★
Sandler replaces Murtagh 1-16, 78G3
Glowa indicted 1-27, 144E3
Reagan at GOP dinner 2-11, 109F2
Norton on Cleaver Defns Fund 2-17, 272E1
FBI thefts of SWP rptd 3-17, 3-28, 3-29, 234A3, 569B2
Humphrey upstages candidates 4-1, 233C2
DeSapio pleads not guilty 5-24, 442B3
Beame endorses Carter 5-26, 390B3
Cunningham, law partner indicted 5-26, 6-7, 442E2
Nadjari jurisdictn limited 6-3; Cunningham, DeSapio other indictmts dismissed 8-12—12-22, 1016E1

1977

Finances
Rail svc aid budgeted 1-17, 33C1
Debt repaymt talks 2-8—3-9, payback plan OKd 3-10, 193A1-F2
Adams for more transit aid 2-25, 213D3
US aid pledged 3-1—3-11, loan released 3-11, 193G2-G3
Munic rehiring planned 5-16, 384C2
SEC rpt chrgs offcl decptn 8-26; Beame scores, other reactn 8-26—8-28, 665C2, D3
'84 Olympics bid lost 9-25, 828C3
MAC legality upheld 10-3, 760C3
Fscl '77 budget deficit data vary 10-4, 881A2
Moody's rates notes low; sale canceled, Beame scores 11-10; Goldin bars new sale 11-13, 881A1

Labor
Secondary strikes curbed 2-22, 149E3
Banks chrgd re job bias 2-23, 279G1
Schl cleaners strike ends 2-28, 153C3
US Sup Ct bars minority labor compensatn case review 2-28, 175D2
Unionists jam Stevens mtg 3-1, 153E3
Saccharin worker layoffs set 3-10, 177B1
Constructn union hiring rule voided 3-21, 279D2
Dock protest 4-14—4-18, 324D2
Jobless data rptd 5-16, 384B2, D2
Teachers union fined 7-20, 558D2
Teachers assigned by race 9-7, plan challenged 10-31, 837A3
ILA strikes containerships 10-1, 778C1
Fscl '77 budget deficit data vary 10-4, 881C2
Public note sale canceled 11-10, 881E1
ILA strike ends 11-29, 916C1

Obituaries
Mark, Julius 9-7, 788F1
Powell, Clilan 9-22, 788C2
Shor, Toots 1-22, 84F3

Politics & Government—*See also 'Crime' and 'Finances' above*
Axelson named to US post 1-18, 52D3; withdraws 3-9, 191B2
Abzug declines Carter post 2-19, 140B3
Carter visit urged 7-24, 573E1
Primary 9-8; Koch, Bellamy win Dem runoff for mayor, cncl pres 9-19, 723G1
Carter visits, tours S Bronx 10-4—10-5, 760G3
Koch, Bellamy elected 11-8, 855F1, D2

1978

Ala ex-sheriff, 18 others chrgd with fraud 10-27, 992A2
CIA mail-opening damages upheld 11-9, 940D1
Lufthansa cargo terminal robbed 12-11, 1028G2
Wells Fargo truck robbed in Staten I 12-19, 1028E2

Education
Queens schl bd suspended in ethnic data dispute 3-10, 264G1-A2
Student sex survey case review denied by US Sup Ct 3-20, 206C1
Teacher assignmt by race ends 4-7, 264C1
Schl system biggest in US 4-12, 264A1
Queens schl ordrd desegregatd 5-16, 369G1-C2
Schl inspectn for asbestos danger asked 12-21, 1009B2

Environment & Pollution
Blizzards hit 1-20, 2-5—2-7, 105G1
Atlantic sludge sites OKd 3-3, 164A1
Sun Day celebrated 5-3, 322A1
Air quality rated bad 7-5, 513C1
Air quality rpt corrected 7-19, 644B2

Finances
Key figures in fscl crisis listed 86A2-F3
Proxmire, Brooke rptd vs future fed aid 1-4, 87A1
Koch, Carey, other offcls see long-term fed aid need 1-9; Rohatyn warns '79 bankruptcy 1-11, 87F2
Carey budgets $350 mln in aid 1-17; Carey, Koch agree on new state aid 2-6, 87C2
Koch issues recovery plan 1-20, 87D1
GOP attacks Carter budget 1-31, 63C1
Koch meets Carter, gets aid assurances 2-2, 87B1
Sen Banking Com rpt issued; fed aid renewal, recovery plan opposed 2-9, 86E1-87A1
State, city offcls vs Sen com rpt 2-9, 87B1
US loan guarantee bill dvpts 2-14—7-27; Carter signs, details 8-8, 608C1-D3
Carter backs fed aid plan 3-2, 141A1
Carter urban-aid plan reactn 3-27, 218A1
S Bronx offered US aid 4-12, 285E1
Carter cautions re aid 4-25, 307F3
Carey signs control bd-MAC bill 6-2, 608D3
Labor coalitn, city agree on contract 6-5, 609A1
Fscl '79 budget OKd, 'windfall' funds found 6-28, 609C1
US seasonal loan progrm expires, repaymts cited 6-30, 609E1
Investors to lend $2.55 bln 7-27, 609A1

Labor
Key figures in fscl crisis listed 86D3
Fscl recovery plan issued 1-20, 87A2
Sen Banking Com rpt issued; fed aid renewal, recovery plan opposed 2-9, 86B2
Blumenthal proposes long-term loan guarantees 3-2, Carter signs bill 8-8, 608C1, G2
Nursing homes struck 4-4—4-7, 284F3-285A1
Teacher assignmt by race ends 4-7, 264C1
S Bronx offered US aid 4-12, 285G1
Carey signs control bd-MAC bill 6-2, 608E3
Labor coalitn, city agree on contract 6-5, 609A1
Munic legal immunity ended by US Sup Ct 6-6, 447D1-A2
Daily News struck 6-13—6-17, 625A2
Fscl '79 budget OKd, 'windfall' funds found 6-28, 609E1
Ostrer indicted 7-18, 599D1
Tonelli, 4 others indicted 7-19, 598E3
3 newspapers struck 8-9, 625E1
Newspr strike ends, impact rptd 11-6, 864E3-865A2

Obituaries
Leibowitz, Samuel 1-11, 96F2

Politics & Government—*See also other appropriate subheads in this section*
Green upsets Abzug in US House race, Garcia wins Badillo seat 2-14, 108F1
Primary results 9-12, 716B2
GOP tax-cut tour in Bklyn 9-20, 734F3
Diplomatic immunity revised 9-30, 750E3
Carter at Wall St rally 11-2, 862G1

1979

FALN bomb hoax in Dem, GOP hq 10-17, 786A2
Studio 54 drug indictmt 10-23, owners plead guilty to tax chrgs 11-2, 891G2
Cuban mission bombed 10-27, 852D1; 12-7, 947B3
Iranians protest shah 11-4, 843E1
ILA's Scotto convicted 11-15, 890A1
Queens mosque firebombed 11-24, 898B2
Soviet UN missn bombed 12-12, 965C3
Studio 54 drug figure pleads guilty 12-18, 1000E1

Energy—*See also 'Atomic' above*
Gas anti-price gouging drive starts 4-16, 301C2
Gas price violatns rptd 4-27, 324C3
Odd-even gas rationing begins 6-20, 462E2
Gas prices, statn closings rptd 6-23, 479D1
Tug strike impact cited 6-27, 500E3
Gasohol sales test set 8-10, 649G1

Finances
Moody's upgrades note rating 1-16, note sale successful 1-22, 55G3
Conv Cntr architect named 4-21, 375C2
Mayor, offcls get pay hikes 7-27, 580G1
'78 FRB funds cited 9-6, 840G3
Bond ratings listed 9-20, 920E3
Pope's visit cost estimated, fed aid sought 760G3, 761A2
Goldin, Koch doubt long-term borrowing 10-28, 11-8, 920C2
Fscl '79 finances rptd 11-1, GAO study issued 11-2, 920A2, E2

Labor & Employment
ILA's Scotto indicted 1-17, 87G2-C3
NYSE workers settle 2-21, 131C1
Waterfront indictmts continue 3-6, 220B2; 4-9, 292B1
Transit Auth ex-addict ban backed by US Sup Ct 3-21, 231B2
Union printing contract case refused by US Sup Ct 4-2, 281F2
ILGWU pact set 5-30, 402F1
Carter asks fed pay revisn 6-6, 419D2
88-day tug strike ends 6-27, 500D3
Carter cites job rise 9-25, 723G2
Police overtime for Castro visit rptd 10-11—10-14, 779A1
Sears sued by US re bias 10-22, 885D3
Long-term borrowing doubts linked 11-8, 920E2
ILA's Scotto convicted 11-15, 890A1

Medicine & Health
Breast-feeding survey rptd 1-5, 64C2
Abortn protest at St Patrick's 1-22, 63B3
2d opinion surgery plan evaluated 1-29, 140C1
Plastic surgeon loses malpractice suit 5-3, 392A3
Malpractice suit award cut 6-4, 527F2
Hosp closing plan cited 7-27, 580A3

Presidential Campaign
GOP conv bid lost 1-23, 70E3
Newspr Publshrs hear Carter 4-25, 294A2
Dems pick for '80 conv 6-28, 518D1
Carter at Queens town mtg 9-25, 723C2
Kennedy visits 9-27, 12-13, 962A1, G1
Reagan opens pres bid 11-13, 866G2
Brown visits 11-20, 962G2
Mondale opens campaign 11-28, 961C3
'50s CIA biological tests chrgd 12-3, 946A1
R Carter, Mondale campaign, heckled in Harlem 12-5, 918A3
Baker visits 12-20, 983G1

1980

Draft registratn protested 7-21, 597E3
Delta flight hijacked to Cuba 7-22, 617A3
Violinist found slain 7-24, 654A1
Fraunces Tavern bombing suspect convicted 7-30, 2d suspect rptd sentncd 8-4, 601D1, E1
Falcones indicted 7-31; Mafia, pizza indus ties probed 8-24, 714D1, A2
Iranian protesters arrested 7-27, freed 8-5, 586F1
Refugees hijack Eastn jets to Cuba 8-26, 9-8, 704G1-A2
Stagehand arrested in violinist slaying 8-30, indicted 9-7, 713B1
Hoffman surrenders 9-4, 713G1
Cuban UN attache assassinated in Queens 9-11, 685A2
Letelier murder convictns overturned 9-15, 703F3
Redgrave TV film protested 9-30, 835C3
Turkey office bombed 10-12, 794D1
Graivers win '76 jet plane damages 10-15, 826G3
'70 Weatherman bomber sentncd 10-28; '69 fugitive surrenders in Ill 12-3, 928A1, D1
NJ Sen Williams, 3 others indicted in Abscam probe 10-30, 824C3
NYU prof gets 5 yrs 11-13, 997D3
Lennon slain, ex-mental patient chrgd 12-8; reactn 12-9, 933D2-943F3
NY businesswoman, partner convicted 12-21, 997F2

Environment & Pollution
Environmental impact ct reviews limited by Sup Ct 1-7, 15B3
Air quality problem noted 2-19, 145E2
Earth Day celebrated 4-22, 307E3
NJ chem dump burns 4-22, 331B2
Reagan backs Westway projct 10-1, 738D1
Water shortage rptd, comm issues warning 12-1, 947B3, D3

Finances
Gold prices soar above $800 1-2—1-18, round-the-clock trading rptd 1-7, 30F1-E3
City worker contract talks open 1-31, 186D3
NYS offcl sees revenue surplus 2-19, 186B3
US completes 'up-front' loan guarantees 2-21, 186E3
2 financial futures mkts to merge 3-21, 224E1
Fscl '81 balanced budget OKd 6-16; Koch revises recovery plan 8-11, sees Miller on fed loan guarantees 9-10, 742G3-743F1
City worker pacts setld 6-19, 7-3, 518C1
Kennedy scores Reagan on bailout 8-12, 613F3
Pub bond sale moves rptd, Rohatyn opposed 9-10, 743F1
Reagan backs fed aid 9-27, 10-1, 738C1, E1
Carter reaffirms aid pledge 9-29, 739B1
Carter signs funds guarantee 10-1, Miller OKs release 10-2, 826B2
Carter chrgs Reagan 'flipflop' 10-27, 816B3

Labor & Employment
Sovt airline boycotted 1-14, 55C2; 1-18, 45E1
LIRR pres strike bd rpts; '79 agrmt cited 1-14, 53D1
City worker contract talks open 1-31, 186D3
DeLury dies 2-12, 175G3
Transit strike starts 4-1, impact rptd 4-1—4-10, unions fined 4-8, 267D3, 268B1-D2
Transit strike ends 4-11, 289C2
Waterfront racketeer convicted 5-2; 7 sentncd 5-20, 927E2
Deliverers Union head convicted 5-15, 370E3; sentncd 6-26, 656D1
City worker pacts setld 6-19, 7-3, 518A1
Svc Employees Union meets 6-25, 480B1
Transit strike fines hiked 7-2, 518E1
Hooks notes ghetto life 8-13, 611E3
PATH strike ends 9-1, 704D2-C3
Carter addresses ILGWU 9-29, 738G3
Reagan hits jobs issue 10-1, 738B1
Met Opera strike settled 10-25, 883E3

Medicine & Health
Influenza outbreak rptd 2-15, 158A3, C3
Jordan enters hosp 6-12, 442A2
Carter vows Medicaid funds 10-20, 803F1

Politics & Government—*See also other appropriate subheads in this section*
Aiello gets Carter post 1-3, 5G3
US Cong primary results 9-9, 682C2
Detroit census revisn ordrd, NYC suit cited 9-25, 741F2
Census revisn ordrd 12-23, Sup Ct overrules 12-30; '80 figures released, reapportmt seen 12-31, 982E3, G3

Presidential Election (& Transition)
GOP platform hearing set 1-14, 32A1
FALN raids Bush hq 3-15, 208B3-209A1
Koch on pres primary vote 3-25, 221A3
Kennedy addresses union 6-25, 480B1
Urban League hears candidates 8-3—8-6, 597A1
Reagan visits S Bronx 8-5, 597A3

1976

Gross slain 6-6, 442D3
Carter visits 6-23, 452E1
FBI burglaries rptd probed 6-24, 7-29, 569C2, G3
Nadjari dismissed 6-25, 1016D1
Troy pleads guilty 7-1, sentncd 9-29, quits com post 9-30, jailed 10-22, 860B2
Nixon disbarred in NYS 7-8, 493C3
Carter arrives 7-10, 509E1
Dem Natl Conv held 7-12—7-15, 505D1
Carter sees business, labor ldrs 7-22, 550C3, 551E1
Reagan, Schweiker in Bklyn 8-5, 564D2
FBI burglary probe dvpts 8-16—8-22, 633D2, 634A2-B3, 635C1
Connally at VFW conv 8-18, 601E2
Mondale campaigns 8-25, 8-26, 645G2
Carter campaign visit 8-31, 645G1, D2
O'Dwyer loses Sen primary 9-14, 687E2
Mondale campaigns 9-19, 704D3
Carter 'whistlestop' tour 9-20, 704F1, B3
Elliott named econ dvpt dep 10-5, 892G1
Mondale in Columbus Day parade 10-11, 763D3
Ford campaigns, backs US aid 10-12, 763F2
Carter campaigns 10-14, 10-19, 827E1; 10-27, 10-28, 803D2, A3
Ford, Carter at Al Smith fete 10-21, 785E1
Mondale campaigns 10-31—11-1, 827D2
Voters OK 'Las Vegas nites' 11-2, 821G2, 825D3
Carter thanks New York 11-7, 845E3
Christmas named Carter aide 11-23, 881C3
Thomas rejected US post 12-16, 937A2
Steingut indictmt voided 12-17, 972A1
Carter renews vows 12-28, 978C2

1977

Sports
Jets to remain at Shea 2-18, 163D3
Grand Prix Masters set 4-19, 430G3
Jets-Mets dispute settled 5-26, 491A2
NY Nets move to NJ set 7-26, 584C2
Loses '84 Olympics bid Carey blames Grant 9-25, 828G2
SST/Concorde Issues—*See under AVIATION*

1978

Sports
'84 Olympic pact OKd by LA 10-12, 842G3
WTT Apples fold 10-27, 1027A1
Transportation
NE rail offcls resign 1-30; more funds allocated 2-11, projct delays rptd 2-24, 225B1
Conrail safety efforts scored by GAO rpt 3-15, 224F3-225A1
UK air-fare dispute setld 3-17, 206C2, D2
S Bronx offered US aid 4-12, 285G1
LA gets 2-carrier London air svc 6-9, 570E1
US, Israel in air svc pact 7-15, 640C2
US, W Ger air svc pact 10-25, 831F1

1979

Sports
Rodgers win marathon 10-21, 911E3
School Issues
SAT coaching schl study issued 5-29, 785D2
Schl aid denial upheld by Sup Ct 11-28, 944A2
Transportation
$99 cross-country air fares, new routes OKd 1-12, 35E2
Aircraft near-collisn 2-11, FAA updates radar improvemt 3-12, 206G1, C2
Air flights cut back, fuel shortage blamed 2-13, 126D2
Amtrak fare hike set 2-20, 167D1
Iran Air cuts svc 2-25, 144E3
Transit Auth ex-addict ban backed by US Sup Ct 3-21, 231B2
Aircraft near-collisn rpt issued 4-9, 412C2
US-French air svc pact rptd 5-12, 465B3
United offers new LA fare 5-24, 402C2
Kennedy Intl on '78 world's busiest airport list 6-1, 421C1
DC-10s grounded, Laker svc halted 6-6, 421A1
Delta jet hijacked to Cuba 6-11, 442B1
Odd-even gas rationing begins 6-20, 462E2
88-day tug strike ends 6-27, 50003
Subway receipts rptd stolen 7-23, 656E1
Amtrak NYC-KC train ordrd cut 8-29, 868B1
Eastern-Natl merger rejected 9-27, 830B1
State bond issue OKd 11-6, 846G3

1980

Dem natl conv held 8-11—8-14, 609C1-615C1
Mondale campaigns with Koch, Carey 9-15, 780B2
Reagan campaigns 9-27, 10-1, 738A1, E1
Carter campaigns 9-29, 738G3
Jackson stumps with Carter 10-13, 778E3
Carter, Reagan at Al Smith fete 10-16, 803G1-A2
Carter visits 10-20, 803B1, F1
Carter chrgs Reagan 'flipflop' 10-27, 816B3
Reagan cites S Bronx in TV debate 10-28, 814G1
Carter in garment center 10-30, 841B1
Reagan visits 12-9, 956A2
Press & Broadcasting
TV statn license lifted 1-24, 119F2
Cue NY sale agrmt rptd 3-4, 239A2
Saudi film telecast 5-12, Nielsen rating rptd 5-13, 375E3
Redgrave TV film protested 9-30, 835C3
FCC backs WOR-TV move to NJ 11-6, 906E1
School Issues
Hispanic immigrant survey rptd 5-11—5-14, 396D2
Teachers' pact setld 6-19, 518C1
Parochial schl remedial aid case refused by Sup Ct 10-6, 782F2
Sports
Mets sold to Doubleday 1-24, 795G2
Ruiz '79 Marathon run invalidated 4-25, 527F2
ASL NY United moves to Shea, name chng cited 5-28, 771E1
Marathon results 10-26, 890E3
Transportation
LIRR pres strike bd rpts; '79 agrmt cited 1-14, 53D1
Teamsters boycott Sovt plane 1-14, 55C2; 1-18, 45E1
Pan Am revives discount coupons 3-10, 346E3
Transit strike starts 4-1, impact rptd 4-1—4-10, unions fined 4-8, 267D3-268D2
Transit strike ends 4-11, 289C2
Amtrak aid bill signed by Carter 5-30, 427G1
NYC transit strike fines hiked 7-2, 518E1
Delta flight hijacked to Cuba 7-22, 617A3
NY-Peking air svc set 9-17, 707B1
Reagan backs Westway projct 10-1, 738C1
Rockwell Intl subway damages awarded 12-24, 985A3
Welfare & Social Services
Hispanic immigrant survey rptd 5-12, 396F3
Carter vows fed aid 10-20, 803F1

1976

NEW York Cocoa Exchange
US comm warns 9-15, 990D2
NEW York Coffee & Sugar Exchange
US comm warns 9-15, 990D2
NEW York Cotton Exchange
US comm warns 9-15, 990D2
NEW York Daily News—*See DAILY News*
NEW Yorker (magazine)
Sullivan dies 2-19, 192G3
Louis Sissman dies 3-10, 316C1
Drew on pres debate panel 9-23, 700G3
NEW Yorker Hotel—*See HILTON Hotels Corp.*
NEW York Mercantile Exchange
Speculators default on potato futures 5-25; suit filed 5-27, 397C1, E3
Potato future default penalty set 8-31, ct delays setlmt 9-27, 990E1
US comm warns 9-15, 990D2
New potato futures contract OKd 11-2, trading halted 11-3, 990A1
NEW York and New Jersey, Port Authority of—*See PORT Authority, etc.*
NEW York Philharmonic Orchestra
Wins Grammy 2-28, 460D3
NEW York Post (newspaper)
Leonard Lyons dies 10-5, 970C2
Carter endorsement rptd 10-30, 831G2
Murdoch plans purchase 11-19, 887D2

1977

NEW York Clearing House
Job bias charged 2-23, 279G1
NEW York Cocoa Exchange
NY commodity cntr opens 7-5, 521A3
NEW York Coffee & Sugar Exchange
Saccharin ban affects trading 3-9, 177A2
NY commodity cntr opens 7-5, 521G2
Accused re price rules 10-17, 818G2
NEW York Cotton Exchange
Frozen orange juice futures up 1-21, 55B1; 1-31, 76C1
NY commodity cntr opens 7-5, 521G2
NEW Yorker, The (magazine)
Katherine White dies 7-20, 604G3
Arthur Russell Jr dies 12-4, 1024B3
Perry Barlow dies 12-26, 1023G3
NEW York Magazine Co. Inc.
Murdoch gains control 1-7, 48B3
New West—*See separate listing*
New York—*See separate listing*
Village Voice—*See separate listing*
NEW York Mercantile Exchange
NY commodity cntr opens 7-5, 521G2
NEW York Post (newspaper)
Murdoch takes control 12-30-76, names Bolwell editor 1-8, 48C3, G3
NEW York Racing Association (NYRA)—*See HORSE Racing*
NEW York Shipping Association, Inc.
Sup Ct bars longshoremen loading case review 1-10, 57G1
NEW York Shipping Association Inc. v. NLRB
Sup Ct refuses review 1-10, 57G1

1978

NEW York City Ballet
Baryshnikov joins 4-26, 335F3
NEW York Daily News—*See DAILY News*
NEW Yorker, The (magazine)
White wins Pulitzer citatn 4-17, 315B1
Janet Flanner dies 11-7, 972A3
NEW York Life Insurance Co.
Stevens union sets bd bid 9-11; Brown, Finley quit directorships 9-12, 699C2
NEW York Magazine Co., The
New York—*See separate listing*
Village Voice—*See separate listing*
NEW York Post (newspaper)
Strike halts publication 8-9, 625G1
Resumes publicatn 10-5; Times, News strike ends 11-6; impact rptd 864E3-865A2

1979

NEW York City Ballet
Baryshnikov named Amer Ballet dir 6-20, 527E3
NEW York City Transit Authority v. Beazer
Ex-addict ban backed by Sup Ct 3-21, 231D2
NEW York Coffee & Sugar Exchange
El Salvador coffee price squeeze chrgd 3-13, 348B2
NEW York Daily News—*See DAILY News*
NEW Yorker, The (magazine)
Audax Minor dies 10-8, 860D3
S J Perelman dies 10-17, 860C3
Richard Rovere dies 11-23, 932D3
NEW York Hospital-Cornell Medical Center
Shah admitted 10-22, Iranians stage protest 11-4, 843C1, E1
Shah's medical treatmt completed 11-29, 897E1
Shah discharged 12-2, 914A1
NEW York Life Insurance Co.
2d-opinion surgery coverage set 3-19, 218E3
NEW York Mercantile Exchange (NYME)
Maine potato futures trading halted 3-9, CFTC probes 5-9, 348D1
Platinum price soars 10-2—10-3, 740E1
NEW York Post (newspaper)
Bilingual educ oppositn rptd 1-29, 127C2
Morales phone tip rptd 5-25, 431B2
Daily circulatn listed 6-6, 431C1
Connally Mideast peace plan printed 10-12, 783C2

1980

NEW York City Opera
Sills gives final performance 10-27, 908F2
NEW York Clearinghouse Association
FRB backs free-trade zones 11-19, 958E1
NEW York Coffee, Sugar & Cocoa Exchange
Sugar futures soar, world stock fall seen 2-8, 182D1
Sugar price hits 5 1/2-yr high 10-9, 777A2
Prices drop on higher US interest rates 12-10, 932B2
NEW Yorker, The (magazine)
St Clair McKelway dies 1-10, 104C3
Wins Polk award 2-25, 692G3
Kenneth Tynan dies 7-26, 608E3
Whitworth named Atlantic Monthly ed 9-22, 908G2
NEW York Institute of Technology (Old Westbury)
Loses NCAA Div II basketball title 3-15, 240C3
NEW York Insurance Exchange (NYIE)
Opens for business 3-31, 265G3
NEW York Post (newspaper)
Reagan pres endorsemt rptd 11-1, 841G3

1976

NEW York State—*See also NEW York City*
Anti-boycott law signed 1-1, impact studies rptd 10-12, 987B2
'74 LI kidnap convictn cited 124F1
Glowa indicted 1-27, 144E3
Hollander admits Medicaid fraud 2-2; sentncd 5-18, 384C3
A-engineer quits Indian Pt projct, urges closing 2-9, 115E1
GE Ft Edward, Hudson Falls plants scored re PCBs 2-9, Hudson R fishing curbed 2-25, 171E3
Yonkers in default 2-14, rescued 2-17, 994B2
'74 trust case vs 3 oil cos dismissed 3-10, case vs 7 rptd pending 3-11, 413B1
Buffalo rescued 3-12, 994B2
Sovt amb in Glen Cove car crash 3-15, 260A1
Sup Ct bars stay on Medicaid-for-abortns order 4-26, 359D2
Rockville Centre bishop named 5-4, 424C1
US Concorde decisn upheld 5-19, 378G2
Ct curbs plutonium use 5-26, 398A2

1977

NEW York State—*See also NEW York City*
US Sup Ct rules '68 stock transfer tax amendmts illegal 1-12, 57C2
US Sup Ct bars review of New Castle fed grants 1-17, 58C1
Buffalo challenges Canada TV ad deletns 1-17, policy halted 1-21, 61A1
Syracuse schl integratn plan voted 1-25, 112A3
Hudson R oil spill 2-4, 214G2
US-Canada bridge pact signed 2-5, 133B1
Indian land claims rptd 2-7, 197D1
Fed spending inequities chrgd 4-6, 423D3
Moon '75 property tax ruling cited 4-14, 310F1
Buffalo populatn ranking drops 4-14, 388D1
Mail-order mins tax status challenged 4-15, 310B2
'76 blue laws ruling cited 4-21, 388A2
GM engine exchng suit settld 4-25, 326A1
Port Auth mass transit aid curbed 4-27, 382G3

1978

NEW York State—*See also NEW York City*
Offshore drilling challenge refused 2-21, 125F2
Unificatn Church seminary charter denied; '77 solicitatns bar, deportatns cited 2-22, 295G2
Conrail safety efforts scored by GAO rpt 3-15, 224F3-225A1
Buffalo TV statn ordrd dropped by Canada 3-28, 226A2 ★
Honkong Bank to buy Marine Midland 4-5, 263E1-A2
Calif jurisdictn in child-support case denied by US Sup Ct 5-15, 387F3
Alien MD ruling declined by US Sup Ct 5-15, 388A1
Yugo dissident in Garden City 6-6, 504G2
Welfare eligibility case refused by Sup Ct 6-12, 468C1
Con Ed blamed in '77 blackout 7-6, 529F3
'75 abortns rptd 8-10, 744C1
Gannett to sell Rochester TV statn 8-20, 759F3
A-plant delays threaten elec supply 9-11, 702C1

1979

NEW York State—*See also NEW York City*
Buffalo laetrile death rptd 2-1, 138G3
Ford stockholders suit barred 3-8, 202A3
Alimony rule in child custody case backed by US Sup Ct 3-19, 203F2
Rochester museum to get Steichen works 3-24, 375D2
Beauty contest losers to be reimbursed 3-27, 308E3
Amer Assemb meets in Harriman 4-2, 282G2
Frampton 'live-in-partner' suit dismissed 4-17, 289E1
Woolworth takeover stayed 4-20, 304C2; 5-25, bid dropped 5-29, 440C2
Unwed father adoptn consent role backed by US Sup Ct 4-24, 364B1
'78 wiretaps rptd 4-28, 386F3
Sunset Bay derailmt 5-4, 472F3
Medicaid, welfare cuts set 6-19, 561G1
AMA chrgd in chiropractors suit 7-5, 570F2
'78 per capita income rptd 9-16, 746G1, C2

1980

NEW York State
State ct jurisdictn narrowed by Sup Ct 1-21, 93A2
'79 forgn mfg investmt rptd 2-6, 92C3
Civil rights suit filing limit upheld by US Sup Ct 5-19, 440F2
Amer Airlines held immune in DC-10 crash 5-23, 518G3
Ormandy gives final concert at Saratoga Springs 8-23, 908D1
Harrison hotel fire kills 26 12-4, 948G1

1976

7 oil cos, trade assn indicted 6-1, 412F3
Rev Moon property assessed 6-2, 971E1
Nassau, Suffolk Cnty beaches declared disaster area 6-23, Jones Beach stays closed 6-24, 454F2
Schiess sues central NY bishop 7-8, 755E3
Hurricane hits East Coast 8-8—8-11, 595G1
Atlantic offshore lease sale challenged 8-13—8-17, bids accepted 8-25, 648G2-A3
FRB bars Bankers Trust acquisitn 8-19, 667G1
Attica prison strike 8-23—8-28, 656E1
US Sen com rpts Medicaid fraud 8-30, 715B1, F2
Yonkers Raceway sees losses 9-1, 680E3
Medicaid lease fee-splitting barred 9-5, 715B3
GE signs PCB pact 9-8, 691F2-B3
Fiscal '75 per capita income, tax burden rptd 9-15, 10-12, 959D1, B2
Canada ends TV ads tax deductns 9-22, 771D3
Ali decisns Norton 9-28, Athletic Comm rejcts appeal 9-29, 756C2
China A-test fallout rptd 10-5, 790G3
Richardson vows boycott info 10-20, 786G2
Fiscal '76 bankruptcies rptd 10-20, 984C3
Gene research hearing held 10-21, 860E3
H Rap Brown wins parole 10-21, 912C3
US Sup Ct voids Vt tax collectn stay 11-9, 882A3
US Sup Ct bars Concorde landing review 11-15, 882B2
Pocantico site dedicated 11-21, 887G2
Former Attica inmates pardoned 12-30, 995C2

1977

'76 per-capita income table 5-10, 387D2
Mohawk Indians get Clinton Cnty land award 5-13, 632D2
Buffalo econ data table 5-16, 384D2
Gulf uranium cartel probe rptd 6-9, 479B3
Foster care rule voided 6-13, 517D2
Blackout hits Westchester, probes ordrd 7-13—7-14, 537C2
Bethlehem Steel closes Lackawanna plant 8-18, 775D3; 3d ¼ record loss posted 10-26, 836F2
Offshore lease sale OKd by ct 8-25, 650B1
'76 per capita income, tax burden table 9-13, 10-18, 821B2, G2, G3
LI ocean dumping upheld 9-19, 723G3
Hudson R found toxic 9-28, 762A2
MAC legality upheld 10-3, 760C3
Indian Pt A-plant found safe 10-12, 838F2
Buffalo loses Canada TV ad deletn challenge 11-30, 946A2
Pvt schl aid law voided 12-6, 938A3

Crime

Hastings sentenced 1-31, 103D1
'70-76 Westchester pol indictmts rptd 2-10, 162E3
New Rochelle man kills 5, self 2-14, 162E2
Connie Francis suit setld 2-23, 140F3
Liquor authority suspends Foremost 3-7, 215E1
Croat hijacker sentncd 5-12, 451B3
Forced waiver of immunity voided 6-13, 517B2
Political penalty voided 6-13, 517B2
Croats face criminal chrgs 6-16, 497E2
Son of Sam sought 6-26, 532C1; for subsequent developments, see BERKOWITZ, David R.
Holzer indicted 7-12, 10-13, 848F1
5 indep oil cos convicted 8-30, 691A3; fined 9-16, 918F2
Farley cleared by ABC rpt 9-3, 828A2
Crimmins paroled 9-7, 848D1
5 indep oil cos fined 9-16, 918F2
Schenley rebates chrgd 10-6, 860E1
Death penalty provisn voided 11-15, 919B3
Players' agent sentenced 11-28, 1021A2
Vet indicted in horse-switch scandal 12-2, 971A1
Pot law detailed 12-11, 972D3

Fuel-Weather Crisis

FPC OKs emergency gas purchase 1-19, 53G3
Airline diversns re goods shortages OKd 1-19, 54F1
Gas emergency declared 1-19, 54A2
Layoffs rptd 1-22, 54C2; 1-30, 75F3
Blizzard hits Buffalo, Natl Guard called in 1-27; 6 found dead 1-29, 75G2
Full state of emergency declared 1-27, 75B3
Watertown snowfall, dairy losses rptd 1-27—2-1, 76D1
US offers emergency job funds 2-1, 75G3
Buffalo, 9 counties get disaster aid 2-5, 91A2
Layoff total rptd 2-7, 91F2, G2

Labor—*See also 'Fuel-Weather Crisis' above*

Sup Ct upholds pub works jobs rule 1-10, 57E1
Jobless aid for strikers upset 5-24, 463A1; US Sup Ct bars review 6-6, 478G3
NY Bell job loss seen 8-7, 629F2
Bethlehem Steel layoffs rptd 8-18, 9-30, 775D3
US sues re police job bias 9-8, 819B2
Bond issue rejected 11-8, 879G1
Jobless aid for strikers upheld 11-9, 899A2

1978

Firestone suits rptd 9-22, 835F1
Citibank, Chase hike mortgage rates, usury ceiling cited 11-6, 11-9, 919D1, F1
Indian Pt A-plant rating rptd 11-25, 940D3
Redlining study finds race bias 12-7, 942E2-A3
Mortgage rate lid raised, redlining barred 12-8, 962F1
Illegitimate child inheritance law upheld by US Sup Ct 12-11, 981B1

Crime

11 Amex optns traders indicted, move scores 1-5, 4F3-5A1
Bergman sentenced 2-2, 232F3
Carey orders Little extraditn 2-23, appeals ct backs 5-9; Marshall delays 5-30, Sup Ct declines appeal 6-5, 431G1-B2
Death penalty bill clears legislature 3-20; Carey vetoes 4-11, override fails 5-2, 388G2-B3, D3
Testimony thru illegal search backed by US Sup Ct 3-21, 220G3
Chem co indicted 3-23, 243E1
Provenzano convicted for kickbacks 3-25, 232C2
NYC policemen slain, Carey '76 Attica pardon scored 4-5, 388C3
Rep Richmond pleads not guilty to sex chrg 4-6, 265F1-B2; renominated 9-12, 716B2
Abrahams sentenced on probatn violatn 4-20, 283C1
Prison 'strip-frisk' searches ordrd ended 4-22, 440A2
'77 blackout rpt issued 4-23, 396F1
'Son of Sam' pleads guilty 5-8, sentenced 6-13, 500F2
'77 prison populatn rptd up 6-3, 440C1
Little extradicted to NC 6-9, 560E3
Provenzano convicted of murder 6-14, sentncd 6-21, 480B2
NJ curare case-press freedom controversy 6-30—8-28, jailed NY Times rptr freed 8-30, 678F2
Death penalty case refused by US Sup Ct 7-3, 552A2
Provenzano sentncd for kickbacks 7-11, 560E2
W Ger terrorist jailed in Albany 7-16, 577B1
Port Chester '74 disco fire convictn 9-7, 824F2
Croatian killed 9-29, 933E3
Death penalty restoratn appeal declined by US Sup Ct 10-16, 789C2
Vet sentncd in '77 horse switch 11-3, 1028F1
Richmond wins reelectn 11-7, 846E2
Greece Holiday Inn arson 11-26, 971B3
Serbs indicted in Tito murder plot 12-1, 933D3

Environment & Pollution

LI Sound oil, gas spills rptd 1-10, 3-16, 524F1, A2
LI '77 open-space effort rptd 85C2
2d in US defense contracts 2-21, 127D2
Snowpack rptd above normal 3-5, 207C2
Niagara chem dump perils warned 8-2; US declares disaster area, state cleanup aid vowed 8-7, 703A1
Niagara chem dump cleanup costs cited 11-21, 899G2

Finance—*For New York City fiscal crisis, see NEW York City—Finances*

'67, '77 sales-tax rates rptd 1-5, 15E3
State tax revenue data 1-9, 84D2, F3
Carey submits $11.9 bln budget 1-17, 87D2
Carter urban-aid plan reactn 3-27, 3-28 218B1, C1
Income tax relief rptd 5-25, 425D1
Property tax ruled illegal 6-23, 526F1
Property-tax-limit case refused by US Sup Ct 10-30, 832B3

Labor

Sup Ct backs state police alien ban 3-22, 221A1
Buffalo Anaconda strike setld 4-3, 284E3
Coal strike utility billing probe set 5-10, 367A1
Rochester police hiring challenge case declined by US Sup Ct 5-22, 388B2
Extended jobless aid rptd 7-10, 552B3; 8-4, 607D3
Provenzano sentncd for kickbacks 7-11, 560E2
Utica, Elmont Teamster funds scored 8-14, 625E1

1979

Westchester Viet vet study released 9-25, 725A2
Ft Dix (NJ) to stay open 10-10, 809E1
Buffalo '79 living costs ranked 12-28, 991A1

Atomic Energy

James A Fitzpatrick (Scriba) A-plant ordrd shut 3-13, 186F1
R E Ginna (Ontario) A-plant community studied 3-17, 207E3
Central Hudson shareholders defeat A-power delay 4-3, 322F3
Greene City (Cementon) A-plant cancelled 4-5, 261B3
A-protest rptd 4-28—4-29, 322F3
R E Ginna, Indian Pt (Buchanan) A-plant pipe leaks rptd 5-2, 322B3
Shoreham (Brookhaven) protesters arrested 6-3, 416A2
Indian Pt protesters arrested 8-5, 743A1
Energy plan rules out new A-plants 8-7, 609G3
NRC studies site rules, Indian Pt danger noted 9-17, 743A2
Indian Pt plant shutdown urged 9-17, 743B2
'50s fallout, SAT decline linked 9-17, 747C2
West Valley waste storage protested 9-29, 742E3
New Haven reactors rejected 10-12, 807B1
Indian Pt plant security said lax 10-16, 10-20, 807E1
Indian Pt FALN bomb threat rptd 10-18, 786E2
Indian Pt shutdown possible 11-5, 849D1

Crime & Civil Disorders

Drug law challenge declined by US Sup Ct 1-8, 14C3
Graiver ruled dead, bank chrgs dismissed 1-8, 161B1
Attica riot prisoner paroled 2-21, 156E1
'Son of Sam' pre-arrest evidence rptd 2-26, 156F2
Podell, Brasco disbarmt challenges declined by Sup Ct 4-16, 303C1, 416A2
Attica inmate slain in racial brawl 6-3, 548F2
Gun-in-car law upheld by Sup Ct 6-4, 438C3
'Probable cause' in detentns backed by Sup Ct 6-5, 464C2
Provenzano, Konigsberg '78 murder convictns upset 6-7, 491G3
'Open-ended' warrants use curbed by Sup Ct 6-11, 478B3
'78 inmate totals rptd 6-21, 548C2
Ctroom pub access curbed by Sup Ct; reactn 7-2, 515B2, C3
Cocaine trade growth rptd 9-5, 972G2
Trial closure case declined by Sup Ct 11-5, 884E3
Scotto convicted 11-15, 890B2
Conrad pleads guilty to tax evasn 12-18, 1000F1

Energy—*See also 'Atomic' above*

Cementon coal plant planned 4-5, 261B3
'78 per capita gas use rptd 5-27, 395G2
Winter heating fuel supply promised 8-28, 703B2
Odd-even gas rules lifted 9-6, 683F1
Odd-even gas rationing begins 6-20, 462E2
July gas supply use rptd 6-23, 479G1
Canada James Bay hydro projct starts, elec sales cited 10-27, 833F3
Westchester rejcts Con Ed takeover 11-6, 846F3
Utility ad ban, policy statemt cases accepted by Sup Ct 11-26, 919A3

Environment & Pollution—*See also 'Atomic' above*

Bird deaths near Newburgh laid to fertilizer 3-18, 206F3
Niagara chem dump hearings 4-10, 4-11, 281B3
Carter cites Niagara chem dump 6-13, 441F1
Niagara chem dump probe rptd 6-18, 597A2
Olin convicted for Niagara mercury dumping 8-16, 704E1
Hooker chrgd in LI dumping 8-31, 665G3
Army '50 grain blight tests rptd 10-7, 771B1
Olin fined for Niagara dumping 12-10, 947A1
US sues Occidental, Olin re Niagara chem dumps 12-20, 990F1

Finances—*For New York City fiscal crisis, see NEW York City—Finances*

Carey asks $225 mln tax cut 1-3, 13G2
Fscl '78 tax revenue rptd 2-13, 152B2
Lake Placid Olympic costs soar 6-17, 798B2
Housing bond price drops 10-11, 765C1

Labor & Employment

Jobless pay for strikers upheld by Sup Ct 3-21, 231D1
Alien teacher ban backed by US Sup Ct 4-17, 325E3
Sup Ct pretrial press curb rule leaked 5-18, 382A3
Provenzano, Konigsberg '78 murder convictns upset 6-7, 491G3
Rochester GM plant struck 8-23—8-27, 698E2
Lawyer survey rptd 9-17, 787E1
Scotto convicted 11-15, 890B2

1980

Atomic Energy & Safeguards

Carter outlines A-waste storage plan, West Valley site studied 2-12, 128B1
Demonstratns mark 3 Mile I anniv 3-28—3-31, 249B1
Shoreham A-plant protest 9-29, 961C3
West Valley A-waste storage clean-up enacted 10-1, 739D1
Con Ed Indian Pt 2 leak controversy 10-17—10-23; judge backs rate surchrg 12-1, NRC staff seeks fine 12-11, 961C2
2d leak at Indian Pt 2 A-plant 11-3, 961B3

Crime & Civil Disorders

Attica prison violence, overcrowding rptd 1-31, 2-1, 112D3
Abscam probe revealed, Murphy, others linked 2-2, 2-3, 81C1
O'Connell dies 2-27, 176G2
'Scarsdale Diet' MD slain 3-10, suspect chrgd 3-11, 214E3
Warrantless home arrests curbed by Sup Ct 4-15, 305G3
Rape shield law case dismissed by US Sup Ct 5-19, 440C2
Gun control bill signed 6-13, 470G2-C3
Murphy indicted in Abscam probe 6-18, 454F1-E2
Falcones indicted 7-31; Mafia, pizza indus ties probed 8-24, 714D1, A2
Abscam judge quits Murphy case 8-7, 599E3
Hoffman surrenders 9-4, 713A2
Buffalo area black slayings, other racial incidents prompt probe 10-13, 997C1
Police interrogatn chase case declined by Sup Ct 12-1, 918F2
Murphy convicted in Abscam case 12-3, 919D1

Energy—*See also 'Atomic Energy' above*

2d 1/4 gas use target set 3-20, 250G3
Utilities' free speech upheld by Sup Ct 6-20, 555F1-C2
Ct blocks ND synfuels projct 12-8, 962C1

Environment & Pollution

US budget proposes waste clean-up fund 1-28, 73A3
Occidental, Hooker sued re Love Canal dumping 4-28, 331C3
Love Canal dump health defects rptd 5-16; homeowners demand evacuatn 5-19, US OKs, Carey reacts 5-21, 386D3-387E1
Hoffman fugitive yrs recapped 9-4, 713A2
GE OKs Hudson R dump site cleanup 9-24, 825E2
Love Canal relocatn aid enacted 10-1, 739E1
Water shortage rptd, comm issues warning 12-1, 947B3, D3
US toxic waste clean-up bill signed 12-11, 935E3, 936C1

Finances

Fscl '79 tax revenue rptd 2-20, 307B3
NOW bank accounts OKd nationwide 3-31, 246A1
Chase drops mortgage rate to 12% 7-15, 575B1
FRB backs free-trade banking zones 11-19, 958A2

Labor & Employment

LIRR pres strike bd rpts; '79 agrmt cited 1-14, 53D1
LIRR struck 4-1, 267E3-268B1
LIRR setlmt reached 4-11, 289C3
Pub works jobs resident preference case declined by Sup Ct 4-21, 344B2
Longshoreman fatality damages ruling affirmed by Sup Ct 5-12, 426D3
Rochester teachers strike 9-3, 723C3
Carter sees civil svc workers 10-1, 739F1
Stevens, textile union come to terms 10-19, 805B2
Zimco special labor aid OKd 11-5, 870C2

1976

Politics
Primary date set 22A2
US Sup Ct voids campaign rules 1-12, 23D2
Murtagh dies 1-13, 56F3 ★
Sandler replaces Murtagh 1-16, 78G3—79A1
Rep Hastings quits 1-20, 68D3
Thaler dies 2-5, 124F3
Dem wins Hastings' seat 3-2, 166D2
Bayh quits pres race 3-4, 165D2
Primary results 4-6, 244E2
Blumenthal case dismissed 4-13, 271B1
Ford gets 119 delegates 5-24, 374C1
DeSapio pleads not guilty 5-24, 442B3
Cunningham, law partner indicted 5-26, 6-7, 442E2
Nadjari jurisdictn limited 6-3; Cunningham, DeSapio other indictmts dismissed 8-12—12-22, 1016E1
Carter, Brown see delegates 6-14, 432C1, G1
Nadjari dismissed 6-25, 1016D1
Dems broaden delegate slate 6-28, 490B1
Ct disbars Nixon 7-8, 493B3
Dem conv women delegates, table 508D2
Dem conv pres vote, table 7-14, 507D2
Ford claims delegate gains 7-20, 531E3
Ford meets delegates 7-22, 549E3
Reagan, Schweiker visit 8-5, 564C2
Ford, Reagan claim delegate gains 8-7, 8-10, 583A2, E2
GOP pre-conv delegate count 8-14, 583D3
GOP conv scuffle on 16-C 8-17, 600G1
GOP conv pres, vp vote tables 8-18—8-19, 8-19, 599D1, E1, D3
Reagan, Ford seek conv delegates 8-18, 601C3
Reagan scores oppositn 8-19, 615F2
US Sen primary results 9-14, 687C2
Dole, Rockefeller campaign 9-16, 687B1
Mondale in Binghamton 9-20, 704B1
Carter in Buffalo 9-30, 742D3
Mondale in Buffalo 10-10, 763B3
Ford campaigns in suburbs, Yonkers 10-13, 763G2, A3
Carter in Rochester 10-14, 785C2
Carter in Syracuse 10-14, 827E1
Mondale in Albany 10-26, 804B1
Carter in Hempstead 10-28, 803A3
Ford campaigns 10-31, 826C3
Mondale in Buffalo 11-1, 827E2
Election results 11-2: pres 817D1, 818C1, E1, 819A2; cong 813C3, 817E2, 819F3, 828D2, 830F1-D2; state 821G2, 825D3
Steingut indictmt voided 11-15, 972A1
Carter primary spending, contributns rptd 11-17, 938E2-A3
Alex Rose dies 12-28, 1015E2

NEW York Stock Exchange (NYSE)
Dow climbs, hits 1,000 1-2—3-11, 184C2
Sup Ct upholds svc chrg rule 1-12, 24C1
Haack named Lockheed chrmn 2-13, 131E1
Composite index drops from peak 3-11, 185C1
Dow climbs, stalls 3-11—5-28, 413G1-E2
SEC rpts on '75 broker fees, profits 4-2, 348F1
Needham to quit, SEC reforms cited 4-27, 347E3-348F1
Dow climbs to near-high, retreats 6-1—11-10, 846G2

NEW York Times, The (newspaper)
'75 Ecuador drugs article cited 1-13, 28G2
Ignores Carson trial gag order 1-13, 124A2
Nixon wiretap depositn publshd 1-18, 184B1
Rpts Cambodia populatn shift 1-19, 46D2
Rpts unreleased House com findings 1-20—1-28, 92D1-93B3
USSR plans distributn 1-21, 76G2
Best seller list 1-25, 80B3; 2-29, 208E3
Publishes Moynihan cablegram 1-28, 67F2
Rpts N Viet memo on US aid 2-2, 103A2
Harris article on Hearst publshd 2-22, 201C3

1977

Medicine & Health
Drug prescriptn ruling voided 2-22, 150F1
Laetrile rptd OKd by ct 4-17, 376E1
HEW sets Medicaid cut 6-8, 460D3
Contraceptive curbs voided 6-9, 501G1
Abortn ruling vacated 6-27, 538G3
HMOs hailed for cost control 8-5, 643E2
Free abortions continued 10-12, 787A1

Obituaries
King, Carleton 11-19, 952G2
Powell, Clilan 9-22, 788C2
Saypol, Irving 6-30, 532F3
Taylor, Dean 10-16, 872A3

Politics & Government
Legislature schedule rptd 6E2
Rochester v mayor named Carter aide 1-14, 35F2
US Sup Ct backs racial voter redistricting 3-1, 174D3-175D1
Fed role in civil actions curbed 3-22, 231D2, A3
Forced waiver of immunity voided 6-13, 517B2
Buffalo, Albany mayoral results 11-8, 855C3
2 bond issues rejected 11-8, 879F1

Sports
Farley quits Athletic Comm 6-3, ABC rpt clears 9-3, 828A2
NBA aids Nets 6-15, 583E3, 584C1
Nets move to NJ set 7-26, 584F1
House subcom probes TV coverage 11-2, 950A1
Players' agent sentenced 11-18, 1021A2
Vet indicted in horse-switch scandal 12-2, 971A1

SST/Concorde Issues—*See under AVIATION*

NEW York Stock Exchange (NYSE)
'68 stock transfer tax amendmts ruled illegal 1-12, 57D2
Sen subcom rpt scores accountants 1-17, 79A1
Quebec asbestos stocks fall 1-26, 82D1
Kreps rpts net worth 2-25, 148B1
Saccharin ban trading 3-9, 177A2
Amex merger talks fail, optns plan blamed 5-19; Amex asks SEC probe 6-13, 520F3-521C2
Negotiated fees impact rptd 6-6, 521D2
Closed during blackout 7-14, 537A3
Babcock shares close up, McDermott down 8-25, 667A2
Trading value, vol, profits rptd down 8-29; Dow ends decline 9-2, 691D1
Gerber stock falls 9-19, 799F2
Donaldson Lufkin buys Pershing, Wood Struthers 10-11, 800B1
SEC bars optns trading 10-18, 859C3
'72-77 consolidatns rptd 10-19, 799E3
SEC off-bd trading curbs to remin; natl mkt delay scored, ITS cited 12-1, 1004C1
Seat price hits record low 12-12, 1004F1

Dow Jones Industrial Average—*See under STOCKS*

NEW York Stock Exchange et al v. New York State Tax Commission
NYS '68 tax amendmts ruled illegal 1-12, 57C2

NEW York Telephone Co.—*See AMERICAN Telephone & Telegraph Co.*

NEW York Theaters & Producers, League of
Tony awards 6-5, 452G1

NEW York Times, The (newspaper)
Shanahan named to HEW post 1-19, 53B1
USSR renews attack on Wren 2-2, 101D1
Best-seller list 2-6, 120E3; 2-20, 118E3; 4-3, 264F1; 5-1, 356B2; 6-4, 452G1; 7-3, 548C3; 8-14, 643F1; 9-4, 712C3; 10-2, 808C3; 11-6, 872C3; 12-4, 1021F2
Czechs detain Hofmann 2-12—2-13, 114G2
Hofmann disputes Czechs 2-17; papers returned 3-1, 3-16, 220F3
Jick phone interview rptd 2-28, 224G2
Nigeria ousts Darnton 3-12, 258E1
William Laurence dies 3-19, 264B3
Coll costs survey released 3-27, 483D1

1978

UAW asks stay on United Tech bid for Carrier 10-30, stay lifted 11-10, 896E2
UAL maternity leave case refused by US Sup Ct 11-27, 937A2

Politics & Government
Legislature schedule rptd 14F3
Green upsets Abzug in US House race, Garcia wins Badillo seat 2-14, 108F1
Richmond pleads not guilty to sex chrg 4-6, 265F1-B2; renominated 9-12, 716B2
Dems bar pres 'loophole primary' 6-9, 448A3
Primary results 9-12, 716G1
Carter at Buffalo rally 10-28, 831C2
Richmond wins reelectn 11-7, 846E2
Electn results 11-7: cong 846E2-A3, 848F2, 849F1-B2, 851C3; state 845B2, 847C1, 849D1, 853D3, 897D3

Sports
AHL ban on 1-eyed player lifted 2-2, 296F3

NEW York Stock Exchange (NYSE)
'77 composite index loss cited 1-1, 66G3
Amex optns traders indicted 1-5, 5A1
Kennecott price closes up 4-5, 402C3
Record-breaking rally 4-13—4-26, 303A1-E2
Amax trading probe set 9-11, 700E2
Dow drops, margin calls rise 10-16—10-31, rebounds on $ aid 11-1—11-3, 825B1, 826D1-827A1
Top-priced Superior Oil, IBM stocks close up 12-19, 1004A1
Record '78 volume rptd 12-29, 1004C2
CBOE '78 volume, seat price compared 12-29, 1004C3

Dow Jones Industrial Average—*See under STOCKS*

NEW York Stock Exchange v. Heimann
Bank stock sale case refused by Sup Ct 3-27, 241E2

NEW York Theaters & Producers, League of
Tony Awards 6-4, 579E2

NEW York Times, The (newspaper)
Speer interviewed 1-3, 4A3
Best-seller list 1-8, 24C3; 2-5, 116A3; 3-5, 195C3; 4-2, 272A3; 4-30, 356F1; 6-4, 460A3; 7-2, 579B3; 8-6, 620G1
Panama Canal poll cited 1-19, 58D2
Film industry probes rptd 2-4, 2-13, Valenti denies 3-2, 251D2
Haldeman book syndicatn upset by Post scoop 2-16, 2-17, 124C2
Equatorial Guinea envoy interviewed 2-16, 152B3
Borland dies 2-22, 196C2
Pl electn coverage protested 4-11, 269C1
Carter poll standings down on econ issues 4-12, 260A3

1979

Politics & Government—*See also other appropriate subheads in this section*
Legislature schedule rptd 5E3
Carey inaugural 1-1, opens Legis 1-3, 13E2
Rockefeller dies 1-26, 103E3, 104B1
Ex-Rep Hall dies 6-2, 508A3
Kennedy, Carter backers primary date clash rptd 8-2, 593C1
Kennedy in Hyde Park 10-26, Buffalo 11-3, 962A1, C1
Baker seeks '80 primary win 11-1, 829A1
Referenda results 11-6, 846B2, F3, G3, 847A1
Crangle gets Kennedy campaign post 12-20, 983C3

School Issues
Pvt schl reimbursemt bar voided by US Sup Ct 4-2, 281A3
Alien teacher ban backed by US Sup Ct 4-17, 325E3
Integratn study rpts urban lag 5-9, 650F1
Admissns test disclosure law enacted 7-14, 785A3
Suffolk Cnty, Brentwood bilingual programs ordrd 7-18, 7-20, 597C1, D1
Teachers' strikes rptd 9-12, 679B1
SAT decline, '50's A-fallout linked 9-17, 747C2
Lawyer survey rptd 9-17, 787E1

Sports
ASL Eagles move to Albany 2-28, 432F1
Lake Placid Olympic facilities rptd faulty 4-24, costs soar 6-17, 798A2
Harness-racing suspensn voided by Sup Ct 6-25, 540E1
Boxer KOd 11-23, dies 11-28; Athletic Comm suspends boxing, probes death 11-28–12-27, 1004E3

NEW York State Electric and Gas Corp.
New Haven reactors rejected 10-12, 807C1

NEW York Stock Exchange (NYSE)
SEC asks options trading overhaul, surveillance inspectn 2-15; freeze end seen 2-22, 348B3, 349A1, E1
2,100-member union settles 2-21, 131C1
McDonnell Douglas stock drops 6-6, 421A1
Financial futures trading OK asked 6-21, 681D3
A-protesters shutdown plan rptd 8-31, 742G3
A-protesters arrested 10-29, 827E2

Dow Jones Industrial Average—*See under STOCKS*

NEW York Telephone Co. v. New York State Department of Labor
Jobless pay for strikers upheld by Sup Ct 3-21, 231D1

NEW York Terminal Co.
Carter peanut loan scheme alleged 3-11–3-13, spec prosecutor sought 3-13, 183F3-184A2

NEW York Times, The (newspaper)
Best-seller list 1-7, 80A3; 2-4, 120A3; 3-4, 173C3; 4-8, 271F1; 5-6, 356B2; 6-3, 432G1; 7-1, 548A3; 8-5, 620A3; 9-2, 672A3; 10-14, 800A3; 11-4, 892A3
US rights rpt on Israel published 2-8, 107F3, 108A1
Racial poll rptd 2-20, 306D3, E3
'Son of Sam' interviewed 2-22, 156G2
Nixon Admin pub TV moves rptd 2-24, 194B1
Peoples Temple tape copy obtained 3-15, 219F2
Safire hints Carter land sale 'hush money' 3-22, 203A2
Carter poll rating up 3-29, 231D3

1980

Medicine & Health
'77 abortn data rptd 1-9, 23A3
Abortn funding case argued in Sup Ct 4-21, 306B2

Politics & Government—*See also other appropriate subheads in this section*
Legislature schedule rptd 18E1
State of State message 1-9, 270A1
Carter budget cut delay scored 3-17, 201F2
Rockland Cnty political firings barred 3-31, 291A2
Levitt dies 5-6, 448C2
Bessie Buchanan dies 9-7, 755D2
US Cong primary results 9-9, 682D1
Election results 11-4: cong 840F2, 843C3-A4, 845G1, A3, 846A1, A2, A3, 848A3; state 848C3
Census revisn ordrd 12-24, Sup Ct stays 12-30; '80 figures rptd, reapportmt seen 12-31, 983A1, F1

Presidential Election (& Transition)
Mrs Carter in Buffalo 1-31, y
Kennedy campaign said troubled 3-4, 167B1
Ford meets GOP ldrs 3-13, 207F1
Kennedy stresses primary 3-19, 206G3
Pres primary results 3-25, 221A2, A3
Carey backs open conv 8-11, 610A1
Carey praises Carter econ renewal plan, vows reelectn support 8-28, 663E2
Poll sees vote shift 9-5, Liberal Party endorses Anderson 9-6, 681D1
Anderson news conf in Union 9-9, 681B1
Mondale in Buffalo 9-10, 780C2
Reagan in Buffalo 9-11, 699E3
Mondale in Rochester 9-23, 780F2
Anderson ballot access seen assured 9-27, 818C2, D2
Carter in Niagara Falls 10-1, 739D1
Carter in Hempstead 10-16, 802D2
Carter in Rochester 10-29, 816E2, 841A1
Press endorsemts rptd 11-1, 841G3
Election results 11-4, 838C1, 839A2, F3

School Issues
Pvt schl reimbursemt upheld by Sup Ct 2-20, 146B2
Aptitude test disclosure law cited 4-7, 319A1, C1
Rochester teachers strike 9-3, 723C3

Sports
Sovts plan Lake Placid Olympics role 1-20, 45F3
Taiwan Olympic team backed in ct 2-7; decision reversed 2-11, 2-12, team excused from games 2-13, 154F3
Lake Placid Olympic results 2-12—2-24, 154E2-156D1
ASL NY (Albany) Eagles fold 2-13, 771D1
Lake Placid Olympics com debt, bankruptcy threat rptd 6-1, 421A2
US Grand Prix results 10-5, 1002B1
NASL Rochester club put on notice 11-24, terminated 12-8, 1001C1
ASL NY (Albany) Eagles readmittn rptd 12-17, 1001C3

NEW York Stock Exchange (NYSE)
Phila exchng censored 3-13, 334B3
SEC delays decisn on optns trading 3-26, 224B2
Silver price plunges, Hunt empire totters; trading halted in 3 brokerage houses, Hunt-owned energy co 3-27, 223C2
Engelhard trading halted 3-31, 245A1
Phelan elected pres 5-22, 456A3
Batten contract extended 7-2, 600C3
Revlon heir, financier indicted 8-19, 713G3
Natl securities mkt failure scored 9-12, 806G1
Investor survey rptd 12-9, 958A2

Dow Jones Industrial Average—*See under STOCKS*

New York Futures Exchange (NYFE)
ACE merger set 3-21, 224B1
Currency futures trading OKd by CFTC 5-28, 481B2
Treasury futures trading exclusivity OKd by CFTC 7-15; Chicago ct overturns order 7-17—7-18, enforcemt chief quits 7-22, 558G2
Opens; T-bond, currencies traded 8-7; T-bill futures made available 8-14, 616D3

NEW York Theaters and Producers, League of
Tonys presented 6-8, 692G2

NEW York Times, The (newspaper)
Best-seller list 1-13, 40A3; 2-10, 120B3; 3-9, 200A3; 4-6, 280A3; 4-30, 359C3; 6-8, 448A3; 7-13, 568A3; 8-17, 640D3; 9-19, 716A3; 10-12, 796C3; 12-7, 948C3
Abscam probe revealed 2-2, 81B1
Iran chrgs rptr took gifts from shah 2-9, 122B3
Rpts US arms Afghan rebels 2-15; US denies 2-16, 122D3
Kifner, Whitman win Polk awards 2-25, 692E3, G3
Iran readmits newsmen 3-7, 178D2
El Salvador leftist ad run 3-12, 191A3
Mandatory sentnc poll rptd 3-29, 359A2
Salisbury sues US 4-10, 459F1

1976

Reagan interview 3-10, 180B2
Andrew Young interview 4-8, 261C1
Estimates US intellignc costs 4-27, 299C3
Schanberg, Smith win Pulitzers 5-3, 352D3, E3
Carter delegate count 5-4, 322G2
Smith sues Nixon re taps 5-10, 349E2
Bessell interview 5-12, 364F3
Rhoodie interview 5-13, 339B1
Tanner hurt in Beirut 5-16, 355A1
Denies Sovt spy chrg 5-25, 371A3
Pres delegate count 6-1, 390D1
Dr Muir interview 6-3, 484A3
GOP delegate count 6-12, 432F2
GOP delegate count 6-26, 467G2; 7-1, 467D3; 7-10, 513D3; 7-17, 7-20, 531F2, E3; 7-23, 549C3; 7-29, 550E2; 8-2—8-5, 563F2, 564B2, D2
Carter interview 7-7, 490C1
Reed interviewed 7-27, 550B2
Raleigh interviewed 7-29, 545F2
Final Olympic standings table 8-2, 573B3
Ford nominatn clinched 8-16, 601D3
Eur soclst ad scores Argentina violence 8-26, 672C2
Carter interview 9-4, 664C1, F1
Prints Croat hijack demands 9-11, 685E1
Rpts Ford funds probe 9-25, 722F3
Frankel on press debate panel 10-6, 740F2, 741C3
Interviews Vorster 10-18, 793G1
CBS poll: Carter ahead 10-27, 826A1
Carter endorsement rptd 10-30, 831G2

NEW York University (NYU)
Hopper dies 1-19, 56D3
Pope-Hennessey named 5-25, 504E2
Kalman Silvert dies 6-15, 524F3

NEW Zealand—*See also ADB, COMMONWEALTH of Nations, IEA, OECD*
Listed as 'free' nation 1-19, 20C3
Joint US, Australia maneuvers set 2-19, 137D2
SEATO formally disbanded 2-20, 148C1
S Pacific Forum meets 3-8—3-9, 179B2
Australia prime min visits, Anzus backed 3-8—3-11, 187B3
China scores Sovt Indian O buildup 3-13, 265C3
ILO jobless report issued 3-13, 297E3
Total IMF oil loan rptd 4-1, 340B2
Muldoon in France, gets A-test assurances 4-16, 372E3
Delargey named cardinal 4-27, 336C2
Muldoon sees Mao in China 4-30, 439E2
Vs WHO anti-Israel stand 5-19, 355D2
At Timor Assemb meeting 5-31, 423A1
Australia OKs A-ship visits 6-4, 455E3
US' Carter for more ties 6-23, 451F2
Journalists strike 7-14—7-15, 677A3
Austerity budget set 7-29, 589E3
US GOP platform text cites 8-18, 609A3
Govt passes strike measures 8-19, 677G2
US A-ship docks; port workers strike, violence erupts 8-27—9-2, 677E2
Canada sets meat import quota 10-19, 837B1
Suspends forgn exchng 11-28, devalues currency 11-29, 896D1, G2
IMF loan granted 11-29, 1013G1
'77 US beef export pact OKd 12-15, 976B2
Dollar revalued up 2% 12-20, 1013G1
Niue Island—*See separate listing*
Sports
OAU warns Olympic boycott 7-6, 487D3
African, Asian natns quit Olympics 7-9—7-21, 528G2
Olympic results 7-18—7-31, 573D3, 574A3, 576C1
Curbs vs S Africa planned 10-17, 910G2

NGEAN Ros
Cambodia presidium dep chrmn 4-14, 265E1
NGHI, Le Thanh
United Viet planning min 7-3, 502E3
In Politburo 12-19, 967F3
NGHI, Nguyen Van
Rival US refugee groups split 2-20, 176G2
NGHIEM, Col. Tran
Surprised by '75 victory 4-24, 315G2

1977

Rpts on Indochina postwar plight 5-1—5-3, 336C3-337G1
Tennis tourn fee disclosures 5-7, FCC rpts probe 7-8, 548F2
Raskin letter publishd 6-5, 448F3
Shannon named amb to Ireland 6-21, 626E3
Rpts soccer popularity 7-5, 676B3
USSR claims Jews influence 7-22, 589B2
Herbert Matthews dies 7-30, 604D3
CIA mind-control test revealed 8-4, 611A1
FBI-ACLU ties reveals 8-4, 628F1
Assad interview 8-26, 663F1
US-Sovt strategic weapons compared 751C3
CIA links chrgd, denied; CIA file request cited 9-12, 720B3-721C1
Foreman tied to Pa politician, quits 9-12, 920E3
Trib NY files trust suit 9-13, 723D1
Palestinian ad accuses Israel in '67 US ship raid 9-19, 715B1
Rpts US pollutn violatns 9-19, 800B2
S Africa arrests rptr's son 9-23, 825F3
Dayan interview 9-27, 733G2
Markel dies 10-23, 872E2
Sadat interviewed 12-6, 929D2
On most reliable govt news source list 12-10, 1009B1
Audubon libel case review declined 12-12, 960E2

NEW York Times Co.
Vance rpts net worth 2-25, 148E1
New York Times—*See separate listing*
NEW York University (NYU)
Friedricks gets Medal of Sci 11-22, 952A1
NEW York v. Cathedral Academy
NYS pvt schl aid law voided 12-6, 938E3

NEW Zealand—*See also COMMONWEALTH of Nations, IEA, OECD, SEATO*
Dec '75-76 inflatn rate rptd 2-7, 87B2
Hospital drug deaths rptd 2-28, 224E2
Wage increase ordered 3-2, 222D2
'77-78 budget presented 7-21, tax rise protested 7-22, 638G1, E2
200-mi fishing zone declared 9-7, 729A3
Muldoon asks tap powers 9-8, 729D3
Anti-tap protest in Parlt 10-18, Muldoon scores 11-14, 926A1
Newspaper strike 11-14—11-16, 925G3
Foreign Relations (misc.)—*See also 'Monetary, Trade & Aid' below*
UN Assemb member 4A1
N Ireland detainees to immigrate 2-21, 258D2
Queen visits 2-22—3-7, names Holyoake Gov-Gen 3-7, 222A2
Muldoon in UK; affirms S Africa policy, scores Amin 3-31, 258A2
Australia defense pact rptd 5-4, 410F2
ASEAN backs ties 6-27—6-29, 537E1
Muldoon sees ASEAN ldrs 8-6—8-7, 607A2
Indochina refugee quotas eased 8-31, 685E2
Sovts rue assault on envoy 10-18, 926C1
ANZUS alliance cited 11-9—11-10, 925E3
Muldoon in US, sees Carter 11-9—11-10, 925E3
French A-tests rptd 11-23, 11-25, 1013B1
Monetary, Trade & Aid Issues (including all foreign economic developments)
UK lamb trading set 2-22, operatns limited 3-22, 258E1
'76 paymts deficit narrowed 2-28, 222E2
Australia sets textile import quota 4-17, 346A1
Israel gets US arms preference 5-12, 361E1
Australia rebuffs textile quota plea 5-18, 410C2
US sets arms sales policy 5-19, 380G2
IWC cuts whaling quotas 6-24, 496G3
Sovt car imports planned 7-4, 638F2
Muldoon scores farm import curbs 7-21, 638D2
Fiji dock strike ends 8-8, 636C3
200-mi fishing zone declared 9-7, 729B3
Japan OKs more beef imports 10-28, 862A1
Australia livestock banned 11-23, 922G3
Obituaries
Cobham, Viscount 3-20, 264E2
Sports
S Africa compromise agreed 6-8—6-15, 487E1

NFL (National Football League)—*See FOOTBALL*
NFLPA (National Football League Players Association)—*See FOOTBALL—Professional*
NGAPO Ngawangjigme
Asks Dalai Lama to end exile 5-1, 347E1
NGOMA, Maj. Louis Sylvain (Congo premier)
Named premier, 2d vp 4-4, 282E2

1978

Indonesia info min interviewed 4-15, 318B3
3 win Pulitzers 4-17, 315B1, A2-B2
Nixon memoirs excerpted 4-30, 5-1, 319E2
Carter interviewed 4-30, 339E2
Arafat interviewed 5-1, 339B3
US-Israel agrmt on cluster bombs rptd 5-12, 358A3
Kadar interviewed by Oakes 6-10, 534E2
USSR accuses Whitney 6-28, 518C1, D2
Farber in Jascalevich curare case-press freedom controversy 6-30—8-30; jailed for contempt 8-4, freed 8-30, 678C2
Whitney pays fine 8-4, 634B1
Strike halts publication 8-9, 625G1
USSR closes Whitney case 8-18, 651F1; warns 8-24, 670C2
Sex bias suit setld 9-28, 835F2
Farber jailing scored by IAPA 10-13, 829F1
Farber released, fine ended upon Jascalevich acquittal 10-24, 841C2
Carter interview 11-6, 862B1
Strike ends, impact rptd 11-6, 864D3-865A2
Vance interview published 11-25, 925B1
Farber case declined by Sup Ct 11-27, 937E1
Best seller list 12-3, 970G3-971C1
China policy poll 12-19, 976E1

NEW York Times Co.
Cowles Communicatns to liquidate 1-6, 75F3-76A1
New York Times—*See separate listing*
New York Times Syndication Sales Corp.
Haldeman book syndicatn upset by Post scoop 2-16, 124C2
Quadrangle/The New York Times Book Co.
Haldeman book publicatn date upset by Post scoop 2-16, 2-17, 24C2
NEW York Times Co. v. New Jersey
Case declined by Sup Ct 11-27, 937G1
NEW York Times Syndication Sales Corp.—*See under NEW York Times Co.*
NEW York University (NYU)
USSR study programs halted 7-14, 542B2
Bobst dies 8-2, 708A2
NEW York v. Blanks
Death penalty restoratn appeal refused by Sup Ct 10-16, 789C2
NEW York v. James
Death penalty case refused by Sup Ct 7-3, 552A2

NEW Zealand—*See also COMMONWEALTH of Nations, GATT, SOUTH Pacific Forum, OECD*
Abortn law in effect 4-1, repeal petitn rptd in Parlt 5-18, 498A2
Maoris evicted from Bastion Pt 5-25, 498G1
James sails solo around world 6-8, 653D2
Muldoon's Natl Party wins electns, majority reduced 11-25, 924F2
Cook Islands—*See COOK Islands*
Economy & Labor (domestic)
'77 inflatn, jobless rate rptd 3-7; income drop forecast 4-17, 497D3
2 state-owned airlines merge 4-1, 498D2
Meat workers strike 5-25, 498C2
Muldoon presents '78-79 budget; tax cuts, farm aid asked 6-1, 497G2
'77 jobless rise rptd 7-28, 677D1
Foreign Relations (misc.)—*See also 'Monetary, Trade, Aid & Investment' and 'UN' below*
Ulster peace movemt relocatn rptd 4-17, 373F1
Solomons gain independnc 7-7, 549E1
Mideast peace force rptd backed 8-31, 673G1
Monetary, Trade, Aid & Investment
Japan fishing, trade ties disputed 1-25—5-23; 200-mi limit in effect 4-1, accord reached 5-23, 497G3
US arms sales ceiling exempts 2-1, 106E2
'77 paymts deficit rptd 3-7, 497D3
S Korea fishing accord signed, steel deal rptd 3-13, 498F1
USSR fishing accord signed 4-5, 498F1
US '78 arms sales forecast 5-19, 387B1
Lamb exports halted by strike 5-25, 498C2
US hikes meat import quotas 6-8, 428E2
US sets '79 arms sales lid 9-26, 734A2
UN Policy & Developments
ILO rpts '77 jobless rise 7-28, 677D1
Racism conf boycotted 8-26, 676B2
Assemb member 713C3
U.S. Relations—*See also 'Monetary, Trade, Aid & Investment' above*
Mondale visits 5-8, 360B3
Mideast peace force rptd backed 8-31, 673G1

NEZHINSKY, Alexander
Kills tourists 6-27, 519F1
NFC (National Football Conference)—*See FOOTBALL—Professional*
NFL (National Football League)—*See FOOTBALL—Professional*
NFLPA (National Football League Players Association—*See FOOTBALL—Professional*
NGO Dinh Diem—*See DIEM, Ngo Dinh*

1979

A-power poll rptd 4-10, 259G2
Baker wins Pulitzer 4-16, 336B3
US spy satellite data rptd compromised 4-28, 318F2-319A1
US, USSR strategic weapons compared 338G3
Sadat interview 5-12, 360A1
B Carter interview 5-18, 380G3
'78 state gas use rptd 5-27, 395D2
China OKs office 5-30, 406B2
Mrs Javits Iran lobby role detailed 5-30, 408B2
Daily, Sunday circulatn listed 6-6, 431C1
Begin rptdly vowed no new setlmts 6-10, Begin denies 6-11, 436B2
Zimbabwe cmdr interviewed 6-13, 547A1
Mayors Conf rpt cited 6-15, 439D3
Smith wins Nixon tap suit rule 7-12, 611A3
Kennedy interviewed re Chappaquiddick 7-17, 539F1, A2
Iran ousts Ibrahim 7-22, US regrets 7-23, 565F3, 566B1
Mattson named co pres 7-23, 640D3
Carter interview on Palestinians 7-31, 575C1; rights remark clarified 8-17, 607C1
Jascalevich trial costs ordrd paid 8-14, 656E2
S Korea oppositn ldr interviewed 9-16, 710A3
Hooks interviewed 10-11, 780G2
S Korea bars Halloran 10-13, OKs entry 10-14, 803B3
Guatemala leftist ad run 10-26, 814A1
Kennedy leads in poll 11-4, 847D2
Abortn, womens ordinatn poll rptd 11-11, 930A2
Bell interviewed 12-5, 943G2

NEW York Times Co.
Mattson named pres 7-23, 640D3
New York Times—*See separate listing*
NEW York Times v. Sullivan
'State of mind' libel queries backed by Sup Ct 4-18, 302C1
Case cited by Sup Ct 6-26, 540E2
NEW York University (NYU)
Forgn student enrollmt listed 167D3
Buettner-Janusch indicted 10-4, 839G3
NEW York v. Jones
Case declined by Sup Ct 11-5, 884E3
N.Y. v. Tompkins
Case declined by Sup Ct 2-26, 164F3

NEW Zealand—*See also COMMONWEALTH of Nations, GATT, IEA, OECD*
Woman gives birth after hysterectomy 5-16, 392B3
$ devalued 6-21, budget speech rptd 6-22 566G2
A-blast fallout rptd 11-13, rpt disputed 11-14, 882F2
Antarctic DC-10 crash kills 257 11-28, pilot error blamed 11-29, 912B1
Cook Islands—*See COOK Islands*
Foreign Relations (misc.)
China Viet invasn concern voiced 2-18, 123G1
Australia drug probe linked to murdered couple 6-20, 467G2
ANZUS meets on Indochina refugees, scores Viet 7-4—7-5, 495A2, F2
Australia trade, pol union explored 8-19, 8-21, 631G3-632C1
UN membership listed 695A3
UK lamb imports cited 11-14, 873D1
Australia names high comr 12-8, 948E1
In Zimbabwe peacekeeping force 12-23, 976E3
Sovt Afghan invasn opposed 12-30, 974E2
Obituaries
Partridge, Eric 6-1, 508D3

NEZ Perce Indians—*See INDIANS, American*
NFL (National Football League)—*See FOOTBALL–Professional*

1980

'Charlie's Angels' fraud probe rptd 5-1, 376B3
Hispanic-Amer survey rptd 5-11—5-14, 396A2
Oveissi interviewed 6-11, 433F2
US anti-Khomeini broadcasts rptd; US denies 6-29, 490F2
Foreman marries Cianfrani 7-14, 890B2
Kamm, son arrested in Malaysia 9-6; ousted 9-7, 810G1
'74 job bias suit setld 9-17, 746A3
PLO prisoner interviewed, cites Sovt mil training 10-31, 912F2
Canby scores Heaven's Gate 11-19, 906C1
Kemp interviewed 11-23, 897B2
Muskie interview rptd 11-23, 915B2
Presidential Campaign & Election
Reagan age seen as factor in NH 2-17, 128E2
Times/CBS political poll results 2-20, 130D2
Reagan 'basic speech' excerpts 2-29, 207A2
Ford interview rptd 3-2, 167D1
Bush 'basic speech' excerpts 3-3, 208G2
Connally, Kennedy 'basic speech' excerpts 3-7, 3-10, 183A1, 184A2
Times/CBS III primary poll cited 3-18, 206F2
Times/CBS pres poll rptd 4-18, 304E3
Times/CBS pres poll rptd 6-3, 423B1
Reagan interview rptd 6-11, 452F2
Times/CBS protectionism poll rptd 6-26, 515F3
Carter interview rptd 7-17, 549B2
Poll rpts campaign vote shift 9-5, 681F1
Golden in pres TV debate 9-21, 721D3
Post-debate pres poll rptd 9-28, 739C3
Pres poll standings tighten, toss-up seen 10-23, 816A2
Carter pres endorsemt rptd 11-1, 841G3
Electn exit poll results 11-4, 838G2

NEW York Times Co,
Us magazine sale rptd 3-7, 239A2
NEW York University (NYU)
May to become business school dean 3-18, 224E3
'79 endowmt earnings rptd 3-24, 319C2
Buettner-Janusch convicted 7-16, 607F3-608A1; sentenced 11-13, 997D3
NEW York v. Howard
Case declined by Sup Ct 12-1, 918F2
NEW York Zoological Society
Panda finding mission begins 5-12, 398A2

NEW Zealand—*See also ADB, ANZUS, COMMONWEALTH of Nations, GATT, IEA, OECD*
Defns-GNP ratio rptd 2-19, 132G1
Foreign Relations (misc.)
Pacific orgn studied 1-20, 78C2
Anti-Sovt steps rptd re Afghan invasn 1-22, amb expelled 1-24, 100A2
USSR expels envoy 1-29, 119D1
Iran emb closed 2-7, 122C3
Japan joins 4-natn Pacific naval games 2-26, 151C3
US asks Iran crisis support 4-7; 257D2; sanctns 4-13, 281D2; Iran asks neutrality 4-11, 282G1
Olympic com rejects Moscow boycott 5-8, 379B3
Moscow Olympic flag controversy 7-19, 588C1
S Pacific island pact rptd signed 7-24, 576F2
Iran hostage appeal rptd 8-16, 634G3
Muldoon in China 9-11, 706D3
EC limits sheepmeat exports 9-30, 737A3
Government & Politics—*See also other appropriate subheads in this section*
Muldoon overcomes party challenge 10-23, 830B3
Obituaries
Ballantrae, Baron 11-28, 928B2
Sports
Moscow Olympics shift backed 1-22, 45A3, 100D2
Olympic com rejects Moscow boycott 5-8, 379B3
Moscow Olympic flag controversy 7-19, 588C1
U.S. Relations
Pacific naval games start 2-26, 151C3
Iran crisis support asked 4-7, 257D2; sanctns 4-13, 281D2; Iran asks neutrality 4-11, 282G1
Iran hostage appeal rptd 8-16, 634G3

NEY, Roman
Named Polish Politburo alternate 12-2, 910A1
NEZHAD, Eric
Reggae opens 3-27, 392F3
NFL (National Football League)—*See FOOTBALL*
NGOYI, Lillian
Dies 3-12, 280C1

1976

NGOUABI, Marien
Zaire recognizes Angola MPLA 2-28, 163A2
NGUZA, Karl I Bond
Zaire foreign min 2-4, 270C2
NHARI, Thomas
Chitepo murder rpt issued 4-9, 428C2
NIARCHOS, Stavros Spyros
Govt chrgs rptd 9-28, 11-2, 854D1
Govt oil takeover set 12-4, 1004A3

NICARAGUA—*See also CACM, IDB, OAS, SELA*
Russell ct scores rights abuse 1-17, 61D2
Listed as 'partly free' 1-19, 20D3
Somoza in Guatemala, pledges quake aid 2-4, 81F1
Forgn min sees Kissinger in CR 2-24, 177B1
Total IMF oil loan rptd 4-1, 340D2
Guerrilla ldrs killed 6-25, 11-7, 11-9, Cuba rebel aid chrgd 11-16, 926D1
4 get Mex safe conduct 9-10, 926G1
US sugar duties tripled 9-21, 721D3
Cuba exile coalitn rptd 10-19, 779E3

1977

NGOUABI, Marien
Killed 3-18, 220A2
Linked to Biayenda slaying 3-23, 220D2
Plotters sentncd, executed 3-25, 3-26, 282A3
Successor named 4-3, 282D2
Amin on assassinatn 7-4, 512A2
NGUEMA, Francisco Macias (Equatorial Guinea president)
28 rptd executed 7-11, 658F2
NGUESSO, Maj. Denis Sassou
Named defns min, 1st vp 4-4, 282E2
NGUZA Karl-I-Bond
Treason chrgd 8-13, 641D2
Ordrd executed 9-13; spared 9-15, 731C1
NHL (National Hockey League)—*See HOCKEY, Ice*
NHTSA—*See U.S. GOVERNMENT—TRANSPORTATION—National Highway Safety Administration*

NICARAGUA—*See also IDB, OAS*
Guerrillas sentenced; 20 seek Mex asylum 3-2, 168G2
Guerrilla ldr, others rptd killed 4-9, 5-17, 476C1
'61-75 GDP variatns table 5-30, 439B1
Somoza suffers coronary 7-25, Cong bars temporary replacemt 8-18, 656D3
Malaria upsurge rptd 9-4, 747D3
Somoza returns home 9-7, 767A3
Guerrillas attack, map 10-12—10-18; pol support rptd 10-20, 802C1-B3
Pol 'dialogue' asked by priests, execs 10-19—10-26; rejected 10-26, 10-27, 864C2
Cong pres quits 10-21, Somoza rptd grooming son 10-26, 865F1

Foreign Relations (misc.)—*See also 'Human Rights' below*
UN Assemb member 4A1
Somoza backs Panamanian Canal demands 1-18, 46G1
Israel rptd prime arms seller 1-15, 28E3
'75-76 trade, paymts data; table 3-11, 189B1, A2★, B2
'66-75 arms transfers table 4-8, 415B2
CR seizes anti-Somoza plotters 9-25, 767A3
Guerrillas safe in CR, forgn embs 10-12—10-28, 865A1
CR closes border 10-14, chrgs exchngd 10-15—10-16, 802C3
Brazil coffee policy backed 10-21, 876C3
Guerrillas deny Cuba aid 10-26; Somoza chrgs intl communist plot 11-7, 864A3
CR border dispute probed by OAS 10-26, 865E1
Abstains on UN anti-Israel res 10-28, 830G2

Human Rights (including political prisoner issues)
500 pol prisoners rptd 1-1, 3G1
Church chrgs govt terror, asks US pressure 2-6—3-2; US confrms rights abuse, aid cutoff sought 3-4, 168F1-F2
Latin intellectuals ask US aid cutoff 3-25, 476B1
US withholds aid 4-7, rights probe scored 4-19; House com backs cutoff 6-14, 475B3
Student refugees fly to Mex 6-8, 476D1
Bishops chrg Natl Guard 'terror' 6-13, 475F3-476A1
US delays police arms sales 7-17, 572F3
US mil aid amendmt dispute 7-21—8-6, house defeats cutoff move 7-23, 656F2
Amnesty Intl details '76 rights abuse 8-15; '77 decline rptd, US pressure cited 8-16, 656B2
State of seige lifted 9-19, 767G2
US criticism cited re rebel offensive 10-12—10-18, 802F2
Newsmen rptd arrested 10-24, 864A3
Army deserter chrgs abuses 10-26, 865B1
OAS panel bars probe 10-26, 865E1

1978

NGOUABI, Marien (D. 1977)
10 executed for assassinatn 2-7, 115D2
NGUGI wa Thiong'o
Arrest confirmed 1-12, 75D1
Freed 12-12, 968A2
NGUZA Karl-I-Bond
Freed 7-14, 652E2
NHL (National Hockey League)—*See HOCKEY, Ice*
NHTSA—*See U.S. GOVERNMENT—TRANSPORTATION—National Highway Traffic Safety Administration*
NIAGARA Falls, N.Y.—*See NEW York State*
NIAGARA Gazette (Niagara Falls, N.Y. newspaper)
Chem dump area evacuatn funded 8-4, 703D1
NIAGARA River (N.Y.)
Olin indicted 3-23, 243E1
NIAYE, Tabara
Ceddo released 2-16, 618G3

NICARAGUA—*See also GATT, IDB, OAS*
Liberals win munic electns, 80% boycott 2-5, 91D1

Foreign Relations (misc.)—*See also 'UN' and 'Unrest' below*
CR threatens Somoza land expropriatn 2-22, 151A1
Coffee exports to be withheld 3-10, 181B3
Chile bars anti-Somoza protest 9-5, 796B1
CR to seize Somoza estate 9-22, 823E2
Guatemalans burn Somoza restaurant 10-6, 796B3
IMF stays loan 11-1, Venez oil cutoff rumored 11-8, 883G2
OAS panel scores rights abuses 11-17, 1019B1
CR border clashes, ties broken 11-21; Somoza closes border 12-26, 1018G3-1019A1
Trade boycott set by forgn unions 11-24, 1014C2

1979

NGUEMA Mbasogo, Lt. Col. Teodoro (Equatorial Guinea head of state)
Leads Equatorial Guinea coup 8-3, grants amnesty 8-6, 613D3
NGUZA Karl-I-Bond
Reinstated in Zaire Cabt 3-6, 215C2
NHL (National Hockey League)—*See HOCKEY, Ice*
NIAGARA Falls, N.Y.—*See NEW York State*
NIAGARA River (N.Y.)
Olin convicted for mercury dumping 8-16, 704E1
Olin fined for mercury dumping 12-10, 947B1
NIARCHOS, Maria Isabella
Marries 6-15, 527E2
NIARCHOS, Stavros
Daughter marries 6-15, 527E2

NICARAGUA—*See also GATT, IDB, NONALIGNED Nations Movement, OAS*
70% illiteracy rptd 9-1, 689E3

Economy & Labor
Currency devalued 4-6, econ straits detailed 4-10, 270A1*
Rebel junta outlines econ, agri reforms 6-27, 475C3
Banks natlzd; fishing, mining, forestry takeover set 7-25, 574A1, C1
Cruz on bank reserves, govt debts 7-25, 603B2, E2
Reforms decreed, natl health plan outlined 8-9, 615F3-616B1, D1
Large currency notes recalled 8-24, $32.5 mln deposited 8-25-8-26, 689F1-E3
Currency rate set, other decrees issued 9-3, 689E2
Farm works progrm outlined 9-18, 732F1
High jobless rate, labor exodus spur econ crisis; land expropriatn halted 12-3, 950F2

Foreign Relations (misc.)—*See also 'Monetary' and 'UN' below*
Castro: US caused repressn, deaths 1-1, 20B1
Colombia guerrillas rptdly planned amb kidnap 1-7, 115E1
Honduras termed 'friendly', CR guerrilla aid scored 1-9, 21G3
CR gun loan from Venez rptd 3-23, 238A2
UK downgrades ties 3-29, 255A2
CR arms-smuggling rptd 4-5, 254F3
Guerrillas issue 'reconstructn' plan 4-5, 269E3
Panama arms plot indictmts 5-14, 386C3
Mex cuts ties 5-20; dispatches Latin missn, asks support 5-21, 409A1
CR denies rebel offensive launched 5-29, 409A2
Quintana asks OAS invoke mutual defns treaty 5-29, 409C2
Andean Group sends envoys, CR defns warned 6-11, 446F3
Panama prisoner transfer offered 6-12, 446E3
Pilot defects to CR 6-13, 446E2
Rebels invade from CR 6-16-6-17, 461C1
Andean Group lauds rebels 6-16, 461B2
Panama rebel aid probed 6-20, 481B2
Latins oppose OAS peace force 6-21, 460D3
Panama hosts US, rebel mtg 6-27, 475G2
Rebel junta outlines policy, seeks aid 6-27, 475B3, D3
Andean Group, US seek pol solutn 7-4-7-6; rebels score 7-5, 503E3-504E1
Tunisia intercepts PLO arms 7-11, 512E2
Somoza soldrs rptd in Honduras 7-21, Nicaragua invasn plan chrgd 7-28, 573F2
Mex team arrives, Guatemala convoy set 7-21; Cuban aid arrives 7-25, 574B2
200 in El Salvador Emb get safe passage, 72 held 7-26, 574G1
3 junta ldrs visit Cuba 7-26, 574C2
Radicals expelled to Panama 8-16, 636B2
Bill of Rights issued 8-21, 636B2
Eur, Latin arms aid missn set 8-31, 689A3
Cuban mil aid sought 8-31; educ, mil training progrms rptd 9-1, 689B3
Nonaligned movemt joined 9-3, 675E1
El Salvador rebel role chrgd 9-24, 731E3
Paraguay extraditn of Somoza sought 10-9, 794B1
El Salvador proposes ties 10-18, 813E1

Government & Politics—*See also other appropriate subheads in this section*
Legal, pol reforms set 3-9, 255F1
Rebel junta outlines progrm 6-27, 475B3
Cong sessn cancelled 6-28, 475F3
Cong meets, Somoza announces Natl Guard draft 7-7, 512D2
Junta outlines reconstructn progrm 7-11, 512G1
Somoza resigns, leaves for US 7-17, 535D1
Rebels begin reconstructn, form Cabt 7-23; name army gen cmnd 7-29, 573B2

1980

NGUEMA Mbasogo, Lt. Col. Teodoro (Equatorial Guinea head of state)
USSR fish pact expiratn rptd 1-28, 119C1
NHL (National Hockey League)—*See HOCKEY, Ice*
NHONGO, Teurai Ropa
Zimbabwe youth min 3-11, 198C1
NIAGARA Falls—*See NEW York*
NIATROSS (race horse)
Named top trotter 12-17, 1002C2

NICARAGUA—*See also GATT, IDB, NONALIGNED Nations, OAS*

Economy & Labor
'Plan 80' issued; '79 inflatn, '80 goals rptd 1-3, 7E1
Radical press scores '80 plan; paper closed, editor arrested 1-24, 118A1
Journalists' union expels radio commentator 2-2, 118C1
La Prensa struck 4-20, 315C2
Business discontent rptd growing 4-22, 315G2
Land, business confiscatn ended 4-28, 390F1
Sugar price hits 5 1/2-yr high 10-9, 777D2

Foreign Relations (misc.)—*See also 'Monetary', 'UN Policy' below*
Hassan, delegatn in USSR 3-19; E Eur 3-22, 234G2
30 forgn delegatns mark Somoza downfall, Castro presence prompts CR boycott 7-15, 565G2
Iran forgn min cancels visit 7-18, 545E1
Arafat visits 7-21, PLO ties finalized 7-22, 565E3
Somoza assassinated in Paraguay 9-17; Argentina terrorists sought, suspect slain 9-18, 697F2
OAS chief held hostage in El Salvador 9-17, 708E1
Cuban presence spurs Bluefields riots 9-30, UK links chrgd 10-1; deportatns seen 10-2, 792F1
Paraguay cuts ties, Somoza assassinatn links chrgd 10-1, 792B2

Government & Politics—*See also other appropriate subheads in this section*
Civil rights restored 1-3, 7D1
Chamorro quits junta 4-19; Robelo resigns, scores Sandinistas 4-22, 315B2
Council of State expansn set 4-21, 315E2
State of siege ended, electns set 4-28, 390F1
Cncl of State meets, CP excluded 5-4, 390G1
2 moderates join junta 5-18, 390C1
Sandinistas mark Somoza downfall 7-19, 565E2

1976

1977

1978

UN Policy & Developments

Venez asks Cncl rights probe 9-2, 960D3
Assemb member 713C3
UN reps asks Somoza quit 10-5, 777F2
Refugee comr vows Honduras aid 11-6, 883D2
Assemb condemns rights abuses 12-15, 1019D1

Unrest

Oppositn editor Chamorro slain 1-10, 19C3
Chamorro mourned by 1000s 1-10—1-11; riots, arson 1-11—1-12, 72G3
Chamorro murder suspects seized 1-11, testimony rptd contradictory 1-13—1-22, 73D1
Oppositn bars Somoza 'dialogue' 1-15, 73D3
Gen strike called; Chamorro death probe, Somoza resignatn demanded 1-23—1-30; Somoza bars 1-27, 73A2
Student protests dispersed 1-30, 73E2
Church backs gen strike 1-31, 73A3
Chamorro paper leads Somoza ouster drive 2-1, 73F2
6 die in natnwide riots 2-1, 91A2
Forgn newsmen beaten by troops 2-1, 91B2
Guerrillas attack Granada, Rivas; 14 rptd killed 2-2—2-3, 91E1
Guerrillas infiltrate from CR 2-2, 91F1
Somoza calls gen strike 'elitist,' bars resignatn 2-3, 91C1
Managua protesters dispersed 2-6, 91C2
Gen strike ends, 'econ reasons' cited 2-7, 90G3
Venez asks OAS probe rights abuse 2-8, 91F2
Protesters riot in Managua, Granada 2-10, 2-12, 115C3
'Civil war' vs Somoza planned 2-12, 115D3
El Salvador guerrillas bomb emb 2-14, 115G2
Deaths mount in anti-Somoza campaign 2-21—3-1, 150B2
Somoza vows reform 2-26, protests continue 2-26—2-27, 150D3-151A1
Colombia emb bombed 2-26, 151B1
Sandinistas vow to topple Somoza, arms aid rptd 3-2, 192F2
Masaya cease-fire 3-3, Somoza directs relief effort 3-5, 192D2
15 injured in Jinotepe clashes 3-3, 192E2
Top mil aide killed 3-8, guerrillas take credit 3-9, 192A2
Guerrilla attacks continue 3-17—4-14, 376E1
Guerrilla assassin rptd in Mex emb 3-27, 376A2
Venez seeks OAS rights probe, Somoza scores 3-28—5-8, 376A3
Anti-govt unrest continues 3-31—4-28; Somoza yields to hunger strikers 4-19, students 4-28, 375E2
Somoza names Chamorro death probe panel, 4 shun 4-6, 376B2
CR seizes guerrilla ldr 4-13, 376A2
Troops fire on student protesters 5-4, 376D1
Chamorro cousin murdered 5-8, 376E1
Students strike 5-15—5-18, 2d strike smashed 7-11—7-12, 593F1
The Twelve return from exile 7-5, 593E1
Anti-govt violence, 23 die 7-9—7-25, 592G3-593A2
Castro blamed re anti-Somoza campaign 7-22, 593F1
CR denies anti-Somoza unrest stand 7-28, 617F2
30 Natl Guard ldrs rptd fired 8-18, 659G2
Guerrillas invade Natl Palace, kill 6, take hostages 8-22; demands met 8-23, 8-24, 658D3-659B2

1979

Somoza natl debt rptd, theft chrgd 7-25, 574B1
Junta member sees electns in '82 8-8, 636A2
Reforms decreed, ethics code set 8-9, 615E3-616G1
Bill of Rights issued, state cncl set 8-21, 636C1, A2
Recovery decrees issued 9-3, 689E2
Moderates form pol party 9-7, 732A1
Pol party titles curbed 9-18, 732E1
Somoza extraditn sought 10-9, 794A1
Trials set for Somoza, 7000 war prisoners 11-29; spec prosecutor named 12-3, 950A3
Cabt resigns at junta's request 12-4, 950E3

Monetary, Trade, Aid & Investment

Trade boycott dropped by ORIT 1-15–1-16, 28D3
Forgn debt paymt delayed 2-1, 101F2
IMF standby loan sought 4-6, 270A1*; 372F3; protested 4-25, 332E1; 5-10, 373A1; OKd 5-14, 372B3
Forgn banks curbed; Israel, Argentina debt paymt halted 7-25, 574A1
IDB aid rptd 8-2, 8-4, 603D1-G1
OAS pledges $500,000 in aid 8-2, 603F2
IMF loan probe rptd urged 8-6, 603G1
Food export controls decreed, '78 trade cited 8-9, 616D1
Borders sealed during currency recall 8-25–8-26, 689A2
Forgn debt paymts in doubt 9-28, 753D2
US vows aid 10-1, 754C1
Forgn debt being rescheduled; loan graft probed, intl credit extended 11-27, 909C3-910A1
Currency black mkt, food imports spur econ crisis 12-3, 951A1

Sports

Reforms decreed 8-9, 616C1

UN Policy & Developments

Rights comm seeks abuses end 3-13, 255B2
WHO cited re health svc reforms 8-9, 616A1
Membership listed 695A3
Ortega addresses Assemb 9-28, 753D2

Unrest

Guerrillas kill 55 soldiers 1-3–1-5, 8G1
Guerrillas, troops differ on casualties 1-7, 21F3
Labor ldr killed by troops 1-9, 21C3*
Protesters honor slain editor 1-10, 21A3
Guerrillas, troops clash near CR border 1-10, 21F3
Guerrillas, Natl Guard rearm 1-17; clashes near border continue 1-19, 76B3
New plebiscite plan rejctd by Somoza; FAO scores, new oppositn group gains strength 1-19, 76D2-A3
Guerrillas claim Somoza land seizure, redistributn 1-24, 101E2
5 killed in Managua 2-1, 101E2
US issues rights rpt 2-10, 107D2
Latin bishops back Salazar 2-12, 108D3
Guerrilla factns OK unity pact 3-7, business exec support sought 4-5, 254F3
Pol arrests continue 3-9, 255A2
Cotton destructn by guerrillas rptd 3-16, 255B1
Jan-Mar killings tolled 3-21, 4-5, 254C3
Guerrillas issue 'reconstructn' plan 4-5, Somoza names reform coms 4-6, 269C3
Rebels attack in north 4-7–4-9, Somoza denies flight 4-9, 269E2-C3
Heavy fighting continues in north 4-13–4-29, Esteli recaptured 4-14, 331G3
Managua rite for Somoza kin 4-18, 332D1
MDs, nurses stage 1-day strike 4-26, 332F1
Mex chrgs 'genocide' 5-20, 409A1
Heavy fighting renewed; Jinotega raid repelled, 5-pronged attack from CR launched 5-20–5-31, 409F1
Guatemala, El Salvador aid to Somoza chrgd, mercenary recruitmt rptd 6-2, 427F1
Natl Guard, rebel forces compared 6-2, 427F1
CR warned 6-3; rebel aid curbs asks, border policing rejctd 6-4, 427D1
FSLN gen strike starts 6-4, Somoza calls state of seige 6-6, 426F3-427A1
Leon, CR border fighting heavy, other clashes rptd in NW 6-4–6-5, 427B1
US rights missn completed 6-5, 427G1
Panama rebel arms aid chrgd 6-6, 427D1
Fighting reaches Managua; oppositn press burned, looting rptd 6-9–6-13; US evacuates natls 6-11–6-12, 446D2
Rebels attack 4 cities in north 6-11, 446C3
Govt regains control in south, estimates casualties 6-11; rebels offer prisoner swap 6-12, 446D3
Leon falls to rebels, Natl Guard cmdr killed 6-15, 461E2
Rebels launch southn offensive from CR 6-16–6-17, Natl Guard sends reinforcemts 6-18, 461C1
Rebels announce provisional junta 6-17, 461F1
Somoza scores rebel govt, bars resignatn 6-18, 461C2
Govt troops regain control of Managua 6-18, rebel bombing missn fails 6-21, 461D2

1980

Sandinistas bar electns until '85 8-24, 672A2
Somoza assassinated, junta denies death role 9-17; death celebrated 9-18, 697F2, D3
Pol rally banned, oppositn scored 11-9, Managua office attacked 11-10; non-Sandinistas boycott State Cncl 11-12, 874B1

Monetary, Trade, Aid & Investment

'79 exports, '80 target rptd 1-3, 7F1
Mex '80 oil imports seen 1-15, 60B2
Sovt trade pact signed 3-19, 234F2
US aid authrzn OKd 5-19, 410A1
US aid appropriatn OKd 5-31, 709F2
US supplemental appropriatn clears Cong 7-2, Carter signs 7-8, 515E1
US '79-80 aid rptd 7-19, 565B3
Cuba arms shipmts rptd, US blocks aid 8-1; $75 mln released 9-12, 709E2-B3
$582 mln debt rescheduled 9-5, 689C2-A3

Press & Censorship

El Pueblo closed, editors arrested 1-24, 117G3
2 radio commentators ousted 2-1, 2-2, 118B1
La Prensa struck 4-20, 315C2

UN Policy & Developments

Abstains on res vs Sovt Afghan invasn 1-14, 25F2

Unrest

'79 export losses rptd 1-3, 7G1
El Pueblo closed, editors arrested 1-24; 2 radio commentators ousted 2-1, 2-2, 117G3, 118B1
US issues rights rpt 2-5, 87A3
State of siege ended 4-28, 390F1
Larios chrgd in coup plot 9-11, 709C3
Bluefields rioters arrested 9-30, order restored 10-1; deportatns seen 10-2, 792F1
Larios sentncd; 6,000 ex-Guard troops rptd in jail 10-31, 874F1
Business ldr slain 11-17, others rptd jailed 11-18, 887F1

1976

1977

U.S. Relations—*See also 'Human Rights' above*
Solaun confrmd US amb 7-28, 626E3
Somoza hospitalized in US 7-28, 656D3
Somoza ends hospitalizatn 9-7, 767A3
Mil arms sales agrmt rptd set 9-30, 767G2
Rebel ldr asks US end aid 10-26, 864G3

1978

Guerrillas, prisoners flown safely to Panama 8-24, 658E3, 659B1; 22 arrive Cuba 9-1, 690F3
New anti-Somoza gen strike begins 8-25, businesses join 8-27—8-28, 659B2
Managua, Matagalpa bombings, clashes 8-26—8-30, Obando mediates 8-30, 659D2
Mil-civiln plot, 85 arrests rptd 8-28; Somoza: 35 seized 8-29, 659F2
Matagalpa rebels subdued 9-1; strike spreads, backers seized 9-2—9-5, 690E2
Venez asks UN rights probe 9-2; Somoza, govt score 9-4, 9-5, 690D3
Guerrillas launch offensive in Managua, 5 other cities 9-9—9-13; Somoza declares martial law 9-11, calls up Natl Guard 9-12, 705B2
OAS stalls Venez mediatn call 9-11, oppositn ldrs seek forgn role 9-14, 705C3, D3
Venez offers CR troop aid 9-13, 705E3
Jailed oppositn ldr rptd dead, others in hiding 9-14, 705A3
Oppositn groups unite; plan provisnl govt, 3-man comm for cease-fire talks, forgn mediatn effort 9-14, 705B3
Urban revolts crushed, 1500 dead 9-16—9-22; map; Natl Guard atrocities, econ ruin rptd 9-16, 9-19, 756G3-757F2
Guatemala guerrillas kill amb 9-16, 777F1
OAS debates crisis, vs interventn 9-21—9-23, 757C3
Oppositn ldrs freed 9-27, 757B3
Somoza, oppositn OK intl mediatn 9-30, 757G2; team sees Somoza 10-6, oppositn ldrs 10-7, 777D2
Somoza bars resignatn before '81 10-3, 757B3
OAS rights panel visits 10-3—10-7, 777E2
UN reps ask Somoza quit 10-5, 777F2
Venez party scores OAS inactn 10-6, 799C2
Press censorship lifted 10-9, 777F2
Latin church cncl asks Somoza quit 10-13, 823D3
IAPA scores press curbs, Chamorro murder probe 10-13, 829E1, A2
Pol refugees, oppositn ldrs harbored by Mex, other embs 10-13, 10-23, 10-25, 839F1, E3
Siege extended 6 mos, curfew cut 10-13, 839D2
CR, Honduras raid guerrilla camps 10-13, 10-26, 839D3
Venez, Colombia, CR critics scored by Somoza 10-14, 839B3
Guerrillas reject Marxism; demand Somoza exit, for 'pluralistic democracy' 10-16, 823B3
Panama fires col re rebel aid oppositn 10-16, 884D2
OAS censures re CR air raid 10-17, 839A3
Pol talks suspended 10-21; The Twelve quit, FAO submits plan 10-25; talks rptd stalled 10-27, 839D1
Managua, Jinotepe, El Carmen unrest; guerrillas driven into CR 10-30, 839G1
Daily killings rptd 11-2—11-5, Somoza aide shot 11-7, 883F1
Labor group leaves FAO 11-3, 883F2
Somoza bars resignatn; pol talks impasse continues 11-5; US Christns urge US press resignatn 11-8, 883F2, C3
Refugees flee to CR, Honduras, El Salvador; UN unit vows Honduras refugee camp aid 11-6, 883D2
Rights abuses scored by OAS panel 11-17, UN Assemb 12-15, 1019B1
Plebiscite OKd by Somoza, opponents 11-30, terms disputed 12-8—12-27, 1018C2-1019D1
Martial law, censorship lifted 12-7; amnesty signed 12-15, pol prisoners freed 12-16, 1018E2
Guerrillas vs plebiscite 12-11; clash with troops, death toll rptd 12-18, 1018F3
Venez, Panama, CR urged by US to end Sandinista aid 12-11, 1018F3
Pre-amnesty arrests rptd 12-16, 1019B1

U.S. Relations
US urges more freedom, '81 electns without Somoza; Somoza reactn 1-15, 73B3
US to end mil aid 2-1, neutrality spurs anti-Somoza drive 2-5, 91D2
US issues rights rpt, aid cut cited 2-9, 101D3, G3
US proposes '79 arms aid cut 2-22, 127E1
Ramos extraditn sought in Chamorro death probe 4-11, 376C2
US resumes aid 5-16, 376D2
US OKs food, educ aid 5-16, 593D2
Somoza in NY, scores Carter re rights 5-30, visits A-facility 6-22, 593A2
Rights abuse chrgd by US panel 6-24, 490C1
Carter lauds Somoza rights vow, State Dept upset 8-1, 593C2
Natl Guard dismissals seen gesture to Carter 8-18, 659A3
Somoza aide launches govt defense in US 8-31, 690E3
US asks Somoza 'control' troops 9-20, 757F1
US aide visits, Somoza OKs US 'cooperatn' in crisis 9-25, OKs mediatn 9-30, 757G2; mediators see Somoza 10-6, oppositn ldrs 10-7, 777D2
Aid cutoff asked by US congressmen 10-12, 10-13, 823D3, 839G2
OAS Nicaragua censure backed 10-17, 839A3

1979

Natl Guard total casualties rptd 6-20, 461F2
US rptr, aide slain 6-20; Natl Guardsman held, journalists leave 6-21, 461F2
Rebels threaten Inter-Continental Hotel 6-21, 461C3
Rebels abandon Managua, stalled in south 6-28, 476A1
US rptr's slayer confesses 6-30, 512B3
US, Andean Group seek pol solutn 7-4–7-6; junta rejcts 7-5, 503E3-504E1
Rebels continue to threaten Managua, consolidate control in north, advance in south 7-5, 504F1
Natl Guard bombs Leon, Masaya, Rivas 7-8, 512C2
Rebels delay final assault on Managua 7-11, 512A2
Natl Guard surrenders in Grenada, other cities 7-17; guardsmen flee 7-18, 535B2
Rebels take Managua, civil war ends; death toll, refugee count rptd 7-19, 535F1, B3
1,200 Somoza soldrs rptd in Honduras 7-21, invasn plan chrgd 7-28, 573F2
Tribunals to try Somoza soldiers 7-22, 574E1
Managua svcs restored 7-27, 574D1
Curfew, press curbs eased 8-9, 615E3, 616B1
Natl Guard prisoners released 8-11–8-12, Red Cross lauds treatmt 8-15, 616G1
Radicals rally 8-15, 60 foreigners expelled 8-16, 636B2
State of emergency extended 9-18, 732C1
Somoza's nephew, 20 others slain by rightists 10-4; 120 rptd detained 10-10, 793F3
Somoza, son accused in Chamorro death 10-9, 794B1
Crime wave rptd 12-3, security forces reinforced 12-8, 950F3
500-1,000 illegal executns alleged 12-3, 951C1

U.S. Relations
Castro: US caused repressn, deaths 1-1, 20B1
New oppositn group, Somoza vs US role 1-14, 76F3
New plebiscite plan rejctd by Somoza 1-19, 76D2
Carter State of Union Message 1-23, 48F1
US plans mild pressure 2-1, 101D2
US cuts mil ties, emb staff, econ aid 2-8, 255C1
US issues rights rpt 2-10, 107D2
Somoza sets reforms 3-9, 255F1
Somoza visits 4-8–4-9, 269E2, B3
Somoza returns from US 4-18, 332C1
US group protests IMF loan 4-25 Admin OKs 5-14, 373A1 332E1; 40 congressmen 5-10,
US indicts 5 in Panama arms plot 5-14, 386C3
Mex urges US end ties 5-20, 409A1
Heavy fighting near US-owned mines rptd 5-29, 409A2
Viet vet mercenary recruitmt rptd 6-2, 427F1
Rights missn ends, beef boycott proposed; '78, 1st $1/4$ exports rptd 6-5, 427G1-B2
US House Panama subcom hears arms aid chrgs 6-6, 427D1
US citizens evacuate Managua 6-11–6-12, 446B3
Vance asks OAS mediatn, urges pol solutn 6-13, 446G3

1980

U.S. Relations
US issues rights rpt 2-5, 87A3
US aid authrzn OKd 5-19, 410A1
US aid appropriatn OKd 5-31, 709F2
Refugees get 3-mo extensn 6-30, 495B2
US supplemental appropriatn clears Cong 7-2, Carter signs 7-8, 515E1
US delegatn marks Somoza downfall, '79-80 aid cited 7-19, 565E2, B3
$75 mln aid blocked 8-1, released 9-12, 709E2-B3
$582 mln debt rescheduled 9-5, 689G2-A3
Somoza death reactn restrained 9-17, 697F3
Reagan electn reaction 11-5, 841F2
Carter urges 'pluralistic' policy 11-19, 881G2
Reagan policy scored by US amb 12-11, 942C1

1976

NI Chih-fu
In Shanghai post 10-30, 871B3
NICHOLLS, Sir Douglas
Named S Australia gov 5-25, 424A2
NICHOLS, Barbara (Barbara Nickeraurer)
Dies 10-5, 970F2
NICHOLS, Rep. William (D, Ala.)
Reelected 11-2, 821F3, 828F2
NICHOLSON, Jack
Wins Oscar 3-29, 240G2
NICKEL
Australia ocean find rptd 2-26, 154F3
UN Sea Law Conf deadlocked 8-2—9-17, 700F1
NICKEL, Erna & Kurt
Seized on spy chrgs 6-14, 441F3
NICKEL Carbonyl—*See CHEMICALS*
NICKERAURER, Barbara—*See NICHOLS, Barbara*
NICKLAUS, Jack
Named top '75 player 1-16, 123F2
Ties 3d in Masters 4-11, 272G1-A2
Runner-up in British Open 7-10, 716E2
NICKRO, Phil
Montefusco pitches no-hitter 9-29, 756A3
NICOTINE—*See TOBACCO*
NICOUE, Urbain
Sentenced 2-1—2-2, 404C1
NICULESCU, Nicolae
Rumania health min 6-15, 440D2
NICULESCU-Mizil, Paul
Shifted to consumer post 6-15, 440C2
NIDAL, Abou
Blamed for Damascus raid 9-26, 720E3
Linked to radical Palestinians 12-2, 895A1
NIDECKER, John E.
'74 Korea bribe bid rptd 10-29, 900B2
NIEHOUS, William
Kidnaped in Venez 2-27, 208B2
Owens meets kidnap demands 4-6, suspects seized 7-20, 8-3, 592B3
Rptd still alive 8-20, 874C3
Venez kidnap probe stalled 10-9, 874C2

NIGER—*See also AFRICAN Development Bank, NONALIGNED Nations Movement, OAU*
Listed as 'not free' nation 1-19, 20E3
Urgent food aid sought 2-9, 205A3
Cabt shuffled 2-21, 205A3
Coup try foiled 3-15, 205F2
Closer Algeria, Libya ties set 4-8, 372A1
7 executed re Mar coup try 4-21, 483C2
US proposes Sahel aid program 5-1, 318D2
At France-Africa summit 5-10—5-11, 355A3
EC aid set 7-8, 529A3
Olympic withdrawal rptd 7-21, 528B3
Rpt Libya annexes border area 9-9, 696F2
James confrmd US amb 9-23, 808A1
ECOWAS rptd ratified 11-6, 974E2

1977

NI Chih-fu
In Politburo 8-21, 645G2
NICHOLAS, Cindy
Breaks Eng Channel swim mark 9-8, 808B3
NICHOLLS, Sir Douglas
Resigns 5-4, 346D1
NICKEL
Cuba seeks US export 4-20—4-21, 390E1
UN Sea Law Conf adjourns 7-15, US scores rpt 7-20, 572B3
Canada layoffs set 10-20, intl cartel asked 10-21, dumping chrg vs US hinted 10-24, 923F3
Inco to keep ESB 11-11, 918E3
NICKLAUS, Jack
Wins Gleason-Inverrary 2-27; 2d in Masters 4-10, 311C1, C2
Wins Tourn of Champs 4-17, Memorial Classic 5-23; 2d in Pleasant Valley Classic 7-17, 676A1, D1, A2
2d in British Open 7-9, 659A3
3d in PGA Championship 8-14, 659F2
PGA top money winner 10-30, 950G3
NICOLCIOIU, Emil
Dismissed 1-25, 100F1
NIDA (National Institute on Drug Abuse)—*See U.S. GOVERNMENT—PUBLIC Health Service—Alcohol, Drug Abuse & Mental Health Administration*
NIEDERBERGER, Cyril J.
Convicted 2-24, sentncd 3-31, 288G1, A3 *
Gulf indicted 6-15, 504A1
NIEH Jung-chen
In Politburo 8-21, 645G2
Asks Mao creed modificatn 9-9, 694C3
Calls for 'honesty' 744A1
NIEHOUS, William
Kidnap still unsolved 9-25, 867A3 *
NIEKRO, Joe
NL pitching ldr 10-2, 926E3
NIEKRO, Phil
NL pitching ldr 10-2, 926E3
NIELSON, James
Refuses duel 7-6, 615A1
NIELSEN Co., A. C.
TV top 10 list rptd 2-9, 119C1 *
TV viewing decline rptd 12-6, 1021D3
NIEMOLLER, Rev. Martin
Schleyer kidnaped 9-5, 695C2

NIGER—*See also NONALIGNED Nations Movement, OAU*
UN Assemb member 4A1
At France-Africa summit 4-19—4-20, 316F3
Sahel dvpt plan OKd 6-1, 458E3
UN Cncl electns held 10-24, 852F3

1978

US econ aid funds signed 10-18, 862E2
Somoza resignatn rptd sought 10-19, 839E2
Pol talks suspended 10-21, rptd stalled 10-27, 839D1
IMF loan stay, Venez oil cutoff rptd backed by US 11-1, 11-8, 883A3
US Christns urge US press Somoza resignatn, end aid 11-8, 883C3
US mil aid cutoff, econ aid delay cited 11-9, 1018C3
Somoza pressed re plebiscite, oppositn demands 12-7—12-27; US scores 12-27, 1018E2, G2
Trade boycott backed by US unions 12-10, 1014C2
US urges Venez, Panama, CR end Sandinista aid 12-11, 1018F3
Somoza scores re criticism 10-14, 839B3

NICHOLLS, Allan
Wedding released 9-29, 970D3
NICHOLS, Bruce
Wins NCAA tennis title 5-29, 419E2
NICHOLS, George W.
Wins Ala Sen primary 9-5, 699F1
Withdraws from race 10-2, 769F1
NICHOLS, Mike
Drinks Before Dinner opens 11-23, 1031D1
NICHOLS, Rep. William (D, Ala.)
Reelected 11-7, 850B1
NICHOLSON, Jack
Goin' South released 10-6, 970D1
NICKEL
Mich sues Ford Motor re pollutn 2-1, 163D3
Australian mine to close 2-4, 88F1
US House OKs seabed mining bill 7-26, 588F3
NICKLAUS, Jack
2d in LA Open 2-19, 355C3
Wins Inverrary Classic 2-26, 355D3
2d in Doral Open 3-12, 355E3
Wins Tourn Players title 3-19, 355E3
Wins British Open 7-15, 580B2
Wins Phila Classic 7-23, 672D3
PGA top money winner 10-31, 990B3
Wins Australian Open 11-19, 990D2
Named sportsman of yr 12-20, 990A3
NICOTINIC Acid—*See MEDICINE—Drugs*
NIDA (National Institute on Drug Abuse)—*See U.S. GOVERNMENT—PUBLIC Health Service—Alcohol, Drug Abuse & Mental Health Administration*
NIDAL, Abou (Sabry Banna)
Tied to Egypt terror group 4-24, 300E2
PLO asks Iraq return for trial 7-4, 546F3
Fatah ties to slayings 7-13, 7-17, 546D3, F3
Ends feud with Fatah 8-23, 674A1
NIDECKER, John
Testifies on Korean bribes 6-1, 433A1
NIDETCH, Jean
Heinz to buy Weight Watchers 5-4, 364D2
NIEDERBERGER, Cyril J.
Bribery convictn review refused by Sup Ct 11-27, 937C2
NIEDERBERGER v. U.S.
Case refused by Sup Ct 11-27, 937D2
NIEKRO, Phil
Rose closes 44-game hitting streak 7-31, 618F2
NL pitching ldr 10-24, wins Golden Glove Award 11-21, 928G2, B3
NIELDS, John
Questions Park 4-3, 239B2
NIELSEN Co., A. C.
Super Bowl viewing record rptd 1-17, 39F3
NIELSON, Glenn
Announces Pitfield resignatn 6-21, 629A2
NIEMEYER, Oscar
Founds pro-democracy center 8-1, 646E3
NIEMI, Olivia
Sex abuse suit vs NBC dismissed 8-8, 635C2-A3
NIETO, Gen. Alberto Vincente
Quits Argentine post 6-25, 520G3
NIGER—*See also GATT, NONALIGNED Nations Movement, OAU*
Chad peace plan OKd 2-24, 130A2
6 W African natns back ECOWAS 3-18, USSR scores 3-20, 237E1
UN Assemb member 713C3

1979

ABC rptr, aide slain 6-20; Natl Guardsman held, journalists leave 6-21, 461F2
US House probes Panama rebel aid 6-20, 481B2
US urges Somoza ouster, OAS peace force 6-21, 460D3
US envoy meets rebels in Panama 6-27, 475G2
US presses Somoza resignatn 6-28, terms rptd unacceptable 6-29, 475E3, G3
ABC rptr's slayer confesses 6-30, 512B3
US, Andean Group seek pol solutn 7-4—7-6; rebels score 7-5, 503E3-504E1
ISC paymts alleged 7-9, 541F3
Rebels rpt US talks progress 7-12, 512F1
Somoza resigns, leaves for Miami 7-17, 535D1
200 guardsmen hijack plane, fly to Miami 7-18, 535A3
US econ aid rptd 7-19, 574A2
US long-term ties detailed 535C2
Rebels curb bank operatns 7-25, 574B1
Borge meets Pezzullo re arms 7-28, US vs war role 7-30, 573E2, G2
US aid, Red Cross distributn scored 8-4, 603A3
IMF loan probe urged 8-6, 603G1
US bans beef imports 8-6, 616C2
US mil aid to El Salvador debated 8-16, 652E2
Bill of Rights compared 8-21, 636E1
Arms aid sought 8-31, 689A3
US OKs $8.8 mln in aid, limited mil training 9-11, 731E2
3 junta ldrs in US, seek aid 9-24, 731C3
US vows aid 10-1, 754C1
Army officers tour US mil bases 11-11—11-21, 910B1
Currency black mkt rptd thriving 12-3, 951A1

NICHOLLS, Allan
Perfect Couple released 4-5, 528C3
NICHOLS, Dr. Buford
Rpts on breast-feeding 1-5, 64C2
NICHOLS, Jeffrey
On gold price rise 5-27, 435F2
NICHOPOULOS, Dr. George
Presley drug chrgs rptd 12-19, 1005C3
NICKEL
Canada strike continues 5-12, 369F1
NICKLAUS, Jack
Trevino career earnings top $2 mln 6-24, 587C3
Ties for 2d in Brit Open 7-21, 587A1
NICOLE, Anastasia
What the Devil opens 4-16, 712E3
NICOSIA, Steve
In World Series 10-10—10-17, 816D1
NIDA (National Institute on Drug Abuse)—*See U.S. GOVERNMENT—PUBLIC Health Service—Alcohol, Drug Abuse and Mental Health Administration*
NIEHOUS, Donna
Appeals to husband's kidnapers 2-12; Venez closes case 3-1, Owens-Ill drops ransom effort 3-10, 192G3
sband rescued 6-30, 505B3
NIEHOUS, William F.
Wife appeals to kidnapers 2-12; Venez closes case 3-1, Owens-Ill drops ransom effort 3-10, 192F3
Rescued 6-30, news conf 7-1, 505B3
NIEKRO, Joe
NL pitching ldr 9-30, 2d in Cy Young vote 11-7, 955G2, A3
NIEKRO, Phil
NL pitching ldr 9-30, wins Golden Glove Award 11-20, 955G2, 956D1
NIELSEN, Erik
Canada pub works min 6-4, 423F3
NIELSEN, Gifford
Oilers win in playoffs 12-29, 1001A1
NIELSEN, Leslie
City on Fire released 9-14, 819G3
NIELSON, Glenn
Announces Husky sale to Alberta Gas 5-13, 405G2

NIGER—*See also GATT, NONALIGNED Nations Movement, OAU*
Foreign Relations (misc.)
Chad civil war mediatn set 3-1, 153F3
Chad peace pact signed 3-20, 211F1
UN membership listed 695A3
Iran scored for US Emb seizure 11-24, 895D3
U.S. Relations
US issues rights rpt 2-10, 107E3
Student enrollmt in US rptd 167D2
Iran US Emb seizure scored 11-24, 895D3

1980

NICHOLS, Bobby
Nicklaus wins PGA Championship 8-10, 741C2
NICHOLS, Glenn W.
Loses US House electn 11-4, 851F3
NICHOLS, Mary
Scores Reagan remarks 10-9, 779B3
NICHOLS, Mike
Gilda Live released 3-28, 416G2
Billy Bishop opens 5-29, 756B3
Lunch Hour opens 11-12, 892D3
NICHOLS, Rep. William (D, Ala.)
Reelected 11-4, 842A1
NICHOLSON, Jack
Shining released 5-23, 675D3
NICHOPOULOS, Dr. George C.
MD license suspended 1-19, 199C1
Indicted 5-16, 414B2
NICKEL
US curbs French steel imports 11-17, 886B1
NICKLAUS, Jack
2d in Doral Open 3-16, 412G2
Career earnings at $3.4 mln 3-23, 412A3
Watson ties Brit Open record 7-20, 714G2
Wins PGA Championship 8-10, 714B2
NICKLES, Don
In Okla US Sen primary; runoff set 8-26, 683A1
Wins runoff 9-16, 724A3
Elected to US Senate 11-4, 840G2, 845A3, 850B1
NICKS, Carl
In NBA draft 6-10, 447G1
NICOLAIJ, Regina
Arrested 5-6, 411A3
NICOLAZZI, Franco
Vows Venice aid 3-8—3-9, 194C2
NIDING, Gerard
Chrgd in '76 Olympic fraud 10-2, 788E1
NIEKRO, Joe
Astros win NL West playoff 10-6, 795D2
NL pitching ldr 10-6, 926G2
Phillies win NL pennant 10-12, 796C1
NIEKRO, Phil
NL pitching ldr 10-6, wins Golden Glove 12-6, 926E1, G2
NIELDS Jr., John
Gray chrgs dropped 12-11, 940A2
NIELSEN, Arthur C.
Dies 6-1, 528A3
NIELSEN, Leslie
Prom Night released 8-15, 675C3
NIELSEN Co., A. C.
'79-80 TV ratings rptd 4-22, 376A1
'Death of a Princess' rating rptd 5-13, 375E3
'Dallas' episode rating record rptd 11-25, 905B3

NIGER—*See also GATT, OAU*
UN Cncl seat taken 1-1, 12B2
Konutche ends Syria visit 6-26, 525G3
Mondale in African tour 7-17—7-23, 620D2
UN Cncl scores Israel Jerusalem move 8-20, 627C2
Islamic League meets 11-10, 895B2
Libyan role in Chad opposed 12-23—12-24, 979E1

1976

NIGERIA—*See also AFRICAN Development Bank, COMMONWEALTH of Nations, DISARMAMENT—Geneva Committee, OAU, OPEC*
Port clog legislatn rptd 1-5, 102G3
Listed as 'partly free' 1-19, 20D3
New capital, more states set 2-3, 102B3
Mohammed slain, coup try fails 2-13; Obasanjo, Yar Adua appointed 2-14, 141C3, 142C1
Gowon denies coup role 2-13, 192B1
Coup probe ordrd 2-15, ldr arrested 3-5, 191C3
Kano tribal clashes rptd 2-16, 192A1
Defense min, 29 others executed re coup try 3-11, 222B2
Dimka rpts Gowon mtg 3-11, 222D2
Yar Adua backs defense cuts 3-11, 222F2
Cabt shuffled 3-15, 222G2
Austerity budget set; inflatn, other data rptd 4-1, 366A2
'75 oil output down 4-25, 298B3
Ekandem named cardinal 4-27, 336D2
Univ closure, suspensns rptd 5-15, 366E2
Dimka, others executed 5-16, 366F1
Gowon army ouster rptd 5-16, 366G1
Anti-strike law rptd 5-27, 498A3
Const drafted 10-7; local cncls elected 12-28, 1007A3
Free educ rptd 11-10, 1007B3
Foreign Relations (misc.)
Assails Ford letter on Angola, reaffirms MPLA stand 1-7; US rebuts 1-8, 2F2, D3 ★
Equatorial Guinea repressn chrgd 1-7, contract labor evacuated 1-26, 62A1
Anti-US demonstratns rptd 1-11, 16B2
US radio statn ordrd shut 1-16, 103B1
Equatorial Guinea exiles rptd 1-24, 62A2
At intl econ conf 2-11—2-20, 148B1
UK envoy implicated in coup, Nigeria protests 2-16—2-20; envoy recalled 3-4, 191D3
UK newsman expelled 2-16, 192A1
Ford to curb gas imports 2-26, 149D2
Sterling content of reserves cut 3-9, 222B3
UK asked to extradite Gowon 3-12, 222F2
Total IMF oil loan rptd 4-1, 340F2
'75 paymts deficit rptd 4-1, 366B2
Cancels Kissinger visit 4-7, 295A2
US Lockheed data pact 4-20, 286A1
Ghana cancels Kissinger visit 4-28, 295A2
UK vs Gowon extraditn 5-16, 366G1
At Timor Assemb meeting 5-31, 423A1
2 Amers seized in gun plot 6-2, Lockheed link cited 6-19, 498E2
Sovt mil presence rptd 6-13, 467C1
Australian rptd held re gun possessn 6-19, 498F2
Aid to Rhodesia guerrillas rptd 7-6, 488A1
Olympic withdrawal rptd 7-21, 528B3
Decree on industry natlzn rptd 10-29, 1007C3
ECOWAS rptd ratified 11-6, 974E2
'76 US Eximbank loan default rptd 11-11, 915A3
Rhodesia independnc date asked 11-23, 879A2
Exxon unit natlzd 12-23, 1007E3

NIGHT of the Iguana, The (play)
Opens 12-16, 1014F3
NIGHTWORK (book)
On best-seller list 12-5, 972G2
NIKOLIC, Dragomir
4 sentncd re emigre plot 3-12, 223B3
NIKON, Archbishop (Nicolas P. Rklitsky)
Dies 9-4, 1015C2
NILES, Mich.—*See MICHIGAN*

NIMEIRY, Mohammed Gaafar el- (Sudanese president)
19 executed re '75 coup try 1-23—2-22, 502E1 ★
Cabt reshuffle 2-10, 502C1
Backs Eritrea peace efforts 5-31, 457D2
Army revolt crushed 7-2—7-3; led loyal forces 7-3, 501B3
Returns from US, Paris visits 7-2, 501C3
Cites Mahdi role in coup 7-2, 502A1
At OAU summit 7-5, 487G2
Says Libya ties cut 7-6, 501D3
Signs Egypt defns pact 7-13—7-14, 531D2
Ties Libya to coup 7-15, 531C3
Joins Egypt, Saudis vs Libya 7-18—7-19, 531B2
Plotters executed 8-4, 8-5, 592C2
Shuffles Cabinet 8-9, 857E2
Ethiopia rebels free UK newsman 9-6, 674A3
Ex-mins sentenced to die 9-30, 857C2

1977

NIGERIA—*See also COMMONWEALTH of Nations, DISARMAMENT—Geneva Committee, NONALIGNED Nations Movement, OAU, OPEC*
Crude oil price rise rptd 1-5, 12B2
Dissident home burned 2-18; civilian-mil strife rptd 2-19, 258F1
Cabt shuffled 3-15, 393C2
'76 oil output rise rptd 3-21, 227G3
'77-78 budget set, '76-77 econ data cited 3-31, 393F1
Const Assembly elected 8-31, 746A3
Constituent Assemb opens 10-6, 986B3
Foreign Relations (misc.)
UN Assemb member; Elias on World Ct 4A1, F1
Pirates raid forgn freighters 1-9, 48C2
Pan-Africa festival 1-15—2-12, 105D1, 106B1
UN comm scores Israel occupatn rule 2-15, 107F2
Afro-Arab policy statemt scored 3-3—3-5, 170B2
Uganda to move Ghana office 5-24, 429C2
Ethiopia army strength compared 6-25, 547D3
UN conf vs apartheid 8-22—8-26, 661E2
$1 bln Euroloan rptd 9-1, 746C3
UN Cncl elects member 10-24, 852F3
UK, UN Rhodesia reps visit 11-9, 875A3, 876A1
USSR to train officers 11-13, 986A3
Pirates raid Danish ship 11-21; natns protest 11-22, security tightened 11-24, 986E2
Namibia contact group tours 11-21—12-7, 1016E3
France, W Ger gun boat sales rptd 11-23, 986G2
S Africa oil ban asked 12-14, 1016A2
U.S. Relations
Young visits 2-7—2-10, 105C1, C2
US natl freed 3-7, 393E2
US rptr ousted 3-12, 258E1
Garba sees Young, Zaire mediatn role OKd 3-22, 261A1
Young vs US 'cold war' policy 4-11, 271D3
Ashland payoff rptd 5-17, 503B1
UN amb scores Young speech 5-19, 399E2
Young presents Rhodesia plan 8-24, 661F1
Carter apartheid effort lauded 8-25, 662B1
Chase unit rptd in $1 bln loan 9-1, 746C3
Carter visit scheduled 9-23, 738F1
Obasanjo visits DC 10-11—10-12, 797D1
Copter sale set 10-17, 986B3
Carter visit deferred 11-7, 854A1; rescheduled 12-1, 914C2
Namibia contact group tours 11-27—12-7, 1016E3

NIGHTCLUBS—*See RESTAURANTS & Nightclubs*
NIH—*See U.S. GOVERNMENT—PUBLIC Health Service—National Institutes of Health*
NILE River
Zaire invasn seen threat 5-1, 394B1
Sudan canal oppositn rptd 9-7, 844A1
NILSSON, Ulf
WHA final standings 4-7, 310F2

NIMEIRY, Mohammed Gaafar el- (Sudanese president)
Chrgs Ethiopia plot 1-1, recalls amb 1-5, 24A3
Ethiopia seen backing new coup try 62D3
Backs Eritrea separatists 1-30, 98B3
Elected party secy-gen 2-9, 117F2
Names Cabt 2-11, 117F2
Joins Egypt-Syria cmnd 2-27—2-28, 143F2
At Red Sea summit 3-22—3-23, 208F2
Reelected 4-20, 417A1
Visits France 5-17—5-19, 450D1
USSR advisers expelled 5-18, 417A1
Asks US arms 5-24, 400B1
Rightist reconciliatn rptd 7-18, 602C2
Announces gen amnesty 8-8, 619C2
Al-Mahdi, other pardoned 8-13, 711B1
Shuffles Cabt 9-10, 843G3
Greets al-Mahdi 9-28, 843E3
Sees Sadat, hails Israel trip 11-22, 890B3
NIMETZ, Matthew
Named State counselor 1-7, 14C2
NIMITZ Aircraft Carrier—*See ARMAMENTS—Ships*
NIMROD (UK aircraft)—*See ARMAMENTS—Aircraft*
NIN, Anais
Dies 1-14, 84D3
Delta of Venus on best-seller list 8-14, 643F1; 9-4, 712D3
1984 (book)
USSR bars entry 9-6, 765G3

1978

NIGERIA—*See also COMMONWEALTH of Nations, DISARMAMENT—Geneva Committee, GATT, NONALIGNED Nations Movement, OAU, OPEC*
Freedom House lists as partly free 44A2
Govt takes over undeveloped land 3-29, 248D1
'78-79 austerity budget rptd 4-3, 247G3-248C1
Jan oil output drop rptd 4-3, 248B1
Students protest tuitn rise 4-28, 479E1
State mil govs abolished 7-24; pol party ban lifted 9-21, 3 parties emerge 9-22, 758F1
Foreign Relations (misc.)
Garba presses Horn of Africa mediatn 2-9, 100E1
Angola rebels chrg troops sent 2-10, 165D1
UN comm votes res vs Israel 2-14, 99A2
UN Chile rights abuse res abstentn 3-6, 210F1
6 W African natns back ECOWAS 3-18, USSR scores 3-20, 237E1
USSR trade pact signed 3-21, 248E1
Barclays funds withdrawn in S Africa dispute 3-22; '76, '77 data cited 237A2
S Africa chrgs rights abuse 3-31, Obasanjo asks tougher sanctns 4-1, 233G2-234A1
'77 paymts deficit rptd 4-3, 248B1
Consumer import bans rptd 4-4, 248C1
Islamic bank poor-natn aid rise rptd 4-9, 257F2
In Rhodesia mtg 4-15, 290F2
W Ger chancellor visits 6-26—6-27, defends S Africa ties 6-30, 584B1
At Smith-Nkomo mtg 8-14, 740G2
6 forgn ships expelled for unloading violatns 9-2, 758A2
UN Assemb member, named to Cncl 9-19, 713A3, C3
Callaghan, Kaunda meet 9-22, 756A3
USSR backed re Rhodesia 11-24, 911G3
$750 mln loan set 11-30, 934G1
French loan pullout cited 11-30, 934A2
Sports
World Amateur Boxing tourn results 5-6—5-20, 600D2
U.S. Relations
Textron paymt probed by US 2-28, 161C2
Carter visits, Obasanjo asks stronger S Africa sanctns 3-31—4-3, 233B1, F2-234C1
Textron bribe evidence rptd destroyed 5-8, 449B1
IBM quits re local ownership rule; Colgate, Citibank pullouts cited 6-26, 798G2-799B1
ITT paymts chrgd 11-2, 876C1
IBM joint venture rptd 11-6, 906B3
Rhodesia effort scored 11-24, 911G3
NIGER River
Sub-Sahara drought danger rptd 1-3, 24G1
NIGH, Lt. Gov. George (D, Okla.)
Faces primary runoff for gov 8-22, 683C1
Wins runoff 9-19, 737A1
Elected Okla gov 11-7, 853D3, 855G2
NIGHTCLUBS—*See RESTAURANTS*
NIGHT Fever (recording)
On best-seller list 3-8, 196B1; 4-5, 272F3; 5-3, 356D1
NIGRO, Robert
PS Your Cat is Dead opens 3-22, Company 5-7, 887D1, F2
NIH—*See U.S. GOVERNMENT—PUBLIC Health Service—National Institutes of Health*
NIJINSKY, Vaslav (1890-1950)
Ex-partner Karasavina dies 5-26, 440G2
NIKAIDO, Susumu
Tied to Lockheed scandal 1-30, 72E3
NIKODIM, Metropolitan
Dies 9-5, 778G1
NILSSON, Kent
Winnipeg wins WHA title 5-22, 458B2
Named WHA top rookie 7-6, 656D3
NILSSON, Ulf
Signs with NHL Rangers 3-20, 296F1
WHA assist ldr 4-11, 296A2, G2, A3
Winnipeg wins WHA title 5-22, 458B2
NIMEIRY, Mohammed Gaafar el- (Sudanese president)
1st parlt electns rptd 3-21, 497B2
To head Arab summit com 3-28, 215C1
Signs Natl Front pact 4-12, 293A1
Vows continued dvpt 5-24, 479A2
Oppositn party disbands, ldr amnestied 7-3, 595B1
Vs forgn troops in Africa 7-18, 561G1
OAU chrmn, Arab link cited 7-22, 561C2
Takes defns min post in Cabt shuffle 7-29, 595D1

NIMITZ, U.S.S. (aircraft carrier)
US jet drops bomb on Sardinia 2-11, 133E2
NIMRODS (Hawker-Siddeley surveillance planes)—*See ARMAMENTS—Aircraft*
NINE, Louis
Loses US House election 2-14, 108C2

1979

NIGERIA—*See also COMMONWEALTH of Nations, DISARMAMENT–Geneva Committee, GATT, NONALIGNED Nations Movement, OAU, OPEC*
Freedom House lists as partly free 13A1
Oil prices hiked 3-27, surchrg set 3-28, 227C3
Oil prices hiked 5-25, 396D2
Oil prices hiked again 6-28, 473F1
Civiln Senate elected 7-7, 545E1
Civiln House elected 7-14, 636A3
Oil output cut rptd 7-25, 645D2
Shagari elected pres 8-11, vote results challenged 8-18, 636E2
Army size rptd 9-4, 825B3
Shagari electn upheld 9-26; inagurated, govt installed 10-1, 753B3
Oil prices hiked above OPEC limit 11-3, 864D1
Oil price per barrel rptd 12-21, 977B2
Foreign Relations (misc.)—*See also 'UN' below*
Chad ex-pres arrives 3-23, 329C3
Zimbabwe Rhodesia recognitn barred, warns US, UK 5-31, 393G1-B2
Ghana oil shipmts halted 6-29, 524C2
BP oil sales cut 7-12, 545A2; assets natlzd, S Africa, Zimbabwe cited; UK scores 7-31, 584D2-D3
Chad factns meet in Lagos 8-21, 638D2
Barclays boycott rptd ended 9-26, 796D3
UK warned re Zimbabwe solutn 11-15, 881F1
UN Policy & Developments
UN amb scores Westn loans to S Africa 4-2, 270E2
Israel arrests Unifil offcr 6-15; PLO arms smuggling admitted 6-22, 551F3
Membership listed 695A3
Israel sentncs, expels UNIFIL offcr 12-24, 980C1
U.S. Relations
Young, US trade missn visit; oil exports, fertilizer plant deal rptd 9-11–9-15, 720A3, G3

NIGH, Gov. George (D, Okla.)
Abstains in govs' vote on Carter '80 support 7-8, 518D1
NIGHTCLUBS—*See RESTAURANTS*
NIGHT and Day (play)
Opens 11-27, 956E3
NIGHT of the Living Dead (film)
Sequel released 4-19, 528A2
NIH—*See U.S. GOVERNMENT–PUBLIC Health Service–National Institutes of Health*
NIJINSKY, Vaslav (1890-1950)
Massine dies 3-16, 272B3
NILSSON, Kent
Named WHA best sportsman 5-16, 470F2

NIMEIRY, Mohammed Gaafar el- (Sudanese president)
Backs Giscard re Eur ties 5-22, 398D3
Scores Tanzania re Uganda invasn 7-17, 552C2
Ousts Ibrahim 8-12; names Khali vp, takes party ldrship 8-13, 617G3

NIMMO, Robert
Scores Fonda Viet war role 7-20, 593E2
NIMOY, Leonard
Star Trek released 12-8, 1008F1
1984 (book)
USSR OKs book fair entry 9-4, 690D1
1940's Radio Hour, The
Opens 10-7, 956E3
1941 (film)
Released 12-14, 1008A1

1980

NIGERIA—*See also COMMONWEALTH of Nations, GATT, GENEVA Committee, NONALIGNED Nations, OAU, OPEC*
Freedom House lists as free 87D3
Prisoners suffocate in van 3-3, 354E1
'80 budget presented 4-1, 353G3
Foreign Relations (misc.)—*See also 'Oil & Gas', 'UN Policy' below*
UK trade reductn cited 1-16, 59F1
Amnesty Intl evaluates rights record 3-3, 354F1
Africa trade cited 4-1, 243B2
Import curbs eased 4-1, 354A1
Zimbabwe gains indepndnc 4-18, 301E1
Chad refugee total rptd 4-23, 311B2
S Africa warned, A-bomb dvpt hinted 10-3, 792C2
Islamic League meets 11-10, 895B2
Libyan role in Chad stirs controversy 12-23—12-24, 979C1
Oil & Gas Developments
Oil prices hiked 1-2, corrected; US exports cited 1-4, 4G1
Natl oil co dirs' bd suspended in scandal 4-17, probe begun 4-18, 354C1
Forgn cos oil-take disputed 8-8, 620E1
US record inventories rptd 9-5, Admin assured vs shortfall 10-3, 785E3
US warned on S Africa 10-3, 793C2
Africa exports vowed 11-9, 864D2
UN Policy & Developments
Cncl replacemt seated 1-1, 12C2
Leb militia head blames UNIFIL troops for mine blast 4-30, 363A1
U.S. Relations
Mondale visits, signs trade pact 7-23, 620C2
Shagari in US 10-3—10-7; warns on S Africa 10-3, meets Carter 10-7, 792C2

NIGH, Gov. George (D, Okla.)
State of State message 2-19, 404A1
Declares drought 'prayer day' 7-20, 616E1
NIGHTCLUBS—*See RESTAURANTS & Nightclubs*
NIGHT Games (film)
Released 4-11, 416C3
NIH (National Institute of Health)—*See under U.S. GOVERNMENT--PUBLIC Health Service*
NIJBOER, Gerard
Wins Olympic medal 8-1, 624E1
NIJINSKY (film)
Released 3-20, 216D3
NIJINSKY, Romola
Nijinsky released 3-20, 216D3
NIJINSKY, Vaslav (1890-1950)
Nijinsky released 3-20, 216D3
NIKITIN, Igor
Wins Olympic medal 7-28, 624F2
NIKOLAY, Michael
Wins Olympic medal 7-25, 622F3
NILES, John Jacob
Dies 3-1, 280D1
NILSSON, Kent
In NHL All-Star game 2-5, 198G2
NIMETZ, Matthew C.
Israel to build jet fighter 2-25, 180G1
NIMITZ (U.S. aircraft carrier)
Returns to Norfolk, Carter greets crew 5-26, 403F1-B2
Carter mil pay proposal scored 5-28, 424B2
1941 (film)
Heaven's Gate withdrawn from theaters 11-19, 906E1

1976

1975 World Series (TV special)
Wins Emmy award 5-17, 460C2
90 Minutes at Entebbe (book)
Published 7-26, 547F1-C2
NINOMIYA, Kazuhiro
Wins Olympic medal 7-28, 575A1
NIPPON Maru (Japanese sailing ship)
In Operation Sail 7-4, 488A3
NISHIOKA, Takeo
In new party 6-25, 497B3
NISHIYAMA, Takichi
'74 acquittal reversed 7-20, 539D1
NISSAN Motor Corp.
Datsun tops '75 US imports 1-11, 280G1
Buys Australia VW plant 2-12, 137E3
US car dumping chrgs end 5-4, 320F3, 321D2
Australia OKs project 6-10, 438B3
Australia deal set 8-15, 650F1
US rates Datsun fuel-econ 9-22, 766A2
Oct US sales rptd 11-3, 885A3
NITSCHKE, Carola
Sets world swim mark 6-1—6-5, 424G3
NITZE, Paul H.
Briefs Carter on defns 7-26, 551D1
Carter campaign donatn rptd 10-22, 939B1
NIUE Island (New Zealand territory)
S Pacific Forum meets 3-8—3-9, 179B2
NIVEN, David
Horses on best seller list 1-25, 80C3; 2-29, 208E3; 12-5, 972B2
NIX, Rep. Robert N.C. (D, Pa.)
Reelected 11-2, 830D3
NIXON, Peter J.
'77 Concorde flights OKd 5-28, 400C1
Lobbyists oppose Concorde 7-20, 537B2
Qantas admits price cutting 9-23, 749F3

NIXON, Richard Milhous
Chou En-lai dies 1-8, 9A2
Iran CIA aid request rptd 1-26, 93B1
Armstrong confrmd UK amb 1-27, 68B1
N Viet claims econ aid vow 2-1, 103B1
China visit planned 2-6, Ford comments 2-10, 109F3, 117F3
Visits China 2-21—2-29, Admin seeks rpt 3-2, 189A3
China ICBM projct rptd dropped 2-24, 190D1
Testimony on Chile released, Sen Church scores 3-11, 183G2, F3
US sets Taiwan force cut 3-11, 254F2
Ford denies Mideast rpt 3-17, 198F2
'71 wage-price freeze cited 3-19, 215E1
China trip rpt 'useful' 3-22, 215A1
Tanaka denies '72 Lockheed deal 4-2, 286C2
Howard Hughes dies 4-5, 336E1
US-Sovt A-test pact drafted 4-9, 242E2
Rentschler pleads guilty 4-20, 316E3
'72 electn costs, donors rptd 4-25, 688A1
Sen com cites use of intelligence agencies 4-28, 330B2
US-Sovt A-treaty signed 5-28, 387B1
Martha Mitchell dies 5-31, 404C2
'Love letters' called 'hoax' 6-4, 438A2
Sen com rpt cites '72 Iran arms deal 8-1, 581F2
Reactn to Mao death 9-9, 657C2
'70, '71 emergencies ended 9-14, 689C2
Rpt Brezhnev regrets resignatn 9-29, 752D1
'74 Panama Canal toll hike cited 10-5, 793E1
Sup Ct refuses import surchrg challng 11-29, 901A1
Carter appoints Schlesinger 12-23, 956G2
Presidential Campaign Issue
Ford on China trip 2-17, 129G2
Reagan on China trip 3-6, 180E1
Reagan warns GOP vs Ford nominatn 3-9, 180F1
Sen Church scores 3-11, 183F3
Church scores Ford pardon 4-19, 282B1
Carter notes policy shift 6-14, 433C1
Mondale cites pardon 7-15, 507G3, 511F2
Ford defends pardon 7-19, 532A1
Carter scores pardon 7-20, 532G1
Mondale scores farm policy 7-31, 565C1
Carter assails scandal 8-3, 564E2
Carter vs condoning crimes 8-11, 585B2, E2
GOP platform com omits reference 8-12, 583A2
GOP conv 8-15—8-19, 598G2, 599G3, 601B2, 614F3
Cited in Dole biog sketch 614D2-B3
Rptdly watches GOP conv on TV; favors Ford, Connally ticket 8-19, 615G3
Carter chrgs Ford continuity 8-20, 632F1
Mondale scores on housing, educ, arms sales 8-25, 8-28, 645G2, B3
Carter assails morality 9-7, 664F2
Carter lists 9 econ errors 9-15, 686D3
Carter Playboy interview cites 9-20, 704C2
Ford, Carter debate 9-23, 701F2, E3, 703C1
Carter clarifies Playboy remarks 9-24, 724E2
Carter on African policy 9-27, 724B2
Carter sharpens attack 9-30, 10-1, 742E3, G3
Mondale scores Ford, Dole 10-5, 743A3

1977

1977 Gordon Conference on Nucleic Acids—*See NUCLEIC Acids, 1977 Gordon Conference on*
NIPPON Kokan K. K.
Technology edge vs US rptd 8-13, 776B1
US dumping chrgs upheld 10-3, 774C3
NIPPON Steel Corp.
US upholds dumping chrgs 10-3, 774C3
NISHIO, Shunichi
Seizes hostages 3-3—3-4, 201A3
NISSALKE, Tom
Named NBA coach of yr 5-19, 584F3
NISSAN Motor Corp.
Datsun tops '76 US import sales 1-6, 38F3
US import rank cited 4-11, 463G3
Volvo, Saab agree to merge 5-6, 469D3
Datsun 2d in EPA gas ratings 9-19, 723C3
NITRATES & Nitrites—*See CHEMICALS*
NITROSAMINES—*See CHEMICALS*
NITROUS Oxide—*See CHEMICALS*
NITSCHE, Hellmuth
E Ger ousts 8-29, 684E1
NITSCHKE, Karl-Heinz
E Ger ousts 8-29, 684E1
NITZE, Paul H.
Testifies vs Warnke 2-9, 2-28, 172B3
Leaks SALT details 11-1, 996D2
NIUE Island
NZ to set 200-mi fishing zone 9-7, 729B3
NIXON, Norm
In NBA draft 6-10, 584B2
NIXON, Peter
Threatens air controllers 1-11, 42F2
Named Australia transport min 12-19, 982A2

NIXON, Richard Milhous
Ollie Atkins dies 1-9, 84F2
Carter inaugurated 1-20, 26E2
Richardson named amb at large 1-25, 53F1
HEW schl aid cutoffs considered 2-17, 156D3
Sen OKs reorganizatn powers 3-3, 191D3
Germ warfare tests rptd 3-8, 195C3
Carter asks Job Corps funds 3-9, 173G1
DC ct reorganization upheld 3-22, 231E1, A2
Carter reorganizatn powers cleared 3-31, 228B1
Carter assistance offered 4-19, 321E3
Regional mil spending inequities chrgd 4-26, 423B3
Young calls racist 6-3; GOP, Carter score 6-6; Young explains 6-6, 6-7, 443B3-444A1
Alaska pipeline opens 6-20, 476A3
Foreign Policy
Cited in Japan Lockheed trial 1-27, 83C2
Viet aid pledge copy asked 2-22, Nixon denies commitmt 5-14, US releases letter 5-19, 403E2
Chile coup support chrgd 3-9, 219E1
Carter denies cruise missile agrmt 3-30, 225G2
Carter bars shoe import curbs 4-1, 248D3
Rpt vowed normal US-China ties 4-10, 298D2
Latin neglect chrgd 4-17, 296C1
Viets cite aid vow 5-4, 333C1
Brazil policy rejected 5-11, 414F1
Frost TV interviews 5-12, 385D3; 5-19, 405C3; 5-25, 419B3
Hanoi airs aid note 5-22, US chrgs omissns 5-23, 403D3
Hanoi aid opposed 6-2—6-3, 441G1
Korea scandal cover-up chrgd 7-7, 557B1
USSR: Jews influenced electn 7-22, 589C2
Panama Canal pacts signed 9-7, 677E1
USSR drugging of staff suspected 9-21, 721A3
USSR '71 Davis trial invitatn cited 12-15, 1017B2
Frost TV Interviews (& developments)
On Watergate 5-4; reactn, poll rptd 5-4—5-9, 365G3-368A1
Carter thinks violated law 5-12, 381C2
On forgn affairs, Kissinger 5-12, 385D3
On natl security actions, Indochina 5-19, 405C3
On resignatn, Agnew, Allende 5-25, 419B3
Haldeman vs cover-up version 5-26, 420B3
On tapes, Mitchell, news media, Kissinger 9-3, 692G2
Watergate
Ulasewicz sentenced 2-18, 197E2
Sup Ct bars Ehrlichman convictn review 2-22, 150A1
4 Watergate burglars get setlmts 2-22, 157F2
Agnew friend sentncd 4-4, 312C3
Watergate appeals decisn leaked 4-21, 382C2; review denied 5-23, 406E1
Frost TV interview 5-4; reactn, poll rptd 5-4—5-9, 365G3-368A1
Jack Anderson suit rptd 5-4, 423B1
Campaign funds rptd seized 5-6, 482E2
Haldeman vs cover-up versn 5-26, 420B3

1978

NIPPON Kokan K. K.
US '77 dumping ruling revised 1-9, 80E2
Australia iron imports set 5-30, 411F1
NIPPON Steel Corp.
On US trigger prices 1-4, 3B3
US '77 dumping ruling revised 1-9, 80E2
Australia iron imports set 5-30, 411F1
China mill constructn set 12-5, 986D2
NISSAN Motor Corp.
'78 US import price hike rptd 7-17, 665E1
US Datsun prices hiked, $ drop linked 10-29; Nov US sales rptd down 12-6, 935F3
NIT (National Invitation Tournament)—*See BASKETBALL—Collegiate*
NITRATES & Nitrites—*See CHEMICALS*
NITROGLYCERIN—*See MEDICINE—Drugs*
NITROSAMINES—*See CHEMICALS*
NITSCHKE, Ray
Enters Pro Football HoF 7-29, 1025D1
NITZE, Paul H.
Scores SALT 12-5, 12-14, 995G1
NIUE Island—*See SOUTH Pacific Forum*
NIVAR Seijas, Maj. Gen. Neit
Rptd behind vote count suspensn, says situatn 'normal' 5-17, 371D3, F3
Loses army command 8-16, 648F2 ★
Sen rejcts as OAS mil rep 11-9, 881B1
NIVEN, David
Candleshoe released 8-4, 969F3
NIX, Rep. Robert N. C. (D, Pa.)
Defeated in primary 5-16, 389D3
Gray wins seat 11-7, 849E2
NIXON, Norm
NBA assist ldr 4-9, 271G2
NIXON, Peter
On domestic air fare hike 7-13, 555C2
Announces UK air fare cut 10-11, 793B3
Qantas curb on Jews probed 10-18, 836D1
Seeks cut-rate US air fare 11-14, 920F2

NIXON, Richard Milhous
Cong support rating cited 1-7, 12B3
Attends Humphrey rites 1-15, 32A3
Haldeman book chrgs Watergate break-in, cover-up role; other allegatns rptd 2-16—2-17, 124G1-125D1
Park admits contributn 4-3, 239A2
Anderson suit dismissed 4-4, 265B1
FBI probe clears Admin 4-10, 262D1
Broadcasters denied White House tapes by Sup Ct 4-18, 308C1
Ehrlichman freed 4-27, 320B2
Memoir excerpts published, Watergate role cited 4-30, 5-1, 319D2-320A2
Clements wins Tex gov primary 5-6, 362E3
Wallace quits Sen race 5-16, 362B3
China asks '72 communique implemented 5-20, 384G2
Blamed for '72 inflation 5-22, 427B2
Hosts ex-POW receptn 5-27, 513D2
Ex-aide testifies on Korea bribes 6-1, 433A1
RN: Memoirs on best-seller list 6-4, 460C3; 7-2, 579C3; 8-6, 620B2
Honored in Hyden (Ky), warns vs forgn aggressors 7-2, 513A2
Sup Ct voting alignmts shift noted 7-3, 565E3
Snepp book ruling scored 7-7, 527C3
Kalmbach reinstated by Calif bar 7-11, 844B1
Presley offer to aid FBI rptd 7-14, 553E3
Pub seen grading offcls harder 7-26, 682C3
ITT-Hartford merger case cited 7-28, 767G1
Albania scores China re '72 visit 7-30, 635E1
Bobst dies 8-2, 708A2
Carter poll ratings compared 8-10, 8-27, 682C2, D2
Haldeman legal fees to exceed book profits 8-17, 844C1
Carter aides linked to Vesco 'pol fix' 9-1—9-15, 719G3
Cited at JFK death hearings 9-13, 9-14, 749E2
Colson movie premiers 9-24, 844D1
'71 wage-price controls, $-gold actions cited 11-1, 825C1, 826C1
Presidential papers law signed 11-4, 897D2
Cohen wins US Sen seat in Me 11-7, 847D2
Speaks in Biloxi, backs Iran shah 11-11, 900C2
In Paris, comments on Watergate 11-28; at Oxford 11-30, 942A2
Fernandez enters pres race 11-29, 938B3
Lacey dies 12-11, 1032B3
US-China ties agreed 12-14, 973F1, 975B2, D2
'72 Shanghai communique text excerpt 976D2
Buzhardt dies 12-16, 1032D2
Haldeman leaves prison 12-20, 1011A3
Data access upheld by US Appeals Ct 12-21, 1011B3

1979

NIPPON Steel Corp.
China cancels contract 2-26, 181E3
China revives contract 6-12, 484E3
NISSIM, Moshe
Palestinian talks open 5-25, 394A3
NIT (National Invitation Tournament)—*See BASKETBALL–Collegiate*
NITRATES & Nitrites—*See CHEMICALS*
NITROSAMINES—*See CHEMICALS*
NITROUS Oxide—*See CHEMICALS*
NITZE, Paul H.
Scores SALT at Sen hearing 7-12, 536D1
NIXON, Norm
NBA assist ldr 4-8, 290G2
NIXON, Pat (Thelma Catherine Patricia Ryan) (Mrs. Richard Milhous)
Amer Cancer Soc gift rptd 7-11, 527B3
NIXON, Peter
Dropped from Coordinatn Com 2-4, 113D2
Assumes Sinclair portfolio 9-27, 787F3

NIXON, Richard Milhous
Haig associatn cited 1-3, 3A3
Rand study on '75 S Viet collapse issued 1-7, 29E1
Invited to China state dinner 1-17, 29E3
Connally announces pres bid 1-24, 70F2, A3
Rockefeller dies 1-26, 104B1, C2
Sees China dep prime min in DC 1-29, 1-31; return protested 1-29, 66F1, C2
'69-74 pub TV moves disclosed 2-24, 194A1
US blocks H-bomb article, Pentagon Papers controversy compared 3-9, 193G3-194A1
Carter peanut loan probe sought 3-13, 184B2; special counsel named 3-20, 203D1
Grandson born 3-14, 271G2
Pol Pot document on '70 US Cambodia invasn rptd 3-18, 229G2
Kissinger phone records case accepted by Sup Ct 4-16, 302E3
Cited in Carter SALT address 6-18, 458A3
Carter poll rating compared 7-1, 497F2; 7-9, 514E1
Amer Cancer Soc gift rptd 7-11, 527B3
Ruled liable in tap suits 7-12, 611D2
Visits shah in Mex 7-13, 544C2
Cited re Carter Cabt shake-up 7-17–7-20, 529G1, 530B3
White House tapes release OKd 7-24, 561E2
'72 FRB credit policy, '69 Volcker apptmt cited 7-25, 555E2, C3
Magruder starts mktg exec job 8-8, 656G2
Buys NYC apartmt 8-11, 656A3
Butterfield dismissed by Calif Life 8-16, 656F2
San Clemente estate expenses disputed 9-5–9-6, 683B2
Draft Haig com forms 9-10, 680E2
Visits China 9-17–9-22, 751F1
San Clemente cost repaymt asked by Cong 9-26, 883F2
Buys NYC town house 10-5, 860E1
Eisenhower tapes revealed 10-21, 869B1
Viet vet drug dischrgs ordrd upgraded 11-28, 992E1
'Brethren' publicatn stirs controversy 12-2, 988D2
Judge Gurfein dies 12-16, 1008A3
Haig bars pres bid 12-22, 984G1
'71 gold, $ policy cited 12-31, 978F1

1980

NINE to Five (film)
Released 12-19, 1003C2
NIPPON Steel Corp.
USSR OKs deal delay 2-19, 235F3
US protests French-Sovt steel deal 9-19, 728E3
NIPPON Telegraph and Telephone Public Corp. (NTT)
Japan bars open bidding 5-15, 482E1
Japan-US trade talks resume 10-19, 864B3
US, Japan sign procuremt pact 12-19, 995C2
NISSAN Motor Co. Ltd.
UAW pres asks US plants 1-13, 35C2
US Jan sales rptd up 2-5, 127B3
US truck productn plan rptd 2-18, 127D1
US truck plant sought, UAW pres asks car plants 4-17, 288D1
US raises truck import duty 5-20, 384A2
Spain investmt talks rptd 6-4, 467C3
US productn, tariff rise feared 7-1, 7-29, 599G1
Alfa Romeo project OKd 9-20, 751B3
Reagan aide quits campaign post 10-30, 818A1
VW joint project planned 12-3, 924D3
NISSEN, Inge
Old Dominion wins AIAW basketball title, named tourn MVP 3-23, 240B3
NISSIM, Moshe
Israeli justice min 8-13, 653F3
NITRATES & Nitrites—*See CHEMICALS*
NITROPYRENE—*See CHEMICALS*
NITZE, Paul H.
US arms outlay rise urged 5-9, 369A3
NIUE Island
Island trade pact rptd 7-24, 576G2
NIXON, Jeff
NFL '79 interceptn ldr 1-5, 8D2
NIXON, Norm
NBA assist ldr 3-30, 278E3
Lakers win NBA title 5-16, 432C1
NIXON, Pat (Thelma Catherine Patricia Ryan) (Mrs. Richard Milhous)
Becomes NYC resident 2-14, 199C3
NIXON, Peter
Rpts Sovt grain sale limit 6-24, 496A2
Backs Sovt grain embargo 11-18, 900G2
NIXON, Richard Milhous
Sovt grain embargo cited 1-8, 12G3
Ehrlichman Calif bar resignatn accepted 1-19, 199D1
Bush denies '70 campaign gift coverup 2-7, 128E3
Becomes NYC resident 2-14, 199C3
Fscl '69 budget surplus cited 3-31, 243G3
Agnew death fears rptd 4-20, 333D3
Bennett dies 5-4, 448C1
'76 Sup Ct oil import fee ruling cited 5-13, 366C1
Ia schools buy White House uniforms 5-16, 460A3
Taps case accepted by Sup Ct 5-19, 440C1
Trial order petitn rejected by Sup Ct 5-19, 440F1
Watergate tapes go public 5-28, 460F1
Impeachmt lawyer sentencd 6-10, 460B1
Dem platform blames 6-24, 480A1
Helen G Douglas dies 6-28, 528E1
Real War on best-seller list 7-13, 568C3
GOP platform adopted 7-15, 535B3
At shah's funeral, lauds Sadat 7-28—7-29, 571F1
Wm J Baroody dies 7-29, 608B1
Carter pres renominatn acceptance speech 8-14, 613A3
Testifies at FBI ex-offcls' trial 10-29, 884B2
Allen quits Reagan post 10-30, 817E3
'69 nerve gas productn halt cited 12-5, 935B3
Taps case argued in Sup Ct 12-8, 937C2
Haig named secy of state 12-16, 955A2
Sues for pres records 12-17, 963B3
Haig hires atty for confirmatn hearings 12-22, 980C1

1976

Carter scores Ford 10-9, 10-10, 762C2, F2
Mondale, Dole debate Watergate 10-15, 784A1
Ford denies Watergate coverup; Ruff, Levi vs new probe 10-15, 10-20, 784F3
Carter on crime 10-15, health-care 10-19, 785F1
Dole rebuts Dems 10-17—10-27, 804E1-A3
Ford cites re Arab boycott 10-20, 784B3
Ford, Carter debate 10-22, 800D2, 801G2
Mondale hits Watergate 10-29—10-31, 827C2
Watergate Issue—*See also 'Presidential Campaign Issue' above; also WATERGATE*
Cited in Gulf payments rpt 134B1
Newman fined 1-6, 6C3
Tapes custody ruling upheld 1-7, 6E2
Kissinger, Haldeman tap depositns filed 1-12, 3-11, 184B1, A2
Wiretap deposition filed 3-10, 183G3
Woods wins personal items return 4-23, 316E1
Sen com rpts FBI wiretap use 5-9, 344E2
Editor files wiretap suit 5-10, 349E2
Ehrlichman verdict upheld 5-17, 379E1
Disbarred in NY 7-8, 493B3
Milk lobbyist gets 2 yrs probatn 8-20, 1016A1
'76 bid to Grumman chrgd 9-13, 979G1-D3
Mitchell, Haldeman, Ehrlichman convictns upheld; Mardian overturned 10-12, 770E1-E2
Release of tapes OKd 10-26, 849A3
Ehrlichman enters prison 10-28, 849F2
S Korea bribery attempts, lobbying rptd 10-29, 11-7, 899B3, 900A3
Sup Ct accepts papers case 11-29, 900C2
O'Neill named House speaker 12-6, 919E1
Held liable re wiretap 12-16, 980A3-981B1
Ulasewicz convicted 12-23, 981C1
Flying Tiger contributn rptd 12-29, 986F1

NIXON, Mrs. Richard Milhous (Thelma Catherine Patricia Ryan)
China visit planned 2-6, 109F3, 117F2
In China 2-21—2-29, 189A3
Hospitalized with stroke 7-8, 519B2

NJOBA, Cornelius
Lauds Namibia plan 8-20, 654D1

NJONJO, Charles
Warns vs pres successn debate 10-6, 947B2

NKOMO, Joshua
Smith talks continue 1-6—1-8, 1-16, 53F3
In UK 176D2
Smith scores guerrillas 2-6, 176G1
UK envoy in talks 2-24—2-27, 176A2
Smith talks collapse 3-19, 239D3
On UK charter plan 3-23, 240A2
At Zambia mtg 3-24—3-25, 240E2
Sees Kissinger 4-26—4-27, 295F1
Vs chiefs in cabt, hardens stand 5-7, 339E2
Todd house arrest lifted 6-5, 428E2
Arrest rptd sought 6-27, 522B3
OAU told of Rhodesia violence 6-28, 487F3
At conf on ANC rift 9-6—9-7, 661E3 *
Sithole claims ZANU ldrshp 9-9, 733B3
Backs Kissinger plan 9-21, 697E1
Scores UK majority rule plan 9-23, 718F1
Backs ANC factn mtg 9-25; sees Muzorewa 10-1, Schaufele, Rowlands 10-4, 738F2-A3
Asks Rhodesia conf delay, joins Mugabe, sets demands 10-9; UK invites to conf 10-12, 781C1, C2
Names conf delegatn 10-14, 781D2
Vs Smith terms 10-22; arrives Geneva 10-24, warns conf boycott 10-27, 797C1, E1
Independnc bid fails 11-2, 831D3
Vs intl fund, favors Sovt ties 11-8, 843D2
Sees Richard 11-10, 843E1
Conf resumptn delayed 11-13, 862D1
Vs new indepndnc date plan 11-16; Muzorewa denounces 11-17, 861G2
Sees Angola, Mozambique reps; Botswana office bombed 11-19, 879A2
OKs UK independnc date 11-26, offers interim govt plan 11-30, 893B1, F1
ANC chrgs plot 11-27—11-28; UK, Zambia deny 11-28, 11-29, 893C2
Muzorewa scores on electns 12-4, 914B3
Muzorewa-Smith pact seen, Muzorewa scores 12-14, 935G1, B2
Zambia cuts Muzorewa ties 12-19, 1009C3
Asks tea massacre probe 12-22, 1009A2

NL Industries Inc.
Rpts titanium price-fixing talks 12-5, 988A2

1977

Haldeman, Mitchell enter prison 6-21, 6-22, 483F2
US documts custody upheld 6-28, 539D3
Halperin awarded $5 in tap suit 8-5, 652B2
Tapes open for civil suit 10-3, 760B2
Demarco case review refused 10-3, 760C3
Mitchell, Haldeman, Ehrlichman jail terms cut 10-4, 761G3
FBI break-in links probed 12-6, 940F1

NIXON, Mrs. Richard Milhous (Thelma Catherine Patricia Ryan)
Nixon-Frost interview 5-25, 419D3, 420E1

NIZAR, John
Arrest rptd 4-9, 304B3

NJENGA, Michael
Offers Ethiopia aid 9-9, 715G2

NJOBA, Cornelius
Angola refugees barred 1-12, 21E3

NKOMO, Joshua
New ZAPU front rptd 1-6, 3F2
Front-line states back 1-9, 10D3
Sees Richard 1-10, 11E1
Aide killed 1-22; natlst strife cited 1-24, 49D2
Smith rejects UK plan 1-24, 49E1
Vorster bars Smith pressure 1-28, 73B1
Bars Richard mtg 1-30, 72A3
ZAPU kidnaps 400 students 1-30, 73D1
Muller asks pact 2-2, 122A3
At Frelimo cong 2-3—2-7, 137E1
OAU backs Patriotic Front 2-4, 122B3
Army chrgd in cleric deaths 2-7, 85D1
ZAPU urges Geneva talks resumed 2-22, 145A1
Podgorny backs Patriotic Front 3-26, meets 3-28, 247G3
Flies to Angola 3-29, 249D3
Owen sees Mugabe 4-11, 296E1
At front-line mtg 4-17—4-18, 296D3
Sees UK, US reps 5-31, 457E1
Sees US, UK reps 7-7; proposal scored 7-12, 536B1, D1
Muzorewa scores 7-17, 563G3
Civil war fears cited 7-25, 581F3
Zambia office bombing rptd 8-1, 599B3
ZAPU blamed for Salisbury blast 8-7, 624B2
Sees Young on Carib tour 8-9, 646B3
Sets peace terms 8-12, rejcts UK-US const plan 8-15, 624E1
Owen, Young seek new plan support 8-28, 661A2
Vs UK-US plan 9-14, 735B1
Smith sees Kaunda 9-25, mtg detailed 10-26, 810B2, D2
Patriotic Front unity talks delayed 10-3, 810A3
Frictn re Smith-Kaunda mtg rptd 10-30, 875C3
Sees UK, UN reps 10-31, 875B3

NLRB—*See U.S. GOVERNMENT—NATIONAL Labor Relations Board*
NOAA—*See U.S. GOVERNMENT—COMMERCE—National Oceanic & Atmospheric Administration*

1978

NIXON v. Warner Communications Inc.
Broadcasters denied Nixon tapes by Sup Ct 4-18, 308D1

NJONJO, Charles
Sets corruptn drive 10-31, 885A3

NKOMO, Joshua
Facts on 59A1
Sees UK, US reps in Malta 1-30, 59E1, G1
Malta mtg ends 2-1, 120A1
Scores internal setlmt pact 2-16, UK, US reactns 2-17, 119E3
Rhodesia raids Zambia camp 3-5—3-6, 156A1
Addresses UN Sec Cncl on pact 3-9, 192G3
Sees US, UK reps 3-11—3-14, rejects internal pact talks 3-14, 193B1
Muzorewa scores Kaunda support 3-19, 210G2
Sees Young 3-22—3-24, 248D3
Rhodesia interim govt frees supporters 4-13, 290G3
Sees Vance, Owen; asks Anglo-Amer plan chngs 4-14—4-15, 290E2
Mugabe plot denied 4-23, 455C3
ZAPU legalized 5-2, 317E2
Cubans rptd training ZAPU 5-14, 395C3
Vorster backs govt role 5-27, 615C2
Admits Cubans train troops 6-6, 455D2
ZAPU cited re missionary deaths 6-27, 594A3
Sees Schmidt 6-30, W Ger aid hinted 7-6, 584G1
Rhodesia interim govt backs role 7-18, 615C2
Sees Smith 8-14, bars US-UK conf 9-11, 740F2-B3
Front-line ldrs split on Smith mtg 9-2, 740E3
Claims ZAPU downed civiln jet 9-5, 740E3
ZAPU members arrested 9-9, 9-13, party banned 9-14, 741A1, D1
ZANU scores mil effort 9-11, 740C3
Smith mtg cited re Tanzania-Lonrho dispute 9-26, 905F2
Zambia reopens Rhodesia RR 10-10, 783D3
Rhodesia bombs Zambia camp 10-19, 784B2
Rejects new talks 10-20—10-22; disputes Rhodesia Zambia raid claim 10-22, 819D1
Matabele chief asks return 11-8, 884F2
OKs new UK envoy mtg 11-27, 912A1
Claims oil depot attack 12-11, 955C3

NKRUMAH, Kwame
CIA role in '66 coup chrgd 5-8, 367F3

NKUMBULA, Harry
Sets Zambia pres candidacy 8-1, 617E1
Kaunda elected, UNIP rule chng cited 12-12, 989G2

NL (National League)—*See BASEBALL*
NLRB—*See U.S. GOVERNMENT—NATIONAL Labor Relations Board*

NLRB v. Writers Guild of America, West Inc.
Unions curbed on supervisor discipline by Sup Ct 6-21, 509E1

NOAA—*See U.S. GOVERNMENT—COMMERCE—National Oceanic & Atmospheric Administration*

1979

NKOMO, Joshua
Rhodesian dispute role described 170A2
Claims credit for downed Air Rhodesia jet; scores US, UK denunciatns 2-14, 136B3
Rhodesia hits Angola camps 2-26, 170G1
Rhodesians raid Lusaka, home destroyed 4-13, 294B1
E Ger visit re mil aid rptd 6-19, 490F2
Zimbabwe troops raid Lusaka 6-26, 490E2
Detainees rptd freed 7-4, 547F1
Muzorewa repeats amnesty offer 7-10, 546A3
Vs Commonwealth Zimbabwe plan 8-7, 8-9, 589G2, 590C1
To attend UK setlmt conf 8-20, 638E1
London conf opens 9-10; const chng, agenda debated 9-11, 9-12, 675F2, C3, F3
London talks deadlocked 9-13; OKs white const role 9-24, 717F3, 718D1
Vs new UK const proposal 10-8—10-11, unilateral talks begin 10-16, 777B2
OKs UK const plan 10-18; transitn talks deadlocked 10-19—11-2, 844E1
Zimbabwe bars Zambia corn shipmts 11-5, 844F2
Transitn talks continue 11-9—11-14, OKs UK plan 11-15, 881A1, B1
UK offers cease-fire plan 11-16, accepts gen terms 12-5, 936G3-937F1
Salisbury office raided by police 12-14, 960A2
Initials cease-fire 12-17, 960A1, D1
Signs cease-fire, other pacts 12-21, 976A3
Factnal tensn cited 12-22, 976B1

NKRUMAH, Kwame
Limann pol bent cited 6-22, 485B3
Afrifa executed 6-26, 485E2

NLRB—*See U.S. GOVERNMENT- NATIONAL Labor Relations Board*

NLRB v. Baptist Hospital
Case decided by Sup Ct 6-20, 516B2

NLT Corp.
Great Southn acquired 1-17, 88G3

NOAA—*See U.S. GOVERNMENT-COMMERCE-National Oceanic & Atmospheric Administration*

1980

NIXON v. Fitzgerald
Trial order petitn rejected by Sup Ct 5-19, 440G1

NKALA, Enos
Soames bars campaigning 2-10, 118B3
Zimbabwe finance min 3-11, 198D1
Issues budget 4-20, 301A2
ZAPU protests Nkomo threats 7-9, 581E3
Incites Mugabe guerrillas 11-10, 889A1

NKOMO, Joshua
Vs rebel assemb deadline 1-2, 7B3
Returns to Zimbabwe, asks reconciliatn 1-13, 31C2
Registers ZAPU as Patriotic Front; party symbol rejected 1-14, 49B1, D1
Mugabe returns from exile 1-27, 80G1
Smith favors over Mugabe 1-31, 118E3
Carrington chrgs Mugabe voter intimidatn 2-6, 118F2
Bomb blast kills 2 2-24, 162A2
ZAPU starts army integratn 2-25, 198B2
Electns held 2-27—2-29, Mugabe win rptd 3-4; Cabt role seen 3-4, 161C1, C2
Refuses presidency 3-6; named home affairs min 3-11, to oversee immigratn 3-13, 198B1, F1
Walls named army head 4-15, 301C3
Zimbabwe gains indepndnc 4-18, 301F1, G1
Force reductn urged 5-30, 469D1
Denounces ZIPRA rebelln chrgs 6-27; Mugabe excludes from Matabele mtg, rift rptd 7-26, 581A3
Walls resigns army post 7-17, 568D1
Pol violence kills supporter 9-13, 795B2
Rival guerrillas clash 11-10—11-11, 888F3
Supporters arrested 11-21, 946E2

NLRB (National Labor Relations Board)
See under U.S. GOVERNMENT

NLRB v. Longshoremen
Case decided by Sup Ct 6-20, 555G2

NLRB v. Mercy Hospital Association
Case declined by Sup Ct 4-14, 307D1

NN Corp.
Engelhard to buy 6-24, 557D3
Armco wins merger bid 8-20, 745G3

NOAA (National Oceanic and Atmospheric Administration)—*See under U.S. GOVERNMENT--COMMERCE*

NOAH, Yannick
Loses Italian Open 5-25, 607D3

1976

NOBEL Prizes
Jane Kennedy nominatn rptd 3-4, 272D1
Winners plead for Sovt dissident 3-24, 421G2
Announced 10-14—10-21, 839E3
10 laureates score Ford 10-26, 840B2
NOBLE, Dr. Ernest
On Rand alcholism study 6-10, 814G3
NOCETTI Fasolino, Alfredo
Asks Lopez Rega extraditn 3-8, 211G3
Dismissal in Peron probe rptd 5-8, 399B3
NOCKE, Peter
Wins Olympic medal 7-25, 575E2
NODA, Uichi
Named to econ post 11-5, 889F3
NOE, James A.
Dies 10-18, 970F2
NOEL, Jeanie
Arrest rptd 8-17, 624E3
NOEL, Gov. Philip W. (D, R.I.)
Quits platform post 5-14, 357F3
Loses Sen primary 9-14, 704E3
NE govs meet 11-13—11-14, 864B3
NOGUES, Alberto
To be named Paraguay forgn min 3-8, 206B1
NOISE Abatement—*See under ENVIRONMENT*
NOLAN, Gary
In World Series 10-16—10-21, 815E3
NOLAN, Rep. Richard (D, Minn.)
Reelected 11-2, 829F4
NO Man's Land (play)
Opens 11-9, 1014F3
NO Mystery (record album)
Wins Grammy 2-28, 460B3
NONALIGNED Nations Movement (Afghanistan, Angola, Algeria, Argentina, Bahrain, Bangladesh, Benin, Bhutan, Botswana, Burma, Burundi, Cameroon, Cambodia, Cape Verde, Central African Empire, Chad, Congo, Comoros, Cuba, Cyprus, Egypt, Equatorial Guinea, Ethiopia, Gabon, Gambia, Ghana, Guinea, Guinea-Bissau, Guyana, India, Indonesia, Iraq, Ivory Coast, Jamaica, Jordan, Kenya, Kuwait, Laos, Lebanon, Lesotho, Liberia, Libya, Madagascar, Malawi, Malaysia, Mali, Malta, Mauritania, Mauritius, Morocco, Mozambique, Nepal, Niger, Nigeria, North Korea, North Yemen, Oman, Panama, Peru, Qatar, Rwanda, Sao Tome and Principe, Saudi Arabia, Senegal, Seychelles, Sierra Leone, Singapore, Somalia, Southern Yemen, Sri Lanka, the Sudan, Swaziland, Syria, Togo, Trinidad and Tobago, Tunisia, Uganda, United Arab Emirates, Tanzania, Upper Volta, Vietnam, Yugoslavia, Zaire, Zambia and the Palestine Liberation Organization)
Tito woos Latins, Portugal 3-9—3-22, 256C2
Sadat, Tito conf on summit 4-9, 275E2
Angola sets policy 5-23, membership backed 5-31, 455B3
Peru forgn min ousted 7-16, new min to boycott mtg 8-4, 590C3
UN Sea Law Conf deadlocked 8-2—9-17, 700F1
Sri Lanka conf; adopts Korea resolutn, issues communique 8-16—8-20, 621F2
US on Korea stand 8-18, 8-25, 618E3, 626E1
Malta forgn policy cited 9-20, 713E1

NORCROSS, David F.
Wins Senate primary 6-8, 410A1
Loses electn 11-2, 821B2
NORDBERG, William
Dies 10-3, 970F2
NORDEN, Albert
E Ger Politburo enlarged 5-22, 381E2
NORDHEIMER, Jon
Interviews Reagan 3-10, 180B2

NORDLI, Odvar
Norway premr; cabt listed 1-12, 30F1
At Europn socialist conf 1-18—1-19, 48A3; 3-13—3-14, 222F3
NORFOLK, Va.—*See VIRGINIA*
NORMAN, Fred
In World Series 10-16—10-21, 815A3
NORMAN, Neville
Named to econ advisory bd 9-14, 730G1
NORRIS, Clarence (Willie)
Pardoned 10-25, 859G3—860B1
NORRIS, Dr. John
Scores alcohol study 6-9, 443E1
NORRIS Industries, Inc.
'75 arms sales listed 2-6, 147D3
NORSKE Esso, Inc.—*See EXXON*
NORTH, Bill
AL batting ldr 10-4, 796D1
NORTH, Joseph
Dies 12-20, 1015C2

1977

NOBADULA, Mzukisi
Death rptd 12-26, 1016C3
NOBEL Prizes
Announced 10-6—10-14, 951B2
NOBLE, Dr. Ernest P.
Warns pregnant women vs alcohol 6-1, 472E1
NOBRE da Costa, Alfredo
Portugal industry min 3-25, 330E2
NOERGAARD, Ivar
Danish commerce min 2-25, 373D1, E1
NO-Fault Insurance—*See AUTOMOBILES—Insurance Issues*
NOISE Abatement—*See under ENVIRONMENT*
NOLAN, Gary
Traded to Angels 6-15, 644E2
NOLAN, Rep. Richard (D, Minn.)
Farmland fund plan withdrawn 3-11, 195C1
Says farm bill inadequate 9-24, 737B1
Sees Castro on Africa 12-5, US prisoner to be freed 12-13, 1011G2, D3
NOLL, Chuck
Atkinson loses slander suit, Blount suit cited 7-22, 659C1, E1
NOMURA, Shusuke
Seizes hostages 3-3—3-4, 201B3

NONALIGNED Nations Movement (Afghanistan, Angola, Algeria, Argentina, Bahrain, Bangladesh, Benin, Bhutan, Botswana, Burma, Burundi, Cameroon, Cambodia, Cape Verde, Central African Empire, Chad, Comoros, Congo, Cuba, Cyprus, Egypt, Equatorial Guinea, Ethiopia, Gabon, Gambia, Ghana, Guinea, Guinea-Bissau, Guyana, India, Indonesia, Iraq, Ivory Coast, Jamaica, Jordan, Kenya, Kuwait, Laos, Lebanon, Lesotho, Liberia, Libya, Malagasy, Malawi, Malaysia, Mali, Malta, Mauritania, Mauritius, Morocco, Mozambique, Nepal, Niger, Nigeria, North Korea, North Yemen, Oman, Panama, Peru, Qatar, Rwanda, Sao Tome e Principe, Saudi Arabia, Senegal, Seychelles, Sierra Leone, Singapore, Somalia, Southern Yemen, Sri Lanka, Sudan, Swaziland, Syria, Tanzania, Togo, Trinidad & Tobago, Tunisia, Uganda, United Arab Emirates, Upper Volta, Vietnam, Yugoslavia, Zaire, Zambia and the Palestine Liberation Organization)
Tanzania, Kenya affirm policy 3-23, 3-25, 247B3, F3
Belize '75 independnc resolutn cited 5-20, 414C3
Tito asserts Yugo support 8-16—9-8, 709D3-G3
Yugo sees US acceptance 10-4, 785E3
Yugo pres backs 10-19—10-20, 844F2

NON-Nuclear Future, Conference for a
Salzburg mtg 4-29—5-1, 335E1, 403E1
NOORANI, Maulana Shah Ahmed
Arrested 3-18, 223C1
Released 6-3, 450A3
NORDHAUS, William
Named to CEA 1-18, 52E3

NORDLI, Odvar (Norway premier)
North Sea Ekofisk oil well productn halted 4-28—5-2, 336F2
Jovanka Broz at receptn 6-14, 786B1
Party wins one-vote edge 9-12, Norland recount 9-15, 730E1, B2 ★
NORFOLK, Va.—*See VIRGINIA*
NORFOLK Island (Australia territory)
Appeals to UN on pol status 2-9, 132A2
NORFOLK & Western Railway Co.
ICC curbs grain-car deals 8-1, 613C1
NORIN Corp.
Fortune rpts '76 sales rise, Maple Leaf Mills purchase 340C1, 341B1
NORLAND, Donald R.
Named amb to Botswana, Lesotho, Swaziland 4-25, confrmd 6-23, 626B3
NORMAN, Dan
Traded to Mets 6-15, 644D2
NORMAN Jr., George I.
Sup Ct curbs IRS tax seizures 1-12, 57A3
NORMAN, John D.
Linked to child porno 5-15, 432A3
NORMAN, Nelson
Traded to Rangers 12-8, 990C1
NORMAN Thomas: The Last Idealist (book)
Wins Natl Book Award 4-11, 355B2
NORPIPE—*See PHILLIPS Petroleum Co.*
NORRIS, Clarence
Denied compensatn 4-6, 396B3
NORTH America—*See also country names*
Mid-'75 populatn rptd 1-30, 123G2

1978

NOATAK River (Alaska)
Carter protects Alaska lands 12-1, 936G3
NO Beast So Fierce (book)
Film versn released 3-18, 619G3
NOBEL Prizes
'77 peace winners to quit Ulster movemt 4-15, fund dispute rptd 4-17, 373B1
15 winners score Orlov trial 5-19, 401B2
Announced 10-5—10-27, 886B1-B3
Sadat to shun rites 11-30; aides comment 12-1, 12-2; Begin, Sadat aide accept 12-10, 950B3-951A1
NOBILE, Gen. Umberto
Dies 7-29, 620C3
NOBLE, Ray
Dies 4-3, 356C3
NOERGAARD, Ivar
Named Danish environmt min 8-30, 688A1
NOGUCHI, Isamu
Natl Gallery commissn rptd 6-1, 578C3
NOGUERA, Luis R.
Teacher released 5-13, 620A1
NOISE Abatement—*See under ENVIRONMENT*
NOLAN, Dick
Promoted to Saints coach 2-6, 171A3
NOLAN, Rep. Richard (D, Minn.)
Reelected 11-7, 851B2
NOLTE, Nick
Who'll Stop Rain released 8-25, 1030G3

NONALIGNED Nations Movement (Afghanistan, Algeria, Angola, Argentina, Bahrain, Bangladesh, Benin, Bhutan, Botswana, Burma, Burundi, Cambodia, Cameroon, Cape Verde, Central African Empire, Chad, Comoros, Congo, Cuba, Cyprus, Djibouti, Egypt, Equatorial Guinea, Ethiopia, Gabon, Gambia, Ghana, Guinea, Guinea-Bissau, Guyana, India, Indonesia, Iraq, Ivory Coast, Jamaica, Jordan, Kenya, Kuwait, Laos, Lebanon, Lesotho, Liberia, Libya, Malagasy Republic, Malawi, Malaysia, Maldives, Mali, Malta, Mauritania, Mauritius, Morocco, Mozambique, Nepal, Niger, Nigeria, North Korea, Oman, Palestine Liberation Organization, Panama, Peru, Qatar, Rwanda, Sao Tome e Principe, Saudi Arabia, Senegal, Seychelles, Sierra Leone, Singapore, Somalia, Sri Lanka, Sudan, SWAPO, Swaziland, Syria, Tanzania, Togo, Trinidad & Tobago, Tunisia, Uganda, United Arab Emirates, Upper Volta, Vietnam, Yemen, Yemen Arab Republic, Yugoslavia, Zaire, Zambia)
Carter backs Yugo 3-9, 194E1
Carter chrgs Cuba subversn 6-7, 423D3
Yugo scores E-W conflict 6-20, 519F2
UN disarmamt sessn ends, little progress seen 6-30, 523A1
Forgn min mtg; Cuba scored re Africa role, Sovt alliance; bilateral disputes 7-25—7-30, 583G1
SWAPO admitted 10-2, 820D1

NONGOGO (play)
Opens 12-3, 1031F2
NOONAN, Tom
Buried Child opens 11-6, 1031B1
NOONE, Bill
Moliere opens 3-12, 887B2
NOOR al-Hussein, Queen (Jordan) (formerly Elizabeth [Lisa] Halaby)
To wed King Hussein 5-15, 420A3
Marries Hussein, proclaimed queen 6-15, 580B1
NORANDA Mines Ltd.
Copper strike cited 10-20, 805C1
NORDEN, Albert
Scores W Ger article 1-18, 36A2

NORDLI, Odvar
Hails Volvo deal, Sweden-Norway econ pact 12-8, 965B3
Bars Norway EMS entry 12-11, 952D2, E2
NOREPINEPHRINE—*See CHEMICALS*
NORFOLK, Va.—*See VIRGINIA*
NORFOLK Island (Australian territory)
Australia offers home rule 5-8, 369D3
NORFOLK State College (Va.)
HEW OKs Va integratn plan 3-17, 369B1
NORFOLK & Western Railway Co.
Struck 7-10, union pres on issues 7-14, 565F1
US acts to end natl strike 9-26—9-29, strike ends 9-30, 809D2
NORMAL, Ill.—*See ILLINOIS*
NORMAN, Edward
Scores WCC pol bias 11-8, 907D1
NORMAN, Greg
2d in golf World Cup 12-3, 990E2
NORRISH, Ronald George Wreyford
Dies 6-7, 540D3
NORRIS Trophy, James—*See HOCKEY—Awards*
NORTH, Andy
2d in Tourn of Champs 4-16, 355G2
Ties for 2d in Kemper Open 6-4, wins US open 6-18, 580G1, F3
US wins golf World Cup 12-3, 990E2
NORTH, Billy
In World Series 10-10—10-17, 799D3

1979

NOBARI, Ali Riza
On probe of shah's assets 11-26, 897D2
NOBEL Prizes
13 winners cut Sovt links 3-1, 172D2
Announced 10-12–10-18, 857C3
NOERGAARD, Ivar
A-plants deferred 4-9, 276B2
NOFZIGER, Lyn
Resigns from Reagan campaign 8-28, 661E3
NOGUEIRA, Victor
NASL goalkeeping ldr 8-12, 654G3, 655B1
NOISE Abatement—*See under ENVIRONMENT*
NOLAN, Rep. Richard M. (D, Minn.)
Castro explains attack on US 1-7, 40E3
Joins draft-Kennedy move 5-23, 384C2
NOLTE, Nick
North Dallas Forty released 8-1, 820D2
NO More Tears (Enough Is Enough) (recording)
On best-seller list 11-7, 892E3

NONALIGNED Nations Movement (Afghanistan, Angola, Algeria, Argentina, Bahrain, Bangladesh, Benin, Bhutan, Bolivia, Botswana, Burma, Burundi, Cambodia, Cameroon, Cape Verde, Central African Republic, Chad, Comoros, Congo, Cuba, Cyprus, Djibouti, Egypt, Equatorial Guinea, Ethiopia, Gabon, Gambia, Ghana, Grenada, Guinea, Guinea-Bissau, Guyana, India, Indonesia, Iran, Iraq, Ivory Coast, Jamaica, Jordan, Kenya, Kuwait, Laos, Lebanon, Lesotho, Liberia, Libya, Malagasy Republic, Malawi, Malaysia, Maldives, Mali, Malta, Mauritania, Mauritius, Morocco, Mozambique, Nepal, Nicaragua, Niger, Nigeria, North Korea, North Yemen, Oman, Pakistan, Panama, Patriotic Front, Peru, PLO, Qatar, Rwanda, Sao Tome e Principe, Saudi Arabia, Senegal, Seychelles, Sierra Leone, Singapore, Somalia, South Yemen, Sri Lanka, Sudan, Surinam, SWAPO, Swaziland, Syria, Tanzania, Togo, Trinidad & Tobago, Tunisia, Uganda, United Arab Emirates, Upper Volta, Vietnam, Yugoslavia, Zaire, Zambia)
Cambodia-Viet conflict reactn rptd uncertain 1-11, 11B2
Khomeini defines Iran policy 2-24, 145E1
Tito sees Brezhnev, reaffirms committmt 5-16, 379E3
Mex, Cuba discuss Havanna conf 5-17–5-18, 372F2
Coordinating bur mtg; Viet, Egypt disputes cited 6-4–6-11, 437B1
Spain defends Havana conf plans, US unruffled 8-10, 8-13, 654D2
Preparatory summit mtgs 8-28–9-1, 674C3
Cuba denies US rpt on Sovt troop presence 8-31, 657D2; USSR scores US 9-10, 673C2
6th summit held in Havana; new natns admitted, pro-USSR tilt seen 9-3–9-9, 674B2, 675C1-D2
Leb hijackers protest missing Moslem ldr 9-8, 677E3
Burma quits, Cuba summit cited 9-28, 742C2
Nigeria reaffirms ties 10-1, 753C3
Castro in US 10-11–10-14; addresses UN, asks $300 bln aid 10-12, 778B2
NORDHOFF, Charles
Hurricane released 4-11, 528E2
NORDLI, Odvar (Norwegian premier)
Volvo sale blocked 1-26, to meet Sweden premr 1-27, 77C2
Announces Cabt chngs 10-5, 774D1
Carter sees, urges missile plan OK 12-7, 938E1
Wage controls extended 12-18, 996E3
NORFOLK, Va.—*See VIRGINIA*
NORFOLK and Western Railway Co
Railway clerks sign accord 1-8, 87B2
Rock Island takeover ordered 9-26, 722C3
Southn Railway merger talks ended 10-19, 868A2
NORMAN, Greg
2d in Australian Open 11-28, 970C2
NORMAN, Maria
Simpson Street opens 3-5, 292A3
NORMAN, Marsha
Getting Out opens 5-15, 711B3
NORMAN, Tom
Moscone-Milk slayer convicted 5-22, 386A1
NORMA Rae (film)
Released 3-1, 174C3
Top-grossing film 4-4, 271F2
NORRIS Trophy, James—*See HOCKEY–Awards*
NORTH, Billy
NL stolen base ldr 9-30, 955F2
NORTH, Edmund H.
Meteor released 10-19, 1008A1
NORTH Alabama, University of (Florence)
Wins NCAA Div II basketball title 3-17, 239B1
NORTH American Affairs, Coordination Council for
US-Taiwan ties to continue 2-15, 146F1-A2

1980

NOBARI, Ali Riza
Claims shah family plundered 2-26, 137F2
Calls US hostage response 'cool' 11-11, 861A2
NOBEL Prizes
US laureates cut Sovt ties 4-16, 326A3
Announced 10-9—10-15, 889G1
NOEL, William
Charged in GSA scandal 1-15, 112F1
NOFZIGER, Lyn
Reagan retains Brock 6-13, 452A3
Quits Reagan press post 11-30, 935F2
Named pres asst 12-23, 980C2
NOISE Abatement—*See under ENVIRONMENT*
NOLAN, Bob
Dies 6-16, 528A3
NOLAN, Dick
Fired as Saints coach 12-25, 999G1
NOLAN, Leland
Fiendish Plot of Dr Fu Manchu released 8-8, 675E2
NOLAN, Rep. Richard (D, Minn.)
Weber wins seat 11-4, 851E1
NOLES, Dickie
In World Series 10-14—10-21, 812B2
NOLL, Chuck
Steelers win Super Bowl 1-20, 61G2-62C1
NO Lost Love (book)
On best-seller list 5-4, 359D3; 6-8, 448B3
NOLTE, Nick
Heart Beat released 4-25, 416A3
NO More Tears (recording)
On best-seller list 1-2, 40E3
NONALIGNED Nations Movement (Afghanistan, Algeria, Angola, Argentina, Bahrain, Bangladesh, Benin, Bhutan, Bolivia, Botswana, Burma, Burundi, Cambodia, Cameroon, Cape Verde, Central African Republic, Chad, Comoros, Congo, Cuba, Cyprus, Djibouti, Egypt, Equatorial Guinea, Ethiopia, Gabon, Gambia, Ghana, Grenada, Guinea, Guinea-Bissau, Guyana, India, Indonesia, Iran, Iraq, Ivory Coast, Jamaica, Jordan, Liberia, Libya, Malagasy Republic, Malawi, Malaysia, Maldives, Mali, Malta, Mauritania, Mauritius, Morocco, Mozambique, Nepal, Nicaragua, Niger, Nigeria, North Korea, North Yemen, Oman, Pakistan, Panama, Patriotic Front, Peru, PLO, Qatar, Rwanda, Sao Tome e Principe, Saudi Arabia, Senegal, Seychelles, Sierra Leone, Singapore, Somalia, South Yemen, Sri Lanka, Sudan, Surinam, SWAPO, Swaziland, Syria, Tanzania, Togo, Trinidad & Tobago, Tunisia, Uganda, United Arab Emirates, Upper Volta, Vietnam, Yugoslavia, Zaire, Zambia)
Yugo scores USSR Afghan invasn 1-6, 11B1
UN res vs Sovt Afghan invasn backed 1-14, 25D2
NATO rejects united actn re Afghanistan 1-15, 28F1
Carter cites USSR threat 2-25, 139B3
Tito dies 5-4, Castro skips funeral 5-8, 338C2, 339A1
NATO scores Afghan invasn 5-14, 377C2
W Ger sees Sovt Afghan invasn impact 6-30, 489G1
India sets Cambodia ties 7-7, 547G2

NONGONOCOCCAL Urethritis (NGU)—*See MEDICINE--Diseases*
NORAD—*See NORTH American Air Defense Command*
NORFOLK—*See VIRGINIA*
NORFOLK and Western Railway Co.
Southn Railway merger sought 6-2, 427C2
Southn ends Chessie-Seaboard merger oppositn 7-10, 745D3
Southn Railway merger OKd by bd 7-22, 598F3
NORFOLK and Western Railway v. Liepelt
Case decided by Sup Ct 2-19, 131D1
NORFOLK Island (Australian territory)
Pacific cable planned 5-19, 387E3
NORMAN, Petty Officer Craig
Convicted of sex harassmt 7-11, 598F1
NORMAN, Dennis R.
Zimbabwe agri min 3-11, 198B1
NORMAN, Greg
Wins World Match Play tourn 10-14, 972E2
NORMA Rae (film)
Wins Oscars 4-14, 296G1
NORRIS, Mike
AL pitching ldr 10-6, 926F3, G3
2d in AL Cy Young vote 11-12, wins Golden Glove 12-6, 925G3, 926D1
NORTH, Phil R.
Roach replaces as Tandy pres 10-23, 959B3

1976

NORTH American Congress on Latin America
Rpts Peru '70-75 US mil training 1-16, 142C3

NORTH Atlantic Treaty Organization (NATO) (Belgium, Canada, Denmark, France, Great Britain, Greece, Iceland, Italy, Luxembourg, Netherlands, Norway, Portugal, Turkey, U.S., West Germany)
Warsaw Pact troop strength rpt cited 761A2
USSR denounces Angola role 1-6, 2D2
UK budget talks 1-14—1-15, Thatcher backs strong role 1-19, 101D1, F1
A-planning group meets 1-21—1-22, 297G2
Schmidt defends detente 1-29, 158A1
Independent Program Group meets 2-2, 2-9, 297B3
Dutch plane replacemt bribe case opens 2-10, 141D2; acquittal 2-25, 158E2
Italy CP backs membership 2-27, 195F3
Study on Warsaw Pact attack denied 3-16; W Ger asks Close ouster 3-19, 297A2
Civil servants strike 3-18, 4-7—4-8, 297C2
Sovt, Cuba Red Sea buildup rptd 4-5, 242B2
Poland sentences spy 4-10, 268C3
Italy CP backs role 4-18, 297A1
Giscard bars return 5-5, Gaullist claim denied 6-2, 417A3, D3
Italy CP reaffirms support 5-13, 352G1
France reaffirms pol support 5-18, 372C2
Forgn mins meet, score USSR 5-20—5-21, 353A1-354B1
W Ger arrests spies 6-2, 6-5, 442A1
Spain forgn min asks entry 6-3, 459G2
Defns mins meet, France, Greece shun; aid to Portugal, Turkey OKd; Canada Leopard tank buy OKd 6-10—6-11, 449E1
On Cuba troops in Angola 6-13, 467D1
Italy CP repeats assurances 6-15, 446C1
'77-82 goals rptd 7-1, 760C3
France dismisses admiral 7-7, 521F2
Faults scored 7-8—9-3, 760F2-B3
Italy loan ban disclosed 7-19, 530G3
Portugal to seek greater role 7-19, 558E1
Israel arms to Leb rptd 7-20, 527D3
Canada Lockheed deal agreed 7-21, 555B1
Tank purchase issue unresolved 8-4, 581F1
Portugal CP vs brigades 8-5, 774G2
2 arrested as spies in W Ger 8-16, 640B2
French policy dispute rptd 8-26, 637G3
Dutch legislator rptd on tour 9-1, 684D2
Sovt MiG-25 pilot in Japan, asks US asylum 9-6, 696G1
UK ships collide in exercises 9-20, 713A1
Malta forgn policy cited 9-20, 713E1, G1
Holds war exercise 9-20, 760D2
France to cut W Ger troops 10-9, 852G2; strategy scored 10-18, 880D1
Sovt civil defns plans rptd 10-11, 934B1
Eur air quality improvemt rptd 10-16, 934D1
UK spending cuts raise concern 10-17, 880C1
Callaghan warns UK pullout 10-25, 810C1
Greece vs Cyprus mediatn 11-12, 897A3
Spain delegatn ends inspectn tour 11-14, 880E1
A-planning group meets on Sovt missile threat 11-17—11-18, 879D2
France bars jt Eur defns 11-30, 905A3
Defns min mtgs: warn on Warsaw Pact might 12-6, urge spending hikes, Spain observer status 12-7—12-8; forgn mins veto Warsaw Pact A-treaty, membership freeze 12-10, 933A1
European Force Reduction Talks—*See under EUROPE*
Iceland-UK Fishing Issue
Iceland urges NATO role 1-8, bases blocked 1-10—1-11, 50A3
Cncl meets 1-12, 50C3
Luns meets Hallgrimsson 1-14—1-15, Callaghan 1-19, 50D3
Luns mediatn fails 2-1, Iceland cuts UK ties 2-19, 156B1
Interim cod pact signed 6-1, 389D2

1977

NORTH America Bank and Trust Co.
Failed Conn bank purchase cited 3-28, 577C1
NORTH American Soccer League (NASL)—*See SOCCER*
NORTH, Andy
Wins Westchester Classic 8-21, 675F3
NORTH Anna (Va.) Environmental Coalition
A-plant safety cover-up rptd 9-30, 838E1, B2
NORTH Atlantic Shipping Associations, Council of—*See SHIPPING Associations, etc.*

NORTH Atlantic Treaty Organization (NATO) (Belgium, Canada, Denmark, France, Great Britain, Greece, Iceland, Italy, Luxembourg, Netherlands, Norway, Portugal, Turkey, U.S., West Germany)
Gen Sir John Sharp dies 1-15, 84E3
Schmidt-Andreotti talks 1-17—1-18, 65A1
W Ger OKs Indonesia, Turkey arms sales 2-2, 139F2
French seize 4 as Sovt spies 3-22, 255B3
Danish defense budget passed 3-29, 426D2
Italy CP disputes NATO role 4-2, reactn 4-9, 284A2
USSR denies Zaire role 4-7, 266A1
Gundersen named Mil Com chrmn 4-15, 360F1
4-power London talks, USSR warned re Berlin 5-9, 358C2
Luns on Cyprus threat 5-9, 359D1
London mins mtg, Warsaw Pact strength seen 5-10—5-11, 358G2, 359E3
Arms standardizatn progress rptd 5-14, 359F3
USSR scores Berlin warning 5-14, 496F2
USSR defns spending rise, Warsaw Pact strength rptd 5-17, 379E3
Defns spending hike OKd, '76 total cited 5-18, 379C3
Quebec separatists drop exit plan 5-29, 425F2
USSR SS-20 deploymt rptd 6-9, 530G1
Brezhnev, Giscard on French policy 6-22, 495A1
Spain Socialist ldr backs entry 6-23, 507A1
USSR scores Eurocommunism 6-23, 507A2
Denmark, Greenland oil accord rptd 7-13, 672D2
USSR sub exercise rptd 7-28, 591E1
USSR chrgs S Africa A-bomb aid 8-9, 657A1
Dutch army union protests discipline 8-18, 986D2
Sovt-backed firm arms orders rptd 8-19, 700G1
IISS assesses E-W mil balance, NATO problems 9-2, 686E1
Warsaw Pact attack warning time revised 9-2, 700E1
Sovt envoy observes war games 9-13, 700B1
Haig meets Dayan 9-15, 713G2
UK '78-79 defns cuts scored, arms contributn cited 9-16, 957C1
Comecon OKs formal EC talks 9-21, 771C2
Denktash splits with Turkey over independnc 9-24, 946D3
Greece in mil exercise 9-28, 957G1
A-planning group debates neutron bomb, cruise missile 10-11—10-13, 956G2
Malta premr provokes USSR, E Eur walkout in Peking 11-3, 925E2
Greek electn results 11-20, 925C1
Malta threatens Libya defns pact 11-23, 925A3
Defnse mins meet, mil budget hikes urged; France, Greece absent 12-6—12-7, 956E3
Turkey mil aid urged 12-6, 957E1
Sovt hovercraft, T-80 tank threat seen 12-8, 941D3
Forgn mins meet: back SALT pact, detente, score rights abuses, mil buildup 12-8—12-9, 956F3
W Ger Defns Min spy scandal disclosed 12-12, 968C1
European Force Reduction Talks—*See under EUROPE*

1978

NORTH American Soccer League (NASL)—*See SOCCER*

NORTH Atlantic Treaty Organization (NATO) (Belgium, Canada, Denmark, France, Great Britain, Greece, Iceland, Italy, Luxembourg, Netherlands, Norway, Portugal, Turkey, U.S., West Germany)
Algeria pres visits Malta 1-3, 39C2
Warsaw Pact conventional warfare edge seen 1-6, 5B3
Dutch premr backs strong ties 1-16, 90B3
Caramanlis, Ecevit agree to meet 1-23, 2-9, 170C2
Greek premr sees Luns on unified command 1-26, 149C2
USSR air threat seen 1-29, 81B3
Arms standardizatn progress seen 1-31, 82A1
French sentence 5 as USSR spies 2-1, 71B2
Ethiopia protests Somalia aid 2-1, 100E1
Greek '78 defns budget presented 2-16, 149B3
Malta '77 UK base revenue rptd 2-17, 228B3
Warsaw Pact forces compared 2-20, 162D3
Helsinki review conf statemt offered 2-21, 179C2
W Ger probes spy scandal 2-24, 210D3
Turkey to review ties 3-24, 230E2
USSR role in Africa Horn area feared 3-26, 215G1
USSR scores China-EC trade pact 4-4, 302G3
50 UK tanks rptd withdrawn, manpower shortages cited 4-17, 298B3
Nuclear Planning Group meets 4-18—4-19, 298A2
Haig at 26th Bilderberg Conf 4-21—4-23, 302D3
Multiple rocket launch system dvpt rptd 4-25, 299A1
USSR proposes Turkish arms aid 4-26, 477F1
Spain: Canaries navy base not to be in NATO 4-26, 576G3
UK defns chief's remarks on USSR cause uproar 5-1, 329G2
Brezhnev visits W Ger 5-4—5-7, 417E1
Canada aerial defns designer sentncd 5-5, 451D3
Eurogroup sets joint arms programs 5-17, 398G1-B2
Ecevit, Caramanlis link Cyprus setlmt, NATO role 5-17, 5-27, 398B3
Greek, Turkish premrs meet 5-29, 398C2
DC summit: long-term defns plan OKd; Africa role debated, Sovt priorities examined 5-30—5-31, 397A1-398A1
Brezhnev scores Zaire role, long-term defns plan 5-31, 423G1
Hungary scores arms race, shares blame 6-10, 534G2
USSR scores long-term defns plan, Zaire role 6-17, 464F3, G3
Ecevit in Moscow, signs pacts 6-21—6-23; West reassured 6-24, 6-30, 595A2
Iceland electn set back 6-25, Cabt to resign 6-26, 497C2
W Ger neo-Nazis arrested 8-4, 652E1
Icelandic coalitn govt formed 8-31, 688C3, G3, 689A1
E-W mil balance assessed by IISS 9-1, 676G2
W Ger spy scandal disclosed 9-1, smear campaign chrgd 9-5, 725E2, F2
Autumn maneuvers begin, Greece joins 9-5; 18 deaths rptd 10-2, 748B2, D2
USSR says Begin seeks Israel ties 9-6, 673G2
W Ger questns maneuvers 9-23, affirms commitmt 9-27, 748E2-A3
W Ger spy probe dropped 9-26, 868B3
USSR-France tensns cited 10-29, 830G3
Warsaw Pact summit topic 11-22—11-23, 913E2
Eurogroup sets '79 arms list 12-4, 954B3
Defense mins mtg OKs AWACS, Nimrods purchase 12-5—12-6, 954A2
Forgn mins mtg 12-7—12-8; Vance assures re US support 12-9, 954F2
European Force Reduction Talks—*See under EUROPE*
Neutron Bomb—*See under ARMAMENTS*

1979

NORTH American Air Defense Command (NORAD)
Quebec autonomy plans backs membership 6-1, 424B2
NORTH American Irregulars, The (film)
Released 4-12, 528B3
NORTH American Life & Casualty Co.—*See under MUTUAL Life Insurance Co.*
NORTH American Philips Corp.
Viet defoliant suit filed 2-1, 90C1
NORTH American Soccer League Players Association (NASLPA)—*See SOCCER*
NORTH American Van Lines Inc.
Fined by ICC 1-15, 92B1

NORTH Atlantic Treaty Organization (NATO) (Belgium, Canada, Denmark, France, Great Britain, Greece, Iceland, Italy, Luxembourg, Netherlands, Norway, Portugal, Turkey, U.S., West Germany)
Poland defense budget frozen 1-9, 39A3
Westn-natn Turkey aid offer rptd 1-12, 40D2
UK spending plans unveiled 1-17, 59G2
E Ger rpts defectn 1-21, 61E3
USSR '67-77 mil outlay rptd 1-25, 99B3
Northn defns capabilities rptd weak 2-17, 147G3
Canada aerial defns designer cleared 2-20, 189A2
Employe defects 3-5, Luns Nazi link cited 3-6; E Ger spy data rptd 180D3, E3
Murder attempt on UK aide seen 3-22, 228C3
USSR computer sale rptd under review 4-5, 287G2
UK Tories urge greater role 5-15, 358G2
Defense Planning Com mtg backs 3% budget hike, SALT 5-15—5-16, 359G2
Westn natns set Turkey aid 5-30, 397E2
Forgn mins meet, back SALT, A-modernizatn 5-30—5-31, 415D3
Mins warn UK, US vs Zimbabwe ties 5-31, 416A1
Quebec autonomy plan backs membership 6-1, 424B2
Turkey to get USSR A-plant 6-5, 488G2
Schmidt backs modernizatn 6-6, 430A1
W Ger sentncs Lutzes as spies 6-18, 489F3
Haig assassinatn try fails 6-25, 476D2
France backs SALT II 6-28, 497A1
Norway SALT info vow rptd 7-26, 762A2
Spain reaffirms entry commitmt 8-13, 654F2
IISS assesses mil balance 9-4, 825A3
France backs strengthened conventional forces 9-11, 686C2
Turkey grants PLO full status 9-27, 740C3
USSR offers E Ger troop cut, missile freeze 10-6; rejected 10-7, 761D1, C3
UK plans 3% spending rise 11-1, 855D2
Nuclear Planning Group meets 11-13—11-14, 880A2
Defns mins meet 12-11—12-12, forgn mins 12-13—12-14, 959C1-D2
European Force Reduction Talks—*See under EUROPE*
Missile Deployment Issue
USSR SS-20 threat seen, W Ger missile deploymt hinted 2-20, 148A1
USSR SS-21 deploymt rptd 4-23, 340E1
Nuclear Planning Group urges A-modernizatn 4-25, 340A1
Intell error re USSR SS-21 deploymt rptd 5-23, 399E1
Forgn mins back A-modernizatn 5-30—5-31, 415F3
France A-weapon policy cited 5-31, 415G3

1980

NORTH American Air Defense Command (NORAD)
23 AF guards disciplined in Colo drug probe 1-17, 115F3
US computer errors trigger false A-alerts 6-3, 6-6, failed component blamed 6-17, 457D3, 458F1
Canada offered F-18 discount 7-11, 543F3
NORTH American Philips Corp.
GTE TV units purchased 10-2, 985E2
Magnavox Co., The
CBS, RCA sign video disk pact 1-10, 120G1
Zenith joins RCA in video disk pact 3-3, 239D3
Pioneer to enter US video disk mkt 3-26, 376F3
NORTH American Publishing Co.
Cue NY sale agrmt rptd 3-4, 239A2
NORTH American Soccer League (NASL)
See SOCCER
NORTH Anna Power Station—*See VIRGINIA--Atomic Energy & Safeguards*
NORTH Atlantic Treaty Organization (NATO) (Belgium, Canada, Denmark, France, Great Britain, Greece, Iceland, Italy, Luxembourg, Netherlands, Norway, Portugal, Turkey, U.S., West Germany)
Olympic boycott re Afghan crisis discussed 12-30-79 3C1
Canada PCs cite '74 mtg 1-8, 38F1
Canada comm accuses Treu of passing secrets 1-11, 78B3
Afghan crisis, anti-USSR steps discussed 1-15, 28D1
France, W Ger affirm support 2-5, 84G2
USSR backs detente, scores US 2-7, 106D3
Iceland coalitn govt formed 2-8, 117F3
W Ger 3% defns spending hike claimed 2-25, 153D3
Poland sentncs UN employe as spy 3-7, 221A1
Ex-Secy Gen Brosio dies 3-14, 279F1
Norway exercises held, USSR scores 3-14—3-19, 285D3
Japan mil spending compared 3-20, 320A3
UK issues defense white paper 4-2, 274F1, A2, D2
Canada backs stronger ties 4-14, 293E1
OECD OKs Turkey aid 4-15, 295C3
Warsaw Pact parity evaluated 4-29, 327B3
4 natns mark USSR May Day parade 5-1, 354A3
Greece to seek full membership 5-8, 352D2
Norway-Iceland ocean pact set 5-10, 398D2
Defns, forgn mins meet 5-13—5-14; Afghan invasn denounced, increased Eur mil role OKd 5-14, 377B2
Franco-Sovt summit on Afghan 5-19, 378G2, B3
Greece vows readmissn talks 5-23, 407E3
Spain entry, EC membership linked 6-5, 435F3
Italy reaffirms disarmamt support 6-20, 474C2
Schmidt USSR trip plans rptd 6-23, 474F1
Forgn mins meet 6-25—6-26; Afghan invasn, other terrorism condemned; Palestinian rights, disarmamt conf backed 6-26, 489E2
Greece-Turkey talks omit 6-28, 500D2
Iceland critic elected pres 6-30, 498F2
Giscard sees necessity 7-7, 522A1
W Ger lifts navy curbs 7-18, 540G1
Armenians score 7-31, 606B1
Greece links US bases, mil re-entry 8-20, 652D2
'Autumn Forge' maneuvers begin 9-1; Belgium withdraws from Turkish maneuvers 9-15, 696A2
Spain shuffles Cabt, entry talks cited 9-8, 690C2
Turkey coup ldrs reaffirm membership 9-12, 9-16; Belgium quits Turkey maneuvers 9-15, 696B3, F3
Netherlands defense spending hiked 9-16, 709C2
UK Labor Party backs membership, disarmament 10-2, 768C3
UK Tories affirm backing 10-10, 790G2
Greece rejoins mil wing 10-20, 800C1-B2
UK Labor Party ldrs back membership 11-10, 872D2
French spy arrested, 2 Sovt Emb aides expelled 11-13, 921B3
UK govt stresses role 11-20, 901C1
W Ger, US stress defns posture; W Ger hints 3% spending goal problem 11-20, 903G3
UK Labor exit plan spurs rift 11-28, 922A1
Defns mins meet on Sovt mil role in Poland, arms outlays 12-9—12-10, 949B2, C2
Japan arms outlay hike asked 12-12, 953A1
W Ger secy sentncd as spy 12-12, 969A2
W Ger '81 budget hikes mil spending 12-17, 969B1
Missile Deployment Issue
USSR rejects Eur missile reductn talks 1-3, 4A3
Carter cites US policy 1-23, 42A3
Gromyko reaffirms disarmamt interest, asks missile withdrawal 2-18, 124C1
Europn CPs vs missiles 4-29, 327C3
USSR vs nondeploymt offer 5-19, 378B3
US: UK, Italy to get missiles first 6-3, 450A3
A-Planning Group reaffirms modernizatn 6-4, 450E2

1976

U.S. Developments
Kissinger briefs cncl on Angola 1-15, 16D2
Ford State of Union message 1-19, 38A3
Kissinger briefs cncl on Moscow talks 1-23, 61G3
Spain defense pact signed 1-24, 76F3
Bruce quits as amb 1-30, Strausz-Hupe replaces 3-3, 186D2
US to consider German tank 2-12, 183D2
AWACS offer questioned 3-2, 183E2
US rep cites NATO, Warsaw Pact spending data 3-7, 182B2
Kissinger warns vs CP govts 4-7, 259C3; 4-13, 296G3
USSR scores Kissinger statemts 4-18, 277A1
Kissinger addresses mtg 5-20, 353D2
US Sen asks more cooperatn 5-26, 411B3
Defns mins act on US Ger base, AWACS plans, OK Portugal aid 6-10—6-11, 449A2
Rumsfeld presses Greece on ties 6-15, 449F1
US Dem platform text cites 6-15, 478C1, F1
Carter proposals 6-23, 451E3
US inefficiency in Eur rptd 7-8, 760F2
'77 arms bill backs weapon compatibility 7-14, 517D1
US-W Ger tank standardized 8-4, 581D1
US GOP platform text cites 8-18, 609D1, 611B3
Mondale urges arms standardizatn 8-30, 645E3
Ford, Carter debate 10-6, 741B1
US questns NATO equipmt, tactics; Haig defends 10-13—11-15, 879B3
US to send more fighter planes to W Ger, UK 10-27, 879A3, 961G1
Ford extends Haig term 11-11, 879G3
Chrysler wins tank contract 11-12, 942A1
Ford urges Carter mtg 11-22, 881B1
Defns mins defer AWACS decisn, Rumsfeld comments 12-7—12-8, 933C1
Rumsfeld urges Spain observer status 12-7, 933B2
Kissinger addresses, pledges Carter support 12-9, 12-10, 933B2

NORTH Bergen, N.J.—*See NEW Jersey*
NORTH Carolina
9 arrested in pot seizure 1-11, 160D1
Williams freed 1-16, 79A1
'72 Wilmington 10 convictn review denied 1-19, 43E1
'74 Eastern crash damages awarded 1-19, 80A2
Sup Ct sets death sentnc review 1-22, 87G2
A-engineer quits NRC 2-9, 115F1
Kepone cases rptd 2-26, 171C3
New River OKd for US scenic system 3-12, dam project 3-24, 219A3
Sup Ct bars review of homosexual conviction 3-29, 261E3
Cong clears Wrightsville saline water funds 6-7, 434A3
Sup Ct backs Charlotte on union dues 6-7, 435A2; signed 6-22, 982F1

1977

U.S. Developments
F-16 sale review set 1-17, 70C3
Mondale visits hq, vows no cut in US support 1-24, 69B1, D2, 70C1
US rpt on Warsaw Pact manpower, arms gains issued 1-24, 70G1
US defns secy sees spending hike 1-25, 94A3
AWACS purchase deferred 1-27, 71A1
US envoy visits Greece, Turkey 2-17—2-22, 122G1; Cyprus 2-23—2-26, 147A1
Turner confrmd CIA dir 2-24, 148G3
UK rejects AWACS, sets Nimrod dvpt; US scores 3-31, 360C1
Carter arms stand backed 4-1, 247B1
Bennett confrmd amb 4-25, 418C1
21 F-15s sent to W Ger 4-28, 360F1
US mil aid to Portugal signed 4-30, 339A2
F-16 pact set 5-5, 441A2
Carter at London 4-power talks 5-9, addresses mins mtg 5-10, backed 5-14, 358G2, 359E3
W Ger lauds Carter diplomacy 5-11, 359B2
Vance plans USSR civil defns talks, Westn concern noted 5-11, 359G3
Israel gets US arms preference 5-12, 361E1
US-UK mil info exchng OKd 5-16, 380A1
Defense spending, GNP data rptd 5-17, 379F3
'76 defense spending rptd 5-18, 379D3
Carter sets arms-sales policy 5-19, 380G2
US bars Israel-GTE projct 6-22, 511E1
Carter defers neutron bomb decisn 7-12, 533C2
Norway leftists reveal secret talks 8-22, 730D2
IISS scores W Ger troop deploymt 9-2, 686A2
Hart asks NATO overhaul 9-10, 700C1
Turkey arms purchases rptd 9-25, 957F1
Brookings study sees need for focused US buildup 9-26, 858C1
A-planning group debates neutron bomb, cruise missile 10-11—10-12, 956A3
US: mil budget hikes inadequate 12-6—12-7, 956F3
Vance reassures NATO on SALT 12-8—12-9, 956F3

NORTH Benton, O.—*See OHIO*
NORTH Carolina
Legislature schedule rptd 6E2
Coll integratn rules ordrd 1-17, 112B2
Winter rptd worst in 100 yrs 1-22, 54D2
Charlotte low temp cited 2-6, 91D2
Chief Justice Sharp cited 2-12, 140D3
Charlotte-Mecklenburg schl busing success cited 2-15, 112G1
ERA rejected 3-1, 197C2
Coll integratn rules reordrd 4-1, 446D1
Inmate legal aid ordrd 4-27, 383D1
Plea-bargaining review backed 5-2, 406D2
'76 per-capita income table 5-10, 387E2
Shapp fund repaymt ordrd 5-12, 482C2
Wilmington 10 denied retrial 5-20, 531C3
Death penalty in effect 6-1, 594C2
Apple labeling rule voided 6-20, 517E1
Inmate union curbs upheld 6-23, 539C2

1978

U.S. Developments—*See also ARMAMENTS—Neutron Bomb*
Papandreou asks US mil exit 1-4, 22G1
Carter visits hq; vows more consultatn, troops 1-6, 1D1
Sovt conv warfare edge seen in US '77 rpt 1-6, 5C3
Carter-Mitterrand mtg scored 1-6—1-10, 54E1
US alerts to USSR satellite fall 57E1
Carter budgets AWACS adaptn 1-23, 45E1
W Ger gun OKd for US XM-1 tank 1-31, 82A1
US exempts from arms sales ceiling 2-1, 106E2
US tactical buildup urged by Pentagon 2-2, 81A2
Asia, Pacific commitmt affirmed by US 2-20, 126E3
Turkey threatens exit 3-29, US moves to lift arms embargo 3-29—4-6; Greeks angered 4-4, 276A2, F2, 277A1
A-group seeks contd cruise missile dvpt 4-19, 298D2
Vance reassures on cruise missile 4-24, US-USSR talks rptd 4-25, 297E1
GAO backs F-16 review 4-24, 407D2
Haig resignatn threat rptd, denied 4-25, 289E2-B3
US set back in moves to lift Turkey arms embargo 5-3, 5-11, 378D1
Eurogroup sets joint arms programs, F-16 training 5-17, 398G1
US reinforcemt plan presented, AWACS decisn rptd near 5-18—5-19, 398B1
Haig to remain cmdr 5-19, popularity rptd 5-23, 398D3-399B1
US mil constructn authorizatn clears House 5-22, 407A1
Turkey scores US arms embargo, hints USSR ties 5-29—5-30, 397D2
Schmidt sees Carter at DC summit 5-30—5-31, reviews talks 6-1, 519F1
Carter sees Ecevit, Caramanlis 5-31, 398D2
Carter for sustained mil spending, USSR scores 6-7, 424B1, F1
Brown affirms US mil superiority, concedes alliance weakness 6-23, 493A3
Carter optimistic on Eur troop-cut talks 6-26, 491F1
Schmidt cites Carter meeting 7-7, 545G2
Carter urges Cong to end Turkey arms ban 7-20, 549F3
Turkish arms embargo end gets Cong prelim OK 8-1, 587E2, A3, B3
Carter vetoes '79 arms authorzn 8-17, 621B1
Mil constructn funds clear Cong, Admin bid cut 8-21, 662D1
U-2 missns rptd increased 8-22, 748A3
Autumn maneuvers begin 9-5, deaths rptd 10-2, 748C2
US sets '79 arms sale lid, end to Turkey embargo 9-26, 734A2-E2
US plans defns budget rise 11-9, 874F3
US neutral on China arms sales 11-9, 901E3
'80 defns budget hike seen 11-15, 895B2; Carter cites goal 11-30, 916A3
Jackson scores SALT as threat 11-27, 996C2
AWACS purchase OKd 12-5—12-6, US warned vs arms spending decrease 12-6, 954A2, E2
Vance assures re arms, SALT 12-9, 954A3
Carter defends defns budget plans 12-14, 979F3
Treaty cited in US congressmen's suit re Taiwan 12-22, 995C2

NORTH Carolina
Legislature schedule rptd 14F3
'67, '77 sales-tax rates rptd 1-5, 15F3
Wilmington 10 denied convictn review 1-5, 24D2
State govt tax revenue table 1-9, 84D2
Wilmington 10 sentences cut 1-23, Wright paroled 6-1, 560B2
Piedmont Airlines hijack foiled 1-28, 212C2
US rejcts coll integratn plan 2-2, 85D1
Southn Bell pleads guilty 2-13, fined 2-16, 116G2
NY gov orders Little extraditn 2-23, appeals ct backs 5-9; Marshall delays 5-30, Sup Ct declines appeal 6-5, 431G1-B2
Carter at Wake-Forest Univ 3-17, 202C1
'Right-to-die' law rptd 3-18, 597F3

1979

USSR offers missile freeze 10-6; NATO rejcts, Carter backs arms deploymt 10-7, 10-9, 761F1, A3, D3
USSR campaigns vs A-missiles 10-13—11-6, 880F2
China premr backs missiles 11-5, 854D2
USSR warns vs missiles 11-7, 856E2
Nuclear Planning Group backs missiles 11-14, 880A2
USSR warns W Ger 11-21—11-24, 938A3
E Ger scores missiles 12-5, 938D3
Dutch parlt rejects missile plan 12-6, 938C2
W Ger Soc Dems back missiles 12-6, 938E2, G2
Warsaw pact asks arms reductn talks 12-6, 938C3
US seeks Norway, Netherlands, Denmark support 12-7, 938D1
Defns, forgn mins OK Pershing II, cruise deploymt; Dutch, Belgium reservatns cited 12-12, 959C1-B2
USSR, E Ger score deploymt OK 12-13—12-17, 959E2-A3
Dutch govt backed on plan 12-20, 959E2

U.S. Developments—*See also 'Missile Deployment Issue' above*
Haig sets resignatn 1-3, 3A2
Turkey aid offer rptd 1-12, 40D2
A-target chng urged 1-13, 52F3
Carter budgets defns hike, AWACS adoptn 1-22, 42D1, 43A1
Carter State of Union Message 1-23, 47D2
Cong rpts doubt NATO defns capability 2-17, 147E3
Rogers named to replace Haig 2-28, 147C3
Mondale on Norway role 4-17, 299C2
Vance asks unified policy re SALT III 5-30, 415E3
Mins warn vs Zimbabwe ties 5-31, 416A1
Carter backs modernizatn 6-6, 430A1
Carter addresses Cong on SALT II 6-18, 459D1
US 'quick-strike' force planned 6-22, 482C3
France backs SALT II 6-28, 497A1
Vance stresses SALT need 7-9, 7-10, 510B2, C2
Haig backs SALT ratificatn delay 7-26, 643G2
Norway SALT info vow rptd 7-26, 762A2
Vance reaffirms budget hike vow 7-30, 644A1
W Ger threat to AWACS deal rptd 8-1, 586E1
W Ger spending criticized 9-21, 733A2
Pressler backs less US contributns 9-25, 724G1
Carter warns vs SALT rejectn 10-1, 738E1, 739A2
US Defns Dept backs US arms to China 10-3, 789B2
US Sen com SALT reservatn backs mil aid 10-22, 822E2
Brown urges reinforcemt preparatns 12-11, thanks re Iran support 12-12, 959C2
US-Sovt A-arms talks sought 12-12, 959A2
4 US employes killed in Turkey 12-14, 998C1

NORTH Braddock, Pa.—*See PENNSYLVANIA*
NORTH Carolina
Legislature schedule rptd 5E3
Cigaret mfr rise rptd 2-11, 218E2*
Rent collectn bankruptcy laws backed by Sup Ct 2-21, 128G3
Pub schl cost share rptd 3-5, 282E3
Regulatory bds rptd segregated 4-9, 307A2
PCB dumping chrgd 6-4—6-13, disposal disputed 6-5, 597G2-E3
Charlotte rptd hit by gas shortage 6-23, 479C1
Truckers protest 6-28, 479C2
Soul City support withdrawn 6-28, suit filed 8-17, injunctn denied 8-27, 665F1
Hang-glider completes transcontinental flight in Kill Devil Hills 8-16, 656C3

1980

USSR rejected W Ger A-missile freeze offer 6-9; Schmidt gets Carter letter 6-16, seeks mtg 6-18, 450C3-451D1
USSR warns W Ger 6-12, 451D1
UK sets cruise missile sites 6-17, 487D1
US, Italy reaffirm support 6-20, 474C2
W Ger seeks Eur mil balance 6-23, 474F1
Belgium fails to endorse 6-26, 490B1
Schmidt, Brezhnev in talks, negotiatns seen 6-30—7-1; US comments 7-2, 489C1
Schmidt backs French A-weapons 7-11, urges deploymt 7-15, 540A1, C1
UK Trident purchases set 7-15, 544C2, D2
Belgium to accept A-missiles 9-19, 737A2
Troop Reduction—*See MUTUAL and Balanced Force Reduction*

U.S. Developments—*See also 'Missile Deployment Issue' above*
Turkey-US base accord set 1-9, 22B3
US sen urges expanded Mideast oil route protectn role 1-14, 32C1
Carter cites policy 1-23, 42G1, A3
US budgets AWACS plane funds 1-28, 71D1
US compares Japan mil spending 3-20, 219A3
US, Turkey sign base pact 3-29, 255D3
Iran hostage rescue missn scored 4-25, 324C2
Muskie to attend Brussels mtg 5-8, 343B1
Eur mil role increase OKd 5-14, 377D2
US reaffirms disarmamt support 6-20, 474C2
Carter urges Spain entry 6-25, 474C3
US sets disarmamt conf terms 6-26, 489G2
Canada offered F-18 discount 7-11, 543F3
UK Trident purchases set 7-15, 544D2
Brown reassures on A-strategy shift 8-8, 615E3
Greece links US bases, mil re-entry 8-20, 652C2
17,000 airlifted for 'Autumn Forge' maneuvers 9-1, 696B2
Brown scores Dutch, Danish spending 10-3, 737D1
US mil exercise performance scored, UK gen disputes 10-11, 777C1
UK hopeful on Reagan electn 11-5, 841B3
Carter, Schmidt stress defns posture 11-20, 903G3
AWACS dispatched on Poland fears 12-9, 930A1
Europns defend arms outlays; US shore cited 12-9—12-10, 949C2
Muskie lauds mins response to Sovt Poland role 12-12, 949C1
Haig named secy state 12-16, 955C2

NORTH Carolina
Blizzards hit, 4 killed 3-1—3-2, 292B2, C2
Trains collide near Raleigh 4-2, 391F3
Stevens, union come to terms 10-19, 805C1-D2
Charlotte, Greenville busing, housing integratn study rptd 11-16, 989E3
Crime & Civil Disorders
Ft Bragg sex harassment probed 2-10, 189A1
Army recruiting suit rptd filed 4-11, 369D3
KKK Johnston Cnty rally held 4-19, 333G1
Lejune Marines alerted 7-4, 515A1
Road builders bid-rigging scandal rptd 7-5, 655F1, B2
Ga prison escapees recaptured 7-30, 654E1

1976

Police firing upheld 6-10, 552D2
Pvtly insured S&Ls rptd OKd 6-20, 495E1
Blacks win J P Stevens suit 6-25, 944C1
US Sup Ct voids death penalty law 7-2, 491G1
Hurricane Belle damage rptd 8-9, 595E2
New River dams blocked 9-11, 689D1
FSCL '75 per capita income, tax burden rptd 9-15, 10-12, 959D2
US Sup Ct refuses phone equipmt case 12-13, 960F2

Politics
Primary date set 22A2
Reagan campaigns 1-8, 5C1
Primary results 3-23, 213G2
Black Dems meet in Charlotte 4-30—5-2, 343A3
Dem conv women delegates, table 508D2
Dem conv pres vote, table 7-14, 507D2
GOP pre-conv delegate count 8-14, 583D3
Mondale in Black Mt 8-15, 617A3
GOP conv scuffle on 16-C 8-17, 600A2
Primary results 8-17, 633E1
GOP conv pres, vp vote tables 8-18—8-19, 8-19, 599D1, D3
Dole, wife visit 9-1, 646A1
Salisbury honors Mrs Dole 9-2, 666C1
Flaherty wins runoff 9-14, 705E1
Dole in Wilmington 10-6, 763E3
Carter in Winston-Salem 10-19, 827E1
Ford in Raleigh 10-23, 802D3
Southn Bell takes paymts blame, chrgs vs execs dropped 10-25, 939C1
Election results 11-2: pres 818C1, 819B2; cong 822D2, 830D2, 831G1; state 820F2

NORTH Carolina, University of (Chapel Hill)
Loses Peach Bowl 12-31, 1014G2

NORTH Carolina National Bank—*See under NCNB Corp.*

NORTH Dakota
US Sup Ct to hear coal mining environment impact case 1-12, 23G3
State-chartered bank cited 6-10, 437G2
Strip-mining stay reversed 6-28, 569A1
GOP conv results 7-8, 513A3
Dem conv women delegates, table 508D2
Dem conv pres vote, table 7-14, 507D2
GOP pre-conv delegate count 8-14, 583D3
GOP conv pres, vp vote tables 8-18—8-19, 8-19, 599D1, D3
Gov primary results 9-7, 687E3
Fscl '75 per capita income, tax burden rptd 9-15, 10-12, 959B1, C2
Dole campaigns 9-22, 724C3
Canada vs reservoir 10-12, 945G3
Election results 11-2: pres 818C1, 819A1; cong 820D1, 823D3, 828A3, 830F2, 831G1; state 820B3, 823E3

NORTHEAST Bank (Houston, Tex.)
Closed 6-3, 438D1 ★

NORTHEAST Petroleum Industries Inc.
In tanker spill suit 12-22, 969D1

NORTHERN Ireland (Ulster)
Factory closings, unemploymt rptd 3-26, 278F1
Belfast firemen strike 10-1—10-4, 855B1

Anglo-Irish Relations—*See also 'Unrest' below*
Rees meets advisors 1-5, Loyalists 1-5—1-6, 19E2
Paisley urges 'war' on IRA, threatens strike 1-5, 19G2
UK parties differ on troop increase 1-6, 1-7; Wilson for consultatns 1-7, Ulster Protestants vs 1-8, 19C3
Rees-Cooney security talks 1-8, 19F3
Rees to recall Const Conv 1-12, 19G3
Loyalists score SDLP, Const Conv 2-2, 146B3
Const Conv reconvenes 2-3; rift reemerges, SDLP walkout 2-12, 146A3, C3

1977

Coll integratn plan issued 7-5, 630G2
Southn Bell, offcls indicted 8-2, 631A3
Jonesville sniper kills 2, self 9-5, 848G2
'76 per capita income, tax burden table 9-13, 10-18, 821D2
Overtime suit filed vs A&P 9-27, 778D2
Church coll student aid backed 10-3, 760E3
Joan Little escapes Raleigh jail 10-15, seized 12-7, 992A1
J P Stevens fines set 10-27, 899G1
Wilmington 10 cases probed by Amnesty Intl 11-5; pardons sought 12-4, 943A1, B1
5 die in western floods 11-6, 888B3
Raleigh elects woman mayor 11-8, 855D3
Referenda results 11-8, 879B2, G2
ERA econ boycott rptd 11-14, 918E1
Pot law detailed 12-11, 972D3
Stevens chrgd re contract bargaining 12-21, 1005C1

NORTH Carolina, University of
Chapel Hill Campus
NCAA basketball tourn results 3-28, 262E1
2 in NBA draft 6-10, 584A3
Loses Liberty Bowl 12-19, 1020B2
Charlotte Campus
NCAA basketball tourn results 3-26, 3-28, 262F1
Maxwell in NBA draft 6-10, 584B3

NORTH Carolina Prisoners' Labor Union Inc.
Inmate union curbs upheld 6-23, 639C2

NORTH Carolina State University (Raleigh)
Carr in NBA draft 6-10, 584A3
Wins Peach Bowl 12-31, 1020D2

NORTH Dakota
Legislature schedule rptd 6F2
Rpt scores Garrison project 1-7, 60C3
Indiana OKs ERA 1-18, 59C2
FEA orders home heating oil productn hike 1-24, 54G1
Garrison project halted 2-18, 133A1
Carter cuts Garrison $s 2-22, 126E1
'76 per-capita income table 5-10, 387E2, B3
'76 per capita income, tax burden table 9-13, 10-18, 821E1, C2
IJC scores Garrison projct 9-19, 726A1

NORTHEAST Louisiana University (Monroe)
Passman subpoena served 11-30, 915E2

NORTHEAST-Midwest Economic Advancement Coalition—*See under U.S. GOVERNMENT—HOUSE*

NORTHERN Ireland (Ulster)
NZ OKs detainee immigratn 2-21, 258D2
Econ aid announced 8-1, 639A1
O'Fiaich named Cath Primate 8-22, 728E3
Peace Movemt holds first cong 10-8—10-9, 783F3

Anglo-Irish Relations—*See also 'Unrest' below*
Fianna Fail backs UK exit, reunificatn 6-16; UK reactn 6-18, 475E2
Lynch asks united Ireland, UK exit 7-6, 599B1
Queen's safety threatnd 8-7—8-10; Jubilee visit 8-10—8-11, violence 8-12, 638A3-639A1
Mason affirms UK direct rule, Gars exit 9-10, 730A1
SDLP seeks new Irish-UK initiative 9-21, 783A3
Lynch, Callaghan in power-sharing, devolutn talks 9-28, 782A2
Unionists OK UK devolutn talks 10-8—10-9, 783E3

1978

US warns on coll segregatn 3-22, OKs plan 5-12, 368G3, 369C1
Stevens' plant union bargaining ordrd 3-26, 243B2
Health Planning Act upheld by Sup Ct 4-17, 308A3
Stevens-NLRB setlmt excludes state plants 4-28, 324G1
Cong primary results 5-2, 342A3
Anti-gay ruling declined by Sup Ct 5-15, 387E3
Construction pact signed 5-22, 429D3
Primary runoff results 5-30, 426C2
'77 prison populatn rptd up 6-3, 440C1
Little extradited from NY 6-9; indicted 6-18, sentenced 7-12, 560E3
Penal transfer bill enacted 6-16, 560F3
Univ minority rep case sent back by US Sup Ct 7-3, 552C1
Caldwell ABA pensn upheld by Appeals Ct 7-19, 656F1
Carter visits Wilson 8-5, 605F3
Viet papers rptd found in ex-amb's car 9-13, 720A2
Carter visits Asheville 9-22, 736A1
US Sen campaign spending rptd 11-15, 898B1, D1

NORTH Carolina, University of
Chapel Hill Campus
Ford 2d in coll basketball 3-13, 272D2
Ford in NBA draft 6-9, 457F3
Minority rep case sent back by Sup Ct 7-3, 552C1
Election results 11-7: cong 846A2, 848F2, 851B4, 852F3

NORTH Carolina State University (Raleigh)
Texas wins NIT 3-21, 272G1
Sadri loses NCAA tennis title 5-29, 419E2
Wilmington 10 student paroled 6-1, 560D2
Wins Tangerine Bowl 12-23, 1025D2

NORTH Carolina v. Califano
Health Planning Act upheld by Sup Ct 4-17, 308A3

NORTH Central Airlines Inc.
Southn Airways merger set 7-13, 684D1

NORTH Dakota
'67, '77 sales-tax rates rptd 1-5, 15F3
State govt tax revenue table 1-9, 84D2
Mercer Cnty coal gasificatn plant financing plan submitted 6-2, 471B3
Tornadoes 7-5, 654G3
Election results 11-7: cong 848F2, 851C4, 855A1; state 847E1, 855A1, 897C3

NORTHEAST—*See also state names*
Rail projct offcls resign 1-30; more funds allocated 2-11, projct delays rptd 2-24, 225A1
Blizzard paralyzes 2-5—2-7, 105F1-E2
Snowpack rptd above normal 3-5, 207C2
Carter presents urban-aid plan 3-27, 217D2
Housing bias survey rptd 4-17, 285F2
'77 living costs rptd 4-26, 349G1
NOW bank acct use cited 5-1, 5-5, 345G3
'70-77 Fortune 500 hq shift rptd 5-8, 326B1
Fed oil subsidies planned 5-26, 408B1
Fed oil subsidies proposed 6-15, 470G3-471B1
A-plant site review ordrd 6-30, 529G2
A-plant delays threaten elec supply 9-11, 702B1
Carter tours 10-28, 831B2
Lead-free gas shortage rptd 11-21, 939F1
'75-77 migratn of poor from South reverses 12-3, 943B1
City populatn losses rptd 12-6, 942C3
Gas shortage probe rptd 12-6, 962F3
OPEC price hikes to raise '79, '80 utilites rates 12-19, 978D2

NORTHEASTERN University (Boston, Mass.)
Bowers finds death sentencing bias 3-6, 389A1

NORTHEAST Power Coordinating Council
A-plant delays threaten elec supply 9-11, 702B1

NORTHERN Ireland (Ulster)
Firemen vote to end strike 1-12, 17G3

Anglo-Irish Relations—*See also 'Unrest' below*
Mason sees partial UK troop exit 1-4, 7F3
Lynch remarks cause furor 1-8—1-10, interparty talks collapse 1-9, 18A2, B3
Ulster job bias rptd 1-12, Protestants angered 1-13, 18G2
Irish RC primate urges UK end Ulster rule 1-16, 37B2
Cath pol ldr scores UK Parachute Regimt recall 4-3, 268A2
Paisley, Ulster MP protest Westminster mass 7-6, 557E3
Irish RC primate scores jail conditns, Mason refutes 8-1, 630B1

1979

Army recruiting fraud probed 8-19, 649F2
Hurricane David hits 9-4, 690G3
'78 per capita income rptd 9-16, 746E2
Southn Bell pol paymts scored by FCC 9-20, 870G1
Life of Brian furor rptd 10-30, 859C2

Atomic Energy
A-plant plans canceled 1-4, 186D2
Brunswick (Southport) A-plants called unsafe 1-26, 90C3
Perkins (Davie Cnty) A-plant delayed 5-21, 382A1
McGuire (Cowans Ford Dam) reactor licensing delayed 11-5, 849C1

Crime & Civil Disorders
Wilmington 10 case scored by Amnesty Intl 2-1, 85E2
MacDonald murder trial challenge declined by Sup Ct 3-19, 203G2-A3
Viet ex-amb documt possessn prosecutn dropped 3-30, 252F3
Verbal rights waiver backed by US Sup Ct 4-24, 364A2
Little paroled 6-9, 527D3
KKK-Communist clash in China Grove 7-8; Greensboro anti-KKK rally, 5 slain 11-3, 864C2-865C3
Parolee arrested on kidnap chrgs 7-30, 604G3
MacDonald gets life for '70 slayings 8-29, 817F2
KKK activity in Greensboro, Grinesland cited 865B1
14 indicted in Greensboro anti-KKK rally deaths 12-13, 991E3

NORTH Carolina, University of
Chapel Hill Campus
Med Cntr malnutritn study rptd 4-30, 386B3
Bradley in NBA draft 6-25, 507B3
Black woman wins Rhodes scholarship 9-9, 1005G2
Wins Gator Bowl 12-28, 1001B3

NORTH Carolina State University (Raleigh)
Brown in NFL draft 5-3, 335F2
Ritcher wins Outland Trophy 11-25, 1001E2

NORTH Carolina v. Butler
Case decided by Sup Ct 4-24, 364A2

NORTH Central Airlines Inc.
Carter OKs Southn Airways merger 6-5, 465D3

NORTH Dakota
Legislature schedule rptd 5E3
Med malpractice arbitratn rptd 1-28, 139E3
DC voting rep amendmt rejectn rptd 3-19, 204B3
Red River floods 4-26—4-30, 472A2
'78 per capita gas use rptd 5-27, 395A3
'78 per capita income rptd 9-16, 746F1, E2
PCBs contaminate food 9-17, 704A3
Grain handlers strike cost estimated 9-25, 723A1

NORTH Dakota, University of (Grand Forks)
Loses NCAA hockey title 3-24, 356E1

NORTH Dallas Forty (film)
Released 8-1, 820D2
Top-grossing film 9-26, 800G3

NORTHEAST Louisiana University (Monroe)
Natt in NBA draft 6-25, 507A3

NORTHEAST Petroleum Co.
Buckley on heating fuel supply 10-11, 786B3

NORTHEAST Utilities Service Co.
Westinghouse uranium supply suit setld 9-26, 727C3

NORTHERN Baby (race horse)
3d in English Derby 6-6, 448B3

NORTHERN Ireland (Ulster)
Emergency declared re truck, oil tank driver strikes 1-11, 20E3

Anglo-Irish Relations—*See also 'Unrest' below*
UK faulted in US, MPs score 4-19—4-24, 312E2
Atkins named UK secy 5-5, 338G1
Tory govt to seek solutn 5-15, 358C3
US conf plan announced 8-6, 602E1
Thatcher visits 8-29; sees Lynch, UK security aims detailed 9-5, 669D2, G2
Mountbatten funeral held 9-5, 669A1
Security accord set 10-5, 792E3
Thatcher vows support 10-12, 791A1
Eire attitudes polled 10-14, 836D1
UK plans home rule talks, parties score 10-25, 835B3
Eire asks local admin restoratn 11-9, 874E2

1980

MacDonald murder convictn voided 7-30, 654F3
Hunt assaulted in Denver 8-5, 596F3-597A1
6 Klansmen acquitted in '79 Greensboro deaths 11-17; US vows review, other reactn 11-17—11-18, 898D2-C3
Wilmington 10 convictn reversed 12-4, 940C1

Politics & Government—*See also other appropriate subheads in this section*
Canceled bond issue rptd 2-28, 186F1
Pres primary results 5-6, 341F2, 342C1, 405G1
Anderson ballot access challenged 10-27, 818B2
Newspaper pres endorsemts rptd 11-1, 841G3
Election results 11-4: pres 838C1, 839B2, F3; cong 840F2, 845A2, 849F3; state 845C3, 847D1, 849G3
'80 census rptd 12-31, 983F1

NORTH Carolina, University of
Chapel Hill Campus
O'Koren in NBA draft 6-10, 447F2
3d World press coverage study rptd 11-29, 914D1
Wins Bluebonnet Bowl 12-31, 999E3
Charlotte Campus
Kinch in NBA draft 6-10, 447G2

NORTH Carolina State University (Raleigh)
Ritcher in NFL draft 4-29, 336F3
Whitney in NBA draft 6-10, 447F2*

NORTH Dakota
Reagan campaigns 4-17, 327E3
Hunt coal property transfers rptd 5-2, 345A1
Hunts bailout loan collateral listed 5-28, 426D1
Synfuel plant loan OKd 7-18, 553B2
Primary results 9-2, 683C1
Election results 11-4: pres 838C1, 839A1, F3; cong 840F2, 843C4, 845A3, B3, 851A2; state 845D3, 847C1, 851B2
Synfuels plant gets $1.5 bln fed loan 11-19, ct blocks projct 12-8, 961F3
'80 census rptd 12-31, 983F1

NORTH Dakota, University of (Grand Forks)
Wins NCAA hockey title 3-29, 488G3

NORTHEASTERN Oklahoma State University (Tahlequah)
Loses NAIA Div I football title game 12-20, 999B3

NORTHEASTERN University (Boston, Mass.)
Prof indicted in welfare fraud 5-13, 414E3

NORTHERN Border Pipeline Co.
US OKs Canada gas imports, westn pipe leg 7-3, 562E2

NORTHERN Ireland (Ulster)
Catholic job bias rptd 9-10, 708G2-B3

Anglo-Irish Relations—*See also 'Unrest' below*
Home rule talks begin, bog down 1-7, Paisley bars parallel talks 1-11, 39G1-F2
Haughey urges solutn 2-16, reactn 2-17, 133D1
Home rule talks adjournment set 3-19, 232G2-C3
Haughey meets Thatcher 5-21, 389E3
UK home rule plan released, detailed; reactn 7-2, 522B3-523F1
Home rule talks renewed, stalemate rptd 9-22—9-23; Powell vs home rule 9-26, 750F2
Queen's speech omits home role plan 11-20, 901B1

1976

Eur human rights study scores UK, full disclosure urged 2-11—2-12, 147A1
Const Conv fails 3-3—3-4; dissolved, UK affirms rule, militants denounce 3-5, 277D3
UK Labor loses Parlt majority 4-6, 4-7, 267C1
Rees retains post 4-8, 267A1
'16 Easter rebelln marked 4-18, 278E1
London-Dublin judicial accords 6-1, 499B1
Callaghan in Belfast, sees Rees 7-5, 498B3
Eur human rights study issued, UK torture detailed 9-2, 675E1-F2
UK textile plant to close 10-22, 889E3
UK fears intellignc breach 11-18, 946F2
Ulster peace rally in London 11-27, 1008D1

European Community—*See EUROPEAN Community*

Government & Politics—*See other appropriate subheads in this section*
Faulkner retires Protestant Unionist ldrship 8-19, 638E2
Protestant independence plan publshd 11-11, 873B2

Irish Republic Relations—*See also 'Anglo-Irish Relations' above, 'Unrest' below*
Cosgrave rues deaths 1-5, 19D2
Sinn Fein ldr scores Provisional IRA 1-18, 146A2
Cosgrave vows cooperatn vs IRA 2-20, 147A1
Wilson, Cosgrave talks 3-5, 277G3
'16 Easter rebelln marked 4-18, 278E1
IRA warns vs testimony to North 5-31, 499E1
Sinn Fein ldr deported 7-26, 590G1
Sinn Fein talks ended 7-29, 590B2
Parlt declares state of emergency 9-1, opens debate on IRA curbs 9-2, 676F1
Emergency Powers Bill signed 10-16; IRA curbs expanded 10-18, 838A1

Unrest
19 killed in S Armagh area 1-3—1-13, 19F1
IRA warns UK on troops 1-3, UK reacts 1-4, 19C2
UK offcls Ulster bomb targets 1-5, IRA warns 1-14, 146G1
Protestants urge sealed border 1-6, 19F2
UK to send more troops to S Armagh 1-6, SAS unit 1-7, 19A3
UK announces new security steps 1-12, 20B1
14 killed in extremist attacks 1-17—2-9, 146F1
Loyalist spy unit warns IRA 1-18, 146B2
2 IRA members detained 2-8, 146C2
Violence mars '75 truce anniv 2-10, death toll rptd 2-11, 146D1
New Provisional IRA staff chief rptd 2-10, 147D1
IRA hunger striker dies 2-12; UK tightens security; violence, arrests rptd 2-12—2-22, 146C2, C3
S Belfast bomb blast 2-20, 146G2
Belfast, Londonderry riots 2-26—2-28, UK ends pol prisoner status 3-1, 278A1
IRA mortars airport 3-6, army base 3-18, 278B1
6 Protestant extremists killed 3-28—4-3, 278C1
4 UK soldiers killed 3-30—3-31, 278B1
Belfast blasts, IRA member killed 4-3—4-5, 278C1
O'Connell freed 4-9, 278E1
Cath killed by SAS 4-15, Belfast reprisals 4-16; security probe ordrd 4-17, 278C1
Dublin seizes UK troops 5-7, 499F1
Death toll rises 5-15—6-23, 498D3
US Dem platform text cites 6-15, 478E1
UDA bombs Irish hotels 7-4, 499A1
Libya IRA arms aid rptd 7-15, 531E1
Dublin bombing frees IRA member 7-15, 538C3
UK amb slain in Dublin 7-21, 538D2-C3
Sinn Fein ldr arrested 7-23, banned 7-26, 590G1
Sniper kills policeman; Cookstown barracks attacked 7-31, 590B2
Violence marks internmt anniv 8-7—8-10, 590C1
MP holds off IRA mob 8-9, 589G3
Drumm arrested 8-9, 590D1
Londonderry pre-parade violence 8-11, UK troops called in 8-12, 638B2
Belfast children killed, women protest 8-12, 8-14, 638C2
Drumm released 8-27, 679A2
Women stage peace marches 9-11, 9-15, 732B3
New min protested in Belfast 9-13, 732E2
Belfast press offices bombed 9-15, 732A3
Police hq bombed 9-18, 732C3
W Belfast pub shooting 9-24, 774A1
Cath girl killed 9-24, 855B1
IRA attacks women's peace organizers 9-26—10-10, Sinn Fein launches propaganda campaign 10-9, 773C3
Peace worker's son mutilated 9-28, 855A1
IRA bomber dies in UK jail 10-9, 774A1
Ballymena bombing reprisal 10-10, 773G3

1977

Lynch asks UK back reunificatn 10-12, 782E2

European Community—*See under 'E'*

Government & Politics—*See also other appropriate subheads in this section*
Dist cncl electns 5-18, 487D2
Unionists hold party rally 10-8—10-9, 783D3
Irish Independence Party formed 10-8, 783D3

Irish Republic Relations—*See also 'Anglo-Irish' above, 'Unrest' below*
Lynch vs Emergency Powers Act 5-26, 475F2
Cosgrave loses electn 6-16, 475D2
O'Brien speech vs unificatn causes furor 9-18, 782A3
SDLP urges Irish link 9-20, Unionists denounce 9-21, 783G2

Obituaries
Faulkner, Brian 3-3, 264F2

Unrest
12 bombs hit London 1-29, 222B3
UK admits torture tactics 2-7, pledges vs use 2-8; Eur rights ct hearings 4-19—4-22, IRA scored 4-22, 315E2-F3
IRA gunmen sentncd in '75 London slayings 2-10, 222F2
Irish police brutality chrgd 2-15, 782E3
'76 UK patrol cleared in Dublin 3-8, 329A2
IRA attacks on UK businessmen rptd 3-24, 639B1
IRA prisoners end Portlaoise hunger strike 4-22, 487A3
Ulster loyalist strike fails 5-2—5-14, 487F1
IRA rpts UK army capt executed 5-16, 5 chrgd 5-28, 487F2
IRA factions feud 7-27, 7-28, total death toll rptd 7-27, 639C1
Queen's visit stirs violence 8-7—8-12, 638A3-639A1
Lynch sees Callaghan on Ulster Defense Regiment 9-28, 782E2
Amnesty Intl chrgs Irish policy brutality 9-28, govt probe set 10-7, 782C3
Costello killed in Dublin 10-5, 782E3
Irish anti-terrorist detentn law lapses 10-6, 782D3
Corrigan, Williams win Nobel 10-10, 951C2
S Africa min compares situatns 10-21, 825F1
Firemen strike, IRA firebomb Belfast 11-22, 1013B3

1978

UK press, Pardoe urge troop exit 8-14, 9-17; Liberals disavow 9-17, Conservative scores 9-19, 723D1, B2
Gallup poll finds Britons for exit 9-20, 723C2
Callaghan govt seeks Ulster MP support 11-1, 838D1, F1
SDLP backs UK exit 11-4—11-5, 923B2
US peace conf oppositn rptd 11-14, 923F1

European Community—*See EUROPEAN Community*

Foreign Relations (misc.)
Leb arms shipmt rptd seized in Belgium 1-6, 7F3
NZ relocatn projct rptd 4-17, 373F1
IRA, W Ger terrorists linked to UK army base bombings 8-19—8-24, 688E1

Government & Politics—*See also other appropriate subheads in this section*
Interparty talks collapse 1-9, 18A2

Irish Republic Relations—*See 'Anglo-Irish' above, 'Unrest' below*

Unrest
'77 violence rptd down, death data 1-4, 7D3
IRA bombings increase 1-4—1-5, 18E2
Ireland probes '76 UK amb death 1-4, police chrg rptd 1-13, 37C3
IRA arms shipmt rptd seized in Belgium 1-6, 7F3
IRA expose forces pullout of UK agents 1-9, 18F2
Belfast bombings, IRA blamed 1-12, 18D1, 37E2
Unionists ask vigilante action 1-12, 71G2
UK cleared of post-Oct '71 torture chrgs, rights ct rules on Aug-Oct '71 abuses 1-18, 36E3
IRA bombings injure UK, RUC soldiers 1-23, 71B3
2 jailed IRA terrorists marry 1-24, 172E2
'Bloody Sunday' anniv marked in Belfast, Londonderry; 2 UK soldiers wounded 1-26, 71C3
2 UK soldiers wounded in Belfast 2-2, 132B3
Londonderry police find M60 ammunitn 2-3, 132B3
2 UDR officers, 4 others killed in IRA violence 2-4—2-12, 132D3-E3
Belfast restaurant bombing kills 12 2-17; suspects questnd 2-18, IRA claims credit 2-19, 132E1, B2
UK col killed in copter crash 2-17, IRA claims credit 2-18, 132G2
Lynch urges US aid cutoff 2-18, scores US rep on IRA 2-22, 289C1
Londonderry bus depot firebombed 2-19, 132A2
Nairac murder trial postponed 2-20, 132F3
UK bars death penalty restoratn 2-21, 132E2
IRA factn, others condemn Belfast bombing; UK, Ulster Protestants urge restraint 2-19-2-21; Belfast mourns 2-22, 132B2, F2
UK soldiers, police killed in Belfast, Londonderry 2-28—3-3; '78 death total rptd 2-28, 168C1
UK soldier wounded in Belfast ambush 3-6, 2 Caths killed in Protestant reprisal 3-8, 268E1
UK patrol fired on from Irish border 3-13, 268G1
UK soldier dies in Maghera ambush, top IRA suspect captured 3-16, 268C1
1 soldier, 2 civilians wounded in Belfast 3-16, 268G1
US Dems condemn violence, UK rights abuse 3-16, 373A3
IRA M60, other arms found in Belfast 4-3, 268B2
Belfast hosp shooting 4-10, 373A2
Armored car blast kills 3 4-13, 373A2
UDR bus driver killed 4-14, 373B2
Long Kesh IRA prisoner protest rptd 4-14, 373B3
Nobel winners, co-worker to quit peace movemt 4-15; disputes rptd 4-17, 373B1
Armoy cop killed in bombing 4-15, 373C2
Police photographer killed 4-22; suspect kills self, violence erupts 5-10, 373C2, F2; police reveal IRA link 5-11, 474F2
Provisional IRA raids; 15 arrested 4-27, 373D2
Payne wounded 4-27, 373E2

1979

UK offers home rule plans 11-20, Fitt quits SDLP re support 11-22, talks deferred 11-29, 927B3-928B1
Lynch resigns 12-5, 950B2

European Community—*See EUROPEAN Community*

Foreign Relations (misc.)
IRA, Spain Basque cooperatn rptd 1-28, 100C3
Belgium explosn link to IRA disputed 8-28, 641E2
Papal visit barred 8-29, 642B1
7 forgn rptrs arrested, freed 9-4, 669F3
Pope in Eire, pleas for peace 9-30; IRA rejcts 10-2, 760G1-A3

Irish Republic Relations—*See also 'Anglo-Irish' above, 'Unrest' below*
Ireland bars trans-border suspect pursuit, extraditn 9-2, 669E3
Eire attitudes polled 10-14, 836C1
Lynch urges US cooperatn, vs IRA 11-8, seeks reunificatn 11-9, 874A2

Unrest
IRA bombs fuel depots in UK 1-17, 96G3
IRA attacks Belfast bus depot 1-18, 97A1
IRA Eire PO attacks rptd 1-22, 97B1
2 UK undercover agents wounded 1-25, 97C1
UK soldiers to be chrgd in '78 youth's death 2-1, 97C1
11 Prot extremists sentncd 2-20, 190C2
IRA bomb blasts in UK 2-23, 190D2
Keady youths killed by bomb 2-24, 190D2
IRA prisoner treatmt protested 3-5, 190E2
MD chrgs police brutality 3-11, UK probe confrmatn rptd 3-15, 190D1
Guerrilla violence continues 3-19—4-21, 312E3-313A1
IRA linked to UK Dutch amb's murder 3-22, 3-23, 228E2-B3
Tory MP slain, IRA linked 3-30, 254E1
Londonderry, Omagh explosns; IRA blamed 3-31, 4-1, 254D2
Guerrilla violence continues 4-21—7-23, 565C1-C2
UK soldiers cleared re youth's death 7-4, 565A1
US suspends arms sales to police 8-2, 601F3
Marches, violence mark 10th anniv of UK troops arrival 8-11, 8-12, 614C2
Suspected IRA backers arrested in Belfast 8-15, 614G2
IRA kills Mountbatten, kin; UK, Ireland deplore 8-27; Thatcher sees mins 8-28, 641A1
19 Britons killed in IRA Warrenpoint attack 8-27, 641D2
Prot extremists threaten reprisals 8-27, 8-28, 1 killed 8-28, 641F2-642B1
Belgium explosn link to IRA disputed 8-28, 641E2
Papal Armagh visit barred 8-29, 642B1
Ireland chrgs Mountbatten murder suspects, IRA scores UK 8-30, 669F1, B2
Ireland seals border 8-31, 669E2
2 Belfast Catholics killed 9-1, 9-3, 669F2
IRA, forgn rptrs arrested, freed 9-4, 669F3
Guerrilla violence continues 9-11—10-29, 835G3-836C1
Pope pleas for violence end 9-30, IRA rejcts 10-2, 760G1-A3
UK security agrmt reached 10-5, 792E3
Guerrilla violence, arrests mount 11-6—12-17, 994B3
Mountbatten murder suspect convicted 11-23, 909F1-C2
Haughey vows UK security cooperatn, seeks troop exit, vs IRA terrorism 12-7, 950F1
Amnesty Intl cites UK brutality 12-9, 980C2
Thatcher, Carter discuss arms sales 12-17, 968B2

1980

Thatcher meets Haughey 12-8; Paisley warns 12-9, 942F2

European Community—*See EC*

Foreign Relations (misc.)
Italy terrorist, IRA links seen 1-2, 20F2
UK soldiers attacked in W Ger 2-16, 3-1, 3-10, IRA claims credit, notes other forgn violence 2-19, 194A1
Intl parley asked 2-17, 133A2

Irish Republic Relations—*See also 'Unrest' below*
Home rule talks begin 1-7, Paisley bars parallel talks 1-11, 39B2, E2
Haughey urges solutn 2-16, backs intl parley; reactn 2-17, 133D1
Haughey meets Thatcher 5-21, 389E3
UK home rule plan backs links; reactn 7-2, 522G3, 523E1
Powell vs home rule 9-26, 750C3
Thatcher meets Haughey 12-8; Paisley warns 12-9, 942F2

Unrest
UK soldiers accidentally shot in Tullydonnell 1-1, reserve cop killed in Newtonbutler 1-3, 58F3, G3
IRA, Italy terrorist links seen 1-2, 20F2
Beating death discovered 1-4, Belfast bombings, attack rptd 1-5, 59A1
IRA bomb factory found in Ireland 1-5, arms cache 1-14, 59B1
Land mine blast near Castlewellan 1-6, Belfast 1-17, 59B1, C1
Peace movemt figure kills self 1-21, 59D1
Part-time soldier shot 2-2, 194G1
Antique dealer kidnaped 2-8, found dead 2-9, 194G1
UK soldiers attacked in W Ger 2-16, 3-1, 3-10; IRA claims credit, notes other forgn violence 2-19, 194A1
Man shot in W Belfast 2-29, Prot injured by car bomb 3-8, 194F1
Soldiers injured in UK army camp bombings 3-7, 194E1
Orangemen demonstrate vs IRA 3-15, 232D3
UK soldier killed at Crossmaglen 3-15, 232E3
Bombings, other IRA attacks 3-31—6-21, 619C1-A3
Arms cache found 4-25, bombs defused 4-29, 619G1, A2
IRA jailed ill bomber freed 4-30, 619A2
3 IRA gunmen surrender after killing UK soldier 5-2, 619B2
Haughey warns vs violence 5-21, 389B1
IRA renews terror drive vs prison offcls 6-12, 619F2
Newtonbutler Prot rally demands Eire border closed 6-23, 619A3
'75 London bombing organizer sentncd 6-25, 619B3
2 Eire policemen killed by bankrobbers 7-7, 619C3
Dublin police rpt Eire training camp raid 8-5, 619D3
Internment law anniv spurs protests, 4 dead 8-9—8-10, 618G3
Belfast police ambush fails, woman killed 8-16, 708C3
INLA Armagh blast kills 1 8-29, 708C3
Cop kidnaped by IRA 8-31, rptd dead 9-4, 708D3
4 children hurt in Belfast blast 9-3, 708D3
Belfast building bombed 9-17, 830B1
Police reservist murdered 9-23, 830C1
Warrenpoint car bomb injures 7 9-23, 830C1
UK withdraws more troops 10-8, 830A1
2 murdered in Belfast 10-15, 830D1
IRA prisoners ask pol status 10-23, start hunger strike 10-27, 829D3-830A1
Protestant group claims 4 murders 10-29, 994B1
RC man wounded in Belfast 11-14, 994C1
3 women prisoners join hunger strike 12-1, 922C2
London barracks bombed 12-2, IRA Xmas offensive feared 12-3, 922A2
2 wounded at Strabane 12-9, 994C1
Protestant prisoners start hunger strike 12-12, 965F3
IRA prisoners hunger strike prompts Londonderry, Armagh riots 12-13—12-14; 23 inmates join fast 12-15, 965C3
IRA suspect escapes London jail 12-16, 994D1

1976

Cath, UK troop violence mounts; 2 killed 10-12—10-24, 854E1-855A2
O'Connell sentncd in Dublin 10-13, 855C1
Blast kills 3 IRA members 10-16, 854F3
Youths attack Belfast peace march 10-22, 854F3
Protestant militiaman slain 10-26, 854E3
Drumm slain 10-28, buried 11-1, 854B3
Londonderry stores firebombed 12-5, 926A2
Drogheda peace march held 12-5, 926C2
Loyalist com chrgs Protestant politicians 12-12, 1007B1
IRA bombs Belfast 12-13, 1008C1
'76 violence data rptd 12-23, 1007G3
Belfast bombing ends IRA ceasefire 12-28, 1007F3

NORTHERN Natural Gas Co.
Buys North Sea gas 4-7, 521E3
NORTH Korea—*See KOREA (North)*
NORTH Little Rock, Ark.—*See ARKANSAS*
NORTHROP, Judge Edward S.
Bars HEW move vs Md schl funds 3-8, 203D1
NORTHROP Corp.
'75 arms sales listed 2-6, 147B2
Jones renamed chrmn; Paine, pres 2-18, 133C1
Swiss Parlt OKs jet deal 3-16, 314F3
Confirms Iran jet-oil barter talks 5-11, 340B1
Ethiopia F-5E buy rptd 5-14, 364G2
Canada settles suit 9-7, 710G1-B2
Pentagon sets curb on favors 12-9, 982G3
Top fscl '76 defns contractor 12-21, 961A3
Political Payments
Admits Page paymts in Italy 2-20, 362A3
Brazil bribes rptd admitted 2-23, 147F1
Repays Iran agent fee, denies Iran seeks Page penalty deductn 2-23, 156F2
Lockheed accuses; denies chrgs, Pentagon probe set 3-2, 200F2
Rpt Dutch bribe probe widens 4-13, 322C2
SEC lists paymts 5-12, 725G3, 728D2
Bernhard role in '71 W Ger buy rptd 9-2, 684F2
W Ger campaign issue 9-29, 10-1, 754C3
Cannon reelected 11-2, 824D2

1977

U.S. Relations
US vs involvemt 3-16—3-19, 329F1
US aid halt to IRA asked 3-17, 222D3
NY gov scores IRA 4-22, 329G1
US vows peace aid 8-30; Ireland, UK reactn 9-1, 729E3

NORTHERN Natural Gas Co.
FPC splits on Alaska pipe route 5-2, 369B3
NORTH Korea—*See KOREA (North)*
NORTHROP Corp.
Paymts total cited 1-21, 79F1
Backs Concorde landings 3-11, 213F1

1978

Newry job exchng mgr shot 4-27, 373E2
Financial Times Dublin office vandalized 5-5, 373F2
IRA warns of 10-yr war 5-8, 373F1
Londonderry checkpoints dismantled 5-25, 474G2
2 IRA Provisionals get life sentncs 5-26, 474A3
Londonderry post office firebombed, Belfast blasts 5-27, 474B3-C3
Amnesty Intl chrgs police brutality 6-1, inquiry set 6-8; RUC denies chrgs 6-9, 6-14, 474E1
Paisley chrgs Belfast restaurant bombers in Eire 6-4, 474C3
Sinn Fein ldr wounded in Belfast 6-7, 474D3
Checkpoints removed in most towns 6-7, 474D3
UK soldiers kill IRA member, Londonderry youths riot 6-10, 474E3
Twomey sentenced, IRA reorganizatn plans cited 6-10, 474F3
Armagh cop slain, partner kidnaped 6-17, rptd 'executed' 6-19; priest seized 6-18, 474D2
RUC deaths since '69 rptd 6-19, 474F2
3 IRA members, bystander killed in UK troop shootout 6-21, 474G3
Ulster mailman kidnaped, slain 6-25, 630G2
IRA gunman wounded in Belfast 6-27, 630A3
IRA scores RC primate 7-1, 630A2
Police reservist killed in Castlederg 7-4, 630B3
Protesters throw manure in Commons, demonstrate in support of Irish prisoners 7-6, 533A3
UK soldiers kill boy at Dunby arms cache site 7-11, 630B3
IRA blast kills UK soldier in Crossmaglen 7-12, 630E2
Protestants mark Orange Day, ask factnl strife end 7-12, 630F2
6 bombs explode in Belfast 7-16, 630C3
Londonderry bus drivers strike 7-18, 630D3
Englishman sentncd in Dublin for arms smuggling 7-18, 630D3
UK soldier killed near Dungannon, 2d wounded in Belfast 7-19, 630E3
UK soldier, 3 civilians wounded in Belfast blast 7-25, 630E3
Hijacked bus blown up in Belfast 7-27, 630F3
Irish RC primate scores Long Kesh jail conditns, Mason refutes 8-1; inmates plan Eur Rights Comm plea 8-8, 630B1
Police reservist killed in Ballymena, 9-yr death toll rptd 8-3, 630F3
UK sends 500 reinforcemts 8-5, 631A1
6 gun attacks on UK soldiers in Belfast 8-9, 630G3
Internmt 7th anniv marked by violence 8-9, 630G3
UK army bases in Rhine bombed 8-18; IRA, W Ger terrorists linked 8-19—8-24, patrols increased 8-25, 688D1
UDR ex-member killed in Keady 8-19, 722F3
IRA ambush kills worker in Lough Melvin 8-21, 722E3
'71 Belfast tavern bomber sentenced 9-6, 722F3
Prov Sinn Fein ldr released 9-6, 723B1
Prov Sinn Fein editor arrested 9-9, 723B1
Prov IRA ldrship shift rptd, violence rise seen 9-15, 723C1
IRA bombing offensive launched 11-14—11-19, train hijacked 11-20, warden killed 11-26, 923A1
IRA violence continues 11-30—12-21, 1017D2
U.S. Relations
IRA use of US M60 guns rptd 1-19, 1-29, 71D3; ammunitn found 2-3, 132B3
Lynch bids US cut aid 2-18, scores Biaggi IRA link 2-22, 289C1
US Dems condemn violence, UK rights abuses 3-16, 373A3
IRA M60 found in Belfast 4-3, 268B2
2 US reps arrive, seek '79 'peace forum' 11-14, 923E1

NORTH Korea—*See KOREA (North)*
NORTH Park College (Chicago, Ill.)
Wins NCAA Div III basketball title 3-18, 272B2
NORTH Pole—*See ARCTIC Regions*
NORTHROP Corp.
10th in '77 defns contracts 3-28, 224G2
Malaysian sentncd for kickback 6-6, 439E3

1979

U.S. Relations
US legislators seek paramil groups mtg 1-25, 97D1
US House speaker, NY gov, other offcls fault UK; MPs score 4-19—4-24, 312E2
US suspends arms sales to police 8-2, 601F3
Carey asks UK-Ireland conf 8-6, Atkins comments 8-7, 602E1
US rptr arrested, freed 9-4, 669F3
Carter, Pope urge peaceful solutn 10-6, 759D3
Lynch visits US, seeks cooperatn 11-8, 11-9, 874A2
Thatcher, Carter discuss arms sales 12-17, 968B2

NORTHERN Natural Gas Co.
US overchrgs alleged 9-30, 849E3
NORTHERN States Power Co.
Wis A-plant bid rejctd 2-27, 186C2
Tyrone A-plant canceled 7-26, 609F3
Minn A-plant leak 10-2; cold shutdown reached 10-3, probe 10-7—10-9, 786C3
NORTH Korea—*See KOREA (North)*
NORTHLEY, Leland
Indicted re casino skimming 8-23, 851D1
NORTH Park College (Chicago, Ill.)
Wins NCAA Div III basketball title 3-17, 239B1

1980

Protestants end hunger strike 12-17, 994A1
IRA prisoners end fast 12-18, 12-19, 993F2
Protestants, Loyalists claim attacks on Belfast prison offcrs 12-21, 12-30, 994D1, E1
Part-time soldier killed at Armagh 12-28, 994E1
U.S. Relations
Haughey asks US role 2-17, 133A2
GM plant set 2-20, 125A3
Haughey attacks groups aiding IRA 7-27, 604B3
Powell vs home rule 9-26, 750C3

NORTHERN Ireland Aid Committee (N.Y., N.Y.)
Eire scores IRA aid 7-27, 604B3
NORTHERN Michigan University (Marquette)
U of ND wins NCAA hockey title 3-29, 488G3
NORTHERN Tier Pipeline Co.
Carter OKs Alaska oil pipe route 1-18, 56B3
NORTH Park College (Chicago, Ill.)
Wins NCAA Div III basketball title 3-15, 240D3
NORTH Providence—*See RHODE Island*
NORTHROP Corp.
FX jet for export OKd 1-4, 16D3

1976

NORTH Sea
Norway projcts '84 Statfjord yields 1-6, 30B2
UK loan to Burmah Oil rptd 1-13, 173F3
UK oil find rptd 1-19, US consortium yields 51% interest 2-26, 173A3
Ireland oil finds rptd 2-1, 157C1
UK oil field Euroloans rptd 2-4, 2-5, 173E3
1st UK Auk oil shipmt rptd 2-25, 173D3
UK buys Burmah interest in Ninian Field 3-10, 521D3
Dutch increase oil, gas role 3-25, 255E1
US utility buys propane, butane 4-7, 521E3
W Ger buys oil 4-27, 521E3
Conoco find rptd 5-28, 521D3
French-UK talks end 6-24, 481E3
UK, BP to share fields 7-1, 521F3
UK rpts 3 new finds 7-9, 521B3
Norway, BP joint probe set 8-6, 590C2
Norway, UK sign oil pact 9-10, 832E3

NORTH Slope, Alaska—*See ALASKA*
NORTH-South Conference—*See ECONOMIC Cooperation, Conference on International*
NORTH Vietnam—*See VIETNAM (North)*
NORTHWEST Airlines Inc.
'75 zero tax paymt rptd 10-2, 847F1
Ford rejcts transatlantic route 12-28, 992C2
NORTHWEST Guaranty Savings & Loan Association (Seattle, Wash.)
'71 failure cited 2-17, 185F1
NORTHWEST Industries Inc.
SEC lists forgn paymts 5-12, 728D2
Velsicol workers poisoned 12-6, 950B2
NORTON, Eleanor Holmes
Cleaver Defense Fund formed 2-17, 272F1
NORTON, Ken
Loses decisn to Ali 9-28, 756C2

NORWAY—*See also ADB, IEA, NATO, OECD*
Premier quits 1-9; Nordli, cabt named 1-12, 30F1, A2 ★
Listed as 'free' nation 1-19, 20C3
Freighter lost at sea 1-19, 79D3
Jens Bjoerneboe dies 5-9, 404F1
Tanker, US ferry collide in Miss 10-20, 876G1
Economy & Labor (domestic)
Statfjord oilfield dvpt, yield rptd 1-5, 1-6, 30B2
Parlt OKs new state oil co 1-7, 30C2
Price freeze in effect 9-13, 873G2
'77 budget submitted 10-6, 858D2
Oil cleanup sought 11-17, 873E2
'74 tax rate rptd 11-18, 905G1

European Force Reduction Issues—*See under EUROPE*
Foreign Economic Developments
BP unit acquisitn planned 1-7, 30D2
SDR rate rptd 1-15, 14B3
Brazil bauxite operatn begun 1-16, 98G2
Vs World Bank Chile loan 2-3, 99G2
Pledges loan to Portugal 2-5, 142G3
France quits snake float 3-15, 229F1
Canada seal-hunt protests canceled 3-17, 3-24, 250F3
Total IMF oil loan rptd 4-1, 340F2
UK, Iceland cod pact signed 6-1, 389B3
Joint oil probe set with BP 8-6, 590C2
UK Sea oil pact signed 9-10, 832E3
Aug trade deficit rptd 10-4, 873F2
W Ger mark revalued 10-17, 782B1
Foreign Relations (misc.)
Europn socialists meet 1-18—1-19, 48A3; 3-13—3-14, 222F3
Angola MPLA recognized 2-18, 163D1
Anders confrmd US amb 4-1, 262B3
Vs WHO anti-Israel stand 5-19, 355D2
Ship in US Bicentennial event 7-4, 488A3, D3
Argentina refugee asylum rptd 7-19, 571G2
N Korean diplomats expelled 10-18, 799B3

1977

NORTH Sea
UK in Exxon, Shell pact 1-5, 20E3
'76-80 share of world oil supply estimated 1-28, 108B2
Norway Ekofisk well blowout, map 4-23—4-30, productn halted 4-28—5-2, 336D1-C3
Herring fishing banned 7-18, 9-16, 771B3
Danes OK gas line 8-1, 672C1
EC bans Sovt trawlers 9-31, 771F2
Ekofisk blowout blamed on human error 10-10, 967B3
NORTH-South Conference—*See ECONOMIC Cooperation, Conference on International*
NORTH Vietnam—*See VIETNAM*
NORTHWEST Airlines Inc.
Glasgow, Scandanavia routes OKd 12-21, 1006C2
NORTHWEST Energy Co.
Northwest Pipeline Corp.—*See ALCAN Pipeline Co.*
NORTHWESTERN Memorial Hospital (Chicago, Ill.)
Finley undergoes surgery 9-15, 768D2
NORTHWESTERN Steel & Wire Co.
'76 Fortune 500 list drops 341D1
Chrgs Canada dumping 11-3, 836F3
NORTHWESTERN University (Evanston, Ill.)
Said denies Geneva invitatn 11-15, 873E2
Gray named Chicago U pres 12-10, 1021B2
NORTHWEST Georgia Bank (Ringgold)
Lance role probed 9-7, 690B2
NORTHWEST Industries Inc.
Coca-Cola Bottling OKs purchase 10-17, 880A2
Velsicol Chemical Corp.
Tris recall-cost sharing ordrd 5-3, 483D2
Indicted on pesticide data 12-12, 1007E3
NORTHWEST Pipeline Corp.—*See ALCAN Pipeline Co.*
NORTHWEST Power Pool (utility group)
BPA asks 10% power cut 2-11, 244D3
Conservatn efforts lauded 2-15, 152F3
NORTH-West Shelf Joint Venture Companies
Australia OKs gas search 8-24, 704E3
NORTH Yemen—*See YEMEN Arab Republic*
NORTON, Eleanor Holmes
Named EEOC chrmn 5-16, confrmd 5-27, 500A1
EEOC reorgnztn plan rptd 7-20, 669F1
NORTON, Ken
KOs Bobick 5-11, 395E1
Decisns Young 11-5, 970C2
WBC softens threat vs Ali 12-1, 970B2
NORTON Simon Inc.
Avis control purchased 6-27, 519G1
Glass Containers strike ends 10-14, 818F3

NORWAY—*See also IEA, NATO, OECD*
Left-Socialists reveal secret rpt 8-22, 730D2
Labor Party wins 1-vote edge 9-12, Norland recount 9-15, 730E1, B2 ★
Nobel Peace Prizes announced 10-10, 951B2
Economy & Labor (domestic)
'76 GNP rise rptd 2-1, '77 forecast 2-2, 99E2-A3
2.9% wage pact rptd 4-5, 967G1
North Sea Ekofisk oil blowout, map 4-23—4-30, productn halted 4-28—5-2, 336D1-C3
Svalbard fisheries zone declared 6-3, 967G2
Ekofisk blowout blamed on human error 10-10, 967B3
'78 budget presented 10-13, 967F1
'77 GNP growth below forecast 10-13, 967C2
'75 world pay, buying power rank rptd 11-6, 853D3
'77 oil, gas productn forecast 12-9, 967C3

Foreign Relations (misc.)—*See also 'Monetary, Trade & Aid' below*
UN Assemb member 4-11, 99E3
'76 Eur Cncl pact vs terror cited 9G2
In 14-natn sulphur-dioxide pact 1-19, 109F2
6 Sovt spies expelled 1-28, 99A3
USSR ousts 2 diplomats 2-14, 967A3
Spain exiles Basque prisoners 6-6, 6-9, 454B1
Tito's wife at Nordli fete 6-14, 786B1
Eur Cncl to study Turkey rights abuses in Cyprus 9-8, 764G1-A2; rpt shelved, Greece protests 11-3, 946E3
Nigeria pirate raid scored 11-22, 986F2

Helsinki Agreement—*See EUROPE—Security and Cooperation*
Monetary, Trade & Aid Issues (including all foreign economic developments)
UK 200-mi fishing zone in effect 1-1, 21A1
Czech trade visit canceled 1-30, 99C3
SDR defined 87G2
Canada fines fishing vessel 2-22, 147A2
In Canada seal hunt 3-15, 237F3
SAS strike settled 5-9—5-20, 469G2
GATT to probe US ruling on Japan electronic duties 5-23, 416C2
Svalbard fisheries zone declared 6-3, USSR disputes 11-11, 967F2

1978

NORTH Sea
UK '77 paymts surplus rptd 1-17, 132D1
EC fishing policy vetoed by UK 1-30—1-31, 159A1
Norway Ekofisk blowout linked to krone devaluatn 2-10, 134A1
Eur '77 oil output rptd up 2-14, 158D3
Scots get oil exploitatn control 2-22, 131G3
UK oil revenue plans announced 3-21, 227B1
UK offshore oil tax hiked 8-2, 591D3
NATO maneuvers begin 9-5, 748C2, D2
Norway, Sweden sign oil agrmt 12-8, 965B3

NORTH Vietnam—*See VIETNAM*
NORTHWEST—*See also state names*
Drought declared over, reservoirs refilling 3-5, 207B2
NORTHWEST Airlines Inc.
Stewardess pay bias case refused 2-21, 125G3
Pilots strike 4-29—8-15, 680E3
NORTHWEST Airlines v. Laffey
Stewardess bias case review refused 2-21, 125G3
NORTHWESTERN University (Evanston, Ill.)
Minority press employmt survey rptd 4-13, 835C3
Real estate tax-dispute review refused by Sup Ct 5-1, 364E1
NORTHWEST Industries Inc.
Velsicol Chemical Corp.
Mich PBB suit dismissed 10-27, 834E1
NORTH Yemen—*See YEMEN Arab Republic*
NORTON, B. W. L.
Convoy released 6-28, 619C1
NORTON, Eleanor Holmes
EEOC to monitor corps 1-4, 5B1
NORTON, Elizabeth Ann
FBI break-in case refused by Sup Ct 12-4, 959G1
NORTON, Ken
Seeks Spinks fight 3-1, threatens suit vs Arum, Spinks 3-8; WBC names champ 3-18, 211B3—212C1
Loses WBC heavywgt title to Holmes 6-9, 600A1
NORTON Simon Inc.
Avis Inc.
Parking ticket case refused by Sup Ct 10-30, 832F2
NORTON v. U.S.
Case refused by Sup Ct 12-4, 959F1

NORWAY—*See also COUNCIL of Europe, GATT, IEA, EFTA, NATO, OECD*
'76 tanker, ferry collisn rpt issued 5-17, 460B1
Energy conservatn progress cited 6-5, 449E3 ★, 450F1
Nobel Peace Prize announced 10-27, 886C1; accepted 12-10, 950B3
Economy & Labor (domestic)
Austerity measures imposed; credit, bank loans curbed 1-28—1-29, 134C1
Oil field dvpt slowdown forces krone devaluatn 2-10, 133G3
Price freeze imposed 2-12, 134E1
Jobless rate rptd at 1% 2-13, 134A1
'77 inflatn, wage hikes rptd; '75-77 per-unit product cost 2-13, 134B1
'74-77 pvt consumptn, real income rptd 2-14, 134C1
'73-77 wage gain cited 2-27, 189C3
Income per capita rank rptd 5-12, 384F3
'77 per capita GNP ranked 4th 7-18, 624E1
'79 austerity budget presented 10-5, 775C1, 883G3
A-power backed by study com 10-12, 884E1
1st ½ '78 oil productn rptd up 11-14, 871B2
European Force Reduction Talks—*See under EUROPE*
Foreign Relations (misc.)—*See also 'Monetary, Trade, Aid & Investment' and 'UN' below*
Intl group meets in Oslo on Cambodia atrocities 4-21—4-23, 301C2
Eur conservative group formed 4-24, 424C3
Leb army move to south urged 8-8, 638C3
USSR plane crashes 8-28; Moscow scores probe 10-6; flight recorder opened 10-12, 820G1-F2
USSR satellite, radar equipmt in Barentsburg rptd 9-28; sea violatns rptd 10-12, 820D2
Seal kill off Scotland canceled 10-16, 816A2
Helsinki Agreement—*See EUROPE—Security and Cooperation*
Monetary, Trade, Aid & Investment
Krone devalued 8% 2-10, 133F3
'75-77, '77 paymts, trade deficit rptd 2-10, 134C1, D1
S Africa investmt banned 3-11, 193C3
Krone in new SDR basket 4-3, 300G3
US backs F-16 review 4-24, 407E2
EC monetary zone proposed 7-6—7-7, 545B2
Rhodesia rebel aid OKd by WCC 8-10, 650A3
'79 forgn debt rise forecast, poor-natn aid budgeted 10-5, 775E1, 884C1
W Ger mark revalued up 10-16, 798C2

1979

NORTH Sea
UK oil constructn workers' strike expands 1-8, 20D3
Norway-Sweden oil pact imperiled 1-26, 77C2
UK, Norway oil access cited 2-20, 126A3
£ strength, UK oil earnings linked 5-1, 321C1
Allied Chem to buy Eltra 6-28, 560A2
UK revises oil estimate 7-10, 582A2
UK plans more exploratn 7-26, 582F1
UK OKs Scottish gas plant 8-10, 614B2
'79 1st 1/2 world oil output rptd 8-28, 645A2
Canada potential compared 9-11, 728B3
UK bars oil assets sale 9-14, 707G1
France oil access, EC budget contributn opposed by UK 9-17, 719D2, E2
UK ordrs oil cutback 10-29, 836F1
BNOC sets price hike 11-6, 864B2

NORTHWEST Airlines Inc.
DC-10s grounded, travel chaos rptd 6-6, 420G3
NORTHWESTERN Bank (Winston-Salem, N.C.)
Bagley indicted 3-14, 291G3
Bagley acquitted 8-1, 578D2
NORTHWESTERN College (Orange City, Iowa)
Loses NAIA Div II football title game 12-8, 1001F2
NORTHWESTERN University (Evanston, Ill)
Pvt Title IX suit allowed by Sup Ct 5-14, 382D3
Laetrile rptd lethal to rats 7-13, 571C1
NORTHWEST Georgia Bank (Ringgold)
Lance, 3 others indicted in plot 5-23, plead innocent 5-24, 380D2
NORTHWEST Industries Inc.
Agent Orange suit filed 2-1, 90B1
Velsicol Chemical Corp.
Mich PBB indictmt 4-26, not guilty plea 5-7, 597E3
NJ Meadowlands cleanup ordrd 8-26, 704B2
Mich PBB contaminatn rpt issued 10-9, suits settled 10-23, 808G2-D3
NORTH Yemen—*See YEMEN Arab Republic*
NORTON, B. W. L.
More Amer Graffiti released 8-17, 820B2
NORTON, Eleanor Holmes
Comments on racial poll 2-20, 306F3
Scores Sears suit 5-15, 365G3
Backs Weber case Sup Ct ruling 6-27, 477A3
NORTON, Ken
Knoetz fight protested 1-13, 79E2
Shavers KOs 3-23, 412C3
NORTON Simon Inc.
Mahoney heads '78 top-paid execs list 5-14, 347E3

NORWAY—*See also COUNCIL of Europe, GATT, IEA, NATO, OECD*
Tanker fleet safety record rptd 8-15, 608E1
Nobel Peace Prize announced 10-17, 857D3, G3
Economy & Labor
Jan jobless rate up 2-8, 136G2
North Sea oil access cited 2-20, 126A3
Inflatn ceiling threatened by oil prices 5-25, 396D3
'78 per capita GNP ranked 7th 7-24, 575E3
'80 budget presented 10-6—10-7, 774B1
Lapps protest hydro project 10-8—10-12, 796G3
Shipowner fined 12-17, 996F3
Parlt OKs wage controls extensn 12-18, 996D3

European Force Reduction Talks—*See under EUROPE*
Foreign Relations (misc.)—*See also 'Monetary' and 'UN' below*
S Africa '73 pol gifts chrgd 3-21, 213D1
Bhutto executn scored 4-4, 247A2
Sovts opposed by US in Svalbard dispute 4-17, 299D2
SALT monitor role denied 7-26, 762G1
USSR cancels theater tour 10-1, 775B1
USSR vs A-missiles 10-13—10-16, 880G2
Government & Politics—*See also other appropriate subheads in this section*
Rightists gain in local elections 9-17, 709F3
Cabt shuffled 10-5, 774D1
Helsinki Agreement—*See EUROPE-Security and Cooperation*
Monetary, Trade, Aid & Investment
'78 trade deficit rptd 1-24, 136E2
Volvo deal blocked, Sweden econ pacts imperiled 1-26; premrs to meet 1-27, 77G1
Finland '78 trade rptd 2-2, 215G2
Iran oil cutoff impact assessed 2-20, 126A3
Sweden seeks joint oil progrm 3-13, 214A1
Iceland fishing dispute averted 8-18, 796F3
'80 paymts deficit cut seen, oil exports cited 10-6—10-7, 774B1

1980

NORTH Sea
UK oil productn plans rptd 1-4, 7B1
Oil platform capsizes, 123 killed 3-27, 256D1
UK Labor backs oil natlzn 5-31, 429E2
US gas pipe OKd 6-19, 463D2
Norway drillers strike 7-10, govt intervenes 7-16, 565F3; strike ends 8-13, 620E2
Norwegian gas find rptd 7-16, 548D2
UK plans oil output cut 7-23, 563C3
UK plans new oil levy 11-24, 901G1, C2

NORTHWEST Energy Co.
Pacific Resources merger bid 8-18, 746D1
NORTHWESTERN University (Evanston, Ill.)
Faster hay fever treatmt rptd 2-18, 159F3
'79 endowmt earnings rptd 3-24, 319C2
Bennett argues abortn funding in Sup Ct 4-21, 306D3
NORTHWEST Georgia Bank (Ringgold)
Chrgs vs Lance, 3 others reduced 4-9, 292A1
NORTHWEST Industries Inc.
Heineman named First Chicago chrmn 4-28, 456B2
Velsicol Chemical Corp.
Mich seeks PBB dump cleanup 4-17, 331E2
NORTH Yemen—*See YEMEN Arab Republic*
NORTON, Eleanor Holmes
On sex harassmt regulatns 4-11, 441B3
Hails Ford job-bias setlemt 11-25, 899B3
NORTON Simon Museum (Pasadena, Calif.)
Bouts painting bought for record sum 4-16, 472A3
NORTON Sound (U.S. missile test ship)
Lesbian probe set 5-15, scored 6-13, 6-15; 6 rptd chrgd 6-28, 517B3
Sailor convicted of sex harassmt 7-11, 598E1

NORWAY—*See also ADB, COUNCIL of Europe, CSCE, GATT, IEA, MBFR, NATO, OECD*
Nobel Peace Prize announced 10-13, 889G1, A2
Economy & Labor
OECD assesses outlook 2-5, 100E2, G2
Oslo purchasing power rptd low 2-12, 125F3
N Sea drillers strike 7-10; govt intervenes in 3 fields 7-16, impact rtpd 7-17, 565F3; strike ends 8-13, 620E2
'81 budget presented 10-6, 792E3
Energy
N Sea oil platform capsizes 3-27, 256F1
N Sea workers strike 7-10; govt intervenes 7-16, impact rptd 7-17, 565F3; strike ends 8-13, 620E2
N Sea gas find rptd 7-16, 548D2
'81 oil revenue rise seen 10-6, 792F3

Foreign Relations (misc.)—*See also 'Monetary', 'UN Policy' below*
Moscow Olympic boycott rptd backed 2-2, 85C1
Olympic com OKs Moscow participatn 3-30, 259B3
USSR science conf attended 4-13—4-15, 326F2
Sports Fed backs Olympic boycott 4-19, 325F3
USSR May Day parade shunned 5-1, 354G2
Tito funeral held 5-8, 339B1
IOC issues Olympic acceptance list 5-27, 420E3
Iran hostage appeal rptd 8-16, 634G3

Monetary, Trade, Aid & Investment
Debt repaymt, current acct surplus seen 2-5, 100F2
Venez shipping scandal rpt, ex-pres censured 5-8, 411E1
Iceland ocean accord set 5-10, 398B2
EC fishing vessels ordrd out 12-10, 969C3
Sovts vs US arms stockpiling, OK Barents Sea talks 12-22—12-23, 979A2

1976

Sports
Winter Olympics results 2-4—2-15, 158F3-159B2
Summer Olympic results 7-18—7-31, 573E3, 575D1

NORWEIGIAN Ballet
Blair dies 4-1, 484C3
NORWOOD, Janet L.
On labor cost index 6-18, 494E2
On June jobless rate 7-2, 494C1
NOSSITER, Bernard
S Africa details buffer force 2-3, 106A2
NOTRE Dame, University of (South Bend, Ind.)
Mondale speech 9-10, 687C1
Carter addresses 10-10, 762E2
Hesburgh named Carter aide 11-19, 881D3
Wins Gator Bowl 12-27, 1014G2
NOUIRA, Hedi
Libya death plot foiled 3-22, 239C2
Libyan sentncd to die 4-23, 335B1
NOVAK, Robert
Rpts Sonnenfeldt '75 remarks on E Eur policies 3-22; rpt disputed 3-29—4-2, 232G2, 233B1, 245B2
E Eur press scores Sonnenfeldt rpt 4-9—4-14, 277D1, F1
NOVIKOV, Sergei
Wins Olympic medal 7-26, 575A1
NOVO, Guillermo
DINA link chrgd 10-18; denies Letelier death role 10-20, 844F2
Linked to Letelier murder 10-19; '65 indictmt, '74 convictn cited 10-20, 780G2
NOVO, Ignacio
DINA link chrgd 10-18; Letelier death role denied 10-20, 844F2
Linked to Letelier murder 10-19; '65 indictmt cited 10-20, 780G2
NOVOJILOV, Viktor
Wins Olympic medal 7-31, 576D3
NOW—*See WOMEN, National Organization for*
NOWAK, Rep. Henry J. (D, N.Y.)
Reelected 11-2, 830D2
NOWAKOWSKI, Richard
Wins Olympic medal 7-31, 574B1
NOWICKI, Mieczysl
Wins Olympic medal 7-26, 574C2
NOYES, Daniel
'72 campaign gift listed 4-25, 688C1
NOYES, Nicholas
'72 campaign gift listed 4-25, 688C1
NSUBUGA, Emmanuel Cardinal
Named cardinal 4-27, 336B2
NTIRUGIRIMBABAZI, Denys
Sees Kenya finance min 7-22, 559G3
NTSHONA, Winston
Expelled 10-24, 813B2

1977

In 11-natn Portugal loan 6-22, 530B3
IWC cuts whaling quotas 6-24, 496F3
Danes block PVC plants 7-7, 672F1
'77 paymts deficit forecast 7-31, 586D2
Danes OK North Sea gas line 8-1, 672C1; delay rptd 12-9, 967D3
1st ½ trade deficit up 8-1, 967D2
Sweden quits 'snake' 8-29, 709A1
Krona devalued 5% 8-29, 709B1
Sovt Barents Sea fishing talks rptd 9-2, 967G2
US F-16 purchases budgeted 10-13, 967B2
'77 paymts deficit, forgn debt forecast 10-14; Jan-July data rptd 10-27, 967D2

Obituaries
Hambro, Edvard 2-1, 164G2

U.S. Relations
US F-16 sale review set 1-17, 70D3
US team caps N Sea oil well 4-30, 336D1
US F-16 pact set 5-5, 441A2
GATT to probe US electronics rule 5-23, 416C2
Lerner confrmd amb 7-13, 626A3
Secret US talks revealed 8-22, 730D2
F-16 purchases budgeted 10-13, 967B2

NOSEDA, Alfreda
Charged 5-8, 565A1
NOTHLING, Jan. E.
Orders Biko death inquest 10-26, 887A2
NOTRE Dame, University of (South Bend, Ind.)
Carter addresses graduates 5-22, 397B1
Arns gets honorary degree 5-22, 447A3
MacAfee, Browner win Downtown AC trophies 12-8, 950A2, E2
NOTTAGE, Kendall W.
Bahamas community affairs min 7-29, 675D1
NOUR, Abdullah Abdurahman
Defects 7-17, 562E2
NOUIRA, Hedi
Replaces Cabt 12-26, 1019E2
NOVAK, Robert
Scores cruise missile 10-29, 857D3
SALT leaks in article cited 11-8, 996A3
NOVILLO, Horacio
Found dead 1-18, 197F3
NOVO, Guillermo
Flees after Letelier murder testimony 9-10, 743A3
NOVOCAIN (procaine hydrochloride)—*See MEDICINE—Drugs*
NOW—*See WOMEN, National Organization for*
NOYES, Eliot F.
Dies 7-17, 604E3
NOYES, Nicholas H.
Dies 12-25, 1024E2
NQUMAYO, Albert Andrew Muwalo
Sentenced 2-14, 309E2
NRC—*See U.S. GOVERNMENT—NUCLEAR Regulatory Commission*
NRO—*See U.S. GOVERNMENT—DEFENSE—National Reconnaissance Office*
NSA—*See U.S. GOVERNMENT—DEFENSE—National Security Agency*
NSUBUGA, Bishop Dunstan
Amin letter cited 3-5, 308C3

1978

At Brussels monetary summit 12-4—12-5; EMS entry barred 12-11, quits snake 12-12, 952B2
Volvo, Swedish econ pacts signed 12-8, 965F2
North Sea oil seen as hedge vs OPEC price hike 12-18, 978E1
UK air pact OKd 12-22, 1017F1

Obituaries
Lyng, John 1-18, 96F2

Sports
Speed-skating record set 3-12, 316C3

UN Policy & Developments
Leb peace force (Unifil) formed 3-19, 197D2; **for peacekeeping developments, see MIDDLE EAST—LEBANON**
Assemb member 713D3

U.S. Relations
US alerts to USSR satellite fall 57E1
US backs F-16 review 4-24, 407E2
'76 tanker, ferry collisn rpt issued 5-17, 460B1

NOSENKO, Yuri
JFK probe info, CIA imprisonmt rptd 9-15, 749D3
NO Time For Breakfast (film)
Released 9-15, 970D2
NOTRE Dame, University of (South Bend, Ind.)
Wins Cotton Bowl 1-2, ranked 1st 1-3, 8F2, A3
Laetare Medal awarded to Ellis 3-6, 172F3
NCAA basketball tourn results 3-25, 272A1
3 in NFL draft 5-2, 336F3
NOTTE, Robert F.
Loses electn for Essex Cnty exec 11-7, 849D1
NOURI, Sheik Yahya Nasiri
Arrested as plotter 9-12, 693F1
NOUVELLE Cie. de Paquebots, La
Seamen agree to end strike 11-4, 882D1
NOVAK, Robert
Interviews China premr 11-27, 949D2, G2
NOVA Scotia (Canadian province)—*See CANADA*
NOVEMBER People, The (play)
Opens 1-14, 760A3
NOVO, Guillermo
Arrested in Miami 4-14, 287C2
Moved to NY jail 4-28, brother seized 5-4, 370E3
Letelier murder role detailed 6-2, 452A1
Indicted in Letelier murder 8-1, 614A1
Pleads not guilty 8-11, 647F3
NOVO, Ignacio
Seized in Letelier murder case 5-4, bail set 5-8, 370D3
Indicted in Letelier murder 8-1, 614B1
Pleads not guilty 8-11, 647F3
NOW—*See WOMEN, National Organization for*
NOW (Negotiable Orders of Withdrawal)—*See BANKS*
NOWAK, Rep. Henry J. (D, N.Y.)
Reelected 11-7, 851A4
NRC—*See U.S. GOVERNMENT—NUCLEAR Regulatory Commission*
NSA—*See U.S. GOVERNMENT—DEFENSE—National Security Agency*
NUCATOLA, John
In basketball HOF 5-1, 457D3

1979

Shipowner fined 12-17, 996F3

Sports
Waitz in NYC Marathon, sets women's world record 10-21, 911E3

UN Policy & Developments
4 Unifil soldiers die 2-3, 84E3
Cncl mtg on Viet-China war asked 2-22, 142B1
W Bank setlmt res abstentn 3-22, 198F2
Unifil soldier killed 4-18, 277G3
Membership listed 695A3

U.S. Relations
Mondale visits Eur 4-11–4-22, 299C2
SALT II verificatn methods sought 6-28, 497C1
SALT monitor role denied 7-26, 762F1
Carter sees Nordli, seeks A-missile plan support 12-7, 938D1

NORWOOD, Janet
Working women, 2-income families up 2-2, 110D3
On Feb '78-79 jobs gain 3-8, 182B3
On Mar employmt rpt 4-6, 280G2
On Oct producer prices 11-1, 828D1
NOSEDA, Alfredo
Chrgd re Chiasso scandal 2-15, 137E1
Sentenced 7-3, 505E2
NOSENKO, Yuri
Paisley death probe urged 1-24, 55E1
NOTHLING, J. E.
Bars chrgs vs Van den Burgh 1-25, 99D2
NOTRE Dame, University of (South Bend, Ind.)
Wins Cotton Bowl 1-1, '78 rank rptd 1-2, 1-3, 8E2, A3
NCAA basketball tourn results 3-26, 238B3
Manion dies 7-28, 588A3
Ex-pres Cavanaugh dies 12-28, 1008B2
NOTT, John
UK trade secy 5-5, 338G1
On British Airways sales 7-20, 564D3
Backs UK trust legis 10-31, 855D3, F3
NOVAES, Guiomar
Dies 3-7, 272D3
NOVA Scotia (Canadian province)—*See CANADA*
NOVELLO, Don
Gilda Radner Live opens 8-2, 711C3
NOVO Sampol, Guillermo
Letelier murder trial opens 1-9, jury chosen 1-12, 19D2
Letelier trial testimony begins 1-15; Townley testifies 1-18–1-24, 57E3-58A2
Called 'assassin' 2-13, convicted 2-14, 114C2, F2
Sentncd to life 3-23, 234E2
NOVO Sampol, Ignacio
Letelier murder trial opens 1-9, jury chosen 1-12, 19D2
Cited in Letelier trial testimony 1-16, 1-18, 58C1, B2
Convicted 2-14, 114C2
Sentncd to 8 yrs 3-23, 234E2
NOW—*See WOMEN, National Organization for*
NOW (Negotiable Orders of Withdrawal)—*See BANKS*
NOWICKI, Jan
Just Like At Home released 4-19, 528F2
NOW and Then: Poems 1976-78 (book)
Warren wins Pulitzer 4-16, 336G2
NOYCE, Phillip
Newsfront released 5-30, 820D2
NRC—*See U.S. GOVERNMENT–NUCLEAR Regulatory Commission*
NRC Corp.
Amdahl bid to Comten matched, Comten OKs acquisitn 4-23, 440G3
NSA—*See U.S. GOVERNMENT–DEFENSE–National Security Agency*
NTSOELENGOE, Ace
Named to NASL All-Star team 8-27, 776E1
NU Beng
Cambodian health min 1-8, 10B1
NUCLEAR Energy for Environmental Development (NEED)
Sponsors pro-nuclear rally in Calif 10-13, 806D3

1980

Sports
Speed skating championships 1-13, 1-20, 470E1, G1
Moscow Olympic boycott rptd backed 2-2, 85C1
Lake Placid Olympic results 2-12—2-24, 154F2, 155F2-156D1
Olympic com OKs Moscow participatn 3-30, 259B3
Sports Fed backs Olympic boycott 4-19, 325F3
IOC issues Olympic acceptance list 5-27, 420E3
Waitz in NYC Marathon; sets women's world mark 10-26, 890G3

UN Policy & Developments
UNIFIL troops replace Irish in Leb post 4-22, 302D3
Palestinian state Cncl res abstentn 4-30, 325D1
Palestine state Assemb res opposed 7-29, 572F1
Cncl seat replacemt set 11-13, 896E1

U.S. Relations
Iran hostage appeal rptd 8-16, 634G3
Sovts vs US arms stockpiling 12-22—12-23, 979D2

NORWOOD, Janet L.
On June jobless rate 7-3, 513E2
On July jobless rate 8-1, 599D2
On Aug jobless rate 9-5, 683F3
On Sept producer prices 10-3, 783G1-A2
NOSSAL, Sustav
Malaria outbreak rptd 5-31, 478A2
NOTHING Personal (film)
Released 4-18, 416D3
NOTRE Dame, University of (South Bend, Ind.)
'79 endowmt earnings rptd 3-24, 319C2
Ferguson in NFL draft 4-29, 336G3
Hanzlik in NBA draft 6-10, 447G2
Muskie warns of Reagan's 'endless' wars 10-11, 776G3
NOTTNY, Norbert
Wins Olympic medal 7-22, 624B3
NOUIRA, Hedi (Tunisian premier; replaced Mar. 1)
Warns vs govt overthrow 1-30, 90C1
Suffers stroke 2-25, 196G3
Mzali named interim premr 3-1, confrmd 4-23, 316A3 316A3
NOVA Scotia (Canadian province)—*See CANADA*
NOVELLO, Don
Gilda Live released 3-28, 416G2
NOVIKOV, Vladimir N.
Replaced as Sovt dep premr 12-19, 996D2
NOVO Sampol, Guillermo
Letelier murder convictn overturned, new trial ordrd 9-15, 703C3
NOVO Sampol, Ignacio
Letelier perjury convictn overturned 9-15, 703D3
NOW—*See NATIONAL Organization for Women*
NOWAK, Rep. Henry J. (D, N.Y.)
Carter policies scored in rpt 5-29, 455E2
Reelected 11-4, 843A4
NOWAKOWSKI, Richard
Wins Olympic medal 8-2, 622F1
NRA—*See NATIONAL Rifle Association*
NRC (Nuclear Regulatory Commission)—*See under U.S. GOVERNMENT*
NSA (National Security Agency)—*See under U.S. GOVERNMENT--DEFENSE*
NU, U
Returns from exile 7-29, 617C3

1976

NUCLEAR Issues—*See ARMAMENTS, ATOMIC Energy, DISARMAMENT*
NUGENT, David R.
Seized re Phila water threat 11-3, 972D1
NUGENT, Luci Johnson
Campaigns with Carter 10-31, 827B2
NUGENT of Guilford, Lord (George Richard Hodges) (Great Britain)
Outlines drought measures 8-23, 630E2
NUJOMA, Sam
On Angola aid offer 3-6, 206F1
Zambia arrests hostile factn 5-4, 386G2
Seeks USSR, Cuba arms; scores Israel 8-22, 654G2
Asks Vorster talks 9-6, 660D3
At conf on ANC rift 9-6—9-7, 661D3
Says negotiatn possible 9-21, 697E2
In Tanzania 9-23—9-26, Cuba 10-5, 794A1, B1
Asks UN embargo 9-27, sees Kissinger 9-29, 793G3
Vorster rejects talks, hints indirect mtg 10-18, 793E2
NUNEZ Rivero, Capt. Walter
Quits cabt, named navy chief 1-12, 27A1
NUNN Jr., Sen. Sam (D, Ga.)
Honor-code hearing 6-21, scores defns attys 8-27, 670A3
Wild chrgs dismissed 7-24, 566B1
Asks NATO improvemts 11-14, 879D3
NUPEN, Charles
Acquitted 12-2, 927A2
NURIKYAN, Norair
Wins Olympic medal 7-19, 576D2
NURSING Homes—*See 'Hospitals' under MEDICINE*
NUTRITION—*See FOOD*
NYAGAH, Jeremiah
Sees Rwanda finance min 7-22, 559G3
NYERERE, Julius K.
In India; scores Ford Angola letter, backs USSR, Cuba roles 1-18, 36C1
At Zambia mtg on Rhodesia 3-24—3-25, 240E2
Kissinger visits 4-25—4-26, warns on Rhodesia 4-26, 295D1
At conf on ANC rift 9-6—9-7, 661D3
Sees Schaufele 9-8, 681F1
In Kissinger talks 9-15, 681C1
Sees Kissinger 9-21, comments 9-22, 717G2-718C1
Scores UK Rhodesia plan 9-26—9-28, 718C1, C2
Sees Rhodesia black rule 9-28, 718A3
Scores Rhodesia conf 9-30; sees UK, US reps 10-2, 738D3
Natlst accord at conf rptd urged by US 10-26, 797F2, 798A1
Sees Reinhardt 11-6, 843G1
Scores UK 11-10, 843B2
Scores Kenya re EAC 12-7, 974E2
NYSTROM, Lorne
On fed cleaning contracts 4-5, 265A3
NZAMBIMANA, Lt. Col. Edward
Named prime min 11-13, 1012G2

1977

NUCLEAR Exchange Corp.
A-growth standstill rptd 8-1, 717C2
NUCLEAR Fuels Corp.
TVA sues re uranium 11-18, 895G1
NUCLEAR Issues—*See ARMAMENTS, ATOMIC Energy, DISARMAMENT*
NUCLEAR Nonproliferation Treaty—*See under DISARMAMENT*
NUCLEAR Power and Its Fuel Cycle, International Conference on
Salzburg mtg 5-2—5-13, 402D2
NUCLEAR Regulatory Commission—*See under U.S. GOVERNMENT*
NUCLEAR Society, American
A-energy conf ends, US plutonium ban scored 4-13, 334F2
NUCLEAR Suppliers' Group (Belgium, Canada, Czechoslovakia, East Germany, France, Great Britain, Italy, Japan, Netherlands, Poland, Sweden, Switzerland, USSR, U.S., West Germany)
London mtg scores Carter plans 4-28—4-29, 403F1-A2
Safeguard pact OKd 9-21, 717A1
NUCLEIC Acids, 1977 Gordon Conference on
DNA research backed 6-17, 847B1
NUH, Abdul (Mark E. Gibson)
Convicted 7-23, sentencd 9-6, 711A2
NUJOMA, Sam
At Frelimo cong 2-3—2-7, 137E1
Sees Podgorny 3-28, 247G3
Flies to Angola 3-29, 249D3
At front-line mtg 4-17—4-18, 296D3
Scores West re Namibia role 5-16; sees Young, eases stand 5-17, 399F1
Joins Western talks on Namibia 8-8, 639B3
Steyn OKs Namibia return 9-8, 699F3
NUNN Jr., Sen. Sam (D, Ga.)
Bell confrmatn hearings 1-11—1-18, 34C2
Warsaw Pact rpt issued 1-24, 70A2
Urges draft revival 1-24, 94E3
Vs Warnke nomination 2-1, 89A1; 2-22, 172E2
Wild waiver case rejected 5-16, 419A2
NUNZIO, Judge Nicholas S.
Hanafis convictd 7-23, sentncd 9-6, 711A2
NUON Chea
Identified in Cambodia CP post 9-3, 780B1
Pol Pot in China; govt post cited 9-28, 741B3
NURSING Homes—*See MEDICINE—Hospitals*
NUSEIBEH, Hazem
Asks probe of Israel occupatn rule 3-25, 226G3
NUSSER, Hans
Removed as prison dir 10-18, 790G2
NUTRITION—*See FOOD*
NYABADZA, Basil
Killed 4-1, 297C1
NYANDORO, George
Returns to Rhodesia 12-10, 1016E1
NYANGWESO, Gen. Francis
Ousted 2-23, 142D1
NYANZI, Semeo
Defects 2-28, 142D1
NYE Jr., Joseph S.
Named State dep undersecy 1-21, 53D1
Panel scores breeder reactor, plutonium use 3-21, 234G3
Denies US uranium cartel aim 6-29, 624D3 ★
NYE, Stephen A.
Replaced in FTC 4-6, 272B3
NYERERE, Julius K. (Tanzanian president)
Sees Richard 1-7, 1-11, 11D1, F1
Backs Patriotic Front 1-9, 11C1
Elected new party head 1-21, 102B3
2 mins, comrs quit 1-23, 161D2
Young visits re Rhodesia 2-3—2-6, 105C1, B2
Scores Kenya on EAC 2-8, 106D1
Shuffles Cabt 2-13, 161A2
Sees Podgorny 3-23, 247B3
Sees Owen 4-11, 296A2
Sees Canada, US offcls on Rhodesia 8-2—8-13; in Jamaica 8-11—8-12, 623F3
Scores France-S Africa ties 8-20, 662F2, A3
Sees Owen, Young 8-30, 661E2
Kaunda quarrel re UK-US Rhodesia plan rptd 12-18, 1015D3
NYQUIST, Ewald
Syracuse integratn plan voted 1-25, 112B3
NYSTROM, Bob
Agent admits theft 9-20, sentenced 11-28, 1021A2

1978

NUCLEAR Exchange Corp.
Exec chrgd in trust probe 6-2, 449B3
NUCLEAR Issues—*See ARMAMENTS, ATOMIC Energy, DISARMAMENT*
NUCLEAR Nonproliferation Treaty—*See under DISARMAMENT*
NUCLEAR Planning Group—*See NORTH Atlantic Treaty Organization*
NUCLEAR Regulatory Commission (NRC)—*See under U.S. GOVERNMENT*
NUCLEAR Society, American
NM A-waste burial planned 11-15, 961D2
NUCLEAR Suppliers' Group (Australia, Belgium, Canada, Czechoslovakia, East Germany, France, Great Britain, Italy, Japan, Netherlands, Poland, Sweden, Switzerland, USSR, U.S., West Germany)
Australia joins, observer status rptd 2-24, 129C2
NUDEL, Ida
Sentenced 6-21, 504A1
NUEVA (Chilean Island)—*See BEAGLE Channel*
NUJOMA, Sam
Sees Young 3-22—3-24, 248D3
Cancels contact group talks 5-7, 339D1
Shipanga freed 5-25, 476A1
Sees contact group, OKs plan 7-11—7-12, 547C2
Chrgs electn irregularities, asks UN supervisn 12-12, 988D3
NUMAC Gas and Oil Ltd.
Canada uranium fund rptd 9-13, 722B1
NUNN Jr., Sen. Sam (D, Ga.)
Canal pact vote sought 3-9; pact reservatn agreed 3-15, pact OKd 3-16, 177E1, D2, E3
Scores Carter on neutron bomb 4-4, 4-7, 254A1, C1
Votes for 2d Canal pact 4-18, 273B1
Scores Carter re neutron bomb 6-11, 469B3
Wins renomination 8-8, 625D3
Reelected 11-7, 848E1, 852G1
Visits USSR 11-11—11-18, 905A2
Outspent Stokes 96-1 11-15, 898C1
NUNZIO (film)
Released 5-13, 619C3
NUR, Nur Mohammad
Schmidt in Nigeria 6-26—6-27, talks rptd 7-6, 584C1
Loses Cabt post, reassigned 7-10, 538A1
Vs forgn troops in Africa; warns USSR, Cuba 7-18, 561G1-A2
NURSES—*See MEDICINE—Hospitals*
NURSES-AFT, American Federation of—*See TEACHERS, American Federation of*
NURSES' Association, American
AFT to organize nurses 11-29, 961D1
NURSING Homes—*See MEDICINE—Hospitals*
NUTRITION—*See FOOD*
NWOSU, Alex
San Fran wins NCAA soccer title 12-10, 969B2
NYAD, Diana
Begins Cuba-Fla marathon swim 8-13, fails 8-15, 653E1
NYE Jr., Joseph S.
'77 A-export safeguard pact detailed 1-11, 11A2
NYERERE, Emmy
Expelled from univ 3-7, 169F3
NYERERE, Julius K. (Tanzanian president)
Rhodesia role cited 59C2
Sets amnesty 2-6, 169E3
Univ expels son for protest 3-7, 169F3
Sees Young 3-21, 248D3
Frees Babu, others 4-26, 479D2
Scores pan-Africa force, US role; defends Cuba, USSR presence in Africa 6-8, 441G2
Lauds US Angola move, backs Cuba 6-25, 487D3
Vs Nkomo-Smith mtg 9-2, 740E3
Smith scores Patriotic Front support 9-9, 741B1
Chrgs Lonrho Rhodesia support, Smith-Nkomo mtg cited 9-26, 905E2
Sees Kaunda re RR reopening 10-7, 783E3
Vows Uganda defeat 11-2, 860A1
Rejcts Amin pullout offer 11-9, 870C2
NYSE—*See NEW York Stock Exchange*

1979

NUCLEAR Engineering Co.
Nev A-dump ordered closed 7-2, 519A2; reopened 7-24, 561G2
Washn, Nev A-dumps closed 10-4, 10-22, 806G2-C3
NUCLEAR Fuel Services Inc.—*See under GETTY Oil Co.*
NUCLEAR Insurers, American
3 Mile I A-accident compensatn vowed 3-31, 244B2
NUCLEAR Issues—*See ARMAMENTS, ATOMIC Energy, DISARMAMENT*
NUCLEAR Planning Group—*See NATO*
NUCLEAR Regulatory Commission—*See under U.S. GOVERNMENT*
NUEVA (Chilean Island)—*See BEAGLE Channel*
NUGENT, Luci Johnson
Divorce suit rptd 1-19, 79B2
Divorced 8-31, 859B3
NUGENT, Patrick
Divorce suit rptd 1-19, 79B2
Divorced 8-31, 859B3
NUJOMA, Sam
SWAPO rift cited 171G2
Bars UN monitor 1-13; rejcts truce, vows takeover 3-1, 171C2, B3
NUMISMATICS
Viking coin identified 2-7, 138E1
Canada Maple Leaf gold coin on sale 9-6, 684C3
USSR gold coin sales pushed 11-29, 929F1
NUNN, Louie B.
Wins primary for Ky gov 5-29, 420E1
Loses electn 11-6, 846C2
NUNN Jr., Sen. Sam (D, Ga.)
Meets Teng in China 1-9, 27B1
On vet recall plan 4-10, 307D2
Withdraws draft amendmt 6-13, 438F1
For arms hike link to SALT 8-2, 591B1, 7-25, 643F3
Defense budget hike request cited 9-11, 678G1
Votes present on Talmadge denunciatn 10-10, 769G1
On mil recruiting abuses 11-19, 903G3
Carter defense spending plan, SALT linked 12-13, 963A2, D2
Asks SALT vote delay, Carter rejcts 12-16, 979A2
NUREYEV, Rudolf
At 'Lulu' debut in Paris 2-25, 174A1
NURI, Gen. Khajeh
Executed 4-9, 276B3
NURSE (book)
On best-seller list 11-4, 892D3
NURSES—*See MEDICINE-Hospitals*
NURSING Homes—*See MEDICINE-Hospitals*
NUTLEY, N.J.—*See NEW Jersey*
NUTRITION—*See FOOD*
NVF Co.
Sharon Steel buys UV Industries assets 11-26, 986E2
NWOKOCHA, Nnamdi
SIU-Edwardsville wins NCAA soccer title 12-9, 1004A2
NYAD, Diana
Completes Bahamas-Fla swim 8-20, 656E3
NYANDORO, George
Zimbabwe rural dvpt min 5-30, 393E1
NYERERE, Julius K. (Tanzanian president)
US Peace Corps return OKd 1-9, 22F3
Called hypocrite by US rights rpt 2-10, 107F2
Sets demands re Uganda pullout 2-28, 147A1
Disregards Qaddafi warning 3-27, 257F1
Recognizes new Uganda govt 4-12, 288B2
Nimeiry scores re Uganda invasn 7-17, 552C2
On Commonwealth Zimbabwe plan 8-6, 8-7, 590D1
NYSE—*See NEW York Stock Exchange*
NYTOL—*See MEDICINE-Drugs*

1980

NUCLEAR Fuel Cycle Evaluation
Vienna conf ends, plutonium fuel backed 2-27, 220E3
NUCLEAR Issues—*See ARMAMENTS, ATOMIC Energy, DISARMAMENT*
NUCLEAR Regulatory Commission—*See under U.S. GOVERNMENT*
NUDE Bomb (film)
Released 5-9, 675B3
NUDO Seduto (Seated Nude) (painting)
Sold for record sum 5-13, 472G1
NUGENT, Elliott
Dies 8-9, 676D2
NUGENT, Nelle
Morning's at Seven opens 4-10, 392E3
Home opens 5-7, 392C3
NUJOMA, Sam
Might not back UN Namibia plan 6-13, 466C3
NUMAN, Gary
Cars on best-seller list 6-4, 448E3
NUMAN, Henk
Wins Olympic medal 7-27, 623D1
NUMISMATICS
Gold coin set sold for record sum 4-10, 472F2
Hunts bailout loan collateral listed 5-28, 426A1
Franklin Mint, Warner merger set 12-24, 985B1
NUNEZ, Daniel
Wins Olympic medal 7-21, 624E2
NUNEZ, Gen. Manuel
On Uruguay const proposal defeat 11-30, 924F2
NUNEZ, Rear Adm. Walter
Sworn Bolivia defns min 4-7, 272F1
NUNEZ Guardado, Elias
Chrgd in El Salvador alien case 7-19, 560E2
Convicted 10-20, 825F3
NUNN Jr., Sen. Sam (D, Ga.)
Scores Army infantry shortfall 3-10, 267E2
Carter backs mil-pay bill 5-26, 403A2, 424C2
Draft registratn funding signed 6-12, 478E2
Mil benefits authrzn signed 9-8, 765C1
House OKs mil-pay appropriatn amendmt 9-16, 742A1
NURSES—*See MEDICINE--Physicians*
NURSING Homes—*See MEDICINE--Hospitals*
NUSSEIBAH, Hazem
Scores Israel, Jews in UN debate 12-8; Blum chrgs anti-Semitism 12-10, 952A3
NUTRITION—*See FOOD--Diets & Dieting*
NUTRITION and Your Health (booklet)
US dietary guidelines issued 2-4, 157B3
NUVEEN & Co., John
'79 municipal bonds sales rptd up 1-16, 92A3
NVF Co.
On '79 Fortune 500 list 5-5, 291E1
NYAGUMBO, Morris
Zimbabwe mines min 3-11, 198D1
NYAMBUI, Suleiman
Wins NCAA indoor mile, 2-mile runs 3-15; NCAA outdoor 5,000, 10,000-m runs 6-5—6-7, 891F3, 892A1
Wins Olympic medal 8-1, 624E1
NYERERE, Julius K. (Tanzanian president)
Rebuffs Ali 2-3, 85C1
Warns re Zimbabwe rebel electn defeat 2-25; lauds Mugabe win 3-4, 162D1
Amin scores 6-3, 446E2
Reelected 10-26, names Cabt 11-7, 888C1
NYSE—*See NEW York Stock Exchange*
NYSTROM, Bob
Islanders win Stanley Cup 5-24, 487G3

O

1976

OAKAR, Mary Rose
Elected 11-2, 823F3, 825F2, 830B3
OAKES, Judge James L.
Backs race quotas for NY principals 1-19, 42C2
OAKLAND (Calif.) Tribune (newspaper)
Ford endorsement rptd 10-30, 827F3

1977

OAKES, Judge James L.
Backs protectn of journalists' thoughts 11-7, 920D3
OAKLAND, Calif.—*See CALIFORNIA*
OAK Ridge, Tenn.—*See TENNESSEE*

1978

OAKAR, Rep. Mary Rose (D, O.)
Reelected 11-7, 851F3
OAKES, John B.
Kadar interview rptd 6-10, 534E2
OAKIE, Jack (Lewis Delaney Offield)
Dies 1-23, 96B3
OAKLAND, Calif.—*See CALIFORNIA*
OAKLAND Tribune (newspaper)
Gannett plans purchase, circulatn hike seen 5-8, 345G2
OAKLEY, Robert
On Indonesia student detentns 2-8, 122B3
OAK Ridge, Tenn.—*See TENNESSEE*
OAK Ridge Boys (singing group)
Win Grammy 2-24, 316A1

1979

OAKES, Judge James L.
Overturns Bell contempt citatn 3-19, 207E1
OAKLAND (Calif.) Tribune (newspaper)
H-bomb letter cites interviews 9-16, 9-18, 717C1, B2
OAK Ridge, Tenn.—*See TENNESSEE*

1980

OAKAR, Rep. Mary Rose (D, Ohio)
Reelected 11-4, 843F4
OAKES, Gary
Wins Olympic medal 7-26, 624A1
OAKES, Laurie
Rpts Upton criticisms on Gandhi 11-6, 870A3
OAKLAND—*See CALIFORNIA*

1976

OAS—*See ORGANIZATION of American States*
OATS
New support-rate set 10-13, 787G3
OAU—*See ORGANIZATION of African Unity*
OBA, Tetsuo
Diet subpoenas 2-26, testifies 3-1, 190C3
All-Nippon loan probed 3-5, 191F1
OBADA, Maj. Gen. O. E.
Nigeria works min 3-15, 222A3
OBADOV, Slavko
Wins Olympic medal 7-28, 575A1
O'BANNON, Helen
Merril Lynch settles bias suit 6-4, 414E1
OBASANJO, Gen. Olusegun
Nigerian head of state 2-14, 141D3
Orders coup probe 2-15, 191C3
Announces cabt shift 3-15, 222G2
On austerity budget 4-1, 366B2
Dimka, others executed; forgn refuge for Gowan 5-16, 366G1
Sets bank takeovers 7-29, 1007D3
OBENSHAIN, Richard
GOP conv OKs platform plank 8-18, 600C3
OBERHOLTZER, Cmdr. George
On tanker, ferry collisn 10-20, 876C2
OBERSTAR, Rep. James L. (D, Minn.)
Reelected 11-2, 829G4
OBEY, Rep. David R. (D, Wis.)
McNamara letter on OPEC aid cited 1-12, 15D1
Heads House reform task force 6-4, 551D2
Reelected 11-2, 831A4
OBITUARIES—*See DEATHS*
O'BOYLE, Cardinal Patrick
Successor named 4-27, 336E2
O'BRADY, Rory
Ulster arrests 7-23, bans 7-26, 590G1
Barred from Drumm funeral 11-1, 854D3
O'BRIEN, Charles
Indicted 7-7, pleads not guilty 7-11, 570D2
O'BRIEN, Conor Cruise
Expands IRA broadcast curbs 10-18, 838C1
O'BRIEN, Rep. George M. (R, Ill.)
Reelected 11-2, 829A3
O'BRIEN, Robert
Loses Vt primary for gov 9-14, 705B2
O'BRIEN, Most Rev. Henry
Dies 7-23, 656F3
OBROU, Maj. Fidel
Sentenced 2-14, 204C2
Executed 2-14, 288E2
OBSCENITY—*See PORNOGRAPHY & Obscenity*
OBSTETRICIANS & Gynecologists, American College of
'75 price-fixing agrmt cited 11-17, 988G3
OCAMPO, Satur
Arrested 638A3
OCCIDENTAL Petroleum Corp.
Writes off Venez investmt 1-1, 12D3
N Sea oil Euroloans rptd 2-4, 2-5, 173E3
Babcock sentence upheld 2-10, 144G3
Venez bribes rptd 2-14—2-19, 147F1, F3
Hammer pleads guilty again 3-4, 180D3
Hammer, Babcock spared jail terms 3-23, 6-4, 442B2
Venez panel issues bribery rpt 6-8; Hammer scores 6-10, arrests ordrd 7-14, 593B1
Iran to buy shares 6-20, 6-21, 450B2
Iran deal dropped 8-27, 643D1
Watson fined 9-23, 725D2
Hammer sees Brezhnev 10-20, 947E3
Venez drops bribery chrgs 11-16, new compensatn talks asked 11-17, 930C1
UOP Inc.
SEC lists paymts 5-12, 729E1
OCCORSIO, Vittorio
Killed 7-10, 539B1
OCEANS & Oceanography—*See also ocean names*
UN Sea Law Conf impasse 3-15—5-7, 342C1
US urges new intl law 4-8, 342B2
Dem platform text re energy 6-15, 474B3, 475D1
UN Sea Law Conf deadlocked 8-1—9-17, 700E1
GOP platform text 8-18, 608C1, 610E3, G3
Ford, Carter debate 10-22, 801E2, A3
OCHBERG, Dr. Frank M.
Rpts mental illness, econ link 1-26, 159B3
OCHS, Phil
Dies 4-9, 272G3
O'CONNELL, David
Freed 4-9, 278E1
Sentenced 10-13, 855C1

1977

OAS—*See ORGANIZATION of American States*
OAU—*See ORGANIZATION of African Unity*
OBADA, Maj. Gen. O. E.
Nigeria Cabt drops 3-15, 393C2
OBANDO Bravo, Archbishop Miguel
Offers Somoza-oppositn talks role 10-22, 864G2
OBASANJO, Lt. Gen. Olusegun (Nigeria head of state)
Sees Young re Rhodesia 2-10, 105E1, D2
Presents '77-78 budget 3-31, 393F1
Sees Young, new Rhodesia plan leaked 8-24, 661F1
Visits US 10-11—10-12, 797D1
OBENGA, Theophile
Sees Schaufele re ties 7-6, 583B2
OBERLE, Frank
Chrgs govt blacklist firing 1-25, 97A2
Reveals blacklist to Parlt 1-26, links '70 RCMP theft 2-2, 97A1
OBERLIN (O.) College
Knoll fossil find rptd 10-15, 908G1
E Ger author to join faculty 12-19, 984A2
OBEY, Rep. David R. (D, Wis.)
Ethics code adopted 3-2, 173A3
OBITUARIES—*See DEATHS*
OBOTE, Milton
Chrgd in anti-Amin plot 2-16, 138D3
Tribesmen rptd purged 3-28, 308F1
OBOTH-Ofumbi, A. C. K.
Killed 2-16, reactn 2-17—2-21, 138C3, 139A1
Waldheim asks death probe 2-24, 142B1
O'BRIEN, Conor Cruise
Loses parlt seat 6-16, 475C2
Elected to Irish Sen 8-27, 728E3
Speech vs unificatn causes furor 9-18, quits parlt party 9-20, 782A3
O'BRIEN, Danny
Ranger punished for assault 4-5, 310E3 ★
Fines LA player $10,000 12-12, 990G2
O'BRIEN, Davey
Dies 11-18, 952B3
O'BRIEN, Lawrence F.
Fines 2 for NBA playoff brawl 5-27, 490C3
NBA meets on Knicks-Nets dispute 7-14, Nets NJ move agreed 7-26, 584F2, G2
Fines Abdul-Jabbar 10-20, 870F1
O'BRIEN, Peter S.
Fined 7-20, 558E2
O'BRYANT, John D.
Elected to Boston Schl Com 11-8, 855D3
OBSCENITY—*See PORNOGRAPHY and Obscenity*
OBSERVER, The (London newspaper)
Zaire ousts newsman 5-6, 394G1
OBSTETRICS & Gynecology, American Journal of
DES cancer risk rptd less 5-3, 432C1
OCCIDENTAL Life Insurance Co.—*See TRANSAMERICA Corp.*
OCCIDENTAL Life Insurance Co. v. EEOC
Bias-suit time limit barred 6-20, 517D1
OCCIDENTAL Petroleum Corp.
SEC sues, chrgs settled 5-3, 503B3
Peru '78 pipe link seen 5-25, 428A1
Venez sued 5-27, 547B1
Rumania coal deal set 5-30, 468C3
DBCP curbed 9-8, 723E2
OCCUPATIONAL Safety & Health Administration—*See under U.S. GOVERNMENT—LABOR*
OCCUPATIONAL Titles, Dictionary of (book)
Sexist titles dropped 12-17, 979F2
OCEANIA
Australia trade data rptd 6-22, 504F2
OCEANS & Oceanography—*See also ocean names*
Richardson named to UN Sea Law Conf 1-25, 53F1; confrmd 2-24, 148F3
Carter addresses UN 3-17, 185E2
Bruce Heezen dies 6-21, 5328F
UN Sea Law Conf adjourns 7-15, US scores rpt 7-20, 572G2
NSF '78 authoriztn signed 8-15, 689E1
Energy research authorizatn OKd by Cong 10-20, 833G1
Antarctic shelf penetrated 12-9, 971F2
O'CONNELL, Dick
Fired as Red Sox vp, gen mgr 10-24, 989G2

1978

OAS—*See ORGANIZATION of American States*
OATES, Johnny
In World Series 10-10—10-17, 800D2
OATES, Joyce Carol
Elected to Arts Institute 2-7, 316E1
OATS—*For feed grains, see GRAIN*
OAU—*See ORGANIZATION of African Unity*
OBANDO y Bravo, Archbishop Miguel
Shuns Chamorro death probe panel 4-6, 376C2
Acts in guerrilla demands 8-22—8-24, 8-30; 658G3, 659D1, F2
OBASANJO, Lt. Gen. Olusegun (Nigerian head of state)
Sets land takeover 3-29, 248D1
Greets Carter 3-31, asks stronger action vs S Africa 4-1, 233F2-234A1
Rpts '78-79 austerity budget 4-3, 247G3-248C1
Lifts pol party ban 9-21, 758F1
Backs USSR re Rhodesia 11-24, 911G3-912A1
OBED, Elsha
Mattioli KOs 3-11, 379C2
OBENSHAIN, Richard D.
Wins Sen nominatn in Va 6-3, 467A2
Killed in plane crash 8-2, 645A3
OBERAMMERGAU Passion Play
Revision opposed 1-12, 95E2
Classic text retained 3-5, 295C2
OBERLANDER, Henry
Sentncd for fraud 5-31, 824C3
OBERSTAR, Rep. James L. (D, Minn.)
House votes parks bill 7-12, 526G3
Reelected 11-7, 851B2
OBEY, Rep. David R. (D, Wis.)
On HEW fund cuts 6-8, 6-13, 445E2, G2
Reelected 11-7, 852D4
OBIEGLO, Hubert
Convicted as E Ger spy 2-13, 115D1
OBIEGLO, Johanna
Convicted as E Ger spy 2-13, 115D1
OBITUARIES—*See DEATHS*
OBOLENSKY, Serge
Dies 9-29, 778G1
O'BRIEN, Rep. George M. (R, Ill.)
Reelected 11-7, 850F3
O'BRIEN, Lawrence F.
Reinstates Washington 2-1, 271A2
Haldeman book on Watergate rptd 2-16—2-17, 124G2, A3
Suspends Powers 3-2, 271A3
Declares Webster free agent 7-31, 656F1
Warriors OK Barry compensatn terms 9-5, 1027D3
Orders Seattle compensatn for Webster loss 10-29, 1027B3
OBSCENITY—*See PORNOGRAPHY & Obscenity*
O'CALLAGHAN, Gov. Mike (D, Nev.)
Not standing for reelectn 9-12, 936E2
List elected successor 11-7, 857D1
OCASEK, Oliver
Ohio aids Cleveland schls 4-13, 279C2
OCCIDENTAL Petroleum Corp.
Coal, uranium holdings lid backed by FTC aide 4-5, 282F2
Poland trade deal rptd 5-28, 650E2
Husky Oil takeover bid 6-12—7-27; collusn chrgd 6-16, probe launched 6-19, 628E3-629E2
Seeks Mead takeover 8-11, Mead rejects 8-18, 767C2
USSR ammonia plant opened 8-22, 670F1
US sues vs Mead takeover 10-11, trust concessns offered 10-23, US expands suit 10-25, 895A3
SEC probes disclosures 11-28, 1004E3
Ct bars Mead takeover 12-9, ends efforts 12-20, 1004C3
Hooker Chemicals and Plastics Corp.—*See separate listing*
OCCORSIO, Vittorio (d. 1976)
Murder trial opens in Florence 1-30, 133B2
OCCUPATIONAL Safety & Health, National Institute for (NIOSH)—*See U.S. GOVERNMENT—PUBLIC Health Service—Disease Control, Center for*
OCCUPATIONAL Safety & Health Administration—*See under U.S. GOVERNMENT—LABOR*
OCEAN Equipment Corp.
Indicted 3-8, pleads guilty 3-16, 184D3
Fined 10-23, 876C3
OCEANS & Oceanography—*See also ocean names*
UN Sea Law Conf deadlocked 4-6—5-19, 401G2-D3
Hawaii tidal power plant planned 5-3, 321E3
UN Sea Law Conf talks continue 5-23—7-15, US seabed mining bill debated 8-21—9-16, 732C3
Thermal energy use seen remote 6-7, 512B2
Greece, Turkey in seabed talks 7-4—7-6, 624A1
Seabed mining bill clears US House 7-26, 588E3
Seabed mining bill dies 10-15, 785C1
Pollution—*See ENVIRONMENT & Pollution—Air & Water*
OCEAN Thermal Energy Conversion (OTEC)—*See THERMAL Energy*
OCHAB, Edward
Asks pol, econ reforms 1-6, 20D1
O'CONNELL, Martin P.
Canada labor min 11-24, 921E3

1979

OAS—*See ORGANIZATION of American States*
OATES, Joyce Carol
Book awards protest rptd 8-9, 755F3
OATS—*See GRAIN*
OAU—*See ORGANIZATION of African Unity*
OBANDO y Bravo, Archbishop Miguel
Mass marks Chamorro death anniv 1-10, 21B3
O'BANNON, Dan
Alien released 5-24, 528A1
OBASANJO, Lt. Gen. Olusegun (Nigerian head of state; replaced Oct. 1)
Scores Tanzania re Uganda invasn 7-18, 552D2
Replaced by Shagari, sets mil retiremt 10-1, 753D3
OBERON, Merle
Dies 11-22, 932C3
OBEY, Rep. David R. (D, Wis.)
Scores Califano firing, Jordan promotn 7-19, 531A3
OBOTE, Milton
Asks Amin ouster 1-12, 78F1
Rebels vow Amin ouster 2-28, 146E3
Binaisa named president 6-20, 488D3
O'BRIEN, Judge Donald J.
Rules vs transit strike 12-20, 987D2
O'BRIEN, Jack
Most Happy Fella opens 10-11, 956D3
O'BRIEN, James A.
Convicted 2-22, sentncd 3-19, 220F2
O'BRIEN, Lawrence F.
Sets Walton compensatn 9-18, voided 9-19, 1003C2
O'BRIEN, Tim
Discloses Sup Ct rulings 4-16, 4-17, ct worker fired re leaks 4-20, 302G2
Leaks another Sup Ct ruling 5-18, 382A3
O'BRIEN, Tim (author)
Wins Natl Book Award 4-23, 356G1
O'BRIEN, William
Lauds UAW-Chrysler settlemt 10-25, 805F3
OBSCENITY—*See PORNOGRAPHY & Obscenity*
OCASIO, Osvaldo (Jaws)
Holmes TKOs 3-23, 412A3
OCCIDENTAL College (Los Angeles, Calif.)
Hufstedler named Educ secy 10-30, 829A2
OCCIDENTAL Petroleum Corp.
Peru oil find rptd 1-12, 39E2; 2-9 256B1
ITC rules vs Sovt ammonia imports 10-3, quota asked 10-5, 802B3-803B1
Peru orders contract renegotiated 12-7, 951A2
Hooker Chemical Co.—*See separate listing*
OCCUPATIONAL Safety & Health, National Institute for (NIOSH)—*See U.S. GOVERNMENT—PUBLIC Health Service—Disease Control, Center for*
OCCUPATIONAL Safety & Health Administration—*See under U.S. GOVERNMENT—LABOR*
OCEAN Grove, N.J.—*See NEW Jersey*
OCEAN Grove v. Celmer
Case declined by Sup Ct 11-13, 902G1
OCEANS & Oceanography
US project impact rpts ordrd 1-5, 16F3
UN Sea Law Conf yields no accord 3-19—4-27, 360C3
US-China pact set 5-13, 370F1
SALT II pact, communique cite 6-18, 454B3, 458D1
US to challenge coastal sea claims 8-10, 646F1
Obituaries
Cousteau, Philippe 6-28, 508D2
OCEAN Spray Cranberries Inc.
Antitrust action urged by FTC staff 6-20, 985G3
OCHOA, Santiago
Seized in El Salvador emb raid 5-11, 371C1
OCKRENT, Mike
Once A Catholic opens 10-10, 956F3
OCLEPPO, Gianni
Loses Bologna Grand Prix 11-25, 1003G3
OCONEE Nuclear Station—*See SOUTH Carolina—Atomic Energy*

1980

OAS—*See ORGANIZATION of American States*
OATS
Futures trading suspended 1-6, 2C1-E1
OAU—*See ORGANIZATION of African Unity*
O'BANNON v. Town Court Nursing Home
Case decided by Sup Ct 6-23, 554G3
OBERLIN—*See OHIO*
OBESTAR, Rep. James L. (D, Minn.)
Reelected 11-4, 843B2
OBEY, Rep. David R. (D, Wis.)
Reelected 11-4, 844D4
OBITUARIES—*See DEATHS*
OBOTE, Milton
Denies coup role 5-11, party ban lifted 5-14, 375G1-C2
Returns from exile; urges unity, scores Binaisa, Lule, Amin 5-27, 446E1-C2
Amin calls unpopular 6-3, 446D2
Party ousts Cabt rivals 9-17, 731B1
Claims Amin backers invade Uganda 10-7, 794D2
Electns held, outcome uncertain 12-10—12-11, 945G3-946C1
Wins electn 12-13; inaugurated, frees Binaisa 12-15, 968F2, C3
O'BRIEN, Rep. George M. (R, Ill.)
Reelected 11-4, 842F3
O'BRIEN, Lawrence F.
On NBA cocaine use 8-19, 656F2
OBSERVER (London newspaper)
Wage accord reached 8-16, 670B3
O Canada
Proclaimed natl anthem 7-1, 496E3-497C1
OCCIDENTAL Petroleum Corp.
Peru tax debt may be $110 mln 1-8, 21E2
USSR deal seen threatnd 2-25, 139E3
Hammer sees Brezhnev re phosphate embargo 2-27, 165G1
Permian-Charter merger talks dropped 3-17, 385G2
Gold, silver futures trading profits rptd 3-31, 245D1
Nader coalitn attacks 4-17, 308B2
NY sues re Love Canal dumping 4-28, 331C3
Peru contract signed 4-30, 354F1
On '79 Fortune 500 list 5-5, 291B1
Saudi 1.2% interest noted 7-14, 542D3
Abboud named pres, chief operating officer 8-4, 702A1
Hammer sees Brezhnev 10-14, 776C3
Hammer buys Da Vinci ms 12-12, 997F3
Hooker Chemical Co.—*See HOOKER Chemical Co.*
OCCUPATIONAL Safety & Health Administration—*See under U.S. GOVERNMENT--LABOR*
OCEANSIDE—*See CALIFORNIA*
OCEANS & Oceanography
Simulated dive depth record rptd 4-12, 415E3
Norway-Iceland pact set 5-10, 398C2
UN Sea Law Conf yields draft accord 7-28—8-29, 660B1
Canada min cites UN Sea Law accord 9-22, 748G3
OCHOANTESANA Badiola, Juan Angel (alias Kirru)
Identified as ETA hit man 7-7, 367F1
OCLEPPO, Gianni
Czechs win Davis Cup 12-7, 946F3
O'CONNELL, John F.
Dies 2-27, 176G2
O'CONNELL, Susan
Tell Me a Riddle released 12-17, 1003E2
O'CONNELL, Cardinal William (1859-1944)
Jos Kennedy, Swanson affair alleged 10-13, 907G3

1976

O'CONNOR, Colleen
Wins Olympic medal 2-9, 159B1
O DALAIGH, Cearbhall
Signs emergency bill 10-16, 838A1
Emergency bill review scored 10-18—10-21, resigns 10-22, 837D3
Hillery named pres-elect 11-9, 873F1
Donegan shifted to lands min 12-2, 1006C2
ODINGAR, Gen. Noel
Rebels surrender 7-8, 559E3
ODLUM Floyd B.
Dies 6-17, 524C3
O'DONNELL, John J.
St Thomas runway warning rptd 4-29, 335A3 ★
On Canada air strike 6-24, 481E2
O'DRISCOLL, Brian
Injured 7-21, 538F3

ODUBER Quiros, Daniel (Costa Rican president)
Chrgs CP infiltratn 1-16, 123C1
'Vesco Law' repealed 11-2, 1000E2
O'DWYER, Paul
Loses NY Sen primary 9-14, 687E2
OECD—*See ORGANIZATION for Economic Cooperation & Development*
OEKSNES, Oskar
Norway agri min 1-12, 30A2
OESTERREICH, Rolf
Wins Olympic medal 2-7, 159B1
OFER, Avraham
On Galilee land takeover 2-29, 174F3
OFFSHORE Co.—*See under SOUTHERN Natural Resources*
OGAWA, Heishiro
China protests Miyazawa statemt 7-19, 555F2
OGBINAR, Commodore Ernesto
Pl navy cmdr 3-27, 255C3
OGDEN Corp.
Bars boycott compliance 3-18, 747B2
SEC lists paymts 5-12, 728E2
OGILVIE, Richard B.
Chrgs GOP delegate bribes 8-16, 616C1
OGLALA Sioux Indians—*See INDIANS, American*
O'HARA, Rep. James G. (D, Mich.)
Loses Sen primary 8-3, 565G2
OH! Calcutta (play)
Opens 9-24, 1014E3
O'HERRON Jr., Edward M.
Loses NC primary for gov 8-17, 633F1

OHIO
NAACP loses Cleveland schl constructn plea 1-6, 6C2
ERA study disputed 2-13, 172A2
Cleveland violent crime up 3-2, 336D3
Medicaid fraud effort set 3-26, 249F1
Oberlin rector '75 convictn reversed 4-9, new trial denied 6-11, 755A3
Rubber workers strike 4-21, 308C3, G3
Steubenville off US jobless list 5-5, 347E2
VW rejcts Brook Park site 5-28, 987D3
Columbus Anheuser-Busch strike ends 6-6, 436B2
Pvtly insured S&Ls rptd OKd 6-20, 495E1
Eastlake zoning referendum upheld 6-21, 453A1
2 Cincinnati police sentncd 7-6, 524C1
Miners strike spreads 7-26, 553B2
'74-75 Cleveland SATs rptd 9-13, 993G1
Akron integratn praised 9-14, 993A1
Dayton integratn praised 9-14, 993A1
Fiscal '75 per capita income, tax burden rptd 9-15, 10-12, 959B2
UMW conv in Cincinnati 9-23—10-2, 748G1
Fiscal '76 bankruptcies rptd 10-20, 984C3
GM suspends Lordstown productn 10-25, 885B2
Bertsch wins Rockefeller award 11-16,. 911E3
Anti-boycott law cited 12-1, 987B2
Cincinnati employes laid off, '77 budget deficit cited 12-5, 994E2
Flu shot paralysis rptd 12-17, 950E1
Cleveland transatlantic air route rejctd 12-28, 992E2

1977

O'CONNER, Carroll
Wins Emmy 9-11, 1021G3
OCTAVIO, Jose Andres
Scores public admin 5-27, 546E3
OCTAVIO, Gen. Rodrigo
Asks rights restored 2-25, 281E2
ODA, Shigeru
World Ct member 4G1
O'DANIEL, W. Lee
'41 fraud re LBJ Sen bid seen 8-6, 631G2
ODEH, Adnan Abu
Backs Sadat Israel trip 11-22, 890D3, 894E1
O'DONNELL, Kenneth P.
Dies 9-9, 788B2
O'DONOGHUE, Martin
Ireland econ ministry head 7-5, 598F3
ODRIA, Manuel
Immediate electns demanded 8-7, 673C2
ODUBER Quiros, Daniel (Costa Rican president)
Backs Panamanian canal demands 1-18, 46G1
'78 PLN pres candidate named 3-13, 506D2
Vesco pol financing scandal 4-23—6-13, 506A1
Sees Mrs Carter 5-31, lauds 6-5, 454F2, A3
Sees Torrijos, regional ldrs 8-5—8-6; new Panama Canal pact backed, Intl Coffee Fund set 8-6, 606B3, 608A3
At Panama Canal pact signing 9-7, 678C1
Backs CR independenc 9-30, 786D1
ODUM, Eugene P.
Gets ecology award 4-15, 354F1
O'DWYER, Paul
In union protest vs Stevens 3-1, 153G3
Bellamy wins primary runoff 9-8, 723C2
ODYSSEY House Inc. (N.Y.)
Densen-Gerber on child abuse 5-23, 432E3
OECD—*See ORGANIZATION for Economic Cooperation & Development*
OESTERGAARD, Lise
In Danish Cabt 2-25, 373C1, E1
OFER, Avraham
Asks govt aid in corruptn probe, Rabin bars 1-1—1-3; kills self 1-3, 8E1
Govt drops probe 1-9; press, oppositn protest 1-10, 21D1
O'FIAICH, Tomas
Named Irish Cath Primate 8-22, 728E3
OFFICE Equipment
Apr indl output up 5-16, 384B1
OFFICE of Management & Budget—*See BUDGET under U.S. GOVERNMENT*
OGADEN—*See under ETHIOPIA*
OGARKOV, Marshal Nikolai
Named Sovt army staff chief 1-9, 47B3
Named marshal 1-14, 88G1
OGDEN Corp.
Avondale job-bias accord rptd 3 21, 279C2
OGILVY & Mather International Inc.
Foreign paymts rptd 3-30, 233D3
OGLEBAY-Norton Co.
USW strike ended 12-16, 977B3
OGUNLADE, G. A.
Nigeria info comr 3-15, 393D2
OGUTU, Matthew
Kenya hunting banned 5-19, 470D2
OH, Sadaharu
Breaks Aaron HR record 9-3, awarded Medal of Honor 9-5, 748E2
Braves win Japan baseball title 10-27, 927E2
O'HARA, James G.
'76 spec interest gifts rptd 2-15, 128D2
O'HARE International Airport (Chicago)
Mass transit funds OKd 9-19, 778E3
OH, God! (film)
Top-grossing film 10-19, 872G3; 12-7, 1021B3
OHIO
Legislature schedule rptd 6F2
'68 NYS stock transfer tax amendmts ruled illegal 1-12, 57F2
US Sup Ct voids Toledo housing rule 1-25, 80D2
US Sup Ct backs attys fee 2-28, 175D2
Carter call-in from N Benton 3-5, 171D1
Frances Payne Bolton dies 3-9, 264D2
Fed spending inequities chrgd 4-6, 423D3
Cleveland out of '75 largest cities list 4-14, 388B1
Amtrak Cincinnati-Norfolk svc to end 5-3, 368E3
'76 per-capita income table 5-10, 387D2
Cincinnati, Cleveland business confidence rptd; econ data table 5-16, 384E2, D3
Job benefits law upheld 5-31, 461C3
E Cleveland 1-family zoning rule upset 5-31, 461F3
Media ruled liable to performers' suits 6-28, 557F3
Steel cos OK clean-up pacts 6-30, 521C3
UMW wildcat strikes 7-11—9-6, 690G2
Dayton firemen strike 8-8—8-10, 613B3
A-material rptd missing from Portsmouth 8-8, 717A2
Miss America crowned 9-10, 808A3
'76 per capita income, tax burden table 9-13, 10-18, 821C2
Youngstown steel operatns cut back 9-19, 775E3
Legion fever rptd in Columbus 9-23, 748E1
Honda plans Allen Townshp plant 10-11, 859E2
HMO unit certified 10-26, 870A1
Cincinnati challenge of pub works bill minority quota provisn cited 10-31, 979C1
Cleveland mayor elected 11-8, 855F1, F

1978

O'CONNOR, Carroll
Wins Emmy 9-17, 1030F1
O'CONNOR, Judge Earl E.
Dismisses NCAA suit vs Title IX 1-9, 40D2
O'CONNOR, Fred
Hired as 49ers coach 10-31, 1024A3
O'CONNOR, Kevin
Scenes From Country Life opens 3-13, 887A3
O DALAIGH, Cearbhall
Dies 3-21, 252B3
ODINGA, Oginga
Kenyatta dies 8-22, 639B2
Barred from KANU electns 10-28, 885G2
ODIO Benito, Elizabeth
Named CR solicitor gen 3-4, 171A1

ODUBER Quiros, Daniel (Costa Rican president; replaced May 8)
Oppositn candidate elected pres 2-5, vows Vesco expulsn 2-7, 89A3, D3
Carter consults on DR electn 5-19, 414C3
OECD—*See ORGANIZATION for Economic Cooperation & Development*
OESTERGAARD, Lise
Named to Danish Cabt 8-30, 688A1
OFFERGELD, Rainer
Named W Ger econ coop min 2-3, 93A3
Cancels poor natn debts 10-6, 776F2
OFFICE Equipment
IBM sues Xerox 2-23, 510B2
SCM set back in Xerox suit 6-7, 510E1-C2
SCM-Xerox verdicts 7-10, 7-11; damages set 8-9, 8-16, 664G2
Van Dyk-Xerox trial begins 7-12, 664E3
Xerox, IBM settle patent dispute 8-1, 664E2
Distaphone OKs Pitney-Bowes takeover 12-21, 1005E1
SCM Xerox award set aside 12-29, 1005E2
OFFICE of Management & Budget—*See U.S. GOVERNMENT—BUDGET*
O FIAICH, Archbishop Tomas
Urges UK end Ulster rule 1-16, 37B2 ★
Scores Long Kesh jail conditns 8-1, 630B1
OGADEN—*See under ETHIOPIA*
OGARKOV, Marshall Nikolai
In Turkey, arms aid proposed 4-26, 477D1
OGIER, Bulle
Celine & Julie released 2-24, 618G3
OGLEBAY Norton Co.
Medusa merger bid cited 3-16, 283G1
OGLIVIE, Ben
AL batting ldr 10-2, 928D3
OGUMA, Shoji
Canto decisions 1-4, 56B1
OH, Sadaharu
Hits 800th homer 8-30, 780A1
O'HARA, Maureen
Husband killed 9-2, 777F3
O'HARA, Richard
King murder bounty offer alleged 11-29, 938B2
O'HARE International Airport (Chicago, Ill.)
Blizzard closes 1-26—1-27, 105B3

OHIO
Teamster fund bd revised 1-3, 4E2
US Steel to close Youngstown plants 1-3, 4G2
'67, '77 sales-tax rates rptd 1-5, 15F3
US judge backs coed sports 1-9, 40D3
Blizzard hits 1-25—1-26; US disaster, state energy emergency declared 1-26, 2-9; econ losses rptd 1-26—2-11, 105D3, E3
Coal strike threatens power shortage, Carter declares energy emergency 2-11, sees gov 2-16; task force meets 2-15, 104C1-D2
EPA sulfur dioxide rules upheld 2-13, 109G1
Akron abortn ordinance passed 2-28, 744A1
USW backs LTV Youngstown rescue 4-10, 6-21, Bell OKs merger 6-21, 492F3
Coal strike utility billing probe set 5-10, 366F3
Lawyer solicitatn curbed by Sup Ct 5-30, 430C2
Death penalty law voided by US Sup Ct 7-3, 552D1-A2
Steubenville, Cincinnati on bad-air list 7-5, 513D1
EPA denies sulfur dioxide rule stay 7-6, 513E1
Bad-air list corrected 7-19, 644B2
Ford chooses Ontario plant site 8-3, 613C2
Firestone suits rptd 9-22, 835F1
N&W strike ends 9-30, 809E2
Ruppert retrial case refused by Sup Ct 11-6, 874E1
Steel haulers strike 11-11, 1006G1-A2
Earthworm rumor hurts fast-food ch 11-16, 942G1

1979

O'CONNOR, Carmen
GSA scandal sentence scored 5-25, 964G2
O'CONNOR, Carroll
Wins Emmy 9-9, 858D2
O'CONNOR, Christy
Wins PGA Senior tourn 7-8, 587D3
O'CONNOR, Fred
Fired as 49ers coach 1-8, 175F2
O'CONNOR, Kevin
Frequency opens 4-25, 711B3
O'CONOR Jr., Judge Robert
Fines Westland Oil 9-18, 850B1
ODEH, Adnan Abu
Scores Israel peace bid 5-19, 379C1
ODINGA, Oginga
Electn bar protested 11-8, 874D3
Named cotton bd head 11-28, 969B2
ODOM, Steve
NFL '78 punt, kick return ldr 1-6, 80F2, G2
O'DONNELL, Kenneth
Cited in House com draft rpt on JFK 3-16, 204C3
O'DONOGHUE, Michael
Gilda Radner Live opens 8-2, 711C3
O'DONOVAN, Danny
Goldengirl released 6-15, 820C1
O'DONOVAN, Edwin
Wins Oscar 4-9, 336A2
OECD—*See ORGANIZATION for Economic Cooperation & Development*
OERTEL, Charles Henry
Sentenced in GSA scandal 6-1, 964E3
OFFICE Equipment
Xerox plans WUI acquisitn 1-18, 89C1
NCR OKs Comten purchase 1-21, 89F1
2d 1/4 profits rptd down 8-17, 628G2
3d 1/4 profits rptd down 10-31, 923B1
OFFICE of Management & Budget—*See U.S. GOVERNMENT-BUDGET*
OFFICE and Professional Employees International Union (AFL-CIO)
NYSE unit settles 2-21, 131C1
O'FIAICH, Cardinal Tomas
Installed cardinal 6-30, 640D2*
Greets Pope 9-29, 760E1
OGADEN—*See under ETHIOPIA*
OGARKOV, Marshal Nikolai Vasilyevich
Cited in SALT II communique 6-18, 457C1
Scores US SALT opponents 8-2, 644D1
OGILVIE, Major
Alabama wins Sugar Bowl 1-1, 8F2
OGLESBY, Marshall
Tunnel Fever opens 5-10, 712B3
OGOURTSOV, Igor
PEN seeks release 7-21, 554A1
OGUMA, Shoji
Draws with Gonzalez 1-29, 412C3
Gonzalez KOs 7-6, 839A1
OH, Sadaharu
Hits 814th home run 5-20, 1003C1
O'HAIR, Madalyn Murray
Loses 'In God We Trust' suit 3-2, 208C2
Sues to halt Pope's DC mass 9-18, case dismissed 10-3, 760B3
O'HARA, Brian
Sky High opens 6-28, 712D2
O'HARE, Virginia
Wins med malpractice suit 5-3, 392A3
Malpractice suit award cut 6-4, 527F2
O'HARE International Airport (Chicago, Ill.)
Blizzard closes 1-12—1-14, 120F1
DC-10 crash kills 275 5-25, 411C3
'78 world's busiest airport 421C1
DC-10s grounded indefinitely 6-6, 420F2
Serbian hijacks jet 6-20, 491G2
DC-10 crash rpts issued 7-10, 538E3; 12-21, 988G2
Midway Airlines begins svc 11-1, 989E1
O'HEARN Jr., Walter D.
Scotto convicted 11-15, 890D1

OHIO
ITT Cleveland long-distance phone svc OKd 1-4, 15E2
Med malpractice arbitratn rptd 1-28, 139E3
Medicaid '78 abortns rptd 3-8, 315B1
Cincinnati archbp named to '80 Rome synod 5-3, 376A1
Chillecothe derailmt 5-6, 472E3
'78 per capita gas use rptd 5-27, 395G2
Hoover sale blocked 6-11, 560F2
Newfields town project ended 6-28, 665D2
Cambridge motel arson kills 10 7-31, 639F1
Canton air crash kills Munson 8-2, 671A3
'78 per capita income rptd 9-16, 746A2, D2
Attys billbd ad case refused by Sup Ct 11-5, 884B3
Pioneer boarding home fire kills 14 11-11, 954D2
Atomic Energy
Davis-Besse (Oak Harbor) A-plant safety study urged 4-1, 245F1
Davis-Besse A-plant shut by NRC 4-27, 322A1
'50s fallout, SAT decline linked 9-17, 747C2
Zimmer (Moscow) reactor licensing delayed 11-5, 849C1

1980

O'CONNOR, Carroll
Kennedy ad cited 4-22, 304E1
O'CONNOR, Timothy
Loses primary for gov 9-9, 700C3
ODE, Robert
Hostages' letters published 1-18—1-20, 47D3
O'DOHERTY, Kieran
Electronic mail plan OKd, conflict of interest chrgd 4-8, 347B3
O'DONNELL, John
Abstains on Carter endorsemt 8-20, 647A3
O'DONNELL, William T.
Bally gets NJ gambling license 12-29, 988B3
O'DONOGHUE, Michael
Gilda Live released 3-28, 416G2
O'DONOVAN, Danny
Filumena opens 2-10, 392G2
OECD—*See ORGANIZATION for Economic Cooperation & Development*
OERTER, Al
Fails to make US Olympic team 6-25, 891C2
OFFERGELD, Rainer
Sworn W Ger econ cooperatn min 11-5, 925F1
OFFICE Equipment
Xerox machine cancer risks rptd 4-11, 357B1-A3
Japan typewriter duties set by US 4-22, 368B1
Xerox win in Van Dyk trust suit rptd upheld 10-6, 917D3
OFFICE of Management & Budget—*See under U.S. GOVERNMENT*
OFF The Wall (recording)
On best-seller list 2-6, 120G3; 3-5, 200F3; 4-2, 280F3; 4-30, 360A1
OF the Fields, Lately (play)
Opens 5-27, 756F3
OGADEN—*See ETHIOPIA--Ogaden Developments*
OGANESYAN, Sanasar
Wins Olympic medal 7-29, 624E3
OGARKOV, Marshal Nikolai
Sovts plan partial Afghan exit 6-22, 475A2
OGILVIE, Ben
NL wins All-Star Game 7-8, 636E1
AL batting ldr 10-6, 926E3
OGILVIE, Major
Alabama wins Sugar Bowl 1-1, 23D1
OGILVIE, Richard B.
Milwaukee Rd westn track purchase rejected in '79 1-7, 53B1
Milwaukee Rd svc cut set 2-25, ICC spurns reorganizatn plan 3-19, 346A1-C1
OGLOBIN, Dmitir
Sets world speed skating mark 3-29, 470B2
OGUMA, Shoji
KOs Park for WBC flywgt title 5-18, 1000F3
OH, Calcutta (play)
Kenneth Tynan dies 7-26, 608E3
OH, God! Book II (film)
Released 10-3, 836C3

O'HAIR, Madalyn Murray
Son apologizes in schl prayer dispute 5-9, 471F2
O'HARA, Clifford Bradley
Confrmd Panama Canal comr 4-2, 308E3
O'HEANEY, Caitlin
He Knows You're Alone released 9-26, 836A3

OHIO
Blizzards hit, 6 killed 3-1—3-2, 292B2
Tornado hits 4-7—4-8, 391A3
NBA player killed in car crash 5-23, 656A2
Legionnaires disease study rptd 6-9, 527C1
Cleveland Press sold 10-31, 1003D1

Atomic Energy & Safeguards
Babcock plant review ordrd 3-4, 169F2
Babcock '77 Toledo plant accident fine asked 4-10, 332C1
'79 A-plant mishaps rptd 7-14, 551F2
GPU seeks $4 bln from NRC 12-15, 960G3-961A1

1976

Politics
Primary date set 22C2
'72 Nixon spending rptd 4-25, 688A2
Carter in Cincinnati 5-4, 324E1
Ford in Columbus 5-26, 391D1
Carter, Udall campaign 5-27—5-28, 390F1
Carter campgn dvpts 6-3, 6-7, 411C1
Ford, Reagan campaign dvpts 6-5—6-7, 410A2, C2, C3, 430F3
Primary results 6-8, 408F2, 409D1, F2
Dem conv women delegates, table 508D2
Dem conv pres vote 7-14, table 507F1, D2
Hays quits reelectn race 8-13, 636F1
GOP pre-conv delegate count 8-14, 583D3
GOP conv pres, vp vote tables 8-18—8-19, 8-19, 599D1, D3
Mondale in Dayton 8-28, 645B3; Barberton 9-6, 665F2
Carter in Cleveland, Columbus, Springfield 9-8—9-9, 664C1
Dole in Medina 9-19, 703C3
Dole campaigns 9-27—9-28, 724E3
Mondale in Cleveland 9-28, 725C1
Carter in Cleveland 10-9, 762C2
Mondale in Columbus, Cleveland, Canton 10-24—10-31, 803E3, G3, 827D2
Dole in Troy 10-26, 804D2
Ford campaigns 10-28, 803F1; 10-29, 11-1, 826B3, C3
Carter in Cleveland 10-28, 803F2
Ford in Cincinnati 10-28, 848C3
Carter rally in Toledo 10-29, 827E1
Election results 11-2: pres 817D2, 818C1, E1-G1, 819B2; cong 817E1, 819F3, 820D2, 823E3, 825F2, 830F2-B3; state 823G3, 825A3
Carter primary spending rptd 11-17, 938A3

1977

Referenda results 11-8, 879D2-F2
US facilities cited for pollutn 11-25, 944C2
Toledo housing suit case declined 12-5, 939C1
Pot law detailed 12-11, 972D3
Cleveland police dispute 12-15—12-16, 1005F1
Cleveland 'gateway' air svc OKd 12-21, 1006C2

Crime
Hustler publisher sentncd in Cincinnati 2-8, 118A2
Cincinnati couple kidnaps 8 2-11, chrgd 2-13, 163F1
Warrensville Hts hostages freed, Carter talks to captor 3-9, 178B3
Secret info use in death sentencing curbed 3-22, 231D1
Pot decriminalizatn impact rptd 3-31, 332A3
US sues Teamster fund 4-4, 280B2
'76, '77 death row populatn rptd 5-5, 6-7, 594A1, C1
Columbus KKK rally disrupted 7-4, 540D1

Fuel-Weather Crisis
FPC OKs emergency gas purchase 1-19, 53G3
Airline diversns OKd 1-19, 54F1
Rhodes orders Dayton area schl, business closings 1-20, rescinds 1-21; asks voluntary fuel conservatn 1-23, 54A2
Layoffs rptd 1-22, 54C2; 1-30, 75F3
Natl Guard mobilized 1-28—1-29, 75F2
Rhodes leads prayer svc 1-29, 75B3
US offers emergency job funds 2-1, 75G3
US declares emergency status 2-5, 91B2
Columbus low temp cited 2-6, total layoffs rptd 2-7, 91D2, F2
Rhodes asks disaster status 2-8, 92B1
Columbus schls reopen 3-7, 196G2-A3

School Issues
Schls in 8 dists reopen 1-3, 16C2
US Sup Ct upholds teacher on free speech 1-11, 57G3
Cleveland busing plan proposed 1-18, 112F2

1978

Cleveland
Schls in fscl crisis 1-6—4-6, state aids 4-13, 279B2
Energy emergency task force meets 2-15, 104G1
Clean-air rating rptd 2-23, 144D3
'73 auto crash award 5-3, 460D1
Schl levy, bond issues defeated 6-6, 425B1
NHL team merges with North Stars, shifts divisn 6-14, 656F2
Fiscal crisis crows 7-10—8-23, 663F2-F3
Police strike 7-13—7-14, 565D2
'44 LNG blast cited 7-31, 610F1
Mayor Kucinich wins recall vote 8-13, 663A2
Busing plan defered 8-25,, 699D1
Schls get state loan 8-28; teachers strike 9-7, schls fail to open 9-8, 699A1
Teachers settle 10-16, 1008E3
6 cncl members indicted 10-27, 1008F3
Rhodes notes Cleveland vote 11-27, 916C1
Abortn zoning ordinance case refused by Sup Ct 11-27, 937D2
Populatn ranked 12-6, 942G3
Default dvpts: pol squabbling, Muny light issue cited 12-12—12-28, 1008B2-E3
Defaults on notes 12-16, 1008G1-A2
Kucinick's brother arrested 12-18, 1008G3

Politics & Government—*See also 'Cleveland' above*
Legislature schedule rptd 14F3
Gag-order case review barred 1-9, 13E1
State tax revenue data 1-9, 84E2, G3
Primary results 6-6, 448C1
Ex-gov O'Neill dies 8-20, 708C3
Carter visits Columbus 9-23, 736B1
Legis OKs DC voting rep amendmt 10-25, 10-30, 1011F2
Electn results 11-7: cong 846A3, 848F2, 851D4, 854E1; state 847C1, D1, 853D3, 854D1, F1, 915D2
Legis pay hike vote cited 11-29, Carter angry 12-1, Kahn asks rollback 12-4, 934F3, 935B1

School Issues
Cleveland schls in fiscal crisis 1-6—4-6, state aids 4-13, 279B2
Brunswick striking teachers jailed 4-8—4-14, 279G2-A3
Toledo schools struck 4-10, 279G2

1979

Cleveland Fiscal Issues
Bond issue ban refused by Sup Ct 2-21, 128B3
Voters OK tax rise, Muny Light retentn 2-27, 150A1
Kucinch seeks state purchase of notes, vs control bd 2-28, 150F1
FRB clears bank re Cleveland Elec stock buy 3-14, 204D2
Mayor, cncl OK repaymt plan 6-9, 579E3
2d default averted 7-6, 580A1
US House subcom ties default to anti-mayor moves 7-17, 579G2
Muny Light rpts '78 profit 7-29, 580D1
2d default 8-31, some debt repayed 9-26, 3d default averted 10-5, 920F2-C3
Bond ratings listed 9-20, 920F3
Kucinich loses electn 11-6, 846G1, F2

Crime & Civil Disorders
Stolen films seized in Bay Village 1-8, 102E2
'78 Cincinnati Nazi activity cited 1-19, 102B1
City Council pres acquitted 7-18, 580E1
FBI agent slain in Cleveland 8-9, suspect chrgd 8-16, 727E3
Middletown KKK activity cited 865B1
Cincinnati rock concert stampede 12-3, 954G1

Environment & Pollution—*See also 'Atomic' above*
EPA sulphur-dioxide emissns case refused by US Sup Ct 1-15, 32B1
Cleveland bad air quality cited 1-25, 90C2
US Steel, Erie Coke sued re Lorain, Fairport Harbor plant pollutn 1-25, 2-5, 90E2-G2
2d EPA sulphur-dioxide emissns case refused by US Sup Ct 3-19, 203B3
Coal co sues vs clean-air rule 3-22, 206A3
EPA sues Ford plant 3-22, 206C3
EPA upheld re coal use 5-7, 351C1
EPA eases air rule for Cleveland Elec 6-6, 422D3-423C1

Labor Issues
Lawyers' interstate rights limited by US Sup Ct 1-15, 31C3
Dissident steel haulers end strike 4-29, 384C3
Toledo city workers walkout 7-3–7-4, ratify pact 7-5, 599D1
Mansfield GM plant struck 8-23–8-27, 698F2
State workers Soc Security non-participatn cited 9-10, 727B1
Teachers' strikes rptd 9-12, 679B1
Cincinnati papers joint pact OKd 11-26, 1007G1
Youngstown steel layoffs rptd 11-27, 11-28, US aid set 12-3, 941E3

Politics & Government—*See also other appropriate subheads in this section*
Legislature schedule rptd 5E3
John Hollister dies 1-4, 104B3
Fscl '78 tax revenue rptd 2-13, 152B2
Reagan speaks in Columbus 2-18, 124E1
S Africa '78 campaign contributns to Jepsen chrgd, denied 3-21, 213C1
Dayton, Columbus mil depots to close 3-29, 265F3
Akron ex-offcl libel case declined by US Sup Ct 4-23, 346G2
Draft-Kennedy activity in Cleveland rptd 5-23, 384E2
Cleveland mayoral primary results 10-2, 829C1
Voinovich elected Cleveland mayor, other electn results 11-6, 846G1, B2, F2, E3

School Issues
Kent '75 damage suit settled 1-4, 5C2
Integratn study rpts urban lag 5-9, 650F1
Columbus, Dayton busing orders upheld by Sup Ct 7-2, 539E2

1980

Cleveland Fiscal Issues
Fiscal emergency declared, state panel set 1-4, 187D1
Bank default setlmt, bond purchase agreed 7-29, 743B3

Crime & Civil Disorders
FBI 'Miporn' probe rptd 2-14, 136F1
'Pyramid' money schemes rptd 5-17, 655A3
Judge acquitted of sex-bartering, convicted of other chrgs 6-13, 503A2
Cleveland FBI bribe plotters convicted 7-3, 655D2
Inmate cell crowding case accepted by Sup Ct 11-3, 856F2
Flynt Cleveland convictn case accepted by Sup Ct 12-8, 937A2

Energy—*See also 'Atomic Energy & Safeguards' above*
Sohio gas price hike order rescinded 5-1, 366F1
Ct blocks ND synfuels projct 12-8, 962C1

Environment & Pollution
DES in cattle rptd 4-24, 358F1
EPA firms Cleveland Elec air rule 6-17, 494B3
Diamond Shamrock, Chem Recovery toxic waste suits filed 10-7, 825F1

Labor & Employment
Cleveland teachers end strike 1-3, 5A3
Honda to open Marysville plant 1-11, 35F2
Oberlin DJ fired, '79-80 'captivity' cited 2-6, 199D3
Youngstown US Steel plant closings blocked 2-28, 266A2
Harvester strike ends 4-20, 308G2
Youngstown US Steel plant closings upheld 7-25, 575G1
Reagan addresses Teamsters, sees 'Carter depressn' 8-27, 664A2
Teachers strike in Columbus, 3 other districts 9-4, 723F3
Reagan visits Lima auto plant 10-15, 780C1
Youngstown US Steel plant suit ends 11-14, 917A1
Bobbie Brooks '77 bias case setld 12-21, 988C1

Politics & Government—*See also other appropriate subheads in this section*
Legislature schedule rptd 18F1
Ky boundary placemt upheld by Sup Ct 1-21, 93F2
Fscl '79 tax revenue rptd 2-20, 307B3
Ex-Rep McCulloch dies 2-22, 176E2
Census revisn ordrd, Cleveland undercount claimed 9-25, 741G2
Election results 11-4: cong 837E1, 840G2, 843D4, 845A3, 846F1, G1, 851C2; state 845D3, 847G1, F2
'80 census rptd, reapportmt seen 12-31, 983F1

Presidential Election (& Transition)
Citizens' Party conv in Cleveland 4-11—4-13, 288E3
Kennedy in Cincinnati 5-21, 383F1
Kennedy win doubted 5-28, 399E2
Kennedy campaigns 5-29, 401B3
Carter, Reagan in Columbus 5-29, 423C3
Primary results 6-3, 422F2, 423E2, 424C1
Poll rpts voter discontent 6-3, 423B1
Reagan in Columbus, addresses Teamsters conf 8-27, 664A2
Mondale in Cleveland 9-1, Columbus 9-10, 780E1, C2
Reagan in Cleveland 9-10, 681A1, 699C3
Bush in Cleveland, Columbus 9-17, 780G3
Anderson ct battle for ballot access rptd 9-27, 818B2
Carter in Dayton 10-2, 762B2
Reagan in Youngstown, Steubenville 10-7, 10-8, 763E2, 779B2
Reagan in Lima 10-15, 780C1
Mondale in Toledo 10-16, 817B1
Reagan in Cincinnati 10-20, 802B1
Carter in Youngstown 10-20, 803A1
Cleveland TV debate set 10-21, 801F3
Carter, Reagan debate in Cleveland 10-28, 813E1
Press endorsemts rptd 11-1, 841G3
Reagan winds up campaign 11-2, 840A2
Carter rallies held 11-2, 11-3, 841C1, D1
Election results 11-4, 838C1, 839A2, F3

School Issues
Cleveland teachers end strike 1-3, 5A3
US rights comm lauds Dayton, Columbus busing orders 1-15, 36E3
Cleveland busing challenge refused by Sup Ct 3-17, 225F3

1976

OHIO Players (music group)
Love Rollercoaster on best-selling list 1-28, 104G3
Wins Grammy 2-28, 460B3
OHIO State University (Columbus)
Loses Rose Bowl 1-1; '75 rank rptd 1-2, 31B3
Paul Pimsleur dies 6-22, 524D3

OHIRA, Masayoshi
Seeks Miki ouster 5-13, 458G1
Miki asked to quit 8-23, 626D3
Sees Miki re compromise 8-30, 676G3
Uchida heads LDP 9-15, 694E1
LDP secy gen 12-23, 1006E2

OHISHI, Buichi
Loses house seat 12-5, 925E3
OIDOV, Zeveg
Wins Olympic medal 7-31, 576C3
OIL City, Pa.—*See PENNSYLVANIA*
OIL & Gasoline—*See PETROLEUM*
OILS & Fats
FDA requires oils labeling 1-5, 7C2
EEC-Algeria olive oil pact rptd 1-21, 84B3
Group of 77 sets trade guidelines 2-10, 108C1
Pacific exchng closes, US sues 5-10, 348C2
France proposes price stabilizatn fund 5-10—5-11, 355E3
OIL Shale Corp.
'75 consortium pullout cited 8-23, 649D1
OIL Spills—*See 'Oil & Gas Issues' under ENVIRONMENT*
OJARA, Mario
On Peru seaport plan 11-23, 975B2
OJEDA, Gen. Edmundo
Argentina police chief 7-6, 571C3
OJEDA Paullada, Pedro
'75 Levi drug talks rptd 1-19, 61G1
On opium poppy fields 6-8, 419F3, 420A1
Mexico labor min 12-2, 907A1
OKAI, Lt. Gen. Lawrence
Replaced 11-14; retiremt linked to car import fraud 12-3, 1003D2
OKAMOTO, Kozo
Hijackers demand release 6-29, 463D1
Hijackers seek release 9-4, 662G2
OKAWARA, Yorhio
Arrives Australia 3-9, 187E3
O'KELLY, Justice William C.
Sentences Murphy abductor 9-17, 796E3
OKINAWA and other Ryukyu Islands (Japanese territories)
Newsman's '74 acquittal reversed 7-20, 539F1
OKINDA, Jerome
Named min of state 10-19, 1003A2

1977

Rhodes orders Dayton area schl closings 1-20, rescinds 1-21, 54A2
Columbus schls reopen 3-7, 196G2-A3
Columbus schl integratn ordrd 3-8, 217A1
Cincinnati teachers strike 4-13—5-10, 481F2
Dayton busing order backed 4-22, 446D1
Church schls limited aid backed 6-23, 539F2
Dayton busing plan remanded 6-27, 538F2; voided 12-15, 978B3
Kent State gym protested 7-12, 560E1
Columbus integratn plans rejctd 7-29, 631C1
Kent protests continue 7-29—10-25, 820E2-A3
KKK rally in Columbus 9-5, 838C1
Dayton term opens calmly 9-7, 838B1
Kent damage suit retrial ordrd 9-12, 820B3
Cleveland schls kept open by US cts, state legis 10-21—12-7, teachers strike 11-29—12-8, 939E2
Local tax referenda results 11-8, 879E2
Financing system ruled illegal 12-5, 939D3
Sports
Cleveland NHL team rescued 2-23, 164D1
Cleveland NHL team sale OKd 5-12, 430F1
Cleveland Indians refinancing proposal OKd 12-4—12-8, 989G3
OHIO Bureau of Employment Services v. Hodory
Job benefits law upheld 5-31, 461D3
OHIO Edison Co.
Westinghouse settlemt rptd 3-3, 177D2
Westinghouse dispute formerly ends 3-30, 252G1-B2
Westinghouse settlemt cited 12-26, 1003B3
OHIO River
Flow decline rptd 3-8, 244A3
FMC plant shut 3-9, reopened 3-15, 196B3, D3
OHIO State University (Columbus)
Wins Orange Bowl 1-1, '76 rank rptd 1-2, 1-3, 8E3
Brudzinski in NFL draft 5-3, 353B3
Ward wins Downtown AC Trophy 12-8, 950E2

OHIRA, Masayoshi
Backers vs Miyazawa high post 11-28, 932A2

OHLIN, Bertil
Wins Nobel Prize 10-14, 951E3
O'HORTON, Jack
Replaced as Interior asst secy 4-11, 272B3
OIL Chemical and Atomic Workers International Union (AFL-CIO)
Canada farm workers unionize 3-21, 237F2
DBCP exposure curbed 9-8, 723A3
OIL & Gasoline—*See PETROLEUM*
OILS & Fats
UN rpts '76 price drop 2-14, 146B1
Brazil-Iran trade pact 6-23, 524A2
US loans to exporters curbed 10-19, 815D2
OIL Spills—*See ENVIRONMENT—Oil & Gas Issues*
O'KENNEDY, Michael
Named Ireland forgn min 7-5, 599A1
OKHOTSK Sea
USSR sets 200-mi limit 3-1, 147E1
OKINAWA—*See JAPAN*

1978

Cleveland, Columbus, 196 other levy, bond issues defeated 6-6, 425B1
Cleveland fiscal crisis grows 7-10—8-23, 663G2
Columbus busing plan OKd 7-14, 611E1
Dayton busing plan upheld 7-27, 610G3
Cleveland busing plan deferred 8-25, 699D1
Cleveland gets state loan 8-28; teachers strike 9-7, schls fail to open 9-8, 699A1
Cleveland teachers settle 10-16, 1008E3
Bond issue results 11-7, 854F1; 915D2

OHIO State University (Columbus)
Loses Sugar Bowl 1-2, 8D3
Ward in NFL draft 5-2, 336E3
Cook wins US Amateur golf title 9-3, 990F1
Loses Gator Bowl; Hayes punches Clemson player 12-29, Hayes fired 12-30, 1025F2, G2
OHIO University (Athens)
S Africa investmt barred 2-11, 135F1

OHIRA, Masayoshi
Facts on 913A1
Wins LDP electn, premrshp assured 11-27, 912D2
LDP delays confirmatn 12-6; confirmed as premr, forms Cabt 12-7, 945D2
Shelves '78 growth target 12-8, 988G1
Carter call re China ties rptd 12-16, 977D1

OHRALIK v. Ohio State Bar Association
Lawyer suspensn affirmed by Sup Ct 5-30, 430C2
Oil, Chemical and Atomic Workers International Union (AFL-CIO)
Grospiron rptd vs Carter wage curb 11-21, 917B3
OIL and Gas Journal
'78 world oil output rise rptd 12-26, 1000B3
OIL & Gasoline—*See PETROLEUM*
OIL of Wintergreen (methyl salicylate)—*See MEDICINE—Drugs*
OILS & Fats
Palm oil aid curbed by OPIC extensn 4-24, 323A3
Japan, NZ trade accord rptd 5-23, 498A1
Greek EC entry terms set, olive oil curbs noted 12-21, 1017D3
OIL Spills—*See ENVIRONMENT—Oil & Gas Issues*
OJEDA Paullada, Pedro
Urges US rejoin ILO 6-7, 523F3
OKAMOTO, Kozo
PLO raiders sought release 3-11, 175G2
OKCUN, Gunduz
Named Turkey foreign min 1-5, 21E2
Warns US vs peace role 1-20, 170G2
OKEFENOKEE National Wildlife Refuge (Ga., Fla.)
Ga acreage gift accepted 3-14, 186B3
OKHOTSK, Sea of
USSR icebreaker opens new path 6-12, 506B2

1979

Columbus busing order reissued 8-2, 596A3
Dayton, Columbus busing begins peacefully 9-4, 9-6; Cleveland protests staged 9-9, plan effected 9-10, 679A2-A3
Teachers' strikes rptd 9-12, 679B1
Sports
Reds ex-pres Giles dies 2-7, 176B3
NHL-WHA merger set 3-22, Cincinnati team to fold 3-30, 355A3
Dayton WBL team moved 6-12, 526G2
'Trans-America' balloon crashes 10-2, 992A3
OHIO Edison Co.
EPA upheld re coal use 5-7, 351E1
OHIO Edison Co. v. Williams
Case refused by Sup Ct 3-19, 203C3
OHIO State University (Columbus)
Bruce named football coach 1-12, 175D3
NIT results 3-21, 238E3
Cousineau in NFL draft 5-3, 335C1, E2
Wins NCAA golf title 5-26, 587F1

OHIRA, Masayoshi (Japanese premier)
Meets Teng 2-7, 84C1
Carter trade warning rptd 2-10, rpt disputed 2-15; notes surplus cut 2-22, 160E1
Blumenthal sees re trade imbalance 3-5, 160A1
Affirms A-program 4-1, 246F2
In US, sees Carter on trade 5-2—5-3, 320F1-B3
Presents gifts to Asian Society, NYC museum 5-4, 375A2
On Viet refugees 6-18, 460C3
Carter in Tokyo talks re energy, refugees 6-26, 494D1
7-yr econ plan OKd 8-11—8-12, 615B2
Mondale briefs on China talks 9-3, 660B3
Dissolves House, sets electns 9-7; LDP wins, margin reduced 10-7, 762B2
Resigns formally 10-30, challenged by Fukuda 11-2, reelected 11-6, 844B3
Names new Cabt 11-8, 874F2
Warns on Iran excess oil imports 11-16, 879G2
In China, econ pacts signed 12-5—12-7, 939C3
Defends Iran oil purchases 12-11, 933E2
Vows pressure vs Iran 12-17—12-18, 959B1
OHLIN, Bertil
Dies 8-3, 671B3
OHLWARTER, Fritz
Swiss win world 2-man bobsled title 2-18, 392E1
OHMAN, Christopher
Father's Day opens 6-21, 711A3
OIL, Chemical and Atomic Workers International Union (AFL-CIO)
Cyanamid sterilizatn suit threatnd 1-4, 56A3
Gulf pact within US wage guidelines OKd 1-11, 87B1
Back pay rule vs Amer Cyanamid upheld 2-10, 131A1
Carter cites setlmt 2-12, 109E3
Silkwood estate wins A-suit 5-18, 381A2
OIL & Gas Journal
'79 1st 1/2 record world oil output rptd 8-28, 645G1
OIL & Gasoline—*See PETROLEUM*
OIL Spills—*See ENVIRONMENT—Oil & Gas Issues*
OKEECHOBEE, Lake
Fla dam breaks 10-31, 912B3
O'KEEFE, Georgia
Stolen paintings ordrd returned 7-27, 656F1
O'KEEFE, John
Wild Oates opens 1-8, 292F3
O'KENNEDY, Michael
Invited to US Ulster peace conf 8-6, 602E1
On UK-Eire security accord 10-5, 792E3, 793B1

1980

Teachers strike in Columbus, 3 other districts 9-4, 723F3

OHIO, U.S.S. (nuclear submarine)
Deploymt delay seen 10-11, 986F3
OHIO Association of Realtors
Bush addresses 9-17, 780G3
OHIO Independent Dealers for Survival
Sohio gas price hike order rescinded 5-1, 366A2
OHIO State University (Columbus)
Loses Rose Bowl 1-1, '79 rank rptd 1-2, 23B1, D1
Hightower sets 60-yd hurdles mark 2-8, 892E2
US youth jobless rate said higher 2-28, 228A3
NCAA basketball tourn results 3-24, 240A2
Legionnaires disease study rptd 6-9, 527E1
Ransey in NBA draft 6-10, 447C1, F2
Young campaigns for Carter 10-10, racial remark repudiated 10-15, 803D1
Loses Fiesta Bowl 12-26, 999C3
OHIO Transformer Corp.
PCB cleanup device rptd 9-11, 747C2
OHIO v. Kentucky
Case decided by Sup Ct 1-21, 93G2
OHIRA, Masayoshi (Japanese premier; died June 12)
Brown urges defns spending hike 1-14, 31B2
In Australia, sees prime min 1-16, Pacific orgn studied 1-20, 78E1-D2
Scores Sovt Afghan invasn 1-25, 67D3
Fires Kobota 2-3, 99C3
Cited in Connally 'basic speech' 3-7, 184B2
Backs more US troop support 3-20, 3-24, 219F2, B3
Sees Panama pres, canal feasibility study agreed 3-25, 234B3
In DC, meets Carter 5-1; in Mex, oil export hike barred 5-2—5-4, 341B1-A2
At Tito funeral 5-8, 339B1
Loses confidence vote 5-16; Diet dissolved, electns set 5-19, 380F3-381C1
Chinese Premr Hua visits 5-27—6-1, 422A1
Mex oil-trade pact signed 5-28, 409C2*
In hosp 5-31, dies, 6-12; Ito becomes acting premr 6-12, 434C3
LDP wins parlt electns 6-22, 499A1
Mem'l svcs held; Carter, Hua attend 7-9, 506B1, D1
Suzuki named LDP head 7-15, elected premr 7-17, 539F2
Suzuki outlines admin goals 8-18, 635E2

OH Jeff...I Love You Too...but (painting)
Sold for record sum 5-15, 472A2
OHSAKO, Tatsuko
Wins Japan Classic 11-9, 972F2
OH Tak Keun
8 pol prisoners freed 12-11, 968F1
OIL, Chemical and Atomic Workers International Union (OCAW) (AFL-CIO)
Natl strike begins 1-8; industry offer rejctd 2-28, unions back demands 3-1, 187G1
Chem plants cancer study rptd 7-24, 584A3
OIL & Gasoline—*See PETROLEUM*
OILS & Fats
Medit pollutn pact signed 5-17, 381C3
Poland rationing set 11-19, 878G2
OJOK, Brig. Gen. David Oyite
Ousted 5-10, leads Uganda coup 5-11, 375D1-B2
O'KENNEDY, Michael
Presents '80 budget 2-27, 150F3

1976

OKKER, Tom
Wins US Open doubles 9-12, 716C1

OKLAHOMA
US Sup Ct to review beer law 1-12, 24D1
Carter leads Dem caucuses 2-7, 129D1
US Sen seats Bellmon 3-4, 180C2
Tulsa on US jobless list 5-5, 347E2
Reagan ups delegate lead 5-11, 343A1
Death penalty voided 7-6, new law enacted 7-24, 568B3
Efaw draft chrgs dismissed 8-11, 680A3
GOP pre-conv delegate count 8-14, 583D3
Reagan seeks conv delegates 8-17, 601B3
GOP conv pres, vp vote tables 8-18—8-19, 8-19, 599D1, D3
GOP conv delegates back Helms as vp 8-19, 598F2
Phillips tax fraud chrgd 9-2, 725F2
Fscl '75 per capita income, tax burden rptd 9-15, 10-12, 959D2
Ford in Lawton 10-8, 763B2
Dole in Okla City 10-19, 804D1
Election results 11-2: pres 818C1, G1, E2, F2, 819B1; cong 822G2, 830C3
US Sup Ct stays gag order 11-24, 901C2
Flu shot paralysis rptd 12-17, 950E1
US Sup Ct bars beer-buying sex bias 12-20, 960E1

OKLAHOMA (record album)
Wins Hall of Fame award 2-28, 460E3

OKLAHOMA, University of (Norman)
Wins Orange Bowl 1-1, rank rptd 1-2, 31A3
Carter speech 9-13, 686E2
Wins Fiesta Bowl 12-25, 1014G2

OKLAHOMA City, Okla.—*See OKLAHOMA*

OKLAHOMA City Times (newspaper)
Ford endorsement rptd 10-30, 831F2

OKUBO, Toshiharu
Quits Marubeni, testifies on Lockheed payoffs 2-17, 132F1, 191B1
Rptdly rejoins Marubeni 2-20, 191C1
Diet subpoenas 2-26, testifies again 3-1, 190C3
Arrested 6-22, 450A3
Indicted for perjury 7-13, 557B2
Indicted for bribery 8-16, out on bail 8-17, 624A2

OKUN, Arthur
Carter briefing session 7-27, 551C1
Carter econ adviser 12-1, 898G2

OLDER, Judge Charles
Appeals Ct backs Farr 12-6, drops case 12-21, 995C1

OLDEST Living Graduate, The (play)
Opens 9-23, 1014E3

OLDHAM Jr., John
Chrgs vote bribe bid 8-17, 616F1

OLD Lyme, Conn.—*See CONNECTICUT*

O'LEARY, Liam
On '2-tier' mgt bar 2-10, 156F3

O'LEARY, Michael
Bank strike ends 8-24, 735C1

OLENDORF, George
Sentence rptd 7-20, 860F2

OLIN Corp.
Sup Ct bars review of trust case 10-4, 807B3

OLIPHANT, Mark
Aborigine succeeds 5-25, 424A2

OLIVA, Chris Ana Olson de
Killed by army 10-20, 996A2

OLIVEIRA de Arriaga, Gen. Kaulza (ret.)
Freed 1-21, 53G1

OLIVER, Al
NL Batting ldr 10-4, 795F3

OLIVER, Judge John W.
Upholds free agent rule 2-4, 951G3

1977

OKKER, Tom
Wins Richmond WCT 2-6, 430F2

OKLAHOMA
Legislature schedule rptd 6F2
Coll integratn rules ordrd 1-17, 112B2
'75 interstate gas sales rptd 1-28, 76C3
Juvenile ct gag order voided 3-7, 211B2
Foss bank fails 3-10, 578C1
ERA set back 3-14, 279C3
Coll integratn rules reordrd 4-1, 446D1
Laetrile OKd by ct 4-8, 376C1
'76 per-capita income table 5-10, 387F2
Executn by drugs OKd 5-10, 594F1
Oklahoma City, Tulsa business confidence rptd; econ data table 5-16, 384F2, 385B1
3 Girl Scouts slain at camp 6-13, 492E1
State abortn funding rptd 6-20, 787B1
Laetrile legalized 6-21, 508E1
Coll integratn plan issued 7-5, 630G2
US asks farm holdings breakup 8-22, 703G2
Escaped convict sought in Girl Scout murders 8-22, 711E3
'76 per capita income, tax burden table 9-13, 10-18, 821E2
ERA econ boycott rptd 11-14, 918E1

OKLAHOMA, University of (Norman)
'76 football rank rptd 1-2, 1-3, 8E3
Albert record subpoena rptd 12-1, 915F1
Henderson wins Downtown AC Trophy 12-8, 950E2

OKLAHOMA City, Okla.—*See OKLAHOMA*

OKLAHOMA Press Publishing Co.
FCC OKs Gannett purchase 4-14, 395E2

OKLAHOMA Publishing Co. v. District Court
Juvenile gag order voided 3-7, 211C2

OKLAHOMA State University (Stillwater)
Dokes in NFL draft 5-3, 353B3
Miller loses in Heisman voting 12-8, 950B2

O.K. Motor Service
ICC sues 11-3, 861D1

O'KOREN, Mike
Marquette wins NCAA title 3-28, 262B2

OKOT, Bishop Yona
Chrgd in anti-Amin plot 2-16, 138D3

OKUBO, Toshiharu
Lockheed bribe trial starts 1-27, 83D2

O'LEARY, Jean
Miami homosexual rights law repealed 6-7, 446A3

O'LEARY, John
Montreal wins Grey Cup 11-27, 950G2

OLESEN, Kjeld
Danish transport min 2-25, 373C1, E1
On UK SAS flight ban 10-30, 883A1

OLIART, Alberto
Spain industry, energy min 7-5, 545B2

OLIN Corp.
Rpts forgn paymts 1-27, 94E1
Sup Ct backs EPA authority 2-23, 150G2

OLIN Foundation, John M.
Simon named pres 3-1, 396E3

OLIVER, Al
NL batting ldr 10-2, 926C3
Traded to Rangers 12-8, 990C1

OLIVER'S Story (book)
On best-seller list 4-3, 264F1; 5-1, 356B2; 6-4, 452G1; 7-3, 548D3

OLIVIER, George Borg
Replaced as oppositn ldr 1-16, 136D2

1978

OKKER, Tom
Wins WCT doubles title 5-7, 418A3
Wimbledon results 7-8, 539F3

OKLAHOMA
Legislature schedule rptd 14F3
'67, '77 sales-tax rates rptd 1-5, 15F3
NASL '77 Tulsa club move cited 1-5, 23A1
State govt tax revenue table 1-9, 84E2
Tulsa McDonnell Douglas strike 1-13—4-16, 284A3
College integratn plan OKd 2-2, 85D1
ERA boycott evaluated 3-20, 494G2
Girl Scout slaying suspect arrested 4-6, 380D3
Ex-gov Hall released from jail 5-22, 420G3
Construction pact signed 5-22, 429D3
Oral Roberts hosp in Tulsa OKd 5-25, 577A3
'77 prison populatn rptd down 6-3, 440D1
Grasshopper invasn rptd, EPA aid asked 7-13—7-31, 654B3
Primary results, runoff set 8-22, 682G3
Primary runoff results 9-19, 736G3
GOP tax-cut tour in Okla City 9-22, 734F3
Black Fox A-plant protests, 14 arrested 10-7, 11-1, 941E2, F2
Electn results 11-7: cong 845E1, 846G1, 848G2, 851G4-852A1, 855G2; state 847C1, 853D3, 855G2
Natural gas price control suit filed 11-20, 900B1

OKLAHOMA, University of (Norman)
Loses Orange Bowl 1-2, '77 rank rptd 1-3, 8A3, B3
Wilkinson named Cardinals coach 3-2, 171D3
Wrestling rank rptd 3-13, 379A3
Peacock in NFL draft 5-2, 336F3
Roberts wins Outland Trophy 11-25, Sims wins Heisman 11-28, 1025G1, A2

OKLAHOMA City, Okla.—*See OKLAHOMA*

OKLAHOMA State University (Stillwater)
Miller in NFL draft 5-2, 336E3

OKONITE Co.
US sues re price-fixing 9-22, 739A1

OKUBO, Toshiharu
Ties 6 to Lockheed scandal 1-30, 72C3

OKUN, Arthur
Carter offers pay insurance plan 10-24, 805G2

OLAVARRIA, Jorge
Resumen issue seized, takes asylum in Vatican emb 12-3, 953D1

OLAVSEN, Dag
San Fran wins NCAA soccer title 12-10, 969A2

OLBRYCHSKI, Daniel
Landscape After Battle released 2-9, 619F2

O'LEARY, John F.
Ties for 2d in Irish Open 8-27, 672G3
Rpts 3 cos seek gas allocatns 12-3, 939C1

OLEK, Henry
Different Story released 6-13, 619E1

OLIN Corp.
Forgn natn drug trust suit OKd 1-11, 33E3
Indicted for Winchester S Africa sales 3-14, 193G2; fined 3-30, 249E2
Indicted for mercury dumping 3-23, 243E1
Fined again for S Africa firearms sale 6-1, 632G3
Celanese plans takeover 10-3, 767G3
Celanese merger ended 11-10, 897C1

OLINKRAFT Inc.
Indicted for price fixing 1-25, 67B2
Texas Eastern merger set 7-17, 700E3
Johns-Manville offer OKd, Tex Eastn bidding ended 10-27, 896A3
Morgan Stanley sued 11-8, 896D3

OLIPHANT v. Squamish Indian Tribe
Indian ct trials of non-Indians barred 3-6, 162D1

OLIVEIRA, Elmar
Wins Tchaikovsky competitn 7-5, 844A2

OLIVEIRA, Paulo Gomes de
Tortured by security offcls 1-27—2-1, 166D1

OLIVEIRA e Silva, Alberto
Sworn Portugal internal affairs min 1-30, 91C3

OLIVER, Al
AL batting ldr 10-2, 928D3-E3

OLIVER, Judy
2d in US Women's Amateur golf title 8-19, 990E1

OLIVER'S Story (book)
On best-seller list 4-30, 356B2

OLIVER'S Story (film)
Released 12-14, 1030C3

OLIVIER, Claude
Dear Detective released 4-24, 619D1

1979

OKITA, Saburo
Japan forgn min 11-8, 874G2
At energy conf in Paris, US urges sanctns vs Iran 12-10, 933C2

OKKER, Tom
Wins US Natl Indoor doubles 3-4, 391A3
Wimbledon results 7-6, 7-7, 569D3
Loses Tennis Legends 8-12, Carte Blanche Legends 8-26, 734B2, D2

OKLAHOMA
Legislature schedule rptd 5F3
Teacher dismissal backed by US Sup Ct 2-26, 164G3
Ex-Sen Bartlett dies 3-1, 272A2
Carter revisits Elk City 3-24, 230C2
Girl Scout slaying suspect acquitted 3-30, 291E2; dies 6-4, 508A3
Lawton tornado kills 3 4-10, 288F2, A3
Minnow sale ban voided by US Sup Ct 4-24, 364C2
GM scored in Okla City union dispute 7-16, UAW wins organizing vote 7-19, 598D1, G1
GM pressed on Okla City UAW contract 8-23—8-27, 698F2
Teachers' strikes rptd 9-12, 679B1
'78 per capita income rptd 9-16, 746F2

Atomic Energy
Silkwood estate wins A-damages 5-18, 381D1
Black Fox (Inola) A-plant delayed 5-21, 382A1
Black Fox protesters arrested 6-2, 416B2
Silkwood damages award upheld 8-20, 629G3

OKLAHOMA! (play)
Opens 12-13, 1007D2

OKLAHOMA, University of (Norman)
Wins Orange Bowl 1-1, '78 rank rptd 1-2, 1-3, 8D2, B3
NCAA basketball tourn results 3-26, 238A3

OKLAHOMA City, Okla.—*See OKLAHOMA*

OKLAHOMA City, U.S.S. (flagship)
Retirement announced 1-23, 89C3

OKLAHOMA State University (Stillwater)
2d in NCAA golf championship 5-26, 587G1

O.K. MEAT Packing Co.
Settles '78 beef-price suit 10-22, 985E3

OKOLONA, Miss.—*See MISSISSIPPI*

OKUN, Arthur
On '29 Depression, '80s econ forecast 11-1, 827A2

OLD Boyfriends (film)
Released 3-21, 528B3

OLD Dominion University (Norfolk, Va.)
Wins AIAW basketball title 3-25, 239A1
Lieberman named top woman basketball player 3-29, 290F3

OLDOINI, Enrico
Stay As You Are released 12-21, 1008G1

OLD Phantoms (play)
Opens 2-8, 292C2

O'LEARY, John F.
Sees gas shortfall 5-7, 343B1
On winter heating oil supplies 6-29, 514E2
Resigns Energy post 7-9, 514A1

OLESEN, Kjeld
Named Danish forgn min 10-26, 855B1
Sees Vance re NATO missile plan 12-7, 938G1

OLGILVIE, Richard B.
Milwaukee Rd westn embargo OKd 9-26, 867F2

OLIN Corp.
Convicted for mercury dumping 8-16, 704E1
Fined for mercury dumping 12-10, 947A1
US sues re Niagara dump 12-20, 990G1

OLINKRAFT Inc.
Michael chrgs dismissed 4-29, 327D3

OLIVARES, Ruben
Pedroza KOs 7-22, 839B1

OLIVARE Santana, Enrique
Named Mex interior secy 5-17, 408C3, G3

OLIVE, John
Minnesota Moon opens 1-31, 292B2

OLIVER, Al
AL batting ldr 9-30, 955D3

OLIVER, Johnnie L.
Slain 8-9, 727G3

OLIVETTI & Co. SpA, Ing. C.
Brazil metalworkers strike 10-29, 833B2

1980

OKITA, Saburo
In US mil talks 3-20, 3-21, 219F2
Reaffirms Olympic boycott stand 4-15, 283B3

OKKER, Tom
Loses WCT doubles title 1-6, Grand Prix Masters 1-12, 213B2, C2

OKLAHOMA
State ct jurisdictn narrowed by Sup Ct 1-21, 93A2
Tornadoes hit 4-7—4-8, 391G2
DES in cattle rptd 4-24, 358F1
Hunts bailout loan collateral listed 5-28, 426E1
US intrastate gas sale power affirmed 6-6, 552D3
Drought, heat wave hit, death toll rptd 6-23—8-15; Carter declares disaster area 7-16, Nigh asks 'prayer day' 7-20, 616C1, E1, G1, D2
Snowstorm hits 11-16, 948A1
Tulsa busing, housing integratn study rptd 11-16, 989E3

Crime & Civil Disorders
Shooting spurs Idabell racial violence 1-20, murder chrg filed 1-21, 94E1
FBI Brilab probe rptd 2-8—2-9, 111C3

Politics & Government—*See also other appropriate subheads in this section*
Legislature schedule rptd 18F1
Ex-Sen Monroney dies 2-13, 176F2
State of State message 2-19, 404A1
Ex-Rep Belcher dies 8-2, 676A1
US Cong primary results, runoff set 8-26, 682G3
Primary runoff results 9-16, 724A3
Election results 11-4; cong 840G2, 843G4-844A1, 845A3, B3, 850B1; state 845D3
'80 census rptd 12-31, 983F1

Presidential Election (& Transition)
Carter wins Dem caucus vote 3-11, 209B1
Reagan gains delegates 5-3, 342B3
Reagan seconded at conv 7-16, 529F1
Election results 11-4, 838C1, 839B2, F3

OKLAHOMA, University of (Norman)
Wins Orange Bowl 1-1, '79 rank rptd 1-2, 23B1, E1
Sims, Cumby in NFL draft 4-29, 336C3-G3

OKLAHOMA State University (Stillwater)
Wins NCAA team golf title 5-31, 714F3

O'KOREN, Mike
In NBA draft 6-10, 447F1

OKUMA, Masataka
Fears Nissan US productn 7-29, 599G1

OKUN, Arthur
Dies 3-23, 280D1

OLAYAN, Suliman S.
Named to Mobil bd 10-31, joins 12-1, 960D3

OLD Dominion University (Norfolk, Va.)
Lieberman named top '79 female coll athlete 1-8, 104D1
Wins AIAW basketball title, Nissen named tourn MVP 3-23, 240A3
NCAA basketball tourn results 3-24, 240A2
Lieberman named top coll basketball player 3-26, 240G3

OLDFIELD, Brian
US Olympic trials ban voided 6-25, 891B3

OLD Time Gospel Hour (TV show)
Falwell profiled 9-15, 819D3

OLESEN, Kjeld
Vs Olympic boycott 1-22, 68D1

OLIANSKY, Joel
Competition released 12-3, 972D3

OLIVA, Patrizio
Wins Olympic medal 8-2, 622F1

OLIVARES Santana, Enrique
On Chiapas land dispute unrest 6-1, 465A3

OLIVER, Al
AL batting ldr 10-6, 926D3-F3

OLIVER, Michael
New Hebrides rebels linked 6-8, 436E2

OLIVIER, George Borg
Dies 10-29, 876A3

1976

OLSEN, Rear Adm. Kaare
Denies UK MD torture chrg 1-5, 8C2
OLSON, Alice
Releases husband's death files 1-10, 24F3
OLSON, Carl
Daughter killed 10-20, 996A2
OLSON, Frank R. (d. 1953)
CIA documents made public 1-10, 24F3
OLSON Farms Inc.
Sup Ct bars review of judge removal in trust case 11-15, 882G2
OLSSON, Elvy
Named to Swedish Cabt 10-8, 794C2
OLSZEWSKI, Jerzy
Stays Polish forgn trade min 3-27, 268A3
OLSZEWSKI, Kazimierz
Polish deputy premier 3-27, 268F2
Dem conv women delegates, table 508D2
Dem conv pres vote, table 7-14, 507D2
OLSZOWSKI, Stefan
Poland OKs Bonn pact 3-12, 260A2
Stays Polish foreign min 3-27, 268G2
Named to Secretariat 12-2, 926D3
OLYMPIC Airways, S. A.
Prop plane crash kills 50 11-23, 912D2
Pilots bar night flights 11-30, 1004C3
OLYMPIC Games (Liberian tanker)
Spills oil in Del R 12-27, 1014E1
OLYMPICS—*See under SPORTS*
OMAHA, Neb.—*See NEBRASKA*
OMAHA World Herald (newspaper)
Ford endorsement rptd 10-30, 831F2
O'MALLEY, Brian
Dies 4-6, 267C1
O'MALLEY, William
On Yuba HS bus crash 7-22, 595A3

OMAN—*See also ARAB League, NON-ALIGNED Nations Movement*
Iran recalls amb 1-7, 12G3
S Yemen border fighting, Iran troop aid rptd 1-9, 1-14, 52G1 ★
Listed as 'not free' nation 1-19, 20E3
Total IMF oil loan rptd 4-1, 340G2
Cuban guerrilla aid rptd 4-5, 242A2
PFLP rptdly backs guerrillas 365G2
UK to quit bases 7-19, 594E2
Disputes S Yemen on Iran jet incident 11-25, 914A1
Hosts Persian Gulf conf 11-25—11-26, 914B1

OMAR, Khayri Tewfik
Convicted 12-9, hanged 12-18, 954A3
OMEIR, Khairy Tewfik
Survives Amman raid 11-17, 861G1
OMNIUM Shipping Co.
Cargo ship disappears 10-15, 912E1
ONAN, Umit Suleiman
Turkish Cypriot negotiator 4-15, 311B2
ONASSIS, Jacqueline Lee Bouvier Kennedy (Mrs. Aristotle Socrates)
Prince Radziwill dies 6-27, 524D3
Stepfather dies 11-20, 970B1
ONE Flew Over the Cuckoo's Nest (film)
Top-grossing film 1-28, 104F3; 2-25, 208G3; 3-31, 240B3
Wins 5 Oscars 3-29, 240F2
O'NEILL, Col. Keith
Denies '70 Viet massacre 8-2, 571F3
O'NEILL, Louis
Named cultural affairs min 11-26, 903A3
O'NEILL, Michael J.
SEC suit settled 5-10, 359G3-360C1

O'NEILL Jr., Rep. Thomas P. (Tip) (D, Mass.)
Endorses Udall for pres 1-7, 22C3
Scores State of Union speech 1-19, 40B1
Udall Mass primary results 3-2, 165G1
Platform com testimony 5-18, 357C3
Asks Hays to quit posts temporarily 6-2, 433F2
Albert to retire 6-5, 434C3
Reelected 11-2, 829C4
Carter meets cong ldrs 11-17, 864F1
Elected House speaker by Dems 12-6, 919A1
Names whip, deputy 12-8, 981D1

1977

OLSON Jr., A. William
Replaced as asst atty gen 3-18, 211F1
OLSON, H. A. (Bud)
Named to Canada Sen 4-5, 281B3
OLSONITE Corp.
Yarborough named top race driver 12-8, 1020C3
OLSZEWSKI, Kazimierz
Dismissed 12-17, 987F1
OLULEYE, Maj. Gen. J. J.
Nigeria finance comr 3-15, 393D2
OLUTOYE, Maj. Gen. Olufemi
Nigeria Cabt drops 3-15, 393C2
OLYMPIA Brewing Co.
Paymts disclosure rptd 2-4, 215D2
OLYMPIC Committee, U.S. (USOC)
Elects officers, expands athletes rights 4-29—5-1, 491G2
OLYMPICS—*See under SPORTS*
OLYMPIC Sports, President's Commission on—*See under U.S. GOVERNMENT*
OMAHA, Neb.—*See NEBRASKA*
O'MALLEY, Desmond
Named Ireland industry min 7-5, 598G3
O'MALLEY, John
Kruger pays damages 11-18, 935F1

OMAN—*See also ARAB League, NONALIGNED Nations movement*
UN Assemb member 4A1
Oil prices raised, '76 output cited 1-31, 108G2
Rebel ldr, 5 others surrender 10-14, 949A3
Sadat Israel trip backed 11-19, 890B3

OMEN, The (film)
Goldsmith wins Oscar 3-28, 264D1
ONASSIS, Aristotle Socrates (d. 1975)
Estate settlmt rptd 9-20, 808D2
ONASSIS, Christina
Estate settlmt rptd 9-20, 808D2
ONASSIS, Jacqueline Lee Bouvier Kennedy (Mrs. Aristotle Socrates)
Edith Bouvier Beale dies 2-5, 164D2
Estate settlmt rptd 9-20, 808D2
Quits Viking Press 10-13, 927B3
ONCE An Eagle (book)
On best-seller list 2-6, 120G3
O'NEAL, A. Daniel
On Alaska pipeline rates 6-28, 498B1
Report scores ICC 8-3, 651E2
O'NEAL, John F.
Sugar lobby gifts alleged 7-20, 614B1, E1
ONEGLIA, Stewart B.
To screen sex bias laws 7-18, 669D2
O'NEIL, Michael G.
To repay illegal contributns 10-27, 860A2
O'NEILL, Eugene Gladstone (1888-1953)
Son commits suicide 6-23, 1024F2
O'NEILL, Louis
Vows cable TV appeal 1-14, 43C2
O'NEILL, Oona
Commits suicide 6-23, 1024F2
Charlie Chaplin dies 12-25, 1024C1
O'NEILL, Shane
Commits suicide 6-23, 1024F2

O'NEILL Jr., Rep. Thomas P. (Tip) (D, Mass.)
Elected House Speaker 1-4, 5C3
Carter econ plan disclosed 1-7, 5B2
Swears in Mondale 1-20, 25F1
Sikes loses subcom post 1-26, 53G2
Amer Airlines gift rptd 2-9, 112B1
Assassinatn com controversy 2-10—2-21, 127C1
Vs Cong speeches by forgn ldrs 2-17, 127D3
Rptdly backs joint intell com 2-24, 151C2
Gonzalez quits com 3-2, King hearing urged 3-3, 149B1
Stokes named assassinatn com head 3-8, 228E2
Backs cong pub electn funds 3-16, 232E3
Asks halt to US IRA aid 3-17, 222E3
Common-site picket bill fails 3-23, 229D1, C2
Backs Carter arms stand 3-31, 247G1
NE-Midwest base-closing ban asked 4-6, 423A3
Chides Ford for criticism 4-19, 321F3
Names Ashley energy com head 4-21, 321D1
At Carter fiscal mtg 5-2, comments 5-3, 364D2
Defends Carter on TV 5-8, 364A3
Cautns Carter vs vetoes 6-1, 459G2-B3
Carter backs min wage bill 7-12, 534B1
Backs intell com ratio, names Boland chrmn 7-14, 557A2

1978

OLIVIER, Laurence
Betsy released 2-9, 618C3
Boys From Brazil released 10-5, 969E3
OLOITIPTIP, Stanley S. O.
Kenya home affairs min 10-11, 784C3
OLSEN, Erling
Named Danish housing min 8-30, 688A1
OLYMPIC Airways, S. A.
1-day strike staged 3-1, 149G3
OLYMPIC Committee, International (IOC)—*See SPORTS—Olympics*
OLYMPIC Committee, U.S. (USOC)—*See SPORTS—Olympics*
OLYMPICS—*See under SPORTS*
OMAHA, Neb.—*See NEBRASKA*

OMAN—*See also ARAB League, NONALIGNED Nations Movement*
Islamic, Arab poor-natn aid rise rptd 4-9, 257F2
Egypt terror group rptd smashed 4-26, 300D2
Arab fund loan to Sudan rptd 8-17, 925F3
UN Assemb member 713D3

OMENS, Estelle
Bright Golden Land opens 4-3, 760E1
OMOLO Okero, Isaac
Kenya power min 10-11, 784C3
ONASSIS, Aristotle Socrates (d. 1975)
Greek Tycoon released 5-12, 619C2
ONASSIS, Christina
Marries Sovt citizen 8-1, 844E3
ONASSIS, Jacqueline Lee Bouvier Kennedy (Mrs. Aristotle Socrates)
Joins Doubleday 2-13, 172C2
Greek Tycoon released 5-12, 619C2
ONCE In a Lifetime (play)
Opens 6-15, 887C2
ONCE In Paris (film)
Released 10-9, 970E2
ONE Flew over the Cuckoo's Nest (film)
Top United Artists execs quit 1-13, 1-16, 75B3
O'NEAL, A. Daniel
Rebuts moving indus defamatn chrg 6-30, 589F2
Proposes trucking deregulatn 11-7, 12-21, 1007C1, D2
O'NEAL, Ryan
Driver released 7-28, 970B1
Oliver's Story released 12-14, 1030C3
O'NEAL, Tatum
Intl Velvet released 7-19, 970G1
ONE Hundred Years of Solitude (book)
Royalties to fund intl rights group 12-21, 1015C3
O'NEILL, C. William
Dies 8-20, 708C3
O'NEILL, Jennifer
Caravans released 11-1, 969F3 ★

O'NEILL Jr., Rep. Thomas P. (Tip) (D, Mass.)
Park gifts rptd 1-14, 63E3
Seeks Park testimony 1-18, OKd 1-31, 64C1, E1
On Face the Nation 1-22, 64C1
Women's combat bar repeal rptd sought 3-4, 162A2
Scores Ulster violence 3-16, 373B3
Korea rpt chrgs gifts sought, rpt denied 4-4, 239A3
Vance hints Israel broke US arms law in Leb invasn 4-5, 236D2
Vs Turkish arms embargo end 4-5, 276E3
Asks Mideast jet-sale legis delay 4-25, 307B1
On Soc Sec rollback legis 5-17, 5-18, 386C1
Orders Africa aid curbs review 5-22, 383C1
Warns Korea re Kim testimony 5-31, 432D2
Sees CIA evidence on Cuba role in Zaire 6-2, 442F1
On legislative veto 6-22, 466C2
Cleared by Korea probe 7-13, 527A2
Angered by Griffin firing, new post found 7-28—8-7, 605E2
On House tax bill passage 8-10, 604E1
Backs '79 arms authorzn veto 8-17, 621E1
Diggs on com chrmnshps 10-10, 791G3
On Carter inflatn plan 10-24, 806G3
McGarry named to FEC 10-25, 831G2, A3

1979

OLIVIER, Laurence
Wins Oscar 4-9, 336C2
Little Romance released 4-27, 820F1
Dracula released 7-13, 820A1
OLMOS, Edward James
Zoot Suit opens 3-25, 712G3
OLSON, William F.
Burger assails Sup Ct bar admissn 6-25, 541B1
OLYMPICS—*See under SPORTS*
OMAHA World-Herald (newspaper)
Peter Kiewit dies 11-2, 932B3
O'MALLEY, Mary
Once A Catholic opens 10-10, 956F3
O'MALLEY, Thomas D.
Sentncd for extortn, mail fraud 1-18, 79C1
O'MALLEY, Walter F.
Dies 8-9, 671C3

OMAN—*See also ARAB League, NONALIGNED Nations Movement*
Oil price hike rptd sought 2-27, 145B3
UK queen ends visit 3-2, 190D1
OAPEC ouster of Egypt opposed 4-17, 278A2
UN membership listed 695A3
At Persian Gulf security conf, offers shipping plan 10-14—10-16, 804A2
US sets evacuatns, travel curbs 11-26, 894A2
US to seek bases for moves vs Iran 12-18, 958D2
Oil price hike set 12-29, 977D2
O'MEARA, Mark
Wins US Amateur golf title 9-2, 969D3
OMEGA 7
Sovt UN missn in NYC bombed 12-12, 965D3
Cuban missn in NYC bombed 10-27, 852D1; 12-7, 947B3 12-13, 947C1
OMER, Sultan Ahmed
Says N Yemen rebels fight govt S1-1, 158D1
ONASSIS, Jacqueline Lee Bouvier Kennedy (Mrs. Aristotle Socrates)
Sister postpones wedding 5-3, 392B2
Martha's Vineyard home rptd planned 12-20, 1005B3
ON Broadway (recording)
Benson wins Grammy 16, 6E3
ONCE A Catholic (play)
Opens 10-10, 956F3
ONDO, Antonio
Denies Equatorial Guinea coup 8-3, 613F3
O'NEAL, A. Daniel
2 reps soften trucking deregulatn stand 1-9, 111F3
Fitzsimmons asks Carter to fire 1-18, 111G3
On Rock Island RR takeover costs 9-26, 722G2
To leave ICC post 10-4, Gaskins to replace 10-12, 831B1
O'NEAL, Ryan
Main Event released 6-22, 820G1
O'NEILL, Chris
Wins Australian Open 1-3, 103C2
O'NEILL, Jennifer
Innocent released 1-11, 174G2
O'NEILL, Louis
Fired in Quebec Cabt shuffle 9-21, 750B1
O'NEILL Jr., Rep. Thomas P. (Tip) (D, Mass.)
Reelected House speaker 1-15, 30F1, 71A1
On Carter budget 1-22, 70E1
McGarry confrmd to FEC 2-21, 130D3
Gets Blumenthal debt ceiling bill plea 4-2, 251D3
In Dublin, Belfast; faults UK re N Ireland 4-19, 4-20, 312E2, D3
Standby gas rationing plan defeated 5-10, 342D2
Misses Camp David mtg 6-1, 418C2
Wayne backs Canal treaty implementatn 6-7, 481C1
Lauds Carter energy speech 7-15, 534G1
Meets Jordan 7-17, comments 7-18, 531A2
Diggs censured by House 7-31, 578F1
Arms sales to Ulster police suspended 8-2, 602B1
Sees possible Kennedy '80 nomination 9-8, 680E1
On Fla pres caucuses 10-15, 783F1
Iran hostage release urged 11-7, 842C3
Scores Hansen Iran visit 11-26, 895F2
Scores NBC Iran hostage interview 12-11, 935A1

1980

OLIVIER, Laurence
Filumena opens 2-10, 392G2
Jazz Singer released 12-19, 1003B2
OLIZARENKO, Nadezhda
Wins Olympic medals 7-27, 8-1, 624A2, B2
OLLIEL, Alain
Separatists take captive 1-6, turned over to police 1-11, 58C1, A2, C2
OLMSTEAD, George
Chrgd in Bahamas bank looting suit 3-3, 228G3
OLON, John
Dona Rosita opens 3-20, 392F2
OLSEN, Tillie
Tell Me a Riddle released 12-17, 1003E2
OLSON, Allen I.
Wins ND primary for gov 9-2, 683D1
Elected ND gov 11-4, 845D3, 847C1, 851B2
OLSON, Bud
Canada econ dvpt min 3-3, 171F1, A2
OKs Foothills pipe construction 7-22, 577E3
OLSON, James E.
On phone industry deregulatn 4-7, 370E2
AT&T begins reorgn, managemt realigned 8-20, 648G1
OLSZOWSKI, Stefan
Restored to Polish Politburo 8-24, 641E1
Scores econ planners 10-6, 760F2
Moczar reelected to Politburo 12-2, 910A1
OLYMPIC Committee, International (IOC)
For Olympics, see SPORTS--Olympic Games
Killanin bars reelectn bid 5-19, 379A2
Samaranch elected IOC pres, Gurandou-N'Diaye vp 7-16, 590D3
OMAHA—*See NEBRASKA*
OMAN—*See also ARAB League, NONALIGNED Nations*
US to seek mil bases 1-9, 11G1, A2
US base talks rptd begun 1-22, 46D1
Egypt fears S Yemen threat 1-28, 69A3
US base pacts set 4-21, 303A1; 6-4, 436D3
Iran hostage rescue role rptd 4-24, 297A2
Iraq air, troop use rptd blocked 10-3, 758F1
Iraqi planes rptd stationed 10-6, 757D1
US offers air defense aid 10-7, 758D1
Islamic League meets 11-10, 895B2
OMEGA 7
Sovt airline office in NYC bombed 1-13, 55C2
Cuban UN attache assassinated 9-11, 685A2
OMURA, Joji
Meets US defns secy; US asks arms outlay hike, cites Sovt threat 12-11—12-12, 952G3-953B1
Rpts USSR Backfire bomber coastal deploymt 12-11, 953C1
ONASSIS, Christina
Kouris sentncd re Caramanlis article 12-30, 996F3
O'NEAL, Lt. Gov. Dave (R, Ill.)
Wins Sen primary 3-18, 206C3
Loses US Sen electn 11-4, 850C3
O'NEAL, Tatum
Little Darlings released 3-28, 416C3
O'NEIL, Barbara
Dies 9-3, 756D1
O'NEILL, Ralph A.
Dies 10-23, 876A3

O'NEILL Jr., Rep. Thomas P. (Tip) (D, Mass.)
On Kelly GOP conf resignatn 2-21, 143G3-144D1
Scores budget cut calls 3-5, 168D3
Gets Carter rpt on Iran rescue mission 4-27, 321C1
Delays Nicaragua aid 5-13, 410B1
Votes vs 1st '81 budget res 5-29, 424A3
Wilson censured 6-10, 438A2
Asks King Hussein join peace talks 6-17, 450C1
Sees '81 tax cut 7-1, 492C3
Forgn aid motion OKd 7-2, 515E1
Chairs Dem conv 8-11—8-14, 610C3, 611B2
Anderson ruled eligible for fed funds 9-4, 665F2
Reelected; comments 11-4, 837D1, 843D1, 846D1
Warns veto of tax bill 11-12, 866A2
Sees Reagan, vows 'honeymoon' 11-18, 880G2, B3
Redesignated speaker 12-8, 936F2

1976

ONI, Toshiyoshi
Home searched 2-24, 190F2
Diet subpoenas 2-26, testifies 3-1, 190G2-C3
ONISCHENKO, Boris
Disqualified at Olympics 7-19, ordrd home 7-20, 563F1
ONO, Kichiro
Quits broadcast post 9-4, 838E3
ONSAGER, Lars
Dies 10-5, 970G2
ONTARIO, Ore.—*See OREGON*
ON Watch (book)
Reagan quotes 3-31, 232F2
OPEC—*See ORGANIZATION of Petroleum Exporting Countries*
OPERA—*See MUSIC*
OPERATING Engineers, International Union of
Judge bars bias 9-1, 943F3
OPERATION Sail
Ships reach Newport 6-26, NYC 7-4, 488G1, 489E2
USS Eagle in NY photo 7-4, 488C1
OPIATES—*See NARCOTICS & Dangerous Drugs*
OPINION Polls—*See names (e.g., GALLUP, HARRIS); also 'Polls' under POLITICS; country names*
OPINION Research Center, National (Chicago, Ill.)
RC church decline analyzed 3-23, 443F3
OPIUM—*See NARCOTICS & Dangerous Drugs*
OPPENHEIMER, Harry
Asks race reforms 10-5, 928C2
OPPORTUNITIES Industrialization Centers of America
Kissinger addresses natl conf 8-31, 660B3
OPUS Dei
Suarez named Spain premr 7-3, 500B3, F3, 501B1
ORADELL, N.J.—*See NEW Jersey*
ORANGE County, Calif.—*See CALIFORNIA*
ORANGES—*See FRUITS & Vegetables*
ORANTES, Manuel
Loses Connors challenge match 2-29, 716D2
2d in Brit hardct tennis 5-16, 716C2
ORBEN, Robert
Named Ford speechwriter 1-21, 40C3
ORDIA, Abraham
Supports Olympic boycott 7-17, 528C3
ORDINARY People (book)
On best-seller list 12-5, 972F2
ORDONEZ de Londono, Sara
Colombia communicatns min 10-19, 925B1
OREGER, Rev. George
Feared dead 12-5, 1009E2
OREGON
Nov '75 Ontario gunfight cited 7G1
Primary date set 22B2
Sen bars Crater Lake mining 2-4, 135A2
AEC tests on prisoners confrmd 2-28, 316C2
Portland violent crime rptd up 3-2, 336D3
Baptists meet in Portland 5-5, 951A3
Pres campaign dvpts 5-20—5-23, 373B3-G3, 374E1
Primary results 5-25, 373E1-G1, F2, 374D2
Robert Holmes dies 6-6, 524G2
Dem conv women delegates, table 508D2
Dem conv pres vote, table 7-14, 507D2
GOP pre-conv delegate count 8-14, 583D3
Reagan seeks conv delegates 8-17, 601B3
GOP conv pres, vp vote tables 8-18—8-19, 8-19, 599D1, D3
Fscl '75 per capita income, tax burden rptd 9-15, 10-12, 959E2
Carter in Portland 9-27, 724F1, C2
Crater Lake park mining curb signed 9-28, 834C2
Ford in Portland 10-25, 802F3
Election results 11-2: pres 818C1, G1, E2, 819A1; cong 830C3, state 825A3
OREGON, University of (Eugene)
Gov Brown addresses 5-20, 373D3
OREJA, Marcelino
Forgn min 7-8, 523D2
Signs Vatican Concordat revisn 7-28, 753E3
In Canada 11-22—11-23, 962G3
OREJUELA Bueno, Raul
Colombia health min 10-19, 925B1
OREN, Martin
Hearst trial testimony planned 2-4, 114C1
ORFF, Carmina Burana (record album)
Wins Grammy 2-28, 460D3

1977

Admits Korea probe lags 7-18, 556E2
House OKs Carter energy pkg 8-5, 609E2
Vs youth subminimum wage 9-15, 759C2
Sees natural gas deregulatn bar 9-23, 757D1
Korean probe seeks rent records 10-7, 816D3
Cargo preferne defeated 10-19, 815E1
In Cuba, sees US prisoners 10-24—10-28, 896F2
Offshore leasing bill blocked 10-25, 833A3
Consumer agency bill shelved 11-1, 856F2
ONE on One (film)
Top-grossing film 8-31, 712G3
ONETTI, Juan Carlos
Uruguay bans books 10-17, 905A2
OOSTERHUIS, Peter
2d in Canadian Open 7-24, 676A2
OPERA—*See MUSIC*
OPERATION PUSH (People United to Save Humanity)
Jackson at black ldrs mtg 8-29, 702D1
OPERATION Wishbone—*See 'Drug Enforcement Administration' under U.S. GOVERNMENT—JUSTICE*
OPPORTUNITIES Industrialization Centers of America
Sullivan at black ldrs mtg 8-29, 702F1
OPANGO, Col. Joachim Yombi (Congo president)
Named Congo pres 4-3, 282D2
OPEC—*See ORGANIZATION of Petroleum Exporting Countries*
OPIC—*See OVERSEAS Private Investment Corp. under U.S. GOVERNMENT*
OPINION Polls—*See names (e.g., GALLUP, HARRIS); country names*
OPINION Research Center, National (Chicago, Ill.)
'74 poll on women priests cited 5-6, 375B2
Job dissatisfactn rise found 8-9, 632G1
OPIUM—*See NARCOTICS*
OPPENHEIMER, Harry
Young in S Africa 5-21—5-22, 399A3
Manganese deal rptd barred 8-16, 657B2
OPTICS—*See also EYES & Eyesight*
Hardy dies 10-31, 872B2
OPTIONS Trading—*See STOCKS*
OPTOMETRY—*See EYES & Eyesight*
ORAL Roberts University (Tulsa, Okla.)
Roberts in NBA draft 6-10, 584B3
ORANGES—*See FRUITS & Vegetables*
ORANTES, Manuel
Loses German Intl 5-15, 431B1
'Heavyweight championship' fee probe rptd 7-8, 548E2
US Open results 9-11, 787E1
ORCA-Killer Whale (film)
Top-grossing film 8-3, 643B2
ORD, Tommy
Cosmos win NASL title 8-28, 676E2
ORDINARY People (book)
On best-seller list 9-4, 712F3
OREGON
Legislature schedule rptd 6F2
Cottage Grove schls reopen 1-11, 16C2
US Sup Ct reverses '73 land ruling 1-12, 57D3
US Sup Ct limits suspects rights 1-25, 80F1
Snowfall rptd below normal 2-1, 76G3
Drought continues, conservatn urged 2-15, 152E3
'75 aerosol ban takes effect 3-1, 323B2
Pot decriminalizatn impact rptd 3-31, 332A3
'76 per-capita income table 5-10, 387G2
Portland econ data table 5-16, 384G2
Drought persists 6-16, 492A3
Forest fires rptd 8-4, 8-9, 660G2
Rainier A-plant protest 8-8, 702G2
Washington sues 10 oil cos 8-16, 691E3
Oil cos settle fed suit 8-31, 691C3
State oil trust suits rptd merged 9-12, 691G3
'76 per capita income, tax burden table 9-13, 10-18, 821F2
GM cuts '78 Chevette price 9-15, 722F3
Boeing struck in Portland 10-4—11-17, 1005A2
Free abortions continued 10-12, 787A1
HMO unit certified 10-26, 870A1
Champion intl convictn review declined 11-7, 857B2
Bond referenda results 11-8, 879G1, A2
Correctns officer firing case remanded 11-14, 878C3
Pot law detailed 12-11, 972D3
'Guest passenger' law review refused 12-12, 960F2
Striking farmers bar Portland, Seattle grain delivery 12-21, 1003B1
OREGON, University of (Eugene)
Ballard in NBA draft 6-10, 584A3
OREGON v. Mathiason
'73 land ruling overturned 1-25, 80F1
O'REILLY, Kathleen
Consumer Fed of Amer dir 2-13, 217B2
OREJA, Marcelino
On Mideast trade mission 1-27, 101D3
Named to Spain Senate 6-15, 453E1
On full EC entry 7-28, 582D2

1978

In Lynn with Carter 10-28, 831C2
Reelected 11-7, 851C1
Reelected House Speaker 12-4, 958A2
ONGAIS, Danny
Fails in Indy 500 try 5-29, 538C2
ONGUT, Gunes
Named Turkey transport min 1-5, 21F2
ONTARIO (Canadian province)—*See CANADA*
ON the Twentieth Century (play)
Opens 2-19, 887C2
Wins Tonys 6-4, 579A3
OPANGO, Joachim Yhomby—*See YHOMBY Opango, Joachim*
OPEC—*See ORGANIZATION of Petroleum Exporting Countries*
OPERATION PUSH (People United to Save Humanity)
Jackson scores media racism 4-8, 419E3
OPIC—*See U.S. GOVERNMENT—OVERSEAS Private Investment Corp.*
OPIUM War, The (film)
Released 9-14, 970E2
OPPENHEIMER Fund Inc.
Class actn suits curbed by Sup Ct 6-19, 492B2
OPPENHEIMER Fund v. Sanders
Class actn suits curbed by Sup Ct 6-19, 492A2
OPTICIANS Association of America
FTC eyewear ad proposal scored 5-24, 434F1
OPTIONS Trading—*See under COMMODITIES, STOCKS*
OPTOMETRIC Association, American
FTC eyewear ad proposal scored 5-24, 434F1
ORAL Roberts University (Tulsa, Okla.)
Hospital OKd 5-25, 577A3
ORANGE, Alfredo
Panama agri dvpt min 10-12, 884B2
ORANGE Bowl—*See FOOTBALL—Collegiate*
ORANGES & Orange Juice—*See FRUITS & Vegetables*
ORANTES, Manuel
USTA ranks 5th 1-5, 22E3
Connors wins Grand Prix Masters 1-8, 22B3
Defies 'Super Grand Prix', loses Suntory Cup 4-23, 418B3
Wins US Pro title 8-29, 1027B2
ORBAN, Kurt
Scores US steel trigger prices 1-4, 3B3
ORECK Corp.
Trust damage award case refused by Sup Ct 10-30, 832G2
ORECK Corp. v. Whirlpool Corp.
Case refused by Sup Ct 10-30, 832A3
OREFFICE, Paul F.
Named Dow pres, chief exec 5-3, 809G1
OREGON
No state sales taxes rptd 1-5, 15C3
State govt tax revenue table 1-9, 84E2
Rain spurs alum plant production 1-10, 24F1
Marshall Field to buy Portland stores 1-20, 185F1
Wilderness area clears Cong 2-9, 109D2; signed 2-24, 218A2
'Right-to-die' law rptd 3-18, 597F3
Eugene gay rights vote set 4-25, 327B2
Carter news conf in Portland 5-4, 320G3
Primary results 5-23, 406F2
Eugene gay rights law repealed 5-23, 409D3
2 convicted in bombings 7-11, 824A3
Trojan A-plant protested 8-6—8-7, 609B3
US parks bill cleared 10-13, 834C3
Carter in Gresham 11-3, 862B2
Election results 11-7: cong 846A2, 848G2, 852B1, 857C2; state 845G1, 847A1, A2, 853D3, 857G1
Pacific Power to buy RCA Alaska unit 11-30, 935C2
Rideout acquitted of spouse rape, '77 law revisn cited 12-27, 1028C3
Portland jet crash kills 10 12-28, 1031D3
OREGON, University of (Eugene)
Brain protein study rptd 2-18, 334C1
O'REILLY, Kathleen
Scores Cong 3-4, 183E1
OREJA, Marcelino
Visits Iran, China 6-14—6-19, 576A2
OREK, Osman (Turkish Cypriot premier)
Replaces Konuk as Turk Cypriot premr 4-22, 329A1
Cabt mins resign 11-28, 922F2-B3

1979

ONE Man (film)
Released 7-27, 820E2
ONE O'Clock Jump (recording)
Asleep at Wheel wins Grammy 2-16, 336F3
ONGAIS, Danny
Wins Daytona endurance 2-4, 491C1
3d in Indy 500 5-27, 490C3
ON Golden Pond (play)
Opens 2-28, 712G1
ON Human Nature (book)
Wilson wins Pulitzer 4-16, 336G2
ONION Field, The (film)
Released 9-19, 820E2
ON Mount Chimborazo (play)
Opens 5-21, 712G1
ONTARIO, N.Y.—*See NEW York State*
ONTARIO (Canadian province)—*See CANADA*
ONTARIO, Lake
Canada A-plant accident revealed 6-16, 502E1
ON The Yard (film)
Released 1-18, 174C3
ONTKEAN, Michael
Voices released 3-13, 528G3
OPEC—*See ORGANIZATION of Petroleum Exporting Countries*
OPERATION Push (People United to Save Humanity)—*See also JACKSON, Rev. Jesse*
US Arab group gives $10,000 10-13, 780G3
O.P. Murphy Produce v. Agricultural Labor Relations Board
Case refused by Sup Ct 11-5, 884C3
OPTIONS Trading—*See under STOCKS*
OPTOMETRIC Association, Texas
Corp name use curbed by Sup Ct 2-21, 128A3
ORCHESTRAL Association, National
Mozart manuscript sold 7-16, 672G2
ORCHESTRA Rehearsal (film)
Released 8-17, 820F2
OREGON
Legislature schedule rptd 5F3
Rideout, spouse reconciled 1-6, 79D1; divorced 4-20, 392E3
Paper mill strikes end 1-30—5-9, 345D2
Alsea miscarriages, herbicide ban linked 3-1, 167F1
Atiyeh scores Calif gas hike 5-17, 361D2
Marijuana treatmt law signed 6-18, 492B3
'78 inmate totals rptd 6-21, 548C2
Goldschmidt named Transport secy 7-27, 577B1, B2
Forest fires rptd 8-12, 620D1
Scientology church loses fraud suit 8-15, 640D2
'78 per capita income rptd 9-16, 746G2
Portland Timbers sale OKd 10-15, 1004C2
Iranians march in Portland 11-8, 842A3
Atomic Energy
Trojan (Prescott) A-plant called unsafe 1-26, 90C3
Trojan A-plant rptd worst '78 performer 4-15, 322G2
Pebble Springs (Arlington) A-plants delay seen 5-9, 382D1
OREGON Cattleman's Association
Truckers strike impact seen 6-14, 463A1
OREGON Magazine
CIA-disputed article publshd 4-19, 309B3
O'REILLY, Kathleen
Meets with Carter 6-1, 418G1
O'REILLY, Terry
Bruins, fans brawl in NYC 12-24, 1004D1
OREJA Aguirre, Marcelino
In France re ETA curbs 1-12, 61D1
Defends nonaligned conf plans 8-13, 654E2
Meets Arafat in Spain 9-13—9-15, 694D3

1980

O'NEILL, Lt. Gov. William A. (D, Conn.)
Succeeds Grasso as gov 12-31, 990B3
ONE Nation Under God
DC rally held 4-29, 348D3
ONE Step Closer (recording)
On best-seller list 10-8, 796B3
ONE-Trick Pony (film)
Released 10-3, 836D3
ONO, Yoko (Mrs. John Lennon)
Lennon slain in NYC 12-8, 933E2
ONTARIO (Canadian province)—*See CANADA*
ONTARIO (Calif.) International Airport
Amer Airlines jet hijacked to Cuba 4-9, 617A3
ON the Nickel (film)
Released 5-4, 416D3
ONWARD Victoria (play)
Opens 12-14, 1003E3
OO, Brig. Gen. Tin
U Nu returns from exile 7-29, 617D3
OPEC—*See ORGANIZATION of Petroleum Exporting Countries*
OPEL, John R.
Elected IBM chief exec officer 3-25, 224E3
Named IBM chief exec 12-21, 986F2
OPPENHEIMER, Harry
Surveillance chrg cited 1-15, 60E3
OPTICAL Society of America
USSR barred from conf 2-22, 135G1
OPTIONS Trading—*See under STOCKS*
ORANTES, Manuel
Loses Nice Open 3-30, 607A3
In French Open default controversy 6-3, 606G3
USTA, pros settle rules dispute 7-16, 691F3
ORBACH, Jerry
42d Street opens 8-25, 756D3
ORDINARY People (film)
Released 9-19, 836D3
Top-grossing film 10-1, 796G3; 12-3, 948G3
OREGON
Alcan pipeline sectn OKd 1-10, 57A1
Influenza outbreak rptd 2-15, 158C3
Milwaukee Rd RR svc cut set 2-25, 346B1
DES in cattle rptd 4-24, 358F1
Natl Guard conf in Portland 5-7, 369F3
'Pyramid' money schemes rptd 5-17, 655A3
Mt St Helens damage assessed 5-24—7-4, 503C3, F3, 504B3
Mt St Helens eruptns resume 8-7, 10-17, 970C3
U of Ore athletic dept probe delay chrgd 10-13, denied 10-15, 875B3
Fishing indus aid clears Cong 12-4, 955D1; signed 12-22, 982C1, 995B3
Politics & Government
Bush in Eugene 5-14, 366C3
Primary results 5-20, 382E3-383E1, 404B3
Carter in Portland 9-23, 722G3; 11-3, 841D1
Reagan in Portland 11-3, 840A3
Election results 11-4, pres 838C1, 839F3; cong 837E1, 840G2, 844A1, 845B3, 852E2; state 845D3, 847G2, A3
'80 census rptd 12-31, 983D1
OREGON! (book)
On best-seller list 5-4, 359F3
OREGON, University of (Eugene)
Transcript scandal rptd 2-14, 469E2
Pac-10 punishes in transcript scandal 8-11, 875D1, G1
Athletic dept probe delay chrgd 10-13, denied 10-15, 875B3
Salazar wins NYC Marathon 10-26, 890E3
OREGON State University (Corvallis)
Pac-10 punishes in transcript scandal, MacVicar backs 8-11, 875D1, G1, A2
O'REILLY, Terry
Suspended over NYC brawl 1-25, suspensn upheld 1-30, 198C3
OREJA Aguirre, Marcelino
UK accord sets Gibraltar links 4-10, 274G2
Suarez shuffles Cabt 5-2, 355F1
Replaced as Spanish forgn min 9-8, 690C2
Sworn Spain min for Catalonia 10-21, 832C2
ORELLANA, Melvin Rigoberto
Slain 10-10, 829D2

1976

ORFILA, Alejandro
In Chile, lauds Pinochet 3-14—3-17; rebuts Mex criticism 3-19, 310G1
Visits Chile prison camp 6-18, scored 6-21, 464G3, 465B1
Hails Honduras-El Salvador arbitratn pact 10-6, 975F2

ORGANIZATION for Economic Cooperation & Development (OECD) (Australia, Austria, Belgium, Canada, Denmark, Finland, France, Great Britain, Greece, Iceland, Ireland, Italy, Japan, Luxembourg, Netherlands, New Zealand, Norway, Portugal, Spain, Sweden, Switzerland, Turkey, U.S., West Germany)
Rpt disputed OPEC poor natn aid data 1-12, 15E1
Italy econ rpt issued 1-26, 74A3
Rptd drafting business ethics code 3-8, 200G1
Dutch econ rpt issued 3-26, 255F1
Multinatnl code OKd 5-21, 430C3
Mins meet; adopt multinatl code, set growth rate 6-21—6-22, 450C1-B2, 458A1
Spain inflatn rpt cited 7-2, 541A3
'75 incomes, forgn aid ranked 7-12, 581G3
US proposes forgn paymts disclosure bill 8-3, 668A3
US GOP platform text cites 8-18, 611A1
France scores incomes rpt 10-12, 964A2
Rpts '74 tax rates 11-18, 905F1
Sees '77 growth slowdown; Bonn, France dispute 11-22—11-23, 975F3
Terms Irish econ critical 11-29, 1006A2
'75 oil imports down 8% 12-6, 935G3
Oct. 12-mo inflatn rates rptd 12-6, 976A1
'76 intl borrowing rptd 12-22, 976G1

ORGANIZATION of African Unity (OAU) (Algeria, Benin, Botswana, Burundi, Cameroon, Cape Verde, Central African Empire, Chad, Comoro Islands, Congo, Egypt, Equatorial Guinea, Ethiopia, Gabon, Gambia, Ghana, Guinea, Guinea-Bissau, Ivory Coast, Kenya, Lesotho, Liberia, Libya, Malagasy Republic, Malawi, Mali, Mauritania, Mauritius, Morocco, Mozambique, Niger, Nigeria, Rwanda, Sao Tome e Principe, Senegal, Sierre Leone, Somali Republic, Sudan, Swaziland, Tanzania, Togo, Tunisia, Uganda, Upper Volta, Zaire, Zambia)
Nigeria rejcts US plea, reaffirms MPLA stand 1-7, 2A3, D3, 3B1
USSR scores US Angola chrgs 1-8, 2G1
Angola preparatory summit mtg 1-8, 3B1
Angola summit deadlocks 1-10—1-13; reactn 1-11—1-15, 15E2, 16C1
Cuba vows contd MPLA aid 1-11, 16F3
MPLA display mercenaries 1-12, 16G2
Tanzania scores Ford Angola letter 1-18, 36C1
US Angola summit econ pressure disputed 1-23, 1-28, 67E3
MPLA recognized by Sierra Leone 1-29, Cameroon 2-2, 82G2
Recognizes, admits Angola MPLA 2-11, 105C2
Deadlocks on Sahara recognitn 2-26—3-1, 178D3
UN Cncl meets on Angola 3-26—3-31, 228C2
Vs Vorster trip to Israel 275F3
Arab-Africa mtg, Zionism scored 4-19—4-22, 356A1
France to join African Dvpt Fund 5-10—5-11, 355F3
Warns S Africa 6-18, 447G2
Forgn mins meet, Rhodesia tribal violence rptd 6-28, 487E3
Summit in Mauritius 7-2—7-6, 2 protest Sahara resolutn 7-3; motns on Israel raid, S Africa, Afars OKd 7-5, 7-6, 487F2
Amin vs Israel Uganda raid 7-5, 486C1
Libya denies tie to Sudan coup 501F3
UN Cncl meets on Israel Uganda raid 7-9, 515E3
Summer Olympic withdrawals rptd 7-21, 528A3
Uganda asks Kenya dispute mediatn 7-25, Mbuomoua effort set 7-27, 548G2, A3
To probe Libya role in Sudan coup 8-8, 592G2
US GOP platform text cites 8-18, 610F1
OKs Cuba aid to SWAPO 8-30, 660F3
Vs Transkei independnc 10-22, 813F1
Advice to Rhodesia natlsts rptd 11-17, 843B2
Split rptd re Namibia conf 12-21, 1010E3
Zambia ousts UNITA 12-27, 995D3

ORGANIZATION of American States (OAS) (Argentina, Barbados, Bolivia, Brazil, Chile, Colombia, Costa Rica, Dominican Republic, Ecuador, El Salvador, Grenada, Guatemala, Haiti, Honduras, Jamaica, Mexico, Nicaragua, Panama, Paraguay, Peru, Trinidad & Tobago, U.S., Uruguay, Venezuela)
Juridical Com backs Argentina Falkland claim 1-15, 96G3
Guatemala quake aid rptd 2-4, 81F1; 2-10, 120E3

1977

ORFILA, Alejandro
Credited in Paraguay prisoner releases 2-23, 167A3
US presses Uruguay re rights 2-25, 351C3
Guatemala claim to Belize backed 3-1, 190G2
Linked to Graiver, denies illegal 4-19—4-29, 371A3
Retains forgn min post 7-5, 545F1
Uruguay release of forgn newsmen urged 7-15, 7-21, 601E1, G1

ORGANIZATION for Economic Cooperation & Development (OECD) (Australia, Austria, Belgium, Canada, Denmark, Finland, France, Great Britain, Greece, Iceland, Ireland, Italy, Japan, Luxembourg, Netherlands, New Zealand, Norway, Portugal, Spain, Sweden, Switzerland, Turkey, U.S., West Germany)
Rpts '74-75 recessn job data 1-3, 29D3
Rpts Nov. 12-mo consumer price rise 1-7, 29B3
20th Century Fund energy rpt issued 1-11, 170B1
'76 COMECON trade gap rptd 1-26, 123B2
France '76 trade deficit rptd 1-26, 159E2
Rpts on world energy outlook 1-27, 169A3
Mondale sees Van Lennep 1-28, 69C1
Norway '76 GNP rptd 2-1, '77 forecast 2-2, 99F2-A3
Australia '77 inflatn rate forecast 2-3, 96E2
Rpts Dec '75-76 inflatn rates 2-7, 87A2
'76 Poland trade deficit rptd 2-8, 242E1
Finland '77 econ forecast 2-10, 182A2
Econ policy com urges Bonn stimulus pkg 3-1, 243D2
Oil spill safety rules urged 5-1, 336B3
ILO jobless data cited 5-7—5-8, 357F1
Sahel dvpt plan OKd 6-1, 458D3
3d World external debt cited 6-3, 437A3
Vance arrives for summit 6-23, 495B2
Econ rpt issued 7-20, oil deficits blamed for growth curbs 7-31, 586G1-A3
China econ growth rptd 8-16, 635A3
EC mins ask S African code 9-20, 771D1
1st, 2d ¼, '76 oil-use rptd 11-24, 999C1
Labor mins meet on jobless youth 12-15—12-16, 998E3
6-mo rpt urges econ stimulus, lauds US expansn 12-27, 999A1

ORGANIZATION of African Unity (OAU) (Algeria, Angola, Benin, Botswana, Burundi, Cameroon, Cape Verde, Central African Empire, Chad, Comoro Islands, Congo, Djibouti, Egypt, Equatorial Guinea, Ethiopia, Gabon, Gambia, Ghana, Guinea, Guinea-Bissau, Ivory Coast, Kenya, Lesotho, Liberia, Libya, Malagasy Republic, Malawi, Mali, Mauritania, Mauritius, Morocco, Mozambique, Niger, Nigeria, Rwanda, Sao Tome e Principe, Senegal, Seychelles, Sierre Leone, Somalia, Sudan, Swaziland, Tanzania, Togo, Tunisia, Uganda, Upper Volta, Zaire, Zambia)
S Africa rpts Angola war role 1-3, 85F2
Smith UK plan rejectn scored 1-25, 49C2
Liberatn Com Rhodesia mtg opens 1-29, 72A3, C3
Afars students vs French conf 1-30, 88C1
Rhodesia Patriotic Front backed 2-4, 122B3
US rep on Cuban troops in Angola 2-15, 110A2
Waldheim asks Uganda probe 2-24, 142C1
Morocco suspends ties 2-25, 160D1
Guatemala claim to Belize backed 3-1, 190G2
Arab conf preparatory mtgs 3-3—3-5, summit 3-7—3-9, 170D1-D2
Uganda Anglicans ask rights probe unit 3-14, 308A3
Ramphul lauds Young 4-8, 272C2
Libya protests Egypt actns 4-13, 361F2
Amin chrgs Angola violatn re Zaire 4-22, 317C2
Morocco fears rift re Zaire 4-23, 317A2
Afars independnc vote observed 5-8, 363B2
US seeks budget share cut; Panama, Peru score 5-13, 415F1
Eteki sees Young 5-18, 399A2
Transkei summit reps barred 6-22, 512F2
Forgn mins mtg debates summit agenda, asks Mozambique aid 6-23—7-2, 512B2
Djibouti becomes member 6-27, 512F2
Summit in Gabon marked by disunity; resolutns back Patriotic Front, score interventn 7-2—7-5, 512A1
Amin addresses summit, bares plot 7-4, 512G1
Sithole scores Patriotic Front support 7-10, 536D3
Ethiopia urges Ogaden mediatn role 8-2; com meets 8-5, Somalia quits talks re rebel role 8-8; truce urged 8-9, 608D1
Bongo seeks Goldsmith release 8-11, 635B1
Ethiopia scores re Ogaden 9-18, 715D2
UN Cncl electns held 10-24, 852F3

ORGANIZATION of American States (OAS) (Argentina, Barbados, Bolivia, Brazil, Chile, Colombia, Costa Rica, Dominican Republic, Ecuador, El Salvador, Grenada, Guatemala, Haiti, Honduras, Jamaica, Mexico, Nicaragua, Panama, Paraguay, Peru, Surinam, Trinidad & Tobago, U.S., Uruguay, Venezuela)
Venez protests CIA paymt rpt 2-22, 124A2
Orfila credited in Paraguay prisoner releases 2-23, 167A3

1978

ORFILA, Alejandro
Carter consults on DR electn 5-19, 414C3

ORGAN Donation—*See MEDICINE—Surgery*

ORGANIZATION for Economic Cooperation & Development (OECD) (Australia, Austria, Belgium, Canada, Denmark, Finland, France, Great Britain, Greece, Iceland, Ireland, Italy, Japan, Luxembourg, Netherlands, New Zealand, Norway, Portugal, Spain, Sweden, Switzerland, Turkey, U.S., West Germany)
Swedish trade plans rptd 1-10, 21F1
'76 income rpt cited in French electn campaign 2-6, 148E3
Norway paymts deficit, GNP growth scored 2-13, 134E1
Solomon on $ defense policy 2-16, 118B3
Turkey '77 inflatn rate rptd 3-1, 170D2
3d World '77 debt estimate cited 3-11, 301F1
Australia trade curbs, monetary policy scored 4-27, 327F3
Per capita incomes ranked 5-12, 384E3
Comecon '77 debt rise rptd 6-27, 505E1
Sovt-bloc shipping rpt cited 8-24, 670G2-B3
Brazil rptd top bank borrower 8-25, 828C3
Carter inflatn plan backed, '79 paymts gap narrowing seen 11-17, 918B1

ORGANIZATION of African Unity (OAU) (Algeria, Angola, Benin, Botswana, Burundi, Cameroon, Cape Verde, Central African Empire, Chad, Comoro Islands, Congo, Djibouti, Egypt, Equatorial Guinea, Ethiopia, Gabon, Gambia, Ghana, Guinea, Guinea-Bissau, Ivory Coast, Kenya, Lesotho, Liberia, Libya, Malagasy Republic, Malawi, Mali, Mauritania, Mauritius, Morocco, Mozambique, Niger, Nigeria, Rwanda, Sao Tome e Principe, Senegal, Seychelles, Sierre Leone, Somalia, Sudan, Swaziland, Tanzania, Togo, Tunisia, Uganda, Upper Volta, Zaire, Zambia)
Colonial boundary backing cited re Ogaden war 43B3
Iran warned vs Horn of Africa role, S Africa oil sales 1-20, 100G1
US, allies back Ogaden peace effort 1-21, 43F2
Spain king in Libya re Canaries 1-21, Liberatn Com backs separatists 2-21, 136G1
Horn of Africa mediatn effort fails 2-9, 100E1
Spinks-Ali rematch plan protested 3-8, site chngd 3-9, 212G1
Carter presses Ogaden peace role 3-19, 178F2
USSR scores ECOWAS 3-20, 237F1
US, UK back cooperatn 6-5, 441F2
Carter scores Cuba re Zaire 6-14, 443B1
US backs Africa arbitratn 6-20, 487C2
Zaire exiles amnestied 6-24, 652C2
Forgn mins mtg 7-7—7-15; Rhodesia, Comoro delegatns ousted 7-7, 7-8, 561D2
Summit in Sudan; forgn troops debated, resolutns OKd, secy gen elected 7-18—7-22, 561A1-D2
US warned vs Rhodesia sanctns 7-22, 561C1
China, Yugo back Africa border role 8-25—8-27, 675G2
Uganda-Tanzania mediatn offered 11-6, 860A2; Nyerere rejcts 11-9, 870D2

ORGANIZATION of American States (OAS) (Argentina, Barbados, Bolivia, Brazil, Chile, Colombia, Costa Rica, Dominican Republic, Ecuador, El Salvador, Grenada, Guatemala, Haiti, Honduras, Jamaica, Mexico, Nicaragua, Panama, Paraguay, Peru, Surinam, Trinidad & Tobago, U.S., Uruguay, Venezuela)
Venez seeks Nicaragua rights probe, Somoza scores 3-28—5-8, 376B3
DR electns observed 5-16, vote count suspended 5-17, 371C3

1979

ORFILA, Alejandro
Reelected OAS secy gen 10-24, 824D2

ORGANIZATION for Economic Cooperation & Development (OECD) (Australia, Austria, Belgium, Canada, Denmark, Finland, France, Great Britain, Greece, Iceland, Ireland, Italy, Japan, Luxembourg, Netherlands, New Zealand, Norway, Portugal, Spain, Sweden, Switzerland, Turkey, U.S., West Germany; special member: Yugoslavia)
Turkey aid role OKd 2-6, 116E3
'78 trade rise, paymts surplus rptd 2-8, 161B1
IEA OKs 5% oil demand cut 3-2, 162B1
French econ study issued 3-25, 236F1-B2
France OKs econ stimulus steps 4-4, 267B2
Turkey aid package set 5-30, 397F1
Swedish econ seen improving 5-30, 428B3
Finance mins meet, warn on oil price hikes 6-14, 437B2, A3
Tokyo summit sets energy tech group 6-29, 493F2
Rpt warns vs W Ger interest rate hikes 7-10, Bonn disregards 7-13, 586E1
Econ slowdown forecast, oil price hikes linked 7-19, 554E2
World uranium reserves estimated 7-20, 555A1
Canada, Australia econ surveys rptd 8-2, 8-3, 599E3-600A1, 601D1
1st 1/2 inflatn rptd at 11.8% 8-9, 627B1
Japan econ study issued 8-13, 615A3
French knitwear import curbs cited 8-20, 668F3
Ireland econ study rptd 8-28, 688C2
Portual econ slump persists, measures urged 8-30, 710G1
Denmark econ study rptd 9-7, 668F1
Greek econ survey rptd 9-12, 707A3

ORGANIZATION of African Unity (OAU) (Algeria, Angola, Benin, Botswana, Burundi, Cameroon, Cape Verde, Central African Republic, Chad, Comoro, Congo, Djibouti, Egypt, Equatorial Guinea, Ethiopia, Gabon, Gambia, Ghana, Guinea, Guinea-Bissau, Ivory Coast, Kenya, Lesotho, Liberia, Libya, Malagasy Republic, Malawi, Mali, Mauritania, Mauritius, Morocco, Mozambique, Niger, Nigeria, Rwanda, Sao Tome e Principe, Senegal, Seychelles, Sierre Leone, Somalia, Sudan, Swaziland, Tanzania, Togo, Tunisia, Uganda, Upper Volta, Zaire, Zambia)
Amin asks aid vs Tanzania 1-25, 85D3
Uganda-Tanzania peace efforts begin 2-21; Amin asks mediatn, Nyerere issues demands 2-28, 146G3
Pan-African News Agency planned 5-9, 342C1
SALT II communique backs role 6-18, 458B2
Summit in Liberia, conflicts erupt; resolutns, rpt OKd 7-17—7-21, 552D1-B3
PLO delegatn ldr shot 7-25, 552C1
Young urges Israel ties 9-6, 720B3
Sahara com asks Morocco exit 12-5, 981C1

ORGANIZATION of American States (OAS) (Argentina, Barbados, Bolivia, Brazil, Chile, Colombia, Costa Rica, Cuba, Dominica, Dominican Republic, Ecuador, El Salvador, Grenada, Guatemala, Haiti, Honduras, Jamaica, Mexico, Nicaragua, Panama, Paraguay, Peru, St. Lucia, Surinam, Trinidad & Tobago, U.S., Uruguay, Venezuela)
El Salvador leftists seize offices 1-16, gain Mex asylum 1-18, 59F1
Nicaragua plebiscite plan rejctd by Somoza 1-19, 76E2

1980

ORGANIZATION for Economic Cooperation & Development (OECD) (Australia, Austria, Belgium, Canada, Denmark, Finland, France, Great Britain, Greece, Iceland, Ireland, Italy, Netherlands, New Zealand, Norway, Portugal, Spain, Sweden, Switzerland, Turkey, U.S., West Germany; special member: Yugoslavia)
Belgian slowdown, joint Luxembourg current acct deficit seen 1-17, 56C2
Future food shortages seen 1-23, 49C3
W Ger forecasts econ growth 1-30, 197E3
Norway econ assessed 2-5, 100E2
UN dvpt aid fund disputed 2-9, 124C2
Turkey seeks debt restructuring 2-11; W Ger takes aid role 2-19, 135D3, F3
'79 inflatn rptd 2-13, 125B3
Steel conf meets 2-28, 204F2
UK econ downturn predicted 3-3, 172E2
Dutch 1% GNP growth seen 3-3, 173F3-174A1
Turkey aid pkg deferred 3-26, 236A2
Turkey $1.16 bln aid OKd 4-15, 295A3
Paris summit: econ forecasts issued; inflatn curbs, free trade backed 6-3—6-4, 422D1
Yugoslav deficit reductn seen 6-6, 468E3
Nuclear unit warns vs A-plant delays, '79 data rptd 7-8, 509F2
Turkey debt rescheduled 7-24, 568A1
Australia econ forecast rptd 7-29, 617C2
US stays Turkey debt paymts 10-24, 874F3
Steel indus losses seen 10-30, 822E1
UK jobless rise, deeper recessn seen in '82 12-21, 994D2

ORGANIZATION of African Unity (OAU) (Algeria, Angola, Benin, Botswana, Burundi, Cameroon, Cape Verde, Central African Republic, Chad, Comoro, Congo, Djibouti, Egypt, Equatorial Guinea, Ethiopia, Gabon, Gambia, Ghana, Guinea, Guinea-Bissau, Ivory Coast, Kenya, Lesotho, Liberia, Libya, Malagasy Republic, Malawi, Mali, Mauritania, Mauritius, Morocco, Mozambique, Niger, Nigeria, Rwanda, Sao Tome e Principe, Senegal, Seychelles, Sierra Leone, Somalia, Sudan, Swaziland, Tanzania, Togo, Tunisia, Uganda, Upper Volta, Zaire, Zambia, Zimbabwe)
Zimbabwe joins 4-18, 301A2
Obote asks electn observers 5-27, 446B2
Summit in Sierra Leone; W Sahara, other African conflicts condemned, Polisario entry shelved 7-1—7-4, 509D1-B2, D2
Chad peace conf fails 10-18—10-19, 810F1
Chad cease-fire agrmt completed 11-28; premr signs 12-16, 965E1
Split on Libyan Chad role 12-23—12-24, 979B1

ORGANIZATION of American States (OAS) (Argentina, Barbados, Bolivia, Brazil, Chile, Colombia, Costa Rica, Cuba, Dominica, Dominican Republic, Ecuador, El Salvador, Grenada, Guatemala, Haiti, Honduras, Jamaica, Mexico, Nicaragua, Panama, Paraguay, Peru, St. Lucia, Surinam, Trinidad & Tobago, Uruguay, U.S., Venezuela)
El Salvador guerrillas demand rights probe 2-6, 97B1

1976

'75 Cuba embargo end cited 138B2
US vows modernizatn 2-17, 177C2
Orfila in Chile, lauds Pinochet 3-14—3-17; in Bolivia 3-19, 310G1
Spain king addresses 6-2, 459C2
Assemb meets in Chile: Mex boycotts, rights issue stressed, US scored, aid to Paraguay, Bolivia vowed, US backs rights, trade ties 6-4—6-18, 464B2, 465A2
Orfila visits Chile prison 6-18, scored 6-21, 464G3, 465B1
Venez chrgs Uruguay asylum abuse 7-8, 542C2
2 Chile attys exiled 8-6, 711D2
Honduras, El Salvador OK DMZ 8-12, arbitratn 10-6, 975F2
US GOP platform text cites 8-18, 609F3, 610A1
Panama Canal toll hike opposed 8-26, 793E1
Cuba rejects re-entry 9-14, 832G3

Alliance for Progress

US Dem platform text cites 6-15, 478G2

Inter-American Commission on Human Rights

3 members vs Chile inactn 3-5, 310B1, E1
Kissinger on Chile rights abuse 6-8, 465B2
Rights abuse rpt publshd in Chile 6-9, 464G3
Rpts Paraguay pol prisoner abuses 6-9, 557C3
Scores Cuba pol prisoner abuse 6-11, 465G1
Chile resolutn passed 6-18, 464C2

1977

US pressure re Uruguay rights rptd 2-25, 351D3
Ethiopia chrgs Sudan raids 4-11, 328B2
Carter address stresses rights 4-14, 295C2-296C1
Orfila linked to Graiver, denies illegal 4-23—4-29, Permanent Cncl backs 4-27, 371A3, E3
Upcoming Grenada mtg cited 6-5, 6-12, 454B3, 455E2
Rights issue, structural reforms dominate Grenada assemb; Belize, Carib entry issues declined 6-14—6-22, 493C2
Surinam joins 6-14, 494B3
Carter lauds Venez rights stand 6-28, 546G1
US-Panama Canal treaty open for signatures 8-12, 621E1
Panama Canal pacts signed at hq; protocol deposited, text 9-7, 677B1, 683F2
CR, Nicaragua exchng border violatn chrgs 10-15, 802F3
Nicaragua-CR clash probed 10-26, 865E1

Inter-American Commission on Human Rights

US urges budget increase 6-14, 494E1
Rights abuse rpt submitted, pol motivatn denied 6-17, 494D2
Grenada assemb lauds efforts 6-22, 493F2
US, Venez pledge support 7-1, 546D2
Torrijos asks Panama rights probe 9-13, 699F1

1978

Carter consults on DR electn 5-19, 414C3
Gen Assemb opens: Carter stresses rights 6-21; rights abusers scored 6-23, 489D2-490A1, 496B1
Gen Assemb ends; rights, econ resolutns passed 7-1, 505A2
Amer rights conv enacted 7-18, 828E3
Bolivia vote fraud chrgd 7-19, 571G1
Venez call for Nicaragua mediatn stalled 9-11, 705D3
Nicaragua crisis debated, interventn opposed 9-21—9-23, 757C3
Venez party scores Nicaragua inactn 10-6, 799C2
Nicaragua censured re CR air raid 10-17, 839A3
Nicaragua plebiscite terms disputed 11-30—12-27, 1018F2, A3
Beagle Channel peace role urged by US 12-12, 979B3

Defense Board, Inter-American

DR Sen rejcts Nivar as envoy 11-9, 881B1

Human Rights, Inter-American Commission on (IACHR)

Paraguay OKs probe 1-9, 113F1
Nicaragua probe asked by Venez 2-8, 91F2
Uruguay abuses chrgd 3-14, 292A1
Uruguay, Paraguay, Chile rights abuses rptd 6-21, 6-23, 489G2, E3
Uruguay, Paraguay rejct rights rpts 6-28, 6-30, 505D2
Mandate extended; Uruguay, Paraguay, Chile resolutns passed 7-1, 505B2
Paraguay oppositn ldr scores govt 7-6, arrested 7-7, 559D1
Amer rights conv enacted, status strengthened 7-18, 828E3
Team visits Nicaragua 10-3—10-7, 777E2
Argentina OKs probe 10-19, 792B2
Nicaragua abuses scored 11-17, Venez hits OAS inactn 12-14, 1019B1
Chile disappearances probe asked by US offcls 12-8, 1014C1

1979

Dominica admitted 1-19, 101F1
Brzezinski sees ambs, explains US 'globalism' 5-10, 416D3
St Lucia admitted 5-22, 416B3
Nicaragua asks mutual defns treaty invoked 5-29, 409C2
Nicaragua warns CR 6-3, border policing barred 6-4, 427D1
US asks Nicaragua mediatn 6-13, 446F3
Argentina missing persons rptd 6-17, 467C1
US urges Somoza ouster, peace force for Nicaragua; Latins oppose interventn 6-21, 460D3
Somoza resigns, leaves for US 7-17, 535D1
Nicaragua interventn barred, US backs 7-30, 574A1
Nicaragua aid pledged 8-2, 603F2
El Salvador asks electn observers 8-16, 652B2
Paraguay-Somoza ties cited 8-19, 636E2
Carter cites US policy re USSR-Cuban troop issue 10-1, 739A1
Gen Assemb meets: Bolivia access to Pacific, US tin sales, other issues debated; electns held 10-22–10-31, 824E1

Human Rights, Inter-American Commission on (IACHR)

El Salvador rights abuse chrgd 1-22, 58E3-59C1
Argentine rights groups raided, files confiscated 8-10; Amnesty Intl scores 8-13, 611G3
Argentina probe opens 9-6, 683D2
Argentina revises missing persons law 9-12, 728E1
Argentina probe ends 9-18, Timerman expelled 9-25, 728D1
Argentina army rebelln crushed 9-29, 748F3
Gen Assemb res passed 10-30, 824F2

1980

Offices seized in Honduras 8-15, El Salvador 9-17, 708D1
Assemb meets: Carter addresses on rights, Argentina scores, rights res OKd, Bolivia rpt asked 11-19—11-27, 881E2, 913B3

Human Rights, Inter-American Commission on (IACHR)

Argentina rpt issued 4-18, junta scores 4-19, 309D2
Colombia DR Emb hostages visited, DR envoy freed 4-22, 311E3
Colombia DR Emb siege ends 4-27, 335A2
Salvadoran head slain 10-26, 829C2
Carter vows contd US support 11-19, 881G2
Assemb debates rpt, OKs rights res, Bolivia rpt asked 11-19—11-27, 913C3

ORGANIZATION of Arab Petroleum Exporting Countries (OAPEC) (Algeria, Bahrain, Egypt, Iraq, Kuwait, Libya, Qatar, Saudi Arabia, Syria, United Arab Emirates)

1979

Egypt ousted, embargo imposed 4-17, 278G1-A2

ORGANIZATION of Petroleum Exporting Countries (OPEC) (Algeria, Ecuador, Gabon, Indonesia, Iran, Iraq, Kuwait, Libya, Nigeria, Qatar, Saudi Arabia, United Arab Emirates, Venezuela)

1976

Venez oil natlzatn rite 1-1, 12D2
IMF mtg debates aid to poor natns 1-8, aid data rptd 1-12, 14C3
Ecuador reaffirms ties 1-14, 48G3
Paris conf sets poor natn funds, delays price conf 1-26—1-28, 62B2
IEA OKs energy plan 1-30—1-31, 108D1
Occidental Venez bribes rptd 2-14, Flores to quit 2-19, 147G3
Meets on price differentials 4-22—4-23, 298B3
'75 top US oil co profits rptd 437G1
US urges '76 price freeze 5-9, 340D1
Aids UN agri fund 5-11, 389E1
Shihata to head poor natn fund 5-11, 389F1
Holds price freeze 5-28, 389C1
Kuwait, Saudis, Iran cut prices 6-7, 6-9, 6-10; Libya ups 6-8, 407C3
Kuwait backs Saudi ouster 6-8, 407E3
US Dem platform text cited 6-15, 474E3
UK links to £ drop 6-16, 457D3
OAS scores US trade curbs vs Venez, Ecuador 6-18, 464F2
Libya '75 raid role rptd 7-15, 531F1
Meets on aid to poor 8-5—8-6, 643G1
Fails to OK price plan 8-23—8-27, 643F1
US GAO vs synfuel program 8-24, 649A2
1st ½ US deficit rptd 8-26, 668D1
US Admin warns vs boycott legis 9-27, 746C3
Rpt Greece OKs Iran bank 9-29, 854A2
Total US bank deposits rptd, '75 Sen subcom hearings cited 11-10, 915G1
Burns sees 10% price hike 11-11, 865D3
Carter cites mtg 11-15, 864A1
Venez defends price rises 11-16, 929A3
Ford asks restraint 12-1; US warns vs price rise 12-8, 12-9, 934D3
Castro scores price rises 12-2, 1000E3
Oil prices, NY stock prices linked 12-8—12-15, 984E1
Carter urges price restraint 12-14, 12-16, 935C1, 937E2
Meets; separate price hikes set 12-15—12-17; Ford scores 12-17, 934D2-935C1
Iraq, Iran vs Saudis on price hike 12-18, 975A3
IEA sees consumer demand drop 12-20, 975D3
'73-76 revenue surplus rptd 12-22, 976A2
Loans to 6 states OKd 12-23, 975E3

1977

Separate price hikes in effect; Iran, Kuwait feel pinch, set productn cuts 1-1—1-11, 11D3-12C2
Venez pledges Latin credits 1-1, price hike rptd 1-6, 23A2
US tax cut proposed 1-6, 12A3
USSR oil price hike rptd 1-6, 67E3
Saudis asks US consumer price break 1-8, 12C2
Poor natn loan funds allocated 1-10, 12D2
Mex prices compared 1-14, entry pressure seen 1-25, 66G1
Demand for high-priced oil drops 1-20—2-9, 107E3
USSR oil cartel plan rptd 1-24, rejctd 1-29, 108F1
OECD rpts on world energy outlook 1-27, 169C3
'76 revenue surplus rptd; future decline seen 1-28, 108G1
Saudis bar Qatar price compromise plan 2-6, 107G2
Saudi price plan rptd 2-14, 107D3
Poor natn allotmt set 2-28, 227E3
US, Persian Gulf weather aids Iran, Kuwait in price war 3-2, 3-24, 227G2
Cambodia rejects loan 3-3, 183F1
'76 trade data rptd 3-8, 188G2, C3
US FRB asks banker role 3-10, 363C1
W Ger scientist bugging cited 3-16, 259D3
Mex reserves estimate up 3-18, 240E3
IMF role in paymts debt managing, petro$ recycling rptd 3-28, 362F3
US CIA oil forecast 4-18, 294F1
Perez plans tour re price unity 4-19; tours 4-21—5-5; renews plea 5-9, 361G3
US energy plan 4-20, 292D2; reactn 4-22, 320D3
Carter cites at 7-natn summit 5-8, 358C1
Mrs Carter in Ecuador, Venez talks on US trade curbs 6-2, 6-12, 455A1, D2
North-South talks end 6-3, 437A2, D2
US $ strength, petro$ recycling linked 6-21, 502C1
Secret Saudi-US pact rptd 6-27, 474E1
Perez defends policies 6-28, 546A2
Price split ended, '77 freeze seen 6-29—7-5, 535D2
Carter welcomes price freeze 6-30, 515A2, 535A3
Talks held; price differences, '78 freeze discussed 7-12—7-13, 552A2
Price rise rptd feared from US $ drop 8-8, 586B1
IMF rpts '76 paymts balance, '77 forecast 9-11, 700G2
Petro$ investmts, US $ strength linked 9-30, 754A1
Iran backs '78 price freeze 11-16, 897B1, B2
Vance, Venez pres discuss prices 11-23, 912F3-913A1
'76 investmts in US rptd 12-5, 997D3
UAE asks $ replacemt, cites drop 12-6, 933E1
Developing natn investmt hike planned, US banks bypassed 12-7, 997E3
Saudis assure US on prices 12-14, 954D2
US asks Japan share deficit financing burden 12-15, 974F1

1978

GAO urges tougher US stand, Admin warns vs 1-3, 6A1
W Ger '77 trade rptd 1-3, 21D3
Price hike held unlikely 1-12, 2-10; discounting rptd OKd 2-2, 158F2
$ price base shift seen 1-13, 158A3
'77 output rptd up 2-14, Jan down 2-22, 158D2, D3
US fears $ price base shift 3-7, 234C2
'77 petro$ purchases of US securities rptd 3-22, 221E3
Carter urges poor-natn aid 3-29, 233G1
Poor-natn aid rise rptd 4-9, 257G2
US '77 trade deficit share rptd, '74-77 data 4-28, 344F2
US investmt pattern shift rptd 4-28, 344A3
$ kept as price base; Libya, others cite upturn, warn US 5-6—5-7, 341C3
No '78 price hikes seen 5-7, 341D3
Purchasing power decline estimated 341G3
US energy study sees demand exceeding supply in '80s 5-8, 366F2
Oil price freeze, $ base affirmed 5-8, 523A2
Saudi price stand, US jet sale linked 5-15, 357D2
Cutback plan rptd by Kuwait 5-16, denial issued 5-18, 384A1
US blames oil prices for inflatn 5-22, 427C2
US revises '80s output estimate 5-26, 407F3
IEA study sees '85 shortage, import curbs lag 6-5, 449E3 ★, 450C1, E1
Oil price freeze to continue dispite purchasing power loss, pol divisns; currency study group set 6-19, 465C1-B2
Sovt import talks noted 6-29, 635C1
Panel vs $ base, for currency 'basket' 7-21, 640C1
Vienna mtg 10-9—10-11: oil-refining role asked, cutbacks hinted 10-9; rift rptd 10-12, 871B1
US funds IMF program 10-18, 862G2
US $ drop fueled by oil price hike speculatn 10-30—10-31, 825F2
Mex pres in Japan; vows not to join, undersell 11-2, 903G3
1st ¾ '78 productn rptd down 11-14, 871B2
Carter vs price hike 11-17, 899E3-F3
Carter urges restraint 12-12, 957D1
14.5% oil price rise, light crude premiums set; revenues, US $ drop linked, paymt in US $s OKd 12-17; US, world reactn 12-17, 12-18; US impact rptd 12-18, 12-19, 977C2-978F2, 1004G2
Oteiba elected pres 12-17, 977A3 ★
US 2d, 3d ¼ investmts rptd down 12-19, 982F1
Mex '79 price hike set 12-20, 978E2
'78 productn rptd down, Iran unrest blamed 12-26, 1000B3, D3

1979

Indonesia raises prices 1-1, 52F1
Jamaica gas price riots kill 7 1-8–1-10, 21E2
Price hike impact on France cited 1-17, 37F3
CR raises fuel prices, oppositn scores 1-19, 238B2
Saudi denies oil cutback 2-7; Abu Dhabi, Qatar, Libya hike prices 2-15, 2-21; Geneva mtg set 2-19, 126D1-A2
'78 trade, paymts rptd 2-8, 161C1
Kuwait, Venezuela hike prices 2-26; Saudi, Iraq bar 1st ¼ hike 2-27, 145F2
US plans oil conservatn 2-27, 145E3
Iran oil export resumptn set 2-27, 145F3
US Jan trade gap rptd 2-28, 159C2
IEA 5% oil demand cut welcomed 3-2, 161F3-162C1
Algeria, Iraq, Venez crude oil price hikes rptd 3-5, 162D1
Venez vs US trade curbs 3-23, 248F1
9% price rise, surchrgs OKd, productn cut seen 3-27; US, EC, India reactns 3-27, 3-28, 227F2, E3
US $ gains, yen falls on price hike 3-27–5-1, 320G3
US Feb trade gap rptd 3-28, 252G2
Australia vs wheat price cartel model 4-3, 253C1
US ends domestic price controls 4-5, 250C2
Iran hikes output, prices 4-13, 4-15, 279E1
US Mar trade gap rptd 4-27, 325D2
Iran hikes oil prices again 5-10; Venez, Libya 5-16; Abu Dhabi 5-17, 360F2
Price hikes continue 5-20–5-31, 396B2
US Apr trade gap rptd 5-30, 403B1
UNCTAD mtg rptd divided by oil issue 6-3, 417B3
US May trade gap rptd 6-27, 480G3
Base prices hiked to $18, $20 a barrel 6-28; Carter scores, cites impact 6-28, 7-1, 473A1-C2, 494C2
Tokyo summit scores price hike 6-29, 493C1
Canada seeks price hike 6-29, 501C3
Saudis to increase productn 7-2, 495F3
Australia energy measures set 7-3, 522D1
Spain hikes oil prices 7-3, 546C1
Carter aide scores 7-7, 513E3
US energy plan proposed 7-15, lauded 7-16, 533G1, 535A1, C1
Canada raises export prices 7-19, 542E2
OECD sees econ slowdown 7-19, 554F2, B3
US 2d 1/4 GNP drop rptd 7-20, 556F2
Nigeria, Algeria oil output cut rptd 7-25, 7-30, 645C2
US June trade gap rptd 7-29, 577B3
France notes price hike impact 8-2, 614C1
Schlesinger sees $40-a-barrel by '89 8-5, 629A2
AFL-CIO cncl urges natlzn study 8-6, 629C2
Ecuador to retain membership 8-10, 613B3

1980

Mex lifts oil prices 1-2, 4F1
Nigeria hikes oil prices 1-4, 4G1
Libya oil min rptd ousted 1-8, 40E1
Venez sets 6% productn cut 1-14, 102G3
US $ drain rptd offset by gold holdings 1-18, 30B1
France rpts '79 inflatn 1-22, 97F2
Carter links oil prices, US inflatn 1-23, 43B2
Kennedy vs Carter re Persian Gulf defns 1-28, 74D3
US '79 trade gap rptd 1-29, 77B2
AFL-CIO urges US indepndnc 2-18, 146D3
IEA delays import cuts, quotas 2-19, 142D1
Kuwait sets 25% productn cut 2-20, 165G3
Pricing system devised; supply guarantees, poor natn aid backed 2-21—2-22, 142E1
US Jan trade gap rptd 2-28, 167F3
'79 Comecon sales, '80 estimate rptd 3-3, 166C1
Saudi bars US reserve purchases 3-4, 165D3
Saudi sees oil surplus, price reforms 3-5, 165F3
Kennedy 'basic speech' excerpts 3-10, 183C2, F2
US Feb trade gap rptd 3-27, 247D3
French ldr urges 3d World aid 4-14, 312D2
EC vs buying Iran oil 4-22, 298F1
IMF $ support plan shelved 4-24, 302E1
US Mar trade gap rptd 4-29, 328G3
Pricing, productn plans set; Algeria, Iran, Libya voice reservatns 5-7—5-8, 364F2
Saudi hikes prices 8% 5-14, 364F3-365B1
US Apr trade gap rptd 5-28, 401D1
Algeria mtg: $32 a barrel base price set, Saudi, UAE bar price hikes 6-9—6-10, 6 set increases, US scores 6-11, 435D2
US May trade gap rptd 6-27, 492A3
Kuwait seeks 15% of Getty Oil 7-14, 542E3
Iran cuts crude oil price, 5 natns delay hikes 7-17; spot mkt prices drop 7-21, 628B2
US June trade gap rptd 7-29, 574A3
Kuwait UN oil focus warning rptd 8-27, 643B1
US July trade gap rptd 8-27, 666B2
Reagan US pres campaign issue 9-10, 699D3
IMF oil debt role studied 9-15, 695F2
Pricing accord reached: Saudis OK $2 hike, bar productn cut; other members OK freeze 9-18, 694A3
US, Saudi secret mtg 9-18; US stockpiling rptd resumed 10-27, 826C1
Iran-Iraq war prompts halt to planned 10% cut 9-26, 735B1
US Aug trade gap rptd 9-26, 741G1
Quito, Baghdad mtgs postponed re Iran-Iraq war 10-6, 10-8, 759B1, D1
Abu Dhabi lifts oil price $2, other hikes seen 10-15, 775B1
Venez min seeks mtg 10-22, 822B2
US Sept trade gap rptd 10-29, 824G1
Islamic states given preference 11-4—11-6, 865C1

1976

ORGANIZED Crime—*See under CRIME*
ORGAN Pipe Cactus National Monument (Ariz.)
Sen votes mining halt 2-4, 135A2
Mining curbs signed 9-28, 834B2, C2
ORIOL y Urquijo, Antonio Maria de
Kidnaped 12-11, 967D2
ORION Capital Corp.
SEC accuses Seidman re Equity 9-1, 984B3
ORIS, Juma Abdalla
Denies ties to hijackers 7-9, 515G3
ORLANDO, Fla.—*See FLORIDA*
ORLANDO Sentinel-Star (newspaper)
Ford endorsement rptd 10-30, 827F3
ORLOV, Yurv
Forms CSCE monitor group 5-13, detained 5-15, 408G1
ORME, Stanley
UK health, soc sec min 4-8, 267A1
Named UK soc sec secy 9-10, 693F3, 694A1
Assailed by moderate Laborites 11-16, 906C1
ORNE, Dr. Martin T.
Testifies for Hearst 2-25—2-27, 202B1
O'ROURKE, Michael
Escapes jail 7-15, 538C3
ORR, William
Montoya audit irregularities rptd 4-12, 283G3
ORRICK Jr., Judge William H.
Sentences Hearst 9-24, 735G1
Frees Hearst on bail, denies retrial 11-19, 891C2, B3
ORSINI, Dominique
Sentenced 12-17, 971B3
ORTHODOX Jewish Congregations of America, Union of
Meets in DC 11-25—11-28, 912A1 ★
ORTHOPEDIC Surgeons, American Academy of
'75 price-fixing agrmt cited 11-17, 988G3
ORTHO Pharmaceuticals—*See JOHNSON & Johnson*
ORTIGAO, Capt. Ramalho
Scores Mozambique treatmt of Portuguese natls 1-13, 52E1
ORTIZ, Jose
France denies spy ring link 1-9, 45E2-F2
ORTIZ Mena, Antonio
Rpts record '75 IDB loans 5-17—5-19, 465F2, A3
ORTOLI, Francois-Xavier
Scores Tindemans rpt 1-8, 20B2
European Comm meets 12-22—12-23, 977F1
OSANO, Kenji
Lockheed payoffs probed 2-5—2-17, 131E3, 132F1
Lockheed rpt omits 10-15, 838B3 ★
OSCAR Peterson and Dizzy Gillespie (record album)
Wins Grammy 2-28, 460B3
OSCARS—*See 'Awards' under MOTION Pictures*
OSMAN, Ahmed
In France 1-6—1-8, 36G1
OSMAN, Lt. Col. Hassan Hussein
Executed 1-23, 502E1
OSMAN, John
Amin threatens 6-14, 502E2
OSMAN, Osman Ahmed
Replaced as housing min 11-10, 852E1
OSPINA Perez, Mariano
Dies 4-14, 316B1

1977

Venez mtg defers price hike 12-20—12-21; US, EC laud 12-22, 973A1
Debt aid to developing natns urged 12-20, 973B2
W Ger '75 Vienna raider captured 12-20, 1017D3

ORGANIZED Crime—*See under CRIME*
ORIENT Express
Service ends 5-22, 458F3
ORIOL y Urquijo, Antonio Maria de
Kidnapers drop death threat 1-2, 22B3
Rightists suspected in kidnap 1-25, 68B1
Rescued 2-11, 307E1
ORION (anti-submarine aircraft)—*See ARMAMENTS—Aircraft*
ORION Capital Corp.
Equity Funding swindle cited rpt 1-17, 78B3
Equity Funding suit settled 5-11, 408G3
ORLANDO, Stephen
Indicted re Torres 10-20, 820G3
ORLOV, Yuri F.
Arrested 2-10, 117B1
CIA link chrgd 3-4, 226B3
UK atty to defend 4-20, 314E1
US sci acad seeks info 4-27, 315A2
UK atty denied visa 5-4, 436G2
UK atty opens mock trial 6-13, 512D3
Formally chrgd 6-27, 512C3
US bars USSR book pact 12-7, 955E2
ORMET
New USW pact reached 5-24, 422E1
ORNEST, Ota
Sentenced 10-18, 812C1
ORT, John
Boxing scandal rpt issued 9-3, 828A2
ORTEGA, Rafael
Lastra decisns 12-17, 970D3
ORTHODOX Church in America—*See under EASTERN Orthodox Churches*
ORTIZ Jr., Frank V.
Named amb to Barbados, Grenada 6-29, confrmd 7-13, 626C3
ORTIZ Avalos, Roberto
Workers, peasants take hostage 11-10, freed 11-13, 969F3
ORTIZ Mena, Antonio
Submits IDB annual rpt 5-30, scores US rights stand 6-1, 438G2, 439D1
ORTIZ-Patino, Graziella
Kidnaped 10-3, freed 10-13, 871F1
ORTOLI, Francois-Xavier
Gets Eur Comm post 1-7, 74D2
ORWELL, George (Eric Blair) (1903-50)
USSR bars books entry 9-6, 765G3
ORYEMA, Lt. Col. Erenaya
Killed 2-16, reactn 2-17—2-21, 138C3, 139A1
Waldheim asks death probe 2-24, 142B1
OSANO, Kenji
Indicted 1-21, 83F2
OSHA—*See U.S. GOVERNMENT—LABOR—Occupational Safety & Health Administration*
O'SHAUGHNESSY, Niall
In AAU indoor championshps 2-25, 602E3
OSMAN, Ahmed
Named Morocco prime min 10-10, 772E1
OSMENA 3rd, Sergio
Trial delayed 2-7, 100A1
Escapes to US 10-1, 10-2, 803A3
OSORIO, Alfonso
Cabt mins back center-right coalitn 1-21, 68B2

1978

ORGANIZED Crime—*See under CRIME*
ORINASE (tolbutamide)—*See MEDICINE—Drugs*
ORION Capital Corp.
SEC censures Dirks, 4 cos re Equity Funding 9-4, 681G1, A2 ★
ORION 80—*See ARMAMENTS—Tanks*
ORKENY, Istvan
Catsplay opens 4-16, 887C1
ORKNEY Islands—*See GREAT Britain*
ORLANDO, Stephen
Sentncd in Torres case 3-28, appeal rptd 12-14, 991C3
ORLINSKY, Walter
Loses primary for Md gov 9-12, 716F1
ORLOV, Irina
Husband sentenced 5-18, 359D3
ORLOV, Yuri Fyodorovich
Trial opens 5-15; sentenced, US protests 5-18, 359B3
UK mock trial held 5-15, 360A1
West protests sentence 5-19—5-30, USSR defends 5-21, 401C1
US, W Ger scientists cancel USSR trip 6-2, 504C1
Begun sentenced 7-28, 543D1
USSR-France tensns cited 10-29, 830F3
ORME, Charles
Damien released 6-8, 619D1
ORR, Bobby
Retires from hockey, career cited 11-8, 991D1, G1-A2
ORRICK Jr., Judge William H.
Denies Hearst appeal 5-15, 379B3
ORSINI, Dominique
Slain 4-10, 396G2
ORTEGA, Oyden
Panama labor, welfare min 10-12, 884B2
ORTUZAR, Enrique
Details const draft 4-13, 351E1-A2
ORVIS, Herb
Traded to Colts 5-1, 336B2
OSBORNE, John
Rpts on Carter strategy sessn 4-29, 306E3
OSHA—*See U.S. GOVERNMENT—LABOR—Occupational Safety & Health Administration*
O'SHEA, Bernard
Loses primary for Vt gov 9-12, 716D2
OSHEISH, Mahmoud
Chrgs N Yemen invaded S Yemen 7-2, 522B2
OSHIMA, Hiroshi
WWII secret documts rptd decoded 9-10—9-18, 744C3, D3
OSHIMA, Keichi
Study faults govts on energy policy 6-13, 450G2
OSKOIAN, Gregory
Named to bakery, tobacco union post 8-16, 700A2
OSMANY, Maj. Gen. Ataul Ghany
Loses pres electn, chrgs fraud 6-3, 435A1
OSMER, Margaret
Interviews Ehrlichman 4-27, 320F2
OSORES Typaldos, Carlos
Panama forgn min 10-12, 884B2
OSORIO, Guillermo (d. 1977)
'77 death rptd 3-8, 189C1
Ex-DINA chief quits 3-21, 209A3
Autopsy details leaked by US 4-21, 371F1

1979

US oil industry protested 8-22, 10-17, 831F2, A3
US trust suit dropped 8-23, 647C3
US July trade gap rptd 8-28, 646C3
Co-founder dies 9-3, 756C3
IMF links oil price hikes, world econ problems 9-16, 719G3-720D1
Carter links price hikes, US inflatn 9-25, 723G2
US Aug trade gap rptd 9-27, 745E2
IMF scored re oil loans 10-3, 779C3
Kuwait, Iraq hikes prices 10-9, 10-18; Libya, Iran break $23 ceiling 10-15, 781B1
Algeria price hikes top ceiling 10-24, 864G1
Price hikes, US oil co profits linked 10-25, 804E3
US Sept trade gap rptd 10-30, 828B2
Nigeria price hike breaks ceiling 11-3, 864D1
Brown offers pricing plan 11-9, 962E2
Indonesia sets price hikes 11-14, 864A2
Iran assets freeze risk detailed 11-19, 880C1
Iran sets '80 productn cut 11-26, 897B1
US Oct trade gap rptd 11-29, 922D1
Caracas mtg fails to set price 12-17–12-20; chart 12-21, prices soar 12-28–12-30, 977D1-E2
Berti elected pres 12-20, 977A2
Kennedy scores Admin re price hikes 12-20–12-21, 983A3
US Nov trade gap rptd 12-28, 984G3
Gold price rise, US $ drop linked to price hikes 12-31, 978C1, F3

ORGANIZED Crime—*See under CRIME; country names*
ORGOLINI, Arnold
Meteor released 10-19, 1008A1
ORIOL y Urquijo, Antonio Maria de
Kidnapers escape jail 12-17, 997F3, G3
ORION Pictures
Life of Brian denounced by religious groups 8-27, other dvpts 10-24–10-30, 859E1-E2
ORLANDO, Stephen
Wins Torres case appeal 2-6, 156C2
Resentenced 10-30, 839B3
ORLIKOW, David
Wife rptd '71 CIA drug subject 1-29, 95G3
ORLIKOW, Val
CIA '71 drug tests rptd 1-29, 95G3, 96A1
ORLOFF, Tom
Newton murder case ends in 2d mistrial, chrgs dropped 9-27, 818C3, E3
ORLOV, Yuri Fyodorovich
US scientists cut Sovt links 3-1, 172A2
USSR prisoner total estimate rptd 9-14, 697E2
ORMANDY, Eugene
Announces retiremt 4-3, 272F1
O'ROURKE, Thomas
Suicide In B Flat opens 3-13, 292B3
OROZCO, Orlando
Venez urban dvpt min 3-10, 192C3
OROZCO Sepulveda, Gen. Hector
Townley admits lies 1-22, 58G2
ORR, William
Single-sex alimony barred by Sup Ct 3-5, 184D2
ORR v. Orr
Single-sex alimony barred by Sup Ct 3-5, 184C2
ORTA, Jorge
Signs with Indians 12-19, 1002A1
ORTEGA, Humberto
FSLN tactics rptd 332B1
Seeks arms aid 8-31, 689A3
ORTEGA Saavedra, Daniel
Named to Nicaragua provisional junta 6-17, 461A2
Meets US envoy in Panama, plans outlined 6-27, 475A3, C3
Eases curfew, press curbs 8-9, 615E3, 616B1
In US; seeks aid, denies Latin interventn 9-24, 731C3
Repudiates forgn debt 9-28, 753D2
ORTHODOX Rabbis of the United States and Canada
Life of Brian denounced 8-27, 859G1
ORTIN Gil, Gen. Constantino
Assassinated 1-3, 40F1
Funeral 1-4, king scores mil unrest 1-6; murder suspects arrested 1-8, 60F3-61C1
ORTIZ, Rev. Octavio
Killed 1-20, mourning set 1-22, 59E1
ORTIZ de Rosas, Carlos
Named Argentine amb to UK 11-16, 906D2
ORTIZ Molina, Julio
Testimony on soclsts '78 deaths rptd 5-3, 350E2
ORWELL, George (Eric Blair) (1903-1950)
USSR seizes Animal Farm 9-4, 690D1
OSCAR Mayer & Co.
State age bias filings required by Sup Ct, time limit barred 5-21, 400D2
OSCAR Mayer & Co. v. Evans
Case decided by Sup Ct 5-21, 400D2
OSGOOD, Suzanne
Seized in Kennedy's office 11-28, 962D2
OSHA—*See U.S. GOVERNMENT–LABOR–Occupational Safety & Labor Administration*
OSMAN, Ahmed
Resigns as Morocco premr 3-23, 271E1
OSORIO, Alfonso
Forms rightist coalitn 1-16, 61B2
OSSER, Irving A.
Jordan cocaine allegatns rptd 9-16, 9-26, 767E2

1980

Africa members meet, pledge African exports 11-8—11-9, 864D2
Stockpilers warned, US reductn rptd 11-17; IEA disputes data 11-23, 895F2, A3
Sept output at 5-yr low 11-23; Indonesia sees Dec price rise 11-24, UAE backs freeze 11-25, 895C2
US Oct trade gap rptd 11-28, 916A2
IEA sets '81 buying curb 12-9, 932A1
Bali mtg: 'broad' price accord reached, Ortiz term extended 12-15—12-16, 951D1-B3
US Nov trade gap rptd 12-30, 984A2

ORGANIZED Crime—*See CRIME--Organized Crime*
ORGAN Pipe National Monument (Ariz.)
14 El Salvador aliens rescued, 13 dead 7-4—7-5; search continues 7-7, 518E2-C3; 4 held 7-11, 7-19, 560E2
ORLOV, Yuri Fyodorovich
Science conf hears paper 4-13, 326F2
US scientists seek Sovt boycott 4-16, 326A3
ORLOVA, Raisa
CP, writers' union ousts re Sakharov 3-12, 3-15, 181C3
Sovts expel 11-12, 863A2
ORMANDY, Eugene
Gives final concert 8-23, 908D1
ORME Dam (Ariz.)
Constructn appropriatn clears Cong 6-25, 9-10, Carter signs 10-1, 803E2
ORMSBY, Alan
My Bodyguard released 8-1, 675B3
ORMSKERK, Frits
Executed 5-2, 410G2
ORR, Donald
Rozelle defends pass call 1-7, 23G1
ORR, Lt. Gov. Robert D. (R, Ind.)
Elected Ind gov 11-4, 845E2, 847E1, 851A1
ORREGO Villacorta, Eduardo
Wins Lima mayoral electn 11-23, 923B1
ORSINI, Bette Swenson
Wins Pulitzer 4-14, 296F2
ORSTEAD, Hans-Henrik
Wins Olympic medal 7-24, 622F2
ORSZULIK, Rev. Alojzy
Polish bishops warn dissidents 12-12, 976C1
ORTEGA Saavedra, Daniel
Defends El Pueblo closing 1-26, 118A1
Stresses natl unity 7-19, 565D3
ORT Federation, American (ORT)
Iran parlt ousts Jew 8-17, 644A3
ORTIZ, Frank
Spanish amb takes refuge 2-1, 98A3
ORTIZ, Rene G.
Warns on oil stockpiling 11-17, 895F2
OPEC term extended 12-16, 951B3
ORTIZ Mena, Antonio
Reelected IDB pres 11-1, 864E3
OSANN, Edward
Vs Carter dam support 10-1, 803A3
OSBORN, Paul
Morning's at Seven opens 4-10, 392E3
OSBORN, William
Sim opens 6-2, 756G3
OSHA (Occupational Safety & Health Administration)—*See under U.S. GOVERNMENT--LABOR*
OSHIMA, Tsunetoshi
Arrested as spy 1-18, 60B1
OSMANOLIEV, Kanibek
Wins Olympic medal 7-20, 624D2
OSMENA Jr., Sergio
Arrest warrant issued 10-20, 809C1
O Sole Mio (recording)
Pavarotti wins Grammy 2-27, 296F3
OSPINA, Ivan
Escapes prison 6-25, 521A2

1976

OSSOLA, Rinaldo
Sworn Italy trade min 7-30, 573G1
OSTRY, Sylvia
Stats Canada probe rpt issued 11-12, 888E2
OSWALD, Lee Harvey (1939-63)
CIA memos on Cuban links rptd 3-20, 3-21, 217A2
OSWEGO-Peace (Liberian tanker)
Leaks oil in Thames R 12-28, 1014G1
OTERO, Rolando
2 testify at bombing trial 8-17, 8-18, 791F1
OTIS, Amos
AL batting ldr 10-4, 796C1
OTIS Elevator Co.
SEC rpts paymts probe 5-12, 728E2
USSR pact rptd 10-9, 907G3
OTIS McAllister Export Corp.
Arab boycott rpt released 10-18, 786A1
OTTINGER, Rep. Richard L. (D, N.Y.)
Reelected 11-2, 830B2
OTTO, Alexander
Shoots French amb in mishap 11-6, 910A2
OUEDRAOGO, Capt. Mahamadou
Upper Volta transport min 2-9, 269C3
OUELLET, Andre
Ruled in contempt 1-23, 72E1
Mackay chrgs 3 mins interfere 2-20, 188A1
Resigns 3-16, 220D3-221B2
Replaced in Cabt post 9-15, 692F1
Ct rules on appeal 10-20, 851F2
Named urban affairs min 11-3, 851E2
OUELLETTE, Jocelyne
Recount stalled 12-3, 924E1
Wins recount 12-22, 998B3
OULD Ahmed, Mohamed Lamine
SADR prime min 3-5, 178G2
Sees Castro 3-14, 251C3
Morocco arrest warrant 3-26, 277C3
OULD Mustafa, Brahim Ghali
SADR cabt min 3-5, 178A3
OUTLER, Rev. Dr. Albert
Vs homosexuality 5-5, 951A3
OVANDO Candia, Gen. Alfredo (ret.)
Guevara death controversy 4-14—5-13, 415D3
OVEN Fork, Ky.—*See KENTUCKY*
OVINNIKOV, Richard S.
Disputes PLO UN seating 5-4, 320D1

1977

OSSWALD, Albert
'76 resignatn cited 353B1
OSTENRIEDER, Gerda
Sentenced in W Ger for spying 9-23, 968D2
OSWALD, Lee Harvey (1939-63)
De Mohrenschildt found dead 3-29, 228B3
FBI releases assassinatn files 12-1, 12-7, 943D1
OSWALD, Robert L.
ICC suspends 6-8, 500C3
ICC fires 12-8, 1007E1
OTA—*See U.S. GOVERNMENT—TECHNOLOGY Assessment, Office of,*
OTEIFI, Gamal
Out as informatn min 2-1, 83G1
OTERO, Rolando
Sentenced 3-18, 288E3
OTERO Novas, Jose Manuel
Spain premr's office min 7-5, 545C2
OTERO Silva, Miguel
Asks US end Nicaragua aid 3-25, 476C1
OTHER Side of Midnight, The (book)
On paperback best-seller list 8-14, 643A2
OTHER Side of Midnight, The (film)
Top-grossing film 7-6, 548G3; 9-4, 712F3
OTIS Elevator Co.—*See UNITED Technologies Corp.*
OTTAWAY, David
Ethiopia ousts 4-25, 327C3
Ethiopia reentry rptd 9-23, 830F1
OTTAWAY, Mark
Roots sources doubted 4-10, 356C1
OTTOLINA, Renny
Independent pres bid rptd 8-26, 674C2
OUATTARA, Patrice
Upper Volta planning min 1-14, 183A2
OUEDRAOGO, Paul-Ismael
Upper Volta post min 1-14, 183B2
OUR Mims (race horse)
Named top 3-yr old filly 12-13, 970F3
OUTDOOR Recreation, Bureau of—*See under U.S. GOVERNMENT—INTERIOR*
OVERSEAS Private Investment Corp.—*See under U.S. GOVERNMENT*
OVERSEAS Writers (Washington, D.C.)
Brzezinski addresses 10-18, 866D1
OVSHINSKY, Stanford R.
Rpts solar cell advances 7-5, 558E3

1978

OSSOLA, Rinaldo
Named Italy forgn trade min 3-11, 191C1
OSTERMAN, Lester
Crucifer of Blood opens 9-28, 1031C1
OSTLUND, John
Wins primary for Wyo gov 9-12, 736C2
Loses electn for Wyo gov 11-7, 856G1
OSTRER, Louis C.
Indicted 7-18, 599D1
OSTROW, Stuart
Stages opens 3-19, 760D3
OSWALD, Barbara Ann
Shot to death 5-24, 1029F1
OSWALD, Lee Harvey (1939-63)
CIA bid to discredit Warren Comm critics detailed 1-4, 14C3
More JFK assassinatn files released 1-18, 109F3
Cuba consul on '63 emb visit 8-2, 831D1
JFK assassinatn hearings 9-6—9-11, 697D3
JFK assassinatn com ends hearings 9-28, 749B2-750C1
JFK murder film assessed 11-26, 916F1
House com finds JFK plot likely 12-30, 1002B1, C1
OSWALD, Robert L.
ICC fires Kyle 6-7, 570G1
Indicted 9-22, pleads not guilty 9-29; challenges dismissal 9-25, 770E2
Acquitted 12-21, 1007G3
OSWALD, Robin
Held in jet hijacking 12-21, 1029F1
OTA—*See U.S. GOVERNMENT—CONGRESS—Technology Assessment, Office of*
OTEC (Ocean Thermal Energy Conversion)—*See THERMAL Energy*
OTEIBA, Sheik Manae Said al-
Elected OPEC pres, defends price rise 12-17, 977A3★, G3★
OTERO, Rolando
Rptd questioned in Letelier murder probe 4-17, 287E2
OTHELLO (play)
Opens 1-30, 887D2
OTHER Side of the Mountain, The. Part II (film)
Released 3-24, 619C3
Fox fined for 'block booking' 9-12, 759C2
OTIS, Amos
AL batting ldr 10-2, 928E3
OTIS, Arlene
Chrgd in welfare fraud 5-8, 684F3
OTIS Elevator Co.
United Tech takeover cited 9-25, 896G1
O'TOOLE, Stanley
Boys From Brazil released 10-5, 969D3
OTTAWA (Canadian province)—*See CANADA*
OTTAWA, Kan.—*See KANSAS*
OTTER, C. L. (Butch)
3d in Idaho primary for gov 8-8, 625E3
OTTINGER, Rep. Richard L. (D, N.Y.)
Consumer group lauds 3-4, 183D1
GAO rpt scores Conrail safety efforts 3-15, 224F3-225A1
India uranium sale OKd by House 7-12, 551F1
Reelected 11-7, 851F3
OTTOLINA, Renny
Dies in plane crash 3-16, 231A1
Pres poll rptd 3-24, 270A1
OUEDRAOGO, Gerard Kango
Upper Volta Natl Assemb pres 6-9, 479F2
OUEDRAOGO, Macaire
Lamizana elected Upper Volta pres 5-28, 479E2
OUELLETTE, Andre
Canada Urban Affairs Min to disband 11-24, 921C3
OUKO, Robert John
Kenya econ min 10-11, 784C3
OULD Daddah, Moktar (Mauritanian president; deposed July 10)
Deposed 7-10, 535B1
Transfer rptd 7-17, 577G1
OULD Salek, Col. Mustapha (Mauritanian head of state)
Deposes Ould Daddah 7-10, 535C1
Backs peaceful Sahara solutn 7-14, 562C2
Sets freedom guarantees 7-14, 577G1
OUTBOARD Marine Corp.
EPA sues on Johnson PCB pollutn 3-17, 243B1
OUTER Space, Committee on the Peaceful Uses of—*See under UNITED Nations*
OUTLET Co.
FCC OKs WTOP purchase 5-11, 599G3
OUT of the Blue (recording)
On best-seller list 2-4, 116G3
OUTSIDE (Rolling Stone publication)
India confrms rpt of A-device loss 4-17, 288C2
OUZOUNIAN, Richard
Bistro Car opens 3-23, 887B1
OVERSEAS Press Club
Questns Pulitzer photo authenticity 4-17, 315F1
OVERSEAS Private Investment Corp.—*See under U.S. GOVERNMENT*
OVSEPYAN, Elisa
Ends US emb sit-in 11-1, 947A2
OVSHINSKY, Stanford R.
Claims solar cell breakthrough 11-30, scientists cautious 11-30, 12-1, 983E1-D2

1979

OSSINING (N.Y.) Correctional Facility
Cuban defector released 2-21, 442G1
OSSOLA, Rinaldo
Italy Cabt excludes 3-20, 212D1
OSTERMAN, Lester
Getting Out opens 5-15, 711B3
OSWALD, Barbara Ann (d. 1978)
Trapnell sentncd 2-9, 119D2
OSWALD, Lee Harvey (1939-63)
Ruby organized crime link rptd unproven 1-3, 4E1
Author files exhumatn suit 1-9, wins med data access 2-23, 166A3
'Look-alike' dies 1-14, 93C2
New JFK murder film rptd 2-8, 166E1
'63 death threat revealed 2-18, 166D2
House com suspects organized crime link 3-16, 204G3
House com final rpt issued 7-17, 538F1
Exhumatn sought; substitutn theory discounted 10-22, 905A3
OSWALD, Marguerite
Scores son substitutn theory 10-22, 905A3
OSWALD, Robert L.
ICC dismissal backed 3-5, 309D1
OTA—*See U.S. GOVERNMENT-CONGRESS-Technology Assessment, Office of*
O-T-C (Over-the-Counter) Market—*See STOCKS*
OTERO, Jack
Backs Carter reelectn 7-30, 593D3
OTEYEZA, Jose Andres de
10-yr dvpt plan rptd 5-4, 353C3
OTHELLO (play)
Opens 8-8, 712A2
OTRANTO, Strait of
Italian completes swim 7-14, 656F3
OTT, Ed
In World Series 10-10–10-17, 816F1
OTTAVIANI, Cardinal Alfredo
Dies 8-3, 671C3
OTTAWA (Kan.) University
U of New Mex basketball scandal detailed 12-13–12-21, 1003A2
OTTINGER, Rep. Richard L. (D, N.Y.)
Joins draft-Kennedy move 5-23, 384C2
Doubts heating oil supply claims 6-29, 514F2
OUEDDEI, Goukouni (Chadian president)
Heads Chad provisional govt 3-23, 329C3
Heads 3d provisnal govt 8-21, 638D2
OUKO, Robert
Named Kenya forgn min 11-28, 969B2
OVEISSI, Gen. Gholam Ali
Quits as Iran army cmdr, Teheran gov 1-4, 2B3; new gov named 1-6, 11B3
Iran urges assassinatn 5-13, 357G1
OVERLOAD (book)
On best-seller list 2-4, 120B3; 3-4, 173D3; 4-8,
OVERSEAS Private Investment Corp.—*See under U.S. GOVERNMENT*
OVER-the-Counter Market (O-T-C)—*See STOCKS, Bonds & Securities*
OVERTON, Dolph
To buy Liggett US cigaret business 1-26, 283E1
Liggett merger talks end 6-14, 517G1
OVSHINSKY, Stanford R.
Solar dvpt accord with Arco rptd 5-2, 419C1

1980

OSTERMAN, Lester
Watch on the Rhine opens 1-3, 136F3
Lady From Dubuque opens 1-31, 136C3
A Life opens 11-3, 892G2
O'SULLIVAN, Maureen
Morning's at Seven opens 4-7, 392E3
O'SULLIVAN Jr., William
Wins NJ US House primary 6-3, 439A3
OSWALD, Lee Harvey (1939-63)
Justice to reopen JFK probe 1-4, 17F1
O-T-C (Over-the-Counter) Market—*See STOCKS*
OTIS, Amos
In World Series 10-14—10-21, 811F2-812G2
O'TOOLE, Annette
Foolin' Around released 10-17, 836G2
O'TOOLE, Stanley
Nijinsky released 3-20, 216D3
OTTE, Paul
Chrgd re bombings 6-25, 500D3
OTTEY, Merlene
Sets indoor 220-yd dash mark 2-29, 892E1
Wins Olympic medal 7-30, 624B2
OTTINGER, Rep. Richard L. (D, N.Y.)
Reelected 11-4, 843F3
OTTO, Jim
Enters Pro Football HOF 8-2, 999A2
OUEDDEI, Goukouni (Chadian president)
Factional fighting resumes 3-22—3-25, 221E1
Truce efforts fail, fighting intensifies 3-25—4-25, 311E1
Peace conf fails 10-18—10-19, 810G1
Libyans occupy Chad capital 12-16, 965D1
OAU split on Libyan Chad role 12-23—12-24, 979D1
OUELLET, Andre
Canada consumer min, postmaster 3-3, 171A2
Drops chrgs vs butchers 4-11, 372E1
Postal contract ratified 6-2, 444B1
OUINBOLD, Dugarsuren
Wins Olympic medal 7-31, 624D3
OUR Gang (film series)
Allen Hoskins dies 7-26, 608B2
OUTLAND Trophy—*See FOOTBALL--Collegiate*
OUTLAWS (motorcycle gang)
Flamont chrgd in Ga prison escape 7-30, 654F1
OUTSIDER (film)
Released 6-3, 675C3
OVEISSI, Gen. Gholam Ali
Sees Khomeini overthrow 6-11, 433F2
OVERLOAD (book)
On best-seller list 2-10, 120D3
OVER-the-Counter Market (O-T-C)—*See STOCKS*
OVETT, Steve
Sets mile run mark 7-1, 589A2
Ties 1500-m mark 7-15, 589A2
Wins Olympic medals 7-26, 8-1, 589B2, 624A1, E1
Breaks 1500-m mark 8-27, 892G1

1976

OWEN, Gail
Adamson chrgd in Bolles murder 6-21, 483A3, F3
OWEN, Judge Richard
Denies West Pt honor code stay 6-3, 395E1
OWENS, Gail
Cited in Bolles case 11-19, 971E3
OWENS-Illinois Inc.
Venez exec seized 2-27, 208B2
Venez seizes assets 4-6, police intercept ransom 7-20, 592D3, F3
Venez exec rptd alive 8-20; kidnap probe stalled 10-9, 874C3
Bias action vs rptd 9-11, 943G3
Venez natlzatn stalled 11-1, 874D3
OXFORD, Hermann
Quits re terrorist escapes 7-10, 593F3
OXFORD University (England)
Women get 1st Rhodes scholarships 12-19, 993G3
OXFORD University Press Inc.
US files consent decree 7-27, 989A2
OZGA-Michalski, Jozef
Polish State Cncl member 3-25, 268D2
OZONE—*See 'Air & Water' under ENVIRONMENT*

1977

OWEN, David
Named UK forgn secy 2-21, 200F3-201A1
Rhodesia oil-sanctn probe set 4-8, 413D2
In southn Africa, seeks Rhodesia conf 4-11—4-17, 296D1
Jay appointmt scored 5-11, 5-12, 391G3, 392B1
Sees Mondale 5-22, 398E1
On Rhodesia Parlt dissolutn 7-19, 563E3
Sees Vance, Carter on Rhodesia 7-23, 581A3
New Rhodesia plan set 8-12; tours southn Africa with Young 8-26—8-30, 661E1-E2
Gives Smith Rhodesia plan 9-1, 699E2
Visits Spain 9-6—9-7, asks Gibraltar border opening 9-7, 717D3
On EC S Africa ethics code 9-20, 771D1
Smith chrgs deceptn 9-21, 735C1
In USSR re Rhodesia, detente 10-10—10-11, 812F3
Smith scores, lauds Young 10-17, 810F1
Carver briefs 11-10—11-11, 876B1
Rhodesia sanctns renewed 11-11, 876B1
Kaunda bars Rhodesia plan 12-6, 1015C3
OWEN, Judge Richard
Voids NY jobless aid for strikers 5-24, 463A1
Bans Macy Tris clothing sale 8-20, 651G3
OWENS-Illinois Inc.
Mass health agency suit rptd 7-12, 560C1
Strike ends 10-14, 818F3
OXFORD University (England)
Conf honors Levich 7-11—7-13, 551C2
USSR scores Levich conf 8-24, 683G3
OZAYDANLI, Gen. Irfan
Scores govt 2-10, 138B2
OZBUN, Lefteriya
Edgar Smith sentncd 4-25, 396E1
OZONE—*See ENVIRONMENT—Air & Water*

1978

OWEN, David
Sees Belize prime min 1-24—1-25, 94F1
Smith scores upcoming Malta mtg 1-25, 59E2
Sees Rhodesia natlsts in Malta 1-30, 58D3
Malta mtg ends 2-1, 119G3
Meets Sadat 2-9, 98D2
At Namibia conf 2-11—2-12, sees progress 2-13, 113G3
Backs Rhodesia internal setlmt pact 2-16, Nkomo calls 'racist' 2-17, 119B3, G3
Sees Sithole on setlmt pact 2-20—2-21, 119C3
Issues statemt on internal pact 3-3, 155G3
Muzorewa lauds setlmt pact mtg 3-6, 155G2
Sees Vance on pact 3-8, 193D1
Plays down Young remark on UK 3-9, 193G1
Sees Nkomo, Mugabe; pact talks rejctd 3-13—3-14, 193B1
Scores Sovt, Cuban role in Africa 4-5; ambs protest 4-6, 4-7, 259C1
On EC-US A-export talks 4-8, 258A2
Seeks new Rhodesia talks 4-13—4-17, 290D2-E3
Reactn to Saudi whippings 6-15, 516C1
Warns USSR re Shcharansky 7-10, 542B3
Rhodesia sanctns end barred 7-20, 561D1
Rhodesia oil-sanctns violatn study released 9-19, 755G3
New Belize independnc talks begin 9-25, 798A3
Meets China forgn min 10-10—10-13, 796G1
Gives shah UK support 10-22, 828B1
OWEN, Simon
Ties for 2d in British Open 7-15, 580B2
2d in World Match Play 10-16, 990A2
OWENS, John
UMW pensn attachmt case review refused by Sup Ct 4-3, 309B1
OWENS-Illinois Inc.
In Dow Jones indl avg 66F2
Indicted for price fixing 1-25, 67C2
Plead no contest 10-25, 1005A3
OXBERGER v. Winegard
Iowa press info order case refused by Sup Ct 5-15, 388A1
OXFORD Pendaflex Corp.—*See ESSELTE AB*
OXFORD University (England)
Nixon visits 11-30, 942B2
O YOUNG Ho
Serrano KOs 7-9, 600A2
OZ, Dogan
Assassinated 3-24, 230B2
OZAYDINLI, Irfan
Named Turkey interior min 1-5, 21E2
In Gaziantep after violence 1-17, 74A2
Blames right for Malatya bombing 4-19, 378C2
Asks martial law 12-26, 1021E1
OZDEMIR, Mahmut
Named Turkey regional min 1-5, 21G2
OZONE—*See ENVIRONMENT—Air & Water*

1979

OWEN, David
Sees Vance re Rhodesia 2-2—3-3, 98D3
Queen tours Arab states 2-12—3-2, 190C1
Carrington named UK forgn secy 5-5, 338D1
Scores BNOC cutback 7-26, 582F1
Vs center coalitn idea 11-23, 950D1
OWEN, Henry
On Carter-Ohira mtg 5-2, 320A2
OWENS, Artie
NFL '78 kick return ldr 1-6, 80C2
OWENS, Major R.
Speaks at library conf 11-16, 901C1
OWENS-Illinois Inc.
In Dow Jones indl avg 72F1
Niehous case closed 3-1, ransom effort ended 3-10, takeover bid dropped 3-13, 192E3
2 acquitted re price-fixing 4-29, 327C3
Niehous rescued 6-30, 505C3
OWUSU, Victor
Ghana pres runoff vote set 6-22, 485A3
Limann elected pres 7-10, 524F1
OXFAM (British relief group)
Cambodia aid dispatched 10-12, 779B2
Cambodia aid blocked; USSR, Viet role denied 12-20, 978G1
OXFORD University (England)
US black woman wins Rhodes scholarship 9-9, 1005F2
OYSTER Creek Nuclear Power Plant—*See NEW Jersey-Atomic Energy*
OZ, Frank
Muppet Movie released 6-22, 820C2
OZARK, Danny
Fired as Phillies mgr 8-31, 1002F1
OZAYDINLI, Irfan
Quits as Turkey interior min 1-2, 8B1
New interior min named 1-14, 40G2
OZONE—*See ENVIRONMENT-Air & Water*

1980

OWEN, David
Liberals woo Labor dissidents 9-12, 708B2
Williams bars Labor candidacy 11-28, 921F3, 922B1
OWEN, George
'Good faith' muncipal immunity ended by Sup Ct 4-16, 328F2
OWEN, Johnny
Pintor KOs 9-19, dies 11-3, 907A3
OWEN, Judge Richard
Sentences Studio 54 owners 1-18, 64C3
OWEN, Roberts
Appeals to World Ct on hostages 3-18—3-20, 203E3
OWENS, Artie
NFL '79 kick return ldr 1-5, 8C3
OWENS, Burgess
NFL '79 interceptn ldr 1-5, 8D2
OWENS, James
NFL '79 kick return ldr 1-5, 8G3
OWENS, Jesse
Dies 3-31, 280E1
OWENS, Judge Wilbur D.
Rules Sumter Cnty biased 4-7, 309A2
OWENS-Illinois Inc.
In Dow Jones indl avg 76F1
OWEN v. City of Independence
Case decided by Sup Ct 4-16, 328D2
OXFORD Shipping Co.
Supertanker sinks off Senegal 1-17; S Africa oil sale suspected, Shell sues 2-7, 108F2, B3
OXFORD University (England)
Czechs deport prof 3-9, 262D2
Czechs oust 2d prof 4-13, 326D3
OXHOLM, Tom Erik
Wins Olympic medals 2-16, 2-23, 155G3, 156B3
OZAL, Turgut
Seeks Turkey debt restructuring 2-11, 135F3
On OECD aid pkg deferral 3-26, 236D2
Coup ldrs ask econ policy role 9-15, 696C3
Named Turkey dep premr 9-21, 720B3
OZDOWSKI, Jerzy
Named Polish dep premr 11-21, 909C2
OZMEN, Jalip
Armenians kill 7-31, 606A1
OZONE—*See ENVIRONMENT--Air & Water*
OZSVAR, Andras
Wins Olympic medal 8-2, 623E1

P

1976

P-3 ORION—*See 'Aircraft' under ARMAMENTS*
PAAR, Jack
Orben named Ford speechwriter 1-21, 40C3
PAARLBERG, Don A.
Asks retail meat price cut 8-30, 667G3
PACE, Darrell
Wins Olympic medal 7-30, 573F3
PACE, Eric
Iran denies police torture 5-26, 418F2
PACE, Dr. Nicholas A.
Scores alcohol study 6-10, 443D1
PACHECO, Manuel
Testifies on Army meat fraud 5-10, 395D2
PACHECO Areco, Jorge
Loses pol rights 9-1, 678G1
PACIFIC Bancorp.
Rptd on FRB 'problem' list 1-22, 111C3
Community National Bank (Bakersfield, Calif.)
Rptd on comptroller's 'problem' list 1-26, 113E1
PACIFIC Commodities Exchange (San Francisco)
Closes, govt sues 5-10, 348C2
PACIFIC Islands
40 ACP-natns OKd EC pact 2-3, 164D3
Ford acceptnc speech cites 8-19, 612B1
PACIFIC Lighting Corp.
Seeks Australia gas 8-8, 650G1

1977

PAARLBERG, Don
Replaced as Agri asst secy 3-24, 272A3
PABST Brewing Co.
Windham dies 5-11, 452F3
PACIFICA Foundation
WBAI obscenity order voided 3-16, 215E3
PACIFIC Gas & Electric Co.
To test voltage cuts 3-18, 278B1
FPC splits on Alaska pipe route 5-2, 369B3
NRC vs A-plant reopening 8-5, 838D2
PACIFIC Lighting Corp.
Pacific Lighting Gas Development Co.
FPC splits on Alaska pipe route 5-2, 369B3
PACIFIC Lighting Gas Development Co.—*See under PACIFIC Lighting Corp.*

1978

PAAVELA, Paul
Signs Australia uranium accord 7-20, 590E1
PACEPA, Ion
Defects to W Ger 7-28, confrmd 8-8, 650F3
Defectn rptd 8-8, 650F3
W Ger spy scandal disclosed 9-1, 725D2★
Defectn triggers purges 9-1, 9-6, 741B3
W Ger drops spy probe 9-26, 868G2
PACIFICA Foundation
FCC 'Filthy Words' ban upheld by Sup Ct 7-3, 551G2
PACIFIC Gas & Electric Co.
'76 tax nonpaymt rptd 1-27, 65G2
A-plant rejectd by Kern Cnty 3-7, 184F1
Diablo Canyon A-plant protested 8-6—8-7, 609D3
Diablo Canyon protesters convicted 8-30, 941E2
PACIFIC Holding Corp.
Iowa Beef acquisitn plan rptd 11-6, 1005B2
PACIFIC Homes Corp.
United Methodist Calif immunity case declined by Sup Ct 10-16, 789E2
PACIFIC Islands, Trust Territory of (U.S.)
Bikini islanders to relocate, '54 bomb test cited 4-12, 278C2-A3

1979

P-Plane Series—*See ARMAMENTS-Aircraft*
PACCAR Inc.
Seeks Harnischfeger 6-11, 942A3
PACE, Lanfranco
Arrested in Paris 9-14, 709D2
PACIFIC Development Inc.
IRS tax seizure stay denied 1-3, 4C3
PACIFIC Gas & Electric Co.
Shareholders defeat A-power delay 4-18, 322F3
Calif LNG projct OKd 9-27, 769D2
San Luis Obispo pro-nuclear rally 10-13, 806F3
PACIFIC Islands
Palmyra A-waste site disputed 8-21, 743D3
PACIFIC Lighting Corp.
Calif LNG projct OKd 9-27, 769D2

1980

PAASIO, Rafael
Dies 3-17, 280F1
PABON Pabon, Rosemberg
Ends DR Emb siege; flies to Cuba, frees hostages 4-27, 335E1
PACE, Lanfranco
More extensive probe urged 1-2, 20A3
PACHIOS, Harold C.
Loses US House electn 11-4, 848B2
PACHOV, Mintcho
Wins Olympic medal 7-23, 624E2
PACI, Patrizio
Arrested 2-20, 194E3
PACIFIC Christian Junior College (Fullerton, Calif.)
Purdue transcript scandal rptd 1-23, 469E2
PACIFIC Gas & Electric Co.
Alcan pipeline sectn OKd 1-10, 56G3
PACIFIC Historical Review
MacArthur WWII 'gift' dispute rptd 1-30, 1-31, 115F1
PACIFIC Homes Corp.
Methodists settle fraud suit 12-10, 963C3
PACIFIC Islands
Carter sets econ plan 2-14: govs meet, set projcts 2-19—2-22, 495A1
N Marianas lose US citizenship 3-7, 495F1
Self-rule pacts signed 10-31, 11-17, 884C1
PACIFIC Islands Development Council
Created 2-19—2-22, 495D1

1976

PACIFIC Ocean
Bolivians score Chile outlet plan 1-1—1-3; Bolivia, Peru name study panels 1-7, 27A1
Bolivia mil chngs rptd 1-9, 26F3
US, Australia, NZ maneuvers set 2-19, 137D2
France bars atmospheric A-tests 4-16, 372E3
Chile rejects Bolivia seaport plan 11-26, 975G1

PACIFIC Overtures (play)
Opens 1-11, 1014B3
PACIFIC Telephone & Telegraph Co.—*See AMERICAN Telephone*
PACIFIC Vegetable Oil
SEC lists forgn paymts 5-12, 728E2
PACKAGING Corp. of America—*See TENNECO Inc.*
PACKARD, George
Loses Senate primary 4-27, 305B1
PACKARD, Reynolds
Dies 10-15, 970G2
PACKWOOD, Sen. Robert (R, Ore.)
Scott campaign gift rptd 8-30, 980E1
PADDEN, Mike
Reagan gets electoral vote 12-13, 979B1
PADDEN, Thomas J.
Testifies Hearst had gun 2-13, 201B2
PADUCAH (Ky.) Sun-Democrat (newspaper)
Carter endorsement rptd 10-30, 831G2
PAGE, Richard L. (U.S. warship)
In Intl Naval Review 7-4, 488D3
PAGE, Robert
Wins Grammy 2-28, 460D3
PAGE Communications Engineers, Inc.—*See NORTHROP Corp.*
PAGE-Europa S.p.A.—*See NORTHROP Corp.*
PAGES, Jean
Dies 10-21, 970A3
PAHANG Sultan Ahmed Shah, King (Malaysia)
Swears Hussein premr 1-15, 55F2

PAHLEVI, Shah Mohammed Riza (Iran)
Named terrorist target 365G2
CIA Kurd aid request rptd 1-26, 93B1
Northrop repays agent fee 2-23, 156G2
Kurdish leader scores 2-25, 146D1
Signs Pak, Turk econ pact 4-22, 298A2
Seeks US arms relay to Morocco via Jordan 5-22, 458D2
Secret police control rptd 5-28, 418C2
Sees Kissinger, scores US Sen arms rpt 8-6, 581C2
Drops US aircraft barter plan 9-10, 773B3
US civiln force for F-16 jets set 9-16, 773A3
Nixon '72 mtg cited 9-26, 979G3
Signs French A-pact 10-6, 773E2
US Gen Brown remarks rptd 10-17—10-18, clarifies 10-18, 787D1, B2, G2
Asked not to return Sovt defector 10-28, 854C2
UK oil-arms deal signed 11-18, 906B2

1977

PACIFIC Ocean
Australia denies Sovt chrgs on US bases 1-25, 81B2
USSR sets 200-mi limit 3-1, 147E1
US-Bolivia outlet talks 5-16, 414G2
IWC cuts whaling quotas 6-24, 497A1
US, Australia renew base pact 10-19, 800F3
Antarctic shelf penetrated 12-9, 971A3

PACIFIC Stock Exchange
Options trading expanded 3-4, 521E1
SEC limits optns trading, begins probe 10-18, 859C3
SEC scores natl mkt move delay, ITS cited 12-1, 1004F1
PACIFIC Telephone & Telegraph Co.—*see AMERICAN Telephone & Telegraph*
PACKAGING—*See CONTAINERS*
PACKER, Arnold H.
Labor asst secy 3-11, confrmd 3-18, 211F1 ★
PACKWOOD, Sen. Robert W. (R, Ore.)
Sen campaign com chrmn 1-4, 6A2
Votes vs Califano 1-24, 52F2
Backs Javits on Mideast 6-27, 496A1
On abortn funds curb 6-29, 515B3
PACOSTE, Gheorghe
Ousted re miners strike 10-21, 948B1
PADDEN, Mike
Electoral Coll vote counted 1-6, 14G2
PADILLA Fernandez, Roberto
Venez urban dvpt min 1-7, 23E2
Guerrillas attack ranch 9-24, 867D3
PAGANELLI, Robert P.
Replaced as amb to Qatar 8-3, 626G2
PAGARO, Pir of (Pakistan)
Named PNA head 4-24, 313B2
Meets jailed PNA ldrs 4-26, says govt eases stand 4-27, 313F2
On Saudi, UAE mediatn 4-29, 348D3
On prisoner arrest 5-5, 348F3
Rejcts referendum bid 5-13, arrested 5-14; followers protest, freed 5-16—5-18, 378B2
Chrgs dissident arrests 5-23, warns govt 5-24, 450B3
PAGE, Greg
USSR tour results 1-29—2-5, 263B2
PAGE, Mitchell
AL batting ldr 10-2, 927A1
Murray named AL top rookie 11-22, 927G1
PAGE, Richard S.
Named Urban Mass Transport admin 6-13, confrmd 7-1, 626C3
PAHLEVI, Princess Ashraf (Iran)
Escapes assassinatn 9-13, 745F2

PAHLEVI, Shah Mohammed Riza (Iran)
Sees Perez 4-27—4-30, 362D1
Asks Hoveida quit 8-7, instructs Amouzegar govt 8-7, 618E1
Announces prisoner release 8-17, 8-18, 655C3
Tito sees 9-8, 710C1
Sister escapes assassinatn 9-13, 745A3
Visits Carter; on oil prices, arms 11-15—11-16, 897A1
Carter visits 12-31, 1000E3

1978

PACIFIC Maritime Association (PMA)
Maritime Comm labor contract jurisdictn enlarged 3-1, 143C3-144C1
PACIFIC Ocean
USSR satellite falls in Canada 1-24, 57F1
USSR admits satellite error 2-4, 103D1
'45-62 A-test exposure rptd 2-15, 164G1
US affirms mil commitmt 2-20, 126B3
Bolivia breaks Chile ties 3-17, cites outlet impasse 3-19, 216B1
1st woman sails world solo 6-8, 653E2
US hopeful on Bolivia outlet setlmt 6-21, 489C3
US House OKs seabed mining bill 7-26, 588F3
USSR rptd leading shipper 8-1, 670D3
Argentina pres backs Bolivia outlet 10-25, 860C3
Chile sea-access dispute cited re Bolivia Cabt shuffle 11-1, 11-6, 868E3
USSR mil buildup rptd 11-9, 914G1-A2
Indochina refugee island urged 12-12, 956C2
New Beagle Channel talks fail 12-12, 979E2
Sperm whale quota reduced 12-25, 1001A3

PACIFIC Petroleums Ltd.—*See PHILLIPS Petroleum*
PACIFIC Power & Light Co.
RCA plans Alaska phone unit sale 11-30, 935B2
PACIFIC Southwest Airlines (PSA)
San Diego crash kills 150 9-25, 758D2
FAA proposes air-safety rules 12-27, 1006C3
PACIFIC Stock Exchange
LA shift voted down 2-1, 66B3
PACIFIC Telephone & Telegraph Co.—*See AMERICAN Telephone & Telegraph Co.*
PACIFIC Telephone & Telegraph Co. v. California Public Utilities Commission
Case refused by Sup Ct 12-11, 981F1
PACIFIC Western Airlines
Brit Columbia crash 2-11, 271A1
PACIOREK, Tom
AL batting ldr 10-2, 928D3
PACKAGING—*See CONTAINERS*
PACs (political action committees)—*See POLITICS—Campaign Finances; also specific committee names*
PACKWOOD, Sen. Robert W. (R, Ore.)
Scores Carter Canal pact vote deal 3-14, OKs neutrality pact 3-16, 177F2, B3
Votes for 2d Canal pact 4-18, 273B1
PADILLA, Miguel Tobias
Killed by guerrillas 4-11, 285A3
PADILLA Arancibia, Gen. David
Leads junta in bloodless coup; vows July '79 electns, swears Cabt 11-24, 913B1
PAGE, Alan
Placed on waivers, signed by Bears 10-10, 1024G3
PAGE, Geraldine
Interiors released 8-2, 970F1
PAGE Airways Inc.
SEC sues re forgn paymts 4-13, 449G1-C2
PAGUAGA Fernandez, Enrique
Quits UN post, asks Somoza resign 10-5, 777G2

PAHLEVI, Shah Mohammed Riza (Iranian head of state)
Warns Ethiopia vs Somali invasn 1-2, 43G3
Meets Sadat, backs peace moves 1-9; briefs Saudis 1-10, 26C2
Khatemi, Textron paymts probed 1-24—2-28, 161A2
Kenya ties cut 2-18, 137F2
Warns vs Afghan gulf threat, Pak splitup 5-19, 391F1
Pak warned vs Bhutto executn 5-19, 391G1
Hosts Spain king; trade stressed 6-14—6-15, 576B2
Meets Hua, culture pact signed 8-29—8-31, 675A3
Anti-Government Developments—*For complete listing, see IRAN—Unrest*
Anti-govt riots continue, Eur trip postponed 5-8—5-11, 352D3
Teheran protest 5-15; univ riots 5-30—5-31, 6-1, 437E3-438A1
Rights group vs repressn 5-16, 438C1
Warns vs Tudeh takeover 5-31, 438A1
Ousts security chief 6-6, 437C3
Rioters oppose liberal policies 639F3
Changes govt 8-27, 667E3

1979

PACIFIC Ocean
Canada, US draft Atlantic pact 1-23, 95E3
USSR steals US dummy torpedo 8-9, returns 8-10, 636F3
US, Canada in tuna dispute 8-26—9-4, 667D1
Quake hits 9-13, 800G2
Bolivia demands access 10-22, 824F1

PACIFIC Southwest Airlines (PSA)
San Diego '78 crash rpt issued 4-19, 412D2*
PACIFIC Stock Exchange
SEC asks options trading overhaul 2-15, freeze end seen 2-22, 348B3
PACIFIC Telephone & Telegraph Co. v. California Public Utilities Commission
Case refused by Sup Ct 10-1, 768D1; 10-15, 848C1
PACINO, Al
Richard III opens 6-14, 712B2
And Justice for All released 10-19, 1007G2
PACKAGING—*See CONTAINERS*
PACKWOOD, Sen. Robert W. (R, Ore.)
Elected GOP Conf chrmn 1-15, 30C2, 71B2
GOP ldrs meet in Md 2-3—2-4, 86C1
PACs (political action committees)—*See POLITICS—Campaign Finances; also specific committee names*
PADDLEBALL
Hogan wins natl singles title 3-18, 527B2
PADDLEWHEEL Alliance
Ill A-plant protest 6-3, 416D2
PADILLA, Miguel Tobias (d. 1978)
Econ offcl's home bombed 9-27, 749A3
PADILLA Arancibia, Gen. David (Bolivian president; replaced Aug. 6)
At Brazil pres inaugural 3-15, 210D1
Electns held 7-1, 501B2
Guevara electd interim pres 8-6, 600D2
Quells Bolivia army rebelln 10-11, 811E1
Scores mil coup, dismissed as mil cmdr 11-1, 833B1
Loyal troops plan offensive 11-3, anti-Natusch letter publshd 11-5, 852F3
PAGAN, Dylcia
Husband escapes 5-21, 431C2
PAGANO, Rev. Bernard
Cleared in 'gentleman bandit' case 8-23, 953A3
PAGE Airways Inc.
SEC sues Grumman, Gulfstream; case settled 1-4, 16G1
PAGOAGA, Jose Manuel
Wounded in France 1-13, 61D1
PAHLEVI, Prince Abdorreza (Iran)
ISC paymts alleged 7-9, 541F3
PAHLEVI, Princess Ashraf (Iran)
Iran urges assassinatn 5-13, 357E1
Assets identified in Swiss bank 11-26, 897D2
Son assassinated 12-7, 935C1
PAHLEVI, Princess Azzadeh (Iran)
Brother assassinated 12-7, 935C1, F1
PAHLEVI, Shahbanou Farah Diba (Mrs. Mohammed Riza) (Iran)
Iran urges assassinatn 5-13, 357A1, E1-A2
Leaves with shah for Mex 6-10, 445E3
Iran probes assets 11-26, files $56.5 bln damage suit 11-28, 897A2-B3
PAHLEVI, Princess Fatima (Iran)
French fund transfer documented 11-26, 897E2
PAHLEVI, Gholam Riza (Iran)
Iran urges assassinatn 5-13, 357E1-A2
PAHLEVI, Shah Mohammed Riza (Iran)
Riot at sister's US home 1-2, US orders probe 1-4, 3F1
US amb asks Washn advice on departure 1-3, 3C1
Formally names Bakhtiar premier, Natl Front scores 1-4, 2D2, G2
Vacations 1-4—1-5, 2A3
Names Gharabaghi staff chief 1-4, 2B3
US vows Bakhtiar cooperatn 1-4, 3B1
Installs Bakhtiar govt, plans vacatn 1-6, 11D2
Djam rejects war min post 1-6, 11G2
Rallies oppose 1-6—1-11, 11D3
Frees pol prisoners 1-9, 11D3
Asks family to cede assets 1-9, 12B1
US on regency cncl, vacatn plans 1-11, 12E1
Leaves Iran, permanent exile seen; in Egypt, plans US visit 1-16, 25A1
Khomeini hails departure 1-16, 25E2
Khomeini says 'dethroned' 1-19, 49B2
Aide urges vs return 1-21, 49E3
Meets Ford, deplored US policy shift 1-21, 50A1
Ends Egypt visit, in Morocco 1-22; delays trip to US 1-23, 1-24, 49B3
US House panel blames US intell failure 1-24, 67E2

1980

PACIFIC Lutheran University (Tacoma, Wash.)
Wins NAIA Div II football title game 12-13, 999A3
PACIFIC Ocean
Brown pledges US strength 1-12, 31G1
Pacific orgn studied 1-20, 78B2
Storms hit US coast 2-13—2-22, 213F2
Japan joins 4-natn naval games 2-26, 151C3
Cable system planned 5-19, 387E3
Australia questions US A-waste plan 5-21, 405G2, C3
Beagle Channel—*See BEAGLE Channel*

PACIFIC Resources Inc.
NW Energy offers bid 8-18, 746D1
PACIFIC Southwest Airlines (PSA)
San Diego air control zone set 3-22, 347C1
PACIFIC Stock Exchange
New options issues banned 10-10, 986E2
PACILEO v. Walker
Case decided by Sup Ct 12-8, 937D1
PACINO, Al
Cruising released 2-15, 216D2
PACKAGING—*See CONTAINERS & Packaging*
PACKARD, James L.
Chrgs Ore U delays athletic dept probe 10-13, schl denies 10-15, 875C3
PACKWOOD, Sen. Robert W. (R, Ore.)
Wins primary 5-20, 404D3
Reelected 11-4, 840G2, 845B3, 852E2
Named to Sen GOP post 12-2, 915E2
Scores Percy Palestine stance 12-9, 936E1
PACs (political action committees)—*See POLITICS--Campaign Finances*
PADILLA, Mayor Herman (San Juan, P.R.)
On Bush primary victory 2-17, 130C1
PADILLA Lorenzo, Heberto
Leaves Cuba for US 3-16, 231A3
PAGAN, Dylicia Noemi
Arrested 4-4, 308G3
Convicted 7-30, 601D1
Indicted 12-10, 963G3
PAGE, Geraldine
Clothes for a Summer Hotel opens 3-26, 392E2
PAGE, Joe
Dies 4-21, 360F2
PAGELS, Elaine
Gnostic Gospels wins Amer Book Award 5-1, 692F2
PAGOLA, Col. Javier
Dismissed after ETA raid 11-16, 903F2
PAHLEVI, Princess Ashraf (Iran)
Iran publishes Waldheim photo 1-1, 3F3
PAHLEVI, Crown Prince Riza (Iran)
Sadat offers family Egyptian refuge 7-27, 571E1
Claims father's title, US vs 10-31, 859F2
Egypt recognizes Iran 11-1, 859A3

PAHLEVI, Shah Mohammed Riza (Iran)
Iran publishes Waldheim photo 1-2, 3G3
Red Cross jail rpt issued 1-9, 47B2
Iran hostage compromise studied 1-11—1-12, 29E1
Iran asks extraditn 1-12; Iran rpts arrest 1-23, 1-24; Panama denies 1-23, 47B1
Iran ousts US newsmen 1-14, 29G2
Wounded Khomeini aide treated in US 1-17, 30D1
Denies massacre during rule 1-17, 47G1
Militants bar hostage deal 1-24, 47F1
Bani-Sadr on hostage release terms 1-28, 67D1
Kennedy scores Carter, urges UN comm probe 1-28, 74C3
US issues rights rpt 2-5, 87F2
Waldheim presses hostage release 2-7, 88G2
US, UK newsmen chrgd re gifts 2-9, 122B3
US group sees emb militants 2-10, 106C1
Iran sets hostage release terms 2-11—2-13, secret plan OKd 2-13, 105E1
Kennedy scores US entry 2-12, 110B2
Reagan defends 2-14, 128D3

1976

1977

1978

Tied to missing Leb Moslem ldr 8-31, 713E2
Protesters ask ouster 9-7, 693C1
Carter reaffirms support 9-10, 693E2
Ties intl subversn to riots 9-11, 693G1
Moslem ldr scores Carter support 9-13, 740F2
Communist coup plot chrgd 9-16, 740C1
Curbs royal family dealings 9-26, 740A2
Amnesties exiled activists 10-2, 775A1
Vows contd reforms 10-6, 775B1
Carter reaffirms support 10-10, 797A3
Press ban lifted, criticism barred 10-13, 797E2
Gets UK, US assurances 10-22, 10-31, 827G3
Prisoners freed on birthday 10-25, 827D3
Oil workers strike 10-31, 827G1
Son sees Carter 10-31, 828A1
Foes shun coalitn move 857E3
Emami, Cabt quit 11-5; imposes martial rule, vows anti-corruptn drive, electns 11-6, 857D2-G3
US backs mil rule 11-6, 858B2
For special ct to try accused 11-8, 858C1
Khomeini calls business deals invalid 11-9, 858A2
Foes vow contd resistance 11-9, 869F1
Family financial probe set 11-9, 869F1
Vs forgn help vs ouster 11-18, 894A1
Renews free electn vow 11-19, 893F2
Carter backs 11-30, 936E2
Work action cuts oil output 12-4, 929A1
Carter unsure of survival, US denies confidence loss 12-7, 953E3
Isfahan riots 12-10—12-12; supporters rally 12-13, 953F1, B2
Carter reaffirms support 12-12, 953D3
Khomeini warns backers on oil 12-13, 953B3
Names Sadiqi to form new govt 12-17; fails, Natl Front disavows 12-21, 993E1
US intellignc feud rpt cites 12-20, 994D2
Sanjabi asks ouster 12-25, 993G1
Names Bakhtiar to form govt 12-29, 993A1
Departure plans denied 12-29, 993D1
Bakhtiar on status 12-30, 993D1

1979

Khomeini scores oil sale to US 2-1, 67A1
Khomeini: Bakhtiar govt illegal 2-4, 81B2
Bazargan heads provisional govt 2-5, 81C1
US issues rights rpt 2-10, 107D3
Palace seized 2-12, 105A2
Khomeini wins CP backing 2-13, warns leftists 2-19, 125A1, B1
US severs ties 2-16, 125B3
Swiss asked to freeze assets 2-23, 144G3
Leftists fear Khomeini repressn 2-23, 145C1
Egypt Moslems vs Sadat backing 161F3
Swiss bar assets freeze 3-5, 161E1
Bars abdicatn 3-5, to be tried in absentia 3-6, 161F1
Natl Front members form new party 3-7, 180B1
US tap of Khomeini aide rptd barred 3-11, 180D1
Ex-offcls executed 3-13, 179F3
Iran suspends trials, executns 3-16, 199F1
Madani OKs US F-14 repurchase 3-27, 228G3
US offers residency 3-29, leaves Morocco for Bahamas 3-30, 247B3
Scores Hoveida, other executns 4-13, 267E2, G3
Asked to stay out of US 4-19, US denies ban 4-20, 297E3
Qaraneh slain 4-23, 297E1
Iran urges assassinatn 5-13, 357A1, E1-A2
US Sen votes vs executn plan 5-17; Mrs Javits link chrgd, denied 5-21, 388C3, E3
Sadat may offer asylum 5-24, 408G1
Bahamians vs presence 5-30, 408E1
Mrs Javits lobby role bared 5-30, 408C2
Cutler link cited re Iran and rejectn 6-4 425A3
Kin, aides' assets seized 6-7, 469F1
Quits Bahamas for Mex 6-10; US aid, Kissinger mtg rptd 6-11, 445E3
Iran sent assassinatn squad 6-16; Mex denies attack rpt 6-27, 486G2
Egypt offers asylum 6-23, 486A3
Nixon visits in Mex 7-13, 544C2
Moslem figure slain 7-21, 565E3
Linked to seized Iran newspr 8-7, 602C2
Iran cancels US arms deals 8-10, 634D3
Taleghani dies 9-10, 688B1
Personal MD executed 9-24, 814B3
US resumes arms shipmts to Iran 10-5, 773C3
In NY hosp 10-22, gallbladder removed 10-24, tumor rptd 11-5; Iranians protest 11-4; US exit offered 11-8, 843B1
US Emb in Teheran seized, return to Iran demanded 11-4; US refuses 11-5, 11-6, 841A1-C2
Iran chrgs US planned entry 11-8, 841G2; warned US 11-9, 862F2
Egypt offers asylum 11-9, 862A3
'53 coup book rptd recalled in US 11-10, 886F3
Carter vs demand on US hostages 11-12, 861C1
US rejcts UN Cncl debate 11-13, 896C1
D Rockefeller, Kissinger blamed for US entry 11-14, 861C2
Students warn on removal from US 11-16, 877D2
US hostages face spy trial 11-18–11-20 877A2
US rptd aware of trouble re entry 11-18, 879F1
US Emb hostages describe ordeal 11-18, 11-19, 879A2, B2
World reactn to US Emb takeover 11-20–11-27, 895C3
Freed US hostages read captors plea 11-21, 894F2
Wealth assessed, figures in dispute 11-22–11-26, 897B3-898B1
Hansen urges Cong probe 11-25, 895F2
Shariat Madari: extraditn not essential 11-26, 895G3
Gallstone removed 11-26, medical treatmt completed 11-29, 897E1
Iran probes assets 11-26, files $56.5 bln damage suit 11-28, 897A2-B3
Khomeini demands Iranian probe 11-27, 896G1
Carter defends US entry, denies Kissinger role 11-28, 895A1
Mex bars reentry 11-29, 897C1
Egypt renews asylum offer 11-30, oppositn ldr scores 12-4, 914D1
US seeks haven 12-1, 12-3; Egypt, S Africa, 2 Latin natns ruled out 12-5, 914B1
Leaves NY hosp for Tex AF base convalescence 12-2, 913G2
Kennedy scores 12-2, draws fire 12-3, 918F2, B3
NY hecklers seek extraditn 12-5, 918A3
Carter briefs hostage kin 12-7, 934E1
Nephew assassinated 12-7, 935B1
Carter drafts hostage plan 12-8, 934C1
Amnesty Intl scores regime 12-9, 980E2
Reagan backs US asylum 12-10, Connally scores 12-12, 982B2, F3
US Emb hostage interviewed 12-10, 934C3
Chrgd with embezzlemt in Iran 12-11, 935G1
Leaves US for Panama 12-15, thanks govt for asylum 12-16; Panamanians protest 12-18, 957A1, G1

1980

UN probe comm formed 2-17; Khomeini, militants demand extraditn 2-20, 2-21, 122A1, A2
Kennedy vs US complicity with reign 2-18, 130B2
UN probe comm arrives Teheran 2-23; comm told of family plunder 2-26, vows probe 2-28, 137A1, F2, 138D1
'60 Minutes' airs Iran segmt 3-2, govt pressure rptd 3-6, 239B1
US aide's warning re Amer asylum cited 3-4, 164F2
Militants set conditn for UN comm hostage visit 3-5, 164D2
Khomeini sets hostage release terms, UN comm balks 3-10, 177C1
Health worsens 3-11; examined 3-14, operatn delayed 3-16, 204F1
Gen amnesty issued 3-18, 204A2
US urges to stay in Panama, MDs dispute med treatmt 3-21—3-23, 217C1
Iran chrgs US plot vs shah's extraditn 3-22, 217G1
Quits Panama 3-23; in Egypt, gets permanent asylum 3-24; enters Cairo hosp, Sadat visits 3-25, 217A1, A2
Iran vs Egypt move, US fears setback 3-23—3-26, 217D2-218D1
Iran files extraditn request 3-24, 217B1
Spleen removed 3-28, liver cancer rptd 3-31; student protests continue 3-28, 3-31, 242D1
Khomeini scores US re move to Egypt 4-1, 241E1
Egypt Moslems score Sadat 4-4, 273G3
Leaves hospital 4-9, 283E1
Iranian firing squad photo wins Pulitzer 4-14, 317G2
Iran says US blocked query in Panama 4-16; US denies 4-17, 283C1
Timms back US probe 4-21, 299A2
Iran Eurodif ties unresolved 5-2, 409E1
Parsa executed 5-8, 373E1
Bani-Sadr strips Khalkhali of power 5-13, 373D2
UN comm renews hostage mission 5-17; comm rep in Iran 5-26, 393C2
Iran executes secret police agent 5-26, 419G3
New parlt meets 5-28, 394B2
Iran airs US '79 coup plot 6-2, 418F2
Iran repeats demand for return 6-6, 433D1
Leftists, Khomeini backers clash 6-12, 464D3
Anti-Khomeini plot rptd 6-12, 464G3
Khomeini scores Bani-Sadr govt 6-27, 490D1
Undergoes lung surgery 6-30, 490D3
Gen Hatam executed 7-14, 545F2
UK sets armor purchases 7-14, 564B2
Bakhtiar cousin seized in plot 7-17, 545G1
Dies 7-27, state funeral 7-29; reactn 7-27—7-28, 571B1-E2
Iran parlt ousts Jew 8-17, 644A3
Amnesty Intl cites executn pleas 8-28, 671F2
Iran hostage plan asks wealth returned 9-1, 671G1
US ex-amb scores Brzezinski '79 Iran policy 9-6, 694B1
Khomeini asks wealth returned 9-12, 693C1
Reagan urges hostage release concessns 9-13, 700A1
Iran ignored Iraq border pact 9-17, 694C2
Iraq warns US vs arms to Iran 10-25, 820G2
Son claims title 10-31, 859F2
Iran parlt demands property return 11-2, 853B1, B2
Iran gets US response on hostages 11-12, 861E1
Iran asks for wealth for hostage return 12-19, 973A1

1976

PAIEMENT, Lucien
On US bond rejectn 12-9, 945C3
PAINE, Thomas O.
Named Northrop pres 2-18, 133D1
PAINO, Salvador Horacio
Testifies on AAA origins 2-4, 212C1
PAINTERS and Allied Trades, International Brotherhood of (AFL-CIO)
Raftery quits Ford panel 1-8, 4C1
PAINT Industry
Mercury pesticides banned 2-18, 137G1
Sen OKs lead poison bill 2-19, 170F3
Mercury ban lifted 5-31, 571C1
Cong clears lead poison bill 6-7, 434F2

PAINTING & Sculpture
Renaissance frescoes found 1-2, 104D3
Rubens Visitation stolen 1-26, 104C3
Stolen Toulouse-Lautrec returned 1-29, 104B3
France gets pvt collectn 1-31, 124F2
Avignon Picasso theft 1-31, 124G2
Cong clears copyright revisn bill 9-30, 764E3; signed 10-19, 982G1
Obituaries
Albers, Joseph 3-25, 240C3
Badi, Aquiles 5-8, 368D2
Bjoerneboe, Jens 5-9, 404F1
Calder, Alexander 11-11, 970C1
Ernst, Max 4-1, 272F3
Lowry, Laurence 2-23, 192E3
Monnington, Thomas 1-7, 56F3
Ray, Man 11-18, 970A3
Richter, Hans 2-1, 124F3
Rukhin, Yevgeny 5-24, 404D2
Tobey, Mark 4-24, 368B3
Yolpo, Carl 9-25, 892G3

PAISLEY, Rev. Ian D.
Urges UK 'war' on IRA, threatens strike 1-5, 19G2
PAK Bo Hi, Lt. Col.
Rev Moon ends US ministry 9-18, link to KCIA cited 970F3, 971F1
US influence peddling rptd 10-24—11-1, 899A1, A2 ★
PAK Chol
Lauds DMZ tree-falling 8-21, 625F1
PAK Gi Pil
Expelled from Norway 10-18, 799B3
PAKHOMOVA, Ludmila
Wins Olympic medal 2-9, 159B1
PAK Hyong Kyu, Rev.
Released 7-6, 540F1

1977

PAHR, Willibald
Offers Czech dissidents asylum 1-25, 82B3
PAINE Webber Inc.
Davant on Dean Witter-Reynolds merger 10-3, 799F3
PAINTERS and Allied Trades, International Brotherhood of (AFL-CIO)
Buckhardt confrmd to Labor post 3-18, 272F2

PAINTING & Sculpture
Lady Churchill declines aid 2-22, 140E3
Dutch art collectn fire 7-18, 986E1
Alechinsky wins 1st Mellon prize 8-1, 808F2
Picasso estate settled 9-19, 808E2
Rembrandt, other works defaced 10-7, W Ger natl chrgd 10-8, 848E2
Obituaries
Gabo, Naum 8-23, 696F2
Gropper, William 1-6, 84B3
Maeda, Seison 10-27, 872E2
Nash, John 9-23, 788B2
Wolff, Robert 12-29, 1024G3
Zrzavy, Jan 10-13, 872C3

PAIS, Arie
Named Dutch educ min 12-19, 986B1
PAISLEY, Rev. Ian
Loyalist strike fails 5-2—5-14; expelled from MP group 5-4, arrested 5-10, 487A2, C2
Party gains in dist cncl electn 5-18, 487D2
PAK, Feliks
US tour results 1-29—2-5, 263B2
PAK Bo Hi
Named KCIA agent 6-5, 441G3
SEC chrgs 9-28, consent accord rptd 10-3, 774B1, E1

1978

PAHLEVI, Crown Prince Riza (Iran)
Sees Carter 10-31, 828A1
PAINCHAUD, Col. Jacques
Scores Danson 7-10, transferred 7-12, 556G2
PAINT Industry
Du Pont pigmt monopoly chrgd 4-10, 346A1

PAINTING & Sculpture
Sutherland portrait of Churchill rptd destroyed 1-11, 335D2
Rodin sculptures stolen 1-21, 2-20, 335C1
Arts Institute honors 3 2-7, 316D1
Poussin painting slashed 4-3, 335D1
Van Gogh paintings slashed 4-5, 4-25, 335E1, F1
Hals painting smeared 4-11, 335A2
Rubens painting, 9 others stolen 4-21; recovered 4-23, 335A2
Wyeth elected to Sovt Acad, '77 French honor cited 4-24, 335D3
Brussels statue stolen 4-25, 4-27, 335C2
Paris library tapestry stolen 5-12, 579G1
Natl Gallery commissns rptd 6-1, 578B3
Pompeiian statues stolen 6-8, 579E2
Von Hirsch collectn auctioned 6-20—6-27, 578F2, D3
13 French paintings stolen in Marseilles 6-20, 579F1
Patino primitive art collectn auctnd 6-29, 579D1
USSR revokes Rabin citizenship 6-30, 543D1
Brazil museum fire 7-8, 579A2
Degas, Renoir, 20 other paintings stolen from W Ger gallery 7-30, 1029B1
Paris museum Bosch theft 12-13, 1029A1
Rembrandt, 3 other Dutch paintings stolen from San Fran museum 12-25, 1028G3-1029A1
Chicago Cezanne theft 12-27, 1028E3
Obituaries
Bertoia, Harry 11-6, 972F2
De Chirico, Giorgio 11-20, 972A3
Dickinson, Edwin W 12-2, 1032F2
Grant, Duncan 5-10, 440F2
Jennewein, Carl Paul 2-22, 196C3
Koch, John 4-19, 356A3
Linder, Richard 4-16, 356B3
Rattner, Abraham 2-14, 196E3
Rockwell, Norman 11-8, 972E3
Wengenroth, Stow 1-22, 96G3

PAIS, Fernando da Silva
Delgado murder trial opens 10-9, 799E1
PAIS, Jose Santos
Sworn Portugal justice min 1-30, 91C3
PAISLEY, Rev. Ian
Interparty talks collapse 1-9, 18B2
Asks calm after Belfast bombing 2-19, 132D2
Chrgs Belfast restaurant bombers in Eire 6-4, 474C3
Protests Westminster mass 7-6, 557D3
PAISLEY, John A.
Found dead 10-1; Sen panel probe rptd 10-5, suicide suspected 10-20, 10-26, 835D3
Suicide disputed by wife 11-25, 917C2
PAISLEY, Maryann (Mrs. John A.)
Disputes husband's suicide 11-25, 917D2
PAK Bo Hi
Unificatn Church-KCIA link probed 3-22, 203E1
PAK Hwa Choon
Freed by PI rebels 2-2, 248C2

1979

Students link US exit, hostage trial 12-15, 958F1
Iran presses intl ct probe 12-16, 958E1
Khomeini scores Carter for US exit 12-17, 958B1
Panama curbs protests 12-19–12-21, 975B3
PAHLEVI, Riza (d. 1944)
S Africa asylum cited 914C1
PAHLEVI, Princess Shams (Iran)
Citibank fund transfer documented 11-26, 897E2
PAHLEVI Foundation (Teheran) (defunct)
Iran sues shah, wife 11-28, 897B2
Bank Omran
Pahlevi family assets estimated, US investmts rptd 11-26, 897G3
PA. Human Rights Commission v. Pittsburgh Press Co.
Case declined by Sup Ct 6-18, 499E1
PAIGE, Don
Wins IC4A outdoor 800-m, 1500-m runs 5-20, 911B3
PAINT Industry
Du Pont pigment monopoly case dismissed 9-17, 810E1

PAINTING & Sculpture
Australia paintings rptd stolen 1-3, 18F2
Breughel painting stolen in Italy 2-1, 119G1
Greek sculpture stolen from NY Met 2-9, recovered 2-14, 119D1
NYC museums get Rockefeller works 2-9, 173E2
Peabody to sell Inman portraits 2-9, 173F2
Art theft symposium held in Del 2-12–2-14, 119A2
'Last Supper' restoratn rptd 2-27, 173B3
Renoir painting willed to LA museum 3-7, 375G1
US inflatn 'hedge' demand cited 3-16, 264G2
Wyeth paintings sold, donated to SC museum 3-22, 375B2
5 Stuart pres portraits go to Natl Gallery 4-10, Boston library sale of 2 others halted 4-14, 374D3-375C1
Einstein monumt unveiled 4-22, 392E2
Poncet sculpture smashed in NYC 5-6, 375C1
Flemish art stolen from Rome convent 6-3, 656E1
Sonnenberg collectn auction record rptd 6-12, 672D1
Matisse, Picasso works sold for record sums 7-3, 672A1
US arts cncl sets business skills progrm 7-4, 672F2
Time, Control Data to sponsor shows 7-19, 672C2
Princeton gallery ordrd to return stolen paintings 7-27, 656F1
Poncet sculpture rededicated 9-15, 892F2
Picasso retrospective opens in Paris 10-10, 892C1
Michelangelo icon believed found 10-20, 892F1-A2
Church painting sold for record sum 10-25, 891F3
Da Vinci mural believed found 11-1, 892D1
UK art historian named as Sovt spy, controversy ensues 11-15–11-21, 908C2-909F1
Nevelson in Arts Institute 12-7, 1005A3
Obituaries
Adler, Samuel 11-12, 932A2
Dasburg, Andrew 8-13, 671A2
Delaunay, Sonia 12-5, 1008D2
Douglas, Aaron 2-2, 176G2
Ettinghausen, Richard 4-2, 356D3
Garbisch, Bernice Chrysler 12-14, 1008F2
Guggenheim, Peggy 12-23, 1008A3
Kahnweiler, Daniel-Henry 1-11, 104B3
Leach, Bernard 5-6, 432B3
Maze, Paul 9-17, 756G2
Roman, Jo 6-10, 521B2
White, Charles W 10-3, 860G3

PAISLEY, Eddie
Calls father's death murder 6-27, 520E2
PAISLEY, Rev. Ian
Vs US halt of arms sales to Ulster police 8-2, 602C1
Scores IRA march 8-12, 614F2
On home rule talks 10-25, 835F3
PAISLEY, John A. (d. 1978)
Sen panel urges Justice death probe 1-24, 54G3
Death probe dropped by Justice Dept 4-18, 283E3
Sen panel plans death probe 4-30, 368A1
Autopsy questioned 6-27, CIA scored on probe 7-8, 520B2-G2
PAISLEY, Maryann (Mrs. John A.)
Sen panel urges Justice probe husband's death 1-24, 55A1
Husband's death probe dropped 4-18, 283G3
Sen panel to probe husband's death 4-30, 368A1
Husband's autopsy questioned 6-27, 520C2
PAJETTA, Giancarlo
Dropped from Italy CP secretariat 7-10, 525F3
PAK Bo Hi
'77 SEC chrg cited 5-1, 376B3

1980

PAIGE, Don
Wins NCAA indoor 1,000-m run 3-15; IC4A outdoor 800, 1,000-m runs 5-24—5-25, 891F3, 892B2
In US Olympic trials 6-23, 6-29, 891G1, C2
PAINE, Thomas (1737-1809)
Reagan pres nominatn acceptance speech 7-17, 533C2
PAINE Webber Inc.—*See BLYTH Eastman Paine Webber Inc.*
PAINT Industry
OSHA benzene standard rejected by Sup Ct 7-2, 510D3
Resin price trust setlmt reached 7-22, 917D1
Du Pont monopoly case dismissal upheld 10-27, 916F3

PAINTING & Sculpture
Loren collectn claim rptd denied 2-9, 200B2
Cassatt print sold for record sum 2-14, 472B2
Okla State of State message 2-19, 404C1
Titian forgeries chrgd 2-26, 472B3
NYC sculpture smashed again 3-24, 472D3
Bouts painting sold for record sum 4-16, 472G2
Hann icons sold for record sum 4-17, 472A3
NYC record auctns held 5-12—5-16, 471G3-472A2
Hunts bailout loan collateral listed 5-28, 425D3, G3
'Last Supper' crack rptd 6-16, 472E3
Homer oil sold for $1.7 mln 10-17, 997G3-998A1
Calif artist royalties case declined by Sup Ct 11-10, 868C2
Pope scores modern art 11-19, 905A3
Argentina Natl Museum robbed 12-25, 991D1
Obituaries
De Lempica, Tamara 3-18, 280A1
Kandinsky, Nina 9-3, 755E3
Kokoschka, Oskar 2-22, 176A2
Lye, Len 5-15, 448C2
Marini, Marino 8-6, 676B2
Martinez, Maria 7-22, 608D2
Rosenberg, Jakob 4-3, 360B3
Shoumatoff, Elizabeth 11-30, 928D3
Still, Clyfford 6-23, 528E3
Sutherland, Graham 2-18, 176F3
Thompson, Joe 4-21, 360F3
Whitaker, Frederic 3-9, 280F2

PAISLEY, Rev. Ian
Home rule talks begin 1-7, bars parallel talks 1-11, 39A2, F2
Scores Haughey speech 2-17, 133A2
Home rule talks adjournment set 3-19, 232B3
On home rule plan 7-2, 523C1
Home rule talks renewed, stalemate rptd 9-22—9-23, 750F2
Warns vs Ulster moves 12-8, 942G2
PAISLEY, John A. (d. 1978)
Exonerated in Senate probe 4-24, 459C1
PAISLEY, Maryann (Mrs. John A.)
Sen com clears husband 4-24, 459D1
PAK Hung Ju, Col.
Executed 3-6, 195F3

1976

PAKISTAN—*See also ADB, DISARMAMENT—Geneva Committee*
Listed as 'partly free' 1-19, 20D3
Newsmen form new group 1-19, 55G2
Khan released from jail 8-28, 679B2
Tribal revolt crushed 9-3—9-10, 873A3
Building collapses 9-13, 816E1
Political foes jailed 10-30, 873C3

Foreign Relations (misc.)—*See also 'UN Policy' below*
French Mirage purchase cited 1-16, 36C2
Bangladesh rebel ldr identified 156D2
Emigratn curb sought; forgn emigrant totals 2-8, 121G1
Australia wheat deal OKd 2-11, 137F3
At intl econ conf 2-11—2-20, 148B1
Angola MPLA recognized 2-23, 163E2
US vs French A-plant sale 2-23; IAEA OKs plant 2-24, 175C1
Canada A-talks suspended 3-2, 174G3
French A-plant pact signed 3-18, 581C3
Bid to drop India flight ban case 3-27; India bid to renew ties 4-11, 278E2
India fears forgn arms aid 3-31, 278B3
IMF oil loans rptd 4-1, 340D2
Hijacked PI jet lands 4-12, leaves 4-13, 260B3
At Iran, Turk econ summit 4-21—4-22, 298A2
Renewed India ties set 5-12—5-14, 5-18, 356C2
French pres visits US 5-17—5-22, 372A2
Bhutto sees Mao in China 5-27, 439D2
India amb exchng 7-21, rail, air svc renewed 7-22, 538F1, G.*
US, Pak discuss French A-plant 8-8—8-9; France protests 8-9, 581G2
Bhutto reactn to Mao death 9-9, 657E2
India jet hijackers seized 9-11, 685C3 *
Qantas admits price cutting 9-23, 749E3
Ford, Carter debate 10-6, 741D1
Syrian emb raided 10-11, 759C1
France to honor A-sales 10-11, 772D3
France A-plant deal cited 12-16, 1002C3
Canada ends A-aid 12-22, 998C1
Gets OPEC loan 12-23, 975F3

1977

PAKISTAN—*See also CENTO, DISARMAMENT—Geneva Committee*
Agrarian reforms proposed 1-7, 24D2
Malaria upsurge rptd 9-4, 747F3

Foreign Relations (misc.)
UN Assemb, Cncl member 4A1, E1
French A-plant deal set 1-3, 12B3; US scores 1-29, 69B2
Indian hijackers freed 1-5, India protests 1-6, 45F3
UN comm scores Israel occupatn abuses 2-15, 107F2
Iran, Turkey pact signed, RCD revitalized 3-12, 190B2
Saudi, UAE, Libya mediatn efforts fail 4-28—4-29, 5-4, 348B3
Tribesmen hold China workers hostage, seek Peking interventn 4-28—5-4, 349C1
BBC subversn chrgd, UK rejcts protest 4-28, 349A2
Iran, India mil threat chrgd 5-11, 378A2
Australia trade office end urged 6-2, 484E3
France confirms A-plant deal 9-8, 1013A1
Sweden cancels debts 10-12, Iqbal lauds 10-13, 904A1
UN Cncl electns held 10-24, 852F3

Government & Politics—*See also other appropriate subheads in this section*
Electns set 1-7; Assemb dissolved, factns clash 1-9—1-10; 2 Cabt mins quit 1-13, 66E2-A3
40 die in pre-electn riots 202G1
Bhutto party wins electns 3-7, 3-10; foes chrg fraud 3-8, ask resignatn 3-12, 201F3
Post-electn riots 3-11, 3-14, 202C1; 80 die; 4 PNA ldrs arrested 3-16—3-22, 222G3
Bhutto asks Assemb boycott end 3-12, 3-14, 202D1
PNA bars Bhutto talks 3-20, 223E1
Bhutto offers to free PNA ldrs 3-20, Khan refuses 3-21, 223F1
PNA calls gen strike 3-21, 223G1
Karachi bar assn begins ct boycott 3-22, 223G1
Lahore rioting 3-23, 259D1
Punjab attys seized 3-25, govt thwarts protest strike 3-26, 258F3
PNA vs Bhutto peace bid 3-25, Elahi rejcts demands 3-27, 259G1
Assemb opens new session, govt foes stage protest 3-26, 258E3
Assemb reelects Bhutto 3-28, 258A3
Bhutto forms new Cabt, cedes forgn post 3-30, 258A3
Sind Prov Assemb sessn boycotted 3-30, 259C1
Ex-Cabt min loses Assemb seat 3-31, 258D3
PNA chrgs 150 die in riots 4-3, 258D3
4 PPP ldrs quit, set new party 4-8; PPP secy quits 4-13, 305F2
2 ambs quit in protest 4-13, 4-14, 305D2
Govt offers easing of censorship 4-14, Assemb electns 4-15, 305B2
Bhutto asks followers fight back 4-14, 305C2
Bhutto, Cabt meet on crisis 4-15—4-16, 305C2
Lahore riots, PPP, PNA confrontatns 4-15—4-19, 305G2
Hayat loses Parlt seat 4-16, 305G1
Bhutto sets reforms 4-17; PNA, Moslem ldr reject 4-18, 305D1, A2

1978

PAKISTAN—*See also DISARMAMENT—Geneva Committee, GATT*
Police-strikers clash in Multan 1-2, casualties rptd 1-3, 8C1
2 jet hijack attempts foiled 1-21, 3-2, 212E2
A-bomb seen unlikely before '84 1-26, 61C2
TV workers seize facilities 2-16, unions outlawed 4-8, 268F2
Locust plague threat seen 6-12, 465E2
Afghan border floods kill 122 7-9, 655C1
Malaria rptd on rise 8-6, 635G3
4 Amers climb K2 9-6—9-7, 843E2

Foreign Relations (misc.)—*See also 'Monetary, Trade, Aid & Investment' and 'UN' below*
UK prime min visits, sees Zia 1-12—1-13, 37G1
Indian talks on ties 2-6—2-7, 112G3
Bhutto death sentnc reversal pleas rptd 3-22, Zia rejects 3-27, 229A1, B1
Israel: terrorists train in Leb 4-7, 256D3
Afghan ties pledged 5-6, 349F2, A3
Afghan pro-Sovt stance, Baluchistan unrest feared 5-19, 391D1, A2
Iran warns Pak vs Bhutto executn 5-19, 391G1
Afghans seek refuge 6-5, 434G2
Iran names new amb 6-6, 437D3
Iraq consulate raid blocked 8-2, 582C3-583A1
Afghan tribesmen seek refuge 9-24, 738C2
Karachi, Bombay consulates cited 796G3
Iranian amb resigns 827B3
Afghan rebelln rptd 12-5, 943G2

Government & Politics—*See also other appropriate subheads in this section*
Wali Khan, aides cleared 1-1, 8A1
Bhutto backers arrested 1-4, 55G2
Bhutto daughter, wife freed from detentn 1-13, 1-15, 55A3
Zia forms advisory cncl 1-15, 75G1
Govt, prov offcls purged 2-7, 113C1
Political ban set 2-28, extended 3-29, 268E2
Bhutto, others sentncd to death 3-18, appeals 3-25; pro-Bhutto riots 3-18—3-20, 228D3-229C1
Rashid, other bomb plotters rptd arrested 4-7, 268C2
PPP subversn denial rptd 4-9, 268D2
New Cabt named 7-5, 559B1
Pres Chaudhry quits 9-14, Zia assumes pres 9-16, 740C2
Bhutto backers riot 10-2, self-burn victim dies 10-3, 775A2
Bhutto daughter arrested; backers riot, detained 10-4, 775C2
PPP ldrs arrested 10-4, 10-12, 818C2
Bhutto denies '77 electn fraud 10-5, 798E1
Govt blamed re riots 10-8, 775D2
Political parties curbed 10-16, 818B2
Bhutto's wife ordered freed 11-18, 925C3

Monetary, Trade, Aid & Investment
'77 A-export safeguard pact detailed 1-11, 11G1
UK in '72 natlizatn compensatn talks 1-12, 37A2
India in trade talks 2-6—2-7, 113A1
Ethiopia chrgs Somalia aid 2-14, 100C1
Islamic bank poor-natn aid rise rptd 4-9, 257F2
US A-fuel export license deferred 5-20, 408B2
UK cancels debts 7-31, 592E1
France asks A-contract revisn, US pressure cited 8-9; Zia scores, denies China agrmt 8-23, 668A2
Bhutto on Pak A-capability, cites US oppositn to A-deal with France 10-5, 798F1
US F-5E jet deal rptd, US denies 10-6; Pak rptd vs US bid 10-16, 797B1

1979

PAKISTAN—*See also DISARMAMENT—Geneva Committee, GATT, NONALIGNED Nations Movement*
Abdus Salam wins Nobel 10-16, 858C1
Newsman arrested 11-14, sentncd 11-29, 951F1
Jet crash in Saudi kills 156 11-26, 912F1

Atomic Energy & Safeguards
US sees A-arms threat, cuts aid 4-6; Pak denies 4-8, 277B2
India bars A-bomb 4-20, sees Pak threat 5-3, 323D3
US rpts A-bomb materials purchase 5-1, 323E3
Swiss rptd probing A-materials sales 5-2, 342F1
US seeks A-projct halt 8-11, Pak fears covert actn 8-14, 607C3
India warns of A-arms race 8-15, 646C1
A-bomb plan denied by Zia 9-22, 794D2
US-Pak talks inconclusive 10-17—10-18, 794B2

Foreign Relations (misc.)—*See also 'Atomic' above, 'Monetary' and 'UN' below*
Afghan rebel fighting rptd 1-7, 56D2
China dep premr visits 1-20, vows aid vs 'aggressn' 1-22, 59C3
Afghan rebel attacks rptd 1-27, mil aid denied 2-2, 147A3
UK ends immigrant virginity tests 2-2, 96D3
Iran govt recognized 2-12, 106B2
USSR, other natns protest Bhutto death sentnc 2-12; Zia scorns intl clemency pleas 2-14, 116B2, D2
Afghan rebel ldr flees 3-5, 209E2
Shahi ends Iran visit 3-11, 181C3
CENTO quit 3-12, 181B3
USSR chrgs aid to Afghan rebels 3-18, 209D2
Afghan war refugees enter 3-22, 232E3
Afghan rebel aid denied 3-23, 232G3-233A1
Intl protests vs Bhutto executn 4-4, 247G1-A2
Afghan chrgs border raid 4-8, denied 4-9; refugee entries up 4-10, 284A1
USSR naval activity cited 4-12, 313G3
Afghan rebel aid chrgd 4-22, 4-27, 360C2
USSR warns re Afghan rebel aid 6-1; chrg rebel training 6-11, ask India role 6-14, 443C1, D1
Viet offcl defects to China 7-5, 604C1
Afghan war refugees rptd 7-20, 562E1
Afghan links to army revolt 8-5, 599E2
Afghans chrg rebel aid 8-9, 666F2
Nonaligned movemt joined 9-3, 675E1
Afghan pres rptd dead, premr ambushed 9-18, 9-19, 696A1
Afghan links coup try 10-16, 810F3
Iran holds natl in US Emb 11-5, 841E1; frees 11-22, 895A3
W Eur heroin supply role cited 11-11, 972E3
Iran takeover of US Emb opposed 11-16, 878D3
Mecca mosque takeover scored, US role denied 11-21, 893E1
UK library sacked 11-21, 893F1
Afghan refugee data rptd 11-26, 11-28, 966G1
Saudis capture mosque raiders 12-4, 916B1
Sovt Afghan invasn opposed 12-29, 974E2

Government & Politics—*See also other appropriate subheads in this section*
Freedom House lists as partly free 13B1
Bhutto supporters arrested 2-2, univ closed 2-5, 116D2
Islam declared natl law 2-10, 116E2
Prisoner clemencies set 2-10, 116A3
Bhutto sons warn vs executn 2-13, executn stayed 2-14, 116G1
Bhutto clemency pleas ignored 3-29, 4-1; **Bhutto executed 4-4;** protests ensue, Zia defends actn 4-4—4-5, 247A1-A2
Pak Natl Alliance quits govt 4-15, interim govt formed 4-21, 313A3
Bhutto widow heads People's Party 5-4; supporters freed 5-21; wife, daughter released 5-28; daughter vows contd struggle 5-29, 430C2
Bhutto's daughter chrgd 9-1, 794F1
Parties disqualified for electn 10-2; Zia procedure rigging chrgd 10-4, compromise set 10-7, 794G1
Zia postpones electns 10-16, oppositn ldrs detained 10-17, 794C1

Monetary, Trade, Aid & Investment—*See also 'Atomic' above*
Australia wheat deal rptd 1-22, 56F3
US cuts aid, chrgs A-arms threat 4-6, Pak denies 4-8; US jet offer rptd 4-16, 277B2, G2
US studies aid sanctns 8-11, 607F3
US aid resumptn asked 9-22, 794E2

1980

PAKISTAN—*See also ADB, GATT, GENEVA Committee, NONALIGNED Nations*

Atomic Energy & Safeguards
US: A-progrm threatns aid 2-27, 165F2
Swiss reject US A-export protest 9-22, 754D2

Economy & Labor
Defns-GNP ratio rptd 2-19, 132G1

Foreign Relations (misc.)—*See also 'Monetary', 'Soviet-Afghan Issue', 'UN Policy' below*
Islamic conf proposed 1-7; held 1-27—1-29, 67F1, E2
China forgn min visits 1-18—1-21, 44G2
PLO gunman dies in Israel raid 4-7, 260E2
Zimbabwe gains indepndnc 4-18, 301E1
Iran hostage rescue try scored 4-25, 324F1
UK Emb captors free natl 5-3, 337F1
Tito funeral held 5-8, 339B1
Islamic Conf held 5-17—5-22, 395F2
W Ger pol asylum rules rptd tightened 7-31, 581E2, F2
Burma citizenship law rptd proposed 8-13, 617F3
Kashmir violence, 4 killed 8-16, 634G2-A3
Saudi mil base talks rptd 8-19, 653G3
Saudi jet fire kills natls 8-19, 778C1, E1
Nehru, Mountbatten affair alleged 8-27, 890B3
Zia in Iran-Iraq war mediatn missn 9-27—9-30; rpts failure 10-1, 734C1
Australia criticisms re Gandhi raise concern 11-6, 870F2

Government & Politics—*See also other appropriate subheads in this section*
Freedom House lists as not free 87D3
Bhutto's widow, daughter released 4-8, 336C2

Monetary, Trade, Aid & Investment
See also 'Soviet-Afghan Issue' below
Japan aid package signed 9-1, 686F1
Swiss reject US A-export protest 9-22, 754D2
IMF loan OKd, Sovts protest 11-25, 904D3

Obituaries
Ali, Chaudhri Mohammed 12-1, 1003G3
Yahya Khan, Agha Mohammad 8-8, 676G3

Soviet-Afghan Issue
Sovts chrg Afghan rebel training 1-1, 1D2; say US plans arms 1-4, warn Pak 1-7, 10D2
India concerned re US arms sale 1-1, 2F2; 1-5, 12A1 12A1
US offers mil, econ aid 1-12, Zia for no 'strings' 1-15, 27A1

1976

UN Policy & Developments
Cncl member 62F2; 720C1
OKs Cncl pro-Palestine resolutn 1-26, 59G2
Backs rights comm resolutn vs Israel 2-13, 125E2
IAEA OKs French A-plant sale 2-24, 175C1
Palestine com member 2-26, 162C1
IAEA signs French A-plant pact 3-18, 581C3
Asks session on Israel occupatn 3-22, 211E1
Bhutto bid to India to drop ICAO case 3-27, 278F2
Bukhari on WHO anti-Israel stand 5-19, 355D2
OKs Israel Arab land exit 6-29, 464C1
Shuns vote on anti-terror 7-14, 515G3
IAEA dir cites 9-21, 760F3
S Africa arms ban vetoed 10-19, 781D3

Sports
Olympic results 7-18—7-31, 573F3, 574A3

1977

Anti-govt riot toll rptd 4-19, 305E1
2 PPP electn wins overturned 4-20, 313G2-314A3
Govt takes emergency powers, martial law set in 3 cities 4-21, 313A1
Riot death toll 250 313B1
Parlt OKs emergency powers 4-21, 349G1
40 die in clashes 4-22, 313E1
Bhutto, party meet on crisis 4-22, 313F1
Press curbs set 4-23, 313B1, F1
PNA scores martial law 4-23, 313A2
More PNA ldrs arrested 4-24, 313B2
Pir of Pagaro heads PNA 4-24, 313B2
PNA plans anti-Bhutto march 4-24, govt seeks ban 4-27, 313C2
Labor asks mil chiefs aid 4-24, mil chiefs vow govt support 4-27, 313D2
2 envoys quit 4-24, 4-26, 314A1
Pir meets detained PNA ldrs 4-26, says govt eases stand 4-27, 313E2
Gen Tikka Khan in Cabt 4-27, 313D2
Bhutto renews PNA bid 4-28, 4-29, 349A1
Tribesmen join anti-govt drive 4-28—5-4, 349C1
Anti-Bhutto march blocked 4-29, 4-30, 349B1
PNA picks new ldrs 5-3, 348F3
More PNA ldrs arrested 5-5, 348E3
PNA issues 'final' demands 5-5, 348G3
Martyrs' Day marked, anti-Bhutto demonstrations; violence erupts 5-6—5-15, 378C2
Bhutto asks PNA ldr drop demands 5-11, 378A2
Bhutto proposes referendum, PNA vs 5-13; Assemb OKs vote 5-16, 378D1
Pir rejcts referendum bid 5-13, arrested 5-14; followers protest, Pir freed 5-16—5-18, 378B2
3 die in Alipur clashes 5-16, 450B3
Pir chrgs 800 arrests 5-23, threatns unrest 5-24, 450B3
Lahore ct voids martial law 6-2, Sup Ct upholds 6-3, 450F2
PNA ldrs freed 6-2, 6-3, 2,000 freed 6-6, 450G2
Martial law lifted 6-6, PNA talks progress rptd 6-7, 450E2
Bhutto-PNA talks falter 6-14, 6-21, 7-2, 7-4, 509B2
Zia heads army coup; Bhutto, PNA ldrs detained; martial law set, electns vowed 7-5, 509A1, B1 *
Civil servants named 7-7, 509A2
Zia details coup plan, bars Bhutto trial 7-8, 544E3
New martial-law rules issued 7-10, crime rptd down 7-13, 545A1
Bhutto fed force probe rptd 7-13, 545C1
Bhutto release planned 7-14, 545D1
Zia states aims, electn rule 7-27, 599F1
Bhutto, others freed 7-28; martial law scored 7-29, 599E1
Media curbs lifted 8-20, 707B3
Bar assn asks Bhutto arrest 8-28, 707A3
Bhutto arrested on murder chrgs 9-3; 3d murder hinted 9-6, 707B2, G2
Bhutto party to enter electns 9-4, 707B3
Mahmud sentenced 9-5, 707F2
Amnesty Intl lists jailed legislators 9-5, 753A2
Bhutto freed on bail 9-13, rearrested with 10 PPP ldrs 9-17; followers rally 9-18, 730F2
Emergency ended 9-15, 730A3
PPP plans electn strategy 9-18, 730A3
Chief judge orders Bhutto arrest hearing 9-20, ousted 9-22; ruling overturned 9-25, 765A3
Bhutto daughter arrested, wife warned 9-29, 765E2
Electns delayed, martial rule extended 10-1; Bhutto scores 10-3, 765B2, G2
Bhutto formally chrgd 10-11, 803C1
'78 electns pledged 10-13, 802G3
Govt seizes Bhutto trust 10-17, 885G2
Press crackdown 10-23, 11-2, 11-3, 885F2
Martial law, Bhutto detentn upheld 11-10, 885D2
Detentn power extended to provs 11-13, 885C2
Bhutto loses plea 11-20, 987A1
Bhutto barred as Parlt candidate 11-25, 986F3
Security force disbanded 11-30, 968A1
Karachi newsmen strike re new Musawat newspr mgt 12-3; arrested 12-5, freed 12-7; Musawat returned to Bhutto family 12-6, 967E3

U.S. Relations
US urges France to curb A-sales 1-29, 69B2
Amb to US mediates Hanafi seige 3-11, 192A3
US bars tear gas 4-20, Pak scores 4-26, 314C1
US plot chrgd, US denies 4-28, 349E1
Nixon reminisces re '73 India war 5-12, 385E3, 386B2
US interfernc protested 5-14—5-15, 380D1
US Navy transfers 2 ships 5-19, 450E3
US bars A-7 jet sale 6-2, 450C3
Hummel confrmd amb 6-7, 499F3

1978

India trade talks fail 10-7—10-9, 796E3
Trade deficit since '75 cited 796F3
US to renew econ aid, French A-deal cancelatn cited 10-24, 839G3

Press & Censorship
Govt-newspr agrmt on job loss 10-8, 818G2
Jailed newsmen released 10-10, 818A3
Press curbs imposed 10-17, newsprs suspend publicatn 10-18—10-22, 818D2

UN Policy & Developments
Aga Khan quits UN refugee post 12-31-77, 62B1
UN comm votes res vs Israel 2-14, 99A2
FAO fears locust plague 6-12, 465E2
Assemb member 713D3

U.S. Relations
CIA sees no A-bomb before '84 1-26, 61C2
Bhutto death sentnc reversal plea rptd 3-22, 229B1
US columnist's suit vs Nixon dismissed 4-4, 265C1
US policy readjustmt urged 5-19, 391A2
US A-fuel export license deferral rptd 5-20, 408B2
France asks A-contract revisn, US pressure cited 8-9, 668B2
Bhutto on US oppositn to A-plant 10-5, 798F1
India regrets US jet sale, US denies bid 10-6; Pak rptd vs US bid 10-16, 797B1
US to renew econ aid, French A-deal cancellatn 10-24, 839G3
McDonnell Douglas paymts rptd 12-15, 982F2

1979

UN Policy & Developments
Membership listed 695A3
Pol Pot govt seat upheld 9-19, 695C2

U.S. Relations
CIA alleged station chief named 1-4, 17B3
Zia scorns Bhutto clemency plea 2-14, 116B2
Bhutto executn regretted 4-4, 247G1
US cuts aid, chrgs A-arms threat 4-6, Pak denies 4-8; US jet offer rptd 4-16, 277B2, G2
Pak A-bomb materials purchase rptd 5-1, 323E3
US seeks A-projct halt, studies optns 8-11, Pak fears covert actn 8-14, 607C3
Zia asks aid resumptn 9-22, 794E2
McDonnell Douglas sued re overchrg 9-25, US indicts re paymts 11-9, 886F1
A-talks inconclusive 10-17–10-18, 794B2
US pleas for hostages in Iran 11-6, 841C2
Iran takeover of US Emb opposed 11-16, 878D3
US Emb stormed, 2 Amers killed; attack detailed 11-21; Pak ldrs deplore 11-21, 11-24, 893A1, A2-894B1
Anti-US protests spread 11-21, 400 evacuated 11-23, 893F1

1980

Carter gets US Cong backing on arms 1-3, 27B1
US weighs mil aid 1-4, 1F1
Sovts condemned in UN debate 1-5, 2B2
Afghan war refugees total 402,000 1-6, 3C2
US, China in mil aid talks 1-6—1-9, 11B2; US rpts China rebel aid agrmt 1-16, 31A2
Zia warns 'human community' 1-8, 10D3
US pres candidate backs aid 1-9, 13F2
Anti-US rally in India re arms aid 1-9, 27A2
Zia on threat 1-12, warns vs Sovt move 1-15; gen says Pak unprepared 1-16, 27C1
US offers mil, econ aid 1-12, 27A1; Zia calls pkg 'peanuts' 1-17, US delays 2-3, 83D1
Zia vs call for war vs Sovts 1-13, 44B3
UK forgn secy visits 1-16, 27E1
US assures India re Pak aid 1-16, 27G1
Zia rpts Kabul clash 1-17, 44B1
China vows aid 1-18—1-21, 44F2
Carter asks mil, econ aid pkg 1-21; warns USSR 1-23, 41C2, 42D3, 43D3
Sovts claim mil aid to Afghan rebels 1-28, 67G2
India, US confer 1-30—1-31, US arms aid opposed 1-30, 83B3
US missn arrives 2-1; aid vs Sovt invasn vowed, Zia lauds 2-3; US briefs Saudis 2-4—2-5, 83A1-G1
US-Pak '59 defense pact text 83F2
Sovt tanks mass near border 2-4, 85G2
US rights rpt scores Pak 2-5, 87E1
UN res adopted 2-14, 123D3
Afghan subversn chrgd 2-22, 138F2
Brezhnev accuses 2-22, 139E2, F2
Kabul-Peshaware highway closed 2-23, 138C3
US: A-progrm threatns aid 2-27, 165A3
Sovt jet invades air space, warning shot fired 3-1, 164D3
Afghan refugee total at 513,116 3-1, 164E3
More refugees flee to Pak 3-4—3-5; Zia asks intl camp inspectn 3-6, 205D3
US aid offer dismissed 3-5, 165A2
W Ger aid plans cited 3-10, 205E2
Cuba seeks to mediate feud 3-25—3-27; Pak demands USSR quit Afghan 3-27, 271C2
USSR links Afghan exit, foreign mil aid 4-24—4-25, 351G3
Afghan rebel bldg bombed 5-3, 349G2
Afghan plan on Sovt troop exit opposed 5-15, 361E2
Afghans free 16 Pakistanis 5-16, 443E1
US rpts Afghan refugee total 5-17, 387G2
Islamic Conf 5-17—5-22, talks proposed 5-22, 395F2
Afghans cross border re combat 6-15, 508F1
Afghan basketball players defect 6-20, 475D2
Canadian UN offcl freed in Kabul 6-22, 486C2
USSR restates exit conditns 7-2, 507B3
Afghan wrestlers defect 7-6, 590D2
Sovts mine Afghan-Pak passes 7-7, 507F3
Afghan rebels claim 1,200 civilians killed by Sovts 8-17, 650C1
Kabul highway rptd cut 8-26, 650E1
Arms rptd seized 9-1, 686C1
Japan aids Afghan refugees 9-1, 686E1
Afghan rebels clash at Pak base 9-2, 686D1
Afghan copters hit Pak border 9-26, 766A1
Rebel ldr deplores Pak arms refusal 10-2, 766D1
Sovts open new drive near Pak border 10-23, 827E2
Afghan refugees strafed 10-24, 900C1
Sovt annexatn of border area rptd 11-4, 900B1
USSR chrgs rebel aid 12-9, denies Persian Gulf threat 12-10, 930B2, F2

UN Policy & Developments
Sovt Afghan invasn opposed 1-5, 2B2
Sovt Afghan res adopted 2-14, 123D3
Canadian offcl freed in Kabul 6-22, 486C2
Cncl vote on Iraq-Iran war blocked 9-25; action OKd 9-28, 733F2

U.S. Relations
Mil aid weighed 1-4, 1G1; for subsequent developments, see 'Soviet-Afghan Issue' above
China briefs Pak on Brown visit 1-18—1-21, 44A3
US-Pak '59 defense pact text 83F2
US issues rights rpt 2-5, 86A3, 87C1
Gromyko, India score arms plan 2-13, 108G3
US: A-progrm threatns aid 2-27, 165F2
Iran hostage rescue try scored 4-25, 324F1
'79 terrorism deaths rptd 5-11, 365E3
US faults Pak on '79 emb rescue 6-9, 477D3
US A-export protest rejected by Swiss 9-22, 754D2
US Cong fails to bar India uranium sale 9-24, 724A2

1976

PAKISTAN International Airlines
Resumes India flights 7-21, 528G1
Qantas admits price cutting 9-23, 749E3
PAKO Corp.
Chrgd re Arab boycott 10-8, 785D3
PAKRADOUNI, Kerim
Bomb blasts car 12-14, 953F1
PAK Sung Chul
N Korea premier 4-30, 335B2
Asks US exit from South 8-17, 621E3
PALESTINIAN Movement—*See under MIDDLE EAST—ARAB Policies*

PALEVSKY, Joan
'72 campaign gift listed 4-25, 688C1
PALEVSKY, Max
'72 campaign gift listed 4-25, 688C1
PALEY, William S.
Sets resignatn as chief exec 10-13, 892F1
PAL Joey (play)
Opens 6-22, 1014D3
PALLOTTINE Fathers Missionary Society
Fund-raising probed 6-18—10-24, 950E3
PALM, Nancy
GOP conv vp vote table 8-19, 599F3
PALM Beach, Fla.—*See FLORIDA*
PALME, Olof
At Europn socialist confs 1-18—1-19, 48G2; 3-13—3-14, 222F3
Spanish socialist aid set 1-24, 120A2
Regrets Bergman expatriatn 4-28, 368D3
Castro sets Angola troop exit 5-21, 370B3, 371B1
Lauds worker managemt law 6-2, 559G1
Scores Argentina violence 8-26, 672D2
Resigns after Soc Dem defeat 9-20, 714D1
Scores Falldin 10-8, 794A2
PALMER, Arnold
Sets world flight record 5-19, 368F3
PALMER Jr., Gen. Bruce (ret.)
Armed forces study scored 6-7, 454F1
PALMER, Donald D.
Named Togo amb 9-8; confrmd 9-15, 808C1
PALMER, Jim
Gets Cy Young award 11-10, 952C1
PALMER, Dr. Richard E.
AMA backs natl health insurnc 12-7, 931D2

1977

PAK Sung chul
Replaced as premier 12-15, 986C3
PALEONTOLOGY
Oldest fossils of life found 10-15, 908F1

PALESTINE Liberation Organization—*See ARAB League, MIDDLE EAST, NONALIGNED Nations Movement*
PALESTINIANS—*See under MIDDLE EAST; also NONALIGNED Nations Movement; for plane hijackings, see AVIATION—Middle East Incidents; for Lebanon developments, see LEBANON*

PALEY, William S.
Retirement set 4-20, 355G3
Replaced as CBS chief exec 5-11, 532F1
PALLAVICINI, Princess Elvina
Lefebvre scores modernism 6-6, 470G3
PALLOTTINE Fathers Missionary Society
RC editor fired 2-11, 471G1-A2
PALM Beach, Fla.—*See FLORIDA*
PALMDALE, Calif.—*See CALIFORNIA*
PALME, Olaf
Scores price freeze 4-4, 429F1
At Brandt comm mtg 12-9—12-11, 998A1
PALMEDO, Roland
Dies 3-15, 264C3
PALMER, Jim
NL wins All-Star Game 7-19, 567B2, F2
AL pitching ldr 10-2, 927A1
Lyle wins AL Cy Young Award 10-25, 927D1
PALMER, Richard
Denies Texaco withholds gas 2-23, 152F1
PALMER, Russell E.
On Touche Ross, Lasser merger 8-22, 650F2
PALMER, Sandra
Wins Womens Intl 4-17, 951B1
LPGA top money winner 11-27, 951F1

1978

PAKISTAN International Airlines
2 hijack attempts foiled 1-21, 3-2, 212E2
PAKULA, Alan J.
Comes A Horseman released 11-1, 969G3
PALDEN Thondup Namgyal
Seeks funds for exile move 227C3

PALESTINE Liberation Organization—*See ARAB League, LEBANON, MIDDLE EAST, NONALIGNED Nations Movement*
PALESTINIANS—*See under MIDDLE EAST; for Lebanon developments, see LEBANON*

PALEY, Barbara Cushing (Babe)
Dies 7-6, 620D3
Sister dies 11-4, 972B3
PALEY, William S.
Wife dies 7-6, 620D3
PALLADIUM
Sovt '77 top export to US 3-29, 229G3
PALLAIS Debayle, Luis
Guerrillas take hostage 8-22, freed 8-24, 658F3, 659C1
Defends Somoza on US TV 8-31, 690E3
PALLEY, Ahrn
Quits as Muzorewa aide 12-1, 945E3
PALLOTTINE Fathers Missionary Society
Carcich indicted 1-6, 24G2
Carcich sentenced 5-9, 380F1-A2
PALMA, Riccardo
Killed 2-14, 133D1
PALM Beach, Fla.—*See FLORIDA*
PALMER, Arnold
2d in Victorian Open 2-19, 355C3
PALMER, Gray
Price of Genius opens 6-26, 887F2
PALMER, Jim
NL wins All-Star Game 7-11, 559B3
AL top pitcher 10-2, wins Golden Glove Award 11-21, 928A3, F3
PALMER Jr., Linwood E.
Wins primary for Me gov 6-13, 467A1
Loses electn 11-7, 847E2
PALMER, Richard B.
On Texaco offshore gas find 8-14, 665C3
PALMER, Sandra
2d in Colgate Triple Crown 1-29, 76E1

1979

Evacuatns, travel curbs ordered 11-26, 894A2
Anti-US protest in Rawalpindi 12-2, 915E1
US assures on Afghan coup 12-30; India protests to US 12-31, 974G1-B2
PAKISTAN International Airlines
McDonnell Douglas sued re overchrg 9-25, indicted re paymts 11-9, 886B2
PALACIOS de Vizzio, Sergio
UN Cncl asks Iran free hostages 11-9, rejcts debate 11-14, 862B1, E1
UN Cncl vs US plea on Iran hostages 11-20, 878E2
UN Cncl debate on Iran asked 11-25, 896A1
PALESTINE Liberation Organization (PLO)—*See ARAB League, LEBANON, MIDDLE EAST, NONALIGNED Nations Movement*

PALEY, Grace
Sentenced 2-12, 133A3
PALIN, Michael
Life of Brian released 8-17, 820A2
PALISADES Nuclear Power Station—*See MICHIGAN—Atomic Energy*
PALLAIS Checa, Marcel
Slain 10-4, 793F3
PALLOTTI, Alfredo
Asks A-plant safety guarantees 4-1, 246A2
PALME, Olof
Scores '79-80 budget 1-9, 77G1
A-plant fueling OKd 6-25, 505B2
Nonsocialists win electn 9-16, 697B1
PALMER, Jim
In World Series 10-10—10-17, 816F1
Wins Golden Glove Award 11-20, 956C1
PALMER, John
On Mount Chimborazo opens 5-21, 712A2
PALMER, Patrick
And Justice for All released 10-19, 1007G2
PALMER, Sandra
Ties for 2d in US Women's Open 7-15, 587E1
PALMER v. Feminist Women's Health Center
Case declined by Sup Ct 10-29, 884E1

1980

PAKTIAWAL, Akhtar Mohammed
Vs Sovt Afghan invasn, defects to W Ger 10-25, 827E2
PAL, George
Dies 5-2, 448D2
PALAU, Republic of (U.S. trust)
Self-rule pact signed 11-17, 884C1
PALECKIS, Justas
Dies 1-26, 176G2
PALESTINE Liberation Organization (PLO)—*See ARAB League, NONALIGNED Nations, PALESTINIANS*
PALESTINIANS—*See also ARAB-Israeli Developments, LEBANON—Military*
Libya ends Al Fatah ties 1-5, 107F3
Begin, Sadat meet on autonomy 1-7—1-10, 12E1; for subsequent developments see ARAB-Israeli Developments—Palestinian Autonomy
USSR Afghan invasn backed by PLO factn 1-9, 10C3
Redgrave TV role protested 1-13, 120C2
PLO to boycott Islamic conf 1-22, 67E2
PLO scores Carter Persian Gulf defns pledge 1-25, 65D1
Arafat at Iran anniv rites 2-11, 106B1
Israel says PLO gets Sovt tanks 2-12, 107E3
Shukairy dies 2-26, 176D3
Canada envoy backs PLO ties 2-29, 230C3
French pres tours Arab states, backs rights 3-1—3-10; Arafat hails 3-8, 179G3
PLO vs US disavowal of UN anti-Israel vote 3-5, 163G3
Austria gives PLO aide special status 3-13; Israel protests 3-14, Arafat lauds 3-15, 205G3-206B1
India recognizes PLO 3-26; Arafat visits 3-28—3-29, 260D3
PLO backs anti-Sadat front 4-2, 273C3
PLO gunman dies in Israel raid 4-7, 260E2
PLO at hard-line Arab summit 4-14—4-15, 284F2
PLO scores US hostage rescue try 4-27, 324D2
CIA rpts on '79 terrorism 5-11, 365F3
Jaabari dies 5-29, 448G1
UN women's conf attended 7-14—7-30, 5-yr plan OKd 7-30, 587A2, A3
Gunmen seized in Bakhtiar death try 7-18, 545C1
Arafat tours Moscow Olympic Village 7-20, 590C1
Arafat in Nicaragua 7-21, PLO ties formalized 7-22, 565E3
Khaddoumi scores Camp David pact, US policy at UN 7-22, 572B2
W Ger pol asylum rules rptd tightened 7-31, 581E2
World Bank, IMF dispute status 9-4—9-22; dirs bar observer role 9-19, 719D3-720A1
IMF role in oil debt jeopardized 9-15, 695F2
PLO backs Iraq in Iran war, Arafat mediatn effort cited 9-23, 719E2
W Ger bombing links denied 9-30, 755C1
Redgrave TV film aired by CBS, Jews protest 9-30, 835C3
Israel scores EC re terrorist violence 10-7, 767B3
Curbs tightened re Iran-Iraq war 10-22, 821B2
Arafat addresses UNESCO conf 10-27, 821E3
Redgrave pledges support 11-2, 908F3
PLO at Islamic econ conf 11-4—11-6, 865D1
PLO scores Reagan electn, Carter 11-5, 841D2
US convicts 2 FBI ex-offcls 11-6, 884E2
Arab League summit boycotted 11-25—11-27, 911B1
Syria chrgs Jordan plot vs PLO 11-29; demands Jordan vow backing 12-2, 911E2, G2-A3
Sayegh dies 12-9, 1004D3
Turkey sentncs 4 to die for '79 Egypt Emb raid 12-23, 997A1
PALEY, William S.
Backe quits CBS post, dispute hinted 5-8, 376E1
Names Wyman CBS chief 5-22, 501A2
Jankowski CBS resignatn hoax 5-23, 501A2
PALLOTTO, Marino
Rptd dead in prison cell 8-1, 605G1
PALME, Olof
In Iran hostage mission 5-25—5-26, 394D1
Named Iraq-Iran peace missn envoy 11-11; trip to Teheran, Baghdad ends 11-24, rpts to Waldheim 11-25, 894G2
Rpts agrmt on trapped forgn ships in Persian Gulf 11-26, 913C2
PALMER, Arnold
2d in World Seniors Invitatnl 9-28; wins PGA Seniors tourn 12-7, 972C2, G2
PALMER, Betsy
Friday the 13th released 5-10, 675F2
PALMER v. Chicago Board of Education
Case declined by Sup Ct 1-7, 15E3

1976

PALMIERI, Eddie
Wins Grammy 2-28, 460C3
PALM Springs, Calif.—*See CALIFORNIA*
PALTRIDGE, Shane (d. 1966)
Lockheed payoff chrgd 4-29, 322G1
PANA International Corp.
Arab boycott rpt released 10-18, 786A1
PANACEK, Josef
Wins Olympic medal 7-24, 575B2
PANAGOULIS, Alexandros
Killed 5-1, murder chrgd 5-5, 351D3
Rt-wing group implicated in death 7-9, 538C1

PANAMA—*See also IDB, NONALIGNED Nations Movement, OAS, SELA*
Torrijos in Cuba, signs pacts 1-10—1-15, 52C2
Listed as 'not free' nation 1-19, 20E3
Critics exiled 1-20, business ldrs strike 1-21—1-29, 121B2
Tito on tour 3-9—3-22, 256C2
Tack replaced 4-1, 291A2
Total IMF oil loan rptd 4-1, 340D2
Students riot 9-10, 9-15, 9-20, Boyd denies econ causes 9-22, 792B1, E2, B3
Guatemala-UK Belize talks held 9-21—9-22, 977F3
Econ problems listed 9-27, 792C3
Castro chrgs CIA Aug bombing role 10-15, 780B2
Cuba exiles terrorist plans rptd 10-19, 780C2

Panama Canal & Zone—*See PANAMA Canal*
UN Policy & Developments
Cncl member 62F2; 720C1
OKs Cncl pro-Palestine resolutn 1-26, 59G2
Conf vs US policy 6-11, 431D3
OKs Israel Arab land exit 6-29, 464C1
Abstains on anti-terror resolutn 7-14, 515G3
S Africa arms ban vetoed 10-19, 781D3
Gets UNDOF compromise 11-30, 895D2
Abstains on Waldheim vote 12-7, 914E2, F2
U.S. Relations—*See also PANAMA Canal*
United Brands signs pact 1-8, 52B3
Javits visit rptd 1-11, 52F2
US dislike of Tack rptd 1-16, 291B2
US joint drug drive agreed 1-20, 61A1
Reagan linked to regime critics 1-21, denial rptd 1-23, 121E2

1977

PALMERS, Walter Michael
Kidnaped 11-9, freed 11-13; 2 arrested 11-23, 990F1
3d W Ger kidnap suspect captured 12-20, 1017F3
PALM Oil—*See OILS & Fats*
PALOMINO, Carlos
'77 boxing champion 12-17, 970A3
PALOTAY, Rt. Rev. Sandor
Invites Graham to Hungary 8-13, 732C1
PANA, Gheorghe
At miners strike 8-2, 947F3
PANAGIOTOPOULOS, George
Named Greek trade min 11-28, 925B2

PANAMA—*See also IDB, NONALIGNED Nations Movement, OAS*
Tanker rptd sunk off Cape Cod 1-11, 104E3, 214D3
Boyd quits as forgn min, Gonzalez Revilla replaces 2-9, 379A1
Torrijos vows pol exiles return 9-17, 716F3
Torrijos describes pol stance 9-28, 755G3
Pol repressn scored by attys 10-14, 809G1
Torrijos makes vows re San Blas Indians 11-9, censorship, rights, exiles 11-12, 911D2, A3
Exile total estimated 11-13, 911B3
Economy & Labor (domestic)
Econ plan set 1-3; reactn 1-4, 1-5, 1-14, 46B2
New austerity program set 1-22, 379A3
'76 econ stagnation rptd 4-22, 379F2
'61-75 GDP variatns table 5-30, 439B1
Benefits from Canal pacts detailed 10-21, 809E2
Foreign Relations (misc.)—*See also 'Monetary, Trade & Aid' below*
UN Assemb, Cncl member 4A1, E1
Takes Peru exiles 1-8, 46C3
Peru exiles accepted 1-8, 46C3
El Salvador deports priest 5-6, 373A3
Guatemala severs ties re Belize 5-19; chrgs exchngd 5-20, 5-24, Latin mediatn asked 5-27, 414G2
Belize prime min starts visit 5-20, 414C3
Belize independnc backed 6-16, 494G2
Uruguay release of Mex newsman asked 7-15, 601E1
Cuba frees exile commandos 8-2, 654C2
Torrijos invites OAS rights probe, UN Canal plebescite observance 9-13, 699F1
Spanish king visits 9-16—9-17, 804G3, 805D1
Torrijos begins 10-natn tour 9-24, 755D3; completes tour 10-14, 792B2
UN Cncl electns held 10-24, 852F3

Monetary, Trade & Aid Issues (including all foreign economic developments)
'75-76 trade, paymts table 3-11, 189A2 ★, B2
'66-75 arms transfers table 4-8, 415B2
UNCTAD shipping study rptd 4-17, 337E2
Bahamas Castle Bank to transfer operatns 4-28, 395F3
IWC cuts whaling quotas 6-24, 496G3
Torrijos, Latin ldrs set Intl Coffee Fund 8-6, 608A3
IDB OKs $98-mln hydroelec loan 9-2, 786F1
US aid plan scored 10-14; Torrijos defends 10-20, 10-21, 809B2
Backs Brazil coffee policy 10-21, 876C3
Saudis boycott ships 12-10, 955D1
Panama Canal & Zone—*See PANAMA Canal*
U.S. Relations—*See also PANAMA Canal*
'66-75 arms transfers table 4-8, 415B2
Reagan, Bunker testify on rights record 9-8; Torrijos effort praised 9-13, 699C1-A2
Torrijos in US 9-24—9-27, 755E3; 10-14, 791A3

1978

PALMERI Sr., Ernest
Indicted 10-5, 770F3
PALMERS, Walter
Kidnap suspect arrested in Bulgaria 6-22, 500D1
Swiss jail 2 W Ger terrorists 6-30, 558A3
PALMIERI, Judge Edmund
Fines Fox for 'block booking' 9-12, 759D2
PALMIERI, Sergio
Wounded 4-27, 330F1
PALM Oil—*See OILS & Fats*
PALO, Ia.—*See IOWA*
PALOMINO, Carlos
KOs Sorimachi 2-11, 379A2
KOs Mohatar 3-18, 379C2
PAMMO, Capt. Oscar
Bolivia indus, commerce min 11-24, 913E1
PANAGIOTOPOULOS, George
Visits Albania; signs trade pact, tours ethnic areas 3-28—3-30, 374B2

PANAMA—*See also IDB, NONALIGNED Nations Movement, OAS*
Press curbs rptd by IAPA 10-13, 829A2

Economy & Labor (domestic)
'77 GDP, inflatn up; 14 new banks opened 6-30, 632B2
MDs strike 7-21—8-2, 632E2

Foreign Relations (misc.)
H Torrijos named amb to Spain 3-1, 211E2
UN Chile rights abuse res opposed 3-6, 210F1
El Salvador peasants, students seize emb 4-11—4-18, 723C3 ★
Chile exiles fast 5-23, 452E2
Amer rights conv enacted, ct formed 7-18, 828E3, 829C1
Nicaragua guerrillas, freed prisoners arrive 8-24, 658E3, 659B1
El Salvador guerrilla manifesto publshd 8-25, 722B2, 723F2 ★
Guatemala ties resumed 8-29, 798A3
22 Nicaragua prisoners arrive Cuba 9-1, 690F3
Latin export bank opens 9-8, 828C3
Nicaragua oppositn for forgn mediatn 9-14, 705C3
UN Assemb member 713D3
CR deports Nicaragua guerrillas 10-13, 839E3
Nicaragua emb harbors 11 refugees 10-13, 839F3
Turk Cypriot tourist indus dispute rptd 11-29, 922B3
Nicaragua rebel aid halt urged by US 12-11, 1018F3

Government & Politics—*See also other appropriate subheads in this section*
M Torrijos quits as Spain amb; brother replaces 3-1, 211E2
Pol exiles get amnesty 4-18; Arias returns, scores govt at rally 6-10, 463C3
Torrijos pol party planned 7-8, 632G1
Liberals join govt pol comm 7-28, 632A2
Natl Assemb elected 8-6; Torrijos lauds voters, scores Arias 8-7, 632C1
Torrijos bars presidency, to keep mil post; backs Royo as pres 9-1, 691F3
Royo elected pres 10-11, 764C3; names Cabt 10-12, 884G1
Rightist col removed 10-16, 884C2

Panama Canal & Zone—*See PANAMA Canal*
U.S. Relations—*See also PANAMA Canal*
US issues rights rpt 2-9, 102B1
Carter consults on DR electn 5-19, 414C2
US bank plans refinancing pkg 6-22, 632D2

1979

PALMYRA
A-waste site disputed 8-21, 743D3
PALOMINO, Carlos
Benitez decisns for WBC welterwgt title 1-14, 79B3
PALO Verde Nuclear Generating Station—*See ARIZONA–Atomic Energy*
PANA, Gheorghe
Named Bucharest mayor 1-31, 171B1

PANAMA—*See also IDB, NONALIGNED Nations Movement, OAS*
Freedom House lists as partly free 12G3
Tanker fleet safety record rptd 8-15, 608E1
Coup plot revealed amid strikes 10-24, Royo rejects union demands 10-25, 836A3-837A1
Teachers strike settled 10-31, 875D1

Foreign Relations (misc.)—*See also 'UN' below*
Nicaragua, El Salvador prelates backed 2-12, CELAM documt signed 2-13, 108A3, F3
Japan trade missn moves from El Salvador 3-1, 235E1
Swiss banks block Peoples Temple funds 3-12, 250F1
Mex-CR missn on Nicaragua dispatched 5-21, 409B1
Nicaragua denounces rebel aid 5-27, 409D2
El Salvador rebels accept asylum 5-31, alter plans 6-1, 424E3
Nicaragua chrgs rebel arms aid 6-6, 427D1
Nicaragua rebels offer prisoner transfer 6-12, 446E3
Nicaragua rebel aid probed 6-20, 481B2
US envoy meets Nicaragua rebels 6-27, 475G2
Peoples Temple funds transfer rptd 8-2, 592C3
Nicaragua deports 60 radicals 8-16, 636D2
OAS lauds rights stance 10-30, 824G2
Shah rules out asylum 12-5, 914D1
Shah gets asylum 12-15, thanks govt 12-16; protests rptd 12-18, 957A1
Shah asylum scored by Iran 12-16, 12-17, 958B1
Anti-shah protests curbed 12-19—12-21, 975B3
Obituaries
Pinilla, Jose M 8-10, 671D3

Panama Canal & Zone—*See PANAMA Canal*
UN Policy & Developments
Membership listed 695A3
Pol Pot govt seat opposed 9-19, 695D2
U.S. Relations—*See also PANAMA Canal*
Peoples Temple money rptd banked 1-17, 117G2; Swiss banks block funds 3-12, 250F1; funds transfer rptd 8-2, 592C3
Firestone '72 gold trading chrgd 3-15, 202A2

1980

PALMIERI, Doria
Marries Reagan's son 11-24, 998B1
PALMIERI, Judge Edmund L.
OKs Loews film productn 2-27, 229E1
PALMIERI, Louis
Indicted 3-3, 215E1
PALMIERI, Salvatore
Indicted 3-3, 215D1
PALMIERI, Victor H.
In Bangkok on US relief aid 1-8; in Malaysia, says US to take refugees 1-12, 49G1
Says Cambodia famine averted 1-23, 108A2
On 6-mo refugee reprieve 6-20, 484C3, 485A1
PALMYRA Island (U.S. territory)
US A-waste plan questioned 5-21, 405G2
PAN Am—*See PAN American World Airways*

PANAMA—*See also IDB, NONALIGNED Nations, OAS*

Foreign Relations (misc.)—*See also 'Monetary' below*
Emb in El Salvador seized 1-11; amb, 5 others exchngd for leftists 1-14, 38G3
Iran asks shah extraditn 1-12; Iran rpts arrest 1-23, 1-24; Panama denies 1-23, 47B1
Emb in El Salvador seized again, amb taken hostage 2-13, 117C2
Emb in El Salvador vacated, amb freed 2-14, 149D1
Students occupy El Salvador emb 2-28, 152D1
Peoples Temple funds returned to US 2-28, 170C3
Bahamas bank looting case rptd 3-3, 229A1
Shah in hosp 3-11—3-14, operatn delayed 3-16, 204F1
US asks shah to stay, MDs dispute med treatmt 3-21—3-23, 217C1
Iran chrgs US plot vs shah's extraditn 3-22, 217G1
Shah leaves 3-23, arrives Egypt 3-24, 217A1
Iran files shah's extraditn request 3-24, 217B1
Royo in Japan, sees Ohira 3-25, 234B3
Iran says US blocked probe of shah 4-16; US denies 4-17, 283C1
Colombia leftist-govt mtg proposed 4-19, rejctd 4-21, 311E2, C3
AF plane crashes in El Salvador 6-15, gunrunning denied 6-16, 462C3
US aircraft carrier collides with freighter, 2 killed 7-29, 675D1
Bolivia junta tied to drug trafficking 8-15, 668C1
22 DR stowaways drown on freighter 9-5, crew detained 9-9, 687C3
Iran attacks ships 10-7, 758G2
Reagan US electn reactn 11-5, 841F2
UN Cncl seat won 11-13, 896C1
Cuba ex-offcl asks UN probe prison hunger strike 12-4, 965D2
Bolivia coup condemned by Santa Marta conf 12-17, 992A3
Government & Politics—*See also other appropriate subheads in this section*
Natl cncl electns won by Torrijos party 9-28, voter turnout disputed 9-30, 752F1
Monetary, Trade, Aid & Investment
Japan canal feasibility study agreed 3-25, 234B3
El Salvador leftist arms aid denied 6-16, 462D3
Pan Cafe liquidatn plans rptd 10-3, 777F2

Panama Canal & Zone—*See PANAMA Canal*

1976

Arias return barred 1-29, 121F3
Lockheed payoffs cited 2-4, 130F2
Forgn min sees Kissinger in CR 2-24, 177B1
'75 shrimp import data rptd 5-11, 431G1
CIA 'destabilizatn' plan chrgd, denied 9-17—9-22, 792C1, F1-G2

1977

Students burn US amb's car 10-4, 756G1
Dole chrgs Torrijos drug role 10-13; US clears, concedes brother indicted 10-13—10-15, 792C1
US econ, mil aid plan scored 10-14; Torrijos defends 10-20, 10-21, 809B2
Aid pacts held unconst by Sen Allen 10-28, State Dept disputes 11-15, 912G1
Sens visit; Torrijos vows chngs 11-9—11-12, 911A2
Drug chrgs anger Panama 11-13, Dole to get file on Torrijos' brother 11-16, 912C2

1978

Nicaragua rebel aid halt urged by US 12-11, 1018F3
Guyana cult money rptd found in bank accts, frozen 12-20; USSR rejects bequest 12-18, 1000F1, B2

1979

5 indicted in arms plot 5-14, 386C3
US House probes Nicaragua rebel aid 6-20, 481B2
US envoy meets Nicaragua rebels 6-27, 475G2
Nicaragua troop training set 9-11, 731E2
US scored on Cuba naval maneuvers 10-24, 824C2
US vets arrested in coup plot 10-24, 836C3
Carter thanks for shah asylum 12-15; US econ aid motive, anti-US riots rptd 12-18, 957B1, A2

PANAMA Canal Co.—*See under U.S. GOVERNMENT* (1976)

PANAMA Canal Co.—*See under U.S. GOVERNMENT* (1977)

PANAMA Canal Commission (1977)
Treaty creates; text 9-7, 677D2, 680A1-682G3

PANAMA Canal & Zone

1976

Torrijos, Castro conf on US talks 1-10—1-15, 52C2
'70-75 Peru mil training rptd 1-16, 142D3
US dislike of Tack rptd 1-16, 291B2
No '76 US-Panama pact seen 1-17, 52G2
Panama exiles treaty critics 1-20; business ldrs strike, score Torrijos 1-21—1-29, 121C2
US sends Guatemala quake relief 2-4—2-11, 120C3
Talks resume, impasse rptd 2-7—2-22, 291C2
Colombia backs Panama claim 2-23, 178D1
Torrijos warns vs talks failure 3-7, 291D3
Canal Co strike 3-15—3-20; Torrijos, US press statemts 3-22, 3-25, 291E3-292C1
US ship-measuring system enacted 3-23, 292B1
Tack replaced 4-1, 291B2
US House subcom probes talks 4-6—4-8; Bunker testimony revealed 4-13, White House statemt on treaty aims 4-15, 281D1, 291G2
UN conf vs US policy 6-11, 431D3
OAS urges new US pact 6-18, 464G2
Venez asks US return canal 6-22, 793C1
Fscl '76 traffic, revenues down 7-9, 793F1
US treaty aims rider enacted 7-12, 534A2
Torrijos asks nonaligned support vs US 8-17, 621F3
OAS com vs toll hike 8-26, canal co asks US OK 10-5, 793D1
Students riot; US talks suspensn blamed, residents seized 9-10—9-20; Boyd denounces US, asks new talks 9-22, 792C1-B3
New canal talks set 10-7, deadlock described 10-8; Torrijos warns US 10-11, 792D3
Treaty talks continue, detailed 10-19—10-26; 12-13—12-18, 1008F1
Suit vs canal talks filed 10-26, thrown out 12-18, 1008E2
Canal Zone blasts 10-31—11-1; Torrijos scores US chrgs 11-29, 1008A3
Peru execs vs canal toll hike 11-1; Ford OKs hike 11-18, US shippers score 11-24, 1008C3
Venez again urges US return canal 11-16, 929C3
Soclst Intl seeks US sovereignty recognitn 11-27, 935F3
US panel urges new treaty 12-14, 975A1
U.S. Presidential Campaign Issue
Reagan scores US talks 2-28, secret agrmt denied 3-2, 166C1
Ford rebuts Reagan 3-6; chrgs traded, White House statemts 4-10—4-21; Boyd, Torrijos score candidates 4-13, 4-16, 4-21, 281C1, B3, 291C2
Reagan scores Ford Admin 3-31, 232E3
Goldwater, Rockefeller attack Reagan stand 5-2—5-4, 324G1
Goldwater ad scores Reagan 5-8—5-9, 342B3
Dem platform text cites 6-15, 478G2
Carter states views 6-23, 452A1
Dem conv women delegates, table 508E2
Dem conv pres vote, table 7-14, 507A2
GOP platform com OKs plank 8-13, 582G2
GOP platform text cites 8-18, 609G3
Boyd cites issue 9-22, 792B3
Ford, Carter debate 10-6, 742F1
Torrijos scores Ford-Carter debate 10-7, 792F3

1977

CIA linked to '71 Cuba swine fever 1-9, 19G2
Panama studts burn US flags at mem'l svc 1-9, 46D1
Latin ldrs back Panama demands 1-18, 46F1
Canal Co rpts '76 resignatns 2-1, 379E2
2 US sens back treaty talks 2-2, 379A2
Linowitz joins US team 2-8, apptmt disputed 2-21—3-19, 379B1
Escobar to lead Panama talks 2-9, 379A1
Panama detains treaty opponent 2-11, 2-12, US protests 2-14, 379C2
US treaty talks open 2-14—2-23, 379A1
Carter call-in topic 3-5, 171E1, D2
Panama hires firm to promote treaty 3-24, 379B2
Carter backs treaty talks, Latin A-ban pact 4-14, 295F2, E3
Panama '76 svcs rptd down 4-22, 379G2
US talks continue 5-9—5-11, defns role disputed 5-12—5-18, 378F2
Pitty notes US 'exploitatn' 5-13, 415C2
Videla, Perez back Panama claim 5-13, 547F2
Carter signs Latin A-pact 5-26, 415D3
Treaty talks progress rptd 6-15, defns issue rptd resolved 6-17, 494E2
Carter hopeful on treaty 6-30, 515G1
Carter Miss town mtg topic 7-21, 575C1
Carter: US considering 2d canal 7-21; experts cite econ drawbacks 7-25, 589E3
Carter sees negotiators, writes Torrijos; Escobar reaffirms Panama terms 7-29, 589D2-D3
2 US sens vs treaty talks 7-29, 589G3
Torrijos, regional ldrs meet; back new canal pact 8-5—8-6, 606A3-607A1
Treaty talks resume, econ dispute rptd resolved 8-8, 607A1
Treaty accord reached 8-10, Carter discloses provisns 8-12, 621A1
Castro, Church talks 8-10, 653G3, 654D1
US Sen ratificatn battle looms, House critics score 8-11—8-18, 621F2-622D2
Panama protests rptd 8-11; Escobar defends treaty, ratificatn seen 8-12, 622E2
Young lauds Castro treaty backing 8-11, 646D3
Young, Perez laud new pact 8-12, 647D1
US reps assess Argentina treaty backing 8-18—8-20, 670G1
US conservatives fight ratificatn 8-19—9-7, Sen support rptd unclear 9-7, 678E1-E3
Escobar defines US interventn, warship transit rights treaty terms 8-19, 754A3
US Admin ratificatn campaign gains Sen, labor, business endorsemts 8-20—8-30; mil support sought 8-29, 678F3
Carter defends proposed treaty 8-23, 649F2
Vance-Gromyko mtg delayed 8-31, 751D2
US to downplay Cuba ties 9-1, 685D3
Brazil, Mex treaty support rptd 9-3, 678E1
Carter hemispheric 'summit', treaty support assured 9-6, 677G2-678A1
Carter, Torrijos sign treaties, protocol deposited with OAS 9-7, 677A1; texts 679B2-683E3
Latin ldrs, Trudeau at treaty signing 9-7, 677F2, 678C1
Canal Zone map 9-7, 678A2
Panama students protest treaties, 30 seized in police clash 9-7, 679D1-A2
Canal Zone residents protest treaties, canal employe resignatns seen 9-7, 679A2
Canal Zone gun sales, crime rate up 9-7—9-18, 756E1
Reagan, Bunker testify on treaties, rights issue raised 9-8, 698C3-699E1
Torrijos sets Oct treaty plebiscite 9-9, 698G1
US sens take treaty stands, conservatives plan 'truth squads' 9-9—9-11, 698G2
Mex pres rptd vs treaties 9-9, 716F3
CAB acts on NY-London budget fare 9-9, 9-15, Carter overrules 9-26, 860E2
US Sen vote delayed until '78 9-10, 698E2
USSR, China assess treaties 9-10, 699B2
Torrijos invites OAS rights probe, UN plebesicite observance; US lauds 9-13, 699F1
Treaty error bars taxes for US residents 9-14, 699C2
Kissinger, Rusk defend treaties before House com 9-14, vets vs 9-16; NCC backs 9-14, John Wayne 9-20, 716A3-E3

1978

US troop presence rptd 1-2, 5D2
Baker visits Panama, sees Torrijos 1-3—1-7, 58G1
Vance backs pacts in 'Jan blitz' 1-11—1-13, 58A2
Byrd backs pacts 1-13; Byrd, Baker plan amendmts 1-25, 58G1
Sup Ct bars pact challenge 1-16, 33F2
Anti-pact 'truth squad' tours US 1-17—1-19, 58B2
Carter State of Union Message 1-19, 29B1, B3, 31A3
NYT/CBS poll cited 1-19, 58C2
US Sen com backs pacts, asks defns, transit addenda; Baker, Byrd see ratificatn 1-30, 58A1
Durkin, Leahy back pacts 2-1, 58E1
Carter in TV appeal for pacts 2-1, 58E2
Gallup Poll: US backs pacts 45%-42% 2-2, 58D2
Byrd, Baker ask pact amendmts 2-7, 120C1
US Sen debate opens 2-8—2-10: Torrijos drug link discussed 2-21—2-22; pact critics lose procedural vote 2-22, 120B1-121A1
Reagan scores pacts in TV address 2-8, 121A1
US: Canal revenues will supply all Panama paymts 2-9, 120A2
Carter backs pacts, gets ovation in NH 2-18, 123B3
US Sen pact votes sought 3-9; Carter deals rptd 3-13, Packwood scores 3-14, 177E1, A3
US Sen amends neutrality pact 3-10, 3-13, OKs reservatns 3-15, 3-16, 177G1, G3-178F1
Torrijos scores DeConcini reservatn, Carter placates 3-15; Escobar buys time 3-16, 255B2
US Sen OKs neutrality pact, roll call vote listed 3-16, 177C1, C2, 178F1
Carter lauds vote, sees Apr ratificatn 3-16, 178G1
Panama hints pact chngs OK, study ordrd 3-16, 178A2
Panama oppositn threatens pacts 3-16—4-14, renegotiatn urged 4-6, 255E1, D2, D3
Venez backs US pacts 3-28, 233D1
Harris Poll on pact backing in US rptd 4-3, 256B1
Sen rejcts land transfer amendmt 4-5, 256B1
Torrijos initiates diplomatic maneuvers vs DeConcini reservatn 4-6, 4-7, 4-9; Carter warns 4-7, Byrd discounts 4-8, 255E2
UN delegates rpt Panama circulatn of treaty reservatn note 4-7, 255E2
DeConcini seeks 2d reservatn, OKs 'understanding'; Moynihan, Haskell vote threat rptd 4-13, 255E3-256A1
Canal treaty ratificatn in doubt; Carter Dem ldrship lobby 4-14—4-18, 273B2
US Sup Ct denies treaty stay 4-17, 308G2
US Sen OKs DeConcini, other Canal Treaty reservatns 4-18, 273B1
US Sen ratifies Panama Canal Treaty 4-18, 273A1
Carter, Torrijos hail treaty vote 4-18; Panamanians celebrate, protest 4-18—4-20, 273G2, 274E1
US gen scores pact 4-27, resigns 4-28, 321G2
Treaty challenge review refused by US Sup Ct 5-15, 387G3
Panama revenue up in '77 6-9, 632D2
Anti-treaty rally hears Arias 6-10; 2 killed in anti-Carter rally 6-14; govt bans 2 more rallies, closes univ 6-15, 463C3
Treaty instrumts exchngd by Carter, Torrijos; Latin ldrs attend 6-16; Carter addresses Zonians 6-17, 463F2, 464B1
Carter: pacts good Latin omen 6-21, 489B3
Mil constructn funds cleared by Cong 8-21, 662B2
US backs Alaska oil transport 9-12, 702D1
Treaty negotiator elected Panama pres 10-11, 764D3
Mex oil arrives Japan 11-5, 903F3
Clark loses US Sen reelectn 11-7, 854C2

1979

US Army truck crash kills 16 1-11, 140D3
Carter sees GOP ldrs re treaty legis 6-7, 419D3
US House debates treaty implementatn 6-20–6-21, clears bill 6-21, 481A1-B2
VFW vs US treaty implementatn 8-21, 628D1
Royo lauds Carter re pacts 9-5, 675A2
US House votes down treaty implementatn 9-20; Cong OKs compromise 9-25, 9-26; Carter signs 9-27, 723A1
Tolls hiked 29.3% 9-26, 723B2
US treaty implemented; control ended, admin installed 10-1, 753F3
'80 funds clear Cong 11-15, 11-19, Carter signs 11-30, 920D1
US comm apptmts delayed, treaties violatn chrgd 12-6, 938G3-939E1

1980

Reagan 'basic speech' scores Carter 2-29, 207G2
Japan-Panama 2d canal study agreed 3-25, 234B3
US comm apptmts confrmd 4-2, 308C3
US 5th judicial circuit split 10-14, 918B3
Carter cites treaty adoptn 11-19, 881A3
Shipping increase clogs, US sets improvmt aid 11-24, 895C3-896C1

1976

PANAMA City, Fla.—*FLORIDA*
PAN American World Airways
Panama bars Arias return 1-29, 121F3
Commercial flight marks set 5-2, 5-3, 912F3
Ct voids '75 route swap 6-30, CAB overrules 11-19, 992E2
Drops Lebanon employees 629B2
USSR arrests employe 11-24, 907E3
Ford rejcts CAB transatlantic plan 12-28, 992D2
PANATTA, Adriano
Wins Italian Open tennis 5-30, 656C2
PANCHA Kaysornthon
Shot 4-1, 255F3
PANDOLFI, Filippo
Sworn Italy finance min 7-30, 573E1, F1
PANDREAUD, Robert
On French crime rate 12-7, 1003C1
PANETTA, Leon E.
Burns scores NAACP ruling 8-12, 671F2
Elected 11-2, 824G3★, 829B1
PANGGABEAN, Maraden
Says Fretelin defeated 2-11, 192D1
In Australia talks 4-14, 309A3
PANSAK Vinyaratn
Arrested 10-16, 794E2, C3
PANTCHOULIDZEW, Col. A. E.
Cited in Bernhard probe rpt 8-26, 628B1
PANTOJA, Noel
Orders Occidental bribe case arrests, 7-14, 593C1
PAPADOPOULOS, Despina
Sentenced 6-28, 873C1
Acquitted 12-15, 1004E2
PAPADOPOULOS, George
Tanker runs aground 12-15, 968D3
Wife acquitted 12-15, 1004E2
PAPADOPOULOS, Capt. Georgios
Nantucket oil spill testimony rptd 12-28, 1014B1
PAPADOPOULOS, Tassos
Greek Cypriot negotiator 4-8, 311B2
Wins parlt seat 9-5, 772F1
Asks expulsions halt 10-7, 963B3
PAPAGNO, Rogelio
Rights revoked, arrest ordrd 6-23, 520D1
PAPAGO (U.S. warship)
In Intl Naval Review 7-4, 488D3
PAPALIGOURAS, Panayotis
At Greece-EC talks 7-27, 853E3
On dissolutn of Andreadis holdings 9-8, 854C1
PAPANASTASIOU, Vassilios
W Ger terrorist extradited 10-1, 755A1

1977

US bugging of talks rptd 9-16; US Sen com probes 9-16—9-19, 716A2
Torrijos vows pol exiles return 9-17, 716F3
Spain king backs treaties 9-17, 805D1
US mil chiefs reaffirm treaty support, Carter pressure chrgd 9-20—10-4, 755F1
Cranston sees US Sen ratificatn after Hollings endorsemt 9-20; Byrd sees vote short, rpts mail 4000 to 6 vs 9-24, 755G2
US poll shows public vs pacts 9-21, 755F2
Torrijos begins 10-natn treaty support tour 9-24, 755D3; completes tour 10-14, 792B2
US Sen treaty hearings open 9-26; interventn rights, warship transit terms disputed 9-26—10-5, 754F2
Panamanian treaty backing grows 9-27, 756B1
GOP Natl Com rejects pacts 9-30, 755D3
US Sen panel tap hearings postponed 9-30, 756D1
Dole documt release spurs treaty terms controversy, ethics probe 10-4—10-6, 792B1
US Sen hears mil chiefs dispute USSR, Cuba interest; pub concern wanes 10-9—10-10, 792F1
Dole chrgs Torrijos drug role 10-13, US clears 10-13—10-15, 792C1
Interventn, transit issues clarified by Carter, Torrijos 10-14; Byrd, Dole laud 10-15, 791A3
Panama treaty oppositn detailed, censorship reimposed 10-14—10-23, 809F1-B2
Torrijos defends pacts, US 'defense umbrella' 10-20—10-21, 809C2
Carter topic in Denver 10-22, 817D1
Panama plebiscite OKs treaties; UN, forgn univ observers present 10-23; Torrijos lauds 10-24, 809A1
Plebiscite fraud chrgd 10-23, teacher rptd arrested 10-24, 809D1
Castro sees US ties delayed by treaty controversy 10-26, 896D2
Aid pacts held unconst by Sen Allen 10-28, State Dept disputes 11-15, 912G1
Plebiscite final vote count rptd 10-29, 845A1
GOP oppositn continues 10-29, fund-raising use rptd 10-30, party warned 11-13, 912A1
TV campgn vs pacts begins in 3 southn states 10-29, 912B1
US House treaty OK stressed 11-3, 912A2
Byrd: US opinion 'shifting' 11-8, 911E3
US sens visit Panama, Torrijos vows chngs 11-9—11-12, 911A2
Panama Indians' treaty oppositn examined 11-10, 911C2
US drug chrgs anger Panama 11-13; Dole to get file on Torrijos' brother 11-16, 912C2
UPI: 39 sens favor pacts 11-22, 911G3
Jamaica asks US ratify pacts 12-16, 1019A2
Carter stresses treaty 12-28, 1002B1
PANAMA City, Fla.—*See FLORIDA*
PAN American Building (N.Y.)
Copter tips over, kills 5 5-16, 412A3
PAN American Health Organization
Fred Soper dies 2-9, 164E3
PAN American World Airways (Pan Am)
Indicted for rate-fixing 2-3, 93F2
Pacific fare hike barred 2-9, 324G3
Linowitz role in Panama Canal talks scored 2-21, suit filed 3-16, 379D1
KLM crash in Canary I 3-27, 244C1
Canary I crash suits filed 3-31—4-6; probe opens 4-4, 311B3-312C1
Ozone illness measures rptd 5-6, 369C2
Laker 'Skytrain' svc OKd 6-13, 500G2
UK air svc pact set 6-22, 500G1, D2
US-UK fare cut sought 7-29, 593D1
Loses Dallas-London route, wins 2 others 12-21, 1006E2, A3
PANATTA, Adriano
Wins WCT tourn 4-18, loses doubles title 5-8, 430D2, A3
Australia wins Davis Cup 12-4, 970F1, E2
PANDEY, R. M.
Quits party 2-2, 71F1
PANDIT, Vijaya Lakshmi
Backs Gandhi foes 2-14, 116E1
PANHANDLE Eastern Pipe Line Co.
FPC splits on Alaska pipe route 5-2, 369B3
Trunkline Gas Co.
FPC OKs Algeria LNG imports 4-29, 370B1
PAN Ocean Oil Corp.
Marathon Oil takeover cited in table 880G1
PANT, K. C.
Loses Parlt seat 3-16—3-20, 205C2
PAOLUCCI, Capt. Dominic (ret.)
Acquitted for Iran contract fraud 11-24, 942F2
PAPA, Vincent
Slain 7-26, 642B1
PAPACONSTANTINOU, Constantine
Named Greek dep premr 11-28, 925F1, A2
PAPADONGONAS, Alexandros
Named Greek communicatn min 11-28, 925B2
PAPADOPOULOS, Lefteris
Sentenced to life 8-11, 764D2
PAPA Junior, Jose
Asks democracy 2-2, 281B2
PAPALIGOURAS, Panayotis
Named Greek forgn affairs min 11-28, 925G1, B2

1978

PAN American Games—*See under SPORTS*
PAN American World Airways (Pan Am)
'77 aviation deaths rptd 1-6, 24B1
'76 tax nonpaymt rptd 1-27, 65G2
Lockheed L-1011 jet deal announced 4-4, 264D2
LA gets 2-carrier London svc 6-9, 570D1
Boston-Amsterdam fare experiment 6-15—7-31, stranded travelers get aid 7-16, 640C3
Natl Airlines stock purchase OKd 8-28, merger set 9-7, 700G3
CAB OKs Houston svc 9-1, 701E1
Svc to Moscow, 9 other Eur cities to end 9-7, 701F1
Canary I '77 crash rpt issued 10-18, Dutch score 10-23, 888A2
US, W Ger air svc pact expanded 10-25, 831F1
Australia proposes cut-rate US fare 11-14, 920G2
Eastn seeks Natl merger 12-11, SEC probe rptd 12-22, 1007C3
Australia-US air pact set 12-13, 985G1-A2
Intercontinental Hotels Corp.
China hotels set 11-6, 880A2
PANATTA, Adriano
Loses Italian Open 5-28, 418D2
PANCHEN Lama
At China Consulative Conf 2-24—3-8, 154G2
PANDOLFI, Filippo Maria
Named Italy treasury min 3-11, 191B1
Andreotti wage policy backed 10-31, 883C1
PANETTA, Rep. Leon Edward (D, Calif.)
Reelected 11-7, 850F1
PAOLELLA, Alfredo
Killed 10-11, 817B1
PAON, Robert
Named French budget min 4-5, 245F2
PAPAGEORGIOU, Andreas
Named Cyprus commerce min 3-8, 189A2

1979

PAN American World Airways (Pan Am)
Iran airport strikers ask ban 1-1, 3A1
False ads chrgd 1-10; $99 cross-country fares, new routes OKd 1-12, 35D2, F2
London fare cut urged by CAB 1-23, 87F3
IATA membership ended 1-31, 112A1
Sydney hijack bid foiled 4-4, 266F2
Dutch probe Canary I '77 crash 5-29, 412C2
Half-fare plan takes effect 7-1, 579A1
CAB OKs merger bid 7-10; TXI quits race 7-28, Natl stock purchased 8-2, 578D3
TXI eyes TWA merger 9-13, 830E1
China charter svc pact OKd 9-17, 726D1
Natl stock acquisitns rptd 10-18, CAB OKs merger 10-25, Carter approval sought 10-29, 830A1
Mex ground workers strike 11-1, 874E3
Carter OKs Natl merger 12-22, 989C1
PANANDIKAR, Pau
Birth control problems rptd 8-13, 687A3
PANATTA, Adriano
US wins Davis Cup 12-16, 1003A3
PANAVISION—*See WARNER Communications*
PANAX Corp.
Mich TV licenses granted 5-31, revoked 7-12, 618E2
PANCHEN Lama
Imprisonmt rptd 5-6, 353F1
PAN Ching-hsi
Says Viets mass near Laos-China border 9-6, 660B2
PANDOLFI, Filippo Maria
Defends central bank 3-26, 237C2
Tries to form govt 7-27, 583G2
Abandons bid to form govt 8-1, Cossiga sworn premr 8-5, 602G3
PAPA, Vincent (d. 1977)
2 convicted in slaying 10-23, 840A3
PAPADOULOS, Archbishop Cyril
Guerrillas attack home 7-4, 546F3
PAPALARDO, Conrado
Pinochet, Letelier assassins rptd linked 2-9, 114F3

1980

PAN American World Airways (Pan Am)
Natl merger completed 1-7, Miami-London svc retentn OKd 4-7, 346F2
Ozone illness measures rptd 2-12, 159C1
USSR office reductn set 2-20, 134G3-135A1
Discount coupons revived 3-10, 346D3
Laker Miami-London svc OKd 5-15, 516D2
NYC bldg sold for record price 7-28, 985B3
PANATTA, Adriano
Wins Florence Grand Prix 5-18, 607D3
Loses Geneva Open 9-28, Paris Open 11-2, 947G1, D2
Czechs win Davis Cup 12-7, 946D3
PAN Cafe S.A.
ICO rpts liquidatn plans 10-3, 777F2
PANDAS—*See WILDLIFE*
PANDEY, Kedar
Sworn India irrigatn min 6-8, 445F1
PANDICK Press Inc.
'Insider' stock trading convictn voided by Sup Ct 3-18, 226B2
PANDOLFI, Filippo Maria
Italy treasury min 4-4, 275F3
Replaced as treas min 10-18, 809B1
PANETTA, Rep. Leon E. (D, Calif.)
Reelected 11-4, 842F1
Budget reconciliatn signed 12-5, 936G1
PANFILOV, Alexandr
Wins Olympic medal 7-22, 622E2
PANOV, Valery
Violinist found slain 7-24, 654C1
PANTHEON (magazine)
Titian forgeries chrgd 2-26, 472B3
PAOLETTI, Paolo
Slain 2-5, 99C1

1976

PAPANDREOU, Andreas
Scores US re Turkey pact 3-31, 259D2
Scores govt re MP death 5-2, 351F3
PAPAPOSTOLOU, Col. Demetrios
Sentenced re '75 plot 3-16, 221D3
PAPER & Paper Products
'75 Dutch productn drops 1-6, 102G2
Peru cuts newsprint imports 1-12, 142B2
Dec '75 output rptd up 1-16, 92C1
Canada strikes end 1-21, 47B1
Paperbd indictmts 2-18; cos fined 9-20, stiffer penalties asked 10-5, 885F3; offcls sentenced 11-30, 921D2
Cuba, Colombia sign pact 2-20, 251F3
UK, Japan cos set Paraguay investmt 4-30, 403B3
US GOP platform text cites 8-18, 608B1
5 paper-bag makers indicted 10-29, 886B3

PAPUA New Guinea—*See also ADB, COMMONWEALTH of Nations*
Listed as 'partly free' 1-19, 20D3
Bougainville secessionist raids 1-27, truce 1-28, 123A2
Tribal clashes 2-8, 123B2
Australia aid agrmt rptd 3-4, 172C3
S Pacific Forum meets 3-8—3-9, 179B2
Australia copper deal 3-22, 237D2
Bougainville ends secession try 3-26, 256G2
Total IMF oil loan rptd 4-1, 340D2
Quake hits Indonesia 6-26—6-28, 544A3
Australia trade pact signed 11-8, 997A3
Fraser tours Torres Strait I re seabed pact 11-22—11-24, 961C3
Abstains on UN Gaza resettlemt res 11-23, 878F2
Devalues currency 11-29, 896D1, A3
PARADE (magazine)
Newhouse buys Booth chain 11-8, 910G2
PARAGUAY—*See also IDB, LAFTA, OAS, SELA*
'73 defns budget, mil forces rptd 1-2, 60G2
Listed as 'partly free' 1-19, 20D3
CP ldr arrest, death rptd 1-31, 2-17, 206C1
Forgn debt, GNP data rptd 2-13, 205C3
'75 inflatn rate 6.7%; Alto Parana prices soar 3-5, 205D3
Navy cmdr replaced 3-5, 205F3
Sapena quits as forgn min, Nogues named 3-8, 206B1
Police, guerrillas clash 4-3—4-6; mass arrests rptd 4-10—5-8, 403G1
Pol prisoner abuses chrgd 6-9, 7-12, 557A3
Stroessner reelectn planned 7-16, 557E3
Represssn rptd up in '75-76 10-31, 975D1
Solano Lopez dies 12-14, 1015G2
Listed as not free 12-22, 977B3
Foreign Relations (misc.)
Sidepar, Brazil cos plan steel mill 1-16, 205E3
Russell ct scores rights abuse 1-17, 61D2
Arms, auto smuggling to Argentina rptd 2-4, 3-5, 205G3, 212C1
Bolivia deports 'plotters' 2-4, 237D3
Forgn debt size scored, exports cited 2-13, 205C3
World Bank loan OKd 2-27, 205B3
Stroessner in Uruguay 3-24—3-27, 382D3
Police, Argentine guerrillas clash 4-4—4-6, 403B2
Intl Rights League chrgs Indian abuse, scores US 4-5, 403E2
UK, Japan cos set paper investmts 4-30, 403B3
Yugo dissident kills Uruguay amb 6-8, 542D3
Refugee in Argentina kidnaped 6-11, freed 6-12, 495G3

1977

PAPANDREOU, Andreas
Electn results 11-20, 11-23, 924E3, 925B1
Mavros resigns as DCU head 11-27, 925C2
PAPER & Paper Products
Me Indian land dispute setlmt sought 1-11—1-21, 59A2
Paperbd execs sentncs cut 2-17, 504D1
1st ¼ profits drop rptd 4-28, 668E3
'76 sales rise rptd 340B1
Paper-bag makers convicted 11-23, 918G2-C3
PAPIASHVILI, Avtandil
On Sovt dissidents detentn 8-31, 684B1
PAPILAYA, Max
Killed 6-11, 468F1

PAPUA New Guinea—*See also COMMONWEALTH of Nations*
UN Assemb member 4A1
Seabed border set, Australia suspends talks 2-7, 132C1
Guise quits as gov-gen 2-8, Lokoloko elected 2-18, 203B2
Govt radio ad ban defeated 2-9, 203C2
Queen Eliz visits 3-23—3-26, 280D2, 309A3
Lome Conv membership rptd 3-30, 309A3
1st gen electn 6-18—7-9; fighting follows poll 7-13, 639D1
Currency revalued 8-5, 639C2
Somare elected prime min 8-9, 639F1
NZ to set 200-mi fishing zone 9-7, 729B3
Abstains on UN anti-Israel res 10-28, 830G2
Australia livestock banned 11-23, 922G3

PARAGUAY—*See also IDB, OAS*
UN Assemb member 4A1
Amnesty Intl on pol prisoners 1-1, 3G1
United Liberal party formed 1-24, manifesto rptd 2-7, 202C2
Pol prisoners freed; US, OAS credited 1-27, 2-23, 167G2
Assembly electn 2-6, 202B2
Constitutn amended for Stroessner reelectn 3-7—3-11, 202A2
'75-76 trade, paymts table 3-11, 189B2
'61-75 GDP variatns table 5-30, 439B1
Govt moves vs oppositn rptd 7-8, 9-23, 803E1
Nazi flees Argentina, rptd dead in Asuncion 8-11, 670E3
Nazi war criminal asylum rptd 8-17, 803B2
Stroessner to seek 6th term 9-11, 803D1
In Brazil, Argentina hydroelec talks 9-22—9-23, 794D3; critics rptd arrested 9-23, 803G1
Radical Liberal pres candidate rptd 10-21, 845B1
Amnesty Intl plans campgn 10-28, 905B3
Elec grid frequency chng barred 11-11, 976B1

1978

PAPANDREOU, Andreas
Asks US military exit 1-4, 22G1
Scores US on Turkey arms embargo end 4-4, 277A1
Caramanlis woos DCU 5-11, 374A1
PAPANDREOU, George
DCU split rptd 3-16, 4-11, 374C1
Cardbd mfrs fined 10-13, plead no contest 10-16, 10-25, 1005F2
PAPER & Paper Products
Cardbd mfrs indicted 1-25, 67A2
Harold Zellerbach dies 1-29, 96G3
EPA sets kraft pulp mill pollutn rules 3-22, 263F2, A3
Du Pont pigment monopoly chrgd 4-10, 346A1
NCR plans sale to BAT Industries 5-5, 345B3
Time Inc to buy Inland Container 5-19, 403G2-C3
ICC orders rail freight rates cut back 6-30, 569A3
Olinkraft-Tex Eastn merger set 7-17, 700E3
Union chief Tonelli indicted 7-19, 598D3
Occidental seeks Mead takeover 8-11, Mead rejcts 8-18, 767C2
Intl Paper settles '76, '78 chrgs 8-25, 10-1; 3 other '76 defendants settle 9-25, 10-2, 768C3
'77 defendants sentncd 9-21, 768F2-B3
Abitibi plans Price takeover 9-29, 772C3
US sues vs Occidental-Mead merger, cites copier-paper productn 10-11, expands suit 10-25, 895B3
Olinkraft OKs Johns-Manville offer, ends Tex Eastn bidding 10-27, 896A3
3d ¼ profits rptd down 10-30, 919G2
Union sues Admin re wage-price plan 12-1, 934B2
PAPERWORKERS International Union, United (UPIU) (AFL-CIO)
Union pol organizing backed by Sup Ct 6-22, 508B3
Tonelli, 4 others indicted 7-19, 598E3
PAPLIGOURAS, Panayotis
Resigns as Greek forgn min 5-10, 373E3
PAPP, Joseph
Water Engine opens 1-5, Prayer 1-17, Starving Class 3-2, Runaways 3-9, Catsplay 4-16, All's Well 7-5, Spring Awakening 7-13, Master & Margarita 11-11, Fathers & Sons 11-16, Drinks 11-23, 770B1-G3, 887C1-C3, 1031D1, E1, D2

PAPUA New Guinea—*See also COMMONWEALTH of Nations, SOUTH Pacific Forum*
Currency revalued 1-9, 192C3
Rival tribes riot in Moresby 1-15, 192E3
'78 budget proposed 2-22, 192G2
West New Guinea rebels held 2-27, 192C3
200-mi econ zone set 3-31, 269E3
Students strike 5-7; 90 arrested, univ closed 5-11, 395D3
Australia wartime hangings probe asked 5-8, 350C1
UN Assemb member 713D3

PARADISE Alley (film)
Released 11-10, 970E2

PARAGUAY—*See also IDB, OAS*
Stroessner reelected 2-12, 113D1
Final electn count rptd 2-17, 211G2
State of siege lifted in 3 depts 5-5, 395E3
Stroessner begins new term 8-15, 640F3
Foreign Relations (misc.)—*See also 'Human Rights' and 'Monetary, Trade, Aid & Investment' below*
UN Assemb member 713D3
Nicaragua OAS censure vote abstentn 10-17, 839A3
Chile murder suspect cites Paraguay visas 10-24, 1014F3
Human Rights
Dec '77 prisoner data rptd 1-3, 1-27, 113D2
OAS rights probe OKd 1-9, 'crisis' rptd 1-10, 113F1-A2
Pol prisoners begin hunger strike 6-11, 6 rptd freed 7-7, 559E1
Rights abuse rptd by OAS 6-21, Jamaica scores 6-23, 489G2, E3
OAS rights rpt issued, measures urged 6-28, 7-1; Argana denies chrgs, IACHR probe OKd 6-30, 505B2, D2, B3
Oppositn ldr scores govt 7-6, arrested 7-7, 559C1
Oppositn ldr released 8-8, 640G3
Pol prisoners on hunger strike 9-19, others rptd freed 9-22, 777A3
Oppositn ldr rptd exiled 9-29, 777G2
Press curbs rptd by IAPA 10-13, 829A2
3 pol dissidents return, arrested 11-17, 989F3
Nicaragua abuses scored by UN 12-15, 1019D1
Monetary, Trade, Aid & Investment
Exports value up in '77; trade surplus posted 2-17, 292E3
World Bank OKs road dvpt loan 3-9, 292F3
Hydro project forgn bank loan rptd 3-30, 311C2
Brazil steel loan rptd 5-5, 395E3
US aid cutoff urged by oppositn ldr 7-6, 559D1
Brazil joint hydro projct waters diverted, Eur turbine deal signed; Argentina projcts cited 10-20, 829F2
Obituaries
Chavez, Federico 4-24, 356C2

1979

PAPANDREOU, Andreas
Scores ct ruling on bank strike 8-14, 708G1
PAPER (& Paper Products)
Westn strikes end 1-30–5-9, 345D2
Rumania sets price hikes 3-12, 279E3
GATT pact signed, tariff cuts seen 4-12, 273G1
Crown Zellerbach, Hammermill chrgd re price violatns 4-27, Hammermill cleared 5-17, 385E1
Cardbd mfrs acquitted 4-29, civil setlmts revealed 5-1, 327B3
St Regis Paper struck 5-15, contract ratified 6-23, 598A3
Paperbd trust suit setld 6-28, 647G3
Du Pont pigment monopoly case dismissed 9-17, 810E1
3d 1/4 profits rptd up 10-31, 923C1
Mergers & Acquisitions
Boise Cascade buys Stone Container 1-22, 89E1
Stone Container rejcts Boise bid 1-30, Boise to buy Lone Star unit 4-11, 440E3
Tyco seeks Ludlow 2-9, drops bid 5-3, 560C3
Intl Paper to buy Bodcaw, Weyerhaeuser outbid 3-8, 350A1
Intl Paper buys Bodcaw 8-9, plans oil interest sale 8-10, 664F1
PAPERWORKERS International Union, United (UPIU) (AFL-CIO)
St Regis Paper struck 5-15, pact ratified 6-23, 598A3
PAPP, Joseph
Umbrellas Of Cherbourg opens 2-1, 292E3
New Jerusalem opens 2-15, 712G1
Taken in Marriage opens 2-26, 292D3
Southn Exposure opens 2-27, 292B3
Coriolanus opens 3-14, 292C1; 6-28, 711C2
Sancocho opens 3-28, 712C2
Leave It to Beaver opens 4-3, 712B1
Nasty Rumors opens 4-12, 712F1
Dispatches opens 4-18, 711E2
The Woods opens 4-25, 712G3
Spell #7 opens 7-15, 712E2
Othello Opens 8-8, 712A2
Mercier & Camier opens 10-25, 956D3
Sorrows of Stephen opens 12-11, 1007E2
PAPROSKI, Steven
In Canadian Cabt 6-4, 423G3
Loto Canada sale OKd 8-21, 651D2
PAPUA New Guinea—*See also COMMONWEALTH of Nations*
State of emergency declared 7-23, 616E2-A3
UN membership listed 695A3

PARACEL Islands
China chrgs Viet raid 4-10, asks Viet cede claim 4-26, 298F1, C2

PARAGUAY—*See also IDB, LAFTA, OAS*
Foreign Relations (misc.)—*See also 'Human Rights' below*
Beagle Channel papal mediatn agreed 1-8, 51D3
Letelier murder testimony cites '76 passports 1-18, 58F1
Chile pres tied to Letelier assassins 2-9, 114E3
Stroessner at Brazil pres inaugural 3-15, 210D1
Nazi fugitive loses citizenship, UN extraditn pressure cited 8-8; bounty offered 8-10, 616A3
Somoza arrives 8-19, 636D2
UN membership listed 695A3
Nicaragua seeks Somoza extraditn 10-9, 794B1
Argentina, Brazil dam accords signed 10-19, 845A1
Human Rights
Freedom House lists as partly free 12G3
Jehovah's Witnesses banned 1-4, 22B3
PEN Club condemns 7-21, 554B1
OAS asks comm visit 10-30, 824F2, A3

1980

PAPANDREOU, Andreas
Scores NATO mil wing re-entry 10-20, 800A2
PAPER (& Paper Products)
Paper bag price fixing appeals declined by Sup Ct 1-14, 37E1
'79, 4th 1/4 profits rptd down 2-7, 222A2
Mex in Swedish, Canadian agrmts 5-24, 5-27, 409A3, C3
Antipollutn costs overestimated 6-18, 494F2
Canada contract talks fail 6-20, workers strike 6-27, 7-1, 497G1-F2
Canada contract OKd, strike ends 7-31, 603B2
Canada forest fire losses rptd 8-2, 633A2
Mead rptd guilty of box price fixing 9-15, 917E1
Fine paper trust suits rptd setld 9-29, 12-3, 917A2, B2
Inventory tax ruling impact on publishing rptd 10-5, 836D1
Paperbd trust setlmt case dismissed by Sup Ct 10-20, 807A3
Mergers & Acquisitions
Gulf & Western OKs Brown sale to James River 2-1, 3-27, 385E3
Huyck, Wheelabrator to merge 7-30, 745E3
PAPP, Joseph
Salt Lake City opens 1-23, 136E3
Marie & Bruce opens 2-3, 136C3
Sunday Runners opens 5-4, 392G3
Mother Courage opens 5-13, 392E3
Sea Gull opens 11-11, 892F3
You Know Al opens 11-13, 892G3
Dead End Kids opens 11-18, 1003A3
True West opens 12-23, 1003F3
PAPP, Veronica
Angi Vera released 1-9, 216B2
PAPPAS, George
First Deadly Sin released 10-24, 836G2

PAPUA New Guinea—*See also ADB, COMMONWEALTH of Nations*
Somare govt falls, Chan becomes prime min 2-11, 194F3
Gold, copper dvpt by consortium conditionally OKd 3-10, 194G3
Malaria outbreak rptd 5-31, 478A3
Island trade pact rptd 7-24, 576G2
Troops arrive in Vanuatu 8-18; Espiritu Santo rebellion quelled 8-31, 674B1

PAPUTIN, Viktor S.
Afghanistan death rptd 1-3, 26B2
Role in Afghan coup cited 1-21, 44B2
Afghan role rptd disputed 2-2, 123A3
PARACEL Islands
China claims 1-30, 132C3

PARAGUAY—*See also IDB, OAS*
Human rights record scored 12-10, 978B3
Foreign Relations (misc.)
Colombia envoy seized in DR emb raid 2-27, 141B1
Argentine A-pact cited 3-18, 229E2
IOC rpts Olympic boycott 3-28, 259F3
Colombia DR Emb siege ends, envoy freed 4-27, 335G1
Bolivian mil govt recognized 7-31, 577F1
Somoza assassinated 9-17; Argentina terrorists sought, suspect slain 9-18, 697F2
Nicaragua ties cut, Somoza assassinatn links chrgd 10-1; Somoza Asuncion home attacked 10-2, 792B2
OAS cites poor rights record 11-27, 913B3

1976

PARAMOUNT Pictures Corp.
Adolph Zukor dies 6-10, 444A3
PARBO, A. H.
Rpts Australia copper find 11-18, 902A3
PARDI, Rear Adm. Julio
Argentina social welfare min 3-29, 236C1
PARDO Buelvas, Rafael
Colombia interior min 10-19, 925B1
PAREDES, Adm. Isaias
Loses Cabt post 7-16, 590A3
PAREDES, Juan
Wins Olympic medal 7-31, 574B1
PARENT, Oswald
Recount stalled 12-3, 924E1
Loses recount 12-22, 998C3
PARFET Jr., R. T.
On Upjohn payoffs 3-26, 361E2
PARFITT, Maj. Gen. Harold R.
Settles Panama Canal strike 3-20, 291F3
PARIS, Club of (creditor nations)
Reschedules Zaire debt 6-17, 488A2
PARIS Symphony Orchestra
S Africa TV debuts 1-5, 11B3
PARIZEAU, Jacques
Named finance min 11-26, 903G2
On finance mins conf 12-7, 943A2
PARK, Youngchul
Wins Olympic medal 7-28, 575A1
PARK Chong Kyu
'74 US bribe bid rptd 10-29, 900B2

PARK Chung Hee (South Korean president)
Gulf paymt rptd 134B1, C1
Rpts oil find near Pohang 1-15, 54B1
Kim Ok Son denied passport 2-6, 122B1
Resignation asked 3-1, 176E2
Political foes arrested 3-10, 223B1
3 plotters sentenced 5-3, 334D2
Anti-govt party split 5-25, 440B3
Kim asks N-S cong 7-22, 557F2
On N Korea DMZ attack 8-20, 619D1
18 dissidents sentncd 8-28, 655E1
Imposes social curbs 9-19, 734A1
US influence peddling rptd 10-24, 898E3, 899A1
Shifts Cabt, ousts KCIA head 12-4, 928F2

PARKE, Davis & Co.—*See under WARNER Lambert*
PARKER, Ariz.—*See ARIZONA*
PARKER, Daniel
In Guatemala 2-12—2-16, asks US Cong emergency aid 2-18, 155B3
PARKER, Dave
NL batting ldr 10-4, 795G3
PARKER, Gail Thain
Quits Bennington post 1-29, 271F3
PARKER, John
Sets prison manual probe 9-20, 809B1
PARKER, Thomas
Quits Bennington post 1-29, 271F3

1977

U.S. Relations
Pol prisoners freed; US, OAS credited 1-27, 2-23, 167G2
Todman visits 8-17—8-18, 803B2
Stroessner sees Carter 9-6, at Panama Canal pact signing 9-7, 678A1; 803A2
US sees rights improvemt 9-23, 803A2

PARAMUS, N.J.—*See NEW Jersey*
PARANA River
Brazil, Paraguay, Argentina hydroelec talks 9-22—9-23, 794E3
Paraguay hydro plan critics arrested 9-23, 803G1
Paraguay vs elec grid frequency chng 11-11, 976B1
PARDEE, Scott E.
Rpts '76 forgn exchng mkt tensns, central bank interventns 3-2, 188D3
PARDOE, John
On Healey budget 3-29, 256B3
PARDO Leon, Alberto
Killed by abductors 12-22, 1011A2
PAREDES Bello, Gen. Fernando
Venez defense min 7-15, 566B1
PARENT-Teacher Association, National (PTA)
TV violence outcry rptd 2-9—2-18, 157E3
PARFITT, Maj. Gen. Harold R.
On 2d Panama canal 7-21, 589F3
Sees Dem sens 11-11, 911F2
PARIS, Club of (creditor nations)
Zaire debt rescheduled 7-7, 583D1
PARIS Montesinos, Pedro
Venez youth min 1-7, 23F2
PARIZEAU, Jacques
Govt wage curbs end 1-15, 43G1
PQ info-gathering network rptd 12-7, confrmd 12-9, 965G1, A2
PARK, Ian
Denies exported meat diseased 8-29, 725B2
PARK Chan Hyun
S Korea educ min 12-20, 1017D1

PARK Chung Hee (South Korean president)
Foes urge end to curbs 1-14, 1-26, 116G3 *
US declines Mondale visit 1-28, 70A1
Plans to shift capital 2-10, 116E3
US cong group sees on rights 4-12, 305E3
Foes ask reforms 4-18, 306E1
OKs US troop pullout 5-24—5-26, 441A1
US lobbying scheme detailed 6-5—6-7, 441B3
Lobbying scheme curb rptd 6-20, 556E3
Kim rpts lobbying probe pressure 7-2, 556F3
14 dissidents freed 7-17, foes questn move 7-19, 551C3
In US troop talks 7-25—7-26, 572D1
Park Tong Sun extraditn sought 9-6, 9-8, 687F3
US ex-rep indicted 10-14, 816B1
Lobbying scheme approval chrgd 10-19—10-21, 816E2
Bid to block Kim Hyung Wook testimony chrgd 11-30, 915B1
Reshuffles Cabt 12-20, 1017C1

PARKE, Davis & Co.—*See WARNER Lambert*
PARKER, Judge Barrington
Helms plead no contest 10-31, 838E3
Sentences Helms 11-4, 861E1
PARKER, Dave
NL wins All-Star Game 7-19, 567C2
NL batting ldr 10-2, 926B3, D3
PARKER, Richard B.
Named amb to Leb 2-4, confrmd 2-10, 148F3
Replaced as amb to Algeria 5-9, 418E1
Sees Hoss, Israel shelling end asked 6-16, 510C2
Informs Leb of peace try 10-12, 793A3
PARKER, Tom A.
Elvis Presley dies 8-16, 695F3

1978

U.S. Relations
OAS rights probe OKd 1-9, 'crisis' rptd 1-10, 113A2, B2
Letelier murder suspects identified 3-3—3-6, 188A3
Rights abuse, World Bank loan oppositn linked 3-9, 292F3
US scores Chile on Letelier probe 6-23, 495F3
Oppositn ldr urges US aid cutoff 7-6, arrested 7-7; US ties strained 7-11, 559D1
US amb cited by Letelier murder suspect 10-24, 1014F3

PARANA River
Waters diverted for Itaipu dam 10-20, 829F2
PARAQUAT—*See HERBICIDES*
PARDEE, Jack
Resigns as Bears coach 1-19, signs with Redskins 1-25, 171G2
PARDO Buelvas, Rafael
Assassinated 9-12, 814B3
PARDOE, John
Scores Aldermaston plutonium contaminatn 8-17, 667F2
Urges Ulster troop exit, Liberals disavow 9-17; Conservative scores 9-19, 723D1, B2
On TUC rejectn of econ policy statemt 10-14, 903A2
PARENT, Bernie
NHL goaltending ldr 4-9, 296E2
PARENTS and Teachers, National Congress of—*See NATIONAL PTA*
PARIS, Club of (creditor nations)
Peru forgn govt debt renegotiated 11-4, 1019B2
PARIZEAU, Jacques
Scores insurnc co move 1-6, 16B2
Cuts some sales taxes 4-11, 286G2
Hints new Quebec currency 5-16, 412C3
Chrgs tax cuts aid Ontario 5-17, 391E3
Settles tax cut dispute 6-8, 451B2
Rejects sales tax plan 6-14, 495E1
PARK, Alex
BL ex-exec jailed 8-11, 667A3
PARK, Brad
In NHL top paid player list 4-6, 296G3
Montreal wins Stanley Cup 5-25, 458F1
PARK Chong Kyu
Korea lobbying role chrgd 6-1, 433B1
PARK Choong Hoon
Warns vs US mil pullout 5-29, 399D2

PARK Chung Hee (South Korean president)
Dissidents vs US rights rpt 2-17, ask end to one-man rule 2-24, 135C2
US lobbying role chrgd 3-15, 3-21; denied 3-17, 203D1, F1, A2
Kim candidacy thwarted 4-17, 377G3
Pres electors chosen, assured reelectn 5-18, 377D3
Meets Brzezinski 5-25, 399C2
House seeks Kim Dong Jo testimony 5-31, 432A2
Protectn chief lobbying role chrgd 6-1, 433B1
N Korea vs trade bid 6-23, 497D2
Oppositn ldrs detained 7-5, 538B2
Reelected 7-6, 538A2
Kin tied to housing scandal 7-14, 594F3
US House subcom details lobbying effort, '71 forgn paymts 11-1, 862A3, F3
Inaugurated 12-27, 1022D1

PARKE, Alan
Midnight Express released 10-6, 970C2
PARKE, Davis & Co.—*See under WARNER Lambert*
PARKE, Davis Co. v. Califano
FDA drug seizure case refused by Sup Ct 3-27, 241F1
PARKER, Alan K.
US OKs survey device sale to China 6-9, 436D2
PARKER, Judge Barrington D.
Sets Passman competence test 4-19, 324D1
OKs Townley plea-bargain pact 8-11, 647B3
Bars Westinghouse guilty plea 10-24, fines co 11-20, 961G2
Death threat rptd 12-14, 1015A1
PARKER, Dave
NL batting ldr 10-2; named MVP 11-15, wins Golden Glove Award 11-21, 928E1, D2-F2, B3
PARKER, Justice Michael
Issues rpt on Windscale A-plant 3-6, 227B2
PARKER, Richard B.
Leb asks more UN troops 4-4, 236C1
Wife to leave Beirut 7-27, 581D2
Leb to shift army to south 7-28, 581F1

1979

U.S. Relations
US ex-amb testifies in Letelier trial 2-8, 114F3

PARAMOUNT Pictures Corp.—*See GULF + Western*
PARANA River
Argentina, Brazil, Paraguay dam accords signed 10-19, 845B1
PARAQUAT—*See HERBICIDES*
PARAY, Paul
Dies 10-10, 860B3
PARDOE, John
Stresses electn reform 4-10, 285G2, A3
PAREDES Bello, Gen. Fernando
Venez defense min 3-10, 192C3
PARENT, Paul
Main Event released 6-22, 820G1
PARHAM v. Hughes
Case decided by Sup Ct 4-24, 364B1, E1
PARHAM v. J. L.
Case decided by Sup Ct 6-20, 515E3
PARIS Was Yesterday (play)
Opens 12-19, 1007D2
PARIZEAU, Jacques
Sets asbestos expropriatn bill reading 5-2, 352D2
Vows asbestos co takeover talks 7-25, 563C1
On asbestos co takeover 10-4, 10-9, 771G3
PARK Chan-hee
Decisns Canto for WBC flywgt title 3-18, 412E3
Decisns Igarashi 5-20, 838G3
Draws with Canto 9-9, 839C1

PARK Chung Hee (South Korean president; slain Oct. 26)
Photo 821D1
Kim scores 1-2, police questn 2-10, 116A3
Offers peace talks 1-19, North welcomes 1-25, 69A3
US assures dissidents re rights 3-7, 390A1
Angered at bank scandal 4-13, 287E2
Waldheim confs on N Korea feud 5-5, 342A1
Independents join party 6-7, 470B1
Meets Carter, joint communique issued 6-29–7-1, 494B3-495B1
Kim resignatn call rptd 7-30, paper seized 7-31, 617F3
Carter discloses conversn effort 8-5, 639B2
Oppositn party raid scored 8-11, 617D3
NDP ldr asks resignatn 8-28, 653F3
Kim's NDP ouster protested 9-11, 710A3
Assemb ousts Kim for criticism 10-4, 762B3
Pusan rioters score govt rule 10-16–10-17, 794G2
Gets Carter note on dissent 10-18, 803F2
Slain with 6 bodyguards; Kim, 5 KCIA aides seized 10-26; govt rpts on death 10-26, 10-28, 821A1, F1
Carter lauds 10-27, 822G1
Kim Young Sam deplores death 10-28, 822A1
Funeral held 11-3, 843D3
Foes continue Assemb boycott 11-5, 844B1
Death rpt chrgs Kim coup plot 11-6, 843D2-D3
Election plans set 11-10, Kim Jong Pil named party ldr 11-12, 875B2, E2
Assassinatn trial suspended 12-4, 928F1
Choi elected pres 12-6, 951F3
Chung, others seized 12-12, tied to murder 12-13, 959B3
7 get death for slaying 12-20, 997C1
PARKER, Judge Barrington D.
Gets 2d death threat 1-3, 6B3
Letelier murder trial opens 1-9, jury chosen 1-12, 19G2, A3; data curbed by '78 US-Chile pact 1-23, 75A1
Townley admits lie 1-24, 58E2
Orders cigaret, ad cos obey FTC subpoenas 1-25, 91C3
Sentncs Letelier assassins 3-23, 234F2
Sets wage-rule hearing 5-4, 345G1
Sentences Townley 5-11, 369E2
Bars wage-guide contract denial 5-31, 399A2-F3
Orders Army drug dischrgs upgraded 11-28, 992D1
PARKER, Dave
NL wins All-Star Game, named MVP 7-17, 568D3-569A2
NL batting ldr 9-30, wins Golden Glove Award 11-20, 955D2-F2, 956D1
Pirates win NL pennant 10-5, 797C2
In World Series 10-10–10-17, 816D1
PARKER, Stewart
Spokesong opens 3-15, 712F2

1980

PARAMEDICS—*See MEDICINE--Physicians*
PARFENOVICH, Vladimir
Wins Olympic medal 8-1, 622B2
PARINI, Col. Romano J.
Sentenced for sex harassmt 6-28, 598G1
PARISI, Angelo
Wins Olympic medals 7-27, 8-2, 623D1
PARIS Lights, The All-Star Literary Genius Expatriate Revue (play)
Opens 1-24, 136D3
PARIZEAU, Jacques
On asbestos co purchase 5-8, 371E3-G3
PARK Chan-hee
Oguma KOs for WBC flywgt title 5-18, 1000F3
PARK Choong Hoon (South Korean premier; replaced Sept. 2)
Named S Korea premier 5-21, 395C1
Replaced as premier 9-2, 673B1

PARK Chung Hee (d. 1979)
Aide's death sentnc commuted 1-30, sentnc upheld 5-19, 395G1
US issues rights rpt 2-5, 87C2
687 dissidents amnestied 2-29, 195B3
NDP leadership challenged 3-1, 195E3
Col Pak executed 3-6, Chung sentncd 3-13, 195E3
Students force univ pres ouster 3-19, 375C1
Chon heads KCIA 4-14, 295C1
S Korea widens martial law 5-18, 380F2
Slayer, 4 others executed 5-24, 395F1
Aides arrested re corruptn 7-19, 566E2
Chun promoted to full gen 8-6, 620G2
Cited in Kim Dae Jung trial 8-18, 711F1
Nan Duck Woo named premr 9-2, 673B1
N Korea pres: Chun 'more vicious' 9-25, 737B1
Poet, 7 other pol prisoners freed 12-11, 968A2

PARKER, Alan
Fame released 5-16, 675D2
PARKER, Alton B. (deceased)
Carter concedes early 11-4, 837G1
PARKER, Judge Barrington D.
Letelier murder convictns overturned 9-15, 703D3
Kraft probe suspended 12-12, 989G2
PARKER, Clarence
Executed 4-22, 353A2
PARKER, Jameson
Small Circle of Friends released 3-9, 216F3
PARKER, Robert
Taiwan-China eased ties rptd 4-9, 295E2
PARKER, Scott
Die Laughing released 5-23, 675C2
He Knows You're Alone released 9-26, 836A3

1976

PARKER Hannifin Corp.
Religious-day work ruling affirmed 11-2, 848C1
PARKINSON, C. Jay
Denies '70 anti-Allende aid offer 12-23, 999D2
PARKINSON, Nicholas F.
Australian amb to US 2-1, 97A3
US loan OKd 5-20, 400A1
PARK Soon Nyo
Sentenced 12-15, 1013A3
PARKS & Recreation Areas
Sen OKs end to natl park mining 2-4, 134G1
House OKs Indiana Dunes enlargemt 2-17, 171A1
2 NYS beaches declared disaster area 6-23, Jones Beach stays shut 6-24, 454F2
Valley Forge made natl park 7-4, 489C2
Coastal energy dvpt aid signed 7-26, 566C3
GOP platform text cites 8-18, 607F3
Ford lists as top issue 8-27, 645D1
Ford proposes $1.5 bln plan 8-29, reactn 8-29—8-31, 644C2-E3
Cong clears land conservatn funds 9-13, 745E2-B3; signed 9-28, 982G1
Ford vows expansion 9-15, 686A1
Mondale scores Ford 9-16, 687C2
Ford, Carter debate 9-23, 702F1
Mining curbs signed 9-28, 834B2
Ind Dunes enlargemt signed 10-18, 834B3
Local govt compensatn for fed land acquisitn signed 10-20, 835E1
Ford, Carter debate 10-22, 801F2-B3

PARK Tong Sun (Tongsun Park)
US influence peddling rptd 10-24—12-1, 898E3-900B2
McFall loses US House post 12-6, 919A2
Brademas replaces McFall 12-8, 981F1

PARMA, Jimmy
Arrested 10-14; body rptd found 10-21, 874B2
PAROLE—*See 'Prisons & Prisoners' under CRIME*
PARRA Leon, Bishop Alberto
Seized in Ecuador 8-12, hospitalized 8-15; returns Venez, scores junta 8-23, 693A1
PARRIS Island, S.C.—*See SOUTH Carolina*
PARROTT, Dr. Max H.
On Ill malpractice suit 6-1, 1016C3
PARSKY, Gerald I.
On commodity pacts 6-1, 388E3
Scores UK econ policies 6-22, 458A1
Rptd vs boycott tax penalties 10-7, 787B1
PARSONS, Judge James B.
Fines paperbd cos 9-20, US asks stiffer penalties 10-5, 885F3, 886C2; sentences offcls 11-30, 921D2
S Korea probe rptd 10-30, 11-13, 900A2
PARTRIDGE, Mark
Named Rhodesia conf delegate 10-12, 781D2
PASADENA, Calif.—*See CALIFORNIA*
PASCAL Allende, Andres
'75 CR asylum cited 47F2
In CR, Chile asks extraditn 2-2, 99G3
CR denies extraditn 4-9, 288C3
PASSAGES (book)
On best-seller list 12-5, 972B2
PASSAGE to Ararat (book)
Wins Natl Book Award 4-19, 292D3
PASSAIC River
Great Falls dedicated historic site 6-6, 410B3
PASSMAN, Rep. Otto E. (D, La.)
Defeated in primary 8-14, 633A1
Travel expense probe ends 10-27, 981G3
Huckaby elected 11-2, 822G1
PASTI, Nino
Rptd on CP ticket 5-17, 5-30, 402C3

1977

PARKS, G. Johnny
Named ILWU candidate 4-23, 324A3
Loses ILWU vote 6-23, 481E3
PARKS & Recreation Areas
Ford '78 budget proposals 1-17, 31E3
Cong sets '77 budget levels 3-3, 174E1
Carter proposes youth jobs 3-9, 173F1
Redwood Pk hearings 4-13, 4-14, expansn asked 4-19, 322F3
House OKs strip-mine curbs 4-29, 365E3
Mohawks get NYS Macomb park land 5-13, 632D2
Summer camp porno effort rptd 5-15, 432E2
Sen amends '70 Clean Air Act 6-10, 461B1
Okla Girl Scout campers slain 6-13, 492E1
Minn wilderness, recreatn areas proposed 9-13, 724D1
Alaska plan proposed, ct challenge filed 9-14, 9-15, 739A3, C3
NJ voters OK beach cleanup 11-8, 87C2
PARK Tong Jin
Sees Carter on troop exit 3-9, 202F3
On Park extradtn to US 9-8, 688A1

PARK Tong Sun (Tongsun Park)
Burmah fee, SEC probe rptd 1-19, 55A2
US lobbying scheme detailed 6-5—6-7, 441A3
US employes rptd subpoenaed 6-18, 556B3
Thomson denies KCIA link 7-7, 557A1
Korea lobbying info sharing agreed 8-3, 688D2
House ethics com interview bid rptdly fails 8-20, 688C2
Denies KCIA chrgs 8-24; indicted 9-6, extraditn sought 9-6, 9-8, 687D2
Carter immunity offer rptd 9-17, rejectn seen 9-21, 774G1
SEC chrgs 9-28, consent decree rptd 10-3, 774E1
O'Neill rent records subpoenaed 10-7, 816D3
US ex-Rep Hanna indicted 10-14, 815G3
US interrogatn, bid fails 10-16—10-25, 816D1
'69-76 rice comms detailed 10-19—10-21, 816G2
House asks Korea cooperatn 10-31, Carter rpts immunity offer 11-5, State Dept negotiatns continue 11-30, 915D1, F2
Gift to Passman rptd, denied 11-2, 915C2
'72 diary sought by IRS 11-29, 915A3
US testimony, immunity OKd; Jaworski scores 12-30, 1002A3

PARR, George B. (d. 1975)
LBJ '48 Sen primary fraud chrgd 7-30, 631C2
PARRA Leon, Antonio
Venez health min 1-7, 23E2
PARSONS, Benny
2d in Daytona 500 2-20, 531C2
NASCAR final standing, earnings rptd 11-20, 1020D3
PARSONS, Judge James B.
Cuts paperbd execs sentncs 2-17, 504D1
PARTRIDGE, Mark
Named defns min 3-10, 223F2
Scores UK-US Rhodesia plan 9-8, 699G2
Named Rhodesia agri min 9-18, 824E3
PASCALE, Graziano
Uruguay arrests 7-4, frees 7-14, 601C1
PASQUINI, Eduardo
US sci acad seeks info 4-27, 315A2
PASSAGES (book)
On best-seller list 2-6, 120F3; 3-6, 184F3; 4-3, 264A2; 5-1, 356C2; 6-4, 452A2; 7-3, 548E3, F3; 9-4, 712E3; 10-2, 808F3; 11-6, 872F3
PASSAMAQUODDY Tribe—*See INDIANS American*
PASSMAN, Otto E.
Sex-bias suit OKd 1-3, 59C3
Park gift rptd, 11-2; records subpoenaed 12-2, 915C2
PASTOR, Robert
On Mrs Carter's Latin tour 5-30—6-12, 454F1

1978

PARKER v. Flook
Computer program patents curbed by Sup Ct 6-22, 509B1
PARKES, Phil
NASL goalkeeping ldr 8-6, 655E1, D2
Wins Goalkeepers Cup 8-25, 707A3
PARKINSON, Brian
Apollo wins ASL title 9-10, 707F3
PARKS, Chris
On Jonestown suicides 11-26, 911E1
PARKS, Gerald
On Rev Jones sexual tyranny 11-24, 911A2
PARKS, Patricia
Killed in Guyana cult ambush 11-18, 889E2
PARK Service, National—*See under U.S. GOVERNMENT—INTERIOR*
PARKS & Recreation Areas
Carter budget proposals 1-23, 47E2
Redwood Park expansn clears Cong 2-9, 85D2; 3-21, Carter signs 3-27, 218D1
New wilderness areas clear Cong 2-9, 109C2; signed 2-24, 218A3
RI settles Narragansett claim 3-2, 326G3
Penn Central reorganizatn plan OKd 3-9, 186A1
Alaska bill clears US House 5-19, 386G1
Carter vetoes fish, wildlife authorzn 7-10, 567F3-568B1
House votes $1.3 bln bill 7-12, 526B3
Natl parks $1.2 bln authorzn cleared 10-13, 834G2; signed 11-10, 897A2
Alaska bill dies 10-15, 785A1
Penn Central reorgn ends 10-24, 875G3
NJ, Denver referenda results 11-7, 915C2, F2
Carter protects Alaska lands 12-1, 936F3
PARK Tong Jin
Oppositn to talks with N Korea, US rptd 4-5, 277B3
Vs China Korea stand 5-11, 340A3
PARK Tong Sun (Tongsun Park)
US House seeks testimony 1-4—1-23, Korea OKs 1-31, 63G3
US Justice Dept testimony deal signed 1-10, 1-11, terms rptd 1-13, 63G2-B3
Testifies in Korea 1-13—2-1, total paymts rptd 1-14; US House incumbents seen implicated 1-20, 1-26, 63C2, F2, C3
Dissidents score Korea govt 2-24, 135F2
Testifies to House ethics com 2-28—3-9, 203C3-204A1
Justice testimony re KCIA links rptd 3-1, 203E3
House subcom probes KCIA links 3-16, 203G1, A2
Cited in Hanna guilty plea 3-17, 202F3
Passman indicted 3-31, Park admits paymts 4-3, 239B1, E2
Testifies publicly to House ethics com, denies being S Korea agent 4-3, 4-4; disputed 4-4, 4-5, 239G1-D3
Rice dealer indicted 5-26, 432E3
Korea probe indictmts end seen 6-1, 432A3
US Sen ethics com rpts McClellan gift, 3 others dispute chrgs 6-19, 527D2
US House ethics com cites 4 reps for misconduct, clears O'Neill 7-13, 527B1-B2
3 US reps reprimanded 10-13, 831E3
Sen ethics com terms Korea agent 10-16, 832D1
McFall loses reelectn 11-7, 846D2
PARLOV, Mate
KOs Cuello 1-8, 56C1
PAROLE—*See CRIME—Prisons & Prisoners*
PAROLE Commission—*See under U.S. GOVERNMENT—JUSTICE*
PARRISH, Larry
NL batting ldr 10-2, 928F2
PARSKY, Gerald L.
Loses NYC hotel bid 5-31, 404A2
PARSONS, Benny
3d in Daytona 500 2-19, 538C3
PARSONS, Bob
NFL '77 punting ldr 1-1, 56F3
PARSONS Co., Ralph M.
SEC sues, case settled 8-4, 643C2 ★
PARTEE, J. Charles
Vs discount rate hike 1-6, on dissent 1-9, 28F1
PASCAL, Stephen
Strawberry Fields opens 6-4, 887C3
PASCHALIS, Panalyotis
Israel sentncs for PLO link 7-7, 547G1
PASEDENA, Calif.—*See CALIFORNIA*
PASHAYAN Jr., Charles (Chip)
Wins US House seat 11-7, 850F1, 856C3
PASS, Albert
Boyle convicted again 2-18, 129B1
PASSAGES (book)
On best-seller list 1-8, 24F3
PASSER, Ivan
Silver Bears released 4-20, 619G3
PASSMAN, Otto E.
Park gift testimony rptd 1-14, 63C3
Head paymt chrg rptd 1-27, denied 3-7, 240B2 ★
Indicted 3-31, Park admits paymts 4-3, 239B1, E2
Mental competence test set 4-19, 324D1
Indicted on tax charges 4-28, 324B1
NYC rabbi admits bribing Flood 5-11, 363E2
Korea probe indictmts end seen 6-1, 432A3
PASSMORE, Thomas
Scores Irish RC primate 8-1, 630G1
PASTORA, Eden (Comandante Cero)
Leads Nicaragua guerrilla operatn 8-22—8-24, 659D1-A2
Brother gets Venez emb asylum 10-23, 839G3

1979

PARKER, Viveca
Hitting Town opens 1-6, 292F1
PARKER, William
Rules re dredging scandal 6-11, 468C2
PARKER v. Bergy
Case accepted by Sup Ct 10-29, 884D1
PARKER v. Randolph
Case decided by Sup Ct 5-29, 422A1
PARKER v. Roth
Case refused by Sup Ct 10-15, 847E3
PARKES, Phil
NASL goalkeeping ldr 8-12, 654G3, 655A1
Named NASL top goalie 8-13, 776D1
Named to NASL All-Star team 8-27, 776E1
Whitecaps win NASL title 9-8, 775F2, A3, C3
PARKHURST, Michael
Scores ICC trucking surcharges 6-15, 463B1
PARKINSON'S Disease—*See MEDICINE-Diseases*
PARKLANE Hosiery Co.
SEC suit retrial barred by Sup Ct 1-9, 14B2
PARKLANE Hosiery v. Shore
Case decided by Sup Ct 1-9, 14B2
PARKS Jr., Gordon
Killed in plane crash 4-3, 356F3
PARKS, Hildy
I Remember Mama opens 5-31, 711G3
PARKS & Recreation Areas
Carter budget proposals 1-22, 45D3
Boston Navy Yd renovatn set 2-1, 94A1
US House OKs Alaska bill 5-16, 366E3
PARK Tong-Jin
Hails US troop exit halt 7-21, 567A3
Meets with Vance 11-3, 843F3
Retained as S Korea forgn min 12-14, 997G1

PARK Tong Sun (Tongsun Park)
IRS tax seizure stay denied 1-3, 4C3
US closes Bayh probe 1-5, 4A3
Passman acquitted 4-1, 265B3
Galifianakis indicted 4-10, 283C2
US drops Connell prosecutn 4-16, 283D2
'77 SEC chrg cited 5-1, 376G2
Galifianakis chrg dismissed 8-3, 630A2
US drops indictmt 8-16, 630D1-A2

PARMENTIER, Bernard
Chrgd re pirate broadcasts 8-24, 653D1
PARNELL, Peter
Sorrows of Stephen opens 12-11, 1007E2
PARODI Munoz, Manuel
Arrested in Madrid 8-13, 670F2
PAROLE—*See CRIME-Prisons & Prisoners*
PAROLE Commission—*See under U.S. GOVERNMENT-JUSTICE*
PARRISH, Larry
NL batting ldr 9-30, 955E2
PARRIS Island, S.C.—*See SOUTH Carolina*
PARROT, Jean-Claude
Jailed re '78 strike 5-7, 352D1
NDP scores jailing 11-22–11-25, 927A2
PARRY, L. George
On Phila police probe 4-16, 310E3
PARSONS, Frank
Loses mayoral race 10-30, 829B1
PARSONS, Talcott
Dies 5-8, 432C3
PARTON, Dolly
Wins Grammy 2-16, 336F3
PARTRIDGE, Denny
Homeland opens 4-16, 711F3
PARTRIDGE, Eric
Dies 6-1, 508D3
PARVIN, Theodore
Meteor released 10-19, 1008A1
PASCAGOULA, Miss.—*See MISSISSIPPI*
PASCAL, Stephen
Don Juan opens 4-15, 711E2
PASSAIC, N.J.—*See NEW Jersey*
PASSMAN, Otto E.
4 Korean paymts chrgs dismissed 3-29, acquitted 4-1, 265B3
Ruled liable to sex-bias suit by Sup Ct 6-5, 464A1
Settles sex bias suit 8-23, 649E3
Head convicted of bribery 10-12, sentncd 10-24, 906E1
PASTERNAK, Boris Leonidovich (1890-1960)
Hayward dies 3-18, 272F2
PASTEUR, Louis (1822-95)
Yeast patent ruling cited 3-29, 265A3
PASTORA, Eden (Comandante Cero)
Leads rebel assault in south 6-17, 461D1

1980

PARKER v. Levy
Case cited by Sup Ct 1-21, 93D1
PARKS, Bert
Dropped as Miss America emcee 1-4, replacemt named 3-5, 198G3
PARKS, Hildy
Day in Hollywood opens 5-1, 392F2
PARKS, Patricia (d. 1978)
Layton faces murder chrgs 5-22, 407G3
PARKS, Rosa L.
King Peace Prize award rptd 1-28, 200B1
Gray withdraws as US judge nominee 9-17, 744D2
PARKS & Recreation Areas
State of State messages 1-8, 403F3; 1-9, 483G2, 484E2
Carter budget proposals 1-28, 73G3
Gulf Oil drilling rights affirmed by Sup Ct 3-31, 291A3
Park Svc dir ousted 4-24, 333C2
El Salvador aliens rescued in Organ Pipe Desert 7-4—7-5, 518E2-C3
Alaska lands bill clears Sen 8-19, 631B2
Calif voters OK bond issue 11-4, 847F3
Alaska lands bill clears House 11-12, 866E2
EPA issues new air rules 11-25, 898G1-C2
Lands bill signed 12-2, 915G3-916D1
Fla land donatn rptd 12-19, 987F1
PARK Tong Jin
On US rep's N Korea visit 7-21, 547E1
PARLOV, Mate
Camel decisns for WBC cruiserwgt title 3-31, 320B2
PARNELL, Kenneth Eugene
Chrgd in kidnapings 3-2, 238E2
PARNELL, Kevin (Pat)
Loses US House electn 11-4, 852G1
PAROLE—*See CRIME--Prisons*
PARRIS, Stanford
Elected to US House 11-4, 844A4, 850E2
PARRISH, Lemar
NFL '79 interceptn ldr 1-5, 8G2
PARRISH, Robert
Traded to Celtics 6-9, 447B1
PARRISH, Roy
On Las Vegas hotel fire 11-25, 894C1
PARROT, Jean-Claude
Postal contract ratified 6-2, 444B1
PARSA, Farrokhrou
Executed 5-8, 373E1
PARSIPANNY—*See NEW Jersey, PENNSYLVANIA*
PARSONS, Sir Anthony
Asks Iran-Iraq war end 11-5, 894C3
PARSONS, Benny
Wins LA Times 500; NASCAR top $ winner 11-15, 1002D1, E1
PARTEE, Charles
Not in discount rate vote 7-25, 574G3
PARTON, Dolly
Nine to Five released 12-19, 1003C2
PARTRIDGE, Cliff
NFL '79 punting ldr 1-5, 8F3
PARTSALIDES, Dimitrios
Dies 6-22, 528B3
PARUN, Onny
Loses Austrian Indoor championship 3-23, 607G2
PASANDIDEH, Ayatollah Morteza
Chrgs vote fraud 3-18, 218G1
PASCAGOULA—*See MISSISSIPPI*
PASCALINO, Pietro
Urges anti-terrorist steps 1-11, 59G3
PASCHEK, Frank
Wins Olympic medal 7-28, 624B2
PASHAYAN Jr., Rep. Charles (Chip) (R, Calif.)
Reelected 11-4, 842F1
PASSAMAQUODDY Indians—*See INDIANS, American*
PASSIONE (play)
Opens 5-22, 756F3

1976

PASTORE, Sen. John O. (D, R.I.)
Primary for successor 9-14, 704E3
Chafee wins seat 11-2, 820C1, 821C3
PATAGONIA Corp.
Rptd on FRB 'problem' list 1-22, 111C3
PATAN, Ion
China trade pacts signed 1-29, 117E3
PATASSE, Ange
Named prime min 9-5, 924E2
PATE, James
Quits 1-27, replaced 2-26, 186G1, D2
PATE, Jerry
Wins US Open golf 6-20, 756B3
PATEK, Fred
AL batting ldr 10-4, 796D1
PATEL, Babubhai
Resigns 3-12, backers seized 3-13, 222C1
Arrested 8-9, 624B1
PATEL, H. M.
Vs exec power bill 9-1, 652D1
PATEL, Praful
Scores Malawi re Goans 5-16, 382C2
PATENTS
Sen votes reform 2-26, 181B3
PATERSON, N.J.—*See NEW Jersey*
PATERSON, Basil A.
Carter backs in Dem post 7-12, 513A2, B2
Renamed to Dem post 7-16, 532B3
PATERSON Morning and Evening News
Ford endorsement rptd 10-30, 831F2
PATH of Bliss (religious sect)
Sarkar sentenced 11-29, 952G3
PATINO Ayoroa, Col. Jose (ret.)
Deported to Chile 2-22, 238D1
PATMAN, Rep. Wright (D, Tex.)
Asks bank regulatory audit 1-25, 112B1
Dies 3-7, 240E3
PATO, Octavio
Sets pres bid 5-18, 366D3, 367A1
Ramalho elected pres 6-27, 482D3
Scores Spinola return 8-10, 732F3
PATOLICHEV, Nikolai
Hungary barter pact rptd 4-1, 543B3
Vs US trade policy 11-30, 947B3, D3
PATTEN, Rep. Edward James (D, N.J.)
Reelected 11-2, 830E1
PATTERSON, Rep. Jerry M. (D, Calif.)
Reelected 11-2, 829E1
PATTERSON, William K.
Jailed 9-3—9-17, 700B3
PATTISON, Rep. Edward W. (D, N.Y.)
Reelected 11-2, 830C2

PAUL VI, Pope (Giovanni Battista Montini)—*See 1963, pp. 231G3-232B1 for biog. data*
Vs abortn 1-4, 32D3
Vatican statemt on sex 1-15, 124B2
Scores abortn protest 1-21, 124C2
Warns vs feminism 1-31, 124D2
'42-50 US intellignc ties alleged 1-31, 140D3
Names 2 archbps 2-12, 2-17, 21 cardinals 4-27, 336F1
Birth control ban linked to religion decline 3-23, 443F3
Lauds Cuba progress effort 3-25, 252A1
Names 2 bishops 5-4, 424C1
Urges vote vs CP 5-12, 5-21, 402D3, F3
Installs cardinals 5-24, 423G3
Scores Lefebvre 5-24, 424B1
Spain king renounces bishops veto power 7-16, 541F1

1977

PATE, Jerry
Wins Phoenix Open 1-9, 104C1
Wins Southern Open 10-23, 950E3
Wins Mixed Team tourn 12-4, 950C3
PATEK, Fred
AL batting ldr 10-2, 927A1
PATEL, H. M.
Indian banking min 3-26, 240B1
PATEL, Prabhudas
Quits Congress Party 3-3, 205G2
PATENTS
DNA order lifted 2-24, 184A2
Xerox wins suit vs Canada IBM 7-5, 525B3
Bodine wins United Tech suit 9-28, 860C1
Microbe patent granted 10-6, 847D1
Laser patent to Gould 10-11, 860A1
Inco to retain ESB 11-11, 918E3
PATENT & Trademark Office—*See under U.S. GOVERNMENT—COMMERCE*
PATERSON, Katherine W.
Wins Natl Book Award 4-11, 355B2
PATILINET, Vasile
Named Rumania mines min 12-15, 987A3
PATILLO, Daniel B.
Cited in Lance banking probe 8-18, 625A3
PATINO, Antenor
Niece freed 10-13, 871F1
PATNAIK, Biju
Indian steel min 3-26, 240C1
Corruptn probe asked 4-1, 283D3
PATOCKA, Jan
Rpts Charter 77 support 2-4, 114D3
Sees Dutch foreign min 3-1; detained 3-1—3-2; dies 3-13, 220F2, 264C3
PATOLICHEV, Nikolai S.
US import cut seen 6-11, 530E1
PATRICELLI, Robert E.
Replaced as Urban Mass Transport admin 7-1, 626C3
PATRICK, Harry
Loses UMW pres bid 6-14, 462C3
Miller win certified 7-21, 691B1
PATRICK, Ted
Sentenced 3-28, 287E1
PATRONAGE, Political—*See POLITICS (U.S.); CARTER—APPOINTMENTS; FORD—Politics*
PATT, Gideon
Israel constructn min 6-20, 474E2
PATTEE Canyon—*See MONTANA*
PATTEN, Rep. Edward (D, N.J.)
Named in Hanna indictmt 10-14, 816B1
PATTERSON, Lee Roy
Loses UMW pres bid, steelworkers ties cited 6-14, 462B3, G3
Miller win certified 7-21, 691B1
Miller win affirmed 10-11, 937E2
PATTERSON, Percival
Named foreign min 1-4, 46B1, C1
PATTERSON, Ray
Scores Laker injury to rival 12-12, 990E3
PATTERSON, Red
Demotn by Angel owner rptd 12-17, 990B2
PATTERSON, Russell
Dies 3-17, 264C3

PAUL VI, Pope (Giovanni Battista Montini)—*See 1963, pp. 231G3-232B1 for biog. data*
Leftists score Rome mayor 1-6, 8B3
Names 2 US archbps 1-25, 2-22, 375G2-A3
Mondale visits 1-27, 69C1
Regrets Rhodesia clerics massacre 2-7, 85C1
Sees Spain King, Queen 2-10, 242D3
Traditionalists occupy Paris church 2-27, 471D1
Names US black bishop 3-8, 471B2
On Biayenda death 3-23, 220E2
Female ordinatn review asked 3-23, 374G3
Sees Anglican ldr 4-28—4-29, 374F2
Hungary bishops visit rptd 5-2, sees Kadar 6-9, 492B2
Asks El Salvador min's release 5-8, 373F2

1978

PASTORA, Edgardo
Venez emb gives asylum 10-23, 839F3
PASTORE, Carlos
Exile rptd 9-29, 777G2
PASTORINI, Dan
Oilers win in playoffs 12-24, 12-31, 1024D1, F1
PASTORINO, Carlo
Named Italy tourism min 3-11, 191C1
PASZTOR, Erzsi
Rain & Shine released 12-21, 1030D3
PATAN, Ion
Replaced as Rumania trade min 3-7, 193C2
PATASSE, Ange (Central African Empire premier; replaced July 14)
Replaced 7-14, 596C1
PATE, Jerry
2d in Phoenix Open 1-16, 76D1
Lopez breaks rookie earnings mark 6-18, 580C3
2d in PGA Championship 8-6, 672F2
Wins Southn Open 9-10, 2d in Pacific Club Masters 10-8, 3d in Mixed Team tourn 12-3, 990E1, G1, A2
PGA top money winner 10-31, 990B3
PATENTS & Trademarks
Miller 'Lite' trademark case review barred 1-9, 13C1
Autogiro case review barred 1-23, 65D1
IBM chrgs Xerox patent infringemt 2-23, 510B2
GE gene-spliced microbe patent upheld, '77 Upjohn ruling cited 3-2, 187D1
Patent accord takes effect 6-1, 506B3
SCM set back in Xerox suit 6-7, 510G1, B2
Wis U computer research secrecy order lifted 6-12, 513F3
Poulter dies 6-14, 540E3
Computer program patents curbed 6-22, 509B1
SCM-Xerox verdicts 7-10, 7-11; damages set 8-9, 8-16, 664B3
Xerox, IBM settle dispute 8-1, 664E2
Roberts wins Sears suit 10-2, 844B2
SCM trust award set aside 12-29, 1005E2
PATENT & Trademark Office—*See under U.S. GOVERNMENT—COMMERCE*
PATH Between the Seas: The Creation of the Panama Canal, 1870-1914, The (book)
Wins Natl Book Award 4-10, 315D2
PATIL, Veerendra
Loses Parlt electn to Gandhi 11-5, 861E2
PATINO, Jorge Ortiz
Primitive art collectn auctnd 6-29, 579D1
PATINO Ayoroa, Col. Jose (ret.)
Pres nominatn rptd 5-12, 411F2
PATIO/Porch (play)
Opens 4-13, 887D2
PATOLICHEV, Nikolai Semyonovich
Canada trip rptd canceled 2-14, 111A1
PATON, Lori
FBI mail scrutiny held unconst 11-29, 940B1
PATRICK, Robert
My Cup Runneth Over opens 6-22, 760F2
PATRICK, Ted
Deprogramming suits rptd 4-7, 4-16, 295D3
Moonie loses deprogramming suit 12-29, 1012A2
PATRIOTIC Front—*See RHODESIA*
PATRIOT Missile—*See ARMAMENTS—Missiles*
PATRONAGE, Political—*See under POLITICS*
PATSALIDES, Andreas
Named Cyprus finance min 3-8, 189G1
PATTEN, Caymichael
Choices opens 12-10, 1031C1
PATTEN, Rep. Edward James (D, N.J.)
Cited for misconduct by ethics com re Park gift 7-13, 527C1
Reelected 11-7, 849C1, 851B3
PATTERAKIS, Chris
Loses US House electn 11-7, 856E3
PATTERSON, Eugene
Scores CIA press operatns 1-5, 15B1
PATTERSON, Rep. Jerry Mumford (D, Calif.)
Reelected 11-7, 850B2
PATTERSON, L. Brooks
Loses Sen primary in Mich 8-8, 625G3
PATTERSON, Percival J.
Scores Uruguay, Paraguay, Chile rights abuse 6-23, 489E3
PATTERSON, Richard
Gentleman Tramp released 4-26, 619B2
PATTISON, Rep. Edward W. (D, N.Y.)
Loss reelectn 11-7, 849F1
PATTON, Jr., Gen. George Smith (1885-1945)
Brass Target released 12-21, 1030E2
PAUL VI, Pope (Giovanni Battista Montini)—*See 1963, pp. 231G3-232B1 for biog. data*
Names Czech church ldr 1-10, 17C3
Meets Dayan on Jerusalem status 1-12, 10G2
Meets Sadat 2-13, 98C3
Regrets Belfast bombing 2-20, 132C2
Pleas for Moro release 4-23, 313F3
At Moro state funeral 5-13, 689E2
Scores USSR dissident trials 7-16, 543B1
Mtg with El Salvador archbp rptd 8-5, 723F3 *
Dies 8-6; papal record rptd, photo 601A1
W Ger '76 kidnap plot rptd 8-6, 689A3
Funeral 8-12, 658D2
Successor elected, takes name 8-26, 657B1, F1

1979

PASTORINI, Dan
Steelers win NFL conf title 1-7, 8E3
Oilers win in playoffs 12-23, 12-29, 1000G3, 1001A1
PATE, Jerry
Ties for 2d in Tourn of Champs 4-22, US Open 6-17; 2d in Kemper Open 587A1, C2, A3
PATEK, Freddie
Signs with Angels 12-5, 1002A1
PATEL, H. M.
Sworn India home min 1-24, 97A3
On religious riot deaths 4-18, 314E3
PATENTS & Trademarks
Scholl-Kresge case refused by Sup Ct 1-15, 32A1
Nonpatent royalties upheld by Sup Ct 2-28, 165B2
GE, Upjohn microbe patents reaffirmed 3-29, 265E2
Sears ordrd to pay Roberts 5-31, 466C2
Formica case refused by Sup Ct 6-5, 464F2
MCA, IBM in video disk venture 9-5, 756F1
GE, Upjohn microbe case accepted by Sup Ct 10-29, 884D1
Carter proposes indl innovatn 10-31, 829E3
Korvettes-Shure Bros case refused by Sup Ct 11-5, 884D3
PATERSON, N.J.—*See NEW Jersey*
PATERSON, Katherine
Wins Natl Book Award 4-23, 356B2
PATINKIN, Mandy
Leave It to Beaver opens 4-3, 712B1
Evita opens 9-25, 956A3
PATOCKA, Jan (d. 1977)
Charter 77 picks new ldrs 2-8, 126F3
PATRICK (film)
Released 9-7, 820F2
PATRIOTIC Front—*See NONALIGNED Nations Movement, ZIMBABWE*
PATRONAGE, Political—*See POLITICS*
PATTERSON, Chuck
Old Phantoms opens 2-8, 292D2
PATTON Jr., Gen. George Smith (1885-1945)
Weyland dies 9-2, 756F3

PAUL VI, Pope (Giovanni Battista Montini) (1897-1978)—*See 1963, p. 231G3-232B1 for biog. data*
'Cross of Lourdes' refunds set 1-19, 91C3
John Paul II presents 1st encyclical 3-15, 216G3
'66 Polish visit cancelatn cited 6-2, 413G1
US priest silenced, female ordinatn issue cited 12-1, 1000A1

1980

PASTORINI, Dan
Rozelle defends pass call 1-7, 23G1
PAST Tense (play)
Opens 4-24, 392E3
PATCHETT, Tom
Up the Academy released 6-6, 675F3
PATE, Jerry
2d in Canadian Open 6-22, 715B1
3d in World Series of Golf 8-24, wins US-Japan title 11-9, Brazil Open 11-24, 972A1, F2, G2
PGA top money winner 10-12, 971E3
PATENTS & Trademarks
Upjohn microbe case remanded by Sup Ct 1-14, 37D1
THC patents backed by FDA 2-4, 358C1
Miller 'Lite' case refused by Sup Ct 2-19, 131A1
GE microbe case cited 3-5, 318B1
'Bionic' trademark case declined by Sup Ct 3-31, 291D3
FTC trademark challenge barred 5-28, 702F3
GE microbe patent upheld by Sup Ct; reactn 6-16, 452E3-453A2
Unpatented key ingredient monopolies backed by Sup Ct 6-27, 511C2
W Ger, USSR sign pact 7-1, 489D2
Dem platform plank adopted 8-13, 614C3
Patent law revisn clears Cong 11-21, 915E3
Patent law revision signed 12-12, 982A1
PATERNITY—*See CHILDBIRTH*
PATERNO, Joe
Endorses Bush 4-20, 304E2
PATERSON—*See NEW Jersey*
PATIL, Veerendra
Named India petro min 3-7, 233A1 *
PATMAN, William
Elected to US House 11-4, 844A3, 850B2
PATMAN, Wright
Son elected to US House 11-4, 850B2
PATON, Angela
Passione opens 5-22, 756F3
PATRICK, Gail
Dies 7-6, 608F2
PATRICK, Ted
Convicted 8-29, 727B1
Sentenced 9-26, 857B3
PATRIOTIC Front—*See NONALIGNED Nations, ZIMBABWE*
PATRIOT Missile—*See ARMAMENTS--Missiles*
PATT, Gideon
On Weizman electn tour with Carter 10-28, 830F2
PATTEN, Rep. Edward James (D, N.J.)
Not standing for reelectn 6-3, 439A3
PATTERSON, Rep. Jerry M. (D, Calif.)
Reelected 11-4, 842B2
PATTERSON, Percival J.
W Ger import credit rptd 6-4, 465D1
Loses Jamaican electn 10-30, 854C1
PATTERSON, Dr. Roy
Rpts faster hay fever treatmt 2-18, 159F3
PATTERSON, William A.
Dies 6-13, 528C3
PATTERSON, William L.
Dies 3-5, 280F1
PATTIHIS, Nicos
Named Cyprus agri min 9-9, 749G2
PATTISON, Andrew
Loses Hall of Fame championship 7-14, 691G2
PATWARI, Prabhudas
Ousted as Tamil Nadu gov 10-26, 873F1

PAUL VI, Pope (Giovanni Battiste Montini) (1897-1978)
Vatican issues euthanasia statemt 6-26, 970A2
Humanae Vitae encyclical cited 9-29, 810F2
Papal dispensatn guidelines issued 10-14, 970E1

1976

Suspends Lefebvre 7-24, seeks reconciliatn 8-15; Lefebvre defies ban 8-29, 655D3
Addresses Intl Eucharistic Cong 8-8, 596A3
Disputes Coggan on female ordinatn 8-21, 756A1
Australia banned Masses held 8-31, 691F3
Sees Lefebvre 9-11, publishes letter 11-30, 932F2
Queries Argentina on priest murders 9-27, 996B1
Rhodesian bishop sentncd 10-1, 812F3
Carter cites Butz '74 slur 10-2, 744G1
Asks Wyszynski to retain post 11-1, 932B3
Sees Venez pres 11-20, 929C3
Meets ADL ldrs 11-24, 912D1

PAUL, C. A.
Iran seeks re sugar deal 2-10, 156D3
PAUL, Rep. Ron (R, Tex.)
Defeated 11-2, 822G3, 823A1
PAULING, Linus
Lipscomb wins Nobel 10-18, 840F1
PAULSEN, Erik
Wins world bridge title 5-8, 352G3
PAULSSEN & Gulce Ltd.
Arab boycott rpt released 10-18, 10-20, 786B1, B2
PAUN, Radu
Replaced 6-15, 440C2
PAVLASEK, Peter
Disqualified at Olympics 7-30, 563B2
PAVLOV, Todor
Bulgaria Politburo drops 4-2, 250C1
PAVON, Guillermo
Assassinated 3-29, 264F1
PAVULON—*See 'Drugs' under MEDICINE*
PAWLOWSKI, Jerzy
Poland sentences as spy 4-10, 268B3
PAYETTE, Lise
Named consumer affairs min 11-26, 903A3
PAZ, Juan Carlos
Scores wage hike 1-23, 96E2
PAZ Estenssoro, Victor
Opposes Chile sea outlet plan 1-1, 27F1
PCBs (polychlorinated biphenyls)—*See CHEMICALS*
PEABODY Holding Co.
To buy Peabody Coal 12-14, 985B1
PEACOCK, Andrew
On '76 foreign aid cuts 2-4, 97B2
In NZ, at S Pacific Forum 3-8—3-11, 187B3
Visits US, addresses UN conf 3-11—3-17, 203G3
Visits Indonesia 4-14, 309F2
Angola recognized 4-28, 332D1
On Lockheed payoff chrg 4-29, 322A2
PEARSON, David
Wins Western 500 1-18, 56F2
Wins Daytona 500 2-15, 424A3

1977

Lefebvre scores modernism 6-6, 470F3
Proclaims Neumann a saint 6-19, 731C3
Lefebvre dispute continues 6-20—7-27, 620F1-E2
Benelli, 4 others inducted cardinals; '76 secret apptmt revealed 6-27, 768A3
Rep at charismatic conf 7-20—7-24, 620F3
Names O'Fiaich Irish Primate 8-22, 728F3
Bishops' synod meets 9-30—10-29, 906A1
Sees Panama ldr 10-4—10-6, 792C2
Proclaims Lebanese saint 10-9, 845F3
Offers self as hostage to hijackers 10-17, 789F2
Asks Israel free Capucci 10-30; freed 11-6, 850G2-C3
Ends US excommunicatn for remarried 11-10, 906D3
Sees Gierek 12-1, 987B1
PAUL, Alice
Dies 7-9, 604E3
Honored at ERA march 8-26, 669B2
PAUL, Gabe
Saves Yankee mgr's job 6-21, 644C3
Yankees to keep Martin 10-18, 806G3
Resigns as Yankee pres 12-1, 990D2
PAUL, Jerry
'75 contempt convictn review declined 10-17, 797G3
PAUL, Les
Mary Ford dies 9-30, 788B1
PAUL, Ron
'76 spec interest gifts rptd 2-15, 128F2
Sup Ct vs electn challenge 6-6, 479A1
PAUL, Dr. William D. (Shorty)
Dies 12-19, 1024F2
PAUL, Weiss, Rifkind, Wharton & Garrison
Sorenson withdraws CIA nominatn 1-17, 35G1
PAVLICEK, Frantisek
Gets suspended sentence 10-18, 812D1
PAVLOVA, Anna (1881-1931)
Uday Shankar dies 9-26, 788F2
PAVLOVSKY, Col.-Gen. Ivan Grigoryevich
Nigeria officer training set 11-13, 986A3
PAVULON (Curare)—*See 'Drugs' under MEDICINE*
PAWLEY, William Douglas
Dies 1-7, 84D3
PAYIL, Meir
In Israel peace group 10E2
PAYNE, Rev. Dr. Paul C.
Dies 12-2, 1024G2
PAYNE, Virginia
Dies 2-10, 164D3
PAYNER, Jack P.
Bahama tax evidence barred 4-28, 395C3
PAYTON, Walter
Sets one-game rushing record 11-20, 1019D3
Dallas wins in playoffs 12-26, 1019G3
PAZ Galarraga, Jesus Angel
MEP pres candidate named 9-25, 867B3
PCP (Phencyclidine)—*See NARCOTICS*
PCBs (polychlorinated biphenyls)—*See CHEMICALS*
PDFLP (Popular Democratic Front for the Liberation of Palestine)—*See MIDDLE EAST*
PEABODY Coal Co.
Mont coal lease revoked 1-13, 59A1
Kennecott sells 6-30, 520F1
FTC divestiture order cited 520F1
Sale linked to copper indus woes 10-31, 859D1
Kennecott Carborundum deal linked to divestiture 11-16, 880C1
PEABODY Holding Co. Inc.
Peabody Coal Co.—*See separate listing*
PEACE Corps—*See under U.S. GOVERNMENT—ACTION*
PEACH Bowl—*See FOOTBALL—Collegiate*
PEACHEY Property Corp. Ltd.
Miller kills self 9-22, 788G1
PEACOCK, Andrew
Rpts ASEAN review com formed 1-20, vows tariff adjustmts 1-24, 60D2
CIA agents in Australia named 5-17, 5-19, 410G1
Rhodesia info cntr to close 9-20, 762D3
Bars return of Viet refugees 11-30, 1018E2
Named Australia forgn min 12-19, 982A2
PEANUTS
Ga drought crop damage rptd 7-28, 659F3
PEARCE, Dennis Robert
Deserts Rhodesia army 2-9, flees to Zambia 3-2, 144E3
PEARLS
'77 fashion wrap-up rptd 6-6, 1022G1

1978

Successor dies 9-28, 746B3; foul play denied 10-12, new pope elected 10-16, 781B1, 782A1

PAUL, Antony
Chrgs Cambodian atrocities 4-21—4-23, 301C2
PAUL, Ron
Regains US House seat 11-7, 852B3, 855D3
PAUL Robeson (play)
Opens 1-19, 760A3
PAULSON, Dan
Comes A Horseman released 11-1, 969G3
PAVEL, Samy
Let's Face It released 7-14, 970G1
PAVELLE Corp.
Berkey wins trust suit vs Kodak 1-21, 67A2
PAVLIDES, Vassos
Arrest rptd 4-11, 288B1
Leads prison siege 9-15—9-19, 894D3
PAYANO Rojas, Gen. Virgilio
DR police cmdr 10-2, 881C1
PAYEDAR, Mustapha
Iran exec affairs min 10-30, 827F3
PAYNE, David
Wounded 4-27, 373E2
PAYNE, Dennis S.
Forever Yours opens 6-21, 887G1
PAYNE, Frederick George
Dies 6-15, 540D3
PAYSON, Joan Whitney (d. 1975)
Met Museum pledge ordrd paid 7-11, 579C2
Daughter becomes Mets chrmn 11-8, 1026E2
PAYTON, Carolyn
Quits as Peace Corps dir 11-24, 915F1
PAYTON, Eddie
NFL '77 punt, kick return ldr 1-1, 56F3, G3
PAYTON, Walter
NFL '77 touchdown, rushing ldr 1-1, 56E2, E3
NFC wins Pro Bowl; named game MVP 1-23, 56G1
Named NFL MVP 1-23, 171D3
PAXTON, Mike
Traded to Indians 3-30, 779C3
PAZ Estenssoro, Victor
Gets Bolivia pres nominatns 5-24, 478G2
Campaign harassmt rptd 7-9, 530C3
Rptd 4th in pres vote count 7-11, 530G2
Scores electn 7-13, asks annulmt 7-15; rptd underground 7-24, 571D1
PAZ Garcia, Gen. Policarpo
Interpol chief seized in drug scandal 4-24, 614E3
Linked to 'mafia' chief in land deal 6-9, 615B1
Leads Honduras mil junta 8-7, 614A3
PAZ Romero, Virgilio
Sought in Letelier murder case 5-4, 370E3
Letelier murder role detailed 6-2, 452B1
FBI offers reward 7-4, indicted 8-1, 614A1
PBBs (polybrominated biphenyls)—*See CHEMICALS*
PCBs (polychlorinated biphenyls)—*See CHEMICALS*
PEACE Corps—*See under U.S. GOVERNMENT—ACTION*
PEACEFUL Uses of Outer Space, Committee on the—*See UNITED Nations—Outer Space, etc.*
PEACH Bowl—*See FOOTBALL—Collegiate*
PEACHES—*See FRUITS & Vegetables*
PEACOCK, Andrew S.
Recognizes Indonesia '76 Timor takeover 1-20, 72G1
On Jan iron, coal import cuts 6-27, 514B2
Lauds Finnish uranium accord 7-20, 590F1
Sees import tariff curb 11-13, 944E1
Chrgs Sovts bug Moscow emb 11-14, 878C3
PEACOCK, Elvis
In NFL draft 5-2, 336F2
PEANUTS
US pesticide sales curbed 2-15, 16B3
PEARLE, Gary
Hooters opens 4-30, 760D2
PEARL of Great Price (book)
Mormons end ban on black priests 6-9, 480B3
PEARSON, Burke
In Recovery Lounge opens 12-7, 1031B2
PEARSON, Drew
NFL '77 pass receiving ldr 1-1, 56F2
PEARSON, Sen. James B. (R, Kan.)
Votes for Panama Canal neutrality pact 3-16, 177F2
Votes for 2d Canal pact 4-18, 273B1
Primary results, retiremt cited 8-1, 606F1
Kassebaum wins seat 11-7, 854E2

1979

PAUL, William
Silkwood estate wins A-suit 5-18, 381C3
PAUL, Hastings, Janofsky & Walker
Janofsky installed ABA pres 8-15, 769B1
PAULINE Fathers (Order of St. Paul the First Hermit)
US crime probe rptd 11-9, 905E3
PAULUS, Arrie (P. J.)
Scores black labor reforms 5-11, 373F2
PAUL v. Davis
Case cited 4-23, 346A3
Quits labor confederatn 5-17, 447D2
PAWLEY, Howard
Named Manitoba NDP ldr 1-13, 57C3
PAXSON, Jim
In NBA draft 6-25, 507B2
PAYIL, Meir
Knesset defeats no-confidence motion 7-4, 496D2
PAYNE-Gaposhkin, Cecelia
Dies 12-6, 1008D3
PAYTON, Carolyn
Peace Corps successor named 3-29, 310F2
PAYTON, Eddie
NFL '78 punt, kick return ldr 1-6, 80C2, D2
PAYTON, Walter
NFL '78 touchdown, rushing ldr 1-6, 80E1, E2
PAZ Estenssoro, Victor
Bolivia pres bid rptd 3-16, 233E2
2d in Bolivia electn 7-1, 501F1
Guevara elected interim pres 8-6, 600B2, G2, B3
Natusch heads mil coup 11-1, 833A1
Gueiler replaces Natusch 11-16, 888F2
At Bolivia Cabt swearing 11-19, 907B2
PAZ Romero, Virgilio
Letelier murder testimony cites 1-18, 58E1, A2
3 convicted re Letelier 2-14, 114D2
PAZZI, Bruno
Stockbrokers score apptmt, strike 1-17, 38F3
PBBs (polybrominated biphenyls)—*See CHEMICALS*
PCBs (polychlorinated biphenyls)—*See CHEMICALS*
PCDF (dibensofuran)—*See CHEMICALS*
P.C. Pfeiffer Co. v. Ford
Case decided by Sup Ct 11-27, 919B3
PEABODY College for Teachers (Nashville, Tenn.)
Vanderbilt merger OKd 3-19, 209D1
PEACE Corps—*See under U.S. GOVERNMENT—ACTION*
PEACE and Freedom Party
Viet War era CIA surveillnc rptd 3-9, 207C2
PEACH, Blair
Dies 4-24, 313B1
PEACHES & Herb (singing group)
Reunited on best-seller list 5-2, 356G2; 5-30, 448E3
2 Hot on best-seller list 5-2, 356B3
PEACOCK, Andrew S.
At ANZUS conf, backs Viet Cambodia exit 7-4–7-5, 495F2
UK A-pact signed 7-24, 562G2
PEALE, Stanton
Jupiter moon theory rptd 3-17, 216G2
PEANUTS
Carter Family Business—*See CARTER–PERSONAL*
PEARCE, Eddie
2d in Texas Open 10-7, 970F1
PEARCE, Maj. Richard H.
Returns from Cuba 11-21, 924F1
Charged as deserter 12-19, 965G3
PEARL River (Miss.)
1000s homeless in flood 4-17, 288D3
PEARSON, Burke
Poet & the Rent opens 5-9, 712A2
PEARSON, Dennis
NFL '78 kick return ldr 1-6, 80G2
PEARSON, Drew
Steelers win Super Bowl 1-21, 62F3-63A2
PEARSON, Drew (1897-1969)
CIA '63 Castro death plot rptd confrmd 5-2, 367E3

1980

PAUL, John
2d in Daytona endurance 2-3, 637G3
PAUL, Rep. Ronald E. (R, Tex.)
Votes for Abscam evidence request res 2-27, 143A3
Draft registratn funding signed 6-12, 478F2
Reelected 11-4, 844B3
PAUL, Steven
Falling in Love Again released 11-21, 972D3
PAULEN, Adrian
Backs Moscow Olympics officiating 7-31, 589B3
PAULINE Fathers (Order of St. Paul the First Hermit)
Gannet News Svc wins Pulitzer 4-14, 296B2, F2
PAUL Richard (yacht)
Atlantic sailing record set 8-1, 908A1
PAUL Robeson: Tribute to an Artist (film)
Wins Oscar 4-14, 296A2
PAVAROTTI, Luciano
Wins Grammy 2-27, 296F3
PAVLOV, Ivan Petrovich (1849-1936)
Gantt dies 2-26, 176C1
PAVLOV, Pavel
Wins Olympic medal 7-24, 624B3
PAWLOWSKI, Janusz
Wins Olympic medal 7-31, 623C1
PAYNE, Jim
Ka-Boom! opens 11-20, 1003C3
PAYNE, Steve
In NHL All-Star game 2-5, 198F2
PAYNER, Jack
Cts power to suppress evidence curbed 6-23, 554B3
PAYSAN en Blouse Bleue (Peasant in a Blue Shirt) (painting)
Sold for record sum 5-13, 472G1
PAYTON, Walter
NFL '79 touchdown, rushing ldr 1-5, 8E2, E3
PAYTON v. New York
Case decided by Sup Ct 4-15, 305G3
Case cited by Sup Ct 10-6, 782D3
PAZ Estenssoro, Victor
Siles rivalry continues 4-7, 272D2
Electns held 6-29; Siles leads, lacks majority 7-3; coalitn movemt mounts 7-4, 508F3, 509A1
Quits pres race 7-9, 543C1
PAZ Garcia, Brig. Gen. Policarpo (Honduran president)
Liberals win upset in assemb vote 4-20, 313G3
Cedes power to assembly, remains interim pres 7-20, 564C2
PAZ Zamora, Jaime
Survives plane crash 6-2, 728D1
Joins Bolivia oppositn ldr in Lima 9-16, 728C1
PBBs (polybrominated biphenyls)—*See CHEMICALS*
PB: The Paul Brown Story (book)
Author fined 1-22, 175C3
PCBs (polychlorinated biphenyls)—*See CHEMICALS*
P.C. Pfeiffer Co. v. Ford
Case cited by Sup Ct 1-14, 37F1
PEACE Corps—*See under U.S. GOVERNMENT–ACTION*
PEACOCK, Andrew
On need for aid to Cambodia 5-27, 397B2
Loses Australia Labor dep ldr bid 10-30, named indl relatns min 11-2, 857G2
Scores strikers pay settlmts 11-26; Victoria accord attacked 12-2, 940C2, F2
PEANUTS
Midwest, South drought damage rptd 6-23—8-15, 616C2
PEARCE, Diana
On busing, housing integratn study 11-16, 989C3
PEARCE, Maj. Richard H.
Sentenced as deserter 1-30, 94E3
Sentence overturned 2-28, 189E1
PEARLE, Gary
Tintypes opens 10-23, 892F3
PEARSON, Bennie
Rpts foiled countercoup 5-14, 381F3

1976

PEARSON, Lester
Diefenbaker accuses JFK 10-4, 837E1
PEARSON, Nathan W.
Rpt on Gulf Oil paymts detailed 133A2
PEART, Frederick
Europn Parlt backs beef policy 2-12, 163G3
Tours drought areas 8-17, studies aid 8-19, 630G2, A3
Named UK lord privy seal 9-10, 693D3, 694A1
PEASE, Donald James
Elected 11-2, 823F3, 830A3
PEAVEY Co.
India sues 5-3, 333E2
PECHMAN, Joseph A.
Carter econ advisor 12-1, 898G2
PECKINPAH, Judge Denver
Newsmen jailed 9-3—9-17, 700D2
PEDENOVI, Enrico
Assassinated 4-29, 333A3
PEDER Skram (Danish warship)
In Intl Naval Review 7-4, 488D3
PEDINI, Mario
Sworn Italy culture min 7-30, 573G1
PEIREZ, Lawrence
Accuses Austrian exec 3-10, 380A3
PEIVE, Jan
Dies 9-17, 970A3
PELEJERO, Raimon
Concerts banned 2-6, 144E2
PELL, Sen. Claiborne (D, R.I.)
Church 3d in RI 6-1, 390A1
PELSHE, Arvid Y.
Politburo named 3-5, 195C2
PELTIER, Leonard
Canada extraditn ordrd 12-17, 999B1
PEMCOR Inc.
Rola-Jensen Co.
Pa plant illness identified 11-5, 911B2
PEMJEAN, Enrique
Chile expulsn cited; on threat to Soria 12-15, 963E2
PENASQUITOS Ranch
Teamsters fund loan rptd 12-29, 991B1
PENDLETON, Clarence M.
On marines assault, KKK 11-29, 983D1
PENFIELD, Wilder G.
Dies 4-5, 316C1
PENG Chung
Attacked in Nanking posters 7-19, 555C2
In Shanghai post 10-30, 871B3
PENG Teh-huai
Mao ties cited 2-8, 117F2
Cited in Mao biog 659E1
Cited in Mao death announcemt 659C2
PENGUIN Books Inc.
US files consent decree 7-27, 989A2
PENICILLIN—*See 'Drugs' under MEDICINE*
PENIDO Burnier, Rev. Joao Bosco
Killed by police 10-12, 836C1
Repercussns of murder 10-22, 10-29, 11-5, 850F2
PENKOVSKY Papers, The (book)
CIA authorship rptd 4-26, 299E1
PENN Central Co.
Penn Central Transportation Co.
Ford signs aid bill 2-5, 110A1
House votes Conrail funds 2-18, 152C1
Record '75 loss rptd 3-5, 235B3
Chessie, Southern drop Conrail role 3-23, 235E2
Conrail begins operation 4-1, 235E1
PENN-Md. Steamships Corp.
Arab boycott rpt released 10-18, 786B1
PENN Nouth
On cabt resignations 4-7, 250A2
Replaced as premier 4-14, 265D1

PENNSYLVANIA
Mellon role in Gulf shakeup rptd 1-15, 132E3
US Sup Ct voids police misconduct rule 1-21, 42C3
Pittsburgh teachers end strike 1-26, 95G2
Housing agency rescued 2-2, 994C2
Steel workers win Trade Act aid 3-1, 4-16, 348A3
Anti-busing bill vetoed 3-19, 203B3
Asbestos rptd in Phila water 4-30, 349F1
Pittsburgh radiatn subjects recalled 5-12, 384B2
French pres in Phila 5-19, 372D2
Phila budget, tax hike voted 5-27, 994C2
VW plans New Stanton plant 5-28—10-5, 987D3
7 oil cos, trade assn indicted 6-1, 412F3
Veneris US visit rptd 6-29, 484F2 ★
Ford in Valley Forge, designates as US park; in Phila 7-4, 489B1, B2
Queen Eliz visits Phila 7-6, 489E2
Amer Legion conv in Phila 7-21—7-24, mystery disease kills 23 7-27—8-5, 573C2
Intl RC cong meets in Phila 8-1—8-8, 596B2
Mystery disease probe continues 8-6—8-31, 656D2-A3
Rumanian officer defects in Phila 8-7, 907B3

1977

PEART, Ernest
Jamaica workers min 1-4, 46C1
PEAT Marwick Mitchell & Co.
Sen subcom staff rpt scores 1-17, 78C3
Pot decriminalizatn survey rptd 3-31, 332B3
Rptd largest acctg firm 8-22, 650G2
PEAVEY Co.
Fined 2-8, 113E1
PECHORA River (USSR)
A-blast course diversn seen 2-8, 88B2
PEDRO, Purificacion
Rptd killed 7-31, 618E3
PEER, Dr. Lyndon
Dies 10-8, 872F2
PEERPARK Corp.
Diet supplemt recall ordrd 9-22, 820D1
PEIJNENBURG, Rinus
Named Dutch sci min 12-19, 986B1
PELE (Edson Arantes do Nascimento)
Beckenbauer named NASL MVP 8-18, 676F3
Cosmos win NASL title 8-28, 676F2
Honored at last game, career highlighted 10-1, 827C2, E2
PELED, Mattityahu
Rpts Israel-PLO contacts 1-2, 10D2
PELLICER, Carlos
Dies 2-16, 164E3
Asks US end Nicaragua aid 3-25, 476C1
PELSHE, Arvid Yanovich
Revolutn anniv fete photo 11-7, 865D2
PELTIER, Leonard
Convicted 4-18, sentncd 6-2, 491G3
PELTZ, Philip
Berkowitz tapes impounded, seeks removal from Son of Sam case 8-16, 642A1
P.E.N. Club, International
Goma arrives Paris 11-20, 948C1
PENA Jaquez, Toribio
Freed in amnesty 9-2, 710D2
PENG Chung
In Politburo 8-21, 645G2
PENICILLIN—*See MEDICINE—Drugs*
PENN Central Co.
Sen subcom rpt scores auditors 1-17, 78B3
2 cleared in '69 rail scheme 3-11, 1 convicted 3-30, 491E3
ICC curbs rail grain-car deals 8-1, 613C1
PENN Central Transportation Co.—*See PENN Central Co.*
PENN-Dixie Steel Corp.
Unit chrgs Canada dumping 11-3, 836F3
PENNEY Co. Inc., J. C.
Kreps to quit as dir 1-10, 34B3
Axelson named to Treas post 1-18, 52D3; withdraws 3-9, 191A2
Tsanas sentenced 8-5, 848A2
Fyrol FR-2 warning rptd 9-29, 820C2

PENNSYLVANIA
'68 NYS stock transfer tax amendmts ruled illegal 1-12, 57F2
US rights comm backs Phila city-suburb busing 2-15, 112E1
Tower City coal mine flooded 3-1, 204C3
Pitts area utilities, Westinghouse settle uranium dispute 3-3, 177B2
Westinghouse dispute formally ends 3-30, 252G1-B2
Conrail line cuts set 3-31, 325F2
Fed spending inequities chrgd 4-6, 423D3
Phila on '75 10 largest cities list 4-14, 388A1
Phila schl sex bias affirmed 4-19, 342C3
'76 blue laws ruling cited 4-21, 388A2
'76 per-capita income table 5-10, 387D2
Pitts '77-78 NHL season set 5-12, 430G1
Pitts, Phila econ data rptd; table 5-16, 384D2, 385A1
US Sup Ct refuses youth mental health rights case 5-16, 419A1
VW seeks 2d US car plant 6-15, 463G3
Neumann canonized 6-19, 731B3
Medicaid abortn fund curb upheld 6-20, 516D2
Steel cos OK clean-up pacts 6-30, 521C3
Venez pres visits Phila 7-1, 546C2
UMW wildcat strikes 7-11—9-6, 690G2
Phila stock exchng shut 7-14, 537B3
Johnstown flood kills 68 7-19—7-20, disaster declared 7-21, 603G3

1978

PEARSON, John
Saudi sentence rptd 6-15, 516D1
PEASE, Rep. Donald James (D, O.)
Reelected 11-7, 851E3
PEARY, Rear Adm. Robert Edwin (1856-1920)
Daughter dies 4-16, 356A3
PEAT Marwick Mitchell & Co.
Issues '77 financial data; ranked 1st 1-30, 84B1
PECH Cheang
Rpts Viet raids, doubts major drive 6-28, 548G1
PECK, Gregory
Boys From Brazil released 10-5, 969E3
PECKHAM, Judge Roger F.
Newsroom searches by police backed by Sup Ct 5-31, 430B1
PECKINPAH, Sam
Convoy released 6-28, 619C1
PEDINI, Mario
Named Italy educ min 3-11, 191B1
PEDROZA, Eusebio
TKOs Lastra 4-16, 379D2
Decisns Solis 11-27, 969G1
PEERCE, Larry
Other Side of Mountain released 3-24, 619C3
PEGASUS (U.S. satellite)—*See ASTRONAUTICS—Satellites*
PEI, I. M.
Natl Gallery additn opens 6-1, 578E2
PEI, Mario
Dies 3-2, 252C3
PELE (Edson Arantes do Nascimento)
Bogicevic signs with Cosmos 1-4, 23A2
Brazil fans score coach 6-7, 520D3
PELL, Sen. Claiborne (D, R.I.)
Carter backs reelection 2-17, 123E1
Votes for Panama Canal neutrality pact 3-16, 177E2
Votes for 2d Canal pact 4-18, 273B1
Personal finances rptd 5-19, 385D2
Wins primary 9-12, 716G2
Reelected 11-7, 847F3, 848C3
PAC contributions rptd 12-24, 1008E1
PELLEGRINO, Dr. Edmund
Becomes Cath Univ pres 9-1, 844D1
PELTASON, John
On Sup Ct Bakke ruling 6-28, 482A3
PENA, Rui
Sworn Portugal admin reforms min 1-30, 91C3
Quits Cabt 7-24, govt falls 7-27, 593F2
PENA Gomez, Jose Francisco
Sees soclist govt, Cuba ties 5-20; Guzman rebuffs 5-21, 414F2
PENA Rivas, Silvio
Seized in Chamorro murder 1-11, testimony rptd contradictory 1-13—1-22, 73D1
PENCE, Judge Martin
Rules vs GTE in trust suit 3-1, 510B3
PENG Teh-huai (deceased)
Poster lauds 11-24, 949G1
Rehabilitatn rptd 12-11, 950D1
Cleared 12-22, rites held 12-24, 1015G1
PENKOV, Victor
Expelled from France 7-15, 649F3
PENN Central Co.—*See PENN Central Corp.*
PENN Central Corp. (formerly Penn Central Co.)
Judge OKs reorganizatn plan 3-9, 185F3-186F1
Alleghany, NY Central '60 proxy fight cited 3-24, 402B3
Loews buys 3 NYC hotels 5-31, 404A2
Grand Central office complex barred by Sup Ct 6-26, 566G3
Reorganizatn ends; officers, subsidiaries named 10-24, 875F3
PENN Central Transportation Co.—*See PENN Central Corp.*
PENN Central v. N.Y.C.
Grand Central office complex barred by Sup Ct 6-26, 567A1
PENNCO (Pennsylvania Co.)—*See PENN Central Co.*
PENN Dixie Industries Inc.
Castle, 2 others indicted 10-10, 808F2

PENNSYLVANIA
'67, '77 sales-tax rates rptd 1-5, 15F3
NASL '77 Phila expansn cited 1-5, 23B1
Coal shortage rptd 2-11, Carter sees gov 2-16, 104D1, D2
9th in US defense contracts 2-21, 127D2
Coal strike mtg 2-23, 122E3
Phila sludge-dump sites OKd 3-3, 164A1
Phila-London air fare agreed 3-17, 206D2
Johnstown flood cited re US disaster funds 4-4, 261D3
Penn Relays 4-29, 692F3
Coal strike utility billing probe set 5-10, 366F3
Phila sued on pollutn 5-17, 5-24, 409G1
Harrisburg 'tug-of-war' injures 70 6-13, 460G2
Phila makes bad-air list 7-5, 513C1
Pinto collisns kill 3 7-6, 7-8, 569C3
House votes parks bill 7-12, 526E3
Bad-air list corrected 7-19, 644B2
Marrow transplant order denied 7-26, 597F2; patient dies 8-10, 708B3
Derry copter crash kills 7 9-4, 758A3
Penn Central base to stay in Phila 10-24, 876B1
US, W Ger air svc pact expanded 10-25, 831F1
Honesdale hotel arson 11-5, 971C3
FCC orders Phila TV statn studios in NJ 11-9, 1030D2

1979

PEARSON, Peter
One Man released 7-27, 820E2
PEASLEE, Richard
Teibele & Her Demon opens 12-16, 1007F2
PEAT, Marwick, Mitchell & Co.
Insurgents elected top execs, '79 revenues cited 10-10, 851E3
PEATE, Patricia Flynn
Madman & Nun opens 1-18, 292B2
PEBBLE Springs Nuclear Plant—*See OREGON—Atomic Energy*
PECCI, Victor
Loses French Open 6-10, 570E1, D2
Loses Washn Star Intl 7-22, 734B2
PECK, Wiley
In NBA draft 6-25, 507B2
PECKFORD, Brian
Named Newfoundland premr 3-17, 233F3
PCs up majority in Parlt vote 6-18, 467G3
PEDROZA, Eusebio
TKOs Kobayashi 1-9, 79C3
KOs Olivares 7-22, 839B1
PEERCE, Larry
Bell Jar released 3-20, 528C1
PEETE, Calvin
Wins Greater Milwaukee Open 7-15, 2d in Quad Cities 7-22, 587E3
PEI, I. M.
To design NYC Conv Cntr 4-21, 375B2
JFK library dedicated 10-20, 807D3, 905E1
PELAEZ, Emmanuel
Named Romulo asst 7-23, 567A1
PELE (Edson Arantes do Nascimento)
Mazzei named Cosmos tech dir 6-5, 655B2
PELL, Sen. Claiborne (D, R.I.)
Rules Com chrmn 1-23, 71E2
Finances disclosed 5-18, 383D2
PELLECCHIA, Ralph
Indicted 2-22, 155G3
PELLETIER Jr., Lawrence
Arrested for theft, murder 4-17, 316G1
PENA, Eduardo
Loses LULAC pres electn 6-17, 810F1
P.E.N. Club, International
Conf ends; 6 Latin natns chrgd re rights, Wastberg named pres 7-21, 553G3
US unit joins book awards protest 11-25, 1007A2
PENG Chen
Imprisonmt rptd 5-6, 353F1
China Cong vice chrmn 7-1, 502F2
Promotn to Politburo rptd 9-28, 750C3
PENINSULA Times-Tribune, The (Palo Alto, Calif.) (newspaper)
Hansen article features, H-bomb diagram reprinted 8-30, 713D2, 714B1
Hansen H-bomb letter cites 9-16, 9-18, 717C3
PENNA, Joao Camilo
Brazil indus min designate 1-19, 95D1
PENN Central Corp.
Marathon Mfg purchase set 8-10, 664D1
Reorganizatn challenges declined by Sup Ct 10-1, 768E1
PENN Dixie Industries Inc.
Castle convicted 8-29, 655F3, 656A1*
PENNEY Co. Inc., J. C.
Ex-chrmn Hughes dies 3-22, 272G2
PENNINGTON v. Kansas
Case refused by Sup Ct 2-21, 128C3
PENN Nouth
With Sihanouk in China 1-6—1-8, 10D3

PENNSYLVANIA
ITT Phila long-distance phone svc OKd 1-4, 15E2
Food Fair closes 123 supermkts 1-27, 131G2
Connellsville fire 4-1, 316A3
Dissident steel haulers end strike 4-29, 384C3
N Braddock derailmt 5-6, 472D3
Jobs-wanted ad case declined by Sup Ct 6-18, 499E1
VW 2d US plant planned 7-26, 663E3
Wheeling-Pittsburgh loan cited 8-28, 682D1
Hurricane David hits 9-7, 690B1
Phila plans papal altar, ACLU threatens suit 9-13, 760C3
'78 per capita income rptd 9-16, 746D2
Phila bond ratings listed 9-20, 920E3
Conrail freight wreck kills 2 10-1, Phila commuter trains collide 10-16, 912E3
Coalport mining accident, woman dies 10-2, 860G2
Pope in Phila; upholds celibacy, female ordinatn ban 10-3—10-4, 757D1, 758B3; visit cost estimated 761A1
Ft Dix (NJ) to stay open 10-10, 809E1
VW's New Stanton car plant cited 10-12, 785A1
Jones & Laughlin Steel US aid cited 11-28, 941G3
Phila '79 living costs ranked 12-28, 991A1

1980

PEASE, Rep. Donald James (D, Ohio)
Reelected 11-4, 843E4
PEATE, Patricia Flynn
Of the Fields opens 5-27, 756F3
PECI, Patrizio
Role in Red Brigades arrests rptd 4-15, 294F3; 4-27, 353E1
Christn Dem vp's son sought 5-13, 408D1
PECK, Kimi
Little Darlings released 3-28, 416C3
PECKFORD, Brian
Vs Canada const 'patriatn' 9-8, 706A1
Scores '81 budget proposal 10-29, 858C3
PEDROZA, Eusebio
Decisns Nemeto 1-22, 320A3
Decisns Lockeridge, retains title; post-fight drug tests negative 10-4, 1001A1
PEER v. Griffeth
Case declined by Sup Ct 4-14, 307F1
PEETERS, Pete
In NHL All-Star game 2-5, 198A3
PEGG, Stuart
Fined 2-11, 134D3
PEHRSON, Wilfred R.
Dies 10-14, 876B3
PEIGNEUR, Lake
'Swallowed' in salt-mine collapse; illus 11-20, 970C2, E2
PEKO Wallsend
Queensland coal conversn project rptd set 10-2, 748A2
PELADEAU, Pierre
Phila Journal strike ends 1-25, 115G2
PELEN, Perrine
Wins Olympic medal 2-21, 155A3
PELL, Sen. Claiborne (D, R.I.)
Higher educ authrzn clears Cong 9-18, 9-25, signed 10-3, 803C3
Clears Admin in B Carter affair 10-2, 764F1
PELTIER, Leonard
Sentenced 1-23, 349D1
PENA Gomez, Jose Francisco
Scores fuel price hike 5-31, 462D2
PENDLETON, Austin
John Gabriel Borkman opens 12-18, 1003C3
PENG Zhen (Peng Chen)
Outlines forgn tax plan 9-2, 677D2
PENN, Judge John Garrett
Jenrette convicted in Abscam trial 10-7, 783B1
PENN Central Corp.
GK Technologies merger set 7-7, 745E3
$2.11 bln US setlmt rptd 11-17, 985B3
GK Technologies merger dropped 11-25, 985G1
New Haven RR reorgn challenge refused by Sup Ct 12-15, 957D2
PENN Central Transportation Co.—*See CONRAIL*
PENN-Dixie Industries Inc.
Bankruptcy filed 4-7, 985F3
PENNEY Co. Inc., J. C.
Credit restrictions rptd 3-27, 222G2
Japan TV dumping case setld 4-28, ct blocks 5-9, 368D1
FRB credit controls end hailed 7-3, 513C2

PENNSYLVANIA
Blizzards hit, 2 killed 3-1—3-2, 292A2
Tornadoes hit 3 cities 5-12, 391F2
Phila panel blocks draft registratn 7-18, 597F3
Ormandy gives final concert 8-23, 908D1
Natl securities mkt failure scored 9-12, 806E2
Snowstorm hits 11-17, 947G3

1976

Yablonski slayers sentncd 9-3, 816B3
'74-75 Phila, Pittsburgh SATs rptd 9-13, 993G1
Fscl '75 per capita income, tax burden rptd 9-15, 10-12, 959B2
New Legion disease probe set 9-30, 815D1
China A-test fallout rptd 10-5, 790G3
3 die after flu shots 10-11; progrms halted 10-12—10-17, resumed 10-18, 795F1
Kallinger gets life sentnc 10-14, 972E1
US Sup Ct accepts Phila schools sex-segregatn case 10-18, 867C3
Phila bank sold 10-21, 940G1
3 seized in Phila water threat 11-3, 972D1
Kittanning plant illness identified 11-5, 911A2
Middletown youth curfew review denied 11-15, 882E2
Legion disease hotel closes 11-18, probe scored 11-23—11-24, 911B2, F2
6 coal cos indicted 11-19, 989C2
Reading homeowner tax bias rule review denied 11-29, 900G3
Flu shot paralysis rptd 12-17, 950E1
Del R oil spill 12-27, 1014E1
Pittsburgh transatlantic air route rejctd 12-28, 992E2

1977

Johnstown glass factory blast 7-25, 604B1
Phila Eagles owner loses financial control 8-8, 659A1
Johnstown flood, July rental income loss linked 8-17, 629A2
Bethlehem Steel Johnstown plant rptd closed 8-18, 775D3
State employes sick-in 8-19; budget passed, Phila fscl crisis eased 8-20, 666B1
New youth job corps cntr rptd open 8-31, 692E2
Hosp oxygen, anesthesia mixup rptd fatal 9-10, 748G1
'76 per capita income, tax burden table 9-13, 10-18, 821B2
Phila landing rights for Concorde proposed 9-23, 738B2, C3
Abortn funding curbed 10-12, 787A1
US Steel Homestead plant rptd closed 10-13, 775A3
Bethlehem loss linked to Johnstown plant closing 10-26, 836F2
Pitt pub works bill challng minority quota provisn cited 10-31, 979C1
Soc Sec benefits seizure dispute declined 11-7, 857C2
ILA dock strike ends 12-1, 916C1
Pitts 'gateway' air svc OKd 12-21, 1006C2

Crime

Boyle convictn upset 1-28, 95D3
Saxe sentenced in Phila 2-11, 140G1
6 coal cos fined 3-21, 2 execs indicted 6-2, 520G2
Ex-House Speaker Fineman jailed 6-10, 484D1
Phila LEAA office to close 6-20, 630E2
5 indep oil cos convicted 8-30, 691G2; fined 9-16, 918F2
Police rights vs traffic violators extended 12-5, 939A1

Fuel-Weather Crisis

Steel layoffs rptd 1-17, 37D2
Shapp declares gas emergency 1-18, orders schls closed 1-26, 54B2
FPC OKs emergency gas purchase 1-19, 53G3
Airline diversns OKd 1-19, 54F1
Natl Guard mobilized 1-28—1-29, 75F2
Carter in Pittsburgh 1-30, 75B3
US offers emergency job funds 2-1, 75G3
US declares emergency status 2-5, 91B2
Layoff total rptd 2-7, 91F2

1978

Bruceton coal-gas conversn plant closed 12-1, 962G3-963A1
Phila populatn ranked 12-6, 942E3

Crime & Civil Disorders

Boyle gag-order case remanded 1-9, 13F1
Lloyd Carr fugitive served Pa jail term 1-14, 83D2
Flood, Eilberg probes rptd 2-8, 2-19, 3-9, 239G3-240A3
Boyle convicted again 2-18, 129A1
Cianfrani begins jail term 2-20, 172A3
Phila radicals blockaded 3-8, surrender 5-7, 410D1-C2
Death penalty case refused by Sup Ct 7-3, 552A2
Phila radicals routed; cop killed, 12 chrgd 8-8, 645D1
Flood indicted 9-5, 685B1
Ex-Rep Clark indicted 9-5, 685D1
Eilberg chrgd by ethics com 9-13, 697F1
Flood indicted again 10-12, 792A1
Eilberg indicted 10-24, pleads not guilty 11-1, 835C2
Eilberg loses reelectn; Flood, Diggs win 11-7, 846D2, E2

1979

Atomic Energy

3 Mile Island (Middletown) A-plants called unsafe 1-26, 90D3
Radium waste sites alleged 3-5, 187B2
Beuver Valley (Shippingport) A-plant ordrd shut 3-13, 186E1
A-plant communities studied 3-17, 207D3
3 Mile I accident 3-28; radiatn released; explosn, meltdown feared 3-28—4-3; Carter visits 4-1, 241A1-246C1
3 Mile I A-plant diagrams 242A1, 243A3
China Syndrome impact seen 3-29, 4-1, 243C1, 246D3
3 Mile I accident sparks intl concern 3-31—4-5, 246C1-C3
3 Mile I accident sparks protests, reassessmts 3-31—4-8, 261G2-262B1
3 Mile I errors, clean-up detailed; crisis declared over 4-4—4-9; Carter forms probe panel 4-5, 259D2-261G2
Carter vows 'full account' re 3 Mile I 4-5, 251A1
3 Mile I Europn reactn continues 4-6—4-13, 276E1-E2
Carter reaffirms US commitmt, vows 3 Mile I panel apptmts 4-10, 263A3
NRC plans safety rules review 4-10, warns 34 A-plants 4-12; advisory com proposes chngs 4-17, 275A2
Carter names 3 Mile I comm 4-11; reactor shutdown starts, other dvpts 4-13—4-18; Met Ed rate hike suspended 4-19, 274E2-275F1
3 Mile I NRC transcripts released 4-12, 275D2
GPU cuts dividend 4-26; 3 Mile I reaches shutdown, NRC orders other Babcock plants closed 4-27, 321D3-322D2
NRC, 3 Mile I operators testify 4-30, 5-7; blast danger, radiatn levels rptd 5-1, 5-5, 344E1-E2
3 Mile I radiatn estimate hiked 5-3, 344C1
DC A-protest 5-6, 343B3
3 Mile I safety benefit seen 5-7, 373G3
3 Mile I comm halts probe 5-17, gets subpoena power 5-17, 5-21, 417F2-F3
Cattle deaths near 3 Mile I rptd 5-20, 382E1
Met Ed blamed for 3 Mile I accident 6-5, 518A3
GPU gains credit line 6-19, 519A1
NRC shuts undamaged 3 Mile I reactor No 1 7-2, extends order 8-9, 629D3-G3
3 Mile I clean-up proposed 7-17; NRC urges water purificatn method 8-14, 629F2-D3
NRC: 3 Mile I preventable 8-2, 609E1
3 Mile I property values rptd unaffected 8-20; evacuation size, costs rptd 9-23, 743G2-D3
Met Ed fined $155,000 10-26, 826F1-E2
3 Mile I comm final rpt: Met Ed scored, no serious health effects seen 10-30, 825G3
Met Ed license challenged, rate hike asked 11-1, 826E2
3 Mile I coal shift studied 11-5, 849C2
Carter on 3 Mile I comm rpt 12-7, 940F1-E2

Crime & Civil Disorders

Cianfrani granted '80 parole 1-11, 102A3
Lewisburg jail conditns scored 2-1, 85F2
Flood mistrial declared 2-3, 102A2
Eilberg pleads guilty 2-24, 152C2
Eilberg law practice suspended 3-29, 272A1
Phila bar unit assails police 4-19, 310B3
Ex-Rep Clark sentncd 6-12, 442G2
Truckers' strike sparks Levittown riot 6-23, 6-24, 479D2
Bell signs Phila police brutality complaint 8-10; US files chrgs, Rizzo calls suit political 8-13, 610E1-E2
Priest cleared in 'gentleman bandit' case 8-20, look-alike sentncd 11-30, 953F2
Seagram unit admits to liquor bd bribery 9-27, 809E3
SBA minority-aid abuse rptd 9-28, 947A3
Boyle sentncd again 10-11, 840D1
Phila police brutality suit dismissed 10-30, 831B3
Pauline Fathers US probe rptd 11-9, 905F3
'60s drug tests on Holmesburg inmates rptd 11-25, 947E1
Mennonite farmer acquited in abductn case 12-4, 932D1

Energy—*See also 'Atomic' above*

Standby gas rationing rejctd by US House 5-10, 342G2
'78 per capita gas use rptd 5-27, 395G2
Winter heating fuel supply promised 8-28, 703C2
Odd-even gas rules lifted 9-6, 683F1

1980

Atomic Energy & Safeguards

Rogovin 3 Mile I study issued 1-24, Sen rpt released 7-2, 550F3
3 Mile I radioactive water leaks 2-11, 128E1
Bechtel to repair 3 Mile I 2-12, 128G1
Babcock A-plant review ordrd by NRC 3-4, 169E2
3 Mile I gas venting proposed 3-12, Middletown residents oppose 3-20, 248B3
GPU sues Babcock & Wilcox 3-25, 249C1
3 Mile I anniv marked by demonstratns 3-28, 249A1
3 Mile I health studies rptd 4-2, 4-15, 4-17, 332G1-B3
Babcock fine asked by NRC 4-10, 332B1
3 Mile I containmt bldg entry fails 5-20, NRC OKs gas venting 6-10, 440F3, 441B1
3 Mile I gas venting danger seen 6-18; radioactive water spilled 6-27, krypton vented 6-28—7-11; containmt bldg entered 7-23, 550C2-E3
GPU asks 3 Mile I cleanup aid, revises estimates 8-9, 649A3
3 Mile I accident cited in Kennedy conv speech 8-12, 614F1
NRC staff backs 3 Mile I cleanup 8-14, 649D2
3 Mile I containmt bldg entered again 8-15, 649F1
Va A-plant gets operating license 8-20, 648E3
Maine votes to keep A-plant 9-23, 723D2
3 Mile I cleanup costs revised 11-10; NRC lists GPU aid optns 11-28, Phila Electric backs cost sharing 12-10, 961B1
GPU seeks $4 bln from NRC 12-8, 960F3-961A1

Crime & Civil Disorders

Flood resigns 1-31, pleads guilty 2-26, 190F1-B2
Abscam probe revealed; Myers, Lederer, Murtha, others linked 2-2, 2-3, 81A2, B2
Phila bankruptcy scandal indictmts 2-12, 502D2
Bahamas bank looting case rptd 3-3, 229B1
Mafia ldr slain 3-21, 237B2
Phila radicals convicted in '78 cop killing 5-8, 414A1
Atty conflict of interest probes backed by Sup Ct 5-12, 426G2
Cianfrani released from prison 5-16; marries 7-14, 890A2
Myers, Lederer, other pub offcls indicted in Abscam probe 5-22, 5-27, 5-28, 402C2-B3
Criden indicted, Murtha named in Abscam probe 6-18, 454G1-B2
Phila rptr cited for Abscam silence 7-10, 554A2
Youths riot at Ft Indiantown Gap refugee cntr, 50 jailed at Lewisburg 8-5, 591B3
Abscam judge quits Myers, Lederer cases 8-7, 599E3
Myers loses Abscam entrapmt plea 8-8, 684G2
Mafia, pizza indus ties probed 8-24, 714D1
Myers, Johanson, Criden convicted in Abscam trial 8-31, 684B2
Schwartz, Jannotti convicted 9-16, 740B2
Lottery fraud chrgs rptd 9-19, 786B3
Redgrave TV film protested 9-30, 835C3
Appeals ct backs Abscam tapes broadcast 10-1; Sup Ct refuses stay, tapes aired 10-14, 781D2
Myers expelled from House 10-2, 740B1
Hayes pretrial press exclusn case refused by Sup Ct 11-17, 882F1
Schwartz, Jannotti convictns dismissed 11-26, 919G1

Energy—*See also 'Atomic Energy' above*

Coal mine inspectn case declined by Sup Ct 1-7, 15F3
LTV coal properties sold 3-25, 385C3
Phila refined oil tax dropped, co 'contributns' set 6-10, 743F3

1976

Politics
Primary date set 22A2
Carter campaigns 4-8, 261D1
Carter polls blacks 4-10—4-11, 261E2
US Rep Barrett dies 4-12, 305B1, 315F3
Carter news conf in Phila 4-23, 305A2
Primary results 4-27, 304E3-305G1
Kearns dies 6-11, 484E3
Dem delegate tiff setld 6-29, 490A1
Ford in Valley Forge, Phila 7-4, 489B1, B2
Govs Conf at Hershey 7-5—7-6, 492G2
Dem conv women delegates, table 508D2
Dem conv pres vote, table 7-14, 507D2
Reagan visits 7-15—7-16, 531G2
Reagan names Schweiker running mate 7-26; Ford retains delegate support 7-27—7-29, 549C2, 550F2
Reagan delegate gains rptd 8-2, 8-3, 564B2
Ford delegate gains rptd 8-10, 583A2, F2
GOP pre-conv delegate count 8-14, 583D3
Reagan, Ford seek conv delegates 8-15, 8-18, 601G2, C3
GOP conv pres, vp vote tables 8-18—8-19, 8-19, 599D1, D3
Reagan scores oppositn 8-19, 615F2
Carter in Phila, Scranton, Pittsburgh 9-7—9-8, 663G3-664A1
Carter 'whistlestops' 9-20, 704F1, B3
Ford, Carter debate in Phila 9-23, 700E2
Ford, Carter in Phila 9-24, 724A1
Mondale campaigns 9-30, 725D1
Rizzo recall vote barred 9-30, 994D1
Carter in Pittsburgh 10-2, 743A1, 744F1
Mondale visits 10-25—10-26, 803G3, 804A1; 11-1, 827E2
Ford campaigns 10-26—10-28, 802G3-803F1
Dole in Erie 10-26, 804E2
Carter campaigns 10-27, 10-28, 803E2, G2; 10-29, 827E1
Election results 11-2: pres 817D2, 818C1, E1, G1, A3, 819A2; cong 817E2, 820B1, C1, D2, 821A3, 828B3, 830D3
Rizzo delivers Dem vote 11-2, 818A3
Carter primary spending rptd 11-17, 938A3
Shapp Presidential Campaign—*See SHAPP, Milton J.*

PENNSYLVANIA, University of (Philadelphia)
Alcoholism rpt publshd 8-8, 814E3
Blumberg wins Nobel med prize 10-14, 840C1
Gyorgy awarded Science Medal 10-18, 858E3
PENNSYLVANIA State University (University Park)
'75 football rankings 1-2, 31C3
Loses Gator Bowl 12-27, 1014G2
PENN Ventilator Co.—*See FREEPORT Minerals*
PENNZOIL Corp.
Duval, sales unit indicted 6-29, 748E1
PENRICE, Rev. James
Vs Canada female ordinatn 11-29, 932D1
PENSACOLA, Fla.—*See FLORIDA*

1977

Politics & Government
Legislature schedule rptd 6F2
Offcls die in Harrisburg plane crash 2-24, 204D3
Pittsburgh mayoral results 11-8, 855G1, A3
Pittsburgh referendum OKd 11-8, 879A3
Flaherty eyes race for gov 11-26, 914D2

PENNSYLVANIA, University of (Philadelphia)
Radio station loses license 4-4, 395A3
Loren Eiseley dies 7-9, 604A3
Mundheim confrmd to Treasury post 8-2, 626B3
Pneumonia vaccine gets FDA OK 11-21, 907B1
PENNSYLVANIA Power Co.
Westinghouse settlemt rptd 3-3, 177D2
Westinghouse dispute formally ends 3-30, 252G1-B2
Flaherty confrmd dep atty gen 4-5, 272G2
FEC orders Shapp repay funds 5-12, 482C2
Phila rptr quits, tied to Cianfrani 9-12, 920E3
Shapp defends ouster of black 9-28, 800C2
Jacquin settles chrgs re liquor bd gifts 10-17, 860G1
Westinghouse settlmt cited 12-26, 1003B3
PENNSYLVANIA State University (University Park)
Malley sets 3000-mtr steeplechase mark 6-9—6-11, 602B3
Mueller gets Medal of Sci 11-22, 952B1
Wins Fiesta Bowl 12-25, 1020B2
PENNSYLVANIA v. Mimms
Police rights vs traffic violators extended 12-5, 939A1
PENNZOIL Co.
Gulf of Mex gas probe set 2-17, 151F3
Duval ups copper price 3-18, 209C2
Duval chrgs dismissed 6-10, 483D3, F3
Oil rig copter crash 12-8, 1023F2
PENOBSCOT Tribe—*See INDIANS, American*

1978

Labor
Anthracite pact ratified 4-30, 324E2
Phila workers strike 7-14—7-21, 565C2
Allentown opositn to postal pact rptd 7-21, 565A1
US Steel job bias found 8-3, 811B3
Phila Teamster fund scored 8-14, 625E1
Phila teachers strike 9-1—9-7, 698A3
Firestone suits rptd 9-22, 835F1
New Stanton VW plant struck 10-9—10-15, 809C3
Steel haulers strike 11-11, 1006G1-A2
Connellsville employees adultery firing case declined by US Sup Ct 12-11, 981A1
Marston Dismissal Controversy—*See MARSTON, David*
Politics & Government—*See also 'Crime' above*
Legislature schedule rptd 14F3
State tax revenue data 1-9, 84E2, F3
DeLuca named temp Phila dist atty 1-24, 62D2
Carter sees gov 2-16, 104D2; 2-23, 122E3
Flood gets Lions Club award 3-16, 240A3
Vaira succeeds Marston as Phila atty 3-23, 243B3
Primary results 5-16, 389A3
Ex-gov Fine dies 5-21, 440F2
GOP tax-cut tour in Phila 9-20, 734F3
Carter visits Aliquippa 9-23, 736A1
Electn results 11-7: cong 846E2, A3, 848C3, 849C2, 852B1; state 845G1, 846B3, 847D1, 849B2, 853D3, 897E3
House rejcts DC voting rep amendmt 11-14, 878G1
House control shifts to GOP 11-28, 915B3

PENNSYLVANIA, University of (Philadelphia)
Riedel '76 death sentencing study confrmd 3-6, 389B1
NCAA basketball tourn results 3-27, 272C1
Polymer with elect conductivity rptd 5-18, 654D1
PENNSYLVANIA Co. (Pennco)—*See PENN Central Co.*
PENNSYLVANIA State University (University Park)
'77 football rank rptd 1-3, 8A3
Wins women's lacrosse title 5-28, 540B2
PENNSYLVANIA v. Moody
Death penalty case refused by Sup Ct 7-3, 552A2
PENSACOLA, Fla.—*See FLORIDA*

1979

Environment & Pollution—*See also 'Atomic' above*
US sues vs Youngsville warehouse PCB storage 3-9, 206E3
Pittsburgh area cleanups set by Colt unit 5-7, US Steel 5-22, 385B2-B3
Phila sewage suits settled 5-30, 704C2
Pittsburgh area cleanup suit setld by US Steel 7-23, 704F2
Medicine & Health—*For radiation hazards, see 'Atomic' above*
Abortn control law voided by US Sup Ct 1-9, 14A1 1-26, 90D3
Amish polio outbreak rptd 6-5, vaccine sent 6-9, 472E1
Child mental commitmt rules backed by Sup Ct 6-20, 515F3
AMA chrgd in NY chiropractors suit 7-5, 570A3
PPA pneumonia outbreak in Pittsburgh hosp cited 11-1, 971C2
Holmesburg inmate drug tests rptd 11-25, 947E1
Politics & Government—*See also other appropriate subheads in this section*
Legislature schedule rptd 5F3
Fscl '78 tax revenue rptd 2-13, 152B2
Kennedy, Green campaign in Phila 10-22, 808B1
Baker seeks '80 primary win 11-1, 829A1
Green elected Phila mayor 11-6, 846G1, A3
Flood sets '80 resignatn 11-7, 900C2
Connally in Pittsburgh 11-15, 982F3
Fed funds control case declined by US Sup Ct 3-5, 185D1
Pittsburgh fiscal status rptd 3-20, 204B2
State employee leaves OKd 4-2, 245A3
Phila mayoral primary results 5-15, 363C2
Mayors Conf in Pittsburgh 6-9—6-13, 439F2-440B1
Phila loses Dem conv 6-28, 518F1
Ex-Rep Granahan dies 7-10, 588G2
Carters visit Carnegie 7-12, 513F2
School Issues
Integratn study rpts urban lag 5-9, 650F1
Wilson Coll closing barred 5-26, 482C1
Pvt schl transport challenge dismissed by Sup Ct 6-25, 540C2
Pittsburgh busing rptd set 9-2, 679E3
Teachers' strikes rptd 9-12, 679B1
Sports
Phila gets WBL team 6-12, 526G2

PENNSYLVANIA, University of (Philadelphia)
NCAA basketball tourn results 3-26, 238F2, B3
'60s drug tests of Holmesburg prisoners rptd 11-25, 947E1
PENNSYLVANIA Life Co.
Southn Pacific to buy Ticor 3-28, 283E1
PENNSYLVANIA State University (University Park)
Loses Sugar Bowl 1-1, '78 rank rptd 1-2, 1-3, 8C2, E2
Ramsey wins women's intercollegiate squash title 3-4, 527D2
A-plant communities studied 3-17, 207D3
Dorney in NFL draft 5-3, 335F2
Wins women's lacrosse title 5-13, 507C3
3d in NCAA soccer 12-9, 1004G1
Wins Liberty Bowl 12-22, 1001A3

1980

Environment & Pollution
Union Corp sued re PCBs 4-24, 331E3
Shenango OKs Neville I plant curbs 8-22, 825C2
3 cos sued for PCB dumping 10-9, 825B1, D1
Water shortage rptd, comm issues warning 12-1, 947B3, E3
US Steel fined 12-22; Clairton deadline extended 12-30, 987C1, E1
Labor & Employment
Phila Journal strike ends 1-25, 115F2
Phila police, fire layoffs set 2-4, effected 3-1, 187B1
Steel talks in Pittsburgh 2-5, 289F1
Docker injury benefits backed by Sup Ct 6-23, 555B1
Phila ILA workers reject pact 9-18, OK 10-2, 826F2, A3
Politics & Government—*See also other appropriate subheads in this section*
Legislature schedule rptd 18F1
Ex-Rep Muhlenberg dies 1-19, 104C3
Fscl '79 tax revenue rptd 2-20, 307B3
Sen primary results 4-22, 304D3
Detroit census revisn ordrd, Phila suit cited 9-25, 741F2
Election results 11-4: cong 840C3, 844B1-A2, 845A3, 846A1, A2, D2, 848D2; state 847G1
GOP govs meet in Phila 11-17, 880G1
'80 census rptd, reapportmt seen 12-31, 983F1
Presidential Election (& Transition)
GOP platform hearing set in Phila 1-14, 32A1
Reagan in Pittsburgh 4-10, 288B2
Carter, Kennedy campaign 4-18—4-22, 304F1
Reagan, Bush campaign 4-20—4-21, 304E2
Pres primary results 4-22, 303G3-304A3
Carter at Phila town mtg 5-9, 367D1, F2
Lewis named to GOP post 6-13, 452B3
Kennedy conv speech cites 3 Mile I 8-12, 614F1
Reagan visits shipyd 8-19, 629A2
Mondale in Westmoreland Cnty 9-1, Phila 9-30, 780D1, C2
Carter tours Phila 9-3, 699A1
Bush in Pittsburgh 9-5, Phila 9-25, 780D3, 781D1
Reagan visits Erie 9-11, 699E3
Anderson in Harrisburg 9-23, 722C3
Reagan in Wilkes-Barre 10-1, Pittsburgh 10-2, 738F1, G1, C2
Carter in Lansdowne 10-2, 762D2, F3
Reagan in Phila area 10-7, 763E2
Carter in Yatesville 10-15, 778G3
Kennedy visit rptd 10-22, 817E1
Anderson in Phila 10-29, 816E1
Carter in Pittsburgh, Phila 10-29, 816C2, 841A1
Reagan winds up campaign 10-30, 10-31, 840A1, A2
Press endorsemts rptd 11-1, 844E1
Mondale in Phila 11-2, 841C1
Election results 11-4, 838C1, 839A2, F3
Press & Broadcasting
Phila Journal strike ends 1-25, 115F2
Phila Bulletin sold to Charter Media 4-10, 376F3
Charter Media dissolved; Eller retains Phila Bulletin 9-30, 836B2
Pres press endorsemts rptd 11-1, 844E1
NYC TV statn move to NJ backed 11-6, 906A2
Refugee Issues
Ft Indiantown Gap processing cntr opens 5-18, 380E1
Ft Indiantown Gap resetlmt lags 6-2, 420F1
Carter orders criminals expelled 6-7, 435D1
Ft Indiantown Gap gays await processing 7-7, 514G2
Youths riot at Ft Indiantown Gap 8-5, troops quell violence 8-6, 591G2
Ft Indiantown Gap youth dies 8-19, violence continues 8-28; resetlmt problems grow 8-29, 684E3
Ft Indiantown Gap to send Ark camp 'hard-core' refugees 9-25, 725D3
Refugee aid to states clears Cong 9-25, 10-1, Carter signs 10-10, 785B1
School Issues
Phila teachers strike 9-2, 723B3
Sports
NASL Phila club move to Montreal set 12-8, 1001F1
PENNSYLVANIA, University of (Philadelphia)
'79 endowmt earnings rptd 3-24, 319C2
Klein wins Nobel 10-15, 890A1
PENNSYLVANIA State University (University Park)
Clark in NFL draft 4-29, 336E3
Wins Fiesta Bowl 12-26, 999C3
PENNZOIL Co.
Gulf coast leasing bids set records 9-30, 785B2
PENOBSCOT Indians—*See INDIANS, American*
PENSACOLA—*See FLORIDA*

1976

PENSIONS & Retirement
Muskie rebuts Ford 1-21, 40A2, D2
'77 budget proposals 1-21, 66F2
W Ger ratifies pact with Poland 3-12, 260F1
Cong clears SCORE funds 5-13, 393D1
Time struck 6-2, 398D1
Guild ends Time strike 6-21, 454E2
Teamster fund probe, tax status rptd 6-24—7-7, 492B2
Sup Ct affirms mandatory retiremt 6-25, 552C1
GE pact reached 6-27, Westinghouse 7-20, 536F3, 537C1
Sen OKs tax revisions 8-6, 586C1, D1
GOP platform text cites 8-18, 606E2
Ford signs options tax bill 9-3, 708D1
Pa VW pact signed 9-15, 987G3
Cong clears tax revisns 9-16, 705D3, F3, 706B1
Cong hikes vet benefits 9-20, 806G3; signed 9-30, 982G1
Fed 'kicker' repealed 10-1, 834A2
Ford-UAW contract ratified 10-12, 789F1
Jobless benefits revisn signed 10-20, 788F1
Teamsters fund data rptd 12-28, 990E3
Social Security—*See SOCIAL Security under U.S. GOVERNMENT*

PENTACOSTAL Church
Washn (DC) clerics sentncd 9-17, 776F2
PENTAGON—*See DEFENSE, Department of, under U.S. GOVERNMENT*
PENTAGON Papers Controversy—*See WATERGATE*
PENTATHALON
Sovt star disqualified 7-19, Olympic results 7-22, 563F1, 575B1
PENTERIANI, Renato
Kidnaped 6-16, 446B1
PENTHOUSE (magazine)
Sovt laser use rpt denied 11-23, 961A2
PEOPLE (magazine)
Guild begins strike 6-2, 398C1
Guild ends strike 6-21, 454C2
PEOPLE'S Downtown National Bank of Miami (formerly Capital National Bank of Miami)
Lefferdink sentenced 4-26, 384G2
PEOPLE'S Party
Final pres vote tally 12-18, 979B2

1977

PENSIONS & Retirement
Exxon age-bias judgemt reversed 1-30, 279A1
NYC debt repaymt dvpts 2-8—3-11, 193C1-G3
IBM repurchases stock 2-22—3-9, 409B2
Carter plans mil study 3-1, 148F2
Farmland fund proposal withdrawn 3-11, 195A1
Teamsters to revise fund posts 3-13, 195C1-C2
'Double dipping' questioned re HEW hirings 3-23—3-26, 236B2
US sues to protect Nev union fund 3-30, 261F3
US sues Ohio Teamster fund 4-4, 280B2
Armed forces amendmt fails 4-25, 324C1
Teamsters fund trustees quit 4-29, fiduciary named 6-17; organized crime loans revealed 7-18, 558A2
Cong sets '78 targets 5-17, 405B1
Pentagon backs cutbacks 5-26, 420D3
Mil svc credit backed 6-6, 478G2
Mil manpower cost panel named 6-27, 499A3
Bank managemt concentratn chrgd 6-28, 578B2
2 copper cos in strike setlmt 7-1, 558F1
AT&T, CWA phone pact agreed 8-6, 613A3
Poll on top US concerns 8-10, 632C2
'78 mil funds bill signed 9-21, 834D1
Mandatory retiremt curb voted by House 9-23, 737C2
Mil cost cuts urged 9-25, 777B3
NYC fscl '77 budget deficit data vary 10-4, 881C2
Steelworkers OK can pacts 10-31, 837B1
Vets old-age, non-mil disability hike OKd by Cong 11-3, 877E3
Teamster kickback chrg dropped 11-11, 928C1
Coal workers strike 12-6, 937A2
Early retiremt plan backed 12-12, 960G1-D2
Social Security—*See under U.S. GOVERNMENT*

PENTAGON—*See U.S. GOVERNMENT—DEFENSE*
PENTAGON Papers Controversy
Canada Viet mission cover-up rptd 1-14, 97B3
Sorensen '73 testimony cited 1-15, 35D1
Nixon scores Ellsberg 5-19, 406B1
PENTECOSTAL Church
Charismatic conf held 7-20—7-24, 620A3, E3
PENTHOUSE (magazine)
Hustler publisher convicted 2-8, 118C2
Rpts CIA plots vs Jamaica ldr; CIA denies 11-2, 884F1
PEOPLE (magazine)
Margaret Trudeau interview 3-28, 281E3
PEOPLES Gas Co.
Natural Gas Pipeline Co. of America
FPC splits on Alaska pipe route 5-2, 369B3
PEOPLE'S Republic of China, U.S. Committee on Scholarly Communication with—*See SCHOLARLY Communication, etc.*

1978

PENSIONS & Retirement—*See also U.S. GOVERNMENT—SOCIAL Security Administration*
Ohio Teamster fund bd revised 1-3, 4E2
Miner jurisdictn case review barred 1-9, 13E2
CBO mil pensn revisns proposed 1-11, 52F3
US sues to regain Teamster funds 2-1, 83B1
New CPIs described 222B2, C2
Mfrs Hanover ousts bd member 3-7, 163B1
Mandatory retiremt curb clears Cong 3-23, signed 4-6, 238E2
Teamster ldr convicted in kickback case 3-25, 232B2
Minn law backed by Sup Ct 4-3, 308D3
UMW attachmt case review refused by Sup Ct 4-3, 309B1
Mil pension overhaul proposed by pres comm 4-10, 280E3-281F1
McDonnell Douglas strike ends 4-16, 284F2
Military pensn rule review declined by Sup Ct 4-17, 308C3
Sex-based pensn plans barred by Sup Ct 4-25, 322A3
Teamster chief's son, 2 others acquitted 4-28, 324C2
Methodists settle fraud suit 5-21, 480F3
Union insurnc scheme chrgd 6-15, 560G2-D3
Minn law voided by US Sup Ct 6-28, 567B1
Teamster ldr sentncd for kickbacks 7-11, 560E2
ABA player's pensn upheld by NC ct 7-19, 656F1
Teamster funds scored 8-14, 625C1
Tax rules revisn clears 10-15, 786D1
Calif retiremt home immunity case declined by Sup Ct 10-16, 789F2
DC pensn reform vetoed 11-4, 897E2
Carter eases fringe benefit test for wage rule 12-13, 957F1, E2
Brown urges mil pensn reform 12-14, 1009C2
Coal Strike Issue
UMW bargaining cncl rejcts tentative contract terms 2-12, 104B3
P&M pact rejected by miners 2-26, 160A1
UMW: key strike issue 3-8, 159F3
UMW, operators in new tentative accord 3-14, 182D1
Fiscal Crises—*See NEW York City—Finances*

PENSKE, Roger
CART group rptd formed 12-28, 1028B2
PENTAGON—*See U.S. GOVERNMENT—DEFENSE*
PENTAGON Papers Controversy
Ehrlichman freed 4-27, 320B2
PENTECOSTALISTS
USSR group in US emb sit-in 6-27, 543B2
USSR group continues US emb sit-in 11-1, 947B2
PENZIAS, Arno A.
Wins Nobel Prize 10-17, 886A2
PEOPLE'S Advocate
Calif voters OK Gann amendmt 6-6, 425F1
PEOPLES Gas Co.
Coal gasificatn plant financing plan submitted 6-2, 471A3
PEOPLES Temple
Rev Jones photo 890A1
Blakely affidavit filed; Rev Jones, Jonestown (Guyana) abuses described 6-15, 891C3
Map of Guyana 889C1
US Rep Ryan, others arrive Guyana; see US emb, Jones reps 11-15; arrive Jonestown commune 11-17, 889A1-A2
Ryan, 4 others killed in ambush; Jonestown mass murder-suicides; US, cult survivors rpt 11-18, 889A2-890C3
Rep Ryan photo 891A2
Photo of victims' bodies 909A1
US wounded flown home 11-19, 890D1
S Amos, children found dead 11-19, 890D3
Layton rptd under arrest 11-20, 889D2, 890A2, C2, C3
Guyana denies blame, releases Jones's refs from Mrs Carter, Mondale, Califano 11-20; cult ties cited 11-21, 890C1
US Temple attys rescued 11-20, 890C3
Death toll rptd 11-21, 11-24, 890F1
US sends mil aid teams, US bodies flown home 11-21, 890D3
US denies cult probe neglect, cites Ryan briefings; Mrs Carter denies remembering Jones 11-21, 891E1, E2-A3
Jones, San Fran mayor pol ties cited 11-21, 891B2
Calif Temple seemed doomed; pol facts on Jones, New West article rptd 11-21, 892A2
Layton chrgd in US delegatn deaths 11-22; Beikman held in Amos murders 11-25, 910E2
Jonestown bodies removed, flown to US 11-24—11-26; identified, embalmed 11-26—11-30, 909D1, 910C1-C2
Guyana govt admits high death toll, silent on Jones's ties; oppositn scores 11-24, 909E2
US defends pre-suicide probes 11-24, 910A1
Body removal costs US $3 mln 11-24, 910D1

1979

PENSIONS & Retirement
SEC role barred by Sup Ct 1-16, 32F1-D2
Carter budget proposals 1-22, 41G2, 43G2; table 42E2
Rail pensn excluded from divorce pact by Sup Ct 1-22, 53G3
Forgn svc retiremt rule upheld by Sup Ct 2-22, 151A1
Engineers pensn paymts case refused by Sup Ct 2-26, 164D3
Business rpts US rule compliance costs 3-14, 230A3
Baseball umpires' pensn plan extended 5-18, 569F2
St Regis Paper contract ratified 6-23, 598B3
Loeb settles suit 7-9, 640E3
UAW-Big 3 contract talks begin 7-16, 598D1
Mil retiremt plan proposed 7-19, 628E1
ABA backs armed forces divorce law chngs 8-15, 769A1
UAW wins major increases in GM pact 9-14, 698G1
Mail fraud crackdown set 9-19, 921C3
Ill judge law challenge refused by Sup Ct 10-9, 784F1
Minn law voided by Sup Ct 10-15, 847E3
Ford ratifies UAW contract 10-22, 806A1
Uniroyal sex bias suit setld 10-23, 885F2
UAW wins Chrysler increase, OKs deferral 10-25, 805G2, E3
Sen subcom urges safeguards 11-26, 905B1
Methodist legal immunity cases declined by Sup Ct 11-26, 919E2
Gulf+Western sued by SEC 11-26, 923F1
Sachs to pay Teamsters debt 12-10, 965C1
Social Security—*See under U.S. GOVERNMENT*

PENSON, Boris
Release cited 4-29, 317D2
PEN Sovan
Denies famine rpts 10-12, 811A2
PENTAGON—*See U.S. GOVERNMENT–DEFENSE*
PENTAGON Papers Controversy
Judge Gurfein dies 12-16, 1008A3
PENTECOSTALISTS
USSR natl cncl formed 9-5, 690F2
PENTHOUSE (magazine)
Ex-employe, Jordan link rptd 9-28, 767E3
PEOPLES Temple
USSR rptdly turned over cult money to Guyana 1-1, 117C3
Justice Dept bars body transfer 1-6, 588 rptd unclaimed 2-1, 117E2
IRS probes pol activities 1-13, 117F3
Buford, Guyana disclose cult money location 1-17, 1-23, 117G2
FBI documts to be probed by grand jury 1-17, 117D3
Justice Dept sues re body removal costs 1-22, 117D2
Assets to be dissolved 1-23, Jonestown kin sue 1-28, 117B2*
FBI radio message transcripts rptd 1-29, 118B1
Jones, 28 followers '78 cremation cited 2-1, 117G2
S Jones retracts 'confessn' 2-2, 117G3
Guyana const formatn slowed 3-2, 299E3
Guyana dismisses Layton chrgs 3-7, 220E1
Swiss banks block funds 3-12, 250E1
Jones aide commits suicide 3-13, 220C1
Property auctioned 3-14, 220F1
Tape transcript excerpts rptd 3-15, 219F2
GOP wins Ryan's House seat 4-3, 265F1
Calif bodies transfer, burials set 4-19, 4-21; 546 bodies rptd unclaimed 4-21, 336C1
State Dept rpt finds cult probe neglect 5-3, 335D3
GAO rpts body recovery cost 5-17, 404C3
Swiss rpt funds transfer 8-2, 592B3

1980

PENSIONS & Retirement
ERISA cases declined by Sup Ct 1-14, 37A1
Va shipyd, USW pact signed 1-31, 251E2
Pension funds investmt change cited 2-19, 2-21, 127A1
Maddox pension bill fails 2-27, 200A1
USW steel pact set 4-15, 289C1
Pre-ERISA insured pensn benefits backed by Sup Ct 5-12, 426B3
Baseball contract dispute setld 5-23, 402A2
Mandatory pensns urged 5-23, 404F1
ILA dock pact setld 5-27, 482A2
DC fscl recovery plan proposed 7-19, '80 budget deficit rptd 9-30, 742G2, E3
AT&T pacts reached 8-9, 648D1
Carter pres renominatn acceptance speech 8-14, 613A2
AT&T begins reorgn, OKs pensn plan consolidatn 8-20, 648C2
Union investmt role urged by AFL-CIO cncl 8-21, 647D3
Teamster fund probe scored by GAO 8-25, 704C3
UAW-AMC contract set 9-17, 725E1
Multi-employer plan reform clears Cong 9-18, 9-19, signed 9-26, 856C3
Mil pensn divorce case accepted by Sup Ct 10-20, 807A3
Rail pensn revisn backed by Sup Ct 12-9, 936G3
Methodists settle Pacific Homes fraud suit 12-10, 963C3
Social Security—*See under U.S. GOVERNMENT*

PENTAGON—*See under U.S. GOVERNMENT*
PENTATHLON
Moscow Olympic results 7-24, 623E1
PENTHOUSE (magazine)
Guccione wins libel case 3-1, 239B2
Guccione libel award cut 4-17, 405A3
PENTHOUSE International
Newsconcorp
'Caligula' ruled not obscene in Boston 8-1, 640B2
PENZIAS, Arno A.
Cuts Sovt ties re dissidents 4-16, 326A3
PEOPLE (magazine)
NY businesswoman, 2 partners indicted 1-10, 216G1
Us magazine sale rptd 3-7, 239B2
PEOPLE'S Business Commission
Vs GE microbe patent Sup Ct ruling 6-16, 453F1
PEOPLES Energy Corp.
ND synfuels plant gets $1.5 bln fed loan 11-19, ct blocks projct 12-8, 962A1
PEOPLES Temple
$10 mln in assets located in Panama, 3 other Latin natns 2-6; $6 mln returned to US 2-28, 170C3, E3
2 defectors, daughter slain 2-26, 190A3
US mil computer failure rptd 3-10, 210D2
Layton wins trial delay 4-1, Beikman sentncd for murder attempt 4-8, 313B3
Layton acquitted of attempted murder, Beikman appeals sentence 5-22, 407F3-408B1
Beikman murder chrgs rptd dropped 9-20, 751B1

1976

PEOPLE'S Trust of New Jersey—*See UNITED Jersey Banks*
PEORIA, Ill.—*See ILLINOIS*
PEPIN, Jean-Luc
Meets execs on inflatn plan 8-9, 623A3, F3
PEPITONE, Byron V.
Rpts draft registratn, lottery ended 1-23, 68A3
PEPPER, Rep. Claude Denson (D, Fla.)
Reelected 11-2, 829C2
PEPSICO, Inc.
USSR deal signed 8-18, 679E2
Execs rptd in Cuba, exiles protest 9-27, 791D2
PERALTA Ballabriga, Bishop Francisco
Scores Vitoria killings 3-5, 207G1
PERCY, Sen. Charles H. (R, Ill.)
Ford lists as potential VP 1-22, 41A2
Scores Lockheed payoffs 2-4, 130A3
With Ford in Ill 3-6, 180C1
Ford urges regulatory reform 5-13, 347A1
VP prospect cited 8-10, 584D1
Scott campaign gift rptd 8-30, 980F1
Brown dismissal rptd asked 10-20, 787C3

PEREDA Asbun, Col. Juan
Says Latin leftists aid ELN 4-8, 416C1
Says amnesty excluded 'extremists' 6-6, 415B3
On state of siege 6-9, miners strike 6-19, 456A2, E2

PEREIRA de Araujo Neto, Benvenuto
Loses pol rights 8-4, 850F3
PEREIRA da Silva, Armenio
Killed 1-1, 11A1

1977

PEOPLE United to Save Humanity—*See OPERATION Push*
PEPIN, Jean-Luc
Resigns 5-6, 346B3
Unity task force chrmn 7-5, 542D1
PEPITONE, Byron V.
Quits as Selective Svc dir 3-9, 211A2
PEPPERDINE University (Malibu, Calif.)
Odum gets ecology award 4-15, 354G1
PEPSICO, Inc.
Pizza Hut takeover cited in table 880G1
Stock falls 3-9, saccharin substitute rptd 3-10, 177B1, A2
Indicted 3-30, fined 5-19, 504G1-A2
Joan Crawford dies 5-10, 452F2
Lee Way Motor Freight Inc.
Record bias award ordrd 10-11, 818G3
PERALTA Azurdia, Col. Enrique
Guatemala pres candidate 10-16, 869D1
PERALTA Mendez, Gen. Ricardo
Chrgs constant rights abuse 7-14, 673B1
Guatemala pres candidate 10-16, 869D1
PERCY, Sen. Charles H. (R, Ill.)
At India pres funeral 2-13, 116B1
Backs Lance on finances 7-25, 574A2
Asks Lance resignatn, spec prosecutor 9-5, 689G3-690A1
Powell apologizes 9-14, 701B3
Apologizes to Lance 9-15, 700C3
Testifies re Lance 9-17, 718D3
Urges actn vs liquid protein 11-23, 992D3
PERDUE, Arthur
Dies 6-27, 532E3
PERDUE Inc.
Arthur Perdue dies 6-27, 532E3

PEREDA Asbun, Gen. Juan
Banzer to name interim pres 11-10, 901D3
Named AF chief 11-30, navy backs pres bid 12-22, 1009A3

PEREIRA dos Santos, Gen. Adalberto
Sees Carter 9-6, at Panama Canal pact signing 9-7, 678A1

1978

Jones sexual tyranny, '73 lewdness arrest rptd 11-24, 911G1-D2
Press curbed at death site 11-25, 909F2
Cult suicide resistance rptd 11-26, 911D1
1st survivors return to US 11-27, 11-29; others held re murders 11-28, 910C2
US cult, Sovt emb links rptd 11-27, 11-28, 910B3
San Fran mayor slain 11-27, 920D2
Sovt, other world press reactn 11-28, 11-30, 911D2
Final death toll 911 11-30, 909D1
More survivors return to US 12-2—12-6; FBI, Calif grand jury query 12-8; grand jury probe stayed 12-13, 955D1, F1
Beikman, Layton murder hearings 12-4; Layton indicted in Ryan murder 12-8, takes 'full responsibility' 12-13, 955A2
Carter on rights abuse 12-6, 934D1
Death ritual tape rptd found 12-8, 954E3
592 victims identified in US 12-8; 1st bodies leave Del air base 12-9, 955F2
Poison murders rptd 12-11, 955C1
Coroner's jury queries Rhodes; detained survivors live in fear 12-14, 955D2
Swiss bank acct withdrawals by Buford, Lane rptd 12-15, denied 12-16; Panama accts located, part sought by US 12-20, 1000E1
Stephan Jones confesses in Beikman trial 12-18, Guyana indicts 12-19, 1000A1
USSR rejects Jonestown bequest 12-18, 1000A2
Ryan murder probe resumes, Guyana survivors queried 12-21—12-27, Buford claims Oct defectn 12-21, 1000D1
More Guyana survivors return to US 12-21—12-29, 1000C2
Guyana jury rules Jonestown deaths murder, blames Jones; Guyana probe ends 12-22; US to issue death certificates 12-23, 999D3

PEOPLE United to Save Humanity—*See OPERATION Push*
PEPE, Luigi
Wounded 7-10, 574E1
PEPPER, Rep. Claude Denson (D, Fla.)
Mandatory retiremt age hiked 4-6, 238F2
Reelected 11-7, 850G2
PEPSICO Inc.
USSR vodka sales deal expanded 1-10, 20D3
FTC bars bottler limits 4-25, 346C1
Philip Morris to buy 7-Up 5-15, 364B3
Wilson Sporting Goods Co.
Women's pro basketball league begins play 12-9, 1027G2
PERALTA Azurdia, Col. Enrique
Pres vote count delayed by violence, fraud chrgs 3-5—3-9, 168A2
Disputes electn results 3-10—3-11, offcl figures rptd 3-14, 190F1
Lucas named pres-elect by Cong 3-13, 190E1
PERALTA Mendez, Gen. Ricardo
Scores climate of violence 2-15, 168A3
Pres vote count delayed by violence, fraud chrgs 3-5—3-9, 168A2
Disputes electn results 3-10—3-11, offcl figures rptd 3-14, 190F1
Lucas named pres-elect by Cong 3-13, 190E1
PERATIS, Kathleen
Hails Navy sea duty rule 7-27, 589E1
PERCEVAL (film)
Released 10-6, 1030C3
PERCY, Sen Charles H. (R, Ill.)
Votes for Panama Canal neutrality pact 3-16, 177F2
On Begin Sen com appearance 3-21, 199G1
Wins renomination 3-21, 207G1
Votes for 2d Canal pact 4-18, 273B1
Personal finances rptd 5-19, 385D3
Reelected 11-7, 848F1, 853G1-A2
PEREDA Asbun, Gen. Juan (Bolivian president)
3 set oppositn pres bids 4-10—5-12; rptdly leads race 4-21, leftist disunity cited 5-11, 411F2
Pres electn held, fraud chrgd 7-9; leads vote count, oppositn scores electns 7-11, 530D2
Campaign harassmt rptd 7-9, 530C3
Electn annulled 7-19; seizes power 7-21, swears Cabt 7-24, 570C3-571E1
Post-coup detainees ordrd freed 7-26, 617C2
Sets '80 electns, bars pres bid 8-6, 617A2
State of siege lifted; natl security, govt svc laws revoked 8-11, 671G1
US resumes mil aid 8-15, 671A2
Videla visits, backs sea outlet 10-25, 860C3
Cabt quits 11-1, mil controls new Cabt 11-6, 868D3
Army officers seized in 'plot' 11-2, 868D3
Presses anti-corruptn campgn 11-15, 11-21, offcl oppositn cited 11-24, 913F1
Ousted in bloodless coup 11-24, 913B1
PEREDO, Oswaldo ('Chato')
Arrest in Bolivia rptd 9-1, 691F2
PERELMAN, S. J.
Wins Natl Book Award 4-10, 315A3
PERENHA, Capt. Itamar
Runs for cong; scores Figueiredo, jailed 6-16, 556D1

1979

PEOPLE United to Save Humanity (PUSH)—*See OPERATION Push*
PEORIA, Ill.—*See ILLINOIS*
PEPIN, Jean-Luc
Unity Task Force rpt issued 1-25, 74C3
PEPPERIDGE Farms Inc.
PCB contaminated cakes destroyed 9-17, 704E3
PEPPERMINT Soda (film)
Released 7-15, 820G2
PEPSICO Inc.
Iran interests natlzd 7-5, 503A3
PEQUEA Valley School District v. Pa. Department of Education
Case dismissed by Sup Ct 6-25, 540C2
PERCY, Sen. Charles H. (R, Ill.)
Finances disclosed 5-18, 383E2
H-bomb letter published 9-16, 9-18, 713B2; text of letter, diagram 714D1-717E3
On 'lost' Army guns 10-4, 852C1
GIs Agent Orange exposure rptd 11-24, 904C2

PEREDA Asbun, Gen. Juan (ret.)
Siles pres bid rptd 3-16, 233F2

PEREIRA, Aristides (Cape Verde Islands president)
Young urges Israel dialogue 9-5, 720B3
PEREIRA Magro, Acacio
Portugal trade min 7-30, 603E3
PERELMAN, S(idney) J(oseph)
Dies 10-17, 860C3

1980

PEPIN, Jean-Luc
Canada transport min 3-3, 171A2
PEPPER, Rep. Claude Denson (D, Fla.)
Reelected 11-4, 842A3
PEPSICO Inc.
'79 top TV advertiser 4-4, 376B2
Lee Way Motor Freight Inc.
Job bias suit settled for $2.7 mln 1-10, 17C2
PERCY, Sen. Charles H. (R, Ill.)
GAO rpt scores costly sewer projects 1-19, 54D2
Visits Moscow, forsees arms talks 11-26—11-28; reactn 11-28, 11-30, 914G3, 915C1
Palestinian state support rptd; comments 12-5; Reagan aides, others score 12-7, 12-9, 931B1
'Confident' of arms talks 12-12, 950A3
PEREN, Roger
USSR opposes as amb 1-29, 119E1
PERE Ramos, David
Held hostage in El Salvador 1-11, freed 1-14, 38G3-39A1
Held hostage again 2-13, 117C2
Freed 2-14, 149D1

1976

PERES, Shimon
Warns Syria on Leb interventn 1-8, 1D2
On Arab detainees 1-13, 35F1
Rpts Syria warning effective 1-23, 59E2
Israel welcomes Leb refugees 1-25, 59C2
Rptd irked at Rabin statmt on US arms bid 106G2
Abstains on Avineri appointmt 2-15, 126A1
In Sinai, hails pact 2-19, 145G1
Warns Arab rioters 3-16, 210C3
Briefs Cabt on Syria troops in Leb 4-11, 258B1
On W Bank election results 4-13, 258B3
Wary of Leb interventn, warns Syria 4-28, 296F1
Newsmen barred from Ramallah 5-3, 319E3
Weighs anti-riot moves 5-18, 354D2
Abstains on Arab grievance com formatn 5-23, 370E1
Vs defense budget cut 6-20, 459G3
Rpts food aid to Leb civilns 6-24, 527G3
Ties Amin to hijackers 7-4, 485A2
Backed Dayan mission to Uganda 7-10, 515D1
Orders med aid for Leb 8-6, 578E2
Denies Leb coast blockade 8-17, 618G2
On Christn-Palestinian clash 9-1, 642A1
On KLM hijacker landing demand 9-5, 662B3
On Hebron shrine clash 10-3, 737D2, G2
Vs Israeli troops in Leb 10-26, 798F2
Vs Syrian, Palestinian troops in south Leb 10-27, 798A3
Doubts Sadat peace bid 11-16, 878E1
Warns vs Syria border actn 11-21, 877G1
PERETZ, Anne
'72 campaign gift listed 4-25, 688C1
PERETZ, Martin
'72 campaign gift listed 4-25, 688C1
PEREZ, Carlos Andres
At oil natlzatn rite 1-1; sees 'social democracy' 1-2, 12E2
On SELA 1-12, 60B3
Sees Canada prime min 1-29—2-2, 116F2
Issues Occidental paymts rpt 2-14, 147F3
Sees Kissinger 2-16—2-17, 177B2, E2
Guerrilla kidnapers score 2-28, 208F2
Declined nonaligned invite 3-26, 256C2
Addresses intl soc dem conf 5-23, 449A3
Asks US return Panama Canal 6-22, 793C1
Defends arrests of deps 8-5, 592E3
Mesa, Herrera arrests scored 8-12, 874F2
Gives Letelier widow condolences 9-29, 780G3
Scores Cuba jet sabotage 10-8, vows info 10-16, 779G3
Cuban exile contacts rptd 10-21, 780F2
Cuba exile ties cited 10-24, 843E3
Addresses UN; tours W Eur, USSR 11-16—11-30, 929G2-930C1
Addresses Socialist Intl 11-28, 935D3
PEREZ, Leonora M.
Chrgd with murder 6-16, out on bond 6-30, 503D3
PEREZ, Romona Teresita
Seconds Ford nominatn 8-18, 597G2
PEREZ, Tony
NL wins All-Star game 7-13, 544C2
In World Series 10-16—10-21, 815D2
PEREZ Beotegui, Ignacio (Wilson)
Release asked 12-11, 967E2
PEREZ Guerrero, Manuel
On North-South talks impasse 7-18, 530E1
North-South conf delayed 12-9, 976G3
PERIODICAL Correspondents' Association
Sup Ct declines review of case vs Consumer Rpts 1-12, 24G1
PERK, Mayor Ralph (Cleveland)
GOP seeks Mayors Conf posts 6-30, 493A2
PERKINS, Rep. Carl D. (D, Ky.)
Reelected 11-2, 829F3
On Ky mine blast rescue 11-19, 892C1
PERKUS, Cathy
On FBI role in SWP burglaries 7-14, 570B1
PERLE, Richard N.
Rockefeller chrgs CP ties 4-15, regrets 4-27, 305E3
PERLINGER, Col. Luis (ret.)
Rptd arrested 5-17, 399C1

1977

PERES, Shimon
Seeks premiership 1-11, 48B2
Says Egypt troops left Sinai for riot duty 1-21, 62G2
Warns Syria vs troop moves 1-25, 71G3
Eban quits premier race 2-3, 135G1
Warns US re Ecuador jet sale bar 2-7, 87C3
Meets Waldheim 2-10, 86F2
Vance visits 2-16—2-17, 121C1
On US bomb sale ban 2-19, 121F1
Rabin renominated 2-23, 135D1
Denies hawk views, seeks Mapam aid 4-8, 267C2
Allon defers electn race 4-9, 267B2 ★
Replaces Rabin as Labor candidate 4-10, 267B2
On Egypt Sinai exchanges 4-19, 297G1
Assumes premier powers 4-22, 329E2
Says Arabs block peace 4-25, 316F1
Labor ousted in electns 5-17, 377B1
Rejcts Likud unity bid 5-19, 377F1
Sadat on Begin electn win 5-20, 401D3
Leb mil role rptd asked 8-22, 648F1
Vs US-Sovt Geneva plan 10-2, 750E1
Sadat speech reply 11-20, 889C2
Vs Begin peace plan 12-28, 994G2
PEREZ, Adela
Chrgs peasant executns 2-22; probe ordrd 2-23, 255D1
PEREZ, Carlos
Jailed in Spain 1-30, 101G3
PEREZ, Carlos Andres (Venezuela president)
Christmas pardons rptd 1-1, 3F1
Sets oil credits to Latins 1-1, 23B2
Creates new Cabt posts 1-4; swears Cabt 1-7, 23C2
Backs Panamanian canal demands 1-18, 46G1
CIA paymts rptd 2-19; chrgs protested, Carter regrets 2-19—2-24, 124F1, 151A2
Lauds Carter rights stand 2-27, 142F2
Backs tax reform 3-11, 547E1
Backs US A-policy, Brazil ties worsen 4-1, 547A3
Seeks OPEC price unity 4-19, tours OPEC states 4-21—5-5, renews plea 5-9, 361G3
US envoy visits 5-10—5-12, 414E1
Videla visits 5-11—5-14, 547G1-F2
Sees Mrs Carter 6-12, 455D2
Visits US, sees Carter 6-27—7-2, 546D1
OPEC price split ended 6-29—7-5, 535E2
Sues Cuba exile Bosch 7-4, 868B1
Sets austerity measures 7-11, 565F2
Shuffles Cabt 7-15, 565G3
Pinerua wins AD '78 pres nominatn 7-17, 566E1
Carter canal treaty advice rptd 7-27, 590D1
Sees Torrijos, regional ldrs 8-5—8-6; new canal treaty backed, Intl Coffee Fund set 8-6, 606B3, 608A3
Sees Young, lauds canal treaty 8-12, 647B1
Copei platform scores 8-18, 674G1
Backs Dutch Antilles indepndnc 8-19, 949G2
At Panama Canal pact signing 9-7, 678D1
Spanish king visits 9-8—9-10, 805A1
Cuba exiles tried in mil ct 10-10, 868A1
In Brazil 11-16—11-20; A-policy backing rptd 11-25, 912D3
Sees Vance, bars price freeze effort 11-23, 912F3-913A1
Urges OPEC price hike, poor natn debt aid 12-20, 973B2
PEREZ, Jaime
Torture rptd 2-15, 352A1
PEREZ, Leonora M.
Convicted 7-13, 568F2
New trial ordrd 12-19, 991G2
PEREZ Arreola, Evaristo
Strike closes UNAM 6-20, 528D2
PEREZ Esquivel, Adolfo
Arrested 4-4, UN panel protests 6-20, 522G3
PEREZ Guerrero, Manuel
Venez intl econ min 1-7, 23F2
PEREZ y Perez, Gen. Enrique
Gets key army post 11-4, backs Balaguer reelectn 11-5, 969D3
PERKINS, Rep. Carl D. (D, Ky.)
'76 spec interest gifts rptd 2-4, 128G3, 129E2
Carter backs min wage bill 7-12, 534B1
Schl meal bill signed 11-10, 897G2
PERKINS, Susan Yvonne
Crowned Miss America 9-10, 808A3
PERKINS, Wilmot
Castro visit criticism rptd 10-23, 884A1
PERLER, Meinrad
Arrested 4-24, 350G2

1978

PERES, Shimon
In Austria, sees Sadat 2-11, 98F2
Vs Cabt re W Bank, Gaza 6-19, 461G1
Contacts with Sadat rptd 6-21, 489D1
Israel Cabt vs Sadat mtg 7-16, clashes with Begin 7-19, 546D2, B3
Party questns Begin health 7-20, 563D2
Backs Camp David summit pacts 9-18, 712E3
PERETTE, Carlos
Detained re econ criticism 4-23, 611D3
PEREYRA, Carlos Julio
Sent poisoned wine 9-6, 799F1
PEREZ, Angel
Indicted in oil pricing scheme 9-14, 718B3
PEREZ, Carlos Andres (Venezuelan president)
Orders Ottolina plane crash search 3-16, 231B1
Carter visits 3-28—3-29, 233C1
Seeks Nicaragua rights probe by OAS, Somoza scores 3-28—5-8, 376B3
Carter consults on DR electn 5-19, 414C3
Tax reform plan OKd 5-26, 559D2
At Panama Canal pact instrumnts exchng 6-16, 463F2, 464A1
Nicaragua pres scores 9-5, 690D3
Hosts Spain premier 9-7—9-9, 821E3
Nicaragua oil cutoff vow rptd 11-8, 883C3
Herrera elected pres, AD to control Sen 12-3, 952C3
Resumen issue seized, editor takes asylum in Vatican emb 12-3, 953D1
Scores OAS inactn on Nicaragua rights abuse 12-14, 1019C1
PEREZ, Leonora M.
Chrgs dropped 2-1, 116D2
PEREZ, Col. Simeon
Rptd kidnaped 3-3, 248A2
PEREZ, Tony
NL batting ldr 10-2, 928F2
PEREZ Reyes, Hector
Sees Balaguer reelectn, explains vote count suspensn 5-18, 372A1
PEREZ Rodriguez, Col. Juan
Assassinated 7-21, 575E3
PEREZ Valladares, Ernesto
Panama treas, finance min 10-12, 884B2
PEREZ Vega, Gen. Reynaldo
Killed by guerrillas 3-8, 192A2
PEREZ y Perez, Maj. Gen. Enrique
Lauds Balaguer, electoral bd chides 1-20, 94C2
Remains army cmdr 8-16, 648F2
Loses army post, named Spain amb 9-3, 774B2
Sen rejects UK post apptmt 11-9, 881B1
Retiremt forced 11-17, 989A3
PERJURY—*See under CRIME*
PERKINS, Rep. Carl D. (D, Ky.)
Reelected 11-7, 850E4
PAC contributions rptd 12-24, 1008D1
PERKINS Jr., Mahlon F.
Pleads guilty 9-21, sentncd 10-17, 808D2
PERLE, George
Elected to Arts Institute 2-7, 316E1
PERLMAN, Itzhak
Wins Grammy 2-24, 316C1

1979

PERES, Shimon
Scores Kreisky, Brandt re Arafat visit 7-8, 511C3
PERESSE, Ange
Sentncd 10-20, 835E2
PEREVEDENTSEV, Viktor
Urges birth rate increase 10-10, 857D1
PEREZ, Carlos Andres
Owens-Ill drops Niehous ransom effort 3-10, 192F3
Herrera scores admin 3-12, 192C2
'78 Dutch Antilles visit cited 11-13, 882F3
PEREZ, Charlie
On Mex deportatn protest 3-10, 308E1
PEREZ, Tony
Signs with Red Sox 11-20, 1002A1
PEREZ Alfonzo, Juan Pablo
Dies 9-3, 756C3
PEREZ Olivares, Enrique
Named Caracas gov 3-10, 192C3
PEREZ Vega, Gen. Reynaldo (d. 1978)
Nicaragua spec prosecutor named 12-3, 950D3
PERFECT Couple, A (film)
Released 4-5, 528C3
PERILLI, Ivo
Till Marriage Do Us Part released 7-20, 820E3
PERJURY—*See Under CRIME*
PERKINS, Anthony
Winter Kills released 5-17, 528G3
Romantic Comedy opens 11-8, 956G3
Black Hole released 12-21, 1007A3
PERKINS, Bill
On Silkwood A-suit impact 5-18, 381C3
PERKINS, Rep. Carl D. (D, Ky.)
Education Com chrmn 1-24, 71C1
Sponsors jobs bill 5-23, 384A2
PERKINS, James A.
Forgn-language study urged 11-7, 944F1
PERKINS, Ray
Hired as Giants coach 2-22, 175D2
PERKINS Nuclear Station—*See NORTH Carolina-Atomic Energy*
PERLER, Meinrad
Chrgd re Chiasso scandal 2-15, 137E1
PERLMAN, Clifford S.
Underworld ties cited 6-26, 520D1
PERLMAN, Itzhak
Wins Grammy 2-16, 336G3

1980

PERES, Shimon
Meets Carter, gives W Bank plan 4-24, 324G3
Visits Egypt 11-7—11-9, 863F2
Gives peace plan at Labor Party conv 12-17; reelected chrmn, to run vs Begin 12-18, 966E1
PEREZ, Carlos Andres
Censured 5-8, 411C1
In Nicaragua, marks Somoza downfall 7-19, 565F2
PEREZ Esquivel, Adolfo
Awarded Nobel Peace Prize 10-13, 889A2
PEREZ Heras, Joaquin
Wins Olympic medal 8-3, 622G2
PEREZ Llorca, Jose Pedro
Suarez shuffles Cabt 5-2, 355E1
Named Spain forgn min 9-8, 690C2
Addresses CSCE Madrid prep talks 9-9, 679B3
France terrorism talks rptd 11-27, 923D2
PEREZ-Perez, Crecencio
Hijacks Delta jet to Cuba 9-17, returned to US for trial 9-18, 704B1, B2
PERINI North River Associates v. Fusco
Case remanded by Sup Ct 1-14, 37F1
PERJURY—*See under CRIME*
PERKINS, Anthony
Ffolkes released 4-18, 416F2
PERKINS, Rep. Carl D. (D, Ky.)
Reelected 11-4, 842F4
PERLMAN, Clifford S.
Caesars gets NJ gambling license 10-25, 988A3
PERLMAN, Stuart Z.
Caesars gets NJ gambling license 10-25, 988A3

1976

PERNA, Edoardo
On CP confidence abstentn 8-5, 589F2
PERON, Eva Duarte de (Mrs. Juan Domingo) (1922-52)
'51 Dutch bribes rptd 3-12, 254E3
Buried 10-2, 997B2
PERON, Juan Domingo (1895-1974)—See 1974, p. 538D3 for biog. data
Testament com named 1-5, testament publshd 1-7, 26B2
'51 Dutch bribes rptd 3-12, 254E3
Ivanissevich dies 6-5, 524G2
Cited re Spinola-Eanes link 8-11, 733B1
Buried 12-19, 997A2
PERON, Maria Estela (Isabel) Martinez de (Mrs. Juan Domingo)
Names Peron testament com 1-5, 26B2
Mil ldrs block provincial takeovers 1-8, 26E1
Scores leftist guerrillas 1-9, 7F2
Party ldrs bar reelectn bid 1-13, 1-20, 71B3
Shuffles cabt 1-15—1-16; pol, mil, labor ldrs score 1-16—1-27, 71A2
Replaces labor, econ mins 2-3, 154F2
Pol ldrs ask quit; bans TV progrm, closes La Opinion 2-10, 154E2
Closes Cong 2-16, bars reelectn bid 2-18; labor, mil ldrs seek resignatn, new cabt 2-19—2-23, 154E1
Fires defense min 2-23, 211F3
Impeachmt bid fails 2-26, Luder rejects Cong sessn re fitness 3-4, 211E3
Modifies econ plan 3-10, 212A3
Bomb attack blocked 3-18, 212D1
Govt overthrown; arrested 3-24, 211E2
New pres, cabt sworn 3-29, 236A1
Junta freezes bank acct 3-30, 236D3
Denies funds misuse 4-30, prelim chrgs filed 5-6, 399E2
Funds misuse chrgs rptd 6-4, 6-18, goods frozen 7-1, 520E1
Ivanissevich dies 6-5, 524G2
Pol rights revoked 6-23, 520B1
Indicted for embezzlemt 10-25, 997B1
PERPER, Martin H.
Defeated 11-2, 823B1
PERPICH, Rudy
Anderson to seek Sen seat 11-10, 865C1
PERRAULT, Raymond
Stays Canada Sen ldr 9-14, 692C2
PERRINI Guala, Aldo
Rptd tortured to death 3-5, 207D3
PERRY (Tony) Awards, Antoinette
Presented 4-18, 460C2
PERSIAN Gulf
Iran vs plan to rename 1-7, 12G3
Japan-Iran oil plant set 1-7, 141A2
Cuba troops rptd in area 4-5, 242F1
Forgn mins conf 11-25—11-26, 914B1

1977

PERNIA, Julio Cesar
UNO nominates for pres 8-7, 727A2
PERON, Juan
Jose Ber Gelbard dies 10-4, 872A2
PERON, Maria Estela (Isabel) Martinez de (Mrs. Juan Domingo)
Detention continues 1-1, 3B1
Caraballo seized 4-14, 345B3
PEROVIC, Mileta
Rptd seized 11-22, 1018B3
PERREAULT, Gil
NHL season ldr 4-3, 262F3
PERROTA, Rafael
Rptd kidnaped 7-15, 595F2
PERRY, Jack
Scores Miller 8-26, 691B1
PERRY, Judge Sam
Rules in Black Panther suit 4-15, 6-21, 540E2
PERRY, William
Arms dvpt, procuremt consolidated 4-25, 343A3
More arms contract competitn planned 11-21, 942E1
PERRY (Tony) Awards, Antoinette
Presented 6-5, 452C1
PERSHING & Co.
Donaldson Lufkin buys 10-11, 800A1
PERSIAN Gulf
Saudi port projct cited 1-10, 78G2-A3
Bahrain ends US base pact 7-1, 511G3
PERSONS, Maj. Gen. Wilton B. (ret.)
Dies 9-5, 788C2
PERTAMINA—See under INDONESIA
PERTSCHUK, Michael
Named to FTC 3-25, confrmd 4-6, 272B3

1978

PERNIA, Julio Cesar
Rebuffs leftist unity plan 4-28; pres bid rptd weak 5-28, 413F2, A3
Runs 3d in pres vote 6-4, 443D2
PERON, Juan Domingo (d. 1974)
Police disperse followers 7-1, 793A2
PERON, Maria Estela (Isabel) Martinez de (Mrs. Juan Domingo)
Convicted of embezzlemt 2-20, 208E2
Moved to house arrest 8-28, 793F1
PEROSIO, Beatriz
Kidnaped 8-8, 792G3
PEROVIC, Mileta
Sentenced 4-13, 292G1
PERPICH, Gov. Rudolph G. (D, Minn.)
Names Mrs Humphrey to husband's Sen seat 1-25, 52G2
Reserve Mining to stay 7-7, 553D3
Wins primary 9-12, 716D1
Loses reelectn 11-7, 854B3
PERRAULT, Gilles
Dossier 51 released 12-12, 1030F2
PERREAULT, Gil
Wales Conf wins NHL All-Star game 1-24, 76D3
NHL top paid player 4-6, 296F3
NHL scoring ldr 4-9, 296E2
PERRY, Fred
Borg wins 3d consecutive Wimbledon title 7-8, 539G3
PERRY, Gaylord
NL pitching ldr 10-2, wins Cy Young Award 10-24, 928F1, G2
PERRY, William
Sees cruise missile defns edge 6-1, 407F2
Lauds cruise missile test 6-21, 493A2
Sees cruise missile improvemts 11-14, 1020E3
Rpts USSR look-down radar test, discounts cruise missile defns 12-26, 1020C3
PERRY (Tony) Awards, Antoinette
Presented 6-4, 579F2
PERSHIN, Viktor
In US to study grain shipmt delays 3-2, 151E2
PERSIAN Gulf
Iran fears Afghan threat 5-19, 391E1
US, USSR clash on arms sales, talks stalled 12-5—12-15; US rift rptd 12-19, 996C3

PERTINI, Alessandro (Sandro) (Italian president)
Elected Italian pres 7-8, sworn 7-9, 558A1
Scores USSR dissident trials 7-12, 543B1
8,000 convicts amnestied 8-4, 724B3
PERTRAMER, Brunhild
Released in Moro case 3-20, 247B2
PERTSCHUK, Michael
Defends children's TV ad curbs 4-26, says Hollings wary 4-27, 347F2, A3
On big merger rise 7-27, 767D1-A2
Banned from FTC children's ad probe 11-3, 941A3

1979

PERLMUTTER, Nathan
Vs Young meeting with PLO rep 8-15, 606A2
Denies pressure for Young resignatn 8-19, 624A2
PERON, Eva Duarte (Mrs. Juan Domingo) (1919-1952)
Evita opens 9-25, 956A3
PERON, Juan Domingo (1895-1974)
Argentina Nazi fugitive asylum cited 8-8, 616F3
Evita opens 9-25, 956A3
Argentina bans union pol activity 11-16, 887E2
Campora granted safe passage 11-20, 906B2
PERON, Maria Estela (Isabel) Martinez de
3 rights groups raided 8-10, 612A1
Campora granted safe passage 11-20, 906C2
PEROT, H. Ross
Claims Iran prison rescue 2-19, 125E3
PERREAULT, Gil
Soviets win Challenge Cup 2-11, 118G2
PERRIN, Vincent
Travel Act bribery convictn upheld by Sup Ct 11-27, 919E3
PERRINE, Valerie
Magician of Lublin released 11-9, 1008A1
Electric Horseman released 12-21, 1007C3
PERRIN v. U.S.
Case decided by Sup Ct 11-27, 919F3
PERRONE, Dominic
Italy expels 2-14, 136D1-A2
PERRY, Elizabeth
Frequency opens 4-25, 711B3
PERRY, Fred
Borg named '78 top player 1-18, 103G2
PERRY, Commodore Matthew C(albraith) (1794-1858)
Carter visits Shimoda 6-27, 494B2
PERRY, Rod
NFL '78 interceptn ldr 1-6, 80G1
PERRY, William Haggin
Coastal wins Belmont Stakes 6-9, 448B2
PERSHING Missile—See ARMAMENTS–Missiles
PERSIAN Gulf
US 'quick-strike' mil force planned 6-21, 482C3
Iran oil productn drop, weather linked 8-24, 645C2
6 states hold security conf 10-14–10-16, 804G1-A3
PERSIAN Gulf Organization for Development in Egypt (Kuwait, Qatar, Saudi Arabia, United Arab Emirates)
Disbanded 4-27, 319D2
PERSKY, Lester
Hair released 3-13, 528D2
Yanks released 9-19, 820G3
PERSONNEL Administrator v. Feeney
Case decided by Sup Ct 6-5, 421D1
PERSONNEL Management, Office of—See under U.S. GOVERNMENT

,**PERTINI, Alessandro (Sandro) (Italian president)**
Asks La Malfa to form govt 2-22, 155F1
La Malfa gives up Cab; bid 3-2, Andreotti asked again 169B3
Swears new Cabt 3-21, 212D1
Andreotti submits resignatn 3-31, dissolves parlt 4-2, 254F2
Asks Craxi to form govt 7-9, 525F2, D3
Pandolfi tries to form govt 7-27, 583A3
Cossiga govt sworn 8-5, 602F3
Scores Czech dissident trial 10-23, 802D2
Sees China premr, new NATO missiles backed 11-5, 854D2, E2
Sees Vance on Iran 12-11, 933G2
PERTSCHUK, Michael
Sees merger dangers 5-7, 349C2

1980

PERLMUTTER, George
Nothing Personal released 4-18, 416D3
PERMIAN Corp.—See OCCIDENTAL Petroleum
PERON, Isabel Martinez de
'76 arrest order lifted 12-24, 991F1
PERPETUAL Federal Savings & Loan (Washington, D.C.)
Mortgage rate rptd at 17% 3-7, 222D3
PERRAULT, Raymond J.
Canada Senate ldr 3-3, 171F1, B2
PERRIN, Dr. Pierre
Viets capture 6-25, release 6-29, 508G2
PERRY, Judge Joseph Sam
Voids Treasury futures trading curbs 7-17, denies appeal 7-18, 558D3
PERRY, Lester
Remains in Cuba 10-27, 828D3
PERRY, Nick
Chrgd in lottery fraud 9-19, 786C3
PERRY, Rod
Steelers win Super Bowl 1-20, 61G3-62C1
PERRY, Vernon
Steelers win NFL conf title 1-6, 8E1
PERRY, William J.
Rpts US tank detector system 3-21, 267D1
On MX deploymt chng 5-6, 369E2
Testifies on 'stealth' plane disclosure 9-4, 666A1
MX distortn rptd 10-5, 897D1
PERSHING, Gen. John J. (1860-1948)
Gen Simpson dies 8-15, 676B3
PERSHING Missile—See ARMAMENTS–Missiles
PERSIAN Gulf
Iran warns vs oil blockade 1-11, 29D2
Sovt surveillance ship sighted 1-22; vietn withdraws 1-23, 46D1
Carter warns USSR area vital to US 1-23, 41A1, 42F2
Tass scores Carter warning 1-24, 43A3
Arabs score Carter State of Union pledge 1-25, 1-26, 65B1
Egypt scores Sovt Afghan invasn, Saudi stand 1-28, 69G1, A3
Kennedy scores Carter Doctrine 1-28, 74E2, F2, E3
GOP rebuts Carter Doctrine 1-28, 75C1
Carter admits defense weakness 1-29, 65A1
US envoy warns Sovts on move 1-31; Vance, Byrd rebut remark 2-1, 2-2, 83C2
Pentagon rpt on US defense ability issued 2-1, 83E3
USSR denies aims, scores US 2-2, 84D2
Saudis back US on defense 2-4—2-5, 83G1
Carter asks draft registratn 2-8, 110G2
US assault force dispatched 2-12, 106G1
US' Connally backs mil presence 2-20, 129F3; 3-7, 184G3
W Europe gets US defns plan 2-22, 139D2
Carter weighs force 4-1, 247C1
UK weighs stockpiling 4-2, 274A2
US jets deployed in Egypt 7-10, 548A2
US, Somalia sign mil base pact 8-21, 645B3, D3
Hormuz Strait access seen threatnd 9-24, 718C1; for subsequent developments, see IRAN—Iraqi War
Bush scores Carter policy 9-25, 781D1
US deploys missile cruiser 10-11, 773E2
Carter, Reagan TV debate 10-28, 813G2
French set mine-sweeping force 10-28, 821E2
Sadat vs Reagan policy shift 11-23, 894A2
NATO defns mins urged to up arms outlays 12-9—12-10, 950B1
Brezhnev offers peace plan 12-10; US rejects 12-11, 930D1
    Iran-Iraq War—See IRAN–Iraqi War
PERSKY, Bill
Serial released 3-28, 416E3
PERSON, Chris
Wins IC4A 400-m hurdles 5-25, 892B2
PERSSON, Stefan
Islanders win Stanley Cup 5-24, 487F3
PERTINI, Alessandro (Sandro) (Italian president)
Air controllers stage job actn 3-12, 194B2
Cossiga Cabt resigns 3-19, 212G2
Magistrates demand protectn 3-22, 233B2
Carter visits Rome 6-19—6-21, 474A2
Visits Bologna after bombing 8-2, 605D1
Loren tax case appeal rptd 9-10, 908C1
Forlani agrees to form govt 10-2, 751G2
Scores quake relief efforts 11-26, 943D2
PERTSCHUK, Michael
Lauds FTC funding agreemt 4-30, 348A2
FTC child ad probe refused by Sup Ct 6-16, 511D3

1976

Pol ldrs rptd seized 7-19—7-30, 590F3
Emergency extended 8-1, 652B3
Leftist mil plotters, pol dissidents arrested 8-13—8-27, 652C2
Student protesters seized 8-23, 8-27, 652F2-A3
'70 quake casualties cited 11-27, 932A1

Economy & Labor (domestic)
'74 defns budget rptd 1-2, 60G2
Austerity measures set 1-12, scored 1-23, 2-2—2-3, 142D1, A2
Graphic workers strike 1-15—1-24, 142D2
Mineworkers strike 1-19—1-20, 142C2
'13 strike decree revoked 2-4, 142D2
Sporadic strikes protest austerity 3-1—6-25, 499E2-B3
Ousted newspr dirs rptd vs austerity 3-19, 499G3
New austerity measures set 6-28, 6-30, protested, emergency declared 7-1—7-5, 499G1
Pvt bus driver strike continues 7-1, 499D2
Strikes end, schls reopen 7-7—7-15; protests continue 7-12, union ldrs seized 7-19—7-30, 590E3
Mil rebelln fails 7-9, 591B1
Mine strike averted, ldrs arrested 8-16, 8-27, 652A3

Foreign Relations (misc.)
Belaunde begins visit 1-4; lauds Morales 1-5, 55A3
Panel to study Chile-Bolivia sea outlet plan 1-7, 27C1
Magazine imports banned 1-10, 55C3; 1-12, 2-3, 142B2, E3
'75 trade, reserves rptd, imports cut ordrd 1-12, 142F1
French Mirage purchase cited 1-16, 36C2
Venez to buy iron ore 1-20, 142F2
At intl econ conf 2-11—2-20, 148B1
In US talks on Cuba Angola role 2-18, 178B1
Forgn exchng shortage rptd 2-19, 178A1
Angola MPLA recognized 2-23, 163D1, 178C1 ★
UN multinatl panel meets 3-2—3-12, 297F3
Total IMF loan rptd 4-1, 340D2
Radical killed in Argentina 4-3, 264F1
Bolivia: 'seditionaries' aid guerrillas 4-8, 416C1
Zileri returns from Argentina 5-14, 500C1
Haya de la Torre at intl soc dem mtg 5-23—5-25, 449B3
Amb murdered in Jamaica 6-15, 522C2
Import subsidies cut 6-30, 499B2
Blanco expelled 7-10, in Sweden 7-11, 590F3
Forgn bank loan talks rptd 7-30, 8-4, 590F2
Sovt plane deal rptd 8-19, 652C3
Barua on 3d World debt moratorium demand 10-2, 778F1
Chile rejects Bolivia seaport plan 11-26, 975G1
Bolivia seeks neutrality re Chile war; Sov arms imports cited 12-7, 975D2

1977

Economy & Labor (domestic)
Soc property enterprises curbed 1-7, 46E3-47A1
Wage hike set 1-26, Lima teachers score 2-9, 428C2
Indl community law modified 2-2, CP scores 2-17, 428G1
Econ plan issued 2-6, 241B1
Mil housing allowance rptd set 2-11, 428D2
Petroperu details Amazon costs 3-14, 428A1
Sugar industry emergency set 3-17, 428E1
Anchovy fishing resumes 4-14, suspended 5-6, 428D1
Govt sets '77-78 dvpt plan 5-9, 427D3
Barua quits in austerity plan dispute 5-13, 427C2
Trans-Andean oil pipe opens 5-25, 427F3
Sol devalued 5-26, 427E2
'61-75 GDP variatns table 5-30, 439B1
Austerity program set 6-10, protested 6-13—6-21, 488F1-C3
Sol devalued 6-11, 488B2
Tanguis quits, austerity plan dispute continues 7-6, 563D2
Sol devaluatn disputed 7-6—7-15, 563D2-B3
Students, workers riot 7-11—7-12, 563A2
Gen strike paralyzes Lima 7-19, 563B1
'Minidevaluatns' ended 7-20, 618F2
Strikers ordrd dismissed 7-21—7-24; state miners protest 7-25, church scores 7-26, 618F2
Morales acts to defuse austerity protests 7-28, 618C2
Copper miners strike 8-2, 673D2
July strike ldrs released, union offices remain closed 8-24, 784E2
'74-76 econ projct credits rptd 9-1, 784G3
'77 budget deficit curb, sol devaluatn, price hikes set 9-30, 784A3
Natlizatn, land redistributn, other reform guidelines issued 10-9, 784E1
Sol floated 10-10, 785A2

Foreign Relations (misc.)—*See also 'Monetary, Trade & Aid' below*
UN Assemb member 4A1
Panama, Mexico take exiles 1-8, 46C3
Argentine pres visits; protests 3-3—3-6, 259D1
Ecuador fears arms buildup 6-2, 454C3
Chile hijackers land in Lima 7-5, 537B2
Chile border buildup rptd 8-31, 785C1
Morales at Panama Canal pact signing 9-7, 678A1
Belize independnc backed at UN 11-28, 969A3

Government & Politics—*See also other appropriate subheads in this section*
Pres sees civilian rule 1-1, 21B2
Velasco urges civilian govt 2-3, 241G2
Pol, econ plan issued 2-6, reactn rptd 2-25, 241B1
'78 munic electns seen 2-12, 241D1
Morales to stay as pres after army retiremt 4-22; Apra backs, asks 'open dialogue' 5-7, 488C3
Apra protests voter registratn delay 4-22, 488F3
Econ min quits 5-13, replaced 5-17, 427C2, B3
New econ min quits 7-6, 563D2
Civilian rule vowed for '80 7-28, 618A2
Morales asks debate on '78 vote plan; AP, Odristas ask immediate electns 8-7; Belaunde scores assemb plan 8-25, 673A2
Vannini: electns won't be 'like before' 10-3, 784F1

1978

Economy & Labor (domestic)
'77 inflatn at 32.4% 1-13, 353D2
Steel strike spurs Chimbote, Lima unrest; CGTP strike threats 1-15—2-10; strike rptd setld 2-3, 134F1-C2
Farms hit by drought, low rice crop seen 4-28, 353D2
Teachers strike 5-8—7-27; miners 8-4, emergency declared 8-22, 668F3
Austerity measures set 5-11, 353C1
Price hikes set 5-15; riots, gen strike ensue; emergency declared, strike ldrs seized 5-15—5-23, 393G3
Econ, industry mins replcd 5-15, 394D2
Leftist ldrs deported for gen strike role 5-25; 77 teachers fired, 6-6, peasants group banned 6-9, 475E1, A2
Local industry rptd in default 6-2, 669B2
Teachers strike detainees freed 7-14, 668E3
Health workers strike 7-14—8-12, 669C1
Press natlizatn abandoned; stock sale, ex-owner compensatn set 7-21, Comercio ex-owner to appeal 7-22, 691G3-692A1
Govt, IMF reach new pact 8-7; price rises, state employe dismissals seen 8-18, 669D1
Miners ordrd back to work 8-30, strike broken 9-4—9-8, 775E2
Lima govt workers strike 9-6, health workers 9-19—9-20, 775D3
Anti-inflatn progrm credits authorized by IMF 9-19, 776D1
Govt newspaper workers strike 9-20, 775F3
Cuzco paralyzed by strike 9-21, 775E3
Price hikes set 10-12, protested 10-23—11-10, 1019E1-A2
Real wages, price drops rptd 12-15, 1019B2

Foreign Relations (misc.)—*See also 'Monetary, Trade, Aid & Investment' below*
Ecuador border attacks chrgd 1-18; mil chiefs meet, declare amity 1-20, 216A2
Abstains on UN Chile rights abuse res 3-6, 210F1
Bolivia breaks Chile ties 3-17, cites sea outlet dispute 3-19, 216C1
Richter Prada back from USSR 4-9, 353A2
Leftists deported to Argentina 5-25, 475E1
Amer rights conv enacted, ct formed 7-18, 828E3, 829C1
Argentina AAA seen as terrorist model 8-29—9-15, 776B1
Colombian newsman kidnaped 9-3—9-10, 776B1
UN Assemb member 713D3
Chile fears Argentina war role 11-2, 860B3
Spain king visits 11-22—11-26, 967G2, D3

Government & Politics—*See also other appropriate subheads in this section*
Morales: army to retain power after electns 134E2
Morales retires from army, retains presidency 1-30; prime min retires 1-30, replaced 1-31, 134F2
Parties register for June Assemb electns 2-3, 134C2
Cabt shuffle 5-15, 394E2
Assemb vote delayed 5-19; leftists seized, media curbed 5-19, 5-20, 394E1
12 leftist ldrs deported 5-25, Rodriguez arrested 6-18, 475E1
Constituent Assemb elected 6-18, APRA leads vote 6-22, 475A1
Pol exiles return in amnesty; const guarantees restored 7-14, 668E3
Constituent Assemb final vote returns 7-15, 668C3

1979

Economy & Labor
Wage hike granted, unions ask more; rice, gas prices hiked 1-3, 39B2
Emergency declared 1-5, hundreds seized 1-6–1-8; gen strike begins 1-9, called off 1-10, 39D1
Striking garbagemen prosecuted 1-12, 39D2
Justice Dept workers strike 2-5, 255A3
Iron miners strike 2-9, 255G2
Textile strike clash kills 3 2-9, 255G2
Northeast oil find rptd, productn forecast 2-9, Petroperu rptd near bankruptcy 3-16, 256B1
Copper miners strike 3-13–3-30, emergency declared 3-15, 255C2
Journalists protest 3-19–3-23, 255E3
Aeroperu pilots, technicians strike 5-7, 411F2
Teachers' strike 6-4, supporters arrested 6-7, 504A2
Anchovy catch drops; '78, '79 fish-meal output data rptd 7-3, 555C1
Strike protests 30% price hikes, govt calls 'illegal' 7-19, 566B3
Jan-June COL up 80% 7-19, 566E3
Vicuna policy debate rptd 7-26, 584E3

Foreign Relations (misc.)—*See also 'Monetary' below*
Chile spy executed, amb expelled; land dispute cited 1-20, 51F3
UN membership listed 695A3

Government & Politics—*See also other appropriate subheads in this section*
Freedom House lists as partly free 13B1
Richter Prada sworn prime min, Garcia Bedoya forgn min 2-2, 101G2-A3
Haya de la Torre ill in US 3-12, 255A3
Leftist assemblyman arrested 3-16, freed 3-20, 255E2
Proposed constitutn rejectd, Assemb disbands 7-15, 545C2

1980

Economy & Labor
Econ laws set; min wage hiked, income tax cut 1-1, 21A2
Crops hit by drought; sugar harvest hurt, losses estimated at $400 mln 2-8, 234D3
Striking phone workers occupy Spanish Emb 2-8, 234G3
Cocaine crackdown launched, Tingo Maria stages gen strike 3-28, 277E1
'79 oil earnings rptd, '80 forecast 4-30, 354F1
'80 inflatn, unemploymt rptd 5-18, 390E2
Belaunde vows econ expansn, defns cuts 7-28, 579G3, 580B1

Foreign Relations (misc.)—*See also 'Monetary' below*
Cuban Emb shooting rptd, amb recalled 1-18, 103C1, 261A2
Spanish Emb occupied by strikers 2-8, amb heads talks 2-11, 234G3
Colombia amb eludes DR emb raiders 2-27, 141C1
7,000 Cubans seek asylum in Havana Emb 4-1—4-6; Andean Group debates resetlmt, Lima offers sanctuary 4-9—4-10, 261G1
Colombia envoy in DR Emb talks 4-9, 293E3*
1,000 Cuban refugees offered asylum 4-16, arrive in Lima 4-17, 285B1
Cuba refugee policy shift scored 4-16, 285F1
Cuba refugee flights suspended 4-18, CR offers 10,000 asylum 4-20; marchers rally 4-19, flights resume 4-24, 300C2-D3
Cuban refugees picked up by US flotilla 4-21—4-24, 300E3
Colombia DR Emb siege ends, envoy freed 4-27, 335G1
Moscow Olympic participatn set 5-8, 379B3
450 Cubans remain in Havana Emb, talks rptd underway 5-29, 397B1
442 Cubans leave Havana Emb 6-2, 33 detained 6-5, 420D2
Bolivian ldr sued for campaign plagiarism 7-12, 543E1
CR protests Cuba refugee policy, shuns Nicaragua fete 7-15, 565A3
Forgn delegatns at Belaunde inauguratn, border dispute setlmt vowed 7-28, 579E3, 580B1
Argentina pres snubbed; intell operatns disclosed, probe seen 7-28, 580C1
Bolivia coup condemned 7-29, 577D1
Cuban refugees storm jet at Lima airport 8-29, surrender 8-30, 672B2
Bolivia oppositn ldrs surface in Lima 9-15, 9-16, 728B1
Honduras, El Salvador sign peace pact 10-30, 872C3
Cuba ex-offcl asks UN probe hunger strike 12-4, 965D2
Bolivia coup condemned by Santa Marta coup 12-17, 992A3

Government & Politics—*See also other appropriate subheads in this section*
Belaunde elected pres 5-18, 390A2
Belaunde inaugurated; outlines goals; guarantees human rights, press freedom 7-28, 579E3
Munic electn results 11-23, 923A1

1976

Press & Censorship
Magazine imports banned 1-10, 55C3; 1-12, 2-3, 142B2, E3
Graphic workers strike 1-15—1-24, 142D2
Lima newspr dirs replaced 3-15, 499F3
Marka rpts harassmt 3-20, 499D3
Morales scores Velasco 4-30, 500A1
Marka execs, Zileri, others amnestied 5-7, 499E3, 500B1
12 magazines closed 7-3, 499C3
Journalists rptd seized 7-19, 590F3
Govt to retain press control 7-21, 591C1
Urrutia seized 8-17, Roncagliolo arrest ordrd 8-25, 652D2

U.S. Relations
Magazines, comics banned 1-10, 55C3; 2-3, 142F3
Marcona natlzatn cited 1-12, 142A2
'70-75 US mil training rptd 1-16, 142B3
Kissinger visits, students protest 2-17—2-18, 177A1, G3
'75 imports from US up 3-19, 466B1
Ship in US Bicentennial event 7-4, 488B3
US bank loan talks rptd 8-19, 652E3
US triples sugar duties 9-21, 721D3
Marcona natlzatn paymts OKd 9-23, 1013A2
Execs vs Panama Canal toll hike 11-1, 1008D3
'75-76 US bank loans cited 11-10, 915F1
US arms imports cited 12-7, 975E2

1977

Constituent assemb '78 vote set 10-4, reactn 10-5; pol plan issued 10-9, 784D1
Molina '78 premrship set 10-4, 784B2
'78 electn law decreed 11-16, 1015D2
Velasco dies 12-24, 1024F3

Human Rights—*See also 'Press & Censorship' below*
Late '76 amnesty rptd 1-1, 3D1
US rpts abuses 1-1, 51E1
Leftist mil officers, labor ldrs expelled 1-8, 1-14, 46A3
Leftist arrests rptd 2-10, 3-11; Ledesma kidnap 2-10, 241D2, F2
Pre-dawn curfew shortened 2-16, 241D2
Students seized in raid 2-21, most rptd freed, 1 dead 2-26, 241E2
US rpts on rights 3-12, 241A3
Repressn vs intellectuals rptd 4-1, 488G3
Lima curfew lifted, natl emergency remains 4-7; 9-mo deaths, arrests rptd 4-8, 488F3
Mrs Carter in talks 6-3, Morales statemt 6-4, 455C1
RC bishops score repressn 7-13, 563B2
Lima gen strike arrests rptd 7-19, 563C1, E1
Soclist ldr arrested 8-20—8-31, 784D2
July strike ldrs released 8-24, 784E2
State of emergency lifted 8-28, 673G1

Monetary, Trade & Aid Issues (Including all foreign economic developments)
USSR arms purchases cited 1-1, 1-10, 2A3, D3
US backs contd aid 1-1, 51F1
Pol, econ plan stresses forgn investmt 2-6, 241C1, C2
US, Aeroperu settle rebate case 2-18, 324G3
US modifies duty-free list 2-28, 189E3
New forgn oil co pacts set 3-3, 428B1
'75-76 trade, paymts table 3-11, 189A2 ★, B2
'66-75 arms transfers table 4-8, 415A2, F2
IMF loan terms stirs controversy 4-13—5-17, 427D2
'77-78 forgn investmt drop seen 5-9, 427D3
US banks offer $200 mln loan 5-17, 427C3
Ecuador, Venez import cuts seen 5-25, 427G3
Occidental '78 pipe link seen 5-25, 428A1
Imports cut; forgn financing effort, bank devaluatns set 6-10; IMF reactn rptd 6-17, 488G1-D2
IMF loan terms controversy continues, sol devaluatn disputed 7-6—7-15, 563D2-B3
'Minidevaluatns' ended, IMF estrangemt seen 7-20, 618F2
Forgn exchng reserves drained, '77 trade deficit forecast 7-28, 618D2
Miners strike US copper co 8-2, 673D2
Multinatl bank operatns authorized 8-17, local bankers score 9-16, 785A2
Central Bank pres sees US bankers 8-19, IMF ldrs 8-22—8-23, 785F1
Gulf Oil '75 natliztn pay agreed 8-24, 785C2
Cocaine traffic rptd 8-29, 972F1
Forgn debt crisis detailed; exports, reserves drop; arms purchases, US '70s loan curbs cited 8-31, 9-1, 784D3
Morales sees Carter, Blumenthal re econ crisis 9-7—9-8, 785G1
Morales: IMF biased vs 3d World 9-8, 785E1
Saenz sees US, IMF offcls re debt crisis 9-26—9-30, 785G1
State copper co seeks forgn investmt 9-29, 785C2
IMF loan agreemt rptd 9-30, 784F2, 785F1
Sol devaluatn set 9-30, 784B3
Sol floated 10-10, 785A2
Cheap exports blamed for US copper industry woes 10-31, 859A1
IMF OKs 90 mln SDRs line 11-18, 1015C2
In Zaire, Zamibia copper cutback agrmt 12-7, 975A1
US rejects loan request 12-15, lauds IMF pact 12-17, 1015G1

Obituaries
Velasco Alvarado, Juan 12-24, 1024F3

Press & Censorship
Ban on 7 magazines lifted 1-1, 21G1
2 magazines resume publicatn; Equis-X asks dem socialism 1-14, 47B1
'Natl debate' on pol, econ plan seen unlikely, leftist ban cited 2-25, 241E1, G1
Church rights rpt censored 3-18, 241B3
Gen strike protests censorship 7-19, 563E1
UK journalist questioned 9-6, 784E2
Ban on 6 more magazines lifted 9-28, 784C2
Lima press 'socializatn' rptd 10-9, 784F1
Magazine censorship ends 12-18, 1015D2

U.S. Relations—*See also 'Monetary, Trade & Aid' above*
US rpts rights abuses 1-1, 51E1
US rpts on human rights 3-12, 241A3
Shlaudeman confrmd amb 5-25, 500B1
Mrs Carter visits, arms control discussed 6-3—6-6, 454E1, 455A1
Morales vows '80 electns 7-28, 618D2
Morales sees Carter 9-6, at Panama Canal pact signing 9-7, 678A1

1978

Constituent Assemb prelim mtgs 7-18—7-27, Haya de la Torre elected pres 7-27; Assemb opens, Morales vows cooperatn 7-28, 668G2
Leftists attacked by terrorists 8-29—9-15, 775F3
Belaunde sets pres bid 10-3, 776C1

Monetary, Trade, Aid & Investment
Forgn debt rptd at $4.17 bln 1-13, default seen 3-14, 353G1
'77 trade gap rptd down 1-20, 353C2
IMF aid barred, banks rejct loan refinancing 3-10; talks rptd 5-11, 353E1, B2
USSR resets arms paymts 4-9, 353A2
Sol devalued, investmt incentives set 5-11, 353D1
IMF austerity measures implemented 5-15, Morales warns 5-20, 394A1, G1
Finance offcls see intl bankers 5-23—5-24, 394C2
Local industry rptd in default 6-2, 669B2
Forgn debt rptd at $8.2 bln 6-23, 669A2
8-natn Amazon pact signed 7-3, 829C2
Forgn banks defer $185 mln paymts 7-19, 669A2
Govt, IMF reach new pact 8-7, 669D1
Chrysler operatns cited 8-10, 623F2
US copper co halts shipmts re strike 8-17, 669B1
IMF pact cited 9-8, forgn exchng losses rptd 9-15, 775A3
IMF clears $311 mln in loans 9-19, 776D1
Copper indus troubles cited 10-20, 805B1
Forgn govt debt renegotiated by Paris Club 11-4, forgn bank debt renegotiatn sought 11-6, 1019B2
Spain king in copper trade talks 11-22—11-26, 967A3

Press & Censorship
20 pol publicatns banned 5-19, 7 resume 6-14, 475G1
Media curbed, pol publicatns banned 5-20, 394F1
Marka chrmn deported, ed flees 6-2, 475A2
Proletarian Voice rptd bombed 9-3, 776A1
Colombian rptr kidnaped 9-3—9-10, 776B1
Govt newspaper workers strike 9-20, 775F3
IAPA scores curbs 10-13, 829E1, A2

Sports
World Cup soccer finals, sidelights 6-1—6-25, 519F3, 520F1, C3

1979

Monetary, Trade, Aid & Investment
Forgn bank debt rescheduled 1-2, 22C3
Occidental oil find rptd 1-12, 39E2; export hike seen 2-9; Petroperu debts rptd 3-16, 256C1
Copper export revenues plummet 3-13—3-30, 255D2, F2
Forgn debt prepaymt agreed; '80 external debt, paymts surplus forecast 11-26, 951C2
US oil co contracts ordrd renegotiated; '79 productn, earnings rptd 12-7, 951A2

Obituaries
Beltran Espantoso, Pedro Gerardo 2-16, 176E2
Haya de la Torre, Victor Raul 8-2, 671C2

Press & Censorship
7 magazines closed 1-5, 39F1; 255D3
2 more magazines closed 2-15, journalists protest 3-19—3-23, 255D3
La Prensa ex-owner dies 2-16, 176E2
New magazine seized 3-5, 3-12, 256A1

U.S. Relations
Occidental oil find rptd 1-12, 39E2; 2-9, 256C1
US issues rights rpt 2-10, 107E3
Haya de la Torre ill in US 3-12, 255A3
Cargo ship rams barge in US 8-30, 800D1
US cocaine trade growth rptd 9-5, 972A3
US oil co contracts ordrd renegotiated 12-7, 951A2

1980

Monetary, Trade, Aid & Investment
Tariffs revised, new imports OKd 1-1, 21C2
Occidental says back taxes at $110 mln re new law 1-8, Belco not affected 1-9, 21E2-C3
Sugar imports seen 2-8, 234F3
$80 mln lost in silver futures speculatn, Minpeco shakeup ordrd 2-15, 152F1
Sovt fighter plane purchase rptd 3-12, 213D1
Argentine A-pact cited 3-18, 229E2
Occidental, Belco sign new oil contracts 4-30, 354F1
Belaunde vows forgn investmt, oil exploratn; Sovt fighter purchase cited 7-28, 579G3
Amazon pact signed 10-28, 865C2

Sports
Moscow Olympic participatn set 5-8, 379B3

U.S. Relations
Occidental says back taxes at $110 mln re new law 1-8, Belco not affected 1-9, 21E2-C3
Occidental, Belco sign new oil contracts 4-30, 354F1
US revises Cuba refugee policy 5-8, 361C1
Carter lauds Belaunde electn 5-18, 390A3
Mrs Carter at Belaunde inauguratn 7-28, 579E3
Cuban refugees storm Braniff jet, demand flight to Miami 8-29; surrender 8-30, 672B2

1976

PESANTES, Armando
Ecuador forgn min 1-14, 48G3, 49A1
PESTICIDES & Herbicides
Mercury compounds banned 2-18, 137F1
EPA urges toxic chem law 2-26, 171C3
US cncl issues pollutn rpt 2-27, 171A2
Allied Chem indicted re Kepone, other suits pending 5-7, 349A1
Mercury paint ban lifted 5-31, 571C1
Pesticide bill vetoed 8-13, 646F2
GOP platform cites 8-18, 603F1
Allied Chem fined re Kepone 10-5, 767D3
Tex leptophos poisoning sparks probe 12-6, 950B2
PESUT, Frane
Hijacks TWA jet 9-10, arraigned 9-13, 685C2
PETER, Friedrich
Rpt Wiesenthal ends Nazi hunt 1-9, 97D3
PETERS, Jean
Howard Hughes dies 4-5, 336F1
PETERSON, Ben
Wins Olympic medal 7-31, 576E3
PETERSON, Charles
Dies 8-4, 892D3
PETERSON, Elly
Scores ERA foes 2-25, 172F1
PETERSON, John
Wins Olympic medal 7-31, 576D3
PETERSON, Russell W.
Cuts off UN debate on Panama Canal 6-11, 431E3
PETKOVIC, Momir
Wins Olympic medal 7-24, 576A3
PETROCHEMICALS—*See PETROLEUM*
PETROCHILO, Vice Admiral Socrate
Named French naval tests chrmn 1-22, 139E1
PETRODOLLAR Issue—*See OPEC and OPEC country names*
PETROFUNDS Inc.
SEC sues 5-26, 984E2
PETROLEUM Marketing Corp.—*See COMMONWEALTH Oil Refining Co.*

1977

PERUYERO, Juan Jose
Slain 1-7, 163D1
PESTICIDES
EPA sets water-pollution curbs on DDT, others 1-3, 95A2
Allied Chem Kepone fine cut, Va endowmt set 2-1, 95B1
Science group analysis rptd 2-22, 183E3
SEC sues Allied Chem re Kepone 3-4, 252E2
Fluorocarbon ban exemptn rptd 5-11, 387A2
Carter environment message 5-23, 404D2
DDT cited re malaria upsurge 9-4, 747F3
DBCP curbed 9-8, 723D2
Allied-Va Kepone suits settled 10-13, 800C1
Medit natns reach pollutn pact 10-21, 876D2
Australia develops insectidal esters 11-7, 945F1-A2
Clean-water bill revised 11-10, 900E2
NY Times-Audubon libel case review declined 12-12, 960E2
Velsicol indicted on heptachlor, chlordane data 12-12, 1007C3
Clean-water revisns clear Cong 12-15, 959D1; signed 12-28, 1001A3
PESUT, Frane
Convicted 5-5, 451A3
Sentenced 7-20, 642C2
PETERSON, Esther
Named consumer affairs adviser 4-4, 354D2
PETERSON, Peter G.
Sen forms ethics panel 1-18, 77B3
To head Lehman Bros Kuhn Loeb 11-28, 1004A3
PETRESCU, Gheorghe
Named Rumania state secy 1-25, 100E1
PETRIC, Jaksa
Kidnap plot vs chrgd 6-16, 497D2
PETRIE, Sir Charles
Dies 12-13, 1024G2
PETRODOLLAR Issue—*See OPEC and OPEC country names*
PETROLANE Inc.
Rpts payoffs 4-7, 503E1

1978

PERVUKHIN, Mikhail Georgievich
Death rptd 7-25, 620D3
PESESHKPOUR, Mohsen
Scores Teheran 'massacre' 9-12, 693C2
Calls martial law illegal 9-17, 740D1
PESMAZOGLU, Ioannis
DCU resignatn rptd 4-11, 374A1
PESTICIDES
Carter budgets pollutn controls 1-23, 47C2
Benzene exposure rule issued 2-2, 85C3
EPA curbs sale of 2,000 2-15, 163A3
Chem-spill fines set by EPA 3-3, 163F3
Fluorocarbon aerosols banned, some insecticides exempt 3-15, 186B2
DBCP rule set by OSHA 3-15, 186F2-A3
Methoxychlor, malathion rptd non-carcinogenic 3-21, 3-24, 727D3
Chlordimeform ban eased 3-30, 263D3
E Africa locust spraying begun 6-6, 465F2
Colo aids grasshopper spraying 7-12, EPA bars higher-potency insecticide 7-13, 654D3
Mosquito immunity rptd 8-6, 635F3
DBCP curbs asked by EPA 9-19, 719C2
Environmtlists score Carter 12-20, 1009E1
PETERS, Donald
Named in US Teamster fund suit 2-1, 83E1
PETERS, John
Eyes of Laura Mars released 8-4, 970C1
PETERSEN, Erika
Hooters opens 4-30, 760D2
PETERSON, Esther
Scores consumer agency defeat 2-8, 82G1
Carter bolsters consumer office 4-27, 347D3
PETERSON, Lawrence E.
Gamma ray spectral line rptd 2-25, 293G2
PETERSON, Martha D.
USSR bares expulsn 6-12, 476A3
PETERSON, Oscar
Wins Grammy 2-24, 315F3
PETERSON, Ronnie
2d in world driving title 9-10, 968C3
Dies 9-11, 778A2
PETERSON, Russell
Rpts solar energy study, backs incentives 6-23, 493D3
PETERSON, Judge William
Dismisses PBB suit 10-27, 834C1
PETE'S Dragon (film)
Top-grossing film 1-4, 24G3
PETRIC, Damir
Flees W Ger, seeks Swedish asylum 8-30, 925F3
PETRIE, Daniel
Betsy released 2-9, 618C3
PETRILLI, Serge
Convicted 5-3, 396B1

1979

PESTICIDES
Fla plant blast injures 15 6-7, 572B3
Hooker Calif dumping, well pollutn rptd 6-18; US, state probe 6-19, 6-21, 597G1
Hooker sued for Mich waste clean-up 6-22, 597C2
US bans Nicaragua beef 8-6, 616C2
Hooker chrgd in NY suit 8-23, 665G3
Hooker settles Mich dump suit 10-24, 808F3
PETER Pan (play)
Opens 9-6, 956F3
PETERS, Bernadette
Jerk released 12-14, 1007E3
PETERS, Jon
Main Event released 6-22, 820G1
PETERS, Michael
Comin' Uptown opens 12-20, 1007D2
PETERSBURGH, Va.—*See VIRGINIA*
PETERSEN Jr., Brig. Gen. Frank E.
Promoted 2-23, 272C1
PETERSON, Anders
Silent Partner released 5-10, 528E3
PETERSON, Don
Almost Perfect Affair released 4-26, 528B1
PETERSON, Esther
To head Consumer Affairs Cncl 9-26, 902C3
PETERSON, Jack
Crosses US in hang-glider 7-9–8-16, 656C3
PETERSON, James K.
Acquitted re price-fixing 4-29, 327C3
PETERSON, Oscar
Wins Grammy 2-16, 336E3
PETERSON, Russell W.
Installed Natl Audubon pres 4-1, 272D1
PETREE, Richard W.
Calls Unifil res one-sided 6-14, 436B3
Deplores UN Assemb vote vs Israel-Egypt pact 11-29, 979G2
PETREE, Robert
Surrenders 5-7, 392F2
PETRELLI, Col. Siegfried
Spy arrest announced 6-21, 490A1
PETRI, Rep. Thomas E. (R, Wis.)
Elected to Cong 4-3, 265A2

1980

PERVY, Aleksandr
Wins Olympic medal 7-24, 624E2
PESHKIN, Dr. M. Murray
Dies 8-17, 676D2
PESTICIDES
Maine State of State message 1-2, 269E2
US budgets regulation fund 1-28, 73B3
Lilly Ind plant case declined by Sup Ct 2-19, 131E1
Mex tomatoes found toxic 2-20; 3 packing plants closed, border checks stiffened 3-12, 233A3
Ct limits children's harvest work, US study plan cited 3-20, 227C1, F1
Memphis area illness probed 4-2, 331B3
DDT noted in Medit pollutn pact 5-17, 381C3
Lindane use curbs sought 7-3, 519C3
US banned item export curb set 8-2, 599C3
Cong amends control program 12-4, 955E1
US program extensn signed 12-17, 982C1
PETALS on the Wind (book)
On best-seller list 7-13, 568C3; 8-17, 640G3; 9-14, 716D3
PETER, Prince (Greece)
Dies 10-16, 876C3
PETER Grimes (recording)
C Davis wins Grammy 2-27, 296F3
PETERS, Jon
Die Laughing released 5-23, 675C2
PETERS, Leonard
Back in the Race opens 4-17, 392C2
PETERSON, Donald
Named Ford president 3-13, 224C3
Confrms Ford-Toyota productn talks 7-9, 556G2
PETERSON, Eric
Billy Bishop opens 5-29, 756B3
PETERSON, Oscar
Wins Grammy 2-27, 296E3
PETER the Great (book)
On best-seller list 12-7, 948E3
PETILLO, Carol
MacArthur WWII 'gift' dispute rptd 1-30, 1-31, 115F1, G1
PETKOVA, Maria
Wins Olympic medal 8-1, 624C2
PETREE, Richard W.
Vs UN vote on Israel trade sanctns 12-15, 952G2
PETRI, Louis
Dies 4-7, 360G2
PETRI, Rep. Thomas (R, Wis.)
Reelected 11-4, 844C4
PETRITSCH, Gerhard
Wins Olympic medal 7-25, 623D2
PETRO-Canada
Newfoundland Ben Nevis drilling halted 8-22, 668E3
Oil chiefs reject Ottawa plan 11-5, 871A3

PETROLEUM & PETROLEUM PRODUCTS

1976

PETROLEUM (& Petroleum Products)—
Note: Items involving two or more countries and all Arab developments are listed here. See also ENERGY; see also specific country, organization (e.g., OPEC) and company names
Africa—*For OPEC developments, see OPEC*
Gulf Angola operatns halt cited 1-30, 82D2
US OKs Gulf Angola operatns 2-21, 163E1
Gulf, Texaco pay Angola royalties 3-11, 3-17, Gulf to resume Cabinda operatns 4-5, 287E2
Nigeria productn rptd 4-1, 366B2
Uganda halts shipmts to Rwanda 4-7, 502F2
Rhodesia sanctn violatns by Mobil, others chrgd 6-21, 621D1
Uganda chrgs Kenya blockade 7-16, dispute widens 7-17—7-28, 548F1-C3
Rwanda-Kenya mtg 7-22, 559G3
Kenya deliveries to Uganda rptd resumed 8-17, 874D1
Gulf rpts Angola output 8-19, 649G2
BP plans S Africa investmt rise 8-26, 714B1
Mobil denies Rhodesia violatns 8-27, 698C2
No Mobil violatns rptd re Rhodesia sales 10-17, 855E3
Nigeria natlizes Exxon unit 12-23, 1007E3

1977

PETROLEUM (& Petroleum Products)—
See also specific country, organization (e.g., OPEC) and company names
'76, '77 major US mergers, table 880F1
PR deposits tied to statehood 1-5, 16A3
Ford energy message 1-7; urges Cabt-level dept 1-11, 14A3-F3
20th Century Fund energy study issued 1-11, 170C1
Arco buys Anaconda 1-12, 55F2
Oil supplies rptd depleted 1-14, 37A2
DOT rpts transportatn consumptn 1-15, 58G2
Ford budget proposals 1-17, 31C2-B3
Cold weather, fuel shortages persist; emergency actns taken 1-18—1-26, 53B3-54E3
FEA orders home heating oil productn hike 1-24, 54F1
Heating oil reserves rptd down 1-27, 2-2, 76G1
Carter fireside chat 2-2, 75E1
Oil cos accused re fuel shortage, probe ordrd 2-3—2-26, 151D3-152D2
Heating oil record use rptd 2-4, 92A1
Carter sees sacrifices, undue profits curb 2-8, 88B3
Heating oil reserves data 2-9, 91F3; 2-17, 152F2
Carter budget revisns 2-22, 125B2, C2
AFL-CIO to seek cargo share 2-22, 153D2
Carter on reserve supplies data 2-23, 126D3
Carter asks energy dept 3-1, 148F1
Carter call-in topic 3-5, 171C1-E1
Record exploratn budgets set 3-8, '76 drilling rptd 3-10, 196F2
Feb refinery output rptd down 3-9, 196E2
'76 energy use rptd 3-13, 196A2
US '76, '71-76 elec power data rptd 3-23, 3-25, 277F1, B2
New gas output process rptd 3-23, 278G1
Carter asks US plutonium ban 4-7, 268C1
GM drops rotary engine projct 4-12, 409D1
Carter energy plan 4-18, 4-20, 289A1-290B3, 294D2-295C3; fact sheet 291B1-293C3
CIA forecast pessimistic 4-18, 294C1
Cong, other Carter plan reactn 4-20—4-24, 290B3, 293G1-294B1, C2, 320F3

1978

PETROLEUM (& Petroleum Products)—
See also company and organization (e.g., OPEC) names
Exxon cited again for overchrgs, issues denial 1-11, 14B2
NAACP scores Carter energy plan 1-11, 68F1
IRS revokes forgn tax paymt credit 1-16, 69D1
Sun Oil buys Becton shares 1-17; Wms Act violatn chrgd, Cong chrmn ask probe 1-27, 65F3
Shortage in '80s disputed 1-18, 52C3
Co rebates to consumers barred 1-20, 108F3
Carter budgets stockpiling, exploratn, indus controls 1-23, 46E1, D2, E2, 47F2
'77 4th ¼ profits rptd down 2-7, 282E3
'77 US output up 2-14, 158E3
McDermott pleads guilty, fined 2-22, 142F2
'64-78 spending-pattern chngs reflected in new CPIs 222D2
Texaco fined for '77 Tex fire 3-2, 212F3
States curbed on tanker regulatn 3-6, 161D3
Heating aid funds signed 3-7, 160F2
Crude oil tax passage seen unlikely 3-7, 3-8, 220E1
Penn Central reorganizatn plan OKd 3-9, 186A1
New fuel standards for light trucks issued 3-15, 284F1-B2
Energy bill deadlocked in cong gas deregulatn talks 3-22, 220C1
Crude oil tax revenue for Soc Sec proposed 4-2, 241C1
FTC aide backs lid on cos' coal, uranium holdings 4-5; Justice Dept proposal rptd 4-6, 282D2, A3
'77 proven reserves rptd down; crude output, exploratn up 4-10, 282B1, F1
Gas tax deductn end backed by House com 4-17—4-19, 305G3
Jan-Mar demand rptd 4-20, 282A2
Cong actn on energy plan taxes rptd 4-21, 305C1, E1
1st ¼ '77, '78 profits rptd down 4-27, 403E2
Carter seeks solar optns 5-3, 321F3
'77 indus sales return rptd 5-8, 325B3
Energy study forecasts consumptn, imports rise 5-8, 366A2
'77 top-paid execs ranked 5-15, 364F3

1979

PETROLEUM (& Petroleum Products)
Pipe ownership curb urged 1-4, 55E2
Reserves estimate revised, Green R Basin fund cited 1-5, 17E1
Dec '78 gasoline producer prices rptd 1-11, 32C3
Gulf, oil workers OK pact 1-11, 87B1
Carter sees price rise 1-17, 30B1
'78 demand rptd slowed 1-18, 35G3
Adams backs '85 gas mileage standard 1-19, 87E3
Carter budget proposals 1-22, 45A2, C2, F2, E3; table 42G2
'78 4th 1/4 profits rptd up 1-25, Carter remark scored 1-26, 70F1-A2
Carter orders fed agency fuel-saving 2-6, 82C3
Oil firms rpt sales cutbacks 2-6, 2-8, 83A1, B1
Carter urges conservatn 2-12, 109C3
Oil firms plan more productn, sales cutbacks; airlines cancel flights 2-13–2-21, 126A2 2-15, 153B2
Environmt cncl sees use cut 2-20, 132D2
Carter asks conservatn powers 2-26, plans cautn 2-27, 145B3
Mobil, Amoco, Cities svc set allocatns 2-27, 2-28, 146B1
Exxon, other firms to curb sales 3-1–3-13, 183G2-C3
House com OKs Alaska lands bill 3-1, 187E1
Gasoline price controls eased 3-2, 162F1
Calif fuel price law challenge declined by Sup Ct 3-5, 185E1
4 fuel-short airlines cut flights 3-6, 3-7, 162A2
GAO scores conservatn actn, oil cos 3-7, 182D2
Fuel shortage, price hikes threaten auto use 3-10, 187D3
Oil record use rptd 3-12, 183B2
Sohio cancels Calif-Tex pipe 3-13, El Paso denies bar 3-14, 183D1
Cost pass-through rule cited 3-16, 264B3
Tenneco fined in La bribe case 3-17, 239B3
Feb gas prices up 2% 3-25, 252F1
Conservatn lag rptd 3-28, 227G3
A-accident impact seen 4-1, 246B3
Forest land dvpt proposed 4-16, 282G1

1980

PETROLEUM (& Petroleum Products)
Exxon rptd '79 gas selling ldr 1-2, 90D3
State of State messages 1-7—1-15, 404D2, A3, 404E1; 1-9—2-6, 268D3, 269B1, A2, B3, 270B1, F2; 1-9, 1-10, 1-14, 483B1, A3, C3
Oil workers strike 1-8; industry offer rejctd 2-28, unions back demands 3-1, 187G1
Dec '79 gas producer prices rptd 1-10, 15A1
US long-term supply cited 1-15, 60A2
'79 consumptn, productn drop, supplies rptd 1-17, 90A2
Carter State of Union proposals 1-21, 1-23, 41A1, D2, 42C1, 43F1, D3
'79 record profits rptd; chart 1-23—1-31, 90F2-F3
Dec, '79 CPI, gas, heating oil prices rptd up 1-25, 75C2
'80-81 oil price rise forecast 1-30, 74D2
Mobil TV ad rejectn rptd 1-31, 120D1
Brookings economists back rationing 2-6, 2-7, 126F2
Jan gas prices rptd up 2-22, 144G1
FTC trust procedure case accepted by Sup Ct 2-25, 187E3
Fed leasing lottery suspended, scandal hinted 2-29; resumptn ordrd 4-7, 330B2
Carter asks more coal-fired utilities 3-6, 169A3
Feb producer prices rptd 3-7, 182B2
Oil supplies at record high 3-7; Feb deliveries, demand down, unleaded gas use up 3-12, 250A3
Gasohol seen as world food productn threat 3-15, 251A1
'79, 4th 1/4 profits rptd up 3-19, 222E1
Vt tax on Mobil forgn dividends backed by Sup Ct 3-19, 249F2
US sets 2d 1/4 gas use targets, '80 consumption drop 3-20, 250C3
Feb gas prices rptd up 3-25, 222B2
Ashland unveils gas refining advance 3-31, 251E1
Gulf natl park drilling rights affirmed by Sup Ct 3-31, 291A3
Mobil wins $154.2 mln jet fuel contract 4-1, 248C2
Credit controls modified by FRB 4-2, 263F2
Mar producer prices rptd 4-4, 263B1
State-local '79 tax collectns rptd 4-17, 307D2

1976

1977

Carter defends energy plan 4-22, 321D1
FEA regulatn case review refused 4-25, 342D3
1st ¼ profit drop rptd 4-28, 668E3
Carter energy plan scored 4-30—6-8, GOP TV rebuttal 6-2, 408F2, 443E1-G2
'76 sales return rptd 340B2
FEA proposes coal conversn 5-9, 369A1
'76 pipe deaths rptd 5-12, 412G2
Carter on fuel crisis 5-17, 381B3
Sen votes energy dept 5-18, 405C2, E2
Carter, Cong tussle over energy plan 6-9—6-14, 460E1-C2
Carter warns vs energy lobby 6-10, 460A3
FTC oil cos info rule review rejctd 6-13, 517E1
'81-84 gas mileage standards set 6-26, 522E1
NY commodity trading cntr opens 7-5, 521G2
Gas rationing studied 7-10, 538C2
ARCO to mkt more efficient motor oil 7-11, 558D3
Seadock superport project threatened 7-12, 559A2
'Enhanced recovery' prospects revised down 7-17, 559C1
Carter backs gas-tax plan 7-22, 575B2
'78 FEA funds signed 7-26, 592F3
Seadock pres scores govt controls 7-26, Tex aid seen 7-27, 724G3-725A1
Carter urges conservatn 7-28, 574C3
2d ¼ drillings rise rptd 7-28, 627G3
Loop superport license signed 8-1, 724B3
Energy Dept created 8-4, 591F2, G2
House OKs Carter energy pkg 8-5, 609F2-610C3
Gulf buys Kewanee 8-9, 612E2
Washington state sues 10 cos 8-16, 691E3
Tenneco buys Phila Life 8-25, 650G3
McDermott wins Babcock bidding war 8-25, 666F3
5 indep cos convicted 8-30, 691G2; fined 9-16, 918F2
6 cos settle trust case 8-31, 691C3
Sen OKs weakened coal-conversn bill, bars acquisitn curbs 9-8, 702B3, F3
6 state suits rptd merged 9-12, 691F3
Gas-guzzler ban OKd by Sen 9-13, 703C1
Carter wellhead tax opposed in Sen 9-19—9-26, 757E1
Gas-guzzler tax opposed, 4¢-gal extensn backed by Sen com 9-20, 757E2, F2*
Ashland OKs Commonwealth stock purchase 9-22, 723B1
Great Western Sunshine takeover OKd 10-4, 799A1
Carter scores industry, reactn 10-13, 772E2, F3
Research bill clears Cong 10-20, 833F1, A2
Energy tax bill clears Sen 10-31, 832C1-F3
Carter criticism softer 11-8, 854D1
Schlesinger comments draw fire from House 11-21—11-23, 916G3-917A1
Winter shortage plan announced 12-1, 942A3
Calif-Tex pipe OKd 12-2, 942D3
Hunt oil suit case declined 12-5, 938E3
Exxon cited for overchrgs 12-27, 1008C2

1978

Petro-Lewis Plans to buy Shenandoah 5-15, 403G3-404A1
Lobbyist's role in energy policy questnd 5-15, 408E2-C3
Justice Dept backs 15% lid on cos' coal holdings, 10% on uranium reserves 5-15, 471C2
Carter lauds TVA 5-22, 386B3
Price hikes, inflatn linked 5-22, 427C2
Schlesinger forecasts supplies, plans E Coast subsidies 5-26, 407E3-408C1
Tex refinery blast kills 7 5-30, 460F2
Oil shortage forecasts conflict 6-5, 449E3 ★ -450A2
Exxon sued for overchrg 6-8, 450A3
Gas price hike urged by Sawhill 6-13, 450D2
Md refiner-run gas statn ban upheld by Sup Ct 6-14, 491F3
Schlesinger sets new rules for Calif, proposes E Coast subsidies 6-15, 470B3-471B1
Pipeline ownership curb backed by Sen subcom 6-21, 471C1
Alaska job preference law voided by Sup Ct 6-22, 508F3
Computer program patents curbed by Sup Ct 6-22, 509C1
Energy Dept offers standby gas ration plan 6-22, 511F1
Solar energy study rptd 6-23, 493F3
Crude oil taxes rptd studied 6-29, 512D1
Crude oil overchrgs laid to 5 cos 7-2—8-4; Gulf suit setld 7-27, 610A2-C3
Coal conversn bill clears Sen 7-18, 549G3-550F1
Coal slurry pipe bill defeated 7-19, 550A2
1st ½ productn, consumptn rptd 7-19, 590B1
Carter urges crude oil tax 7-20, 549D3
Conoco pricing probe rptd 7-21, ex-offcl pleads no-contest 8-9, 610D3
Fuel tax deductns cut by House com 7-27, 587A1
Mo rejcts gasoline tax hike 8-8, 626C1
Regulatory overhaul asked by ABA 8-8, 626E2
Occidental seeks Mead takeover 8-11, bid rejctd 8-18, 767C2, B3
US strategic-reserve storage plans scored 8-16, 701A3
Solar, renewable energy draft study issued 8-25, 718C2; final study rptd, spending hike backed 12-12, 983C1
Co movt into other energy fields rptd 9-8, 700D2
Energy Dept emergency plans faulted 9-11, 701F2
7 indicted in Fla pricing scheme 9-14, 718G2-C3
La oil reserve fire 9-21—9-26, 738E1
Aug CPI rise rptd 9-26, 752D1
Sen OKs natural gas bill 9-27, 733E1
US sues vs Occidental-Mead merger 10-11, 895A3, G3
Carter energy bill clears Cong 10-15, 786D2, F2, 787G1-F2; signed 11-9, 873A1
Penn Central reorgn ends 10-24, 875G3
Oct producer prices rptd up 11-2, 864A2
Diamond Shamrock to buy Falcon Seaboard 11-2, 1005A2
Calif voters OK Sohio lease 11-7, 857B1
Tex securities regulatn case refused by Sup Ct 11-13, 874C3
1st ½ '78 productn rptd 11-14, 871B2
Energy Dept fuel rules unveiled, '79 decontrol seen 11-15, 919F3-920B1
Premium unleaded gas shortage, price hikes rptd 11-20—11-21, 939E1
Shell trust probe rptd 11-28, 939C3
Shell monopoly suit filed 11-30, 939D3
Shell, Amoco begin rationing 12-1; 3 others seek OK 12-3; artificial shortage discounted 12-4, 938F3-939E1
Gas shortage probe rptd, rationing studied 12-6, 962E3
Nov producer prices rptd 12-7, 957G3
House subcom staff rpt chrgs 'middleman' price fraud 12-10, 983B3
Carter vows actn vs industry abuses 12-12, 983E2
'75-76 pricing cost pass-on upheld 12-13, 983F2
Jet fuel shortage feared 12-14, 983G3-984B1
'79 gas, fuel oil price hike seen 12-18, 978B2
AAA rpts '78 gas price rise 12-19, 1010F1
Occidental ends Mead takeover fight 12-20, 1004C3

1979

1st 1/4 gas demand rise rptd 4-22, 343E1
Carter sees climbing prices, gas shortage; home-oil reserve ordrd 4-25, 300D1
EPA fines Texaco in Calif gas-switching 4-26, 301D2
1st 1/4 profits rptd; chart 4-27, 301F1-C2
Carter urges Cong OK standby controls 4-30, 324F2-A3
'78 reserves rptd down 4-30, 324A3
Arco unit, Energy Conversn in solar dvpt accord 5-2, 419C1
Apr gas producer prices rptd up 5-3, 325D1
Energy shortage poll rptd 5-4, 343F1-B2
Carter vows farm supplies 5-4, 346D3
Carter orders Calif gas shortage probe, backs rationing 5-5, 347D1
May gas supplies seen tightening, shortfall explained 5-7, 342G3
Jan-Apr wholesale gas price rise rptd 5-7, 343E1
'78 Fortune 500 data rptd 5-7, 305E1
Calif odd-even gas rationing begins 5-9, 342B3
Standby gas rationing defeated, temp controls clear Cong 5-10, 342A2
Oil platform collapses 5-10, 472G3
Carter scores House on gas ration defeat, calls for Cong plan 5-11; criticizes pub on shortage 5-15, 361A1
FTC, Justice probe oil firm-shortage link 5-15, 361E2
US air fares rise 5-15, 465E3
Carter sees Brown, hikes Calif gas allocatn 5-16; Ore gov scores, summer shortfall warned 5-17, 361F1-E2
House OKs Alaska land bill 5-16, 366G3
State-local '78 auto fuel tax revenues up 5-16, 386C2
Diesel fuel shortage seen 5-18, 361G2-D3
Exxon unveils energy-saving device 5-18, 404B2
Sohio reaffirms Calif-Tex pipe cancellatn 5-24, 396F1
Diesel fuel allocatn rules adopted 5-25, 395C2
Apr CPI rise rptd 5-25, 402D3
Retail gas price rise rptd 5-26, 395D3
'78 state gas use rptd; chart 5-27, 395D2-A3
Gold price soars, oil fears cited 5-27–6-11, 435E2-A3
June gas supplies cut 5-29–5-30, 395B3
States get gas sales regulatn power 5-29, 395G3-396A1
Carter sees execs 5-31, Indianapolis Dems 6-2, 417G3-418F1, G2
Calif energy plan proposed 5-31, 418F3
No-lead gas output incentives set 6-4, 418A3
May producer prices rptd up 6-7, 422B2
Truckers strike re fuel prices, shortage 6-7, 462D3
Connally on energy crisis 6-11, 439F3
Inflatn, energy problems linked 6-13, 463A2
Mich oil facility fire 6-16, 572C3
Odd-even gas rationing spreads to E Coast, Tex 6-19–6-21; Mobil asks standby plan 6-21, 462C2-C3
Gasohol tax exemptn proposed 6-20, 498F1
Diesel fuel allocatn rule canceled; trucker demands noted 6-22, 479C3, D3
Gas shortage spreads; cos rpt July allocatns 6-23–6-27, 479B1
Md sues US re gas allocatn 6-26, 479G1
May CPI rise rptd 6-26, 480C3
House OKs synthetic fuel bill 6-26, 498G1
Schlesinger, Carter on US consumptn 6-27, 6-28, 494B1
US prices seen affected by OPEC hikes 6-28, 473F1
Heating oil supplies reviewed 6-28–6-29, 514E2
Admin meets truckers' demands 6-29, 516G2
Carter vacatn cancelatn, gas crisis linked 7-1, 497A3
Carter calls NE govs re gas 7-2, 497C3
June producer prices rptd up 7-6, 516G3
Mondale on Admin plans 7-8, 517E3
Carter orders temp controls 7-10, 514B2
Summer intercity bus svc expansn OKd 7-12, 579C2
Carter outlines 6-pt energy program to cut forgn oil imports, US use 7-15, 7-16; reactn 7-15–7-17, 532A1-534F1
Amtrak raises fares 7-15, 726C3
Spot mkt purchases rptd 7-16, 494E2
Gas price rise OKd, other rules revised 7-16, 557F2
1st 1/2 productn rptd 7-19, 557D2
Schlesinger fired, gas crisis linked 7-20, 530E1
Tenneco seeks UV assets 7-23, 770B3
Gas rationing veto amendmt OKd in House, Carter scores 7-25, 557A2
Kennedy-Durkin energy plan unveiled 7-25, 557D3
June CPI rise rptd 7-26, 556F3
Retail slowdown, gas shortage linked 7-27, 648G3
Chrysler sales drop, gas crisis linked 7-31, 576B3
Energy, Justice Depts clear cos of hoarding, rpt Feb-May shortage data; probe continues 8-6, 628A3

1980

Mar CPI rptd 4-22, 305C2
1st 1/4 profits rptd; chart 4-22—4-30, 331B1
Getty Oil in pay-TV film venture 4-22, Justice Dept to probe 4-24, 376D2
Sohio gas price hike order rescinded 5-1, 366F1
Hunt silver bailout set 5-2, 344G3
'79 Fortune 500 data rptd 5-5, 290A3, 291A1, D1
Indus solar monopoly denied 5-5, 554A1
Gasoline price case refused by Sup Ct 5-12, 426C2
Apr indl output down 5-16, 384C3
Land-grant exchng ban upheld by Sup Ct 5-19, 440A2
Apr CPI rptd 5-23, 400B3
Hunts bailout loan collateral listed 5-28, 425C3, 426C1, E1
Pre-1920 shale mining claims upheld by Sup Ct 6-2, 513C1
Calif voters reject profits tax 6-3, 439D2
Wis out-of-state earnings tax backed by Sup Ct 6-10, 511E3
Phila refining tax dropped, co 'contributns' set 6-10, 743F3
Carter submits standby gas rationing plan 6-12, 551E3
GE microbe patent upheld by Sup Ct; reactn 6-16, 452F3-453A2
Cong com OKs stockpiling 6-16, 552G1
Synfuel bill clears Cong 6-19, 6-26, 479C2; Carter signs 6-30, 494G1-A2
May CPI rptd 6-24, 481B1
Texaco chrmn to quit bd 6-30, 600B3
Duncan sees energy conservatn acceptance 7-6; 1st 1/2 imports, consumptn rptd down 7-24, 553A1
US auto rules reviewed 7-8, 505E1
5 cos cut gas prices 7-9, 553F1
Conn tax pass along ban voided 7-9, 553D3
Wholesale gas price cuts rptd 7-11—8-27, 666G2
Oil cos absolved in '79 shortage 7-17, 552B1
June CPI rptd 7-23, 556E1
Getty Oil pay-TV film plan draws trust suit 8-4, 639D3
July producer prices rptd 8-15, 630C3
Cos cut gasoline prices, revive dealer rebates 9-1—9-23, 786A1
Record inventories rptd 9-5, Admin assured vs shortfall 10-3, 785D3
US wage-price guidelines revised 9-19, 764D3
Aug CPI rptd 9-23, 741C1
Tesoro paymts case setld 11-21, 957D3
Nov farm prices rptd 11-28, 938B2
Stockpiling bill clears Cong 12-1, 954E2; signed 12-12, 982B1
Toxic waste clean-up signed 12-11, 936A1, C1
FTC trust complaint challenge curbed by Sup Ct 12-15, 957E1
Watt sees dvpt conflict 12-22, 980A1
'80 heating oil futures up 12-31, 984G3

1976

Alaska Pipeline—*See ALASKA—Oil & Gas*
Arab Boycott Issue—*See under BUSINESS*

1977

Alaska Pipeline—*See ALASKA—Oil & Gas*
Exports and Imports (U.S.)
USSR oil price rise rptd 1-6, 67C3
Dec '76 imports rptd down 1-28, 92G1
Jan imports rise rptd 2-8, 91G3
New England import aid ordrd 2-10, 152B3, D3
Wkly imports up 2-17, 2-24, 152G[illegible]
Jan imports record rptd 2-28, 154[illegible]
Wkly oil imports rptd 3-9, 196C2
'76 imports total rptd 3-13, 196B2
Cart[illegible] import cuts 3-17, 191A1
'76 [illegible] imports, prices rptd 3-28, [illegible]
Ca[illegible]nergy plan sets imports cut goal [illegible] 4-20, 289E2, 290A3
US House OKs Japan oil export ban 4-20, 323E3
US 1st ¼ Venez imports up 4-26, 547A1
Mar imports rptd 4-27, 339B3
Tax deductn delay clears Cong 5-16, 382C1; Carter signs 5-23, 417F3
Apr imports drop rptd 5-26, 445F1
US imports poll rptd 6-2, 464G2-A3
US OKs exports to Japan 6-12, 460D1
BIS links imports, trade gap 6-12, 502F1
Imports rise, 1st ¼ paymts deficit linked 6-22, 502A1
May imports rptd 6-27, 502B2
Alaska exports to Japan barred 7-10, 538B1
US tanker cargo preference backed 7-11, 538A2
OECD issues econ rpt 7-20, '77 data rptd 7-31, 586G1-A3

1978

Alaska Pipeline—*See ALASKA—Oil & Gas*
Exports and Imports (U.S.)
GAO urges tougher US stand, Admin warns vs 1-3, 5F3
London Times links imports, $ drop; cites Carter policies 1-4, 27B3
Carter energy bill plea 1-12, 12A1, D1
Carter State of Union Message 1-19, 30A2, B2, 31G2
'77, Dec imports rptd 1-30, 127F2
US '77 Saudi imports up 2-11, 113F2
$ weakness, imports linked 2-24—3-6, 118D3-119A1; 3-2, 140G3
Jan imports rptd up 3-3, 221A3
US imports, $ drop linked 3-7, 234C2
Fed Reserve chrmn backs import curbs 3-15, 181C1
Import fee backing by Blumenthal rptd 3-24, 220B2
Mar, 1st ¼ imports rptd 3-26, 344C2
USSR '77 top export 3-29, 229G3
Feb imports rptd 3-31, 262F1
Carter cites imports cost, vows cutback 4-11, 260D1, F1
Carter threatens import curbs 4-11, 304A2
Venez import demands rptd down, forgn competitn cited 4-16, 331G3
1st ¼ imports rptd down 4-20, 282A2
Blumenthal asks price freeze; vows $ defns, energy policy enactmt 4-21, 523A2
Carter sees energy bill progress, delays interventn 4-25, 307A3

1979

AFL-CIO cncl urges natlzn study 8-6, 629C2
July producer prices rptd 8-9, 621D2
Texaco to test gasohol sales 8-10, 649F1
2d 1/4 profits rptd up 8-17, 628A3
Diesel allocatn to farmers vowed by Carter 8-22, 622A3
UAW holds energy job actn 8-22, oil industry protested 10-17, 831B2-B3
July CPI rise rptd 8-25, 646D2
Northeast govs get fed reassurance on heating fuel 8-28, 703G1-C2
CAB grants 9.5% air fare hike 8-31, clarifies rule 9-4, 725E3
Carter calls import reliance security threat 9-3, 661F1
9 states, DC lift odd-even rules 9-3–9-10, Calif retains 9-7, 683E1
Sohio 1st 1/2 profits up 9-6, 686G3
Aug gasoline, heating oil producer prices rptd up 9-7, 681A1
Carter asks heating oil price freeze 9-8, 9-12, oil cos respond 9-16–9-19; Dem House Caucus asks controls 9-19, 703A1-G1
Amtrak rpts May-June record ridership rptd 9-8, 726A3
US daily consumptn data cited 9-11, 706F2
Oil exec scores Carter 'amateurs' 9-12, 702F3
GAO rpts on '79 shortage 9-13, Energy Dept plans review 9-14, 702A3
Tree rptd diesel fuel source 9-15, 1000B2
Highway Trust Fund shortfall seen 9-17, 726A2
Heating fuel inventories rptd up 9-19, 703C2
2d 1/4 paymts gap, oil imports linked 9-20, 701G2
Calif cnties drop odd-even rules 9-20–10-2, 850D1
Aug CPI, gas, heating oil prices rptd up 9-25, 725D2
Sept producer prices rptd up 10-4, 766E1
Army OKs E Coast refinery 10-4, 769G3-770F1
Heating fuel storage goal rptd met 10-11, 786A3
House ends gas price controls 10-12, reverses decisn 10-24, 848E3
Odd-even gas rules reimposed in Calif 10-13, 870C1
Standby gas rationing clears Cong 10-17, 10-23, Carter signs 11-5, 848A3
RFK's son scores co profits 10-20, 807G3
3d 1/4 profits rptd up; chart 10-22–10-26, 804C2-F3
Chevron cuts gas prices 3¢ 10-26, 804G3
Sept CPI rise rptd 10-26, 827G3
CAB OKs 3.7% air fare hike 10-26, 830B3
Price hikes, world econ problems linked 10-29, 11-1, 826D3, 827A1
Socal 3d 1/4 profits rptd 10-31, 849E2
Oct producer prices rptd 11-1, 828D1
Consumptn cut urged in Sen 11-8, 843B1
Brown offers energy plan 11-8, 847G2
Texaco sets chem venture 11-14, 941D3
Carter urges govs aid conservatn 11-16, 879A3
Mobil exec joins Kennedy campaign 11-19, 962C2
Proven reserves rptd 11-21, 953B1
Oct CPI rise rptd 11-27, 903A3
Nov producer prices rptd 12-6, 921E3
Hunt-Coastal States suit review declined by Sup Ct 12-10, 988G1
Kennedy scores Carter 12-20–12-21, 983G2
CAB OKs 3.3% fare hike 12-20, 989B1
Nov CPI gasoline prices rptd up 12-21, 984E2
Finch on crisis solutn 12-24, 984F1
New England living costs, oil dependence linked 12-28, 990G3
Alaska Pipeline—*See ALASKA—Oil & Gas*
Carter Decontrol & Tax Plans
Carter ends domestic price controls; asks windfall profits tax, other measures 4-5, 250B2-251A1
Carter seeks profits tax 4-10, 263C2
Carter scores tax foes 4-23, 4-25, 300G1, A2
Cong gets tax plan; Ullman, consumer advocate react 4-26, 300G3-301F1
Kennedy scores, Carter rebuts 4-30, 324A2
Energy Dept denies decontrol-overchrg claims linked 5-2, 343E2
Poll finds decontrol opposed, profits tax backed 5-4, 343A2
AFL-CIO sets fight 5-8, 345C2
House Dems oppose decontrol 5-24, 395G1
Carter warns vs inactn 5-25, 401A2
Consumerists see Carter, protest decontrol 6-1, 418F1-A2
Carter sees GOP ldrs 6-7, 419D3
Mayors Conf backs 6-13, 439F2-A3
Solar energy bank proposed 6-20, 498E1
House OKs weaker profits tax 6-28, 541A2
Govs Assn backs plans 7-10, 518B1
Carter stresses profits tax passage to fund energy program 7-15, 7-16, 532F2, D3, 534C1
Carter defends profits tax 7-24, 7-25, 557G1, C2

1980

Alaska Pipeline—*See ALASKA—Oil & Gas*
Carter Decontrol & Tax Plans
Budget proposals 1-28, 70A1, B1, 72A1, G3
GOP scores 1-28, 75A2
Windfall profits tax clears Cong 3-13, 3-27, Carter signs 4-2, 244B2-E3
Anti-inflatn plan unveiled 3-14, 201E1
Revised budget proposals 3-31, 243G2
Oil import fee blocked by Dist Ct 5-13, 366A1
Oil import fee bar OKd by Cong 6-4, 6-5; Carter vetoes 6-5, veto overridden 6-5, 6-6, 436G2-437B2
Oil import fee proposal dropped 6-19, 551D3
Dem platform drafted 6-24, 479G2
Conn oil tax pass along ban voided 7-9, 553F3
GOP platform plank proposed 7-10, 506C3; adopted; text 7-15, 536D3
Windfall profits tax suit filed 10-14, 960D2
Windfall profits item in budget reconciliatn clears Cong 12-3, signed 12-5, 936G1

1976

International Developments—*See also other appropriate subheads in this section and under ENERGY; also NORTH Sea; for oil crisis effect, see other economic headings (e.g., BALANCE of Payments, ECONOMY, MONETARY Developments) and country names*
Norway OKs BP unit acquisitn 1-7, 30C2
US rpt disputes China export role 1-8, 10A1
China-N Korea pipelines completed 1-8, 78B1
Sovt price to Hungary up 1-15, 101D2
EC urges minimum oil-import price 1-16, 84G3
Japan-US-Dutch consortium rptd 1-16, 208C3
Sovt-Greek deal rptd 1-19, 73B2
US-Canada pipe delay rptd 1-20, treaty initialed 1-28, 116C3
Sweden-Pl deal signed 1-21, 104B1
Japan to up Chinese imports 1-22, 208C3
IEA OKs energy plan 1-30—1-31, 108D1
Canada refinery bankruptcy dvpts 2-13—3-12, 221C2
Yugo-US Dow Chem deal 3-26, 256G1
Hungary-Sovt barter pact rptd 4-1, 543A3
Rpt China-Japan trade falls 4-5, 265D3
S Viet-forgn co talks rptd 4-24, 352A2
'75 world output down 4-25, 298A3
Australia dvpt projct set 4-29, 332B1
N Viet vows forgn cooperatn 5-7, 367D2
IEA OKs cooperatn pact 5-20—5-21, 372F3
'75 USSR exports to West up 5-24, 655B3
Canada opens Sarnia-Montreal pipeline 6-6, 6-15, 438D3
Petro-Canada buys ARCO unit 6-7, 417C1
W Ger-Poland petrochem pact 6-11, 442F1
Canada cuts US exports 6-11, 481B3
Greece, Turkey Aegean dispute flares 6-17—7-13, 538D1
7-nation econ summit declaratn 6-28, 462D2
US, Finns in Sovt drill deal 7-16, 540E2
Canada plans BC-Alberta pipe 7-16, 587E3
Aegean dispute grows, UN debates 7-29—8-16, 622D1, D2
US firm rpts Scotland find 8-19, 675F2
Nonaligned conf urges France embargo 8-20, 621D3
Canada cuts export levies 9-1, 710F1
Aegean feud continues 9-1—9-25, talks resume 11-2, 845A1—B2
US, Canada exchngs set 9-2, 650D2
Canada ups US export prices 9-10, cuts quota 9-14, 710D1
Rumania Greek search rptd 9-28, 854F1
USSR cuts Czech exports 10-4, 851B3
'77 importers paymts deficit seen 10-5, 778E1
Canada oil export cuts rptd 10-13, 11-23; levies adjusted 11-1, 11-10, 945F2

1977

June imports rptd 7-27, 585C1
Carter scores imports 7-28, 574C3
US $ depreciatn strategy rptd, OPEC price rise feared 8-8, 585E1-G1, 586B1
July imports drop 8-25, 651C2
US cargo preference bill stirs price dispute 8-27, 8-29, 9-9, 719E3-720B1
US 1st ½ imports from USSR rptd 9-12, 766B2
US 2d ¼ paymts deficit, imports linked 9-21, 722F2
Imports seen causing $ drop 9-29, 754C1
Carter threatens import tariff 10-2, 757A2
IEA OKs '85 consumptn lid 10-5—10-6, US cuts seen key 10-7, 793F3-794C1
Cuba oil products reach US 10-20, 896B3
Carter cites imports, asks energy bill actn 10-27, 813G1
Sept imports rptd 10-27, 818C1
Carter address to natn stresses 11-8, 854C2
Oct imports rptd 11-28, 933A2
Carter links $ drop, imports 12-20, 997A3
Nov deficit rptd 12-28, 1003G1

Foreign Developments—*See also 'Exports and Imports' above, 'Payments Issues' below*
Ecuador buys local Gulf assets 1-1, 7G2
OPEC price hikes, productn chngs in effect 1-1—1-11, 11D3-12C2
UK in Shell, Exxon N Sea pact 1-5, 20E3
Venez exports rptd; Exxon to continue present level 1-6, 23G1
Venez exports rptd 1-6, 23G1
Saudis seek US co proof on consumer price break 1-8, 12C2
Mex sets output, export hikes 1-14; OPEC entry pressure seen 1-25, 66D1
EC, 3 Arab natns sign pact 1-18, 73G3
Arab oil demand drops 1-20—2-9; Yamani comments 2-9, 107E3
Saudi-French deal signed 1-24, 50F1-B2
Rpt USSR seeks cartel plan 1-24, rebuffed 1-29, 108F1
OECD rpts on world energy outlook 1-27, 169A3
'76-80 world demand from OPEC estimated 1-28, 108A2
Oman raises prices 1-31, 108G2
Irish dispute UK Rockall rights 2-3, arbitratn set 2-17, 329B2
Saudis rejct OPEC price compromise 2-6, 107G2
Mobil to build Saudi pipeline 2-8, 108C2
Qatar completes Shell takeover 2-9, 108E2
US vs Israel Suez drilling 2-14, 107B2
Saudi price plan rptd 2-14, 1st ¼ output estimated 2-16, 107D3, 108A1
4 buyers rptd picked for extra Saudi oil; Saudi scores rpt 2-15, 108B1-E1
Aramco in consumer price break pact 2-15, 108E1
Asia '76 econ growth rptd 2-16, 147C2
Mex exploitatn, export hike rptd 2-18, 240F3
Sovt-India deal signed 2-19, 161E1
EC '76 econ growth rptd 2-22, 146C2
ASEAN trade pact signed 2-24, 145A3
Iran Feb exports rptd up 3-2, purchase agrmts honored 3-8, 227A3
US firms get Libya natlizatn damages 3-2, 488E1
Peru sets new forgn co pacts 3-3, 428B1
'76 trade data rptd 3-8, 188G2, B3
Saudi Feb output rptd up 3-10, 227E3
Latin trade, paymts table 3-11, 189A2 ★ D2
Greek petrochem plant set 3-14, 203A2
Mex petrobond issue set 3-14, 240G3
Mex reserves estimated 3-18, 240C3
US-Japan energy talks 3-21—3-22, 209A3
'76 regional output rptd up 3-21, 227F3
Kuwait Feb output rptd up 3-24, 227B3
Brazil to cut imports 3-26, 268F3
IMF paymts debt managing role rptd 3-28, lending facility backed 4-29, Saudis rpt role 5-3, 5-4, 362A3
Gulf Angola plants seen protectd by Cubans 4-11, 271G3
Mex petrobonds oversubscribed 4-18, sale 4-29, 528C1
Venez seeks OPEC price unity 4-19—5-5, 362A1
Rumania in Black Sea find; imports cited 4-20, 468E3

1978

Schmidt scores US imports 4-28; sees Carter 5-30—5-31, reviews talks 6-1, 519A2
Energy study forecasts imports rise 5-8, 366A2
US Sen debates forgn policy link 5-15, 357C2
Schlesinger outlines policies 5-26, 408F1-A2
Apr imports rptd 5-26, 429B1
US imports forecast 6-5, 449E3 ★, 450C1
Schlesinger sets new rules for Calif, proposes E Coast subsidies 6-15, 470B3-471B1
1st ¼ paymts deficit widens 6-21, 469F3
Carter warns Cong on import fees 6-22, 511F2
May imports rptd 6-27, 507F1
Sen votes bar to import fee, Admin scores 6-27, 511B3, 523A3
Crude import fees, quotas rptd studied 6-29, 511G3
Schmidt links import cuts, $ weakness 7-7, 545G2
Carter vows import cuts at Bonn summit 7-16—7-17, 554A1
US to review sales to USSR 7-18, 542G1
Coal conversn import cuts estimated 7-18, 550A1
1st ½ imports rptd down 7-19, 589G3-590B1
Carter denies productn equipmt licensing linked to USSR policy 7-20, 549D2
June imports rptd down 7-26, 607C1
USSR technology sale rules issued 7-31, 634E2
USSR equipmt sale OKd 8-9, 634D2; 9-6, 743D1
July imports rptd 8-29, 680C1
Iranian oil purchases cited 9-10, 693F2
GAO vs Alaska exports to Japan 9-12, 702D1
Carter vows import cuts at IMF-World Bank mtg 9-25, 731G2
Aug imports rptd 9-27, 752G1
USSR equipmt sale rptd 9-29, 821A1
US equipmt sale cited re Carter 'export consequences' order 10-10, 804A3
Carter plan clears Cong 10-15, 786F2
Sept imports rptd 10-26, 804D3
Carter signs plan, backs import curbs 11-9, 873C1
Oct imports rptd 11-29, 918D3
Oil equipmt sale to USSR OKd 12-4, 966E1
Nov imports rptd 12-18, 1003G2

Foreign Developments—*See also 'Exports and Imports (U.S.)' above*
US '75 investmts in Canada rptd 1-10, 70C3
French-Ivory Coast offshore drilling accord 1-11—1-15, 71C1
US revokes forgn tax paymt credit 1-16, 69D1
Canada metric conversn set 1-16, 89C1
China '77 trade hits record 1-16, 89E2
France '77 imports rptd 1-16, 149E1
US, Canada to study joint storage 1-17, 53C3
Shortage in '80s disputed 1-18, 52E3
OAU warns Iran vs S Africa sales 1-20, 100G1
Spain '77 imports near $5 bln 1-21, 395A1
Belize drilling by Exxon cited 1-25, 94A2
Ecuador '77 exports down 2-3, 148G2
Venez offers forgn buyers discounts 2-3, 332A1
'77 noncommunist output rptd up; OPEC non-OPEC, Eur, Mex, Saudi data cited 2-14, 158C3
Japan, China sign pact 2-16, 103E3
Egypt, 2 US cos sign pact 2-16, 139A3, B3 ★
Chile-Argentina Beagle Channel dispute cited 2-20, 216G1
OPEC Jan output rptd down 2-22, 158D2
Mexico '77 sales up 2-27, 331B1
UK oil revenue plans announced 3-21, 227B1
US use of Sinai base for USSR surveillnc rptd 3-26, 215G1
Israel starts Sinai operatns 3-26, 215B2
Argentina find rptd 3-27, new areas opened 4-17, forgn investmt up 4-24, 310A3
Arab poor-natn aid rise rptd 4-9, 257B2
Australia import warning, '85 cost cited 4-10, 265D3
Canada budgets exploratn 4-10, 266F1
Bolivia paymt to Gulf Oil rptd 4-14, 478A3
'76 Belize find by Mex rptd 4-21, 354B2
Venez-Brazil deal signed 4-28, 332B1
Japan to hike stockpile 5-3, 341G2
China find rptd 5-6, 436E2
CIA '77 Sovt study assessed 5-21, 384E1
Argentina-Chile Beagle Channel talks fail 5-22—11-2, 860E2
Sudan discoveries rptd 5-24, 479A2
New Zealand plans gas duty 6-1, 497C3
Gabon productn drop cited 6-1, 596B2
Shortage forecasts conflict, import curbs lag 6-5, 449E3 ★ -450A2
Petro-Canada, Occidental in Husky bidding war 6-10—7-27; Alberta Gas wins control 6-27, 628E3-629E2
Trilateral Comm study sees no '80s shortage 6-13, 450E2
Spain trade deficit with Iran cited 6-16, 576B2
Turkey, USSR in trade, exploratn agrmts 6-21—6-23, 595E2
USSR imports seen, OPEC talks rptd 6-26; natural gas exports forecast 8-13, 634F3
US Sen ratifies UK tax pact 6-27, 588D3
Brunei output, revenue cited 534A1

1979

Carter asks profits tax passage 7-31, 592F2
AFL-CIO cncl vs phased decontrol, backs profits tax 8-6, 629D2
Carter stresses tax on Miss R boat trip 8-17–8-24, 622D2
Carter decontrols heavy crude, seeks profits tax exemptn 8-17, 629C1
Mondale offers more mass-transit aid 8-22, 726B1
Carter links windfall tax, co profits 10-25, 804E2
Kennedy scores Carter 11-3, 12-13, 962C1, A2
Kennedy attacks Carter 11-7, 847E1
Sen OKs profits tax 12-17, 961A1

Foreign Developments (Including U.S. international news)—*See also 'Mergers' below*
Indonesia raises prices 1-1, 52F1
Mex proven reserves doubled in '78 1-2, 22A3
Iran vs sale to Israel, S Africa 1-3, 2D2; 1-11, 11C3
Iran pipe reopens 1-5, heating oil reaches Teheran 1-6, 12A1
Israel ties Egypt pact to Sinai oil access 1-5, 51B2
UK constructn workers' strike expands 1-8, 20E3
Jamaica ups prices 1-8, Manley links to OPEC hike 1-10, 21D2
Hungary ups gas prices 1-8, 101A2
S Africa stockpile rptd 1-9, 22B1
UK Texaco tank drivers end strike 1-11, 20B3
N Ireland declares emergency strike 1-11, 30E3
Canada prov sets stock giveaway 1-11, 37A3
Occidental Peru find rptd 1-12, 39E2; 2-9, 256C1
Carter confident despite Iran unrest 1-17, 26C2
Carter on Mex prospects 1-17, 30B1
USSR '78 plan shortfall rptd 1-19, 60G1, B2
CR raises fuel prices, oppositn scores 1-19, 238B2
Iran gas cutoff forces USSR switch 1-23, 50B2
Australia aborigine rights probed 1-24, 94G2
Japan '78 imports drop rptd 1-24, 98D2
USSR-US '79 ship rate rptd set 1-25, 60A3
Norway-Sweden pact imperiled 1-26, 77C2
Saudi 1st 1/4 output rise seen 1-30, 69F3
US '78, Dec imports rptd 1-30, 71D3
Khomeini scores US sales 2-1, 67A1
Iran crisis forces oil co sales curbs 2-6, 2-8, 83A1, B1
Schlesinger terms Iran oil crisis serious 2-7, Blumenthal challenges 2-8, 82F2-B3
France supplier search speedup ordrd 2-7, 82D3
Iran cutoff causes gold, US $, Dow fluctuatn 2-7–2-8, 83C1-C2
Saudi denies cutback 2-7; Abu Dhabi, Qatar, Libya hike prices 2-15, 2-21; OPEC mtg set 2-19, 126D1-A2
ICI Australia petrochem plans rptd 2-8, 94C3
'78 trade data rptd 2-8, 161B1
Canada prov OKs output rise 2-12, 153A3
Iran oil cutoff impact assessed 2-13–2-21, 126A2-C3
Carter, Mex pres in talks 2-14–2-16, 124F1, C3
Exxon cuts Canada deliveries, 2-15, 153B2
Iran seeks export resumptn 2-19, 125D2
Portugal '78 imports rptd 2-20, 212F3

1980

Foreign Developments (including U.S. international news)—*See also 'Mergers', 'U.S. Presidential' below; also PERSIAN GULF*
Canada hikes prices 1-1, 6F1
Mex lifts prices, US exports cited 1-2, 4F1
French energy measures OKd 1-2, 6F2
Canada's Clark seeks higher prices 1-2, Trudeau vs gas excise tax 1-12, 37G3, 38C1
Saudi supply, Exxon US sales rptd linked 1-2, 90F3
Newfoundland find confrmd 1-3, 6D1
Nigeria hikes prices, US exports cited 1-4, 4G1
UK productn plans rptd; '79, '80 output estimated 1-4, 7B1
Spain hikes prices 1-7; sets conservatn plan 1-8, 22F1
Peru tax impact on US cos rptd 1-8, 1-9, 21E2-C3
Canada co sets merger 1-9, 19D1
Brazil-Iraq accord signed 1-9, 95E2
Turkey-Iran deal rptd 1-10, 22C3
Mex spill continues, total loss rptd 1-10, 60D2
Iran warns vs sanctns, threatens cutoff 1-11, 29C2
Chile '78, '79 import costs rptd 1-14, 19A3
Algeria plans conservatn 1-14, 55G2
Venez sets 6% productn cut, US multinatl sale curbed; '79 data, '80 estimates rptd 1-14, 102E3
Mex '80 productn, exports seen up 1-15, 60F1-B2
Saudi, USSR, Mex long-term supplies cited 1-15, 60A2
Mex oil field discovered 1-15, 60B2
Shah blames intl cos for overthrow 1-17, 47A2
Carter rejects Canada pipe route 1-17, 56B3
US '79 import drop rptd 1-17, 90D2
Liberia supertanker sinks off Senegal 1-17; S Africa oil sale suspected, Shell sues 2-7, 108D2
Australia stock gains linked 1-18, 56D1
W Ger imports seen 1-18, '79 data cited 1-30, 103B2, G2
Carter sets import ceiling, seeks dependence end 1-23, 41A1, D2, 42C1, 43F1
USSR '79 output shortfall rptd 1-25, 79B3
Turkey sets product price hikes, new exploratn rules 1-25, 80B1, C1
Japan '79 import costs rptd 1-25, 100B1
US '79 oil costs, imports rptd 1-29, 77C2
Canada raises US export price 2-1, 79C1
USSR high prices, E Eur econ slowdown linked 2-4, 166A3
Norway econ growth seen 2-5, 100E2
UK cites US fiber import curbs 2-5, 125A2
Canada '79 chem profits rptd up 2-7, 116C2
IEA delays import cuts, quotas 2-9, 142B1
Australia shale oil projct rptd 2-12, 116F1
USSR expert vs dvpt methods 2-13, 235C3

1976

Standard Oil retrial bid re Samoa eased 10-18, 867G2
US confrms China computer sale 10-28, 832F2-B3
Australia sees USSR threat 11-4, 850B2
Aegean truce agreed 11-11, 897G1
French trade deficit rises 11-18, 964D2
OECD '75 imports down 12-6, 935G3
Schmidt on price rise, paymts aid 12-16, 968B2

Latin America—*For Venezuela domestic and foreign developments, see 'Oil' under VENEZUELA; for OPEC developments, see OPEC*
Bolivians vs Chile land deal 1-3, 27E1
Anglo yields Ecuador oil unit 1-16, 49F1
Argentina vs UK Falkland exploitatn 1-20, 96F3
Cuba productn plans, Sovt imports rptd 3-2, 251G3
Bolivia gets UK loans 3-12, 4-14, 416E1
Bolivia gets intl bank loan 6-18, 456B3
Argentina opens fields to pvt dvpt 7-27, 554D1
Texaco pays Ecuador back taxes 8-20, 872E1
Ecuador to buy Texaco-Gulf pipeline 9-17, 872E1
USSR hikes Cuba price 9-30, 772D1
Gulf pays Ecuador back taxes 9-30; sellout talks begin 10-25, 872A1

Middle East—*See also 'Arab Boycott' under BUSINESS*
Japan-Iran oil pact 1-7, 141G1
Libya seeks oil independence 1-15, 205E2
Egypt buys Greek tankers 1-16, 73D2
Algeria-N Viet pact signed 1-17, 46A1
OPEC delays price conf 1-26—1-28, 62B2
Iran revenue drops, Westn firms scored 2-3, 101F3
Libya chrgs Tunisia re Gabes find 3-22, 239F2
NATO supplies from Mideast cited 4-5, 242B2
OPEC meets on prices 4-22—4-23, 298B3
'75 output down 4-25, 298A3
Israel-US deal signed 5-4, OKd 5-6, 338A3
US asks price freeze 340C1
Iran, US jet firms seek barter deal 5-9, 5-11, 340A1
OPEC holds price freeze 5-28, 389C1
Kuwait, Saudis, Iran cut prices 6-7, 6-9, 6-10; Libya ups 6-8, 407C3
US Dem platform text 6-15, 476F2
Iran to buy Occidental shares 6-20, 6-21, 450B2
7-natn econ summit declaratn 6-28, 462D2
OPEC meets on aid to poor states 8-5—8-6, 643G1
US-Iran pact signed 8-7, 581B2
US GOP platform text 8-18, 610C1
Nonaligned conf urges Israel embargo 8-20, 621D3
OPEC fails to OK price plan 8-23—8-27, 643F1
Iran, Occidental drop deal 8-27, 643D1
Japan to aid Iran project 8-27, 643E1
Israel bars Amoco drilling in Suez 8-31, 9-4, 9-6; US protest 9-6, 663D2
Israel, US meet on Amoco Suez feud 9-8, 9-13; Israel orders probe of Amoco rpt leak 9-29, 759G2-C3
Carter deplores blackmail 9-30, 742G3
Ford, Carter debate 10-6, 740E2, 741D3
Ford on Arab embargo 10-20, 784F2
Egypt reactn to US electns 11-4, 826C2
Price hike fears, US stock price drop linked 847B1
US FRB sees 10% OPEC price hike 11-11, 865D3
Carter urges price restrnt 11-15, 864A1
UK, Iran deal signed 11-18, 906F1
Soclst Intl topic 11-28, 935D3
Ford asks OPEC restraint 12-1; US warns vs price rise 12-8, 12-9, 934D3
Castro scores OPEC 12-2, 1000E3
OPEC prices, NY stock prices linked 12-8—12-15, 984E1
Carter urges OPEC restraint 12-14, 12-16, 935C1, 937E2
OPEC sets separate price hikes, 12-15—12-17, Ford scores 12-17, 934D2-935C1
Iraq, Iran vs Saudis on price hike 12-18, 12-20, 975A3
IEA sees OPEC consumer drop 12-20, 975D3
6 states get OPEC loans 12-23, 975E3

1977

UN unit estimates reserves 4-26, 362E2
Venez 1st ¼ output up 17% 4-26, 547A1
India-USSR pact set 4-27, 348F1
Viet-French oil agrmt rptd 4-28, 329C1
7-natn summit backs paymts fund, use cuts 5-7—5-8, 357A2, D2
Saudi rpt on May output 5-10, 362A2
Canada land-use rules rptd 5-10, 8-10, 634A2
Saudis rptdly to up '77-82 output; Aramco figures 5-11, 362F1
Fire halts major Saudi pipeline 5-11—5-12, sabotage suspected 5-12, 362B2
Saudi fire out 5-13; casualties, losses rptd 5-15, 5-19, 402B2
US Rhodesia-Mobil probe inconclusive 5-16, 413F2
Egypt threatens US embargo re Israel 5-22, Saudis deny 5-24—5-25, 401F3
Zambia asks US Rhodesia embargo 5-23, 400A1
Peru trans-Andean pipe opens 5-25, 427F3
Occidental sues Venez 5-27, 547B1
Egypt to ask Israel compensatn 5-29, 496D1
29 cos sued for Rhodesia sanctn violatns 5-31, 413C2
Iraq protects oil fields 5-31, 440F2
Canada OKs Beaufort Sea search 6-1, 425E3
North-South talks end 6-3, 437A2-G2
Canada units to quit Mackenzie drilling 6-4, 466C3
S Korea-Japan pact effected 6-8, 467G1
World Ct to hear Libya-Tunisia dispute 6-10, 497F2
Sovt '76 sales to West, COMECON rptd 6-11, 513F1
Iraq-Turkey pipeline opened 6-11, 565B2
Commonwealth rptd vs S Africa-Rhodesia trade 6-16, 486D3
Mex hikes reserves estimate 6-22, 528D1
Brazil, Iran sign trade pact 6-23, 524F1
Brazil cuts Jan-May consumptn 6-24, 524B2
Secret US-Saudi pact rptd 6-27, 474E1
OPEC price split ended 6-29—7-5, 535D2
Venez petrochem industry reorganizatn rptd 7-8, 565E3
Uruguay '76 import data rptd 7-8, 601G2
Denmark, Greenland accord rptd 7-13, 672A2
Eng Channel offshore rights setld 7-18, 625C1
US studies 2d Panama canal 7-21, 589E3
Spain import costs raised 7-25, 582A2
Danes OK North Sea pipeline 8-1, 672C1
ASEAN preference agrmt 8-5, 607D1
Bell asks trust probe aid 8-8, 629G3
USSR output drop forecast 8-8, 948D3
Trinidad earnings stir indl dvpt 647B1
Australia hikes prices 8-16, 670F3
Zambia sues 17 cos re Rhodesia sanctns 8-22, 662D1
Trinidad attracts investors 8-22, 905G3
Peru offers Gulf compensatn 8-24, 785C2
USSR pipe constructn rptd 9-17, 949D1
Rich, poor nations econ growth rates rptd 9-18, 717B3
Kuwait nationalizes US co 9-19, 805G3
Libya setles with US firms 9-26, 772C2
Eng Channel offshore rights dispute erupts 9-29, 10-12, 772F1-B2
Gandhi arrested in French bid-rigging scandal 10-3, 765A1
IEA OKs '78 consumptn lid 10-5—10-6, 793F3-794C1
US urges Nigeria price curbs 10-12, 797G1
Sakhalin oil find announced 10-12, 853E3
Commonwealth presses S Africa on Rhodesia embargo 10-19, 876B1
S Africa stockpiling rptd 11-2, 887C2
Australia depletn forecast 11-3, 862F1
Iran backs '78 price freeze 11-16, 897B1, B2
Canada prov royalty tax ruled illegal 11-23, 923D3
OECD rpts 1st, 2d ¼ '76 use 11-24, 999C1
Israel finds Suez gulf oil 11-25, 955E1
Mex $17 bln dvpt program rptd 12-1, 967E1
Israel-Rumania trade rptd 12-10, 987C3
3d World use discouraged 12-11, 975A3
Saudi assures US on OPEC prices 12-14, 954D2
USSR '78 output goal set 12-14, 987F3
US asks Japan share deficit financing burden 12-15, 974F1
UN asks S Africa ban 12-16, 1016G1
China '77 output up 12-26, 1010D3

1978

Libya, Malta talks, price cuts agreed 7-3—7-4, 592E2
Australia '77 productn, imports rptd 7-5, 514E2
Uganda shortages rptd, Kenya paymts delay cited 7-10, 616B3
E Ger-Brazil deal rptd 7-13, 649D1
Canada settles Inuit claim 7-14, 556G1
Iran-S Africa link scored by OAU 7-22, 561F1
UK hikes offshore tax, offers new blocks 8-2, 591D3
Australia domestic tax hike proposed 8-15, 628A2, C2
Mex oil wealth sparks US hopes 8-24, reserves rise rptd 9-1, 690B1
S Africa embargo asked by UN racism conf 8-26, 676A2
US co sued re Indonesian bribe 8-30, 737C1
UK releases Rhodesia sanctions violatns study 8-31, 9-19; reaction 9-2—9-28, 755G3-756F3
Japan crude stockpile fund set 9-3, 694D1
Japan offers China dvpt loans 9-6, 695E2
Canada-Viet exploratn pact rptd 9-7, 686G3
Latin '77 econ decline linked 9-10, 828E2
Venez, Cuba, USSR, Spain in transport pact 9-15, 822C1
Australia find rptd 9-21, 738D3
Canada prov ordrd to pay interest on illegal tax 10-3, 773B2
Norway '78 revenues revised down 10-5, 775F1
Bolivia gets World Bank loan 10-8, 840D3
Ecuador boom rptd over 10-9, 798D3
Zambia-Rhodesia RR reopened 10-10, 783B3
China find rptd 10-12, 871A3
Nicaragua scores Venez prices 10-14, 839C3
US cites China potential 10-16, 871F2
BP retracts Rhodesia swap denial 10-22, 838E2
French seamen's strike causes shortages 10-23—11-4, 882F1
Mex, Japan sign loan pacts 10-30—11-4; Japan gets Mex shipmt 11-5, 903E3
Iran workers strike, exports cut 10-31, 827G1
Iran shortage grows 11-6, 11-7; Japan faces cutback 11-7, 857F3, 858C2
Ghana workers strike 11-6, 882A2
Canada buys US-owned unit 11-10, 11-20, 901A2
Mex claims new reserves, sees '80 export hike 11-13, 903E2
'73-77 consumptn, 1st ½ '78 productn rptd 11-14, 871G1-B2
Australian delivery strike ends 11-15, 921A1
Carter vs OPEC price hike 11-17, 899E3
Spain-Mex shipmt talks 11-17—11-22, 967A3
Canada price rise OKd 11-27, 944A2, E2
Iran strikes cut output 12-4, 929A1; output worsens 12-12; Moslem exile ldr warns buyers 12-13, anti-Israel stand cited 953F2, A3
France, China sign trade pact 12-4, 986A2
Norway, Sweden sign pact 12-8, 965A3
Canada price hikes OKd 12-8, 985E3
UK urges Rhodesia trade violatns probed 12-15, 987A3
Chile price rise seen 12-15, 1014A2
OPEC raises prices 14.5%, sets light crude premiums, OKs paymt in US $s 12-17; US, world reactn 12-17, 12-18, US impact rptd 12-18, 12-19, 977C2-978F2
Iran gen strike 12-18; exports end 12-26, rationing starts 12-28; output at record low 12-31, 993G2
Mex '79 price hike set 12-20, 978E2
'78 world output rise rptd 12-26, 1000B3

1979

St Lucia transhipmt terminal, free port planned 2-21, 181E2
Brown, Schlesinger see US defns of Mideast interests 2-25; remarks clarified 2-26, 2-27, 143D3-144B1
Iran exports urged, forgn debt cited 2-25, 144F3
Kuwait, Venezuela hike prices 2-26; Saudi, Iraq bar 1st ¼ hike 2-27, 145F2
China cancels Japan deals 2-26, 181F3
Iran export resumptn set 2-27, Westn consortium sale barred 2-28, 145F3
Price hikes, Dow fall linked 2-27, 166C2
Egypt, Israel talks; treaty rptd linked 2-28, 143B1
US Jan imports rptd, seasonal figures revised 2-28, 159E1, G1
Indl natns OK 5% demand cut, OPEC welcomes 3-2, 161F3-162C1
Iran exports resume, output cut 3-5, 161B3
Algeria, Iraq, Venezuela crude oil price hikes rptd 3-5, 162D1
US $ stability linked to price hikes 3-5, 320F3
Price rise effect on US econ warned 3-7, 182D2
EC backs 5% import cut 3-13, 180G1
W Eur inflatn rise seen 3-13, 180B2
Canada co ordrd to import oil 3-13, 210G2
Swedish energy bill rptd 3-13, 213E3, 214A1
Arabs urge boycott vs US 3-14, 178D1
USSR-India aid pact signed 3-14, 200A2
USSR ups oil price 3-21, 228A1
Venez vs US OPEC trade curbs 3-23; Mondale in talks 3-23—3-24; productn hike OKd 3-24, 248F1, A2
Israel, Egypt, US settle Sinai oil issue 3-24—3-25; treaty signed 3-26, 221C1, F2, 226G3
S Africa Mideast imports rptd 3-26, 270F2
OPEC sets 9% price hike, surchrgs 3-27, 227F2
Canada electn issue 3-27, 3-28, 266C3, E3
US Feb imports rptd down, Iran cutoff cited 3-28, 252F2
S Africa offshore search funds hiked 3-28, 270B2
Australia Exmouth Plateau drilling rptd 3-28, 233D1
Arafat asks US, Egypt boycott 3-28, 248F2
W Ger links oil prices, inflatn 3-29, 334A1
Producer natns see US A-accident impact 4-1, 246B3
France, Mex sign cooperatn pact 4-1—4-4, 372F1
Intl air fare rise set 4-3, 324D1
Carter asks tariff end 4-5, 250D3
France '81-86 goals rptd 4-5, 267C2
Saudi cutback set 4-9, US Sen estimates '80s cut 4-14, 279A1
US chrgs 2 execs re '76 Qatar bribe, Lance '78 influence role alleged 4-9, 305E3-306C1
Iraq halts Sudan shipmts 4-10, 278A2
Canada offers US oil pipe routes 4-10, 284E2
W Eur hit by shortages, govt measures rptd 4-12—5-29, 396F2-G3
Iran rpts output, price hikes 4-13, 4-15, 279E1
US concerned re Indian O tanker routes 4-16, 314A1
OAPEC ousts Egypt, imposes embargo 4-17, 278G1-A2
US Mar imports, exports rptd 4-27, 325B2
W Ger sets auto fuel, other conservatn steps 4-30, 5-16, 373B3-F3
£ strength, UK N Sea earnings linked 5-1, 321C1
Mex 10-yr dvpt plan rptd 5-4, 353D3
Australia profits rptd down 5-8, 351E3
Iran hikes oil prices again 5-10; Venezuela, Libya 5-16; Abu Dhabi 5-17, 360F2
Forgn-flag tanker case refused by US Sup Ct 5-14, 383E1
Mex, Cuba trade talks 5-17—5-18, 372F2
Spain fuel prices rptd 5-17, 428C1
Australia shortages seen 5-18, 368D2
Iran cuts Japan exports 15% 5-18, 389C2
Gas prices in W Eur, other natns rptd 5-19, 5-20, 396G3
Swiss imports cited 5-20, 390F3
Oil price hikes continue 5-20—5-31, 396B2
Japan asks Sunday gas statn closings 5-21, 389B2
Sovt bloc natns face shortages, USSR warns 5-21—5-24; 1st ¼ Comecon imports rptd 5-31, 397B1
IEA renews use cutback vow 5-22, 380E1
US import subsidy announced 5-25, EC natns score 5-30—6-2, 417G1
Colombia, Venez OK offshore talks 5-26—5-28, 398C2
Venez '78 revenue rptd 5-28, 429E3
Saudi budget plans rptd 5-29, 427A3
US Apr imports rptd 5-30, 402G3-403A1
Canada co divestiture issue cited 5-30, 424D1
Nigeria cutoff to US, UK feared; export total cited 5-31, 393A2
Mex 1st ¼ productn rptd 6-1, 487C2
Mex oil well blows out 6-3—6-16, 462A2, A3
UNCTAD divided by issue 6-3, 417A3
IEA-Sweden aid rptd 6-4, 396E2
Australia bars barrier reef drilling 6-4, 423F1

1980

Canada electn issues cited 2-18, 2-19, 121D1, C2, E2
AFL-CIO urges OPEC independnc 2-18, 146D3
Newfoundland finds rptd 2-20, 2-21, 148G1
US oil tanker subsidies repaymt backed by Sup Ct 2-20, 170E2
Canada '79 4th 1/4 profits up 2-22, 211E2
W Ger defns spending hike plan linked 2-25, 153E3
Canada stock gains linked 2-27, 128F1
Ireland plans levy hike 2-27, 150G3
US Jan oil costs, imports rptd 2-28, 167D3
US-Saudi talks, reserve purchases barred 3-1—3-4; US stockpiling stalled 3-5, 165B3
Kuwait OKs Sovt, Comecon sales 3-2; '79 Comecon imports, '80 estimate rptd 3-3, 166B1
Saudi sees intl surplus, OPEC price reforms 3-5, 165F3
Saudi productn capacity increase planned; output, consumptn rptd 3-5, 166A1
Brazil imports costs forecast 3-5, 191A2
Iran oil fields bombed 3-6—3-8; daily productn cited 3-9, 178A2
Australia levy plans rptd 3-6, 210F2
Australia tanker drivers strike 3-8—3-9, 190G2; accord scored 3-14, 229B3
Canada stock mkt fall, Mobil offshore doubts linked 3-10, 191D3
Carter proposes oil-import fee 3-14, 201E1
Gasohol productn seen as world food threat 3-15, 251C1
US links Iraq exports, Italy A-aid 3-17, 220D3
Australia com backs fuel stockpiling 3-18, 229E3
Mex bars GATT entry 3-18, 234C1
Mex lifts '80 productn target, '79 export earnings rptd 3-18, 234G1
USSR price hikes re Hungary cited 3-24, 274E3
UK plans gas tax hikes 3-26, 232E1, G1
US Feb oil costs, imports rptd 3-27, 247B3
N Sea oil platform capsizes 3-27, 256D1
Canada cuts tar-sands prices 3-28, 272C3
French-Cuban exploratn accord rptd 4-1, 253A3
French use cut announced 4-2, 254C1
US-Mex talks 4-2—4-3, 315A2
US-Iran sanctns threaten Japan econ 4-8, 276B2, F2
Saudis rptdly weigh UK exports end 4-10, 294C1
Canada ownership rise, new price policy vowed 4-14, 293A1, B1
Japan trade deficit linked 4-15, 314F3
Portugal bans Iran trade, '79 3d 1/4 imports cited 4-17, 281F2
Japan-Iran talks fail 4-17, price hike barred 4-19; trade threatened, alternate supplies seen 4-20, 298D3
Nigeria oil co probe begun 4-18, 354B1
US drivers rptd buying Canada gas 4-21, 334E3
EC bars Iran oil purchase 4-22, 298F1
Saudis weigh UK trade curbs 4-22, 313E2
Greece-US pact signed 4-22, 352F2
Rumania-Iran pact rptd 4-23, 298B2
Japan substitutes for Iran rptd found 4-25; US offers aid 5-1, 341F1
Canada OKs Hunts property transfer to Engelhard 4-28, 345D1
US Mar oil costs, imports rptd 4-29, 328F3
Peru, 2 US cos sign new contracts 4-30, 354F1
Mex-Japan talks 5-2—5-4, 341G1
OPEC sets pricing, productn plans 5-7—5-8, 364F2
Mobil protests Saudi film telecast 5-8, 375C3
Australian drilling spurs Aborigine protests 5-8, 371B1; 8-11, 617G2
Libya threatens US, UK cutoff 5-9, 373A3
Libya expels, detains US co employes 5-12, 5-13, 373F3
Saudi hikes prices 8% 5-14, 364F3-365B1
Canada plans 5 projects; Atlantic coast self-sufficiency seen 5-16, 406F1, G1
Mex in French, W Ger, Swedish, Canadian talks; trade agrmts signed 5-16—5-28, 409G1, C2
Medit pollutn pact signed 5-17, 381D3
Newfoundland productn delay rtpd 5-20, 429C1
Iran pipeline saboteurs executed 5-22, 5-23, 419F3
US Apr oil costs, imports rptd 5-28, 401B1
Mex '80 exports, US share rptd 5-28, 409B2
Mex-Japan 3-yr pact signed 5-28, 409C2*
DR hikes price 5-28, taxi drivers strike 5-29—6-3, 462F1
USSR-W Ger pact set 5-29, 411C2
Alberta vs Ottawa price proposals 5-30, 428E3
UK Labor backs North Sea natlzn 5-31, 429E2
E Ger gas cash sales limited 6-1, 431C3
Jamaica rpts Venez, Iraq credits 6-4, 465E1
Rumanian conservatn urged, Sovt exports cited 6-4, 465F3
OPEC sets $32 a barrel base price 6-9—6-10; Kuwait, Venez, Iraq, Qatar, Algeria, Libya set price hikes, US scores 6-11, 435D2

1976 1977 1978

1979

US-Canada oil-sands study pact signed 6-4, 444D2-A3
France stresses Westn policy in US talks 6-5, 485A1
Turkey to get USSR oil 6-5, 488A3
Schmidt, Carter in talks 6-6, 430B1
Japan proposes Mex pipeline 6-8, 487E3
UK to hike gas tax, sell BP shares 6-12, 445E2, G2
Turkey sets new exchng rate, hikes prices 6-12, 447B1, D1
EC Comm proposes plan 6-13, 437F1
OECD warns re price hikes 6-14, 437B2, A3
S Africa curbs press 6-14, 469D3
Amax Australia Aborigine land drilling OKd 6-18, 467G1
China rpts '78 crude oil output 6-18, 484A3
China, W Ger sign pact 6-19, 637G3
EC leaders back import lid 6-22, 476C1
NZ plans pvt exploratn 6-22, 566B3
Italy hikes diesel, heating oil prices 6-26, 486G3
Comecon denies shortage, USSR productn lag cited 6-26–6-29, 497B2
US May imports rptd 6-27, 480E3
Iraq threatens Canada cutoff 6-27, 502B2
OPEC hikes base prices to $18, $20 a barrel; Carter scores 6-28, 473A1-C2
Tokyo summit sets '79-85 targets, intl energy tech group 6-28–6-29, 493A1-F2
Libya threat on export halt rptd, clarified 6-29–6-30, 496B1
Canada seeks price hike 6-29, 501B3-502A1
Saudis to increase productn 7-2, 495E3
Australia measures set 7-3, 522C1
Greece sets conservatn steps 7-3, 543G3, 544A1
Spain hikes prices, Libya import data rptd 7-3, 546C1
W Ger program detailed 7-4, 506C1-B2
Iran natlizes Shell Group interests 7-5, 503A3
OPEC scored by Carter aide 7-7, 513E3
China-US trade pact signed 7-7, 523G2
Iran pipelines bombed 7-7–7-10, mil protectn asked 7-11, 524F3
China to sell to Pl 7-8, 567C1
US confrms Saudi output hike 7-9, 536D3
UK revises N Sea estimate 7-10, 582A2
Canada rptd top gasoline user 7-11, 542B3
Iraq to hike French exports 7-11, 564C1
Brazil sets import ceiling 7-11, hikes prices 8-1, 871B2
Egypt, Israel agree on sales 7-12, 511A3
Nigeria cuts sales to BP 7-12, 545A2
US denies Saudi arms aid link 7-13, 536B3
Australia refinery struck 7-14, 542E1
Spot mkt situatn rptd 7-16, 494D1
USSR export freeze seen 7-18, 1st 1/2 productn rptd 7-20, 568F1
Canada ups export prices to US 7-19, 542D2
OECD sees econ slowdown 7-19, 554E2
US 1st 1/2 imports rptd 7-19, 557D2
Israel hikes prices 7-19, 566C1
Clark Oil settles Mideast paymt chrgs 7-19, 985F2
Pl notes price rise impact 7-23, 567A1
Tenneco seeks UV assets 7-23, 770B3
Nigeria, Algeria output cut rptd 7-25, 7-30, 645D2
UK plans BNOC cuts, more N Sea exploratn 7-26, 582B1
Mex productn, reserves data rptd 7-26, 636A1
Rumania hikes gas price 7-27, demands Westn money paymts 8-1, 645D3, G3
US bank loan to Mex rptd, '78 Brazil loan cited 7-28, 584E1, D2
US June imports rptd 7-29, 577G2
Spain 10-yr energy plan OKd; oil import, consumptn data rptd 7-30, 585E2
IATA members agree on air fare hikes 7-30, 721G3
BP natlzd by Nigeria 7-31, 584D2-D3
US links Palestinian autonomy talks progress 8-1, 575B1
DR riots re gas prices 8-1, 575G3
France notes OPEC price impact 8-2, 614C1
Canada OKs oil-sands plant 8-3, 651D1
Schlesinger sees $40-a-barrel OPEC price by '89 8-5, 629A2
Israel chrgs Mideast peace link 8-7, US denies 8-8, 591A2, E2
OECD links 2d 1/4 inflatn hike 8-9, 627C1
Ecuador exploratn planned 8-10, 613A3
Japan urges conservatn 8-11–8-12, price impact noted 8-13, 615G2, A3
CR strike halts productn 8-14, 667D3
Arafat warns Carter 8-20, 659A2
US kerosene, diesel fuel sale to Iran set 8-21; Carter defends 8-22, 622C3
Australia levy, discovery tax break set 8-21, 631G2, F3
Australia, NZ trade union explored 8-21, 632A1
Mex policy scored re well biowout 8-21, 635E3-636B1
Iran productn drop, gold price rise linked 8-22, 645B3
OPEC trust suit dropped 8-23, 647C3
China offshore oil find rptd 8-24, 664E3

1980

Saudi bars price hike; links productn cut, US stockpiling 6-10, 435F2, A3
US 1st 1/4 paymts gap rptd 6-19, 455C1
Venice summit vows reliance end, sets '90 goal, OKs IEA aims 6-22—6-23, 473A1-474E1
Australia plans hydrogen cars 6-22, 496F2
IMF sees poor natn debt rise 6-24, 477B3
US May oil costs, imports rptd 6-27, 492F2
Dutch bar S Africa embargo 6-27, 499G1
Italy OKs gas price hike 7-2, 523E3
World glut cuts Eur, OPEC prices 7-4—8-12, 628F1-D2
Canada backs moderate price rise 7-6, 543C2
China '79 rig collapse rptd 7-6, 621E3
Australia-Exxon shale-oil accord set 7-7, 520B1
Shell-Saudi petro complex deal agreed 7-9, 524G2
Mobil wells off Newfoundland rptd productive 7-10, 7-11, 544B1-D1
Norway N Sea drillers strike 7-10, govt intervenes 7-16, 565F3; strike ends 8-13, 620E2
Canada levy raised 75% 7-11, 543C3
Taiwan 1st 1/2 costs rptd 7-11, 567F2
Libyan-B Carter deal rptd 7-14, 542D2
US blames Iran for '79 shortage 7-17, 552C1
UK plans N Sea output cut 7-23, 563C3
US 1st 1/2 imports rptd down 7-24, 553A1
Canada talks fail 7-25, prices hiked 7-31, 577A2, F2
Guyana forgn dependence cited 7-25, 791C2
Mex, Brazil in trade talks 7-27—7-31, 605A3
Peru vows investmt, exploratn 7-28, 579G3
US June costs, imports rptd 7-29, 574F2
UK Labor asks N Sea profits aid indus 7-29, 578G1
US, W Ger, Japan synfuel pact signed 7-31, 666D2
Mex, Venez sign Latin supply guarantee 8-3, 605C3
Nigeria disputes forgn cos oil-take 8-8, 620E1
Liberian tanker runs aground off Tex 8-9, 621A3
Canada '79 profits rptd up 8-12, 618A1
World Bank '80 forecast grim, price hikes seen 8-17, 628F2
OPEC June output rptd at 41/2-year low 8-17, 666B2
Iraq June productn rptd 8-17, 666D2
Israel links Sinai fields withdrawal, US aid request 8-20, 662G3
Libya disputes Malta-Italy offshore project 8-21, 709E1
Mobil halts Newfoundland Ben Nevis drilling 8-22, 668D3
Canada co gets Japan loan 8-23, 651C1
China oil min scored re '79 accident 8-24, fired; vice premr censured 8-25, 651B3
Muskie, Rao address UN aid talks 8-25, 642A3, C3, 643A1
Dutch rpt Arab boycott threat 8-26, 643F2
France port blockade concessns offered 8-26; navy opens blockade 8-27, 651D3
Kuwait UN oil focus warning rptd 8-27, 643C1
US July oil costs, imports rptd 8-27, 666A2
US price controls, EC polyester duties linked 9-1, 662B3
Mex reserves, productn levels rptd 9-1, 729C3
US Aug imports show record drop; Jan-Aug decline rptd 9-6, 785A3
Brazil rig accident cuts productn 20% 9-7, 731A3
France plans tax hike 9-10, 688D1
Australia electn issue 9-11, 727D3
IMF role in oil debt studied 9-15, 695D2
GATT links oil prices, global trade lag 9-16, 695F3
IMF revises SDR valuatn method 9-17, 695B2
OPEC reaches price accord: Saudis OK $2 hike, bar productn cut; other members OK freeze 9-18, 694A3
US, Saudi secret talks 9-18; US stockpiling rptd resumed 10-27, 826B1
Iraq, Iran jets hit oilfields, exports stopped 9-21—9-24, end to oil glut seen 9-24; Iran warns Hormuz Strait block, US seeks contd flow 9-24, 717E1, 718B1-A3
World Bank '80 loans rptd 9-22, 720D1
US Aug oil costs, imports rptd 9-26, 741F1
World Bank, IMF set poor natn aid 9-30, 761D2-D3
Canada prov delays price hike 9-30, 788B1
Spain sets subsidy cut 9-30, 793A3
France plans less use 10-1, 749D3
Sovts pledge COMECON exports 10-1, 753B3
IEA pledges oil stock depletn, reserves estimated 10-1, 759A2
Australia coal conversn project rptd set 10-2, 748A2
Brazil rpts Sovt purchase, deals with 6 other natns 10-2; hikes gas prices 10-3, 759E1-A2
Canada talks fail again 10-2, 787C3
US import shortfall measures rptd 10-3, 785D3
Nigeria warns US on S Africa 10-3, 792C2

1976

1977

1978

1979

Iran productn shortfall denied 8-24, 645B2
1st 1/2 world output rptd 8-28, 645F1
US July import rise rptd 8-28, 646G2
Carter sees no Arab oil threat 8-30, 659C1
Australia alcohol fuel projct rptd 8-30, 666D3
US-Iran kerosene deal jeopardized 9-2, 708C3
Hungary price controls dropped 9-3, 741G2
Rumania eases gas paymt rule 9-3, 741G3-742A1
Exporter-natn aid asked by poor countries, Iraq OKs 9-4, 675G1
Angola-Texaco oil pact signed 9-4, 705G2
Egypt to sell Sinai oil to Israel 9-5, 658G1
Petro-Canada breakup studied 9-5, 684E3
E-W Ger deal set 9-5, 796A3
Iran productn rptd down 9-5, 708E3
BP profits soar 9-6, 686F3
Nigeria US exports cited 9-11, 720G3
Canada offshore potential seen 9-11, Newfoundland strike rptd 9-21, 728F2, B3
Intl cong in Rumania 9-11, 728B3
10th World Petro Cong meets 9-12, 703A1
W Ger Cabt OKs conservatn steps 9-12, 733E2
Iran cutoff impact in US rptd 9-13, 702B3, E3
Beaufort Sea find discounted 9-13, 728C3
UK bars North Sea oil assets sale 9-14, 707F1
France N Sea access, EC budget contributn opposed by UK 9-17, 719D2, E2
Dutch plan gas tax hike 9-18, conservatn progrm 9-19, 730C3, 731B1
China reserve estimate raised 9-18, 2d offshore find rptd 10-10, 790D1
UK supply forecast revised down 9-18, 752A2
Canada cuts US exports 9-19, 706D2
Young: Africa victimized by Mideast conflict 9-20, 721A2
Czech hikes prices 9-20, 9-23, 741F3
Concorde program ended 9-21, 721A3
Newfoundland find, Dow rise linked 9-21, 745C3
France plans exploratn aid 9-21, 752B1
Dutch Shell refinery struck 9-24, 731A2
Carter links OPEC price hikes, inflatn 9-25, 723G2
Saudi productn level to continue 9-26, '80 cutback set 10-4, 781E1
US strategic reserve purchases rptd cut 9-26, 9-27, 781G1
US Aug import rise rptd 9-27, 745D2
Canada to sell crown co 9-28, 749G2
Dutch Shell refinery strike ends 9-28, 815C1
Belgium to hike gas prices 10-2, 832B3
Mideast oil money, gold price rise linked 10-3, 740B1
Saudi sees reactn re $ weakness, inflatn 10-3, 779B3
USSR, E Ger sign pact 10-5, 761C2
Norway plans gas tax hike 10-6–10-7, 774C1
Venez '78 earnings rptd 10-6, 837C3
Kuwait, Mex hike prices 10-9; Libya, Iran break OPEC ceiling 10-15; Iraq rise rptd 10-18, 781B1
Jamaica import costs forecast 10-9, 996B1
Swedish import hike seen 10-10, 795E2
Connally links Mideast policy, oil flow 10-11, 783A2
Persian Gulf states meet on security 10-14–10-16, 804A2
Petro-Canada stock giveaway urged 10-14, 812B1
UK to sell BP stock 10-16, 792D2
Volcker links price hikes, living standard drop 10-17, 10-28, 940C3
Algeria price hikes top OPEC limit 10-24, 864G1
UK orders N Sea cutback 10-29, 836F1
Canada prov threatns cutoff 10-29, 853E2
US Sept imports rptd 10-30, 828G1
Canada hikes US prices 10-31, 864F1
Nigeria hikes prices over OPEC ceiling 11-3, 864D1
UK's BNOC sets price hike 11-6, 864B2
Taiwan econ growth decline linked to prices; Jan–Sept consumptn cut 11-6, 952G2, C3
Venez, Brazil export agrmt 11-6–11-7, 953G1
Iran cutoff threat seen in US Sen 11-8, 843B1
Iran 5% export cut confirmed 11-8, 843F1
Brown offers OPEC pricing plan 11-9, 962E2
Australia find 11-10–11-11, 888G1
US bans Iran purchase; US, forgn import data rptd 11-12, 861A1, D1, D2
Canada prime min seeks price rise, cites US 11-12, 888B3
Indonesia sets price hikes 11-14, 864A2
Iran ends sales to US cos, US rpts allies' support 11-15; Iran hints $ paymt shift 11-19, 11-20, 879E2-C3
UK moves up tax collectn 11-15, 889F2
Rumania Black Sea find rptd, '78 output drop cited 11-19, 910A2
USSR reserves called world's largest 11-19, 928G3

1980

Saudi, Kuwait, UAE export boosts rptd set 10-5—10-6, 758D3
OPEC postpones mtgs re Iran-Iraq war 10-6, 10-8, 759D1
Norway '81 revenue rise seen 10-6, 792F3
Iraq, Iran oil fields bombed 10-8, 10-15, 773G1-C2
Abu Dhabi lifts price $2, other OPEC hikes seen 10-15, 775B1
US-Israel agrmt set 10-15, signed 10-17, 775E3
US defends Saudi AWACS shipmt 10-19, 798C3
Iraq seeks Iran fields 10-21; cuts off Khuzistan, hits petrochem plants 10-22, 799C2, A3
Sovt productn, '81 projectn rptd 10-22, 798C2
Venezuela raises fuel-oil prices, US impact cited 10-27, 822F1
Saudis plan $2 premium on excess productn, Kuwait seeks $5; UAE, Qatar up productn 10-28, 822C2
Canada energy plan set 10-28, oppositn heated 10-29—10-30, 858C1-E3
US Sept oil costs, imports rptd 10-29, 824F1
India protester's blockade smashed 11-2, 873E1
OPEC gives Islamic states preference 11-4—11-6, 865C1
Canada oil chiefs reject Ottawa plan 11-5, 11-7, 871A3
Italy tax scandal probe rptd set 11-5—11-6, 873D2
US 3d 1/4 imports rptd 11-6, 867F2
Alberta sets Mar '81 oil cutback 11-7, 885G2
Africa OPEC members pledge Africa exports 11-9, 874D2
OPEC warns stockpilers, US reductn rptd 11-17; IEA disputes data 11-23, 895F2, A3
Japan costs widen trade gap 11-18, 902B1
Canada oil sands projects stalled 11-18—11-19, 920D3
Mex sets export limits 11-19; studies domestic price hikes 11-20, 902C2
Iraq resumes oil pumping 11-20, 894A2
Iran renews Kharg I terminal use 11-21, 894C2
OPEC Sept output at 5-yr low, price surge rptd 11-23; Indonesia sees Dec OPEC price rise 11-24, UAE backs freeze 11-25, 895C2
Panama Canal congestn, trade increase linked 11-24, 895D3
UK plans new N Sea oil levy 11-24, 901G1, C2
Australia strike settlmt accord scored 11-26, 940D2
US Oct oil costs, imports rptd 11-28, 916G1-A2
USSR sets 11th 5-yr plan 12-1, 945A2
Saudi exec joins Mobil bd 12-1, 960D3
Sweden rpts huge Sovt find, USSR denies 12-5, 951B3
IEA sets '81 oil buying curb 12-9, 932A1
North Sea oil bolsters UK pound 12-10, 932G1
Beagle Channel accord proposed 12-12, 978E3
Iraq rations gas 12-13, halts pipeline deliveries 12-19, 978G1
OPEC in 'broad' price accord 12-15—12-16, 951D1
Brazil '81 costs forecast 12-17, 991D3
Saudi '80 revenue rptd 12-19, 983G2
US Nov oil costs, imports rptd 12-30, 984G1

1979

Iran daily revenue rptd $70 mln 11-20, 897B1
Arab League vs oil as weapon 11-20, 916C2
Venezuela estimates Orinoco tar field reserves; proven reserves, '79 productn rptd 11-21; US comments 11-26, 953A1
US's Miller in Persian Gulf 11-23–11-28, 896A3
Iran bars US $ paymts 11-23, hostile natns boycott ordrd 11-25, '80 productn cut set 11-26, 897D3
Brazil raises gas prices 58% 11-23, imports to exceed $7 bln 11-26, 907B2, E2
Mex Nov output up 6.9%; US export hike barred; Spain, Israel sales cited 11-23, 909G2
Israel returns oilfield to Egypt, US supply treaty effected 11-25, 916E2
Iran '73-78 revenue diversn chrgd 11-26, 897F2, F3
China finds rptd 11-26, 918F1
Australia grants exploratn permits, reclassifies offshore field 11-27, 925F2
Japan import costs, current acct deficit linked 11-27, 996F2
USSR urges conservatn 11-27; rpts shortfall, '80 target 11-28, 928C3, E3
Carter sees dependnce as security threat 11-28, 894D3
US Oct imports rptd 11-29, 922A1
Saudis cut off Italy shipmts re payoffs scandal 12-5, 995B3
S Korea trade deficit rptd 12-5, 997B2
Japan, China sign pact 12-6, 939E3
Brazil '79 import costs, '80 estimate rptd 12-7, 948A3
Peru orders US contracts renegotiated; '79 productn, earnings rptd 12-7, 951A2
Japan defends Iran trade 12-11, 933E2
Canada price, excise tax hikes budgeted 12-12, defeated 12-13, 936C3, D3
US drilling co sues Iran 12-13, 976D2
Saudi, 3 others hike prices 12-13, 977F1
Japan to cut Iran imports 12-14, 958D3
Iran '79 revenues, output rptd; '80 1st 1/4 forecast 12-17, 976B1
OPEC mtg fails to set price 12-17–12-20; chart 12-21, prices soar 12-28–12-30, 977D1-E2
UK ends Zimbabwe sanctns violatn probe 12-19, 976D3
Kennedy scores Admin re OPEC hikes 12-20–12-21, 983A3
US Nov imports rptd 12-28, 984E3
UN sanctns vs Iran exempt oil sales 12-31, 974A3

Mergers & Acquisitions
Ashland unit holdings sold 2-4, 560E3
Deutsche BP-Veba deal OKd 3-5, 214F3
Mobil outbid for Bodcaw 3-8, 350C1
Mobil merger bid for Gen Crude OKd 3-28, 282G3
Indiana Standard to buy Cyprus Mines 4-11, 560B3
Alberta Gas sets Husky takeover 5-13, 405F2
Exxon in Reliance Elec talks 5-18, 404E2
Exxon bids on Reliance 6-21, completes purchase 9-24, 770F1-D2
Allied Chem to buy Eltra 6-28, 560A2 621D2
Sun, Becton stock purchase ruled illegal 7-9, 541E2
BP share sales planned 7-24, 564F3
Sun Co purchase of Elk R Resources set 7-31, 986B3
Marathon Mfg-Penn Central merger set 8-10, 664D1
Placid to buy Intl Paper oil interests 8-10, 664A2
Reserve Oil accepts Denison Mines bid 8-14, Getty Oil bid 10-31, 986B3
Great Canadian, Sun Oil merge 8-22, 651A2
Continental buys Fla Gas 8-28, 986C3
Mobil suit fails 12-7; Shell acquires Belridge Oil 12-10; Mobil, Texaco sue 12-11, 942D1
Tenneco to acquire Southwestn Life 12-11, 986A3
Charter Co to bid for ERC Corp 12-21, 986C3

1980

Mergers & Acquisitions
Union Pacific, MoPac set merger 1-8, 52E3
Canada gas, whiskey cos merge 1-9, 19D1
Gulf Resources rejects Placid offer 2-26, 385A3
Mobil, Texaco drop Belridge litigatn 3-6, 385D3
Occidental drops Permian sale talks 3-17, 385G2
Standard Oil (Ind) to buy LTV assets 3-25, 385C3
Smith Intl to acquire Galveston-Houston 3-26, 385B3
Engelhard acquires Hunts' Beaufort Sea holdings 3-31, 244F3; property transfer cleared 4-28, 345D1
Charter Media buys Phila Bulletin 4-10, 376F3
Seagram accepts Sun bid for Tex Pacific 4-11, 385B2
Exxon buys Arco shale oil project 5-13, 553G2
Getty Oil buys ERC 6-5, 557F2
Smith, Galveston-Houston deal fails 6-9, 557E2
BP plans Selectn Trust takeover 7-7, 523A2
Rhone-Poulenc sells petrochem units 7-9, 522C2
Kuwait seeks 15% of Getty, Saudi interest in Occidental noted 7-14, 542A3
Kuwait bid for Getty rejctd 7-18, 556G3
Petro-Canada to buy Newfoundland refinery 8-1, 633B1
Alaska Interstate, C&K agree 8-18, 745F3
NW Energy to buy Pacific Resources 8-18, 746D1
Esmark sells 3 Vickers units 8-26, 745D2-A3
Aramco takeover by Saudis confrmd 9-4, 661G3; cited 9-18, 725A2
Tex Pacific, Sun merger complete 9-12, 985A1
Union Pacific, MoPac, Westn Pacific file 9-15, 745C2
Schlumberger, Mfg Data Systems agree 9-18, 746B1
Charter Media dissolved 9-30, 836B2
Barber Oil liquidates, Petro-Lewis buys unit 10-2, 986A1
Sohio to buy US Steel coal assets 12-2, 985B2
Mapco, Earth Resources merger set 12-5, 985E1
Tenneco, Houston Oil merger set 12-9, 985A2

1976

North Sea Finds—*See NORTH Sea*

1977

Offshore Developments (U.S.)
Andrus backs offshore drilling controls 1-18, 35A1
Offshore lease renewal tied to productn 3-15, 195F3
Carter energy plan sets goals 4-18, 4-20, 292F2

1978

Offshore Developments (U.S.)
Carter budgets rents, royalties 45G2
Atlantic lease sales delayed 1-30, 108D2
NJ drilling challenge refused 2-21, 125E2-B3
NJ (Baltimore Canyon) well rptd dry 6-2, 6-5, 449C3

1979

Offshore Developments (U.S.)
NJ (Baltimore Canyon) wells rptd dry 1-10, 17A2; 2-14, 186E3; 3-13–5-16, 361D3
NJ (Baltimore Canyon) find seen 1-17, 55C2
Carter budgets rents, royalties 1-22, 42F2

1980

Offshore Developments (U.S.)
Mass (Georges Bank) lease bids rptd accepted 1-7, 18A1
Mass State of State message 1-14, 483C3
Carter budget proposals 1-28; table 70F1, 74A1

1976

Petrodollar Issue—*See under MONETARY Developments*
Political Payments Issue—*See under BUSINESS; also company names*
Pollution (including oil spills)—*See 'Oil & Gas Issues' under ENVIRONMENT*
Producer-Consumer Talks
US backs IEA energy plan 1-30—1-31, 108D1
Intl econ conf 2-11—2-20, 148B1
U.S. Developments (domestic)—*See also 'U.S. Presidential Election' below*
Ford State of Union message 1-19, 37E3, 39D2
'77 energy research budgeted 1-21, 64A3, C3
Dec, '75 CPI 1-21, 90C1
Dec, '75 imports, costs rptd 1-27, 91D1
'75 4th ¼ corp profits down 2-3, 215A3
Jan CPI rptd 2-20, 168D2
Ford legis proposals 2-26, 149E2
Jan oil shipmts rptd 2-27, 168D3
Feb WPI drop cited 3-4, 199F1
NY ct dismisses '74 trust case vs 3 cos 3-10; case vs 7 rptd pending 3-11, 413B1
Feb CPI down 3-19, 215A2
House com vs Ford budget estimates 3-23, 231E2
Feb imports rptd down 3-26, 230A2
'75 crude oil reserves down 3-30, 285D1
Cong opens Navy reserves 3-31, 246G2-C3
'75 energy use data rptd 4-4, 285A1-D1
Naval reserves bill signed 4-5, 982E1
Oil rig sinks off Tex 4-15, 544D3
ERDA stresses energy conservatn 4-19, 284G3
Mar CPI rptd 4-21, 306G1, C2
Mar oil shipmts down 4-26, 307E1
Alaska offshore lease sale 4-26, 648E3
'75 top 500 indls ranked 437A1-G1
Ford urges regulatory reform 5-13, 346G3
April CPI rptd 5-14, 375E1
Alaska pipe problems assessed 5-21—9-10, cost estimate raised 6-30, 690F2-691B2
SEC sues Petrofunds 5-26, Geo Dynamics 6-1, 984D2
7 oil cos indicted 6-1, 412C3
Ky Standard Oil rpts antibusing threats 6-14, 453F1
Sup Ct upholds import tariff 6-17, 452A3
Sup Ct declines entitlemts progrm review 6-21, 569E1
May CPI rptd 6-22, 453B3
May import drop rptd 6-28, 494D3
FEA controls end 7-1, 534A1
June WPI rptd 7-9, 519E1
May, June CPI rptd 7-21, 536D2
Coastal states impact aid signed 7-26, 566G2
June imports rptd 7-27, 568C1
Navy reserve dvpt funds signed 7-31, 623D1
La refinery blast 8-12, 816A2
Atlantic offshore lease sale challenged 8-13—8-17, bids accepted 8-25, 648C2-F3
Price rise, incentive bill signed 8-14, 622F2
July CPI rptd 8-20, 635G1
Colo oil-shale leases suspended 8-23, GAO vs synfuel progrm 8-24, 648G3
July imports rptd 8-26, 668D1
Aug WPI rptd 9-2, 667D3
Indl output index revised 9-16, 709E1
Elec car veto overridden 9-17, 708A1
Synfuel loan bill defeated 9-23, 883B3
Aug imports rptd 9-27, 770D1
Offshore leasing bill defeated 9-28, 883E2
Divestiture bill not cleared 10-2, 883G2
James Noe dies 10-3, 970F2
Sept CPI rptd 10-21, 805G2
Sept imports rptd 10-28, 833D2
Klein scores import bulge 10-28, 833E2
NE aid plan urged 11-14, 864F3
Tex cuts output 11-18, 12-16, 991C3
Oct CPI rptd 11-19, 885A1
Gas price decontrol proposed 11-23, Ford backs 12-29, 991F2-A3
Oct, 10-mo imports rptd 11-29, 958C2
FEA vs Alaska surplus export 11-30, 991E3
Final Alaska pipeline sectn laid 12-5, 991F3 ★
FEA proposes stockpile plan 12-15, 991D3

1977

Lease sales delayed 5-17, Andrus defends 5-19, 6-3, 498F3
Carter on offshore dvpt 5-23, 404C2
Global rpts paymts 6-2, 503F2
Gulf leases canceled 6-8, 499C1
Carter for Atlantic probes 7-22, 575G1
E Coast lease sale OKd by ct 8-25, 650A1
Leasing bill blocked in House com 10-25, 833C2
Gulf of Mex rig copter crash 12-8, 1023F2
Payments Issues
Burmah fee to S Korea's Park rptd 1-19, 55A2
Jones '76 guilty plea re Gulf gift cited 2-16, 111G3
Shell rpts '75 forgn paymts 2-16, 233B3
Gulf: sales unaffected by crackdown 2-28, 233E1
Petrolane rpts forgn paymts 4-7, 503D1
McDermott rpts pol paymts 4-12, 503A3
SEC sues Occidental 5-3, 503B1
Sup Ct declines Wild waiver case 5-16, 419A2
SEC opens some files; Ashland paymts rptd 5-17, 503A1
Global rpts paymts 6-2, 503F2
BP admits overseas paymts 6-3, 526A2
Gulf indicted re IRS gifts 6-15, 504A1; pleads guilty, fined 11-22, 944A1
Exxon settles chrgs 10-25, 818D1-A2
Phillips pleads guilty, fined 11-22, 944B1
Pollution (including oil spills)—*See ENVIRONMENT—Oil & Gas Issues*
Prices (U.S.)
Nov '76 prices rptd 1-14, 37E2
Ford orders price decontrol 1-19, Carter rescinds 1-24, 55C1
Dec '76 CPI hike rptd 1-19, 78B1
Jan CPI rise rptd 2-18, 129C3
Westinghouse links uranium, oil prices 3-3, 177D3
Feb CPI rise rptd 3-18, 215C1
Mar CPI rise rptd 4-21, 324C2
Apr WPI rise rptd 5-5, 383A3, C3
Apr CPI rise rptd 5-22, 406B3
Schlesinger urges price role 5-25, 443G2
May CPI rise rptd 6-22, 482B1
June CPI rptd 7-21, 554C2
July CPI rptd 8-19, 651E1
Nov CPI rise rptd 12-21, 977E1

1978

Leasing chngs clear Cong 8-22, 662F2-663A1
Fed estimate of reserves cited 8-22, 662G2
Tax law revisn clears 10-15, 786E1
3 NJ (Baltimore Canyon) wells rptd dry 12-6, 12-11, 12-27, 1010B1
Pollution (including oil spills)—*See ENVIRONMENT—Oil & Gas Issues*

1979

Ashland unit holdings sold 2-4, 560E3
Mass (Georges Bank) lease ban lifted 2-20, 186F3
NJ (Baltimore Canyon) lease bids low, reserve estimate cited 2-28, 186C3
NJ (Baltimore Canyon) find rptd 6-5, new well dry 7-6, 518D2
Calif lease bids placed 6-29, 518B2; accepted 8-7, 649E1
Tex port OKd 7-2, 518F2
Gulf of Mex lease bids placed 7-31, accepted 8-28, 664D3
NJ (Baltimore Canyon) wells rptd dry 9-27, 10-3, 867C2
Tex supertanker port OKd 10-15, 769B3
Mass (Georges Bank) lease sale delayed 11-6, OKd 11-9, 867E1-A2
Gulf of Mex lease bids placed 11-27, 942F3
Shell accident liability case refused by Sup Ct 12-3, 964D2
Gulf of Mex lease bids accepted 12-10, 990C2
Alaska (Beaufort Sea) lease sale held 12-11, 990D2
Mass (Georges Bank) lease sale OKd bids placed 12-18, 990G1
Pollution (including oil spills)—*See ENVIRONMENT-Oil & Gas Issues*
Price Violations
Sun Co chrgd 1-3, 17D1
Wage-price noncompliance rptd 2-6, 127G3
Kerr-McGee OKs price refund 2-8, 112G3
Gas anti-price gouging drive starts 4-16, 301C2
150 gas price violatns rptd 4-27, 324C3
7 oil firms accused 5-2, 343B2
Amerada Hess chrgd 5-17, 385A2
Amerada Hess chrgd, other refiners warned; Jan-May hikes noted 5-30, 396C1
Gulf cleared re Vepco 6-12, 580A3
Energy Dept actions 7-19–10-25, 849B3
Mobil refund agreed 9-18, 849F3
Westland fined 9-18, 850A1
Cities Svc accepts penalties 11-1, 850B1
Mobil, 8 others accused 11-6, 849F2
Shell, 4 others accused 11-8, 905E2
Amerada Hess, 3 others accused 11-14, 905G2-A3
8 cos accused 11-18–12-11, 943B1
Getty OKs settlemt 12-4, 943G1-A2
Mobil overchrg action said improper 12-4, 990B3
Energy Dept actions 12-10–12-19, 990E2-A3

1980

Calif leasing pressed, '81-85 reoffering sale planned 3-28, 330C3
La oil leasing rights denied by Sup Ct 4-28, 369C1
Andrus OKs leasing speedup 6-17, 552E2
Alaska lease curbs lifted 7-3, 7-8; leases OKd 7-9, 552E3
13 die in Mex Gulf hurricane evacuatn 8-9, 621F2
Gulf Coast leasing bids set records 9-30, 785G1
Exxon Beaufort Sea find rptd 10-3, 785E2-A3
Beaufort sea leases upheld 10-14, 960B3
Leasing overhaul ordrd 10-31, 960G2
Persian Gulf Issue—*See PERSIAN Gulf*
Pollution (including oil spills)—*See ENVIRONMENT--Oil*
Price Violations
Standard Oil (Ind) settles chrgs 2-14, 189F3
11 cos cited for '79 noncompliance, Mobil chrgd 2-25, 189C3
Crown Central chrgd 3-7, Murphy Oil 3-25, 248E2
Carter scores Mobil, seeks punitive measures 3-28, 4-1; defns contract awarded 4-1, contract ban set 4-4, 248F1-E2
Mobil settles price case 4-24, 309E1
Phillips, Sun setlmts OKd 9-25, 9-26, 960E1
Coalitn sues over setlmts 10-8, 960G1
Standard Oil (Ind) setlmt OKd 12-3, 960C1
U.S. Presidential Campaign
Connally backs Iran 'disruptns' 1-3, 5F1
Anderson urges 50 cents per gal tax 1-5, 4D3
GOP platform proposals urge NATO role, US independnc 1-14, 32C1, F1
Kennedy urges rationing, GOP scores 1-28, 74E2, E3, 75G1
Kennedy urges 'recontrol', conservatn 2-2, 91D1, E1
GOP candidates debate in NH 2-20, 129F3
Reagan 'basic speech' excerpts 2-29, 207G3
Connally 'basic speech' excerpts 3-7, 184F2, B3
Kennedy 'basic speech' excerpts 3-10, 183C2, E2
Dem platform drafted 6-24, 479G2
GOP platform proposed 7-10, 506C3; adopted; text 7-15, 536D3, 537B1, F1
Reagan seeks gas allocatn rule repeal 7-12, 535E1
Reagan acceptance speech 7-17, 532B2, 533E2
Dem conv keynote speech 8-11, 612A2*, D2
Dem platform planks voted 8-13, 611F2
Carter acceptance speech 8-14, 612E1, F3, 613F1
Anderson platform offered 8-30, 665C2
Anderson scores US Arab oil dependnc 9-4, 682A1
Reagan scores forgn dependnc 9-10, 699D3
Anderson, Reagan TV debate 9-21, 721E3, 722A1
Carter seeks to end forgn dependnc 10-14, 779G1
Carter, Reagan TV debate 10-28, 814B1, 815D1

1976

Coleman to OK 2 superports 12-17, 991G3
Nov imports rise rptd 12-28, 983B3
Consumptn rptd at record high 12-29, 991A3

U.S. Presidential Election
Shriver issues program 1-7, 22G2
Reagan sees ldrs on funding, backs depletn allowance 4-5, 4-6, 281F2
Black Dems draft plank 5-1, 343F3
SEC lists corp paymts 5-12, 725G3, 726C1
Reagan scores US curbs 5-14, 356F3
Dem platform vs cos' holdings in other energy interests 6-15, 432C3
Dem platform text 6-15, 474B3-475G2
Carter gives breakup views 7-1, 490E2
Udall urges big-oil breakup 7-14, 506D1
Mondale tax record cited 512G3
Carter vows tax reform cautn 7-22, 550D3
Carter vs industry breakup 8-9, 585C1
Carter vs 'vertical divestiture'; for 'accountability' 8-17, 617G1
GOP platform text 8-18, 607D2
Phillips tax fraud chrgd 9-2, 725F2
Cong clears historic sites preservatn funding 9-13, 745B3
Carter proposes Cabt-level energy dept 9-21, 704G2
Ford, Carter debate 9-23, 702E2
Carter vows fair allocatn, deplores Arab blackmail 9-30, 742E3
'75 corp tax data rptd 10-2, 10-14, 847A2
Ford, Carter debate 10-6, 740E2, 741D3
Ford donatns cited 10-22, 938F3
Carter backs Atlantic offshore exploratn 10-30, 827G1
Egypt reactn to Carter win 11-4, 826C2
Oct WPI rptd 11-4, 846C2
Carter urges OPEC price restraint 11-15 864A1; 12-14, 12-16, 935C1, 937E2

PETROLEUM Institute, American (API)
Rpts crude oil reserves down 3-30, 285D1
Eased clean-air rules upheld 8-2, 570A3
PETROV, Boris
Robbed 10-14, USSR protests 10-19, 857A2
PETTIS, Rep. Shirley N. (R, Calif.)
Reelected 11-2, 829E1
PETTY, Richard
2d in Daytona 500 2-15, 424A3
PEUGEOT S. A.
US ends car dumping probe 5-4, 321D2
Citroen merger cleared 10-1, 773B1
PEYK (Turkish warship)
In Intl Naval Review 7-4, 488D3
PEYSER, Rep. Peter A. (R, N.Y.)
Rpts IRS probes Rev Moon 6-1, 971B1
NYC gets flu vaccine funds 6-6, 443B2
Loses NY Sen primary 9-14, 687F2
Caputo elected 11-2, 821G2
PEZARAT Correia, Brig. Gen. Pedro
Quits as southn mil cmdr 8-12, 733D2
PFEIFFER, Jane Cahill
Commerce post declined 12-14, 12-16, 936D1, 937C1
PFIZER Inc.
Rpts foreign payoffs 3-19, 362C1
SEC lists forgn paymts 5-12, 728E2
'69 trust suit ends in mistrial 8-17, 988B3
Sup Ct bars review of trust case 10-4, 807B3
PHAGNA Bong Souvannavong
Prison escape barred 4-26, 333F3
PHAKATI, Jane
Rptd detained 8-27, 653F1
PHARAON, Ghaith R.
Detroit bank acquisitn OKd 12-19, 983G3

1977

PETROLEUM Association of America, Independent
Carter energy plan reactn 4-21, 319E3
PETROLEUM Institute, American (API)
Rpts oil supplies depleted 1-14, 37A2
Rpts wkly fuel reserves drop 1-19, 54A3; 1-27, 2-2, 76G1
Rpts Jan imports, reserves 2-8, 2-9, 91F3
Rpts wkly oil stocks, imports 2-17, 2-24, 152F2, B3; 3-9, 196C2
Rpts Feb refinery output 3-9, 196E2
Carter energy plan 4-20, 292E3
Rpts 2d ¼ drillings rise 7-28, 628A1
On Carter oil industry attack 10-13, 772F3
PETROLEUM Marketing Corp.—*See COMMONWEALTH Oil Refining Co.*
PETROVIC, Dusan
Dies 7-21, 604F3
PETRUS, Bernardus
Namibia police torture chrgd 12-16, 1017B1
PETTY, Richard
Yarborough wins Daytona 500 2-20, 531C2
NASCAR final standing, earnings rptd 11-20, 1020D3
PETUKHOV, Valery
Toth chrgd 7-12, 564A2
PEUGEOT S. A.
EPA fuel-econ ratings issued 9-19, 723C3
Argentina exec slain 12-16, 981F3
PEYREFITTE, Alain
Named justice min 3-30, 239E1
Defends Croissant extraditn 11-25, 969C1
PEZZULLO, Lawrence A.
Named amb to Uruguay 7-1, confrmd 7-13, 626C3
PFEIFFER, Dr. Carl
CIA mind-control tests revealed 8-1—8-9, 611D1
PFLP (Popular Front for the Liberation of Palestine)—*See LEBANON, MIDDLE EAST*
PGA (Professional Golfers Association)—*See GOLF*
PHAN Hien
In US talks, asks post-war aid 5-3—5-4, 333B1
In US talks, gives MIA list 6-2—6-3, 441E1
PHARAON, Ghaith R.
To buy Lance bank shares; Houston, Detroit bank ownership cited 12-27, 1003E2

1978

PETROLEUM Industry Research Foundation Inc.
Energy-GNP link rptd down in '77 4-20, 282B2
Sees no oil shortage before 2000 6-5, 449E3 ★ -450B1
PETROLEUM Institute, American (API)
Benzene exposure rule scored 2-2, 85D3
'77 data rptd 4-10, Jan-Mar 4-20, 282C1-B2
Lobbyist's role in energy policy questnd 5-15, 408F2-C3
Jan-June imports, other data rptd 7-19, 589G3-590B1
Law firm dual-rep case refused by Sup Ct 11-6, 874A1
Mex claims huge new reserves 11-13, 903F2
Gas supplies rptd adequate 12-1, 939A1
PETRO-Lewis Corp.
Shenandoah Oil purchase planned 5-15, 403G3-404A1
PETROV, Gen. Vasily Ivanovich
Rptd in Ethiopia 2-24, 137E1
PETROV, Vladimir
USSR wins world hockey title 5-14, 458D3
PETRY, Heinz
Iran completes Krupp paymts 7-27, 617C1
PETTIS, Jerry L. (d. 1975)
Lewis wins US House seat 11-7, 856F3
PETTIS, Rep. Shirley (R, Calif.)
Lewis wins seat 11-7, 856F3
PEUGEOT-Citroen, P.S.A.
To buy Chrysler Eur units 8-10, 623C2-F3
UK OKs Chrysler sale 9-28, 764D1
PEVERALL, John
Deer Hunter released 12-14, 1030F2
PEYREFITTE, Alain
Renamed French justice min 4-5, 245F2
Scores Chirac 12-15, Gaullist rift rptd 12-19, 987D2
Gaullists suspend 12-20, 1016D3
PEYROT, Yves
Faces of Love released 7-7, 970C1
PEYSER, Peter A.
Wins US House seat 11-7, 849A2, 851F3
PFEIFFER, Jane Cahill
Named NBC chrmn, RCA dir 9-13, 759B3
PFIZER Inc.
Forgn natn tetracycline trust suit OKd 1-11, 33E3
PFIZER Inc. v. Government of India
Foreign natn trust suit OKd 1-11, 33A3
PFLP (Popular Front for the Liberation of Palestine)—*See MIDDLE EAST*
PGA (Professional Golfers' Association)—*See GOLF*
PHARAON, Ghaith R.
Lance bank deal linked to loan repaymts, Abedi role rptd 2-13, 204D3

1979

PETROLEUM Association of America, Independent
Jan-Apr wholesale gas price rise rptd 5-7, 343E1
PETROLEUM Institute, American (API)
Oil co pipe divestiture scored 1-4, 55G2
'78 oil demand rptd slowed 1-18, 35G3
Smog rule protested 1-26, 90F1
OTA oil shortage forecast disputed 3-10, 188B1
1st 1/4 gas demand rise rptd 4-22, 343E1
'78 oil reserves rptd down 4-30, 324B3
DiBona on Carter mtg 5-31, 418E1
1st 1/2 oil imports, productn rptd 7-19, 557D2
Swearington scores Carter 'amateurs' 9-12, 703A1
Heating fuel inventories rptd up 9-19, 703C2
DiBona vs industry protest 10-17, 831D2, F2
DiBona defends 3d 1/4 profits 10-25, 804E2
PETRONE, Joe
Hired as Drillers coach 7-23, fired 9-19, 1004E2
PETROVA, Totka
Banned from track 10-26, 912A1
PETTI, Deborah
Enchanted Pig opens 4-23, 711F2
PETTY, Richard
Wins Daytona 500 2-20, 490F3
Wins 7th NASCAR Gr Natl title; top $ winner 11-18, 1005A2
PEUGEOT-Citroen, P.S.A.
Spain exec kidnaped 2-21, 192C1
Lorraine plant plans rptd 4-25, 299B3
PEYREFITTE, Alain
Goldman death probe backed 9-26, 772A3
On Boulin suicide note chrgs 10-31, 835D1, G1
Boulin successor named 11-8, 872G3
PEYREFITTE, Roger
Nest of Vipers released 9-7, 820C2
PEYROT, Yves
Your Turn, My Turn released 1-27, 175A1
PEZZULLO, Lawrence A.
Presses Somoza to quit 6-28, 475E3, G3
Urcuyo challenges peace plan 7-17, 535A2
US to continue Nicaragua econ aid 7-19, 574A2
Meets Borge 7-28, bars US war role in Nicaragua 7-30, 573E2, G2
PFEFFER, Kirk
2d in NYC Marathon 10-21, 911E3
PFEIFFER Co., P. C.
Onshore dockers injury benefits upheld by Sup Ct 11-27, 919C3
PFISTER, Hank
Australian Open results 1-3, 103D2
PFLP (Popular Front for the Liberation of Palestine)—*See MIDDLE EAST*
PGA (Professional Golfers' Association)—*See GOLF*
PHANTASM (film)
Released 6-1, 820G2
PHARAON, Ghaith R.
Cited re Lance '78 oil deal influence chrg 4-9, 306B1

1980

PETROLEUM Association of America, Independent
Windfall profits tax suit filed 10-14, 960D2
PETROLEUM Institute, American (API)
'79 US consumptn, productn drop, supplies rptd 1-17, 90A2
US oil supplies, Feb deliveries rptd 3-12, 250A3
Windfall oil profits tax scored 4-2, 244F2
Oil indus solar monopoly denied 5-5, 554A1
1st 1/2 oil imports, gas consumptn rptd down 7-24, 553A1
US record oil inventories rptd 9-5, 795G3
Jan-July oil import decline rptd 9-6, 785C3
PETRO-Lewis Corp.
Doric Petroleum merger set 8-26, 745F2
Barber Oil unit bought 10-2, 986A1
PETROMAR Services
Hunts interest rptd 5-28, 426E1
PETRO Processors of Louisiana Inc.
La chem-dump suit names 7-15, 559A1
PETROU, Pandelis
Slain 1-16, 150D3
PETROV, Alexei
Warning on Polish unions rptd 9-27; E Ger, Czechs publish 9-30, 752F3, 753D1
PETROV, Boris N.
Death rptd 8-26, 676E2
PETROV, Petar
Wins Olympic medal 7-25, 623G3
PETRUSEVA, Natalya
Wins world speed title 1-13, sets 1000-m mark 3-27, 470E1, B2
Wins Olympic medals 2-14, 2-17, 156B1
PETTINE, Judge Raymond J.
Upholds gay prom date 5-28, 471C1
PETTITI, Louis-Edmond
On UN comm to probe shah 2-17, 122B1
PETZOLD, Barbara
Wins Olympic medal 2-18, 155C3
PEUGEOT S.A. (formerly P.S.A. Peugeot-Citroen)
Chrysler productn talks, finance deal rptd 2-6, 127D2
Research collaboratn set 4-22, 303B3
Chrysler to sell imports 6-2, 457C1
Chrysler engine deal confrmd 7-17, 541E2
Fiat project set 9-15, 751F3*
PEYREFITTE, Alain
Assemb OKs crime bill 6-21, 497F3
Le Monde editors chrgd 11-7, 872C1
PEYSER, Rep. Peter A. (D, N.Y.)
Abscam evidence request res defeated 2-27, 143G2
Reelected 11-4, 843F3
PEZZOLI, Walter
Killed 12-11, 966C3
PEZZULLO, Lawrence A.
At Sandinistas anniv fete 7-19, 565F2
Scores Reagan Latin policy 12-11, 942C1
PFAFF, Jean-Marie
W Ger wins Eur Soccer Championship 6-22, 771F2
PFEFFER, Thomas
Wins Olympic medal 7-24, 623D2
PFEIFFER, Jane Cahill
Sees Silverman 7-7, relieved of duties 7-8; resigns as NBC chrmn, RCA dir 7-10, 582B1
PFEIL, Mark
Wins Tallahassee Open 4-21, 714F3
PFISTER, Hank
Wins French Open men's doubles 6-7, 606F3
PGA (Professional Golfers' Association)
See GOLF
PHARAON, Ghaith R.
Holding in Occidental noted 7-14, 542D3

1976

PHARMACEUTICAL Manufacturers Association
Prescriptn drug panel formed 11-30, 931G2
PHARMACOLOGY—*See 'Drugs' under MEDICINE*
PHARRIS (U.S. warship)
In Intl Naval Review 7-4, 488D3
PHAT, Huynh Tan
Vows to punish govt foes 5-25, 441G2
United Viet deputy premier 7-3, 502F3
PHELPS Dodge Corp.
Australia mining deal rptd 7-28, 571G3-572B1
'75 zero tax paymt rptd 10-2, 847F1
PHICHAI Rataku
Assures on US mil exit 7-19, 541G3
PHILADELPHIA, Pa.—*See PENNSYLVANIA*
PHILADELPHIA Bulletin (newspaper)
Rpts Scott tax notice 9-12, 980F1
PHILADELPHIA Daily News
Carter endorsement rptd 10-30, 831B3
PHILADELPHIA Gear Overseas Corp.
Arab boycott rpt released 10-20, 786A2
PHILADELPHIA Inquirer (newspaper)
Auth wins Pulitzer 5-3, 352E3
Ford endorsement rptd 10-30, 831F2
PHILADELPHIA Orchestra
Wins Hall of Fame award 2-28, 460E3
PHILANTHROPY
Wm Blakely dies 1-5, 56A3
H R MacMillan dies 2-9, 160E3
Sup Ct void NJ canvassers curb 5-19, 393C3
A Rockefeller Mauze dies 5-27, 404B2
GOP platform text 8-18, 608B2
CAB accuses Flying Tiger 12-29, 986F1
PHILIP Morris Inc.
DR paymts detailed, denied 12-28, 1001B2
PHILIPPEAUX, Adolfo
Arrest rptd 3-26, 236D3

PHILIPPINES, Republic of the—*See also ADB, ASEAN*
Listed as 'partly free' 1-19, 20D3
Marcos bars vote, keeps powers 1-21, 75A3
2 priests deported 103C2
Troops detain strikers 1-30, 103B2
Mil command shakeup 3-27, 255B3
Macapagal vs Marcos rule 4-1, 255C2
RC group chrgs torture 4-23, 313C3
Rebel-govt clashes rptd 4-26, 313A3
Sin named cardinal 4-27, 336C2
Typhoon Olga hits 5-20, Luzon declared disaster area 5-24, 404E2
Rebels hijack jet 5-21, free 14 5-22; troops attack, 13 die, 3 rebels held 5-23, 383B3
Manila decreed capital 5-31, in effect 6-24, 500F1
Air Manila jet crashes in Guam 6-4, 736A2
Aquino trial starts, bars defense 8-3; boycotts 8-11, 695D1
Quake hits, emergency declared 8-17—8-20, 619G1
Quake toll at 8,000 8-22, 638B3
Rebels kill 7 8-23, 9-4, 695C1
NPA leaders captured 8-26, 638F2
3 CP officials rptd seized 638A3
Marcos to keep martial law; 25 seized rebels appear 8-27, 694G3
Amnesty Intl chrgs torture 9-15, probe vowed 9-28; 6 ordrd punished 9-29, 751C3
Anti-referendum dvpts 9-29, 10-10, 10-13, 839C1
Vote boycott asked 9-30, protest march thwarted 10-3, 752A1
Prisoners start hunger strike 10-2, 751F3
Referendum backs martial law 10-16—10-17; results 10-18, 839B1
6 die in Jolo blast 10-17, 839C1
Soldiers ousted for torture 11-8, 855B2
Priest seized, radio statns shut 11-19, 890E1
Communists raid Mabalacat 11-24, 1009D1
Rebel peace talks set in Libya 11-27; talks held, pact ends revolt 12-15—12-23; cease-fire 12-24; plebiscite set 12-27, 1008B3

Foreign Relations (misc.)
Natls quit S Vietnam 1-3, 11G3
Australia in SE Asia talks 1-16—1-17, 46B1, D1
Swedish oil pact signed 1-21, 104B1
Group of 77 mtg held; Marcos pledge to UNCTAD fund 2-10, 107G3
SEATO formally disbanded 2-20, 148C1
Sovt sugar purchase data disputed 3-12—3-15, 278B2
Macapagal denied US asylum 4-1, 255C2
Total IMF oil loan rptd 4-1, 339F3, 340E2
Jet hijacked 4-7, arrives Libya 4-13, hostages freed 4-14, 260B2

1977

PHARMACOLOGY—*See MEDICINE—Drugs*
PHELAN, John
Third in mayoral vote 11-8, 855C3
PHELPS Dodge Corp.
Raises copper price 3-21, 209C2
Strike begins 7-1, 558G1
Copper prices cut 7-2, 7-20, 577D2
3d ¼ loss rptd 11-2, 859G1
PHELPS Stokes Fund (N.Y.)
Smythe confrmd amb to Cameroon 5-9, 418A2
PHENCYCLIDINE (PCP)—*See NARCOTICS*
PHENFORMIN (Meltrol)—*See MEDICINE—Drugs*
PHILADELPHIA, Pa.—*See PENNSYLVANIA*
PHILADELPHIA Inquirer (newspaper)
2 win Pulitzer 4-18, 355F2
Foreman tied to state sen 8-27, quits NY Times 9-12, 920E3
PHILADELPHIA Life Insurance Co.
Tenneco buys 8-25, 650F3
PHILADELPHIA Orchestra
Leopold Stokowski dies 9-13, 788G2
PHILADELPHIA Stock Exchange
Options trading expanded 3-4, 521E1
Shut 7-14, 537B3
SEC limits optns trading, begins probe 10-18, 859C3
SEC scores natl mkt move delay, ITS cited 12-1, 1004F1
PHILANTHROPY
White House backs phone ad curbs 10-21, 921C1
Obituaries
Coleman, John 2-23, 164D2
Jain, Shanti Prasad 10-27, 872D2
Lilly, Ely 1-24, 84C3
Murphy, Charles 9-20, 788A2
PHILCO-Ford
Indonesia contract rptd 1-25, 182C3
PHILIP, Prince (Duke of Edinburgh) (Great Britain)
Arrives Australia 3-7, 199D1
Daughter rptd pregnant 4-8, 396A3
In Canada 10-14—10-19, 822A2
In Bahamas 10-20, 844A3
PHILIP II, King (Macedon) (382-336 B.C.)
Tomb found 11-24, 952D1
PHILIP Morris Inc.
In USSR deal 1-17, 47F2
Indonesia exit rptd planned 4-18, 392A3

PHILIPPINES, Republic of the—*See also ASEAN, SEATO*
Bishops meet 1-25—1-29, score govt 2-6, 99D3
2 Marcos plotter trials delayed 2-7; 4 others sentncd 2-10, 100A1
Pilot slays 7 in robbery plot 3-31, 312F3
Tenant ldr arrested 4-25; torture chrgd, freed 5-13, 468D2
6 die in govt-CP rebel clash 5-6, 468C3
Mil cts to be phased out 6-3, 468B2
Aquino chrgs views silenced 7-6, 619A1
Right group chrgs torture 7-31, 618B3
Martial law eased 8-22; Marcos warns extensn 8-26, 665C1
Rights abuse protested by 2000 8-25, 664G3
55 prisoners freed 8-27, 665D1
Aquino trial witness, 4 others slain 9-1, 746G3-747A1
Amnesty Intl lists jailed legislators 9-5, 753B2
Marcos plotters flee jail 10-1—10-2, 803A3
Sison captured 11-10, 1019B2
Manila hotel fire, typhoon 11-13—11-14, 928F3
Aquino, 2 others get death sentence 11-25; new trial ordrd 11-28, 947A1
Mental hosp blaze 12-16, 1023A3

Foreign Relations (misc.)
UN Assemb Member 4A1
In USSR sugar deal 1-18, 47F2
IMF loan set 2-4, 87F2
Australia uranium sought 3-8, 218C1
Moslem pact reached in Libya 3-20, 341C3
CP rebels get China arms 6-11, 468B3
Viet refugees barred 6-19, 497F1
World Food Cncl meets 6-20—6-24, 513C3
ICJ chrgs rights abuses 7-31, 618B3
Malaysian Sabah claim dropped 8-4, 607G1

1978

PHARES, Robert A.
Loses primary for Neb gov 5-9, 363D1
PHARMACEUTICAL Manufacturing Association (PMA)
Drug law revisns scored 3-16, 231G1-A2
PHEGLEY, Roger
In NBA draft 6-9, 457G2
PHELPS Dodge Corp.
'76 tax nonpaymt rptd 1-27, 65G2
US sues re price fixing 9-22, 768G3
PHILADELPHIA, Pa.—*See PENNSYLVANIA*
PHILADELPHIA Electric Co.
'76 tax nonpaymt rptd 1-27, 65G2
PHILADELPHIA Inquirer, The (newspaper)
Wins Pulitzer pub svc medal, 2 rptrs honored 4-17, 315A1, D1
PHILADELPHIA Journal (newspaper)
'77 debut cited 1-9, 75F3
PHILADELPHIA Newspapers Inc. v. Jerome
Pa gag-order case remanded 1-9, 13F1
PHILADELPHIA v. New Jersey
NJ waste dumping law voided by US Sup Ct 6-23, 566B2
PHILANTHROPY
Pallottine priest indicted 1-6, 24A3
Payson museum pledge ordrd paid 7-11, 579C2
Obituaries
Fosburgh, Mary Cushing 11-4, 972B3
Koussevtizky, Olga 1-5, 96E2
Meadows, Algur Hurtle 6-10, 540C3
Rockefeller 3d, John D 7-10, 620D3
PHILCO Overseas Services—*See FORD Motor Co.*
PHILIP Morris Inc.
WTA ends Va Slims pact 4-21, 419B2
7-Up takeover sought 5-1, 5-11; bid OKd, '77 earnings cited 5-15, 364F2-C3
Liggett forgn operatns purchased 7-26, 718C1
Miller Brewing Co.
'Lite' trademark case review barred 1-9, 13C1
'77 sales, 'Lite' beer success cited 5-15, 364B3
PHILIPPE, Claudius C.
Dies 12-25, 1032D3

PHILIPPINES, Republic of the—*See also ASEAN*
86 mayors purged 1-15, 55B3
Marcos calls for Assemb electns 1-17; Liberals to boycott 2-3, reverse decisn 2-16, 268G3
Electns, Marcos party wins 4-7; fraud chrgd 4-8, 4-9; seized protesters freed 4-11, 268G2
Govt drive vs Communist rebels rptd 4-15, 290C2
Local electns postponed 5-26, 455C1
Imelda Marcos gets new Cabt post 6-1, 475G2
Oppositn ldrs freed 6-3, 455A1
631 detainees amnestied 6-10, 475E2
Marcos chooses Cabt 6-11, 475F2
Marcos sworn premr, Natl Assemb convenes, 6-12, 475C2
AF jet crashes in storm 9-14, 758B3
Typhoon Rita hits 10-27, 314 rptd dead 11-6, 972C2

Foreign Relations (misc.)—*See also 'Monetary, Trade, Aid & Investment' below*
Spratly isle occupied, China protests 3-11, 290F1
Forgn newsmen tied to electn unrest 4-10; 2 get Marcos protest 4-11, 269A1
UN Assemb member 713D3
Cambodia dep premr visits 10-19, 803F2
China-US ties lauded 12-16, 977D1
Viet refugee boat barred 12-27, 997F2
Monetary, Trade, Aid & Investment
Viet trade missn ended 21B3
USSR offers PI A-plant 1-5, 2-14, 134B3

1979

PHENYLPROPANOLAMINE—*See MEDICINE-Drugs*
PHI Delta Kappa (national honor society)
Test scores of future teachers drop 10-4, 810G1
PHILADELPHIA, Pa.—*See PENNSYLVANIA*
PHILADELPHIA Inquirer, The (newspaper)
Cramer wins Pulitzer 4-16, 336B3
Sunday circulatn listed 6-6, 431D1
'60s drug tests of Holmesburg prisoners rptd 11-25, 947E1
PHILADELPHIA Orchestra
Ormandy announces retiremt 4-3, 272F1
PHILADELPHIA Stock Exchange
SEC asks options trading overhaul 2-15, freeze end seen 2-22, 348B3
PHILANTHROPY
Ford Foundatn names new pres 1-30, 78D3
J Rockefeller lifetime donatns total $94 mln 7-10, 656B3
Emory U gets $100 mln gift 11-8, 902C2
Obituaries
Belmont, Eleanor 10-24, 860A2
Brown, John N 10-9, 860A2
Knowles, John H 3-6, 272A3
Rosenwald, Lessing J 6-24, 508E3
Sawyer, Charles 4-7, 356G3
Strauss, Anna Lord 2-23, 176F3
PHILATELY
US inflatn 'hedge' demand cited 3-16, 264G2
Kenny fined in Cook I stamp schmeme 6-2, 648C2
Haas collectn sold for record sum 8-14, 672G1
PHILBY, Kim
Spy ring scandal reopened 10-28, 10-29, 873G3
Blunt named 4th spy 11-15, 908D2-B3
PHILIP, Prince (Duke of Edinburgh) (Great Britain)
Tours Arab states 2-12—3-2, 190C1
PHILIP Morris Inc.
FTC subpoena compliance ordrd 1-25, 91D3
Navratilova wins Avon title 3-25, 391B2
Fortune rpts '78 rank, 7-Up acquisitn cited 5-7, 305B1
PHILIPPINE Airlines
China, Taiwan flights OKd 7-8, 567D1
Chrmn named in McDonnell Douglas paymts chrg 11-9, 886D2

PHILIPPINES, Republic of the
Cabt shuffled, econ ills cited 7-23, 566G3-567A1
Probe of Macapagal, others set 9-7, suspended 9-12, 710A1
Cardinal Sin tells of unrest 9-7, 710C1
Marcos vs end to martial law 9-10, 9-14; vs Aquino release 9-14, 710D1-G1
Macapagal probe resumes 9-19, 815E1
Students protest 9-26, 24 arrested 10-10, 815G1
1,602 prisoners freed 9-27, 815A2
Atomic Energy & Safeguards
Westinghouse project halted 6-15, 487G3

Foreign Relations (misc.)—*See also 'UN' below*
Viet boat people evacuated 1-8, 51F2
Canada, Australia to admit Viet refugees 2-12, 109A1
Civil war refugees flee to Malaysia 3-5, 193C1
216 Viet refugees flown to Canada 4-5, 299G1
Island offered for Viet refugee processing 5-16, 379B2
More Indochina refugee admissns barred 6-30; US, Japan seek aid 7-2, 495A2

1980

PHELAN Jr., John J.
Elected NYSE pres 5-22, 456A3
PHELPS Dodge Corp.
USW strike settled 10-8, 805D2
Alusuisse buys Consolidated Alum share 11-23, 985C2
PHILADELPHIA—*See MISSISSIPPI, PENNSYLVANIA*
PHILADELPHIA Inquirer, The (newspaper)
Wins Pulitzer 4-14, 296C2, F2
Schaffer cited for silence on Abscam source 7-10, 554A2
Foreman marries Cianfrani 7-14, 890B2
Carter pres endorsemt rptd 11-1, 844E1
PHILADELPHIA Bulletin, The (newspaper)
Sold to Charter Media 4-10, 376F3
Charter Media dissolved; Eller retains ownership 9-30, 836C2
Charter Co acquires from Eller 11-6, 907G1-A2
PHILADELPHIA Electric Co.
Gilkeson backs utility cost sharing 12-10, 961E1
PHILADELPHIA Journal (newspaper)
4-day strike ends 1-25, 115F2
PHILADELPHIA Stock Exchange
SEC censures on policing practices 3-13, 224F2-B3
SEC ends optns trading ban 3-26, 224B2
Natl securities mkt failure scored 9-12, 806F1
New options issues banned 10-10, 986E2
Wetherill retires, Giordano elected pres 12-18, 959A2
PHILADELPHIA Symphony Orchestra
Ormandy gives final concert 8-23, 908D1
PHILANTHROPY
Charity solicitatn limit voided by Sup Ct 2-20, 170A2
Harper's bought 7-9, 582A3
Obituaries
Reynolds, Julia 11-28, 1004B3
Stern, Edith 9-11, 756D2
Westheimer, Irvin F 12-30, 1004F3
PHILATELY
US halts Moscow Olympic commemorative sale 3-11, 206A2
British Guiana stamp sold for record sum; photo 4-5, 472C2, D2
Liechtenstein cancels Olympic stamp issue 5-2, 379D2
PHILBY, Kim
Honored by USSR 7-15, 566G2-B3
PHILCO—*See GENERAL Telephone & Electronics Corp. (GTE)*
PHILIP, Prince (Duke of Edinburgh) (Great Britain)
Awards Templeton prize 5-13, 471D2
PHILIP Morris Inc.
Miller Brewing Co.
'Lite' trademark case refused by Sup Ct 2-19, 131A1

PHILIPPINES, Republic of the—*See also ADB, ASEAN*
Economy & Labor
Manila purchasing power rptd low 2-12, 125E3
Defns-GNP ratio rptd 2-19, 132G1
Aquino family farm expropriated 5-7, 354E2
8 union ldrs arrested 9-9, 710B1

Foreign Relations (misc.)—*See also 'UN Policy' below*
Pacific orgn studied 1-20, 78C2
China claims Spratly, Paracel I 1-30, 132D3
US-bound Viet refugees arrive in Bataan 2-22, 141B2
Chile pres cancels 11-day Asian tour 3-22, cuts ties 3-24; assassinatn plot revealed 3-25, 230F3-231E1
Moscow Olympics role canceled 3-28, 259F3
Chile ties restored 4-2, 311D2
Vatican issues clergy reassignmt plan 7-22, 970G1

1976

Libya bars hijackers asylum 4-15, hostages return to PI 4-16, 313B3
Marcos at UNCTAD conf, Kenyatta boycotts 5-5, 320G1
Marcos in Moscow, Sovt ties set 5-31—6-2, 440F1
Fishermen die in US Navy test bombings 6-14, 6-18, 6-28; PI asks halt 7-13, US agrees 7-14, 539B2
2 nurses chrgd in US VA hosp deaths 6-16, 503E3
Amnesty Intl chrgs torture 6-26, govt to probe 6-27, 500D1
Vietnam sets ties 7-12, 593D2
Libya rebel arms aid rptd 7-15, 531F1
US GOP platform text cites 8-18, 609A3
Ford quake aid offer rptd 619C2
US triples sugar duties 9-21, 721D3
IMF-World Bank mtgs in Manila 10-4—10-8, 777A1
Forgn press scored 10-22, 855G1
US newsman ousted 11-2; forgn newsmen protest 11-5; security cited 11-6, 855D1
Canada immigratn rptd 11-3, 851E1
2 US clerics ousted 11-18, 11-20, 890C1
US base pact agrmt disputed 12-1—12-6, PI rejcts offer 12-4, 926D2
Islamic States Conf aids rebel pact 12-15—12-23, 1008F3

PHILIPS' Gloellampenfabriken, N.V.
Off Arab blacklist 3-24—4-3, 242C1
PHILLIPS, Dr. Robert
Dies 9-20, 1015D2
PHILLIPS Exeter (N.H.) Academy
Reagan visits 2-10, 109B2
PHILLIPS Petroleum Co.
SEC lists paymts 5-12, 725G3, 728E2
Tax fraud chrgd 9-2, 725F2

1977

World Law Conf held 8-22—8-26; dels in rights protest 8-25, 664B3
Libya denies aid to rebels 10-17, 824F2
E Ger trade pact set 12-7, 1000B2

Moslem Rebellion
Rebel peace talks held 2-5—3-3; impasse rptd 3-5, new try set 3-10, 202D2
Qaddafi tied to rebel revolt 3-10, 202A3
Govt, rebels set for new clashes 202B3
Moslem autonomy pact agreed in Libya 3-20; Marcos rpts agrmt 3-26, reassures Christns 3-29, 241C3
Voters bar southn autonomous region 4-17, final returns 4-23; map 330C1
Moslems reject plebiscite 4-20, 330G1
Govt-rebel talks resume 4-21, collapse 4-30; rebels asked to give up 6-11, 468F2
Sept toll updated 803G2
24 die in terror blast, govt drive vs rebels 9-20; fighting spreads 9-21, 746D3
Govt, rebels seek combat halt 10-1—10-2, 803G2
53 die in Basilan clash 10-2, 803G2
33 troops slain on Jolo 10-10, govt massacre chrgd 10-12, 803E2
Govt-rebel clashes 10-12—10-26, 824G1
Libya denies aid to rebels 10-17, 824F2
Communists join Moslem rebels 10-19, 824C2
Jan-Oct casualty toll 10-20, 824D2
11 die near Zamboanga 10-26, 885C3
Govt captures Moslem camp 11-1, 885B3
5-yr civiln death toll rptd 11-7, 885D3

U.S. Relations
US rpts rights abuses, urges contd mil aid 1-1, 51G1
Marcos scores US rights rpt, threatens to end mil ties 1-7; eases stand 1-24, 83G2
US chrgs GTE paymts 1-12, 79F2-D3
CIA paymts to Magsaysay rptd 2-19, 124F1
US modifies duty-free list 2-28, 189E3
US issues rights rpt 3-12, 187B1, C1
US pressure frees tenant ldr 5-13, 468D2
US arms aid authorized 8-4, 668C1
Rights abuses chrgd, PI defends 8-21, 8-25, 664G3
US mil base talks 9-22—9-23, joint statemt 9-24, 824F2-B3
Marcos plotters escape to US 10-1—10-2, 803A3
US vs Aquino convictn 11-27, gets trial record 11-28, 947D1

PHILLION, Romeo
Lie detector ban upheld 3-22, 237C3
PHILLIPS, Jackson
On Moody's NYC note rating 11-10, 881D1
PHILLIPS, Capt. Mark
Son born 11-14, christened 12-22, 1021E2
PHILLIPS, Peter Mark Andrew
Born 11-14, christened 12-22, 1021E2
PHILLIPS, Rubel L.
Convicted 1-29, 103F1 ★, G1
Sentenced 3-11, 203A3
PHILLIPS, Sam
Elvis Presley dies 8-16, 695E3
PHILLIPS Petroleum Co.
Gulf of Mex gas probe set 2-17, 151F3
Gasoline output process rptd 3-23, 278G1
North Sea Ekofisk oil slick dissolved 5-2, 336E2, A3
Alaska pipeline opens 6-20, 476B3; ICC set rates 6-28, 498F1
Seadock support rptd 7-19, 559F2
Danes OK Norpipe gas line 8-1, 672E1
Washington state sues 8-16, 691E3
US trust suit setld 8-31, 691D3
Ekofisk blowout blamed on human error 10-10, 967B3
Helium dispute case declined 10-31, 11-28, 919F2
Pleads guilty, fined re pol paymts 11-22, 944B1
PHILLIPS Petroleum Co. v. Ashland Oil Inc.
Helium dispute case declined 10-31, 11-28, 919A3
PHILLIPS-Van Heusen Corp.
'76 Fortune 500 list drops 341D1

1978

US ct OKs tetracycline trust suit 1-11, 33D3
Westinghouse A-contract fee rptd 1-13; Marcos orders probe, Herdis group sale 1-16, 38C2
US queries Westinghouse A-plant 2-8, 2-14, 134C3
US rights rpt notes aid level 2-9, 101D3
A-fuel export license deferral rptd 5-20, 408B2
Australia safeguards pact signed 8-7, 666G1
China oil claims cited 10-16, 871G2
Trade missn rptd in Japan 10-18, 798D1
Mex pres in oil talks 11-4—11-5, 904B1
US mil base-econ aid pact signed 12-31, 1000F2

Moslem Rebellion
Govt drive pressed on Jolo, Mindanao 1-17—1-28, 73E3-74A1
Rebels seize exec 1-20, free 2 forgn kidnap victims 2-2, 3-12, 248A2
Jolo cmdr, rebels surrender 2-26, 3-1; hq bombed, col rptd held 3-3, 248F1
43 die in rebel ambush 4-13, 290B2
Rebels seize 56 hostages 4-30; rescue drive launched 5-1, hostages freed 5-23, 439G3
Islamic conf urges govt rebel talks, govt OK cited 650G1
Rebel attacks 7-4, 8-13; drive rptd widened 7-30, 650E1

U.S. Relations—*See also 'Monetary, Trade, Aid & Investment' above*
US troop presence rptd 1-2, 5D2
US issues rights rpt, aid level noted 2-9, 101D3, 102E1
2 newsmen chrgd re electn rptg 4-11, 269C1
Mondale visit debated in US 4-28, 360C3
Mondale visits; sees Marcos, govt foes, stresses rights 5-2—5-3, 360D3
ITT paymts chrgd 11-2, 876C1
McDonnell Douglas paymts rptd 12-15, 982F2
US-China ties lauded 12-16, 977D1
US alerts naval force for shift to Iran 12-29, 993C1, 994D1
Mil base pact signed 12-31, 1000F2

PHILIPS' Lamps Holdings
Brazil workers strike 5-17—5-23, 412C1
PHILLIPS, Claude
Sued on Amoco Cadiz spill 9-13, 749C1
PHILLIPS, Ethan
Modigliani opens 5-17, 760E2
PHILLIPS, Louis
Ballroom in St Patrick's opens 12-1, 1031A1
PHILLIPS, Rubel L.
Fraud convictn review denied by Sup Ct 10-2, 751E2
PHILLIPS Petroleum Co.
UK hikes offshore oil tax 8-2, 591G3
Pacific bought by Petro-Canada 11-10, 11-20, 901B2

1979

China trade pact signed, '78 data cited 7-8, 567B1
Indochina refugee asylum vowed at intl conf 7-20—7-21, 549D1
85 Viet refugees rptd shot 7-22, 550A2
Viet refugees land 9-3—10-9, 763F3
Taiwan extends offshore zones 9-6, 733F3
Spratly Islands annexed 9-7, 660B3
Iran frees natls in US Emb 11-22, 895A3

UN Policy & Developments
Viet refugee plan OKd 3-30, 299G1
UNCTAD mtg held 5-7—6-3, 417A3
Membership listed 695A3

U.S. Relations
US naval move cited 1-2, 3E1
CIA alleged agent named 1-4, 17C3
US issues rights rpt 2-10, 107D2
Viet refugees get asylum 2-12, 109A1
US warship leaves for Arabian Sea 3-7, 157E2
Laetrile shipmt recalled 3-8, 196A1
Ford stockholders suit barred 3-8, 202A3
Westinghouse A-projct suspended 6-15, 487G3
US asks Indochina refugee asylum 7-2, 495D2
US denies spy aid 8-9, 664D2
Mondale in refugee talks 9-1, 660A3
Marcos vs Aquino release 9-14, 710E1
Macapagal scores Carter 9-15, 815F1
Students protest 9-26, 815A2
McDonnell Douglas paymts alleged 11-9, 886G1, D2
Anti-US protest dispersed 11-30, 915C1, D1

PHILLIPS, Charles
NFL '78 interceptn ldr 1-6, 80D1
PHILLIPS, John
Cited in H-bomb letter 9-16, 9-18, 717A2
PHILLIPS, Peter
Warriors opens 5-22, 712D3
PHILLIPS, Richie
Baseball umpires' strike setld 5-18, 569D2
PHILLIPS, Thomas L.
On Raytheon-Beech Aircraft merger 10-2, 785C1
PHILLIPS Petroleum Co.
US files overchrg suit 1-5, 17B1
Gas allocatns cut 30% 2-21, 126C2
July gas supplies rptd 6-25, 479E1
Gasohol marketing test cited 8-10, 649G1
'79 heating oil price freeze attempt seen 9-19, 703E1
3d 1/4 profits rptd up 10-25, 804D3
Australian exploratn lease won 11-27, 926A1

1980

Panamanian freighter, US aircraft carrier collide 7-29, 675E1
Iranians demonstrate in Manila 8-8, 635A2
Malaysian Sabah State claim dropped 10-31, 902E3

Government & Politics—*See also other appropriate subheads in this section*
Info min ousted 1-17, 100B3
Marcos party wins local electns 1-30; fraud charged 2-4, 100A3
Marcos ordrs electn fraud probe 2-6; admits party fraud 2-11, 152D2
2 quit ruling party 2-11; 4 groups seek merger 2-12, 152E2
Aquino freed from detentn 5-8, 354D2
Marcos protesters chrgd 7-5; subversn crackdown set 7-20, 566B1
Marcos murder plot chrgd 8-5, 672E3
Aquino asks return to democracy 8-20, 673D3
Anti-Marcos group formed 8-29, 672A3
Marcos rpts son's life threatened 11-16, 902A3

Sports
Moscow Olympics role canceled, funding blamed 3-28, 259F3
Arrozal loses WBA flywgt challenge 6-29, 1000G3

UN Policy & Developments
Cncl seat taken 1-1, 12B2

Unrest
Moslems attack Mindanao cities 2-23, 3-9; Marcos issues warning 2-26, asks peace talks 3-18, 235A1
Freedom march 7-4, dissenters chrgd 7-5; arrests ordrd 7-20, 566B1
Aquino warns of violence 8-4, 8-20, 672C3
Underground group chrgd 8-5, 672G3
Iranians protest in Manila 8-8, 635A2
Manila area anti-govt blasts 8-22, 672C3
8 union ldrs arrested 9-9, 710B1
Manila terrorist bombings 9-12; Marcos orders crackdown 9-13, 709E3
20 die in terrorist bombings 9-20—9-26; Marcos links Aquino 9-20, 752E2
US tourism conf warnings issued 10-1, 10-4, parley bombed 10-19; arrests ordrd 10-20, martial law extensn threatened 10-21, 809D1-A2
Manila area bomb blasts 10-4, 10-11; new curbs decreed 10-11, 809A2
Marcos death plot chrgd 10-28, 23 arraigned 11-3, 874D2
US tourism conf delegate admits bombing, 3 others held 10-31, 874A2
Moslem rebellion rptd ending 10-31, 902D3

U.S. Relations
MacArthur WWII 'gift' dispute rptd 1-30, 1-31, 115E1
US Persian Gulf troop deploymt rptd 2-12, 106C2
US-bound Viet refugees arrive in Bataan 2-22, 141B2
US gonorrhea epidemic rptd 4-9, 584G3
US OKs Westinghouse A-reactor 5-6, 440E3
Aquino flies to US for med treatmt 5-8, 354D2
US aircraft carrier, Panamanian freighter collide, 2 killed 7-29, 675E1
Aquino in US, sees anti-govt violence 8-4, 8-20, 672C3
US natl chrgd in Marcos murder plot 8-5, 672F3
Iranians demonstrate at US Emb 8-8, 635A2
US woman killed in Manila bombing 9-12, 709F3
Marcos warns foes vs US role 9-20, 752B3
Westinghouse plant constructn resumes 9-25, 752C3
Manila tourism conf warnings issued 10-1, 10-4; parley bombed 10-19, arrests ordrd 10-20, 809D1
Marcos on tourism conf bombing suspects 10-31, 874A2, C2
Marcos's son's life rptd threatnd 11-16; Marcos asks US protectn 11-17, 902A3

PHILLIP, Peter Winston
Arrested 6-3, 420C2
PHILLIP, Strachen
Killed 6-20, 498D2
PHILLIPS, Bum (Oail Andrew)
Fired as Oilers coach, gen mgr 12-31, 999F1
PHILLIPS, Dayton
Dies 10-23, 876C3
PHILLIPS, Howard
Political role profiled 7-11—9-15, 819G1
PHILLIPS, James
Executed 4-22, 353G1
PHILLIPS, Janice
Convicted of mail fraud 2-9, 157C2, F2
PHILLIPS, John Aristotle
Loses US House electn 11-4, 848C1
PHILLIPS, Lincoln
Brand breaks NASL shutout mark 7-3, 770A1
PHILLIPS Petroleum Co.
N Sea oil platform capsizes, 123 killed 3-27, 256G1
Wholesale gas price cut rptd 8-8, 666D3
Price setlmt OKd 9-25, 960E1

PHILLIPS-Van Heusen Corp.
US-China textile pact opposed 9-18, 707D1

1976

PHILOSOPHY
Martin Heidegger dies 5-26, 404G1-A2
Gilbert Ryle dies 10-6, 932G3
PHOENIX, Ariz.—*See ARIZONA*
PHOENIX Gazette (newspaper)
Ford endorsement rptd 10-30, 827F3
PHOSPHATES and Phosphorus
Rebels cut Sahara transit belt 1-26, 58A3
Spain sells Sahara stake to Morocco 2-9, 107C3
Morocco export decline cited 4-6, 458A3
Morocco, Mauritania to share Sahara deposits 4-14, 277A3
France proposes price stabilizatn fund 5-10—5-11, 355E3
PHOSVEL (lepthophos)—*See PESTICIDES*
PHOTOGRAPHS (& Photography)—*See also ILLUSTRATIONS*
Austria-US deal rptd 1-30, 97F3
Paul Strand dies 3-31, 272G3
Pulitzer Prizes awarded 5-3, 352E3
Cunningham, White die 6-24, 524D2, G3
Charles Peterson dies 8-4, 892D3
Ray Man dies 11-18, 970B3
PHUMIPHOL Aduldet, King (Thailand)
Dissolves Parlt 1-12, 30C3
Proclaims Seni Cabt 4-21, 315D1
Reappoints Seni to form Cabt 9-25, 754G1
OKs new Cabt 10-22, 813D2
PHYSICIANS—*See under MEDICINE*
PHYSICIANS National Housestaff Association
NLRB rejects petitions 3-22, 220F1

PHYSICS
New atomic particle observed 2-8, 124A1
Bethe wins Niels Bohr award 5-6, 504D3
2 share Nobel Prize for subatomic particle 10-18, 840F1
Bethe gets Science Medal 10-18, 858C3
Wu gets science medal 10-18, 858G3
Obituaries
Heisenberg, Werner 2-1, 124D3

PIASECKI, Boleslaw
Polish State Cncl member 3-25, 268D2
PIATIGORSKY, Gregor
Dies 8-6, 892D3
PICACHY, Lawrence Trevor Cardinal
Named cardinal 4-27, 336C2
PICARIELLO, Richard J.
Indicted 7-14, 796B3
PICASSO, Pablo (1881-1973)—*See 1973, p. 410A2 for biog. data*
Avignon art theft 1-31, 124G2
PICCIONI, Attilio
Dies 3-10, 240F3
PICHAI Rataku!
Sets Laos border pact 8-3, 678A1
PICKERING, Charles
Named GOP platform subcom chrmn 8-9, 583B1
Reagan vs vp draft move 8-19, 598D2
PICKERING, Thomas R.
In talks on Leb crisis 6-22, 448B2
PICKERING, William H.
Awarded Medal of Science 10-18, 858F3
PICKLE, Rep. J. J. (Jake) (D, Tex.)
Reelected 11-2, 830D4
PIEDMONT Driving Club (Atlanta, Ga.)
Bell scored re membership 12-20, to quit 12-22, 956F3

1977

PHILOSOPHY
Jan Patocka dies 3-13, 220F2
Ernst Bloch dies 8-3, 696D2
PHIPPS, Frank
Scores Castro visit to Jamaica 10-16, 883G3
PHIRI, W. J.
Zambia home affairs min 8-2, 674F3
PHOENIX, Ariz.—*See ARIZONA*
PHOENIX Container Lines
Rebates cited 1-5, 6C3
PHOSPHATES (& Phosphorous)
EC, 3 Arab natns sign pacts 1-18, 73G3
Morocco rpts Sahara dvpt 3-6, 337C2
Morocco-USSR pact rptd 6-6, 513B3
PHOTOGRAPHS (& Photography)—*See also under ILLUSTRATIONS*
Ollie Atkins dies 1-9, 84F2
S Africa black wins award 2-22, 160G3-161A1
Pulitzer Prizes awarded 4-18, 355G2
Polaroid instant movies unveiled 4-26, 409A1
Child porno rptd widespread 5-15—5-23 432C2-G3
USSR censors US exhibit 8-18, 657F2
Polaroid ends S Africa sales 11-22, 934D2
PHOTOVOLTAIC Research—*See SOLAR Energy*
PHS—*See U.S. GOVERNMENT—PUBLIC Health Service*
PHUMIPHOL Aduldet, King (Thailand)
Escapes bomb blast 9-22, 747G1
Assailants arrested 10-10, 827G1
Mil seizes power 10-20, 827D1
PHYSICIANS—*See under MEDICINE*

PHYSICS
Space test backs relativity 1-7, 170E3
NSF '78 authorizatn signed 8-15, 689E1
Nobel won by Van Vleck, Anderson 10-11, 951G2
Medal of Sci awarded 11-22, 952A1
Obituaries
Beams, Jesse 7-23, 604E2
Budker, Gersh 7-6, 604F2
Coolidge, Albert 8-31, 696E2
Gregory, Bernard 12-25, 1024A2
Hardy, Arthur 10-31, 872B2
Kompfner, Rudolf 12-3, 1024C2
Schild, Alfred 5-24, 425E3
Vereschagin, Leonis (rptd) 2-23, 164F3

PIAZZA Tanguis, Walter
Peru econ min 5-17, 427B3
Sets austerity program 6-10, 488F1-D2
Quits econ post 7-6, 563D2
IMF loan agreemt rptd 9-30, 784A3
PICASSO, Jacqueline (Mrs. Pablo)
Husband's estate rptd setld 9-19, 808E2
PICASSO, Pablo (1881-1973) —*See 1973, p. 410A2 for biog. data*
Estate rptd settled 9-19, 808E2
PICHAI Wasanasong
Arrested 3-28, 243C2
PICKANDS Mather & Co.
USW strike ends 12-16, 977B3
PICKETING—*See LABOR*
PIECE of the Action, A (film)
Top-grossing film 10-19, 872G3; 12-7, 1021B3
PIEDMONT Airlines Inc.
William Magruder dies 9-10, 788F1
PIEDRAHITA Cardona, Jaime
Leftists nominate for pres 7-16, 727G1

1978

PHILOSOPHY
Harvard revises curriculum 5-2, 348D2
Obituaries
Gilson, Etienne 9-19, 778D1
PHIL Woods Six—Live From the Showboat, The (recording)
Group wins Grammy 2-24, 315F3
PHOENIX, Ariz.—*See ARIZONA*
PHOSPHATES (& Phosphorous)
Morocco-USSR constructn pact 1-31, 95F1
Poland-Occidental deal rptd 5-28, 650E2
PHOTOGRAPHY—*See also ILLUSTRATIONS—Photographs*
Berkey wins trust suit vs Kodak 1-21, 67C1
Kodak damages awarded to Berkey 3-22, 205A1
Black, white female consumers compared 4-12, 812C1
2 win Pulitzers 4-17; spot photo mix-up setld 4-21; feature photo authenticity questnd 4-21, 4-22, 314F2, 315F1, B2
Rhodesia Pulitzer-sparked atrocity probe rptd halted 4-22, 455C2
Avedon imposter sentenced 5-5, 380B2
JFK murder film assessed 9-26, 916E1
Shroud of Turin studied 10-4, 11-7, 926C1-F1, F2
Obituaries
Kanaga, Consuelo 2-28, 196C3
Smith, W Eugene 10-15, 888F3
PHOTOSYNTHESIS
US, Japan plan joint research 9-6, 695D3
PHS—*See U.S. GOVERNMENT—PUBLIC Health Service*
PHYSICIANS—*See under MEDICINE*

PHYSICS
Molecular sieve dvpt rptd 2-9, 293C3
Fractional chrg (quark) experiments rptd 2-16, 293A3
USSR CP ousts Polikanov 2-21, 275D3
Ferromagnetism in superfluid helium 3-A rptd 3-16, 293E3
Hydrogen storage study rptd 4-8, 293G3
US physicists protest Orlov sentence 5-20—5-26, 401C1
China dvpt plan outlined 5-28, 436F1
US, W Ger cancel USSR trip re Orlov 6-2, 504B1
Weinberg/Salam unified field theory confirmatn rptd 6-12, 654A2
Mass of subatomic particle 'Upsilon' measured 7-5, 654E2
Fusion research advance rptd 8-12, 653F2
US, Japan plan joint research 9-6, 695D3
Kennedy meets Levich in USSR 9-9, 743B1
'79 NASA authorzn signed 9-30, 750C3
Polikanov arrives Denmark 10-10, 946F3
Nobels to 3 announced 10-17, 886C1, A2
US-China talks rptd set 11-6, 871D2
Zenon metallic conversn rptd 11-25, 1023C3
Levich emigrates 11-30, 946F2
Gravity wave evidence rptd 12-14, 12-16, 1023D3
Obituaries
Alikhanian, Artemi 2-25, 196B2
Goudsmit, Samuel A 12-4, 1032G2
Moureu, Henri 7-20, 620C3
Sawyer, Ralph A 12-6, 1032E3
Siegbahn, Manne 9-26, 778A2

PIANCONE, Cristoforo
Kills Turin cop, captured 4-11; alleged interview rptd 4-28, 329C3
Turin apartmt searched 5-12, 393A3 ★
PIANO Bar (play)
Opens 6-8, 887E2
PICARDO, Robert
'Tribute opens 6-1, 887D3
PICASSO, Pablo (1881-1973)—*See 1973, p. 410A2 for biog. data*
Paintings destroyed in Brazil museum fire 7-8, 579A2
PICCARDO, Ralph (Little Ralphie)
Provenzano convicted 3-25, 232F2 ★
Provenzano, Konigsberg convicted 6-14, 480C2
PICCO, Giovanni
Wounded by terrorists 3-24, 247D2
PICKER, David V.
Oliver's Story released 12-14, 1030C3
PICKERING, Charles W.
Loses Sen primary in Miss 6-6, 448B1
PICKETING—*See LABOR*
PICKETT Jr., John O.
Named Islanders fscl mgr 6-6, refinancing plan OKd 8-10, 656D2
PICKLE, Rep. J. J. (Jake) (D, Tex.)
Reelected 11-7, 852A3
PICTON (Chilean Island)—*See BEAGLE Channel*
PIEDMONT Airlines
Hijack attempt foiled 1-28, 212C2
PIEDRAHITA, Jaime
Rebuffs leftist unity plan 4-28, pres bid rptd weak 5-28, 413F2, A3
Runs 5th in pres vote 6-4, 443D2

1979

PHILOSOPHY
Herbert Marcuse dies 7-29, 588B3
Fuller in Arts Institute 12-7, 1005A3
PHOENIX, Ariz.—*See ARIZONA*
PHOENIX, Ill.—*See ILLINOIS*
PHOENIX Steel Corp.
Fed aid rptd blocked 8-28, 682F1
PHOSPHATES (& Phosphorous)
Hooker-USSR deal rptd 8-5, 597F2
PHOTOGRAPHS—*See under ILLUSTRATIONS*
PHOTOGRAPHY
Steichen works to go to Rochester museum 3-24, 375D2
GATT pact signed, tariff cuts seen 4-12, 273A2
Berkey trust award reversed 6-25, 517C2-A3
Argus sues Kodak, 2 others 8-28, 986B1
Pope's US visit gets record coverage 10-1—10-7, 760E3
Obituaries
Halsman, Philippe 6-2, 508A3
PHOTOGRAPHY, International Museum of (Rochester, N.Y.)
Steichen works entrusted 3-24, 375D2
PHUOC, Nguyen Van
On sunk boat 7-31, 626F1
PHYSICIANS—*See under MEDICINE*
PHYSICIANS, American Academy of Family
2d-surgical opinion backed 2-5, 218G3
PHYSICIANS, American College of
Blue Cross hosp test paymt curbs backed 2-6, 138B2

PHYSICS
Levich gets City Coll post 3-2, 272E1
Solid hydrogen rptd formed 3-2, 290C1
Solar neutrino theory rptd 4-12, 691E3
Einstein monumt unveiled 4-22, 392E2
Magnetic confinemt fusion advance rptd 6-14, 692E1
Laser fusion advance rptd 6-16, 692B1
Stratospheric ozone levels studied 6-22, 692D1
Gluon existence, quantum chromodynamics confrmatn claimed 8-28, 692D3
Antimatter detected from space 10-15, 1000B2
Nobels to 3 announced 10-16, 858C1
UK spy scandal reopened 10-28, 10-29, 874A1
Obituaries
Gabor, Dennis 2-8, 176A3
Haworth, Leland J 3-5, 272E2
Tomonaga, Shinichero 7-8, 588E3

PIANO Teacher, The (short story)
Nest of Vipers released 9-7, 820C2
PIASECKI, Boleslaw
Dies 1-1, 104F3
PICASSO, Pablo (1881-1973)
Kahnweiler dies 1-11, 104B3
Massine dies 3-16, 272B3
Painting sold for record sum 7-3, 672C1
Retrospective opens in Paris 10-10, 892C1
PICCINELLI, Franco
Shot 4-24, 331B3
PICCOLI, Flaminio
Confrms Cervone contact with Red Brigades 2-7, 97F3
PICH Cheang
On Pol Pot govt shakeup 12-27, 977F2
PICKER, David V.
Bloodline released 6-28, 819F3
Jerk released 12-14, 1007E3
PICKERING, Thomas R.
Rpts Pak A-bomb materials purchase 5-1, 323F3
Cited in H-bomb letter 9-16, 9-18, 715F2
PICKETT, Rev. O. Eugene
Named Unitarian pres 4-29, 376A2
PICKFORD, Mary
Dies 5-29, 432D3
PICNIC At Hanging Rock (film)
Released 2-22, 174D3
PICTON (Chilean Island)—*See BEAGLE Channel*
PIERCE, Donald
Flying Paster wins Santa Anita Derby 4-1, 448D3
PIERCE, Frederick S.
Promoted to ABC vp 4-30, 334F3
PIERCE, Judge Lawrence Warren
Named to wiretap ct 5-18, 442D3
PIERCE Packing Co.
PCB feed grain contaminatn rptd 9-17, 704C3
PIERPONT Morgan Library (N.Y., N.Y.)
Mozart manuscript purchased 7-16, 672G2

1980

PHILOSOPHY
Obituaries
Barthes, Roland 3-25, 279D1
Fromm, Erich 3-18, 279G2
Kaufman, Walter 9-4, 755E3
Randall Jr, John H 12-1, 1004B3
Sartre, Jean-Paul 4-15, 360C3
PHIRI, Wilted
Named Kaunda aide 12-4, 969F2
PHOENIX (recording)
On best-seller list 2-6, 120G3; 3-5, 200F3
PHOENIX Foundation
New Hebrides separatist role chrgd 6-3, 422B3; 6-8, 436C2
PHOSPHATES (& Phosphorous)
ILA loads Sovt cargo 2-1, 169F1
US halts USSR shipments, '79 sales cited 2-25, 139D3
US exec sees Brezhnev re embargo 2-27, 165G1
PHOSPHOROUS Trichloride—*See CHEMICALS*
PHOTOGRAPHS—*See under ILLUSTRATIONS*
PHOTOGRAPHY
Kodak raises film prices 1-8, 31A1
Berkey trust appeal refused by Sup Ct 2-19, 130F3
Land retires as Polaroid chief exec 3-7, 225B1
Pulitzer awarded 4-14, 317E2
Ctroom cameras case accepted by Sup Ct 4-21, 344E1
Newsroom searches curb signed 10-14, 835A2
Ctroom cameras case argued in Sup Ct 11-12, 882A2
Obituaries
Beaton, Cecil 1-18, 104F1
Healy, Giles G 2-29, 279D3
PHOTOPLAY (magazine)
Us magazine sale rptd 3-7, 239B2
PHS (Public Health Service)—*See under U.S. GOVERNMENT*
PHYSICIANS—*See MEDICINE--Physicians*
PHYSICS
New particle type rptd 1-31, 415B2
Antigravitational force rptd proposed 3-8, 415C2
Organic superconductor rptd 4-5, 415C3
Neutrino mass proposed 4-30, 416G1
Tokamak fusion advance rptd 7-17, 715B3
High temperature superconductor rptd 9-4, 716B2
Nobels to 2 announced 10-14, 889B3
Obituaries
Matthias, Bernd 10-27, 876F2
Robert, Richard 4-4, 360B3
Van Vleck, John 10-27, 876E3

PIAGET, Jean
Dies 9-16, 756E1
PIATEK, Mary Lou
Loses Richmond Intl 7-27, 691A3
PICARD, Camille
Wins Quebec by-electn 11-17, 900B3
PICASSO, Pablo (1881-1973)
Loren art collectn claim rptd denied 2-9, 200B2
Painting sold for record sum 5-12, 472B1
PICCOLI, Flaminio
Chosen Christian Dem party secy 3-6, 194E2
Backs Cossiga, scores CP probe 6-3, 6-3, 430C2
PICHARDO, Ulises
OAS office occupied in Honduras 8-15, 708F1
PICKETT, Cindy
Night Games released 4-11, 416D3
PICKLE, Rep. J. J. (Jake) (D, Tex.)
Reelected 11-4, 844A3
PICKWICK International Inc.
Lester named CBS video divsn pres 1-31, 239E3
PIERCE Jr., Samuel R.
Named HUD secy 12-22, 979E2

1976

PIERRE, S.D.—*See SOUTH Dakota*
PIERRE, Simon
Named rural, agri dvpt min 8-20, 926C1
PIERRE-Brossolette, Claude
Replaced as Giscard pres aide 7-28, 556A1
Seconds Ford nominatn 8-18, 598A1
PIERRE-Louis, Raoul
Haiti educatn min 4-1, 267E2
PIERRE-Louis, Wilner
Haiti trade min 9-7, 1005D3
PIERSON, Frank
Wins Oscar 3-29, 240A3
PIGNEDOLI, Cardinal Sergio
On anti-Zionist declaratn 2-7, 272F2
PIGOTT, Jean
Elected 10-18, 808D2
PIGUET, Frank L.
Indicted 5-7, 349E1
Acquitted 9-2, 767F3
PIKE, Rep. Otis G. (D, N.Y.)
Deplores censorship vote 1-29, 92A2
Scores intellignc rpt curbs 2-2, 150D2
Intellignc reforms offered 2-10, 150E1, B2
Accuses CIA, Rogovin 3-9, Bush rebuts 3-16, 216G3-217C1
Testifies in Schorr probe 7-19, 748E3
Reelected 11-2, 830F1
PILLARD, Charles H.
Quits Ford panel 1-8, 4C1
PIMENOV, Pyotr
Chrgs US CSCE violatns 5-25, 408D1
PIMSLEUR, Paul
Dies 6-22, 524D3
PINCUS, Mathilde
Wins Tony 4-18, 460F2
PINDER, Peggy
GOP platform text cites 8-18, 602D2
Seconds Dole nominatn 8-19, 599F1
PINELL, Hugo
Found guilty 8-12, 656C1
PINE Valley Country Club (Clementon, N.J.)
Ford golf outings rptd 9-21, 9-23, 722G2, B3
PINHEIRO de Azevedo, Vice Adm. Jose
Announces cabt 1-2, 1-6, 11A2
Sees farm ldrs 1-30, 143F1
Confirms pres candidacy 5-18, 366D3, 367A1
Campaign dvpts 5-27—6-27; stricken 6-23; Eanes elected 6-27, 482C3-483E1
PINHO Freire, Gen. Anibal
Resigns mil cncl seat 8-12, 733E2
PINIELLA, Lou
In World Series 10-16—10-21, 815D2
PINIGIN, Pavel
Wins Olympic medal 7-31, 576D3
PINKHAM, Fred O.
AID asst admin 3-17; confrmd 4-1, 262D3
PINOCHET Ugarte, Gen. Augusto
2 OK advisory roles 1-2, 1-4; Frei rejcts 1-2, scores 1-3, 8E2
Mil discontent, staff chngs rptd 1-3—1-10, 47D1
'75 censorship decree scored 1-9, 47F3
Church econ aid unit set 1-16, 47B3
Sees church ldrs 1-20, bishop lauds 1-21, 100D2
Scores Frei 1-21; denies mil rift, junta backs 1-28, 99D3
Signs prisoners' rights decree 1-28; ICJ scores 2-2, 100D1
Cabt quits 3-5; shuffled 3-8, 288F2
OAS secy gen lauds 3-16, explains 3-19, 310G1
Argentina CP cites repressn 3-29, 236A3
Visits Uruguay 4-21—4-24, 382D3
Scores UN rights abuse chrgs 4-24, 310E1
Addresses OAS mtg 6-4, 464A3
Says Chile creditworthy 6-30, 871G1
Lunches with bishops 8-18, 711B2
Rpt US rules out Letelier death role 10-12, 780E3
Rejects US aid 10-19, 870G3

PINTO, Edras
Arrested 12-20, 999E2
PINTO, Adm. Javier
Loses navy command 1-6, 26G3
PINTO de Magalhaes, Gen. Altino
'75 FLA ultimatum rptd 2-10, 143A3

1977

PIERRE, Percy A.
Named Army asst secy 4-25, confrmd 5-9, 418G1
PIGGOTT, Lester
Alleged wins Arc de Triomphe 10-2, 971A2
PIGNATARI, Francisco (Baby)
Dies 10-27, 872F2
PIGS—*See LIVESTOCK*
PIKE, Rep. Otis G. (D, N.Y.)
Assassination panel revived 2-1, 77F1
Vs Treas loans to Soc Sec 10-27, 814F3
PIKE Grain Co.
Fined 2-8, 113E1
PILLSBURY Co.
Calif weight-labeling rules curbed 3-29, 277B1
PILLSBURY, Madison & Sutro
On 5 largest law firms list 5-16, 383A2
PIMEN, Patriarch
Vs female ordination 9-25, 845B3
PIMIENTO, Msgr. Jose de Jesus
Scores govt 8-9, 727F2
PINAR, Blas
Pol cohorts seized 3-13—3-14, 307D2
PINCUS, Robert
Tried in absentia 2-10, 100B1

PINDLING, Lynden O. (Bahamas prime minister)
PLP wins electns, returned to office 7-19, 578F3
Names new Cabinet 7-29, 675C1
At Panama Canal pact signing 9-7, 678C1
Salary increased 10-29, 844A3

PINERUA Ordaz, Luis
Wins AD '78 pres nominatn 7-17, 566C1
Copei nominates Herrera Campins 8-18, Ottolina bid effect seen 8-26, 674B2, E2
PINGEL, Jurgen
Sentenced in W Ger for spying 12-6, 968F2
PINGEL, Karim
Sentenced in W Ger for spying 12-6, 968F2
PINIELLA, Lou
In World Series 10-11—10-18, 806G2
PINKNEY, Arnold R.
On schl financing problem 10-19, 939G2
PINK Panther Strikes Again (film)
Top-grossing film 2-2, 120D3

PINOCHET Ugarte, Gen. Augusto (Chile president)
Renews Antarctic claim 1-5, 18B3
Vatican scores 1-9, 18D3
Pol parties banned 3-11, 219A3
Plans limited electns by '85 7-9, US lauds 7-11, 635F2
Eyzaguirre scores secret police 8-11, 635E2
Secret police abolished 8-12, 635G1
Sees Todman 8-12, 635B2
Rptdly foils disappearnc probe 9-5, 743D1
Sees Carter 9-6, at Panama Canal pact signing 9-7, 678A1
UN rights probe rptdly OKd 9-7, 743B1
Denies Letelier death link 9-7, 743C3
Defends rule, bars early pol chng 9-11, 742B3
'85 electn plan oppositn rptd 9-16, 743F1
Banishes labor ldrs 12-4, 1019B1

PINTO Cohen, Gustavo
Venez agri min 7-15, 566B1

1978

PIERSON, Frank C.
Eubie opens 9-20, 1031E1
King of Gypsies released 12-19, 1030B3
PIERSON, Lynn
Marijuana use OKd 7-13, 598D3
PIERSON, Robert H.
Retires as Adventists pres 10-20, 907A3
PIERSON, Warren Lee
Dies 1-12, 96C3
PIGEON, Louis-Philippe
Rules re Quebec probe 10-31, 879C3
PIKE, Douglas
Warns vs anti-Cambodia force 8-21, 659E3
PIKE, Rep. Otis G. (D, N.Y.)
Not standing for reelectn 9-12, 716C2
Carney wins seat 11-7, 849A2
PILLAY, Moonsamy
Death rptd 1-2, 20F2
PILLIOD Jr., Charles
Sees Carter, backs inflatn plan 4-20, 361G3
PILLSBURY Co.
Weight Watchers purchase bid cited 5-4, 364E2
Green Giant acquisitn agreed 9-18, 752C3
PINA, Joao Almeida
Stays Portugal housing min 11-18, 1022B1
PINDLING, Lynden O. (Bahamian prime minister)
Creates Cabt com on investmt 3-6, 194F1-A2

PINE Bluff, Ark.—*See ARKANSAS*
PINEDA, Alvaro (d. 1975)
Brother killed in horse race 5-3, 539D3
PINEDA, Robert
Killed in horse race 5-3, 539C3
PINERA, Jose
Chile labor min 12-26, 1014D2
PINERUA Ordaz, Luis
Leads Herrera in pres poll 7-15, 559C2
Ties Herrera in pres poll 9-29, 799B2
Loses pres vote 12-3, concedes 12-5; returns incomplete 12-8, 952A3
Herrera declared pres-elect in final vote count 12-11, 990A1
PINIELLA, Lou
AL batting ldr 10-2, 928D3
In World Series 10-10—10-17, 800C1
PINKUS, William
Children excluded from porno rule by Sup Ct 5-23, 405A3
PINKUS v. U.S.
Children excluded from porno rule by Sup Ct 5-23, 405G2

PINOCHET Ugarte, Gen. Augusto (Chilean president)
Plebiscite protests, oppositn rptd 1-2; vote backs rule 1-4; domestic, forgn reactn 1-5, 1-8, 16F2-17C2
Banishes Christian Dems 1-14; US protests 1-17; ruling rptd 1-31, 210B1
Sees Videla on Beagle Channel dispute 1-19, 2d mtg put off 1-24, 101B2
Sees Videla re Beagle Channel 2-20, 216E1
Poll shows public support 3-4—3-6, 209F3
Backs US in Letelier murder probe 3-6, 188F2
Lifts state of siege 3-9, 209E3
'Goodwill' to Bolivia cited 3-19, 216C1
Ex-DINA chief quits as aide 3-21, 209G2
Leigh vs, seeks civiln rule 3-26; rift downplayed 3-29, 267A2
Commutes Lazo jail term 3-27, 267F1
Lifts night curfew 3-31, 267E1
Vows Letelier probe cooperatn 4-5, US pressure cited 4-9, 266F3
Sets amnesty for pol prisoners 4-5, 267A1
Orders new const by yr's end 4-5, 267D1
Names civilians to Cabt 4-12, 4-21; denies mil rift, US pressure 4-16, 4-21, 350E3
Mrs Townley: urged Letelier probe cooperatn 5-2; US sources confirm 5-5, 370G3-371A1
Beagle Channel talks fail 5-22—11-2, 860F2
'Disloyalty' to Townley seen by ex-DINA men 5-23, 452G1
Sees US labor ldrs 5-23, 452C3
US Letelier probe rptd embarrassmt 6-5, 4352E1
Washn Post asks resignatn 6-10, 452A2
Upholds mil govt 6-17, 478B3
US coup plot chrgd 6-23, 496A1
Leigh scores rule 7-18; Cabt scores Leigh 7-20, junta fires 7-24, 572D2
AF gens replaced 7-25; seen in total control 7-29, 591G1-C2
Asks 'proof' for extraditing Letelier suspects; denies role, says govt not imperiled 8-2, 613G3, 614G1
Contreras friendship denial rptd 9-21, 755E3
Trade boycott set by forgn unions 11-24, US offcls back 12-8, 1014E1
Scores trade boycott 12-6, shuffles Cabt 12-26, 1014D1, C2
US offcls ask intl disappearances probe 12-8, 1014D1
New Beagle Channel talks urged 12-12, 979A3
PINS and Needles (play)
Opens 7-6, 760A3
PINTER, Rabbi Lieb
Flood paymt chrg rptd 1-27, 240C2
Pleads guilty to bribery tax chrgs 5-11, 363C2
Sentenced 6-22, 500E3

1979

PIERSON, Frank C.
Whoopee opens 2-14, 292F3
PILGRIM Station—*See MASSACHUSETTS–Atomic Energy*
PILLIOD Jr., Charles J.
Sees Kahn, wage-guide compliance urged 4-20, 345A1
PILLSBURY Co.
Burger King donates $2 mln to Olympics 5-15, 798E1
PILON v. Bordenkircher
Case remanded by Sup Ct 10-9, 784C1
PIMENTEL, Col. Rosario
Arrested 9-25, plot exposed 9-26, 751F3
PINAR, Blas
Basque speech sparks riot 12-2, 929C2
PINCAY, Laffit
Affirmed wins Santa Anita Handicap 3-4, 448C3
Affirmed wins Woodward Stakes 9-23, Jockey Gold Cup, sets earning record 10-6, 876F2, F3
Earns $8 mln 12-9, named top jockey 12-11, 1005C1
PINCUS, Warren
Tip Toes opens 3-26, 712A3

PINDLING, Lynden (Bahamian prime minister)
Curbs land sales to forgners 12-7, 948A2

PINERA, Jose
Sees labor ldrs 1-2, offers new union freedoms 1-3, 6F2
Cancels Group of 10 mtg 1-12, 29B1
Defends new labor decrees 7-9, 523B2
PINERUA Ordaz, Luis
Party loses munic electns 6-3, 429A3
PINES, Wayne
Urges sleep aid, nose spray ban 5-1, 354C3
On methapyrilene drug recall 6-8, 471A2
PINILLA, Col. Jose M.
Dies 8-10, 671D3
PINNER, Uli
Loses W Ger Grand Prix 7-22, 734B2

PINOCHET Ugarte, Gen. Augusto (Chilean president)
Trade boycott dropped by ORIT 1-15–1-16, 28E3
Letelier case data curbed in '78 US-Chile pact 1-23, 75C1
Letelier extraditns seen unlikely 2-7, 114C3
Linked to Letelier assassins 2-9, 114E3
Mrs Letelier lauds Cuban convictns 2-14, 114A3
Addresses natn; bars civil rule, scores US ldrship 9-11, 685B2
US trade boycott studied 10-1, 750D2

PIN Sovan
Cambodian vice pres 1-8, 10A1
PINTASSILGO, Maria de Lurdes (Portuguese premier)
Named Portugal caretaker premr 7-19, 545F2
Names Cabt 7-30, sworn 8-1, 603C3
Econ measures seen 8-30, 710D2
Socialists lose assemb electns 12-2, 916G3
PINTO, Carlos Mota
Sets China ties 2-8, 134C3
PINTO, Pvt. Daniel
Censorship re '78 murders ended 9-14, claims chrgs false 9-19, 802E1
PINTO, Paolo
Swims Strait of Otranto 7-14, 656F3
PINTOR, Lupe
Decisns Zarate for WBC bantamwgt title 6-3, 838G3

1980

PIERRE, James
Executed 4-22, 353A2
PIEST, Robert (d. 1978)
Gacy convicted 3-12, gets death sentence 3-13, 214B2
PIGEON, Louis-Philippe
Lamer replaces at Sup Ct 3-28, 273C2
PIGNEDOLI, Cardinal Sergio
Dies 6-15, 528C3
PILGRIM, Michael (St. Lucian prime minister)
On Hurricane Allen damage 8-4, 621B2
PILLSBURY, Sarah
Wins Oscar 4-14, 296A2
PILLSBURY Co., The
Wyman named CBS chief 5-22, 501A2
PINANGO, Jose
Wins Olympic medal 8-2, 622E1
PINARD, Yvon
Canada privy cncl pres 3-3, 171C2
Announces Parlt early recall 9-18, 728C2
PINCAY Jr., Laffit
Codex wins Santa Anita Derby 3-30, 447G3

PINDLING, Lynden O. (Bahamian prime minister)
In UK 5-10, 371F2

PINE Bluff—*See ARKANSAS*
PINERO, Manuel
2d in Brazil Open 11-24, 972G2
PINEY River—*See VIRGINIA*
PINK Floyd (singing group)
Wall on best-seller list 1-2, 40F3; 2-6, 120G3; 3-5, 200F3; 4-2, 280F3; 4-30, 360A1; 6-4, 448F3
Another Brick in the Wall on best-seller list 3-5, 200E3; 4-2, 280F3; 4-30, 359G3
PINKOWSKI, Carey
Wins 6,000-m Penn Relays 4-25, 892C2
PINKOWSKI, Josef (Polish premier)
Named Polish premier 8-24, 641F1
In USSR, affirms ties 10-30, 859G3-860C1
Meets union ldrs 10-31, 860D1
On agriculture problems 11-12, 879A1
PINNA, Franco
French arrest 3-28, 255E1

PINOCHET Ugarte, Gen. Augusto (Chilean president)
Chile econ recovery plan detailed 1-14, 19C3
French CP compares Sakharov 2-20, 149D3
Cancels 11-day Asian tour 3-22, severs Pl ties 3-24; assassinatn plot alleged 3-25, 230F3-231E1
Dismisses forgn min 3-25, names replacemt 3-28, 255G3
Restores Pl ties 4-2, 311D2
Draft const submitted to junta 7-11, 563B1
Removes security chief 7-24, 603E2
Sets draft const vote 8-8; oppositn surfaces, mil rule scored 8-27, 9-2, 669B2
Internal security shakeup, dir quits 8-11; 20 arrested 8-12, 618A3
Draft const approved by voters 9-11; reactn 9-11—9-12, 706B2
Favors Pope's Beagle Channel plan 12-12, 978G3

PINTO Balsemao, Francisco (Portuguese premier)
Sworn Portugal dep min of state 1-3, 21D3
Named Soc Dem ldr 12-13, Portuguese premr 12-22, 995G3
PINTOR, Lupe
KOs Owen 9-19, Owen dies 11-3, 907A3

1976

PIPER, John Anthony
Named amb to Algeria 2-18, 155B1
PIPPIN (play)
Long runs listed 12-31, 1015A1
PIRATES of Penzance (play)
Opens 5-6, 1014C3
PIRES, Abilio
Natl Assemb scores release 7-30, 733G1
PIRES Veloso, Brig. Gen. Antonio
Resigns mil cncl seat 8-12, 733E2
Oporto home bombed 9-3, 733E1
PIROMALLI, Girolamo
Acquitted in Getty kidnap 7-29, 816C3
PIRONIA, Eduardo Cardinal
Named cardinal 4-27, 336C2
PISTON, Walter
Dies 11-12, 970A3
PITA, Col. Juan
Kidnaped 5-30, 399A1
PITCHESS, Peter
On Calif weapons cache 12-11, 952E3
PITCHLYNN, John F.
Marine racism charged 6-4, 435B3
PITHOUD, Nadia
Seconds Ford nominatn 8-18, 598A1
PITMAN, Harry
Wins Durban electn 5-5, 422E3
PITNEY-Bowes Inc.
Bars boycott compliance 3-18, 747B2
PITTSBURGH, Pa.—*See PENNSYLVANIA*
PITTSBURGH, University of
Radiation subjects recalled 5-12, 384B2
Dorsett wins Heisman 11-30, 969D2
PITTSBURGH Press (newspaper)
Ford endorsement rptd 10-30, 831F2
Backs Gilmore death plea 11-15, 891C2
PLAMBECK, Juliane
Escapes from jail 7-7, 593E3
PLANK, Herbert
Wins Olympic medal 2-5, 158D3
PLANNED Parenthood Federation of America, Inc.
Sup Ct rules on abortion 7-1, 519B1
Medicaid abortn curb voided 10-22, Sup Ct bars stay 11-8, 848G1, B2
PLANNING Association, National
Rpts US-Canada ties strained 7-26, 587A3
PLASTICS
Beverage bottle challenged 4-21, 308A2
Dow rptd in E Ger pact 11-26, 1002A1

1977

PIPER Aircraft Corp.
Chris-Craft damages voided 2-23, 150B2
PIRES, Telmo
Americans win ASL title 9-4, 827B3
PIR of Pagaro—*See PAGARO, Pir of*
PISARKIEWICZ, Steve
In NFL draft 5-3, 353B2
PISKULYN, Anatoly
Wins triple jump 7-1—7-2, 602F2
PISTOLESI, Angelo
Killed 12-28, 1014E2
PITA da Veiga, Adm. Gabriel
Quits Cabt 4-12, mil crisis resolved 4-13, 285G2
PI Ting-chun
'76 death cited 7-25, 706A2
PITTS, Dr. Robert F.
Dies 6-6, 532E3
PITTSBURGH, Pa.—*See PENNSYLVANIA*
PITTSBURGH, University of
Wins Sugar Bowl 1-1; ranked 1st 1-2, 1-3, 8D3
Dorsett in NFL draft 5-3, 353D2, A3
Wins Gator Bowl 12-30, 1020C2
PITTSBURGH Courier, The (newspaper)
George Schuyler dies 8-31, 788E2
PITTSBURGH Museum of Art
Mellon art prize winner rptd 8-1, 808G2
PITTSTON Co.
Brink's sued 6-21, 520D3
PITTY Velazquez, Nander
Scores US re OAS budget cut 5-13, 415C2
PIUS X International Society Seminary—*See ROMAN Catholic Church—Traditionalist Movement*
PIVAVAROV, Yuri Sergeyevich
Spain expulsn cited 7-4, 546B1
PIZZA Hut Inc.
Pepsico takeover cited in table 880G1
PJERREGAARD, Ritt
Danish educatn min 2-25, 373E1
PLACE, Mary Kay
Wins Emmy 9-11, 1022A1
PLAINS, Ga.—*See GEORGIA*
PLAINS, Kan.—*See KANSAS*
PLAMBECK, Juliane
2 W Ger terrorists captured 12-20, 1017G3
PLANETS—*See ASTRONAUTICS*
PLANNED Parenthood Federation of America, Inc.
Abortn alternatives proposed, teenage pregnancy data rptd 7-19, 786D3, E3
PLANTS
New life form identified 11-2, 907G3
PLASTICS (& Plastic Products)
'76 sales, stockholder returns rptd 340B2, A3
Medit natns reach pollutn pact 10-21, 876D2

1978

PINUERA Ordaz, Luis
Pres race poll rptd 3-24; campaign opens 4-1, 269G3
PIONEER (U.S. Interplanetary probe series)—*See ASTRONAUTICS—Interplanetary Projects*
PIONEER Bowl—*See FOOTBALL—Collegiate*
PIPER, Harold D.
USSR seizes notes 3-2, US protests 3-8, 180E1
USSR chrgs slander 6-28, issues statemt 7-3, 518C1-F2
Sovt ct convicts 7-18, 575D2
Fine paid 8-4, 634B1
USSR closes case 8-18, 651F1; gets warning 8-24, 670C2
PIRANHA (film)
Released 8-4, 970F2
Top-grossing film 8-30, 708A2
PIRONI, Didier
Wins LeMans 6-11, 538G2
PI Shu-shih, Archbishop Ignatius
Dies 5-16, 440C3
PISIER, Mari-France
Celine & Julie released 2-24, 618G3
PITCHFORD, Maria Elaine
Acquitted of self-abortn 8-30, 743B2
PITFIELD, Ward C.
Quits Husky Oil bd 6-20, 629G1
PITNEY-Bowes Inc.
Dictaphone OKs takeover bid 12-21, 1005E1
PITT, Lord
Comm urges Bermuda independnc 8-2, 603G3
PITTARD, Timothy
Fined in Rhodesia arms scandal 7-23, 616A2
PITTI Palace (Florence, Italy)
Rubens painting, 9 others stolen 4-21; recovered 4-23, 335A2
PITTMAN, Portia
Dies 2-26, 196E3
PITTSBURGH, University of
'77 football rank rptd 1-3, 8A3
Holloway in NFL draft 5-2, 336F3
Loses Tangerine Bowl 12-23, 1025D2
PITTSBURGH & Lake Erie Railroad—*See PENN Central Corp.*
PITTSBURGH Testing Laboratory
Chrgd in W Va scaffold collapse 6-8, 459E3
PITTSBURG & Midway Coal Mining Co.—*See under GULF Oil Corp.*
PITTSTON Co.
Carter sees Camicia on coal strike 2-24, 122G3
Brinks Inc.
Fined on trust chrgs 4-22, 511D1
NYC airport robbery 12-11, 1028A3
PITTSTOWN, N.J.—*See NEW Jersey*
PITTWAY Corp.
BRK smoke detector fine agreed 11-6, 942E1
PITYANA, Dimza
Freed, banning continues 3-10, 193E2
PIUS X, Pope (Giuseppe Sarto) (1835-1914)
Venice patriarchy cited 658F1
PIUS XII, Pope (Eugenio Pacelli) (1876-1958)—*See 1958, p. 335D2 for biog. data*
Papal electn cited 8-26, 658C2
PJERREGAARD, Ritt
Named Danish educ min 8-30, 688A1
PLAGAR, Barclay
Hired as Blues coach 2-16, 458B3
PLAGIARISM—*See LITERATURE*
PLAIN, Belva
Evergreen on best-seller list 9-4, 708B1; 10-9, 800A3; 11-6, 887F3; 12-3, 971A1
PLAINS, Ga.—*See GEORGIA*
PLAINS Monitor (newspaper)
Flynt '77 purchase cited 187B1
PLANCHON, Roger
Dossier 51 released 12-12, 1030F2
PLANETS—*See ASTRONAUTICS, ASTRONOMY; planet names*
PLANNED Parenthood Federation of America, Inc.
Abortns rptd down 6-20, 743C3
PLANTS
DBCP pesticide curbs asked 9-19, 719D2
PLAQUEMINE, La.—*See LOUISIANA*
PLASTER, Walter E.
Chrgd in '75 Joyvies cover-up 12-14, 991D2
PLASTERS' and Cement Masons' International Association of the United States and Canada, Operative (AFL-CIO)
Union insurnc scheme chrgd 6-15, 560B3
PLASTICS
US acrylonitrile rule issued 1-16, 85F3
Benzene exposure rule issued 2-2, 85C3
Du Pont pigment monopoly chrgd 4-10, 346A1
'77 indus profit rise rptd 5-8, 325A3
US acrylonitrile rule finalized 9-29, 754A1
Benzene exposure rule upset 10-5, 834A1
Mich PBB contaminatn rptd 10-9, 769E2
OPEC seeks mfg role 10-9—10-11, 871D1
Diamond Shamrock to buy Falcon Seaboard 11-2, 1005A2
Borg-Warner, Firestone to merge 11-28, 935E1
PLASTOW, David
On Japan auto exports 2-8, 112A3

1979

PINYIN (Chinese transliteration system)
Introduced 1-1, 75D2
PIONEER, Ohio—*See OHIO*
PIONEER (U.S. Interplanetary probe series)—*See ASTRONAUTICS—Interplanetary Projects*
PIOUS, Minerva
Dies 3-16, 272D3
PIPERNO, Franco
Threatnd in Curcio letter 8-10, 635F2
Arrested in Paris 8-18, 709E2
PIRASTEH, Rostam
Iran to review forgn contracts 2-4, 82C2
PIRES, Gen. Walter
Brazil army min designate 1-19, 95E1
PIRIE, Robert B.
On '79 enlistmt gap 10-25, 903D3
Backs female combat role 11-13, 868D2
PIRVULESCU, Constantin
12th CP cong held 11-19—11-23, scores Ceausescu 11-23, 11-23, 910D1
PISIER, Marie-France
Love On The Run released 4-5, 528A3
PITALUA, Alfredo
Watt KOs for WBC lightwgt title 4-17, 412F3
PITCHFORD, Dean
Umbrellas Of Cherbourg opens 2-1, 292F3
PITLIK, Noam
Wins Emmy 9-9, 858E2
PITTORINO, Victoria
Marries brother 5-25, sentncd for incest 7-31, 656B2
PITTSBURGH, Pa.—*See PENNSYLVANIA*
PITTSBURGH, University of
Marcuso radiatn safety studies asked 1-30, 90E3
Heart disease preventn study rptd 3-19, 219C1
Sternglass on 3 Mile I radiatn 3-29, 243A1
Sternglass scores 3 Mile I A-accident 4-7, 261C1-D1
Ulcer drug-sperm study rptd 5-3, 354E3
Wins Fiesta Bowl 12-25, 1001A3
PITTSBURGH School District v. Pa. Department of Education
Case dismissed by Sup Ct 6-25, 540C2
PLACID Oil Co.
Intl Paper oil interests purchase set 8-9, 664A2
PLAGER, Barclay
Quits as Blues coach 12-8, 1004F1
PLAIN, Belva
Evergreen on best-seller list 8-5, 620D3; 9-2, 672D3; 10-14, 800D3
PLANETS—*See ASTRONAUTICS, ASTRONOMY; planet names*
PLANNED Parenthood Federation of America, Inc.
Minn funds ban upset 2-23, 310D2
PLANTE v. Gonzalez
Case refused by Sup Ct 1-22, 54G1
PLANTS
2 herbicides banned 3-1, 167E1-C2
James Crockett dies 7-11, 588E2
Canada acid rain perils noted 7-26, 581G2
Tree rptd fuel source 9-15, 1000B2
PLASTICS
Formica trademark case refused by Sup Ct 6-5, 464G2
PLASTIC Surgery—*See MEDICINE-Surgery*

1980

PIONEER (U.S. Interplanetary probe series)—*See ASTRONAUTICS--Interplanetary Projects*
PIONEER Electronics Corp.
U.S. Pioneer Electronics Corp.
Video disk mkting planned 3-26, 376E3
PIPERNO, Franco
More extensive probe urged 1-2, 20A3
PIQUET, Nelson
Wins US Gr Prix West 3-30, forced out of Canadian Gr Prix 9-28, 1001G3
PIRIE, Robert B.
Recruiters to stress unemploymt 6-11, 458C2
PIRONI, Didier
3d in Canadian Gr Prix 9-28, 1002A1
PISANO, Giorgio
Chrgs Bisaglia oil tax evasn role 10-28, 873A3
PITINKIN, Mandy
Wins Tony 6-8, 692B3
PITTMAN, John
Zimbabwe min freed in murder case 12-8, 946B2
PITTSBURGH—*See PENNSYLVANIA*
PITTSBURGH, University of
Football '79 rank rptd 1-2, 23C1
May wins Outland Trophy 11-20, 999G2
Green 2d in Heisman Trophy vote 12-1, 999F2
Wins Gator Bowl 12-30, 999E3
PITTSTON Co.
San Fran Brink's truck robbed 8-15, 654G2
'50 Boston Brinks robber dies 9-27, 756B2
Clinchfield Coal finded $100,000 12-4, 962G3
PLACID Oil Co.
Gulf Resources rejects offer 2-26, 385A3
$1.1 bln Hunt silver bailout set 5-2, 344G3
Hunts bailout loan paid 5-27, collateral listed 5-28, 425E2, C3, 426F1
PLAGE, La (The Beach) (painting)
Sold for record sum 5-13, 472G1
PLAGE au Pouldu, La (painting)
Sold for record sum 5-13, 472G1
PLAIN, Belva
Random Winds on best-seller list 6-8, 448B3; 7-13, 568E3; 8-17, 640E3; 9-14, 716B3
PLAIN Dealer, The (Cleveland newspaper)
Reagan pres endorsemt rptd 11-1, 841G3
PLAMBECK, Juliane
Dies in auto crash 7-25, 581C1
PLANET Petroleum Co.
Hunts interest rptd 5-28, 426E1
PLANETS—*See ASTRONAUTICS, ASTRONOMY*
PLANK, Doug
Fined for 'unnecessary violence' 10-21, 998B3
PLANNED Parenthood Federation of America Inc.
Medicaid abortn funding limit scored 6-30, 492A2
PLANTS
Lindane use curbs sought 7-3, 519D3
Photosynthesis step rptd replicated 7-17, 715G3
Plant Variety Protectn Act amendmt clears Cong 12-8, signed 12-22, 980G3
PLASTICS
'79 Fortune 500 data rptd 5-5, 291D1
Medit pollutn pact signed 5-17, 381C3
Mex-W Ger plant set 5-21, 409F2

1976

PLATT, Judge Thomas
Rules on Soc Sec bias 5-12, 413E3
PLATTE City, Mo.—*See MISSOURI*
PLAYBOY (magazine)
Fair '75 interview cited 43D2
Carter interview disclosed 9-20, 704F1
Carter explains interview, regrets LBJ remark 9-24, 9-27, 724C2
Carter, Butz remarks compared 10-3, 744D2
Dole assails Carter remarks 10-6, 763F3
Baptist ldr scores Carter interview 10-10, 763D2
Dole, Mondale debate Carter interview 10-15, 783F3
Ford: refused interview 10-20, 784D3
Ford, Carter debate 10-22, 800C3, D3
Carter wins electn 11-2, 818B3
PLAY the Red (race horse)
2d in Preakness 5-15, 368G3
PLISSONNIER, Gaston
Addresses Sovt CP Cong 2-28, 195G3
PLOEG, Adrianus
Rptd approached by Lockheed 9-1, 684B2
PLUMB, Sir Henry
Asks EEC drought aid 6-19, 548D3
PLUMB, John
Wins Olympic medal 7-25, 574C2
PLUMBING and Pipe Fitting Industry of the United States and Canada, United Association of Journeymen & Apprentices of the (AFL-CIO)
Ward quits Ford panel 1-8, 4C1
PLUMMER, Chester M.
Killed by White House guard 7-25, 860E1
PLUMPTRE, Beryl
Quits AIB 6-10, denies rift 6-11, 439A1
AIB replacemt named 8-9, 750B2
PLUTO (planet)—*See ASTRONOMY*

PLUTONIUM
'45-47 tests on humans rptd 2-22, 272B3
Canada cites '74 India incident 2-25, 175C1
US ct curbs commercial use 5-26, 398G1
US OKs reactor sale to Spain 6-21, fuel sale to India 7-21, 739C2
7-natn waste conf opens 7-12, 739A2
GAO rpts missing A-fuel 8-5, 739B3
Taiwan fuel reprocessing rptd 8-29, 732E1
Ford, Carter debate 10-22, 801A3
Ford urges tighter A-curbs, Carter statemt 10-28, 848D3

PLYUSHCH, Leonid I.
In Vienna, rpts pol patients 1-11, arrives Paris 1-12, 30E2
Details Sovt asylum stay 2-3, 122C1
French CP ldr scores Sovt repressn 2-4, 119B2
Letter to French CP confrmd 2-4, 122D1
Tverdokhlebov sentncd 4-15, 292A2
PNEUMOCONIOSIS (black lung disease)—*See 'Heart & Lungs' under MEDICINE*
POAGE, Rep. William Robert (Bob) (D, Tex.)
Reelected 11-2, 830D4
PODDAR, Srikumar
Loses passport 7-12, 538B2
PODGORNY, Nikolai V.
Politburo named 3-5, 195C2
Pl ties set 6-2, 440G1
Sees Venez pres 11-24—11-26, 929E3
POETRY
2 Mao poems published, text 1-1, 9D2
Ashbery wins Natl Book Award 4-19, 292D3
Ashbery wins Pulitzer 5-3, 352C3
Natl Arts Inst admits Brooks, awards Tate 5-19, 504C3
E Ger dissident exiled 11-16, 905A2
Obituaries
Bosco, Henri 5-4, 368E2
Lukonin, Mikhail 8-5, 892C3
Maluf, Chafic 12-27, 1015A2
Qazi Nazrul Islam 8-29, 1015F1
Sissman, Louis 3-10, 316C1
POHLE, Rolf
Extradited from Greece 10-1, 754G3
POISONS & Poisoning—*See substance names*
POISON Tree, The (play)
Opens 1-8, 1014B3
POITIER, Sidney
Weds Shimkus 1-23, 271E3

1977

PLATINUM
NY commodity trading cntr opens 7-5, 521G2
Bophuthatswana declared independent 12-5, 935D2
PLAYBOY (magazine)
Entertainers spoof Carter 1-19, 26F2
Hustler publisher sentncd 2-8, 118C2
Young interview stirs 'racism' controversy 6-3—6-7, 443B3-444A1
PLAYER, Gary
2d in Gleason-Inverrary 2-27, 311C2
2d in Memphis Open 6-12, 676F1
PLAZA, Galo
Civiln rule delayed 4-5, 347C3
PLEA Bargaining—*See COURTS*
PLO (Palestine Liberation Organization)—*See LEBANON, MIDDLE EAST*
PLOURDE, Archbishop Joseph Aurele
Grants gen absolutn 3-15, 375B2
PLUMMER, Christopher
Wins Emmy 9-11, 1022A1
PLUMMER, James W.
Replaced as AF undersecy 7-21, 626A3
PLUTON (French missile)—*See MISSILES*

PLUTONIUM—*For atomic safeguards issue, see ATOMIC Energy—Industrial Use*
Pakistan to buy French A-plant 1-3, 12C3
Energy research budgeted 1-17, 31G2
US rpts material missing 8-4, 8-8, 717D1

PLYTAS, George
Greek culture, science min 11-28, 925B2
PNEUMONIA—*See MEDICINE—Diseases*
POAGE, Rep. W. R. (D, Tex.)
Sugar lobby gifts alleged 7-20, 614B1, D1
PODGORNY, Nikolai V.
In Africa 3-23—4-2, 247G2, 249D3
Sees Castro 4-4—4-6, 249F3
Hosts Mengistu 5-4, 390G3
Ousted from Central Com, party rise cited 5-24, 412A2
Retires, Brezhnev elected pres 6-16, 469C2, F2
PODIATRY—*See MEDICINE*
PODIATRY Association, American (APA)
Ill unit sued re fee-fixing 2-15, 156B3
Mayoral successor elected 4-5, 252E3
PODRABINEK, Alexander
Rpts Lithuania anti-Russian riot 10-30, 955D3
Rpts Klebanov arrest 12-20, 1017C2
POELKER, Mayor John H. (St. Louis, Mo.)
Medicaid abortn curb upheld 6-20, 516D2
POELKER v. Doe
St. Louis abortn fund curb upheld 6-20, 516D2
POETRY
E Ger dissident leaves 8-29, 684D1
Awards
Eberhart wins Natl Book Award 4-11, 355A2
Merrill wins Pulitzer 4-18, 355D2
Aleixandre wins Nobel 10-6, 951F2
Obituaries
Biddle, Katherine 12-30, 1024A1
Galich, Alexander 12-15, 1024F1
Lowell, Robert 9-12, 788E1
Pellicer, Carlos 2-16, 164E3
Prevert, Jacques 4-11, 356E3
Untermeyer, Louis 12-18, 1024E3
POIRER, Jean
On RCMP MP files 8-17, 653D2
POISONS & Poisoning—*See specific substances (e.g., ARSENIC)*

1978

PLATA, Sgt. Benjamin Rodolfo
Sentncd in '75 land reform murders 2-2, 194C2
PLATINUM (play)
Opens 11-12, 1031F2
PLATT, Henry B.
On diamond surcharge 4-27, 319C1
PLATT, Polly
Pretty Baby released 4-5, 619C3
PLAYBOY (magazine)
NFL ex-cheerleaders score team managemt 11-1, 1024B1
PLAYBOY of the Weekend World, The (play)
Opens 11-16, 1031F2
PLAYER (singing group)
Baby Come Home on best-seller list 2-4, 116F3
PLAYER, Gary
Wins Masters 4-9, Tourn of Champs 4-16, Houston Open 4-23, 355E2
2d in Lancome Trophy tourn 10-22, 990C2
PGA top money winner 10-31, 990B3
PLAYERS (play)
Opens 9-6, 887E2
PLAYS—*See THEATER*
PLAZA Hotel (N.Y., N.Y.)
Kennecott proxy vote held 5-2, 403A1
PLEASENCE, Donald
Halloween released 10-15, 970E1
PLESKOW, Eric
Resigns from United Artists 1-13, 75A3
PLESSY Co. Ltd
ICAO picks US bad-weather landing system 4-19, 319A3
PLO (Palestine Liberation Organization)—*See ARAB League, LEBANON, MIDDLE EAST, NONALIGNED Nations Movement*
PLOCK, Gary
Loses NCAA tennis title 5-29, 419E2
PLOTKIN, Norman
Scenes From Country Life opens 3-13, 887A3
PLUMBING and Pipe Fitting Industry of the United States and Canada, United Association of Journeyman and Apprentices of the (AFL-CIO)
Ward on '77 top-paid labor ldrs list 5-15, 365G1
PLUMMER, Christopher
Drinks Before Dinner opens 11-23, 1031D1
PLUTO (planet)—*See ASTRONOMY*
PLUTONIUM—*For atomic safeguards issue, see ATOMIC Energy—Industrial Use*
US, UK researchers rpt safe reprocessing technique 2-27, 144F2
US weighs A-material ban 4-3, 277C2
UK A-reprocessing plant OKd 5-15, 437G2
US A-fuel export license for Pak deferred 5-20, 408C2
Japan breeder research pact with France, W Ger rptd 6-23, 548G3
UK research facility shut 8-24, 667D2
Australia waste causes concern; UK denies negligence, offers aid 10-5—10-10, 771G2
Argentina plans processing plant 10-17, 840B3
GAO links A-plants, arms productn 10-23, 900F1
Australia waste monitoring centralized 11-9, 900D2
UK research center safety study released 11-21, 964E3
PLYTAS, George
Loses Athens mayoralty 10-22, 816E2
PNEUMOCONIOSIS (black lung disease)—*See MEDICINE—Heart & Lungs*
POAGE, Rep. W. R. (D. Tex.)
Not standing for reelectn 5-6, 363A1
Leath wins seat 11-7, 855D3
POCHIN, Sir Edward
Aldermaston safety study released 11-21, 964F3
PODRABINEK, Alexander
Arrested 5-14, 504D1
Gets internal exile 8-15, 634G1
Sovt MD backs abuse chrgs 8-16, 670F3
Sentence upheld 11-23, 947G1
POENISCH, Walter
Marathon swim ends 8-15, 653E1
POETRY
Awards
Arts Institute honors 2 2-7, 316E1
Nemerov wins Natl Book Award 4-10, Pulitzer 4-17, 315C1, A3
Obituaries
Baldwin, Faith 3-19, 252C2
Damas, Leon 1-22, 96E1
Highet, Gilbert 1-20, 96C2
Kuo Mo-jo 6-12, 540B3
Martinson, Harry E 2-11, 196D3
McGinley, Phyllis 2-22, 196D3
Wheelock, John Hall 3-22, 252F3
Zukofsky, Louis 5-12, 440G3
POETZSCH, Anett
Wins world figure-skating title 3-10, 316D3
POINTS, Anthony
Loses Okla US Sen primary 8-22, winner denies gay chrg 8-23, 683B1
PO I-Po
Rehabilitated 12-22, 1015G1
POLA, Claude
Avalanche released 8-28, 969B3

1979

PLATER, Alan
All Things Bright & Beautiful released 3-8, 528B1
PLATH, Sylvia
Bell Jar released 3-20, 528D1
PLATINUM
Canada strike continues 5-12, 369F1
Price soars, drops 10-2–10-3, 740E1
PLATT, Judge Thomas C.
Sentences FBI ex-agent 1-17, 92C3
PLAYER, Gary
Ties for 2d in Greater Greensboro Open 4-8, US Open 4-17, 587B1, C2
PLAYS From Africa (play)
Opens 1-14, 292D2
PLENUM Publishing Corp.
USSR signs 10-yr deal 9-10, 690B2
PLO (Palestine Liberation Organization)—*See ARAB League, LEBANON, MIDDLE EAST, NONALIGNED Nations Movement*
PLOTKIN, Jerry
Taken hostage in Iran 11-29, 895G2
PLUMMER, Christopher
Murder By Decree released 2-8, 174B3
Silent Partner released 5-10, 528F3
Hanover Street released 5-17, 528E2

PLUTONIUM
French-W Ger custody dispute setld 5-16, 380B1
W Ger A-reprocessing plant blocked 5-16, 411A1
Silkwood Okla estate wins A-damages 5-18, 381D1; damages award upheld 8-20, 630A1
H-bomb letter, diagram cites 9-16, 9-18, 715F3, 716A1, 717D2

PLYMOUTH, Mass.—*See MASSACHUSETTS*
PNEUMONIA—*See MEDICINE—Diseases*
PODELL, Bertram L.
Disbarmt challenge declined by Sup Ct 4-16, 303C1
PODELL v. The Joint Bar Association
Case declined by Sup Ct 4-16, 303C1
PODGORNY, Nikolai Viktorovich
Pol career ends; facts on 3-4, 237D2
POEHL, Karl Otto
Named Bundesbank chief 9-19, 733G2-C3
POET and the Rent, The (play)
Opens 5-9, 712A2
POETRY
Blake book sold for record sum 6-13, 672E1
PEN Club cong ends 7-21, 553G3
Awards & Honors
Warren wins Pulitzer 4-16, 336G2
Merrill wins Natl Book Award 4-23, 356B2
Elytis wins Nobel 10-18, 857G3
Obituaries
Bishop, Elizabeth 10-6, 860B2
Tate, Allen 2-9, 176G3
POETZSCH, Anett
Wins Eur figure-skating title 2-3, 392B1
POHER, Rev. Jacques
Censured 12-18, 999B3
POINT Beach Nuclear Plant—*See WISCONSIN—Atomic Energy*
POINT Conception, Calif.—*See CALIFORNIA*
POINT Reyes Light (newspaper)
Wins Pulitzer 4-16, 336D2, A3
POIRET, Jean
Cage aux Folles released 5-12, 528F1
POISONS & Poisoning—*See specific substances (e.g., ARSENIC)*

1980

PLATINUM
Price hits record high 1-17, 30F3
W Ger sets bank curbs 1-23, 103D2
PLATSHORN, Robert Elliot
Convicted 2-4, 270D3
PLAYBOY (magazine)
'Playmate of Yr' found slain 8-15, 713D3
PLAYBOY Enterprises Inc.
Audit, repayments revealed 2-12, 558B2
Marine dischrgd for pose 2-21, 189D1
PLAYER, Gary
Ballesteros wins Masters 4-13, 412A2
Praises Nicklaus 8-10, 714D2
PLAYING for Time (TV film)
Redgrave role protested 1-13, 120B2
CBS airs film, Jews protest 9-30, 835B3
PLESHETTE, Suzanne
Oh, God! Book II released 10-3, 836D3
PLEVEL, Edward
Chrgd in lottery fraud 9-19, 786C3
PLOWRIGHT, Joan
Filumena opens 2-10, 392G2
PLUGGED Nickle (race horse)
Wins Wood Memorial 4-19, 448A1
PLUNKETT, Elzavan U.
Charged in GSA scandal 1-15, 112F1
PLUNKETT, Jim
Raiders win playoffs 12-28, 999E1
PLUTO (planet)
New moon theory rptd 4-22, 416D1

PLUTONIUM
US breeder reactor oppositn cited 2-26, 149E2
W Ger reprocessing plant permit sought 2-27, 154A1
Vienna conf backs fuel use 2-27, 220D3
Italy aid to Iraq seen; US concern noted 3-17, disputed 3-18, 220A3
Colo A-plant protests held 4-19—4-20, 441F1
Extractant chem dvpt rptd 9-12, 9-13, 716F2

PNEUMO Corp.
LTV Corp merger set 8-28, 746B1
PNEUMONIA—*See MEDICINE--Heart & Lungs*
POCHINCHUK, Pyotr
Wins Olympic medal 7-24, 623G3
PODBORSKI, Stephen
Wins Olympic medal 2-14, 155F2
PODLUZHNYI, Valery
Wins Olympic medal 7-28, 624C1
POE, James
Dies 1-24, 176A3
POEHL, Karl Otto
On interest rate hikes 2-29, 153A3
POETRY
2 Sovt poets quit Writers Union 1-12, 46G3
Padilla emigrates to US 3-16, 231A3
Awards & Honors
Justice wins Pulitzer 4-14, 296E2
Obituaries
De Moraes, Vinicius 7-9, 608F1
Hayden, Robert 2-25, 176E1
Reynolds, Julia 11-28, 1004B3
Rukeyser, Muriel 2-12, 176B3
Wright, James 3-25, 280G2
POETZSCH, Anett
Wins Olympic medal 2-23, 155F3
Wins world figure skating title 3-15, 470B2
POHL, Dan
2d in Crosby Pro-Am 2-3, 412C2
POHL, Frederik
JEM wins Amer Book Award 5-1, 692F2
POHL, Karl Otto
Discount, Lombard rates hiked 4-30, 356C1
POIKOLAINEN, Tomi
Wins Olympic medal 8-2, 622C1
POITIER, Sidney
Stir Crazy released 12-12, 1003D2

1976

POLAND—*See also COMECON, DISARMAMENT-Geneva Committee, WARSAW Pact*
Listed as 'not free' nation 1-19, 20E3
Const amendmts draft publshd 1-24; Wyszynski scores 1-25; amendmts adopted 2-10; oppositn rptd 2-10, 3-19, 267G3
Sejm elected, Cath ldr dropped 3-21; new State Cncl, Cabt listed 3-25, 3-27, 268A2, A3
Catholic MP dropped from Sejm 3-21, 268A3
Quake tremors rptd 5-6, 352B3
Food price hike set 6-24, riots force repeal 6-25, CP rallies back govt 6-26—6-28, 482A2
Prince Radziwill dies 6-27, 524D3
CP press vs agri methods 7-7, 522F2
Subsidized housing ends 7-8, 522G2
Meat, produce prices rise 7-13, 522E2
Food rioters sentncd 7-19, 7-20, asks clemency 7-20, 543C3
53 rioters arrested 7-29; church appeals issued 9-10, 9-26; sentences cut 9-27, 811B1
Sugar rationed 8-16; meat price ceiling set 9-27, 811A2
Meat thieves sentncd 8-17, 811C2
Julian Kulski dies 8-18, 656F3
Auto prices hiked 9-1, 811D2
Gierek food shortages, forms price comms 9-3; Central Com OKs plan 9-9, 811E1
Coal rationed 9-8, 966D1
Food-price hikes cut 9-17, 811G1
Brutality vs food rioters chrgd 10-14—12-6, 966F1
Wyszynski asked to continue 11-1, 932B3
Train crash kills 25 11-3, 912B2
Plane hijacked to Vienna 11-4, 907G1
Church scores atheism stand 11-28, 966A2
Central Com meets; CP, govt posts shuffled 12-1—12-2, 926C3
Gierek on 5-yr plan 12-1; Sejm OKs 12-18, 966G3
Wyszynski backs workers 12-12, 966A2
Drought caused grain crop fall 12-31, 977D3
European Force Reduction Issues—*See under EUROPE*
Foreign Relations (misc.)
US inspects Polish grain cargo 1-17—1-19, 44A1
Italy cattle shipmts suspended 1-29, 74G2
Charter chngs cite Sovt ties 2-10, 268B1
US grain shipmt grade disputed 2-26, 3-12, 247F3
To join A-safeguards group 3-13, 243G2
Shuns China fete for Egypt vp 4-19, 275G2
'75 Sovt trade rptd 5-5, 340F3
Addresses E Ger SED Cong 5-19, 381A2
Gierek at E, W Europe CP conf 6-29—6-30, 461D2
Ship in US Bicentennial event 7-4, 488A3
Forgn investor rules eased 7-8, 522F2
Italy CP asks clemency for food rioters 7-20, 543D3
China regrets ouster of newsman 8-24, 674E1
Sovt space program set role 9-14, 684D1
Swedish—US spy device rptd 9-14, 734G1
Rpt US, UK, France return Danzig gold 9-28, 907F1
Ford, Carter debate 10-6, 741C3
Ford debate gaffe stirs controversy 10-7—10-12, 762A1-763F1
Dole defends Ford record 10-15, 783E3
Gierek in USSR, signs aid pact 11-9—11-15; trade rise seen 11-16, 907C1
Coal exports rptd 11-17, 966E1
'75 trade deficit rptd 11-18, 977D1
Canada grain deal OKd 11-24, 889B1
W Ger backs coal project 12-8, 966E1
Jaroszewicz visits UK, signs econ pact 12-15—12-17, 966C1

1977

POLAND—*See also COMECON, DISARMAMENT—Geneva Committee, WARSAW Pact*
Gierek sees Wyszynski 10-29, Cath populatn cited 885F3
Church scores sexual permissiveness 12-4, 987E1
Dep premr, 2 mins ousted 12-17, 987F1
Economy & Labor (domestic)
Econ plan revised, consumer goods stressed 1-21, 66A3
'76 econ growth rptd 2-8, 242E1
'76 food-price rioters rptd freed 3-24, 242A1; 4-22, 314D2
Bad harvest, food shortages rptd 10-7, 885E3
Gierek sees Wyszynski 10-29, 886A1
Pvt shopowners trade rules eased 11-10, 987G1
Poor grain harvest cited 11-15, 916F2
Foreign Relations (misc.)—*See also 'Human Rights' and 'Monetary, Trade & Aid' below*
UN Assemb member; Lachs on World Ct 4A1, G1
Denmark ousts consul 1-10, 62B1
In 14-natn sulphur-dioxide pact 1-19, 109B3
Spain ties rptd renewed 1-27, 242C2
Australia jails Karasinski 2-15, 425A2
Spain hijacked jet lands 3-14, 224E3
Iraqi Kurds free 4 hostages 3-29, 256F3
Malta premr provokes walkout in Peking 11-3, 925G2
W Ger chancellor visits 11-21—11-25, 926E1
Gierek in Italy 11-28—12-1, sees Pope 12-1, 987B1
Egypt closes consulates, cultural cntrs 12-7, 929B1, 930B1
Dutch sentence war criminal 12-14, 986C1
Helsinki Agreement—*See EUROPE—Security and Cooperation*
Human Rights
Police brutality probe asked 1-8, 24E2
Govt eases stand vs dissidents 1-20, 66F3
Intellectuals back Czech dissidents 2-1, 82F2
Dissident homes rptd searched 2-22, 242B1
'76 food-price rioters rptd freed 3-24, 242A1; 4-22, 314D2
21 seek Dutch asylum 3-26, 315A1
Human rights group formed 3-27, 242C1
27 in Denmark ask W Ger asylum 5-3, 15 OKd 5-4, 427C1
Dissident student dies 5-7; protests 7 seized 5-15—5-19, 436F3
Dissident protester freed 6-8, 513D1
Prelates in rights plea, press scored 6-9, 513B1
Amnesty frees '76 rioters 7-23, 639E2
Bishops score media 9-18, 752D3
Workers Defns Com chngs name, widens activities 10-3, 752C3

1978

POLAND—*See also COMECON, DISARMAMENT—Geneva Committee, GATT, WARSAW Pact*
CP central com conf 1-9—1-10, 20B1
Culture minister resigns 1-26, 95A2
1st Pole in space 6-27, 506A1; ends flight 7-5, 622C3
Krakow cardinal elected Pope 10-16, 781A1, E2
Salyut space visit cited 11-2, photos rptd taken from orbit 11-3, 861B1, E1
Independence day marked 11-9, 1019F2
Independence rally 11-11, 925D3
Economy & Labor (domestic)
CP members ask reforms 1-6, 20C1
Price hikes seen, min wage raised 1-9, 20A1
GNP '77 increase rptd 2-6, 115F3
Gasoline, alcohol prices hiked 3-20, 5-28, 535C2
'77 growth, average wage rptd 5-15, 535A2
Meat prices raised 6-1, 650C2
Farmers protest pensn plan, Gierek vows review 10-5, 904E1
European Force Reduction Talks—*See under EUROPE*
Foreign Relations (misc.)—*See also 'Monetary, Trade, Aid & Investment' and 'UN' below*
At USSR maneuvers 2-6—2-10, 103C2
Iraq chrgs pro-Israel stand 416F1
Nazi extraditn from Brazil rptd sought 6-8, 477C2
Czech, Polish dissidents mark '68 Sovt invasn 8-15, 635F1
E Ger hijacks plane to W Berlin 8-30, 894F3
Czech, Polish dissident contact rptd 10-7, 868G3
Cosmonaut Salyut visit cited 11-2, 861B1
Anti-USSR slogans at rally 11-11, 925D3
Helsinki Agreement—*See EUROPE—Security and Cooperation*
Human Rights
CP members ask reforms 1-6, 20C1
Min rptdly admits censorship excessive 2-24, 180A3
Dissidents held re study group 3-5, 180G2
Dissidents join writers' union 4-8, 276D1
Rights group chrgs police brutality 4-12, 276E1
Dissidents, Czech Charter 77 mtg rptd 8-15, 635F1
Bishops score censorship 9-17, 749F1
Czech, Polish dissident contact rptd 10-7, 868G3
Pope's Christmas message rptd censored 12-21, 1019D2

1979

POLAND—*See also COMECON, DISARMAMENT-Geneva Committee, GATT, WARSAW Pact*
Warsaw bank blast kills 49 2-15, 212D2
Auschwitz photos issued 2-22, 193D1
Eastn floods rptd 4-8, 289A1
Economy & Labor
'79 budget defns spending freeze rptd 1-9, 39F2
Westn banks to monitor 1-11, 59E3-60C1
'79 growth slowdown set 1-11, 60B1
Bad weather cripples econ 1-31, 120C2
CP member asks free discussn 5-4, 374A3
Alcohol sales banned for Pope's visit 6-1—6-4, 414C2
Econ growth rptd stagnant 7-29, 741F3
European Force Reduction Talks—*See under EUROPE*
Foreign Relations (misc.)—*See also 'Monetary' and 'UN' below*
Cambodia downfall rptd lauded 1-10, 11B2
Czech dissident sentncd 1-11, 62C2
E Ger '78 hijacker freed in W Berlin 5-28, 430E2
USSR border rptd closed re Pope 6-2, extra press fee canceled 6-2, 414F1, C2
Nazi's extradtn denied by Brazil 6-20, 483A3
Ger invasn anniv marked, new dissident party seeks Sovt power end 9-1, 802F2
USSR troop deploymt rptd 761F2
USSR dominatn scored by dissidents 12-10, 939A2
Zimbabwe allows newsman 12-17, 960B2
Helsinki Agreement—*See EUROPE-Security and Cooperation*
Human Rights
Freedom House lists as partly free 12G3
Czech dissident sentenced 1-11, 62C2
Bible availability cited 3-13, 238E1
Kuron, Michnik arrested, 'flying' univ harassmt cited 4-18, 374G2
CP member asks free discussn re econ 5-4, 374A3
Kuron, Michnik freed 5-25, 414D2
Pope backs religious freedom, curbs cited 6-2, 6-5, 413E1, D2
Czech dissident arrests scored 7-5, 802E2
New party formed at Warsaw rally 9-1, 802E2
UN seeks employe detentn info 10-29, 939B2
Unoffl independnc rally held 11-11, organizers sentncd 12-10, 939G1
Mass, rally mark '70 riots 12-17-12-18, 980C3

1980

POLAND—*See also COMECON, CSCE, GATT, GENEVA Committee, MBFR, WARSAW Pact*
Airliner crash kills 87 3-14, 213E3; engine failure seen 3-31, 256B3
Milosz wins Nobel 10-9, 889D2
Economy & Labor—*See also 'Labor Unrest' below*
'79 data rptd 2-8, 166G1
Econ problems, Politburo shuffle linked 2-11—2-15, 152G2, D3
Meat price hikes spur labor unrest 7-1—7-11; food shortages seen, wage hikes pledged 7-9, 7-11, 566E1, 658D1
Problems, data revealed, Politburo denies 11-12; govt sets overhaul 11-19, 878D2
Kania, Walesa confer 11-14, 878B1
'81 econ plan announced 12-19, 976D3
Foreign Relations (misc.)—*See also 'Labor Unrest', 'Monetary', 'UN Policy' below*
USSR Afghan invasn rptd 1-10, 11A1
W Ger offcl's visit cancellatn cited 1-30, 103F1
USSR, detente backed 2-11, 152A2
Italy CP rejects Paris CP parley 4-2, 254C3
Zimbabwe gains independnc 4-18, 301F1
Europn CPs meet 4-28—4-29, 327B2
Franco-Sovt summit held 5-19, 378G2
E Ger gas cash purchases barred 6-1, 431D3
Canada immigratn records rptd found 8-20, 651A2
Sovt ties reaffirmed 9-4, 658G2, C3
USSR lauds Kania promotn 9-6, 678A3
Kania: Sovt ties 'paramount' 9-6, 678C3
W Gers arrest alleged spy 9-9, 889D1
Nazi kills self in Brazil 10-3, 810E1
Warsaw Pact mins meet Kania, other Polish ldrs 10-19—10-20, 800D2
E Ger restricts travel 10-28, curbs scored 10-30, 828G3, 860C1
Kania, Pinkowski in USSR, ties affirmed 10-30, 859G3
Czechs curb travel 11-20, 879C1
E Ger border shut 12-1, 910F2
US scores USSR Persian Gulf peace plan 12-11, 930C2
Government & Politics—*See also other appropriate subheads in this section*
8th CP cong: Politburo shuffled, premr removed 2-11—2-15, 152G2
Sejm electn turnout high 3-23, 262F3
Pol reforms demanded by strikers 8-17; Gierek rejects, govt negotiator replaced 8-21, 625A1, 658F1
Babiuch, other ldrs ousted; Pinkowski named premr 8-24, 641A1, E1, 658D2
Gierek hospitalized 9-5; Kania named party chief, Jagielski 1st dep 9-6, 678E2, C3
CP concedes reforms needed 9-14, 9-15, 710B2
Politburo member ousted 9-19, 720F2
CP Central Com meets 10-4—10-6; 8 purged 10-6, 760C2-E3
CP, govt shakeup 11-17—11-18, 878A2
Cabt shuffled 11-21, local CP ldrs dismissals rptd 11-22; 4 Politburo men purged 12-2, 909B1, B2
Human Rights—*See also 'Labor Unrest' below*
Draft law eased, Jehovah's Witnesses benefit 1-23, 88C1
UN employe sentncd as spy 3-7, 220G3
Katyn protester kills self 3-20, 262E3
Czestochowa bishop bars vote 3-20, boycott fails 3-23, 262F3
Czech, Polish dissident lectures compared 4-2, 262D2
UN employe's sentence upheld 4-14, 326G3
Worker's 2d trial rptd 4-21, 381D2
Publisher rptd cleared 5-15, 381B2
4 sentncd for copier acquisitn 6-12, 500G3
RC Sunday mass broadcast 9-21, 720G2
Labor Unrest
Gdansk workers protest 1-30, 1-31, 88A1
Meat price hikes spur strikes 7-1—7-11, 566E1, 658D1
Gierek warns pay hikes inflationary 7-9, 566F1, 658D1

1976

1977

Gierek sees Wyszynski 10-29, 886A1
Dissident journals seized 12-7, 12-19, 987C2

1978

1979

1980

Strikes spread, some pay hikes won 7-15—8-12, 626B1, 658D1
Politburo forms workers' rights comm 7-18, 626D1
Gdansk shipyd workers strike, demands include pol reforms 8-14; unrest spreads thru Baltic 8-15—8-19, 625A1, 658E1
Babiuch TV plea to workers 8-15, 625D1
Strike com demands include trade unions, end to censorship 8-17, 8-19, 625F1, C2, 658F1
Gierek vows pay hikes, rejcts pol reforms, delays W Ger trip 8-18, 625G1
USSR rpts on unrest 8-19, jams Westn broadcasts 8-20, 626B2, 658F1
Sovt bloc, Vatican, US, Polish-Amer reactn 8-19—8-21, 626F2-627B1
Kuron, 17 other dissidents arrested 8-20—8-21, 625C2, 658F1
Schmidt cancels E Ger trip 8-22, Strauss urges Polish loans withheld 8-24, 642E2, 658F1
Govt recognizes strikers 8-23, phones reconnected 8-24; talks held, strike spreads 8-23—8-27, 641B1
Babiuch, other ldrs ousted 8-24, 641A1, 658D2
Dissidents still held 8-25, 641C2
Sovts rpt Babiuch resignatn 8-24—8-25, call crisis 'internal affair' 8-26, score strikers 8-27, 642B1, 658D2
E Eur reactn 8-25, 642G1
Wyszynski urges calm 8-26, 641D2, 658D2
Gdansk strike ldr pleas for labor restraint, govt warns workers 8-28, 657C1
Wyszynski counseling rptd distorted by govt 8-28, 657F1
Silesia coal miners walkout, send reps to Gdansk 8-29, 657B1, G1, 658E2
Gdansk strike ldrs see agreemt, Szczecin talks deadlocked 8-29, 657B2
USSR scores strike setlmt, chrgs subversn; E Eur reactn mixed 8-29—9-3, 658D3-659B1
Gdansk, Szczecin prelim strike accord reached; free trade unions, other demands granted 8-30, 657C2, 658E2
Strike accord formally concluded, final sessn televised 8-31, 657B1, G2-658A1, F2
US unions aid strikers, Admin cautns 8-31, 9-4, 659G2
Gdansk, Szczecin, other strikers return to jobs 9-1—9-3, 657A1, 658B1, A2
Silesia miners strike continues 9-1; accord reached 9-2, 15,000 stay out 9-3, 657B1, 658B1-C2, F2
Kuron, 17 other dissidents freed 9-1, 658A2
ILO praise workers 9-1, 659G3
Reagan, Carter praise strikers 9-1, 664D2
Carter, Reagan statemts scored by Sovts 9-2, 659E2
W Ger campaign issue 9-3—9-5, 690E3
Old, new unions vie for support 9-4, 658A3; defectn rate rptd high 9-6, 679A1
US union OKs worker fund 9-4; Warsaw protests 9-9—9-10, Admin disavows 9-11, 679F1-D2
France union rift widens 9-4, 688E1
Chronology 7-1—9-4, 658C1
UK TUC cancels visit 9-5, 668F2
CP shakeup; Kania named party chief, Jagielski 1st dep 9-6, 678E2, C3
Kania vows strike accord implementatn 9-6; visits Gdansk 9-8, Silesia 9-9, 678A3-679A1
Work stoppages continue, agri co-ops seek redress 9-11, 679B1
Carter lauds strike dignity 9-12, 710C3
CP concedes reforms needed 9-14, 9-15, 710C2
S Africa chrgs SWAPO support 8-29, US denies 9-9, 710D1
Union regulatns issued 9-15, federatn formed 9-17, 9-18, 710D1
W Ger RR workers strike, cite Gdansk 9-17, 731F1
16 strikes rptd ongoing; Politburo member ousted 9-19, 720E2, F2
RC Sunday mass broadcast 9-21, 720G2
Free trade unions register; ldrs see Jagielski 9-24, 720C2
Sovts warn unions 9-25, 9-27; E Ger, Czechs echo 9-30, 752F3; 10-8—10-9, 761C1-G1
Jagielski warns on new strike 10-1; unions hold 1-hour stoppage 10-3, 760E3, 761B1
Govt sees continued crisis 10-4—10-6, 760F2, C3
Portugal CP electn loss linked 10-5, 760E1
E Eur warnings increase, mil interventn hinted 10-8—10-21, 831B1
Warsaw Pact communique issued 10-20, 800C2
Union registratn conditns scored 10-24, 830D3
E Ger restricts travel 10-28, curbs scored 10-30, 829B1, 860C1
USSR affirms govt support, aid sought 10-30, 860A1
Pinkowski meets labor ldrs, Walesa affirms strike deadline 10-31, 860D1
E Ger, Czech criticism continues 11-5, 860G1-B2
CP warns vs strike 11-7; authorities prepare for unrest 11-8—11-9; Sup Ct backs unions, strike averted 11-10, 862B2-B3
Kania, Walesa meet 11-14, 878B1
Walesa urges end to strikes 11-15; Gdansk sit-in ends, Czestochowa strike threat off 11-17, 878E1

1976

Sports
Olympic results 7-18—7-31, 573C3, 574B1-576B3
Olympic athlete disqualified 7-30, 563B2

West German Relations—*See 'Eastern European Policy' under GERMANY, Federal Republic of*

1977

Monetary, Trade & Aid Issues (including all foreign economic developments)
UK 200-mi fishing zone in effect 1-1, 21A1
Sovt oil price rise rptd 1-6, 67C3
Westn trade debt rptd 1-21, 66E3
'76 OECD trade gap rptd 1-26, 123C2
'76 trade deficit rptd 2-8, 242D1
Westn debt rptd mounting 2-13—4-13, 335C3
US adopts fishing agrmt 2-21, 173D3
A-supplier natns score Carter plans 4-28—4-29, 403F1-A2
Chase rpts $350 mln copper loan 8-31, 886A1
A-suppliers natns OK export safeguards 9-21, 717D1
More grain imports seen 10-7, 885E3
Canada wheat purchase rptd 11-9, 987B2
US grain sales cited 11-15, 916F2
Carter OKs more agri aid 12-30, 1001A2

U.S. Relations—*See also 'Monetary, Trade & Aid' above*
Carter visit scheduled 9-23, 738F1
Carter visit deferred 11-7, 854A1; rescheduled 11-29, 914B2
Carter visits 12-29—12-30, 1000E3, 1001B1

1978

Monetary, Trade, Aid & Investment
US retirees exchng rate lowered 1-1, facts on 20D1
Swedish fishing zones set 1-1, 21A2
'77 A-export safeguard pact detailed 1-11, 11B2
EC imposes steel dumping levies 1-23, 80B2
Zloty exchange rate adjusted 2-1, 95G1
UK reassigns shipbldg order 2-5, 112A3
'77 imports, exports rptd 2-6, 115G1
Australia joins A-supplier group 2-24, 129C2
Zloty float rptd 4-5, 535G2
Cobalt purchases rptd up 5-24, 382D2
Occidental trade deal rptd 5-28, 650E2
Westn debt estimated, considered good credit risk 6-1, 535F2
'77 trade deficit down 6-15, 535E2
USSR plane order rptd 7-5, 650D2
US favored natn trade status cited 7-8, 534D2
Shipping competitn vs EC rptd 7-11, 670C3
US bars clothespin import curbs 10-2, 805E1
Westn debt estimated 11-28, 999A2

Sports
World Amateur Boxing tourn results 5-6—5-20, 600D2
World Cup soccer finals, sidelights 6-1—6-25, 519F3, 520F1

UN Policy & Developments
UNDOF mandate renewed 5-31, 400B2
Assemb member 713D3
UNESCO press declaratn lauded 11-22, 931E1

U.S. Relations—*See also 'Monctary, Trade, Aid & Investment' above*
Carter State of Union Message 1-19, 31B3

1979

Monetary, Trade, Aid & Investment
US agri loan OKd, aid total rptd 1-6, 39B3
Westn banks to monitor econ 1-11, 59E3-60C1
'78 trade deficit rptd 2-21, 212C2
'78 Westn debt rptd 3-16, 3-20, 200E3, 212A2
US, UK, Canada banks sign loan 3-30, 279G2
Fiat deal signed 6-18, 487F1-A2
Fiat announces investmt plan 9-12, 709C2
EC ball bearing dumping probe opened 9-20, 719E2
US bank branches cited 11-15, 882C3

Obituaries
Piasecki, Boleslaw 1-1, 104F3

Roman Catholic Church
Facts on govt restrictns 413E2
Macharski rptd named Krakow archbp 60G2
Pope visit plan rptd 1-24, 60G2
Pope arrives, St Stanislaus anniv cited; meets Gierek 6-2, on E Eur RC freedom 6-3, addresses bishops 6-5, visits Nazi death camps 6-7, 413A1-414D1, G1
Sovt reactn to Pope's visit 6-3, 414E1
Pope ends visit 6-8–6-10, 435E1
Macharski, Rubin installed cardinals 6-30, 640B2

UN Policy & Developments
Membership listed 695B3
Assemb seeks employe detentn info 10-29, 939B2

U.S. Relations
Agri loan OKd, aid total rptd 1-6, 39B3
CIA issues Auschwitz photos 2-22, 193D1
US banks sign loan 3-30, 279G2
US A-accident media coverage rptd 4-11, 323D1

1980

E Eur, Sovts score 11-16—11-30, 910E1
2 unionists arrested 11-21, Warsaw workers protest 11-24, gen strike urged 11-25—11-26; unionists freed, Walesa urges moderatn 11-27, 909B1-B2
RR, sugar strikes settled 11-26, 909F1
Kania scores unionists 12-1, 910B1
USSR orders E Ger border shut 12-1, 910F2
E Ger-Polish border shut 12-1; reserves rptd active, Sovts deny 12-2, 910F2
US, EC warn USSR vs Poland mil interventn 12-2, 12-3, 910G2, B3
CP warns nation 12-4, 909A1
Moscow summit mtg issues warning 12-5, 929A1
Sovt invasn preparatn rptd complete 12-7; US dispatches AWACS 12-9, 929F2, 930B1
E Eur press attacks resume 12-8—12-10, Tass rpt denied; govt scores dissidents, army urges reform 12-8, 929A1
Sovts hint mil action, claim US 'fanning war psychosis' 12-11, 929A1
NATO mins warn Sovts 12-9—12-12, 949A1
US Sen Percy says warned Brezhnev 12-12, 950C3
Church warns dissidents 12-12, urges moderatn 12-14; defns com ldr scores church 12-20, 976A1
Parlt speaker warns vs forgn interventn 12-13, 976F1
Farmers rally to form union 12-14, 976G1
Walesa urges unity at '70 riot rites 12-16, 12-17; says unions want talks, not strikes 12-17, 976B2
Castro scores workers' movemt 12-17, 12-20, 992F3
Walesa urges chrgs vs Moczulki dropped 12-22, 976E1
USSR aid sought by Czyrek 12-26, Jagielski 12-29, 976G2

Monetary, Trade, Aid & Investment
Copper, silver '79 exports cited 2-26, 166A2
COMECON to keep fixed prices for Sovt commodities 5-29, 451F1
EC butter imports suspended 7-9, 566F1
Westn banks grant loans 8-12, 8-22, 642C2
W Ger urged to withhold loans 8-24, 642F2
US 22% credit hike asked 8-27, Carter urges Westn aid 8-29; W Ger, USSR reactn 9-3, 9-4, 659C1
US unions aid strikers, Admin cautns 8-31, 9-4, 659G2
USSR hard currency loan rptd 9-3, 658G2, A3
US union OKs worker aid 9-4; Warsaw protests 9-9—9-10, Admin disavows 9-11, 979F1-D2
USSR currency credits rptd, Westn debt paymts pledged 9-8, 679E1
USSR aid talks held, food, mfrd goods increase pledged 9-10—9-11, 679C1
US grants $670 mln grain credit 9-12, 710F2
USSR increased food, goods aid sought 10-30, 860B1
'81 grain imports seen, sugar imports cited 11-12; food exports halted 11-14, 879A1, B1
US loan sought, grain credit rise proposed 11-13, 879B1
Czechs curb currency exchng 11-20, 879C1
Kania reveals $1.3 bln USSR aid 12-1, 910B1

Obituaries
Jantar, Anna 3-14, 214B1
Kaminska, Ida 5-21, 448B2
Walsh, Stella 12-4, 1004F3

Soviet Relations—*See 'Labor Unrest' above*

Sports
Moscow Olympic results 7-20—8-3, pole vault mark set 7-30, 588A3, 589C1, 622F1-624F3
Chess Olympiad results 12-7, 972B3

UN Policy & Developments
Rights comm Afghan res opposed 2-14, 123E3
Dvpt plan employe sentncd as spy 3-7, 220G3; sentnc upheld 4-14, 326G3
World Ct demands Iran free US hostages 5-24, 393C1

U.S. Relations
Statemt on Polish unrest; Polish-Amers score passivity 8-21, 626C3, 627A1
CP scores strike setlmt 8-29, 659A1
US unions aid strikers, Admin cautns 8-31, 9-4, 659G2
Reagan, Carter praise strikers 9-1, 664D2
Carter, Reagan strike statemts scored by Sovts 9-2, 659E2
US union OKs worker aid 9-4; Warsaw protests 9-9—9-10, Admin disavows 9-11, 679F1-D2
US grants $670 mln grain credit 9-12, 710F2
Milosz wins Nobel 10-9, 889D2
US loan sought; grain credit rise proposed 11-13, 879B1
US vs Sovt invasn 12-2, 910G2; 12-19, 950E1
US rpts Sovt invasn preparatn complete 12-7; US AWACS dispatched 12-9, 929F2, 930B1
Muskie lauds NATO warning to Sovts 12-12, 949C1
Sen Percy: warned Brezhnev 12-12, 950C3

1976

POLANYI, Michael
Dies 2-22, 192F3
POLAROID Corp.
Austria camera deal rptd 1-30, 97F3
POLETTI, Ugo Cardinal
Scores Franzoni CP support 6-17, 446D1

POLICE
Chicago racial quotas set 1-5, 6G1
CIA aid to DC area police rptd 1-11, 1-13, 24A3
Sup Ct declines Mass questionaire rule review 1-12, 24F1
Mich unit ordrd disbanded 1-18, 45E1
Ford State of Union message 1-19, 38A2
Sup Ct voids Pa misconduct rule 1-21, 42C3
Warrantless arrests upheld 1-26, 87A2
Ford on 'brutality' issue 2-14, 130A1
Handgun study rptd 2-17, 170C2
Sup Ct gives libel immunity 3-23, 218C3
Chrgd re FBI thefts 3-28, 3-29, 234D3
Sup Ct upholds grooming codes 4-5, 262B2
Sup Ct voids NJ canvasser curb 5-19, 393C3
Sup Ct upholds job test rule 6-7, 435A1
NC firing upheld 6-10, 552F2
Dem platform text 6-15, 474A1, D1
Sup Ct upholds Mo bargaining law 6-21, 553A1
Sup Ct rules on wages 6-24, 468B2
Warrantless 'doorway' arrests upheld 6-24, 553B1
Sup Ct upholds Mass retiremt law 6-25, 552E1
2 Ohio officers sentncd 7-6, 524C1
Fed cts criminal appeals limited 7-6, 534B3
Warrantless alien interrogatn upheld 7-6, 534G3
Traffic violatn auto search upheld 7-6, 535C1
Howe convicted 7-23, 552B1
Detroit recalls 450 8-16, other dept dvpts 8-20—9-28, 776B2, C2
NYC protests staged 9-26, 4 arrested 10-6, 991D2
Ford at chiefs conv 9-27, 723D3
Survivor benefits bill signed 9-29, 834D2
Sup Ct upholds Mass unpaid duty rule 10-12, 848A3
Sup Ct to review mandatory death sentence 11-29, 900F2
NYC PBA wins '75 increase 12-22, 991A2

POLICE, International Association of Chiefs of
Ford addresses 9-27, 723D3
POLICH, Dr. J. Michael
Alcohol study scored 6-9, 6-10, 442F3-443E1
POLIO (infantile paralysis)—*See 'Diseases' under MEDICINE*
POLISH American Congress
ABC joke case review denied 2-23, 170A1
POLISH Americans
ABC joke case review denied 2-23, 170A1
Ford, Carter at conv 9-24, 724A1
Ford, Carter debate 10-6, 741D3
Ford debate gaffe stirs controversy 10-7—10-12, 762A1-763F1, B3
Buffalo honors Pulaski 10-10, 763B3
Ford at Buffalo mass 10-31, 826C3
POLITICAL Assassinations—*See under CRIME*
POLITICAL Rights Defense Fund
Perkus on SWP burglaries 7-14, 570B1

1977

POLANSKI, Roman
Indicted for rape 3-24, 262D1
Pleads guilty 8-8, mental exam ordered 9-19, 732C3
POLAROID Corp.
Instant movies unveiled 4-26, 409A1
S Africa sales ended 11-22, 934D2
POLGAR, Thomas
Viet evacuatn scored in Snepp book 11-18, 898C1
POLICE—*See also country names*
France rpts INTERPOL role in Daoud release 1-11, 9A2
Saxe sentenced 1-17, 140E1
US Sup Ct limits suspects rights 1-25, 80E1
Chicago hiring goals accepted 2-6, 279A3
US Sup Ct voids SC informant curb 2-22, 150B1
US issues terrorism rpt 3-2, 484C1
Miranda rule review sidestepped 3-23, 275B3
Chesimard convicted, sentncd for '73 NJ slaying 3-25, 288C3
Va death penalty bill signed 3-29, 594E1
Chicago spying disclosed 5-11, 388D2
LA hq rptd kiddie porno operatn 5-15, 432A2
US Sup Ct backs Mo deadly force law 5-16, 419F1
LA, NYS sued re job bias 6-2, 9-8; LA cities OK quotas 6-29, 819F1-E2
Mandatory death sentncs curbed 6-6, 478C2
1-man lineups upheld 6-16, 518D1
Chicago cops win Panter suit 6-21, 540E2
NYS death penalty bill vetoed 7-12, 594F2
NYC blackout injuries 7-13—7-14, 537A3
Bus riders' 'bill of rights' set 8-8, 627C2
FHWA truck inspectns intensify 9-8, 778D3
Pay hikes, property tax boosts linked 9-12, 722B1
House mandatory retiremt curb votes 9-23, 737E2
Castroville (Tex) marshal convctd 9-29, 821C1
Chicago promotn quota case review refused 10-3, 760A3
Ill break-in case review declined 10-3, 760B3
4 Houston ex-police indicted re Torres 10-20, 820F3
NJ harassmt case review refused 10-31, 835C2
NY death penalty provisn voided 11-15, 919C3
State police meal stipends ruled taxable 11-29, 919D1
Search, seizure rights in traffic violatns extended 12-5, 938G3-939B1
Cleveland dispute 12-15—12-16, 1005F1

POLIO (infantile paralysis)—*See MEDICINE—Diseases*
POLITICAL Payments—*See BUSINESS—Payments Issues*
POLITICAL Science Association, American
Davidson tenure policy chngd 5-6, 472B1

1978

POLANSKI, Roman
Flees US on morals chrg 2-1, 116A2
POLARIS—*See ARMAMENTS—Ships*
POLESHCHUK, A. S.
Named as Sovt spy 3-30, 247F3

POLICE—*See also country names*
Tex marshal sentenced in '75 Morales slaying 2-18, 991E3
Phila radicals blockaded 3-8—5-7, 410D1-C2
Md restores death penalty 3-10, 388F3
NYS death penalty bill clears legislature 3-20; Carey vetoes 4-11, override fails 5-2, 388A3
Witness found thru illegal search backed by Sup Ct 3-21, 220G3
State policy alien ban backed by US Sup Ct 3-22, 221A1
3 Houston ex-cops sentncd in Torres case 3-28, appeal rptd 12-14, 991B3
2 NYC officers slain, Attica ex-inmate arrested 4-5, 388C3
Mandatory retiremt curb exempts 4-6, 238F3
Phila Inquirer, 2 rptrs win Pulitzers 4-17, 315A1, D1
Spinks avoids drug indictmt 4-18, 379B1
Ill juvenile suspect rights case review refused by Sup Ct 4-24, 322F2
NM press info order review refused by Sup Ct 5-15, 388B1
Rochester (NY) hiring challenge case declined by Sup Ct 5-22, 388B2
Newsroom searches backed by Sup Ct 5-31, 429E3
4 Houston ex-cops chrgd in '77 Webster death cover-up 6-3, 991F2
LA plans layoffs 6-7, 425B3, D3
Double jeopardy doctrine reversed by Sup Ct 6-14, 468B3
Murder scene search warrants backed, hosp interrogatns curbed by Sup Ct 6-21, 509D2
NYC 'runaway' father search rptd 7-3, 685A1
Cleveland strike 7-13—7-14, 565D2
US drops dual prosecutn of Dallas cop in '73 Rodriguez case 7-14, 991C3
Phila radicals routed; cop killed, 12 chrgd 8-8, 645D1
Memphis strike 8-10—8-18, 644C2
Wichita strike 9-14—9-20, 753E1
Neb 'deadly force' case refused by US Sup Ct 10-16, 789C2
DC pensn reform vetoed 11-4, 897F2
Cities' power over suburbs backed by Sup Ct 11-28, 937C3
Auto search power broadened by Sup Ct 12-5, 959C2
Newark layoffs planned 12-11, 1012E1
Press search shield bill proposed 12-13, 1029C3
Houston ex-chief convctd of extortn 12-14, 991A2
2 Houston ex-cops chrgd in '75 Joyvies cover-up 12-14, 991D2
Tenn gov's aide arrested 12-15, 1011F1
Cleveland layoffs canceled 12-28, 1008E3

POLIAKOFF, Stephen
Strawberry Fields opens 6-4, City Sugar 6-5, 887D1, C3
POLIDAN, Ronald
Black hole rptd in constellatn Scorpio 6-22, 654D2
POLIDENT—*See MEDICINE—Dentistry*
POLIKANOV, Sergei M.
Ousted by CP 2-21, 275D3
Arrives in Denmark 10-10, 946F3
POLIOMYLETIS (infantile paralysis)—*See MEDICINE—Diseases*
POLIS, Joel
Family Business opens 4-12, 760B2
POLISH Americans
Bench jokes upset audience 1-7, 195B1
POLITICAL Action Committees (PACs)—*See POLITICS—Campaign Finances; also specific committee names*
POLITICAL Payments—*See BUSINESS—Payments Issues*
POLITICAL Prisoners—*See HUMAN Rights; country names*
POLITICAL Science
Obituaries
Lasswell, Harold D 12-18, 1032B3
POLITICS (non-U.S.)—*See country names*

1979

POLIAKOFF, Stephen
Hitting Town opens 1-6, 292F1

POLICE—*See also country names*
Houston ex-chief sentncd 1-29, 79C1
3 Houston ex-cops win Torres case appeal 2-6, 156B2
Rock Springs (Wyo) chief faces murder trial 2-7, 156A1
New Orleans strike 2-8—3-4, 165E3-166C1
Ill prison gang rule broken 2-24, 196D3
Hartford crime-control progrm rptd 2-25, 156F3
'Son of Sam' pre-arrest evidence rptd 2-26, 156F2
Hayes pleads guilty to drug sale 3-14, sentncd 3-22, 335B3
Tenneco fined in La bribe case 3-17, 239C3
Carter urges restricted newsroom searches 4-2, 264D3
Phila brutality chrgd 4-16, Rizzo denies 4-17; bar unit assails 4-19, 310B3-G3
2 San Fran offcrs win libel case vs newspr 4-18, 4-19, 334B2
Ala woman slain 6-22, 2,000 protest 7-20, 869C3
Toledo (O) contract rejctd 7-3, 599E1
LA Cnty deputies end 'sickout' 7-12, 599E1
Textile union sues Ga offcls 7-18, setlmt rptd 8-1, 598G3
Hawaiian police end 'sickout' 7-18, 599F1
ABA rejects 3d party search limits 8-9, 8-15, 768D3
US basketball coach sentncd in Pan Am Games assault 9-10, 798E3
Bell signs Phila brutality complaint 8-10; US files chrgs, Rizzo calls suit political 8-13, 610E1-E2
Mass death penalty bill signed 8-14, 990A1
NYC bank protectn ordrd 8-22, 656C1
Pope in 6 cities, overtime costs estimated 10-1—10-7, 761A2
Castro protected in NYC 10-11—10-14, 779A1
Ill mayor slain, strike cited 10-16, 840D2
Phila brutality suit dismissed 10-30, 831B3
3 Houston ex-cops resentncd 10-30, 839B3
Newark manpower ordinance cited 11-13, 921A2
Newark hiring ordinance vetoed 11-15, override fails 11-20, 992F1
Cleaver murder chrgs rptd dropped 12-3, 1006E1
Supreme Court Rulings
Random car checks barred 3-27, 263D1
Buian damage case declined 4-23, 346G2
Verbal rights waiver backed 4-24, 364A2
'Probable cause' in detentns backed 6-5, 464B2
'Open-ended' warrants use curbed 6-11, 478A3
PR search law voided 6-18, 499A2
Warrantless phone surveillnc upheld 6-20, 516C1
Youth 'Miranda rights' limited 6-20, 516B2
Luggage search warrants backed 6-20, 516C2
'Good faith' arrest backed 6-25, 540B1
Mass driver license suspensn rule upheld 6-25, 540G1
Juvenile 'Miranda rights' case remanded 6-25, 540B2
Tex identificatn law convictn voided 6-25, 540D2
Rights violatn proof in false arrest suits backed 6-26, 540G3
'78-79 Sup Ct term ends, voting alignmts rptd 7-2, 558A1
Va men's room surveillnc case declined 10-1, 768G1
'Exclusionary rule' case refused 10-1, 768A3
Motorist 'Miranda rights' case declined 10-9, 784D1
Extended searches curbed 11-28, 944E2-C3
POLICE, Fraternal Order of the—*See FRATERNAL Order of the Police*
POLIOMYELITIS (infantile paralysis)—*See MEDICINE—Diseases*
POLISH-American Congress
Weber case Sup Ct ruling scored 6-27, 477F2
POLISH Americans
Pope holds mass in Chicago 10-5, 759F2
POLITICAL Action Committees (PACs)—*See POLITICS—Campaign Finances; also specific committee names*
POLITICAL Power: USA/USSR (book)
USSR bars book fair entry 9-4, 690D1
POLITICAL Science
Intl Pol Sci Assn meets 8-12—8-18, 637A1
POLITICAL Science Association, International
Conf held in Moscow 8-12—8-18, 637A1
POLITICAL Studies, Joint Center for
Black voter registratn drive launched 10-25, 808G1

1980

POLANSKI, Roman
Tess released 12-12, 1003E2
POLAROID Corp.
Land to retire as chief exec officer 3-7, 225B1
POLETTI, Angelo
Duran wins WBC welterwgt title 6-20, 772B3
POLIACIK, Dusan
Wins Olympic medal 7-26, 624F2
POLICE
Cleaver gets 5 yrs probatn 1-3, 64F3
B McQueen sues for false arrest 1-4, 199A3
State of State messages 1-8, 1-9, 404A1, E1
Phila layoffs take effect 3-1, 187B1
Chicago strip search suit setld 3-26, 404C2
'58 Ala church bomber sentncd 5-14, 405C1
Miami cops cleared in black exec's '79 death 5-17, riots erupt 5-17—5-19, 382F2
5 Miami cops suspended 5-22—5-23, 401E3
NAACP warns re brutality 5-29, 460A2
Md ct voids Tichnell death sentnc 6-10, 869F1
NYC pact setld 7-3, 518B1, E1
Rights violatns deplored 7-9, 519G1
Mobile (Ala) strike 7-14—7-24, 576D1
DC fscl recovery plan proposed 7-19, 742A3, E3
Chattanooga racial disorders erupt 7-22—7-26, 575G3
Idaho TV statn raided, Mich print shop search cited 7-26, 582A2, D2
Dade Cnty ex-cop indicted 7-28, 576B1
Detroit layoffs rptd 9-8, 743G2
US weighs China police gear request 9-20, 788F2
Blacks protest Miss shooting 10-4, 884E3
Buffalo area black slayings prompt probe 10-13, 997C1
Newsroom searches curb signed 10-14, 835F1-C2
LA settles job bias suit 11-21, 926A3
Amnesty Intl scores US brutality 12-10, 978F2
Supreme Court Rulings
'Miranda rights' waiver proof backed 1-21, 93C3
Car box search case refused 3-24, 265C2
Ctroom ID in illegal arrest backed 3-25, 265A3
Warrantless home arrests curbed 4-15, 305F3
'Good faith' municipal immunity ended 4-16, 328F2
Ctroom cameras case accepted 4-21, 344E1
LA purposeful bias case declined 4-28, 369B2
Interrogatn defined 5-12, 386B2
'Exclusionary rule' narrowed 5-27, 453C2
Panther Chicago shootout retrial order declined, legal fees award voided 6-2, 513A1
Jail informant use curbed 6-16, 511A3
Donated porno warrants required 6-20, 555G1
Illegal search protectn narrowed 6-25, 541A1
'79-80 Sup Ct term ends, decisns cited 7-2, 540E2
Arrest warrant 3d party searches case accepted 10-6, 782C3
La itinerant worker registratn ruling affirmed 10-20, 807A3
Ctroom cameras case argued 11-12, 882A2
NYS interrogatn chase case declined 12-1, 918F2

POLIO—*See MEDICINE--Diseases*
POLIOMYELITIS (infantile paralysis)—*See MEDICINE--Diseases*
POLISH-Americans
Reagan tells ethnic joke 2-16, apologizes 2-18, 128B2
US passivity re Polish strikers scored 8-21, 627A1
Reagan meets Chicago group 9-8, 699C3
US grants Poland $670 mln grain credit 9-12, 710B3
Reagan seeks support 10-7, 763E2
POLIT, Cornelia
Wins Olympic medal 7-27, 623B3
POLITICAL Action Committees (PACs)—*See POLITICS--Campaign Finances*
POLITICAL Science
Obituaries
Morgenthau, Hans 7-19, 608E2

POLITICS (U.S.)

1976

POLITICS (U.S.)—*See also state names; also appropriate headings under U.S. GOVERNMENT*
Hatch Act repeal clears Cong 3-31, 234A2; Ford warns of veto 4-3, 245F1
Equal-time rules upheld 4-12, 282D1
Hatch Act revision vetoed 4-12, 284D1
'72-74 women's role rptd up 4-27, 379E3
Pol groups, individuals cited as FBI probe target 4-28, 330E1-B3
Hatch Act veto sustained 4-29, 346E1
Sup Ct voids NJ canvassers curb 5-19, 393C3
Dem platform text cites pol rights 6-15, 472E1
Dems OK platform plank on Hatch Act 7-13, 509C2
Business Political Payments Issue—*See 'Political Payments' under BUSINESS*
Campaign Finances & Practices—See also 'Finances' under CARTER, 'Funds' under FORD—POLITICS; also FEDERAL Election Commission under U.S. GOVERNMENT
Pres contenders get US funds 1-2, more paymts OKd 1-8, 22C3
McCarthy, Reagan vs Common Cause code 1-9, 22G3
Jones pleads guilty 1-29, 134D1
Sup Ct upholds pub financing, disclosure; voids spending limits, FEC 1-30, 86C1-87A2
Babcock sentence upheld 2-10, 144G3
Bayh rpts campaign debt 3-4, 165E2
Matching fed funds total rptd 3-4, 180B3
Hammer pleads guilty again 3-4, 180F3
Wild indicted 3-12, acquitted 7-27, 566A1
Hammer, Babcock spared jail terms 3-23, 6-4, 442B2
Sup Ct rejcts plea for US matching funds 4-23, 306C1
Book on '72 costs, donors rptd 4-25, 687G3 ★
Matching funds end hurt Dems in Pa 4-27, 305E1
SEC lists cos chrgd 5-12, 725E3-729F2
Matching funds resumed 5-21, 391F2
Udall ends campaigning 6-14, 432C1
Dem platform text 6-15, 471G1
Campaign debts rptd 6-16, 491C1
9 denied fed funds 6-23, 490E3 ★
Cella convctd 6-24, sentnc rptd 7-20, 860D2
Total FEC paymts rptd 7-1, 490G3
Fed funds for Carter ticket OKd 7-20, 565A3
Carter backs cong electn financing 8-11, 585A3
Fed funds for Ford ticket OKd 8-24, 688A3
CBS rpts Nixon Grumman bid 8-27, 979E3
Pres nominatn costs rptd 8-28, 688D2
FEC OKs TV debate funding 8-30, 644D1
Scott campaign gift to 3 sens rptd 8-30, 980E1
Phillips tax fraud chrgd 9-2, 725G2
Dole denies Gulf irregularities 9-6, 9-8, 665D3
Ex-Grumman exec accuses Nixon 9-13; denied 9-15, 9-16, 979G1-D3
Ford probe rptd, Kent Cnty com records subpoenaed 9-21, 9-25; Nessen, Ford, other statemts 9-21—9-30; Justice Dept referral rptd 10-1, 722E1-723G2
Watson fined 9-23, 725D2
SIU gifts to LBJ, Nixon cited 9-25, 723A1
Sup Ct bars review of Chestnut, Gross convictns 10-4, 766D1
Carter lists '70 donors 10-17, 804E3
Major lobbyist, individual donatns rptd 10-22, 938B3
S Korea gifts probed 10-24—12-1, 898D3-900B2
Gurney acquitted of final chrg 10-27, 845F3
GOP surplus reported 12-6, 938E1
Continental Oil rpts paymts 12-16, 986D1
CAB chrgs Flying Tigers, 4 others cited 12-29, 986E1
FEC certificatns, surplus rptd 12-31, 979E1, F2
Corruption Issues—*Note: Initial incident only listed; for subsequent developments, see personal names. See also 'Campaign Finances' above; also BUSINESS—Political Payments; WATERGATE*
Md ex-official sentncd 1-9, 32F2
Bailey cleared in Conn 1-12, 271D1
Mich ex-judge sentenced 1-26, 95E3
Hinshaw convicted 1-26, 95F3
Glowa indicted 1-27, 144E3
Chrgs vs Scott probed 2-4, 133E3
Addabo, Leggett probed 2-19, 171D1
Callaway chrgd 3-12, 197G1
Clay travel expenses queried 3-23, 247E1
Sikes chrgd 4-7, 286F2
Blumenthal case dismissed 4-13, 271B1
Rentschler pleads guilty 4-20, 316E3
Moore, aide acquitted 5-5, 342E3
DeSapio pleads not guilty 5-24, 442B3
Hays admits affair with aide 5-25, 392B2
Cunningham indicted 5-26, 6-7, 442E2
Helstoski indicted 6-2, 414C3
Ariz reporter slain, land frauds linked 6-2—6-22, 483G2
Chrgs vs Young rptd 6-11, 433E3
Sex chrgs vs Gravel rptd 6-12, 434B1
Howe arrested 6-12, 434G1-B2

1977

POLITICS (U.S.)—*See also state names; also appropriate headings under U.S. GOVERNMENT*
'69-75 campus attitudes rptd 1-14, 157F1, G1
AFL-CIO seeks Hatch Act revisn 2-22, 153D2
Carter asks Hatch Act chng 3-22, 210D2, F2
Sup Ct backs govt employe agency shops 5-23, 444D1
House eases Hatch Act 6-7, 442G2
Business Payments—*See BUSINESS—Payments*
Campaign Finances & Practices—*See also 'Corruption' below; also BUSINESS—Payments*
'76 electn complaints rptd 1-4, 59F2
Spec interest gifts detailed 1-15, 2-4, 2-15, 128C1-129F2
Spec interest gifts to cong fiscal coms rptd 3-7, 232D2
Cong pub electn fund bills introduced 3-7, 3-16, 232C3
Carter seeks changes 3-22, 210D2-F2
Fund raising for personal use OKd 3-24, 233A1
Corp double jeopardy bar upheld 3-28, 276G3
Mondale urges pub funds bill support 3-31, 251B1
AP reporter wins Pulitzer 4-18, 355F2
GOP outspent Dems in '76 4-28, 482C1
FCC reverses air time stand 5-6, 376G1
Nixon funds rptd seized 5-6, 482E2
Shapp funds repaymt ordrd 5-12, 482B2
Clark electn law challenge rejctd 6-6, 478F3
Paul electn challenge refused 6-6, 479A1
Carter backs pub financing of Sen campaigns 7-28, 574F3
Dem cargo preference support, maritime contributns linked 8-1—8-29, 719A3
Sen pub finance bill killed 8-2, 592B2
Lance '74 practices queried 8-18, 625F3, 626A1; E1; **for subsequent developments, see LANCE, Thomas B.**
Carter to reimburse bank for plane use 8-24, 649E3
Maritime contributns list rptd 10-3, 815D1
GOP seen exploiting Canal issue 10-30, 912A1
Mendelsohn Interior nominatn withdrawn 11-11, 877B2
McCarthy lawyer fee case declined 12-5, 939B1
AFL-CIO sued by US 12-16, 980A1
Corruption—*See also BUSINESS—Payments; KOREA (South)—U.S.—Korean Political Payments; WATERGATE*
Carter conflict-of-interest code issued 1-4, 4C2
Ex-Miss road dir convicted 1-8, 60D1
Callaway probe dropped 1-11, 59D2
Ford seeks new ethics code 1-17, 33F3
Sen ethics com set 1-18, House code proposed 1-31, 77E2
Sikes loses subcom post 1-26, 53E2
Hastings sentenced 1-31, 103D1
'70-76 indictmt data rptd 2-10, 162C3
Jones, Hansen guilty pleas cited 2-16, 111G3
Carter aides rpt net worth 2-25, 147B3-148F1
House adopts ethics code 3-2, 173B2-C3
House forms ethics com 3-9, 191C2
Carter asks electn fraud penalties 3-22, 210B3
2 Mass state sens sentncd 3-23, seats vacated 3-31, 4-4, 252G3; Di Carlo loses 5-24, 446F3
Sen adopts ethics code 4-1, 251A2
Carter backs spec prosecutor bill 5-3, 338F1
Tonry resigns 5-4, indicted 5-12, 418A3

1978

POLITICS (U.S.)—*See also state names; also appropriate headings under U.S. GOVERNMENT*
Business Payments—*See BUSINESS—Payments*
Campaign Finances & Practices—*See also 'Corruption' below*
Pub funding bill rebuffed by House 3-21, 202D3
Mendelsohn suit setld 4-18, named US aide 6-10, 446F3-447B1
Lance chrgd re '74 gov race 4-26, 324E3
Corp free speech backed by Sup Ct 4-26, 343D2
Cong electn funds rejected 7-19, 550E2-C3
'Reverse check-off' by unions barred 7-21, 565F2-A3
Tax deductns cut by House com 7-27, 587A1
FEC fund-raising rpt issued, pol actn coms (PACs) noted; 'PAC democracy' feared 9-7, 753F1-G2
Tax credit increase clears 10-15, 786C1
Sen races won by big spenders 11-15, 898A1
PAC gifts to cong com chrmn rptd 12-24, 1008A1
Corruption—*See also BUSINESS—Payments Issues; KOREA (South)—U.S.-Korean Political Payments*
Marston dismissal controversy 1-10, 1-12, 12C2; Bell ousts 1-20, 32F1; **for subsequent developments, see MARSTON, David**
Byington chrgs rptd 1-12, quits CPSC 2-8, 185F2
Flood, Eilberg probed 1-27—3-15, 239G3-240A3
Pa ex-state sen begins jail term 2-20, 172A3
Agnew case papers released 3-3, 164E3
Ala treasurer indicted 3-21, 379G3
Rep Diggs indicted 3-23, 220C2
Gurney trial press-curbs review declined by Sup Ct 4-17, 308D2
Ga ex-offcls acquitted, Carter testimony cited 4-21, 309E3
NYC rabbi admits bribing Flood 5-11, 363C2; sentenced 6-22, 500E3
S Africa influence-buying rptd 5-13, denied 6-14, 498D3
Flood, Eilberg win primaries 5-16, 389E3
Okla ex-gov released from jail 5-22, 420G3
Ala treas convicted 5-24, 6-25, sentncd 6-8; ousted from office 6-9, 886F3

1979

POLITICS (U.S.)
State com structure law backed by Sup Ct 6-4, 439C1
Campaign Finances & Practices—*See also 'Corruption' below*
Boston referendum spending case refused by Sup Ct 1-8, 14A3
SWP wins rpt exemptn 1-9, 13D3
Fla Const 'sunshine' amendmt review refused by Sup Ct 1-22, 54F1
Carter State of Union Message 1-23, 46F3
Sen delays outside income limit 3-8, 185F2
Sen again votes income limit delay 3-18, 281E1
FEC clears Carter primary spending 4-2, 265A1
PAC '78 spending rptd up 5-10, Common Cause deplores 5-15, 363E1-C2
Crane on pres bid debt 5-16, 363E3
Tiernan heads FEC 5-17, 401C3
House com defeats electn financing bill 5-24, 401D2
Carter '76 campaign ad financing probed 5-25, 401A3
Carter campaign billed $50,203 6-4, 419G2
Labor '78 cong campaign gifts rptd 6-13, 595B1
Udall told to repay '76 electn funds 6-18, 595E1
GOP credit card plan blocked 6-21, 595G1
Carter '76 campaign ad financing improprieties denied 6-22, 500B2
Pres campaign funds rptd 7-12, 593G3-594B1
Reagan pres funds rptd 7-26, 594C1
FEC clears Carter general electn financing 8-21, 661G3
Cong financial disclosure statemts studied 9-1, 701C3-702B1
FEC completes '76 election audits, Wallace repayment noted 9-5, 724A2
Kennedy pres funding challenged 10-4, 783A3
Kennedy finance dir named 10-24, 847G1
Connally bars matching funds 12-12, 982B3
Reagan scores fed funds 12-13, 982B2
FEC OKs LaRouche funds 12-18, 984A2
Corruption—*See also BUSINESS—Payments Issues; KOREA (South)—U.S.-Korean Political Payments; SOUTH Africa—Information Ministry Scandal*
More GSA kickback pleas rptd 1-3, 1-26, 92F3
Tenn parole-selling probe continues 1-4, 36F1-B3; **for subsequent developments, see TENNESSEE**
Mandel conviction upset 1-11, 17G3; reclaims office 1-15, 56D1
Pa ex-state sen granted '80 parole 1-11, 102A3
Fla ex-insurnc comr sentncd 1-18, 79C1
Mitchell paroled 1-19, 176D1
Diggs, Flood drop subcom chairs 1-23, 1-25, 71G2
Connally announces pres bid 1-24, 70A3
Tenn ex-comr sentncd 1-26, 156E2
Haldeman discloses '75 CBS-TV interview fee 1-27, 176C1
Food stamp program probe rptd 2-2, 93B3
Flood mistrial declared 2-3, 102A2
Eilberg pleads guilty 2-24, 152C2
Diggs expulsn rejctd, ethics com to study case 3-1, 165E2

1980

POLITICS (U.S.)
Govt political firings barred by Sup Ct 3-31, 291G1-E2
Pope bars priests' role 5-4; Drinan, Cornell comply 5-5, 5-6, 341A2
Campaign Finances & Practices—*See also POLITICS--Corruption*
Bush, Kennedy funds OKd by FEC 1-2, 1-4, 5B2
Calif lobbyist ban case refused by Sup Ct 1-21, 93G2
Bush denies '70 campaign gift coverup 2-7, 128E3
Connally sponsors natl telethon 2-14; fund shortage, spending rptd 2-20, 2-22, 129C1
Reagan fund status cited 2-28, 143C2
Baker, Dole, Crane, Brown lose matching funds 3-13, 209C1
Pres spending limit upheld by Sup Ct 4-14, 306E3
Independent pres bid problems cited 4-24, 303F3
Kennedy supporters' petitn rejctd by Sup Ct 4-28, 369A2
Bush ends pres bid 5-26, 398F2-G3
Common Cause sues vs 'indepndnt' pres com spending 7-1, 493B1
Evangelical Christian pol actn profiled 7-11—9-15, 819B1, C2
GOP platform adopted 7-15, 535C3, 537C1
Dem platform plank OKd 8-12; Carter hedges, conv adopts 8-13, 611B1, E1; text excerpt 615C1
Gravel loses Alaska primary 8-26, 683B2
Talmadge wins Ga Sen runoff 8-26, 683D2
Reagan fund raising coms upheld by fed ct 8-28, 681G1
Anderson ruled eligible for fed funds 9-4, 665C2
Anderson bank loan plan fails 10-2, abandoned 10-15; Dem, GOP spending cited 10-15, 818D1
PAC donatns case accepted by Sup Ct 10-6, 782A2
Burger stays GOP campaign aid ruling 10-17, Sup Ct continues 10-21, 856D1
Anderson ballot access costly 10-27, 818A2
Trade assn PAC funds soliciting ban challenge refused 11-3, 856E2
GOP gain in state legislatures 11-4, 847B2
Anderson, Carter, Reagan paymts certified 11-13, 866F1
Corruption
Mandel, wife sued 1-4, 18D2
GSA scandal chrgs continue 1-15; Sen hearing 1-19, 112C1
Flood resigns 1-31, pleads guilty 2-26, 190F1-B2
Helstoski cleared of '76 chrgs 2-27, 228B1
GSA scandal funds recovery suits filed 3-17, 228F1
Ill atty gen convicted of tax evasn 3-19, 215A3
State legislators' immunity curbed by Sup Ct 3-19, 249E3
Vesco grand jury ends, no indictmts brought 4-1, 251B3
Mandel appeal refused by Sup Ct 4-14, 307A1
Wilson found guilty of financial misconduct 4-16, censure asked 4-24, 333F3
GSA kickback scandal indictmt, convictn totals rptd 5-2; ex-offcl indicted 5-9, 495A2
Pa ex-state sen released from prison 5-16, marries 7-14, 890A2
Mandel begins prison sentence 5-19, 471E2

1976

2 Calif city offcls sentncd 6-21, 860C2
Ex-SBA official sentncd 6-25, 596G1
Nadjari dismissed 6-25, 1016D1
McVeigh, others indicted re Alaska vice 7-8, 816F2
Moritt indictmt transferred 8-12, 1016A2
Dunphy pleads guilty to FBI property misuse 8-13, 666F3
Passman bribes rptd 8-16, 633B1
Kelley admits favors, gifts 8-31, 666C2
Spec prosecutor's office not cleared 10-2, 884D1
Troy jailed 10-22, 860B2
S Korea influence peddling rptd 10-24—12-1, 898D3-900B2
House travel expense probe ends 10-27, 981F3
DiFalco chrgs dismissed 11-4, 1016A2
Steingut indictmt voided 11-15, 972A1
Brust indictmt dismissed 12-1, 1016B2
Mandel mistrial declared 12-7, 922E2
Hastings convicted 12-17, 982C1
Saypol indictmt dismissal seen 12-20, 1016C2
Mercorella chrgs dismissed 12-22, 1016F1

Democratic Party—*See also 'Campaign Finances' above, 'Democratic Party Convention', 'Presidential Election Campaign' and 'Presidential Nomination Campaign' below; also 'Democrats' under U.S. GOVERNMENT, subheads CONGRESS, HOUSE, SENATE*
Bailey cleared in Conn scandal 1-12, 271F1
Mayors hold forum 4-1, 233C2
Equal-time rules upheld 4-12, 282F1
Blacks draft platform 4-30—5-2, 343A3, 358A1
Platform hearings 5-17—5-20, 357G2
Party identificatn poll 5-27, 565B1
Hays asked to quit post 6-2, agrees 6-3, 433G2, A3
Carter vs 'wish box' platform 6-3, 411C1
James Farley dies 6-9, 444A1
Moss on effect of Howe arrest 6-14, 434B2
Platform OKd by com 6-15, 432F2
Platform text 6-15, 469A1 ★ -478F3
Carter asks Strauss to stay 6-18, 452E1
Carter sees Natl Com; Strauss, other officers reelected 7-16, 532F2
Carter sees Natl Com panel 8-4, 564D3
Carter sees Steering Com 8-23, 631D2
Carter sees state chrmn 8-31, 645B2
Sup Ct bars equal-time review 10-12, 765E3
Strauss resigning 11-8, 845F3
NE govs meet 11-13—11-14, 864A3
Strauss named Carter aide 11-19, 881D3
Chicago Mayor Daley dies 12-20, 969B3

Democratic Party Convention (N.Y.)
Platform text 6-15, 469A1 ★ -478F3
Carter, women compromise re representatn 7-11—7-15, 509E3
Opens, Glenn, Jordan keynote 7-12, 505D1, 508B1-509D1
Women delegates, Dems abroad representatn, table 508A2
Black leaders pacified 7-12, 513E1
Platform action, Hatch Act revisn, platform OKd; Humphrey speaks 7-13, 505D1, 509F1
Carter wins on 1st ballot 7-14, 505F1
State, Dems abroad roll-call votes, table 7-14, 507A2
Carter names Mondale vp choice, ratified 7-15, 506G1
Carter acceptance speech 7-15, 506D3; text 510A1-511A3
Mondale acceptance speech 7-15, 507F2; text 511B1
Carter, Mondale photo 505A1
Debate on rules 7-15, 513D2
Delegates compared 8-7, 8-8, 8-17, 616A2

Elections (congressional)
GOP loses NY seat 3-2, 166D2
95th Cong electn results 11-2, 819B3, 820F1, 828A1-831B3
Meeds wins Washn count 11-16, 865D1
Mikva wins in Ill 11-19, 882A1

1977

Ga state sen acquitted 5-20, 424D1
Ex-Pa House speaker jailed 6-10, 484D1
NYS political penalty voided 6-13, 517B2
Tonry loses La primary vote 6-25, 501E1
Carter Miss town mtg topic 7-21, 575E1
Tonry gets 1-yr sentence 7-28, 603A3
LBJ '48 Sen primary fraud chrgd 7-30; denied 8-1, 8-3; '41 Sen bid fraud seen 8-6, 631G1, F2
Garmatz indicted 8-1, 603C3
Mo House ex-speaker sentncd 8-16, 712A2
Md Gov Mandel, 5 others convicted 8-23, 652A1
Rptr tied to Pa politician quits 9-12, 920E3
Mandel, 5 others sentncd 10-7, 807D2
Young cleared re Thevis, Kasemehas allegatns cited 10-19, 861E3
Bilandic fires accuser 11-21, 944C2
ICC offcl under probe fired 12-8, 1007E1
Hawaii mayor's trial folds 12-27, 1008E1

Democratic Party—*See also 'Campaign Financing' above; also 'Democrats' under U.S. GOVERNMENT, subheads CONGRESS, HOUSE and SENATE*
Carter picks Curtis as chrmn 1-6, 14D2
Natl com endorses Curtis, fills other posts 1-21, 53A2
White House reception 1-21, 53A2
Strauss confrmd trade negotiator 3-29, 272D3
Carter urged to consult with state units 4-1, 250G3
Carter scores liberals' criticism 5-12, McGovern replies 5-13, 380F3, 381D2
Carter clarifies Caddell memo, denies liberal threat 5-12, 381C1
Israel cites '76 platform 6-28, 495C3
Jewish ties chrgd 7-22, 589C2
Natl Com boycott vs non-ERA states rptd 11-14, 918C1
Curtis resigns as chrmn 12-7, 960A3
Memphis favored as '78 conv site 12-9, 960C3
White named chrmn 12-28, 1005D3

Elections (congressional)
GOP wins Minn seat 2-22, 128A1 ★
Ga special electn, runoff set 3-15, 191G3
Fowler wins Ga runoff 4-5, 252A1
GOP wins Washn seat 5-17, 382F1
GOP wins La seat 8-27, 693B1

1978

Brooke admits false loan disclosure 5-26, 406B1; wins primary 9-19, 736F3; loses reelectn 11-7, 847F2
AFL-CIO fined $10,000 6-12, 509C3
Carter com, Ga bank fined for '76 plane use 6-26, 509A3
Carter asks Gartner resignatn 6-26; Gartner denies interest conflict, bars resignatn 6-28, 513F2
Talmadge repays expense claims 8-18, denies wrongdoing 8-18, 8-19, 643G3
GSA indictmts seen 8-30, 685E1
Admin linked to Vesco 'pol fix', denials issued 9-1—9-15; Anderson revises article 9-11, 719G3
Flood indicted 9-5, 685B1
Ex-Rep Clark indicted 9-5, 685E1
Eilberg chrgd by ethics com 9-13, 697F1
GSA probe coordinator named 9-20; 18 indicted 9-29, 4 plead 10-4, 753A3-G3
ICC ex-offcl indicted 9-22, pleads not guilty 9-29; challenges dismissal 9-25, 779E2
Diggs convicted 10-7, 791D3-792A1
Flood indicted again 10-12, 792A1
Eilberg indicted 10-24, pleads not guilty 11-1, 835C2
6 Cleveland cncl members indicted 10-27, 1008F3
Flood reelected, Eilberg defeated 11-7, 846D2, E2, 849D2
Flaherty loses Pa gov bid 11-7, 849B2
Gurney loses US House bid 11-7, 849E3
Diggs reelected 11-7, 854B1
Anaya loses US Sen bid 11-7, 855D2
Dymally loses Calif lt gov reelectn 11-7, 856F2
Talmadge testifies on finances before grand jury 11-8; Sen panel chrgs rules violatns, hearing set 12-19, 981C3
GSA probe dir named 11-13, Alto steps down 11-14, 899E1-B2
Diggs sentenced 11-20, 900A2
IRS offcl's bribery convictn review refused by Sup Ct 11-27, 937C2
Diggs subcom chair threatnd, Wilson, Roybal, Flood unaffected by House Dem ethics rule chng OK 12-6, 958B2
Tenn gov's aides arrested 12-15, 1011E1
More GSA kickback indictmts 12-16, 12-21, 1011B1
Brooke ethics com probe to end 12-19, 982A1
ICC ex-offcl acquitted 12-21, 1007G3

Democratic Party—*See also U.S. GOVERNMENT—CONGRESS—Democrats*
White installed as chrmn 1-27, 87G2
'53, '78 cong compositn compared 1-30, 107E2
Korea contributns claimed 3-21, 3-22; denied 3-21, 203B2
Ill cnty clerk electn ballot case refused by Sup Ct 3-27, 241F2
Kissinger testifies on Korea contributns 4-20, 280D1
Natl com revises pres nominatn rules 6-9, 448D2
'68 conv FBI informants rptd 7-3, 507E3
UAW to reassess ties 7-19, 611B2
White on Carter prospects 7-26, 682A3
Cong campaign fund raising rptd 9-7, 753G1
White on electn results 11-8, 845B1
Carter, Meany on electn results 11-9, 875A2, C2
Midterm conf in Memphis 12-8—12-10; Carter downplays dissent 12-12, 956D1-C3, D3

Elections (congressional)
Green, Garcia win NY seats 2-14, 108F1-C2
Results 11-7, 845B1-846A3, 847C2-857C3; 96th Cong listed 848B1, 850A1-852D3
Warner Va Sen win confrmd 11-27, 915A3
Thorsness wins SD recount 12-19, 1008F1

1979

Carter trustee buys land from Billy 3-1, 'hush money' hinted 3-22, 203G1
Carter peanut loan scheme alleged 3-11–3-13, spec prosecutor sought 3-13, 183F3-184B2
GSA kickback scandal sentncs handed down 3-14–4-24, 367F2-B3
Carter peanut probe spec counsel named, GOP scores limits 3-20, 203A1
Grant of immunity broadened by Sup Ct 3-20, 204A1
Brooke cleared by ethics com 3-20, 208F2
IRS bribe convictn 3-26, 239E3
Ill atty gen indicted 4-9, 291B3
Carter: unaware of peanut loan illegalities 4-10, 263F3
B Carter, NBG deny peanut loan, '76 campaign link 4-11, 301C3
Podell, Brasco disbarmt challenges declined by Sup Ct 4-16, 303C1
Carter probe spec counsel gains more power, GOP reacts 4-23, 301G2-B3
Marston wins Phila mayoral primary 5-15, 363E2
GSA kickback scandal sentences continue 5-23–12-17, controversy 5-25–5-30, 964E2-965A1
NJ ex-offcls subject to rejailing by Sup Ct 6-4, 439A1
Ex-Rep Clark sentncd 6-12, 442G2
Cong immunity broadened by Sup Ct 6-18, 498C3
Helstoski indictmt rule backed by Sup Ct 6-18, 499A1
Diggs admits funds misuse, accepts censure 6-29, 515D1; censured 7-31, 578D1
Cleveland cncl pres acquitted 7-18, 580E1
Mandel convictn reinstated 7-20, 604D3
Leach pleads not guilty to vote buying 7-24, 561D1
Minchew pleads guilty to fraud 7-30, 702B2
Horgan quits in NJ HFA scandal 8-9, 747B3
Diggs sued by US 8-16, 649G3-B1
Vesco jury foreman quits, claims cover-up 8-29, 647E2; Heymann, Carter deny chrgs 8-31, juror resignatn rejected 9-7, 725F2-E3
Talmadge denunciatn voted by Sen com 9-14, 702B1
Talmadge denounced by Sen 10-10, 769B1
Minchew sentenced 10-10, 769A2
Flood, Passman briber convicted 10-12, sentncd 10-24, 906D1
Leach acquitted 11-3, 900E2
Diggs convictn upheld 11-14, 900F2
GAO 'fraud hotline' rptd effective 12-9, 947B2
Wilson chrgd re House rules 12-13, 945E2

Democratic Party—*See also 'Presidential Nomination Campaign' below; also under U.S. GOVERNMENT, subheads CONGRESS, HOUSE AND SENATE*
Carter aide sees 'new realities' 1-4, 3C2
Carter addresses Dem Natl Com 5-25, 401D1
R Carter addresses Women Dems 7-12, 514E1
Carter energy program reactn 7-15, 7-16, 534G1, A3
JFK backed McNamara pres bid 9-23, 748A3
Chicago-Cook Cnty patronage ruled illegal 9-24, 770D3
FALN bomb hoax in NYC 10-17, Chicago device defused 10-18, 786A2, C2
White on electn results 11-6, 846A2
Natl Com meets 11-9, 961D2

Elections (congressional)
GOP wins 2 seats in Calif, Wis 4-3, 265E1-A2

1980

Talmadge finances probe dropped 5-30, 427E3-428A1
Diggs convictn review confused by Sup Ct 6-2, Diggs resigns 6-3, 428A1
Wilson loses primary 6-3, 439A2
Chicagoan indicted in ERA bribe probe 6-5, chrgs denied 6-6, 441C3
Wilson censured 6-10, 438F1-E2
Nixon impeachmt lawyer sentenced 6-10, 460C1
Diggs enters prison 7-24, Justice Dept drops suit 8-4, 908D3
Treas offcl guilty of conflict of interest 7-28, fined 9-15, 927B3
Ill atty gen sentncd 7-29, 654F2
FBI ex-offcls convicted 11-6, 884G1; sentncd 12-15, 963F2; chrgs vs ex-dir dropped 12-11, 940G1

Democratic Party—*See also 'Presidential' subheads below*
White rebuts Brock Carter criticism 1-2, 5D1
Tower links intl decline 1-14, 32B1
Kennedy campaign urges White resignatn 5-5, 366E3-367A1
Platform drafted 6-24, 479F2
Carter addresses natl com 8-15, 629C3
White assails Reagan Klan remark 9-2, 664A1
Carter on future role 11-12, 865G1-F2
Eizenstat offers advice 12-4, 938B3
Reagan makes Cabt-level apptmt 12-22, 979F2

Democratic Party Convention (N.Y., N.Y.)
Dem delegate count table 6-4, 596A2
Platform drafted 6-24, Kennedy vows floor fight 6-25, 479F2-480D1
Open conv move forms, Carter popularity dips 7-25—7-31; Kennedy, Anderson meet, hold news conf 7-31, 570E1-D3
Carter adamant vs 'open conv' 8-1, 8-4, 596A3
Byrd joins open-conv bid 8-2, 596F2
Govs neutral on open conv 8-3—8-5, 595F3
Carter, Kennedy aides OK agrmt 8-5, 596D1
Kennedy ends bid after open conv move fails 8-11, 609C1, E1
Udall keynote address 8-11, 612A2*
Moynihan addresses 8-11, 612C3
Kennedy wins econ, other platform planks 8-12, 609D1, 610F2-611C1
Kennedy speech stirs conv 8-12, 609D1, 610D1; text excerpts 613D2-614B3
Carter renominated on 1st ballot, blacks make token challenge 8-13—8-14, 609C1, 611G2-E3
Hooks, Brown speak 8-13, 611E3
Carter issues platform statemt; Kennedy endorses, conv adopts 8-13, 609D1, 611C1; text excerpts 614C2-615C3
Carter, Kennedy photo 8-14, 609A1
Mondale acceptance speech 8-14, 612B1
Carter acceptance speech 8-14, 609E1, 611G2, 612D1-A2; text excerpts 612E2-613C3

Elections (congressional)
GOP wins Ill seat 1-22, 50D3
Tauzin wins La seat 5-17, 404D3
Hutchinson wins W Va seat 6-3, 439C3
97th Cong results 11-4, 837D1, 840B1*, 842A1*-844E4, 845F1-847A1, 848B1-852C3
'82 reapportmt set 12-31, 982E3, 983C1

1976

Elections (gubernatorial)
Results 11-2, 820E2, 831B2

Elections (mayoral)
Rizzo recall vote barred 9-30, 994D1

Elections (misc.)
State results 11-2, 820F3-825F1

Elections (presidential)
Carter wins 11-2, 817D1
Popular, electoral vote table 818A1; map 819A1
Teeter: 'nonpartisan media events' 11-29, 917D3
Electoral College votes 12-13, 979A1
Final tally rptd 12-18; table 979C1, A2

Elections (primaries)
Iowa results 1-19, 40G3
Miss results 1-24, 94F3
NH results 2-24, 148E1
Mass, Vt results 3-2, 164G2
Fla results 3-9, 179D1
Ill results 3-16, 196D2-D3
NC results 3-23, 213G2
Incumbent pres defeats rptd 3-24, 231D3
NY, Wis results 4-6, 244F2-245E1
Pa results 4-27, 304E3
Tex results 5-1; Ind, Ga, Ala, DC 5-4, 322D2-323F2
Neb, W Va results 5-11, 342D1-E3
Mich, Md results 5-18, 356D2, 357E1-A2
Ore, Ida, Nev, Ky, Tenn, Ark results 5-25, 373D1, 374A2
RI, SD, Mont primary results 6-1, 389E2-390A3, 411F1
NM, Miss results 6-1, 411E1 ★
Calif, Ohio, NJ results 6-8, 408F2-410B1
Mo, Mich results 8-3, 565C2-A3
Tenn results 8-5, 633G1
La results 8-14, 633A1
NC results 8-17, 633E1
GOP platform text cites 8-18, 603F3
Mo nominee successor named 8-21, 633D1
Ariz, Fla, Conn, ND results 9-7, 687G2-F3
NY results 9-14, 687C2
RI, Mass, Minn, Nev, NH, NC, Utah, Vt, Wis, Wyo results 9-14, 704E3-705D2
NJ special primary 9-21, 725B2
Washington results 9-21, 804C3
Hawaii results 10-2, 764D2

Polls
Gallup: Ford effort lags 1-7, 21G2
Gallup: Carter leads Ford 3-15, 197D1
Gallup, Harris: Carter leads Ford, Reagan 4-12—8-1, 564A3
Gallup: Dems outnumber GOP 5-27, 565B1
Gallup: Ford leads Reagan with GOP, independents 7-18, 7-28, 565B1
AP, Washn Post compare conv delegates 8-7, 8-8, 8-17, 616A2
Washn Post, Gallup, Harris: Ford leads Reagan, Schweiker ticket 8-11, 8-12, 583F2
Gallup: Carter lead drops, Southn base firm 8-25, 8-28, 9-1, 644G1
Gallup: Ford leads in 1st debate 9-30, 725F1
Gallup: Carter lead: 8% 9-30, 725B2
Gallup: Carter lead up after 2d debate 10-15, 764B2
Gallup: Carter leads 6 pts 10-21, 804B3
Ford, Carter debate 10-22, 799F3, 800G2
Electn eve forecasts 10-27—11-1; Gallup statemt 11-3, 825F3
Ford on Carter decline 10-28, 803G1
Caddell analyzes electn 11-5, 11-11, 845G1
Tester: pres electns 'nonpartisan media events' 11-29, 917D3

Presidency—*See also FORD, Gerald*
One 6-yr term proposed 11-29, 917G2

Presidential Campaign TV Debates
Ford asks Carter debate, Carter agrees 8-19, 599E2
League of Women Voters sets dates 8-19, 632E3
Ford suggests earlier dates, Carter rep vs 8-24, 632G3-633A1
Negotiators meet 8-26, 632C3

1977

Elections (gubernatorial)
NJ, Va results 11-8, 855E1, A2-D2
Coleman wins in Amer Samoa 11-22, 943E3

Elections (mayoral)
Richmond (Va) elects black 3-8, 252C3
Conway elected in St Louis 4-5, 252E3
Soglin reelected in Madison (Wis) 4-5, 252F3
Bradley reelected in LA 4-6, 252B3
Bilandic wins in Chicago 6-7, 446B3
Jackson reelected in Atlanta 10-4, 879E1
NYC, Cleveland, Detroit, other results 11-8, 855F1, D2-E3
New Orleans elects black 11-12, 879C1
McConn wins in Houston 11-22, 900B3

Elections (misc.)
Miami homosexual rights law repealed 6-7, 446E2
State, city gen results 11-8, 855G1, F2, D3; bond issues, non-binding referendums 879F1, F2

Elections (presidential)
Cong: Carter wins Electoral Coll vote 1-6, 14F2

Elections (primaries)
Mass state sen 5-24, 446F3
NJ vote results 6-7, 446C3
Va results 6-14, 465A1
La cong results 6-25, 501E1
LBJ '48 Sen primary fraud chrgd 7-30; denied 8-1, 8-3, 631G1
NYC mayor 9-8; Koch wins Dem runoff 9-19, 723G1

Presidency—*See also CARTER, Jimmy; FORD, Gerald*
Carter asks voting change 3-22, 210C2
Carter backs spec prosecutor bill 5-3, 338F1
Nixon on pres rights 5-19, 405C3

1978

Elections (gubernatorial)
Results 11-7 845C1-E3, 846B3, 847B2-849C3, 852F1-857G2; govs listed 853D2

Elections (mayoral)
Gibson reelected in Newark 5-9, 363G1
Results 11-7, 848A2

Elections (misc.)
Cleveland rejects schl-tax hike 4-6, 279D2
St Paul repeals gay rights law 4-25, 327A2
Wichita, Eugene repeal gay rights laws 5-9, 5-23, 409D3
Calif property-tax cut amendmt OKd 6-6; text 425A1-426F1
Ohio schl-tax issues defeated 6-6, 425B1
Cleveland mayor wins recall vote 8-13, 663A2
State results 11-7, 847E2-849F3, 852F1-857C3, 898A1; legis 845C1, 847D1, 897A3-898A1; referenda 845E2, 847D1-B3
55% of bond issues OKd 11-7, 915A2
VI results 11-7, 915E3
Pa House shifts to GOP 11-28, 915B3
Black state legis losses rptd 11-28, 915C3

Elections (presidential)
'76 election data 4-13, 285A2

Elections (primaries)
Ill results 3-21, 207E1-A2
NC, Ind results 5-2, 342A3, C3
Tex results 5-6, 362D3-363B1
W Va, Neb results 5-9, 363B1, D1
Pa results 5-16, 389A3
Ky, Oregon results 5-23, 406D2
Ark results, NC runoff 5-30; Tex runoff 6-3, 426G1-G2
Calif, NJ, Miss, Ohio, Iowa, SD, Mont, NM results 6-6, 425C1, 447C3-448D2
Dem natl com revises rules 6-9, 448F2
Me, SC, Ark runoff, Va results 6-13, 466G3-467B2
Miss, SC runoff results 6-27, 510C1
Kan, Tenn results 8-1, 8-3, 606D1
Ga, Ida, Mich, Mo results 8-8, 625B3
Alaska, Okla results 8-22, 682D3, G3
Ga runoff results 8-29, 683E1
Ala results 9-5, 699E1
Del results 9-9; Fla, NH, Wis, Airz, Wyo, Colo, Nev 9-12; La 9-16; Mass, Wash, Okla runoff 9-19, 732C1-737A1
Minn, Md, NY, Vt, Conn, RI results 9-12, 715G3-716A3
Ala runoff results 9-26, Fla 10-5, 769D1, G1
Hawaii results 10-7, 791C3
Alaska results final 10-20, 831D2

Obituaries
Allen, Clifford 6-18, 540D2
Allen, James 6-1, 432E1
Bolin, Wesley 3-4, 186F3
Byron, Goodloe E 10-11, 888G2
Humphrey, Hubert 1-13, 32E2
Ketchum, William 6-24, 540B3
Metcalf, Lee 1-12, 96A3
Metcalfe, Ralph H 10-10, 888C3
Miller, Izette Jewel 11-15, 972D3
Montoya, Joseph 6-5, 540C3
Steiger, William A 12-4, 1032E3

Patronage
Carter backs judges merit selectn 11-8, 873F2-C3
SBA abolitn asked 11-20, 919C3

Presidency—*See also CARTER, Jimmy*
Dems chng nominatn rules 6-9, 448D2
Nixon data access upheld 12-21, 1011B3

1979

Elections (gubernatorial)
Ky, Miss results 11-6, 846G1, C2, E2
Treen elected in La 12-8, 946C3

Elections (mayoral)
GOP wins in KC (Mo) 3-27, 231A3
Byrne wins in Chicago 6-14, 444C3 4-3, 251G3
Skornicka wins in Madison 4-3, 265C2
Cockrell wins in San Antonio 4-7, 265B2
McNichols wins in Denver 5-15, 363A3
Arrington wins in Birmingham 10-30, 829B1
Results 11-6, 846G1, F2-D3
Chandler wins in Memphis 11-15, 904F3
McConn wins in Houston 11-20, 904E3
Feinstein wins in San Fran 12-11, 946E3

Elections (misc.)
VI rejects const 3-6, 167F3
San Antonio city cncl 4-7, 265B2
Miami rejcts anti-smoking law 5-8, 350C3
Dade Cnty (Fla) rejects tax cut 9-18, 724B2
NJ, Miss state results 11-6, 846A2, E2
Referenda results 11-6, 846B2, D3, G3
Houston city cncl 11-6, 904E3

Elections (primaries)
Chicago mayor 2-27, 149E3-150A1
Gary mayor 5-8, 363F2-A3
Phila mayor 5-15, 363C2
Ky governor 5-29, 420C1
Miss governor 8-7, 8-28, 680E2
Cleveland mayor 10-2, 829C1
La gov 10-27, 946D3

Obituaries
Bartlett, Dewey F 3-1, 272A2
Breckinridge, John B 7-29, 588D2
Brundage, Percival F 7-16, 588D2
Cain, Harry Pulliam 3-3, 272B2
Capehart, Homer E 9-3, 756B2
Cavanagh, Jerome Patrick 11-27, 932C2
Duffy, F Ryan 8-16, 671B2
Fortson Jr, Ben 5-19, 432F2
Gatherings, E C (Took) 5-22, 432G2
Granahan, Kathryn O'Hay 7-10, 588G2
Hall, Leonard 6-2, 508A3
Hebert, F Edward 12-29, 1008B3
Lloyd, Sherman P 12-15, 1008C3
Manion, Clarence E 7-28, 588A3
McMillan, John L 9-2, 756A3
Morton, Rogers 4-19, 356E3
Murdock, Abe 9-15, 756C3
Potter, Charles Edward 11-23, 932D3
Richards, James P 2-21, 176C3
Rockefeller, Nelson A 1-26, 103E3
Saltonstall, Leverett 6-17, 508E3
Sawyer, Charles 4-7, 356G3
Short, Dewey 11-19, 932E3
Tugwell, Rexford Guy 7-21, 588E3

Presidency—*See also CARTER, Pres. Jimmy*
Bell for 6-yr term 1-25, 110G1-A2
Carter favors 6-yr term 4-27, 326E1
Sen rejects direct vote 7-10, 514G3-515D1

Presidential Nomination Campaign—*See also 'Campaign Finances' above; for candidates' campaigns, see personal names and issues in Index*

1980

Elections (gubernatorial)
Results 11-4, 837D1, 845C2, 847A1, 848B1-852G3

Elections (mayoral)
Maier reelected in Milwaukee 4-1, 247B2

Elections (misc.)
Fla OKs property tax cut, ct amendmt, Miami Beach redvpt 3-11, 184G1-185C1
Me voters ban slot machines 3-11, 185C1, A2
Saco (Maine) repeals property tax ceiling 4-29, 744A1
Calif ballot issues 6-3, 439C2
San Fran OKs revenue hike 6-3, 744A1
San Fran OKs at-large vote 8-19, 632A3
Me votes to keep A-plant 9-23, 723C2
State results 11-4, 847E1-852G3

Elections (presidential)
Reagan wins 11-4, 837C1
Popular, electoral vote tables; map 838A1, 839A1, D3
Electoral College votes 12-15, 956F1

Elections (primaries & caucuses)
Iowa caucus results 1-21, 50D1
Ark caucus results 2-2, 92A1
Maine caucus results 2-10, 109B1
PR primary results 2-17, 130A1; 3-16, 208B2
NH results 2-26, 142D2
Mass, Vt results 3-4, 166B2
SC results 3-8, 183E3
Fla, Ga, Ala results 3-11, 182G3
Okla, Hawaii, Washn, Alaska Dem caucus results 3-11, Del 3-12, 209A1
Ill results 3-18, 206B2-F3
NY, Conn results 3-25, 221A2
Wis, Kan results 4-1, 246E1
La results 4-5, 264F3
Pa results 4-22, 303G3, 304A3, D3
Mich Dem caucus results 4-26, 327D2
Tex results 5-3, 342A2
Okla, Mo, Ariz, Minn, Guam GOP selectn 5-3, 342B3
Ind, NC, Tenn, DC results 5-6, 341F2-342A2, 405G1
Md, Neb results 5-13, 366D2
Mich, Ore results 5-20, 382E3-383G1, 404B3
Ark, Ida, Ky, Nev results 5-27, 399B1-F2
Calif, NJ, NM, RI, SD, Ohio, Mont, W Va, Miss, Ia results 6-3, 422D2-424C1, 439G1-E3
Jenrette wins SC runoff 6-24, 496F1
GOP plans study 7-15, 535A2
Mich, Kan, Mo, Ga results 8-5; Tenn 8-7; Okla, Alaska, Ga runoff 8-26; Ala, ND 9-2, 682E2-683E2
NY results 9-9, 682D1
Fla, Conn, Ariz, Colo, Nev, NH, RI, Utah, Vt, Wis results 9-9, 700F1-D3
Wash, Mass, La, Okla runoff results 9-13, 9-16, 724A2-B3
Hawaii results 9-20, 745D1
Ala runoff results 9-23, 745F1
Fla runoff results 10-7, 807C3

Obituaries
Belcher, Page 8-2, 676A1
Bennett, John C 5-4, 448C1
Buchanan, Bessie 9-27, 755D2
Casey, Joseph E 9-2, 755D2
Coe, Frank 6-2, 528D1
Colmer, William M 9-9, 755F2
Dewey, Charles S 12-26, 1004C†
Donnell, Forrest C 3-3, 279B2
Douglas, Helen G 6-28, 528E1
Ewing, Oscar R 1-8, 104E2
Fallon, George H 3-21, 279E2
Hass, Eric 10-2, 876A2
Kean, Robert Winthrop 9-21, 755F3
Levitt, Arthur 5-6, 448C2
Longley, James B 8-16, 627A2
Lowenstein, Allard 3-14, 214C2
McCormack, John W 11-22, 928G2
McCulloch, William 2-22, 176E2
McFarlane, William 2-18, 176E2
Monroney, Mike 2-13, 176F2
Muhlenberg, Frederick A 1-19, 104C3
Phillips, Dayton 10-23, 876C3
Runnels, Harold L 8-5, 676F2
Slack, John M 3-17, 280C2
Sundstrom, Frank L 5-23, 448A3

Presidency—*See also CARTER, Pres. Jimmy*
Cong chrgd re weakened office 1-14, 32E1
Nixon sues for records 12-17, 963A3

Presidential Election—*See also other appropriate subheads in this section; for individual campaigns and issues, see personal names and subjects in Index*

1976

FEC OKs pres, vp debates 8-30; ground rules set 9-1, 644A1
McCarthy, Maddox threaten suits 9-2, 664F1
Carter sees tie as victory 9-4, 664F1
More ground rules rptd 9-8, 700F3
2d, 3d debates set 703A2
3d-party challenges rejctd 9-17, 9-20, 703D2
Networks OK ground rules 9-18, 9-20, 703B2
1st Ford-Carter debate 9-23, 700E2-703A2
Experts, poll rate debate 9-24, 9-30, 725D1
Ga gov vs Ford re Medicaid remark 9-25, 725G1
2d debate 10-6, 740B2-742G2
Reactn to Ford E Eur remark 10-7—10-12, Ford admits error 10-12, 762A1, A3, G3; 10-27, 910B1
Ford: 'quiz show' 10-7, 763G1
Ford scores on Panama Canal stand 10-7, 792F3
Dole admits 2d debate damage 10-8, 763G3
Ford lists Carter 'errors' 10-9, 763C2
Sup Ct bars equal-time review 10-12, 765D3
Carter lead up after 2d debate 10-15, 764B2
Dole, Mondale debate 10-15, 782E1-784E1
3d debate 10-22, 799E2-802C3
Dole scores Carter Yugo remark 10-26, 804F2
Carter: key to victory 11-2, 845D1
Carter aide minimizes Ford E Eur remark 11-11, 845E2
Carter sees unifying result 11-22, 880G3
Presidential Election—*See also 'Campaign Finances' and other appropriate subheads in this section; for individual campaigns and issues, see personal names and subjects in Index*
State primary dates table 22A2
Gallup poll results 1-7, 21G2
Byrd declares Dem bid 1-9, 21D3
Carter leads Dems in Iowa 1-19, 40G3
Calif GOP primary rule upheld 1-19, 42G3
Shapp hits Ford plan 1-20, 40A3
Sanford withdraws 1-23, 95C1
Wallace wins in Miss caucuses 1-24, 94F3
Carter leads Okla caucuses 2-7, 129D1
Bentsen withdraws 2-10, 129G1
Sup Ct bars GOP delegate rule review 2-23, 170A1
NH primary results 2-24, 148E1
Mass, Vt primary results 3-2, 164G2-165B2
Bayh withdraws 3-4, 165C2
FCC rules on pol ad cases 3-4, 180E2-A3
Fed conventn funds rptd 3-4, 180D3
Fla primary results 3-9, 179D1
Shapp ends bid 3-12, 197C2
Brown enters Calif primary 3-12, 197F2
Gallup poll results 3-15, 197D1
Natl black conv plans ticket; Bond, Dellums decline bids 3-15—3-20, 214E2
Ill primary results 3-16, 196D2-G3
Church announces candidacy 3-18, 197D2
Shriver releases delegates 3-22, 214C2
NC primary results 3-23, 213G2
Incumbent primary defeats rptd 3-24, 231D3
NY, Wis primary results 4-6, 244F2-245E1
Harris ends natl effort 4-8, 261G2
Delegate box score 4-9, 261A1
Equal-time rules upheld 4-12, 282E1
Pa primary results 4-27, 304E3
Humphrey rules out campaign 4-29, 305F2
Delegate count rptd 4-30, 324G2
Tex primary results 5-1; Ind, Ga, Ala, DC 5-4, 322D2-323F2
Jackson ends 'active' bid 5-1, 324F2
Black Dems hear candidates 5-2, 343A3
Neb, W Va, Conn vote results 5-11, 342D1-G3
Reagan ups delegate lead 5-11, 343A1
Dem platform hearings 5-17—5-20, 357G2
Mich, Md primary results 5-18, 356D2, 357E1
Kennedy denies interest 5-20, 357D2
Ore, Ida, Nev, Ky, Tenn, Ark vote results 5-25, 373D1, 374A2
Dem, GOP delegate selectn bias chrgd 5-27, 413F3
RI, SD, Mont vote results 6-1, 389E2-390A3
GOP delegate count 6-1, 390D1; 6-12, 432F2; 6-26, 467G2; 7-1, 467D3; 7-10, 513D3; 7-17, 7-20, 531F2, E3; 7-23, 549C3; 7-29, 550E2; 8-3, 563F2; 8-5, 564D2
Calif, Ohio, NJ vote results 6-8, 408F2-409F3
Primary delegates totaled 6-8, 409A3
Carter 1st ballot nominatn seen 6-9, 408F2
Dems unite behind Carter; Church, Udall withdraw 6-10—6-16, 431F2-432A2
Reagan sweeps Mo delegates 6-12, 432B2
Amer party, Natl Black Pol Assemb name candidates 6-18, 490C3
Reagan gains 16 delegates in 5 states 6-19, 450E2
Dems plan '80 conv rules 6-20, 451G1-C2
GOP platform guidelines issued 6-21, 451E1

1977

1978

1979

Detroit named GOP '80 conv site 1-23, 70A3
Connally announces bid 1-24, 70F2
AFL-CIO GOP pres bid support seen unlikely 2-21, 149F1
Weicker announces bid 3-12, 185A3
Kennedy ahead in Dem. pres poll 4-26, 384E2
Bush enters pres race 5-1, 326B1
Dole enters pres race 5-14; Crane renews bid, Weiker quits 5-16, 363B3-F3
Draft-Kennedy move launched 5-23, 384B2
Ford rules out bid 5-25, 594D2
Reagan to change vp selectn 5-27, 594E1
Anderson enters pres race 6-8, 439C2
Carter confident vs Kennedy pres bid 6-12, 440D1
ADA opts for Kennedy 6-24, 482C2
NAACP maps pol activism 6-25, 559D3
NYC chosen Dem '80 conv site 6-28, 518D1
Govs back Carter for '80 7-8, 518B1
NWPC discusses '80 conv tactics 7-13–7-15, 578A3
Brown state legis rebuffs detailed 7-13–8-8, pres com formed 7-30, 593E1-B3
Carter Cabt shake-up, reelectn bid linked 7-17–7-20, 529B1, 530A1; Carter denies 7-20, 556D1
Urban League vs 'dumping' movemt 7-22, 560E1
Jackson sees Kennedy '80 bid 7-24; Carter responds 7-25, 556B2-D2
Volcker nominatn linked 7-25, 555E2
McGovern backs Kennedy '80 bid 7-26, 556A2
Byrd defends Carter '80 reelectn 7-28, 593E3
6 union ldrs endorse Carter 7-30, 593B3
Carter-Kennedy primary tension rptd 8-2, Mass legis bars date chng 8-6, 592G3-593E1
Pressler com formed 8-2, 594E2
Kraft named Carter campaign com dir 8-10, 608F2
GOP disputes Carter on Miss R boat trip 8-17, 8-19, 622A2, D2
Tex gov discounts Kennedy '80 run 8-19, 627D3
Cranston vs Carter '80 renominatn 8-20, 627B3
Reagan aide resigns 8-28, 661E3
Mondale '80 pres race suggested 9-5, 662B1
Kennedy considers '80 race 9-6–9-11, 679E3-680A2
Libertarians set ticket 9-8, 680F2
Draft Haig com forms 9-10, 680C2
Reagan forces win Calif primary procedural fight 9-16, 724B1
Kennedy gets Secret Svc protectn 9-20, 723G3
Draft Ford movemts start 9-20, 10-12, 783F2
Pressler enters race 9-25, 724E1
Carter comments on Kennedy ldrship 9-25, sends letter 9-26, 723B3-F3
Kennedy campaigns 9-27–11-3, 961E3
NEA endorses Carter 9-28, 782F2
Carter news conf 10-9, 766G3-767D1
Fla Dem caucuses 10-13, Carter win rptd 10-19, 783B1
Kennedy Chicago hq bomb defused 10-18, 786C2
Kennedy gets endorsemts 10-19, 10-30, 847B2-D2
Ford bars '80 GOP bid 10-19, 808D1
Carter in SW 10-10–10-11, Midwest 10-15–10-16, NJ 10-25; with Kennedy at JFK library dedicatn 10-20, rivalry intensifies 10-22, 807C2-808D1
Carter DC Dem rally held 10-24, 961E2
Kennedy DC hq opened 10-29, 847F1
Thomson announces 3d party bid 10-31, 829D1
Baker enters GOP race 11-1, 828D3
Iowa, Me straw-vote results 11-3, 866G2-B3
Kennedy poll lead rptd 11-4, 847D2
Carter expects Cabt role 11-5, 961F2
Carter, Kennedy Ia debate set 11-6, 866A3
Strauss named Carter campaign com head 11-6, 961A2
Kennedy announces Dem bid 11-7, 847B1
Brown enters Dem race 11-8, 847E2
White endorses Carter 11-8, 961C2
Natl Com meets 11-9, 961D2
Reagan announces GOP bid 11-13, 866C2
Reagan bars GOP debates 11-14; Connally seeks at Ia forum 12-12, 982C1, E3
Carter labor support sought 11-15, 885E1
Fla straw vote results 11-17, 11-18, 887C1
FCC upholds Carter ad bid 11-20, 918G3
Reagan tops GOP polls 11-25, 982D1
Carter on Iran crisis impact 11-28, 895C1
Mondale, Carter kin campaign 11-28–11-30, 961B3-E3
Carter enters race 12-4, 918A2, F2, A3
Brown asked to Ia debate 12-4, 962A3
Carter takes poll leads 12-11, 962C3
SALT delay asked, Carter rejcts 12-16, 979A2
Haig decides vs bid 12-22, 984G1
Finch declares bid 12-24, 984E1
Carter to skip Ia debate 12-28; reactn 12-28–12-31, 983E2

1980

Evangelical Christian role profiled 7-11—9-15; voters surveyed, Falwell ministry detailed 9-15, 818C3-819F3
Reagan gets Klan endorsemts 7-30, 9-2, 664E1
Carter revives in polls 8-17, 8-19, 630B1
VFW endorses Reagan 8-18, 629D1
Carter offers econ renewal plan; Reagan scores; Carey vows support; other reactn 8-28, 663A1-D3
FEC issues campaign rules 9-5, Admin sets Cabt guidelines 9-8, 681D2
NY Liberal Party endorses Anderson 9-6, 681D1
Carter rejcts 3-way debate 9-9, controversy ensues 9-9—9-10, 680D2
Kraft steps down re cocaine probe 9-14, 700B1
Reagan seeks equal TV time 9-18, 698A3
Carter seeks Reagan debate 9-18, 698E3
Reagan, Anderson TV debate; Carter absence noted 9-21, 721C2-722E2
Carter uses warmonger theme 9-22—9-23; Reagan, Anderson protest 9-23, 722F2
Post-debate poll findings 9-23—9-28, 739F2
2d pres debate plans falter 9-25, vp debate canceled 9-29, 739F3
Anderson ballot access costly, 43 state ballots gained 9-27, 818B2
Dems for Reagan formed 9-29, 738F2
Commoner uses vulgar radio ad 10-15, 818A3
Carter, Reagan debate set 10-21, 801F3
Polls indicate toss-up 10-23—10-27, 816G1
Mondale sees close Carter win 10-26, 816C3
Carter, Reagan TV debate 10-28, 813A1-815E3
Reagan aide quits post 10-30, 817E3
Press endorsemts rptd 11-1, 841D3
NRA endorses Reagan 11-1, 844F1
Reagan, wife electn photo 11-4, 837A1
Reagan wins landslide; Carter concedes, pledges transitn aid 11-4, 837C1-838G3
Popular vote table 838A1; electoral vote table, map 839A1, D3
NBC defends projectns 11-5, Carter on early concessn 11-12, 865E3, 866D1
Electoral College votes 12-15, 956F1
Presidential Nomination Campaign
See also other appropriate subheads in this section; for individual campaigns and issues, see personal names and subjects in Index
Ia GOP debate held; Des Moines Register poll cited 1-5, 4C2, E2
Carter leads polls 1-8, 1-9, 13F1, F3
Pressler drops out 1-8, 13F3
Ia poll results 1-11, 33D1-A2
Kennedy, Brown, Mondale debate in Ia 1-12, 32C2
Carter, Bush win Iowa caucuses 1-21, 50D1
Reagan drops GOP debate ban 1-30, 91G2
Ark GOP caucus results 2-2, 92A1
Maine Dem caucus results 2-10, 109B1
Dole quits PR GOP primary 2-13; Bush wins 2-17, results challenged 2-19, 130A1
Anderson publicity problem rptd, strategy detailed 2-15, 129D2
More Ark GOP delegates picked 2-16, 130F1
NH gun control forum 2-18, GOP pres debate 2-20, 129G2, G3
Kennedy, Reagan slip in Times/CBS poll 2-20, 130D2
NH limited GOP debate dispute sparked 2-23, 143C1
NH primary results 2-26, 142D2
Ford considers bid, Reagan challenges 3-2, 167C1-A2
Mass, Vt primary results 3-4, 166B2
Baker drops out 3-5, 166E2, 167A2
Connally 'basic speech' excerpts 3-7, 184B2, 185E1
Reagan wins SC primary 3-8, 183E3
Connally ends bid 3-9, 183F3
Kennedy 'basic speech' excerpts 3-10, 183A1, 184A2
Fla, Ga, Ala primary results 3-11, 182G3
Okla, Hawaii, Washn, Alaska, Dem caucus results 3-11, Del 3-12, 209A1
Ill GOP forum held 3-13, 206E2
Carter '79 ad bid upheld by ct 3-14, 221F3
Ford declines race 3-15, 207C1
Dole quits GOP race 3-15, 208C1
FALN raids Carter, Bush hqs 3-15, 208A3-209A1
Carter wins PR primary 3-16, 208B2
Ill primary results, delegate count cited 3-18, 206B2-207A1
NY, Conn primary results 3-25, 221A2, A3
Gallup Poll results 3-31, 4-1, 246E3-247B1
Wis, Kan primary results 4-1, 246E1-A3
Brown quits race 4-1, 246C2, B3
La primary results 4-5, 264F3
Candidates address editors 4-7—4-10, 264G3-264E3
Commoner named Citizens' Party candidate 4-13, 288A3
Thomson ends run 4-14, 288F3
Crane withdraws 4-17, 304B3
Poll finds 50% dissatisfied with Carter, Reagan choice 4-18, 304E3
Pa primary results 4-22, 303G3-304A3
Anderson announces independent bid 4-24, 303D2
Mich Dem caucus results 4-26, 327D2

1976

Stassen seeks support 6-25, 467E3
Minn, Mont, Ida, NM GOP conv results 6-26, 467F1
Dem credentials hearings end 7-1, 489F3
ND, Colo conv results 7-8—7-10, 513A3
Utah, Conn GOP conv results; delegate selectn completed 7-17, 531D2
Reagan names Schweiker running mate, text 7-26; delegate reactn rptd 7-27—7-29, 549C2-550A3
Buckley candidacy promoted 8-11, 8-12, 584A3
GOP pre-conv delegate count 8-14, 583E3
Amer Indep Party picks Maddox 8-27, 666D1
Southn govs urge regional primaries 9-1, 671A3
Press endorsemts rptd 10-30, 11-8, 827D3
Carter wins narrow victory 11-2, Ford concedes 11-3, 817D1-819D2
Stock mkt reactn 11-3—11-4, 826B1
Forgn pol, econ 11-3—11-4, 826C1-F2
Electoral College votes 12-13, 979A1
Final tally rptd 12-18; table 979C1,A2

1980

Kennedy supporters' petitn rejctd by Sup Ct 4-28, 369A2
White readies Carter campaign 5-2, Kennedy backers assail 5-5, 366E3-367A1
Tex primary results 5-3, 342A2
Reagan delegate count grows 5-3, 342B3
Ill gov endorses Reagan 5-4, 342D3
NY gov asks open Dem conventn 5-5, 342E3
Tenn, Ind, NC, DC primary results 5-6, 341F2-342A2
Byrd urges Carter debate 5-10, 367A1
Md, Neb primary results 5-13, 366D2
Kennedy seeks Carter debate 5-15, 383A2
Carter, Reagan tied in polls 5-19—6-23, 452G1
Mich, Ore primary results 5-20, 382E3-383G1
Jackson: Reagan may win 5-22, 399E3
Bush quits race 5-26, 398E2-399B1
Ark, Ida, Ky, Nev primary results 5-27, 399B1-F2
Carter bars Anderson debate, Reagan favors 5-27, 399A3
Carter leads Kennedy 2 to 1 6-1, 452G1
Calif, NJ, NM, RI, SD, Ohio, Mont, W Va, Miss primary results; Carter gains delegate majority 6-3, 422D2-424C1
Polls rpt voter discontent 6-3, 423A1
Carter, Kennedy vote totals 6-4, 596A2
Carter bars Kennedy debate 6-5, 423F1
Voter discontent rptd 6-18, 493A3
Anti-draft group vows conv protests 6-24, 478C3
GOP to study primary system 7-15, 535A2
Dem open conv move forms, Carter popularity dips 7-25—7-31; Kennedy, Anderson meet, hold news conf 7-31, 570E1-D3

Republican Party—*See also 'Campaign Finances' and 'Presidential Nomination Campaign' above, 'Republican Party Convention' below; also 'Republicans' under U.S. GOVERNMENT, subhead HOUSE*

1976

Rockefeller sees Ga GOP 4-15, 305D3
Party identificatn poll 5-27, 565B1
Platform guidelines issued 6-21, 451E1
Rules, platform com actns 8-8—8-13, 582C1-583A2; 8-15, 600B1
Platform text 8-18, 602A1-611C3
Smith reelected Natl Com chrmn 8-20, Connally rejctn rptd 8-22, 631D1
Ford sees SD ldrs 8-29, 644F3
Dole addresses Tex conv 9-11, 687A1
Smith resigns 11-22, 882B1
GOP govs meet 11-29—11-30, 917F2-D3
Natl com leaders see Ford 12-6, 938E1
Ford, Reagan, Rockefeller, Connally meet, plan unity 12-9, 938A1

1977

Republican Party—*See also 'Campaign Financing' above; 'Republicans' under U.S. GOVERNMENT, subheads CONGRESS, HOUSE and SENATE*
Brock elected GOP natl chrmn 1-14, 40F3
Ford on role, '80 bid 3-25, 236C2
Carter energy taxes scored 4-25, 320F3
Natl com ends mtg, scores Carter energy plan 4-30, 443A2
TV reply to Carter energy plan 6-2, 443D1
Natl Com rejcts Panama Canal pacts 9-30, 755D3
Canal pact controversy continues 10-29, 10-30; party warned vs divisn 11-13, 912A1

1978

Republican Party—*See also U.S. GOVERNMENT—CONGRESS—Republicans*
Jackson addresses natl com 1-20, 568D2
State of Union rebuttal 1-26, Carter budget 1-31, 62F3-63G1
'53, '78 cong compositn compared 1-30, 107E2
Korea contributns rptd 3-22, 203B2
Ill cnty clerk electn ballot case refused by Sup Ct 3-27, 241F2
Black ldrs interviewed on vote issues 4-10, 568F2-B3
Va US Sen nominees picked 6-3, 467G1
Hooks addresses natl com 7-21, 568A2
Crane announces pres bid 8-2, 606C1
GSA aide reassignmt called 'payoff' 8-5, 605D3
Va US Sen nominee successor named 8-12, 645A3
DC voting amendmt backed by ldrs 8-22, 661B2
1st in cong campaign fund raising 9-7, 753F1
Cross-country blitz staged for tax-cut bill 9-20—9-22, 734D3
Tax cut bill clears Cong, scored 10-15, 785D2
Brock scores Carter anti-inflatn plan 10-24, 807A1
State legis gains rptd 11-7, 897A3
Brock on electn results 11-8, 845B1
GOP govs meet 11-27—11-28, 915G3
Fernandez announces pres bid 11-29, 938G2

1979

Republican Party—*See also 'Presidential Nomination Campaign' above; also U.S. GOVERNMENT, subheads CONGRESS, HOUSE and SENATE*
Brock scores B Carter remarks 1-11, 31E2
State of Union reactn 1-24, 48F1-B2
GOP poll ratings 3-4, 3-10, 185D3
FALN bomb hoax in NYC 10-17, Chicago device defused 10-18, 786A2, C2
Gaylord on electn results 11-6, 846A2
Govs meet in Austin 11-18, 983F1
Tidewater Conf held; SALT debated, fed spending curb sought 2-3–2-4, 86A1-B2
Carter forgn policy scored 2-16, 2-18, 124D1
Natl Com scores Carter defns policy 3-1, 165A3
Midwest offcls meet 3-10, 185F3
Carter energy program reactn 7-16, 7-17, 534G1-A3
FRB money policy, '72 electn linked 7-25, 555E2
Natl com asks US intell overhaul 8-6, 610C3

1980

Republican Party—*See also 'Presidential' subheads above*
Brock vs Carter forgn policy 1-1, 5A1
Platform hearings open 1-14, 1-15, 31G2
State of Union reactn 1-28, 75C1
'81 counter-budget proposed 4-1, 244F1
Pres campaign spending limit upheld by Sup Ct 4-14, 306E3
Reagan retains Brock 6-13, 452G2-B3
DC hq taps suspected 6-21, 6-24, 480D3
Natl com meets; Brock renamed chrmn, Heitman chosen co-chrmn 7-18, 549D2, F2
AFL-CIO seeks enhanced role 12-5, 938G3

Republican Party Convention (Kansas City, Mo.)

1976

Reagan, Ford delegates compared 8-7, 8-8, 8-17, 616A2
Platform com OKs planks 8-8—8-13, 582F2-583A2
Rules com acts on pre-ballot vp selectn, other issues 8-9—8-11, 582C1
Conv rules com vs Reagan vp proposals 8-15; delegates defeat 16-C, OK other com proposals 8-17, 600B1
Ford, Reagan seek delegates 8-15—8-18 601E2
Rhodes named permanent chrmn 8-17, 601G1
Press sees Ford nominatn 8-16, 8-17, 601D3
Reagan delegate count 8-16, 601E3
Opens; Baker keynotes, Rockefeller, others speak 8-16, 601F3
Buckley ends pres bid 8-16, 615E3
Delegate vote bribes chrgd 8-16, 8-17, 616C1
Ford wins 16-C rules test 8-17, 600B1
NY delegatn scuffle on 16-C 8-17, 600G1
Rhodes, Connally address 8-17, 601G1
Ford, Reagan nominated 8-18; Ford wins 8-19, 597E1
Pres, vp vote tables 8-18—8-19, 8-19, 599A1, A3
Platform text 8-18, 602A1-611C3
Sears, Reagan assess campaign 8-18, 8-19, 615E2-E3
Schweiker offers to withdraw, Reagan rejects 8-18, 615D3
Ford sees Reagan, advisers re vp 8-19, 598E1, B3
Dole wins vp nominatn 8-19, 598B2-599F1
Ford accepts nominatn, asks Carter debate 8-19, 599F1; text 611C1-612E3
Reagan addresses 8-19, 599A2; text 613F1
Dole accepts nominatn 8-19, 599C2; text 612E1
Reagan farewell to supporters 8-19, 615C2
Nixon's views rptd 8-19, 615G3
Ford, Dole photo 597A1 ★

Republican Party Convention (Detroit, Mich.)

1980

GOP delegate count table 6-28, 506A2
Detroit workers strike 7-2, 518G1
Platform com meets 7-7—7-10; bars ERA support, seeks US abortn ban amendmt 7-9, 506G1-D3
Carter Detroit visit scored 7-14, 505B2
Opens, C Young greets 7-14; others address 7-14—7-17, 529C1, 531B3
VP hopefuls address 7-14—7-16, 530A3
Reagan arrives in Detroit 7-14, 532F1
Ford addresses 7-14, Kissinger, Hooks 7-15, Vander Jagt keynotes 7-16, 534G1-535D1
Rules Com rejects PR delegate rise, other proposals 7-14; rpt adopted 7-15, 535A2
Ford sees Reagan re vp spot 7-15, 7-16, talks fail 7-16, Bush selectn rptd 7-17, 529D2, 530A1, 532G1
Reagan sees Kissinger, women, blacks, jobless groups 7-15, 533A3-534B1
Reagan nominated by Laxalt, wins vote 7-16, Bush gets vp spot 7-17, 529C1, E1, 534C1
Reagan acceptance speech; text 7-17, 531A1, F3, 532A2-533G2, 534F3
Carter congratulates Reagan; seeks debate, Reagan accepts 7-17, 532D1
Reagan, Ford, Bush photo 7-17, 529A1

Third Parties

1976

Third Parties—*See also COMMUNISM, U.S.*
McCarthy names running mate 2-5, 95B1
FBI thefts of SWP rptd 3-17, 569B2; **for subsequent developments, see SOCIALIST Workers Party**
Nazi 'kill' list rptd 6-14—6-16, 453F1
Amer Party, Black Pol Assemb name pres candidates, 6-18, 6-19, 490C3
Maddox heads Amer Indep ticket 8-27, 666D1
McCarthy, Maddox threaten debate suits 9-2, 664F1
McCarthy, Maddox, Camejo debate challenges rejctd 9-17, 9-20, 703D2

1977

Third Parties—*See also COMMUNISM, U.S.*
Soclst Workers Denver probe ends 1-6, 15D3
Mich eligibility rules upheld 3-21, 230C3
McCarthy pres debate suit review declined 4-4, 341D3
Ill Natl Soclst rally ban upset 6-13, 517G2; swastika display barred 7-12, 560A2
Natl States Rights Party chrmn indicted 9-26, 907D3
Nazi tape request denied 12-21, 1008A2

1978

Third Parties
Ill Natl Soclst swastika display OKd 1-27, 68F3; **for subsequent developments, see NATIONAL Socialist Party of America**
FBI informant case declined by Sup Ct 6-12, 468D1
Election results 11-7, 849A3, 856D2
SWP mail scrutiny held unconst 11-29, 940A1

1979

Third Parties—*See also COMMUNISM (U.S.)*
SWP wins funds rpt exemptn 1-9, 13D3
FBI ex-agent's statemt in SWP trial sought 1-16, 92B2
Ill electn law struck down by Sup Ct 2-22, 150D1
Peace Party CIA surveillnc rptd 3-9, 207C2
SWP informant case rule overturned 3-19, 207E1
Citizens Party formed, platform issued 8-1, 594E3-595A1
SWP sets '80 pres ticket 8-22, 680G2
Libertarians set '80 pres ticket 9-8, 680F2

1980

Third Parties
LaRouche wins 2% of NH vote 2-26, 142F2
LaRouche wins 3% of Conn vote 3-25, 221D3
Citizens' Party holds conv 4-11—4-13, picks pres ticket 4-13, 288A3
Thomson ends bid 4-14, 288F3
Anderson announces independent bid 4-24, 303E3; for complete coverage, see ANDERSON, Rep. John
LaRouche wins 13% of Mich vote 5-20, 383G1
Clark urges Anderson quit pres race 8-20, 682B1

1976

Carter addresses NY Liberal Party 10-14 827E1
McCarthy poll results rptd 10-21, 804C3
Maddox vote results 11-2, 818F2
Final pres vote tally 12-18; table 979C1, B2
Alex Rose dies 12-28, 1015E2

Vice Presidency—*See also ROCKEFELLER, Nelson*
Carter for post-conv selectn period 7-15, 506F2
Ford backs pre-conv selectn 8-20, 631G1
Mondale, Dole debate 10-15, 782F1-784E1
Carter, Ford debate 10-22, 801B2

Voting Rights (& other voting issues)
Sup Ct on OK of reapportionmt plans 3-3, 219B1
Sup Ct backs one-member dists 3-3, 219D1
DC Cong vote blocked 3-23, 234F1
Sup Ct rules on redistricting plans review 3-30, 262C1
Multilingual electns ordered 4-21, 307D3
Blacks urge postcard registratn 5-1, 343E3
Dem platform text 6-15, 472F1
Carter for univ registratn 7-15, 510A3
Mondale record cited 512B3
Dems plan registratn drive 7-16, 532G2
House OKs mail registratn 8-9, bill not cleared 10-2, 883E1
GOP platform text 8-18, 603F3
Dems launch registratn drive 8-23, 631E2
Carter sees Atlanta registrars 8-30, 645A2
Carter vows registratn at 18 9-10, 686C2
Ford, Carter debate 10-22, 802A1
Carter urges turnout 10-26, 10-27, 803B2, E2
Sup Ct backs Conn primary vote rule 12-6, 920D3

Watergate Issue—*See WATERGATE*

1977

Vice Presidency—*See also MONDALE, Walter*
Ford urges pay hike 1-17, 33D3
Pay raise takes effect 2-20, 127D2
Carter asks voting change 3-22, 210C2
Carter backs spec prosecutor bill 5-3, 338F1

Voting Issues
Byrd position cited 1-4, 6A1, C1
Sup Ct backs racial redistricting 3-1, 174C3-175D1
Carter asks universal registratn 3-22, 210C2, A3
Mondale urges registratn bill 3-31, 251B1
Colo alien voting law review denied 4-18, 342D1
Miss reapportnmt plan rejected 5-31, 461B3
Atty Gen powers upheld 6-20, 517A1
Sup Ct rulings scored 10-31, 878G3, 879B1
Registratn issues lose in Ohio, Washn 11-8, 879F2
Hinds Cnty (Miss) apportnmt case refused 11-28, 919F2

Watergate Issue—*See under 'W'*

1978

Vice Presidency—*See MONDALE, Walter*

Voting Issues
Carter State of Union Message 1-19, 30G2
Crime code revisn clears Sen 1-30, 64A3
Cities subject to US electn law 3-6, 162F1
'76 pres vote data 4-13, 285A2
Corp free speech backed by Sup Ct 4-26, 343D2
Carter on vote decline 11-6, 862F1
Voter turnout declines 11-7, 915G2-A3
Cities' power over suburbs backed by Sup Ct 11-28, 937G2
Ga schl bd pol rule struck down by Sup Ct 11-28, 937E3

Watergate Issue—*See WATERGATE*

1979

Citizens Party support urged at A-protest 9-23, 742A3
SWP-Bell contempt case declined by Sup Ct 10-9, 783D3
Thomson announces Const Party pres bid 10-31, 829D1
2 Nazis arrested in NC slayings 11-3, 864F3
Electn results 11-6, 846A3, C3

Voting Issues
Boston referendum spending case refused by Sup Ct 1-8, 14A3
Miss legis redistricting ordrd by Sup Ct 3-26, 231C1
Carter urges black vote 5-20, 384F2-A3
Mich HS voter turnout law signed 8-14, 724D2
Black registratn drive launched 10-25, 808G1
Wayne Cnty (Mich) govt reorgnztn referendum accord reached 11-1, 921D1, E1

1980

NY Liberal Party endorses Anderson 9-6, 681D1
Javits to run on NY Liberal line 9-9, 682F1
Anderson ballot access costly, 43 states gained 9-27, 818B2
Anderson bank loan plan fails 10-2, abandoned 10-15, 818E1
Commoner uses vulgar radio ad 10-15, 818A3
Clark on 50 state ballots; ideology cited 10-28, 818E2
Anderson, Clark press endorsemts rptd 11-1, 841E3, 844F1
Pres popular vote table 11-4, 838A2
Javits loses reelectn 11-4, 845G1, 848B3
Anderson FEC paymt $4.1 mln 11-13, 866F1

Voting Issues
Kan State of State message 1-15, 403B3
SC reapportionmt suggestd 2-14, 185A2
Sumter Cnty (Ga) ruled biased vs blacks 4-7, 309A2
SC reapportionmt suit filed 4-18, 349A2
At-large local electns upheld by Sup Ct 4-22, 343A2
Voting Rights Act provisn upheld by Sup Ct 4-22, 344C1
Latin registratn surveyed 5-20, 396F3
'82 House reapportmt seen 12-31, 982E3, 983C1

1976

POLLACK, Andrea
Sets world swim mark 6-1—6-5, 424G3
Wins Olympic medals 7-19, 7-22, 575A3
POLLACK, James A.
On Martian sky 7-21, 526C2
POLLAK, Burglinde
Wins Olympic medal 7-26, 576F1
POLLARD, Robert D.
Rpts NRC resignatn 2-9, 115E1
POLLOCK, Jackson (1912-56)
Mark Tobey dies 4-24, 368B3
POLLS & Surveys—*See names (e.g., GALLUP, HARRIS); also 'Polls' under POLITICS; country names*
POLLUTION—*See ENVIRONMENT*
POLSKY, Justice Leon B.
Dismisses DeSapio indictmt 12-17, 1016B2
POLYANSKY, Dmitri S.
Dropped from Politburo 3-5, 195F1
Ousted as agri min, replaced 3-16, 206B2
Named amb to Japan 4-17, 314B1
POLYCHLORINATED Biphenyls (PCBs)—*See CHEMICALS*

1977

POLLACK, James
Dies 3-15, 264D3
POLLACK, Judge Milton
Lifts Port Auth Concorde ban 5-11, 368B1-D2
Appeals ct upsets Concorde ruling 6-14, 463E1
Overturns Concorde ban; reactn 8-17, 627D1-B2
NY Concorde ruling upheld 9-29, 738D3
POLLS & Surveys—*See names (e.g., GALLUP, HARRIS); country names, subjects*
POLLUTION—*See ENVIRONMENT & Pollution*

POL Pot (Tol Saut) (Cambodia premier)
Rpt heads CP 8-19; apptmt formally rptd 9-25, 741C2
In China, cites Cambodian conditns 9-28, 741G2
Ends China trip, '75 visit disclosed 9-28—10-2, 779E3, 780A1
On evacuatn move 10-2, 779E3
Denies widespread killings 840C3

POLYAKOV, Nikolai
Sees Fahmy on Libya ties 4-27, 5-5, 361B3
POLYANSKI, Dmitri
Vs Japan fishing protest 3-8, 250D1
POLYCHLORINATED Biphenyls (PCBs)—*See CHEMICALS*

1978

POLK, James (1795-1849)
Carter vetoes '79 arms authorzn 8-17, 621F1
POLL, Martin
Somebody Killed Her Husband released 9-29, 970C3
POLLACK, Judge Milton
Sentences Beasley 5-31, 404E2
POLLAK, Emile
Dies 1-6, 96C3
POLLARD, Bob
Traded to Cardinals 1-31, 172D1
POLLARD, Jim
In basketball HOF 5-1, 457D3
POLLENTIER, Michel
Tour de France suspends, fines 7-16, 692D2
POLLOCK, Richard
Scores rpt on A-waste storage 3-15, 184A1
POLLOCK, Sam
Resigns as Canadiens gen mgr, vp 9-6, 991A1
POLLS & Surveys—*See names (e.g., GALLUP); also country, subject names*
POLLUTION—*See ENVIRONMENT & Pollution*
POLON, Vicki
Girlfriends released 8-16, 970D1

POL Pot (Tol Saut) (Cambodian premier)
Asks N Korea aid vs Viets 1-3, 4E1
Viet denies 'federatn' plan 1-18, 43C1
Teng ends Cambodia visit 1-22, 80G1
In Thai talks 1-30—2-2, 61C1
Vs Viet federatn plan 3-16, 201B3
Chrgs Viet aggressn 4-13, 277E3
Chrgs Sovt buildup in Viet 11-5, 894B2
Rebel front scores 12-3, 12-4, 933F1, B2

POLYANSKI, Dmitri
Japan vs peace bid 2-22, 121G3
Vs Japan-China peace pact 6-19, 637G1
POLYBROMINATED Biphenyls (PBBs)—*See CHEMICALS*
POLYCHLORINATED Biphenyls (PCBs)—*See CHEMICALS*

1979

POLK County, Ark.—*See ARKANSAS*
POLLACK, Sydney
Electric Horseman released 12-21, 1007C3
POLLARD, Robert
Asks A-plant shutdown 1-26, 90A3
Asks NY A-plant shutdown 9-17, 743C2
POLLARD, William
Heads black delegatn to Israel 10-14—10-17, 780C3
POLLOCK, Jackson (1912-1956)
Matisse work sold for record sum 7-3, 672B1
POLLOCK, Richard
On 3 Mile I comm final rpt 10-30, 826E1
POLLOCK, Capt. Thomas S.
AF plane lost 4-12, feared dead 5-5, 404B3
POLLS & Surveys—*See names (e.g., GALLUP); also country, subject names*
POLLUTION—*See ENVIRONMENT*
POLO, Marco (1254?-1324?)
China premr visits home 11-6, 854C2

POL Pot (Tol Saut) (Cambodian premier; replaced Dec. 27)
Sees 'life-or-death struggle' 1-5, 1D2
Sovt bloc lauds downfall 1-9, Rumania scores 1-10, 11F1
Heng chrgs massacres 1-25, 68E3
Vietnam friendship pact signed 2-18, 123B2
Vs Cambodia-Viet pact 2-18, 142B2
Loyalists press drive 2-21, 2-22, 142D1
Document on '70 US Cambodia invasn rptd 3-18, 229G2
Hq taken, escape to Thailand rptd 4-5, 278F3
Rptd alive, in Cambodia 5-14, 360E2
Seeks right-wing alliance 5-31, 6-2, 443D3
Viets: China seeks comeback 6-1, 474F2
Nonaligned mtg admits rep 6-4, 437D1
Thais ask halt to refugee flow 6-12, 436B1
Gets death sentnc 8-19, 666F3
US, China vs peace role 8-28, 644F2
Khieu in Cuba, nonaligned summit bars 8-30, 674C3, 675D1
UN rep retains Assemb seat 9-21, 741F1
Sihanouk discloses exile group formatn 10-4, 811B2
Cambodia relief aid reaches forces 10-17, 779E2
UK ends govt ties 12-6, 978G3
Replaced as premr 12-27, 977E2

POLSKY, Abe
Devour the Snow opens 5-13, 711D2
POLYANSKY, Dmitri
Japan vs Kurile buildup 2-5, 85A3
POLYBROMINATED Biphenyls (PBBs)—*See CHEMICALS*
POLYCHLORINATED Biphenyls (PCBs)—*See CHEMICALS*

1980

POLK Memorial Awards, George
Presented 2-25, 692D3
POLLACK, Alan M.
H Ford kickback suit settled 1-11, 225D3
POLLACK, Andrea
Wins Olympic medal 7-24, 623C3
POLLACK, Irving M.
Thomas replaces 10-21, 960B1
POLLACK, Judge Milton
Bars Colombia kidnap liability 1-6, 18A2
Sentences LaChance 6-26, 656E1
POLLAN, Clayton
Dies 9-13, 756F1
POLLIO, Claudio
Wins Olympic medal 7-29, 624C3
POLLOCK, Jackson (1912-56)
Painting sold for record sum 5-16, 472A2
POLLOCK, Richard
On '79 A-plant mishap rpt 7-14, 551D2
POLLUTION—*See ENVIRONMENT*
POLOVCHAK, Walter
Granted asylum in US 7-19, 7-21, 560C1

POL Pot (Tol Saut)
Sihanouk scores rule 2-22, 141C2
Successors refute excesses 2-28, 181F1
Cambodia '70-79 populatn drop rptd 5-24, 397E2
UN conf on Cambodia aid excludes reps 5-26, 397C2
Rebels ambush train 6-10, 475G3
UN women's conf delegate shunned 7-17, 587C2
UN rep keeps Assemb seat 10-13, 775B2
Ieng on exile govt ouster, planned reforms 11-29, 913E2-A3

POLUDNIAK, Stephen
Convicted in extortn scheme 10-24, 890C1
POLYBROMINATED Biphenyls (PBBs)—*See CHEMICALS*
POLYCHLORINATED Biphenyls (PCBs)—*See CHEMICALS*

1976

POLYSAR Ltd.
Trudeau on rebates 11-26, 904G1
POMPIDOU, Georges Jean Raymond (1911-74)
Rpt Chalandon backs Eur defns group 1-15, 126D2
De Broglie killed in Paris 12-24, 1002E2
POMPONIO Jr., Louis
Convctd, bros acquitted 6-6; sentncd 6-25, 860F2
PONCE, Camilo
Dies 9-14, 1015D2
PONCET, Jean-Francois
French forgn min secy 1-12, 49D2
PONIATOWSKI, Michel
Reinforces riot police 3-5, 204C3
Chirac scores coalitn foes 6-6, 418A1
Renamed interior min 8-27, 650D3, F3
Croats surrender TWA jet 9-12, 685A2
Orders raid vs newspaper 12-6, 964C1
PONOMAREV, Boris Nikolaevich
Politburo, Secretariat named 3-5, 195D2, F2
PONS, Lily
Dies 2-13, 160G3
PONSTEEN, Herman
Wins Olympic medal 7-22, 574B2
PONTECORVO, Gillo
Rptd on CP ticket 5-17, 5-30, 402D3
PONTES, Paulo
Dies 12-28, 1015D2
POOLTARAT, Payao
Wins Olympic medal 7-31, 574A1
POOR Murderer (play)
Opens 10-20, 1014E3
POPE-Hennessey, Sir John
NY Met Museum apptmt rptd 5-25, 504D2
P & O Petroleum
Scotland oil find rptd 8-19, 675A3
POPISIL, Frantisek
Olympics penalize for drug use 2-7, 158B3
POPOV, Hristos
US seizes boat 9-30, 910D2
POPOV, Ivan
Bulgaria Politburo drops 4-2, 250C1
POPOVIC, Srdja M.
Yugo sentences 3-10, 223F3
Wins sentence suspensn 5-26, 543B1

POPULATION—*See also BIRTHS*
Bulgaria census results rptd 1-3, 104C2
US '74 farm populatn down 1-12, 216E2
Freedom House survey rptd 1-19, 20D2
Ford seeks curbs on CIA spying 2-18, 127A2
Australia Sept '75 total rptd 3-15, 204D1
India data rptd 4-16, 290E1
July '75 US male, female data rptd 4-27, 379F3
'75 Australia data rptd 5-18, 400D1
'75 US growth rptd 7-31, 911G1
Australia rpt notes decline 10-1, 749B3
US farm populatn drop rptd 10-5, 10-18, 833F1
Mid-decade census bill signed 10-17, 834F3
Global growth rate down 10-28, 863G1
Ward Allen dies 12-17, 1015A1

POQUETTE, Tom
AL batting ldr 10-4, 796B1, C1
PORGY and Bess (play)
Opens 9-26, 1014E3
PORGY and Bess (record album)
Wins Hall of Fame award 2-28, 460E3
PORK—*See MEAT*

PORNOGRAPHY & Obscenity
Danish crackdown rptd 1-26, 101A1
Canada law review urged 3-25, 250D3
Sup Ct upholds theater zoning 6-24, 478G3
Australia smuggling ring rptd 7-8, 537E1
GOP platform text 8-18, 604G1
Sup Ct bars review of art fund rules 10-18, 867B3; Calif theater, bookstores 11-1, 868A1

PORPOISES—*See WILDLIFE*
PORRO, Alfred A.
Indicted 6-2, 414D3
PORSCHE A.G.—*See VOLKSWAGENWERK*
PORT Authority of New York and New Jersey
US OKs Concorde test, Carey scores 2-4, 94C2, D3
Bars Concorde flights 3-11, 378A3
US Sup Ct bars Concorde landing review 11-15, 882B2

1977

POLYGAMY—*See MARRIAGES*
POLYSAR Ltd.—*See CANADA Development Corp.*
POLYVINYL Chloride (PVC)—*See CHEMICALS*
POMA, Roberto
Kidnaped 1-27, body found 2-25, 182B1
POMERO, Vincente
Czechs detain 4-2—4-3, 314B3
POMPANO Beach Fla.—*See FLORIDA*
PONCE, Camilo
Backers score police raid 9-1, 842B2
PONCELET, Christian
Wins Sen seat 9-25, replaced in Cabt 9-26, 744G2
PONIATOWSKI, Michel
Police versn of de Broglie murder questnd 1-5—1-9, 44A1
Ousted from Cabinet 3-30, 239D1
Named Giscard envoy 5-13, 391A3
PONS Llobet, Jose Luis
Freed from prison 7-17, 582C3
PONTIAC, Mich.—*See MICHIGAN*
PONTO, Jurgen
Slain 7-30, 601A3
Schleyer kidnaped 9-5, 695E1, A2
Replaced as Dresdner Bank hd 9-9, 969D2
Slayers linked to Schleyer murder 10-20, 791B2
Suspect captured 11-10, 887E3
Baader atty linked to suspects 11-18, 969A1
POOLE, Harry
Joins AFL-CIO exec cncl 12-12, 961G1
POORTVLIET, Rien
Gnomes on best seller list 12-4, 1021A3
POPE, Evans & Robbins
New coal-burning plant set 3-4, 278D1
POPPIES—*See OPIUM*
POPULAR Front for the Liberation of Palestine (PFLP)—*See MIDDLE EAST*

POPULATION
Sovt Jan total 257.9 mln 1-22, 101A3
Mid-'75 world data rptd 1-30, 123F2
US science group meets 2-21—2-25, 183A3, G3
Afars & Issas data 221E2
Canada '76 data rptd 3-25, 237D2
US '75 10 largest cities rptd; table 4-14, 387B3, 388A1
Soc Security tax hike asked 5-9, 364A1
Egypt problems studied 5-11—5-12, 390A3
Bahama Islands data 579E1
Luxembourg concerned re birthrate decline 7-21, 745A3
US '76 data rptd 7-25—12-13, 962G2-C3
US '78 planning aid signed 8-4, 668F1
Rumania Jan '77 census rptd 9-22, 948B2
US House creates com 9-24, 833G3-834A1
US forgn aid funds clear Cong 10-19, 815E2; Carter signs 11-1, 834D1
POPULATION Council
Birth pill-smoking risk rptd 3-29, 287E3
Abortn alternatives proposed 7-19, 786D3
POPULATION Crisis Committee
Wm Gaud Jr dies 12-5, 1024G1
PORCARI, Luciano
Hijacks jet 3-14, arrested 3-16, 224B3
PORGY and Bess (play)
Wins Tony 6-5, 452E1
PORK—*See MEAT*
PORNOGRAPHY and Obscenity
Hustler publisher sentncd 2-8, 118A2
Sup Ct bars retroactive prosecutns 3-1, 175E1
Argentina bans Emanuelle 3-1, 198C1
FCC '75 NYC order voided 3-16, 215D3-216B1
Pa radio statn loses license 4-4, 395A3
Child abuse arrests 4-11, 4-26; abuse schemes rptd 5-15—5-18; House legis hearings 5-20, 5-27, 432G1-G3
Sup Ct upholds Iowa convictn 5-23, 444C2
Ad role in trials upheld 6-6, 478B3
Sup Ct restores Ill law 6-9, 501B3
Mafia control rptd nationwide 6-19, 7-3, 568B2
FCC cable TV rule ordrd suspended 9-1, 846B2
Nastase barred from '78 Davis Cup 10-3, 1020B3
Calif nightclub license revocatn case review refused 10-17, 797F3
Young cleared re Thevis 10-19, 861D3
Sup Ct rulings scored 10-31, 879B1
Washn referendum curbs OKd 11-8, 879G2
PORPOISES—*See WHALES & Porpoises*
PORT Authority of New York and New Jersey
Concorde flights delayed 2-3, Carter backs trial 2-16, 131F2
Concorde noise study rptd 4-9, FAA endorses 4-14, 368E2
Mass transit aid curbed 4-27, 382G3
Judge lifts Concorde ban; reactn 5-11, 368B1-D2
Appeals ct backs Concorde ban 6-14, 463E1
Concorde ban overturned; reactn 8-17, 627D1-B2
NY Concorde ruling upheld 9-29, 738D3
Concorde JFK landings delay rejctd 10-6; Marshall issues stay 10-7, Sup Ct denies 10-17, 797A3

1978

POLYMERS—*See CHEMICALS*
POMARICI, Ferdinando
Quits in kidnap controversy 1-22, 133B3
POMPIDOU, Georges Jean Raymond (1911-74)
France in UN Leb peace force 3-19, 197F2
Chaban-Delmas wins Assemb post 4-3, 245B3
PONCIA, Vini
Song wins Grammy 2-24, 315G3
PONCIANO, Edgar
Guatemala agri min 7-21, 722C3 ★
PONIATOWSKI, Michel
Loses reelectn 3-19, 201D1
PONOMAREV, Boris Nikolaevich
Carter warns re Ethiopia role 1-25, 43D3
PONTIAC, Ill.—*See ILLINOIS*
PONTO, Jurgen (d. 1977)
Yugo arrests 4 W Ger terrorists 5-11, 438G3
Slaying suspect killed 9-6, 724F3
Speitel captured 9-24, 885A1
POOLE, Alec
3d in Daytona endurance 2-5, 538D3
POOLE, Mick
NASL goalkeeping ldr 8-6, 655D2
POORTVLIET, Rien
Gnomes on best-seller list 1-8, 24E3; 3-5, 195E3; 4-2, 272C3; 4-30, 356A2; 12-3, 971B1
POPE, John Russell (1874-1937)
Natl Gallery additn opens 6-1, 578A3
POPESCU, Peter
Last Wave released 12-18, 1030B3
POPULAR Front for the Liberation of Palestine (PFLP)—*See MIDDLE EAST*
POPULAR Library Books—*See CBS Inc.*

POPULATION
USSR Jan populatn rptd 1-4, 230F1
Mex '77 growth 3.6% 2-26, 331B1
W Ger decline rptd 8-16, 725A3
Cleveland loss cited 8-23, 663F3
Black urban growth at standstill 11-30, 943F1
'75-77 migratn of poor from South reverses 12-3, 943A1
US top 20 cities ranked, losses rptd 12-6; table 942A3, D3
US House com notes illegal immigratn 12-20, 1010C2

POPULATION Research, Office of—*See PRINCETON University*
PORCH (play)
Opens 11-14, 1031G2
PORGY & Bess (recording)
Houston Grand Opera wins Grammy 2-24, 316C1

PORNOGRAPHY & Obscenity
Canada prov film censorship upheld 1-19, 111A2
Child porno curbs clear Cong 1-24, 82D3; 2-6, 218A2
US crime code revisn clears Sen 1-30, 64G2
Flynt shot, mistrial declared 3-6, 186G3
Ga obscenity convictn overturned by Sup Ct 3-21, 220E3
Md obscenity rule review declined by Sup Ct 4-24, 322F2
Child abuse extensn signed 4-24, 323C3
Thevis flees jail 4-28; govt witnesses slain 10-25, arrested 11-9, 971B2
Film distributor sentenced 5-19, 396G3
Children excluded from jury definitn by Sup Ct 5-23, 405G2-F3
Port of entry case declined by Sup Ct 5-30, 430B3
Solzhenitsyn scores West 6-8, 444E2
FCC 'Filthy Words' ban upheld by Sup Ct 7-3, 551F2
FCC renews WGBH license 7-20, censorshp role rejctd 7-21, 599E1
NFL ex-cheerleaders score team managemt 11-1, 1024B1
PORSCHE, Ferdinand (1875-1951)
VW halts 'beetle' productn 1-19, 74D3
PORT Arthur, Tex.—*See TEXAS*

1979

POLYGAMY—*See MARRIAGE*
POMERANCE, Bernard
Elephant Man opens 1-14, 292D1
PONCET, Antoine
Sculpture smashed in NYC 5-6, 375D1
Attends sculpture rededicatn 9-15, 892F2
PONIATOWSKI, Michel
Rpts Bakhtiar in France 3-30, 247C3
PONOMAREV, Boris Nikolaevich
On US-USSR mil strength 4-17, 314A2
PONTI, Alex
Killer Fish released 12-7, 1007F3
PONTI, Carlo
Convicted of currency-smuggling 1-23, 79B1
POORTVLIET, Rien
Gnomes on best-seller list 1-7, 80B3*; 2-4, 120C3
POP Muzik (recording)
On best-seller list 10-3, 800E3; 11-7, 892E3
POPOV, Yevgeny
Union bars reinstatemt 12-17, 980F2
POPULAR Front for the Liberation of Palestine (PFLP)—*See MIDDLE EAST*

POPULATION
US populatn up in '78 1-1, 18B3
English, Welsh populatn down 1-11, 38F1
US illegal alien issue detailed 1-29, 127D1, G1
China '77 data rptd 5-14, 370A3
W Ger populatn drop seen 6-26, 489D2
Carter OKs pol '80 Census hiring 8-9, 631E1
China plans zero growth 8-13, 652C1
India data rptd 8-13, 687E3
US '78 populatn rptd 9-16, 746C3
USSR birth rate rise urged; populatn, male-female ratio rptd 10-10, 857D1
Urban fscl policy chngs predicted 10-24, 920A2
Calif OKs spending link 11-6, 846E3
E Timor populatn down 9.2% 12-15, 994F3

POPULATION Crisis Committee
World abortn figures rptd 4-29, 547A3
PORK—*See MEAT*

PORNOGRAPHY & Obscenity
Lawyers' interstate rights limited by Sup Ct 1-15, 31C3
Flynt convctd in retrial 3-28, 240C1
'Open-ended' warrants use curbed by Sup Ct 6-11, 478A3
Norfolk (Va) law challenge dismissed by Sup Ct 6-25, 540A2
Neb case jury challenge refused by Sup Ct 10-1, 768F1
Thevis, 2 others convicted 10-21, 818G1
Spain rally denounces 11-18, 952B2

PORTASH, Joseph
Grant of immunity broadened by Sup Ct 3-20, 204A1

1980

POLYTARIDES, Antonio
Letelier murder trial testimony ruled inadmissible 9-15, 703F3
POMERANCE, Rafe
On scenic area air rules 11-25, 898B2
Denounces Watt apptmt 12-22, 979G3
POMPIDOU, Georges Jean Raymond (1911-74)
Fontanet shot 2-1, dies 2-2, 97D2
PONCET, Antoine
Sculpture smashed again in NYC 3-24, 472D3
PONIATOWSKI, Michel
Impeachmt sought 4-14, 312E2
PONOMAREV, Boris Nikolaevich
Europn CPs meet 4-28—4-29, 327B3
PONTI, Carlo
Art collectn claim rptd denied 2-9, 200B2
PONTO, Jurgen (d. 1977)
Murder suspect arrested 5-5, 411B3
PONTOIL
Supertanker bound for Genoa sinks 1-17; S Africa oil sale suspected, Kuwait warns 2-7, 108B3
POOLE, Mick
Arrows win MISL title 3-23, 771A2
POOLEY, Don
2d in Atlanta Classic 6-8, 715B1
Wins BC Open 8-31, 972G1
POPE, Dr. Kenneth S.
'79 women survey rptd 1-9, 78C1
POPESCU, Aurel
Defects to Austria 7-3, 548D3
POPEYE (film)
Released 12-12, 972F3
POPOV, Leonid
Soyuz 35 launched 4-9, 365G1
Salyut 6 docks with Soyuz 36 5-27, 397C3
Remains on Salyut 6 6-9, 477D1
Soyuz 37 team boards Salyut 6 7-24, 547G3
Cuba-Sovt team in Soyuz trip 9-18—9-26, 737E2
Ends record flight 10-11, 777B3
POPOV, Leonid M.
Filatov rptd alive 9-23—9-24, 753F3
POPOV, Vladimir I.
French athletes deliver rights appeal 8-2, 590F2
POPULATION
US populatn up in '79 1-2, 54G3
State of State messages 1-14, 268G3; 1-15, 484B1, A2
USSR '79 total rptd 1-25, 79E3; 2-9, 152E3
US Hispanic immigrants surveyed 5-11—5-20, 396A2
Cambodia '70-79 data rptd 5-24, 397D2
US median age at 30 yrs 6-21, 519E1
Venice summit urges 3d World growth curbs 6-23, 474A1
Canada, US data compared 7-16, 562A3
Global forecast gloomy 7-23, 573F1, A2
US census revisn ordrd for Detroit, other cities claim undercount 9-25, 741C2
US Sup Ct extends NJ census data stay 12-15, 857C3
US census revisn ordrd for NY 12-23, Detroit rule stayed 12-24; Sup Ct bars stays 12-30; '80 figures released, table 12-31, 982D3, 983C1

PORK—*See MEAT (& Meat Products)*

PORNOGRAPHY & Obscenity
FBI 'Miporn' probe rptd 2-14, 136C1
Tex film restraints voided by Sup Ct 3-18, 226E3
Abortn funding cases argued in Sup Ct 4-21, 306B3
Thevis firearm convictn case refused by Sup Ct 4-21, 344B2
DC Christian rally held 4-29, 348E3
Donated porno warrants required by Sup Ct 6-20, 555G2
Evangelical Christian pol actn profiled 7-11—9-15, 818E3
US Families Conf urges legal action 7-12, 601C2, F2
'Caligula' ruled not obscene in Boston 8-1, 640B1
Conn phone harrassmt law challenge declined by Sup Ct 12-1, 918G2
Flynt Cleveland convictn case accepted by Sup Ct 12-8, 937A2

PORPOISES—*See WHALES & Porpoises*
PORSCHE AG
Schutz named pres, chief exec 12-3, 959D3
PORT Authority of New York and New Jersey
USSR to end Kennedy Aeroflot flights 2-4, 114F3
O'Hara confrmd Panama Canal comr 4-2, 308E3
PATH strike ends 9-1, 704D2

1976

PORT Barre, La.—*See LOUISIANA*
PORT Charlotte, Fla.—*See FLORIDA*
PORTER, Dwight
Replaced as amb to IAEA 2-6, 110C2
PORTER, Sylvia
Money Book on best-seller list 12-5, 972D2
PORTER, William J.
In talks on Leb crisis 6-22, 448B2
PORTLAND, Me.—*See MAINE*
PORTLAND, Ore.—*See OREGON*
PORTLAND (Me.) Express (newspaper)
Ford endorsement rptd 10-30, 827G3
PORTLAND Oregonian (newspaper)
Ford endorsement rptd 10-30, 831F2
PORTLAND Oregon Journal (newspaper)
Carter endorsement rptd 10-30, 831B3
PORTOS, Ampy
Named interior min 8-20, 926B1
PORTRAIT of the Assassin (book)
Cited in Ford biog sketch 613F3
PORTS—*See HARBORS & Ports*

PORTUGAL—*See also NATO, OECD*
Sensi named cardinal 4-27, 336B2
African Relations—*See also ANGOLA—Portuguese Relations, MOZAMBIQUE*
Guinea-Bissau freezes bank assets, Lisbon suspends paymts 3-1, 543F2
Malawi expels Goans 5-16, 382C2
Azores—*See under 'A'*
Economy & Labor (domestic)
'76 deficit budget released 1-1, 11D2
Unions vs price hikes 1-6, 11F2
Govt sells gold 1-6, 11G2
Price-wage curbs set 1-8, 75G3
Land reform curbed 1-9, 75D3
Farmers score land seizure, Lopes Cardoso 1-11, 75F3
Elec power curbs take effect 1-12, 76A1
CDS denounces govt, parties 1-13, 53B1
Agri protests continue 1-30—2-1; Rev Cncl backs reform law, Lopes offers compromise 2-10, 143E1
Govt defends agri reform law 1-31; farmers protest 2-1, 143F1 ★
Labor unrest 2-11—3-16, 367D2
Const OKd 4-2, enacted 4-25, 367C1
Eanes platform rptd 6-4, 483A2
Eanes, Soares set goals 7-14, 7-23, 558B1
Inflatn, jobless data rptd 7-24, 558B1
CDS to woo Cath workers 7-24, 558A3
Govt program proposed 8-2, Assemb OKs 8-11; CP scores 8-5, 774B2
Austerity, mil cncl membership rules linked 8-13, 733C2
Austerity plan set, labor reforms vowed 9-9; CP denounces 9-10, 774B1
Govt begins land return to farmers; reaction, 9-21—9-27, 811D2-B3
Labor reforms set, CP control curbed 10-1, 774F1
Bakery workers strike 10-15, 811D3
AF fires 15 workers 10-23, 811E3
'77 budget, econ plan OKd 12-29, 1013B2

Foreign Relations (misc.)
W Ger killed 1-1, 11A1
Rev Cncl to curb foreigners 1-7, 11G1
Melo Antunes in Hungary, Czech 1-12—1-16, Brussels 1-28, 143B1
Campinos in Yugo trade talks 1-13, 143B1
IMF oil loans rptd 1-13, 4-1, 340A1
Europn socialists meet 1-18—1-19, 48A3-C3
Southn socialists meet, Soares absent 1-24—1-25, 120B1, E1
W Ger forgn min begins visit, vows loan 2-4; EEC pledge cited 2-5, 142G3, 143A1
Swiss, Norway pledge loans 2-5, 142G3
Spinola in Switz 2-7; probe rptd 4-7, expelled 4-8, 315B1
Melo Antunes sees Spain min 2-12, 143C1
MFA papers used in Spain mil trial 3-8—3-9, 314F2
Tito on tour re nonaligned conf 3-9—3-24, 256C2
Europn socialists meet, pledge aid 3-13—3-14; CP, PPD denounce 3-15, 222D3
Const vs imperialism 4-2, 367D1

1977

Concorde noise alternatives offered 10-8, protests staged 10-9, 10-17, 819E3
Concorde NYC operatns begin, noise data cited 10-19, 10-20, 819C3
Aircraft noise rule set 12-14, Byrne vetoes 12-27, 1006F3
Sagner buys Nation 12-22, 1004F3
PORTELA, Petronio
Reform timetable upsets MDB 12-13, 964C1
PORTER, Gareth
Urges Viet, Laos food aid 12-16, 989C1
PORTER, Dr. Jane
Drug death study rptd 2-28, 224F2
Smoking linked to early menopause 6-25, 620D1
PORTER, Keith Roberts
Gets Medal of Sci 11-22, 952B1
PORTER, William J.
Replaced as amb to Saudi 6-7, 500D1
PORTLAND, Ore.—*See OREGON*
PORTSMOUTH, O.—*See OHIO*

PORTUGAL—*See also NATO, OECD*
TAP Madeira crash 11-19, 928G2
Bombs explode in Oporto 11-19, 5 other towns 11-25, near Lisbon CP hq 12-1, 947B3
Azores—*See AZORES*
Economy & Labor (domestic)
Jobless rate 14% 1-30, 330E3
Dec '75-76 inflatn rate rptd 2-7, 87C2
15% wage hike limit set 2-12, 330D2
Unions oppose govt on dismissal law 2-17, 330F3
Soares sets austerity progrm 2-25; workers, housewives protest 3-3, 3-24, 330B2
Technocrats join Cabt 3-25, 330E2
'76 GDP grew 5% 3-28, 331A1
Pvt indl investmt down 4-1, 330E3
Govt lags in returning expropriated cos 4-12, 330F3
Eanes warns Soares re crisis 4-25, 330G2
Austerity progrm protests 6-22, 530A3
Land reform law passed 8-10, protested 8-29—9-8, OKd by Rev Cncl 9-17, 886D2-C3
New austerity steps set 8-25, scored 8-26; spending cuts decreed 10-26, 886C1
35% inflatn rate cited 8-25, 886E1
Austerity support asked 11-15, oppositn rejects 11-30; govt falls 12-8, 947E1-B3

Foreign Relations (misc.)—*See also 'Monetary, Trade & Aid' below*
UN Assemb member 4A1
Cuba role in Angola detailed 1-9, 19B1
Angola executes 2 for technician's death 1-15, 86B2 ★
In 14-natn sulphur-dioxide pact 1-19, 109B3
Socialist ldr at Israel Labor Party conv 2-22, 135F1
EC entry formally filed 3-28, 269B2
Mozambique ousters rptd 6-1, 467F2
Forgn min quits, Soares takes post 10-10, 886E3
Yugo pres visits 10-17—10-19, 844E2
CP ldr backs USSR, scores Eurocommunism 10-28, 886F3
France drops plan to bar immigrant families 10-30, 1013D1
Africa refugees arrive despite ban 11-6, 886G3-887B1

1978

PORT Chester, N.Y.—*See NEW York State*
PORTELL, Jose Maria
Assassinated, ETA takes credit 6-28, 537D2
PORTER, Bruce
Nayatt School opens 5-12, 887C2
PORTER, Cole (1893-1964)
Gay Divorce opens 3-9, 760C2
PORTER, George
Norrish dies 6-7, 540D3
PORTER, Kevin
Sets assist record 2-24, NBA ldr 4-9, 271A2, G2
PORTER, Marina Oswald
Testifies at JFK death hearings 9-13, 9-14, 749D2
PORTER, Stephen
Man & Superman revived 12-17, 1031D2
PORTER, William J.
On Korea lobbying intell rpts 3-15, 203F1
PORTERS, Brotherhood of Sleeping Car (AFL-CIO)
Merges with BRAC 2-28, 185B2
PORTES Gil, Emilio
Dies 12-10, 1032D3
PORTLAND, Me.—*See MAINE*
PORTLAND, Ore.—*See OREGON*
PORTLAND General Electric Co.
Trojan A-plant protested 8-6—8-7, 609B3
PORTLAND State University
Williams in NBA draft 6-9, 457F3
PORTRAIT of a Rabbi (painting)
Stolen from San Fran museum 12-25, 1028G3
PORTRAIT of Madame Leriaux (painting)
Stolen from W Ger museum 7-30, 1029B1
PORTS—*See HARBORS & Ports*
PORTSMOUTH, Me.—*See MAINE*
PORTUGAL—*See also COUNCIL of Europe, EFTA, GATT, NATO, OECD*
Economy & Labor (domestic)
Lisbon expenses rated 1-14, 28B3
Austerity pact signed by CDS, Soclsts 1-19, 91F3
CP '77 labor restraint rptd 1-21, 92E1
Austerity plan OKd by Assemb 2-12, '78 budget submitted 3-15, 229C1
Civil servants, teachers strike 3-10, 229G1
Law on seized small firms OKd 3-11, 229A2
Real wages down 18% in '77 3-23, 229F1
1st ¼ inflatn at 27%; '77 rate, '78 forecast compared 3-30, 331E2
Transport, elec rates hiked 4-4; food prices raised 4-7, 331D2
Pensn benefits, min wage raised 4-5, 331D2
Austerity budget OKd by Assemb 4-13, 331G1
GNP grew 6.9% in '77; govt to hold to 3% in '78 4-14, 331F2
Eanes asks austerity, pvt sector recovery role 4-25, 331G2
Eanes scores Soares govt 5-28, 594B1
Govt split on health plan, MDs strike rptd 6-16, 593E3
Govt falls, farm issue cited 7-24—7-27, 593E2, D3, 594B1
Premr-designate da Costa outlines policy 8-9, 632A3
Da Costa sets austerity program 9-7, Assemb rejects 9-14, 757E3
Communist-run collectives ordrd to return seized land 10-11, 799C1
Land restitutn suspended after clashes 10-16, Assemb defeats anti-govt res 10-19, 830E2
European Force Reduction Talks—*See under EUROPE*
Foreign Relations (misc.)—*See also 'Monetary, Trade, Aid & Investment' below*
Costa Gomes at Dutch neutron bomb protest 3-18—3-19, 255C1
Eur conservative group formed 4-24, 424C3
Italy abortn reform enacted 5-18, 378G1
Angola expels Martins 5-31, 594D1
Egypt recalls amb 6-19, 473A2
Cuba Eritrea role rptd opposed 6-21, 584B3
Mozambique OKs 80 natls return 7-2, 596A3
French pres visits 7-19—7-21, 667B2
Thomaz ends Brazil exile 7-23, 594E1
Angola refugees rptd leaving 8-10, 645E3
UN Assemb member 713D3

1979

PORTELLA, Eduardo
Brazil educ min designate 1-19, 95E1
PORTELLA, Petronio
Brazil justice min designate 1-19, 95E1
PORTER, Darrell
NL wins All-Star Game 7-17, 569B1
AL batting ldr 9-30, 955E3
PORTER, J. Robert
Slain 8-9, 727F3
PORTER, Kevin
Reaches 1000-assist mark 3-29, leads NBA 4-8, 290G2, B3
PORTLAND, Me.—*See MAINE*
PORTLAND, Ore.—*See OREGON*
PORTMAN, Richard
Wins Oscar 4-9, 336B2
PORTOCARRERO Lemus, Leoncio
Arrested in Panama coup plot 10-24, 836E3
PORTRAIT of the Artist as a Young Man (film)
Released 4-21, 528C3
PORTSMOUTH, N.H.—*See NEW Hampshire*
PORTSMOUTH, Va.—*See VIRGINIA*

PORTUGAL—*See also COUNCIL of Europe, GATT, NATO, OECD*
Alcohol consumptn rptd up 3-9, 218B3
Economy & Labor
Eanes asks new sacrifices 1-1, 22D3
Farm seizure compensatn set 1-11, 212C3
'78 inflatn rptd down 1-18; govt sets '79 wage ceiling, CP scores 2-1, 212E2
Agri Min budget hiked 60% 2-20, 212G3
'79 budget proposals protested in parlt 6-4, 427C2
RR workers strike 6-6, 427D2
Econ slump persists; GDP, inflatn forecasts revised 8-30, 710G1

European Force Reduction Talks—*See under EUROPE*
Foreign Relations (misc.)—*See also 'Monetary' and 'UN' below*
China ties set 2-8, 134C3
Mota Pinto at Brazil pres inaugural 3-15, 210E1
Hijacked Spanish plane refuels 8-4—8-5, 604A1
Mex conservatives score Soares visit 10-30, 874G3
Israel emb attack; envoy escapes, bodyguard killed; PLO denies role 11-13, 882B1
Spain, W Ger AD aid, ties rptd 12-2, 917B1
Spanish guerrillas seek refuge 12-17, 997C3

1980

PORTELLA Nunes, Petronio
Dies 1-6, 104E3*
PORTER, Cole
Happy New Year opens 4-27, 392A3
PORTER, Darrell
Leaves Royals for alcohol, drug treatmt 3-14; returns 4-26, 637E1
NL wins All-Star Game 7-8, 636B2
In World Series 10-14—10-21, 811F2, 812G2
PORTER, Douglas
SAT coaching study rptd 5-15, 559C3
PORTER, Rep. John E. (R, Ill.)
Elected to US House 1-22, 50D3
Reelected 11-4, 842E3
PORTER, Katherine Anne
Dies 9-18, 756G1
PORTER, Stephen
Major Barbara opens 2-26, 392D3
PORTLAND—*See OREGON*
PORTLAND International Airport
Mt St Helens eruptns force closing 5-25, 6-13, 503F3
PORTLAND Oregonian (newspaper)
Hilliard on pres TV debate panel 10-28, 813F1
PORTNOV, Aleksandr
Wins Olympic medal 7-23, 623E3
PORTOCARRERO Somoza, Hope
At husband's funeral 9-17, 721D1, A3
PORTRAIT of Juan de Pareja (painting)
Sale record cited 5-13, 472F1
PORTRAITS (book)
On best-seller list 3-9, 200B3; 4-6, 280B3; 5-4, 359C3; 12-7, 948F3
PORTS—*See HARBORS & Ports*

PORTUGAL—*See also COUNCIL of Europe, CSCE, GATT, MBFR, NATO, OECD*
N Sea oil platform capsizes 3-27, 256F1
Azores—*See AZORE Islands*
Economy & Labor
Austerity budget submitted, gold reserves revalued 4-2, 277F2-B3
Eanes vetoes new econ laws, blocks Sa Carneiro budget 4-11, 315A3
Eanes vetoes revised econ laws 5-21; Sa Carneiro denounces mil cncl, vows reforms 5-23, 410D1
Airline pilots strike 6-23, Eanes acts to end dispute 7-14, 580E1

Foreign Relations (misc.)—*See also 'Monetary', 'UN Policy' below*
USSR tie review set 1-15, 28B2
Iran asks neutrality on US hostages 4-12, 282F1
France asks EC expansn slowdown, entry delay seen 6-5, 435E3-436D1
Anti-Sovt steps re Afghan urged, Iran release of hostages backed 6-26, 475C1
4 Sovt diplomats expelled 8-20, 'unacceptable activities' cited 8-21, 689A3
Sovt aggressn, CP electn loss linked 10-5, 760E1
5 Cubans defect at Lisbon airport 10-18, 828E3

1976

EC aid set 4-6, 276E2
W Ger head cites CP 4-15, 503D1
Cuba emb blast 4-22, rightists claim credit 4-23, Cuba scores 4-24, 367B2
Cuba Oporto consulate bombed 4-22, 371F1
Soclsts score Chile 'fascism' 5-25, 449C3
W Ger cites mil aid 6-11, 449D2
Schmidt apology to France re Salazar rptd 7-5, 521A2
Soares sets forgn policy goals 7-19, 558E1
PIDE agents escape to Spain, France 733A2
Forgn exchng, other curbs proposed 8-2, set; W Eur aid sought 9-9, 774D1, D2
Cunhal scores Eur ties, EC entry plan 8-5, 774F2
Cuba emb bombing arrests rptd 8-9, 733D1
Argentina violence scored 8-26, 672E2
Cuba trade pact rptd 9-14, 811G3
Medeiros on EC entry bid 9-20, 812F2
Cncl of Europe admits 9-22, 733F2
Import curbs decreed 10-8, 811B3
Cuba chrgs CIA role in emb blast 10-15, 780A2
Canada immigratn rptd 11-3, 851E1
Eur loan rptd pending 11-23, 966B3
Soares addresses Soclst Intl 11-28, 935D3
Venez pres visits, oil pact signed 11-29—11-30, 930B1

Government & Politics—*See also other appropriate subheads in this section*
Cabinet appointments 1-2, 1-6, 11A2
Spinola interview 1-3, 11C2
Mil rule extensn proposed 1-13, parties denounce 1-18, 52D3-53B1
Legis electn campaign begins 1-16, 52G3
Defns costs to stay high 1-16, army manpower cut 1-23, 143B3
Listed as 'partly free' 1-19, 20D3
Cunhal scores electoral chng 1-24, 76C1
Mil, pol ldrs sign pact 2-26, 367E1
Const OKd 4-2, enacted 4-25, 366C3, 367B1
Soclsts win Assemb vote, vow minority govt 4-25; bar alliances 4-30, 366F2
Soares vs pres bid 5-2, backs Ramalho 5-12, 366E3
4 set pres bids 5-12—5-18, 366D3-367B1
Carvalho sets pres bid 5-27, scores Pinheiro 5-29, Eanes 6-21, 483C1, C2
Ramalho platform rptd 6-4, 483A2
Pinheiro stricken 6-23; interim premr named 6-24, 482D3
Eanes elected 6-27, to name Soares premr 6-28, 483A1
Soares rejcts coalitn 7-2; pol parties, church ldrs pledge support 7-7—7-23, 558B2
Eanes sworn pres 7-14, mil chief 7-15; installs Soares, minority Cabt 7-23, 558A1
Eanes installs army chief, warns vs mil politics 7-19, 558F2
Spinola returns, 8-10; rise of right, Spinola tie to Eanes cited 8-10—8-12, 732D3
Mil cncl sets membership rules 8-12, 733B2
PPD name chng held pol move 10-4, 812D1
Soares to 'respect' Dec vote 10-5, 812E1
Anti-PIDE law voided 10-11, 858E2
Socialists win elections 12-12, 966C2
Listed as free 12-22, 977C3

Macao—*See under 'M'*
Madeira Island—*See under 'M'*
Portuguese Timor—*See TIMOR*
Press & Censorship
Republica ordrd returned to owners 1-28, 143C2
Le Monde Diplomatique launched 2-8, 143E2
Sao Tome e Principe—*See under 'S'*

Sports
Olympic results 7-18—7-31, 573E3, 575A2, 576A1
Timor—*See TIMOR*
Unrest—*See also 'Economy & Labor' above*
Oporto, other violence 1-1—1-2, 1-7; CP denounces 1-3, 10F3
Anti-leftist bombings in north 1-13—1-19, 53A2
Carvalho seized in '75 plot 1-19; CP linked 1-20, denies chrgs 1-21, 53B1
2 Salazar aides, others freed 1-21, 1-23, 53F1
Lisbon riot kills 1 1-21, 76A1
2 bomb blasts, Cunhal urges govt curbs 1-23, 76B1
Pre-electn violence 2-22—5-1, 367A2
Carvalho freed 3-3, 383G2
Sanches Osorio returns 3-3, 383A3
Cuba emb blast 4-22, rightists claim credit 4-23, Cuba scores 4-24, 367B2

1977

Government & Politics—*See also other appropriate subheads in this section*
Rosa quits re son's arrest 1-3, 21F2
PIDE officer sentncd 1-5; reactn 1-6, 21C2
Cabt shifts set 3-25, 330E2
Forgn min quits; Soares takes post 10-10, 886E3
Ex-secret police chrgd in '65 Delgado murder 10-19, 887C1
CP ldr chrgs govt repressn 10-28, 886F3
PSD ldr quits 11-7, 886C3
Lisbon CP hq area bomb blast 12-1, 947C3
Socialist govt falls 12-8, 947E1-B3

Helsinki Agreement—*See EUROPE—Security and Cooperation*
Monetary, Trade & Aid Issues (including all foreign economic developments)
UK 200-mi fishing zone in effect 1-1, 21A1
Ford budgets loan plan 1-17, 31G1
US grants $300 mln loan 2-14, 330B3
Escudo devalued, import curbs set 2-25, 330B2
US urges Westn aid 4-1; Soares in US talks 4-20—4-22, 330B3
Paymts deficit up; currency, gold reserves depleted 4-2, 4-25, 330E3
'76, Jan-Feb trade deficit soars 4-20, 330D3
Tourism up 4-20, 331A1
Eanes vs IMF loan reliance 4-25, 330A3
US OKs mil aid 4-30, 339G1
US in loan talks 5-16, 398B2
New forgn investmt code OKd 6-20, 530C3
US, 10 other natns OK $750 mln loan 6-22, 530B3
New austerity steps set 8-25; oppositn scores, cites IMF terms 8-26; govt vs IMF terms 11-15, 886C1
Escudo downward float set 8-25—9-12, 886D1, A2
Jan-June paymts deficit rise cited 8-25, 886E1
Angola sets mine share natlztn 9-1, 779C1
EC natns uneasy re entry 10-6, 867A2
Soares defends IMF talks 12-6, govt falls 12-8, 947E2, A3
Sports
US Cosmos open intl soccer tour 9-4, 827F2

1978

Government & Politics—*See also other appropriate subheads in this section*
Cunhal scores Soclst-CDS pact 1-20, 92D1
Soares forms new govt 1-26, Cabt sworn 1-30, 91A3
Eanes scores govt re soc problems 5-28, 594B1
Martins seized on return from exile 5-31, 594D1
Govt split on health plan, MD strike rptd 6-16, 593E3
Anti-fascist bill passed 6-16, CDS asks veto 6-19, 593E3
Leftist extremists arrested 6-22, 594E1
Soc Dems recall ex-pres, OK rightist program 7-3, 593G3
Thomaz returns from exile 7-23, 594E1
CDS leaves Cabt 7-24, 593E2
Govt falls, Soares fired, CDS-Soclst dispute cited 7-27; Eanes seeks new govt 7-28, warns politicians 8-1, 593E2-594C1
Coalitn bid fails 8-6; da Costa named premr-designate; Soares, leftists score 8-9, 632F2
Da Costa, Cabt sworn 8-28, 8-29, 671F3
Da Costa govt falls after progrm rejectn 9-4; Eanes warns new electns 9-22, meets pol ldrs 9-26, 757D3-758C1
New electoral law passed 10-2, 777B3
Delgado murder trial opens 10-9, 799D1
Mota Pinto named premr 10-25, 830B2
Mota Pinto names Cabt 11-18, parlt OKs program 12-13, 1022B1
Helsinki Agreement—*See EUROPE—Security and Cooperation*
Macao—*See MACAO*
Monetary, Trade, Aid & Investment
Austerity pact OKd 1-19; IMF, EC talks renewal vowed 1-30, 91G3
Govt austerity plan OKd by Assemb 2-12, '78 budget submitted 3-15, 229C1
US signs $300 mln loan pact 3-2, 229G1
IMF talks resume 3-29; paymts deficit, escudo actn OKd 4-3, 331B2
'77 forgn debt rptd $4.3 bln 3-30, 331F2
'78 austerity budget OKd by Assemb 4-13, 331B2
'77 trade deficit hit $2.73 bln 4-14, 331F2
Angola cooperatn OKd 6-26, 562A2
IMF pact backed by new govt 9-7, govt falls 9-14, 758A1
US releases $100-mln of loan 10-4, 777D3
Greek EC entry terms set 12-21, 1017G3

1979

Government & Politics—*See also other appropriate subheads in this section*
Parlt censures govt 6-4; Mota Pinto resigns, govt falls 6-7, 427B2, 545F2
Parlt dissolved, electns asked 7-13; Pintassilgo named caretaker premr 7-19, 545F2
Pintassilgo names Cabt 7-30, sworn 8-1, 603C3
Rightists win assemb electns, Sa Carneiro to form govt 12-2, 916F3-917F1, 953A2
Rightists wins municipal electns 12-16, 968F2

Helsinki Agreement—*See EUROPE—Security and Cooperation*
Monetary, Trade, Aid & Investment
EC entry sacrifices cited by Eanes 1-1, 22D3
Farm seizure compensatn set 1-11, 212E3
'78 trade, current acct deficits rptd down 1-30, 212G2, A3
IMF talks resume, no pact reached 2-7—3-6, 212B3
Agri min in UK, aid sought; '78 credits cited 2-20, 212E3
Renault expansn progrm rptd 5-24, 409A3
Intl banks lend $300 mln; '78 debt drop, export, reserve rise cited 5-25, 409E2-A3
'79 current accts deficit rise seen 8-30, 710B2

UN Policy & Developments
Cncl mtg on China, Viet asked 2-22, 142B1
WHO rpts alcohol consumptn up 3-9, 218B3
Israel setlmt policy opposed in comm rpt 7-14, 551B2
Membership listed 695B3

1980

Government & Politics—*See also other appropriate subheads in this section*
Mil council end rptd set 1-2, 22A1
Sa Carneiro Cabt sworn, mil excluded 1-3, 21C3
Sa Carneiro, Eanes clash; mil cncl role disputed 3-4—4-1, 277A2, B3
AD names Soares pres candidate 4-11, leftists protest 4-19, 315B3
Sa Carneiro denounces mil cncl, vows const reforms 5-23, 410F1
AD wins Assembly vote, gains 8 seats 10-5; Sa Carneiro sees Eanes defeat 10-6, 760B1
Eanes scores left 10-14; Soares quits Soclst post 10-19, 809C2
Sa Carneiro, Eanes exchng chrgs 11-21; pres campaign opens, AD supporters storm Eanes hq 11-22, 902F3
Sa Carneiro, defns min die in Lisbon plane crash 12-4, 923D1
Eanes reelected pres 12-7, AD govt resigns 12-8, 944A2
Pinto Balsemao named party ldr 12-13, premier 12-22, 995G3

Monetary, Trade, Aid & Investment
$350 mln in loans sought, gold reserves revalued 4-2, 277G2-B3
Iran trade banned, oil imports cited 4-17, 281F2
Obituaries
Abecassis, Snu 12-4, 923E1
Amaro da Costa, Adelino 12-4, 923D1
Caetano, Marcello 10-26, 876A1
Gouveia, Antonio Patrico 12-4, 923D1
Sa Carneiro, Francisco Manuel Lumbrales de 12-4, 923D1

UN Policy & Developments
Palestinian state res abstentn 4-30, 325D1
Cncl seat replacemt set 11-13, 896E1

1976

Campaign violence 6-5, 6-17, 483B1
Carvalho backers form front 7-5; '75 coup chrgs revived 7-13, 558G2
Natl Assemb vs PIDE releases 7-30; trials set 7-31, 733E1
Mil comm rpts pol torture, arrests since '74 coup 8-1, 733A2
Rightist bombing suspects rptd seized 8-9, 8-12, 733C1
Bombs explode in Oporto 9-3, 733D1
Carvalho scores govt 10-3, seized 10-23; leftists protest 10-25, 811G3
Cuba chrgs CIA role in emb blast 10-15, 780A2
Capts queried re mtg, Lourenco chrgs rightist agitatn 10-22, 812C2
Carvalho freed 11-12, 966E2

U.S. Relations
Protests US on Cuba Azores stop 1-23, 106C2
Northrop rpts payoffs 2-20, 362C3
Carvalho scores US 5-29, 483E1
Rumsfeld backs NATO aid 6-11, 449C2
US Dem platform text cites 6-15, 478D1
Ship in US Bicentennial event 7-4, 488A3, C3
Soares seeks closer ties 7-19, 558E1
Cunhal scores US dependency 8-5, 774F2
US aid pacts signed 8-13; US OKs tariff concessns 8-31, 811E3
US GOP platform text cites 8-18, 609F1
Azores AF base talks planned 9-5, 812A2
Soares seeks more US aid 9-9, 774D1
US pres campaign debate issue 10-6, 740G3, 741C1
Ford scored re debate claim 10-8, 812E2
CIA chrgd re Cuba emb blast 10-15, 780A2
Dole, Mondale debate 10-15, 783G3
Azores ldrs US trip blocked 812B2
New US loan set 11-16, another rptd pending 11-23, 966G2

PORTUGUESE Guinea—*See GUINEA-Bissau*
PORTUGUESE Timor—*See TIMOR*
PORTUONDO, Jose Antonio
Vatican accepts amb credentls 3-25, 252B1
POSADA, Estanislao
Asks Lopez reelectn move 1-4; Lopez rejcts 1-7, 31B1
POSADA, Luis
Arrested, terrorist plans confiscated 10-6, 780E2
Arrest confrmd 10-14, CIA ties rptd 10-20, 779D3, 880E1
FBI contact confrmd 10-25, 844A2
Venez indicts 11-2, 843F2, D3, 844B1
POSNER, Michael
Vs govt spending cuts 7-28, 572F3
POSTON, Ersa
Accuses Waldheim on UN jobs 10-11, 760A2
POTASH
US producers indicted 6-29, 748A1
Canada natlzn cited 8-12; US suit scored 9-21, 750B2 ★
US, Canada price fixers named 8-30, 673E2
Canada prices rptd 9-1, 750D2
POTASH Co. of America—*See IDEAL Basic Industries*
POTATOES—*See FRUITS & Vegetables*
POTLATCH Corp.
Trust suit dvpts 2-18—10-5, 886D1, E2; Kepford plea cited 11-30, 921D3
POTOK, Chaim
In The Beginning on best seller list 1-25, 80B3; 2-29, 208E3; 12-5, 972G2
POTTECK, Uwe
Wins Olympic medal 7-18, 575A2
POTTER, David S.
Replaced as Navy undersecy 9-8, 808C1
POTTINGER, J. Stanley
Brief on busing review filed 5-14, 377C3
On FBI burglaries probe 6-30, 569E2
POULOS, Leah
Wins Olympic medal 2-7, 159A1
POULTRY —*See LIVESTOCK*
POVEDA Burbano, Vice Adm. Alfredo
Heads Ecuador junta 1-11, 28E1
Drug trade linked 1-12, Dutch rptr ousted 1-13, 28G2
New cabt sworn 1-14, 48F3
POVERTY—*See also SOCIAL Services; country names*
US health rpt issued 1-12, 32E1
'77 budget proposals 1-21, 62B3, 63C2, 65B1, 66A2
Revenue sharing study made public 3-2, 187C1
Cong clears ACTION funds 5-13, 393D1; signed 5-27, 982F1
Free trial transcripts curbed 6-10, 552G2
Cong extends depressed area aid 9-29, 765E1; signed 10-12, 982G1
World Bank on world poor, stresses aid 10-4; chart 777B2, 778A1
Developing Nations—*See under 'D'*
Food Stamp Program—*See under FOOD*
Housing—*See under 'H'*
Medicaid—*See under MEDICINE*
Presidential Election
Humphrey scores anti-DC talk 3-24, 233E1
Black Dems draft plank 5-1, 343D3
Carter stresses commitmt 6-14, 433C1, D1
Dem platform text 6-15, 469F2, D3, 471E2, 472E3, 474C2, 476E3, G3
Mondale actn on legal aid cited 512A3
Carter seeks understanding 8-22, 631A3
Carter on LBJ 9-24, 724A3
Carter attacks Ford 10-4, 743D1
Ford, Carter debate 10-22, 801C3
Welfare—*See under 'W'*

1977

U.S. Relations—*See also 'Monetary, Trade & Aid' above*
Mondale expresses support for Soares 1-27, 69F2
Soares in US 4-20—4-22, 330B3
Mondale sees Eanes, Soares 5-16, 398A1, A2
US arms aid authorized 8-4, 668C1
US Cosmos open intl soccer tour 9-4, 827F2

POSADA Carriles, Luis
Tried in mil ct re '76 bombing 10-10, 868C1
POST, Rev. Avery Denison
Elected Church of Christ pres 7-4, 642F2
POST, Sandra
2d in LPGA Championship 6-12, 951C1
LPGA top money winner 11-27, 951F1
POSTAL Service, U.S.—*See under U.S. GOVERNMENT*
POSTAL Workers Union, American (AFL-CIO)
Andrews joins AFL-CIO exec cncl member 12-12, 951G1
POTASH
Canada prov defends policy 1-6, 18B1
Price-fixing chrgs dismissed vs Potash Co 2-25, 5 others 6-10, 483C3
Canada prov vote backs policy 6-8, 466F3
POTASH Co. of America—*See IDEAL Basic Industries*
POTATOES—*See FRUITS & Vegetables*
POTOMAC Associates (Wash., D.C. research group)
Cuba ties polled 8-8, 654F1
POTTER, John
Chrgs ZANU in cleric killings 2-7, 85C1
POTTINGER, J. Stanley
Replaced as asst atty gen 3-4, 211E1
POULSON, John
Cordle quits Parlt 7-22, 581D1
POULTRY & Poultry Products
Sup Ct upholds drivers bargaining right 1-11, 58A1
Price rise, soybean trading linked 4-18, 301B2
Arthur Perdue dies 6-27, 532E3
Nitrate data ordrd by FDA 8-31, 820C1
POVEDA Burbano, Vice Adm. Alfredo (Ecuador president)
At Panama Canal pact signing 9-7, 678C1
POVERTY—*See WELFARE and Poverty*

1978

U.S. Relations
US troop presence rptd 1-2, 5C2
US alerts to USSR satellite fall 57E1
$300 mln loan pact signed 3-2, 229G1
Pan Am to end Lisbon svc 9-7, 701G1
US releases $100-mln of loan 10-4, 777D3

PORTUGAL, Apolinario Vaz
Stays Portugal agri min 11-18, 1022B1
POST, Sandra
Wins Winners Circle title 4-2, 355F3
Lopez wins LPGA Champnshp 6-11, 580A3
Wins Lady Stroh's Open 8-24, 672F3
LPGA top money winner 11-20, 990C3
POST, Ted
Go Tell Spartans released 9-23, 970E1
POSTAL Rate Commission—*See under U.S. GOVERNMENT*
POSTAL Service, U.S.—*See under U.S. GOVERNMENT*
POSTAL Workers Union, American (AFL-CIO)
New contract negotiated 7-21, 564F2
Contract revised 9-15, OKd 10-11, 765G3
POTASH
Canada prov purchases rptd 3-27, prorationing policy rules illegal 10-3, 773D1-A2
Canada prov tax upheld by ct 11-17, 922D1
POTATOES—*See FRUITS & Vegetables*
POTLACH Corp.
'76 trust suits setld 10-2, 768D3
POTTS, Annie
Corvette Summer released 8-4, 970A1
POTVIN, Denis
Wales Conf wins NHL All-Star game 1-24, 76D3
In NHL top paid player list 4-6, 296G3
POUGH, Ernie
Traded to Giants 4-17, 336G1
POULLAIN, Ludwig
Fired, Halstenberg resigns 1-17, 55D1
Dismissal upheld 6-1, 456F3
POULTER, Thomas C.
Dies 6-14, 540E3
POULTRY
PCB contaminated chickens destroyed 4-12, 727D3
Natl Mktg Assn trust immunity denied by Sup Ct 6-12, 468A1
Nitrite additives linked to cancer 8-11, FDA proposes phase-out 8-31, 727G3
US-Japan trade talks fail 9-5—9-7, 695A1
POUND, Ezra Loomis (1885-1972)
Zukofsky dies 5-12, 440G3
POUSSIN, Nicolas (1594-1665)
Painting slashed 4-3, 335D1
POVEDA Burbano, Vice Adm. Alfredo (Ecuadorean military junta chief)
Hails vote on new const 1-15, 111D3
Seeks Peru border strife setlmt 1-18, 216B2
POVERTY—*See WELFARE and Poverty*

1979

PORTUGAL, Apolinario Vaz
In UK, agri aid sought 2-20, 212E3
PORTUGUESE Macao—*See MACAO*
POSEIDON Adventure (film)
Sequel released 5-24, 528D1
POSEIDON Submarine-Launched Ballistic Missile—*See ARMAMENTS, subheads Missiles and Ships & Submarines*
POSNER, Victor
Sharon Steel buys UV Industries assets 11-26, 986F2
POSPELOV, Pyotr (Peter) N.
Death rptd 4-24, 356F3
POST, Sandra
2d in Arden Classic 2-18, Orange Blossom Classic 2-26, 2-18, 220E3, F3
Ties for 2d in Honda Civic Classic 3-18; wins Winners Circle 4-8, Lady Michelob tourn 5-13, 587A2, C2, F2
Wins KC Classic 9-20; 2d in Mary Kay Classic 9-30, Mizuno Classic 11-3, 970E1, F1, B2
LPGA top money winner 11-30, 969G2
POSTAL Service, U.S.—*See under U.S. GOVERNMENT*
POSTOL, Theodore
Cited in H-bomb letter 9-16, 9-18, 714F1, A3, 716F3-717G1
POTAMKINA, Victor
Richard III opens 6-14, 712B2
POTATOES—*See FRUITS & Vegetables*
POTOFSKY, Jacob S.
Dies 8-5, 671D3
POTOMAC, Md.—*See MARYLAND*
POTTER, Charles Edward
Dies 11-23, 932D3
POTTSTOWN (Pa.) Mercury, The (newspaper)
Kelly wins Pulitzer 4-16, 336B3
POTTSVILLE (Pa.) Republican, The (newspaper)
Gaul, Jaspin win Pulitzer 4-16, 336E2, A3
POTVIN, Denis
Named NHL top defenseman 6-12, 470C2
POULTRY
Carter proposes regulatory reform 3-25, 230A2
GATT pact signed 4-12, 273F2
Truckers' strike harm feared 6-18–6-28, 479A3
Antibiotics in feed rptd risky 6-25, 734G3
PCB limits cut 6-28, 571C2, E2
PCB feed grain contaminatn rptd 9-17, 704A3
POURIER, Miguel
Heads Dutch Antilles interim govt 7-6–11-13, 882E3
POVEDA Burbano, Vice Adm. Alfredo (Ecuadorean military junta chief)
Roldos wins pres bid 4-29, 329F3
POVERTY—*See WELFARE and Poverty*

1980

U.S. Relations
US backed re Afghan crisis 1-15, 28B2
Iran asks neutrality on US hostages 4-12, 282F1
Carter visits 6-26, 474C3, 475B1

PORTUGALOV, Nikolai
Backs detente, scores US 2-7, 106D3
PORUSH, Menahem
Vs kidney transplant for Arab girl 2-8, 107C2
POSADA, Luis
Acquitted in '76 Cuba jet bombing 9-26, 794A3
POST, Sandra
2d in Whirlpool Championship 2-3, Bent Tree Classic 2-24, 412D2, E2
Wins Wheeling Classic 8-3, 972E1
LPGA top money winner 10-12, 971F3
POSTAL Service, U.S.—*See under U.S. GOVERNMENT*
POSTELL, Charles
Indicted 8-27, 712F2-D3
Cleared 11-12, 927A1
POSTELL, Judi
Indicted 8-27, 712F2-D3
Cleared 11-12, 927A1
POSTLEWAIT, Kathy
2d in Sunstar Classic 3-9, 412G2
POSTREKHIN, Sergei
Wins Olympic medals 8-1, 8-2, 622B2, C2
POTATOES—*See FRUITS & Vegetables*
POTTERY
Maria Martinez dies 7-20, 608D2
POTTS, Jack Howard
Ga executn stay issued 6-28, Sup Ct extends stay 6-30, 511F1
POTVIN, Denis
Islanders win Stanley Cup 5-24, 487D3
POULOS-Mueller, Leah
Sets world speed skating mark 1-21, 470F1
POULTRY
Maine State of State message 1-2, 269C2
US to buy Sovt-bound chickens 1-21, 44C3
US purchase affects budget 1-28, 73C2
US dietary guidelines issued 2-4, 157B3
Chicken teeth rptd grown 3-8, 415D2
USSR tight feed supplies seen 4-9, 316A1
Iowa farm cancer study rptd 4-15, 357E3
Mar CPI rise rptd 4-22, 305C2
May farm prices rptd up 5-30, 425D1
South drought damage rptd 7-21, 616A2
July farm prices rptd 7-31, 575D1
July producer prices rptd 8-15, 630B3
POUND, Dick
Vs Canadian Olympic boycott 4-14, 283A3; 4-22, 325C3
POUYAN, Anowshiravan
Arrest rptd 7-17, 545A3
POVERTY—*See WELFARE & Poverty*

1976

POWELL, Enoch
Fears race war 5-24, 482F1

POWELL, Jody (Joseph Lester)
Carter scores critics 5-27, 390F2
Vs Ford debate move 8-24, 632G3-633A1
Debate negotiatns open 8-26, 632C3
Scores Ford park plan 8-29, 644D3
Carter regrets LBJ remark 9-22, 704D2
On Carter tax stand 10-14, 785D2
On transition study 11-11, 845F2
Carter names as press secy 11-15; facts on 864C1
Visits White House 11-16, 864D1
Rpts Lance transitn duties 11-26, 898E2
On steel price hike 11-29—12-2, 897D3
Carter sees econ aides 12-1, 898B2
On Carter B-1 stand 12-2, 942E1
On defns spending cuts 12-28, 978E1
On Mondale status 12-28, 978F2
Pres isolation a concern 12-30, 978C3

POWELL, John
Wins Olympic medal 7-25, 575G3

POWELL Jr., Justice Lewis F(ranklin)—*For Supreme Court developments not listed here, see SUPREME Court under U.S. GOVERNMENT*
Rules on campaign law 1-30, 87A2
Backs disability cutoff procedures 2-24, 169C2
Vs retroactive seniority 3-24, 218A2
Backs govt access to bank records 4-21, 331C1
Candidates' funds plea rejctd 4-23, 306D1
Backs drug convictn ruling 4-27, 349C2
Backs FPC job bias powers 5-19, 393B3
Backs RR fund ruling 6-17, 552F3
Backs some church-coll aid 6-21, 452F3
Vs local-zoning referendum 6-21, 453D1
Vs summary ruling on police bargaining 6-21, 553A1
Holds US wage laws not binding on states 6-24, 468D2
Vs patronage ouster bar 6-28, 468E3
Vs press gag order 6-30, 491F3
Backs death penalty 7-2, 491C2
For fed cts criminal appeals curb 7-6, 534D3
Vs sympathy strike ruling 7-6, 535G1
Vs utilities trust ruling 7-6, 569F1
Stays 3 executns 7-22, 568F2
Vs carry-back tax ruling 11-2, 867C2
Vs Austin busing plan 12-6, 920E2
Vs pregnancy benefits 12-7, 920E1

1977

POWELL, Dr. Cilian B.
Dies 9-22, 788C2

POWELL, Jody (Joseph Lester)
On conflict-of-interest code 1-4, 4D2
Press apptmt cited 1-14, 35D3
Carter backs Concorde trial 1-16, 131E2
Warnke appointmt backed 2-3, 2-4, 89C1
On concussion bomb sale 2-17, 121D1
On CIA forgn paymts rpt 2-18, 123C3
On Carter-Sakharov letter 2-18, 137E2
On alleged intell com watch 2-25, 150G3
On Carter-Post mtg 2-28, 151B3
On Carter Mideast terms 3-7, 3-8, 165E1, A2
Carter backs NY Concorde tests 3-9, 212E3
On Carter NYC aid pledge 3-11, 193B3
On Califano hirings 3-23, 236B1
Defends gay rights mtg 3-27, 278G2
Carter not to reprimand Brown 3-28, 232C1
Defends US arms proposals 3-31, 4-4, 246B3, 247D1
On Carter thrift 5-5, 359A3
On new warhead deploymt 6-1, 462B1
On US-Cuba 'interest sectns' 6-2, 455C3
Nixon, Ford not 'racists' 6-6, 443E3
On Korea probe prosecutor 6-9, 442G2
On Cong energy measures 6-10, 6-14, 460F1, C2
On Toth detentn 6-14, 475C1
On Carter tax return 6-24, 499C2
On Shadrin case 7-14, 564E2
On GOP cargo preference chrgs 8-1, 719D3
On Lance probe, Carter use of bank plane 8-18, 626C1, F1
Defends Carter, Lance overdrafts 8-23, 649D2
Says Carter to reimburse bank for plane use 8-24, 649F3
On July econ indicator drop 8-30, 669C1
On Ulster aid pledge 8-30, 729F3
On Lance charges 9-6, 690D1
Saw FBI rpt on Lance 9-12, 701D3
Apologizes to Percy 9-14, 701B3
Corrects Carter recollectn re Lance 9-22, 718G1
On Gromyko-Carter mtg 9-27, 750F3
On Carter-Obasanjo mtg 10-11, 797F1
On Meyer resignation 10-20, 814D2
On Carter, Shah A-plant mtg 11-16, 897G1
Schlesinger energy bill comments defended 11-23, 917B1
Curtis to resign Dem post 12-7, 960A3
Carter confers with blacks 12-14, 960D1

POWELL Jr., Justice Lewis F(ranklin)—*For Supreme Court developments not listed here, see U.S. GOVERNMENT—SUPREME Court*
Upholds restrictive suburban zoning 1-11, 15C1
Vs steelworkers electn ruling 1-12, 57F3
Jurek executn delayed 1-17, 40B3
Backs expanded govt taps 1-18, 58C2
Backs racial voter redistricting 3-1, 175D1
Vs retroactive porno prosecutns 3-1, 175A2
Backs Mich electn rules 3-21, 230C3
Sidesteps Miranda rule review 3-23, 276B1
Vs intra-group grand jury bias 3-23, 276E2
Backs schl spankings 4-19, 342F1
Backs illegitimate children's rights 4-26, 382B3
Vs govt employe agency shop rule 5-23, 444F1
Backs Medicaid abortn curbs 6-20, 516E2
Overturns 'Schwinn doctrine' 6-23, 539A2
Vs performers' media suits 6-28, 558A1
Vs Coker executn for rape 6-29, 557E2
Hears Bakke case arguments 10-12, 835B1
Upholds Nazi tape restraint 12-21, 1008A2

1978

POWELL, Enoch
On tax vote 5-9, 415A2

POWELL, Jody (Joseph Lester)
Rpts Jordan legal separatn 1-9, 96B1
On crude oil tax 3-8, 220G1
On Begin-Carter talks 3-23, 214B3
On Callaghan-Carter mtg 3-23, 226D3
Soc Sec tax cut opposed 4-5, 240E3
Rpts on Cabt, staff sessn 4-17, 306G2, D3
Scores Carter inflatn plan critics 5-8, 361C3
Silent on discount rate hike 5-11, 361D2
Rpts Carter Mideast jet sale lobbying 5-15, 357D1
Denies Mideast jet sale vendetta 5-16, 358D1
Defines Rafshoon staff job 5-18, 386C3
On Carter address to Ill legislature 5-26, 404E3
Rebuts Gromyko on Zaire 5-27, 422F1
Scores Sen oil import fees vote 6-27, 511D3
Young rebuked for remarks re US 'pol prisoners' 7-12, 7-15, 542D3, G3
Harris cancels cong testimony 8-7, 605A2
On US troops to Mideast 8-30, 9-7, 673G1, C2
Denies Vesco 'pol fix' 9-10, 720B1
On econ goals 11-28, 980F1
On Carter '80 budget mtgs 12-4, 936E3
Assures Iran on US support 12-7, 953F3
On Brezhnev note to Carter 12-21, 995A2

POWELL Jr., Justice Lewis F(ranklin)—*For Supreme Court developments not listed here, see U.S. GOVERNMENT—SUPREME Court*
Not in Miller 'lite' trademark rule 1-9, 13D1
Vs trust suits by forgn natns 1-11, 33D3
Vs prosecutors plea-bargaining rule 1-18, 65A1
Vs Wis remarriage law 1-18, 65C1
Backs Multistate Tax Compact 2-21, 126G1
Vs personal holding co tax rule 2-22, 126G2
Not in FPC rate review rule 2-27, 143C2
Vs Maritime Comm labor contract jurisdictn 3-1, 144B1
Rules on oil tanker regulatn 3-6, 162C1
Vs damages for suspended students 3-21, 220C3
Vs NH gov flag-lowering curb 3-24, 221E2
Vs judicial immunity in sterilizatn case 3-28, 241E3
Not in A-plant rulings case 4-3, 280B3
Vs Minn pensn funds law 4-3, 309A1
Vs Ark defendants rights rule 4-3, 309B1
Denies broadcasters Nixon tapes 4-18, 308G1
Vs clergy pub office ban 4-19, 309D1
Backs corp pol free speech 4-26, 343A3
Not in Va judicial inquiry case 5-1, 363E3
Backs utility customer hearings 5-1, 364B1
Backs Calif jurisdictn in child-support case 5-15, 387G3
Vs exclusn of children from porno rule 5-23, 405E3
Sets atty solicitatn rules 5-30, 430D2
Backs newsroom searches by police 5-31, 430F1
Not in natural gas diversn case 5-31, 431D1
Not in Alaska pipe rates case 6-6, 447D2
Vs alien deportatn trial 6-6, 447F2
Denies poultry group trust immunity 6-12, 468B1
Backs FBI informant case review 6-12, 468E1
Vs lengthening double jeopardy protectn 6-14, 468G3
Not in Md gas statn ban case 6-14, 492G1
Backs Tellico Dam vs rare fish 6-15, 468C2
Vs Iowa business tax formula 6-15, 468E2
Backs Freedom of Info in NLRB cases 6-15, 468G2
Backs class actn suit curbs 6-19, 492C2
Backs union pol organizing 6-22, 508D3

1979

POVEY, Terry
Iran expels 9-5, 708B3

POWELL, Anthony
Wins Oscar 4-9, 336A2

POWELL, Dick
Death tied to '53 A-test 8-4, 630D1

POWELL, Jack
Wild Oates opens 1-8, 292G3

POWELL, Jody (Joseph Lester)
On B Carter remarks 1-11, 31E2
Denies Vance-Brzezinski rift re China, USSR ties 1-16, 27F2
Says Carter unaware of Lance banking favors 1-18, 31A2
On Carter Viet dispute remark 2-20, 123F3
Begin scores press briefing on pact talks 3-13, 177C2
On Carter peanut probe 3-20, 203F1
Scores OPEC 9% hike 3-27, 227E3
3 Mile I NRC transcripts released 4-12, 275G2
On summer gas supplies 5-17, 361C2
Bars comments on Lance indictmt 5-23, 380D3
On House Dem res vs oil decontrol 5-24, 395B2
Ct bars wage-guide contract denial 5-31, 399A3
Carter sees oil execs 5-31, 418C1
Cited in SALT II summit communique 6-18, 457C1
Announces Carter energy address 7-2, cancels 7-4, 497B3, C3
Downplays Eizenstat memo 7-7, 513F3
On Jordan appointmt, Cabt, staff shake-up 7-18, 529C2
Cited re Califano firing 7-20, 556D1
Carter OKs pol '80 Census hiring 8-9, 631E1
With Carter on Miss R boat trip 8-17–8-24, 622E2, 623A1
Denies Studio 54 visit 8-24, 647A2
On Kennedy '80 plans 9-8, 680B1
On Jordan cocaine probe 9-20, 767B3
On Fla Dem caucuses 10-14, 783E1
On Curran probe findings 10-16, 782G3
Scores oil co 3d 1/4 profits 10-22, 804D2
Denies secret tapes 10-29, 869F1
On FBI probe of KKK slayings 11-6, 865D3
On Iran oil sales end, US allies' support 11-15, 879F2
Scores House hosp cost-control bill defeat 11-15, 883C1
Jordan cocaine probe spec prosecutor named 11-29, 900G3-901A1
On Carter Taiwan defns treaty ruling 11-30, 919G1
On Kennedy Iran remarks 12-3, 918E3
On Carter fund-raiser cancelatn 12-4, 918G2
On shah's departure to Panama 12-15, 957C1
Vs Kennedy energy remarks 12-21, 983C3

POWELL, Josephine (Mrs. Lewis Franklin)
Husband reports finances 6-15, 464C3

POWELL Jr., Justice Lewis Franklin—*For Supreme Court developments not listed here, see U.S. GOVERNMENT—SUPREME Court*
Backs Boston referendum spending case review 1-8, 14C3
Vs SEC role in pensn plans 1-16, 32B2
Not in Energy Comm rate relief case 1-16, 32F3
Backs corp name curbs 2-21, 128F2
Vs Blue Shield drug plan trust rule 2-27, 165A2
Backs single-sex alimony 3-5, 184F2
Surgery 3-15, tumor rptd benign 3-22, 231G2
Vs jobless pay for strikers 3-21, 231A2
Vs LA fire dept bias case finding 3-27, 263A2
Absent from Weber case argumt 3-28, 262E3
Backs racial 'steering' suits 4-17, 325D3
Backs NYS alien teacher ban 4-17, 325E3
Backs 'state of mind' libel queries 4-18, 302F1
Backs covert US entries for 'bugging' 4-18, 346F1
Backs unwed father adoptn consent role 4-24, 364C1
Not in verbal rights waiver case 4-24, 364A2
Not in mental hosp commitmt ruling 4-30, 364A3
Vs pvt Title IX suit 5-14, 382F3
Vs mutual fund dirs' power 5-14, 383D1
Vs pretrial body-cavity searches 5-14, 383B2
Not in fair-mkt property acquisitn case 5-14, 383B3
Vs fed ct welfare suits 5-14, 384A1
Financial disclosure delay cited 5-15, 382C2
Backs state age bias filing time limit 5-21, 400G2
Not in securities law case 5-21, 400D3
Vs state parole discretn 5-29, 421B3
Not in co-defendant confessns case 5-29, 422B1
Vs NY gun-in-car law 6-4, 438E3
Not in NJ ex-offcls rejailing case 6-4, 438G3
Vs sex-bias suits vs congressmen 6-5, 464D1
Not in 'probable cause' detentns case 6-5, 464F2
Backs schls right to bar disabled 6-11, 478B2
Not in ICC rail rate suspensn case 6-11, 478E3
Reports finances 6-15, 464C3
Not in Cong legal immunity case 6-18, 499A1

1980

POWELL, Enoch
Vs home rule 9-26, 750A3

POWELL, Jeffrey
Weatherman fugitive surrenders 7-8, 576E3

POWELL, Jody (Joseph Lester)
Scores Kennedy grain embargo stance 1-8, 12G3
Iran hostage letter cited 1-17, 47F3
Scores Kennedy Iran criticism; Kennedy rebuts 2-13, 109G2, C3
Denounces Kennedy statemt on shah 2-18, 130C2
Announces inflatn policy review 2-25, 144G2
'60 Minutes' Iran segmt pressure rptd 3-6, 239D1, E1
On Carter budget cut delay 3-17, 201F2
Denies Carter note to Khomeini 3-29, 241D2
Lauds USOC boycott vote 4-12, 283C2
Rpts Carter financial data, scores Kennedy 4-15, 305C1, E1
On Mobil price setlmt 4-24, 309F1
On Carter Muskie comment 5-9, 367E1
On Apr CPI 5-23, 400G2
Scores Australia Olympic com boycott rejectn 5-23, 421B1
Carter bars Anderson debate 5-27, 399A3
On Carter delegate status 5-28, 399D1
On Jordan, Watson shift 6-11, 438G3
Qualifies Carter hostage rescue statement 6-12, 506G3
On prosecuting Clark 6-16, 459G3
On '81 tax cut 6-30, 492E3
On B Carter controversy 7-22—7-31, 548G3, 569F1, D2, 570A1
On B Carter secret cable 8-1, 595F1
On Muskie A-strategy shift controversy 8-11, 615E2
On econ planks fight 8-12, 610A3
Calls NSC Africa memo forgery 9-17, 726F3-727B1
Warns Sovts vs Poland mil interventn 12-2, 910G2

POWELL Jr., Justice Lewis Franklin—*For Supreme Court developments not listed here, see U.S. GOVERNMENT--SUPREME Court*
Backs mil petitn limits 1-21, 93C1
Backs Dallas busing case review 1-21, 93E2
Vs Ohio boundary placemt 1-21, 93F2
Backs contd abortn aid order stay 2-19, 130B3
Backs total plaintiff class lawyer fees 2-19, 131B1
Vs pvt coll faculty unions 2-20, 146E1
Not in Calif dual seniority case 2-20, 146B3
Backs fed gun law prior convictn limit 2-27, 188A3
Vs Calif wine pricing law 3-3, 210F1
Backs Cleveland busing challenge review 3-17, 225G3
Vs 'insider' stock trading convictn 3-18, 226D2
Vs Tex habitual-offender law 3-18, 226C3
Backs Tex porno film restraints 3-18, 226F3
Backs state legislators' immunity 3-19, 250A1
Vs class actn 'moot' standard redefinitn 3-19, 250D1, E1
Backs inmate mental health hearings 3-25, 265F2
Backs govt political firings 3-31, 291D2
Backs 'good faith' municipal immunity 4-16, 328A3
Backs at-large local electns 4-22, 343D2
Vs Voting Rights Act provisn 4-22, 344D1
Backs Wilmington (Del) busing case review 4-28, 368F3
Backs La oil leasing royalties 4-28, 369D1
Gets 'Great Ldrs' award, refutes Sup Ct media image 5-1, 368F2
Vs EEOC class actn process avoidance 5-12, 426C2
Vs pre-ERISA insured pensn benefits 5-12, 426C3
Finances rptd 5-15, 555C3
Backs narrow Ga death law applicatn 5-19, 440A1
Vs land-grant exchng ban 5-19, 440B2
Vs fed unincorporated business trust suits 5-19, 440F2
Backs shopping cntr petitn access 6-9, 512E2
Backs defendants pre-arrest silence testimony 6-10, 512C1
Backs Calif zoning ordinances 6-10, 512F1
Vs GE microbe patent 6-16, 453D1
Vs state sales preference 6-19, 554G2

1976

POWER! (book)
On Bestseller list 12-5, 972D2
POZEGA, Irina
Sentenced as Sovt spy 5-25, 542C3
PRADO International, S. C.
Chrgd re Arab boycott 10-19, 786E1
PRAPHAS Charusathien
Returns to Thailand 8-15; protests 8-17—8-21, deported 8-22, 640C1 ★ -A2
Thanom return barred 8-31, 677C3
Rpt Laos trains rebels 9-3, 677E3
Sa-Ngad named defense min 10-4, 754E1
PRATESI, Pieto
Rptd on CP ticket 5-17, 5-30, 402D3
PRATT, Judge John H.
OKs Lockheed consent decree 4-13, 285A3
Declares mistrial in Mandel case 12-7, 922E2
PRATT, John Lee
Bequests rptd 1-9, 80C2
PRATT, Judge Philip
Nurses chrgd in '75 hosp deaths 6-16, 503E3
PRATT & Whitney Aircraft Divison—*See under UNITED Technologies Corp.*
PRECHT Banados, Rev. Cristian
Heads church aid unit 1-16, 47B3
Rpts prisoner torture continues 1-26, 100A2
PREGNANCY—*See BIRTHS*
PREJUDICE—*See MINORITIES*
PRENTICE, Reginald
Retains Cabt post 9-10, 694B2
Quits as overseas min 12-21, 1004F1
PRENTICE-Hall Inc.
US files consent decree 7-27, 989A2
PRESCRIPTION Drug Use, Joint Commission on
Formed 11-30, 931G2
PRESIDENT Kruger (S. African warship)
In Intl Naval Review 7-4, 488C3
PRESQUE Isle, Me.—*See MAINE*

1977

POWELL, Marvin
In NFL draft 5-3, 353A2
POWERINE Oil Co.
US trust suit setld 8-31, 691D3
POWERS, Francis Gary
Dies 8-1, 696E3
POWERS, John R.
Dies 7-19, 604F3
POWERS, Pamela (d. 1968)
Miranda rule review sidestepped 3-23, 275B3
POWERS, Richie
NBA referees strike 4-10—4-25, 332C1
POWs (prisoners of war)—*See under U.S. GOVERNMENT—ARMED Forces*
PRABHUPADA, Swami—*See BHAKIVENDANTA, A. C.*
PRAPHAS Charusathien
Returns to Thailand 1-8, 47C3
PRATT, Judge John H.
Orders integratn rules for 6 state colls 1-17, 112B2 ★
Reordrs integratn guidelines 4-1, 446C1
Coll integratn plan issued 7-5, 630A3
Orders US worker pay bias suit costs 8-23, 670A1
Bars US coal-leasing plan 9-27, 1007C2
PRATT, Judge Philip
Nurses convicted in '75 VA Hosp deaths 7-13, 568G2
Upsets convictns of VA nurses 12-19, 991G2
PRATT & Whitney Corp.
Southern Air Ga crash 4-4, 286C3
PREGNANCY—*See BIRTHS*
PRENTICE-Hall Inc.
At USSR book fair 9-6—9-14, 765E3
PRESBYTERIANS
Davidson tenure policy chngd 5-6, 471G3
Charismatic conf held 7-20—7-24, 620D3
Rev Payne dies 12-2, 1024G2
Presbyterian Church in the U.S. (Southern)
Revised doctrine rejctd 2-11, 309E3
United Presbyterian Church in the U.S.A. (Northern)
Southern merger set back 2-11, 309E3
PRESLEY, Elvis Aron
Dies 8-16, 695C3
Facts on 695C3
Records sold out 8-18, 696C1
2 mourners killed 8-18, 696G1
Book orders set record 8-20, 696D1
Papers sell out death editns 8-22—8-24, 696E1
Father named executor 8-22, 696A2
PRESLEY, Lisa Marie
Named son's executor 8-22, 696A2
PRESLEY, Minnie Mae
Named in son's will 8-22, 696A2
PRESLEY, Vernon
Named son's executor 8-22, 696A2

1978

Vs Ark prison attys' added fees 6-23, 566A2
Backs press prison data access 6-26, 566D3
Backs Bakke med schl admissn, race-based affirmative actn principle; opinion excerpt 6-28, 481B1-482F1, 483F1
Vs juvenile case reviews 6-28, 567A2
Vs NM water rights 7-3, 522C2
Voting alignmts shift noted 7-3, 565E3-566C1
Denies LA Bustop appeal 9-9, 699A1
Backs GA schl bd pol rule 11-28, 937F3
Backs stockbroker liability case review 12-4, 959E1
Backs broader police auto search power 12-5, 959G2
Not in Mass drunk rights waiver ruling 12-11, 980G3

POWELL Jr., Wesley
Loses primary for NH gov 9-12, 736F1
POWER, Phil
Loses Sen primary in Mich 8-8, 626A1
POWERS, Richie
Suspended in zone defns dispute 3-2, 271A3
POWs (prisoners of war)—*See under U.S. GOVERNMENT—ARMED Forces*
POYNTER, Nelson
Dies 6-15, 540F3
PRADO Salmon, Col. Gary
Bolivia planning min 11-24, 913E1
PRAI, Jacob
PNG holds rebels 2-27, 192D3
PRAMOON Chanchamnong, Gen.
Rpts Laos refugees forced back; UN, US distressed 2-16, 139D3, G3-140A1
PRANTL, Gen. Amaury
Fired from intellignc post, arrested 6-25, 6-28, 537G2
PRATT, Judge John H.
Bars postal strike 8-26, 766B1
PRATT & Whitney Aircraft Division—*See under UNITED Technologies Corp.*
PRAVDA (Soviet CP newspaper)
US reviews reporters status 6-30, 7-5, 518F2
PRAYER For My Daughter, A (play)
Opens 1-17, 760B3
PRECHT, Rev. Cristian
Lauds amnesty, asks actn on missing persons 4-25, 351B3
PREGNANCY—*See CHILDBIRTH*
PREMADASA, Ranasingle (Sri Lankan prime minister)
Named Sri Lanka prime min 2-6, 116C1
PRESA, Ernesto Eugenio
Confesses in murder case 10-21, 881F2
PRESBYTERIAN Church in the U.S.—*See under PRESBYTERIANS*
PRESBYTERIANS
Presbyterian Church in the U.S. (Southern)
Female clergy survey rptd 3-23, 295B2
'77 membership loss, contributn rise rptd 6-2, 907D3
United Presbyterian Church in the U.S.A. (Northern)
Gay ordinatn study issued 409G3
Assemb opens 5-16, ordinatn of gays opposed 5-22, 409E3, 410A1
PRESCOTT, Robert W.
Dies 3-3, 252C3
PRESENT Danger, Committee on the—*See COMMITTEE on the Present Danger*
PRESLEY, Elvis Aron (1935-77)
Offer to aid FBI rptd 7-14, 553D3-554B1
Death anniv marked 8-16, 644A3
PRESQUE Isle, Me.—*See MAINE*

1979

Not in Helstoski indictmt rule case 6-18, 499B1
Not in accountants suits case 6-18, 499D1
Not in warrantless phone surveillnc case 6-20, 516G1
Backs youth probatn officer consultatn right 6-20, 516C2
Backs end to AFDC-UF welfare plan 6-25, 540A1
Not in W Va youth suspect press case 6-26, 541A1
Not in Weber case ruling 6-27, 477C2
Not in dockworker negligence case 6-27, 558C2
Not in criminal evidence standard case 6-28, 558B3
Backs ctroom pub access curbs 7-2, 515F2
'78-79 Sup Ct term ends, voting alignmt rptd 7-2, 558A1
Vs Ohio busing orders 7-2, 539B3
Vs power to void state convictns 7-2, 559A1
Vs Ga laws in church land dispute 7-2, 559C1
Vs Washn Indian fishing treaties 7-2, 559F1
Vs Mass abortn-consent law 7-2, 559A2
At ABA conv, comments on trial closures 8-13, 630B3
Urological surgery rptd 8-31, 744G3
Backs onshore dockers injury benefits 11-27, 919D3
Hears govt minority constructn grants case argumts 11-27, 945C1
Vs NYC schl aid denial 11-28, 944E2
Vs Taiwan treaty case review 12-13, 940C1

POWER, Donald C.
Dies 3-11, 272E3
POWERS, Noyes Thompson
Argues Weber case in Sup Ct 3-28, 262F3, 263A1
POWERS That Be, The (book)
On best-seller list 6-3, 432B2; 7-1, 548C3
POWs (prisoners of war)—*See under U.S. GOVERNMENT-ARMED Forces*
PO Yi-po
China dep premier 7-1, 502E2
Promotion rptd 9-28, 750E3*
PRAMOJ, Kukrit
Thai electns held 4-22, 314D2
PRAMOJ, Seni
Thai electns held 4-22, 314E2
PRATS Gonzalez, Gen. Carlos (d. 1974)
Townley testimony on murder role curbed 1-23, 75C1
PRATT, Judge Carlisle E.
Frees Maoist protesters 11-14, 904G3
PRATT, Elmer (Geronimo)
FBI sets murder convictn probe 9-24, 886F2
PRATT, Judge John H.
OKs FTC data disclosure to states 3-28, 308C2
Rules on Exxon-Reliance merger 8-17, 770B1
PRATT v. Wescott
Case decided by Sup Ct 6-25, 539E3
PRATT & Whitney Aircraft Division—*See under UNITED Technologies Corp.*
PRECHT, Henry
Memo on shah's entry to US rptd 11-8, 841G2
PREFONTAINE, Steve (1950-75)
Virgin breaks 10000-m run mark 6-17, 911A2
PREGERSON, Judge Harry
Barry pleads guilty to tax evasn 6-12, 527B3; sentncd 7-10, 656D2
PREGNANCY—*See CHILDBIRTH*
PRESBYTERIANS
Baptism rites agrmt reached 3-31, 375G2
Ga laws in land dispute backed by Sup Ct 7-2, 559C1
Carter discloses Park conversn effort 8-5, 639C2
United Presbyterian Church in the U.S.A. (Northern)
Barbour dies 1-10, 104E2
PRESBYTERIAN-University Hospital (Pittsburgh, Pa.)
PPA pneumonia outbreak cited 11-1, 971C2
PRESCOTT, Ore.—*See OREGON*
PRESCOTT National Park (Ariz.)
Fire destroys 19,200 acres 7-2, 572D3
PRESLEY, Elvis Aron (1935-77)
Poster dispute refused by Sup Ct 2-21, 128E3
Estate probated 3-24, 272G1
MD drug chrgs rptd 12-19, 1005C3
PRESLEY, Lisa Marie
Father's estate probated 3-24, 272G1

1980

Backs utilities' free speech 6-20, 555A2
Vs donated porno warrants 6-20, 555B3
Vs cts power to suppress evidence 6-23, 554D3
Vs magistrates pretrial role 6-23, 555A1
Vs broader right to sue states 6-25, 540F3
Backs Medicaid abortn funding limits 6-30, 491G3
Backs minority constructn grants 7-2, 510D1, G1
Not in open criminal trials case 7-2, 510F2
Vs OSHA benzene standard 7-2, 510G3
'79-80 Sup Ct term ends, voting alignmts rptd 7-2, 540C2
5th judicial circuit split, backing cited 10-14, 918D3
Stays BN-Frisco rail merger 11-21, 937A3
Not in EPA clean water enforcemt case 12-2, 918E1
Vs FTC trust complaint challenge 12-15, 957F1

POWELL, Peter
Final Countdown released 8-1, 675E2
POWELL, Robert
39 Steps released 5-2, 416F3
POWELL, Wesley
Loses Sen primary 9-9, 700F2
POWERS, Lt. Col. John A. (Shorty)
Dies 1-1, 104E3
POWERS, O. E.
Resigns McGraw-Edison post 12-8, 959F3
PPG Industries Inc.
EPA guidelines appeals ct review backed by Sup Ct 5-27, 453F3
EPA accuses of fuel-switching 11-25, 899C3
PRADO, Sergio
Ousted as radio commentator 2-1, 118B1
PRAIRIE Grain Co.
Heller kills self 1-31, elevator scandal rptd 2-25, suit filed 3-12, 237G3
Grain fraud probe rptd 5-14, 414F2
PRATT, Elmer (Geronimo)
Denied parole 2-5, 215A2
2 protest appeal denial 5-11, 667E1
PRATT, Judge George C.
Redefines Abscam term 8-20, 684E2
Rep Myers, co-defendants convicted in Abscam trial 8-31, 684C2
Appeals ct backs Abscam tapes broadcast 10-1; Sup Ct refuses stay, tapes aired 10-14, 781G2
PRATT, Judge John
Dismisses suit vs USOC 5-16, 379C3
USOC suit dismissal upheld 5-23, 421A2
PRATT & Whitney—*See UNITED Technology*
PRECIADO, Mateo
Chrgd in El Salvador alien case 7-19, 560E2
PRECIADO Navarro, Mateo
Convicted 10-20, 825F3
PREGERSON, Judge Harry
Bribe plot, Heymann letter rptd 2-8, organized crime summit rptd canceled 2-13, 111G3-112A1
Bars NFL franchise rule 2-22, injunctn stayed 2-22, 2-29, 175A2
PREGNANCY—*See CHILDBIRTH*
PREMINGER, Otto
Human Factor released 2-8, 216A3
PREM Tinsulanonda, Gen. (Thai premier)
Thai premier 3-3, forms Cabt 3-12, 196D3
Meets China premr on Cambodia conflict 10-30, 952B1
PRENTICE-Hall Inc.
Photocopy co sued 2-5, 119G3
Photocopy suit rptd setld 3-21, 376D3
PRESBYTERIANS
US rep reassured re Taiwan treatmt 1-24, 102F2
Taiwan Rev Kao sentncd 6-5, 468B1
Presbyterian Church in the U.S. (Southern)
Protestant unity mtg ends, common ministry OKd 1-24, 156G2
United Presbyterian Church in the U.S.A. (Northern)
Protestant unity mtg ends, common ministry OKd 1-24, 156G2
Intercommunion poll rptd 4-4, 413A3
S Korea arrests, frees US MDs 6-28, 499F3
PRESENZANO, Angelo
Galante link cited 3-3, 215F1
PRESLEY, Elvis Aron (1935-77)
MD license suspended 1-19, 199C1
MD indicted 5-16, 414B2
Lennon slain 12-8, 934B3

1976 1977 1978 1979 1980

PRESS

1976

PRESS—*See also specific newspapers, magazines, wire services*
Ford interviewed in St Louis 1-5, 3G2
Carson case gag order reversed 1-30, 124A2
Craft unions cross Washn Post picket line 2-16, 2-23, 153E3
Firestone settles on safety ads 2-16, 186B3
AFL-CIO urges Washn Post arbitratn 2-23, 149F1
Lewine named to Gridiron Club 3-5, 272A1
NLRB: journalists not professionals 4-5, 249C1
Sup Ct bars review of Church libel suit 4-5, 262A2
NLRB rules on ethics code 4-8, 272C2
Sup Ct bars Time privacy suit review 5-24, 393B2
Guild strikes Time Inc 6-2, 398D1
Ariz reporter slain 6-2, 483F2; **for subsequent developments, see BOLLES, Don**
3 chrgd re threat to NY wkly 6-7, 442A3
Quinlan story rights sold 6-10, 423A3
Guild ends Time strike 6-21, 454C2
Sup Ct voids Neb gag order, bars review of 3 other cases 6-30, 491C3-492D1
Guild wins Washn Post vote 7-22, 553D3
4 Calif newsmen jailed re info source 9-3—9-17, 700C2
Atlanta editor's kidnaper sentencd 9-17, 796E3
UMW conv ousts 'CP' press 9-25—9-27, 748F2
Cong clears copyright revisns 9-30, 765G3
Ariz crime probed 10-2, 849B2
Sup Ct bars review of NH magazine fund curb 10-18, 867A3
Hartford Times folds 10-20, 849F1
Nixon tapes release OKd 10-26, 849A3
Newhouse buys Booth chain 11-8, 901F2
Australian to buy NY Post 11-19, 887D2
Sup Ct stays Okla gag order 11-24, 901C2
Nation rptd sold 11-28, 901C3
Unificatn Church sets NYC daily 12-14, 971F1
LA newsman wins source disclosure test 12-21, 995C1
Nation sale fizzles 12-21, 995E1
Suit for Kissinger papers access planned 12-28, 980G2

Awards
Pulitzer Prizes 5-3, 352D3
Bolles wins Ariz U award 12-9, 971G3

Intelligence Issues
Sup Ct vs review of Consumer Rpts bar 1-12, 24G1

1977

PRESS—*See also specific newspapers, magazines, wire services*
Jurek executn filming protested 1-3, 40D3
Australian control of Post takes effect 12-30-76; gains NY Mag control 1-7, 48B3
Ford State of Union message 1-12, 13A2
Gilmore executn film barred 1-17, 40A3
Tarver named AP chrmn 1-18, 140E2
Kansas City Star Co sold 2-15, 216F1
Newhouse Booth purchase cited 2-18, 274E2
Sup Ct bars operating agreemt rule review 2-22, 150G1
Cross-media ownership barred 3-1, 216B1
US issues terrorism rpt 3-2, 484A1
Okla juvenile ct gag order voided 3-7, 211C2
IRE rpts Ariz drug trade 4-3, 332G3
Washn Post pressmen plead guilty 4-14, 345F1-A2
Gannett Okla, Mo deals OKd 4-14; Speidel merger set 5-10, 395C2
JFK-King probe chrmn on CIA ties 4-24, 4-28, 339D2
Child porno series rptd 5-15—5-18, 432E2
Burger disputes critics 5-17, 419A3
Nixon-Frost interview 5-25, 420E1
Baltimore papers settle trust suit 5-26, 504A2
FCC revokes '76 Telpak order 6-1, OKs AT&T pvt rates 6-1, 6-8, 465D1
RC editor fired re press freedom 6-16, 471E1-B2
Gen Starry scores 6-17, 482G3
Wyo libel jurisdictn review refused 6-20, 517C1
Emmy academies end dispute 7-12, 583C3
AT&T to maintain Telpak 7-21, FCC '75 'end-link' order upheld 8-5, 631C3, G3
ABA issues ad rules 8-10, 630G1
LA Times ad policy challenged 8-17, 658C3
Presley death editns sell out 8-22—8-24, 696E1
IHT sues Trib NY 8-24, 723F1
Nixon-Frost interview 9-3, 692G3
CIA links charged 9-12, 720F2-721C1
NY Times rptr tied to Pa politician quits 9-12, 920E3
Trib NY sues NY Times, IHT, intl Trib 9-13, 723D1
Filmmakers get 1st Amendmt rights 9-23, 921D2
Carter seeks more pub broadcast funds 10-6, 846E1
White House backs phone ad curbs 10-21, 921D1
Ida secret news source case review refused 10-31, 835E2
IRE cited re Bolles case convictns 11-6, 871E2
Fla libel case review refused 11-7, 857D2
Journalists' thoughts protected 11-7, 920F2
Seattle, Spokane newsmen elected mayors 11-8, 855B3
MCA acquires New Times 11-10, 1004E3
FBI releases Cointelpro files 11-21, 940C3
Rinaldi, Glover, Fadell libel cases refused 11-28, 919A3
Korean influence plan rptd 11-29, 914A3
CIA curbs news media contacts 11-30, 941C1 ★, A1
Kissinger loses transcript ruling 12-8, 962F2
Most reliable govt news sources listed 12-10, 1008G3
NY Times-Audubon libel case review declined 12-12, 960E2
Tex farmers bar Lubbock paper delivery 12-21, 1003B1
NFL denies censorship effort 12-22, 1020G1
Colby, other CIA ex-offcls defend ties 12-27, 1005E3

Awards
Pulitzer Prizes 4-18, 355E2
Graffis inducted into golf HOF 8-23, 675E3

1978

PRESS—*See also specific newspapers, magazines, wire services*
CIA exploitatn detailed in House hearings, editors seek curbs 1-4, 1-5, 14G2
Ohio, SC gag-order cases review barred, Pa case remanded 1-9, 13E1
Trib debuts in NYC 1-9, Learsy elected chrmn 1-17, 75C3
Bolles killers sentenced 1-10, 24B2
FCC bars Telpak rate hike exemptn 1-18, 84F1
Carter asks intell curbs 1-24, 49G2; legis introduced in Sen 2-9, 107B1
Gag rule eased in US crime code revisn 1-30, 64G2
Gannett buys 2 Wilmington papers 1-30, 109D3
Time to buy Washn Star 2-3, 109F2
Washn Post scoops Haldeman book 2-16, NY Times syndicatn, Newsweek plans upset; excerpts highlighted 2-16—2-17, 124C2, E3, 125B1
Chicago Daily News folds 3-4, 195E1
Washn Star sale completed 3-16, 270B3
Fla tape curb challenge refused by Sup Ct 3-20, 206B1
Student sex survey case review denied by Sup Ct 3-20, 206C1
Korea influence effort chrgs cited 3-21, 203G2
Anderson suit vs Nixon dismissed 4-4, 265B1
Trib ceases publicatn 4-5, 270A2
Media racism scored, minority job data cited 4-7—4-8, 419E3
Carter addresses editors soc 4-11, 259E2, 260D3
Lance scores coverage 4-12, 324F3-325A1
Minority employmt survey rptd 4-13, 835B3
Gurney trial press-curbs review declined by Sup Ct 4-17, 308C2
Broadcasters denied Nixon tapes by Sup Ct 4-18, 308C1
Burger warns re media 'empires' 4-26, 343G3
Nixon memoirs excerpted 4-30, 5-1, 319D2-320A2
Va judicial inquiry law voided by Sup Ct 5-1, 363G2-E3
Gannett plans Combined purchase, circulatn hike seen 5-8, 345E2
Iowa, NM info order review refused by Sup Ct 5-15, 388A1, B1
Newsroom searches by police backed by Sup Ct 5-31, 429E3
Allbritton quits as Washn Star publisher 5-31, 672D2
FCC cross-media ban backed by Sup Ct 6-12, 467B3
NY Daily News struck 6-13—6-17, 625A2
Prison data access curbed by Sup Ct 6-26, 566G2-D3
NY Times rptr in NJ curare case-press freedom controversy 6-30—8-30; jailed for contempt 8-4, freed 8-30, 678C2
Tex executn filming case declined by Sup Ct 7-3, 552D2
Carter complains of security leaks 7-11, 524E2
FBI admits 4 media informants 7-13, 554B1
'More' ceases publicatn, merges with Columbia Journalism Review 7-21, 672G1
3 NY papers struck 8-9, 625E1
ABA backs gag-order guidelines 8-9, 626C3
Talmadge scores for coverage of finances 8-19, 644E1
Gannett to sell TV statn 8-20, 759F3
NJ curare case-press freedom controversy continues 8-30—10-6; MD acquitted, NY Times rptr freed 10-24, 841C2
Anderson rpt on Vesco 'pol fix' denied by Admin 9-10, revises article 9-11, 719D3
Women gain locker room access 9-25, 1026A3
NY Times settles sex bias suit 9-28, 835F2
NY Post resumes publicatn 10-5; Times, News strike ends 11-6; impact rptd 864E3-865A2
Hearst press launches editorial pardon pleas 10-8, 824C1
IAPA rpts press freedom, scores jailing of NY Times rptr 10-13, 829F1, A2
Synanon threats probed 10-15, 842A1
Murdoch plans new NY tabloid 10-18, 865F1
Hagar in barroom brawl 11-11, Martin chrgd 11-12, 1026E2
New Times to halt publicatn 11-15, 1029G3
St Louis papers struck 11-20, 1006A2
NY Times press freedom case declined by Sup Ct 11-27, 937E1
Bolles state witness jailed 12-9, 992D2
Search shield bill proposed 12-13, 1029B3
Nixon data access upheld by Appeals Ct 12-21, 1011B3

Awards
Pulitzer Prizes 4-17, photo mix-up settled 4-21, 314D2-315B2

1979

PRESS—*See also specific newspapers, magazines, wire services*
Washn Star pacts renegotiated 1-1, 5E1-C2
Graham steps down as Washn Post publisher, son succeeds 1-10, 78C3
St Louis newsprs resume 1-14, 1-15, 87E2
Lawyers' interstate rights limited by Sup Ct 1-15, 31C3
Carter warns staff re leaks 2-12, 109G3-110B1
Wichita TV rptr contempt convictn review refused by Sup Ct 2-21, 128C3
Rptrs phone bill subpoena case refused by Sup Ct 3-5, 184E3
Judge blocks H-bomb article 3-9, 193C2-194A1; 3-26, 230A1
Newton chrgs persecutn 3-24, 239F1
Carter proposes restricted newsroom searches 4-2, 264D3
Lance grand jury dismissal motn rejctd 4-13, 327G3
Sup Ct rulings disclosed 4-16, 4-17, Ct worker fired re leaks 4-20, 302F2; 5-18, 382B3
'State of mind' libel queries backed by Sup Ct 4-18, reactn 4-18, 4-23, 301F3, 302B2
Calif paper loses libel case 4-18, plaintiffs win damages 4-19, 334B2
Ore Magazine prints CIA-disputed Uganda article 4-19, 309B3
1st Amendmt legal fund set 4-23, 302E2
Newspr Publishers meet in NY 4-25, 294B2
St Regis Paper strike 5-15—6-23, 598B3
Sup Ct office access curbed 5-18, 382G2
Marshall decries 'state of mind' libel ruling 5-27, 422D1
Top circulatn papers listed 6-6, 431B1
Crane scores Manchester Union articles 6-8, 594G1
Justice Dept admits H-bomb documt security error 6-8, judge continues to block H-bomb article publicatn 6-15, 713C1, E1
W Va youth suspect law voided by Sup Ct 6-26, 541A1
Ctroom pub access curbed by Sup Ct; reactn 7-2, 515G1, C3
'78-79 Sup Ct voting alignmts rptd 7-2, 558B1
H-bomb article hearing order denied by Sup Ct 7-2, 559A1
Loeb settles pensn fund suit 7-9, 640E3
Carter energy speech reviewed 7-16, 7-17, 534C3-E3
Mattson named NY Times Co pres 7-23, 640D3
Trial closure efforts rptd up 8-4; Burger, Powell comment 8-8, 8-13, 630C2-C3
Sen com spy rpt leak probed 8-9, 664E2
ABA rejects 3d party search limits 8-9, 8-15, 768D3
NY Times ordrd to pay NJ curare case trial costs 8-14, 656E2
Radio deregulatn proposed 9-6, 858G3
Stevens, Blackmun comment on trial closures 9-8, 745B1
Judge bans H-bomb letter publicatn 9-15; Wis, Chicago papers defy ban 9-16, 9-18, 713B1, B2; text of H-bomb letter, diagram 714D1-717E3
Justice Dept ends effort to stop H-bomb article publicatn 9-17, 713A1
3 scientists deny H-bomb letter chrgs 9-17, 714B2
1st Amendmt insurnc plan set 9-27, 859E2
Pope's US visit gets record coverage 10-1—10-7, 760E3
UPI press partnerships sale rptd 10-4, 859F2-A3
Va trial closure case accepted by Sup Ct 10-9, 783F3
Brennan criticizes 10-17, 848C1
Minneapolis Star prostitutn expose 10-18, 887G1-B2
Bishop executn witnessed 10-22, 817B2
Wall St Journal daily circulatn lead rptd 11-7, 1007F1
'Brethren' excerpts stir controversy 12-2, 988A2
NM newspapers libel case refused by Sup Ct 12-3, 964A2
Gannett claims news chain circulatn lead 12-12, 1007E1

Awards & Honors
Pulitzer Prizes 4-16, 336C2

1980

PRESS
Postal rate challenge declined by Sup Ct 1-7, 15F3
Times Mirror Conn divestiture ordered 1-24, 120B1
Phila Journal strike ends 1-25, 115F2
UPI financing plan fails 1-31, 120C1
Nader libel case declined by Sup Ct 2-19, 131E1
B Heiden scores Olympic pressure 2-20, 155E1
CIA admits use of journalists 2-21, 189A3
Des Moines Register privacy case refused by Sup Ct 2-25, 188A1
Bolles killers convictns overturned 2-25, 214B3
N Amer Newspaper Alliance disbanded 2-29, replaced 3-3, 239D2
Penthouse publisher wins libel case 3-1, 239B2
Kissinger records access blocked by Sup Ct 3-3, 209D3
Newspr Ed Soc holds conv 4-7—4-10, 263G3-264E3
CIA use of journalists backed by Turner 4-10, Carter 4-12; Sen OKs intell oversight bill 6-3, 458E3, G3
Salisbury sues US 4-10, 459F1
Penthouse publisher's libel award cut 4-17, 405A3
Anderson death plot revealed in Liddy book excerpts 4-21, 333B3
Postal rate hike proposed for '81 4-21, 347C2
Powell refutes Sup Ct media image 5-1, 368F2
Mobil protests Saudi film telecast 5-8, 375B3
NY Deliverers Union head convicted 5-15, 370E3; sentncd 6-26, 656D1
Nixon taps case accepted by Sup Ct 5-19, 440E1
Food ad rules set by FTC 5-21, 703E2
Cable-TV news network debuts 6-1, 501A3
Calif voters OK source protectn 6-3, 439E2
Schl censorship power upheld 6-13, 582G3
Harper's to cease publicatn 6-17, 501A1
Pretrial data secrecy rule oppositn rptd 6-19, 632C1
Open criminal trials backed by Sup Ct 7-2, 510C2-C3
'79-80 Sup Ct term ends, decisns cited 7-2, 540E2
Kingman quits as sportswriter 7-2, 637C2
Berkeley Barb folds 7-3, 582E3
Pa rptr cited for Abscam silence 7-10, 554A2
Ex-NY Times rptr marries Cianfrani 7-14, 890B2
Carter aides took oaths re leaks 7-16—7-17, 549G1
Idaho TV statn raided by police, Mich print shop search cited 7-26, 582B2, D2
Idaho prosecutor defends TV tapes raid 7-28, statn sues 8-1, 732A3
Garvey article reprint OKd 8-14, 637D2
Ga rptr indicted in 'death row' escape 8-27, 712F2-D3
Felker Daily News post rptd 8-27, 732G3
Reagan scores 'stealth' plane disclosure; Brown, Perry testify on leaks 9-4, 665E3
Hoffman fugitive yrs recapped 9-4, 713B2
NYC black media gets NSC Africa memo 9-16, Admin calls forgery 9-17, 726E3-727B2
NY Times settles '74 bias suit 9-17, 746A3
CIA agents bill defeated by Sen 9-30, 982B2
Appeals ct backs Abscam tapes broadcast 10-1; Sup Ct refuses stay, tapes aired 10-14, 781C2
Calif corp 'pub figures' libel case refused by Sup Ct 10-6, 782E2
UPI eds hear Christopher 10-7, 758C1
Mass rape trial press exclusn case remanded by Sup Ct 10-14, 782B1
Newsroom searches curb signed 10-14, 835F1-C2
Bolles killer convicted 10-17, 860E3
Ga rptr cleared in 'death row' escape 11-12, 927A1
Bolles killer sentenced 11-14, 926B3
Pa pretrial exclusn case refused by Sup Ct 11-17, 882F1
Will hosts Reagan dinner 11-20, 897G2
Flynt Cleveland convictn case accepted by Sup Ct 12-8, 937A2

Awards & Honors
Polk Memorial presented 2-25, 692D3
Pulitzer Prizes 4-14, 296B2

1976

Kissinger, Haldeman file Halperin case depositns 1-12, 3-11; Nixon depositn released 3-10, 184A1, B2
CIA manipulatn rptd 1-16, 1-17; House com rpt leaked 1-23, 92C2
House com asks CIA contacts bar 2-10, 150B2
CIA limits media contacts 2-11, 150A3
Schorr admits leaking House com rpt 2-12; House votes probe 2-19, CBS suspends 2-23, 150D3-151A2
Schorr dismissal urged 2-17, 216F3
Ford seeks law vs security leaks 2-18, 127D3
House com leak probe underway 3-2, 216E3
Contd CIA contacts chrgd 4-26, 299B1
Sen com rpts FBI media efforts 4-28, 330G2
Smith sues Nixon re taps 5-10, 349E2
Sovt press ties 3 US newsmen to CIA 5-25, 5-26, 371G2
House com hearings on Schorr probe 7-19, 7-20; Schorr, others subpoenaed 8-25; probe dropped 9-22, 748A3
Nixon, 2 aides held liable re Halperin wiretap 12-16, 980C3

International Developments—*For internal issues, including censorship, see country names*
7 die in Beirut press office raid 1-3, 82D3
Ecuador ousts Dutch UPI rptr 1-13, 28F2
Angola Unita bar Westn newsmen 1-14, 16B3
Israel defers forgn censorship plan 1-20, 34B3
USSR to make more Westn dailies available 1-21, 76F2
Le Monde launches Portugal editn 2-8, 143E2
Nigeria ousts UK newsman 2-16, 192A1
Sovt press ties 3 US newsmen to CIA 5-25, 5-26, 371G2
Angola ousts 3 journalists 6-9—6-16, 480B3
Jamaica scores US press 6-20, 522G1
Malaysia, Singapore arrest plotters 6-22, 497F3
US newsman sues Sovt press 6-25, 559B1
Latin natns meet, OK regional agency 7-12—7-21; IAPA scores 7-23, 619C3
Developing natns OK news pool 7-13, 619A3
Japan newsman's '74 acquittal reversed 7-20, 539D1
BBC closes India office 8-5, 621D1
Angola ousts US journalist 8-15, 649G2
China regrets Polish ouster 8-24, 674E1
UK newsman freed in Ethiopia 9-6, 674F2-A3
S Africa accuses Briton 9-7, 662B2
Yugo scores US criticism 9-12, 685D2
India lifts forgn curbs 9-18, 700B3
S Africa sentences Britons 9-29, 733F3
Greece sentncs US journalist 10-4, 873D1
Thais curb forgn press 10-11, 775E3
Venez ousts 3 US rptrs 10-22, 844E1
Pl scores forgn press 10-22, 855G1
S Africa curbs newsmen 10-26, 11-7; intl group scores 12-9, 927D2, G2
Pl ousts US newsman 11-2; forgn newsmen protest 11-5; security cited 11-6, 855D1
French journalists visit China 11-2, 871D3
UNESCO shelves Sovt plan 11-6, 842G1
Argentina holds, frees Spanish newsman 11-7, 997A1
UK ordrs 2 US rptrs ousted 11-15, 11-17, 946B2
UNESCO panel OKs news plan 11-22, 879B1
UNESCO OKs press pool plan 11-26, 896B1
UNESCO shelves press plan 11-29, 895E3
US comm cites Helsinki gains 12-2, Ford scores Sovt bloc 12-8, 934F1, D2
S Africa frees UK newsman 12-9, 1010B3
Israel ends Palestinian rptr's detentn 12-10, 954F1
Syria seizes Leb papers 12-15—12-20, 953C2
Freedom House sees govt control threat 12-22, 977E2
E Ger ousts W Ger newsman 12-22, 1001D3

1977

International Developments—*For internal issues, including censorship, see country names*
Syria ends Leb office occupatn 1-3, 2A2
India lifts BBC ban 1-6, 45G3
Czechs chrg UK journalist 1-23, 82G3
Leb ends forgn curbs 1-25, 72C2
USSR ousts AP newsman 2-4; US retaliates 2-5, 101C1
Czechs detain US, Bonn newsmen 2-4—2-14, 114G2
Botswana sentncs 3 Rhodesia newsmen 2-8, 85A2
Yugo scores dissident coverage 2-10, 2-15, 139F2
US sets Agee, Hosenbell expulsns 2-16, 134A2
Czech detentns disputed 2-17, papers returned 3-1, 3-16, 220E3
Czechs oust 2 French journalists 3-2, attack 2 others 3-3, 220D3, E3
Nigeria ousts US rptr 3-12, 258E1
Czechs hold Spain rptr 4-2—4-3, seize Canada journalist's notes 4-24, 314A3
Zaire ousts AP rptr 4-4, 261B1
Czechs set forgn censorship 4-8, 314F2
Kenya ousts UK rptr 4-13, 393E1
UNESCO parley 4-18—4-20, 319E2
Morosi wins Australia libel suit 4-22, 326A2
Ethiopia ousts Western rptrs 4-25, 327C3
Zaire ousts 7 Eur newsmen 5-6, 394G1
Venez chrgs Argentina abuses 5-11, 547C2
Goldsmith drops Pvt Eye libel suit 5-16, 527B1
UK chrgs 3 5-24; Hosenball, Agee expelled 5-27, 6-3, 526C3
US chrgs Sovt bloc curbs 6-6, 473E1
USSR holds US rptr 6-11—6-15, 474C3
Canada rpt scores violence 6-15, 485G1
Uganda arrests Canada rptr 6-22, frees 7-10, 600A3
UK Beaverbrook chain sold 6-30, 526F3-527B1
Uruguay Excelsior, AP arrests controversy 7-4—7-21, 601C1
Bulgaria rptr gets French asylum 7-7, 606G2
USSR chrgs US rptr 7-12, 564E1
CAE holds US, UK rptrs 7-14—8-15, 634E3
Italy CP paper to open US bur 7-20, 581F2-A3
Rhodesia ousts UK rptr 8-2, 599F2
US distributes Panama Canal 'fact sheet' 8-4, 590B1
US Cong comm scores USSR 8-5, 606C2
Westn rptrs tour Ogaden 8-13—8-14, 648B3; 8-20—8-24, 684D2; 9-14, 715C2
Young backs press curbs 8-14, IAPA scores 8-16, 647G1
Agee CIA expose planned 8-19, 654G2
Ethiopia OKs US rptr reentry 9-23, 830F1
Westn rptrs tour Ogaden 9-27, 756A2
US newsmen score S Africa curbs 10-10, 10-21, 825C2
S Africa upholds appeal of UK editor 11-25, 935D1
China expels Canada rptr 11-27, 946B2
UN OKs Palestine newsletter 12-2, 931E1
Helsinki review conf adjourns 12-22, 997D2

1978

International Developments—*For internal issues, including censorship, see country names*
E Ger bars W Ger rptr 1-4, closes Der Spiegel office 1-10, 11G2
CIA exploitatn scored 1-5, 15B1
Uruguay frees Mex newsman 1-5, 136F3
Begin chrgs Egypt anti-Semitism 1-21—1-23; Egypt press denies 1-24, 41E1, A2, G2-42D1
S Africa detains forgn rptrs 1-22, 54G3
UK propaganda unit disbanded 1-27, 71E2
Nicaragua troops beat forgn rptrs 2-1, 91C2
Pak, India OK journalist exchng 2-6—2-7, 113B1
Cyprus chrgs UK newsman 2-22, drops case 2-24, 138E2
USSR seizes US rptr's notes 3-2, US protests 3-8, 180D1
Pl ties forgn newsmen to electn protest 4-10; 2 get protest 4-11, 269A1
S Africa bribery attempts rptd 4-17, 377D3
S African rptr asks US asylum 4-20, 314C3
USSR bars US photo transmissn 4-20, 360B1
L'Express control bought by UK financier 4-27, 352A3
Czechoslovakia ousts AP rptr 5-1, 439B3
CIA '75 Angola propaganda rptd 5-8, 367G2
E Ger scores W Ger rptrs re protest coverage 5-11, 504E2
DR scores US electn coverage 5-23, 414B3
USSR seizes 3 Westn rptrs 5-24, 416F2
Egypt recalls 30 journalists 5-26, 414D3
Egypt warns forgn newsmen 6-7; Arab group scores Sadat 6-21, 473D2
Solzhenitsyn scores West 6-8, 444B3
UPI Leningrad bur rptd closed 6-12, 476B2
Ugandan envoy loses Danish libel suit 6-18, 688B1
USSR files slander chrg vs 2 US rptrs 6-28, rptrs issue statemts 7-3, 518B1-F2
US reviews USSR rptrs status 6-30, 7-5, 518F2
Czech ousts W Ger rptr 7-4, 635E1
Malta bans UK rptrs 7-9, closes radio statn 7-16, 592A3
USSR convicts 2 US rptrs 7-18, 575C2
US rptrs pay USSR fines 8-4, 634A1
Czechs oust Belgian rptr 8-10, 691B3
Malawi bars forgn rptrs 8-14, 677G1
USSR closes US rptrs case 8-18, 651E1; warns 8-24, 670C2
Colombia rptr kidnaped in Peru 9-3—9-10, 776B1
USSR detains 3 Westn newsmen 9-4, 947C2
Cuba exile eds visit Havana 9-7, 687E1
USSR expels Austrian rptr 9-30, 821E1 ★
IAPA scores Argentina abuses 10-9, 792B3
IAPA ends assemb; adopts rights resolutns, rates freedom 10-13, 829D1-B2
UK drops maj secrets chrgs vs 3 10-23, 838A3; sentncs re other chrgs 11-17, 924E1
S Africa role in Washn Star '74 purchase bid rptd 11-1, 868D2
Calif newsmen arrive Guyana 11-15; 3 killed in cult ambush 11-18, bodies flown home 11-21, 889A1, G1, E2, 891C1
UNESCO backs free press 11-22; text 931C1, C2-932F2
Guyana bans forgn rptrs from Jonestown 11-25, murder-suicide reactn rptd 11-28, 11-30, 909F2, 911D2
2 US rptrs in Cambodia 12-9, escape gunman 12-23, 997A2

1979

Foreign Developments (including U.S. international news)—*See also 'Mergers' below; for internal issues including censorship, see country names*
US-China pact signed 1-31, 65D1
LA Times rptr slain in Iran 2-10, 105B2
S Africa bribe chrgs rptd 3-10, 191B1
Israel scores US coverage of Carter Mideast missn 3-13, 177B2
IAPA holds annual mtg; pres backs Peru journalist hunger strike 3-21, 255G3
4 Westn rptrs believed killed in Uganda 4-9, 257D2
E Ger curbs Westn rptrs 4-14, 285E2; ousts W Ger 5-14, 370E3
Rhodesian electn observed 4-17—4-21, 293A2
US protests UK rptr's chrg of Sovt abuse 4-20, 390F1-A2
Eur rights ct rules vs UK censorship 4-26, 331A1
4 Westn rptrs' bodies found 4-26, 429F1
Africa news agency planned 5-9, 342C1
USSR ousts W Ger newsmen 5-16, 410B2
4 US papers to open China offices 5-30, 406B2
E Eur coverage of Pope in Poland rptd 6-2, 413B2
Poland press fee rptd canceled 6-4, 414C2
E Ger curbs info flow 6-28, 568G2
Iran ousts LA Times rptr 7-1, 525D2
USSR extends UK rptr's visa 7-10, 636G3
S Africa link denied by US publisher 7-18, 567G1
OAU backs pan-Africa news agency 7-21, 552F2
PEN Club cong ends 7-21, 553G3
Iran ousts NYT rptr 7-22, sets forgn curbs 7-23, 565F3
Iran ousts NBC 4-man TV crew 8-6, 602D2
Iran widens forgn curbs 8-13, IJC scores 8-14, 614F3
Iran ousts newsmen 8-16, 9-1, new rules set 9-3, AP office ordered closed 9-4, 670G1
W Ger rptr arrested as spy 8-16, 742E2
Iran ousts 5 W Eur rptrs 8-21, 635A2
Sovts chrg Iran distortn re Afghan role 8-22, 666G2
7 rptrs arrested, freed in N Ireland 9-4, 669F3
Iran expels 15th forgn newsman 9-5, 708B3
Iran expels Wall St Journal rptr 9-26, 814B3
US co runs ads to free 2 execs in El Salvador 10-10, 790D3
S Korea bars US rptr 10-13, OKs entry 10-14, 803B3
USSR rptr flies to US after Japan defectn 10-24, 856D3
Guatemala leftist ads run 10-26, 813E3
Mecca mosque coverage curbed 11-20, 899D1
Pak newsman sentncd 11-29, 951F1
UK editor rpts death threat in Argentina 12-4, leaves 12-16, 12-4, 966E2
Zimbabwe lifts forgn rptr curbs 12-13; admits Polish newsman 12-17, 960B2
W Ger rptr sentenced in E Ger 12-14, 980F3

Mergers & Acquisitions
S Africa chrgd re Washn Star '74 purchase bid; info sale barred in UK, US 3-21, 213F1, G1
S Africa Washn Star purchase bid confrmd 4-2, 270C1; 6-4, 427D3
Esquire sale to Tenn firm rptd 5-1, 334D2

1980

Foreign Developments (including U.S. international news)—*See also 'Mergers' below; for internal issues including censorship, see country names*
Iran bars CBS-TV 29A3
Iran ousts US newsmen; warns UK, W Ger rptrs 1-14; defends move 1-15, 29D2-A3
Israel, Egypt trade newspapers 1-18, 48B3
Afghanistan ousts US newsmen 1-17, 26A3
Australia ousts Sovt rptr 1-22, 100D2
Tanzanians assail Ali 2-3, 85C1
Iran chrgs US, UK rptrs took gifts from shah 2-9, 122B3
US sets Sovt rptr ceiling 2-22, 140A1
Iran to readmit US newsmen 2-26; AP invited 2-27; 2 US newsmen turned back 2-28, 138E1-A2
Iran readmits more US rptrs 3-7, 178C2
Iran hostage film purchase offer rejctd by US TV networks 4-10, 282C3
Haiti law stifles criticism 4-11, 294E2
US widens sanctns vs Iran, exempts rptrs 4-17, 281C1
AP rptrs seized in Leb 4-18, 302A3
Algeria bars rptrs from Berber region 4-19, 334D1
Iran ousts US newsmen 4-23, 378E2
UK, Leb rptrs seized in Iran Emb in London 4-30, 324B3
Iran arrests US free lancer 5-6, 434B1
Regional econ unity hosted 5-9, 410B2
Bolivia detains US rptr 6-9, 443F2
S Africa bars forgn newsmen from riot areas 6-16, 466A1
Sovt Olympic crackdown 7-13—7-23, 590B1, D1
Leb offcl slain 7-23, 579F2
S Korea detains journalists 7-24; rptrs fired, 172 periodicals banned 7-30, 620B3
Last 2 US newsmen, 3 UK rptrs flee Iran 7-25, 572C1
UK press confidentiality ruling 7-30, 634G1
US journalist detained in Bolivia 8-6—8-12, 668D1
US Iran invasn plan rptd 8-16; publicatn decision 'anguishing' 8-18, 635A1
Malaysia ousts US rptr, son 9-7, 810G1
Spain to ease curbs 9-8, 690B3
UNESCO conf: world info order backed, 3d World states score Westn news svcs 9-23—10-28, 821F2; 3d World coverage study rptd 11-29, 914C1
UK press confidentiality case dropped 9-30, 750F3
Iraq expels 3 forgn newsmen 10-2; extends order 10-10, 774D3
France expels US journalist 10-3, 790B2
Zimbabwe announces curbs 10-24, 833B3
S Africa rptr released 10-26, 887F3
Le Monde editors chrgd 11-7, 872C1
Uruguay arrests UK rptr 11-7, frees 11-10, 888B3
Australia censors articles on US ties 11-8, 885B1
Poland bars Westn rptrs 11-9, order rescinded 11-10, 862A3
Turkish left-wing paper banned 11-11, 874C3
Polish union ldr cites problems 11-14, 878E1
Korea orders media regrouping 11-14, 888B1
Iran ends forgn press ban 11-15, 879E3
Turkish left-wing paper ban lifted 11-20, 924F1
S African striking black journalists fired 11-27, 967E3
Haiti arrests Duvalier critics 11-28—11-30, 922E2
Australia censorship upheld by High Ct 12-1, 919E2
Australian banned articles publshd 12-2, 991F2
Israel sets W Bank curbs 12-14, 977C1
Hua scored in Chinese press 12-16, 12-30, 975C3

Mergers & Acquisitions
Thomson, Newsco bid for FP Publicatns 1-2—1-11, Thomson wins 1-11, 38G1
Atlantic Monthly sale rptd 3-1, 239F1
Cue NY sale agrmt rptd 3-4, 239G1
Us magazine sale rptd 3-7, 239A2
Washn Star purchase bid disclosure ordrd 3-17, 278C1

1976

Obituaries
Baukhage, Hilmar 2-1, 124C3
Bolles, Don 6-13, 484G2
Cogley, John 3-28, 272E3
Donnelly, Tom 2-10, 192D3
Herzberg, Joseph 2-12, 160D3
Johnson, Malcolm 6-18, 524G2
Lisagor, Peter 12-10, 1015A2
Lyons, Leonard 10-5, 970C2
Mariano, Frank 8-8, 892C3
McKelway, Benjamin 8-30, 680G3
North, Joseph 12-20, 1015C2
Reichmann, John A 2-2, 124F3
Reynolds, Packard 10-15, 970G2
Satyukov, Pavel 11-17, 970B3
Sissman, Louis 3-10, 316C1
Sullivan, Frank 2-19, 192G3
Thomson of Fleet, Lord 8-4, 816G3
Vishniak, Mark 11-30, 1015A3

Presidential Election (& transition)—*For TV debates, see under POLITICS*
Wallace scores coverage 1-9, 22E2, F2
Reagan chrgs 'distortion' 1-12, 22C1
Ford sees NH editors 1-22, 41A2
Reagan aide chrgs 'distortn' 2-7, 130C1
Shapp scores coverage 3-12, 197D2
Equal-time rules upheld 4-12, 282E1
Ford sees Harte-Hanks editors 4-19, 281A2
Brown sees Washn Post staff 5-6, 343E2
Ford at LA press club 5-25, 374B1
Reagan at Sacramento press club 6-2, 410B1, D2
Carter sees Hearst, Time editors 7-22, 551E1
Carter sees 3 groups in DC 8-4, 564D3
Women cover Carter church class 8-15, 617D1
Ford clinches nominatn 8-16, 8-17, 601D3
Mondale sees ethnic editors 8-25, 645F2
Carter gives Washn Post, NYT, Baltimore Sun interviews 9-4, 664C1
Carter Playboy interview disclosed 9-20, 704F1; **for subsequent developments, see PLAYBOY**
Mondale at Time conf 9-26, 724F3
Dole at UPI conv 10-8, 763G3-764A1
Pres endorsemts rptd 10-30, 11-8, 827D3
Carter news conf 11-4, 819D2
Carter: coverage fair 11-5, 845E1
Carter news conf 11-15, 863D2-864C1, B2
Powell named Carter press secy 11-15; with Nessen 11-16, 864C1
Carter news confs 12-14, 12-16, 936D1, B3; 12-20, 957A1
Carter, Cabt confs 12-27—12-29, 978D1-E2

Presidential Debates—*See under POLITICS*

Presidential News Conferences—*See PRESS under FORD*

1977

Obituaries
Atkins, Ollie 1-9, 84F2
Batchelor, C. D. 9-5, 787F3
Bliven, Bruce 5-27, 452E2
Bowles, Heloise 12-28, 1023G3
Gainza Paz, Alberto 12-26, 1024F1
Habe, Hans 9-30, 788C1
Howe, Quincy 2-17, 164A3
Kleinschmidt, Edward 8-9, 696A3
Lacerda, Carlos 5-21, 452D3
Laurence, William 3-19, 264B3
Lewis, Ross 8-6, 696A3
Love, Philip H 8-17, 696B3
Markel, Lester 10-23, 872E2
Marshall, Slam 12-17, 1024E2
Matthews, Herbert 7-30, 604D3
McCarroll, Marion 8-4, 696D3
Mowrer, Edgar Ansel 3-2, 264C3
Powell, Clilan 9-22, 788C2
Powers, John 7-19, 604F3
Schuyler, George 8-31, 788E2
Thieriot, Chas deYoung 3-21, 264F3
Vorhees, Melvin 2-6, 164F3
Wheaton, Anne 3-23, 264G3
White, Katherine 7-20, 604G3

Presidential News Conferences (& Interviews)—*See PRESS under CARTER*

1978

Obituaries
Alexander, Eben Roy 10-30, 888D2
Bliss, George 9-11, 777F3
Borland, Hal 2-22, 196C2
Earl, Johnrae 1-10, 96F1
Ewing, Donald M 9-2, 778C1
Flanner, Janet 11-7, 972A3
Francois-Poncet, Andre 1-8, 96A2
Freeman, Harry 1-13, 96A2
Frick, Ford C 4-8, 356F2
Jacobs, Paul 1-3, 96D2
Kiernan, Walter 1-8, 96D2
Mullin, Willard 12-21, 1032C3
Poynter, Nelson 6-15, 540F3
Rockwell, George L 3-3, 252D3
Smith, W Eugene 10-15, 888F3
Utely, Freda 1-21, 96F3

Presidential News Conferences (& Interviews)—*See CARTER—PRESS*

1979

Rolling Stone, Look merge 5-7, 430F3
Look ends tie to Rolling Stone 7-3, 640B3
Gannett buys, sells Tenn papers 7-5, 618B3
Cincinnati papers joint pact OKd 11-26, 1007G1
Gannett buys Calif paper 12-12, 1007E1

Obituaries
Barth, Alan 11-20, 932B2
Beltran Espantoso, P 2-16, 176E2
Bernstein, Theodore M 6-27, 508D2
Capp, Al 11-5, 932C2
Franzblau, Rose N 9-2, 756D2
Kiewit, Peter 11-2, 932B3
Larsen, Roy E 9-10, 756F2
Minor, Audax 10-8, 860D3
Morris Jr, Joe Alex 2-10, 105B2, 176D3
Muir, Malcolm 1-30, 104E3
Newhouse, Samuel I 8-29, 671B3
Robb, Inez 4-4, 356F3
Rovere, Richard H 11-23, 932D3
Viannson-Ponte, Pierre 5-7, 432G3

Presidential News Conferences (& Interviews)—*See CARTER—PRESS*

1980

Phila Bulletin sold to Charter Media 4-10, 376F3
Chattanooga (Tenn) papers partially join 5-12, Civiletti OKs 9-2, 732E2
Saturday Review sold 5-20, 582C3
Gannett purchase of NM paper rescinded 6-30, 582D2-A3
Harper's sold to philanthropies 7-9, 582A3
Thomson, Southam Canada paper closings spur deals 8-27, 668G2-D3
Tex Monthly buys New West 8-27, 732E3
Charter Media dissolved 9-30, 836C2
2 London evening papers to merge 10-1, 750D3
London Times offered for sale 10-22, 808A3
Times Mirror Co to buy Denver Post 10-22, 857C1
Cleveland Press sold 10-31, 1003D1
Chattanooga (Tenn) papers' pact gets final OK 11-6, 907E1
Phila Bulletin acquired by Charter Co 11-6, 907G1-A2

Obituaries
Agar, Herbert 11-24, 928F1
Bates, Lucias C 8-22, 676A1
Beckman, Aldo 9-10, 755C2
Fischetti, John R 11-18, 928D2
Healy Jr, George W 11-2, 928F2
Johnson, Gerald W 3-23, 279F3
Lieb, Fred 6-3, 528D2
McClean, Robert 12-5, 1004F2
McKelway, St Clair 1-10, 104C3
McWilliams, Carey 6-27, 528F2
Mueller, Merrill 12-1, 1004B3
Pollan, Clayton 9-13, 756F1
Rubin, Morris H 8-8, 676E2
Shea Jr, George E 4-27, 360E3

Presidential News Conferences (& Interviews)—*See under CARTER*

U.S. Presidential Election (& Transition)
Kennedy chrgs Carter misuse 2-14, 130B2
Anderson publicity problem rptd 2-15, 129E2
Reagan assails ethnic joke rpt 2-18, 128C2
Candidates address eds 4-7—4-10, 263G3-264E3
Reagan scores rpts 4-10, 288B2
Kennedy addresses LA Press Club 5-15, 383B2
Reagan sees Ebony, Jet editors 8-5, 597B3
Carter, Reagan ad budgets rptd 9-4, 665B3
Mondale warns vs subpoenas 9-18, 780B2
Black journalists hear Anderson 9-29, 739E2
Endorsemts rptd 11-1, 841D3

1976

PRESS Club, National—*See NATIONAL Press Club*

1977

PRESS Club, National—*See NATIONAL Press Club*

1978

PRESS, Frank
GAO issues A-satellite hazards rpt 2-6, 103G1
E Coast boom study to be reviewed 3-15, 187D2
Heads science mission to China 7-6—7-10, 564C2-B3
USSR trip canceled re Shcharansky 7-8, 542B1

PRESS Club, National—*See NATIONAL Press Club*

PRESSEAU, Richard
Disputes '72 APLQ raid purpose 1-13, 35F2

1979

PRESS, Frank
Leads science group in USSR 2-5–2-7, 100D1
To visit Brazil 3-22, 248B1

1980

PRESS, Frank
A-blast mystery rpt cited 1-23, 49A3
US-Japan science pact signed 5-1, 341C1

PRESS Institute, International
Turkey paper ban plea 11-20, 924F1

PRESS, Richard
Horowitz & Mrs Washn opens 4-2, 392C3
Lesson From Aloes opens 11-17, 1003D3

1976

PRESSER, William
Resigns Teamsters post 10-7, 990G3
PRESSLER, Rep. Larry L. (R, S.D.)
Reelected 11-2, 830A4
PRESSNER Trading Corp.
Sued 5-27, 397E3
PRESTES, Luis Carlos
Chrgs MDB-PCB ties 2-8; MDB denies 2-10, 287G3
PRESTOL (Dominican Republic warship)
In Intl Naval Review 7-4, 488C3
PREUS, Rev. David
Vs Mo Synod ousters 5-29, 776F3
Scores Mo Synod 10-10—10-11, 932D2
PREUS, Rev. Jacob A. O.
Ousts 4 dist pres, dispute widens 4-2—9-30, 776B3
Scores ALC 10-10—10-11, 932C2
PREYER, Rep. (Lunsford) Richardson (D, N.C.)
Reelected 11-2, 830E2
PRIA Olavarrieta, Joaquin
Vs import, export duties 9-13, 694C3
PRICE, Rep. Charles Melvin (D, Ill.)
Reelected 11-2, 829A3
PRICE, George (Belizean prime minister)
In UK re Belize independnc 1-5, 55B2
At Guatemala-UK talks 9-21—9-22, 977F3
PRICE, William J.
Testifies on busing 6-14, 453F1
PRICE-Fixing—*See ANTITRUST*
PRICES—*See under ECONOMY*
PRICHARD, Edward
Testifies at privacy comm probe 2-13, 151G2
PRIEMER, Petra
Wins Olympic medal 7-19, 575B3
PRIESTNER, Cathy
Wins Olympic medal 2-6, 158G3
PRIETO, Arnaldo
Corruptn expose cites 8-3—8-5, 851C1
PRIMARIES—*See 'Elections' under POLITICS*
PRIMATESTA, Archbishop Raul Francisco Cardinal
Asks Cordoba kidnap moves 1-12, 26B1
AAA sends death threat 3-13, 212A2
Sees Videla 7-22, 571C2
Munoz protest bishops expulsns 8-16, 692G3
PRINEAS, Peter
GOP conv vote bribe chrgd 8-17, 616G1
PRINSLOO, Gen. Gert
On township riot deaths 6-21, 447B2, D2
Denies riot death rpts 8-4, 579C2
Asks press curbs 10-27, 927A3
PRINTING and Graphics Communications Union, International (AFL-CIO)
15 members indicted 7-14, 7-21, 553C3
PRIOR, James
Pledges Tory-union accord 10-6, 791F3
PRISONS & Prisoners—*See under CRIME; country names*
PRITCHARD, Rep. Joel M. (R, Wash.)
Reelected 11-2, 831A1

1977

PRESSER, William
US sues Ohio union fund 4-4, 280C2
PRESSLER, Rep. Larry (R, S.D.)
Sup Ct remands Cong pay hike suit 5-16, 419G1
PRESTES, Beatriz
Kidnaped 1-11, 42C1
PRESTES, Carlos Alberto
Children kidnaped 1-11, 42D1
PRESTES, Enrique
Kidnaped 1-11, 42C1
PRESTIN, Vladimir
Detained 3-2, US protests 3-3, 226E2, A3
PREVERT, Jacques
Dies 4-11, 356F3
PREYER, Rep. (Lunsford) Richardson (D, N.C.)
Vs Sprague firing 2-10—2-21, 127A1, D1
Named Ethics com chrmn 3-10, 191F2
De Mohrenschild found dead 3-29, 228C3
PRICE, George (Belizean prime minister)
Starts Panama visit, Torrijos affirms Belize stand 5-20, 414A3, C3
10-yr UK defense pact sought 5-20, 415C1
UDP scores, fears leftist ties 7-11, 553C2
Warns of Guatemala invasn 11-18, 969A3
PRICE, James
Griffin cleared in '73 slayings 11-5, 871B3
PRICE, Rep. Charles Melvin (D, Ill.)
'76 spec interest gifts rptd 2-4, 128G3, 129D2
Cited in Park indictmt 9-6, 688D1
Named in Hanna indictmt 10-14, 816B1
PRICE Jr., Raymond K.
On Nixon-Frost interview 5-5, 367F3
PRICE-Fixing—*See ANTITRUST Actions*
PRICES—*See under ECONOMY*
PRICE Waterhouse & Co.
Sen subcom staff rpt scores 1-17, 78C3
Stronger SEC regulatn backed, earnings disclosed 5-10, 519B3
Big 8 acctg firms ranked 8-22, 650G2
PRIDE of the Peacock, The (book)
On paperback best-seller list 8-14, 643A2
PRIESTS' Councils, National Federation of
Female ordinatn backed 3-23, 374G3
PRIETO Figueroa, Luis Beltran
Venez pres candidate 9-25, 867G2
PRIGOGINE, Ilya
Wins Nobel Prize 10-11, 951B3
PRINCE of Our Disorder, A: The Life of T. E. Lawrence (book)
Wins Pulitzer 4-18, 355D2
PRINCETON (N.J.) University
Hosts IC4A indoor track championships 3-7, 603B1
'77-78 costs rptd 3-27, 483G1
Goheen confrmd amb to India 4-25, 418D1
Anderson wins Nobel Prize 10-11, 951G2
PRINS, Marthinus Johannes
Presides at Biko inquest 11-14, 887C2
Police cleared by Biko inquest 12-2, 933F3
PRINZE, Freddie
Dies 1-29, 84E3
PRIOR, James
Vs closed union shops 10-11, 863E3
PRIO Socarras, Carlos
Sees Vance, vs US-Cuba talks 2-25, 180B3
Dies 4-4, 356F3
PRISONERS of War—*See under U.S. GOVERNMENT—ARMED Forces*
PRISONS, Bureau of—*See under U.S. GOVERNMENT—JUSTICE*
PRISONS & Prisoners—*See under CRIME*
PRITCHARD Jr., Charles M.
Indicted 3-10, 203E3
PRITCHARD, William C.
Indicted 3-10, 203E3
PRITCHARD & Baird Inc.
Pritchards indicted 3-10, 203F3

1978

PRESSER, Jackie
Named in US Teamster fund suit 2-1, 83E1
'76 earnings rptd 2-20, 365A2
PRESSER, William
To resign as Ohio Teamster fund trustee 1-3, 4F2
Named in US Teamster fund suit 2-1, 83E1
PRESS Institute, International
Indonesia press ban protested 1-24, 72B1
PRESSLER, Rep. Larry (R, S.D.)
Cong pay-hike suit dismissal backed 1-16, 33F2
Wins US Sen primary 6-6, 448A2
Elected 11-7, 846G1, 848C3, 855A1
PRESTES, Luis Carlos
MDB endorsemt scored by govt 11-14, 921D2
PRETTY Baby (film)
Released 4-5, 619C3
PREUSCH, Robert W.
Settles pensn fund fraud suit 5-21, 480F3
PREYER, Rep. (Lunsford) Richardson (D, N.C.)
Assassinatn com hears testimony re King 8-14—8-18, 641C1, C2
JFK assassinatn hearings open 9-6, 697D3
Oswald's widow testifies re JFK death 9-13, 9-14, 749E2
Says King conspiracy possible 9-24, 898E1
Reelected 11-7, 851B3
PRIBILOF Islands, Alaska—*See ALASKA*
PRICE, Rep. Charles Melvin (D, Ill.)
Cleared by ethics com re Park gift 7-13, 527A2
Reelected 11-7, 850F3
Scores Selective Service 12-3, 984C1
PRICE, David
Kerr phones 8-14, Munro scandal spurs resignatn 9-9, 721C3
PRICE, George (Belizean prime minister)
In UK, sees forgn secy 1-24—1-25, 94F1
3 Carib natns in Belize defns accord 3-10, 211C2
Vows non-pol independnc talks 6-2, 478D2
PRICE, Reynolds
Early Dark opens 4-25, 760B2
PRICE, Richard
Bloodbrothers released 9-27, 969D3
PRICE, Vincent
Diversns & Delights opens 4-12, 887F1
PRICE Fixing—*See ANTITRUST*
PRICEL
Dymo foils takeover 5-12, 404C1
PRICE of Genius, The (play)
Opens 6-26, 887E2
PRICE Paper Co. Ltd.
Abitibi plans takeover 9-29, 772C3
PRICES and Price Indexes—*See appropriate subheads under ECONOMY; also commodity names*
PRICE Waterhouse & Co.
Issues '77 financial data; ranked 2d 84D1
PRIETO, Arnaldo
Collective bargaining OKd by govt 10-27, 879B2
PRIMA, Louis
Dies 8-24, 708C3
PRIMARIES—*See POLITICS—Elections (primaries)*
PRIME Time (recording)
Basie fund wins Grammy 2-24, 315F3
PRIMUS, Matter of
Nonprofit atty soliciting backed by Sup Ct 5-30, 430D2
PRINCE, Donald J.
Loses electn for Calif treas 11-7, 856A3
PRINCE, Harold
On 20th Century opens 2-19, 887C2
Little Night Music released 3-7, 619A3
PRINCE Edward Island (Canadian province)—*See CANADA*
PRINCE and the Pauper, The (book)
Film version released 3-2, 619C1
PRINCETON (N.J.) University
Goldberg named Cal tech pres 3-6, 172E3
Population Research rpt issued 4-15, 295D1
Black hole rptd in constellatn Scorpio 6-22, 654D2
Cigaret smoking rptd down 7-5, 727D1
Fusion research advance rptd 8-12, 653F2
PRINSLOO, Gert
Biko family sues 1-3, 20B3
PRINZ, Rosemary
Tribute opens 6-1, 887D3
PRIOR, James
Backs free mkt pay policy 10-10, 763C3
Lauds Vauxhall anti-strike votes 10-25, 816F1
PRISONERS of War (POWs)—*See under U.S. GOVERNMENT—ARMED Forces*
PRISONS—*See under CRIME*
PRISONS, Bureau of—*See under U.S. GOVERNMENT—JUSTICE*
PRITCHARD, Rep. Joel M. (R, Wash.)
Reelected 11-7, 852A4
PRITCHETT, James
Unicorn in Captivity opens 11-15, 1031C3

1979

PRESSLER, Sen. Larry (R, S.D.)
Pres bid tested 8-2, 594E2
Financial disclosure statement studied 9-1, 702B1
Enters GOP pres race 9-25, 724E1
PRESSMAN, Edward R.
Old Boyfriends released 3-21, 528C3
PRESSMAN, Michael
Boulevard Nights released 3-22, 528E1
PRESTON, Rich
Named WHA playoff MVP 5-20, 470G2
Winnipeg wins WHA title 5-20, 448B1*
PREVIN, Andre
Farrow divorces 1-31, 79B2
Every Good Boy opens 7-30, 711F2
PREYER, Rep. (Lunsford) Richardson (D, N.C.)
Loses health subcom chair 1-30, 86C3
PRICE, The (play)
Opens 4-19, 712B2
PRICE, Rev. Charles
On prayer bk revisn 9-12, 755A2
PRICE, Rep. Charles Melvin (D, Ill.)
Armed Svcs Com chrmn 1-24, 71C1
PRICE, George (Belizean prime minister)
UDP Dec '78 munic electn win rptd 1-19, 78B1
PUP wins parlt electns 11-21, 906G3-907C1
PRICE, Sir Leslie
China wheat deal rptd 1-22, 56E3
PRICE, Lonny
Class Enemy opens 6-18, 711C2
PRICE, Michael P.
Whoopee opens 2-14, 292F3
PRICE, Richard
Wanderers released 7-13, 820F3
PRICE Fixing—*See ANTITRUST Actions*
PRICES and Price Indexes—*See appropriate subheads under ECONOMY; also commodity names*
PRIDA, Dolores
Beggars Soap Opera opens 7-23, 711D1
PRIESAND, Sally J.
Resigns NY post 2-2, 176F1
PRIMARIES—*See POLITICS—Elections (primaries)*
PRINAIR (Puerto Rican International Airlines)
St Croix crash kills 8 7-24, FAA grounds 10-25, 830F2
PRINCE, Harold
Sweeney Todd opens 3-1, 292C3
Evita opens 9-25, 956A3
PRINCE Edward Island (Canadian province)—*See CANADA*
PRINCESS Daisy (book)
Paperback rights sale sets record 9-12, 755D3
PRINCETON, N.J.—*See NEW Jersey*
PRINCETON Gallery of Fine Arts
O'Keefe stolen paintings ordrd returned 7-27, 656G1
PRINCETON University
Rutgers football rivalry to end 1-20, 175D3
Gengler 2d in women's intercollegiate squash champs 3-4, 527D2
Taylor named to 3 Mile I probe 4-11, 275C1
Magnetic confinemt fusion advance rptd 6-14, 692E1
H-bomb letter printed 9-16, 9-18, Taylor denies chrgs 9-17, 714A1, C2; text of letter 714D1-717E3
Lewis wins Nobel Prize 10-17, 858G1
PRINTING & Engraving, Bureau of—*See under U.S. GOVERNMENT–TREASURY*
PRIOR, James
UK employment secy 5-5, 338F1
Sees union ldrs 6-25, 502F3
Govt proposes union curbs 7-9, 524B3
Urges trade union reforms 12-7, 949B2
PRISONER of Zenda, The (film)
Released 5-15, 820G2
PRISONERS of War—*See under U.S. GOVERNMENT–ARMED Forces*
PRISONS—*See under CRIME*
PRITCHARD, Rep. Joel M. (R, Wash.)
Vs neighborhoods panel rpt 3-15, 208B3
PRITIKIN, Nathan
Pritikin Program on best-seller list 6-3, 432B2; 7-1, 548C3; 8-5, 620C3; 9-2, 673C3; 10-14, 800C3
PRITIKIN Program, The (book)
On best-seller list 6-3, 432B2; 7-1, 548C3; 8-5, 620C3; 9-2, 673C3; 10-14, 800C3

1980

PRESSER, Jackie
Reagan transitn role queried, backed 12-15, 12-18, 955E3
PRESSLER, Sen. Larry (R, S.D.)
Ends pres bid 1-8, 13F3
Rejected Abscam bribe offers 2-3, 82A1, E1
PRESSMAN, Michael
Those Lips released 9-9, 836G3
PRESSON, H. Kent
Sees personal bankruptcy filing rise 3-25, 263C3
PRESTON, Billy
With You I'm Born Again on best-seller list 4-2, 280E3; 4-30, 359G3
PRETENDERS (recording)
On best-seller list 6-4, 448F3
PRETENDERS (singing group)
Album on best-seller list 6-4, 448F3
PRETTYMAN Jr., E. Barrett
Hired as Abscam spec counsel 2-13, 143E2
PREYER, Rep. (Lunsford) Richardson (D, N.C.)
Loses reelectn 11-4, 849G3
PRICE, Rep. Charles M. (D, Ill.)
Reelected 11-4, 842A4
PRICE, Marian
Freed 4-30, 619A2
PRICE Fixing—*See ANTITRUST Actions*
PRICE Indexes—*See under ECONOMY*
PRICE Waterhouse & Co.
Bahamas bank looting suit rptd 3-3, 229B1
Statistics Canada cleared 4-1, 272G3, 273B1
PRIDMORE, Coleman Blair
Acquitted 11-17, 898G2
PRIESTLEY, Jack
First Deadly Sin released 10-24, 836G2
PRIMARIES—*See POLITICS--Elections*
PRIME Rate—*See BANKS--Interest Rates*
PRIMER on Alcoholism (book)
Marty Mann dies 7-22, 608D2
PRINCE, Harold
Wins Tony 6-8, 692A3
PRINCESS Daisy (book)
On best-seller list 2-10, 120B3; 3-9, 200A8; 4-6, 280A3; 5-4, 359C3; 6-8, 448B3
PRINCETON (N.J.) University
Photocopy co sued by univ press 2-5, 119G3
Photocopy suit rptd setld 3-21, 376D3
'79 endowmt earnings rptd 3-24, 319B2
Boyd dies 5-28, 448C1
Walter Kaufman dies 9-4, 755E3
Fitch wins Nobel 10-14, 889C3
H Dodds dies 10-25, 876C1
PRINSENDAM (Dutch ocean liner)
Burns, 470 flee 10-4, 769C2
PRIOR, James
Cautns re labor reform 2-3, 98C1
Urges steel strike mediator 3-3, 193B3
Wage curbs rptd rejected 6-7, 444E3
June unemploymt sets mark 6-24, 498E1
PRISONS—*See CRIME--Prisons*
PRITCHARD, Rep. Joel M. (R, Wash.)
Reelected 11-4, 844A3
PRITIKIN, Nathan
Pritikin Program on best-seller list 2-10, 120D3; 4-6, 280C3
PRITIKIN Program, The (book)
On best-seller list 2-10, 120D3; 4-6, 280C3

1976

PRIVACY Issues—*See HUMAN & Civil Rights*

PRIVETTE, Coy C.
Wins primary runoff spot 8-17, 633F1
Loses runoff 9-14, 705E1
PROANO Tafur, Col. Rodolfo
Gets amnesty 1-28, 363C3
PROBLEM of Slavery in the Age of Revolution: 1770-1823, The (book)
Wins Natl Book Award 4-19, 292D3
PROFESSIONAL Educators of Los Angeles
Suit vs faculty desegregatn plan rptd 5-22, 453E2
PROFESSIONAL Golfer's Association of America (PGA)—*See GOLF*
PROHIBITION Party
Final pres vote tally 12-18, 979C2
PROJECT Haven—*See BAHAMA Islands*
PROKOFIEV, Yevgeny
On freer forgn press access 1-21, 76A3

1977

PRIVACY Issue—*See also MAIL Surveillance, WIRETAPPING*
IRS seizures curbed 1-12, 57G1
FBI watch on women's groups rptd 2-6, 423D1
Lawyers Guild suit vs US rptd 3-2, 423F1
Natl ID card studied, poll opposes 4-24, 4-27, 370B3, D3
SEC to open some corp payoff files 4-27, 502G3
CIA watch on Anderson rptd 5-4, 422G3
52 file suit in New Haven 5-12, 422D3
Sup Ct declines 2 freedom of info cases 5-16, 419C1
143 suits vs US rptd 5-22, 422A3
Natl Sci Acad exempt from disclosures 5-23, 444B3
FBI investigative guidelines sought 6-6, 481B1
NY contraceptive curbs voided 6-9, 501C2
Natl crime data svc under review 6-16, 480B3
ACLU files released by FBI 6-19, 481B1
Justice Dept warrantless searches curbed 6-21, 539A1
FBI raids Scientology offices 7-8, raids ruled illegal 7-27, 628A2
US comm submits rpt 7-12, 632B1
Libel suit vs NBC dismissed 7-12, 643C1
CIA mind-control tests revealed 8-1—8-9, 610D3
FBI-ACLU ties revealed 8-4, 628E1
Mondale addresses ABA conv 8-8, 630B1
US to keep Rhodesia info office open 8-26, 699B3
NY Times CIA file bid cited 9-12, 720E3
Police break-in case declined 10-3, 760B3
FBI domestic spying curb rptd 11-9, 861E2, F2
FBI Cointelpro papers released 11-21, 940C3
FBI Scientology search warrant ruled valid 12-1, use of documts blocked 12-8, 940G1, F2
Police rights vs traffic violators widened 12-5, 939B1
FBI probe attys clash with Bell 12-7, 940B1
Kissinger loses transcript ruling 12-8, 962F2
NIOSH med-data access upheld 12-22, 1008F2

PRIVATE de Garilhe, Dr. Michael
Antiviral drug rptd 8-10, 675B3
PRIVATE Eye (London magazine)
Goldsmith drops libel suit 5-16, 527B1
PROANO, Bishop Leonidas
Scores labor repressn 10-5, 823E3
PROCAINE Hydrochloride (Novocain)—*See MEDICINE—Drugs*
PROCTOR & Gamble Co., The
Folger ups coffee prices 2-25, 168F3; 3-14, 209F1; 3-30, 319C1
On '76 Fortune 500 list 340F1
Folger cuts coffee prices 5-12, 6-2, 458C1
Folger cuts coffee price 10-14, 876G2
PRODUCTIVITY—*See LABOR*
PROFESSIONAL Golfers' Association of America (PGA)—*See GOLF*
PROJECT Haven—*See BAHAMA Islands*
PROJECT Max (USAF computer system)—*See U.S. GOVERNMENT—AIR Force*
PROJECT Seafarer—*See SEAFARER, Project*

1978

PRIVACY Issue—*See also MAIL Surveillance, WIRETAPPING; also country names*
IRS computer projct rptd dropped 1-9, 15D1
Carter defines intell agency curbs, reactn 1-24, 49A3
Agnew case files released 3-3, 164F3
FBI destroying old criminal files 3-15, 186C3
Scientology challenge of FBI raid ruling rejctd 3-20, 205C3
IRS agent liability case review denied 3-20, 206B1
Fla press curb challenge refused by Sup Ct 3-20, 206B1
Student sex survey case review denied by Sup Ct 3-20, 206C1
Testimony thru illegal search backed by Sup Ct 3-21, 220G3
Gray, 2 other FBI ex-offcls indicted; disciplinary actn vs LaPrade, 68 agents asked 4-10, 261E3-262D1
LaPrade chrgs pol influence 4-13, 285B1
Broadcasters denied Nixon tapes by Sup Ct 4-18, 308C1
NY prison 'strip-frisk' search end ordrd 4-22, 440A2
OSHA warrantless searches curbed by Sup Ct 5-23, 405B2
Newsroom searches by police backed by Sup Ct 5-31, 429E3
Arson probe search warrants backed by Sup Ct 5-31, 431E1
Mine safety inspectn case remanded by Sup Ct 6-5, 431E2
FBI informant case declined by Sup Ct 6-12, 468D1
Wis U computer research secrecy order lifted 6-12, 513F3
Freedom of Info in NLRB cases barred by Sup Ct 6-15, 468F2
Cong immunity case refused by Sup Ct 6-26, 566F2
Press prison data access curbed 6-26, 566G2-D3
Evidence hearing rules drawn by Sup Ct 6-26, 566D3
FBI informants rptd at '68 Dem conv 7-3, 507E3
Sup Ct '77-78 voting trend noted 7-3, 566C1
Bell cited for contempt in FBI informants case 7-6, 507A2; order stayed 7-7, 524G3
LaPrade fired 7-6, 507G2
FBI '77 Scientology raids upheld 7-6, 554E1
Women rptrs gain locker room access 9-25, 1026B3
Presidential-papers act signed 11-4, 897D2
FBI urges file disclosure delay 11-8, 877F3-878A1
Douglas FBI file detailed 11-14, 877C3
A-plant ratings released 11-25, 940B3
Gray, 2 other FBI ex-offcls' dismissal motion denied 11-30, 939D3
FBI penalizes 4 in break-ins 12-5, 939F2
Police auto search power broadened by Sup Ct 12-5, 959F2
Pub employees adultery dismissal case declined by Sup Ct 12-11, 981A1
Press search shield bill proposed 12-13, 1029B3
Nixon data access upheld by Appeals Ct 12-21, 1011B3

PROCTER & Gamble Co., The
In Dow Jones indl avg 66F2 ★
Lowers Folger coffee price 3-9, 181C3
On '77 Fortune 500 list 5-8, 325F1
Folger sets Uganda coffee boycott 5-16, 416D3
PROCUNIER v. Navarette
Limited immunity for prison offcls backed 2-22, 126C2
PRODUCER Price Index (wholesale finished, intermediate, crude goods index)—*See ECONOMY—Prices*
PRODUCTIVITY—*See LABOR—Wages, Hours & Productivity*
PROFESSIONAL Football Writers of America—*See FOOTBALL*
PROFESSIONAL Golfers' Association (PGA)—*See GOLF*
PROFESSIONAL Groups—*See also groups names (e.g. AMERICAN Medical Association)*
PAC gifts to cong com chrmn rptd 12-24, 1008B1
PROGESTIN—*See MEDICINE-Drugs*
PROKES, Michael
Held in Guyana murder probe; rpts Jonestown-Sovt tie 11-28, 910F2, B3, 911A1
Contacts FBI in US, subpoenaed to Calif grand jury 12-28, 1000E2

1979

PRIVACY Issue—*See also country names*
A-test cancer link rptd ignored by PHS 1-8, 17B2
CIA UFO probe detailed 1-12, 93A1
Mil dischrg suit filed 1-19, 53F1
Fla Const 'sunshine' amendmt review refused by Sup Ct 1-22, 54F1
Tex abortn record access case declined by Sup Ct 1-22, 54A2
'50s CIA files made public, 'disposal' problems detailed 1-22, 55G1-C2
Carter seeks data disclosure curbs 1-25, 70C2
FBI agent's dismissal rescinded 1-26, 92F2
Calif ct OKs respirator removal 2-15, 291C2
Viet War era domestic spying rptd 3-9, 207B2
CIA considered ESP spies in '50s 3-11, 208D2
Bell contempt citatn overturned 3-19, 207E1
FBI informant loss rptd, disclosures scored 3-22, 232C2
Carter proposes legis 4-2, 264C3
Kissinger phone records case accepted by Sup Ct 4-16, 302B3
Reverse Freedom of Info suits curbed by Sup Ct 4-18, 345D3
US covert 'bugging' entry upheld by Sup Ct 4-18, 346B1
State Dept rpt finds Guyana cult probe neglect 5-3, 336A1
'Open-ended' warrants use curbed by Sup Ct 6-11, 478C3
Julius Rosenberg article publshd 6-16, 466C1
FDA Laetrile ban upheld by Sup Ct 6-18, 498B3
Warrantless phone surveillnc backed by Sup Ct 6-20, 516C1
Luggage search warrants backed by Sup Ct 6-20, 516C2
CIA spying on antiwar activists rptd 7-16, 561A2
Nixon tapes release approved 7-24, 561F2
FBI charter proposed 7-31, 599B2
ABA rejcts 3d party search limits 8-9, 8-15, 768D3
Viet vet study released 9-25, 725F1
Va men's room surveillnc case declined by Sup Ct 10-1, 768G1
NSA upheld on withholding data 10-29, 945C3
FBI memo re '50s Kissinger link disclosed 11-3, 870C2
Calif Laetrile ban declined by Sup Ct 11-13, 902F1
Extended searches curbed by Sup Ct 11-28, 944E2-C3

PRIVATE Account (race horse)
3d in Travers Stakes 8-18, 876G3
PRIVITERA v. California
Case declined by Sup Ct 11-13, 902E1
PROANO, Bishop Leonidas
Denies Pope scored 'liberatn theology' 2-1, 108C3
PRO Arts Inc. v. Factors Etc. Inc.
Presley poster dispute refused by Sup Ct 2-21, 128E3
PROCTER & Gamble Co., The
In Dow Jones indl avg 72F1
On '78 Fortune 500 list 5-7, 304E1
PROCTOR, Eugene
Sentncd in GSA kickback scandal 3-24, 3-26, 367A3
PROCTOR v. State Farm Mutual Automobile Insurance Co.
Auto insurnc wage rate ruling voided by Sup Ct 3-5, 184F3
PRODI, Romano
Italy Cabt excludes 3-20, 212D1
PRODUCER Price Index (wholesale finished, intermediate, crude goods index)—*See ECONOMY-Prices*
PRODUCTIVITY—*See LABOR—Wages, Hours & Productivity*
PROFESSIONAL Golfers' Association—*See GOLF*
PROFFER, Carl
USSR denies visa 8-29, 690B1
PROFFER, Ellendea
USSR denies visa 8-29, 690B1
PROFITT, Nicholas
Arrives Iran 8-15, ousted 8-16, 670D2
PROGRESSIVE, The (magazine)
Judge blocks H-bomb article 3-9, Knoll scores 3-14, 193A3-194A1; 3-26, 230A1
Justice Dept admits H-bomb documt security error 6-8, judge continues to block article publicatn 6-15, 713C1, E1
H-bomb article hearing order denied by Sup Ct 7-2, 559A1
Hansen H-bomb letter published 9-16, 9-18, 713G2; text 714E1-717E3
Justice Dept ends effort to stop H-bomb article publicatn, Knoll lauds 9-17, 713A1, G1
PROKES, Michael
Commits suicide 3-13, 220C1

1980

PRIVACY Issue
Terkel files case refused by Sup Ct 1-7, 15G3
FBI Seberg probe rptd extensive 1-9, 55C1
Canada freedom of info legis asked 1-11, 78G2
Medicaid abortn aid ban voided 1-15, 35D3
Agee suit by US asked 2-5, ct OKs 4-2, 268E2
IRS handwriting orders upheld by Sup Ct 2-20, 170E1
Charity solicitatn limit voided by Sup Ct 2-20, 170D2
Des Moines Register case refused by Sup Ct 2-25, 188A1
Kissinger records access blocked by Sup Ct 3-3, 209B3
Fed funded group info access curbed by Sup Ct 3-3, 210B1
Freedom of Info ct order bar backed by Sup Ct 3-19, 250B1
Dow chrgs EPA spying 3-25, 387B3
Salisbury sues US 4-10, 459F1
Warrantless home arrests curbed by Sup Ct 4-15, 305F3
Fonda-Hayden data case refused by Sup Ct 5-12, 426A3
DEA detainmt procedure backed by Sup Ct 5-27, 454A1
Illegal search protectn narrowed by Sup Ct 6-25, 541A1
'79-80 Sup Ct term ends, decisns cited 7-2, 540E2
US GOP platform text 7-15, 536C3
Canada freedom of info legis introduced 7-16, 562E3
Arrest warrant 3d party searches case accepted by Sup Ct 10-6, 782C3
Newsroom searches curb signed 10-14, 835F1-C2
Arab boycott data released 10-20, 801B1
Laetrile ban challenge declined by Sup Ct 10-20, 807G1
La itinerant worker registratn ruling affirmed by Sup Ct 10-20, 807D2
Ferrigno wins suit 11-3, 890E2
2 FBI ex-offcls convicted 11-6, 884G1
Conn phone harassmt law challenge declined by Sup Ct 12-1, 918G2
Med records bill defeated by House 12-1, 982C2
2 Scientologists sentncd 12-19, 997B3

PRIVATE Account (race horse)
Wins Widner Handicap 3-1, 447F3
PRIVATE Benjamin (film)
Top-grossing film 12-3, 948G3
PROCTER & Gamble Co., The
In Dow Jones indl avg 76F1
'79 top TV advertiser 4-4, 376A2
FTC ends detergent indus probe 5-12, 703A2
Rely tampon, toxic-shock syndrome linked 9-17; recall ordered 9-22, 726G2-E3
Harness retires; Smale, Butler replace 12-9, 959B1
PRODUCER Price Index—*See ECONOMY (U.S.)—Price Indexes*
PRODUCTIVITY—*See LABOR (U.S.)—Wages, Hours & Productivity*
PROEBER, Martina
Wins Olympic medal 7-21, 623F3
PROFESSIONAL Golfers' Association (PGA)—*See GOLF*
PROGRESSIVE, The (magazine)
Morris Rubin dies 8-8, 676E2

1976

PROSTITUTION
Howe arrested 6-12, chrgs entrapmt 6-13, 434G1-A2
9 indicted in Alaska scheme 7-8, 816F2-A3
Howe convicted 7-23, 552A1
Howe conviction upheld 8-24, 636E2
Brazil death squads linked 12-26, 997G3

PROTESTANTISM
'75 US church attendance rptd 1-3, 32A3
Rabbis seek Vatican-Israel ties 2-8, 272A3
Northern Ireland Dispute—*See NORTHERN Ireland*

PROTOCOLS of the Elders of Zion, The (book)
Argentina circulatn rptd 8-15—8-30, 672B2
PROVENZANO, Anthony (Tony Pro)
Indicted 6-23, 460A1
Fed charges dismissed 10-29, 971B1
PROVIDENCE, R. I.—*See RHODE Island*
PROVIDENCE Bulletin (newspaper)
Ford endorsement rptd 10-30, 831F2
PROVIDENCE Journal (newspaper)
Ford endorsement rptd 10-30, 831F2
PROVOST, Terry
Held in Indian shooting 5-5, 384F2
PROXMIRE, Sen. William (D, Wis.)
Criticisms of AF waste rptd 1-1, 6D3
GAO rpt scores defns contracting 1-11, 70G3-71C1
On bank regulatory reform 1-12, 111G1, F2
Gets FDIC bank 'problem' list 1-23, 112B2
Rockwell's Pentagon guests listed 2-3, 3-17, 200F3, 201A3
Burns offers bank data compromise 2-6, 112E1
Sees bank undercapitalizatn 2-6, 113C2
Questns Pentagon Sovt arms spending data 3-5, 182G1
On US bribe disclosure plan, intl pact 3-5, 200E1
Rickover vs Navy shipyd paymts 6-7, 453G3
Richardson letter on forgn paymts legis 6-11, 668E3
Banking com OKs anti-bribery bill 6-22, 668B3
GAO scores Treas anti-bias action 7-1, 943D3
Unopposed in primary 9-14, 705C2
Sen OKs anti-bribery bill 9-15, 708B1
Chrgs Korea bid-rigging 10-27, 982A2-A3
Reelected 11-2, 820D1, 824A1, 828D3
Scores Burns re money policy 11-11, 865C2
PRUDENTIAL Federal Savings Association
Sued for home-loan sex bias 4-15, 285G1
PRUDKOV, Oleg
Accuses US newsmen 5-26, 371D3
PRYOR, Gov. David (D, Ark.)
Seconds Mondale at conv 7-15, 506B3
Reelected 11-2, 820A3, 821F3, 831C1
PRYOR, Richard
Wins Grammy 2-28, 460C3
PSYCHOLOGY
Shaffer dies 7-20, 716F3
Martha Wolfenstein dies 11-30, 1015B3

1977

PROPANE—*See GAS, Natural*
PROPRANOLOL (Inderal)—*See MEDICINE—Drugs*

PROSTITUTION
'70-76 indictmts of pub offcls rptd 2-10, 162C3
Child abuse arrests 4-11, 4-26; abuse schemes rptd 5-15—5-18, House legis hearings 5-20, 5-27, 432G1-G3
Mafia control rptd 5-16, 568E1
CIA mind-control test revealed 8-1—8-9, 611C1
PROTECTIONISM—*See FOREIGN Trade*
PROTEIN, Liquid—*See FOOD*

PROTESTANTISM
Carter role re S Korea rights urged 4-19, 305C3
Charismatic conf held 7-20—7-24, 620A3, D3
Northern Ireland Dispute—*See NORTHERN Ireland*

PROUST, Marcel (1871-1922)
'77 fall fashions rptd 7-29, 1022E1
PROVENZANO, Anthony (Tony Pro)
Kickback chrg dropped 11-11, 928C1
Reindicted 12-19, 991B3
PROVIDENCE, R.I.—*See RHODE Island*
PROVIDENCE College
Dorm fire kills 7 12-13, 1023B3
PROWSE, Russell
On Australia SRD rate hike 2-3, 113E2
PROXMIRE, Sen. William (D, Wis.)
On Sovt mil aims estimate 1-5, 40B1
Asks tax cut 1-6, 12D2
Questns Harris 1-10; Lance, Harris confirmed 1-20, 34C1, F2
'76 special interest contributns rptd 1-15, 128F3, 129D1
Votes vs Bell 1-25, 52A3
Jt Chiefs deny Sovt mil edge 1-30, 70E2, B3
Vance backs boycott curbs 2-28, 167D1
Rpts on defns industry hiring 4-12, 344C1
B-1 cost estimate hiked 5-18, 421B1
Sen bars HEW-Labor funds cut 6-28, 515G2
Accuses Lance, Lance vows compliance 7-15, 574A1
Issues USSR defns spending rpt, sees tech lag 8-22, 673E3
Scores contractor's gifts to mil, space 10-24, 920C2
PRUDENTIAL Insurance Co. of America
Minority, women job-hiring goals rptd 1-10, 278C3
Sup Ct declines employer records case 5-16, 419D1
PRYCE, Jonathan
Wins Tony 6-5, 452D1
PRYOR, Gov. David (D, Ark.)
Names Hodges to Sen seat 12-10, 1005A3
PRYOR, Greg
Traded to Red Sox 12-14, 990G1
PSYCHIATRY—*See MEDICINE—Mental Health*
PSYCHOLOGICAL Association, American
Non-ERA state boycott rptd 11-14, 918C1 ★
PSYCHOLOGY
David Krech dies 7-14, 604C3
Aleksandr Luria dies 8-16, 696C3
William Sheldon dies 9-19, 788F2
D Slesinger dies 10-13, 872G2

1978

PROLL, Astrid
Arrested in UK 9-15, 725A2
PROMISE, The (book)
On best-seller list 6-4, 460D3
PROMISE, The (play)
Opens 3-8, 760B3
PRONOVOST, Marcel
Fired as Sabres coach 12-4, 991D1
PROPANE—*See GAS, Natural*
PROPRANOLOL (Inderal)—*See MEDICINE—Drugs*
PROPERTY Taxes—*See TAXES*
PROPOSITION 13 (Jarvis-Gann Amendment)—*See TAXES—Reform & Tax Cut Proposals*
PROPPER, Eugene M.
2 Chileans sought in Letelier murder probe 2-21, 146C2
In Chile; identifies Letelier murder suspects 3-20, 209B3
Townley, Fernandez questnd 4-1, 266B3
Visits Chile 5-22—5-25, interior min scores 5-26, 452D1
Death threat rptd 12-14, 1015A1
PROSTITUTION
Child abuse curbs clear Cong 1-24, 82D3; 2-6, 218A2
US rep pleads not guilty 4-6, 265F1-B2
Child abuse extensn signed 4-24, 323C3
Victimless crime study issued 9-11, 842B2
PROTECTIONISM—*See FOREIGN Trade*

PROTESTANTISM—*See also specific denominations*
Angola populatn cited 87E3
US '53, '78 cong membership compared 1-30, 107F2
Israel conversn study asked 2-1, 294B2
Argentina orders non-Catholics register 2-14, 208E1
Laity role rptd expanding 2-19, 294C3
China curbs rptd eased 2-26, 294E1
Female clergy survey rptd 3-23, 295A2
French survey rptd 3-24, 352G2
E Ger clergy score schl mil drills 6-25, 648G2
Westminister mass protested 7-6, 557D3
'Test-tube baby' reactn rptd 7-25, 597E1
E Ger pastor kills self 9-17, 840F3
E Ger synod rptd vs student mil training 9-21, 840G3
Latin church cncl meets, asks Nicaragua pres resign 10-13, 823D3
Church ldr asks US oust Somoza 11-8, 883E3
Northern Ireland Dispute—*See NORTHERN Ireland*

PROTHRO, Tommy
Fired as Chargers coach 9-25, 1024A3
PROUVOST, Jean
Dies 10-17, 888D3
PROVAL, David
Nunzio released 5-13, 619C3
PROVENZANO, Anthony (Tony Pro)
Convicted in kickback case 3-25, 232B2
Convicted of Castellito murder 6-14, sentncd to life 6-21, 480B2
Sentenced for kickbacks 7-11, 560D2
PROVENZANO, Josephine
Gets Teamsters post 6-23, 560F2
PROVENZANO, Salvatore
Niece gets Teamsters post 6-23, 560F2
PROVIDENCE (R.I.) University
Mullaney to coach Brown 4-3, 272G2
PROXMIRE, Sen. William (D, Wis.)
Vs NYC fed aid renewal 1-4, crisis role cited 86E2, 87A1
Queries Miller re Textron-Iran paymt 1-24—2-28, vs FRB confirmatn 3-2, 3-3, 161E1-B3
Asks Sun Oil Becton purchase probe 1-27, 66B1
Scores Carter on arms sales plan 2-1, 106A3
Votes for Panama Canal neutrality pact 3-16, 177E2
Votes for 2d Canal pact 4-18, 273B1
GAO clears Lockheed on overbilling chrg 6-22, 493C3
Scores Navy 'bailout' of Gen Dynamics, Litton 7-6, 528B3
Vs '79 arms authorzn 7-11, 526B3
NYC aid compromise reached 7-13, Carter signs bill 8-8, 608C1, B3
Endangered Species Act revised 7-19, 551F2
Calls for SBA abolitn 11-20, 919C3
PRUDENTIAL Insurance Co. of America
MacNaughton sets retiremt 2-15; Beck succeeds as chrmn, chief exec 9-1, 808G3
PRUITT, Greg
NFL '77 rushing ldr 1-1, 56B3
PRYOR, Gov. David (D, Ark.)
Faces Sen primary runoff 5-30, 426G1
Wins runoff 6-13, 467E1
Wins US Sen seat 11-7, 846G1, 848C1, 855G1
Outspent Kelly 71-1 11-15, 898D1
PRYOR, Rashard
Blue Collar released 2-9, 618D3
PSA—*See PACIFIC Southwest Airlines*
PSYCHIATRY—*See MEDICINE—Mental Health*
P.S. Your Cat Is Dead! (play)
Opens 3-22, 887F2
PTA, National—*See NATIONAL PTA*

1979

PROMISE, The (film)
Released 3-7, 528D3
PROMISES in the Dark (film)
Released 11-2, 1008B1
PROPERTY Taxes—*See TAXES*
PROPHECY (film)
Released 6-15, 820A3
Top-grossing film 6-27, 548G3
PROPOSITION 13 (Jarvis-Gann Amendment)—*See TAXES—Reform & Tax Cut Proposals*
PROPOXYPHENE (Darvon)—*See MEDICINE & Health—Drugs*
PROPPER, Eugene M.
Letelier murder trial opens 1-9, jury chosen 1-12, 19A3
Letelier case data curbed by '78 US-Chile pact 1-23, 74G3
PROPRIETARY Association
Methapyrilene drugs recalled 6-8, 471F1

PROSTITUTION
Wyo '78 investigatn cited 2-7, 156B1
Newton murder case ends in mistrial 3-24, 239D1
Iran executns held 7-12–7-13, 544C3
Tax loss on illegal income estimated 8-31, 665A3
NYC rpt reviewed 10-9, 'John Hour' debuts 10-23, 887E1
Minneapolis press expose 10-18, 887G1-B2
'Hillside Strangler' sentncd, accomplice chrgd 10-19, 10-22, 818G2
Australia sets new drug unit 11-6, 870D2

PROTESTANTISM—*See also specific denominations*
'78 church attendance rptd 1-5, 24D1
RC abortn stand scored by NY clergy 1-23, 63B3
Mozambique oppositn rptd 2-8, 215B3
China schl reimbursemt set 3-16, 218A1
Baptism rites agrmt reached 3-31, 375F2
2 PR mins arrested in Navy protest 5-19, 385D3
Burundi expels missnaries 6-12, 470D1
US religious tolerance gains rptd 8-4, 639C3
Pope in US, holds ecumenical prayer svc 10-7, 760A1
Abortn, womens ordinatn poll rptd 11-11, 930A2

PROTOPOPOV, Oleg
Defects to Switzerland 9-18, 721B3
Gets Swiss asylum 10-30, 939G3
PROVENZANO, Anthony (Tony Pro)
Indicted re racketeering 2-22, 155F3
'78 Castellito murder convictn upset 6-7, 491F3
Sentenced re extortion 7-10, 548E1
PROVIDENCE (R.I.) College
In Big East basketball conf 5-29, 526G3
PROVO, Utah—*See UTAH*
PROWSE, Philip
Chinchilla opens 6-4, 711B2
PROXMIRE, Sen. William (D, Wis.)
Banking Com chrmn 1-23, 71C2
Scores SALT treaty 3-4, 258A2
Neighborhoods panel issues rpt 3-15, 208B3
Libel suit rights broadened by Sup Ct 6-26, 540F2
Votes vs trade bill 7-23, 646G3
Votes vs Miller Treas apptmt 8-2, 627B2
Praises Volcker policies 9-26, 745A2
Asks Textron probe 10-31, 923G2
Scores Carter Chrysler rescue plan 11-1, 845G2
Criticizes Goldschmidt 12-6, 984D1
PRUITT Jr., Sherman
Indicted on paymts chrg 11-9, 886A2
PRYOR, Sen. David (D, Ark.)
In USSR re SALT 8-28–8-30, 658D1
PRYOR, Richard
Richard Pryor Live released 2-15, 174E3
PSORIASIS—*See MEDICINE–Diseases*
PSYCHIATRY—*See MEDICINE–Mental Health*
PSYCHOLOGICAL Association, American
SAT decline, '50s A-fallout linked 9-17, 747B2

1980

PROLL, Astrid
Sentenced, freed 2-22, 154E1
PROM Night (film)
Released 8-15, 675C3
PROPERTY Tax—*See TAXES*
PROPOXYPHENE (Darvon)—*See MEDICINE--Drugs & Health-Care Products*
PROPP, Brian
In NHL All-Star game 2-5, 198G2

PROSTITUTION
Va sterilizatn program rptd 2-23, 158E3
Libertarian pres candidate cites stance 10-28, 818A3
Nev voters endorse legalization 11-4, 847D3

PROTESTANTISM—*See also specific denominations*
'79 church attendance rptd 1-4, 8C1
US Bible reading survey rptd 1-18, 157A2
Rev Buttrick dies 1-23, 104A2
Swiss reject church-state separatn 3-2, 233C1
Citibank ties cut re S Africa loans 3-24, 277G3
US intercommunion poll rptd 4-4, 413E2
US evangelicals profiled 7-11—9-15, 815F3
Pope in W Ger, seeks ecumenical ties 11-15—11-19, 904F3-905A3
Consultation on Church Union (COCU)
Unity mtg ends, common ministry OKd 1-24, 156B2

PROVIDOKHINA, Tatyana
Wins Olympic medal 7-27, 624A2
PROXMIRE, Sen. William (D, Wis.)
Asks Miller-Textron spec prosecutor 2-8, 2-10, 145E1-B2
Vs tax cut 2-27, 168G2
Miller spec prosecutor rejctd 3-11, 185D2, G2
Vs Carter anti-inflatn plan 3-17, 201E2
Settles libel suit 3-24, pays legal costs 5-29, 470D3
Eximbank loan policy hearings 5-10—5-13; urges GAO probe 10-1, 989C1, E1
Probes Hunt bank deals; scores Comex, studies FRB regulatn 5-29—5-30, 425E1-B3
Scores intell oversight bill 6-3, 458C3, F3
Fla banks tied to drug money 6-5, 502A1
Vs NYC loan guarantees 9-10, 743F1
Housing, community dvpt authrzn clears Cong 9-30, signed 10-8, 804C2
On NYC loan oppositn 9-30; Carter signs funds guarantee 10-1, funds released 10-2, 826B2, E2
PRUDENTIAL Insurance Co. of America
FBI Brilab probe rptd 2-8—2-9, 111B3
Tex Brilab indictments 6-12, 454A3
PRUDHOE Bay—*See ALASKA*
PRUITT, Mike
NFL '79 rushing ldr 1-5, 8B3
PRUNEYARD Shopping Center v. Robins
Case decided by Sup Ct 6-9, 512A2
PRUSSIAN State Museum (West Berlin)
Titian forgeries chrgd 2-26, 472B3
PRYOR, Richard
Burned in blast 6-9, released from hospital 7-25, 638C1
In God We Trust released 9-26, 836C3
Stir Crazy released 12-12, 1003D2
PSINAKIS, Steve
Chrgd in Marcos murder plot 8-5, 672F3
PSYCHIATRY—*See MEDICINE--Mental Health*
PSYCHOLOGY—*See also MEDICINE--Mental Health*
Jean Piaget dies 9-16, 756E1

1976

PUBLIC Broadcasting, Corporation for—*See BROADCASTING, Corporation for Public*
PUBLIC Broadcasting Service (PBS)
Grossman elected pres 1-8, 80F2
Muskie rebuts Ford message 1-21, 40F1
OKs to pres debate rules 9-18, 703C2
PUBLIC Citizen Litigation Group
Backs Reagan protest re Kissinger 5-14, 359E1
PUBLIC Citizens Forum
Carter addresses 8-9, 584E3, 585A2
PUBLIC Employes, Coalition of American
AFSCME quits AFL-CIO unit 2-15, 154B1
PUBLIC Health Association, American
Carter addresses 10-19, 785B2
PUBLIC Interest Research Group
Scores bank diversificatn 7-5, 495B2-A3
PUBLIC Opinion, American Institute of—*See GALLUP Poll*
PUBLIC Service Electric & Gas Co.
Offshore A-plant OKd 4-9, 284A2
PUBLIC Service of New Mexico
SEC lists paymts 5-12, 728E2
PUBLIC Utilities—*See UTILITIES, Public*

PUBLIC Works—*See also CONSTRUCTION, ROADS*
House OKs pub works bill 1-29, 93C3; Ford vetoes 2-13, 127E3; comments 2-17, 129B3; Sen sustains 2-19, 135C2
Ford vs pub works funds 1-31, 87F3
Sen OKs expanded bill 4-13, 283B1
Dem platform text 6-15, 469D3
Cong OKs revised pub works bill 6-23, Ford vetoes 7-6, 518B2
Mayors back bill 7-1, 493E1
'77 water, power funds signed 7-12, 517E1
Revised pub works bill veto overridden 7-22, 533E2
Cong OKs funds 9-22, 727F3; signed 10-1, 982F1
Cong extends depressed area aid 9-29, 765E1; signed 10-12, 982G1
'77-78 army engineer projects signed 10-22, 835A2
Mayors urge jobs prgrm 12-14, 937A3

PUBLISHING Industry—*See also LITERATURE, PRESS*
Canada-Reader's Digest ad tax agrmt 2-3, 116E3
Sen OKs copyright revisn 2-10, 152C2
Canada ad tax bill OKd, Time halts editn 2-25, 188G2
FTC rules vs Britannica co 3-26, 235E3
US files consent decree vs 21 7-27, 989D1
GOP platform text 8-18, 608B2
Cong clears copyright revisns 9-30, 764E3; signed 10-19, 982G1
Obituaries
Joseph, Richard 9-30, 970B2
Kern, Harold 2-19, 192E3
Kirchwey, Freda 1-3, 56E3
Leventhal, Albert 1-6, 56E3
Lippincott, Joseph 10-22, 970C2
Newman, Cecil 2-7, 160G3
Snyder, Jerome 5-2, 524F3

1977

PUBLIC Affairs Analysts Inc.
Panama Canal treaty promotn rptd 3-24, 379B2
PUBLIC Broadcasting Corp. (PBC)
Wallis electd chrman 3-9, 396D3
PUBLIC Broadcasting Service (PBS)
Powell on MacNeil-Lehrer Rpt 8-23, 649D2
Carter seeks more funds 10-6, 846B1
PUBLIC Citizen Inc.
Claybrook confrmd to Transport post 4-6, 272G2
Health Research Group
Files DES suit 4-25, 431B3
Phenformin ban rptd asked 7-25, 603D2
FAA rejects flight crew smoking ban 9-1, 778F3
DBCP curbed, plea cited 9-8, 723B3
PUBLIC Citizens Litigation Group
A-plant accident liability limit voided 3-31, 277D2
PUBLIC Gas Association, American
'76 gas price hikes upheld 6-16, 464D2
PUBLIC Grain Elevator of New Orleans Inc.
Fined 2-8, 113E1
PUBLIC Health Association, American
Abortn alternatives proposed 7-19, 786D3
PUBLIC Health Service—*See under U.S. GOVERNMENT*
PUBLIC Interest Campaign
Natl Sci Acad exempt from disclosures 5-23, 444B3
PUBLIC Interest Research Group
Hudson R found toxic 9-28, 762A2
PUBLIC Justice, Committee for
Backs FBI curbs 2-15, 157C3
PUBLIC Opinion—*See specific poll names (e.g., GALLUP, HARRIS); country names*
PUBLIC Policy Research, American Enterprise Institute for
Ford joins 3-25, 236A3
Ford addresses 12-20, 976D3
PUBLIC Relations
John Hill dies 3-17, 264G2
PUBLIC Service Co. of New Hampshire
Seabrook A-plant constructn halted 3-31, 344C3
Seabrook A-plant OKd 6-17, 498E2
PUBLIC Transit Association, American
Adams backs mass-transit fund 10-12, 860C3
PUBLIC Utilities—*See UTILITIES, Public*
PUBLIC Works—*See also ROADS*
Carter plans jobs boost 1-7, 5G1
US Sup Ct upholds NY jobs law 1-10, 57E1
Ford '78 budget proposals 1-17, 33D2
Carter revises econ aid plan 1-27, 52F1; submits to Cong 1-31, 75A2
Carter plan debated 2-1—2-4, 89E2, C2
Sen creates new com 2-4, 90F1, D3, 91C1
House, Sen OK prelim expansn bills 2-24, 3-10, 174G1
Cong sets new '77 budget levels 3-3, 174D1
Carter energy plan 4-20, 290G1; fact sheet 292C1
Expansn bill clears Cong 5-3, 365E1; Carter signs 5-13, 380D3
Econ aid funds clear Cong 5-5, 365E2; Carter signs 5-13, 380D3
Carter, Cong water projct differences eased 6-15, 459E3
CETA extensn signed 6-15, 500F3
'78 appropriatns clears Cong 7-25, 592F2; Carter signs 8-8, 609D2
Expansn bill minority quota provisn challenged 10-31, 978F3-979C1
AFL-CIO urges job prgrams 12-12, 961C1
PUBLISHERS, Association of American (formerly American Book Publishers Council)
Douglas Black dies 5-15, 452D2
Knowlton hosts USSR dissidents 9-8, 766B1
US bars USSR book pact 12-7, 955D2
PUBLISHING Industry—*See also LITERATURE, PRESS*
Solzhenitsyn forms Vt firm 1-21, 140F3
Hustler publisher sentncd 2-8, 118A2
Paperback record sum rptd 3-1, 356A2
Doubleday sued by Haley 3-16, black writer 4-22, 356D1, G1
1st ¼ profits rptd up 4-28, 668F3
Haley sued 5-24, 643E1
Johnson rptd 2d largest black-owned firm 6-1, 519F3
Time to buy Book-of-the-Month 7-5, 519D2
Presley record book ordr rptd 8-20, 696D1
USSR hosts book fair 9-6—9-14, 765C3
J Onassis quits Viking 10-13, 927B3
Reader's Digest sex-bias suit setld 11-4, 979A2
US bars USSR pact 12-7, 955C2
Time plans cable-TV purchase 12-22, 1004C3
Nation magazine sold 12-22, 1004F3
Lippincott OKs Harper & Row bid 12-23, 1004D3
Obituaries
Amaury, Emilien 1-2, 84E2
Black, Douglas 5-15, 452D2
Foley, Martha 9-5, 788A1
Gainza Paz, Alberto 12-26, 1024F1
Jain, Shanti Prasad 10-27, 872D2
Kaminstein, Abraham 9-10, 788C1
Mardersteig, Giovanni 12-27, 1024D2
Moorhouse, Clifford 2-17, 164D3
Russell Jr, Arthur 12-4, 1024B3
Thieriot, Chas deYoung 3-21, 264F3
Thorman, Donald 11-30, 952F3

1978

PUBLIC Broadcasting, Corporation for
Fleming named pres 9-14, 759E3
PUBLIC Broadcasting Service (PBS)
Minow named chrmn 2-5, 335F2
Moyers interviews Carter 11-13, 914D2
PUBLIC Citizens Inc.
Health Research Group
HEW anti-smoking plan scored 1-11, 23G2
PUBLIC Debt—*See under U.S. GOVERNMENT—BUDGET*
PUBLIC Health Service—*See under U.S. GOVERNMENT*
PUBLIC Opinion—*See specific poll names (e.g., GALLUP, HARRIS); country names*
PUBLIC Relations
Venez pol parties hire US experts 5-5, 395G1
Rafshoon to join Carter staff 5-18, 386E3
Obituaries
Sonnenberg, Benjamin (rptd) 9-18, 778A2
PUBLIC Service Co. of Colorado
FTC credit-chrg setlmt rptd 5-3, 434G1
PUBLIC Service Co. of New Hampshire
Seabrook A-plant protested 6-24—6-26, 494C1
Seabrook A-plant halt ordrd 6-30, 529E3
Seabrook A-plant constructn OKd 8-10, 609G2
Seabrook work order upheld 8-22, 941E1
NH rejcts Seabrook bond guarantee, shutdown seen 12-8, 1009G2-B3
PUBLIC Service Electric & Gas Co.
Offshore A-plant contract canceled 12-19, 1009D3
PUBLIC Utilities—*See UTILITIES, Public*

PUBLIC Works
AFL-CIO offers stimulus plan 2-20, 141F3
Paymt bond coverage for sub-subcontactors denied 2-22, 126A3
Humphrey-Hawkins bill passes House 3-16, 182C2
Carter unveils urban-aid plan 3-27, 217B3
Hart on arms bill 7-12, 526E2
Endangered Species Act revised 7-19, 551A2
Budget cleared after cong dispute 9-23, 733G3
Minority business quotas upheld by NY ct 9-23, 811E2
Carter threatens veto 9-28, 751G3
Carter vetoes bill, House upholds veto 10-5, 765A1-D2, 769B2
Humphrey-Hawkins bill cleared 10-15, 808A1; Carter signs 10-27, 873A2
Carter cites veto 11-6, 862C1
Chicago sex bias suit setld 11-17, 1006G2

PUBLISHERS, Association of American
Presents Natl Book Awards 4-10, 315C2
PUBLISHER'S Weekly (magazine)
Best-sellers list 9-4, 708B1; 10-9, 800A3; 11-6, 887F3

PUBLISHING Industry—*See also LITERATURE, PRESS*
Rizzoli Rome office firebombed 1-4, 19C2
Cowles Communicatns to liquidate 1-6, 75F3-76A1
US sues CIA ex-analyst Snepp 2-15, 129C1
CBS makes IMS bid 2-15, rejected 2-22, 185B1
Burger warns re media 'empire' 4-26, 343G3
Time Inc to buy Inland Container 5-19, 403G2-C3
Mgt gains for women rptd 5-22, 554F3
Dymo OKs Esselte takeover 5-26, 404B1
US sues CBS, seeks Fawcett divestiture 6-1, 510E3
Popular Library, Fawcett '76 sales rptd 6-1, 510F3
Puzo paperback rights sold for record sum 6-16, 620C2
Snepp to lose book profits, Random House scores 7-7, 527F2
'More' ceases publicatn, merges with Columbia Journalism Review 7-21, 672G1
Benchley book record movie price rptd 9-1, 759D2
Book club FTC complaint rptd setld 9-7, 702G1
Roots plagiarism suit dismissed 9-21, 759A3
Search shield bill proposed 12-13, 1029D3
Haley settles Courlander plagiarism suit 12-14, 1029E3
Obituaries
Ascoli, Max 1-1, 96C1
Emmerich Sr, John Oliver 8-17, 708F2
Fischer, John 8-18, 708F2
Poynter, Nelson 6-15, 540F3
Prouvost, Jean 10-17, 888D3

1979

PUBLIC Broadcasting, Corporation for (CPB)
Carnegie Comm rpt urges chngs 1-30, 78D2
Nixon Admin moves disclosed 2-24, 194C1, B2
Fleming on Pay Advisory Com 10-16, 829F2
PUBLIC Broadcasting Service (PBS)
Nixon Admin moves disclosed 2-24, 194D1
US House coverage begins 3-19, 208E1
Reorganizatn approved 6-25, 588C1
PUBLIC Citizens Inc.
3 Mile I A-probe urged 4-5, 260B3
Health Research Group
HEW rejcts Darvon ban 2-15, 138A3
Lawsuits curbed by judge 3-14, 308A2
PUBLIC Health Service—*See under U.S. GOVERNMENT*
PUBLIC Interest Law Center (Philadelphia, Pa.)
Phila police scored 4-19, 310B3
PUBLIC Opinion—*See specific poll names (e.g., GALLUP, HARRIS); country names*
PUBLIC Service Co. of Colorado
Ft St Vrain A-plant dispute rptd settled 4-3, 344E2
PUBLIC Utilities—*See UTILITIES, Public*
PUBLISHERS, Association of American
Presents Natl Book Awards 4-23, 356F1
Natl Book Award chngs set 6-27; writers protest, dirs defend 8-8, 8-9, 755F3-756C1
US cancels Moscow emb receptn 9-2; Hoffman scores book seizures 9-4, 690B1, G1
PEN Club joins book awards protest 11-25, 1007A2

PUBLISHING Industry—*See also LITERATURE, PRESS*
W Ger cos fined for price-fixing 2-7, 101B1
Flynt convictd in retrial 3-28, 240C1
Natl Book Award chngs set 6-27; writers protest, dirs defend 8-8, 8-9, 755F3-756C1
Time Inc to sponsor art show 7-19, 672C2
USSR hosts intl book fair; publshrs barred, deals set 9-4—9-10, 689F3-690C2
Krantz paperback rights sold for record sum 9-12, 755D3
Harcourt Brace sues Goldwater 9-14, 859G3
Press freedom insurnc plan set 9-27, 859F2
Arnheiter libel cases declined by Sup Ct 10-29, 884A2
McGraw-Hill recall of Iran book rptd 11-10, 886F3
PEN Club joins book awards protest 11-25, 1007A2
Novelist libel case refused by Sup Ct 12-3, 964F1
Mergers & Acquisitions
Amer Express seeks to buy McGraw-Hill 1-9, 15G3
Mattel to buy Westn Publishing 1-9, 16B1
Amer Express bid rejctd by McGraw-Hill 1-15, tender offer filed 1-16, 53B2-C3
McGraw-Hill rejcts sweetened Amer Express bid 1-31; proxy battle dropped 2-23, offer expires 3-1, 151B3
S Africa '74 Washn Star bid rptd 3-21, 213F1; 4-2, 270C1
Rolling Stone, Look merge 5-7, 430E3
McGraw-Hill buys Data Resources 8-28, 682F3

1980

PUBLIC Broadcasting Service (PBS)
'Death of a Princess' protested 5-8, aired 5-12; US cts rule on telecast 5-9, 5-12; Nielsen rating rptd 5-13, 375E2-376A1
Moyers moderates pres TV debate 9-21, 721C3
Grossman plays down RCTV-BBC deal 12-11, 1002E3
PUBLIC Citizens Inc.
Litigatn Group cited re children's work curbs 3-20, 227F1
Health Research Group
US to curb Darvon productn 4-24, 358E2
PUBLIC Health Association, American
MD sentncd in Koch assault 6-6, 639G2
PUBLIC Health Service—*See under U.S. GOVERNMENT*
PUBLIC Opinion Research Institute
Israelis vs new setlmts 3-25, 219B2
PUBLIC Relations
Doris Bernays dies 7-11, 608D1
PUBLIC Service Electric & Gas Co.
Salem A-plant gets start-up license 4-16, 332F1
PUBLIC Utilities—*See UTILITIES, Public*

PUBLIC Works
Appropriatn clears Cong 6-25, 9-10, signed 10-1, 803D2
Summer jobs progrm rptd 6-30, 496A1
Boston settles US job bias suit 12-5, 962B3

PUBLISHERS, Association of American
Presents Amer Book Awards 5-1, 692E1

PUBLISHING Industry
Photocopy co sued 2-5, 119F3
Macmillan chrmn resigns, successor named 2-11, 224G3
Playboy audit, repayments revealed 2-12, 558B2
Snepp CIA disclosure limits upheld by Sup Ct 2-19, 130C3
Penthouse publisher wins libel case vs Hustler owner 3-1, 239B2
Britannica sales practices case refused by Sup Ct 3-17, 226E1
Photocopy suit rptd setld 3-21, 376D3
Snepp rehearing denied by Sup Ct 4-14, 307E1
Penthouse publisher's libel award cut 4-17, 405A3
Amer Book Awards presented 5-1, 692E1
Polish dissident rptd cleared 5-15, 381B2
Snepp novel rptd submitted for CIA OK 6-13, 517A1
Harper's to cease publicatn 6-17, 501A1
Canada paperworkers strike 6-27, 7-1, 497E2
Berkeley Barb folds 7-3, 582F3
Whitworth named Atlantic Monthly ed 9-22, 908F2
Inventory tax ruling impact rptd 10-5, 835F3
Newsroom searches curb signed 10-14, 835A2
Amer Book Awards revamped 10-19, 906A2
Australia bans articles, book on US ties 11-8, 11-9, 885D1; High Ct upholds 12-1, 919E2
Inventory tax ruling amendmt discarded by House 12-13, 982F2
Mergers & Acquisitions
Thomson, Newsco bid for FP Publicatns 1-2—1-11, Thomson wins 1-11, 38G1

1976

PUERTO Ricans
NYC soc club blaze 10-24, 876E2
Key support for Carter win 11-2, 818G2

PUERTO Rico
Russell ct scores US 1-17, 61C2
Dem platform text 6-15, 472B2
Sup Ct voids alien engineer bar 6-17, 552E3
Ford arrives, warns Cuba 6-26, 462A3
7-nation econ summit held 6-27—6-28, 461F2, 530D3, 557A1
Dem delegate tiff re status 6-29, 490A1
Independnc rally in Phila 7-4, 489C1
Dem conv women delegates, table 508E2
Dem conv pres vote, table 7-14, 507D2
Summer Olympic results 7-18—7-31, 573F3, 574A1
Jose Gallardo dies 7-18, 656E3
Govt wiretapping scandal 7-30—11-27, 994E3
GOP pre-conv delegate count 8-14, 583D3
GOP conv rules com OKs delegatn chng 8-17, 600F2
Reagan seeks conv delegates 8-17, 601B3
GOP conv pres, vp vote tables 8-18—8-19, 8-19, 599D1, D3
GOP platform text 8-18, 605D3
Nonaligned conf for independnc 8-20, 621D3
Cuban exile killed 10-25, 844C3
Election results 11-2, 825F1
US House Dem ldrs elected 12-6, 919C1
Tanker runs aground 12-28, 1014A2
Ford urges statehood, reaction 12-31, 994F2-D3

PUEY Ungpakorn
Leaves Thailand 10-7, 813E3
PULASKI, Casimir (d. 1779)
Buffalo parade honors 10-10, 763B3, C3
PULITZER Prizes
Awarded 5-3, 352B3
PULLAI, Arpad
Replaced 10-27, 947A1
PULLEN, Kay
Joins Mrs Ford's staff 1-21, 40D3
PULLMAN Inc.
SEC lists paymts 5-12, 728F2
China fertilizer plant open 10-25, 832D3

1977

PUEBLO West, Colo.—*See COLORADO*
PUERTO Rican Independence Movement
FBI Cointelpro campaign rptd 11-21, 941A1
PUERTO Ricans
3 chrgd in '76 NYC blaze 1-2, 1-11, 140A2
FALN linked to NYC FBI, other blasts 3-21, 261A2
Chicago riots 6-4—6-5; Bilandic sees ldrs 6-6, jobs set 6-7, 464A3
FALN claims Chicago blast 6-4, 464E3
FALN bombs 2 NYC office bldgs 8-3, dud found 8-8, 613D3, G3
Figueroa pardoned 10-6, 808A2
FBI Cointelpro papers released 11-21, 941A1

PUERTO Rico
Romero Barcelo inaugurated 1-2, 16F2
Statehood proposal linked to oil rights 1-5, 16A3
Ford proposes statehood legis 1-14, 36C2
US sees contd Cuba independnc drive 2-16, 180G2
Tennis tourn results 3-6, 548E2
Venceremos in Cuba 4-8—4-11, 283F2
Carter backs Latin A-pact 4-14, 295F2; signs 5-26, 415D3
House curbs porpoise kill 6-11, 443A1
Diamond dealer murders probed 7-28—10-19, 871D3
Drought aid OKd 8-24, 659D3
Ashland OKs Commonwealth stock purchase 9-22, 723C1
FBI Cointelpro papers released 11-21, 941A1
FALN—*See separate listing*

PULICH, Judge Martin
Sentences Yoshimura 3-17, 288A3
PULITZER Prizes
Awarded 4-18, 355C2

1978

Rothermere, Viscount 7-12, 620F3
Wheelock, John Hall 3-22, 252F3

PUCCIO, Thomas
Announces Tonelli indictmt 7-19, 598G3
PUEBLO Indians—*See INDIANS, American*

PUERTO Rico
US troop presence rptd 1-2, 5D2
San Juan bus drivers strike 1-10, 116B1
No jobless benefits cut seen 1-26, 51B2
Power co strike, sabotage rptd 1-29; Romero comments 2-2, 115G3
Guerrillas bomb bank branch 2-8, 116B1
Schl bus accident kills 11 2-15, 270F3
3 bank branches, 2 San Juan dept stores bombed 2-16, 129F1
US welfare benefits exclusn upheld by Sup Ct 2-27, 143A1
Wallenda falls to death 3-22, 252F3
Statehooders San Juan hq bombed 5-5, 627E2
Cepeda sentncd for pot smuggling 6-14, 1026F2
Extended jobless aid rptd 7-10, 552A3; 8-4, 607C3
Munoz Marin campgns vs statehood 7-17, 627A2
PDP pres quits 7-19, new pres chosen 7-25; statehood issue cited 7-26, 627A1
US to back statehood referendum results 7-25, 627G1-A2
Soclst youths killed by cops 7-25, 627B2
Socialists seized in shooting, holdup 7-27, 627D2
US poll opposes statehood 7-28, 627F1
Un panel calls colony 9-13, Dellums scores '67 vote 9-15, 979C3
Trade missn rptd in Japan 10-18, 798D1
Lufthansa to serve San Juan 10-25, 831F1

PUGET Sound
Washn oil tanker regulatn curbed 3-6, 161E3
PUIG Antich, Salvador (d. 1974)
Catalan actors sentncd 3-7, 250G1
PUKA, Charles
Rptd held in USSR 4-12, 275G2
Leaves USSR 4-28, 360A1
PULITZER Prizes
Awarded 4-17, photo mix-up settled 4-21, 314D2-315B2
PULLING Your Own Strings (book)
On best-seller list 6-4, 460C3; 8-6, 620B2; 9-4, 708C1
PULP and Paper Workers, Association of Western
Sues Admin re wage-price plan 12-1, 934B2

1979

Macmillan accepts Mattel bid 8-30; spurns, accepts ABC offer 10-16; ABC ends talks 11-22, 942A3
Random House to be sold by RCA 9-6, 682D2
CMT-Paramount deal called off 9-12, 942F2
Murdock ends Herald takeover bid 11-22, 906G2
Obituaries
Kahn, Albert E 9-15, 756E2
Larsen, Roy E 9-10, 756F2
Muir, Malcolm 1-30, 104E3

PUERTO Rican International Airlines—*See PRINAIR*

PUERTO Rico
Cuba offers US prisoner, jailed PR natlsts trade 1-7, 40F3
Med malpractice arbitratn rptd 1-28, 139C3
Cuban exile slain 4-28, 350G2
Soclst youths '78 deaths disputed 4-30–5-3, US probe ordrd 5-2, 350F1-G2
US-Canada naval maneuvers 5-9–5-19, fishermen protest 5-16, 5-19, 385B3
Luggage search law voided by Sup Ct 6-18, 499A2
US basketball coach arrested in Pan Am Games assault 7-8, convctd 8-22, sentncd 9-10, 798D3
US commutes sentncs of 4 PR natlsts, Cuba prisoner trade denied 9-6, 666D1-B3
PR natlsts freed 9-10, return to San Juan 9-12, 682G3
Cuba releases 4 US prisoners 9-17, 706C3
US welfare held discriminatory 10-11, 786F2
Castro scores colonialism 10-12, sees 2 US reps 10-13, 778G2, 779F1
FALN, 2 other groups bomb govt bldgs; protest naval trial 10-18, 786A2
Baker seeks '80 primary win 11-1, 829A1
Vieques protester found dead in cell 11-11, probes ordrd 11-18, 11-23, 904A3
Terrorist activity rptd up 11-15, 882A2
Natlst ambush kills 2 US sailors 12-3, 924G2
Navy patrol attacked again 12-9, 947D3
Obituaries
Figueroa Cordero, Andres 3-7, 272D2
Marques, Rene 3-22, 272B3
Sports
WBC welterwgt title bout 1-14, 79A3
Boxing title bouts 2-18, 3-25, 412D3, F3
Pan Am Games hosted 7-1–7-15, 798E2
Cepeda hired by White Sox 11-20, 1002F3

PUGET Sound
Indian salmon fishing treaties upheld by Sup Ct 7-2, 559D1
PUGET Sound (U.S. aircraft carrier)
Navy fire probe rptd 7-5, 519G3
PUJOL, Jose A.
Indicted in arms plot 5-14, 386E3
PULFORD, Bob
Replaced as Black Hawks coach, to remain gen mgr 6-9, 470D3
PULITZER Prizes
Awarded 4-16, 336C2
PULLEY, Andrew
Loses Chicago mayoral race 4-3, 251G3
Heads '80 SWP pres ticket 8-22, 680G2
PULLING Your Own Strings (book)
On best-seller list 10-14, 800D3; 11-4, 892D3
PULLMAN Inc.
Pullman Kellog, Nigeria deal signed 9-13, 721A1
Amtrak 'Superliner' unveiled 10-12, 868F1
PULLMAN Kellog—*See PULLMAN Inc.*
PULP and Paper Workers, Association of Western
'78 strikes end 1-30–5-9, 345D2

1980

Doubleday buys NY Mets 1-24, 795A3
Newhouse to buy Random House 2-6, 386D1
Atlantic Monthly sale rptd 3-1, 239F1
Cue NY sale agreemt rptd 3-4, 239G1
Us magazine sale rptd 3-7, 239A2
Chattanooga (Tenn) papers partially join 5-12, Civiletti OKs 9-2, 732E2
Financial World buys Saturday Review 5-20, 582D3
Harper's rescued 7-9, 582B3
Tex Monthly buys New West 8-27, 732E3
Source Telecomputing, Reader's Digest merge 9-24, 746F1
McGraw-Hill takeover case declined by Sup Ct 11-3, 856A2
Warner to buy Franklin Mint 12-24, 985B1
Obituaries
Grayzel, Solomon 8-12, 676E1
Kenney, Douglas 9-1, 755F3
Kirkus, Virginia 9-10, 755F3
MacAusland, Earle 6-4, 528D2
Martin Jr, William T 10-13, 876F2
Mingo, Norman 5-8, 448D2
PUCCIO, Thomas P.
Confirms Abscam term redefinition 8-20, 684E2
Williams, 3 others indicted in Abscam probe 10-30, 824D3
PUCHKOV, Alexandr
Wins Olympic medals 7-27, 624B1
PUERTO Rico
Marta Casals Istomin gets Kennedy Cntr post 2-26, 199C2
2d 1/4 gas use targets set 3-20, 250F3
Welfare aid rate backed by Sup Ct 5-27, 453C3
Reps at US Families Conf 6-5, 442B3
Crime & Civil Disorders
Vieques bombing, airline plot foiled 1-7; Navy Lt, 2 others arrested 1-25, 94A1
Navy maneuvers off Vieques disrupted 1-19, 94D1
3 Army instructors attacked 3-12, 190D1
FALN raids US pres campaign hq 3-15, 208A3-209A1
11 FALN suspects arrested in US 4-4; houses raided, execs hit list seized 4-7, 4-8, 308F3-309E1
Cops cleared in '78 killings 4-25, 348G2
Navigatn statns bombed, air traffic rerouted 7-14, 559F3
8 FALN suspects convicted 7-30; 2 others sentncd, 1 rptd extradited 8-4, 601C1
US Navy ambush suspects murdered 8-11, 9-11, 1 rptd missing 9-8; natlst probe set 9-19, 786A2
15 steal $2.4 mln 11-21, terrorists suspected 11-24, 971G2
Obituaries
Munoz Marin, Luis 4-30, 360E2
Politics & Government—*See also other appropriate subheads in this section*
Romero loses reelectn 11-4, recount called 11-5, 852D3
Romero declared winner in recount 12-18, 988G1
Presidential Election (& Transition)
Dole quits GOP primary 2-13; Bush wins 2-17, electn results challenged 2-19, 130A1
FALN raids US offices 3-15, 208A3-209A1
Carter wins Dem primary 3-16, 208B2
GOP rules vs delegate rise 7-14, 535B2
Dem platform plank adopted 8-13, 615E1
Refugee Issues
Hispanic immigrants in NYC surveyed 5-11—5-14, 396G2, F3
Carter sets resetlmt camp 9-18, 742B2
Resetlmt camp constructn begins 9-27, suits filed 9-29, 9-30, 742C2
Resetlmt camp to be opened 9-23, 725E3-726A1
Camp Allen blocked by legal battles 10-1—10-24, 825A3
Camp Allen ban lifted, security tightnd 11-3, 869C2
Camp Allen blamed for Romero reelectn defeat 11-4, 852G3
Camp Allen blocked again 12-18, 988B2
Sports
Olympic com vs boycott 4-18, 325D3
Sports feds get Olympic boycott choice 5-24, 421F1
Boxing team in Moscow for Olympics 6-29, 588A2
PUERTO Rico, University of (San Juan)
2 Army instructors attacked 3-12, 190D1
PUFE, Margitta
Wins Olympic medal 7-24, 624G1
PUGET Sound
Ferry strike ends 4-16, 308B3
PUIKKONEN, Jari
Wins Olympic medal 2-23, 155D3
PUJOL, Jordi
Party wins upset in Catalonia 3-21, 235F1
Suarez names ally to Cabt post 9-8, 690F2
PULITZER Prizes
Awarded 4-14, 296B2
PULLMAN Inc.
McDermott bids for control 6-30; Wheelabrator bids 8-21, buys control 9-25, 784G2
Rockwell NYC subway damages awarded 12-24, 985A3

1976

PUMA, Velasco, Gen. Raul
Loses Cabt post, arrested 1-9; scores Duran 1-11, 28A2
Gets amnesty 1-28, 363C3
PUNA, Nzau
Rpts FNLA-Unita clashes 1-10, 1-22, 58A1
PUNXSATAWNEY, Pa.—*See PENNSYLVANIA*
PURSELL, Carl D.
Elected 11-2, 823E2, 829D4
PUSCH, Alexander
Wins Olympic medal 7-23, 574F2
PYCIAK-Peciak, Janusz
Wins Olympic medal 7-22, 575B1
PYKA, Tadeusz
Polish deputy premier 3-27, 268F2
PYM, Francis
Shadow cabt agri min 1-15, 101C2
PYTLAK, Shirley
'73 warning on Teton Dam cited 423D1
PYTTEL, Roger
Sets world swim mark 6-1—6-5, 424G3

1977

PUREX Corp.
Calif land holding breakup asked 8-22, 703G2
PURTZER, Tom
Wins LA Open 2-20, 311G1
PUSH, Operation—*See OPERATION PUSH*
PUSHKIN, Alexander Sergeyevich (1799-1837)
Moscow rights vigil 12-10, 955G3
PUTTEMANS, Emil
5000-mtr run mark broken 7-5, 603D1
PYJAS, Stanislaw
Found dead 5-7, 436F3
Cardinal scores press rpts 6-9, 513C1
PYKE, Neal
Sets 20-km walk mark 7-1—7-2, 602E2
PYPE, Antoon
Sentence upheld 4-25, 314B3

1978

PULZ, Penny
2d in Winners Circle 4-2, 355F3
LPGA top money winner 11-20, 990C3
PUNITIVE Medicine (book)
Podrabinek gets internal exile 8-15, 634A2
PURDUE University (Lafayette, Ind.)
Wins Peach Bowl 12-25, 1025E2
PURDY, Andrew
At JFK death hearing 9-27, 750F1
PUROLATOR Inc.
Armored car unit fined on trust chrgs 5-4, 511E1
PURSELL, Rep. Carl D. (R, Mich.)
Reelected 11-7, 851D1
PURTELL, William A.
Dies 5-31, 440C3
PURVIANCE, Edna
Woman of Paris released 4-13, 620D1
PUTNA, John
San Fran wins NCAA soccer title 12-10, 969B2
PUTNAM, Mayor Helen (Petaluma, Calif.)
On developers' fee 7-21, 611E2
PUTNAM'S Sons, G. P.
Puzo paperback rights sold for record sum 6-16, 620D2
PUTTNAM, David
Duellists released 1-14, 619F1
Midnight Express released 10-6, 970C2
PUVOGEL, Hans
Resigns over '36 Nazi thesis 3-23, 477F2
PUZO, Mario
Paperback rights sold for record sum 6-16, 620C2
Fools Die on best-seller list 10-9, 800A3; 11-6, 887F3; 12-3, 971A1
Superman released 12-14, 1030E3
PYATKUS, Viktoras
Sentenced 7-13, 541E2

1979

PULZ, Penny
Wins Corning Classic 5-27, 587A3
PUNCH, Angela
Newsfront released 5-30, 820D2
PUNGAN, Vacile
Israel gets bid to mediate PLO, Syria feud 8-31; Israel rejects 9-2, 659C2
PURDUE University (Lafayette, Ind.)
Loses NIT 3-21, 238E3
NCAA basketball tourn results 3-26, 238B3
H C Brown wins Nobel 10-16, 858B1
Wins Bluebonnet Bowl 12-31, 1001C3
PUROLATOR Inc.
3 security guards robbed, killed 4-16, 316E1
PURSCH, Dr. Joseph
Rpts Valium abuse 9-10, 734G2
PURTZER, Tom
2d in BC Open 9-2; wins US-Japan individual title 11-11, 970C1, C2
PUSH (People United to Save Humanity)—*See OPERATION Push*
PUTNAM, Dr. Tracy J.
Merritt dies 1-9, 104D3
PUZO, Mario
Krantz paperback rights sold for record sum 9-12, 755E3
Fools Die on best-seller list 11-4, 892C3
P.V.M.—*See FOOD–Diets*
PYE, Richard
On 3 Mile I A-accident 4-5, 260G2
PYM, Francis
Tories set Africa policy 4-11, 285C3
UK defense secy 5-5, 338E1

1980

PURCELL, Mel
Wins NCAA doubles tennis title 5-26, 607D1
Loses US Clay Cts 8-10, 691B3
PURDUE University (Lafayette, Ind.)
Football '79 rank rptd 1-2, 23C1
Transcript scandal rptd 1-23, 469C2, E2
NCAA basketball tourn results 3-24, 240E1, A2
Carroll in NBA draft 6-10, 447A1, E2
Liberty Bowl won 12-27, 999D3
PURSELL, Rep. Carl D. (R, Mich.)
Reelected 11-4, 843E1
PURTZER, Tom
Ties for 2d in Hope Desert Classic 1-14, 412B2
2d in Memphis Classic 6-29, 715B1
PUTNAM, David
Foxes released 2-29, 216E2
PUTNAM, Hayes & Bartlett Inc.
EPA cleanup study rptd 6-18, 494B2
PUZO, Mario
Fools Die on best-seller list 1-13, 40D3
PYKA, Taduesz
Ousted 8-24, 641F1
PYM, Francis
Reveals A-weapons plans 1-24, 79F1
Saudi visit rptd canceled 4-23, 313A3
On Sovt A-superiority 6-4, 450F2
UK sets cruise missile sites 6-17, 486G3
On armor purchases 7-14, 564A2
On Trident purchases 7-15, 544C2, E2
Plans arms for svcwomen 12-2, 922F1-A2
PYRAMID Schemes—*See CRIME–Bribery, Fraud & Extortion*
PYROMAGLOU, Kominos
Dies 7-2, 608F2
PYTTEL, Roger
Wins Olympic medals 7-20, 7-23, 623F2

Q

1976

QABUS bin Said, Sultan (Oman)
S Yemen border clashes rptd 1-14, 52G1 ★
QADDAFI, Col. Muammer el- (Libyan head of state)
Egypt chrgs plot ordrd 3-9, 205A2
Tunisian death plot chrgd 3-22, 239D2
Sees Chirac in Libya 3-22, 239C3
Report gets Sovt arms 4-4, 275D1
Libya, Niger, Algeria set closer ties 4-8, 372A1
Tunis rpts assassinatn try 4-19, 334F1
Meheishi denounces 4-22, 334E1
Tunis death plot chrgd 4-22, 335C1
On 'tenuous' Egypt ties 5-25, 467B2
Tied to Sudan coup 7-6, 501E3
Rpt foes hijack jet 7-6, 539A2
Arafat tells of Leb crisis 7-11, 514A3
World terrorist network rptd 7-15, 531D1
Sudan links to coup 7-15, 531C3
Sadat ties to Sudan coup 7-22, 547B3
Chrgs Egypt troops mass 7-25, 547C3
Egypt chrgs sabotage 8-8, 588G2
Addresses nonaligned conf 8-18, 621G3
Tied to Egypt jet hijack 8-23, 629C2
Denies Egypt chrgs 9-2, 682D3, 683A1 ★
Gets Arafat plea vs Syria 10-13, 758D2
Pl rebel-govt talks set 11-17, 1009C1
Visits Brezhnev 12-6—12-9, 949B1
Meets Agnelli in Moscow 12-9, 965D1

1977

QADDAFI, Col. Muammer el- (Libyan head of state)
Claustre thanks 2-1, 84D2
Sees Castro 3-1—3-10, 249A2
Govt, country names chngd 3-3, 348E2
Tied to Pl revolt 3-10, 202G2
Pl Moslem pact reached 3-20, Marcos sees agrmt observed 3-29, 241C3, G3
Amnesty Intl chrgs sentences chngd 3-24, 348B3
'75 coup plotters executed 4-2, 348A3
Chrgs Egypt mistreats Libyans 4-13, 361F2
Egypt: 'plot' smashed 4-15, 361F2
Chrgs Egypt mil plot 5-1, 361D3
Egypt chrgs deportatns 5-2, 361F3
Proposes union with Tunisia 6-2, 497G2
Urges closer US ties 6-12, 488B1
Carter sees Palestine state tied to Jordan 7-6, 509G2
Sadat scores re clashes 7-22, 569E1
Boumedienne mediates Egypt feud 7-24—7-25, 569F2
Vs US peace moves 10-18, 793G1
Offers Sahara kidnap mediatn 11-2, 852C2
Vs Sadat visit to Israel 11-16, 874C1
At Tripoli anti-Sadat mtg 12-2—12-5, 929B2
Fahmy discloses arms vow 12-3, 930E2

1978

Q (recording)
Brothers Johnson win Grammy 2-24, 315G3
QADDAFI, Col. Muammer el- (Libyan head of state)
Asks Palestinian peace role 2-3, 78B3
Visits Tunisia 2-6, 170F1
Chad peace plan OKd 2-24, 130B2
Copter crash 3-6, plot hinted 3-28, arrests rptd 3-29, 228D1
In Algeria 5-31—6-6, shifts stance on Polisario 6-3, 562D2
In Malta, vows mil aid 7-3—7-4, 592E2
Tied to missing Leb Moslem ldr 8-31, 713D2
Castro visits in stopover 9-19, 776G3
Asks Hussein rejct summit pact 9-22, 730C1
Hardliners conf ends, oil funding disputed 9-24, 730B1
Arms bid for Iran revolt rptd 12-29, 993F2

1979

QADDAFI, Col. Muammer el- (Libyan head of state)
Threatns Tanzania raid 3-27, aid to Amin rptd 3-31, 257F1
At Malta fete re UK troop exit 3-31, 269D2
'71, '75 A-bomb bids rptd 4-14, 299C3
B Carter confrms Libya financed '78 trip 4-15, 300C1
Oil export halt threat rptd, clarified 6-29—6-30, 496B1
Egypt ties to Emb raid in Turkey 7-16, 536A3
Urges forgn emb takeover 9-2, 688F2
Tied to missing Leb Moslem ldr 9-8, 677E3
US black group honors 9-16, 694B3
Sadat fears Saudi link 10-10, 801F2
PLO hq under seige 12-6, offcls protest 12-9; Israel policy scored 12-10, 937B3
Scores Arafat 12-11, cuts PLO ties 12-22, 980C1

1980

QADDAFI, Col. Muammer el- (Libyan head of state)
Syria says Israel plans attack 2-23, 140C3
At hard-line Arab summit 4-14—4-15, 284G2
2 execs killed in Rome 4-19, 5-10, 373D3
Warns exiles to return, oppositn crackdown seen 4-26, 353A3
US ousts 4 natls 5-11, 373G2-C3
UK arrests 3 for 2 Libyan murders 5-12, 373D3
Dissidents warned 6-7, 451B3
Exiles attacked in Italy 6-11, 451A3
Rptdly backs anti-Sadat move 6-11, 6-22, 451D3
UK expels envoy 6-13, 463G2
Carter rpts on brother's Libyan role 8-4, 593E3, F3
B Carter probe opens 8-4, 595G2
Tobruk mutiny rpt denied 8-18, 652B3
Proposes Syria merger 9-1, Syria OKs 9-2, 660D3
In Syria merger talks 9-8—9-9; unity OKd 9-10, 697D1
Leb missing Moslem ldr rptd jailed 9-9, 709C1
W Ger neo-Nazi link chrgd 9-30, 755D1
Backs Iran vs Iraq, asks Saudi aid; Iraq cuts Libya ties 10-10, 774A2
Scores Saudis for US AWACS 10-19, Saudis cut ties 10-28, 820C3
Carter hits Reagan A-arms stance 10-29, 816C2
Meets Assad, merger delayed 12-16—12-18, 978B2

1976

QANTAS Airways Ltd.
Australia gets Eximbank loan 4-13, 264F3
Rpts '75 losses, admits price cutting 9-23, 747D3

1977

QALYUM Khan, Abdul
Resigns 1-13, 66G2-A3
QANTAS Airways Ltd.
S Africa flights halted 9-20, 762C3

1978

QANTAS Airways Ltd.
'77 profit rptd 3-6, 225F2
UK air fare cut announced 10-11, 793C3
Curbs on Jews probed 10-18, 836D1; Syria drops demand 10-20, 900E3
Australia-US cut-rate fare pact set 12-13, 985G1-A2

1979

QANTAS Airways Ltd.
Asian fare policy oppositn rptd 1-5, 6D1
QARANEH, Maj. Gen. Mohammed Wali
Named Iran armed forces staff chief 2-12, 105F2
Dissolves Imperial Guard 2-17, rpts army discipline restored 2-20, 125A2
Bans US intell posts 2-21, 145C2
US listening post taken over 3-1; 161E2
Resigns as armed forces chief 3-27, 247E2
Slain 4-23, 297C1
Motahari slain 5-1, 321E1
Khomeini vs newspr article 5-10, 358B1
QASSEMLOO, Abdul Rahman
Iran orders arrest 8-19, 635D1
Vows 'all-out war' 8-25, 653D2
Arrest sought 9-4, 688A2

1980

QADDANI, Gen. Ali Majid
Saudi defns resignatn cited 1-1, 22E1
QADIR, Abdul
Killed 9-1, 686C1
QANTAS Airways Ltd.
Australia-US svc increase set 7-30, 617F2

1976

QATAR—*See also ARAB League, NON-ALIGNED Nations Movement, OPEC*
Iran recalls amb 1-7, 12G3
Listed as 'not free' nation 1-19, 20E3
Sadat visits, gets aid vow 2-27, 162C1
Joins Egypt aid fund 8-21, 630A1
Listed as partly free 12-22, 977B3

1977

QATAR—*See also ARAB League, NONALIGNED Nations Movement, OPEC*
UN Assemb member 4B1
Saudis reject oil price compromise 2-6, 107G2
Completes Shell takeover 2-9, 108E2
Black Africa funds vowed 3-7, 170A2
Gulf group aids Egypt 3-25, 390D3
Venez pres visits 4-21—4-23, 362A1
Intl consortium OKs Egypt aid 5-11—5-12, 390C3
Leb hijacker surrenders 6-29, 525C2
Killgore confrmd US amb 8-3, 626G2
Assad visits re Cairo conf 12-11, 954F2

1978

QATAR—*See also ARAB League, NONALIGNED Nations Movement, OPEC*
Econ dvpt plans rptd slowed 2-20, 122E1, G1
France signs AIO arms pact; US, UK deals cited 3-14, 237C1 ★
Islamic, Arab poor-natn aid rise rptd 4-9, 257D2, F2
Arab fund loan to Sudan rptd 8-17, 925F3
UN Assemb member 713D3

1979

QATAR—*See also ARAB League, NONALIGNED Nations Movement, OPEC*
Oil prices raised 2-15, 126D1-A2
Doha jet crash kills 45 3-14, 240C3
Egypt recalls envoy 4-7, 278D1
US chrgs 2 execs re '76 oil bribe 4-9, 305E3-306C1
Egypt ties cut 4-25, 296E1
Egypt aid group disbanded 4-27, 319D2
Arab arms plant in Egypt to close 5-14, 359F3
Oil prices hiked again 5-26, 396C2; 6-28, 473C1
UN membership listed 695B3
At Persian Gulf security conf 10-14—10-16, 804A2
US sets evacuations, travel curbs 11-26, 894A2
Oil prices hiked 12-13, price per barrel rptd 12-21, 977G1, B2

1980

QATAR—*See also ARAB League, NONALIGNED Nations, OPEC*
French pres tours Arab states 3-1—3-10, 180B1
Japan oil trade seen 4-20, 299D1
IOC bans from Moscow Olympics 5-27, 420D3
Oil price hike set 6-11, 435G2
Syria seeks backing for Libya merger 9-10, 697G1
Oil productn hike rptd 10-5, 775C1
Algeria quake aid rptd 10-11, 776E1
Oil productn increase rptd 10-28, 822E2

1976

QAZI, Nazrul Islam
Dies 8-29, 1015F1
QUADROS, Waldir Jose de
Torture chrg vs army rptd 9-10, 850D3
QUAINTON, Anthony
Amb to CAR 12-10-75; confrmd 2-4, 110C2
QUANBECK, Alton H.
Study vs B-1 publshd 2-8, 183B2
QUARLES Jr., John R.
Policy permits new plants 11-10, 869B1
QUARRIE, Donald
Wins Olympic medals 7-24, 7-26, 575F3, G3
QUAX, Dick
Wins Olympic medal 7-30, 576C1
QUAYLE, J. Danforth
Elected 11-2, 823C2, 829B3
QUEENS, N.Y.—*See NEW York City*
QUIE, Rep. Albert Harold (R, Minn.)
Reelected 11-2, 829F4
QUIETO, Roberto
Montoneros protest abductn 1-13, 26C1
QUIJANO, Raul
Argentina forgn min 1-16, 71C2
UK ship fired on 2-4, 220E2
QUILLEN, Rep. James H. (Jimmy) (R, Tenn.)
Reelected 11-2, 830B4
QUINLAN, Joseph T. & Julia
Daughter wins right to die 3-31, 292C2
Sells magazine story rights 6-4, 423G2
QUINLAN, Karen Anne
Wins right to die 3-31, 292C2
Off respirator 5-22, moved 6-10, 423D2
Magazine buys story rights 6-4, 423A3
Sup Ct bars review of case 11-1, 867F3
QUINN, Robert E.
Loses US House electn 11-2, 823C1
QUINN, Thomas
AMC fined $4 mln 1-5, 5F3
QUINN, William F.
Wins Sen primary 10-2, 764D2
Loses Senate race 11-2, 825B1
QUINN, William J.
SEC sues, settles 6-29, 984A2
QUIROGA Santa Cruz, Marcelo
Greets Mrs Torres in Mex 6-7, 456F2
QUIROS Guardia, Alberto
Arrested 1-15, exiled 1-20, 121B2

1977

QOBOZA, Percy
Arrested 10-19, 803F3; US press protest 10-10, 10-21, 825C2
QUAINTON, Anthony
Protests Randal, Goldsmith detentn 8-16, recall rptd 8-17, 635C1
QUAKER State Oil Refining Corp.
On '76 Fortune 500 list 341C1
QUANTICO, Va.—*See VIRGINIA*
QUARLES Jr., John R.
EPA orders Ford halt productn 2-8, 113C1
Replaced as EPA dep admin 3-4, 211D1
QUAX, Dick
Sets 5000-mtr run mark 7-5, 603D1
QUEEN of Angels Chapel (Dickinson, Tex.)
Lefebvre consecrates 7-10, 620F2
QUEENS, N.Y.—*See NEW York City*
QUERO Morales, Constantino
Venez Investmt Fund pres 1-7, 23F2
Replaced as state min 7-15, 566A1
QUIE, Dr. Paul
On drug-resistant pneumonia 10-21, 847A2
QUIETO, Roberto
Guerrillas rptd in disarray 1-3, 16G3
QUINCY, Mass.—*See MASSACHUSETTS*
QUINLAN, Joseph T. & Julia
Daughter rptd in stable conditn 3-31, 355A1
QUINLAN, Karen Anne
Conditn rptd stable 3-31, 355A1
QUINN, Archbishop John R.
Named SF archbp 2-22, installed 4-26, 375A3
Electd Bishops Conf pres 11-15, 906C3
QUINTAL, Joseph Roland
RCMP probe overseer 10-25, 841B2
QUIROGA Santa Cruz, Marcelo
Bolvia amnesty excludes 12-21, 1010A1

1978

QOBOZA, Percy
Freed from detention 3-10, 193D2
QUADRANGLE/The New York Times Book Co.—*See under NEW York Times Co.*
QUAGLINO, John P.
Murder case refused by Sup Ct 10-2, 751C2
QUAGLINO v. California
Case refused by Sup Ct 10-2, 751C2
QUAKERS—*See FRIENDS, Religious Society of*
QUALITY Paperback Book Club—*See BOOK-of-the-Month Club*
QUARTETS for Strings (recording)
Juilliard Quartet wins Grammy 2-24, 316C1
QUAX, Dick
5000-mtr run mark broken 4-8, 600F2
QUAYLE, Anthony
Somersaults opens 1-9, 760A2
QUAYLE, Rep. Dan (R, Ind.)
Reelected 11-7, 853A3
QUEBEC (Canadian province)—*See CANADA*
QUEBECOR Inc.
Phila Journal '77 debut cited 1-9, 75F3
QUEEN (singing group)
2 recordings on best-seller list 2-4, 116F3, G3
QUEENS, N.Y.—*See NEW York City*
QUEMOY (Taiwan-held Islands)
Peking ends shelling 12-31, 995D1
QUERN v. Mandley
State emergency-welfare standards backed by Sup Ct 6-6, 447E2
QUESADA Hernandez, Estela
To be CR labor min 3-4, 170G3
QUICK, Dr. Armand J.
Dies 1-26, 96C3
QUIE, Rep. Albert H. (R, Minn.)
Wins primary for gov 9-12, 716D1
Elected Minn gov 11-7, 853F2, 854B3
QUILEUTE Indians—*See INDIANS, American*
QUILLEN, Daniel
Wins Field Medal 8-15, 1023F2
QUILLEN, Rep. James H. (Jimmy) (R, Tenn.)
Reelected 11-7, 852C2
QUILLOIN v. Walcott
Father's role in adoptns limited 1-10, 13C3
QUINLAN, Karen Ann
Med care cost rptd 4-10, 597D3
Ends 2d yr off respirator 5-14, 597B3
QUINN, Anthony
Greek Tycoon released 5-12, 619D2
Caravans released 11-1, 969F3 ★
QUINOFORM (clioquinol)—*See MEDICINE—Drugs*
QUINONES, Capt. Carlos
Chile mining min 12-26, 1014D2
QUINTANILLA, Pedro J.
Arrest rptd 9-4, 690C3

1979

QUADROPHENIA (film)
Released 11-2, 1008B1
QUAKER Oats Co.
'75 FTC trust suit cited 10-9, 810B1
QUALITY Meat Packing Co.
Settles '78 beef-price suit 10-22, 985E3
QUANTICO, Va.—*See VIRGINIA*
QUARLES, William
Describes ordeal as hostage 11-18, freed 11-19, 878A1, G1-B2
QUAYLE, Rep. Don (R, Ind.)
Chrysler bill defeated 12-18, 981F2
QUEBEC (Canadian province)—*See CANADA*
QUEBECAIR
Turboprop crash kills 17 3-29, 240D3
QUEENS, N.Y.—*See NEW York City*
QUERN v. Zbaraz
Case accepted by Sup Ct 11-26, 919A2
QUICK Point Pencil Co.
Nonpatent royalties upheld by Sup Ct 2-28, 165B2
QUIJADA, Manuel
Venez development min 3-10, 192C3
QUILLEN, Dale Marden
Indicted 3-15, 309E2
QUINE, Richard
Prisoner of Zenda released 5-25, 820A3
QUINLAN, Karen Ann
Calif respirator ruling cites 2-15, 291D2
QUINLAN, Kathleen
Taken in Marriage opens 2-26, 292D3
Promise released 3-7, 528D3
Runner Stumbles released 11-16, 1008D1
QUINN, Grady
At HS prom with gay date 5-3, 392C3
QUINN, Archbishop John R.
Named to '80 Rome synod 5-3, 376A1
QUINN, Tom
Scores Sohio pipe cancelatn 3-13, 183G1
QUINTANA, Francisco
Lauds Honduras, scores CR rebel aid 1-9, 21G3
QUINTANA, Julio C.
Asks OAS to invoke defns treaty 5-29, 409C2
QUINTERO, Jose
Faith Healer opens 4-4, 711G2
QUINTET (film)
Released 2-8, 174D3
QUIRT, John
Article rpts on Prop 13 7-2, 499F2

1980

QIN Jiwei
Heads Peking mil cmnd 2-29, 171F3
QUAD Cities Nuclear Power Station—*See ILLINOIS--Atomic Energy & Safeguards*
QUAIL, George
Panel rejects Ciskei statehood 2-12, 134A2
Ciskei votes on Statehood 12-4, victory rptd 12-17 996C1
QUARRIE, Donald
Wins Olympic medal 7-28, 624B1
QUARRYMEN, The (singing group)
Lennon slain 12-8, 934B3
QUAYLE, Dan
Elected to US Sen 11-4, 840F1, 845A2, 850F3
QUDES, Abdul Manaf
Defects to US 9-6, 705C1
QUEBEC (Canadian province)—*See CANADA*
QUEEN (singing group)
Crazy Little Thing on best-seller list 2-6, 120F3; 3-5, 200E3; 4-2, 280E3
Game on best-seller list 9-10, 716F3; 10-8, 796B3
Another One Bites the Dust on best-seller list 9-10, 716E3; 10-8, 796A3; 12-3, 948B3
QUEEN, Jeanne
Sees Giscard 4-23, 299C2
QUEEN, Richard I.
Mother sees Giscard 4-23, 299C2
Hospitalized 7-7; Iran release ordered 7-10, freed 7-11; arrives Switz, W Ger 7-12, US 7-18, 539E1
Sees Carter 7-19, details captivity 7-21, 545G2
Rpts mock hostage executn 7-24, 572A1
QUEEN for a Day (TV series)
Bailey dies 2-1, 175E3
QUESADA, Gen. Elwood
Financial Gen deal set 7-25, 600F3
QUESADA Zamora, Graciela Calderon
Jailed in US 6-30, 514D2
QUEZON, Manuel Luis (1878-1944)
MacArthur WWII 'gift' dispute rptd 1-30, 1-31, 115E1
QUICK Change (play)
Opens 10-30, 892D3
QUIE, Gov. Albert H. (R, Minn.)
State of State message 1-24, 269A3
QUI Huizuo
Gang of 4 trial defendant 11-20—12-29, 975E2
QUILLEN, Rep. James H. (Jimmy) (R, Tenn.)
Reelected 11-4, 844C2
QUINN, Jane Bryant
Panelist in pres TV debate 9-21, 721C3
QUINN, John
On Rockefeller pub defender plea 9-22, 908C3
QUINN, Archbishop John R.
Challenges birth control ban 9-29, 810E2
QUINN, Pat
Named NHL top coach 6-6, 488D1
QUINTERO, Jose
Clothes for a Summer Hotel opens 3-26, 392E2
QUIRICO, Judge Francis
Orders life aid in 'Right-to-Die' case 1-24, 158G2
QUIROGA Santa Cruz, Marcelo
Electns held 6-29, gains rptd 7-3, Siles coalitn weighed 7-4, 508G3-509A1
Slain 7-17, 546C3
QUISENBERRY, Dan
AL pitching ldr 10-6, 926G3
Royals win AL pennant 10-10, 796A1
In World Series 10-14—10-21, 811F3-812A3

R

1976

RAAB, Selwyn
Carter, Artis convicted 12-21, 1015E3
RABASA, Emilio
Resignatn linked to Spain ties 1-8, 75G2
Cited re campaign vs Excelsior 7-8, 620B2
RABB, Ellis
Wins Tony award 4-18, 460D2
RABBINICAL Council of America
Backs Vatican statemt on sex 1-26, 124C2
Vatican recognitn of Israel urged 2-8, 272G2
Wurzburger installed pres 5-26, 932E2
RABBIS, New York Board of
Carter addresses 8-31, 645D2
RABIES—*See 'Diseases' under MEDICINE*
RABIN, Yitzhak (Israeli premier)
Vs UN Cncl peace role 1-4, 1-11, 18C3
Secret Hussein talks rptd 1-12, 19D1
US Golan setlmt protest rptd leaked 34D3
Rpts censorship plan deferred 1-20, 34B3
Warns Leb vs interventn, scores Vatican 1-25, 59D2
Syria scores US UN veto 1-26, 59F3
In US, presses for contd aid 1-27—1-29, 60B1-B2
Back from US trip, rpts agrmt 2-6; Parlt debates US arms statmt, wins confidence vote 2-9, 106E2
On Avineri appointment 2-15, 126B1
Cabt backs US peace moves 2-22, 145B1
Meir joins party ldrship, Zarmi withdraws resignatn 3-5, 253B3
Sharon quits as adviser 3-21, 253D3
Vs Scranton UN speech 3-26, 227A3
Ties riots to CP, wins confidence vote 3-31, 227F1

1977

RAAB, Enrique
Arrested 4-16, 345C3
RABBIS, Central Conference of American
New home prayer book issued 3-7, 471A3
Abraham Feldman dies 7-21, 604B3
RABBITT, Richard J.
Convicted 7-28, sentenced 8-16, 712A2
RABBO, Jaber Abed
Hanged 1-6, 2D2
RABIN, Leah (Mrs. Yitzhak)
Illicit US bank fund admitted 3-15, 3-20, 4-8, 266F3
Fined 4-17, 329F2
RABIN, Oskar
Arrested 9-12, 753D1

RABIN, Yitzhak (Israeli premier; replaced June 21)
Studies Ofer corruptn probe, bars role 1-1—1-3; Ofer kills self 1-3, 8E1
Gets mandate for new govt 1-4; parlt ends, new electns set 1-5, 8B2
Peres seeks to unseat 1-11, 48B2
Vows Daoud trial 1-16, 27G3
Meets Waldheim 2-10, 86F2
Vance visits 2-16—2-17, 121C1
Renominated 2-23, 135D1
Meets Carter 3-7—3-8; reaffirms setlmt terms 3-8, 3-9, 165A1, E2
Egypt scores Carter mtg 3-10, 166D1
On Carter withdrawal proposal 3-13, 187E2
Denies Carter plan Rogers revival 3-14, backs Carter on overall setlmt 3-15, 187G2
Tied to illicit US bank fund 3-15, 3-20, 4-8; admits lied, quits electn race 4-8, 266E3
Vs Carter on Palestine 'homeland' 3-17, 187G3

1978

RABBINICAL Alliance of America
Hecht opposes gay rights 5-18, 410B1
RABBIT Test (film)
Released 4-8, 619D3
Top-grossing film 4-26, 356C1
RABIES—*See MEDICINE—Diseases*
RABIN, Oskar
Citizenship revoked 6-30, 543D1

RABIN, Yitzhak
Vs Begin stand on Res 242 3-9, 156A3

1979

RABB, Judge Roger
Vs wage-guide contract denial 6-22, 480F2
RABBINICAL Alliance of America, The
Life of Brian denounced 8-27, 859G1
RABBINICAL Council of Syrian and Near Eastern Sephardic Communities of America, The
Life of Brian denounced 8-27, 859G1
RABEN, H.
On Canary I '77 jet crash 5-29, 412C2
RABIES—*See MEDICINE–Diseases*
RABII, Lt. Gen. Amir Hussein
Arrested 2-11, 105G1
Executed 4-9, 276B3

RABIN, Yitzhak
Book excerpt on '48 war deleted 10-22, Allon disputes 10-24, 823G1

1980

RABIES—*See MEDICINE--Diseases*

RABIN, Yitzhak
Vs Weizman party role bid 11-22, 902A1
Peres defeats for Labor ldrship 12-18, 966E1

1976

On Ford aid veto threat 4-8, 258B2
Meets Vorster 4-9, 275F3
Sets 'red line' for Syrian troops in Leb 4-14, 258B1
Cautions Syria on Leb role 4-15, 274C1
In W Bank, assures Israeli settlers 4-20, 274F2
Heads group to study Arab grievances 5-23, vs Arab Galilee demands 5-24, 370D1, F1
On Syrian invasn of Leb 6-2, 385A2
Vs Syria, PLO control of Leb 6-15, 429G3
To head hijacking talks 7-1, 463A2
Briefs parlt on Uganda raid 7-4, 485F1
US lauds Uganda raid 7-4, 486G1
Vs Dayan mission to Uganda 7-10, 515E1
Links Amin to hijacking 7-11, 515B2
Denies Leb arms aid 7-22, 527E3
90 Minutes at Entebbe publshd 7-26, 547G1
Amin asks Entebbe paymt 8-19, 663C3
Sees US amb on Suez oil feud 9-8, 9-13, 759G2
On Allon troop exit plan 9-17, 699B3
Galilee Arabs score Koenig rpt stand 9-22, 738D1
Bars W Bank setlmts transfer 9-29, 738A1
Ordrs probe of Amoco rpt leak 9-29, 759A3
On US arms for Israel 10-10, 759G1
Cabt meets on Hebron unrest 10-10, 799B1
Bars Christian meeting 10-25, 798E2
No-confidence vote loses 10-26, 854F2
On US electn results 11-3—11-4, 826A2
Sees Ribicoff 11-11, doubts Sadat peace bid 11-11—11-17, 878C1
Vs Syrians, Palestinians near border, for Leb army control 11-23, 887B2; 11-28, 894C2
For Geneva conf talks 11-27, 894F2
Addresses Soclst Intl 11-27, 935C3
Vows Leb border force 11-29, 894G2
Egypt vs peace plea 12-2, 894A3
Wins confidence vote 12-14, ousts NRP 12-19; quits, sets early electns 12-20, 964B3
RABINOWITZ, Yehoshua
Submits budget 2-24, 157E1
US oil deal OKd 5-6, 338D3
Vs defns budget cut 6-20, 459G3
RABKIN, David
Arrested 7-29, 592D1
Charged in S Africa 9-7, 662B2
Sentenced 9-29, 733G3
RABKIN, Susan
Arrested 7-29, 592D1
Charged in S Africa 9-7, 662B2
Sentenced 9-29, 733G3
RABOTOSON, Francois de Paul
Named educ min 8-20, 926B1
RACHMANINOFF Piano Concerto No. 2 in C Minor (record album)
Wins Hall of Fame award 2-28, 460E3
RACICOT, Normand
Loses recount 12-1, 924D1
RACISM—*See also MINORITIES; geographic headings; for UN Zionism resolution, see JEWS*
UNESCO conf postponed 1-15, 36E2
UN ECOSOC debate resumes 4-13—4-30, 320F2
RADAR
Australia AF to get new equipmt 5-12, 380B2
RADIATION—*See 'Environmental Hazards' under ATOMIC Energy, 'Radiation Hazards' under ENVIRONMENT, 'Cancer' under MEDICINE*
RADICALS & Radicalism—*See group names (e.g., SDS, WEATHER Underground); country names*
FBI Developments—*See 'Intelligence Investigations' under U.S. GOVERNMENT—FEDERAL Bureau of Investigation*
RADIO, Celestin
Named pub works min 8-20, 926B1
RADIO Free Europe—*See BROADCASTING, Board for International under U.S. GOVERNMENT*
RADIO Liberty—*See BROADCASTING, Board for International under U.S. GOVERNMENT*
RADIOLOGY, American College of
Bars price-fixing 11-17, 988F3
RADNAY, John P.
SEC suit settled 5-11, 360B3
RADULOVIC, Ljubomir
Sentenced 3-12, 223B3
RADZIWILL, Lee Bouvier (Mrs. Stanislas)
Prince Radziwill dies 6-27, 524D3
RADZIWILL, Prince Stanislas
Dies 6-27, 524D3
RAFAEL, Farid
Leb finance min 12-9, 913D2
RAFAEL, Gideon
Protests UK UN vote 3-27, 227C3
RAFIE, Abdel Meguid al-
Residence shelled 5-13, 337E2
RAFTERY, S. Frank
Quits Ford panel 1-8, 4C1
RAGEN, Michael E.
Named in grain fraud 3-11, 247D3
Fine rptd 11-11, 990G2
RAGTIME (book)
On best seller list 1-25, 80B3; 2-29, 208E3; 12-5, 972F2
RAHALL, Nick Joe
Elected 11-2, 823F1, 831A3
RAHMAN, Obaidur
Arrested 11-29, 923E2
RAHMAN, Maj. Gen. Ziaur
Split with Tawab rptd 5-2, 332G1
Chrgs India aids rebels 9-25, 755B1
Electns postponed 11-21, 923G2
Takes full powers, arrests pol ldrs 11-29, 11-30, 923D2

1977

Vs Palestine Natl Cncl stand 3-20, 208E1
Peres replaces as Labor candidate 4-10, 267B2
Fined 4-11, 267A2
Wife fined 4-17, 329F2
Takes leave, Peres assumes power 4-22, 329E2
Sadat on Begin electn win 5-20, 401D3
Chrgs new US Mideast plan 5-29, 440B2
Begin becomes premier 6-21, 474G1
Vs Begin peace plan 7-19, 549G2
In Begin clash on US stand 7-23, 7-25, 7-27, 570G2, D3-G3
3 W Bank towns legalized 7-26, 570B1
Leb mil role rptd asked 8-22, 648E1
Greets Sadat 11-19, 889C1
RABINOWITZ, Yehoshua
Tied to kickback chrg 2-14, 135C2
RACAL Electronics Ltd.
Wins Milgo takeover battle 2-17, 275A1
RACHIDI, Hlaku Kenneth
Biko dies 9-12, 707E3
Arrested 10-19, 803G3
RACKER, Efraim
Gets Medal of Sci 11-22, 952B1
RACKETEERING—*See CRIME—Organized Crime*
RACINE, Wis.—*See WISCONSIN*
RACISM—*See HUMAN & Civil Rights, MINORITIES*
RACKMAN, Rabbi Emanuel
Elected Bar-Ilan Univ pres 3-2, 354B2
RADCLIFFE, Viscount (Cyril John)
Dies 4-2, 356G3
RADER, Dave
Traded to Cubs 12-8, 990E1
RADIATION—*See also ATOMIC Energy—Industrial Use*
US emb discounts Sovt microwave threat 1-4, 22F1
US emb employe tests ordrd 1-19, 1-21, 161G1-A2
Fluorocarbon aerosol warning ordrd 4-26, 323A2
Breast X-rays curbed 5-10, 431C2
Fluorocarbon ban proposed 5-11, 387G1
US rules out Sovt microwave harm 6-27, 530D1
Nobel won for radioimmunoassay 10-13, 951C3
'57 Nev A-test, cancer link probed 12-13, 1022C3
RADICALS & Radicalism—*See also country names*
Saxe sentenced 2-11, 140E1
Rudd, other Weathermen surrender 3-25—9-15, 839C1
Sacco, Vanzetti vindicated 7-19, 652G2
Chicago 7 figure named to OSHA 9-30, 808B2
RADICE, Lucio Lombardo
Disputes Italian NATO role 4-2, 284A2
RADIO—*See BROADCASTING*
RADIO, Celestin
Malagasy labor min 8-8, 772D1
RADIO Free Europe—*See U.S. GOVERNMENT—BROADCASTING, Board for International*
RADIO Liberty—*See U.S. GOVERNMENT—BROADCASTING, Board for International*
RADULESCU, Dan
Ousted re miners strike 10-21, 948B1
RAFAEL Rodriquez, Carlos
Angola war role rptd 1-31, 86B1
RAFSHOON, Gerald
Carter on mtg re poll drop 10-27, 814A1
RAGHURAMAIAH, Kotha
Quits Cong Party 5-6, 392B2
RAHIM Khan, Abdul
Quits amb post 4-13, 305E2
RAHMAN, Maj. Gen. Ziaur
Mushtaque sentenced 2-26, 183D1
Sworn pres 4-21, 309F1
Vote backs martial law 5-29, 451D2
Says army coup crushed 10-2, 763D2
Bans 3 parties 10-14, 805E2

1978

RABORN Jr., William F.
On Kennecott bd rival slate 3-27, 402G3
RACHIDI, Hlaku Kenneth
Rptd freed, banned 12-19, 989C2
RACHKOV, Valery
Wins World Amateur Boxing tourn 5-6—5-20, 600E2
RACISM—*See also MINORITIES*
UN conf censures Israel, S Africa; 12 Westn natns quit 8-14—8-26, 676G1-C2
RACISM & Racial Discrimination, UN Decade for Action to Combat—*See under UNITED Nations*
RACKETEERING—*See CRIME*
RACKMIL, Gladys
Platinum opens 11-12, 1031F2
RADAR
Carter budgets aircraft jamming equipmt 1-23, 45F1
USSR satellite falls in Canada 1-24, 57C1
USSR rptdly questnd US statns 2-28, 298E1
USSR look-down test rptd 12-26, 1020C3
FAA proposes air-safety rules 12-27, 1006E3, F3
RADIATION—*See ARMAMENTS—Atomic Weapons & Tests, ATOMIC Energy—Industrial Use, MEDICINE, subheads 'Cancer' and 'Radiation Hazards', MICROWAVES*
RADICALS & Radicalism—*See country, group, personal names*
RADIO—*See BROADCASTING, ELECTRIC & Electronics and PRESS*
RADIO City Music Hall Corp.
Rescued 4-13, 293C1
RADIO Free Europe—*See U.S. GOVERNMENT—BROADCASTING, Board for International*
RADIOLOGICAL Protection, International Commission on (ICRP)
UK safety study released 11-21, 965A1
RADIO Shack—*See TANDY Corp.*
RADZHABOV, Akper
Rptd sentenced 5-15, 416G2
RAE, Mike
Traded to Buccaneers 9-12, 1024D3
RAFFERTY, Gerry
Baker Street on best-seller list 6-7, 460F3; 7-5, 579G3
City to City on best-seller list 6-7, 460G3; 7-5, 580A1
RAFFERTY, Kevin
Wounded in Belfast 6-7, 474D3
RAFFILL, Joseph C.
Sea Gypsies released 4-26, 619E3
RAFFILL, Stewart
Sea Gypsies released 4-26, 619E3
RAFSHOON, Gerald R.
To join Carter staff 5-18, 386C3
Cancels Costanza TV appearnc 7-25, 606A1
RAHALL, Rep. Nick Joe (D, W. Va.)
Beats Hechler in primary 5-9, 363D1
Reelected 11-7, 852C4
RAHMAN, Maj. Gen. Ziaur (Bangladeshi president)
UK prime min visits 1-4—1-5, 37C1
Reelected 6-3, denies vote fraud 6-5, 435A1
Forms new Cabt 6-29, 538D1
RAI Guevara, Milton
DR min without portfolio 8-16, 648D2
RAILROAD Passenger Corp., National—*See AMTRAK*

1979

RABIN Memoirs, The (book)
Israel deletes excerpt 10-22, 823F1
RABINOWITZ, Victor
Lauds Sterns '57 spy chrg dismissal 3-22, 232E1
RABINOWITZ, Yehoshua
Dies 8-12, 671E3
RACISIM, Committee Against
KKK clash in Calif 8-19, 866A2
RACKETEERING—*See CRIME*
RADAR
Carter budgets aircraft 1-22, 42B3, 43B1
FAA updates NY area improvemt 3-12, 206G1
Air controllers score computer safety 11-20, 988F3-989A1
RADELAT, Paul
Beggars Soap Opera opens 7-23, 711D1
RADEMAKERS, Fons
Max Havelaar released 1-20, 174A3
RADER, Stanley R.
Worldwide Church put in receivership 1-3; barred from office 1-8, 23A3, E3
RADIATION—*See also ARMAMENTS–Atomic Weapons; ATOMIC Energy–Industrial; MEDICINE, subheads 'Cancer' and 'Radiation Hazards'*
Ultraviolet impact on aging rptd 3-20, 290G1
Solar ultraviolet radiatn, stratospheric ozone levels linked 6-22, 692D1
Ozone level study rptd 11-17, 1000E2
RADIATION, White House Interagency Task Force on Ionizing—*See under U.S. GOVERNMENT*
RADIO—*See BROADCASTING, ELECTRIC & Electronics and PRESS*
RADIO Free Europe—*See U.S. GOVERNMENT–BROADCASTING, Board for International*
RADIUM
Colo waste sites rptd 3-5, 187F1
RADIX, Kendrick
Seeks forgn ties 3-16, US overtures rptd 3-24, 236B3
RADNER, Gilda
Gilda Radner Live from NY opens 8-2, 711B3
RADO, James
Hair released 3-13, 528D2
RADOSH, Ronald
Julius Rosenberg article publshd 6-16, 466B1
RADZIEVSKY, Gen. Alexei
Dies 9-3, 756D3
RADZIWILL, Lee Bouvier
Postpones wedding 5-3, 392B2*
RAE, Robert
Scores bank rate hike 7-24, 562G3
RAFFERTY, Tony
Completes Death Valley run 7-15, 656D3
RAFI, Mohammad
Jail term reduced 10-8, 787F2
RAFSANJANI, Ayatollah Hasheimi
Shot 5-25, US blamed 5-26, 407D2*
Named dep interior min 7-19, 565F2
RAFSHOON, Gerald R.
3 Mile I NRC transcripts released 4-12, 275G2
Ga pastor joins staff 4-15, 300F3
Carter '76 campaign ad financing probed 5-25, 401B3; improprieties denied 6-22 500C2; FEC clears 8-21, 661G3
Curran probe clears on '76 ad finances 10-16, 782F3
RAFSHOON Advertising Agency Inc.
Carter '76 campaign ad financing probed 5-25, 401A3; improprieties denied 6-22, 500B2; FEC clears 8-21, 661G3
Curran probe clears on '76 ad finances 10-16, 782F3
RAGNI, Gerome
Hair released 3-13, 528D2
RAGONE, Stanley
On North Anna coal shift study 10-15, 807A2
RAGSDALE, George
NFL '78 kick return ldr 1-6, 80G2
RAHIMI, Lt. Gen. Amir
Arrested 2-11, 105G1
Executed 2-16, 125E1
RAHIMI, Brig. Gen. Saif Amir
Defies dismissal order 7-9, 525F1
RAHMAN, Hassam Abdel
Vs UN Palestinian film 8-28, 643D2
RAHMAN, Maj. Gen. Ziaur (Bangladeshi president)
Party wins parlt electns 2-18, sets martial law end 2-19, 172F3
Martial law lifted 4-7, 328G2
India accords reached 4-18, 328C2
RAHMIN, Abdulla
Sovt encroachmt in Sinkiang chrgd 9-29, 803A2
RAHWAY, N.J.—*See NEW Jersey*

1980

RABINOWITZ, Geraldine
FBI bribe plotters convicted 7-3, 655F2
RACINE, Ralph
Hart KOs, injures 5-17; Canada launches probe 7-7, 907D3
RACISM—*See also MINORITIES*
US UN women's conf motion withdrawn 7-28, conf adopts 5-yr plan 7-30, 587E2, A3
Bush scores Carter 9-17, 780G3
RC bishops family life conf opens 9-26, 810C3
Carter repudiates Young remark 10-15, 803D1
Carter, Reagan TV debate 10-28, 814A2
Carter hits Reagan debate statemt 10-29, 816D2
Miami riots linked 12-6, 963D1
RACKETEERING—*See CRIME–Organized*
RACKMIL, Gladys
West Side Story opens 2-14, 136G3
Perfectly Frank opens 11-30, 1003E3
RACOONS
Fla student to get rabies shots 2-9, 200A2
RACZ, Andrew
On Hunt group bond issue 3-26, 223C1
RACZ, Lajos
Wins Olympic medal 7-23, 624A3
RACZ International Inc.
Hunt silver-backed bond issue evaluated 3-26, 223C1
RADAR
US 'stealth' fighter said to evade detectn 8-20, 630B2
Reagan scores 'stealth' plane disclosure; Brown, Perry testify on leaks 9-4, 665D3
Sovt ABM system rptd updated 9-14, 730A3
RADCLIFFE College (Cambridge, Mass.)
Jordan dies 6-3, 528C2
RADIATION—*See also appropriate subheads under ARMAMENTS, ATOMIC Energy, MEDICINE*
Medit pollutn pact signed 5-17, 381C3
ESA satellite venture fails 5-23, 397A3
RADICH, Otto
Machado replaces as ASL com 12-17, 1001B3
RADIO—*See under BROADCASTING*
RADIO Liberty
Moslem broadcast dissatisfactn rptd 6-29, 490G2
RADIO-Television News Directors' Association
Frederick rptd honored 7-7, 638F2
RADNER, Gilda
Gilda Live released 3-28, 416G2
Lunch Hour opens 11-14, 892E3
First Family released 12-25, 1003G1
RADOFF, Franklin
Calif MD felony chrgs dismissed 12-29, 997C2
RAE, Mike
Rams win NFL conf title 1-6, 8G1
RAE, Robert
Scores Ottawa budget, energy plan 10-29, 858D2
RAFEEDIE, Judge Edward
Drops 3 chrgs in La Scola insulin-slaying 12-29, 997A2
RAFI, Mohammad
On Afghan rebel-army clashes 1-28, 67F2
RAFSANJANI, Ayatollah Hasheimi
Chosen parlt speaker 7-29, 571B3
Accepts US Cong hostage plea, scores policies 7-29, 571G3
US hostage debate delayed 8-4, 587C1
Gets Westn natns hostage plea 8-16; rebuffs appeal 8-17, 634C3
Hostage kin ask mtg 9-8; text of letter aired 9-15, 693F2
Demands US apology, cites Khomeini omission 9-15; cuts parlt debate on hostages 9-16, 693C2, E2
Restates demand on hostages 9-22, 719A3
Vs Iraq truce bid 9-29, 733F1
Warns of hostage trials 12-22; denounces Reagan, US 12-29, 974A1, D1
RAFT, George
Dies 11-24, 928C3
RAGE of Angels (book)
On best-seller list 7-13, 568A3; 8-17, 640E3; 9-14, 716A3; 10-12, 796D3
RAGING Bull (film)
Released 11-14, 972G3
RAHALL, Rep. Nick Joe (D, W.Va.)
Reelected 11-4, 844C4

1976

RAILROADS—*See also 'Rail' under ACCIDENTS; also specific lines; country names*
Ford State of Union message 1-19, 37D3, F3, 39C2, D2
US budget proposals 1-21, 66A1
Cong clears revised aid bill 1-28, 68D3
Ford signs aid bill 2-5, 109G3
'74, '75 food mktg costs rptd 2-11, 216A2
Grain co fraud claimed 3-16, 247G3
Carter urges US jobs 4-23, 305D2
1st ¼ profits rptd 4-29, 376C3
Black caucus drafts plank 5-1, 343F3
Default on potato futures 5-25, delivery chng asked 5-26, 397F1, B3
Dem platform text 6-15, 469G1, 474B2, 475B1
Sup Ct upholds ICC fund powers 6-17, 552F3
SEC sues Milwaukee Corp, settles 6-29, 984G1
Safety bill signed 7-8, 919D3
Lester Schoene dies 7-19, 656G3
Miners strike forces cutbacks 7-27, 553B2
2d ¼ profits rptd 7-28, 708F3
James Symes dies 8-3, 892G3
'77 funds OKd 8-4, 646B2; Ford signs 8-14, 982F1
GOP platform text 8-18, 607E1, A2
Pa VW pact signed 9-15, 988A1
Carter 'whistlestop' tour 9-20—9-21, 704F1, A3
'75 corp tax paymts rptd 10-2, 10-14, 847A2, C2
'77-78 aid signed 10-19, 834D2
3d ¼ profits rptd down 10-28, 866F2
New potato futures contract OKd 11-2, 990B1
Mayors urge rail rehabilitatn 12-14, 937A3
Amtrak—*See AMTRAK*
Conrail—*See CONRAIL*

RAILROADS, Association of American
Ailes named to Ford bd 2-17, 127E1

RAILSBACK, Rep. Thomas F. (R, Ill.)
Blocks gun control bill 3-2, 170G1
Vs Connally vp selectn 8-5, 584F2
Reelected 11-2, 829A3

1977

RAILROADS—*See also ACCIDENTS—Rail; also specific lines, country names*
DOT issues future trends rpt 1-15, 58A3
Ford '78 budget proposals 1-17, 33C1
ICC acts re gas shortage 1-24, 54E1
Carter urges retiremt prgrm rebates 1-27, 52C1
'76 4th ¼ profits rptd 2-8, 301D1
Milwaukee Road-BN merger bid rejctd 2-16, 213E2
Carter budget revisions 2-22, 125C3
Cong sets new '77 budget levels 3-3, 174E1
2 Penn Central ex-offcls cleared 3-11, 1 convicted 3-30, 491E3
Carter energy plan 4-18, 295A1
BN setls SEC complaint 4-28, 368F3
1st 2d ¼ profit rise rptd 4-28, 7-28, 668C3, F3
SEC 'betterment' accounting barred 4-29, 369B1
Rehabilitatn loan funds clear Cong 5-5, 365F2; Carter signs 5-13, 380D3
Orient Express ends svc 5-22, 458F3
Coal slurry bill deferred 6-27, 516A1, E1
NYC blackout halts 7-13—7-14, 537F2
Milwaukee Rd stock purchase OKd 7-15, 593C2
ICC curbs grain-car deals 8-1, 612G3
O'Neal rpt scores ICC 8-3, 651A3
Sen OKs coal transport aid 9-8, 702F3
FRA to buy C&NW stock 9-9, 778B3
Chicago mass transit funds OKd 9-19, 778E3
Grain shipping price policy curbed 10-3, 760D2
Health regulatn dispute review refused 10-3, 760E2
ICC OKs 5% freight rate hike 11-10, 899D3
Commuter line aid bill signed 11-16, 900A1
Brae Corp seeks Green Bay line 11-22; ICC OKs BN bid 11-30, BN drops offer 12-1, 1007B1
Winter fuel shortage guidelines set 12-1, 942A3
BN, Frisco OK merger 12-5, 1007D1
Coal strike begins 12-6, 937D1
White cos win minority-earmarked contract 12-13, 979C1
Milwaukee Rd bankrupt 12-19, 1006G3
Amtrak—*See separate listing*
Conrail—*See separate listing*

RAILROADS, Association of American
3d ¼ losses rptd 11-10, 899E3
High coal loadings rptd 12-6, 937D1

1978

RAILROADS—*See also specific lines, country names*
Coal slurry study issued 1-18, 49A1-A2
Carter budget proposals 1-23, 47B3
NE rail offcls resign 1-30; more funds allocated 2-11, projct delays rptd 2-24, 225A1
'77 4th ¼ profits rptd down 2-7, 282E3
Coal car shortage in West rptd 2-15, 104C2
Pullman porters join BRAC 2-28, 185B2
Penn Central reorganizatn plan OKd 3-9, 185F3-186F1
1st ¼ '77, '78 profits rptd down 4-27, 403D2
ICC rate rules backed by Appeals Ct 5-5, 433G3
Fed coal land leasing cautn urged 5-15, 471E2
Record 1st ¼ loss rptd 5-27, 433C3
ICC fines lines in freight-car shortage 6-15, 7-3, 569A2
Grand Central office complex barred by Sup Ct 6-26, 566G3
ICC orders freight rates cut back 6-30, 569F2-A3
Norfolk & Westn Rwy struck 7-10, 565F1
Coal slurry pipeline bill defeated 7-19, 550A2, C2
4 unions OK new pact 7-21, 565B1
LNG safety measures urged 7-31, 610A1, C1
ICC revises freight-car svc order 7-31, cuts rail fines 8-11, 643E2
US acts to end expanded N&W Rwy strike 9-26—9-29, strike ends 9-30, 809A2
Milwaukee Rd wins BN merger appeal 10-5, 812B2
Zambia reopens Rhodesia rte 10-6, 783E2
US study predicts decline 10-10, 812D1
Tax cut bill clears 10-15, 786E1
Sept indl output rise, RR strike linked 10-17, 790E2
Penn Central reorg ends 10-24, 875F3
ICC proposes trucking deregulatn; indus, cong ldrs leery 11-7—12-31, 1007E1
Chessie, Seaboard merger set 11-16, 897A1
Rate hike request trimmed to 7% 11-24, 6½% OKd 12-11, 1007G2-B3
Rail clerk strike stay renewal denied by Sup Ct 11-27, 937E2
'78 coal output rptd down, strike linked 12-20, 1010A2
Accidents—*See ACCIDENTS—Rail*
Amtrak—*See AMTRAK*
Conrail—*See CONRAIL*
Safety Issues
High carbon wheels curbed 3-23, 365D3
Roadbed, track maintenance aid hiked, '77 derailmts cited 4-15, 365E3
Tank-car deadlines advanced, other measures planned 5-9, 365G2

RAILROADS, Association of American
Coal study backed 1-18, 49F1
Record 1st ¼ loss rptd 5-27, 433C3
4 unions OK new pact 7-21, 565A1
Rate hike request trimmed to 7% 11-24, ICC Oks 6½% 12-11, 1007G2-B3

RAILROAD Signalmen, Brotherhood of (AFL-CIO)
New contract set 7-21, 565E1

RAILSBACK, Rep. Thomas F. (R, Ill.)
ERA rescissn amendmt rejected by House 8-15, 661F2, G2
Reelected 11-7, 850F3

1979

RAILROADS
US deregulatn plan rptd 1-15, 35C3
Carter budget proposals 1-22, 41G2, 45B1
Carter State of Union Message asks deregulatn 1-23, 46G3
ICC limits truckers' trust immunity 2-28, 167B1
US deregulatn bill introduced 3-23, shippers assail 6-6, 579D2
Yard noise rules proposed 4-16, 282A1
1st 1/4 profits rptd up 4-27, 385E1
Milwaukee Rd borrowing OKd 5-4, svc cut denied 6-1, 465F1
Diesel fuel allocatn rules adopted 5-25, 395D2
A-waste transport rules set 6-15, 610C1
Auto-Train withdraws fed loan applicatn 8-21, Seaboard extends pact 8-24, 726A2
Mondale offers more mass-transit aid 8-22, 726C1
Milwaukee Rd embargoes westn track 11-1, Carter signs aid bill 11-4, embargo lifted 11-5, 867E2-C3
NY bond issue OKd 11-6, 846G3
Southn Railway fined 11-12, 868F1-A2
ICC svc funds clear Cong 11-15, 11-19, Carter signs 11-30, 920E1
Milwaukee Rd bailout ruled legal 11-25, 989A2
Rock I takeover order extended 11-28, reorganizatn plan filed 12-28, 989B2
Auto-Train financing plan OKd 12-7, 989A3
ICC authority curb proposed 1-15, 35E3
Accidents—*See ACCIDENTS—Rail*
Amtrak—*See AMTRAK*
Conrail—*See CONRAIL*
Foreign Developments (including U.S. international news)
UK strike threatnd 1-9, 20C3; staged 1-23, 59B2
Spain workers strike 1-11–1-16, 61E1
UK-France channel tunnel planned 2-9, 135A3
French workers strike 3-6–3-7, 189F3
USSR line completed 6-22, 504F2
UK rail workers warn vs rail cuts 6-25, OK pay accord 6-26, 486D1
Israel-Egypt svc restoratn weighed 7-12, 511A1
CR labor unrest halts svc 8-14, 667C3
French workers strike 8-22, 633G1-634A1
Zimbabwe cuts Zambia links 10-12, 11-5, 11-18, 844F2, 899C2
Australia plans electrificatn 11-12, 888C1
Canada vows chem transport legis 11-13, 872B1
S Africa admits Zimbabwe mil role 11-30, 937C2
Australia backs electrificatn projcts 12-4, 947G3
China, Japan sign pact 12-7, 939E3
Labor Issues—*See also 'Foreign' above*
Religious worker union dues case refused by Sup Ct 1-8, 14E3
N&W Rwy, clerks OK accord 1-8, 87B2
Railway clerks settle 1-13, 87F1-A2
Pensn excluded from divorce pact by Sup Ct 1-22, 53G3
Carter averts dispatchers strike 5-8, contract accord reached 5-31, 598E2
Punitive damages vs unions barred by Sup Ct 5-29, 421C3
Rock Island struck 8-28, 8-29, Carter orders cooling-off period, ICC action 9-20; judge stalls bankruptcy 9-21, ICC orders takeover 9-26, 722A1-C3
Ill GM plant targeted for UAW strike 9-10, 698C1
Rock Island svc resumes 10-5, judge orders reorganizatn plan 10-10, contract accord reached 10-22, 830C3
Mergers & Acquisitions
Shareholders back Chessie-Seaboard merger 2-13, 205E3
Seaboard cleared of trust chrgs 2-22, 205G3
Southn Pacific to buy Ticor 3-28, 283D1
Paccar seeks Harnischfeger 6-11, 942G2
Penn Central to buy Marathon Mfg 8-10, 664D1
Southn Railway, N&W end merger talks 10-19, 868A2
Safety Issues
Jan-Sept '78 tank car derailmts rptd 4-9, 472C3
Canada vows chem transport legis 11-13, 872B1
Supreme Court Rulings
Religious worker union dues case refused 1-8, 14E3
Pensn excluded from divorce pact 1-22, 53G3
EEOC curb on BN data upheld 2-21, 128F3
ICC freight fee case refused 3-19, 203D2
US land grant easemt right curbed 3-27, 263B2
Punitive damages vs unions barred 5-29, 421C3
ICC freight rate suspensn power backed 6-11, 478D3
Penn Central reorganizatn challenges declined 10-1, 768E1

RAILROADS, Association of American
RR-yard noise rules proposed 4-16, 282C1

1980

RAILROADS
ICC orders BN refund 1-4, Sup Ct refuses stay 1-14, 37A3
Milwaukee Rd gets fed loan; Westn track purchase rejected in '79 1-7, 52G3
LIRR pres bd rpts; '79 agrmt cited 1-14, 53D1
State of State messages 1-15, 484F1; 2-19, 404C1
Carter asks deregulatn 1-21, 43F3
Rock I liquidatn ordrd 1-25, bids rptd 2-4; svc extensn asked 2-14, 131F1
Carter budget proposals 1-28, 73B1
Tax liability in worker compensatn backed by Sup Ct 2-19, 131C1
Rock I service extended 2-22, 147F3
Milwaukee Rd svc cut set 2-25, ICC spurns reorganizatn plans 3-19, 345E3-346E1
Carter seeks deregulatn legis 3-14, 201F1
Rock I svc continues 3-31, judge warns ICC on paymt 4-1, 345C3
LIRR struck 4-1, 267E3-268B1; pact reached 4-11, 289C3
'79 profits rptd up 4-23, 345B3
Rock I aid bill clears Cong 5-22, Carter signs 5-30, 427E1
Rock I svc cutback urged 5-27, 598B3
Rock I svc extended 5-30, 427B2
Rock I abandonmt OKd, worker aid law upset 6-2; Sup Ct bars ruling 7-2, rail law study 11-10, 868E2
Auto-Train financial, svc difficulties detailed 7-31—9-26, DC investors rescue attempt rptd 11-26, 958C2-D3
Dem conv keynote speech cites deregulatn 8-11, 612A2*, D2
ICC curbs collective rate fixing 8-13, 616E2
PATH strike ends 9-1, 704D2-C3
Deregulatn clears Cong 9-30, 10-1; signed 10-14, 783D3-784D1
A-fuel tariffs case declined by Sup Ct 10-6, 782D2
Itel rpts huge '79 loss 10-16, 784F1
Pensn revisn backed by Sup Ct 12-9, 936G3
New Haven RR reorgn challenge refused by Sup Ct 12-15, 957D2
Accidents—*See ACCIDENTS—Rail*
Amtrak—*See AMTRAK*
Conrail—*See CONRAIL*
Foreign Developments (including U.S. international news)
S Africa troops guard Zimbabwe links 1-6, Mugabe scores 1-8, 31D3
S Africa troops to leave Zimbabwe 1-26, 80D2
UK OKs Channel tunnel concept, bars funding 3-19, 212A2
UK pay pact set 4-17, 313D1
UK pact revisn OKd 4-29, 335C3
E, W Ger pact signed 4-30, 355C3
Mex-French projct agreed 5-18, 409D2
Canada Liberals back freight rate freeze 7-4—7-6, 543E2
Brit Rail plans sales 7-15, 544E1
Polish strikes 7-16, 7-23, 626C1, F1
China pledges Tanzam aid 9-2, 731B2
W Ger workers strike 9-17, 731F1
W Ger workers end strike 9-25, 300 rptd quit 9-29, 794G3
S Africa RR bombed 10-15, 793A2
E Ger-Polish svc suspended 11-26, 910G1
Mergers & Acquisitions
Union Pacific, MoPac set link 1-8, 52B3
Union Pacific to buy Westn Pacific 1-21, 131B2
Milwaukee Rd track sales set 3-19, 4-1, 346E1
BN, Frisco merger OKd 4-17, 345D2
Santa Fe, Southn Pacific merger set 5-15, 427A3
Southn Railway, N&W seek merger 6-2, 427C2
Southn Pacific to buy Rock I segment 6-10, 598E3
Southn Railway, N&W bds OK merger 7-22, 598F3
Union Pacific, MoPac, Westn Pacific file 9-15, 745G1
Trans Union OKs Marmon Group merger 9-22, 746F1
Chessie, Seaboard merger OKd 9-24, 745A3
BN merger stayed by Powell 11-21; appeals ct OKs link 11-24, Sup Ct lifts stay 11-25, 937G2-A3

RAILROADS, Association of American
'79 industry profits rptd up 4-23, 345B3

RAILSBACK, Rep. Thomas F. (R, Ill.)
Reelected 11-4, 842F3

1976

RAILWAY, Airline and Steamship Clerks, Freight Handlers, Express and Station Employes, Brotherhood of (AFL-CIO)
Rejects Conrail labor plan 3-23, 235G2
RAILWAY Association, U.S.—*See CONRAIL*
RAIMON—*See PELEJERO, Raimon*
RAISON, Timothy
In new UK shadow Cabt 11-19, 1004G1
RAJAONAH, Pierre
Killed 7-30, replaced 8-20, 926C1
RAJNAI, Klara
Wins Olympic medal 7-30, 574A2
RAKOTOMALALA, Lt. Col. Joel
Malagasy premr 1-11, 55E2
Killed 7-30, replaced 8-20, 926A1
RAKOTOMAVO, Bruno
Named forgn affairs min 8-20, 926B1
RAKOTONIANA, Justin
Named prime min 8-20, 926A1
RAKOTOVOA, Adriantina
Named communicatns min 8-20, 926B1
RAKOWSKI, Mieczyslaw
Wife protests Polish charter chng 2-10, 268G1
RALEIGH, N.C.—*See NORTH Carolina*
RALEIGH, C. Barry
China visit rptd 7-29, 545F2
RALL, Fritz-Josef
Heads govt Lockheed probe 3-15, 270D1
RALL, Gunter
Rptd cleared of Lockheed bribe 2-11, 132F2
RALLIS, George
Gets Greek educatn post 1-5, 73D2
RAMADAN, Milod el-Sadik
Denies shooting rpt 4-19, 334C1
Egypt ousts 6-30, 547E3
RAMBLA, Maria Dolores (d. 1974)
Slayer guillotined 7-28, 588F3
RAMETTA, Giovanni
Sought for contempt 1-7, 43D3
Indicted 7-13, 990B3
RAMGOOLAM, Sir Seewoosagur
At France-Africa summit 5-10—5-11, 355A3
OAU summit opens 7-2, 487G2, A3
Loses electns 12-20, 1013F1
RAMIREZ, Pedro Felipe
Forced to leave Colombia 2-1, 118A3
RAMIREZ, Raul
2d in Washn Star tourn 7-27, 716B2
2d in Volvo Int tennis 8-9, 656B2
RAMIREZ Sanchez, Illich (Carlos)
Link with Uganda hijacker rptd 7-5, 485G2, 486A1
Libya terrorists training rptd 7-15, 531B2
Rptd in Belgrade 9-6—9-10; denied 9-17, 722B1
RAMIREZ Vazquez, Pedro
Mexico pub works min 12-2, 907A1
RAMOS, Maj. Gen. Fidel
Retired 3-27, 255B3
RAMOS, Julio
Protests Uruguay emb abductn 6-28—7-7, 542C2
RAMOS Horta, Jose
Chrgs Australia, Indonesia block UN missn 2-10, 122F3
RAMPHAL, Shridath
Commonwealth plans Mozambique aid 3-4, 175F2
RAMPHELE, Dr. Mamphela
Arrested 8-13, 624B3
RAMPTON, Gov. Calvin L.
Matheson wins seat 11-2, 824B3
Stays Gilmore executn 11-11, 891C1
RANARD, Donald K.
On S Korea lobbying 11-13, 899D3
RANCUDO, Maj. Gen. Jose
Ousted as PI AF cmdr 3-27, 255C3
RANDALL, Rep William J. (D, Mo.)
Skelton wins seat 11-2, 823B3

1977

RAILWAY Association, U.S.—*See CONRAIL*
RAINBOLT II, John V.
On Brazil coffee prices 2-23, 169D1
RAINIER, Prince (Monaco)
Daughter's engagemt announced 8-25, 808B3
RAINIER, Ore.—*See OREGON*
RAISE the Titanic! (book)
On best-seller list 2-6, 120E3; 3-6, 184E3; 4-3, 264G1; 11-6, 872E2; 12-4, 1021A3
RAKEL, Bob
LA player injures rival 12-9, 990B3
RAKOTOARIJAONA, Lt. Col. Desire
Malagasy prime min 8-8, 772D1
RAKSAK Watanapanich
Arrested 3-28, 243C2
RALEIGH, N.C.—*See NORTH Carolina*
RALLIS, George
Named Greek econ min 11-28, 925A2
RAM, Jagjivan
Quits Cabt, Cong Party; forms new party 2-2, 71C1 ★ -A2
Pandit backs Gandhi foes 2-14, 116F1
Desai named prime min 2-14, 205E1
Rpt govt foes still held 2-20, 160C1
Named to Cabt, balks 3-26; relents 3-27, 239E3
Sworn defense min 3-26, 240A1
CDP joins Janata Party 5-1, 348C2
RAMACHANDRAN, P.
India energy min 3-26, 240C1
RAMALHO, Thales
Backs Geisel on US aid bar 3-6, 168C1
RAMAN, Gopalakrishnan
Singapore chrgs plot 2-16, 223E3
RAMAYANA Restaurant (N.Y.)—*See under INDONESIAN Enterprises*
RAMIREZ, Raul
Loses Miami Grand Prix 2-13, King Tour 5-1, 430F3, 431A1
Loses US Open doubles match 9-9, 787B2
RAMIREZ, Socorro
Socialst Bloc to back pres bid 8-10, 727A2
RAMIREZ Sanchez, Illich (Carlos)
Rpt French police sought revenge 9B2
Krocher-Tiedemann captured 12-20, 1017E3
RAMOS, Cesar
Young decisns Foreman 3-17, 263C1
RAMPHAL, Shridath
At Commonwealth finance mins conf 9-21—9-24, 936D2
RAMPHUL, Radha Krishna
Lauds US Amb Young 4-8, 272B2
RAMSBOTHAM, Sir Peter
Jay appointmt scored 5-11, 5-12, 391G3, 392A1
Declares state of emergency 12-2, 935E2
RANAGHAN, Kevin
On charismatic conf 7-20—7-24, 620C3
RANDAL, Jonathan C.
Detained in CAE 7-14—7-21, 634E3
RAND Corp.
Rpts US populatn shift 2-24, 183G3
Peak-load elec pricing urged 3-11, 277D3
White confrmd Defns asst secy 5-9, 418A2
Volunteer mil rpt issued 9-25, 777E2
Urban policy rpt studied 12-7, 959G3

1978

RAILWAY, Airline and Steamship Clerks, Freight Handlers, Express and Station Employes, Brotherhood of (BRAC) (AFL-CIO)
Pullman porters join 2-28, 185B2
Norfolk & Westn Rwy struck 7-10, 565F1
4 other unions OK pact 7-21, 565E1
'70 Northwest strike cited 8-15, 680G3
US acts to end expanded strike 9-26—9-29, strike ends 9-30, 809B2
Strike stay renewal denied by Sup Ct 11-27, 937E2
RAILWAY Association, U.S.—*See CONRAIL*
RAIN—*See STORMS & Floods*
RAINER, Ove
Backs Sweden A-power 6-14, 691A2
RAINIER III, Prince (Monaco)
Daughter married 6-28, 6-29, 580D1
RAIN and Shine (film)
Released 12-21, 1030D3
RAISIN River (Mich.)
Ford sued re pollution 2-1, 163C3
RAJSICH, Dave
Traded to Rangers 11-10, 1026B1
RAKAS v. Illinois
Police auto search power broadened by Sup Ct 12-5, 959D2
RALLIS, George
Named Greek forgn min 5-10, 373E3
Sees Turkish threat 5-16, 398F2
Greek EC entry terms set 12-21, 1017B3
RALSTON Purina Co.
PCB contaminated animal feed recalled 4-12, 727C3
Dean vows wage-price compliance 11-1, 863B3
RAM, Jagjivan
Singh quits Janata posts, party split seen 4-29, 374D3
Says India to buy UK-French jet 10-7, 797A1
RAMIREZ, Manuel Antonio
Shot at by guerrillas 9-18, 823A3
RAMIREZ, Raul
USTA ranks 8th 1-5, 22E3
Connors wins Grand Prix Masters 1-8, 22B3
Loses Amer Airlines Games 2-19, Volvo Classic 3-18, Rotterdam WCT 4-9; wins Monte Carlo WCT 4-16, 419A1-C1
Loses Player Classic 6-18, 540C1
Wimbledon results 7-8, 539F3
US Open results 9-10, 707C1
RAMIREZ, Socorro
Colombia pres bid rptd weak 5-28, 413F2
Runs 6th in pres vote 6-4, 443D2
RAMIREZ, Col. Victor
Bolivia labor min 11-24, 913E1
RAMIREZ Lima, Col. Samuel Humberto
Assassinated 6-20, 497G1
RAMIREZ Mercado, Sergio
On Nicaragua oppositn comm; seeks forgn mediatn 9-14, 705C3
RAMIS, Harold
Animal House released 7-27, 970D2
RAMLJAK, Aldo
Scores govt econ policies 8-25, 793E2
RAMOS, Domingo
Traded to Rangers 11-10, 1026B1
RAMOS, Dr. Pedro
Chamorro murder role alleged 1-13—1-22, 73E1
Nicaragua judge seeks US extraditn in Chamorro death case 4-11, 376C2
RAMSAY, Remak
Rear Column opens 11-19, 1031A3
RAMSBOTHAM, Peter
UK comm urges Bermuda independnc 8-2, 603G3
RAMSEY, Craig
NHL scoring ldr 4-9, 296E2
RAMUS, Al
Goin' South released 10-6, 970D1
RANDALL, Murray
Refutes King murder bounty 11-29, 938B2
RANDALL, Robert
Wins marijuana use for glaucoma 5-19, 728F3
RAND Corp.
Study rpts black-white wage gap narrowed 5-8, 810G2
MD malpractice claims studied 6-8, 577F3

1979

RAILWAY, Airline and Steamship Clerks, Freight Handlers, Express and Station Employes, Brotherhood of (BRAC) (AFL-CIO)
Norfolk & Westn accord signed 1-8, 87B2
39-mo contract setld 1-13, 87F1
Conrail pact agreed 3-23, 262F2
Otero backs Carter reelectn 7-30, 593D3
Rock Island struck 8-28, Carter orders cooling-off period 9-20; takeover set, pay issue settled 9-26, 722F1-B3
Rock Island svc resumes 10-5, accord reached 10-22, 830C3, G3
RAILWAY Association, U.S.—*See CONRAIL*
RAILWAY Labor Conference, National
Railway clerks settle 1-13, 87F1
RAIN—*See STORMS & Floods*
RAITT, Bonnie
At Diablo Canyon A-protest 4-7, 262A1
Performs at NYC A-protest 9-23, 742G2
RAJAGOPLAM Sampatkumar
Scores Viet refugee drowning 4-2, 299E1
RAJI, Parviz
Mrs Javits lobby role bared 5-30, 408C2
RAKOFF Alvin
City on Fire released 9-14, 819G3
RALSTON Purina Co.
Sen Danforth finances rptd 5-18, 383F3
RAM, Husang
'78 Wis bank interest rptd 11-26, 898A1
RAM, Jagjivan
Vs A-bomb for India 4-20, 323D3
Janata feud cited 6-26, Dharia backs as ldr 7-18, 544G1, C2
Gives up Cabt try 7-22, 573B1
Heads Janata Party 7-27, 573A2
Scores Parlt dissolutn 8-20, 634A3
RAMACHANDRAN, R. G.
Gandhi bars parlt race 5-20, 411E2
RAMADAN, Taha Yasir
Iraqi 1st vice premr 7-16, 544F3
RAMAGE, Rob
In NHL entry draft 8-9, 655A3
RAM Good (race horse)
3d in Queen's Plate 6-30, 876D3
RAMIREZ, Ramiro
Sancocho opens 3-28, 712C2
RAMIREZ, Raul
Loses libel case 4-18, 334C2
RAMIREZ, Raul (tennis player)
Loses Wimbledon men's doubles 7-7, 570D1
RAMIREZ Mercado, Sergio
Named to Nicaragua provisional junta 6-17, 461F1
Meets US envoy in Panama, plans outlined 6-27, 475A3
Scores US on aid policy 8-4, 603A3
Announces export controls, ethics code 8-9, 616D1, G1
Rpts 32.5 mln currency recall 8-26, 689C2
In US, seeks aid 9-24, 731C3
Announces trials for Somoza, 7000 war prisoners 11-29, 950B3
RAMIS, Harold
Meatballs released 7-3, 820A2
RAMPHAL, Shridath
Commonwealth conf held 8-1—8-7, 589E1
RAMSEY, Gail
Wins natl women's intercollegiate squash champs 3-4, 527C2
RAMSEY, Steve
NFL '78 punting ldr 1-6, 80C2
RANCHO Seco Nuclear Generating Station—*See CALIFORNIA—Atomic Energy*
RAND, Sally
Dies 8-31, 671E3
RAND Corp.
S Viet '75 collapse study rptd 1-7, 29C1-B3

1980

RAILWAY, Airline and Steamship Clerks, Freight Handlers, Express and Station Employes, Brotherhood of (BRAC) (AFL-CIO)
Kroll abstains on Carter endorsemt 8-20, 647A3
RAILWAY Association, U.S.—*See CONRAIL*
RAILWAY Carmen of America, Brotherhood of (AFL-CIO)
PATH strike ends 9-1, 704E2
RAILWAY Labor Executives' Association
Sup Ct bars pleas re Rock I ruling 7-2, 11-10, 868G2
RAIN—*See STORMS & Floods*
RAINBOW Warrior (research ship)
Spain impounds 6-18; escape prompts adm's dismissal 11-15, 903B3
RAISE the Titanic (film)
Released 8-1, 675D3
RAITCHEV, Valentin
Wins Olympic medal 7-30, 624D3
RAJAI, Mohammed Ali (Iranian premier)
Named premier 8-9, parlt OKs 8-11, 619G3-620A1
Amnesty Intl scores executns 8-28, 671E2
US asks hostage release 8-31, 671E1
Names Cabt, Bani-Sadr vs 8-31; parlt delays OK 9-2, 671C2
Scores UK detentn of Iranians 9-4, 671A3
Bani-Sadr OKs 14 Cabt mins 9-7, parlt approves 9-10, 688G3*
Scores Muskie hostage plea 9-9, 688C3
US not optimistic on hostages 9-12, 693G1-A2
Blames US for Iran-Iraq war 9-29, 733F1
US assures on AWACS to Saudis 10-1, 734D3
Meets Sovt amb 10-4; Sovt arms bid rejected 10-5, 758B3
Scores Iraqi unilateral truce 10-5, 758D2
USSR denies arms bid 10-8, 774F2
Vs Waldheim truce plan 10-13, 774A2
To present case vs Iraq to UN 10-15, 774D1
Carter, Muskie seek NYC mtg 10-16, 799G3
UN Cncl speech scores truce, US, Iraq; US denies chrgs 10-17—10-19, 798D2, B3
Iraq says seeks US spare parts 10-18, 799C2
Says US set to meet hostage terms 10-22, 799E3
Asks quick US reply on hostage terms 11-4, 853E3
Indifferent to US electn 11-5, 853G3
Calls UN peace mission 'waste' 894B3
Says US response re hostages unclear 11-22, 912C3
Confirms govt gets hostage control 12-1, 913B1
Seeks more war funds 12-3, 913E1
Revises hostage demand 12-27, 973B2
RAKER, Lee
Virginia wins NIT 3-20, 240F2
RAKHMANOV, Sultan
Wins Olympic medal 7-30, 624G2
RAKOFF, Alvin
Death Ship released 4-25, 416F2
RAKOWSKI, Mieczyslaw
Sees CP reforms 9-14, 710B2
RALEIGH—*See NORTH Carolina*
RALKOV, Gheorghi
Wins Olympic medal 7-23, 624B3
RALLIS, George John (Greek premier)
Aegean Sea air dispute ended 2-22, 2-23, 150A3
Elected premr 5-8, 352B2, C2
Wins confidence vote 5-23, 407D3
RAM, Jagjivan
Quits Janata Party 3-7, 232E3
Joins Congress oppositn 4-8, 275A2
RAMACHANDRAN, M. G.
Coalition wins Tamil Nadu vote 6-2, 445F1
RAMADAN, Mohammed Mustafa
Killed 4-11, 353A3
RAMADAN, Taha Yasin
Seeks Iran oil fields capture 10-21, 799D2
RAMAO, Emmanuel
Chrgs vs Beikman rptd dropped 9-20, 751B1
RAMBALDI, Carlo
Wins Oscar 4-14, 296A2
RAMERA, Carlos de
Held hostage in El Salvador 2-5, 97A1
Freed 2-18, 149C1
RAMIREZ, Jack
Wins primary for Mont gov 6-3, 439G2
Loses gov electn 11-4, 847E1, 851G3
RAMIREZ, Raul
Wins WCT doubles title 1-6, 213C2
Loses Florence Grand Prix 5-18, French Open men's doubles 6-7, 606F3, 607D3
RAMIREZ, Santos Lino
Captured 10-14, 872G3
RAMIREZ Mercado, Sergio
On Cncl of State expansn 4-21, 315F3
RAMOS, Hipolito
Wins Olympic medal 8-2, 622E1
RAMP, James (d. 1978)
Phila radicals convicted 5-8, 414E1
RAMPLING, Charlotte
Stardust Memories released 9-26, 836F3
RAMSEY, Chuck
NFL '79 punting ldr 1-5, 8B3
RANDAL, Jonathan
Arrives Teheran 2-25; expelled 2-28, 138A2
RANDALL, Florence Engel
Watcher in the Woods released 4-16, 416G3
RANDALL Jr., John H.
Dies 12-1, 1004B3

1976

RAND Corp.
Alcohol study scored 6-10, 442E3-443E1
Alcoholism study backed 8-8, 814D3
RANDOLPH, Sen. Jennings (D, W. Va.)
Dem conv pres vote, table 7-14, 507E3
Scores forest bill 9-30, 834B1
RANDOLPH, Leo
Wins Olympic medal 7-31, 574A1
RANDOLPH, Willie
In World Series 10-16—10-21, 815A3
RANDOLPH Institute, A. Philip
Rustin heads Cleaver Defense Fund 2-17, 272E1
RANDOM House Inc.
US files consent decree 7-27, 989A2
RANDRANTO, Marius
Named labor min 8-20, 926C1
RANGEL, Rep. Charles B. (D, N.Y.)
Carter meets black leaders 7-12, 513C2
Reelected 11-2, 830B2
RANGEL, Jose Vicente
Chrgs police torture leftists 8-6, 874A3
RANKIN, Judy
2d in LPGA championshp 5-30, 424C3
RANKIN, William E.
Elected to Summa bd 8-4, 596D3
RANUCCI, Christian
Guillotined 7-28, 588E3
RAO, C. Rajeswara
Scores Congress Party 1006G1
RAPE—*See under CRIME*
RAPHAEL, Yitzhak
Removed from Cabt 12-19, 964C3
RAPID City, S.D.—*See SOUTH Dakota*
RARICK, John R.
Loses Indep Party bid 8-27, 666D1
Defeated 11-2, 822A2
RARIVOSON, Justin
Named econ, trade min 8-20, 926B1
RAS al Khaima—*See UNITED Arab Emirates*
RASCOVICH, Mark
Dies 12-10, 1015D2
RASHID, Hussein Mohammed al-
Seized in hijack try 8-11, 579A1
Sentenced 11-16, 861D2
RASHID, Lt. Col. Khandakur Abdur
Visits Dacca, stay denied 4-20—4-30, 332A2
Rpts army split 5-2, 332F1
RASHIDOV, Sharaf R.
Politburo alternate member 3-5, 195D2
RASKATOV, Vladimir
Wins Olympic medal 7-22, 575E2
RASKIN, Marcus
Chrgs Chile in Letelier murder 9-21, 710F2
RASPE, Jan-Carl
Cited in Baader-Meinhof trail 1-27, 77B3
Meinhof found hanged 5-9, trial adjourned 5-13, 383A2
RASPERRY, John
FBI-terrorist ties chrgd 1-11, 42F1
RAST, L. E.
Southn Bell pol paymts admitted 10-25, 939D1
RATH, Fritz Josef
Rptd at US Lockheed hearings, clears Rall 2-11, 132G2
RATHBONE, Monroe J.
Dies 8-2, 816F3
RATIANI, Georgi
Chrgs US interference 4-18, 276G3
RATSIRAKA, Capt. Didier
Announces pol amnesty 1-1, 55E2
Sworn pres 1-4, names premr 1-11, 55E2
Names Cabt 8-20, 926A1
RAUBENHEIMER, A. J.
Named S Africa forestry min 1-22, 76F1
RAUSCH, Bishop James
Letelier burial mass in DC 9-26, 781A1
RAUSCHER, Dr. Frank J.
Cancer-agent unit set 3-29, 384A2
Backs breast X-ray 8-22, 680A1
Quits 9-20, named Cancer Soc vp 11-1, 876D1
RAVEL: Concerto for Left Hand and Concerto for piano in G, Faure: Fantaisie for Piano & Orchestra (record album)
Wins Grammy 2-28, 460D3
RAVEL: Daphnis et Chole (record album)
Wins Grammy 2-28, 460D3
RAVENS, Karl
Loses Lower Saxony revote 2-6, 157G2
RAWLS, Nancy W.
Replaced as Togo amb 9-15, 808C1
RAW Materials
Intl econ conf 2-11—2-20, 148B1
Hungary-Sovt barter pact rptd 4-1, 543A3
UNCTAD conf opens 5-5, 320F1
Kissinger addresses UNCTAD 5-6, 317C1, C2, 318A1
France proposes price stabilizatn fund 5-10—5-11, 355F3
Eur, Latin soc dems issue declaratn 5-25, 449G2
UNCTAD OKs commodity fund, vs US bank plan 5-30, US scores 6-1, 388E2, B3
Parsky on commodity pacts 6-1, 388E3
EC producers aid set 7-8, 529G2
Intl econ conf deadlocked 7-8—7-10, 7-12—7-17, 530D1
Canada exports to Japan cited 836A3
W Ger-Poland credit deel rptd 11-4, 907F1
UK Oct costs up 11-8, 853A3
Poland-USSR pact signed 11-15, 907D1
Soclst Intl holds cong 11-26—11-28, 935D3

1977

RANDLE, Lenny
Slugs mgr 3-28, punished 4-5, 310E3 ★
Pleads no contest 7-19, fined 7-28, 644G2
Sued by ex-Ranger mgr 9-21, 768D2
RANDOLPH, Sen. Jennings (D, W. Va.)
'76 spec interest gifts rptd 1-15, 128F3
On Carter energy plan 4-20, 293G1
Sees UMW strikers 8-5, 690B3
Minimum wage bill signed 11-1, 834C1
RANDOLPH, Willie
NL wins All-Star Game 7-19, 567E2
In AL playoff 10-5—10-9, 807A2
In World Series 10-11—10-18, 806G1
RANDOLPH Institute, A. Philip
Rustin at black ldrs mtg 8-29, 702F1
RANDOLPH-Macon College (Ashland, Va.)
Loses NCAA basketball title 3-19, 262D2
RANDOM House Inc.—*See under RCA*
RANG, Gerard
Arrested 3-10, 288E2
RANGEL, Jose Vicente
MAS nominates for pres 7-30, 674C2
RANKIN, J. Lee
FBI releases JFK assassinatn files 12-7, 943F1
RANKIN, Judy
2d in LPGA Championship 6-12, 951C1
LPGA top money winner 11-27, 951E1
RANUCCI, Christian (d. 1976)
Carrien guillotined 6-23, 543G1
RAO, C. Rajeswara
On CP protests 1-1, 8C1
RAO, J. Vengal
Quits Cong Party 5-6, 392B2
Mins quit in protest 12-1, 966C1
RAPE—*See under SEX Crimes*
RAPOPORT, Miguel
Executed 2-5, 197G3
RAPPAPORT, Bruce
Indonesia ct litigatn 1-18, 2-7, 2-24; Sutowo probe rptd 3-29, 304G2
Pertamina debt settled 8-11, 637C3
RARE Joel (race horse)
Cauthen sets earnings mark 10-24, 970B3
RAS al Khaima—*See UNITED Arab Emirates*
RASHID, Rao
Suspension rptd 545C1
RASHID el-Tahir Bakr
In Egypt, defns pact activated 1-15—1-16, 62D3
RASKIN, Marcus
Scores Chile econ policies 6-5, 448E3
RASPE, Jan-Carl
Sentenced 4-28, 352G1
Hunger strike ends 9-2, Schleyer kidnapers ask release 9-6, 9-8, 695B2
Baader atty arrested 9-30, extradited 11-16, 968E3
Hijacked jet freed 10-18, 789B1
Kills self 10-18, reactn 10-18—10-20, 789C1, 790D2-791E1
Schleyer slain 10-18, 791F1
Suicide rpt issued 10-26; buried 10-27, 868D1
Lufthansa jets threatened 11-5, 868A3
More explosives found 11-11, 888C2
RAST, L. E.
Indicted 8-2, 631B3
RASU Maritima S. A.
Gets ct injunctn vs Pertamina 2-7, revoked 2-24, 304F3
RATANOV, Anatoly
USSR cuts Somalia arms 10-19, 829G2
RATHER, Dan
Camera Never Blinks on best-seller list 9-4, 712E3
RATH Packing Co., The
Calif weight-labeling rules curbed 3-29, 277B1
'75, '76 losses rptd 340C2
RATSIRAKA, Didier (Malagasy president)
Names new Cabt 8-8, 772D1
RATTIGAN, Sir Terence
Dies 11-30, 952B3
RATTLEY, Jessie
Blacks meet re govt 'neglect' 8-29, 702F1
RATTRAY, Carl
Jamaica justice min 1-4, 46C1
RATZINGER, Msgr. Joseph
Inducted as cardinal 6-27, 768B3
RAU, Doug
In World Series 10-11—10-18, 806A3
RAUSCH, Archbishop James S.
Named Phoenix archbp 1-25, installed 3-22, 375G2
At bishops conf 5-3—5-6, 375E1
RAVENTOS, Joan
On meeting with king 6-21, 507B1
RAWLS Jr., Wendell
Wins Pulitzer 4-18, 355F2
RAW Materials
EC '76 econ growth rptd 2-22, 146C2
ASEAN trade pact signed; US, Japan talks urged 2-24, 145G2
Unctad commodity talks deadlocked 4-3, 297C3
India eases import curbs 4-28, 392D2
7-natn summit backs N-S talks, commodity fund 5-7—5-8, 357C2
N-S talks end 6-3, 437A2, F2, A3
S Korea ends import curbs 6-14, 470G2
Unctad common fund talks fail 12-1, Perez cites re poor natn debt rise 12-20, 973D2, 974E2

1978

RANDLE, Lenny
Lucchesi settles suit 12-8, 1026F2
RANDOLPH, A. Philip
Union merges with BRAC 2-28, 185C2
RANDOLPH, Sen. Jennings (D, W. Va.)
Votes vs Panama Canal neutrality pact 3-16, 177F2
Votes vs 2d Canal pact 4-18, 273B1
Wins primary 5-9, 363B1
Carter makes campaign visit 5-26, 404G3
Carter visits home town 10-7, 769B2
Reelected 11-7, 846B2, 848E3, 854F1
PAC contributns rptd 12-24, 1008F1
RANDOLPH, John F.
Wins cong primary in NY 9-12, 716C2
Loses US House electn 11-7, 849A2
RANDOM House Inc. (of RCA Corp.)
Snepp ruling scored 7-7, 527B3
RANELLI, J.
Halloween Bandit opens 12-18, 1031A2
RANGEL, Rep. Charles B. (D, N.Y.)
Backs gas price compromise 8-17, 677B3, D3
Reelected 11-7, 851E3
RANGEL, Jose Vicente
3d in pres vote 12-3, returns incomplete 12-8, 952B3
Herrera declared pres-elect in final vote count 12-11, 990A1
RANKIN, Jacob
Killed 7-4, 630B3
RANKIN, Judy
3d in LPGA Championship 6-11, 580A3
Wins LI Classic 8-13, 672F3
RANK Organization Ltd.
Japan joint plant set 8-23, 667C3
RANNEY, Frank H.
Named in US Teamster fund suit 2-1, 83E1
RAPE—*See under SEX Crimes*
RAPID City, S.D.—*See SOUTH Dakota*
RAPP, Paul
Avalanche released 8-28, 969B3
RAPP, Vernon
Fired as Cardinals mgr 4-25, 355C2
RAS al Khaima—*See NONALIGNED Nations Movement, UNITED Arab Emirates*
RASH, Steve
Buddy Holly Story released 7-21, 969E3
RASHAD, Ahmad
NFL '77 pass receiving ldr 1-1, 56F2
RASHID, Sheik Mohammad
Arrested 4-7, 268C2
RASPE, Jan-Carl
Atty smuggled guns into prison 1-12, 21G3
Experts confirm suicide 1-23, 115A1
Parlt com rpt affirms suicide 2-23, 152A2
Stuttgart prosecutor's office affirms suicide 5-8, 354D1
Eur rights ct rejcts jail abuse chrgs 7-19, 651A3
Memorial rally 10-18, 885G1
RATCHFORD, William R.
Wins US House seat 11-7, 847C2, 850D2
RATCHFORD v. Gay Lib
Mo univ challenge refused 2-21, 125C3
RATTNER, Abraham
Dies 2-14, 196E3
RAU, Johannes
N Rhine-Westphalia premr 9-19, 725G3 ★
RAUH, Joseph
Scores Sen block of job-bias bd 9-21, 720B3
RAUSCHENBERG, Robert
Elected to Arts Institute 2-7, 316D1
RAUTZHAN, Lance
In World Series 10-10—10-17, 800C1
RAVAIOLI, Aldo
Shot 7-6, 517B2
RAVAN, Robert
Mr Joyce opens 4-23, 760F2
RAVENEL, Charles D. (Pug)
Wins Sen primary in SC 6-13, 467C1
Loses US Sen electn 11-7, 852G3
RAVENS, Karl
Resigns as W Ger housing min 2-3, 93F2
RAVENSCROFT, Vernon
Loses Idaho primary for gov 8-8, 625E3
RAWLINS, Lester
Wins Tony 6-4, 579F2
RAWLS, Lou
Wins Grammy 2-24, 315G3
RAW Materials—*See also specific kinds*
Mex, China in 3d World aid talks 10-24—10-30, 903D3

1979

RANDLE, Lenny
Traded to Pirates 6-28, 1002A3
RANDOLPH, A(sa) Philip
Dies 5-16, 432E3
RANDOLPH, Sen. Jennings (D, W. Va.)
Environmt Com chrmn 1-23, 71D2
Labor '78 campaign gifts rptd 6-13, 595E1
RANDOLPH, Willie
AL batting ldr 9-30, 955E3
RANDOLPH Institute, A. Phillip
Rustin visits Israel 10-14—10-17, 780D3
RANDOM House Inc. (of RCA Corp.)
Bernstein barred from USSR fair 8-23, 689F3
RCA to sell 9-6, 682D2
Arnheiter libel cases declined by Sup Ct 10-29, 884A2
RANGEL, Rep. Charles B. (D, N.Y.)
Carter hosp cost plan faces hurdles 2-13, 110C1
At hosp cost bill ceremony 3-6, 163C2
RANIER Bancorporation
Columbia U sells stock 3-23, 271A1
RANKIN, Judy
2d in Corning Classic 5-27, Lady Stroh 7-1, Mayflower 7-8, 587A3-E3
Wins Westn Union Intl 8-13; 2d in Columbia Savings Classic 9-9, 970A1, D1
LPGA top money winner 11-30, 969G2
RANKINS v. Commission on Professional Competence
Case dismissed by Sup Ct 12-10, 988G1
RANSOHOFF, Martin
Wanderers released 7-13, 820F3
RAPE—*See under SEX Crimes*
RAPE of Love (film)
Released 9-23, 820A3
RAPID-American Corp.
Schenley Industries Inc.
SEC setlmt rptd 2-16, 131E3
RAPPAPORT, Michele
Old Boyfriends released 3-21, 528C3
RARITAN River (N.J.)
US files pollutn suit 2-7, 129G3
RAS al Khaima—*See UNITED Arab Emirates*
RASCOE, Judith
Portrait of the Artist released 4-21, 528D3
RASHAD, Ahmad
NFL '78 receiving ldr 1-6, 80F1
NFC wins Pro Bowl; named game MVP 1-29, 79G3
RASKOB, John Jacob (1879-1950)
USSR to get former estate 7-13, 568C2
RASMUSSEN, Norman C.
'75 A-safety rpt called unreliable 1-19, 54C2
UCS asks A-plant shutdown 1-26, 90B3
3 Mile I A-accident raises safety issues 3-28, 241F1
RATHJENS, George
Hansen H-bomb letter published 9-16, 9-18, reactn 9-17, 713G2, 714C2; text of letter 714D1-717E3
RATIA, Armi
Dies 10-3, 860C3
RAT'S Nest
Opens 2-2, 292D2
RATTRAY, Alfred E.
Vs Nicaragua interventn 6-21, 461A1
RAUCH, Robert
Vs EPA coal-use rule 5-25, 404B1
Vs easing of Ohio air rule 6-6, 423B1
RAUCH, Sheila Brewster
Marries Joseph Kennedy 2d 2-3, 176B1*
RAVETCH, Irving
Norma Rae released 3-1, 174C3
RAVITCH, Richard
Chrgs Syrian abuse of Jews 2-22, 148B2
RAWLINGS, Flight Lt. Jerry (Ghanaian head of state); replaced Sept. 24)
Coup attempt fails 5-15; chrgs econ exploitatn 5-28, 425A2
Ousts Akuffo 6-4; named head of state; vows electns, civiln rule 6-5, 425G1
Acheampong executed 6-16, 468D3
Akuffo, Afrifa, 4 others executed; anti-corruptn drive rptd 6-26, 485F2
Vows executns halt 6-30, 524B2, D2
Limann backs anti-corruptn fight 7-11, 524A2
Limann takes office 9-24, 721D2
RAWLS, Lana Jean
Jordan cocaine allegatns rptd 9-16, 9-26, immunity bid noted 9-28, 767E2, D3
RAWLS, Lou
Jordan cocaine allegatns by ex-wife rptd 9-16, 9-26, immunity bid noted 9-28, 767F2, D3
RAW Materials—*See COMMODITIES*

1980

RANDOLPH, Sen. Jennings (D, W. Va.)
On toxic waste clean-up 11-24, 898E1
RANDOLPH, John
American Clock opens 11-20, 1003A3
RANDOLPH, Leo
TKOs Cardona for WBA junior featherwgt title 4-4, 1000F3
RANDOLPH, Lillian
Dies 9-12, 756A2
RANDOLPH, Willie
NL wins All-Star Game 7-8, 636D1, G1, A2
RANDOM House Inc. (of RCA Corp.)
Newhouse purchase OKd 2-6, 386D1
RANDOM Winds (book)
On best-seller list 6-8, 448B3; 7-13, 568B3; 8-17, 640E3, 9-14, 716B3
RANGEL, Rep. Charles B. (D, N.Y.)
Reelected 11-4, 843E3
RANKIN, Jill
Old Dominion wins AIAW basketball title 3-23, 240C3
RANKIN, Judy
2d in Honda Civic Classic 3-16, 412A3
RANSEY, Kelvin
In NBA draft; traded to Trailblazers 6-10, 447C1, F1
RANSOHOFF, Martin
Change of Seasons released 12-17, 1003G1
RAO, P. V. Narasimha
Named Indian forgn min 1-14, 39F3
In US talks 1-30—1-31, 83A3
Announces Cambodia ties 7-7, 547F2
Addresses UN aid talks 8-25, 642D3
RAPHAELSON, Samson
Jazz Singer released 12-19, 1003B2
RAPPAPORT, Paul
Dies 4-21, 360A3
RAPPER'S Delight (recording)
On best-seller list 1-2, 40E3; 2-6, 120F3
RARITAN River (N.J.)
Edison dump to be covered 1-30, 93D3
RAS al Khaima—*See UAE*
RASHAD, Ahmad
NFL '79 receiving ldr 1-5, 8F2
RASHCHUPKIN, Viktor
Wins Olympic medal 7-28, 624C1
RASHEED, Hakeem Abdul (Clifford Jones)
Convicted of mail fraud 2-9, 157B2, F2
RASMUSSEN, Hans Kjeld
Wins Olympic medal 7-26, 623D2
RATEBZAD, Anahita
Slain 7-21, 602D1
RATHER, Dan
Named CBS anchorman 2-15, 198E3
Denies tie to Afghan gang slayings 8-4, 602E1
RATTLEY, Jessie M.
Addresses cities conv 12-1, 914E3
RAUH, Carl
Vesco grand jury ends 4-1, 251B3
RAVELO Renedo, Fernando
Accompanies DR Emb captors to Cuba 4-27, 335G1
RAVENAL, Charles
Loses US House electn 11-4, 850E1
RAVENITE Social Club (N.Y., N.Y.)
Galante slaying probe figures indicted 3-3, 215F1
RAVISHANKAR University (Raipur, India)
Galaxy formatn study rptd 8-14, 716B1
RAVIV, Dan
Rpt claims '79 Israel A-test 2-21; Israel cancels credentials 2-24, 141F3

1976

RAY, A. N.
Upholds political jailings 4-28, 313C2
RAY, Dixy Lee
Wins gov primary 9-21, 804C3
Elected 11-2, 820C3, 825D1, B2, 831D2
RAY, Elizabeth
Hays admits affair 5-25, 392C2
House to cooperate in probe 6-9, 433B3
Chrgs of sex with Gravel rptd 6-12, 434B1
Washn Fringe Benefit cited 6-12, 434D1
Hays quits reelectn race 8-13, 636G1
Hays suits dismissed 10-26, Justice Dept drops chrgs 12-8, 982B1
RAY, Franklin Edward
Kidnapped 7-15, 560C1
RAY, James Earl
Appeal denied 5-10, 384F2
Transferred to new jail 8-13, 640D3
Sup Ct bars review of guilty plea rule 12-13, 960D2
RAY, Man
Dies 11-18, 970A3
RAY, Gov. Robert D. (R, Iowa)
In Iowa 1-17, trials in straw vote 1-19, 41C1
Ford lists as potential VP 1-22, 41A2
Leads Ford forces 6-18, 451D1
On platform guidelines 6-21, 451E1
Outgoing Govs Conf chrmn 7-6, 493B1
GOP platform com actn 8-8—8-13, 583A1-E1
VP prospect cited 8-10, 584C1
RAYTHEON Co.
'75 arms sales listed 2-6, 147C2
US cancels Jordan missile order 4-15, 274C3
RAZAFIMAHATRATRA, Victor Cardinal
Appointed cardinal 4-27, 336C2
RAZAK, Abdul
Dies 1-14, 55F2
Australian ldr at funeral 1-16, 46B1
RAZAKABOANA, Rakoto
Named finance min 8-20, 926B1
RCA Corp.
Vows no boycott compliance 3-18, 747B2
Conrad quits, Griffiths named 9-16, 708G1
Fluke rpts boycott noncompliance 11-2, 986A3
Hertz Corp.
FTC trust suit setld 7-12, 989A3
National Broadcasting Co. (NBC)
Young dies 1-12, 56G3
Muskie rebuts Ford message 1-21, 40E1
Bush on Meet the Press 2-22, 151F1
Reagan on Meet the Press 3-7, 180A2
Reagan paid TV address 3-31, 232G3
Walters moves to ABC 4-22, 504A2
Goldwater on Meet the Press 5-2, 324A2
TV man detained in W Bank 5-7, 338G2
Airs Kissinger interview 5-17, 359B1
Wins Emmy sports award 5-17, 460C2
Giscard on Meet the Press 5-23, 372E2
Carter on Meet the Press 7-11, 509E1
Reagan on Today 7-22, 549F3
Sees Ford nominatn 8-17, 601E3
OKs pres debate rules 9-18, 703C2
Newman moderates pres debates 9-23, 700G2
Scranton on Meet the Press 10-3, 744C2
Valeriani on pres debate panel 10-6, 740F2
Berger on pres debate panel 10-15, 782B3
Friedman on Meet the Press 10-24, 809F3
Pres vote issues polled 11-2, 818B3
OKs US programming pact 11-17, 869D1
FCC probe requested 11-23, 901D1
Carter on Today show 12-3, 916E2
R Document, The (book)
On best-seller list 12-5, 972G2
READ, John C.
Labor asst secy 4-26; confrmd 5-12, 412A2
READER'S Digest (magazine)
Canada publicatn agrmt rptd 2-3, 116E3
Ford, Carter interviews 9-19, 704A1
READING, Pa.—*See PENNSYLVANIA*
READING Anthracite Coal Co.
Indicted 11-19, 989E2
READING Railway System
Chessie drops out of Conrail 3-23, 235E2
Conrail begins operation 4-1, 235E1

1977

RAY, A. N.
Retires as chief justice, Beg named 1-29, 71A3
RAY, Gov. Dixy Lee (D, Wash.)
Cloud-seeding progrm starts 2-28, 153E1
RAY, James Earl
Justice Dept findings cited 2-2, 77A2
Justice Dept issues King rpt 2-18, 149G1
King hearing proposed 3-3, 149E1
New bullet tests set 3-17, sees House com lawyers 3-22, 228A3
Escapes jail 6-10, recaptured 6-13; conspiracy discounted 6-14, 459A1
Sentenced for escape 10-27, 848C1
RAY, Rabi
Released 1-5, 45D3
RAYI, Hassan
Hanged 1-6, 2E2
RAYTHEON Co.
Israel missile sale to Chile rptd 1-8, 28E3
Falcon Seaboard purchase set 6-22, 519C2
RAZA Kasuri, Ahmed
Quits Pak ruling party 4-8, 305F2
RAZA Khan, Amer
Arrested 3-25, 258G3
RAZOUK, Brig. Gen. Abdul Hamid
Slain 6-18, 496E2
RCA American Communications Inc.—*See under RCA*
RCA Corp.
Princeton lab employe spy role rptd 1-7, 41C3
Rptd vs TV import curbs 3-14, 208E3
Solar cell advance rptd 7-5, 559B1
USSR claims Jews influence 7-22, 589B2
Bethlehem tops record loss 10-26, 836G2
National Broadcasting Co. (NBC)
Sadat on 'Today' 1-3, 10G1
FCC sets probe 1-14, 119E1
Ford contract rptd 1-29, 236C3
Moscow Olympics pact signed 2-1, Satra sues 2-14, 130G3, 131E1
Czechs detain Collitt 2-4, 114B3 ★
Sex-bias suit accord rptd 2-13, 279C1
Violence curb pledged 2-14, 157E3
Kissinger contract rptd 2-17, 131B2
Czechs return Collitt papers 3-1, 220F3
Califano on Meet the Press 3-20, 236A1
Emmy broadcast cancelled 4-15, 355B3
Energy producers on Meet the Press 4-24, 319B3, G3, 320A1
Giscard on 'Today' 5-9, 358E2
To show Christ film yrly 5-16, 395E2
Ben Grauer dies 5-31, 452A3
GOP energy plan TV rebuttal 6-2, 443D1
Schlesinger on Meet the Press 7-10, 538C1, E2
Emmy academies end dispute 7-12, 583C3
'Scottsboro' libel suit dismissed 7-12, 643B1
USSR claims Jews influence 7-22, 589B2
TV job bias study refuted 8-15, 643A1
Howard fired as NBC-TV pres, sports unit formed 8-22, 658A3
Sex-bias suit settled 8-31, 979C2
CIA links charged, denied 9-12, 720B3, F3, 721D1
Ali fight sets TV viewing record 9-29, 827D3
House subcom probes TV sports 10-4, 11-2, 949E3, 950C1
CBS reorganizes 10-17, 846A2
NFL record TV pact rptd 10-26, 950F1-A2
Trust accord OKd 12-1, 918B3
Satra drops Olympic suit 12-9, 971D2
On most reliable govt news source list 12-10, 1009C1
Random House Inc.
Boycotts USSR book fair 9-6—9-14, 765F3
Secret publicatn of book on Viet evacuatn rptd 11-18, 897D3
RCA American Communications Inc.
Viacom satellite pay-TV pact rptd 10-25, 921D1
RCA Records
Presley records sold out 8-18, 696C1
RCD—*See REGIONAL Cooperation for Development*
RCMP (Royal Canadian Mounted Police)—*See under CANADA*
READ, Benjamin H.
Named State undersecy 7-25, confrmd 8-3, 626D3
READ, William
Loop license signed 8-1, 724E3
READER'S Digest (magazine)
Laird chrgs USSR ABM violatns 11-23, 997D1
READER'S Digest Association Inc.
Sex bias suit settled 11-4, 979A2
READING Anthracite Coal Co.
Fined, Dougan chrgs dropped 3-21, 520B3

1978

RAY, James Earl
King murder plot alleged 7-26, 589A3
House com hearings 8-14—8-18, testifies 8-16—8-18, 641A1
Confessn alleged by UK ex-cop, atty denounces 8-18, 641B3
Cowden retracts alibi 8-18, 642B1
Preyer on King conspiracy evidence 9-24, 898E1
Married 10-13, 844D3
House com hearings resume 11-9—11-17, testimony declined 11-10, 898D1-D3
House com hearings end: family plot, bounty offer alleged; Lane assailed 11-17—12-1, 937G3-938F2
Seeks FBI King tapes 12-12, 1002A3
Tenn gov's aides arrested 12-15, 1011A2
House com finds King plot likely 12-30, 1002C1, E2
RAY, Jerry
King plot role alleged 11-27, denied 11-30, 938A1
Seeks FBI King tapes 12-12, 1002B3
RAY, John
King plot role alleged 11-27, denied 11-30, 12-1, 938A1, E1
Arrested for burglary, assault 11-27, 938F1
RAY, Jole
Dies 5-13, 440D3
RAY, Rabi
Quits Janata post 7-2, 516G1, E2
RAY, Gov. Robert D. (R, Iowa)
Wins renomination 6-6, 448E1
Reelected 11-7, 853E2, 854C2
RAY, Satyajit
Chess Players released 5-17, 619A1
RAYMOND Motor Transport v. Rice
Wis truck-length limit voided 2-21, 126E1
RAYTHEON Co.
United Engineers in A-plant constructn accord 4-18, 281B3
United Engineers chrgd in W Va scaffold collapse 6-8, 459E3
RAY v. Atlantic Richfield Co.
States curbed on oil tanker regulatn 3-6, 161E3
RAZAF, Anzy
Eubie opens 9-20, 1031E1
RCA Corp.
Pfeiffer named dir 9-13, 759B3
USSR color TV deal rptd 10-5, 821A1
Alaska phone unit sale set 11-30, 935B2
National Broadcasting Co. (NBC)
Silverman to head 1-20, 75D2
Sadat interview broadcast 2-5, 77B2
'Holocaust' aired 4-16—4-19, NBC rpts 120 mln viewers 4-20, 316G1
Sex abuse suit OKd by Sup Ct 4-24, 322A2
Sex abuse suit dismissed 8-8, 635B2-A3
Carter poll ratings 8-10, 682C2
Poll rpts econ pessimism growing 8-13, 679E2
ERA poll rptd 8-16, 661B3
Independent news producers sue 9-11, 759G1
Pfeiffer named chrmn 9-13, 759B3
Fla slayer loses TV violence suit 9-26, 759G2
McGovern on Meet the Press 10-15, 784G2
Kahn on Meet the Press 11-5, 863G2
2 Calif newsmen in Guyana cult probe missn 11-15—11-17, killed 11-18, bodies returned 11-21, 889E2, 891C1
SBA loan guarantee to Brokaw rptd 11-16, 919D3
Fall TV lineup dropped 11-29, 1030C1
Vance on Meet the Press 12-17, 973D2
Random House Inc.—*See separate listing*
Sarnoff Laboratory (Princeton, N.J.)
Solar cell advance questnd 11-30, 983C2
READ, John Kingsley
Racial slurs stir dispute 1-6, 18E1
REA Express Inc. (defunct)
Kole pleads guilty 1-16, sentenced 3-31, 310C1
Bankruptcy case review refused by Sup Ct 3-20, 206A1

1979

RAY, David L.
Worldwide Church receivership lifted 3-17, 376C2
RAY, Gov. Dixy Lee (D, Wash.)
Closes Hanford A-dump 10-4, 806G2-A3
Announces Hanford A-dump reopening 11-19, 885D3-886A1
RAY, James Earl
Parole deal rptd too costly 1-18, escape convictn upheld 2-21, 156D2
House com final rpt issued 7-17, 538C1
Caught in jail break 11-5, 891E2
RAY, Jerry
House com final rpt issued 7-17, 538D1
RAY, John
House com final rpt issued 7-17, 538D1
RAY, Nicholas
Dies 6-1, 508D3
RAY, Rabi
Sworn India health min 1-24, 97A3
Resigns 7-12, 544A2
RAYE, Martha
Concorde Airport '79 released 8-3, 820A1
RAYMOND, Bill
Mercier & Camier opens 10-25, 956D3
RAYMOND, Cindy
Sentenced 12-6—12-7, 1000D1
RAYMOND, Gen. Claude
Haitian defense min 11-13, 874G1
RAYNE, Fred
Kidnaped Beckman execs freed 11-7, 872F2
RAYSES, Vidamantas
Alcoholism study rptd 1-5, 289C3
RAYTHEON Co.
9th in '78 defns contracts 8-1, 609C1
Beech Aircraft merger set 10-2, 785A1
Amana franchise terminatn case refused by Sup Ct 10-29, 884C1
RCA Corp.
CIT purchase sought 7-5, bid fails 7-10, 517E1
Records unit staff firings cited 8-10, 618E1
CIT merger set 8-17, unit sales sought 9-6, 682A2-E2
Satcom III contact lost 12-10, 991D1
Conrad pleads guilty 12-18, 1000F1
National Broadcasting Co. (NBC)
Carter interviewed 1-13, 31F2
Wage-price compliance rptd 2-6, 128C1
Schlesinger on Meet the Press 2-25, 143F3
Klein quits as program chief, Currlin replaces 3-5, 334G3
Goodman retiremt plan rptd 3-8, 335A1
Ex-offcl pleads guilty 3-28, expense acct scandal grows 4-19, 334E2
Salant vice chrmn apptmt rptd 3-29, 335A1
Carson won't quit Tonight Show 5-2, 334B3
Energy shortage poll rptd 5-4, 343F1-B2
Kennedy interviewed re Chappaquiddick 7-17, 539F1
Natl Sports Festival held 7-21—8-1, 799C1
ABC-TV affiliates rptd on par 7-31, 588B2
Iran ousts 4-man TV crew 8-6, 602D2
Jaffe linked to KGB 8-11, 611B2
Small named news div pres 8-28, 756G1
Carter job rating poll rptd 9-13, 680A2
ABC wins TV rights to '84 LA Olympics 9-25, 797C3
'77 trust setlmt challenge refused by Sup Ct 10-1, 768C2
FCC scores children's TV 10-30; NAB responds 11-1, 858B3
Iran emb hostage interviewed 12-10; networks, Admin score 12-11, 12-10, 934A3
'77 trust setlmt challenge refused again by Sup Ct 12-10, 988A2
Random House Inc.—*See separate listing*
RCA Global Communications Inc.
FCC unit rejects Postal Svc satellite leasing plan 10-18, 921F2
RCA Global Communications Inc.—*See under RCA Corp.*
READER'S Digest (magazine)
Nixon Admin pub TV moves disclosed 2-24, 194C2
Libel suit rights broadened by Sup Ct 6-26, 540B3
REA Express Inc. (defunct)
Kania indicted for funds misuse 3-8, 239F3

1980

RAY, Gov. Dixy Lee (D, Wash.)
State of State message 1-15, 484B1
Backs big business 4-17, 308D2
Defeated in primary 9-16, 724A2
Spellman wins seat 11-4, 852B3
RAY, Donald W.
Indicted in Brilab probe 6-12, 454F2
Acquitted 10-23, 971C2
RAY, James
In NBA draft 6-10, 447F1
RAY, John
On UK fiber curb 2-5, 125A2
RAY, Gov. Robert D. (R, Iowa)
State of State message 1-15, 269A2
RAYFIELD, Allen L.
Named GTE Communicatns pres 7-2, 600G2
RAYMOND, Alex
Flash Gordon released 12-5, 972E3
RAYMOND, Gen. Claude
Dismissed from Haiti Cabt 4-26, 336A1
RAYTHEON Co.
9th in '79 defns contracts 5-28, 403F1
RCA Corp.
Valente becomes pres 1-1, fired 6-18, 582G1
CBS video disk pact signed 1-10, 120F1
Satellite rental plans rptd, missing Satcom insurnc claims cited 2-20, 160C3
Zenith joins in video disk pact 3-3, 239C3
Lloyd's Satcom liability cited 3-31, 266F1
Pfeiffer resigns as dir 7-10, 582B1
National Broadcasting Co. (NBC)
Rozelle defends Oilers call 1-7, 23A2
CBS, RCA sign video disk pact 1-10, 120A2
Carter on Meet the Press 1-20, 45C2, 50G1
Moscow Olympic boycott $ loss rptd 1-20, 45E3
Mobil TV ad rejectn rptd 1-31, 120E1
Abscam probe revealed 2-2, 81B1
Iran chrgs Lewis took gifts from shah 2-9, 122B3
Iran readmits newsmen 3-7, 178C2
Carter ad bid upheld by ct 3-14, 222C1
Moscow Olympics coverage barred, $61 mln rptd lost 3-28, 259D1
Iran hostage film purchase rejctd 4-10, 282C3
Revised Olympic coverage hinted 4-14, 283F2
Bush on Meet the Press 4-20, 328C2
'79-80 Nielsen ratings rptd, CBS regains lead 4-22, 376B1
Olympic telecast plans dropped, loss estimated at $22 mln 5-6, 379D3
Carson contract signing rptd 5-6, 470G3
CBS, US settle trust dispute 5-8, 501C3
Kennedy on Meet the Press 6-1, 422G3
Managemt realigned, Segelstein named TV pres 6-3, 501D2
Kalb, Mudd get posts 6-18, 7-1, 638F2
Pfeiffer sees Silverman 7-7, relieved of duties 7-8; resigns as chrmn 7-10, 582B1
Frederick rptd honored 7-7, 638E2
Barnes on Meet the Press 7-27, 570G1
Pres poll rptd 8-19, 630B1
ABC settles US trust suit 8-22, 732F1
Mugabe on Meet the Press 8-24, 674G2
Kirkland on Meet the Press 8-31, 659C3
'Shogun' aired 9-15—9-19, top ratings rptd 9-24, 835E2-B3
Reagan equal-time bid rejctd 9-19, 723B1
Post-debate pres poll rptd 9-26, 739B3
Appeals ct backs Abscam tapes broadcast 10-1; Sup Ct refuses stay, tapes aired 10-14, 781F2
Pres poll standings tighten, toss-up seen 10-27, 816A2
Pol airtime case accepted by Sup Ct 11-3, 856D2
Pres electn projectns defended 11-5, 865E3
News copter missing in Carib 11-13, 869D3
McCarthy TV film libel case refused by Sup Ct 12-1, 918D2
ABC, CBS in cultural cable-TV deals 12-2, 12-10, 1003C1
Muskie, Brown on Meet the Press 12-21, 973F1
Random House Inc.—*See RANDOM House*
READER'S Digest (magazine)
Kennedy's Chappaquiddick account questioned, aide rebuts 1-14, 32F3-33B1
READER'S Digest Association Inc.
Source Telecomputing merger rptd 9-24, 746F1
READING Co., The
Emerges from bankruptcy 12-31, 985G3
REAGAN, Nancy (Mrs. Ronald)
Makes racial gaffe in Ill 2-17, 128D2
Photo with husband 11-4, 837A1
Fetes DC ldrs 11-18, 880E3
Visits White House 11-20, 897E2
At DC dinner 11-20, 897F2
REAGAN, Ronald P.
Makes NY ballet debut 10-10, 908A3
Marries 11-24, 998B1

REAGAN, RONALD WILSON

1976

REAGAN, Ronald Wilson
Campaigns in NH, NC; stresses detente, budget, Angola 1-5—1-8, 4B3-5E1
Campaign in Fla, Midwest, NH; dogged by press on budget proposal 1-9—1-15, 21G3-21C2

1977

REAGAN, Ronald Wilson
Gets Electoral Coll vote 1-6, 14G2
Brock elected GOP natl chrmn 1-14, 40F3
Rebuts Carter energy plan 6-2, 443F1
Conservatives to fight Panama Canal treaty 8-15, 622B1

1978

REAGAN, Ronald Wilson
Scores Canal pacts in Denver 1-19, 58C2
Scores Canal pacts in TV address 2-8, 121A1
Poll standings 5-11, 5-24, 404C3
Bell wins NJ Sen primary 6-6, 447F3

1979

REAGAN, Ronald Wilson
Scores Carter forgn policy 2-18, 124E1
Leads GOP polls 3-4, rated 2d in Midwest 3-10, 185E3
Weicker cites poll results 5-16, 363G3
Sees vp selectn change 5-27, 594E1

1980

REAGAN, Ronald Wilson
Calls Lennon slaying 'tragedy' 12-9, 934B2
Cities
Visits Mayors Conf, rpts urban advisory panel formatn 6-8, 438A3

1976

Vs Common Cause campaign code 1-9, 23A1
In Iowa 1-17, trails in straw vote 1-19, 41C1
Panama Canal cited as campaign issue 1-17, 52A3
In NH, concedes budget plan flaw 1-19, 41E1
Shapp scores Ford budget plan 1-20, 40A3
Panama chrgs dissident link 1-21, denies 1-23, 121D2
Ford scores budget plan 1-22, 41B2
Ford campaigns vs 2-6—2-10, 109C1, C3
Shifts Soc Sec stance 2-7, chrgs Ford distortn 2-18, 130B1
In NH, NYC; scores forgn policy 2-10—2-11, 109A2
Ford chrgs extremism 2-13, 2-17, 129D2, D3
Reveals Ford cabt bid 2-20, 148G2
Ford challenges budget plan 2-23, 149B3
Issues financial statement 2-25, 148C3
Denounces Ford on defense 3-4, 165E3
Downgrades Fla, Ill primaries 3-4—3-10, 180G1
Loses equal-time bid 3-4, 180G2-A3
Ford defends forgn policy 3-5, 179E3
Continues forgn policy criticism 3-6, warns vs Watergate candidate 3-9, 180D1
Ford rebuts on defense 3-6, 291D2
Rebuts Kissinger 3-11, 198B1
Ends Ill campaign, Ford replies to chrgs 3-12, 196G3
Kissinger campaign role scored 3-13, 198C1
Hits Ford forgn policy 3-22; cancels Wis appearances, plans TV address 3-23, 214C1
Ford replies to forgn policy chrgs 3-24—3-29, 231C3-232B1
Humphrey scores 3-24, 233E1
TV address scores Ford econ, forgn policies 3-31, 232B2
Morton discounts TV address 3-31, Kissinger rebuts 4-1, 233A1
Ford rebuts TV address, backs Kissinger 4-2, 4-7, 245G1, C2
Defends TV address, offers Ford debate 4-2, 245B2
Trades chrgs with Ford on defense, forgn policy 4-4—4-21; Panama offcls score 4-16, 4-21, 280E3, 281E2, 291C2
Sees oil leaders 4-5, 4-6, 281F2
Delegate box score 4-9, 261B1
Ford fight intensifies, Rhodesia policy an issue 4-28—5-2, scores Kissinger 4-30, 323G2
Goldwater, Rockefeller attack Panama Canal stand 5-2—5-4, 324G1
Ford seeks '77 defns budget hike 5-4, 394E1
Ups delegate lead, sees 1st-ballot win 5-6; in Idaho 5-11, Ky 5-12, 342G3
Ford delays Sovt A-pact signing 5-12, 371F2
In Mich 5-14, 356E3
Carter: sways Ford forgn policy 5-14, 390E3
Kissinger wants to leave 5-16, 359C1
Ford seeks busing rule review 5-18, 377G2
In Nev, Ark, Tenn, Kan, Ore; on Viet, TVA 5-19—5-23, 374E1
Ford gets 119 NY delegates 5-24, 374C1
Says law aids defendants 5-26, 391A2
Sen OKs arms authorzn 5-26, 411D2
Carter scores critics 5-27, 390F2
Stresses aim to sway GOP policy 5-28, 391B2
On Humphrey, Carter 6-1, 391C2
Rhodesia remarks disputed 6-2—6-6, 410B1
Speaks vs schl busing 6-2, 410D2
Nofziger vs Ford ads 6-5, 410B2 ★
Primary campaign wind-up 6-6, 6-7, 410C3, E3
Delegate box score 6-8, 409B3
Wins 18 of 19 Mo delegates 6-12, 432B2
Aide projects win 6-16, 450F3
In Des Moines 6-18, 451D1
Gains 16 delegates in 5 states 6-19, 450E2
US vetoes Angola UN entry 6-23, 455C2
Scores Ford tactics 6-25, 6-28, 467B3
Minn, Mont, Ida, NM conv results 6-26, 467F1
Trails Carter, Ford in polls 6-27—8-1, 564F3
Goldwater endorses Ford 6-30, 467F3
GOP delegate count 7-1, 467D3
Dems see as 'tough' opponent 7-6, 489E3
TV talk scores Ford, Carter 7-6, 490F2
ND, Colo conv results 7-8—7-10, 513A3
Ford: qualified for pres 7-9, 513E3
In NJ, Pa 7-14—7-16; rpts delegate gains, Thurmond endorsemt 7-17—7-20, 531G2
Conn, Utah conv results, delegate selectn completed 7-17, 531D2
AFL-CIO cncl backs Dem ticket 7-19, 532D2
Woos delegates 7-22—7-25; names Schweiker running mate, text 7-26; disenchantmt rptd 7-27—7-29, 549C2-550A3
Claims delegate gains 8-2—8-3; starts campaign swing 8-4—8-5, 563G2-564D2
Ends 5-state campaign swing 8-7, delegate gains claimed 8-10—8-14, 583B2
Ford delegates compared 8-7, 8-8, 8-17, 616A2
GOP platform com OKs planks 8-8—8-13, 582F2-583A2
GOP conv rules com acts on pre-ballot vp selectn, other issues 8-9—8-11, 582C1

1977

Asks Canal pact vote 8-23, vows ratificatn fight 8-25, 678G2
Scores Canal pacts in Sen testimony 9-8, 698C3-699B1
Torrijos invites to Panama 9-28, 756A1
Uses Canal issue as fund raiser 10-30, 912A1

1978

Citizens for the Republic listed top PAC fund-raiser 9-7, 753A2
Backs Kemp-Roth bill 9-22, 734G3
Bell loses US Sen bid, Curb elected Calif atty gen 11-7, 849B1, 856F2
On new China policy 12-16, 976D1

1979

Crane scores Loeb articles 6-8, 594B2
Leads Carter in poll 7-1, 514D1
Scores Carter energy speech 7-16, 534G2
Pres campaign funds rptd 7-26, 594C1
Nofziger resigns 8-28, 661E3
Bars USSR ties re Cuba troops 9-11, 674A2
Scores SALT II 9-15, 739D3
Wins Calif primary procedural fight 9-16, 724B1
NH draft Ford movement starts 9-20, 783G2
Thomson enters pres race 10-31, 829E1
Baker enters '80 race 11-1, 828F3, 829A1
4th in Me straw poll 11-3, 866B3
Opens pres bid 11-13, 866C2
Opens campaign touring, bars GOP debates; set speech noted 11-14, 982B1, F1
Kemp named policy dvpt head, other staff changes cited 11-14, 982D2
Wins Fla straw vote 11-17, 887D1
Leads GOP polls 11-25, 982D1, E1
Defends shah 982A2
Trails Carter, Kennedy in polls 12-11, 962D3
Connally bars US matching funds, vs on la forum, shah 12-12, 982D3, E3
Vs campaign-fund law 12-13, 982B2
Connally switches strategy 12-15, 982F2, B3

1980

Addresses Urban League; backs 'enterprise zones', 'homesteading' 8-5, 597G1
Visits S Bronx 8-5, 597A3
Kennedy says 'no friend' 8-12, 610B1, 613E3
Debates with Anderson 9-21, 721E2, 722C1
Backs fed aid to NYC 9-27, 10-1, 738C1, E1
Carter quotes anti-NY remark 9-29, 739B1
NYC funds release OKd 10-2, 826D2
Carter warns vs divisiveness 10-6, 762E3
Deplores Carter campaign 'hysteria' 10-7, 763D2
Carter softens attack 10-9, 778C2
Mondale denounces tax cuts 10-16, 817B1
Carter chrgs 'flipflop' on NYC aid 10-27, 816B3
Debates with Carter 10-28, 814G1-C2
Anderson answers debate questns 10-28, 816A1
Sends message to Natl League 12-1, 914D2

Courts

Vows to study female Sup Ct apptmts 7-15, 533E3
Clarifies positn on apptmts 9-30, 738C3
Vows to name woman to Sup Ct 10-14, Carter scores 10-15, 779A1, D3
Sees Sup Ct members 11-19, 881D1

Defense & Armed Forces—*See also 'Disarmament' below*

Scores appeasemt, seeks rearmamt 1-29, 91C3
Admits gaffe re Viet vets GI benefits 4-10, 288A2
Sets up advisory panel 4-20, 304C3
Urges defns buildup 5-29, 423G3
Draft registratn funding signed 6-12, 478C2
Carter scores spending progrm 6-22, 646F2
Anti-draft group cites draft oppositn 6-24, 478D3
Nominatn acceptance speech notes 7-17, 531D1, 532A1, 533B1
Addresses vets; urges strong defenses, mil pay hike 8-18, 8-20; VFW endorses 8-18, 629A1-A2, 630A2
Urges maritime program 8-19, 629A2
Anderson attacks policies 8-19, 629F3
US ICBM vulnerability seen 8-20, 630A2
US 'stealth' fighter said to evade radar 8-20, 630D2
Scores 'stealth' plane disclosure 9-4, 665D3
Mondale hits 'big stick' 9-5, 9-23, 9-24, 780A2, F2
Proposes 5-yr plan 9-9, 699A2
Debates with Anderson 9-21, 721E2, 722A1
Deplores Carter warmonger theme 9-23, 722F2
Deplores US weakness 9-24, 723A1
Carter hits A-arms stance 10-2, 10-6, 762B2
Carter attacks stand 10-9—10-14, 778D2, G2, D3, 779A2
Muskie warns of 'endless' wars 10-11, 776G2-C3
Carter assails on A-superiority 10-16, 10-19, 802E2, A3
Pledges peace thru strength 10-19—10-20, 801F2-802D1
Debates with Carter 10-28, 813B1, A2, C2-814A1, B3, 815G2, B3, C3
Anderson answers debate questns 10-28, 815G3
Carter presses 'war-and-peace' issue 10-29, 816B2
Carter plans spokesman role; on Reagan policy support 11-12, 865F2, A3
Carter on A-policy support 11-12, 865A3
Gets intelligence briefing 11-19, 881E1
Nerve gas funds omitted from '81 defns appropriatn 12-5, 935B3

Disarmament

Carter blasts on A-arms race 9-2, 664A3
Mondale hits stand 9-23, 780F2
Would redo SALT 9-30, 738E3
Carter assails SALT stand 10-1, 739A2; 10-2, 10-6, 762B2
Carter attacks arms control stand, SALT oppositn 10-8—10-10, 778B2, F2, D3
Muskie scores SALT views 10-16, 776A2, D2
Carter assails policies, sees 'nuclear precipice' 10-16, 10-19, 802D2
Pledges SALT III talks 10-19, 801C2, 802A1
Mondale calls 'warmonger', scores SALT stance 10-26, 816D3
Debates with Carter 10-28, 813A1, E1, A2, 814F2, B3, 815G2
Anderson answers debate questns, backs SALT II 10-28, 816C1
Carter hits SALT, A-arms stands 10-29, 816C2
Plans Sovt policy shift 11-6, 839D2
Percy in Moscow, forsees SALT talks 11-26—11-28; reactn 11-28, 11-30, 914F3-915A2
Percy 'confident' of new talks 12-12, 950A3

Economy

Addresses newspaper editors 4-8, 264F2
Dogged by agri parity issue 4-9, 288F2-A3
Sets up advisory panel 4-17, 304C3
Scores 'cheap food' policy 4-17, 4-18, 327E3-328A1
Scores Carter econ policy 5-2, 344C3
Vs Carter re econ 5-29, 6-3, 423C3, G3
Carter scores tax-cut talk 6-10, 438G2
Pvt anti-inflatn com sets policy 6-21, 481E1

1976

VP nominatn discounted, consultatn vowed 8-10, 584A2
GOP vp selectn polled 8-11, 8-12, 583G2-584B1
Buckley candidacy promoted 8-11, 8-12, 584B3
Pre-conv delegate count 8-14, 583A3
Conv rules com vs vp proposals 8-15, delegates defeat 16-C 8-17, 600B1, A2
Seeks GOP delegates at conv 8-15—8-18, 601E2
Laxalt on delegate count 8-16, 601E3
Delegate vote bribes chrgd 8-16, 8-17, 616D1
Nominated 8-18, 598A1
GOP conv pres, vp vote tables 8-18—8-19, 8-19, 599A1, E3
Wins forgn policy plank 8-18, 600G2
Vs Schweiker offer to withdraw 8-18, 615D3
Ford wins pres nominatn 8-19, 597F1-598E1
Sees Ford on vp selectn, backs Dole 8-19, 598E1, C2
Tex, Fla, Okla backers favor Helms as vp 8-19, 598F2
Addresses GOP conventn 8-19, 599A2; text 613F1
Ford acceptnc speech cites 8-19, 611F1
Farewell speech to supporters, Times interview 8-19, 615C2-A3
Nixon rptdly favors Ford 8-19, 616A1
Ford backs early running mate selectn 8-20, 631G1
Rockefeller on platform 9-16, 687B1
Dole visits 9-25, 724E3
With Dole in New Haven 10-2, 743B2
Father visits at Yale 10-2, 743B3
At GOP event with Ford 10-7, 763A2
Ford, Carter debate 10-22, 800G2
Meets Ford on GOP unity 12-9, 938A1
Electoral vote rptd 12-13, 979B1
FEC certificatn total rptd 12-31, 979G2

Campaign Funds

Gets US campaign subsidy 1-2, 22E3
Fed fund total listed 3-4, 180C3
Loses Sup Ct funds plea 4-23, 306C1
Fed funding resumed 5-21, 391D3
Campaign debt rptd 6-16; fed fund total 7-1, 491B1, C1
Still eligible for fed funds 6-23, 490G3
Nominatn costs rptd 8-28, 688E2

Primary Results

Ford edges in NH primary 2-24, reactn 2-25, 148E1, F2
Loses Mass, Vt primaries 3-2, 164G3, 165G1-A2
Ford edges in Fla primary 3-9, 179D1, E2
Loses Ill primary 3-16, 196D2, E3
Wins NC primary 3-23, 213G2
Loses Wis primary 4-6, 245C1
Wins Tex primary 5-1, reactn 5-2; wins in Ind, Ga, Ala 5-4, 322D2-G3, 323B1
Ford wins DC primary 5-4, 322G2, 323F2
Wins Neb primary, loses W Va 5-11, 342D1, B3
Loses in Mich, Md 5-18, 356D2, 357F1
Loses in Ore, Ky, Tenn, wins Ark, Ida, Nev 5-25, 373E1, G1, E2, 374A2
Wins in SD, Mont, loses RI 6-1, 389F2, 390C1, A2
Wins Calif, loses Ohio, NJ 6-8, 408F2-409E3

1977

1978

1979

1980

Carter scores tax cut, balanced budget 6-22, 646F2
Proposes tax-cut plan 6-25, Sen Dems reject amendmt 6-26, 480A2-F2
Sen again rejects tax plan 6-30, 492D3
Issues car-industry plan 7-12, 535D1
Vows econ growth 7-15, 534B1
Nominatn acceptance speech notes 7-17, 531D1, B2, G2, 532A2, D2
Addresses Urban League, scores recessn 8-5, 597B2
Carter pres renominatn acceptance speech 8-14, 612E1, F3
Kennedy denounces policies 8-25, 646B3
Sees 'Carter depressn' 8-27; defends remark, vows actn 9-1, 664A2, C2
Scores Carter econ renewal plan 8-28, 663C2
Anderson platform scores 8-30, 665A1
Hits issue in Midwest 9-8, 699B3
Proposes 5-yr plan 9-9, 699A2
Releases steel indus plan 9-16, 699F2-A3
Debates with Anderson 9-21, 721E2, D3, 722F1
Outlines farm policy, scores inflatn 9-30, 738A3
Carter scores Chrysler aid oppositn 10-1, 739A2
Gives housing aid plan 10-2, 738E2
Assails Carter credit policy 10-2, 763C1
Carter calls proposals inflationary 10-6, 762G2-B3
Chrgs govt data doctored 10-6, 763A3
Carter attacks 'dream' 10-12, 779A1
Carter scores tax plan 10-14, 779F1
Pledges farm price supports 10-14, 780B1
Bush vows fewer regulatns 10-15, 817F2
Prime rate rise continues 10-17—11-6, 867B2
Carter scores proposals, denies CPI tampering 10-24, 816F2
Hits Carter record, gives 8-pt plan 10-24, 10-29, 817G1-E2
Mondale: weak on issues 10-26, 816D3
Debates with Carter 10-28, 813B1, D1, A2, E2, 814B1, 815G2, E3
Anderson answers debate questns 10-28, 816A1
Presses issue in campaign windup 10-29—11-3, 840A1
Plans quick actn 11-6, 837F2, 839B3
Aides on budget plans 11-12, 866C2
Meets with advisory panel 11-16, 881B2
Cong sees spending cuts 11-20, 896C2
Aides urge budget cuts, inflatn controls 11-23, 897F1-E2
Declares econ 1st priority 12-1, 914D2
'81 deficit cuts doubted 12-2, 916G2
Chrysler rebates, Ford subsidies offered 12-5, 938D2
Emergency action studied 12-17, 956B1
Schutlze attacks advisers 12-19, 980D3
UAW urges crisis meeting 12-20, 980E2
Emergency opposed by Carter, Burns 12-24, 980B3
Emergency act said unlikely 12-28, 980G2-A3

Education

Backs evolutn teaching chngs 8-22, 646D2
Backs parochial schl tax credits 10-1, 738F1
Carter calls proposals inflationary 10-6, 762B3
Backs voluntary schl prayers 10-7, 763E2
Vs 'federalized' role 10-13, 779C3, 780A1
Backs antibusing measures 11-18, 880F3
Renews antibusing views 12-11, 956E2

Energy

Scores auto regulatn 5-15, 383B1
Backs deregulatn 5-29, 424A1
Seeks gas allocatn rule repeal 7-12, 535E1
Nominatn acceptance speech notes 7-17, 531D1, 532A1, A2, B2
Carter pres renominatn acceptance speech 8-14, 612E1, F3
Carter rebuts attack 9-10, 699C1
Scores Admin policy 9-10, 9-11, 699E3
Debates with Anderson 9-21, 721E2, F3-722A1
Sen panel OKs Synfuels Corp appointmts 9-25, 725A3
Offers 8-pt econ plan 10-24, 817D2
Debates with Carter 10-28, 813D1, 814B1, 815D1,
Anderson answers debate questns 10-28, 816A1, D1

Environment & Pollution

Kennedy says 'no friend' 8-12, 610B1, 613F3
Backs eased pollutn rules 9-16, 699G2
Air pollutn remarks disputed 10-7—10-9, 779B2-D3
Carter hits 'tree' pollutn 10-22, 802F3
Debates with Carter 10-28, 815F1-A2
Anderson answers debate questns, scores 'trees' comment 10-28, 816D1
NRA endorses 11-1, 844G1

Foreign Issues

Welcomes Carter Sovt mistrust 1-2, 5E1
Scores US Iran policy 1-7, 1-8, Sovt grain embargo 1-7, 1-10; clarifies Afghan arms remark 1-9, 1-10, 13D2-D3
Vs Carter on Afghan crisis reaction 1-19, 50C3
Scores Carter re Iran, Afghan 1-24, 1-27, suggests Cuba blockade 1-27, 91A3, B3
Vs US apology to Iran; defends shah 2-14, 128D3
Assails Carter forgn policy 2-15, 128B3
Addresses newspaper editors 4-8, 264F2
Carter defends USSR stand 4-10, 264A1
Denies Olympic boycott shift, admits Viet vet gaffe 4-10, 288A2
Sets up advisory panel 4-20, 304C3
Favors '2-China' policy 5-18, Peking scores 6-13—6-15, 452B3

1976 | 1977 | 1978 | 1979 | 1980

Canada forgn min opposes 6-1, 429C2
Vs car import quotas 7-12, 535F1
Nominatn acceptance speech notes 7-17, 532B1, D2, 533A1-B2, E2
Castro scores 'Big Stick' policy 7-19, 565C3
Anderson rpts forgn concern 7-20, 550B1
PLO scores Israel stand 7-22, 572C2
Carter pres renominatn acceptance speech 8-14, 612A1, 613B1
Backs US-Taiwan ties, triggers China rift 8-16—8-26, 645E2
Urges US strength 8-18, 8-20, 629B1, E1
Lucey scores Taiwan stance 8-25, 646F3
Woodcock scores Taiwan remarks 8-26, 664C3
Praises Polish strikers 9-1, 664D2
USSR scores statemts on Poland unrest 9-2, 659E2
Vows Japan auto import curbs 9-2, 664F2
Addresses B'nai B'rith, assails Carter Mideast policies 9-3, 681A3
Mondale scores policies, notes China gaffe 9-3—9-24, 780F1, G1, D2, F2
Anderson scores Israel policy 9-4, 682B1
Hua vs 2-China policy 9-7, 678A1
Urges Iran hostage release concessns 9-13, 699G3
Carter scores Iran hostage statemt 9-15, 699E1
Backs eased Mex immigratn rules 9-16, 699F3
Deplores Carter warmonger theme 9-23, 722F2
Blames US for Iran-Iraq crisis 9-24, 723A1
Scores Sovt grain embargo, backs farm exports 9-30, 738B3
Vows Israel UN support 10-1, 738B2
Carter warns vs divisiveness 10-6, 762E3
Castro criticism cited 10-13, 789F1
Brezhnev: no pres preference 10-14, 776D3
Advocates firm policy 10-14, 779F3
Carter scores Sovt Afghan invasn response 10-16, 802F2
Asserts peace priority 10-19, 801C2-802B1
Bush hails strong Israel stand 10-19, 817D3
Stresses peace theme on tour 10-20, 802B1
Hits hostage issue 10-20—10-22, 802D1
Carter ridicules Iran hostage stance 10-21, 10-22, 802C3
Mondale calls 'dangerous', questns Israel stance 10-26, 816D3, E3
Carter chrgs Sovt grain embargo 'flipflop' 10-27, 816B3
Debates Iran hostages, other issues with Carter 10-28, 813D1, 814D2-B3, 820B3
Avoids Iran hostage issue 11-2, 840A2
Forgn reactn to electn 11-5, 11-6, 841B2, 853F3
Plans policy shift, cautns Iran; names bispartisan advisory panel 11-6, 837F1, 839C1, D2
Aide warns vs Kim Dae Jung executn 11-18, 944G2
Briefed by CIA dir 11-19, 881D1
Carter affirms rights stance 11-19, 881F2
Meets with Schmidt 11-20, 897F2
Meets Schmidt on NATO, arms 11-20; Schmidt rpts to parlt 11-24, 903G3-904A2
Sadat fears Arab policy shift 11-23, 894E1
Muskie: USSR seeks better ties 11-23, 915A2
Sovts warned vs Poland mil interventn 12-2, 910A3
Palestinian autonomy talks suspended 12-4, 912B3
US for Iran hostage talk speedup 12-4, 912G3-913A1
Backs Camp David process 12-7, 930B3
Percy support of Palestine state disavowed by aides 12-7, 931D1
Haiti aid, Duvalier support seen 12-8, 942F3
Geneva tin accord stalled 12-8, 979D3
Latin policy scored by US El Salvador amb 12-9, US Nicaragua amb echoes 12-11, 941F3-942E1
Castro cautious on Admin policy 12-17, 12-20, 992F3
Scores Iran re hostages 12-24, 12-28; parlt speaker replies 12-29, 974B1
US reminds Iran of inauguratn date 12-30, 973G2

Labor & Employment

On trust laws for unions 4-22, 328A1
Scores Carter on jobless rate 6-6, 437A3
Scores auto layoffs 7-12, 535G1
Vows more jobs, meets unemployed workers 7-15, 534B1
Addresses Urban League 8-5, 597F1
Kennedy says 'no friend' 8-12, 610B1, 613E3
AFL-CIO cncl scores 'antipathy' 8-20, 647B3
At Teamsters conf, sees 'Carter depressn' 8-27; defends remark, vows jobs 9-1, 664G1-C2
Mondale attacks record 9-1, 10-9, 780D1, F2
Sees Detroit auto execs, workers; scores imports, fed regulatns 9-2; Admin disputes 9-3, 664E2
Proposes 5-yr plan 9-9, 699B2
Sees Gleason, other union ldrs in Buffalo 9-11, 699E3
Hits jobs issue 10-1—10-2, 738A1
Carter scores re unions 10-1, 739F1
Visits steelworkers 10-2, 738C2
Carter warns vs jobs policy 10-6, 762D3
Carter scores min wage, jobless benefits stands 10-10, 778D2

1976 1977 1978 1979 1980

Visits Ohio auto plant, scores Carter 10-15, 780C1
Bush vows pvt minority hiring 10-16, 817A3
Carter ridicules 'secret plan' 10-22, 802F3
Kennedy scores farm workers record 10-22, 817D1
Hits Carter record, cites 'misery index' 10-24, 10-29, 817G1-B2
Carter chrgs min wage 'flipflop' 10-27, 816B3
Debates with Carter 10-28, 813C1, E1, 814B1, E1, G1, B2, 815G2, D3
Proposes ombudsman 11-3, 840B3
Wins blue-collar vote 11-4, 837D2, 838A3
Readies fed hiring freeze 11-6, 837F1, 839B3
Visits Teamsters hq 11-18, 880D3
Renews youth min wage support 12-11, 956E2

Medicine & Health

ABA repudiates GOP abortn plank 8-6, 744F1
Carter scores Medicare, Medicaid oppositn 10-1, 739A2; 10-10, 778C3, D3
Debates with Carter 10-28, 813B2, 814C2, 815D2
Reaffirms abortn stand 11-6, 839C3

Minorities

Young racial remark repudiated by Carter 10-15, 803D1
Wins endorsemts from Abernathy, other blacks 10-16—10-22, 802B2
Debates racial issue with Carter 10-28, 814A2
Carter hits debate statemt 10-29, 816D2
Wins ethnic vote 11-4, 837D2, 838A3
Backs antibusing measures 11-18, 880F3
Vows to speak out vs racism 12-1, 914G2
Meets black ldrs in NYC 12-9, DC, vows rights defense 12-11, 956A2-F2
Meese at black conf 12-14, 956G2
Names Black to Cabt 12-22, 979E2

Personal

Vows checkup for senility 6-11, 452E2
Rpts '79 tax data 7-31, 570D3-571A2
Son makes NY ballet debut 10-10, 908A3
Carter says age not issue 10-29, 816E2
Ends Calif vacatn 11-14, 881A2
Son marries 11-24, 998B1
Returns to Calif 12-13, 956C2

Politics—*See also 'Transition Developments' below*

GOP Ia debaters score absence; Des Moines Register poll cited 1-5, 4D2, F3, G3
Connally scores 1-8, 13D3
Trails Carter in poll 1-11, 33D1
Ia poll lead cut in half 1-11, 33D1; visits 1-19, 50C3
Bush beats in Iowa caucus 1-21, 50D1
Steps up campaign pace 1-22—2-5, 91F2-D3
Drops ban vs debate 1-30, 91G2
Wins six Ark delegates 2-2, 92A1
Assails Bush in NH 2-5, 2-6, 128F2
Connally campaigns in SC 2-14, 129A2
Tells ethnic joke 2-16, apologizes 2-18, 128A2
Gains one Ark delegate 2-16, 130G1
Wife makes racial gaffe in Ill 2-17, 128D2
Age seen as factor in NH 2-17, 128E2
Bush wins PR primary 2-17, 130B1
NH gun control forum 2-18, GOP pres debate 2-20, 129B3, G3
Slips in Times/CBS poll 2-20, 130E2
NH limited GOP debate dispute sparked 2-23, 143C1
Wins NH primary 2-26, 142D2-143A1, F1
Fires Sears, 2 other campaign aides 2-26; scored 2-28, 143B1, G1-C2
Campaign fund status cited 2-28, 143C2
'Basic speech' excerpts 2-29, 207A2
Ford considers pres bid; responds 3-2, 167C1-A2
Wins Vt primary, 3d in Mass 3-4, 166E2-E3
Wins SC primary 3-8, 183E3
Connally sees win 3-9, 184B1
Trails Carter in poll 3-9, 208B1
Wins Fla, Ga, Ala primaries 3-11, 182G3
In Ill GOP forum 3-13, 206E2
Ford vs pres bid 3-15, 207D1
Wins Ill primary, delegate count cited 3-18, Anderson stresses oppositn 3-19, 206B2, G3-207B1
Wins NY primary, 2d in Conn; delegate strength near 33% 3-25, 221A2-D3
Connally endorses 3-25, 221F2
Gallup Poll results 3-31, 4-1, 246E3-247A1
Wins Wis, Kan primaries 4-1, 246E1-A3
Wins La primary 4-5, 264F3, G3, 265A1
Addresses newspr eds on econ, forgn crises 4-8, 264F2
Kennedy likens Carter 4-10, 264B3
Scores critical press rpts 4-10, 288A2
Terkel: same as Carter 4-11, 288D3
Thomson endorses 4-14, 288F3
Crane backs 4-16, Rhodes 4-20, 304B3
Sets up advisory panels 4-17, 4-20, 304C3
Poll finds 50% dissatisfied with Carter, Reagan choice 4-18, 304E3, 305B1
Baker backs 4-20; campaigns in Pa 4-20—4-21, Bush scores 4-21, 304E2, G2
Anderson scores 4-20, 4-25, 425B1, C1
Loses Pa primary 4-22, 304A1, B1, C2
Anderson quits GOP race 4-24, 303E2, G3
Sears: Anderson could win 4-29, 328E1
On Carter move to campaign 4-30, 328A2

1976	1977	1978	1979	1980

Wins Tex primary 5-3, 342A2
Delegate count grows 5-3, 342B3
Thompson endorses 5-4, 342D3
Wins Tenn, Ind, NC primaries 5-6, 341F2-342A2
Wins Md, Neb primaries 5-13, 366D2-D3
Tied with Carter in polls 5-19—6-23, 452G1
Loses Mich, wins Ore primaries 5-20, 382E3-383E1
Kennedy warns Carter 5-21, 383F1
Jackson sees possible win 5-22, 399E3
Bush ends pres bid 5-26, 398F2-399B1
Wins Ida, Ky, Nev primaries 5-27, 399A2-F2
Ford endorses 5-27, 399C2
Would debate Carter, Anderson 5-27, 399B3
Kennedy: Carter a clone 5-30, 422G3
Polls rpt discontent 6-3, 423B1, C1
Wins 9 primaries 6-3, 423B2-424C1
Ford meets, pledges cooperatn 6-5, 423A2
Keeps Brock as GOP head 6-13, 452G2-B3
Kennedy attacks 6-14, 480F1
Voter discontent rptd 6-18, 493B3
Anderson scores 6-20, 493B2
Delegate count table 6-28, 506B2
Skips NAACP conv 6-30—7-4; Kennedy scores Reaganism 7-2, 515E2, F2
GOP platform drafted 7-7—7-10, 506G2-D3
Arrives in Detroit 7-14, 532F1
Sees Ford re vp spot 7-15, 7-16, talks fail 7-16, Bush selectn rptd 7-17, 529D2, 530A1, 532G1
Sees Kissinger, women, blacks 7-15, 533A3-534B1, 535C1
Kissinger, Vander Jagt address conv 7-15, 7-16, 534G1, C3
GOP platform adopted 7-15, 535A3
Dems strategy set 7-15, 549C3
Nominated by Laxalt, wins conv vote 7-16, Bush gets vp spot 7-17, 529C1, E1, 534C1
Nominatn acceptance speech; text 7-17, 531A1, F3, 532A2-533G2, 534F3
Carter congratulates on nominatn, seeks debate; accepts 7-17, 532D1
Photo with Ford, Bush 7-17, 529A1
Biog sketch 530C2, C3
Talks 'crusade' to natl com 7-18, 549D2
Campaigns in Detroit, Houston 7-19, 549E2
Carter scores Ford vp 'debacle' 7-19, 549D3
Campaign com appointmts rptd 7-22, 549A3
Leads in Calif poll 7-30, 570C2
Gets Klan endorsemts 7-30, 9-2, 664E1
Kennedy, Anderson meet; hold new conf 7-31, 570D2
At Miss fair, backs states' rights 8-3, 597B3
Visits Jordan 8-4, addresses Urban League 8-5, 597F1, D2
Sees Chicago black ldrs 8-5, 597B3
Udall scores in Dem keynote speech 8-11, 612A2*
Kennedy Dem conv speech 8-12, 610D1, 613G3
Kennedy: defeat 'imperative' 8-13, 611B2
Graham scores 'politics of nostalgia' 8-13, 611B3
Dems warned vs 'out Reaganing Reagan' 8-13, 611D3
Brown assails pres bid 8-13, 611F3
Carter pres renominatn acceptance speech 8-14, 612A1, E2-613C3
Mondale renominatn acceptance speech 8-14, 612B1
To ignore 'distorted' chrgs 8-16, 629C2
Carter revives in polls 8-17, 8-19, 630B1
Kennedy attacks 8-21, 629C3
Lucey scores conservatism 8-25, 646F3
Fund raising coms upheld by fed ct 8-28, 681G1
Ex-aide convicted 8-29, 727B1
Visits Detroit, notes Carter in Klan 'birthplace' 9-1; remark stirs furor, offers clarificatn 9-2, 663D3, 664E2
Campaign ad budget rptd 9-4, 665B3
Poll sees vote shift in NY 9-5, Liberal Party endorses Anderson 9-6, 681F1
FEC issues campaign rules 9-5, Admin sets Cabt guidelines 9-8, 681A3
Carter rejcts 3-way debate 9-9, decisn scored 9-10, 680D2
Bush rebuts Dem attacks 9-11, 780F3
Addresses Italian-Amers in DC 9-13, 699E3
Carter says 'under wraps' 9-15, 699C1
Scores Dem 'legis chaos' 9-15, 699F3
Carter deplores racism 9-16, clarifies 9-18, 698A2
Tours Tex border towns 9-16, 699F3
Equal TV time sought 9-18, 698A3
Carter seeks one-on-one debate 9-18, 698E3
Equal-time bid rejected 9-19, 723B1
Debates on TV with Anderson, notes Carter absence 9-21, 721C2-722E2
Deplores Carter use of warmonger theme 9-22—9-23, 722F2
Tours South 9-22—9-24, 722A3, G3-723A1
Post-debate poll findings 9-23—9-28, 739F2
Declines 2d TV debate 9-25, 739F3
Dems for Reagan formed 9-29, 738F2
Woos Dem voters 10-1—10-2, 738A1
Carter in broadscale attack 10-1, 739A2
Deplores Carter campaign 'hysteria' 10-7, 763C2
In Pa, Ohio 10-7, 763E2

1976 | 1977 | 1978 | 1979 | 1980

Carter admits attacks 'ill-advised' 10-8, shifts tone 10-9, 778A2, C2
Carter: 'bad' for US 10-10, 778D3
Commoner uses vulgar radio ad 10-15, 818A3
Wins endorsemts from Abernathy, other blacks 10-16—10-22; McCarthy 10-23, 802B2
Shares dais with Carter in NY 10-16, 803G1-A2
TV debate with Carter set 10-21, 801F3
Carter questns ability 10-21, 802G3
Carter 'incompetent' 10-22, 10-23, 802A2
Kennedy scores record 10-22, 817F1
Poll standings tighten, indicate toss-up 10-23—10-27, 816G1
Carter chrgs 'flipflop' on issues 10-27, 816A3
Debates Carter on TV 10-28, 813A1-815E3
Anderson answers debate questns on cable TV 10-28, declares 'draw' 10-29, 815F3
Allen conflict-of-interest chrgd 10-28, quits campaign post 10-30, 817E3
Finishes strong 10-29—11-3, 839C3-840B3
Press endorsemts rptd 11-1, 841D3
NRA endorses 11-1, 844F1
FEC paymt $29.4 mln 11-3, 866G1
Photo with wife 11-4, 837A1
Elected pres in landslide; breaks Dem coalitn, wins Sen control 11-4, 837C1-838B3
Carter concedes 11-4, vows 'fine transitn' 11-4—11-5, 837E2, 838B3
Popular vote table 838A2; electoral vote table, map 839A1, D3
Laxalt reelected 11-4, 852A1
Forgn reactn to electn 11-5, 11-6, 841B2-D3
NBC defends electn projectns 11-5, Carter on early concessn 11-12, 865F3, 866D1
Meets with Brock 12-10, 956B2
Electoral College votes 12-15, 956F1

Religion

Addresses fundamentalists; notes evolutn 'flaws', backs teaching chngs 8-22, 646B2
Breakfasts with Krol 9-8, 699B3
Evangelical Christian votes profiled 9-15, 819A2
Debates with Anderson 9-21, 721F2, 722G1
Backs tuitn-tax credits 10-1, 738F1
Backs voluntary schl prayers 10-3, 763E2
Carter warns vs divisiveness 10-6, 762E3
Deplores Carter campaign 'hysteria' 10-7, 763D2
Carter drops attack 10-9, 778D2
Wins RC, Jewish vote 11-4, 837D1, 838A3
Visits Cardinal Cooke 12-9, 956A2

Taxes

Mondale denounces plan 10-16, 817B1
Carter hits massive cuts 10-24, 816G2
Scores Carter policies, offers 8-pt plan 10-24, 817C2
Debates with Carter 10-28, 813D1, E1, E2, 814D1, 815A3
Anderson answers debate questns 10-28, 816A1, B1
Readies swift cuts 11-6, 837F2, 839B3
Renews pledge for cuts 11-16, 881C2
Aides urge personal, business cuts 11-23, 897D2
Renews cities' plan 12-1, 914F2

Transition Developments

Holds press conf 11-6, 839C1
Names bipartisan forgn policy panel 11-6, 839F2
Names Casey, Meese to head transitn team 11-6, 839A3
Carter has no advice, plans to help 11-12, 865G2-A3
Names Baker, Meese to top White House posts 11-14, 881E1-A2
Sees Connally, Clements 11-15, 11-16, 881A2
In DC: sees exec, legis, judicial ldrs; fetes local offcls 11-17—11-19, 880F1-881E1
Visits White House 11-20, 897E2
Conservative columnist hosts DC dinner 11-20, 897F2
Ends DC trip 11-21, 897G2
Cabt speculatn rptd 11-26—11-30, 935B2
Haig State apptmt seen; Byrd, Baker comment 12-6, 12-9, 935F1-B2
Visits NYC, DC: meets black ldrs, Cardinal Cooke 12-9—12-13, 956A2-F2
Fills 8 Cabt posts 12-11, 934G3
Presser's role queried, backed 12-15, 12-18, 955E3
Named Haig secy of state 12-16; US, forgn reactn 12-16—12-17, 955G1
Names Donovan Labor secy 12-16, 955F2
Named Deaver, Friedersdorf aides 12-17, 955C3
Fills 4 more Cabt posts 12-22, 979E2, F3
Names Agri secy, 4 white house aides 12-23, 980E1, A2

Welfare & Social Services

Carter scores proposals 6-22, 646F2
ABA repudiates GOP abortn plank 8-6, 744F1
Kennedy says 'no friend' 8-12, 619B1, 613F3
Carter pres renominatn acceptance speech 8-14, 612F1, F3, 613A2
'Antipathy' scored by AFL-CIO cncl 8-20, 647B3
Carter scores Soc Sec stand 9-3, 699B1
Vows strong Soc Sec system 9-7, 699A3
Mondale scores record 9-10—10-2, 780D2, F2

1976 **1977** **1978** **1979** **1980**

1980

Carter calls proposals inflationary 10-6, 762B3
Carter scores Soc Sec oppositn 10-10, 10-14, 778C3, 779A2
Vows to preserve Soc Sec 10-10, 780B1
Carter ridicules 'secret plan' 10-22, 802E3
Mondale scores record 10-26, 816G3
Carter chrgs 'flipflop' on Soc Sec 10-27, 816B3
Debates with Carter 10-28, 813B2, 814C2, 815A2
Reaffirms abortn stand 11-6, 839C3
Renews states control support 12-11, 956E2
Women
Vows to study Sup Ct apptmts 7-15, 533E3
ABA repudiates GOP abortn plank 8-6, 744F1
Clarifies positn on ct apptmts 9-30, 738C3
Vows Sup Ct apptmt 10-14, Carter scores 10-15, 779A1, D3
Debates with Carter 10-28, 813B2, 814B2, 815C2, A3
Cong electn results 11-4, 846E2
Reaffirms abortn stand 11-6, 839C3
Mrs Dole named pres asst 12-20, 980C2
Makes Cabt-level apptmt 12-22, 979F2

1976

REAGAN, Mrs. Ronald (Nancy Davis)
GOP conv cheers 8-16, 615F1
REAL Estate—*See also HOUSING, TAXES*
Major banks on 'problem' list 1-11, 110F3, 111C1
63 savings & loan banks on 'problem' list 2-17, 185B2
Hamilton files bankruptcy 2-20, 167A1, G1
Sikes conflict of interest chrgd 4-7, 286B3
Fla wetlands dvpt denied 4-16, 284G2
Ford urges regulatory reform 5-13, 347A1
IRS probe of Rev Moon rptd 6-1, property assessed 6-2, 971C1
Ariz bombing tied to land frauds 6-2—6-21, state reforms rptd spurred 6-22, 483G2
Iran, Occidental deal signed 6-20, 450C2
Sup Ct upholds local zoning referendum 6-21, 452G3
Bank diversificatn scored 7-5, 495C2
NY bars Medicaid fee-splitting 9-5, 715B3
18 indicted in Ariz fraud 9-14, 859D3
Zeckendorf dies 9-30, 970D3
Clean air amendmts not cleared 10-2, 883D2
Sup Ct bars review of bias case 10-4, 807G2
New Orleans bank fails 12-3, 939E3
Teamsters fund lists loans 12-28, 991A1
REAL Estate Appraisers, American Institute of
Sued for home-appraisal bias 4-16, 285D2
REAL Estate Appraisers, Society of
Sued for home-appraisal bias 4-16, 285D2
REAP, Harold
Kunstler to ask chrgs dropped 1-17, 79D1
REASONER, Harry
Walters to co-anchor news 4-22, 504B2
REBELO Teixeira, Celestino
Killed 1-1, 11A1
RECESSION—*See ECONOMY*
RECONNAISSANCE
US denies Sovt laser use vs surveillnc craft 11-23; Sovt 'hunter-killers' rptd 12-18, 961A2
RECORDING Arts and Sciences, National Academy of
Grammys presented 2-28, 460F2
RECORDINGS & Recording Industry—*See also MUSIC*
Nixon tapes release OKd 10-26, 849A3
RECREATION—*See also PARKS & Recreation Areas, SPORTS*
Sup Ct bars review of health spa bias 4-5, 262G1
Ford signs youth funds bill 4-15, 282D2
GOP platform text cites 8-18, 605G3
Oct '75-76 CPI rptd 11-19, 885A1
Bell pvt club membership disputed 12-20—12-22, 956E3
Nov '75-76 CPI rptd 12-21, 958A2
RECRUITMENT and Training Program Inc.
Green wins Rockefeller award 11-16, 911E3
RECZI, Laszlo
Wins Olympic medal 7-24, 576A3
REDBANK Shipping Co.
Tanker spills oil in Del R 12-27, 1014E1

1977

REAL, Judge Manuel L.
Rules on Calif damages law 1-4, 312E1
REAL Estate—*See also HOUSING, TAXES*
Vatican land holdings scored 1-6, 8C3
Miami rpts Quebec deals 1-13, 43A2
Sup Ct bars review of New Castle (NY) grants 1-17, 58C1
NM Rio Rancho, Amrep convictns 1-24, 156B2; 4 sentncd 3-10, 203B3
Great Westn settles land-fraud cases 1-26, 156C1
Ind exec kidnaped 2-8—2-10, 162G1
'76 Cong gifts rptd 2-15, 128G1
US Steel unit trust rule voided 2-22, 149E2
McCulloch pleads guilty 2-22, 156F1
Irvine Co takeover battle rptd 3-3, 274E3
Gulf + Westn plans Madison Sq Garden takeover bid 3-7, 275D1
Goldwater conflict of interest chrgd 3-21, 210A2
Sen ethics code adopted 4-1, 251B3
Sioux reservatn land laws upheld 4-4, 341G3
Norin '76 sales rptd 340C1
'76 tax revenues rptd 5-4, 388E1
Urban business confidence rptd 5-16, 385A1
'75 Fed Reserve actns scored 5-24, 406G3
Irvine won by Taubman group 5-20, 519D1
Greenspun wins Summa damage suit 6-3, 472C2
Housing inflatn analyzed 9-12, 721G3
Great Western Sunshine takeover OKd 10-4, 799A1
Conn welfare law re sales upheld 10-17, 797F3
Calif land owners dispute declined 11-7, 857E2
Tex voters OK vet loans 11-8, 879D2
Appraisers OK anti-bias rule 11-11, 898A3
Obituaries
Miller, Eric 9-22, 788G1
Murphy, Charles 9-20, 788A2
REAL Estate Appraisers, American Institute of
Anti-bias agrmt OKd 11-11, 898A3
REAL Estate Appraisers, Society of
Anti-bias suit remains 11-11, 898B3
REALTORS, National Association of
'76 Cong gifts rptd 2-15, 128G1
REAPPORTIONMENT—*See POLITICS—Voting Issues*
REBAYE, Salem Ali
At Red Sea summit 3-22—3-23, 208F2
REBELO, Jorge
At Frelimo cong 2-3—2-7, 137D1
REBMANN, Kurt
On Schleyer kidnap 9-6, 695A2
REBOZO, Charles G. (Bebe)
Cuba to free nephew 8-11, 653D3
RECESSION—*See ECONOMY—Inflation & Recession*
RECHNITZER, Carlos
Vesco wins libel suit; fraud trial ordrd 9-12, 767D1
RECLAMATION, Bureau of—*See under U.S. GOVERNMENT—INTERIOR*
RECONNAISSANCE
US satellite destructn by USSR rptd possible 10-4, 777A2
RECONNAISSANCE Office, National—*See under U.S. GOVERNMENT—DEFENSE*
RECORDS & Recordings
Motown leads black-owned firm list 6-1, 519F3
Presley record sold out 8-18, 696C1
RECREATION—*See also CLUBS; PARKS & Recreation Areas*
'60-61, '72-73 family spending compared 5-10, 423E2
May CPI rptd 6-21, 482C1
June CPI rptd 7-21, 554D2
July CPI rptd 8-19, 651F1
RECTOR, Richard
NBC cancels Emmy broadcast 4-15, 355B3

1978

REAL Estate—*See also HOUSING, TAXES, WILLS & Estates*
Zoning laws linked to segregatn 1-8, 13F3
RI settles Narragansett claim 3-2, 326E3
Penn Central reorganizatn plan OKd 3-9, 185G3-186A1
US halts Australia land sales 5-1, 327F2-D3
Suit chrgs Ford scheme 5-16, 390G3
Petaluma (Calif) developers fee rptd 7-21, 611D2
Realtors Pol Actn Com ranked 6th-top PAC fund-raiser 9-7, 753B2
Fla land fraud indictmts 10-10, 808G2
Penn Central reorg ends 10-24, 875G3
Obituaries
MacArthur, John 1-6, 96G2
REALTORS Political Action Committee, National Association of
6th-leading PAC fund-raiser 9-7, 753B2
REAR Column (play)
Opens 11-19, 1031A3
REASONER, Harry
ABC sets news show chngs 4-19, move to CBS set 5-12, 419A3, C3
REBATES—*See BUSINESS—Payments Issues*
REBILLON, Gisele
Bonjour Amour released 6-11, 618D3
REBMANN, Kurt
Says Baader atty smuggled guns into prison 1-12, 21G3
Police dispute Baader gun smuggling 1-17, 115B1
SPD spy probe dropped 9-26, 868G2 ★
RECESSION—*See ECONOMY—Inflation & Recession*
RECHNITZER, Carlos
Vesco indicted 3-16, 269C3
Vesco fraud chrgs dismissed 4-30, 354F2
RECINOS, Roquelino
Guatemala health min 7-21, 722C3 ★
RECONNAISSANCE
US resumes photo flights over Cuba 11-16, 1016G1
RECORDING Arts and Sciences, National Academy of
Grammys presented 2-24, 315D3-316D1
RECORDS & Recordings—*See also MUSIC*
Record cos denied Nixon tape access by Sup Ct 4-18, 308C1
FCC 'Filthy Words' ban upheld by Sup Ct 7-3, 522G2
Best Sellers—*See under MUSIC*
RECREATION—*See also CLUBS, PARKS & Recreation Areas*
Carter vs business tax break 2-17, 123A2
S Bronx offered US aid 4-12, 285G1
Pa 'tug-of-war' injures 70 6-13, 469G2
REDACK, Jay
Rabbit Test released 4-8, 619D3
RED Army Faction (RAF)—*See GERMANY—Terrorism*
RED Brigades—*See ITALY—Terrorism & Unrest*

1979

REAL Estate
Carter seeks property bias curbs 1-25, 70C2
C&O to buy Liggett US cigaret business 1-26, 283E1
Buckley, Sitco partners settle SEC chrg 2-7, 132C1
Chase REIT files for bankruptcy 2-22, 131G1-E2
Land appraisal reimbursemt ruling reversed by Sup Ct 2-26, 164E3
Nev ad rule affirmed by Sup Ct 3-5, 184G3
Bi-state agency immunity curbed 3-5, 185C1
Holzer convicted of grand larceny 3-15, 239F2; sentncd 5-3, 431A3
Talcott financial troubles cited 3-19, 205F2
US land grant easemt right curbed by Sup Ct 3-27, 263B2
Rockefeller Williamsburg estate willed to foundatn 4-13, 672E2
Racial 'steering' suits allowed by Sup Ct 4-17, 325A3
Govt relocatn aid curbed by Sup Ct 4-17, 325G3
Colo land sale refunds set 5-8, 595G3
PAC top '78 spenders cited 5-10, 363F1
Fair-mkt property acquisitn backed by Sup Ct 5-14, 383B3
C&O, Liggett merger talks end 6-14, 517G1
Ga laws in church dispute backed by Sup Ct 7-2, 559C1
Penn Central to purchase Marathon Mfg 8-10, 664D1
3 Mile I values rptd unaffected 8-20, 743G2-B3
Chrysler unit sold 8-22, 663D2
Fla land fraud convictn 8-29, 655G3
Calif drug profit investmt cited 9-5, 972F2
Landrieu to sell interests 9-12, 700G2
Horizon sales scored by FTC 10-3, 903E1
Brown seeks selective credit 11-9, 962F2
Pahlevi family investmts in US rptd 11-26, 897E3-898B1
Bahamas 1st 1/4 boom rptd, forgn sales curbed 12-7, 948F1
REAL Life (film)
Released 3-1, 174E3
RE-ARRANGEMENTS (play)
Opens 3-9, 292E2
REBATES—*See BUSINESS-Payments Issues*
REBHAN, Herman
Hails UK engineers' pact 10-4, 773B1
RECESSION—*See ECONOMY-Inflation & Recession*
RECONNAISSANCE
USSR flights over Viet-China battle zone rptd 2-21, 122B1
US U-2 SALT verificatn seen 4-3, 258D2
Turkey-US dispute U-2 flights 5-7–5-29, 397B3; 6-24, 6-27, 488B2
U-2 SALT verificatn talks rptd 6-21, optns sought 6-28, 497B1
USSR troops in Cuba rptd 8-31, 657C1
US drops U-2 plan for SALT 9-12, 762E1
US rpts A-blast off S Africa 10-25, 824B3
RECORDS & Recordings
Industry slump rptd 8-8, CBS fires staff 8-10, 618D1
Kerkorian trust suit dismissed 8-14, 756D1
Cocaine use cited 9-5, 972G2
Best Sellers—*See MUSIC*
RECREATION
US wilderness proposal scored 1-4, 16D2
Southn Railway fined 11-12, 868G1-A2
RED Army Faction (RAF)—*See GERMANY-Terrorism*
RED Brigades—*See ITALY-Terrorism*

1980

REAL, Judge Manuel
Overturns Calif A-plant laws 4-23, 332A1
REAL Estate—*See also HOUSING (U.S.)*
Brokers ruled subject to trust suits by Sup Ct 1-8, 16C1
Union Pacific, MoPac set merger 1-8, 52E3
Md convictn appeals declined by Sup Ct 1-21, 93B3
Carter tax proposal 1-28, 70A2
Bahamas bank looting suit rptd 3-3, 229A1
Indian land 'inverse condemnatn' barred by Sup Ct 3-18, 226F3
Indian land managemt fed liability limited 4-15, 306F1
Govt desert land retentn backed by Sup Ct 4-16, 328C3
Mandatory civil jury case refused by Sup Ct 4-28, 369G1
Hunts bailout loan collateral listed 5-28, 425C3, F3, 426E1
Calif zoning ordinances backed by Sup Ct 6-10, 512F1
Tishman dies 6-18, 528F3
Penn Central, GK Technologies merger set 7-7, 745E3
Pan Am sells NYC bldg for record price 7-28, 985B3
Reagan rpts '79 tax data 7-31, 571A2
ABC ties to Spelling-Goldberg rptd probed by SEC 8-7—8-8, 640F1
NRC staff backs 3 Mile I cleanup 8-14, 649F2
Detroit tax revenue drop seen 9-8, 743F2
NYC recovery plan revised, 20% tax hike asked 9-10, 743D1
Sup Ct bars extended judicial immunity 11-17, 882B1
Japan eases forgn investmt rules 12-1, 966F3
Reading emerges from bankruptcy 12-31, 985G3
REALITY...WHAT A Concept (recording)
Williams wins Grammy 2-27, 296G3
REALLY Rosie (play)
Opens 10-12, 892E3
REALTORS, National Association of
'79 Nov used home sales rptd 1-9, 15F2
REAL War, The (book)
On best-seller list 7-13, 568C3
REASONER, Harry
Files for divorce 6-30, 639A1
REASONER, Kathleen
Husband files for divorce 6-30, 639A1
REAY, Trisha
Sneezing record rptd 4-29, 471D1
REBMANN, Kurt
Rpts neo-Nazis chrgd 6-25, 500C3
Munich bomber allegedly killed 9-28, 754F3
RECESSION—*See ECONOMY--Inflation & Recession*
RECONNAISSANCE
A-blast mystery off S Africa unsolved in US rpt 1-23, 49B3
Turkey bars USSR consultatn re U-2 7-4, 526C1
RECORDS & Recordings
Decca merger set 2-14, 132D3
NY record co indicted 2-28, 237B3
Benjamin Selvin dies 7-28, 608C3
Calif artist royalties case declined by Sup Ct 11-10, 868E2
Lennon slaying sparks Beatles music sales 12-9, 934B1
Warner, Franklin Mint merger set 12-24, 985B1
Best Sellers—*See under MUSIC*
RECREATION
NJ State of State message 1-8, 403F3
Water pollutn control benefits seen 4-21, 308C1
REDBOOK (magazine)
Charter Media dissolved; Charter Co retains ownership 9-30, 836C2

1976

RED Cross, International (International Red Cross Committee & League of Red Cross Societies) (ICRC)
Guatemala quake aid rptd 2-10, 120E3
Ends Angola refugee aid 3-27, 228F1
Leb aid efforts fail 7-4—7-5, 487C1
Leb evacuatn plan fails 7-21, 527B3; 7-23, 546D2
Removes Tel Zaatar wounded 8-3, 8-4, 561B1
Delays Leb camp evacuatn 8-6, 877E1
US GOP platform text cites 8-18, 609F3
Kennedy: Cuba denies prison access 8-28, 791A2
Ends Viet foreigner evacuatn 9-14, 696G2
On Leb war destructn 12-2, 913G1
S Africa jail inspectn rptd 12-8, 927C1
REDFEARN, Timothy
Arrested 7-14, tied to Denver SWP break-in 7-30, 569G2-B3 ★
FBI sets informants review 8-11, 633G3
REDFIELD, William
Dies 8-17, 892D3
REDISTRICTING & Reapportionment—*See 'Voting Rights' under POLITICS*
REDLANDS, Calif.—*See CALIFORNIA*
REDLINING—*See HOUSING*
REDONDO, Nicolas
Police interrogatn rptd 4-16, 314D1
RED River of the North
Canada protests Lonetree Reservoir 10-12, 945G3
RED Sea
Cuba troops rptd in area 4-5, 242F1
REED, Sir Carol
Dies 4-25, 368A3
REED, Clarke
Scores Reagan vp choice 7-27, endorses Ford 7-28, 550B2, D2
Warns Ford vs liberal vp choice 8-12, 582E1
REED, Joe
Wallace wins Ala primary 5-4, 323C2
REED, John H.
Replaced in Transport post 2-5, 110D2
Amb to Sri Lanka, Maldives 4-26; confrmd 5-26, 412A2
REED, Thomas C.
Orders Swedish spy-device sale probe 9-14, 734E1
Defends B-1 12-2, 942F1
REEG, Frederick J.
Armed forces study scored 6-7, 454F1
REES, Merlyn
Meets Loyalists, Wilson on security needs 1-5—1-6, 19E2
In Cooney security talks 1-8, 19F3
To recall const conv 1-12, 19G3
Const conv reconvenes 2-3—2-12, 146A3, D3
Dissolves Const Conv, affirms UK rule 3-5, 277D3
Retains post 4-8, 267A1
Callaghan visits Belfast 7-5, 498B3
Deports Sinn Fein head 7-26, 590G1
Sinn Fein talks ended 7-29, 590B2
On Eur human rights rpt 9-2, 675C2
Named UK home secy 9-10, 693D3, 694A1
2 US rptrs ordrd ousted 11-15, 11-17, 946E2
REES, Sgt. Michael
Suspensn rptd 5-28, 435E3
REFUGEES—*See IMMIGRATION & Refugees; country names*
REGAN, Thomas F.
Convctd 6-5, sentncd 6-25, 596G1
REGENSTEIN, Lewis
Sees Carter 12-16, 937C2
REGISTER Publishing Co.
Hartford Times folds 10-20, 849G1
REGO, Armando
Natl Assemb scores release 7-30, 733G1
REGO, Raul
On Republica return order 1-28, 143D2
Scores PIDE releases 7-30, 733G1
REGUERA Guajardo, Andres
Informatn min 7-8, 523D2
REGULA, Rep. Ralph S. (R, O.)
Reelected 11-2, 830A3

REHNQUIST, Justice William H(ubbs)—*For Supreme Court developments not listed here, see SUPREME Court under U.S. GOVERNMENT*
Backs IRS emergency procedure 1-13, 23F3
Rules on campaign law 1-30, 86B3, 87A2
Vs retroactive seniority 3-24, 218A2
Backs drug convictn rule 4-27, 349B2
Vs drug price ad ruling 5-24, 393A2
Vs aliens' civil svc rule 6-1, 414B2
Vs silence on arrest ruling 6-17, 552C3
Vs guilty plea ruling 6-17, 552D3
Backs some church-coll aid 6-21, 452F3
Vs Serbian Church ruling 6-21, 553B1
Rules US wage laws not binding on states 6-24, 468B2

1977

RED Cross, International (International Red Cross Committee and League of Red Cross Societies)
Rpts on Chile pol prisoners 1-1, 3C1
Gets protest on Israel jails 1-19, 72E2
Rhodesia asks kidnap probe 2-1, 73G1; supervises mtg 2-6, 85G1
San Salvador protesters evacuated 2-28, 181A3
Israel-Egypt Sinai exchngs 4-14, 4-19, 297F1
Mex '68 massacre records rptd missing 5-20, 529G2
Chile disappearances protested 6-23—6-27, 493A2
W Ger plans terrorist autopsies 10-18, 790C3
French plea on Sahara rptd 11-3, 852C2
REDDY, Jagmohan
To probe corruptn 4-18, 304A2
REDDY, K. Brahamananda
Named Cong Party pres 5-6, 392A2
To shun Gandhi probe hearing 12-5, 966C2
Gandhi quits party exec com 12-18, 984D2
Suspends Urs 12-26, exec com splits 12-27, 1013E3
REDDY, Neelam Sanjiva (India president)
Nominated India pres 7-7, chosen 7-21, 637G2
Retains party presidency 10-15, 801G1
REDFEARN, Timothy J.
Probe ends 1-6, sentnc rptd 1-9, 15D3
REDISTRICTING & Reapportionment—*See POLITICS—Voting Rights*
REDLINING—*See HOUSING*
RED River of the North
Rpt scores Garrison-Lonetree project 1-7, 60E3
US halts projct 2-18, 133A1
RED River Waterway (La.)—*See RIVERS & Waterways*
RED Sea
4 natns hold security conf, score Israel 3-22—3-23, 208D2
Djibouti strategic role cited 506A3
Somalia scores USSR 9-14, 715A3
Israel seeks free use 10-10, 769B2
REDWOOD National Park (Calif.)
Admin seeks expansion 4-19, 322F3
REED, Nathaniel Pryor
Replaced as Interior asst secy 4-1, 272A3
REES, Merlyn
Sets Agee, Hosenball expulsns 2-16, 134A2
3 chrgd under Secrets Act 5-24, 526E3
Backs Natl Front march 8-14, 637B1
REESE, Don
Put on waivers 8-1, sentncd for drug sale 8-10, 659A2
REFAC Technology Development Corp.
On Gould laser patent value 10-24, 860B1
REFUGEES—*See IMMIGRATION & Refugees; country names*
REFUGEES, Office of the High Commissioner for—*See under UNITED Nations*
REFUSE—*See WASTE, Solid*
REGHAYE, Kamel
Morocco trade min 10-10, 772F1
REGIONAL Cooperation for Development (RCD) (Iran, Pakistan, Turkey)
Revitalized 3-12, 190B2
REGULATORY Agencies, U.S.—*See under U.S. GOVERNMENT*

REHNQUIST, Justice William H(ubbs)—*For Supreme Court developments not listed here, see U.S. GOVERNMENT—SUPREME Court*
Vs steelworkers electn rule 1-12, 57F3
Backs racial voter redistricting 3-1, 175D1
For Soc Sec widower benefits rule 3-2, 192A2
Rules on death sentencing 3-22, 231A1, C1
Extends 'comity' to civil actns 3-22, 231F2
For Miranda rule review 3-23, 276D1
Watergate appeals decisn leaked 4-21, 382C2; case refused 5-23, 406E1
Backs porno trials ad role 6-6, 478D3

1978

RED Cross, International (International Red Cross Committee and League of Red Cross Societies)
Nicaragua riot deaths 2-26, 150E2, G2
Nicaragua unrest rptd 3-3, 192D2
Nicaragua hunger strikers ask better treatmt for pol prisoners 4-4—4-27, 375B3
Rhodesia workers killed 5-18, 455B2
Chile office occupied 5-22—6-9, 452E2
Zaire Kolwezi death toll rptd 5-27, 441B2; 5-30, 417G2; 6-16, 478A2; 7-10, 652E1
Viet Chinese evacuatn to Taiwan set 6-20, 464A3
Nicaragua fighting rages 8-30, 659E2
Angola, S Africa swap prisoners 9-2, 742A2
On Leb war losses 761F2
Guatemala protesters wounded 10-10, 796D3
REDDITT, Edward A.
Testifies at House com King hearings 11-10, 898E2
REDDY, K. Brahamananda
Vows to retain presidency 1-3; rebel factn ousts 1-4, 7F2, C3
Quits as Cong Party pres 2-27, 169B1
REDDY, Neelam Sanjiva
Asks end to violence 4-14, 415E3
REDEKER, Quinn K.
Deer Hunter released 12-14, 1030F2
REDFORD, Robert
Speaks at NYC Sun Day rally 5-3, 322A1
REDGRAVE, Vanessa
Wins Oscar 4-3, 315C3
REDLINING—*See under HOUSING*
REDMOND, Marge
Shay opens 3-7, 887B3
REDPATH Industries Ltd.
Fined record sum 10-6, 794F3
RED Sea
Israel discloses Ethiopia aid 2-6, 100B1
USSR chrgs Ethiopia access bar sought 3-15, 215F3
US surveillnc flights from Israel Sinai base rptd 3-26; US denies 3-27, 215F1, G1
REDWOOD National Park (Calif.)
Expansn clears Cong 2-9, 85D2; 3-21, Carter signs 3-27, 218D1
REED, Alina
Eubie opens 9-20, 1031E1
REED, Oliver
Crossed Swords released 3-2, 619D1
REED, Pamela
Starving Class opens 3-2, 887C3
All's Well opens 7-5, 760B1
REED, W. Vernie
On '77 top-paid labor ldrs list 5-15, 365G1
REED, Willis
Fired as Knicks coach 12-11, 1027E2
REEL, Arthur
Crane's Way opens 7-12, 760G1
REES, Merlyn
Analyzes Ilford by-electn 3-4, 167A3
London race riot probe asked 6-11, 452F3
Sees W Ger min 9-4—9-5, 688B2
Orders prison inquiry 11-2, 867G1-B2
REESE, Jim
Loses Tex Cong primary runoff 6-3, 426F2
REEVE, Christopher
Superman released 12-14, 1030E3
REEVES, Dan
Allen hired as Rams coach 2-1, 171F2
REFORMED Church in America
Howard elected NCC pres 11-4, 907F1
REFUGEES—*See IMMIGRATION & Refugees (U.S.); INDOCHINA; other region, country names*
REFUGEES, Office of the High Commissioner for—*See under UNITED Nations*
REFUSE—*See WASTE, Solid*
REGAN, Joe
Taxi Tales opens 12-29, 1031A3
REGGIANI, Serge
Cat & Mouse released 5-6, 618F3
REGINA XI (Regina B. de Liska)
Colombia pres bid discounted 5-28, 413G2
Runs 8th in pres vote 6-4, 443E2
REGULA, Rep. Ralph S. (R, O.)
Reelected 11-7, 851F3
REGULATORY Agencies (& Issues)—*See under U.S. GOVERNMENT*

REHNQUIST, Justice William H(ubbs)—*For Supreme Court rulings not listed here, see U.S. GOVERNMENT—SUPREME Court*
Vs Pa gag order case rule 1-9, 13G1
Backs EPA asbestos rule curb 1-10, 13A3
Vs trust suits by forgn natns 1-11, 33D3
Backs Wis remarriage law 1-18, 65D1
Vs Mo univ Gay Lib case refusal 2-21, 125E3
Backs med student ouster 3-1, 143F2
Vs curbs on oil tanker regulatn 3-6, 162B1
Vs Indian ct trials of non-Indians 3-6, 162D1
Backs testimony thru illegal search 3-21, 220G3

1979

RED Cross, International (International Red Cross Committee and League of Red Cross Societies)
Arab torture chrgs denied by Israel 2-7, 2-11, 108D2
Israel-PLO prisoner swap aided 3-14, 178F2
Rhodesia war scored 3-20, 286B3
3 Mile I A-accident evacuatn rptd 4-2, 245A3
Nicaragua rebels offer prisoner swap 6-12, 446E3
Nicaragua guardsmen seek refuge 7-18, aid vowed 7-19, 535A3, 536A1
Somoza soldiers in Honduras rptd 7-21, 573G2
Guatemala relief convoy set 7-21, 574B2
Somoza soldiers to be tried by junta 7-22, 574G1
Cambodia missn confrms famine, torture 8-3, 600B3
Nicaragua junta scores US aid policy 8-4, 603A3
Nicaragua prisoners released 8-11–8-12, treatmt lauded 8-15, 616A2
El Salvador asks jail inspectns 8-16, 652B2
Cambodia food, medicine airlifted 8-29, 9-8, 684F1
Cambodia relief agrmt set 9-26, 740G3-741A1; US backs 10-9, 767A2
Cambodia relief aid starts 10-13–10-14, 779G1
El Salvador vows pol prisoner probe 10-18, 813D1
US vows Cambodia food aid 10-24, 811F1; Pnompenh rejcts plan 10-27, 823D3
E Timor famine aid rptd 10-30, 838C2
Fla dam break evacuatn rptd 10-31, 912B3
Bolivian coup deaths rptd 11-7, 853C1
Cambodia relief called inadequate 11-25, 917E2
Cambodia aid rptd blocked 12-17, Pnompenh refutes 12-24, 977D3
REDDY, Neelam Sanjiva (Indian president)
Asks Chavan form new govt 7-18, 544D1
Chavan, Ram end Cabt try 7-22; Singh asked 7-26, sworn prime min 7-28, 573B1
Ends Parlt, sets electns 8-22, 634A3
Mourns Mountbatten death 8-27, 641B2
REDFORD, Robert
Electric Horseman released 12-21, 1007C3
REDGRAVE, Vanessa
Agatha released 2-8, 174C2
Yanks released 9-19, 820G3
REDI
Dalai Lama return allowed 7-18, 563C3
REDISTRICTING & Reapportionment—*See POLITICS–Voting Rights*
RED Lake, Minn.—*See MINNESOTA*
RED River
Minn, ND, Manitoba floods 4-26–4-30, 472A2
RED Sea
Whaling banned, sanctuary set 7-11, 554C2
RED Wing, Minn.—*See MINNESOTA*
REED, Alan
Convicted in '77 Papa slaying 10-23, 840A2
REED, Oliver
Class of Miss MacMichael released 1-26, 528A2
REED, Pamela
Seduced opens 2-1, 292A3
Getting Out opens 5-15, 711B3
Sorrows of Stephen opens 12-11, 1007E2
REED, Thomas C.
Criticizes SALT 4-11, 295E1
REES, Merlyn
Estimates 250,000 layoffs 1-27, 75D3
Asian immigrant virginity tests halted 2-2, 96D3
Cautns MPs re terrorists 4-2, 254C2
Vs proposed immigratn curbs 11-14, 873G1
REES-Mogg, William
On proposed Times intl wkly 4-20; stops publicatn 4-29, 330D3, F3
REFORMED Churches
Baptism rites agrmt reached 3-31, 375F2
REFUGEES—*See IMMIGRATION & Refugees; INDOCHINA; other region, country names*
REFUGEES, Office of the High Commissioner for—*See under UNITED Nations*
REFUSE—*See WASTE, Solid*
R. E. GINNA Nuclear Power Plant—*See NEW York State–Atomic Energy*
REGULATORY Agencies (& Issues)—*See under U.S. GOVERNMENT*

REHNQUIST, Justice William Hubbs—*For Supreme Court developments not listed here, see U.S. GOVERNMENT—SUPREME Court*
Backs Pa abortn control law 1-9, 14A2
Backs SEC suit findings retrial 1-9, 14E2
Backs Mo women jury exclusn law 1-9, 14A3
Backs rail pensn in divorce pact 1-24, 54C1
Backs single-sex alimony 3-5, 184E2
Backs Ill right-to-counsel rule 3-5, 185B2
Backs muffler assn tax break 3-20, 203F3
Backs jobless pay for strikers 3-21, 231F1

1980

RED Cross, International (International Red Cross Committee and League of Red Cross Societies)
Cambodia backlog rptd 1-2, 12D2
Rpts on shah's jails issued 1-9, 47B2
Colombia bullring collapse kills 222 1-21, 80E3
Waldheim presses for Iran release of US hostages 1-30, 2-4, 88G2
Thai border statn operatn suspended 2-7, 108G1
Cambodia famine disaster averted 2-10, 108D1
Cambodia relief shipmts disputed 3-10, rice seed airlifted 4-4, 261G3, 262A1
Chad truce efforts rptd 3-25, 311B2
2 aides visit US hostages in Iran 4-14; rpt 4-14, 4-15, 282B2
Colombia DR Emb takeover ends 4-27, 335D1
Iran to hand over dead US raiders 4-28, 323G1
US raiders bodies returned to US 5-6, 337A2
Cambodia relief aid halted 6-17, renewal OKd 7-12, 591C2
Viets capture 2 offcls 6-25, release 6-29, 508F2
Cambodia aid resumed 8-4, 644F3
Algeria quake aid effort starts 10-11; casualties rptd 10-14, 776C1, E1
E Timor relief barred 12-9, 943D1
Cambodia food aid ended 12-16, 951E3
Flag display by trapped ships in Iran waterway barred 12-29, 978F1
RED Diamond V (U.S. freighter)
731 Cubans arrive in US, capt arrested 6-3, 420B2
REDDY, Neelam Sanjiva (Indian president)
Asks Gandhi to form govt 1-10, 11F3
REDFIELD, Peter S.
Itel terminatn agrmt rptd 10-16, 784B2
REDFORD, Robert
Ordinary People released 9-19, 836D3
REDGRAVE, Vanessa
TV role protested 1-13, 120B2
'Playing for Time' aired by CBS, Jews protest 9-30, 835C3
Backs Israel destructn, pledges PLO support 11-2, 908F3
REDISTRICTING & Reapportionment—*See POLITICS--Voting Issues*
RED Sea
Jordan Dead Sea canal plan rptd 8-30, 661A2
REED, John S.
On Santa Fe, Southn Pacific merger proposal 5-15, 427D3
REED, Ron
Phillies win NL pennant 10-12, 796C1
In World Series 10-14—10-21, 811G3
REED, Stanley F.
Dies 4-3, 360A3
REED, Thomas C.
Heads Draft Ford Com 3-6, 207E1
REES-Mogg, William
Times strike ends 8-29, 670A3
REEVE, Christopher
Somewhere in Time released 10-3, 836F3
5th of July opens 11-6, 892C3
REEVE, Gordon
On Tex chem workers cancer rate 7-24, 584D2
REEVES v. Stake
Case decided by Sup Ct 6-19, 554E2
REFORMED Church in America
Intercommunion poll rptd 4-4, 413A3
REFUGEES—*See IMMIGRATION & Refugees*
REFUGEES, Office of the High Commissioner for—*See under UNITED Nations*
REFUSE—*See WASTE, Solid*
REGAN, Donald T.
Named Treas secy 12-11, 935A1
Birk gets Merrill Lynch posts 12-17, 959E1
REGAN, Gerald
Canada labor, sports min 3-3, 171B2
NS Liberal paymts rptd 3-17, explains 3-19, 253E1
Minumum wage hike rptd 8-11, backs 8-20, 650G3, 651C1
REGELSON, Lev
Sentenced 9-24, 863D2
REGGAE (play)
Opens 3-27, 392F3
REGIONAL Primate Research Center (Seattle, Wash)
Kin recognitn study rptd 6-19, 715C2
REGISTRATION and the Draft, Committee Against (CARD)
Rallies planned 6-24, 478G2
Amnesty for evaders asked 8-4, 597F3
Draft registration statistics disputed 8-26, 9-4, 683E2
REGOZZY, Kristina
Wins Olympic medal 2-17, 155F3
REGULA, Rep. Ralph S. (R, Ohio)
Reelected 11-4, 843F4
REGULATORY Agencies & Issues—*See under U.S. GOVERNMENT*
REHNQUIST, Justice William Hubbs—*For Supreme Court developments not listed here, see U.S. GOVERNMENT--SUPREME Court*
Vs inmate escape justificatn 1-21, 92F3
Backs Dallas busing case review 1-21, 93E2
Vs Ohio boundary placemt 1-21, 93F2
Backs contd abortn aid order stay 2-19, 130B3
Backs Berkey trust appeal review 2-19, 130G3
Vs total plaintiff class lawyer fees 2-19, 131C1
Backs IRS handwriting orders 2-20, 170F1

1976

Dissents re pvt schl bias 6-25, 479F1
Dissents re rights laws application to whites 6-25, 479C2
Vs union overtime bar 6-25, 552B2
Vs patronage ouster bar 6-28, 468F3
Bars contd schl rezoning 6-28, 468G3
Vs press gag order 6-30, 491F3
Vs parent, husband abortn consent 7-1, 518E3
Vs black-lung law provision 7-1, 568F3
Ct upholds death penalty, voids NC, La laws 7-2, 491G2, C3
Backs sympathy strikes 7-6, 535E1
Vs utilities trust ruling 7-6, 569F1
Rejects tuna fishers appeal 11-12, 902D1
Vs MD office abortn rule 11-29, 900D3
Vs Gilmore executn stay 12-3, 952D2
Vs Austin busing plan 12-6, 920E2
Vs jury death sentence ruling 12-6, 920C3
Vs pregnancy benefits 12-7, 920B1
Vs Okla beer-buying rule 12-20, 960D1

REIBMAN, Jeanette
Loses US Sen primary 4-27, 305B1
REICHLER, Paul
Westn Elec bias damages ordrd 10-22, 943E2
REICHMANN, John A.
Dies 2-2, 124F3
REID, Charlotte
Quits FCC 5-27, 412B2
Replaced on FCC 9-8, 807G3
REID, Kerry Melville
Loses Federatn Cup tennis 8-29, 716A2
REID, Ogden R.
On Hudson R PCB pollutn 2-9, 171F3
REID, Patrick
Heads Ontario Liberal wing 4-25, 350D2
REID, Willie Mae
Sup Ct bars equal-time review 10-12, 765E3
REIDHAAR, Donald
On Calif U reverse bias case 11-11, 882A2
REIDINGER, Charles
Testifies on Army meat fraud 5-10, 395E2
REIMAN, Pavel
Dies 11-1, 932F3
REIMANN, Hans
Wins Olympic medal 7-23, 575E3
REIN, Bert W.
Testifies vs Concorde 1-5, 5C3
REINHARDT, John A.
Vs Sovt UNESCO press plan 10-27, 842C2
Sees Kaunda, Nyerere 11-5—11-6, 843G1
To Geneva 11-17, 862E1
REJAN, K. R. Sundar
Arrested 10-25, 837E2
REKOLA, Esko
Sworn Finnish finance min 9-29, 750D3
RELAXATION Response, The (book)
On best seller list 1-25, 80C3; 2-29, 208F3; 12-5, 972C2

1977

Backs contraceptive curbs 6-9, 501D2
Backs Fla retroactive death sentnc 6-17, 518C2
Backs curbs on inmate unions 6-23, 539E2
Vacates Dayton busing ruling 6-27, 538F2
Vs US custody of Nixon papers 6-28, 539G3
Orders Vendo contract dispute award 6-29, 557E3
Backs maternity leave seniority rights 12-6, 938E2

REID, Kerry
Wins Australian Open 1-9, 103E3
REINHARDT, John E.
Named USIA dir 1-7, 14G1
RELIEF & Works Agency—*See under UNITED Nations*

1978

Vs NH gov flag-lowering curb 3-24, 221E2
Vs cities' liability under trust law 3-29, 280D2
Backs ct A-plant ruling curbs 4-3, 280A3
Vs Ark defendants rights rule 4-3, 309B1
Vs clergy pub office ban 4-19, 309D1
Vs sex-based pensn plan bar 4-25, 322E3
Vs engineers fee code 4-25, 323C1
Vs corp pol free speech 4-26, 343E3
Backs lawyer competency case review, scores majority 5-1, 363G3
Vs utility customer hearings 5-1, 364B1
Curbs SEC trading suspensns 5-15, 387E1
Backs fed tap power 5-15, 387F2
Vs tax liability in bankruptcy 5-22, 388E1
Backs OSHA warrantless searches 5-23, 405F2
Vs lawyer solicitatn 5-30, 430F2
Vs presumptn-of-innocence jury chrg 5-30, 430B3
Backs natural gas diversn 5-31, 431C1
Vs arson probe search warrants 5-31, 431E1
Backs munic legal immunity 6-6, 447A2
Vs alien deportatn trial 6-6, 447F2
Backs Skokie Nazi rally delay 6-12, 447B3
Vs '75 double jeopardy doctrine 6-14, 468C3
Vs lengthening double jeopardy protectn 6-14, 468G3
Backs Tellico Dam vs rare fish 6-15, 468D2
Vs IRS summons power 6-19, 492A3
Backs hosp interrogatns 6-21, 509F2
Vs union pol organizing 6-22, 508D3
Vs computer program patent curbs 6-22, 509D1
Vs Ark prison reform, attys fees 6-23, 566F1-A2
Backs NJ waste dumping law 6-23, 566C2
Vs evidence hearing rules 6-26, 566F3
Backs Bakke med schl admissn, vs race-based affirmative actn principle 6-28, 481F1, C2
Backs US offcls' legal immunity 6-29, 567E2
Vs gypsum price fixing ruling 6-29, 567C3
Vs insurnc cos policyholder trust suits 6-29, 567D3
Backs Ohio death penalty law 7-3, 552F1, G1
Voting alignmt shift noted 7-3, 565E3-566C1
Rejects LA Bustop appeal 9-8, 698F3
Backs cities' power over suburbs 11-28, 937B3
Backs broader police auto search power 12-5, 959F2
Vs FRB bank-holding co power 12-11, 980F3

REICHARDT, Louis
Climbs K2 in Pakistan 9-6, 843E2
REID, John M.
Canada fed-prov min 11-24, 921D3
REID, Kerry
Loses Family Circle Cup 4-16, 419B2
Loses US Open doubles title 9-9, 707G1
US wins Federatn Cup 12-3, 1026G3, 1027A1
REID, Mike
2d in Pensacola Open 10-30, 990C2
REID, Ptolemy
Jonestown cult ties cited 11-21, 891G1
Admits high Jonestown death toll, oppositn scores 11-24, 909G2
REID, Robert H.
Czech ousts 5-1, 439B3
REID, Rose Marie
Dies 12-18, 1032D3
REIDERS, Dr. Frederic
Jascalevich acquitted in curare murder case 10-24, 841A2
REIDSVILLE, Ga.—*See GEORGIA*
REILLY, J. J.
Hydrogen storage study rptd 4-18, 293G3 ★
REINER, Rob
Wins Emmy 9-17, 1030F1
REINHARDT, Alexandra
2d in Houston Exchng Clubs Classic 10-22, 990C2
REINHARDT, John E.
Vs UNESCO vote on Israel 11-29, 931G1
REISTRUP, Paul
Resigns as Amtrak pres 3-29, 284C2
Boyd named Amtrak pres 4-25, 349A2
REISZ, Karel
Who'll Stop Rain released 8-25, 1030G3
REITMAN, Ivan
Animal House released 7-27, 970D2
REITZ, Ken
Forsch pitches no-hitter 4-16, 355A2
RELAXIN—*See HORMONES*
RELDAN, Robert R.
Convicted in murder plot 4-26, 380F2
RELIANCE Electric Co.
To buy Fed Pacific Elec 12-18, 1005A2
RELIEF & Works Agency, UN (UNRWA)—*See under UNITED Nations*

1979

Backs random car checks by police 3-27, 263G1
Vs LA fire dept bias case finding 3-27, 263B2
Vs racial 'steering' suits 4-17, 325D3
Vs reverse Freedom of Info suits 4-18, 346A1
Vs unwed father adoptn consent role 4-24, 364E1
Backs Okla minnow sale ban 4-24, 364D2
Backs Calif cargo container taxes 4-30, 364C3
Not in mutual fund dirs' case 5-14, 383D1
Backs pretrial detentn curbs 5-14, 383A2
Discloses finances 5-16, 382C2
Backs state age bias filing time limit 5-21, 400G2
Backs some punitive damages vs unions 5-29, 421E3
Backs Green death sentence 5-29, 421F3
Vs sex-bias suits vs congressmen 6-5, 464F1
Vs 'probable cause' in detentns 6-5, 464F2
Backs broader Cong legal immunity 6-18, 498G3
Vs luggage search warrants 6-20, 516C2
Backs end to AFDC-UF welfare plan 6-25, 540A1
Backs Wolston libel suit right 6-26, 540E3
Backs rights violatn proof in false arrest suits 6-26, 540G3
Backs Weber affirmative actn challenge 6-27, 477A2
Vs unwed mothers survivors' aid 6-27, 558G1
Vs eased criminal evidence standard 6-28, 558B3
Backs ctroom pub access curbs 7-2, 515F2
'78-79 Sup Ct term ends, voting alignmt rptd 7-2, 558A1
Vs Ohio busing orders 7-2, 539B3
Vs power to void state convictns 7-2, 559A1
Vs Washn Indian fishing treaties 7-2, 559F1
Vs Mass abortn-consent law 7-2, 559B2
Calif utilities refund stay refused 10-1, 768C1
Backs 'exclusionary rule' case review 10-1, 768A3
Hears govt minority constructn grants case argumts 11-27, 945D1
Vs NYC schl aid denial 11-28, 944E2
Backs extended searches 11-28, 944B3
Vs pub access to waterways 12-4, 988B1
Vs Taiwan treaty case review 12-13, 940C1

REID, Kate
Bosoms & Neglect opens 5-3, 711F1
REID, Kerry
Loses Family Circle tourn 4-15, 391C3
US wins Federatn Cup 5-6, 391E2
REINER, Carl
Jerk released 12-14, 1007E3
REITER v. Sonotone
Case decided by Sup Ct 6-11, 478E2
REITMAN, Ivan
Meatballs released 7-3, 820A2
REITSCH, Hanna
Dies 8-30, 671E3
REITZ, Ken
NL batting ldr 9-30, 955F2
REKSTEN, Hilmar
Fined 12-17, 996F3
RELIANCE Electric Co.
Exxon seeks merger; '78 assets, Fortune 500 ranking cited 5-18, 404C2
Exxon makes offer 6-21; ct OKs, limits control 8-17, suit dropped 9-19, purchase completed 9-24, 770F1-D2
RELIANCE Group Inc.
Sharon Steel buys UV Industries assets 11-26, 986D2
CTI International Inc.
Gelco purchase set 7-16, 560C2

1980

Backs charity solicitatn limit 2-20, 170D2
Vs fed worker illegitimate child aid 2-26, 188G1
Vs Kissinger records access 3-3, 209F3
Vs fed funded group info access 3-3, 210C1
Backs Cleveland busing challenge review 3-17, 225G3
Backs Tex habitual-offender law 3-18, 226A3
Backs Tex porno film restraints 3-18, 226F3
Backs state legislators' immunity 3-19, 250A1
Vs class actn 'moot' standard redefinitn 3-19, 250E1
Not in mutual fund insurnc case 3-24, 265G1
Backs inmate mental health case dismissal 3-25, 265F2
Backs govt political firings 3-31, 291D2
Backs welfare benefits hearing case review 4-14, 307F1
Backs warrantless home arrests 4-15, 306E1
Backs 'good faith' municipal immunity 4-16, 328B3
Vs multiple sentencing curbs 4-16, 328C3
Hears abortn funding cases 4-21, 306A3
Backs at-large local electns 4-22, 343D2
Vs prisoners right to sue 4-22, 343G3
Backs Mo workman's compenstan law 4-22, 344A1
Vs Voting Rights Act provisn 4-22, 344D1
Backs Wilmington (Del) busing case review 4-28, 368F3
Backs La oil leasing royalties 4-28, 369D1
Vs EEOC class actn process avoidance 5-12, 426C2
Vs pre-ERISA insured pensn benefits 5-12, 426C3
Backs Ga death penalty applicatn 5-19, 440B1
Vs land-grant exchng ban 5-19, 440B2
Vs EPA guidelines appeals ct review 5-27, 453F3
Backs shopping cntr petitn access 6-9, 512C2
Backs use of jail informants 6-16, 511C3
Vs Ala death penalty rule 6-20, 555E1
Vs utilities' free speech 6-20, 555C2
Vs Ill non-labor picketing rights 6-20, 555E2
Vs container pact ban refusal 6-20, 555G2
Vs donated porno warrants 6-20, 555B3
Vs broader right to sue states 6-25, 540F3
Narrows illegal search protectn 6-25, 541C1
Backs oil spill rpts 6-27, 511B2
Backs Medicaid abortn funding limits 6-30, 491G3
Vs Sioux $122.5 mln award 6-30, 511D1
Vs DEA detainmt procedure 6-30, 511A2
Vs govt minority constructn grants 7-2, 510A2, B2
Vs open criminal trials 7-2, 510C3
'79-80 Sup Ct term ends, voting alignmts rptd 7-2, 540B2
Vs inmate legal fees ruling 11-10, 868F1
Ctroom cameras case argued 11-12, 882D2
Backs Ky 10 Commandmts schl law 11-17, 881F3
Backs rail pensn revisn 12-9, 937A1
REICE, Rich
Stoners win ASL title 9-18, 771B1
REICHHOLD Chemicals Inc.
Paint-resin price trust setlmt reached 7-22, 917E1
REID, Mike
3d in Greater New Orleans Open 4-27, 412E3
PGA top money winner 10-12, 971E3
REID, Ptolemy (Guyanan prime minister)
Named prime min 10-6, 791G1
REID v. Georgia
Case decided by Sup Ct 6-30, 511G1
REILLY, Charles Nelson
Charlotte opens 2-27, 392D2
REILLY, Phil
2d in 6,000-m Penn Relays 4-25, 892D2
REIN, Robert E. (Bo)
Presumed dead in aircrash 1-11, Stovall replaces as LSU football coach 1-12, 175A3
REINDERS, Ralf
Sentenced 10-13, 833B1
REINER, Carl
Roast opens 5-8, 392G3
REINES, Frederick
Neutrino mass proposed 4-30, 416G1
REINFELDT, Mike
NFL '79 interceptn ldr 1-5, 8C2
REINISCH, Rica
Wins Olympic medals 7-23, 7-27, 623B3
RELIANCE Electric Co.
Sharon Steel, UV Industries deal final; suits cited 9-26, 746C2
RELIANCE Universal Inc.
Paint-resin price trust setlmt reached 7-22, 917E1

1976

RELIGION—*See also specific denominations; country, group names*
'75 US church attendance rptd 1-3, 32A3
House com asks CIA contacts bar 2-10, 150B2
CIA limits clergy contacts 2-11, 150B3
Sup Ct bars review of snake handling case 3-8, 219C2
Sup Ct upholds retroactive seniority 3-24, 218B2
FBI probe targets cited 4-28, 330E1
Ford lauds US diversity 7-5, 488G3
Rudolf Bultmann dies 7-30, 816E3
Intl Eucharist Cong 8-1—8-8, 596E2
Luther Weigle dies 9-2, 1015B3
Biased soc clubs lose tax exemption 10-20, 835F1
Religious-day work ruling affirmed 11-2, 848B1
Samuel Cavert dies 12-21, 1015C1
Presidential Election (& transition)
Carter asserts views 6-6, 410F3
Carter seeks 'men of faith' 6-19, 452B1
Carter likens self to JFK 9-6, 664C2
Mondale on pol choices 9-10, 687E1
Carter Playboy interview disclosed 9-20, 704B2
Carter on Playboy interview 9-24, 9-27, 724C2
Church taxatn disputed 10-2, 743C2
Ford, Carter debate 10-22, 800E3
School Issues—*See EDUCATION*

REMFRY, Keith
Wins Olympic medal 7-31, 575B1
REMI, Richard Christian
Named youth min 8-20, 926C1
RENARD, Pierre
Mediates in hijacking 6-28, 463B1
Denied access to hijackers 7-4, 485C2
Uganda frees hijacked jet 7-21, 547E1
RENAUDOT, Prix (literature award)
Presented 11-15, 911G3
RENAULT, Regie Nationale Des Usines
US ends car dumping probe 5-4, 321D2
Algeria constructn pact rptd 7-16, 902C2
US car price hike set 8-16, 988D1
Peugeot-Citroen merger rptd 10-1, 773B1
Argentina exec killed 10-10, 996F1
Turkey plant to close 12-24, 1012A1
RENDULIC, Gen. Zlatka
On Yugo mil threat 1-11, 55E1

RENE, Albert
To be Seychelles prime min 6-28, 483F2

RENSSELAER Polytechnic Institute (Troy, N.Y.)
Low to become pres 3-19, 232A2
RENT—*See HOUSING*
RENTSCHLER, William M.
Pleads guilty 4-20, 316E3
REPORTERS' Committee of the Freedom of the Press
Schorr House com rpt leak disputed 2-12—2-24, 150F3-151B1
Kissinger donates records 12-20, 12-28, 980G2

1977

RELIGION—*See also specific denominations; country, group names*
'69-75 student study issued 1-14, 157A2
Carter quotes Micah 1-20, 25E2
Church groups in Stevens protest 3-1, 153G3
Proselytism scored 3-28—3-30, 492C2
U of Chicago conf 4-18, 492E2
'76 church attendnc rptd up 4-26—4-29, 470B3
Christ TV film to be shown yrly 5-16, 395E2
Workers rights limited 6-13, 517C3
UK ed fined for blasphemy 7-12, 617E3
EEOC plans reorganizatn 7-20, 669A2
Carter Miss town mtg topic 7-21, 575F1
Real estate appraisers OK anti-bias rule 11-11, 898B3
Dead Sea scroll analyzed 11-12, 1022F3
US jobs bill backed 11-14, 877B1
Mental patient drug case refused 11-28, 919B3
School Issues—*See under EDUCATION*

RELIGIOUS Cults
Jews for Jesus scored 3-13, 3-28—3-30, 492D2
Krishna indictmts dismissed 3-17, 287G1
NY denies Moon property tax exemptn 4-14, 310D1
NY mail-order mins tax status challenged 4-15, 310B2
Jewish trends conf 4-18, 492E2
Gallup rpts trends 4-26—4-29, 470C3
Polygamist ldr slain 5-10, 6 chrgd 9-27, 847F3
Church of Christ backs 7-5, 642F2
Deprogramming Issues
ACLU aide scores abuses 2-5, 287E1
Calif ct rulings 3-24, 3-28, 286F3; parents lose custody 4-11, 310B1
Patrick sentncd in Denver 3-28, 287E1
REMBRANDT Harmens van Rijn (1606-69)
Man chrgd re defaced works 10-8, 848F2
REMI, Richard Christian
Malagasy foreign min 8-8, 772D1
REMY, Jerry
AL batting ldr 10-2, 927A1
Traded to Red Sox 12-8, 990F1
RENAULT, Regie Nationale Des Usines
Volvo, Saab agree to merge 5-6, 469D3
Argentina workers strike 10-11—10-14, 981B1

RENE, France Albert
Ousts Mancham 6-5, 450F3
Chrgs Mancham countercoup plan 6-8, 489C1
US, UK recognize govt 6-13, 489B1

RENEGOTIATION Board—*See under U.S. GOVERNMENT*
RENO (Nev.) Evening Gazette (newspaper)
3 win Pulitzer 4-18, 355G2
RENOUF, Harold
Named AIB head 4-28, 346B3
RENT—*See HOUSING*
REPORTERS Committee for Freedom of the Press
Kissinger loses transcripts ruling 12-8, 962F2

1978

RELIGION—*See also specific denominations; country, group names*
Oberammergau vs revised Passion Play 1-12, 95E2; retains classic text 3-5, 295C2
Carter asks intell curbs 1-24, 49G2; legis introduced in Sen 2-9, 107B1
Laity role rptd expanding 2-19, 4-7, 294B3
Church-bond investor losses rptd 2-27, 295F3
Church '76, '77 membership, contributns rptd 3-3, 6-2, 6-12, 907B3
Flynt '77 conversn cited 187C1
Gutenberg Bibles sold 3-10, 4-7, 295D2
Sup Ct stays NH flag lowerings 3-24, 221A2; denies stay extensn 4-24, 322G2
French survey rptd 3-24, 352G2
Tenn clergy pub office ban upset by Sup Ct 4-19, 309C1
Lobbying curbs OKd by House 4-26, 323A2
'Test-tube baby' reactn rptd 7-25, 597E1
Shroud of Turin exhibited 8-26—10-8, studied 10-4—11-14; photo 926A1-C3
Obituaries
Kelso, James L 6-28, 540A3
School Issues—*See under EDUCATION*
RELIGIOUS Cults
Laity ldrship role cited 2-19, 294C3
NY denies Moon seminary charter; '77 solicitatns bar, deportatns cited 2-22, 295G2
US House subcom probes Moon-KCIA link 3-15, 3-22, 203D1
Moon subpoenaed by House subcom, US exit rptd 6-6, 433C1
Utah ldr suicide rptdly 8-2, 685D3
US House subcom chrgs Moon abuses, asks interagency probe 11-1, 862C3, G3
Deprogramming Issues
Scientology member, Moonie sue Patrick 4-7, 4-16, 295D3
Moonie loses suit vs Patrick 12-29, 1012G1
Peoples Temple—*See separate listing*
REMAINDER Man (race horse)
3d in English Derby 6-7, 539C2
REMAR, James
Early Dark opens 4-25, 760B2
REMBRANDT Harmens van Rijn (1606-69)
Portrait of Rabbi stolen 12-25, 1028G3-1029A1
REMEK, Capt. Vladimir
Launched into space 3-2, docks with Salyut 3-3, 157E2
Returns to Earth 3-10, 181B1
REMINGTON Arms Co.—*See under DuPONT de Nemours & Co., E.I.*
RENALDO and Clara (film)
Released 1-25, 619D3
RENAUD, Pierre
Denies PQ forgn funding 2-3, 129A3
RENAULT, Regie Nationale Des Usines
AMC plans joint productn, distributn; '77 US sales cited 3-31, 283F3-284B1
Strikes hit plants 5-25—6-27, 532G3
Rumania expansn rptd 6-14, 651A1
Basque office bombed 6-30, 649B2
Peugeot to buy Chrysler Eur units 8-10, 623D2
RENDRA, W. S.
Arrested 5-1, 632B1
RENE, France Albert (Seychelles president)
21 arrested re plot 4-29, 378C3
Sets 5-yr econ plan 6-5, 596B3
Sets 1-party electns 6-20, 596B3
9 accused plotters freed 7-3, 596C3
Warns US, USSR vs Indian O mil expansn 8-7, 8-20, 692B1
S Africa trade ban rptd 8-21, 670B1
RENEGOTIATION Board—*See under U.S. GOVERNMENT*
RENFIELD, Elinor
Shay opens 3-7, 887B3
RENNER, Jack
2d in Greater Greensboro Open 4-2, 355G3
RENOIR, Pierre August (1841-1919)
Portrait of Leriaux stolen 7-30, 1029B1
RENT—*See HOUSING*
RENZ, Father Wilhelm
Convicted in exorcism death 4-21, 379E3
REPLAY (film)
Released 7-10, 970F2
REPORTER, The (magazine)
Ascoli dies 1-1, 96C1

1979

RELIGION—*See also denominations; country, group names*
Gallup '78 church attendance poll rptd 1-5, 24C1
Graham backs financial disclosure law 1-17, 102E1
'Cross of Lourdes' refunds set 1-19, 91B3
IRS exempts church bingo 1-26, 102C1
'In God We Trust' currency suit dismissed 3-2, 208C2
Dead Sea Scroll contents told 3-2, 217G2
Bible smuggling in E Eur rptd 3-13, 238E1
China church reimbursemt set 3-16, 217G3
Baptism rites agrmt reached 3-31, 375F2
India anti-conversion bill scored 4-14, 376D3
Church membership rise rptd 5-4, 639F3
Fair-mkt property acquisitn backed by Sup Ct 5-14, 383B3
Carter sees ldrs at Camp David 7-6—7-11, 513F2; thanks participants 7-30, 608F3-609A1
WCC mtg ends, sci rift eased 7-24, 640C1
US tolerance gains rptd 8-4, 639C3
Life of Brian denounced 8-27, other dvpts 10-24—10-30, 859D1-E2
Church-state legal challenges rptd 9-13—10-3, 760A3
Shroud of Turin age test awaited 11-21, 931E2
School Issues—*See under EDUCATION*

RELIGIOUS Cults
Krishna sued re solicitatns 1-25, 102F1
4 acquitted in polygamist's '77 death 3-20, 240A2
Moon church bank fraud chrgd 5-1, 376D2
Moon church bank fraud chrg setld 6-6, 547E2
Krishna solicitatn rights case refused by Sup Ct 11-26, 919F2
REMAR, James
Warriors released 2-9, 174F3
REMIRO, Joseph M.
Murder convictn upheld 2-27, 156C1
RENAULT, Regie Nationale des Usines
AMC sales pact signed 1-10, 131E2
Mack Trucks share purchased 3-19, 3-20, 236E2, 283B1
Lorraine plant plans rptd 4-25, 299B3
Portugual expansn progrm rptd 5-24, 409A3
Iran interests natlzd 7-5, 503A3
Argentine mkt share rptd 7-20, 562G1
AMC interest purchase set; '78 sales, Mack truck purchase cited 10-12, 784F2
Volvo share purchase set 12-19, 993G3-994C1

RENE, France Albert (Seychelles president)
Arrests rptd re plot chrg 11-20, 969C2

RENFREW, Judge Charles
Named dep atty gen 11-20, 946A3
RENGER, Annemarie
Loses W Ger pres bid 5-23, 410G2
RENNER, Jack
2d in Greater Hartford Open 8-14; wins Westchester Classic 8-19, 969F3, 970A1
RENOIR, Jean
Dies 2-13, 176D3
Father's painting willed to LA museum 3-7, 375G1
RENOIR, Pierre Auguste (1841-1919)
Son dies 2-13, 176D3
Painting willed to LA museum 3-7, 375G1
RENOUF, Alan
Fraser scored in book 8-24, 650G2
RENOUF, Harold
Named NCI dir 3-2, 168D2
RENSSELAER Polytechnic Institute (Troy, N.Y.)
Low to head air safety panel 12-19, 988F3
REN Wanding
Arrested 4-4, 312G1
RENZETTI, Joe
Wins Oscar 4-9, 336B2
REPLOGLE, Rear Adm. Thomas H.
Guantanamo maneuvers begin 10-17, 781G2
REPOLE, Charles
Whoopee opens 2-14, 292F3
REPORTERS Committee for Freedom of the Press
Landau scores Sup Ct 'state of mind' libel ruling 4-18, 302C2
Landau scores ctroom access ruling 7-2, 515D3
Trial closure efforts rptd on rise 8-4, 630C2

1980

RELIGION—*See also denominations; country, group names*
'79 church attendance poll rptd 1-4, 7F3
Medicaid abortn aid ban voided 1-15, 35E3
US Bible reading survey rptd 1-18, 157F1
Airwave evangelism symposium held 2-6—2-7; broadcast growth, TV revenues rptd 2-25, 413C1-D2
CIA use of clergy admitted 2-21, 189A3
Swiss reject church-state separatn 3-2, 236C1
US intercommunion poll rptd 4-4, 413E2
CIA use of clergy backed by Turner 4-10; Sen OKs intell oversight bill 6-3, 458E3, 459B1
Conservative Christians hold DC rally 4-29, 348C3-349B1
Chicago theologian wins Templeton prize 5-13, 471D2
Medicaid abortn funding limits upheld by Sup Ct 6-30, 492A1
FCC revokes Faith Center TV license 10-10, 907B1
School Issues—*See EDUCATION--Religious Issues*
U.S. Presidential Election (& Transition)
Fundamentalist pol role profiled 7-11—9-15; voters surveyed, Falwell ministry detailed 9-15, 818C3-819F3
Reagan addresses fundamentalists; notes evolutn 'flaws', backs teaching chngs 8-22, 646B2
Reagan, Anderson TV debate 9-21, 721F2, 722G1
Anderson scolds fundamentalists 9-29, 739C2
Reagan disavows fundamentalist dogma 10-3, 763F2
Carter warns vs Reagan win 10-6, 762E3
Reagan deplores Carter 'hysteria' 10-7, 763D2
Carter drops Reagan attack 10-9, 778D2

RELIGIOUS Broadcasters Association, National
Anderson addresses 9-29, 739D2
Reagan addresses 10-3, 763F2
RELIGIOUS Cults
Tex witches' priest acquitted of '77 murder 2-1, 238E1
Pope warns vs African rites, voodoo 7-5, 538E1
Deprogramming Issues
Patrick convicted for Ariz abductn 8-29, 727B1
Patrick sentenced 9-26, 857B3
Peoples Temple—*See PEOPLES Temple*
RELIGIOUS Roundtable
Political actn profiled 7-11—9-15, 819G1
REMBRANDT Harmens van Rijn (1606-69)
Rosenberg rptd dead 4-7, 360B3
REMICK, Lee
Tribute released 12-13, 1003F2
RENALDO, Duncan
Dies 9-3, 756B2
RENAULT, Regie Nationale des Usines
Research collaboratn set 4-22, 303A3
AMC loan set 7-1, 556B3
AMC stake increased; rescue plan rptd, finance unit set 9-24, 724C3
Lepeu replaces Sick at AMC 9-29, 959E2
AMC rpts aid crucial 11-19, 883C2
AMC sets credit agrmt 12-11, 938A3

RENE, France Albert (Seychelles president)
Curfew eased 1-11, 40E1

RENFREW, Charles B.
Signs Civiletti probe 8-7, 595E2
RENFRO, Mike
Steelers win NFL conf title 1-6, 8F1
Rozelle defends pass call 1-7, 23G1
Disputed catch film unveiled 1-16, 62G1
RENNER, Jack
2d in Busch Classic 9-28, 972C2
RENNERT, Peter
Loses NCAA singles tennis title 5-26, 607D1
RENOIR, Pierre Auguste (1841-1919)
Painting stolen in Argentina 12-25, 991E1
RENSSELAER Polytechnic Institute (Troy, N.Y.)
Low asks FAA overhaul 6-26, 519B1
High temperature superconductor rptd 9-4, 716B2

1976

REPTILES
Australia smuggling ring rptd 7-8, 537E1
REPUBLICAN Party—*See under POLITICS*
REPUBLIC Corp.
SEC rpts paymts probe 5-12, 728F2
REPUBLIC National Bank of N.Y.
IMF gold purchase rptd 6-3, 430F2
IMF gold buyer 9-15, 739E3
REPUBLIC of New Africa (U.S. organization)
Williams freed 1-16, 79C1
REPUBLIC of Texas Corp.
Rptd on FRB 'problem' list 1-22, 111C3
Republic National Bank (Dallas)
Rptd on comptroller's 'problem' list 1-26, 113E1
N Sea oil Euroloans rptd 2-5, 173F3
REPUBLIC Shipping Co.
Boycott rpt released 10-19, 786D1
REPUBLIC Steel Corp.
Fined 5-4, 379F2
Hikes prices 6% 11-29, 897F2
Reserve Mining Co.—*See separate listing*
REQUE Teran, Gen. Luis
Controversy over Guevara, Zenteno deaths 4-14—5-23, 415C3
RESEARCH for Better Schools Inc.
Violence study released 3-18, 263E1
RESERVE Forces—*See under U.S. GOVERNMENT—ARMED Forces*
RESERVE Mining Co.
Judge in pollutn case removed 1-6, 25C2
Fined 5-4, 379C2
Clean-up deadline set 7-7, 570D3
RESLER, Rex
Cited in Sen rpt on Callaway 10-5, 745C1, E1

RESOURCES, Natural—*See also ENVIRONMENT, PARKS, FORESTS and other related subjects*
Wildlife Federatn rpt issued 1-18, 45A1
'77 budget proposal 1-21, 63F1, 64G2
Fscl '77 US budget estimate tables 231A1, 358B2
US adopts strip-mine rules 5-11, 359D2-B3
Sup Ct backs Cheyenne mineral rights 5-19, 394A1
Eur, Latin soc dems issue declaratn 5-25, 449G2
Dem platform text 6-15, 474B3, 475D3
Local-zoning referendum upheld 6-21, 453A1
Cong clears coal lands bill 6-21, Ford vetoes 7-3, 518C1
Brown TV speech topic 6-25, 468G1
Strip-mining stay reversed 6-28, 568G3
Carter land-use record cited 512D2
Coastal land-use aid signed 7-26, 566G2
Coal land leasing veto overridden 8-3, 8-4, 566E2
GOP platform text 8-18, 607D3, F3
Cong clears land conservatn funding 9-13, 745E2-B3; Ford signs 9-28, 982G1
Cong sets '77 budget levels, table 9-16, 706B2
Natl parks mining bill signed 9-28, 834B2
Strip-mining, youth jobs bills not cleared 10-2, 883A1, F2, 884B1
UN world econ rpt issued 10-13, 760D1, A2
Planning bill vetoes 10-19, 919B2
Land-use bill signed 10-21, 834C1
Ford, Carter debate 10-22, 801D2-B3

RESSMEYER, Rev. Rudolph P. F.
Ousted as dist pres 4-2; resigns 9-14, 776B3, G3
RESTAURANTS—*See FOOD*
RETHBERG, Elisabeth
Dies 6-6, 444G2
RETIREMENT—*See PENSIONS & Retirement*

1977

REPUBLICAN Party—*See under POLITICS*
REPUBLIC Steel Corp.
Steelworkers OK contract 4-9, 273G2
Steel price hiked 5-6, rolled back 5-11, 385E1
Pollutn clean up pacts set 6-30, 521C3
Reserve Mining Co.—*See separate listing*
RESCISSIONS, Fund—*See U.S. GOVERNMENT—BUDGET—Impoundment & Rescission*
RESERVE Forces—*See under U.S. GOVERNMENT—ARMED Forces*
RESERVE Mining Co.
Ct backs dump site 1-31, 95D2
USW strike ends 12-16, 977B3
RESERVOIRS—*See DAMS & Reservoirs*
RESNIZKY, Nehemias
Son kidnaped 7-28, rescued 8-3, 670A3

RESOURCES, Natural—*See also ENVIRONMENT, PARKS, WATER and other related subjects*
Ford energy message 1-11, 14F3
Sup Ct reverses '73 Ariz land ruling 1-12, 57C3
Cong actn sought in Maine Indian land claim 1-14, 59C1-A2
Ford '78 budget proposals 1-17, 31E3
Carter inaugural 1-20, 25G2, 27C1
Carter statemt to world 1-20, 26G1, A3
Land use in drought control urged 2-21, 183A3
Carter budget revision 2-22, 125F2
Sovt Soyuz 24 lands 2-25, 170F2
Carter asks energy dept 3-1, 148A2
Carter addresses UN 3-17, 185E2
Scientists rpt scores EPA 3-21, 252D2
Army dredging case review declined 4-25, 342D3
Cong sets '78 budget target 5-17, 405A1
Carter environmt message 5-23, 404B2, F2
Young Adult Conservatn Corps authorized 8-5, 609C2
Water projct bill signed 8-8, 609D2
UN deserts conf 8-29—9-9, 770C1
3 youth job corps cntrs rptd open, youth-adult progrm begun 8-31, 692E2
Minn wilderness proposed 9-13, 724D1
Populatn com set by House 9-24, 834A1
Japan on Canada investmts 9-27, 780A3
Coal-leasing plan barred by ct 9-27, 1007C2
Geothermal ownership case review declined 10-31, 835A3
Wetlands control resolved in clean-water bill revisn 11-10, 900C2, F2
Wetlands provisn clears Cong 12-15, 959E1; signed 12-28, 1001A3

RESTAURANTS & Nightclubs—*See also FOOD*
Pepsico Pizza Hut takeover cited in table 880G1
Toots Shor dies 1-22, 84F3
Eugenie Brazier dies 3-3, 264E2
Mafia infiltration rptd 5-16, 568E1
Ky nightclub fire 5-28, 429D2
Miami homosexual rights law repealed 6-7, 446F2
Ivory Coast nightclub blaze 6-9, 604G1
Ky nightclub fire rpt issued 6-10; death toll rises 6-12—7-29, damage suits rptd 7-29, 740A1, C1
Lou Walters dies 8-15, 696G3
House backs full min wage tip credit 9-15, 795F1
Great Western Sunshine takeover OKd 10-4, 799A1
Calif liquor license revocatn case review refused 10-17, 797F3
Min wage bill cleared 10-20, 795A3
Viacom-RCA satellite pact rptd 10-25, 921E1
RESTREPO, Fernando
Kidnap rptd 3-13, 255G1
RETAIL Clerks International Union (AFL-CIO)
Housewright dies 9-19, 788C1
Wynn joins AFL-CIO exec cncl 12-12, 961G1
RETAIL Trade—*See BUSINESS*
RETAIL, Wholesale and Department Store Union (AFL-CIO)
Heaps joins AFL-CIO exec cncl 12-12, 961G1
RETIREMENT—*See PENSIONS & Retirement; also U.S. GOVERNMENT—SOCIAL Security*

1978

REPRODUCTION—*See CHILDBIRTH*
REPUBLICAN Governors Association—*See GOVERNORS Association, Republican*
REPUBLICAN Party—*See under POLITICS*
REPUBLIC Steel Corp.
'76 tax nonpaymt rptd 1-27, 65G2
Price hike held to 3%, future price lid pledge hedged 6-14, 470F2, G2
Reserve Mining Co.—*See separate listing*
REQUIEM (recording)
Chicago Symphony wins Grammy 2-24, 316C1
RESEARCH-Cottrell, Inc.
Chrgd in W Va scaffold collapse 6-8, 459D3
RESEARCH Council, National—*See NATIONAL Academy of Sciences*
RESEARCH Industries Corp.
DSMO OKd for cystitis 3-20, 231G2
RESERVE Mining Co. (of Republic Steel Corp.)
To stay in business 7-7, 553E2
RESERVOIRS—*See DAMS & Reservoirs*
RESNICK, Patricia
Wedding released 9-29, 970D3
RESOLUTIONS, Congressional—*See under U.S. GOVERNMENT—CONGRESS—Legislation*
RESORTS International
Atlantic City casino opens 5-26, 6-day take rptd 6-5, 434B2
Water-based land claims barred by Sup Ct 5-31, 431E1
NJ casino profits rptd 10-4, gambling violatns chrgd 10-6; crime rise linked 11-10, 920B1-G1

RESOURCES, Natural—*See also ENVIRONMENT, PARKS, WATER and other related topics; also resource names*
Mondale tours West re land policies 1-9—1-13, 34D1, G1
Carter budget proposals 1-23, 44F2, 47D2, 48G1; table 45D2
GOP attacks Carter budget 1-31, 63C1
'77 environmental decline rptd 85A2-C2
New wilderness areas clear Cong 2-9, 109C2; signed 2-24, 218A2
Okefenokee Refuge expanded 3-14, 186B3
Carter policy scored by Colo sen 5-2, 342B2
Carter on Indian land claims 5-4, 321C1
Cong '79 budget target res cleared 5-17, 385F2
Indians protest in DC 7-15—7-23, 568E3
Land bur '79-82 authorzn signed 8-20, 697C2
Grazing-land law revisn cleared 10-11, 807D2
NJ OKs Green Acres referenda 11-7, 915C2
Carter protects Alaska lands 12-1, 936F3

RESTAURANTS & Nightclubs
Johnrae Earl dies 1-10, 96F1
Carter State of Union Message 1-19, 30G2
Carter vs business tax break 2-17, 123A2
Pulitzer awarded for '77 Ky nightclub fire coverage 4-17, 315A2
S Africa apartheid eased 6-4, 536G1-A2
'77 nightclub fire indictmts barred 8-2, 972C1
'78 disco dressing rptd 8-4—8-11, 10-27—11-3, 1029F2
July CPI rise rptd 8-29, 679B3
NYC '74 disco arsonist convicted 9-7, 824F2
NY newspr strike ends 11-6, 865G1
Kan alcohol referendum results 11-7, 854G2
Earthworm rumor hurts fast-food chains 11-16, 942F1
Microwave oven safety scored 12-11, 936B3
Hershey to buy Friendly's 12-26, 1005A1-A2
RESTON, James
Addresses laity conf 2-19, 294E3
Carter interview 11-6, 862B1
RESURRECTION City—*See BLACK Americans—Welfare & Poverty*
RETAIL Clerks International Association (AFL-CIO)
Wynn on '77 top-paid labor ldrs list 5-15, 365F1
RETAIL Federation, American
Hears Kahn on Carter inflatn plan 11-15, 917C3
RETAIL Trade—*See also BUSINESS—Statistics, DEPARTMENT & Variety Stores, TAXES—Business Tax Issues; company names*
Mgt gains for women rptd 5-22, 554F3
NY newspaper strike ends 11-6, 865G1
RETARDATION, Mental—*See MEDICINE—Mental Health*
RETIREMENT—*See PENSIONS & Retirement*

1979

REPORTERS Committee for Freedom v. AT&T, et al
Case refused by Sup Ct 3-5, 184F3
REPRODUCTION—*See CHILDBIRTH*
REPRODUCTIVE Services Inc. v. Walker
Case declined by Sup Ct 1-22, 54A2
REPUBLICAN Party—*See under POLITICS*
RESEARCH—*See also specific subjects*
Carter urges privacy bill 4-2, 264D3
RESENDE, Eliseu
Brazil transport min designate 1-19, 95D1
RESERPINE—*See MEDICINE—Drugs*
RESERVE Forces—*See under U.S. GOVERNMENT—ARMED Forces*
RESERVE Oil & Gas Co.
Accepts Denison merger bid 8-14, Getty Oil bid 10-31, 986B3
RESNICK, Patricia
Quintet released 2-8, 174D3
RESNIKOFF, Robert
Light Shines opens 1-11, 292G1
RESOLUTIONS, Congressional—*See under U.S. GOVERNMENT—CONGRESS—Legislation*
RESORTS International
NJ casino fined 1-3, 'card-counters' barred 2-1, 152D1
NJ casino granted permanent license 2-26, 151F3
NJ hikes gambling tax, '78 earnings rptd 9-18, 851G1

RESOURCES, Natural
Wilderness proposal scored 1-4, 16B2
Carter budget proposals 1-22, 45D3; table 42F2
Carter State of Union Message 1-23, 46G2, 47C2, 48A1
Farm land rptd lost to dvpt 1-25, 90D2
Carter proposes Cabt-level dept 3-1, 164B1
House com OKs Alaska lands bill 3-1, 187E1
Carter proposes wilderness bill 4-16, 282E1
Cabt-level dept plan dropped 5-15, 365A2
House OKs Alaska land bill 5-16, 366E3
West mounts 'Sagebrush Revolt' 7-13—9-7, 704C1
Continental buys Fla Gas 8-28, 986C3

RESTAURANTS & Nightclubs
Illegal alien issue detailed 1-29, 127E1
Boston Navy Yd renovatn set 2-1, 94A1
Studio 54 owners indicted 6-28; Jordan denies cocaine use 8-24, Landau disputes 8-28, 647D1-E2
USSR hikes prices 7-2, 504E2
Holiday Inns completes Trailways sale 8-21, to buy Harrah's 9-4, 682C2-F2
Studio 54 cocaine rpt disputed 8-31, 767E2
Imperial Group to buy Howard Johnson 9-10; Calif bar seen 10-12, 924B3-E3
Studio 54 drug indictmt 10-23, owners plead guilty to tax chrgs 11-2, 891G2
RESTORING the American Dream (book)
On best-seller list 10-14, 800C3; 11-4, 892C3
RETAIL Clerks International Association (AFL-CIO)
Meat Cutters merger set 1-26, 130F3; merges 6-6, 419F3
RETAIL Federation, American
Hackler trade nominatn rptd blocked 8-3, 647C1
RETAIL Trade—*See also BUSINESS—Statistics, DEPARTMENT & Variety Stores, TAXES—Business Tax Issues; company names*
Tex, NJ blue law cases declined by Sup Ct 1-22, 54E1
Hartz Mt settles FTC complaint 8-28, 903B1
RETIREMENT—*See PENSIONS & Retirement*

1980

REPRODUCTION—*See CHILDBIRTH*
REPUBLIC Airlines Inc.
Jet hijacked to Cuba 8-16, 631C3
REPUBLICAN National Committee v. Federal Election Commission
Case decided by Sup Ct 4-14, 306E3
REPUBLICAN Party—*See under POLITICS*
REPUBLIC Steel Corp.
W Va coal miners strike 2-21—3-3, 170A1
USW contract settled 4-15, 289B2
Prices cut 7-10, 575F2
Reserve Mining Co.—*See RESERVE Mining Co.*
RESEARCH Equity Fund Inc.
Mutual fund insurnc case refused by Sup Ct 3-24, 265F1
RESEARCH Equity Fund v. Insurance Co. of North America
Case refused by Sup Ct 3-24, 265E1
RESERVE Mining Co. (of Republic Steel Corp.)
Ends Lake Superior dumping 3-16, 227A1
RESERVOIRS—*See DAMS & Reservoirs*
RESNICK, Patricia
Nine to Five released 12-19, 1003C2
RESORTS International Inc.
6th Atlantic City casino opens; '79, '80 revenues rptd 12-12, 98F2, E3

RESOURCES, Natural
State of State messages 1-7—1-10, 403D2, D3, F3; 1-15, 268G3
Japan-Australia cooperatn seen 1-16, 78E1
Australia stocks make gains 1-18, 56C1
Carter asks Alaska lands protectn 1-21, 43F3
Carter budget proposals 1-28, 73D3; table 70F1
US extends Alaska lands order 2-12, 131F2-B3
US global forecast gloomy 7-23, 573F1
US Dem platform planks adopted 8-13, 615G1
Alaska lands bill clears Sen 8-19, 631B2-A3
NJ bond issue OKd 11-4, 847A1
Alaska lands bill clears House 11-12, 866E2-C3
New scenic area air rules issued 11-25, 898G1-C2
Alaska lands bill signed 12-2, 916A1
Calif desert plan issued 12-22, 986G3-987C1

RESTAURANTS & Nightclubs
Canada fire kills 42 1-1, 24C2
Studio 54 owners sentenced 1-18, 64B3
Smoking risk to nonsmokers rptd 3-26, 318B2
NY transit strike impact cited 4-10, 268D2
Jordan cleared re Studio 54 chrg 5-28, 402C3
Imperial Group completes Howard Johnson deal 6-17, 557C3
ABA urges sex bias end 8-6, 744A2
McDonald's acquitted in trust suit 9-29, 917B3
RESURRECTION, The (painting)
Sold for record sum 4-16, 472G2
RESZKO, Wojciech
Wins Olympic medal 7-27, 623D1
RETAIL Trade—*See also BUSINESS—Statistics, DEPARTMENT & Variety Stores, TAXES—Business Tax Issues*
Britannica sales practices case refused by Sup Ct 3-17, 266D1
Credit card use rptd tightened 3-27, 222D2
Credit controls modified by FRB 4-2, 263F2
NY transit strike impact cited 4-10, 268D2
Credit card issuers rptd cautious on FRB moves 5-27, 400G1
Shopping cntr petitn access backed by Sup Ct 6-9, 512A2
FRB ends credit controls 7-3, 513C2
RETIREMENT—*See PENSIONS*
RETIREMENT Fund Trust v. Johns
Case declined by Sup Ct 1-14, 37A1

1976

RETURN of the Pink Panther (film)
'75 top rental film 1-7, 32F3
REUSS, Rep. Henry S. (D, Wis.)
Asks bank regulatory reform 1-25, 112A1
Vs loan to Chile 3-19, 3-23; McNamara defends 4-12, 310E2
Bank reform bill split 3-30; com acts on 2 4-30, 5-3; House OKs FRB bill 5-10, 345D1
Forgn-bank bill dies 7-29, 940B3
On Fed Reserve bds make-up 8-15, 667C1
Reelected 11-2, 831A4
Meets Burns, sees FRB-Carter cooperatn 11-12, 865B2
REUTERS (news agency)
CIA manipulatn rptd 1-23, Colby denies 1-26, 92G2
Nigeria ousts newsman 2-16, 192A1
Waldheim: misquoted on Uganda raid 7-8, 516A2
Developing natns OK press pool 7-13, 619A3
Cited in Schorr probe 7-20, 748F3
REVEL, Jean-Francois
'Totalitarian' publicatn rptd 1-20, 119A3
REVENUE Sharing—*See under U.S. GOVERNMENT—BUDGET*
REVERE Copper & Brass Inc.
Sues Jamaica 1-13, 51G1
REVERSE Discrimination
AT&T damages ordrd 6-9, compensatory promotn plan upheld 8-27, 944G1
Conn liability in bias case affirmed 6-28, 569C1
Reagan chrgs Ford, Carter bias 7-6, 490F2
Sup Ct bars Washn labor suit review 10-12, 848G2
Sup Ct stays Calif U admissns ruling 11-15, 882C1
Calif U to appeal admissns ruling 11-19, 995E2
Sup Ct bars La HS case review 11-29, 900E3
NJ Sup Ct voids hiring quotas 11-30, 943C2
REX (play)
Opens 4-25, 1014C3
REXHAM Corp.
Trust suit dvpts 2-18—10-5, 886D1, E2
REYES, Cornelio
Resigns 10-13, 924G3
REYES, Edmundo M.
Pl orders US newsman probe 11-6, 855F1
REYES, Col. Rafael
Assassinated 2-11, 212E1
REYES Heroles, Jesus
Mexico interior min 12-2, 906F3, G3
REYNOLDS, Frank
Pres debate panelist 9-23, 700G3
REYNOLDS, Gene
Wins Emmy award 5-17, 460B2
REYNOLDS, Hal
On World Bank loans to Chile 12-21, 999G1
REYNOLDS, James J.
Scores Panama Canal toll hike 11-24, 1008C3
REYNOLDS, Judge John
Orders Milwaukee schl integratn 1-19, 42B3
REYNOLDS, Milton
Dies 1-28, 80F3
REYNOLDS, Robert M.
Loses electn 11-2, 825F1
REYNOLDS, Ron
Loses Durban electn 5-5, 422E3
REYNOLDS Industries Inc., R. J.
Admits US, forgn paymts 5-28, 9-10, 689F2
Sea-Land Service Inc.
Rebates, paymts rptd 5-28—9-13, 689A3 ★
REYNOLDS Metals Co.
Brazil bauxite operatn begun 1-16, 98G2
Duvaliers' embezzlemt rptd 4-9, 267F2
Admits forgn paymts 6-2, 690D2
Raises can-metal prices 11-30, 898F1
Australia refinery set 12-9, 961G3
REZAI, Reza
Keykavoussi shot in Paris 11-2, 1002G2
REZANTSEV, Valery
Wins Olympic medal 7-24, 576B3
RHINE, International Commission for the Protection of the
Pollutn treaties signed 12-4, 977G1

RHODE Island
Primary date set 22B2
Food stamp ineligibility rate rptd 2-11, denied 2-12, 129B1
Providence revenue sharing bias cited 3-2, 187E1
US Sup Ct rules vs convicts' silence right 4-20, 331F2
Primary results 6-1, 389E2-390A3
Ships in Newport for Bicentennial 6-26, 489E1
Queen Eliz visits Providence 7-11, 489G2
Dem conv women delegates, table 508D2
Dem conv pres vote, table 7-14, 507D2
GOP pre-conv delegate count 8-14, 583D3
GOP conv pres, vp vote tables 8-18—8-19, 8-19, 599D1, D3
Primary results 9-14, 704E3
Fscl '75 capita income, tax burden rptd 9-15, 10-12, 959A2
Dole in Providence 10-25, 804B2
Election results 11-2: pres 818C1, E1, 819A2; cong 820B1, 821C3, 828B3, 830G3, 831C2; state 820B3, 821D3
Amer Bank & Trust fails 11-16, 940F1
Flu shot paralysis rptd 12-17, 950E1

1977

REUSCH, Dale R.
Attacked at Ohio KKK rally 7-4, 540D1
REUSCHEL, Rick
NL pitching ldr 10-2, 926E3
REUSS, Rep. Henry S. (D, Wis.)
'76 spec interest gifts rptd 2-4, 128G3, 129A2
Vance backs rights amendmt 3-23, 211A1
Chrgs questionable FRB actns 5-24, 406D3
REUTEMANN, Carlos
Final Grand Prix standing 10-23, 870E3
REUTERS (news agency)
Czech police attack Requette 3-3, 220D3
Ethiopia ousts rptr 4-25, 327C3
Rpts Israel beatings 7-7, 511F2
CIA links charged 9-12, 720B3
REUTHER, Walter Philip (1907-70)
UAW to study AFL-CIO reentry 5-19, 408G1, D2
REVELLI-Beaumont, Lucino
Kidnaped 4-13, ransomed 7-11, 543C2
REVELO Contreras, Bishop Rene
Chrgs El Salvador priests re Marxism 10-4, Vatican rebukes 10-8, 844E3
REVENUE Sharing—*See under U.S. GOVERNMENT—BUDGET*
REVERE Copper & Brass Inc.
New USW pact reached 5-24, 422E1
US aid to Jamaica resumed 9-12, 11-9, 884D2
US vs mill sale to Alcan 12-9, 1004E3
Ormet—*See separate listing*
REVERING, Dan
Traded to A's, Kuhn may block 12-9, 990A1
REVERSE Discrimination
Detroit police file suit 1-4, 278A3
Soc Sec widower benefits rule voided 3-2, 192G1
Carter call-in on jobs 3-5, 171E1
Califano backs quotas 3-17, 217B3
Soc Sec benefits test voided 3-21, 230E1
Soc Sec old-age benefits bias upheld 3-21, 230G1-D2
Califano backs down on quotas 3-31, 235B2
Califano backs 'goals' 6-5, 445F3
Bakke brief filed 9-19; Sup Ct hears arguments 10-12, orders more briefs 834F2-835G1
Pub works bill minority-quota provisn challenged 10-31, 979A1
REVLON Inc.
Bergerac '76 pay rptd 5-23, 408D3
Hair dye linked to cancer 10-17, 962G3
USV Pharmaceutical Corp.
Phenformin sales barred 7-25, 603B2
REY, Brig. Carlos Alberto (ret.)
Arrested 5-4, 371B1
Freed from jail 6-13, 522D3
REYES, Manuel Humberto
Cuba frees 8-2, 654A2
REYES, Tomas
'Plot' chrgd 3-11, denied 3-13, 219C3
REYE'S Syndrome—*See MEDICINE—Diseases*
REYNOLDS, David P.
On Jamaica unit assets sale 3-31, 258A1
REYNOLDS, Judge John W.
Sets Milwaukee schl integratn goal 3-11, 216F3
REYNOLDS 3rd, Richard S.
Loses primary for lt gov 6-14, 465B1
REYNOLDS Industries Inc., R. J.
Burmah Oil takeover cited in table 880F1
Indonesia exit rptd planned 4-18, 392A3
American Independent Oil Co.
Kuwait nationalizes 9-19, 805G3
Aminoil USA Inc.
Offshore oil lease rptd renewed 3-15, 195G3
Sea-Land Service Inc.
Rebates case setld, recipients named 1-5, 6B2
REYNOLDS Metals Co.
Jamaica buys unit assets 3-31, 257F2, D3
New USW pact reached 5-24, 422E1
Aluminum prices hiked 6-21, 577G1
Australia refinery canceled 7-7, 523F1-A2
REYNOLDS Securities International, Inc.
Thomas Staley dies 9-13, 788F2
Dean Witter merger set 10-3, 799G2
RHEE, Jhoon
Named KCIA agent 6-5, 6-6, 442B1, C1 ★
RHEE, Syngman (Lee Sung Man) (1875-1965)
CIA payments rptd 2-19, 124F1
RHINELANDER, John B.
Replaced as HUD undersecy 3-23, 272B3
RHODE Island
Legislature schedule rptd 6F2
Indian land claims rptd 2-7, 197D1
Conrail line cuts set 3-31, 325F2
Fed spending inequities chrgd 4-6, 423D3
'76 per-capita income table 5-10, 387C2
Providence business confidence rptd; econ data table 5-16, 384D2, A3
Sup Ct backs US fishing laws 5-23, 444C2
NY jobless aid for strikers upset 5-24, 463D1
Prov gay rights march 6-26, 560E2
'76 per-capita income, tax burden table 9-13, 10-18, 821B2
Anti-abortn amendmt rptd sought 10-6, 786B3

1978

RETURN From Witch Mountain (film)
Released 7-14, 970G2
REUSCH, Dale
Loses primary for Ohio gov 6-6, 448C1
REUSS, Rep. Henry S. (D, Wis.)
Backs US aid to NYC 2-14, 608D2
Scores US bank loans to Chile 4-12, 312B2
Harris cancels testimony 8-7, 605F1
Gas pricing plan clears conf com 8-17, 677C3
Reelected 11-7, 852C4
Open Market Com case declined by Sup Ct 11-27, 937F2
REUSS v. Balles
Case declined by Sup Ct 11-27, 937F2
REUTEMANN, Carlos
Wins US Grand Prix events 4-2, 10-1; 4th in world driving title 9-10, 968C3, E3
REUTERS (news agency)
Cyprus presses chrgs vs Biermann 2-22, drops case 2-24, 138E2
REUTERSHAN, Paul
Dies 12-14, 984D1
REVENGE of the Pink Panther (film)
Released 7-19, 970A3
Top-grossing film 7-26, 620D1; 8-30, 708G1
REVENUE Sharing—*See under U.S. GOVERNMENT—BUDGET*
REVERING, Dave
Kuhn cancels Blue sale to Reds 1-30, 194B3
REVERSE Discrimination
Ala State hiring bias ruled 5-1, 348B3
House votes quota curbs 6-13, 445G3
Bakke med schl admissn ordrd, race-based affirmative actn principle upheld by Sup Ct; reactn, opinion excerpts 6-28, 481A1-483A1, E1-487C2
Harvard admissns program described 483A1
AT&T bias case declined by Sup Ct 7-3, 552A1
Calif contractors case sent back by Sup Ct 7-3, 552B1
Univ of NC minority rep case sent back by Sup Ct 7-3, 552C1
Pub works minority business quota provisn upheld 9-23, 811E2
Weber job-bias case accepted by Sup Ct 12-11, 980E2-D3
EEOC issues guidelines 12-12, 1006B2
Calif fire dept ratio plan overturned 12-26, 1006F2
REVILL, Jack
At JFK death hearing 9-26, 750B1
REYES, Albert
Fight for Barbara opens 11-27, 1031F1
REYES Heroles, Jesus
Sees Sinaloa gov 2-15, 290A1
Amnesty bill enacted 9-28, vows more releases 10-1, 817G2
REYNOLDS, Burt
End released 5-10, 619G1
Hooper released 8-4, 970E1
REYNOLDS, Craig
Traded to Astros 12-8, 1026D1
REYNOLDS, Frank
ABC news show chngs set 4-19, 419B3
REYNOLDS, James G.
Unopposed in RI US Sen primary 9-12, 716G2
Loses US Sen electn 11-7, 847F3
REYNOLDS Industries Inc., R. J.
Sea-Land pleads guilty re rebates, fined 4-11, 449E2
HMO rptd successful 5-10, 578E1
Philip Morris to buy 7-Up 5-15, 364B3
SEC paymts chrgs settled 6-6, 449C2
Del Monte merger sought 8-3, bid OKd 9-25, 752A3
REYNOLDS Metals Co.
NW alum productn resumed 1-10, 24F1
REZAEI, Ali
Sought for corruptn 11-17, 893B3
REZNOWSKI, Lorne
Elected Soc Credit ldr 5-7, 392A1
REZUN, Vladimir
Defects to UK 676G1

RHODE Island
Legislature schedule rptd 14F3
'67, '77 sales-tax rates rptd 1-5, 15B3, F3
State govt tax revenue table 1-9, 84E2
Blizzard hits 2-5—2-7, 105F1, D2
Carter visits, backs Pell reelectn 2-17, 123D1, F1
Narragansett land claim settled 3-2, 326E3
A-sub work stoppage feared 3-13, 224A2
Porno film distributor sentncd 5-19, 396G3
Extended jobless aid rptd 7-10, 552B3; 8-4, 607D3
Primary results 9-12, 716G2-A3
Election results 11-7: cong 846A2, 847F3, 848C3, 852A2; state 847C1, G3, 853E3, 915E2
Asbestos danger in schls cited 12-21, 1009C2
Moonie loses deprogramming suit 12-29, 1012A2

1979

REUNITED (recording)
On best-seller list 5-2, 356G2; 5-30, 448E3
REUSCHEL, Rick
NL pitching ldr 9-30, 955G2
REUSS, Rep. Henry S. (D; Wis.)
Banking Com chrmn 1-24, 71C1
Abandons FRB membershp aid bill, scores bankers 4-24, 303D1, C2
Urged Nicaragua IMF loan probe 8-6, 603A2
Scores FRB re money supply errors 10-30, 828A3
Vs prime rate rise 10-31, scores banks re hikes 11-7, 11-16, 940G3, 941A1
REUTER, Thomas
Sentncd for Israel '76 jet plot 9-11, 677D2
REUTERSHAN, Paul (d. 1978)
Viet defoliant suit filed 2-1, 90A1
REUTHER, Walter (1907-70)
Harry Bennett dies 1-4, 104F2
REVCO D. S. Inc.
Woolworth merger talks disclosed 4-17, ended 4-23, 304C1
REVENUE Sharing—*See under U.S. GOVERNMENT—BUDGET*
REVERCOMB, (William) Chapman
Dies 10-6, 860C3
REVERSE Discrimination
Weber job-bias case argued in Sup Ct 3-28, 262B3
DiLeo case declined by Sup Ct 4-23, 346D2
Govt minority constructn grant case accepted by Sup Ct 5-21, 400F3
Weber affirmative actn challenge rejctd by Sup Ct, reactn; majority opinion excerpts 6-27, 477A1-478E1
KKK protesters arrested in Ala 8-12, 631C1
Connally scores 11-15, 982G3
Govt minority constructn grants case argued in Sup Ct 11-27, 944F3
REVLON Inc.
Technicon purchase set 9-6, 664A1
REVOLUTIONARY Communist Party
Anti-Teng DC protesters arrested 1-29, 66E1; freed 11-14, 904G3
REY, Antonio
Simpson Street opens 3-5, 292A3
REY, Fernando
Quintet released 2-8, 174D3
REYES, Hamlet
Beagle Channel papal mediatn agreed 1-8, 51D3
REYES, Maj. Gen. Juan Tomas
Named DR mil attache in Mex 1-12, 62D2
REYES Evora, Gen. Tomas
Arrested 9-25, plot exposed 9-26, 751F3
REYES Heroles, Jesus
Ousted as Mex interior secy 5-16, 408B3, D3
REYNOLDS, Ed
Klansmen arrested in NJ 11-24, 991D3
REYNOLDS, Judge John
OKs Milwaukee desegregatn setlmt 5-4, 596E2
REYNOLDS, Jonathan
Tunnel Fever opens 5-10, 712B3
REYNOLDS, Ray
Jupiter moon theory rptd 3-17, 216G2
REYNOLDS Industries Inc., R. J.
Ordrd to obey FTC subpoena 1-25, 91D3
Bagley chrgd re stock fraud 3-14, 3-15, 292A1
US regulatory costs rptd 3-29, 230C3
Fortune rpts '78 rank, Del Monte acquisitn cited 5-7, 305B1
Bagley acquitted 8-1, 578D2
Sea-Land Service Inc.—*See separate listing*
REY Prendes, Julio Adolfo
Rejects leftist demands 12-14, 968F1
REZNOWSKI, Lorne
Quits Socred ldrshp 2-22, 189E1
Roy replcs as Socred ldr 3-30, 254B1
RHEE, Syngman (1875-1965)
Cited re Pusan riots 10-16—10-17, 794G2

RHODE Island
Legislature schedule rptd 5F3
Capital punishmt law overturned 2-19, 188B2
Jobless pay for strikers upheld by Sup Ct 3-21, 231E1
Winter heating fuel supply promised 8-28, 703C2
Odd-even gas rules lifted 9-6, 683F1
Teachers' strikes rptd 9-12, 679B1
'78 per capita income rptd 9-16, 746A2, C2

1980

RETURN of the Secaucus Seven, The (film)
Released 9-14, 836E3
REUSS, Rep. Henry S. (D, Wis.)
Reelected 11-4, 844C4
REUSS, Jerry
Pitches no-hitter 6-28, 636B3
NL wins All-Star Game 7-8, 636C2
NL pitching ldr 10-6, 926F2, G2
2d in NL Cy Young vote 11-4, 925F3
REUTEMANN, Carlos
2d in Canadian Gr Prix 9-28, 1002A1
REUTERDHAN, Donald E.
On NY Insurance Exchng 3-31, 266E1
REUTERS (news agency)
3d World coverage study rptd 11-29, 914D1
REUTHER, Walter Philip (1907-70)
George Meany dies 1-10, 14E3
Fraser reelected UAW head 6-4, 457A2
REVEL, Jean-Francois
Marchais defends war record 3-8, 193F1
REVENUE Sharing—*See under U.S. GOVERNMENT--BUDGET*
REVERSE Discrimination
Constructn contract Indian preferncs barred by Sup Ct 5-27, 454B1
Govt minority constructn grants upheld by Sup Ct 7-2, 510A1
REVIGLIO, Franco
On Caltagirone tax debt 3-12, 255G1
Lists alleged tax evaders 3-19, 233E1
Italy finance min 4-4, 275F3*
Oil tax scandal probe rptd set 11-5—11-6, 873D2
REVLON Inc.
Revson indicted 8-19, 713F3
REVOLUTIONARY Communist Party
US, Sovt aides assaulted at UN mtg 4-30, 325G1
REVOLUTIONARY May Day Brigade
Alamo occupied, other protests rptd 3-20, 485A2
REVSON, Charles Haskell (1907-75)
Son indicted 8-19, 713A1
REVSON, John
Indicted 8-19, 713F3
REXCUS Consolidated Inc.
Pa bankruptcy scandal indictmts 2-12, 502F2
REY, Thierry
Wins Olympic medal 8-1, 623B1
REYES, Lt. Col. Jose
Chrgd in Pl plot 10-28, 874E2
REYNOLDS, Burt
Smokey & the Bandit II released 8-15, 675E3
REYNOLDS, Clarke
Night Games released 4-11, 416D3
REYNOLDS, James J.
LIRR strike bd rpts 1-14, 53E1
REYNOLDS, Julia
Dies 11-28, 1004B3
REYNOLDS, Richard S.
Dies 10-5, 876D3
Mother dies 11-28, 1004B3
REYNOLDS Metals Co. Inc.
Australia alumina plant planned 2-8, 95E1
USW pact settled 5-30, 482F2
Richard Reynolds dies 10-5, 876D3
REY-Shahri, Hojatolislam
On Anti-Khomeini plot 6-12, 465A1
RHINE, Joseph Banks
Dies 2-20, 176B3

RHODE Island
Influenza outbreak rptd 2-15, 158C3
Gay prom date upheld 5-28, 471C1
Teachers strike in Cumberland, Woonsocket, N Providence 9-3, 723E3
Crime & Civil Disorders
FBI 'Miporn' probe rptd 2-14, 136F1
Police interrogatn defined by Sup Ct 5-12, 386B2
Politics & Government—*See also other appropriate subheads in this section*
Legislature schedule rptd 18F1
State of State message 1-2, 270D1
Pres primary results 6-3, 423E2, 424C1
Primary results 9-9, 700G2
Mondale in Warwick 9-24, 780F2
Election results 11-4: pres 838D1, E1, 839A2, F3; cong 840C3, 844A2, 846C2, 848G3; state 845D3, 847D1, 848G3
'80 census rptd 12-31, 983F1

1976

RHODEN, Harold
On Hughes will 12-14, 971D2
RHODES, Cecil (1853-1902)
1st women scholars named 12-19, 993E3
RHODES, Gov. James A. (R, Ohio)
Ohio ERA study disputed 2-13, 172A2
Campaigns for Ford 6-7, 410D3
RHODES, Rep. John J. (R, Ariz.)
On State of Union speech 1-19, 40B1
On Angola aid cutoff 1-27, 69E1
On HEW-Labor funds veto override 1-28, 69E2
Scores environmt target list 3-25, 219F3
Scores House reforms 7-1, 551C3
Addresses GOP conv as permanent chrmn 8-17, 601G1
Reagan backers demonstrate 8-18, 598D1
Declares Ford pres nominee 8-19, 597G1-E2
Reelected 11-2, 824D1, 828F3
Reelected minority ldr 12-8, 981D3

1977

RHODEN, Rick
In World Series 10-11—10-18, 806F1
RHODEN, Harold
Dummar admits lying 1-11, 120E1
RHODES, David
CIA mind-control tests probed 9-20, 721B2
RHODES, Frank H. T.
Named Cornell U pres 2-16, 140F2
RHODES, Gov. James A. (R, Ohio)
Acts in fuel crisis 1-20—1-23, 54A2; 1-29, 75B3
Asks disaster status 2-8, 92A1
Kent State suit retrial ordrd 9-12, 820B3
Signs schl borrowing bill 12-7, 939C3
RHODES, Rep. John J. (R, Ariz.)
O'Neill elected Speaker 1-4, 5D3
'76 spec interest gifts rptd 2-15, 128A2, F2
Pay raises take effect 2-20, 127A3
Backs Central Ariz Project 3-21, 210F1
Scores Carter forgn policy 3-31, 247G1
Scores Carter energy taxes 4-25, 320G3
Urges Korea spec prosecutor 6-9, 442F2
Scores intell com party ratio 7-14, 557A2
Lauds Jaworski appointmt 7-20, 556F2
Scores Dems on cargo preferne 8-1, 719B3
Carter on 'inept' remark 10-27, 813F2
RHODES, Zandra
'77 Punk fashion rptd 1022F1

1978

RHODE Island, University of (Kingston)
NCAA basketball tourn results 3-27, 272C1
RHODES, George
Stop the World opens 8-3, 887C3
RHODES, Gov. James A. (R, Ohio)
Blizzard hits Ohio 1-25—1-26; declares energy emergency, rpts cleanup costs 1-30, 2-9, 105F2, C3, D3
Coal strike forces fed energy emergency 2-11, sees Carter 2-16, 104G1, D2
Renominated 6-6, 448C1
Clean-air moratorium denied 7-6, 513E1
Reelected 11-7, 853D3, 854D1
Notes Cleveland vote 11-27, 916C1
RHODES, Rep. John J. (R, Ariz.)
Rebuts Carter State of Union Message 1-26, 63E1
Rebuts Carter budget proposals 1-31, 63D1
Vs Mideast jet sale 4-25, 307C1
Scores '79 budget target res 5-17, 385E2
Sees CIA evidence on Cuba role in Zaire 6-2, 442F1
Vs A-carrier cut 9-7, 677D2
On tour for Kemp-Roth bill 9-20—9-22, 734F3
Reelected 11-7, 850C1, 855F1
Reelected minority leader 12-4, 958G1
Backs full China ties 12-16, 976A1
RHODES, Odell
Survives Guyana cult mass suicide 11-18, tells troops of Jones's plan 11-19, 890C2-A3
Guyana coroner's jury queries 12-14, 955D2

1979

RHODE Island, University of (Kingston)
Williams in NBA draft 6-25, 507B3
RHODES, Cecil John (1853-1902)
Rhodesia name chng proposed 1-2, 7G2
RHODES, Gov. James A. (R, Ohio)
Kent State '75 damage suit settled 1-4, 5E2
Kucinich vs control bd 2-28, 150F1
RHODES, Rep. John J. (R, Ariz.)
Loses House speaker electn 1-15, 30G1
House minority ldr 71B1
Scores State of Union Message, budget 1-24, 48G1
GOP ldrs meet, reject balanced budget amendmt 2-4, 86G1
On Carter mtg 6-7, 419E3

1980

RHODE Island v. Innis
Case decided by Sup Ct 5-12, 386B2
RHODES, Gov. James A. (R, Ohio)
Neutral in GOP pres race 3-10, 208B1
Endorses Reagan 4-20, 304B3
With Reagan in Cleveland 9-10, 699C3
RHODES, Rep. John J. (R, Ariz.)
Rebuts Carter State of Union 1-28, 75D1
On Kelly GOP conf resignatn 2-21, 143E3
Vs Carter anti-inflatn plan 3-17, 202E1
On GOP budget proposal 4-1, 244G1
Addresses GOP conv 7-15, 531D3, E3
Reelected 11-4, 842B1, 851B3
Sees Reagan 11-18, 880G2
Michel succeeds in GOP post 12-8, 936A2

RHODESIA

1976

RHODESIA
Cabt shuffled 1-13, Wrathall sworn pres 1-14, 53D3
Banana freed 1-15, 53G3
Listed as 'not free' nation 1-19, 20E3
Guerrilla-govt clashes 4-1—4-15, 295C3
Jan-Apr white emigratn total 523D1
ANC members arrested 4-4, 4-11, 295E3
Rebels halt transit, 3 killed 4-19, security tightnd 4-20, 295A3
Guerrilla actns, casualties rptd 4-26—5-12, 339B2
Mil svc extended 5-1, 5-5, 339F1
Guerrilla-govt clashes, casualties 5-6—6-13, 427B3-428F1
Salisbury-Umtali RR attacks 5-15, 6-13, 428D1
Todd house arrest lifted 6-5, 428D2
State of emergency renewed 6-24; ANC ban, Nkomo arrest sought 6-27, 522A3
Govt sets spending hike 7-6, 523E1
Emigrants' currency cut 7-15, 6-mo white losses rptd 8-1, 591B2
Tobacco subsidy cut rptd 8-25, 713A3
8 ANC members sentncd 8-30, 661B3
7-mo emigratn data rptd 8-31, 733D3
Guerrilla attacks 9-2—9-14, 713B2
Death penalty extended 9-8, 713D2
Smith shuffles Cabt 9-9, 713E2
RC comm chrgs atrocities 9-30, bishop sentncd 10-1, 812D3
Muzorewa returns 10-3, 738B3
Guerrilla activity rptd 10-5—10-17, 812G2-D3; 10-12—11-7, 855G2
Zero econ growth seen 10-17, 855C3
Rpt students join rebels 10-30, 855C3
Salisbury squatters evicted 11-6, 1010D1
ZANU factns clash 11-15—11-27, 1009B3
Airfield constructn rptd 11-25, 1009A3
Guerrilla-govt clashes, casualities rptd 11-30—12-28, 1009B2
Mil duty extended 11-30, 1009F3
Price boycotts rptd 12-13, bus strikers jailed 12-24, 1010A1
Guerrillas massacre tea workers 12-19, probe asked 12-20—12-22, 1009E1
African Relations—*For political developments in majority rule issue, see 'Majority Rule Issue' below*
Zambia factn backers riot 1-12, 54A1
Zambia invokes emergency powers 1-28, 77E3
Mozambique border clashes mount 2-6—2-29, total losses rptd 175E3
Zambia warns of warfare 2-15, 175E3
Rhodesians kill 24 guerrillas 2-24, 175G3
Mozambique arrests 16, Rhodesia shuts Maputo RR link 2-27, 175D2
Mozambique: Pafuri attack 'act of war', shuts border, sets sanctns 3-3, 175D1
Rhodesia, UK, Commonwealth, S Africa, Zambia reactn to sanctns 3-3, 3-4, 175A2, E2-E3, 176B1
Mozambique transport link dependence rptd 3-3, 175C2
Mozambique Feb mtg with 4 African ldrs rptd 3-4, 175F1
Guyana weighs Mozambique aid role 3-6, 253C2
Zambia sees war, asks UK force; cites Mozambique, Tanzania aid 3-19, 3-29, 240B2
Chitepo murder rpt issued 4-9, ZANU guerrilla chrgd 4-21, 428G1-C2
Zambia chrgs ZANU guerrilla in Madekurozwa murder 4-14, 428C2
3 S Africa tourists killed, main road shut 4-19, 295A3
Tanzania: war has begun 4-26, 295D1
Zambia, Mozambique back guerrillas 4-26, 295E1

1977

RHODESIA (Zimbabwe)
RC black bishop named 2-22, 375A3
Smith sets race reforms, Chirau backs 2-23, 123B1
Lamont sentnc cut 2-24, deported 3-23, 223B3
Natlists arrested 6-30, 536D2
Colored family fights evictn 7-24, Smith vs evictn 7-29, 599D2
Facts on coloreds 599E2
RC comm members seized 8-30, freed 9-4, 9-23; nun deported 9-22, 811G1
RC comm, Amnesty Intl chrg atrocities, torture 9-21; probe OKd 9-29, 811A2
Schls rptd closed re white emigratn, black kidnaping 9-30, 10-5, 811F2
Deportatn news banned 10-7, 811F1

1978

RHODESIA (Zimbabwe)—*See also GATT*
Black newspr closed 10-2, 784E1

1979

RHODESIA—*See ZIMBABWE Rhodesia*

1980

RHODESIA—*See ZIMBABWE*

1976

Walls warns guerrilla pursuit into Mozambique 5-1, 339A2
Road to S Africa reopened 5-3, 339D2
Botswana border RR sabotage foiled 5-5, 339C2
Mozambique border clashes 5-6—6-13, 427E3-428D1
2 killed on road to S Africa 5-17, compulsory convoy ordrd 5-23, 428F1
Botswana RR attacks 5-23, 6-13, 428E1
Zambia OKs guerrilla raids 5-28, chrgs Lusaka bombings 6-13; Rhodesia confrms 3d front 6-10, warns Zambia 6-12, 427C2, D2
Mozambique base bombed 6-10, 427A2
Sovt-run guerrilla camps in Tanzania cited 6-14, 428D1
Mobil sanctn violatns chrgd 6-21, 621G1
Guerrilla strife in Tanzania rptd 6-28, 7-2, 487F3
Rpt Nigeria aids guerrillas via Mozambique 7-6, 488A1
Angola confirms death for mercenaries 7-9, 519C3
Mozambique border violence continues 7-10, 7-13, 523C1
Raids Mozambique 8-8, chrgs retaliatn 8-10, 8-11, 580G1
Guerrilla activity rptd 8-12—9-1, Mozambique scored 8-15, 661F2-B3
Botswana rpts guerrilla search 8-12, 661G2
Kaunda seeks arms vs whites 8-19, 622A1
Muzorewa asks armed struggle 8-19, 661F3
UN scores Mozambique raid 8-20, Rhodesia asks probe 8-24, 661A2
5 nations conf in Tanzania re ANC rift 9-6—9-7, 661C3, E3 ★
5 state ldrs rptdly ask US rebel aid 9-14, 681C1
28 Mozambique guerrillas killed 10-1, 812G3
Mozambique attack rptd 10-18, 812D3
Mozambique attack kills 4 10-30, Rhodesia retaliates 10-31—11-2, police comr sees guerrilla setback 11-3, 855C2
Mozambique hits Umtali 11-3; Rhodesia border raid losses rptd 11-4, 855F2
Air strikes in Mozambique rptd 11-11—12-17, 1009F2
USSR rebel aid via Tanzania, Mozambique rptd 11-18, 1009E3
Botswana bars rebel asylum 12-7, rpts raid 12-20, 1009D3

British Relations—*See also 'Majority Rule' below*
UK lauds Mozambique sanctions 3-3, 175F2
Zambia asks mil interventn 3-29, 240B2
UK vs UN rights stand 4-30, 320D3

Foreign Relations (misc.)—*See also 'Majority Rule Issue' below*
'75 tourism data rptd 4-20, 295C3
Sovt-run guerrilla camps rptd 6-14, 428D1
USSR rebel aid rptd 11-18, 1009E3
Swiss priest arrested 12-8, 1010C1

1977

British Relations—*See also 'Majority Rule' below*
Oil-sanctn probe set 4-8; rpt accuses oil cos 4-25, 413D2
Lonrho sues 29 oil cos 5-31, 413C2
Mozambique raid scored 6-1, 413B2
BBC rptr ousted 8-2, 599F2
US renews sanctns 11-11, 876A1

Economy & Labor (domestic)
Bus strikers freed 12-29-76; svc renewed, boycott continues 1-4, 3B3
Bus boycott slows 1-7, 11A3
Party caucus backs Smith land reform plan 1-14, Frost scores 1-17, 49F2
Steel distributn, capital expenditures rptd down; mines closed 1-27, 73C2
Taxes raised, '77 budget deficit projctd 2-24, 144F3
'76 GNP rptd 5-6, 413G2
New budget presented 9-21, 824D3
$ devalued; banks warn 10-13, 824F3

Emigration
Jan-Nov '76 white emigratn rptd 1-17, 29G1
'76 white emigratn rptd 1-26, 50A1
Jan-Feb white emigratn rptd 3-24, 296G3
Catholic exodus rptd 4-3, 297C1
Mar-May white emigratn rptd 6-27, 536D2
Jan-June white emigratn rptd 7-30, 599C3
Jan-Aug data rptd 9-26, 811E2
Sept, 9-mo white losses rptd 11-1, 911F1
Nov slowdown rptd 12-22, 1016F1

Foreign Relations (misc.)—*See also 'Majority Rule', 'Military Developments' and 'Monetary, Trade & Aid' below*
Canada ousts Cuba spies 1-10, 17E2; Cuba clarifies chrg 1-21, 42E3
Swiss priest sentncd 1-12, 11F2
Argentina land for immigrants rptd 1-16, 29F1
Patriotic Front ldrs at Frelimo cong 2-3—2-7, 137E1
Swiss priest's sentence cut 4-6, 297B1
UN OKs info office ban 5-27, 457F1
Mozambique refugees score Frelimo 6-9, 456C3
Intl nonrecognitn cited 506B3
UN com asks communicatns boycott; scores repressn, agression 8-8, 662C1
Australia to close info center 9-20, 762E3
Botswana scored re Rhodesia family assault 10-9, 811B1
'77 UN, Swedish, other refugee aid rptd 12-13, 1000A2
Australia pro-apartheid min fired 12-21, 982D2

Government & Politics—*See other appropriate subheads in this section*
Mil post created 3-7, Cabt shuffled 3-10, 223F2
Ruling party expels anti-reformists 4-29, 414A1
De Kock quits Parlt 7-1, 536A3
Frost quits Rhodesian Front 7-2, Smith scores 7-3, 536F2-A3

1978

British Relations—*See also 'Majority Rule' below*
UK natls kidnaped by guerrillas 8-1, 8-20, 741C2
Oil sanctns violatn study released 8-31, 9-19; reactn 9-2—9-28, 755G3-756F3
BP chngs denial of sanctn violatns 10-22, 838E2
Callaghan backs sanctn violatns probe 12-15, 987A3

Economy & Labor (domestic)
Salisbury expenses rated 1-14, 28B3
'77 indl output drop rptd 2-26, 249F1
Standard Bank sees crisis, cites '77 GDP drop 3-22, 249A2
Tax collectn lags, 750 schls rptd closed 6-16, 455B3
'78 budget presented, deficit doubled 7-20, 616C1
'77 GDP rptd down 7-26, 616E1
4 strikers killed in mine riot 8-15, 741A3

Emigration
'77 total rptd 1-28, 59G3
Jan-Apr slowdown rptd 5-30, 455D3
May-July totals rptd 6-29—8-29, 741F2
Aug, Sept data rptd 11-2, 867E3
Oct white loss sets record 11-27, 946C1
Nov data rptd 12-28, 1019F3

Foreign Relations (misc.)—*See also 'Majority Rule', 'Military Developments' and 'Monetary, Trade, Aid & Investment' below*
Censorship imposed on forgn rptrs 1-7, 20G1
Zambia border closing cited 3-8, 170C1
OAU mtg bars transitn govt reps 7-7, 561F2

1979

1980

1976

1977

1978

1979

1980

1976

Majority Rule Issue
Smith-Nkomo talks continue 1-6—1-8, 1-16, 53F3
Muzorewa ANC backers riot 1-12, 54A1
Smith sees guerrilla war, rpts clashes 2-6, 176D1, F1 ★
EC backs self-determinatn 2-23, 164C3
Greenhill sees Smith, Nkomo on const talks 2-24—2-27; Callaghan rpts to Parlt 3-2, 176A2
Guyana backs united front, weighs Cuba aid role 3-6, 253C2
Smith-Nkomo talks collapse 3-19, 239D3
Smith, Nkomo ask setlmt role 3-19, 3-20, 239E3, 240G1
US warns Cuba 3-22, 2-23, 214D3
UK proposes charter plan 3-22, Smith rejects 3-23, 240B1
4 African ldrs in ANC talks 3-24—3-25, 240D2
USSR vows non-interference 3-25, 228F3
Cuba denounces repressn 3-29, 228A3
EC reaffirms self-determinatn 4-1—4-2, 276B1
EC backs UK policy 4-1—4-2, 276B1
EC embargo aid set 4-6, 276D2
Tanzania lauds US assurance 4-26, 295D1
Nkomo sees Kissinger 4-26—4-27, 295F1
US backs majority rule, offers power transfer aid, vows chrome imports actn; Smith deplores 4-27, 293B1, C2, 294D1-D2, 295E2
4 blacks named to Cabt 4-27, 295B2
Smith scores UK 4-27, 295E2
US offers to mediate 4-28, 293D2
US policy debated in US 4-28, 4-30, 323B3
Chiefs in Cabt opposed 5-4, 5-7, 339D2
Nkomo hardens stand 5-7, 339E2
S Africa bars mil role 5-13, 339A1 ★
US debate continues 6-2—6-6, 410B1
Todd house arrest lifted 6-5, 428F2
Smith sees Vorster in Pretoria 6-13—6-14, 427G1
US Dem platform text scores 6-15, 478E3
Mobil, others chrgd re sanctn violatns 6-21, 621D1
S Africa bars sanctns 6-22, 446G2
EEC, W Ger on S Africa 'responsibility' 6-22, 447B3
Kissinger-Vorster mtg 6-23—6-24, 446F2, G2
ANC asks talks renewed 6-27, Msika bars 7-12, 522C3
Govt rejcts major race reforms 7-2, partitn plan outlined 7-7, 522E3
US continues peace efforts, backs majority rule 7-7—7-9, 523A1
Mozambique rebel terms rptd 7-8, 523B1
Smith rejects reform plan 7-23, 591D1
Kissinger backs UK plan 8-2, sees Callaghan 8-5; Smith asks US talks 8-4, 580F2
S Africa min backs US efforts 8-13, 653B2, 661C1, E1
Kaunda seeks nonaligned arms vs whites 8-19, 622A1
Nonaligned for black rule 8-20, 621D3
ANC factional strife rptd 8-23, 661E3
Zimbabwe Reformed African Natl Cncl formed 8-23, 662A1
Smith on Rhodesian govt stand 8-25, 661F1
Kissinger vs white rule 8-31, Vorster rebuts 9-1, 660A3
Smith scores ANC 9-2, 661G1
ANC rift deepens 9-6—9-7, 661E3 ★
Vorster accord on US-UK plan rptd 9-9, 660B2
ANC reps score Kissinger 9-9, 681G1
Sithole quits ANC, scores disunity 9-9, 733A3
Kissinger optimistic 9-11; sees Tanzania, Zambia ldrs 9-15, 9-16, 681A1
Smith vs majority rule 9-13, 681D2
S Africa vows no pressure 9-13, 9-14, 681E2, G2
US rebel aid urged 9-14, 681C1
Smith sees Vorster in Pretoria 9-14, 681C2
Party cong backs Smith 9-15—9-17, 698F1
Kissinger sees Smith in Pretoria 9-19, UK reactn 9-21, 697B1, 698D1
Welensky, Todd on US, UK roles in crisis solutn 9-19, 698A2
Kissinger sees African ldrs on Vorster-Smith talks 9-20—9-23; Nyerere, Mobutu comment 9-21, 9-22, 717G2
Nkomo backs Kissinger 9-21, 697E1
Cabt meets 9-21—9-22, Smith meets parlt caucus on UK plan 9-23, 717A2
UN Assemb press scores minority rule 9-21, 719A1
ANC reps score plan 9-23, 9-25, 718F1
Smith accepts proposal, cites US, S Africa pressure; terms listed 9-24, 717A1
Kissinger, UK laud Smith 9-24, 717B2
Kissinger denies US policy chng rpt 9-24, 781A2
US, Vorster pressure rptd 9-25, 9-27, 717F1
USSR scores Kissinger 9-25, 718B3
Nkomo will meet natlsts on differences 9-25, 738G2

1977

Anti-reformists form party 7-4; moderate whites 7-5, 536B3
Parlt dissolved, vote set 7-18, 563C3
'77-78 budget rptd 8-25, 730C3
Smith sweeps vote, blacks boycott 8-31, 661A1
Cabt shuffled 9-18, 824D3
Parlt opens, law & ordr stressed 9-20, 824C3
Majority Rule—*For foreign economic sanctions, see 'Monetary, Trade & Aid' below*
Richard sees Smith on UK plan 1-1; visits S Africa, front-line states 1-2—1-6, 3G1
Richard continues front-line shuttle; Tanzania backs UK role, Patriotic Front rejcts 1-7—1-12, 11D1
Front-line states meet, back Patriotic Front 1-8—1-9; ANC scores 1-9, 10D3
White oppositn groups unite 1-10, 11F2
US mission rptd urged 1-10, 11A3
Geneva conf reopening postponed 1-11, 11G1
Van der Byl warns of separate setlmt 1-12, 11A2; casualties rptd 1-13, 73D2
Smith scores Richard shuttle, asks US setlmt role 1-14, 29C1
London ZANU backs Sithole, chrgs Mugabe-CIA link 1-14, 29D1
Richard sees Vorster 1-19, Kissinger plan compromise seen 1-20, 28G3
US urged Vorster press Smith 1-20, 29B1
Nkomo aide killed 1-22; natlst strife cited 1-24, 49D2
US, UK warn Smith vs separate pact 1-23, 1-26, 49G1
Smith bars new UK plan, Richard scores 1-24, 49A1
Banana arrested 1-25, 50B1
US setlmt role seen 1-26; Vance bars separate pact 1-31, 72D3
Rhodesia Front ldrs OK racial reform plan 1-27, 73E2
Vorster bars Smith pressure 1-28, 72G3
African ldrs, Patriotic Front score Richard 1-29—1-30; shuttle ends 1-31, 72G2
OAU Liberatn Com mtg opens 1-29, 72C3
Young starts shuttle 2-1, 72G3
Young in UK, Africa; US role backed 2-2—2-12; Carter comments 2-13, 105A1
Muller vs Smith setlmt plan 2-2, 122A3
Smith backs internal pact 2-4, seeks Vorster support 2-9—2-10, 122F2-A3
OAU backs Patriotic Front 2-4, 122B3
ZAPU urges Geneva talks resumed 2-22, 144G3
Black land purchase OKd 3-4; Smith challenges critics 3-15, party backs 3-16, 223A2
Afro-Arab summit backs 3-7—3-9, 170G1
Kaunda scores West, lauds USSR 3-25, 247E3
Podgorny backs Patriotic Front 3-26, sees Nkomo 3-28; Sithole scores 3-28, 247A3, De, G3
Nkomo flies to Angola 3-29, 249D3
Castro, Neto back rebels 4-2, 249C3
Owen tours region, seeks new Geneva parley, US role 4-11—4-17; US OKs 4-14, 296D1
Front-line states meet, back force 4-17—4-18, 296D3
Rhodesia Front backs Smith setlmt powers 4-18, 296E3
Young sees Sithole 5-13, 399A1
Maputo UN conf: Westn moves, natlsts backed 5-16—5-21; Mugabe disputes 5-16, 399B1
UK-US team tours region 5-17—6-1, 457B1
Vorster backs US, UK on Geneva parley 5-20, Mondale news conf 5-22, 398C1, E1
1st black purchase of white-owned land rptd 5-22, 414C1
Commonwealth conf backs 6-9, 6-10, scores Africa aid 6-16, 486C3, 487C1
OAU backs Patriotic Front 7-5, 512F1
US-UK team tours again 7-5—7-10; Smith statemt 7-12, 536A1
Sithole returns, backs UK-US team 7-10, 536C3
Muzorewa returns, scores Patriotic Front 7-17, 563F3
Smith dissolves Parlt, sets vote; scores US-UK effort 7-18; reactn 7-19, 563C3
Owen sees Vance, Carter; plan defended 7-23, 581A3
Muzorewa sets '78 majority rule plan 7-24, 581C3
Front-line states ask Patriotic Front unity 7-25, 581D3
S Africa scores UK 7-28, backs Smith 8-4, 599B2
Nyerere sees Canada, US offcls 8-2—8-13, 623F3
Vorster hits US policy 8-5, 639B3
Muzorewa loses backers 8-8—8-21, 662C2
Nkomo sees Young on Carib tour 8-9, 646B3
Nkomo sets peace terms, UN peace force cited 8-12, rejcts UK-US const plan 8-15, 624E1
Vance, Owen set new plan 8-12, tour southn Africa 8-26—8-30, 661E1-E2
Smith electn win evaluated 8-31, 661C1
Smith gets US-UK plan 9-1; Smith, defns min score, cite UN peace force; black moderates welcome 9-2, 699D2-A3
UK resident comr Carver rptd named 9-2, 810A1
Mugabe, Nkomo score UK-US plan 9-14, 735B1

1978

Majority Rule—*For foreign economic sanctions, see 'Monetary, Trade, Aid & Investment' below*
Smith, black ldrs resume talks 1-3; Muzorewa boycotts 1-27, OKs return 1-31, 59F2
Carver, Chand tour southn Africa 1-6—1-9, 59F1
Muzorewa rptd vs Malta mtg 1-16, 59E2
Smith scores Malta mtg 1-25, 59D2
Patriotic Front-internal black conflict cited 59C3
UK, US reps see Patriotic Front in Malta 1-30, 58D3
Facts on principal figures in dispute 59A1
Malta mtg ends; UK plan barred, UN role OKd 2-1, 119G3
Internal setlmt pact OKd by Smith, 3 black ldrs 2-15; transitn govt planned 2-16—2-20; US, UK, Patriotic Front react 2-15—2-21, 119B2-G3
Internal pact signed; text; US, UK, Patriotic Front statemts 3-3, 154A3-156A1
Internal pact debated, rejctd by UN Cncl 3-6—3-14, 192E3
Internal pact scored by Carter 3-9, 161C1
US, UK rift, domestic pressures re pact rptd 3-9—3-10, 193E1
Internal pact talks rejctd by Patriotic Front despite US, UK urging 3-14, 193B1
US, UK, govt reps meet 3-17—3-18, 210D2
Muzorewa hailed at rally; on US, UK, Africa support of internal pact 3-19, 210D2
Cncl of state sworn 3-21, 210A2
Patriotic Front discounts Muzorewa rally 3-21, 210G2
Young sees African ldrs, Patriotic Front 3-21—3-24; at front-line mtg 3-25—3-26, 248G2, D3
Front-line natns meet: US, UK scored; Malta follow-up asked 3-25—3-26; Muzorewa denounces 3-26, 248D2
US scores internal pact 3-27, 248B3
Carter asks majority rule 4-1; says US, UK seek conf with govt, Patriotic Front, front-line states, UN 4-2; Rhodesia blacks reject 4-3, 233G2, 234B1
Political detainees freed 4-6, 4-13, 290E3
Vance, Owen seek new Patriotic Front-interim govt talks 4-13—4-17, 290D2-E3
Pol executns rptd abolished 4-14, 291A1
Cncl of ministers sworn 4-14, 291A1
Students arrested in anti-govt rally 4-24, sentncd 4-26, 318B1
US-UK talks rejected by interim govt 4-25, 318A1
Black min ousted 4-28; govt split threatened, probe set 4-28—5-2, 317E1, G2
ZAPU, ZANU legalized; guerrilla amnesty, detainee releases vowed 5-2, 317E2
Muzorewa boycotts pro-govt rally 5-10, 377A1
UANC stays in govt despite black ouster 5-14, 376D3
Zambian pres in UK, US; scores interim govt 5-15—5-23, 395C2
Rival black moderates clash at rally 5-20, 455E3
ZAPU rally scores internal pact 5-27, Nkomo bars setlmt 6-5, 455E2
Vorster backs Nkomo role 5-27, 615C2
US, UK reps in southn Africa re talks 6-2—7-18, 615A2
US asks USSR cooperatn 6-7, 424B1
Black MPs rptd vs setlmt 6-14, 615F3
Smith scores US, UK resistance to interim govt 6-15, 455A3
US backs negotiatns 6-20, 487G1
W Ger chancellor backs peace talks 6-26—6-30; sees Nkomo 6-30, aid hinted 7-6, 584F1
Gabellah urges US support, scores Young 6-30, 615E2
Broadcasting Corp blacks resignatn rptd 7-15, 615F3
Nkomo role rptd backed by interim govt 7-18, 615C2
Whites boo Smith 7-19, by-electn support drops 7-21, 616A1
Interim govt sets electn schedule 7-25, Smith confrms 8-2, 615D1-A2
US: Namibia setlmt aids 7-27, 562D1
Muzorewa ends US, UK tour, gets no support 8-5, 615F2
Partial desegregatn ordrd 8-8, 615A3
WCC OKs Patriotic Front fund 8-10, members protest 8-18, 8-22, 650F2
Muzorewa wins UANC confidence vote 8-13, 650B3
Muzorewa rebel photo scored 8-13, defended 8-16, 650D3
Smith, Nkomo meet 8-14, front-line ldrs split 9-2; Nkomo bars US-UK conf 9-11, 740F2-E3
Independence delay seen 9-6, 9-14, 741E1
ZAPU members arrested 9-9, 9-13; ZAPU, ZANU banned 9-14, 741A1, D1
Smith scores UK, US, Tanzania for Patriotic Front backing 9-10, 741B1

1976

'Front-line' states score UK plan, ask UN conf outside Rhodesia 9-26, 718D1
US: African ldrs accept plan 9-26, 9-27, 718G1
Africa, Rhodesia conflict re proposal, terms 9-26—9-28, US admits 'major details' not accepted 9-27, 718B2
ANC reps meet 9-27, 10-1, 738A3
Rhodesia scores US, asks UK mediatn 9-28, 718F2
Kissinger sees progress 9-28, 718A3
Nyerere sees black rule 9-28, 718A3
USSR, US trade chrgs 9-28, 9-30, 719C1
UK sets conf on interim govt, cites Smith role; Africans hail 9-29, 717D2, 718F1
Machel, Nyerere score conf plan 9-29, 9-30, 738D3-739A1
Smith OKs conf plan 9-30, 738B2
ZIPA scores plan, vows contd war 9-30, 739A1
Muzorewa chrgs US promotes Nkomo, backs conf 10-3, 738B3
UN rep to chair conf 10-4, 738E2
Rowlands, Schaufele see Smith; see ANC factn heads 10-4; Rowlands: conf set 10-5, 738E2
Smith, Crosland dispute conf aim 10-5—10-11, 781B2
US, UK, S Africa discuss Rhodesia fund 10-5—10-7, 781G2
US presidential campaign debate topic 10-6, 741D2
Brezhnev scores US, UK 10-7, 865E3
Nkomo, Mugabe ask conf delay, set demands 10-9; Nkomo modifies demands 10-10, 781D1, A2
Broomburg OKs conf 10-11; Smith warns natlsts 10-13, 781G1
UK names conf members 10-12; delegatns named 10-12—10-15, 781C2
Canada for intl fund 10-15, 843D2
UK sets conf opening 10-16, 781B1
African ldrs meet, ask Sithole conf role 10-17; UK invites Sithole 10-18, 781F2
Rpt US seeks business role 10-18, 781B3
Vorster backs Smith 10-18, 793B2
Muzorewa delegates released 10-19, 797G1
Smith in Geneva 10-21, sees Richard 10-22, 10-23, asks Kissinger role 10-25, 797G1
Nkomo on US proposals 10-22, 797E1
ANC ldrs arrive Geneva 10-24, 10-25, warn conf boycott re UK-Smith 'plot' 10-27, 797B1
Kissinger: Rhodesia plan negotiable 10-24, 797D2
US weighs conf role 10-24; Schaufele joins Wisner 10-27, 797F2
Muzorewa meets Richard, sees setlmt 10-25, 797F1
Smith-natlst-US conflict cited; rpt US urged Nyerere, Kaunda influence 10-26, 797E2, G2
Conf opens 10-28, 797A1
Richard conf with Muzorewa ends 10-29, 831F3
Schaufele arrives 10-30, 831G3
US, Rhodesia, natlst positns cited 831G3
Vorster backs Kissinger plan 10-31, 832B1
Smith to leave, van der Byl to head delegatn 11-1, 831E3
Rhodesia rejects natlst demands 11-2, 831C3
S Africa reactn to US electns 11-3—11-4, 826D2
Smith leaves conf, scores natlsts, UK 11-3; backs majority rule 11-5, 842C3
Van der Byl replaces Smith 11-3, optimistic 11-4, 843B1
Conf cited re Mozambique raid 11-3, 855F2
UK proposes indepndnc date 11-4; Richard sees reps 11-5—11-7, factn ldrs 11-10, 843C1
Schaufele to US 11-4; Reinhardt sees Kaunda, Nyrere 11-5—11-6, 843G1
Mugabe, Nkomo reject intl fund 11-4, 11-8; Nkomo favors Sovt ties 11-8, 843C2
Front-line natns back war 11-6, 843A2
OAU advice to natlsts rptd 11-7, 843B2
Richard sees Callaghan, Crosland; meets black reps 11-10, 843D1
Nyerere scores UK inactn 11-10, 843B2
18-mo transitn rptd OKd 11-11, 843F1
Front-line natns rptdly seek conf delay 11-14, 862D1
Conf resumes; Richard asks flexible independnc date 11-15; Nkomo, Mugabe reject 11-16; Muzorewa scores Nkomo, Mugabe 11-17, 861E2
Reinhardt to replace Schaufele 11-17, 862E1
Conf end date proposed, shorter transitn seen 11-18, 862C1
Nkomo, Mugabe see Angola, Mozambique reps 11-19, 879A2
Nkomo Botswana office bombed 11-19, 879B2
Smith rpts US mil assurances 11-19, US denies 11-19—11-20, 879C2
Sithole leaves for front-line talks 11-20, 879G1
Richard see Crosland 11-22, offers tentative indepndnc date 11-23, 879E1
Tanzania, Nigeria back US indepndnc date 11-23, 879A2
Nkomo, Mugabe OK independnc date 11-26; interim govt talks open 11-29, natlsts present plan 11-30, UK OKs role 12-2, 893A1
ANC chrgs pro-Nkomo plot 11-27—11-28; UK, Zambia deny 11-28—11-29, 893C2
Rebel reps arrive in Geneva 12-1, 914A3
Blacks seek US role 12-3, 915A1

1977

Chikerema returns 9-18, backs Smith transitn terms 9-19, 735F1-B2
West scored re 'selective morality' 9-20, 824C3
Smith chrgs UK-US decptn, defers internal setlmt plan 9-21, 735C1
Front-line states OK UK-US plan, drawbacks cited 9-24, 734B3
Smith sees Kaunda, Nkomo cited 9-25; Kaunda details mtg 10-26, 810F1
Smith on universal suffrage, army 9-26, 10-17, 810C1
Smith invites UK, UN reps re peace force 9-28, 810A1
UN envoy named 9-29, 809F2
Patriotic Front unity talks delayed 10-3, 810A3
Carter cites in UN speech 10-4, 751F3
USSR backs UK plan 10-10—10-11, 812F3
Nigeria ldr in US 10-11, 10-12, 797E1, A2
Smith urges independt US role 10-17, 810D1
Kaunda backs Patriotic Front rule; on electns 10-21, 810E2
UK, UN reps tour region 10-30—11-9, 875G2
Patriotic Front frictn re Smith-Kaunda mtg rptd 10-30, 875C3
UK rep briefs Owen 11-10—11-11, 876B1
Smith OKs majority rule, seeks talks with moderates 11-24; reactn 11-25—11-26, 910E2
Patriotic Front disunity rptd, Zambia backs rule 11-25, 910A3
Smith, black ldrs meet; white parlt bloc debated 12-2—12-29, 1015E2
Zambia bars UK-US role, backs Patriotic Front 12-6; Tanzania quarrel rptd 12-18, 1015B3
Muzorewa aide ends Zambia exile 12-10, 1016E1

Military Developments

Guerrilla attacks, casualties rptd 1-3, 1-6, 3F2
New guerrilla front rptd 1-6, 3E2
US mercenary, Rhodesian soldier desert to Botswana 1-7, 11C2
Guerrilla escapes custody 1-9, 11G2
Mozambique downs patrol plane 1-12, 11E2
Botswana files UN complaint 1-12, van der Byl asks debate role 1-13, 73G1
Guerrilla, civiln casualties rptd 1-13, 1-27, 73D2
S Africa threatens troop role 1-16, 29B1
ANC members hanged, Muzorewa scores 1-17, 29E1
29 guerrillas rptd killed 1-20, 50B1
ZAPU rptd seizing recruits, total estimated 1-21, 49E2
Crosland warns re Sovt, Cuba armed role 1-25, 49B2
Call-ups extended 1-27, 73A2
ZAPU kidnaps 400 students 1-30; Botswana denies kidnap 1-31, 2-1; Red Cross probe asked 2-1, 73C1
Mozambique border clashes 1-31—2-16, 144D3
Rebels kill 7 clerics 2-6; ZANU chrgd; govt, church score 2-7—2-8, 85A1
Kidnaped students stay in Botswana 2-6, Mozambique training set 2-8, 85F1-A2
Rebels burn Nyashanu missn 2-8, 85E1
Botswana sentncs 3 newsmen 2-8, 85A2
Guerrilla clashes, casualties rptd 2-9—2-26, 144A3
3 US natls desert 2-9, S Africa rpts arrest 3-2, 144D3
Defns min quits re call-ups 2-11, manpower bd set 2-15, 123F1-A2
Botswana buffer zone set 2-16, 70 youths defect 2-18—2-20, 144C3
Botswana raid rptd, UN missn probes 2-19, 144A3
Call-ups increased 2-28, 144G2
Missionary's body found 3-1, other casualties rptd 3-7, 3-11, 223G2
Mil post created 3-7, defns min named 3-10, 223F2
Castro bars troops 3-21, 249G2
Botswana natls arms chrgs dropped 3-22, 297E1
Total war losses rptd 3-24, Mar casualties 3-31, 297A1
Army chrgd in civilian death 4-1, missionaries flee 4-3, 297C1
'Protected villages' begun 4-6, 297D1
USSR arms in Mozambique rptd; rebel, army totals cited 4-24, 456E3
RRs bombed 5-3, 6-5, 456G3
Civilians die in guerrilla clash 5-6, 413C1
Anti-rebel drive deaths rptd 5-9, 413D1
Botswana raid 5-16; US chrgs pressure tactic 5-18, 399B2
Zambia declares war 5-16, clash 5-18; Rhodesia paymts suspended 5-24, 413A1
US, S Africa urge guerrilla war end 5-20, 398C1
Mozambique invaded, town held 5-29—6-2, 413E1
Mozambique raid backed 6-2; troop exit completed, arms shown 6-4, 456F2
Zambia shells Kariba 6-4, 457A1
Blacks made lieutenants 6-9, 6-10, 457B1
2d Mozambique raid rptd 6-10, 456B3
Mozambique chrgs attack 6-17; denied 6-18, 536F2
Ousted US missionary rpts wide rebel support 6-22, 536E2
Mozambique accused re raids 6-29; UN asks Mozambique defense aid 6-30, 536E1
June casualties rptd 7-1, 536C2
Botswana-Zambia rebel link chrgd 7-7, 536B2

1978

WCC SWAPO grant rptd 9-26, 742E2
Smith-Nkomo mtg cited re Tanzania-Lonrho dispute 9-26, 905F2
US tour by Smith, black ldrs; all-party talks OKd 10-7—10-20; US visit scored by Front, UN, Kaunda 10-8—10-23, 818D3
Carter on US role 10-10, 767A1
Racial laws abolished 10-10, 783E3
Nkomo bars new talks, backs force 10-20—10-22, 819D1
WCC grants protested, total cited 10-25, 11-4, 906F3, 907B1
Electns delayed 10-29, Matabeleland demand cited 11-1, 867B2
Smith sees US trip 'victory' 10-29, 867D2
Ndiweni quits re Matabeleland seats, asks Nkomo return 11-8, 884E2-A3
Ndebele-Shona conflict cited 11-8, 884A3
Exec cncl sees Botha in Pretoria 11-15; warning re vote delay rptd 11-23, 912A2
Electns delayed 11-16, 893G1
Defense min quits 11-18, 912D2
UK's Hughes to seek new talks 11-23; Kaunda, Obasanjo score 11-24; Smith, Nkomo OK mtg 11-28, 911E3
Cabt role for whites set 11-30, Muzorewa aide quits 12-1, 945A3
Regional divisn planned 11-30, 945F3-946A1
UK resident comr Carver quits 11-30, 946A1
White co-min quits, scores internal setlmt 12-27, 1019G2

Military Developments

USSR, China front line state aid cited 59B1, C1, C2
Jan death total rptd 1-4—1-31, 59F3
Censorship imposed on forgn rptrs 1-7, scored 1-8, 20G1
Rebel amnesty offered 1-20, censorship rptd 1-23, 59E3
Protected village rules tightnd 1-29; facts on villages 156D1
Feb casualties rptd 2-5—3-1, 210C3
Black draft set 2-10, 156F1
Smith, black ldrs OK rebels in new army 2-16, 119E2
Botswana troops, civilians killed 2-27, 156C1
Salisbury bomb blasts 3-4, 156D1
Zambia raid by govt kills 38 rebels 3-5—3-6, 156A1
USSR, Cuba role in Zambia raid rptd 3-12; UN condemns raid 3-17, 210B3
RC clergy deaths, other data rptd 3-13, 249C1
Troops, guerrillas clash on Mozambique border 3-19—3-25, 249B1
Mugabe claims civiln areas control 3-20, 210A3
Civilns lose Rhodesia cmnd control 3-20, 249C1
400 students abducted to Botswana 3-29, most return 3-31, 248F3
Zambia raid rptd 3-29—3-30, 249A1
UK warns USSR, Cuba vs role 4-5, 259E1
Pulitzer awarded for photo coverage 4-17, authenticity questnd 4-21, 4-22, 315F1, B2
Atrocity probe sparked by Pulitzer photo rptd halted 4-22, 455C2
ZANU denies Mugabe plot 4-23, 455B3
ZAPU denies assassinatn plot 4-24, 455F2
Guerrilla war mounts; UK, other civilians slain 5-8—6-10; Jan-May death toll 6-12, 455C1-B2
Cuba rptd training ZAPU 5-14, 395B3
Cuba advisers rptd by Nkomo 6-6, 455D2
Smith admits war difficulty; scores US, UK 6-15, 455G2
Rebel slayings, massacres 6-15—7-31, 594B2
Black school closings, civiln govt breakdowns rptd 6-16, 455A3
2 RC missionaries rptdly ordrd out 6-30, 594G2
Mugabe bars peaceful solutn, OAU backing seen 7-18, 561B2
Smith, UANC trade chrgs re war 7-18, 7-19, 615C3
Salisbury clashes 7-21—7-22, 594C2
Mozambique camps raided 7-30—7-31, Sithole defends 8-2, 594F1
Jan-July deaths rptd 7-31, 594B2
Kapwepwe vows Zambia border opening 8-1, 617F1
UK natls kidnaped 8-1, 8-20, 741C2
Rebel attacks near Salisbury rptd 8-6, 8-21, 8-23, 741C2
Sithole backers rptd killed 8-10, 741D2
Commercial jet downed, massacre chrgd 9-3; Nkomo claims credit 9-5, 740E3
Protected villages dismantling begun 9-8, 741A2
Martial law set 9-10; ZANU, ZAPU banned 9-14, 741A1, D1
ZANU scores Nkomo mil effort 9-11, 740C3
Black draft set 9-16, 741D2
Mozambique guerrilla bases hit 9-20—9-23, Zambia raids rptd 9-25, 741F1
Martial law extended 10-5, 784A3
Umtali hit by rebels 10-15, Mozambique raided in retaliatn 10-18, 784G1
Black schl closures rptd up 10-16, 784C2
Botswana troop clash 10-16, 784C2

1979

1980

1976

Muzorewa scores Mugabe, Nkomo 12-4, asks whites join ANC 12-5; independnc delay seen 12-9, 914B3
Smith scores Richard 12-5; returns to Geneva, stalemate continues 12-8, 914F2
Crosland, Kissinger confer 12-10—12-11, Parlt gets plans 12-14, 935E1
Smith scores UK, leaves Geneva 12-12; plans natlst talks 12-13, 12-14, 935C1
Muzorewa scores Smith, patriotic front 12-12, 935A2
Geneva talks adjourned 12-14, 935A2
Zambia cuts Muzorewa ties 12-19, 1009C3
Richard in US, offers new plans 12-21—12-22; Rhodesia scores 12-23, 974A2
Blacks quit Cabt, form party 12-29, 1009G3

U.S. Relations—*See 'Majority Rule Issue' above*
US warns vs Rhodesia travel 5-13, 339C1
Mobil denies chrgs 8-27, 698C2
US analysts rpt Rhodesia zero econ growth, no Mobil violatns 10-17, 855C3
Viet veterans rptd in army 12-9, 1009F3

1977

Zambia OKs Cuba, Somalia aid 7-8, 536F1
WCC chrgs army atrocities 7-8, 536A2
Zambia rpts fighting 7-11, 536G1
Black family massacred 7-15, UK rptr ousted 8-2, 599F2
Troop-rebel kill ratio down 7-20, 599B3
Casualties rptd 7-22, 599B3
Rebel forces union asked 7-25, 581D3
Zambia ZAPU office bombed 7-31, 599B3
Victoria Falls hotel attacked, rebel group ambushed 7-31, 624F2
Zambia chrgd re attack 8-5, 624E2
Salisbury store bombed 8-6, Muzorewa blames ZAPU 8-7, 624G1
Builder killed in shootout 8-6, 624D2
Salisbury RR bombed 8-8, 624D2
2 missionaries killed 8-9, 624C2
Salisbury bomb blast 8-13, 662B2
2 whites die in ambush 8-14, 662C2
Rebels kill 16 blacks 8-20, 662B2
Mozambique, Zambia, Botswana clashes rptd 8-31—9-25, 810C3
Black workers rptd kidnaped 9-6, 811F1
RC comm, Amnesty Intl chrg atrocities, torture 9-21, 811A2, D2
Defns budget hiked 9-21, 824D3
Casualty totals rptd 9-30, 811E1
War death total since '72 rptd 10-12, 911G1
Black govt forces expanded; black, rebel strength rptd 10-21, 811C1
Mozambique claims aircraft hits 11-14, 911F1
Troops raid Mozambique, kill 1,200 11-23—11-27; UK, US, Muzorewa score 11-29, 911A1
Atrocity probe ordered 11-23, 1016B1
US rptr details atrocities 12-2, 1015F3-1016C1
Air base hit from Mozambique 12-17, 1016C1
Victoria Falls hotel attack 12-17, 1016D1
'77 death total 2,477 12-28, 1016D1

Monetary, Trade & Aid (including all foreign economic developments)
US to press chrome sanctns 1-31, 72F3
UN chrgs Sovt bloc sanctn violatns 2-10, 122D3
Forgn earnings rptd down 2-24, 144G3
Carter backs econ sanctns 3-17, 186E1
US bans chrome imports 3-18, 191C1
UK oil sanctn probe set 4-8; oil cos chrgd 4-25, 413D2
'76 trade surplus rptd 5-6, 414A1
US ends Mobil probe 5-16, 413E2
Zambia asks US oil embargo 5-23, 400A1
Zambia suspends paymts 5-24, 413C1
UK co sues sanctn breakers 5-31, 413C2
Japan chrome imports chrgd 6-28, 512C2
Mozambique, S Africa ports cited re US '76 chrome imports 7-26, 582A1
Japan agrees to US chrome ban 8-3, 662E1
UN com asks more sanctns 8-8, 662C1
Zambia sues oil cos re sanctn breaking 8-22, 662D1
Trade positn cited re $ devaluatn 10-13, 824F3
Commonwealth presses S Africa on oil bar 10-19, 876B1
UN embargoes cited 11-4, 851D1
UK renews sanctns 11-11, 876A1
UN S Africa oil ban asked 12-14, 1016B2

U.S. Relations—*See also 'Majority Rule' and 'Monetary, Trade & Aid' above*
US mercenary desertn confrmd 1-7, 11C2
3 US natls desert 2-9, S Africa rpts arrest 3-2, 144D3
Sovt arms in Mozambique rptd 4-24, 456E3
Young rejects mil role 5-16, 399B2
Mondale urges guerrilla war end 5-20, 398C1
UN OKs US Rhodesia office closure 5-27, 457F1
Mozambique raid scored 6-1, 413B2
US missionary deported 6-21, 536E2
Rhodesia US office to remain open 8-26, 699A3
US nun deported 9-22, 811G1
2 black Rhodesia reps rptd barred 9-25, 811G2
Smith lauds Young 10-17, 810F1
Mozambique refugee aid set 12-2, 1000C1

1978

Zambia ZAPU camp bombed 10-19, 784A2
Zambia raids rptd ended 10-21; Nkomo disputes death toll, says raids continue 10-22, 819F1
Zambia rpts 31 killed 10-25, 830A1
Zambia gets UK arms 10-27, 10-28, 829E3-830A1
Draft scored by students, UANC 10-27, 830A1
Pvt UANC, ZANU armies rptd 10-28, farmers complain 11-7, 867C3
Martial law rptd over ½ populatn 10-31, 867B3
2d Zambia strike, US scores 11-2, 867G2
Rhodesia-Zambia RR sabotage rptd 11-2, 867A3
Zambians attack Rhodesia whites 11-7, Kaunda denounces 11-13, 893E2
Martial law extended 11-10, 893C2
Salisbury attack staged 11-12, 893D2
Troop, guerrilla clashes intensify 11-16, 893A2
Zambia sets arms spending rise 11-20, 912B1
Martial law in 75% of natn 11-24, 955F3
Zambia race tensn cited 11-26, 912F1
Salisbury oil depot hit 12-11, Smith scores 12-13, 955B3
Mozambique arms depots hit 12-11, 955D3
US confirms probe of copters, Cessna rpts 12-13, 955E3
5 black civilns killed 12-16, 1019F3
Zambia army camps bombed 12-21, 50 casualties rptd 12-27, 1019B3
'78 casualties, total since '72 rptd 12-21, 1019C3
RC missionary killed 12-26, 1019E3

Monetary, Trade, Aid & Investment
Swiss ban 3d party deals 1-1, 22E2
USSR, China, front line state aid cited 59B1, C1, C2
US S African unit fined for sales 1-12, 38B3
US chrome import ban cited 1-29, 80G3
Dollar devalued vs US $, S Africa rand 4-2, 249E1
Tanzania ousts Lonrho 6-2, 479C2
W Ger hints Patriotic Front aid 7-6, 584F1
Muzorewa seeks sanctns end 7-17; US, UK bar 7-20; OAU warns US 7-22, 561C1
Euromarket loan rptd 7-20, 616D1
3 fined in arms swindle 7-20, 616G1-C2
'77 paymts deficit up, exports drop 7-26, 616E1
US Cong backs trade sanctns conditnl end 8-2, 588B1
WCC OKs Patriotic Front fund 8-10, 650F2; SWAPO grant rptd 9-26, 742E2
UK oil-sanctions violatn study released 8-31, 9-19; reactn 9-2—9-28, 755G3-756F3
Conditns for econ sanctns end signed 9-26, 734D1, C2
Zambia to reopen rail rte 10-6, front-line natns react 10-7, Nkomo 783E2
BP chngs violatn denial 10-22, 838E2
WCC grants protested, total cited 10-25, 11-4, 906F3, 907B1
Dutch chrome cargo impoundmt rptd 12-13, 965D2
US copters rptd in use, mfr denies sale 12-14, 1019G3
Sanctn violatns probe backed by UK 12-15, 987A3

Obituaries
Dupont, Clifford W 6-28, 540E2
Wrathall, John James 8-31, 708G3

U.S. Relations—*See also 'Majority Rule' and 'Monetary, Trade, Aid & Investment' above*
Censorship imposed on rptrs 1-7, 20C2
Pulitzer awarded for mil coverage 4-17, photo authenticity questnd 4-21, 4-22, 315F1, B2
Pulitzer-sparked atrocity probe rptd halted 4-22, 455C2
Missionary killed 6-15, 594C3
Zambia raid scored by US 11-2, 867A3
US airline fined re pilot training 12-8, 955G3-956A1
US probes copter, Cessna rpts 12-13, 955E3

1979

1980

1976

RHODES Scholars
1st women named 12-19, 993E3

RHOODIE, Eschel
Bars mil role in Rhodesia 5-13, 339A1 ★

1978

RHOODIE, Deneys
Info Dept probers chrg misconduct 12-5, 946E1

RHOODIE, Eschel M.
Quits as S Africa info secy 6-15, 498G2
Named in press scandal 11-2, 868A2
Info Dept probers chrg misconduct 12-5, 946E1

1979

RHODIA Inc.
DES banned in animal feed 6-28, 571B3

RHOODIE, Eschel Mostert
Govt seizes property 1-8, 22D1
Gets van den Bergh job offer, disclosures averted 3-7; chrgs rptd 3-10, 190F3
Van Zyl's passport seized 3-14, 191G1
Arrest sought 3-16; BBC airs Westn-natn bribe chrgs 3-21; US, Vorster deny 3-21, 3-22, 212G3-213C2
Erasmus comm clears Vorster 4-2, 270D1

1980

RHODES v. Chapman
Case accepted by Sup Ct 11-3, 856F2

RHOODIE, Eschel Mostert
Fraud convictn reversed 9-29, 753E1

1976

RIAD, Mahmoud
Sahara mediatn fails 3-2, 178C3
Arab peace force opposed 6-15, 429E2
On Leb peace force 6-20, 448F2
On Leb mediatn breakdown 7-8, 514F2
Syria, PLO talks rptd 7-27, 546G1
Syria OKs Leb summit 8-24, 628B3
Meets PLO offcl on truce 8-31, 663A1
On new Leb peace force 10-26, 798C1
Libya troops to quit Leb 11-29, 894B2
RIBEIRO, Archbishop Antonio Cardinal
Backs govt 7-22, 558E2
RIBICOFF, Sen. Abraham A. (D, Conn.)
Scores Sovt Jewish policy 3-22, 246A1
Endorses Carter 6-7, 411B1
On US India A-blast aid 8-8, 581D3
Scores Ford re anti-boycott legis claim 10-7, 787A1
Israel A-plant visit barred 11-8, 878F1
Ends Israel visit 11-11; in Cairo, gets Sadat peace bid 11-11—11-14, 878A1
Vs Treas boycott guidelines 12-8, 987D2
RICARDO, Hernan
Arrested 10-7, CIA tie chrgd 10-15; bombing confessn rptd 10-18, 779D3, 780E1
Suicide attempt rptd 10-22, 844D1
FBI contact confrmd 10-25, 844A2
Trinidad deports 10-26; Venez indicts 11-2, 843F2, 844A1
RICE
China-Sri Lanka deal rptd 1-2, 78D1
'75 Guyana-Carib trade rptd 1-30, 252F3
Sen OKs rice productn bill 2-3, 135D2; Ford signs 2-16, 982D1
US OKs Portugal credit 8-13, 811F3
Passman sale abuse rptd 8-16, 633C1
US probes S Korea trade abuses 10-24, 899B1, D1
RICE, Jim
AL batting ldr 10-4, 796D1
RICE, Rev. Patrick
Arrested 10-11, deported 12-3, 996B1
RICHARD, Clement
Air group bars aid offer 9-22, 730G2
RICHARD, Ivor
Vs UN rights stand 4-30, 320D3
To chair Rhodesia conf 10-4, 738E2
Replacemt at conf asked 10-9, 781E1
Opens Rhodesia conf 10-28, 797A1
Sees Callaghan, Crosland in UK; meets conf reps 11-10, 843D1
Conf delay rptd asked 11-14, 862E1
On independnc date, interim govt plan 11-15; suggests conf end date 11-18, 861E2
Sees Crosland 11-22, offers indepndnc date 11-23, 879E1
Smith scores 12-5, sees in Geneva 12-8, 914G2
Adjourns Rhodesia conf 12-14, 935A2
Sees Kissinger, Vance in US, offers new plan 12-21—12-22; Rhodesia scores 12-23, 974A2
RICHARD, James Rodney
NL pitching ldr 10-4, 796A1
RICHARDS, Dr. Elizabeth
Hearst mental exams disputed 1-15, 1-23, 69F3, 70A1
RICHARDS, Rev. J. L.
Carter funds returned 8-10, 585B3
RICHARDS, Mark
Gets new Justice post 1-14, 78G3
RICHARDS, Dr. Renee
Barred from US Open 8-27, 716E1
Loses S Orange semifinals 8-27, 716E1
RICHARDSON, Elliot L(ee)
Ford lists as potential vp 1-22, 41G1
Replaced as amb to UK 1-27, 68B1
Sworn Commerce secy 2-2, 110E1
Heads payoff probe 3-21, 262E2
Ford advocate in Calif 5-24, 374A1
Letter on Admin pol paymts legis sparks SEC controversy 6-11—6-17, 668F3
Vs public works bill 6-28, 493F1
Press conf on Admin paymts bill 8-3, 668G2
VP prospect cited 8-10, 584D1
VP poll rptd 8-11, 583F3
GOP conv pres, vp vote tables 8-18—8-19, 8-19, 599E1, F3
Ford wins pres nominatn 8-19, 597F1
Ford sees Reagan re vp choice 8-19, 598F1
Sen OKs anti-bribery bill 9-15, 708D1
On Arab boycott rules, Ford stand 10-20, 786E2-B3
Signs Rumania pact 11-21, sees Ceausescu 11-22, 907D2
In Yogoslavia 11-25—11-27, 1012C1
In Turkey on quake aid 11-28, 897D1
RICHARDSON, James
Sets Lockheed contract review 2-13, 250G2
Lockheed deal fails 5-18, 363E1
Lockheed Cabt repercussns 6-1—6-8, 416C2
NATO OKs W Ger Leopard tank buy 6-10—6-11, 449B2
Lockheed deal revised 7-21, 555A1
Stays defense min 9-14, 692B2
Resigns, replaced 10-13, 790D1
Replaced 11-3, 851E2
RICHARDSON Co., The
Rubber strike cited 648B1
RICHARDSON-Merrell Inc.
Rpts foreign payoffs 2-23, 362F1
SEC rpts paymts 5-12, 728F2
Merrell National Laboratories
Flu immunizatn plan delayed 9-1, 656C3
RICHEY, Judge Charles R.
Votes porpoise protectn 5-11, 398B2
Sentences Bortnick kidnapers 7-21, 544D1
RICHMOND, Va.—*See VIRGINIA*
RICHMOND, Rep. Frederick W. (D, N.Y.)
Reelected 11-2, 830A2

1977

RIAD, Mahmoud
Mediates Egypt-Libya feud 7-24—7-25, 570A1
Quits re Sadat Israel trip 11-17, 890C2 ★
RIBICOFF, Sen. Abraham A. (D, Conn.)
'76 spec interest gifts rptd 1-15, 128F3
Protests Sovt Jew jailing 2-19, 226A2
On Walsh-Califano dispute 3-23, 235G3
Backs Carter Mideast moves 6-29, 496C1
Lance cleared on finances 7-12—7-25, 573F3-574B2
Lance cleared in banking probe 8-18, 625A2, C3, 626B1
Asks Lance resignatn 9-5, 689G3-690A1
Com to probe Lance 9-6, 690B1
Lance hearings 9-9—9-15, 700B3
Regrets press 'lies' re Lance 9-15, 700C3
Testifies re Lance 9-16, 718F3
RICARDO, Hernan
Tried in mil ct re '76 crash 10-10, 868C1
RICCARDO, John
Vs Carter energy plan 4-24, 320D1
RICE
UN rpts '76 price drop 2-14, 146B1
ASEAN trade pact signed 2-24, 145A3
Carter farm plan outlined 3-23, 214D1
Cambodia '76 crop decline rptd 5-2, 337B1
S Korea lobbying effort detailed 6-5, 441D3
World Food Cncl seeks intl reserve 6-23, 513E3
ASEAN preference agrmt 8-5, 607D1
Carter asks farmer-reserve 8-29, 666E2
Farm bill signed, target prices detailed 9-29, 736D2, C3, F3
Viet shortage rptd 10-1, US bars aid 12-16, 988D3, 989D1
US ex-rep indicted in Korea probe 10-4, 815G3
Park Tong Sun paymts described 10-19—10-21, 816G2
'77 disaster aid ceiling lifted by Cong 10-25, 833C3
RICE, Jim
AL batting ldr 10-2, 926F3-927A1
RICE Growers Association of California
Park Tong Sun paymts detailed 10-19—10-21, 816A3
RICE University (Houston, Tex.)
Kramer in NFL draft 5-3, 353C3
Rossini gets Medal of Sci 11-22, 952B1
RICHARD, Ivor
Sees Smith on UK plan 1-1; visits S Africa, front-line states 1-2—1-6, 3G1
Continues shuttle, delays Geneva conf 1-7—1-12, 11D1
Smith scores shuttle 1-14, 29C1
Sees Vorster 1-19, Kissinger plan compromise seen 1-20, 28G3
Offers Rhodesia plan 1-21, Smith rejects 1-24, 49A1
Warns Smith vs separate pact 1-23, 49G1
African ldrs, Rhodesia natlsts score 1-29—1-30; shuttle ends 1-31, 72G2
Sees Young 2-2, 2-11, 105B1
Young racism chrg stirs controversy 4-5—4-7, 272F1
RICHARD, Jim
NL pitching ldr 10-2, 926E3
RICHARDS, Gene
NL batting ldr 10-2, 926D3
RICHARDS, Dr. Renee
USTA rejects sex test 4-12, 354C1
Wins Port Washn Cup 4-17, 430E3
Ct OKs US Open play 8-17, loses doubles match 9-11, 787B2, C2
RICHARDS, Richard
Brock elected GOP natl chrmn 1-14, 40F3
RICHARDSON, Elliot L(ee)
Named amb at large 1-17, 53F1; nominated 2-22, confrmd 2-24, 148F3
OKs Gen Dynamics fed loan guarantee, cites Burmah paymt to Park 1-19, 55D1-F2
Nixon-Frost interview 5-25, 420E1
Scores UN Sea Law Conf rpt 7-20, 572C3
RICHARDSON, Jack E.
Named Australia ombudsman 3-17, 280D3
RICHARDSON, Dr. John A.
Sentenced 5-16, 508E2
RICHARDSON, Lee
Reelected Consumer Fed pres 2-13, 217B2
RICHARDSON, Peter
To retire 9-22, 762E3
RICHARDSON, Ronald James
El Salvador disappearance rptd 3-26, 373F3
RICHEY, Cliff
Loses Pacific Championship 4-3, 430D3
RICHMOND, Rep. Frederick W. (D, N.Y.)
Accuses Brazil re coffee prices 2-22, 169C1
Rpts coffee demand down 4-22, 319D1
Sees Castro re Africa role 12-5; US prisoner to be freed 12-13, 1011G2, D3
RICHMOND, Julius B.
Named HEW asst secy 6-9, confrmd 6-28, 626D3
RICHMOND, Va.—*See VIRGINIA*
RICHMOND Corp.
Continental takeover cited in table 880G1
OKs Continental purchase bid 4-12, 274C3
RICHMOND-San Rafael Bridge (Calif.)
Water pipeline laid 6-7, 492B3

1978

RIAD, Mahmoud
Asks UN actn vs Israel Leb invasn 3-15, 174G3
Hints Arab moves vs Egypt 11-6, 859F1
RIB Cage (play)
Opens 5-28, 887F2
RIBEIRO, Antonio Goncalves
Stays Portugal interior min 11-18, 1022B1
RIBICOFF, Sen. Abraham (D, Conn.)
Kin slain in Israel 3-11, 175A2
Vs pro-Israel lobby 3-13, 176C3
Votes for Panama Canal neutrality pact 3-16, 177E2
Rpts Navy-Gen Dynamics sub accord 3-23, 224B2
Backs Cabt-level Educ Dept 4-14, 279F1 ★
Votes for 2d Canal pact 4-18, 273B1
Visits USSR 11-11—11-18, 905C1
RICCARDO, John J.
Names Iacocca Chrysler pres 11-2, 936B1
RICE
Peru crop decline seen 4-28, 353C2
Colombia '77 trade data rptd 5-19, 414F1
Laos to get US aid 6-1, 400F1
Korean Bribery Scandal—*See also KOREA (South)—U.S.-Korea Political Payments*
Korea lobbying scheme cited 3-17, 203B1
Ex-Rep Passman indicted re Korea paymts 3-31, Park testifies 4-3—4-4, 239E1, E2
US dealer chrgd 5-26, 432E3
RICE, Homer
Hired as Bengals coach 10-2, 1024A3
RICE, Jim
AL batting ldr 10-2, named MVP 11-7, 928D1, D3-F3
RICE University (Houston, Tex.)
Hughes Mormon will ruled fake 6-8, trial costs rptd 6-12, 458G3, 459A1
RICH, Lorimer
Dies 6-2, 540F3
RICHARD, Prince (Duke of Gloucester) (Great Britain)
At Solomons independnc fete 7-7, 549E1
RICHARD, Jim
NL pitching ldr 10-2, 928G2
RICHARD, Rafael
Cited in '72 Torrijos drug indictmt 2-21, 120G2
RICHARDS, Gene
NL batting ldr 10-2, 928E2
RICHARDS, Gerald
Living At Home opens 12-11, 1031C2
RICHARDS, Golden
Cowboys win Super Bowl 1-15, 39E3
Traded to Bears 12-5, 1024E3
RICHARDS, Keith
Heroin sentnc suspended 10-24, band OKs benefit 10-26, 842E1
RICHARDS, Lloyd
Paul Robeson opens 1-19, 760A3
RICHARDS, Martin
Boys From Brazil released 10-5, 969D3
RICHARDS, Ganley, Fries & Preusch
Pensn fund fraud suit settled 5-21, 480F3
RICHARDSON, Elliot L.
Agnew case papers released 3-3, 164G3
Defends US seabed mining bill 8-21—9-16, 732D3
RICHARDSON, Gary
Unopposed in Okla cong primary 8-22, 683D1
RICHARDSON, Howard
Thread of Scarlet opens 12-8, 1031B3
RICHARDSON, Mike
In NBA draft 6-9, 457F2
RICHARDSON, Tony
Joseph Andrews released 4-13, 619F2
RICHEY, Judge Charles R.
Cuts Nader '73 'bumping' case award 1-10, 67F3-68A1
RICHEY, Cliff
Wins S African Open 4-10, 419C1
RICHIE, John Simon—*See VICIOUS, Sid*
RICHMOND, Rep. Frederick W. (D, N.Y.)
Pleads not guilty to sex chrg, 20 reps back 4-6, 265F1-B2
Wins primary easily 9-12, 716B2
Reelected 11-7, 846E2, 851E3
RICHMOND, Dr. Julius
Hits 'tolerable' cigaret rpt 8-10, 726C3
RICHMOND (Va.) News Leader (newspaper)
MacNelly wins Pulitzer 4-17, 315B2

1979

Arrested in France 7-19, 567D1
Plea rejctd 8-8, extradited 8-23, 755B1
Trial opens 9-21, sentncd 774F1
RHYS, Jean
Dies 5-14, 432E3
RIAD, Mahmoud
League mtg on Yemen clashes asked 2-25, 144C2
Quits Arab League post 3-22, 248A3
RIAHI, Taghi
Named Iran defns min 3-30, 247D2
Mil police cmdr defies dismissal order 7-9, 525G1
Quits Iran post, goes to France 9-28, 752C2
RIASHENTSEV, Uri
Strider opens 5-31, 712F2
RIBICOFF, Sen. Abraham (D, Conn.)
Govt Affairs Com chrmn 1-23, 71D2
Manages Educ Dept bill 4-30, 326D2
Sen retiremt set 5-3, 326G1
Resources Dept plan dropped 5-15, 365A2, D2
Votes vs Talmadge denunciatn 10-10, 769F1
Carter submits trade reorganizatn plan 10-25, 803C1
RICARDO, Benny
NFL '78 kicking ldr 1-6, 80F1
RICCARDO, John J.
On Chrysler '78, '79 finances 2-26, 188F1
On Chrysler 2d 1/4 loss, fed aid plea 7-31, 576A1-B3
Lands Carter loan guarantee offer 8-9, 662F2
Salary cut 8-30, 662G3
Rpts Chrysler Jan-Aug cost savings 8-31, 662A3
On Miller loan talks 9-15, 699C1
Sets resignatn 9-17, Iaccoca named successor 9-20, 699B3
RICE
Herbicide ban excludes 3-1, 167B2
India-USSR pact signed 3-14, 200A2
Liberians protest price hikes 4-14—4-15, 279F3
Cambodia famine feared 4-22, 4-28, 318B2
Cambodia famine confrmd 8-3, 600D3; 8-23, 684B2
RICE, Homer
Fired as Bengals coach 12-17, 1001E1
RICE, Rev. Howard L.
Elected United Presby moderator 5-23, 547D2
RICE, Jim
NL wins All-Star Game 7-17, 568F3-569C1
AL batting ldr 9-30, 955D3-F3
RICE, Tim
Evita opens 9-25, 956A3
RICE University (Houston, Tex.)
Eisenhower secret diary rptd 9-16, 9-17, 748A1
Eisenhower tapes revealed 10-21, 868G3
RICH, David Lowell
Concorde Airport '79 released 8-3, 819G3
RICHARD, J. R. (James Rodney)
NL pitching ldr 9-30, 955G2
RICHARD Pryor Live in Concert (film)
Released 2-15, 174E3
RICHARDS, I(vor) A(rmstrong)
Dies 9-7, 756D3
RICHARDS, James Prioleau
Dies 2-21, 176E3
RICHARDS, Martin
Sweeney Todd opens 3-1, 292C3
RICHARDS, Renee
Loses Greater Pittsburgh Open 9-16, 734E2
RICHARDS, Brig. Gen. Thomas C.
Confines senior cadets for prank 2-21, lifts order 2-23, 207B3
RICHARDSON, Elliot L.
US seabed mining legis backed 3-19, 360E3
RICHARDSON, Karl
Wins Grammy 2-16, 336D3
RICHARDSON, Lee
Father's Day opens 6-21, 711A3
RICHARD III (play)
Opens 6-14, 712B2
RICHERT, William
Winter Kills released 5-17, 528G3
RICHEY, Judge Charles R.
Washn Star pacts renegotiated 1-1, 5B2
Denies Park tax seizure stay 1-3, 4C3
Drops Galifianakis chrg 8-3, 630A2
Convicts Scientologists as spies 10-26, 839B2
Sentences Scientologists 12-6—12-7, 1000C1
RICH Kids (film)
Released 8-17, 820B3
RICHMOND, Va.—*See VIRGINIA*
RICHMOND, David
Big Bad Burlesque opens 8-14, 711E1
RICHMOND, Rep. Frederick W. (D, N.Y.)
Financial disclosure statement studied 9-1, 702A1
RICHMOND, Dr. Julius B.
Issues smoking rpt 1-11, 23A1
Gay aliens curb lifted 8-14, 632A2
RICHMOND, Ted
5th Musketeer released 9-7, 820B1
RICHMOND News Leader, The (newspaper)
Va trial closure case accepted by Sup Ct 10-9, 784A1
RICHMOND Newspapers Inc.
Va trial closure case accepted by Sup Ct 10-9, 783G3
RICHMOND Newspapers v. Virginia
Case accepted by Sup Ct 10-9, 783F3

1980

RIAHI, Taghi
Quits as broadcast head 6-19, 464C2
RIBERA, Adolfo
Museum art stolen 12-25, issues appeal 12-27, 991E1
RIBICOFF, Sen. Abraham (D, Conn.)
Backs Carter in conv rules fight 8-11, 609G2
Primary results for seat 9-9, 700C2
Dodd wins seat 11-4, 845B3, 848B1
RIBOUD, Philippe
Wins Olympic medal 7-28, 622B3
RICA, Jose Miguel de la
Rpts INI '79 losses 2-21, 196F2
RICARDO, Hernan
Acquitted in '76 Cuba jet bombing 9-26, 794A3
RICE
Peru crop hit by drought 2-8, 234E3
Cambodia shipmts disputed 3-10, famine renewal feared 3-21; airlift begins 4-4, 261E3, G3, 262A1
US-Japan export pact set 4-12, 314G2
Unpatented key ingredient monopolies backed by Sup Ct 6-27, 511C2
RICE, Emmett
Backs discount rate reductn 5-28, 400D2
RICE, John
Vs austerity measures 6-2, 445B1
RICE, Tim
Wins Tony 6-8, 692A3
RICE, Victor
On Massey-Ferguson equity plan 12-13, 992F1
RICE University (Houston, Tex.)
'79 endowmt earnings rptd 3-24, 319C2
Cooper in NFL draft 4-29, 336F3
RICHARD, J. R.
NL wins All-Star Game 7-8, 636D1
Suffers stroke 7-30, recovery seen 8-4, 636E3
RICHARDS, Gene
NL batting, stolen base ldr 10-6, 926F2
RICHARDS, Martin
Goodbye Fidel opens 4-23, 392G2
RICHARDSON, Bill
Loses US House electn 11-4, 852B1
RICHARDSON, Elliot L.
Lauds UN Sea Law Conf 8-29, 660D1
RICHARDSON, Henry Handel
Getting of Wisdom released 8-5, 675F2
RICHARDSON, Michael Ray (Sugar Ray)
NBA assist, stolen-ball ldr 3-30, 278E3, 279A1
RICHARDSON, Thomas (Sandy)
Dies 9-27, 756B2
RICHARDSON-Merrell Inc.
Dow Chem buys drug unit 11-3, 985E2
RICHERT, Wanda
42d Street opens 8-25, 756D3
RICHEY, Judge Charles R.
Awards female bindery workers back pay 5-20, 442C1, F1
RICHMOND—*See VIRGINIA*
RICHMOND, Rep. Frederick W. (D, N.Y.)
Reelected 11-4, 843E3
RICHMOND, Fredericksburg and Potomac Railroad Co.
Auto-Train svc cut rejected 9-26, 958B3
RICHMOND, Dr. Julius B.
Rpts female lung cancer rise, cites smoking risks 1-14, 40A2
Issues dietary guidelines 2-4, 157C3
RICHMOND Newspapers Inc.
Open criminal trials backed by Sup Ct 7-2, 510F2-C3
RICHMOND Newspapers v. Virginia
Case decided by Sup Ct 7-2, 510D2-C3
Case cited by Sup Ct 10-14, 782B1

1976

RICHTER, Annegret
Wins Olympic medals 7-25, 7-28, 576F1, G1
RICHTER, Burton
Wins Nobel Prize 10-18, 840F1
RICHTER, Hans
Dies 2-1, 124F3
RICHTER, Ulrike
Sets world swim mark 6-1—6-5, 424G3
Wins Olympic medals 7-21, 7-25, 575G2
RICHTER Prada, Gen. Pedro
Peru army staff chief 7-16, 590G2
RICKOVER, Adm. Hyman G.
Rptdly backed Navy takeover of shipyds 4-8, 309C2
House OKs '77 arms bill 4-9, 283A2
On US, Sovt naval strength 5-5, 394F2-B3
Vs overrun paymts 6-7, 453G3
Cited in Carter biog 512B1
RIDGEWAY, Rick
US team climbs Mt Everest 10-8, 876C3
RIEDEL, Rev. Robert J.
Ousted as dist pres 4-2, leaves synod 10-1, 776C3, G3
RIEGLE Jr., Rep. Donald Wayne (D, Mich.)
Wins Sen primary 8-3, 565F2
Elected senator 11-2, 820A1, 823E2, 828G1
RIESSEN, Marty
Wins US Open doubles 9-12, 716C1
RIFAI, Zaid al-
On Parlt electns 2-5, 83B3
Denies W Bank influence bid 2-9, 107A1
Says US Hawk deal off 4-14, 274B3
Resigns 7-13, 949A3
Meets Leb Christns 11-1, 841G1
RIFKIND, Simon H.
ABA forms Rosenberg unit 1-8, 70F2
RIFLE Association, National (NRA)
House com recommits handgun ban 3-2, 170E1
RIGERT, David
Wins Olympic medal 7-26, 576E2
RIGHT and the Power, The (book)
On best-seller list 12-5, 972C2
RIGHTS of Man, International League for the—*See INTERNATIONAL League for Human Rights*
RINALDO, Rep. Matthew J. (R, N.J.)
Reelected 11-2, 830E1
RINCON Puentes, Gen. Federico
Rpt Lockheed papers cite bribe 8-24, 740A2
RINCON Quinones, Gen. Ramon (d. 1975)
4 assassins sentncd 1-30, 118A2
RING, Bona Malwal Madut
Sudan info min 2-10, 502D1
RINGEL, Erwin
On W Eur suicide rates 11-22, 944G3
RINGER, Robert J.
Winning on best seller list 1-25, 80C3; 2-29, 208F3; 12-5, 972C2
RINGGOLD, Timothy
Seeks West Pt honor code stay 6-1, 395D1
RINN, Hans
Wins Olympic medal 2-7, 159G1
RIPON Society
GOP delegate rule review denied 2-23, 170A1
Vs Dole as vp 8-19, 598F2
RISENHOOVER, Rep. Theodore M. (D, Okla.)
Reelected 11-2, 830C3
RISKIEV, Rufai
Wins Olympic medal 7-31, 574D1
RISSER, James
Wins Pulitzer Prize 5-3, 352E3
RITTER, Judge Willis W.
Sup Ct refuses trust suit removal case 11-15, 882F2
RIVADENEIRA, Luiz
Poveda linked to drug trade 1-12, 28A3
RIVERA, Juanito
Leads Communist raiders 11-24, 1009D1
RIVERA Terrazas, Luis
Rightists ask ouster 4-20—5-4, 419F2
RIVERO Vasquez, Luisa Rondon de
Occidental chrgs dropped 11-16, 930E1

1977

RICHMOND Unified School District v. Berg
Sup Ct orders case examined 12-6, 938A3
RICHTER Scale—*See also EARTHQUAKES*
Revised 2-14, 161B3
RICKOVER, Vice Adm. Hyman G.
With Carters on A-sub 5-27, 417D3
RIDGWAY, Rozanne
Named amb to Finland 5-3, confrmd 5-25, 500B1
RIEGLE Jr., Sen. Donald Wayne (D, Mich.)
Abstains on Bell confrmatn 1-19, 34D1
Votes vs Bell 1-25, 52A3
In Panama: links pact support, rights 11-9—11-12, 911C2, E3
RIES, Judge Bernard
Rules vs J P Stevens 12-21, 1005D1
RIESSEN, Marty
Loses La Costa Intl 3-29, 431B1
REITIG, Wolfgang
Sentenced in E Berlin for spying 11-23, 968E2
RIGHT-to-Die—*See MEDICINE—Death Issues*
RIGHETTI, Alfio
Spinks decisions 11-18, 970C3
RIGHT to Life Group, National
Rally vs women's conf 11-19, 918A1
RILEY, Judge Paul
Voids Ohio schl finance law 12-5, 939D3
RINALDI v. Holt, Rinehard & Winston
Libel case refused 11-28, 919A3
RINALDI v. U.S.
Dual fed-state prosecutns curbed 11-7, 857B2
RING (magazine)
ABC issues boxing scandal report, Loubet comments 9-3, 828D1-D2
RINGER, Robert J.
Looking Out for Number One on best-seller list 8-14, 643A2; 9-4, 712E3; 10-2, 808E3; 11-6, 872D3; 12-4, 1021A3
RINGO, Jim
Fired as Bills coach 12-23, 1020B2
RIO Rancho Estates Inc.—*See AMREP Corp.*
RIORDAN, Bill
'Heavywt championship' fee disclosures 5-8, FCC rpts probe 7-8, 548G2
House subcom probes TV sports coverage 11-3, 950C1
RIO Tinto Zinc Corp. Ltd.
Linked to uranium cartel 4-25, 479F2
TVA sues re uranium 11-18, 895F1
UK denies Westinghouse legal evidence 12-1, 1003D3
RITCHARD, Cyril
Dies 12-18, 1024G2
RITSCHARD, Willi
Elected Swiss pres 12-7, 1018D1
RITTENBAND, Judge Laurence J.
Ordrs Polanski mental exam 9-19, 732C3
RITTER, Judge Willis W.
Grants Gilmore delay, ruling reversed 1-17, 40C2
RIVAS Posada, Rafael
Natl Univ closed 4-27, 347G3
RIVE, Louis
Halts French phone deal 11-25, 934C2
RIVERO Milan, Fernando E.
Canada bars return 1-12, 42G3
RIVERS, Mickey
AL batting ldr 10-2, 926F3
In AL playoff 10-5—10-9, 807A2
In World Series, desires trade 10-11—10-18, 806G1, E2
RIVERS, Richard R.
Holds Japan trade talks 11-17—11-21, press scores US recalls 11-23, 931B2
RIVERSIDE Church (N.Y.)
Coffin elected min 8-14, 808B2

1978

RICHTER, W. D.
Invasn of Body Snatchers released 12-21, 1030A3
RICHTER Prada, Gen. Pedro
Heads Peru joint chiefs 1-31, 134A3
USSR resets Peru debt paymts 4-9, 353A2
RICHTER Scale—*See EARTHQUAKES*
RICKMAN, Thomas
Hooper released 8-4, 970F1
RICKOVER, Adm. Hyman G.
Doubts Portsmouth cancer findings 2-28, 164D3, E3
Disputes Gen Dynamics on sub costs 3-14, 224G1
RIDEOUT, Greta
Husband acquitted of rape 12-27, 1028C3
RIDEOUT, John
Acquitted of raping wife 12-27, 1028C3
RIDGEWAY, Edmund (deceased)
Family OKs 7-Up sale 5-15, 364A3
RIDGEWAY, Rick
Climbs K2 in Pakistan 9-7, 843F2
RIEDEL, Dr. Marc
Bowers confrms death sentencing bias 3-6, 389B1
RIEGLE Jr., Sen. Donald Wayne (D, Mich.)
Votes for Panama Canal neutrality pact 3-16, 177E2
Votes for 2d Canal pact 4-18, 273B1
RIESSEN, Marty
Loses US Open doubles title 9-9, 707G1
RIFFE Jr., Vernal G.
Ohio aids Cleveland schools 4-13, 279C2
RIFKIN, Stanley Mark
Robs LA bank by phone 10-25; arrested 11-5, chrgd 11-20, 992A1
RIGG, Diana
Little Night Music released 3-7, 619A3
RIGHETTI, Dave
Traded to Yankees 11-10, 1026B1
RIGHT-to-Die—*See MEDICINE—Death Issues*
RIGHT-To-Work—*See LABOR—Unions*
RIGHT to Work Committee, National
AFL-CIO fined $10,000 6-12, 509E3
RILEY, Richard A.
Firestone, Borg-Warner to merge 11-28, 935F1
RILEY, Richard W.
Faces SC primary runoff for gov 6-13, 467D1
Beats Harvey in SC runoff 6-27, 510D1
Elected SC gov 11-7, 847B1, 853B1, E3
RILEY v. Illinois
Juvenile suspect rights rule review refused by Sup Ct 4-24, 322G2
RINALDO, Rep. Matthew J. (R, N.J.)
Reelected 11-7, 851B3
RING (magazine)
FCC faults ABC boxing tourn 4-25, 379E1
RINGER, Robert J.
Looking Out For Number #1 on best-seller list 7-2, 579E3; 8-6, 620C2
RIO Mimbres (N.M.)
NM water rights backed by Sup Ct 7-3, 552C2
RIOS Camerena, Alfredo
Arrest for corruptn cited 3-21, 289B3
RIOTS—*See under CRIME*
RIPLEY, Dan
Tully breaks indoor pole vault record 1-7, 76A3
Sets pole vault mark 6-8—6-10, 600B3
RISENHOOVER, Rep. Theodore M. (D, Okla.)
Loses primary 8-22, 683D1
Synar wins US House seat 11-7, 855A3
RISI, Dino
Viva Italia released 7-9, 970C3
RITCHIE, Michael
Bad News Bears released 7-14, 969C3
RITCHIE, Roland
Upholds Nova Scotia film censorship 1-19, 111A2
RITT, Martin
Casey's Shadow released 3-17, 618F3
Begelman chrgd with forgery 3-31, 251D1
RITTER, Donald L.
Wins US House seat 11-7, 849E2, 852D1
RITTER, Phil
Beaten 9-21, Synanon role probed 10-15, 842A1
RITTER, Judge Willis W.
Dies 3-4, 252C3
RIVAS, Noel
Arrest rptd 9-4, 690C3
RIVERA, Col. Luis
Bolivia health min 11-24, 913E1
RIVERA Caminero, Vice Adm. Francisco
Replaced as navy staff chief 8-16, 648E2
RIVERDELL Hospital (Oradell, N.J.)
Jascalevich case-press freedom controversy 6-30—8-30, 678C2
RIVERS, Joan
Rabbit Test released 4-8, 619D3
RIVERS, Mickey
In World Series 10-10—10-17, 800B1

1979

RICHMOND Times-Dispatch, The (newspaper)
Va trial closure case accepted by Sup Ct 10-9, 784A1
RICHTER, Detlef
W Gers win world 4-man bobsled title 2-25, 392F1
RICHTER, W. D.
Dracula released 7-13, 820A1
RICHTER Prada, Gen. Pedro (Peruvian prime minister)
Sworn prime min, war min, army cmdr 2-2, 101G2
Sets mtg with protesting journalists 3-21, cancels 3-22 256A1
RICKETS—*See MEDICINE—Diseases*
RICKIE Lee Jones (recording)
On best-seller list 5-30, 448F3
RIDDICK, Steven
Shares indoor sprint medley mark 2-23, 911E2
RIDE a Cock Horse (play)
Opens 3-18, 292E2
RIDEOUT, Greta
Reconciled with husband 1-6, 79D1
Divorced 4-20, 392E3
RIDEOUT, John
Reconciled with wife 1-6, 79D1
Divorced 4-20, 392E3
RIEKERT, Pieter
Fewer black curbs urged 5-8, 373B2
RIESCHBIETER, Karlos
Brazil finance min designate 1-19, 95B1
RIESEL, Victor
Johnny Dio dies 1-12, 176F2
RIESSEN, Marty
Loses Baltimore Grand Prix 1-21, 391F2
RIFKIN, Ron
Goodbye People opens 4-30, 711D3
RIFKIN, Stanley Mark
Rearrested in 2d wire-transfer scheme 2-13; pleads guilty to '78 theft 2-22, sentncd 3-26, 239G1
Canadian sentncd in wire-transfer scheme 9-24, 840C3
RIGBY, Harry
Mtg By the River opens 3-28, 712D1
I Love My Wife opens 5-15, 711F3
RIGGINS, John
NFL '78 rushing ldr 1-6, 80E2
RIGGS National Bank (Washington, D.C.)
Contreras funds transfer probed 10-9, 772A2, B2
RIGHT Stuff, The (book)
On best-seller list 11-4, 892C3
RIGLER, Chuck
Resigns Dole staff 12-6, 983C2
RIJSBERGEN, Wilhelmus (Wim)
Signs with Cosmos 4-3, 655E1
Named to NASL All-Star team 8-27, 776E1
RILEY, Larry
Songs From City Streets opens 4-9, 712E2
RILEY, Richard A.
Sees Kahn, wage-guide compliance urged 4-20, 344G3
RILEY, Gov. Richard W. (D, S.C.)
Orders A-dump cutback 10-31, 851B2; 885G3-886A1
RINGER, Robert J.
Restoring Amer Dream on best-seller list 10-14, 800C3; 11-4, 892C3
RINGLING Brothers-Barnum & Bailey Combined Shows Inc.
Emmett Kelly dies 3-28, 270G2
RING My Bell (recording)
On best-seller list 7-4, 548E3; 8-1, 620E3
RIO Grande Ranches of Colorado
Land sale refunds set 5-8, 596A1
RIOS, Eduardo
Labor min cancels Group of 10 mtg 1-12, 29B1
RIOS, Rosemary
Beggars Soap Opera opens 7-23, 711D1
RIO Tinto-Zinc Corp.
UK offers trust legis 10-31, 855F3
RIOUW Islands—*See INDONESIA*
RIPERTON, Minnie
Dies 7-12, 588C3
RISCHBIETER, Karlos Heinz
Trade cncl revived 8-17, forgn investmt rptd 10-2, 871A1, E1
Sees inflatn over 70% 11-26, 907E2
RISE (recording)
On best-seller list 10-3, 800E3; 11-7, 892E3
RISEBROUGH, Doug
Montreal wins Stanley Cup 5-21, 447C3
RISEN, E. David
Sky High opens 6-28, 712D2
RISSER, James
Wins Pulitzer 4-16, 336A3
RITCHER, Jim
Wins Outland Trophy 11-25, 1001E2
RITCHIE, Michael
Almost Perfect Affair released 4-26, 528B1
RITT, Martin
Norma Rae released 3-1, 174C3
RITZMAN, Alice
2d in Sarah Coventry Open 6-17, 587B3
RIVEAU, Philippe Robert
Arrested in Salameh slaying 1-26, 69C2
RIVERA, Jose Antonio de (d. 1939)
Rally commerates 11-18, 952C2
RIVEROS, Gen. Santiago Omar
Retiremt expected 12-7, 947F3
RIVERS, Mickey
Traded to Rangers 8-1, 1002B3
RIVERSIDE Church (N.Y., N.Y.)
Coffin scores Iran sanctns 12-23; sees hostages 12-24–12-25, forgn min 12-27, 975B1

1980

RICKS, Columbus
Job bias suit filing time limit upheld by Sup Ct 12-15, 957B2
RIDDICK, Steve
Sets indoor sprint medley relay mark 2-29, 892F1
RIDDICK v. New York
Case decided by Sup Ct 4-15, 305G3
Case cited by Sup Ct 10-6, 782D3
RIDE Like the Wind (recording)
On best-seller list 4-30, 359G3
RIECKEHOFF, German
Vs PR Olympic boycott 4-18, 325D3
RIEDEL, Petra
Wins Olympic medal 7-23, 623B3
RIESSEN, Marty
Wins US Open mixed doubles 9-7, 691F2
RIFLE Association, National
Anderson answers TV debate questn 10-28, 816B1
RIGGINS, John
NFL '79 touchdown, rushing ldr 1-5, 8E2, E3
RIGHT Stuff, The (book)
Wins Amer Book Award 5-1, 692A2
RIIHIVUORI, Hilkka
Wins Olympic medals 2-15, 2-18, 155C3
RILEY, Richard A.
Firestone retiremt, replacemt set 9-1, 702D1
RILEY, Gov. Richard W. (D, S.C.)
State of State message 1-16, 483E3
US suggests reapportionmt 2-14, 185A2
RIMAWI, Kassem el- (Jordanian prime minister; resigns Sept. 28)
Jordan prime min 7-3; quits, Badran named 8-28, 698G1
RINALDO, Rep. Matthew J. (R, N.J.)
Reelected 11-4, 843B3
RINGLING Bros. v. Mikos
Case refused by Sup Ct 3-24, 265A2
RIOTS & Civil Disorders—*See under CRIME*
RIPON Society
Pres campaign spending limit upheld by Sup Ct 4-14, 306F3
RISCHBIETER, Karlos Heinz
Resigns 1-15, 95C2
RISE (recording)
Albert wins Grammy 2-27, 296C3
RISE of Theodore Roosevelt, The (book)
Morris wins Pulitzer 4-14, 296E2
Wins Amer Book Award 5-1, 692C2
RISS, Sheldon
Really Rosie opens 10-12, 892E3
RISSNER, Danton
Up the Academy released 6-6, 675F3
RITCHER, Jim
In NFL draft 4-29, 336F2
RITCHIE, Michael
Divine Madness released 9-25, 836E2
RITTENBERG, Sidney
Named to China sci post 3-17, 231C2
RITTER, Rep. Don L. (R, Pa.)
Reelected 11-4, 844D1
RITTER, John
Hero at Large released 2-8, 216G2
RITZ Associates
NJ casino project, Abscam linked 2-5, 111A1-C1
Williams, 3 others indicted 10-30, 824A3
RIVAR Sacconi, Jose Manuel
DR Emb siege ends, hostages freed 4-27 335B2
RIVAS Rodriguez, Manuel de Jesus
Slain 11-3, 871F3
RIVER, The (recording)
On best-seller list 12-3, 948C3
RIVERA Rosado, Angela
PR cops cleared in husband's '78 death 4-25, 348B3
RIVERA y Damas, Arturo
Scores leftist ldrs murders 11-28, 921A2
RIVERS, Larry
Drawings & Digressns wins Amer Book Award 5-1, 692B2
RIVERS, Mickey
AL batting ldr 10-6, 926D3, F3
RIVERSIDE—*See CALIFORNIA*
RIVERSIDE Methodist Hospital (Columbus, O.)
Legionnaires disease study rptd 6-9, 527E1

1976

RIVERS—*See specific names*
RIVERS, Mickey
AL batting ldr 10-4, 796B1, C1
In World Series 10-16—10-21, 815E3
RIVLIN, Alice M.
On fscl '77 budget optns 3-15, 230D3
On econ recovery, productivity 8-2, 647A2
Carter econ adviser 12-1, 898G2
RIZK, Assad
Leb labor min 12-9, 913D2
RIZZO, Mayor Frank L. (Philadelphia, Pa.)
US Sup Ct voids police misconduct rule 1-21, 42E3
Jackson loses primary 4-27, 305D1
Endorses Carter 6-10, 432F1
Recall vote barred 9-30, 994D1
Pledges to help Carter 11-1, 827E2
Carter elected 11-2, 818A3
Rpts Bellevue-Stratford demolitn 11-10, 911G2
RKLITSKY, Nicolas P.—*See NIKON, Archbishop*
RKO General Inc.—*See under GENERAL Tire & Rubber*
ROA, Raul
Rejects Cuba OAS reentry 9-14, 832G3
ROACH, Barbara
US team climb Mt Everest 10-8, 876B3
ROACH, Gary
US team climbs Mt Everest 10-8, 876B3
ROACH, Joseph
Testifies on Nantucket oil spill 12-30, 1014B1
ROADS & Highways
US budget proposals 1-21, 65F3
Energy dvpt loans urged 2-26, 149E2
Aid authorizatn signed 5-5, 919A3
US Cong clears added funds 5-19, 411F3
Dem platform text 6-15, 469G1, 474A2, E2
Carter legis record cited 512C2
Cong OKs '77 funds, ceiling 8-4, 646A2; Ford signs 8-14, 982F1
GOP platform text 8-18, 607F1
Guatemala IDB loan set 10-13, 1005E1
Transitn ¼ fed spending rptd down 10-27, 866D1
US-Canada pact rptd 11-12, 945E3
NE govs seek plan 11-14, 865A1
Sup Ct refuses Miss constructn case 11-29, 901C1
Accidents—*See ACCIDENTS*

1977

RIVERS & Waterways—*See also specific names*
Flow decline rptd 3-8, 244G2
US water rights in Calif upheld 4-4, 253C1
Carter backs Tenn-Tombigbee, Red R waterways 4-18, 299D3
Carter environmt message 5-23, 404F2
43 rivers below normal levels 6-16, 492G2
US seeks Alaska acreage 9-15, 739B3
ND irrigatn projct scored 9-19, 726B1
Grain shipping price policy curbed 10-3, 760D2
RIVLIN, Alice M.
On CBO poverty rpts 1-13, 1-17, 80C3, 81A1
On Carter goals 2-15, 126F1
RIZA, Iqbal
Quits as emb aide in Paris 4-26, 314B1
RIZIK, Francis
Palestinian atrocities chrgd 4-18, 297F2
RIZZO, Mayor Frank L. (D, Phila.)
Budget passed 8-20, 666F1
Rptr tied to Pa politician quits 9-12, 920F3
ROACH, Archbishop John R.
Gives inaugural prayer 1-20, 25F1
ROADS & Highways
Ex-Miss offcl convicted 1-8, 60D1
DOT issues future trends rpt 1-15, 58A3
Ford '78 budget proposals 1-17, 32F2, 33C1, F1
Carter budget revisions 2-22, 125G2
Cong sets new '77 budget levels 3-3, 174E1
Carter energy plan 4-20, 291E2, C3
Carter defends energy plan 4-22, 321B2
FHWA proposes metric signs 4-27, 369D1
Metric signs plan dropped 6-24, 522G1-A2
NYC blackout affects lights 7-3—7-14, 537F2
Canada sets metric signs 9-6, 705D2
W Ger seeks Berlin link 10-5, 984E1
NC, Dallas referenda OKd 11-8, 879B2, D2
Police rights vs traffic violators extended 12-5, 938G3-939B1
US urban policies scored 12-7, 959G3
Accidents—*See ACCIDENTS*

1978

RIVERS & Waterways—*See also specific names*
States curbed on oil tanker regulatn 3-6, 161E3
Amazon pact signed by 8 natns 7-3, 829C2
Parks bill voted 7-12, 526C3
Parks bill cleared 10-13, 834G2
Inland Waterways authorzn signed 10-21, 897C2
RIVETTE, Jacques
Celine & Julie released 2-24, 618G3
RIZA, Crown Prince—*See PAHLEVI, Crown Prince Riza*
RIZZO, Mayor Frank L. (Phila, Pa.)
Orders radicals blockaded 3-2, 410A2
RMI Co.
Indicted on price fixing 9-28, 768D2
RN: Memoirs of Richard Nixon (book)
On best-seller list 6-4, 460C3; 7-2, 579D3; 8-6, 620B2
ROACH, John F.
Paradise Alley released 10-10, 970F2
ROADS & Highways
Carter State of Union Message 1-19, 32A1
Carter budget proposals 1-23, 47G2
Adams issues policy statemt 2-8, 109F1
World Bank OKs Paraguay loan 3-9, 292F3
E-W Ger talks progress rptd 6-24, 622A3
Camp David summit pact OKs Sinai-Jordan link 9-17, 712B2
Carter scores road bill 9-28, 751G3
Hwy, mass transit Cong actn cited 10-15, 784G3
Carter road bill backing for energy votes rptd 10-16, 786G3
Carter signs fund bill 11-8, 875D2
Environmentalists score Carter 12-20, 1009E1
ROBARDS Jr., Jason
Wins Oscar 4-3, 315C3
Comes A Horseman released 11-1, 969G3
ROBBERY—*See under CRIME*
ROBBINS, Hargus (Pig)
Wins Grammy 2-24, 316A1
ROBBINS, Harold
Betsy released 2-9, 618C3
Dreams Die First on best-seller list 9-4, 708D1

1979

RIVERS & Waterways—*See also specific names*
'79-81 budget outlays table 42F2
Tenn-Tombigbee projct upheld 3-13, 188A3
House OKs Alaska bill 5-16, 366F3
Pub access curbed by Sup Ct 12-4, 987G3-988C1
RIVEST, Jean-Claude
Wins by-electn 4-30, 329D1
RIVLIN, Alice M.
Vs Admin '79 econ forecasts, sees $40 bln deficit, asks deep cuts 1-25, 48E3
RIZZO, Mayor Frank L. (Phila, Pa.)
Police shielding chrgd 4-16, denies 4-17, 310D3, G3
Mayoral primary results 5-15, 363E2
Chrgd in police brutality complaint, calls suit political 8-13, 610E1, C2
Plans papal altar with city funds, ACLU threatens suit 9-13, 760C3
Phila police brutality suit dismissed 10-30, 831C3, E3
Green elected mayor 11-6, 846B3
RKO General Inc.—*See GENERAL Tire & Rubber Co.*
ROA, Raul
Scores Sihanouk in UN debate 1-11, 10E2
ROACH, Max
Glorious Monster opens 7-10, 711C3
ROADS & Highways
Carter budget proposals 1-22, 45G1
Carter backs 55-mph limit 2-12, 109D3
Adams outlines urban-aid policy 2-13, 129B2
US land grant easemt right curbed by Sup Ct 3-27, 263B2
Admin moves on striking trucker demands 6-21—6-27, 479C3
Admin meets truckers' demands 6-29, 516A3
W Ger bars speed limit 7-4, 506C1
Mass transit, highway agencies merger dropped; Trust Fund shortfall seen 9-17, 726F1
Va men's room surveillnc case declined by Sup Ct 10-1, 768G1
Md, Me bond referenda OKd 11-6, 847B1
Zimbabwe cuts Zambia links 11-18—11-19, 899D2
Chicago aid funds rptd 12-4, 984C1

1980

RIVERS & Waterways
GOP platform proposals urge supplier natn route protectn 1-14, 32C1
Carter budget outlays, table 1-28, 70F1
Tenn-Tombigbee project, other funds clear Cong 6-25, 9-10; signed 10-1, 803C2, F2
Calif OKs water projct 7-18, 632A2
Israel plans Medit-Dead Sea canal; map 8-24, 643F2
Jordan Dead Sea-Red Sea canal rptd 8-30, 661G1
Alaska lands bill signed 12-2, 916A1
RIVLIN, Alice M.
On fed budget deficits 3-5, 168B2
RIZK, Edmund
Kidnaped 2-13; freed 3-9, 179E3
RIZZO, Frank L.
Phila radicals convicted 5-8, 414A1
RIZZO, Patti
2d in US Woman's Amateur golf championship 8-17, 714E3
RKO General Inc.—*See under GENERAL Tire*
ROACH, John
Guardsman opens 1-3, 136B3
ROACH, John V.
Named Tandy pres 10-23, 959B3
ROADS & Highways
State of State messages 1-9, 1-14, 483D3, 484C2; 1-15, 403A3; 1-24, 1-25, 269A3-G3
Carter budget proposals 1-28, 73D1
Afghan-Pak highway closed 2-23, 138C3
E, W Ger pact signed 4-30, 355C3
Mt St Helens damage assessed 5-24—7-4, 503E3, 504A3
Anderson urges urban aid 6-9, 438F3
Tex heat wave damage rptd 6-23—8-15, 616D1
SE builders bid-rigging pleas, probe rptd 7-5, 655F1
Jerusalem project OKd 7-18, 572G3
Heat wave damage final rpt 9-7, 857C2
Reagan backs NYC Westway projct 10-1, 738C1
Alaska bond issue OKd 11-4, 847A2
EPA halts Calif, Ky aid 12-11, 963B1

1976

ROARK, Capt. William M.
Vietnam rpts killed 9-6, 678B3
ROBALINO, Cesar
Ecuador finance min 1-14, 49A1
ROBALLOS, Rodolfo
Testimony links to AAA 2-4, 212C1
ROBBER Bridegroom, The (play)
Opens 10-10, 1014E3
ROBBERIES—*See under CRIME*
ROBBINS, A. H.
Rpts foreign payoffs 4-27, 362E1
ROBBINS & Myers Inc.
Sup Ct upholds EEOC complaint deadline 12-20, 960D1
ROBERTO, Holden
At OAU summit 1-10—1-13, 16F1
Scores US arms aid 1-11, 16F2
MPLA northn drive rptd 1-15, 16E2
Denies FNLA northn collapse 1-16, 35F2, B3
Secret FNLA police force rptd 2-8, 106F1
Mobutu recognizes MPLA 2-28, 163A2
ROBERTS, Justice Burton B.
Dismisses '74 case vs 3 oil cos 3-10, 413D1
ROBERTS, David
Bell sets pole-vault mark 5-29, 424D3
Wins Olympic medal 7-26, 576A1
ROBERTS, John
Sworn Canada affairs secy 9-15, 692F1
ROBERTS, Neal
Testifies re Bolles murder 7-15, 859C3
ROBERTS, Rep. Ray (D, Tex.)
Reelected 11-2, 830C4
ROBERTS, Robin
Named to Hall of Fame 8-9, 816C1

1977

ROBARDS, Jason
Wins Oscar 3-28, 264C1
ROBB, Charles S.
Wins primary for lt gov 6-14, 465B1
Elected 11-8, 855G1
ROBB, Judge Roger
DC ct reorganizatn upheld 3-22, 231A2
ROBBERIES—*See under CRIME*
ROBBINS, Alan
Loses LA mayoral race 4-6, 252B3
ROBBINS, Harold
Lonely Lady on best-seller list 4-3, 264A2; 5-1, 356D2; 6-4, 452B2
ROBBINS, Jerome
At Pele tribute 10-1, 827D2
ROBBINS, Spencer E.
SEC chrgs 9-28, consent accord rptd 10-3, 774C1
ROBERT, Jacques
Hijacks French jet, seized 9-30, 807C3
ROBERT Hall Clothes—*See UNITED Merchant & Manufacturers*
ROBERTO, Holden
CIA payments rptd 2-19, 124F1
ROBERTS, Albert
Scored re Poulson scandal 7-26, 581G1
ROBERTS, Anthony
In NBA draft 6-10, 584B2
ROBERTS, Cecil E.
Scores Miller 8-26, 691B1
ROBERTS, Clifford
Kills self 9-29, 788C2
ROBERTS, Dave
Brock sets stolen base mark 8-29, 748E3
ROBERTS, Harry
Mandatory death sentnc voided 6-6, 478D2
ROBERTS, John
Unity task force chrmn 7-5, 542D1
ROBERTS, Neal A.
Named in Bolles murder testimony 1-15, 1-26—1-27, 162A1, F1
Arrested 2-14, 162G1
ROBERTSON, Carol (d. 1963)
'63 bomber convicted 11-18, 907B3

1978

ROBBINS, Jerome
Baryshnikov joins NYC Ballet 4-26, 335F3
ROBBINS, Matthew
Corvette Summer released 8-4, 970A1
ROBBINS, Rex
Players opens 9-6, 887E2
ROBBINS, Justice Sydney L.
Toronto transit strike ends 9-15, 722A1
ROBELO Callejas, Alfonso
Shuns Chamorro death probe panel 4-6, 376C2
On Nicaragua oppositn comm 9-14, 705D3
ROBERSON, Jim
Dismissed from Indiana basketball team 12-12, 1028B1
ROBERSON, Vern
Traded to 49ers 4-17, 336E1
ROBERT, Yves
We Meet In Paradise released 5-22, 620B1
ROBERT F. Kennedy Memorial Stadium (Washington, D.C.)
Redskins trust liability case refused by Sup Ct 6-12, 468F1
ROBERTS, Cecil
On Guyana cult bequest to USSR 12-17, 1000B2
ROBERTS, Dave
Rose begins 44-game hitting streak 6-14, 618F2
ROBERTS, Doris
Cheaters opens 1-15, 760F1
ROBERTS, Eric
King of Gypsies released 12-19, 1030B3
ROBERTS, Sir Gilbert
Dies 1-1, 96D3
ROBERTS, Greg
Wins Outland Trophy 11-25, 1025A2
ROBERTS, Leon
AL batting ldr 10-2, 928D3
ROBERTS, Oral
Hospital OKd 5-25, 577A3
ROBERTS, Peter M.
Wins Sears patent suit 10-2, 844B2
ROBERTS, Rep. Ray (D, Tex.)
Reelected 11-7, 852E2
ROBERTSON, Cliff
Begelman chrgd with forgery 3-31, 251D1
ROBERTSON, George
Wins Hamilton by-electn 6-1, 437E1
ROBERTSON, James R.
Dies 8-1, 708D3
ROBERTSON, John Home
Elected MP in UK by-electn 10-26, 867D1

1979

ROBACZYNSKI, Mary Rose
Freed in mercy deaths 3-29, 291F1-A2
ROBARDS, Jason
Hurricane released 5-17, 528E2
ROBARTS, John
Unity Task Force rpt issued 1-25, 74C3
ROBB, David
NASL scoring ldr 8-12, 654F3
ROBB, Inez
Dies 4-4, 356F3
ROBB, Lynda Bird Johnson (Mrs. Charles Spittal Robb)
Named women's panel head 5-9, 351G1-A3
ROBB, Judge Roger
Named to special prosecutor panel 1-12, 56F1
ROBBERY—*See under CRIME*
ROBBOY, Dr. Stanley J.
Rpts DES risk less 3-6, 196C1
ROBELO Callejas, Alfonso
Named to Nicaragua provisional junta 6-17, 461G1
Meets US envoy in Panama, plans outlined 6-27, 475A3
Visits Cuba 7-26, 574C2
Scores US on aid program 8-4, 603A3
Announces currency recall 8-24, 689B2
Announces currency rate, other decrees 9-3, 689E2
In US, seeks aid 9-24, 731C3
ROBERT Kennedy and His Times (book)
Wins Natl Book Award 4-23, 356A2
ROBERTS, Dave
Traded to Pirates 6-28, 1002A3
ROBERTS, George
NFL '78 punting ldr 1-6, 80B2
ROBERTS, Greg
Clark wins Lombardi Award 1-18, 175G2
ROBERTS, Howard
Comin' Uptown opens 12-20, 1007C2
ROBERTS, Peter M.
Sears ordered to pay profits 5-31, 466C2
ROBERTS, Rachel
Picnic At Hanging Rock released 2-22, 174D3
Once A Catholic opens 10-10, 956F3
ROBERTS, Rep. Ray (D, Tex.)
Veterans' Affairs Com chrmn 1-24, 71F1
ROBERTS, Tom
Paintings rptd stolen 1-3, 18F2
ROBERTS, Tony
Murder at Howard Johnson's opens 5-17, 712F1
Losing Time opens 9-30, 956C3
ROBERTSON, John
Nottingham Forest wins Eur Champions' Cup 5-30, 776G2

1980

ROADWAY Express Inc. v. Piper
Case decided by Sup Ct 6-23, 555B1
ROA Kouri, Raul
Cuban UN attache assassinated 9-11, 685B2
ROAST (play)
Opens 5-8, 392G3
ROBARDS Jr., Jason
Raise the Titanic released 8-1, 675D3
ROBB, Judge Roger
Overturns Letelier murder convictns 9-15, 703F3
ROBBERY—*See under CRIME*
ROBBINS, Gale
Dies 2-18, 176B3
ROBBINS, Harold
Memories on best-seller list 9-14, 716D3; 10-12, 796F3
ROBBINS, Jerome
West Side Story opens 2-14, 136G3
ROBELO Callejas, Alfonso
Quits junta, scores Sandinistas 4-22, 315B2
Shuns Cncl of State mtg 5-4, replaced on junta 5-18, 390C1
Party rally banned 11-9, oppositn boycotts State Cncl 11-12, 874C1, F1
ROBERT, Jean-Jacques
Vanuatu rebellion role rptd 11-21, 903E3
ROBERTS, Clinton
Wins SD US House primary 6-3, 439B3
Elected to US House 11-4, 844C2, 851F2
ROBERTS, Judge Jack
OKs Austin busing plan 1-3, 5C3
ROBERTS, John
Canada science, tech min 3-3, 171B2
Scores US acid rain policy 6-23, 486F2
ROBERTS, Oral
TV revenues rptd 2-25, 413A2
ROBERTS, Pat
Elected to US House 11-4, 842D3, 851C1
ROBERTS, Rachel
Dies 11-26, 928C3
ROBERTS, Rep. Ray (D, Tex.)
On Carter VA MD pay hike veto 8-26, 649F3
Hall wins seat 11-4, 850B2
ROBERTS, Richard
Dies 4-4, 360B3
ROBERTS, Tanya
Gets Charlies Angels role 6-17, 638C2

1976

ROBERTSON, Michael
Unopposed in Mass Sen primary 9-14, 705B1
ROBESON, Paul
Dies 1-23, 80F3
ROBIDEAU, Robert
Acquitted 7-16, 640E2
ROBINSON, Arnie
Wins Olympic medal 7-29, 576B1
ROBINSON Jr., Judge Aubrey E.
Red #2 dye ban in effect 2-12, ct challenge continues 2-13, 137D1
Grants Woods' request 4-23, 316E1
Rejcts pres debate suits 9-17, 703D2
ROBINSON, Charles W.
Dep State secy 4-1; confrmd 4-7, 262E3
ROBINSON, David Glen
Sentenced 1-28, 124D1
ROBINSON, Frank
Rehired as mgr, quits as player 10-4, 815G3
ROBINSON, Glenn O.
Replaced on FCC 9-8, 808D1
ROBINSON, James
Dock strike ends 8-10, 623D2
ROBINSON, Rep. James Kenneth (R, Va.)
Reelected 11-2, 831A1
ROBLEDO, Angel
Loses cabt post 1-15; dismissal scored 1-16, 71B2, F2
Labor ldrs ask new cabt 2-20, 154C2
ROBLES, Ivan & Winston
Arrested 1-15, exiled 1-20, 121A3
ROBLES Linares, Jesus
Mex water resources min 12-2, 907A1
ROBLES Piquer, Carlos
Cousin arrested 2-26, 314B3
Refusal of Cabt post rptd 7-6, 523B2
ROBSON, John E.
Ford rejcts CAB proposal 12-28, 992C2
ROCA, Blas
Elected Natl Assemb pres 12-2, 1000D3
ROCCA, Peter
Wins Olympic medals 7-19, 7-24, 575C2
ROCHE, Josephine A.
Dies 7-29, 716E3
ROCHESTER, N.Y.—*See NEW York State*
ROCHESTER (N.Y.), University of
Whipple dies 2-1, 124G3
ROCHESTER (N.Y.) Democrat & Chronicle (newspaper)
Ford endorsement rptd 10-30, 831F2
ROCHESTER (Minn.) Post-Bulletin (newspaper)
Ford endorsement rptd 10-30, 827G3
ROCHESTER (N.Y.) Times-Union (newspaper)
Ford endorsement rptd 10-30, 831F2
ROCKABYE Hamlet (play)
Opens 2-17, 1014B3
ROCKEFELLER, David
On Chase solvency 1-11, 110A3, 111A1
ROCKEFELLER, Fifi
On Ky pres ballot 5-25, 374C2
ROCKEFELLER IV, John D.
Wins primary for gov 5-11, 342C3
Elected 11-2, 817E2, 820B3, 823D1, 831E2
ROCKEFELLER Jr., John D. (1874-1960)
Daughter dies 5-27, 404B2
ROCKEFELLER Sr., John D. (1839-1937)
Pocantico site dedicated 11-21, 887A3
ROCKEFELLER, Nelson A(ldrich)
Citibank on 'problem' list 1-11, 111B1
Ford lists potential vps 1-22, 41G1
At AFL-CIO meeting 2-11—2-12, 149A1
On revenue sharing 2-24, 149F3
'75 CIA memo re JFK death plot rptd 3-20, 3-21, 217C2
Visits Australia 3-30—3-31, 249F2
Wins 'uncommitted' NY del bloc 4-6, 244G2
Sen apology for remarks vs Jackson aides 4-27, 305D3
Vs Reagan re Panama Canal 5-2, 5-3, 324D2
Ford gets 119 NY delegates 5-24, 374D1
Marks Bicentennial 7-2, 7-4, 489F1-A2
Testifies at GOP platform com hearing 8-9, 583G1
VP prospect cited 8-10, 584D1
VP poll rptd 8-11, 583F3
Addresses GOP conv opening 8-16, 601F3, 615B1
GOP conv scuffle on 16-C debate 8-17, 600G1
Nominates Dole as GOP vp 8-19, 598C3-D3
With Ford in Vail 8-27, 645A1, F1
Campaigns with Dole in NY 9-16, 687B1
Ford donatns rptd 10-22, 938F3
Ford dedicates Pocantico site 11-21, 887A3
Meets Ford on GOP unity 12-9, 938A1
At Daley funeral service 12-22, 969D3
ROCKEFELLER Awards
Announced 11-16, 911C3

1977

ROBERTSON, Norman
On Carter rebate plan withdrawal 4-14, 271G1
ROBERTSON, Oscar
Havlicek becomes 3d all-time NBA scorer 11-14, 991D1
ROBERTSON Co., H. H.
'76 Fortune 500 list drops 341D1
ROBERTS v. Louisiana
Sup Ct curbs automatic death sentncs 6-6, 478D2
ROBINSON, Brooks
Retires 8-21, honored 9-18, 768E2
ROBINSON, Charles W.
Replaced in State post 2-24, 148D3
ROBINSON, Eric
Named Australia finance min 12-19, 982A2
ROBINSON, Frank
Fired as Indian mgr 6-19, joins Angels 7-11, 644G1
Firing by Angels rptd 12-17, 990A2
ROBINSON, Jackie (1919-72)
NL wins All-Star Game 7-19, 567B2
ROBINSON, Jacob
Dies 10-24, 872G2
ROBINSON, Jerry
Wins Downtown AC Trophy 12-8, 950E2
ROBINSON, Len (Truck)
Storen fired as Hawks pres 9-27, 870B3
ROBINSON, Luis
Hijacks bus, slays 2 7-4; chrgd 7-5, 568D3
ROBINSON, Paul
Laser enrichmt of uranium waste rptd 12-17, 975F2
ROBINSON, Thomas
On Ethiopia food supply 8-23, 684E3
ROBISCH, Dave
Traded to Lakers 12-13, 991A1
ROBISON, James
Arrested 1-15, Adamson testifies 1-26—1-27, 161F3, 162C1
Named in bomb chrg 2-14, 162G1
Convicted of Bolles murder 11-6, 871B2
ROBOTHAM, Robert
Urges uranium ban 1-3, 7C1
Quits as CAB chrmn 211A2
ROCARD, Michel
Giscard scores US talks 4-2, 255D2
ROCCA, Antonino
Dies 3-15, 264D3
ROCHA e Silva, Mauricio
To lead repressn fight 7-22, 633C1
ROCHE, Mal
Named ASL rookie of yr 9-8, 827C3
ROCHE, Tony
US wins World Cup 3-11—3-13, 431G1
Australia wins Davis Cup 12-4, 970E2, F2
ROCHESTER, N. Y.—*See NEW York State*
ROCHESTER, University of (N.Y.)
Wallis elected PBC chrmn 3-9, 396D3
ROCHFORD, James
Chicago police spying disclosed 5-11, 388E2
ROCKALL (British Island)
Denmark protests UK fishing limits 1-29, 115G2-A3
Irish dispute UK oil rights 2-3, arbitratn set 2-17, 329B2
ROCKEFELLER, David
Curbs S Africa loans 4-19, 350C2
At 25th Bilderberg conf 4-21—4-24, 359C3
Gardner quits Rockefeller fund 8-23, 927D3
ROCKEFELLER 3rd, John D.
Gardner quits Rockefeller fund 8-23, 927D3
ROCKEFELLER IV, Gov. John D. (D, W.Va.)
Carter visits 3-17, 191B1
ROCKEFELLER, Laurence S.
Gardner quits Rockefeller fund 8-23, 927D3
ROCKEFELLER, Nelson A(ldrich)
Assassination plot jury deadlocks 3-10, 261F2
Gardner quits Rockefeller fund 8-23, 927D3
ROCKEFELLER Brothers Fund
Gardner resigns 8-23, 927D3

1978

ROBERTSON, Robbie
Last Waltz released 4-25, 619G2
ROBESON, Paul Bustill (1898-1976)
'Paul Robeson' opens 1-19, 760A3
ROBEY, Rick
Ky wins NCAA basketball title 3-27, 272D1
In NBA draft 6-9, 457F2
ROBINS, Eva
Named to coal-strike bd of inquiry 3-6; hearings held 3-8, deadlock rptd 3-9, 159B2, E3
ROBINSON, Judge Aubrey
Issues Taft-Hartley order 3-9, 159C2
Denies Taft-Hartley extensn 3-17, 217C1
N&W Rwy strike decisns 8-27, 9-29, 809B2, G2
ROBINSON, Bill (Bojangles) (deceased)
Bill Bailey death rptd 12-17, 1032C2
ROBINSON, CWO Donald K.
On Chesapeake Bay collisn 10-20, 908E3
ROBINSON, Edward J.
Indicted re land fraud 10-10, 808F2
ROBINSON, Eric
Fraser fires Cabt min 8-7, defends actn 8-8, 612A2
Fraser denies Withers scandal link 8-21, 703C2
ROBINSON, Frank
Named Orioles coach 2-11, 195D1
To manage Rochester Triple-A club 5-8, 355D2
Doby named White Sox mgr 6-30, 560F1
ROBINSON, Gregory
Arrives Guyana 11-15, visits cult commune 11-17, killed 11-18, body flown home 11-21, 889A1-F2, 891C1
ROBINSON, James
Drops chrgs vs 2 in '75 Mich VA Hosp deaths 2-1, 116C2
ROBINSON, Rep. James Kenneth (R, Va.)
Reelected 11-7, 852D3
ROBINSON, Larry
Montreal wins Stanley Cup, named playoff MVP 5-25, 458E1, G1
ROBINSON, Len (Truck)
NBA rebound ldr 4-9, 271G1, F2
On NBA all-star team 6-13, 457C3
ROBINSON, Max
ABC news show chngs set 4-19, 419B3
ROBINSON, Richard
Piranha released 8-4, 970F2
ROBINSON, Ron
Lauds Sup Ct Bakke ruling 6-28, 482B3
ROBISON, James
Sentenced 1-10, 24B2
ROBLES Martinez, Jesus
Estate broken up by govt 9-1, 817E3
ROBSON, Mark
Dies 6-20, 540F3
ROCHA, Carlos
Dismissed 12-9, 985D1
ROCHE, Tony
US wins World Cup 3-9—3-12, 252D1
Lobsters lose WTT title 9-21, 1027F1
ROCHEFORT, Jean
We Meet in Paradise released 5-22, 620C1
ROCHESTER, N.Y.—*See NEW York State*
ROCHESTER, University of
Fractional chrg (quark) experimt rptd 2-16, 293A3
Lincoln letter donated 4-15, 335G2
Shroud of Turin carbon 14 test rptd set 11-14, 926F1
ROCHESTER v. Waldert
Case refused by Sup Ct 10-30, 832C3
ROCKEFELLER, David
Sees Carter, backs inflatn plan 4-20, 361G3
Trilateral Comm study faults govts on energy policy 6-13, 450A3
Scores Carter 'export consequences' order 10-10, 804B3
ROCKEFELLER IV, Gov. John D. (D, W. Va.)
Sees Carter on coal strike 2-23, 122E3
Named coal indus panel chrmn 5-26, 405A1
ROCKEFELLER 3rd, John D.
Dies 7-10, 620D3
Art collection willed 7-20, 628C1
ROCKEFELLER, Nelson A(ldrich)
CIA probe comm rptdly heard Black Panther surveillnc chrg 3-17, 243F2

1979

ROBERTSON, Scotty
Named interim Bulls coach 2-16, 290D3
ROBERTSON, William
Chinchilla opens 6-4, 711B2
ROBEY, Rick
Traded to Celtics 1-16, 526D2
ROBIN, Leo
Dancing in Dark opens 1-21, 292D1
ROBIN and the Seven Hoods (film)
FBI seizes stolen copy 1-8, 102F2
ROBINSON Jr., Judge Aubrey E.
US drops case vs ITT exec 2-8, 88E1
Orders DC-10s grounded 6-5, 420A3
DC-10 order reversed 7-10, 538C3
OKs Nixon tapes release 7-24, 561F2
ROBINSON, Bill
In World Series 10-10—10-17, 816D1
ROBINSON, Cliff
In NBA draft 6-25, 507B2
ROBINSON, Daniel
Rpts Flood jury favored acquittal 2-5, 102B2
ROBINSON, Derek
Scores BL job cut plan 9-10, 686B3
BL fires, strikes ensue 11-19, interim accord reached 11-27, 994G1
ROBINSON, Don
Pirates win NL pennant 10-5, 797D2
In World Series 10-10—10-17, 816C1
ROBINSON, CWO Donald K.
'78 Chesapeake Bay collisn rpts issued 1-20, 140F3; 2-26, 3-2, 240E3
Convicted for '78 collisn 11-3, sentncd 11-5, 887A3
ROBINSON, Edward G. (1893-1973)
Manny opens 4-18, 712C1
ROBINSON, Edward J.
Convictn cited 8-29, 656A1
ROBINSON, Eric L.
Resigns from Cabt 2-22, 133C2
Reinstated in Cabt 2-25, 168C1
ROBINSON, James
GM settles emissns dispute 6-5, 441A3
ROBINSON 3rd, James D.
Amer Express, McGraw-Hill file suits 1-18, 1-19, 53F2, A3
Amer Express bid for McGraw-Hill expires 3-1, 151E3
ROBINSON, Jerry
In NFL draft 5-3, 335G1
ROBINSON, John
On Mex oil blow out clean-up 8-16, 608B2
ROBINSON, Larry
Soviets win Challenge Cup 2-11, 118A3
Montreal wins Stanley Cup 5-21, 447B3
ROBINSON, Len (Truck)
Traded to Suns 1-12, 526C2
ROBINSON, Richard
Scores Brown on ex-POW appt 7-13, 593D2
ROBINSON, Ronn
Tip Toes opens 3-26, 712A3
ROBMAN, Steven
Says I opens 2-20, 292F2
ROBSON, Karen
Picnic At Hanging Rock released 2-22, 174D3
ROBUSTELLI, Andy
Young replaces as Giants operatns dir 2-14, 175C2
ROCARD, Michel
Vs Mitterrand at Soclst cong 4-6—4-8, 267E2
ROCHA, Hugo
Denies Unifil lax vs PLO raids 7-27, 592C1
ROCHA Patino, Gen. Hugo
Named Bolivia army chief 11-25, 907F1
ROCHESTER, N.Y.—*See NEW York State*
ROCHESTER (N.Y.), University of
Cancer diagnosis secrecy study rptd 2-26, 218E1
Laser fusion advance rptd 6-16, 692B1
ROCHIN, Aaron
Wins Oscar 4-9, 336B2
ROCKEFELLER, Abby Aldrich (1875-1948)
Son Nelson dies 1-26, 104G1
ROCKEFELLER, David
Brother dies 1-26, 104A2
Shah asked to stay out of US 4-19, 297G3
Iran blames for shah's US entry 11-14, 861C2
Role in shah's US entry rptd 11-18, 879G1
Hosts dinner for Thatcher 12-18, 968D2
Sets Chase retiremt 12-19, 986B2
ROCKEFELLER, Happy (Margaretta Fitler Murphy) (Mrs. Nelson Aldrich)
Husband dies 1-26, 104C2
Husband's will filed 2-9, 173F2
ROCKEFELLER Jr., John D. (1874-1960)
Son Nelson dies 1-26, 104G1
ROCKEFELLER 3rd, John D. (1906-78)
Brother dies 1-26, 104A2
Williamsburg estate willed to foundatn 4-13, 672E2
Lifetime donatns total $94 mln 7-10, 656B3
ROCKEFELLER IV, Gov. John D. (D, W. Va.)
Coal hearings planned 4-10, 263G2
ROCKEFELLER, Laurance
Brother dies 1-26, 104G1
ROCKEFELLER, Mary Todhunter Clark
Ex-husband dies 1-26, 104B2
ROCKEFELLER, Michael (1938-61)
Father dies 1-26, 104B2
ROCKEFELLER, Nelson Aldrich
Dies 1-26, funeral 1-29; facts on 103E3-104E2
Will filed, museums get art 2-9, 173E2
Shrivers buy DC mansn 7-20, 656B3
Marshack publicity job rptd 11-13, 1005A3
ROCKEFELLER, Winthrop (1912-73)
Brother dies 1-26, 104A2

1980

ROBERTSON, Lillie
Guardsman opens 1-3, 136B3
ROBERTSON, Rev. Pat
Political role profiled 9-15, 818F3
ROBERTSON, Paul
TV revenues rptd 2-25, 413A2
ROBERTSON, Robbie
Carny released 6-13, 675B2
ROBERTSON, Scotty
Hired as Pistons coach 6-5, 656F3
ROBERTS v. U.S.
Case decided by Sup Ct 4-15, 306A2
ROBESON, Paul (1898-1976)
Elected to Recording Arts HOF 2-27, 296C3
ROBINS, John
Death Ship released 4-25, 416F2
ROBINSON, A. R. N.
Party wins Tobago parlt vote 11-24, 923B3
ROBINSON Jr., Judge Aubrey E.
Blocks Carter oil import fee 5-13, 366A1
Dismisses steel trigger price return suit 5-16, 455E3
Cong overrides Carter veto of oil import fee bar 6-5, 6-6, 437E1
Oil import fee proposal dropped 6-19, 551D3
ROBINSON, Curtis Lee
Convicted, sentence suspended 10-2, 884F3
ROBINSON, Derek
BL bars reinstatemt 2-7, 117B3
BL workers reject strike 2-20, 150D1
ROBINSON, Eric
Ousted from Australia Cabt 11-2, 857F2
Sparkes scores 11-11, 885B2
ROBINSON, Francis
Dies 5-14, 448E2
ROBINSON, Frank
Wills hired as Mariners mgr 8-4, 926A2
ROBINSON, Gregory (d. 1978)
Layton faces murder chrgs 5-22, 407G3
ROBINSON, James
Adamson convicted 10-17, 860G3
ROBINSON, Rep. James Kenneth (R, Va.)
Reelected 11-4, 844D3
ROBINSON, John
Defends USC athletic admissns policy 10-29, 875F2
ROBINSON, Larry
In NHL All-Star game 2-5, 198F2
Named NHL top defenseman 6-6, 488C1
ROBISON, James
Murder convictn overturned 2-25, 214B3
Political role profiled 9-15, 818F3
ROBOZ, Thomas N.
US-China textile pact 9-18, 707F1
ROBSON, Michael
39 Steps released 5-2, 416F3
ROCA, Roberto
Salvadoran leftists launch offensive 12-26, 993D2
ROCARD, Michel
Soclsts meet 1-12—1-13, 57G3
Pres bid noted 6-30, 522E1
Withdraws pres bid, backs Mitterrand 11-8, 886B2
ROCHE, Mal
Named ASL top Amer player 9-8, 771F1
ROCHESTER—*See New York*
ROCHESTER (N.Y.), University of
'79 endowmt earnings rptd 3-24, 319B2
Marxist historian denied Md faculty post 6-12, 638D3
Alan Valentine dies 7-14, 608E3
ROCHEV, Vasily
Wins Olympic medal 2-14, 155A3
ROCKEFELLER, David
Nixon becomes NYC resident 2-14, 199D3
Iran chrgs plot vs shah's extraditn 3-22, 217G1
Chase replacmt named 6-25, 600D2
ROCKEFELLER IV, Gov. John D. (Jay) (D, W. Va.)
State of State message 1-9, 484B2
Reelected 11-4, 845F3, 847D1, 850G2
ROCKEFELLER, Nelson Aldrich (1909-79)
Kissinger records access blocked by Sup Ct 3-3, 209D3
Ford on pres-vp frictn 7-14, 530D1
Grandson arrested for drunk driving 8-18, 908C3
ROCKEFELLER, Steven C.
Arrested on drunk driving chrgs 8-18, denied pub defender 9-22, 908B3

1976

ROCKEFELLERS, The (book)
On best-seller list 12-5, 972C2
ROCKEFELLER University (N.Y.)
Malaria parasite cultured 6-1, 423A3
ROCK Island, Ill.—*See ILLINOIS*
ROCKETS—*See ARMAMENTS—Missiles*
ROCKVILLE, Md.—*See MARYLAND*
ROCKVILLE Centre, N.Y.—*See NEW York State*
ROCKWELL International Corp.
Pentagon guest lists issued 2-3, 3-17; Currie, Middendorf censured 3-16, 200A3
'75 arms sales listed 2-6, 147B3
Rpts foreign paymts 4-9, 362E2
SEC lists paymts 5-12, 728F2
3 employes slain in Iran 8-28, 652F1
Defense bill delays B-1 9-22, 707D1
Ford visits B-1 plant 10-7, 763A2
Limited B-1 contract awarded 12-2, 942E1
Pentagaon sets curb on favors 12-9, 982G3
Top fscl '76 defns contractor 12-21, 961B3
RODGERS III, Harry W.
Mistrial declared 12-7, 922C3
RODGERS, William
Named UK transport secy 9-10, 693E3, 694A1
RODGERS, William A.
Mistrial declared 12-7, 922C3
RODHELM Reiss Inc.
Air Manila crash kills 46 Kentron employes 6-4, 736B2
RODINA, Irina
Wins Olympic medal 2-7, 159B1
RODINO Jr., Rep. Peter Wallace (D, N.J.)
Scores gun control bill vote 3-2, 170A2
Carter mtg re vp spot set 7-8, 489F3; declines 7-12, 506A2
Nominates Carter at conv 7-14, 505F2
Mondale scores GOP ticket on Watergate 10-5, 743E3
Parades with Mondale 10-10, 763C3
Reelected 11-2, 830E1
RODMAN, Charles G.
Named Grant trustee 4-13, 984F3
RODMAN, Peter
At Kissinger-Vorster mtg 6-23—6-24, 446C3
RODRIGUEZ, Aniceto
At intl soc dems mtg 5-23—5-25, 449C3
RODRIGUEZ, Carlos Rafael
Rpts on Cuba advisers in Angola 1-10, 138F1
Vows contd MPLA aid 1-11, 16E3
With Castro in E Eur, Africa 3-6—3-16, 251A3
RODRIGUEZ, Emilio
Acts re Basque unrest 9-16—9-20, 775A1
RODRIGUEZ, Fernando
Murdered 6-15, 522C2
RODRIGUEZ, Hector
Wins Olympic medal 7-30, 574G3
RODRIGUEZ, Jorge Antonio
Arrested 7-20, dies 7-25; torture chrgd 7-27, 592B3
Police seized in torture death 8-6, 874A3
RODRIGUEZ, Col. Manuel Alfonso
Seized in US 5-15, arraigned 5-16; replaced as mil chief 5-22, 401F1-E2
Sentenced 11-23, 1012C3
RODRIGUEZ Aponte, Salvador
Mari Bras asks dismissal 8-2, 994G3
RODRIGUEZ Couceiro, Jose Antonio
Argentina detains 11-7, 997A1
RODRIGUEZ de Valcarcel, Alejandro
Dies 10-22, 1015E2
RODRIGUEZ Fabregat, Enrique
Dies 11-21, 970B3
RODRIGUEZ Lara, Gen. Guillermo
Hands over power 1-9, formally ousted 1-11, 28D1
'75 plotters amnestied 1-21, 1-22, 4-10, 363B3, D3
Civilian state govs named 3-8, 363A3
RODRIGUEZ Rey, Brig. Gen. Luis
Suspended 10-27, Lockheed paymt rptd 11-6, 909E1
ROE, Rep. Robert A. (D, N.J.)
Reelected 11-2, 830E1
ROEHLISBERGER, Juerg
Wins Olympic medal 7-28, 575A1
ROEL, Santiago
Mexico forgn min 12-2, 906G3

1977

ROCKEFELLER Foundation (N.Y.)
Soper dies 2-9, 164E3
ROCKEFELLER University (N.Y.)
Uhlenbeck gets Medal of Sci 11-22, 952C1
ROCKETS—*See ARMAMENTS—Missiles*
ROCKWELL International Corp.
Layoffs seen re B-1 veto 6-30, 514F3
ROCKY (film)
Top-grossing film 2-2, 120D3; 3-9, 184D3; 4-6, 264E1; 4-27, 356E2; 6-1, 452C2
Wins Oscars 3-28, 264B1
ROCKY Mountain Spotted Fever—*See MEDICINE—Diseases*
RODGERS 3rd, Harry W.
Convicted 8-23, 652F1, A2
Sentenced 10-7, 807D2 ★
RODGERS, William A.
Convicted 8-23, 652F1, A2
Sentenced 10-7, 807D2
RODINO Jr., Rep. Peter Wallace (D, N.J.)
'76 spec interest gifts rptd 2-4, 128G3, 129D2
On Nixon-Frost interview 5-4, 367C3
RODRIGUEZ, Juan
Zarate TKOs 12-2, 970D3
RODRIGUEZ, Ruben Alfonso
Vote fraud chrgd 2-21, 181B2
RODRIQUEZ, Santos
Death rptd 9-29, 821D1
RODRIGUEZ Figueroa, Gen. Leonidas (ret.)
Expelled 1-8, 46A3, C3
RODRIGUEZ Verdes, Jesus
Expelled 1-12, 42F3
ROE, Rep. Robert A. (D, N.J.)
Loses primary for gov 6-7, 446C3
ROEL, Santiago
Sees US envoy Young 8-7—8-8, 646C2
ROELO, Alonso
Asks Somoza-opposítn 'dialogue' 10-26, 864D2

1978

ROCKEFELLER Center Inc.
Radio City Music Hall Corp.—*See separate listing*
ROCKEFELLER Commission
CIA spying on Black Panthers rptd 3-17, 243F2
ROCKEFELLER Foundation (N.Y.)
Study backs breeder reactors 5-10, 346B3
Rockefeller 3d dies 7-10, 620D3
ROCKEFELLER University (N.Y.)
Lederberg named pres 1-18, 172A2
ROCKETS—*See ARMAMENTS—Missiles*
ROCKFORD Files, The (TV series)
Wins Emmy 9-17, 1030F1
ROCKWELL, George L.
Dies 3-3, 252D3
ROCKWELL, George Lincoln (1918-67)
Father dies 3-3, 252D3
ROCKWELL, Norman
Dies 11-8, 972E3
ROCKWELL, Willard F.
Dies 10-16, 888D3
ROCKWELL Jr., Willard F.
Father dies 10-16, 888D3
ROCKWELL International Corp.
6th in '77 defns contracts 3-28, 224F2
Rockwell dies 10-16, 888D3
Indicted on price fixing 11-1, 935A3
ROCKY (film)
Top United Artists execs quit 1-13, 1-16, 75B3
RODENTS
Ala rabies epidemic rptd 11-10, 992E2
RODERICK, David M.
'77 trigger price remark cited 1-3, 3F2
Scores trigger plan 12-28, 1005B3
RODGERS, Bill
Wins Boston Marathon 4-17, 692G2
RODGERS, Mary
Working opens 5-14, 887E3
RODGERS, Richard
Gives Arts Inst $1 mln endowmt 5-1, 335E3 ★
RODHE, Birgit
Swedish dep educ min 10-18, 822A3
RODIN, Auguste (1840-1917)
Sculptures stolen 1-21, 2-20, 335C1
RODINO Jr., Rep. Peter Wallace (D, N.J.)
LEAA revision proposed 7-10, 525D1
Conservative group rates low 10-24, 865B3
Reelected 11-7, 851B3
RODNINA, Irina
Wins world figure-skating title 3-9, 316E3
RODRIGUEZ, Brenda Domecq de
Kidnaped 10-30, rescued 11-12, 926C3
RODRIGUEZ, Carlos Alberto
Murdered 9-18, 823A3
Univ offcls seized in murder 10-21, 881E2
RODRIGUEZ, Carlos Rafael
Denies US chrgs on Zaire 5-30, 418E1
RODRIGUEZ, Jorge Antonio (d. 1976)
Intell agents jailed for death 2-3, 395B2
RODRIGUEZ, Gen. Leonidas (ret.)
Arrest ordrd 5-25, seized 6-18, 475E1
RODRIGUEZ, Ruben Alfonso
Assassinated 9-16, 823G2
RODRIGUEZ, Santos (d. 1973)
US drops dual prosecutn of Dallas cop 7-14, 991D3
RODRIGUEZ Arevalo, Reyes
Sets Honduras pres bid 1-20, 94E3
RODRIGUEZ Sahagun, Agustin
Named Spain indus min 2-24, 394G2
RODRIGUEZ Soldevilla, Jose
DR health min 8-16, 648D2
RODRIGUEZ Varela, Alberto
Argentina justice min 11-6, 865D2
ROE, Rep. Robert A. (D. N.J.)
Reelected 11-7, 851A3

1979

ROCKEFELLER Commission
CIA domestic spying disclosed 3-9, 207D2
ROCKEFELLER Foundation (N.Y.)
Knowles dies 3-6, 272A3
ROCKETS—*See ARMAMENTS–Missiles*
ROCKETT, Pat
Traded to Blue Jays 12-5, 1002E2
ROCK Island and Pacific Railroad—*See CHICAGO, Rock Island and Pacific Railroad*
ROCK Springs, Wyo.—*See WYOMING*
ROCKWELL Jr., Willard F.
On '78 top-paid execs list 5-14, 347F3
ROCKWELL International Corp.
Rockwell on '78 top-paid execs list 5-14, 347F3
ROCKY II (film)
Released 6-15, 820B3
Top-grossing film 6-27, 548G3
ROCKY Flats Nuclear Weapons Facility—*See COLORADO–Atomic Energy*
ROCKY Mountain News, The (Denver, Colo. newspaper)
Child abuse study rptd 1-21, 93E3
RODAK, Michael
Issues financial disclosures for 8 Sup Ct justices 5-15, 5-16, 383B2
Sup Ct workforce data rptd 6-11, 464G1
RODBERG, Leonard S.
Sees jobs gain in solar energy use 4-21, 419B1
RODDAM, Frank
Quadrophenia released 11-2, 1008B1
RODDENBERRY, Gene
Star Trek released 12-8, 1008F1
RODERICK, David M.
In Peking for US Steel talks 1-1, contract signed 1-5, 7E1
On EPA cleanup pact 5-22, 385D2, F2
Rpts Texaco chem venture 11-14, 941D3
On plant closings, layoffs 11-27, sets '80s strategy 12-5, 941D2, B3
RODGERS, Bill
Wins Boston Marathon, sets Amer record 4-16; wins NYC Marathon 10-21, 911C3, E3
RODGERS, Peter
On E Timor famine 11-6, 856E1
RODGERS, Richard
I Remember Mama opens 5-31, 711G3
Oklahoma! opens 12-13, 1007D2
Dies 12-30, 1008D3
RODGERS, William
Callaghan bars wage-price freeze 1-30, 75E3
Channel tunnel planned 2-9, 135B3
RODINO Jr., Rep. Peter Wallace (D, N.J.)
Judiciary Com chrmn 1-24, 71D1
RODNINA, Irina
Not in world figure-skating champs 3-14, 391G3
RODRIGUES, Julio V.
Chrgd with arson 3-30, 316C3
RODRIGUEZ, Luis
Black hole at galaxy cntr seen 3-31, 290E1
RODRIGUEZ, Paul
Loses parlt electn 11-21, 907C1
RODRIGUEZ, Ricardo
Panama Canal Comm member 12-6, 939D1
RODRIGUEZ Cristobal, Angel
Found dead in jail 11-11, probes ordrd 11-18, 11-23, 904B3
Natlst ambush kills 2 US sailors 12-3, 924B3
RODRIGUEZ Garcia, Alfonso
Arrested 7-27, 585C3
RODRIGUEZ Morales, Claudio
PR natlst exchng denied 9-6, 666A2*
Released 9-17, 706G3
RODRIGUEZ Navarro, Reinaldo
Venez labor min 3-10, 192C3
RODRIGUEZ Sahagun, Agustin
Cancels Armed Forces Day 5-27, 428G2*
ROEL Garcia, Santiago
Ousted as Mex forgn secy 5-16, 408B3
US amb to Mex resigns 10-8, 793C3

1980

ROCKEFELLER Center Inc.
Cable-TV unit wins BBC rights 12-11, 1002C3
ROCKEFELLER Family Fund
USW dissident funding suit refused by Sup Ct 3-31, 291B3
ROCKEFELLER Foundation (N.Y.)
Lyman named pres 1-26, 200D1
ROCKEFELLER University (N.Y.)
Dr Wm Stein dies 2-2, 176D3
'79 endowmt earnings rptd 3-24, 319C2
ROCKESTRA Theme (recording)
Wings win Grammy 2-27, 296C3
ROCKETS—*See ARMAMENTS–Missiles*
ROCKFORD Files, The (TV series)
Garner assaulted 1-16, 200E1
ROCKHILL Native (racehorse)
3d in Belmont Stakes 6-7, 447A3
ROCKLAND County—*See New York*
ROCKLER, Walter J.
On Nazi search deadline 1-16, 228F2
ROCKWELL Jr., Willard F.
SCM proxy contest defeat rptd 11-24, 985C3
ROCKWELL International Corp.
Job bias suit settled 9-26, 746G3
Serck trust suit setlmt reached 10-1, 917G1
Ex-chrmn rptd in SCM proxy contest 11-24, 985C3
NYC subway damages awarded 12-24, 985A3
ROCK With You (recording)
On best-seller list 1-2, 40F3; 2-6, 120F3
ROCKY Flats Nuclear Weapons Facility—*See COLORADO–Atomic Energy & Safeguards*
ROCKY II (film)
'79 top domestic rental film 2-6, 120G2
ROCKY Mountain Junior College (Billings, Mont.)
Purdue transcript scandal rptd 1-23, 469E2
ROCKY Mountain News (Denver, Colo.)
Reagan pres endorsemt rptd 11-1, 841G3
RODDENBERRY, Gene
Star Trek on best-seller list 1-13, 40C3
RODELL, Fred
Dies 6-4, 528D3
RODERICK, David M.
Withdraws dumping complaint 9-30, 740F3
RODGERS, Bill
Wins Cherry Blossom, sets US record 3-30; wins Boston men's title, scores Ruiz 4-21, 527A2
Scores USOC boycott vote 4-12, 283E2
5th in NYC Marathon; Salazar breaks record 10-26, 890F3
RODGERS 3rd, Harry W.
Appeal refused by Sup Ct 4-14, 307B1
RODGERS, William
Labor split on cruise missiles 6-17, 487B1
Scores Trident purchase 7-15, 544E2
Liberals woo Labor dissidents 9-12, 708B2
Williams bars Labor candidacy 11-28, 921F3, 922B1
In Labor shadow Cabt 12-4, 942E2
RODGERS, William A.
Appeal refused by Sup Ct 4-14, 307B1
RODGERS v. U.S.
Case refused by Sup Ct 4-14, 307C1
RODINO Jr., Rep. Peter Wallace (D, N.J.)
Vs Abscam evidence request res 2-27, 143A3
Wins primary 6-3, 439A3
Reelected 11-4, 843B3
RODNEY, Donald
Arrested 6-24, brother's death controversy continues 10-6, 791A2
RODNEY, Walter
Killed 6-13, 469F1
Brother arrested 6-24, death controversy continues 10-6, 791A2
RODNINA, Irina
Regains Eur figure skating title 1-23, withdraws from world competitn 3-12, 470F2
Wins Olympic medal 2-17, 155F3
RODRIGUEZ, Alicia
Sentenced 8-4, 601E1
Indicted 12-10, 963F3
RODRIGUEZ, Guillermo
Kate Smith estate feud setld 9-4, 908C2
RODRIGUEZ, Ida Luz
Arrested 4-4, 308G3
Convicted 7-30, 601D1
Indicted 12-10, 963F3
RODRIGUEZ, Jose
Wins Olympic medal 8-1, 623B1
RODRIGUEZ, Kathryn
Kate Smith estate feud setld 9-4, 908C2
RODRIGUEZ, Simon
Freed 3-30, 253E2
RODRIGUEZ Arias, Alfredo
Heartaches of a Pussycat opens 3-19, 392A3
RODRIGUEZ Macias, Silvano
Arrested in El Salvador alien case 7-11, 560F2
RODRIGUEZ Sahagun, Agustin
Denies mil coup plot rumor 1-25, 101B2
ROE, Rep. Robert A. (D, N.J.)
Reelected 11-4, 843B3
ROEDER, Lt. Col. David M.
Iranians hint Viet war crimes trial 1-4, 29G3
ROEG, Nicholas
Bad Timing released 9-21, 836D2
ROELOFSE, Eugene
Biko MD's probe squashed 6-29, 525D1
ROEMER, Charles (Buddy)
Faces La US House runoff 9-13, 724G2
Elected to US House 11-4, 842F3, 849D3
ROEMER II, Charles E.
Indicted in Brilab probe 6-17, 454E3, G3

1976

ROGER, Col.
France denies spy ring link 1-9, 45D2
ROGERS, Rep. Paul G. (D, Fla.)
Reelected 11-2, 829C2
ROGERS, William D.
At mtg re Rhodesia fund 10-5—10-7, 781B3
ROGERS, William P.
Japan newsman's '74 acquittal reversed 7-20, 539F1
ROGOV, Alexander
Wins Olympic medal 7-30, 574E1
ROGOVIN, Mitchell
Denies threats vs Pike 3-9, 217C1
Cited in Schorr probe testimony 7-20, 748F3
ROHATYN, Felix G.
Presents NE aid plan 11-14, 864D3
Visits Carter 12-28, 978D2
ROHLFING, Frederick W.
Loses election 11-2, 825C1
ROHM & Haas Co.
SEC lists paymts 5-12, 728F2
ROHMER, Eric
Wins Cannes film award 5-28, 460G1
ROJAS Pinilla, Gen. Gustavo (d. 1975)
Electn results 4-20, 310G3
ROJO Lugo, Jorge
Mexico agri reform min 12-2, 907A1
ROLA-Jensen Co.—*See PEMCOR Inc.*
ROLFE, Sidney E.
Dies 3-10, 240F3
ROLLAND, Hector
UDR backs capital gains tax 6-9, 418E1
ROLLING Stone (magazine)
Hearst's pre-arrest life rptd 4-25, 368E1
Butz resigns re racist remark 10-4, 743G3
ROLLINS, John
'72 campaign gift listed 4-25, 688B1
ROLLINS Inc.
Admits Mexico payoff 3-3, 419D3
SEC lists paymts 5-12, 729A1
ROLLNICK, Gabriele
Escapes from jail 7-7, 593E3
ROLLS-Royce Ltd.
US car dumping chrgs end 5-4, 320F3, 321D2
Sovt contract rptd 12-24, 1011A2

ROMAN Catholic Church—*See also PAUL VI, Pope*
Vatican statemt on sex 1-15, Rabbinical Cncl backs 1-26, 124B2, C2
Pl deports 2 priests 103C2
Polish dvpts 1-25, 2-10, 3-21, 3-25, 268A1, D1, D2, A3
Pope names 2 archbps 2-12, 2-17, 21 cardinals 4-27, 336G1
'Albanianism' upheld 3-17, 332A1
Laos govt accuses 3-29, 267E3
Pl torture chrgd 4-23, 313C3
Vatican vs CP electns 5-11—5-25, reactn 5-24, 6-1, 402D3
Algeria bans pvt schls 5-12, 455C1
New cardinals installed 5-24, 423G3
Pope scores traditionalism, Lefebvre 5-24, 424B1
Portugal Archbp backs govt 7-22, 558E2

1977

ROENICKE, Gary
Traded to Orioles 12-7, 990E1
ROESCH, Otto
Named Austria defns min 5-31, 425D1
ROGALSKY, Ivan N.
Arrested 1-7, 41A3
ROGERS, Gen. Bernard W.
Lauds volunteer army, women's role 4-6, 343F1
S Korea missile exit starts 4-14, 306A2
Gen Starry reprimanded 6-17, 483A1
ROGERS, Bill
2d in Kemper Open 6-5, 676E1
ROGERS, Maj. Gen. Charles C.
Army ROTC enrolmt rptd up 5-20, 421C2
ROGERS, Dilworth T.
Age-bias judgmt reversed 1-30, 279A1
ROGERS, Rep. Paul G. (D, Fla.)
DNA bill stalled 10-24, 846A3
On med student transfer rule 12-7, 959A3
ROGERS, Steve
NL pitching ldr 10-2, 926E3
ROGERS, William J.
Scores Panama Canal pact 9-16, 716D3
ROGERS, William P.
Rabin on Carter Mideast plan 3-14, 187G2
Nixon-Frost TV interview 5-12, 386A1
Lies re Viet peace talks chrgd 5-14, 403B3
At Panama Canal pact signing 9-7, 677E1
ROGNONI, Giancarlo
Arrested in Spain 2-22, 307B2
ROHATYN, Felix G.
On NYC debt repaymt plan 3-4, 3-10, 193A2, C2
ITT suit settled 3-4, 194C3
ROHM & Haas Co.
Hercules buys Warren-Teed 7-19, 650F3
ROHR Industries Inc.
'75, '76 losses rptd 340C2
ROHRER, Glen Roy
On US E Eur spying 1-7, 19G3
RO Jae Hyun, Gen.
S Korea defense min 12-20, 1017E1
ROJAS, Julio
Freed 1-27, 'house arrest' chrgd 2-16, 167D3
ROJO Lugo, Jorge
Cts to resolve land disputes 1-3, 65F2
ROLLING Stone (magazine)
Jack Ford joins staff 2-24, 354C2
CIA press links rptd 9-12, 720F2-721C1
ROLLING Stones (music group)
Margaret Trudeau at concert 3-5, 281D3
ROLLING Thunder (film)
Top-grossing film 10-19, 872G3
ROLLINS, Hazel R.
Named FEA asst admin 7-14, confrmd 8-4, 626D3
ROLLINS, Wayne
In NBA draft 6-10, 584B2
ROLLINS Environmental Services Inc.
Chemical plant blast 12-8, 1023D3
ROM-Amer Pharmaceuticals Ltd.
FDA approval bid dropped 6-2, 508D3

ROMAN Catholic Church—*See also PAUL VI, Pope*
Vatican land speculatn scored 1-6, 8B3
Episcopal female ordinatn scored 1-11, 119B3
Anglican-Cath comm urges papal primacy 1-18, 119D3
Pl bishops meet 1-25—1-28, assail govt 2-6, 99D3
Vatican study bars female ordinatn 1-27, 119C2
Vatican boosts Sovt bloc broadcasts 2-16, 471E2
Canada archbp gives absolutn 3-15, 375B2
S Korean priests protest govt 4-18, 306E1
Anglican ldr sees Pope, urges intercommunion 4-28—4-29, 374F2

1978

ROGER, Guy
Convicted 5-3, 396B1
ROGERS, Gen. Bernard W.
Gen Singlaub resigns 4-28, 321G2
On discipline actns vs blacks 8-15, 683F1
ROGERS, Bill
Wins Hope Desert Classic 2-13, 355C3
2d in Western Open 7-3, 672C3
ROGERS, George
UK-Scandinavia air pacts OKd 12-22, 1017C2
ROGERS, Harry
Named Canada comptroller-gen 2-20, 145E3
Macdonell lauds apptmt 11-23, 921F3
ROGERS, Kenny
Wins Grammy 2-24, 316A1
ROGERS, Rep. Paul (D, Fla.)
Hosp cost lid rejected by com 7-18, 550G3
ROGERS, Ray
Mitchell quits Stevens bd, cites union pressure 3-21, 205E1
ROGERS, Sharon
Loses Sen primary in W Va 5-9, 363B1
ROGERS, Steve
Rose gets 3000th hit 5-5, 559G3
NL pitching ldr 10-2, 928F2
ROGERS, Wayne
Once In Paris released 11-9, 970E2
ROGERS, William P(ierce)
Disputes Haldeman on '69 Sovt policy 2-16, 124B2
ROGNONI, Pedro
Accepts Panama Canal pacts 4-20, 274A2
ROGNONI, Virginio
Named Italy Interior min 6-13, sworn 6-14, 558B2
ROHATYN, Felix G.
NYC fiscal crisis role cited 86B3
Sees '79 NYC bankruptcy 1-11, 87F2
Blumenthal proposes NYC long-term loan guarantees 3-2, Carter signs bill 8-8, 608C1, F2
ROHDE, Helmut
Resigns as W Ger educ min 2-3, 93F2
ROHMER, Eric
Perceval released 10-6, 1030C3
RO Jae Hyun
In US mil talks, cites N Korea threat 7-26—7-27, 595B1
ROJINSKI, Serge
Sentenced 7-25, 649G2
ROLAND, Jim
Named ASL MVP 8-7, 707G3
ROLANDIS, Nicos
Named Cyprus forgn min 3-8, 189F1, A2
Scores US on Turkey arms embargo end 4-5, 277F1
ROLAND Missile—*See ARMAMENTS—Missiles*
ROLDOS, Jaime
Wins pres vote 7-16, to face Duran in runoff 7-18, 556F3
Home fired on 7-17, 557D1
Cotopaxi pres votes rptd annulled 8-8, 671A3
Electoral ct quits, chrgs vote fraud; new vote count, early runoff set 9-22, 777D1
CFP local offcls take office 9-29, 777D1
Bomb blasts hit backers 9-29, 777E1
Pres runoff set, vote annulmt overruled 10-5; scores lateness 10-13, 881B2
To face Duran in runoff 11-15, 989C3
Murder plot chrgs vs Americans dropped 12-22, 1021D3
ROLF, David E.
Stockbroker liability case refused by Sup Ct 12-4, 959B1
ROLLE, Darrell
In Cabt com on investmt 3-6, 194A2
ROLLING Stone (magazine)
India confrms Outside rpt of '65 A-device loss 4-17, 288C2
ROLLING Stones (singing group)
Some Girls on best-seller list 7-5, 580A1; 8-2, 620F1; 9-6, 708F1; 10-11, 800F3; 11-8, 888D1
Miss You on best-seller list 8-2, 620F1; 9-6, 708E1
Richards' heroin sentnc suspended 10-24, benefit OKd 10-26, 842E1
ROLLNICK, Gabriele
Arrested in Bulgaria, extradited 6-22, 500B1
ROLLS-Royce Ltd.
Pan Am buys L-1011 engines 4-4, 264F2
Brit Airways orders Boeing 757s 8-31, 684A2

ROMAN Catholic Church
Czech ldr named, church admin boundaries revised 1-10, 17C3
China curbs rptd eased 2-26, 294D1
French survey rptd 3-24, 352G2
Irish bishops ease stand vs contraceptive sales 4-5, 289A2
4 convicted in W Ger exorcism death 4-21, rites curbed 5-1, 379D3
Moro family appeal cited 5-10, 337D2
Pope at Moro funeral 5-13, 689E2
Italy abortn law denounced 5-18, 375D1
W Ger archbp kidnap plot foiled 6-7, 439A3
Kadar notes eased ties 6-10, 534C3
Prince Michael denied church marriage 6-16, 580F1
Westminster mass protested 7-6, 557E3
Pope scores USSR dissident trials 7-16, 543B1

1979

ROENICKE, Gary
In World Series 10-10–10-17, 816D2
ROETTGER, Judge Norman C.
Enjoins Knoetze visa revocatn 1-11, 79G2
ROGERS, Gen. Bernard W.
Named NATO cmdr 2-28, 147C3
Urges limited draft 3-13, 307A2
Meyer elevated to Army chief 5-2, 347G2
Sees Sovt mil dominance in '80s 6-15, 460C1
On Army 'quick-strike' force 6-21, 482C3
Army reserve recruiting failure rptd 8-23, 649D3
ROGERS, Bill
2d in Doral Open 3-18, Byron Nelson 5-13, 587G1, F2
2d in World Series of Golf 9-30, Tex Open 10-7; wins World Match Play title 10-14, 969B3, 970F1, G1
PGA top money winner 11-30, 969F2
ROGERS, Buddy
Mary Pickford dies 5-29, 432D3
ROGERS, Lee
Wilson chrgd re kickbacks 12-13, 945F2
ROGERS, Michael
Killer Fish released 12-7, 1007F3
ROGERS, Rosemary
Insiders on best-seller list 2-4, 120C3; 3-4 173F3
ROGERS, Steve
NL pitching ldr 9-30, 955G2
ROGERS, William Pierce
On Mex-Fla vegetable growers rift 7-19, 553E2
ROGNONI, Virginio
Moro parlt probe OKd 2-9, 136B1
Special anti-kidnaping measures barred 9-12, 709E2*, G2
ROGOVIN, Mitchell
NY disco owner pleads guilty to tax chrgs 11-2, 891C3
ROHL, Randy
Takes gay date to HS prom 5-3, 392C3
ROLAND, Robert
Vs waste cleanup bill 6-13, 441C2
ROLAND Missile—*See ARMAMENTS–Missiles*
ROLDOS Aguilera, Jaime (Ecuadorian president)
US alleged murder plotters freed 1-5, 62A3
Wins Ecuador pres bid 4-29, 329D3*
Spain premr visits 8-9–8-13, 613D2, 654D2
Sworn pres; pledges econ dvpt, social justice 8-10, 613C2-C3
Cabt resigns 11-29; meets Bucaram 12-4, names new Cabt 12-9, 967A3-968A1
ROLF, Ida P.
Dies 3-19, 272E3
ROLLE, Esther
Wins Emmy 9-9, 858E2
ROLLER Boogie (film)
Released 12-19, 1008C1
ROLLING Stone (magazine)
Look partial merger completed 5-7, 430E3
Look ends tie, Wenner fired 7-3, 640B3
ROLLING Stones (singing group)
Jagger divorce final 11-2, 1006C1
ROLLINS, Howard E.
GR Point opens 4-16, 711E3
ROLLS-Royce Ltd.
Colne plant strike continues 1-8, 20C3
Strikes spur lockout 9-19, 729G3
NEB members resign over transfer to Industry Dept 11-20, 949C3
ROMAN, Jo
Kills self 6-10, 521B2

ROMAN Catholic Church
Pope presents 1st encyclical 3-15, 216E3
Pope upholds free choice 4-22, 376C1
Pope names state secy, finance dir 4-30, 376E1
Pope installs 14 new cardinals 6-30, 640A2, B2*
Pope visits Ireland, US; reaffirms traditional stance on birth, marriage issues, priestly celibacy, female ordinatn 10-1–10-7, 757F1-760C1
Coll of Cardinals mtg ends; Vatican $20 mln deficit rptd 11-9, 931C1
Shroud of Turin age test awaited 11-21, 931G2
Jesuits ordrd to curb liberal theology 12-7, 999C3

1980

ROENNING, Froede
Wins Olympic medal 2-19, 156A1
ROETHLISBERGER, Juerg
Wins Olympic medal 7-28, 623C1
ROGERS, Gen. Bernard
Greece rejoins NATO mil wing 10-20, 800E1
ROGERS, Bill
2d in Tallahassee Open 4-21, 714F3
2d in Byron Nelson Classic 5-11, 412G3
Wins Japan Open 9-7, 972G1
ROGERS, Darryl
Hired as Ariz State football coach 1-17, 175F2
ROGERS, David
Charlie & Algernon opens 9-14, 892B3
ROGERS, George
Wins Heisman Trophy 12-1, 999D2
South Carolina loses Gator Bowl 12-30, 999E3
ROGERS, Gil
Mecca opens 2-2, 136D3
ROGERS, Harold
Elected to US House 11-4, 842E4, 849B3
ROGERS, Jim
Loses US House electn 11-4, 852F1
ROGERS, Kenny
Kenny on best-seller list 1-2, 40F3
Wins Grammy 2-27, 296D3
Lady on best-seller list 12-3, 948A3
Greatest Hits on best-seller list 12-3, 948B3
ROGERS, Rosemary
Lost Love, Last Love on best-seller list 12-7, 948F3
ROGERS, Roy
Nolan dies 6-16, 528A3
ROGERS, Steve
NL pitching ldr 10-6, 926G2
ROGERS, William D.
Heads El Salvador murder probe 12-6—12-7, 941E2
ROGERS, William P.
Campaigns with Reagan 8-20, 802C1
ROGNONI, Virginio
Italy interior min 4-4, 275F3
Submits resignatn on quake controversy, Forlani refuses 11-27, 943F2
ROGOSIN, Roy M.
Quick Change opens 10-30, 892D3
ROGOVIN, Mitchell
3 Mile I study issued 1-24, 550G3
Anderson bank loan plan fails 10-2, plan abandoned 10-15, 818F1
ROHATYN, Felix G.
Vs NYC pub bond sale 9-10, 743B2
ROHMER, Sax
Fiendish Plot of Dr Fu Manchu released 8-8, 675E2
ROHM & Haas Co.
Unpatented key ingredient monopoly backed by Sup Ct 6-27, 511C2
ROJAS, Ricardo
Wins Olympic medal 8-2, 622A2
ROJAS Galdames, Rene
Named Chile forgn min 3-28, 256A1
ROJAS Marcos, Alejandro
Andalusian vote called 'moral victory' 2-28, 174C3
Sees Suarez, Andalusian autonomy set for '81 10-23, 832E1
ROLAND, Nicholas P.
Charged in GSA scandal 1-15, 112F1
ROLANDIS, Nicos
Cabt shuffled 9-9, 749F2
ROLAND Missile—*See ARMAMENTS--Missiles*
ROLDOS Aguilera, Jaime (Ecuadorian president)
Calls plebiscite on const reforms, sets new party 4-11, 312A1
Gains parlt support, cancels plebiscite 5-19, 462G2
Condemns Bolivia coup 7-29, 577D1
Attends Santa Marta conf 12-17, 992A3
ROLLE, Esther
Horowitz & Mrs Washn opens 4-2, 392C3
ROLLING Stones (singing group)
Emotional Rescue on best-seller lists 8-13, 640B3
Jagger French manor house purchase rptd 9-18, 908A3
ROLLINS College (Winter Park, Fla.)
White wins AIAW singles tennis title 6-11, 607E1
ROLLS-Royce Motors
Vickers merger set 6-25, 498G1
ROMAN, Albino
Held hostage in El Salvador 9-17, 708E1
ROMAN, Federico Euro
Wins Olympic medal 7-27, 622F2

ROMAN Catholic Church
Priests barred from politics 5-4, 341A2
Vatican issues statemts on euthanasia 6-26, clergy reassignmt 7-22, 970E1-C2
Bishops family life conf opens 9-26; birth control, annulmts, other issues debated 9-29—10-6, 810C2
Pope scores wedded lust 10-8, controversy ensues 10-11, 10-22, 810C3
Pope sets dispensatn guidelines 10-14, issues social justice encyclical 12-2, 969F3-970E1

1976

Lefebvre suspended 7-24, defies ban 8-29, 655D3
Franzoni defrocked 8-4, 951B2
Scores Milan abortions 8-13, 840E3
Uganda expels 2 Canadian priests 8-13, 874D2
Pope, Coggan dispute female ordinatn 8-20, 756A1
Australia banned Masses held 8-31, 691F3
Lefebvre sees Pope, continues defiance 9-5—11-14; Vatican plea issued 11-30, 9232F2
Hungary church-state dialogue urged 9-18, 947B1
Wyszynski backs workers 9-26, 811D1
Rhodesian bishop sentenced 10-1; Pope regrets 10-2, 812D3
Pope asks Wyszynski to continue 11-1, 932B3
Pl priest seized, radio statns closed; '72-76 total rptd 11-19, 890D1
Poland anti-church stand scored 11-28; Wyszynski backs workers 12-6, 12-12, 966A2
Rhodesia missionaries killed 12-5, 1009D2
Rhodesia arrests Swiss priest 12-8, 1010C1

Jesuits—*See under 'J'*
Latin Developments—*See also 'Church Developments' under BRAZIL, CHILE*
Argentina archbp urges kidnap measures 1-12, 26B1
Argentina rightists vow executns 1-26, 96C1
2 Argentina priests slain 2-13, 2-14; archbp threatened 3-13, 212G1

1977

Pope sees Hungary bishops 5-2, Kadar 6-9, 492B2
Pl bishops seek torture probe 5-13, 468D2
Italy abortn bill defeated 6-7, 527A3
Turkish amb slain 6-9, 565G1-A2
4 inducted as cardinals; '76 inductn revealed 6-27, 768G2
O'Fiaich named Irish Primate 8-22, 728E3
Bishops' synod meets 9-30—10-29, 906A1
Lebanese monk canonized 10-9, 845F3
Israel frees Capucci 11-6, 850G2-C3
Pl CP chrmn captured 11-10, 1019C2

African Developments
Rhodesia missionary killer escapes 1-9, 11G2
Rhodesia sentncs Swiss priest 1-12, 11F2
S Africa church schls desegregate 1-17, 67E1
Police accused in S Africa unrest 1-25, 100A3
Rhodesia rebels slay 7 2-6, burn missn 2-8, 85A1
Rhodesia priests aid kidnaped students 2-6, 85G1
Southn Africa bps back COs 2-9, score apartheid 2-10, 100D2
S Africa integratn set 2-11, schl plan challngd 2-16, 2-22, 145B1
Rhodesia names black bp 2-22, 375A3
Rhodesia missionary's body found 3-1, 223G2
Cardinal Biayenda slain, Pope rues 3-23, 220C2
Rhodesia deports bishop 3-23, 223B3
S Africa schl integratn pact set 3-28, 350B1
Rhodesia missn exodus rptd 4-3, Swiss priest's sentnc cut 4-6, 297B1, C1
Ghana bishops ask civln rule 4-13, 598B2
Namibia students kidnaped 4-20, 349F2
S African bp arrested 4-21, 350B1
Gantin inducted as cardinal 6-27, 768B3
S Africa colored schls to integrate 7-31, 600A2
2 Rhodesia missionaries killed 8-9, 624C2
Rhodesia jails clerics 8-30, frees 9-4; deports nun 9-22, 811G1, C2
Uganda permits freedom 9-20, 805D2
S Africa arrests Mkhtshwa 10-19, 803G3

Latin American Developments—*See also CHILE—Church Developments*
Nicaragua terror chrgd 2-6—3-4, 168F1-G2
Peru group scores Argentine rights abuse 3-3, 259D2
US study on Brazil abuses rptd 3-7, 168A1

1978

'Test-tube baby' reactn rptd 7-25, 597F1
Spain const draft bars state religion 7-27, 706B1
Pope Paul VI dies 8-6; record rptd; photo 601A1; funeral 8-12, 658D2
W Ger '76 papal kidnap plot rptd 8-6, 689A3
Cardinals convene 8-25, praise conclave unity 8-27, 658G1
Cardinal of Venice elected Pope John Paul I 8-26; photo, biog data 657A1-658F1
Vatican aides reappointed 8-28, 658F1
Nikodim dies during papal audience 9-5, 778G1
Polish bishops score censorship 9-17, 749F1
Pope John Paul I dies 9-28, buried 10-4; papal impact noted 746B3
Pope John Paul I's death tied to foul play 10-6, Vatican denies 10-12, 782E1
Cardinal of Krakow elected Pope John Paul II 10-16; photo, biog data 781A1-782A1
Cardinal electioneering rptd 10-16, conclave disunity 10-19, 782B1
Papal ordinatn plans rptd 10-18, Vatican apptmts held open 10-19, 782A1
Spain const OKd, state religion abolished 12-6, 966C3
Poland rptdly censors papal message 12-21, 1019D2

African Developments
Angola closes RC radio, scores bishops 1-27; religious compositn noted 87D3
Rhodesia clergy deaths, other data rptd 3-13, 249C1
Rhodesia missionaries killed 6-2, 455A2
Botswana cleric detained in S Africa 6-26—8-7, 633A3
Rhodesian missionaries killed 6-27; 2 ousted 6-30, 594G2, C3
Equatorial Guinea ban rptd 6-30; Vatican murder chrgs cited 7-24, 596F1
S Africa bishops ask unionists release 7-4, 633F2
Namibia govt ousts priest 7-14, 547B3
'64 papal visit cited 8-6, 601B2
Rhodesia missionary killed 12-26, 1019E3

Ecumenical Developments
US poll backs church activity 3-2, 295C1
Papal efforts cited 8-6, 601A2
Pope John Paul I backs movemt 8-27, 658A1

Helsinki Agreement—*See EUROPE—Security and Cooperation*
Latin American Developments
Chile bishops score plebiscite 1-2, 16E3, F3
UK cardinal scores El Salvador arms sale 1-13, 75B1
Nicaragua bishops back gen strike 1-31, 73A3
Honduras officers sentncd in '75 murders 2-2, 194C2

1979

Vatican censures liberal theologians 12-18, 999B2-C3

African Developments
Rhodesia missionary found dead, total death toll rptd 1-3, 7E3
Mozambique rift rptd 2-8, 215A3
Burundi expels missnaries 6-12, 470D1
Zimbabwe rebel kidnap rptd 7-23, 638C2
Zimbabwe missnaries freed 9-11, 718C2
Guinea archbp Tchidimbo freed 10-6, 796A3

Asian Developments
Pak pres scorns Bhutto clemency plea 2-14, 116B2
Jesuits seek return to China 3-16, 218C1
Vatican rejcts Chinese bishop 8-17; Pope seeks ties, church recognitn disputed 8-19—8-21, 639D2-C3
Pl Archbp vs martial law 9-7, 9-14, 710C1
India's Mother Teresa wins Nobel Peace Prize 10-17, 857E3
Pope in Turkey, seeks Eastn Orthodox reunificatn 11-28—11-30, Islam ties 11-29, 930A3

Ecumenical Developments
Pope presents 1st encyclical 3-15, 217D2
Baptism rites agrmt reached 3-31, 375F2
Pope in US, holds prayer svc 10-7, 760A1
Pope in Turkey, seeks Eastn Orthodox reunificatn 11-28—11-30; sees Dimitrios I 11-29, joint statemt 11-30, 930A3

European Developments
Spain Concordat ended 1-3, 61C2
USSR forgn min sees Pope 1-24, 60E2
Moro kidnaping link chrgd 2-7, 97E3
Pope in Poland 6-2—6-7, 413A1-414D1; 6-8—6-10, 435E1
Flemish art stolen from Rome convent 6-3, 656E1
Papal N Ireland visit barred 8-29, 642B1
Pope in Ireland, pleas for end to violence 9-29—10-1, 757C1, 760D1-A3
Michelangelo icon believed found 10-20, 892G1-A2
Czech dissident sentenced 10-23, 802B2
Pope in Turkey, seeks Eastn Orthodox reunificatn 11-28—11-30, Islam ties 11-29, 930A3
W Ger liberal theologian censured 12-18, 999B2
Dutch theologian faces heresy chrgs 12-18, 999A3
French Dominican priest disciplined 12-18, 999B3

Latin American Developments
Beagle Channel mediatn agreed 1-8, envoy returns to Vatican 1-9, 51B3
El Salvador priest, youths killed 1-20; archbp scores govt 1-21, sets mourning 1-22, 59D1
El Salvador chrgd by OAS rights panel 1-22, 58E3
Colombia priest detained 1-24, 115A2

1980

African Developments
Pope in Africa: affirms traditional stance, backs Africanization 5-2—5-10; Zaire mass violence, priests barred from politics 5-4, 341B2, 363B1-364A1

Asian Developments
Clergy reassignmt plan issued 7-22, 970G1

Ecumenical Developments
Dutch bishops bar intercommunion 1-31, 156C3
Pope seeks improved W Ger ties 11-15—11-19, 904F3-905A3

European Developments
Dutch bishops hold Vatican synod 1-14—1-31; traditionalism affirmed, doctrinal disputes cited 1-31, 156G2
W Ger liberal theologian's ouster backed by 7 colleagues, Vatican controversy detailed 2-5, 157A1
Turkey envoy deaths cited 2-6, 197C2
Swiss reject church-state separatn 3-2, 233C1
Polish bishop shuns parlt vote 3-20, 262G3
Ukrainian church ldr named 3-27, 413E3
W Ger setlmt with liberal theologian reached 4-10, 364A2
Turkey amb attacked 4-17, 316G1-A2
USSR detains priest 4-18, 431A2
Pope in France 5-30—6-2, sees Giscard 5-31, addresses UNESCO 6-2, 476F2-477B1
Clergy reassignmt plan issued 7-22, 970F1
Pope backs Polish strikers 8-20, cardinal's message aired 8-21, 625G2, 626B3
Polish cardinal addresses natn, urges calm 8-26, 641D2, 658D2
Poland strike plea distortns chrgd 8-28, 657F1
Poland strike accord reached 8-30, formalized 8-31, 657E2, G2
Yugo lauds Poland strike role 8-31, 659B1
Poland CP shakeup 9-6, 678G2
W Ger bishops enter pol debate 9-13, 712C1
Poland Sunday mass broadcast 9-21, 720G2
Italy Soclst scores abortn stand 10-25, 873B2
Pope in W Ger; seeks ecumenical ties, affirms traditionalism 11-15—11-19; youth ldrs denounce 11-19, 904F3-905A3
Layman named Polish dep premr 11-21, 909B2
Pope visits Italy quake area 11-25, 893B2
Italy quake relief dispute rptd 12-11, 944B1
Polish bishops warn dissidents 12-12, urge moderatn 12-14, 976A1
Polish offcls at '70 riot rites 12-16, 12-17, 976E2, G2

Latin American Developments
Brazil clergy attacks rptd, violence debated 1-11, 95A3
Colombia envoy seized in DR emb raid 2-27, 141B1
Bolivia leftist priest slain 3-22, 272G1
El Salvador archbishop assassinated 3-24, 220E1
Ukrainian church ldr named 3-27, 413E3

1976

US reps chrg Chile repressn vs Christian Dems 3-17; Zalaquett exiled 4-12, 310C2, D2
Vatican receives Cuba amb 3-25, 252B1
Colombia anti-Marxist vote urged 4-16, 311A1
Paraguay chrgs guerrilla links, priest arrests rptd 5-8, 403A2, C2
Argentina refugee list stolen 6-10, 496D1
Argentinians killed 7-4, 495D3
Paraguay bishops score govt 7-12, 557A3
Argentina deaths protested 7-14, 7-22, 2 more priests slain 7-21, 571B2
Argentina bishop dies 8-4; foul play seen 8-6, 9-2, 672E1
Ecuador seizes, expels forgn bishops 8-12—8-14, 692B3-693B1
Argentina ban on Nazi publicatns urged 8-15, 672B2
Argentina arrests US priest; expels 8-19; priest chrgs terrorism 9-2, 672C1
Colombia MD strike opposed 9-12, 731A1
Pope queries Argentina on deaths 9-27, 996C1
Guyana takes over schls 10-1, 1005D2
Argentina arrests, expels Irish priest 10-11—12-3, 996B1
'75-76 repressn rptd up 10-31, 975D1

Middle East Developments—*See 'Vatican' under MIDDLE EAST—INTERNATIONAL Developments*

Northern Ireland Dispute—*See NORTHERN Ireland*

Obituaries
Cogley, John 3-28, 272E3
Dopfner, Julius Cardinal 7-24, 716A3
Lercaro, Giacomo Cardinal 10-18, 970B2
O'Brien, Henry 7-23, 656F3

Spanish Developments—*See SPAIN*

U.S. Developments
'75 church attendance rptd 1-3, 32A3
Bishops challenge abortn law 1-7, 32C3
Religious decline analyzed 3-23, 443F3
2 bishops appointed 5-4, 424C1
Quinlan story rights sold 6-10, 423A3
Pallotine Fathers' fund-raising probed 6-18—10-24, 950E3
Intl Eucharistic Cong 8-1—8-8, 596B2
'Legion' disease rptdly hits 2 at Eucharistic Cong 8-6, 656F2
Bishops protest Ecuador expulsns 8-20, 692B3-G3
Carter sees bishops in DC 8-31, 645C2, D2; Phila church bars 9-7, 664A1
Ex-nun to wed FBI dir 9-4, 680F2
Bishops meet Ford re abortn stand 9-10, 686D1
Bishops assert pol neutrality 9-16, 686G1-B2
Rausch celebrates Letelier mass 9-26, 781A1
Butz remark re Pope cited 10-2, 744G1
Ford, Carter at NYC fete 10-21, 785E1
'Call to Action' conf 10-21—10-23, 859B1
Bishops Conf meets 11-8—11-11, 859E1
Carter support cited 11-11, 845D2
PI ousts 2 missionaries 11-18, 11-20, 890C1
Pope meets Jewish ldrs 11-24, 912D1
Tenn bishop grants absolutn 12-5, 12-12, 951E1-B2

1977

El Salvador priest killed 3-12; church asks probe, chrgs terror 3-17, 207B1
Peru rights rpt issued 3-18, 241B3
El Salvador church asks torture end 4-23, priest attacked 5-11, 373B3, C3
El Salvador guerrilla kidnap plea 4-27, 373D2
El Salvador expels Panama priest 5-6, 373A3
Argentine bishops score abuses 5-7, 388F3
Brazil student protests backed 5-8—5-19, 447G2
Bolivia rights panel formed 5-14, abuses detailed 5-15, 414E2, F2
Brazil holds 2 US missionaries 5-15—5-18, Mrs Carter sees 6-8, 455A2
Brazil archbp honored in US 5-22, 447A3
Nicaragua bishops chrg 'terror' 6-13, 475F3
El Salvador Jesuits threatened 6-21; Jesuits defy, govt takes precautns 7-17—7-21, 580B1
Brazil legalizes divorce 6-23, 525A1
Brazil educator acquitted 6-24, 525C1
El Salvador archbp shuns inaugural, scores govt 7-1; asks prisoner release 7-3, 542F2-A3
El Salvador chrgs Jesuits aid 'leftist terrorism' 7-1, 542G2
Peru bishops score repressn 7-13, 563B2
Lefebvre in Colombia, Chile, Argentina 7-20—7-26, 620F1
Peru bishops vs govt re strikers 7-26, 618A3
Brazil expels US missionary 7-27, police beating denied 8-6, 633F2
Mex drive vs priests chrgd 8-4, 746G1
El Salvador church asks 'persecutn' end 9-1, 710D2
Brazil rights rally smashed 9-18, 740C3
Brazil archbps score univ raids 9-25, 9-27, 840G1
El Salvador bishop chrgs priests re Marxism 10-4, Vatican rebukes 10-8, 844E3
Ecuador labor repressn scored 10-5, 823E3
Nicaragua priests ask pol 'dialogue' 10-19—10-26; rejected 10-26, 10-27, 864C2
Guyana sugar strikers' food rptd seized 11-4, 869G1

Northern Ireland Dispute—*See NORTHERN Ireland*

Obituaries
Carroll, Coleman 7-26, 604G2
Coleman, John 2-23, 164D2
Conway, William Cardinal 4-17, 356G2
Keller, James 2-7, 164C3
Lucey, Robert 8-1, 696B3
Staffa, Dino Cardinal 8-7, 696F3
Thorman, Donald 11-30, 952E3
Traglia, Luigi Cardinal 11-22, 952F3

Polish Developments
Polish bishops score media 9-18, 752D3
Wyszynski sees Gierek 10-29, 885F3
Gierek sees Pope 12-1, 987B1
Clergymen score sexual permissiveness 12-4, 987E1
Wyszynski sees Mrs Carter 12-30, 1001B2

Spanish Developments—*See SPAIN*

Traditionalist Movement
Traditionalists occupy Paris church 2-27, Lefebvre celebrates mass 5-22, 471A1
Lefebvre preaches vs modernism in Geneva 5-30, Rome 6-6, 470E3
Lefebvre warned vs ordinatns 6-20, defies order 6-26, 6-29; papal reactn rptd 7-9, 620C2
Tex church consecrated 7-10, 620F2
US membership cited 7-10, 620A3
Lefebvre in Latin Amer 7-12—7-26, 620F1

U.S. Developments
Bernardin defends female ordination bar 1-27, 119F2
Tenn bp '76 absolutn scored 2-8, 3-25, reactn 4-26, 375E2
Priests back female ordinatn 3-23, 374G3
Proselytism scored, cult trends evaluated 3-28—5-13, 490C2
Carter role re S Korea rights urged 4-19, 305C3
Cath Press Assn conv 4-26—4-29, 470B3
NLRB dispute case refused 5-2, 406C2
Bishops Conf meets; excommunicatn rule dropped, 'Call to Actn' statemt issued 5-3—5-6, 375A1
Female ordinatn support rptd up 5-6, 375A2
Brazil archbp honored 5-22, 477A3
Black installed Miss bishop 6-6, 471B2
Editor fired over press freedom 6-16, 471D1-B2
Neumann canonized 6-19, 731B3
Lefebvre consecrates Tex church; US traditionalist membership cited 7-10, 620F2
Charismatic conf 7-20—7-24, 620A3, D3
Excommunicatn for remarriage ended 11-10, 906D3
Bishops conf OKs new catechism, debates controversial topics, elects new ldr 11-14—11-17, 906E1-C3
Mrs Carter sees Polish cardinal 12-30, 1001B2

1978

Argentina orders non-Caths register 2-14, 208E1
Brazil priests' amnesty demand rejected 2-23, 165F2
El Salvador archbp says rights abuses continue 2-26, 152E2
Argentina prisoner release pressed 3-21, 4-10, 286B1
El Salvador peasant groups deny communism 3-30, 245E1
Brazil archbp sees Carter 3-31, 233E2
Nicaragua archbp shuns Chamorro death probe panel 4-6, 376C2
Nicaragua protesters occupy churches 4-8—4-28, 375C3
El Salvador church seizure sparks govt-RC dispute 4-11—4-18, 723B3 ★
Chile OKs amnesty 4-19, actn on missing asked 4-25, 351E2, A3
Chile rights yr launched 4-25, 351C3
Colombia pres campaign ends 5-28, 413B2
Guatemala bishop on rural clashes 6-1, 497D1
Brazil press censorship ends 6-9, 555D2
Guatemala priest killed 6-30, union ldr 7-22, 722C2 ★, 723E2-F2
UN rights comm ends Chile probe 7-27, 591D2
Pope mtg with El Salvador archbp rptd 8-5, 723F3 ★
'64 papal visit cited 8-6, 601B2
Nicaragua bishops mediate in guerrilla demands 8-22—8-24, fighting 8-30, 658G3, 659D1, F2
Chile bishops ask data on 433 disappearnces 10-12, 795F3
Brazil church backs anti-inflatn petitn 10-13, 836F3
El Salvador church rpts arrests, torture 10-13, 881A3
Chile banned union workers backed 10-23, 1014G2
El Salvador priest killed 11-29, archbp denies guerrilla chrg 12-19, 987A1
Venez editor takes asylum in Vatican emb 12-3, 953D1
Pope asks more Beagle Channel talks 12-12, 979D2; mediatn set 12-22, envoy named 12-23, arrives Argentina 12-26, 999A3

Middle East Developments
Pope meets Israel defns min on Jerusalem 1-12, 10G2
Pope sees Sadat at Vatican 2-13, 98B3
Israel '77 conversn law repeal sought 3-1, 294G1
Leb Christn ldr asks end to Syrian attacks 7-2, 502G2
'64 papal visit cited 8-6, 601A2
Israel asks aid vs Syria in Leb 8-28, 674G1

Northern Ireland Dispute—*See NORTHERN Ireland*

Obituaries
Feeney, Leonard 1-31, 96G1
Frings, Joseph Cardinal 12-17, 1032G2
John Paul I, Pope 9-28, 746B3
Paul VI, Pope 8-6, 601A1
Pi Shu-shih, Ignatius 5-16, 440C3

U.S. Developments
Pallottine priest indicted 1-6, 24G2
'53, '78 cong compositn compared 1-30, 107F2
Laity conf 2-19, broader church role rptd 4-7, 294B3
Poll shows diversity within church 3-2, 294G3
Ellis gets Laetare Medal 3-6, 172F3
House rebuffs Admin schl aid plan 3-20, 202C3
Schl enrollmt drop halted 3-20, 348C3
Fertility rate rptd down 4-15, 295D1
Mondale sees PI bishop 5-3, 360E3
Pallottine priest sentenced 5-9, 380F1-A2
'76 membership growth rptd 6-12, 907B3
'65 papal visit cited 8-6, 601B2
US cardinals support cited re John Paul II's electn 10-16, 782C1
Cornell loses US House seat 11-7, 854A2
Rev McCoy asks US press Somoza resignatn 11-8, 883E3

1979

Pope in DR, Mex 1-25–1-31; opens CELAM mtg 1-27, plays down church pol role 1-28, 67A3
Papal attack on 'liberatn theology' denied 2-1, 2-3, 108B3, F3
Nicaragua, El Salvador prelates backed 2-12, 108D3
CELAM mtg ends; bishops ask repressn, injustice end 2-13, 108E2-B3
PR bishop arrested in Navy protest 5-19, 385D3
Guyana priest slain 7-15, 814G1
El Salvador priests stage hunger strike 8-19, 652B3
Argentine missing persons law scored 9-12, 728G1
El Salvador archbp pleads for calm 10-16, 790D2
Bolivian peace efforts fail 11-3, 852G3

Middle East Developments
Capucci named Melkite inspector, Israel reassured 5-7, 376B3*
Pope backs Camp David accords, urges 'just' Palestinian solutn 10-2, 10-6, 758F1, 759D3
Clergy visit Iran hostages 12-24–12-27, 975B1-B2

Northern Ireland Dispute—*See NORTHERN Ireland*

Obituaries
Bengsch, Alfred Cardinal 12-13, 1008A2
Cavanaugh, John Joseph 12-28, 1008B2
Coughlin, Charles E. 10-27, 860A2
DiJorio, Alberto 9-5, 756B2
Drake, Bernard 7-15, 814G1
Furey, Francis James 4-23, 356E3
McIntyre, James Francis 7-16, 588B3
Ottaviani, Alfredo 8-3, 671C3
Piasecki, Boleslaw 1-1, 104F3
Sheen, Fulton J 12-9, 1008E3
Villot, Jean Cardinal 3-9, 272G3
Wright, John 8-10, 671G3 1-1, 104F3

U.S. Developments
'78 church attendance rptd 1-5, 24D1
Abortn stand protested by NY Jewish, Prot clerics 1-22, 63B3
China church reimbursemt set 3-16, 218A1
Church schl labor interventn barred by Sup Ct 3-21, 231D2
Clergy malpractice insurnc OKd 4-9, 376D1
Abortion survey rptd 4-22, 315G1
'80 Rome synod delegates named 5-3, 375G3
PR bishop arrested in Navy protest 5-19, 385D3
Nuns set Md hq sale 7-2, 640G2
Galante funeral controversy rptd 7-16, 548D3
'77-78 membership loss rptd 7-17, 640A1
Religious tolerance gains rptd 8-4, 639C3
Vatican criticism of sexual ethics book rptd 8-11, 640F2
Tex-Viet refugee mediatn sought 8-15, 660E1
Del priest cleared in 'gentleman bandit' case 8-23, 953F2
Life of Brian denounced 8-27, 859A2
Church-state issues challenged by Pope's visit 9-13–10-3, 760A3
Pope in US, affirms traditionalist stance 10-1–10-7; addresses UN 10-2, sees Carter 10-6; photos 757A1-760C1, E3-761A2

1980

Violence mars Romero funeral 3-30, 253C3
Pope lauds Romero 4-3, 341D3
Romero's successor chosen, offers leftist mediatn 4-8, 351G2
Colombia DR Emb siege ends, envoy freed 4-27, 337G1
Priests barred from politics 5-4, 341B2
El Salvador univ stormed 6-26; admin bars transfer, asks church role 6-30, 521B3
Pope in Brazil; urges econ, social reforms 6-30—7-11; mass marred by violence 7-9, 537A2-538F2
Clergy reassignmt plan issued 7-22, 970F1
Bolivia churches raided, 11 priests missing 7-23, 577C1
Bolivia deposed pres gets refuge 8-1, 602C3
Chile cardinal rpts death threats 8-4, 603D3
Bolivia archbp denounced 8-17, 9-3, rights abuses chrgd 9-10, 686C3
DR sugar dispute setld 9-5, 687B3
Brazil priest vs mass request 9-7, Brazil ousts 10-30, 870G3
Bolivia deposed pres gets exit OK 9-15, 728A1
Bolivia deposed pres leaves for Paris 10-4, 787C2
US bishops urge El Salvador aid cutoff 11-8, 872A1
El Salvador leftists kidnaped from Jesuit school, slain 11-27, 921E1
US nuns found slain in El Salvador 12-4, 921B1
El Salvador govt linked to nuns murders 12-6, 941F2
Pope offers Beagle Channel solutn 12-12, 978C3-979A1

Middle East Developments
Capucci sees US Emb militants in Iran 2-8, 106D1
Bugnini in Iran crisis mediatn group 4-5, 258D1
Iran gets papal plea on US ties 4-12, Khomeini replies 4-15, 282A2
Iran OKs repatriatn of dead US raiders 4-28, 323G1; Capucci arranges transfer 4-29—5-6, 337A2
Pope urges peace 6-21, 474D2
Iran blames Pope re US jailings 8-3, 587A1
Iranians demonstrate at Vatican 8-8, 635A2

Obituaries
Espinal Camps, Luis 3-22, 272G1
Pignedoli, Sergio 6-15, 528C3
Romero y Galdamez, Oscar Arnulfo 3-24, 220E1
Vagnozzi, Egidio 12-26, 1004E3

Traditionalist Movement
Pope Latin mass support rptd 3-21; Lefebvre holds outlawed mass 4-7, oppositn rptd 4-26, 364A1

U.S. Developments
'79 church attendance rptd 1-4, 8B1
DC archbp named to Vatican educ post 1-15, 199B2
Bible reading survey rptd 1-18, 157A2
Citibank ties cut re S Africa loans 3-24, 277G3
Ukrainian church ldr named 3-27, 413E3
Intercommunion poll rptd 4-4, 413E2
Priests barred from politics 5-4; Drinan, Cornell drop electn bids 5-5, 5-6, 341B2
Cuban refugee resetlmt lag rptd 6-2, 420G1
Cuban refugee resetlmt costs rptd 6-20, 485A1
Carter visits Pope 6-21, 474D2
Medicaid abortn funding limits upheld by Sup Ct, Cook lauds ruling 6-30, 492A1, A2
US evangelicals profiled 7-11—9-15, 815F3
Clergy reassignmt plan issued 7-22, 970F1
Iran blames Pope re US jailings 8-3, 587A1
Mother Teresa ends visit 8-7, 638F1
Reagan breakfasts with Krol 9-8, 699B3
Anti-abortionists lose Mass primary 9-16, 724C2
Reagan, Anderson debate church, state role 9-21, 722G1
Mondale addresses NY conf 9-23, 780E2
Quinn challenges birth control ban 9-29, 810E2

1976

ROMANKOV, Alexander
Wins Olympic medal 7-21, 574E2
ROMANOV, Grigory V.
Named to Politburo 3-5, 195A2
ROMANUS, Sven
Named to Swedish Cabt 10-8, 794B2
ROME, Club of—*See CLUB of Rome*
ROMEO Lucas, Gen. Fernando
Heads Natl Emergency Com 2-4, 81E1

ROMERO, Col. Carlos Humberto
Named PCN pres candidate 7-5, 1012D3

ROMERO Barcelo, Carlos
Elected PR gov 11-2, 825F1
Electn win linked to tap scandal 11-27, 995B1
On PR statehood proposal 12-31, 994A3
ROMERSA, Michael
Pleads guilty 1-20, 78G2
Sentenced 3-9, 271C2
ROMNEY, Vernon B.
Wins Utah primary for gov 9-14, 705F1
Loses election 11-2, 820C3, 824B3
ROMO, Oswaldo
Chile torture chrgd 2-10, 310D1
ROMULO, Carlos P.
Asks US Navy bombing halt 7-13, 539C2
Denies US base pact agrmt 12-5, 12-6, 926G2
RONCAGLIOLO, Rafael
Arrest ordered 8-25, 652E2
RONCALIO, Teno
Reelected 11-2, 824D3, 831A4
RONSTADT, Linda
Wins Grammy 2-28, 460A3
ROOKER, Jim
NL pitching ldr 10-4, 796A1
ROOLVINK, Bauke
Admits Dutch paymts 1-11, 134A2
ROONEY, Rep. Fred B. (D, Pa.)
Reelected 11-2, 830F3

1977

ROMANENKO, Lt. Col. Yuri
Soyuz launched 12-10, docks with Salyut 12-11, 999E1
ROMANOW, Roy
Defends Saskatchewan dvpt policy 1-6, 18B1

ROMERO, Gen. Carlos Humberto (ret.) (El Salvador president)
Elected pres 2-20, denies fraud 2-21, 181A2, E2, F3
US probes vote fraud 3-9, 206C3
Inaugurated; archbp boycotts rite 7-1, offers talks 7-3, 542D2-A3
Scores rightist violence 7-18, 580E1
Church asks 'persecutn' end 9-1, 710E2
At Panama Canal pact signing 9-7, 678C1 ★

ROMERO Barcelo, Carlos
Inaugurated 1-2, 16F2

ROMERO y Galdamez, Archbishop Oscar Arnulfo
Asks priest murder probe, chrgs terror 3-17, 207D1
Shuns inaugural, scores govt 7-1; seeks reconciliatn 7-3, 542F2-A3

ROMM, Dr. May E.
Dies 10-15, 872G2
ROMMEL, Manfred
Permits Baader gang burial 10-27, 868F1
ROMULO, Carlos
In US base talks 9-22—9-23, 824B3

1978

ROMANENKO, Lt. Col. Yuri
Soyuz 27 docks with Salyut 1-11, 11E2
Breaks US space endurance mark 3-4, 157D2
Returns to Earth 3-16, 180D3
ROMANUS, Gabriel
Swedish soc welfare min 10-18, 822G2
ROMANUS, Sven
Swedish justice min 10-18, 822G2
ROME, Harold
Pins and Needles opens 7-6, 760A3
ROMERAL Jara, Alejandro—*See FERNANDEZ Larios, Armando*
ROMERO, Gen. Carlos Humberto
Peasants vs mil repressn 3-30, 245E1
US aides find rights abuse worse 8-5, 723B3 ★
Guerrillas score govt 8-25, 723F2 ★

ROMERO, Juan de Jesus
Dies 7-30, 620E3

ROMERO y Galdamez, Archbishop Oscar Arnulfo
Chrgs rights abuses continue 2-26, 152E2
Trades chrgs with El Salvador govt 4-14, 4-16; papal support rptd 8-5, 723E3 ★
Scores police killings 12-19, 987A1

ROMERO Barcelo, Carlos (Puerto Rico)
On power strike, sabotage 2-2, 116A1
Statehooders seen winning Dem primary 7-26, 627E1
US poll on PR status rptd 7-28, 627F1
ROMMEL, Field Marshal Erwin (1891-1944)
Son fails in state post challenge 8-16, 725F3
ROMMEL, Manfred
Fails in state post challenge 8-16, 725F3
ROMULO, Carlos P.
Ties forgn newsmen to electn protest 4-10, 269B1
On ASEAN-Communist ties 8-4, 603B3
RONALD Reagan's Citizens for the Republic
PAC top fund-raiser 9-7, 753A2
RONCALIO, Rep. Teno (D, Wyo)
On fed mining-impact loan rate hike 7-11, 697E2
Not standing for reelectn 9-12, 736D2
Cheney wins seat 11-7, 856A2
RONDEAU, Gilbert
Sentenced in arson case 10-6, 794G2
RONDOU, Rene
Merged bakery, tobacco union exec VP 8-16, 700B2
RONO, Henry
Sets 5000-mtr run mark 4-8, 3000-mtr steeplechase mark 5-13, 6-1—6-4, 10000-mtr run mark 6-11, 3000-mtr run mark 6-27, 600F2, G3
RONSTADT, Linda
Living in USA on best-seller list 10-11, 800F3; 11-8, 888D1
ROONEY, David
Influence peddling chrgd 1-31, held on assault 2-1, 88A2
ROONEY, Rep. Fred B. (D, Pa.)
Loses reelectn 11-7, 849E2
ROONEY, Mickey
Married 8th time 7-28, 844D3

1979

Priest-penitent case declined by Sup Ct 10-1, 767E3
Minn lobbyist named in prostitutn expose 10-18, 887A2
Ill papal mass crowd figures disputed 10-21, 931C2
Pauline Fathers crime probe rptd 11-9, 905E3
Abortion, womens ordinatn polls rptd 11-11, 930G1
Bishops reject prayer change 11-14, 930B1
Jesuit priest silenced, ordrd relocated; female ordinatn issue cited 12-1, 999F3
Detroit auxilary bishop in Iran 12-24–12-27, 975B1-B2
ROMANOV, Grigory V.
Career imperiled re scandal 929D1
ROMANTIC Comedy (play)
Opens 11-8, 956G3
ROMERAL Jara, Alejandro—*See FERNANDEZ Larios, Capt. Armando*

ROMERO, Gen. Carlos Humberto (El Salvadoran president; ousted Oct. 15)
Security law repealed 3-1; raids, repressn continue 3-4–3-22, businessmen voice concern 3-9, 234F3, 235E1
Frees 2 BPR ldrs 5-11, bars negotiatns 5-12, 371C1, E1
Calls for natl forum on unrest 5-18, 388A1
Natl forum on violence opens 5-24, 406D3
BPR militants end emb seige 6-1, 424E3
Calls gen amnesty; asks Red Cross, OAS rights role 8-16, 652G1
Brother slain 9-6, violence ensues 9-8–9-8, 686B1
US urges early electns 9-14, 707E1
Cancels Independnc Day festivities 9-15, 707B1
Rebels raid residence 9-23, 729F2
Deposed, seeks Guatemala refuge 10-15, 790F1
Junta outlines progrm 10-18, names Cabt 10-22, 813A1, F1
Leftist unrest resumes 10-25–10-30, 834C2
ROMERO, George A.
Dawn of Dead released 4-19, 528B2
ROMERO, Jose Ernesto
Killed by guerrillas 2-10, 234D3
ROMERO, Jose Javier
Slain 9-6, 686B1
ROMERO, Pedro
Dismissed as Zamora warden 12-19, 997F3
ROMERO Barcelo, Carlos
Vs release of PR natlsts 9-6, 666F1
PR natlsts freed 9-10, return to San Juan 9-12, 683D1
ROMERO y Galdamez, Archbishop Oscar Arnulfo
Priest slain 1-20, sets mourning 1-22, 59D1
Latin bishops back 2-12, 108D3
Scores repressn 3-22, 235A1
Urges pol prisoners freed 5-12, 371D1
Leads hunger strike 8-19, 652B3
Pleads for calm after mil coup 10-16, 790D2
Pol prisoner probe vowed 10-18, 813D1
ROMO, Enrique
In World Series 10-10–10-17, 816C1
ROMULO, Carlos P.
Pelaez named asst 7-23, 567A1
RONBECK, Sissel
Named Norway consumer min 10-5, 774F1
RONDEAU, Gilbert
Prison term lengthened 9-11, 685B1
RONSTADT, Linda
In Africa with Gov Brown 4-7, 271E3
ROOKER, Jim
In World Series 10-10–10-17, 816C1

1980

Reagan backs tuition tax credits 10-1, 738F1
Reagan wins vote 11-4, 837D1, 838A3
Bishops urge El Salvador aid cutoff 11-8, 872A1
Dorothy Day dies 11-29, 928C2
Nuns found slain in El Salvador 12-4, 921B1
Reagan meets Cardinal Cooke 12-9, 956A2

ROMANENKO, Yuri
In Soyuz space trip 9-18—9-26, 737D2
ROMANKOV, Aleksandr
Wins Olympic medal 7-23, 622A3
ROMEO, Max
Reggae opens 3-27, 392F3

ROMERO, Gen. Carlos Humberto
Junta changes rptd 1-9, 20A1
Rightist coup attempt fails 5-2, 372E2

ROMERO, Eduardo
Tax fraud scandal rptd 8-4, 603B3
ROMERO, Julio Cesar
Cosmos win NASL title 9-21, 770C2
ROMERO Barcelo, Gov. Carlos (D, P.R.)
Cops cleared in '78 killings 4-25, 348A3
On refugee resetlmt camp 9-23, 725G3; 9-30, 742E2
Loses reelectn 11-4, recount called 11-5 852D3
Declared winner in recount 12-18, 988G1

ROMERO y Galdamez, Archbishop Oscar Arnulfo
Assassinated 3-24, 220E1
Violence mars funeral 3-30, 253C3
Pope lauds 4-3, 341D3
Successor chosen 4-8, 351G2
US nuns found slain 12-4, 921B1

ROMPKEY, William
Canada revenue min 3-3, 171C2
ROMUALDEZ, Eduardo
Chile-Pl ties restored 4-2, 311D2
RONCONI, Susanna
Arrested 12-4, 944G1
RONDEAU, Jean
Wins LeMans 6-15, 637A3
RONDON, Ernesto
Chrgd in Pl plot 10-28, 874E2
RONNE, Capt. Finn
Dies 1-12, 104F3
RONSTADT, Linda
Mad Love on best-seller list 3-5, 200F3; 4-2, 280F3
ROONEY, David
Cleared re influence chrgs 4-3, 273F1

1976

ROOS, J. L.
Killed 7-15, 539F2
ROOSA, Robert V.
Carter econ adviser 12-1, 898A3
ROOSEVELT, Franklin Delano (1882-1945)—*See 1945, pp. 121-122 for biog. data*
Sen com cites use of intelligence agencies 4-28, 330B2
LA wiretap rptd 5-9, 344F2
James Farley dies 6-9, 444A1
Quoted at Dem conv 7-12, 508G3, 510E1, 511C2, E2
Carter in Warm Springs 9-6, 664G1
Bill ends '33 emergency 9-14, 689B2
Ford, Carter debate 10-6, 741F1
Mondale, Dole debate 10-15, 783C3
Dem coalition cited 11-11, 845D2
ROOSEVELT, Theodore (1858-1919)
Ford vote-loss precedent cited 322F2
ROOTS (book)
On best-seller list 12-5, 972D2
ROPER, Burns
Predicts Carter over Ford 11-1, 825F3
ROREM, Ned
Wins Pulitzer Prize 5-3, 352D3
ROSA, Walter
Portugal industry min 1-6, 11C2
Portugal industry min 7-23, 558G1
ROSACK, Ted
Hijacker killed in Denver 4-19, 383E3
ROSANI, Danuta
Disqualified at Olympics 7-30, 563B2
ROSARIO Resources Corp.
DR to buy more mining shares 12-15, 1001F2
ROSAS, Gen. Cesar
Peru min without portfolio 2-3, 142B3
ROSATO, Joe
Newsmen jailed 9-3—9-17, 700B3
ROSE, Alex
Dies 12-28, 1015E2
ROSE 3rd, Rep. Charles G. (D, N.C.)
Reelected 11-2, 830E2
ROSE, George
Wins Tony 4-18, 460D2
ROSE, Herb
Quits JLP, chrgs plot 6-18, 522C1
ROSE, Michael T.
Vs cadet readmissn plan 8-23, 670F2
ROSE, Pete
NL wins All-Star game 7-13, 544A2
NL batting ldr 10-4, 795F3, G3
In World Series 10-16—10-21, 815D2
ROSEBURY, Theodor
Dies 11-25, 1015E2
ROSELL de la Lama, Guillermo
Mexico tourism min 12-2, 907A1
ROSEN, Jess Michael
Testifies on grain fraud 3-11, 247B3
ROSENBAUM, Richard M.
Ford gets 119 NY delegates 5-24, 374D1
Seconds Ford nominatn 8-18, 597G2
ROSENBERG, Ethel & Julius (d. 1953)
ABA forms unit 1-8, 70F2
Judge to see case papers 1-13, 70B2
ROSENSTIEL, Lewis
Dies 1-21, 80G3
ROSENTHAL, Rep. Benjamin S. (D, N.Y.)
Subcom probes bank regulatory agencies 1-12—2-3, 111D3, 112E2-C3
GAO scores FDA on stocks 1-19, 44D3
Subcom votes comptroller probe 2-26, Smith bars 3-5, 185G3
Urges boycott compliance halt 10-20, 786F2
Reelected 11-2, 830G1
ROSENTHAL, Harold W.
Killed in hijack try 8-11, 578B3
ROSENTHAL & Co.
Commodity comm chrgs fraud 10-21, 990C2
ROSENZWEIG, Harry
Chargd re Ariz land deal 6-2, denies 6-14, 484A1
ROSEWALL, Ken
2d in Alan King tennis 5-16, 716B2

1977

ROOSEVELT, Franklin Delano (1882-1945)—*See 1945, pp. 121-122 for biog. data)*
Carter gives 'fireside chat' 2-2, 75B1
New minimum wage enacted 11-1, 834C1
Eccles dies 12-18, 1024D1
ROOSEVELT Raceway (Westbury, N.Y.)
George Morton Levy dies 7-19, 604C3
ROOTES, Sir Reginald
Dies 12-20, 1024A3
ROOTES Group
Reginald Rootes dies 12-20, 1024A3
ROOTS (book)
On best-seller list 2-6, 120F3; 2-20, 118E3; 3-6, 184F3; 4-3, 264G1; 5-1, 356C2; 6-4, 452A2; 12-4, 1021A3
Wins Natl Book Award citatn 4-11, 355B2
Wins special Pulitzer 4-18, 355B2
Haley sued 5-24, 643D1
ROOTS (TV film)
TV viewing record set 1-23—1-30, 118B3; table 2-9, 119B1
TV segment missing in USSR emb fire 9-2, 766E1
Wins Emmy 9-11, 1022A1
Ohio kidnaper blames series 9-12, 712A2
ROQUE, Julio
Killed 5-29, 522F3
RORER-Amchem Inc.
Rpts forgn payoffs 3-9, sued 3-16, 503B2
ROSA, Walter
Quits Cabt 1-3, 21F2
ROSAS Cresto, Gen. Cesar
Social property deemphasized 1-7, 46G3
ROSCA, Nicolae
Ousted re miners strike 10-21, 948B1
ROSCHMANN, Eduard (alias Federico Wegener)
Argentina OKs extraditn to W Ger 7-4, 614C3
Rptd dead in Paraguay 8-11, Interpol confirms 8-13, 670D3
ROSE, Rep. Charles G. (D, N.C.)
Scores USAF computer project 4-27, 421F2
ROSE, Pete
NL batting ldr 10-2, 926C3, D3
ROSE, Rosa
RCMP barn burning probed 11-1, 902D3
ROSEBAUGH, Rev. Lawrence
Detained 5-15—5-18, sees Mrs Carter 6-8, 455A2
Brazil denies police beating 8-6, 633F2
ROSEN, Al
Paul resigns as Yankee pres 12-1, 990E2
ROSEN, Arthur H.
More US-China exchng visits set 3-13, 220F1
ROSEN, Morris
On 3d World A-plant safety 5-3, 403B1
ROSENBAUM, Francis N.
Convicted 3-30, 491F3
ROSENBERG, Ethel & Julius (d. 1953)
Irving Saypol dies 6-30, 532F3
ROSENBERG, William G.
Replaced as FEA asst admin 5-12, 418E1
ROSENBLOOM, Carroll
Rozelle gets new contract 2-17, 163C3
ROSENDAHL, Vice Adm. Charles E. (Ret.)
Dies 5-14, 452E3
ROSENFIELD, James H.
Named CBS-TV pres 10-17, 846G1
ROSENNE, Meir
Named Israel Cairo conf envoy 11-28, 909E2
At Cairo conf 12-14—12-15, 953G1
ROSENSTOCK, Barry
Rptd subpoenaed 6-18, 556C3
ROSENTHAL, Rep. Benjamin S. (D, N.Y.)
Scores Dixon anti-Nader slur 1-17, 96B1
On antiboycott bill 4-20, 323G2
Vs Egypt air aid plan 9-15, 698E1
ROSENZWEIG, Harry
Mafia ties alleged 3-13—3-20, 568A2
ROSENTHAL, Harold (d. 1976)
US ties 4 natns to terror groups 5-8, 380E1
ROSLAVLEVA, Natalia
Dies 1-2, 84E3

1978

ROONEY, Ruth (Mrs. David)
Held on assault chrg 2-1, 88E2
ROOSEVELT, Franklin Delano (1882-1945)—*See 1945, pp. 121-122 for biog. data*
Carter State of Union Message 1-19, 30C1
Willkie's widow dies 4-16, 356F3
Natl Gallery additn opens 6-1, 578E2
ROOSEVELT Hotel (N.Y., N.Y)
Loews buys 5-31, 404A2
ROOTS (book)
Alexander plagiarism suit dismissed 9-21 759A3
Courlander suit setld 12-14, 1029E3
ROOTS (TV film)
Super Bowl viewing record rptd 1-17, 39G3
'Holocaust' aired 4-16—4-19, 316G1
ROSCOE, Judith
Who'll Stop Rain released 8-25, 1030G3
ROSE, Alex
Wanna Hold Your Hand released 4-21, 619E2
ROSE 3rd, Rep. Charles G. (D, N.C.)
Reelected 11-7, 851C3
ROSE, George
Kingfisher opens 12-6, 1031B2
ROSE, Jacques
Paroled 7-17, 556D3
ROSE, Patrick
Bistro Car opens 3-23, 887B1
ROSE, Paul
Brother paroled 7-17, 556E3
ROSE, Pete
Gets 3000th hit 5-5, 559F3
Hits in 44 straight games 6-14—7-31, 618E2-A3
NL batting ldr 10-2, 928E2-F2
Signs with Phillies 12-5, 1025D3
ROSE, Philip
Angel opens 5-10, 760C1
My Old Friends opens 12-2, 1031E2
ROSE, Reginald
Somebody Killed Her Husband released 9-29, 970C3
Wild Geese released 11-11, 970E3
ROSE, Lt. Gov. Robert (D, Nev.)
Wins primary for Nev gov 9-12, 736E2
Loses electn as Nev gov 11-7, 857E1
ROSE Bowl—*See FOOTBALL—Collegiate*
ROSEN, Martin
Watership Down released 11-3, 1030F3
ROSEN, Nathaniel
Wins Tchaikovsky competitn 7-4, 844A2
ROSEN, Pinhas
Dies 5-3, 440D3
ROSENBAUM, David
Family Business opens 4-12, 760B2
ROSENBERG, Alan
Prayer For My Daughter opens 1-17, 760B3
ROSENBERG, Ben
Tribute opens 6-1, 887D3
ROSENBERG, Edgar
Rabbit Test released 4-8, 619D3
ROSENBERG, Seymour
Indicted 2-16, 116E2
ROSENBLOOM, Carroll
Knox quits as Rams coach 1-12, 171E2
ROSENNE, Meir
On rejectn of Egypt peace plan 7-11, 521C1
ROSENTHAL, Rep. Benjamin S. (D, N.Y.)
On oil tax credit revocatn 1-16, 69A2
Vs US stand on Israel use of US arms in Leb 4-5, 236E2
Vs Turkish arms embargo end 4-5, 4-6, 276A3, E3
Reelected 11-7, 851D3
ROSKELLEY, John
Climbs K2 in Pakistan 9-7, 843F2

1979

ROOSEVELT, Archibald B.
Dies 10-13, 860D3
ROOSEVELT, (Anna) Eleanor (Mrs. Franklin Delano) (1884-1962)
Cong subcom '40s appearance cited 2-7, 112F1
Hickok friendship rptd 11-5, 860C1
ROOSEVELT, Franklin Delano (1882-1945)
Rockefeller dies 1-26, 103G3
US-Nicaragua long-term ties detailed 535D2
Tugwell dies 7-21, 588E3
Mayoral Cabt apptmt cited 7-27, 577E1
Secret records of mtgs alleged 10-29, 869D1
Reagan borrows phrase 11-13, 866F2
Possible cancer disclosed 12-2, 925E2
ROOSEVELT Jr., Franklin Delano
Vs FDR cancer theory 12-2, 925C3
ROOSEVELT, Kermit
Iran book rptd recalled 11-10, 886F3
ROOSEVELT, Theodore (1858-1919)
Archibald Roosevelt dies 10-13, 860D3
Grandson's Iran book rptd recalled 11-10, 887B1
ROOTS: The Next Generations (TV series)
Wins Emmy 9-9, 858E2
RORER Group Inc.
Daylin drops Narco takeover bid 1-24, 88E3
ROSA, Michael (d. 1978)
Police chief chrgd in murder 2-7, 156A1
ROSARIO Polanco, Gen. Aurelio
DR mil attache in Colombia 1-12, 62E2
Arrested 9-25, plot exposed 9-26, 751F3
ROSARIO Resources Corp.
Sought by Amax 10-22, 986D3
ROSE, Alex
Norma Rae released 3-1, 174C3
ROSE, Cristine
Miracle Worker opens 1-6, 292C2
ROSE, Dexter
Fired re US kickbacks, flees Jamaica 1-29, 101B2
ROSE, Edward
Prisoner of Zenda released 5-25, 820A3
ROSE, Jack
Lost & Found released 7-13, 820F1
ROSE, Pete
Sets NL singles mark 8-5, 619F2
NL batting ldr 9-30, 955D2-F2
Ryan becomes top-paid player 11-19, 1001F3
Named Player of Decade 12-29, 1003E1
ROSE, Philip
Comin' Uptown opens 12-20, 1007C2
ROSE, The (film)
Released 11-17, 1008C1
ROSE Bowl—*See FOOTBALL-Collegiate*
ROSEBROOK, Jeb
Black Hole released 12-21, 1007A3
ROSEMONT, Ill.—*See ILLINOIS*
ROSEN, Robert L.
Prophecy released 6-15, 820A3
ROSENBERG, Alan
Kid Champion opens 8-27, 712A1
ROSENBERG, Ben
Faith Healer opens 4-4, 711G2
ROSENBERG, Julius & Ethel (d. 1953)
Fuchs retiremt rptd 2-1, 78E3
New Republic article publshd 6-16, 466A1
Sons seek FBI files preservatn 6-26, 521A1
ROSENBERG, Judge Louis
Steel haulers end strike 1-18, 87D2
ROSENBERG, Stuart
Amityville Horror released 7-27, 819D3
ROSENBLOOM, Carroll
Drowns 4-2, 356G3
ROSENBLUM, Ralph
Great Bank Hoax released 3-22, 528C2
ROSENDAL, Silvios (Netherlands Antilles premier)
Resignation rptd 11-13, 882D3
ROSENFIELD, Maurice
Goodbye People opens 4-30, 711D3
ROSENGREN, Jack W.
Judge blocks H-bomb article 3-9, 193E3
ROSENTHAL, Rep. Benjamin S. (D, N.Y.)
Issues Library of Cong rpt 2-12, 127E3
Vs FRB Cleveland bank rpt 3-14, 204F2
FTC sees oil firm-shortage link 5-15, 361E2
Tours SE Asia refugee camps 8-4—8-7, visits Hanoi 8-8—8-9; links Viet ties, refugee aid 8-11, 607B2
ROSENTHAL, Leslie W.
Wheat speculatn alleged, London optns chrgs cited 3-21, 202E1
ROSENTHAL & Co.
Wheat speculation alleged, London optns chrgs cited 3-21, 202G1
ROSENWALD, Lessing J.
Dies 6-24, 508E3
ROSE v. Mitchell
Case remanded by Sup Ct 7-2, 558E3
ROSEWALL, Ken
Wins Tennis Legends tourn 4-22, 391C3
Wins Tennis Legends championship 8-12, Carte Blanche Legends 8-26, 734B2, D2
ROSKELLY, John
Climbs Gauri Sankar 5-12, 392F2

1980

ROOSEVELT, Franklin Delano (1882-1945)
Douglas dies 1-19, 51C1
MacArthur WWII 'gift' knowledge rptd 1-30, 1-31, 115A2
Reed dies 4-3, 360A3
Reagan pres nominatn acceptance speech 7-17, 533D2, G2
Kennedy Dem conv speech 8-12, 610B1, 613D1, G1
Carter pres renominatn acceptance speech 8-14, 614C2, A3
Reagan hits Carter record 10-29, 817A2
Dem coalitn broken 11-4, 837D1
Shoumatoff dies 11-30, 928D3
ROOSEVELT, Julius K.
Scores USOC boycott vote 4-12, 283D2
ROOSEVELT, Theodore (1858-1919)
Daughter dies 2-20, 176C2
Carter concedes early 11-4, 837G1
ROOTS (TV film)
'Shogun' aired by NBC 9-15—9-19, top ratings rptd 9-24, 835G2-B3
'Dallas' episode viewing record rptd 11-25, 905C3
ROPER Organization Inc., The
Pres poll rptd 6-17, 452B2
ROPES, Bradford
42d Street opens 8-25, 756D3
ROSA, Luis
Sentenced 8-4, 601E1
Indicted 12-10, 963F3
ROSARIO Resources Corp.
Hudson Bay seeks merger 1-10; Amax signs to buy 2-4, 385D3
ROSCH, Eberhard
Wins Olympic medal 2-16, 155D3
ROSE 3rd, Rep. Charles G. (D, N.C.)
Reelected 11-4, 843B4
Loses as House Dem Caucus chrmn 12-8, 936E2
ROSE, Dexter
Jamaica sues US grain shippers 2-4, 99G2
ROSE, Joe
West wins E-W Shrine Game 1-5, 62A2
ROSE, Juan Williams—*See TOWNLEY, Michael Vernon*
ROSE, Mayor Pat (Chattanooga, Tenn.)
Imposes curfew 7-24, hears grievances 7-26, 575G3, 576A1
ROSE, Pete
Receives Player of Decade award; Aaron boycotts fete, chrgs racism 1-28, 637G1
NL wins All-Star Game 7-8, 636B2
NL batting ldr 10-6, 926E2, F2
In World Series 10-14—10-21, 811G2-812G3
ROSE, The (recording)
On best-seller list 7-9, 568E3, F3
ROSEMONT—*See ILLINOIS*
ROSEN, Barbara (Mrs. Barry)
Sees Giscard 4-23, 299C2
ROSEN, Barry
Iranians call spy 1-22, 47G3
Iran newspr closes 2-3, 88E2
Wife sees Giscard 4-23, 299C2
ROSEN, Juan Jose
Warns police vs 'blackmail' 10-21, 832A2
ROSEN, Kenneth
On mortgage rate rise 3-7, 222B3
ROSEN, Judge Max
Blocks draft registratn 7-18, 597G3
ROSENBERG, Alan
Happy Birthday Gemini released 5-2, 416A3
ROSENBERG, Ethel & Julius (d. 1953)
Douglas dies 1-19, 51D1
ROSENBERG, Irene
Onward Victoria opens 12-14, 1003E3
ROSENBERG, Jakob
Death rptd 4-7, 360B3
ROSENBERG, Phillip
Wins Oscar 4-14, 296A2
ROSENBERG, Rick
Hide in Plain Sight released 3-21, 216G2
ROSENBLOOM, Carroll (1907-79)
Steelers win Super Bowl 1-20, 61B3
ROSENBLOOM, Georgia
Steelers win Super Bowl; Rams takeover cited 1-20, 61B3
ROSENBLOOM, Steve
Steelers win Super Bowl; Rams ownership ouster cited 1-20, 61B3
ROSENBLUM, Victor G.
Abortn funding cases argued in Sup Ct 4-21, 306D3
ROSENFIELD, Lois
Barnum opens 4-30, 392D2
ROSENFIELD, Maurice
Barnum opens 4-30, 392D2
ROSENSTEIN, Nettie
Dies 3-13, 280G1
ROSENTHAL, Rep. Benjamin S. (D, N.Y.)
Heads Hunt silver trading probe 3-31, 245A2
Regulators debate commodity futures trading curbs, seeks Hunts' testimony 4-14—4-15, 289G3, 290B2
Nader backs Corporate Democracy Act 4-17, 308A2
Hunts threatened with contempt 4-29, testify 5-2, 345G1
Forgn investmt said dangerous 8-7, 601G3-602A2
Reelected 11-4, 843D3
ROSENTHAL, Leslie
Nominated CBT chrmn 11-24, 960A1
ROSENWALD, Julius (d. 1932)
Daughter dies 9-11, 756D2
ROSEWALL, Ken
Wins Tennis Legends tourn 5-4, 607C3
ROSHOLT, Mike
Lauds black union recognitn 11-7, 903D1

1976

ROSOLIO, Shaul
Cabt OKs Galilee action 4-4, 258D2
ROSS, Christopher
Asks US natls quit Leb 6-18, 447G3
ROSS, Hugh
Wins world bridge title 5-8, 352G3
ROSS, Robert
Rpts Cuban exile plot vs Castro 8-17, 791G1
ROSS, William
Quits Cabt 4-8, 266G3
ROSSETTI, Nadyr
Scores govt 3-20, fired 3-29, 287D3
ROSSI, Andre
Foreign trade min 8-27, 650F3, G3
On Aug trade deficit 9-17, 772E3
ROSSI, Francois
Drug dealers convicted 12-9, 971F2
ROSSI, Opilio Cardinal
Appointed cardinal 4-27, 336B2
ROSSNER, Bernhard
Trial opens 5-6, 503F1
ROSTENKOWSKI, Rep. Daniel (D, Ill.)
Reelected 11-2, 829F2
Named deputy whip 12-8, 981E1
ROSWELL, N.M.—*See NEW Mexico*
ROTARY International
Austrian opposed as pres 3-10, 3-11, 380F2
Davis elected pres 6-14, 484D2
ROTH Jr., Sen. William V. (R, Md.)
Reelected 11-2, 820D1, 821A1, 828D1
ROTHCHILD, John
Arrives Venez 10-21, ousted 10-22, 844F1
ROTHSCHILD & Sons, N. M.
Buys IMF gold; London bullion trading cited 9-15, 739E3, G3
ROTUE, Henri
Loses electn 10-18, 808D2
ROUDEBUSH, Richard
Carter disavows 'dumping' memo 8-13, 616F3
ROUSEK, Robert
Shifted from White House 1-21, 40D3
ROUSH, Rep. J. Edward (D, Ind.)
Loses reelectn 11-2, 823C2
ROUSSEAUX, Claude-Pascal—*See MEDJEBER, Smail*
ROUSSELOT, Rep. John H. (R, Calif.)
Reelected 11-2, 829D1
ROWAN, Robert D.
Sentenced 6-30, 523G3
ROWING—*See BOATING*
ROWLANDS, Edward
Seychelles independence set 1-22, 271A1
Rhodesia asks mediatn 9-28, 718G2
Sees African ldrs 10-2—10-4, says conf set 10-5, 738E2-D3
ROY, Mike
Dies 6-26, 524E3
ROY, William R.
Cited in Dole biog sketch 614C3 ★
ROYAL Dutch/Shell Group of Companies—*See also appropriate subheads under SHELL International Petroleum Co.*
French coastal oil traces rptd 1-31, 139G2
1st UK Auk shipmt rptd 2-25, 173D3
US utility buys N Sea gas 4-7, 521E3
Admits Italy bribes 4-13, 267F1
Australia dvpt project set 4-29, 332C1
N Viet vows forgn cooperatn 5-7, 367A3
Rhodesia sanctn violatns chrgd 6-21, 621A2
UK invites for N Sea talks 7-1, 522A1
Shell International Petroleum Co.—*See under 'S'*
ROYAL Family, The (play)
Wins Tony award 4-18, 460D2
ROYAL Opera (Covent Garden) (London)
Wins Grammy 2-28, 460D3
ROYBAL, Rep. Edward R. (D, Calif.)
Reelected 11-2, 829C1
ROYER, Jean
Wins Parlt seat 5-9, 350B3

1977

ROSOVSKY, Henry S.
Yale pres offer rejected 12-20, 1021D2
ROSS, Diana
Wins Tony 6-5, 452E1
ROSS, Donald
Inducted into golf HOF 8-23, 675E3
ROSS, Nellie Tayloe
Dies 12-10, 1024A3
ROSS, Thomas B.
Named Defns asst secy 1-19, 52G3; nominated 2-15, confrmed 3-4, 211F1
ROSSELLI, John (d. 1976)
House assassinatn com hearing 3-16, 228F2
ROSSELLINI, Roberto
Dies 6-3, 532F3
ROSSI, Andre
Visits Canada 1-9—1-12, 43D1
Named foreign trade min 3-30, 239A2
ROSSI, Walter
Protests follow death 9-30, 1014C2
ROSS Ice Shelf Project—*See ANTARCTIC Regions*
ROSSINI, Frederick D.
Gets Medal of Sci 11-22, 952B1
ROSTAND, Edmond (1868-1918)
Son dies 9-3, 788D2
ROSTAND, Jean
Dies 9-3, 788D2
ROSTENKOWSKI, Rep. Daniel (D, Ill.)
'76 spec interest gifts rptd 2-15, 128B2
ROSTOW, Eugene
Scores Califano on quotas 3-31, 235E2
ROTAN Mosle Financial Corp.
Duncan confrmatn recommended 1-13, 34D3
ROTH, Robert H.
Surrenders 3-25, sentncd 9-13, 839E1
ROTH Jr., Sen. William V. (R, Del.)
Vs Sen ethics code 4-1, 251F3
Vs Lance's 'overpromises' 7-15, 574C1
Queries Lance 9-17, 718E2
ROUBANIS, Lady Sarah Spencer Churchill
Raped, robbed 1-6; suspects held 1-10, 258D1
ROUDEBUSH, Richard L.
Replaced as VA admin 2-25, 148E3
ROUMELL, Judge Thomas
Dismisses '74 Mich DES suit 5-16, 431F3-432B1
ROUSSELOT, Rep. John H. (R, Calif.)
Pay raises take effect 2-20, 127G2
ROUX, A. J. A.
On S Africa A-bomb capacity 2-16, 160A2
ROUX, Maj. Gen. Jannie
Biko death rpt queried 9-15, 735C2
ROW, Howard E.
On Wilmington busing plan 8-5, 630F3
ROWLAND, Roland W.
Smith sees Kaunda 9-25, 810D2
ROWLANDS, Ted
In Belize talks 7-26—7-28, troop exit barred 7-28, 706E2
Reaffirms Belize indepndnc backing on Latin tour 9-8; Guatemala scores 9-23, 767B1
ROWLING, Wallace
Scores Holyoake appt 3-7, 222C2
ROWNY, Lt. Gen. Edward L.
Arrives USSR 3-26, in arms talks 3-28—3-30, 225D2
ROY, Leopold
Lie detector ban upheld 3-22, 237D3
ROYAL American Shows
Canada '75 payoffs rptd 12-6, 12-8, 965B2
ROYAL Canadian Mounted Police—*See CANADA—RCMP*
ROYAL Dutch/Shell Group of Companies—*See appropriate subheads under SHELL International Petroleum Co.*
Kuwait purchase cutbacks rptd sought 1-20, 107F3
Qatar completes takeover 2-9, 108E2
To buy extra Saudi oil 2-16, 108B1, D1
General Atomic Co.—*See separate listing*
ROYAL Plate Glass Co.
Factory blast 7-25, 604B1

1978

ROSOVSKY, Henry S.
Harvard revises curriculum 5-2, 348C2
ROSS, Diana
Wiz released 10-25, 970F3
ROSS, Herbert
California Suite released 12-21, 1030E2
ROSS, Katharine
Betsy released 2-9, 618C3
ROSS, The Rev. Dr. Roy
Dies 1-8, 96D3
ROSS, Stanford G.
Named Soc Security comr 8-24, 664B1
ROSS, Steven J.
On '77 top-paid execs list 5-15, 364F3
ROSS, Thomas
Rpts gen purpose missile studied 9-26, 738C1
Defends cruise missile 10-23, 877E2
ROSSANIGNO, Giorgio
Shot 5-7, 393B2
ROSS Diaz, Alvin
Arrested in Miami 4-14, 287C2
Moved to NY federal jail 4-28, 370E3
Letelier murder role revealed, moved to DC for trial 6-2, 451F3
Indicted in Letelier murder 8-1, 614A1
Pleads innocent re Letelier 8-11, 647F3
ROSSMAN, Mike
TKOs Galindez for light heavywgt title 9-15, 726C2
ROSSNER, Judith
Attachments on best-seller list 9-4, 708D1
ROSTENKOWSKI, Rep. Dan (D, Ill.)
Reelected 11-7, 850D3
ROSTROPOVICH, Mstislav
Citizenship revoked 3-15, 179B3
ROTH, Edwin J.
On Atlantic City crime rise 11-10, 920F1
ROTH, Toby
Wins US House seat 11-7, 852D4, 854A2
ROTH, Werner
Cosmos win NASL title 8-27, 707E2
ROTH Jr., Sen. William V. (R, Del.)
Votes vs Panama Canal neutrality pact 3-16, 177G2
Votes vs 2d Canal pact 4-18, 273B1
Sen rejects mil constructn funds cut 8-3, 662D2
GOP stages cross-country blitz for tax-cut bill 9-20—9-22, 734D3-735B1
Admin tax cut bill cleared 10-15, 785B2
ROTHERMERE, Viscount (Esmond Cecil Harmsworth)
Dies 7-12, 620F3
ROTHKOPF, John William
Ex-associate sentenced 1-27, 232B3
ROTTEN, Johnny
Pistols guitarist accused of murder 10-12, 842D1
ROULAND, Jean-Paul
Dear Detective released 4-24, 619D1
ROUSSELOT, Rep. John H. (R, Calif.)
Reelected 11-7, 850G1
ROUX, Abraham
In US A-talks 6-25—6-29, 537A1
Rpts US uranium contracts canceled 11-4, 904D2
ROVIRA, Alejandro
Scores Jamaica rights abuse chrgs 6-23, 489F3
Scores OAS rights abuse rpt 6-28, 505A3
Replaced as forgn min 7-8, 577A2
ROWAN, Robert D.
Convictn review denied by Sup Ct 11-6, 874D1
ROW Chin Hwan
Korean lobbying role chrgd 6-1, 433B1
ROWE Jr., Gary Thomas
Chrgd agent-provocateur 7-9, 7-11; violence, cover-up probed 7-12, 527E3-528B2
Indicted 9-20, 720D2
ROWLAND, Roland W.
Tanzania ousts Lonrho 6-2, 479C2
Tanzania seizes Lonrho holdings 9-16, Smith-Nkomo mtg role cited 9-26, 905F2
ROWLANDS, Ted
Belize talks with Guatemala vp rptd 7-6, 538F1
ROWLES, Polly
Show-off opens 5-18, 760D3
ROY, Bill
Wins Sen primary in Kan 8-1, 606F1
Loses US Sen electn 11-7, 854E2
ROY, Willy
Named Sting coach 6-16, 707D3
ROYAL Dutch/Shell Group of Companies
Super tanker spill fouls French coast 3-17, 201D3; wreckage spreads 3-23—3-29, 238B1
Coal, uranium holdings lid backed by FTC aide 4-5, 282F2
Brunei oil output, revenue cited 534A1
Indonesia coal pact cancelled 7-24, 631G3
UK hikes offshore oil tax 8-2, 591G3
Rhodesia sanctns-breaking study issued 9-19, 756B1-E3
Japan faces Iran oil cutback 11-7, 858D2
General Atomic Co.—*See separate listing*
Shell International Petroleum Co.—*See separate listing*
ROYBAL, Rep. Edward (D, Calif.)
Cited for misconduct by ethics com re Park gift 7-13, 527D1
Reprimanded in Korean scandal 10-13, 831D3-832A1
Reelected 11-7, 850G1, 856C3
Exempted from House ethics rule chng 12-6, 958D2

1979

ROSS, Donald
Says Carter warned on A-energy 5-7, 344B1
ROSS, Judith
Rich Kids released 8-17, 820B3
ROSS, Katharine
Legacy released 9-28, 820F1
ROSSA, Guido
Killed 1-24, 98C1
ROSS Diaz, Alvin
Letelier murder trial opens 1-9, jury chosen 1-12, 19D2
Letelier trial testimony begins 1-15, Townley discounts murder role 1-18—1-24, 57E3-58E2
Letelier murder boast cited by FBI informer 1-30, 75D1
Called 'assassin' 2-13, convicted 2-14, 114C2, F2
Sentncd to life 3-23, 234E2
ROSSMAN, Andy
Galindez KOs brother 4-14, 412A3
ROSSMAN, Mike
Galindez KOs for WBA light heavywgt title 4-14, 412F2
ROSS Roy
Chrysler drops account 3-1, 188D1
ROSTENKOWSKI, Rep. Dan (D, Ill.)
House chief dep majority whip 71A1
Misses Camp David mtg 6-1, 418C2
Financial disclosure statemt studied 9-1, 701D3
Chicago aid funds rptd 12-4, 984D1
ROTH, Eric
Concorde Airport '79 released 8-3, 820A1
ROTH, Philip
Book awards protest rptd 8-9, 755F3
ROTH Jr., Sen. William V. (R, Del.)
On Paisley death probe 1-24, 55B1
On Carter trade reorganizatn plan 10-24, 803C1
Chrysler aid compromise set 12-19, 981G2
ROTHMAN, Carole
Minnesota Moon opens 1-31, 292B2
ROTHSCHILD & Sons Ltd., N. M.
London gold price role described 2-7, 83C1, G1
ROTOW, Dimitri A.
Justice Dept admits H-bomb documt security error 6-8, ends effort to stop H-bomb article publicatn 9-17, 713E1
Cited in H-bomb letter 9-16, 9-18, 717A2
ROTTON, Alan H.
FBI dismissal rptd 10-17, kills self 10-18, 787A3
ROUGEAU, Weldon J.
Sears ends fed contract work 4-24, 366B1
ROUGH and Tumble (race horse)
3d in Grand Natl 3-31, 448A3
ROUHANI, Shahruar
Sanjabi scores govt role 4-17, 277F1*
ROUSSET-Rouard, Yves
Little Romance released 4-27, 820F1
ROVERE, Richard H.
Dies 11-23, 932D3
ROWE, Mass.—*See MASSACHUSETTS*
ROWE Jr., Gary Thomas
Extraditn OKd 2-7, 120C1
FBI sued over '65 Liuzzo murder 7-5, 521C1
ROWEN, James
Loses Madison mayoral vote 4-3, 265C2
ROWLEY, John F.
Tenneco fined in bribe case 3-17, 239C3
ROWNY, Lt. Gen. Edward L. (ret.)
Scores SALT, retiremt cited 7-12, 536D1, 8-1, 643D3
ROY, Charles
Loses by-electn 4-30, 329B1
ROY, Fabien
Named Soc Credit head 3-30, 254A1
ROYAL Dutch/Shell Group of Companies
Iran oil crisis forces sales curbs 2-8, 83B1
Iran interests natlzd 7-5, 503A3
BP Nigeria project cited 7-12, 545C2
Nigeria natlizes BP assets 7-31, 584F2, A3
Shell Canada heads tar sands consortium 8-3, 651E1
UK OKs Scottish gas plant 8-10, 614A2
Dutch refinery, chem plant struck 9-24, reopening announced 9-27, 731A2
Dutch refinery strike ends 9-28, 815C1
UK orders N Sea cutback 10-29, 836F1
General Atomic Co.—*See separate listing*
Shell International Petroleum Co.—*See separate listing*
ROYER, Rep. William H. (R, Calif.)
Elected to US House 4-3, 265E1

1980

ROSON, Juan Jose
Named Spain interior min 5-2, 355E1
ROSS, Dana Fuller
Oregon on best-seller list 5-4, 359F3
ROSS, Diana
Upside Down on best-seler list 9-10, 716E3; 10-8, 796A3
ROSS, Herbert
Nijinsky released 3-20, 216D3
I Ought to be in Pictures opens 4-3, 392D3
ROSS, Jay
Flees Iran 7-24, 572C1
ROSS, Thomas B.
Scores Sen com study on Iran missn 6-5, 419F1
ROSS Diaz, Alvin
Letelier murder convictn overturned, new trial ordrd 9-15, 703C3
ROSSELLINI, Franco
Caligula released 2-2, 216C2
ROSSI, Paolo
3-yr soccer suspensn ordrd 5-18, 409C1
ROSSO, Roberto
Arrested 12-4, 944E1
ROSTENKOWSKI, Rep. Dan (D, Ill.)
Reelected 11-4, 842D3
ROSTKER, Bernard D.
Sees prosecutn for draft registratn evaders 7-31, 597D3
Draft registratn statistics rptd 9-4, 683E2, B3
ROTARY Clubs
Hoffman fugitive yrs recapped 9-4, 713B2
ROTARY International
Bush addresses Mich club 9-18, 781A1
ROTH, Lillian
Dies 5-12, 448F2
ROTH, Rep. Toby (R, Wis.)
Reelected 11-4, 844D4
ROTH Jr., Sen. William V. (R, Del.)
Backs tax cut 2-27, 168G2
Reagan unveils tax-cut plan 6-25, 480C2
GOP platform adopted 7-15, 536B1
Carter cites tax plan 8-14, 613A2
ROTHMAN, Melvin
Sentences Campbell, Brown 3-7, 230A3
ROTHSCHILD, Baron Alain de
On French anti-Semitism 10-4, 767A3
ROTHWAX, Judge Harold J.
Sentences '70 Weatherman bomber 10-28, 928E1
ROTSKER v. Goldberg
Case accepted by Sup Ct 12-1, 918E1
ROUILLAN, Jean-Marc
Arrested 9-13, 750F1
ROUKEMA, Marge S.
Elected to US House 11-4, 843A3, 846C2, 848F2
ROULEAU, Claude
Chrgd in '76 Olympic fraud 10-2, 788F1
ROUNDS, David
Wins Tony 6-8, 692C3
ROUSSELOT, Rep. John H. (R, Calif.)
Reelected 11-4, 842G1
Loses as House GOP caucus chrmn 12-8, 936C2
ROUSSEV, Yanko
Wins Olympic medal 7-23, 624E2
ROUTHIER, Sir Adolphe (deceased)
O Canada proclaimed natl anthem 7-1, 496E3
ROWE Jr., Gary Thomas
FBI informants probe rptd, Liuzzo murder indictment cited 2-18, 227A3
Cleared 12-15, 990B1
ROWLANDS, Gena
Gloria released 10-1, 836A3
ROY, Fabien
Loses by-electn 3-24, 230F3
Resigns as Canada Socred ldr, scores Clark 11-3, 885E3-886A1
ROYAL Bank of Canada
Profit increase rptd 9-5, 687A1
Frazee, Finlayson promotns rptd 9-5, 687B1
Nicaragua debt rescheduled 9-5, 689G2
Prime rate raised 11-3, 871B2
ROYAL Dutch/Shell Group of Companies
Liberian supertanker sinks off Senegal 1-17; S Africa oil sale suspected, Shell sues 2-7, 108A3
Australia alumina plant planned 2-8, 95E1
Wage pact rptd set 6-17, 465B3
Norwegian N Sea gas find rptd 7-16, 548D2
Nigeria disputes oil-take 8-8, 620F1
Australian gas project rptd set 10-1, 748F1
Shell Oil Co.—*See SHELL Oil Co.*
ROYAL Trustco Ltd.
Campeau sets takeover bid 8-27, bid fails 10-2, 766E3-767A1
ROYBAL, Rep. Edward R. (D, Calif.)
Reelected 11-4, 842G1
ROYER, Rep. Bill (R, Calif.)
Loses reelectn 11-4, 852B2

1976

ROYSTER, Jerry
Montefusco pitches no-hitter 9-29, 756G2
ROZELLE, Pete
Player draft ruled illegal 9-8, 736D3
ROZHDESTVENSKY, Lt. Col. Valery
Soyuz 23 aborted 10-16, 839D3
RUBBER (& Rubber Products)
China-Sri Lanka deal rptd 1-2, 78D1
Group of 77 sets trade guidelines 2-10, 108C1
Firestone settles on safety ads 2-16, 186A3
Goodyr, Firestone trust suits dropped 3-2, 988G2
Big 4 firms struck 4-21, 308C3
FTC probes chrgs vs Gen Tire 4-27, 360C2
France proposes price stabilizatn fund 5-10—5-11, 355E3
SEC sues Gen Tire, settles 5-10, 359C3
Mex tire cos admit payoffs 5-19, 419B3
May indl output linked to strike 6-16, 479C3
June income slowdown rptd 7-20, 568B2
2d ¼ profits rptd 7-28, 708F3
Goodyear, Firestone strikes end 8-28, 8-29, 647A3
URW pacts with Uniroyal, Goodrich, Mansfield set 9-7, 9-8, 10-10, 866F3
3d ¼ profits rptd down 10-28, 866F2
Canada Polysar rebates rptd 11-26, 904A2; govt defends 11-29, 11-30, 924A1
Forgn paymts studies issued 12-18, 12-20, 985G1
RUBBER, Cork, Linoleum & Plastic Workers of America, United (URW) (AFL-CIO)
Strike; boycott backed by AFL-CIO 4-21, chem union 4-27, 308E3
Strikes vs Goodyear, Firestone end 8-28, 8-29, 647A3
Uniroyal, Goodrich, Mansfield pacts set 9-7, 9-8, 10-10, 866F3
Sept indl output, strike linked 10-15, 806A2
RUBENS, Peter Paul (1577-1640)
Visitation stolen 1-26, 104C3
RUBIN, Ira
Wins world bridge title 5-8, 352G3
RUBIN, Miles
'72 campaign gift listed 4-25, 688D1
RUBIN, Vitali
Exit visa denied 2-16, OKd 6-3, 421D2
RUBINSTEIN, Arthur
Wins Grammy 2-28, 460D3
Gets Medal of Freedom 4-1, 504B3
RUCKAUF, Carlos
Loses cabt post 2-3, 154G2
Rights revoked, arrest ordrd 6-23, 520C1
RUCKELSHAUS, William D.
Rptd Ford vp prospect 8-10, 584D1
Cited re FBI burglaries 8-18, 634F2 ★
Ford selects Dole as vp 8-19, 598F1, G2
Pres debate talks open 8-26, 632C3
RUDD, Eldon
Elected to US House 11-2, 824D1, 828F3
RUDEL, Hans-Ulrich
At pilots mtg 10-23; 2 gens dismissed 11-1, 930D3
RUDER & Finn, Inc.
Mrs Javits quits 1-27, 160A2
RUDI, Joe
Sold to Red Sox 6-15, Kuhn voids 6-18, 444B3-F3
Signs contract 12-5, 951D3
RUE, Harrison B.
Indicted 10-29, 886C3
RUEHROLD, Ute
Wins Olympic medal 2-7, 159A2
RUFF, Charles F. C.
Clears Ford of funds misuse 7-16—10-14, 761D1
Rptd probing Ford funds 9-21, 9-25, Justice Dept referral rptd 10-1, 722F1 ★ -723G2
Watson pleads guilty, fined 9-23, 725E2 ★
Bars Ford coverup probe 10-15, 784G3
RUFFINI, Attilio
Sworn Italy transport min 7-30, 573E1, G1
RUGGIERI, Pasquin
Killed 9-25, 773A1
RUGGIERI, Xavier
Killed 9-25, 773A1
RUIZ, Rear Adm. Alario
Retired 3-27, 255C3
RUIZ-Gimenez, Joaquin
To defend Camacho 4-1; Dem Coordinatn backed 4-4, 269B1 ★
On new Cabt 7-8, 523G2
RUKHIN, Yevgeny
Leningrad artists detained 5-20, 421E3
Dies 5-24, 404D2

1977

ROYO, Aristides
Rpts Panama Canal accord 8-10, 621D1
ROZELLE, Pete
Atkinson loses slander suit 7-22, 659D1
Issues memo on violence 9-15, 1019B3
Admits NFL officiating error 10-30, 1020E1
ROZEMA, Dave
AL pitching ldr 10-2, 927A1
ROZENDAL, S. G. M.
Wins electn 6-17, 566D1
RSN Projects Inc.
Indicted 3-30, fined 5-19, 504G1-A2
RUBAYA Ali, Salem
At Tripoli anti-Sadat mtg 12-2—12-5, 929B2
RUBBER (& Rubber Products)
Intl buffer stock plan rejctd 1-23, 169E2
SEC sues Uniroyal 1-27, 93C3
Canada Polysar admits illegal rebates 2-8, 114B2
UN rpts '76 price up 2-14, 146B1
Asia '76 econ growth rptd 2-16, 147C2
Tire-grading case review denied 3-21, 230E2
1st, 2d ¼ profits rptd up 4-28, 7-28, 668C3, F3
Worker benzene exposure curbed 4-29, 345D1
'76 sales, stockholder returns rptd 340B2, A3
Goodyr Tire-Egypt agrmt rptd 5-16, 390E2
Beasley indicted, Firestone paymts cited 10-25, 818C2
3d ¼ profit rise rptd 10-27, 11-14, 918B2
Goodyr settles paymnts chrgs 12-21, 1005A1
RUBELLA (German measles)—*See MEDICINE—Diseases*
RUBENSTEIN, Jorge
Death rptd 12-10, 982C1
RUBIN, Judge Carl B.
Voids Dayton busing plan 12-15, 978B3
RUBIO Diaz, Jose Manuel
Body found 3-1, 223G2
RUBY, Jack (1912-67)
FBI releases JFK assassinatn probe files 12-7, 943A2
RUCHS, Juergen
E Ger ousts 8-29, 684E1
RUDA, Jose Maria
World Ct member 4G1
RUDD, Mark
Surrenders 9-14, 9-15, dischrgd in NYC 10-13, 839C1
RUDENKO, Mikola
Arrested 2-5, 117E1
Sentenced 7-1, 512C3
RUDIN, Lewis
Backs NY Concorde ruling 5-11, 368D2
RUDNICKI, Walter
Oberle ties blacklist, '73 firing 1-25, 97A2
Libel suit cited 6-13, 541A3
RUE, Harrison B.
Convicted 11-23, 918A3
RUFFELS, Ray
Apples win WTT title 8-27, 787E3
RUFFINI, Attilio
Replaces Lattanzio 9-18, 729C1
RUGGIERO, Frank D.
Scores Panama Canal treaties 9-16, 716C3
RUIZ, Julian
Dies 8-4, 696E3
RUIZ, Maria del Carmen
Release by Cuba confirmed 10-13, 896F2
RUIZ Castro, Fred
Defends martial law 8-21, 665B1
RULE, Elton H.
Sets ABC News budget hike 5-10, 395B2
Top '76 salaries rptd 5-23, 408D3

1978

ROYKO, Mike
Chicago Daily News folds 3-4, 195G1
ROYO, Aristides (Panamanian president)
Torrijos backs for pres 9-1, 691G3
Elected Panama pres 10-11, 764C3
Names Cabt 10-12, 884G1
Natl Guard deputy cmdr fired 10-16, 884D2
ROZELLE, Pete
To study NFL appeals ct 9-17, 1024A1
RRR (reduced residual radiation) Bomb—*See ARMAMENTS—Atomic Weapons*
RTSKHILADZE, Viktor
Arrested 1-25, 180F1
RUBAYA Ali, Salem (South Yemeni president)
Tied to N Yemen pres murder 6-24, link denied 6-25, 498E3, 499B2
Deposed, executed 6-26, 498E3
Ismail purges ruling group 6-28, 522D2
N Yemen says backers fighting govt force 7-4, 522D2
Army troops resist disbandmt 10-20, fighting rptd 10-21, 885E3
RUBBER (& Rubber Products)
Benzene exposure rule issued 2-2, 85C3
Goodyr buys Chile tire co 2-9, sets job cuts 3-29, 312C2
'64-78 spending pattern chngs reflected in new CPIs 222E2
1st ¼ '77, '78 profits rptd down 4-27, 403D2
'77 indus profit rise rptd 5-8, 325A3
ICC orders rail freight rates cut back 6-30, 569A3
Firestone tire recall sought 7-8, 8-31, suits rptd 9-22; recall set 10-20, 834D3
'77-78 2d ¼ corp profits drop rptd 7-28, 642B3
ASEAN-US talks on prices 8-3—8-4, 603G2
FTC complaint vs Bridgestone Tire rptd setld 9-14, 942A1
Firestone, Borg-Warner to merge 11-28, 935D1
Intl rubber talks fail 12-8, 998B2
RUBBER Gun, The (film)
Released 4-24, 619E3
RUBELLA (German measles)—*See MEDICINE—Diseases*
RUBENS, Herbert
Forever Yours opens 6-21, 887G1
RUBENS, Peter Paul (1577-1640)
'3 Graces' stolen 4-21, recovered 4-23, 335A2
RUBENSTEIN, Amnon
Amit joins DMC splinter group 9-13, 798F3
RUBICAM, Raymond
Dies 5-8, 440D3
RUBIES
Australian field found 11-23, 920F3
RUBIN, Bernard G.
Indicted 6-15, 560G2
RUBIN, Judge Carl
Backs coed sports 1-9, 40D3
RUBIN, Ellis
Scores Hunt-JFK murder link 11-4, 898F3
RUBIN, Gail
Slain in PLO raid 3-11, 175A2
RUBINSTEIN, Artur
Wins Grammys 2-24, 316D1
RUBIROSA, Porfirio (1909-65)
Flor de Ora Trujillo dies 2-15, 196G3
RUBIROSA Fermin, Guillermo
Killed by police 3-26, 292C2
RUBY, Earl
Testifies at JFK death hearing 9-26, 750B1
RUBY, Jack (1912-67)
More JFK assassinatn files released 1-18, 109F3
JFK death hearings end 9-28, 750A1
RUCKER, Bo
Native Son opens 3-27, 760G2
RUDD, Rep. Eldon (R, Ariz.)
Reelected 11-7, 850C1, 855F1
RUDDY, Albert S.
Matilda released 6-22, 619B3
RUDIN, Rabbi James A.
Vs NCC stand on Israel cluster bombs 5-12, 358C3
RUDOLPH, Wilma
Run'ers' opens 5-3, 887A3
RUE, Harrison B.
Sentenced 9-21, 768A3
RUEDA Sierra, Agustin
Killed 3-13; protests held at funeral 3-20, 249A3
RUEFF, Jacques Leon
Dies 4-23, 356D3
RUFFELS, Ray
Loses US Open mixed doubles title 9-10, 707A2
RUFFINI, Attilio
Named Italy defense min 3-11, 191B1
RUIZ Jr., Israel
Vs NYS death penalty veto override 5-2, 388D3
RUIZ, Roberto
Arrested in drug scandal 7-4, 614F3
RUIZ Perez, Carlos Humberto—*See MARTINEZ Montenegro, Roberto*
RULE, Elton H.
On '77 top-paid execs list 5-15, 364F3

1979

ROYO Sanchez, Aristides (Panamanian president)
Lauds US re Canal pacts 9-5, 675A2
Threatens canal takeover 9-21, treaty implementatn enacted 9-27, 723F1
Marks Canal treaty implementatn 10-1, 753G3
Coup plot revealed 10-24, rejcts strikers demands 10-25, 836D3-837A1
Carter thanks for taking shah 12-15; shah holds news conf 12-16, 957C1, E1
ROZELLE, Pete
Admits Super Bowl officiating error 2-22, 175C3
ROZOVSKY, M.
Strider Opens 5-31, 712F2
RS-Missile Series (Soviet strategic intercontinental ballistic missiles)—*See ARMAMENTS—Missiles*
RUBBER (& Rubber Products)
URW 'Big 4' contract talks, wage guides in dispute 2-2—5-9; Uniroyal struck 5-9, 344B3
Tire grading order upheld 2-8, 111D2
Radial tire grading ordrd 3-13, 208C3
GATT pact signed, tariff cuts seen 4-12, 273G1
Uniroyal to sell Eur operatns 4-17, 560F3
Borg-Warner, Firestone drop merger 4-24, 349C3
Wage-guide ruling sought 5-2, hearing set 5-4, 345E1-A2
Firestone '78 loss, tire recall linked 5-7, 305F1
URW links Uniroyal setlmt, wage-guide contract denial bar 5-31, 399D3
URW sets pact with Goodrich 6-15, Uniroyal 6-18, 480C1
Synthetic rubber cited 7-8, 517C3
UNCTAD trade pact reached 10-5, 781A3
Uniroyal sex bias suit setld 10-23, 885F2
3d 1/4 indus profit drop rptd 10-31, 923B1
RUBBER, Cork, Linoleum & Plastic Workers of America, United (URW) (AFL-CIO)
'Big 4' contract talks, wage guides in dispute 2-2—5-9; Uniroyal struck 5-9, 344B3
Wage-guide ruling sought 5-2, hearing set 5-4, 345E1-A2
Ct bars wage-guide contract denial, Uniroyal setlmt seen 5-31, 399D3
Goodrich pact set 6-15, Uniroyal 6-18, 480C1
RUBELL, Steve
Indicted 6-28; Jordan denies cocaine chrg 8-24, Landau disputes 8-28, 647E1-E2
Jordan cocaine use rpt disputed 8-31, 767E2
Pleads guilty in tax case 11-2, 891A3
RUBENS, Peter Paul (1577-1640)
'Moses' stolen from Rome convent 6-3, 656F1
RUBENSTEIN, Artur
At 'Lulu' debut in Paris 2-25, 174A1
RUBIN, Jeff
Men in White opens 7-11, 712E1
RUBIN, Cardinal Ladislao
Installed cardinal 6-30, 640C2
RUBINSTEIN, Jerold H.
Break a Leg opens 4-29, 711G1
RUBINSTEIN, Richard P.
Dawn of Dead released 4-19, 528B2
RUBSTIC (race horse)
Wins Grand Natl steeplechase 3-31, 448A3
RUBY, Jack (1912-67)
Oswald organized crime link rptd unproven 1-3, 4E1
Anonymous '63 death threat vs Oswald revealed 2-18, 166F2
Crime links detailed 7-17, 538A2
RUDD, Paul
Bosoms & Neglect opens 5-3, 711F1
RUDEL, Julius
Wins Grammy 2-16, 336G3
RUDELL, John P.
Sentenced in GSA scandal 6-25, 964E3
RUDER & Finn Inc.
Mrs Javits link to shah denied 5-21, 388F3; Iran role detailed 5-30, 408E2
RUDOLPH, Marvin (Mendy)
Dies 7-4, 588C3
RUEL, Claude
Hired as Canadiens coach 12-12, 1004E1
RUFF, Howard J.
How To Prosper on best-seller list 4-8, 271A2; 8-5, 620C3; 9-2, 672C3; 10-14, 800B3; 11-4, 892C3
RUFFINI, Attilio
Army joins anti-terror effort 5-9, 372D1
RUKAVISHNIKOV, Maj. Nikolai
In Soyuz 33 flight 4-10—4-12, 279B2
RULE, Elton H.
Pierce promoted to ABC vp 4-30, 334F3
On '78 top-paid execs list 5-14, 347F3

1980

ROYO Sanchez, Aristides (Panamanian president)
Iran asks shah extraditn 1-12; replies, denies shah arrest 1-23, 47B1
In Japan, sees Ohira; canal feasibility study agreed 3-25, 234B3
Attends Santa Marta conf 12-17, 992A3
ROZELLE, Pete
Defends Oilers call 1-7, 23F1
Stingley lawyer seeks Tatum suspensn 1-10, 175G2
Admits 2 officiating errors 1-16, 62G1
On Raiders LA move attempt 1-18, 62C1
Fines Brown for autobiography chrgs 1-22, 175B3
Raiders agree to play in LA 3-1, 175F1
Fines NFL players for 'unnecessary violence' 10-21, 998A3
RUBBER (& Rubber Products)
Uniroyal to shut 2 plants 1-22, 52G2-A3
Uniroyal tire recall set 3-7, 348C2
Firestone cited for job bias 3-21, 251G2
'79 Fortune 500 data rptd 5-5, 291D1
Firestone fined 5-13, tire recall set 7-3, 702B2
S Africa strikers fired 6-25, 499D2
Firestone US contracts voided 7-15, 560B2
Mansfield Tire liquidates 9-19, 985F3
Goodyear names Mercer chief exec 12-2, 959B2
RUBBER, Cork, Linoleum & Plastic Workers of America, United (URW) (AFL-CIO)
Bommarito vs natl accord 5-6, 385B2
RUBELL, Steve
Sentenced 1-18, 64B3
Grand jury clears Jordan 5-28, 402D3
RUBENS, Peter Paul (1577-1640)
Loren art collectn claim rptd denied 2-9, 200B2
RUBICON Chemical Corp.
La chem-dump suit names 7-15, 559A1
RUBIN, Jerry
To join investmt firm 7-30, 638G2
RUBIN, Mann
First Deadly Sin released 10-24, 836G2
RUBIN, Morris H.
Dies 8-8, 676E2
RUBINSTEIN, Helena (d. 1965)
Sutherland dies 2-18, 176F3
RUBINSTEIN, John
Children of a Lesser God opens 3-30, 392E2
Wins Tony 6-8, 692B3
RUBIO, Manuel
Convicted 7-2, 568C2
RUDD, Rep. Eldon (R, Ariz.)
Reelected 11-4, 842C1, 851C3
RUDMAN, Warren
Wins Sen primary 9-9, 700F2
Elected to US Senate 11-4, 840E2, 845A2, 848E2
RUELAS, Eleazar
Ariz alien case mistrial declared 7-29, retrial sought 8-29, 713E3
RUFF, Howard J.
How To Prosper on best-seller list 2-10, 120E3; 3-9, 200D3
RUFFINI, Attilio
Signs Yugo EC trade pact 4-2, 365B3
RUHLE, Vern
Phillies win NL pennant 10-12, 796D1-E1
RUHN, Melita
Wins Olympic medal 7-25, 623A1
RUI, Bernard
Convictn rptd 6-18, 522G2
RUIZ, Henry
On '80 econ plan 1-3, 7E1
RUIZ, Rosie
Boston Marathon win disputed 4-21; '79 NYC run invalidated 4-25, loses Boston title 4-29, 527C2-G2
RUKAVISHNIKOVA, Olga
Wins Olympic medal 7-24, 624F1
RUKEYSER, Muriel
Dies 2-12, 176B3
RULE, Elton H.
Spelling-Goldberg ties probed by SEC 8-7—8-8, 640F1

1976

RUMANIA—*See also COMECON, DISARMAMENT—Geneva Committee, WARSAW Pact*
Listed as 'not free' nation 1-19, 20E3
Balkan natns meet 1-26—2-5, 213E3
China trade pact signed 1-29, 117D1, E3
Ceausescu at Sovt CP Cong 2-24—3-5, 195B3, 196C1
Joins Arab boycott 3-11, 242D1
Australia coal deal rptd 4-6, 250A1
Ceausescu visit to Greece rptd 4-8, 333B2
Reps at Czech CP Cong 4-12—4-16, 289G1
Sonnenfeldt doctrine scored, US assures on policy 4-13, 277D1
Yugo sentences Cominformists 4-14, 542G3
IMF OKs SDR purchase 4-27, 420D3
Eur CPs meet, cong set 5-4—5-6, 341F1
US Gen Tire paymts chrgd 5-10, 360B1-B2
At E Ger SED cong 5-18—5-22, 381B2
Culture cong meets; Ceausescu eases Sovt, Eur CP mtg stance 6-2—6-4, 420C2
Defns, other mins replaced 6-15, 440A2
Ceausescu at E, W Eur CP conf 6-29—6-30, 461D2
Ship in US Bicentennial event 7-4, 488A3
Prisoner amnesty declared 7-6, emigre pardons rptd 7-7, 907G2
Angola envoy killed 7-12, 649F2
Ship officer in US bicentennial asks asylum 8-7, 970B3
Swiss expel emb aide 8-16, 640B1
2 sentenced for indl spying 8-29, 907A3
Ceausescu in Yugo 9-8—9-10, 734G2
Role in Sovt space program set 9-14, 684D1
Greek oil search rptd 9-28, 854F1
US pres campaign controversy 10-6, 741C3; 10-7—10-12, 762A1-763F1
EEC textile pact rptd 11-12, 907C2
US Cong fact-finders rptd barred 11-21, 880G1
Richardson visits, signs trade pact 11-21—11-22, 907C2
Brezhnev visits, asks unity 11-22—11-24, 907A2
Defns offcl in Peking 11-22, 907C2
Italy trade credit rptd 12-1, 1010F1
Moldavian ldr visits 12-3—12-7, 1010E1

European Force Reduction Issues—*See under EUROPE*

Obituaries
Bodnaras, M Emil 1-24, 160C3

Sports
Olympic results 7-18—7-31, 5 athletes defect 7-28—8-4, 562C2, 563D1, 573C3, 574C1-576E3

UN Policy & Developments
Cncl member 62F2; 720C1
OKs Cncl pro-Palestine resolutn 1-26, 59G2
Joins Group of 77 108C1
Palestine com member 2-26, 162C1
WHO com rpts Israel health data 5-10, 338F2

1977

RUMANIA—*See also COMECON, DISARMAMENT—Geneva Committee, WARSAW Pact*
Party shuffled, Mrs Ceausescu promoted 1-25, 100D1
Ceausescu's son rptd CP youth ldr 1-27, 100E1
Quake hits 3-4; USSR, other aid noted 3-8—3-13, death toll rptd 3-15, 204E1
Quake damage rptd 5-9, 468F3
Gerovital dvpt cited 5-20, 508C3
Single party-state ldr cited 6-16, 469F2
Jan '77 populatn census rptd 9-22, 948B2
Crime rptd up, amnesties blamed 12-5, 987G2
CP congress opens 12-7, 987D2

Economy & Labor (domestic)
'76 indl output, '77 forecast rptd 1-1, 100A2
'76 econ data rptd 2-10, 468G3
Work-week cut rptd delayed 3-11, 468F3
Black Sea oil found 4-20, 468E3
Coal miners strike, Ceausescu vows reforms 8-1—8-3; troops sent, reprisals rptd 9-1, 947D3
Mining mins ousted 10-21, 948B1
Constructn, trade mins rptd ousted 11-23, 948A2
'81-85 econ plan presented 12-7, 987D2
Mines min ousted 12-15, 987A3

Foreign Relations (misc.)—*See also 'Human Rights', 'Monetary, Trade & Aid' and 'UN Policy' below*
Spain ties rptd renewed 1-27, 242C2
USSR, other quake aid rptd 3-8—3-13, 204A2, C2
Eurocommunism, Spain CP backed 7-5, 513F2
Israel premr visits 8-25—8-29, 663C2
Sadat ends visit 11-3, 850A2
Ceausescu rptd Begin-Sadat go-between 11-16, 873C2
Israel thanks Ceausescu 11-18, 895B1
Goma arrives Paris 11-20, 948C1

Helsinki Agreement—*See EUROPE—Security and Cooperation*

Human Rights (including emigration)
Writer rptd ousted 1-14, 100A2
'76 Swiss asylum bids rptd 1-25, 138A1
NCC suspends Archbp Trifa 2-4, 119F3
Dissidents issue rights plea 2-8, Ceausescu scores 2-17, 137E1
Jews chrg visas denied 2-20, 315B1
Udrescu gets US asylum 2-24, 315B1
Dissident emigratn rptd 2-26, Westn emb contact blocked 4-2, 315E1
Goma chrgs dissident abuses, cites rights plea 3-13; arrest rptd 4-13, 314G1
Gen amnesty declared, Goma freed 5-9, 437A1
Press self-censorship set 6-30, 567E1
Rights movemt rptd abating, emigratn cited 9-3, 752F3
UNESCO protests treatmt of offcl 10-8, 948D1
Goma in Paris 11-20, asks West rights pressure 11-24, 948C1

Monetary, Trade & Aid Issues (including all foreign economic developments)
US adopts fishing agrmt 2-2, 173D3
Tech aid asked 3-11; USSR plans quake aid 3-13, 204A2
US coal sale set 5-30, 468C3
Neutron bomb ban plea shunned 8-8, 640A3
Canada A-pact set 10-24, 982D3
Israel trade expansn rptd, '77, 78 forecast 12-10, 987B3

Obituaries
Lupescu, Magda 6-29, 532C3

Sports
Czechs keep hockey title 5-8, 430C2
Nastase barred from '78 Davis Cup 10-3, 1020A3

UN Policy & Developments
Assemb, Cncl member 4A1, E1
Secretariat chrgs Rhodesia sanctn violatns 2-10, 123A1
UNESCO protests treatmt of offcl 10-8, 948D1
Cncl electns held 10-24, 852F3

1978

RUMANIA—*See also COMECON, DISARMAMENT—Geneva Committee, GATT, WARSAW Pact*
'77 quake death toll rptd 1-29, 480A2
Secret police offcl's defectn triggers purges 9-1, 9-6, 741B3

Economy & Labor (domestic)
Price hikes set, econ reform rptd 5-10, 651B1
Mil budget curbs backed; econ growth lag, '77 mine strike cited 11-29—12-1, 929F2
Mil spending cut set, '79 budget rptd 12-20, 1020A1

European Force Reduction Talks—*See under EUROPE*

Foreign Relations (misc.)—*See also 'Human Rights', 'Monetary, Trade, Aid & Investment' and 'UN' below*
Hungary, Rumania CP ldrs meet 2-16—2-19, tensns rptd 2-23, 180D2
Ceausescu visits UK; detente, disarmamt discussed 6-13—6-16, 515F2
Secret police dep min defects in W Ger 7-28, confrmd 8-8, 650F3
Albania details China dispute, cites '68 pact proposal 7-30, 635E1
USSR scores China Premr Hua re visit 8-5, 8-21, 8-27; Ceausescu reassures Brezhnev 8-7, 675D3-676A1
Hua visits, seeks to counter USSR influence 8-16—8-21; communique issued 8-18, 674G2-675A2
Defector implicates W Ger offcls in spy scandal, chrgs disputed 8-31—9-6, 725C2, D2 ★
Albania scores Hua trip 9-3, 678B1
W Ger spy probe dropped 9-26, 868B3
Indepndnc from Sovt bloc, Hua trip cited 11-25, 913F2
Ceausescu affirms Warsaw Pact stand 11-29—12-1, Brezhnev scores 12-5, 929F2-930F1
USSR scores defns, China policies at intl CP conf 12-15, 1020C1

Government & Politics—*See also other appropriate subheads in this section*
CP, govt posts shuffled 3-7, 193B2
Mil budget curbs win support 11-29—12-1, 929F2
60th anniv marked 12-1, 929F2
Mil spending cut set, '79 budget rptd 12-20, 1020A1

Helsinki Agreement—*See EUROPE—Security and Cooperation*

Human Rights
Hungarian minority held mistreated 1-24; dissident rpts exile 3-1, 180A2
Facts on Hungarian minority 180C2
US rep scores visa curbs 4-11, protesters picket Ceausescu 4-13, 291G1-A2
Carter, Ceausescu end talks 4-13, 291F1
Hungarian minority mistreatmt protested 4-25, dissident poet scored 5-7, 360E1 ★
UNESCO offcl rptd back at post 5-18, 360A2
UK protests rights abuses 6-13, 515D3
Transylvania unrest cited re mil spending curbs 12-1, 930D1

Middle East
Sadat visits, seeks Mideast peace backing 2-12, 98A3
PLO raiders sought amb hostage 3-12, 175F2
Dayan meets Ceausescu 4-3—4-4, lauds talks 4-5, 235D3
Carter lauds Ceausescu '77 go-between role 4-11, ends talks 4-13, 291D1
UK lauds peace role 6-14, 515C3
Israel, Egypt ties cited 12-9, 965F3

Monetary, Trade, Aid & Investment
EC steel dumping probe begun 1-23, 80C2
EC seeks steel export agrmt 3-2, 158C2
US trade expansn agreed 4-13, 291F1
Ceausescu in UK 6-13—6-16, jet deal signed 6-15, 515F2
Renault expansn deal rptd 6-14, 651A1
UK '77 trade rptd 6-15, 515B3
Articles vs Comecon rptd 6-27, 505C1
US favored-natn trade status cited 7-8, 534D2
China econ, tech cooperatn backed 8-18, agrmt signed 8-21, 675C1
US bars clothespin import curb 10-2, 805E1
Canada reactor sales set 12-15, 1013F2

UN Policy & Developments
UNESCO offcl rptd back at post 5-18, 360A2
Amb rptd purged 9-6, 741C3
Assemb member 713D3

1979

RUMANIA—*See also COMECON, DISARMAMENT–Geneva Committee, GATT, WARSAW Pact*

Economy & Labor
Cabt shuffled 1-31, 171B1
Agri reform, '78 output rptd 2-6, 170F3
Price rises, cuts set 3-12, 279E3
Planning comm head named 3-30, 279D3
Gas price hiked 7-27, 645G3
Black Sea oil find rptd, '78 productn drop cited 11-19, 910A2, C2
'81-85 5-yr plan rptd 11-19, 910C2

European Force Reduction Talks—*See under EUROPE*

Foreign Relations (misc.)
Aides in Cambodia escape to Thailand 1-8, 10A1
Poland defense outlay frozen 1-9, 39F2
Viet scored re Cambodia invasn 1-10, 11E1
China Viet invasn stand causes Sovt bloc split 2-19, USSR denounces 2-21, 122E2
IMF OKs loan 4-6, 374B3
W Bank, Gaza health probe set 5-23, 398F2
Westn money for gas demanded; Hungary, Czech ordr travel ban 8-1, 645D3, F3
Israel-PLO-Syria feud mediatn offered 8-31; Israel rejects 9-2; Arafat mtg cited 659B2*
Czech gas paymt rule eased 9-3, 741G3-742A1
Intl oil conf held 9-11, 728B3
10th World Petro Cong meets 9-12, 703A1
UN membership listed 695B3
EC ball bearing dumping probe opened 9-20, 719E2
USSR troop absence rptd 761G2
E Ger fete unattended by Ceausescu 10-7, 761E2
W Ger expropriatn pact set 10-12, 910E2
Oil import data cited 11-19, 910A2, B2
Sovt-bloc indepndnc stressed 11-19, 910B2
Taiwan trade bar affirmed 11-28, 952B3

Government & Politics—*See also other appropriate subheads in this section*
Cabt shuffled 1-31, 171B1
Govt posts shuffled 3-30, 279D3
CP purge planned 9-18–9-19, 910C2
12th CP cong held 11-19–11-23, Pirvulescu scores Ceausescu 11-23, 910C1

Helsinki Agreement—*See EUROPE–Security and Cooperation*

Human Rights
Dissident worker charter released 3-5, rights crackdown rptd 3-28, 334D1
Bible availability cited 3-13, 238E1

Sports
World Gym Championships results 10-5–10-9, 1005B2
3 women banned from track 10-26, Marasescu protest rptd 11-15, 912A1

1980

RUMANIA—*See also COMECON, CSCE, GATT, GENEVA Committee, MBFR, WARSAW Pact*
Ceasusescu cites indus growth, urges energy conservatn 6-4, 465F3
Defense budget rptd cut 9-11, 689C3

Foreign Relations (misc.)
USSR scored re Afghan invasn 1-1, 11A1
UN res vs Sovt Afghan invasn shunned 1-14, 25F2
Gromyko visits re Afghan support 1-31—2-2, 108F3, 109A1
USSR Afghan support barred 2-6—2-7, 109A2
EC ties pact initialed 2-12, 109A2
In UK talks, Sovt Afghan move scored 3-14, 205G1
China joins IMF 4-17, 302E2
New Iran trade deal 4-23, 298G1
Iran hostage rescue try scored 4-25, 324D1
Europn CPs meet 4-28—4-29, 327C2
Tito funeral held 5-8, 339B1
Ceausescu urges export drive; debt estimated 6-4, 465D3
Poland unrest, defense budget cut rptd linked 9-11, 689C3
Iran attacks ships 10-7, 758G2
Poland CP unions scored 10-21, 831B1

Government & Politics—*See also other appropriate subheads in this section*
Mrs Ceausescu named dep premr 3-29, 412B1

Human Rights
Horodinca defects to US 2-24, 142A3
Horodinca's wife asks asylum 3-6, 221C1
20 defect to Austria 7-3, 548C3

Sports
Moscow Olympic results, disputes mar women's gymnastics 7-20—8-3, 588A3, 589D2-B3, 622E1-624C3
Chess Olympiad results 12-7, 972B3

1976

WHO vs rpt on Israel 5-17, 355A2
OKs Israel Arab land exit 6-29, 464C1
Abstains on anti-terror res 7-14, 515G3
S Africa arms ban vetoed 10-19, 781D3

RUMOR, Mariano
Named in oil co payoffs 4-11, 267C2
Denies link to Lockheed 4-22, 298A1
CP asks resignatn 6-11; denies paymts 6-13, 445C2
New govt excludes 7-30, 573D1
RUMSFELD, Donald H(enry)
At NATO A-group mtg 1-21—1-22, 297A3
Defends defns budget, issues Cong rpt 1-27, 68D1
Iran arms purchase drop seen 2-4, 102F1
Discounts 'padding' memo, defends budget 2-4, 116B1
Backs cruise missiles 2-6, 183F1
Censures Currie, Middendorf 3-16, 200G2
Named to business probe panel 3-21, 262E2
On review of training practices 5-2, 378E1
Asks more '77 Navy funds 5-4, 394B1
At NATO defns mins mtg 6-10—6-11, in Greece 6-15, 449F1, C2
In Kenya, Zaire 6-15—6-19, 466F3
Rptd Ford vp prospect 8-12, undergoes surgery 8-13, 584G1
GOP conv vp vote table 8-19, 599F3
On Sovt A-arms 9-27, 961F1
Currie corp favors chrgd 10-14, new curbs proposed 12-9, 983A1
Defends Brown, scores remarks 10-18, 787E1, A3
Chrysler wins tank contract 11-12, 941G3-942A3
At NATO mtg 11-17—11-18, 879F2
Briefs Carter 11-22, 881C1
At NATO defns mtg 12-7—12-8, 933G1
RUNNELS, Rep. Harold L. (D, N.M.)
Reelected 11-2, 824F2, 830F1
RUNNER Stumbles, The (play)
Opens 5-18, 1014D3
RUPP Jr., Paul
Dies 8-3, 565D2
RUPP 3rd, Paul
Dies 8-3, 565D2
RUPPE, Rep. Philip E. (R, Mich.)
Reelected 11-2, 829E4
RURAL Affairs
'75 environmtal rpt issued 1-18, 45C1
Cable TV loans urged 1-26, 135C3
Postal closings delayed 3-5, 186F3
Dem platform text 6-15, 474A2, C2
'77 dvpt funds signed 7-12, 533C3
Mondale scores GOP 7-31, 565E1
GOP platform text 8-18, 602G3
Dole identifies with 8-22, 631C2
Carter in Iowa 8-25, 632C1
Air pollutn threat rptd 12-8, 943D1
Migrant Workers—*See under AGRICULTURE*
RUSANOVA, Liubov
Wins Olympic medals 7-21, 7-24, 575A3
RUSEK, Antonin
Freed 12-10, 1012B3
RUSEVSKI, Ace
Wins Olympic medal 7-31, 574B1
RUSH, Kenneth A.
Croats surrender TWA jet 9-12, 685A2
RUSHER, William A.
Maddox named pres nominee 8-27, 666E1
RUSSELL, Bertrand Arthur William (3d Earl of Russell) (1872-1970)
2d Tribunal meets, disbands 1-10—1-17, 61B2
Tribunal witness found dead in Argentina 5-20, 399A2
RUSSELL, Judge Donald S.
Extends EEOC probe powers 1-23, 70E3
RUSSELL, Rosalind
Dies 11-28, 932F3
RUSSI, Bernhard
Wins Olympic medal 2-5, 158D3
RUSSIAN Orthodox Church—*See under EASTERN Orthodox Churches*
RUSSIANS, The (book)
On best-seller list 12-5, 972B2
RUSSO, Rep. Martin A. (D, Ill.)
Gun control bill recommitted 3-2, 170G1
Reelected 11-2, 829F2
RUSSO, Miguel
Convicted 12-9, 971F2-C3
RUSTAMOVA, Zebeniso
Wins Olympic medal 7-30, 573F3
RUSTIN, Bayard
At Sovt Jews' rights conf 2-17—2-19, 206B3
Cleaver Defense Fund formed 2-17, 272E1
RUSTIN, Mohammed
Named as hijacker 9-4, 662F2
RUSU, Stefan
Wins Olympic medal 7-24, 576A3
RUTGERS University (New Brunswick, N.J.)
Alcoholism rpts back Rand 8-8, 814D3
RUTHERFORD, Johnny
Wins Indy 500 5-30, 424F2
RUTILE
Australia to end Fraser I mining 11-11, 888A2
RUZICKA, Leopold
Dies 9-26, 932G3

1977

U.S. Relations
Westn debt rptd amounting 2-13—4-13, 335C3
US adopts fishing agrmt 2-21, 173D3
Udrescu gets US asylum 2-24, 315B1
US warning on 2d quake discounted 3-10, 204B2
Dissident contact barred at US emb 4-2, 315F1
Coal sale set 5-30, 468C3
CP neutron bomb ban plea 8-8, 640A3

RUMANIAN Orthodox Church—*See EASTERN Orthodox Churches*
RUMOR, Mariano
2 ex-mins indicted 1-29, 116A3
Ex-mins face Lockheed trial 3-10, 284D1
RUMSFELD, Donald H.
Searle pres 4-17, 396G3
RUN Dusty Run (race horse)
Seattle Slew wins Triple Crown 6-11, 491B1-D1
RUPP, Adolph F.
Dies 12-10, 1024B3
RURAL Affairs
US populatn shift rptd 2-24, 184A1
Sen amends '70 Clean Air Act 6-10, 461B1
Carter on gas-tax plan 7-22, 575C2
'78 dvpt funds signed 8-12, 688B3, C3
Health clinic aid clears Cong 11-29, 938F1; signed 12-13, 1001G2
RURAL Electrification Administration—*See under U.S. GOVERNMENT—AGRICULTURE*
RUSAKOV, Konstantin V.
Named Central Com secy 5-24, 412C2
RUSH, Alvin
Defends TV sports coverage 11-2, 949F3
RUSH, Bob
In NFL draft 5-3, 353B2
RUSH, Ian
Rebate knowledge denied 7-7, 542C1
RUSH, Kenneth A.
France warns vs Concorde ban 3-7, 212F2
Replaced as amb to France 6-7, 499E3
RUSIE, Amos (d. 1942)
Inducted into baseball HOF 8-8, 643G3
RUSK, Dean
Defends Panama Canal pacts 9-14, 716A3
RUSSELL Jr., Arthur J.
Dies 12-4, 1024B3
RUSSELL, Bill
In World Series 10-11—10-18, 806F1
RUSSELL, Rev. David
Sentenced 2-17, 145A2
RUSSELL v. Texas
Felony probatn loss review declined 11-14, 878B3
RUSSIA—*See UNION of Soviet Socialist Republics*
RUSSIAN Orthodox Church—*See under EASTERN Orthodox Churches*
RUSSO, Anthony
Sorensen withdraws CIA nominatn 1-17, 35D1
RUSSO, Giuseppe
Killed 8-21, 1014C3
RUSSO, Rep. Martin A. (D, Ill.)
'76 spec interest gifts rptd 2-15, 128E2
RUST, John Edward
Execution set 3-18, 594D1
RUSTIN, Bayard
Blacks meet re govt 'neglect' 8-29, 702F1
RUTGERS University (New Brunswick, N.J.)
NY Nets move to NJ set 7-26, 584G1
Gross dies 10-11, 872B2
RUTHERFORD, Johnny
Indy 500 results 5-29, 531G1
Final USAC standing, earnings rptd 10-31, 871A1
RUTIGLIANO, Sam
Named Browns coach 12-28, 1020A2
RUTTER, Dr. William J.
Rpts insulin gene reproductn 5-23, 451D3
RUZZ, Abou al-
Hijackers release 7-10, 535B2

1978

U.S. Relations
Ceausescu visits US 4-11—4-18, sees Carter 4-12—4-13, 291C1-A2
US favored-natn trade status cited 7-8, 534D2
Defector rptd questnd by US 8-8, 650F3; W Ger spy scandal disclosed 9-1, 725D2 ★
Pan Am to end Bucharest svc 9-7, 701G1
Blumenthal visits, support re mil spending stance seen 12-8—12-9, 965C3-966A1
RUMOURS (record album)
Wins Grammy 2-24, 315E3
RUMSFELD, Donald H.
Brown presents defns posture statemt 2-2, 81B1
RUNAWAYS (play)
Opens 3-9, 887G2
RUN'ERS' (play)
Opens 5-3, 887A3
RUNNELS, Rep. Harold L. (D, N.M.)
Reelected 11-7, 851C3, 855D2
RUNNING and Being (book)
On best-seller list 7-2, 579D3
RUNNING On Empty (recording)
On best-seller list 3-8, 196C1; 4-5, 272G3; 5-3, 356E1
RUPERT, Gene
Players opens 9-6, 887E2
RUPP, Adolph (1901-77)
Ky wins NCAA basketball title 3-27, 272G1
RUPPE, Rep. Philip E. (R, Mich.)
Primary results, retiremt cited 8-8, 626B1
Davis wins seat 11-7, 854B1
RUPPERT, James U.
Murder retrial case refused by Sup Ct 11-6, 874E1
RUPPERT v. Ohio
Case refused by Sup Ct 11-6, 874E1
RURAL Affairs
Carter budgets MD svcs 1-23, 48D2
MD shortage rptd 4-6—4-7, forecast bleak 7-23, 577C3
New TVA chrmn takes over 5-19, 390C2
Admin health plan announced 10-2, 770D1
Public works veto upheld 10-5, 765C1
RUSHVILLE, Ind.—*See INDIANA*
RUSKIN, Jeanne
Halloween Bandit opens 12-18, 1031A2
RUSSELL, Bill
Dodgers win NL pennant 10-7, 779D1
In World Series 10-10—10-17, 800B1
RUSSIA—*See UNION of Soviet Socialist Republics*
RUSSIAN Orthodox Church—*See under EASTERN Orthodox Churches*
RUSSO, Rep. Martin A. (D, Ill.)
Reelected 11-7, 850D3
RUSSO, Salvatore
Wounded 7-19, 574A2
RUSTIN, Bayard
Vs Carter urban-aid plan 3-30, 218D1
At pro-Shcharansky, Ginzburg rally 7-10, 542B3
RUTGERS University (New Brunswick, N.J.)
Texas wins NIT 3-21, 272A2
Loses Garden State Bowl 12-16, 1025B2
RUTHERFORD, Johnny
2d in Daytona endurance 2-5, 538D3
2d in Schaefer 500 6-25, 538E3
RUTHVEN, Dick
Stargell becomes all-time strikeout ldr 8-6, 779D3
Phillies lose NL pennant 10-7, 779A1
RUTLEDGE, Jeff
Alabama wins Sugar Bowl 1-2, 8E3
RUVALDINO, Roberto
Lujan TKOs 3-18, 379C2
RUZICI, Virginia
Loses German championship 5-21, 419D1
Loses Italian Open 5-27, 418E2
Wins French Open 6-11, 540E1
Loses Canadian Open 8-19, 1027B2

1979

U.S. Relations
US A-accident media coverage rptd 4-11, 323C1
US bank branches cited 11-15, 882C3
Black Sea drilling aid cited 11-19, 910A2

RUNCIE, Rev. Robert
Named Archbp of Canterbury 9-7, 755E2
RUNNER Stumbles, The (film)
Released 11-16, 1008D1
RUNNING
Rafferty crosses Death Valley 7-15, 656D3
RUNNING (film)
Released 11-2, 1008D1
RUPEREZ, Javier
Kidnaped 11-11, ETA claims credit 11-12, 875F2
Freed by ETA 12-12, 952C2
RUPERT, Michael
Festival opens 5-7, 711A3
RURAL Affairs
US ups poverty levels 4-9, 283E3
Malnutritn rptd down 4-30, 386G2
Carter proposes mental health plan 5-15, 365E1
Pope in Iowa, lauds rural values 10-4, 759B1, D1-A2
RUSK, Dean
At Teng luncheon in Atlanta 2-1, 83F2
Carter on Sovt troops in Cuba 10-1, 737B2
RUSSELL, Rev. David
Chrgd re ban violatn 12-10, 969E1
RUSSELL, Judge Donald S.
Mandel conviction upset 1-11, 18C1
RUSSELL, John
Comin' Uptown opens 12-20, 1007C2
RUSSELLVILLE, Ark.—*See ARKANSAS*
RUSSIA—*See UNION of Soviet Socialist Republics*
RUSSIAN Orthodox Church—*See under EASTERN Orthodox Churches*
RUSSIAN Soviet Federative Socialist Republic—*See USSR-Republics*
RUSSO, Aaron
Rose released 11-17, 1008C1
RUSSO, Basil M.
Cleveland defaults again 8-31, 920G2
RUSTIN, Bayard
Backs Rhodesia electn 4-21, 293E2
Visits Israel 10-14—10-17, 780D3
RUTGERS University (New Brunswick, N.J.)
Princeton football rivalry to end 1-20, 175D3
Bailey in NBA draft 6-25, 507A3
Newhouse Law Cntr dedicated, Brennan scores press 10-17, 848D1
RUTH Jr., George Herman (Babe) (1895-1948)
Mays in Baseball HOF 8-5, 618E3
RUTH Jr., Henry
Hired by Jordan 9-4, 767E2
RUTLEDGE, Jeff
Alabama wins Sugar Bowl 1-1, 8F2
RUTLEDGE, Kevin
Ariz State fires Kush, suit cited 10-13, 1001C3
RUZICI, Virginia
Loses Detroit Avon tourn 2-25, 391C2

1980

U.S. Relations
Rumania envoy defects 2-24, 142A3; wife asks asylum 3-6, 221C1
Iran hostage rescue try scored 4-25, 324D1

RUMBO (racehorse)
2d in Ky Derby 5-3, 447A2
RUMBOUGH, Maj. Gen. William S.
Dies 12-2, 1004C3
RUML, Jiri
15 Charter 77 members arrested 6-1, 431C3
RUMMEL, William James
Tex habitual-offender law upheld 3-18, 226G2
RUMMEL v. Estelle
Case decided by Sup Ct 3-18, 226D3
Case cited by Sup Ct 3-31, 291G2
RUMMENIGGE, Karl-Heinz
W Ger wins Eur Soccer Championship 6-22, 771F2
RUMSFELD, Donald H.
Addresses GOP conv 7-14, 530B3
RUNCIE, Most Rev. Robert (Archbishop of Canterbury)
Enthroned 3-25, 364D2
Meets Pope 5-9, 363B3
RUNNELS, Dorothy
Loses US House election 11-4, 852C1
RUNNELS, Rep. Harold Lowell (D, N.M.)
Dies 8-5, 676F2
Skeen wins seat 11-4, 852C1
RUNNING
Heart attack risk rptd reduced 2-14, 158A2
Rodgers scores USOC boycott vote 4-12, 283E2
Woman sets UK distance record 8-15, 638C3
RUNYON, Damon (1884-1946)
Little Miss Marker released 3-21, 216C3
RUOFF, Bernie
Edmonton wins Grey Cup 11-23, 999D2
RUPIPER, Rev. Darrell
Visits US hostages in Iran 4-6, 258D2
RURAL Affairs
Carter State of Union topic 1-23, 43A2, F2
Presidential Election (& Transition)
Carter warns vs Reagan win 10-6, 762E3
Reagan deplores Carter 'hysteria' 10-7, 763D2
Carter softens Reagan attack 10-9, 778C2
RUSH v. Savchuk
Case decided by Sup Ct 1-21, 93A2
RUSSELL, Bill
Abdul-Jabbar named NBA MVP 5-29, 656B3
RUSSELL, Bill E.
Reuss pitches no-hitter 6-28, 636B3
RUSSELL, Dale
Arrows win MISL title 3-23, 771B2
RUSSELL, Rev. David
Sentncd re ban defiance 2-28, 195A3
RUSSELL, Hugh
Wins Olympic medal 8-2, 622E1
RUSSELL, R. Robert
On '79 oil co price abuses 2-25, 189D3
Sees continued inflatn 3-25, 222C2
On June producer price rise 7-8, 513E3
RUSSELL, Theresa
Bad Timing released 9-21, 836D2
RUSSELLVILLE—*See ARKANSAS*
RUSSIA—*See UNION of Soviet Socialist Republics*
RUSSO, Rep. Martin A. (D, Ill.)
Reelected 11-4, 842D3
RUSSO, Vincenzo
Italy regional affairs min 4-4, 275G3
RUSSO, William
Paris Lights opens 1-24, 136E3
RUSTIN, Bayard
At Cambodia border aid vigil 2-6, 108C2
RUSU, Stefan
Wins Olympic medal 7-24, 624A3
RUTGERS University (New Brunswick, N.J.)
Crib death heredity link rptd 2-28, 358C3
RUTHERFORD, Mayor James W. (Flint, Mich.)
Print shop police raid cited 7-26, 582D2
RUTHERFORD, Johnny
Wins Indy 500 5-25, 637E2
2d in Pocono 500 6-22, 638A1
CART membership cited 6-30, 1002A2
Named top driver; earnings cited 12-5, 1002E1
RUTHERFORD, Stephen
In Statue of Liberty protest 5-11, 667D1
RUTHVEN, Dick
NL pitching ldr 10-6, 926G2
Phillies win NL pennant 10-12, 796A2
In World Series 10-14—10-21, 812E1
RUTILE
Australia bans Sovt export 1-28, 116E1
Australia lifts Sovt embargo 2-12, 148A1
RUTKOWSKI, Tadeusz
Wins Olympic medal 7-30, 624G2
RUTLEDGE, Howard
Wins Okla US House primary 8-26, 683C1
Loses US House electn 11-4, 850C1
RUZICI, Virginia
Loses Women's Italian Open 5-11, French Open 6-7, 606B3, 607C3
Wins Austrian Grand Prix 7-27, 691A3
Loses Women's Dutch Indoors 11-16, 947E2

1976

RWANDA—*See also AFRICAN Development Bank, NONALIGNED Nations Movement, OAU*
- Listed as 'not free' nation 1-19, 20E3
- Uganda blocks oil shipmts 4-7, 502F2
- At France-Africa summit 5-10—5-11, 355A3
- Amb to Uganda sees Amin 7-16, 548F1
- Kenya chrgs Uganda seized oil shipmt 7-16, 548A2
- Kenya oil mtg 7-22, 559F3
- World Bank OKs credit 12-16, 1013C2

RYAN, Hewson A.
- On Uruguay aid 8-4; transfer rptd 9-20, 814C2

RYAN, Most Rev. Joseph T.
- Succeeded 5-4, 424D1

RYAN, Rep. Leo J. (D.-Calif)
- On Teton Dam collapse 9-25, 736C1
- Reelected 11-2, 829B1

RYAN, Nolan
- AL pitching ldr 10-4, 796D1

RYBAKOV, Victor
- Wins Olympic medal 7-31, 574B1

RYBAKOV, Yakov R.
- Named to Secretariat 10-26, 839E2

RYBICKI, Jerzy
- Wins Olympic medal 7-31, 574C1

RYDBECK, Olof
- Named UN Sahara envoy 2-1, 107A3
- Ends Sahara missn 2-17, 178D2

RYE
- New support-rate set 10-13, 787G3

RYLE, Gilbert
- Dies 10-6, 932G3

RYON, Luann
- Wins Olympic medal 7-30, 573F3

RYSTE, Ruth
- Norway soc affairs min 1-12, 30A2

1977

RWANDA—*See also NONALIGNED Nations Movement, OAU*
- UN Assemb member 4B1
- Uganda drops US exit ban 3-1, 141B2
- Uganda mercenary aid rptd 3-28, 308G1
- At France-Africa summit 4-20—4-21, 316F3

R-W Service System
- ICC sues 11-3, 861D1

RYAN, John J.
- Indicted 8-2, 631B3

RYAN, Dr. Kenneth
- Chrgs unneeded hysterectomies 5-9, 732E2

RYAN, Rep. Leo (D, Calif.)
- Vs US Concorde policy 9-8, 9-23, 738F2, A3

RYAN, Nolan
- AL pitching ldr 10-2, 927A1

RYAN, Richie
- Presents '77 budget 1-26, 64C2

RYBACHENKO, Vladimir
- France ousts as spy 2-11, 159D3

RYDER, Lord
- To sue Daily Mail 5-24, quits Natl Enterprise Bd 7-1, 526G1

RYOR, John
- Scores SAT study 8-24, 739B2

RYUMIN, Valery
- On Soyuz 25 missn 10-9—10-11, 771C3

1978

RWANDA—*See also GATT, NONALIGNED Nations Movement, OAU*
- UN rights comm condemns Israel 2-14, 99A2
- UN Assemb member 713D3
- Cholera outbreak, Belgium aid rptd 10-12, 927E2
- Polisario recognitn cited 11-10, 999G2

RYAN, Claude
- Rebuts Levesque re separatism plan 10-11, 837E1

RYAN, Hermine Braunsteiner
- W Ger war crimes trial criticism rptd 1-30, 114B3
- Deportatn cited 10-30, 872E2

RYAN, Rep. Leo J. (D, Calif.)
- Photo 891A2
- Petitns for Hearst pardon 9-26, 824B1
- Reelected 11-7, 850E1
- Arrives Guyana 11-15, Jonestown cult commune 11-17; killed 11-18, Carter lauds 11-19, body flown home 11-21, 889A1-891B3
- Guyana chrgs Layton 11-22; cultists held as witnesses 11-28, 910E2
- FBI murder probe cited 12-8, 955D1
- Calif grand jury queries Guyana survivors 12-8, probe suspended 12-13, 955G1
- Layton indicted 12-8, takes 'full responsibility' 12-13, 955B2
- Grand jury probe resumes 12-21—12-27, 1000D1

RYAN, Nolan
- AL pitching ldr 10-2, 928G3

RYDER, Lord
- BL ex-exec jailed 8-11, 667A3

RYDER, Richard
- Piano Bar opens 6-8, 887E2

RYMAN, John
- Scores Rees re London race riot 6-11, 452F3

RYOR, John
- On Propositn 13 7-5, 525G3

1979

RWANDA—*See also GATT, NONALIGNED Nations Movement, OAU*
- Franco-African summit hosted 5-21—5-22, 398D3
- CAE student massacre probe rptd 8-6, 601A3
- UN membership listed 695B3

RYABOV, Yakov P.
- Moved to Planning Comm post 4-17, 314D1

RYALL, George Francis Trafford (Audax Minor)
- Dies 10-8, 860D3

RYAN, Claude
- Wins by-electn 4-30, 329A1
- Scores referendum delay 6-21, 484A1
- Hails PQ by-electn defeat 11-14, 889B2

RYAN, Elizabeth (Bunny)
- Dies 7-6, King breaks Wimbledon mark 7-7, 570C1

RYAN, Gordon M.
- Settles SEC chrg 2-7, 132B1

RYAN, John
- Rejects Knight resignatn 8-24, 799A1

RYAN, Leo J. (d. 1978)
- Layton chrgs dismissed 3-7, 220E1
- Jonestown tape copy rptd 3-15, 219B3
- GOP wins seat 4-3, 265F1

RYAN, Nolan
- NL wins All-Star Game 7-17, 568D3
- AL pitching ldr 9-30, 955G3
- Signs with Astros, becomes top-paid player 11-19, 1001E3

RYAN, Thomas
- Suspended in Morales escape 5-21, 431A2

RYDELL, Mark
- Rose released 11-17, 1008C1

RYKIEL, Sonya
- '79 fashion roundup rptd 1006D2

RYUMIN, Valery
- Soyuz 32 launched 2-25, 163F1
- Soyuz 33 linkup fails 4-10—4-12, 279B2
- Space endurance record set 7-15, 553E1
- Ends record flight 8-19, 626D2

1980

RWANDA—*See GATT, NONALIGNED Nations, OAU*

RYAN, Claude
- On Quebec Liberal const reform 1-10, 19B1
- Scores referendum campaign violence 5-2, 350A3
- Broadbent scores 5-11, 372D2
- On referendum defeat 5-20, 377F1
- On '76 Olympic contributns 6-6, 444G1

RYAN, Hermine Braunsteiner
- US deportatn cited 1-16, 228F2

RYAN, Leo J. (d. 1978)
- Layton trial delayed 4-1, 313D3
- Layton faces murder chrgs 5-22, 407F3

RYAN, Nolan
- NL pitching ldr 10-6, 926G2
- Phillies win NL pennant 10-12, 796G1
- Winfield signs record pact with Yankees 12-15, 999G3

RYBAKOV, Viktor
- Wins Olympic medal 8-2, 622F1

RYBICKI, Jerzy
- Wins Olympic medal 8-2, 622A2

RYKIEL, Sonya
- '80 fashion roundup rptd 998A2

RYUMIN, Valery
- Soyuz 35 launched 4-9, 365G1
- Soyuz 6 docks with Soyuz 36 5-27, 397C3
- Remains on Salyut 6-9, 477D1
- Soyuz team boards Salyut 7-24, 547G3
- Cuba-Sovt team in Soyuz trip 9-18—9-26, 737E2
- Ends record flight 10-11, 777B3

S

1976

SAAB, Edouard
- Killed in Beirut 5-16, 354D3

SAAB-Scania Aktiebolag
- US ends car dumping probe 5-4, 321D2
- Car price hike set 8-16, 988D1

SAALFIELD, Albrecht
- '72 campaign gift listed 4-25, 688D1

SABAH al-Salem al-Sabah, Sheik
- Sahara plea rptd 1-29, 58D2 ★
- Dissolves Natl Assemb 8-29, 642G1
- At Riyadh peace conf 10-17—10-18, 778A3

SABATA, Jaroslav
- Freed 12-10, 1012B3

SABATELLA, Paul
- Sentenced 3-9, 271C2

SABENA Belgium World Airlines
- Sex bias in pay barred 4-8, 276C3

SABETI, Parviz
- Denies police torture 5-26, 418F2

SABHARWAL, Pran
- Loses press certificatn 2-14, 139C3

SABIN, Dr. Albert
- Ford asks flu vaccine drive 3-24, 224B2
- Polio vaccine danger rptd 9-23, 776B1

SABOTAGE—*See ESPIONAGE*

SABRY, Moussa
- Gets press post 3-28, 333F1

SACCUCCI, Sandro
- Arrested 6-1, 403B1

SACH, Pham Van
- Rival US refugee groups split 2-20, 176B3

SACHS, Dennis N.
- On Teton Dam collapse 7-15, 736E1

1977

SAAB-Scania, A. B.
- Volvo merger agreed 5-6, 469B3
- Volvo merger called off 8-28, 709E1

SAAR, John
- Rpts Singlaub vs Korea policy 5-19, 403G3, 404E1

SABA—*See NETHERLANDS Antilles*

SABAH, Sheik Saad Abdullah
- Sovt mil aid pact signed 4-13, 394D3

SABAH al-Ahmed al-Sabah, Sheik
- Mediates Egypt-Libya feud 7-24—7-25, 570A1
- Meets Assad, rues Arab rift 12-9, 954A3
- Dies 12-31, 1019A2

SABBE, Osman Saleh
- Chrgs govt asks Cuba aid 3-8, 239B1

SABICH, Vladimir (Spider) (d. 1976)
- Longet sentncd 1-31, 102E3

SABINE Pipe Line Co.—*See under TEXACO Inc.*

SABOTAGE—*See ESPIONAGE*

SABRI, Yussef
- Riot role denied 1-23, 62E2

SABRY, Moussa
- Defends Sadat vs Sovts 2-22, 144F2 ★

SABUNI, Col. Juma
- Named in slaying of 2 Amers 9-2, 709C3

SA Carneiro, Francisco
- Quits as oppositn ldr 11-7, 886C3
- Soares scores 12-6, 947G2

SACCHARIN—*See SWEETENERS, Artificial*

SACCO, Nicola (d. 1927)
- Vindicated 7-19, 652E2-A3

SACHR, Lt. Gen. Vilem
- Demotion rptd 4-7, 314C2

1978

SA-11 (Soviet missile)—*See ARMAMENTS—Missiles*

SAAB-Scania, A.B.
- Brazil workers strike 5-12—5-16, 5-19—5-23, 412A1, F1

SAAD, Michael
- Bleacher Bums opens 4-24, 760E1

SAARINEN, Eero (1910-1961)
- Eames dies 8-21, 708E2

SABAH, Sheik Ali Khalifa al-
- Rpts OPEC cutback plan 5-16, 384B1
- Heads OPEC currency study 6-19, 465B2
- OPEC panel backs currency 'basket' 7-21, 640C1
- Hints oil cutback 10-9, 871E1

SABAH, Sheik Sabah al-Ahmed al-
- Asks Leb pres to stay on 7-9, 522C1

SABATA, Jaroslav
- Arrest rptd 10-7, 868G3

SABBAGH, Hassib
- Seeks PLO-Christn accord 11-13, 870B1

SABBE, Odman Saleh
- Rebel factn, Saudi backing cited 372G2

SABELLICO, Richard
- Gay Divorce opens 3-9, 760C2

SABETI, Parveez
- Rpt ousted from Savak post 10-29, 827B3

SABO, Martin Olav
- On Proposition 13 7-6, 526A1
- Wins US House seat 11-7, 851A2, 854D3

SABOTAGE—*See ESPIONAGE, TERRORISM*

SABRY, Moussa
- Ties Arafat to radicals 2-27, 138B2

SA Carneiro, Francisco
- Reelected Soc Dem pres 7-3, 593G3-594A1
- Mota Pinto named premier 10-25, 830D2

SACCHARIN—*See SWEETENERS, Artificial*

SACHS A.G.
- Guest takeover halted by W Ger ct 2-23, 211B1

SACHS, Ann
- Man & Superman revived 12-17, 1031D2

SACHS, Norman
- My Old Friends opens 12-2, 1031E2

SACKLER, Howard
- Gray Lady Down released 3-10, 619B2
- Jaws 2 released 6-16, 619E2

SACKS, Ezra
- FM released 4-28, 619A2

1979

SAAB-Scania, A.B.
- Brazil metalworkers strike 3-13—3-27, 328C3

SAADATMAND, Hassan
- Executed 5-9, 353D2

SAAD Muhammad, Matthew
- KOs Johnson for WBC light heavywgt title 4-22, 412G3
- Decisns Conteh 8-18, 839C1

SAAR, Pap Koll
- Israel arrests 2-18, 157A2
- Israel sentences 5-10, 341A3

SABAGHIAN, Mohammed Hashem
- Gets Iran interior min post 2-12, 105F2*
- Curbs rallies 8-14, 614F3
- Chrgs Iraq, Israel aid Kurds 9-1, 670C1
- On Kurdish ambush 10-9, 773G3

SABAH, Sheik Ali Khalifa al-
- OPEC mtg set 2-19, 126G1

SABAN, Lou
- Hired as West Pt football coach 1-4, 175A3

SABATA, Jaroslav
- Sentenced 1-11, 62C2
- Sentence extended 5-10, 782F1

SABEEL, Imam Sheik Mohammed Ibn
- Mecca mosque seized 11-20, 898D3

Sa CARNEIRO, Francisco Manuel Lumbrales de
- AD wins assemb electns, to form new govt 12-2, holds news conf 12-3; facts on 916G3-917F1, 953A2
- AD wins municipal elections 12-16, 968F2

SACASA, Juan B. (deceased)
- US-Nicaragua long-term ties detailed 535E2

SACCHARIN—*See SWEETNERS, Artificial*

SACHS, Allan D.
- Completes Argent deal 12-10, organized crime probe rptd 12-12, 965B1

SACKHEIM, William
- In-Laws released 6-15, 820D1

SACKLER, Howard
- Saint Jack released 4-26, 528E3

1980

SAAB-Scania, A.B.
- Lundvall rptd dead 9-22, 756C1

SAADE, Pedro
- Disrupts Navy maneuvers 1-19, 94D1

SAAD Muhammad, Matthew
- TKOs Conteh 3-29, 320C3
- KOs Mwale 11-29, 1001B1

SAAVEDRA Lamas, Carlos (1878-1959)
- Perez wins Nobel Peace Prize 10-13, 889C2

SABAH, Sheik Ali Khalifa al-
- Threatens to blacklist Pontoil 2-7, 108C3
- OKs oil sales to USSR, Comecon 3-2, 166B1
- Proposes OPEC pricing compromise 9-18, 694C3

SABBE, Osman Saleh
- Chrgs govt depopulatn effort 3-8, 274D1

SABIN, Dr. Albert B.
- Brazil polio drive stalled 4-16, 310G1-C2

SABO, Rep. Martin Olav (D, Minn.)
- Reelected 11-4, 843B2

SABRI, Maj. Gen. Mohammed
- Named Saudi AF head 1-1, 22D1

SABYROV, Shamil
- Wins Olympic medal 8-2, 622E1

SA CARNEIRO, Francisco Manuel Lumbrales de (Portuguese premier)
- Cabt sworn, excludes mil 1-3, 21C3
- Clashes with Eanes 3-4—4-1, 277A2, B3
- Submits '80 austerity budget 4-2, 277F2
- Eanes vetoes new econ laws, blocks budget 4-11, 315A3
- Soares gets AD pres nod 4-11, 315C3
- Denounces mil cncl, vows const reforms 5-23, 410F1
- Giscard asks EC expansn delay 6-5, 435F3
- Carter sees 6-26, 475B1
- AD wins Assembly vote, gains 8 seats 10-5; Eanes defeat seen 10-6, 760B1
- Eanes oppositn cited 10-14, 809F2
- Scores Eanes, backs Carneiro 11-21, 902F3
- Dies in Lisbon plane crash 12-4, 923D1
- Eanes reelected 12-7, AD govt resigns 12-8, 944B2, D2
- Pinto Balsemao named premr 12-22, 995G3

SACCHARIN—*See SWEETNERS, Artificial*

SACCHI, Robert
- Sam Marlowe released 10-3, 836E3

SACKHEIM, William
- Competition released 12-3, 972D3

SACKLER, Howard
- Goodbye Fidel opens 4-23, 392G2

SACKS, Ezra
- Small Circle of Friends released 3-9, 216F3

1976

SACRAMENTO, Calif.—*See CALIFORNIA*

SADAT, Anwar el- (Egyptian president)
Backs PLO at Geneva conf 1-13, 18G3
Blames Syria, Leb for civil war 1-25, 2-3, 83D2
Seeks Sahara setlmt 1-27, 58C2
Rpts Kissinger peace moves ended 1-27, 'secret' US Sinai agrmt 2-29, 162E1-B2
Fulbright award rptd 1-28, 160D2
In Arab oil natns, gets aid vows 2-21—2-29, 162C1
PLO sees no Geneva conf 2-27, 162C2
US sen rpts Egypt aid pressure 2-28, 161D1
US seeks jet sales 3-3, 161E1
Asks Sovt pact end, lauds US; cites MiG parts ban 3-14, 193A1
Reorganizes press 3-14, 3-19, 3-28, 333E1
Ford denies '75 border agrmt 3-17, 198G2
India confrms MiG parts ban 3-17, 275C3
US hails Sovt break 3-19, USSR assails 3-22, 227C3
Calls emergency mtg on Leb 3-28, 226D2
In 6 Eur natns; comments on Sovt break, Leb crisis, Israel A-power 3-29—4-12, 274D3-275E2
Lauds W Bank electn results 5-1, 319G2
Syria talks renewal sought 5-23, 370C2
Chamoun denies Egypt arms buy 5-24, 369E2
Says Syria blocks peace 6-4, 406G1
In Leb crisis talks 6-21, 448F3
Assad summit seen 6-24, 449A1
Arafat warns of Syria threat to Beirut 7-8, 514C3
Signs Sudan defense pact 7-13—7-14, 531D2
Joins Sudan, Saudis in pact vs Libya 7-18—7-19, 531B2
Ties Libya to Sudan coup 7-22, 547B3
Qaddafi threatens break 7-25, 547D3
Arafat disavows Syria peace pact 7-30, 578A1
Scores Qaddafi 8-13, 8-15, 629D3, G3
Egypt gets Arab fund aid 8-21, 630C1
Chrg Libya vs renominatn 8-24, 629B3
Renominated 8-25, reelected 9-16, 734F3
Meets Leb ldrs 9-18, blamed for impasse 9-20, 698B3
Vows aid to Sarkis 9-23, 699C2
Vs Syria Leb drive, questns Damascus raid rpt 9-28, 720B2, D2
Asks Arab summit on Leb 9-29, 737B2
Gets Arafat plea vs Syria drive 10-13, 758D2
Sworn for 2d term 10-16, 852E1
At Riyadh peace conf 10-17—10-18, 778A3
Centrists win electns 10-28, 11-4, 852D1
Multiple parties restored 11-11, 852A2
Meets US congressmen 11-11—11-17, 877G2
Meets Assad, Syria union set 12-18—12-21, 954D2
Backs Palestine-Jordan tie, Israel exit, Leb conf role 12-29, 12-30, 973A1

1977

SADAT, Anwar el- (Egyptian president)
Israel weighs Jordan-Palestine plan 1-2; renews plan 1-3, 10E1
Wants PLO at Geneva conf 1-4, 10A2
Meets Hussein, PLO peace role backed 1-14—1-15, 50C1
Deals with food riots 1-20, 43F3
Tito visit canceled 1-20, 43F3
Econ policies backed vs Sovt criticsm 1-23, 62C2
Decrees political curbs 2-3, 83B1
Khaddam visits 2-3, Syria pol cmnd formed 2-4, 87A1
Hussein vs plebiscite 2-5, 115D3
Plebiscite OKs curbs 2-10, 115A3
Sees Vance, asks Jordan-PLO link 2-17; PLO reactn 2-18, 121B1, G1, 124F2
USSR vs memoirs 2-19, Egypt replies 2-22, 144A2
PLO, Jordan OK link 2-22—2-23, 122D1
Saudi cited as CIA liaison 2-22, 124A3
Sudan joins Egypt-Syria cmnd 2-27—2-28, 143F2
Egypt to get 50 Sovt MiGs 2-27, 144F1
Hosts Afro-Arab summit 3-7—3-9, 170D1
Carter Mideast views scored 3-10, 166G1
Vs Carter on Israel borders 3-12, 187C2
Says Arabs back PLO-Jordan tie 4-3, 245B2
Meets Carter; seeks US aid, gives peace views 4-4—4-5; rpts differences 4-6, 245A1
On Rabin resignatn 4-9, 267G2
Peres says impedes peace 4-25, 316F1
Qaddafi chrgs mil designs 5-1, 361E3
Zaire gets pilots 5-2, 394A1
Egypt, Israel increase war games 5-9, 361B2
Nixon reminisces 5-12, 386A2
Forgn investmts increase 5-16, 390C2
Warns Israel to withdraw 5-18, 378A1
Meets Arab ldrs on Israel electn 5-19, sees no chng 5-20, 401D3
Asks Israel oil compensatn 5-29, 496D1
Begin asks peace talks 6-21, 474C2
Thanks China for arms 6-25, 496D2
Told Carter Israel ties impossible 7-2, 509G1
Backs Begin call for Oct Geneva talks 7-4; Begin replies 7-5, 509D1
Moslem sect vows 'war' vs 7-7, 526A1
Meets Hussein, PLO-Jordan tie backed 7-9—7-10, 534G2
Carter lauds peace moves, Hussein mtg 7-12, 533E2
Says USSR cut mil deals, Saudis to fund defense 7-16, 550B1
On Israel war bodies return 7-17, 550A2
Vs Israel peace plan 7-20, 549D2
On Libyan clashes; scores Qaddafi, Sovts 7-22, 569E1
Orders Libya cease-fire 7-24, 569D2
Meets Vance; OKs Israel-Arab pre-Geneva mtg 8-1—8-2; assures Arafat 8-4, 588B2
Israel backs mtg plan 8-3, Assad vs 8-4, 588G2, D3
Meets Vance, notes Sinai pact expiratn 8-11, 605G2
Dayan: favors peace pact; Begin: no moderate 8-11, 623B3
Sovt, Czech cotton trade curbed 8-14, 636A3
Confrms Moslem-Copt strife 9-28, 863D2
Meets Arafat on Geneva 10-18—10-19, 793B1
Asks US OK PLO at Geneva 10-19, 793A1
Changes Cabt 10-25, 824A1
Suspends Sovt debt repaymt; bans cotton to USSR, Czechs 10-26, 811F3
Yugo visit delayed 10-27, 844E2
Ends Rumania, Iran, Saudi visit 11-3, 850A2
For pre-Geneva agenda 11-4, Israel vs 11-6, 850G1-B2
Urges Geneva talks, vows visit to Israel parlt 11-9, 850D1
US lauds Geneva peace call 11-10, 850D2
Asks US Palestine prof as Geneva rep 11-12, 873D2
Arab League delays Geneva decisn 11-12—11-14, 874F1, B2
In Ismailia 11-18, 890A2

Israel Visit (& aftermath)
In Begin exchng on Israel visit 11-11, 11-12, 11-14; gets formal invitatn 11-15, accepts 11-17, 873A1
US, Arab, Sovt reactn 11-15—11-16, 873F2
Sees Assad 11-16, 873G1
Ceauscescu go-between role rptd 11-16, 873C2
Arab reactn to visit 11-17—11-22, 890D2-D3, 894E1
US, Sovt reactn to visit 11-17—11-22, 894E2
Begin thanks Ceausescu 11-18, 895B1
Arrives Israel 11-19; tours Jerusalem, addresses Knesset 11-20, 889A1
Knesset speech text 11-20, 891A1-893D1
Holds news conf with Begin, final communique released 11-21, 889D2-890F1
Hailed upon return to Egypt 11-21, 890F1
Sees Nimeiry, trip hailed 11-22, 890B3
EC backs visit 11-22, 894G3
Syria info min rules out Geneva conf 11-25, 909B2

1978

SACRAMENTO, Calif.—*See CALIFORNIA*

SADAT, Anwar el- (Egyptian president)
Asks Carter to pressure Israel 1-2; Begin scores 1-3, 2D2, B3
Meets Carter on Palestinians; Begin lauds talks 1-4, 1C1, 2A2, 3A1
Shah meets, backs peace moves 1-9; briefs Saudis 1-10, 26C2
Meets Israel defense min 1-11, 10D1
Carter: views 'almost identical' 1-12, 12G1-A2
Sees 'no hope' for Israeli talks 1-12, 1-13, 26A2
Suspends Pol Com talks, recalls delegatn 1-18, 25A1
Israel Cabt scores talks suspensn 1-18, 25B2
US asks Israel talks renewal 1-18, 25F2
Arab hardliners score 1-19, 1-22, 42D1
Meets Vance, vs Israel talks renewal 1-20, 41D1
Begin on talks breakdown, chrgs Egypt press anti-Semitism 1-21—1-23; press denies chrgs 1-24, 41E1, B2, 42B1
On Israel talks suspensn 1-21, 41F1
Rpts private Israel talks 1-25, 41C1
Offers Somalia aid; scores USSR, Cuba role 1-26, 2-6, 99F3
Asks US Jews back peace moves 1-29, ADL denied reply 2-1, 60B3
Meets US aide on peace moves 1-30—2-1, 60D1
In Morocco, seeks Hassan backing 2-2, 60F1
Algiers summit; hardliners map strategy, Iraq boycotts 2-2—2-4, 78E2
In US, presses peace drive 2-3—2-8; sees Carter, aides at Camp David 2-4—2-5, 77A1-B2
New Wafd Party reinstated 2-3, 131E1
Chrgs Israel intransigence, asks US Jewish ldrs aid 2-6, 77C2
Asks US cong for arms 2-7, Begin opposes 2-8, 78A1, C1
In 6-natn Eur tour, seeks Mideast peace initiative support 2-9—2-13, 98C2-C3
US rights rpt lauds regime 2-9, 102A2
Sebai slain in Cyprus 2-18, 117C1
US aide resumes mediatn 2-21—3-6; sends Begin note 3-2, gets reply 3-6, 156D3
Cuts ties with Cyprus 2-22, 118A2
Cyprus urges ties renewal 2-23, 138F2
Carter lauds for Cyprus raid 2-23, US denies taking sides 2-26, 138G2
PLO scores Palestinian stand 2-24, 2-28, 138C2
Vs Sovt arms to Syria 2-25, 139G2
French jet order rptd 3-1, 139B2
Carter for Begin-Sadat talks 3-2, 140E3
Israel, US dispute Res 242 3-4, 3-6—3-9, 156C2
Vs PLO raid on Israel 3-14, 176B1
Vs Israel Leb invasn 3-16, 174G3
Begin hopes for talk renewal 3-22, 199E1
Arab League seeks to end rift on peace stand 3-27—3-29, 215A1
Meets Weizman 3-30—3-31; asks Begin flexibility, lauds US role 4-5, 235F2, C3
Heykal says peace moves failed 415C1
US aide in Cairo re talks renewal 4-21—4-25, 299B3
Carter lauds peace progress 4-25, 307A2
US reassures Egypt on Carter Palestine statemt 5-1, 339B3
Asks Cabt shift 5-1, 3 ousted 5-7, 392B3
Proposes Jordan, Egypt get W Bank, Gaza 5-10, 424F2
Sets referendum to curb foes 5-14, voters back plan 5-21; lauds results 5-23, 392F1
Lauds US Sen jet pkg OK 5-16, 358C2
US asks peace talks renewal 5-19, 424D2
Cracks down on critics 5-26, 5-28, defends move 5-30, 414D3, 415C1
Warns Israel of peace lag 5-30, 6-6; Israel scorns deadlines 5-30, 5-31, 424F1
Assemb enacts pol curbs 6-1, 436E3
Threatens war re Israel occupatn, cites Israel separate peace plan rejectn 6-7; Israel scores threat 6-7, 6-8, 461G2
Threatens to oust forgn newsmen 6-7; Arab press group scores 6-21, 473D2
UK lauds Rumania peace role 6-14, 515D3
Amb to Portugal ordrd recalled, scores Sadat policies 6-19, 473A2
On Israel W Bank, Gaza stand 6-20, 461E2
Peres contacts rptd 6-21, 489D1
US Sen Javits scores 6-22, 461D2
Weizman says 'sincere' 6-23, 489G1
Egypt plans W Bank, Gaza proposal 6-24; Israel rejects 6-25, Begin comments 6-27, 488E3
Gives Mondale peace plan; OKs Egypt-Israel conf 7-3; plan detailed, text 7-5, 501A1, E1, C2, 502C1
Arrives Vienna 7-7; meets Peres, OKs Kreisky-Brandt peace plan 7-9, 521A2
Israel vs peace plan 7-9, 7-11; disappointed 7-10, 521A1, G1
Premiership takeover seen 7-12, 573G1
Meets Weizman, gives new peace plan 7-13; Israel defers actn on plan, scores Weizman, Peres mtgs 7-16, 7-19, 546A2, D2, B3
Calls Weizman, Peres talks 'successful' 7-14, 546C2
Preference for Weizman, Peres over Begin seen 7-16, 546G2
Calls Begin 'obstacle' to peace 7-22, 563B1
Begin bars El Arish, Mt Sinai return 7-23, 563E1
Israel mil missn ousted 7-26, 562G2
Meets Atherton 7-28—7-30, 581E2

1979

SACRAMENTO, Calif.—*See CALIFORNIA*
SACRAMENTO Union (newspaper)
McGoff purchase, S Africa link confirmed 6-4, 427E3
SADAT, Anwar el- (Egyptian president)
Iran's shah visits 1-16, 25C1
US issues rights rpt 2-10, 107C3
Meets US defns secy; asks US arms, bars Israel pact concessns 2-16—2-18, 143B3
Balks at high-level Israel talks 2-25; Begin hints at Carter mtg 2-26, bars Khalil talks 2-27, 142F2, B3
PLO says 'isolated' by Iran revolt 2-26, 144A2
Warns Islamic radicals 3-1, 161C3
Carter in Cairo talks 3-8, 157A1
Assad warns vs Israel pact 3-8, 157G1
Carter in Egypt 3-8—3-10, 3-13; OKs Israel pact 3-13, 177A1, A2
Arafat shuns in pact protest letter to Arabs 3-11, 178E1
Saudi rptdly warned of aid cutoff 3-11, 178F1
Carter lauds on Israel pact 3-14, 177F2
Saudi warns vs Israel pact signing 3-18, 197D2
Brzezinski briefs on Saudi, Jordan talks 3-18, 197G2
Hails Knesset OK of peace pact 3-22, 197G1-A2
Meets Begin, Sinai oil turnover OKd 3-25, 221F2
Signs Israel peace treaty 3-26, 221A1
Arafat scores for Israel pact 3-26, 222C2
Vs separate US-Israel pact 3-28, 222B1
In Bonn, seeks econ aid 3-29; returns to Cairo 3-31, 250A1
Arab League hopes for overthrow 3-31, 248E2
Meets Begin in Cairo, OKs agrmts 4-2—4-3; lauds progress 4-4, 248E3
Greets US trade missn 4-17, 296C1
Referendum OKs electns 4-19; ends parlt, sets vote date 4-21, 295B3
Deplores PLO raid on Israel 4-22, 296B3
Sees Weizman on Sinai exit 4-25—4-27, 320D1
Assails Saudi, discounts econ impact 5-1; Riyadh refutes 5-2, 319E1
Told Hassan of plea re Jerusalem 5-3, 360G1
Arab group vows to 'bring down' 5-10, 341E2
Says Saudis will renege on US jet deal 5-12, 360A1
US role to end Saudi feud rptd 5-20, 378C3
Begin: vowed open border 5-24, 394E2
May offer shah Egypt asylum 5-24, 408G1
Visits El Arish 5-26, 394C1
Israel border opening announced 5-27, 394B3
Vs Israel settlers in El Arish 5-28, 395C1
Gaza supporter slain 6-1, 414A3
Dayan visits, reaffirms hold on W Bank, Gaza 6-4, 415G2
Announces China arms deal 6-5, 415A3
Party wins parlt electns 6-7, 6-14, 468A3
Offers shah asylum 6-23, 486A3
Sees Strauss, Palestinian role in autonomy talks urged 7-2, 511C2
Meets Begin on Palestinian autonomy 7-10—7-11, Begin hails mtg 7-12, 511F2
OAU speech prompts Arab walkout, backs provisional Palestinian govt 7-18, 552F1
Sees UNTSO feud resolved 7-24, 551A2
Bodyguard tied to PLO aide's death 7-26, 625E2
Scores exploiters, plotters rptd arrested 8-17, 633D1
Vs US plan on UN Palestine res 8-18, 623E2
UN delegate backs Palestinian res 8-23, 642B2
Vows Morocco mil aid 9-2, 697A2
Meets Begin; Sinai patrols, oil sale OKd 9-4—9-6, 658D1
Briefs Strauss on autonomy talks progress; hopeful on Jordan, PLO role 9-9, 676E2, A3
Carter phones on Camp David anniv 9-17, 695F1
Meets Jesse Jackson 10-1, 763E1
US arms shipmts displayed 10-6, 762F3
Chrgs Saudi 'hate campaign', fears Libya link; Faud denies accusatns 10-10, 801E2-802A1
Offers shah asylum, scores Khomeini 11-9, 862B3
Visits Mt Sinai 11-19, 881E3
Renews shah's asylum offer 11-30; oppositn ldr scores 12-4, bid ruled out 12-5, 914D1
Sees Linowitz 12-9, 938B1

1980

SACO—*See MAINE*
SACRAMENTO—*See CALIFORNIA*
SACRAMENTO River
$5 bln water plan adopted 7-18, 632A2
SADAT, Anwar el- (Egyptian president, premier)
In Begin autonomy talks 1-7—1-10, 12E1
Vs Sovt Afghan invasn, cuts emb staff; scores Saudis 1-28, 69E1
Meets Linowitz on autonomy talks 1-29, 89D2
Jurists vs 'law of shame' 2-15; law aired 2-21, 148F3
Egypt to buy US F-15s, F-16s deferred 2-21, 140D2
Carter invites 3-19; in talks on autonomy impasse 4-10, 260F2, B3
Backs deadline for autonomy talks 3-21, 219E1
Gives shah permanent asylum 3-24; discounts Iran protests, US fears 3-25, 217B2
Honors DeBakey for shah's operatn 3-28, 242F1
Exile front seeks overthrow 4-2, 273B3
Moslems score re Copts, shah, Israel pact 4-4, 273G3
Carter meets Begin on Palestinian autonomy 4-15—4-16; talks speedup OKd 4-16, 284F1
On US hostage rescue try 4-25, 324F1
Suspends autonomy talks, meets US aide 5-8; gets Carter plea 5-13, OKs talks renewal 5-14, again suspends 5-15, 362D1
Plans Cabt shift, scores Copts 5-14; revamps Cabt, takes premiership 5-15, 389G1
Charter changes voted, pres term limit lifted 5-22, 406E3
Libya warns dissidents 6-7, 451C3
Carter seeks autonomy talks renewal 6-8, 434D1
Iran exiled gen mtg rptd 6-11, 434A1
Qaddafi rptdly backs coup vs 6-11; martial law near Libya border reimposed 6-16, 451C3
US anti-Khomeini broadcasts rptd 6-29, 490A3
Visits hospitalized shah 6-29, 491A1
Anderson visits 7-12, 549G3
Announces shah's death 7-27, leads state funeral 7-29; Nixon lauds 7-28, 571C1, F1
Vs Israel vote on Jerusalem as capital 7-30, 572F3
Asks Carter, Begin delay autonomy talks re Jerusalem issue 8-3; gets replies 8-4, 8-8, 585A1, F1
Begin autonomy talks exchngs rptd 8-11, 8-12, 627C1
Asks new 3-way summit 8-15, Begin cool 8-19, 627F1
Decrees 1-month meat sale ban 9-1, 691C1
Sees US aide on autonomy talks, OKs renewal 9-3, 660C2
Qaddafi: 'Arab unity' move opposes 9-8, 697F1
Khomeini scores US link 9-12, 693E1
Party wins Consultative Cncl electn 9-25, 769G1
US-Egypt-Israel summit delayed 10-15, 775B3
Recognizes Iran; scores Iraq, Syria, Libya 11-1, 859A3
Regrets Carter electn defeat 11-5, 841C2
Israel oppositn ldrs visit 11-7—11-9, 863E2
Islamic League meets 11-10, 895A2
Warns Reagan on Arab policy 11-23, 894E1
Syria chrgs Hussein hostile 11-29, 911D2
Linowitz urges Reagan back summit 12-7, 930D3
Reaffirms Camp David process 12-18; US lists obstacles 12-19, 952C3

1976

SADEK, Salem Ould
Rpts Sahara death toll 11-6, 974C3
SADLI, Mohammed
OPEC holds price freeze 5-28, 389D1
SADLOWSKI, Edward
USW conv backs Abel 8-30—9-3, 669B3
SADR, Iman Mussa al-
Arafat pressed truce 3-31, 225E2
Meets US mediator 4-1—4-2, 241E2
SADRUDDIN Agha Khan, Prince—*See AGHA Khan, Prince Sadruddin*
SAED, Maj. Gen. Hanna
Offers amnesty 3-10, 209F1
SAEED, Mohammed Nur
Arrested 7-8, 543E3 ★
Admits Libya coup role 8-4, executed 8-5, 592D2
SAENZ de Pazos, Luis
Lockheed paymt rptd 11-6, 909G1
SAFAIE, Kohsrow
Slain 5-4, 365E2
SAFER, John
'72 campaign gift listed 4-25, 688B1
SAFEWAY Stores Inc.
Skaggs dies 5-8, 484G3
SAFFORD, Ariz.—*See ARIZONA*

1977

Asks pre-Geneva Cairo mtg, bares secret US pacts 11-26, 909A1
Israel accepts Cairo conf 11-26, envoy named 11-28, 909D2
Syria rejcts Cairo conf, sets Tripoli mtg 11-27, 11-28; 909F1-A2
Hussein: trip split Arabs 11-28, 909D2
US hesitates, accepts Cairo conf 11-29; hails breakthrough 11-30; presses Arab, USSR attendance 12-1, 910B1, 913A2-C3
USSR rejcts Cairo conf 11-29, 910E1
UN names Cairo conf envoy 11-29, 910A2
Tripoli conf vs peace stand 12-2—12-5, cuts ties with 5 states 12-5, 929A1
Scores Sovt, Arab critics, lauds US 12-6; closes Sovt-bloc cntrs 12-7, 929C2, 930B1
Cairo rally backs Israel visit 12-8, 930A2
Sees Hussein on Arab rift 12-8, 930B2
Meets Vance, vows overall peace setlmt 12-10, 953E2
Carter: PLO 'negative' 12-15, 954C3
PLO: would bar Begin W Bank plan 12-19, 995B3
Meets Israel defense min 12-20—12-21, 993G1
Begin Ismailia summit hits impasse; new talks set 12-25—12-26; Begin airs plan rejected by Sadat 12-28, 993A1-994A3
Vs Carter Palestinian stand 12-29, 994D3
Carter visit hinted 12-31, 1000E3

SADRUDDIN Agha Khan, Prince—*See AGHA Khan, Prince Sadruddin*
SADLOWSKI, Edward
McBride leads in union vote 2-8, files protest 2-18, 130B3
Steelworkers OK contract 4-9, 273C3, E3
US ends union vote probe 11-11, 899G2
SAEED, Gen. Hanna
Replaced as army head 3-28, 227D1
SAEED Kirmani, Ahmed
Ousted as amb to Egypt 4-24, 314A1
SAENZ Barsallo, Gen. Alcibiades
Named Peru econ min 7-6, rptdly contacts IMF 7-12, 563A3
Sees US, IMF offcls 9-26—9-30, 785G1
IMF agreement rptd 9-30, 784A3
SAFEWAY Stores Inc.
Sued on cereal ads 6-30, 613B2
SAFIRE, William
Full Disclosure on best-seller list 9-4, 712D3

1978

Bars new Israel talks 7-30, US rebukes 7-31, 581E2
Meets Fahd 7-30—7-31, 582D1
US sens chrg hard line 8-1, 582E1
Vance chrgs pressure vs Israel 8-4, 602B2
Meets Vance 8-7—8-8; OKs summit talks with Carter, Begin; comments 8-8, 601G2, E3
At Camp David summit talks with Carter, Begin 9-6—9-7, 673A1
Camp David summit ends; signs pacts with Carter, Begin; photo 9-17, 709B1
Text of agrmts 9-17, 711A1-712C3
Carter details pacts to US Cong, lauds role 9-18, 709E2
Carter: summit faced collapse, confrms 9-18, 710D1
Forgn min, amb to US quit in summit pact protest 9-18, 710F3, 712C1
USSR denounces pact role 9-18, 712E2
Links 2 summit pacts 9-19, for Israel pact in 2 mos 9-20, 710D3
Saudi, Jordan noncomittal on pacts 9-19; PLO, other Arab states score 9-19, 9-20, 712D1
Begin notes setlmts dispute, Golan, E Jerusalem compromise 9-20, 710E2-F2
Briefs Morocco king on summit, asks Syria role 9-20—9-23; welcomed in Cairo 9-23, 730A3
Camp David summit letters released 9-22, 729F1; text 730C2-G3
Says US-Egypt policy identical on Jerusalem 9-22, 892G3
Hussein 'shattered' by separate peace initiative 9-23, 730E1
Ends ties with Arab hardline states 9-24, 729G2
Begin backs on Sinai setlmt demand 9-25, 729F1
Carter: backed Sarkis Leb govt 9-28, 745D1
Defends summit pacts, names new premr 10-2; removes war min, staff chief 10-3, 746A2
Presides over new Cabt 10-5, 774G2-B3
Vs Syrian, Palestinian oppositn to Camp David pacts; Syrian Leb role 10-10, 762E1
Carter links W Bank issue, peace talks 10-10, 766E3
Says Egypt to alter Israel pact draft 10-25, 802C3
Ex-dep prime min named as Westinghouse payoff recipient 10-26, 961B3
Heeds Carter plea vs talks delegatn recall 10-27, 858G2
Wins Nobel Peace Prize 10-27, 886D1
Shuns Arab summit delegatn 11-4, 859B2
Asks W Bank linkage to Israel pact 11-7, 858C3
Seeks Israel pact text chng 11-9, 858C3
Says talks collapse possible 11-9, 892C3
Hassan: Carter gave vow on E Jerusalem, W Bank 11-10; US denies 11-12, 892E3-893B1
Asks Israel cede Gaza Strip 11-14, 892D3
W Bank protest vs peace moves 11-19, 893E1
Message backs Palestinian solidarity 11-29, 951F2
Begin gets new pact stand 11-30; aide meets Carter, Vance 12-1—12-2, 930F2
To shun Nobel award rites 11-30; aides comment 12-1, 12-2; aide accepts prize 12-10, 950B3
Regrets Meir death 12-8, 1032G1
Meets Vance, OKs new Israel pact draft 12-10—12-12, 950C2
Carter lauds on Israel-Egypt pact draft 12-14, 951C1
Egypt denies Israel pact chng 12-15, 978D3
Says Arab oppositn helps Begin block pact 12-25, 997F3

SADDINGTON-Poole, Lily
Detained as Saudi trial witness 6-15, 516D1
SADIQI, Gholam Hussein
Named to form Iran govt 12-17; fails, Natl Front disavows 12-21, 993E1
SADLOWSKI, Edward
Union legal fee liability case review denied by Sup Ct 4-17, 308D3
USW sues 9 foundatns 4-19, 310A1
Steelworkers chng electn rules 9-21, 737F2
SADR, Imam Moussa
In Libya 8-25, rptd missing 8-31; Beirut protest strike 9-15, 713B2
SADRUDDIN Aga Khan, Prince—*See AGA Khan, Prince Sadruddin*
SAENZ de Inestrilla, Capt. Ricardo
Arrest in anti-govt plot rptd 11-21, 967F2
SAETA Airlines
Plane hijacked to Cuba 1-18, 212A3
SAFEGUARD Industry Inc.
US halts Australia land sales 5-1, 327A3
SAFE House (play)
Opens 4-13, 760C3
SAFEWAY Stores Inc.
FTC complaint rptd setld 1-10, 348A1
SAFFIR, Leonard
Learsy elected Trib chrmn 1-17, 75E3
Trib ceases publicatn 4-5, 270A2
SAFIRE, William
Wins Pulitzer Prize 4-17, 315B2
Full Disclosure on best-seller list 8-6, 620C2

1979

SAD Eyes (recording)
On best-seller list 10-3, 800E3
SADR, Imam Moussa
Qaddafi tied to disappearance 9-8, 677C3
SADR, Reza
Named Iran commerce min 2-19, 125D2
SAEDI, Golam H.
Cycle released 2-12, 174D2
SAENZ, Josephine
Ex-husband's will filed 6-20, 527C3
SAFECO Insurance Co.
MD-managed plan cuts hosp costs 6-14, 570D3
SAFEWAY Stores Inc.
Black employé firing case declined by Sup Ct 2-21, 128D3
PCB contaminated eggs destroyed 9-17, 704D3
SAFIRE, William
Hints Carter land sale 'hush money' 3-22, 203A2

1980

SADAT, Hassan
Iran oil min release demanded at OPEC mtg 12-15, 951G2
SADDLER, Donald
Happy New Year opens 4-27, 392A3
SADLOWSKI, Edward
USW suit vs foundatn funding refused by Sup Ct 3-31, 291C3
SADR, Ali Reza
Warns vs oil blockade 1-11, 29C2
SADR, Imam Moussa
Rptd jailed in Libya 9-9, 709B1
SADR, Immam Mohammed al-Bakr
Beirut Shiites protest rptd executn 4-15, Khomeini accuses Iraq 4-22, 300A2, C2
SADRI, John
Loses Australian Open, fined 1-2, 213E1
SAENZ de Inestrillas, Capt. Ricardo
Sentenced for '78 coup plot 5-7, 355A2
SAFEWAY Stores Inc.
Retail prices frozen 3-6, 349C1
SAFEWAY Stores v. Meat Prices Investigators
Case refused by Sup Ct 10-14, 782A1
SAFI, Abdul Qader
Rpts Sovt Afghan drive 10-2, 766C1

1976

SAGINAW, Mich.—*See MICHIGAN*
SAGINAW News, The
Newhouse buys Booth chain 11-8, 901B3
SAGRES II (Portuguese sailing ship)
In Operation Sail 7-4, 488A3

SAHARA, Western (formerly Spanish Sahara)
France indicates Morocco support 1-6—1-8, 36G1
Morocco gets US arms 1-7, orders French jets 1-15, 1-16, 36A2, D2
Morocco, Mauritania troops rout Polisario 1-8—1-11, 36F1
Cuba adviser aid rptd 1-10, 138G1
Spanish troop withdrawal ends 1-12, 36E1
Polisario downs Morocco jet 1-21, takes Mauritania town 1-23, 58D2
El Aium clashes rptd 1-23, Morocco reinforces 1-26, 58F2
Polisario rpts Farsaya clashes; Mauritania, Morocco deaths 1-23, 58A3
Morocco denies napalm attacks 1-23, 58D3
Cuba, N Viet Polisario aid rptd 1-25, 58F2
Bou Craa transit belt rptd cut 1-26, 58A3
Moroccans rout Algerians 1-27—1-29, 58D1
Arab natns seek Morocco-Algeria setlmt 1-27—1-29, 58B2
Morocco summons forgn ambs 1-28, 58B2
Morocco envoy sees Kissinger 1-29, 107G2
France vs independnc, denies Algeria dispute 1-31, 107D2
Arab diplomatic efforts continue 2-1—2-6, 107A3
UN envoy named 2-1, 107A3
Amgala casualties disputed 2-1, 2-2, Morocco occupies Tiferiti 2-5, 107B3
Kissinger scores Cuba role 2-5, 138C1
Spain sells phosphate stake to Morocco 2-9, 107C3
Algeria bars Morocco flights 2-15, 178C3
Amgala control disputed, other fighting rptd 2-16—2-18, 179B1
UN envoy ends missn 2-17, 178D2
Spain leaves, scores Morocco-Mauritania annexatn 2-26, 178G1
UN spurns El Aiun mtg 2-26, 178C2
OAU deadlocks on recognitn 2-26—3-1, 178D3
Polisario proclaims SADR 2-27, Morocco scores 2-29, 178E2
Arab League mediatn fails 3-2, 178C3
SADR forms govt 3-5, 178G2
SADR recognized by Malagasy, Burundi 3-5, Algeria 3-6, 178G2
Morocco, Mauritania sever Algeria ties 3-7, 178A3
Castro backs Polisario 3-12, sees Ould Ahmed 3-14, 251C3
Morocco issues SADR arrest warrants 3-26, 277B3
Algeria, Libya, Niger for independnc 4-8, 372C1
Morocco, Mauritania divide territory 4-14, 277F2-B3
Morocco, Mauritania battle Polisaro rebels 4-15—4-27, 341E3-342A1
Morocco promotes officers 4-26, 342A1
Morrocco, Maurjtania boundary map corrected 4-27, 341G3
Moroccan casualties rptd 5-5, 5-8, 466D3
US arms relay to Morocco sought 5-22, 458E2
Polisario ldr killed in Mauritania attack 6-8, successor named 6-21, 466A3
Algeria accused re Polisario ldr's death 6-25, 643C2
Laroussi opens 3d Polisario cong 8-26, 643B2
Morroco, Mauritania death toll 6,500 11-6, 974C3
Ore RR destroyed in clash 12-27, 974B3
SAHARAN Arab Democratic Republic (SADR)—*See SAHARA, Western*
SAHEL, Club des Amis du
US asks intl aid for Sahel 5-1, 318E2
SAID, Mohammed
Peace force attacked 7-25, 546G2
St. CHARLES Grain Elevator Co.—*See ADNAC, Inc.*
St. CHRISTOPHER'S Hospital for Children (Philadelphia, Pa.)
Interns unionizatn barred 3-22, 220F1
St. CLAIRE'S Hospital (Denville, N.J.)
Quinlan off respirator 5-22, moved 6-10, 423F2, G2
St. GERMAIN, Rep. Fernand Joseph (D, R.I.)
Reelected 11-2, 821C3, 830G3
St. JOE Minerals Corp.
Australia mining deal rptd 7-28, 571G3-572B1
St. KITTS (St. Christopher)-Nevis —*See CARIBCOM, WEST Indies*

1977

SAGAN, Carl
Dragons of Eden on best-seller list 7-3, 548E3; 8-14, 643G1; 9-4, 712E3; 10-2, 808E3; 11-6, 872E3
SAGNER, Alan
Vs NY Concorde ban end 8-17, 627F1
Group buys Nation mag 12-22, 1004F3
SAHARA (desert)
Winds, weather chngs linked 2-21, 183G2

SAHARA, Western (formerly Spanish Sahara)
Polisario rpts '76 Mauritania fighting 1-1, 88A1
Algeria rpts 105,000 refugees, asks aid 1-21, 88A1
Morocco, Mauritania deaths rptd 2-20—4-21, 337A2
Morocco econ dvpt plans rptd 3-6, 337C2
Polisario shows prisoners, US, W Eur arms 3-28, 337B2
Algeria refugee total disputed 4-6, 337D2
French killed, captured in Polisario raid 5-1, families quit Mauritania 5-2; France, Algeria trade chrgs 5-3—5-8; Polisario warn foreigners 5-21, 440G2-E3
Polisario hits Bou Craa 5-31; 129 Spanish leave, mining halted 6-2—6-3, 513G2
Morocco-USSR phosphate pact OKd, Algeria, Polisario protest rptd 6-6, 513B3
Algeria frees 6 French natls 6-19, 567A1
OAU summit divisns cited 7-2—7-5, 512D1, G1
Mauritania envoy shot in Paris 7-7; Morocco, Mauritania accuse Algeria 7-7—7-8, 543B2
Zouerate hit 7-16, Morocco sends troops 7-18—7-19; Morocco presence, Mauritanian weakness rptd 7-21, 591B2
Polisario-Mauritania clashes 8-31, 9-5, 717F3
2 French natls, 15 Mauritanians kidnaped 10-25, Algeria 'deplores' 10-26, France expels Polisario backers 10-29, 831F2
Polisario claims RR attack 10-26, 831C3
Polisario rpts attacks in Morocco, Mauritania 10-26, 11-4, 852A3
French natl kidnap data rptd 10-28, 831D3
France pressures Algeria on kidnaped natls 10-30, reinforces Senegal garrison 11-1, seeks Red Cross, Libya aid 11-3, 852A2
Morocco threatens Polisario pursuit 11-6, Algeria warns vs incursns 11-7, 852F2
French envoy in Polisario talks, kidnap victims rptd alive 11-7, 852E2
Arab League delays move on Algeria-Morocco feud 11-12—11-14, 874C2
Polisario, Mauritania casualties rptd 11-22—12-18, 998D3
Polisario rpts French jets hit 12-2, 12-14, 12-18; France denies air role, admits 12-23, 998B3
French natls freed, Polisario cites gratitude re Soclst support 12-23, 998G2

SAHEL—*See AFRICA*
SAID, Ali
Says Sutowo detained 3-29, 304G2
Sutowo cleared of chrgs 9-23, 747F1
SAID, Edward W.
Denies bid to Geneva 11-15, 873E2
SAILING—*See BOATS & Boating*
St. BONAVENTURE (N.Y.) University
Wins NIT basketball tourn 3-20, 262E2
St. ELIZABETH'S Hospital (Wash., D.C.)
'65 pneumonia linked to Legion fever 1-18, 81A2
St. EUSTATIUS—*See NETHERLANDS Antilles*
St. GERMAIN, Rep. Fernand Joseph (D, R.I.)
Opens Lance probe 9-6, 690D1
SAINT-Jean, Gen. Iberico (ret.)
Graiver probe role rptd 4-22, 371F2
St. KITTS (St. Christopher)-Nevis—*See WEST Indies*

1978

SAGAN, Carl
Wins Pulitzer Prize 4-17, 315C1
Dragons of Eden on best-seller list 6-4, 460D3

SAHARA, Western (formerly Spanish Sahara)
Algeria orders France trade cut 1-11, 11D3
Jan-Mar Polisario attacks rptd; Morocco, Mauritania casualties 1-18—4-13, 278B3
Facts on conflict 278E3
Spain warned on Morocco fishing pact 2-20, 278D3
Algeria blames Spain for Canaries unrest 4-20, 576E3
French jets raid Polisario 5-3—5-4, 562F2
Libya shifts stance towards Polisario 6-3, 562D2
Mauritania coup linked to Polisario gains, Moroccan, French dependence 7-10, 535E1
Polisario orders Mauritania cease-fire 7-12, Ould Salek backs solutn 7-14, 562B2
OAU names com 7-22, 561E1
Morocco, Algeria dispute at nonaligned conf 7-25—7-30, 583A3
Mauritania backs Polisario autonomy 7-27; Morocco rejectn rptd 8-17, 676D2
France presses mediatn effort, Algeria rejcts compromise 8-1, 676F2
Polisario conf held, Mauritania cease-fire backed 9-26—10-1, 999C2
Morocco chrgs Algerian attack 10-3, 999F2
Mauritania-Polisario talks rptd 10-13, 10-19, 999B2
Tanzania recognizes Polisario 11-10, 999G2
Polisario attacks Spanish, Moroccans 11-28—12-11, 999E2

SAHEL—*See AFRICA; country names*
SAIAS, Luis
Sworn Portugal agri min 1-30, 91C3
Govt falls over farm issue 7-24—7-27, 593F2, D3, 594B1
SAIFUDIN
Replaced as Sinkiang ldr 1-29, 89A2
SAIKHANOV, Lt. Col. Aziz
Killed 6-29, 519A1
SAILING—*See BOATS & Boating*
SAIL On (recording)
Imperials win Grammy 2-24, 315G3
ST. ALBAN, Dominique
Replay released 7-10, 970G2
St. ALBIN, Gen. Roger
Haiti mil staff chief 9-15, 777G1
St. CHRISTOPHER (St. Kitts)-Nevis-Anguilla—*See CARIBBEAN Community*
St. GERMAIN, Rep. Fernand Joseph (D, R.I.)
Wins renomination 9-12, 716A3
Reelected 11-7, 852A2
On banking reform bill passage 11-12, 1002F3
ST. JOE Paper Co.
Indicted for price fixing 1-25, 67D2
St. JOHN'S University (N.Y., N.Y.)
Johnson in NBA draft 6-9, 457G3
St. KITTS (St. Christopher)-Nevis-Anguilla—*See also CARIBBEAN Community*
Robt Bradshaw dies 5-24, 440D2

1979

SAGAN, Carl
Broca's Brain on best-seller list 9-2, 672C3
SAGER, Carole Bayer
They're Playing Our Song opens 2-11, 292E3

SAHARA, Western (formerly Spanish Sahara)
Mauritania sets Polisario talks 5-3, 323G3
Mauritanian pres resigns 6-4, 417F1
OAU backs UN electns 7-20, 552B2
Morocco warns Mauritania vs pullout, US weighs arms aid 8-2, 592B2
Mauritania signs Polisario pact, ends war role 8-5, 592G1
Spain defends nonaligned conf plans 8-10, 8-13, 654E2
Morocco annexes Tiris el-Gharbia 8-11; scores Mauritania, backs Algeria talks 8-19, 626B3
Polisario rpts major Moroccan clash 8-13, 626G3
Mauritania, Algeria restore ties 8-14, 626G3
Polisario ambushes Moroccans at Lebuirate 8-24, rpts 800 slain 8-25, 697B2
Morocco gets Egypt aid vow 9-2, arms 9-8, 697G1
Morocco rpts Smara battle, chrgs Algeria troops 10-9—10-10, 804D1
US OKs Morocco arms sale 10-22; US rep, Algeria score 10-22, 10-23, 803F3
OAU com asks Morocco exit 12-5, 981C1
Zak outpost clash rptd 12-9, 981A2

SAHIBI, Yadollah
Named Iran state min 2-19, 125D1
SAIF, Capt. Abdullah Mohammed
Cited as N Yemen rebel fighter 3-1, 158E1
SAILING, *See BOATS & Boating*
St. BONAVENTURE (N.Y.) University
In Big East basketball conf 6-26, 526F3
St. CHRISTOPHER (St. Kitts)-Nevis-Anguilla—*See CARIBBEAN Community*
St. CLAIR, James
Defends Ocean Spray 6-20, 986B1
St. CROIX—*See VIRGIN Islands*
St. GEORGE, Utah—*See UTAH*
SAINT Jack (film)
Released 4-26, 528E3
St. JAMES, Susan
Love At First Bite released 4-12, 528G2
St. JOHN-Stevas, Norman
UK chancellor of Lancaster 5-5, 338G1
OAS admits 5-22, 416B3
St. JOHN'S University (N.Y., N.Y.)
In Big East basketball conf 5-29, 526G3
St. JUDE Children's Research Hospital (Memphis, Tenn.)
Leukemia study rptd 2-9, 139A2
St. KITTS (St. Christopher)-Nevis-Anguilla—*See also CARIBBEAN Community*
St Lucia diplomatic svc seen 2-19, 181A3

1980

SAGAN, Carl
Cosmos on best-seller list 12-7, 948E3
SAGEMAN, Robert E.
Named AT&T Intl pres, chief exec 8-20, 648A2
SAGINAW—*See MICHIGAN*
SAGINAW (Mich.) News (newspaper)
Petykiewicz wins Polk award 2-25, 692E3
SAGUY, Maj. Gen. Yehoshua
Backs Israel Leb raid 8-19, 628A1
SAHABI, Yadollah
Backs talks with US 9-30, 769C1
SAHARA, Western (formerly Spanish Sahara)
Morocco breaks with Cuba over Polisario 4-23, attacks 2 Cuban tankers off Africa 7-12, 563C2
OAU summit condemns conflict, Polisario entry shelved 7-1—7-4, 509D1
Spain recognizes Polisario; fishermen freed 12-17, 995C3

SAHINKAYA, Gen. Tashin
In Turkey mil junta 9-21, 720C3
SAILING (recording)
On best-seller list 8-13, 640B3; 9-10, 716E3
ST. AGNES Hospital (White Plains, N.Y.)
'Scarsdale Diet' MD slain 3-10, 214G3
ST. BERNARD, Keith
Eludes police 6-19, 498B2
St. CHARLES County—*See MISSOURI*
SAINT-GAUDENS, Augustus (1848-1907)
Gold coin set sold for record sum 4-10, 472F2
ST. GERMAIN, Rep. Fernand J. (D, R.I.)
Reelected 11-4, 844A2, 849B1
SAINT JAMES, Susan
How to Beat the High Cost of Living released 7-11, 675A3
ST. JOHN International Inc.
Jamaica names in grain fraud suit 2-4, 99C2

1976

St. LAWRENCE Seaway
Oil spill 6-23, 859D2
St. LOUIS, Mo.—*See MISSOURI*
St. LOUIS Globe Democrat (newspaper)
Ford endorsement rptd 10-30, 827G3
St. LOUIS Post-Dispatch (newspaper)
Carter endorsement rptd 10-30, 831G2
St. LUCIA (British colony)—*See CARIBBEAN Community, COMMONWEALTH of Nations*
St. MARY'S Episcopal Church (Denver, Col.)
Cuts natl ties re women 11-28, 932F1
St. PAUL, Minn.—*See MINNESOTA*
St. PETERSBURG, Fla.—*See FLORIDA*
St. PETERSBURG Times (newspaper)
Carter endorsement rptd 10-30, 831G2
St. PHILLIP'S Pentecostal Church (Washington, D.C.)
Clerics sentncd in food stamp swindle 9-17, 776F2
St. REGIS Paper Corp.
Trust suit dvpts 2-18—10-29, 886D1, G1, Van Keuren plea cited 11-30, 921D3
Indicted again 10-29, 886D3
St. SIMON'S Island, Ga.—*See GEORGIA*
St. STEPHEN and the Incarnation Church (Washington, D.C.)
Cheek rejects compromise 4-4, forms separate unit 5-9, 755C3
St. VINCENT (British colony)—*See CARIBBEAN Community*
SAIRAFI, Mohammed Ali
Ousted re sugar deal 2-10, 156C3
SAIT, Ebrahim Sulaiman
Claims riot deaths 10-27, 810E2

SAKHAROV, Andrei D.
Melchuk loses post 3-26, 314A1
Detained at Dzhemilev trial 4-14—4-16, 292C1
Scores Uruguay rights abuse 5-10, 441B2
Wife in Sovt CSCE monitor group 5-13, 408B2
Vs Iran return of Sovt defector 10-28, 854C2 ★
Bukovsky, Corvalan exchgd 12-18, 955C3
At Jewish culture conf 12-21, 966E3
SAKHAROV, Yelena Bonner (Mrs. Andrei)
Detained at Dzhemilev trial 4-14—4-16, 292C1
In CSCE monitor group 5-13, 408B2
SALAM, Saeb
Vs Christian pres 2-11, 107B2
Vs Leb reforms 2-15, 125F1
Syria-bound jet attacked 3-19, 210C1
Scores Jumblat admin plans 4-24, 296E1
Meets Gemayel 8-7, Khativ scores 8-8, 578B1
OKs halt to civln shelling 8-18, 629B1
SALAMAH, Abu Hassan
Meets Christian ldrs 9-4, 663C1
SALANT, Richard S.
Pres debate rules OKd 9-20, 703C2
On Schoor resignatn 9-28, 749A2
SALAZAR, Antonio de Oliveira (d. 1970)
Aides freed 1-21; others 1-23, 53F1
Schmidt apology to France rptd 7-5, 521A2
SALEH, Harris
Becomes Sabah chief min 6-6, 419E1
SALEM, Mamdouh
Nasser cleared of '67 theft chrg 2-4, 119C1
Syria talks called off 5-19, 370A2
In Syrian talks 6-23—6-24, 449D1
Links Qaddafi to hijack 8-23, 629C2
Rpts bus strike arrests 9-20, 735A1

SALIM, Salim A.
Scores S Africa arms ban veto 10-19, 781F3
SALINAS, Cesar Augusto
Killed 6-25, 926G1
SALISBURY, Md.—*See MARYLAND*
SALISBURY, N.C.—*See NORTH Carolina*
SALK, Dr. Jonas
Ford asks flu vaccine drive 3-24, 224B2
On polio-vaccine danger 9-23, 776B1
SALMAN, Salah
Leb interior min 12-9, 913E2
Newspaper seizure protested 12-17, 953E2
SALMAN, Talal
Protests newspaper seizure 12-17, 953E2
SALMON, Gov. Thomas P. (D, Vt.)
On hurricane damage 8-11, 595D2
Wins Sen primary 9-14, 705A2
Loses Senate election 11-2, 821D3
NE govs meet 11-13—11-14, 864B3
SALOMON, Richard
'72 campaign gift listed 4-25, 688C1
SALOMON Brothers
Kaufman asks bank regulatory reform 1-12, 111G2
SALONEN, Neil A.
On Manhattan Cntr purchase 9-8, 971E1
SALONGA, Jovito
Asks referendum boycott 10-13, 839D1
SALT (Strategic Arms Limitation Talks)—*See 'U.S.-Soviet Developments' under DISARMAMENT*

1977

St. LAURENT, Yves
'77 fall fashions rptd 7-29, 1022E1
St. LAWRENCE River
Flow decline rptd 3-8, 244A3
St. LAWRENCE Seaway
Bridge pact signed 2-5, 133B1
Carter-Trudeau toll talks 2-21—2-23, 132C3
Canada, US set toll hike 12-16, 982D3
St. LAWRENCE Seaway Development Corporation—*See under U.S. GOVERNMENT—TRANSPORTATION*
St. LOUIS, Mo.—*See MISSOURI*
St. LOUIS—San Francisco Railway Co.
BN merger OKd 12-5, 1007D1
St. LUCIA (British colony)—*See also COMMONWEALTH of Nations, WEST Indies*
OAS fails to act on entry 6-21, 494B3
St. MAARTEN—*See NETHERLANDS Antilles*
St. PAUL (Minn.) Pioneer Press (newspaper)
ICC trucking probe rptd 6-3, 500D3
St. REGIS Paper Co.
Co, offcls acquitted 11-1, 11-23, 918A3
SAJON, Edgardo
Arrested 4-1, Lanusse protests 4-4, 345G2
Questioned in Graiver scandal 4-22, 371A3
SAKAI, Hiroichi
Chrgs Boeing kickback 2-14, 136E1
SAKHALIN Island
Oil find announced 10-12, 853E3

SAKHAROV, Andrei D.
Warned 1-25; US defends, controversy ensues 1-27—2-1, 83E3-84E1
US gets plea, other dissidents seek support 1-28, 84E1
Gets Carter reply 2-17, 137B2
Brezhnev scores Carter on rights 3-21, 226D1
Turchin leaves USSR 10-14, 812C2
Sovt harrassmt rptd 11-10, 11-16; US labor union visit blocked 12-1, 955F2
Stepdaughter, husband emigrate 11-12, 955C3
Honored by B'nai B'rith 11-20, 955G1
Westn attys plan pub trials for Shcharansky, others 11-28, 955C2
AFL-CIO hears appeal 12-12, 961D1

SAKS, Gene
Wins Tony 6-5, 452C1
SALAMAN, Frank
Sentenced 5-16, 508E2
SALANT, Richard
Disputes CIA-link 9-12, 721C1
SALAS, Luis
Chrgs LBJ '48 Sen primary fraud 7-30; denied 8-1, 8-3, 631B2
SALBY, Jay
Sentence commuted 1-25, 139D3
SALCEDO Bastardo, Jose Luis
Venez secy of pres 1-7, 23F2
Venez sci, tech min 7-15, 566B1
SALEH, Mahmoud
Slain 1-3, 9C1

SALEM, Mamdouh (Egyptian premier)
Food price hike set 1-17, 43D3
Rejects Kaissouni resignatn 1-19, 43E3
Ties Leftist Party to riots 1-29, 83E1
Cabt shift tied to riots 2-1, 83F1
Anti-Copt law dropped 9-12, 863E2
Gives up interior post 10-25, 824C1
Sovt-bloc cntrs closed 12-7, 930B1

SALERNO, Anthony
Mistrial declared 12-15, 992G1
SALGADO, Salomon
Killed 2-11, 182B1
SALI, Usman
Sought in killings 10-10, 803E2, F2
SALIM, Emil
On Hughes Aircraft payoffs 2-14, 182C3
SALIM Mussallm al Awar Bait Said
Surrenders 10-14, 949A3
SALK Institute (La Jolla, Calif.)
Guillemin wins Nobel 10-13, Medal of Sci 11-22, 951D3, G3
SALMAN, Salah
On Chuf area fighting 8-23, 647B3
SALMONELLA—*See MEDICINE—Diseases*
SALOMON Brothers
Dean Witter, Reynolds merger set 10-3, 799B3
Cited in Lehman Bros, Kuhn Loeb merger 11-28, 1004G2
SALOTH Sar—*See POL Pot*
SALT (Strategic Arms Limitation Talks)—*See DISARMAMENT—U.S.-Soviet Developments*

1978

St. LAURENT, Larry
Bares jobless overpaymts 5-5, 350A3
St. LAURENT, Yves
'78 high chic fashion rptd 8-4—8-11, 10-27—11-3, 1029B2, D2, E2
St. LAWRENCE Sugar Ltd.
Fined record sum 10-6, 794F3
St. LOUIS, Mo.—*See MISSOURI*
St. LOUIS Art Museum
Rodin sculptures stolen 1-21, 2-20, 335C1
St. LOUIS Globe-Democrat (newspaper)
Closed by strike 11-20, 1006A2
St. LOUIS Post-Dispatch (newspaper)
Closed by strike 11-20, 1006A2
Dudman escapes slaying in Cambodia 12-23, 997A2
St. LUCIA (British colony)—*See CARIBBEAN Community, COMMONWEALTH of Nations*
St. PAUL, Minn.—*See MINNESOTA*
St. PAUL Fire & Insurance Co. v. Barry
Policyholder trust suits backed by Sup Ct 6-29, 567D3
St. REGIS Paper Co.
'77 trust acquittal cited 9-21; settles '78 chrgs 768A3, E3
St. VINCENT (British colony)—*See CARIBBEAN Community*
SAINZ Jimenez, Hernan
Named CR finance min 3-4, 171A1
SAITO, Kunikichi
Japan LDP secy gen 12-7, 945F2

SAKHAROV, Andrei Dmitrievich
Stepson rptdly gets visa 2-4, 180A2
Held re Orlov trial entry 5-18, 359E3
Sees Kennedy 9-9, 743B1
Apartmt ransacked 11-29, KGB blamed 12-2, 947D1

SAKI (Hector Hugh Munro) (1870-1916)
Playboy of Weekend World opens 11-16, 1031G2
SAKS Fifth Avenue—*See B.A.T. Industries—International Stores Holdings*
SALAM, Abdus
Unified field theory confirmatn rptd 6-12, 7-8, 654A2
SALAMA, Ali
Clashes with Assemb dep speaker 2-15, 131A2
SALAMANDERS
Magnetic orientation rptd 1-19, 334C1
SALANT, Richard S.
Leonard to head CBS News 7-14, 599A3

SALEH, Col. Ali Abdullah (North Yemeni president)
Elected N Yemen pres 7-17, 559A1
Mil coup crushed 10-15, 799B1
Plotters executed 11-15, 885B3
SALEH, Jasem
Executed 6-26, 499B1
SALEM, Mamdouh (Egyptian premier; resigns Oct. 2)
Egypt curbs Palestinians 2-27, 138D1
Ousts econ min, 2 others 5-7, 392G2
Sadat plan to assume post rptd 7-12, 573G1
Says all Egypt backs Sadat on summit pact 9-19, 730A2
Resigns as premier 10-2, 746C2
SALES, Roland
Arkansas wins Orange Bowl, sets rushing record 1-2, 8C3
SALES Tax—*See TAXES*
SALHI, Kheireddine
Quits PSD central com 1-11, 74D1
SALI, Usman
Govt presses search 1-27, 73F3
Govt bombs Jolo 3-3, 248A2
SALINAS, Francisco
Beaten by Nicaragua troops 2-1, 91C2
SALISBURY, Harold
Fired as S Australian police chief 1-17, scores Dunstan 1-20, 53F1
SALLEH, Datuk Harris Ben Mohhamed
Page Airways paymt chrgd 4-13, 449B2
SALMAN, Salah
Ties Israel to Beirut clashes 4-12, 256G1
Vs Israel Leb pullback 4-12, 256F2
SALMON, Gen. Angel
Cabt quits 11-1, 868E3
Army officers seized in 'plot' 11-2, 868D3
SALMON River (Ida.)
Carters take raft trip 8-22—8-24, 664E1
SALONEN, Ahti
Kekkonen reelected 1-16, 36G2
SALONEN, Neil
Denounces Unificatn Church chrgs 11-1, 862G3, 863A1
SALT (Strategic Arms Limitation Talks)—*See DISARMAMENT—U.S.-Soviet Developments*
SALT, Waldo
Coming Home released 2-15, 619B1

1979

St. LAURENT, Yves
'79 fashion roundup rptd 1006G1, B2, E2
St. LOUIS, Mo.—*See MISSOURI*
St. LOUIS Globe-Democrat (newspaper)
Publication resumed 1-15, 87E2
St. LOUIS Post-Dispatch (newspaper)
Publication resumed 1-14, 87E2
St. LOUIS-San Francisco Railway Co.
Rock Island takeover ordered 9-26, 722C3
St. LOUIS University
Hickey in basketball HOF 4-30, 526E3
Midwest quake threat rptd 11-15, 954C1
St. LUCIA—*See also COMMONWEALTH of Nations, OAS*
4-natn diplomatic svc, Barbados defns pact seen 2-19, 181A3
Independence attained 2-21; fete marred by oppositn boycott, unrest 2-21—2-22; facts on 181A2
152d UN member 9-18, 695A2, A3
St. PAUL, Minn.—*See MINNESOTA*
St. PETERSBURG, Fla.—*See FLORIDA*
St. PIERRE, Suzanne
Weds Eric Sevareid 6-30, 527E2
St. REGIS Paper Co.
3 unions strike 5-15, ratify contract 6-23, 598A3
St. VINCENT—*See also COMMONWEALTH of Nations*
St Lucia diplomatic svc seen 2-19, 181A3
Mt Soufriere erupts, residents evacuated 4-13—4-18, 399C1
Independence OKd, set 7-9, 568B3
Independence gained, data rptd 10-27, 825C1
US sets Carib policy 11-29, 960E3
Labor Party wins electns 12-5, 951A3, D3
Union, Palm Island rebelln crushed 12-7—12-8, 951G2
SAITSEV, Alexander
Not in world figure-skating champs 3-14, 391G3
SAKHAROV, Andrei Dmitrievich
Identifies '77 subway blast suspect 1-30, 100F2
Sup Sovt bid rptd barred 2-2, 100F1
USSR seizes US books 9-4, 690D1
Rpts Nekipelov arrest 12-7, 939F1

SAKS, Gene
I Love My Wife opens 5-15, 711F3
SALAM, Abdus
Wins Nobel Prize 10-16, 858C1
SALAME, Col. Walter
Leads Bolivia army rebelln 10-11, 811D1
SALAMEH, Ali Hassan (Abu Hassan)
Assassinated 1-22, 51A1
Israel town blasted in reprisal 1-28, 69B2
SALAND, Ronald
Amityville Horror released 7-27, 819D3
SALANT, Richard S.
NBC vice chrmn apptmt rptd 3-29, 335A1
SALAZAR, Abel
Cited in Ecuador pol murder 1-12, 62F2
SALAZAR, Antonio de Oliveira (1889-1970)
Neto dies 9-10, 705D2
Sa Carneiro oppositn cited 12-2, 917D1
SALAZAR, Maj. Gonzalo
Chrgs police in '74 lime kiln murders 7-5, 523B1
SALAZAR, Bishop Manuel
Latin bishops back vs Somoza 2-12, 108D3
SALAZAR, Maj. Pablo Emilio
Nicaragua invasn plan chrgd 7-28, 573F2
SALEH, Ali Abdullah (North Yemen president)
Signs Yemen unification plan 3-29, 250C1*

SALEK, Col. Mustapha Ould
Resigns as Mauritania head of state 6-4, 417D1
SALEM, N.J.—*See NEW Jersey*
SALES Tax—*See TAXES*
SALGADO, Germanico
Ecuador indus min 12-9, 967F3
SALIM, Salim Ahmed
Elected UN Gen Assemb pres, backs PLO 9-18, 695G1
Asks Poland for UN worker detentn info 10-29, 939B2
Pleas for US hostages in Iran 11-20, 878F2
SALINGER, Pierre
Arrested in N Ireland, freed 9-4, 669F3
SALLID, Otis
Glorious Monster opens 7-10, 711C3
SALMON—*See FISHING Industry*
SALOMON Brothers
IBM bond issue loss rptd 10-11, 765E1
SALOTH Sar—*See POL Pot*
SALT (Strategic Arms Limitation Talks)—*See DISARMAMENT—U.S.-Soviet Developments*
SALT, Waldo
Wins Oscar 4-9, 336A2

1980

ST. LAURENT, Yves
'80 fashion roundup rptd 998E1-C2
St. LOUIS—*See MISSOURI*
ST. LOUIS Globe-Democrat (newspaper)
Reagan endorsemt rptd 11-1, 841G3
ST. LOUIS Post-Dispatch (newspaper)
Carter endorsemt rptd 11-1, 341G3
ST. LOUIS-San Francisco Railway Co.
BN merger OKd by ICC 4-17, 345D2
BN merger stayed by Powell 11-21; appeals ct OKs link 11-24, Sup Ct lifts stay 11-25, 937G2-A3
ST. LUCIA—*See also COMMONWEALTH of Nations, OAS*
Hurricane Allen kills 16 8-4, 621B2
St. MARTIN'S Press—*See MACMILLAN Press*
ST. MARY'S College (Notre Dame, Ind.)
Reagan visits 4-22, 328A1
St. PAUL—*See MINNESOTA*
ST. PAUL Chamber Orchestra
Wins Grammy 2-27, 296F3
St. PETERSBURG—*See FLORIDA*
ST. PETERSBURG (Fla.) Times (newspaper)
Orsini, Stafford win Pulitzers 4-14, 296F2
ST. VINCENT and the Grenadines—*See also COMMONWEALTH of Nations*
UN joined 9-16, 736E1
US offshore bank fraud indictments 10-20, 860A3
SAITO, Kunikichi
Quits Cabt in scandal, replaced 9-19, 752E1

SAKHAROV, Andrei Dmitrievich
Asks USSR Afghan withdrawal, vs Olympics 1-2, 46A3
Rpts Lithuanian natlst arrest 1-14, 46F3
Expelled from Moscow; Kirillin resignatn linked 1-22, 46F2, E3
Outcry grows 1-22—2-5; issues statemt, text 1-28, 85F3-86A2, B2
Intl protests grow 2-18—3-11, 181F2-A3
Chrgs police brutality 2-18, 181C3
French CP scores 2-20, 149D3
Protests sci acad mtg bar 3-4, retains membership 3-6, 181D2, B3
Police block Moscow apartmt 3-4, 3-5, 181B3
Orlova censured re support 3-12, 3-15, 181C3
Science conf hears paper 4-13, 326F2
US scientists seek Sovt boycott 4-16, 326A3
Perez wins Nobel Peace Prize 10-13, 889C2

SALANT, Richard S.
NBC managemt realigned 6-3, 501F2
SALAZAR, Alberto
Wins NYC Marathon 10-26, 890E3
SALAZAR, Roberto
Home attacked 4-25, quits planning post 5-2, 372G2
SALAZAR Aguello, Jorge
Slain 11-17, 887G1
SALEM (Liberian supertanker)
Sinks off Senegal 1-17; S Africa oil sale suspected, Shell sues 2-7, 108D2
SALIERI, Antonio (deceased)
Amadeus opens 12-17, 1003G2
SALIM, Salim Ahmed
Replaced as UN Assemb pres 9-16, 736E1
Named Tanzania forgn min 11-7, 888F1
SALINAS, Jose Manuel
Threatens Cordova gen strike 8-30, 673E3
SALISBURY, Harrison
Sues US over alleged probe 4-10, 459F1
SALK, Dr. Jonas
Brazil polio drive stalled 4-16, 310A2
SALLAY, Andras
Wins Olympic medal 2-17, 155F3
SALMON, Jorge
Chrgs Banzer campaign plagiarism 7-12, 543F1
SALNIKOV, Vladimir
Wins 3 Olympic gold medals 7-22—7-24, 588G3, 623G2, A3
SALNIKOV, Yuri
Wins Olympic medal 7-27, 622G2
SALOMON Brothers
Kaufman backs wage-price controls 2-21, 144E3
'79 univ endowmt earnings compared to bond index 3-24, 319E1
Kaufman predicts prime rate drop, bond mkt rallies 4-16, 286E2-A3
SALONGA, Jovito
Arrested 10-20, 809G1
SALT (Strategic Arms Limitation Talks)—*See DISARMAMENT—U.S.-Soviet Developments*
SALTIK, Gen. Haydar
In Turkey mil junta 9-21, 720C3
Mil arrests rptd over 11,000 10-28, 832G2
SALTIMBANQUE (Acrobat) Seated with Arms Crossed (painting)
Sold for record sum 5-12, 472B1

1976

SALT Lake City, Utah—*See UTAH*
SALT Lake Tribune (newspaper)
On Gilmore case 11-7, 891B2
SALVANT, Achille
Haiti social affairs min 4-1, 267E2
SALYUT (Soviet space laboratory series)—*See 'Manned Flight' under ASTRONAUTICS*
SAM (surface-to-air missile)—*See 'Missiles' under ARMAMENTS*
SAMAK Sundaravej
Says rebels get Laos training 9-3, 677E3
Named interior min 10-22, 813F2
Chrgs Viet invasion plan 12-8, 949C3
SAME Time Next Year (play)
Long run listed 12-31, 1015A1
SAMMARRAYE, Abdel Razzak
Killed 7-3, named as hijacker 7-5, 485C1, F2
SAMOA, American—*See AMERICAN Samoa*
SAMOA, Western—*See WESTERN Samoa*
SAMPSON, Nikos Giorgiades
Arrest asked 1-28, faces Makarios plot chrg 2-3, 155D1
Arrested 3-16; sentncd 8-31, 858E1
SAMUELS, Howard J.
Carter liaison to mayors 11-7—11-8, 845A3
SAN Antonio, Tex.—*See TEXAS*
SAN Antonio Express (newspaper)
Carter endorsement rptd 10-30, 831B3
SANCHES Osorio, Jose
Returns to Portugal 3-3, 383A3
SANCHEZ, Phillip
Replaced as Honduras amb 9-8, 807E3
SANCHEZ, Archbishop Robert F.
Ecuador expels 8-14, 692D3
SANCHEZ, Maj. Ruben (ret.)
Bolivia chrgs plot 2-19, 238B1
Escapes arrest 4-2, 416A1
SANCHEZ Mejorada, Jorge
Vs import, export duties 9-13, 694B3
SANCHEZ Montero, Simon
Freed 8-4, 753G2
SANDA, Dominique
Wins Cannes film award 5-28, 460F1
SANDBURG, Carl (1878-1967)
Mondale quotes 7-15, 511F3
SANDERS, Carl E(dward)
Cited in Carter biog sketch 512D1-A2
SANDERS Associates Inc.
SEC lists paymts 5-12, 729A1
SAN Diego, Calif.—*See CALIFORNIA*
SAN Diego (U.S. warship)
In Intl Naval Review 7-4, 488D3
SAN Diego Gas and Electric Co.
Utah project dropped 4-14, 284C2
SAN Diego Tribune (newspaper)
Ford endorsement rptd 10-30, 827F3
SAN Diego Union (newspaper)
Chrgs FBI backed rt-wing terrorists 1-11, 42A1
SANDLER, Judge Leonard H.
Replaces Murtagh 1-16, 78G3
Glowa indicted 1-27, 144F3
DeSapio pleads not guilty 5-24, 442B3
Dismisses Brust indictmt 12-1, 1016B2
Sees Saypol indictmt dismissal 12-20, 1016C2
Dismisses Cunningham, Mercorella indictmts 12-22, 1016E1
SANDOVAL Alarcon, Mario
Rightist coalitn controls Cong 7-18, 1005C1
SANEYEV, Victor
Wins Olympic medal 7-30, 576C1
SANFORD, Terry
Gets US campaign subsidy 1-2, 22D3
Common Cause rpts code backing 1-9, 23A1
Ends '76 pres bid 1-23, 95C1
Fed fund total listed 3-4, 180C3
Fed fund total rptd 7-1, 491B1
FEC certificatn total rptd 12-31, 979G2
SAN Francisco, Calif.—*See CALIFORNIA*
SAN Francisco, University of (Calif.)
Wins NCAA soccer title 12-5, 969G2
SAN Francisco Chronicle (newspaper)
Spann interview rptd 7-26, 551G1
SA-Ngad Chaloryu, Adm.
Assures on US mil exit 7-19, 541G3 ★
Becomes defense min 10-4, 754E1
Heads Thai mil govt, suspends charter 10-6, 754A1
Names civln premier 10-8, 775F2
Assures nation on purge 10-11, 775C3
Announces charter comm 10-11, 775D3
Named defense min 10-22, 813E2
SAN Giorgio (Italian warship)
In Intl Naval Review 7-4, 488C3
SANGUINETTI, Alexandre
Brother loses French naval post 1-22, 139D1
Scores Giscard policies 6-3, 417D3
SANGUINETTI, Vice Admiral Antoine
Scores new mil code, CSCE conf 1-16—1-19; ousted 1-22, 139D1
Dismissed 7-7, 521D2
SANGUMBA, Jorge
Vows guerrilla warfare 2-9, 105G1
SANITAS Service Corp.
SEC lists paymts 5-12, 726B1, 729A1

1977

SALT Lake City, Utah—*See UTAH*
SALVATION Army
Brown named pres 5-5, 532G1
Recalls Uganda missionaries 9-21, 805E2
SALYUT (Soviet space laboratory series)—*See ASTRONAUTICS—Manned Flight*
SAM (surface-to-air missile)—*See ARMAMENTS—Missiles*
SAMAK Suntoravej
Mil seizes power 10-20, 827C1
SAMBWA Pida Mbagui
Dismissed 8-11, 641F2
SAMMONS, Dr. James H.
Hysterectomies disputed 5-9, 732A3
Rebuts Califano on health cost 6-19, 479B1
SAMOA, American—*See AMERICAN Samoa*
SAMOA, Western—*See WESTERN Samoa*
SAMPSON, William
Arrested 2-14, kills self 2-15, 160E2
SAMSON, Joan
Auctioneer on best-seller list 3-6, 184G3
SAMSON, Robert
Quebec RCMP panel gets break-in memo 11-11, 903B2
SAMUELS, Michael A.
Replaced as amb to Sierra Leone 6-23, 626A3
SAMUELSSON, Dr. Bengt
Wins Lasker Award 11-16, 927A3
SANAN Khachornprasart, Lt. Col.
Gets life sentence 4-21, 331E2
SAN Antonio, Tex.—*See TEXAS*
SANBORN, Rev. Donald
Tex church consecrated 7-10, 620G2
SANCHEZ, Manuel Antonio
Killed 2-17, 182B1
SANCHEZ Covisa, Mariano
Arrested 2-22, protest staged 2-23, 307B2
SANCHEZ de Leon, Enrique
Spain health, soc sec min 7-5, 545C2
SANCHEZ Parodi, Ramon
Heads Cuba 'interest office' in US 9-1, 685E3
SANCHEZ Zapata, Victor
Freed 8-24, 784E2
SANDBURG, Carl (1878-1967)
Widow dies 2-18, 164E3
SANDBURG, Lilian
Dies 2-18, 164E3 ★
SANDEMAN, Ian
Anti-reform party formed 7-4, 536B3
SANDERS, Greg
Named NIT MVP 3-20, 262E2
SANDERSON, Fred
Warns vs US wheat productn cuts 8-29, 666D3
SAN Diego, Calif.—*See CALIFORNIA*
SAN Francisco, Calif.—*See under CALIFORNIA*
SAN Francisco, University of (Calif.)
Hartwick wins NCAA soccer title 12-4, 1020E3
SAN Francisco Chronicle, The (newspaper)
Thieriot dies 3-21, 264F3
SA-Ngad Chaloryu, Adm.
Coup try fails 3-26, 243E1
Leads mil coup 10-20; on electn plans 10-21; heads ruling group 10-22, 826G3-827F1
SANGER, Fred
Viral DNA sequence completed 2-24, 184C1
SANGSTER, Robert
Alleged wins Arc de Triomphe 10-2, 971A2
SANGUMBE, George
Backs S Africa aid, rpts Alves seeks union 6-26, 522C2
SANGUYO, Benjamin
Slain 9-1, 747A1
SANHEDRIN (race horse)
Seattle Slew wins Triple Crown 6-11, 491B1, D1
SANITATIONMEN
Detroit workers strike 7-6, 558G2

1978

SALT Lake City, Utah—*See UTAH*
SALT & Salt Mines
US oil reserve storage plans scored 8-16, 701A3
SALVAN, Col. Jean-Germain
Wounded 5-2, 340A1
SALVATION Army
Female clergy survey rptd 3-23, 295A2
UK missionaries killed in Rhodesia 6-7, 455A2
WCC membership rptd suspended 8-22, 650B3
WCC rebel aid oppositn cited 10-25, 906E3
SALYUT (Soviet space laboratory series)—*See ASTRONAUTICS—Manned Flight*
SAM (surface-to-air missile)—*See ARMAMENTS—Missiles*
SA Machado, Vitor
Quits Cabt 7-24; govt falls 7-27, 593F2
SAMATER, Mohamed Ali
Rpts 6 officers executed 4-11, 353A3
SAMAWI, Qassem al-
Escapes death try 8-2, PLO accused 8-3, 582D3-583A1
SAME Time, Next Year (film)
Released 11-22, 970A3
SAMOA, American—*See AMERICAN Samoa*
SAMOA, Western—*See WESTERN Samoa*
SAMORE, Cardinal Antonio
Named Beagle Channel mediator 12-23, in Argentina 12-26, 999A3
SAMUEL Johnson (book)
Wins Natl Book Award 4-10, 315D2
Wins Pulitzer 4-17, 315C1
SAN Andreas Fault, Calif.—*See CALIFORNIA*
SAN Antonio, Tex.—*See TEXAS*
SANCHEZ, Federico—*See SEMPRUN, Jorge*
SANCHEZ Baret, Vicente
Sworn DR interior min 8-16, 648C2
SANCHEZ Barsallo, Gen. Alcibiades
Replcd as Peru econ min 5-15, 394D2
SANCHEZ Parodi, Ramon
Invites exiles to Cuba for pol talks 11-4, 880C3
SANCHEZ Ramos, Gen. Juan
Assassinated 7-21, 575E3
SANCHEZ Teran, Salvador
Named Spain transport min 2-24, 394G2
SAN Clemente, Calif.—*See CALIFORNIA*
SANDBURG, Carl
Chicago Daily News ceases publicatn 3-4, 195G1
SAND Castle (film)
Wins Oscar 4-3, 315D3
SANDERS, Frankie
In NBA draft 6-9, 457G2
SANDERS, Col. Harland
Libel suit dismissed 3-14, 420E3
SANDERS, John
NFL '77 interceptn ldr 1-1, 56G2
SANDERS, Tom (Satch)
Named Celtic coach 1-3, 40F3
Fired as Celtics coach 11-14, 1027E2
SANDERSON, Derek
Makes NHL comeback 3-15, scores 200th goal 3-16, 296D3
SANDHU, Anna
Marries James Earl Ray 10-13, 844D3
SANDIA Laboratories (Albuquerque, N.M.)
Antimatter rptd in Earth galaxy cntr 5-6, 653E3
SAN Diego, Calif.—*See CALIFORNIA*
SAN Diego Gas & Electric Co.
Sundesert A-plant voted down 4-13, 281F2
SANDIFORD, William
Chrgd in PC MP tap 4-3, 244A2
SANDINO, Cesar Augusto (1895-1934)
Protesters mark death 2-21, 150C2
Rebellion marked 5-4, 376D1
SANDOVAL, Richard
In World Amateur Boxing tourn 5-6—5-20, 600D2
SANDOVAL Alarcon, Mario
Govt-MLN split rptd 3-9, 168F2
SAN Francisco, Calif.—*See under CALIFORNIA*
SAN Francisco, Fine Arts Museum of
Rockefeller art bequeathed 7-20, 628D1
SAN Francisco, University of
2 in NBA draft 6-9, 457G3
Wins NCAA soccer title 12-10, 969G1
SAN Francisco Examiner (newspaper)
Murphy editorial seeks Hearst release 10-8, 824C1
Robinson in Guyana cult probe missn 11-15—11-17, killed 11-18, body returned 11-21, 889E2, 891C1
SAN Francisco State University—*See CALIFORNIA State University—San Francisco Campus*
SANG, Samantha
Emotion on best-seller list 3-8, 196A1; 4-5, 272F3
SANGUINETTI, Alexandre
Scores Giscard Eur policy 11-12, 902F2
Attacks Chirac 12-13, 987C2, E2
SANGULIAN, Ivan
Named Metros coach 6-13, 707C3
SANITATION Workers
Phila workers strike 7-14—7-21, 565C2
New Orleans strike 7-18—7-21, 565C2
Cities' power over suburbs backed by Sup Ct 11-28, 937A3

1979

SALT Lake City, Utah—*See UTAH*
SALTONSTALL, Leverett
Dies 6-17, 508E3
SALTZ, Amy
Voice of My Own opens 5-2, 712C3
SALVATION Army
Holz installed natl cmdr 3-28, 272D1
SALYUT (Soviet space laboratory series)—*See ASTRONAUTICS—Manned Flight*
SAMBWA Pida Nbagui
Named in McDonnell Douglas paymts chrg 11-9, 886D2
SAMINI, Kazem
Named Iran health min 2-13, 106A1
SAMOA, Western—*See WESTERN Samoa*
SAMORE, Cardinal Antonio
Beagle Channel mediatn agreed 1-8, returns to Vatican 1-9, 51B3
SAMPSON, William
Slain in NC 11-3, 864D3
SAMSON, Robert
Dare testifies on '72 APLQ break-in 7-4, 522D3
SAMUELSON, Peter
Man, Woman & Bank released 9-28, 820G1
SAN Antonio, Tex.—*See TEXAS*
SANCHEZ, Archbishop Roberto
Named to '80 Rome synod 5-3, 376A1
SANCHEZ, Rodolfo
Decisns Jurietti 10-7, 839D1
SANCHEZ Casas, Jose Maria
Arrested 10-14, 795B1
5 Grapo guerrillas escape jail 12-17, 997D3
SANCHEZ Gonzalez, Juan
New oil find announced 2-9, 256C1
SAN Clemente, Calif.—*See CALIFORNIA*
SANCOCHO (play)
Opens 3-28, 712B2
SAND, Ulf
Named Norway finance min 10-5, 774E1
SANDER, Helke
All-Round Reduced Personality released 4-23, 528A1
SAN Diego, Calif.—*See CALIFORNIA*
SAN Diego, University of
New shock therapy tested 3-1, 290B1
SAN Diego Evening Tribune, The (newspaper)
Staff wins Pulitzer 4-16, 336A3
SAN Diego Union, The (newspaper)
Mex immigratn study rptd 2-12, 127A3
SANDINO, Gen. Augusto Cesar (1895-1934)
US-Nicaragua long-term ties detailed 535D2, D3
SANDSTROM v. Montana
Case decided by Sup Ct 6-18, 499G1
SANFORD, Rick
In NFL draft 5-3, 335G1
SAN Francisco, Calif.—*See CALIFORNIA*
SAN Francisco, University of
Newell in basketball HOF 4-30, 526D3
Cartwright in NBA draft 6-25, 507A3
SAN Francisco Examiner (newspaper)
Loses libel judgmt 4-18, plaintiffs awarded $4.56 mln 4-19, 334B2
SANGSTER, Jimmy
Legacy released 9-28, 820E1
SANGUILLEN, Manny
In World Series 10-10—10-17, 816B2
SANITATION Workers
Hawaii workers end strike 12-3, 922A3

1980

SALT Lake City Skyline (play)
Opens 1-23, 136E3
SALT (sodium chloride)
US issues dietary guidelines 2-4, 157A3
La mine collapse 'swallows' lake 11-20, 970C2
SALVAGE, Lynn D.
Mello named First Women's pres 6-12, 600A3
SALVATION Army
Chamberlain dies 3-24, 279G1
SALVI, Paolo
Cossiga innocence upheld 7-27, 579C1
SALYUT (Soviet space laboratory series)
See ASTRONAUTICS--Manned Flight
SAMADZADEH, Ali Akbar
Slain 5-5, body found 5-7, 337C1
SAMARANCH, Juan Antonio
Elected IOC pres 7-16, 590D3
SAMBITO, Joe
Phillies win NL pennant 10-12, 796F1
SAM Marlowe, Private Eye (film)
Released 10-3, 836E3
SAMOA, Western—*See WESTERN Samoa*
SAMOYOA, Salvador
Joins rebels 1-8, 20B1
Arrested 5-27, chrgs rptd 6-7, 444E3
SAMPSON, Dinorah
Paraguay home attacked 10-2, 792C2
SAMPSON, Ralph
Virginia wins NIT, named tourn MVP 3-20, 240F2, A3
SAMSON, Susan Madden
Hide & Seek opens 5-4, 392B3
SAN Bernardino—*See CALIFORNIA*
SANCHEZ, Ladaslad
Judges middlewgt title bout 3-16, 320D2
SANCHEZ, Pablo
Arrest protested, wins CP support 10-21, 832G1, B2
SANCHEZ, Rafael
Kills DR amb in Columbia 11-16, 889C1
SANCHEZ, Raul Augusto
Freed 4-22, 311G3
SANCHEZ, Salvador
TKOs Lopez for WBC featherwgt title 2-2, 320F2
TKOs Lopez 6-21, 1000G3
SANCHEZ Gordillo, Juan Manuel
Leads Andalusia hunger strike 8-14—8-19, 653G1
Gets Andalusia jobs aid pledge 8-22, 673D2
SANCHEZ Mesas, Victor
Held hostage in El Salvador 2-5, 97A1
Freed 2-12, 149C1
SANCHEZ Parodi, Ramon
Cuba to free US prisoners 10-13, 789B1
SANCHEZ Tera, Salvador
Pledges Andalusia jobs aid 8-22, 673D2
SANDALO, Roberto
Terrorist tipoff scandal threatens coalitn govt 5-29—6-3, 430B1
Cossiga innocence upheld 7-27, 578G3, 579D1
SANDERS, Harland (Colonel Sanders)
Dies 12-16, 1004C3
SANDERS v. U.S.
Case decided by Sup Ct 6-20, 555A3
SAN Diego—*See CALIFORNIA*
SANDIFORD, William
Guilty in '77 MP bugging fraud 4-28, 335A1
SANDINO, Gen. Augusto Cesar (1895-1934)
Nicaragua marks Somoza downfall 7-19, 565D3
SANDLER, Barry
Mirror Crack'd released 12-18, 1003C2
SANDOZ Ltd.
McCormick rejects takeover offer 3-18, 386C1
SANDRICH, Jay
Seems Like Old Times released 12-19, 1003D2
SANDRINI, Luis (Felipe)
Dies 7-5, 608G2
SANDS, Dorothy
Dies 9-11, 756C2
SANDURSKI, Adam
Wins Olympic medal 7-31, 624E3
SANEYEV, Viktor
Wins Olympic medal 7-25, 623G3
SANEZ de Santamaria, Gen.
Removed as govt rep to Basques 10-21, 832D2
SAN Francisco—*See CALIFORNIA*
SAN Francisco, University of
'78 NCAA soccer title vacated 11-18, '80 title won 12-14, 1001C3
SAN Francisco Examiner & Chronicle (newspaper)
Reagan pres endorsemts rptd 11-1, 841F3
SAN Francisco International Airport
Brink's truck robbed 8-15, 654G2
SAN Francisco Museum of Fine Arts
Cassatt print bought for record sum 2-14, 472B2
SANGER, Frederick
Wins 2d Nobel Prize 10-14, 889G2
SANGER, Jonathan
Elephant Man released 10-3, 836F2
SANITATION Workers
DeLury dies 2-12, 175G3
Detroit workers strike 7-2, 518G1, strike ends 7-12, 542G1
NYC pact setld 7-3, 518B1, E1
Mobile (Ala) strike 7-14—7-24, 576D1

1976

SAN Jose, Calif.—*See CALIFORNIA*
SAN Jose Mercury, The (newspaper)
Ariz crime probed 10-2, 849B2
SANJUAN, Pedro
Dies 10-18, 970B3
SAN Leandro, Calif.—*See CALIFORNIA*
SAN Marino
Listed as 'free' nation 1-19, 20C3
SAN Rafael, Calif.—*See CALIFORNIA*
SAN Simeon, Calif.—*See CALIFORNIA*
SANSINENA (Liberia tanker)
Explodes in LA harbor 12-17, 969F1
SANSOM, William
Dies 4-20, 524E3
SANTA Ana, Calif.—*See CALIFORNIA*
SANTA Barbara, Calif.—*See CALIFORNIA*
SANTA Fe International Corp.
SEC lists paymts 5-12, 729A1
Forgn paymts policy cited 12-18, 985A2
SANTA Monica, Calif.—*See CALIFORNIA*
SANTANA Machado, Luiz
Arrest confirmed 3-9, 288B1
SANTINI, Rep. James (D, Nev.)
Unopposed in primary 9-14, 705C1
Reelected 11-2, 824D2, 830C1
SANTOS Silva, Antonio
To keep govt post 1-6, 11B2
SANTUCHO, Mario Roberto
Killed 7-19, 571E1
Mil ldrs rptd elated by death 8-9, 671F3
SAN Yu
Plotters arrested 7-2, 543D2
SAO Tome e Principe (Portuguese territory)—*See also NONALIGNED Nations Movement, OAU*
Listed as 'partly free' 1-19, 20D3
At France-Africa summit 5-10—5-11, 355A3
SAPENA Pastor, Raul
Quits as forgn min 3-8, 206B1
SARAGAT, Giuseppe
Named CIA aid recipient 1-31, 140C3
Social Dems oust Tanassi 3-12—3-16, 254B2
SARASIN, Rep. Ronald A. (R, Conn.)
Seconds Ford nominatn 8-18, 597G2
Reelected 11-2, 829A2
SARASOTA, Fla.—*See FLORIDA*
SARBANES, Rep. Paul Spyros (D, Md.)
Wins Senate primary 5-18, 357A2
Dem conv speaker 7-13, 509E3
AFL-CIO donatn rptd 10-22, 938D3
Elected senator 11-2, 819F3, 821D1, 828G1
SARETT, Lewis H.
Gets Medal of Science 10-18, 858F3
SARGENT, Francis W.
Cited in Dole biog sketch 614A3
SARGENT, Dr. William
Claims Hearst 'brainwashed' 1-29, 70D1
SARKAR, Prabhat Ranjan
Gets life prison term 11-29, 952G3

SARKIS, Elias (Lebanese president)
Meets US mediator 4-3, 241E2
Moslems seek electn delay 4-27, 296B1
Moslems back Edde as pres 4-30, 319B1
Assad seeks new candidate 319C1
Elected pres; Franjieh delays resignatn, Moslems score 5-8, 337A1, E1
Seeks war end 5-8—5-12, 337C1
Shootout at hotel 5-8, 337F2
Moslems offer cooperatn 5-10, 5-11, 337A2
US envoy lauds 5-11, 337C2
Holds peace talks 5-20, 369B2
France offers peace force 5-21, 369B1
Sees factional ldrs 5-27—5-28; asks new ceasefire 5-31, 385D2
Sees Jumblat 6-2, 385E1
Syria sets withdrawl terms 6-13, 429A2
Libya premier mediates 6-15, 429A3
US amb slain 6-16, 425B1
Rpt Israel arms Christians 7-3, 487B1
To head peace dialogue 7-29, 547B1
Sees Franjieh on power shift 8-19, 628B3
Meets US aides 8-22—8-24, 628G3
In peace plan talks 8-26—8-27, 662F3
Sees Assad on ties 8-31, peace plan rptd 9-3, 662G3
Meets Al Fatah official 9-4, 663C1
Franjieh Cabt shift scored 9-15, 682A3
In truce talks 9-17, 9-19; sees Sadat 9-18, 698F2, C3
Takes office 9-23, 699E1

1977

SAN Jose, Calif.—*See CALIFORNIA*
SAN Jose State University
Faumuina in NFL draft 5-3, 353B3
SAN Marino
Helsinki Agreement—*See EUROPE—Security and Cooperation*
SANSON, Chris
IRS cleared in Miami probe 1-6, 16D1
SANTA Catalina Island—*See CALIFORNIA*
SANTA Fe, N. M.—*See NEW Mexico*
SANTA Fe Industries, Inc.
Antifraud rules expansn barred 3-23, 276A3 ★
SANTA Fe National Forest
12,000 acres burn 6-16—6-22, A-lab threatened 6-18, 660F3
SANTA Fe-San Vel Corp.
Wins minority contract 12-13, 979C1
SANTA Monica Mountains
Satellite constructn dispute declined 11-7, 857E2
SANTISTEBAN, Carlos
Resignatn rejected 5-13, 427A3
Quits Central Bank in monetary dispute 7-11, 563G2
SANTUCHO, Mario Roberto (d. 1976)
Videla escapes blast 2-18, 197D3
Mattini succeeds as ERP ldr 7-20, 595D3
SANYO Electric Co. Ltd.
US TV productn cited 3-28, 319A1
US TV operatns cited 12-14, 974B2
SAN Yu, Gen.
Followers rptd purged 10-8, 779C3
SAO Tome e Principe (Portuguese territory)—*See also NONALIGNED Nations Movement, OAU*
UN Assemb member 4B1
IMF admits 9-30, 754D2
Cuba medical aides rptd 11-17, 896G1
SANTORO, Jennifer
Murdered 7-22, suspect indictd 9-7, 712F1
SAOUMA, Edouard
Sees new Sahel famine 9-19, 770G1-A2
SAPIR, Pinhas (d. 1976)
Tied to Yadlin kickback chrg 2-14, 135B2
SARBANES, Sen. Paul Spyros (D, Md.)
'76 spec interest gifts rptd 2-15, 128C2
Scores Thurmond re Panama Canal debate 10-4, 755E2
In Panama, undecided on pacts 11-9—11-12, 911C2, E3
SARKAR, Prabhat Ranjan
Ananda Marga attacks rptd 11-28, 12-1, 966A3

SARKIS, Elias (Lebanese president)
Meets on Christn hq blast 1-4, 2F1
Meets Assad, cooperatn set 2-2, 72A2
OKs Palestinian pullback pact 2-25, 143B2
Weighs UN troop use 2-27, 143C2
Butros sees crisis 3-1, 143D2
Deploys police to south 3-12, 188B2
Cabt meets on Jumblat death 3-16, 188F1
Christians ask protectn 3-18, 3-19, 208B2
League force extended 3-27, 227C2
Names new army head 3-28, 227C1
Gets Christn plea to halt fighting 4-7, 266D2
Names new security heads 4-11, 297A3
Pro-Palestinian stand chrgd 4-18, 297G2
Seeks PLO curbs 4-19, 316F2
Sees Mohsen on Palestinian shift 4-22, 316A3
Vs Palestinian presence 5-27, 439F3
Vows '69 Cairo pact enforcmt 6-8, 440A1
Meets Vance 8-2, 588C3
Chuf area peace rptd vowed 8-22, 647F3
Christns warn re support 8-27, 697C2
Seeks to end fighting 9-22, 714C3
US informs of peace try 10-12, 793A3
Sees Assad on peace moves 11-5, 850C1
Begin invites to Israel 11-15, 873G1

1978

SAN Joaquin Valley Nuclear Project
Kern Cnty voters reject 3-15, 184D1
SANJABI, Karim
Vs Shah coalitn govt plea 857E3
Arrested 11-11, 869C2
Released 12-6, 929C2
Vs role in Sadiqi govt 12-17, 993E1
Asks shah ouster 12-25, 993G1
SAN Jose, Calif.—*See CALIFORNIA*
SAN Marino
Gen electn held 5-28; Christian Dem, CP coalitn dispute unresolved 5-28, 5-30, 438D1
Ghironzi corruptn chrgs rptd 5-30, 438F1
CP reach accord with Soclsts 6-23, coalitn leads new regime 7-17, 575F1
USSR dissident trials scored 7-18, 575B2
Helsinki Agreement—*See EUROPE—Security and Cooperation*
SANTA Barbara, Calif.—*See CALIFORNIA*
SANTA Clara Pueblo v. Martinez
Indian tribal authority backed by Sup Ct 5-15, 387A3
SANTA Cruz II (Argentine freighter)
Chesapeake Bay collisn 10-20, 908C3
SANTA Fe Industries Inc.
Atchison, Topeka & Santa Fe Railroad
ICC fines in freight-car shortage 6-15, 569B2, E2
ICC reduces fine 8-11, 643F2
SANTAMARIA, Mongo
Record wins Grammy 2-24, 316B1
SANTANA, Frank
Iowa wins NCAA wrestling title 3-18, 379G2
SANTINI, Rep. James (D, Nev.)
House subcom probe cited 1-11—1-13, 40B2
Reelected 11-7, 851E2, 857G1
SANTOFIMIO Botero, Alberto
Wins Sen seat despite jailing 2-26, 147E1
SANTONE, Ellis
This Room opens 6-15, 760E3
SANTORO, Antonio
Killed 6-6, 453D2
SANTOS, Antonio de Almeida
Sworn Portugal dep premier 1-30, 91B3
SANTOS, Francisco Antonio
Arrested 9-3, 774A2
SANTOS, Gonzalo
Estate broken up by govt 9-1, 817E3
SANZ, Capt. Alberto
Bolivia urban, housing min 11-24, 913E1
SAO Tome e Principe (Portuguese territory)—*See also NONALIGNED Nations Movement, OAU*
UN Assemb member 713D3
SAOUMA, Edouard
Fears E Africa locust plague 6-12, 465E2
SAQQAF, Salem al-
Executed 11-15, 885C3
SARAGAT, Giuseppe
On Moro death, Berlinguer refutes 5-9, 338E1
SARANDON, Susan
King of Gypsies released 12-19, 1030B3
SARASIN, Rep. Ronald (R, Conn.)
Nominated for gov 9-12, 716F2
Loses electn 11-7, 847C2
SARAVIA, Col. Rolando
Bolivia peasant affairs min 11-24, 913E1
SARAZEN, Gene
Sues PGA over exemptn rule 1-23, 76F1
SARBANES, Sen. Paul Spyros (D, Md.)
Votes for Panama Canal neutrality pact 3-16, 177E2
Vs Turkish arms embargo end 4-5, 276E3
Votes for 2d Canal pact, ratificatn role cited 4-18, 273B1, F2
On Turkish arms ban end 5-11, 378A2
SARDINIA—*See ITALY*
SARGENT, Alvin
Straight Time released 3-18, 619G3
Wins Oscar 4-3, 315C3
SARID, Yossi
Rpts Ethiopia ousts natls 2-18, 138B1
SARKIS, Elias (Lebanese president)
Gets protest on PLO arms 1-25, 79F2
Sets Syria peace agrmt 2-11—2-12; Leb Parlt OKs joint mil ct 2-14, 99A1, C1
Talks to Assad on Israel invasn; scores Israel 3-15, 174D3, E3
Meets Waldheim 4-17, 274F2
Renames Hoss to form Cabt 4-28; rpts failure, reinstates Cabt 5-15, 359D1
Meets UN aide 5-20—5-21, 383E2
Syria OKs troop role in south 5-31—6-1, 462C3
Warned on troops to south 6-5, 463A1
Syria scores Christian policy 6-28, 502D2
Threatens to quit over Syria demands 7-6, 502B3
Syria demands Christians obey 7-9, 522B1
Vows to resign 7-9, Chamoun vs decisn 7-12, 522B1
Syrian pres questns on resignatn 7-12, to stay on 7-15, 547A1
Syria backs Leb army in south 8-3, 583F1
Chamoun ties to US-Syria plot 8-31, 674F2
Carter: Begin, Sadat back govt 9-28, 745D1
Seeks to prolong truce 10-1, 745G2
In French talks on peace 10-2, 745G1
Meets Arab ldrs on peace plan 10-2, 10-12, 783B1, F1

1979

SANJABI, Karim
Bars Iran regency cncl apptmt 1-13, 25G1
Named Iran forgn min 2-13, 105G2
Quits Cabt 4-15, scores Khomeini rule 4-16—4-17, 276G3-277G1
Yazdi named forgn min 4-24, 297B2
SAN Luis Obispo, Calif.—*See CALIFORNIA*
SAN Luis Valley Ranches Inc.
Colo land sale refunds set 5-8, 596A1
SAN Onofre Nuclear Generating Station—*See CALIFORNIA-Atomic Energy*
SAN Rafael (Calif.) Independent-Journal, The (newspaper)
Gannett buys 12-12, 1007E1
SANTA Cruz II (Argentine freighter)
Chesapeake Bay collisn rpts issued 1-20, 140F3; 2-26, 3-2, 240F3
SANTA Fe Industries Inc.
Atchison, Topeka RR takeover of Rock Island ordered 9-26, 722C3
SANTA Fe International Corp.
Iran sued 12-13, 976D2
SANTAMARIA, Col. Efrain
Rpts Nicaragua rebel raid repelled 5-23, 409F1
SANTINI, Rep. James (D, Nev.)
Threatens NCAA curbs 1-10, 103F1
SANTOS de Andrade, Joaquim
On strike arrests 10-29, 833G1
SANTOS Zelaya, Gen. Jose (deceased)
US-Nicaragua long-term ties detailed 535C2
SAOMA, Edouard
Hails FAO conf results 7-20, 554E1
SAO Tome e Principe—*See also NONALIGNED Nations Movement, OAU*
UN membership listed 695B3
SARAGAT, Giuseppe
Named Italy dep premr 3-7, 169E3
Backs martial law 5-3, 331D2
SARANDON, Chris
Woods opens 4-25, 712G3
SARANDON, Susan
Short of Paradise released 10-5, 1008F1
SARAVA (play)
Opens 2-11, 292F2
SARBANES, Sen. Paul Spyros (D, Md.)
Financial disclosure statement studied 9-1, 702B1
SARCINELLI, Mario
Chrgd re bank dealings 3-26, 237A2
Suspended from bank post 4-17, 313D2
Favorable ct ruling rptd 11-14, 909D2
SARGENT, Bill
Knockout opens 5-6, 712A1
SARGENT, Joseph
Goldengirl released 6-15, 820C1

SARKIS, Elias (Lebanese president)
Vs Israel peace bid 5-7, 341E1
Meets Assad re unrest 5-14—5-15, 378G2
Accepts Hoss resignatn 5-15, 378G2
Asks Hoss to form new govt 7-2, Cabt announced 7-16, 671D1
Asks Arab aid in Leb fighting 8-24, 643D1
Meets with US black leaders 9-18, 694G1
Clashes with Arafat at Arab League summit 11-21, 11-22, 916B2
Seeks to bar Iran volunteers 12-10, 937A3
Bars Iran volunteers in Leb 12-18, Syria reassures 12-20, 980A1

1980

SAN Jose—*See CALIFORNIA*
SAN Marino—*See CSCE*
SANTA Barbara (Calif.) News-Press (newspaper)
McClean dies 12-5, 1004F2
SANTA Clara—*See CALIFORNIA*
SANTA Fe—*See NEW Mexico*
SANTA Fe Industries Inc.
South Pacific RR merger set 5-15, 427A3
Southn Pacific merger canceled 9-12, 745D2
SANTA Fe New Mexican, The (newspaper)
Gannett purchase ordrd rescinded 6-30, 582D2-A3
SANTANGELO, Betty
NY drug dealer sentenced 6-30, 503G1
SANTINI, Rep. James (D, Nev.)
On USSR metals buying 2-5, 85E1
Reelected 11-4, 843F2, 852B1
SANTUCCI, John J.
Loses NY US Sen primary 9-9, 682C2
SANWA Bank
Nicaragua debt rescheduled 9-5, 689A3
SANYAMA, Oliver
Slain 1-22, 80C2
SAO Tome e Principe—*See NONALIGNED Nations, OAU*
SAPIELO, Piotr
Poles arrest 11-21, free 11-27, 909C1, F1
SARASOTA—*See FLORIDA*
SARATOGA, U.S.S. (aircraft carrier)
Overhaul scheduled 9-30, 780C2
SARAZIN, Gene
Nicklaus wins PGA Championship 8-10, 714D2
SARGENT, Alvin
Ordinary People released 9-19, 836D3
SARGENT, Joseph
Coast to Coast released 10-3, 836D2
SARKINSIAN, Yurik
Wins Olympic medal 7-21, 624E2

SARKIS, Elias (Lebanese president)
Accepts Hoss resignatn, names Solh 7-20, 579C3
Names Wazan premr 10-22, 874A1

1976

Makes truce moves 9-23—9-24, 9-26, 720E2
Moves into pres palace 9-24, 720G2
In truce talks 10-4, 737F1
Truce agrmt backs govt 10-9, 758A2
At Riyadh peace conf 10-17—10-18, 778A3
To head Arab peace force 10-18, 778C3
Holds mtg on Riyadh pact 10-20, 779C1
Names Hajj Arab force cmdr 11-4, 841D1
Meets US charge 11-5, 841E2
Asks Arab peace force OK 11-7—11-8; Christns agree 11-9, 841C1
Lauds Arab peace force 11-21, 877C1
Israel for Leb border role 11-29, 894E2
Extends arms collectn deadline 12-5, 913A1
Names Hoss premier 12-8, 913C2
Edde protests death try 12-13, 953C1

SARMIENTO, Camila
Ransomed 6-14, 731C2

SARMIENTO, Rafael
Peron embezzlmt chrg rptd 6-18, 520G1

SARMIENTO, Brig. Gen. Samuel
Named Pl AF head 3-27, 255C3

SARMIENTO, Yolanda
Pleads guilty 11-5, 971A3

SARNOFF, Robert W.
Conrad quits RCA 9-16, 708C2

SARTORIUS, Nicolas
Arrested 11-22, 909C1

SARTRE, Jean-Paul
44 linked to CIA 1-13, 1-14, 49C3, G3
Pleads for Sovt dissident 3-24, 421A3

SASSER, James R.
Wins Tenn Sen primary 8-5, 633G1
Elected 11-2, 819F3, 822C3, 828C3

SASSOON, Vidal & Beverly
Yr of Beauty on best-seller list 12-5, 972B2

SATHANANTHAN, Sheila
Sentenced 2-5, 123C2

SATO, Takayuki
Arrested 8-20, 628C2
Indicted 9-10, 740A3

SATPATHY, Nandini
Loses Orissa post 12-16, 1006D1

SATTERFIELD III, Rep. David Edward (D, Va.)
Reelected 11-2, 830G4

SATYUKOV, Pavel A.
Dies 11-17, 970B3

SATZ, Jay
On Pa mystery disease 8-5, 573A3

SAUDI Arabia—*See also ARAB League, NONALIGNED Nations Movement, OPEC*
Middle East jet crash kills 82 1-1, 79G3
Listed as 'not free' nation 1-19, 20E3
'75 oil output down 4-25, 298B3

Foreign Relations (misc.)
Iran recalls amb 1-7, 12G3
French Mirage purchase cited 1-16, 36C2
Sahara diplomatic efforts continue 2-1—2-6, 107A3
Nasser cleared of '67 theft chrg 2-4, 119C1
At intl econ conf 2-11—2-20, 148B1
Consortium-backed Italy loan rptd 2-16, 141A1
India fears Pak arms aid 3-31, 278B3
Total IMF oil loan rptd 4-1, 340G2
At Timor assemb meeting 5-31, 423A1
Joins Egypt, Sudan vs Libya 7-18—8-19, 531B2
Libya recalls amb re Sudan, Egypt alliance 7-25, 547D3
Joins Egypt aid fund 8-21, 630A1
Egypt plans French missile resale 8-27, 675B1
In Pl-rebel talks 12-15—12-23, 1008G3
Iraq, Iran vs oil price hike 12-18, 12-20, 975A3
Forgn paymts rptd accepted 12-20, 985A3
Middle East Conflict—*See MIDDLE EAST*

1977

SARKIS, George
US warns on Syrian moves 1-26, 72A1

SARMIENTO, Yolanda
Sentenced 1-21, 103B1

SARSANEDAS, Rev. Jorge
El Salvador deports 5-6, 373A3

SAS—*See SCANDINAVIAN Airlines System*

SASSER, Sen. James (D, Tenn.)
Visits Panama 11-9—11-12, 911C2

SAT (Scholastic Aptitude Test)—*See EDUCATION*

SATELLITES—*See under ASTRONAUTICS*

SATHE, V. P.
On corruptn probe 4-1, 283D3

SATO, Takayuki
Lockheed bribe trial opens 1-31, 83E2

SATPATHY, Nandini
Quits party 2-2, 71E1
Arrested 9-17, 801G2-A3

SATRA Corp.
Sues NBC over Moscow Olympics 2-14, 131E1
Drops suit vs NBC, IOC 12-9, 971D2

SATTY, Nora
Sup Ct upholds maternity leave seniority rights 12-6, 938D2

SATURDAY Evening Post, The (defunct magazine)
Boeing rpts consultant 1-5, ct backs secrecy 2-25, 215C3
Ollie Atkins dies 1-9, 84F2

SAUD al-Faisal, Prince (Saudi Arabia)
Vs Israel on setlmts 9-3, 685E1

SAUDI Arabia—*See also ARAB League, NONALIGNED Nations Movement, OPEC*
'77-82 econ dvpt plan cited 1-10, 78A3
Surplus revenue estimated 363A2
Cholera outbreak rptd 9-26, 748A1

Arab-Israeli Conflict—*See MIDDLE EAST*
Foreign Relations (misc.)—*See also 'Oil Developments' below*
UN Assemb member 4B1
Western investmts cited 1-17, 107C3
French pres visits 1-22—1-25, 50F1-D2
Egypt econ aid vowed 1-22, 62F2
Ethiopia chrgs rebel link 2-4, 98A3
Waldheim visits 2-5—2-6, 86E2
Israel boycott eased 2-18, 167E2
Black Africa funds vowed 3-7, 170A2
Castro for alliance on Djibouti 3-10—3-16, 249D2
Gulf group aids Egypt 3-25, 390D3
Morocco fears Zaire interventn 4-18, 317A2
Arab monetary fund created 4-18, 318B1, C1
Khalid in UK for treatmt 4-25—4-27, 362B1
Ethiopia hijack foiled 4-26, 328D1
Pak feud mediatn 4-28, 348B3
In IMF lending facility plan 5-3, 5-4, 363E1
Intl consortium OKs Egypt aid 5-11—5-12, 390C3
Egypt rpts defense finance agrmt 7-16, 550B1
Ethiopia amb defects 7-17, 562E2
Zaire aid revealed 7-19, 583C1
Somalia arms aid rptd 9-1, 684A3
Somali ldr visits, aid offer rptd 9-14, 715A3
W Ger thanks re hijacked jet rescue 10-20, 789F2, 790G1
Somalia arms aid rptd 10-22, 830B1
Sadat ends visit 11-3, 850A2
Assad visits re Cairo conf 12-8—12-9, 954F2
Boycott vs Israel extended 12-10, 955C1
Lebanon Civil Strife—*See LEBANON*

1978

Escapes palace shelling 10-4, 746D1
Meets Assad re truce 10-7—10-9; in Saudi 10-9—10-10, UAE 10-10, 761E1
French shocked at peace plan rebuff 10-7, 761B2
Chamoun vs talks with Assad 10-9, 761A2
Beirut Moslems strike vs peace plan 10-10, 761A2

SARLAI, Imre
Rain & Shine released 12-21, 1030D3

SARNOFF Laboratory—*See under RCA Corp.*

SARRAZIN, Michael
Caravans released 11-1, 969F3 ★

SASAKI, Hideyo
Tied to Lockheed scandal 1-30, 72E3

SASAKI, Ryosaku
Interviews Teng 11-26, 950B1

SASKATCHEWAN (Canadian province)—*See CANADA*

SASSER, Sen. James R. (D, Tenn.)
Votes for Panama Canal neutrality pact 3-16, 177E2
Votes for 2d Canal pact 4-18, 273B1

SAT (Scholastic Aptitude Test)—*See SCHOLASTIC Aptitude Test*

SATAN in Goray (book)
Singer wins Nobel Prize 10-5, 886G1

SATELLITES—*See under ASTRONAUTICS*

SATO, Shoji
In China peace pact talks 7-21—8-12, 637C1

SATO, Takayuki
Tied to Lockheed scandal 1-30, 72E3

SATTERFIELD III, Rep. David Edward (D, Va.)
Reelected 11-7, 852D3

SATURDAY Evening Post, The (magazine) (defunct)
Norman Rockwell dies 11-8, 972E3

SATURDAY Night Fever (film)
Top-grossing film 1-4, 24G3; 2-1, 116E3; 3-1, 195G3; 3-29, 272E3; 4-26, 356C1

SATURDAY Night Fever Soundtrack (recording)
On best-seller list 2-4, 116G3; 3-8, 196B1; 4-5, 272G3; 5-3, 356E1; 6-7, 460G3

SAUD, Sultan ibn Abd al-Aziz Al (Saudi Arabia)
Vance sees on summit pacts 9-22, 731D1

SAUD al-Faisal, Prince (Saudi Arabia)
On Carter-Khalid talks 1-4, 2B3
Vs US F-15 conditns 5-12, 358F2
Fears Africa communist role 5-31, 441A2
French Leb peace plan offered 10-3, 745A2
Vs forgn power role in Leb 10-16, 783C1

SAUDI Arabia—*See also ARAB League, NONALIGNED Nations Movement, OPEC*
Princess, lover executns confirmed 2-1, 172G3
Arms-mfg city rptd planned 2-18, 199G1
Econ dvpt rptd slowed 2-20, 122E1

Arab-Israeli Conflict—*See MIDDLE EAST*
Foreign Relations (misc.)—*See also 'Oil Developments' below*
Shah briefs on Sadat talks 1-10, 26E2
Somalia arms sources rptd 1-24, 44C1
Ethiopia protests Somalia aid 2-1, 2-14, 100D1
Somalia gets French-made tanks 2-8, 100A1
Israel deplores US jet sale 2-14—2-15, 97F1
France signs AIO arms pact; US, UK deals cited 3-14, 237C1 ★
Rial added to new SDR basket 4-3, 300E3, F3
Islamic, Arab poor-natn aid rise rptd 4-9, 257C2, F2
Ethiopia rebel support cited 4-27, 372G2
Saudis see stepped-up Sovt expansn 5-13, 358E2
2 UK workers whipped 5-15; other natls rptd arrested, sentenced 6-15—6-21, 515E3
Saud in Paris, fears Africa communist role 5-31, 441A2
Zaire aid rptd backed 6-1, 441G1
Zaire aid mtg observed 6-13—6-14, 478A1
N Yemen pres slaying deplored, warns vs interventn 6-24, 499B2
S Yemen pres executed 6-26, 499D1
Yamani in Canada 6-29, 635B1
Leb pres asked to stay 7-6, 502B3
UK workers fired 7-17, 631A1
Arab fund loan to Sudan rptd 8-17, 925F3
Canada orders Bell Co bias ended 9-11, guidelines issued 9-21, 772F3
UN Assemb member 713E3

1979

SARNEY, Jose
Sees democracy in 2 yrs 3-13, 210A1

SARNO, Geraldo
Col Delmiro Gouveia released 4-30, 528A2

SARTAWI, Isa
Met with US amb 8-22, 625B1

SARTRE, Jean-Paul
Leftist writer slain 9-20, 772B3

SASSER, Sen. James R. (D, Tenn.)
Votes vs Talmadge denunciatn 10-10, 769F1
Tours Cambodia refugee camps in Thailand 10-21—10-23; in Cambodia, proposes food convoy 10-24; rpts to Carter 10-26; Cambodia vs plan 10-27, 823C3-824E1
Rpts gas raids vs Laos rebels 11-3, 979B1
GAO 'fraud hotline' rptd effective 12-9, 947G1

SASSOU-Nguesso, Col. Denis (Congolese head of state)
Congo head of state 1-8, 85F3

SAT (Scholastic Aptitude Test)—*See SCHOLASTIC Aptitude Test*

SATCOM (U.S. communications satellite series)—*See ASTRONAUTICS—Communications Projects*

SATELLITES—*See under ASTRONAUTICS*

SATIE, Erik (1866-1925)
Massine dies 3-16, 272B3

SATMAR Hasidim—*See JEWS*

SATOWAKI, Cardinal Joseph Asjiro
Installed cardinal 6-30, 640D2

SATTER, David
USSR extends visa 8-3, 636G3

SATURDAY Night Fever Soundtrack (recording)
Wins Grammy 2-16, 336D3

SATURDAY Night Live (TV series)
Gilda Radner Live opens 8-2, 711C3

SATURN (planet)
Voyager II passes Jupiter 7-9, 552B3
Pioneer 11 flies by; photo 9-1, 696F1

SAUD al-Faisal, Prince (Saudi Arabia)
Saudi to drop '80 oil productn 10-4, 781F1

SAUDI Arabia—*See also ARAB League, NONALIGNED Nations Movement, OPEC*
Budget plans rptd 5-29, 427E2
'78 per capita GNP ranked 10th 7-24, 575E3
Pak jet crash kills 156 11-26, 912F1
Shiite unrest denied 12-2—12-3, 916C1
Money reserves said less, theft rumor rptd 12-12, 968B3

Arab-Israeli Conflict—*See MIDDLE EAST*
Foreign Relations (misc.)—*See also 'Mecca Mosque Takeover' and 'Oil' below*
Teng fears Iran chain reactn 2-7, 84C1
N Yemen mil aid plan rptd 2-8, 89D2
UK queen tours 2-17, 190C1
Yemen border clashes spur troop alert, mediatn accepted 2-24—2-28, 144B2
N Yemen arms shipmt speeded by US 2-26, 144F2
Egypt recalls envoy 4-7, 278D1
Pak denies A-bomb chrg 4-8, 277F2
Egypt ties cut 4-23, 296D1
Egypt aid group disbanded 4-27, 319D2
Egypt assails tactics, discounts econ impact 5-1; Saudi refutes 5-2, 319E1
Unifil troops Leb exit cited 5-7, 341A2
Air Canada pact signed, Arab boycott clause rptd 5-7, 467F3
US talks on Egypt jet funding rptd 5-8, 341D2
Sadat sees no US jet deal 5-12, 360A1
Arab arms plant in Egypt to close 5-14, 359E3
Taiwan-N Yemen jet pilot deal aided 5-29, 395G1
Canada phone pact threatnd 6-19, 467E3
US delays F-5 jet sale to Egypt 7-6, 512A1
Libya fete attended by royalty 9-1, 688C3
Canada envoy tours Mideast 9-9—10-20, Bell deal rptd cancelled 10-18, 833D2, A3
UN membership listed 695B3
Egypt chrgs 'hate campaign', fears Libya link; Faud denies accusatns 10-10, 801E2-802A1
At Persian Gulf security conf 10-14—10-16, 804G1
UK MPs admits affair with Khashoggi's ex-wife 12-15, 994A3

1980

SARTI, Adolfo
Italy educ min 4-4, 275F3

SARTRE, Jean-Paul
Dies 4-15, 360C3

SARVARI, Assadulah
Wounded in shootout 2-7, 123A3

SASAKI, Ryosaku
Parlt defense panel formed 4-7, 314C3

SASSON Taeil, Victor
DR Emb siege ends, hostages freed 4-27, 335B2

SASSOU-Nguesso, Col. Denis (Congolese head of state)
Meets Pope 5-5, 363E2

SAT—*See SCHOLASTIC Aptitude Test*

SATCOM (U.S. communication satellite series)—*See ASTRONAUTICS—Communications Projects*

SATELLITES—*See under ASTRONAUTICS*

SATTERFIELD, Rep. David E. (D, Va.)
Bliley wins seat 11-4, 850E2

SATURDAY Evening Post, The (magazine) (defunct)
Wm T Martin dies 10-13, 876F2

SATURDAY Night Fever Soundtrack (recording)
NY record co indicted 2-28, 237D3

SATURDAY Review (magazine)
Sold 5-20, 582C3

SATURN (planet)
Vogager 1 flies by, findings detailed 11-12, 932C2-933A1

SATURN 3 (film)
Released 2-15, 216D3

SAUCIER, Kevin
In World Series 10-14—10-21, 812C2

SAUD al-Faisal, Prince (Saudi Arabia)
Briefed on Palestine autonomy talks 2-2, 89D2
In Hunt silver-backed bond group 3-26, 223B1
To quit Aramco bd 7-8, 662G1
On US air defns gear for Saudis 10-5, 758C1

SAUDI Arabia—*See also ARAB League, NONALIGNED Nations, OPEC*
Armed forces shifted; '79 mil, admin resignatns cited 1-1, 22C1
Tighter Islamic law enforcemt, other anti-unrest moves rptd 2-5, 195A1
Jidda rptd most expensive city 2-12, 125E3
Jet fire kills 301 8-19, 778B1*
Human rights record scored 12-10, 978B3

Arab-Israeli Conflict—*See ARAB-Israeli Developments*
Foreign Relations (misc.)—*See also 'Iran-Iraq War', 'Oil & Gas' below*
Olympic role canceled re Afghan crisis 1-6, 3B1
Islamic conf proposed 1-7; held 1-27—1-29, 67E2
USSR Olympics boycott cited 1-18, 28C3
Egypt: Sovts use air space for S Yemen arms aid 1-28, 69A2
US defns rpt cites Moscow port targets 2-1, 84A2
Persian Gulf defns role cited by US 2-1, 84C2
Sovt threat to Pak seen 2-5, 83G1-A2
Egypt to buy US F-15s, F-16s deferred 2-25, 140D2
French pres visits, sees Khalid 3-10, 180D1
W Ger note sale set 3-24, 236E2-A3
Turkey aid vow seen 3-26, 236E2
IOC boycott list rptd 3-28, 259F3
UK film on Saudi princess strains ties, '79 trade cited 4-10, 4-11, 294B1
Australia bars film telecast 4-15, 309F3
UK film dispute spurs amb ouster order 4-23, trip cancellatns 4-25, 313C2-B3
UK regrets film 5-21, 407A3
US co contracts to UK barred 5-21, 407B3
UK ties restored 7-28, 578A3
World Bank loans frozen over PLO issue 8-2, 592A2
Israel holy war urged; Iraq, Algeria mtgs cited 8-14, 627F2
Pak mil base talks rptd 8-19, 653G3
Israel scorns war threat 8-28, 660B3
PLO status in World Bank, IMF disputed, funding cutoff threatened 9-4—9-22; dirs bar observer role 9-18, 719F3
Syria seeks backing for Libya merger 9-10; supports 9-14, 697G1-C2

1976

UN Policy & Developments—*See UN DEVELOPMENTS under MIDDLE EAST*

U.S. Relations

Stevenson rpts on visit 2-28, 161B1
No funding for Hawk missile sale seen 4-4, 242E1; Jordan: deal off 4-14, 274B3
Zarb visits, asks oil price freeze 340C1
US suit vs Gen Tire setld 5-10, 360F1
To get US air defns systm 7-31, 561F1
Embargo threat linked to boycott bill, missile sale 9-26, 9-27, 746G2
Arms sales a US pres campaign issue 9-30, 725D1, 742F3
Carter arms sales data disputed 10-8, 764A1
Forgn paymts rptd accepted 12-20, 985A3
SEC sues Amer Hosp 12-29, 986A2

1977

Oil Developments—*See also OPEC*

5% price rise in effect 1-1, productn rise OK rptd 1-2, 11F3, 12E1
US consumer price break urged 1-8, 12C2
French accord signed 1-24, 50F1-A2
Iran, Iraq, Kuwait exports drop 1-26, 2-9, 107G3
OPEC price compromise barred 2-6, 107G2
Mobil to build pipeline 2-8, 108C2
Bad weather cuts output 2-9, 1st ¼ forecast 2-16, 108A1
Yamani price plan rptd 2-14, 107D3
Buyers rptd picked for extra oil; Yamani scores rpt 2-15, 108B1-E1
Output drop aids Iran 3-2, Kuwait 3-24, 227G2
Feb output rise rptd 3-10, 227E3
'76 output rise rptd 3-21, 227G3
US CIA oil forecast 4-18, 294F1
US energy plan cites 4-18, 294A3
Venez pres visits 4-25—4-27, 362A1
Yamani on May productn 5-10, 362A2
'77-82 increase seen 5-11, 362F1
Fire halts major pipeline 5-11—5-12, sabotage suspected 5-12, 362B2
Fire deaths rptd 5-15, losses 5-19, 402B2
Embargo vs US barred 5-24—5-25, 401F3
Backs N-S 'oil dialogue' 6-3, 437D2
USSR '76 exports rptd 6-11, 513G1
Secret US-Saudi pact rptd 6-27, 474E1
Oil price linked 7-1, 535D2
Iran backs '78 price freeze 11-16, 897B1, B2
US assured on prices 12-14, 954C2
Surplus, output cut cited 12-21, 973D1

U.S. Relations —*See also 'Oil Developments' above; for Arab-Israeli conflict, see MIDDLE EAST—U.S. DEVELOPMENTS*

Bechtel boycott suit settled 1-10; Jubail port, '77-82 econ dvpt plan cited 1-10, 78G2-A3
Vance visits; PLO, trade ties stressed 2-19, 121G2-122A1
Adham cited as CIA liaison 2-22, 124G2
Uganda drops US exit bar 3-1, 141B2
Carter plans mtg 3-8, 165A2
Carter sees Fahd 5-24—5-25, 401F3
West confrmd amb 6-7, 500D1
Secret pact rptd, US denies 6-27, 474C1
Carter seeks arms sales curbs 7-28, 574B3
Vance visits, PLO shift hinted 8-7—8-9, 605C1
Carter visit scheduled 11-29, 914B2
Vance visits, Cairo conf backed 12-14, 954C2

1978

Oil Developments—*See also OPEC*

Yamani vs '78 price rise 1-12, 158G2
US revokes oil co tax credits 1-16, 69D1
US '77 imports rptd up 2-11, 113F2
'76, '77 output rptd 2-14; Jan data 2-22, 158E2, E3
US jet deploymt plans rptd 2-16, 139A2
US forgn policy, oil link debated 5-15, 357C2
US ties, OPEC price freeze linked 6-19, 465G1
US study of USSR imports backed 6-29, 635B1
US vs oil import hike 9-12, 702E1

U.S. Relations—*See also 'Oil Developments' above; also MIDDLE EAST—ARMAMENTS—Egypt-Israel-Saudi Plane Package*

Carter in talks 1-3 1C1, 2A3
US mil constructn projcts exempt from arms ceiling 2-1, 106E2
US '77 trade rptd up 2-11, 113E2
Pharaon-Lance bank deal, Abedi role cited 2-13, 204D3
US bank holding co, SEC sue Adham 2-17, 3-18; SEC settles 3-19, 204B2, B3
US architects to design arms complex 2-18, 199G1
US rpts dvpt plans slowed 2-20, 122E1
US on reactn to PLO Israel raid 3-13, 176E1
AIO arms pact cited 3-14, 237C1 ★
US pub relatns firm rptdly hired 3-31, 236F3-237B1
Arms sales cutback urged 7-16, 564A2

1979

Mecca Mosque Takeover

Islamic militants seize mosques, issue demands 11-20; govt forces retake shrine 11-24, 898G2-899C1
Mosque seizure rpts vary, press blackout blamed 11-20, 11-30, 899D1
Iran chrgs US, Israel role; prompts Pak raid on US Emb 11-21, 893C1
Pak scores 'extremists', denies US role 11-21, 893E1
Anti-US protests spread 11-22–11-23, 894B1
Khomeini repeats chrgs vs US, Israel 11-24, 895B2
Siege ends, 130 rptd dead 12-4, 916A1
Govt calls raid 'political', implicates USSR, S Yemen; US confrms Saudi acct 12-16, 996G3

Obituaries

Baroody, J 3-4, 272A2

Oil & Gas Developments

1st 1/4 output rise seen 1-30, 69F3
Production cutback denied 2-7, 126F1
US stresses need for close ties 2-12, 142E2
EC rpts Iran shortfall coverage 2-13, 126F2
1st ¼ price hike barred 2-27, 145A3
Iraq reverses moderate stance, crude oil price hike rptd 3-5, 162E1
Prices hiked 3-27, 227B3
Productn cutback set 4-9, US Sen estimates '80s cut 4-14, 279A1
Budget plans rptd 5-29, 427A3
Nigeria 2d top US exporter 5-31, 393A2
Prices hiked; West warned re US $ drop, oil conservatn urged 6-28, 473C1-A2
Productn increase set 7-2, 495E3
US confrms output hike 7-9, 536D3
US denies arms aid link 7-13, 536B3
Tankers collide off Tobago 7-19, 553D3
Reserve estimate cited 8-3, 651A2
US denies Mideast peace link 8-8, 591B2
'79 1st 1/2 world oil output rptd 8-28, 645A2
Productn level to continue 9-26, '80 cutback set 10-4, 781E1
US strategic reserve purchases rptd cut 9-26, 9-27, 781G1
Khayl sees reactn re inflatn, $ weakness 10-3, 779B3
Connally links Mideast peace 10-11, 783A2
Iran shortfall replacemt seen 11-12, 861E2
Proven reserves rptd 11-21, 953B1
Italy oil cut off by Petromin re scandal 12-5, payoffs denied 12-14, 995B3
Prices hike 12-13, per barrel price rptd 12-21, 977F1, B2
Kennedy scores Carter re price hike reactn 12-21, 983B3

U.S. Relations—*See also 'Mecca Mosque Takeover' and 'Oil' above*

Grumman admits paymts 1-3, 16F1
US jets to visit 1-10, 12B2; visit ends 1-23, 50F1
N Yemen mil aid plan rptd 2-8, 89D2
US issues rights rpt 2-10, 107A3
Defns Secy Brown visits, vows allied jet sale 2-10–2-12; Saudis bar mil base 2-26, 143C2, B3
Fahd cancels visit 2-22–2-24, 143F1
US speeds N Yemen arms shipmt 2-26, 144F2
Student enrollmt in US rptd 167E2
US sends warships 3-5, offers F-15s for N Yemen 3-7, 157E2-158A1
US orders AWACS 3-8, 2 sent 3-9, 179D1
US missn seeks Egypt-Israel pact support 3-17–3-18, 197B2
Ties chng seen 4-9, 279C1
US neutral on Egypt feud 5-2, 319B2

1980

IMF revises SDR valuatn method, riyal dropped from currency 'basket' 9-17, 695C2
Libya asks US AWACS removal 10-10, 774C2
France naval aid set 10-14, 790C1
Uganda invasn role denied 10-15, 832G3
Palestinian curbs rptd tightened 10-22, 821B2
Islamic '81 conf set 11-6, 865D1
Mediates Syria-Jordan feud 11-30—12-2, 911F2-A3
Turkey cuts Israeli ties 12-2, 912C1
Jordan-Syria feud mediatn set 12-5, border troops withdraw 12-10—12-11, 931A3
'80 yen, mark buying rptd 12-19, 983G2

Iran-Iraq War

US air defns aid asked 9-26, 4 AWACS arrive 10-1, 734A3; more defns gear sent 10-5, 758A1
Oman role rptd blocked 10-3, 758G1
US AWACS surveillance rptd 10-8, 773G2
Qaddafi asks Iran backing 10-10, 774B2
Jordan King visits, asks Iraq support 10-11—10-12; Saudis bar direct aid 10-13, 774G2
Iran: US AWACS aid Iraq 10-17; US denies 10-17—10-19, 798E2, B3
Libya-Saudi exchng on US AWACS 10-19, 10-22; Libyan ties cut 10-28, 820C3
Ports open for Iraq war supplies 11-20, 894D2

Mecca Mosque Takeover

Armed forces shakeup linked 1-1, 22D1
63 raiders executed 1-9, 22B1
Islamic law enforcemt moves linked 2-5, 195B1

Oil & Gas Developments

Exxon '79 US gas sales rptd linked 1-2, 90F3
Long-term oil supply cited 1-15, 60A2
US Pentagon rpt cites oilfield vulnerability 2-1, 84A2, C2
US pres hopeful's 'basic speech' excerpts 2-29, 207G3
US energy secy in talks, Yamani bars reserve purchases 3-1—3-4; US stockpiling stalled 3-5, 165B3
Intl oil surplus, OPEC price reforms seen 3-5, 165F3
Productn capacity increase planned; output, consumptn rptd 3-5, 166A1
UK export suspensn weighed 4-10, 294C1
Australia film oppositn linked 4-15, 310B1
UK trade curbs weighed 4-22, 313E2
Prices hiked 8% 5-14, 364F3-365B1
World glut cuts Eur, OPEC prices 7-4—8-12, 628F1
Aramco dirs named 7-8; takeover completed, bd members listed 9-4, 661G3
Shell to co-build Jubail petro complex 7-9, 524G2
Occidental 1.2% interest noted 7-14, 542D3
Productn cut impact evaluated 8-17, 662D2
US record inventories rptd 9-5, Admin assured on shortfall 10-3, 785E3
IMF oil debt role studied 9-15, 695F2
OPEC pricing accord reached; OKs $2 hike, bars productn cut 9-18, 694A3
Aramco takeover cited 9-18, 725A2
US energy secy, Yamani in secret talks 9-18; US stockpiling rptd resumed 10-27, 826E1
Brazil oil sales rptd 10-2, 759A2
Export hike rptd set 10-5—10-6, 758D3
France reliance cited 10-14, 790F1
$2 premium on extra productn set 10-28, 822C2
Olayan joins Mobil bd 12-1, 960D3
Sovt oil find debunked 12-5, 951D3
Price hike OKd 12-15, OPEC in 'broad' accord 12-16, 951F1, A2
'80 revenue rptd 12-19, 983G2

U.S. Relations—*See also 'Oil & Gas' above*

Bases to US refused 1-9, 11B2
Carter Persian Gulf defns vow lauded 1-26, 65D1
US policy scored by Egypt 1-28, 69A2
US briefs on Palestine autonomy talks 2-2, 89D2
US briefs on Pak defense talks; Persian Gulf defense backed 2-4—2-5, 83G1-B2
US issues rights rpt 2-5, 87F2
Connally bank connectn, '78-79 fund transfers rptd 2-11, 129A2
US $ sale re W Ger note purchase cited 3-24, 236G2
Hunt silver debts rptd 5-2, 345D1
US broadcast of Saudi film protested 5-8, aired 5-12; cts rule on dispute 5-9, 5-12, 375E2-376A1
US co contracts to UK barred 5-21, 407B3

1976

SAUD al-Faisal, Prince (Saudi Arabia)
Seeks Egypt, Syria talks renewal 5-23, 370C2
Oil embargo threat rptd 9-26, denied 9-27, 746G2
SAUER, Walter C.
Replaced as Eximbank vp 7-29, 807G3
SAUNDERS, Harold H.
Censured for leak 3-12, 198D2
SAUNIER-Seite, Alice
French univ state secy 1-12, 49D2 ★
Students protest educ reforms 3-17—4-23, talks pledged 4-12, 312B1
SAURA, Carlos
Wins Cannes film award 5-28, 460E1
SAUVAGNARGUES, Jean
Disputes '77 EEC budget priorities 4-5, 276F1
On A-export safeguards 4-8, 372C3
Denies Leb mil role offer 5-26, 385F2
Defends govt defense policy 6-2, 417D3
Vs hijackers demands 6-29, 463E1
Signs Sovt A-safeguards pact 7-16, 540E2
SAUVE, Jeanne
Stays communicatns min 9-14, 692C2
SAVAGE, Royce H.
Jones pleads guilty 1-29, 134E1
SAVANE, Landing
Pardoned 4-3, 591F3
SAVANNAH, Ga.—*See GEORGIA*
SAVANNAH (U.S. warship)
In Intl Naval Review 7-4, 488D3
SAVCHENKO, Victor
Wins Olympic medal 7-31, 574C1
SAVELYEV, Sergei
Wins Olympic medal 2-5, 159C1
SAVIMBI, Jonas
At OAU Angola summit 1-10—1-13, 16F1
Vows FNLA support 1-18, 35G2
Appeals for Westn aid 1-29, 57C1
Mocks Zaire mercenary ban 2-3, 82C1
SAVINGS Associations, U.S. League of
Sued for home-loan bias 4-16, 285D2
SAVING The Queen (book)
On best seller list 2-29, 208E3; 12-5, 972F2
SAVLOFF, Guillermo
Found dead 1-21, 96A2
SAWA, Yuji
Arrested 6-22, 450B3
Indicted 7-13, 557B2
SAWYER, Harold S.
Elected 11-2, 823E2, 829D4
SAWYER, James G.
Indicted 5-7, 349E1
SAWYER, James G.
Charges dropped 10-5, 767F3
SAXBE, William D.
Metzenbaum wins Sen race 11-2, 819F3
SAXE, Susan
Mistrial declared 10-13, 816B2
SAYED, Abdel Wahab al-
Slain 12-24, 973F2
SAYEH, Hamed al-
In Egypt econ post 11-10, 852F1
SAYEM, Abu Sadat Mohammed
Postpones electns 11-21, 923F2-A3
SAYPOL, Justice Irving H.
Indictmt dismissal seen 12-20, 1016C2
SCAIFE, Richard Mellon
'72 campaign gift listed 4-25, 688A1
SCALIA, Vito
Named CIA aid recipient 1-31, 140C3
SCANDANAVIAN Airlines System (SAS)
Lockheed payoffs rptd 2-4, 130D3
SCARBOROUGH, Edward
Scores armed forces study 6-7, 454F1
SCEARCE, James F.
Fed Mediatn Svc dir 3-16; confrmd 4-7, 262E3
Aids in Calif cannery pact 7-27, 570D1
SCHAFER, William
Harris dismissed from murder case 10-22, 859G2

1977

Pharaon to buy Ga bank shares 12-27, 1003E2
Carter begins world tour 12-29, 1000G3

SAUNDERS, Harold H.
Keeps US intell post 1-21, 53E1
SAUVE, Jeanne
Vs LaMarsh rpt proposals 6-16, 485F2
SAVANG Vatthana
Arrested 3-12, 201C3
SAVANNAH, Ga.—*See GEORGIA*
SAVANNAH Foods & Industries Inc.
'76 Fortune 500 list drops 341D1
SAVARD, Raymond
Wins election 5-24, 410B3
SAVCHENKO, Viktor
US tour results 1-29—2-5, 263G1
SAVIMBI, Jonas
S Africa pro-UNITA role rptd 1-3, 85F2
SAVIN, Maj. Gen. Vitaly
Scores poor youth training 8-20, 673G3
SAVINGS Associations, U.S. League of
Redlining curb scored 11-9, 898G2
Anti-bias suit remains 11-11, 898C3
SAVINGS Bonds—*See U.S. GOVERNMENT—TREASURY*
SAVINGS & Loan Associations (S & Ls)—*See BANKS*
SAWAKI, Masao
Assures GATT on trade surplus 11-29, 933C2
SAWHILL, John
Panel scores breeder reactor, plutonium use 3-21, 234F3
SAWIN Hiranyasiri, Maj.
Leads troops in coup try 3-26, 243F1 ★
Gets life sentence 4-21, 331E2
SAXBE, William B.
Replaced as amb to India 4-25, 418D1
SAXE, Susan
Pleads guilty 1-17, sentncd 2-11, 140E1
SAYD Maudoodi, Maulana
Vs Bhutto reforms 4-18, 305B2
SAYED, Abu
Hijacks jet 7-8, surrenders 7-10, 535C1
SAYEM, Abu Sadat Mohammed
Quits, Rahman sworn 4-21, 309F1
SAYERS, Gale
Named to football HOF 1-17, 164A1
Inducted into HOF 7-30, 659A1
SAYERS, Capt. Hugh (d. 1973)
Slayers' sentncs confrmd 5-2, 374E2
Burrows executed 12-2, 935G2
SAYPOL, Irving. H.
Dies 6-30, 532F3
SBA—*See U.S. GOVERNMENT—SMALL Business Administration*
SCANDINAVIA—*See also country names*
Carter expands air svc 12-21, 1006D2
SCANDINAVIAN Airlines System (SAS)
Strike settled 5-9—5-20, 469G3
UK bans some flights 10-30, 882G3
SCANLON, Hugh
Leyland strikers reject 3-11, 256F1
SCANLON, Robert
Uganda arrests 6-10, 508C1
Escape rptd 9-22; death rptd 10-9, 805F1
SCARGILL, Arthur
Grunwick strike violence 7-11, 543D3
SCHACT, Hjalmar
US germ warfare use rptd 3-9, 195B3

1978

Boeing chrgd re payoffs, Adham cited 7-28, 642G3, 643A1
Hosp Corp paymts chrgd, Amer Hosp suit cited 10-26, 876E3-877C1

SAUDI Arabian Airlines
UK pilot, flight attendant held on alcohol chrgs 6-15, 516D1
SAUD Ibn Abdul Aziz al Faisal al Saud (Saudi Arabian King) (1902-69)
Great grandaughter executed 2-1, 172F3
SAUNDERS, Harold
Meets Hussein, W Bank ldrs; talks anger Israelis 10-17—10-19, 802A2
SAUNIER-Seite, Alice
Named French univ min 4-5, 245G2
SAUSAITIS, Vintsas
Rptd sentenced 2-21, 151E3
SAVAGE, John
Deer Hunter released 12-14, 1030F2
SAVANNAH, Ga.—*See GEORGIA*
SAVCHENKO, Viktor
Wins World Amateur Boxing tourn 5-6—5-20, 600E2
SAVE-the-Redwoods League
Drury dies 12-14, 1032F2
SAVINGS Associations, U.S. League of
Redlining curb protested 5-18, 410F2
SAVINGS & Loan Associations (S&Ls)—*See BANKS*
SAVINGS and Savings Banks—*See under BANKS*
SAVINO, Antonio
Arrested 10-1, 817E1
SAWHILL, John
Study faults govts on energy policy 6-13, 450D2
SAWI, Abdel Moneim el-
In Cyprus to get Sebai body 2-19, 117F2
On Cyprus commando attack 2-20, 117E2
SAWYER, Rep. Harold S. (R, Mich.)
Reelected 11-7, 851E1
SAWYER, Kenneth T.
Resigns as NE rail projct dir 1-30, 225C1
SAWYER, Ralph A.
Dies 12-6, 1032E3
SAXE, Bacon, Bolan & Manley
Cohn represents Bolan in suit vs Ford 4-25, 390B3
SAXON, David
Lauds Sup Ct Bakke ruling 6-28, 482A2
SAXON, Don
Diary of Anne Frank revived 12-18, 1031D1
SAYED, Abu
Assassinated 3-8, 157C2 ★
SAYED, Sayed Ali
Clashes with Wafd member 2-15, 131A2
SAYER, Leo
Song wins Grammy 2-24, 315G3
SAYLES, John
Piranha released 8-4, 970F2
SBA—*See U.S. GOVERNMENT—SMALL Business Administration*
SCANDINAVIA—*See also country names*
USSR denies use of spy trucks 3-15, 291E2
UK air pact OKd 12-22, 1017F1
SCANDINAVIAN Airlines Systems (SAS)
UK air pact OKd 12-22, 1017A2, B2
SCARDINO, Donald
Angel opens 5-10, 760C1
King of Hearts opens 11-22, 1031C2
SCENES From Country Life (play)
Opens 3-13, 887A3
SCHACHT, Dr. Lawrence
Aids Guyana cult mass suicide 11-18, 890E2
Body identified in US 11-27; autopsy planned 11-29, 910E1, G1
SCHACHTER, Steven
Water Engine opens 1-5, 760G3
SCHACKELFORD, Leroy J.
To head new BRAC unit 2-28, 185C2
SCHADOCK, Horst
Arrested 1-4, 21E3
SCHADOCK, Marie-Luise
Arrested 1-4, 21E3

1979

Vance says ties deteriorate 5-8, 341B2
Sadat sees no US jet deal 5-12, 360A1
US role to end Egypt feud confrmd 5-20, 5-21, 378B3
US delays F-5 jet sale to Egypt 7-6, 512A1
Strauss sees Hussein, Fahd 7-7, 511D2
ISC paymts alleged 7-9, 541F3
US to give more arms aid 7-13, 536B3
Miller tours Persian Gulf, discusses Iran crisis 11-23—11-28, 896A3
US seeks bases for moves vs Iran 12-18, 958D2
IBM notes bought 12-27, 986G1

SAULZINGER, Boris
Shame of Jungle released 9-14, 820C3
SAUNDERS, Harold
Urges US arms aid to Morocco 8-2, 592C2
Disputes Israel defns min on Leb bombing 9-18, 693E2
Jesse Jackson briefs on Mideast trip 10-8, 763F1
Briefs Iran hostage kin 12-7, 934F1
SAUNDERS, Robert M.
Pleads guilty 3-13, 239G3
SAUVE, Jeanne
On Canada tech grants 4-17, 311B3
SAVAGE, John
Hair released 3-13, 528D2
Onion Field released 9-19, 820E2
SAVARD, Serge
Montreal wins Stanley Cup 5-21, 447D3
SAVICH, Rene
Wine Untouched opens 6-22, 712F3
SAVILLE, Victor
Dies 5-8, 432F3
SAVIMBI, Jonas
Chrgs Cuba kidnaps children 11-5, 981C2
SAVINGS Associations, U.S. League of
Automatic funds shift voided 4-20, 303B3
Carter bank law reform proposal scored 5-22, 403B2
SAVINGS and Savings Banks—*See under BANKS*
SAWYER, Charles
Dies 4-7, 356G3
SAWYER, Rep. Harold S. (R, Mich.)
Challenges JFK, King findings 1-26, 91F1
SAYS I, Says He (play)
Opens 2-20, 292F2
SBORGI, Rossella
Attacked 5-23, car bombed 6-1, 426C3
SCALES, DeWayne
LSU suspends from basketball 3-5, 291B1
SCALZONE, Oreste
Threatnd in Curcio letter 8-10, 635F2
SCANDINAVIA
Viking artifact identified 2-7, 138E1
Mondale tours 4-11—4-21, 299B2
SCANLON, Richard S.
Brass Ring opens 7-2, 711F1
SCARDINO, Don
Holeville opens 12-4, 956B3
SCARED Straight (film)
Wins Oscar 4-9, 336B2
Wins Emmy 9-9, 858E2
SCARSDALE Medical Diet, The Complete (book)
On best-seller list 3-4, 173E3
SCA Services Inc.
US sues re NJ pollutn 2-7, 130B1
Earthline Corp.—*See EARTHLINE Corp.*
SCAVENGER Hunt (film)
Released 12-25, 1008E1
SCHNACKE, Judge Robert
IBM wins Transamerica trust suit 10-18, 851F2
SCHAEFER, Mayor William D. (Baltimore, Md.)
Reelected 11-6, 846D3

1980

US faults Pak for '79 emb rescue 6-9, 478A1
Saudis seek extra gear for F-15s 6-16; US weighs request 6-17, 450F1
F-15 gear talks 6-26; US sens vs 7-8; Saudis score 7-9, 538G2
Financial Gen deal set 7-25, 600E3
Jet fire kills US natls 8-19, 778E1*
US debates forgn bank takeovers 8-28, 9-17, 806A3
US air defns aid vs Iran asked 9-26; 4 AWACS arrive 10-1, 734A3
Carter scores 'politics' at IMF-World Bank mtg 9-30, 762A1
US sends more defns gear 10-5, 758A1
US AWACS rpt on Iran-Iraq war 10-8; US sends refueling planes 10-11, 773F2
Libya asks 4 AWACS removal 10-10, 774C2
Iran scores AWACS shipmt 10-17; US reassures 10-17—10-19, 798E2, B3
Carter vs some F-15 gear 10-24, US says undecided 10-27; Saudi scores 10-30, 821A1-F1
Carter reelectn rptd favored 10-27, 826G1
Olayan joins Mobil bd 12-1, 960D3
SAUDI Arabian Airlines
Jet fire at Riyadh airport kills 301 8-19, 778B1*
SAUER, Dr. Louis W.
Dies 2-10, 176C3
SAUL Jr., B. F.
Financial Gen deal set 7-25, 601A1
SAUNDERS, George
Scores $1.8 bln MCI award 6-13, 457A1
SAUNDERS, Harold
Shuns Sen com Mideast vote probe 3-20, 218F2
SAUNDERS, Vince
Loses US House electn 11-4, 852B1
SAUVE, Bob
NHL goaltending ldr, clinches Vezina Trophy 4-6, 296A1, E1
SAUVE, Jeanne
Canada Commons speaker 2-29, 171C2
SAVAGE, Frank
Carter names to Synfuels Corp bd 9-13, Sen panel OKs 9-25, 725F2
Carter names to interim Synfuels Corp bd 10-5, 786F2
SAVAGE, John
Inside Moves released 12-19, 1003A2
SAVAGE, Peter
Raging Bull released 11-14, 972G3
SAVCHENKO, Viktor
Wins Olympic medal 8-2, 622A2
SAVE the Maine Yankee Committee
Maine votes to keep A-plant 9-23, 723F2
SAVETTI, Carlo
A-dvpt support rptd 1-9, 20D3
SAVIANO, Nick
Loses Cologne Cup 11-2, 947C2
SAVINGS and Loan League, National
FHLBB mortgage, funds infusn moves backed 4-3, 266F3
SAVINGS Associations, U.S. League of
Banking deregulatn bill signed 3-31, 245G3
FHLBB mortgage, funds infusn moves backed 4-3, 266F2
Interest rules suit filed 6-16, 516A3
SAVINGS & Savings Banks—*See under BANKS*
SAWETAWILA, Sithi
US vows arms 6-27, 491C3
SAWHILL, John C.
Outlines coal-fired utilities plan 3-6, 169E3
Named Synfuels Corp chrmn 9-10, Sen panel OKs 9-25, 699C1, 725D2
Sen confirmatn blocked 10-1, Carter names to interim bd 10-5; Energy Dept resignatn effective 10-8, 786F2-A3
SAWYER, Rep. Harold S. (R, Mich.)
Reelected 11-4, 843E1
SAWYER, Mary
Australian Open results 1-1, 213G1
SAXON, James J.
Dies 1-28, 104F3
SAXON Theatre Corp.
'Caligula' ruled not obscene in Boston 8-1, 640B2
SAYEGH, Fayez A.
Dies 12-9, 1004D3
SAYLES, John
Return of the Secaucus 7 released 9-14, 836E3
SAZAK, Gun
Killed 5-27, funeral held 5-30, 445B3
Corum riots linked 7-4—7-5, 544E3
Erim slain 7-19, 567C3
SBA (Small Business Administration)—*See under U.S. GOVERNMENT*
SCAMARDO, Arthur Vincent
Reunited with brother 6-29, 638B3
SCANDINAVIA
'79 inflatn rptd down by OECD 2-13, 125D3
Coca-Cola boycotted 4-16, 463D3
Dutch to probe S Africa sanctns 6-27, 499A2
SCARDAMAGLIA, Elio
Immortal Bachelor released 2-22, 216A3
SCARDAMAGLIA, Francesco
Immortal Bachelor released 2-22, 216A3
SCARDINO, Don
He Knows You're Alone released 9-26, 836A3
SCARSDALE Medical Group (N.Y.)
'Scarsdale Diet' MD slain 3-10, 215B1
SCA Services Inc.
NJ dump suit partly setld 1-30, 93G3
Earthline Corp.—*See EARTHLINE Corp.*
SCHAEFFER, Col. Thomas
Fellow hostage calls spy 4-9, 282C3

1976

SCHAFFER, Gloria
Unopposed in Conn primary 9-7, 687E3
Loses electn 11-2, 820E1, F3, 825G2
SCHALLER, Johanna
Wins Olympic medal 7-29, 576G1
SCHANBERG, Sydney H.
Wins Pulitzer 5-3, 352D3
SCHAPIRO, Meyer
'38 letter from Chambers cited 3-18, 218D1
SCHATZ, Judge Albert G.
OKs Omaha desegregatn plan 4-27, 453D2
SCHAUFELE Jr., William E.
At Kissinger-Vorster mtg 6-23—6-24, 446C3
Begins Africa tour 7-7, 523A1
Scores Ethiopia 8-7, 674E2
In Tanzania, Zambia 9-8—9-9, 681F1
Sees African ldrs 9-28, 718G2; 10-2—10-4, 738E2-D3
Rpt ordered to Geneva 10-27, 797F2; arrives 10-30, 831G3
To return to US 11-4, 843G1
Reinhardt to replace 11-17, 862E1
SCHEEL, Walter
Meets Sadat 3-29—4-2, 275A1
SCHEIBLICH, Christine
Wins Olympic medal 7-24, 575F1
SCHENLEY Industries, Inc.
Rosenstiel dies 1-21, 80G3
SCHERER, Mario
Torture death rptd 6-9, 557D3
SCHERER Garcia, Julio
Govt campaign vs Excelsior chrgd 7-7—7-29, ousted 7-8, 620C1
SCHERING-Plough Corp.
Rpts foreign payoffs 2-17, 362C1
SEC lists paymts 5-12, 729A1
SCHEUER, Rep. James H. (D, N.Y.)
On Arab boycott compliance 9-7, 747A1
Reelected 11-2, 830A2
SCHIESS, Rev. Betty Bone
Sues Cole 7-8, 755E3
SCHIFF, Dorothy
Australian to buy Post 11-19, 887D2
SCHINDLER Bros. Steel
Fined 4-10, 988E3
SCHIRMER, Katherine
Carter transition aide 11-23, 881B3
SCHLAAK, Evelin
Wins Olympic medal 7-29, 576A2
SCHLAFLY, Phyllis
Scores ERA on child care 2-13, 172G1
SCHLEBUSCH, A. L.
Named S Africa pub works min 1-22, 76E1
SCHLEI, Marie
W Ger forgn aid min 12-15, 968A2
SCHLESINGER, James Rodney
US-Japan defense com set 1-19, 51G2
Views Mao body 9-13, continues China tour 9-14, 711F3
Confers with Carter 10-3, 743E1
Named energy aide 12-23, 956F2
Bio sketch 957G3
SCHLITZ Brewing Co., Jos.
SEC sues Emersons 5-11, 360F2
Uihlein dies 11-12, 970C3
SCHMELZER, Norbert
Admits Gulf paymts 1-11, 134A2
SCHMIDT, Alexander M.
Red #2 dye banned 1-19, 44B2
FDA probe rpt scored 5-23, 392E1
On aerosol warning labels 11-23, 901G3

1977

SCHALLY, Andrew V.
Wins Nobel Prize 10-13, 951D3
SCHARDT, Arlie
Scores US Concorde policy 9-23, 738G2, B3
SCHAUFELE Jr., William E.
Sees Carter on Amin exit bar 2-25, 141C1
Named amb to Greece 6-23, confrmd 7-13, 626E3
Sees Congo min re ties 7-6, 583B2
Sen testimony causes uproar 7-12, Greece rejcts as envoy 7-22, 598F2
SCHECKTER, Jody
3d in US Grand Prix; final standing 10-23, 870C3, E3
SCHECTER, Jerrold
On US Viet initiative 2-11, 110A2
SCHECTER, Joel
UN desert conf protest 8-30, 770D1
SCHEEL, Walter (West German president)
Names Lambsdorff econ min 10-7, 969B2
Speaks at Schleyer funeral 10-25, 868C2
SCHEERSBERG A—*See KERKYRA*
SCHELLING, Dr. Thomas
On US death views 2-25, 183F3
SCHENLEY Industries Inc.
NYS chrgs rebates 10-6, 860E1
SCHERMAN, Harry
Book-of-Month Club sold 7-5, 519E2
SCHERMERHORN, Willem
Dies 3-12, 264E3
SCHIESS, Karl
Baader trial adjourned 3-17, 260C1
SCHIFF, Dorothy
Australian takes over Post 12-30-76, 48C3
SCHIFF, John M.
Kuhn Loeb plans Lehman merger 11-28, 1004A3
SCHILD, Alfred
Dies 5-24, 425F3
SCHILLER, Lawrence
Gilmore executed 1-17, 40A3
SCHILY, Otto
Asks Baader suicides probe 10-18, 790A3
SCHINDLER, Rabbi Alexander M.
Assured on US Mideast views 3-9, 166A1
On Carter Israel policy 6-11, 6-13, 474B1
Vs US-Sovt Geneva plan 10-2, 750F1
Doubts US Mideast policy 10-26, 831C1
SCHINDLER, Steve
In NFL draft 5-3, 353B2
SCHIPPERS, Thomas
Dies 12-16, 1024B3
SCHLAFLY, Phyllis
Addresses anti-ERA rally 11-19, 917G3
SCHLESINGER, James R.
Sees gas pipeline execs 1-21, 53D3
Sworn in 1-23, 52E2
At energy seminar 3-17, 191A1
Vs plutonium use 3-25, 234C2
Defends Carter energy plan 4-24, 319C3
GOPs score energy 4-25, 321A1
Backs coal slurrying 5-5, 516D1
Suits vs US spying rptd 5-22, 422C3
Backs administered pricing 5-25, 443G2
US bars Alaska oil trade with Japan; confrms US gas rationing study 7-10, 538B1, C2
Named Energy secy, confrmd 8-4, 591C2
In Canada gas pipe talks 9-1—9-2, 687C1
Signs Canada pipe pact 9-20, 725C3
Warns Sen re oil import fee 10-2, 757A2
Sees Carter plan key to IEA oil use goal 10-5—10-6, 794B1
Energy bill comments draw fire from House 11-21—11-23, 916C3-917C1
Natural gas compromise killed 12-22, 1002A2
SCHLEYER, Hanns-Martin
Kidnaped, guards slain 9-5; ransom asked 9-6—9-8, 694C1
Kidnap, search dvpts 9-9—10-18; slain 10-18, manhunt begun 10-20, 789D1, 790C1, 791E1-A3
Krabbe sought for kidnap role 10-21, state funeral 10-25, 868B2
Dutch tycoon kidnaped 10-28, 871E1
Dutch capture kidnap suspect 11-10, 887E3
4th Baader-Meinhof member kills self 11-12, 888A2
Baader atty linked to suspects 11-18, 969A1
2 W Ger terrorists captured 12-20, 1018A1
SCHLITZ Brewing Co., Jos.
TV violence curbs ordrd 2-16, 157F3
SEC sues 4-7, 503E3
SCHLOSSER, Herbert S.
Satra sues 2-14, 131F1
SCHLOSSTEIN, Ralph
At League of Cities conf 12-4, 959D3

1978

SCHAFFNER, Franklin J.
Boys From Brazil released 10-5, 969D3
SCHARER, Erich
Wins 2-man bobsled championship 2-5, 2d in 4-man title 2-12, 316F3
SCHECHNER, Richard
Cops opens 3-28, 760F1
SCHECHTER, David
Runaways opens 3-9, 887G2
SCHEEL, Walter (West German president)
Asks Nazis studies 3-5, 477E2
Sees Brezhnev on ethnic Gers, Nazis 5-4, 417G1
Plea to free Hess rptd rejctd by USSR 6-11, 477E3
Admits past Nazi membership 11-11, 872E1
SCHEIDER, Roy
Jaws 2 released 6-16, 619E2
SCHEUER, Rep. James H. (D, N.Y.)
Reelected 11-7, 851D3
Urges illegal alien curbs, scores Carter plan 12-20, 1010B2, A3
SCHIAVETTI, Felice
Wounded 4-7, 330C1
SCHILLER, Bob
Wins Emmy 9-17, 1030F1
SCHINDLER, Rabbi Alexander
Deplores Siegel resignatn; vs Carter, Brzezinski on Mideast 3-9, 176G2
SCHIZOPHRENIA—*See MEDICINE—Mental Health*
SCHLAFLY, Phyllis
ERA extensn clears Sen; sees ct challenge 10-6, 788G1
SCHLEBUSCH, Alwyn L.
In S Africa Cabt shuffle 1-25, 55D1
SCHLEI, Marie
Resigns W Ger econ post 2-3, 93E2
SCHLESINGER, James R.
Sees govs on energy policy 2-26, 144G3
Clinch R A-project halt held illegal 3-10, 183D2
Backs A-plant licensing chngs 3-17, 205F2, A3
Clinch R A-projct compromise proposal rptd 3-17, 3-23, 242A1, C1
On coal industry study 3-25, 217A2
In pvt cong conf re energy plan 4-12, 304A2
Lauds gas price accord 4-21, 305B1
Oil lobbyist's role in energy policy questnd 5-15, 408F2, C3
Details energy policies: sees '80s oil shortage, E Coast aid; renews uranium contracts 5-26, 407E3-408A2
Sets new oil rules for Calif, proposes E Coast aid 6-15, 470B3-471B1
Offers standby gas ration plan 6-22, 511F1
On oil import fee 6-22, 511A3
Sen votes oil import fee bar; sees import quotas possible 6-25, 511F3
On Carter breeder research, gas vote link 8-25, 678D1
Draft solar study issued 8-25, 718B2
Vs USSR oil equipmt sale 9-6, 743D1
In China energy talks 10-25—11-5, rpts US aid offer 11-6, 871C2
Sees more energy proposals in '79 11-9, 873C1
Unveils fuel rules, sees '79 decontrols 11-15, 919F3-920A1
EPA fuel test questioned 11-21, 939C2
SCHLESINGER, Kurt
Thread of Scarlet opens 12-8, 1031B3
SCHLEYER, Hanns-Martin (d. 1977)
W Ger admits hunt error 3-7, pol controversy ensues 3-7—4-6, 332B2-C3
Dutch protest for Baader-Meinhof 3-14, 192A2
Moro kidnap link rptd 3-20, 200C1
Swiss host 4-natn terrorism mtg 4-8—4-9, 438C2, F2
Dutch rule on extraditn of Folkerts, 2 others 5-8, 354C1, 454C3
Moro case compared 5-10, 337E2
Yugo arrests 4 W Ger terrorists 5-11, 438G3
Boll loses libel suit 5-30, 439E2
Rpt issued, police effort scored 6-3—6-4; Maihofer resigns 6-6, 456A3
Free Dems lose 2 state electns 6-4, 456F2
Baumann resigns 7-3, 651E2
Terrorism law upheld by high ct 8-8, 651C3
Kidnap suspect killed, 3 others arrested 9-6, 724D3
UK arrests terrorist suspect 9-15, 725B2
Speitel captured 9-24, 885A1
Folkerts extradited 10-17, 885D1
Yugo bars extraditn of suspects 11-17, 906A2
SCHLITZ Brewing Co., Jos.
Indicted for kickbacks, tax fraud 3-15, 223C2
SEC upheld on disclosure power 6-8, chrgs settled 7-9, 642D3
Pleads no contest, fined 11-1, 877C1
SCHMAUTZ, Bobby
Montreal wins Stanley Cup 5-25, 458D1
SCHMIDT, Alexander M.
Drug seizure case refused by Sup Ct 3-27, 241G1

1979

SCHAFFEL, Robert L.
Sunnyside released 6-1, 820D3
SCHARER, Erich
Swiss win world 2-man bobsled title 2-18, 392E1*
SCHATZBERG, Jerry
Joe Tynan released 8-17, 820C3
SCHATZEDER, Dan
Traded to Tigers 12-7, 1002F2
SCHECKTER, Jody
Wins Belgian Gr Prix 5-13, Monoco Gr Prix 5-27, Italian Gr Prix, world title 9-9, 1005D1
SCHEEL, Walter
Carstens elected pres 5-23, 410G2
SCHEIDER, Roy
Last Embrace released 5-3, 528G2
All That Jazz released 12-20, 1007F2
SCHELL, Maximilian
Black Hole released 12-21, 1007A3
SCHELL, Orville H.
Scores Argentine justice 5-26, 467C1
SCHENKEN, Howard
Dies 2-20, 176E3
SCHETTINI, Italo
Rptd killed 3-30, 269F1
SCHEUER, Rep. James H. (D, N.Y.)
Illegal alien issue detailed 1-29, 127C1
SCHICK, Rene (deceased)
US-Nicaragua long-term ties detailed 535F2
SCHICK Products—*See WARNER-Lambert Co.*
SCHIFFMAN, Suzanne
Love On The Run released 4-5, 528A3
SCHILLEBEECKX, Rev. Edward
Vatican heresy chrgs rptd 12-18, 999A3
SCHINDLER, Richard T.
Sought re investmt fraud 2-13, 119C3
SCHINDLER & Associates, R. T.
Investmt fraud plea bargains rptd 2-13, 119C3
SCHISSEL, Jack
Grand Tour opens 1-11, 292E1
Bent opens 12-2, 1007C2
SCHLEBUSCH, Alwyn L.
Named S Africa justice min 6-14, 469A3
Dismisses censor chief 10-5, 774A3
SCHLESINGER Jr., Arthur M.
Wins Natl Book Award 4-23, 356A2
Addresses ADA 6-23, 482E2
SCHLESINGER, Helmut
Named Bundesbank vp 9-19, 733C3
SCHLESINGER, James R.
With Teng in Houston 2-2, 83G2
Warns on Iran oil cutoff 2-7, Blumenthal disputes 2-8, 83D1
CIA apptmt rptd studied 2-22, 133B1
Sees US defns of Persian Gulf interests 2-25, Admin clarifies remarks 2-26, 2-27, 143F3-144B1
On oil conservatn powers 2-26, 145B3
Judge blocks H-bomb article 3-9, 193D3
Rpts record US oil use, repeats resignatn offer 3-12, 183D2
Calif-Tex pipe canceled 3-13, 183E1
DC A-protesters ask dismissal 5-7, 344B1
At IEA mtg 5-22, 380G1
On Calif-Tex pipe cancellatn 5-25, 396A2
No-lead gas output incentives set 6-4, 418B3
Defends US oil policy 6-27, 494C1
Resignation predicted 7-8, 514A1
Dismissal rumored 7-17, fired 7-19, 529C1-530F1
Sees $40-a-barrel oil by '89 8-5, 629A2
Named to Georgetown U post 9-1, 859E3*
SCHLESINGER, John
Yanks released 9-19, 820G3
SCHLEYER, Hanns-Martin (d. 1977)
Murder suspect killed 5-4, 374E2
Heissler arrest rptd 6-10, 490E1
Murder suspect chrgd 11-5, 998E3
Swiss arrest murder suspect 11-20, 998C3
SCHLITZ, Don
Wins Grammy 2-16, 336F3
SCHLUMBERGER Ltd.
Fairchild purchase set 5-21, 440D3
SCHMERTZ, Herbert
Joins Kennedy campaign 11-19, 962C2
SCHMIDT, Heinrich
Acquitted of war crimes 4-19, 333E3

1980

SCHAFFER, Frank
Wins Olympic medal 7-30, 624C1
SCHAFFER, Jan
Cited for silence on Abscam source 7-10, 554A2
SCHALLER, George B.
In Panda-finding mission 5-12, 398A2
SCHAPER, W. H. (Herb)
Dies 9-8, 756C2
SCHARY, Dore
Dies 7-7, 608A3
SCHATZ, Judge Albert G.
Dismisses Oglala Sioux Black Hills suit 9-11, 704C2
SCHATZ, Henry Lee
Escapes Iran 1-28, 66E2
Escape described 2-1, 88D3*; 2-12, 106F1
SCHAUS, Nicholas
Loses US House electn 11-4, 848D1
SCHEEDER, Louis W.
Charlie & Algernon opens 9-14, 892B3
SCHEERER, Robert
How to Beat the High Cost of Living released 7-11, 675A3
SCHELLER, Robert
Genetech stock holding value tops $1 mln 10-14, 806C1
SCHENKER, Joel W.
Horowitz & Mrs Washn opens 4-2, 392C3
SCHENLEY, William
La Scola insulin-slaying chrgs reduced 12-29, 990B2
SCHERER, Cardinal Alfredo Vicente
'79 attack rptd 1-11, 95C3
SCHERING A.G.
Iran takeover rptd 7-9, 546E2
SCHERING-Plough Corp.
Interferon rptd produced in lab 1-16, 62E3
Interferon productn talks rptd 3-5, 317D3
Unit settles job bias case 12-14, 962D3
SCHIAVONNE, Ronald
Donovan named Labor secy 12-16, 955G2
SCHIAVONNE Construction Co.
Donovan named Labor secy 12-16, 955F2
SCHIFFMAN, Dr. Phillip L.
Crib death heredity link rptd 2-28, 358E3
SCHINE, G. David
McCarthy TV film libel case refused by Sup Ct 12-1, 918D2
SCHIZOPHRENIA—*See MEDICINE—Mental Health*
SCHLAFLY, Phyllis
On Ill ERA rejectn 6-18, 482D3
Reagan ties scored by Lucey 8-25, 646F3
On electn results, sees ERA end 11-4, 846B3
SCHLAUDEMAN, Harry
Warns Peru vs Cuban refugee exit 8-29, hijackers surrender 8-30, 672F2
SCHLEBUSCH, Alwyn L.
Const chng, nonwhite cncl backed 5-8, 374A1
Named S Africa vp 8-26, 690A1
To head S Africa multiracial cncl 10-2, 793A1
SCHLECHT, Otto
Makes econ forecast 1-30, 197C3, D3
SCHLESINGER Jr., Arthur M.
Helps Cuban poet immigrate to US 3-16, 231C3
SCHLEYER, Hanns-Martin (d. 1977)
Swiss sentence murder suspect 9-26, 755D1
SCHLICHTER, Art
Ohio State loses Fiesta Bowl 12-26, 999C3
SCHLONDORFF, Volker
Tin Drum released 4-11, 416F3
SCHLOTHAUER, Walter
Named ASL top Amer rookie 9-8, 771F1
SCHLUMBERGER Ltd.
Unitrode divestiture OKd 3-4, 558A1
Mfg Data Systems merger set 9-18, 746B1
SCHMIDT, Carmela
Wins Olympic medals 7-22, 7-24, 623D3

SCHMIDT, Helmut (West German chancellor) [1976]
On CDU victory in Lower Saxony 1-15, 77C2
At Europn socialist conf 1-19, 48A3, C3
Iran univ pact rptd 1-20, 102A2
Urges Poland pact ratificatn 1-29, 77C3
Defends 'Ostpolitik,' detente 1-29, 157G3
On CDU Lower Saxony win 2-6, 157A3

SCHMIDT, Helmut (West German chancellor) [1977]
Sees Andreotti, backs IMF loan 1-17—1-18, 64F3
Mondale visits 1-25, 69C1
Baader trial adjourned 3-17; meets pol ldrs, denies tap role 3-18, 260B1, B2
Econ stimulus pkg OKd 3-23, 243E2
Sees Vance on arms talks, Brazil A-pact 3-31, 247A1, 268A3

SCHMIDT, Helmut (West German chancellor) [1978]
Rejcts US econ stimulus pressure 1-19, 93E3
Sees Caramanlis, backs EC entry 1-31, 149E2
Leber resigns, Cabt reshuffled 2-3, 93B2, A3
Vogel asks local curbs on Nazis 2-4, 114C2

SCHMIDT, Helmut (West German chancellor) [1979]
At 4-natn Guadeloupe summit; endorses SALT, rptdly cautns vs China sales 1-5—1-6, 12E2, C3, 40C2
Shipbuilding aid proposed 1-21, 77G3
4% '79 econ growth seen 1-23, 62A1
Budget OKd by parlt 1-26, 77E2
At 'Lulu' debut in Paris 2-25, 174A1
Nazi contd prosecutn backed 3-8, 214D3

SCHMIDT, Helmut (West German chancellor) [1980]
Sees Giscard re Afghan 1-9, 10G2
Sees US offcl, backs detente 1-16, 28G1
Wage restraint call, energy remarks rptd 1-18, 103A2
Genscher urges Soviet policy change re Olympics 1-28, 68F1
Mtg with E Ger premr postponed 1-30, 103E1

1976

Sees Giscard 2-12—2-13, 229D1
Hails Poland pact 3-12, 260A2
Meets Sadat 3-29—4-2, 275A1
SPD loses state vote 4-4, 270D1
On European CPs 4-15, 503C1
Bars printers mediatn role 4-30, 352E2
Gierek visits 6-8—6-11, 442D1
Addresses SPD conventn 6-19, 502G3
Sees Vorster 6-25, 447D3 ★
At 7-natn econ summit 6-27—6-28, 461G2, 462E1, G1
Apology to France rptd 7-5, 521G1
French ldr visits 7-6, 521E1
Visits US 7-15—7-17, 530E2
Discloses Italy loan ban 7-16, 530D3
Italy loan ban repercusns 7-20, 557B1
Parlt OKs antiterror law 7-29, 593B3
Protests E Ger border incidents 8-11, 8-13, 630D3, G3
Bernhard role in '71 jet buy rptd 9-2, 684F2
Sees Kissinger on S Africa 9-7, 660F2
Backs Rhodesia compensatn 9-8, 681B2
Trades pol payoff chrgs 9-29, 10-1, 754C3
SPD-FDP coalitn wins electns 10-3, sets goals 10-4, 754B2-F3
Focke resigns min 10-15, 857B3
SPD gains seat in recount 10-20, 857A3
US election reactn 11-3—11-4, 826E1
CSU votes to split with CDU 11-19, 930E2
Addresses Socialist Intl 11-26, 935B3
Carstens elected Parlt pres 12-14, 968B3
Reelected chancellor 12-15, presents program 12-16, 968E1

SCHMIDT, John
Named in grain fraud 3-11, 247D3
SCHMIDT, Kathryn
Wins Olympic medal 7-24, 576F1
SCHMIDT, Mike
NL batting ldr 10-4, 795F3, G3
SCHMIDT, Wolfgang
Wins Olympic medal 7-25, 575G3
SCHMITT, Bishop Adolf Gregor
Killed 12-5, 1009D2
SCHMITT, Harrison Hogan
Wins Senate primary 6-1, 411E1 ★
Elected 11-2, 817E2, 819D3 ★, 824E2, 828D2
SCHMUECKER, Toni
VW OKs US plant 4-23, 321E2
SCHMULEW, Derek Paul
Dutch asylum rptd 11-12, 927F3
SCHNABL, Karl
Wins Olympic medals 2-7, 2-15, 159E1
SCHNEIDER, Paula J.
Women in Amer rpt issued 4-27, 379C3
SCHOCKEMOEHLE, Alwin
Wins Olympic medal 7-27, 574D2
SCHOENDIENST, Albert (Red)
Dismissed as Cardinal mgr 10-5, 816B1
SCHOENE, Lester P.
Dies 7-19, 656G3
SCHOENFELD, Rabbi Fabian
Backs Vatican sex statemt 1-26, 124D2
Urges Vatican ties with Israel 2-8, 272G2
Wurzburger succeeds 5-26, 932E2
SCHOENFELD, James L.
Arrested 7-29, 560B1
Chowchilla trial moved 11-10, 876E3
SCHOENFELD, Richard A.
Surrenders 7-23, 560C1
Chowchilla trial moved 11-10, 876E3
SCHOOL Integration Issue—*See under EDUCATION*
SCHOONMAKER, Frank
Dies 1-11, 56G3
SCHORR, Daniel
Admits leaking House com rpt 2-12; House votes probe 2-19, CBS suspends 2-23, 150D3-151A2
CBS dismissal urged 2-17, 216F3
House probe underway 3-2, 216E3
House com hearings 7-19, 7-20; subpoenaed 8-25, refuses testimony 9-15; probe dropped 9-22, 748A3
SCHOTTLAND, Stanley A.
Indicted 10-29, 886C3

1977

Carter asks Portugal aid 4-1, 330C3
At Buback funeral 4-13, 286D2
Affirms A-export policy 4-21, 4-26, 334A1
At 25th Bilderberg conf 4-21—4-24, 359C3
Senghor visits 5-3, 394F1
At 7-natn econ summit, sees Carter 5-7—5-8, 357B1-G1, F2, 358D1, E1, 359E1
At 4-power NATO talks 5-9, min mtg 5-10, 358C2
Loses '73 power challenge 5-26, censure motion defeated 6-21, 601G3
Sees Giscard 6-16—6-17, A-data exports halted 6-17, 566C3
In Canada 7-6—7-12, US 7-13—7-14, 566G1, F2
Rptdly OKs mark revaluatn 7-21, 552G1
Ponto slain 7-30, 601D3
US reflationary proposals rptd rejctd 8-8, 585B2
Kappler jail escape delays Andreotti mtg 8-15, 637E3
Brandt warns of Nazi revival 8-19, 658G1
Scores Schleyer kidnap 9-5; orders probe, asks talks 9-6—9-8, 695F1
Cabt passes 3 anti-terrorist bills 9-8, 695D2
Lufthansa jet hijacking dvpts 10-17—10-20, 789C2, E2, 790D1, F1
Sees Callaghan, JET site vote agreed 10-18; UK chosen 10-25, 853A1
OKs UK mil 'offset paymt' terms 10-18, 926F2
Addresses parlt on terrorists 10-20, 791A1, E2
At Schleyer funeral 10-25, 868C2
Visits Poland 11-21—11-25, 926E1
Meets Andreotti in Verona 12-1, 1014G3
Scores $ drop, cites EC $ purchases in '77 12-6, 932C3

SCHMIDT, Herman J.
Calls Carter 'unfair' 10-13, 772G3
SCHMIDT, Mike
NL batting ldr 10-2, 926C3, D3
SCHMIDT, Rodolfo
Links Orfila, Graiver 4-23, 371B3
SCHMIDT, Waldemar
Young decisns Foreman 3-17, 263C1
SCHMITT, Sen. Harrison H. (R, N.M.)
Vs Sen ethics code 4-1, 251D3, F3
SCHMUCKER, Toni
VW seeks 2d US plant 6-15, 463G3
SCHNEIDER, Gerd Richart
Captured by Dutch police 11-10, 887F3
Schubert kills self 11-12, 888D2
SCHNEIDER, John A.
Replaced as CBS broadcast pres, becomes senior vp 10-17, 846F1
SCHNEIDER, Mark
Chile loans blocked 6-28, 493C1
SCHOEFFLER, Paul
Dies 11-21, 952C3
SCHOEMAN, Hendrik
Asks sex laws repeal 7-5, 564B1
SCHOENFELD, James L.
Pleads guilty 7-25, 642D1
Convicted 12-15, 992D1
SCHOENFELD, Richard A.
Pleads guilty 7-25, 642D1
Convicted 12-15, 992D1
SCHOLARLY Communication with the People's Republic of China, U.S. Committee on
China rejcts exchng bid 6-28, 505F3
SCHOLASTIC Aptitude Test (SAT)—*See EDUCATION*
SCHOLTEN, Bishop Dominic
Arrested 4-21, 350B1
SCHOLZ, Father Dieter
Rhodesia jails 8-30, frees 9-23, 811C2
SCHOOL Integration Issue—*See under EDUCATION*
SCHOOL Lunch Program—*See FOOD—School Meals*
SCHOOLS—*See EDUCATION*
SCHORER, Mark
Dies 8-11, 696F3
SCHOTTLAND, Stanley A.
No contest plea cited 11-23, 918B3

1978

In French summit 2-6—2-7, 122B1
Sees Sadat in Hamburg 2-9, 98E2
Sees Blumenthal, bars '78 growth rate hike 2-13, 119C1
Urges newspaper strike setlmt 2-15, 250E2
Testifies at Defns Min spy probe 2-24, 210D3
Defends Schleyer hunt 3-13, Cabt resignatn sought 3-16, 332G2, A3
Sees Giscard, Sovt uranium deal discussed 4-2, 258C2
On EC growth target, econ stimulatn 4-7—4-8, 257D3
Husak visits W Ger 4-10—4-14, detente support pledged 4-11, 332F3
Clarifies neutron bomb stand, warns US vs policy shifts 4-12, 254A3
Anti-terror laws repassed 4-13, 332A2
Scores US oil imports, econ policy 4-28, clarifies comments 4-29, 519B2
Sees Brezhnev in Bonn 5-4—5-7, joint communique issued 5-7, 417A1
Sees Carter 5-30—5-31, briefs parlt 6-1, 519F1
Backs US warning to USSR on Africa 5-31, 397A2
Free Dems lose 2 state electns 6-4, 456C2, D2
Sees Genscher, names Baum interior min 6-6, 456C3
Sees Giscard on EC monetary zone 6-23, presents plan at Bremen summit 7-6—7-7; UK, US, others wary 7-7—7-18, 545D1-546B1
In Nigeria, Zambia 6-26—6-30; defends S Africa ties 6-30, 584B1
Carter visits 7-14—7-15, 544G3-545C1
At 7-natn Bonn econ summit, vows stimulus measures 7-16—7-17, 543C3, G3, 544F1
Announces W Ger econ stimulus plan 7-28, 583E3-584A1
Filbinger quits over Nazi chrgs 8-7, 616G3
Disputes SPD spy scandal 9-6, 725G2
'79 budget presented 9-20, 906C1, E1
Ex-aide sentncd for espionage 10-5, 776D3
Coalitn wins Hesse vote 10-8, 776G2
Highway to Berlin OKd 11-16, 905G3
France backs limits on EC Parlt 11-21, 902A2
Parlt OKs $7.8 bil econ stimulus 11-24, 925E2
Hails Irish EMS entry 12-15, 979C2

SCHMIDT, Kate
AAU suspends 6-23, 692E2
SCHMIDT, Kurtis J.
Arrested re A-sub plot 10-4, 824F1
Charges dropped 10-19, 992E1
SCHMIDT, Mike
Wins Golden Glove Award 11-21, 928A3
SCHMIEGE, Calvin H.
Indicted 3-23, 243F1
SCHMITT, Sen. Harrison Hogan (R, N.M.)
Votes vs Panama Canal neutrality pact 3-16, 177G2
Weicker quits ethics com re Korea probe 4-14, 279E3
Votes vs 2d Canal pact 4-18, 273B1
SCHMUCKER, Toni
Warns UAW re VW contract 10—19, 809G3
SCHMUDE, Jurgen
Named W Ger educ min 2-3, 93A3
SCHNEIDER, Bert
Gentleman Tramp released 4-26, 619B2
Days of Heaven released 9-13, 970A1
SCHNEIDER, Gerd
Dutch backers stage protest 3-14, 192G1 ★
Dutch OK extraditn 5-8, 354C1
Extradited to W Ger 10-13, 885B1
SCHNEIDER, Harold
Days of Heaven released 9-13, Goin' South 10-6, 970A1, E1
SCHNEIDER, Mark L.
El Salvador rights abuse rptd worse 8-5, 723A3 ★
SCHNEIDER, Romy
Woman at Her Window released 6-9, 620C1
SCHNELLENBACH, Karen
Penn State wins women's lacrosse title 5-28, 540C2
SCHOENBERG, Arnold (1874-1951)
Quartets for Strings wins Grammy 2-24, 316C1
SCHOENFELD, James L.
Sentenced for Chowchilla kidnap 2-17, 232C3
SCHOENFELD, Richard A.
Sentenced for Chowchilla kidnap 2-17, 232C3
SCHOESSLING, Ray
On '77 top-paid labor ldrs list 5-15, 365E1, F1
SCHOLASTIC Aptitude Test (SAT)
Verbal scores stabilize 9-16, 754G1
SCHONAU, Horst
Wins 4-man bobsled championship 2-12, 316F3
SCHOOL Integration Issue—*See under EDUCATION*
SCHOOLS—*See EDUCATION*
SCHOTTLAND, Stanley A.
Sentenced 9-21, 768B3
SCHRADER, Leonard
Blue Collar released 2-9, 618D3
SCHRADER, Paul
Blue Collar released 2-9, 618D3

1979

SPD-FDP gain in regional electns 3-18, 214A3
Sadat visits, seeks econ aid 3-29, 250A1
Carstens elected pres 5-23, 410B3
CDU-CSU alliance faces split 5-24, 5-28, 489E1
Meets Carter in US, endorses SALT 6-6, 430A1
FDP backs A-power 6-16, 489G2
Lutzes sentncd as spies 6-18, 489F3
At Tokyo energy summit 6-28—6-29, 493B1
Strauss wins CDU support 7-2, 505G3-506A1
Stresses coal in energy address 7-4, 506A1
Carter rptdly urged Israeli setlmts actn 7-9, 511B2
Carter energy plan assessed 7-16, 534F3
Sees US offcls re $, mark rates 9-29, 779E3
Reactn to US-Sovt conflict on SALT, Cuba troops rptd 10-3, 738B1
Skeptical re USSR troop cut plan 10-7, 761E3
Backs A-missile delay 10-14, 880C3
Sees China premr 10-22, 853F3, 854A1
Bundesbank hikes discount rate 10-31, 838E1
Gromyko sees, warns vs NATO missiles 11-21–11-24, 938A3
Addresses Soc Dems, plans '80 mtgs with Brezhnev, Honecker 12-4; gets strong support 12-6, 938D2
Sees Vance on Iran 12-11, 933G2

SCHMIDT, Kate
AAU reinstatemt cited 11-28, 956F1
SCHMIDT, Mike
NL wins All-Star Game 7-17, 568D3-569A1
NL batting ldr 9-30, wins Golden Glove Award 11-20, 955E2, F2, 956D1
SCHMIEGE, Calvin H.
Convicted 8-16, 704F1
Fined, put on probatn 12-10, 947B1
SCHMITT, Sen. Harrison Hogan (R, N.M.)
Scores SALT treaty 4-5, 258G1
Talmadge denunciatn asked 9-14, 702A2
Talmadge denounced by Sen 10-10, 769E1
Replaced on Sen Ethics Com 10-31, 945A3
SCHNACKE, Judge Robert H.
Bans H-bomb letter publicatn 9-15, suit dismissed 9-17, 714C1, A2
SCHNEIDER, Alan
Loose Ends opens 6-6, 712C1
SCHNEIDER, Barry
Roller Boogie released 12-19, 1008C1
SCHNEIDER, Paul
Just a Little Less opens 5-20, 712A1
SCHNEIDERMAN, Dr. Marvin
Details cancer death rates 3-5, 195B3
SCHOENMAN, Ralph
Ousted from Iran 3-5, 199C2
SCHOLASTIC Aptitude Test (SAT)
Coaching schl study issued 5-29, 785A2
Test scores rptd down 9-8, 785E1; 10-4, 810B2; '50s A-fallout linked 9-17, 747A2
SCHOLL Inc.
Kresge dispute refused by Sup Ct 1-15, 32A1
SCHOLL v. Kresge
Case refused by Sup Ct 1-15, 32B1
SCHOLTEN, Willem
Some Dutch troops vs Unifil svc 2-1, 84G3
Asks US A-missile delay 11-13, 880D2
SCHOOL Meals—*See under FOOD*
SCHOOLS—*See EDUCATION*
SCHRADER, Leonard
Old Boyfriends released 3-21, 528C3
SCHRADER, Paul
Hardcore released 2-8, 174F2
Old Boyfriends released 3-21, 528C3
SCHRAGER, Ian
Indicted 6-28; Jordan denies cocaine chrg 8-24, Landau disputes 8-28, 647E1-E2
Pleads guilty in tax case 11-2, 891A3

1980

US amb's pol gaffes rptd 1-30, 200D2
Semiannual mtg with Giscard ends, Sovt Afghan exit asked 2-5; USSR sees US pressure 2-6, 84F2-D3
Vance asks backing vs Sovt Afghan invasn 2-20, 139A2
Meets Carter in US, discusses Afghan 3-5, 205B2
Seeks talks with E Ger 3-20, 236B3
Hints Olympic boycott support 3-20, 259D3
French Olympic boycott decisn delay seen 3-23, 259E3
Backs UK re EC budget 3-28, 242B3
Meets E Ger offcl, trade expansn set 4-17, 303B2
Sees war threat, regrets US plight 4-20, 303C1
Backs US hostage rescue try 4-25, 324B2
Budget suplmt approved 4-30, 355G3
At Tito funeral 5-8, 339B1
Sees Mex pres 5-20, joint statemt issued 5-21, 409F2
Says USSR rejects A-missile freeze offer 6-9; Carter letter vs 6-16; seeks mtg 6-18, 450B3-451D1
Sees Carter, vs USSR trip criticism 6-21, 473E1
Outlines USSR trip plans 6-23, 474E1
Visits Moscow, discusses A-missiles, urges Afghan exit 6-30—7-1, 489A1-B2
Backs French A-weapons, Eur world role 7-11, 539G3
Anderson visits 7-14, 550A1
Cancels E Ger trip 8-22, 642E2, 658G1
Brezhnev asks US arms talks 8-22, 679E3
Carter urges Poland aid 8-29, reactn 9-3, 659C1, C2
Campaign chrgs rptd 9-3—9-5, 690D3
Scores RC bishops pol letter 9-13, 712C1
US briefs on hostages in Iran 9-19, 719C3
Vs US plan for intl force to protect Gulf oil 9-26, 735E2
SPD-FDP coalition wins elections 10-5; sets goals 10-7, 759G2, 760A1
Scores E Ger entry fee hikes 10-12, 794C3
Sworn W Ger chancellor 11-5, 925E1
Meets Pope 11-15, 905E1
Meets Reagan 11-20, 897F2
Visits US; meets Carter, Reagan 11-20; addresses parlt on mtg, co-determinatn legis 9-24, 903G3-904G2
Mannesman restructuring rptd 12-1, 925C1
SCHMIDT, Mike
NL batting ldr 10-6, 926E2, F2
In World Series 10-14—10-21, named Series MVP 10-21, 811C2-812F3
Named NL MVP 11-26, wins Golden Glove 12-6, 925B3, 926E1
SCHMIDT, Terry
NFL '79 interceptn ldr 1-5, 8G2
SCHMITT, Sen. Harrison Hogan (R, N.M.)
Suit filed vs pres com spending 7-1, 493D1
Reagan funding drive upheld 8-28, 681A2
SCHMITZ, John G.
Loses Calif US Sen primary 6-3, 439A2
SCHMUDE, Jurgen
Sworn W Ger educ min 11-5, 925F1
SCHNEIDER, Alan
Lady From Dubuque opens 1-31, 136C3
SCHNEIDER, Claudine
Unopposed in RI US House primary 9-9, 700G2
Elected to US House 11-4, 844A2, 846C2, 849B1
SCHNEIDER, Peter
Knife in the Head released 4-23, 416B3
SCHNEIDER, Petra
Wins Olympic medal 7-26, 623E3
SCHOENDIENST, Red
Named interim Cardinals mgr 8-29, 926C2
SCHOENMAKER, Lex
Cosmos win NASL title 9-21, 770G1
SCHOLASTIC Aptitude Test (SAT)
Aptitude test study disputed 1-14, 36F2
Aptitude test data to be disclosed 4-7, 318E3
Coaching rptd helpful 5-15, 599B3
Test score decline continues 10-4, 786C2
Scientific literacy study rptd 10-22, 990F1
USC coach backs athletic admissns policy 10-29, 875F2
SCHOLEY, Robert
Urges end to steel strike 3-9, 193F2
Steel strike settled 4-1, 254C2, F2
SCHONROCK, Sybille
Wins Olympic medal 7-21, 623C3
SCHOOL Meals—*See under FOOD*
SCHOOLS—*See EDUCATION*
SCHORR, Daniel
Rpts Trigon-Kissinger spy controversy 10-4, 754A1, D1
SCHORSCH Jr., Irvin G.
Named in PCB suit 4-24, 331F3
SCHORSCH, John B.
Named in PCB suit 4-24, 331F3
SCHRADER, Paul
American Gigolo released 2-1, 216A2
Raging Bull released 11-14, 972G3
SCHRAGER, Ian
Sentenced 1-18, 64B3
Grand jury clears Jordan 5-28, 402E3

1976

SCHREIBER, Sol
Nantucket oil spill hearing 12-28—12-31, 1031F3
SCHROEDER, Rep. Patricia (D, Colo.)
Questns AWACS offer 3-2, 183E2
Reelected 11-2, 824E1, 829F1
SCHROEFFER, Joseph Cardinal
Named cardinal 4-27, 336C2
SCHUBERT, Rainer
E Ger jails 1-26, 85E1
SCHUBERT: Trios Nos. 1 & 2 (record album)
Wins Grammy 2-28, 460D3
SCHULTZE, Charles L.
At Carter econ mtg 12-1, 898A3
SCHRUMP, Raymond C.
Addresses GOP conv 8-17, 615G1-B2
SCHULMAN, Samuel
'72 campaign gift listed 4-25, 688B1
SCHULTZ, Arnaldo
Release from prison rptd 1-23, 53A2
SCHULTZ, Dietrich
On spy arrests 6-14, 441F3
SCHULTZ, Karl
Wins Olympic medal 7-25, 574C2
SCHULTZ, Klaus
Censured re terrorist escape 7-23, 593G3
SCHULTZE, Charles L.
Briefs Carter on econ 7-27, 551B1
Designated CEA chrmn 12-16, 936A3, 937A1
Biog sketch 937E1
SCHULZ, Rev. Larold K.
Chrgs Rhodesia sanctn violatns 6-21, 621E1
SCHULZE, Rep. Richard T. (R, Pa.)
Reelected 11-2, 830D3
SCHUMANN, Margit
Wins Olympic medal 2-7, 159G1
SCHUT, Ruby (Ruby Bates)
Dies 10-27, 1015F2
SCHWARCZENBERGER, Ildiko
Wins Olympic medal 7-24, 574G2
SCHWARTZ, Edwin
Letters on Colombia bribes publshd 2-8, 147E2
SCHWEIKER, Sen. Richard S. (R, Pa.)
Reagan names running mate, text 7-26; delegate disenchantmt rptd 7-27—7-29, 549C2-550A3
In SC 7-29, briefs press 7-30, 564F1
Reagan claims delegate gains 8-2—8-3, starts campaign swing 8-4—8-5, 563G2-564C2
Ends 5-state campaign swing 8-7, 583E3
GOP vp polls rptd 8-11, 8-12, 583F2-584B1
Buckley candidacy promoted 8-11, 8-12, 584C3
GOP platform com OKs planks 8-13, 583D1
Sears on vp choice 8-18, 615C3
Offers to withdraw, Reagan rejects 8-18, 615D3
GOP conv vp vote table 8-19, 599F3
Reagan bids supporters farewell 8-19, 615C2
SCHWEITZER, Albert (1875-1965)
Carter, Ford debate 10-22, 800E3

SCIENCE & Technology—*See also specific science*
Fscl '77 US budget estimate tables 231A1, 358B2
White House office re-created 5-11, 346A1
Ford OKs '77 ERDA funds 7-12, 517F2
Carter acceptance speech 7-15, 510F2
GOP platform text 8-18, 608D1
Cong sets '77 budget levels table 9-16, 706B2
Jan Peive death rptd 9-17, 970A3
'77 NSF authorizatn signed 10-11, 835A2
Medal of Science awards 10-18, 858B3
Nobel laureates score Ford 10-26, 840B2
US rpts post-Helsinki gains 12-8, 934C2

1977

SCHREIBER, Gov. Martin James (D, Wis.)
Sworn gov 7-7, 560B3
SCHREYER, Ed
Loses Manitoba electn 10-11, 823D1
SCHROEDER, John
Loses San Diego Open 1-30, 104C1
2d in Colonial Natl tourn 5-15, 676D1
SCHUBERT, Ingrid
Explosives discovered 11-10, hangs self 11-12, ruled suicide 11-13, 888G1
SCHULTZ, William
A-plant accident liability limit voided 3-31, 277F2
SCHULTZE, Charles L.
Confrmatn recommended 1-18, confrmd 1-20, 34B1, 35A1
Council seats filled 1-18, 52E3
Sworn 1-23, 52E2
Econ plan hearings 1-27—2-4, 52A1, 89C2
On wage, price monitoring 1-31, 90B1
Rpts personal finances 2-25, 148D1
Quits as Econ Policy Group co-chrmn 3-15, 211A2
Backs rebate plan end 4-14, 270G3
On steel price hike 5-8, 5-9, 385E1, A2
Scores steel price hike 7-21, 577B1
SCHULZ, Edwin J.
Convicted 1-29, 103F1 ★, G1
Sentenced 3-11, 203A3
SCHUMACHER, E. F.
Dies 9-4, 788D2
SCHUMANN, Jurgen
Slain by hijackers 10-16, 789G1
SCHUPPAN, Vernon
2d in Le Mans 6-12, 531B2
SCHUSCHNIGG, Kurt von
Dies 11-21, 952C3
SCHUT, Ruby Bates (d. 1976)
Libel suit vs NBC cited 7-12, 643C1
SCHUTZ, Klaus
Resigns 4-29, Stobbe replaces 5-2, 352D3
SCHUYLER, George S.
Dies 8-31, 788E2
SCHWANKE, CWO Glen W.
Wounded 7-13, N Koreans return 7-16, 552F2, F3
SCHWARTZ, Brian
Held 2-26—3-1, arrives Kenya 3-2, 141C2
SCHWARTZ, Judge Charles
Sentences Tonry 7-28, 603A3
SCHWARTZ, Dr. Daniel W.
Declares Berkowitz insane 8-30, 848D3
SCHWARTZ, Judge Murray
Delays Wilmington desegregatn 8-5, 630D3
SCHWARZER, Judge William
IAM, Lockheed ruling 12-15, 1005E2
SCHWEIKER, Sen. Richard S. (R, Pa.)
Backs cong electn funds bill 3-7, 232D3
Scores germ warfare tests 3-8, 195D2
Visits China 4-9—4-17, 298D2
SCHWER, Francis
Killed by guerrillas 10-20, 921B3
SCHWINN & Co., Arnold
'Schwinn doctrine' overturned 6-23, 539E1
SCIARROTTA, Anthony
Indicted 2-4, 103A1
SCIENCE, American Association for the Advancement of (AAAS)
Annual mtg 2-21—2-25, 183C2-184C1, F1
SCIENCE, National Medal of
Awarded 11-22, 951G3-952C1
SCIENCE for the People
DNA safety debated 10-6, 846D3
SCIENCE Foundation, National—*See U.S. GOVERNMENT—NATIONAL Science Foundation*
SCIENCE News (magazine)
Rpts gas productn drop 2-26, 152B2
Rpts on DNA recombinatn 10-8, 846F3
SCIENCES, National Academy of—*See NATIONAL Academy, etc.*

SCIENCE & Technology—*See also specific science*
US budget table item 1-17, 32F2
AAAS annual mtg 2-21—2-25, 183C2-184C1, F1
Carter keeps Ford budget 2-22, 125B2
Iran, Pak, Turkey sign pact 3-12, 190C2
Scientists rpt scores EPA 3-21, 252B2
Carter for Latin training programs 4-14, 296A1
Cong sets '78 budget target 5-17, 405A1
Oxford conf honors Levich 7-11—7-13, 551C2
USSR scores Levich conf 8-24, 683G3
China '78 parley rptd set 9-22, 781D1
Medals of Sci awarded 11-22, 951G3-952C1

1978

SCHREIBER, Gov. Martin J. (D, Wis.)
Lauds A-plant moratorium 8-17, 665B3
Wins primary 9-12, 736A2
Loses reelectn 11-7, 846C3, 854G1
SCHREYER, Edward
Canada gov gen 12-7, 963B3
SCHROEDER, Barbet
Celine & Julie released 2-24, 618G3
Perceval released 10-6, 1030D3
SCHROEDER, John,
2d in San Diego Open 1-29, 76E1
SCHROEDER, Rep. Patricia (D, Colo.)
Chrgs House job bias, other abuses 9-21, 720C3
Reelected 11-7, 850C2
SCHROTER, Herbert
Schmidt ex-aide sentncd 10-5, 776D3
SCHUBERT, Steve
NFL '77 punt return ldr 1-1, 56F3
SCHUITEMA, Fritz
Kidnaped in El Salvador 11-24, Philips meets guerrilla demands 12-21, 986B3
Freed 12-30, 1021E3
SCHULTZ, Dave
NHL penalty minutes ldr 4-9, 296E2
SCHULTZ, Dwight
Water Engine opens 1-5, 760G3
SCHULTZ, Michael
Sgt Pepper's released 7-21, 970B3
SCHULTZE, Charles L.
On wage, price policy 1-20, 48D3
Tax-cut plan scaled back 5-12, 361C1
Issues cotton dust rules 6-19, 471D3, G3
Natl health plan delay urged 6-26, 491F2
Named to labor-pact panel 8-7, 624D2
Kahn named Wage-Price Cncl chrmn 10-25, 806D2
At St Louis wage-price forum 11-1, 863A3
Scores Long VAT proposal 12-3, 962D2
On OPEC price hike impact 12-17, 978C1
SCHULZ, Adelheid
Eludes police 8-21, rptd apprehended 9-6, 724F3
SCHULZE, Rep. Richard T. (R, Pa.)
Reelected 11-7, 852C1
SCHUMACHER, Joel
Wiz released 10-25, 970E3
SCHUMAN, Edward
Rubber Gun released 4-24, 619E3
SCHUMANN, Robert (1810-56)
Fantasie-Stucke wins Grammy 2-24, 316D1
SCHURTI, Manfred
2d in Daytona endurance 2-5, 538D3
SCHUSTER, Hans-Emil
Asteroid finds near Earth rptd 3-12, 293D3
SCHWAIGHOFER, Hans
Oberammergau vs revised Passion Play 1-12, 95G2
SCHWARTZ, Judge Murray
Orders Wilmington busing plan 1-9, 15F2-A3
SCHWARTZ, Stephen
Working opens 5-14, 887E3
SCHWEIKER, Jim
Awarded Pulitzer 4-17; photo mix-up rptd, quits UPI 4-21, 314F2
SCHWEIKER, Sen. Richard S. (R, Pa.)
Votes vs Panama Canal neutrality pact 3-16, 177G2
Votes vs 2d Canal pact 4-18, 273B1
Scores Sen com rpt on Marston 4-25, 5-4, 343A1
Visits USSR 11-11—11-18, 905A2
SCHWENDLER, William
Dies 1-14, 96E2
SCHWEPPES Ltd.—*See under CADBURY Schweppes Ltd.*
SCIARROTTA, Anthony
Acquitted 4-28, 324D2
SCIENCE, American Association for the Advancement of (AAAS)
A-plant radiatn-cancer link argued 2-17, 164B2, G2
Gamma ray spectral line rptd 2-25, 293G2
Cocaine preference by monkeys rptd 8-11, 771A2
Margaret Mead dies 11-15, 972D3
SCIENCE Foundation, National—*See U.S. GOVERNMENT—NATIONAL Science Foundation*
SCIENCES, National Academy of—*See NATIONAL Academy of Sciences*
SCIENCE & Technology—*See also specific science*
France-China accord 1-21, 71F1
Carter budget proposals 1-23, 44E2; table 45D2
Pak, India OK exchng 2-6—2-7, 113B1
Helsinki review conf ends 3-9, 179D1
China conf held, drive launched 3-18—3-31, 436C1
US Educ Dept proposed 4-14, 279D1
Harvard revises curriculum 5-2, 348D2
Cong '79 budget target res cleared 5-17, 385E1
Nobel winners score Orlov sentence 5-19, 401B2
Turkey, USSR sign pact 6-21—6-23, 595E2
Carter revises secrecy rules 6-29, 508F1
US scientists visit China 7-6—7-10, 564C2-C3
China, Libya sign pact 8-9, 691F2
US, Japan talks end 9-6, 695B3
France-China pact signed 10-20, 814B1
US-China acad exchng set 10-22, 814E1

1979

SCHREIBER, Terry
Devour the Snow opens 5-13, 711D2
SCHREYER, Edward
Pawley named Manitoba NDP ldr 1-13, 57C3
Gets Trudeau resignatn 6-4, 423D3
Canada Indians vs Const patriatn 7-2, 523A1
Meets Indian reps 7-19, 632G2
Reads Throne speech 10-9, 788F1
House dissolved, electns set 12-14, 936A3
SCHRODER, Ricky
Champ released 4-3, 528G1
SCHROEDER, John
2d in Citrus Classic 3-4, 220F3
SCHROEDER, Dr. John Speer
Rpts heart-transplant survivals 5-6, 355D1
SCHUCKIT, Marc
Alcoholism study rptd 1-5, 289C3
SCHUITEMA, Fritz
El Salvador '78 ransom rptd 3-23, 235G1
SCHULMAN, Jack M.
Cleveland defaults again 8-31, 920A3
SCHULTZ, Henry E.
Dies 5-5, 432F3
SCHULTZ, Michael
Scavenger Hunt released 12-25, 1008E1
SCHULTZ, Theodore W.
Wins Nobel Prize 10-17, 858G1-B2
SCHULTZE, Charles L.
Backs hosp cost-control bill 3-9, 194B3
Warns rubber industry on wage-guide compliance 4-20, 345A1
Defends wage hike limit 5-10, 362D2
Carter econ team rptd revamped 6-4, 463E1
On 3d 1/4 econ rebound 10-19, 805F1
SCHULZ, Brigitte
Sentncd for Israel '76 jet plot 9-11, 677D2
SCHUMANN, Manfred
Swiss win world 2-man bobsled title 2-18, 392E1
SCHUSTER, Alan
Big Bad Burlesque opens 8-14, 711E1
SCHWANTNER, Joseph
Wins Pulitzer 4-16, 336G2
SCHWARTZ, A. R.
Calls pres primary bill 'dead' 5-22, 594A3
SCHWARTZ, Arthur
Dancing in Dark opens 1-21, 292D1
SCHWARTZ v. Gilsterx
Case refused by Sup Ct 10-1, 768G1
SCHWARZENEGGER, Arnold
Villain released 7-20, 820E3
SCHWEIKER, Sen. Richard S. (R, Pa.)
Vs hosp cost-control bill 3-9, 194C3
Scores SALT treaty 4-5, 258G1
Rhodesia sanctns res voted 5-15, 359A2
Finances disclosed 5-18, 383E2
Reagan to chng vp selectn 5-27, 594F1
SCHWEIZERISCHE Aluminum AG (Alusuisse)
Maremont acquired 7-30, 770G2
SCIENCE, American Association for the Advancement of (AAAS)
Masters addresses 1-5, 17F1
Frozen sperm study rptd 1-7, 64E2
Stakman dies 1-22, 104G3
SCIENCE Foundation, National—*See U.S. GOVERNMENT-NATIONAL Science Foundation*
SCIENCES, National Academy of—*See NATIONAL Academy of Sciences*

SCIENCE & Technology
Major research dvpts rptd 1-4-3-31, 289B3-290G1
Carter budget proposals 1-22, 46A2; table 42F2
US-China pact signed 1-31, 65C1
US, Mex sign cooperatn pact 2-16, 124D3
US scientists cut Sovt links 3-1, 172A2
More research dvpts rptd 3-21-8-28, 691A2-692G3
US seeks more Brazil ties 3-22, 248B1
Canada tech weakness seen 3-24, 234D1
USSR-Australia ties to be resumed 4-3, 253D1
Carter urges innovatn, dvpg natn aid 4-23, 300A3
US-China cooperatn pact set 5-13, 370E1
WCC mtg ends, sci rift eased 7-24, 640C1
More research dvpts rptd 9-1-12-13, 1000A2-F2
China-Italy pacts OKd 11-6, 854D2
USSR mil seen aided by US trade 11-8, 856E3-857D1

1980

SCHREIBER, Avery
Silent Scream released 2-2, 216E3
SCHREIBER, Ed
Loses US House electn 11-4, 851D3
SCHREYER, Edward
Reads Throne Speech 4-14, 292F3
SCHROEDER, Rep. Patricia (D, Colo.)
On Somali refugee problem 4-6, 274C1
Reelected 11-4, 842C2, 851D3
SCHROTER, Martina
Wins Olympic medal 7-26, 623B2
SCHUBERT, Ingrid (d. 1977)
Amnesty Intl cites case 5-28, 411F2
SCHUBERT, Steve
NFL '79 punt return ldr 1-5, 8F3
SCHULLER, Gunther
Elected to Arts Inst 12-5, 998C1
SCHULLER, Robert
TV revenues rptd 2-25, 413B2
SCHULTZ, Frederick
Backs discount rate reductn 5-28, 400E2
Not in discount rate vote 7-25, 574G3
SCHULTZ, George P.
Pvt anti-inflatn com sets policy 6-21, 481E1
Says econ plan has 'socko' 11-16, 881C2
SCHULTZ, Pierre
Convictn rptd 6-18, 522G2
SCHULTZ, Susanne
Wins Olympic medal 7-26, 623B3
SCHULTZE, Charles L.
Budget forecasts recession 1-28, 69C2
On Feb producer price rise 3-7, 182D2
On May producer price index 6-6, 437E3
Sees House Dems re taxes 6-26, 480C3
Scores econ 'Dunkirk' talk 12-19, 980D3
SCHULZ, Bill
Wins Sen primary 9-9, 700D2
Loses US Sen electn 11-4, 851A3
SCHULZE, Rep. Richard T. (R, Pa.)
Reelected 11-4, 844C1
SCHUMAKER, Larry
Loses SD US Sen primary 6-3, 439B3
SCHUMER, Charles
Elected to US House 11-4, 843E3
SCHUSTER, Bernd
W Ger wins Eur Soccer Championship 6-22, 771D2
SCHUTZ, Peter W.
Named Porsche pres, chief exec 12-3, 959D3
SCHWAB, Jack
Dies 3-17, 280A2
SCHWAB'S Drug Store
Founder dies 3-17, 280A2
SCHWADA, John
Fires Miller as Ariz State athletic dir, hires Knox 1-3, 175E2
SCHWARTZ, Bernard L.
Vs Carter anti-inflatn plan 3-15, 202F1
SCHWARTZ, Bruce
Canterbury Tales opens 2-12, 136A3
SCHWARTZ, George X.
Indicted in Abscam probe 5-22, 402A3
Convicted 9-16, 740B2
Conviction dismissed 11-26, 919A2
SCHWARTZ, Sidney
Sees NYC revenue surplus 2-19, 186B3
SCHWARY, Ronald L.
Ordinary People released 9-19, 836D3
SCHWEIGERT, Jack
Wins Honolulu mayoral primary 9-20, 745E1
SCHWEIKER, Sen. Richard S. (R, Pa.)
GOP retains seat 11-4, 846A1, 848D3
Named Health secy 12-11, 935C1
SCHWINDEN, Lt. Gov. Ted (D, Mont.)
Wins primary for gov 6-3, 439G2
Elected gov 11-4, 845G2, 847D1, 851G3
SCHWINGER, Julian Seymour
Cuts Sovt ties re dissidents 4-16, 326B3
SCHYGULLA, Hanna
Wrong Move released 1-25, 216G3
SCIARRA, John
NFL punt return ldr 1-5, 8F3
SCIENCE, American Association for the Advancement of (AAAS)
Dinosaur extinctn theory rptd 1-1, 415F1
Maternity smoking, drinking risks rptd 1-4, 23D3
Stuttering, genetics link rptd 1-5, 63C3
New drug rptd effective vs heroin addictn 2-2, 160A2

SCIENCE & Technology
Major research dvpts rptd 1-1—5-4, 415D1-416B2
US bars tech equipmt to USSR for Afghan invasn 1-4, 1D1; 1-9, 9F1
Australia suspends Sovt exchngs re Afghan invasn 1-9, 9E2
Canada, Portugal end high-tech exports to USSR 1-11, 1-15, 28A2
US rejects USSR tech export licenses 1-11, 28C2
Japan, Australia discuss 1-16, 78B2
USSR warned re Sakharov exile 1-22—1-24; Tass rebuts 1-25, 85G3, 86G1
US defense posture rptd 1-25, 66B2
Carter budget proposals 1-28, 69D3, 71C3; table 70F1
Illegal US sales to USSR probed 2-14, 135B1
Intl protests over Sakharov grow 2-18, 2-24, 881F2-A3
Japan-US USSR steel deal delayed 2-19, 235F3
USSR scientists barred from 2 US confs 2-22, 135D1
OPEC links supply guarantees, tech transfers 2-22, 142G1

1976

SCIENCE News (magazine)
WMO urges limited SST fleet 1-17, 104A3
SCIENTIFIC American (magazine)
Jerome Snyder dies 5-2, 524F3
SCIENTIFIC Unions, International Council of
DNA research com formed; conv cited 10-14, 891D3
SCIENTISTS, Union of Concerned
Pollard to become DC rep 2-9, 115E1
NRC suit vs S Africa A-deal rptd 5-30, 388F1
SCOLA, Ettore
Wins Cannes film award 5-28, 460F1
SCORSESE, Martin
Wins Cannes film award 5-28, 460F1
SCOTIA Coal Co.—*See BLUE Diamond Coal*
SCOTLAND—*See GREAT Britain*
SCOTT, Ed
Loses US House race 11-2, 824E1
SCOTT Jr., Sen. Hugh D(oggett) (R, Pa.)
McCloy rpt on Gulf illegal paymts cites; US probes 2-4, 133E3
Lauds State of Union address 1-19, 39G3
Primary vote results 4-27, 305A1
Backs Ford 5-11, 343F1
Names intellignc com members 5-20, 377D1
Vs Treen platform amendmt 8-13, 582G3
Cited in Dole biog sketch 614G2
Campaign gift to 3 sens rptd 8-30, 980E1
IRS notice rptd sent 9-12, 980D1, F1
Sen com ends Gulf gifts probe 9-15, 980A1
Heinz wins seat 11-2, 820C1, 821A3
SCOTT, J. Donald
Sentenced 11-30, 921A3
SCOTT Jr., John (Jack)
Cited in Hearst trial 2-9, 114F2, A3
SCOTT, Louis
Arrested 11-3, 972D1
SCOTT, Norman
Thorpe denies homosexual ties 1-29, '71 probe rptd 2-6, 174C2
S Africa implicated in Thorpe scandal 3-9—3-13, 252E2-A3
Thorpe releases letters 5-9, resigns 5-10, 351A1
Thorpe 'coverup' detailed 5-12; libel suit dropped 5-14, 364G3
SCOTT, Sen. William L. (R, Va.)
Scores detente resolutn 3-22, 245G3
Hugh Scott campaign gift rptd 8-30, 980E1
SCOTT, Sir Winston
Dies 8-9, 892E3
SCOTT Paper Co.
Vows no boycott compliance 3-18, 747B2
SCOTTSBORO, Ala.—*See ALABAMA*
SCOTTSDALE, Ariz.—*See ARIZONA*
SCOUNDREL Time (book)
On best-seller list 12-5, 972B2

1977

SCIENCE and Technology Policy, Office of—*See under U.S. GOVERNMENT*
SCIENTIFIC American (magazine)
US-Sovt strategic weapons compared 751C3
SCIENTIFIC Control Corp.
Merrill Lynch paymt ordrd 10-11, 859G2
SCIENTISTS, Federation of American
US wheat productn cuts opposed 8-29, 666D3
SCIENTISTS, Union of Concerned
A-plant closings asked 11-5, Mich unit shut 11-18, 917D1, B2
SCIENTOLOGY, Church of
FBI raids offices 7-8, raids ruled illegal 7-27; sues FBI 7-18, 8-15, 628A2
Min jailed for contempt 7-29, freed 9-14, 940D2
FBI search warrant ruled valid 12-1, use of documts blocked 12-8, 940G1, F2
SCOTIA Coal Co.—*See BLUE Diamond Coal*
SCOTLAND—*See GREAT Britain*
SCOTT, Charlie
Traded to Lakers 12-27, 1021A1
SCOTT, Most Rev. Edward
On euthanasia rpt 8-17, 732C2
SCOTT, George
NL wins All-Star Game 7-19, 567F2
AL batting ldr 10-2, 926G3
SCOTT Jr., Hugh D(oggett)
Baker elected minority ldr 1-4, 6F1
SCOTT, Hugh L.
Seadock project threatened 7-12, 559D2
Doubts Seadock future 7-26, 724F3
SCOTT, Norman
Murder plot alleged 10-19, Thorpe denies link 10-27, 883G1
SCOTT, Sen. William (R, Va.)
Votes vs Young 1-26, 52C3
Argentina visit rptd 8-30, 670C2
SCOTTISH Aviation
Nationalized 4-29, 526B3
SCOTTSBORO, Ala.—*See ALABAMA*

1978

Obituaries
Davis, Francis 4-16, 356E2
Keldysh, Mstislav V 6-24, 540A3
Poulter, Thomas C 6-14, 540E3
SCIENCE and Technology Policy, Office of—*See under U.S. GOVERNMENT*
SCIENTIFIC and Technical Committee—*See under UNITED Nations*
SCIENTISTS, Federation of American
E Coast booms linked to Concorde 3-15, 187G1
SCIENTISTS, Union of Concerned
PI A-plant safety questnd 2-14, 134E3
NRC A-plant ratings released, safety progrm scored 11-25, 940C3, E3
A-reactor safety test scored 12-10, 961A2
SCIENTISTS' Institute for Public Information
Power plant size, efficiency study rptd 6-2, 408D3
SCIENTOLOGY, Church of
Founder sentenced, fined 2-14, 232G3
FBI search warrant ruling review denied by Sup Ct 3-20, 205D3
Marks deprogramming suit rptd 4-7, 295D3
FBI '77 LA raids upheld 7-6, 554E1
11 indicted, spy effort chrgd 8-15, 644B3
SCM Corp.
Xerox trust suit set back 6-7, 510E1-C2
Xerox trust verdicts 7-10, 7-11; damages set 8-9, 8-16, 664G2
Xerox award set aside 12-29, 1005D2
SCOLA, Ettore
Viva Italia released 7-9, 970C3
SCOOT, Oz
Mahalia opens 6-5, 887B2
SCORSESE, Martin
Last Waltz released 4-25, 619G2 ★
SCOTLAND—*See GREAT Britain*
SCOTT, Allen
Joseph Andrews released 4-13, 619F2
SCOTT, Charlie
Traded to Nuggets 6-26, 656B1
SCOTT, Freddie
Traded to Lions 5-1, 336B2
SCOTT, George C.
Movie, Movie released 11-22, 970C2
SCOTT, Harold
Mighty Gents opens 4-16, 760E2
SCOTT, Hugh
Gulf illegal paymt rptd 6-2, 449E1
SCOTT, James
NFL '77 pass receiving ldr 1-1, 56F2
SCOTT, Norman
Thorpe, 3 others arrested in murder plot 8-4, 614A2
Thorpe faces 2d murder chrg 9-2, 688C2
Thorpe pretrial hearings 11-20—12-4; testifies 11-29, 12-4, 945A1-C2
Thorpe trial ordered 12-13, 987D3
SCOTT, Oz
Nongogo opens 12-3, 1031F2
SCOTT, Paul
Dies 3-1, 252E3
SCOTT, Ridley
Duellists released 1-14, 619F1
SCOTT, Sen. William L. (R, Va.)
Says pub vs Canal pacts 2-8, 120F1
Votes vs Panama Canal neutrality pact 3-16, 177G2
Votes vs 2d Canal pact 4-18, 273B1
Vs warrantless tap curbs 4-20, 306G1
Scores Sen com rpt on Marston 5-4, 343B1
Not standing for reelectn 6-13, 467A2
Endangered Species Act revised 7-19, 551F2
ERA amendmts defeated 10-3, 788C1
SCOTT, Wilton E.
To retire as Tenneco chrmn 6-30, 809C1
SCOTTI, Vincenzo
Named Italy labor min 3-11, 191C1
SCOTT v. U.S.
Fed tap power broadened by Sup Ct 5-15, 387E2

1979

Obituaries
Blodgett, Katharine 10-12, 860B2
Sugiura, Kanematsu 10-21, 860F3
SCIENTIFIC American (magazine)
US, USSR strategic weapons compared 338G3
SCIENTIFIC Inc.
US sues re NJ pollutn 2-7, 130B1
Earthline Corp.—*See EARTHLINE Corp.*
SCIENTISTS, Federation of American
MX 'racetrack' deployment plan scored 9-7, 678B1
SCIENTISTS, Union of Concerned—*See UNION of Concerned Scientists*
SCIENTISTS for Orlov and Scharansky (SOS)
Sovt links cut 3-1, 172B2
SCIENTOLOGY, Church of
'50s CIA files made public, 'disposal' problems detailed 1-22, 55G1-C2
CIA considered ESP spies in '50s 3-11, 208E2
'76 documts seizure upheld by Sup Ct 5-14, 383A3
Titchbourne wins fraud suit 8-15, 640E2
Army '64 hallucinogen test rptd 9-24, 727F1
8 convicted in spy case 10-26, 839B2
CIA NYC biological tests chrgd 12-3, 946A1
9 sentenced 12-6–12-7, 1000B1
SCOON, Paul
Grenada affirms Commonwealth ties 3-25, 236F3
SCOPOLIMINE (Hyoscine)—*See MEDICINE–Drugs*
SCOTIA Coal Co.—*See BLUE Diamond Coal*
SCOTLAND—*See GREAT Britain*
SCOTT, Aubrey
Right-to-counsel doctrine clarified by Sup Ct 3-5, 185A2
SCOTT, David
Feinstein elected mayor 12-11, 946F3
SCOTT, Doug
Named Australia trade min 12-8, 948E1
SCOTT, George
Traded to Royals, signing with Yankees cited 6-14, 1002A3
SCOTT, George C.
Hardcore released 2-8, 174F2
SCOTT, Jake
NFL '78 interceptn ldr 1-6, 80G1
SCOTT, Jonathan
W Ger firm to buy A&P share 1-16, 53E3
SCOTT, Michael
One Man released 7-27, 820E2
SCOTT, Norman
Thorpe acquitted 6-22, 485D3-486C1
SCOTT, Oz
Spell #7 opens 7-15, 712E2
SCOTT, Ridley
Alien released 5-24, 528A1
SCOTT, Rodney
NL stolen base ldr 9-30, 955F2
SCOTT, Tom
Edmonton wins Grey Cup 11-25, 1001G1
SCOTT, Wilfred
Fishing dispute setld 6-7, 465A1
SCOTT, William J.
Indicted re tax evasn 4-9, 291B3
SCOTTO, Anthony M.
Indicted 1-17, 87G2-C3
Convicted 11-15, 890A1
SCOTTO, Marion
Husband, cousin indicted 1-17, 87C3
SCOTT Paper Co.
Paper workers strike ends 2-20, 345A3
Rolls back prices 4-16, 385G1
SCOTT v. Illinois
Right-to-counsel doctrine clarified by Sup Ct 3-5, 185A2

1980

EC warns US vs trade war 2-28, 204F2
US tightens Sovt tech export curbs 3-18, 204E3
Sovt bloc barter deal rise cited 4-1, 285C3
USSR Jews hold conf 4-13—4-15, 326D2
US scientists seek Sovt boycott 4-16, 326A3
US-Greek pact signed 4-22, 352E2
US, Japan sign research pact 5-1, 341C1
Australia-China pact signed 5-7—5-11, 338A1
Research dvpts rptd 5-10—9-18, 715E1-716A3
Argentina-Brazil agrmts signed 5-15—5-17, 405D2
Mex-W Ger cooperatn pacts renewed 5-21, 409F2
Eur cos push tech sales to USSR 5-22, 431A1
US OKs China tech sales 5-29, 397D3
Unpatented key ingredient monopolies backed by Sup Ct 6-27, 511C2
USSR, W Ger sign tech pact 7-1, 489D2
Carter offers econ renewal plan 8-28, 663C2
US scientific literacy lag rptd 10-22, 990C1
Islamic econ conf 11-4—11-6, 865C1
Pope issues social justice encyclical 12-2, 970A1
Natl Science Foundatn authrzn clears Cong 12-2, 953G2; signed 12-12, 982B1
Beagle Channel accord proposed 12-12, 978E3
Obituaries
Bullard, Edward 4-3, 360C1
Rappaport, Paul 4-21, 360A3
SCIENTIFIC Inc.
NJ dump suit partly setld 1-30, 93G3
Earthline Corp.—*See EARTHLINE Corp.*
SCIENTISTS, Union of Concerned—*See UNION of Concerned Scientists*
SCIENTOLOGY, Church of
2 sentenced 12-19, 997B3
SCIORTINO, Samuel Orlando
LA judge bribe plot rptd 2-8, 112B1
SCM Corp.
Japan typewriter duties set 4-22, 368C1
Proxy contest rptd defeated 11-24, 985C3
SCOPES, John T. (d. 1970)
Kerr dies 6-27, 528A2
SCORSESE, Martin
Raging Bull released 11-14, 972G3
SCOTT, Allan
Awakening released 10-31, 972C3
SCOTT, Douglas
Sinclair takes over Cabt post 8-18, 650E2
SCOTT, Freddie
NFL '79 receiving ldr 1-5, 8F2
SCOTT, George C.
Changeling released 3-28, 416E2
Tricks of the Trade opens 11-16, 892G3
Formula released 12-19, 1003A2
SCOTT, James
Robbery convictn appeal refused 1-14, 320F3
SCOTT, Jonathan L.
Resigns as A&P chrmn 4-29, 456D2
SCOTT, Michael
Happy New Year opens 4-27, 392A3
SCOTT, Peter
In Panda-finding mission 5-12, 398A2
SCOTT, Rodney
NL batting, stolen base ldr 10-6, 926E2, F2
SCOTT, Steve
In US Olympic trials 6-29, 891B2
SCOTT, Tom
Edmonton wins Grey Cup; ties CFL receiving mark 11-23, 999C2
SCOTT, W. Eugene
FCC revokes Faith Center TV license 10-10, 907C1
SCOTT, William J.
Loses Ill Sen primary 3-18, 206D3
Convicted of tax evasn 3-19, 215A3
Sentenced 7-29, 654F2
SCOTTI, Vincenzo
Italy European affairs min 4-4, 275F3
SCOTTO, Anthony M.
Sentenced 1-22, 64D2
7 ILA offcls sentenced 5-20, 927A3
SCOTT Paper Co.
Fine paper trust suit setld 9-29; acquittal rptd in 2d suit 12-3, 917A2, C2

1976

SCOWCROFT, Lt. Gen. Brent
Named to payoff probe 3-21, 262F2
Nixon rpts on China trip 3-22, 215B1
At emergency mtg on Leb 6-16, 425C2
On Ford E Eur remark 10-7, 762E3
SCRANTON, Pa.—*See PENNSYLVANIA*
SCRANTON, William W(arren)
Named US amb to UN 2-25, 150C1; confrmd 3-3, 186C2
Vs Israel occupatn policy 3-23, vetoes UN resolutn 3-25, 211A2 ★
Israel scores occupatn policy speech 3-26, 227A3
Clarifies Angola stand 3-26; scores Cuba, Sovt interventn 3-31, 228C2
Backs Cncl role in Leb 3-30, 226C2
Defends Zionism in ECOSOC debate 4-28, 320G2
Vs UN stand on Israel occupatn policy, warns Israel on setlmts 5-26; denies feud 5-27, 406D3 ★
Backs Rhodesia majority rule 7-9, 523B1
Lauds Israel Uganda raid 7-12, 516D1
Bids Pa delegates back Ford 7-29, 550A3
Rptd Ford vp prospect 8-10, 584D1
On plan to veto Viet UN membership 9-13, 682E1
For Butz resignation 10-3, 744C2
On S Africa arms ban veto 10-19, 781D3 ★
Vetoes Viet UN membership 11-15, 862C3
Abstains on Angola UN entry; vs Cuba role 11-22, 879D1
Vs UN Palestine panel rpt 11-23, 878B3
Vs Assemb resolutns on Geneva conf 12-9, 914E1
Reaffirms peace efforts in Mideast, Africa 12-22, 955B1
SCRIPPS-Howard Newspapers
Carter meets editors 8-4, 564E3
SCRIVENER, Christiane
French consumers state secy 1-12, 49D2
SCUDDER, Dr. John
Dies 12-6, 1015F2
SCULPTURE—*See PAINTING & Sculpture*
SDRs (Special Drawing Rights)—*See IMF*
SDS—*See STUDENTS for a Democratic Society*
SEABROOK, N.H.—*See NEW Hampshire*
SEADOCK Inc.
Coleman to OK superport 12-17, 992E1
SEAFARERS International Union of North American (AFL-CIO)
Ford funds probe rptd 9-25, 722F3
LBJ, Nixon campaign donatns cited 9-25, 723A1
Ford cleared 10-14, 761E2
SEAGA, Edward
Rptdly gains US allies re Cuba denunciatn 5-14, 522B2
On state of emergency 6-23, 522E1
Scores detentns 12-15, 965C3
SEAGRAM Co. Ltd.
Seagram & Son, Inc., Joseph E.
Bronfman cosponsors Carter mtg 7-22, 550G3
Bronfman case verdict 12-10, 952B3
SEA-Land Service Inc.—*See under REYNOLDS Industries*
SEALS—*See WILDLIFE*
SEAMANS Jr., Robert C.
OKs fast breeder dvpt 1-2, 115F2
Stresses conservatn efforts 4-19, 284F3
Scores GAO synfuel rpt 8-24, 649D2
SEARLE & Co., G. D.
Rpts forgn payoffs 1-9, 2-20, 361D3
Vows no boycott compliance 3-18, 747B2
SEC lists paymts 5-12, 729A1
SEARS 4th, John P.
Forecasts win for Reagan 6-16, 450F3
Claims Reagan majority 7-19, 7-20, 531G2, G3
On Schweiker choice 7-27, 550A1
Claims Reagan delegate gains 8-2, 564A2
Asks pre-ballot vp selectn 8-9, 582C1
Vs Buckley candidacy 8-11, 584B3
Backs platform com planks 8-13, 582F2
Rpts Reagan delegate count 8-13, 583C2
Denies delegate bribe chrgs 8-16, 616E1
On Reagan campaign 8-18, 615A3
GOP conv vp vote table 8-19, 599F3
SEARS Roebuck & Co.
Allstate Insurance Co.
'74 zero tax paymt rptd 10-2, 847G1
On air bag ruling 12-6, 921F1
SEATO—*See SOUTHEAST Asia Treaty Organization*
SEATTLE, Wash.—*See WASHINGTON*
SEATTLE Times, The (newspaper)
Ariz crime probed 10-2, 849D2
SEAVER, Tom
NL wins All-Star game 7-13, 544B2
NL pitching ldr 10-4, 796A1
SEBA, Yousef el-
Quits Cabt to assume press post 3-28, 333F1
SEBELIUS, Rep. Keith G. (R, Kan.)
Reelected 11-2, 829D3
SEBILLEAU, Pierre
Dies 11-6, 910G1
SEBURGO Silva, Rear Adm. Sergio
Chile mil staff chief 1-6, 47D1
SECOMSKI, Kazimierz
Named deputy min 12-2, 926C3
SECONDE, Reginald
Backs MD re Chile torture chrg 1-1, 8D2

1977

SCRANTON, William W.
Intell Oversight Bd member 5-5, 462F2
US confrms PLO mtg, denies missn role 7-19, 550C2
PLO contact rptd 7-20, 550A2
SCRIPPS Co., The E. W.
Scripps-Howard Broadcasting Co.
Zacchini suit vs WEWS-TV OKd 6-28, 557G3
SCRIPPS-Howard Broadcasting Co.—*See under SCRIPPS Co.*
SCULLY, Todd
Sets 2-mile walk mark 2-25, 602E3
SCULPTURE—*See PAINTING & Sculpture*
SDRs (Special Drawing Rights)—*See IMF*
SEABED Issue—*See OCEANS & Oceanography*
SEABOARD Allied Milling Corp.
Calif weight-labeling rules curbed 3-29, 277B1
'76 Fortune 500 list drops 341D1
SEABORN, Blair
Viet missn cover-up rptd 1-14, 97C3
SEABROOK, N.H.—*See NEW Hampshire*
SEACOAST Products, Inc.
US fishing laws backed 5-23, 444A2
SEADOCK Inc.
3 firms withdraw 7-12, 559A2
SEAFARER, Project
Cong authorizes funds 7-14, 576B1
Mich site backed 12-15, local oppositn rptd 12-16, 977D3-978B1
SEAGA, Edward
Replacement seen 3-25, 258B1
SEAGRAM Co. Ltd.
Seagram & Son, Inc., Joseph E.
2 in Bronfman case sentncd 1-6, 103C1
Admits dubious paymts 10-14, 818B2
SEA-Land Service Inc.—*See under REYNOLDS Industries*
SEALS—*See WILDLIFE*
SEARCH for Noah's Ark (film)
Top-grossing film 2-2, 120D3
SEARCH & Seizure—*See PRIVACY*
SEARLE, Daniel D.
Elected chrmn 4-17, 396G3
SEARLE & Co., G. D.
Rumsfeld elected pres, Searle chrmn 4-17, 396G3
SEARS Roebuck & Co.
TV violence curbs ordrd 2-15, 157F3
SEAT Belts—*See AUTOMOBILES—Safety Issues*
SEATTLE, Wash.—*See WASHINGTON*
SEATTLE Slew (race horse)
Wins Triple Crown 6-11, NYS ownership probe rptd 6-16, 490G3
Named top horse 12-13, 970F3, G3
SEATO—*See SOUTHEAST Asia Treaty Organization*
SEAVER, Tom
Sets strikeout mark 6-7, traded to Reds 6-15, 644B2
NL wins All-Star Game 7-19, 567D2
NL pitching ldr 10-2, 926E3
SEAWELL, William T.
On US-UK air svc pact 6-22, 500D2
Pan Am route scores Carter on 12-21, 1006E2
SEBULIBA, Mark
Death rptd 8-17, 641A2
SEC—*See U.S. GOVERNMENT—SECURITIES & Exchange Commission*
SECOND International Sakharov Hearings
Westn attys plan pub trials 11-28, 955B2

1978

SCOVILLE Jr., Herbert
MAP missile plan oppositn rptd 9-23, 738A1
SCOWEN, Reed
Wins Quebec by-electn 7-5, 514G2
SCREEN Writers Guild
Arthur Sheekman dies 1-12, 96E3
SCRIPPS Clinic and Research Foundation (La Jolla, Calif.)
Allergy suppressant rptd 3-11, 334D2
SCRUGGS Jr., James L.
Loses US House electn 11-7, 849C3
SCRUPLES (book)
On best-seller list 4-2, 272B3; 4-30, 356G1; 6-4, 460B3; 8-6, 620A2; 9-4, 708B1
SCULLY, Todd
Sets 20-kilomtr walk mark 6-8—6-10, 600C3
SCULPTURE—*See PAINTING & Sculpture*
SDRs (Special Drawing Rights)—*See IMF*
SEABED Issue—*See OCEANS*
SEABOARD Coast Line Industries Inc.
Chessie merger set 11-16, 897A1
SEABOARD Coast Line Industries Inc.
Louisville & Nashville Railroad Co.
Tenn derailmt 2-23, propane blast 2-24; US prelim probe rptd 3-6, 196C1
SEABROOK, N.H.—*See under NEW Hampshire*
SEABROOK Natural Guard
A-plant halt hailed 6-30, 529C3
SEACOAST Antipollution League
NH A-plant site review ordrd 4-28, 347B1
SEADER, Richard
Diary of Anne Frank revived 12-18, 1031D1
SEAFARERS' International Union (AFL-CIO)
Hall on '77 top-paid labor ldrs list 5-15, 365G1
SEAGRAM Co. Ltd.
Seagram & Son, Inc., Joseph E.
SEC sues re paymts, case setld 9-8, 961E3
SEA Gypsies, The (film)
Released 4-26, 619E3
SEA-Land Service Inc.
Pleads guilty on rebates, fined 4-11, 449E2
FMC rebate case setlmt cited 9-18, 752F3
SEALS—*See WILDLIFE*
SEAMAN, Kim
Traded to Cardinals 12-5, 1026C1
SEAMANS Jr., Robert C.
Named MIT dean 4-26, 420D1
SEAR, Judge Morey L.
Fines McDermott 2-22, 142E2
SEARCH & Seizure—*See PRIVACY*
SEARLE, John
Dies 1-21, 96E3
SEARLE & Co., G. D.
Ex-pres Searle dies 1-21, 96E3
SEARLS, Hank
Jaws 2 on best-seller list 6-4, 460C3; 7-2, 579D3; 8-6, 620C2
SEARS Roebuck & Co.
In Dow Jones indl avg 66F2
TV ads withdrawn, PTA advisory cncl set 5-12, 599B3
Cushman dies 6-12, 540E2
Roberts wins patent suit 10-2, 844B2
Oreck trust case refused by Sup Ct 10-30, 832A3
Canada merger plan blocked 12-18, 986B1
SEARS Roebuck & Co. v. San Diego County District Council of Carpenters
Unions held subject to trespass laws by Sup Ct 5-15, 387B2
SEATRAIN Lines Inc.
Trinidad joint shipping co set 1-13, 100A3
States curbed on oil tanker regulatn 3-6, 161G3
Indicted 3-8, pleads guilty 3-16, 184B3
FMC rebate chrgs setld for $2½ mln 9-18, 752D3
Fined 10-23, 876B3
SEATTLE, Wash.—*See WASHINGTON*
SEATTLE Slew (race horse)
Syndicated as stallion 2-18, 539C3
Affirmed wins Triple Crown 6-10, 538G3, 539F1
Wins Marlboro Cup 9-16, 1028D1
Named top older male horse 12-12, 1028C1
SEAVER, Tom
Pitches no-hitter 6-16, 559G3
NL pitching ldr 10-2, 928G2
SEAWITCH (book)
On best-seller list 8-6, 620C2
SEBAI, Youssef el-
Slain 2-18, funeral 2-19, 117C1, 118C2
Egypt curbs Palestinians 2-27, 138C1
Sadat on PLO raid vs Israel 3-14, 176C1
Slayers sentncd to death 4-4, 236E3
Egypt terror group rptd smashed 4-24, 300E2
PLO ties Iraq, Nidal to death 7-4, 546G3
Slayers spared 11-14, 870G1
SEBELIUS, Rep. Keith G. (R, Kan.)
Reelected 11-7, 850D4
SEC—*See U.S. GOVERNMENT—SECURITIES & Exchange Commission*
SECOND Generation (book)
On best-seller list 10-9, 800A3; 11-6, 887F3
SECOND Ring of Power, The (book)
On best-seller list 2-5, 116C3; 3-5, 195E3

1979

SCOWEN, Reed
On Quebec cos exit 9-5, 750D1
SCRANTON 3rd, Lt. Gov. William
On 3 Mile I A-accident 3-28, 242F1
SCRANTON, William Warren
Rejects Mideast amb post 296A1
Backs IBM case judge's ouster 7-19, 610B3
SCREEN King (race horse)
3d in Preakness 5-19, 448G2
SCRIBA, N.Y.—*See NEW York State*
SCRIPPS Clinic and Research Foundation (La Jolla, Calif.)
Benzaldehyde cancer research rptd 1-28, 139D1
SCRIPPS Co., The E. W.
UPI press partnership sale rptd 10-4, 859G2
SCRIVER, Peter
Linked to Salameh slaying 1-24, 69D2
SCRUGGS, Earl
Lester Flatt dies 5-11, 432E2
SCRUPLES (book)
On best-seller list 6-3, 432C2; 7-1, 548C3; 8-5, 620D3
Paperback rights sold for record sum 9-12, 755F3
SCULPTURE—*See PAINTING & Sculpture*
SCYPION, Wilford
KOs Classen 11-23, Classen dies 11-28, 1004E3
SDRs (special drawing rights)—*See IMF*
SEABOARD Coast Line Industries Inc.
Shareholders back Chessie merger 2-13, 205E3
ICC clears of trust chrgs 2-22, 205G3
RR extends Auto-Train pact 8-24, 726A2
Louisville & Nashville Railroad Co.
Tenn-Tombigbee projct upheld 3-13, 188B3
Train derails near Crestview (Fla), residents evacuate 4-8, 472E3
SEABOARD World Airlines Inc.
Flying Tiger merger set 7-18, 579D1
Justice Dept asks Flying Tiger merger ban 10-2, shareholders OK deal 10-19, 830B2
SEABROOK, N.H.—*See NEW Hampshire*
SEADRIFT, Tex.—*See TEXAS*
SEAFARERS' International Union (AFL-CIO)
Hall backs Carter reelectn 7-30, 593D3
SEAGA, Edward
Denies anti-govt coup chrg 1-10, 21E2
SEAGRAM Co.
Seagram & Sons Inc., Joseph E.
Bribery plea set 9-27, 809E3
SEA-Land Service Inc. (of Reynolds Industries)
Indicted re price fixing 6-1, 423D2; pleads no contest, fined 6-8, 442B2
SEA-Launched Cruise Missile (SCLM)—*See ARMAMENTS—Missiles*
SEA Quest International
Concepcion find rptd 1-1, 24G1
SEARCH for the Manchurian Candidate, The (book)
Publicatn cited 1-29, 96B1
SEARS, John P.
Nofziger resigns, clash cited 8-28, 661F3
Campaign staff chngs cited 11-14, 982D2
SEARS Roebuck & Co.
In Dow Jones indl avg 72F1
US sued over bias laws 1-24, 92B1
On wage-price compliance 2-6, 128D1
Thompson settles FTC dishwasher ad chrg 4-15, 308F3
Fed contract work ended 4-24, 366A1
Price rollback rptd 4-27, catalogue price cuts set 4-30, 363C1
Bias suit vs US dismissed 5-15, 365A3
Roberts profits paymt ordrd 5-31, 466C2
Ex-chrmn Rosenwald dies 6-24, 508E3
TV set repair recall set 8-31, 903D1
Dishwasher ads faulted by FTC 10-16, 903A2
US files job-bias suits 10-22, 885C3
SEASON To Unravel, A (play)
Opens 1-25, 292G2
SEATON, George
Dies 7-28, 588D3
SEATRAIN Lines Inc.
5 Teamsters indicted 2-22, 155F3
Indicted re price fixing 6-1, 423D2; pleads no contest, fined 6-8, 442B2
Provenzano, 3 others sentenced 7-10, 548E1
SEATTLE, Wash.—*See WASHINGTON*
SEBERG, Jean
Found dead 9-8, FBI admits '70 slander 9-14, 704G3
SEC—*See U.S. GOVERNMENT—SECURITIES & Exchange Commission*
SECOBARBITAL (Seconal)—*See MEDICINE—Drugs*
SECOND Generation (book)
On best-seller list 1-7, 80A3; 10-14, 800C3; 11-4, 892D3
SECOND Thoughts (play)
Opens 5-4, 712C2

1980

SCREEN Actors Guild
TV, film actors strike 7-21, 684A3
TV, film actors end strike 10-23, 805C3
SCRIPPS Co., The E.W.
UPI financing plan fails 1-31, 120C1
Cleveland Press sold 10-31, 1003E3
SCUDELLARI, R. D.
Architect's Eye wins Amer Book Award 5-1, 692C2
SCULPTURE—*See PAINTING & Sculpture*
SDRs (special drawing rights)—*See INTERNATIONAL Monetary Fund (IMF)*
SEABOARD Coast Line Industries Inc.
NC train wreck 4-2, 391G3
Chessie merger set 9-24, 745A3
Auto-Train svc cut rejected 9-26, 958B3
SEABORD World Airlines Inc.
CAB OKs Flying Tiger merger 5-8, 516F1-A2
SEABROOK—*See NEW Hampshire*
SEAFARERS' International Union (AFL-CIO)
Hall dies 6-22, 526G1
SEAGA, Edward Phillip George (Jamaican prime minister)
Jamaican econ woes detailed 4-7, 276D1
5 slain at party fund-raiser 4-20, 336C1
Role in coup attempt denied 6-23, 498G3
Condemns violence 7-18, 579A2
Manley sets Oct 30 electn 10-5, 791F3
Elected 10-30, sworn 11-1: facts on 854B1
SEAGRAM Co. Ltd., The
Sun bid accepted for Tex Pacific 4-11, 385B2
Sun, Tex Pacific merger completed 9-12, 985A1
Paul Masson Vineyards
Winery strike ends 9-22, 747B3
SEA Gull, The (play)
Opens 11-11, 892E3
SEALS, Judge Woodrow
Orders Tex aliens schooling 7-21, 576A2
SEARLE & Co., G. D.
Interferon productn rptd up 3-5, 317C3
SEARS, John P.
Reagan fires as campaign chief 2-26; scores 2-28, 143B1, F1-C2
Ford consults 3-7, 207E1
SEARS Roebuck & Co.
In Dow Jones indl avg 76F1
Indicted on Japan TV rebates 2-26, 251G3
Brennan to replace Swift as pres 3-12, 225B1
Credit restrictions rptd 3-27, 222G2
USOC funds linked to Olympics boycott 4-3, 260A1
Japan TV dumping case setld 4-28, ct blocks 5-9, 368D1
Appliance performance claim order rptd 5-19, 703D2
Ala bias suit dropped 5-22, 485D1
FRB credit controls end hailed 7-3, 513C2
Telling named pres 10-7; exec chngs rptd 11-19, 959F2
SEATRAIN Lines Inc.
Disclosure suit settled 2-8, 558B1
Oil tanker subsidies repaymt backed by Sup Ct 2-20, 170G2
SEATRAIN Shipbuilding Corp. v. Shell Oil Co.
Case decided by Sup Ct 2-20, 170F2
SEATTLE—*See WASHINGTON (state)*
SEATTLE (Wash.) University
Faculty sex-bias Title IX case accepted by Sup Ct 12-1, 918C2
SEAWOLF (U.S. nuclear submarine)
Reactor rptd lost 6-17, 458F2
SEBALD, William J.
Dies 8-10, 676G2
SEBASTIAN, John
Dies 8-18, 676A3
SEBASTIANI, August
Dies 2-16, 176C3
SEBE, Lennox
Ciskei votes on statehood 12-4; victory rptd 12-17, 996A1
SEBERG, Jean (1938-79)
FBI probe rptd extensive 1-9, 55C1
Ex-husband kills self 12-2, 1004G1
SEC (Securities & Exchange Commission)—*See under U.S. GOVERNMENT*
SECORD, Al
Fined over NYC brawl 1-25, 198C3

1976

SECRET Army Organization
Newspaper rpts FBI backing 1-11, 42A1
SECRET Service—*See TREASURY under U.S. GOVERNMENT*
SECRET Service (play)
Opens 4-12, 1014C3
SECURITIES—*See STOCKS, Bonds & Securities*
SECURITIES Dealers, National Association of
Disciplines 2 re boycott 8-11, 747C2

SECURITY, National—*See also specific related subjects (e.g., DISARMAMENT, WIRETAPPING); appropriate subheads under U.S. GOVERNMENT*
Carter Cabt unit set up 12-29, 978E2
Defense Issue—*See DEFENSE under U.S. GOVERNMENT*
Intelligence Investigations & Irregularities—*See also under U.S. GOVERNMENT, subheads CENTRAL Intelligence Agency and FEDERAL Bureau of Investigation*
Mansfield sees Cong action 1-19, 40A1
Muskie rebuts Ford 1-21, 40E2
House com urges reforms 2-10, disbands 2-11, 150E1-B2
Ford revises intell command, seeks ban on bugging, info leaks, human drug tests 2-17; issues exec order, legis 2-18, 127A1, G2
Kissinger scores attacks 3-11, 197E3
Kissinger censures aides on leaks 3-12, 198B2
Sen com issues rpt, chrgs US irregularities, urges tighter controls; text excerpts 4-26, 298D2-304E3
Intellignc costs estimated 4-27, 299C3
Sen com issues domestic rpt, sets reforms 4-28; text 324C3-331C1
Sen creates permanent intellignc com 5-19, 376D3
Mondale oversight com role cited 513G1
Ford, Carter debate 9-23, 703E1
Watergate—*See under 'W'*

SECURITY and Cooperation in Europe, Conference on—*See under EUROPE*
SECURITY National Bank—*See 'Chemical Bank' under CHEMICAL New York Corp.*
SECURITY New York State Corp.
Rptd on FRB 'problem' list 1-22, 111C3
SEC lists paymts 5-12, 729A1
SECURITY Pacific Corp.
Rptd on FRB 'problem' list 1-22, 111C3
Security Pacific National Bank (Los Angeles)
Rptd on comptroller's 'problem' list 1-26, 113D1
Arab boycott noncompliance rptd 10-24, 986G2
SEDILLO, Arthur
US probes Mex prisoner abuse 1-15, 75A2
SEDKI, Gamaleddin
Signs China MiG parts pact 4-21, 275F2
SEDMAK, Michael
Rptd in Yugoslav jail 7-26, 559G2
SEDYKH, Yuri
Wins Olympic medal 7-28, 576B1
SEELYE, Talcott W.
Succeeded as amb to Tunisia 3-3, 186B2
Named amb to Leb; meets with Kissinger, 4 ambs on crisis 6-22, 448G1
Recalled for consultatns 7-27, 546A1
Leb Arab Army protects 8-2, 578G2
SEGARD, Norbert
French posts state secy 1-12, 49C2
SEGER, Adolf
Wins Olympic medal 7-31, 576D3
SEIBERLING Jr., Rep. John F. (D, O.)
Reelected 11-2, 830A3
SEIBOLD, Werner
Wins Olympic medal 7-21, 575A2
SEIDMAN, L. William
Named to payoff probe 3-21, 262F2
SEC accuses firm 9-1, 984F2-B3
Mondale chrgs women work bias, denies 10-22, 803F3
SEIDMAN & Seidman
SEC accuses 9-1, 984F2-B3
SEIXAS, Dr. Frank B.
On new alcoholism test 12-3, 950E3
SEKOU Toure, Ahmed
Sees Castro, Neto, Cabral 3-15—3-16, 251E3
Benin, Togo re open border 3-27, 372D1
SEK Sam Ieth, Gen.
Cambodia asks Thais return 9-4, 734F3
SELA—*See LATIN American Economic System*
SELASSIE, Emperor Haile (Ethiopia) (1892-1975)
Ex-guard cmdr killed 2-15, 173A1
Rptd smothered 6-21, 457A3
SELF-Portrait in a Convex Mirror (book)
Wins Natl Book Award 4-19, 292D3
Ashbery wins Pulitzer 5-3, 352C3
SELSKY, Oleg
Paris paper links to CIA 1-13, 49E3
SELTMANN, Monica
Sets world swim mark 6-1—6-5, 424G3

1977

SECRETARIAT (race horse)
Missing mare rptd found by FBI 12-9, 971A2
SECRET Service—*See under U.S. GOVERNMENT—TREASURY*
SECURITIES—*See STOCKS, Bonds & Securities*
SECURITIES Dealers, National Association of
SEC bars optns trading 10-18, 859C3
SECURITIES Dealers Automated Quotations, National Association of—*See NASDAQ*
SECURITIES & Exchange Commission—*See under U.S. GOVERNMENT*
SECURITIES Industry Association
Off-bd trading curbs to remain 12-1, 1004C1
SEC scores natl mkt move delay, cites ITS 12-1, 1004E1

SECURITY, National—*See also specific related subjects (e.g., PRIVACY Issue, WIRETAPPING); also U.S. GOVERNMENT, subheads CENTRAL Intelligence Agency and FEDERAL Bureau of Investigation*
Leak penalties debated 3-9, 212C1
Sen panel expires 3-31, 251F3
Nixon OKs pres illegal acts 5-19, 405C3
FBI probes rptd down 6-6, 481A1
Cargo preference debated 7-11—9-9, 720E1
Visa curbs eased 8-17, 667D2

SECURITY and Cooperation in Europe, Commission on—*See under U.S. GOVERNMENT*
SECURITY & Cooperation in Europe, Conference on—*See under EUROPE*
SECURITY National Bank—*See CHEMICAL New York Corp.—Chemical Bank*
SEDATIVES—*See NARCOTICS & Dangerous Drugs*
SEGAL, Erich
Oliver's Story on best-seller list 4-3, 264F1; 5-1, 356B2; 6-4, 452G1; 7-3, 548D3
SEGARS, Joseph M.
S Africa restaurant bars 1-26, 67E2
2d envoy rptd barred 2-5, 101B1
SEGHI, Phil
Fires Robinson as Indian mgr 6-19, 644G1
SEGUY, Georges
Vows union actn 4-25, 328G3
SEIBERLICH, Rear Adm. Carl
Rpts '77 Navy desert rate 10-27, 858A2
SEIN Win, U
Replaced as Burma premier 3-29, 243B3
Rptd purged 10-8, 779D3
SEITZ, Peter
Backs NBA 11-man rosters 11-4, 870C1
SEKHAR, Chandra
Freed 1-12, 45C3
SELASSIE, Emperor Haile (Ethiopian head of state)(1892-1975)
Great-grandchildren escape Ethiopia 8-5, 649D1
Family arrives in US 9-24, 808E1
SELECTIVE Service System—*See under U.S. GOVERNMENT*
SELLERS, Jon
Bolles murder affidavit filed 1-15, 161G3
SELLIER Jr., Charles E.
Lincoln Conspiracy on best-seller list 11-6, 872F3
SELUZHKO, Gennadi
Hijacks jet 7-10, surrenders 7-12, 537F1
Sentenced 11-10, 988E2

1978

SECRETARIAT (race horse)
Affirmed wins Triple Crown 6-10, 539F1
SECRET Service—*See under U.S. GOVERNMENT—TREASURY*
SECRIST, Ronald
Dirks censured re Equity Funding 9-4, 681B2
SECURITIES—*See STOCKS, Bonds & Securities*
SECURITIES Dealers, National Association of (NASD)
'78 O-T-C mkt boom rptd 12-29, 1004D2
SECURITIES Dealers Automated Quotations, National Association of—*See NASDAQ*
SECURITIES & Exchange Commission (SEC)—*See under U.S. GOVERNMENT*
SECURITIES Investor Protection Corp.
Investor protectn bill signed 5-21, 386E2 ★

SECURITY, National—*See also specific related subjects (e.g., PRIVACY, WIRETAPPING); also U.S. GOVERNMENT, subheads CENTRAL Intelligence Agency and FEDERAL Bureau of Investigation*
Smith Act repeal clears Sen 1-30, 64C3
GOP sens score Carter 5-3, 342F2
Carter revises classificatn rules 6-29, 508B1
Carter complains of leaks to Cong ldrs 7-11, 524E2-F3
SECURITY & Cooperation in Europe, Commission on—*See under U.S. GOVERNMENT—CONGRESS*
SECURITY and Cooperation in Europe, Conference on—*See under EUROPE*
SECURITY Council—*See under UNITED Nations*
SECURITY Pacific Corp.
Chrmn Larkin to retire, Flamson named 10-17, 809F1
Security Pacific National Bank (Los Angeles)
$10.2 mln robbed by phone 10-25, computer consultant arrested 11-5, 991G3-992D1
SECURITY Pacific National Bank—*See SECURITY Pacific Corp.*
SECURITY Supporting Assistance—*See FOREIGN Aid (U.S.)*
SEC v. Sloan
SEC trading suspensns curbed by Sup Ct 5-15, 387C1
SEDITION—*See SECURITY, National*
SEDOV, Leonid Ivanovich
Admits A-satellite reentry error 2-4, 103D1
SEEGER, Pete
At Seabrook A-plant protest 6-24—6-26, 494E1
SEEVER, Frank
Do Lord Remember Me opens 4-4, 887G1
SEGAL, Erich
Oliver's Story on best-seller list 4-30, 356B2
Oliver's Story released 12-14, 1030C3
SEGAL, George
Great Chefs of Eur released 10-6, 970E3
SEGAL, Henry
Indicted 7-19, 598F3
SEGALL, Harry
Heaven Can Wait released 6-27, 619D2
SEGER, Bob
Stranger in Town on best-seller list 6-7, 460G3; 8-2, 620G1
SEGRETTI, Donald H.
Law practice suspensn ends 1-27, 172G2
SEGUIN, Pierre
6th Cross kidnaper alleged 11-2, 880C1
SEIBERLING Jr., Rep. John F. (D, O.)
Reelected 11-7, 851F3
SEIDENBERG, Jacob
Named to RR strike bd 9-28, 809C2
SEIFERT, Harold
Wins 4-man bobsled championship 2-12, 316G3
SEIFFERT, Wolfgang
Defects to W Ger 4-21, 333F1-C2
SEIGNIOUS Jr., Lt. Gen. George M. (ret.)
Named ACDA head 10-20, 804A2
SEITH, Alex R.
Wins US Sen primary in Ill 3-21, 207G1
SEKGAPANE, Norman Pagaman
Cervantes TKOs 8-26, 969E1
SELASSIE, Emperor Haile (Ethiopia) (1892-1975)
US issues rights rpt 2-9, 101E3
USSR role in Ethiopia rptd 'decisive' 12-2, 1016F2
SELBY, David
Rib Cage opens 5-28, 887G2
SELDES, Marian
Death Trap opens 2-26, 760A2
SELECTIVE Service System—*See under U.S. GOVERNMENT*
SELF-Portrait in Gray Hat (painting)
Slashed 4-25, 335F1
SELKE Trophy, Frank—*See HOCKEY—Awards*
SELLERS, Arlene
Silver Bears released 4-20, 619G3
SELLERS, Peter
Revenge of Pink Panther released 7-19, 970A3
SELMA, Ala.—*See ALABAMA*
SELTZER, David
Damien released 6-8, 619D1
SELWYN-Lloyd, Lord of Wirral (John Selwyn Brooke Lloyd)
Dies 5-17, 440E3

1979

SECRETARIAT (race horse)
Kentucky Derby legacy rptd 5-5, 448F2
Gen Assemb wins Travers Stakes 8-18, 876F3
SECRETARY of Public Welfare v. Institutionalized Juveniles
Case decided by Sup Ct 6-20, 515F3
SECRET Service—*See under U.S. GOVERNMENT-TREASURY*
SECURITIES—*See STOCKS, Bonds & Securities*
SECURITIES Dealers, National Association of (NASD)
O-T-C mkt explained 72C3
SEC asks options trading overhaul 2-15, freeze end seen 2-22, 348B3, 349E1
SECURITIES & Exchange Commission—*See under U.S. GOVERNMENT*

SECURITY, National—*See also specific related subjects (e.g., PRIVACY); also U.S. GOVERNMENT subheads CENTRAL Intelligence Agency and FEDERAL Bureau of Investigation*
Carter vs proposed balanced budget amendmt 1-17, 29D2
Carter State of Union Message 1-23, 47E2, 48D1
WWII secret file released 2-3, 2-6, 93F1
Trial secrets legis rptd planned 2-8, 88G1
H-bomb article blocked 3-9, 193C3; 3-26, 230A1
H-bomb documt security error admitted 6-8, article publicatn bar continues 6-15, 713C1, E1
H-bomb article hearing ordered by Sup Ct 7-2, 559A1
H-bomb letter published 9-16, 9-18, 713B1, B2; text, diagram 714D1-717E3
US ends effort to stop H-bomb article publicatn 9-17, 713A1
Baker voices concern 12-19, 983D1

SECURITY & Cooperation in Europe, Conference on—*See under EUROPE*
SECURITY Council—*See under UNITED Nations*
SECURITY National Bank—*See under SECURITY Pacific Corp.*
SECURITY Pacific Corp.
Security Pacific National Bank (Los Angeles)
Poland econ monitor plan set 1-11, 59G3
Viet ex-amb documt possessn prosecutn dropped 3-30, 252F3
Computer consultant sentncd 3-26, 239G1
SEDCO Inc.
Mex oil blowout role rptd 8-21, 636B1; liability unclear 8-23, 689C1
Mex oil blowout suits filed 9-13–9-18, Clements link probed 9-22, 718G2
Tex, US file oil blowout cleanup suits 10-18, 10-23, 809D2
SEDUCED (play)
Opens 2-1, 292G2
SEDUCTION of Joe Tynan (film)
Released 8-17, 820C3
Top-grossing film 9-26, 800G3
SEEGER, Charles L.
Dies 2-7, 176F3
SEEGER, Pete
Father dies 2-7, 176F3
Performs at NYC A-protest 9-23, 742G2
SEEVERS, Gary L.
CFTC resignatn cited 9-5, 681C2
SEGAL, George
Lost & Found released 7-13, 820F1
SEGUY, Georges
Assails govt 8-7, 633A3
Urges labor unity 9-5, 668A3
CFDT joint progrm set 9-19, 729B3
SEIBERLING, Henrietta Buckler
Dies 12-6, 1008E3
SEIDERS, Glenn A.
On 3 Mile I A-accident 4-3, 246B1
SEIDMAN, Cliff
Eyes on the Harem opens 4-24, 711G2
SEIGNIOUS, Lt. Gen. George M. (ret.)
Confrmd ACDA dir 3-1, 272C1
Cited in SALT II communique, Carter Cong address 6-18, 457C1, 458E3
Backs SALT, scores Gromyko threat 6-30, 496E3
Backs SALT ratificatn 7-10, 510E2
SEKO, Toshihiko
2d in Boston Marathon 4-16, 911C3
SELBY, John D.
Scores NRC fine 11-9, 867C1
SELDEN, Albert W.
Utter Glory opens 5-13, 712C3
Comin' Uptown opens 12-20, 1007D2
SELECT Brands Industries
Corenswet franchise terminatn case refused by Sup Ct 10-29, 884B1
SELECTIVE Service System—*See under U.S. GOVERNMENT*
SELKE Trophy, Frank—*See HOCKEY-Awards*
SELLERS, Arlene
Cuba released 12-21, 1007B3
SELLERS, Peter
Prisoner of Zenda released 5-25, 820A3
SELMA, Ala.—*See ALABAMA*
SELTZER, David
Prophecy released 6-15, 820A3

1980

SECRETARY of HUD v. Karlen
Case decided by Sup Ct 1-7, 15A3
SECRETARY of the Navy v. Huff
Case decided by Sup Ct 1-21, 93B1
SECRET Service—*See under U.S. GOVERNMENT--TREASURY*
SECURITIES—*See STOCKS*
SECURITIES Dealers, National Association of (NASD)
O-T-C mkt explained 76C3
SECURITIES & Exchange Commission—*See under U.S. GOVERNMENT*
SECURITIES Industry Association
FRB OKs commercial paper bank sales 9-29, 986B2
DeNunzio named chrmn 11-6, 959B2

SECURITY, National—*See also specific related subjects (e.g., PRIVACY); also U.S. GOVERNMENT subheads CENTRAL Intelligence Agency and FEDERAL Bureau of Investigation*
Carter aides rptdly took oaths re leaks 7-16—7-17, 549G1
Allen gets Reagan post 12-23, 980A2

SECURITY and Cooperation in Europe, Conference on—*See CSCE*
SECURITY Council—*See under UNITED Nations*
SECURITY Pacific Corp.
Flamson named chrmn, Moody pres, chief exec 12-16, 959F1
SEDALIA—*See MISSOURI*
SEDYKH, Yuri
Wins Olympic medal 7-31, 624D1
SEEBIRT, Cmdr. James
Drops lesbian chrgs vs 4 8-21, 898G3
SEEMS Like Old Times (film)
Released 12-19, 1003D2
SEFF, Sherie
Ka-Boom! opens 11-20, 1003C3
SEGAL, Erich
Change of Seasons released 12-17, 1003G1
SEGAL, Fred
Change of Seasons released 12-17, 1003G1
SEGAL, George
Last Married Couple released 2-8, 216B3
SEGAL, Jerry
Die Laughing released 5-23, 675C2
SEGAR, E. C.
Popeye released 12-12, 972F3
SEGELSTEIN, Irwin
Named NBC TV pres 6-3, 501D2
SEGER, Bob
Against the Wind on best-seller list 4-2, 280F3; 4-30, 360A1; 6-4, 448F3; 7-9, 568F3
SEGNANA, Remo
Reveals oil tax evasn rpt 10-30, 873B3
SEGOTA, Branko
Arrows win MISL title 3-23, 771A2
SEGUY, Georges
Fishermen backed, wider strike threatened 8-27, 652A1
SE Hong Jang
Wins Olympic medal 7-29, 624C3
SEIBERLING Jr., Rep. John F. (D, Ohio)
Reelected 11-4, 843E4
SEIF, Juseiman bin
Executed re mosque raid 1-9, 22C1
SEITZ, Franz
Tin Drum released 4-11, 416F3
SEJDI, Saban
Wins Olympic medal 7-31, 624D3
SEKERAMAYI, Sidney
Zimbabwe lands min 3-11, 198D1
SELACRYN—*See MEDICINE--Drugs & Health-Care Products*
SELECTED Poems (book)
Justice wins Pulitzer 4-14, 296E2
SELECTIVE Service System—*See under U.S. GOVERNMENT*
SELIMOV, Nermedin
Wins Olympic medal 7-30, 624C3
SELLERS, Peter
Dies 7-24, 608B3
Fiendish Plot of Dr Fu Manchu released 8-8, 675E2
SELMI Bank A.G.
Fraud scandal rptd 7-28, 581F1
SELVIN, Benjamin B.
Dies 7-28, 608C3
SELZER, Edgar Karl
Seized in DR emb raid 2-27, 141B1; freed 3-6, 180F2

1976

SEMERDJIEV, Krastio
Wins Olympic medal 7-26, 576F2
SEMINEX—*See CONCORDIA Seminary*
SENCER, Dr. David J.
On Pa mystery disease 8-5, 573E2
Defends Legion disease probe 11-23—11-24, 911D2
On swine flu program halt 12-17, 950F1
SEND In the Clowns (song)
Wins Grammy 2-28, 460A3
SENEGAL—*See also AFRICAN Development Bank, NONALIGNED Nations Movement, OAU*
Ethiopia warned vs MPLA ties 1-11, 16B1
Listed as 'partly free' 1-19, 20D3
Sea limits extended 2-5, 591F3
Backs UN rights comm resolutn vs Israel 2-13, 125E2
Natl sentenced in CAR 2-14, 204C2
UN Palestine com member 2-26, 162C1
Total IMF oil loan rptd 4-1, 340E2
Multiparty, pres successn amendmts adopted 4-1; oppositn scores 6-11, 591D2
Former premr, others pardoned 4-3, 491D3
Arab-Africa mtg 4-19—4-22, 355G3
Thiandoum named cardinal 4-27, 336B2
Kissinger visits 5-1—5-2, 318C2, C3
US proposes Sahel aid progrm 5-1, 318D2
WHO com rpts Israel W Bank, Gaza health data 5-10, 338F2
At France-Africa summit 5-10—5-11, 355G2
WHO vs rpt on Israel 5-17, 355A2
Backs IAAF S Africa expulsn 7-22, 562B2
ECOWAS rptd ratified 11-6, 974E2
Progressive Union at Soclst Intl cong 11-26—12-28, 935A3
In Pl-rebel talks 12-15—12-23, 1008G3
SENET, Daniel
Wins Olympic medal 7-21, 576E2
SENGHOR, Leopold Sedar (Senegalese president)
Warns Ethiopia vs MPLA ties 1-11, 16B1
Pres successn amendmt adopted 4-1, oppositn scores 6-11, 591E2, B3
Urges Arab-Africa cooperatn 4-19, 356C1
Kissinger visits 5-1—5-2, 318C3
At France-Africa summit 5-10—5-11, 355G2, C3
SENI Pramoj
Kukrit chrgs party pressure 1-12, 30D3
Says govt lax on corruptn 1-12, 30D3
To replace Kukrit as premr 4-4, 255D3
House OKs Cabt 4-17, king proclaims 4-21, sworn 4-22, 315D1
Wins confidence vote 4-30, 335C2
Assures on US mil exit 7-19, 541G3
Praphas returns 8-15, resignatn asked 8-19, 640D1, G1
Takes defense post 8-25, 677C3
Asks Thanom to leave 9-21; quits 9-23, renamed 9-25, names new Cabt 10-5, 754E1
Ousted in coup 10-6, 753F3, 754A1
In protective custody 775E2
Viets score Thai govt 10-17, 795E1
SENSI, Giuseppe Maria Cardinal
Named cardinal 4-27, 336B2
SEPELEV, Yuri
Yugo holds Sovt offcl as spy 4-6, 256C1
SEQUENTIALS—*See BIRTH Control & Family Planning*
SERACHE, Nat
Detained 11-7, 927F2
SERAPHIN, Jean-Jacques
Named health min 8-20, 926B1
SERBIAN Orthodox Church—*See under EASTERN Orthodox Churches*
SEREGNI, Gen. Liber (ret.)
Rptd rearrested 1-11, 55G3
Leftists lose pol rights 9-1, 678G1
SERGIPE (Brazilian warship)
In Intl Naval Review 7-4, 488D3
SERRANO, Humberto
Cited re Scherer ouster 7-7, 620F1
SERVAIS, Jean
Dies 2-17, 192G3
SERVAN-Schreiber, Jean-Jacques
Wins Lorraine election 1-6, 49A3
SERVICE Employes International Union (AFL-CIO)
NY apartment strike ends 5-19, 379B1
Mass workers strike 6-21—6-24; OK pact 12-4, 921G1
SERWANIKO, John
Rptd dead 10-7, 874C2

1977

SEMYONOV, Alexei
Expelled from schl 11-10, 955F2
SENATE, U.S.—*See under U.S. GOVERNMENT*
SENCER, Dr. David J.
Asked to resign 2-4, 103C3
Successor named 4-5, 287D3
SENEGAL—*See also NONALIGNED Nations Movement, OAU*
UN Assemb member; Forster on World Ct 4B1, F1
Giscard visits 4-19—4-23; France-Africa summit held 4-20—4-21, 316C3
Senghor meets Schmidt 5-3, 394E1
Senghor scores forgn interventn in Africa 5-3, 394E1
Sahel dvpt plan OKd 6-1, 458F3
Cohen confrmd US amb 6-23, 626D3
Conservative party formed 9-9, 710F3
New Sahel famine seen 9-19, 770A2
W Ger asks more Dakar airport security 10-23, 868D3
France reinforces garrison 11-1, 852A2, D2
SENGHOR, Leopold Sedar (Senegalese president)
Asks joint Africa defense 4-20, 316C3
Sees Schmidt; scores forgn role in Africa 5-3, 394E1
OKs conservative party creatn 9-24, 710G3
SENIOR Citizens—*See AGE and Aged Persons*
SENKTUTTUVAN, Arun
Arrested 2-15, admits anti-govt article 3-12, 223D3
Freed, loses citizenship 4-13, 309B3
SENN, Gen. Hans
Rpts on A-shelters 11-14, 904G2
SEPARATIONS—*See DIVORCES & Separations*
SEREGNI, Gen. Liber (ret.)
Detention rptd 3-23, 351C2
SERRAT, Oscar
Kidnaped 11-10, freed 11-11, 922G1, B2
SERRATIA Marcescens—*See CHEMICAL & Biological Warfare*
SERVAN-Schreiber, Jean-Jacques
Wins Lorraine electn 1-6, 63A2
Sells L'Express shares 3-16, 255D3
Elected Radical Party head 5-15, 449G3
Soclst alliance sought 10-20, 924E2
SERVICE Employes—*See MAINTENANCE Employes*
SERVICE Employes International Union (AFL-CIO)
Strikes NYC schools 2-23—2-28, 153C3
SETHI, P. C.
Arrested 8-15, 637D2
Arrested 10-3, 765C1
SETO Inland Sea (Japan)
Tanker accident 4-6, 1000B1
SETON, Mother Elizabeth Ann Bayley (1774-1821)
Neumann canonized 6-19, 731C3
SETON Hall University (South Orange, N.J.)
Mosley in NBA draft 6-10, 584B3
SETOYAMA, Mitsuo
Vows anti-hijacking moves 10-8, 801F3
Named Japan justice min 11-28, 932B2

1978

SEMBENE, Ousmane
Ceddo released 2-16, 618G3
SEMI-Tough (film)
Top-grossing film 1-4, 24G3; 2-1, 116E3
SEMPRUN, Jorge (Federico Sanchez)
Carrillo refutes book 1-21, CP ldrs rptd shaken 2-24, 136B2
Woman at Her Window released 6-9, 620C1
SEMYONOV, Alexei
Visa OK rptd 2-4, 180A2
SENATE—*See under U.S. GOVERNMENT; for legislation, see under U.S. GOVERNMENT—CONGRESS*
SENEGAL—*See also GATT, NONALIGNED Nations Movement, OAU*
Freedom House lists as partly free 44A2
UN rights comm OKs Israel res 2-14, 99A2
Senghor wins reelectn 2-26, 152F3
At W African mtg; backs ECOWAS, upgrades ties 3-18; USSR scores 3-20, 237D1
UN Leb troops (Unifil) slain 5-1, 5-5, 339F3; **for peacekeeping developments, see MIDDLE EAST—LEBANON**
Guinea ties restored 5-5, 445A2
French raids vs Polisario rptd 5-5, 562F2
S Africa econ pressure rptd asked 6-2, 633B2
US aids Zaire rescue 6-5, airlifts peace force 6-6, 441C1, D1
Zaire pan-Africa force rptd backed 6-8, 442D1
UN Assemb member 713E3
IMF loan rptd, drought damage cited 10-30, 885C3
UNESCO backs free press 11-22, 931D1
SENER, Ahmet
Named Turkey state min 1-5, 21E2
SENGHOR, Leopold Sedar (Senegalese president)
Wins reelectn 2-26, 152F3
SENIOR Citizens—*See AGE & Aged Persons*
SENKAKU Islands
China boats anchor 4-12, Japan protests 4-14, chrgs denied 4-15; boats rptd out 4-16, 278C1
China rptdly drops claim, Taiwan reaffrims claim 8-12, 637E1, E2
SENSENBRENNER, F. James
Wins US House seat 11-7, 852D4, 854A2
SENSITIVE Prince (race horse)
Loses Kentucky Derby 5-6, 539B1
SEPAMLA, Sipho
Passport denial rptd 6-10, 536D3
SEPARATIONS—*See DIVORCES & Separations*
SEPTIEN, Rafael
NFL '77 kicking ldr 1-1, 56F2
SEPTIOGLU, Ali Riza
Named Turkey state min 1-5, 21E2
SEPT. 30, 1955 (film)
Released 3-31, 619E3
SERAGUDDIN, Fuad
Heads New Wafd Party 2-17, 131D1
New Wafd Party dissolves 6-2, 436G3
SERBAN, Andrei
Master & Margarita opens 11-11, 1031D2
SEREGNI, Gen. Liber (ret.)
Sentencd for 'conspiracy' 5-26, 537E3
SGT. Pepper's Lonely Hearts Club Band (film)
Released 7-21, 970B3
SERLY, Tibor
Dies 10-8, 888E3
SERONEY, John Marie
Freed 12-12, 968G1
SERPENT'S Egg, The (film)
Released 1-27, 619F3
SERRANO, Sammy
Decisns Martinez 2-18, 379B2
KOs O Young Ho 7-9, 600A2
SERRANO Suner, Ramon
Denies WWII spying for Japan 9-17, 744F3
SERVAN-Schreiber, Jean-Jacques
Small govt parties form electn accord 1-10, Gaullists break pact 1-11, 54C3
Narrowly wins reelectn 3-19, 201C1
Goldsmith buys control of L'Express 4-27, 352B3
Loses Assemb seat 6-30, 533A2
Loses by-election 10-1, 815A2
SERVANT and Mistress (film)
Released 6-6, 619F3
SERVICE Armament Co. v. U.S.
Antique gun tax rule declined by Sup Ct 5-22, 388B2
SERVICE Employes International Union (AFL-CIO)
NYC nursing home strike 4-4—4-7, 284F3-285A1
SERVOMATION Corp.
GDV takeover bid OKd 8-31, 700A2
SESAME Street (TV program)
Record wins Grammy 2-24, 316B1
SETTE, Pietro
Offers chem indus rescue plan 10-26, 817D2

1979

SEMALL, Paul
Traded to Cubs 6-26, 1002A3
SEMPLE Jr., Lorenzo
Hurricane released 4-11, 528E2
SENATE—*See under U.S. GOVERNMENT*
SENECA, S.C.—*See SOUTH Carolina*
SENECA, Ill.—*See ILLINOIS*
SENEGAL—*See also GATT, NONALIGNED Nations Movement, OAU*
Freedom House lists as partly free 13B1
Israel arrests Unifil soldier 2-18, 157A2
IMF grants loan, '78 drought cited 3-30, 411G2
Israel sentncs soldier 5-10, 341A3
W Bank, Gaza health probe set 5-23, 398F2
CAE student massacre probe rptd 8-6, 601A3
Zaire troop exit rptd 8-14, 733G3
UN membership listed 695B3
Pol Pot govt UN seat upheld 9-19, 695C2
Young, US delegatn visit; Israel ties barred 9-20, 720A3
SENGHOR, Leopold Sedar (Senegalese president)
Sees Young, rejects Israel ties 9-20, 721F1
SENIOR Citizens—*See AGE & Aged Persons*
SENNA, Orlando
Col Delmiro Gouveia released 4-30, 528A2
SEPARATION—*See DIVORCE*
SEPE, Angelo J.
Arrested 2-17, 155B3
SEPTEE, Moe
Richard III opens 6-14, 712B2
SEPTIEN, Rafael
NFL '78 kicking ldr 1-6, 80F1
Steelers win Super Bowl 1-21, 63D1
SEQUOIA National Forest (Calif.)
Fires destroy 630 acres 9-11—9-23, 799E3
SEQUOYAH Nuclear Power Plant—*See TENNESSEE-Atomic Energy*
SERAPHINE, Oliver (Dominica prime minister)
Sworn prime min; vows govt probe, Grenada ties 6-29, 502D3
US sets Carib policy 11-29, 960E3
SERBAN, Andrei
Umbrellas Of Cherbourg opens 2-1, 292E3
SEREGOS, Nicholas
Scotto convicted 11-15, 890D1
SERRA, J. Tony
Newton murder case ends in 2d mistrial, chrgs dropped 9-27, 818E3
SERRA, Raymond
Manny opens 4-18, 712C1
SERRANO, Apolinaro
Slain 9-30, 790B3
SERRANO, Sammy
Decisns Valdez 2-18, 412D3
SERRATIA—*See BACTERIA*
SERRAULT, Michel
Cage aux Folles released 5-12, 528F1
SERVICE Employees International Union (AFL-CIO)
Boston U strike ends 4-22, 327A1
SERV-U Meats Inc.
Settles '78 beef-price suit 10-22, 985E3
SETON Hall University (South Orange, N.J.)
In Big East basketball conf 5-29, 526G3
SETRAKIAN, Ed
Seduced opens 2-1, 292A3
SETTE, Pietro
Nominated holding co head 1-8, 20G3

1980

SEMENENKO, Serge
Dies 4-24, 360E3
SEMPLE Jr., Lorenzo
Flash Gordon released 12-5, 972E3
SEMYONOV, Vladimir
Signs W Ger econ pact 7-1, 489C2
SENATE—*See under U.S. GOVERNMENT*
SENDAK, Maurice
Really Rosie opens 10-12, 892E3
SENEGAL—*See also GATT, NONALIGNED Nations, OAU*
Liberian supertanker sinks off coast 1-17, 108D2
Senghor visits US 4-4—4-6, 336D2
Mondale in African tour 7-17—7-23, 620D2
Islamic League meets 11-10, 895B2
Libyan Chad role opposed 12-23—12-24, 979E1
SENGHOR, Leopold Sedar
In US 4-4—4-6, 336D2
SENIOR Citizens—*See AGE & Aged Persons*
SENSENBRENNER, Rep. F. James (R, Wis.)
Reelected 11-4, 844D4
SEPARATION—*See DIVORCE & Separation*
SEPER, Cardinal Franjo
Issues papal dispensatn guidelines 10-14, 970C1
SEPTIEN, Rafael
NFL '79 kicking ldr 1-5, 8F2
SERAPHINE, Oliver (Dominican prime minister; replaced July 21)
Party loses electn, replaced as prime min 7-21, 635G3
SERASINO, Roberto
Killed 12-11, 966C3
SERBAN, Andrei
Sea Gull opens 11-11, 892F3
SERCK Ltd.
Rockwell trust suit setlmt reached 10-1, 917G1
SERIAL (film)
Released 3-28, 416E3
SERIKOV, Shamil
Wins Olympic medal 7-24, 624A3
SERRANO, Sammy
TKOs Kazama 4-3, 320C3
SERRANO Pinto, German
Banana workers' strike setld 1-17, 117E1
SERREAU, Genevieve
Heartaches of a Pussycat opens 3-19, 392A3
SERVICE Employees International Union (AFL-CIO)
Kennedy addresses conv 6-25, 480B1
SETHNA, H. N.
US delays A-shipmts 3-13, 182C1

1976

SEVENTH Day Adventists
Carter interview cited 10-2, 743C2
SEVILLA Quintana, Juan Alberto
'75 torture cited 6-1, 501B2
SEWAGE—*See under ENVIRONMENT*

SEX—*See also CRIME—Rape; PORNOGRAPHY; also other related subjects (e.g., HOMOSEXUALITY)*
Vatican issues statemt 1-15, Rabbinical Cncl backs 1-26, 124B2, C2
Sup Ct bars 'proof' rule review 3-1, 170D1
Sup Ct bars review of sex educ suit 4-5, 262B2
Bishops Conf backs Vatican code 11-8—11-11, 859F1
Sup Ct refuses Va sex case 11-29, 901A1
Tenn bishop grants absolutn 12-5, 12-12, 951F1-B2

SEYCHELLES (British colony)—*See also NONALIGNED Nations Movement*
UK sets independnc date 1-22, 270F3
Mancham at France-Africa summit 5-10—5-11, 355F2, A3
Becomes free republic 6-28, 483E2
Joins Commonwealth 6-28, 799D2
Becomes UN member 9-21, 719A1

SEYMOUR, Capt. Rufus A.
McClure dies 3-13, 378C1
Reprimanded 9-1, 942D2
SHACKELFORD, Robert L.
Cited re FBI burglaries 8-18, 634F2
SHACKLEFORD, Rufus
Amer Party vp candidate 6-19, 490C3
SHACKLETON, Lord
Falklands visit rptd 1-13, 26G1
SHADDICK, Peter R.
Sentencing postponed 3-9, 271C2
SHAFEI, Mohammed Zaki
Replaced in econ post 11-10, 852F1
SHAFER, Capt. Walter R.
Acquitted 5-12, 941G2
SHAFFER, Laurance Frederic
Dies 7-20, 716F3

1977

SEVAREID, Eric
Retires 11-30, 1021E2
SEVENTH-Day Adventists
Harry Willis Miller dies 1-1, 84D3
SEVER, John
Wins Birmingham by-electn 8-18, 655A1
SEVILLA Sacasa, Guillermo
Rptd Somoza choice to succeed 10-21, 865G1
SEWAGE—*See ENVIRONMENT—Air & Water*
SEWARD Peninsula—*See ALASKA*
SEWELL, Joe
House subcom sets TV family hour hearings, '76 ruling cited 2-9, 158A1
Inducted into baseball HOF 8-8, 643G3
SEX
S Africa interracial laws debated 7-5, 7-7, 564A1
US bishops vs new RC study 11-16, 906C2
Polish church scores permissiveness 12-4, 987E1

SEX Crimes
Polanski indicted for sodomy 3-24, 262D1
Child abuse arrests 4-11, 4-26; abuse schemes rptd 5-15—5-18; House legis hearings 5-20, 5-27, 432G1-G3
Hyde Amendmt abortn scope defined 7-27, 8-4, 786C2
Abortn funds for incest clear Cong 12-7, 958F2, A3
Rape
Francis suit rptd setled 2-23, 140E3
Calif woman acquitted 3-4, 262B1
Miranda rule review sidestepped 3-23, 275A3
Polanski indicted 3-24, 262D1
Va death penalty bill signed 3-29, 594E1
Scottsboro figure denied compensatn 4-6, 396B3
Slain Girl Scout molested 6-13, 492F1
Executn for rapist barred 6-29, 557C2
Hyde Amendmt abortn scope defined 7-27, 8-4, 786C2
Polanski pleads guilty 8-8, mental exam ordered 9-19, 732C3
Wis judge recalled 9-7, 712A1
'76 FBI data rptd 9-27, 847E3
Abortn funds clear Cong 12-7, 958F2, A3
Moore convictn reversed 12-12, 960G2
Calif strangler sought 12-14, 992B1

SEYCHELLES—*See also COMMONWEALTH of Nations, NONALIGNED Nations Movement, OAU*
UN Assemb member 4B1
Dvpt plan announced 1-1, 24G2
At France-Africa summit 4-20—4-21, 316F3
LeMelle confrmd US amb 5-9, 418F1
Mancham ousted 6-5, USSR aid denied 6-6, 450F3-451C1
Stores reopen 6-7, curfew cut 6-12, 489D1
Absent from Commonwealth conf 6-8—6-15, 487F1
Rene denies Sovt aid, chrgs Mancham countercoup plan 6-8, 489C1
US, UK recognize new govt 6-13, 489B1
SEYMOUR, Steven
Misinterprets Carter 12-29, 1001A2
SHADOW Box, The (play)
Wins Pulitzer Prize 4-18, 355D2
SHADRIN, Blanka
Seeks husband's release 7-14, 564B2
US blamed in husband's disappearance 8-17, 641B1
SHADRIN, Nikolai (Nikolai Artamonov)
Release sought 7-14, 564B2
US blamed for disappearance 8-17, 640D3
SHAFIZADEH, Abraham
Body found 7-29, identified 10-19, 871D3

1978

SETTLE, Mary Lee
Wins Natl Book Award 4-10, 315D2
SEVENTH-Day Adventists
USSR jails ldr 3-14, 275C3
Blacks refused separate role, Wilson elected pres 10-20, 907F2
SEVEN-Up Co.
Philip Morris seeks takeover 5-1, 5-11; bid OKd, '77 earnings cited 5-15, 364F2-B3
SEWAGE—*See ENVIRONMENT—Air & Water*

SEX Crimes
Carter backs abortn funds for incest 2-17, 123G2-A3
Mo univ sodomy case review refused 2-21, 125C3
US Rep Richmond pleads not guilty 4-6, 265F1-B2
Calif suit vs NBC OKd by Sup Ct 4-24, 322A2
Child abuse extensn signed 4-24, 323C3
Abortn funds for incest barred by House 6-13, 445C3
Calif suit vs NBC dismissed 8-8, 635B2-A3
Richmond wins renominatn 9-12, 716B2
Richmond reelected 11-7, 846E2
'74 Houston slayer's sentnc reversed 12-20, 992B2
Rape
HEW issues abortn rules 1-26, 116E1
US crime code revisn clears Sen 1-30, 64F2
Polanski flees US 2-1, 116A2
Carter backs abortn funds 2-17, 123G2-A3
NYS death penalty bill clears legislature 3-20; Carey vetoes 4-11, override fails 5-2, 388A3
Indian retrial backed by Sup Ct 3-22, 221D1
Ark convictns reversed by US Sup Ct 4-3, 309B1
Okla Girl Scout slaying suspect arrested 4-6, 380D3
Calif suit vs NBC OKd by Sup Ct 4-24, 322D2; dismissed 8-9, 635D2, F2
Child abuse extensn signed 4-24, 323C3
Lawyer competency case declined by Sup Ct 5-1, 363F3
3 Frenchmen convicted 5-3, 396B1
NH law case refused by Sup Ct 6-5, 431B2
Abortn funds curbed by House 6-13, 445C3
S Africa '76-77 data rptd 7-20, 670E1
Arkansas football players suspended 12-14, 1025B3
Oregon man acquitted of spouse rape 12-27, 1028C3
SEX Pistols (punk rock band)
Sid Vicious accused of murder 10-2, 842C1

SEYCHELLES—*See also COMMONWEALTH of Nations, NONALIGNED Nations Movement, OAU*
Freedom House lists as partly free 44F1
21 arrested in plot 4-29, Kenya role chrgd 5-8, 378C3
5-yr econ plan set 6-5, 596B3
Rene sets 1-party electns 6-20, 596B3
9 accused plotters freed 7-3, 596C3
Rene warns US, USSR vs Indian O mil activity 8-7, 8-20, 692B1
Emergency rptd ended, detainees freed 8-8, 692D1
S Africa trade ban rptd 8-21, 670B1
UN Assemb member 713E3

SEYMOUR, W. W.
Secy-treas of new BRAC unit 2-28, 185C2
SEYRIG, Delphine
Faces of Love released 7-7, 970C1
SHABA Invasion—*See under ZAIRE*
SHABANGU, Samuel
S Africa arrests 6-21, dies 6-29; negligence chrgd 7-1, 633G2
SHABARUDDIN Chik
Australia sugar talks ended 1-11, 34C3
SHADDICK, Peter R.
Named Franklin co-conspirator 7-13, 681D1
SHADOW, The (radio show)
Bret Morrison dies 9-25, 778F1
SHADOW Dancing (recording)
On best-seller lists 6-7, 460B3; 7-5, 579G3, 580A1
SHAER, Musleh
Execution confirmed 2-1, 172G3
SHAFFER, Anthony
Death On Nile released 9-29, 970B1
SHAFFER, Beverly
Film wins Oscar 4-3, 315D3

1979

SEVAREID, Eric
Weds 6-30, 527E2
SEVENTH-day Adventists
Rail worker union dues case refused by Sup Ct 1-8, 14E3
Bradford elected N Amer church ldr 1-11, 78D3
Vegetarian diet study rptd 2-22, 140G1
USSR emigratn rptd backed in US 2-26, 172F2
USSR sentences ldr 3-23, 238C1
Membership rise rptd 5-4, 640A1
IAM firing case declined by Sup Ct 6-4, 439A2
SEVEN-Up Co.—*See PHILIP Morris*
SEVERINI, Robert
Chairs world radio conf 9-27–12-6, 1006B3
SEWANEE Review, The (journal)
Allen Tate dies 2-9, 176G3
SEWELL, Duane
Cited in H-bomb letter 9-16, 9-18, 714F1, 717D1-B3
SEWELL, John
Fired as Surf coach 5-17, 1004D2
SEX
B Bardot: films 'gone too far' 9-28, 860A1
Ft Dix fraternizatn scandal rptd 12-3, 924A1
SEX Crimes
Chicago man indicted in mass murder 1-8, 24G2
Child abuse data rptd 1-26, 93D3
US suspends Hong Kong aide 2-10, 109E1
Siblings marry 5-25, sentncd for incest 7-31, 656B2
Mass anti-abortn law omits incest 6-12, 547A3
Houston sex slayer convicted again 6-27, 819C1
S Africa racial law chng sought 9-25, 774B2
Va men's room surveillnc case declined by Sup Ct 10-1, 768A2
'Hillside Strangler' gets life 10-19, 10-22, accomplice chrgd 10-19, 818F2
Rape
Oregon couple reconciled after trial 1-6, 79D1; divorced 4-20, 392E3
'73-77 survey rptd 1-18, 119A1
La juvenile trial jury ban refused by Sup Ct 2-21, 128B3
Va prisoner gets setlmt 3-17, 316D2
Okla Girl Scout slaying suspect acquitted 3-30, 291E2; dies 6-4, 508A3
Neb ct backs bail denial 4-4, 310A2
Smith Va death penalty challenge declined by Sup Ct 5-21, 400F3
Green death sentnc vacated by Sup Ct 5-29, 421E3
Little paroled 6-9, 527D3
Hines '78 convctn protested by blacks 6-9, 865G3
Mass anti-abortn law omits 6-12, 547A3
Mont homicide convictn reversed by Sup Ct 6-18, 499F1
Mass man sentncd for rape of wife 9-24, 819F1
2d 1/4 rise rptd 10-9, 819B3
Neb bail case refused by Sup Ct 10-15, 847E3
Neb slayer acquitted in retrial 10-17, 890G3
Abortion funding cases accepted by Sup Ct 11-26, 919B2

SEYCHELLES—*See also COMMONWEALTH of Nations, NONALIGNED Nations Movement, OAU*
Whaling banned, Indian O sanctuary set 7-11, 554C2
UN membership listed 695B3
Students protest training plan 10-11, 969D2
Arrests rptd re Rene plot chrg, France, S Africa implicated 11-20, 969C2

SEZGIN, Ismet
Named Turkey finance min 11-12, 876E1
SHABER, David
Warriors released 2-9, 174F3
Last Embrace released 5-3, 528F2
SHADLE, Eugene D.
Sentncd in GSA kickback scandal 3-14, 367F2
SHAFAQAT, Gen. Jaafar
Named Iran war min 1-11, 11G2
SHAFER, David
Viable ape hybrid rptd 7-21, 692C2
SHAFER v. Penn Central Corp.
Case refused by Sup Ct 10-1, 768E1
SHAFFER, Paul
Gilda Radner Live opens 8-2, 711C3
SHAFIE, Ghazali bin
Asks US to set up refugee camps 6-26, 474D1
Vs US refugee rescue missn 7-30, 575D2
SHAFIE, Manoucher
Pahlevi family Ga real estate projct rptd 11-26, 897E3
SHAGARI, Shehu Usman Aliyu (Nigerian president)
Elected Nigeria pres 8-11, 636E2
Electn upheld 9-26, inaugurated 10-1, 753B3
Envoy in UK re Zimbabwe 11-15, 881F1

1980

SEVENTH-day Adventists
USSR ldr dies in prison 1-27, 87G3
SEVER, Engin
Slain 12-17, 991C2
SEVERE Mercy, A (book)
Wins Amer Book Award 5-1, 692F2
SEWALL, John
Loses reelectn 11-11, 900D3
SEWERYN, Marek
Wins Olympic medal 7-22, 624E2
SEX
RC bishops family life conf opens 9-26, 810C2, C3

SEX Crimes
NBA player arrested for sex abuse 1-2, sentncd 6-4, 656G1
Neo-Nazi ex-ldr arrested 1-10, 55D3
Parole offcls immunity upheld by Sup Ct 1-15, 51F1
GI sentenced for harassment 3-6, 1891A1
Gacy convicted 3-12, gets death sentence 3-13, 214C-C2
Ohio judge acquitted of sex-bartering 6-13, 503A2
Iran firing squad executns 7-14, 7-20—7-21, 545G2
Ore U sodomy indictmts cited 10-15, 875C3
Libertarian pres candidate cites stance 10-28, 818A3
Pa pretrial press exclusn case refused by Sup Ct 11-17, 882F1
Rape
Jones arrested 1-31, complaint dropped 2-1, 320D3
Hines '78 convictn overturned 3-18, 215E2-A3
India feminist actn cited 4-9, 275G2
Multiple sentencing curbed by Sup Ct 4-16, 328B3
Abortn funding cases argued in Sup Ct 4-21, 306C2
NYS shield law case dismissed by Sup Ct 5-19, 440C2
Canada ct questioning broadened 6-27, 520C3
Abortn funding limits upheld by Sup Ct 6-30, 491G2
US, Canada rates compared 7-16, 562C3
Mandatory sentncs rptd up 8-29, 359E1
'79 US data rptd 9-24, 971D1, F1
Mass press exclusn case remanded by Sup Ct 10-14, 782B1
Hines declared unfit for retrial 11-21, 927F1

SEYCHELLES—*See also COMMONWEALTH of Nations, NONALIGNED Nations, OAU*
Students sentenced 1-6, curfew eased 1-11, 40E1

SEYMOUR, Jane
Somewhere in Time released 10-3, 836F3
SHABER, David
Those Lips released 9-9, 836G3
SHADMEHR, Gen. Mohammed Hadi
Airmen end protest; backs Bani-Sadr as armed forces head 2-19, 122F2
Named mil affairs adviser 6-19, 464E2
SHADOW, The (radio program)
Enlow dies 5-18, 448E1
SHAFFER, Anthony
Wicker Man released 3-26, 416G3
SHAFFER, Paul
Gilda Live released 3-28, 416G2
SHAFFER, Peter
Amadeus opens 12-17, 1003G2
SHAFIR, Herzl
Admits rights abuses 12-30, ousted 12-31, 994D3
SHAGAN, Steve
Formula released 12-19, 1003A2
SHAGARI, Shehu Usman Aliyu (Nigerian president)
Launches oil co probe 4-18, 354C1
In US 10-3—10-7: issues S Africa warning, hints A-bomb dvpt 10-3; meets Carter 10-7, 792C2

1976

SHAH, J. C.
Denies A-plant leak 2-7, 156D2
SHAHAM Inc.
Cited in Grumman-Iran feud 140D1
SHAHEEN Natural Resources Co.
Newfoundlnd refinery in receivership 2-13, bankrupt 3-12, 221C2
SHAHI, Agha
India ties set 5-12—5-14, 356A3
SHAITO, Ibrahim
Leb health min 12-9, 913E2
SHAKA, Bassan al-
Rpts W Bank-Jordan trade curb 8-11, 699F3
SHALAGIN, Boris
US newsman chrgs libel 6-25, 559C1
SHALE—*See 'U.S. Developments' under PETROLEUM*
SHAMPOO (film)
'75 top rental film 1-7, 32F3
Grant wins Oscar 3-29, 240A3
SHAMSABADI, Abolhassan
Alleged slayers rptd arrested 5-17, 365B3
SHANKER, Albert
AFSCME quits AFL-CIO unit 2-15, 154C1
Cleaver Defense Fund formed 2-17, 272F1
Endorses Carter 7-22, 551E1
HEW scored re principal selectn stand 11-9, 922B1
SHANNON, Daniel J.
Teamsters fund lists loans 12-28, 991B1
SHAPIRO, Irving S.
Named Carter adviser 11-19, 881D3
Briefs Carter 12-1, 898A3
SHAPIRO, Stuart H.
Loses MD malpractice suit 6-1, 1016C3
SHAPP, Gov. Milton J. (D, Pa.)
Common Cause rpts code backing 1-9, 23A1
Hits Ford plan 1-20, 40A3
9th in Mass primary 3-2, 165B1
Reaffirms '76 pres bid 3-4, 166C2
Fed fund total listed 3-4, 180D3
4th in Fla primary 3-9, 179G1
Ends pres bid 3-12, 197C2
Vetoes anti-busing bill 3-19, 203B3
Pa primary results 4-27, 304F3, 305D1
FEC funds released 5-21, 391E3
Tenn primary results 5-25, 374E2
RI primary results 6-1, 390C2
Endorses Carter 6-10, 432E1
FEC ends fed funds 6-23, 490F3
Fed fund total rptd 7-1, 491B1
Dem conv pres vote, table 7-14, 507E2
Sign Pa VW pact 9-15, 987F3
NE govs meet 11-13—11-14, 864B3
FEC certificatn total rptd 12-31, 979G2
SHAQA, Bassam al-
Scores Nablus slaying 5-16, 354D1
SHARAF, Sherif Abdul Hamid
Scores US UN veto 1-26, 59F3
Defends anti-Zionism stand 4-28, 320B3
SHARARE, Farouk al-
Emb raiders sought 10-11, 759D1
SHARJA—*See UNITED Arab Emirates*
SHARON, Maj. Gen Ariel
Quits as Rabin adviser 3-21, 253D3
SHARP, Ian
Named to econ advisory bd 9-14, 730F1
SHARP, Mitchell
Resigns 9-12, replaced 9-15, 692C1
SHARP, Rep. Philip R. (D. Ill.)
Reelected 11-2, 829C3
SHARPHORN, Capt. Daniel H.
Seeks honor code review 5-18, 394F3, 395D1
Scores honor-code proceedings 8-4, 670B2
SHARPS Pixley Inc.
IMF gold purchase rptd 6-3, 430G2
Buys IMF gold; London bullion trading cited 9-15, 739E3, G3
SHARY, Valeri
Wins Olympic medal 7-24, 576E2
SHATTUCK, John Howard Francis
Named ACLU DC dir 9-6, 680F2 *
SHAW, Irwin
Nightwork on best-seller list 12-5, 972G2
SHAW, Sir Patrick
Replaced as amb to US 2-1, 97A3
SHAW, Dr. Spencer
New alcoholism test rptd 12-3, 950C3
SHAW, Tim
Wins Olympic medal 7-22, 575E2

1977

SHAH, J. C.
To probe corruptn 4-18, 304A2
Gandhi govt probe begins 9-29, 765A2
Gandhi boycotts probe 11-21, 12-2, 966E1
SHAHIN, Issa Abdel Hamid
Demoted to state min 10-25, 824B1
SHAKAR, Bassam
Kahane spurs W Bank riot 4-17, 335A3
SHAKESPEARE, William (1564-1616)
China lifts ban 5-25, 449D3
SHALL We Tell the President? (book)
J Onassis quits Viking 10-13, 927B3
SHAMGAR, Meyer
Conf OKs rights proposal 8-23, 664F3
SHAMIR, Yitzhak
Elected parlt speaker 6-13, 474F2
SHANAHAN, Eileen
Named HEW asst secy 1-19, 53B1
SHANKAR, Ravi
Brother dies 9-26, 788E2
SHANKAR, Siddahrtha
Loses Cong Party pres race 5-6, 392A2
SHANKAR, Uday
Dies 9-26, 788E2
SHANKER, Albert
Fined $250 7-20, 558D2
Heads new AFL-CIO dept 12-7, 961F1
SHANNON, Daniel
Testifies before Sen panel 10-31, 837C2
SHANNON, William V.
Named amb to Ireland 6-20, confrmd 6-21, 626E3
SHAPIRO, Ed
Hare Krishna indictmts dropped 3-17, 287A2
SHAPIRO, Irving S.
Rptdly backs Miller selectn 12-28, 1000B3
SHAPP, Gov. Milton J. (D, Pa.)
Acts in gas emergency 1-18, 1-26, 54B2
Offcls die in air crash 2-24, 204D3
FEC orders fund repaymt 5-12, agrees 5-13, 482B2
Pa budget passed, fscl crisis eased 8-20, 666D1
Defends ouster of black 9-28, 800C2
Govs' panel visits DC 11-29, 960A1
SHARAF, Abdul Hamid
Vs separate pact with Israel 8-14, 623E3
Meets Carter 9-28, 734A1
SHARARA, Samir Mohammed Hassan
Hijacks jet, surrenders 6-29, 535B2
SHARIF, Bassam
Scores Jordan, Egypt 7-14, 534G3
SHARIF, Mohammed
Seeks mil aid vs govt 4-24, 313D2
SHARJA—*See UNITED Arab Emirates*
SHARMA, S. D.
Loses Parlt seat 3-16—3-20, 205C2
SHARMAN, Bill
NBA final standings 4-10, 331D3
SHARON, Maj. Gen. Ariel (ret.)
Party wins 2 parlt seats 5-17, 377D1
Israel agri min 6-20, 474E2
Submits new setlmt plan 9-2, 685F1
Vs US peace plan 9-25, 733B2
Greets Sadat 11-19, 889C1
SHARON Steel Corp.—*See D W G Corp.*
SHARP, Gen. Sir John
Dies 1-15, 84E3
SHARP, Mitchell
Seaborn Viet missn cover-up rptd 1-14, 97B3
SHARP, Justice Susie
Bird named Calif justice 2-12, 140C3
SHARPE, John (Bermuda prime minister)
No confidence move fails 2-11, 4 Cabt mins resign 2-15, 374C2
Resigns 8-26, 675E1
Replaced as prime min 8-29, 969C3
SHARPLES, Richard (D. 1973)
Slayers' sentences confrmd 5-2, 374E2
Burrows executed 12-2, 935G2
SHASIN, Valentin D.
Dies 3-22, 306C3
SHAVERS, Earnie
Ali decisions 9-29, 827C3
Ali match telecast probed 11-2, 949F3
SHAW, Irwin
Beggarman on best-seller list 12-4, 1021G2
SHAW, Kristien
Apples win WTT title 8-27, 787E3, F3
SHAW, Lawrence Timothy (Buck)
Dies 3-19, 264E3

1978

SHAH, Capt. Ahmed
Sentncd for Northrop kickback 6-6, 439E3
SHAH, J. C.
Orders Gandhi contempt trial 1-11, 37A3
Condemns Gandhi rule 5-15, 374F2
SHAH, Syed Riaz Hussain
Chrgd with involuntary servitude 3-2, 396E3
SHAHEEN Jr., Michael E.
Carter, Bell cleared on Marston ouster 1-24, 62D2
SHAHI, Agha
Meets India forgn min 2-6—2-7, 113A1
Assured on UK-French jet sale to India 10-16, 797D1
SHAH of Iran—*See PAHLEVI, Shah Mohammed Riza*
SHAHOOD, Judge George
Burke pleads guilty on 2 chrgs, no contest on 3d 9-26, 734C3
SHAHPUR, Gen.
Arrested for Afghan coup plot 8-17, 671F1
SHAKESPEARE, William (1564-1616)
Othello opens 1-30, 887E2
All's Well That Ends Well opens 7-5, 760B1
Henry IV opens 11-27, 1031A2
SHANER, John Herman
Goin' South released 10-6, 970D1
SHANGHAI Communique (1972)
Partial text 976D2
Cited in statemts on US-Peking ties 12-15—12-17, 973F1, A2, 976A2
SHANKER, Albert
AFT to organize nurses 11-29, 961B1
SHANNON, Daniel
Sued by US on Teamster pensn funds 2-1, 83C1
SHANNON, James M.
Wins US House seat 11-7, 847C3, 851C1
SHAPARD, Virginia
Leads Ga US House primary, runoff set 8-8, 625C3
Wins primary runoff 8-29, 683E1
Loses electn 11-7, 852F2
SHAPIRO, Irving
Sees Carter, backs inflatn plan 4-20, 361G3
SHAPIRO, Mel
Stop the World opens 8-3, 887C3
SHAPIRO, Peter
Wins Essex Cnty exec electn 11-7, 849D1
SHAPP, Gov. Milton J. (D, Pa.)
Sees Carter on coal strike 2-23, 122E3
SHARBAUGH, H. Robert
Replaced as Sun chief exec 9-9, 809C1
SHARIAT Madari, Ayatollah Haj Seyyed Kazem
To ask natl electns 7-12, 574B1
Denies link to Abadan fire 8-20, 639E3
Asks anti-govt resistance 9-13, 9-14, 740E1
Warns govt on reforms 11-1, 827F3
SHARIF Emami, Jaffar—*See EMAMI, Jaffar Sharif*
SHARJA—*See NONALIGNED Nations Movement, UNITED Arab Emirates*
SHARKEY, Susan
Strawberry Fields opens 6-4, 887D3
SHARON, Ariel
Questns Sinai setlmt halt 2-13, 98A2
Setlmt policy retained 2-26, 138D3
Reversed order on settlmt 3-7, 157F1
W Bank setlmts move canceled 8-14, 639B1
SHARP, Edwin
FBI admits media informants 7-13, 554B1
SHARP, Rep. Philip R. (D, Ind.)
Reelected 11-7, 850B4
SHASTEEN, Donald E.
Wins US Sen primary in Neb 5-9, 363F1
Loses electn 11-7, 854F3
SHATTUCK, John
Notes 95th Cong gains 10-20, 981A3
SHAVERS, Earnie
Holmes decisions 3-25, 600B1
SHAW, Gaylord
Wins Pulitzer Prize 4-17, 315A2
SHAW, George Bernard (1856-1950)
My Astonishing Self opens 1-18, 760F2
Man & Superman revived 12-17, 1031D2
SHAW, Irwin
Beggarman, Thief on best-seller list 9-4, 708D1
SHAW, Robert
Dies 8-28, 708D3
Force 10 released 12-21, 1030G2
SHAW, Stan
Boys In Company C released 1-31, 618D3

1979

SHAHEEN Jr., Michael E.
Denies Vesco probe cover-up 8-29, 647A3
SHAHI, Agha
Ends Iran visit 3-11; Pak quits CENTO 3-12, 181B3
In US A-talks 10-17—10-18, 794B2
SHAH of Iran—*See PAHLEVI, Shah Mohammed Riza (Iran)*
SHAKA, Bassam
Tied to W Bank terrorism; ouster ordrd, ct delays 11-8; W Bank protests, mayors quit 11-11—11-15; Israel widens chrgs 11-15, 881C2
Deportatn appeal ordrd 11-22, hearing held 11-29; freed, reinstated 12-5, 916A3
Israeli-Arab W Bank clashes 11-27—12-22, 979C3
SHAKEMAN, Michael L.
Chicago patronage ruled illegal 9-24, 770E3
SHAKER, Saadun
Iraqi interior min 7-16, 544F3
SHAKESPEARE, William (1564-1616)
Coriolanus opens 3-14, 292C1; 6-28, 711C2
Umbatha opens 4-9, 712B3
Richard III opens 6-14, 712B2
Othello opens 8-8, 712A2
SHAKE Your Body (Down to the Ground) (recording)
On best-seller list 5-30, 448E3
SHAKIBA, Mohammad Rashid
Denies unrest in Sanandaj 8-19, 635C1
SHAKRI, Gen. Hossein
Iran armed forces chief 7-21, 565G2
SHALALA, Donna E.
On urban displacemt 2-13, 132A3
SHALE Oil
Carter outlines proposals 4-5, 250E3
Admin plans previewed 7-8, 517E3
Carter seeks Energy Sec Corp 7-15, 532C2, 534B1
SHAME of the Jungle (film)
Released 9-14, 820C3
SHAMROCK Broadcasting Co.
Starr Broadcasting acquisitn OKd 6-8, 588G1
SHAMROCK Meats Inc.
Settles '78 beef-price suit 10-22, 985E3
SHAPIRO, Arnold
Wins Oscar 4-9, 336B2
SHAPIRO, Irving
Scores Carter Cabt shake-up 7-19, 531B2
Backs IBM case judge's ouster 7-19, 610B3
On du Pont monopoly case dismissal 9-17, 810D1
SHAPIRO, Mel
Bosoms & Neglect opens 5-3, 711F1
SHAPOSHNIKOVA, Natalia (Natasha)
Wins Spartakaide gymnastics title 7-26, 799E1
SHARIAT Madari, Ayatollah Haj Seyyed Kazem
Listed in Moslem hierarchy 297A3
Vs referendum plan 3-11, 179E3
Plea for Afghan Moslem rebels cited 3-22, 233B1
Backs amnesty for ex-offcls 5-13, 357C1
Taleghani dies 9-10, 688A1
Vs US Emb takeover 11-26, 895F3
New charter protested, home attacked 12-5; backers seize Tabriz 12-6, 915A3
Defies Khomeini, backs Azerbaijan autonomy 12-7; supporters rally, violence erupts 12-7—12-13, 935E3
Mofateh slain 12-18, 958B3
Backers seize 9 hostages 12-27, stage rally 12-30; release asked 12-31, 975E3
SHARIF, Omar
Bloodline released 6-28, 819F3
SHARJA—*See NONALIGNED Nations Movement, UNITED Arab Emirates*
SHARKEY, Bill
Knoetze KOs, fight protested 1-13, 79D2
SHARON, Ariel
Votes vs Israel-Egypt pact 3-22, 197B1
Vs death penalty for terrorists 4-29, 319F3
Palestinian talks open 5-25, 394A3
Urges more W Bank, Gaza setlmts 5-30, 415B2
Says US seeks Palestinian state 6-15, 474D3
SHARON Steel Corp.
Buys UV Industries assets 11-26, 986C2
SHARPS Pixley Inc.
London gold price role described 2-7, 83C1, G1
SHATNER, William
Star Trek released 12-8, 1008F1
SHAVERS, Earnie
KOs Norton 3-23, 412C3
Holmes TKOs 9-28, 838C3
SHAW, Bernard
Marries Patricia Hearst 4-1, 271G2
SHAW, Frank
Frisco Kid released 7-6, 820C1
SHAW, George Bernard (1856-1950)
Candida opens 3-6, 711A2
SHAW, Robert
In NFL draft 5-3, 335G1

1980

SHAHEEN, John
Petro-Canada to buy refinery 8-1, 633C1
SHAHI, Agha
US offers econ, mil aid 1-12, 27B1
US aid offer dismissed 3-5, 165A2
SHAH of Iran—*See PAHLEVI, Shah Mohammed Riza*
SHAIB, Musa
Slain 7-28, 579A3
SHAKA, Bassam
Bomb blast maims 6-2; blames Israel 6-3, 417B1
Jordan treats 5-6; US offers aid, Israel scores bid 6-10, 434F2
Returns home 7-9, 547A2
Meets 2 Israeli CP parlt members 9-25, 736F3
SHAKESPEARE, William (1564-1616)
Ages of Man wins Grammy 2-27, 296G3
Twelfth Night opens 12-16, 1003F3
SHAKHRAI, Sergei
Wins Olympic medal 2-17, 155F3
Wins world figure skating title 3-12, 470B2
SHALE Oil—*See PETROLEUM (& Petroleum Products)*
SHALLO, Karen
We Won't Pay! opens 12-17, 1003G3
SHAMANSKY, Bob
Elected to US House 11-4, 843E4, 846G1, 851D2
SHAMBERG, Michael
Heart Beat released 4-25, 416A3
SHAMIR, Yitzhak
Named Israel forgn min 3-9, confirmed 3-10, 179A3
Cabt vs shift to defns post 5-27, 429E3
On Saudi peace proposal 5-28, 395D2
Dutch assure no EC Mideast peace move 6-4, 418E1
Protests French-Iraqi A-deal 7-28, 573A3
Protests US UN vote on Jerusalem 8-21, 643C2
Scores EC re terrorist violence 10-7, 767B3
Vs Weizman electn tour with Carter 10-28, 830E2
Palestinian autonomy talks suspended 12-4, 912B3
SHAMSA, Dr. Mansour
Visits US hostages 4-14, 282E2
SHAMS Ardakani, Ali
Ends Iran boycott of UN 10-15, 774D1
SHAMUYARIRA, Nathan M.
Zimbabwe info min 3-11, 198D1
On Zimbabwe press curbs 10-19, 833D3
SHANER, John Herman
Last Married Couple released 2-8, 216B3
SHANGE, Ntozake
Mother Courage opens 5-13, 392E3
SHANK, Duane
Vows pres conv draft protests 6-24, 478D3
SHANKAR, P. Shiv
Named Indian law min 1-14, 39F3
SHANKER, Albert
Carter gets AFT endorsemt 8-21, addresses conv 8-22, 646G2
SHANKER, Mark
First Deadly Sin released 10-24, 836G2
SHANNON, Rep. James M. (D, Mass.)
On oil import fee bar 6-5, 437A2
Wins renominatn despite RC bid vs abortn 9-16, 724D2
Reelected 11-4, 843C1
SHANNON & Luchs Co. v. U.S.
Case declined by Sup Ct 1-21, 93B3
SHAPIRO, Debbie
Perfectly Frank opens 11-30, 1003E3
SHAPIRO, George
In God We Trust released 9-26, 836C3
SHAPIRO, Irving S.
Named Econ Revitalizatn Bd co chrmn 8-28, 663C2
SHAPOSHNIKOVA, Natalya
Wins Olympic medals 7-25, 589A3, 622G3, 623A1
SHARAF, Abdul Hamid (Jordanian prime minister; died July 3)
Dies 7-3, 608C3
Rimawi named prime min 7-3, Badran 8-28, 698G1
SHARIAT Madari, Ayatollah Haj Seyyed Kazem
Backers clash in Qom, Tabriz 1-4—1-6, 4A1
Denies tie to Moslem People's Party 1-5, 4C1
Tabriz unrest continues 1-7—1-9; visitors barred 1-8, curfew imposed 1-10, 20A2
Tabriz followers riot vs executns 1-12, 30B1
SHARIF, Abu
Quits as guard cmdr 6-17, 464B2
Replaced as Rev Guard cmdr, named dep 6-29, 490C2
SHARJA—*See UAE*
SHARKEY, Ray
Idolmaker released 11-14, 972F3
SHARON Steel Corp.
UV Industries deal final; SEC probe, Reliance suits cited 9-26, 746B2
SHARP, Don
39 Steps released 5-2, 416F3
SHARP, Rep. Philip R. (D, Ind.)
Reelected 11-4, 842C4
SHATTUCK, John
Scores Abscam probe tactics 2-6, 82F2
SHAW, Mayor Clay (Ft. Lauderdale, Fla.)
Wins US House primary 9-9, 700B2
Elected to US House 11-4, 842G2, 849E2
SHAW, George Bernard (1856-1950)
Major Barbara opens 2-26, 392D3
Heartbreak House opens 4-29, 392B3
SHAW, Sam
Gloria released 10-1, 836A3

1976

SHCHARANSKY, Anatoly
Shchelokov sees 10-21, 856G3
Freed 11-8, 966D3
SHCHELOKOV, Nikolai A.
Sees Jewish dissidents 10-21, 856G3
SHCHERBITSKY, Vladimir V.
Politburo named 3-5, 195D2
SHEAR, David
Wins Rockefeller award 11-16, 911F3
SHEARER, William K.
Maddox gets Amer Indep Party pres bid 8-27, 666E1
SHEEHAN, Edward R. F.
Kissinger, Ford act on leaks article 3-12, 3-17, 198B2
SHEEHAN, William
Westin quits ABC 1-26, 160E2
SHEEHY, Gail
Passages on best-seller list 12-5, 972B2
SHEET Metal Workers' International Association (AFL-CIO)
Carlough quits Ford panel 1-8, 4C1
SHEHAN, Lawrence Cardinal
Intl Eucharistic Cong 8-1—8-8, 596B3
SHEHU, Mehmet
Myftin named deputy 10-13, 850B1
SHEINKMAN, Jacob
Clothing, textile unions merge 6-3, 436G1
SHELDON, Georgiana H.
Civil Svc v chrmn 2-3; confrmd 2-26, 186C2
SHELDON, Sidney
Stranger on best-seller list 12-5, 972E2
SHELL International Petroleum Co.
In Australia gas deal 8-8, 650B2
BAC, Iran deal signed 11-18, 906A2
Shell Oil Co. (U.S.)
'74 NY trust case rptd pending 3-11, 413F1
In Viet oil talks 4-24, 352B2
Colo oil shale leases suspended, consortium breakup cited 8-23, 648G3, 649D1
SHELL Oil Co.—*See under SHELL International Petroleum Co.*
SHELLY, Mary Josephine
Dies 8-6, 892E3
SHEMTOV, Victor
On Kadum closure move 5-9, 338G1
SHENANDOAH (play)
Long run listed 12-31, 1015A1
SHEP, Lee
Sentenced 4-12, 316B3

1977

SHAWA, Rashid al-
Fears move for W Bank Arab rights 8-15, 623B2
SHCHARANSKY, Anatoly
CIA link chrgd 3-4, press interview blocked 3-7; arrested 3-15, 226B3-E3
Treason chrgd 6-1; US protests 6-2, denies CIA link 6-6, 436E1
Toth questned re contacts 6-15, 475D1
Levich questioned 7-20, 551G2
Axelrod arrested 9-21, 753C1
To face treason chrg 10-28; US voices concern 10-31, 11-17, 955A2
Honored by B'nai B'rith 11-20, 955G1
Westn attys plan pub trials 11-28, 955B2
Defense atty expelled 12-4, 956C1
US bars USSR book pact 12-7, 955E2
US sci acad asks trial observers 12-15, 1017E1
Detentn extended 12-15, 1017G1
SHCHARANSKY, Natalia
Asks US aid re husband 11-20, 955A2
SHEARMAN & Sterling
On 5 largest law firms list 5-16, 383A2
SHEARSON Hayden Stone Inc.
Weill on Dean Witter-Reynolds merger 10-3, 799F3
SHEEHAN, William
Replaced as ABC News pres 5-2, 395A2
Disputes ABC-CIA link 9-12, 720E3
SHEEHY, Gail
Passages on best-seller list 2-6, 120F3; 3-6, 184F3; 4-3, 264A2; 5-1, 356C2; 6-4, 452A2; 7-3, 548E3, F3; 8-14, 643A2; 9-4, 712E3; 10-2, 808F3; 11-6, 872F3; 12-4, 1021A3
SHEEP—*See LIVESTOCK*
SHEIK, Mohammed Adan
Backs Ogaden truce 9-20, 756E2
SHEIL, Glenister
Australia vets affairs min 12-19, 982B2
Fired for pro-apartheid stand 12-21, 982B2
SHELDON, Sidney
Stranger in the Mirror on best-seller list 4-3, 264A2; 5-1, 356D2
Other Side of Midnight on best-seller list 8-14, 643A2; 9-4, 712F3
SHELDON, William Herbert
Dies 9-19, 788F2
SHELL Chemical Co.—*See under SHELL International Petroleum Co.*
SHELLEDY, James E. (Jay)
Ida secret news source case review refused 10-31, 835F2
SHELL International Petroleum Co.
In UK N Sea pact 1-5, 20E3
Canada operatns end cited 6-4, 466D3
Australia OKs NW Shelf gas search 8-24, 704E3
Shell Chemical Co.
DBCP product curbed 8-12, 723E2
Shell Oil Co. (U.S.)
US revokes Mont coal leases 1-13, 58F3
US forgn paymts rptd 2-16, 233B3
US gas probe set 2-17, 151F3
On '76 Fortune 500 list 340E1, C3
Lonhro sues re Rhodesia sales 5-31, 413C2
FTC info order review rejctd 6-13, 517G1
Seadock backing rptd 7-19, 559F2
Loop license signed 8-1, 724E3
Washington state sues 8-16, 691E3
Zambia sues re Rhodesia sanctns 8-22, 662D1
SHELL Oil Co.—*See under SHELL International Petroleum Co.*
SHELL Oil v. Dartt
Age bias filing time extended 11-29, 919B2
SHEMTOV, Victor
Questns rights for W Bank, Gaza Arabs 8-15, 623A2
SHEN Chang-huan
Vs US Peking stand 7-2, 514A1
SHENKER, Morris
Bramlet found slain 3-17, US sues 3-30, 261F3
SHENOUDA III, Pope Anba (Coptic)
Arrives NY 4-14, 471F2
Egypt drops anti-Copt law 9-12, 863E2
SHEPARD, Dr. Charles C.
On Legion fever bacteria 1-18, 81E1

1978

SHAWHAN, April
History of Amer Film opens 3-30, 760D2
SHAY (play)
Opens 3-7, 887A3
SHAY, Dorothy
Dies 10-22, 888E3
SHAZLI, Lt. Gen. Saad Eddin al-
Egypt ordrs recall; scores Sadat 6-19, defies return 6-20, 473A2
SHCHARANSKY, Anatoly
Lawyer rptd named 2-24, 179G3
Roommate rptd linked to CIA 3-6, 179D3
Beilin visa OK rptd 3-7, 180G1
Wife called imposter 3-8, 180A1
Sovt lawyer rptd rejected 3-15, 275G3
Toon warns USSR 4-3, 275E3
Swap rptd discussed, US discounts 4-24, 318F2
Trial set 7-7, US cancels visits 7-8, 542A1
Trial starts 7-10, sentncd 7-14; US, other protests 7-10—7-18, 541A1-543C1
Carter rebukes Young for remarks on US 'pol prisoners' 7-12—7-15, 542E2
Vance gives Gromyko protest note 7-12, sees wife 7-13, 543E2
Carter deplores convictn 7-20, 549C2
US observer manhandled by emb guard 7-20, 575C3
US cancels 3d offcl trip 7-25, 575C3
Family sees Kennedy 9-9, 743B1
SHCHARANSKY, Leonid
At brother's trial 7-10—7-14, 541B1, F1
SHCHARANSKY, Natalia (Avital)
Called imposter 3-8, 180A1
Dutch premier vows aid 7-11, 543C1
Sees Vance 7-13, 543F2
Asks US Cong support 7-17, 542E1
SHEA, John
Safe House opens 4-13, 760C3
SHEAR, Bob
2d In Garden State PGA 10-22, 990B2
SHEEHAN, George
Running & Being on best-seller list 7-2, 579D3
SHEEHY, Gail
Passages on best-seller list 1-8, 24F3
SHEEKMAN, Arthur
Dies 1-12, 96E3
SHEEP—*See LIVESTOCK*
SHEET Metal Workers' International Association (AFL-CIO)
A-plant constructn accord excludes 4-18, 281C3
New RR pact set 7-21, 565E1
SHEETZ, Jack A.
Named in US Teamster fund suit 2-1, 83F1
SHEKHAR, Chandra
Narain scores Janata ldrship 6-29, 516A2
Gets plea on Aligarh riot, gives rpt 10-15, 797G1
SHELBY, Richard C.
Wins US House seat 11-7, 849B3, 850B1
SHELDON, Sidney
Bloodline on best-seller list 3-5, 195D3; 4-2, 272A3; 4-30, 356F1; 6-4, 460A3; 7-2, 579B3; 8-6, 620A2; 9-4, 708B1
SHELKOV, Vladimir A.
Arrested 3-14, 275C3
SHELL International Petroleum Co.
Australia unit to close nickel mine 2-4, 88F1
Shell Oil Co.
On '77 Fortune 500 list 5-8, 325F1
Brittany hq bombed 5-29, 474C1
Pipeline divestiture urged by Sen subcom 6-21, 471E1
Interstate gas sale probed 6-22, 471A2
Crude oil '73-74 price violatns chrgd 7-2, 610E2
Lead-free gas productn rptd down 11-20, 939G1
FTC trust probe rptd 11-28, 939C2
Gas sale monopoly suit filed, chrgs denied 11-30, 939D3
Gas rationing begins 12-1, eased 12-6, 938F3
NJ offshore well rptd dry 12-11, 1010B1, D1
SHELL Oil Co.—*See under SHELL International*
SHELTON, Lonnie
Sent to SuperSonics as Webster compensatn 10-29, 1027C3
SHELTON, Sally A.
El Salvador rights abuse rptd worse 8-5, 723A3 *
SHELTON, Timothy
Cops opens 3-28, 760F1
SHEN, C. Y.
In Kuomintang Party shift 1-6, 38C2
SHEN, James C. H.
Leaves amb post in US 12-29, 995A1
SHENANDOAH Oil Corp.
Petro-Lewis plans purchase; Union Pacific pact, '77 losses cited 5-15, 403G3-404A1
SHEN Chang-huan
Scores Japan-China pact 8-12, 637D2
Resigns as forgn min 12-16, 974C2
SHENEFIELD, John H.
Stiff trust penalty imposed 2-3, 142D2
Vs LTV-Lykes merger, overruled 6-21, 492E3
On '71-77 merger rise 7-28, 767D1-A2
On merger notificatns, probes 10-4, 767C1
On trust voluntary disclosure plan 10-4, 768F1-C2
SHEPARD Jr., Alan
Gets space medal of honor 10-1, 861C2

1979

SHAWA, Rashid al-
PFLP threatens 6-3, 414G2
SHAY, Michele
Coriolanus opens 6-28, 711C2
SHCHARANSKY, Anatoly
US scientists cut Sovt links 3-1, 172A2
SHCHERBITSKY, Vladimir Vasilyevich
Gets Supreme Sovt seat 3-4, 237G2
SHEA, John
Sorrows of Stephen opens 12-11, 1007E2
SHEA, Mary
Sets 10000-m run mark 6-16, 911B2
SHEARER, Bob
2d in West Lakes Classic 10-28, Australian PGA 11-1, 970A2, B2
SHEARER, Harry
Real Life released 3-1, 174E3
SHEARSON Hayden Stone Inc.
Loeb Rhoades merger set 5-14, 366A3
SHEDD, Jacqueline Phillips
Wins Oscar 4-9, 336B2
SHEEHAN, Neil
Arnheiter libel cases declined by Sup Ct 10-29, 884A2
SHEEN, Archbishop Fulton J.
Dies 12-9, 1008E3
SHEEN, Martin
Apocalypse Now released 8-15, 819D3
SHEEP—*See LIVESTOCK*
SHEINKMAN, Jacob
Urges shoe-import bid 3-6, 207C1
SHELDON, Sidney
Bloodline on best-seller list 3-4, 173F3; 4-8, 271B2; 5-6, 356E2; 7-1, 548D3
Bloodline released 6-28, 819E3
SHELKOV, Vladimir A.
Sentenced 3-23, 238C1
SHELLEY (play)
Opens 4-14, 712D2
SHELLEY, Carole
Elephant Man opens 1-14, 292E1
SHELLEY, Percy Bysshe (1792-1822)
Shelley opens 4-14, 712D2
SHELL International Petroleum Co.
1st $^1/_4$ oil profits rptd 4-27, 301B2
On '78 Fortune 500 list 5-7, 304F1
Australia profits rptd down 5-8, 351F3
3d 1/4 oil profits rptd up 10-25, 804D3
Shell Oil Co.
US files overchrg suit 1-5, 17B1
Ohio EPA sulphur-dioxide emissns case refused by US Sup Ct 1-15, 32B1
NJ offshore well rptd dry, Atlantic search abandoned 2-14, 186E3
Refinery reductn set 2-21, 126B2
Energy Comm gas productn power denied by Sup Ct 2-22, 150F3
May gas allocatn rptd cut 5-7, 343A1
June gas supplies cut 5-30, 395D3
US overchrgs alleged 11-6, 849G2; 11-8, 905F2; 11-18, 943F1; 12-19, 990E2
Accident liability case refused by Sup Ct 12-3, 964D2
Belridge Oil acquired 12-10; Mobil, Texaco sue 12-11, 942D1
SHELL Oil Co.—*See under SHELL International Petroleum Co.*
SHELL Oil Co. v. Deukmejian
Case declined by Sup Ct 3-5, 185E1
SHELL Oil Co. v. Olsen
Case refused by Sup Ct 12-3, 964E2
SHELL Oil Co. v. U.S. Environmental Protection Agency
Case refused by Sup Ct 1-15, 32B1
SHELTON, Chad (d. 1978)
Harper sentncd to death 11-7, 891B1
SHELTON, Lonnie
Sonics win NBA title 6-1, 506G3
Webster '78 compensatn voided 9-19, 1003C2
SHELTON, Robert
KKK activity rptd 7-22, 865G2
SHENEFIELD, John H.
Oil co pipe ownership bar asked 1-4, 55G2
On natl trust comm rpt 1-16, 88D2
Backs Kennedy merger-limit bill 3-8, 202F2
Merger curbs rptd backed 5-7, 349F2
On oil firm-shortage probe 5-15, 361F2

1980

SHAWA, Rashid al-
Meets US aide, vs autonomy talks 1-30, 89B2
Quits as Gaza mayor 6-2, 417F1
Withdraws resignatn 6-5, 547C2
Meets Begin on Kawasmeh, Milhem ouster 10-21, 822A3
SHAWCROSS, William
Wins Polk award 2-25, 692G3
SHAWN, Wallace
Marie & Bruce opens 2-3, 136C3
SHAYEVICH, Rabbi Adolf
Installed in Moscow 4-12, 431D1
SHAZLI, Saad Eddin al-
Heads anti-Sadat front 4-2, 273B3
SHCHARANSKY, Anatoly
US scientists seek Sovt boycott 4-16, 326A3
SHEA Jr., George E.
Dies 4-27, 360E3
SHEARSON Loeb Rhoades Inc.
NYSE halts trading 3-27, 223C2
Ford electn to bd rptd 5-22, 456A3
SHEEHAN, Daniel
3 Mile I gas venting danger seen 6-18, 550D3
SHEEHAN, Francis
Quits Anderson campaign 8-28, 665C3
SHEEN, Martin
Final Countdown released 8-1, 675F2
SHEEPMEAT—*See MEAT (& Meat Products)*
SHEFFIELD, James E.
Named US dist judge 4-9; tax probe leak halts Sen hearing 8-27, bars withdrawal 9-9, 744D3
SHEHATI, Ahmed
Warns dissidents 6-7, 451B3
SHEHU, Fecor
Rptd Albania interior min 5-2, 356E2
SHEHU, Mehmet
Rptd replaced as defns min 5-2, 356E2
SHEIK, Gen. Abdul Rahman
Saudi security forces head 1-1, 22D1
SHELBY, Rep. Richard C. (D, Ala.)
Reelected 11-4, 842B1
SHELDON, Sidney
Rage of Angels on best-seller list 7-13, 568A3; 3-17, 640F3; 9-14, 716A3; 10-12, 796D3
SHELKOV, Vladimir A.
Dies in prison 1-27, 87G3
SHELLEY, Norman
Dies 8-18, 676A3
SHELLEY: Also Known As Shirley (book)
On best-seller list 8-17, 640F3; 9-14, 716B3; 10-12, 796E3
SHELL Oil Co. (of Royal Dutch Shell)
'79 profit rptd 1-31, 90F2
Mobil, Texaco drop Belridge litigatn 3-6, 385D3
1st 1/4 profit rptd, Belridge acquisitn cited 4-23, 331D1-G1
On '79 Fortune 500 list 5-5, 290F1
Solar production rptd 5-5, 554D1
US offshore leasing schedule scored 6-17, 552A3
Saudi petro complex deal agreed 7-9, 524G2
UK gasoline prices cut 8-11, 628G1
Gasoline prices cut 9-11, 786B1
Gulf coast leasing bids set records 9-30, 785B2
Canada oil sands operatn threatnd 11-19, 921A1
Shell Chemical Co.
La chem-dump suit names 7-15, 558G3
SHE Loves Me (recording)
Lennon slain 12-8, 934C3
SHENANGO Inc.
Pa plant pollutn curbs OKd 8-22, 825C2
SHENG-Dean Chen
Taiwan wins Little League title 8-30, 796G2

1976

SHEPHERD, Jack
Adams Chronicles on best-seller list 12-5, 972D2
SHEPHERD of Spalding, Lord (Malcolm Newton) (Great Britain)
Resigns from Cabt 9-10, 693C3
SHERATON Corp. of America—*See INTERNATIONAL Telephone & Telegraph*
SHERER Jr., Albert W.
Replaced as amb to Czech 4-28, 412E1
US vetoes Angola UN entry 6-23, 455E1, G1
Vetoes Israel Arab land exit 6-29, 464D1
SHERIFF, Ahmed Fuad
Dies 8-6, 892E3
SHEVARDNADZE, Eduard
Rpts Georgian harvest damage 3-23, 321E3
SHIFFMAN, Theodore
Sentencing rptd 7-20, 860E2
SHIHATA, Ibrahim F. I.
To head OPEC poor nation fund 5-11, 389F1
SHIINA, Etsaburo
Backs Miki ouster 5-13, Miki bars reconciliatn talks 5-26, 458G1, B2
SHIKONGO, Hendrik
Sentenced 5-12, 386B2
SHIMADA, Adm. Shigetaro
Dies 6-7, 524E3
SHIMKUS, Joanna
Weds Poitier 1-23, 271E3
SHINE, Michael
Wins Olympic medal 7-25, 575F3
SHINING Star (recording)
Wins Grammy 2-28, 460B3
SHIN Jik Soo
Ousted as KCIA head 12-4, 928F2
SHIPLEY, Rep. George Edward (D, Ill.)
Travel expense probe ends 10-27, 981G3
Reelected 11-2, 829A3

SHIPS & Shipping—*See also 'Marine' under ACCIDENTS; also HARBORS & Ports; appropriate headings under U.S. GOVERNMENT; also country, company names*
Nigeria port legis rptd 1-5, 102G3
Major US banks on 'problem' list 1-11, 110F3
5 Armada ships found 1-11, 124C3
Egypt buys Greek tankers 1-16, 73D2
Argentina fires on UK ship 2-4, 220D2
US-Israel co default rptd 2-9, 173G3
Laos-N Viet talks 2-11, 121E1
Australia to OK US navigatn base 2-17, 137C2
USSR-Cape Verde pact rptd 3-6, 404D1
Pacific Forum meets 3-8—3-9, 179C2
Finnish seamen, dockworkers strike 3-9, 4-3, 266C1
Australia OKs US base 3-23, 237D1
New ship-measuring system for Panama Canal ordrd 3-23, 292B1
Japan dockworkers strike 4-10—4-16, 290C3
Iran, Pak, Turkey set RCD co 4-22, 298C2
Finnish dock strike ends 5-3, 355A2
UK govt wins natlzn ruling 5-27, 410G3 ★
Sea-Land rebates, paymts rptd 5-28—9-13, 689A3
UK defers natlzn plans 6-7, 407B3
Dem platform text 6-15, 476D2
China cancels Japan talks 7-16, 555E2
US-Sovt rate pact 7-19, 558D3
US protests Sovt grain shipmts 8-17, 655E2
GOP platform text 8-18, 611A1
US A-ship in NZ spurs dock strike 8-27—9-2, 677E2
Probe of MEBA, SIU gifts to Ford rptd 9-21, 9-25, 722G1-F2, F3
US-Sovt grain shipping talks 9-30—10-7, 856A3
'76 Panama Canal traffic down 10-5, 793F1
Arab boycott rpts released 10-18—10-20, 785F3
USSR seeks Atlantic conf entry 10-22, 948C1
UK govt wins natlzn, dock worker debate limit votes 11-8, 852G3, 853A1, C1
US OKs E Ger ship's entry 889F1
France, UK set cooperatn 11-12, 880C2
Panama Canal tolls hiked 11-18, US shippers score 11-24, 1008C3

1977

SHERATON Hawaii Corp.—*See INTERNATIONAL Telephone & Telegraph Corp.*
SHERCK, Douglas
Deserts Rhodesia army 2-9, arrested 3-2, 144E3
SHERIF Hussein Mohamed
On Somali union, troop data 8-1, 608C1
SHERLOCK, William
Killed 2-24, 204D3
SHERMAN, George
At Cairo conf 12-14—12-15, 953G1
SHERRY, Norm
Fired as Angel mgr 7-11, 990A2
SHERWIN-Williams Co.
Saccharin ban scored 3-9, 176E3
SHEYENNE River
ND irrigatn project scored 1-7, 60E3
ND projct scored 9-19, 726E1
SHIHATA, Ibrahim F. I.
On OPEC investmt plans 12-7, 997E3
SHIKONGO, Hendrik
Freed 3-17, 349B3
SHING Chang
Rpts on DNA recombinatn 10-8, 846E3
SHINN, Robert
Leaves Uganda 3-1, 141B2
SHIPPING Associations, North Atlantic Council of
E Coast dock protest ends 4-18, 324F2 ★

SHIPS (& Shipping)—*See also ACCIDENTS—Marine; also HARBORS & Ports; appropriate headings under U.S. GOVERNMENT; also country, company names*
Sup Ct bars longshoremen loading case review 1-10, 57F1
Ford '78 budget proposals 1-17, 33B2
Tidal marine auditors sued 2-16, 156C2
Carter budget revision 2-22, 125C3
AFL-CIO to seek oil cargo share 2-22, 153D2
E Coast dock protest 4-14—4-18, 324D2
ILWU's Bridges retires 4-18, 324G2
US Coast Guard authorizatn clears Cong 6-21, 501B1
US subsidized ships to transport Alaska oil 6-24, 498G1
US tanker cargo preference backed by Admin 7-11, 538A2
US cargo preference debated 7-11—9-9, 719A3
Ex-Rep Garmatz indicted 8-1, 603C3
ILA strikes E, Gulf ports 10-1, 777G3
Cargo preference loses in House 10-19, 815A1
Maritime subsidy authorizatn cleared, rebate language eased 11-1, 856B2; signed 11-12, 1001E2
Lykes 3d ¼ shipping rptd profitable 11-4, 943B3
Oct exports drop, strike linked 11-28, 933G1
ILA strike ends 11-29, 915F3
ILA aide sentenced 12-2, 937E3
Dock strike impact on Nov trade deficit cited 12-28, 1003F1
Foreign Developments (including U.S. international news)—*See also other appropriate subheads in this section; also WATERS, Territorial*
Nigeria pirates rptd 1-9, 48C2
Sweden to settle US-Sovt disputes 1-11, 29F3
Japan rejcts EC plan 1-17, trade talks rptd settled 1-18; comm study issued 1-24, 73F2
Belgium-Zaire talks 1-17—1-24, 200A1
Australia-Japan dispute 1-17—2-21, deals set 2-16, 3-15, 253E1-F2
Gen Dynamics wins US loan guarantee, Burmah paymt to Park cited 1-19, 55D1-F2
Greek '76 paymts gap narrows 2-10, 135B1

1978

SHEPARD, Sam
Starving Class opens 3-2, 887B3
Days of Heaven released 9-13, 970A1
Buried Child opens 11-6, 1031B1
SHEPHERD, Mark
US trade missn arrives Japan 10-2, asks trade boost 10-5, 10-13, 797C3, 798B1
SHERIN, Edwin
Somersaults opens 1-9, 760A2
1st Monday in Oct opens 10-3, 1031F1
SHERK, Cathy
Wins Canadian, US Women's Amateur golf titles 8-12, 8-19, 990E1
SHERMAN, Arthur
November People opens 1-14, 760A3
SHERMAN, John W.
Convicted 7-11, 824A3
SHERMAN, Richard M.
Magic of Lassie released 8-3, 970B2
SHERMAN, Robert
Convoy released 6-28, 619C1
Magic of Lassie released 8-3, 970B2
SHERMAN Antitrust Act—*See ANTITRUST*
SHERO, Fred
Quits as Flyers coach 5-22, OKs Rangers contract 6-1, 458G2
SHERWOOD, David J.
Named Prudential pres 7-11, 809A1
SHETLAND Islands—*See GREAT Britain*
SHEVARNADZE, Eduard Ambrosievich
Heckled at language protest 4-14, 275B2
USSR Politburo alternate 11-27, 924D3
SHEVCHENKO, Arkady Nikolayevich
Renounces Sovt citizenship 4-10; CIA, FBI links rptd 4-21, defects to US 4-26, 302A2
Wife kills self 5-8, 440E3
Denies CIA financed gifts 10-13, 844A3
SHEVCHENKO, Leongina I. (Mrs. Arkady)
Kills self 5-8, 440E3
SHEVIN, Robert
Faces primary runoff for Fla gov 9-12, 736C1
Loses runoff 10-5, 769G1
SHIBA, Lt. Col. Ali
Takes power in N Yemen 6-25, 499G1
SHIDIAK, Maj. Sami
Under Christian guard 6-19, 462G2
Ordrd back to Beirut 7-31, 581D1
To be tried for aiding Israel 10-22, 803D1
SHIELDS, Brooke
Pretty Baby released 4-5, 619D3
SHIKUKU, Martin
Freed 12-12, 968G1
SHILLING, Gary
On 3d ¼ profit rise, '79 recessn fears 10-30, 919E2
Carter inflatn plan, $ drop linked 11-1, 826C3
SHIMP, David
Transplant order denied 7-26, 597F2
SHINING, The (book)
On best-seller list 2-5, 116D3; 3-5, 195F3
SHIPANGA, Andreas
Freed 5-25, forms party 6-19, 475G3
SHIPLEY, Rep. George Edward (D, Ill.)
Crane wins seat 11-7, 853B2
SHIPP, Larry
Sets indoor 60-yd high hurdles mark 1-13, Nehemiah breaks 1-27, 76E2, B3

SHIPS (& Shipping)—*See also HARBORS & Ports; appropriate headings under U.S. GOVERNMENT; also country, company names*
Maritime Comm labor contract jurisdictn enlarged 3-1, 143C3-144C1
Farrell acquires Amer Export 888A3
Longshoremen heart study released 3-24, 597G3
State stevedoring tax OKd by Sup Ct 4-26, 344B1
22 indicted on port corruptn 6-7, 480D2
Lykes-LTV merger OKd 6-21, 493E1
Reynolds seeks Del Monte 8-3, bid OKd 9-25, 752B3
RR decline predicted, barge user chrgs urged 10-10, 812E1
Inland Waterways authorzn signed 10-21, 897C2
OSHA to consolidate rules 10-24, 833G3
Carter vetoes malpractice bill 11-4, 897G2

Accidents—*See ACCIDENTS—Marine*
Foreign Developments (including U.S. International news)—*See also 'Safety Issues' below*
France, Ivory Coast cargo pact 1-11—11-15, 71C1
Caricom dvpt plans fail; Jamaica-Mex, Trinidad-US cos planned 1-13, 100F2-A3
W Ger dock strike ends 1-30, 93E3
UK reassigns Polish order 2-5, 112A3
Israel discloses Ethiopia aid 2-6, 100B1
Nigeria in USSR deal 3-21, 248E1
Australia union blocks African ship 4-4, 243E3
Australia ports hit by job actns 4-9—5-2, 349F3-350B1; congestn continues 5-22, 411A2; dock setlmt rptd 6-5, 450F3

1979

SHEPARD, Sam
Seduced opens 2-1, 292A3
Suicide In B Flat opens 3-13, 292B3
Wins Pulitzer 4-16, 336E2, G2
SHEPARD, Thomas Z.
Wins Grammy 2-16, 336G3
SHERATON Boston Hotel (Boston, Mass.)
Fire 3-29, 316C3
SHERIN, Edwin
Losing Time opens 9-30, 956C3
SHERMAN, Gary
Comin' Uptown opens 12-20, 1007C2
SHERMAN, Geoffrey
Ride A Cock Horse opens 3-18, 292E2
SHERMAN, Martin
Bent opens 12-2, 1007C2
SHERPA, Dorje
Climbs Gauri Sankar 5-12, 392F2
SHERPA, Pema
Climbs Annapurna 5-8, 392G2
SHEVCHENKO, Arkady Nikolayevich
Marriage rptd 1-8, 79D1
SHEVEY, Betsy
Warriors opens 5-22, 712D3
SHIBUMI (book)
On best-seller list 7-1, 548A3; 8-5, 620B3
SHIELDS, Brooke
Just You & Me Kid released 7-27, 820E1
SHIMADA, Mitsuhiro
Kills self 2-1, 98E2
Grumman denies Japan bribes 2-6, 305D3
SHIMAZU, Kiyoshi
My Love released 1-4, 174B3
SHIMERMAN, Armin
I Remember Mama opens 5-31, 711G3
SHINDO, Kaneto
My Love released 1-4, 174B3
SHIN Hyon Hwack (South Korean premier)
Named S Korea premr 12-10, 997G1
SHIN Sun Ho
Arrest rptd, bank chiefs ousted 4-13, 287B2-D2
Sentenced 9-14, 710D3
SHIPANGA, Andreas
Facts on 171F2
SHIPPINGPORT, Pa.—*See PENNSYLVANIA*

SHIPS (& Shipping)
Carter budget proposals 1-22, 45F1
Admin drafting legis 1-25, 70D2
NLRB to probe Va shipyd vote 3-2, 187C2
Tenn-Tombigbee projct upheld 3-13, 188A3
Va shipyd strike suspended 4-22, 306C2
Calif cargo container taxes voided by Sup Ct 4-30, 364A3
Diesel fuel allocatn rules adopted 5-25, 395D2
Cong OKs anti-rebate bill 6-5, 465F3
NY tug strike ends 6-27, 500D3
Tex offshore port OKd 7-2, 518F2
Grain handlers strike 7-6—9-25, 722D3-723A1
Curran told to repay NMU benefits 7-27, 744G2
Ingalls shipyds damaged by hurricane 9-12, 691F1
Tex supertanker port OKd 10-15, 769B3
N Orleans reliance cited 11-29, 921G1

Accidents—*See ACCIDENTS—Marine*
Foreign Developments (including U.S. international news)—*See also 'Safety' below*
Spanish galleon rptd found 1-1, 24E1
W Ger urges shipbldg aid 1-21, 77E3
USSR, US petro coke rate OKd 1-25, 60A3
USSR ship ban OKd by FMC 1-29; USSR warns 2-14; Justice, State Depts sue 3-6, 213G2
Hong Kong chrgs Viet boat capt 2-4, 109D1
US-China pact rptd 2-23, 146F2
USSR ship ban delayed by US ct 4-6, 287A3
Bahrain bars Egypt ships 4-17, 278A2
French dock dispute persists 4-24—4-30, 330E1

1980

SHEPARD, Sam
True West opens 12-23, 1003F3
SHEPARD, Thomas Z.
Wins Grammy 2-27, 296G3
SHEPLEY, James R.
Replaced as Time pres 5-15, 456E2
SHERIN, Edwin
Goodbye Fidel opens 4-23, 392G2
SHERMAN, John W. F.
Executed 4-22, 353A2
SHERMAN, Roger
Urges NRC reactor licensing resumptn 1-9, 17C1
SHERMAN, Stanford
Any Which Way You Can released 12-17, 1003F1
SHERRILL, Bishop Henry Knox
Dies 5-11, 448F2
SHEUER, Rep. James H. (D, N.Y.)
Reelected 11-4, 843D3
SHEVELOVE, Burt
Happy New Year opens 4-27, 392A3
SHIBAYEV, Sergei
Ginzburg family arrives NY 2-2, 87F3
SHIBUMI (book)
On best-seller list 7-13, 568D3; 8-17, 640G3
SHIELDS, Brooke
Blue Lagoon released 6-20, 675G1
SHIH Ming-teh
Tried for '79 riot 3-18—3-28, gets life sentence 4-18, 316G1
10 sentncd for harboring 6-5, 468B1
SHIMBERG, Hinks
A Life opens 11-3, 892G2
SHIN Byong Hyun
On '80 econ lag 11-12, 944B1
SHINE, Richard
On bribery guidance offer 3-24, 227A2
SHIN Hyon Hwack (South Korean premier; replaced May 21)
Vows S Korea reforms, urges calm 5-15, 380C3
Quits as premier 5-20, 380D2
New Cabt replaces 5-21, 395C1
Unaffected by purge 11-12, 874B3
SHINING, The (film)
Released 5-23, 675D3
Top-grossing film 5-28, 448G3; 7-2, 568G3
SHINN, Richard
Stevens, ACTWU mtgs rptd 10-20, 805G1-D2
SHIN Pyong Hyon
Named S Korea dep premr 9-2, 673C1
SHIPLEY, Carl L.
Auto-Train investmt plan rptd 11-26, 958A3
SHIPOMEX
Supertanker sinks off Senegal 1-17, 108G2

SHIPS (& Shipping)
Washn State of State message 1-15, 484F1
Oil tanker subsidies repaymt backed by Sup Ct 2-20, 170E2
Va shipyd pact signed 3-31, 251B2
Tampa Port reopened 5-21, 391F1
Container pact ban refusal affirmed by Sup Ct 6-20, 555E2
Dem platform plank adopted 8-13, 614C3
Reagan urges maritime program 8-19, 629A2
Saratoga overhaul set, Phila jobs seen 9-30, 780C2
Barber Oil liquidates 10-2, 986A1
Fishing indus aid clears Cong 12-4, 955B1; signed 12-22, 982C1, 955B3

Accidents—*See ACCIDENTS—Marine*
Foreign Developments (including U.S. international news)
ILA boycotts Sovt ships, ILWU shuns boycott 1-8, 9D1
US acts re ILA boycott 1-19, 45B1
ILA Sovt boycott end asked 1-28, cts back 1-29, 2-1, ILA loads ships 1-29, 2-1, 169B1
'79 cargo ship losses rptd 2-18, 108E3
US oil tanker subsidies repaymt backed by Sup Ct 2-20, 170E2
Spain '79 losses rptd 2-21, 196G2
EC warns US vs trade war 2-28, 204F2
Australia labor unrest rptd 3-11, 190G3
French dockers strike 3-20, 231G3
Japan-Panama 2d canal study agreed 3-25, 234C3

1976

Venez, UK pact signed 11-23, 929D3
USSR-Libya pact signed 12-6, 949B1
US-Sovt talks fail 12-8, 947F3
Polish-UK pact signed 12-15—12-17, 966D1
Forgn paymts study rptd 12-20, 985D2

Military Issues—*See 'Ships & Submarines' under ARMAMENTS*

SHISKIN, Julius
On Feb jobless rate 3-5, 198D3
On Mar jobless rate 4-2, 263B1
On Apr jobless rate 5-7, 347B2
On July jobless rate 8-6, 586A3
On Oct jobless rate 11-5, 846F1
SHIYA, Jamil
In Syrian Cabt 8-8, 594G2
SHOBEK, Michaiah
Hanged for '74 murder 10-19, 1012D2
SHOES—*See CLOTHING*
SHOOTING (sport)
Olympic results 7-19—7-24, trapshooter disqualified 7-19, 563B2, 575G1, B2
SHOPOV, Atanas
Wins Olympic medal 7-26, 576F2
SHORE, Peter
UK environment min 4-8, 266F3
Retains Cabt post 9-10, 693F3, 694A1
SHORT, Edward
Quits UK Cabt 4-8, 266G3

1977

Ireland sets fishing vessel curbs 2-15, 146B3
Asia '76 econ growth rptd 2-16, 147D2
Red Sea summit 3-22—3-23, 208E2
US-USSR pact OKd 3-30, 306C2
UNCTAD 'flags-of-convenience' study rptd 4-17, 337D2
'68 uranium loss rptd Israeli plot 5-30, 416D3
6 Swedish shipyds merged 6-22, 709F1
UK natlizes shipbldg 7-1, 526C2-A3
Japan-Australia sugar dispute idles ships 7-15, 578D3; 8-4, 615D2
US ends blacklist of forgn ships making Cuba stops 9-7, 781D3
France asks 'organized free trade' 9-15—9-16, 1012D3
Australia OKs US navigatn statn 9-23, 762B3
US-USSR extend rate pact, grain shipmts rptd 10-17, 948D3
Nigeria pirates raid Danish ship 11-21, 986E2
Saudis add 16 forgn ships to Israel blacklist 12-10, 955C1
St Lawrence toll hikes set 12-16, 982D3

Military Issues—*See ARMAMENTS—Ships & Submarines*

Payments Issues
Sea-Land case setld, rebate probe continues 1-5, 6B2
Gen Dynamics wins US loan guarantee, Burmah paymt to Park cited 1-19, 55D1-F2
ARA Svcs rpts rebates 1-28, 94E1
'76 maritime union cong gifts rptd 2-15, 128F1
Singer kickbacks rptd 3-10, 233F2
US Lines settle SEC chrgs 6-6, 651B1
Sony settles FMC chrgs 8-19, 650G3-651A1

Safety Issues—*See also ACCIDENTS—Marine*
US oil tanker safety rules tightened 1-18, 214D2
US-Sovt pact terms set 2-7, 161A1
Liberia oil tanker fails US inspectn 2-7, 214E3
Carter asks oil tanker safety rules 3-18, 214G1-D2
Maritime worker compensatn law affirmed 6-17, 518E2
Liberia tightens standards 7-19, 736A2

SHIPTON, Eric
Dies 3-28, 264F3
SHIPTON, Roger
Scores PNG border stand 2-7, 132G1
SHISKIN, Julius
On '76 work force growth, Dec jobless rate 1-12, 37A3
On jobless rate 8-5, 611A3
On June-Aug finished-goods index 9-1, 692C1
On Sept jobless rate 10-7, 776B3
On Nov employmt 12-3, 961A3
SHLAUDEMAN, Harry W.
Named amb to Peru 5-13, confrmd 5-25, 500B1
SHOES
US import curbs disputed 1-6—4-5, Carter bars 4-1, 248C1
Australia sets NZ import quotas 4-17, extends quotas 5-2, 345G3; NZ plea rebuffed 5-18, 410C2
Taiwan, S Korea OK prelim US export pacts 5-14, 5-16, 416C2
Ward Melville dies 6-5, 532D3
Fashion wrap-up rptd 6-6, 7-29, 1022G1
Taiwan, Korea export pacts signed 6-14, 6-21, 587E2
US industry gets fed aid 7-20 587B2
US makers rptdly join importers ranks 8-8, 587F2
IMF on Taiwan, Korea pacts with US 9-26, 753F3
Canada curbs imports 12-1, 982G3
SHOE Workers of America, United (AFL-CIO)
Scores Carter import ruling 4-2, 248B2
SHOR, Bernard (Toots)
Dies 1-22, 84F3

1978

Helsinki naval conf on peacetime cooperatn 5-16—5-18, 424F3
USSR insurnc bias vs US chrgd 6-9, 499D3
USSR opens new Arctic path 6-12, 506A2
Swedish shipyd closings planned 6-17, 691A1
UK shipbldg losses rptd 6-27, 573A3
UK A-sub workers strike 7-7—8-13, 650A1
Sovt-bloc growth rptd, West concerned 7-11—8-24, 670G2-E3
Australia strikes disrupt ports 8-11—9-7, 686F1
Nigeria expels forgn ships 9-2, 758A2
Japan Apr-June, Aug exports rptd down 9-8, 9-13, 694C2, D2
USSR rate-cutting scored by EC 9-11, defended 9-11, 9-17, 820A3, D3
Australia dockers close major ports 9-12—9-16, 738E2
USSR co gets US show-cause order re rates 9-13, 820F2
Camp David summit pact affirms navigatn rights 9-17, 712A2
2 forgn-flag carriers fined by US 10-1, 752F3
French dock strike 10-23, 816A1
Indonesia seamen end strike 11-4, 882D1
Japan cos settle US rebate chrgs 11-8, 961F3
E, W Ger transport pact OKd 11-16, 906B1
Belgium vows shipbldg aid 11-24, 921F1

Military Issues—*See ARMAMENTS—Ships & Submarines*

Payments Issue
Garmatz indictmt dropped 1-9, 15G3
Rebate probe delay barred 2-3, 184D3
Maritime Comm rebate fine total cited 184F3
Seatrain, Ocean Equipmt, Tenna offcl indicted 3-8, plead guilty 3-16, 184B3
Sea-Land pleads guilty, fined 4-11, 449E2
Reynolds settles SEC chrgs 6-6, 449D2
22 indicted on port corruptn 6-7, 480D2
Seatrain fined, other setlmts rptd 9-18, 10-1, 752E3
2 forgn-flag carriers fined by US 10-1, 752F3
Seatrain, Ocean Equipmt fined 10-23, 876B3
Japan cos settle rebate chrgs 11-8, 961F3

Safety Issues—*See also ACCIDENTS—Marine*
France issues tanker rules 3-23, 238G1
US warns Liberia 4-3, 234E1
US warns asbestos workers 4-6, 326G2
US Coast Guard progrm cut from fscl '79 budget 5-2, 344G1
Helsinki naval conf discusses rescue operatns 5-16—5-18, 424F3
France acts to curb oil spills 6-4—7-5, 524A1
Carter signs Coast Guard '79 authorizatn 6-30, 525C2
France sues US on Liberia tanker spill 9-13, 749D1
US tanker safety law signed 10-17, 807B3

SHIRAZI, Ayatollah
Violence in Meshed 12-31, 993D2
SHIRLEY Heights (race horse)
Wins English Derby 6-7, 539A2
SHISKIN, Julius
On Feb jobless rate 3-10, 221F3
Dies 10-28, 888E3
SHIYANGA, Toivo
Killed 2-7, 114B1
SHOEMAKER, Willie
Hawaiian Sound 2d in English Derby 6-7, 539B2
SHOES
Venez bans consumer imports 4-6, 332C1
Quebec ends sales tax 4-11, 286G2
'77 indl productivity drop rptd 6-14, 470A1
Interco settles FTC chrgs 7-14, 768E3
'78 high chic fashion rptd 8-4—8-11, 10-27—11-3, 1029B3
Interco outbid by Amer Can for Fingerhut purchase 8-14, 718E1
Australia import tax proposed 8-15, 628C2
Australia import tax scored 8-17, 646A2
Addidas founder dies 9-18, 778B1
SHOPOV, Valkan
Dismissed from Bulgaria agri post 4-29, 530G3
SHORE, Peter
Windscale A-reprocessing plant OKd 3-22, 227B2
SHORT, Peter
Named Aztecs coach 8-2, 707C3
SHORT, Purvis
In NBA draft 6-9, 457F2

1979

Calif tax on Japan cargo containers voided 4-30, 364A3
Environmt accord set by UN Sea Law Conf 5-13, 360F3
Forgn-flag oil tanker case refused by US Sup Ct 5-14, 383E1
Brazil-China maritime pact signed 5-22, 443C3
Colombia dock strike 5-29, 563E3
US indicts 7 cos re US-Eur freight rates 6-1, 423A2; fines levied 6-8, 442A2
UNCTAD pact rptd 6-3, 417D3
Canal treaty implementatn bill clears US House 6-21, 481D1
Iran industries natlzd 7-5, 503F2
Japan ships shun Viet waters 7-15, 550B1
Brit Shipbldrs denatlzn deferred 7-23, 564F3
French dockworkers' pact OKd 7-25, 564A1
Australia dock strike ends 8-8, 612A1
US to challenge coastal sea claims 8-10, 646F1
CR strike disrupts port of Limon 8-14, 667D3
Scotland shipyd closings, job cutbacks planned, protests sparked 8-16, 634B1
'France' sails to W Ger after labor blockade 8-19, 633D3
Rotterdam port struck 8-23, 653B3
Sovt-Greek port accord rptd signed 9-11, 708C1
Rotterdam port strike ends 9-24, 731E1
Panama Canal tolls hiked 29.3% 9-26, 723B2
US resumes spare parts shipmts to Iran 10-5, 773C3
Dutch tugboat strike ends 10-13, 815A1
USSR ban lifted by US 10-16, 815F2
UK trust legis proposed, US law targeted 10-31, 855E3
Iran ship boycott spreads 11-13, 879C1
Norway shipowner fined 12-17, 996F3

Military Issues—*See ARMAMENTS—Ships & Submarines*

Mergers & Acquisitions
C&O to buy Liggett US cigaret business 1-26, 283E1
C&O, Liggett merger talks end 6-14, 517G1
Congoleum-Fibic merger OKd 9-21, 942A2

Payments Issue
ILA's Scotto indicted 1-17, 87G2-C3
5 Teamsters indicted re Seatrain racketeering 2-22, 155F3
ILA, other E Coast indictmts continue 3-6, 220A2
Dock indictmts mount 4-9, 292B1
Atlantica consortium fine rptd 10-31, 985G2
ILA's Scotto convicted 11-15, 890A1

Safety Issues—*See also ACCIDENTS—Marine*
US Coast Guard training faulted 1-20, 140E3
Tanker spill rpt urges tougher steering gear rules 3-8, 162C2-163A1
US tanker inspectn progrm rptd effective 3-20, 200E3-201A1
Dockworker negligence suits backed by Sup Ct 6-27, 558B2
'74-78, 1st 1/4 '79 oil spill data; tanker safety records rptd 8-15, 608A1
Onshore dockers injury benefits upheld by Sup Ct 11-27, 919B3

Suez Canal Issue—*See MIDDLE EAST—SUEZ*

SHIRAZI, Hujaat al-Islami Razi
Shot 7-15, 544A3
SHIRE, Talia
Old Boyfriends released 3-21, 528C3
Prophecy released 6-15, 820A3
Rocky II released 6-15, 820C3
SHITIKOV, Aleksei P.
On U-2 flights 5-28, 397F3
SHOEMAKER, Bill (Willie)
Named Spectacular Bid jockey 6-23, race results 7-1—10-6, 876F2-A3, E3
SHOES
Scholl-Kresge case refused by Sup Ct 1-15, 32A1
Shoe workers union merges; US, Canada import lid urged 3-6, 207A1
GATT pact signed, tariff cuts seen 4-12, 273G1, 274F1
'79 fashion roundup rptd 1006F2
Interco to buy Ethan Allen 8-13, 664B1
SHOE Workers of America, United (AFL-CIO)
Clothing workers merger OKd 3-6, 207A1
SHOMAN, Assad
PUP Dec '78 munic electn loss rptd 1-19, 78C1
SHOMRON, Maj. Gen. Dan
On El Arish pullout 5-25, 394B1
SHOOTER, R. A.
UK smallpox rpt released 1-3, 7B2
SHORE, Howard
Gilda Radner Live opens 8-2, 711C3
SHOREHAM, N.Y.—*See NEW York State*
SHORENSTEIN, Carole J.
Grand Tour opens 1-11, 292E1
SHORT, Dewey
Dies 11-19, 932E3

1980

Lloyd's '79 cargo liability cited 3-31, 266F1
Sweden shipyd bill urged 4-9, 410B3
Liberia to continue registratn business 4-15, 284D3
Venez shipping scandal rptd, ex-pres censured 5-8, 411C1-A2
Sweden dockers strike 5-12, 365F1
Australia harbor pilot strike rptd 5-16, 371F1; ends 5-21, 405C3
Finland strike end rptd 5-23, 407A1
Mystery freighter intercepted off Cuba 7-4, 514G3
UK fiscal '80 losses rptd 7-31, 578E2
Polish Gdansk shipyd strike 8-14—8-22, 625A1; 8-23—8-27, 641A1
Australia dockers strike 8-18—8-26, 650F2
W Ger line insolvency rptd 8-18, 674E1
French union ldr threatens wider strike 8-27, 652B1
Polish strike continues 8-28—8-31, accord reached 9-1, 657A1-658A1, E2
Antarctic fishing pact signed 9-11, 721C1
US-China pact signed 9-17, 707A1, C1
17 Haitians jailed for hijacking 9-17, 726B1
ILA OKs pact, affirms Sovt boycott 9-18, 826F2, D3
Persian Gulf shipmts seen threatnd 9-24, 718B1; for subsequent developments, see IRAN—Iraqi War
S Africa system strained 10-15, 793D2
Sovt freighter seized in Canada debt dispute 10-22, 828F2
Brit Shipbldrs '81 aid hike seen 11-6, 886C3
Panama Canal congestn linked to traffic increase, vessel size 11-24, 895C3-896C1

Military Issues—*See ARMAMENTS—Ships*

Payments Issue
Seatrain settles disclosure suit 2-8, 558B1
Bethlehem Steel, ex-offcl plead guilty in bribe cases 7-24, 8-7, 600E1, A2

Safety Issues
Waterway constructn injury case remanded by Sup Ct 1-14, 37F1
OSHA cites Va shipyd 2-27, 147C3
Liberia to continue registratn business 4-15, 284D3
Longshoreman fatality damages ruling affirmed by Sup Ct 5-12, 426D3
Onshore docker state injury benefits backed by Sup Ct 6-23, 555B1

SHIRAZI, Ayatollah Hujaat al-Islami Razi
Treated in US for wounds 1-17, 30D1
SHIRE, David
Wins Oscar 4-14, 296G1
SHIRE, Talia
Windows released 1-18, 216G3
SHOBEK, Michaiah (d. 1976)
'76 hanging cited 1-29, 132A2
SHOCKLEY, William B.
Rpts sperm bank donatns 2-28, 990D2
SHOES
'Bionic' trademark case declined by Sup Ct 3-31, 291D3
Australia import tariffs kept 8-15, 632F2-D3
Natl files for bankruptcy 12-11, 985F3
'80 fashion roundup rptd 998C2
SHOGUN (book & TV film)
TV film aired by NBC 9-15—9-19, top ratings rptd 9-24, 835F2
On best-seller list 10-12, 796E3
SHOGUN Assassin (film)
Top-grossing film 12-3, 948G3
SHOOTING (sport)
Soviets dominate Moscow Olympics 7-20—7-26, 588G2, 623C2
SHOPE, Dani Lee
'79 sentence cited 2-27, 238E3
SHORE, Peter
Scores EC budget compromise 6-2, 421B3
Left advances at Labor Party conf 9-29—10-3, 768E1
SHOREHAM—*See NEW York State*

1976

SHORTER, Frank
Wins Olympic medal 7-31, 576E1
SHRIVER, Rep. Garner E. (R, Kan.)
Loses reelectn 11-2, 823D2
SHRIVER Jr., (Robert) Sargent
Gets US campaign subsidy 1-2, 22E3
Issues economic plan 1-7, 22F2
Common Cause rpts code backing 1-9, 23A1
5th in Iowa precinct vote 1-19, 41B1
3d in Miss caucuses 1-24, 94F3
5th in NH primary 2-24, 148F1, B3
Mass, Vt primary results 3-2, 165B1, A2
Fed fund total listed 3-4, 180D3
3d in Ill primary, quits race 3-16, 196E2, 197F1
Releases delegates 3-22, 214C2
Wis primary vote 4-6, 245D1
FEC ends fed funds 6-23, 490F3
Fed fund total rptd 7-1, 491B1
FEC certificatn total rptd 12-31, 979G2
SHRONTZ, Frank A.
Succeeded in AF post 3-10, 232F1
SHTEMENKO, Gen. Sergei
Dies 4-23, 368A3
Gribkov replaces 10-12, 858G2
SHTERN, Dr. Mikhail
Nobel winners plead for release 3-24, 421A3
SHTERYANOV, Boycho
Bulgaria Komsomol scored 3-29—4-2, 250D1
SHUCK, Peter H.
On ABA ad actn 2-18, 136G3
SHUKLA, Vidya Charan
Defends press curbs 1-28, 74B1
Forgn press curbs lifted 9-18, 700B3
SHUMAKOV, Alexey
Wins Olympic medal 7-24, 576F2
SHUMLIN, Boris T.
Rpts '75 Jewish emigratn 1-22, 76B3
SHUN Hyung Shik
S Korea constructn min 12-4, 928G2
SHURE Brothers Inc.
Chrgd re Arab boycott 10-20, 786F1
Chrgd re Arab boycott 11-3, 986C3
SHUSTER, Rep. E.G. (R, Pa.)
Reelected 11-2, 830E3
SHUVAL, Zalman
US oil deal OKd 5-6, 338C3
SIAGE, Riad
Vs Israel, S Africa at UN racism debate 4-27, 320F2
SIAM Kraft Paper Co.
US sues Kearns, Bostwick 8-9, 709D3
SICKLE Cell Anemia—*See 'Blood' under MEDICINE & Health*
SICLAIT, Henri
Liberal purge rptd 4-6, 4-9, 267F2
Dismissed 9-7, expelled 9-24, 1005B3
SIDDICK, Abba
Claims credit for Malloum plot 4-13, 270F3
SIDDIQUI, Kader
Bangladesh rebel leader 156C2
SIDELL, William
Quits Ford panel 1-8, 4C1
SIDIAK, Victor
Wins Olympic medal 7-22, 574F2
SIEGEL, Siegrun
Wins Olympic medal 7-26, 576F1
SIERRA Club
Utah power projct dropped 4-14, 284E2
NRC suit vs S Africa A-deal rptd 5-30, 388F1
Strip-mining stay reversed 6-28, 568G3
Eased clean-air rules OKd 8-2, 570A3
Backs Ford park plan 9-1, 644C3
McCloskey sees Carter 12-16, 937C2

SIERRA Leone—*See also AFRICAN Development Bank, COMMONWEALTH of Nations, NONALIGNED Nations Movement, OAU*
Listed as 'partly free' 1-19, 20D3
Recognizes Angola MPLA 1-29, 82G2
UN Palestine com member 2-26, 162C1
IMF oil loans rptd 3-5, 4-1, 339G3, 340E2
Stevens reelected pres 3-26, govt chngs rptd 5-20, 503B3
IMF OKs loan 9-20, 1013C2
ECOWAS rptd ratified 11-6, 974E2
SIGCAU, Chief Botha
Named pres 10-19, 813A2
SIGHO, Isic—*See MASEKO, Isaac*
SIGMA Ltd.
Chrysler sets merger 11-3, 856E1
SIHANOUK, Prince Norodom (Cambodia)
Ends foreign tour; chairs cabt mtg 1-3, 8B1
Hails new charter 1-5, 8B1
Wins Natl Assemb seat 3-20, resigns as chief of state 4-5, 250F1-A2
Replaced as chief of state 4-14, 265D1
SIITONEN, Hannu
Wins Olympic medal 7-26, 576A1
SIKES, Rep. Robert L. F. (D, Fla.)
Conflict of interest chrgd 4-7, 286F2
Ethics Com votes inquiry 4-28, 309D2
Reprimanded by House, denies intent 7-29, 551D3
Wins renomination 9-7, 687D3
Reelected 11-2, 820B2, 829B2

1977

SHOSTAK, Eliezer
Israel health min 6-20, 474E2
SHOVELTON, Patrick
Warns US on Concorde 4-22, 368B2
Signs US air svc pact 7-23, 593C1
SHOWTIME Entertainment Inc.—*See under VIACOM*
SHREVEPORT, La.—*See LOUISIANA*
SHRONTZ, Frank A
Replaced as Defense asst secy 4-25, 418F1
SHTERN, Mikhail
Freed 3-14, 226D3
Arrives Vienna 4-13, 314C3
SHUE, Gene
Fired as 76er coach 11-4, 991B1
SHUKLA, Vidya Charan
Rpts press curbs lifted 1-20, 45G2
Loses Parlt seat 3-16—3-20, 205C2
SHUMATE, John
Traded to Pistons 11-23, 991C1
SHUSTER, Rep. Bud (R, Pa.)
Introduces air-bag res 6-30, 522B1
SHUSTER, George N.
Dies 1-25, 84F3
SHUTT, Steve
NHL season ldr 4-3, 262D3, F3
SIBERT, William C.
Sentenced 12-21, 1009F1
SIBON, Capt. Guy
Malagasy defense min 8-8, 772D1
SICOURI, Lucien
Vs AECL agent disclosure 1-25, 114D1
SIDI Baba, Dey Ould
Elected Morocco parlt pres 10-17, 869A2
SIDI Ould Sheikh Abdallahi
Mauritania econ min 8-4, 772E1
SIEBERT, Paul
Traded to Mets 6-15, 644F2
SIEDLE, Robert L.
Death detailed 9-2, 709A3
SIEGMAN, Rabbi Henry
Backs Trifa suspensn 2-5, 120B1
SIEMER, Deanne C.
Named Defense gen counsel 4-1; confrmd 4-25, 418G1
SIERRA, Julian
Expulsion rptd 1-14, 46C3
SIERRA Charter Corp.
US sues vs union loans 3-30, 261G3
SIERRA Club
Lauds Carter plutonium ban 4-7, 268F1
Carter energy plan reactn 4-21, 320A2
Sues TVA on air pollutn 6-22, 521C3

SIERRA Leone—*See also COMMONWEALTH of Nations, NONALIGNED Nations Movement, OAU*
UN Assemb member 4B1
Students protest 1-30, emergency declared 2-1, 139F3
APC wins electns 5-6, 470F2
Linehan confrmd US amb 6-23, 626A3
Cuba mil aides rptd 11-17, 896G1
Bauxite base price OKd 12-7, 975E1

SIEVERTS, Frank
Viets return US bodies 9-30, 795G1
SIGCAU, Chief Botha
Opens Assemb 3-9, 350E2
SIILVASVUO, Lt. Gen. Ensio
Named UN Cairo conf envoy 11-29, 910A2
At Geneva conf 12-14—12-15, 953E1, C2
SIKES, Rep. Robert L. F. (D, Fla.)
Loses subcom post 1-26, 53E2
SIKMA, Jack
In NBA draft 6-10, 584A2
SIKORSKY Aircraft Division—*See UNITED Technologies*

1978

SHORT, Robert (Bob)
Denies '68 Korea gift to Dems 3-21, 203B2
Tax-cut plan disputed 7-21, 735B1
Wins US Sen primary in Minn 9-12, 715G3
Loses electn 11-7, 854A3
SHORT People (recording)
On best-seller list 2-4, 116F3
SHOSTAK, Eliezer
Vs summit pact in Cabt vote 9-24, 729C1
SHOTTS, Ron
Wins Okla primary for gov 8-22, 683C1
Loses electn 11-7, 855G2
SHOW-Off, The (play)
Opens 5-18, 760C3
SHREVEPORT, La.—*See LOUISIANA*
SHRIVER, Pam
Loses US Open 9-10, 707A1, D1
SHROUD of Turin
Exhibited 8-26—10-8, studied 10-4—11-14; photo 926A1-C3
SHUKLA, Vidya Charan
Sanjay Gandhi starts jail term 5-5, 375B1
SHUKRI, Saddi Rahman al-
Held in Naif murder 7-12, 582A3
SHUKRY, Gen. Nabil
Leads Cyprus airfield raid 2-19, details 2-21, 117G2
SHUMWAY, Norman D.
Wins US House seat 11-7, 850F1, 856B3
SHUSTER, Rep. E. G. (R, Pa.)
Reelected 11-7, 852C1
SHUTT, Steve
Montreal wins Stanley Cup 5-25, 458F1
SHYER, Charles
Goin' South released 10-6, 970D1
SIANI, Mike
Traded to Colts 7-21, 1024D3
SIBIR (Soviet ship)
Opens new Arctic path 5-25—6-12, 506A2
SICKLE Cell Anemia—*See MEDICINE—Blood*
SID-Ahmed, Mohammed
Egypt probes, exit barred 5-28, 415A1
SIDLER, Maren
Sets shot put mark 6-8—6-10, 600C3
SIEGBAHN, Manne
Dies 9-26, 778A2
SIEGEL, Mark
Quits Carter staff, vs Mideast stand 3-8, 3-9, 176C2
Jewish ldr deplores resignatn 3-9, 176A3
SIEMENS A.G.
Italy violence 5-4, 5-8, 393A2, C2
SIERRA Club
Carter gets high rating 12-20, 1009F1

SIERRA Leone—*See also COMMONWEALTH of Nations, GATT, NONALIGNED Nations Movement, OAU*
Girl held as 'slave' in US 3-2, 396E3
6 W African natns back ECOWAS 3-18, USSR scores 3-20, 237E1
UK cancels debts 7-31, 592E1
UN Assemb member 713E3

SIGCAU, Chief Botha
Dies 12-1, 1032E3
SIGMA Delta Chi
SC gag-order case review denied 1-9, 13F1
SIGMA Delta Chi v. Martin
SC gag-order case review barred 1-9, 13F1
SIGN of Four, The (book)
Crucifer of Blood opens 9-28, 1031C1
SIGNORET, Simone
Madame Rosa released 3-19, 619A3
SIILASVUO, Lt. Gen. Ensio P.H.
In Israeli talks on Leb peace force, refugees 3-21, 3-22, 197E2
Gets Israel Leb pullback plan 4-6, 236A1
Israel OKs more Leb pullbacks 4-18, 274G2
Leb protests Unifil statemt on Haddad 6-14, 462D2
Christns OK Unifil deploymt 8-30, 713E1
SIJEYO, Wasonga
Freed 12-12, 968G1
SIKES, Rep. Robert (D, Fla.)
US A-carrier cut 9-7, 677E2
SIKORAL, Richard G.
Gives Letelier murder details 6-2, 452C1

1979

SHORTER, Frank
Virgin breaks 10000-m run mark 6-17, 911A2
SHOSSETT, Ronald
Alien released 5-24, 528A1
SHOUT, The (film)
Released 11-9, 1008E1
SHREVEPORT, La.—*See LOUISIANA*
SHRIVER, Eunice Kennedy
Buys Rockefeller DC mansn 7-20, 656B3
With brother in Iowa 11-12, 962D1
SHRIVER, R. Sargent
Buys Rockefeller DC mansn 7-20, 656B3*
SHROPSHIRE, Noble
Marquis of Keith opens 3-13, 712D1
SHROUD of Turin
Age test awaited 11-21, 931E2
SHUCK, Robert E.
Rpts draft registratn renewal costs 1-4, 15D1
SHUKLA, Vidya Charan
Sentncd in censorship case 2-27, 193A1
SHUKRI, Ibrahim
Vs asylum for shah 12-4, 914E1
SHULMAN, Max L.
Convicted of IRS bribe 3-26, 239E3
SHUMLIN, Diana
Grand Tour opens 1-11, 292E1
SHUMLIN, Herman
Dies 6-14, 508E3
SHURAFA, Suliman al-
Expelled from Libya 12-9, 937C3
SHURE Brothers Inc.
Korvettes patent case refused by Sup Ct 11-5, 884D3
SHURE Brothers Inc. v. Korvettes
Case refused by Sup Ct 11-5, 884D3
SHUSTER, Rep. E. G. (R, Pa.)
House GOP Policy Com chrmn 71B1
SHUSTER, Michael D.
Convicted 2-22, sentncd 3-19, 220F2
SHUSTER, Rosie
Gilda Radner Live opens 8-2, 711C3
SHUTT, Steve
Montreal wins Stanley Cup 5-21, 447C3
SHYRE, Paul
Paris Was Yesterday opens 12-19, 1007E2
SIAM, Gulf of
Boat people rescue cited 7-28, 575B2
SIBEKO, David
Assassinated 6-12, 476G3
SIBSON & Co.
'78 top-paid execs listed 5-14, 347G3
SICK, Wilson
On AMC-Renault deal 10-12, 784C3
SIDLER, Maren
Sets shot put mark 6-17, 911C2
SIEGEL, Don
Escape from Alcatraz released 6-21, 820B1
SIEGMAN, Henry
Denies Jewish role in Young UN resignatn 8-16, 606B2; 8-19, 624G1
SIEMENS A.G.
Spain issues A-plant permit 8-25, 670C3
Argentine A-plant contract rptd 10-1, 749C1
SIEPI, Cesare
Carmelina opens 4-8, 711A2
SIERRA Club
US wilderness proposal scored 1-4, 16C2
Carter scored re Tellico Dam bill 9-26, 766E3
Calif LNG projct opposed 9-27, 769A3
SIERRA Leone—*See also COMMONWEALTH of Nations, GATT, NONALIGNED Nations Movement, OAU*
Freedom House lists as partly free 13B1
UN membership listed 695B3

SIGALOS, John
New JFK murder film rptd 2-8, 166F1
SIGCAU, Chief Botha (d. 1978)
Transkei pres elected 2-19, 215D3
SIGNAL Cos. Inc.
Renault buys interest in Mack Trucks 3-19, 3-20, 236E2, 283B1
Renault interest in Mack Trucks cited 10-12, 784G3
SIHANOUK, Prince Norodom (Cambodia)
Freed from house detentn 1-5, 10G2
In Peking 1-6—1-8; on Pol Pot govt, Viet conflict 1-8; in NY for UN debate 1-9, 10F2
In UN Cncl debate 1-11—1-12, 10G1-E2
To stay in West, gets US bid 1-18, 68G3
Visits Teng in DC 1-31, 66D2
Sees Cambodia return 2-11, 2-13; Viets rebuff, China welcomes 2-13, 142C2
Asks end to Cambodia-Viet war 3-19, 229E2
Pol Pot seeks backing vs Viets 5-31, 6-2, 443E3
Asks nonaligned natns bar Khieu, Heng recognitn 8-22, 675A1
Rpts guerrilla group formatn, to seek US aid 10-4; plans US visit 10-12, 811B2
Asks US to bar Cambodia aid 10-11, 811F2
SIKMA, Jack
NBA rebound ldr 4-8, 290F2
Sonics win NBA title 6-1, 506G3
SILAI, Ileana
Banned from track 10-26, 912A1

1980

SHORT, Bobby
Vanderbilt drops River House suit 6-12, 639G1
SHOUMATOFF, Elizabeth
Dies 11-30, 928D3
SHRAR, Majed Abu
Fatah takes credit for Israel raid, says seeks Jordan base 6-9, 434C2
SHREVEPORT—*See LOUISIANA*
SHRIVER, Pam
Loses US Open women's doubles 9-6, 691F2
Loses New South Wales champ 12-7, 947A3
SHUE, Gene
Quits as Clippers coach 5-1, hired as Bullets coach 5-27, 656D3
SHUH-Shin Li
Taiwan wins Little League title 8-30, 796G2
SHUKAIRY, Ahmed
Dies 2-26, 176D3
SHUKLA, Vidya Charan
Congress-I wins electn; gains Parlt seat 1-3, 1-6, 11E3
Cleared of film theft 4-11, 294A3
Sworn Indian supplies min 6-8, 445F1
SHULL, Leon
On disaffectn with Carter 6-15, 480G1
SHULTZ, George P.
Bars Reagan Cabt apptmt 11-28, 935D2
Named Bechtel pres 12-2, 959D3
SHUMWAY, Forrest N.
On Ampex acquisitn 2-19, 385G3
SHUMWAY, Rep. Norman D. (R, Calif.)
Reelected 11-4, 842F1
SHURE, Michael
Pleads guilty 7-31, 639C3
Gets probation 10-7, 890E1
SHUSTER, Rep. E. G. (R, Pa.)
Links Abscam, Dem majority 2-5, 82B2
Reelected 11-4, 844C1
Loses as House GOP whip 12-8, 936C2
SHUSTER, Rosie
Gilda Live released 3-28, 416G2
SHWAN, Azad
On Iraqi Kurds autonomy fight 10-1, 735F2
SICK, Wilson W.
Demoted 9-29, 959E2
SIDE Effects (book)
On best-seller list 12-7, 948E3
SIDEL, William
Confirmed Panama Canal comr 4-2, 308E3
SIDESHOW: Kissinger, Nixon and the Destruction of Cambodia (book)
Shawcross wins Polk award 2-25, 692G3
SIDLER, Maren
Ties natl champ career shot-put mark 6-14, 892B1
SIDORENKO, Aleksandr
Wins Olympic medal 7-27, 623A3
Vassallo beats Olympic swimming time 7-30, 834G2
SIEGEL, Barry
Windows released 1-18, 216G3
SIEGEL Auction Galleries, Robert A. (N.Y., N.Y.)
British Guiana stamp sold for record sum 4-5, 472D2
SIEGMAN, Rabbi Henry
Scores NCC PLO support 11-6, 864F1
SIERRA Club
UN Sea Law Conf yields draft accord 7-28—8-29, 660C1

SIERRA Leone—*See also COMMONWEALTH of Nations, GATT, NONALIGNED Nations, OAU*
US co chem waste dump plan rejctd 2-20, 154A2
Stevens hosts OAU summit, notes shortcomings 7-1—7-4, 509E1, B2
Chad peace conf fails 10-18—10-19, 810G1
Libyan Chad role controversy 12-23—12-24, 979C1

SIERRA Nevada (Venezuelan freighter)
Overpaymt chrgd, Perez censured 5-8, 411E1
SIERRA Torres, Manuel de la (Marques de Urquijo)
Slain with wife 8-1, 605E3
SIGNAL Cos. Inc.
Agrees to buy Ampex 2-19, 385F3-386A1
Greathouse quits UAW post 6-4, 457B2
Ampex deal set again 10-13, signed 10-29, 985F1
SIGNAL of Distress, The (painting)
Sold for $1.7 mln 10-17, 998A1
SIGNORELLO, Nicola
Italy Merchant Marine min 4-4, 275G3
SIHANOUK, Prince Norodom (Cambodia)
In US, backing for Cambodia armed group denied 2-22, 141B2
US rep visits N Korea 7-18, 547B1
SIKMA, Jack
NBA rebound ldr 3-30, 278E3
SILAGH, Valentin
Wins Olympic medal 8-2, 622A2

1976

SILBERMAN, Laurence H.
Hits US re Toth 7-23, 559D2
Tito scores 7-31, 594E1
Yugo chrgs Croat support 9-12, 685A3
Denies asked Toth to resign 9-22; resigns 11-17, 910B2
SILES Salinas, Louis Adolfo
Scores Chile sea outlet plan 1-1, 27F1
SILES Zuazo, Hernan
Scores Chile sea outlet plan 1-1, 27F1
SILKIN, John
Named UK agri secy 9-10, 693D3, 694A1
SILLARS, James
Scottish Labor Party meets 1-18, 73D1
SILVA Cunha, Joaquim da
Release from prison rptd 1-23, 53A2
SILVA Henriquez, Cardinal Raul
Asks forgn priests stay 1-23, 100B2
Bishops score harassmt re Montealegre visit 7-29, 711D2
Excommunicates 4 8-17, 711A2
SILVA Marques, Armando
Wins Olympic medal 7-20, 575A2
SILVA Munoz, Federico
Suarez named premier 7-3, 500E3
Refusal of Cabt post rptd 7-7, 523C2

1977

SILAS, Paul
NBA final standings 4-10, 331D3
SILBERMAN, Laurence H.
Replaced as amb to Yugo 6-7, 499E3
SILES Salinas, Luis Adolfo
Heads Bolivia rights panel 5-14, 414F2
Pres bid seen, scores Banzer 11-11, 901D3
SILES Zuazo, Hernan
Bolivia amnesty excludes 12-21, 1009G3
SILK, Andrew D.
S Africa arrests 9-23; leaves, denies ouster 9-24, 825F3
SILK, Leonard
S Africa arrests son 9-23, 825F3
SILKIN, John
EC farm price-rise blocked 3-29, 269A3
SILKIN, Samuel
Ct upholds S Africa boycott injunctn 1-27, 98F3
Defends UK in torture trial 4-21, 315B3
S Africa boycott ruling upset 7-26, 617B3
SILKWOOD, Karen
Filmmaker given 1st Amendmt protectn 9-23, 921E2
SILMARILLION, The (book)
On best-seller list 10-2, 808C3; 11-6, 872C3; 12-4, 1021F2
SILVA, Carlos Rafael
Venez educatn min 1-7, 23E2
SILVA, Fred
NFL officiating scored 12-18, 1020G1
SILVA Arantes, Aldo
Torture examinatn barred 2-16, 186C3
SILVA Henriquez, Cardinal Raul
Sees Todman 8-12, 635C2
SILVA Luongo, Luis Jone
Venez finance min 7-15, 566A1

1978

SILBERT, Earl J.
Townley plea-bargain pact OKd 8-11, 647D3
SILES Salinas, Luis Adolfo
Nominated for pres 5-3, 411F2
SILES Zuazo, Hernan
Sets pres bid 4-10, leftist unity bid fails 5-11, 411E2, A3
Chrgs pres vote fraud 7-9; 2d in vote count, scores electns 7-11, 530F2
Campaign harassmt rptd 7-9, 530C3
Scores electn 7-13, asks annulmt 7-15; stages hunger strike 7-18—7-19; rptd underground 7-24, 571D1
Asks new electns, threatens strikes 7-29; oppositn ldrs shun 7-30, 617B2
Followers seized in foiled 'coup' 10-29, 840C3
Homes of kin bombed 11-23, backs new mil junta electn plan 11-24, 913B2
SILICON—*See CHEMICALS*
SILIKOFF, Dr. Irving
PBB test rptd 10-9, 769B3
SILKIN, Samuel
Backs sanctns vs pay hike excesses 2-6, 131A3
SILMARILLION, The (book)
On best-seller list 1-8, 24C3; 2-5, 116A3; 3-5, 195D3; 4-2, 272B3
SILVA Henriquez, Cardinal Raul
Launches church rights year 4-25, 351C3
Bishops ask data on 433 missing 10-12, 795F3
SILVA Ruete, Javier
Named Peru econ min 5-15, 394D2
Signs new IMF pact 8-7, 669E1
SILVEIRA, Antonio Azeredo da
Says Carter not invited 3-30, 233C2

1979

SILAS, Paul
Sonics win NBA title 6-1, 506G3
SILBERT, Earl J.
Letelier case data curbed by '78 US-Chile pact 1-23, 75A1
Lauds Letelier case convictns 2-14, 114G2
Defends Letelier case plea-bargaining 3-23, 234G2
Scores Gasch GSA sentencing 5-25, 964F2
SILENT Partner, The (film)
Released 5-10, 528E3
SILES Salinas, Luis Adolfo
Bolivia pres bid rptd 3-16, 233F2
SILES Zuazo, Hernan
Bolivia pres bid rptd 3-16, 233E2
Leads in Bolivia electn 7-1, 501F1
Guevara elected interim pres 8-6, 600B2
SILICON—*See CHEMICALS*
SILINS, Ints
Hit at human rights mtg 11-9, 874D1
SILK, Leonard
Clarifies Carter Palestinian-rights remark 8-17, 607C1
SILKIN, John
Scores EC farm policy 2-21, 154D2
SILKWOOD, Karen (d. 1974)
Estate wins A-damages 5-18, 381D1
A-damages award upheld 8-20, 629G3
SILMARILLION, The (book)
On best-seller list 1-7, 80B3; 4-8, 271C2
SILVA, Rodolfo
On IDB Nicaragua loan 8-4, 603D1
SILVEIRA, Antonio Azeredo da
Named amb to US 3-23, 248C1

1980

SILAS, James
NBA free-throw ldr 3-30, 278D3
SILAS, Paul
Hired as Clippers coach 5-21, 656E3
SILENT Scream (film)
Released 2-2, 216E3
SILES Zuazo, Hernan
Paz rivalry continues 4-7, 272D2
Electns held 6-29; leads vote, lacks majority 7-3; Soclst alliance weighed 7-4, 508D3-509A1
Paz quits pres race 7-9, 543C1
Mil seize power 7-17, resistence urged 7-20, 546E2, C3
Forms clandestine govt, urges 'passive resistence' 7-30, 577A2
Scores mil takeover, urges resistence 8-6, 602F3
Brazil offers family asylum 8-12, 668G1
Surfaces in Peru 9-15, Paz joins 9-16, 728B1
SILKWOOD, Karen (d. 1974)
3 Mile I gas venting danger seen 6-18, 550D3
SILLS, Beverly
Gives final performance 10-27, 908E2
SILUNDUKA, T. George
Zimbabwe posts min 3-11, 198C1
SILVA, Chris
We Won't Pay! opens 12-17, 1003G3
SILVA Henriquez, Cardinal Raul
Death threat rptd 8-4, 603D3
SILVA Ruete, Javier
On Peru econ reform 1-1, 21E2

SILVER

1976
SILVER
UK price gains 3-3, 175B3
Pacific exchng closes, US sues 5-10, 348C2

1977
SILVER
Peru-Chile border buildup rptd 1-10, 2A3
Hunts seek Sunshine Mining takeover 3-21, 275C1
Record Mar, 1st ¼ trading rptd 4-18, 301C2
Hunt trading cited 4-28, 341A3
Futures contract trading cited 7-5, 521F2
Great Western Sunshine Mining takeover OKd 10-4, 798G3

1979
SILVER
USSR hikes jewelry prices 7-2, 504D2
Price soars 10-2, 740D1
NY price soars, trade squeeze cited 12-31, 978F2, A3

1980
SILVER
Prices soar 1-8—1-17; Kodak hikes prices 1-8, substitutes sought 1-11; Comex moves to curb speculatn 1-8, 1-10, 30F3
Comex suspends futures trading, doubles margin requiremt 1-21; Chicago Bd sets curbs 1-22, 68A3
W Ger sets bank curbs 1-23, 103D2
Mex bans mine stock trading 1-24, levies sales tax 1-25, 68E3
Comex eases futures trading curbs 1-30, 2-13, Chicago Bd restrictns upheld 2-11, 114B1, E1
Peru futures trading losses, Minpeco shakeup rptd 2-15, 152F1
Poland '79 exports rptd 2-26, 166A2
Hunt group plans bond sales 3-26, 222F3
NY price plunges; Hunt group suffers huge losses, margin calls cause stock mkt turmoil 3-27, 223E1
Hunts use oil assets to settle Engelhard debt 3-31, 244F3
Occidental profits from futures trading hedge 3-31, 245D1
Hunt trading, Bache ties probed 3-31—4-2; additional debts rptd, shakeup seen 3-31, 245G1-B3
Hunt trading debts repaid 4-8, 4-16, Canada OKs Engelhard setlmt 4-28, 345D1
Sunshine Mining offers silver-backed bonds 4-11, 265C3
Regulators debate speculatn curbs 4-14—4-15, 289F3
Hunts $1.1 bln trading bailout set 5-2, 344F3
Hunts testify at House, Sen probes; chrg SEC manipulatn 5-2, 345F1
Hunts bailout loans paid 5-27, collateral listed 5-28, 425E2, B3-426F1
Hunt bank deals probed by Sen com; Comex scored, FRB regulatn studied 5-29—5-30, 425D1-B3
Hunt's daughter acquires NM stake 6-24, 685D3
Sovt Aug purchases rptd 9-24, 730E3
Hunts liquidate Bache holdings 10-21, 867J3
Sunshine Mining strike ends 11-8, 883D3
CFTC sets tighter commodity trading rules 11-25, 899C1
Price drops on higher US interest rates 12-10, 932A2
'80 futures price down 12-31, 985A1

SILVER Bay—SIMKO

1976
SILVER Bay, Minn.—*See MINNESOTA*
SILVER Convention (music group)
Wins Grammy 2-28, 460C3
SILVERMAN, Tanya Melish
Vs GOP platform on abortn 8-17, 8-18, 601F1
SILVERT, Kalman H.
Dies 6-15, 524F3
SIM, Alastair
Dies 8-20, 892F3
SIMANTS, Erwin Charles
Sentenced to death 1-29, 492C1
Sup Ct voids gag order 6-30, 491E3-492C1
SIMEONI, Edmond
Corsicans demand release 4-3, 50D2
Trial opens 5-17, 401E2
Sentenced 6-22, 482A1
Brother leads wine depot raid 8-24, 693F2
SIMEONI, Max
Leads wine depot raid 8-24, 693F2
SIMEONI, Sara
Wins Olympic medal 7-26, 576G1

1977
SILVER Iodide—*See CHEMICALS*
SILVER Streak (film)
Top-grossing film 2-2, 120D3; 3-9 184D3
SIMANTS, Charles
Executn set 3-18, 594D1
SIMEONI, Edward
Freed from jail 1-14, backs non-violence 8-14, 744E3
SIMEONI, Max
At UPC rally 8-14, surrenders 9-27, 744F3-745A1
SIMKO, Svetozar
Defectn rptd 2-24, 220B3

1978
SILVER Bears, The (film)
Released 4-20, 619G3
SILVER Bullet Band
Stranger in Town on best-seller list 6-7, 460G3; 8-2, 620G1
SILVERMAN, Fred
To head NBC 1-20, replaced 2-1, 75D2
Pfeiffer named NBC chrmn, RCA dir 9-13, 759D3
Drops NBC fall TV lineup 11-29, 1030C1
SIMEONOV, Vladimir
Found dead 10-2, 748A1

1979
SILVER, Joan Micklin
On The Yard released 1-18, 174C3
SILVER, John Micklin
Head Over Heels released 10-19, 1007D3
SILVER, Ralph D.
On The Yard released 1-18, 174C3
SILVERMAN, Fred
Salant apptmt rptd 3-29, 335B1
Carson won't quit Tonight Show 5-2, 334D3
SILVERMAN, Stanley
Coriolanus opens 6-28, 711C2
SILVESTRI, Joseph
Testimony on NJ HFA kickbacks rptd 8-9, 747C3
SILVEX—*See HERBICIDES*
SILVIA, Queen (Sweden)
Gives birth to son 5-13, 392G3
SIMANTS, Erwin Charles
Acquitted in retrial 10-17, 890E3
SIMARD, Jean
Guilty in dredging fraud 5-5, 352B2
Sentenced 6-11, 468C2

1980
SILVER, Dorothy
Killings opens 6-5, 756E3
SILVER Bullet Band (singing group)
Against the Wind on best-seller list 4-2, 280F3; 4-30, 360A1; 6-4, 448F3; 7-9, 568F3
SILVERHEELS, Jay (Tonto)
Dies 3-5, 280A2
SILVERMAN, Fred
NBC realigns managemt, Segelstein promoted 6-3, 501D2
Sees Pfeiffer 7-7, relieves of duties 7-8; Pfeiffer resigns 7-10, 582C1
SILVERMAN, Harold L.
Loses US House electn 11-4, 848B2
SILVESTRI, Joseph
Named Abscam middleman 2-5, 111C1
Indicted in Abscam probe 6-18, 454G1, A2
SIM, Cpl. Stephen
Wounded in attack 3-10, 194D1
SIMEONI, Edmond
Separatists demonstrate 1-26, 97A3
Corsica comments rptd 8-12, 670D2
SIMEONI, Sara
Wins Olympic medal 7-26, 624A2
SIMIONESCU, Maria
Disputes mar women's Olympic gymnastics 7-24, 7-25, 589F2, A3
SIMKINS, George
Deplores NC KKK acquittals 11-18, 898C3

1976

SIMMONNOT, Philippe
Dismissed 5-9, 537E3
SIMMONS, Ted
NL batting ldr 10-4, 795G3
SIMMONS Co.
Vows no boycott compliance 3-18, 747B2
SIMON, J. C.
Convicted 3-13, sentncd 3-29, 292F3
SIMON, Ladjilav
Wins Olympic medal 7-31, 576E3
SIMON, Maria
Remains uncaptured 695A1
SIMON, Mircea
Wins Olympic medal 7-31, 574D1
SIMON, Paul
50 Ways on best-selling list 1-28, 104G3
Wins Grammys 2-28, 460F2
SIMON, Rep. Paul (D, Ill.)
Reelected 11-2, 829B3
SIMON, William E.
Use of AF planes rptd 1-1, 6E3
On IMF monetary accord 1-8, 14F2
Orders IRS paymts probe expanded 2-10, 134D2
In Italy talks 3-7—3-10, 253F3
Named to payoff probe 3-21, 262E2
Orders positive Hughes ID 4-5, 336A1
Defends IRS on Montoya audit 4-12, 283F3
IMF, World Bank staff protest wage actn 4-28, 340E1
In Chile 5-7—5-8, 464E3
Backs Ford in Calif 5-24, 374A1
On trade deficit 5-30, 396A2
Scores UNCTAD re intl bank bar 6-1, 388F2, B3
Sees Spain finance min 6-15—6-16, 501G2
Scores UK econ policies 6-22, 458A1
On 7-natn econ summit 6-28, 6-30, 462F1, B2
Strauss deplores GOP admin 7-12, 508G3
Italy loan ban disclosed 7-18, 530E3
Protests Toth detentn 7-23, 559E2
Sees Australia prime min 7-27, 554F1
Rptd Ford vp prospect 8-10, 584D1
GOP vp poll rptd 8-11, 583F3
Ford sees Reagan re vp choice 8-19, 598F1
GOP conv vp vote table 8-19, 599F3
Vs World Bank funds hike 10-5, 777E2-778E1
Rptd vs Arab boycott tax penalties 10-7 787B1
Carter, Ford debate 10-22, 800E3
Denies £ devaluatn conditn for UK loan 10-24, 809E3
Briefs Carter 11-22, 881D1
Sees Brezhnev, scores trade curbs 11-30, 947B3
Brezhnev not to 'test' Carter 12-3, 916A3
Backs UK IMF loan 12-16, 1003F3
SIMONET, Henri
On EEC oil-import pricing 1-16, 85A1
SIMON & Schuster Inc.—*See GULF & Western Industries Inc.*
SIMONSEN, Mario Henrique
Rpts '75 trade deficit down 1-6, 27E2
Rpts '75 COL up 29.4% 1-16, 98D2
SIMPLOT, Jack Richard
Co sued 5-27, 397G3
Potato futures default penalty set 8-31, ct delays setlmt 9-27, 990E1
SIMPLOT Industries Inc.
Sued re potato futures default 5-27, 397D3
Potato futures default penalty set 8-31, ct delays setlmt 9-27, 990E1
DR to buy more Rosario shares 12-15, 1001F2
SIMPSON, Richard
Replaced as consumer comm chrmn 5-26, 412E1
SIMS, Frank E.
Fined 12-22, 1016E2
SIMS, Rep. Steven D. (R, Ida.)
GOP conv vp vote table 8-19, 599F3
SIMS, Walter
Loses Fla Sen primary 9-7, 687C3
SIN, Jaime Cardinal
Named cardinal 4-27, 336C2
SINATRA, Frank
Marries Barbara Marx 7-11, 640F3
SINATRA, Mrs. Nancy
Ex-husband remarries 7-11, 640F3
SINCLAIR, Ian
Heads new cabt com 1-14, 26G2
Issues drought study 9-8, 709F2-E3
SINCLAIR, W. R.
On air safety comm 6-28, 481G2
SINDERMANN, Horst
SED Cong held 5-18—5-22, 381B2, E2
Named peoples chamber pres 10-29, 889D1
SINGAPORE—*See also ADB, ASEAN, COMMONWEALTH of Nations, NONALIGNED Nations Movement*
Australia in SE Asia talks 1-16—1-18, 46C1
Listed as 'partly free' 1-19, 20D3
Australia wheat deal rptd 3-11, 187D3
Premr sees Mao in China 5-12, 439D2
Australia OKs '77 Concorde flights 5-28, 400D1
Arrests newsmen as plotters 6-22, 497F3
US GOP platform text cites 8-18, 609A3
Sets UN seabed treaty terms 8-27, 700B2
Thais bar Thanom return 8-31, 677C3
UN Assemb condemns apartheid 11-9, 842G2
Socialist Intl withdrawl rptd 11-27, 935G2
Ruling party wins electns 12-23, 1013D2

1977

SIMMONDS, Robert
Admits MP tapped 9-20, 742A2
RCMP '73 PQ raid revealed 10-28, 840F3
SIMMONS, Ted
NL batting ldr 10-2, 926C3
SIMON, Norton
BN settles SEC complaint 4-28, 369A1
SIMON, William E.
On $12.5 bln tax cut proposal 1-4, 5C2
Vetoes housing tax shelter ban 1-5, 36E2
Named Olin Foundatn pres 3-1, 396E3
Elected USOC treasurer 4-29, 491B3
SIMON & Co., Charles E.
Rpts '70-76 business paymts total 1-21, 79D1
SIMONS, Jim
Wins New Orleans Open 4-24, 676B1
SIMONS, Lawrence B.
Named HUD asst secy 3-11, confrmd 3-23, 272C3
SIMONS, Marlise
Panama Canal talks impasse 5-17—5-18, 378B3
SIMONSEN, Mario Henrique
Calmon de Sa named industry min 2-9, 281D2
SIMONSON, Judge Archie
Defeated in recall electn 9-7, 712A1
SIMPLOT, Jack Richard
Fined for tax evasion 5-20, 491D3
SIMPLOT Industries Inc.
Simplot fined 5-20, 491D3
SIMPSON, O. J. (Orenthal James)
Has knee surgery 11-9, 1019C3
Payton breaks rushing record 11-20, 1019D3
SIMPSON Timber Co.
Redwood Pk expansn asked 4-19, 323A1
SIMS Motor Transport Lines
ICC sues 11-3, 861D1
SINAI—*See MIDDLE EAST, subheads ARAB-Israeli Developments and EGYPT-Israel Peace Moves*
SINAI, Stuart
Indicted 2-4, 103A1
SINATRA, Frank
Mother dies 1-6, 84G3
SINATRA, Natalie (Dolly)
Dies 1-6, 84G3
SINCLAIR, Ian
Bars wool floor-price drop 3-15, 236E3
Denies CIA funded NCP 5-4, 372C1
Blames strikes on UK immigrants 8-5, 632B3
Clarifies chrgs vs UK immigrants 9-12, 762A3
Scores UK immigrants 10-9, 800A3
On sheep disease in North 11-14, 881D3
Drops plan to kill diseased cattle 11-28, 945E1
Australia primary indus min 12-19, 982A2
SINGAPORE—*See also ASEAN, COMMONWEALTH of Nations, NONALIGNED Nations Movement*
UN Assemb member 4B1
Socialist supporter sentncd 1-8, 223F3
9 govt critics seized 2-15; plot chrgd 2-16, Senkuttuvan admits role 3-12, 223D3
'76 econ growth rptd 2-16, 147C2, G2
Newsman rearrested 3-12, 223C3
More Viets seek refuge 3-25, 243F3
Senkuttuvan freed, loses citizenship 4-13, 309B3
UNCTAD shipping study rptd 4-17, 337E2
W Ger min sees Lee on rights 4-28, 394F3
Newsman freed 4-29, 394F3
Viet refugees barred 6-12, 497F1
Amnesty Intl lists lawmakers held 9-5, 753B2
Br Airways Concorde pact rptd 10-24, 905D3
Hijacked Viet jet lands 10-29, 848C2
Colgate Far East golf tourn 11-13, 951E1
Viet hijackers jailed 12-15, 991G3

1978

SIMMONS, Matty
Animal House released 7-27, 970D2
SIMMONS, Ted
NL batting ldr 10-2, 928F2
SIMMONS Co.
OKs Gulf+Westn merger bid 10-15, 808A2
SIMON, Brigitte
French Open results 6-11, 540F1
SIMON, Herbert A.
Wins Nobel Prize 10-16, 886E2-B3
SIMON, Melvin
Somebody Killed Her Husband released 9-29, 970C3
SIMON, Neil
Cheap Detective released 6-22, 619A1
California Suite released 12-21, 1030E2
SIMON, Paul
NASL Phila club ownership cited 1-5, 23C1
SIMON, Rep. Paul (D, Ill.)
Reelected 11-7, 850A4
SIMON, Peter
PS Your Cat is Dead opens 3-22, 887F2
SIMON, Roger L.
Big Fix released 10-6, 969C3
SIMON, William E.
Backs Jarvis tax-cut plan 9-26, 735E3
Orioles purchase bid rptd 12-21, 1026F2
SIMONS, Jim
Wins Memorial Tourn 5-21, 580E3
SIMON & Schuster Inc.—*See under GULF + Western Industries Inc.*
SIMPSON, Alan K.
Wins US Sen primary in Wyo 9-12, 736C2
Elected 11-7, 846G1, 848F3, 856F1
SIMPSON, Bill
NFL '77 interceptn ldr 1-1, 56G2
SIMPSON, Keith
In NFL draft 5-2, 336F2
SIMPSON, Canon Mary
Preaches in Westminster 4-2, 294D2
SIMPSON, O. J. (Orenthal James)
Traded to 49ers 3-24, 336C1
SIMPSON, Ralph
Traded to 76ers 8-16, 655G3
SIMS, David
NFL '77 touchdown ldr 1-1, 56B2
SIN, Jaime Cardinal
Meets Mondale 5-3, 360E3
SINAI—*See MIDDLE EAST, subheads ARAB-Israeli Developments—Israeli Occupation Policies and EGYPT-Israel Peace Moves*
SINAI, Stuart
Acquitted 4-28, 324D2
SINCLAIR, Ian
Asks 200-mi fishing zone 4-13, 286E2
Accepts UK A-waste aid 10-10, 771C3
Rpts govt mfg subsidy cut 11-13, 944D1
SINDONA, Michele
Barone arrested 1-11, 19G2
Barone resigns bank post 3-10, 454C2
Italy rejcts appeal 4-3, US orders extraditn 5-19, 454F1
Bordoni extradited to US 6-2, 454C2
Named Franklin co-conspirator 7-13, 681D1, F1
Extraditn upheld by US ct 11-15, 906A3
SINDONOLOGY
Shroud of Turin exhibited 8-26—10-8, studied 10-4—11-14; photo 926A1-C3
SINGAPORE—*See also ASEAN, COMMONWEALTH of Nations, GATT, NONALIGNED Nations Movement*
US info leaks cited in Viet spy chrgs 1-31, 68E3
Australia trade barriers scored 2-15, 121F2
Australia '77 gold imports rptd 3-15, 208F3
Vietnamese refugees ask Australia, US asylum 4-9, 265B3
Singapore Airlines to buy Boeing jets 5-9, 365E2
New US amb rptd 6-6, 448G1
UN Assemb member 713E3
China dep premr visits 11-12—11-14, 894G1

1979

SIMMS, Phil
In NFL draft 5-3, 335F1
SIMON, Neil
They're Playing Our Song opens 2-11, 292E3
Maggie Smith wins Oscar 4-9, 336A2
Chapter Two released 12-14, 1007A3
SIMON, Rep. Paul (D, Ill)
Asks US-USSR airlift aid to Cambodia 11-1, 863B3
SIMON, William E.
Williams buys Baltimore Orioles 8-2, 619B1
SIMONOV, Konstantin
Dies 8-28, 671F3
SIMONS, Col. Arthur D. (ret.)
Dies 5-21, 432F3
SIMONS, Jim
Ties for 2d in Greater Milwaukee Open 7-15, 587E3
2d in Buick Open 9-16, 970D1
SIMON & Schuster Inc.—*See under GULF + Western*
SIMONSEN, Mario Henrique
Brazil planning min designate 1-19, 95B1
Sets new econ measures 2-2, 210F1
Figueiredo sworn pres 3-15, 210F1
Resigns Brazil planning post 8-10, 612A3
Delfim sets econ reforms 8-15, 870F3
SIMONTON, Tex.—*See TEXAS*
SIMPSON, Sen. Alan K. (R, Wyo.)
Scores SALT treaty 4-5, 258G1
SIMPSON, Marguerite (Mrs. O. J.)
Husband files for divorce 3-9, 271G3
SIMPSON, O. J. (Orenthal James)
Files for divorce 3-9, 271G3
Cousineau in NFL draft 5-3, 335D1
SIMPSON, Ralph
Traded to Nets 2-7, 526E2
SIMPSON Street (play)
Opens 3-5, 292A3
SIMS, Billy
Oklahoma wins Orange Bowl 1-1, 8B3
White wins Heisman Trophy 12-3, 1001D2
SIMS, David
NFL '78 touchdown ldr 1-6, 80B1
SIN, Jaime Cardinal
On unrest, urges martial law end 9-7, 9-14; asks Aquino release 9-14, 710C1
SINAI—*See under MIDDLE EAST*
SINCLAIR, George
Ian Sinclair quits Cabt 9-27, 787D3
SINCLAIR, Ian
China wheat deal rptd 1-22, 56F3
Cabt operatns streamlined 2-4, 113D2
Quits Cabt post, denies chrgs 9-27, 787G2
Fraser shuffles Cabt 12-8, 948D1
SINCLAIR, James
On gold price rise 6-4, 435G2; 12-31, 978A1
SINCLAIR, J. Frederick
Madson pleads guilty to espionage 9-25, 747G3; sentncd 10-26, 831G3
SINDONA, Michele
US ex-offcl discloses loan 1-9, 205D3
3 Franklin ex-offcls convicted 1-23, 205B3
Indicted 3-19, 205C2
Rptd missing 8-3, kidnap feared 8-6, 635A3
Reappears, enters NY hosp 10-16, 793E2
SINGAPORE—*See also ASEAN, COMMONWEALTH of Nations, GATT, NONALIGNED Nations Movement*
Australia air policy oppositn rptd 1-5, 6D1
Rhodesia chrgd re illegal US copters 1-5, 7F3
Viet SE Asia policy scored at UN 1-13, 28G1
Waldheim in refugee talks 5-11—5-12, 379D2
More Indochina refugee admissns barred 6-30; US, Japan seek aid 7-2, 495A2
Pol Pot Cambodia forces backed 8-30, 674D3
Viet refugees land 9-3—10-9, 763F3
UN membership listed 695B3
UNCTAD rubber accord reached 10-5, 781B3

1980

SIMMER, Charlie
NHL scoring ldr 4-6, 295G3, 296D1
SIMMONS, Ted
NL batting ldr 10-6, 926E2
SIMMONS v. U.S.
Case cited by Sup Ct 6-25, 541E1
SIMON (film)
Released 2-29, 216E3
SIMON, Neil
I Ought to be in Pictures opens 4-3, 392D3
Seems Like Old Times released 12-19, 1003D2
SIMON, Norton
Wife buys Bouts painting for record sum 4-16, 472A3
SIMON, Paul
NY record co indicted 2-28, 237D3
One-Trick Pony released 10-3, 836D3
SIMON, Rep. Paul A. (D, Ill.)
Reelected 11-4, 842A4
SIMON, Rita J.
Female white-collar crime study rptd 1-21, 215G3
SIMON, William E.
Heads Reagan advisory panel 4-17, 304C3
Pvt anti-inflatn com sets policy 6-21, 481E1
Addresses GOP conv 7-14, 530B3
Bars Reagan Cabt apptmt 11-28, 935C2
SIM: One Night with a Lady Undertaker from Texas (play)
Opens 6-2, 756G3
SIMONIS, Adrianus
At Dutch bishops synod 1-14—1-31, 156G3
SIMONS, Jim
2d in Greater Hartford Open 7-27, 715E1
SIMPSON, John
Wins Kan US Sen primary 8-5, 682E3
Loses US Sen electn 11-4, 851B1
SIMPSON, Peter
Prom Night released 8-15, 675C3
SIMPSON, Scott
Wins Western Open 7-6, 715C1
2d in Hall of Fame tourn 9-14, 972A2
SIMPSON, Gen. William Hood
Dies 8-15, 676B3
SIMPSON Thatcher & Bartlett
Vance resumes practice 6-11, 471A2
Vance elected US Steel dir 8-7, 702C1
SIMS, Billy
Oklahoma wins Orange Bowl 1-1, 23E1
In NFL draft, hints Canada move 4-29, 336E2, C3
Detroit contract rptd 8-27, 998G2
SINAI—*See under ARAB-Israeli Developments*
SINATRA, Frank
Offers Chrysler aid 6-11, 457F1
First Deadly Sin released 10-24, 836G2
SINCLAIR, Donald
King chrgd in Tex church murders 6-22, 568G2
SINCLAIR, Ian
Chrgd re business fraud 4-29, 334B2
Acquitted 8-14; rejoins Cabt 8-18, 650C2
SINCLAIR, Stanley (d. 1979)
King chrgd in Tex church murders 6-22, 568G2
SINDONA, Michele
Convicted in Franklin Bank fraud, extraditn sought by Italy 3-27, 237D1
Fraud suit ruling refused by Sup Ct 4-21, 344A2
Bordoni sentenced 4-23, 415B1
SINDONA v. Tisch
Case refused by Sup Ct 4-21, 344A2
SINGAPORE—*See also ADB, ASEAN, COMMONWEALTH of Nations, GATT, NONALIGNED Nations*
Pacific orgn studied 1-20, 78C2
US amb's pol gaffes rptd 1-30, 200C2
Pan Am revives discount coupons 3-10, 346E3
Moscow Olympic boycott joined 5-3, 379D2
Viet refugees arrive 6-10, 476C1
Pol Pot govt UN Assemb seat backed 10-13, 775C2
More Viet refugees arrive 11-19, 952E1

1976

SINGER, Dr. Margaret T.
Testifies in Hearst trial 2-9, 114B3
Testimony for Hearst barred 3-1, 202D1
SINGER Co.
Italy layoffs rptd 1-30, 141D1
'75 record loss rptd 437C2
SEC lists paymt 5-12, 729B1
Sup Ct refuses computer evidence case 11-29, 900E3
SINGH, Jagjit
Dies 8-7, 892F3 ★
SINGH, Charan
Announces birth-control plan 4-16, 290C1
SINNATHAMBY Rajartnam
Urges Asean cooperatn 2-10, 108B2
SINNO, Salvatore
Named in Provenzano indictmt 6-23, 460E1
SIOUX Falls, S.D.—*See SOUTH Dakota*
SIOUX Indians—*See INDIANS, American*
SIRACUSA, Ernest
Scores VOA rpt on Uruguay torture 4-21, 382G3
Vs Uruguay mil aid ban 10-18, 814E1
SIRICA, Judge John J.
Special mail fees hiked 4-9, 287B2
US to curb pocket-veto use 4-13, 284E1
Mondale scores GOP ticket on Watergate 10-5, 743E3
Major Watergate convictns upheld; Mardian's upset 10-12, 770F1, E2
SIRIT, Oscar
Slain 2-16, 125B2
SISANA Sisan
On Laos 'cultural revolution' 4-11, 267E3
Laos bans birth control 9-9, 735F1
SISAY Habte, Maj.
Rptd executed 7-13, 523D3
SISCO, Joseph J.
Quits as State undersecy 2-23, 186C2
SISK, Rep. B. F. (D, Calif.)
Vs assassination panel 9-17, 729G2
Reelected 11-2, 829B1
SISSMAN, Louis E.
Dies 3-10, 316C1
SITHOLE, Rev. Ndabaningi
Quits ANC, claims ZANU ldrshp 9-9, 733A3
Scores majority rule plan 9-23, 718G1
Vs Nkomo-Mugabe alliance 10-10, 781F2
ZANU endorsement rptd 10-10, 781F2
In Tanzania 10-13, 781F2
Rhodesia conf role urged 10-15, 10-17; UK invites 10-18, 781E2, F2
In Geneva 10-25, 797F1
OKs flexible independnc date 11-15, 862A1
Intra-ZANU clashes rptd 11-15—11-27, 1009B3
Independnc date set 11-26; natlsts ask new interim plan 11-29, 893C1, F1
SIVARD, Ruth L.
Arms spending study released 2-29, 182G3
1600 Pennsylvania Avenue (play)
Opens 5-4, 1014C3
SIZOV, Gennadi F.
Addresses CP Cong 2-25, 195D1
SIZWE Banzi Is Dead (play)
Transkei expels actors 10-24, 813B2
SKAF, George
Gets 3 Leb Cabt posts 9-15, 682F2
SKAGGS, Marion B.
Dies 5-8, 484G3
SKALA, Carole Jo
3d in LPGA championship 5-30, 424C3
SKATING, Ice
Winter Olympic results 2-5—2-13, 158E3, 159A1
SKELLY Oil Co.
In Viet oil talks 4-24, 352B2
SKELTON, Ike
Elected 11-2, 823B3
SKELTON, Norman
Resignatn urged 4-9, 351G1
SKELTON, Red
Orben named Ford speechwriter 1-21, 40C3
SKIING
Gabl dies 1-18, 56C3
Winter Olympic results 2-5—2-13, 158D3, 159C1, E1
Italy cable car falls 3-9, 384E1
Colo gondolas fall 3-26, 384F1
Mittermaier retires 5-31, 424G1
SKINNER, Scott
Loses Vt Sen primary 9-14, 705A2
SKOLNIK, Barnet D.
Mistrial in Mandel case 12-7, 922D3
SKOWRON, Edward (deceased)
Named in Provenzano indictmt 6-23, 460E1
SKRICEK, Rheinhard
Wins Olympic medal 7-31, 574C1
SKRZYLEWSKI, Andrzej
Wins Olympic medal 7-24, 576B3
SKUBITZ, Rep. Joe (R, Kan.)
Reelected 11-2, 829E3

1977

SINGAPORE Airlines
Br Airways Concorde pact rptd 10-24, 905D3
SINGER Co., The
Questionable paymts rptd 3-10, 233F2
Jones sentncd re '72 pol gift 4-4, 312C3
SINGER v. U.S. CIVIL Service Commission
Sup Ct voids rule 1-10, 57B1
SINGH, Charan
India home affairs min 3-26, 240A1
Ex-offls face probe 4-1, 4-7, 283G2
Lists emergency rule jailings 4-5, 283E3
Asks assemb electns 4-18, 304D2
Asks 9 state assembs ended 4-29, 348B2
SINGH, Col. Iqbal
Assaulted 9-15, suspect arrested 9-18, 779F1
SINGH, Kewal
Jethmalani seeks India return 2-1, 71F2
SINGH, Moni
Arrested 10-13, 805F2
SINGH, N. K.
Arrested 8-15, 637D2
SINGH, Nagendra
World Ct vice pres 4F1
SINGH, Ravindra Prasap
To run vs Sanjay Gandhi 2-15, 116G1
Wins Parlt seat 3-16—3-20, 205B2
SINGH, Surinder
Arrest sought 8-23, 655F2
SINGH, Swaran
Named Cong Party interim pres 4-15, 392B2
SINGLAUB, Maj. Gen. John K.
Chrgs N Korea ambush 5-9, 411A3
US policy criticism rptd 5-19, loses post 5-21, testifies 5-25, 403G2-404G1
Carter explains action 5-26, 417A2
Assigned to Ft McPherson 5-27, 417D2
Mil chiefs coercion re Panama Canal pacts chrgd 9-20, 755G1
SINGLETON, Ken
AL batting ldr 10-2, 926F3
SIOUX Falls, S.D.—*See SOUTH Dakota*
SIOUX Indians—*See INDIANS, American*
SIRACUSA, Ernest V.
Replaced as amb to Uruguay 7-13, 626C3
SIRICA, Judge John J.
Natl Sciences Acad exempt from disclosures 5-23, 444B3
Cuts Watergate sentences 10-4, 761G3
Retires from full-time duty 10-4, 927E3
SIRIKIT, Queen (Thailand)
Aide killed 2-16, 138E1
Escapes bomb blast 9-22, 747G1
Assailants arrested 10-10, 827G1
Samak opposed by mil 10-20, 827D1
SISK, Rep. B. F. (D, Calif.)
Offshore leasing bill blocked 10-25, 833G2
SISON, Jose Maria
Captured 11-10, 1019B2
SITHOLE, Rev. Ndabaningi
London ZANU backs 1-14, 29D1
OAU backs Patriotic Front 2-4, 122C3
Zapu urges Geneva talks resumed 2-22, 145A1
Scores Sovts 3-28, 247G3
Owen rejects conf bar 4-11, 296F1
Sees Young 5-13, 399A1
Returns, backs UK-US team 7-10, 536C3
Scores Smith settlemt plan 7-19, 563F3
Muzorewa backers quit UANC 8-8—8-21, 662E2
Lauds UK-US plan 9-2, 699A3
Kaunda backs Patriotic Front 10-21, 810F2
Sees UK, UN reps 11-4, 875D3
OKs Smith majority-rule talks 11-25, 910B3
Sees Smith re majority rule 12-2—12-29, 1015F2
SIX Men (book)
On best-seller list 11-6, 872E3
16th STREET Baptist Church (Birmingham, Ala.)
'63 bomber convicted 11-18, 907G2
SIXTY Minutes—*See CBS Inc.*
SIYOVELWA, Peter Saldi
Resigns 1-23, 161D2
SKELLY Oil Co.
Getty takeover cited in table 880G1
SKIING
Callaway probe dropped 1-11, 59E2
Colo gets drought relief 1-29, 77A1
Sabich slayer sentncd 1-31, 102E3
Colo cloud-seeding rptd 2-21, 153C1
Roland Palmedo dies 3-15, 264C3
SKINNER, Judge Walter Jay
Sentences 2 Mass sens 3-23, 253A1
SKOCHILOV, Anatoly
Death rptd 7-7, 604F3
SKOKIE, Ill.—*See ILLINOIS*
SKOLNIK, Barnet D.
Joins FBI probe 12-13, 979C3

1978

SINGAPORE Airlines
Boeing jet buy set 5-9, 365E2
SINGER, Isaac Bashevis
Wins Nobel Prize 10-5, 886F1-A2
SINGER Co., The
'76 tax nonpaymt rptd 1-27, 65G2
Colombia store bombed 10-9, 814C3
Rockwell, Textron indicted re price fixing 11-1, 935B3
SINGH, Charan
Quits Janata posts 4-29, 374C3
Vs govt handling of Gandhi case 6-28; Cabt asks resignatn 6-29, quits 6-30, 516F1
Lal chrgs plot in ouster, govt purges 7-4; Lal restored in Janata compromise, Singh calls off rally 7-8, 7-9, 631C3
Mishra quits over ouster 7-6, 631E3
SINGLAUB, Maj. Gen. John K.
Scores Carter, recalled to DC 4-27, resigns 4-28; Goldwater backs 5-1, 321D2-B3
Continues Carter Admin criticism 6-2, 433A2
SINGLETON Jr., Judge John V.
Fines cardbd mfrs 10-13, 1005G2
SINNO, Salvatore (Big Sal)
Provenzano, Konigsberg convicted 6-14, 480C2
SIRICA, Judge John J.
Ehrlichman freed 4-27, 320B2
Voids Navy sea duty bar 7-27, 589C1
SISK, Rep. B. F. (D, Calif.)
Vs S Korea food aid cutoff 6-22, 467F2
Cong electn funds rejected 7-19, 550B3
Coelho wins seat 11-7, 856E3
SISK, T. Edward
Arrested in parole payoff 12-15, 1011F1
SISLEY, Alfred (1840-99)
Paintings stolen in Marseilles 6-20, 579F1
SISSLI, Noble
Eubie opens 9-20, 1031E1
SISSON, Rosemary Anne
Candleshoe released 8-4, 969F3
SITHOLE, Rev. Ndabaningi
Facts on 59B2
Scores Muzorewa walkout 1-27, 59B3
OKs majority-rule pact 2-15, in transitn govt talks 2-16—2-20; sees Owen 2-20—2-21, 119B2-B3, C3
Signs majority-rule pact 3-3, 154A3
Sworn state cncl member 3-21, 210A2
Detainee releases revealed 4-6, 290F3
Council of ministers sworn 4-14, 291B1
Sees Owen, Vance 4-17, 290E3
Black min ousted 4-28; govt split threatened, probe set 4-28—5-2, 317G1, C2
Govt split averted dispite black ouster 5-14, 376G3
Rival pro-govt groups clash 5-20, 455E3
Supporters rptd killed 7-15, 7-22, 594D2
Defends Mozambique raids 8-2, 594A2
WCC grants Patriotic Front aid 8-10, 650A3
Supporters rptd killed 8-10, 741D2
Bars US-UK conf 8-30, 740B3
Denies knowing of Smith-Nkomo mtg 9-2, 740A3
Announces black draft 9-16, 741E2
In US tour 10-7—10-20, 818D3
Armed backers rptd 10-28, scored 11-7, 867C3
Plays down electn delay 10-30, 867F2
Sees Botha 11-15; warning vs vote delay rptd 11-23, 912B2
Agrees to electn delay 11-16, 893B2
Backs Cabt role for whites 11-30, 945D3
SITTLER, Daryl
Wales Conf wins NHL All-Star game 1-24, 76D3
SITTLER, Robert
Buddy Holly Story released 7-21, 969E3
SIXTY Minutes—*See CBS Inc.*
SIZOO, J. A.
Black ldr cited in FBI '64 memo on King conspiracy 5-29, 410A3
SJOBERG, Lars-Erik
Named WHA top defenseman 7-6, 656D3
SKARMETA, Antonio
Calm Prevails released 4-6, 618E3
SKATING, Ice
Heiden wins speed-skating title 2-26, sets records 3-2, 3-12, 316A3
World figure-skating championships 3-9—3-11, 316D3
SKEEN, Joe
Wins primary for NM gov 6-6, 448C2
Loses electn 11-7, 855F2
SKELTON, Rep. Ike (D, Mo.)
Reelected 11-7, 851C2
SKIBUTZ, Rep. Joe (R, Kan.)
Whittaker wins seat 11-7, 854F2
SKIING
World Alpine championships 1-29—2-5, 316D2
4 die in Squaw Valley tram car fall 4-15, 460A2
SKINNER, Anita
Girlfriends released 8-16, 970D1
SKINNER, Judge Walter J.
Rules on Mass Indian land claim 1-6, 6F1
Curbs NH gov on flag lowerings 3-22, 221B2
Dismisses Wampanoag land claim 3-24, 327A1
SKOKIE, Ill.—*See ILLINOIS*
SKOTAREK, Alex
Named Roughnecks coach 6-25, 707D3
SKUBITZ, Rep. Joe (R, Kan.)
Primary results, retiremt cited 8-1, 606F1

1979

SINGAPORE Airlines
Entebbe hijack case declined by US Sup Ct 4-30, 364G3
SINGER, Issac Bashevis
Magician of Lublin released 11-9, 1007G3
Teibele & Her Demon opens 12-16, 1007F2
SINGER, John
Dies in shooting 1-18, 94B1
SINGER Co., The
'75 record loss cited 10-30, 845G3
SINGER and Friedlander Ltd.
Cuban bond sale abandoned 11-8, 872G1
SINGH, Charan (Indian prime minister; resigned Aug. 20)
Sworn India dep prime min 1-24, 97G2
Announces fscl '79 budget 3-1, 169F2
Janata feud cited 6-26, 544G1
Asked to form govt 7-26; sworn prime min 7-28, names Cabt 7-28, 7-30, 573A1
Warns Pak vs A-arms race 8-15, 646C1
Quits 8-20, heads caretaker govt 8-22, 634G2
SINGH, Lallan P.
On Naga attacks 1-5, 97F2
SINGH, Sher
Rpts USSR A-plant bid rejctd 5-2, 323F2
SINGH, Siri Sat Nam
Second Thoughts opens 5-4, 712C2
SINGLAUB, Maj. Gen. John K. (ret.)
Warns Carter of Sovt challenge 1-12, 15B1
Criticizes SALT 4-11, 295F1
SINGLETON, Ken
AL batting ldr 9-30, 2d in MVP vote 11-21, 955B2, E3
In World Series 10-10—10-17, 816B1
SINOPOLI, Mario
'78 deficit rptd; scores black mkt, pub employees 6-26, 486E3
SIOUX Falls, S.D.—*See SOUTH Dakota*
SIOUX Indians—*See INDIANS, Americans*
SIPE, Brian
NFL '78 passing ldr 1-6, 80A1
SIRETTA, Dan
Tip Toes opens 3-26, 712A3
SIRHAN, Sirhan Bishara
Parole hearing denied 11-7, 953B3
SIR Ivor Again (race horse)
3d in Flamingo Stakes 3-24, 448C3
SIRICA, Judge John J.
Curbs Nader group suits 3-14, 308A2
SIRS, Bill
Warns vs steel plant closings 7-12, 543G1
SIRT, Gen. Walid Mahmoud
Sentenced 8-7, executed 8-8, 602F2
SISK, T. Edward
Indicted 3-15, 309D2
SISTER Sledge (singing group)
We Are Family on best-seller list 5-30, 448E3; 7-4, 548E3
SISTERS of Charity (Emmitsburg, Md.)
China reimbursemt set 3-16, 218B1
SISTERS of Mercy of the Union
Md hq sale announced 7-2, 640G2
SISTERS and Strangers (book)
On best-seller list 9-2, 672D3
SITHI Sawetawila, Air Marshal
Rpts Cambodian refugees mass near border 9-9, 684E2
SITHOLE, Rev. Ndabaningi
Rhodesian dispute role described 170B3
Whites OK draft const 1-30, 77B1
Asks Smith quit politics 2-22, 170D1
Gabellah quits ZANU 3-5, 170F1
Disputes Muzorewa electn 4-24, 293B1
Boycotts new Parlt 5-7, 354C1; Cabt 5-30, 393E1
ZANU mtg; ends Assemb boycott 7-31, 586A3
On Commonwealth Zimbabwe plan 8-6, 589E2
Muzorewa on govt-ZANU clash 8-17, 638B2
SITKOVETSKY, Dmitri
Wins Kreisler violin contest 9-19, 892F2
SIXTY Minutes—*See CBS*
SKAARE, Kolbjorn
Identifies Viking artifact 2-7, 138E1
SKAGGS, Dave
In World Series 10-10—10-17, 816A3
SKAGGS Co.
Amer Stores takeover set 3-14, 283C1
SKALA, Carole Jo
2d in LPGA Team tourn 9-16, 970E1
SKATING, Ice
Hoffman, Poetzsch win Eur titles 2-1—2-3, 392B1*
Tickner, Fratianne win US titles 2-3—2-4, 392A1
Heidens win world speed-skating titles 2-4, 2-11, 2-15; set world marks 2-11, 2-17, 392B1
World figure-skating championships 3-14—3-17, 391D3-392A1
Lake Placid Olympic facilities rptd faulty 4-24, 798D2
USSR champions defect 9-18, 721B3
Obituaries
Chalfen, Morris 11-4, 932D2
SKERRITT, Tom
Alien released 5-24, 528A1
SKILLINGS, Thomas
Viet defoliant suit filed 2-1, 90C1
SKINNER, Al
Traded to 76ers 2-7, 526F2
SKINNER, Cornelia Otis
Dies 7-9, 588D3
SKOKIE, Ill.—*See ILLINOIS*
SKOLIMOWSKI, Jerry
Shout released 11-9, 1008E1
SKORNICKA, Joel
Elected Madison mayor 4-3, 265C2

1980

SINGH, Charan
Gandhi wins electn 1-3, 1-6, violence rptd 1-3, 1-4, 11D3, 12D1
Vs state assemb dissolutn 2-18, 133F2
SINGH, Lallan P.
Unrest hits Assam 3-24—4-7, 275D1
SINGH, Zail
Defends detention law 12-16, 966D1
SIOUX Falls—*See SOUTH Dakota*
SIOUX Indians—*See INDIANS, American*
SIRICA, Judge John J.
Bennett dies 5-4, 448C1
SIRS, Bill
Predicts steel pact 2-1, 98A1
Dismisses steelworkers' vote 3-9, 193F2
SISLER, Dr. Frederick D.
Dies 3-2, 280B2
SISMAIL, Mohammed
Named Tamil Nadu gov 10-26, 873F1
SISSON, Rosemary Anne
Watcher in the Woods released 4-16, 416G3
SITAL, Sgt. Badressein
Arrested 1-30, leads coup 2-25, 153D2
Ousted from mil cncl 8-18, 653A3
SITHI Sawetawila, Air Marshal
Named Thai forgn min 2-11, 3-12, 196F3
Protests Viet attack 6-24, 475B3
On Viet incursn 6-26, 508D1
Vs Viet Thai-Cambodia DMZ plan 7-18, 591F1
SITHOLE, Rev. Ndabaningi
Party symbol rejected 1-14, 49D1
Supporter slain 1-22, 80C2
SITKA—*See ALASKA*
SIX Years with God: Life Inside Rev. Jim Jones's Peoples Temple (book)
Author slain 2-26, 190D3
SKACHKO, Tatiana
Wins Olympic medal 7-31, 624B2
SKALBANIA, Nelson
NHL OKs Flames purchase 6-24, 488A2
SKATING, Ice
Petruseva wins women's world speed title 1-13, 470E1
Heiden sets 2 world speed records, 1-13, 1-19, Poulos-Mueller sets 1 1-21, 470F1
US figure skating championships 1-17—1-19, 470E2
Stenshjemmet wins Eur speed title 1-20, 470G1
Rodnina, Zaitsev regain Eur pairs title 1-23, Cousins wins men's crown 1-24, 470F2
Heiden retains men's sprint title, Enke takes women's crown 2-10, 470A2
Lake Placid Olympics results 2-14—2-23, 155E3-156B1
US pairs team withdraws from Olympics 2-15, 154B3
E Heiden wins 5 Olympic gold medals, sets records 2-15—2-23; sister wins medal, scores press 2-20, 155A1, D1
Heiden loses world speed title to Van der Duim 3-2, 470C1
E Gers, Sovts win world figure skating titles 3-12—3-15, 470B2
Petruseva, Oglobin set world speed marks 3-27, 3-29, 470B2
SKEEN, Joe
Elected to US House 11-4, 843C3, 852B1
SKELTON, Rep. Ike (D, Mo.)
Reelected 11-4, 843D2
SKIING
Lake Placid Olympic results 2-14—2-23, 155F2-D3
Mahre wins Olympic medal 2-22, 154D3
Wenzels win World Cup 3-2, 3-11, 469F3
Klammer injured 3-3, 470A1
Vermont wins NCAA title 3-8, 470B1
Moser retires 3-16, 470A1
SKOBLIKOVA, Lidiya
Heiden wins 5 Olympic gold medals 2-15—2-23, 155A1
SKOUDIS, Vitaldas
Arrest rptd 1-14, 46F3
SKRZECZ, Pawel
Wins Olympic medal 8-2, 622A2

1976

SLACK, Rep. John M. (D, W. Va.)
Reelected 11-2, 831A3
SLAPSTICK (book)
On best-seller list 12-5, 972G2
SLBM (submarine launched ballistic missiles)—*See 'Missiles' under ARMAMENTS*
SLEEPING Murder (book)
On best-seller list 12-5, 972G2
SLEPAK, Vladimir
Exit visa denied 2-16, 421E2
Sees Shchelokov 10-21, arrested 10-25, 856G3, 857B1
Freed 11-8, 966D3
SLOAN-Kettering Institute for Cancer Research (N.Y.)
Boyse gets Adler Prize 2-11, 272C1
A Rockefeller Mauze dies 5-27, 404B2
SLONIMSKI, Antoni
Polish charter chng protest cited 268F1
SLUSARSKI, Tadeusz
Wins Olympic medal 7-26, 575G3
SLUTTEN, Kjell
At boat collisn probe 10-23, 876A2
SLUTZKY, Arthur
Sentenced 3-9, 271C2
SLY Fox (play)
Opens 12-14, 1014F3
SMART, L. Edwin
To become TWA pres 9-22, 892G1
SMETNANINA, Raisa
Wins Olympic medals 2-7, 2-10, 159D1
SMIESZEK, Karlheinz
Wins Olympic medal 7-19, 575G1
SMIRNOV, Andrey
Wins Olympic medal 7-25, 575F2
SMIT, H. H.
Named S Africa colored min 1-22, 76F1
SMITH, A. J.
Says students join rebels 10-30, 855C3
SMITH, Becky
Wins Olympic medal 7-24, 575C3
SMITH, Carlvin
Acquitted, '74 convictn cited 2-6, 124F1
SMITH, David
Shifted to finance min 1-13, 53E3
Rpts emigrant currency cut 7-15, 591B2
Sees Kissinger 9-19, 697C1
Rhodesia conf delegate 10-12, 781D2
SMITH, David Frederick (Fred)
Dies 8-14, 656G3
SMITH, David S.
Amb to Sweden 3-18; confrmd 4-1, 262E3
SMITH, Donald G.
Slain 8-28, 652G1
SMITH, Don S.
Vs FPC gas rate hike 7-27, 635C3
SMITH, Ernest B.
Quits Hong Kong airways post 2-11, 132G2
SMITH, Frederick
Named DLP ldr 9-24, 962F1
SMITH, Gerald L. K.
Dies 4-15, 316C1
SMITH, H. Allen
Dies 2-23, 192G3
SMITH, Hedrick
Files tap suit vs Nixon 5-10, 349E2
Russians on best-seller list 12-5, 972B2

SMITH, Ian Douglas (Rhodesian prime minister)
Nkomo talks continue 1-6—1-8, 1-16, 53F3
Shuffles cabt 1-13, 53D3
Sees guerrilla war, rpts more clashes 2-6, 176E1
Sets UK cooperatn on const talks 2-20, sees envoy 2-24—2-27, 176A2
EC backs Rhodesia self-determinatn 2-23, 164D3
Nkomo talks collapse 3-19, 239D3
Appeals for UK setlmt role 3-19, 3-20, 239E3, 240G1
Rejects UK charter plan 3-23, 240B1
Kaunda urges UK interventn 3-29, 240D2
Names blacks to Cabt; on security, censorship steps; scores US, UK 4-27, 295B2

1977

SKYTRAIN—*See LAKER Airways*
SLATER, Courtenay M.
On Mar WPI rise 4-7, 274D1
On Mar trade deficit 4-27, 339A3
On July indicators 8-30, 669B1
SLAUGHTER, William
Rpt scores air safety enforcemt 11-28, 965C3
SLAYTON, Donald
Lauds shuttle flight tests 10-26, 908D3
SLBM (submarine launched ballistic missile)—*See ARMAMENTS—Missiles*
SLEEPING Murder (book)
On best-seller list 2-6, 120E3; 3-6, 184E3
SLEEPING Pills—*See NARCOTICS & Dangerous Drugs*
SLEEPWEAR—*See CLOTHING*
SLEPAK, Vladimir
CIA link chrgd 3-4, press interview blocked 3-7, 226B3
SLESINGER, Donald
Dies 10-13, 872G2
SLOAN-Kettering Institute for Cancer Research (N.Y.)
Rpt scores laetrile 6-15, 508A2
Heroin for pain relief studied 7-1, 992F3
SLOVIK, Antoinette
Appeal rejected 8-13, 808F1
SLOVIK, Pvt. Eddie (deceased)
Widow's appeal denied 8-13, 808F1
S&Ls (Savings & Loan Associations)—*See BANKS*
SMALE, Ted
Urges business role vs apartheid 8-14, 657A2
SMALL, Hugh
Jamaica youth dvpt min 1-4, 46C1
SMALL Business Administration—*See under U.S. GOVERNMENT*
SMALLPOX—*See MEDICINE—Diseases*
SMAYDA, Theodore
Scores NH A-plant OK 6-17, 498D3
SMEAL, Eleanor
Elected NOW pres 4-24, 532F1
SMIRNOV, Lt. Cmdr. Valery
Canada chrgs indl spying 7-20, 579F3
SMIT, Jeanne-Cora
Killed 11-23, 934E3
SMIT, Robert
Killed 11-23, 934E3
SMITH, Bryan
Traded to Expos 12-7, 990D1
SMITH, Cyril
Vs Liberal Labor pact 9-28, 745E1
SMITH, David
Hikes taxes 2-24, 144F3
Sets Rhodesia budget 9-21, 824D3
Rhodesia $ devalued 10-13, 824F3
SMITH, David N.
Seeks to buy Lance bank stock 7-26, 574C2
SMITH, David S.
Replaced as amb to Sweden 8-3, 626G2
SMITH, Don S.
Backs Arctic Gas Alaska plan 5-2, 369D3
SMITH Jr., Edgar Herbert
Convicted 4-1, sentenced 4-25, 396E1
SMITH, Gerard
Gives France S Africa A-test data 8-17, 663D3
SMITH, Grant
Randal freed 7-21, 634G3

SMITH, Ian Douglas (Rhodesian prime minister)
Sees Richard on UK plan 1-1, 3A2
Scores Richard shuttle, asks US setlmt role 1-14, 29C1
Land reform OKd 1-14; Frost scores 1-17, 49G2
Muzorewa scores rebel hangings 1-17, 29E1
Kissinger plan compromise seen 1-19, US asks Vorster pressure 1-20, 29A1
UK, US vs separate pact 1-23, 1-26, 49G1
Rejects UK plan 1-24; guerrilla war, forgn interventn seen 1-24—1-26, 49A1, B2
Party ldrs OKs race reform plan 1-27, 73E2
US vs separate pact 1-31, 72E3
Muller vs internal pact 2-2, 122A3
Backs internal pact 2-4, seeks Vorster support 2-9—2-10, 122F2

1978

SKYHORSE, Paul
Acquitted 5-24, 396B2
SKYLAB (U.S. orbiting laboratory)—*See under ASTRONAUTICS*
SKYLITSIS, Aristidis
Loses Piraeus mayoralty 10-22, 816F2
SLA—*See SYMBIONESE Liberation Army*
SLACK, Rep. John M. (D, W. Va.)
Reelected 11-7, 852B4
SLADE, Bernard
Tribute opens 6-1, 887D3
Same Time, Next Year released 11-22, 970A3
SLADE, Catherine
Black Body Blues opens 1-24, 887B1
SLAVE of Love, A (film)
Released 8-14, 1030D3
SLBM (submarine launched ballistic missile)—*See ARMAMENTS—Missiles*
SLEPAK, Maria
Arrested, hospitalized 6-1, 503F3
Gets suspended sentence 7-26, 634F1
SLEPAK, Vladimir Solomonovich
Sentenced 6-21, 503E3
Wife gets suspended sentence 7-26, 634F1
SLOW Dancing in the Big City (film)
Released 11-8, 970B3
SLOWHAND (recording)
On best-seller list 3-8, 196B1; 4-5, 272G3; 5-3, 356E1
S&Ls (Savings & Loan Associations)—*See BANKS*
SMALL Business Administration—*See under U.S. GOVERNMENT*
SMALLPOX—*See MEDICINE—Diseases*
SMART, William
Firing to be probed by NRC; GAO review sought 3-29, 242G1
SMID, Tomas
Loses Monte Carlo WCT 4-16, 419C1
SMILES OF A Summer Night (film)
Little Night Music released 3-7, 619A3
SMIT, Robert (d. 1977)
Botha scores press chrgs 12-7, 989E1
SMITH, Al
Nordiques win WHA All-Star game 1-17, 76F3
WHA goaltending ldr 4-11, 296G2
Winnipeg wins WHA title 5-22, 458B2
Named WHA top goalie 7-6, 656C3
SMITH, Alexis
Casey's Shadow released 3-17, 618F3
Platinum opens 11-12, 1031F2
SMITH, Anne
Lobsters lose WTT title 9-21, 1027F1
SMITH, Barbara B.
Opposes ERA 5-5, 907D2
SMITH, Bubba
Suit vs NFL ends in mistrial 2-1, 172B1
SMITH, C. Arnholt
FDIC paymt case refused by Sup Ct 10-16, 789C1
SMITH, Cyril
Vs Thorpe reelectn bid 8-5, 614G2
SMITH, David Collville
Muzorewa claims insult 1-27, rpts apology 1-31, 59G2
Announces $ devaluatn 4-2, 249E1
SMITH, Floyd
Named WHA Stingers coach 7-27, 656G3
SMITH, Frank
Indicted 10-5, 770F3
SMITH, Gerard C.
In S Africa re A-talks 6-25—6-29, 537A1
SMITH, Hamilton O.
Wins Nobel Prize 10-12, 886E2

SMITH, Ian Douglas (Rhodesian prime minister)
Facts on 59A1
Internal talks resume 1-3; Muzorewa boycotts 1-27, to return 1-31, 59F2
Scores Malta parley 1-25, 59D2
OKs internal setlmt pact 2-15, in transitn govt talks 2-16—2-20, 119B2-B3
Signs internal pact 3-3, 154A3
UN rejcts internal pact 3-14, 192E3
Sworn state cncl member 3-21, 210A2
Front-line natns score US, UK on internal pact 3-26, 248E2
US scores internal pact 3-27, 248C3
US, UK seek new peace conf 4-2; blacks reject 4-3, 234B1
Detainee releases revealed 4-6, 290F3
Council of ministers sworn 4-14, 291B1
Sees Vance, Owen in Salisbury 4-17, 290F2, D3

1979

SKVORTOV, Alexander
Soviets win Challenge Cup 2-11, 118B3
SKY High (play)
Opens 6-28, 712D2
SKYLAB (U.S. orbiting laboratory)—*See under ASTRONAUTICS*
SKYTOEN, Lars
Named Norway industry min 10-5, 774F1
SLADE, Bernard
Romantic Comedy opens 11-8, 956G3
SLATER, Courtnay M.
On 3d 1/4 econ rebound 10-19, 805E1
SLATER, Pamela
Electroshock technique rptd 3-1, 290B1
SLBM (submarine launched ballistic missile)—*See ARMAMENTS–Missiles*
SLCM (sea-launched cruise missile)—*See ARMAMENTS–Missiles*
SLEEP Breathing (apnea)—*See MEDICINE–Heart*
SLOAN, Donald R.
Elected Peat Marwick chrmn 10-10, 851F3
SLOANE, Harvey
Loses primary for Ky gov 5-29, 420D1
SLOANE Inc., W. & J.—*See CITY Stores Co.*
SLOVIK, Antoinette
Dies 9-7, 756D3
SLOVIK, Pvt. Eddie (deceased)
Widow dies 9-7, 756D3
SLOZIL, Pavel
Loses Austrian Grand Prix 7-29, 734B2
S&Ls (Savings & Loan Associations)—*See BANKS*
SMALL, Vice Adm. Bill
6th Fleet personnel shortage rptd 11-22, 904D1
SMALL, William J.
Named NBC News pres 8-28, 756G1
SMALL Business Administration—*See under U.S. GOVERNMENT*
SMALLEY, Roy
NL wins All-Star Game 7-17, 568E3
SMALLPOX—*See MEDICINE–Diseases*
SMARTEN (race horse)
2d in Travers Stakes 8-18, 876G3
SMEAL, Eleanor (Ellie)
Scores vets' job-prefernc ruling 6-5, 421C2
Barred from Carter mtg 12-13, 961A3
SMID, Tomas
Wins W Ger Grand Prix 7-22, 734B2
SMIGHT, Jack
Fast Break released 3-1, 174E2
SMITH, Andrew
Main Event released 6-22, 820G1
SMITH, Ballard
To assume Padres operatn 8-24, 1003B1
SMITH, Billie
In World Series 10-10—10-17, 816C1
SMITH, Bobby
Named NHL top rookie 6-12, 470E2
SMITH, Bradford
On Voyager I findings 3-10, 216A1
SMITH, C. Arnholt
Convicted 5-4, 5-7, sentncd 5-31, 442C2
$29.9 mln damage judgemt rptd 12-24, 991F3
SMITH, Charlie
Dies 10-5, 860E3
SMITH, David Collville
Zimbabwe finance min 5-30, 393E1
SMITH, David Harold
GSA scandal sentence scored 5-25, 964G2
SMITH, Don
In NFL draft 5-3, 335F1
SMITH, Judge Donald S.
Sentences '78 DC protesters 2-22, 133A3
SMITH Jr., Edgar Herbert
Buckley admits misled in '57 case 1-22, 78G3
SMITH, Gerard C.
Seeks Pak A-projct halt 8-11, 607D3
SMITH, Hedrick
Nixon, aides held liable in tap suit 7-12, 611A3
SMITH, Helen
Resigns Dole staff 12-6, 983D2
SMITH, Homer
Replaced as West Pt coach; '78 firing, recruiting chrgs cited 1-4, 175B3

SMITH, Ian Douglas (Rhodesian prime minister; replaced May 29)
Rhodesian dispute role described 170A2
Backs black rule 1-11, 39G3
Const draft approved 1-30, 77A1
To stay in politics; Sithole, others score 2-22, 170B1
Final Parlt speech scores UK 2-28, 170A1
Muzorewa defends pol role 4-29, 332D2
Thatcher wins UK electn 5-3, 338B2
Zimbabwe min without portfolio 5-30, 393C1, E1
Mugabe lauds US trade ban 6-8, 434C3
Muzorewa defends Cabt role 7-10, 546G2
ZANU asks retiremt 7-31, 586E3
Commonwealth Zimbabwe plan opposed 8-7, 589E2, 590C1

1980

SKYDIVING
Miss woman survives parachute failure 5-11, 471E1
SKY'S the Limit, the (book)
On best-seller list 12-7, 948E3
SLACK, John M. (D, W. Va.)
Dies 3-17, 280C2
Hutchinson wins seat 6-3, 439D3
Staton wins seat 11-4, 850A3
SLACK, Warner
On SAT coaching study 5-15, 559C3, D3
SLADE, Bernard
Tribute released 12-13, 1003F2
SLATER, Courtenay M.
On Jan trade gap 2-28, 167D3
On 1st 1/4 GNP 4-18, 305G2
On 3d 1/4 GNP rise 10-17, 804A3
On Sept indicators, recessn 10-30, 824C1
SLATER, Herbert L.
Canada industry min 3-3, 171E1, A2
SLIM, Taieb
Asks Iraq, Iran to end war 9-23, 718D3
SLIPYJ, Josef Cardinal
Successor named 3-27, 413E3
SLIWINSKI, Marian
Ousted from Polish Cabt 11-21, 909D2
SLOAN-Kettering Institute for Cancer Research (N.Y.)
FDA OKs Laetrile testing 1-3, 23F2
Interferon lung cancer study rptd 5-28, 526E2
SLOT Machines—*See GAMBLING*
SLUPIANEK, Ilona
Wins Olympic medal 7-24, 624G1
SLURRY Power Station—*See VIRGINIA–Atomic Energy & Safeguards*
SLUSARSKI, Tadeusz
Wins Olympic medal 7-30, 624D1
SMAIL, Doug
ND wins NCAA hockey title 3-29, 488G3
SMALL, Ronald Hugh
Sees intl bankers in NY, aid request rejctd 4-7, 276A1
Sees forgn bankers, reaches debt agrmt 4-15, 314D2
Loses Jamaican electn 10-30, 854D1
SMALL, William J.
NBC managemt realigned 6-3, 501E2
SMALL Business Administration—*See under U.S. GOVERNMENT*
SMALL Circle of Friends, A (film)
Released 3-9, 216F3
SMEAL, Eleanor (Ellie)
Sets natl ERA drive 1-13, 54B3
Scores electn results for women 11-4, 846F2
SMETANINA, Raisa
Wins Olympic medal 2-15, 155C3
SMID, Tomas
Wins German Indoor championship 3-16, 607G2
Wins Italian Indoor 11-23, 947F2
Czechs win Davis Cup 12-7, 946D3
SMILEY'S People (book)
On best-seller list 1-13, 40A3; 2-10, 120B3; 3-9, 200B3; 4-6, 280B3
SMIRNOV, Vladimir
Wins Olympic medal 7-23, 622A3
SMIT, Hennie
Scores 'black' intellect 6-5, 653A1
SMITH Jr., Albert L.
Wins Ala US House primary 9-2, 682E2
Elected to US House 11-4, 842B1, 849F1
SMITH, Anne
Wins French Open women's doubles 6-6, Wimbledon women's doubles 7-5, 606A3, E3
US wins Wightman Cup 11-1, 947A1
SMITH, Rev. Dr. Bailey
Disparages Jewish prayers 8-22, religious ldrs denounce 9-18, 9-19, 811A1
Jewish prayer stance cited 10-11, 811G1
SMITH, C. Arnholt
Jury award upheld 1-18, 55D2
SMITH, Christopher H.
Elected to US House 11-4, 843A3, 848A3
SMITH, David
Zimbabwe commerce min 3-11, 198B1
SMITH, Denny
Wins Ore US House primary 5-20, 404C3
Elected to US House 11-4, 844B1, 846E1, 852F2
SMITH, Don
NFL '79 punt return ldr 1-5, 8C3
SMITH, Elliot
On ACE, NYFE merger 3-21, 224E1
SMITH, Eric
Named ASL top rookie 9-8, 771F1
SMITH, Greg
39 Steps released 5-2, 416F3
SMITH, Sgt. Gregory
In Rodney death controversy 10-6, 791B2
SMITH Jr., Harry J.
Named in Jamaican grain fraud suit 2-4, 99C2
SMITH, Howard K.
Carter, Reagan TV debate moderator 10-28, 813F1
SMITH, Ian Douglas
Backs Nkomo over Mugabe 1-31, 118E3
Rhodesian Front wins white seats 2-14; on Mugabe win 3-4, 161F1, E2
Shuns Zimbabwe indepndnc rite 4-18, 301G1
Urges Zimbabwe whites cooperatn 8-31, 674B3

1976

Cabt appointmts scored 5-4, 5-7, 339D2
Sees Vorster in Pretoria 6-13—6-14, 427G1
On Vorster-Kissinger talks 6-27, 522D3
Rejects reform plan 7-23, 591D1
Asks US talks 8-4, 580F2
Vs majority rule timetable 8-25, outside talks 9-2, 661F1
Shuffles Cabt 9-9, 713E2
Vs majority rule 9-13, 681D2
Sees Vorster in Pretoria 9-14, 681C2
Meets govt officials on UK plan 9-21—9-22, 9-23, OKs plan 9-24, 717A1
OKs conf 9-31, sees Rowlands, Schaufele 10-4, 738B2
Disputes Crosland on conf aim 10-6; UK invites to conf, names delegatn 10-12, 781A2, C2
ANC: UK delegatn extensn 10-9, 781F1
Warns nationalists 10-13, 781G1
Vorster backs 10-18, 793B2
In Geneva 10-21, sees Richard 10-22, 10-23, asks Kissinger role 10-25, 797G1
ANC chrgs UK plot 10-27, 797C1
To leave Geneva 11-1, bars natlst demands 11-2, 831D3
Leaves conf 11-3; backs majority rule 11-5, 842C2
Says US vows mil support; US denies 11-19—11-20, 879C2
Natlsts ask new interim govt plan 11-30, 893F1
Scores Richard 12-5; returns Geneva 12-8, 914F2
Scores UK 12-10, leaves conf 12-12; plans natlst talks 12-13, 12-14, 935C1, A2
Blacks quit Cabt, form party 12-29, 1009G3

SMITH, James E.
On Citibank, Chase 'problem' status 1-11, 110E2, D3
Proxmire asks testimony 1-12, 111F2
Testifies on bank 'problem' list 2-6, 113F1-D2
On GAO audit plan 2-9, 112D2
Hamilton Natl declared insolvent 2-16, 167E1
Proxmire scores 2-17, 3-1, 185D2
Bars House subcom probe, asks GAO aid 3-5, 185G3-186A1
Vows expense acct reimbursemt 3-7, 185D3
SMITH, James McCoy (Yazoo)
Football player draft ruled illegal 9-8, 736B3
SMITH, Jan H.
Paris group in A-plant deal 5-28, 387G2
SMITH, John
UK home rule min 4-8, 267A1
SMITH, John
Bars prisoner deals 10-20, 836D3
SMITH Jr., Judge John Lewis
Delays postal closings 3-5, 186G3
Delays food-stamp cutback 6-15, 435A1; 6-19, 454B3
Holds Nixon, 2 aides liable in Halperin tap suit 12-16, 980A3-981B1
SMITH 2d, John Thomas
Commerce counsel 1-27; confrmd 2-26, 186C2
SMITH, Joseph A.
Indicted 5-7, 349E1
Charges dropped 10-5, 767F3
SMITH, Kent
'72 campaign gift listed 4-25, 688B1
SMITH, Kingsbury
Brezhnev interview rptd 12-29, 978B3
SMITH, Mary Louise
Reelected GOP chrmn 8-20, 631F1
Resigns GOP post 11-22, 882B1
SMITH, Rep. Neal (D, Iowa)
Natural gas regulatn extended 2-5, 108C2
Reelected 11-2, 827D3
SMITH, R. B.
Cited in Bernhard probe rpt 8-26, 628A1
SMITH, Robert S.
Replaced as Ivory Coast amb 9-30, 808D1
SMITH, Shannon
Wins Olympic medal 7-20, 575B3
SMITH, Stuart
Backs Ontario Liberal split 4-25, 350E2
SMITH, Rep. Virginia (R, Mont.)
Reelected 11-2, 830C1
SMITH, Walter (Red)
Wins Pulitzer 5-3, 352E3
SMITH, Worthington L.
SEC sues, settles 6-29, 984B2

1977

Cowper quits 2-11, manpower bd set 2-15, 123A2
Botha named S Africa forgn min 2-11, 160E3
ZAPU urges Geneva talks resumed 2-22, 145A1
Sets race reforms 2-23, 123B1
Land reform OKd 3-4; critics challenged 3-15, party backs 3-16, 223A2
Mugabe vs conf role 4-11, 296F1
Sees Owen, for US conf role 4-13, 4-15—4-17, 296D2-B3
Rhodesia Front backs re const setlmt 4-18, 296E3
Party expels anti-reformists 4-29, 414A1
Scores Frost resignatn 7-3, 536G2-A3
Sithole returns 7-10, 536D3
On US-UK proposals 7-12, 536D1
Dissolves Parlt, scores US-UK proposals 7-18, 563C3
Owen sees Vance, Carter 7-23, 581B3
Vs Muzorewa vote plan 7-24, 581D3
Seeks 'facts' on colored family's evictn 7-29, 599D2
S Africa backs 8-4, 599B2
Scores Salisbury bombing 8-6, 624B2
Muzorewa loses supporters 8-8—8-21, 662E2
Nkomo demands removal 8-12, 624F1
Bomb explodes near office 8-13, 662B2
New US-UK plan leaked 8-24, 661F1-A2
Sweeps Rhodesia vote, vows internal settlemt try 8-31, 661A1
Gets UK-US plan 9-1, scores 9-2, 699D2
Shuffles Cabt 9-18, 824D3
Chikerema backs transitn plan 9-19, 735G1-B2
Chrgs UK-US plan deceptn, defers internal setlmt plan 9-21, 735C1
Kaunda seeks dismissal assurance 9-24, 734C3
Sees Kaunda 9-25, 810F1
On universal suffrage, army 9-26, 10-17, 810C1
Invites UN, UK reps 9-28, 810A1
OKs probe of RC comm, Amnesty Intl chrgs 9-29, 811E2
Urges independt US role 10-17, 810C1
Kaunda backs Patriotic Front 10-21, 810F2
Patriotic Front frictn re Kaunda mtg rptd 10-30, 875C3
Sees UK, UN reps 11-6, 875D3
OKs majority rule, seeks talks with moderates 11-24; reactn 11-25—11-26, 910E2
Mozambique raid scored 11-29, 911F1
Sees black ldrs re majority rule 12-2—12-29, 1015E2

SMITH, Jerry (Butch)
USSR tour results 1-29—2-5, 263B2
SMITH, Jerry Lee
Obscenity convictn upheld 5-23, 444D2
SMITH, Joan Irvine
Irvine Co takeover bid rptd 3-3, 274D3
Group wins Irvine 5-20, 519D1
SMITH Jr., Judge John Lewis
Dismisses suits vs FBI re King 1-31, 77C2
Halperin awarded $5 in tap suit 8-5, 652C2
Rules vs Kissinger transcript rights 12-8, 962D2
SMITH, Judge Joseph
Blocks Amtrak redcap svc end 9-12, 778A3
SMITH, (Edward) Mayo
Dies 11-24, 952D3
SMITH, Lt. Gen. Oliver P. (ret.)
Dies 12-25, 1024C3
SMITH, Oscar
Kidnaped 2-11, 198B3
Wife asks probe 4-11, 388C3
SMITH, Philip
Named natural resources min 3-10, 223F2
SMITH, Reggie
NL batting ldr 10-2, 926C3
In World Series 10-11—10-18, 806F1
SMITH, Richard J.
Avis sold to Norton Simon 6-27, 519G1
SMITH, Gen. Robert (ret.)
SEC Korea paymts probe rptd 11-29, 915D3
SMITH, Sam
Gilmore executed 1-17, 40F2
SMITH, Stan
Loses Springfield Championship 2-13, 430C3
S Africa Davis Cup match protests 4-15—4-17, 353G2
SMITH, Timothy
Wins Ashfield by-electn 4-28, 374A1

1978

Black min ousted 4-28; govt split threatened, probe set 4-28—5-2, 317G1, D2
Govt split averted dispite black ouster 5-14, 376G3
Nkomo bars settlemt 6-5, 455E2
Black MPs rptd vs settlemt 6-14, 615G3
Admits cease-fire failure 6-15, 455G2
Scores blacks re truce failure 7-18, UANC rebuts 7-19, 615C3
Whites boo speech 7-19; by-electn support drops 7-21, 616A1
On arms-buying scandal 7-23, 616B2
Confirms electn schedule 8-2, 615A2
Sees Nkomo 8-14, 740F2-E3
Sets martial law, scores forgn backing of Patriotic Front 9-10, 741A1
Bans ZAPU, ZANU; sees indep endnc delay 9-14, 741D1
Nkomo mtg cited re Tanzania-Lonrho dispute 9-26, 905F2
US visa denied 10-1, granted 10-3; tours US, OKs all-party conf 10-7—10-20, 818D3
Zambia reopens Rhodesia RR 10-10, 783C3
WCC grants to Muzorewa, others cited 10-25, 906G3
Announces electn delay 10-29, 867B2
Sees Botha 11-15, warning vs vote delay rptd 11-23, 912B2
Backs electn delay, denies guerrilla link 11-16, 893B2
OKs new UK envoy mtg 11-28, 912A1
Cabt role for whites set 11-30, 945D3
On oil depot attack 12-13, 955C3
Hayman scores 12-27, 1019A3

SMITH, Jim
NFL '77 kick return ldr 1-1, 56C3
SMITH, John
NFL '77 kicking ldr 1-1, 56C2
SMITH Jr., Joseph (d. 1839)
Great-grandson installed Mormon ldr 4-5, 294G2
Mormons end ban on black priests 6-9, 480B3
SMITH, Keely
Louis Prima dies 8-24, 708C3
SMITH, Kennard
CIA ex-offcl's suicide disputed 11-25, 917D2
SMITH, Justice L. Kingsley
Rules property tax illegal 6-23, 526F1
SMITH, Lloyd H.
On Kennecott bd rival slate 3-27, 402G3
SMITH, Maggie
Death On Nile released 9-29, 970B1
California Suite released 12-21, 1030E2
SMITH, McNeill
Loses US Sen primary in NC 5-2, 342B3
Reelected 11-7, 850C4
SMITH, Ozzie
NL stolen base ldr 10-2, 2d in top rookie poll 11-20, 928A2, F2
SMITH, Randy
East wins NBA All-Star game, named game MVP 2-5, 271D3
NBA scoring ldr 4-9, 271E2
SMITH, Raymond F.
USSR guard manhandles 7-20, 575B3
SMITH, Reggie
NL batting ldr 10-2, 928E2
In World Series 10-10—10-17, 799D3
SMITH, Stan
Loses United Bank Classic 2-26, 419A1
Loses WCT doubles title 5-7, 418A3
Loses Kent championship 6-10, 540C1
Wins US Open doubles title 9-9, 707G1
US wins Davis Cup 12-10, 1026F3
SMITH, Tommy
Named Aztecs coach 6-5, fired 8-2, 707C3
SMITH, Rep. Virginia (R, Neb.)
Reelected 11-7, 851E2, 854F3
SMITH, W. Eugene
Dies 10-15, 888F3
SMITH, W. Wallace
Succeeded as Mormon ldr 4-5, 294G2
SMITH, Wallace B.
Installed Mormon ldr 4-5, 294F2

1979

Attends London conf 9-10, 675F2
Rejects UK const offer 9-14, Muzorewa rift revealed 9-15-9-16, 718B1, F1
US Sen aides' London conf role rptd; UK denies protest 9-20, 718G1
Quits London conf, seeks white support vs const 10-6; returns 10-12, 778D1

SMITH, Jackie
Steelers win Super Bowl 1-21, 63D1
SMITH, Jim
Spenkelink executed in Fla 5-25, 400C1
SMITH, John
Concorde debt canceled 2-22, 154B2
SMITH Jr., Judge John Lewis
Dismisses Hancho Kim indictmt 6-15, 521A2
'76 liability rule affirmed 7-12, 611E2
Sentences Minchew 10-10, 769A2
SMITH, Kathleen (d. 1974)
Newton murder case ends in 2d mistrial, chrgs dropped 9-27, 818D3
SMITH, Maggie
Wins Oscar 4-9, 336G1
Night & Day opens 11-27, 956E3
SMITH, Marvin L.
CIA 'interest' in Letelier killer rptd 1-11, 19E3
SMITH, Matthew
Sentenced in GSA scandal 12-17, 965A1
SMITH, Michael M.
Va death penalty challenge declined by Sup Ct 5-21, 400F3
SMITH, Rep. Neal (D, Iowa)
Small Business Com chrmn 1-24, 71E1
SMITH, Randy
Walton compensatn set 9-18, 1003D2
SMITH, Robert
NBA free-throw ldr 4-8, 290F2
SMITH, Robert H.
Settles SEC charge 4-9, 588A2
SMITH, Sandy
Slain in NC 11-3, 864D3
SMITH, Stan
Loses Hall of Fame 7-15, US Open doubles title 9-8; wins Cleveland Grand Prix 8-20, 734G1, A2, D2
Wins Austrian Grand Prix 10-29, 1003E3
US wins Davis Cup 12-16, 1003A3
SMITH, Stephen
Opens Kennedy hq 10-29, 847F1
SMITH, Stuart
Rpt scores A-plant safety 4-27, 352B3
SMITH, Tommy
Mennea breaks 200-m dash record 9-12, 799A2
SMITH, Waddell
Edmonton wins Grey Cup 11-25, 1000G1
SMITH, Wayne
Walks out on Castro speech 9-3, 674E2

1980

SMITH, J. Lucian
'79 resignatn cited 5-30, 600D2
SMITH, Jaclyn
NY actress to join Charlies Angels 6-17, 638D2
SMITH, James
Argues ctroom cameras case in Sup Ct 11-12, 882C2
SMITH, Jerry Paul
Acquitted 11-17, 898F2
SMITH, Jim
Steelers win Super Bowl 1-20, 62A1
SMITH, Joe
Dem platform backs MX 6-24, 479C3, E3
Introduces anti-MX plank 8-13, 611D2
SMITH, John
NFL '79 kicking ldr 1-5, 8B2
SMITH Jr., Judge John Lewis
Grants judges 12.9% pay hike 3-24, 250G1
SMITH, Jonathon
ATFA formatn cited; TAC OKs paid amateur meets 6-28, 891C3
SMITH, Kate
Estate feud settled 9-4, 908C2
SMITH, Lonnie
In World Series 10-14—10-21, 811G2, 812B1
SMITH, M. J.
2d in Sun City Classic 3-2, 412F2
SMITH, Mary Louise
On Reagan mtg 7-15, 533E3
SMITH, Rep. Neal (D, Iowa)
Reelected 11-4, 842C4
SMITH, Ozzie
Wins Golden Glove Award 12-6, 926E1
SMITH, Roger B.
Named GM chrmn, chief exec 9-9, 701F3
SMITH, Ron
Steelers win Super Bowl 1-20, 61F3-62C1
SMITH, Sherman
NFL '79 touchdown ldr 1-5, 8B2
SMITH, Stacey
Retains US ice dancing title 1-19, 470E2
SMITH, Stan
Wins Frankfurt WCT tourn 3-23, 607A3
Loses Wimbledon men's doubles 7-5, 606G2
Wins US Open men's doubles 9-6, 691F2
SMITH, Stephen
Rebuts Chappaquiddick article 1-14, 32F3, 33B1
SMITH, Steve
US Olympic trials ban voided 6-25, 891A3
SMITH, Rep. Virginia (R, Neb.)
Reelected 11-4, 843E2
SMITH, Virginia B.
Buckley cancels commencemt appearance 5-19, 471B2
SMITH, Wayne S.
Havana anti-US protest draws 1 mln 5-17, 380B2
On stranded Cuba refugees 11-19, 883F2
SMITH, William French
Named atty gen 12-11, 935D1
SMITH, William L.
Sworn comr of educ 1-9, 18D2
SMITH Jr., William Reece
Installed ABA pres 8-6, 744A2

1976

SMITH International Co.
SEC lists paymts 5-12, 729B1
SMITHSONIAN Institution—*See under U.S. GOVERNMENT*
SMITH & Wesson—*See BANGOR Punta Corp.*
SMOKEY Bear
Dies 11-9, 995G2
SMOKING—*See 'Smoking-Health Link' under TOBACCO*
SNAKE River Valley
Teton Dam collapse rpts 7-15, 9-25, 736E1
SNAKES—*See REPTILES*
SNAPE, Richard
Named to econ advisory bd 9-14, 730F1
SNEAD, J. C.
Wins Kaiser Intl golf 9-26, 756A3
SNEAD, Sam
Nephew wins Kaiser Intl golf 9-26, 756A3
SNEED, Melita
Wounded 6-6, 442E3
SNELLING, Richard Arkwright
Wins Vt primary for gov 9-14, 705B2
Elected 11-2, 820D3, 821D3, 831D2
SNOWDON, Earl of (Antony Armstrong-Jones)
Separates from Margaret 3-19, 252A3
SNOW White & the Seven Dwarfs (film)
Dec '75 top grossing film 12-31-75, 32G3
SNYDER, Rep. (Marion) Gene (R, Ky.)
Scored by environmt group 3-25, 220A1
Releases Bunker canal testimony 4-13, 281D1, 291B3
Vs Panama Canal treaty rider 6-29, 534B2
Reelected 11-2, 829E3
SNYDER, Gerald
Stats Canada probe rpt cites 11-12, 888E2
SNYDER, Jerome
Dies 5-2, 524F3
SOAMES, Sir Christopher
China-EEC trade talks rptd set 1-27, 84C3
Signs Canada pact 7-6, 496E3
SOARES, Rev. Francisco
Assassinated 2-13, 212G1
SOARES, Mario
At Europn socialist confs 1-18—1-19, 48A3; 3-13—3-14, 222F3
Scores mil rule proposal 1-18, 53A1
Not at socialist mtg 1-24—1-25, 120E1, F1
Bars Socialist pol alliances 4-30, 366B3
Rptdly rejectd pres bid 5-2, backs Eanes 5-12, 366E3
To be named premr 6-28, 482G3
Rejcts coalitn 7-2; pol parties, church ldrs back 7-7—7-23, 558B2
Named premr 7-16, sworn 7-23; sets forgn policy goals 7-19, 558A1
Introduces govt program 8-2; Natl Assemb OKs 8-11, 774B2
Links Spinola return to rise of right 8-12, 732F3
Cncl sets membership rules 8-12, 733C2
US aid pacts OKd 8-13, 811F3
Scores Argentina violence 8-26, 672E2
At Azores assemb inaugural 9-4; US base talks set 9-5, 812F1, A2
Sets austerity measures 9-9; CP scores 9-10, 774B1
Backs agri min 9-22, 811G2
Cabt sets labor law chngs 10-1, 774F1
Carvalho scores 10-3, 812A1
To 'respect' Dec vote 10-5, 812E1
At Madeira assemb inaugural 10-23, 812C2
US loan set 11-16, 966A3
Addresses Soclst Intl 11-28, 935D3
Sees Perez 11-29, 930B1
Soclsts win electns 12-12, 966D2

1977

SMITHERMAN, William C.
Navajo ldr indicted 2-9, 162E3
SMITHKLINE Corp.
Chrgd re Arab boycott 1-7, 167G1
Ulcer drug rptd OKd by FDA 8-23, 748D2
SMITH, Kline and French Laboratories—*See SMITHKLINE Corp.*
SMITH & Nephew Associated Cos. Ltd.
Textile co ends S Africa black union pact 7-19, 600D2
SMITHSONIAN Institution—*See under U.S. GOVERNMENT*
SMITH v. U.S.
Convictn upheld by Sup Ct 5-23, 444D2
SMITH & Wesson—*See BANGOR Punta Corp.*
SMITHYMAN, Christopher
Sovts apologize for assault 10-18, 926C1
SMOKEY and the Bandit (film)
Top-grossing film 8-3, 643B2
SMOKING—*See TOBACCO—Smoking-Health Link*
SMOOT, Lewis
S African co joint bid 10-17, 979E1
SMOOT Construction Co.
Loses govt contract 12-13, 979E1
SMYTHE, Mabel Murphey
Named amb to Cameroon 4-25, confrmd 5-9, 418A2
SNAIL Darter—*See FISH*
SNEED, Ed
Wins Tallahassee Open 4-17, 675G3
SNEED, Michael
Rpts on child porno 5-15—5-18, 432G2
SNEGIRYOV, Gely
Rptd jailed 9-26, 753B1
SNEIDER, Richard L.
S Korean dissident scores 4-20, 306A1
Hosts receptn, S Korea vs dissidents presence 5-26, 441B1
Demonstratn vs US pullout 5-26, 441D1
SNEPP, Frank
Book scores Viet evacuatn 11-18, 897D3-898B2
SNEVA, Tom
2d in Indy 500 5-29, 531G1
Wins Schaefer 500 6-26, 871C1
Wins USAC championship 9-4; final standing, earnings rptd 10-31, 870F3
SNOW—*See WEATHER*
SNOW, C. P.
Presents Natl Book Awards 4-11, 355G1
SNOW, John W.
Replaced in Transport post 4-6, 272G2
SNOW, Judge Marcellus
Rules on Mormon suit 3-10, 310G1
SNOWMOBILES
Carter environmt message 5-23, 404F2
SNYDER Jr., Judge Daniel J.
Bars USW strike injunctn 7-29, 593A3
SNYDER, Rep. Marion G. (Gene) (R, Ky.)
Scores Panama Canal pact 8-17, 622C2
SNYMAN, Maj. Harold
Testifies at Biko inquest 11-14—11-15, 887C2
SOARES, Mario (Portuguese premier)
Lauds Rosa resignatn 1-3, 21F2
Scores leniency for PIDE 1-6, 21E2
Mondale phones support 1-27, 69F2
Sets econ austerity program 2-25, 330B2
Adds technocrats to Cabt 3-25, 330E2
Portugal asks EC entry 3-28, 269D2
Eanes warns on econ crisis 4-25, 330G2
Sees Mondale 5-16, 398A2
Sets new austerity measures 8-25, 886D1
Assumes forgn min post 10-10, 886E3
PSD ldr quits 11-7, 886D3
Seeks econ austerity support 11-15, oppositn rejcts 11-30; govt falls 12-8, 947E1-B3

1978

SMITH Act of 1940
Repeal clears Sen 1-30, 64C3
SMITHSONIAN Institution (Washington, D.C.)
National Gallery of Art—*See separate listing*
SMITH v. Collin
Case refused by Sup Ct 10-16, 789C2
SMOG—*See ENVIRONMENT—Air & Water*
SMOKE Detectors
Pittway OKs CPSC fine 11-6, 942E1
SMOKING—*See TOBACCO*
SMOKING & Health, Office on—*See under U.S. GOVERNMENT—HEALTH, Education & Welfare*
SMOLEY, Sandy
Loses US House electn 11-7, 856D3
SMOTHERS, Dick
Presley offer to aid FBI rptd 7-14, 554A1
SMOTHERS, Tom
Presley offer to aid FBI rptd 7-14, 554A1
SMYTHE Trophy—*See HOCKEY—Awards*
SNAIL Darter—*See FISH*
SNEAD, J. C.
Ties for 2d in US Open 6-18, 580A2
SNEAD, Sam
Sues PGA over exemptn rule 1-23, 76G1
Wins Legends of Golf title 4-30, 356B1
SNELLING, Gov. Richard Arkwright (R, Vt.)
Unopposed in primary 9-12, 716D2
Reelected 11-7, 847G3, 853E3
SNEPP, Frank W.
US sues re book 2-15, 129C1
US suit noted re Stockwell book 5-8, 367B3
US wins book suit, to get profits; Random House scores 7-7, 527F2
Viet documt possessn by ex-amb rptd probed 9-13, 720B2
Colby CIA book publshd uncut 11-19, 917B2
SNEVA, Tom
2d in Indy 500 5-29; 3d in Schaefer 500 6-25, 538B2, F3
Wins USAC title 12-24, 1028C2
SNOW—*See STORMS & Floods*
SNOW, C. P. (Charles Percy) (Baron Snow of Leicester)
Leavis dies 4-14, 356B3
SNOWBELT States—*See NORTHEAST, MIDWEST; state names*
SNOWDON, Earl of (Antony Armstrong-Jones)
Divorced 5-24, 420D3
SNOWE, Olympia J.
Wins US House seat 11-7, 846F2, 847F2, 851A1
SNYDER, Rep. (Marion) Gene (R, Ky.)
Reelected 11-7, 850E4
SNYDER, Nancy
5th of July opens 4-27, Cup Runneth Over 6-22, 760C2, E2
SOARES, Mario (Portuguese premier)
Communists score CDS pact 1-20, 92D1
Forms new govt 1-26; Cabt sworn 1-30; vows IMF, EC talks resumptn 1-30, 91A3
Civil servants, teachers strike 3-10, 229G1
Raised pensn benefits, min wage 4-5, 331C2
Eanes scores govt 5-28, 594B1
Sees Giscard in Lisbon 7-19—7-21, 667B2
CDS leaves Cabt 7-24, govt falls 7-27; stays on as caretaker 7-28—8-1, 593E2-A3, 594A1
Scores da Costa apptmt as premr 8-9, 632F2, B3
Scores new govt 9-11; govt falls 9-14; criticism of Socialists, party dissensn rptd 9-23, 757G3, 758C1

1979

SMITH College (Northampton, Mass.)
S Africa stock divestiture rptd 3-24, 271C1
SMITH Corp., A. O.
No-contest plea cited 10-22, 986E1
SMITHKLINE Corp.
Ulcer drug-sperm study rptd 5-3, 354F3
Ulcer drug OKd by FDA panel 6-1, 471C2
SMITHSONIAN Institution (Washington, D.C.)
National Gallery of Art—*See separate listing*
National Portrait Gallery—*See separate listing*
SMITH-Sonneborn, Joan
Ultraviolet impact on aging rptd 3-20, 290G1
SMITH v. Arkansas State Highway Employees
Case decided by Sup Ct 4-30, 364E3
SMITH v. Daily Mail Publishing Co.
Case decided by Sup Ct 6-26, 541B1
SMITH v. Maryland
Case decided by Sup Ct 6-20, 516C1
SMITH v. Virginia
Case declined by Sup Ct 5-21, 400F3
SMOG—*See ENVIRONMENT & Pollution-Air & Water*
SMOKING—*See TOBACCO*
SMOKING & Health, Action on—*See ACTION on Smoking & Health*
SNAIL Darter—*See FISHING*
SNAKES
World record for sitting set 5-13, 392C3
SNEAD, Sam
Shoots round below age 7-22, 587E3
SNEED, Ed
2d in Heritage Classic 4-1, Masters 4-15, 587B1, B2
SNELLING, Gov. Richard Arkwright (R, Vt.)
Govs vs budget amendmt 2-26, 150A2
Gets reassurance on heating fuel supply 8-28, 703C2
Seeks Ford '80 pres race 10-12, 783G2
SNIDER, Duke
Sentenced 12-6-12-7, 1000D1
SNIDER, Conway
Rpts Mars surface water 8-9, 692C3
SNOW Leopard, The (book)
Wins Natl Book Award 4-23, 356A2
SNYMAN, J. H.
Dismissed 10-5, 774A3
SNYMAN, Peter
Sets world record for snake sitting 5-13, 392C3
SOAMES, Lord (Christopher)
UK lord pres of council 5-5, 338E1
Named Zimbabwe gov 12-7, 937G1
Arrives Salisbury, takes office 12-12, 936F3, 937A2
Halts executns, raids; orders pol detainee review 12-13, 960G1, B2
Lifts Zambia embargo 12-17, 960F1
Lifts Patriotic Front pol ban, other decrees 12-21, 976G3
Sets '80 electns 12-28, 976A1
Orders anti-infiltratn actns 12-29, 976G3
SOARES, Jair
Brazil soc welfare min designate 1-19, 95E1
SOARES, Mario
Mex visit scored 10-30, 874G3
Socialists lose assemb electns 12-2, 917C1
Socialists lose municipal electns 12-16, 968G2

1980

SMITH International Inc.
To acquire Galveston-Houston 3-26, 385B3
Galveston-Houston deal fails 6-9, 557E2
SMITH Kline Corp.
FDA Selacryn probe rptd 1-25, 64A1
SMITHSONIAN Institute (Washington, D.C.)
Hughes flying boat to be dismantled 5-22, 560G2
SMITH Transfer Corp.
MR&R Trucking Corp.
Fla deregulates trucking 7-1, 558F2
SMOKEY and the Bandit, II (film)
Released 8-15, 675E3
Top-grossing film 9-3, 716G3
SMYTH, Martin
Orangemen demonstrate 3-15, 232D3
SMYTHE, Conn
Dies 11-18, 928E3
SNEAD, Sam
2d in Legends of Golf 4-27, 412E3
Trevino clinches Vardon Trophy 9-21, 971D3
SNELL, Dr. George
Wins Nobel 10-10, 889F3
SNELL, Peter
Wicker Man released 3-26, 416G3
SNELL, Ray
In NFL draft 4-29, 336G2
SNELLING, Gov. Richard Arkwright (R, Vt.)
State of State message 1-10, 270C2
Wins renominatn 9-9, 700B3
Reelected 11-4, 845E3, 847E1, 849D1
SNEPP, Frank W.
CIA disclosure limits upheld by Sup Ct 2-19, 130C3
Rehearing denied by Sup Ct 4-14, 307E1
Novel rptd submitted for CIA OK 6-13, 517A1
SNEPP v. U.S.
Case decided by Sup Ct 2-19, 130C3
Rehearing denied by Sup Ct 4-14, 307F1
SNEVA, Tom
2d in Indy 500 5-25, 637G2
3d in Pocono 500 6-22, 638A1
CART membership cited 6-30, 1002A2
SNIDER, Duke (Edwin Donald)
Elected to Baseball HOF 8-3, 796B2
SNIDER, Paul
Found slain 8-15, 713D3
SNOW, C(harles) P(ercy)
Dies 7-1, 608D3*
SNOW, George
Missing in Carib copter crash 11-13, 869E3
SNOWE, Rep. Olympia J. (R, Me.)
Reelected 11-4, 843A1, 848B2
SNOW Leopard, The (book)
Wins Amer Book Award 5-1, 692A2
SNOW White and the Seven Dwarfs (film)
FBI 'Miporn' probe rptd 2-14, 136B2
SNYDER, Keith S.
Wins NC atty gen primary 5-6, 405G1
SNYDER, Rep. Marion Gene (R, Ky.)
Reelected 11-4, 842E4
SOAMES, Lord (Christopher)
Rejects rebel assemb deadline extensn 1-2, 7B3
OKs transitn role for regular, auxiliary forces, S Africa troops 1-6; Mugabe scores 1-8, 31B3
Nkomo lauds 1-13, 31E2
Rpt on 1st mo issued, ZANU truce violatns chrgd 1-15, 48F3
Extends emergency state 1-18, 48D3
Rpts S Africa troops to leave 1-26, 80D2
Mugabe scores 1-27, 80A2
Assumes extra power 2-5; bars ZANU candidate 2-10, 118G2
Mugabe escapes assassinatn 2-11, 118C3
Warns re ZANU vote exclusn 2-12; Mugabe sees 2-26, 162A3
Electns held 2-27—2-29; asks calm 3-3; UK lauds role 3-4, 162B1, E1
Get Mugabe Cabt list 3-11, 198A1
Ends martial law 3-20, 301F3
SOAPS & Detergents
FTC ends detergent indus probe 5-12, 703A2
Detergent carcinogen OKd 5-27, 526C3
SOARES, Mario
Shuns Sa Carneiro-Eanes rift 3-4—4-1, 277B3
Carter sees 6-26, 475C1
Soclsts retain 73 seats 10-5, 760B1
Eanes cites dismissals 10-14; quits Soclst post 10-19, 809C2
Eanes seeks Soclst support 11-22, 903B1

1976

SOBERON, Guillermo
Scores 'porros', police probe 4-28, 419G2
SOBRINO Aranda, Luis
Asks Peron quit 2-10, 154E2

SOCCER
Olympic results 7-31, 575B2
Argentina World Cup offcl killed 8-19, 672B1
San Fran wins NCAA title 12-5, 969F2
SOCIALISM, International—*See also country names*
Europn socialists meet in Denmark 1-18—1-19, 48F2
Southn socialists meet in Paris 1-24—1-25, 120B1
Kissinger lobbying efforts rpts 2-5, 120B2
Austria soclsts urge 3d world liberatn support 3-11—3-13, 380D2
Bordaberry rptd vs ties 3-12, 4-11, 382A3
Europn socialists meet in Portugal 3-13—3-14, 222D3
Eur, Latin soc dems meet in Venez 5-23—5-25, 449E2-C3
Eur, Latin reps at Spain PSP cong 6-5—6-6, 459C1
Blazej Vilim dies 9-23, 1015A3
Soclst Intl meets in Geneva 11-26—11-28, 930A1, 935E2

SOCIALIST International
Meets in Geneva, Brandt elected pres 11-26—11-28, 930A1, 935E2
SOCIALIST Labor Party
Final pres vote tally 12-18, 979C2
SOCIALIST Party U.S.A.
Final pres vote tally 12-18, 979C2
SOCIALIST Workers Party
'73 NY suit vs FBI bares new thefts evidence 3-17, 6-26, 569B2, C3
FBI '60s NY office thefts, police role chrgd 3-28, 3-29, 234A3
Sen intellignc com cites as FBI target 4-28, 330F1
Denver office burglarized 7-7, Justice Dept to probe 7-27, 569G2-B3 ★
FBI agent admits NY theft role 7-29, 569G3
'73 FBI suit dvpts 7-30—8-15, 634C3
Cited re FBI restructuring 8-11, 8-16, 633C2, C3
Camejo pres debate challenge rejctd 9-20, 703F2
Sup Ct bars equal-time review 10-12, 765E3
Final pres vote tally 12-18, 979B2
SOCIAL Security—*See under U.S. GOVERNMENT*

1977

SOBERON, Guillermo
Rejcts UNAM strike demands 6-20, 528B2
SOBHUZA II, King (Swaziland)
Dissolves parlt 3-22, 394G3

SOCCER
US popularity rptd 7-5, 676B3
NASL season ends, final standings 8-7, 676C3
Cosmos set attendance record 8-15, 676A3
Beckenbauer named NASL MVP 8-18, 676F3
Cosmos win NASL title 8-28, 676C2
Cosmos world tour 9-4—9-20, 827F2
Americans win ASL championship 9-4, 827B3
Roche named ASL rookie of yr 9-8, 827C3
Pele honored 10-1, 827C2, E2
China team tours US 10-6—10-10, 827A3
NASL Tightens forgn-player limit 10-22, 1020G3
Hartwick wins NCAA title 12-4, 1020E3

SOCIALISM, International
Eur ldrs meet, back Czech dissidents 1-29—1-30, 82D3
Reps at Frelimo cong 2-3—2-7, 137D1
SOCIALIST International
Reps at Israel Labor Party conv 2-22, 135F1
Chile econ sanctns asked 8-31, 743B2
SOCIALIST Workers Party
Denver probe ends 1-6, 15D3
SOCIAL & Rehabilitation Service—*See U.S. GOVERNMENT—HEALTH, Education & Welfare*
SOCIAL Security (& Administration)—*See under U.S. GOVERNMENT*

1978

SOBERS, Ricky
NBA assist ldr 4-9, 271G2
SOBHUZA II, King (Swaziland)
Electns held 10-27, 1022A2
SOBLESKI, Carol
Casey's Shadow released 3-17, 618F3
SOBUKWE, Robert
Dies 2-27; funeral, Buthelezi stoned 3-11, 193C3, 196E3
SOCAL—*See STANDARD Oil Co. of California*

SOCCER
Cosmos sign Bogicevic 1-4, 23A2
NASL expansn completed 1-5, realignment playoff format set 1-10, 23A1, C1
Argentina World Cup plans rptd 2-17, 4-7, 4-12, 285C3, 310C3
NASL coaching chngs 5-16—8-2, 707B3
World Cup tourn, sidelights 6-3—6-25, Argentina wins, photo 6-25, 519D3-520G3
Cosmos set season-game attendance record 6-21, 655G1
NASL season ends; final standings, statistical ldrs 8-6, 655D1, A2
Cosmos win NASL title 8-27, Tueart named playoff MVP 8-31, 707A2
ASL attendance rise rptd 8-29, 708A1
Apollo wins ASL title 9-10, 707E3
NASL OKs Caribous sale, Atlanta move 10-3, 969A3
Kissinger named NASL bd chrmn 10-4, 969C2
NASL Diplomats sale rptd 10-5, 969F2
FIFA to ban Best 10-10, 969D2
Hudson signs with Sounders 10-16, 969D2
Messing signs with MISL Arrows 11-16, 969E2
Marinho joins Cosmos 11-25, 969C2
San Fran U wins NCAA title 12-10, 969G1

Awards & Honors
Roland named ASL MVP 8-7, 707G3
Waiters named NASL top coach 8-14, 707F2
Ethertington named NASL top rookie 8-17, 707G2
NASL All-Star team announced 8-20, 707A3
Flanagan named NASL MVP, top offensive player 8-21, 707F2, G2
Alberto named NASL top defensive player 8-21, 707G2
Chinaglia wins NASL top scorer award 8-23, 707G2
Parkes wins NASL Goalkeepers Cup 8-25, 707A3
Lenarduzzi named top NASL N Amer player 8-25, 707A3
Tueart named NASL playoffs MVP 8-31, 707E2
John named ASL top rookie 9-5, 707G3
Lawther named ASL top coach 9-10, 707G3

Obituaries
Zamora, Ricardo 9-7, 778C2

SOCCER Reporters Association, Professional
Tueart named NASL playoff MVP 8-31, 707E2
SOCIALIST International
Peres at Eur conf 2-11, 98G2
SOCIALIST Workers Party (SWP)
FBI informant case declined by Sup Ct 6-12, 468D1
Bell cited for contempt in FBI informants case 7-6, 507A2
Bell contempt order stayed 7-7, 524G3
FBI mail scrutiny held unconst 11-29, 940A1
SOCIAL Security (& Administration)—*See under U.S. GOVERNMENT*

1979

SOBELL, Sir Michael
Troy wins Irish Derby 7-1, 876D3
SOBELL, Morton
Julius Rosenberg article publshd 6-16, 466D1
SOBERS, Ricky
NBA free-throw ldr 4-8, 290F2
SOCAL—*See STANDARD Oil Co. of California*

SOCCER
MISL season ends 3-18, 432B1
UK drug probe clears teams 3-28, 655D2
Cosmos set season-game attendance record 4-22, 654C3
NASL season ends; final standings, statistical ldrs 8-12, 654A3, C3
ASL season ends 8-26, 776C2
Cosmos dethroned in playoffs 8-29, 9-1, 775D3
FIFA readmits mainland China 10-14, 1004F2
Mecca mosque militants ask ban 11-20, 899B1

Awards & Honors
Zungul named MISL MVP 3-22, Messing named playoff MVP 3-25, 3-22, 432D1
Fabbiani named NASL top scorer 8-13, 776D1
Parkes named NASL top goalie 8-13, 776D1
Cruyff named NASL top offensive player 8-25, NASL MVP 9-5, 776B1
Dempsey, Mijatovic named NASL top defensive players 8-25, 776C1
Liekoski named NASL top coach 8-25, 776C1
NASL All-Star teams announced 8-27, 776E1
Hulcer named NASL top rookie 8-30, 776D1
Davis named NASL top N Amer player 9-5, 776D1
Ball named NASL playoff MVP 9-8, 775D3
McDermott named ASL top rookie 9-11, 776F2
Garcia named ASL MVP 9-13, 776E2
Ehrlich named ASL top coach 9-15, 776F2
Filby, Arber named ASL title game MVPs 9-16, 776D2

Player & Executive Developments
ASL Eagles move to Albany 2-28, 432F1
Mueller joins Strikers 3-6; Rijsbergen, Neeskens sign with Cosmos 4-3, 6-11, 655E1
Best suspensn lifted 3-28, 655C2
NASLPA strike, INS warns forgn players 4-13—4-18; NLRB orders owners to bargain 5-3, 431B3-432B1
NASL coaching chngs 5-15—10-9, 1004D2
Cruyff signs with Aztecs 5-22, plays 1st game 5-23, 655B1
Firmani fired by Cosmos 6-1, signs with Americans 6-18, 655F1
Kliveca named Cosmos interim coach 6-1, Mazzei tech dir 6-5, 655A2
Whitecap, Cosmos players fight 7-15, 775E3
Lancers beat Tea Men 8-11, NASL to probe suggested goal fix 8-17, 776F1
NASL owners meet: sale of 3 teams OKd, rosters cut, games increased, other actns 10-15—10-16, 1004B2
Cousy firing forecast 11-19, quits as ASL comr 11-20, 1004A3

Winners
Nottingham Forest wins Eng League Cup 3-17, Eur Champions' Cup 5-30, 776F2
Arrows win title 3-25, 432B1
Arsenal wins FA Cup 5-1, 776A3
Borussia wins UEFA Cup 5-2, 5-16, 776A3
Barcelona wins Cup-Winners' Cup 5-9, 776A3
Whitecaps win NASL title 9-8, 775D2
Gold wins title 9-16, 776C2
SIU-Edwardsville wins NCAA title 12-9, 1004G1-A2

SOCIALIST International
Meets; Arafat sees Kreisky, Brandt 7-6—7-8, 511B3
SOCIALIST Workers Party (SWP)
Funds disclosure exemptn backed 1-9, 13D3
FBI ex-agent's trial statemt sought 1-16, 92D2
Bell contempt citatn overturned 3-19, 207E1
Bell contempt case declined by Sup Ct 10-9, 783D3
Iranian students fight US visa probe 11-21, 898E1
Iranian student probes ruled illegal 12-11, 935F2
SOCIALIST Workers Party v. Attorney General
Case declined by Sup Ct 10-9, 783F3
SOCIAL Security Administration—*See under U.S. GOVERNMENT*

1980

SOARES Carneiro, Gen. Antonio
Named AD pres candidate 4-11, leftists protest 4-19, 315C3
Party wins Assembly electn 10-5, Sa Carneiro sees pres victory 10-6, 760G1
Pres chances said stronger re Soares resignatn 10-19, 809F2
Sa Carneiro backs, scores Eanes 11-21, 902G3
Sa Carneiro killed 12-4, 923D1
Loses Portuguese pres electn 12-7, 944A2
SOCAL—*See STANDARD Oil Co. of California*

SOCCER
Italy scandal rptd 3-6, 194F2
Afghan players defect to W Ger 3-26, 271A2, 475E2
Milan team demoted 5-18, 409B1
Hunts' bailout loan collateral listed 5-28, 425E3
Moscow Olympic results 8-2, 623E2
NASL season ends; final standings, statistical ldrs 8-24, 769D3, 770B1, C3
ASL season ends 9-8, 771C1
British fans riot in Madrid 9-17, 771E3
Honduras, El Salvador ties restored; '69 'soccer war' cited 10-30, 872D3
USF vacates '78 NCAA title 11-18, 1001F3
Italy players rptd acquitted 12-22, 12-24, 995E1

Awards & Honors
Zungul named MISL MVP 3-19, 771B2
Hinton named NASL top coach 9-6, 1001A3
Roche named ASL top Amer player 9-8, 771F1
Ehrlich named ASL top coach 9-8, 771F1
Gorleku named ASL MVP 9-8, 771F1
Smith, Schlothauer named ASL top rookies 9-8, 771F1; Durgan, NASL 9-13, 1001A3
Brand named NASL top N Amer player 9-15, 1001A3
Davies named NASL MVP 9-16, 1001G2
McDermott, Tipping named ASL title game MVPs 9-18, 771G1
Chinaglia named NASL playoff, Soccer Bowl MVP 9-21, 770E2

Player & Executive Developments
ASL Skyhawks fold 1-29, 771D1
ASL Eagles fold 2-13, 771D1
Cruyff signs with Diplomats 2-26, 770A3
Jansen traded to Diplomats 3-6, 770B3
Van der Elst signs with Cosmos 4-3, 770B3
ASL Fire folds 4-19, 771D1
Fernando signs with Aztecs 4-23, 770C3
ASL NY United moves to Shea, name chng cited 5-28, 771E1
Cosmos suspend Neekens 9-11, 770A2
NASL NLRB order refused by Sup Ct 10-14, labor pact set 12-5; owners, player reps ratify 12-12, 12-18, 1001D2
NASL revises point system 10-21, 1001B2
NFL cross-ownership ban backed 11-18, 999A1
NASL retrenches: 3 clubs dropped, 3 moved, divisns realigned 11-24, 12-8; dispersal draft held, Cryuff reverts to Cosmos 12-15, 1001C1-B2
Machado named ASL com 12-17, 1001B3
ASL Eagles readmissn rptd 12-17, 1001C3

Winners
ASL title, Stoners 9-18, 771B1
Challenge Cup, Cosmos 5-26, 770E3
Cup-Winners' Cup, Valencia 5-7, 771A3
English FA Cup, West Ham United 5-10, 771C3
English League Cup, Wolverhampton 3-15, 771E3
Eur Champion's Cup, Nottingham Forest 5-21, 771A3
Eur Championship, W Ger 6-22, 771B2
MISL title, Arrows 3-23, 771G1
NASL title, Cosmos 9-21, 770E1-E2
NCAA title, USF 12-14, 1001C3
UEFA Cup, Eintracht 4-30, 5-14, 771B3

SO Chong Hwa
Named S Korea interior min 9-2, 673C1
SOCIALIST International
3 members visit Iran 5-25—5-26, 394C1
SOCIALIST Labor Party (SLP)
Eric Hass dies 10-2, 876A2
SOCIAL Security Administration—*See under U.S. GOVERNMENT*

1976

SOCIAL Services—*See also specific subjects (e.g., WELFARE)*
Ford '77 budget receipts, outlays table 63F1
Fscl '77 US budget estimate tables 231B1, 358F1, C2
Ford State of Union message 1-19, 39E2, G2
Cong clears ACTION funds 5-13, 393D1
US Dem platform text 6-15, 472E3, 474G1, E2, 475A3
Carter backs more US aid 7-6, 492F3
Carter briefed 8-16, 617F1
Cong sets '77 budget levels, table 9-16, 706C2
Block grants to states bill not cleared 10-2, 883A1, 884A2
Dole, Mondale debate 10-15, 782G1, 783C2
Ford scores Carter 10-19, 784D2
Transitn ¼ fed spending rptd down 10-27, 866D1

SOCIETE Anonyme Louis-Dreyfus et Cie Louis Dreyfus Corp. (N.Y.)
India sues 5-3, 333E2
Soviet grain sale 5-4, 321C3
Ex-supervisor indictmt rptd 8-23, 990D3

SOCIETY of Independent Gasoline Marketers of America—*See GASOLINE Marketers, etc.*

SOCIETY of Jesus—*See JESUITS*

SOCIOLOGY
Lazarfeld dies 8-30, 680F3

SOCRATES (469-399)
Jail rptd found 2-1, 124A3

SODER, Karin
Named to Swedish Cabt 10-8, 794B2

SOEDERGREN, Ben
Wins Olympic medal 2-14, 159C1

SOFIA, Queen (Spain)
Attends Jewish service 5-28, 459A3
Visits DR, US 5-31—6-1, 459A2-C3
At meml mass for Franco 11-20, 909A1
Venez pres visits 11-28, 930A1

SOILIH, Ali
Elected Comoro pres 1-2, names premr 1-6, 119A1

SOKUPA, Silumko
Arrested 8-13, 624B3

SOLANA, Fernando
Mexico industry min 12-2, 907A1

SOLANKI, Madhav Sinh
Gujarat chief min 12-24, 1006C1

SOLANO Lopez, Miguel
Dies 12-14, 1015G2

SOLAR Energy—*See SUN*

SOLARI Yrigoyen, Hipolito
Kidnaped 8-18, rescued 8-30, 672G1

SOLARZ, Rep. Stephen J. (D, N.Y.)
Rpts Rhodesia rebel demands 7-8, 523B1
Reelected 11-2, 830A2

SOLDATOV, Alexander
Sovts seek to bar Leb Moslem defeat 7-13, 514D3

SOLER, Miguel Angel
Rptd seized 1-31, rumored dead 2-17, 206C1

SOLI, Salvatore
Convicted in Knight murder 5-20, sentenced, chrgd in 2d death 504B1

SOLIAH, Stephen
Freed on bail 1-15, 70A2
2 defense motns denied 2-9, 114F3
Toback testifies 4-23; acquitted 4-27; Toback comments 4-30, 368G1
Life with Hearst rptd 4-25, 368E1

SOLID Wastes—*See under ENVIRONMENT*

SOLODOVNIKOV, Vasiliy
In Zambia as Sovt amb 8-10, 950B1

SOLOMENTSEV, Mikhail S.
Politburo alternate member 3-5, 195E2

SOLOMIN, Vayile
Wins Olympic medal 7-31, 574B1

SOLOMON, Harold
2d in US Pro tennis 8-31, 716G1

1977

SOCIAL Services—*See also specific subjects (e.g., WELFARE)*
CBO issues poverty rpt 1-13, 80B3
Ford '78 budget requests 1-17, 30B1
US Sen forms new com 2-4, 91D1
CBO on Carter goals 2-15, 126F1
Carter illegal alien plan 8-4, 592A1

SOCIETE Anonyme Louis-Dreyfus et Cie Louis Dreyfus Corp. (N.Y.)
ICC curbs rail grain-car deals 8-1, 613D1

SOCIETY of Independent Gasoline Marketers of America—*See GASOLINE Marketers, etc.*

SOCIETY of Jesus (Jesuits)—*See ROMAN Catholic Church*

SOCIETY of St. Pius X—*See ROMAN Catholic Church—Traditionalist Movement*

SODETANI, Judge Toshimi
Fasi trial folds 12-27, 1008G1

SODOMY—*See SEX Crimes*

SOEGAARD, Poul
Named Denmark defense min 10-3, 882G3

SOEMITA, Willy
Sentenced for corruptn 9-9, 767B3

SOFIA, Queen (Spain)
Sees Pope 2-10, 242D3

SOFT Drink Industry—*See BEVERAGES*

SOHARDJONO, Maj. Gen.
Tied to Hughes kickback 1-25, 182E3

SOHN Ho Young
US defection rptd 9-27, 774B2
US rep rptd probed re defection tip-off 10-28, 816F3
Confirms Korea influence plan documt 11-29, bid to block Kim testimony 11-30, 914C3, G3

SOILIH, Ali (Comoro Islands president)
Referendum backs 10-28, 868G3

SOISSON, Jean-Pierre
Elected Repub Party pres 5-20, 449E3

SOKO, Axon
Out as Zambia mines min 4-24, 490B2

SOKOINE, Edward (Tanzania prime minister)
Named Tanzania prime min 2-13, 161A2

SOLAR, Ricardo
Killed by guerrillas 10-23, 921B3

SOLAR Energy
US research budgeted 1-17, 31B3
French open power plant 1-25, 159E3
Carter budget revision 2-22, 125D2
Ford-Mitre study 3-21, 234B3
US research lab set 3-24, 278F1
UN Sri Lanka experiment rptd 3-30, 298D3
Carter presents energy plan 4-18, 4-20, 289B1, E2, 290G2, 294B3, 295A2; fact sheet 291F1, B3, 292E1, G1, 293B3-E3
Carter energy plan reactn 4-20, 320A2, B3
A-opponents for use 4-29—5-1, 403E1
Greece sets tax benefits 5-18, 487D3
Solar cell advances rptd 7-5, 558E3
House OKs Carter energy pkg 8-5, 610B1
Sen votes demonstratn projcts 9-13, 703F1
Research authorizatn OKd by Cong 10-20, 833C1, F1
Tax credit OKd by Sen 10-31, 832A3
Scientists endorse A-power 11-16, 936G3
World dvpt urged 12-11, 975G2

SOLARI Yrigoyen, Hipolito
Exiled 5-1, 388E3
Carter encouragemt rptd 9-2, 922F1

SOLAUN, Mauricio
Named amb to Nicaragua 7-8, confrmd 7-28, 626E3

SOLDATOV, Alexander
Leb weighs UN troop case 3-1, 143D2

SOLID Waste—*See WASTE, Solid*

SOLITRON Devices, Inc.
Sup Ct declines case review 3-21, 230G2

SOLOMON, Anthony M.
Named Treas undersecy 1-18, 52D3
US steel import, industry aid plan rptd 12-6, 931C3

SOLOMON, Arthur P.
New house costs rptd soaring 3-3, 178A2

SOLOMON, Harold
US beaten in Davis Cup 4-29—5-1, 353E3
US Open results 9-11, 787E1

1978

SOCIAL Services—*See also agency names under U.S. GOVERNMENT; also specific subjects (e.g. WELFARE)*
Cong '79 budget target res OKd 5-17, 385F1, A2, A3
State claims setlmt signed 6-12, 465F3
Kennedy scores Carter budget plans 12-10, 956F1
Carter soothes NAACP ldrs on budget plans 12-11, 980B2

SOCIETE General—*See EUROPEAN-American Banking Corp.—European-American Bank & Trust Co.*

SOCIETE Generale de Banque (Paris bank)
8th in '77 world ranking 11-8, 914B1, D1

SOCIETE Marcel Dassault-Breguet Aviation
French govt to acquire interest 3-8, 313E1
French Assemb OKs acquisitn 12-8, 987G2

SODOMY—*See SEX Crimes*

SOEGAARD, Poul
Named Danish defns min 8-30, 688A1

SOELKNER, Lea
Wins world skiing title 2-3, 316G2

SOFIA, Queen (Spain)
Visits Iran, China 6-14—6-19, 576A2
With king in Latin Amer 11-17—11-26, 967B3

SOFIANOS, Chrysostomos
Named Cyprus educ min 3-8, 189A2

SOFT Drink Industry—*See BEVERAGES*

SOHIO—*See STANDARD Oil Co. (Ohio)*

SOILIH, Ali (Comoro Islands president; ousted May 13)
Trial for alleged plotters demanded 1-22, 94B2
Coup ousts 5-13, 371G1
Killed 5-29, 445B2
OAU mtg bars Comoros 7-8, 561F2
Mercenary rptd removed from govt 7-23, 596D1
Mercenary quits Comoros 9-27, 798B3

SOISSON, Jean-Pierre
Named French youth, sport min 4-5, 245G2

SOK Kheang
Leaves Hanoi emb post 1-3, 4E1

SOLAR Action Inc.
Sun Day celebrated 5-3, 321C3-322B1

SOLAR Energy
Carter budgets research 1-23, 46G1
Research authorizatn clears Cong 2-8, 107A3; 2-25, 218B2
Govs urge more fed funding 2-27, 145A1
Environmt cncl rpt issued; major role, govt backing urged 4-12, 281E3-282B1
Energy bill conferees back low-interest loans 4-21, 305G1
Sun Day celebrated; Carter vows natl strategy, spending hike 5-3, 321C3-322B1
New TVA chrmn backs growth 5-19, 390C2
On-site use, economics studied by Cong unit 6-23, 493D3
Small business loan aid signed 7-4, 512E1
Fed draft study released 8-25, 718G1; final study rptd, spending hike backed 12-12, 982G3
US, Japan plan joint research 9-6, 695D3
Pub works bill vetoed, upheld 10-5, 765E1
US bars satellite power program 10-11, 861G1
Energy bill clears Cong 10-15, 787C2, E2
Solar cell breakthrough claimed 11-30, scientists cautious 11-30, 12-1, 983E1-D2
Carter questns oil industry acquisitns 12-12, 983E2

SOLAR Energy Research Institute (Golden, Colo.)
Carter visits on Sun Day 5-3, 321C3

SOLARZ, Rep. Stephen J. (D, N.Y.)
Chrgs Cambodian killings 4-19, 301E2
Sees Castro, Zaire role denied 6-13, 442F2-A3
Says Cuba to free dual citizens 8-17, 687E1
Reelected 11-7, 851E3

SOLID Waste—*See WASTE, Solid*

SOLIS, Enrique
Pedroza decisns 11-27, 969G1

SOLO, Robert H.
Invasn of Body Snatchers released 12-21, 1030A3

SOLOMON, Anthony M.
On $ defense policy 2-6, 2-16, 118G2

SOLOMON, Beth
2d in Amer Cancer Society tourn 2-13, 355B3

SOLOMON, Freddie
Traded to 49ers 4-17, 336E1

SOLOMON, Gerald B.
Wins US House seat 11-7, 849G1, 851G3

SOLOMON, Harold
Wins N Amer Zone Davis Cup matches 3-17, 3-19, 252B1
Wins King Classic 4-30, 419C1
Wins Louisville Intl 7-30; loses US Pro title 8-29, S Africa Grand Prix 12-4, 1027A2, B2, D2

1979

SOCIAL Services—*See also agency names under U.S. GOVERNMENT; also specific subjects (e.g. WELFARE)*
Carter restores some budget cuts 1-2–1-5, 3C3
Carter State of Union Message 1-23, 48A1
Carter defends budget 1-26, 70A1
Illegal alien issue detailed 1-29, 127E1
Drug abuse costs rptd 2-12, 140C2
Weicker sees as priority 3-12, 185C3
Carter urges privacy bill 4-2, 264F3

SOCIOLOGY
Talcott Parsons dies 5-8, 432C3

SODERBERG, C. Richard
Dies 10-17, 860E3

SODERHOLM, Eric
Traded to Yankees 11-13, 1002C3

SOETEMAN, Gerald
Max Havelaar released 1-20, 174A3

SOFIA, Queen (Spain)
At requiem mass for slain gen 3-6, 191F3

SOFT Drink Industry—*See BEVERAGES*

SOFT Lenses Inc.
Long-wear contact lenses OKd 6-13, 572E1

SOGLIN, Mayor Paul (Madison, Wis.)
Aide loses in mayoral vote 4-3, 265C2

SOHN Joo Hang
Quits S Korea Assemb 10-13, 794C3

SOLAR Energy
Satellite power program backed 1-10, 36B1
Carter asks budget rise 1-22, 45D2
Admin drafting dvpt legis 1-25, 70D2
Mex, US sign cooperatn pact 2-16, 124D3
Swedish energy bill rptd 3-13, 213F3
Carter asks greater use 4-5, 250F3
Jobs gain seen 4-21, 419A1
Elec conversn dvpt accord rptd 5-2, 419C1
Calif energy plan proposed 5-31, 419A1
French projct revived 6-18, 485F1
Carter presents natl plan 6-20, 498A1
Admin plans previewed 7-8, 517E3
Carter offers 6-pt energy plan 7-15, 7-16, 532C2, D3, 534B1
Citizens Party platform backs dvpt 8-1, 595A1
Solar cell silicon productn method rptd 8-27, 649A1
World radio conf held 9-27–12-6, 1006D3
House OKs Energy Dept authrzn bill 10-24, 848G3
Cong OKs alternative fuels program 11-9, 883G1

SOLARZ, Rep. Stephen J. (D, N.Y.)
Vs Rhodesia sanctns end 4-24, 294A1
Gets Kriangsak letter re refugees 6-30, 550G1
Vs Morocco arms sale 10-22, 804C1

SOLDATI, Francisco
Killed 11-13, 906F2

SOLDIER of Orange (film)
Released 8-16, 820D3

SOLOMON, Anthony
Seeks Iran sanctns in W Ger 12-6, 934A1

SOLOMON, Harold
Wins Baltimore Grand Prix 1-21, 391F2
Loses W Ger Open 5-20, 570C2
Loses Forest Hills Invitatnl 7-17, 734A2
Wins Paris Open 11-4, loses London Grand Prix 11-18, 1003F3, G3

1980

SOCIAL Services
State of State messages 1-14, 270B2; 1-15, 483D2
Cuban, Haitian refugee assistance set 6-20, 484F2-485D1

SODA—*See BEVERAGES*

SOEGAARD, Poul
US scores Danish mil spending 10-3, 737D1

SOFINSKY, Vsevolod
New Zealand expels 1-24, 100A2

SOFT Drink Industry—*See BEVERAGES*

SOHIO—*See STANDARD Oil Co. of Ohio*

SOKIROKO, Viktor
Sentence suspended 10-1, 863B2

SOKOINE, Edward (Tanzanian prime minister, resigned Nov. 7)
Msuya replaces as prime min 11-7, 888E1

SOKOLOV, Igor
Wins Olympic medal 7-24, 623D2

SOLAR Energy
State of State messages 1-10, 403E3, 483B1
CEA ex-chrmn urges use 1-14, 32F1
NAS sees limited use 1-14, 53G3
Carter asks dvpt funds 1-23, 43G1
Carter budget proposals 1-28, 72A1
Kennedy urges 'energy bank' 2-2, 91D1
Kennedy 'basic speech' excerpts 3-10, 183F2
France sets new energy measures 4-2, 254D1
US-Mex talks 4-2—4-3, 315A2
Citizens' Party seeks dvpt 4-13, 288D3
Rappaport dies 4-21, 360A3
Oil indus monopoly denied 5-5, 554A1
Synfuel bill clears Cong 6-19, 6-26, 479C2; Carter signs 6-30, 494G1-A2
Dem platform planks adopted 8-13, 611F2, 615F1
Carter pres renominatn acceptance speech 8-14, 613F1

SOLAR Energy Research Institute (Golden, Colo.)
Rappaport dies 4-21, 360A3

SOLAR Maximum Mission Observatory (U.S. satellite)—*See ASTRONAUTICS--Satellites*

SOLARZ, Rep. Stephen J. (D, N.Y.)
Visits N Korea 7-18, sees more ties 7-20; South reacts 7-21, 547A1
Reelected 11-4, 843E3

SOLARZANO, Roberto
Resigns 4-9, 351G2

SOLH, Takieddin (Lebanese premier)
Named Leb premier 7-20, 579C3

SOLID Waste—*See WASTE, Solid*

SOLLMANN, Melitta
Wins Olympic medal 2-17, 156C1

SOLO, Robert
Awakening released 10-31, 972C3

SOLODUKHIN, Nikolay
Wins Olympic medal 7-31, 623B1

SOLOMON, Anthony
Named NY Fed chief 1-21, 52B2

SOLOMON, Rep. Gerald B. (R, N.Y.)
Reelected 11-4, 843G3

SOLOMON, Harold
Wins Baltimore Grand Prix 1-20, W Ger Open 5-18; Grand Prix of Tennis 4-27, 607E2, B3, D3
French Open results 6-6—6-8, 606B3
Threatens US Open boycott 7-12, settles USTA rules dispute 7-16, 691E3
Wins Assn of Tennis Pros tourn 8-24, 691C3
Wins Sabra Classic 10-12, 947A2

1976

SO Long (play)
Opens 4-27, 1014C3
SOLOVIEV, Mikhail
France expels 10-14, 852F2
SOLOW, Herbert
'38 letter from Chambers cited 3-18, 218D1
SOLOWAY, Paul
Wins world bridge title 5-8, 352G3
SOLTI, George
Wins Grammy 2-28, 460D3
SOLVENTS—*See CHEMICALS*
SOLZHENITSYN, Alexander Isayevich
On French TV 3-9, USSR protests 3-10, 424E1
UK airs warning vs communism 3-24, 424F1
Rptd working at Stanford U 5-4, 424D1
Rptdly asks permanent US visa 6-22, moves to Vt 9-9, 680B3
GOP conv adopts platform 8-18, 600D3; text 608C3

SOMALI Republic (Somalia)—*See also AFRICAN Development Bank, ARAB League, NONALIGNED Nations Movement, OAU*
Afars rebel ldr rptd arrested 1-14, 85G3
Listed as 'not free' nation 1-19, 20E3
Afars oppositn collusn chrgd 1-23, 85G3
Afars expels immigrants 2-2, 86B1
Afars border clash with French troops, France recalls amb 2-4, 85G2, B3
Northrop rpts payoffs 2-20, 362C3
Barre at Sovt CP Cong 2-24—3-5, 195B3
Cuba troop presence rptd 4-5, 242G1
Kenya cites Sovt arms aid 4-25, 295B1
Sovt, Cuba mil presence rptd 6-13, 467C1
Kenya-US F-5 sale set 6-15—6-17, 467B1
Sup Cncl dissolved, Soclst Party assumes power 7-1, 1013E2
OAU backs Ethiopia re Afars 7-6, 487E3
Olympic withdrawal rptd 7-21, 528B3
Ethiopian hotel attacked 8-4, 581C1
Guerrillas free French tourist 8-17, 674B3
Ethiopia blames for civil war, asks talks 9-12, 1002G1
Australia sees USSR oil threat 11-4, 850B2
Smallpox cases cited 11-17, 911A1
Kenya wildlife killing rptd 12-14, 947F2
In Pl-rebel talks 12-15—12-23, 1008G3

SOMARE, Michael
Arranges Bougainville truce 1-28, 123B2
Australia aid agrmt rptd 3-4, 172D3
Rpts Australia copper deal 3-22, 237D2
Rpts Bougainville secessn agrmt 3-26, 256G2
Seeks Australia seabed pact 11-25, 961D3
SOMERS, Albert T.
Cited as Carter advisor 4-23, 305F2
SOMETHING'S Afoot (play)
Opens 5-27, 1014D3
SOMMER Jr., A. A.
Quits SEC post 3-6, 232A2
SEC sues Geo Dynamics 6-1, 984D2
SOMOZA Debayle, Gen. Anastasio
In Guatemala, pledges quake aid 2-4, 81F1
Cuba guerrilla aid chrgd 11-16, 926F1

1977

SOLOMON, Samuel J.
Dies 12-8, 1024C3
SOLOVIEV, Yuri
Dies 1-16, 84G3
SOLOVYOV, Vladimir
Exit from USSR rptd 6-9, 512E3
SOLZHENITSYN, Alexander Isayevich
Forms publishing firm 1-21, 140F3
Dissident funding rptd 2-2, 101C2
Dissident fund dir ousted 11-6, 956C1

SOMALI Republic (Somalia)—*See also ARAB League, NONALIGNED Nations Movement, OAU*
Amnesty Intl lists jailed lawmakers 9-5, 753C2
Foreign Relations (misc.)—*See also 'UN Policy' below*
French pact on Afars rptd 1-7, 88C1
Smallpox spreads to Kenya 2-5, 224B1
Afro-Arab summit backs natlists 3-7—3-9, 170G1
Castro visits, urges Africa federatn 3-12—3-14, unscheduled stop rumored 3-16—3-17, 249F1, B2, F2
Djibouti independenc set 3-19, 221F2
At Red Sea summit 3-22—3-23, 208D2
Podgorny visits 4-1—4-2, 247A3, 248C1
USSR aid rptd, Ethiopia dispute cited 4-16, 328B1
Arab monetary fund created 4-18, 318C1
US ties to intl terror groups 5-8, 380D1, A2
USSR aid to Ethiopia scored 5-15, 428F2
Africa Horn federatn barred; Ethiopia, Djibouti dispute cited 5-18, 428E2
US to challenge USSR role 6-10, 460D2
Ethiopia chrgs RR bombing, Djibouti annexatn 6-16, 486E1
Djibouti Repub proclaimed 6-27, 506F2
Kenya chrgs raids, denied 6-30, 512E2
Horn of Africa alliances shift 7-6, 588F1
Zambia OKs aid vs Rhodesia 7-8, 536F1
USSR adviser ouster denied 7-18, ties backed 7-28, 588A1
Kenya border pact vowed 7-20, 588C1
US offers arms aid 7-26, Ethiopia scores 7-27, 587G3
US, UK arms aid OKd 7-28, 608A2
USSR rptdly urges cease-fire 8-4, 608G1
China arms aid offer rptd 8-16, 649B1
USSR cooperatn pact rptd 8-17, Sovt arms shipmts resume 8-18, 649A1
USSR support of Ethiopia scored 8-19, 648G3
Barre in Moscow 8-29—8-31, 684A3
US, France, UK cancel arms sales; Arab offers rptd 8-31—9-2, 684F2
USSR arms-flow halt scored 9-7, 715B3
Ethiopia ties broken 9-8, 715B2
Barre in Saudi, aid offer rptd 9-14, 715A3
US arms aid deceptn chrgd 9-19, 715C3
USSR scores Ogaden role 9-28, cuts arms aid 10-19; Barre denounces 10-21; other arms aid cited 10-22, 829G2
Kenya ties worsen 10-15—10-20; facts on border area 830A2
W Gers rescue hijacked jet 10-18, 'deal' denied 10-19, 789A1, B2, 790C2; 10-22, 830C1
USSR aides ousted, Cuban ties ended 11-13; US lauds 11-14, Moscow scores 11-15, 874D3
Kenya OKs Ethiopia port use 11-30, 998B2
Carter, Shah seek end to Ethiopia conflict 12-31, 1001A1
Ogaden Developments—*See under ETHIOPIA*
UN Policy & Developments
UN Assemb member 4B1
Young sees Barre 2-5, 105D1
UNCTAD shipping study rptd 4-17 337E2

SOMARE, Michael (Papua New Guinea prime minister)
Guise to challenge 2-8, 203B2
1st gen electn 6-18—7-9, 639D1
Elected prime min 8-9, 639F1

SOMATOSTATIN—*See HORMONES*
SOMDA, Albert
Upper Volta labor min 1-14, 183B2
SOMERO, Pentti
Protests devaluatn 9-1, 764E3
SOMMERS, Tom
Firing by Angels rptd 12-17, 990B2

SOMOZA Debayle, Gen. Anastasio (Nicaraguan president)
Backs Panamanian canal demands 1-18, 46G1
Church chrgs terror, asks US pressure 3-2, 168C2

1978

SOLOMON, Jay
Griffin dismissal strains O'Neill-White House ties 7-28—8-7, 605E2
Sees GSA indictmts 8-30, briefs Carter 9-4; Washn Post details allegatns 9-3—9-5, 685E1
Kirbo to monitor GSA probe 9-7, 715E1
Testifies on abuses, lists reforms 9-19, 714B2
18 indicted in GSA probe 9-29, 753C3
Names new GSA probe dir 11-13, Alto steps down 11-14, 899F1, B2
SOLOMON, Brig. Gen. Robert B.
Gen Singlaub resigns 4-28, 321A3
SOLOMON Islands
Facts on 549D1
Independnc from UK effected; US, other forgn offcls observe 7-7, 549D1
UN Assemb admits 9-19, 713G2 ★, E3
SOLORZANO, Valentin
Guatemala econ min 7-21, 722C3 ★
SOLOVYOV, Alla
Sentenced 9-7, 742C3
SOLTI, Georg
Record wins Grammy 2-24, 316C1
SOLZHENITSYN, Alexander Isayevich
USSR fund admin rptd sentncd 4-16, 275F2
Addresses Harvard commencemt, text excerpts 6-8, 444A2 ★ -G3
Ginzburg sentenced 7-13, 541C2, F2
SOMALIA—*See SOMALI Republic*
SOMALI Republic (Somalia)—*See also ARAB League, NONALIGNED Nations Movement, OAU*
Army strength rptd 2-11, 99D3
Plot vs Barre rptd 2-28, 269G1
Army rptd badly damaged 3-17, 215G2
Cholera precautions taken 3-24, 270E1
Army revolt crushed 4-9, 269E1
20 rptd killed in revolt, 6 executed 4-11, 353F2
Locust plague rptd, aerial spraying begun 6-6, 465C2, F2
'77 smallpox case cited 8-2, 636B1
Army officers sentncd 9-12, 758B2; executed 10-26, 885D3
Amnesty declared 10-23, 885E3
Foreign Relations (misc.)—*See also ETHIOPIA—Ogaden*
Barre asks US, W Eur aid 1-16, US rejcts 1-17, 43A3
W Ger OKs credits 1-21; Egypt arms purchase rptd, other sources cited 1-24, 44A1
US issues rights rpt 2-9, 101F3
Egypt plane downed by Kenya 2-15, 137D2
Hostages seized in Cyprus, hijackers denied landing 2-18, 117G1, A2
Italy CP rep sees Barre, Sovt peace plan denied 2-20—2-22, 137G2
Ethiopia demands all forgn terr claims renounced 3-10, 178A3
US envoy visits 3-18—3-23, aid pact signed 3-19, 215D2
Kenya, Tanzania food imports banned 3-24, 270E1
UK scores Sovt aid 4-5, 259D1
Islamic, Arab poor-natn aid rise rptd 4-9, 257F2
Barre in China, pact signed 4-13—4-18, 353E2
Lufthansa '77 hijacker sentncd 4-25, 353F3
Kenya invasn plan rptd foiled 5-8, 758B2
Papal role in '77 W Ger hijacking cited 8-6, 601E2
Cuban role in Africa scored 8-14—8-26, 676C2
Arab fund loan to Sudan rptd 8-17, 925F3
UN Assemb member 713E3
Ogaden Developments—*See under ETHIOPIA*

SOMBROTTO, Vincent
Wins union pres vote 10-10, 766D2
SOMEBODY Killed Her Husband (film)
Released 9-29, 970B3
Top-grossing film 10-4, 800G3
SOME Girls (recording)
On best-seller list 7-5, 580A1; 8-2, 620F1; 9-6, 708F1; 10-11, 800F3; 11-8, 888D1
SOMOZA, Gen. Jose
Exile asked by forgn mediators 12-21, rejcts 12-22, 1018A3

SOMOZA Debayle, Gen. Anastasio (Nicaraguan president)
Chamorro assassinated 1-10, 19F3
Rioters blame for Chamorro murder 1-11—1-12, denies role 1-13, 72G3, 73F1

1979

SOLOMON, Jay
Muellenberg named GSA inspector gen 1-30, 92E3
Resigns as GSA head 3-21, 232B2
Freeman confirmed 6-27, 965A3
SOLOMON Islands—*See also COMMONWEALTH of Nations*
Freedom House lists as free 12F3
UN membership listed 695B3
SOLOVYEV-Sedov, Vasily
Dies 12-2, 1008F3
SOLZHENITSYN, Alexander Isayevich
Hayward dies 3-18, 272F2
Ginzburg to join 4-29, 317G2
USSR seizes US books 9-4, 690D1

SOMALI Republic (Somalia)—*See also ARAB League, NONALIGNED Nations Movement, OAU*
Barre sees better USSR ties 1-21, 85F3
US scored re arms delay 2-7, 193A2
OAPEC ouster of Egypt opposed 4-17, 278A2
Islamic conf suspends Egypt 5-9, 360E1
UN membership listed 695B3
US to seek bases for moves vs Iran 12-18, 958D2
Ogaden Developments—*See under ETHIOPIA*

SOMARE, Michael (Papua New Guinea prime minister)
Sets state of emergency 7-23, 616F2-A3

SOMETHING Short of Paradise (film)
Released 10-5, 1008F1
SOMINEX—*See MEDICINE-Drugs*
SOMOZA, Gen. Jose
Blocks Nicaragua rebels at Rivas 5-31, 409A2

SOMOZA Debayle, Gen. Anastasio (Nicaraguan president; resigned July 17)
Protestors honor slain editor 1-10, 21A3
Says US influence nil 1-14, 76F3
Trade boycott dropped by ORIT 1-15—1-16, 28E3

1980

SOLOMON Islands—*See also ADB, COMMONWEALTH of Nations*
Island trade pact rptd 7-24, 576G2
SOLOVAY, Leonard
Happy New Year opens 4-27, 392A3
SOLTI, Sir Georg
Wins 3 Grammys 2-27, 296F3

SOMALI Republic (Somalia)—*See also ARAB League, NONALIGNED Nations, OAU*
US to seek mil bases 1-9, 11G1
People's Assemb opens; '79 const, electns cited 1-24, 103G2
US-Kenya base 'understanding' rptd 2-22, 142C2
US mil base pact snag rptd 4-21, 303A1
US mil base pact signed 8-21, 645B3
US House subcom scores mil pact 8-28, 661B3
Ethiopia scores US mil pact 9-12, 735G3
UN refugee aid increase sought 9-21, 736C1
US House subcom OKs mil pact 9-30, 735B3
Zimbabwe scores US bases 10-9, 795C1
Kenya, Ethiopia urge land claims end, arms shipmt ban 12-4; Assemb sessn called 12-7, 933E1
Ogaden Developments—*See under ETHIOPIA*

SOMARE, Michael (Papua New Guinea prime minister; replaced Mar. 11)
Govt falls 3-11, 194F3

SOMARRIBA, Leonardo
Arrest rptd 11-18, 887C2
SOMERS, Suzanne
Nothing Personal released 4-18, 416D3
SOMERSET—*See NEW Jersey*
SOMERVILLE—*See MASSACHUSETTS*
SOMEWHERE in Time (film)
Released 10-3, 836F3
SOMMAI Huntrakul
Thai finance min 2-11, 196G3

SOMOZA Debayle, Gen. Anastasio
Junta shuts radical press 1-24, 118B1
US issues rights rpt 2-5, 87A3
Ex-amb freed by DR Emb captors 4-4, 293B3

1976

SOMSAK Tanthansen
Killed 12-22, 1013D3

1977

Latin intellectuals ask US aid cutoff 3-25, 476B1
US offcl scores Natl Guard 4-7, 475C3
Suffers coronary 7-25, hospitalized in US 7-28; Cong bars temporary replacemt 8-18, 656D3
Amnesty Intl details '76 terror, rpt scored 8-16, 656E2
Temporary Natl Guard head 8-18, 656E3
Returns Nicaragua 9-7; lifts state of siege 9-19, 767A3
CR seizes plotters 9-25, 767A3
Target of guerrilla offensive 10-12—10-18, 802D2
Oppositn asks drop mil cmnd 10-20, 802B3
Cong pres quits 10-21; choice for successors rptd 10-21, 10-26, 865F1
Rejects pol 'dialogue' 10-26, guerrillas ask ouster 10-27, 864C2
Rebels ask US end aid 10-26, 864G3
Chrgs intl CP plot, Cuba rebel aid 11-7, 864A3

SOMOZA Debayle, Brig. Jose
Temporary Natl Guard head 8-18, 656E3

SOMOZA Portocarrero, Anastasio
Rptdly being groomed for pres 10-26, 865G1

SOMPHOT Plyaoui
Sentenced in absentia 5-10, 393C3

1978

Evaluates US ties 1-15, 73C3
Pledges 'pol dialogue', oppositn rejcts 1-15, 73D3
Gen strike called, resignatn demanded 1-23—1-30, 73A2
Bars resignatn, scores strike 1-27, 1-28, 73B2
Church backs strike 1-31, 73A3
Chamorro paper leads drive for ouster 2-1, 73F2
US to halt mil aid 2-1, neutrality spurs oppositn drive 2-5, 91D2
Calls gen strike 'elitist', bars resignatn 2-3; strike ends 2-7, 90G3
CR aid to rebels chrgd 2-3, 91G1
Party wins munic electns, 80% boycott 2-5, 91D1
Managua protesters dispersed 2-6, 91C2
Guerrillas plan 'civil war' 2-12, 115E3
El Salvador guerrillas bomb emb 2-14, 115A3
Deaths mount in nationwide protests 2-21—3-1, 150B2
CR threatens land expropriatn 2-22, 151A1
Vows pol, econ reforms 2-26; protests continue 2-26—2-27, 150D3-151A1
Sandinistas vow to topple 3-2, 192F2
Directs Monimbo relief effort 3-5, 192F2
Top mil aide killed by guerrillas 3-8, 192C2
Anti-govt unrest continues 3-31—4-28; yields to hunger strikers 4-19, students 4-28, 375E2
Scores Venez rights probe request 4-4, 5-8, 376B3
Names Chamorro death probe panel, 4 shun 4-6, 376B2
US resumes aid 5-16, 376E2
In US, scores Carter 5-30, visits A-facility 6-22, 593A2
The Twelve return from exile 7-5, 593E1
23 die in anti-govt violence 7-9—7-25; gen strike 7-19, Castro blamed 7-22, 592G3-593A2
CR denies Nicaragua unrest role 7-28, 617F2
Carter lauds rights vow, State Dept upset 8-1, 593C2
Fires Natl Guard ldrs 8-18, 659G2
Guerrillas invade Natl Palace, hold kin 8-22; demands granted 8-23, 8-24, 658F3, 659B1, A2
New gen strike begins 8-25, businesses join 8-27—8-28, 659B2
Mil-civiln plot rptd 8-28, rpts 35 arrests 8-29, 659F2
Vows pres term completn 8-29, 659B2
Aide defends govt in US 8-31, 690E3
Matagalpa rebels subdued 9-1; strike spreads, backers seized 9-2—9-5, 690A3
Scores Venez pres 9-5, 690D3
Chile bars student protest 9-5, 796B1
Guerrillas launch offensive in Managua, 5 cities 9-9—9-13; martial law declared 9-11, Natl Guard called up 9-12, 705B2
Oppositn ldrs unite, seek provisional govt 9-14, 705B3
Guatemala guerrillas kill amb 9-16, 777G1
Faces econ collapse 9-19, 757G1
US asks 'control' troops 9-20, 757F1
CR to seize estate 9-22, 823E2
Sees US aide, OKs US 'cooperatn' in crisis 9-25; OKs intl mediatn 9-30; bars resignatn before '81 10-3, 757G2
Sees OAS rights team 10-4, 777E2
UN reps ask resignatn 10-5, 777G2
Sees intl mediating team 10-6, 777E2
Guatemalans burn restaurant 10-6, 796B3
Lifts press censorship 10-9, 777F2
Latin church cncl asks resignatn 10-13, 823D3
IAPA scores press curbs 10-13, 829E1
Extends siege 6 mos, cuts curfew 10-13, 839D2
US congressmen ask aid cutoff 10-13, 839G2
CR seizes guerrillas 10-13, 839E3
Scores Venez, Colombia, CR, US critics 10-14, 839B3
Guerrillas demand exit, for 'pluralistic democracy' 10-16, 823C3
US rptdly wants resignatn 10-19, 839E2
Pol talks suspended 10-21; The Twelve quit, FAO submits plan 10-25; talks rptd stalled 10-27, 839D1
IMF delays loan, US blamed 11-1; Venez oil cutoff plan rptd 11-8, 883G2, C3
Labor group leaves FAO 11-3, 883G2
Bars resignation 11-5, 883F2
Aide killed by guerrillas 11-7, 883C2
US Christians ask ouster 11-8, 883C3
Plebiscite agreed 11-30, terms disputed 12-8—12-27; US scores 12-27; sees Latin mil ldrs 12-29, 1018C2-1019D1
Lifts martial law, censorship 12-7; signs amnesty 12-15, prisoners freed 12-16, 1018E2
Closes CR border 12-26, 1019A1

SOMOZA Debayle, Luis (d. 1967)
Chamorro assassinated 1-10, 19F3

SOMOZA Garcia, Gen. Anastasio (d. 1956)
Chamorro assassinated 1-10, 19D3

SOMOZA Obregon, Jose
Guerrillas take hostage 8-22, free 8-24, 658F3, 659C1

SOMOZA Portocarrero, Maj. Anastasio
Exile asked by forgn mediators 12-21, father rejcts 12-22, 1018A3

SON, Hoang Bich
In Viet-China refugee talks 8-8, 602C3
Vs China stand at talks 9-26, 747E3

SONAR
Poulter dies 6-14, 540E3

SONATA for Piano No. 18 in E Flat Major, Op. 31, No. 3 (recording)
Rubenstein wins Grammy 2-24, 316D1

1979

New plebiscite plan rejected; FAO scores new oppositn group gains strength 1-19, 76D2-A3
Guerrillas claim land seizure, redistributn 1-24, 101F2
US plans mild pressure 2-1, 101D2
US cuts back ties, regrets 2-8; sets legal, pol reforms 3-9, 255C1
US issues rights rpt 2-10, 107D2
Latin bishops back Salazar 2-12, 108E3
Guerrillas rptd united 3-7, 254G3
UN asks rights abuse end 3-13, 255B2
UK downgrades ties 3-29, 255A2
Guerrillas issue 'reconstructn' plan 4-5, govt reform coms named 4-6, 269C3
Visits US, denies fled Nicaragua 4-8–4-9, 269E2, B3
Lang killed 4-16, funeral 4-18, 332E1
Returns from US 4-18, 332C1
IMF OKs standby loan 5-14, 372C3
Mex cuts ties 5-20, 409A1
Denounces Latin rebel aid 5-27, 409D2
Rebels rptd blocked at Rivas 5-31, 409G1
Warns CR on rebel aid 6-3, 427E1
Threatens strikers 6-4, declares state of seige 6-6, 426F3-427A1
US beef boycott proposed 6-5, 427A2
Fighting reaches Managua 6-9–6-13, 446G2
Estimates rebel, govt casualties 6-11, 446D3
Sees Andean Group envoys 6-11, 446E3
Vance asks OAS mediatn, urges pol solutn 6-13, 446F3
Rebels launch southn offensive from CR 6-16–6-17, 461D1
Scores rebel govt, bars resignatn 6-18, 461C2
US House probes Panama rebel aid 6-20, 481B2
US urges ouster, Latins vs OAS interventn 6-21, 460D3
Rebel junta outlines programs 6-27, 475B3, C3
US presses resignatn 6-28, terms rptd unacceptable 6-29, 475E3, G3
Cong sessn cancelled 6-28, 475F3
Rebels abandon Managua 6-28, 476B1
US, Andean Group propose pol solutn 7-6, 503E3, 504A1
Rpts 50,650 Guard draft 7-7, 512D2
ISC paymts alleged 7-9, 541F3
Junta outlines reconstructn progrm 7-11, 512G1
Resigns, leaves for US 7-17, 535D1
Successor challenges power transfer 7-17, flees 7-18, 535A2
Rebels take Managua, civil war ends 7-19, 535F1
US long-term ties detailed 535F2
1,265 soldrs rptd in Honduras 7-21, son's invasn plan chrgd 7-28, 573F2
Rebels rpt natl debt, personal theft 7-25, 574B1
Expelled from Bahamas 8-2, 600E1
IDB aid loan rptd 8-4, 603E1
IMF loan probe urged 8-6, 603B2
US bans beef imports 8-6, 616D2
Junta sets reforms 8-9, 616A1
Natl Guard prisoners released 8-11–8-12, 616A2
El Salvador calls gen amnesty 8-16, 652A2
In Paraguay 8-19, 636D2
Bill of Rights issued 8-21, 636A2
Large currency notes recalled 8-25–8-26, rate set 9-3, 689A2.E2
Nicaragua repudiates forgn debt 9-28, 753D2
Nephew slain 10-4, 793F3
Chamorro death role chrgd, extraditn sought 10-9, 794A1
Spain '76-77 loan graft probed 11-27, 909F3
To be tried in absentia 11-29, 950C3

SOMOZA Debayle, Luis (deceased)
US-Nicaragua long-term ties detailed 535F2

SOMOZA Garcia, Gen. Anastasio (1896-1956)
US-Nicaragua long-term ties detailed 535E2
Family power ended 7-19, 536B1

SOMOZA Portocarrero, Lt. Col. Anastasio
US-Nicaragua long-term ties detailed 535E3
Nicaragua invasn plan chrgd 7-28, 573F2
Chamorro death role chrgd, extraditn sought 10-9, 794A1

SON, Hoang Bich
Sees US reps in Hanoi 8-9, 607A2

1980

US OKs 3-mo extensn for refugees 6-30, 495B2
Sandinistas, 30 forgn delegatns mark downfall 7-19, 565E2
El Salvador Emb refugees in CR 7-26, 633E3
Sandinistas delay electns until '85 8-24, 672A2
Nicaragua debt rescheduled 9-5, 689C2
Larios arrested in Nicaragua 9-11, 709C3
Assassinated in Paraguay 9-17; Argentina terrorists sought, suspect slain 9-18, 697F2
Junta denies death role 9-17, Nicaraguans celebrate 9-18, 697D3
Buried in Miami, 4000 at rite 9-20; biog data 721D1, G1
Paraguay cuts Nicaragua ties, assassinatn link chrgd 10-1; Paraguay home attacked 10-2, 792B2
6,000 ex-troops rptd jailed in Nicaragua 10-31, 874G1

1976

SONDHEIM, Stephen
Song wins Grammy 2-28, 460A3
SONEIRA, Federico
Leaves Cabt post 6-12, 440E3
SONG Yu Bo
Jailed 2-8, 122A1
SONNENFELDT, Helmut
'75 remarks on US policy re Sovt-E Eur ties rptd 3-22; rpt disputed 3-29—4-1, 232G2, 233B1, 245B2
E Eur press scores 4-9—4-14, 277D1
Kissinger on E Eur policy 5-20, 354A1
Kissinger on E Eur independnc 6-25, 466F2
SONODA, Isamu
Wins Olympic medal 7-28, 575A1
SON Sen
Retains Cabt post 4-14, 265D1
SORENSEN, Theodore Chaikin
Named CIA dir 12-23, 956F2
Biog sketch 958B1
SORGHUM
Argentina drought rptd 1-17, US export credits planned 1-28, 96B3
US support-rate raised 10-13, 787G3
SORIA, Carmelo
Found dead 7-16, UN probes 12-14, 963B2
SORIA, Sixto
Wins Olympic medal 7-31, 574D1
SORIANO, Gen. Jose
Peru min without portfolio 2-3, 142B3
SOR Thon
In Cambodia presidium 4-14, 265E1
SORY, Abdoulaye
Guinea exchange min 12-11, 1005G1
SOTHEBY Parke Bernet, Inc.
1st woman auctioneer named 1-27, 272B1
SOTOMAYOR Cardia, Mario
Portugal educ min 7-23, 558G1
SOUK Bouavong, Prince
Prison escape barred 4-26, 333F3
SOUSA, Daniel
Police rptd in Death Squad murders 10-11, 850C2
SOUSA Gomes, Antonio
Portugal econ min 7-23, inexperience scored 7-24, 558A2
SOUSA Lopes, Carlos
Wins Olympic medal 7-26, 576A1

1977

SONNENBERG, Guenther
Captured 5-3, 601E3
SONODA, Sunao
Named Japan forgn min 11-28, 932B2
SON of Sam (.44-caliber killer)—*See BERKOWITZ, David R.*
SON Sen
Cambodia CP post identified 10-3, 780B1
SONY Corp.
US TV productn cited 3-28, 318G3
US TV dumping ruling cites 4-18, 318A3
US rebate chrgs setld 8-19, 650G3-651A1
US TV operatns cited 12-14, 974B2
SOO Line Railroad—*See CANADIAN Pacific*
SOPER, Dr. Fred L.
Dies 2-9, 164E3
SORENSEN, Theodore Chaikin
Confrmatn hearings, oppositn rptd 1-15—1-18; withdraws 1-17, 35B1
SORG, Judge Herbert
Dismisses Navajo fraud case 5-17, 492C1
SORGHUM
Drought hits Tex High Plains 3-24, 244F3
Carter cuts '78 acreage 11-15, 916C2
SORKIN, Richard
Admits thefts from players 9-20, sentenced 11-28, 1021A2
SORSA, Kalevi
Forms new govt 5-11, 391C1
Jobs program proposed 6-20, '78 budget presented 9-17—9-18, 764B3
SOSA, Elias
In World Series 10-11—10-18, 807A1
SOUMOKIL, Josine
Moluccan mediatn fails 6-9, 468G1
SOURIS River
ND irrigatn project scored 1-7, 60E3
US halts ND projct 2-18, 133A1
ND projct scored 9-19, 726E1
SOUTER, David
Asks NH A-protester penalties 5-5, 410B1

1978

SONDHEIM, Stephen
Company opens 5-7, 887D1
SONMOR, Glen
Hired as North Stars coach 11-18, 991C1
SONNENBERG, Benjamin
Death rptd 9-18, 778A2
SONNENBERG, Gunter
Sentenced 4-26, 353G3
SONNER, Leo
Refused exit by USSR 11-7, 884B3
Cleared 12-1, 966E1
SONNINO, Sergio
Kidnapped 1-4, 19D2
SONODA, Sunao
In Sovt peace talks 1-9—1-10, 28D3
LDP ldrs rptd vs China peace talks 4-7, 278B2
Asks Australia ease import curbs 6-27, 514G1
Enters China peace pact talks 8-8, signs 8-12, 637C1
Corrects Fukuda on Korea remark 10-18, 802B1
Japan-China peace pact implemented, text states role 10-23, 801B1, F1
Retained as forgn min 12-7, 945E2
SON of Sam (.44-caliber killer)—*See BERKOWITZ, David Richard*
SORDI, Alberto
Viva Italia released 7-9, 970D3
SORGHUM—*See GRAIN*
SORIA, Oscar
Chuquiago released 4-18, 619A1
SORIA, Sixto
Wins World Amateur Boxing tourn 5-6—5-20, 600D2
SORIMACHI, Ryu
Palomino KOs 2-11, 379A2
SORVINO, Paul
Slow Dancing released 11-8, 970B3
SOSA, Ruth Chica Rendon de
Guatemala welfare min 7-21, 722C3 *
SOSSI, Mario
'77 kidnap cited 3-18, 200G1
SOTHEBY Parke Bernet & Co. (London)
Von Hirsch collectn auctnd 6-20—6-27, 578D3
Patino art collectn auctnd 6-29, 579E1
SOTOODEHNIA, Ahmad
Iran plans A-cutback 10-22, 816B3
SOUTH—*See also state names*
Industrializatn cited re black-white wage gap decrease 5-8, 810D3
'75-77 migratn reversal rptd 12-3, 943B1

1979

SONDHEIM, Stephan
Sweeney Todd opens 3-1, 292C3
SONEGO, Rodolfo
Wifemistress released 1-6, 174G3
SONG Chen-ming
China oil finds rptd 11-26, 918F1
SONGS From the City Streets (play)
Opens 4-9, 712D2
SONGS of Innocence and Experience (book)
Sold for record sum 6-13, 672E1
SONNENBERG, Benjamin (1901-1978)
Art collectn auctn record rptd 6-12, 672D1
SONODA, Sunao
Indochina refugee aid hiked 7-2, 495E2
SON Sann
Heads Cambodia natlst front 10-12, 779C2
SONS of Italy Supreme Lodge
Carter at Baltimore conv 8-7, 592F3
SONY Corp.
Video recorder copyright trial opens 1-22, 120E2
Video recorder use upheld 10-2, 858F2
SOPER, Mark
Warriors opens 5-22, 712D3
SOPHIA, Living and Loving (book)
On best-seller list 4-8, 271A2; 5-6, 356D2
SOPHIE'S Choice (book)
On best-seller list 7-1, 548A3; 8-5, 620B3; 10-14, 800B3
SOREL, Louise
Later opens 1-15, 292G1
SORG, Judge Herbert Peter
Dies 3-11, 272E3
SORROWS of Stephen (play)
Opens 12-11, 1007E2
SORSA, Kalevi
Replaced as Finnish premr 5-26–5-27, 406F3
SOTHEBY & Co.
Glass bowl auctioned for record sum 6-4, 672D1
Wilson sets retiremt 11-11, 892D2
Sotheby Parke Bernet
Sonnenberg collectn auctn record rptd 6-12, 672E1
Church painting sold for record sum 10-25, 891B1
SOTO, Pedro Juan
Son's death disputed 4-30–5-3, probe ordrd 5-2, 350A2
SOTO Arrivi, Carlos (d. 1978)
Death disputed 4-30–5-3, probe ordrd 5-2, 350A2
Natlst ambush kills 2 US sailors 12-3, 924B3
SOUL City, N.C.—*See NORTH Carolina*
SOUL City Co.
HUD withdraws new town support 6-28, suit filed 8-17, injunctn denied 8-27, 665E1

1980

SONDHEIM, Stephen
West Side Story opens 2-14, 136G3
Wins Grammy 2-27, 296G3
SONG of the South (film)
Top-grossing film 12-3, 948G3
SONG Zhenming
Scored re '79 oil rig accident 8-24, fired 8-25, 651B3
SONJU, Norm
Heads NBA Dallas expansn group 2-2, 119D2
SONMEZ, Fikri
Army seized Fatsa; arrested 7-11, 544A3, C3
SONODA, Sunao
Named Japan health min 9-19, 752E1
SOON to Be a Major Motion Picture (book)
Published 9-2, 713E2
SOPHIE'S Choice (book)
Wins Amer Book Award 5-1, 692G1
On best-seller list 8-17, 640G3; 9-14, 716D3; 10-12, 796F3
SORGHUM
USSR-Argentine 1st 1/4 trade rptd 4-15, 336G1
SORVINO, Paul
Cruising released 2-15, 216D2
S.O.S. Band (singing group)
Take Your Time on best-seller list 7-9, 568E3; 8-13, 640B3
SOTHEBY & Co.
Cassatt print sold for record sum 2-14, 472B2
Bouts painting sold for record sum 4-16, 472G2
Sotheby Parke Bernet
Record art auctns held 5-12—5-16, 471G3-472A2
Homer oil sold for $1.7 mln 10-17, 997G3-998A1
SOTO, Mario
NL pitching ldr 10-6, 926G2
SOTO, Pedro Juan
PR cops cleared in son's '78 death 4-25, 348B3
SOTO Arrivi, Carlos (d. 1978)
Cops cleared in slaying 4-25, 348A3
SOUDAN, Frederick
Supertanker sinks off Senegal 1-17; Shell sues, chrgs fraud 2-7, 108F2, B3
SOUKHOROUTCHENKOV, Sergei
Wins Olympic medal 7-28, 622F2
SOUPCON (film)
Released 3-26, 416E3
SOURCE Telecomputing Corp.
Reader's Digest merger rptd 9-24, 746F1

SOUTH AFRICA, REPUBLIC OF

1976

SOUTH Africa, Republic of
1st TV broadcast; '75 TV set sales rptd 1-5, 11A3
Zulus settle pol struggle 1-15—1-19, shift capital 1-19, 76A2
Listed as 'partly free' 1-19, 20D3
Cabt shuffled 1-22, 76D1
Apartheid liquor law eased 3-8, 206A2
Zulu chief asks majority rule 3-14, 428C3
Sharpeville massacre protesters arrested 3-18, 428G3
Increased arms spending set 3-31, 429A1
New port opened 4-1, 429E1
Meteorite shower cited 4-21, 443D3
Alleged guerrilla recruiters rptd arrested 4-26, chrgd 5-14, 428F3
PRP wins Durban by-electn 5-5, 422D3
Policemen chrgd in Mdluli death 6-11, 428E3
Soweto blacks in language protest 6-16, violence spreads 6-17—6-19; Vorster warns, pub events banned 6-18, 425F1, 426D3
Map of riot area 6-16—6-19, 426A2
Rpt on colored role rejctd 6-18, 639E2
Bantu min meets Soweto ldrs 6-19; looting rptd, rioting resumes 6-19—6-22; Graaf scores govt 6-24, 447B1-B2
Riot death, damage data rptd 6-19—6-23, 447B2
Black riot toll 6-25, 500G1
Arrest total, new arrests rptd 6-25, 7-1, 500C2
Kruger: black rioting organized 6-25, 500F2
2 black leaders seized 6-29, 500D2
Mass funeral denied 6-30, symbolic rite held 7-3, 500E2
Forced Afrikaans language use dropped 7-6, 500F1
Soweto release pleas rejctd 7-10, children freed 7-15, 539A3
Police smash Indians protest 7-13, 539E3
Black tribes clash in gold mines 7-14, 7-19, 539F3
Riots spread in black townships; schls closed, reopened 7-15—7-22, 539E2
Bank rate raised 7-21, 540A1
Indian sociologist banned 7-24, 592G1
Ncokazi ordrd arrested 7-26, 592B2
Journalists, others seized 7-29; reactn 7-29—8-2, 592C1
Pub mtg ban lifted 8-1, schl attendance disputed 8-2, 579F2

1977

SOUTH Africa, Republic of
'76 Jan-Sept emigratn rptd 1-8, 21D3
'76 schl make-up exam set 1-12, 21A3
Cath schls desegregate 1-17, Anglicans to follow 1-24, 67E1
End to pass-law jailings urged 1-26, 67G2
Vorster bars pass-law end 1-28, 100D3
Cath bps back COs 2-9, score apartheid 2-10, 100D2
Caths set integratn plan 2-11, challenges pvt schl rules 2-16, 2-22, 145B1
Black photographer wins award 2-22, 160G3-161A1
Censorship bill withdrawn 3-23, press code set 4-2, 349C3
Cath schl integratn pact set 3-28, 350B1
White paper on coloreds issued 4-19, 349F3
Stellenbosch univ to admit nonwhites 6-11, 469G1
Baboon heart implant fails 6-20, 619B3
Interracial sex laws debated 7-5, 7-7, 564A1
Colored cncl ordrs schl integratn 7-31, 600A2
Jan-May emigratn, '76 Jan-May data rptd 8-3, 640G1
Johannesburg businessmen ask race reform 8-8, 8-14, 657G1
Women's rights rally halted 8-16, 640A2
Drug-resistant pneumonia rptd 9-2, 847B2
Gold mine cave-ins 9-3, 768G3
New black paper published 10-31, 935G1
Pass law revisn set 11-3, facts on 852E1

Atomic Energy & Safeguards
US, France see A-bomb capacity 2-16, 2-17, 160F1
USSR warns West vs A-sales 3-29, 248B1
US denies uranium cartel agrmt 6-29, 624F3
USSR chrgs A-bomb capacity 8-9, 8-14, 656G3
US asks A-safeguards 8-20, France warns vs test 8-22; Botha, Vorster deny progrm 8-21, 8-23, 656F3
Carter rpts A-bomb reassurance 8-23, 649E2
A-test rptly headed off by US, USSR 8-28—8-29, 663A3
Horwood backs A-bomb, Botha reassures US 8-30, 663F3
Cyclotron constructn set 9-15, 825A3
Vorster denies assurance to Carter 10-23; US rebuts 10-24, issues Vorster letter 10-25, 825D2
UN votes arms ban, Pretoria condemns; text 11-4, 851D1

1978

SOUTH Africa, Republic of—*See also GATT*
Racial makeup rptd 20D3
'77 emigratn loss rptd 2-27, 193F3
Cape Town buses rptd desegregated 3-1; theaters, opera houses natnwide 3-10, 193E3
Church segregatn ended 3-17; 26 theaters integrated 6-6; other apartheid chngs rptd 6-4—6-27, 536E1, F1 * -C2
Blacks denied passports 6-9, 6-10, 536B3
Apartheid reform bill OKs black home leases, passbook revisns, ends 'bantu' use 6-14, 535G3
Racial attitude poll rptd 6-15, 6-22, 536C2
Church cncl scores apartheid 7-12, 633G1
'76-77 crime rate rptd 7-20, 670D1
Afrikaner-black mtg rptd 8-17, 669A3

Atomic Energy & Safeguards
US sees A-bomb potential 1-26, 61B2
Enriched uranium productn expanded 2-13, US '75 sale bar cited 135A1
US A-fuel export license deferral rptd 5-20, 408B2, C2
US urges non-proliferatn treaty OK, hints fuel supply 6-25—6-29, 536F3
US cancels uranium contracts, non-proliferatn treaty bar cited 11-4, 904C2

1979

SOUTH Africa, Republic of—*See also GATT*
Mixed couple freed re Immorality Act chrg 9-28, 774E2
Airport toilets integrated 9-30, 774E2
Anglicans vote apartheid bar 12-7, 969D1
Permanent desegregatn permits OKd 12-10, 969B1

Atomic Energy & Safeguards
A-plant protests staged 4-2, 246B2
US envoys ousted as spies 4-12, 287A1
US rpts A-blast 10-25; denies, suggests Sovt sub mishap 10-26, 10-27, 824B3

1980

SOUTH Africa, Republic of—*See also GATT*
'75 Rift Valley epidemic cited 3-2, 318B3
Mine elevator accident 3-27, 256E3
Dutch Reformed Church apartheid rift 5-10, 374F1
Bus-train collisn kills 67; tractor-truck collide, 17 die 6-7, 769B3

Atomic Energy & Safeguards
'79 A-blast mystery unresolved 1-23, 49A3
'79 A-blast laid to Israel A-test; denied 2-21, 141E3
Scientist sentncd for espionage 6-3, 466D3
'79 A-blast dispute continues 7-14, 548E2
Valindaba uranium capacity disclosed 9-30, 753G2
Nigeria hints A-bomb dvpt 10-3, 792C2
Taiwan uranium deal cited 10-17, 831E2

1976

New riots hit Soweto, other black townships 8-4—8-12; Vorster, Kruger stand firm 8-9—8-13, 579E1-580G1
Student ldr dies in police custody 8-5, 591G3
Cape Town, Soweto violence spreads to 3 black townships 8-12—8-23; Buthelezi comments 8-15, 8-17, 639D1
Black ldrs seized 8-13, other arrests rptd 8-17, 624F2
Muller backs race policy reform 8-13, 653B2
Black housing curbs eased 8-14, 8-20; racial separatn reaffirmed 8-19, 8-20, 639B3
Press restraints threatened 8-14, 639F3
Church mixed marriage stand disputed 8-18, 8-19, 639E3
Rand devaluatn feared 8-18, 654D3
Riot death toll at 234 8-21, 638E3
Tribal chiefs meet, score govt 8-21, 639C2
Soweto strike call 8-22; absenteeism rptd high, new violence erupts 8-23—8-25, 638D3
Cape Province univ reopened 8-23, 639D1
Strife, gold price fall linked 8-23, 643C1
'75-76 GNP rise rptd 8-23, 655A1
Soweto violence flares 8-26, 8-30, 652F3
Johannesburg strike ends 8-26, police chrgd re Zulu attacks 8-28, 653A1
Violence in other townships 8-26—8-30, 653F1
Soweto 8-23—8-27 death toll rptd 8-27, 652G3
Vorster admits problems, denies crisis 8-27, Buthelezi scores 8-29, 653B1
Kruger sets Bantu mtg, rpts detainee data 8-27, 653D1
Reserves decline rptd 8-27, 714A1
Black newsman's arrest confrmd 9-1, 662C2
Cape Town, black township unrest continues 9-2—9-8; public mtg ban renewed 9-2, 662A1
Soweto violence flares 9-3, 9-6—9-8, 662A2
Transvaal train collisn 9-6, 840E3
Cape Town violence 9-9—9-12, 695A3
Coloreds get concessns 9-10, 695C3
Vorster addresses Natl Party cong on govt admin 9-13, 681E2
2d Soweto strike 9-13—9-15, 695A2; ends 9-16, 713C3
Govt acts vs money outflow 9-13, 713F3
Cape Town blacks, coloreds strike 9-15, 695F2; 9-16, 713D3
Soweto violence rptd 9-15—9-17, 713B3
Blacks sent to tribal area 9-15, 714B1
Detainee total rptd 9-20, 713E3
Johannesburg, Soweto, other township unrest 9-23, 9-27, 733E3
4 reporters detained 9-23, journalist denied bail 10-8, 794E1
Business execs, press seek race reform 10-5—11-9; urban black fund set 11-19, 928G1
Vorster sees tribal chiefs, rejects conf demands 10-8, 793G2
Buthelezi group plans anti-govt front; 3 white parties unite 10-8, 793C3
Cape Town, Soweto violence 10-12—10-17, 794C1
Gas sales curbed 10-13, 856C1
Vorster vs black pol role, 'outdated' apartheid 10-18, 793G1
20 die in tribal clash 10-18, 794E1
Detainee total up 10-19, 794E1
New Soweto unrest, teacher, student arrests 10-22—10-24, 832C1
Cape Town violence 10-25, 832E1
Bophutatswana, other independnc plans cited 813F1
Actns vs rptrs rptd 10-26—11-19; 2 freed 11-21, 12-8; detentns protested 12-9, 927D2
Police acquitted re Mdluli 10-28, 927D2
Strike call fails, school burned 11-1, exam boycott empties schools 11-2; arrests 11-2, 11-3, 855F3
Soweto teachers rptd freed 856A1
Kriel, Kruger on unrest 11-3, 11-5, 856B1
Auto sales rptd down 11-4, 856F1
Editors ask reform 11-8—11-9, 927D2
Draft-dodger total rptd 11-12, 927G3
9 killed in tribal clash 11-14, 927B1
Union ldrs banned 11-16—11-18; cncl ldr scores 11-30, 927A3
Oppositn parties plan union 11-17, 928B1
Buthelezi scores student strikes 11-18; forms party 11-29, 928C1
Studnt refugee total rptd 11-19; exiles offer guerrilla training 11-24, 927E1
Hotel bar integratn rptd 11-20, 928E2
Johannesburg church groups raided, Coggan protests 11-25, 927B2
Mosalas seized 11-25; freed 12-8, 927C2
Cape Town townshp violence 11-27—12-6, 926G3
Cape Town studnts, lecturer acquitted 12-2, 927G1
Johannesburg diner bombed 12-7, Kruger on urban warfare 12-8, 927B1
Kruger on Red Cross jail probe, detainee releases, Soweto schls reopening 12-8, 927C1
Transvaal Prov death toll rptd 12-11, 1010B2
Mayson, other detainees freed; 2 deaths rptd 12-12—12-29, 1010C2-G2
Student ldrs sentenced 12-21, 1010G2
Cape Town black violence 12-25—12-28; tribal clashes rptd 12-30, 1010A2, C2
Compulsory black educ, free books set 12-30, 1010B3

1977

Bophuthatswana—*See separate listing*

Defense & Armed Forces (domestic issues)
Draft hike set 1-21, 67B1
'76 draft dodger total rptd 1-21, 67C1
'77-78 defns budget hiked 3-30, 284G3
Draft extended, air base set 4-21, 350B2
75% arms sufficiency rptd 4-28, 350C2
Botha: self-sufficient re arms 10-25, 851E2

Economy & Labor (domestic)—*See also 'Unrest' below*
'76 CPI rpt up 10.8% 1-25, 100C3
Small bank aid set 2-22, 160E3
Tax hike set 3-7, 242F1
'77-78 budget hikes defns 3-30, 284G3
Jobless data rptd 4-28, 350F1
Businessmen ask black manager ban end 7-26, 600C2
Black miners get pay rise, white pay rptd 7-28, 600B2
Chrome productn cited 8-3, 662A2
Anglo-Amer manganese deal rptd barred, productn data cited 8-16, 657B2
Oil stockpiling rptd 11-2, 887C3
Govt productn powers activated 11-11, 887G2
Job bias code issued by business ldrs 12-7, 1016B3
Black job curbs eased 12-14, 1016G2-A3

1978

Bophuthatswana—*See BOPHUTHATSWANA*

Economy & Labor (domestic)
De Beers sets diamond surchrg 3-28, 4-27, 319A1
'78 budget presented 3-29, 249B2
'77 growth, inflatn, jobless rptd 3-29, 249D2
Gold mine riot crushed 5-21, 456B1
Steel, machine-tool industries, postal svc end racial job bias 6-8, 6-27, 536B2
Whites back equality in wages 6-15, 6-22, 536F2
Unionists release asked by bishops 7-4, 633F2
Zulus seek labor code 7-13, 633E1
Black unemploymt estimated 7-22, 670C1

1979

Bophuthatswana—*See BOPHUTHATSWANA*

Economy & Labor
Migratory labor law explained 270F3
Oil search expanded 1-4, 22C1
Bank rate cut 2-6; rand revalued 2-8, central bank float set 2-27, 171C3
Oil info ban planned 2-20, 126B3
White miners protest integratn 3-7, 171F3; end walkout 3-14, 191A2
'79 budget presented; '78 GNP, inflatn rptd 3-28, 270F1
Black labor rights backed by comm 5-1, govt accepts 5-2, 332F2
Unions back black reforms, conservatives boycott mtg 5-11, 373E2
Mineworkers quit confederatn 5-17, 447D2
Gas price rptd at $1.76 per gal 5-19, 397A1
Black migrants get reprieve 7-16, 567B2
US co recognizes black union 8-29, 732G2
Botha in Soweto; cancels debt, vows improvemts 8-31, 732B3
White union ldr bans lifted 9-17, 732F2
Migrant blacks get union rights 9-25, 732C2
2 US cos fire 1,325 blacks 11-21–11-22, paper mill struck 11-23, 899C3
Job reservatn ended in car, constructn fields 12-1, 969A1
AF to accept black pilots 12-12, 969B1

1980

Bophuthatswana—*See BOPHUTHATSWANA*

Economy & Labor
Ford rehires black strikers 1-9; activist detained 1-10, 60C3, G3
'80 gold productn seen 1-21, 101C1
Johannesburg stores integrate cafeterias 2-15, 195E1
Ford black pay scored, unionizatn lauded 2-27, 195A2
Budget presented 3-26, 277D3
Constructn trades opened to blacks 4-11, 374D1
6,000 Durban black strikers fired 5-28, 466D2
Auto workers strike ends 6-25, 499B2
Johannesburg black municipal workers strike 7-24—7-31; 1,200 deported, strike broken 8-1, 690D1-B2
'79 gold productn rptd 8-27, 685C3
'80 econ growth projectn cited; transportatn said strained 10-15, 793C2
Black labor law chngs proposed 10-30, 887C2
Radical black union recognized 11-5, indl group lauds 11-7; govt detains union ldrs 11-11, 903C1
Striking black journalists fired 11-27, 967E3

1976

Angola Developments
USSR denounces Angola role 1-6, 2D2
Nigeria repudiates US plea 1-7, 2B3, 3A1
OAU deadlocks on Angola role 1-10—1-13, 15D3
Black Caucus rep scores US alignmt 1-11, 16A2
Cuba vows contd MPLA aid 1-11, 17A1
MPLA display mercenaries 1-12, 16G2
Battalion rptd in Angola 1-12, 16A3
Angola refugees denied entry 1-13, 16B3
Press lauds OAU summit 1-15, 16E1
Fighting rages along southn front 1-15—1-23, seeks mil stalemate 1-21, 35C2, C3
MPLA estimates S Africa forces 1-19, 1-20, 35D3
Portugal resumes refugee airlift 1-22, 53F2
Novo Redondo defeat 1-23, 57D1
Unita rpts troop exit, alert 1-25, 57F2
Botha confrms troop exit, defends role 1-26, 57G1
Vorster no-confidence motn defeated 1-30, 162C3 ★
UN Cncl censures S Africa 1-31, 103D2
Troops rptd at Huambo 2-1, 82A2
Buffer force rptd 2-3, oppositn scores 2-5, 106G1
2 soldiers killed in south 2-7, 106B2
Deplores UN refugee aid bar 2-12; UN stance rptd 3-25, 228F1
MPLA offers guarantees 2-13, demands forces quit south 2-19, 162B3
Cuba, Angola aid offers to Namibia rptd 2-23—3-6, 206D1
Austria vs interventn 3-12, 380E2
Sovt-UK talks 3-15—3-19, 229A1
Castro sees African ldrs 3-15—3-16, 251E3
UK, Sovt, UN mediatory roles rptd 3-21, 3-25, 3-26, 228A1
Troop exit ends 3-27, 227G3
Ends refugee aid 3-27, 228C1
Refugees flee to Namibia 3-27, 3-29, 228G1
UN Cncl censures 3-31, 228A2
Cunene project pact rptd 4-6, 287C2
Buffer zone set 5-19, 386C1
US mercenary linked to S Africa group 6-28, 480G1
Angola confirms death for mercenaries 7-9, 519C3
Israel aid to S Africa chrgd 8-22, 654A3
Southn Angola massacre chrgd 9-28, 734A3
SWAPO rptd in anti-Unita drive 11-10, 862G1
Neto chrgs attacks, S Africa denies 11-11, 862D2
Rpt 8000 refugees to Namibia, some forced to return 11-12, 862B2
Namibia rpts refugee shootings 12-10, 995F3
UN comr chrgs S Africa sets attack 12-10, 995G3

Foreign Relations (misc.)—*See also 'Angola' above, 'Namibia' below*
Amb to Brazil recalled 1-2, 11C3
Briton killed in Namibia 1-2, 11D3
Jamaicans protest IMF talks 1-7, 51B1
SDR rate rptd 1-15, 14B3
French Mirage purchase cited 1-16, 36C2
IMF OKs standby loan 1-21, 76E2
UN Cncl asks Namibia electns 1-31, 103D2
Cuba, Angola aid offers to Namibia rptd 2-23—3-6, 206D1
UK stock mkt reactn to Mozambique-Rhodesia rift 3-3, 175B3
Vorster on Mozambique Rhodesia border closing 3-4, 175B3
UK anti-Liberal plot alleged 3-9—3-10, denied 3-13, 252E2-A3
Gold swap deals rptd 3-17, 429C1
Cuba scores repressn 3-29, 228A3
Plot vs UK Liberal youth ldr chrgd 3-31—4-9, 351E1
Vorster in Israel; Arabs, USSR score 4-8—4-12, 275D3
Rhodesia road shut 4-19, 295A3; reopened 5-3, 339D2
Guerrilla-training network rptd 4-26, 428G3
Syria scores at UN ECOSOC racism debate 4-27, Israel defends 4-29; UK vs UN rights stand 4-30, 320F2, C3, D3
Scored at UNCTAD conf 5-5, 320D2
Bars Rhodesia mil role 5-13, 339A1 ★
EC asks mercy for SWAPO doomed 5-17, 386C2
Rhodesia RR attacked 5-23, 6-13, 428E1
Rhodesia sets road convoy 5-23, 428F1
Paris consortium in A-plant deal 5-28, US uranium role rptd 6-1, 387F1, 388D1
1st IMF gold auction held 6-2, 430G2
US Dem platform text cites 6-15, 478B3-E3
UN, OAU vs riot actions, apartheid 6-18, 6-19, 447F2
Vorster in W Ger; sees S Africa ambs 6-21—6-22, Schmidt 6-25, 447D3 ★
Muller in W Ger, Rhodesia peace role stressed 6-22, 447A3
UN com rpts on black deaths 6-23, 447C2
Rhodesia ANC asks govt talks 6-27, 522C3
OAU scores rioting 7-5, vs Bantusan recognitn 7-6, 487A3, D3
Rhodesia road ambush 7-13, 523D1
Zambia chrgs border attack 7-16, 539G3
Import deposit set; paymts deficit, gold fall cited 7-21, 540A1
UN condemns Zambia raid 7-30, press rpt 8-16, 653E2, A3
2 French warships bought 7-31, 714C1
French A-plant deal signed 8-6, 630G3

1977

Foreign Relations (misc.)—*See also 'Atomic Energy' above, 'Monetary, Trade & Aid', 'Namibia' and 'UN Policy' below; also RHODESIA—Majority Rule*
Canary I airline office bombed 1-3, 22C3
Angola war role detailed 1-3, 85B2
Newsman flees to Botswana 1-5, 3D3
Malagasy detains plane 1-19, 29A3
Podgorny in southn Africa; backs rebels, warns vs A-sales 3-23—4-1, 247A3, 248B1
NZ reaffirms sports policy 3-31, 258A2
Castro backs 'liberatn struggle' 4-2, 249C3
Lesotho trade rptd 4-9, 490E1
Front-line states back overthrow 4-17—4-18, 296D3
Vorster sees Houphouet-Boigny 5-22, 398F1
Angola rebel training chrgd 6-28, 600C1
Rhodesian rep to emigrate 7-1, 536A3
Botswana-Zambia rebel link chrgd 7-7, 536C2
Rescue team rpts on Mozambique mine deaths 8-8, 768E3
Angola sets mine share natlztn 9-1, 779C1
13 Westn envoys at Biko funeral 9-25, 735D3
Nigeria ldr lauds US effort 10-12, 797A2
W Ger, Dutch ambs recalled 10-25, 825C1
UK editors appeal upheld 11-25, 935D1
Australia pro-apartheid min fired 12-21, 982C2

Government & Politics—*See also other appropriate subheads in this section*
6 in UP quit oppositn caucus 1-19, 67C1
Parlt opens, pres addresses, sets draft hike 1-21, 66G3
Botha named forgn min 2-11, 160D3
Johannesburg munic electns 3-2, 242A2
Botha wins Parlt seat 5-11, 428C3
Nonwhite govt role backed by mins 5-24, 5-26, Vorster rejects 5-27, 428A3
Soweto black cncl members resign 6-2, 469E1
Oppositn parties regroup 6-28, 6-29, 529C3

1978

Foreign Relations (misc.)—*See also 'Atomic Energy' above; 'Monetary, Trade, Aid & Investment', 'Namibia' and 'UN' below*
Banned editor flees to Botswana 1-3, 8E1
5 forgn newsmen detained 1-22, 54G3
Scandinavian natns bar cultural ties 3-11, 193C3
Malagasy ct sentences 2 natls 3-22, 230G3
Botswana troops kill 2 natls 3-27, 596A1
Vorster chrgs Nigeria rights abuse 3-31, Nigeria scores apartheid 4-1, 233G2-234A1
Afrikaner church cuts Dutch ties 4-4, 269G2
Forgn influence-buying fund probe ordrd 5-8, 377B3; Info Dept abolished 6-15, 498F2
African moderates harden views 6-2, 633B2
Passports denied blacks 6-9, 6-10, 536C3
Canary separatists bomb airline office 6-21, 576F3
Angola threat chrg re Cuba troops 6-25, 487E3
Botswana cleric held re refugee activities 6-26—8-7, 633A3
Swazi offcl dies in custody 6-29, negligence chrgd 7-1, 633G2
Malawi backs contd ties 6-30, 535A1
Angola trades prisoners 9-2, 742A2
ZAPU claims army officers aboard downed Rhodesia jet 9-5, 740G3
Angola mobilizes vs rptd aggressn threat 11-7, 925C3
Angola chrgs 'undeclared war' 11-11, 906C2
Botswana soldier cleared in death of 2 natls 11-13, 906D2
Rhodesia ldrs visit 11-15, Botha warning vs vote delay rptd 11-23, 912A2
Influence-buying organizatns bare govt funding 11-21, 11-24, 946A2
Zambia whites' origin cited 11-26, 912G1
Angola cites threat re Cuban troops 12-13, 985A1

Government & Politics—*See also other appropriate subheads in this section*
Freedom House lists as partly free 44A2
Nonwhites plan united front 1-11, 20B3
Asian, colored power-sharing plan rptd shelved 1-24, 92F2
Vorster shuffles Cabt 1-25, 55A1
Parlt opens 1-27, 92G2
Buthelezi campaigns for KwaZulu electns 1-29, 92C2
Soweto electn held, by-electns set 2-18, 134F3
Nonwhites form party, seek apartheid end 3-14, 229A3

1979

Foreign Relations (misc.)—*See also 'Information Ministry Scandal', 'Monetary', 'Namibia' and 'UN' below*
Rhodesia conf failure warning issued 1-17, 39F3
Rhodesia air svc rptd cut 2-18, traffic to get mil escort 2-27, 170D3
Smith retiremt urged 2-22, 170E1
Iran cuts ties 3-4, 161A3
Mahlangu clemency pleas rptd 4-6, 270C3
UK Tories set policy 4-11, 285D3
Zimbabwe prime min visit rptd 6-20, 490D2
Dominica probe pledged 6-29, 502D3
Angola rpts '76-79 raid toll 8-2, 617F2; poisonous gas use 8-3, 617A3
Commonwealth conf cites refugees, racism 8-7, 590E2
Biko atty leaves 8-10, rptd in Botswana 8-12, 617D2
Israel ties discounted by Young 9-7, 720D3
Forgn blacks denied union rights 9-25, 732E2
Nigeria opposes racism 10-1, 753C3
Sovt sub mishap seen as A-blast cause 10-27, 824E3
Angola chrgs attacks 10-31, 875F1
Seychelles chrgs plot 969C2
Zimbabwe cuts Zambia rail link 11-18, Zambia blames Pretoria 11-25, 899D2, B3
Amb to El Salvador kidnaped 11-28, 908G1-A2
Zimbabwe troop exit sought by Patriotic front, mil role admitted 11-30, 937E1, B2
US weighs asylum for shah 12-1, shah rules out 12-5, 914B1, D1
UK sees Zimbabwe accord impact 12-18, 968C2

Government & Politics—*See also other appropriate subheads in this section*
Mulder quits Parlt 1-24, 99B2
New constitutn shelved 3-30, 270A3
Black curbs cut urged 5-8, 373B2
Vorster resigns 6-4, 427B3
Cabt shuffled, Kruger named to Sen 6-14, 469F2
Press curb bill dropped, restrictns enacted 6-14, 469B3
Viljoen named pres 6-19, 469A3
Mulder rptd forming new party 6-29, 567B2
3 black ldrs meet 7-30, 617A2

1980

Foreign Relations (misc.)—*See also 'Monetary', 'UN Policy' below*
Zimbabwe OKs S Africa transitn role 1-6, Mugabe scores 1-8, 31B3
Zimbabwe troops to leave 1-26, 80D2; exit begins 1-30, 118G3
Persian Gulf defns role cited in US rpt 2-1, 84G1
Black homelands consolidatn rptd planned 2-9, 134G2-A3
Mozambique arms smuggling seen 2-16, 195C2
'79 blast laid to Israel A-test; denied 2-21, 141E3
Zimbabwe's Mugabe vows noninterference; Botha on electn 3-4, 161C2, 162C1
El Salvador church ldr pleas for kidnaped amb 4-8, 351A3
Zimbabwe gains indepndnc 4-18, 301F1
Port Eliz protester flees to Lesotho 5-6, 374A3
Angola denies attack on bombers 6-13, 466A3
El Salvador amb rptd alive 6-23, 497C3
Angola protests raids 6-26, Pretoria denies civiln deaths 6-27, 7-2; troop exit disputed 6-28, 7-1, 524D3
Zimbabwe cuts ties 6-27, informs OAU 7-4; Pretoria recalls senior staff 7-8, 509D2
Angola raids scored by OAU 7-1, 509A2
Mozambique seizes rebel arms 7-10, 565F1
UK distance running record set by Johannesburg woman 8-15, 638B3
UK amb named 8-26, 689G3-690A1
Zimbabwe tie cut finalized 9-3, 691A1
Canada min scores apartheid 9-22, 748G3-749A1
Nigeria scores aparthied, hints A-bomb dvpt 10-3, 792C2
El Salvador amb rptd dead 10-9, 789B3
Botha in Taiwan 10-13—10-17, 831D2
Zimbabwe scores press 10-19, 833E3
Zambia coup backing chrg denied 10-27, 833F2-B3

Government & Politics—*See also other appropriate subheads in this section*
Natl Security Dept reorgn linked to domestic spying chrg 1-15, 60D3
'79 hanging total rptd 2-7, 134C3
Pretoria, Bloemfontein black visit limits rptd eased 2-7, 195G1
Homelands consolidatn bill issued 2-9, 134G2-A3
Ciskei advised vs statehood 2-12, 134G1
Botha plans black ldr conf 2-15, 174C2
Botha scores Treurnicht 3-7, Cabt ouster bid fails 3-11, 3-12, poll backs 3-16, 255B2

1976

IMF loan set 8-6, 655B1
Zambia border clash 8-7, 653A3
Indian students seized 8-12, 624C3
Muller backs race policy reform, US lauds 8-13, 653B2, 661C1
Nonaligned conf backs black rule, urges sanctns 8-19, 8-20, 621D3, 622A1
July trade deficit up 8-20, 654B3
12-mo paymts deficit, capital investmt data rptd 8-23, 654D3
Botswana replaces rand 8-23, 857E3
BP investmt plans rptd 8-26, 714B1
Mobil denies chrgs re Rhodesia 8-27, 698C2
3 Britons in conspiracy chrg 9-7, 662B2
UN cites Israel ties 9-8, 682D2
SWAPO rep scores Kissinger 9-9, 681G1
Vorster, Muller vow no pressure vs Rhodesia 9-13, 9-14, 681E2, G2
Vorster, Smith meet on Rhodesia 9-14, 681C2; Vorster, Smith, Kissinger meet 9-17—9-20, 697A1, E2
UN Assemb pres scores 9-21, 719A1
IAEA dir cites 9-21, 760F3
USSR, US trade chrgs re role 9-28, 9-30, 719B1
3 Britons sentenced 9-29, 733F3
US rpts on Mobil oil to Rhodesia 10-17, 855D3
Vorster backs Smith 10-18, 793B2
UN arms ban resolutn vetoed 10-19, 781C3
UN asks Transkei ban 10-26, 799F1
9-mo trade deficit rptd 10-26, 856C1
Vorster backs Smith 10-31, 832B1
Israel coal deal rptd 10-31, 928A1
Chrysler-Illings merger set 11-3, 856D1
UN asks West, Israel bar mil aid 11-5, 842B3
UN vs apartheid 11-9, 842F2
France to end A-sales 11-9, 928A1
Buthelezi in US, asks blacks aid 11-9; lauds Carter 11-18, 928F1
Draftee gets Dutch asylum 11-12, 927F3
IMF loan set 11-12, 1011A1
Venez scores apartheid, cuts trade ties 11-16, 929B3
US aid to student refugees rptd urged 11-24, 927F1
Botswana bars rebel asylum 12-7, 1009D3
UK editor freed 12-9, 1010B3
French A-plant deal set 12-16, 1002E3
Natl killed in Rhodesia 12-20, 1009C2
UN condemns Lesotho border pressure 12-22, 954B3

Namibia (South-West Africa)—*See also 'Angola' above*
Rpt SWAPO kills 2 1-2, 11D3
Zambia invokes emergency powers 1-28, 77E3
UN Cncl asks electns 1-31, 103D2
EC backs self-determinatn 2-23, 164C3
Cuba, Angola aid offers rptd 2-23—3-6, 206D1
Const conf adjourns 3-19, 386D2
SWAPO attacks rptd 3-24—5-18, 386F1
USSR denies role 3-25, 228F3
Angola-S Africa pact respects boundary 4-6, 287E2

1977

Bantustan oppositn vowed 7-16, 600F2
New Repub Party founder quits 7-22, 600G2
New Soweto black cncl formed 7-26, 600C1
Asian, colored power-sharing plan proposed 8-20, 657C1
Natl Party OKs power-sharing 8-23; coloreds rejct 9-12, 708B2
Liberal oppositn merges 9-5, 708C2
Black township self-govt planned 9-16, 747C1
Vorster calls early electns 9-20, 747A1
Namibia Parlt ties dissolved 9-28, 770B3
Botha quits educ office 10-3; Graaff replaced as party ldr 10-5, 826A1
Vorster wins electns 11-30, backs apartheid 12-2, 934G1
Bophuthatswana independnc declared 12-5, 935A2

Monetary, Trade & Aide Issues (Including all foreign economic developments)—*See also 'UN Policy' and 'U.S. Relations' below*
Israel arms sales rptd 1-8, 28D3, E3
UK unions plan boycott 1-13, 1-15, 29A2
Chad sets boycott 1-16, 29G2
ICFTU boycott fails 1-21, 67A3
UK ct upholds boycott injunctn 1-27, 98F3
Import-deposit plan ended 2-1, 100C3
IMF SDR defined 87G2
'76 trade deficit rptd down 2-7, 100B3
USSR warns West vs A-sales 3-29, 248B1
Import surchrg, capital flow rules set 3-30, 285A1
Zaire aid rpt denied 4-9, 265F2
Uranium cartel role rptd 4-25, 479F2
Mobil-Rhodesia oil info rptd withheld from US 5-16, 413E2
IWC cuts whaling quotas 6-24, 496G3
Angola oppositn group seeks aid; chrgs black natns 'hyprocrisy' 6-26, 522C2
UK firm ends black union pact; other pacts noted 7-19, 600D2
Angola chrgs UNITA aid 7-26, 675A1
Tanzania asks US arms embargo 8-6, 624B1
Tanzanians protest French policy 8-18, 662E2
Owen sees business, labor ldrs re apartheid 8-29, 661C2
Capital outflow rules eased 8-29, 708G1
Qantas halts Johannesburg flights 9-20, 762C3
EC adopts ethics code 9-20; investmts, exports rptd 9-23, 770C3
Israel steel sales rptd 10-10, 887D3
Canada chrgs steel dumping 10-18, 863A1
Commonwealth urges Rhodesia oil bar 10-19, 876B1
EC protests black bans 10-27, Pretoria rejects 10-28, 853B2
3-mo paymts surplus rptd down 11-1, 887C3
France cancels navy sales, '70-76 trade data 11-8, 883B1
Govt productn powers activated 11-11, 887A3
Australia livestock disease confrmd 923A1
French phone deal halted 11-25, 934C2
Canada cuts formal econ ties 12-19; '76 trade total rptd 1016C2

Namibia (South-West Africa)
Angola refugees barred 1-12, 21E3
Conf reopens, draft const proposed, SWAPO boycotts 1-18, 67A2
UN comr rptd named 109D3
Nujoma at Frelimo cong 2-3—2-7, 137E1
Angolans flees to Ovambo 2-21, 145C2
12 die in SWAPO clash 2-25, 145B2
US backs SWAPO isolatn call 2-28, 145A2
Afro-Arab summit backs blacks 3-7—3-9, 170G1
'76 SWAPO assassins freed 3-17, 349A3
Castro bars troops 3-21, backs 'liberatn struggle' 4-2, 249A3, C3

1978

Buthelezi rptd Zulu electn victor 3-14, 229B3
Natl party wins Springs by-electn 4-5, 269B3
2d Soweto electn 4-15; cncl sworn 4-18, 314B2-B3
New black party formed 4-30, ldrs detained 5-4, 377B2
Forgn influence-buying fund probe ordrd 5-8, 377B3; Info Dept abolished, Rhoodie quits 6-15, 498F2
6 mln blacks rptdly lost citizenship 6-12, 536E3
Blacks back democracy, free enterprise system 6-15, 6-22, 536B3
Zulu party conv 7-13, 633E1
Vorster links Info Dept scandal, Mulder 9-1, 742F1
Vorster quits as prime min 9-20, Botha replaces 9-28; Vorster named pres 9-29, 741D3, 742D1
Info Dept newspaper funding scandals erupt 10-29—11-2, 867F3, 868D2
Info Dept probe testimony released 11-2, judge fired 11-7; new hearings open 11-6, 868F1
Mulder resigns in Info Dept scandal 11-7, 868D1
Parlt Info Dept probe set, oppositn boycotts 11-7, 904G3
Info Dept judicial probe papers confiscated 11-9—11-10, 904F3
Mulder quits party post 11-11, 905B1
Cabt shuffled, moderates favored 11-14, 904A3
Pvt organizatns bare funding 11-21, 11-24, 946A2
Transvaal hardliner elected ldr 11-25, 946C2
Info Dept probe mandate extended 12-1, rpt issued 12-5, 946D1
Info Dept secret projcts limit set, Botha warns press 12-7, 989A1
Parlt defeats govt resignatn motn 12-7, 989F1

Monetary, Trade, Aid & Investment—*See also 'Atomic Energy' above, 'U.S. Relations' below*
US unit fined for Rhodesia sales 1-12, 38B3
Japan threatens fishing agrmt 2-22, 498E1
EC seeks steel export agrmt 3-2, 158C2
Scandinavian natns ban investmt 3-11, 193B3
Malawi '77 imports rptd 3-15, 535B1
Nigeria withdraws Barclays funds 3-22, 237A2
UK Midland Bank loan policy rptd 3-25, 237C2
De Beers sets diamond surchrg 3-28, 4-27, 319A1
Nigeria asks tougher sanctns 4-1, 233G2
Rhodesia devalues $ vs rand 4-2, 249E1
Rand dropped from new SDR basket 4-3, 300E3
Australia union blocks ship 4-4, 243E3
Credit rating rptd damaged by apartheid 4-23, 377G1-A2
Canada business code issued 4-28, 377F1
UN Assemb backs econ sanctns 5-31, 339C1
W Ger defends trade ties 6-30, 584E1
Church cncl asks forgn investmt revisn 7-12, 633G1
Zulus to press forgn cos for reforms 7-13, 633E1
OAU scores Iran re oil 7-22, 561F1
Thai trade ban rptd 8-7, 670A1
Seychelles trade ban rptd 8-21, 670B1
UK rpt on Rhodesia oil-sanctns violatn released 9-19, 756A1, C1, B2
SWAPO gets WCC grant 9-26, 742E2
UN warns sanctns re Namibia plan rejectn 9-29, 819F2
Zambia reopens Rhodesia RR link 10-10, 783F2-B3
Rhodesia violatn denial statemt chngd by BP 10-22, 838E2
WCC grants protested, total cited 10-25, 906F3
Iran oil workers strike 10-31, 827D2
Canada arms sales suspected 11-6—11-7, 904E2

Namibia (South-West Africa)
Facts on 114A1
SWAPO, army clash rptd 1-29, 114D1
Ovambo health min assassinated 2-7, 114B1
Torture rpt released 2-10, 114A1
Westn contact group meets, Botha walks out 2-11—2-12; progress seen 2-13, 113G2
SWAPO, troops clash; 17 rptd killed 2-19—2-22, 229G2
SWAPO abducts 119 students 2-21—2-22, 229F2
Young sees Nujoma 3-22—3-24, 248D3

1979

Steyn removed as Namibia head, Viljoen replaces 8-1, 585G1
Johannesburg by-electns 8-29, 733B1
New oppositn ldr named 9-3, 733A1
Venda independence declared 9-13, 732G1-B2
Marriage, sex law chngs sought 9-25, 774B2
By-electns show rightist swing 10-3, 774F2
Censor chief ousted 10-5, 774A3
Natl Party loses by-electn 11-8, 889E3
Botha bars majority rule, coloreds denounce 11-9, 889G3

Information Ministry Scandal
Rhoodie property seized 1-8, 22D1
Rand Daily Mail fined 1-17, 99D2
Mulder quits Parlt 1-24, 99B2
Van den Bergh avoids chrgs 1-25, 99C2★
Van den Bergh sees Rhoodie, disclosures averted 3-7, 190E3
Rhoodie chrgs listed, cites US, forgn bribes; Vorster implicated 3-10; rpt censored 3-12, 191B1
Van den Bergh's passport seized 3-14, 191G1
Rhoodie arrest sought 3-16; BBC airs Westn-natn bribe chrgs 3-21, Vorster scores 3-22, 212G3-213A2
US House com bars bribe probe 3-21, 213B2
Botha bars resignatn 3-22, 213B2
US lobbying rptd heavy 3-23, 213D2
Erasmus comm clears Vorster 4-2, 270B1
Mulder expelled from Natl Party 4-6, 270F1
Erasmus comm issues final rpt, Vorster quits 6-4, 427B3
Press curb bill dropped, restrictns enacted 6-14, 469C3
Mulder summoned on contempt chrg 7-3, 567A2
US probes media links 7-12, 618F2
McGoff denies Pretoria links 7-18, 567G1
Rhoodie arrested in France, extraditn sought 7-19, 567D1
Rhoodie plea rejctd 8-8, extradited 8-23, 755B1
Mulder cleared of contempt 8-30, 732F3
Rhoodie trial opens 9-21, sentncd on fraud chrgs 10-8, 774F1

Monetary, Trade, Aid & Investment
Iran vs oil sale 1-3, 2D2; cutoff anticipated 1-4, 1-9, 22A1; sales bar set 1-11, 25G1
UK fears sanctns pressure 1-17, 39F3
Rand float set, trading halted 1-24, reopened 1-29, 99F1
Iran oil cutoff impact assessed, info ban planned 2-20, 126B3
US univ stock divestitures rptd 3-10—3-24, 270G3; 4-26—5-3, 332G3
Mideast oil imports rptd 3-26, 270F2
'78 paymts surplus rptd 3-28, 270G1
'72-78 Westn loans rptd 4-2, 270C2
UK Tories bar sanctns 4-11, 285B3
Rhodesia to seek contd aid 4-29, 332C2
US black rights ldr scores forgn investmt 8-1, 617G1
Nigeria cuts BP oil re tanker 7-12, 545A2; natlizes BP assets, sales linked 7-31, 584E2, B3
US co recognizes black union 8-29, 732G2
Krugerrand cited re Canada gold coin sale 9-6, 684D3
Israel arms embargo compliance cited 9-7, 720D3
Venda aid cited 9-13, 732B2
Nigeria ends Barclays boycott 9-26, 796D3
2 US cos fire 1,325 blacks 11-21—11-22, 899C3
Krugerrand rptd preferred to USSR coin 11-29, 929G1

Namibia (South-West Africa)
Political parties described 171E2
UN envoy reopens talks, Nujoma bars monitors 1-13; Waldheim urges cease-fire 2-26, 171B2
Botswana border clash 1-14, 171C3
Carter State of Union Message 1-23, 48F1
SWAPO launches raid from Angola 2-13; Nujoma rejcts cease-fire, vows takeover 3-1, 171A3
Pretoria rejcts UN plan 3-5, raids SWAPO Angola bases 3-6, 171D1

1980

Vorster hits Botha policies 3-12, 255G2
Natl Party wins by-electn 5-7, 374E1
Nonwhite pres advisory cncl, const change backed 5-8, 373G3
Buthelezi backs black community cncls 5-10, 374C1
Botha abandons black cncl 8-8, 652E3
Botha shuffles Cabt 8-26; scores hardliners 9-2, supporter wins by-electn 9-3, 689E3
Mafeking given to Bophuthatswana 9-19, 753A2
New Broederbond head chosen 9-26, 753E2
Multiracial cncl named 10-2, 793A1
Apartheid chngs proposed 10-30, 887C2
Ciskei votes on statehood 12-4, victory rptd 12-17, 996A1

Information Ministry Scandal
2 publishers fined 2-11, 134D3
McGoff loses documt disclosure suit 3-17, 278B1
Rhoodie convictn reversed 9-29, 753E1

Monetary, Trade, Aid & Investment
Two-tier currency system cited 101A1
Ford rehires black strikers 1-9, 60C3
Liberian supertanker sinks off Senegal 1-17; oil sale suspected, info blackout ordrd 2-3; Kuwait warns, Shell sues 2-7, 108A3
Gold price benefits noted 1-18, 30F2
Rand rpt up on gold rise; '80 gold income seen 1-21, 100G3-101C1
Anglo-Amer buys Consolidated Gold 2-12, 398A3
Ford scored re black pay, integratn role lauded 2-27, 195A2
Gold price benefits noted, forgn exchng controls eased, imports surchrg ends 3-24, 277D3, F3
US churches cut Citibank ties 3-24, 277G3
US-Canada co guilty of arms sales 3-25, 278F1
9 African natns seek econ indepndnc 4-1, 243D1
Dutch bar oil embargo, to probe econ sanctns 6-27, 499F1
OAU asks investmt exit 7-1—7-4, 509G1
Canada arms seller fined 8-14, 618F2
Zimbabwe maintains trade missn 9-3, 691A1
IMF revises SDR valuatn method 9-17, 695C2
'80 imports rptd up; business concerned 10-15, 793A2
Taiwan uranium deal, trade cited 10-17, 831E2, A3

Namibia (South-West Africa)
SWAPO, troop clashes intensify 2-3—2-16, 195E2
Casualty total rptd 3-24, 374A3
SWAPO wrecks power line 4-16, 4-20, 374G2
Botha pledges legis powers for assemb 5-1, troop turnover 5-13, 374E2
UN talks delayed, assurances re SWAPO sought 5-12, 374B2
UN peace plan backed at black African summit in Zambia 6-2, 462C3
SWAPO bases in Angola attacked, May incursns cited, UN peace plan seen imperiled 6-13, 466F2-C3

1976

US urges independence 4-27, 293B1, F1, 294D2
Zambia holds SWAPO members, Nujoma support cited 5-4, 386G2
2 SWAPO members get death 5-12, 386G1-C2
Vorster OKs SWAPO const conf role 5-17, SWAPO wing bars 5-31, 386D2
Const conf resumes 6-2, 386F2
SWAPO losses rptd 6-14, 7-30, 654A3
US Dem platform text cites 6-15, 478D3
W Ger scores govt policy 6-22, 447D3
Kissinger-Vorster mtg 6-23—6-24, 446F2
Angola confirms death for mercenaries 7-9, 519C3
Govt presses anti-guerrilla drive, deaths rptd 7-10—7-17, 539G3
Const conf resumes 8-3, indep set 8-18; UN, US, others score conf plan 8-19—8-26; S Africa modifies 8-20, 653B3-654E2
SWAPO seeks USSR, Cuba arms; scores Israel 8-22, 654G2
Mudge bids troops stay 8-27, 660G3
UN warns on Cuba, USSR role 8-30, 660F3
OAU OKs Cuban aid to SWAPO 8-30, 660F3
Kissinger hits white rule 8-31, Vorster rebuts 9-1, 660A3
Const conf reopens 8-31, 661B1
Torture charge rptd 8-31, 661B1
Vorster: SWAPO legitimate 9-5, 660F2
SWAPO asks talks 9-6, 660D3
Nujoma in Tanzania on ANC rift 9-6—9-7, 661D3, E3 ★
Kissinger-Vorster agrmt on UN conf rptd set 9-7, 660G2, E3
Vorster bars govt-SWAPO talks 9-8, 697G2
SWAPO rep scores Kissinger 9-9, 681G1
US rebel aid urged 9-14, 681C1
Const conf asks SWAPO role 9-14, '77 independnc 9-16, 698A1
Kissinger sees Tanzania, Zambia ldrs 9-15—9-16, 681B1; sees Vorster 9-19, 697E2
Zambia backs gen conf 9-17, 698C1
SWAPO pres sees negotiatn 9-21, 693E2
Nyerere hits const conf, asks UN role 9-21, 718B1
Nujoma in Tanzania 9-23—9-26, Cuba 10-5, 794A1, B1
Nujoma asks UN embargo, 9-27; sees Kissinger 9-29, 793G3
USSR scores US mediatn 9-28, 719C1
Angola refugee flight rptd 9-28, 734A3
SWAPO rpts attacks 9-30, 794B1
World Bank aid offer rptd 10-8, 794B1
Vorster on Geneva conf role, SWAPO talks 10-18, 793C2
UN arms ban vetoed 10-19, 781C3
Const conf com breaks down 10-19, 10-21; resumes, const plan OKd, adjourns 10-22, 832E1
Const conf resumes 11-9, adjourns 12-8; OAU, SWAPO divisns rptd 12-21, 12-22, 1010C3
SWAPO asks Angola aid 11-11, 862E2
UN backs black struggle, recognizes SWAPO 12-20, 955B1

1977

Nujoma sees Podgorny 3-28, flies to Angola 3-29, 247G3, 249D3
Amnesty Intl torture rpt denied 4-4, 349G2
Vorster rejcts Westn independnc plan, UN compliance 4-7, 285B1
Angola refugees rptd 4-13, 424B2
Owen sees SWAPO reps 4-15, Neto 4-17, 296A3, C3
Front-line states back overthrow 4-17—4-18, 296D3
UN rpt scores forgn cos re bias 4-19, 349G2
RC missn students kidnaped 4-20, 349F2
21 die in Angola border clashes 4-26, 349E2
Vorster sees Westn talks progress 4-29, 349C2
2 escape SWAPO prison camp 5-1, 349E2
West rejcts Turnhalle const 5-8—5-10, Vorster OKs concessns 5-9, 400D1
Maputo UN conf: Westn moves, natlsts backed 5-16—5-21; Nujoma disputes 5-16, sees Young 5-17, 399B1
Whites back Turnhalle const 5-17, 400C2
Vorster sees Mondale, electn pledge affirmed 5-18—5-20; UK briefed 5-22, 398A1
SWAPO member hanged 5-30, 457E2
New Westn plan OKd, Turnhalle const out 6-8—6-10, 457F1
Commonwealth conf backs majority rule 6-10, 486C3
SWAPO scores Westn plan 6-11, 457B2
Vorster vows Walvis Bay retentn 6-14, 457D2
Angola refugees rpt UNITA town recapture 6-27, 522B2
OAU backs West effort 6-28, 512D2
Zambia rpts fighting 7-11, 536G1
Angola town recapture confrmd 7-21, 675B1
12 die in SWAPO clashes 8-3, 8-14, 639E3
Vorster hits US policy 8-5, 639B3
Nujoma joins Westn talks 8-8, 639B3
SWAPO OKs Westn plan, continuing SWAPO-Pretoria disputes cited 8-19, 699E3
Independnc plan effected, admin gen takes office 9-1; SWAPO vote talks OKd 9-8, 699B3, C3 ★, F3 ★
Pretoria takes over Walvis Bay; US, UN score 9-1, 699G3
Pretoria-Westn parley stalled re troop cuts 9-22—9-26, 770D2
White party splits 9-28, 770A3
S Africa Parlt ties dissolved, white party breaks natl ties 9-28, 770B3
Carter UN speech remarks 10-4, 751F3
UN presence rptd OKd 10-4, 1016F3
Nigeria ldr lauds US effort 10-12, 797A2
Turnhalle const conf dissolved 10-12, 876F1
Apartheid, security laws ended 10-14—11-11, 876D1
Major SWAPO clashes 10-27—10-29, 11-10, 876E1
UN Assemb condemns 'illegal occupatn' 11-4, 851E1
Westn contact group fails to win SWAPO concessns, Pretoria troop-exit talks stalled 11-21—12-7, 1016D3
3 soldiers rptd killed in clash 12-9, 1017B1
Police torture chrgd 12-16, denied 12-18, 1017A1

1978

Front-line natns back Westn indep plan 3-26, 248G2
Herero chief killed in tribal clash, Mar casualties rptd 3-27; SWAPO denies role 3-28, 229C2
Violence rptd 3-28—4-22, 299C2
Westn natns revise plan 3-31, 299D1
Angola refugees rptd 4-4, 265E2
UK warns USSR, Cuba vs role 4-5, 259E1
Tribes clash at Herero chief's rites 4-8—4-9, 269C2
Emergency powers granted to Steyn 4-8; SWAPO rpts 10 held 4-25, 299B2
Vorster sees Westn contact group 4-23; OKs independnc plan, UN role detailed 4-25, 299C1
UN Assemb spec sessn opens 4-24, econ sanctns backed 5-3, 339C1
SWAPO issues independnc plan terms 4-28, 339E1
Troops raid Angola SWAPO camps 5-4; death toll rptd 5-6, 5-7, 338A3
Jan-May troop, SWAPO deaths rptd 5-5, 339A1
UN Cncl scores Angola raid 5-6, 339B1
Nujoma cancels Westn contact group talks 5-7, 339D1
Angola raid censure by US scored 5-12, 475E3
Shipanga freed 5-25, forms party 6-19, 475G3
Angola raid prisoners freed 5-27, 475E3
US asks USSR role in peaceful solutn 6-7, 424B1
SWAPO to resume talks 6-11, 475C3
Angola raid scored by UN refugee comr, WHO 6-16, 475D3
Voter regis set by Pretoria 6-20, 475A3
US backs negotiatns, Angola contacts 6-20, 487G1, B3
RR sabotaged 6-21, 475F3
US envoy in Angola 6-21—6-26, 488A1
ILO entry OK rptd 6-24, 547E3
SWAPO rep held in voter protest 6-25, 547B3
Voter registratn opens 6-26, total rptd 7-11, 547G2
W Ger backs Westn plan 6-26—6-30, 584F1
Steyn assumes censorship power 7-3, 547D3
US envoy's Angola visit rptd success 7-8, 547G2 ★
2 SWAPO ldrs freed 7-9, 547D3
SWAPO OKs Westn indep plan 7-12, 547B2
Churchmen ousted 7-14, 547B3
Walvis Bay talks disputed 7-15, 7-17, 547E2
Mugabe backs Westn plan 7-18, 561B2
SWAPO reps reimprisoned 7-26, 633G3
UN backs Westn plan, Botha warns re Walvis Bay 7-27, 561G2
Facts on Walvis Bay 562B1
Pretoria OKs UN missn, defers indep plan OK re Walvis Bay 7-28, 7-31; Ahtisaari delegatn arrives 8-6, 633D3
SWAPO, troops clash, 8 rptd killed 8-13, 669E2
Troops raid Zambia SWAPO camps 8-23—8-26, 669C2
Ahtisaari leaves, no progress seen 8-23, 669E2
UN Racism conf vs indep recognitn 8-26, 676A2
Waldheim presents settlmt plan, 7,500 troops asked 8-30, 741G3
Angola, S Africa swap prisoners 9-2, 742A2
Vorster quits, UN plan rejctd 9-20, 741D3, 742A1
Steyn sets electns, parties plan boycott 9-20, 742B1
SWAPO vows increased struggle 9-22, 742C1
SWAPO gets WCC grant 9-26, 742E2
UN Cncl OKs Waldheim plan, warns vs rejectn 9-29; S Africa Cabt replies 10-3, 819E2
SWAPO joins nonaligned movt 10-2, 820D1
S Africa-sponsored electns rescheduled 10-3, DTA, govt bar further delay 10-14, 10-17; SWAPO, Natl Front, SWAPO-Dems bar vote 10-15, 819G2-820C1
UN contact group in Windhoek 10-14; sees Botha, Steyn; new talks OKd 10-16—10-18, 819D2, G2, 820A1
Ahtisaari talks to reopen 10-19, 819E3-F3
Botha to accept UN-sponsored vote results 10-19, 819G3
WCC grants protested, total cited 10-25, 906F3
UN Cncl warns sanctns re electns 11-13, 904A2
Botha sees Waldheim, Vance 11-27, Carter 11-30; Pretoria to retain Namibia control 12-2, 988F3-989A1
Windhoek bomb blasts 12-2, 12-5, 988B3
Tjongarero, SWAPO reps arrested 12-3, 988C3
Electns 12-4—12-8, DTA wins 12-15, 988G2
Vote registratn coercn chrgd by church group 12-5, 988E3
Electn irregularities chrgd by Nujoma UN supervisn asked 12-12, 988D3
Namibia assemb meets; OKs UN plan, sets terms 12-20—12-22, 1020F1
Pretoria OKs UN plan, '79 electns seen 12-22, 1020D1
SWAPO vp, 5 others freed 12-27, 1020A2

Obituaries

Diederichs, Nicolass 8-21, 708E2
Sobukwe, Robert 2-27, 196E3

South-West Africa—*See 'Namibia' above*

1979

UN contact group sees Botha 3-19–3-22, Pretoria asks more control over SWAPO bases 5-7, 354D2
UK Tories urge rebel support end 4-11, 285D3
US 'regrets' envoy ouster 4-12, Pretoria denies talks pullout sought 4-14, 4-14, 287C1, G1
39 SWAPO ldrs arrested 4-27, US scores 5-1, 354F2
Constituent assemb gets lawmaking power 5-8, 354B2
Natl assemb opens 5-21, 447C2
UN Assemb opens debate 5-23; S Africa barred; US, 18 other Westrn natns oppose ouster 5-24, 409C3
UN Assemb votes Cncl actn, contact group abstains 5-31, 428A1
Angola SWAPO camps raided 7-4–7-6, 585G1
Apartheid rptd ended 7-13, 585F1
Steyn removed as admin gen, Viljoen replaces 8-1, 585G1
Angola rpts refugee casualties 8-2, 617F2
Commonwealth conf topic 8-7, 590E2
Assemb gets legis powers 8-13, 617B3
UN opens talks re demilitarized zone 11-12, S Africa joins 11-13–11-16, 889B3
Cuba rptd training children 12-4, 12-10, 981B2
Pretoria partially OKs UN plan 12-5, 969G1

Obituaries

De Klerk, Jan 1-23, 104G2

1980

Angola protests raids 6-26; Pretoria denies civiln deaths, admits SWAPO operatn 6-27, 7-2; UN censures 6-27, 524D3
Pretoria sets defense force 8-1, 711A1
Viljoen recalled in Cabt shift 8-26, 689F3
UN, Waldheim SWAPO support chrgd 8-29; US denies 9-9, 710D3
US backs majority rule 10-7, 792G2
UN cease-fire talks fail 10-20—10-24, 831A3
Alliance parties lose electns 11-14, 967A3
UN talks schedule agreed 11-24, 967F1

Obituaries

Fouche, Jacobus Johannes 9-23, 755A3
Ngoyi, Lillian 3-12, 280C1

1976

Sports
Brazil bars yacht race 1-2, 11C3
OAU vs NZ rugby ties 7-6, 487E3
31 natns quit Olympics 7-9, 528A3
US gymnastics tour confrmd 7-20, 528E3
IAAF expels 7-22, 562B2
Mixed intl teams, matches OKd 9-23, 793D3
White rugby players warned 10-12, 793F3
NZ plans curbs 10-17, 910G2

Transkei—*See TRANSKEI*

1977

Sports
Davis Cup matches 4-15—4-17, 353F2
NZ compromise agreed 6-8—6-15, 487E1
US Open demonstratn 9-11, 787A3
UN asks intl boycott 12-14, 1016C2

Transkei—*See TRANSKEI*
UN Policy & Developments—*See also 'Namibia' above*
UN Assemb member 4B1
Diederichs scores UN 1-21, 67B1
UN rights com chrgs cited 3-11, 207A2
UN conf condemns apartheid 8-22—8-26, 661E2
UN sanctn support asked by US Black Caucus 10-21, 825C1
UN econ, permanent arms sanctns vetoed; apartheid res OKd 10-31, 851F2
UN votes arms ban, Pretoria condemns; text 11-4, 851C1
Assemb votes anti-apartheid resolutns 12-14, 1016B2
Assemb votes oil, investmt bans 12-16, 1016G1

Unrest (domestic)—*See also 'Namibia' above*
Soweto schls reopen, other townships patrolled 1-5, 3B3, D3 ★
Cape Town journalist flees 1-5, 3D3
Soweto house explodes 1-7, RR blast link probed 1-9, 21B3
Cape Town schls bombed 1-10, 95 arrested 1-12, 21F2
2 detainees rptd dead, '76 total cited 1-11, 21C3
Police accused in black unrest 1-25, 100A3
2 detainee deaths probed 1-27, 100F3
Blacks disrupt exams 2-1—2-9, return to schl 2-10, 100B2
2 more detainee deaths 2-15, 2-24, 160E2
Anglicans score apartheid, priest sentenced 2-17, 145F1
'76 riot rpt blames aprtheid 2-17, 160D2
Bishop arrested 2-21, 350B1
Thloloe rptd held 3-2, 349E3
Soweto rent riots 4-27—4-28, rises deferred 4-29, 350C1
Coloreds protest rent rises 5-2, 350A2
Mandela banished 5-19, 399G3
Miners riot re pay 5-1, 469B2
Soweto patrolled, student ldr arrested 6-10; incidents rptd 6-10—6-14, 469C1
2 Johannesburg whites killed 6-13, 469A1
12 die in '76 Soweto anniv riots 6-15—6-21, 489E1-C2
200 students arrested in Johannesburg protest, 2 die in Soweto riot 6-23—6-24, 529A3
Breytenbach acquitted 7-15, 564D1
Blacks boycott schools, battle police 7-25—8-1, 599D3
Mandela chrgd 7-28, 600A1
8 held re Johannesburg attack 7-28, 600B1
Miners get pay hike 7-28, 600B2
Black student boycott spreads 8-1—8-16, 640D1
2 more detainee deaths, torture rptd 8-1—8-4, 640F1
Cape Town shantytown demolitn protested 8-8—8-12, 639F3
Black student ldr Biko arrested 8-18, hunger strike rptd 9-5, 707D3, 735A3
Soweto student killed 8-19, govt takes over schls 9-1, 708E1
Soweto teachers quit 9-6, 708D1
2 sentncd re Mandela trial 9-7, 825G3
Biko dies in jail 9-12; protests, probe urged 9-13—9-15, 707C3-708D1
Biko death questnd 9-14—9-17; Kruger admits irregularities 9-17, 735B2
Vorster regrets Biko death 9-16, calls early electn 9-20, 747C1
Soweto blacks hold Biko meml svc 9-18, 735B3
Progressives ask Kruger ouster, detentn law repeal, death probes 9-19, 735A3
Biko death violence 9-21, 9-23, 9-25, 735F3
Biko buried, forgn envoys attend 9-25, 735C3
Soweto terrorist killed, urban terrorist group cited 9-26, 825B3
Kingwilliamstown crowd dispersed 9-28, 825E3
MD dies in detentn 9-29, 935C1
Youth killed in Queenstown 10-2; rpt 6 die in Port Eliz 10-15, 825E3
Bantu educ min quits 10-3; boycott spread, teacher returns rptd 10-22, 826A1
Biko death rpts spur govt-press clashes 10-7—10-12, 804D2
Press closings scored in US 10-10, 10-21, 825C2
Black groups banned, 2 papers closed, ldrs seized; foes denounce 10-19; Vorster defends 10-20, 803C3, 804A1 ★ -C2
Kruger blames US 10-21, 825E1

1978

Sports
Lamb named to Davis Cup team 2-12, Moore quits 2-28, 251C3
Spinks-Ali rematch plan protested 3-8, site chngd 3-9, 212B1, E1
Scandinavian natns bar ties 3-11, 193C3
US Davis Cup protests 3-17—3-19, loses N Amer Zone title 3-19, 251A1-252C1
S Africa Open results 4-10, 419C1
Spinks-Ali US rematch signed 4-11, 378F3
Davis, Federatn cups barred 4-16, 419F2
US blacks ask intl ban 7-6, 632E3
S Africa Grand Prix results 12-4, 1027D2

Transkei—*See TRANSKEI*
UN Policy & Developments—*See also 'Namibia' above*
Arms embargo compliance lags 4-28, 377A2
Assemb backs econ sanctns 5-3, 339C1
ILO entry OK rptd 6-24, 547E3
Racism conf censures, 12 Westn natns quit 8-14—8-26, 676G1-C2
Assemb member 713E3
Canada arms sales suspected 11-6—11-7, 904E2
Assemb chrgs Israel mil ties 11-27, 931A3

Unrest (including political protests & detentions)—*See also 'Namibia' above*
Asian detainee rptd dead 1-2, 20F2
Banned editor flees 1-3, 8E1
Biko family sues officials 1-3, 20A3
Anti-apartheid white killed 1-8, 20D2
6 injured in Port Eliz riot 1-8, 20F2
Cape Town shanty demolitn begun 1-16, 39A1
Soweto schl opening boycotted 1-17, 39C1
Amnesty Intl chrgs routine torture 1-19, 39D1
Newsmen held re Soweto mtg 1-22, 55A1
Soweto electn boycott urged 1-22, 55A1; 1-29, 92D2
4 lose appeals in Mandela case 1-23, Mandela gets suspended sentences 2-9; banning explained 114D1
Schl boycott end urged 1-29, probe pledged 2-1; students return 2-1, 2-5, 92D2
Kruger vows detainee protectn 1-31, 92G1
Biko case actn vs police barred 2-2, 92F1
'77 detainee death ruled suicide 2-7, 92A2
Soweto electns boycotted 2-18, 134F3
Black editor, 9 others freed 3-10, 193D2
Port Eliz bomb kills 1 3-10, 193D3
Amnesty Intl chrgs MDs torture 3-11, 180C3
Buthelezi stoned at Sobukwe funeral 3-11, 193C3
Indian detainee death ruled suicide 3-15, 229D3
2 black detainees die 3-19, 7-13; 6 policemen face murder chrgs, 3 suspended 7-20, 633C2
Motlana, 2 other blacks freed 3-23, 229C3
6 sentenced in ANC terrorism trial 4-7, 269D1
Rptr asks US asylum 4-20, 314C3
'77 nonpol detainee deaths rptd 4-24, 377F2
Suburban guerrillas, arms captured 5-2; 10-month total rptd 5-4, 377E2
AZAPO ldrs arrested 5-4, 377D2
Black newspaper offcl arrested 5-5, 377E2
Black policeman executed 5-16, 456F1
Biko police probe rptd; 'errors' admitted, case closed 5-17, 455F3
Detainee torture denied, '77 deaths rptd 5-17, 456B1
Gold mine riot crushed 5-21, 456B1
Duma acquitted, Mayet arrested; black journalist arrests since '76 cited 5-29, 456C1, E1
Cape Town squatters camp raided, 50 arrested 6-5, 456E1
2 Cape Town academics convicted 6-13, 456G1
Black newspaper banned 6-15, 535C3
Racial attitudes polled 6-15, 6-22, 536E2, A3
Soweto '76 riot marked 6-16; cops break up crowd 6-17, warn Motlana 6-19, 535A3-F3
RC bishops ask unionists release 7-4, 633F2
Black detainee dies 7-10, probe set 7-11, 535F3; 3 policemen transferred 7-21, 633E2
Church cncl paper 'understands' violence 7-12, 633A2
Pretoria multiracial theater bombed 7-18, Natl Front disclaims role 7-19, 633B3
'76 Soweto riot cost rptd 7-31, 670B1
Motlana banned 9-6, 742D2
Biko friends, family rptd arrested 9-12, 742D2
Cape Town squatter camp raid kills 3 9-14, 742B2
Police cleared re black detainee death 10-3, 820D1

1979

Sports
US revokes Knoetze visa 1-9, judge enjoins 1-11; Knoetze KOs Sharkey, fight protested 1-13, 79D2
Villenueve wins Gr Prix 3-4, 1005E1
Runners banned from Boston Marathon 4-12, 911D3
Snake sitting record set 5-13, 392C3
Tate decisns Coetzee for WBA heavywgt title 10-20, 838F2

Transkei—*See TRANSKEI*
UN Policy & Developments—*See also 'Namibia' above*
Angola raid toll rpt 8-2, 717F2
Israel arms embargo compliance cited 9-7, 720D3
Assemb pres scores on rights 9-18, 695B2
Membership listed 695C3
Castro addresses Assemb, scores racism 10-12, 778G2
Cncl condemns Angola attacks 11-2, 875G1

Unrest—*See also 'Namibia' above*
White miners protest integratn 3-7, 171F3; end walkout 3-14, 191A2
Mdluli widow gets damages 3-19, 213D2
Crossroads squatters to get homes 4-5, 270D3
Mahlangu hanged for '77 Johannesburg attack; clemency pleas ignored, students protest 4-6, 270B3
Black unrest prompts labor reforms 5-2, 332F3
Soweto police statn attacked 5-3, 373G1
Soweto 11 sentenced 5-11, 373C1
Pan-Africa Cong UN rep slain in Tanzania 6-12, 476G3
Kruger loses justice post 6-14, 469G2
Pan-Africa Cong activists sentenced 6-26, 476E3
Biko family wins setlmt 7-27, 585E1
US black rights ldr backs civil disobedience 8-1, 617G1
Biko atty leaves 8-10, rptd in Botswana 8-12, 617D2
Botha in Soweto 8-31, 732E3
White union ldr bans lifted 9-17, 732F2
Soweto police statn attacked, 2 die 11-2, 875G1
2 US cos fire 1,325 blacks 11-21—11-22, paper mill struck 11-23, 899C3
Anglican priest chrgd 12-10, 969E1
Mandela backers jailed 12-13, 969F1

1980

Sports
Johannesburg woman sets UK distance running record 8-15, 638B3
2d in World Amateur Team golf tourn 10-12, 972E2
Borg, McEnroe decline match offer 10-16, 947E1
WBA heavywgt title bout held, riots erupt 10-25, 887E3, 1000E3
Rival Gr Prix circuit set 10-31, 1002C1
Mathebula wins WBA flywgt title 12-13, 1001B1

Transkei—*See TRANSKEI*
UN Policy & Developments
Sovt Afghan invasn res shunned 1-14, 25F2
Environmt Progrm ends ties 4-28, 374G1
Namibia talks delayed 5-12, 374B2
Namibia peace plan backed at black African summit 6-2, 462C3
Namibia peace plan seen imperiled 6-13, 466C3
Dutch to probe sanctns 6-27, 499B2
Botha denies Angola raids, Cncl censures 6-27, 524F3
Waldheim scores Angola raids 7-1, 509A2
Women's conf in Denmark 7-14—7-30, 587G1
Canada arms seller fined 8-14, 618F2
Waldheim, Cncl SWAPO support chrgd 8-29; US denies 9-9, 710D3
Canada min scores apartheid 9-22, 748G3-749A1
Namibia talks fail 10-20—10-24, 831A3
Namibia talks schedule agreed 11-24, 967F1

Unrest—*See also 'Namibia' above*
Ford rehires black strikers 1-9, 60C3
Port Eliz blacks demonstrate 1-10, 60F3
ANC seizes bank, 5 die 1-25, 100C3
Bank seizure arrests rptd 1-31; gunman buried 2-9, 134B3
Arms cache found in Natal 2-16; ANC rebel strike rptd 2-18, 195B2
3 banned re Port Eliz protest 2-27, 195G2
Anglican priest sentncd 2-28, 195G2, A3
Soweto '76 riot rpt presented 2-29, 174C1-C2
Booysens police statn attacked 4-4, 278F1
Colored students protest spending inequalities 4-21—4-24, 356F2
Botha vows educ spending review 5-5, colored schl boycott wanes; Indian, black support cited 5-6—5-13, 374B3
Port Eliz protester flees to Lesotho 5-6, 374A3
Cape Town police break up colored march 5-24, kill 2 pupils 5-28, 466C2
6,000 Durban black strikers are fired 5-28, 466D2
Botha vows crackdown 5-30, 466A2, E2
Synthetic fuel plants bombed, ANC claims responsibility 6-1, 466A2-B2
A-scientist convicted 6-3, sentncd 6-10, 466D3
Cape Town coloreds riot, 30 die 6-16—6-18, 465G3
Forgn press barred from Cape Town riots 6-16, 466A1
US cautions restraint in riots 6-18, 466G1
Hendrickse blames coloreds lack of pol platform 6-19, 466E1
Auto workers strike ends 6-25, 499B2
Biko MD's probe squashed 6-29, 525C1
Political ban extended 6-30, 525F1
Johannesburg black municipal workers strike 7-24—7-31; 1,200 deported, strike broken 8-1, 690D1-B2
Schl normalizatn steps set 9-5; 77 boycotted schls closed 9-23, 753C2
Soweto blacks, police clash; RR bombed 10-15, 793E1-A2
Soweto church goers arrested 10-19, 887G3
Weaver boxing win spurs riots, 2 killed 10-25, 887E3
ANC-linked rptr released 10-26, 887F3
Port Eliz police kill 4 rioters 11-5, 887D3
White soldiers held in black child's death 11-7, 887C3
3 natlsts sentncd to death 11-26, 968B1

1976

U.S. Relations—*See also 'Namibia' above; also 'Majority Rule Issue' under RHODESIA*
US scores apartheid 4-27, 293B1, 294F2
US A-aid hearings 5-26—5-29, uranium deal rptd 6-1, 388D1
US computer sales rptd 5-26, 388A2
Kissinger, Vorster cite scheduled mtg 6-17, 6-18, 426D1, 427D1 ★
Mobil unit accused on Rhodesia sanctns 6-21, 621G1
Vorster sees Kissinger in W Ger 6-23—6-24, 446E1-447A1
US Angola mercenary linked to S Africa group 6-28, 480G1
Ship in US Bicentennial event 7-4, 488C3
US aide begins 6-natn tour 7-7, 523A1
Kissinger on new policy 8-2, 580D3; Muller replies, US State Dept comment 8-13, 653D2
US black-power ideology scored 8-19, 639E3
US blacks ask actn vs 8-23, 8-25, 654E2
Vorster meets Kissinger in Zurich 9-4—9-6, US-UK Rhodesia plan accord rptd 9-9, 660B2
Kissinger sees Vorster, black ldrs on problems 9-17—9-20, 697A1, C2
US sugar duties tripled 9-21, 721D3
USSR, US trade chrgs re role 9-28, 9-30, 719B1
US abstains in UN Transkei vote 10-26, 799G1
Reactn to Carter electn 11-3—11-4, 826D2
Newsday disputes death toll 12-11, 1010B2

1977

Biko prelim autopsy rpt cited 10-21, 825F1
Crackdown protests, 150 arrested 10-21, 825D3
Eng-language press to defy govt 10-22, 825B2
Kruger on bannings, detentns, paper reopenings 10-23, 825G1
Biko autopsy rpt leaked 10-25, judicial inquest ordrd 10-26, 887E1
Biko inquest opens 10-27, testimony rptd 11-14—11-15, 887D1, C2
US House res condemns repressn, Biko death 10-31, 852D1
Kruger confrms Biko autopsy rpt 11-9, 887B2
600 arrested in Pretoria township raids 11-10, 887E2
Black rioters, Cape Town police clash 11-15; Johannesburg bomb blasts 11-24, 12-6, 934F3
Detainee suicide announced 11-18, studnt killed at funeral 11-26, 935B1
Kruger pays rptr damages for false arrest 11-18, 935F1
Natl Party candidate, wife slain 11-23, 934B2, E3
Detainee total rptd 11-29, 935A1
Biko inquest clears police 12-2; US, oppositn press score 12-2—12-3, 933F3
Biko kin, others seized in Soweto raid 12-2, 934E1
Johannesburg suburb bomb blast 12-8, 1016D3
Port Eliz unrest 12-19—12-26, detainee death rptd 12-26, 1016C3

U.S. Relations—*See also 'Atomic Energy' above; also RHODESIA—Majority Rule*
US OKs sealskin imports 1-3, 21F3
Restaurant bars US envoy 1-26, 67E2; 2d envoy barred 2-5, 101A1
US backs diplomatic isolatn 2-28, 145A2
US firms to promote equality 3-1, 160G2
US natl arrested 3-2, 144E3
US bars Rhodesian chrome 3-18, 191E1
Young backs econ sanctns 4-5, 272C2
Namibia plan rejected 4-7, 285C1
Young remarks scored, visit in doubt 4-14—5-11, 399D3
Davis Cup match protests 4-15—4-17, 353F2
Chase curbs loans 4-19, 350C2
Namibia compromise seen 4-29, 349C2
Namibia const concessns OKd 5-9, 400D1
Rhodesia-Mobil oil info bar rptd 5-16, 413E2
Mondale sees Vorster 5-18—5-20, briefs UK 5-22, 397G2, 398E1
Young visits 5-21—5-22, statemts scored 5-23, 399A3, F3
Vorster scores US policy 5-22, 398F1
Carter clarifies US policy 6-10, 460G2
Envoy, poet detained 6-10, 469A2
21 US firms join equality plan 6-20, 535G3
Vance asks apartheid end 7-1; Botha reactn rptd 7-4, 535B3
US econ boycott urged 7-5, 642F2
US sues re sugar lobby gifts 7-20, 614A1
US '76 Rhodesia imports rptd 7-26, 582A1
Vorster hits US policy 8-5, 639G2
Tanzania asks US arms embargo 8-6, 624B1
US envoy's wife scored, recall asked 8-10, US defends 8-11—8-12, 640B1
Young at UN apartheid conf, Carter message lauded 8-22—8-26, 662A2
Walvis Bay takeover scored 9-1, 700A1
US Open apartheid protest 9-11, 787A3
US scores student ldrs death 9-13, 708B1
Vorster scores US policy 9-16, 747C1
Namibia conf stalled 9-22—9-26, 770D2
Andrew Silk arrested 9-23; leaves, denies ouster 9-24, 825F3
Envoys at Biko funeral; Ashe, cong send regrets 9-25, 735D3
Carter cites Namibia in UN speech 10-4, 751F3
US press closings scored 10-10, 10-21, 825C2
Israel steel sales rptd 10-10, 887E3
Nigeria ldr lauds US effort 10-12, 797A2
Constructn firm, black US co make joint bid 10-17, 979E1
US vs black crackdown 10-19; Vorster defends 10-20, 803D3, 804F1
US recalls amb for talks 10-21, 825A1
Black Caucus backs sanctns 10-21, Young backs 10-24, 825C1
Kruger blames US re unrest 10-21, 825E1
Young, Carter confer on sanctns 10-24, 851D3
Carter backs arms ban, bars spare parts 10-27, 851G3-852C1
US vetoes UN econ, permanent arms sanctns; OKs apartheid res 10-31, 851F2
US House OKs Biko res 10-31, 852D1
US House res condemns repress, Biko death 10-31, 852D1
Naval attache exit set 11-2, commercial envoy leaves 11-4, 852D1
US amb returns 11-5, 852C1
NCC urges investor boycott 11-10, 934C3
Namibia tour fails to win SWAPO concessns 11-21—12-7, 1016E3
Polaroid ends sales 11-22, 934D2
US cos open chamber of commerce unit 11-23, investmt data rptd 12-4, 934A3
Biko inquest rpt, kin arrests scored 12-2, 934D1
US abstains on UN oil, investmt bans 12-16, 1016A2

1978

Police-rebel shootouts rptd 10-27, 10-30, 904E3
3 policemen sentncd in black detainee death 11-3, 904C3
Koornhof tours Cape Town camp 11-21, delays destructn 11-30, 989G1
Mayet, Rachidi rptd freed, banned 12-19, 989C2

U.S. Relations—*See also 'Atomic Energy' above*
S Africa unit fined for Rhodesia sales 1-12, 38B3
NAACP asks US business boycott 1-16, 38E3
Ford sees Vorster 1-16, backs investmt 1-19, 38G3
US cos equality pledge rptd ignored 1-20, 38F3
US Sen subcom urges business tax credits, guarantees ended 1-25; Eximbank '77 total rptd 2-9, 135A2
US bars chrome alloy duty hike 1-29; '77 imports cited 80F3
US labor, educ institutns cut financial ties 1-29, 2-11, 135F1, G1
US hosts Namibia conf 2-11—2-12, 113G2
US bars mil, police exports 2-17, 135D1
US auto union investmt ban rptd 3-6, 193B3
Citibank halts loans, '74-76 data cited 3-11, 193F3
Olin indicted for firearm sales 3-14, 193G2; fined 3-30, 249E2; 6-1, 632G3
Davis Cup protests in US 3-17—3-19, N Amer Zone title 3-19, 251A3-252C1
Chem Bank rpts loan bar 3-21, BankAmer backs loans 3-22, 237D2
Young sees Nujoma 3-22—3-24, 248D3
Front-line natns back Namibia plan 3-26, 248G2
Vorster scores US rights stand 3-31, Carter urges majority rule 4-1, 233G2-234A1
Paymts to US reps alleged 4-17, 377C3
Rptr asks US asylum 4-20, 314C3
Credit rating rptd damaged by apartheid 4-23, 377G1-A2
Namibia plan OKd by Vorster 4-25, 299C1
2 univs OK stock divestitures 4-30, 5-3, 377D1-E1
Eximbank credit ban backed by House com 5-1, Sen com rejcts 5-3, 377B1
CIA liaison in '75 Angola war rptd 5-8, 367F2
Angola raid censure scored 5-12, 475E3
US bars Peace Corps from hospitals 5-15, 633A1
African moderates urge US econ pressure 6-2, 633B2
Miami U cancels stock divestiture 6-3, 633B1
Columbia U sets bank stock sale 6-6, 633C1
Carter asks USSR role in Namibia solutn 6-7, 424B1
Black passport denial rptd 6-10, 536D3
Pol influence-buying denied by Info Min 6-14, 498D3
3 univ divestitures rptd 6-18, 633D1
Vance backs Namibia talks, scores apartheid 6-20, 487G1, F2, B3
US envoy in Angola 6-21—6-26, 488A1
Sullivan expands corp guidelines 7-5, 632F3
NAACP OKs sanctns call 7-6, 632D3
US envoy's Angola visit rptd success 7-8, 547G2 ★
Namibia plan OKd by SWAPO 7-12, 547C2
Zulus back Sullivan labor code 7-13, 633F1
Chrysler unit merger cited 8-10, 623D3
Quaker group to sell stock 8-15, 669G3
US investmt rptd up, '77 total rptd 8-29, 669E3
GM sets integratn plan 8-29, 742G2
Church group ends bank ties 9-21, 742F2
Washn Star deal probed 11-1—11-2, 868D2
UN abstentn on Namibia electn warning 11-13, 904B2
Carter cites repression 12-6, 934C1

1979

U.S. Relations
US revokes Knoetze visa 1-9, judge enjoins 1-11; Knoetze KOs Sharkey, fight protested 1-13, 79E2
Carter State of Union Message 1-23, 48F1
US rights rpt omits 2-10, 107A2
Columbia U sells stock, other coll divestitures rptd 3-10–3-24, 270G3
US rpts A-plant protest 4-2, 246A2
Mahlangu clemency plea rptd 4-6, 270C3
UK Tories urge rebel support end re Namibia 4-11, 285E3
3 envoys ousted as spies 4-12, US ousts 3 S Africans 4-13, 286E3, 287C1
3 more univs sell stock 4-26–5-3, 332G3
US Sen vote to end Rhodesia sanctns hailed 5-16, 359C2
US vs UN Namibia debate ouster 5-25, 409F3
US unoffcl Zimbabwe envoy named 6-25, 490C2
US black rights ldr ends visit, controversy spurred 8-1, 617D1-D2
Kellogg unit recognizes black union 8-29, 732G2
Young discounts Israel ties 9-7, 720D3
Castro scores US policy role 10-12, 778G2
US rpts A-blast 10-25, Pretoria denies 10-26, 10-27, 824B3
US abstains on UN vote 11-2, 875G1
2 US cos fire 1,325 blacks 11-21–11-22, 899C3
US weighs asylum for shah 12-1, shah rules out 12-5, 914B1, D1

Venda—*See VENDA*

1980

U.S. Relations
Ford rehires black strikers 1-9, 60C3
US distrusts gold mkt 1-18, 30F2
'79 A-blast mystery unresolved 1-23, 49A3
Pentagon cites role vs Sovt subs 2-1, 84G1
US issues rights rpt 2-5, 87E2
'79 blast laid to Israel A-test; denied 2-21, 141E3
Ford scored re black pay, integratn role lauded 2-27, 195A2
McGoff loses documt disclosure suit 3-17, 278B1
US churches cut Citibank ties 3-24, 277G3
US-Canada co guilty of arms sales 3-25, 278F1
US univ sells Standard Oil stock 4-13, 374A2
US cautns restraint in riots 6-18, 466G1
'79 A-blast dispute continues 7-14, 548E2
US denies R Botha UN chrgs 9-9, 710F3
US gets Nigeria oil warning 10-3; Carter pledges Namibia majority rule 10-7, 792C2
Reagan electn reactn 11-5, 841G2

Venda—*See VENDA*

1976

SOUTH African Nonracial Olympic Committee
- Supports games boycott 7-17, 528C3

SOUTH Bend, Ind.—*See INDIANA*

SOUTH Boston Defense League
- Levi busing rule protest rptd 5-31, 392D1

SOUTH Carolina
- A-engineer quits NRC 2-9, 115F1
- Parris I Marine facility probed 5-25—6-9, 435F2
- Dem conv women delegates, table 508D2
- Dem conv pres vote, table 7-14, 507D2
- Schweiker in Columbia 7-29, news conf 7-30, 564G1, C2
- Edwards asks GOP conv rule chng 8-9, 582G1
- Marine abuse convictns rptd 8-12, 586G3
- GOP pre-conv delegate count 8-14, 583D3
- GOP conv pres, vp vote tables 8-18—8-19, 8-19, 599D1, D3
- Carter, Dole in Darlington 9-6, 663F3, 666C1
- Fscl '75 per capita income, tax burden rptd 9-15, 10-12, 959D2
- Fallout rptd from China A-test 10-5, 791A1
- Ford in Columbia 10-23, 802E3
- Carter campaigns 10-26, 803D1, C2
- Election results 11-2; pres 818D1, 819B2; cong 822B3, 830G3-A4
- US Sup Ct declines atty ethics case 12-13, 960D3

SOUTH Dakota
- Primary date set 22C2
- US Sup Ct to hear coal mining environment impact case 1-12, 23G3
- Indian ldr shot 5-5, 384E2
- Primary results 6-1, 389E2, 390A1, D2
- Strip-mining stay reversed 6-28, 569A1
- Dem conv women delegates, table 508D2
- Dem conv pres vote, table 7-14, 507D2
- 2 cleared in Oglala '75 FBI deaths 7-16, 640E2
- Mondale in Pierre 7-31, 565C1
- Means acquitted 8-6, 640E2
- GOP pre-conv delegate count 8-14, 583D3
- GOP conv pres, vp vote tables 8-18—8-19, 8-19, 599D1, D3
- Ford in Rapid City 8-29, 644F3
- Carter in Sioux Falls 9-15, 686D3
- Fscl '75 per capita income, tax burden rptd 9-15, 10-12, 959C2
- Dole campaigns 9-23, 724D3
- Election results 11-2; pres 818D1, 819A1; cong 824A1, 830A4
- Peltier extraditn set 12-17, 999C1

SOUTHEAST Asia—*See ASIA; country, organization names*

SOUTHEAST Asian Nations, Association of—*See ASSOCIATION of Southeast Asian Nations*

SOUTHEAST Asia Treaty Organization (SEATO) (Australia, France, Great Britain, New Zealand, Philippines, Thailand, U.S.)
- Formally disbands 2-20, 148C1

SOUTHEAST Missouri State University (Cape Girardeau)
- Dole campaign stop 10-18, 804G1

SOUTHERN Bell Telephone & Telegraph Co.—*See under AMERICAN Telephone & Telegraph*

SOUTHERN California, University of (USC) (Los Angeles)
- New artery x-ray tech rptd 1-21, 159D2
- Cancer, estrogen links rptd 6-3, 460G3
- Naber wins 4 Olympic medals 7-19—7-24, 562C3
- Ford visits 10-7, 762G3
- Bell 2d in Heisman balloting 11-30, 969E2
- Loses Liberty Bowl 12-20, 1014G2

1977

SOUTHAM, Robert
- Vs LaMarsh rpt proposals 6-15, 485E2

SOUTH America—*See LATIN America*

SOUTH Bend, Ind.—*See INDIANA*

SOUTH Braintree, Mass.—*See MASSACHUSETTS*

SOUTH Carolina
- Legislature schedule rptd 6F2
- Gen Dynamics loan guarantee saves Charleston jobs 1-19, 55F2
- Winter rptd worst in 100 yrs 1-22, 54D2
- Indian land claims rptd 2-7, 197D1
- Sup Ct voids police informant curb 2-22, 150C1
- Carter call-in 3-5, 171C1
- Barnwell A-plant aid barred 4-7, 267C3; Church scores 5-2, 335A1
- '76 per-capita income table 5-10, 387F2
- Charleston tourism rptd; econ data table 5-16, 384E2, A3
- Offshore oil sales delayed 5-17, 498F3
- Textile mill wins Tris ban exemptn 5-18, 483E2
- Death penalty bill signed 6-8, 594D2
- Atty Gen voting rights powers upheld 6-20, 517B1
- Tris ban upset 6-23, recall enjoined 6-26, 560D1
- Carter addresses southn legislators in Charleston 7-21, 550E2; USSR reactn 8-3, 590D1
- '76 per-capita income, tax burden table 9-13, 10-18, 821D2
- Overtime suit filed vs A&P 9-27, 778D2
- ERA econ boycott rptd 11-14, 918E1
- Chas rpts mysterious blasts 12-2—12-22, 1008G3

SOUTH Carolina, University of (Columbia)
- Loses coll baseball title 6-18, 568A1

SOUTH Dakota
- Legislature schedule rptd 6F2
- Coll team to go to Cuba 3-5, 181C1
- Snowstorm hits 3-10—3-12, 204A3
- Indian ldr convictn review denied 3-21, 230F2
- Marijuana law impact rptd 3-31, 332A3
- Coll team in Cuba 4-4—4-9, 282B3
- Sioux reservatn land laws upheld 4-4, 341G3
- Bergland rpts on drought conditns, '76 effects cited 4-18, 376F3
- '76 per-capita income table 5-10, 387E2, B3
- Sioux Falls econ data table 5-16, 384F2
- Indian ldr sentncd for '75 FBI deaths 6-2, 491G3
- Abortn ruling vacated 6-27, 538G3
- '76 per-capita income, tax burden table 9-13, 10-18, 821F1, D2
- Anti-abortn amendmt rptd sought 10-6, 786B3

SOUTH Dakota, University of (Vermillion)
- Basketball team in Cuba 4-4—4-8, 282C3

SOUTH Dakota State University (Brookings)
- Basketball team in Cuba 4-4—4-8, 282C3

SOUTHEAST Asian Nations, Association of—*See ASSOCIATION of Southeast Asian Nations*

SOUTHEAST Asia Treaty Organization (SEATO) (Australia, France, Great Britain, New Zealand, Philippines, Thailand, U.S.)
- Secy gen wants ASEAN ties 514B2
- Disbands 6-30, 514A2

SOUTHERN Airways
- 70 die in Ga crash 4-4, 286A3, 311F2

SOUTHERN Bell Telephone Co.—*See AMERICAN Telephone & Telegraph Co.*

SOUTHERN California, University of (USC) (Los Angeles)
- Wins Rose Bowl 1-1; '76 rank rptd 1-2, 1-3, 8E3
- Ford lecture-seminar set 3-25, 236B3
- 3 in NFL draft 5-3, 353D2, A3
- Med Cntr rpts burn patient death choice 8-11, 712D2
- Wins Bluebonnet Bowl 12-31, 1020C2

1978

SOUTH African Airways
- US blacks urge landing rights ban 7-6, 632E3

SOUTH America—*See LATIN America*

SOUTH Carolina
- Legislature schedule rptd 14F3
- '67, '77 sales-tax rates rptd 1-5, 15F3
- Gag-order case review barred 1-9, 13F1
- State govt tax revenue table 1-9, 84E2
- Teacher tests backed 1-16, 33D2
- Stevens-NLRB setlmt excludes plants 4-28, 324G1
- Barnwell A-plant protest, 250 arrested 4-29—5-1, 347C1
- Construction pact signed 5-22, 429D3
- Nonprofit atty solicitn backed by Sup Ct 5-30, 430D2
- Charleston ILA offcl indicted 6-7, 480F2
- Primary results, runoff set 6-13, 467C1
- Abortns rptd down 6-20, 743C3
- Riley wins gov runoff 6-27, 510D1
- Hilton Head pool accident electrocutes 4 6-27, 636F3
- Carter visits Columbia 9-22, 736A1
- Mellon Bank immunity case refused by US Sup Ct 10-10, 789F2
- Election results 11-7: cong 846A2, A3, 848C3, 852B2, G3; state 845G1, 847B1, 853B1, E3
- Inmate suits judicial-aid case refused by Sup Ct 11-13, 874C3

SOUTH China Sea
- China oil find rptd 5-6, 436E2
- Canada-Viet oil exploratn pact rptd 9-7, 687A1

SOUTH Dakota
- Legislature schedule rptd 14G3
- '67, '77 sales-tax rates rptd 1-5, 15F3
- State govt tax revenue table 1-9, 84E2
- Calif bars Banks extraditn 4-19, 327E1
- Primary results 6-6, 448G1
- Indians protest '73 Wounded Knee trials 7-18, 569C1
- Grasshopper invasn rptd 7-31, 654B3
- Election results 11-7: cong 845D1, 846G1, 848C3, 852C2, 855A1, C1; state 845G1, 847A1, E1, 853E3, 855B1, C1, 897B3
- Rapid City radio statn purchase rptd 11-16, 919D3
- GOP loses cong recount 12-19, 1008F1

SOUTHEAST—*See also state names*
- '77 living costs rptd 4-26, 349G1
- '70-77 Fortune 500 hq shift rptd 5-8, 326B1
- 1st ¼ pay hikes rptd 5-30, 429F1

SOUTHEAST Asia—*See ASIA; country names*

SOUTHERN Airways
- North Central Airlines merger set 7-13, 684D1

SOUTHERN Baptist Convention—*See under BAPTISTS*

SOUTHERN Bell Telephone Co.—*See AMERICAN Telephone & Telegraph*

SOUTHERN California, University of (USC) (Los Angeles)
- Naber wins Sullivan Award 2-7, 780F2
- Loses NCAA swimming title 3-26, 780A3
- Matthews in NFL draft 5-2, 336F3
- Edwards sets track marks, named AAU outdoor champ MVP 6-1—6-4, 6-8—6-10, 600A3, F3
- Wins NCAA outdoor track champ 6-1—6-4, 600F3
- Wins NCAA baseball title 6-8, 560F1
- Laffer Curve cited 7-3, 735G1

1979

SOUTH African Airways
- Rhodesia air svc rptd cut 2-18, 170D3

SOUTH Carolina
- MD abortn prosecutn ban voided by US Sup Ct 3-5, 185B1
- Greenville museum gets Wyeth works 3-22, 375B2
- Ft Jackson to gain training functn 3-29, 265E3
- Brascan-Woolworth takeover stayed 4-20, 304C2; delayed 5-25, bid dropped 5-29, 440F2
- Fla kidnap victim rescued 7-30, 604G3
- Parris I sgt convicted re assault 8-18, 868E3
- Army recruiting fraud probed 8-19, 649F2
- Hurricane David batters Charleston 9-4, 690G3
- '78 per capita income rptd 9-16, 746E2
- Life of Brian furor rptd, Thurmond role cited 10-24, 859C2
- Iranians protest in Charleston 11-9, 863C1
- Southn Railway fined 11-12, 868A2
- Greenville coll suspends Iranians 11-21, 898E2

Atomic Energy
- Ocenee (Seneca), H B Robinson (Hartsville) A-plants called unsafe 1-26, 90C3
- Ocenee A-plant safety studies urged 4-1, 245F1
- Oconee A-plants ordrd shut by NRC 4-27, 321G3
- H B Robinson A-plant pipe leaks rptd 5-2, 322B3
- A-dump cited 7-24, 561B3
- A-facilities protested 10-1, 742C3
- A-dump curb threatens cancer research 10-23, 806B3
- A-dump cutback ordrd 10-31, 851B2, 885G3-886A1

Politics & Government
- Legislature schedule rptd 5F3
- Ex-Rep Richards dies 2-21, 176E3
- DC voting rep amendmt rejectn rptd 3-19, 204B3
- Regulatory bds rptd segregated 4-9, 307A2
- Rep Jenrette denies drug role probe 8-8, 650B1
- Ex-Rep McMillan dies 9-2, 756A3
- Kennedy in Charleston 11-9, 962C1
- Reagan in Columbia 12-13, 982C2
- Thurmond, Edwards endorse Connally 12-27, 982F2

SOUTH Carolina, University of (Columbia)
- Sanford in NFL draft 5-3, 335G2
- Loses Hall of Fame Bowl 12-29, 1001B3

SOUTH China Sea
- US naval move cited 1-2, 3E1
- US Navy rescues boat people 7-23, 549E1; 7-27, 7-30, 575G1
- Refugee decline, rescues rptd 7-31—8-22, 625E3-626A2
- US patrols sight 7 boats 8-25—8-28, 154 rescued 9-3, 659G2

SOUTH Dakota
- Legislature schedule rptd 5F3
- Med malpractice arbitratn rptd 1-28, 139E3
- Gay couple attends Sioux Falls prom 5-3, 392C3
- Sioux awarded $100 mln re Black Hills 6-13, 464D3-465A1
- Sioux child custody case refused by Sup Ct 6-18, 499B2
- Black Hills A-protest held 7-7, 743C1
- Interior Dept seeks to protect primitive areas 9-7, 703C3
- '78 per capita income rptd 9-16, 746F1, E2
- Grain handlers strike cost estimated 9-25, 723A1
- Mail order finance chrg case refused by Sup Ct 10-1, 768B2
- Milwaukee Rd embargoes track 11-1—11-5, 867G2
- Sioux Black Hills compensatn case accepted by Sup Ct 12-10, 988F1

SOUTHEAST Asia—*See ASIA; country names*

SOUTHEASTERN Community College (Whiteville, S.C.)
- Right to bar disabled backed by Sup Ct 6-11, 478F1

SOUTHEASTERN Community College v. Davis
- Case decided by Sup Ct 6-11, 478F1

SOUTHERN Airways
- Carter OKs North Central merger 6-5, 465D3

SOUTHERN Baptist Convention—*See under BAPTISTS*

SOUTHERN Baptist Theological Seminary (Louisville, Ky.)
- Baptism rites mtg ends 3-31, 375C3

SOUTHERN Bell Telephone Co.—*See AMERICAN Telephone & Telegraph*

SOUTHERN California, University of (USC) (Los Angeles)
- Wins Rose Bowl 1-1, '78 rank rptd 1-2, 1-3, 8B2, G2
- Cancer study rpts job hostility 2-10, 139A3
- Forgn student enrollmt listed 167D3
- Barry in basketball HOF 4-30, 526F3
- Primary care MD study rptd 6-14, 570G3
- Robinson in NBA draft 6-25, 507B3
- Hufstedler named Educ secy 10-30, 829A2
- White wins Heisman Trophy 12-3, 1001D2

1980

SOUTHAM Inc.
- Winnipeg Tribune closing spurs Thomson deals 8-27, 668A3

SOUTH Bend—*See INDIANA*

SOUTH Carolina
- Blizzards hit, 2 killed 3-1—3-2, 292B2
- Stevens, union come to terms 10-19, 805C1-D2
- Deering Milliken '56 labor dispute setld 12-3, workers OK 12-14, 956D2

Atomic Energy
- Ala A-dump planned 1-16, 54D1
- Carter outlines A-waste storage plan, Barnwell site studied; Wiley to head advisory panel 2-12, 128B1, D1
- Babcock plant review ordrd 3-4, 169F2

Crime & Civil Disorders
- Waterfront racketeers sentenced 1-11, 64B2
- Abscam probe revealed, Jenrette linked 2-2, 2-3, 81A2
- Jenrette indicted in Abscam probe 6-13, 454C1; wins primary runoff 6-24, 496F1
- 2 Cuban refugees hijack Delta jet 9-17, Havana returns 9-18, 704B1, B2
- Jenrette convicted for Abscam, US House expulsn hearings open 10-7, 782D3; resigns from House 12-10, 962E1

Energy—*See also 'Atomic Energy' above*
- State of State message 1-16, 483E3

Politics & Government—*See also other appropriate subheads in this section*
- Legislature schedule rptd 18F1
- State of State message 1-16, 483E3
- US suggests reapportionmt 2-14, 185A2
- US files reapportionmt suit 4-18, 349A2
- Jenrette wins runoff 6-24, 496F1
- Election results 11-4; cong 840C3, 844B2, 845A3, 846A2, 850D1; state 845D3
- Jenrette resigns from House 12-10, 962E1
- Edwards named Energy secy 12-22, 979G2, F3

Presidential Election (& Transition)
- Reagan in Charleston 1-9, 13D2
- Connally in Spartanburg 1-11, 91F3
- Reagan to enter GOP debate 1-30, 91G2
- Reagan in Greenville, assails Bush on gun control 2-6, 128G2
- Connally sponsors natl telethon 2-14, fund shortage rptd 2-20, 129D1, E1
- Reagan wins primary 3-8, 183E3
- Bush kicks off campaign 9-1, 780B3
- Carter tours 10-31, 841B1
- Election results 11-4, 838D1, 839B2, F3

SOUTH Carolina, University of (Columbia)
- Rogers wins Heisman Trophy 12-1, 999D2
- Loses Gator Bowl 12-30, 999E3

SOUTH China Sea
- USSR naval squadron entry rptd 2-5, 84E2

SOUTH Dakota
- DES in cattle rptd 4-24, 358F1
- State sales preference upheld by Sup Ct 6-19, 554F2
- Drought damage rptd 6-23—8-15, 616B2
- Sioux Falls schls religion case refused by Sup Ct 11-10, 868G1

Indian Issues
- Indian activist sentenced 1-23, 349E1
- Sioux Black Hills compensatn upheld by Sup Ct 6-30, 511B1
- Ogala Sioux seek Black Hills compensatn 7-18, 560F1-B2; suit dismissed 9-11, 704C2

Politics & Government—*See also other appropriate subheads in this section*
- Legislature schedule rptd 18F1
- Abscam probe revealed, Pressler rejects offers 2-3, 82A1, E1
- Primary results 6-3, 423F2, 424C1, 439B3
- McGovern backs open conv 8-11, 610B1
- Reagan tours farm area, pledges price supports 10-14, 780B1
- Election results 11-4: pres 838A1, 839A1, F3; cong 837D2, 840C3, 844B2, 845A2, 851E2; state 845E3, 847G2, D3
- '80 census rptd, reapportmt seen 12-31, 983G1

SOUTHEAST Asia—*See ASIA--See also country, organization names; also related headings*

SOUTHERN California, University of (USC) (Los Angeles)
- Wins Rose Bowl 1-1, '79 rank rptd 1-2, 23B1, D1
- Transcript scandal rptd, Pac-10 launches probe 3-18, 469C2, G2
- 3 in NFL draft 4-29, 336E3-G3
- Zumberge named pres 5-21, 471A1
- 3d in NCAA tennis 5-22, Van't Hof wins singles title 5-26, 607C1
- Wins AIAW tennis team title 6-7, 2 win doubles title 6-11, 607D1
- Pac-10 punishes in transcript scandal 8-11, 875D1, F1
- Faulty athletic admissns revealed 10-13, coaches comment 10-15, 10-29, 875C2
- Moore's son kills self 10-15, 890A2

1976

SOUTHERN California Edison Co.
Utah project dropped 4-14, 284C2
SOUTHERN Christian Leadership Conference (SCLC)
Cited in FBI Cointelpro papers 4-5, 248C2
Carter gets Abernathy endorsemt 4-13, 261D2
New King death probe asked 4-29, 345A1
FBI '62 probe cited 5-5, 344B1
SOUTHERN Governors Conference—*See GOVERNORS, U.S.*
SOUTHERN Independent School Association
Vs pvt schl desegregatn 1-5, 263D2
SOUTHERN Natural Resources Inc. Offshore Co.
SEC lists paymts 5-12, 728D2
SOUTHERN Overseas Corp.
Arab boycott rpt released 10-18, 786B1
SOUTHERN Railway Co.
Conrail labor talks fail 3-23, 235E2
SOUTHERN Yemen—*See YEMEN, People's Democratic Republic of*
SOUTH Korea—*See KOREA (South)*
SOUTH Loop National Bank (Houston)
Chartered 3-3, 167C2
SOUTH Pacific Forum (Australia, Cook Islands, Fiji, Nauru, New Zealand, Niue Island, Papua New Guinea, Tonga, Western Samoa)
Mtg backs A-free zone, US presence 3-8—3-9, 179A2
SOUTH Texas State Bank (Houston)
Declared insolvent 3-3, 167C2
SOUTH Vietnam—*See VIETNAM (South)*
SOUTH-West Africa—*See 'Namibia' under SOUTH Africa*
SOUTHWESTERN Bell Telephone Co.—*See AMERICAN Telephone & Telegraph*
SOUVATTHANA, Col.
Anti-govt group formed 4-21, 350F1
SOVIET Jewry, National Conference on
Scores Sovt UN missn incident 4-2, 259G3
SOVIET Union—*See UNION of Soviet Socialist Republics*
SOWINSKI, Rose Marie
Killed 3-15, 260A1
SOYBEANS
EC sets milk-substitute plan 3-6, OKs revisn 4-14, 276F2
US exports rptd down 3-26, 230F1
US sales to USSR rptd 7-2, 7-6, 540A2
New support-rate set 10-13, 787G3
SPACE & Space Flight—*See ASTRONAUTICS*
SPAGGIARI, Albert
Arrested 10-27, 876G3
SPAHIU, Xhafer
Albania industry, mines min 10-14, 949G1

1977

SOUTHERN Christian Leadership Conference (SCLC)
King suit dismissed 1-31, 77D2
Abernathy loses US House race 3-15, 192B1
Carter scored at 20th anniv mtg 8-18, 702A2
Lowery at black ldrs mtg 8-29, 702E1
Westinghouse settlmt cited 12-26, 1003B3
SOUTHERN Co.
Ala Power pensn credit for mil svc backed 6-6, 478A3
Westinghouse, Ala Power settle 9-21, 895C2
SOUTHERN Concrete Co.
Sup Ct bars US Steel case review 2-22, 149B3
SOUTHERN Illinois University (Carbondale)
Nathanson denied USSR visa 10-3, 766C2
Hartwick wins NCAA soccer title 12-4, 1020E3
SOUTHERN Newspaper Publishers Association
Tarver named AP chrmn 1-18, 140E2
SOUTHERN Pacific Co.
Calif land holdings breakup asked 8-22, 703G2
SOUTHERN Peru Copper Corp.
Toquepala miners strike 8-2, 673D2
SOUTHERN Railway Co.
Claytor named Navy secy 1-19, 52G3; confrmd 2-11, 148D3
SOUTHERN States—*See SUNBELT States*
SOUTH Korea—*See KOREA (South)*
SOUTH Korean National Airline
Airbus use cited 5-24, 441F2
SOUTH Moluccan Issue—*See under INDONESIA*
SOUTH Pacific Forum (Australia, Cook Islands, Fiji, Nauru, New Zealand, Niue Island, Papau New Guinea, Tonga, Western Samoa)
NZ to set 200-mi fishing zone 9-7, 729B3
SOUTH Pole—*See ANTARCTIC Regions*
SOUTH Vietnam—*See VIETNAM*
SOUTH-West Africa—*See SOUTH Africa—Namibia*
SOUTHWEST Airlines
Braniff, Tex Intl indicted 8-16, 629C3
SOUTHWESTERN Bell Telephone Co.—*See AMERICAN Telephone & Telegraph Co.*
SOUTHWORTH, Warren
Rpts on KY nightclub blaze 6-10, 740A1
SOUTH Yemen—*See YEMEN, People's Democratic Republic of*
SOUZA, Flora M.
Health care fraud chrgd 3-8, 235B3
SOVFRACHT (USA) Inc.
USSR ownership cited 10-31, 949A2
SOVIET Bloc—*See COMMUNISM and Communist Countries*
SOVIET Union—*See UNION of Soviet Socialist Republics*
SOYBEANS
Carter proposes loan rate 3-23, 214F1
Record Mar, 1st ¼ trading rptd 4-18, 301B2
Price fluctuatns rptd 4-22—4-29, 341F2
Hunts sued on futures trading 4-28, 341E1
Hunts countersue 5-4; ct lifts trading ban 5-6, backs comm curbs 6-7, 464B1
April WPI rise rptd 5-5, 383B3
Brazil-Iran trade pact 6-23, 524A2
Ala, Ga drought damage rptd 6-23, 7-28, 659F3
US export rise rptd 6-27, 502A2
Spain import costs raised 7-25, 582A2
Rhodesia subsidies rptd 8-25, 730E3
Hunt trading ruled illegal 9-28, 858E3
SPAAK, Antoinette
Elected FDF chrmn 6-15, 561D1
SPAAK, Paul-Henri (1899-1972)
Daughter elected FDF chrmn 6-15, 561D1
SPACE & Space Flight—*See ASTRONAUTICS*
SPAGGIARI, Albert
Escapes 3-10, 288E2

1978

SOUTHERN California Edison Co.
Refund case refused by Sup Ct 10-16, 789A2
SOUTHERN California Edison Co. v. Public Utility Commission of the State of California
Case refused by Sup Ct 10-16, 789A2
SOUTHERN Christian Leadership Conference (SCLC)
Lowery doubts FBI '64 memo on King conspiracy 5-29, 410D3
Lowery scores Carter 12-4, 936D3
SOUTHERN Co., The
'76 tax nonpaymt rptd 1-27, 65G2
SOUTHERN Methodist University (Dallas, Tex.)
Meadows dies 6-10, 540C3
SOUTHERN Missouri State University (Springfield)
Loses NAIA baseball title 6-1, 560A2
SOUTHERN Motor Carriers Association v. ICC
Case refused by Sup Ct 10-10, 789D3
SOUTHERN Motor Carriers Rate Conference
ICC voids freight-rate hike 11-27, 1007E2
SOUTHERN Pacific Co.
Chessie, Seaboard set rail merger 11-16, 897C1
SOUTHERN Pacific Transportation Co.
ICC fines in freight-car shortage 7-3, 569B2
ICC reduces fine 8-11, 643F2
SOUTHERN Peru Copper Corp.
Miners strike 8-4; shipmts suspended 8-17, govt declares emergency 8-22, 669B1
SOUTHERN Railway System
Va derailmt kills 6 12-3, 972D1
SOUTHERN Sun Hotels Corp.
Spinks-Ali rematch plan protested 3-8, site chngd 3-9, 212E1
Spinks-Ali US rematch signed 4-11, 378F3
SOUTHERN University (Baton Rouge, La.)
Sanders in NBA draft 6-9, 457G3
SOUTH Korea—*See KOREA (South)*
SOUTHLAND Royalty Co.
Natural gas diversn curbed by Sup Ct 5-31, 430F3-431D1
SOUTH Moluccan Issue—*See under INDONESIA*
SOUTH Pacific Forum (Australia, Cook Islands, Fiji, Nauru, New Zealand, Niue Island, Papua New Guinea, Tonga, Western Somoa)
NZ, Japan settle fishing dispute 5-23, 498C1
SOUTH Park Independent School District v. U.S.
Case declined by Sup Ct 12-4, 959A2
SOUTH Vietnam—*See VIETNAM*
SOUTHWEST—*See also state names*
Rainstorm, floods hit 3-3—3-5; drought declared over 3-5, 207B2, D2
Justice Dept backs oil, gas cos' coal reserves lid 5-15, 471D2
City populatn gains rptd 12-6, 942C3
SOUTH-West Africa—*See SOUTH Africa—Namibia*
SOUTHWESTERN Bell Telephone Co.—*See AMERICAN Telephone & Telegraph*
SOUTHWIRE Co.
Sued re price fixing 9-21, 769C1
SOUTH Yemen—*See YEMEN, People's Democratic Republic of*
SOUTTER, Michel
Faces of Love released 7-7, 970C1
SOVIET Bloc—*See country names; COMECON, COMMUNISM, WARSAW Pact*
SOVIET Union—*See UNION of Soviet Socialist Republics*
SOYBEANS
US pesticide sales curbed 2-15, 16B3
Paraguay '77 output up 2-17, 292E3
USSR '78 orders rptd 3-2, 151G2
Farm aid, set-aside paymts clear Sen 3-21, 218G2
Carter proposes loan rate hike 3-29, 219D2
E Ger-Brazil deal rptd 7-13, 649D1
CBCP pesticide curb asked 9-19, 719D2
SOYUZ (Soviet spacecraft series)—*See ASTRONAUTICS—Manned Flight*
SPACE & Space Flights—*See ASTRONAUTICS*
SPAETH, Lothar
Named W Ger state premr 8-16, 725E3

1979

SOUTHERN Christian Leadership Conference (SCLC)
Williams ousted as exec dir 4-10, 283F1
Lowery leads Ala marches 6-9, 7-20, 865F3, 869D3
Lowery on Young UN resignatn 8-15, asks black-Jewish mtg with Carter 8-16, 606G1, A2
Meets PLO, Israeli, US Jewish ldrs; backs PLO 8-21, 623F3-624D1
NAACP backs PLO contacts 9-11, 677G1
Levison dies 9-12, 756G2
Ldrs visit Lebanon 9-18—9-20; Israel rebuffs visit 9-20, 694F1, E2
Leb visit ends, Arafat invited to US 9-21, 763C2
Arafat invitation withdrawn 10-11, 780F3
Jordan vs support for PLO 10-14, 780E2
SOUTHERN Co.
Alabama Power Co.
Uranium supply suit setlmt cited 5-15, 366B2
SOUTHERN Exposure (play)
Opens 2-27, 292A3
SOUTHERN Illinois University (Edwardsville)
Wins NCAA soccer title 12-9, 1004G1-A2
SOUTHERN Natural Resources Inc.
Mex natural gas purchased 10-18, 814F3
SOUTHERN Pacific Co.
Ticor Corp purchase set 3-28, 283D1
ITT offers long-distance phone svc 4-23, 350F3
Southern Pacific Transportation Co.
Union dues case refused by Sup Ct 1-8, 14F3
SOUTHERN Pacific Transportation Co. v. Burns
Case refused by Sup Ct 1-8, 14F3
SOUTHERN Peru Copper Co.
Miners strike 3-13—3-30, 255D2, F2
SOUTHERN Railway Co.
N&W merger talks ended 10-19, 868A2
Fined $1.9 mln 11-12, 868F1-A2
SOUTHERN Railway Co. v. Seaboard Allied Milling Corp.
Case decided by Sup Ct 6-11, 478E3
SOUTHERN Railway System
Seaboard cleared of trust chrgs 2-22, 206A1
SOUTHERN Regional Council
Rpts Southn bds segregated 4-9, 307F1-A2
All-white club judicial membership surveyed 9-19, 901E2
SOUTHERN Studies, Institute for (Chapel Hill, N.C.)
Schl integratn study rptd 5-9, 650D1
SOUTH Florida Auto Auction
Miami pot ring rptd broken 5-1, 492G3
SOUTH Korea—*See KOREA (South)*
SOUTHLAND Royalty Co.
Gen Crude merger bid rejctd 3-28, 283A1
SOUTHPORT, N.C.—*See NORTH Carolina*
SOUTH Texas Project
Uranium supply suit setlmt cited 5-15, 366B2
SOUTH-West Africa—*See SOUTH Africa—Namibia*
SOUTHWEST Airlines
Braniff pays trust fine 2-23, 206D2
SOUTHWESTERN Bell Telephone—*See AMERICAN Telephone & Telegraph*
SOUTHWESTERN Life Corp.
Tenneco purchase set 12-11, 986A3
SOUTHWICK, Tom
On Kennedy Secret Svc protectn 9-20, 724A1
SOUTH Yemen—*See YEMEN, People's Democratic Republic of*
SOUVANNA Phouma
Rpts ex-aides detained, admits Thai exodus 3-24, 331C3
SOUVREMENNIK Theater
Norway, Sweden tour canceled 10-1, 775B1
SOVEREIGN State Capital Corp.
Smith convicted 5-7, sentncd 5-31, 442E2
SOVIET Bloc—*See COMMUNISM; country, organization names*
SOYBEANS
'78 record US harvest cited 9-21, 722E1
SOYUZ (Soviet spacecraft series)—*See ASTRONAUTICS—Manned Flight*
SPACE & Space Flights—*See ASTRONAUTICS*

1980

SOUTHERN California Edison Co.
Gould named chrmn 4-18, 456C2
SOUTHERN Christian Leadership Conference (SCLC)
Va ERA rally held 1-13, 54C3
Wrightsville (Ga) rallies held 4-12, 4-19, 333C1, D1
Abernathy, Williams endorse Reagan 10-16, 802B2
SOUTHERN Methodist University (Dallas, Tex.)
Zumberge named USC pres 5-21, 471B1
Loses Holiday Bowl 12-19, 999B3
SOUTHERN Mississippi, University of (Hattiesburg)
Wins Independence Bowl 12-13, 999A3
SOUTHERN Pacific Co.
Santa Fe merger set 5-15, 427A3
ICC OKs Rock I segment deal 6-10, 598E3
Santa Fe merger canceled 9-12, 745D2
SOUTHERN Poverty Law Center
Anti-KKK suit filed 11-4, 884G3-885A1
SOUTHERN Railway System
N&W merger sought 6-2, 427C2
Chessie-Seaboard merger oppositn ended 7-10, 745D3
N&W merger OKd by bd 7-22, 598F3
Hall replaces Crane as chief exec 9-29, 959C2
SOUTH Pacific Forum (Australia, Cook Islands, Fiji, Kiribati, Nauru, New Zealand, Niue Island, Papua New Guinea, Solomon Islands, Tonga, Tuvalu, Vanuatu, Western Samoa)
Island trade pact rptd signed 7-24, 576F2
SOUTH-West Africa—*See SOUTH Africa--Namibia*
SOUTHWEST Bank of St. Louis
Prime rate cut to 13% 5-28, 12% 6-9, 438B1, D1
SOUTHWESTERN Louisiana, University of (Lafayette)
Toney in NBA draft 6-10, 447F2
SOUTHWEST Legal Foundation
Powell gets 'Great Ldrs' award, refutes Sup Ct media image 5-1, 368G2
SOUTHWEST National Bank of Miami
Drug money link denied 6-5, 502E1
SOVERN, Michael I
Named Columbia U pres 1-7, 200C1
SOVIET Bloc—*See COMMUNISM*
SOVIET Union—*See UNION of Soviet Socialist Republics*
SOWELL, Thomas
Addresses black conservatives conf 12-14, 956A3
SOYBEANS
Futures trading suspended 1-6, 2C1
US Jan farm prices rptd down 1-31, 92F2
Ia grain elevator scandal rptd 2-25, 237F3
US crop 'diversn' paymt plan dropped, price rise cited 2-29, 169B1
US Mar farm price drops rptd 3-31, 263F3
USSR-Argentine 1st 1/4 trade rptd 4-15, 336G1
Sovt purchase of US soy meal in W Eur rptd 5-23, US scores 6-2, 431B1
US sales to W Ger, Dutch up 40% 5-23, 431D1
US drought damage rptd 6-23—8-15, 616C2
US July farm prices rptd 7-31, 575D1
US drought damage final rpt 9-7, 857A3
US grants Poland $670 mln credit 9-12, 710G2
US Sept farm prices rptd up 9-30, 741B2
Futures prices hit 3-year highs 10-28, 855D1
US Oct farm prices rptd 10-31, 883C1
SOYUZ (Soviet spacecraft series)—*See ASTRONAUTICS--Manned Flight*
SPACEK, Sissy
Heart Beat released 4-25, 416A3
SPACE Research Corp.
S Africa arms sales admitted 3-25, 278F1
Fined for S Africa arms sales 8-14, 618F2
SPACE & Space Flights—*See ASTRONAUTICS*
SPADACCINI, Teodoro
Accused re Moro affair 1-2, 20G2
SPAHIU, Xhafer
Replaced as Albania industry min 5-2, 356E2

SPAIN

1976

SPAIN—*See also IEA, OECD*
5 Armada ships found 1-11, 124C3
Iranian jet crashes 5-9, 404B3
Oil tanker explodes 5-12, 384C1
Woman acquitted of adultery 10-9, 909A3
Pedro Sanjuan dies 10-18, 970B3
Adultery law protested 11-16; 2 women sentncd 11-24, 909F2

1977

SPAIN—*See also ESA, IDB, IEA, OECD*
Freighter, US Navy launch collide 1-17, 104B3
Italian hijacks jet 3-14—3-16, 224A3
Aleixandre wins Nobel 10-6, 951F2
Contraceptive, adultery reforms set 10-25, 867B1

1978

SPAIN—*See also COUNCIL of Europe, GATT, IDB, IEA, OECD*
A-bomb capability seen unlikely before '84 1-26, 61C2
Adultery penalties ended 2-2, 136A3; law published 5-30, 576B3
Contraceptives sale, ad bill OKd 4-26; 70% use rptd 6-23, 576F2
Abortn debate set, 310,000 illegal abortns rptd 4-26, 576A3
Gas truck blast kills 150 7-11, 636D1
Contraceptive law enacted 10-12, 822B2

1979

SPAIN—*See also COUNCIL of Europe, GATT, IDB, IEA, OECD*
17th century galleon rptd found off DR 1-1, 24E1
Greek oil tanker spill rptd 1-1, 201A1
Valdepenas flood kills 24 7-2, 638G3
Saragossa hotel fire kills 80 7-13, 572F2
Abortionist, accomplices sentncd 12-11, 952D2

Atomic Energy & Safeguards
A-plant protests rptd 3-12, 192A2
A-oversight plans, protests rptd 4-9, 276D2
A-security cncl, 3 new plants planned 5-16; parlt debate rptd 5-17, 428C1

1980

SPAIN—*See also COUNCIL of Europe, CSCE, GATT, IDB, IEA, OECD*
Ortuella school blast kills 64 10-23, 948F2-A3

Atomic Energy & Safeguards
$1.4 bln set for dvpt 1-8, 22B2
OECD rpts A-plant cancellatns 7-8, 509A3
A-plant permit rptd issued, A-power role downscaled 12-3, 923E2, A3

1976

Canary Islands—*See CANARY Islands*

Church Developments

Priest leads amnesty march 1-1, arrested 1-7, 12B1
Workers group members arrested 1-15, 54G2
Priest asks king set amnesty 2-17, 144C2
Workers slain in Vitoria church 3-3, priests score 3-5, 206G3
Priests back worker unionizatn 3-28, 269D2
Queen attends Jewish svc 5-28, 459A3
Basque bishops score torture, violence 6-6, 501E2
Suarez, Opus Dei link cited 7-6, 500B3, F3, 501B1
King renounces bishop veto power 7-16, 541F1
Archbp asks broad amnesty 7-25, 753B3
Vatican Concordat revised 7-28, 753D3
US marriage annulmts rptd 10-15, 909D3

Economy & Labor (domestic)—*See also 'Unrest' below*

Coalitns seek bargaining rights 1-14, 54E2
Constructn workers sign pact 1-15, 54C3
Peseta revalued 2-9, 422B3
Cabt OKs min wage rise 3-18; equal pay, pensn reform 4-6, 269A2, B2
Church backs worker unionizatn 3-28, 269D2
UGT holds cong 4-15—4-18, 314C1
Parlt OKs labor guarantees 4-22, 314F1
Cabt backs unionizatn 5-7, 422B1
Anti-inflatn rally smashed 6-22, 501G1
May COL rptd 6-29, annual inflatn rate 7-2, 541A3
Arias dismissed 7-1, Suarez replaces 7-3, 500C3, 501B1
Martin Villa sworn interior min; Carriles, finance min 7-8, 523E2
Unemploymt hits 5.5% 7-29, 929E1
'77 electn plan unveiled 9-10; unions reject 9-15, 752D3-G3
Basque, Catalan data cited 774G3
Austerity program set 10-8, scored 10-10, 928C3
OECD incomes rpt cites 10-12, 964C2
Sept living cost up 1.8% 10-29, 929F1
Drought cattle, grain loss rptd 12-31, 977D3

Foreign Economic Developments

SDR rate rptd 1-15, 14B3
French Mirage purchase cited 1-16, 36C2
Brazil bauxite operatn begun 1-16, 98G2
EC lifts ban on trade talks 1-20, 84D3
Swiss arms embargo lifted 1-21, '75 sales data rptd 1-22, 104D1
Phosphate stake sold to Morocco 2-9, 107C3
At intl econ conf 2-11—2-20, 148B1
IMF oil loans rptd 2-23, 4-1, 339G3, 340B2
Giron vs EC entry 3-21, 269G1
US bars shoe import curb 4-16, 322C1
IDB entry set 6-3, 465D3
IMF grants loan 6-16, intl loan rptd sought 6-23, 501F2
US OKs reactor sale 6-21, 739B2
$1 bln intl loan confrmd 7-13, 541B3
Suarez reaffirms EC entry bid 7-13, 541C3
$1 bln intl loan signed 8-9, 929G1
Austerity measures set 10-8, 928C3
Lockheed paymts rptd 10-15—11-8, 909D1
King opens Ford plant 10-25, 929A2
Canada signs tax pact, trade data rptd 11-23, 962G3
'76 paymts deficit, debt forecast 12-1, 929F1

Foreign Relations (misc.)

Mex '75 overture rptd 1-8; terms for ties set 1-10, 75E2
France denies Algeria spy chrg 1-9, links spies to anti-Basque unit 1-11, Ortiz chrg rptd 1-13, 45E2, D3
European socialists meet 1-18—1-19, 48A3; 3-13—3-14, 222F3
Equatorial Guinea exiles rptd 1-24, 62A2
Southn socialists meet 1-24—1-25, 120B1, G1
Emb bombed in Colombia 1-30, 118E1
Areilza sees Portugal min 2-12, 143C1
OKs UN Medit pollutn pact 2-16, 126C3
Angola MPLA recognized 2-25, 163D1
Argentina asks Lopez Rega extraditn 3-8, 211G3
UMD trial includes Portugal mil evidence 3-8—3-9, 314F2
Reps at Czech CP Cong 4-12—4-16, 289G1
W Eur labor reps at UGT cong 4-15—4-18, 314F1
W Ger head cites CP 4-15, 503D1
Gonzalez at intl soc dems mtg 5-23—5-25, 449B3
Queen cancels religious freedom speech 5-28, 459A3
Royal couple visits DR 5-31—6-1, 459B2
Reaffirms EEC, NATO entry bids 6-3, 459F2

1977

Basques—*See 'Government' and 'Unrest' below*

Canary Islands—*See CANARY Islands*

Church Developments

Jubany, priests back amnesty 1-1, 1-2, 22F2
King, Queen see Pope 2-10, 242D3
Fascist groups oppose 3-2, 307G2
Basque bishops back protesters 3-11, 331A2

Economy & Labor (domestic)—*See also 'Unrest' below*

Dec '75-76 inflatn rate rptd 2-7, 87B2
Govt sets package, scored 2-22, 307A3
Strikes allowed 3-9, union organizing OKd 3-30, 286D1, E1
Gonzalez sets PSOE goals 6-23, 506G3-507A1
Econ program set 7-12, new dep premr cited 7-13, 545G2
Price controls decreed 7-19; austerity progrm set 7-24; fuel, coffee prices raised 7-25, 582F1
Tax study shows poor pay most 8-21, 866F3
Econ, tax plan OKd by govt, oppositn 10-8—10-9; worker, business reactn 10-12—11-4; pact signed 10-25, 866C3-867E1
60s agitators amnestied 10-14, 826E1
30% inflatn, 6% jobless rate rptd 10-25, 866E3

Foreign Relations (misc.)—*See also 'Monetary, Trade & Aid' below*

UN Assemb member; de Castro on World Ct 4B1-F1
Suarez cancels Mideast trip 1-26, sends Oreja 1-27, 101D3
Sovt-bloc ties renewed 1-27, 2-9, refugee return in questn 2-14, 242C2
Socialist rep at Israel Labor Party conv 2-22, 135F1
Rightists arrested 2-22, 3-5, 307A2, F2
Bulgaria exiles ask CP support 2-23, 314C2
Eurocommunists meet in Madrid 3-2—3-3, 242E3
Argentine seized in student murder 3-2, 307F2
Fascist groups oppose USSR 3-2, 307G2
Mexico ties renewed 3-28, 242A3
Sahara captured arms displayed 3-28, 337B2
Czechs hold rptr 4-2—4-3, 314B3
Mex amb apptmt stirs controversy 4-7—5-11, 529G1
Zaire ousts newsmen 5-6, 394G1
Sahara role scored 5-21, 440E3
Sahara mine town raided, natls leave 6-2—6-3, 513G2
Gonzalez backs NATO entry 6-23, 507A1
USSR scores Eurocommunism 6-23; CP, Carrillo respond 6-25, 6-27, 507F1

1978

Basques—*See 'Government' and 'Unrest' below*

Canary Islands—*See CANARY Islands*

Economy & Labor (domestic)

Cabt team replaced 2-24; austerity act reaffirmed 3-6, farm price hikes set 3-21; business, pol pressures cited 4-10, 394F2
Babcock receivership rptd; auto, steel losses forecast 3-10, 394F3
'77 inflatn 26.4%, jobless at 7½% 3-10, 394G3
Workers protest unemploymt 4-5, 258F2
Custom workers job slowdown 6-23, 532F3
Const draft sets labor rights, econ initiatives 7-27, 706C1
Steel, shipbldg indus restructured 8-29, 822F1
Jobless rate rptd up 10-25, 822D1
Inflatn at 17% annual rate 10-25, 822D1
Ford productn problems cited re UK strike 11-22, 923D2
Stock mkt rptd down 12-25, 1001C2

European Community Relations

EC imposes steel dumping levies 1-23, 80B2
EC negotiator named 2-10; Spain entry review delayed 2-14; Jenkins visits 4-27—4-28, 395C1
EC seeks steel export agrmt 3-2, 158C2
French pres backs entry, cites problems 6-29, 649D1-A2
UK oppositn ldr asks entry 10-21, 821F2
Greek entry terms set 12-21, 1017G3

Foreign Relations (misc.)—*See also 'European Community' above, 'Monetary, Trade, Aid & Investment' below*

King in Libya 1-21, 136G1
France, W Ger OK ESA rocket launcher 2-6—2-7, 122B1
Italy joint mil exercise rptd 2-11, 133F2
Book chrgs Eurocommunists aided Stalin purges 2-24, 136D2
Playwright flees to France 2-27, 250A2
Panama replaces amb 3-1, 211E2
Algeria blames Spain for Canary unrest, Sahara dispute cited 4-20, 576E3
Eur conservative group formed 4-24, 424D3
ESA communicatns satellite launched 5-12, 384D3
Italy abortn reform enacted 5-18, 378G1
Turkish amb's wife, 2 others slain 6-2, 476D3
King in Iran 6-14—6-15, China 6-16—6-19, 576A2
French pres visits 6-28—7-1, Basques protest 6-30, 649D1-C2
ETA ex-ldr ambushed in France, wife killed 7-3, 537E2
France access cut by Basque protests 7-12, 576D1
Suarez visits Venez, Cuba 9-7—9-10, 821D3

1979

Dockworkers boycott A-cargo 5-17, 390G2
A-protests staged 6-2—6-3, 416G1
A-protester killed 6-3, Basques riot 6-5, 428G1-A2
Lemoniz A-plant bombed 6-13, 504E3
A-security cncl, plant constructn OKd by parlt 7-30, 585C2
2 A-plant permits issued 8-25; mayors protest, 25,000 stage march 8-28—9-1, 670A3, D3
A-factory bombed 11-13, 875A3

Basques—*See 'Government' and 'Unrest' below*

Canary Islands—*See CANARY Islands*

Economy & Labor

RR, auto, other strikes 1-11—1-18, 61E1
Strikes continue, govt wage ceiling holds 1-23—1-24, 100C3
Madrid metal workers win 16% raise 2-7; other workers strike 2-20—3-8, 192E1
Govt wins electn 3-1, 191A3, C3
Dockworkers boycott A-cargo 5-17, 390G2
GM plant employmt estimated 6-6, 428B2
Westn wage rates compared 9-19, 697D3
Trade unions rally, issue demands 10-15, 795C1

Energy—*See also 'Atomic' above*

Iran oil cutoff impact assessed 2-20, 126G2
Parlt debate on conservatn, pricing, other measures rptd 5-17, 428C1
Gas price rptd at $2.40 per gal 5-19, 397A1
Oil products price hiked 7-3, 546C1
Libya oil imports rptd 7-4, 546F1
Natural gas finds rptd; '79 imports, consumptn seen 7-10, 546F1
Parlt OKs '77-87 plan; oil imports, use rptd 7-30, 585C2

Foreign Relations (misc.)—*See also 'Monetary' and 'UN' below*

Oreja, French in talks on ETA 1-12; ldr wounded 1-13, 61D1
ETA, IRA cooperatn rptd 1-28, 100B3
France arrests 23 Basques, bars future asylum 1-30, 100B3
France deportatn of Basques protested 2-5, 192B1
French execs kidnaped 2-5—3-1, 192C1
China Viet invasn scored by CP 2-19, 122A3
Belgium tourists hurt in bomb blast 6-30, 504G3
Paris-Madrid train attacked 7-2, 505C1
Equatorial Guinea ties set 8-5, 614B1
Suarez in Brazil 8-6—8-8, Ecuador 8-9—8-13, DR 8-14, 613D2, 654F1-G2
Nazi fugitive eluded '70 capture 8-8, 617B1
Basques protest French refugee status 8-30, 670G3
Libyans occupy Madrid Emb 9-3, 688F2
Arafat, PLO delegatn visit 9-13—9-15, 694C3
Israel non-recognitn explained 9-14, 695C1
Suarez delays Latin trip 9-25, 754C2
Suarez in France; EC entry, Basque issue discussed 11-26—11-27, 952D1
Portugal pol party aid rptd 12-2, 917B1

1980

Canary Islands—*See CANARY Islands*

Economy & Labor

Fuel price hikes spark protests 1-7, govt vs demands, sets energy conservatn 1-8, 22F1
INI '79 losses rptd 2-21, mandatory rescues overturned 2-29, 2-21, 196E2-C3
'79 jobless rate soars, govt benefits rptd 3-5, 196F1-A2
Coca-Cola workers strike 4-25, consumers boycott 5-1, 463E3
Suarez survives censure motion 5-30, 431C2, G2
SEAT '79, 1st 1/4 data rptd 6-4, 467D3
Bilbao metalworkers disrupt Basque parlt 6-26, 567C1
Labor costs rptd 8-12, 698E1
Andalusia hunger strike protests unemployment 8-14—8-19, 653F1
Andalusia jobs aid pledged, hunger strike ends 8-22, 673C2
Cordoba gen strike threatened 8-30, jobless workers barricade roads 8-31, 673E2
Suarez shuffles Cabt 9-8, 690B2
Suarez sets econ plan, Villa pledges devolutn 9-17, 711E3
'81 budget submitted, econ data rptd 9-30, 793E2
Police threaten strike over Basque policy 10-21, 832G1
Basque munic strike 12-9, 968C2

Energy—*See also 'Atomic' above*

Fuel price hikes spark protests 1-7; govt vs demands, sets conservatn 1-8, 22F1
Mex '80 oil imports seen 1-15, 60B2
N Sea oil platform capsizes 3-27, 256F1
Petroleum subsidy cut set 9-30, 793A3

Foreign Relations (misc.)—*See also 'Monetary' below*

Italy terrorist, Basque links seen 1-2, 20F2
CP scores USSR re Afghanistan 1-6, 2G2
Eurocommunism seen hurt by French CP pro-Sovt stand 1-7, 1-11, 57A3
Sakharov exile scored by CP 1-24, 86A1
Equatorial Guinea seeks closer ties 1-28, 119D1
Guatemalan emb seized, amb flees 1-31; ties severed 2-1, 98B2, F2
El Salvador emb seized, amb held 2-5, 96G3
Gibraltar talks, EC entry linked 2-6, 133C1
Emb in Peru occupied by strikers 2-8, amb heads talks 2-11, 234G3
El Salvador amb freed 2-12, demands met 2-17, emb vacated 2-18, 149C1
Sovt arrested as spy 2-14, another leaves for Moscow 2-16, 141A3
Olympic com rejcts Moscow boycott 3-22, 259C3
Europn CP parley boycott rptd 4-2, 254F3
Gibraltar links set by UK accord 4-10, 274G2
Iran asks neutrality on US hostages 4-12, 282F1

1976

US Jews ask Israel ties 6-3, 459A3
King visits UN hqs 6-4, 459B3
Eur, Latin leftists at PSP cong 6-5—6-6, 459B1
Exiled CP ldr at E, W Eur CP conf 6-29—6-30, 461C2
Libya hijacker surrenders on Majorca 7-6, 539A2 ★
Suarez in France 7-13, 541C3
Bomb explodes at Dutch emb 7-20, 541D2
CP meets in Rome 7-28—7-31, mil bases opposed, French, Ital ties cited 7-31, 753F1
W Ger aid to right rptd 7-30, 753E1
Portugal PIDE agents flee to 733A2
Sovts step up CP, other contacts 8-23, 753A2
IAEA dir cites 9-21, 760F3
ETA press conf in France protested 10-6, 774B3
Argentina to ask Lopez Rega extraditn 10-25, 997F1
Cuba airline office bombed 11-7, 844A3
Argentina detains newsman 11-7, 997A1
NATO tour rptd 11-14, 880E1
Socialist conv OKd 11-27, 908E3
Venez pres visits 11-28, 930A1
Gonzalez addresses Soclst Intl 11-28, 935D3
NATO observer status asked 12-7, 933A2

Government & Politics—*See also 'Unrest' and other appropriate subheads in this section*
Oppositn groups seek legitimacy 1-14, 54D2
Electns postponed 1-15, 54A3
Listed as 'partly free' 1-19, 20D3
Ex-Soclst ldr returns, ex-CP ldr asks entry 1-22, 77F1
Juan Carlos confrms electn delay 1-27, 77D1
Mild reforms set, reactn 1-28—1-29, 143G3
Christian Dems meet 1-29, ask elected constituent assemb 1-31—2-1, 144E1, F1
Cabt OKs indoor 'legal' mtgs 2-6, 144G1
King visits Catalonia 2-16—2-18, 144B2
King warns Cncl re reforms 3-4, Cabt OKs penal reform 3-18, 269E1
Cabt OKs more pol freedom 3-5, 207B2
Rightists oppose pol reforms 3-21, 269G1
2 key mil cmdrs named 3-28, 314B3
Oppositn groups merge, ldrs jailed 3-29—4-7, 268F3 ★
Petitns ask new Catalonia mayors, cncls 4-3, 269G2
Legis process speeded 4-24; reformer-rightist struggle rptd 4-27, 314A2
Cabt proposes bicameral legis 5-7, 422B1
Rightists score reformers 5-13, 422D1
Franco rally blocked 5-17, holidays chngd 5-19, 422F1
Cortes eases pol mtg curbs 5-25, 421F3-422B1
Fraga asks pol pacts 6-2, mtgs with oppositn rptd 6-4, 459D1
PSP cong; Morodo scores reforms 6-5—6-6, 459A1
Oppositn ldrs vs CP ban 6-8, 459E3
Cortes OKs pol parties, delays penal reform 6-9, 458B3
Don Juan backs king 6-14, 459E1
Rpt UMD members transferred 6-25, 501F1
Poll: 43% for legalizatn of all parties 6-30, 501D1
Arias fired 7-1, Suarez named premr, reactn 7-3, 500A3
Rpt Reformists, oppositn ldrs refuse Cabt posts 7-6, 523A2
New Cabt sworn, opposition rptd 7-8, king addresses 7-9, 523G1
Cortes OKs penal reform 7-14, 541C1
Cabt seeks pol amnesty, '77 electns, other reforms 7-17; oppositn ldrs laud 7-18, 540E3
Govt shuns Civil War anniv 7-18, 541C2
CP holds pub mtg 7-28—7-31, 753E1
Amnesty decreed 8-4, limits scored; 3 profs reinstated 8-7; 170 rptd freed, Basque, CP releases noted 8-20; exile returns OKd 8-26, 753B2
Suarez sees Gonzalez on reforms 8-11; sees Tierno 9-5, mil chiefs 9-8, 752E3
Carrillo secret visits rptd 8-15, rpt passport denied 8-26, 753A3
Rpt most jailed CP members freed 8-30, 753G1
All CP prisoners rptd freed 8-30, 753A2
Rightists warn Suarez vs pol chng 8-31, 753B1
Reform bill, '77 electn plan set 9-10; CP, Dem Coordinatn, mil chiefs oppose 9-15, 9-19, 9-20, 752F2
Basque, Catalan self-rule demands increase 774E3-775C1
Catalan Day OKd 9-11, 774F3
Suarez replaces defns min 9-22, 753A1
Araluce stand re Basques rptd 10-4, 774E3
Rightists form Popular Alliance 10-9, 908G2
Rodriguez de Valcarcel dies 10-22, 1015E2
Pol reform bill passed, referendum set 11-18, 908A2
Rightists, Juan Carlos pay homage to Franco 11-20, 908F3-909A1
Castiella y Maiz dies 11-25, 970D1

1977

African island rule cited 506B3
Hungary, Rumania back CP 6-30, 7-5, 513F2
Sovt agent seized 7-2, expelled 7-4, 546A1
Sovt bloc on Eurocommunism 7-3—7-24, 590A3
USSR renews Carrillo attack, backs CP 7-6, 545C3
Leftists bomb French emb bldg 7-11—7-12, 546C1
PSOE ldr backs Argentine guerrillas 7-23, 595B3
Basque rebel detentn in France protested 8-18—8-24, vanishes after release 10-7, 826E2
Soclst ldr in Chile, sees rights improvemt 8-28—8-31, 743C2
Owen visits 9-6—9-7, asks Gibraltar border opening 9-7, 717D3
King in Venez, Central Amer 9-8—9-17, 804F3-805E1
Panama ldr visits re Canal 10-1—10-3, 792C2
UN pollutn conf ends, Medit pact reached 10-21, 876B2
W Ger asks more airport security 10-23, 868D3
France drops immigrant family bar plan 10-30, 1013D1
USSR bars Carrillo speech 11-3, 865G2
Gibraltar—*See GIBRALTAR*

Government & Politics—*See also 'Unrest' and other appropriate subheads in this section*
Carrillo sees oppositn 1-4, negotiatn com named 1-7, 22G2-A3
Castilian name law dropped, new decree set 1-10, 68G1
Suarez meets oppositn 1-11, 68G1
Vega promoted, Campano gets new post; mil budget hike OKd 1-15, 68C2
Basque concessns OKd 1-18—1-19; 2 prov govs quit 1-20, 68E1
Cabt mins back center-right coalitn 1-21, 68A2
Pol assn law reformed, mil role barred 2-8, 102D1
CP asks legal recognitn 2-11, issues candidates list 2-21; Sup Ct remands case 4-1, 285C3
Ibarruri asks to return 2-18, 285C3
10 parties legalized 2-18, 2-23; PSOE quits oppositn negotiating team 2-25, 285E3
Basque juntas restored 3-5, 331G1
Natl Movement dissolved 4-1, 285D2, G3
CP legalized 4-9; navy min quits 4-12, mil crisis resolved 4-13, 285C2
CP Central Com meets 4-14, 285B3
Army vs CP legalizatn 4-14, Alvarez Zalba fired 4-20, 306G3
June electns set 4-15, 306E3
Cortes members ask CP debate 4-18, 3 quit 4-19, 307C1
Arias to run for upper house 4-22, Suarez for lower 4-25, 331B1
Suarez-Fraga rivalry noted 4-26, 331D1
UCD wins parlt electns; King names 41 sens, parlt pres 6-15, 453A1-E2
Suarez to form new govt 6-17; sees UCD ldrs, rifts rptd 6-23—6-24, 506C3
Cortes Basques back autonomy 6-19, 507D1
King meets Catalan Socialists, vows more autonomy 6-21, 507B1
Paris exile govt dissolved 6-21, 507E1
PSOE claims 'victory', asks munic electns 6-23, 506E3
Old Cortes mandate ends 6-30; new Cortes opens, ldrs elected 7-13, 545C2
New Cabt named 7-4, sworn, allegiance oath revised 7-5, 545E1-C2
Basque, Catalan autonomy cited re new regional min 7-5, 545B2
Soclst vote cited re new econ progrm 7-13, 545B3
Socialist ex-mayor leaves hiding 7-17, 582F3
King addresses Cortes, asks new const; PSOE scores 7-22, 582B1
Final electn returns rptd 7-22, 582E1
'Basque freedom march' ends 8-28, 826F2
Catalonia Generalitat restored 9-29; Tarradellas sworn pres 10-24, 843A1
Catalonia, Catalan provs maps 843A2
Pol reforms signed by govt, oppositn 10-25, 866C3, 867A1
Basques get limited autonomy 12-31, 1017B3
Helsinki Agreement—*See EUROPE—Security and Cooperation*
Monetary, Trade & Aid Issues (including all foreign economic developments)
UK 200-mi fishing zone in effect 1-1, 21A1
De Broglie linked to '69 Matesa affair 1-5, 44A2
Andorra asks financial review 1-5, 47G3
Forgn investmt rules eased 1-25, 307F3
Oreja leaves for Arab talks 1-27, 101D3
IMF SDR defined 87G2
Sovt gold claim unresolved 2-9, 242E2
Capital smuggling from Spain, '76 tourism income rptd 2-14, 308A1
Cuba trade protocol signed 2-20, 242C3
Export, tourism promotn set 2-22, 307B3
US adopts fishing agrmt 3-3, 173D3
Liberia ship scrapped 3-10, 214E3
US bars shoe import curbs 4-1, 248E2, B3
Schlitz tax avoidance chrgd 4-7, 503G3

1978

WWII spying for Japan rptd 9-10—9-18, ex-forgn min denies 9-17, 744E3
UN Assemb member 713E3
DR names Perez y Perez amb 9-30, 774B2; apptmt rejected 11-9, 881B1
King in Mex, Peru, Argentina 11-17—11-30, 967G2
DR retires Perez y Perez 11-17, 989B3
Basque terrorist killed in France 12-21, 1022F1

Government & Politics—*See also other appropriate subheads in this section*
Freedom House lists as free 44E1
Secret police files ordrd destroyed 1-13, 136G2
Basque leftist party recognized 1-18, 135D3
CP chief refutes critical book 1-21, party ldrs rptd shaken 2-24, 136A2
Cabt shuffled 2-24, 394F2
Theater censorship ended 3-3, 250B2
Basques march on natl day 3-26, 250D1
CP cong; Carrillo reelected chief, 'Leninist' label dropped 4-19—4-23, 821C3
PSOE, PSP merge 4-30, 821B3
PSOE wins 2 Sen seats 5-18, 821B3
PSOE drops 'Marxist' label 5-22, 821D3
PSOE overtakes UCD in poll 6-15, 821A3
New const OKd by lower house 7-21, 576A1
Const draft sets parliamentary monarchy, other provisns rptd 7-27, 705F3
Mil promotn reform set 9-27, 822G1
UCD cong, Suarez reelected head; problems noted 10-19—10-21, 821E2
Const OKd by parlt 10-31, premr, oppositn ldr 12-5, referendum 12-6, 966G2
Franco rule lauded 11-17, 11-19, 967B2
King signs new Constitutn 12-27, 1022G1
Electns set for Mar '79 12-29, 1022G1

Helsinki Agreement—*See EUROPE—Security and Cooperation*
Monetary, Trade, Aid & Investment—*See also 'European Community' above*
'77 trade deficit $7.6 bln, oil cost high 1-21, 395A1
IMF OKs $295 mln in credits 2-7, 395B1
Ethiopia chrgs Somalia aid 2-14, 100C1
Sahara rebels warn on Morocco fishing pact 2-20, 278D3
Forgn debt $14 bln in '77, debt servicing $3.2 bln 2-23, 395A1
Argentina gets $340-mln loan 3-8, 310B3
Peseta in new SDR basket 4-3, 300F3
Eastern buys airbuses 4-6, 264C3
King in Iran, China for trade talks 6-14—6-19; Iran export data rptd 6-16, 576A2
Forgn banks admitted 6-16, 822E1
French truckers protest customs slowdown 6-23, 532F3
French Mirage jet purchase rptd 6-26, 649B2

1979

Government & Politics—*See also other appropriate subheads in this section*
Vatican Concordat ended 1-3, 61C2
Rightist coalitn formed 1-16, 61A2
Suarez scores PSOE 2-27, govt wins electns 3-1, 191B2
Suarez wins confidence vote 3-30, names minority Cabt 4-5, 256F1
Basques boycott parlt 3-30—4-5, 256B2
Left scores in munic vote 4-3; Communist ldr appeals to Soclsts 4-4, 256B2
PSOE ldr quits in Marxist rift 5-20, 390C2
King marks Armed Forces Day 5-27, 428G2*
Basque home-rule bill drafted 7-17, 545D3-546B1
Public security tightened 7-29, 585G3
PSOE drops Marxist line 9-29; moderates win control, Gonzalez reelected ldr 9-30, 754F2
Basques, Catalans approve home rule 10-25, 837B1
Galicia limited home rule OKd by parlt com 11-22, 929D2

Helsinki Agreement—*See EUROPE—Security and Cooperation*
Monetary, Trade, Aid & Investment
Forgn bank activities OKd 1-26, 100E3
'78 trade gap rptd 1-31, 100G3-101A1
Iran oil cutoff impact assessed 2-20, 126G2
Steel pricing cited in US ruling on Polish dumping 4-18, 299C1
GM plant agrmt rptd 6-6, 428A2
GM expansn plans detailed 6-11, 555F1
'78 tourism rptd; July, Aug data 505B1
Libya oil imports rptd 7-4, 546F1
Natural gas imports forecast 7-10, 546B2
10-yr energy plan sets oil import cuts 7-30, 585E2
Brazil RR, mining deals rptd 8-3; trade parity sought, '78 gap noted 8-6, 654A2
Equatorial Guinea aid pledged 8-5, 614B1
W Ger, US cos get A-plant contracts 8-25, 670C3

1980

500 Cuban refugees offered asylum 4-16, 285C1
Europn CPs meet 4-28—4-29, 327C2
Tito funeral held 5-8, 339B1
Olympic boycott backed 5-22, Olympic com rejects 5-23, 421F1
ESA rocket test fails 5-23, 397G2
France asks EC expansn delay 6-5, reactn 6-6; mil poll on entry rptd 6-12, 435E3-436D1
EC, NATO entry backed by US 6-25, 474C3
French premr visits, Suarez receptn cool 7-2—7-3, 567G1
Cuban tankers escorted to Canaries 7-14, 562E2
ESA plans comet probe 7-15, 548A1
Suarez in Peru for Belaunde inauguratn 7-28, 579F3
Westn labor costs compared 8-12, 698E1
Iran hostage appeal rptd 8-16, 634G3
Suarez shuffles Cabt, NATO talks cited 9-8, 690C2
UK soccer fans riot in Madrid 9-17, 771E3
Iraq ousts newsman 10-2, 775A1
UN Cncl seat won 11-13, 896E1
2 Basques die in bar attack 11-21; France protests 11-27, 923D2
Cuba ex-offcl asks UN probe prison hunger strike 12-4, 965D2
Bolivia coup condemned by Santa Marta conf 12-17, 992A3
Polisario recognized; fishermen freed 12-17, 995C3
Government & Politics
Basques, Catalans begin home rule 1-11, 101D2
Basque autonomy policy shifted, Cabt min quits 1-16, Basque party boycotts Natl Assemb 1-18, 101F2
Madrid gen dismissed 1-24, mil coup plot rumor rptd linked 1-25, 101A2
Andalusia autonomy vote falls short; CP, Soclst gains seen 2-28, 174E2-E3
Basque parties win regional vote 3-9, 196B1
Moderates win upset in Catalonia 3-21, 235E1
Basque parlt opens 4-1; Bilbao metalworkers disrupt sessn 6-26, Garaicoetxea backers march 7-3, 567C1
Suarez shuffles Cabt 5-2, 355A1
Suarez sets autonomy timetable 5-20; Soclsts call censure motn 5-21, Suarez survives vote 5-30, 431B2
Suarez shuffles Cabt again 9-8, Soclsts score 9-10, 690B2
Suarez wins confidence vote 9-17, 711E3
Basque, Catalonia mins sworn; spec rep removed 10-21, 832C2
Andalusian autonomy set for '81 10-23, 832E1
Cabt debates Basque terrorism 10-24, 832E2
Mil coup rumors abound 11-22, 903A3
Police, terrorist links debated 11-26, 923C2
Suarez in Basque region 12-9—12-11, 968B2
Galicia autonomy vote passes 12-21, 996F2
Basques win right to tax, expanded police powers 12-30, 996D2

Monetary, Trade, Aid & Investment
Mex '80 oil imports seen 1-15, 60B2
GM plants set 2-20, 125A3
Coca-Cola plant struck 4-25, 463E3
EC dumping chrgs cited 5-6, 412B1
Fiat balks at SEAT acuisitn; Japan, W Ger talks rptd; '79 exports cited 6-4, 467A3
French produce dispute spurs violence, truckers block border 6-16—6-20, 525A3
French premr sees Suarez on EC entry 7-2—7-3, 567G1
Canada fines S Africa arms seller 8-14, 618A3
Suarez shuffles Cabt, EC entry talks cited 9-8, 690E2
Toyota-SEAT talks rptd 10-8, 793A3*

1976

Oppositn asks referendum guarantees 11-27, Suarez meets ldrs 11-29, 908A3
Socialist conv OKd 11-27, 908E3
Oppositn, govt '77 electn talks set 12-9, 967B2
Referendum OKs free electns 12-15, 967F1
Police chiefs replaced 12-23, 1011G2
Political ct closed 12-30, 1011F2

Press & Censorship
Cambio-16 names alleged CIA agents 1-14, 77C1 ★
Magazines ask cabt quit 3-11, 3-12, 207B1
Oppositn press conf barred 3-29; ldrs seized re BBC talks 4-3, 268G3, 269D1
Areilza TV interview banned 4-12, 269A2
Cuadernos torture rpt suppressed, Cambio rpts Amnesty Intl chrg 6-1, 501G1
Censorship protested 7-11, 523A3
Press scores adultery trial 10-9, 909B3
Sabado Grafico head indicted re Lockheed rpt 10-15; Cambio 16 rpts OKd 10-28, 909B2
Oppositn parties ask campaign access 11-27; state TV OKs equal time, bars CP 11-30, 908C3

Sahara—*See SAHARA*

Sports
Olympic results 7-18—7-31, 573E3, 574A2, 576G3

Unrest (domestic)—*See also 'Church' and 'Press' above*
Amnesty marches, petitions rptd 1-1—1-4, 1-6, priest arrested 1-7, 12A1
Fraga on strike laws 1-1, 12C1
Basque, Catalan assemblies formed 1-2, 12D1
Right-wing group formed, bombing rptd 1-5, 12G1
Madrid subway strike 1-5—1-6, soldiers operate 1-7, 12B2
Camacho sees changes 1-6, 12C2
Madrid strikes, protests continue; arrests mount 1-10—1-20; postal, RR workers drafted 1-14, 1-19, 54B2, C3, G3
ETA kidnaps Arrasate heir 1-14, 55A1
Barcelona port struck 1-15, 54G3
Asturias, Santander job actns rptd 1-16, 55A1
Strike com formed, Alonso arrested 1-17, 54A3
Arias charges subversion 1-19, 54E3
Barcelona protests crushed 2-1, 2-8, 144B2
Bilbao workers march, Madrid teachers strike 2-1, 144D2
Valladolid, Vitoria strikes halted 2-3, 144D2
Govt revises anti-terror law 2-6, 144G1
Raimon concerts banned 2-6, 144E2
ETA slays Galdacano mayor 2-9, mechanic 2-10, 144F2
Barcelona munic workers strike 2-16—2-18, 144C2
Strikes, violence increase 2-24—3-15, 206G3
Herreros Robles seized 2-26, 314B3
Pol protests murders continue 3-1—4-19, 269C2
UMD members tried 3-8—3-9, sentncd 3-10; Diez protests 3-11; Cordoba seized 3-13, 2 others sought 3-15, 314D2
Phone workers strike 4-2—4-5, 269A2
Basque UGT delegates rptd arrested 4-16, 314D1
Police roundups, May Day clashes 4-25—5-1; torture alleged 5-13, 422A2
2 slain at Carlist rally 5-9, Prince Sixto ousted 5-14, 422F2
Communist labor ldr, 2 others freed 5-25, 422F2
2 oppositn ldrs arrested 6-3, 459F1
Basque rightist slain 6-9, 458C3
Garcia Trevijano gets bail 6-12, 459G1
Madrid rally smashed, Catalan soclsts rally 6-22, 501G1
'76 pol arrest data rptd 6-24, 501E1
Police torture trials rptd 6-30, 501E2
Police, amnesty demonstrators clash 7-5—7-11, 541E2
Strikes cited re Arias ouster 7-6, 501B1
Postal workers strike 7-6—7-10, 541G2
12 hurt in bombings 7-17—7-18; leftists claim credit 7-19, 541G1
Bomb explodes at Dutch emb 7-20, 541D2
Amnesty, Galicia freedom protesters arrested 7-25, 753C3
Bomb blasts hit 5 cities, 2 die 7-31, 775G1
Police kill 3 students; riots, strike protest 8-13—10-1, 775D1, F1

1977

US rpts Mar fishing violatns 270C2
US A-fuel control rptd sought 4-13, 268C2
US reactor sale agreed 5-17, 398C2
US co to lease Airbus 5-24, 441D2
N-S conf $1 bln aid plan backed 6-3, 437E2
Peseta devalued 7-12, 545F2
Govt asks full EC membership 7-28, 582C2
'77 paymts deficit forecast 7-31, 586D2
Gold, forgn reserves up 8-26, 867F1
Venez, Central Amer pacts OKd 9-8—9-17, 804G3-805E1
EC entry backed by Soclists 9-23; Suarez confers with EC ldrs 11-3—11-4, members rptd uneasy 11-6, 867G1
Econ plan signed by govt, oppositn 10-25, 866D3, 867A1

Obituaries
Ruiz, Julian 8-4, 696E3
Xavier, Prince 5-7, 452F3

Unrest (domestic)
Protesters ask amnesty; rightists threaten Basque editors 1-1—1-6; oppositn talks readied 1-7, 22C2, G2
Kidnapers drop Oriol death threat 1-2, 22B3
Boy killed in Bilbao amnesty protest 1-9; strikes, riots 1-10—1-12, 68D1
Madrid factory guards wounded, GRAPO leaflets found 1-10, 68C1
7 die in Madrid amnesty protests 1-23—1-24; rightists chrgd, workers strike 1-25, 67F3
Villaescusa kidnaped, GRAPO takes credit 1-24, 68C1
Madrid strike violence; rights curbed, other emergency measures rptd 1-26—1-30, 101A3
Oriol, Villaescusa rescued 2-11, GRAPO arrests rptd 2-12, 2-14, 307D1
'76 strikes worst in 40 yrs 2-15, 308B1
Farmers strike 2-21—3-1, govt price vow rptd 3-23, 307D3
Socialist rep at Israel Labor Party conv 2-22, 135F1
Crackdown on rightists, 11 seized re Madrid killings 2-22—3-14, 307A2
Suarez death threat by rightists rptd 3-2, 307E2
Basques, police clash 3-8—3-15, 4-10, prisoners rptd tortured 4-3, 331E1-D2
Strikes, union organizing OKd 3-9, 3-30, 286D1, E1
New amnesty decreed 3-17, 68 pol prisoners rptd freed 4-6, 286F1
Workers strike re econ, labor policies 4-15, 306F3
May Day rallies smashed 5-1, 454C1
Basque amnesty strikes, violence 5-12—5-19, 453F2
US emb cultural center bombed 5-16, 398C2
Basque exec kidnaped 5-20, pol prisoners exiled 5-22—6-9, 454A1
Barcelona, other bombings 6-4—6-13, 453G2-454A1
Bombings precede electns 6-15, 453E2
Basque hostage killed 6-18, govt scores ETA 6-22, 507C3
Barcelonia gay rights protesters dispersed 6-26, 560F2
3 terrorists freed 7-17, non-pol prisoners riot 7-18—7-21, 582E2-D3
GRAPO youths seize radio transmitter, botch broadcast 7-18; Madrid terrorists explode 5 bombs 7-25, 582D3
6600 prisoners rptd freed under '76 amnesty 7-20, 582C3
GRAPO members seized 8-5, 10-10; anti-Suarez plot cited 10-10, 826B3
King, premr escape bomb plot 8-17; leftists blamed 8-20, 826G2
Basque clashes re autonomy, French detentn of exec murder suspect 8-18—8-24, 826D2
Legislator assaulted 8-27; Cortes reactn 9-12—9-15, 826E3
Riots mar Catalan 'natl day' march 9-11, 843F2
Publicatn bombed in Barcelona 9-20, Madrid papers strike 9-23, rightists seized 10-9—10-10, 826C3

1978

French pres visits 6-28—7-1 649D1-C2
Peugeot to buy Chrysler unit 8-10, 623C2
Suarez in Venez trade talks; indl pacts cited 9-7—9-9, 821F3
Suarez in Cuba trade talks, '59 property-natlzn paymt OKd 9-9—9-10; 4-way oil pact with Venez, USSR rptd 9-15, 822A1
UK OKs Chrysler sale to Peugeot 9-28, 764E1
UK Airbus role OKd 10-24, 902B3
King signs Mex, Peru, Argentina econ, tech cooperatn pacts 11-17—11-30, 967A3
Mex '79 oil price hike set 12-20, 978F2

Obituaries
Carita, Maria 9-6, 778A1
De Madariaga, Salvador 12-14, 1032E2
Mercader, Ramon 10-18, 888B3
Zamora, Ricardo 9-7, 778C2

Spanish Sahara—*See SAHARA*

Sports
Nations Cup won 5-15, 419D1
World Cup soccer finals, sidelights 6-1—6-25, 519F3, 520B3
Smash '78 tennis results 10-29, 1027C2

Unrest (domestic)
Basque guerrillas set bombs 1-7, 2-5—2-6; independnc, pol party amnesty demanded 1-31, 135B3
Catalonia bombings 1-15, 1-22—1-23; others unreported 1-26, 136B1
2 die in prison revolts 1-17—1-30, 249C3
Carrero killers get amnesty 1-20, 135F3
Barcelona ex-mayor, wife killed 1-25, 135G3
Barcelona carnival banned 2-2, 136E1
Basque A-plant protests 2-25—2-26, 3-1; 2 die in bombing 3-17, 249E3-250A1
ETA blamed for death of policeman, right-wing mayor 3-5, 3-16, 250C1
Catalan actors sentenced 3-7, 250F1
Prison guards kill anarchist 3-13; protests 3-20; prison chief slain, GRAPO claims credit 3-22, 249G2-B3
ETA vows fight vs 'middle-class state' 3-20, 250B1
2 Basque cops die in ETA attacks, protesters arrested 5-9—5-14, 537C2
Basque soc sec office bombed 6-12, 537C2
Basque cop killed 6-21, 537C2
Basque editor slain 6-28; ETA ex-ldr shot in France, wife killed 7-3, 537D2
Basques protest Giscard visit 6-30, 649B2
2 Basque cops wounded; Pamplona leftists, rightists clash, San Sebastian marchers riot 7-5, 537F2
Basque riots, strikes flare 7-8—7-11; govt laments, vows probe 7-11, 531C1-B2
Basque riots, strikes continue; police violence rptd 7-12—7-13, 7-16, 576C1
Gen, aide killed; pol ldrs score terrorists 7-21; rightists ask coup 7-22, 575E3
Basque town compensated for police violence 7-22, 706D2
GRAPO denies killing gen, aide 7-24; 10 seized in prison chief's murder 7-27, 706G1
4 security officers slain 8-28; GRAPO, ETA credited 8-29, 706E1
Police score govt, 5 ldrs suspended 8-30, 2 fired 8-31, 706B2
ETA ldr shot as informer 8-30, 706D2
9 police chiefs fired 9-12, 821D2
More Basque cops killed; cops mutiny, govt arrests 9-25—10-22, 821F1
Parlt asks terrorism crackdown 11-8, Madrid march backs 11-10; judge killed 11-16, mourners ask army rule 11-17; rally lauds Franco 11-19, 967G1
Basque violence continues 11-15—12-5, 967C1
Anti-govt plot by security offcrs rptd 11-16—11-21, 967C2
Madrid cop killed 12-21, 1022E1
Basque terrorist killed in France 12-21, 1022F1
Death penalty abolished 12-23, 1022F1

1979

Fiat announces investmt plan 9-12, 709C2
Mex oil imports rptd 11-23, 909B3
French trade talks 11-26—11-27, 952A2
Nicaragua '76-77 loan graft rptd, other debts cited 11-27, 909E3, 910A1

Obituaries
Martin-Artajo, Alberto 9-1, 756A3
Valles, Lorenzo Gonzales 9-23, 754G1

Sports
Soccer Cup-Winners' Cup results 5-9, 776A3
El Cordobes returns to bull ring 7-22, 656F3
US wins Ryder Cup 9-16, 969E3

UN Policy & Developments
Membership listed 695C3

Unrest
ETA kills cop, 2 army officers 1-2—1-3; govt anti-ETA drive cited 1-4, 40E1
Rightist offcrs score govt 1-4, unauthorzd patrols scored 1-6, 60F3-61A1
Basque, Madrid assassinatns continue 1-6—1-13, Sup Ct justice killed 1-9, 60C3
Cop kills youth 1-6, Ortin death probe arrests 1-8, 61C1
ETA ldr wounded in France 1-13, 61D1
ETA suspect dies of wounds 1-25, 100A3
ETA, IRA cooperatn rptd 1-28, 100B3
3 Basque civil guards injured, ETA blamed 1-29, 100G2-A3
23 Basques arrested by French 1-30, 100B3
Govt sets anti-terror legislatn 2-1, 192A1
Lt col slain by ETA, '79 assassinatns reach 30 2-4—3-9, 191G3
Basques protest French deportatns 2-5, 192B1
French execs kidnaped 2-5—3-1, 192C1
ETA backers win 4 Cong seats 3-1, 191E2, A3
Army gen killed 3-5; king, queen attend requiem mass 3-6, 191E3
Madrid cop killed 3-10, Feb murder plot vs Suarez rptd foiled 3-13, 192D1
A-protests rptd 4-9, 276D2
Gen, 2 cols assassinated 5-25, 428D2
Madrid bomb blast kills 8 5-26; Armed Forces Day fetes cancelled 5-27, anti-terror campaign vowed 5-28, 428E2
'79 death toll at 65 5-26, 428A3
A-protester killed 6-3, Basques riot 6-5, 428G1-A2
2 Madrid cops killed, '79 total rptd 6-4, 428C2
Lemoniz A-plant bombed, workman killed 6-13, 504E3
Basque bombs damage govt bldgs 6-14, 504D3
Basques bomb resorts 6-26—7-3, 504F3
Madrid-Paris train attacked 7-2, 505C1
Parlt member shot 7-3, 505D1
Basque home-rule bill drafted 7-17, 545E3-546B1
2 terrorists arrested 7-27, '79 death toll rptd 585C3, D3
Basques bomb Madrid airport, RR statns; 5 die; govt ups security 7-29, 585E3
3 hijack plane to Switz 8-4, surrender 8-5, 603F3
2 terrorists captured 8-13—8-14, 670E2-A3
A-plant permits protested 8-28—9-1, 670D3
Basques protest French policy 8-30; violence erupts, gen strike called 9-1—9-3, 670F3
ETA assassinates mil gov, other offcls; rightists retaliate 9-19—9-29; Suarez delays US, Latin tour 9-25, 754F1-E2
20 GRAPO suspects arrested 10-13—10-14, 795B1
Abortion law protested 10-20—10-21, trial suspended 10-26, 875B3

1980

Obituaries
Gil-Robles, Jose Maria 9-14, 755A3

Press & Censorship
El Pais editor sentncd for 'insults' 5-9, 410B2
Suarez shuffles Cabt, curbs eased 9-8, 690B3

Sports
Olympic com rejcts Moscow boycott 3-22, 259C3
Valencia wins Cup-Winners' Cup 5-7, 771A3
Olympic boycott backed 5-22, Olympic com rejects 5-23, 421F1
Jones wins Gr Prix 6-1, 1002B1
Samaranch elected IOC pres 7-16, 590D3
Moscow Olympic results 7-20—8-3, 588B3, 622C2, D2, D3, 623F2, 624F3, G3
British soccer fans riot 9-17, 771E3

Unrest
Basque, Italy terrorist links seen 1-2, 20F2
8 GRAPO querrillas sentncd 1-7, 101F3-102A1
Basque police chief assassinated 1-10, 101E2
Basque bombing kills 4 1-20, rightists claim credit 1-21, 101B3
Mil coup plot rumor rptd 1-25, 101B2
6 cops killed in Basque ambush 2-1, rightists claim 2 revenge deaths 2-2—2-3, 101C3
Sovt linked to extremists 2-16, 141B3
Madrid gov bans demonstrations 2-18, 196D2
5 rightists sentncd in '77 Atocha massacre, Falange Party protest 3-4, 196B2
'78 coup plotters sentenced 5-7, 355G1
Suarez survives censure motion 5-30, 431E2, G2
ETA bomb beach resorts, rightists threaten retaliatn 6-25, 500G1
Bilbao metalworkers disrupt Basque parlt 6-26, Garaicoetxea backers march 7-3, 567C1
Suarez in French talks on ETA 7-2—7-3, 567C1
Basque bombs force evacuatn of Malaga resort 7-4, security tightened 7-5, ETA presents demands 7-6, 566G3
Police magazine names 3 top Basque terrorists 7-7, 567E1
4 killed in San Sebastian gun battle, '80 death toll rptd 7-13, 567E1
Basque bomb kills civil guard, injures 34 7-22; ETA threatens Canaries 7-23, San Sebastian, Bilbao govt bldgs bombed 7-25, 580E2
Gen escapes death try 7-29, 605G3
Marques, wife slain by Basques 8-1, 605E3Y
Andalusia hunger strike, SOC backs 8-14—8-19; radicals claim arson attacks 8-18, 653F1
Andalusia hunger strike ends, jobs aid pledged 8-22, 673C2
GRAPO ldr killed 8-29, gen assassinated in alleged revenge 9-2, 673G2
Cordoba gen strike threatened 8-30, violence erupts 8-31, 673E2
Police score Basque terror policy, ask Roson resignatn 10-21; CP, conservative ldrs vow aid 10-22, 832G1
UCD member slain in Basque region 10-23, Cabt debates terrorism 10-24, 832D2
ETA attacks spawn rightist backlash 11-16—11-23; '80 death toll rptd 11-21, 903B2
Basque bar attack kills 2 11-21; France protests 11-27, 923D2
Leftist infiltratn rptd, mil coup rumors abound 11-22, 903G2-A3
Police, terrorist links debated 11-26, 923C2
Suarez Basque visit spurs ETA moves 12-10, 968C2

1976

Air controllers begin slowdown 8-13, 775B2
Police smash Corunna protest 8-29, 775E1
Basque student killed 9-8; strikes protest 9-9, 9-13—9-15; Martin Villa sees mayors 9-16—9-20, 775A1
Police smash Catalan march 9-12, 775E1
Postmen strike 9-23—10-4, 775A2
Basques hold gen strike 9-27, 775C1
Royal adviser killed 10-4; 100 rptd seized, rightists riot 10-5—10-6; ETA claims credit 10-6, 774G2
Strikes protest austerity program 10-12—11-26, 928E3
Leftists arrested 10-21—11-28, 909A1
Neo-fascists attack bookstores 11-12, 909D2
Oriol kidnapped 12-11, 967D2
Fernandez Miranda forced from car 12-20, 967C2
Carrillo arrested 12-22, 967A3; protests 12-23, 12-29, freed on bail 12-30, 1011E2
Mil trials for terrorists ended 12-30, 1011F2

U.S. Relations

Alleged CIA agents named 1-14, 77C1 ★
Defense pact signed 1-24, 62A1, 76D1
US bars shoe import curb 4-16, 322C1
Royal couple visits 6-1—6-5, 459A2-C3, D3
US warns vs CP legalizatn 6-8, 6-19, 459C3
US Dem platform text cites 6-15, 478D1
Villar Mir in US 6-15—6-17, 501G2
US Sen ratifies defns pact 6-21, 534F2
US OKs reactor sale 6-21, 739B2
Ship in US Bicentennial event 7-4, 488A3, B3
Cortes com OKs defns pact 7-23, 541D3
US support re CP ban, center-right funding denied 7-30, 753C1
CP ldr scores mil bases 7-31, 753G1
US GOP platform text cites 8-18, 609G1
Lockheed paymts rptd 10-15—11-8, 909D1
US marriage annulmts rptd 10-15, 909D3
Base treaty aid signed 10-18, 834B3
Rumsfeld asks NATO observer status 12-7, 933A2

1977

Policeman slain, protested 9-27, army coup asked 9-28, 826C3
Basque ETA factn abandons violence 10-1; 2d factn to continue 10-4, 826C2
Anti-terrorism bill backed 10-8, detailed 10-12, 826G1
Basque ldr slain 10-8, ETA takes blame 10-9, 826B2
New amnesty bill OKd 10-14; COs freed 1st 10-21, 826D1
Barcelona riots on Companys death anniv 10-15, 843G2

U.S. Relations—*See also 'Monetary, Trade & Aid' above*

US-ESA flight set 2-16, 170C3
Fascist groups oppose US 3-2, 307G2
Mondale sees Suarez, King; emb unit bombed 5-17, 398B2
Gonzalez vs bilateral security pact 6-23, 507A1
US producer indicted 7-12, 848G1
US arms aid authorized 8-4, 668C1
Soclst ldr urges US role in Chile 8-28—8-31, 743D2
ESA satellite launching aborted 9-13, 735G3

1978

U.S. Relations

US troop presence rptd 1-2, 5C2
CIA sees no A-bomb before '84 1-26, 61C2
Joint mil exercise rptd 2-11, 133F2
US launches ESA satellite 5-12, 384D3
Schlitz settles paymts chrgs 7-9, 642D3
Peugeot to buy Chrysler unit 8-10, 623C2
WWII spying for Japan rptd 9-10—9-18, ex-forgn min denies 9-17, 744E3
US shipping rebate fine rptd 10-1, 752G3
ITT unit linked to forgn paymts 11-2, 876E1
Carter lauds const referendum 12-7, 967B1

1979

ETA fear, low electn turnout linked; death claims cited 10-25, 837D1, F1
ETA slays Basque worker 10-27, gen strike held 10-29, 837A2
Forgn affairs secy kidnaped 11-11, ETA claims credit 11-12, 875F2
A-factory bombed 11-13, 875A3
Pro-Franco rally in Madrid 11-18, 952B2
Suarez in French talks on Basque terror 11-26–11-27, 952F1
FN backers battle Cordoba, Basque foes 12-2, 929A2
Anti-terrorism law extended 12-3, 929C2
Galicia limited home rule protested 12-4, 929F2
Ruperez freed by ETA 12-12, 952C2
5 Grapo guerrillas escape jail 12-17; warden dismissed, prison offcls protest 12-19, 997C3
'79 Grapo killings rptd 12-17, 998B1

U.S. Relations

Chrysler workers strike 1-15, 61G1; OK pact 1-24, 100D3
US bank activities OKd 1-26, 100E3
US A-accident linked to A-protests 4-9, 276A2, D2
Polish steel dump ruling 4-18, 299C1
GM talks 6-5, plant agrmt reached 6-6, 428A2
GM expansn plans detailed 6-11, 555F1
ITT unit to aid paymts probe 8-8, 648F1
Suarez sees Vance on nonaligned conf 8-10, US unruffled 8-13, 654D2, C2
GE gets A-plant contract 8-25, 670D3
Suarez delays visit 9-25, 754C2

1980

U.S. Relations

CP scores Sovt Afghan invasn criticism 1-6, 2G2
Amb to Guatemala takes refuge 2-1, 98A3
GM plants set 2-20, 125A3
Iran asks neutrality on US hostages 4-12, 282F1
Coca-Cola plant struck 4-25, 463E3
Ford, SEAT productn compared 6-4, 467F3
US ship impounded 6-18, escape prompts Adm's dismissal 11-15, 903A3
Carter visits, backs NATO, EC membership 6-25, 474C3,D3Y
Iran hostage appeal rptd 8-16, 634G3

1976

SPAIN, Jayne Baker
Replaced in Civil Svc post 2-26, 186C2
SPAIN, John
Found guilty 8-12, 656C1
SPANDAU (book)
On bestseller list 12-5, 972C2
SPANISH Americans—*See HISPANIC Americans*
SPANISH Civil War (1936-39)
Spain pensns Republican vets 4-7, 269B2
SPANISH Sahara—*See SAHARA*
SPANN, Mrs. Gloria
Carter queried on son 7-26, 551F1
SPANN, William Carter
Carter queried on jailing 7-26, 551F1
SPANOS, Maj. Anastasios
Sentence cut 4-22, 333A2
SPANOS, Harry V.
Wins NH primary for gov 9-14, 705D1
Loses election 11-2, 820F3
SPAULDING, Anthony
Wins Jamaica House seat 12-15, 965B2
SPAVENTA, Luigi
Rptd on CP ticket 5-17, 5-30, 402D3
SPECIAL Drawing Rights (SDRs)—*See IMF*
SPECK, Richard
Denied parole 9-15, 860A2
SPECTER, Arlen
Loses Pa Sen primary 4-27, 305A1
SPEER, Albert
Spandau on best-seller list 12-5, 972C2
SPELLMAN, Rep. Gladys N. (D, Md.)
Reelected 11-2, 829A4
SPELLMAN, John
Wins GOP gov primary 9-21, 804D3
Loses election 11-2, 820C3, 825D1
SPENCE, Rep. Floyd (R, S.C.)
Reelected 11-2, 830A4
SPENCE, Richard D.
Conrail offcls named 3-3, 235B3
SPENCER, Stuart
Ford acting campaign chrmn 3-13, 197C2
Bids Reagan withdraw 3-16, 196F3
SPENCER, William I.
Bars testimony on Citibank 1-16, 111E3

1977

SPANISH Americans—*See HISPANIC Americans*
SPANISH Sahara—*See SAHARA, Western*
SPANN Jr., William B.
Installed ABA pres 8-10, 630A2
SPARBER, Michael
Sentenced 10-21, 991E3
SPARKMAN, Sen. John Jackson (D, Ala.)
'76 spec interest gifts rptd 1-15, 128F3, 129C1
Backs Panama Canal talks 2-2, 379A2
Backs Javits Mideast peace criticism 6-27, supports Carter moves 6-29, 496B1, C1
SPARKMAN v. Carter
Sup Ct refuses review 1-10, 57A2
SPAULDING, Anthony
Jamaica housing min 1-4, 46C1
Leaves PNP mtg 9-16, 884F2
SPEARS, Judge Adrian A.
Dismisses Braniff, Tex Intl chrgs 2-24, 629D3
SPECIAL Drawing Rights (SDRs)—*See IMF*
SPECTATOR Bird, The (book)
Wins Natl Book Award 4-11, 355A2
SPEED—*See NARCOTICS*
SPEER, Edgar B.
Sees Admin offcls on imports, price hikes 5-5, 385D2
Rpts on White House mtg on steel woes 10-13, 775F2
SPEIDEL Newspapers Inc.
Gannett OKs merger 5-10, 395C2
SPEITEL, Angelika
Sought in Ponto slaying 7-30, 601C3
Linked to Baader atty 11-18, 969A1
SPENCER-Churchill, Lady Clementine (Baroness of Chartwell)
Declines financial aid 2-22, 140D3
Dies 12-12, 1024D3

1978

SPANARKEL, Jim
Ky wins NCAA basketball title 3-27, 272F1
SPANISH Americans—*See HISPANIC Americans*
SPANISH Sahara—*See SAHARA, Western*
SPANN, Scott
At US-USSR swimming meet 4-15—4-16, 780B3
SPANN Jr., William B.
Disputes Burger on trial lawyers 2-10, 108B1
Scores legal aid plan rejectn 8-7, 626C2
SPARKMAN, Sen. John Jackson (D, Ala.)
Votes for Panama Canal neutrality pact 3-16, 177E2
Votes for 2d Canal pact 4-18, 273B1
Wallace quits Sen race 5-16, 362G2
Doubts CIA evidence on Cuba role in Zaire 6-9, 442D2
Gets Israeli plea on Leb Christns 8-7, 638D2
Not standing for reelectn 9-5, 699A2
Ala vote results 9-26, 769E1
Heflin wins seat 11-7, 849A3
SPASSKY, Boris
Fischer to end retiremt 10-20, 843D2
SPEARS, Niall
Attack by Nicaragua guardsmen rptd 11-6, 883B2
SPECIAL Drawing Rights (SDRs)—*See IMF*
SPECK, Richard
Confesses '66 Ill slayings 3-6, 172D3
SPECTACULAR Bid (race horse)
Named top 2-yr old colt 12-12, 1028C1
SPECTER, Arlen
Loses primary for Pa gov 5-16, 389C3
SPEER Jr., Edgar B.
US Steel Youngstown plants to close 1-3, 4A3
Sees Carter on coal strike 2-24, 122F3
SPEERS, Jerrold B.
3d in primary for Me gov 6-13, 467A1
SPEITEL, Angelika
Wounded, captured 9-24, 884F3-885A1
SPELLMAN, Rep. Gladys N. (D, Md.)
Reelected 11-7, 851B1
SPENCE, Rep. Floyd (R, S.C.)
Reelected 11-7, 852B2
SPENCER, Capt. Harry
Backs ship duty for women 11-1, 877A3
SPENCER, Jim
In World Series 10-10—10-17, 800D2
SPENCER, Thomas D.
Gives Rochester U Lincoln letter 4-15, 335G2
SPENCER-Churchill, Lady Clementine (Baroness of Chartwell) (Mrs. Winston) (1885-1977)
Destroyed '54 Churchill portrait 1-11, 335E2
SPENDTHRIFT Farm (Ky.)
Seattle Slew syndicated as stallion 2-18, 539C3
Equine VD dvpts 3-15—7-13, 539F2
SPENGLER, Pierre
Crossed Swords released 3-2, 619C1
Superman released 12-14, 1030E3

1979

SPANARKEL, Jim
In NBA draft 6-25, 507B2
SPANISH Americans—*See HISPANIC Americans*
SPANISH Sahara—*See SAHARA, Western*
SPANN, Gloria Carter
Arrested 2-24, 271B3
SPANN, William Carter
Paroled 12-24, 1006B1
SPANN, Willie Carter
Marriage rptd 4-4, 271B3
SPARKS, Christopher
Iraq to review sentnc 7-5, 583C2
SPARKS v. Parker
Case declined by Sup Ct 10-1, 768B2
SPAULDING, William
Details CIA probe of UFOs 1-12, 93B1
SPECIAL Delivery (film)
Wins Oscar 4-9, 336B2
SPECIAL Drawing Rights (SDRs)—*See IMF*
SPECTACULAR Bid (race horse)
Wins Fla Derby 3-6, Flamingo Stakes 3-24, 448C3
Wins Kentucky Derby 5-5, Preakness 5-19; loses Belmont Stakes, injury blamed 6-9, 448G1
Wins Marlboro Cup 9-8, 2d in Jockey Gold Cup 10-6, 876E2, G2
Named top 3-yr old 12-11, 1005D1
SPECTROFUGE Corp. v. Beckman Instruments
Case refused by Sup Ct 2-26, 164C3
SPEIER, Jackie
GOP wins US House seat 4-3, 265G1
SPEITEL, Angelika
Gets life sentence 11-30, 998G3
SPELCE, Neal
Hails Tex A-bond issue OK 4-7, 261D3
SPELL #7 (play)
Opens 7-15, 712E2
SPENCE, Gerald
Silkwood estate wins A-suit 5-18, 381B3
SPENCER, Brenda
Pleads guilty in schl slayings 10-1, 819E2
Sentenced 11-30, 953G3
SPENKELINK, John Arthur
Death penalty appeal refused by Sup Ct 3-26, 230G2
Death warrant signed, stays denied 5-19–5-25, executed in Fla 5-25; Young comment draws fire 5-25–5-26, 399G3, 400D1
SPENKELINK v. Wainwright
Case refused by Sup Ct 3-26, 230G2

1980

SPAIN, James W.
Signs Turkey bases, aid pact 3-29, 255A3
SPALDING, Harry
Watcher in the Woods released 4-16, 416G3
SPANISH Sahara—*See SAHARA, Western*
SPANN, William Carter
Reimprisoned 2-13, 200D2
SPARKES, Robert
Scores Queensland Liberals 11-11, 885A2
SPARTANBURG—*See SOUTH Carolina*
SPAZZALI, Sergio
Arrest rptd 4-20, 408A2
SPECIAL Drawing Rights (SDRs)—*See INTERNATIONAL Monetary Fund (IMF)*
SPECTACULAR Bid (race horse)
Sets stud price, winnings marks 3-11, 6-8, 447E3
Named top horse, best older horse; trainer wins Eclipse Award 12-17, 1002C2
SPECTER, Arlen
Wins Pa US Sen primary 4-22, 304D3
Elected to US Sen 11-4, 840C3, 845A3, 848D3
SPEEDBOAT Racing—*See BOATS & Boating*
SPEIGEL, Michael
Weatherman fugitive surrenders 7-8, 576E3
SPELLING, Aaron
'Charlie's Angels' fraud probe rptd 5-1, 376B3
ABC ties rptd probed by SEC 8-7—8-8, 640D1
LA DA ends 'Charlie's Angels' probe 12-2, 1002E2
SPELLING-Goldberg Productions
'Charlie's Angels' fraud probe rptd 5-1, 376B3
ABC ties rptd probed by SEC 8-7—8-8, 640B1
LA DA ends 'Charlie's Angels' probe 12-2, 1002F2
SPELLMAN, Rep. Gladys N. (D, Md.)
Reelected 11-4, 843B1
SPELLMAN, John
Wins Washn primary for gov 9-16, 724B2
Elected Wash gov 11-4, 845F3, 847C1, 852B3
SPENCE, Rep. Floyd (R, S.C.)
Reelected 11-4, 844B2
SPENCER, Brenda
Father marries cellmate 3-26, 638G3
SPENCER, Stuart
On Ford draft movemt 3-6, 207E1
SPENCER, Wallace
Marries daughter's cellmate 3-26, 638G3

1976

SPICER, Keith
Scores bilingualism progrm 3-31, 250C2
'74 bilingualism evaluatn cited 8-14, 637F1
SPINELLI, Altiero
Rptd on CP ticket 5-17, 5-30, 402C3
Chrgs govt agreed to loan ban 7-20, 557A1
SPINKS, Leon
Wins Olympic medal 7-31, 574D1
SPINKS, Michael
Wins Olympic medal 7-31, 574D1
SPINOLA, Gen. Antonio de (ret.)
News interview 1-3, 11C2
Arrives in Switz 2-7; W Ger expose probed 4-7, expelled 4-8, 315B1
Carvalho on Ramalho link 6-21, 483D1
Returns Portugal 8-10, 732D3
SPIRIDONOV, Alexei
Wins Olympic medal 7-28, 576B1
SPIRO, Herbert J.
Equatorial Guinea ties cut 3-15, 239A1
SPITZ, Mark
Pyttel sets world swim mark 6-1—6-5, 424G3
SPLITTORFF, Paul
Yankees win pennant 10-14, 796G1
SPOONER, Frank
Loses elecn 11-2, 822G1

SPORTS—*See also specific sport*
Cable TV curbs scored by House unit 1-26, Justice Dept 2-5, 135B3, D3
US youth progrms funded 4-15, 282D2
IAAF expels S Africa 7-22, 562B2
Jobless benefits revisn signed 10-20, 788E1
'60-75 equipmt purchases rptd 11-23, 959G2
Olympic Games
Montreal games set 1-28, plumbing problem cited 1-29, 99F1
Innsbruck winter games, RFE coverage barred 2-4—2-15, 158F2
Trudeau vs federal aid 3-5, 238C3
Canada Olympic coins stolen 3-30, 250G3
Quebec takes over Olympic village 4-6, 288B2
Australia natl anthem set 5-4, 349G3
Canada debt measures 5-11—6-30, bldg fraud chrgd 6-30, 529F1
TV shows win Emmys 5-17, 460C2
Hubbard dies 6-23, 524G2
OAU threatens boycott 7-6, 487D3
African, Asian natns quit Montreal games 7-9—7-21; Waldheim appeals 7-18, 528G2
Canada disputes Taiwan role, US scores 7-11—7-17, Taiwan quits 7-16, 528F3
Montreal games open 7-17, 528E2
Swimming, gymnastic highlights 7-18—7-25, 562B3, 563B1
Results, final medal standings 7-18—7-31, 573B3-576G3
5 athletes disqualified 7-19—7-30; blood doping rumored 7-29, 563F1, C2
Guyana sprinter denied entry 7-22, 562F1
6 E Eur athletes defect 7-28—8-4, USSR rpts death threat 7-31, 562C2
Montreal games end 8-1, 562D1
Sovt defector to return 8-17, 655C2
NZ plans curbs vs S Africa 10-17, 910A3
Montreal to pay debt 12-23, US loan signed 12-31, 998D3

1977

SPETH, James Gustave
Named to environmt cncl 3-7, confrmd 4-4, 272C3
A-plant licensing halt backed 9-29, 794A3
SPICE Islands—*See MOLUCCAS*
SPICKERMAN Sr., John F.
To quit pension post 3-13, 195E1
SPIERS, Ronald I.
Named amb to Turkey 4-15, confrmd 5-25, 500B1
SPINELLI, Thomas
Indicted 2-24, 155G2
Pleads guilty 3-3, 540A3
SPINKS, Leon
Decisns Righetti, '78 Ali fight set 11-18, 970C2, C3
SPIVEY, W. Graydon
Named in A&P overtime suit 9-27, 778E2
SPLITTORFF, Paul
In AL playoff 10-5—10-9, 807G1
SPOKANE, Wash.—*see WASHINGTON*
SPONG, Mason
On boy scout sex abuse 5-15, 432G2

SPORTS—*See also specific sport*
NCAA conventn 1-10—1-12, 104G1
US panel issues amateur study 1-13, 68B3
AMF rpts paymts 2-8, 93G3
Cuba-US talks seen 2-15, 110F1
Carter call-in on Cuba games 3-5, 171C2
US OKs Cuba games 3-5, 3-8, 181C1
Gulf + Westn plans Madison Sq Garden takeover 3-7, 275D1
FCC pay-TV rules voided 3-25, Sup Ct appeal OKd 4-14, 376D2, F2
NZ reaffirms S Africa policy 3-31, 258A2
More US-Cuba games sought 4-11, 283A2
Emmy academies end dispute 7-12, 583C3
NBC unit formed 8-22, 658C3
Nader group to aid fans 9-27, 820F1
House subcom probes TV coverage 10-4, 11-2—11-3, 949C3
ABC wins Emmy awards 11-6, 1022B1
Abercrombie stores closed 12-14, 980D3
S Africa boycott asked by UN 12-14, 1016C2
Obituaries
Dewey, Godfrey 10-18, 872F1
Ferris, Daniel 5-2, 452A3
Olympic Games
US panel issues study 1-13, 68B3
NBC to air Moscow games 2-1, '76 ABC costs cited 2-3, 130G3
Satra sues NBC over rights 2-14, 131E1
USOC elects officers, expands athletes rights 4-29—5-1, 491G2
Australia picks natl song 5-21, 447A2
LA picked for '84 games 9-25, 828G2
House subcom queries NBC deal 10-4, 950C1
'72 Munich attack cited 10-18, 790B1
Satra drops suit vs NBC, IOC 12-9, 971D2

1978

SPERM Banks—*See CHILDBIRTH*
SPERRY & Hutchinson Co.
Bigelow-Sanford ex-pres dies 11-25, 972G3
SPERRY Rand Corp.
USSR computer sale barred 7-18, 542F1
SPICA, John
Denies King murder plot info 7-26, 589C3
SPICKERMAN, John
Named in US Teamster fund suit 2-1, 83F1
SPIEGELER Noriega, Gen. Otto
Keeps Cabt defense post 7-21, 722D3 ★
SPIEGELMAN, Robert
Guaranteed income study rptd 5-19, 720E3
SPIELBERG, Steven
Close Encounters on best-seller list 1-8, 24F3; 2-5, 116D3; 3-5, 195F3
SPIKES, Dr. John
Rpts new marijuana test 8-29, 728C3
SPIKINGS, Barry
Deer Hunter released 12-14, 1030F2
SPINER, Brent
History of Amer Film opens 3-30, 760D2
SPINKS, Leon
Decisns Ali for heavywgt title 2-15, 171B1-C2
Title bout defns in dispute, Ali rematch set 2-17—3-16; Nev comm suspends 3-9, WBC withdraws title, names Norton champ 3-18, 211B3-212D1
Ali rematch plan protested 3-8, site shifted 3-9, 212E1
Arrested on auto, drug chrgs 3-19, 4-21; avoids indictmt, pays fine 5-18, 379A1
Ali rematch contract signed 4-11, 378E3
Ali decisns for 3d heavywgt title 9-15, TV viewing mark rptd 9-20, 726B1
SPITLER, Linda Kay
Judicial immunity in sterilizatn case backed by Sup Ct 3-28, 241G2
SPITSBERGEN (Norwegian Island)
USSR-Norway tensn rptd 10-12, 820C2
SPLEEN—*See MEDICINE—Surgery*
SPOCK, Benjamin
At Seabrook A-plant protest 6-24—6-26, 494E1
Arrested in Seabrook protest 9-12, convicted 12-7, 941B1
SPOKANE, Wash.—*See WASHINGTON*
SPORN, Philip
Dies 1-24, 96F3
SPORTING Goods
'77 indus profit drop rptd 5-8, 325A3
SPORTING News, The (magazine)
NFL '77 statistical ldrs rptd 1-1, 56G2
SPORTS—*See also specific sport*
AIAW meets, chngs scholarship rules 1-7—1-11, 40F2
NCAA suit vs Title IX dismissed 1-9, 40C2
US judge backs coed sports 1-9, 40C3
Carter vs business tax break 2-17, 123A2
US blacks ask S Africa ban 7-6, 632E3
Amateur sports bill, omnibus funds clear Cong 10-15, 842C2-C3; signed 11-8, 1003B1
NJ OKs Sports Auth bond refinancing 11-7, 915C2
African Games
Egypt team attacked in Algiers 7-22, Libyans ousted 7-23; Egypt to boycott 5 states 7-24, 573C1
Olympic Games
NCAA conventn proposal 1-11—1-13, 40F1
USSR in Coca-Cola deal 3-14, 230A1
NCAA rejoins USOC 4-15, 842C3
Canada to continue lottery funding 7-6, 531E2
US OKs USSR crime equipmt sale 7-6, 10-13, 905C2
USSR '80 site protested re Shcharansky trial 7-17, 542D1
Carter vs US boycott in '80 7-20, 549C3
IOC OKs '84 LA pact 10-9, LA approves 10-12, 842F3
Amateur sports bill, omnibus funds clear Cong 10-15, 842D2-C3; signed 11-8, 1003B1
Pan American Games
Amateur sports bill, omnibus funds clear Cong 10-15, 842F2-C3; signed 11-8, 1003B1

1979

SPERANZO, Dimicius
Killed in hijack bid 4-4, 266F2
SPERLICH, Harold K.
Chrysler positn cited 9-20, 700C1
SPERLING, Herbert
Acquitted in '77 Papa slaying 10-23, 840A2
SPERRY Rand Corp.
USSR computer talks rptd 2-8, French deal set 3-27, 237B3
USSR computer sale cleared 3-29, 287F2
SPHEERIS, Penelope
Real Life released 3-1, 174E3
SPIEGEL Inc.
Mail order finance chrg case refused by Sup Ct 10-1, 768B2
SPIEGEL Inc. v. South Dakota
Case refused by Sup Ct 10-1, 768C2
SPIEGLAR Noriega, Gen. Otto
Army staff chief slain 6-10, 445C3
SPIELBERG, Steven
1941 released 12-14, 1008A1
SPIERENBURG, Dirk
EC Comm reforms proposed 9-24, 719F3
SPIERS, Ronald
Turkish-US prisoner transfer accord signed 6-7, 488B3
SPIESS, Gerry
Crosses N Atlantic in 10-ft craft 7-24, 656C3
SPINGHAR, Maj. Gen Abdul Majid
Seized as Afghan coup ldr 10-16, 810F3
SPINOLA, Gen. Antonio de (ret.)
Sa Carneiro link cited 12-2, 917E1
SPIRITS Having Flown (recording)
On best-seller list 2-14, 120F3; 3-7, 174E1; 4-4, 271E2
SPOKESONG (play)
Opens 3-15, 712F2
SPORTING News, The (newspaper)
Hodges named top coll basketball coach 3-24, 290G3
Weaver named top mgr 10-17, 956B1
Golden Glove winners named 11-20, 956B1
Rose named baseball Player of Decade 12-29, 1003E1

SPORTS
NCAA vows Title IX fight, rejcts reforms 1-8-1-10, 102B3-103G1
AIAW conventn 1-8-1-10, 103G1
World Univ Games held 9-8-9-13, 799F1
Title IX guidelines issued 12-4, 1000F2
Land speed record rptd set 12-18, 1006D1
Olympic Games
Hayes pleads guilty 3-14, sentncd 3-22, 335C3
Tass to buy French computer 3-27, 237A3
Lake Placid facilities rptd faulty 4-24, costs soar 6-17, 798A2
'Olympathon' to net $3 mln 4-29, 798F1
Newell in basketball HOF 4-30, 526E3
Burger King donates $2 mln to US com 5-15, 798E1
LA mayor urges fed aid for '84 games 5-28, 798D1
2d Natl Sports Festival held 7-21-8-1, 799B1
USSR holds Spartakaide 7-21-8-5, 799E1
LA com projects '84 Olympic costs 8-15, Coca-Cola sponsorship rptd 8-20, 798A1
USSR gold medalists defect 9-18, 721C3
ABC wins TV rights to '84 LA games 9-25, 797C3
'68 press coverage cited 760F3
PLO accepts '80 invite, IOC 'astonished' 10-2, 798G1
USSR gold medalists get Swiss asylum 10-30, 939G3
Coe, Moses expense paymts probe rptd 11-12, Coe named to UK team 11-13, 956B2
Taiwan sues over 2 China plan 11-15, IOC OKs plan 11-26, 1000C3
Pan American Games
Held 7-1-7-15, 798E2
US basketball coach arrested in assault 7-8, convicted 8-22, sentenced 9-10, 798B3, D3

1980

SPETH, Gus
Warns re water supply 2-19, 145C2
Urges tighter chem controls 6-29, 494G2
SPIERS, Ronald
US-Turkey bases accord set 1-9, 22A3
SPIKE, The (book)
On best-seller list 7-13, 568B3; 8-17, 640E3; 9-14, 716B3
SPINELLI, Ann
Famous Potatoes wins Amer Book Award 5-1, 692D2
SPINNERS (singing group)
Working My Way Back to You on best-seller list 4-2, 280E3
SPITZ, Mark
Heiden wins 5 Olympic gold medals 2-15—2-23, 155B1
Dityatin wins 8th Olympic medal 7-25, 588F3
SPLENDID Girl (race horse)
Sets speed record 5-14, 447D3
SPLITTORFF, Paul
Royals win AL pennant 10-10, 796A1*
In World Series 10-14—10-21, 812F3
SPOONER, Mary Helen
Arrested in Bolivia 8-6, freed 8-12, 668D1
SPORTING News, The (newspaper)
Auerbach named NBA top exec 5-29, 656D3
Top baseball mgr named 11-1, Golden Glove winners 12-6, 926C1, D1

SPORTS—*See also specific sport (e.g., TENNIS)*
AIAW conventn 1-6—1-10, 103E3
NCAA conventn 1-7—1-8, 103B3
Coll transcript scandal spreads; FBI, NCAA probes rptd 1-23—5-23, 469B2-D3
NCAA wins Title IX appeal 4-19, 469D3
NCAA aid limit case declined by Sup Ct 5-12, 426B3
UNM ex-coach acquitted of US chrgs 6-20, 875E3
Cable-TV blackout restrictn cited 7-22, 583B2
Ariz ex-football coach, others indicted 7-24, state probe asked 10-16, 875G2
NCAA probe of UCLA basketball team 'rewards' rptd 7-27, 875C3
Copyright royalty fees divided 7-29, 640F2
Pac-10 punishes 5 schls in transcript scandal 8-11, 875C1
USC reveals faulty athletic admissns 10-13, coaches comment 10-15, 10-29, 875C2
Ore U athletic dept probe delay chrgd 10-13, denied 10-15, 875B3
Cross-ownership ban backed 11-18, 998D3-999A1
Olympic Games (Lake Placid)
Taiwan competitn controversy 1-15—2-12, team excused from games 2-13, 154D3
Sovts to attend games 1-20, 45F3
Results; medal standings 2-12—2-24, 154E2-D3, 155F2-G3
Transportatn problems mar games 2-13—2-18, 155C2
Heiden wins 5 skating gold medals 2-15—2-23, 155A1
US hockey team tops Sovts 2-22, wins gold medal 2-24, 155E1
Organizing com debt, bankruptcy threat rptd 6-1, 421A1
Olympic Games (Los Angeles)
Olympic flag controversy 7-16—8-3, 588F1
Olympic Games (Montreal)
Canada chrgs '76 Olympics contractor 5-9, 406E2
Montreal mayor blamed for '76 debt 6-5, 444C1
Quebec Liberals keep '76 gifts 6-6, 444G1
Montreal mayor scores '76 debt rpt 6-14, 461A3
Canada '76 fraud chrgs rptd 10-2, 788D1
Olympic Games (Moscow)
NATO discusses boycott in response to Sovt Afghan invasn 3C1
Sakharov asks boycott 1-2, 46A3
US weighs boycott 1-4, 1E1; 1-7—1-18, 28E2
Saudis announce boycott 1-6, 3B1
Greece to seek permanent site 1-18, 45C3
Muhammad Ali club for Moscow boycott 1-18, 45D3

1976	1977	1978	1979	1980

1980

Carter urges site shift, asks USOC cooperatn 1-20, 45B2
NBC-TV boycott $ loss seen 1-20, 45E3
US Cong backs boycott, other dvpts 1-22—1-31, 67E3-68G1
NZ supports boycott 1-22, 100D2
Carter affirms USSR boycott threat 1-23, 41B2, 42D2
US House com backs Carter stand 1-23, 45G3
Islamic conf asks boycott 1-29, 67A2
Boycott movemt grows 2-1, 2-2; Ali rebuffed in Tanzania 2-3, 84G3
French, W Ger boycott oppositn softens 2-6, 84A3
USSR scores US 2-7, 106D3
Vance addresses IOC 2-9, IOC backs Moscow Olympics; reactn 2-12, 107B1
W Ger backs US 2-10, 106B3
Australia stresses boycott effort 2-12, 148C1
Carter firm on boycott 2-13, 110B1
Italy CP scores US boycott 2-17, 134E1
Trudeau on boycott conditns 2-19, 121F2
EC split re boycott 2-19, 124A1
USSR dissident crackdown, other pol moves rptd 2-27, 3-18, 259F1, 262E1
W Ger-US communique backs boycott 3-5, 205B2
US halts stamp, postcard sales 3-11, 206A2
Carter asks voluntary products ban 3-12, 206G1
US, GB, Australia, 9 other natns OK alternate games; TV financing studied, Soviets discount 3-18, 206C1
W Ger oppositn seeks firm stand, Schmidt hints boycott support 3-20, 236E3, 259D3
Carter adamant on US boycott 3-21, 3-22, threatens emergency powers 4-10, 258E2
Coca-Cola ends USSR shipmts 3-21, 259E1
Eur coms rebuff US boycott 3-22, 259B3
French boycott decisn delay seen 3-23, 259E3
UK, Canada, Norway coms OK participatn 3-25, 3-30, 259E2
Carter sets mandatory products ban; NBC coverage barred, $61 mln rptd lost 3-28, 259B1
IOC lists boycotting natns 3-28, 259E3
PI to miss games, funding blamed 3-28, 259F3
Vance rebuffs allies on boycott stand 3-31, 259G3
Sears links USOC funds to boycott 4-3, 260A1
Reagan on US boycott 4-8, 264A3
US newspr eds vs Carter curbs 4-9; Carter reasserts stance 4-10, 264E1, F1
Reagan denies view change 4-10, 288C2
Iran sets boycott 4-11, 325D3
USOC backs boycott; Admin lauds, athletes score 4-12, 283E1, C2
Sovts score USOC boycott vote 4-13, 283B3
NBC hints revised coverage 4-14, 283F2
Australia lauds USOC boycott vote 4-14, 283G2
Canada Olympic com favors boycott 4-14, 283A3
W Ger endorses boycott, French boycott seen 4-14, 283D3
Japan reaffirms pro-boycott stand 4-15, 283B3
W Ger vs participatn 4-17, 303B2
PR com vs boycott 4-18, 325D3
Norway Sports Fed backs boycott 4-19, 325F3
Canada backs boycott, Olympic com scores 4-22, 325A3
Gambia, China set boycott terms 4-22, 4-24, 325F3
USOC sued by athletes 4-23, 325F2
Canada com OKs boycott 4-26; W Ger joins, Weyer scores IOC 5-15, 379B2
Bolivia bows out, blames econ 5-2, 379D2
Liechtenstein cancels stamp issue 5-2, 379D2
Singapore joins boycott 5-3, Argentina 5-8, 379D2
NBC drops telecast plans, estimates loss at $22 mln 5-6, 379D3
Killanin meets with Brezhnev 5-7, Carter 5-15, 379E1
NZ com rejects boycott, Peru OKs participatn 5-8, 379B3
Swiss com rejects boycott, leaves optns 5-10, 379B3
French com rejects boycott 5-13, US assails decisn 5-14, 379F2
USOC suit dismissed 5-16, 379C3
UK indep boycott spreads 5-17, 379E2
Killanin rejects reelectn bid 5-19, 379A2
Burma bows out, lacks athletes 5-19, 379F2
Italy warns athletes vs participatn 5-19, com defied 5-20, 379A3
5 Eur coms OK participatn 5-20, 379A3
IOC moves vs boycott 5-21—5-23, Killanin asks Carter, Brezhnev mtg 5-23, 325B2
Turkey backs boycott 5-22, Olympic com OKs 5-23, 421E1
Israel com OKs boycott 5-22, 421E1
Spain backs boycott 5-22, Olympic com rejects 5-23, 421F1
Australia com rejects boycott; Fraser, US score 5-23, sports feds, athletes bar participatn 5-28, 421A1
USOC suit dismissal upheld 5-23, 421G1
US, USSR dispute boycott effect 5-24, Killanin extends invitatn deadline 5-26, IOC sees 85 nations attending 5-27, 420B3

1976

SPORTS Illustrated (magazine)
Rpts Kulagin interview 1-5, 56C2
Snyder dies 5-2, 524F3
Sup Ct bars privacy suit review 5-24, 393C2
Guild begins strike 6-2, 398C1
Guild ends strike 6-21, 454C2
Evert named athlete of yr 12-3, 969A3
SPRIGGS, Harry
Nigeria arrest rptd 6-2, 498E2
SPRINGER, William L.
Named to FEC 5-17; confrmd, sworn 5-21, 391G2
SPRINGFIELD, Ill.—*See ILLINOIS*
SPRINGFIELD, Mo.—*See MISSOURI*
SPROAT, Iain
Moderate Laborites assail leftists 11-16, 906D1
SPROCK, Pvt. Paul B.
Hospitalized 5-28, 435F3
SPROSTONS Guyana Ltd.—*See ALCAN Aluminium*
SPROUSE, James M.
Loses primary for gov 5-11, 342D3
SQUARE Deal Trucking Co. Inc.
Bortnick kidnaped 1-12—1-17, 159F3
SQUIBB Corp.
'69 trust suit ends in mistrial 8-17, 988B3
SQUIRES, Hilary
Todd house arrest lifted 6-5, 428E2
Renews state of emergency 6-24, 522A3
Rhodesia conf delegate 10-12, 781D2
SRILAK Sivarat
Arrested 10-15, 794E2

SRI Lanka (formerly Ceylon)—*See also ADB, COMMONWEALTH of Nations, NONALIGNED Nations Movement*
China aid, trade pacts rptd 1-2, 78D1
Listed as 'partly free' 1-19, 20D3
Goonetillake, daughter sentncd 2-5, 123C2
Total IMF oil loan rptd 4-1, 340E2
Reed confrmd US amb 5-26, 412A2
Olympic withdrawal rptd 7-21, 528B3
Peru to boycott nonaligned natns mtg 8-4, 590C3
Nonaligned natns conf 8-16—8-20, 621F2
Amerasinghe becomes Assemb pres 9-21, 718D3
Univ employes strike 11-11, studnt killed 11-12, demonstratns banned 11-22, 890F1
Offers UN Assemb Geneva conf amendmt 12-6, 914B2
Amerasinghe addresses UN 12-22, 955A1
Listed as free 12-22, 977B3
OPEC loan signed 12-23, 975E3

1977

SPORTS Illustrated (magazine)
Names Cauthen sportsman of yr 12-14, 970E3
SPRAGUE, Richard A.
Boyle conviction upset 1-28, 95F3
House assassinatn com revived 2-2, 77E1
Gonzalez fires, com balks 2-10—2-21, 126G3
Gonzalez quits com 3-2, 149A1
Questions Ray 3-22, 228A3
Resigns from com 3-29, 228A2
SPRAY, Dr. Selwyn
Rhodesia ousts 6-21; rpts rebel support 6-22, 536E2
SPRINGFIELD Newspapers Inc.
FCC OKs Gannett purchase 4-14, 395E2
SPRINGS Mills Inc.
Tris ban exemptn affirmed 5-24, 483E2
Tris ban upset 6-23, recall enjoined 6-26, 560D1
SPRINGSTEAD, Marty
Orioles forfeit vital game 9-14, 748B3
SPYING—*See ESPIONAGE*
SPY Who Loved Me, The (film)
Top-grossing film 8-3, 643B2; 8-31, 712G3; 9-28, 808G3; 10-19, 872G3
SQUIRE, Clark
Chesimard convicted, sentncd 3-25, 288D3
SQUIRES, Hilary
Rhodesia deportatn news banned 10-7, 811F1

SRI Lanka (formerly Ceylon)—*See also COMMONWEALTH of Nations, NONALIGNED Nations Movement*
Emergency laws invoked 1-5; bus workers join rail strike, censorship set 1-10, 22D3
Unions OK strike end 1-15; strikes end 1-17, 68F2
Govt warns emergency rule 1-25, 68B3
Partl recessed 2-12, emergency ends 2-15, 137D3
Govt foes vs parlt recess 2-15, 137F3
4 Freedom Party parlt members quit 2-15, 137G3
Subasinghe quits Cabt, Freedom Party 3-1, 183G1
Radical Party formed 183A2
New Socialist Front formed 4-10, 309C3
Bandaranaike, party lose electns 7-21; Jayewardene sworn prime min 7-23, 571B3
Post-electn riots 7-23—7-25, 571E3
Tamil-Sinhalese riots, 54 die 8-15—8-23, 657C3, G3
Tamils asked to drop secessn 8-18, 658A1

1978

SPORTS Car Club of America
CART backing rptd 12-28, 1028B2
SPORTS Illustrated (magazine)
Woman rptr gains locker room access 9-25, 1026C3
Nicklaus named sportsman of yr 12-20, 990A3
SPRAGUE, Richard A.
Boyle convicted again 2-18, 129B1
SPRATLY Islands
PI occupies islet 3-11, 290F1
Taiwan rescues Viet refugees 12-4, 932C3
SPRING Awakening (play)
Opens 7-13, 887B3
SPRINGER, Ashton
Eubie opens 9-20, 1031E1
SPRINGER, Axel
Named in S Africa press scandal 11-2, 868F2
SPRINGFIELD, Ill.—*See ILLINOIS*
SPRINGSTEEN, Bruce
Darkness on best-seller list 7-5, 580A1
SPROUL, Allan
Dies 4-9, 356D3
SPUNGEN, Nancy
Killed, boyfriend chrgd 10-12, 842C1
SPYING—*See ESPIONAGE*
SPY Who Loved Me, The (film)
Top United Artists execs quit 1-13, 1-16, 75B3
SQUAW Valley, Calif.—*See CALIFORNIA*
SQUIBB Corp.
Forgn natn tetracycline trust suit OKd 1-11, 33E3
Weicker Sr dies 11-25, 972G3
SQUIBB & Sons, E. R.—*See SQUIBB Corp.*
SQUID—*See FISH*
SQUIRES, Hilary
Criticizes Hove 4-19, 317F1
Rhodesia defense min 11-18, 912D2
SREDNICKI, Henryk
Wins World Amateur Boxing tourn 5-6—5-20, 600E2

SRI Lanka (formerly Ceylon)—*See also COMMONWEALTH of Nations, GATT, NONALIGNED Nations Movement*
Freedom House lists as free 44A2
Parlt member shot 1-27, 293A1
Freedom Party shuns assemb mtg 2-2, 92F3
Jayewardene becomes pres, govt system shifted 2-3, 92E3
Premadasa named prime min, other Cabt members reapptd 2-6, 116C1
Amerasinghe elected UN Sea Law Conf pres 4-6, 401C3
Tamil anti-terror drive set 4-19, 292G3
UK cancels debts 7-31, 592E1
UN Assemb member 713E3
UK co tea policies opposed in Australia 9-29, 754E3
Strikes banned 10-2, 758C2
183 Indonesians die in jet crash 11-15, 908G1
Hurricane hits 11-24, 972D2

1979

SPRATLY Islands
China asks Viet exit 4-26, 298F1
85 Viet refugees rptd shot 7-22, 550A2
PI annexatn rptd 9-7, 660B3
SPRINGER, Ashton
Whoopee opens 2-14, 292F3
SPRINGFIELD, Mass.—*See MASSACHUSETTS*
SPRY, Robin
One Man released 7-27, 820E2
SQUADRON, Howard
Vs SCLC on PLO 8-21, 624D1
SQUASH Racquets
Tournaments
Natl women's intercollegiate champs, Ramsey 3-4, 527C2
North Amer open, Khan 1-14, 527A2
US amateur, Surtees 1-21, 527A2
US women's open, McKay 2-11, 527C2
Women's intl open, McKay 1-28, 527B2
SQUIRES, Harry
Electroshock technique rptd 3-1, 290B1
SRI International (formerly Stanford Research Institute) (Menlo Park, Calif.)
Solar cell silicon productn method rptd 8-27, 649A1

SRI Lanka (formerly Ceylon)—*See also COMMONWEALTH of Nations, DISARMAMENT–Geneva Committee, GATT, NONALIGNED Nations Movement*
Tamil separatist curbs enacted 7-19, 604A2
UN membership listed 695A3

1980

Japan com OKs boycott 5-24, 421D1
PR feds get boycott choice 5-24, 421F1
Uganda, Jordan reverse pro-boycott stands 5-24, 5-25, 421G1
IOC bans 4 natns 5-27, 420D3
Individual participatn barred by IOC 6-10, 588G1
Sovts seize auto license plates 6-14, 467C2
Afghan basketball players defect to Pak, soccer player defectns cited 6-20, 475D2
US track & field trials held 6-21—6-29, 891F1
PR boxing team arrives for games 6-29, 588A2
Afghan wrestlers defect to Pak 7-6; Afghan athletes deny defectn plans 7-21, 590B2
Carter rptd grateful for Japan boycott 7-8, 506E1
Sovts crack down on forgn press 7-13—7-23, 588A1, 590B1, D1
Killanin rips boycott 7-18, pleads for intl peace 8-3, 590E3
Games held despite boycott; some natl flags, anthems missing 7-19—8-3, 587E3, 588B1
Soviets set medal record 7-20—8-3, Dityatin wins 8 7-25, 588A1, 590B1
Swimming, track, boxing highlights 7-20—8-2, 588G3-589E1
Arafat tours Olympic Village 7-20, 590B1
Results, final medal standings 7-20—8-3, 587E3-588B1, A3, 622C1-624G3
Disputes mar women's gymnastics 7-21—7-25, 589D2-B3
Australian triple jump disallowed 7-25; IAAF backs Sovt officiating 7-31, 589B3
Soviet men's basketball team loses 7-26, 7-27, 588G2-D3
Coe, Ovett in track duels 7-26, 8-1, 589F1-C2
US salutes team 7-26—7-30, Carter defends boycott 7-30, 590B3
US Swimming Championship times compared 7-29—8-2, 834D2
French athletes deliver rights appeal 8-2, 590E2
No drug use found 8-3, 590G2-B3
Strict security measures detailed, anti-US TV film aired 8-9, 588A1, 589F3-590B1
Carter cites boycott in pres renominatn acceptance speech 8-14, 613C1
Olympic Games (Sarajavo)
ABC wins rights to '84 winter games 1-24, 206F1
SPORTS Illustrated (magazine)
Errico convicted 5-19, 447B3
SPOTTISWOODE, Roger
Terror Train released 10-3, 836G3
SPRAGUE, Ronald
Testifies at B Carter probe 8-20, drug links rptd under investigatn 8-21, 647B2
SPRATLY Islands
China claims 1-30, 132C3
SPRING, Earle
Life aid ordrd in 'Right-to-Die' case 1-24, 158D2
SPRINGFIELD—*See ILLINOIS, MASSACHUSETTS, MISSOURI*
SPRING of the Tiger, The (book)
On best-seller list 6-8, 448D3
SPRINGSTEEN, Bruce
River on best-seller list 12-3, 948C3
SPRUCE Goose (aircraft)
Dismantlement set 5-22, 560G2
SPUZICH, Sandra
Wins Barth Classic 9-7; ties for 2d in Mixed Team tourn 12-14, 972B1, A2
SQUADRON, Howard
Vs Carter disavowal of UN anti-Israel vote 3-4, 164D1
SQUIBB Corp.
DES liability case declined by Sup Ct 10-14, 781F3

SRI Lanka (formerly Ceylon)—*See also ADB, COMMONWEALTH of Nations, GATT, GENEVA Committee, NONALIGNED Nations*
H Jayewardene on UN comm to probe shah 2-17, 122B1
W Ger pol asylum rules rptd tightened 7-31, 581F2
A-treaty review conf ends; US, UK, USSR implementatn failure cited 9-7, 696C1
State of emergency set 10-14; parlt ousts Bandaranaike, nephew 10-16, 810A1
Obituaries
Amerasinghe, Hamilton 12-4, 1004A1
Kotelawala, John 10-2, 876C2

1976

SST (supersonic transport)—*See under AVIATION*
SS-20—*See 'Missiles' under ARMAMENTS*
STABLER, Wells
Spain warned on CP 6-8, 459E3
STACK, Ella
Backs Stretton on cyclone relief 11-21, 902F2
STAEBLER, Neil
Renamed to FEC 5-17; confrmd 5-18, sworn 5-21, 391C3
STAFFORD, Sen. Robert T. (R, Vt.)
Named to intelligence com 5-20, 377E1
Wins renomination 9-14, 705A2
Reelected 11-2, 820D1, 821D3, 828C3
STAFFORD Miller Export Inc.
Chrgd re Arab boycott 10-8, 785D3
STAGG, Francis
Dies 2-12, buried 2-21; violence erupts 2-12—2-22, 146C2, C3
STAGGERS, Rep. Harley O. (D, W.Va.)
Reelected 11-2, 831A3
STAHL, Lesley
Cited re Schorr actions 9-23, 749F1
STAHR, Elvis
Sees Carter 12-16, 937C2
STALIN, Joseph (Josef Vissarionovich Djugashvili (1879-1953)—*See 1953, pp. 73G-74J for biog. data*
Brezhnev named field marshal 5-8, 421G1
Cited in Mao biog 659C1
Lysenko dies 11-20, 970D2
STAMATIS, George
Greek Interior min 1-5, 73D2
Asks riot probe 12-16, 1004D2
STAMBUL, Dr. Harriet B.
Alcohol study scored 6-9, 6-10, 442F3-443E1
STAMMATI, Gaetano
Italian finance min 2-11, 140B2
Sworn Italy treas min 7-30, 573F1
Sets new austerity measures 10-15, 838D1
STANDARD Oil Co. (California)
Australia dvpt projct set 4-29, 332C1
On '75 Fortune 500 list 437B1
Trust suit retrial bid eased 10-18, 867G2
Chevron Oil Co.
Italy exec shot 4-21, 297D1
STANDARD Oil Co. (Indiana)
'74 NY trust case vs Amoco rptd pending 3-11, 413F1
SEC lists paymts 5-12, 729C1
Ky antibusing threats rptd 6-14, 453F1
Colo oil shale leases suspended 8-23, 648G3
Israel curbs Amoco Suez drilling 8-31, 9-4, 9-6, 663D2
US, Israel meet on Amoco Suez feud 9-8, 9-13, 759G2
Israel newspr leaks Amoco rpt document 9-28, Israel probes 9-29, 759A3
STANDARD Oil Co. (N.J.)—*See EXXON*

1977

Pol ldrs tied to riots 8-23, arrested 8-24, 657E3
Tamils relocated 8-24, 8-25, 657F3
Jayewardene peace plea 8-29, 674D1
Violence ends, curfew lifted 8-31, 674C1
Malaria upsurge rptd 9-4, 747F3
Pres-type govt OKd 10-5, law signed 10-20, 843C3
Former rebels freed 11-2, 843B3
Foreign Relations (misc.)
UN Assemb member 4B1
Intl rubber buffer stock plan rejctd 1-23, 169G2
UNESCO energy experiment rptd 3-30, 298D3
Sweden cancels debts 11-8, 904A1
SSI (Supplemental Security Income)—*See U.S. GOVERNMENT—SOCIAL Security Administration*
SST (supersonic transport)—*See AVIATION—SST/Concorde*
STABLER, Ken
Raiders win Super Bowl 1-9, 24E3
Oakland wins in playoffs 12-24, 1019F3
STACY, Hollis
Wins US Womens Open 7-24, 951A1
Wins Muscular Dystrophy Open, sets LPGA record 9-5, 951D1
LPGA top money winner 11-27, 951F1
Wins Mixed Team tourn 12-4, 950C3
STAFF, George L.
Fired 6-16, 520C1
STAFFA, Dino Cardinal
Dies 8-7, 696F3
STAFFORD, Sen. Robert T. (R, Vt.)
Hansen elected conf secy 1-4, 6A2
STAGGERS, Rep. Harley O. (D, W. Va.)
'76 spec interest gifts rptd 2-4, 128G3, 129B2
STAKHANOV, Alexei G.
Dies 11-5, 952D3
STALEY, Anthony
Named Australia post min 12-19, 982A2
STALEY, Thomas F.
Dies 9-13, 788F2
STALIN, Joseph (Joseph Vissarionovich Djugashvili) (1879-1953)—*See 1953, pp. 73G-74J for biog. data*
Brezhnev vows repressn end 5-24, 433F2
Brezhnev elected pres 6-16, 469E2
USSR natl anthem revised 9-1, 766C2
Tatar natlst freed 12-22, 1017C2
STALLINGS, Richard Lee
CIA Australia role cited 5-4, 372B1
STAMATIS, George
Knifing attempt foiled 1-18, 182E2
Named Greek justice min 11-28, 925B2
STANDARD Chartered Bank Ltd.
Bank of Calif takeover rejctd 3-1, 155A2
STANDARD Oil Co. (Indiana)
Amoco Gulf of Mex gas probe set 2-17, 151F3
Carter energy plan reactn 4-24, 319B3
On '76 Fortune 500 list 340E1
FTC info order review rejctd 6-13, 517G1
Swearingen on Carter attack 10-13, 773A1
STANDARD Oil Co. (N.J.)—*See EXXON*
STANDARD Oil Co. (Ohio)
Frances Payne Bolton dies 3-9, 264D2
Alaska pipeline opens 6-20, 476C2, B3
ICC sets Alaska pipeline rates 6-28, 498C1, F1
Calif-Tex pipe OKd 12-2, 942D3
STANDARD Oil Co. of California
To mkt extra Saudi oil 2-16, 108C1, D1
World Ct awards Libya natlizatn damages 3-2, 488E1
On '76 Fortune 500 list 340E1
Employe stock plan cited 5-6, 409G1
Saudi fire forces sale cut 5-19, 402C2
Lonrho sues re Rhodesia sales 5-31, 413C2
FTC info order review rejctd 6-13, 517G1
Washington state sues 8-16, 691E3
Libya paymt pact rptd 9-26, 772C2
Replies to Carter attack 10-13, 773B1
California Asiatic Oil Co.
Australia OKs NW Shelf gas search 8-24, 704E3
Caltex Petroleum Co.—*See separate listing*

1978

SSI (Supplemental Security Income)—*See U.S. GOVERNMENT—SOCIAL Security Administration*
SS-Missile Series (Soviet strategic intercontinental ballistic missiles)—*See ARMAMENTS—Missiles*
SST (supersonic transport)—*See AVIATION—SST/Concorde*
STAATS, Elmer B.
Rpts volunteer force costs 2-6, 82C1
Says Clinch R breeder halt illegal 3-10, 183D2
On fraud in fed spending 9-18, 714G3
STABILE, Joseph
Indicted 9-15, 11-6; resigns, pleads guilty 11-9, 886B3
STABLER, Ken
NFL '77 passing ldr 1-1, 56A2
NFC wins Pro Bowl 1-23, 56E1
STACK, Edward J.
Wins US House seat 11-7, 849F3, 850G2
STACY, Hollis
Wins Birmingham Classic 4-16, 355G3
2d in Lady Tara tourn 4-30, 356B1
2d in Peter Jackson Classic 6-4, 580F3
Wins US Women's Open 7-23, 672G2
LPGA top money winner 11-20, 990C3
3d in Mixed Team tourn 12-3, 990E1
STADOL (butorohanol tartrate)—*See MEDICINE—Drugs*
STAEBLER, Neil
Replaced on FEC 10-25, 831B3
STAEDEL Museum (Frankfurt, West Germany)
Paintings smeared 4-11, 335A2
STAFFORD, Sen. Robert T. (R, Vt.)
Votes for Panama Canal neutrality pact 3-16, 177F2
Votes for 2d Canal pact 4-18, 273B1
STAGES (play)
Opens 3-19, 760D3
STAGGERS, Rep. Harley O. (D, W. Va.)
Reelected 11-7, 852B4
PAC contributions rptd 12-24, 1008E1
STAINED Glass (book)
On best-seller list 7-2, 579C3
STAINLESS Steel—*See STEEL*
STALIN, Joseph (Joseph Vissarionovich Djugashvili) (1879-1953)—*See 1953, pp. 73G-74J for biog. data*
Callaghan compares Shcharansky, Ginzburg trials 7-10, 542C3
Canada press cites 'sincerity' 11-30, 911A3
STALLONE, Sylvester
F.I.S.T. released 4-26, 619A2
Paradise Alley released 10-10, 970F2
STALLWORTH, John
Steelers win in playoffs 12-30, 1024F1
STAMFORD, Conn.—*See CONNECTICUT*
STAMFORD Advocate (newspaper)
Dolan wins Pulitzer 4-17, 315A2
STAMMATI, Gaetano
Named Italy pub works min 3-11, 191B1
STANBACK, Haskel
NFL '77 rushing ldr 1-1, 56E3
STANDARD Brands Inc.
Reggie candy bar debuts 4-13, 779G3
STANDARD Chartered Bank Ltd.
To buy Calif bank 6-8, 553B1
STANDARD Fruit & Steamship Co.—*See under CASTLE & Cooke Inc.*
STANDARD Oil Co. (Indiana)
On '77 Fortune 500 list 5-8, 325F1
Pipeline divestiture urged by Sen subcom 6-21, 471E1
6th-ranked cash-rich US co 9-18, 716E3
Amoco International Oil Co.
Supertanker spill fouls French coast 3-17, 201D3; wreckage spreads 3-23—3-29, 238B1
French sen comm rpts on supertanker spill costs, probe bd ends hearings 7-1, 524C1
Supertanker spill suit 9-13, 749C1
Lead-free gas allocatn begins 12-1, 939B1
Amoco Production Co.
Crude oil '73-76 overchrgs alleged 7-21, 610C3
STANDARD Oil Co. (N.J.)—*See EXXON*
STANDARD Oil Co. (Ohio) (Sohio)
Rebates to consumers barred 1-20, 109A1
Long Beach (Calif) voters OK lease 11-7, 857B1
STANDARD Oil Co. of California (Socal)
In Dow Jones indl avg 66F2
On '77 Fortune 500 list 5-8, 325E1
Amax bars takeover bid 9-7, trading disclosures spur NYSE probe 9-8, 9-11, 700B2
9th-ranked cash-rich US co 9-18, 716E3
Chevron Oil Co.
UK hikes offshore oil tax 8-2, 591G3

1979

SS-GB (book)
On best-seller list 5-6, 356C2
SSI (Supplemental Security Income)—*See U.S. GOVERNMENT-SOCIAL Security Administration*
SS-Missile Series (Soviet strategic intercontinental ballistic missiles)—*See ARMAMENTS-Missiles*
SST (supersonic transport)—*See AVIATION-SST/Concorde*
STABILE, Joseph
Sentenced 1-17, 92B3
STACK, William
Calls '76 Carter campaign ad financing 'ethical' 6-22, 500C2
STACY, Hollis
2d in Sunstar Classic 3-11, 220G3
Wins Mayflower Classic 7-8, 587D3
2d in Patty Berg Classic 8-26, 970B1
STAEBLER, Neil
McGarry FEC apptmt upheld 1-8, 130D3
STAFFORD, Auxiliary Bishop J. Francis
Named to '80 Rome synod 5-3, 376B1
STAFFORD, Jean
Dies 3-26, 272F3
STAGGERS, Rep. Harley O. (D, W. Va.)
Commerce Com chrmn 1-24, 71D1
MD, nursing schl fund cuts trimmed 3-6, 163E3
STAKMAN, Elvin Charles
Dies 1-22, 104F3
STALEY, Anthony
On communicatns satellite 10-18, 852C2
STALIN, Joseph (Joseph Vissarionovich Djugashvili) (1879-1953)
Kapler death rptd 9-15, 756F2
STALLINGS, C. M.
On Va A-plant sabotage 5-8, 386D2
STALLONE, Sylvester
Rocky II released 6-15, 820C3
STALLWORTH, John
Steelers win Super Bowl 1-21, 62F3-63A2
STAMFORD, Conn.—*See CONNECTICUT*
STAMP, Terence
Divine Nymph released 10-12, 1007C3
STAMPER, M. T.
On '78 top-paid execs list 5-14, 347F3
STAMPS—*See PHILATELY*
STANDARD Chartered Bank Ltd.
US OKs Calif bank purchase 3-16, 205C1
STANDARD Life & Accident Insurance Co.
Justice Dept cites '77 Sup Ct tax case errors 10-8, 848A2
STANDARD Oil Co. (Indiana)
US files overchrg suit 1-5, 17B1
Gas allocatn studied 2-14, 126A2
Cyprus Mines purchase set 4-11, 560B3
1st 1/4 oil profits rptd 4-27, 301B2
US overchrg claims denied 5-2, 343B2
US gas shortfall explained 5-7, 343D1
On '78 Fortune 500 list 5-7, 304F1
Swearington on Carter mtg 5-31, 418D1
July gas supplies rptd 6-27, 479F1
Gasohol marketing test cited 8-10, 649G1
Swearingen scores Carter oil policy 9-12, 702G3
US overchrgs alleged 10-18, 849C1
3d 1/4 profits rptd up 10-25, 804C3
Amoco International Oil Co.
Gas allocatns announced 2-28, 146C1
'79 heating oil price rise seen 9-16, 703D1
STANDARD Oil Co. (N.J.)—*See EXXON*
STANDARD Oil Co. (Ohio) (Sohio)
Oil sales cutback set 3-9, 183A3
Calif-Tex pipe canceled 3-13, El Paso denies bar 3-14, 183D1
1st 1/4 oil profits rptd 4-27, 301B2
US overchrg claims denied 5-2, 343B2
Fortune rpts '78 rank, sales gain 5-7, 305A1
Calif-Tex pipe cancellatn reaffirmed 5-24, 396F1
1st 1/2 profits up 9-6, 686G3
3d 1/4 profits rptd up 10-25, 804D2, D3
US overchrgs alleged 11-6, 849G2; 12-19, 990E2
STANDARD Oil Co. of California (Socal)
In Dow Jones indl avg 72F1
Iran oil crisis forces sales curbs 2-6, 83A1
1st 1/4 oil profits rptd 4-27, 301B2
US overchrg claims denied 5-2, 343B2
Calif gas shortage explained 5-7, 343C1
On '78 Fortune 500 list 5-7, 304E1
July gas supplies rptd 6-26, 479F1
3d 1/4 profits rptd 10-31, 849E2
US overchrgs alleged 12-10, 990A3; 12-19, 990E2
Chevron Standard Ltd.
Newfoundland find rptd 9-21, 728F2
Chevron U.S.A. Inc.
Gas supply cutback set 2-15, 126B2
May gas allocatn rptd cut 5-7, 343B1
Gas prices cut 3¢ 10-26, 804G3
US overchrgs alleged 11-6, 849G2; 12-11, 943C1

1980

SSEMOGERERE, Paul
Electns held, outcome uncertain 12-10—12-11, 945E3, 946C1
SS-GB (book)
On best-seller list 4-6, 280D3
STAATS, Elmer
Chrysler loan guarantees OKd 5-10, 383C2
Scores US probe of Teamsters 8-25, 704E3
STABLER, Ken
NFL '79 passing ldr 1-5, 8A2
Raiders win playoffs 12-28, 999E1
STACK, Rep. Edward J. (D, Fla.)
Loses primary 9-9, 700B2
Shaw wins seat 11-4, 849E2
STACK, Norman
Gold coin set sold for record sum 4-10, 472F2
STACKHOUSE, Ron
In NHL All-Star game 2-5, 198A3
STACKPOOLE, Henry Devere
Blue Lagoon released 6-20, 675G1
STACK'S Rare Coin Co.
Gold coin set sold for record sum 4-10, 472G2
STACY, Hollis
Wins Women's Intl 5-4, 412F3
2d in US Women's Open 7-13, 714B3
2d in Patty Berg Classic 8-17, 972F1
STADLER, Craig
Wins Hope Desert Classic 1-14, Greater Greensboro 4-6, 412B2, B3
2d in Kemper Open 6-1, 714G3
PGA top money winner 10-12, 971E3
Ties for 2d in Mixed Team tourn 12-14, 972B1
STAFFELDT, Judge Harold
Ford Ind Pinto crash evidence rptd restricted 3-13, 185G3-186D1
STAFFORD, Charles
Wins Pulitzer 4-14, 296F2
STAFFORD, Joseph D.
Escapes Iran 1-28, 66E2
Escape described 2-1, 88D3; 2-12, 106E1
STAFFORD, Kathleen F. (Mrs. Joseph D.)
Escapes Iran 1-28, 66E2
Escape described 2-1, 88D3; 2-12, 106E1
STAFFORD, Sen. Robert T. (R, Vt.)
On toxic waste clean-up fund 11-24, 898B1
STAFFORD v. Briggs
Case decided by Sup Ct 2-20, 170A3
STAGGERS, Rep. Harley O. (D, W.Va.)
SEC natl securities mkt plan failure scored 9-12, 806D1
RR deregulatn bill signed 10-14, 783E3
Benedict wins seat 11-4, 850A3
STAHL, Bruce
Sets 50-m freestyle mark 4-10, 834G3
STAINED Glass (book)
Wins Amer Book Award 5-1, 692F2
STALEY, Anthony
Ethnic broadcast unit planned 1-24, 116B1
STALIN, Joseph (Joseph Vissarionovich Djugashvili) (1879-1953)
French CP issues rights rpt 2-20, 149E3
China orders portrait removed 8-16, 651F2
STALLWORTH, John
NFL '79 receiving ldr 1-5, 8C2
Steelers win Super Bowl 1-20, 61F3-62C1
STAMMATI, Gaetano
Venice aid vowed 3-8—3-9, 194D2
STAMPS—*See PHILATELY*
STAND, The (book)
On best-seller list 2-10, 120E3; 3-9, 200C3
STANDARD Brands Inc.
Liggett merger bid dropped 5-14, 557B3
STANDARD Fruit & Steamship Co.—*See under CASTLE & Cooke Inc.*
STANDARD Oil Co. (Indiana)
Exxon '79 US gas selling lead rptd 1-2, 90E3
'79 profit rptd 1-25, 90G2, C3
US price violatn chrgs setld 2-14, 189G3
To buy LTV coal properties 3-25, 385C3
1st 1/4 profit rptd 4-22, 331D1, G1
On '79 Fortune 500 list 5-5, 290E1, 291B1
Wholesale gas price cut rptd 8-8, 666D3
Exxon Beaufort Sea find rptd 10-3, 785F2
Price setlmt OKd 12-3, 960C1
Amoco International Oil Co.
Australia tanker strike accord scored 3-14, 229B3
Credit bias suit setld 4-29, 370B3
Gasoline prices cut 9-11, 786A1
STANDARD Oil Co. of California (Socal)
In Dow Jones indl avg 76F1
'79 profit rptd 1-31, 90F2
FTC trust procedure case accepted by Sup Ct 2-25, 187E3
Wesleyan U sells stock 4-13, 374A2
1st 1/4 profit rptd 4-30, 331D1, G1
On '79 Fortune 500 list 5-5, 290E1
Saudi hikes prices 8% 5-14, 365B1
Wholesale gas price cut rptd 8-8, 666D3
Saudi completes Aramco takeover, bd members listed 9-4, 662B1, A2
OPEC pricing agrmt impact seen 9-18, 695B1
Haynes retires, Keller replaces 9-24, 959A3
FTC trust complaint challenge curbed by Sup Ct 12-15, 957E1
Chevron Standard Ltd.
Newfoundland find confrmd 1-3, 6D1
Chevron U.S.A.
Gasoline, other oil product prices cut 9-18, 786B1

1976

STANDARD & Poor's Corp.
Index drops from peak 3-11, 185C1
Detroit notes rptd downgraded 3-24, 994D2
STANFIELD, Robert
PC elects Clark ldr 2-23, 188B2
STANFORD University (Palo Alto, Calif.)
Solzhenitsyn rptd at work 5-4, 421D1
Chile frees Flores 8-5, 711F2
Richter wins Nobel 10-18, 840F1
2 get Science Medals 10-18, 858D3, F3
STANLEY, Fred
In World Series 10-16—10-21, 815A3
STANLEY, Justin A(rmstrong)
Vs judges' pay raise suit 2-16, 136G2
Rptd named ABA pres 8-11, 640G3
STANLEY Home Products Inc.
SEC lists paymts 5-12, 729C1
STANMARK, Ingemar
Wins Olympic medal 2-10, 158D3
STANS, Maurice
Hammer, Babcock spared jail terms 3-23, 6-4, 442E2
STANTON, Rep. James (D, Ohio)
Loses Senate primary 6-8, 409D3
STANTON, Rep. John William (R, Ohio)
Reelected 11-2, 830A3
STAPLETON, Judge Walter K.
Delaware starts football lottery 8-26, 736E3
STARBROOK, Dave
Wins Olympic medal 7-28, 575A1
STARK, Rep. Fortney H. (D, Calif.)
Reelected 11-2, 829A1
STARKEY, Judge John R.
Issues gag order 1-13, reversed 1-30, 124A2
STARCKMANN, Georges
Libya binocular fraud rptd 12-25—12-30, 1007A1
STARKWEATHER, Charles (d. 1959)
Companion paroled 6-8, 442C3
STARLIGHT International
Cited in Grumman-Iran feud 140D1
STARR, Roger
Scores HUD urban aid program 1-8, 25A2
STAR Stations Inc.
Sup Ct lets stand FCC ruling 5-24, 393E2
STASIAK, Ludomir
Polish State Cncl member 3-25, 268D2
STASSEN, Harold E.
Seeks pres support 6-25, 467E3
STATE, County and Municipal Employes, American Federation of (AFSCME) (AFL-CIO)
Quits AFL-CIO dept 2-15, 154A1
DC local sues ACTION 6-2, 414C1
NYC hospital strike 8-4—8-7, 648C1
Mass workers OK pact 12-4, 921G1
STATE-Federal Relations (U.S.)—*See also BUDGET, SUPREME Court and other appropriate headings under U.S. GOVERNMENT; also specific subjects; state names*
Dem platform text 6-15, 471G2, 472A1-E1, 474G2
Carter statemts 6-29, 468D1; 7-6, 492D3
Ford urges ldrship leeway 7-17, 531F2
GOP platform text 8-18, 602F1
Economic Assistance Programs—*See 'State-Local Aid' under U.S. GOVERNMENT—BUDGET*
STATE Legislators, National Conference of
Hears Mondale 9-2, Dole 9-3, 665A3, G3
STATEN Island Community College (N.Y.)
Birenbaum elected Antioch pres 4-12, 504F2
STATE of Maine (U.S. warship)
In Intl Naval Review 7-4, 488E3

1977

STANDARD & Poor's Corp.
Carter energy plan reactn 4-21, 320G1
SEC rpt chrgs NYC '74-75 financial deceptn 8-26, 665C3
500 stock index rptd at '68 level 8-29, 691G1
Moody's rates NYC notes low, sale canceled 11-10, 881B1
STANESCU, Ion
Named Rumania dep min 1-25, 100F1
STANFORD University (Palo Alto, Calif.)
Babcock confrmd asst atty gen 3-4, 211D1
'77-78 costs rptd 3-27, 483G1
Hook, Bettelheim vs quotas 3-31, 235E2
Forrest rpts new pain killer 3-31, 288D1
DNA recombinatn rpt 10-8, 846F3
Taube gets Medal of Sci 11-22, 952B1
Wins Sun Bowl 12-31, 1020D2
STANGELAND, Arlan
Wins US House seat 2-22, 128A1 ★
STANHOUSE, Don
Traded to Orioles 12-7, 990D1
STANISHEV, Dimitar
Named to Bulgaria Central Com 5-12, 451F2
STANISLAUS River
US water rights upheld 4-4, 253C1
STANKY, Eddie
Hired as Ranger mgr 6-22, quits 6-23, 644B3
STANLEY, Rev. David
Quits biblical comm 1-30, 119A3
STANLEY, Justin A.
Vs fed no-fault auto insurnc standards 7-18, 595A1
STANLEY Cup—*See HOCKEY*
STAPLETON, Ruth Carter
At charismatic conf 7-20—7-24, 620G3
STAPLETON, Judge Walter K.
OKs '77 Del football lottery 8-12, 659F1
STAREK, Gerald
Sentenced 3-14, 203E2
STAR Is Born, A (film)
Top-grossing film 3-9, 184D3
Song wins Oscar 3-28, 264D1
STARKEY, Judge John
Berkowitz found fit for trial 10-21, 848B3
STARNES, John Kennett
RCMP '72 raid knowledge chrgd 11-2, 903E1
STARR, Bart
Named to football HOF 1-17, 164B1
Inducted into HOF 7-30, 659A1
STARR, Chauncy
Says breeder reactor safe 3-26, 235A1
STARR, Richard C.
Kidnaped 2-14, abductors rptd dead 2-24, 255F1
STARRY, Lt. Gen. Donn A.
Reprimanded for speech 6-17, 482E3
STAR Wars (book)
On paperback best-seller list 8-14, 643A2; 9-4, 712E3; 10-2, 808F3
STAR Wars (film)
Top-grossing film 6-1, 452C2; 7-6, 548G3; 8-3, 643B2; 8-31, 712G3; 9-28, 808G3; 10-19, 872G3; 12-7, 1021B3
Tops Jaws in domestic rentals 11-19, 1021B3
STASI, Mario
Chrgs Brazil tortures minors 2-13, 168D1
STATE, Department of—*See under U.S. GOVERNMENT*
STATE, County & Municipal Employes, American Federation of (AFSCME) (AFL-CIO)
Wis state workers strike 7-3—7-18, 558F2
Detroit city workers strike 7-6, 558G2
STATE-Federal Relations (U.S.)—*See also BUDGET, SUPREME Court and other appropriate headings under U.S. GOVERNMENT; also specific subjects; state names*
Carter call-in topic 3-5, 171D1
Fed role in state civil actns curbed 3-22, 231A3
Fed utility rate rules opposed in Sen 9-14, 757D2
Economic Assistance Programs—*See U.S. GOVERNMENT—BUDGET—Revenue Sharing & Grants-In-Aid*

1978

STANDARD & Poor's Corp.
'77 index loss cited 1-1, 66G3
Calif bond ratings suspended 6-8, 426D1
Cleveland ratings suspended 7-10, 663A3
Cash-rich US cos ranked by Compustat 9-18, 716E3
SRI International (formerly Stanford Research Institute) (Menlo Park, Calif.)
Guaranteed income study rptd 5-19, 720E3
Poulter dies 6-14, 540E3
STANFORD University (Palo Alto, Calif.)
Lederberg named Rockefeller U pres 1-18, 172B2
Saudi econ dvpt plans slowed 2-20, 122G1
Pollard in basketball HOF 5-1, 457D3
2 in NFL draft 5-2, 336E3, F3
Wins NCAA team tennis title, McEnroe wins singles title 5-29, 419D2
Newsroom searches by police backed by Sup Ct 5-31, 429F3
Unified field theory confirmatn rptd 6-12, 7-8, 654A2
Mammalian gene transfer rptd 10-28, 1023B3
Wins Bluebonnet Bowl 12-31, 1025F2
STANG, P. D.
Antimatter rptd in Earth galaxy cntr 5-6, 653E3
STANGELAND, Rep. Arlan (R, Minn.)
Gets low Cong Watch rating 10-28, 865A3
Reelected 11-7, 851B2
STANGL, Bishop Josef
4 convicted in exorcism death 4-21, 379E3
STANISLAUS, St. (d. 1079)
Poland rptdly censors refs 12-21, 1019D2
STANLEY Cup—*See HOCKEY—Winners*
STANS, Maurice
Fernandez enters pres race 11-29, 938B3
STANTON, Rep. John William (R, O.)
Reelected 11-7, 851E3
STAPLETON, Jean
Wins Emmy 9-17, 1030F1
STAPLETON, Ruth Carter
Flynt '77 conversn cited 187C1
STARBLANKET, Noel
Vs const reform plan 8-29, 755F1
STARBUCK, Lesley
Forever Yours opens 6-21, 887G1
STARGELL, Wilver (Willie)
Surpasses Mantle strikeouts 8-6, 779D3
NL batting ldr 10-2, 928E2
STARGER, Martin
Autumn Sonata released 10-8, 969B3
STAR Is Born, A (film)
Evergreen wins Grammy 2-24, 315E3
STARK Jr., Rep. Fortney H. (D, Calif.)
Scores Soc Sec rollback vote 5-17, 386B1
House OKs seabed mining bill 7-26, 589B1
Reelected 11-7, 850E1
STARK, Ray
Casey's Shadow released 3-17, 618F3
Cheap Detective released 6-22, 619A1
California Suite released 12-21, 1030E2
STARKEY, Grenville
Shirley Heights wins English Derby 6-7, 539C2
STARNES, John Kennett
On PQ forgn funding, infiltratn probe 2-2, 129B3
STARVING Class, The (play)
Opens 3-2, 887B3
STAR Wars (film)
Wins Oscars 4-3, 315B3
$10.1 mln grossed 7-21—7-23, world rental mark rptd 8-2, 672B1
Top-grossing film 7-26, 620D1
Fox fined for 'block booking' 9-12, 759C2
STAR Wars (recording)
Wins Grammy 2-24, 315G3, 316B1
STASSEN, Harold E.
Loses Sen primary in Minn 9-12, 716D1
Clinton elected Ark gov 11-7, 855G1
STATE, Department of—*See under U.S. GOVERNMENT*
STATE, County & Municipal Employes, American Federation of (AFSCME) (AFL-CIO)
Wurf scores Carter fed pay hike plan 4-11, 260G2 ★
Propositn 13 topic at conv 6-26, 6-28, 526C1
AFT to organize health-care workers 11-29, 961C1
STATE-Federal Relations (U.S.)—*See BUDGET, SUPREME Court and other appropriate headings under U.S. GOVERNMENT; also specific subjects; state names*
STATE Legislatures, National Conference of
Propositn 13 topic at conv 7-6, 526A1
Boe on DC voting amendmt 8-22, 661D2
STATEN Island, N.Y.—*See NEW York City*

1979

STANDARD & Poor's Corp.
Amer Express seeks McGraw-Hill 1-9, 16A1
Chrysler debt rating lowered 8-1, 576D2
Cleveland defaults again 8-31, 920A3
Chicago bond rating lowered 9-19, 920C3, F3
Munic bond ratings listed 9-20, 920E3
Chicago schl bd rating drops 11-16, 943E3
STANDING, John
Legacy released 9-28, 820F1
STANFIELD, Robert
PCs win Canadian electns 5-22, 377G2
Heads Canada Mideast study 6-23, 502G1
Tours Mideast 9-9—10-20, 833C2
STANFORD University (Palo Alto, Calif)
Walsh hired by 49ers 1-9, 175F2
Flory cuts Sovt links 3-1, 172D2
Carter cites '78 press case 4-2, 264E3
Kennedy to become provost 4-17, 310A3
Med cntr heart transplants rptd 5-6, 355D1
Kennedy named provost 6-16, 527F3
H-bomb letter printed 9-16, 9-18, Teller denies chrgs 9-17, 713G2, 714B2; text of letter 714D1-717E3
Cohen on 'laughing gas' 10-24, 971G2
STANGE, Jurgen
Prisoner exchange rptd 7-20, 586D2
STANGL, Franz (1908-71)
Brazil '67 extraditn cited 8-8, 617C1
STANHOUSE, Don
Orioles win AL pennant 10-6, 797E2
In World Series 10-10—10-17, 816F1
Signs with Dodgers 11-17, 1001G3
STANISLAUS, St. (d. 1079)
Pope to visit Poland 1-24, 60G2
Pope arrives Poland 6-2, 413A1, G1, 414A2
STANLEY, Bob
NL wins All-Star Game 7-17, 568G3
STANLEY Cup—*See HOCKEY-Winners*
STANLEY Gibbons International
Haas stamp collectn purchased for record sum 8-14, 672A2
STAPLETON, Maureen
Lost & Found released 7-13, 820F1
STAR Dental Manufacturing Co.
Magruder starts mktg exec job 8-8, 656A3
STARGELL, Wilver (Willie)
NL batting ldr 9-30, named co-MVP 11-13, 955F1, E2
Pirates win NL pennant 10-5, 797C2
In World Series 10-10—10-17, named Series MVP 10-17, 815F3
STARK Jr., Rep. Fortney H. (D, Calif.)
Joins draft-Kennedy move 5-23, 384C2
Proposes FBI hq name chng 10-30, 886D3
STARK, Ray
Chapter Two released 12-14, 1007B3
Electric Horseman released 12-21, 1007C3
STARNES, John Kennett
Testimony on RCMP issued 3-28, 253C3
Allmand cites '76 letter re RCMP '72 break-in 4-3—4-5, 311A3
Dare testifies on '72 APLQ break-in 7-4, 522C3
STARR, Michael H.
Settles SEC chrg 2-7, 132B1
STARR, Peter H.
Buckley settles SEC chrg 2-7, 132B1
Settles SEC charge 3-27, 588A2
STARR Broadcasting Group Inc.
Buckley, Sitco partners settle SEC chrg 2-7, 132B1
2 ex-execs settle SEC chrgs 3-27, 4-9, 588G1
Shamrock transfer OKd 6-8, 588F1
STAR Trek (film)
Released 12-8, 1008F1
STAR Wars (film)
FBI seizes stolen copy 1-8, 102F2
Fox pres resigns 6-7, 588B1
Top-grossing film 8-29, 672G3
STATE, County & Municipal Employes, American Federation of (AFSCME) (AFL-CIO)
Wurf backs oil industry protest 10-17, 831D2
STATE Department—*See under U.S. GOVERNMENT*
STATE-Federal Relations (U.S.)—*See BUDGET, SUPREME Court and other headings under U.S. GOVERNMENT; also specific subjects; state names*
STATE Industries Inc.
No-contest plea cited 10-22, 986E1

1980

STANDARD Oil Co. of Ohio (Sohio)
'79 profit rptd 1-31, 90F2
1st 1/4 profit rptd 4-23, 331A2
US rescinds price hike order 5-1, 366F1
Alaska refiners paymt plan rptd, prices hiked 7-7, 553E2
Wholesale gas price cut rptd 8-8, 666D3
Gasoline prices cut 9-11, 786A1
Gulf coast leasing bids set records 9-30, 785B2
US Steel coal assets deal set 12-2, 985B2
BP Oil Inc.
Gasoline prices cut 7-9, 553F1
STANDARD & Poor's Corp.
Moody's lowers Chicago bond rating 1-31, 186B2
'79 univ endowmt earnings compared to index 3-24, 319E1
Milwaukee city, cnty bond ratings maintained 6-13, 743G3
Detroit bond rating lowered 8-6, 743A3
NYC pub bond sale moves rptd 9-10, 743A2
Boston bond rating lowered 12-2, 939C2
STANFEL, Dick
Hired as interim Saints coach 12-25, 999G1
STANFIELD, Robert
Mideast rpt backs PLO ties 2-29, 230C3
STANFORD University (Palo Alto, Calif.)
'79 football tie with USC cited 1-2, 23B1
Lyman sets resignatn 1-26, 200D1
Wins AIAW swim title 3-22, 835B1
Wins NCAA tennis title 5-22, Rennert loses singles title 5-26, 607C1
Multon loses AIAW singles tennis title 6-11, 607E1
D Kennedy named pres 6-13, 638D2
Sup Ct '79-80 term analyzed by Gunther 7-2, 540B3
Pac-10 transcript scandal penalties avoided 8-11, 875B2
Newsroom searches curb signed 10-14, 835G1
Berg wins Nobel 10-14, 889F2
STANISLAVSKY (Soviet freighter)
Seizure rptd in Canada debt dispute 10-22, 813D1, 814B1, 815D1
STANLEY Cup—*See HOCKEY, Ice--Winners*
STANTON, Rep. John William (R, Ohio)
Reelected 11-4, 843E4
STANWOOD Corp.
US-China textile pact opposed 9-18, 707F1
STAPLETON, Dave
AL batting ldr 10-6, 926D3
2d in AL top rookie vote 12-2, 926B2
STAPLETON, Jean
To quit TV series 4-2, 471B3
STARDUST Memories (film)
Released 9-26, 836F3
STARGER, Martin
Marionettes released 11-7, 972F3
STARK Jr., Rep. Fortney H. (D, Calif.)
Joins open-conv move 7-25, 570G1
Reelected 11-4, 842E1
STARK, Nathan
On nursing homes patients rights 7-9, 583G3
STARK, Ray
Seems Like Old Times released 12-19, 1003D2
STARKIE, Martin
Canterbury Tales opens 2-12, 136A3
STARNES, John Kennett
RCMP '71 suspect list rptd sent abroad 2-28, 192C1
'70s sabotage unit rptd 4-20, 350B3
STAROSTIN, Anatoly
Wins Olympic medal 7-24, 623E1
STARR, Bart
Steelers win Super Bowl 1-20, 62C1
STARR, Richard
Freed 2-11, returns to US 2-12, 117A1
STARR, Ringo
Lennon slain 12-9, 934A2, B3
STARSKY and Hutch (TV series)
'Charlie's Angels' fraud probe rptd 5-1, 376A3
LA DA ends 'Charlie's Angels' probe 12-2, 1002F2
STAR Trek (book)
On best-seller list 1-13, 40C3
STAR Trek-The Motion Picture (film)
Top-grossing film 1-9, 40G3
Heaven's Gate withdrawn from theaters 11-19, 906D1
STAR Wars (film)
Williams named Boston Pops conductor 1-10, 199F2
FBI 'Miporn' probe rptd 2-14, 136B2
Sequel released 5-21, 675D2
Sequel summer boxoffice gross rptd 9-10, 732D2
STASZESKY, Frank
Urges NRC reactor licensing resumptn 1-9, 17D1
STATE, County & Municipal Employees, American Federation of (AFSCME)
Endorses Kennedy 4-2, 247G1
Kennedy addresses conv 6-10, 438D3
Detroit workers strike 7-2, 518G1, strike ends 7-12, 542G1
Carter platform statemt 'meaningless' 8-13, 611A2
STATE, Department of—*See under U.S. GOVERNMENT*
STATE Chief Justices, Conference of
Burger '79 judiciary study rptd 1-3, 51A3
STATE Farm Mutual Automobile Insurance Co.
State ct jurisdictn narrowed by Sup Ct 1-21, 93C2
STATE Governments, Council of
Mandatory sentnc study rptd 3-29, 359D1
STATE Legislatures, National Conference of
Carter addresses 3-28, 248F1

1976

STATES (U.S.)—*See also STATE-Federal Relations (U.S.); also specific subjects; state names* Ford urges PR statehood, reaction mixed 12-31, 994F2-D3

STATE University of New York (SUNY) Binghamton Campus
Dole heckled 9-16, 687B1
STAUB, Rusty
AL batting ldr 10-4, 796C1
STAUBACH, Roger
In Super Bowl 1-18, 56B1
GOP conv vp vote table 8-19, 599F3
STEARNS, Monteagle
Ivory Coast amb 9-17; confrmd 9-30, 808D1
STECHER, Renate
Wins Olympic medals 7-25, 7-28, 576F1, G1
STEED, Rep. Tom (D, Okla.)
Reelected 11-2, 830C3
STEEL, David
Elected Liberals leader 7-7, 521F2
STEELE, John D.
Arrested 1-11, 160E1

STEEL & Iron—*See also company, country names*
Peru iron natlzatn cited 1-12, 142A2
Argentina-Venez trade pact 1-14, 96D3
Paraguay-Brazil plant deal rptd 1-16, 205E3
US trade comm import rulings 1-17, 3-2; Ford threatens quotas 3-16, 212D3, 213B3
ECSC OKs minimum price scale 1-20, 85A1
Japan curbs steel exports to EEC 1-20, 85B1
EEC scores US policy 1-21, 85C1
Mex-Brazil iron venture set 1-23, 75C1
Mauritania compensates Miferma 1-28, 104F2
4 Japan steel firms OK merger 1-28, 208D3
US '75 4th ¼ profits rptd 2-3, 215A3
Australia-Japan talks 2-4—2-15, 137D3
Venez to buy Peru iron ore 2-10, 142F2
Cuba, Colombia set trade pact 2-20, 251F3
Eur, Japan cos defer Australia projct 2-24, 154D3
Pa workers win Trade Act aid 3-1, 4-16, 348A3
US Feb productn rptd 3-16, 199A3
EC aid to British Steel set 3-25, 529A3
China-Japan deal rptd off 4-5, 265D3
9 firms fined 4-10, 988D3
Japan specialty firms merge 4-26, 419C1
US 1st ¼ profits rptd 4-29, 376C3
Ford eases flatware import curbs 4-30, 322D1
Angola natlizes Portugal co 5-6, 371A2
Ford sets specialty steel quotas 6-7; Japan OKs pact 6-9; EEC scores 6-14, 430E3-431E1

1977

STATES (U.S.)—*See also STATE-Federal Relations (U.S.); also specific subjects; state names*
Legislature mtgs set 6C2
'76 per-capita income up, table 5-10, 387B2
Fscl '76 spending, revenue rptd 9-2, 740C1
'76 per-capita income data revised, table 9-13, 10-18, 821E1
Energy conservatn credit bill OKd by Sen 10-31, 832G2

STATE Street Bank and Trust Co. (Brighton, Mass.)
Saxe sentenced 1-17, 140F1
STATE University of New York (SUNY)
Boyer named to US post 1-19, 52G3
Oneonta Campus
NCAA basketball tourn results 3-19, 262E2
STEARNS, Ky.—*See KENTUCKY*
STECHER, Fred R.
Citicorp to drop USAC sponsorship 6-24, 531F2
Settles USAC dispute 6-26, new pact set 9-21, 871C1
STEEL, David
Labor pact rptd 3-22, govt wins no-confidence vote 3-23, 239C2
On Saffron Walden by-electn 7-8, 544D1
Liberals extend pact with Labor 7-26, 637A2
Backs Liberal-Labor pact 9-28, 745G1
Welcomes Thorpe probe 10-20, 883D2
Proportional EC rep defeated 12-13, reactn 12-15, 1013C2
STEELE, Alfred (1902-59)
Joan Crawford dies 5-10, 452G2

STEEL & Iron—*See also company, country names*
US Dec '76 WPI rptd 1-12, 38C3
US gas shortage forces layoffs 1-17, 37D2
'76 4th ¼ profits rptd 2-8, 301D1
USW talks open 2-14, 130D3
EC '76 indl output rptd up 2-22, 146D2
Wean forgn paymts rptd 3-8, 233E2
Sharon Steel ends Foremost takeover bid 4-5, 275D1
US steelworkers OK contract 4-9, 273D2
1st, 2d ¼ profits rptd down 4-28, 7-28, 668B3, E3
Speer sees Admin offcls on imports, price hikes 5-5, 385D2
Prices hiked 5-6—5-12, Admin reactn 5-6—5-11, forgn competitn noted 5-6—5-9, 385D1
Productn, utilizatn rate rptd 5-9, 385F2
Urban business confidence rptd 5-16, 385A1
Steelworkers contract worth estimated 6-1, 481G2
Steel bar price-fixing chrgd 6-6, 504B1
Lockheed Navy overbilling chrgd 6-13, 482A3
UN Sea Law Conf issues rpt re mining 7-19, US scores 7-20, 572B3
Prices hiked 7-21, 7-22, Schultze scores 7-21, 577A1
1st ½ steel earnings drop rptd 7-26, 7-27, 612E1
USW strikes ore ranges 8-1, 593E2
Conrail 2d ¼ loss rptd 8-4, 612G3
Carter orders industry study 8-5, 612C1
July WPI rptd up 8-11, 629B1
July indl output down 8-15, 628E3
Industry layoffs, plant closings rptd 8-18—10-12, 775B3

1978

STATES (U.S.)—*See also GOVERNORS (U.S.); also specific subjects; state names*
Legislature schedule rptd 14D3
'67, '77 sales-tax rates rptd 1-5, 15A3
Mondale tours 7 Westn states 1-9—1-13, 34C1
Tax revenue up, table 1-9, 84B2, F2
Panama Canal treaties challenge denied 1-16, 33F2
Multistate Tax Compact upheld 2-22, 126F1-A2
Carter unveils urban-aid plan 3-27, reactn 3-27—3-30, 217C2-218D1
Cities trust law liability upheld by Sup Ct 3-29, 280F1-E2
3d ¼ spending rptd up, 2d ¼ revised 10-20, 864C1
Election results 11-7, 845A1-857C1, 897G3-898A1
Black state, legis post losses rptd 11-28, 915C3

STATTEL, Robert
Henry IV opens 11-27, 1031A2
STAUB, Rusty
AL batting ldr 10-2, 928E3
STAUBACH, Roger
NFL '77 passing ldr 1-1, 56D2
Cowboys win Super Bowl 1-15, 39G2
Injured in Cowboys playoff 12-30, 1024E1
STAVERMAN, Larry
Hired as Kings interim coach 1-8, 272F2
Replaced as Kings coach 5-10, 656C1
STAVOLA, Charlie
Ballroom at St Patrick's opens 12-1, 1031A1
STAYIN' Alive (recording)
On best-seller list 2-4, 116F3; 3-8, 196A1; 4-5, 272F3; 5-3, 356D1
STEADMAN, Richard
Urges upgrading of Joint Chiefs 7-12, 528C2
STEAVER, Gregory
Found after abductn 4-30, 414C1
STEED, Rep. Tom (D, Okla.)
Reelected 11-7, 852A1
STEEL, American Institute for Imported—*See IMPORTED Steel, etc.*
STEEL, Danielle
Says Liberals to end Labor pact 5-25, 452G3
Promise on best-seller list 6-4, 460D3
STEEL, David
Tax vote rptd 5-11, 415A2
Labor narrowly wins confidence vote on Healey's salary 6-14, 496C3
ICC orders rail freight rates cut back 6-30, 569A3
Hails Penistone by-electn 7-13, 557E2
Liberals vs Thorpe reelectn bid 8-5, 614G2
Scores Callaghan electn delay 9-7, 704F3
Urges Rhodesia sanctns-breaking probe 9-13, 756B3
STEEL Haulers, Fraternal Association of (FASH)
Strike called 11-11, 1006F1-A2
STEEL Institute, American Iron &—*See IRON & Steel Institute, American*

STEEL & Iron—*See also company names*
US Steel plans Youngstown plant closing 1-3, 4G2
BSC '77 losses rptd 1-10, govt cuts investmt 1-17, 36G2
Budd reveals Thyssen takeover bid 1-12, 66D1
Iron workers 'prehire' picketing curbed 1-17, 33G3
Mauritania ore-dvpt loan rptd 1-27, 95E1
'77 4th ¼ profits rptd down 2-7, 282E3
US Steel hikes prices 3-29, Admin scores 3-29—3-30; price undercut, rolled back 3-30—4-3, 262C3
1st ¼ '77, '78 profits rptd unchngd 4-27, 403D2
Brazil loan to Paraguay rptd 5-5, 395F3
'77 Fortune list rpts industry losses 5-8, 325B3, C3
Southn iron workrs sign pact 5-22, 429E3
US Steel vs Admin price restraint plea 5-24, Strauss, Bosworth score 5-31, 6-19, 428D1
Lykes Ind plant shutdown warned 5-24, 492G3
Bethlehem holds price hike to 3%, Admin lauds 6-12; Big 3 adopt hike 6-13—6-15, 470B2
'77 indl productivity rptd 6-14, 470B1
Bell backs LTV-Lykes merger 6-21, 492C3
Lockheed cleared on Navy overbilling chrg 6-22, 493B3
Belgian steel strike 6-22—6-27, 612F3
Iran completes Krupp paymts 7-27, 617B1
'77-78 2d ¼ corp profit rise rptd 7-28, 642C3
Penn Dixie ex-offcl indicted 10-10, 808F2

1979

STATES (U.S.)—*See also specific subjects; state names*
Legislature mtgs set 5B3
Fscl '78 tax revenues up 2-13, 152G1
Bi-state agency immunity curbed by Sup Ct 3-5, 185C1
Ct immunity curbed by Sup Ct 3-5, 185C1
FTC data disclosure OKd 3-28, 308C2
Debt collectn priority defined by US Sup Ct 4-2, 281G2
'78 tax revenues up 5-16, 386G1
'78 per capita income rptd 9-16, 746C1
'71-77 tax collectns rptd up 10-21, 990B3

STATE University of New York—*See NEW York, State University of*
STATEVILLE Correctional Center (Joliet, Ill.)
Gang rule broken by Ill police 2-24; arms, drugs rptd seized 3-3, 196D3
STAUB, Rusty
Traded to Expos 7-20, 1002B3
STAUBACH, Roger
NFL '78 passing ldr 1-6, 80D1
Steelers win Super Bowl 1-21, 62G3-63A2
NFC wins Pro Bowl 1-29, 79F3
Robbed 1-30, 175A3
STAY As You Are (film)
Released 12-21, 1008G1
STEADY Growth (race horse)
Wins Queen's Plate 6-30, 876C3
STECHER, Donald Webster
Arrested in Salameh slaying 1-26, 69C2
STEEL, David
Liberals back Tories in confidence vote 3-28, 228F1
Liberals meet 9-25—9-29; addresses conf 9-28, 792D1
STEEL Haulers, Fraternal Association of (FASH)
Strike ended 1-18, 87C2

STEEL & Iron
Steel haulers end strike 1-18, 87C2
'78 4th 1/4 profit rise rptd 2-7, 201B3
Dissident steel haulers end strike 4-29, 384C3
Pittsburgh area cleanups set by Colt unit 5-7, US Steel 5-22, 385B2-B3
Laclede chrgd re price violatns 5-17, 385A2
US Steel prices hiked 6-12, rolled back 7-2; raised 10-1, 11-29, 942A1
Wheeling-Pittsburgh gets fed aid; rivals score, suit filed 8-28, 681F3
Georgetown, Wis Steel fed aid cited, Phoenix aid rptd blocked 8-28, 682F1
US Steel settles SEC suit 9-27, 941F2
Cameron fine rptd 11-1, 923B3
US Steel sets chem venture 11-14, 941D3
US Steel sets plant closings, layoffs, '78-79 earnings cited 11-27; '80s strategy rptd 12-5, 941C2-D3
Jones & Laughlin to close Youngstown plant; US aid cited 11-28, 941G3

1980

STATES (U.S.)—*See also state names*
Legislature mtgs set 18C1
'67-77 elected offcls drop rptd 1-2, 5D3
State of State messages 1-2—2-6, 268B3-270C3; 1-7—1-15, 2-19, 403B2-404F1; 1-9—4-8, 482F3-484A3
GOP platform proposals urge fed responsibility shift 1-14, 32G1, A2
State ct jurisdictn narrowed by Sup Ct 1-21, 93F1
Fscl '79 tax revenue rptd 2-20, 307G2
Carter anti-inflatn plan sets fed spending cuts 3-14, 201C1
'79 tax collectns rptd 4-17, 307B2
US intrastate gas sale power affirmed 6-6, 552B3
Reagan seeks fed shift 6-8, 438A3
Burger warns vs ct systems 'merger' 6-10, 632D1
Standby gas rationing plan submitted by Carter 6-12, 551G3
Sales preference backed by Sup Ct 6-19, 554E2
Right to sue broadened by Sup Ct 6-25, 540C3
Reagan affirms states' rights 8-3, 597B3
Govs score fed ties 8-5, 596B1
Carter deplores Reagan states' rights stance 9-16, clarifies 9-18, 698B2
Refugee aid bill clears Cong 9-25, 10-1, Carter signs 10-10, 785B1
Election results, GOP gain in legislatures 11-4, 845C2, 847A1-852G3
Reagan backs soc svcs control 12-11, 956E2
Revenue sharing program amended 12-12, 955A1

STATON, Mick
Loses W Va spec US House electn 6-3, 439C3
Elected to US House 11-4, 844C4, 850A3
STATUE of Liberty
2 climbers protest Black Panther ruling 5-11, 667D1
STAUBACH, Roger
NFL '79 passing ldr 1-5, 8D2
STAUFFER Chemical Co.
Del toxic waste suit filed 10-9, 825B1
STAVANGER Drilling Co.
N Sea oil platform capsizes, 123 killed 3-27, 256G1
STAVRINAKIS, George
Named Cyprus labor min 9-9, 749G2
STAYNER, Steven
Found in Calif 3-1, 3 arrested 3-2, 238D2
STEAGALD v. U.S.
Case accepted by Sup Ct 10-6, 782D3
STECYK, Wladyslaw
Wins Olympic medal 7-30, 624C3
STEED, Rep. Tom (D, Okla.)
Okla primary results 8-26, 683B1
McCurdy wins seat 11-4, 850C1
STEEL, David
Backs cruise missile decision 6-17, 487D1
Addresses Liberal party, woos Labor dissidents 9-12, 708G1
Scores pub sector pay lid 11-7, 886E3

STEEL & Iron
Bethlehem chairmen named 1-31, 224F3
US Steel Ohio plant closings blocked 2-28, 266A2
Penn-Dixie files for bankruptcy 4-7, 985F3
USW contract settled 4-15, 288G3
USW pact termed within US guidelines 4-23, 385C1
Carter optimistic on indus 5-14, 367G3
May jobless rate rptd 6-6, 437F2
Productn drop, layoffs rptd 6-10, 575A3
Antipollutn costs overestimated 6-18, 494D2
US prices rptd cut 7-1, 7-10, 575F2
Cong OKs jobless aid bill 7-2, Carter signs 7-8, 515G1
Bethlehem, ex-offcl plead guilty in bribe cases 7-24, 8-7, 600E1, A2
US Steel Ohio plant closings upheld 7-25, 575G1
Klutznick vs indus tax breaks 8-1, 575C3
Dem platform plank adopted 8-13, 614C3
Shenango OKs Pa plant pollutn curbs 8-22, 825C2
Bethlehem bribe fines set 8-25, 857E3
Reagan releases indus plan 9-16, 699F2-A3
Carter cites worker recalls 9-18, 698D3
CF&I settles job bias suit 9-22, 746D3
Carter unveils indus aid plan 9-30, 740G2-D3; Reagan scores 10-2, 738C2
Reagan in Ohio 10-7, clarifies pollutn stance 10-9, 763E2, 779C2, A3
US Steel OKs Utah plant pollutn controls 10-16, 825A2
Bethlehem ex-offcl sentenced 10-27, says bribes 'condoned', civil suit ruling rptd 12-8, 957F3, 958B2
US Steel Ohio plant suit ends 11-14, 917A1

1976

Price hike instituted 6-14, 646D3
France vs joint Europn co 7-6, 521G1
Price hike set 8-13; Armco defers 8-26; hike rescinded, GM reactn 8-30, 646B3, 647C1
Can co contracts extended 8-18, 670C1
Italy Sovt sale OK rptd 8-20, 752D2
Dow falls re prices 8-26, 846G3
Ford cites price decision 9-8, 665A2
Australia-Japan ore deal rptd 9-23, 770E3
'75 corp tax data rptd 10-2, 10-14, 847F1, C2
'64 antitrust suit cited 10-5, 886A1
Coke oven emissns curb set 10-20, 847E3-848A1
Dow drop, price hikes linked 11-10—12-31, 984D1
UK, France plan cooperatn 11-12, 880C2
Venez, UK pact signed 11-23, 929D3
Prices hiked 6% 11-24—11-29; Wage Cncl study set 11-24, rpt issued 12-2; Carter, other reactn 11-29—12-2, 897C2-898E1
Carter vs price rise 12-3, 917A2

1977

US cos in Indian plant aid 8-24, 655B2
Allegheny wins Chemetron control 9-8, 880C2
Bethlehem to clean up Md plant 9-22, 762E1
Wage-price panel analyzes industry 10-7, 776F1
US Steel plant closing, anti-pollutn costs cited 10-13, 775A3
British Steel Apr-Sept record losses rptd 10-20, 883D2
US Steel rpts 3d ¼ loss 10-25, 836A3
Bethlehem posts record 3d ¼ loss 10-26, 836E2
3d ¼ net loss rptd 10-27, 918A2, C2
LTV, Lykes rpt 3d ¼ losses 10-28, 11-4; plan merger 11-4, 943F2-D3
Pitts OKs pollutn referendum 11-8, 879A3
Sweden to merge 3 firms 11-8, sets specialty indus aid 11-9, 903C3
Coal strike begins 12-6, 937D1
USSR '78 output goal set 12-14, 987G3
USW ore-range strike ended 12-16, 977C2
Wheeling-Pitt ups prices 12-18, US Steel undercuts 12-22, Admin reactn 12-18—12-22, 1003B2

Trade Issues
Sovt-India deal signed 2-19, 161E1
US bars Rhodesian chrome 3-18, 191G1
US protectionist trade policy feared 248E1, E3-249E1
Cuba seeks US iron export 4-20—4-21, 390E1
Australia scores EC protectionism 7-4, 595E3
Countervailing duty request refused 7-10, 587D1
US, Japan chrome pact rptd 8-3, 662G1
Japan tech advance rptd 8-13, 775G3-776A1
GATT scores US, EC import curbs 9-12, 717F2
France asks 'organized free trade' 9-15—9-16, 1012D3
'75 Japan EC trade curb pact cited 9-19, 775A2
US record June imports cited 9-19, 775C2
'76 rise in Japan exports to US cited 9-19, 775C2
Japan export growth, govt aid rptd 9-19, 776C1
US Steel files dumping chrgs vs Japanese 9-30; Gilmore chrgs upheld 10-3, 774B3, 775A1
Japan sets US mktg pact terms 10-4; Eurofer backs export limit 10-10, 775D1
S Africa-Israel trade rptd 10-10, 887D3
EC min vs trade curbs 10-11, 775F1
Carter sees intl woes, vs voluntary trade curbs 10-13, 775F1
Carter vows actn vs dumping, bars trade curbs; backs tax, pollutn rule ease 10-13, 775D2
McBride backs import curbs 10-13, 775A3
US cos chrg Japan, India dumping 10-17; Eur mfrs chrgd 10-20; Canada 11-3, 836B3
Canada chrgs Japan, W Ger, S Africa dumping 10-18, 862G3
US probes dumping chrgs vs Japan, France, India 10-19, 11-22, 933F2
Sept imports rptd up 10-27, 818C1
Copper, steel indus woes compared 10-31, 858G3, 859B1
Armco chrgs UK dumping 12-5, 932C1, 933A3
US offers trigger price plan to curb Japan imports, aid US industry 12-6, 931B3
US cos dumping chrgs tallied 12-6, 932C1
'73-76 import US mkt share rptd 12-6, 932E1
Armco backs US import plan, vows no new dumping chrgs 12-7, 932C1
EC curbs imports 12-20, 998B1

1978

French Assemb OKs rescue plan 10-11, 815B3
Allegheny drops chem unit sale plan 10-24, 897F1
Brazil loan set by Japan banks 10-25, 837A1
Lykes-LTV merger probe by FTC asked by Kennedy 11-9, rejctd 11-21; shareholders OK merger 12-5, 935C2
Mfrs back Admin price guidelines 11-9, US Steel hikes prices 11-14, 1006C1
Steel haulers strike 11-11, 1006F1-A2
Belgian steel rescue plan set 11-24, 921C1
W Ger strike 11-28, 925F1

Trade Issues
Trigger price list issued 1-3, reactn 1-4, 3B2
US Jan-Nov '77 imports, mkt share rptd 1-3, 3G2
Trigger plan scored in FTC rpt 1-7, 80G2
Japan '77 dumping ruling revised 1-9, 80C2
Carter backs specialty steel import quotas 1-18, 80C3
Japan '77 exports down 1-20, 44B3
EC imposes dumping levies vs 7 suppliers, probes 6 others 1-23, 80A2
Carter bars chrome alloy duty hike 1-29, 80E3
US bars nut, bolt import curbs 2-10, 181A2
US '77 record imports rptd 2-14, 158D1
Japan, China sign pact 2-16, 103D3
EC imposes Australian steel duty 2-16, 129C2
Canada sets gas pipe specificatns 2-20, 130B1
Trigger plan takes effect 2-21, 158C1
Canada dumping measures rptd 2-21, 244G2-B3
US comm orders Japan minimum price 2-23, Carter overrules 4-24, 444B1
EFTA OKs EC export curbs; '76, 9-mo '77 sales rptd 2-28, 158F1
US Steel drops Japan dumping suit, backs trigger plan 3-1, 158A1
EC seeks export curbs with Japan, Comecon, other natns 3-2, 158C2
NZ, S Korea deal rptd 3-13, 498F1
Japan bars Australia iron curbs 3-20, 208A3
US Feb imports rptd up, trigger price linked 3-31, 262G1
Mar US imports rptd down 4-26, 344D2
Japan vows US export cuts 5-3, 341F2
Japan to import Australia iron 5-25, 411D1
Apr US imports rptd 5-26, 429C1
Zenith import duty rebuffed by Sup Ct 6-21, 491B3
US May imports rptd down 6-27, 507F1
Australia notes Japan import cuts 6-27, revised iron contracts asked 7-4, 514B2
Carter bars stainless steel utensil tariff hike 7-2, 805F1
Australia curbs steel imports 7-10, 530G1
Australia coal strike halts Japan exports 7-13, 555E1
US rpts Japan export curbs affirmed 7-17, 544A2
US July imports rptd up 8-29, 680C1
Japan Apr-June exports rptd down 9-8, 694C2
Carter to seek intl pact, dumping end 9-20, 715A3
Australia rpts China iron ore order, Japan import lag 9-29, 754C2-E2
Australia export plan set 10-24, 836B1
US OKs ferrochrome tariff hike 11-2, 999B1
US '78 trigger price hikes rptd, '79 hike set 11-9, 1005F3
France-China pact signed 12-4, 986A2
Bethlehem, US Steel in China iron-ore deals 12-4, 12-6, 986F2
Japan to build China mill 12-5, 986D2

1979

Foreign Developments (including U.S. international news)—*See also* **'Mergers' and 'Trade' below**
W Ger strike widens 1-3, 8D1; workers OK pact 1-10, 22F1
UK '78 output down 1-11, 38D1
French labor unrest 1-12–2-6, 96F1-B2
USSR '78 output rptd 1-19, 60F1, A2
French labor unrest persists 2-16, 2-21–2-28, 135B1, 154A1; 3-3, 3-7–3-8, reorgn plan halted 3-8, 189C3
USSR-India pact signed 3-14, 200B2
Paris protest spurs riots 3-23, 235F3
Andean Group OKs Venez indl plan 5-26–5-28, 398B2
Mex 1st ¼ productn rptd 6-1, 487C2
Japan proposes Mex projct 6-8, 487E3
China rpts '78 steel output 6-18, '79 forecast 6-21, 484A3, D3
Iran industries natlzd 7-5, 503F2
French reorgn pact set 7-24, 564G1
W Australia strike ends 8-3, 666E3
Taiwan indl dvpt projcts rptd 11-6, 952D3
Nippon, Armco in USSR pact 12-17, 997C2

Mergers & Acquisitions
Natl Steel plans United Financial purchase 3-6, 205A2
Australia co to buy Kaiser Steel Hamersley shares 6-4, 562B3
Sacilor-Pompey merger planned 7-25, 564C2
Marathon Mfg-Penn Central merger set 8-10, 664D1
Bliss & Laughlin rpts AEA Investors bid 8-10, 942B2
Sharon Steel buys UV Industries assets 11-26, 986D2

Trade Issues
US Steel China contract signed 1-5, 7D1
UK-China equipmt deal rptd 1-5, 12B3
Japan '78 exports drop rptd 1-24, 98D2
US '78 trade gap rptd 1-30, 71D3
China cancels Nippon deal 2-26, 181E3
Australia sets Japan price rise 3-6, 188E2
USSR stainless deal rptd 3-26, 237D3
Admin vows more trade protectn 3-29, 298G3
GATT pact signed, more tariff cuts barred 4-12, 274F1
US rules Polish steel dumped 4-18, 299A1
US to end specialty steel curbs 6-12, 466A2
China revives Nippon deal 6-12, 484E2
Carter submits trade bill to Cong 6-19, sets tariff cuts 6-21; House OKs bill 7-11, 541F1-A2
Australia exports halted 7-14, 542E1
Turkey imports set 7-31, 637E1
Trigger prices hiked 11-20, 965E3
US Steel links import prices, econ woes 11-27, 941D2

1980

Flat-rolled steel trust probe droped 12-8, 986D1

Foreign Developments (including U.S. international news)—*See also 'Trade' below*
UK steelworkers strike 1-2, 6D3
USSR '79 output drop rptd 1-25, 79B3
Turkey sets price hikes 1-25, 80B1
UK strike widens 2-1—2-3, 97E3
Spain '79 losses rptd 2-21, 196G2
Canada '79 4th 1/4 corp data rptd 2-22, 211E2
Brit Steel annual 1 bln pound loss seen 3-6, 193B3
UK steelworkers OK vote on pay offer 3-9, 193D2
Australia strike rptd 3-11, 191A1
African dependence on S Africa cited 4-1, 243A2
UK strike setld, loss estimated 4-1, 254B2
Australia coal job dispute begins 5-2, 350C2
Krupp rpts '79 profits 6-11, 446B3
Kuwait interests in W Ger cos rptd 6-25, 562E1
EC productn cut OK rptd 7-29, 628F3
Brit Steel record loss rptd 7-30, 578B2
Poland gets USSR loan 9-3, 658A3
Brit Steel aid hike set 9-26, 750D2
EC sets productn cutback plan 10-30, 821F3-822D1
OECD forecasts further indus losses 10-30, 822E1
Brit Steel '81 aid hike seen 11-6, 886C3
Polish productn drop rptd 11-12, 878B3
Mannesman restructuring rptd 12-1, 924G3
Brit Steel recovery plan outlined 12-10; wage curbs sought 12-11, layoffs set 12-12, 965E2

Mergers & Acquisitions
Armco, NN Corp merger set 8-20, 745G3
LTV, Pneumo agree 8-28, 746B1
Sharon Steel, UV Industries deal final 9-26, 746B2
Allegheny Ludlum sells unit 11-12, 985D1
US Steel to sell coal assets to Sohio 12-2, 985B2

Trade Issues
EC-Australia steel accord rptd set 2-5, 132A1
USSR OKs Nippon, Armco deal delay 2-19, 235F3
EC warns vs US curbs at OECD conf 2-28, EC-US talks failure seen 3-14; '78, '79 data 204C2
US rejects 2d 1/4 trigger price increase, warns vs dumping suits 3-19, 204B3
US Steel files dumping complaint, trigger price suspended 3-21, US mkt withdrawals rptd 3-24, 225C1
EC comm bars trade war with US, rejects US Steel suits 3-27, 242C3
French-Cuba accord rptd 4-1, 253A3
Europns resume US orders 4-2, 262B3
EC fines French, W Ger cos 4-3, 262G2
US sets import probe 4-10, 367E3
US finds import damage 5-1, 456B1
China, Australia in talks 5-7—5-11, 388A1
Trigger price return suit dismissed 5-16, 455E3-456A1
Mex-Swedish projcts agreed 5-24, 409A3
Reagan backs trigger price 9-16, 699G2
US protests Franco-Sovt deal 9-19, 728D3
Carter proposes new trigger price mechanism 9-30, 740G2-D3
US Steel ends dumping complaint 9-30, 740E3
US curbs French imports 11-17, 886B1
Trigger price hiked 11-18, 884G2

1976

STEELMAN, Rep. Alan W. (R, Tex.)
Wins Sen primary 5-1, 323B1
GOP conv vp vote table 8-19, 599F3
Loses Sen electn 11-2, 822E3
STEELWORKERS of America, United (AFL-CIO)
Ford threatens steel quotas 3-16, 212F3, 213B1
Sympathy strike injunctns barred 7-6, 535G1
Can co contracts extended 8-18, 670A1
Conv backs Abel, Mondale addresses 8-30—9-3, 665C3, 669A3
Product picketing rule vacated 10-4, 807A2
Coke oven emissns curb set 10-20, 847E3
Identifies Pa plant illness 11-5, 911A2
STEERS, Newton Ivan
Elected 11-2, 821E1, 829A4
STEFAS, George
Surrenders re MP death 5-3, 352A1
STEGALL, Mrs. Bruce
Williams freed 1-16, 79B1
STEIGER, Rep. Sam (R, Ariz.)
Chrgd re Ariz land deal 6-2, denies 6-14, 483B3, 484A1
Wins Ariz Sen primary 9-7, 687G2-A3
Loses Sen electn 11-2, 824B1
STEIGER, Rep. William A. (R, Wis.)
Reelected 11-2, 831A4
STEIN, Jules
Wins Oscar 3-29, 240B3
STEINBERG, Saul
'72 campaign gift listed 4-25, 688B1
STEINEM, Gloria
Kreps quotes 12-20, 957A2
STEINGUT, Robert
Indictment voided 11-15, 972A1
STEINGUT, Stanley
Indictment voided 11-15, 972A1
STEINKE, Robert A.
Scores S Africa detentns 12-9, 927E2
STENNIS, Sen. John C. (D, Miss.)
Backed Bentsen in caucuses 1-24, 95A1
Permanent intelligence com created 5-19, 377B1
Wins primary 6-1, 411G1
Com ends Scott probe 9-15, 980A1
With Carter in Miss 9-17, 704E1, G2
Reelected 11-2, 820D1, 822C2, 828B2
STENSEN, Sten
Wins Olympic medals 2-11, 2-14, 158F3, G3
STEPANOV, Sergei
Robbed 10-2; dies 10-24, 857G3
STEPANOV, Svyatoslav
US bar cited 11-17, 907D3
STEPANSKAYA, Galina
Wins Olympic medal 2-5, 158G3
STEPHENS, Mohammed Fuad
Dies in air crash 6-6, 419D1
STEPHENS Jr., Rep. Robert G. (D, Ga.)
Barnard wins seat 11-2, 822E1
STERILIZATION—*See BIRTH Control*
STERLING Drug Inc.
Rpts forgn payoffs 3-9, 361G3
SEC lists paymts 5-12, 729C1
STERN, Susan
Dies 7-31, 892F3
STERN & Co., Henry
Chrgd re Arab boycott 10-8, 785D3

1977

STEELWORKERS of America, United (USW) (AFL-CIO)
Sup Ct voids electn rule 1-12, 57E3
Canada arsenic pollutn chrgd 1-16, 61F1
McBride leads pres vote 2-8, Sadlowski files protest 2-18, 130B3
Contract talks open 2-14, 130E3
Contract OKd 4-9, 273D2
Aluminum pacts reached 5-24, 421F3
Contract worth estimated 6-1, 481G2
Canada arsenic rpt scored 6-6, 448D1
UMW election issue 6-14, 462G3
Kennecott pact concluded 7-18, 558G1
Strikes ore ranges 8-1, 593E2
McBride backs steel import curbs 10-13, 775A3
40-month can pacts OKd 10-31, 837A1
US ends pres vote probe 11-11, 899F2
Backs US steel import, industry aid plan 12-6, 932B1
Ore-range strike ended 12-16, 977C2
STEELWORKERS v. Usery
Union officer eligibility curbs barred 1-12, 57E3
STEFANOPOULOS, Constantine
Named to Greek post 11-28, 925B2
STEGNER, Wallace
Wins Natl Book Award 4-11, 355A2
STEICHEN, Edward (1879-1973)
Sister dies 2-18, 164E3
STEINBRENNER, George
Yankee mgr keeps job 6-21, 644D3
Yankees to keep Jackson 10-17, 806F3
STEMMLER, James A.
Loses St Louis mayoral race 4-5, 252F3
STENNETT, Renaldo (Rennie)
NL batting ldr 10-2, 926B3
STENNIS, Sen. John C. (D, Miss.)
'76 spec interest gifts rptd 1-15, 128F3
For draft revival 1-25, 94F3
Warnke hearings 2-22, 2-23, 172E2, A3
Sees Carter on SALT 5-18, 401B1
Backs neutron bomb 7-1, 534C3
Opposes Panama Canal pacts 9-11, 698A3
SALT subcom chrgd re leaks 11-8, 996A3
STENVIG, Mayor Charles (Minneapolis, Minn.)
Loses reelectn 11-8, 855F1, A3
STEPAN, Alfred
On Cuba-US profs mtg 11-9, 896C3
STEREOPHONIC Equipment—*See ELECTRIC & Electronic Indusries*
STERLING Drug Inc.
Updates forgn paymts rpt 1-3, 94B1
STERN (W. Ger. magazine)
Zaire ousts rptrs 5-6, 394A2
STERN, Leon
Berkowitz found fit for trial 10-21, 848E3

1978

US hikes nut, bolt import duties 12-26, 998D3
Trigger plan scored by US Steel 12-28, 1005B3
US 11-mo imports rptd up 12-28, 1005E3
Eur steel plate dumping probed; Natl, Armco chrgs withdrawn 12-28, 1005G3-1006B1
STEELWORKERS of America, United (USW) (AFL-CIO)
Striking miners get $1 mln in aid 3-10, 182E2
Anaconda strike ends 4-3, 284C3
McBride backs LTV Youngstown rescue 4-10, 6-21, 493B1
Legal fee liability case review denied by Sup Ct 4-17, 308D3
9 foundatns sued 4-19, 309G3
Cleared of bias at US Steel 8-3, 811C3
Conv held; Carter, Meany address wage controls, other topics 9-17—9-20, 715E1
Conv dels ban outside electn aid 9-21, 737C2
Weber reverse job-bias case accepted by Sup Ct 12-11, 980A3
STEERS, Rep. Newton Ivan (R, Md.)
Loses reelectn 11-7, 848A3
STEEVES, Lt. David (d. 1965)
'57 plane wreckage identified 10-12, 843E3
STEGER, Judge William
Asbestos workers get $20 mln setlmt 2-8, 326D3
STEIGER, Rep. William A. (R, Wis.)
Carter vs tax proposal 6-26, 491B2
Backs House com tax cut bill 7-27, 586E3
Reelected 11-7, 852D4, 854B2
Dies 12-4, 1032E3
STEIN, Joseph
King of Hearts opens 11-22, 1031C2
STEINBERG, William
Dies 5-16, 440E3
STEINBRENNER 3rd, George M.
Martin scores 7-23, quits 7-24; rehires Martin for '80 7-29, 618A1
STEINER, Daniel
On Harvard-CIA secret ties 12-1, 962A3
STEINGUT, Stanley
Asst indicted in labor probe 7-19, 598F3
STENBORG, Helen
In Recovery Lounge opens 12-7, 1031B2
STENDAHL, Krister
Submits Harvard '79 resignatn 7-3, 844E1
STENHOLM, Charles W.
Wins US House seat 11-7, 852B3, 855D3
STENMARK, Ingemar
Wins world skiing titles 2-2, 2-5, 316D2
STENNIS, Sen. John C. (D, Miss.)
Votes vs Panama Canal neutrality pact 3-16, 177F2
Votes vs 2d Canal pact 4-18, 273B1
On '79 arms authorzn 7-12, 526C2
Son loses US House electn 11-7, 582F3
STENNIS, John Hampton
Loses US House electn 11-7, 582G2
STEPHANSKY, Ben S.
Rpts Paraguay rights 'crisis' 1-10, 113B2
STEPHEN (Istvan) I, King (Hungary) (975-1038)
US returns crown to Hungary 1-6, 7A2
STEPHEN, C. M.
Vs Gandhi rule condemnatn 5-15, 374B3
STEPHENS, Jackson T.
Financial Gen sues 2-17, 204B3
SEC chrgs 3-18, settles 3-19, 204C2
STEPHENS Inc.
Financial Gen sues 2-17, 204B3
SEC chrgs 3-18, settles 3-19, 204C2
STEPHENSON, Bette
Sees Munro on Quebec labor law 7-12, 571D3
STEPHENSON, Jan
2d in World Ladies tourn 4-16, 355G3
Wins Women's Intl 5-8, 580D3
STEPHENSON, Judge Roy L.
FCC cable-TV access rules voided 2-24, 195E2
STEPHENSON, Wayne
Wales Conf wins NHL All-Star game 1-24, 76E3
STEPTOE, Dr. Patrick C.
'Test-tube baby' delivered 7-25, 596F3
STEREOPHONIC Equipment—*See ELECTRIC & Electronic Industries*
STERILIZATION—*See BIRTH Control & Family Planning*
STERKEL, Jill
Sets 400-m freestyle relay record 8-26, 780G1
STERLING, Jan
November People opens 1-14, 760A3
STERN, Eric
Company opens 5-7, 887D1

1979

STEELWORKERS of America, United (USW) (AFL-CIO)
HEW radiatn safety studies asked 1-30, 90E3
NLRB to probe Va shipyd vote 3-2, 187C2
Weber reverse job-bias case argued in Sup Ct 3-28, 262D3
McBride named to 3 Mile I probe 4-11, 275C1
Suit vs foundatns dismissed 4-19, 306A2
Va shipyd strike suspended 4-22, 306C2
NLRB dismisses Va shipyd vote chrgs 5-4, orders bargaining 6-26; appeal set 7-3, 560G3
Canada nickel strike continues 5-12, 369G1
Weber affirmative actn challenge rejctd by Sup Ct, reactn; majority opinion excerpts 6-27, 477E1-478E1
McDonald dies 8-8, 671G2
STEEN, Reiulf
Named Norway trade min 10-5, 774F1
STEENS, Miss.—*See MISSISSIPPI*
STEICHEN, Edward (1879-1973)
Works to go to Rochester museum 3-24, 375D2
STEICHEN, Joanna T. (Mrs. Edward)
Husband's works to go to Rochester museum 3-24, 375D2
STEIGER, Rod
Wife loses estate claim 7-5, 527D3
Amityville Horror released 7-27, 819D3
STEIGER, Sherry (Mrs. Rod)
Loses claim on husband's estate 7-5, 527D3
STEIGER, William A. (d. 1978)
Petri wins House seat 4-3, 265A2
STEIN, Jack C. (deceased)
NJ HFA kickback scandal rptd 8-9, 747D3
STEIN, Jeff
Kids Are Alright released 6-15, 820E1
STEIN, Joseph
Carmelina opens 4-8, 711A2
STEIN, Sandor
Fast Break released 3-1, 174E2
STEINBERG, David
Short of Paradise released 10-5, 1008F1
STEINBERG, Louis
Convicted 2-7, 119A3
Sentncd 2-25, 156A2
STEINBRENNER 3rd, George M.
Martin returns as Yankees mgr 6-19, 619A2
Martin in brawl 10-23, fired 10-28; Kuhn, MacPhail warn 11-29, 12-13, 1002B1
STEINEM, Gloria
Vs Carter firing of Abzug 1-13, 30A3
Speaks at NARAL press conf 1-21, 63A3
Speaks at NWPC conv 7-13–7-15, 578C3
STEINLAUF, Steven
Bent opens 12-2, 1007C2
STELLMAN, Martin
Quadrophenia released 11-2, 1008B1
STELLO, Victor
On Mich utility fine 11-9, 867A1
STELMACH, Dr. W. Jack
Backs 2d-surgical opinion 2-5, 218G3
STENERUD, Jan
NFL '78 kicking ldr 1-6, 80C1
STENNETT, Rennie
Signs with Giants 12-12, 1002A1
STENNIS, Sen. John C. (D, Miss.)
Armed Services Com chrmn 1-23, 71C2
For Canal treaty implementatn 9-25, 723A2
Votes vs Talmadge denunciatn 10-10, 769G1
Abstains on Armed Svcs Com SALT vote 12-20, 979E1
STENVIG, Charles
Loses vote for Minneapolis mayor 11-6, 846C3
STEPHENSON, Jan
Ties for 3d in Women's Kemper 4-1, 587B2
STEREOPHONIC Equipment—*See ELECTRIC & Electronic Industries*
STERILIZATION—*See BIRTH Control & Family Planning*
STERLING, Judge Ross N.
Resentences 3 Houston ex-cops in Torres case 10-30, 839B3
STERLING Drug Inc.
Heart failure pill rptd effective 5-8, 472D1
STERN, Alfred K.
'57 spy chrgs dropped 3-22, 232C1
STERN, Judge Herbert
Frees E Ger hijacker 5-28, 430E2
STERN, Leonard
Just You & Me Kid released 7-27, 820D1
STERN, Martha Dodd (Mrs. Alfred K.)
'57 spy chrgs dropped 3-22, 232C1
STERN, Sandor
Amityville Horror released 7-27, 819D3
STERN, Sol
Julius Rosenberg article publshd 6-16, 466B1
STERN, Steven Hillard
Running released 11-2, 1008D1

1980

STEELWORKERS of America, United (USW) (AFL-CIO)
Va ERA rally held 1-13, 54C3
US Steel Ohio plant closings blocked 2-28, 266B2
Va shipyd pact signed 3-31, 251B2
Foundatn dissident funding suit refused by Sup Ct 3-31, 291C3
Basic steel pact settled 4-15, 288G3
Pact termed within US guidelines 4-23, 385C1
Aluminum pact setld 5-30, 482D2
Copper strike drags on 7-1—10-24; Kennecott, Phelps Dodge settle 8-27, 10-8, 805D2
Sunshine Mining strike ends 11-8, 883E3
Copper strike ends 11-21, 987E3
STEEP, Marc
Retained in UAW post 6-4, 457C2
STEEPLES, Lemuel
Killed in Polish jet crash 3-14, 214A1
STEFANSON, Bert
Sentenced 8-18, 714C1
STEFFENS, Lincoln (1866-1936)
Ella Stewart dies 8-5, 676C3
STEIB, Dave
NL wins All-Star Game 7-8, 636B2
STEIN, Bert
Supertanker sinks off Senegal 1-17, 108G2
STEIN, Dr. William Howard
Dies 2-2, 176D3
STEINBRENNER 3rd, George M.
Howser quits as Yankee mgr; Michael replaces 11-21, 926F1
STEINHAUER, Euguene
Scores Ottawa Indian plan 9-30, 828E1
STEIN v. Conference of Federal Savings and Loan Associations
Case decided by Sup Ct 3-17, 226D1
STELLO Jr., Victor
Babcock fine asked 4-10, 332D1
Seeks Con Ed fine 12-11, 961F2
STENDER, Fay
Dies 5-21, 448G2
STENHOLM, Rep. Charles W. (D, Tex.)
Reelected 11-4, 844B3
STENMARK, Ingemar
Wins Olympic medals 2-19, 2-22, 155F2
2d in World Cup skiing 3-11, 469F3
STENSHJEMMET, Kai Arne
Wins Eur speed skating title 1-20, 470G1
Wins Olympic medals 2-16, 2-21, 155G3, 156A1
STEPANOV, Yuri
Defectn rptd in Rome 1-23, 88F1
Returns to USSR 4-1, 262A2
STEPHENSON, Jan
Wins Sun City Classic 3-2, 412F2
STEPTOE, Dr. Patrick C.
US 'test-tube baby' clinic OKd 1-8, 24G1
STERILIZATION—*See BIRTH Control*
STERKEL, Jill
Sets 50-yd, 100-yd butterfly marks 3-20-3-21, 50-yd freestyle mark 3-22, 835C1
Sets 50-m freestyle mark 4-10, 835A1
STERLING Heights—*See MICHIGAN*
STERN (West German magazine)
Crane sues 7-16, 890C2
STERN, Edith Rosenwald
Dies 9-11, 756D2
STERN, Leonard B.
Nude Bomb released 5-9, 675B3
STERN, Robert A. M.
Architect's Eye wins Amer Book Award 5-1, 692C2

1976

STERNER, Michael
Replaced as Emirates amb 9-23, 807F3
STERNSTEIN, Joseph
Gen Brown dismissal rptd asked 10-20, 787C3
STEROIDS—*See 'Drugs' under MEDICINE*
STERRE, Dr. Allen
On new arthritis strain 11-21, 911B3
STETIN, Sol
Clothing, textile unions merge 6-3, 436G1
STEUART, David
Scores US potash suit 8-30, 673E2
STEUBENVILLE, O.—*See OHIO*
STEVANOVIC, Milivoje
Sentenced for emigre plot 3-12, 223A3
STEVE Lobell (race horse)
Wins Hambletonian 9-4, 716F2
STEVENS, Justice John Paul—*For Supreme Court developments not listed here, see SUPREME Court under U.S. GOVERNMENT*
Not in import tax ruling 1-14, 23C3
Not in campaign law ruling 1-30, 87A2
For hearing on homosexual case 3-30, 261C3 ★
Not in city-state housing rule 4-20, 308B3 ★
Abstains from convict silence ruling 4-20, 331G2
Not in defendants rights rulings 5-3, 359B2
Not in drug price ad rule 5-24, 393A2
Rules on alien job rights, Medicare benefits 6-1, 414G1-C2
Vs fed employe job bias suit rule 6-1, 414G2
Not in A-waste regulatn rule 6-1, 414B3
Vs implicatns of police job ruling 6-7, 435E1
Upholds NC police firing 6-10, 552E2
Vs trial transcript ruling 6-10, 552A3
Vs silence on arrest ruling 6-17, 552C3
Vs RR funds ruling 6-17, 552F3
Vs some church-coll aid 6-21, 452F3
Vs local-zoning referendum 6-21, 453D1
Vs Serbian Church ruling 6-21, 553B1
Vs US wage rule re states 6-24, 468F2
Upholds anti-porno zoning 6-24, 479A1
Not in retiremt ruling 6-25, 552F1
Not in New Orleans vendor ruling 6-25, 552F1
Vs union overtime bar 6-25, 552B2
Vs prison transfer ruling 6-25, 552B2
Patronage ousters barred 6-28, 468C3, D3
Vs illegitimates benefits rule 6-29, 568E3
Vs pres gag orders 6-30, 492A1
Vs parent abortion consent 7-1, 518E3
Backs death penalty 7-2, 491C2
Vs sympathy strike rule 7-6, 535F1
For review of jobless pay for strikers rule 10-4, 807F2
Ford cites apptmt 10-22, 802C2
Not in religious-day work ruling 11-2, 848E1
Vs parole revocation hearing rule 11-15, 882D2
Vs prisoner med care ruling 11-30, 920F3
Vs Gilmore executn stay 12-3, 952D2
For pregnancy benefits 12-7, 920F1, A2
Vs EEOC complaint delay ruling 12-20, 960C1

STEVENS, Siaka
Reelected 3-26, govt chngs rptd 5-20, 503B3
STEVENS, Sinclair
Loses PC ldrship bid 2-23, 188F2
STEVENS & Co., J. P.
AFL-CIO rpts unionizatn plans 2-23, 149E1
Unionizatn, boycott set 6-3, 436E1

1977

STERNEBECK, Sigrid
Sought in Ponto slaying 7-30, 601C3
STERNER, Michael
At Cairo conf 12-14—12-15, 953G1

STEVENS, Justice John Paul—*For Supreme Court developments not listed here, see U.S. GOVERNMENT—SUPREME Court*
Vs Miranda rights limitatn 1-25, 80B2
Vs Chris-Craft award ruling 2-23, 150C2
Upholds water pollutn curbs 2-23, 150E2
Backs racial voter redistricting 3-1, 175C1
Vs Soc Sec widower benefits rule 3-2, 192D1, G1
Rules on death sentencing 3-22, 231B1
Backs 'comity' for civil actns 3-22, 231F2
Sidesteps Miranda rule review 3-23, 276B1
Vs porno trial ad role 6-6, 478D3
Vs Fla retroactive death sentnc 6-17, 518D2
Backs US custody of Nixon papers 6-28, 539E3
Backs Omaha, Milwaukee busing orders 6-29, 557A3
Hears Bakke case arguments 10-12, 834G3, 835F1
Vs police rights extensn in traffic violatns 12-5, 939A1
Backs maternity leave seniority rights 12-6, 938F2
Vs phone surveillnc ct orders 12-7, 939C2

STEVENS, Sayre
China econ outlook rptd 8-15, 635C3
STEVENS, Siaka P. (Sierra Leone president)
Declares emergency 2-1, 139F3
STEVENS, Sinclair
Scores budget proposal 3-31, 254A2
STEVENS, Sen. Ted (Theodore F.) (R, Alaska)
Elected minority whip 1-4, 6A2
Delays Panama Canal pact judgmt 8-11, 622G1
STEVENS & Co., J. P.
Unionists protest at annual mtg 3-1, 153E3
Ct finds in contempt 8-31, 724F1
Labor-law fines set 10-27, union sues 11-1, 11-10, 899B1
Chrgd by NLRB law judge 12-21, 1005C1

1978

STERNSTEIN, Rabbi Joseph P.
Responds to Sadat peace plea 1-29, 60C3
STETSON, John C.
AF Acad dean rptd dismissed 4-21, 420D1
STEUBENVILLE, O.—*See OHIO*
STEVENS, Ann (Mrs. Ted)
Killed in air crash 12-4, 1032A1

STEVENS, Justice John Paul—*For Supreme Court developments not listed here, see U.S. GOVERNMENT—SUPREME Court*
Vs Pa gag order case rule 1-9, 13G1
Vs EPA asbestos rule curb 1-10, 13A3
Backs trust suits by forgn natns 1-11, 33A3
Backs 'prehire' union picketing 1-17, 34B1
Vs Wis remarriage law 1-18, 65C1
Not in Wis truck-length limit case 2-21, 126E1
Vs limited immunity for prison offcls 2-22, 126E2
Vs fed constructn paymt bond rule 2-22, 126A3
Rules on oil tanker regulatn 3-6, 162C1
Vs state police alien ban 3-22, 221C1
Vs jury instructn on silent defendant 3-22, 221F1
Vs judicial immunity in sterilizatn case 3-28, 241D3
Backs Nixon tape access to broadcasters 4-18, 308B2
Vs tax breaks in lease-back deals 4-18, 309B2
Vs ban on clergy in pub office 4-19, 309D1
Backs sex-based pensn plans bar 4-25, 322C3
Vs engineers fee code 4-25, 323B1
Vs utility customer hearings 5-1, 364B1
Backs trespass laws vs unions 5-15, 387B2
Vs tax liability in bankruptcy 5-22, 388E1
Backes OSHA warrantless searches 5-23, 405F2
Backs exclusn of children from porno rule 5-23, 405E3
Vs presumptn-of-innocence jury chrg 5-30, 430B3
Vs newsroom searches by police 5-31, 430A2
Backs natural gas diversn 5-31, 431C1
Vs munic legal immunity 6-6, 447G1
Skokie seeks Nazi rally delay 6-9, vs stay 6-12, 447B3
Backs '75 double jeopardy doctrine 6-14, 468E3
Backs Md refiner-run gas statn ban 6-14, 492D1
Vs IRS summons power 6-19, 492A3
Backs union supervisor discipline 6-21, 509D2
Vs class actn certificatn appeals 6-21, 509F2
Backs computer program patent curbs 6-22, 509C1
Backs Ark prison reform, attys fees 6-23, 566A2
Backs press prison-data access 6-26, 566C3
Backs Bakke med schl admissn, vs race-based affirmative actn; opinion excerpt 6-28, 481C1-C2, 486B3
Backs US offcls' legal immunity 6-29, 567F2
Backs FCC 'Filthy Words' ban 7-3, 551C3
Voting alignmt shift noted 7-3, 565F3-566C1
Backs coll sex-bias ruling 11-13, 874C2
Backs cities' power over suburbs 11-28, 937D3
Vs broader police auto search power 12-5, 959C3
Vs Calif auto franchise law 12-5, 959G3
Vs FRB bank-holding co power 12-11, 980F3

STEVENS, Roger L.
Death Trap opens 2-26, 760A2
STEVENS, Sinclair
Chrgs C$ speculatn 5-20; retracts 5-24, 412F3
Scores Chretien tax rebate letter 8-1, 613E3
STEVENS, Susan
Price of Genius opens 6-26, 887F2
STEVENS, Sen. Ted (Theodore F.) (R, Alaska)
Votes vs Panama Canal neutrality pact 3-16, 177G2
Votes vs 2d Canal pact 4-18, 273B1
House OKs Alaska lands bill 5-19, 386C2
Unopposed in primary 8-22, 682G3
Seeks Civil Svc reform chngs 8-24, 661E3, G3
Amateur sports omnibus funds cleared 10-15, 842C3
Reelected 11-7, 848C1, 856B2
Outspent Hobbs 148-1 11-15, 898C1
Injured in air crash, wife killed 12-4, 1032A1
STEVENS & Co., J. P.
Contempt rule review refused, stiff fines seen 2-21, 125F3
Finley forced off bank bd by unions 3-7, 163A1
Annual meeting 3-7, 163D1
Avon chrmn quits bd, cites union pressure 3-21, 205D1

1979

STERNGLASS, Dr. Ernest A.
Scores 3 Mile I A-accident 4-7, 261C1
Links SAT decline, '50s fallout 9-17, 747A2
STERNHAGEN, Frances
On Golden Pond opens 2-28, 712G1
STERZING, Carl B.
Rock Island RR firing rptd 10-5, 830D3
STETSON, John C.
Cites pilot drain, morale loss 2-15, 130E2
WWII women pilots get vet benefits 3-9, 307D3
STEVENS, Greer
Wins Wimbledon mixed doubles 7-7, 570D1
Wins US Open mixed doubles title 9-9, 734A2

STEVENS, Justice John Paul—*For Supreme Court developments not listed here, see U.S. GOVERNMENT—SUPREME Court*
Vs limited lawyers' interstate rights 1-15, 31F3
Not in SEC pensn plans case 1-16, 32F1
Not in foster care benefits case 2-22, 151C1
Backs job-testing data disclosure 3-5, 184D3
Vs Ill right-to-counsel rule 3-5, 185C2
Backs muffler assn tax break 3-20, 203F3
Backs jobless pay for strikers 3-21, 231F1
Absent from Weber case argumt 3-28, 262F3
Backs cable TV pub-access rule 4-2, 281B2
Backs IRS tap evidence 4-2, 281E2
Vs NYS alien teacher ban 4-17, 325E3
Vs remanding music license fee case 4-17, 326B1
Vs covert US entries for 'bugging' 4-18, 346G1
Vs unwed father adoptn consent role 4-24, 364D1
Vs verbal rights waiver 4-24, 364C2
Backs pvt Title IX suit 5-14, 382E3
Vs pretrial detentn curbs 5-14, 383A2
Vs Scientology documts seizure 5-14, 383A3
Vs fed ct welfare suits 5-14, 384A1
Discloses finances 5-15, 382E2
Backs state age bias filing time limit 5-21, 400G2
Vs state parole discretn 5-29, 421A3
Backs some punitive damages vs unions 5-29, 421E3
Vs co-defendant confessns 5-29, 422B1
Backs NY gun-in-car law 6-4, 438D3
Backs NJ ex-offcls rejailing review 6-4, 439B1
Backs pol party state com structure law 6-4, 439D1
Vs broader Cong legal immunity 6-18, 498G3
Vs child mental commitmt rules 6-20, 516B1
Backs youth probatn officer consultatn right 6-20, 516C2
Vs 'good faith' arrest 6-25, 540E1
Vs rights violatn proof in false arrest suits 6-26, 541A1
Not in Weber case ruling 6-27, 477C2
Vs dockworker negligence suits 6-27, 558C2
Vs eased criminal evidence standard 6-28, 558B3
Vs FRB Open Mkt rpt disclosure delay 6-28, 558C3
Backs ctroom pub access curbs 7-2, 515F2
'78-79 Sup Ct term ends, voting alignmt rptd 7-2, 558A1, C1
Votes to void Rose case convictns 7-2, 558G3
Vs Mass abortn-consent law 7-2, 559C2
Comments on trial closures 9-8, 745A1
Vs curb on advisers investor suits 11-13, 902D1
Backs VA malpractice ruling 11-28, 944F3
Vs appointed lawyers legal immunity 12-4, 987F3
Vs Taiwan treaty case review 12-13, 940C1

STEVENS, Leslie
Buck Rogers released 3-29, 528E1
STEVENS, Roger L.
Wings opens 1-28, 292G3
Carmelina opens 4-8, 711A2
STEVENS, Sinclair
Canada treas bd pres 6-4, 423F3
Sets govt hiring freeze 6-8, 444A1
'79 trade deficit forecast 7-24, 613F1
On decentralizatn cutback 7-27, 581E3
Orders '79-80 pub svc cuts 8-15, 632C1
On crown corps sale plan 9-28, 749E2
Plans CDC sell-off 11-19, 908B1
Rpts Statistics Canada probes 12-10, 967E2
STEVENS, Sen. Ted (Theodore F.) (R, Alaska)
Reelected Sen minority whip 1-15, 30B2, 71B2
Sen income limit delayed 3-8, 185F2
Scores Tex pipe cancellatn 3-13, 183F1
Sees Carter 'mental problem' 7-20, 531B3
Votes vs Talmadge denunciatn 10-10, 769G1
STEVENS & Co., J. P.
Textile union '77 suits dismissed 7-18, 8-6, 598C3
Textile union files Ga suit 7-18, 598E3

1980

STEUBENVILLE—*See OHIO*
STEVENS, Greer
Loses Avon tourn 1-20, 607C2
Loses Players Challenge 7-20, 691G2
STEVENS, Jimmy
Leads New Hebrides separatist revolt 5-28, forms provisional govt 6-3, 422A2, B3
On unrest 6-8, 436G1
Phoenix Foundatn, US exec's links rptd 6-8, 436D2
UK, French troops land on Espiritu Santo 7-24, 580G3
Arrested, rebellion quelled 8-31, 674B1, D1
Sentenced 11-21, 903C3

STEVENS, Justice John Paul—*For Supreme Court developments not listed here, see U.S. GOVERNMENT--SUPREME Court*
Backs parole offcls immunity 1-15, 51G1
Vs citizenship revocatn law 1-15, 51F2
Vs mil petitn limits 1-21, 93E1
Vs narrowed state ct jurisdictn 1-21, 93D2
Vs CIA disclosure limits 2-19, 130F3
Vs NYS pvt schl reimbursemt 2-20, 146E2
Not in Calif dual seniority case 2-20, 146B3
Vs IRS handwriting orders 2-20, 170A2
Backs Kissinger records access 3-3, 210A1
Vs Tex habitual-offender law 3-18, 226C3
Vs Vt tax on forgn dividends 3-19, 249C3
Vs govt political firings 3-31, 291B2
Vs warrantless home arrests 4-15, 306A1
Backs Indian land managemt fed liability 4-15, 306G1
Vs govt desert land retentn 4-16, 328D3
Hears abortn funding cases 4-21, 306F2
Backs at-large local electns 4-22, 343F2
Not in Wilmington (Del) busing case 4-28, 368G3
Vs police interrogatn definitn 5-12, 386A3
Vs Atlanta schl integratn ruling 5-12, 386C3
Vs EEOC class actn process avoidance 5-12, 426C2
Backs narrow Ga death law applicatn 5-19, 440A1
Vs narrowed 'exclusionary rule' 5-27, 453E2
Vs EPA guidelines appeals ct review 5-27, 453F3
Vs DEA detainmt procedure 5-27, 454A1
Not in Panther Chicago shootout trial cases 6-2, 513B1
Vs state sales preference 6-19, 554G2
Vs Ala death penalty 6-20, 555D1
Vs container pact ban refusal 6-20, 555G2
Backs donated porno warrants 6-20, 555A3
Rules on lawyer legal fee penalty 6-23, 555B1
Vs oil spill rpts 6-27, 511B2
Vs unpatented key ingredient monopolies 6-27, 511D2
Vs Medicaid abortn funding limits 6-30, 492E1
Vs govt minority constructn grant quota 7-2, 510A2
Backs open criminal trials 7-2, 510B3
Vs OSHA benzene standard 7-2, 510F3
'79-80 Sup Ct term ends, voting alignmts rptd 7-2, 540D2
Hears Nixon taps case 12-8, 937E2
Vs lenient sentence appeal 12-9, 936F3
Vs job bias suit filing time limit 12-15, 957C2
Vs NJ census data stay extensn 12-15, 957D2
Not in census ruling 12-30, 982G3

STEVENS, Robert P.
Charged in GSA scandal 1-15, 112F1
STEVENS, Roger L.
Istomin named artistic dir 2-26, 199D2
Lunch Hour opens 11-12, 892E3
STEVENS, Siaka (Sierra Leone president)
Rejects US co chem waste dump plan 2-20, 154A2
Closes OAU summit, scores failure in Chad 7-4, 509B2
STEVENS, Sen. Ted (Theodore F.) (R, Alaska)
Rebuts Carter State of Union 1-28, 75D1, F1, A2
Alaska lands bill passes Sen 8-19, 631E2, F2
Alaska lands bill clears House 11-12, 866B3
Named Sen GOP whip 12-2, 915E2
STEVENS, Tony
Perfectly Frank opens 11-30, 1003D3
STEVENS, Whitney
ACTWU agrmt announced 10-19, 805G1-D2
STEVENS & Co., J. P.
Textile union agrmt announced 10-19, 805B1-D2
Plants union access case refused by Sup Ct 10-20, 807A2

1976

STEVENSON 3rd, Sen. Adlai E. (D, Ill.)
Returns from Mideast, airs Arafat peace plan 2-28, 161B1
Daley delegates win 3-16, 196D3
5th in Dem delegate count 4-9, 261B1
Named to intelligence com 5-20, 377D1
Releases pres delegates 6-9, 408G3, 409A3
Carter mtg re vp spot set 7-8, 489F3; sees Carter 7-12, 506B2
STEVENSON, Adlai E(wing) (1900-65)—*See 1965, p. 249F2-C3 for biog. data*
Cited as FBI probe target 4-28, 330F1
STEVENSON, Teofilo
Wins Olympic medal 7-31, 574D1
Elected to Natl Assembly 11-2, 1001B1
STEVENSON, William
90 Minutes at Entebbe publshd 7-26, 547F1
Man Called Intrepid on best-seller list 12-5, 972A2
STEWART, Andy
Vs inflatn plan protest 8-12, 623E3
STEWART, Donald
Backs home-rule plan 1-13, 73C1
STEWART, Jack
On convicts riot 9-29, 789C3
STEWART, Mary
Touch Not the Cat on best-seller list 12-5, 972F2

STEWART, Justice Potter—*For Supreme Court developments not listed here, see SUPREME Court under U.S. GOVERNMENT*
Rules on campaign law 1-30, 87A2
Backs shopping cntr pickets ruling 3-3, 218E3
Backs city-suburb housing plan 4-20, 308D2
Backs FPC job bias powers 5-19, 393G2
Vs teacher dismissal ruling 6-17, 552D3
Vs RR funds ruling 6-17, 552F3
Vs some church-coll aid 6-21, 452F3
Holds US wage laws not binding on states 6-24, 468D2
Vs sex-show zoning 6-24, 479A1
Vs private schl bias 6-25, 479C1
Vs union overtime bar 6-25, 552B2
Backs patronage ouster bar 6-28, 468E3
Vs nonlawyer judge rule 6-28, 492F1
Vs press gag order 6-30, 492A1
Vs black-lung law provision 7-1, 568F3
'72 vote vs death penalty cited, backs in '76 7-2, 491B2, C2
Vs tax case evidence rule 7-6, 535B1
Vs car search ruling 7-6, 535C1
Backs sympathy strikes 7-6, 535E1
Vs utilities trust ruling 7-6, 569F1
For housing bias ruling review 10-4, 766B1
Vs plea-bargain confessn ruling 11-1, 867E3
For carry-back tax break curb 11-2, 867A2
Vs pregnancy benefits 12-7, 920E1
For worker contract debate curb 12-8, 960C2
Vs divorced mothers benefits 12-13, 940E3
Vs EEOC complaint delay ruling 12-20, 960C1

1977

STEVENSON Jr., Adlai (1900-65)
Arvey dies 8-25, 696C2
STEVENSON 3rd, Sen. Adlai E. (D, Ill.)
Sen OKs reorganizatn plan 2-4, 90D1
Vance backs boycott curbs 2-28, 167D1
Sen ethics code adopted 4-1, 251D3
Goldman confrmd FEA asst admin 5-12, 418E1
On Sen role in Korean lobbying 8-8, 688D2
STEVENSON, Coke R.
LBJ '48 Sen primary fraud chrgd 7-30, 631B2
STEVENSON, John R.
Replaced in diplomatic post 2-24, 148F3
STEWART, George D.
Jet hijacker demands release 10-20, 807G3
STEWART, Mary
Touch Not the Cat on best-seller list 9-4, 712F3

STEWART, Justice Potter—*For Supreme Court developments not listed here, see U.S. GOVERNMENT—SUPREME Court*
Sup Ct voids steelworkers electn rule 1-12, 57F3
Vs secondary strike curb 2-22, 149G3
Backs racial voter redistricting 3-1, 175D1
Rules on Mich electn law 3-21, 230D3
Vs 'comity' for civil actns 3-22, 231A3
Sidesteps Miranda rule review 3-23, 276A1
Watergate appeals decisn leak disputed 4-28, 382E2
Backs pre-'64 seniority bias 5-31, 461F2
Vs Kent State gym ban 9-3, 820G2
Hears Bakke case arguments 10-12, 834F3
Vs NYS private schl aid law 12-6, 938C3

1978

Textile union declared bargaining rep at NC plant 3-26, 243B2
NLRB suit setld 4-28, 324E1-C2
Textile union sets NY Life bd bid 9-11; Brown, Finley quit directorships 9-12, 699C2
STEVENSON 3rd, Sen. Adlai E. (D, Ill.)
Links Korea loan, lobbying probe aid 2-22, 204B1
On Miller confirmatn hearing 2-28, 161B3
Votes for Panama Canal neutrality pact 3-16, 177E2
Weicker quits ethics com re Korea probe 4-14, 279E3, G3
Votes for 2d Canal pact 4-18, 273B1
Visits USSR 11-11—11-18, 905A2
STEVENSON, Kenneth
On Shroud of Turin study 11-7, 926A1
STEVENSON, Teofilo
Wins World Amateur Boxing tourn 5-6—5-20, 600D2
STEWARD, Douglas Day
Other Side of Mountain released 3-24, 619C3
STEWART, Alice
Links A-plant radiatn to cancer 2-17, 164B2
STEWART, Bennett
Wins US House seat 11-7, 850C3, 853B2
STEWART, Donald
Faces Ala US Sen primary runoff 9-5, 699G1
Wins runoff 9-6, Martin to oppose 10-2, 769D1, F1
Elected 11-7, 846E1, 848C1, 849A3
STEWART, Michael
Hello Dolly opens 3-4, 887A2

STEWART, Justice Potter—*For Supreme Court developments not listed here, see U.S. GOVERNMENT—SUPREME Court*
Vs EPA asbestos rule curb 1-10, 13A3
Backs 'prehire' union picketing 1-17, 34B1
Backs prosecutors' plea-bargaining power 1-18, 64G3
Vs Wis remarriage law 1-18, 65C1
Not in FPC rate review rule 2-27, 143C2
Vs NH gov flag-lowering curb 3-24, 221E2
Vs cities liability under trust law 3-29, 280C2
Vs Minn pensn fund law 4-3, 309A1
Vs clergy pub office ban 4-19, 309E1
Vs Va judicial inquiry law 5-1, 363D3
Vs trespass laws union rule 5-15, 387D2
Vs tax liability in bankruptcy 5-22, 388E1
Backs exclusn of children from porno rule 5-23, 405E3
Vs newsroom searches by police 5-31, 430G1
Not in natural gas diversn case 5-31, 431D1
Backs poultry group trust immunity 6-12, 468C1
Vs IRS summons power 6-19, 492G2
Backs union supervisor discipline 6-21, 509C2
Vs Hughes estate dispute interventn 6-22, 509A1
Vs computer program patent curbs 6-22, 509D1
Vs NJ waste dumping law 6-23, 566C2
Vs press prison-data access 6-26, 566B3
Backs Bakke med schl admissn, vs race-based affirmative actn principle 6-28, 481F1, C2
Vs Minn pensn funds law 6-28, 567D1
Backs US offcls' legal immunity 6-29, 567F2
Vs insurnc cos policyholder trust suits 6-29, 567D3
Vs FCC 'Filthy Words' ban 7-3, 551E3
Voting alignmt shift noted 7-3, 565F3-566C1
Stays NJ Sup Ct Farber ruling 9-26, 841E2
Backs coll sex-bias ruling 11-13, 874C2

1979

STEVENSON 3rd, Sen. Adlai E. (D, Ill.)
Bars reelectn bid 3-30, 265D2
Vs arms hike link to SALT 8-3, 591D1
On Talmadge denunciatn 9-14, 702C1
Talmadge denounced by Sen 10-10, 769E1
Replaced on Sen Ethics Com 10-31, 945A3
Criticizes Goldschmidt 12-6, 984D1
STEVENSON, Cyril
On Somoza expulsn from Bahamas 8-4, 600F1
STEVENSON, John R.
Named Natl Gallery pres 5-3, 375F1
STEVENSON, Karen
Wins Rhodes scholarship 9-9, 1005F2
STEWART, Amil
Knock on Wood on best-seller list 5-2, 356A3
STEWART, Bill
Slain in Nicaragua 6-20, 461F2
STEWART, Sen. Donald (D, Ala.)
Finances disclosed 5-18, 383G3
STEWART, Mary
Last Enchantment on best-seller list 9-2, 672A3; 10-14, 800A3; 11-4, 892B3
STEWART, Michael
Grand Tour opens 1-11, 292E1
I Love My Wife opens 5-15, 711F3

STEWART, Justice Porter—*For Supreme Court developments not listed here, see U.S. GOVERNMENT—SUPREME Court*
Vs SEC suit findings retrial 1-9, 14D2
Not in Energy Comm rate relief case 1-16, 32F3
Backs rail pensn in divorce pact 1-24, 54C1
Backs A&P milk price actn 2-22, 150D3
Not in gas output regulatn case 2-22, 150F3
Backs Blue Shield drug plan trust rule 2-27, 165E1
Vs job-testing data disclosure 3-5, 184C3
Backs muffler assn tax break 3-20, 203F3
Backs broader grant of immunity 3-20, 204C1
Vs LA fire dept bias case finding 3-27, 263A2
Hears Weber case argumt 3-28, 263C1
Vs racial 'steering' suits 4-17, 325D3
Vs 'state of mind' libel queries 4-18, 302F1
Backs covert US entries for 'bugging' 4-18, 346A2
Vs unwed father adoptn consent role 4-24, 364E1
Backs unwed father damage suit bar 4-24, 364F1
Backs verbal rights waiver 4-24, 364B2
Vs mutual fund dirs' power 5-14, 383D1
Backs fed ct welfare suits 5-14, 384A1
Discloses finances 5-15, 382D2
Vs innocence instructn refusal 5-21, 400E3
Vs NY gun-in-car law 6-4, 438E3
Backs vets' job-preferne law 6-5, 421F1
Vs sex-bias suits vs congressmen 6-5, 464E1
Powell reports finances 6-15, 464D3
Vs broader Cong legal immunity 6-18, 498G3
Not in natural gas diversn case 6-18, 499C2
Vs warrantless phone surveillnc 6-20, 516F1
Backs end to AFDC-UF welfare plan 6-25, 540A1
Backs eased criminal evidence standard 6-28, 558A3
Vs FRB Open Mkt rpt disclosure delay 6-28, 558C3
Backs ctroom pub access curbs 7-2, 515D2
Vs Dayton (O) busing order 7-2, 539B3
'78-79 Sup Ct term ends, voting alignmt rptd 7-2, 558A1, C1
Vs power to void state convictns 7-2, 559A1
Vs Ga laws in church land dispute 7-2, 559C1
Vs Washn Indian fishing treaties 7-2, 559F1
Vs Mass abortn-consent law 7-2, 559B2
Backs curb on investor suits vs advisers 11-13, 902B1
Hears govt minority constructn grants case argumts 11-27, 945E1
Vs NYC schl aid denial 11-28, 944E2
Vs extended searches 11-28, 944G2
Vs Taiwan treaty case review 12-13, 940C1

1980

STEVENS (J.P.) & Co. v. National Labor Relations Board
Case refused by Sup Ct 10-20, 807B2
STEVENSON 3rd, Sen. Adlai E. (D, Ill.)
Sen primary results 3-18, 206C3
Vs anti-Anderson moves 6-24, 493A3
Dixon wins seat 11-4, 845B3, 850B3
STEVENSON, Teofilo
Wins 3d Olympic gold medal 8-2, 589E1, 622A2
STEWART, Andrew
Rpts PSAC strike vote 9-22, dissidents ask resignatn 10-8, 807G3, 808A2
STEWART, Rep. Bennett (D, Ill.)
Loses primary 3-18, 206B3
Washington wins seat 11-4, 846D3
STEWART, Bill (d. 1979)
News copter missing in Carib 11-13, 869E3
STEWART, Judge Charles E.
Sentences Scotto 1-22, Anastasio 1-23, 64D2, B3
STEWART, Donald Ogden
Dies 8-2, 676B3
STEWART, Sen. Donald W. (D, Ala.)
US dist judges named 1-10; controversy ensues 5-19—9-17, 744C2
Chairs Hunt silver probe 5-2, 345B2
In Ala US Sen primary; runoff set 9-2, 682F2
Loses primary runoff 9-23, 745F1
Denton wins seat 11-4, 846A1, 849F1
STEWART, Douglas Day
Blue Lagoon released 6-20, 675G1
STEWART, Edward
Wins Oscar 4-14, 296A2
STEWART, Ella Winter
Dies 8-5, 676C3
STEWART, Frank
Executed 4-22, 353A2
STEWART, George R.
Dies 8-22, 676C3
STEWART, Mary
Last Enchantment on best-seller list 1-13, 40B3
STEWART, Michael
Kirschschlager reelected pres 4-30, 392D2
STEWART, Milton D.
Small business paper work costs rptd 1-3, 17E3
STEWART, Justice Potter—*For Supreme Court developments not listed here, see U.S. GOVERNMENT--SUPREME Court*
Vs citizenship revocatn law 1-15, 51E2
Vs mil petitn limits 1-21, 93E1
Backs Dallas busing case review 1-21, 93E2
Backs Calif dual seniority system 2-20, 146A3
Vs govt damage suits geographic relevance 2-20, 170C3
Backs hazardous work refusals 2-26, 188E1
Vs fed worker illegitimate child aid 2-26, 188G1
Not in forgn dividends tax case 3-19, 249D3
Vs class actn 'moot' standard redefinitn 3-19, 250D1, E1
Backs inmate mental health case dismissal 3-25, 265F2
Backs govt political firings 3-31, 291D2
Backs 'good faith' municipal immunity 4-16, 328B3
Hears abortn funding cases 4-21, 306C3
Backs at-large local electns 4-22, 343D2
Vs Voting Rights Act provisn 4-22, 344D1
Backs Wilmington (Del) busing case review 4-28, 368F3
Backs La oil leasing royalties 4-28, 369D1
Defines police interrogatn 5-12, 386E2
Vs pre-ERISA insured pensn benefits 5-12, 426C3
Finances rptd 5-15, 555C3
Backs narrow Ga death law applicatn 5-19, 440A1
Vs narrowed 'exclusionary rule' 5-27, 453F2
Backs SEC fraud intent proof 6-2, 512D3
Vs pre-1920 oil shale mining claims 6-2, 513D1
Not in Wis out-of-state corp earnings tax case 6-10, 512B1
Vs container pact ban refusal 6-20, 555G2
Vs magistrates pretrial role 6-23, 555A1
Backs Medicaid abortn funding limits 6-30, 491G3
Vs govt minority constructn grants 7-2, 510A2, B2
Ctroom cameras case argued 11-12, 882D2
Backs Ky 10 Commandmts schl law 11-17, 881G3
Vs job bias suit filing time limit 12-15, 957C2
Vs NJ census data stay extensn 12-15, 957D2
Stays Detroit census revisn 12-24, 982G3

1976

STEWART, Ron
Rangers dismiss 1-7, 56E2
STEYN, Marais
S Africa cabt shifted 1-22, 76A2
STILL Crazy After All These Years (record album)
Wins Grammy 2-28, 460G2
STILWELL, Gen. Richard
Protests N Korea DMZ deaths 8-19, 625C2
STIMMEL, Dr. Barry
New alcoholism test rptd 12-3, 950C3
STIRN, Olivier
On Afars schl bus attack 2-4, 85B3
Visits Mayotte 2-20—2-21, 205A1
On Mayotte dept status 4-12, 538A3
Guadeloupe volcano erupts 8-30, 643D3
STOCKING, George
On A-waste explosion 8-30, 671A1
STOCKMAN, David A.
Elected 11-2, 823F2, 829D4

STOCKS, Bonds & Securities—*See also city, company, country names*
Dow climbs, hits 1,000 1-2—3-11, 184C2-185C2
Sup Ct lets stand NYSE svc chrg rule 1-12, 24C1
Ford State of Union message 1-19, 38A1, 39G1
GAO critical of FDA 1-19, 44D3
Dec. '75 dividends rptd 1-19, 91E2
'77 budget proposals 1-21, 62D3, 63A3, D3
Ford scores Reagan extremism 2-17, 129F2
House votes US debt financing 2-25, 170C3
Standard & Poor, NYSE indexes drop from peak 3-11, 185C1
Dow climbs, stalls 3-11—5-28, 413G1-E2
Detroit notes purchased 3-24, 994D2
SEC rpts on NYSE '75 broker fees, profits 4-2, 348F1
Needham quits NYSE post 4-27, 347F3-348F1
'75 Fortune top 500 indls ranked 437C1, D2
1st ¼ US, forgn bond sales up 5-17, 397A1-B1
Dow fluctuatns 6-1—11-10, 846G2
Merrill Lynch settles job bias suits 6-4, 414D1
Dem platform text 6-15, 469E3
Ford submits forgn paymts bill 8-3, 668F2
GOP platform text 8-18, 602F3
Ford signs options tax bill 9-3, 708D1
Dow reactn to electn 11-3—11-4, 826B1
Dow ends yr up 11-10—12-31, 984B1
NE govs seek aid 11-14, 864E3
Legal Issues
Vesco, 6 others indicted 1-14, 78A2
US Financial ex-chrmn sentncd 2-3, 124D1
Sup Ct bars suits vs auditors 3-30, 262E1
Former Eximbank offcls sued 8-9, 709B3
2 cos disciplined re boycott 8-11, 747C2
Figueres sued in NY 9-22, 1000G2
Rosenthal & Co chrgd 10-21, 990C2
CR repeals 'Vesco Law' 11-2, 1000E2
Gulf shareholder suits setld 11-18, 939F1
'75 stock fraud sentncs cited 11-20, 885D3
Home-Stake fines rptd 12-22, 1016C2

1977

STEWART, Sherwood
US beaten in Davis Cup 4-29—5-1, 353D3
STEYN, Marthinus T.
Assumes Namibia post 9-1, OKs SWAPO vote talks 9-8, 699C3 ★, F3 ★
Ends Namibia apartheid, security laws 10-14—11-11, 876D1 ★
STILZ, Richard
US to return seized Scientology papers 7-20, 628D2
Boyce sentenced 9-12, 732G3
STING, The (film)
Top-grossing film 6-1, 452C2
STINGL, Josef
On Jan jobless rise 2-4, 139A2
STIPE, Gosset, Stipe & Harper
Swine flu damage claims rptd 3-21, 224B2
STIRLING Jr., David
Convicted 1-29, 103F1 ★, G1
Sentenced 3-11, 203G2
STIRLING, William G.
Convicted 1-29, 103F1 ★, G1
Sentenced 3-11, 203A3
STIRLING Homex Corp.
Ex-offcls convicted 1-29, 103F1 ★, G1; sentncd 3-11, 203F2
STIRN, Olivier
French Guiana dvpt plan rptdly fails 8-3, 728A2
STOBBE, Dietrich
Elected W Berlin mayor 5-2, 352G3
STOCK Car Auto Racing, National Association for (NASCAR)—*See AUTOMOBILE Racing*

STOCKS, Bonds & Securities—*See also city, company, country names*
Carter sets conflict-of-interest code 1-4, 4E2
Ford asks tax changes 1-4, 5B3
'68 NYS transfer tax amendmts ruled illegal 1-12, 57C2
Sen forms ethics com 1-18, House code proposed 1-31, 77A3
Utility stocks hit 3-yr high 1-24, 54E3
Econ indicator index described 1-28, 92E3; **for data, see 'Statistics' under BUSINESS**
Stirling Homex ex-offcls convctd 1-29, 103F1 ★, G1; sentncd 3-11, 203G2
NYC debt repaymt dvpts 2-8—3-11, 193A1-G3
AT&T stocks, debt outstanding rptd 2-14, 156C1
SEC Arab boycott policy reversal rptd 2-18, 167E1
Price hike, merger rise linked 2-18, 274C2
Carter budget revision 2-22, 124E3
Carter aides rpt net worth 2-25, 147B3-148D1
Maine sells bonds 2-25, 197B1
Unionists jam Stevens mtg 3-1, 153E3
Bond investmt scheme indictmts 3-3, 204C1
ITT-Hartford suits setld 3-4, 194B3
SEC sues Allied Chem 3-4, 252E2
Saccharin ban trading 3-9—3-10, 177G1
Sup Ct bars fed antifraud rules expansn 3-23, 276G2 ★
Ogilvy & Mather slush fund rptd 3-30, 233D3
Sen ethics code adopted 4-1, 251A3
1st ¼ Eurobond trading rptd 4-13; Euro-yen issue made 4-19, 318C1
Bond prices up on rebate end 4-14, 271C2
Carter energy plan reactn 4-21, 320G1
AT&T sets employe stock plan 5-6, 409E1
Equity Funding lawsuit setld 5-11, 408G3
NYSE-Amex merger talks fail 5-19, 520F3-521C2
Negotiated fee impact rptd positive 6-6, 521C2
Du Pont-Christiana merger OKd 6-16, 518A1
Del seizure law voided 6-24, 539C3
Graham fund holdings rptd 6-26, 732A1
Secret US-Saudi pact rptd 6-27, 474D1
Index data misuse chrgd 6-28, 554E2
Holzer indicted 7-12, 848G1
NYC blackout closes mkts 7-14, 537B3
Milwaukee Rd stock purchase OKd 7-15, 593C2

1978

STEWART, Rod
Foot Loose on best-seller list 2-4, 116G3
STEWART, Ron
Fired as Kings coach 4-20, 458B3
STEWART, Sherwood
Loses N Amer Zone Davis Cup match 3-18, 252B1
Loses US Open doubles title 9-9, 707G1
STEYN, Marthinus T.
Rpts Namibia student abductn 2-22, 229F2
Gets emergency powers 4-8, 299B2
At Kapuuo funeral 4-9, 269E2
Sets Namibia voter regis 6-20, 475A3
Assumes censorship power 7-3, 547D3
UN ends Namibia missn 8-23, 669F2
Sets Namibia electns 9-20, 742B1
Sees contact group 10-16, 819A3
STIEGLITZ, Alfred (1864-1964)
Kanaga dies 2-28, 196C3
STIEVE, Terry
Traded to Cardinals 1-31, 172D1
STIGWOOD, Robert
Grease released 6-16, 619C2
Sgt Pepper's released 7-21, 970B3
Moment by Moment released 12-21, 1030C3
STILL, Art
In NFL draft 5-2, 336E2
STILL, Clyfford
Elected to Arts Institute 2-7, 316D1
STILL, William
Dies 12-3, 1032F3
STINGER Missile—*See ARMAMENTS—Missiles*
STINGLEY, Darryl
Paralyzed 8-12, 1023G3
STINSON, George
Sees Carter on coal strike 2-24, 122F3
STIPE, Gene
Loses Okla Sen primary 8-22, 683A1
STIRLING, Alexander
Iraq ousts 7-27, 582G2
STIRLING Jr., David
Fraud convictn review denied by Sup Ct 10-2, 751E2
STIRLING, William G.
Fraud convictn review denied by Sup Ct 10-2, 751E2
STIRLING Homex Corp.
Ex-offcls convictns review denied by Sup Ct 10-2, 751E2
STIRLING v. U.S.
Case denied by Sup Ct 10-2, 751E2
STIX, John
Family Business opens 4-12, 760B2
STOBBE, Dietrich
Lauds E, W Ger transport pacts 11-16, 906A1
STOCKMAN, Rep. David A. (R, Mich.)
Reelected 11-7, 851E1

STOCKS, Bonds & Securities—*See also city, state, country, company names*
Econ indicator index described 128B1
Discount, fed fund rates described 679B1
Thyssen bid for Budd hikes price 1-6, 1-12, 66B2
Cowles Communicatns to liquidate 1-6, 75F3-76A1
Carter budgets RR purchases 1-23, 47D3
Autogiro patent case review denied 1-23, 65E1
Pacific Exchng bars LA shift 2-1, 66B3
Church-bond investor losses rptd 2-27, 295F3
Canada asks bond sales in US 3-2, 188C1
Penn Central reorganizatn plan OKd 3-9, 185G3-186F1
Curtiss-Wright, Kennecott proxy fight 3-13—5-24; '60 Alleghany battle cited 3-24, 402A1-403D1
'77 petro$ purchases of US securities rptd 3-22, 221E3
Carter presents urban-aid plan 3-27, 217C3
Bank stock sale case refused by Sup Ct 3-27, 241D2
Bankers Trust stock sale case refused by Sup Ct 3-28, 241F3
Burns urges bond sale for $ defns 3-31, 235C2
UK proposes NY bond issue 4-11, 267F2
Merrill Lynch to buy White Weld 4-14, 283B2
Carter links price rise to energy bill, inflatn progress 4-25, 307B3
Corp pol free speech backed by Sup Ct 4-26, 343C3
OPEC investmt in US rptd 4-28, 344A3
Corp execs '77 appreciatn rights rptd 5-15, 364D3, 365A1
SEC trading suspensns curbed by Sup Ct 5-15, 387C1
Investors protectn measure signed, broker-adviser separatn delayed 5-21, 386D2
Miami U cancels sale 6-3, 4 other univ divestitures rptd 6-6, 6-18, 633B1-D1
Brokerage-exec pay curbs pressed by Admin 6-6, 428B1
Class actn suits curbed by Sup Ct 6-19, 492B2
Occidental-Husky collusn chrg probed 6-19, 629G1
Chrysler raises equity cash for dvpt plan 6-20, 623G3-624A1
Class actn certificatn appeals curbed by Sup Ct 6-21, 509G2

1979

STEWART, Ralph
Joins PCs 3-7, 189C1
STEWART, Rod
Da Ya Think I'm Sexy on best-seller list 2-14, 120E3; 3-7, 174E1; 4-4, 271D2
Blondes Have More Fun on best-seller list 2-14, 120F3; 3-7 174D1; 4-4, 271E2
STEWART, Sammy
In World Series 10-10–10-17, 816G2
STEWART, Sherwood
Loses Grand Prix doubles 1-7, 103D3
STEWART-Warner Corp.
Tax acctg methods limited by Sup Ct 1-16, 32G2
STEYN, Marthinus T.
Removed as Namibia head, Viljoen replaces 8-1, 585A2
STICKLES, Robert
Resigns Chicago schl post 12-4, 943G3
STIEGLITZ, Alfred (1864-1964)
Widow's stolen paintings ordrd returned 7-27, 656G1
STIER, Ed
On Mafia evidence 5-23, 508F1
STIGWOOD, Robert
Evita opens 9-25, 956A3
STILES, George
Light Shines opens 1-11, 292G1
STILLER, Werner
Identified as E Ger defector 1-24, 61E3
Spy arrests continue 1-31, 77D3
CDU infiltratn, E Ger spy data rptd 3-13, 180A3, D3
STILWELL, Gen. Richard G. (ret.)
Criticizes SALT 4-11, 295E1
STINGER Missile—*See ARMAMENTS–Missiles*
STINGL, Josef
Rpts W Ger jobless drop 1-5, 8F1
STITT, Milan
Runner Stumbles released 11-16, 1008D1
STIX, John
Price opens 4-19, 712B2
Dark at the Top opens 11-29, 956A3

STOCKS, Bonds & Securities
Arbitrage, bond, O-T-C, security, stock, tender offer defined 72D2
9 US exchanges listed 72B3
SEC suit retrial barred by Sup Ct 1-9, 14B2
US to end Series E, H bond sales in '79 1-10, 133D1-A2
US '78 savings bond record sales rptd 1-10, 133G1
SEC role in pensn plans barred by Sup Ct 1-16, 32F1-B2
UV Industries to liquidate 1-18, 131F3
SEC suit vs Hughes settled 1-19, 88A2
Carter budget proposals 1-22, 42C1, 45E1
Buckley, Sitco partners settle SEC chrg 2-7, 132A1
Shareholders back Chessie-Seaboard merger 2-13, 205E3
Cleveland bond issue ban declined by Sup Ct 2-21, 128B3
Seaboard cleared of trust chrgs 2-22, 206A1
Columbia U sells bank stock, other coll divestitures rptd 3-10–3-24, 270G3; 4-26–5-3, 332G3
Johns-Manville broker sentncd 3-13, 239D3
Bagley indicted 3-14, SEC chrgs 3-15, 291G3
Bank divd paymt ceiling set 3-16, 264D2
US savings bond sales suspended 4-2, 251C3
Moody's lowers Chrysler debt rating 4-12, 7-31, 576C2
Edper seeks Brascan control 4-30–5-1, 5-30, 440E2, A3
Moon church bank fraud chrgd 5-1, 376D2
'78 Fortune 500 rpts investor return data 5-7, 304B3, 305A2
Mutual fund dirs' power backed by Sup Ct 5-14, 382G3
Corp execs '78 appreciatn rights rptd 5-14, 347D3, 348A1
Shearson, Loeb Rhoades to merge 5-14, 366A3
Securities law broker protectn backed by Sup Ct 5-21, 400C3
McDonnell Douglas stock drops 6-6, 421A1
Edper completes Brascan takeover 6-14, 6-29, 542D3
Customer suits vs accountants curbed by Sup Ct 6-18, 499C1
SEC scores United Tech-Carrier takeover 6-25, shareholders back merger 7-5, 541A3

1980

STEYN, Marais
Named S Africa UK amb 8-26, 689G3-690A1
STILL, Clyfford
Dies 6-23, 528E3
STILLER, Jerry
Passione opens 5-22, 756F3
STIMSON, Henry L. (1867-1950)
MacArthur WWII 'gift' knowledge rptd 1-30, 1-31, 115A2
STIMSON, Sara
Little Miss Marker released 3-21, 216C3
STINGER Missile—*See ARMAMENTS--Missiles*
STINGLEY, Darryl
Lawyer seeks Tatum suspensn 1-10, 175G2
STINTON, Colin
Twelfth Night opens 12-16, 1003F3
STIR Crazy (film)
Released 12-12, 1003D2
STIRN, Olivier
French-Cuba trade accord rptd 4-1, 253B3
STITT, Milan
Back in the Race opens 4-17, 392C2
STOCK, Leonard
Wins Olympic medal 2-14, 155F2
STOCKMAN, Rep. David A. (R, Mich.)
Reelected 11-4, 843E1
Named Budget dir 12-11, 935B1
Reagan studies budget cuts 12-17, 956D1
STOCKPORT—*See IOWA*

STOCKS, Bonds & Securities
Margin explained 899G1
Arbitrage, bond, O-T-C, security, stock, tender offer defined 76D2
Money market, mutual funds defined 223A3
Saco (Me) '79 default rptd 1-7, 54E1
'79 municipal bonds sales rptd up 1-16, 92A3
Kennedy urges dividend controls 1-28, 74F3
Chicago bond, note rating lowered by Moody's 1-31, 186A2
Garrett dies 2-3, 176C1
Kennedy for dividends freeze 2-6, 90G3
FRB sets new monetary supply terms 2-7, 113G3
Bond price drop rptd, finance structure seen threatnd 2-19, 2-21, 126E3
US completes NYC 'up-front' loan guarantees 2-21, 186E3
City, state canceled bond issues rptd 2-26, 2-28, 186D1
SEC censures Phila exchng 3-13, 224F2-B3
Stocks retreat, bonds gain following Carter anti-inflatn plan 3-17, 203A2-C3
FRB money mkt reserve rule contested 3-20; mkt growth detailed 3-21, 223E2
Mutual fund insurance case refused by Sup Ct 3-24, 265E1
'79 univ endowmt earnings rptd 3-24, 319E1
Hunt group sets silver-backed bond issue 3-26, 222F3
Hunts sell equity to meet margin calls on silver 3-27, 223C2
Top 10 money mkt funds chart 3-31, 223F3
Hunt shares in Bache probed 3-31—4-2, 245B2
Bush attacks Admin 4-7, 264D2
Sunshine Mining offers silver-backed bonds 4-11, 265C3
Bond mkt rallies on Kaufman prime rate drop predictn 4-16, 286E2-A3
Chrysler loan guarantees OKd 5-10, 383B3
FRB rejcts money mkt reserve rule plea 5-22, 400G1
Ford electn to Shearson Loeb bd rptd 5-22, 456A3
Phelan elected NYSE pres 5-22, 456A3
Money mkt rates down on FRB credit moves 5-23, 400F1
Hunts' bailout loan collateral listed 5-28, 426E1
NYSE unit awaits futures trading OK 5-28, 481D2

1976

STOCKTON, Dave
Wins PGA open golf 8-16, 656A2

1977

SEC sues IDS, brokers; most settle 7-19, 612A3
Arbitragers hike Babcock price, McDermott shares drop 8-25, 667A2
SEC rpt chrgs NYC '74-75 financial deceptn 8-26; Beame scores, other reactn 8-26—8-28, 665C2, D3
US Steel Chicago plants closing feared 8-26, 775C3
Municipal bond yields rptd down 9-6, 691E2
FRA to buy C&NW stock 9-9, 778B3
Gerber stocks fall 9-19, 799F2
Ashland OKs Commonwealth purchase 9-22, 723B1
Koreans, Diplomat Bank, others chrgd by SEC 9-28, 774B1
Dean Witter-Reynolds merger set, reactn 10-3, 799G2
Utah State U broker dispute review declined 10-11, 774A3
Donaldson Lufkin buys Pershing, Wood Struthers 10-11, 799G3
Merrill Lynch paymt ordrd re Scientific Control stock 10-11, 859F2
'72-77 brokerage co consolidatn rptd 10-19, 799D3
Admin warns FRB on tight money impact 10-20, 798C3
Burns links Admin policy, mkt decline 10-26, 817F2
Graham assn gift annuities OKd 10-26, 845C1
Loeb Rhoades, Hornblower merger planned 10-27, 1004A3
Low prices, merger activity linked 11-4, 879F3
State, city bond referenda results 11-8, 879F1
Levitt voted Amex chrmn 11-10, 859C3
NYC notes get lowest rating; pub sale canceled, Beame scores Moody's 11-10; Goldin bars new sale 11-13, 881A1, G1
Brae seeks Green Bay purchase 11-22, BN drops bid 12-1, 1007B1
Lehman Bros, Kuhn Loeb merger planned 11-28, 1004F2-A3
Players' agent sentenced 11-28, 1021A2
SEC: off-bd trading curbs to remain 12-1, 1004C1
Natl mkt move delay scored; ITS cited 12-1, 1004E1
BN, Fresco OK stock exchng 12-5, 1007D1
NYSE seat price hits low 12-12, 1004F1
AMEX, NASDAQ '77 index closings rptd 12-30, 1003G3

Dow Jones Industrial Average
Closings, vol table 1-3—1-21, 38A2; 1-24—2-11, 93A3; 2-14—3-4, 154A2; 3-7—3-25, 215A2; 3-17—5-25, 408B1; 3-28—4-15, 274A2; 4-18—5-27, 408A2; 5-31—6-17, 464A2; 6-20—7-8, 521A2; 7-11—8-5, 593B3; 8-8—8-26, 651A2; 8-29—9-23, 722A2; 9-26—10-21, 799A2*; 10-24—11-18, 880A3; 11-21—12-9, 941E2; 12-12—12-30, 1004A1
Dow drops re tight money policy 3-17—5-25, 408B1
Falls 4-4, rallies on rebate end 4-14, 271A2
Carter energy plan reactn 4-21, 320G1
Drop linked to June trade deficit, Bethlehem Steel dividend cut 7-27, 593C3, D3
Sagging mkt caps 12-yr decline 8-29, 9-2, 691C1
'77 loss rptd 12-30, 1003F3

Options Trading
CBOE, Amex war rptd 2-17, 521F1
Options trading expanded 3-4, 521E1
NYSE-Amex merger talks issue 5-19, 520G3
Options trading explained 5-23, 520G3
Amex asks SEC probe NYSE plan 6-13, 521C2
SEC limits trading, begins probe 10-18, 859B3

STOCKTON, Charles W.
Sunspots, weather linked 2-21, 183D2

STOCKTON, Dick
Wins US Pro Indoor title 1-3, 103F3
Loses Phoenix Open 1-9, 104C1
WCT tourn results 2-20—5-15, 430D2, G2
US beaten in Davis Cup 4-29—5-1, 353C3

1978

Gartner bars resignatn re Andreas gift 6-28, 513G2
N Central, Southn airlines merger set 7-13, 684D1
TXI, Pan Am purchase of Natl Airlines stock OKd 8-17, 8-28; Pan Am, Natl set merger 9-7, 701A1
Kaiser-Medusa deal canceled 8-22, 700C3
2d ¼ employmt costs cite broker fees 8-30, 680B2
Western, Continental airlines merger set 8-31, 684C1
SEC censures Dirks, 4 cos re Equity Funding 9-4, 681F1
NYSE to probe Amax trading 9-11, 700E2
Meany links inflatn, big divds 9-18, 715D2
Business cash holdings, stock repurchases linked 9-18, 716F3
Del Monte OKs Reynolds merger 9-25, 752B3
Kennecott victory over Curtiss-Wright voided, new electns ordrd 9-28, 752D2
Margin calls fuel NYSE selloff 10-16—10-31, 826F2
Bond trading on capital mkt explained 10-18, 790F3
Penn Central reorgn ends 10-24, 876A1
US to sell yen-, mark-, franc-denominated bonds to aid $ 11-1, 825G1
Carter signs Conrail aid bill 11-1, 875D3
Morgan Stanley sued re Olinkraft arbitrage 11-8, 896D3
Celanese-Olin merger ended, stock price drop cited 11-10, 897D1
Tex securities-regulatn case refused by Sup Ct 11-13, 874C3
Trucking freight-rate hike voided 11-27, 1007F2
Stockbroker liability case refused by Sup Ct 12-4, 959B1
Natl merger bids rptd 12-11, SEC probe rptd 12-22, 1007B3
IBM sets 4-for-1 stock split 12-19, 1003F3
World stock mkt gains rptd; graphs 12-25, 1001C1

Crime
Vesco case review barred 1-9, 13A2
Mattel offcls indicted 2-16, 116E2
Columbia Pictures ex-pres indicted 3-31, stockholder suits rptd 4-1, 251C2
Vesco fraud chrgs dismissed by CR 4-30, 354F2
Admin linked to Vesco 'pol fix' 9-1—9-15, 719G3
Stirling Homex convictn review denied by Sup Ct 10-2, 751E2
SEC charges Houston U ex-aide 10-5, 770B3

Dow Jones Industrial Average
Avg described 66C1
'77 loss compared with other indexes 1-1, 66G3
Closings, vol table 1-3—1-31, 66E1; 2-1—2-28, 142A2; 3-1—3-31, 223A2
$ fears cause Dow drop 1-6—1-11, 28G1
Closings, vol table 4-3—4-28, 303E2; 5-1—5-31, 403A2; 6-1—6-30, 493E1
Kennecott price closes up 4-5, 402C3
Record-breaking rally 4-13—4-26, 303A1-E2
'77 Fortune 500 rpts investor return data 5-8, 325D3-326B1
Closings, vol table 7-3—7-31, 606B2
Closings, vol table 8-1—8-31, 664A2
Closing, vol table 9-1—9-29, 737A2
Aug rise, Sept drop cited in Aug indicators index 10-1, 752D2
Closings, vol table 10-2—10-31, 826A2
Dow down on Carter anti-inflatn plan, prime rate fears 10-16—10-31, rebounds on $ aid steps 11-1—11-3, 825B1, 826D1-827A1
Closings, vol table 11-1—11-30, 918A2
Closings, vol table 12-1—12-29, 1004E2
Graph of '78 performance 12-25, 1001C1
'78 avgs rptd 12-29, 1004B2

New York City Finances—*See under NEW York City*

Options Trading
NY indicts 11 Amex traders, Amex scores; SEC '77 probes cited 1-5, 4F3-5A1
'78 vol record, CBOE seat price rptd 12-29, 1004B3

STOCKTON, Dave
Ties for 2d in US Open 6-18, 580A2

STOCKTON, Dick
USTA ranks 9th 1-5, 22E3
Loses Birmingham WCT 1-15, 418F3
French Open results 6-11, 540F1

1979

FRB Open Mkt rpt disclosure delay backed by Sup Ct 6-28, 558C3
1st 1/2 mergers rptd 7-2, 500F23
Look ends tie to Rolling Stone, fires Wenner 7-3, 640C3
Sun, Becton purchase ruled illegal 7-9, 541E2
Loeb settles pensn suit 7-9, 640F3
UAW opens Big 3 contract talks 7-16, backs Chrysler fed aid 7-18, 598D1, F1
S&P lowers Chrysler debt rating 8-1, 576D2
Bagley acquitted 8-1, 578D2
Chrysler omits dividend 8-2, 576E3
Kerkorian trust case dismissed 8-14, 756C1
Auto-Train withdraws fed loan applicatn 8-21, Seaboard extends pact 8-24, 726D2
Legislators' incomes studied 9-1, 701D3, F3
UAW wins stock optns in GM pact 9-14, 698C2
Municipal bond ratings listed 9-20, 920E3
IBM bonds sold 10-4; price drops, loss rptd 10-11, 765D1
Margin calls explained, linked to Dow drop 765E2
Bond mkt down on FRB credit moves; Treas, NY housing bonds drop 10-10, 10-11, 765A1
Cornfeld acquitted of IOS fraud 10-15, 817F3
SEC fraud powers case accepted by Sup Ct 10-15, 848B1
Wall St observes '29 crash 10-29, economists comment 10-29, 11-1, 826B3-827D2
Bond house failures, investmt losses tied to FRB money supply data error 10-30, 828F2-A3
Chrysler omits dividend again 11-1, 846D1
Eurofranc bond interest rate rptd 11-9, 872A3
Investor suits vs advisers curbed by Sup Ct 11-13, 901G3
Wien Air stock sale to HFC rptd, Alaska Air sues 11-20; CAB rejcts Alaska NW sale 12-20, 989F1
Sun sets Becton divestiture 12-19, 985G1
Chrysler aid plan OKd 12-21, 981E3
Saudis buy IBM notes 12-27, 986G1

Dow Jones Industrial Average
Average described 72D1-C2
Jan closing, vol table 1-2–1-31, 72A1
Feb closing, vol table 2-1–2-28, 166A2
Dow falls on Iran oil fears 2-7, 83E1
Mar closing, vol table 3-1–3-30, 230C3
Apr closing, vol table 4-2–4-30, 325D2
May closing, vol table 5-1–5-31, 402A3
June closing, vol table 6-1–6-29, 481C2
Chrysler, Esmark dropped from index; IBM, Merck added 6-28, 481E2
July closing, vol table 7-2–7-31, 578B2
Carter Cabt shake-up affects mkt 7-18–7-20, 530C1, 531F3
Mkt rallies on Volcker nominatn 7-25, 555C2
Aug closings, vol table 8-1–8-31, 648D2
Sept closing, vol table 9-3–9-28, 745A3
Oct closing, vol table 10-1–10-31, 827A3
Dow at '79 high 10-5; drops on FRB credit moves, record vol 10-8–10-11, 764D1, 765F1
Nov closing, vol table 11-1–11-30, 903B2
Dec closing, vol table 12-3–12-31, 985A2

Options Trading
Stock options trading described 348D2
SEC censures Hutton, employes 2-6, 349G1
SEC rpts on trading growth, abuses; asks overhaul 2-15, 348C2-349G1
SEC sees freeze end 2-22, 348A3

STOCKTON, Dick
Loses US Natl Indoor doubles 3-4, 391A3
Loses World Invitatn 5-20, 570C2

1980

DIDC sets money mkt interest rules 5-28, S&Ls file suit 6-16, 516B3
MGM to split film, hotel units 5-30, 501F2
Milwaukee city, cnty bond ratings lowered 6-13, 743G3
Chrysler offers $500 mln note sale 6-24, 481E2
Gannett purchase of NM paper rescinded 6-30, 582E2-A3
FRB ends money mkt reserve rule 7-3, 513A2
DC recovery plan proposed 7-19, 742F3
Cleveland default setlmt, bond purchase agreed 7-29, 743B3
Ex-Yippie joins investmt firm 7-30, 638A3
Detroit bond rating lowered 8-6, 743A3
NYFE opens, 1st day's trading rptd 8-7, 616D3
NYC recovery plan revised 8-11, fed loan guarantees sought 9-10, 743D1
Auto-Train trading halted 8-18, 958F2
AT&T begins reorgn, OKs Bell unit minority shares purchase 8-20, 648D2
NYC pub bond sale moves rptd 9-10, 743F1
SEC natl securities mkt plan failure scored 9-12, 806D1
'79 securities indus rptd strong 9-28, 806B2
FRB OKs commercial paper bank sales 9-29, 986B2
Genentech issue success rptd 10-14, 805F3
McGraw-Hill takeover case declined by Sup Ct 11-3, 856A2
Housing bonds tax exemptns rptd revoked 11-10, 989C2
NFL cross-ownership ban backed 11-18, 998D3
Boston bond rating lowered 12-2, 939C3
Budget reconciliatn signed 12-5, 936G1
NYSE investor survey rptd 12-9, 958A2
New Haven RR reorgn challenge refused by Sup Ct 12-15, 957D2

Crime & Stock Manipulation
Dickinson ct damages action dropped 2-14, 558A2
Gen Dynamics settles SEC suit 2-27, 558C1
United Tech settles SEC Carrier suit 3-6, 558E1
'Insider' trading convictn voided by Sup Ct 3-18, 226A2
Vesco grand jury ends 4-1, 251B3
Ala black dist judge nominee accused 5-19, withdraws 9-17, 744A3
SEC fraud intent proof required by Sup Ct 6-2, 512A3
ABC ties to Spelling-Goldberg rptd probed by SEC 8-7—8-8, 640A2
Revlon heir, financier indicted 8-19, 713F3
Columbia sued by Kerkorian 9-30, shareholders 10-7; dirs countersue 10-2, 10-20, 906D2

Dow Jones Industrial Average
Average described 76D1-C2
Jan closing, vol table 1-2—1-31, 76A1
Feb closing, vol table 2-1—2-29, 167C2
Feb-Mar closings chart 2-18—3-20, 202A1, D1
Mar closing, vol table 3-3—3-31, 248C1
Dow plummets on Carter anti-inflatn plan 3-17, 203G2
'79 univ endowmt earnings compared 3-24, 319E1
Hunt margin calls shake mkt, rumors spark late rally 3-27, 223A2
Apr closing, vol table 4-1—4-30, 329A3
May closing, vol table 5-1—5-30, 401A2
June closing, vol table 6-2—6-30, 495D3
July closing, vol table 7-1—7-31, 575A2
Aug closing, vol table 8-1—8-29, 666A3
Sept closing, vol table 9-1—9-30, 764A2
Oct closing, vol table 10-1—10-31, 824A2
Nov closing, vol table 11-3—11-28, 916A3
Prices surge on Reagan win 11-5, plunge on prime rate rise 11-6, 844F3, 845D1
Dec closing, vol table 12-1—12-31, 984B3

Foreign Developments (including U.S. international news)
Japan exchng hits record high average 1-14, 100C1
Canada exchngs cut hrs; Jan records cited 2-4, 96B2
Canada exchngs resume normal hrs 2-11, 116F3
Australia hikes bond rate 3-2, 210G3
Bahamas bank looting case rptd 3-3, 229B1
Canada mkt drops again 3-17—3-27, recovers 3-28, 253B1
Canada exchng offcl chrgd 5-5, 406C3
Canada record govt bond redemptn noted 5-16, 388E3
Canada mkt up 5-21, 377A2
Hong Kong exchng merger set 5-27, 398B3
W Ger sets pre-war bond redemptn 6-3, 446F3
Kuwait bid for Getty Oil rejctd 7-18, 556G3
Group of 10 studies IMF bond sale 9-15, 695G2
Japan eases forgn investmt rules 12-1, 966F3

Options Trading
Trader arrested in 'boiler room' swindle 1-2, 94B3
SEC eases ban 3-26, 224A2
Regulators debate speculatn curbs 4-14—4-15, 290A1
4 exchngs ban new issues 10-10, 986D2

1976

STOESSEL Jr., Walter J.
Briefs emb personnel on taps 2-6, 122E2 ★
Rptd ill 2-16, 196C3
Protests Sovt emb harrassmt 3-24, Sovt counterchrgs rptd 3-26, 229C3 ★
Underground A-test pact drafted 4-9, 242C3
Initials underground A-pact 5-12, 371F2
STOICHEV, Trendafil
Wins Olympic medal 7-24, 576E2
STOKES, Rep. Louis (D, Ohio)
Wins 6 pres delegates 6-8, 409D1, G2
Reelected 11-2, 830B3
STOL (short takeoff and landing) Aircraft—*See 'Aircraft' under ARMAMENTS*
STOLERU, Lionel
French manual labor min 1-12, 49D2
STOLTZFUS, William A.
Replaced as amb to Kuwait 4-28, 412F1
STOMMA, Stanislaw
Sejm drops 3-21, 268A3
STONE, Galen L.
Amb to IAEA 1-20; confrmd 2-6, 110C2
STONE, Irving
Greek Treasure on best seller list 1-25, 80B3; 12-5, 972F2
STONE, W. Clement
'72 campaign gift listed 4-25, 688A1
STONEHOUSE, John
Quits Labor Party 4-7, 267B1
Trial begins 4-27, 313D1
Convicted, sentenced 8-6, 589A1
Resigns from Parlt 8-27, 676A1
Tories win seat 11-4, 853E1
STONER, O. G.
Oppositn asks probe 11-25, 924B2
STONES, Dwight
Sets high jump record 6-5, 444G3
Wins Olympic medal 7-31, 576D1
STOP ERA
Schlafly scores child care 2-13, 172G1
STOPFORTH, Lawrence
Reassigned 6-1, threatens libel 6-8, 416B2
STOPH, Willi
E Ger Politburo enlarged 5-22, 381E2
Replaced; named mins cncl chrmn 10-29, 889D1
STOPPARD, Tom
Travesties wins Tony 4-18, 460D2
STORHOLT, Jan Egil
Wins Olympic medal 2-13, 158F3

STORMS & Floods
China aid to Sri Lanka rptd 1-2, 78D1
Typhoon hits Philippines 5-20, 404E2
Teton R Dam bursts 6-5, 423B1
Japan peninsula flooded 7-11, 796C2
Ford OKs Idaho dam victims aid 7-12, 517E3; 9-7, 665C1
Venez, Mex floods rptd 7-18, 7-21, 544B3
Colo canyon flood 7-31, 595E2, G2 ★
Flood research aid signed 8-3, 567A1
Hurricane Belle hits East 8-8—8-11, 595G1
Colo canyon flood probe rptd 8-10, death toll at 138 8-22, 756G1
US GOP platform text 8-18, 603E1
Typhoon Fran hits Japan 9-8—9-13, 796B2
Teton Dam probe rpt issued 9-25, 736C1
Hurricane Liza cracks Mex dam 10-1, 840D2
Australia floods rptd 10-5, 770D3
Dike bursts in Colombia 10-6, 816F1
'72 Indian famine cited 10-28, 863A2
Australia '74 cyclone relief scored 11-4, probe ordrd 11-18, 902D2
UN backs weather manipulatn treaty 12-10, 955D1

1977

STOCKTON, Herbert R.
Indicted 6-6, 504C1
STOCKWELL, John
Backs Snepp Viet evacuatn chrgs 11-22, 898G1
STOESSEL Jr., Walter J.
Replaced as Sovt amb 1-18, 47A2; 6-7, 500C1
STOKES, John
Lance testifies 9-15, 701A2
STOKES, Rep. Louis (D, Ohio)
Named assassinatn com chrmn 3-8, 228E2
Fears Ray escape plot 6-11, 459D1
STOKOWSKI, Leopold
Dies 9-13, 788G2
STOL (short takeoff and landing planes)—*See AVIATION—Aircraft*
STOLL, Caroline
Loses Port Washn Lionel Cup 4-17, 430E3
STOLL, Willy Peter
Linked to Baader atty 11-18, 969A1
2 W Ger terrorists captured 12-20, 1017G3
STONE, Sen. Richard B. (D, Fla.)
Sen Panama Canal hearings open; on treaty interpretatn dispute 9-26, 754G2, D3
STONER, Harry H.
Vendo contract dispute award ordrd 6-29, 557D3
STONER, J. B.
Indicted 9-26, 907D3
STONES, Dwight
High jump mark broken 7-2, 602A3
STOP ERA
Rallies vs women's conf 11-19, 917G3
STOREN, Mike
Fired as Hawks pres 9-27, 870B3
STOREY, Carl E.
Sentenced 3-14, 203E2

STORMS & Floods
Persian Gulf wind storm 227G2, C3
Blizzard hits Midwest, East 1-28—1-29, 75E2
Dust storm hits Colo 2-23, 153F1
Pa coal mine flooded 3-1, 204C3
New blizzard hits Midwest 3-10—3-12, 204A3
UN Water Conf held 3-14—3-25, 250F1
Australia '74 cyclone mem'l unveiled 3-26, 280E2
Bangladesh tornado kills 900 4-1, 312E2
South, Appalachia hit 4-3—4-6, 311E2
Ga hailstorm downs Southern Air jet 4-4, 286A3, 311F2
Johnstown (Pa) flood 7-19—7-20, 603G3
Taiwan typhoons hit 7-25, 7-31, 928D3
US flood aid authorized 8-2, 667D3
Southern Calif hit 8-15—8-17, 747F2
Kan City (Mo) hit 9-12—9-13, 768C3
Athens, Piraeus hit 11-2—11-3, 888D3
Northern Italy hit 11-5—11-10, 888E3
Ga dam bursts 11-6, 888F2
N Carolina floods kill 5 11-6, 888B3
India cyclones 11-12, 11-19, 928A2
Pl typhoon hits 11-13—11-14, 928F3

1978

STOCKWELL, John
Book on CIA publshd, '75 Angola role disclosed 5-8, ex-dir Colby responds 5-14, 367A2-368C1
STOICHKOV, Grigor
Named Bulgaria agri min 4-29, 530G3
STOJANOVIC, Mirko
Fired as Stompers coach 5-16, 707C3
STOKES, John
Loses US Sen electn 11-7, 852G1
Nunn outspent 96-1 11-15, 898C1
STOKES, Rep. Louis (D, Ohio)
Assassinatn com funds OKd 3-13, 183B1
Abortion funding curb OKd 6-13, 445F3
King assassinatn hearings 8-14—8-18, 641C2, E2, F2
JFK assassinatn hearings open 9-6, 697E3
JFK death hearings end 9-28, 749C2
Reelected 11-7, 851F3
Denies King murder plot 11-17, 898C3
Asks JFK murder film review 12-30, 1002D1
STOKKOS, Pavlos
Fired as dep police chief 2-22, 138D2
STOLL, Willy Peter
Eludes police 8-21, killed 9-6, 724D3, F3
STOLZ Jr., Irwin W.
Tonelli indicted 7-19, 599B1
STOMMELEN, Rolf
Wins Daytona endurance 2-5, 538C3
STONE, Edward Durell
Dies 8-6, 708E3
STONE, Jack
Pleads guilty 7-20, 599A1
STONE, Jeremy J.
Links E Coast booms to Concorde 3-15, 187G1
STONE, Olivier
Midnight Express released 10-6, 970C2
STONE, Peter
Silver Bears released 4-20, 619G3
Great Chefs of Eur released 10-6, 970D3
STONE, Sen. Richard (D, Fla.)
Votes for Panama Canal neutrality pact 3-16, 177E2
Votes for 2d Canal pact 4-18, 273B1
Personal finances rptd 5-19, 385D3
On US-China ties 12-17, 976C1
STONE, Robert
Who'll Stop Rain released 8-25, 1030F3
STONE Associates, Edward Durell
Saudi arms complex commissn rptd 2-18, 199A2
STONE Container Corp.
Indicted for price fixing 1-25, 67D2
Price fixing plea, fine rptd 10-16, 1005B3
STONES, Dwight
Joy breaks indoor high jump mark 1-13, 76F2
Sets indoor high jump mark 2-24, 600E3
Suspended by AAU, files suit 6-23, 692E2
STONE & Webster, Inc.
A-plant constructn accord set 4-18, 281B3
STOP ERA
ERA extensn clears Sen; Schlafly sets ct challenge 10-6, 788G1
STOPFORTH, Lawrence H.
Wins libel suit 4-13, 286G3
STOP the World I Want To Get Off (play)
Revival opens 8-3, 887C3
STORCH, Arthur
Tribute opens 6-1, 887D3
STOREY, David
Cromwell opens 7-12, 887E1
STORHOLT, Jan Egil
2d in speed-skating championship 2-26, 316B3
STORMS & Floods
Hartford arena roof collapses 1-18, 95B3
NE blizzards 1-20, 2-5—2-7, 105F1
Midwest blizzard 1-25—1-26, 105E2
Scottish Highlands blizzards 1-28—1-30, 132G3
US '77 environmtl decline rptd 85C2
Calif rainstorm, floods 2-10; LA cloud-seeding probe ordrd 2-14, 105F3-106B1
N Mex, Ariz, Calif rainstorms 3-3—3-6, 207D3
NE snowpacks rptd 3-5, Colo record rptd 3-14, 207C2
US disaster fund supplemt signed 4-4, 261C3
Mozambique floods rptd 4-10, 331F1
India tornado kills 500 in Orissa, 100 in W Bengal 4-16, 479C3
Ala, Ark, Miss, La tornadoes hit 4-17—4-18, 5-1, 479G2
Fla tornadoes kill 2 5-4, 479A3
Poland '77 floods cited 5-15, 535B2
Kan tornadoes kill 18 5-31, 6-17, 479B3
Carter proposes flood control 6-6, 426D3
US lightning, flash flood data 6-24, 7-4, 655A1
ND, Minn tornadoes kill 9 7-5, 654G3
Minn flash floods kill 8 7-6, 654G3
Afghan-Pak floods kill 122, 7-9, 655C1
LNG safety measures urged 7-31, 610A1
Tex flash floods kill 26 8-8, 654E3
Alpine floods kill 23 8-8, 655B1
India floods kill 450 8-13, 655C1
India floods kill 1,200 9-19, 759D1
Pl typhoon 10-27, 314 rptd dead 11-6, 972C2
NJ OKs flood control bond issue 11-7, 915D2
Sri Lanka hurricane 11-24, 972D2
La, Ark, Miss tornadoes kill 4 12-3, 972G1-B2

1979

STODDARD, Thomas
Chrgd re fraud 2-5, 96F2
STODDARD, Tim
In World Series 10-10—10-17, 816F2
STOJANOVIC, Mike
NASL to probe suggested goal fix 8-17, 776A2
STOKER, Bram (1847-1912)
Dracula released 7-13, 820A1
STOKES, Bobby
NASLPA strike, 4-13—4-18, INS warning rescinded 4-17, 4-13, 432A1
STOKES, Rep. Louis (D, Ohio)
Says Oswald organized crime link unproven 1-3, 4E1
STOLL, Caroline
Loses Vienna Open 5-20, wins Berlin Intl 5-27, 570D2
STOMMELEN, Rolf
2d in LeMans 6-10, 490D3
STONE, James M.
Confrmd as CFTC head 4-11, vs options trading resumptn 9-5, 681A2, D2
STONE, Ken
NFL '78 interceptn ldr 1-6, 80G1
STONE, Oliver
Wins Oscar 4-9, 336A2
STONE, Sen. Richard (D, Fla.)
Vs Libya jet sale 3-2, 250A2
Finances disclosed 5-18, 383D2
Scores Nicaragua junta ldrs 9-24, 731E3
STONE, Steve
In World Series 10-10—10-17, 816A3
STONE, Ward
NYS bird death cause noted 3-18, 206G3
STONE Container Corp.
Boise Cascade offer rptd 1-22, 89E1
Boise Cascade bid rejctd 1-30, 440F3
STONES, Dwight
Reinstated by AAU 11-28, 956D1
STONE v. Powell
Case cited by Sup Ct 7-2, 558F3
STONE & Webster Inc.
Stone & Webster Engineering Corp.
5 A-plants ordrd shut 3-13, 186A2
NRC orders 33 A-plants inspected 6-25, 519A1
STOPFORTH, Lawrence H.
Goyer wins libel appeal 3-30, 253F3
STOPPARD, Tom
Despair released 2-15, 174D2
Every Good Boy opens 7-30, 711F2
Night & Day opens 11-27, 956E3
STORAGE Technology Corp.
Memorex bid rejected 10-28, 942D2
STORIES of John Cheever, The (book)
On best-seller list 2-4, 120B3; 3-4, 173D3
Cheever wins Pulitzer 4-16, 336E2, G2
Natl Book Awards rptd 4-23, 356G1

STORMS & Floods
Australia cyclone 1-1—1-2, 18C2
Midwest blizzards 1-12—1-14, 1-24—1-27, 120E1
E Eur blizzards 1-31, 120C2
Brazil floods kill 204 2-7, 120B2
US '78 flood statistics 2-11, 120A2
DC area, Baltimore blizzard 2-18—2-19, 176A2
La, Ill, Miss, Ala floods 3-15—4-18, 288D3-289A1
'78 tornado data rptd 4-1, 288C3
Poland, USSR floods 4-8, 289A1
SW tornadoes hit 4-9—4-11, 288F2
Mo declared disaster area 4-21, 472D2
Fla record rainfalls 4-25, 472G2-A3
Minn, ND, Canadian prov floods 4-26—4-30, 472A2
Tenn flash floods 5-4, 472D2
Carter asks flood projct cost-sharing 5-16, 365G2, A3
W Va floods rptd 5-16, 472F2
India floods kill 600 5-17, 472A3
Indonesia floods rptd 5-26, 6-13, 472B3
Texas floods 6-2, 472E2
Brazil frost rptd 6-4, 430F1
Jamaica flood drowns 32 6-24, 638E3
Japan floods kill 22 6-26—6-30, 639A3
Spanish flood kills 24 7-2, 638G3
La hurricane 7-11, 639B3
Indonesia tidal wave kills 539 7-22, 638F3
Tex, La tropical storm 7-24—7-28, 638D3
India flood kills 15,000 8-11, 620A1
Irish Sea storm drowns 18 yachtsmen 8-14, 799F3; rpt issued 12-10, 955C1
Hurricane David hits Carib, eastn US; 1,100 rptd dead 8-30—9-7, 690A3
Hurricane Frederic ravages Gulf Coast 9-12, disaster aid rptd 9-14, 691C1
Indonesia tidal waves kill 100 9-13, 800F2
Hurricane Frederic loss rptd 10-5, 954F2
Fla dam breaks 10-31, 912A3

1980

STOCKWELL, John
US suit re Angola opens 3-3, 268A3
Settles US suit 6-25, 516D3-517A1
STODDARD, Tim
AL pitching ldr 10-6, 926G3
STOFFERAHN, Kenneth
Wins SD US House primary 6-3, 439C3
STOKER, Bram
Awakening released 10-31, 972C3
STOKES, Rep. Louis (D, Ohio)
Justice to reopen JFK murder probe 1-4, 17F1
Myers expulsn delay fails 10-2, 740E1
Reelected 11-4, 843F4
STOLARSKY, Paul
My Mother, My Father opens 1-9, 136D3
STOLERU, Lionel
Turkish workers protest 3-3, 193D1
STOLLE, Fred
Loses Tennis Legends tourn 5-4, 607C3
STOLOFF, Morris
Dies 4-16, 360E3
STOLON, Samuel
Indicted 2-28, 237D3
STOMMELEN, Rolf
Wins Daytona endurance 2-3, 637E3
STONE, James M.
Testifies on Hunt silver trading 3-31, 245G1
Urges futures trading speculatn curbs 4-15, 290A1, C2
STONE, Ken
NFL '79 interceptn ldr 1-5, 8G2
STONE, Louise
Husband acquitted of murder 2-1, 238F1
STONE, Loy Dean
Acquitted of murder 2-1, 238E1
STONE, Marvin
Carter, Reagan TV debate panelist 10-28, 813F1
STONE, Milburn
Dies 6-12, 528E3
STONE, Sen. Richard (D, Fla.)
Faces primary runoff 9-9, 700F1
Defeated in runoff 10-7, 807C3
Hawkins wins seat 11-4, 846A1, 849D2
Named Reagan forgn policy advisor 11-6, 839G2
STONE, Steve
NL wins All-Star Game 7-8, 636C1
AL pitching ldr 10-6, 926G3
Wins Cy Young Award 11-12, 925G3
STONER, J. B.
Extradited to Ala 1-11, 55A3
At Wrightsville (Ga) rally 4-12, 333C1
Convicted, sentenced 5-14, 405A1
STONER, Tom
Loses Ia US Sen primary 6-3, 439D3
STONES, Dwight
Woodward ties high jump mark 6-7, 892A1
STONE v. Graham
Case decided by Sup Ct 11-17, 881B3
STOPPARD, Tom
Human Factor released 2-8, 216A3
STORARO, Vittorio
Wins Oscar 4-14, 296A2

STORMS & Floods
Australia town hit by cyclone 1-10, 56A1
Calif, Ariz storms, flooding 2-13—2-22, disaster declared 2-20—2-21, 213F2
US water problems noted 2-19, 145F2
Mid-Atlantic, South hit by blizzards, tornadoes 3-1—3-2, 292G1
Venice flood aid vowed 3-8—3-9, 194C2
Tornadoes hit Midwest 4-7—4-8; Mich, Pa, Mo 5-12—5-13, 391B2, G2
Gulf of Mex storms 4-25—4-28, 326D1
Fla Straits thunderstorms 5-2, 339E2
Mt St Helens erupts 5-18, 382A1
Tornadoes hit Grand I (Neb) 6-3, disaster declared 6-4, 527A3
Carter visits Grand I (Neb) 6-10, 439D1
Mex scores US hurricane tests 6-19, bars spotter planes 7-1, 524D2
Canada rain eases drought 6-27, 520B2, E2
Hurricane Allen rips Carib, Tex Gulf Coast 8-4—8-11; damage rptd 8-13, 621G1
USSR grain productn drop rptd linked 9-7, 711C3
Washn flood threats rptd 10-29, 970D3
US snowstorms kill 16 11-16—11-17, 947F3

1976

STORM Warning (book)
On best-seller list 12-5, 972A3
STORROW Jr., James J.
The Nation sale set 11-28, 901C3
Nation sale fizzles 12-21, 995E1
STOVE, Betty
Runner-up in US Open 9-12, 716D1
STOVER, Fred
Dem conv pres vote, table 7-14, 507E3
STRACHAN, Rod
Wins Olympic medal 7-25, 575F2
STRAND, Paul
Dies 3-31, 272G3
STRANGER In the Mirror, A (book)
On best-seller list 12-5, 972E2
STRATEGIC Arms Limitation Talks (SALT)—*See 'U.S.-Soviet Developments' under DISARMAMENT*
STRATEGIC Studies, Institute for—*See INSTITUTE for Strategic Studies*
STRATTON, Rep. Samuel S. (D, N.Y.)
Reelected 11-2, 830C2
STRAUB, Gilbert R. J.
Indicted 1-14, 78C2
STRAUSS, Franz Josef
Denies Lockheed payoff rpts 2-13, 132D2
US Sen subcom ends probe 3-10, 200B2
Lockheed letter termed forgery 9-22, files rptd missing 9-17, 740B1
On pol payoff chrg 9-29, 754C3
CDU loses electns 10-4, 754C2
CSU votes split with CDU 11-19, 930C2, F2
CDU, CSU reunite 12-12, 968G2
STRAUSS, Robert S.
Scores Morton appointmt 1-14, 21C3
Seeks ruling on Morton role 1-22, 41F2
Predicts Dem unity 5-3, 323F3
Carter asks to stay on 6-18, 452E1
Dem govs back Carter 7-6, 492D3
Dem Conv speaker 7-12, 508C1, G3
Reelected, Carter lauds 7-16, 532A3
Vote drives helped Carter 11-2, 818A3
To quit Dem post 11-8, 845F3
Carter meets cong ldrs 11-17, 864E1
Named Carter adviser 11-19, 881D3
At Daley funeral service 12-22, 969D3
STRAUSZ-Hupe, Robert
Amb to NATO 2-23; confrmd 3-3, 186D2
Replaced as amb to Sweden 4-1, 262E3
STREAMERS (play)
Opens 4-21, 1014C3
STREET, Anthony
Rpts revised jobless benefits 3-23, 237F1
Secret papers leaked 7-17, 537G1
On jobless relocatn plan 9-12, 730A1
Rpts Sept jobless down 10-11, 789D2
STREETER, Edward
Dies 3-7, 484G3
STREIDT, Ellen
Wins Olympic medal 7-29, 576A2
STRELOW, Roger
EPA vs Concorde 1-5, 5E2
STRELSIN, Alfred A.
Dies 8-25, 892G3
STRETTON, Maj. Gen. Alan
Scores Darwin '74 cyclone relief 11-4, probe ordrd 11-18, 902D2
STRICKLAND, Sp. 5 David
ELF frees 1-9, 31E1
STRICKLER, Ulrich J.
Indicted 1-14, 78C2

1977

STORM Warning (book)
On best-seller list 2-6, 120F3
STORROW Jr., James J.
Sells Nation magazine 12-22, 1004G3
STOUGAL, Lubomir
Austria trade talks open 11-22, 936G2
STOVE, Betty
Wins Bridgestone doubles 4-10, 430D3
Loses Wimbledon 7-1, 548G1
Wins US Open doubles title, other results 9-7, 9-11, 787A2, E2
STRADA, Vittorio
USSR bars 9-6, relents 9-7, 766C1
STRAIGHT, Beatrice
Wins Oscar 3-28, 264C1
STRAIT of Johore
Hijacked jet crashes 12-4, 992B2
STRANGE, Curtis
2d in Hartford Open 8-7, 676C2
2d in Pensacola Open 10-23, Mixed Team tourn 12-4, 950C3, F3
STRANGER In the Mirror, A (book)
On best-seller list 4-3, 264A2; 5-1, 356D2
STRATEGIC Air Command—*See under U.S. GOVERNMENT—AIR Force*
STRATEGIC Arms Limitation Talks (SALT)—*See DISARMAMENT—U.S.-Soviet Developments*
STRATEGIC Studies, Institute for—*See INSTITUTE for Strategic Studies*
STRATOS, Christoforos
Named Greek interior min 11-28, 925B2
STRATTON, June
Loses Port Washn Lionel Cup 4-17, 430F3
STRATTON, Rep. Samuel S. (D, N.Y.)
Singlaub testifies 5-25, 404E1
Chrgs Joint Chiefs' Canal pact backing forced 9-20; denied 9-27, 755F1
Backs US Concorde proposal 9-23, 738C3
STRAUSS, Franz Josef
Eastern to lease Airbus 5-24, 441D2
Cleared in Lockheed probe 6-22, 602E1
Seeks Saudi help re hijacking 789E2
STRAUSS, Robert S.
Carter picks Dem post successor 1-6, 14D2
Curtis seated 1-21, 53A2
Named trade rep 3-11, confrmd 3-29, 272C3; sworn 3-30, 249D1 *
Free trade policy rptd 3-30, 3-31, 249D1 *
To seek Taiwan, S Korea shoe-import pacts 4-1, 248D1
Ends Japan TV export talks 4-8, 318E3
On sugar subsidies 5-4, 457F3
Japan OKs TV export limit 5-20, 415E3, 416G1
To review beef import quotas 6-1, 454G2
Aide holds US-Japan trade talks 11-17—11-21, Japan press scores 11-23, 931B2, G2
On Japan trade proposals 12-15, 974A1
STRAUSZ-Hupe, Robert
Replaced as NATO amb 4-25, 418C1
STREET, Anthony
On pub employe strike ban 8-19, 652C3
Australia indus relatns min 12-19, 982A2
STREET, Victoria Price
Libel suit vs NBC dismissed 7-12, 643C1
STREISAND, Barbra
Song wins Oscar 3-28, 264D1

1978

STORY, Marguerite
Ousted over electn fraud 7-25, 591C3
STORY, Ted
Unicorn in Captivity opens 11-15, 1031C3
STOSSEL, Dr. Thomas P.
Discounts Sovt emb microwave harm 11-20, 924G3
STOTT, Michael
Stockbroker liability case refused by Sup Ct 12-4, 959C1
STOVE, Betty
Loses Washn Va Slims 1-8, Seattle Va Slims 2-12, 419F1, G1
Wins US Open mixed doubles 9-10, 707G1
STP Corp.
FTC suit settled 2-9, 348C1
STRAIGHT Time (film)
Released 3-18, 619G3
STRAIT of Magellan—*See MAGELLAN, Strait of*
STRAIT of Tiran—*See TIRAN, Strait of*
STRAM, Hank
Fired as Saints coach, gen mgr 1-31, 171A3
STRANG, Lord of Stonesfield (William Strang)
Dies 5-27, 440F3
STRANGER, The (recording)
On best-seller list 3-8, 196B1; 4-5, 272G3
STRANGER In Town (recording)
On best-seller list 6-7, 460G3; 8-2, 620G1
STRATEGIC Arms Limitation Talks (SALT)—*See DISARMAMENT—U.S.-Soviet Developments*
STRATEGIC Materials—*See U.S. GOVERNMENT—DEFENSE*
STRATEGIC Studies, International Institute for—*See INSTITUTE for Strategic Studies, International*
STRATTON, Rep. Samuel S. (D, N.Y.)
Vs Korea aid-warning res 5-31, 432E2
Reelected 11-7, 851G3
STRAUB, Gov. Robert (D, Ore.)
Wins primary 5-23, 406G2
Loses reelectn 11-7, 857A2
STRAUSS, Franz-Joseph
Tap chrgs spur controversy 1-13—1-17, 74B2
Leber linked to new tap scandal 1-24, 74G2
Missing aide reappears 2-15, 115E1
Asks Nazi-era amnesty 8-14, 651E3
Scores budget proposal 9-21, 906D1
STRAUSS, Robert S.
Lauds US-Japan trade pact 1-13, 27B1
On nut, bolt imports 2-10, 181C2
On CB radio tariff hike 3-28, 443E3
Steel price jawboning role rptd 4-3, 263D1
Named Carter anti-inflatn plan coordinator 4-11, 259F2
Backs GM, Ford price hikes 4-28, 5-9, 362C2, F2
Govt-purchasing controls ordrd 5-18, 405A2
Hails steel price hike restraint 6-12, 470C2
Rpts Japan export curb pledge 7-17, 544A2
Griffin added to staff 8-3, 605C3
Named to labor-pact panel 8-7, 624D2
Addresses Natl Govs Assn 8-29, 682B1
US TV statns protest Canadian tax law 8-29, 686B3
In Japanese trade talks 9-5—9-7, 695D1
On Carter copper trade decisn 10-20, 805A1
Kahn named anti-inflatn chief 10-25, 806D2
On fasteners duty hike 12-26, 998E3
STRAWBERRY Fields (play)
Opens 6-4, 887C3
STRECK, Ron
Wins Texas Open 9-17, 990A2
STREEP, Meryl
Wins Emmy 9-17, 1030G1
Deer Hunter released 12-14, 1030F2
STREET, Anthony
On Dec '77 jobless rise 1-6, 53E2
Sets tech impact study 8-29, 721B2
Australia indl relatns min 11-30, 943F3
STREETCAR Named Desire, A (play)
Tandy wins Tony 6-4, 579G2
STREISAND, Barbra
Wins Grammys 2-24, 315E3
You Don't Bring Me Flowers on bestseller list 11-8, 888D1; 12-6, 971D1
Greatest Hits on best-seller list 12-6, 971E1
STRICKLAND, Ted
Nominated for Colo gov 9-12, 736D2
Loses electn 11-7, 855F3

1979

STORY, Ted
Suicide In B Flat opens 3-13, 292B3
STORY of the Chair (film)
2 sentncd for destructn 2-27, 193B1
STOVALL, Lt. Gov. Thelma L. (D, Ky.)
Loses primary for gov 5-29, 420E1
STOVE, Betty
Loses Wimbledon women's, mixed doubles 7-7, 570C1, E1
Wins US Open doubles title 9-8, loses mixed doubles title 9-9, 734G1, A2
Loses Women's Stockholm Open 11-6, 1003F3
STRAIGHT, Beatrice
Promise released 3-7, 528D3
Bloodline released 6-28, 819F3
STRAIT of Hormuz—*See HORMUZ, Strait of*
STRANGE, Curtis
Wins Pensacola Open 10-21, 970G1
STRASBERG, Lee
And Justice for All released 10-19, 1007G2
Boardwalk released 11-14, 1007A3
Going in Style released 12-25, 1007D3
STRASBERG, Susan
In Praise of Older Women released 2-8, 174A3
STRATAS, Teresa
Complete 'Lulu' debuts in Paris 2-25, 174C1
STRATEGIC Arms Limitation Talks (SALT)—*See DISARMAMENT-U.S.-Soviet Developments*
STRATEGIC Studies, International Institute for—*See INSTITUTE for Strategic Studies, International*
STRATTON, Rep. Samuel S. (D, N.Y.)
Vs S Korea troop pullout plan 1-3, 39C1
STRAUB, Karel
Killed 3-22, 228E2
STRAUS, R. Peter
Resigns as VOA head 10-1, 771D1
STRAUSS, Anna Lord
Dies 2-23, 176F3
STRAUSS, Franz Josef
CDU-CSU alliance faces split 5-24, 5-28, 489E1
Wins CDU support 7-2, 505G3
Poehl Bundesbank appt scored 9-19, 733A3
Loss in electn dispute rptd 10-5, 796A2
STRAUSS, Peter
Wins Emmy 9-9, 858E2
STRAUSS, Robert S.
Taiwan, S Korea OK color-TV export limits 1-17, 160B2
Halts Japan trade talks 3-29, 229D3
In econ missn to Egypt, Israel 4-17—4-18, 296C1
Named US Mideast amb 4-24, comments 4-25, 295G3-296C1
Leonard named deputy 5-12, 379B1
To start Mideast post early 5-18, 378D3-379A1
In China textile talks 5-26—5-31, rpts collapse 5-30, 405D3
Signs US-Japan sales pact 6-2, 416C1
Specialty steel trade curbs phaseout set 6-12, 466A2
Trade bill introduced, oppositn neutralized 6-19, 541F1
In Mideast, Palestinian autonomy agenda plan OKd 7-1—7-8, 511D1
Hackler nominatn rptd blocked 8-3, Askew named 8-8, 647C1
Says US vs Res 242 chng 8-13, 606C3
Israel, Egypt vs UN Palestine res plan 8-17—8-19; returns to US 8-20, rpts on talks 8-20—8-22, Carter denies feud on Mideast role 8-22, 623A2-D3
In Egypt, Israel; briefed on autonomy talks, other issues 9-9—9-13; sees Bethlehem mayor 9-11, 676E2
On Jordan cocaine chrgs 9-21, 767C3
J Jackson briefs on Mideast trip 10-8, 763F1
Hails Palestinian autonomy mtg agrmt 10-26, 823A1
Quits as Mideast envoy, named Carter campaign com chrmn 11-6, 961A2
Linowitz named Mideast successor 938A1
At Natl Com mtg 11-9, 961D2
Hits Kennedy Iran remarks 12-3, 918E3
Sees Carter gains 12-4, 918D2
STRAVINSKY, Igor Fedorovich (1882-1971)
What the Devil opens 4-16, 712E3
STREEP, Meryl
Taken in Marriage opens 2-26, 292D3
Manhattan released 4-24, 528B3
Joe Tynan released 8-17, 820C3
Kramer vs Kramer released 12-19, 1007F3
STREET, Anthony
Dropped from Coordinatn Com 2-4, 113C2
STREISAND, Barbra
You Don't Bring Me Flowers on best-seller list 1-10, 80E3
Greatest Hits on best-seller list 1-10, 80F3
Main Event released 6-22, 820G1
Main Event/Fight on best-seller list 9-5, 672E3*
No More Tears on best-seller list 11-7, 892E3
STRELZIK, Hans-Peter
Family flees to W Ger 9-16, 697B3
STREMFELJ, Andrej
Climbs Everest 5-13, 392A3
STRICK, Joseph
Portrait of the Artist released 4-21, 528D3
STRICKLAND, Gail
Nasty Rumors opens 4-12, 712F1
STRICKLER, Dan
Flying Blind opens 11-15, 956B3

1980

STORR, Vernall
Hanged 1-29, 132B2
STOUFFER Inn (Harrison, N.Y.)
Fire kills 26 12-4, 948A2
STOUGHTON, Blaine
NHL scoring ldr 4-6, 295G3, 296D1
Declared free agent 10-3, 1000F2-A3
STOVALL, Jerry
Named LSU football coach 1-12, 175B3
STOWE, John R.
Indicted in Abscam probe 6-13, 454D1
Trial opens 9-5, convicted 10-7, 782D3
STRACK, Dave
Asks expanded Ariz athletic dept fraud probe 10-16, 875G2
STRANGE, Curtis
Wins Houston Open 5-4, 412F3
2d in Quad Cities Open 7-20, 715D1
Wins Westchester Classic 8-17, Mixed Team tourn 12-14, 972A1, F1
PGA top money winner 10-12, 971E3
STRANGELAND, Rep. Arlan (R, Minn.)
Reelected 11-4, 843B2
STRASSELS, Paul N.
All You Need to Know About the IRS on best-seller list 4-6, 280B3; 5-4, 359E3
STRATEGIC Arms Limitation Talks (SALT)—*See DISARMAMENT--U.S.-Soviet Developments*
STRATTEN, Dorothy
Found slain 8-15, 713D3
STRATTON, Rep. Samuel S. (D, N.Y.)
Joint Chiefs score Carter defns budget 5-29, 424F2
Reelected 11-4, 843G3
STRAUB, Jurgen
Wins Olympic medal 8-1, 589C2*, 624E1
STRAUB, Peter
Ghost Story on best-seller list 5-4, 359E3; 6-8, 448D3
STRAUSS, Franz Josef
Scores weak Moscow Olympics, joint French Afghan stands 3-20, 236E3
SPD wins North Rhine-Westphalia electn 5-11, 390D3
Warns Giscard on Eur role 7-9, 522B1
Urges Polish loans withheld, scores Schmidt 8-24, 642F2
Campaign chrgs rptd 9-3—9-5, 690D3
RC bishops enter pol debate 9-13, 712C1
Scores govt re Munich blast 9-27; links Qaddafi, neo-Nazis 9-30, 755A1, D1
Schmidt coalition wins elections 10-5, 759A3, C3, 760A1
STRAUSS, Robert S.
On Kennedy campaign 4-23, 304B2
Carter ends campaigning ban 4-30, 328B2
On Carter Tex delegate strength 5-3, 342A3
Carter gains delegate majority 6-3, 422F2
Jordan joins campaign com 6-11, 439A1
Vs open conv 7-30, 570B3
Dem govs neutral on open conv 8-4, 596A1
FEC issues campaign rules 9-5, Admin sets Cabt guidelines 9-8, 681E2
On pres debate controversy 9-9, 680F2
Cites Iranian issue 11-4, 838E2
STRAWBERRY, Darryl
Drafted by Mets 6-3, 636G3
STREEP, Meryl
Wins Oscar 4-14, 296G1
STREET, Anthony
Scores wage hike 1-8, 37D2
Vs tanker strike accord 3-14, 229B3, C3
On labor policy 9-18, 766C2
Australia forgn min 11-2, 857G2
On A-reprocessing terms 11-27, 920A1
Deplores Turkish murders 12-17, 991C2
STREISAND, Barbra
No More Tears on best-seller list 1-2, 40E3
Guilty on best-seller list 10-8, 796B3; 12-3, 948B3
Woman In Love on best-seller list 10-8, 796B3; 12-3, 948B3
STREKALOV, Gennady
Launched into space 11-27, 914A2
Ends flight 12-10, 933B1

1976

STRIKES—*See under LABOR; also country names*
STRIP-Mining—*See MINES & Mining*
STROESSNER, Gen. Alfredo (Paraguayan president)
In Uruguay 3-24—3-27, 382D3
Reelectn planned 7-16, 557E3
STROKES (cerebrovascular disease)—*See 'Diseases' under MEDICINE*
STROMBERG Carlson Corp.—*See under GENERAL Dynamics Corp.*
STROUGAL, Lubomir
Kreisky visits 2-17—2-19, 289D2
Czech Presidium member 4-16, 289B2
On harvest, grain imports 9-13, 750A3
STROUP, Robert
Loses electn 11-2, 823D3
STRYDOM, Justice J. J.
Sentences SWAPO members 5-12, 386C2
STUART, Judge Hugh
US Sup Ct voids gag order 6-30, 491D3-492C1
STUBBS, Rev. Aelred
On Mohapi death 8-6, 592A1
STUBBS, William L.
Seconds Ford nominatn 8-18, 598A1
STRUCTURAL Metals Inc.—*See COMMERCIAL Metals Co.*
STUCKEY, Rep. W. S. (D, Ga.)
Evans wins seat 11-2, 822E1
STUDDS, Rep. Gerry E. (D, Mass.)
Reelected 11-2, 829C4
STUDENT National Coordinating Committee (SNCC) (formerly Student Nonviolent Coordinating Committee)
Cited in FBI Cointelpro papers 4-5, 248C2
STUDENT National Medical Association
Carter addresses 4-16, 281D3
STUDENTS for a Democratic Society (SDS)
Fine arrested for '70 Wis bombing 1-7, 32E2
Sen intelligne com cites as target 4-28, 330F1
Fine sentenced 8-6, 776G2
STUDENT Unrest—*See under EDUCATION*
STUECKELBERGER, Christine
Wins Olympic medal 7-30, 574D2
STUKALIN, Boris I.
Central com full member 3-5, 195A3
STUMP, Bob
Elected to US House 11-2, 824C1, 828F3
STURDEVANT, Michael
Convicted in '75 Menominee takeover 4-21, 316G3
STURZ, Herbert
Wins Rockefeller award 11-16, 911D3
SUAREZ, Adolfo
On referendum 12-14, 967G1
SUAREZ, Eugenio
Indicted re Lockheed rpt 10-15, 909C2
SUAREZ Gonzalez, Adolfo
Named premr, reactn 7-3, sworn 7-5, asks cooperatn 7-6, 500B3
Reformists, oppositn ldrs bar Cabt posts 7-6, protest 7-8, 523A2
Cabt sworn 7-8, 523G1
In France, reaffirms EC entry bid 7-13, 541C3
Cabt plans pol amnesty, '77 electns 7-17, 540E3
Shuns Civil War anniv 7-18, 541C2
Sees Gonzalez 8-11, Tierno 9-5, mil chiefs 9-8, 752E3
Rightists warn vs pol chng 8-31, 753B1
Rpts '77 electn plan 9-10, 752F2
Replaces defense min 9-22, 753A1
Gets rpt on Lockheed paymts 11-6, 909E1
Pol reform bill passed 11-18, 908B2
Meets oppositn ldrs re referendum 11-29, 908D3
SUAREZ Morales, Rodrigo
Leads Conservative faction 3-8, 363A3
SUBARU Co.
EPA fuel-econ ratings 9-22, 766B2, E2, 769D1
SUBMARINE Launched Ballistic Missiles (SLBM)—*See 'Missiles' under ARMAMENTS*

1977

STRIKES—*See under LABOR; also country names*
STRIP-Mining—*See MINES & Mining*
STROESSNER, Gen. Alfredo (Paraguayan president)
Pol prisoners freed; US, OAS credited 1-27—2-23, 167C3, E3
Const amended for reelectn 3-7—3-11, 202A2
Nazi protectn rptd 8-17, 803C2
Sees Carter 9-6, at Panama Canal pact signing 9-7, 678A1
To seek 6th term 9-11, 9-23, 803D1
Carter rptd favorably impressed 9-23, 803A2
STROH, Nicholas W.
Death detailed 9-2, 709A3
STROLLA, Michael
Indicted 2-24, 155G2
Pleads guilty 3-3, 540A3
STROM, Earl
NBA referees strike 4-10—4-25, 332C1
STRONG, Capt. S. Birney (ret.)
Dies 12-18, 1024D3
STROUD, Jay
Wilmington 10 denied retrial 5-20, 531E3
STROUP, Keith
Backs pot decriminalizatn 3-14, 332C2
STRUGGLE Against World Imperialism
Claims W Ger hijack credit 10-13, 789C1
STUART, Bettyann
Loses US Open doubles match 9-11, 787B2
STUDEBAKER-Worthington Inc.
Rpts forgn paymts 5-4, 503D2
STUDENTS for a Democratic Society (SDS)
Ex-FBI offcl indicted 4-7, 275A2
Rudd surrenders 9-14, 9-15, 839C1
STUDENT Unrest—*See under EDUCATION*
STULBERG, Louis
Dies 12-14, 1024D3
STURGIS, Frank A.
Nixon com to pay $50,000 2-22, 157G2
STURM Freightways
ICC sues 11-3, 861C1
STYDAHAR, Joe
Dies 3-23, 264F3
SUAREZ, Elsa—*See GUTIERREZ, Elsa*
SUAREZ Esquivel, Dionisio
Jailed 9-10, 743A3
SUAREZ Gonzalez, Adolfo (Spanish premier)
Oppositn names negotiating team 1-7, 22A3
Sees oppositn leaders 1-11, 68G1
Cancels Mideast trip 1-26, 101D3
Curbs rights 1-28, urges calm 1-29, 101A3, 102B1
Death threat rptd 3-2, 307E2
Natl Movement dissolved 4-1, 286A1
CP legalized 4-9, rightists rptd reassured 4-10, 285E2, A3
Army vs CP legislatn 4-14; fires Alvarez 4-20, 307A1
To run for lower house 4-25, 331B1
Fraga rivalry noted 4-26, 331D1
UCD wins vote, elected to parlt 6-15, 453A1-E2
Asked to form new govt 6-17, sees UCD ldrs 6-23—6-24, 506C3
Gonzalez asks munic electns 6-23, 506G3
New Cabt sworn 7-5, 545F1
Briefs PSOE ldr on econ plan 7-12, 545B3
Cortes ldrs elected 7-13, 545C2, E2
Prison riots quelled 7-21, 582A3
Bomb plot foiled 8-17; leftist groups blamed 8-20, 826G2
Catalonia Generalitat restored 9-29, 843D1
GRAPO murder plot rptd 10-10, 826B3
Signs pol, econ pacts 10-25, 866C3
Sees EC ldrs on entry 11-3—11-4, 867G1
SUBASINGHE, Tikiri Banda
Quits Cabt, Freedom Party; Radical Party formed 3-1, 183G1
SUBMARINE Launched Ballistic Missile (SLBM)—*See ARMAMENTS—Missiles*
SUBMARINES—*See ARMAMENTS—Ships & Submarines*
SUBRAMANIAM, Chidambara
Resolutn backs Gandhi 10-15, 801B2

1978

STRIKES—*See under LABOR; also country names*
STRIP Mining—*See MINES & Mining*
STROESSNER, Gen. Alfredo (Paraguayan president)
Rptdly OKs OAS rights probe 1-9, 113F1-A2
Reelected 2-12, 113D1
Final electn vote count rptd 2-17, 211G2
Begins new pres term 8-15, 640F3
Oppositn ldr rptd exiled 9-29, 777G2
Diverts Parana waters for Itaipu dam, signs Eur turbine deal 10-20, 829G2
3 pol dissidents return, arrested 11-17, 989F3
STRONG, Maurice
Backs Abitibi takeover of Price 9-29, 772E3
STROUSE, Charles
Record wins Grammy 2-24, 316B1
Broadway Musical opens 12-21, 1031A1
STROUT, Richard Lee
Wins Pulitzer citation 4-17, 315A1
STRUMUR, Gudrum
Arrested in Bulgaria, extradited to W Ger 6-22, 500B1
STUART Little (book)
White wins Pulitzer citatn 4-17, 315B1
STUDDS, Rep. Gerry E. (D, Mass.)
US assurance on F-15s to Saudi rptd 4-10, 257G1
Reelected 11-7, 851D1
STUDENT, Gen. Kurt
Dies 7-1, 620F3
STUDENT Unrest—*See under EDUCATION*
STUMP, Rep. Bob (D, Ariz.)
Reelected 11-7, 850C1, 855F1
STUMP, Judge Harold D.
Immunity in sterilizatn case backed by Sup Ct 3-28, 241G2
STUMP v. Sparkman
Judicial immunity in sterilizatn case backed by Sup Ct 3-28, 241F2
STUSSY, Jan
Film wins Oscar 4-3, 315D3
SUAREZ, Adolfo
Giscard visits 6-28—7-1, 649E1
SUAREZ Esquivel, Jose Dionisio
Sought in Letelier murder case 5-4, 370E3
Letelier murder role detailed 6-2, 452A1
FBI offers reward 7-4, indicted in Letelier murder 8-1, 614A1
SUAREZ Gonzalez, Adolfo
Replaces Cabt econ team 2-24; Fuentes named econ aide 3-6; business, pol pressures cited 4-10, 394F2
Catalan actors sentncd 3-7, 250B2
Basques march on natl day 3-26, 250E1
Visits Canaries, plans navy base 4-26, 576F3
PSOE wins 2 Sen seats 5-18, 821B3
Scores gen's assassinatn 7-21, 575G3
Visits Venez, Cuba 9-7—9-10, 821D3
Reelected UCD chief at party cong 10-19—10-21, 821E2
Anti-govt plot by security offcrs rptd 11-16—11-21, 967D2
Backs new const 12-5; referendum OKs 12-6, 966D3, 967A1
Sets electns for Mar '79 12-29, 1022G1
SUBMARINES—*See ARMAMENTS—Ships & Submarines*

1979

STRIDER (play)
Opens 5-31, 712F2
STRIKES—*See under LABOR*
STRIKE the Main (race horse)
2d in Flamingo Stakes 3-24, 448C3
STROBBE, Dietrich
SPD-FDP gain in electns 3-18, 214C3
STROESSNER, Gen. Alfredo (Paraguayan president)
At Brazil pres inaugural 3-15, 210D1
Mengele loses citizenship 8-8, 616E3
STROKES—*See MEDICINE–Brain*
STRONG, Ken
Dies 10-5, 860E3
STRUTHERS, Sally
Wins Emmy 9-9, 858D2
STUART, Gilbert (1755-1828)
5 pres portraits go to Natl Gallery 4-10, Boston library sale of 2 others halted 4-14, 374D3-375C1
STUBBE, Peter
Hired as Earthquakes coach 5-19, 1004E2
STUDEBAKER-Worthington Inc.
McGraw-Edison to acquire, '78 income rptd 7-24, 682F2-A3
STUDIO 54
Owners indicted 6-28; Jordan denies cocaine use 8-24, Landau disputes 8-28, 647D1-E2
Jordan cocaine rpt disputed 8-31, 767E2
NY drug dealer indicted 10-23, owners plead guilty to tax chrgs 11-2, 891G2
Jordan cocaine probe spec prosecutor named 11-29, 900E3
NY drug dealer pleads guilty 12-18, 1000E1
STUDS Lonigan (book)
Farrell dies 8-22, 671C2
STUKALIN, Boris Ivanovich
Defends book seizures 9-4, 690E1
STUPP, Jack
Arrested re stock fraud 1-10, 37C2
STYNE, Jule
Teibele & Her Demon opens 12-16, 1007F2
STYRON, William
Sophie's Choice on best-seller list 7-1, 548A3; 8-5, 620B3; 9-2, 672A3; 10-14, 800B3
Book awards protest rptd 8-9, 755F3
STYX (singing group)
Babe on best-seller list 11-7, 892E3
Cornerstone on best-seller list 11-7, 892F3
SUAREZ Esquivel, Jose Dionisio
Letelier murder role cited 1-18, 58A2
3 convicted re Letelier 2-14, 114D2
SUAREZ Gonzalez, Adolfo (Spanish premier)
Scores PSOE 2-27, govt wins electns 3-1, 191C2
Feb murder plot rptd foiled 3-13, 192D1
Wins confidence vote 3-30, names minority Cabt 4-5 256F1
Left scores in municipal vote 4-3, 256B2
Marks Armed Forces Day 5-27, 428G2
In GM talks 6-5, plant agrmt reached 6-6, 428A2
Basque home-rule bill drafted 7-17, 545E3, 546B1
10-yr energy plan OKd by parlt 7-30, 585A3
Visits 3 Latin natns; trade, nonalignmt discussed 8-6—8-14; sees Vance 8-10, 613D2, 654F1-G2
Meets Arafat 9-13—9-15, 694D3
Meets on Basque unrest 9-23; delays US, Latin trip 9-25, 754A2, C2
Basques, Catalans approve home rule 10-25, 837B1
In France; EC entry, Basque issue discussed 11-26—11-27, 952D1
SUAREZ Mason, Gen. Guillermo
Retiremt expected 12-7, 947F3
SUBMARINE Launched Ballistic Missile (SLBM)—*See ARMAMENTS–Missiles*
SUBMARINES—*See ARMAMENTS–Ships*

1980

STRNISKO, Julius
Wins Olympic medal 7-30, 624E3
STROESSNER, Gen. Alfredo (Paraguayan president)
Somoza assassinated 9-17: Argentine terrorists sought, suspect slain 9-18, 697B3
STROHBACH, Herman
Drawings & Digressns wins Amer Book Award 5-1, 692B2
STRONG, Michael
Dies 9-17, 756E2
STRYCKER'S Bay Neighborhood Council v. Karlen
Case decided by Sup Ct 1-7, 15A3
STUCKEY, Jim
In NFL draft 4-29, 336F2
STUDDS, Rep. Gerry E. (D, Mass.)
Reelected 11-4, 843D1
STUDIO 54
Owners sentenced 1-18, 64B3
Jordan cleared re cocaine chrgs 5-28, 402C3
NY drug dealer sentenced 6-12, 503F1-A2
STUKOLKIN, Ivar
Wins Olympic medal 7-24, 623A3
STULZ, Percy
UNESCO protests E Ger arrest 6-6, arrest confirmed 6-10; sentenced as spy 9-6, 708A1
STUMP, Rep. Bob (D, Ariz.)
Reelected 11-4, 842C1, 851C3
STYLIANOUS, Petros
Named Cyprus interior min 9-9, 749G2
STYRON, William
Sophie's Choice wins Amer Book Award; boycotts ceremony 5-1, 692G1
Sophie's Choice on best-seller list 8-17, 640G3; 9-14, 716D3; 10-12, 796F3
STYX (singing group)
Babe on best-seller list 1-2, 40E3
Cornerstone on best-seller list 1-2, 40F3
SUAREZ, Felipe
In Iran hostage mission 5-25—5-26, 394D1
SUAREZ Gonzalez, Adolfo (Spanish premier)
Andalusian autonomy vote falls short, govt policy rift cited 2-28, 174A3
UCD set back in Basque vote 3-9, 196E1
Moderates win upset in Catalonia 3-21, 235E1
Shuffles Cabt 5-2, 355A1
'78 coup plotters sentenced 5-7, 355G1
At Tito funeral 5-8, 339B1
Sets autonomy timetable 5-20; censure motn called 5-21, survives vote 5-30, 431B2
Giscard asks EC expansn delay 6-5, 435F3
Carter sees 6-25, 475B1
French premier visits 7-2—7-3, 567G1
In Peru for Belaunde inauguratn 7-28, 579F3
Andalusia hunger strike 8-14—8-19, 653E2
Shuffles Cabt again 9-8, Soclsts score 9-10, 690B2
Presents econ plans, wins confidence vote 9-17, 711E3
'81 budget submitted, econ plan cited 9-30, 793F2
Basque, Catalonia mins sworn 10-21, 832C2
Sets Andalusian autonomy for '81 10-23, 832E1
UCD member slain in Basque region 10-23, Cabt debates terror campaign 10-24, 832D2
Opens Madrid CSCE review conf 11-12, 863B1
Visits Basque region 12-9—12-11, 968B2
Attends Santa Marta conf 12-17, 992A3
Basques win right to tax, expanded police powers 12-30, 996E2
SUAZO Cordova, Robert
Named Honduras assembly ldr, pres victory seen 7-20, 564C2
SUBIC, Joseph
Hostages' letters publshd 1-18—1-20, 47B3, D3
On Iran TV, admits spying 4-9, 282B3
SUBMARINES—*See ARMAMENTS--Ships*
SUBSCRIPTION Television Association
Formed 7-15, 639G3

1976

SUBURBS—*See CITIES & Suburbs*

SU Chen-hua
Heads Shanghai leadership 10-30, 871A3

SUDAN—*See also AFRICAN Development Bank, ARAB League, NONALIGNED Nations Movements, OAU*
ELF frees 2 Americans 1-9, 31D1
Listed as 'not free' nation 1-19, 20E3
19 executed re '75 coup try 1-23—2-22, 502E1 ★
UNESCO literacy drive fails 2-4, 85C2
Cabt shuffled 2-10, 502C1
Total IMF oil loan rptd 4-1, 340E2
Plot in south rptd crushed 4-12, 502B1
Ethiopia delegatn visits 5-31, 457D2
Sovt mil presence rptd 6-13, 467C1
Army revolt crushed 7-2—7-3; 300 killed 7-4; Libya linked in UN protest 7-5; ties cut 7-6, 501B3
Nimeiry returns from US, France 7-2, 501C3
Coup aftermath arrests 7-7, 501G3
Alleged coup ldr arrested 7-8, 543E3 ★
Nimeiry in Cairo, signs defense pact 7-13—7-14, 531D2
Nimeiry ties Libya to coup 7-15, 531C3
Amb to Uganda sees Amin 7-16, 548F1
Joins Egypt, Saudis vs Libya 7-18—7-19, 531B2
Sadat ties Libya to coup 7-22, 547B3
Libya recalls amb to Saudi re alliance 7-25, 547D3
Coup plot trials end 8-2, 98 executed 8-4, 8-5; reactn 8-4—8-8, 592C2
Cabt shuffled 8-9, 857E2
Libyan invasn plan chrgd 8-13, 629G3
Ethiopian rebels free UK newsman 9-6, 674A3
Exiled ex-mins, others sntncd 9-30, 857C2
Eritreans free 3 Britons 10-2, 1002B2
Viral fever hits 10-7, 795G2
OPEC loan signed 12-23, 975E3
Middle East Conflict—*See MIDDLE EAST*
Sports
Olympic withdrawal rptd 7-21, 528B3
Backs IAAF S Africa expulsn 7-22, 562B2

SUDHARMONO
Rpts anti-Suharto plot 9-22, 735A1

SUDOMO, Adm.
On post-'65 coup deaths 12-1, 949F2

SUEZ Canal—*See MIDDLE EAST*

SUFFOLK County, Mass.—*See MASSACHUSETTS*

SUFFOLK County, N.Y.—*See NEW York State*

SUGAR
'75 price drop rptd 1-21, 90B2
Latin output rptd 5-7, 466C1
Kennedy Admin tap of lobby rptd 5-9, 344G2
Dole record cited 614C2
US warns NY commodity exchng 9-15, 990D2
US triples sugar duties 9-21; '75 output data 721E2, C3
International Developments—*See also country names*
Group of 77 sets trade guidelines 2-10, 108C1
Iran ousts 2 aides re UK deal 2-10, 156D3
Japan-Australia pact 2-26, 155A1
China-Australia deal rptd 3-1, 190F1
Sovt buys upset mkt 3-12—3-16, 278G1
Angola natlizes 3 Portugal cos 5-6, 371A2
Australia-China pact confirmed 6-2, 415A2
Canada loan to Ivory Coast rptd 8-12, 1013A1
'76 world crop consumptn projected 9-21, 721G2
Cuba cites world price drop 9-23, scores US 9-27, Sovt '74, '75 Cuban imports rptd 9-30, 771G3-772E1

1977

SUBURBAN General Hospital (Montgomery County, Pa.)
Oxygen, anesthesia mixup rptd fatal 9-10, 748G1

SUBURBS—*See CITIES, Suburbs & Towns*

SU Chen-hua
In Politburo 8-21, 645G2

SUCREST Corp.
Indicted 3-30, fined 5-19, 504G1-A2
'76 Fortune 500 list drops 341D1

SUDAN—*See also ARAB League, NONALIGNED Nations Movement, OAU*
AF revolt crushed 2-2, 2-6, 117C2
Cabt dissolved 2-8, new Cabt named 2-11, 117E2
Nimeiry reelected 4-20, 417A1
Govt, rightist reconciliatn rptd 7-18, 602C2
Gen amnesty declared 8-8, 619C2
Al-Mahdi, other rebels pardoned 8-13, 711B1
Nile canal oppositn rptd 9-7, 844A1
Cabt shuffled 9-10, 843G3
Nimeiry greets al-Mahdi 9-28, 843E3
AF, Libyan rebels freed 10-17, 843F3
Ethiopian Relations
Ethiopia subversn chrgd 1-1; border alert ordrd 1-2, amb recalled 1-5, 24A3
Eritreans free UK family 1-5, 20A2
Ethiopian soldiers flee Eritrea 1-7, 20G1
Egypt defense pact activated 1-15—1-16, 62D3
Ethiopian mil desertns rptd 1-22, 62B3
Nimeiry backs separatists 1-30, Ethiopia scores 2-2, 2-4, 98A3, B3
Ethiopia refugee total rptd 2-25, 238C3
Cuba, Libya score Ethiopia rebel aid 3-10, 249B2
Ethiopia chrgs attacks 4-11, denied 4-13, 328B2
Eritrea consulate closed 4-23, 327F2
Nimeiry scores Ethiopia 5-17, 450E1
Ethiopia chrgs aggressn 6-24, 547D3
Ethiopia grants exiles amnesty 7-1, 562D2
Ethiopia chrgs infiltratn 7-2—7-5, 512E1
EPLF rpts towns taken 7-10, 562A2
Eritrea rebel factns merge 10-20, 830G1
Foreign Relations (misc.)
UN Assemb member 4B1
Egypt defns pact activated re Ethiopia dispute 1-15—1-16, 62D3
Egypt Food aid rptd 1-23, 62F2
Uganda plane downed 1-30, 20 rescued 2-1, 102C3
Israel AF revolt role chargd 2-6, 117E2
Israel boycott eased 2-18, 167F2
Joins Egypt-Syria cmnd 2-27—2-28, 143F2
Cuba, Libya score Ethiopia rebel aid 3-10, Castro urges Djibouti alliance 3-14—3-16, 249B2, D2
At Red Sea summit 3-22—3-23, 208D2
Uganda mercenary aid rptd 3-28, 308G1
Khalid backs Zaire vs rebels 4-7, 265E2
Morocco fears Zaire interventn 4-18, 317A2
Egypt on Zaire invasn 5-1, 394B1
Nimeiry visits France; scores Libya, Ethiopia, USSR 5-17—5-19, 450D1
USSR mil advisers expelled 5-18, 416G3
USSR emb staff cut ordrd 5-19; USSR recalls amb 5-31, 548C1
Kenya ties improve 7-6, 588E1
Libya ties to Egypt clashes 7-24, 569B2
Sovt plan to subvert rptd 7-25, 569C2
Egypt asks Libya halt 'agitatn' 7-25, 569G2
Libyan natls freed 10-17, 843F3
To renew Libyan ties 11-13, 874C2
Sadat Israel trip backed 11-19, Nimeiry visits Egypt 11-22, 890B3
U.S. Relations
Boeing rpts consultant 1-5, ct backs secrecy 2-25, 215C3
Uganda drops US exit ban 3-1, 141B2
US OKs jet sale 4-7, 327G3
Young visits, arms asked 5-24, 400B1
Bergus confrmd amb 5-25, 499D3
US OKs F-5 jet sale 12-23, 1019C2

SUDHARMONO
On probe vs Sutowo 2-14, 304D3

SUDOL, Ed
Retiremt announced 11-14, 990C2

SUENENS, Leon Joseph Cardinal
At charismatic conf 7-20—7-24, 620F3

SUEZ—*See MIDDLE EAST, subheads EGYPT-Israel Peace Moves and SUEZ*

SUGAR
USSR-PI deal set 1-18, 47F2
Frost damages Fla cane 1-18—1-20, 55B1
UN rpts '76 price drop 2-14, 146B1
Cuba-US talks seen 2-15, 110F1
Cuba-Spain protocol signed 2-20, 242C3
US modifies duty-free list 2-28, 189E3
US trade comm rules injury 3-3, asks quota cut; '76 data cited 3-14, 189C1
Saccharin ban affects trading 3-9—3-10, 177A2
Peru emergency declared 3-17, 428E1
Australia-China deal set 3-30, 236G3
4 NE firms indicted 3-30, fined 5-19, 504G1-A2
Carter faces import curb decision 4-1, 248E1
US volunteers in Cuba 4-8, 283F2
Intl price pact talks 4-18—5-27, 457G3
Hunt trading cited 4-28, 341A3
'76 Amstar sales drop rptd 340C1
Carter bars import quotas, OKs subsidies 5-4, 457D3
France aid to Sudan rptd 5-23, 450F1
Gen Foods sued on cereal ads 6-30, 613D2
Futures contract trading cited 7-5, 521G2

1978

SUBURBS—*See CITIES, Suburbs & Towns*

SUDAN—*See also ARAB League, NONALIGNED Nations Movement, OAU*
Khartoum expenses rated 1-14, 28B3
1st parlt electns rptd 3-21, 479A2
Nimeiry, Natl Front sign pact 4-12, 293A1
Nimeiry vows contd dvpt, cites oil finds 5-24, 479A2
Currency devalued 6-8, 479G1
Oppositn party disbands, ldr rpts amnesty 7-5, 595B1
Cabt, party ldrshp shuffled 7-29, 595D1
Ethiopian Relations
Ethiopia attacks border town 1-2, 3F3
Tessenei retaken, rebel lines threatnd 6-23, 584E2
Cuba troop cut rptd 7-6, 584C3
OAU asks Eritrea solutn 7-22, 561F1
Foreign Relations (misc.)
Uganda smugglers sentenced 1-10, 55C3
Somalia aid pledge rptd 1-26, 99F3
Chad peace plan OKd 2-24, 130A2
Nimeiry to head Arab summit com 3-28, 215C1
Arab fund poor-natn aid rise rptd 4-9, 257F2
Somali army revolt rptd 4-9, 269E1
Pound devalued to aid forgn debt 6-8, 479G2
IMF announces loans 6-29, 595E1
Dutch cancel debts 7-10, 575E1
OAU summit hosted 7-18—7-22, 561C2
UK cancels debts 7-31, 592E1
Arab fund loan rptd 8-17, 925F3
UN Assemb member 713E3
IMF SDR purchase rptd 9-21, 925E3
Leb troop exit plan reaffirmed 10-18, 10-19, 803B1

SUDOMO, Adm.
Pol prisoners to be freed 4-11, 288C3
On Rendra arrest 5-1, 632B1

SUEZ—*See MIDDLE EAST—EGYPT-Israel Peace Moves*

SUEZ, Gulf of
Camp David summit pact affirms navigatn rights 9-17, 712A2

SUFFOLK County, N.Y.—*See NEW York State*

SUGAR
Mauritius IMF loan OKd 2-27, 333D3
FTC proposes children's TV ad curbs 2-28, 4-28, Cong wary 4-26—5-2, 347B2, D2
OPIC extensn bill bars export aid 4-24, 323A3
Colombia '77 trade data rptd 5-19, 414F1
US refiners settle '74 trust chrgs 6-12, 511B1
'77 ind productivity rise rptd 6-14, 470B1
Amstar settles trust suits 7-28, 768G3
ASEAN-US talks on prices 8-3—8-4, 603G2
FDA sets calorie-labeling rules 9-21, 770C1
Canada refineries fined record sums 10-6, 794F3
Australia-Malaysia talks ended 10-11, 34C3; pact setld 2-13, 110A2
US price support bill rejected 10-15, 785C1
FTC children's ad probe curbed 11-3; stay denied, probe affirmed 11-17, 941G2-C3

1979

SUBURBS—*See CITIES, Suburbs & Towns*
SUBWAYS—*See TRANSPORTATION–Mass Transit*

SUDAN—*See also ARAB League, NONALIGNED Nations Movement, OAU*
Freedom House lists as partly free 12G3
Jonglei canal route rptd moved 797A1
Price hike riots 8-8—8-12, 618B1
Foreign Relations (misc.)
Iraq halts oil shipmts 4-10, 278A2
OAPEC ouster of Egypt opposed 4-17, 278A2
Nubians in Ugandan army cited 4-18, 288D1
Islamic conf suspends Egypt 5-9, 360E1
Nimeiry backs Giscard re Eur ties 5-22, 398D3
Uganda refugees rptd 6-8, 489B1
Amin residence, Uganda invasn plan denied 8-9, 637C3
Nimeiry ousts Ibrahim 8-12; names Khali vp, takes party ldrship 8-13, 617G3
UN membership listed 695A3
Saudi denies Egypt chrgs, Iraq unrest role 10-10, 801G2-802A1
U.S. Relations
US issues rights rpt 2-10, 107D3
US vows jet sale, Saudis to fund 2-11, 143C2

SUDDEN Infant Death Syndrome (crib death)—*See CHILDREN–Health & Safety*

SUESS, Rosa
Acquitted re war crimes 4-19, 333E3

SUEZ—*See under MIDDLE EAST*

SUFFOLK County, N.Y.—*See NEW York State*

SUGAR
IMF OKs Nicaragua standby loan 5-14, 372E3
Mex, Cuba trade talks 5-17–5-18, 372F2
Lome pact talks collapse 5-26, 398G3
Australia-EC accord set 5-29, 405A1
China-PI pact signed 7-8, 567C1
Guyana strike prompts pol crisis 7-23–8-28, 687G1
Nicaragua export controls set, '78 trade cited 8-9, 616E1
Gulf+Western-DR probe rptd 8-16, 632D3
Haitian 'slavery' in DR rptd 8-17, 804B3
Futures prices soar 10-12; US bars supports, ISA role 10-23, 808A2
Gulf+Western sued by SEC 11-26, 923F1
Intl price pact OKd by US Sen 11-30, 987D2

1980

SUBURBS—*See CITIES*
SUBWAYS—*See TRANSPORTATION--Mass Transit*

SUDAN—*See also ARAB League, NONALIGNED Nations, OAU*
Foreign Relations (misc.)
Saudis execute mosque raider 1-9, 22B1
Khartoum protest vs Israel-Egypt amb exchng 2-26, 140A2
Chad consul rptd killed 4-8, 311C2
Uganda chrgs invasn support 10-10, 794E2
Islamic League meets 11-10, 895A2
Libyan Chad role opposed 12-23—12-24, 979E1

SUGAR
Cuba crop threatened by fungus, annual productn rptd 1-11, 38G2
US issues dietary guidelines 2-4, 157A3
Cyclamate ban rptd upheld by FDA 2-7, 317D2
Futures price soars, world stock fall seen 2-8, 182D1
Peru crop hit by drought, imports seen 2-8, 234F3
Brazil gasohol program evaluated 3-15, 251C1
Zimbabwe ends tax 4-20, 301B2
May producer prices rptd 6-6, 437D3
Glucose fertilizatn role rptd 7-3, 715G2
Gulf & Westn, DR settle dispute 9-5, 687F2
Price hits 5 1/2-yr high 10-9, 777A2
W Ger wine scandal rptd; France, Luxembourg suspect 11-3, 11-18, 925C2
Iran rationing set 11-9, 879D3
Polish shortage rptd 11-12, 879B1
Price drops on higher US interest rates 12-10, 932B2
Cuba '81-85 plan outlined, '80 setbacks admitted 12-17, 12-20, 992G3
US '80 futures trading up, Dec price drop rptd 12-31, 984G3, 985A1

1976

SUGAWARA, Yasaburo
Wins Olympic medal 7-31, 576D3

SUHARTO (Indonesian president)
Signs ASEAN pact 2-24, 148D2
Revamps Pertamina 3-4, 176F3
Sees Australia forgn min 4-14, 309A3
Signs E Timor prov bill 7-17, 543F3
Rpts E Timor fighting 8-25, 679E1
Plotters arrested 9-22, 735A1
Signs pact with Australia 10-10, 789A2, C2

SUICIDE Prevention, International Association for
Ringel on Eur rates 11-22, 944G3-945A1

SUICIDES—*See DEATHS*

SULE, Anselmo
At intl soc dems mtg 5-23—5-25, 449C3

SULLIVAN, Frank
Dies 2-19, 192G3

SULLIVAN, James L.
Elected Southn Baptist pres 6-15—6-18, 951E2

SULLIVAN, John F.
Asks contract relief 5-4, 454D1

SULLIVAN, John L.
Bailey cleared in Conn scandal 1-12, 271G1

SULLIVAN, Rep. Leonor Kretzer (Mrs. John B.) (D, Mo.)
Chairs canal talk hearings 4-8, 291G2
Gephardt wins seat 11-2, 820D2, 823A3

SULLIVAN, Tom
On Israeli shipping rules 10-19, 786C2

SULLIVAN, William C.
Cleared in Halperin tap case 12-16, 981A1

SULLIVAN, William H.
Macapagal seeks US emb asylum 4-1, 255G2

SULONG, Saleh
Killed 6-6, 419E1

SUMMA Corp.
Hannah dies 1-15, 56D3
Hughes dies 4-5, admin named 5-5, 335C3
Board electns 8-4, 596C3

SUN
Ford State of Union message 1-19, 37G3, 39D2
US energy, space resrch budgeted 1-21, 64D2, A3
US cncl cites solar radiatn 2-27, 171D2
Dem platform text cites solar energy 6-15, 474B3, 475D1
Ford OKs solar energy funds 7-12, 517F1
US Sen OKs tax benefits 8-6, 586F1
Carter backs solar energy dvpt 8-9, 585C1
GOP platform text cites solar energy 8-18, 607D2
GAO urges solar funding 8-24, 649B2, D2
Ford, Carter debate energy 9-23, 702E2
Bethe gets Science Medal 10-18, 858C3
NE govs urge heating dvpt 11-14, 864F3

1977

US sues S Africa lobby 7-20, 614A1
Peru low export prices cited 7-28, 618E2
Subsidy limit dropped from agri bill 8-12, 688C3
DR scores US tariff 8-14, 647F1
US direct subsidies ruled illegal 8-19, 854G3
Guyana strike begins 8-24, 710A3; ldrs seized 9-9, 767D2
Low intl price cited re Peru crisis 8-31, 784E3
Farm bill signed; target prices detailed, tariff backed 9-29, 736D2, C3
Great Western Sunshine Mining takeover OKd 10-4, 799A1
Intl sugar pact OKd, '76 top exporters, US consumptn cited 10-7, 855B1
NY exchng chrgd re prices 10-17, 818G2
Ecuador strike cuts productn 10-18—11-4, 842C1
US loans to exporters curbed 10-19, 815D2
Hawaii fields struck 11-2—11-22, 899D2
Guyana withdraws strikebreakers 11-4, 869F1; strike fails 11-25, 970A1
US sets price-support loan guarantee, ups levies; US productn, '77 import data cited 11-8, 854D3
US price-support plan, '78 food price rise linked 11-17, 916B3

Australia-Japan Developments
Dispute 6-30—7-27, 578B3
Australia-Japan talks fail again 8-4, 615C2
Australia state sues Japan refiners 9-28, 800E2
Pact set 10-26, 839G2-C3

SUGAR Conference, International
Intl price pact talks 4-18—5-27, 458B1

SUGIURA, Dr. Kanematsu
Laetrile findings rptd 6-15, 508C2

SUH Jyong Chul, Gen.
Replaced as S Korea defns min 12-20, 1017E1

SUHARTO (Indonesian president)
Sutowo, aides to be probed 3-29, 304F2
Forgn debt svc estimate rptd 4-18, 392C3
Electn fraud chrgd 5-5, 392E3
At ASEAN summit 8-4—8-5, 607A2
Fretelin given amnesty 8-16, 658G2

SUICIDES—*See DEATHS*

SULLIVAN, Haywood
Ct OKs Red Sox sale 12-6, AL owners veto 12-8, 989F2

SULLIVAN, John M.
Named Fed RR admin 4-29, confrmd 6-23, 625F3

SULLIVAN, Rev. Leon
GM to promote S Africa equality 3-1, 160G2
21 US cos in equality plan 6-20, 535G3
Blacks meet re govt 'neglect' 8-29, 702F1

SULLIVAN, Mike
Loses US House election 2-22, 128B1

SULLIVAN, William C.
Dies 11-9, 952D3

SULLIVAN, William H.
Named amb to Iran 4-7, confrmd 5-25, 500C1

SULZBERGER, Arthur Hays (d. 1968)
CIA collaboratn chrg denied 9-12, 720C3

SULZBERGER, C. L.
Denies CIA work 9-12, 721A1

SULZBERGER, Iphigene Ochs
Denies Times CIA link 9-12, 720D3

SUMITOMO Bank Ltd.

Sumitomo Bank of California
Bank of Calif branches bought 7-6, 578E1; purchase challenged 8-9, 669B3
Calif acquisitns OKd 10-19, 979D2

SUMITOMO Bank of California—*See under SUMITOMO Bank Ltd.*

SUMITOMO Metal Industries Ltd.
US steel dumping chrgs upheld 10-3, 774C3

SUMMA Corp.
Hughes '38 will sought 1-17, 120B2, D2
Hughes estate appraised 3-15, 354G2
Woolbright convicted 4-22, 396G1
Davis dismissal rptd 5-28, 472G2
To pay Greenspun $1 mln 6-3, 472C2
Davis files chrgs vs Lummis 6-8, 472B3

SUMNER, Gerald
Replaced as amb to Jamaica 5-25, 499F3

SUN—*See also SOLAR Energy*
Sunspots linked to weather 2-21, 183C2, G2

1978

SUGAR Beet Growers Federation, National
'74 trust chrgs setld 6-12, 511C1

SUGAR Bowl—*See FOOTBALL—Collegiate*

SUHARTO (Indonesian president)
Dissidents try to meet 1-12, 55F2
7 newspapers banned 1-20—1-23, 55F2
Student dissent suppressed 1-21, 1-26, press ban protested 1-24, 71F3, 72C1
ASEAN head formally quits 2-18, 122B2
Reelected pres 3-22, sworn 3-23, forms new Cabt 3-29, 246E1
Rendra arrested 5-1, 632B1

SUICIDES—*See DEATHS*

SUKAN, Faruk
Named Turkey dep premr 1-5, 21D2

SULAIMAN, Jose
Spinks title bout defns in dispute 2-17—3-16; WBC withdraws title, names Norton champ 3-18, 211B3-212D1

SULFUR Dioxide—*See ENVIRONMENT—Air & Water*

SULFUR & Sulfides
BP finds Australia deposit 5-16, 411C2
Poland-Occidental deal rptd 5-28, 650E2
ICC orders rail freight rates cut back 6-30, 569A3

SULIBARRIA Goitia, Tomas
Wounded by ETA 8-30, 706D2

SULINDAC (Clinoril)—*See MEDICINE—Drugs*

SULLIVAN, Brad
Working opens 5-14, 887E3

SULLIVAN, Charles L.
Loses Sen primary in Miss 6-6, 448B1

SULLIVAN, Rev. Leon
Expands S Africa guidelines 7-5, 632F3
Zulus back labor code 7-13, 633F1

SULLIVAN, Maxine
My Old Friends opens 12-2, 1031E2

SULLIVAN, Mike
2d in Buick Open 6-18, 580F3

SULLIVAN, Patrick D.
Indicted 5-15, 380B3
Charged by SEC 10-5, guilty plea cited 770C3

SULLIVAN, William
Suspends Fairbanks 12-18, reinstates 12-20, 1024E2

SULLIVAN, William C. (d. 1977)
Hunter fined for slaying 1-14, 69C2
Black ldr cited in FBI '64 memo on King conspiracy 5-29, 410A3

SULLIVAN, William H.
Rptd vs US Iran evacuatn 12-6, 954C1

SULLIVAN Award, James E.—*See AMATEUR Athletic Union*

SULTAN Ismail, Ahmed
Rptd Westinghouse payoff recipient 10-26, 11-20, 961B3

SUMITOMO Metal Industries Ltd.
US '77 dumping ruling revised 1-9, 80E2
Australia iron imports set 5-30, 411F1

SUMMA Corp.
Holmes indicted on drug chrgs 3-16, 6-6, 459A2
Meier ordered to repay $7.9 mln 3-29, 459E2

SUMMER, Donna
Thank God It's Fri released 5-19, 620B1 ★
Last Dance on best-seller list 7-5, 579G3; 8-2, 620F1
MacArthur Park on best-seller list 11-8, 888C1; 12-6, 971D1
Live & More on best-seller list 11-8, 888D1; 12-6, 971F1

SUMMER Paradise (film)
Released 3-11, 620A1

SUN—*See also SOLAR Energy*
Weather link studied 5-11, 654C1
Vibratn rptd measured 8-3, 654F2

1979

SUGAR Agreement, International (ISA)
US bars participatn 10-23, 808C2
US Sen ratifies 11-30, 987E2

SUGAR Bowl—*See FOOTBALL–Collegiate*

SUGIURA, Kanematsu
Dies 10-21, 860F3

SUHARTO (Indonesian president)
Meets Waldheim on refugees 5-9, 379D2

SUICIDE In B Flat (play)
Opens 3-13, 292B3

SUITTS, Steve
Rpts Southn bds segregated 4-9, 307F1
Assails all-white club judicial memberships 9-19, 901G2

SUKAN, Faruk
Resigns, chrgs Lockheed bribery cover-up 9-20, 775E1

SULLIVAN, Annie (1866-1936)
Miracle Worker opens 1-6, 292B2

SULLIVAN, Jean
Hitting Town opens 1-6, 292F1

SULLIVAN, John
Vs Rock I reorganizatn plan 10-10, 830F3

SULLIVAN, Thomas P.
Announces Scott indictmt 4-9, 291C3

SULLIVAN, William
Patriots release Fairbanks 4-2, 335A2

SULLIVAN, William C. (d. 1977)
Memoirs rpt FBI suspected Sovt spy 6-24, 521A1

SULLIVAN, William H.
Asks US advice on shah departure 1-3, 3C1
Held hostage in Iran emb raid 2-14, 125E2
Sen com hearing on successor 5-15, 357E2
Laingen named amb to Iran 10-2, 752G2

SULTAN Ibn Abdul Aziz, Prince (Saudi Arabia)
Arab arms plant in Egypt to close 5-14, 359E3

SULZBERGER, Arthur Ochs
Mattson replaces as NY Times Co pres 7-23, 640D3

SUMMA Corp.
Canada sets satellite research grant vs Hughes bid 4-17, 311C3

Air Holdings Corp.
SEC suit vs Hughes Air West stock settled 1-19, 88A2*

SUMMER, Donna
Wins Grammy 2-16, 336E3
Hot Stuff on best-seller list 5-30, 448E3; 548E3; 8-1, 620E3
Bad Girls on best-seller list 5-30, 448F3; 7-4, 548E3, F3; 8-1, 620E3, F3
No More Tears on best-seller list 11-7, 892E3

SUN
Neutrino theory proposed 4-12, 691E3
Radiatn, stratospheric ozone levels linked 6-22, 692D1

1980

SUGAR Hill Gang (singing group)
Rapper's Delight on best-seller list 1-2, 40E3; 2-6, 120F3

SUHARTO (Indonesian president)
Opens OPEC mtg, asks Iran-Iraq peace 12-15, 951D2

SULFINPYRAZONE (Anturane)—*See MEDICINE--Drugs & Health-Care Products*

SULLIVAN, Anne
Wins Cherry Blossom run, sets 10 mile record 3-30, 527G2

SULLIVAN, Barry F.
Named First Chicago chrmn 6-24, 600C2

SULLIVAN, Jo
Perfectly Frank opens 11-30, 1003E3

SULLIVAN, Mike
2d in Hope Desert Classic 1-14, 3d in Phoenix Open 1-20, 412B2
Wins Southern Open 10-5, 972D2

SULLIVAN, Terry
Gacy convicted 3-12, gets death sentence 3-13, 214G1

SULLIVAN, William H.
Scores Brzezinski '79 Iran policy 9-6, 694B1

SULTAN, Arne
Nude Bomb released 5-9, 675B3

SULTAN Ibn Abdul Aziz, Prince (Saudi Arabia)
Meets Brown on F-15 gear 6-26; scores US sens stand 7-9, 538C3

SUMEGI, John
Wins Olympic medal 8-1, 622B2

SUMMA Corp.
Hughes flying boat to be dismantled 5-22, 560G2

SUMMER, Donna
No More Tears on best-seller list 1-2, 40E3
Greatest Hits on best-seller list 1-2, 40F3; 2-6, 120G3
Said born-again 1-25, 199G2
Wins Grammy 2-27, 296B3

SUMMERS, John
Retains US ice dancing title 1-19, 470E2

SUMMERSKILL, Edith Clara
Dies 2-4, 176E3

SUMMIT Venture (Liberian freighter)
Fla bridge collapses 5-9, 391C1

SUMTER County—*See GEORGIA*

SUN
US solar study satellite launched 2-14, 160C2
ESA satellite venture fails 5-23, 397A3
Stellar study questns planet presence 6-29, 715D2
Radiatn drop rptd 8-6, 716D1
Sunspots, gas motions rptd linked 8-7, 716A1

1976

SUNDAY Times (London newspaper)
Thorpe letters publshd 5-9, 351A1
Ethiopian rebels free Swain 9-6, 674F2-A3
S Africa ousts Herbstein 11-7, 927G2
SUNG, Vo Van
Rpts US natls departure plan 7-21, 593B2
SUNG Yoo Bo
Sentenced 5-3, 334D2
SUN of Latin Music (recording)
Wins Grammy 2-28, 460C3
SUN Oil Co.
Pending '74 NY trust case cited 3-11, 413G1
SUNSHINE Boys (film)
Burns wins Oscar 3-29, 240A3
Top-grossing film 3-31, 240B3
SUN Yat-sen
Cited in Mao biog 658D2
SUPERIOR, Lake
Reserve Mining case judge removed 1-6, 25D2
Reserve Mining fined 5-4, 379D2
Reserve Mining deadline set 7-7, 570E3
SUPERMARKETS & Chain Stores
Dec, '75 CPI 1-21, 90B2
'75 4th 1/4 profits rptd 2-3, 215A3
'75 food mktg prices rptd 2-11, 216B2
Sup Ct bars review of unemploymt for strikers 10-4, 807E2
SUPERSONIC Transport (SST)—*See under AVIATION*
SUPREME Council for Sport in Africa
Supports Olympic boycott 7-17, 528C3
SUQUIA Giocoechea, Archbishop Angel
Asks broad amnesty 7-25, 753C3

SURINAM
Listed as 'free' nation 1-19, 20C3
Joins Group of 77 108C1
Reynolds admits paymts 6-2, 690E2

SUSLOV, Mikhail A.
Politburo, Secretariat named 3-5, 195D2, F2
Addresses E Ger SED Cong 5-19, 381F1
SUSANN, Jacqueline (d. 1974)
Dolores on best-seller list 12-5, 972E2

1977

SUNBELT States
Job gains rptd 8-7, 8-10, 629E2, F2
US urban aid debated 12-7, 959E3
SUN Bowl—*See FOOTBALL—Collegiate*
SUNDAY Express, The (London newspaper)
Sold 6-30, 526G3
SUNDAY Times (London newspaper)
Chrgs Israel torture 6-19; Israel denies 7-3, 511A2-A3
Holden found slain 12-7, 1019D1
SUNG Pei-ching
Out as Anhwei party head 6-27, 505B3
SUNG Ping
Named Kansu prov chief 6-22, 505A3
SUNKIST Growers Inc.
FTC accuses of monopoly 6-6, 520E2
SUNNI Moslems—*See ISLAM*
SUNNYVALE, Calif.—*See CALIFORNIA*
SUN Oil Co.
Donahue on Carter attack 10-13, 773A1
SUNSET Laws—*See U.S. GOVERNMENT—EXECUTIVE Branch—Reorganization*
SUNSHINE Mills and Grain, Inc.
Drying room explodes 12-22, 1023A2
SUNSHINE Mining Co.
Hunts seek controlling interest 3-21, 275C1
Hunt acquisition bid cited 4-28, 341B3
Great Western takeover OKd 10-4, 798F3
SUNTHORN Hongladarom
Wants SEATO-ASEAN merger 6-30, 514B2
SUOMI, Verner E.
Gets Medal of Sci 11-22, 952B1
SUPER Bowl—*See FOOTBALL—Professional*
SUPERIOR, Lake
Reserve Mining wins dump site 1-31, 95F2
SUPERIOR Oil Co., The
FTC info order review rejctd 6-13, 517G1
SUPERMARKETS & Chain Stores
Butler dies 10-30, 872C1
SUPERPORTS—*See HARBORS & Ports*
SUPERSONIC Transport—*See AVIATION—SST/Concorde*
SUPPLEMENTAL Security Income (SSI)—*See U.S. GOVERNMENT—SOCIAL Security Administration*
SUPREME Court—*See under U.S. GOVERNMENT*
SURFACE Mining (strip-mining)—*See MINES & Mining*
SURFACE Mining Reclamation & Enforcement, Office of—*See under U.S. GOVERNMENT—INTERIOR*
SURGERY—*See under MEDICINE*

SURINAM (formerly Dutch Guiana)—*See also OAS*
UN Assemb member 4C1
OAS entry official 6-14, 494B3
Young visits, lauds rights record 8-10—8-11, 646E1, C3
Ex-agri min sentncd 9-9, 767B3
Natl Repub Party quits coalitn 9-23, 767B3
Govt wins electns 10-31; incomplete vote count rptd 11-4, 844E1
Final electn vote count rptd 11-6, 905D3
Arron vows econ reforms, bauxite exports cited 11-6, 905E3
Bauxite base price OKd 12-7, 975E1
SURRY, Va.—*See under VIRGINIA*
SUSANN, Jacqueline
Dolores on best-seller list 6-4, 452B2; 7-3, 548F3
SUTHEP Chantana, Col.
On anti-rebel drive 1-10, 47D3

1978

SUNBELT States—*See also SOUTHEAST, SOUTHWEST; state names*
'75-77 migratn reversal rptd 12-3, 943D1
SUN Bowl—*See FOOTBALL—Collegiate*
SUN Co. Inc.
Burtis replaces Sharbaugh as chief exec 9-9, 809C1
Sun Oil Co.
Becton Dickinson shares bought 1-17; Wms Act violatns chrgd, Cong chrmn urge probe 1-27, 65F3
SEC sues to rescind Becton takeover 3-9, 223E1
SUN Day
Celebrated 5-3, 321C3
Solar energy draft study released 8-25, 718A2; final study rptd, spending hike backed 12-12, 983A1
SUNDAY Times (London newspaper)
Publicatn suspended 11-30, 923G3-924E1
SUNDBERG, Jim
Wins Golden Glove Award 11-21, 928A3
SUNG, Vo Van
On Vietnam refugees 12-11, 956B1
SUNG Jen-chiung
Heads China Machine Bldg post 2-26—3-5, 153F1
SUN Life Assurance Co. of Canada
Shareholders OK move 4-25, Quebec parlt scores 4-26, 311D2-A3
Quebec OKs English in hq 7-19, 571G2
SUN Oil Co.—*See under SUN Co.*
SUNSHINE Mining Co.
Idaho corp takeover law ruled unconst 8-10, 700F3
SUN Yun-suan (Taiwan premier)
Named Taiwan premr 5-20, 401G3
Taiwan to up arms outlay 12-18, 974E2
SUOMELA, Pentil
On Pnompenh conditns 1-22, 42C2
SUPER Bowl—*See FOOTBALL—Professional*
SUPERIOR, Lake
'75 ore ship sinkage rpt issued 4-20, 460A1
Reserve Mining to continue operatns 7-7, 553F2
SUPERIOR Oil Co.
Stock rptd highest-priced 12-19, 1004A1
SUPERMAN (film)
Released 12-14, 1030E3
SUPERMARKETS & Chain Stores
Safeway complaint rptd setld 1-10, 348A1
Grocer '77 4th 1/4 profits rptd down 2-7, 282E3
BAT Industries US, Brazil operatns cited 5-5, 345D3
Grand Union, Colonial Stores to merge 8-1, 718A1
July CPI drop rptd 8-29, 679A3
Meany links inflatn, middleman profits 9-18, 715D2
Food Fair files for bankruptcy 10-1, 752G3
SUPERSONIC Transport—*See AVIATION—SST/Concorde*
SUPERSTARS (TV show)
AAU suspends 4 track stars 6-23, 692F2
SUPPLEMENTAL Security Income (SSI)—*See U.S. GOVERNMENT—SOCIAL Security Administration*
SUPREME Court—*See under U.S. GOVERNMENT*
SURFACE-to-Air Missile (SAM)—*See ARMAMENTS—Missiles*
SURGEONS, Association of Military—*See MILITARY Surgeons, Association of*
SURGERY—*See under MEDICINE*

SURINAM (formerly Dutch Guiana)—*See also GATT, OAS*
200-mi waters set 6-11, 559F1
In 8-natn Amazon pact 7-3, 829C2
UN Assemb member 713E3

SURVEILLANCE—*See PRIVACY, WIRETAPPING*
SUSLOV, Mikhail Andreevich
Awards Brezhnev Victory medal 2-20, 151D3

1979

SUN, The (British newspaper)
Film stars' deaths tied to '53 US A-test 8-4, 630B1
SUN, Y. S. (Taiwanese prime minister)
On productivity decline 11-6, 952G2
SUN Co. Inc.
Energy Dept chrgs pricing rule abuses 1-3, 17D1
Carter budgets research 1-22, 46G1
NE fuel allocatns announced 3-1, 183C3
1st 1/4 oil profits rptd 4-27, 301C2
July gas supplies rptd 6-27, 479F1
Becton stock purchase ruled illegal 7-9, 541E2
Elk R Resources acquisitn set 7-31, 986B3
Sun Oil, Great Canadian merger forms Suncor 8-22, 651B2
Carter heating oil price freeze proposal opposed 9-17, 703E1
3d 1/4 profits rptd up 10-25, 804D3
US overchrgs alleged 11-6, 849G2; 11-8, 11-4, 905F2-A3; 12-5, 943F1
Becton divestiture set 12-19, 985G1
SUNCOR Inc.—*See SUN Co. Inc.*
SUNDAY Times (London newspaper)
Eur rights ct rules vs UK censorship 4-26, 331B1
Labor pact reached 10-21, 813E2
Publicatn resumptn set 11-13, 874C1
SUNDBERG, Jim
Wins Golden Glove Award 11-20, 956C1
SUNDE, Karen
Marquis of Keith opens 3-13, 712D1
SUNG, Vo Van
Chrgs US collusn in China invasn 2-19, 121D2
SUN Harvest Inc.—*See under UNITED Brands*
SUNNYSIDE (film)
Released 6-1, 820D3
SUN Oil Co. Ltd.—*See SUN Co. Inc.*
SUNQUIST, Donald
Replacemt in Baker campaign cited 12-3, 983A2
SUNSET Bay, N.Y.—*See NEW York State*
SUNSHINE Mining Co.
Idaho takeover law challenge rejctd by Sup Ct 6-26, 540F3
SUNY—*See NEW York, State University of*
SUN Yen-suan (Taiwan premier)
Vs China bid on autonomy 1-11, 27B1
SUPERIOR, Lake
Grain handlers strike, settle 7-6–9-25, 722D3
SUPERIOR Oil Co.
Gulf of Mex oil, gas lease bid rptd 8-28, 664E3
SUPERMAN (film)
Top-grossing film 1-10, 80G3; 2-7, 120G3; 2-28, 174B2; 4-4, 271F2
Wins Oscar 4-9, 336C2
SUPERMARKETS & Chain Stores
W Ger co to buy A&P share 1-16, 53C3
Clerks, meat cutters unions to merge 1-26, 130G3
Food Fair closes 123 supermkts 1-27, 131G2
Safeway firing case declined by Sup Ct 2-21, 128D3
A&P milk price actn backed by Sup Ct 2-22, 150F2
Skaggs to take over Amer Stores 3-14, 238C1
1st 1/4 profits rptd down 4-27, 385D1
Giant Food rolls back prices 5-9, 385B2
Kroger ads ruled deceptive by FTC 6-21, 596C2
SUPERSONIC Transport—*See AVIATION—SST/Concorde*
SUPERTRAMP (singing group)
Breakfast in Amer on best-seller list 5-2, 356A3; 5-30, 448F3; 7-4, 548F3; 8-1, 620F3; 9-5, 672F3; 10-3, 800F3
Logical Song on best-seller list 7-4, 548E3
SUPPLEMENTAL Security Income (SSI)—*See U.S. GOVERNMENT-SOCIAL Security Administration*
SUPREME Court—*See under U.S. GOVERNMENT*
SURGERY—*See under MEDICINE*
SURINAM (formerly Dutch Guiana)—*See also GATT, NONALIGNED Nations Movement, OAS*
Nonaligned movemt joined 9-3, 675E1
UN membership listed 695A3

SURRY Power Station—*See VIRGINIA–Atomic Energy*
SURTEES, William
Wins US amateur squash champs 1-21, 527A2
SURVEILLANCE—*See PRIVACY, WIRETAPPING*
SUSQUEHANNA River
3 Mile I A-waste dumping scored 3-30, 243E3; 4-4, 260G1; contaminatn rptd 4-15 274G2
3 Mile I water purificatn method opposed 8-14, 629C3
SUSQUEHANNA Valley Alliance
Vs 3 Mile I water purificatn plan 8-14, 629C3
SUTCLIFFE, Rick
Named top NL rookie 11-28, 955C3

1980

SUN Co. Inc.
Dickinson ct damages action dropped 2-14, 558A2
Seagram accepts Tex Pacific merger bid 4-11, 385B2
1st 1/4 profit rptd 4-25, 331E1, A2
On '79 Fortune 500 list 5-5, 290F1
Gasoline prices cut 7-9, 553F1
Wholesale gas price cut rptd 8-1, 666D3
Reagan visits Phila shipyd 8-19, 629A2
Gasoline dealer rebates revived 9-1, 786D1
Sunohio rpts PCB cleanup device 9-11, 747C2
Tex Pacific merger completed 9-12, 985A1
Price setlmt OKd 9-26, 960E1
SUNDAY Runners in the Rain (play)
Opens 5-4, 392G3
SUNDAY Times (London newspaper)
Offered for sale 10-22, 808A3
SUNDBERG, Jim
Wins Golden Glove Award 12-6, 926D1
SUNDSTROM, Frank
Convicted in Kenya murder 9-30, sentence rptd protested 10-13, 10-20, 859C3
SUNDSTROM, Frank L.
Dies 5-23, 448A1
SUNSHINE Highway Bridge
Cutter, tanker collide 1-28, 256E2
Tanker rams; collapses 5-9, 391C1
SUNSHINE Mining Co.
Silver-backed bonds offered 4-11, 265C3
Strike ends 11-8, 883D3
SUN Ship Inc. v. Pennsylvania
Case decided by Sup Ct 6-23, 555C1
SUN Yun-suan (Taiwanese premier)
S Africa prime min visits, uranium deal cited 10-13—10-17, 831E2
SUPERBITY (race horse)
Wins Flamingo Stakes 3-5, 447F3
SUPERIOR, Lake
Reserve Mining ends dumping 3-16, 227A1
SUPERIOR Oil Co.
Gulf coast leasing bids set records 9-30, 785B2
SUPERMAN (film)
'79 top domestic rental film 2-6, 120F2
Williams wins Grammy 2-27, 296G3
SUPERMARKETS & Chain Stores
3 retailers freeze food prices 3-6, 349C1
Canada drops fraud chrgs vs 57 4-11, 372E1
Wood replaces Scott as A&P chrmn 4-29, 456D2
Beef pricing trust case refused by Sup Ct 10-14, 781G3
Col Sanders dies 12-16, 1004C3
SUPREME Court—*See under U.S. GOVERNMENT*
SUPREME Court of Virginia v. Consumers Union
Case decided by Sup Ct 6-2, 512F3
SUPRON, Andrzei
Wins Olympic medal 7-24, 624A3
SURANOV, Oleg
Spain arrests as spy 2-14, 141A3

SURINAM (formerly Dutch Guiana)—*See also GATT, NONALIGNED Nations, OAS*
Army sergeants stage coup, Arron deposed 2-25, 153G1
Mil cncl names civiln wing 2-28, sees Ferrier 3-3, 174F3
Arron, 4 mins surrender rptd 2-29, 174E3
Mil cncl ldr, 7 sgts identified 2-29, 174G3
Mercenaries fail in coup attempt, Dutch ldr executed 5-1—5-2; Sen confrms 5-6, 410F2
Ferrier ousted as pres, Chin assumes post 8-13; mil cncl shakeup rptd 8-18, 653E2
Amazon pact signed 10-28, 865C2*
SURVEILLANCE—*See PRIVACY Issue, WIRETAPPING*
SUSLOV, Mikhail Andreevich
Addresses Polish CP cong, influence increase seen 2-12, 152B2
SUTEVSKI, Vladimir
Arrows win MISL title 3-23, 771A2

1976

SUTOWO, Maj. Gen. Ibnu
Ousted as Pertamina head 3-4, 176F3
SUTTON, Don
NL pitching ldr 10-4, 796A1
SUTTER, Frank H.
Harrises convicted 8-9, 595E3
SUTTLE, Judge D. W.
OKs Braniff job bias setlmt 11-23, 943G2
SUTTON, Percy
Asks fact-finding in Namibia 8-25, 654E2
SUTTON-Pryce, Edward
On rebel, govt casualties 6-10, 427C3
Outlines partitn plan 7-7, 522G3
On Mozambique raid 8-28, 661D2
SUZUKI, Akiyoshi
All-Nippon loan probed 3-5, 191F1
SUZUKI, Zenko
Japan agri min 12-24, 1006B3
SVESTKA, Oldrich
Czech Secretariat member 4-16, 289B2
SVOBODA, Ludvik
Czech Presidium drops 4-16, 289A2
SWAEBE, Geoffrey
Named Abercrombie chief exec 8-6, 984E3
SWAIN, Jon
Eritrean rebels free 9-6, 674F2
SWAINSON, John B.
Sentenced 1-26, 70A3
SWAMY, Subramanian
Parlt to probe defectn 9-2, 676C1
SWANN, Lynn
In Super Bowl 1-18, 56B1

SWAZILAND—*See also AFRICAN Development Bank, COMMONWEALTH of Nations, NONALIGNED Nations Movement, OAU*
Listed as 'partly free' 1-19, 20D3
Angola MPLA recognized 2-23, 163E2
S Africa guerrilla network chrgd 4-26, 428G3
Olympic withdrawal rptd 7-21, 528B3
UN Assemb condemns apartheid 11-9, 842G2
S Africa student refugees rptd 11-19, 927E1
SWEARER, Howard Robert
Named Brown U pres 8-14, 640G3

SWEDEN—*See also ADB, DISARMAMENT—Geneva Committee, IEA, OECD*
Parlt opens, '76 draft budget outlined 1-12, 103D3
Listed as 'free' nation 1-19, 20C3
Bank cuts discount rate 1-29, 104B1
Bergman hospitalized 2-3, tax chrgs dropped 3-24, 271C3 ★
Steel projct revisn rptd studied 2-5, 103F3
Rpt shippers ask govt aid 4-21, 422F3
Bergman, Andersson to leave 4-22; Palme regrets 4-28, 368C3
Workers win managemt role 6-2, 559E1
'75 per capita income rptd 7-12, 581F3
July jobless rate rptd down 8-16, 679G2
Soc Dems defeated; Palme resigns, Falldin to form new govt 9-20, 714D1
Falldin A-plant support cited 9-20, 714A2
Facts on Falldin 714E2
Cabinet named 10-8, 794F1, B2
Falldin reverses A-plant stand 10-8, 794G1
Jan-June indl profits fall 11-11, 1012A3
'74 tax rate rptd 11-18, 905A2
Volvo '77 cutbacks set 12-9, 987C3
Foreign Economic Developments
Gulf paymts detailed 133G3
SDR rate rptd 1-15, 14B3
Pl oil deal signed 1-21, 104B1
US import curbs protested 2-2, 104A1
Vs World Bank Chile loan 2-3, 99G2
Lockheed payoff cited 2-6, 131B1
At intl econ conf 2-11—2-20, 148B1
To join A-safeguards group 3-13, 243F2
France quits snake float 3-15, 229F1
US threatens steel quotas 3-16, 212G3
Total IMF oil loan rptd 4-1, 340G2
US ends car dumping probe 5-4, 321D2
France to join African Dvpt Fund 5-10—5-11, 355F3
Loan to prop UK £ OKd 6-7, 407C2
US sets specialty steel quotas 6-7, 430G1, 431D1
Paris Club defers Zaire debt 6-17, 488A2
'75 forgn aid data rptd 7-12, 582A1
Volvo, Saab OK US price hikes 8-16, 988C1
US spy device purchase rptd 9-14, 734D1
W Ger mark revalued 10-17, 782B1, C1
Volvo delays US plant 12-9, 987A3
In IMF UK loan 12-21, 1004B1
Foreign Relations (misc.)—*See also 'UN Policy' below*
Europn soclsts meet 1-18—1-19, 48G2
Uruguay bans youth group 1-20, 208A1

1977

SUTOWO, Maj. Gen. Ibnu
SEC chrgs shakedown 2-2, 93C2
On Pertamina debts 2-14, 304D3
Faces probe on Pertamina, other chrgs 3-29, 304G2
Pertamina settles SEC chrgs 6-1, 540D2
Cleared of chrgs 9-23, 747F1
SUTTON, Don
NL wins All-Star Game, named MVP 7-19, 567F2
In World Series 10-11—10-18, 806F1
SUTTON, Percy E.
Koch wins mayoral primary 9-8, 723B2
SUWEIDI, Ahmad Khalifa al-
Pak mediatn effort fails 4-28—4-29, returns home 5-3, 248C3
SUZMAN, Helen
Scores power-sharing plan 8-22, 657F1
Scores govt crackdown 10-19, 804E1
SUZUKI, Yasumiro
Oh breaks Aaron HR record 9-3, 748F2
SUZUKI, Zenko
Signs Sovt fishing pact 5-27, 458A3
SVALBARD Islands—*See NORWAY*
SVESHNIKOV, Gennady Vassilievich
Spain arrests 7-2, expels 7-4, 546A1
SWAMY, Subramaniam
Seeks to return to India 2-1, 71F2
Returns to India 160C1
SWANBERG, W. A.
Wins Natl Book Award 4-11, 355B2
SWANN, Lynn
Challenges NFL labor pact 4-25, 491G2
Atkinson loses slander suit 7-22, 659D1
SWASTIKA—*See NAZIS*

SWAZILAND—*See also COMMONWEALTH of Nations, NONALIGNED Nations Movement, OAU*
Southn Africa bps score apartheid 1-10, 100A3
Parlt dissolved 3-22, 394G3
Lesotho trade rptd 4-9, 490E1
Mandela travel OKd 5-24, 400A1
Norland confrmd US amb 6-23, 626B3
US authorizes regional fund 8-4, 668D1
S Africa terrorist captures rptd 9-26, 825C3
Students riot 10-13, 869C2
Oldest fossils of life found 10-15, 908G1
SWEARINGEN, John E.
Scores Carter energy plan 4-24, 319B3
Replies to Carter attack 10-13, 773A1
SWEDEN—*See also DISARMAMENT—Geneva Committee, ESA, IDB, IEA, OECD*
A-waste disposal process rptd 2-8, 470B1
Amsterdam fire kills tourists 5-9, 604B2
Race riot 6-19, Goteborg police probe bias 7-24, 709B1
Parlt bans titles 10-6, 904D1
Nobels announced 10-6—10-14, Ohlin wins 10-14, 951B2, E3
Heroin addictn rptd up 10-17—10-21, 971E3
Aerosol can ban set 11-10, 904E1
4 win Lasker awards 11-16, 927A3
Economy & Labor (domestic)
Record deficit budget presented 1-10, 22G3
'76 factory wages rptd 1-28, 158B3
Dec '75-76 inflatn rate rptd 2-7, 87A2
2-mo price freeze, austerity plan announced 4-4, 429D1
Volvo, Saab agree to merge 5-6, 469B3
Air, media workers strike 5-13, 5-23; pvt sector reaches wage pact 5-26, 469E3
6 shipyds merged 6-22, 709F1
Volvo-SAAB merger called off 8-28, 709E1
Krona devalued 10%, price freeze imposed 8-29, 708C3
'75 buying power rptd down 11-6, 853E3
Govt to merge 3 steel firms 11-8, sets specialty indus aid 11-9, 903C3
Foreign Relations (misc.)—*See also 'Monetary, Trade & Aid' below*
UN Assemb member 4C1
UK 200-mi fishing zone in effect 1-1, 21A1
'76 Eur Cncl pact vs terror cited 9G2
In 14-natn sulphur-dioxide pact 1-19, 109B3
Abstains on UN Israel occupatn rule vote 2-15, 107E2
Socialist rep at Israel Labor Party conv 2-22, 135F1
Terrorist plotters arrested, Baader-Meinhof linked, 2 deported to W Ger 4-1—4-6, 428E3

1978

SUTHERLAND, Donald
Invasn of Body Snatchers released 12-21, 1030A3
SUTHERLAND, Graham
Churchill portrait rptd destroyed 1-11, 335E2
SUTHERLAND, Ian
Zambia sentences 11-23, 912G1
SUTHERLAND, John (deceased)
King murder plot alleged 7-26, 589B3
King murder bounty alleged 11-29, 938A2
SUTTER, Bruce
NL wins All-Star Game 7-11, 559E3
SUTTON, Don
Dodgers win NL pennant 10-7, 779C1
SUZUKI, Takakazu
Kidnaped in El Salvador 12-7, negotiatns for release rptd 12-21, 986D3
SUZUKI, Zenko
WZ trade talks fail 2-22, 498E1
Dropped as LDP secy gen choice 12-6, 945G2
SWADOS, Elizabeth
Runaways opens 3-9, 887G2
SWANSON, Howard
Dies 11-12, 972E3
SWAPO—*See NONALIGNED Nations Movement, SOUTH Africa—Namibia*
SWARTHMORE College (Selinsgrove, Pa.)
Salamander magnetic orientatn study rptd 1-19, 334C1

SWAZILAND—*See also COMMONWEALTH of Nations, NONALIGNED Nations Movement, OAU*
Israeli freed in 3-way swap 4-23, 318C2
US bars Peace Corps from S Africa hospitals 5-15, 633A1
Educ offcl dies in S Africa custody 6-29, negligne chrgd 7-1, 633G2
UN Assemb member 713E3
Electns held 10-27, 1022G1

SWEDEN—*See also COUNCIL of Europe, DISARMAMENT—Geneva Committee, EFTA, GATT, IDB, IEA, OECD*
Heart study rptd 1-7, 598D1
5 jailed in Leijon kidnap plot 1-31, 93A1
Energy conservatn progress seen 6-5, 449E3 ★, 450E1
Boras hotel fire kills 20 6-10, 460G1
Leijon kidnap plotters jail terms extended 6-29, 691E1
Nobels announced 10-5—10-27, 886B1-B3
Atomic Energy & Safeguards
'77 A-export safeguard pact detailed 1-11, 11B2
Australia joins A-supplier group 2-24, 129C2
Goteborg bomb blast protests A-plants 5-31, 440A1
Panel backs A-power 6-14, govt split rptd 6-15, 691F1-A2
A-power issue brings down Falldin govt 10-5, 764F2
Economy & Labor (domestic)
'78-79 budget presented; inflatn, GNP data rptd 1-10, 21C1
Labor talks break down 1-17; moderate wage pact reached 3-11—3-12, 291A2
Volvo '77 profit down, layoffs rptd 1-27, 93E1
'73-77 wage gain rptd 2-27, 189C3
Income per capita rank rptd 5-12, 384F3
Trade unions back A-power 6-14, 691A2
Shipyd closing planned 6-17, 691A1
'77 per capita GNP ranked 3d 7-18, 624E1
June '77-78 world inflatn rates ranked 10-18, 914F1
Foreign Relations (misc.)—*See also 'Monetary, Trade, Aid & Investment' and 'UN' below*
Amb ends Cambodia visit 1-21, calls Pnompenh 'ghost city' 1-22, 43A2; Thai min disputes 2-2, 61E1
France, W Ger OK ESA rocket launcher 2-6—2-7, 122B1
USSR sub patrols protested 3-1, 291A3
S Africa culture, sports ties banned 3-11, 193C3
USSR denies use of spy trucks 3-15, 291E2
Falldin at 26th Bilderberg Conf 4-21—4-23, 302D3

1979

SUTHERLAND, Donald
Great Train Robbery released 2-1, 174F2
Murder By Decree released 2-8, 174B3
Man, Woman & Bank released 9-28, 820A2
SUTTER, Bruce
Gets credit for All-Star Game win 7-17, 569A2
Wins NL Cy Young Award 11-7, 955A3
SUWANNEE River
Hooker phosphate plant pollutn rptd 8-5, 597F2
SVALBARD Islands—*See NORWAY*
SVENSON, Bo
North Dallas Forty released 8-1, 820D2
SVOBODA, Ludvik
Dies 9-20, 756E3
SWADOS, Elizabeth
Dispatches opens 4-18, 711E2
SWANN, Lynn
NFL '78 touchdown, receiving ldr 1-6, 80B1, C1
Steelers win Super Bowl 1-21, 63D1
Rozelle admits Super Bowl officiating error 2-22, 175C3
SWANSON, Maura
Poet & Rent opens 5-9, 712A2
SWAPO—*See NONALIGNED Nations Movement*
SWATUK, Brian
Steady Growth wins Queen's Plate 6-30, 876C3

SWAZILAND—*See also COMMONWEALTH of Nations, NONALIGNED Nations Movement, OAU*
UN membership listed 695A3
S Africa unions bar natls 9-25, 732E2
SWEARINGEN, John E.
Meets with Carter 5-31, 418D1
Scores Carter oil policies 9-12, 702G3
SWEARINGEN, M. Wesley
Claims FBI lied in SWP case, judge seeks statemt 1-16, 92D2
FBI papers at Jonestown to be probed 1-17, 117E3

SWEDEN—*See also COUNCIL of Europe, DISARMAMENT-Geneva Committee, GATT, IDB, IEA, OECD*
Queen gives birth 5-13, 392G3
Wastberg named PEN pres 7-21, 553G3
Nobels announced 10-12—10-18, 857C3
Atomic Energy & Safeguards
USSR '78 A-tests rptd 1-31, 109B2
'78 forgn tests rptd 3-6, 625D3
6 more A-statns, Finland joint progrm sought 3-13, 213D3, F3, 214A1
A-waste plans faulted 3-14, 214B1
2 reactors rptd OKd 3-29, 238E2
US A-accident sparks protests 3-31, 4-3, referendum agreed 4-5, 246D1, G1, C2
A-plant fueling OKd 6-25, 505G1-C2
Program halt studied 10-10, 795A2
Safety study released 11-19, 910G2
Economy & Labor
Volvo '78 earnings rptd up 1-26, 77D2
Indl stimulus pkg proposed 3-9, 287B3
Energy bill rptd 3-13, 213D3-214A1
Econ improvemt seen 5-30, 428B3
'78 per capita GNP ranked 4th 7-24, 575E3
Westn wage rates compared 9-19, 697D3
Foreign Relations (misc.)—*See also 'Atomic' above, 'Monetary' and 'UN' below*
2 rptrs believed killed in Uganda war 4-9, 257F2
Chile refugee relocatn rptd 5-7, 369A3
Indochina refugee admissns hiked 6-21, 474B2
USSR envoy '45 disappearance case reopened 8-4, 690C2
Latin pol refugees occupy Rio consulate, protest Argentina repressn 8-6; UN responds 8-8, 627D1, F1
USSR cancels theater tour 10-1, 775B1

1980

SUTHERLAND, Donald
Nothing Personal released 4-18, 416D3
Ordinary People released 9-19, 836D3
SUTHERLAND, Graham
Dies 2-18, 176F3
SUTTER, Bruce
Awarded $700,000 salary by arbitrator 2-25, 637A1
NL wins All-Star Game 7-8, 636C2
NL pitching ldr 10-6, 926G2
SUTTON, Don
NL pitching ldr 10-6, 926F2
In free-agent draft 11-13, signs with Astros 12-3, 1000C1
SUTTON, Hal
2d in NCAA golf championship 5-31; wins US Amateur 8-31, 714D3, F3
Wins World Amateur Team tourn individual title 10-12, 972E2
SUTTON, Willie (Willie the Actor)
Dies 11-2, 928E3
SUZMAN, Helen
Surveillance chrg cited 1-15, 60E3
SUZUKI, Zenko (Japanese premier)
Heads LDP 7-15, elected premr, names Cabt 7-17, 7-15, 539F2-D3
Outlines admin goals 8-18, 635E2
US VP nominee visits 8-19, 646A1
Vs major defns buildup 9-25, 752B1
Backs liberalized trade 9-26, 967A1
Warns vs Kim Dae Jung executn 11-29, 944C3
Meets US defns secy, US asks arms outlay hike 12-11—12-12, 952G3-953A1
SWAGGART, Jimmy
TV revenues rptd 2-25, 413B2
SWANN, Lynn
Steelers win Super Bowl 1-20, 61E3-62C1
SWANSON, Gloria
Alleges Jos Kennedy affair 10-13, 907E3
SWANSON, Robert A.
Genentech stock offer success rptd 10-14, 805G3
SWANSON on Swanson (book)
Swanson, Jos Kennedy affair alleged 10-13, 907F3
SWANSTROM, Nord L.
Alleged ERA briber indicted 6-5, 441D3, G3
SWANTON, Gerald
Sentenced 5-20, 927G2
SWAPO—*See NONALIGNED Nations*
SWAZILAND—*See also COMMONWEALTH of Nations, NONALIGNED Nations, OAU*
At regional econ unity mtg, S Africa dependnc cited 4-1, 243D1, B2

SWEDEN—*See also ADB, COUNCIL of Europe, CSCE, GATT, GENEVA Committee, IDB, IEA, OECD*
VD epidemic rptd, NGU rise blamed 2-5, 158A1
Nobels announced 10-9—10-15, 889G1
Atomic Energy & Safeguards
'70-79 A-tests rptd 1-17, 31E3
Referendum backs A-power, govt seen imperiled 3-23, 2 A-reactors to start up 3-28, 219C3-220E1
Economy & Labor
'81 budget rptd, GNP growth predicted 1-11, 102A1
Shipyd reorgn bill urged 4-9, 410B3
Lockout plan deferred 4-13, 295D1
Coca-Cola workers strike 4-16—4-18, 463D3
Pub-sector workers strike, locked out 4-25, pvt stoppages begin 5-1, 355C2
Pact ends lockouts, strikes 5-11; dockworkers walk out 5-7, 5-11, 365C1
Labor costs rptd 8-12, 698C1, F1
VAT hike set 8-19, 653B3
VAT hiked 9-6; budget cuts set 9-16, 731A1
Govt wins confidence vote 10-22, 822F3
Foreign Relations (misc.)—*See also 'Monetary' below*
Olympic com rejcts Moscow boycott 3-22, 259C3
Iran asks neutrality on US hostages 4-12, 282F1
USSR science conf attended 4-13—4-15, 326F2
Europn CPs meet 4-28—4-29, 327C2
Tito funeral held 5-8, 339B1
Olympic com OKs Moscow participatn 5-20, 379A3
Mex pres visits 5-22—5-24, 409G1, G2
ESA rocket test fails 5-23, 397G2

1976

'75 Sovt ship mutiny rptd foiled 1-22, 122G2
Offers Chile pol refugees asylum 1-28, 100B1
Angola MPLA recognized 2-18, 163D1
Chile exiles arrive 2-22, 3-6, 288B3, E3
Kaj Bjork in bombed Cambodia town 3-2—3-4, comments 3-6, 238B2
Europn soclsts meet 3-13—3-14, 222F3
Rpts Sovt '75 ship mutineers bombed 5-4, 5-5, 421A2
Bonn tries '75 emb raiders 5-6, 503E1
Castro sets Angola troop exit 5-21, 370B3, 371C1
Peru leftist arrives 7-11, 590G3
Argentina refugee asylum agreed 7-19, 571G2
Argentina violence scored 8-26, 672D2
Sovt defects 10-6, 857D1
N Korean envoys expelled 10-22, 799D2, D3, E3

Sports
Winter Olympics results 2-4—2-15, 158D2-159B2
Summer Olympic results 7-18—7-31, 573D3, 574C2, G2, 575E3, 576B1, G3
Canada Cup hockey results 9-15, 736G3

UN Policy & Developments
Cncl member 62F2; 720C1
Asks broad Mideast resolutn 1-14, 18C2
Abstains on pro-Palestine resolutn 1-26, 59G2
Rydbeck named Sahara envoy 2-1, 107A3
Rydbeck ends Sahara missn 2-17, 178D2
Vs WHO anti-Israel stand 5-19, 355D2
Abstains on Israel Arab land exit res 6-29, 464C1
Backs anti-terror res 7-14, 515F3
S Africa arms ban vetoed 10-19, 781D3

U.S. Relations—*See also 'Foreign Economic Developments' above*
Kissinger anti-CP lobbying rptd 2-5, 120B2
Smith confrmd amb 4-1, 262E3
Kissinger visits 5-24, 370C3
Ship in US Bicentennial event 7-4, 488C3

SWEETENERS, Artificial
FDA to keep cyclamate ban 5-11, 414F3
FDA keeps cyclamate ban 10-4, 876F1
SWIFT & Co.
Argentina official killed 5-28, 398G3
SWIFT & Sons Inc., M.
Chrgd re Arab boycott 10-8, 785C3
SWIMMING & Diving
E Ger set 14 world records 6-1—6-5, 424F3
Olympic results 7-18—7-27, Sovt diver defects 7-29, 562D2, B3, 575C2-E3

1977

Terrorists arrested in Leijon kidnap plot; Baader-Meinhof linked, 2 deported to W Ger 4-1—4-6, 428E3
Baader-Meinhof ldrs sentncd 4-28, 352D3
SAS strike setld 5-9—5-20, 469G3
Sovt plane hijacked to Sweden 5-26, 429B1
Soviet hijackers refused 7-10, 537A2
Leijon kidnap plotters indicted 7-25, 709G1
Ethiopian royal family ask asylum 8-5, 649D1
Eur Cncl to study Turkey rights abuses in Cyprus 9-8, 764G1-A2; rpt shelved, Greece protests 11-3, 946E3
W Eur heroin conf 10-17—10-21, 971E3
'75 W Ger emb raid, Schleyer kidnap linked 10-21, 868E2
Nigeria pirate raid scored 11-22, 986F2

Helsinki Agreement—*See EUROPE—Security and Cooperation*
Monetary, Trade & Aid Issues (including all foreign economic developments)
In UK sterling balances pact 1-10, 20C2
Forgn aid budgeted, loans planned 1-10, 23B1
To settle US-Sovt business disputes 1-11, 29F3
IMF SDR defined 87G2
A-suppliers conf meets 4-28—4-29, 403F1-A2
GATT to probe US ruling on Japan electronics duties 5-23, 416C2
Backs N-S conf $1 bln aid plan 6-3, 437F2
Group of 10 membership cited 438F1
In 11-natn Portugal loan 6-22, 530B3
Zaire debt rescheduled 7-7, 583E1
Danes block PVC plants 7-7, 672F1
'77 paymts deficit forecast 7-31, 586D2
Krona devalued 10%, 'snake' abandoned 8-29, 708C3
Finnish devaluatn protested 9-1, 764C3
A-suppliers conf OKs export safeguards 9-21, 717D1
'76 car exports cited 10-11, 853A3
8 poor natns debts canceled 10-12, reactn 10-13, 903F3
Palme at Brandt intl dvpt comm mtg 12-9—12-11, 998A1
Saudis boycott ships 12-10, 955D1
Mozambique refugee aid rptd 12-13, 1000B2

Obituaries
Von Rosen, Carl Gustaf 7-13, 604G3
Wigforss, Ernst 1-3, 84G3

Sports
Czechs keep hockey title 5-8, 430A2

U.S. Relations
US-Sovt business dispute mediatn agreed 1-11, 29F3
US-ESA flight set 2-16, 170C3
Carter energy message 4-18, 294E3
A-suppliers conf scores Carter plan 4-28—4-29, 403F1-A2
GATT to probe Japan electronics duty rule 5-23, 416C2
Young calls racist 5-25, 417F2; Carter comments 6-10, 460F2
Kennedy-Minott confrmd amb 8-3, 626G2
ESA satellite launching aborted 9-13, 735G3

SWEET, Don
Montreal wins Grey Cup, sets point record 11-27, 950A3
SWEETENERS, Artificial
US, Canada set bans 3-9; reactn 3-9—3-11, 176A3-177B2
Neohesperidine dihydrochalcone, aspartame await US OK 3-10, 177C1
US modifies saccharin ban 4-14, 280B1
Canada delays ban 4-19, 304B1
Ind legalizes saccharin 5-1, 375F3
Netherlands curbs saccharin use 5-9, 531E1
WHO sees no bladder cancer link 5-13, 531D1
US panel rpts cancer risk 6-7, 531A1
Canada links to human cancer 6-17, US FDA delays ban 6-20, 530E3
House votes saccharin ban delay 6-21, 531B1
Saccharin ban delay dropped from agri bill 8-12, 688C3
Saccharin ban delay clears Cong; label warning, more studies ordrd 11-4, 878D1; signed 12-20, 1001F2
SWIG, Mel
Cleveland NHL team rescued 2-23, 164D1
SWIMMING & Diving
AAU long-course champnshps 8-18—8-21, 828E3

1978

Eur conservative group formed 4-24, 424C3
ESA communicatns satellite launched 5-12, 384D3
USSR citizen kills tourists 6-27, 519E1
El Salador guerrillas kidnap exec 8-14; co ransoms 8-25, 722A2, F2 ★
Croat seeks asylum 8-30, 925G3
USSR defector rptd 11-1, 947A1

Government & Politics—*See also other appropriate subheads in this section*
Church-state separatn backed 1-19, 93C1
Deputy premier quits govt 1-31, 93C1
Falldin resigns 10-5, 764F2
Ullsten becomes premr 10-13, names Cabt 10-18, 822C2, F2

Helsinki Agreement—*See EUROPE—Security and Cooperation*
Monetary, Trade, Aid & Investment—*See also 'Atomic Energy' above*
Baltic fishing zones set 1-1, 21A2
Dutch rescue Volvo unit 1-5, 93G1
'78-79 forgn loans proposed 1-10, 21E1
'77 paymts deficit rptd 1-11, 21G1
Volvo '77 exports up 1-27, 93F1
Finland '77 trade surplus rptd 1-30, 90C1
Norway devalues krone 2-10, 133F3
S Africa investmt banned 3-11, 193C3
Krona in new SDR basket 4-3, 300F3
Danish fishermen protest 5-5, 371D2
Brazil Saab workers strike 5-12—5-16, 5-19—5-23, 412A1, F1
US firm OKs Esselte takeover 5-26, 404B1
Ethiopia drought aid rptd 6-4, 465A3
'77 poor natn debt cancellatn cited 7-10, 575F1; 7-31, 592E1
Rhodesia rebel aid OKd by WCC 8-10, 650A3
India rejects jet purchase 10-6, 797B1
Norwegian Volvo deal, econ pact signed 12-8, 965F2
UK air pact OKd 12-22, 1017F1

Obituaries
Hasselblad, Victor 8-6, 708A3
Martinson, Harry E 2-11, 196D3
Peterson, Ronnie 9-11, 778A2
Siegbahn, Manne 9-26, 778A2

Sports
Stenmark wins world skiing titles 2-2, 2-5, 316D2
Speed-skating championships 2-26, 316B3
Scandinavian Cup results 3-8, 419B1
World Cup soccer finals, sidelights 6-1—6-25, 519F3
Borg quits Grand Prix bonus chase 6-2, 540A2
Stockholm Open results 11-14, 1027C2
US wins Davis Cup 12-10, 1026E3

UN Policy & Developments
Chile rights abuse res backed 3-6, 210F1
Leb peace force (Unifil) formed 3-19, 197D2; **for peacekeeping developments, see MIDDLE EAST—LEBANON**
Unifil soldier killed 3-29, 213C2
Ethiopia drought aid rptd 6-4, 465A3
Assemb member 713F3

U.S. Relations—*See also 'Monetary, Trade & Aid' above*
US launches ESA satellite 5-12, 384D3

SWEENEY, Christine M.
Coll sex-bias ruling voided by Sup Ct 11-13, 874F1-C2
SWEET, Don
Montreal loses Grey Cup 11-26, 1025E1
SWEET, Jeffrey
Porch opens 11-14, 1031G2
SWEETENERS, Artificial
Saccharin, cyclamate studies rptd inconclusive 7-19, 7-28, 727B3
SWEET Little Lady (race horse)
McHargue sets earnings mark 12-31, 1028F1
SWEIDA, Khalifa al-
In Arab summit delegatn to Cairo 11-4, 859D2
SWENSON, Chuck
Mouse & His Child released 7-7, 970C2
SWIFT, Al
Wins Washn US House primary 9-19, 736F3
SWIFT, David
Candleshoe released 8-4, 969F3
SWIFT Trail Federal Prison Camp, Ariz.—*See ARIZONA*
SWIMMING & Diving
AIAW chngs scholarship rules 1-7—1-11, 40B3
Caulkins leads US women's resurgence 1-7—8-28, 780A1
Naber wins Sullivan Award 2-7, 780F2

1979

Envoy visits US hostages in Iran 11-10, 862A2
USSR oil reserves rptd 11-19, 928G3
Iranian amb seized 12-19, 975G3

Government & Politics—*See also other appropriate subheads in this section*
'79-80 budget presented 1-9, 77C1
Nonsocialists win electn 9-16, 696E3
Falldin named premr 10-9, confrmd 10-11, 795E1-A2

Helsinki Agreement—*See EUROPE–Security and Cooperation*
Monetary, Trade, Aid & Investment—*See also 'Atomic' above*
Norway Volvo deal blocked, econ pacts imperiled 1-26; premrs to meet 1-27, 77G1
Finland '78 trade rptd 2-2, 215G2
Iran oil cutoff impact assessed 2-20, 126A3
Indl stimulus pkg proposed 3-9, 287D3
W Ger, Algeria LNG deal cancelatns; Scandinavian energy cooperatn sought 3-13, 213F3, 214A1
GATT pact signed, aircraft tariff cuts seen 4-12, 273B2
W Ger ranks exporter labor costs 5-1, 374B2
IEA vs oil-sharing plan 5-22, 380F1; informal agrmt rptd 6-4, 396E2
OECD sees export growth 5-30, 428C3
Renault to buy Volvo share 12-19, 993G3-994C1

Obituaries
Ohlin, Bertil 8-3, 671B3

Sports
World speed-skating champs 2-11, 392C1
Sovts retain world ice hockey title 4-25, 448E1
Eur Champions' Cup results 5-30, 776F2
Swedish Open results 7-22, 734B2
Stockholm Open tennis results 11-6, 11-13, 1003F3, G3

UN Policy & Developments
Membership listed 695A3

U.S. Relations
A-accident protests 3-31, 4-3, 246D1, G1
Mondale visits Eur 4-11—4-22, 299C2
Envoy visits US hostages in Iran 11-10, 862A2
A-accident studied 11-19, 910A3, B3

SWEENEY Todd (play)
Opens 3-1, 292B3
SWEET, Don
Edmonton wins Grey Cup 11-25, 1001G1
SWEETENERS, Artificial
Food-safety law revisns urged, saccharin ban backed 3-2, 195D1, E1
SWIFT, Elizabeth Ann
Detained in US Emb 11-19, 878D2
SWIFT & Co.
PCB contaminated meat products destroyed 9-17, 704E3
SWIMMING & Diving
Pan Am Game results 7-1—7-15, 798G2
Pinto swims Strait of Otranto 7-14, 656F3
Woodhead wins 3 gold medals at Natl Sports Festival 7-21—8-1, 799C1
Nyad completes Bahamas-Fla swim 8-20, 656E3
Vogel defects to W Ger 9-18, 721E3

1980

ESA plans comet probe 7-15, 548A1
Westn labor costs compared 8-12, 698C1
Iran hostage appeal rptd 8-16, 634G3
UK interests in Iran represented 9-9, 689E1
Wallenberg family at Madrid CSCE 11-28, 950D2
USSR oil find rpt denied 12-5, 951B3

Government & Politics—*See also other appropriate subheads in this section*
Falldin wins confidence vote 10-22, 822F3

Monetary, Trade, Aid & Investment
Current acct deficit hike seen 1-11, 102B1
Volvo in Europn auto research effort 4-14, 303B3
Mex oil pact signed, joint projcts studied 5-24, 409G2
Jamaica loan rptd 6-4, 465E1

Obituaries
Lundvall, Bjoern 9-22, 756C1
Wallenberg, Jacob 8-2, 676F3

Sports
Lake Placid Winter Olympic results 2-12—2-24, 154F2, 155F2-156D1
Olympic com rejcts Moscow boycott 3-22, 259C3
Canada Cup hockey tourn cancelled 4-30, 488F3
Olympic com OKs Moscow participatn 5-20, 379A3
Moscow Olympic results 7-20—8-3, 588A3, 622B3-624F3
Stockholm Open results 11-2, 11-10, 947C2, D2

U.S. Relations
3 Mile I cited by A-protesters 3-23, 220B1
Iran asks neutrality on US hostages 4-12, 282F1
Coca-Cola plant struck 4-16—4-18, 463D3
Iran hostage appeal rptd 8-16, 634G3
Reagan electn reactn 11-5, 841A3

SWEENEY, Dennis
Chrgd in Lowenstein murder 3-18, 214D2
SWEENEY Todd Soundtrack (recording)
Wins Grammy 2-27, 296G3
SWEET, Judge Robert W.
Sets Bethlehem Steel fines 8-25, 957F3
SWEETENERS, Artificial
Cyclamate ban rptd upheld by FDA 2-7, 317D2
Saccharin cancer risk disputed 3-6, 317D1
SWIFT, A. Dean
Brennan to replace as Sears pres 3-12, 225B1
SWIFT, Rep. Al (D, Wash.)
Joins open-conv move 7-28, 570A2
Reelected 11-4, 844A3
SWIFTLY Tilting Planet, A (book)
Wins Amer Book Award 5-1, 692D2
SWIMMING & Diving
NCAA OKs women's title tourns 1-8, 103C3
U of Oregon transcript scandal rptd 2-14, 469F2
Stanford wins AIAW title 3-22, 835B1
U of Calif wins NCAA title 3-29, 835A1
US Indoor Championships 4-9—4-12, 834E3
Wickham bars Olympic participatn 5-28, 421D1
USSR, E Ger dominate Moscow Olympics 7-20—8-3, 588E2, 623E2-F3

1976

SWINE Flu—*See under MEDICINE*
SWINKELS, Eric
Wins Olympic medal 7-24, 575B2
SWISSAIR
Lockheed payoffs rptd 2-4, 130D3
SWISS Bank Corp. (Zurich)
IMF gold buyer 9-15, 739E3
SWISS Credit Bank (Zurich)
IMF gold buyer 9-15, 739E3
SWITZER, Barry
Sooners top collegiate team 1-2, 31A3

SWITZERLAND—*See also ADB, IEA, OECD*
Cuts in deposit rates, withholding tax rise rptd 1-8, 31G1
Listed as 'free' nation 1-19, 20C3
'75 wholesale price index falls 1-21, 104G1
Abortn referendum gains 1-25, 104E1
'75 alien residents drop 2-3, 104C1
Voters rejct worker participatn, tax reform 3-21, 314D3
Jura assemb sworn 4-12, 315A1
Quake tremors rptd 5-6, 352B3
Anda dies 6-13, 524C2
Tops '75 incomes list 7-12, 581F3
Lefebvre ordains 13 10-31, 932A3
Voters rejct shorter workwk, OK govt price, anti-inflatn plans 12-5, 1011D3
Oct '75-76 inflatn rate rptd 12-6, 976B1
Furgler elected pres 12-8, 1011F3
Longest road tunnel completed 12-16, 1011D3

Foreign Economic Developments
US air pact rptd ended 1-9, 31G1
French Mirage purchase cited 1-16, 36C2
'75 Spanish arms embargo lifted 1-21, 104E1
'75 arms sales rptd up 1-22, 104D1
Lockheed payoffs cited 2-4, Weisbrod denies Dutch role 2-10, 130F2, D3, 131A3
Pledges loan to Portugal 2-5, 142G3
At intl econ conf 2-11—2-20, 148B1
Dutch Lockheed probe OKd 2-25, 254A3
Parlt OKs US jet deal 3-16, 314F3
Australia loan OKd 3-23, 237F2
Total IMF oil loan rptd 4-1, 340G2
Paris group in S Africa A-plant deal 5-28, 387A2
IMF gold purchases rptd 6-3, 430F2
IDB entry set 6-3, 465D3
Loan to prop UK £ OKd 6-7, 407A2
Paris Club defers Zaire debt 6-17, 488A2
Hungary revalues vs franc 7-6, 925C2
Spain signs intl bank loan 8-9, 929A2
US scored re gold price drop 8-26, 643B1
1 sentncd in Sovt drug case 9-3, 857F1
IMF gold purchasers named 9-15, 739D3
Franc gains vs $ 9-30, 721D2; 10-20, 782B2
Franc reactn to US electn 11-3, 826F2
Lockheed paymts rptd smuggled into Spain 11-6, 909A2
Rhine pollutn pacts signed 12-4, 977A2
In IMF UK loan 12-21, 1004A1

Foreign Relations (misc.)
USSR to make more dailies available 1-21, 76A3
E Ger refugee operatns detailed 1-26, 85F1-A2
Spinola arrives 2-7; pol activity probed 4-7, expelled 4-8, 315B1
Angola MPLA recognized 2-18, 163D1

1977

Records, Women's
Boglioli, 100-mtr butterfly 8-18—8-21, 828F3
Browne, 1500-mtr freestyle 8-21, 828E3
Caulkins, 200-mtr ind medley, 400-mtr ind medley, 100-mtr breaststroke 8-18—8-21, 828E3
Hogshead, 200-mtr butterfly 8-18—8-21, 828F3
Jezek, 200-mtr backstroke 8-18—8-21, 828F3
Nicholas, Eng Channel 9-8, 808B3
Treible, 200-mtr breaststroke 8-18—8-21, 828F3

SWINE Flu—*See MEDICINE—Diseases*
SWISHER, Steve
Traded to Cardinals 12-8, 990E1
SWISS Credit Bank
3 Chiasso officers arrested 4-24, 350F2-B3
Chiasso scandal spreads 4-26—6-20, new bank rules signed 6-2, 564B3, E3
Chiasso scandal cited re bank rules adoptn 8-23, 658F1
3 Chiasso offcls fired 10-31, govt fines $28 mln 11-10, 904F1-D2

SWITZERLAND—*See also ESA, IEA, OECD*
Civil defns A-shelter progrms 1-5, 11-14, 904G2
Voters reject forgn populatn limit, treaty veto 3-13, 350C3
Iberia jet hijacker seized 3-16, 224A3
Lefebvre scores RC modernism 5-30, 471A1
Jeanmaire convctd of spying 6-17, 489C2
Lefebvre ordains priests 6-29, 620C2
Open sector cyclotron use cited 825B3
Natl referendum rejcts abortn, rent, pollutn reforms; backs vote curbs, Zurich euthanasia law 9-25, 766C3-767B1
Tin magnate's niece kidnaped 10-3, freed 10-13, 871G1
Jeanmaire case reviewed 10-27, 904B3
CO mil exemptn rejected 12-4, 1018A1
Pres, 2 Cabt mins chosen 12-7, 1018D1
Jet crashes off Madeira 12-18, 1023E2

Bank Issues
Weisscredit bank ordrd shut 3-2, 489D3
3 Chiasso bank officers arrested 4-24, 350F2-B3
Chiasso scandal spreads 4-26—6-20, new bank rules signed 6-2, 564A3, E3
Leclerc bank fails 5-9, 489B3
Scandal closes Hervel, offcrs sought 8-15, 658B1
Union Bank dir chrgd 8-15, 658D1
Bankag to be liquidated 8-19, 658E1
Bank rules adopted 8-23, 658F1
Lloyds Lugano branch to close 8-24, 658E1
3 Chiasso offcls fired 10-31, Swiss Credit fined $28 mln 11-10, 904F1-D2

Economy & Labor (domestic)—*See also 'Bank Issues' above*
'76 inflatn rate rptd 1-18, 84C2
Dec '75-76 inflatn rate rptd 2-7, 87A2
'76 per capita income cited 4-4, 302F2
'76 inflatn, real wages rptd 4-4, 489E3
Mar CPI rptd 4-13, 489G3
Geneva newspaper strike 4-18—4-20, 350F3
Mar jobless rate rptd 4-19, 490A1
A-power statn ban urged 5-28—5-29, Basel votes plant ban 6-12, 490A1
Value-added tax rejected 6-12, 489G2-B3
Natl referendum rejcts rent reforms 9-25, 766F3
Austerity budget presented 10-21, 904E2
'75 world pay rank rptd 11-6, 853D3
Sept jobless rate, alien drop rptd 12-1, 1018D1
Wealth tax voted down 12-4, 1018A1
GNP rise, inflatn rate rptd 12-22, 1018B1

Foreign Relations (misc.)—*See also 'Monetary, Trade & Aid' below*
'76 Eur Cncl pact vs terror cited 9G2
Rhodesia sentncs priest 1-12, 11F2
Not in 14-natn sulphur-dioxide pact 1-19, 109B3
'76 pol asylum requests down 1-25, 138A1

1978

CPSC pool slide standards cited 2-8, 185A3
Ariz State wins AIAW title 3-18, 780G2
Tenn U wins NCAA title 3-26, 780G2
US-USSR dual meet 4-15—4-16, 780E1, B3
Poenisch ends Cuba-Fla marathon 7-13, 653E1, B2
AAU long-course champnshps 8-2—8-6, 780D2
Nyad begins Cuba-Fla marathon 8-13, fails 8-15, 653E1
Taylor ends Bahamas-Fla marathon 8-15, 653E1, A2
US wins world champnshp 8-18—8-28, 780F1, A2

Records, Men's
Babashoff, 400-m freestyle relay 8-22, 780C2
Gaines, 400-m freestyle 8-22, 780C2
McCagg, 400-m freestyle relay 8-22, 780C2
Montgomery, 400-m freestyle relay 8-22, 780C2
Vassallo, 400-yd, 400-m ind medley 4-6, 8-4, 8-21, 780B2, D2, A3

Records, Women's
Caulkins, 200-yd breaststroke, ind medley 1-7, 4-7; 400-yd ind medley 1-8, 4-6; 200-m ind medley, 400-m medley relay 8-2, 8-20; 400-m ind medley 8-23; 400-m freestyle relay, 200-m butterfly 8-26, 780D1-G1
Elkins, 400-m freestyle relay 8-26, 780G1
Hogshead, 200-m butterfly 4-6, 780B3
Jezek, 200-m backstroke 8-24, 780B2
Linehan, 400-m freestyle 8-2, 780E2
Sterkel, 400-m freestyle relay 8-26, 780G1
Wickam, 800-m freestyle 2-23, 780F2
Woodhead, 200-m freestyle 8-3, 8-22; 400-m freestyle relay 8-26, 780G1, B2, E2

SWINE Flue—*See MEDICINE—Diseases*
SWINGFIRE (anti-tank missile)—*See ARMAMENTS—Missiles*
SWISHER, State's Attorney for Baltimore City v. Brady
Juvenile case reviews upheld by Sup Ct 6-28, 567F1
SWISS Credit Bank—*See CREDIT Suisse*

SWITZERLAND—*See also COUNCIL of Europe, EFTA, GATT, IEA, OECD*
Bernese Jura mt blasts linked to separatists 1-24, 75B2
Gun controls tightened 2-9, 151C2
Chaplin's body stolen 3-2, 232D3
Terrorist activity detailed, 2 policemen rptd slain 4-12, 438D2
Chaplin's body recovered 5-17, 380D1
Voters rejct auto ban, abortn reform, daylight savings time 5-28, 558D2
Von Hirsch collectn auctioned 6-20—6-27, 578E2
Alpine flooding kills 23 8-8, 655B1
Quake felt 9-3, 759A1
Jura Canton voted 9-23—9-24, 840C1
Arber wins Nobel Prize 10-12, 886E2
Natl police force referendum rejctd 12-3, 968A1
Blackout hits rural areas 12-19, 1016B3

Bank Issues
Credit Suisse chrmn probed in Italian suit 1-10, secrecy breach denied 1-11, 151C1
Swiss Bank Corp syndicates Venez loan 1-12, 332F1
LeClerc arrested 1-19, 95A2
Credit Suisse to sell Texon holdings 2-10, rpts '77 Chiasso scandal losses 3-1, 151F1-A2
Voters OK wider govt powers 2-27, 151B2
US co buys Credit Suisse et de White Weld stake 4-14, 283D2
Union Bank '79 econ forecast rptd 12-13, 968C1
Guyana cult bank accts cited 12-15—12-16, located in Panama 12-20, 1000E1
Geneva bank robbed 12-27, 1028B3

Economy & Labor (domestic)—*See also 'Bank Issues' above*
Voters OK wider govt powers 2-27, 151A2
Income per capita rank rptd 5-12, 384F3
'77 per capita GNP ranked 2d 7-18, 624D1
June '77-78 inflatn rate ranked world's lowest 10-18, 914F1
'79 GNP growth forecast 12-13, 968C1
Zurich stock mkt gains rptd down; graph 12-25, 1001C2, E2

Foreign Relations (misc.)—*See also 'Monetary, Trade, Aid & Investment' and 'UN' below*
Yugoslav Tito foe chrgs kidnap 1-24, 292A2
'77 pol asylum total rptd 2-1, 151C2
Chad rebels rpt natl captured 2-2, 130C2
At USSR maneuvers 2-6—2-10, 103C2

1979

Records, Men's
Vassallo, 200-m ind medley 7-6, 798A3

Records, Women's
Woodhead, 200-m freestyle 7-3, 798A3

SWINDLER, John B.
Sentncd in GSA kickback scandal 3-24, 3-26, 367A3
SWINE Flu—*See MEDICINE-Diseases*
SWISSAIR
DC-10 grounded indefinitely 6-6, 421B1
SWISS Credit Bank—*See CREDIT Suisse*
SWITCH Partners (race horse)
3d in Santa Anita Derby 4-1, 448D3

SWITZERLAND—*See also COUNCIL of Europe, GATT, IDB, IEA, OECD*
Animal rabies vaccine experimt rptd 2-28, 196E1

Atomic Energy & Safeguards
A-progrm backed in vote 2-18, 136F3
2d A-power vote set, US A-accident impact seen 4-4, 246E1
Pak sales probe rptd set, US request cited 5-2, 342F1
Tighter A-curbs OKd 5-20, 390C3
Argentine A-plant deal rptd 10-1, 749D1
Goesgen A-plant attack rptd 11-4, 876A1

Bank Issues
5 chrgd re Chiasso scandal 2-15, 137C1
Weisscredit Bank offcls convicted 3-1, 155F2
Peoples Temple funds blocked 3-12, 250E1
US indicts Sindona, Bordoni 3-19, 205C2
Geneva to get CP mayor 5-25, 428E3
Chiasso sentncs given 7-3, 505C2
Peoples Temple funds transfer rptd 8-2, 592B3
Secrecy laws challenged 10-8, 795E2
Lending fees, Lombard rate hiked, negative interest rate cut 11-2, 875E3
W Ger robber arrested 11-20, 998D3
Pahlevi family assets identified 11-26, 897E2

Economy & Labor—*See also 'Bank Issues' above*
Weapons spending hike sought 4-11, 391A1
VAT proposal rejctd 5-20, 390G3
Tops '78 per capita GNP list 7-24, 575C3
'80 austerity budget proposed 9-26, 754B3

Foreign Relations (misc.)—*See also 'Atomic' above, 'Monetary' below*
Israel-PLO prisoner swap 3-14, 178G2
Diplomat slain in El Salvador 5-30, 406A3
Indochina refugee conf hosted 7-20–7-21, 549B1

1980

US Championships 7-29—8-2, 834D2
Pac-10 punishes Oregon in transcript scandal 8-11, 875A2

Records (Men's)
Arvidsson, 100-yd butterfly 3-28, 200-yd butterfly 3-29, 100-m butterfly 4-11, 835B1
Barrett, 200-m individual medley 8-1, 834B3
Beardsley, 200-m butterfly 7-30, 834A3
Gaines, 100-m freestyle 4-9, 8-1; 200-m freestyle 4-11, 834D3, F3
Goodell, 800-m freestyle 7-29, 834C3
Lundquist, 100-m breaststroke 4-12, 7-29, 834C3, 835A1
Salnikov, 1500-m freestyle 7-22, 400-m freestyle 7-24, 588G3
Stahl, 50-m freestyle 4-10, 834G3

Records (Women's)
Caulkins, 200-m breaststroke 4-9, 100-m breaststroke 7-29, 400-m individual medley 7-30, 834C3, G3
Krause, 100-m freestyle 7-21, 588G3
Meagher, 100-m butterfly 4-11, 200-m butterfly 7-30, 834B3, F3
Sterkel, 50-yd butterfly 3-20, 100-yd butterfly 3-21, 50-yd freestyle 3-22, 50-m freestyle 4-10, 835A1, C1

SWISS Bank Corp.
Hunt silver debts rptd 5-2, 345C1
Nicaragua debt rescheduled 9-5, 689G2
SWIT, Loretta
Wins Emmy 9-7, 692C1

SWITZERLAND—*See also ADB, COUNCIL of Europe, CSCE, GATT, IDB, IEA, OECD*
Youth riots spur arrests 7-12—7-13, 567A2
Youth riots recur in Zurich 9-4—9-7, 754F2-A3
Longest road tunnel opened 9-5, 754B3

Atomic Energy & Safeguards
Argentina heavy water plant deal opposed by US 3-10—3-11, contract signed 3-14, 229A2
Canada A-deal delay rptd 5-29, 429F1
US A-export protest rejected 9-22, 754C2
US Cong fails to bar India uranium sale 9-24, 723A2

Bank Issues
French customs offcls seized 4-15; Swiss Bank Paris unit searched 5-7, 407B2
Central banks rptd active in forgn exchng mkts 4-30, 436B3
French customs offcls convicted 6-18, 522F2
Auto-Train loan set 8-22, dropped 9-8, 958E2, G2
Forgn deposit curbs ended 8-27, 673B3
Zurich-based bank buys W Ger dept store shares 12-12, 969F1

Economy & Labor
'79 GNP growth rptd 1-10, 102C1
Geneva purchasing power rptd low 2-12, 125F3
Discount, Lombard rates hiked 2-28, 153C3
Commerce suspensn in crises OKd 3-2, 236D1
Labor costs rptd 8-12, 698D1

Foreign Relations (misc.)—*See also 'Atomic Energy' above, 'Monetary', 'UN Policy' below*
Turkey amb attacked 2-6, 197A2
200 Sovt spies alleged 2-18, 141B3
Colombia amb seized in DR emb raid 2-27, 141B1

1976

Sweden drops Bergman chrgs 3-24, 271D3 ★
Israel protests Cannes film 5-14—5-28, 460A2
Vs WHO anti-Israel stand 5-19, 355D2
Pope scores Lefebvre 5-24, 424B1
Hijackers ask prisoner freed 6-29, Amin plea 6-30, 463C1, G1
Lefebvre ordains priests 6-29, 655F3
Argentina refugee asylum agreed 7-19, 571G2
Officer arrested for spying 8-16, 640A1
Sovt, Rumania envoys expelled 8-22, 640B1
Iranian deported as spy 8-30, Gyger recalled 8-31, 735E1
Kissinger-Vorster mtg in Zurich 9-4—9-6, 660B2
Sozhenitsyn move to US rptd 9-9, 680B3
Gen, wife chrgd as Sovt spies 11-10, 1011A3
Soclst Intl meets in Geneva 11-26—11-28, 935E2
Venez pres visits 11-27—11-28, 930A1
Rhodesia arrests priest 12-8, 1010C1
Sovt-Chile prisoner exchng 12-18, 955E2
Menten returned to Netherlands 12-22, 1007B2

Sports
Winter Olympics results 2-4—2-15, 158B3-159B2
Summer Olympic results 7-18—7-31, 573D3, 574E2, G2, 575A1

1977

Rhodesia cuts priest sentnc 4-6, 297B1
To host US interest office' in Cuba 5-30, 455B3
Warner confrmd amb 6-7, 500D1
Viet refugees accepted 6-16, 497E1
UN membership declined 6-30, 565C1
USSR mil exercises observed 7-11, 551C1
US 'interest office' opens in Cuba 9-1, 685C3
Tunisia torture scored 9-1, 867E2
Eur Cncl to study Turkey rights abuses in Cyprus 9-8, 764G1-A2; rpt shelved, Greece protests 11-3, 946E3
W Ger names terrorist negotiator 9-9, 791G2
Austrian kidnap suspects arrested 11-23, 991F1
2 W Ger terrorists captured 12-20, 1017D3

Helsinki Agreement—*See EUROPE—Security and Cooperation*
Monetary, Trade & Aid Issues (including all foreign economic developments)—*See also 'Bank Issues' above*
'76 forgn franc loans rptd 1-4, 48E2
In UK sterling balances pact 1-10, 20C2
'76 record currency interventn, franc rise rptd 1-18, 84F1
'76 trade surplus rptd, watch exports down 1-27, 138B1
Canada Polysar admits illegal rebates 2-8, 114B2
Sovt bloc Rhodesia sanctn violatns chrgd 2-10, 123A1
Spain capital smuggling rptd 2-14, 308A1
US loan repaymt rptd 3-2, 188G3
US execs sentncd for Sovt sales 3-14, 203F2
Mar imports set record, trade deficit up 4-20, 489F3
A-suppliers conf scores Carter plans 4-28—4-29, 403F1-A2
'76 paymts surplus rptd 5-12, 489E3
US asks move to paymts deficit 5-25, 437D3
Australia urges trade office closed 6-2, 484E3
Backs N-S conf $1 bln aid plan 6-3, 437F2
In 11 natn Portugal loan 6-22, 530B3
Zaire debt rescheduled 7-7, 583E1
'77 paymts surplus forecast 7-31, 586E2
French A-plant protest 7-31, 597C2, F2
A-suppliers conf OKs export safeguards 9-21, 717D1
World econ recovery effort cited at IMF-World Bank mtgs 9-26—9-30, 753D3
$ drops vs franc 11-1, 829D2
Jan-Oct paymts deficit rptd 11-16, 1018C1
Nestle-Alcon deal OKd 11-17, 880E1
'77 franc rise vs $ rptd 11-30, 932E3
Wealth tax rejected 12-4, 1018A1
$ closes down vs franc 12-8, 933C1
$ drops 12-30, 997F2

Obituaries
Chaplin, Charlie 12-25, 1024C1

1978

France, W Ger OK ESA rocket launcher 2-6—2-7, 122B1
Begin sees Jewish ldrs in Geneva 2-8, 78D1
Forgn populatn decline rptd 2-10, 151D2
Greek, Turk ldrs meet in Montreux 3-10—3-11, 216D2
4-natn terrorism mtg hosted, 'hot line' set 4-8—4-9; terrorist activity rptd 4-12, 438B2
El Salvador peasants, students seize emb 4-11—4-18, 723C3 ★
Chad rebels free natl 4-14, 287B2
2 W Ger terrorists trial opens 4-25, 353E3
Egypt terror group rptd smashed 4-26, 300D2
ESA communicatns satellite launched 5-12, 384D3
Chile exiles on hunger strike 6-1, 452F2
Club Medit '77 robbery cited 6-11, 473F3
2 W Ger terrorists jailed 6-30, 558F2
Algerian denies Canadian kidnaping 7-6, 531G3

Helsinki Agreement—*See EUROPE—Security and Cooperation*
Monetary, Trade, Aid & Investment—*See also 'Bank Issues' above*
3d party Rhodesian deals banned 1-1, 22E2
$ drop, recovery rptd 1-4, 27E3
'77 A-export safeguard pact detailed 1-11, 11B2
Venez loan rptd 1-12, 332F1
USSR trade pact rptd 1-17, 28G3
'77 $ drop rptd 1-23, 27D2
US $ drops vs franc 2-23, '77 depreciatn cited 118D2, F2
Australia joins A-supplier group 2-24, 129C2
Wider govt trade powers voted 2-27, 151B2
US $ drops vs franc 4-3, 235C1
Merrill Lynch to get Credit Suisse stake 4-14, 283D2
US pledges $ defense 6-13, 523F2
French workers block traffic 6-23, 6-27, 532C3
US $ up vs franc 7-14, 523B3
Italian panel scores Hoffman unit for Seveso '76 blast 7-27, 689E1 ★
Poor natn debts rptd canceled 8-1, 592F1
US $ falls vs franc 8-15, 622F1
Leutwiler scores US $ policy, says franc overvalued 9-27, $ soars 9-28, 732E1
Franc value cut, W Ger mark value boost linked 10-16, 798E2
Brown Boveri in Latin turbine deal 10-20, 829A3
US $ hits new low 10-30; rescue set, $ recovers 11-1, 825B1, G1, D2, G2
US bank robber rptd in Sovt diamond deal 11-5, 992C1
Hungary devalues forint 11-11, 906G2
'79 exports, imports forecast 12-13, 968D1
OPEC $ use seen as aid 12-17, 977F3
US $ closes down vs franc 12-29, 998E2

Sports
Bobsled championships 2-5, 2-12, 316F3

UN Policy & Development
Sovt ILO aide tied to KGB 7-26, ousted 7-31, 676C1
Sovt UN aide gets visa 8-18, 676F1
UNESCO free press text queried 11-22, 931E1
U.S. Relations—*See also 'Bank Issues' and 'Monetary, Trade, Aid & Investment' above*
US launches ESA satellite 5-12, 384D3
Kennedy in Geneva 6-1, 452F2
Miller in Zurich 6-13, 523F2
ITT unit linked to forgn paymts 11-2, 876E1, E2

1979

Mex Emb occupied 8-3, retaken 8-10, 671E1
Spanish plane lands, 3 hijackers surrender 8-5, 604A1
PLO slayer suspect arrested 8-20, 625C2
USSR skating stars defect 9-18, 721B3; get asylum 10-30, 939G3
USSR chess player gets asylum 9-24, 721D3
W Ger terrorist arrested 11-20, 998C3

Government & Politics—*See also other appropriate subheads in this section*
Geneva to get CP mayor 5-25, 428D3
Electns held, 4-party coalitn retains power 10-21, 837D2
Helsinki Agreement—*See EUROPE-Security and Cooperation*
Monetary, Trade, Aid & Investment—*See also 'Atomic' and 'Bank Issues' above*
US sells franc notes to aid $ 1-17, 84G2
US bond offering cited 1-18, 62G1
Forgn capital bars eased 1-24, 78D1
'78 trade deficit down 1-30, 78F1
US $ rises vs franc 2-8, 83B2
Hoffman-La Roche '76 ruling upheld 2-13, 137A1
Iran asks shah's assets frozen 2-23, 144G3
Canada seeks loan 2-28, 153A2
Shah's assets freeze rejctd, Iranian '78 assets rptd 3-5, 161E1
US $ defense rptd 3-7, 159D3, E3
Firestone '72 gold trading chrgd 3-15, 202A2
S Africa '72-78 loans rptd 4-2, 270D2
US tank purchase sought 4-11, 391A1
US $ closes up vs franc 5-1, 321B1
Pak A-sales probe rptd set, US request cited 5-2, 342F1
Oil imports rptd 5-20, 390F3
Alusuisse acquires US auto parts maker 7-30, 770G2
Continental Grain unit fined re boycott violatn 8-27, 648G2
Cuban bond sale abandoned 11-8, 872G1
Tobacco export gains rptd 11-22, 970A3
US $ closes down vs franc 12-27, 978G3

Sports
World 2-man bobsled champs 2-18, 392D1
USSR skating stars defect 9-18, 721B3; get asylum 10-30, 939G3
USSR chess player gets asylum 9-24, 721D3
Swiss Indoor tennis results 10-21, 1003E3

U.S. Relations—*See also 'Bank Issues' and 'Monetary' above*
Swiss couple indicted in US 3-16, 240E1
A-accident impact seen 4-4, 246E1
Hoffman-La Roche NJ unit hikes women's pay 5-13, 482G3
ITT unit to aid paymts probe 8-8, 648F1
Cornfeld trial opens 9-24, acquitted 10-15, 817F3

1980

Iran relayed US notes 3-25, 3-30, 241D1, G2
Amb to Iran in mediatn group 4-5, 258D1
Iran asks neutrality on US hostages 4-12, 282F1
Iran representatn set 4-24, dead US raiders repatriated 5-6, 337B2
Colombia DR Emb siege ends, amb freed 4-27, 335G1, B2
Europn CPs meet 4-28—4-29, 327C2
Cubans attack Havana Emb 5-2, 339F2
Olympic com rejects Moscow boycott 5-10, 379B3
Cuban Emb peril seen 5-15, 361C1, E2
ESA rocket test fails 5-23, 397G2
Guatemala Nestle exec kidnaped 6-17, ransom demand rptd 6-20, 487F2
ESA plans comet probe 7-15, 548A1
Olympic flag controversy 7-24, 588E1
Iran parlt gets US hostage plea 7-29, 571E3
83 Cubans in Havana Emb surrender 8-7, 618E3
Westn labor costs compared 8-12, 698D1
Iran hostage appeal rptd 8-16, 634G3
Guatemala Nestle exec freed 9-10, 731B3
Cubans end Havana Emb occupatn 9-23, 749D2
W Ger terrorist sentenced 9-26, 755D1
Natls flee Dutch ocean liner fire 10-4, 769A3
Iran assets, hostage deal offered 10-20, 800A1

Government & Politics—*See also other appropriate subheads in this section*
Church-state separatn rejected 3-2, 236C1

Monetary, Trade, Aid & Investment
See also 'Atomic Energy', 'Bank Issues' above
Gold reserves rptd 1-18, 30A3
'79 US mfg investmt rptd 2-6, 92D3
Forgn acct interest ban ended 2-20, 153F2
Japan sets yen rescue plan 3-2, 173D2
US $ soars vs franc, central bank intervenes 3-17; profit-taking slows surge 3-19—3-20, 202F3
Hunt group sets silver-backed bond issue 3-26, 223D1
Japan currency swap effected 4-1, 276E2
'79 US investmt rptd 4-8, 329C1
Venez shipping scandal rptd, ex-pres censured 5-8, 411E1
US OKs franc futures trading 5-28, 481C2
Iran gold transfers rptd 6-17, 464A3
Iran takes over Merck unit 7-9, 546E2
Bethlehem Steel pleads guilty in bribe case 7-24, 600E1
Sovt gold sales rptd resumed; Aug silver sales rptd 9-24, 730D3
Algeria quake aid rptd 10-11, 776E1
Brazil Jari project dispute rptd 10-16, 787B3
US $ gains vs franc 11-5, 845B1; 12-10, 932F1
Alusuisse buys Phelps Dodge Consolidated Alum share 11-23, 985C2
US $ up 11% vs franc in '80 12-31, 983E2

Obituaries
Kandinsky, Nina 9-3, 755E3
Piaget, Jean 9-16, 756E1
Sports
Speed skating championships 1-13—1-21, 470F1
Lake Placid Olympic results 2-12—2-24, 154F2, 155F2-156D1
Olympic com rejects Moscow boycott 5-10, 379B3
Moscow Olympic results 7-20—8-3; flag controversy 7-24, 588E1, C3, 622F2, 623D1
UN Policy & Developments
200 Sovt spies at UN offices alleged 2-18, 141C3
UNESCO world info res abstentn 10-25, 821C3, D3
U.S. Relations—*See also 'Monetary' above*
Iran relays US notes 3-25, 3-30, 241D1, G2
Swiss amb in Iran mediatn group 4-5, 258D1
Iran asks neutrality on US hostages 4-12, 282F1
US gets representatn in Iran 4-24, dead US raiders repatriated 5-6, 337B2
Cubans attack Swiss Emb 5-2; US closes interest office, suspends visa procedures 5-4, 339F2
Sindona aide sentenced in NY 5-13, 415C1
US revises Cuba refugee policy 5-14, emb peril seen 5-15, 361C1, E2
Cubans protest US interests 5-17, 380A2
Iran hostage arrives Zurich 7-12, 539E1
US hostage plea delivered to Iran parlt 7-29, 571E3

1976

SY, Gen. Baba
Upper Volta defns min 2-9, 269C3
SYBRON Corp.
SEC lists paymts 5-12, 729C1
SYLVIA L. Ossa (ship)
Vanishes 10-15, 912E1
SYLVIA Porter's Money Book (book)
On best seller list 1-25, 80C3; 12-5, 972D2
SYMBIONESE Liberation Army
Harrises suit filed 1-5, 70G1
Soliah freed on bail 1-15, 70A2
Soliah defense motns denied 2-9, 114F3
Article rpts Harrises' break with Hearst 4-25, 368E1
Soliah acquitted 4-27, 368G1
Harrises appear in ct with Hearst 5-12, 367E3
Harrises convicted 8-9, 595D3
Harrises sentenced 8-31, 679D3
Hearst Case—*See HEARST, Patricia*
SYMES, James M.
Dies 8-3, 892G3
SYMINGTON, Rep. James W. (D, Mo.)
Loses Sen primary 8-3, 565E2
Young wins seat 11-2, 823B3
SYMINGTON, Sen. Stuart (D, Mo.)
Admits CIA contacts 1-23, detailed 1-28, 93F1, C2
Primary results for seat 8-3, 565E2
Danforth wins seat 11-2, 820C1, 823A3
SYMMS, Rep. Steven D. (R, Idaho)
Scored by environmt group 3-25, 220A1
Reelected 11-2, 824G1, 829E2
SYNNERGREN, Stig
Confirms US spy device purchase 9-14, 734D1
SYNTEX Laboratories, Inc.
Sequentials withdrawn 2-25, 224B3
SYRACUSE (N.Y.) Post-Standard (newspaper)
Ford endorsement rptd 10-30, 831F2

SYRIA—*See also ARAB League, NON-ALIGNED Nations Movement*
Listed as 'not free' nation 1-19, 20E3
Assad seeks Sahara setlmt 1-27, 1-29, 58C2
EC trade talks rptd 2-12, 164B3
Kosygin visits 6-1—6-4, 385B2, 406F2
Bomb kills ex-Iraq aide 7-10, Iraq blamed 7-11, 679A3
Ayoubi quits, Khleifawi named 8-1; Cabt formed 8-8, 594F2
Bomb plotters arrested 8-22, 679G2
Turkey border clash 10-14, 858A3
Assad meets Sadat, Egypt union set 12-18—12-21, 954D2
Middle East Conflict—*See MIDDLE EAST*

1977

SYBIL (TV film)
Wins Emmy 9-11, 1022A1
SYMBIONESE Liberation Army
Hearst pleads no contest 4-18, 302C2
Hearst gets probation 5-9, 370E3
Hearst convictn upheld 10-2, 839A1
SYMINGTON, Stuart
Cited in Park indictmt 9-6, 688E1
SYNAGOGUE Council of America
Backs NCC Trifa suspensn 2-5, 120B1
Abraham Feldman dies 7-21, 604B3
L Carter wins prize 9-25, 808A3
SYRACUSE, N.Y.—*See NEW York State*

SYRIA—*See also ARAB League, NONALIGNED Nations Movement*
UN Assemb member 4C1
France arrests Daoud 1-7, 9C2
EC trade pact signed 1-18, 73E3
Khaddam visits Sadat 2-3, pol cmnd formed 2-4, 87A1
Waldheim visits 2-4—2-5, 86E2
Sudan joins Egypt-Syria cmnd 2-27—2-28, 143F2
Assad visits Moscow 4-18—4-22, 297B2, 317C2
Austria defense min quits re arms shipmt 5-30, 424D3
2 Iraqi agents executed 6-13, 457B3
General slain 6-18, 496E2
8 die in Damascus bombings, Iraq blamed 7-4, 7-10, 534F1
Baath Regional Cmnd mtg divisn cited 7-4, 534F2
Hijacked Kuwait jet lands 7-10, 535C1
Somalia arms aid rptd 9-1, 684A3
Cholera outbreak rptd 9-26, 747G3-748C1
Hijacked Japan jet refuels 10-3, 756C3
Hijackers denied landing 10-13, 789F1
Not in UN Medit pollutn pact 10-21, 876B2
Somalia arms aid rptd 10-22, 830B1
Khaddam escapes assassinatn in UAE 10-25; Iraq blamed 10-26, 811B3
Sadat sees Assad 11-16, 873G1
Day of mourning declared 11-19, 890E2
Khaddam in USSR 11-29, 910E1
Egypt recalls amb 12-4, cuts ties 12-5, 929A1, C2
Assad in Saudi, Kuwait, Bahrain, Qatar, UAE; seeks aid vs Cairo conf 12-8—12-11, 954F2

1978

SWP—*See SOCIALIST Workers Party*
SYBERBERG, Hans-Jurgen
Confessns of Winifred Wagner released 3-23, 619C1
SYLVESTER II, Pope (d. 1003)
US returns Hungary crown 1-6, 7A2
SYLVESTER, Victor
Dies 8-14, 708E3
SYMBIONESE Liberation Army (SLA)
Harrises sentncd 10-3, 824A1
SYMINGTON, Stuart
To wed IBM widow 4-12, 420F2
SYMMS, Rep. Steven D. (R, Ida.)
Reelected 11-7, 850C3, 856C1
On Taiwan defns pact suit 12-20, 975C3
SYMPHONY No. 9 in D Major (recording)
Chicago Symphony wins Grammy 2-24, 316C1
SYNANON
Calif woman wins damage suit 9-19; atty attacked by rattler 10-10, 2 members chrgd 10-17, 841F2, D3
Calif probes incidents 10-15, forms task force 10-17, 841G3-842B1
Dederich chrgd in rattler attack 12-3, 971F1
SYNAR, Mike
Wins Okla US House primary 8-22, 683D1
Elected 11-7, 851G3, 855A3
SYNCOPATE (race horse)
McHargue sets earnings mark 12-31, 1028F1
SYPHILIS—*See MEDICINE—Diseases*
SYRACUSE (N.Y.) University
Byrnes in NBA draft 6-9, 457G3

SYRIA—*See also ARAB League, NONALIGNED Nations Movement*
Freedom House lists as partly free 44F1
Assad reelected 2-8, 136F3
Premr Khleifawi quits, Halabi succeeds 3-27; Cabt formed 3-30, 269F3
9 newsmen rptd banned 6-19, 559G1-A2

1979

SWP—*See SOCIALIST Workers Party*
SYCHOV, Vladimir
Rpts dissident electn slate 2-2, electn bid rejctn 2-6, 100E1★, G1★; 2-17, 172D2
SYKES, Richard
Killed, IRA linked 3-22, 228E2-D3
SYLBERT, Paul
Wins Oscar 4-9, 336A2
SYLVANIA—*See GENERAL Telephone & Electronics Corp.*
SYMBIONESE Liberation Army (SLA)
Little murder convictn reversed 2-27, 156C1
Harris convictns review declined by Sup Ct 10-1, 768B1
SYNANON
Pt Reyes Light wins Pulitzer 4-16, 336D2, A3
SYNCTIAL Virus—*See MEDICINE—Diseases*
SYNTHETIC Fuels—*See also specific sources (e.g., SHALE Oil)*
House OKs bill 6-26, 498G1
Admin plans previewed 7-8, 514A1, 517E3
Canada seeks Carter environmt commitmt 7-20, 581E3
Carter accepts slower dvpt 9-11, 702E2
Senate OKs bill 11-8, 961C1
Cong OKs $20 bln dvpt bill 11-9, 883E1
Carter signs dvpt bill 11-27, 920C1
Carter Oil Profits Tax Plan—*For developments not listed here, See PETROLEUM-Carter Decontrol*
Carter seeks Energy Security Corp 7-15, 532B2, C3, 534A1
Carter OKs plan chngs 9-11, 702F2
SYPHILIS—*See MEDICINE—Diseases*
SYRACUSE (N.Y.) University
In Big East basketball conf 5-29, 526G3
Wins Independence Bowl 12-15, 1001G2

SYRIA—*See also ARAB League*
Rights abuse of Jews chrgd 2-22, denied 2-23, 148G1, A3
Atty gen slain 4-11, 488F1
60 army cadets slain 6-16; Moslem Brotherhood blamed, other killings cited 6-22; arrests 6-25, 488B1, E1
15 Moslem extremists executed 6-28, 505G2-B3
Alawite Moslems riot in Latakia 8-30, troops sent 9-1, 710E1
Latakia death toll set at 40 754F3
Neurosurgeon's death rptd 9-1, 710G3
Moslem Brotherhood admits violence planned 9-7, Zaim slain 9-16, 754G3
Reforms announced 9-27, 754D3
Alawite-Sunni clashes 10-19, Apr-Oct death toll 200 10-25, 837F2
Torture, abductns, Jewish emigratn curbs chrgd by Amnesty Intl 10-24, 857A3

1980

Tabatabai slayer flees US 8-6, 671E3
83 Cubans in Swiss Emb interest office surrender 8-7, 618E3
Iran hostage appeal rptd 8-16, 634G3
US A-export rejected 9-22, 754C2
Cubans end Swiss Emb interest office occupatn 9-23, 749D2
US Cong fails to bar India uranium sale 9-24, 723A2
Iran assets, hostage deal offered 10-20, 800A1
SYDNEY Morning Herald (Australian newspaper)
Journalists strike rptd 5-16, 371G1
SYKES, Kym
Wins Drake Relays mile 4-26, 892F2
SYKES, Richard (d. 1979)
IRA claims credit for death 2-19, 194B1
SYLVANIA—*See GENERAL Telephone & Electronics Corp. (GTE)*
SYMBIONESE Liberation Army (SLA)
Hearst probation rptd ended 5-9, 471E3
SYMINGTON, Stuart
Financial Gen deal set 7-25, 600F3
SYMMS, Rep. Steven D. (R, Ida.)
Elected to US Sen 11-4, 840E1, 845A2, 851E3, G3
SYMONETTE, Roland
Death rptd 3-17, 280C2
SYMPHONIES Complete (recording)
Solti, Mallinson win Grammy 2-27, 296F3
SYNANON
Dederich, 2 aides convicted in rattler attack 7-15, 655E3
Dederich gets probatn, aides psychiatric evaluatn ordered 9-3, 860D2, F2
SYNAR, Rep. Mike (D, Okla.)
Reelected 11-4, 843G4
SYNTHETIC Fuels
CEA ex-chrmn urges use 1-14, 32F1
NAS backs dvpt 1-14, 53G3
Carter asks dvpt funds 1-23, 43G1
Carter budget proposals 1-28, 72C1, 73C3
Kennedy urges demonstratn plants 2-2, 91E1
Kennedy 'basic speech' excerpts 3-10, 183F2
Windfall oil profits tax bill signed 4-2, 244F2
S Africa plants bombed 6-1, 466A2
Dvpt bill clears Cong 6-19, 6-26, 479A2; Carter signs 6-30, 494G1-A2
Energy Mobilizatn Bd defeated by House 6-27, 515B2
Canada output up, oil levy raised 75% 7-11, 543C3
ND plant loan OKd 7-18, 553B2
US, W Ger, Japan pact signed 7-31, 666D2
Dem platform planks adopted 8-13, 615F1
Carter pres renominatn acceptance speech 8-14, 612F1, 613F1
Carter names Sawhill, 6 others to Synfuels Corp 9-10, 9-13; Cary withdraws 9-24, Sen panel OKs appointmts 9-25, 699C1, 725D2
Trade assn formatn, operatn rptd 9-21, 725A3
Sawhill Synfuels Corp confirmatn blocked 10-1, Carter names interim bd 10-5, 786E2-A3
Gasohol Competitn Act clears Cong 11-17, 11-19, 953D2
ND plant gets $1.5 bln fed loan 11-19, ct blocks projct 12-8, 961E3
Gasahol Competitn Act signed 12-2, 928A1
SYNTHETIC Fuels Production, National Council of
Formatn, operatn rptd 9-21, 725A3
SYPHUS, Paul
Harrah's gets temp NJ gambling license 11-1, 988D3
SYRACUSE (N.Y.) University
Monk in NFL draft 4-29, 336F3
SYREETA
With You I'm Born Again on best-seller list 4-2, 280E3; 4-30, 359G3
SYRIA—*See also ARAB League, NONALIGNED Nations*
Leading Sunni cleric slain 2-2, 154C2
Patriarch Yacoub dies 6-25, 528G3
Economy & Labor
Defense outlay increased 2-19, 140D3
Gen strike in Aleppo, Hama 3-31, 295G1-B2

1976

UN Policy & Developments—*See also UN DEVELOPMENTS under MIDDLE EAST*
UNESCO literacy drive fails 2-4, 85C2
Shuns pollutn pact signing 2-16, 126C3
Scores Israel, S Africa at ECOSOC racism debate 4-27, 320F2
Asks Israel seat reviewed 10-5, 760B1
U.S. Relations—*See also 'Syria' under MIDDLE EAST—ARAB Policies*
US arms aid bills signed 6-30, 532E3, 533C2
'77 aid funds signed 10-1, 806D3
SZAFRANSKI, Henryk
Polish State Cncl member 3-25, 268D2
SZCERBA, Kazimier
Wins Olympic medal 7-31, 574C1
SZENT-Gyorgyi, Albert
Pleads for Sovt dissident 3-24, 421A3
SZERYNG, Henry
Wins Grammy 2-28, 460D3
SZEWINSKA, Irena
Wins Olympic medal 7-29, 576A2
SZLACHCIC, Franiszek
Dropped as Polish dep premr 3-27, 268E2
SZTANITY, Zoltan
Wins Olympic medal 7-30, 574E1
SZYDLAK, Jan
Named deputy min 12-2, 926C3

1977

Arab-Israeli Conflict—*See MIDDLE EAST*
Cairo Conference—*See MIDDLE EAST—EGYPT-Israel Peace Moves*
Lebanon Civil Strife—*See LEBANON*
U.S. Relations—*For Arab-Israeli conflict, see MIDDLE EAST—U.S. DEVELOPMENTS*
Vance visits 2-20—2-21, 122A1
Carter plans mtg 3-8, 165A2
Carter sees Assad in Geneva 5-9, 360G1-A3
Vance meets Assad 8-4, 588G2
US security aid authorized 8-4, 668D1
Vance briefs on Israel talks 8-11, 605G2
Carter meets Khaddam 9-28, 734A1
US '78 security aid funds cleared 10-19, 815G2; signed 11-1, 834D1
Vance meets Assad, vs Cairo conf 12-13, 954E1
SZEP, Paul
Wins Pulitzer Prize 4-18, 355G2
SZOLD, Robert
Dies 11-9, 952E3

1978

Arab-Israeli Conflict—*See MIDDLE EAST*
Foreign Relations (misc.)—*See also 'UN' below*
2 emb aides slain in London 12-31-77, 3B2
Sovt arms deal rptd 1-11, 42B2
Iraq talks canceled 1-29, 78C3
2 hostages seized in Cyprus 2-18, 117G1
Assad in USSR 2-21—2-22, to get more arms aid 2-24, 139D2
Sadat assails USSR arms aid 2-25, 139G2
Arab fund poor-natn aid rise rptd 4-9, 257F2
Egypt athletes to boycott 7-24, 573C1
Arab fund loan to Sudan rptd 8-17, 925F3
Iraq ousts counselor 8-24, 674E1
Hardliner conf ends; Egypt ties severed, USSR contacts sought 9-24, 729F2
Assad in USSR, Syria to get more arms 10-5—10-6, 762C3
Australia to probe Qantas curb on Jews 10-18, 836E1; Syria drops demand 10-20, 900E3
Iraq frontier opened 10-22, to join forces 10-24—10-26, 803E1, B2
Lebanon Developments—*See LEBANON, MIDDLE EAST—Lebanon*
UN Policy & Developments
Leb peace force support rptd 3-20, 198F2
UNDOF get protest on Israeli violatns 4-2, 236D3
UNDOF mandate renewed 5-31, 400A2
Assemb member 713F3
U.S. Relations—*For Arab-Israeli conflict, see MIDDLE EAST—EGYPT-Israel Peace Moves*
Boeing chrgd re payoffs 7-28, 642G3
Carter signs econ aid authorzn 9-26, 734F1
US econ aid funds signed 10-18, 862D2
SZWARC, Jeannot
Jaws 2 released 6-16, 619E2

1979

Arab-Israeli Conflict—*See MIDDLE EAST*
Foreign Relations (misc.)—*See also 'UN' below*
In Iraqi talks, unity delayed 1-28–1-30, 69F2
Sovt MiG-23 buildup rptd 2-13, 143A3
Assad warns vs Israel-Egypt pact 3-8, 157F1
USSR forgn min visits 3-24–3-26, 222D2
Egypt airline office seized 3-25, 222D2
Egypt chrgs terror plot 4-24, 296E1
Egypt notes Faisal warning 5-1, Saudi denies 5-2, 319A2
Amin presence rptd 5-27, 429F1
Ghana econ exploitatn chrgd 5-28, 425B2
In Iraqi talks 6-17–6-18, joint pol cmnd set 6-19, 462D1
Egypt, Israel linked to Moslem extremists 6-28, 505A3
Egypt ties Assad to emb raid in Turkey 7-16, 536A3
Iraq ties to plot 7-30, 8-5, Assad denies 8-6, 583G1, 602A3
USSR T-72 tank shipmt rptd, Israel arsenal compared 8-28, 643B2
Rumania offers Israel mediatn 8-31, Israel rejects 9-2, 659B2
Libya fete attended by Arab ldrs 9-1, 688C3
Canada envoy tours Mideast 9-9–10-20, 833D2
Israel cites mil threat 9-12, 693D2
USSR links Egypt-Israel treaty, unrest 10-14, 857F2
Assad in USSR, gets arms vow 10-15–10-18; USSR debt rptd canceled 11-3, 857E2
Envoy visits US hostages in Iran 11-10, 862A2
Lebanon Developments—*See MIDDLE EAST–LEBANON*
UN Policy and Developments
Membership listed 695A3
U.S. Relations
US issues rights rpt 2-10, 107B3
US rights rpt disputed 2-22, 148B2
Bomb blasts US Emb 3-25, 222A2
Moslem extremists tied to US 6-27, executed 6-28, 505G2
Jackson visits, meets Assad 10-2, 763E1
US pleas for hostages in Iran 11-6, 841C2
Envoy visits hostages in Iran 11-10, 862A2
US sets evacuatns, travel curbs 11-26, 894A2
SZULZINGER, Picha
Shame of Jungle released 9-14, 820C3
SZYMANKIEWICZ, Joseph (d. 1973)
Spenkelink executed in Fla 5-25, 400A1

1980

Foreign Relations (misc.)—*See also 'Iran-Iraq War', 'UN Policy' below*
2 Sovt aides slain 1-15; 1 wounded 1-16, 102E1
Islamic conf boycotted 1-27—1-29, 67C2
Sovts renew arms commitmt 1-27—1-29, 140D3
Emb in Paris bombed; US, Israel blamed 1-29, 89C3
Israel blamed for antigovt riots 3-17, 213A1
Anti-Sadat front backed 4-2, 273C3
PLO gunman dies in Israel raid 4-7, 260E2
Arab hardliners meet; joint cmnd set, Syria to head 4-14—4-15, 284E2
Egypt-Israel role in US Iran hostage rescue try chrgd 4-25, 297B2
UK Emb captors free natl 5-4, 337F1
Medit pollutn pact signed 5-17, 381D3
Ex-Premr Bitar slain in Paris 7-21, 567C2
Iraq ousts diplomats 8-18, Iraq amb expelled 8-23, 652F2-A3
Israel downs jet over Leb 8-24, 643E1
Libya proposes merger 9-1, Assad OKs 9-2, 660C3
Libya merger talks 9-8—9-9; unity OKd 9-10, Arab backing sought 9-10, 697C1-C2
Begin: unrest prompts Libya unity 9-9, 697D2
Map of Libya merger 9-10, 697A1
Sovt friendship pact signed 10-8, 759D2
Iraq cuts ties 10-10, 774C2
Exiled Iraqi dissidents vow Hussein ouster 11-13, 895B1
Troops mass on Jordan border 11-26; Jordan aid to Moslem Bro'hood chrgd, Hussein defies 11-29, 11-30, 911A2
Israel warns interventn in Jordan feud 11-26, 911E3
Saudis mediate 11-30; Jordan rejects terms for troop exit 12-3, 911F2-A3
Jordan seeks Westn arms speedup 12-1, 911B3
Sovt friendship pact implemented 12-2, 911F3
Assad to attend Jordan feud talks 12-5, border troops withdraw 12-10—12-11, 931F2
Sovt '79 arms sales rptd 12-10, 933A3
Libya merger delayed 12-16—12-18, 978B2
Iraq halts pipeline deliveries 12-19, 978A2
Government & Politics—*See also other appropriate subheads in this section*
Govt leadership purged 1-6, 22D2
New Cabt formed 1-16, 102G1
Human rights record scored 12-10, 978B3
Assad ally slain 12-27; front group claim credit 12-28, 996G2-A3
Iran-Iraq War
Iran plane damage blocks Iraq pipeline 9-27, 735E1
Turkey rptdly bars airlifts to Iran 10-6, 10-8, 774E2
Iraq blamed for Iran war; Syrian, Libyan troops join Iranians 10-7, 757B2
Iraq cuts ties re aid to Iran 10-10, denies aid 10-11, 774C2, D2
Egypt chrgs Arab world split 11-1, 859B3
Hussein scores Iran backing 11-27, 911G1
Lebanon—*See LEBANON*
UN Policy & Developments
UN envoy quits, to form exile group 12-27-79 22F2
Anti-Sovt Afghan res abstentn 1-14, 25F2; res opposed 2-14, 123E3
Daoudy on comm to probe shah 2-17, 122C1
Cncl warned Israel plans attack 2-23, 140B3
World Ct demands Iran free US hostages 5-24, 393B1
Women's conf racism motion withdrawn 7-28, 587G2
Israel ouster sought 9-30, 736B2
Unrest
Moslem Brotherhood claims wide support 213A1
Troops quell anti-govt riots 3-4—3-5, 212D3-213A1
8 in Moslem Brotherhood slain 6-20, 526C1
Assad escapes death try 6-26; Moslem Brotherhood linked, curbs set 7-2, 7-3, 525F3-526B1
Moslem Brotherhood amnesty extended 8-7; mil chief slain 8-16, 673D3
Moslem Brotherhood raided, 45 killed 8-29, 9-3; 900 amnesty takers rptd 9-3, 673G3-674A1
U.S. Relations
US blamed for Paris emb bombing 1-29, 89D3
US issues rights rpt 2-5, 87E2
US blamed for antigovt riots 3-10, 3-16, 3-17, 212F3-213A1
Iran hostage rescue missn scored 4-25, 297A2
SYSTEMS Engineering Laboratories Inc.
Gould merger set 9-8, 746A1
SZALAI, Gyorgy
Wins Olympic medal 7-29, 624G2
SZCZEPANSKI, Maciej
Purged by CP Central Com 10-6, 760D2
SZCZERBA, Kazimierz
Wins Olympic medal 8-2, 622G1
SZOMBATHELYI, Tamas
Wins Olympic medal 7-24, 623E1
SZWARC, Jeannot
Somewhere in Time released 10-3, 836F3
SZYDLAK, Jan
Ousted 8-24, 641F1

T

1976

TABOR & CO.
Delta grain inspector pleads guilty 3-5, 247A3
TACHIKAWA, Tsuneo
Arrested 7-2, 497D2
Trial delayed 9-30, 838D3
TACK, Juan Antonio
Quits govt, replaced 4-1, 291A2
TACONELLI, Dominic
Paris paper links to CIA 1-13, 49F3
TADZHIK Soviet Socialist Republic—*See 'Republics' under USSR*
TAFT Jr., Mayor James L. (Cranston, R.I.)
Wins primary for gov 9-14, 705A1
Loses gov electn 11-2, 820B3, 821D3
TAFT Jr., Sen. Robert A. (R, Ohio)
Campaigns for Ford 6-7, 410D3
Unopposed in primary 6-8, 409D3
AMA donatn rptd 10-22, 938E3
Loses reelection 11-2, 817E1, 819F3, 823E3
TAFT, William Howard (1857-1930)
Ford vote loss precedent cited 322F2
TAGAFA, Seiichi
In new party 6-25, 497B3
TAGGERES, Peter J.
Admits potato futures default 5-27, 398A1 ★
Potato futures default penalty set 8-31, ct delays setlmt 9-27, 990E1
TAHER, Lt. Col. Mohammad Abu
Sentenced to death 7-17, 543B2
TAIANA, Jorge
Rights revoked, arrest ordrd 6-23, 520C1
TAITTINGER, Pierre-Christian
French state secy 1-12, 49D2
Bars jt Eur defns 11-30, 905A3
TAIWAN—*See CHINA, Republic of*
TAKADA, Yuji
Wins Olympic medal 7-31, 576C3
TAKE Me Back (recording)
Wins Grammy 2-28, 460C3
TAKE the 'A' Train (recording)
Wins Hall of Fame award 2-28, 460E3
TAKLA, Philippe
Leb Cabt shift 9-15, 682B3
TAKUR, Chandra
Occidental chrgs dismissed 11-16, 930D1
TALABANI, Jelal
Kurds vow new drive 3-24, 547A3
TALAMANTE, Olga
Freed, deported 3-27, 236F3
TALAMANTEZ, Luis
Acquitted 8-12, 656B1
TALCOTT, Rep. Burt L. (R, Calif.)
On environmt target list 3-25, 219G3
Loses reelectn 11-2, 824G3
TALIJ, Marian
Wins Olympic medal 7-29, 574G3
TALLADEGA (Ala.) College
Herman Long dies 8-8, 816F3
TALLAHASSEE, Fla.—*See FLORIDA*
TALMADGE, Sen. Herman E. (D, Ga.)
Visits Carter 7-24, 551F1
Com ends Scott probe 9-15, 980B1
Carter meets cong ldrs 11-17, 864E1
TALUKDAR, Momin
Arrested 11-29, 923E2
TALVARD, Bernard
Wins Olympic medal 7-21, 574E2
TAMPA, Fla.—*See FLORIDA*

1977

T-80 (USSR tank)—*See ARMAMENTS—Tanks*
TABAN, Steven
Named in slaying of 2 Amers 9-2, 709C3
TABLES—*See under ILLUSTRATIONS*
TACKLYN, Larry
Death sentence confirmed 5-2, 374D2
Executn stay fails, riots erupt 12-1—12-3, hanged 12-2, 935G2
TACOMA, Wash.—*See WASHINGTON*
TAFT Jr., Robert A.
'76 spec interest gifts rptd 2-15, 128D2
TAGAMET (cimetidine)—*See MEDICINE—Drugs*
TAITTINGER, Pierre-Christain
Wins Sen seat 9-25, replaced in Cabt 9-26, 744F2
TAIWAN—*See CHINA, Republic of*
TAKADA, Kenzo—*See KENZO*
TAL, Schlomo
Dealer's body found 9-28, 871B3
TALBOT, Jean-Guy
Named Rangers coach 8-22, 1021F1
TALIADOUROS, Anathassios
Named Greek agri min 11-28, 925B2
TALLIS, Cedric
Paul resigns as Yankee pres 12-1, 990D2
TALMADGE, Sen. Herman E. (D, Ga.)
Bell confrmatn hearings 1-11—1-18, 34C2
'76 spec interest gifts rptd 1-15, 128G3, 129E1; 3-7, 232F2
Sen OKs govt regulatn plan 2-4, 91G1
Health care probe curb chrgd 3-17, 235E3
TAMBO, Oliver
Sees Podgorny 3-28, 247G3; in Angola 3-29, 249D3
At front-line mtg 4-17—4-18, 296D3
TAMIR, Gen. Avraham
At Cairo conf 12-14—12-15, 953G1
TAMIR, Shmuel
Israeli justice min 10-24, 827A2
TAMM, Judge Edward A.
FCC obscenity order voided 3-16, 215F3
TAMPA Bay, Fla.—*See FLORIDA*
TAMURA, Hajime
Resigns 10-4, 756D3
TAN, Hassan
Moluccan mediatn fails 6-9, 468G1
TANAKA, Kakuei
Lockheed bribe trial opens 1-27, 83B2
Japan affirms Kurile claim 4-13, 319E2
TANAKA, Tatsuo
On EC ball-bearing fines 2-8, 109A2
TANANA, Frank
AL pitching ldr 10-2, 927A1
TANASE, Virgil
Ouster rptd 1-14, 100A2

1978

TABALAZA, Lungile
Dies 7-10, probe set 7-11, 535F3; police transferred 7-21, 633E2
Police cleared in death 10-3, 820E1
TABAT, Lou
Spinks decisns Ali 2-15, 171C1
TABLACK, George
Loses Ohio Cong primary 6-6, 448D1
TABLES—*See ILLUSTRATIONS—Charts, Graphs & Tables*
TACOMA, Wash.—*See WASHINGTON*
TACOMA, Marilyn
PBB suit dismissed 10-27, 834E1
TACOMA, Roy M.
PBB suit dismissed 10-27, 834E1
TACOMRON Vibonchai
Canto decisns 11-20, 969G1
TAFT-Hartley Act
Carter invokes 3-6, 159A2; **for subsequent developments, see COAL—Strike**
TAHITI—*See FRENCH Polynesia*
TAHKAMAA, Taisto
Denies USSR mil link proposed 11-15, 894C2
TAIWAN—*See CHINA, Republic of*
TAKADA, Kenzo—*See KENZO*
TAKAIWA, Tan
Message From Space released 11-17, 970B2
TAKASHINA, Takehiko
To head Joint Staff Cncl 7-25, 574F2
TAKAZAUCKAS, Albert
Piano Bar opens 6-8, 887E2
TAL, Schlomo
Convicted of murder 10-6, 824D2
TALAAT, Samih
Ousted as Egypt justice mine 5-7, 392G2
TALBOT, Jean-Guy
Replaced as Rangers coach 6-1, 458B3
TALCOTT National Corp.
Gulf + Western plans purchases, '77 loss cited 5-7, 404E1
TALIDOUROS, Athanasios
Resigns as Greek agri min 5-10, 373E3
TALLADEGA (Ala.) College
Wright paroled 6-1, 560D2
TALLMAN, Lt. Gen. Kenneth L.
Woodward dismissal rptd 4-21, 420C1
Rpts AF Acad 40% drop-out rate 11-20, 916G3-917B1
TALLMAN, William C.
Sees NH A-plant shutdown 12-8, 1009A3
TALLY, Ted
Hooters opens 4-30, 760D2
TALMADGE, Betty
Loses Ga cong primary 8-8, 625C3
Sen panel chrgs ex-husband 12-19, 981E3
TALMADGE, Sen. Herman E. (D, Ga.)
Canal pact vote sought 3-9; gets farm bill backing 3-13, OKs pact 3-16, 177E1, E2, A3
Sen votes farm aid 3-21, 218A3, F3
Votes for 2d Canal pact 4-18, 273B1
Personal finances rptd 5-19, admits small cash gifts 5-21, 385D3, E3
Says Gartner cleared by ethics com 6-28, 513D3
Ex-wife loses primary 8-8, 625C3
Repays expense claims 8-18, denies guilt 8-18, 8-19; probe to continue 8-21, 643G3
Testifies to grand jury re finances 11-8; Sen panel chrgs rules violatns, hearing set 12-19, 981C3
TAM, Rey
Arguello TKOs 4-29, 379D2
TAMMI, Tom
Moliere opens 3-12, 887B2
TAN, Mete
Named Turkey pub health min 1-5, 21E2
TANADA, Lorenzo
Arrested 4-9, release barred 4-11, 268D3
Oppositn ldrs freed 6-3, 455B1

1979

TABANERO Perez, Pedro
Killed 8-14, 670F2
TABATABAI, Sadeq
On US arms deals 8-10, 634E3
TABIA, Ieremia (Kiribati president)
Kiribati president 7-12, 526C1
TABLES—*See ILLUSTRATIONS—Charts, Graphs & Tables*
TABLE Settings (play)
Opens 3-23, 712G2
TABLE Tennis
World championship results 4-30, 527E1
TACOMA, Roy
Velsicol settles PBB contaminatn suit 10-23, 808B3
TADZHIK Soviet Socialist Republic—*See USSR—Republics*
TAGAMET (cimetidine)—*See MEDICINE—Drugs*
TAGGART, David
Good Lads opens 3-27, 711E3
TAGHI, Col. Mohammed
Executed 4-20, 297C3
TAHER, Abdul Hadi
ENI payoffs to Petromin denied 12-5, 995D3
TAHERI, Capt. Monir
Executed 2-23, 144B3
TAIT, Don
N Amer Irregulars released 4-12, 528B3
Apple Dumpling sequel released 8-31, 819E3
TAIWAN—*See CHINA, Republic of*
TAIWAN, American Institute in
Taiwan sets counterpart 2-15, 146F1
US-Taiwan ties bill signed 4-10, 259A3
Cross named head 4-21, 299E2
TAJ, Abbas
Named Iran energy min 2-19, 125D1
TAKE It From The Top (play)
Opens 1-19, 292C3
TAKEN in Marriage (play)
Opens 2-26, 292D3
TAKESHIMA, Masuo
Protests Sovt Kurile buildup 2-5, 85A3
TAKESHITA, Noboru
Japan finance min 11-8, 874G2
In US talks on Iran 12-17—12-18, 959C1
TALBERT, Ray
Indiana wins NIT, named co-MVP 3-21, 238G3
TALBOYS, Brian E.
At ANZUS conf, backs Viet Cambodia exit 7-4—7-5, 495F2
TALCOTT National Corp.
Sindona indicted, financial troubles cited 3-19, 205D2, F2
TALEGHANI, Ayatollah Mahmoud
Seeks end to Kurdish revolt 3-20, 199C1
Kurds' autonomy set 3-25, 228E3
Sons arrested, quits politics 4-12; Khomeini rule protested 4-14—4-17, 277C1
Backs Khomeini, komitehs 4-18—4-19, 297B2
Motahari slain 5-1, 321A2
Vs clergy in govt, bars pres race 6-2, 425E3
Chrgs USSR aids Kurds 8-31, 670C1
Dies 9-10, 687G3-688C1
TALFAH, Adnan Khirallah
Iraqi vice premr 7-16, 544F3
TALLAHASSEE, Fla.—*See FLORIDA*
TALLEY, Salley
Talley's Folley opens 5-3, 712G2
TALLEY'S Folley (play)
Opens 5-3, 712G2
TALMADGE, Sen. Herman E. (D, Ga.)
Hospitalized for alcoholism 1-22, 176E1
Agriculture Com chrmn 1-23, 71C2
Vs proposed Natural Resources Dept 3-1, 164D1
Hosp cost measure cited 3-5, 163B3
Financial disclosure delay rptd 5-18, 383F2
Fortson dies 5-19, 432E2
Financial disclosure statement studied 9-1, 701E3
Senate com votes to denounce 9-14, 702B1
Sen denounces 10-10, 769B1
Minchew sentenced 10-10, 769A2
TAMIR, Shmuel
Denies torture chrgs vs Israel 2-7—2-8, 108A2
Palestinian talks open 5-25, 394A3
TAMOXIFEN—*See MEDICINE—Drugs*
TAN, Chu Van
Arrested 8-2, 604E1

1980

TABAK, Jiri
Wins Olympic medal 7-25, 622F3
TABARLY, Eric
Sets Atlantic sailing record 8-1, 907A1
TABATABAI, Ali Akbar
Slain in US 7-22, 2 suspects seized 7-23, 545B1, B2
DC protesters arrested 7-27, 586G1
3d suspect flees US 8-6, 671D3
Fardust secret visit to US rptd 8-14, 671E3
TABB, Ron
3d in Boston Marathon 4-21, 527B2
TABEYEV, Fikryat
Sovt soldier leaves US Emb in Kabul 9-21, 727B2
TABLES—*See ILLUSTRATIONS—Charts, Graphs & Tables*
TABORI, Kristoffer
Trouble with Europe opens 1-28, 136F3
TACCHELLA, Jean-Charles
Soupcon released 3-26, 416E3
TACKABERRY, Lt. Gen. Thomas H.
To review Pearce desertn sentence 1-30, 94F3
Overturns Pearce desertn sentence 2-28, 189E1
TACOMA—*See WASHINGTON (state)*
TACONITE
Minn plant ends Lake Superior dumping 3-16, 227B1
TADCO Enterprises
Jamaica names in grain fraud suit 2-4, 99C2
TAGUE v. Louisiana
Case decided by Sup Ct 1-21, 93C3
TAHA, Riad
Slain 7-23, 579F2
TAHER, Abdul Hadi
Rpts Aramco takeover completed, retains bd seat 9-4, 662A1, A2
TAHITI
Chile pres cancels Asian tour 3-22, 231A1
TAHITIAN Women Under the Palms (painting)
Sold for record sum 5-12, 472D1
TAHOE, Lake
Taylor killed 11-13, 1002A2
TAIL Gunner Joe (TV film)
Libel case refused by Sup Ct 12-1, 918E2
TAILLIBERT, Roger
Blamed for role in Olympic debt 6-5, 444E1
TAIT, Don
Herbie Goes Bananas released 9-12, 836B3
TAIWAN—*See CHINA, Republic of,*
TAIWAN, American Chamber of Commerce in
Taiwan-China eased ties rptd 4-9, 295E2
TAIWAN, American Institute in
Reagan backs US-Taiwan ties; triggers China rift 8-16—8-26, 645G2, 646G1
TAKALO, Helena
Wins Olympic medal 2-18, 155C3
TAKESHITA, Noburu
Warns on mil spending 3-22, 219A3
TAKE Your Time (Do It Right) (recording)
On best-seller list 7-9, 568E3; 8-13, 640B3
TALBOYS, Brian E.
USSR expels envoy 1-29, 119D1
Muldoon overcomes party challenge 10-23, 830B3
TALEB Ibrahimi, Ahmed
Named Algeria educ min 1-13, 55F3
TALESE, Gay
Thy Neighbor's Wife on best-seller list 6-8, 448C3; 7-13, 568B3; 8-17, 640F3
TALLAHASSEE—*See FLORIDA*
TALLEY'S Folly (play)
Wilson wins Pulitzer 4-14, 296C2, E2
Beatty wins Tony 6-8, 692C3
TALLY, Ted
Coming Attractions opens 12-3, 1003A3
TALMADGE, Sen. Herman E. (D, Ga.)
Justice drops finances probe 5-30, 427E3-428A1
In Ga primary 8-5, wins runoff 8-26, 683B2
Loses reelectn 11-4, 845A2, 849F2
TALMAN Federal Savings and Loan v. Carroll
Case declined by Sup Ct 3-17, 226G1
TALMON, Jacob L.
Dies 6-16, 528F3
TAMAYO Mendez, Arnaldo
In Soyuz space trip 9-18—9-26, 737D2
TAMBORRINO, Gen. Antonio
Sees 10,000 quake deaths 11-27, 943B3
TAMIMI, Sheik Raja Bayud
Israel deports 5-3; W Bank protests; US, UN scores 5-3—5-8; Arafat visits 5-7, 340B2, D3
W Bank return barred 5-11, 362D2
UN censures Israel, Israel ct ordrs explanatn 5-20, 381C1
Israel ct backs ouster 8-19, 627B3
TAMIR, Shmuel
Vs Carter explanatn of US UN vote 3-4, 163D3
In Palestine autonomy talks, calls Jerusalem capital 7-13—7-15, 538G3-539B1
Quits as justice min 7-31, 653E3
TAMM, Felix
Sees recession 4-30, 329F2
TAMM, Yuri
Wins Olympic medal 7-31, 624D1
TAMPA—*See FLORIDA*
TAMPA Bay
Bridge collapse kills 35 5-9, 391C1

1976

TANAKA, Kakuei
Miki OKs China treaty 1-13, 30A1
Lockheed payoffs probed 2-5—2-17, 131C3-132E1
Denies payoff rumors, '72 Nixon deal 4-2, 286B2
Seeks Miki ouster 5-13, 458G1
Arrested 7-27, quits LDP 7-28, 557D1
Chauffeur quizzed 7-31, 8-1, found dead 8-2, 624F2
Secy indicted 8-9, 624A2
Indicted 8-16, out on bail 8-17, 624G1
Ex-aide Hashimoto arrested 8-21, 628F2
Ono visits 8-24; quits broadcast post 9-4, 838E3
Parlt com vs testifying 8-26, 677B1
TANAKA, Tatsuo
Japan intl trade min 12-24, 1006B3
TANANA, Frank
AL pitching ldr 10-4, 796D1
TANASSI, Mario
Named in Lockheed scandal 2-12, 132B2
Social Dems oust 3-12—3-16, 254A2
Lockheed probe rptd 4-2, 298E1
TANDY Corp.
Hinshaw convicted 1-26, 95F3
TANKS—*See under ARMAMENTS*
TANNER, Henry
Wounded in Beirut 5-16, 355A1
TANNER, Roscoe
Loses Birmingham tourn 1-25, 123G2
Wimbledon results 6-29, 504F1
2d in Tennis Week Open 8-29, 716G1
TANNIAN, Philip G.
Dismissed 9-28, 776C2
TAN Sam Oi, Capt.
Rpts executions 5-7, 350C1
TANZANIA—*See also AFRICAN Development Bank, COMMONWEALTH of Nations, NONALIGNED Nations Movement, OAU*
US delays dvpt aid 1-9, 2B1
Nyerere in India; scores Ford Angola letter, backs USSR, Cuba role 1-18, 36C1
Listed as 'not free' nation 1-19, 20E3
Tanzam RR backlog rptd 1-30, 78A1
Mozambique mtg on Rhodesia rptd 3-4, 175G1
Total IMF oil loan rptd 4-1, 340E2
Kissinger in talks 4-25—4-26, 295C1; 5-5, 318C3
S Africa guerrilla training rptd 4-26, 428G3
Kissinger statemt, reactn 4-27, 293C2, 294D2
IBRD suspends EAC loans 5-11, 371F3
400 tribal feuders freed 5-14, 543E3
Sudan mercenary role chrgd 7-6, 501E3
Quits Summer Olympics 7-9, 528G2
China turns over Tanzam RR 7-14, 560A1
East African union threatened 8-4—12-16, Nyerere scores Kenya 12-7, 974E2-B3
Students protest Uganda massacre 8-9, 874G1
Schaufele sees Nyerere 9-8, 681F1
Kissinger arrives 9-14, sees Nyerere 9-15, 681A1
Nyerere sees Kissinger 9-21, 717G2; Schaufele, Rowlands 10-2, 738D3
Zanzibaris appeal convictns 10-18, 1013C3
S Africa rebel training offer rptd 11-24, 927F1

Rhodesian Relations—*See 'African Relations' under RHODESIA*
UN Policy & Developments
Cncl member 62F2; 720C1
US retaliates for Assemb vote 1-9, 2B1
OKs Cncl pro-Palestine resolutn 1-26, 59G2
UNESCO literacy drive fails 2-4, 85C2
OKs Israel Arab land exit 6-29, 464C1
Res vs Israel Uganda raid withdrawn 7-14, 515F3
Shuns vote on anti-terror 7-14, 515G3
S Africa arms ban vetoed 10-19, 781D3, F3

1977

TANASSI, Mario
Indicted 1-29, 116B3
Claims innocence 3-8, trial set 3-10, 284B1
TANKS—*See under ARMAMENTS*
TANNENWALD Jr., Judge Theodore
Park diary rptd sought by IRS 11-29, 915B3
TANNER, Roscoe
Wins Australian Open 1-9, 103D3

TANZANIA—*See also COMMONWEALTH of Nations, EAST African Community, NONALIGNED Nations Movement, OAU*
Tanganyika, Zanzibar parties merge 1-5; Nyerere elected head 1-21, 102B3
2 mins, comrs quit re police brutality 1-23, 161C2
Cabt shuffled 2-13, 161A2, E2
Amnesty Intl lists lawmakers held 9-5, 753C2
Ex-intelligence officer sentncd 10-5, 806A1

Foreign Relations (misc.)
UN Assemb member 4C1
Sweden budgets aid 1-10, 23B1
IMF OKs SDP purchase 1-26, 102B3
Young visits 2-3—2-6, 105C1
IMF OKs trust fund loan 2-4, 87F2
African ldrs celebrate party merger 2-4—2-5, 105C1
Kenya border closed 2-4; US tourists, workers airlifted 2-6—2-11, 106C1
Black Africa funds asked 3-3—3-5, 170A2
Castro visits 3-17—3-21, 249F1, F2
Podgorny visits, loan announced 3-23—3-26, 247G2, B3
Sovt, China, US aid estimates cited 247D3
Young vs US 'cold war' policy 4-11, 271D3
Kenya border shut permanently 4-18, 392E3
Lutheran World Fed meets 6-24, 732E1
Horn of Africa alliances shift 7-6, 588F1
Nyerere sees Canada, US offcls 8-2—8-13; in Jamaica 8-11—8-12, 623F3
US bars arms aid authorizatn 8-4, 668B1
Protest halts de Guiringaud visit 8-18, Nyerere chrgs racism 8-20, 662E2
Namibia plan implementatn readied 8-19, 699F3
Kenya natls ousted 10-5, air links cut 11-1, 913E1
Sweden cancels debts 10-12, 904A1
Cuba advisers rptd 11-17, 896G1
Namibia contact group tours 11-21—12-7, 1016E3

Rhodesian Relations—*See RHODESIA*
Uganda Relations
Anti-Amin plot chrgd 2-16, 138E3
Uganda refugees detail purge 2-23, 141G2
Uganda claims invasn threat 2-24, 141D2
Amin chrgs aggressn 3-8, 170D2
Uganda chrgs plot 5-3; invaders pardoned, given asylum 5-11, 429A2
Uganda rpts Amin, rebels meet 6-8, 487A1
Amin repudiates EAC debts 10-9, 805B2

TAPAJOS, Renato
Arrested 7-27, 633C2

1978

TANAKA, Kakuei
Supports Ohira vs Fukuda 11-27, 912B3
Accused of vote fraud 12-6, 945A3
Backers in Ohira Cabt 12-7, 945E2
TANA River (Kenya)
Kenya dam contracts rptd 4-9, 479D1
TANDY, Charles D.
Dies 11-4, 972F3
TANDY, Jessica
Wins Tony 6-4, 579G2
TANDY Corp.
Charles Tandy dies 11-4, 972F3
TANGANYIKA—*See TANZANIA*
TANGERINE Bowl—*See FOOTBALL—Collegiate*
TANKS—*See under ARMAMENTS*
TANNER, Roscoe
Connors wins Grand Prix Masters 1-8, 22B3
Loses US Pro Indoor 1-29, 418G3
Wins Amer Airlines Games 2-19, 419A1
US wins World Cup 3-9—3-12, 252D1

TANZANIA (formerly Tanganyika and Zanzibar)—*See also COMMONWEALTH of Nations, GATT, NONALIGNED Nations Movement, OAU*
Gen amnesty announced 2-6, '77 rpt on pol detainees cited 169E3
Hominid tracks rptd 3-4, 334A2
Students protest govt pay hikes 3-5; Nyerere's son, others rptd expelled 3-7, 169F3
Cholera epidemic eases; emergency measures, death toll rptd 3-24, 270B1
3 get commuted sentncs re '72 Zanzibar assassinatn 3-31, 251B1
Babu, others freed 4-26, 479D2
Locust threat seen 6-6, 465E2
Foreign Relations (misc.) *See also 'Uganda Dispute' below*
Cambodia visit ended by amb 1-21, 43D2
Uganda seeks improved Kenya ties 2-8, 3-8—3-10, 289D2
Namibia rebel imprisonmt cited 113E3
Zambia hit by port backlog 3-8, 170A1
Kenya closes border 3-22, Somalia bans food imports 3-24, 270E1
Westn indep plan for Namibia backed 3-26, 248G2
Zambia port backlog rptd eased 3-30, 333G2
Shipanga freed 5-25, 475G3
Lonrho ousted re Rhodesia 6-2, 479B2
E Africa locust plague aid asked 6-6, 465C2
Nyerere scores pan-Africa force, US role; defends Cuba, USSR presence in Africa 6-8, 441G2
Namibia rebels OK talks 6-11, 475D3
Angola contact plan lauded 6-25, 487D3
Zambia aid re RR set 6-29, 617G1
Lonrho '67 compensatn set 7-3; natlzatn talks begin 7-25, 635G1
Dutch cancel debts 7-10, 575E1
Westn indep plan for Namibia OKd 7-12, 547F2
UK cancels debts 7-31, 592E1
Lonrho compensatn talks fail, holdings seized 9-16; Rhodesia govt support chrgd 9-26, 905D2
UN Assemb member 713F3
Zambia-Rhodesia rail link opposed 10-7, reopened 10-10, 783F2, C3, E3
Polisario recognized 11-10, 999G2
Rhodesian Relations—*See RHODESIA*
Ugandan Dispute
Uganda rpts invasn 10-12, Nyerere calls 'lies' 10-14, 822F3
Uganda rptdly invades, annexes territory 10-30—11-2, 830G2
Nyerere vows to expel Ugandans 11-2, 860A1
Ugandans consolidate Kagera salient holdings, destroy Taka bridge 11-3; map 860C1
Libya, Kenya offer mediatn 11-5; OAU sees Amin 11-6, 860A2
Amin offers Kagera exit terms 11-8; Nyerere rejcts, bars OAU mediatn 11-9, 870C2
Tanzania mounts counteroffensive 11-10—11-11, refugees flee Ugandan atrocities 11-15, 870D2
Amin rpts troop exit order, forgn pressure cited; Tanzania denies 11-14, 870A2
Tanzania attack rptdly aids Amin domestic popularity 11-15, 870B2
Uganda troop exit confrmd 11-15, westn press tour 11-21, 911D3
Tanzanian counterattack rptd 11-23—11-27, 911B3
U.S. Relations
Angola contact plan lauded 6-25, 487D3
US bars econ aid authorzn 9-26, 734G1
US corn gift rptd 11-15, 870G2
McDonnell Douglas paymts rptd 12-15, 982F2
TAO Chu (d. 1969)
Poster lauds 11-23, 949G1
Rehabilitatn rptd 12-10, 950D1
Rites held 12-24, 1015A2

1979

TANAKA, Kakuei
Lockheed guilty in payoff, fined 6-1, 422G2, D3
TANAKA, Kinuyo
My Love released 1-4, 174B3
TANAKA, Zeizo
Climbs Annapurna 5-8, 392G2
TANASSI, Mario
Convicted 3-1, 155B2
TANDELL, Ron
Tunnel Fever opens 5-10, 712B3
TANDEM Productions
FCC 'family hour' power backed 11-20, 1007C1
TANDY, Spencer
Peter Pan opens 9-6, 956G3
TANGANYIKA—*See TANZANIA*
TANKER Advisory Center Inc.
'74-78, 1st 1/4 '79 oil spill data; tanker safety records rptd 8-15, 608A1
TANKS—*See under ARMAMENTS*
TANNER, Chuck
In World Series 10-10—10-17, 816C1
TANNER, Roscoe
Wins Volvo Tennis 2-18, Volvo Classic 3-17; loses N Orleans Grand Prix 3-25, 391G2, A3
Loses Wimbledon 7-7, 569C3
Loses Assn of Tennis Pros 8-27; US Open results 9-9, 734D1, E2
TANNER, Tony
Class Enemy opens 6-18, 711C2

TANZANIA (formerly Tanganyika and Zanzibar)—*See also COMMONWEALTH of Nations, GATT, OAU*
New hominid species claimed 1-18, 137G3
Hominid footprints rptd 3-21, 691B2
Bus accident kills 60 7-14, 639A2

Foreign Relations (misc.)—*See also 'UN' below*
Grenada coup 3-13, 190C3
Pan-Africanist Cong UN rep killed 6-12, 476G3
Uganda ex-pres freed 7-8, 637G2
Zambia rail, road links cut by Zimbabwe 10-12, 11-18,-11-19, 899D2

Ugandan Dispute—*See UGANDA—Tanzanian-Rebel Conflict*
UN Policy & Developments
Membership listed 695A3
Salim elected Assemb pres 9-18, 695A2

U.S. Relations
Peace Corps return OKd 1-9, 22F3
US issues rights rpt 2-10, 107F2
Young delegatn visits 9-18, 720A3, 721D1
Zimbabwe Rhodesian Relations—*See ZIMBABWE*

1980

TANAKA, Kakuei
Party factn in Cabt 7-17, 539A3
TANAKA, Rokusuke
Japan forgn trade min 7-17, 539B3
TANDY Corp.
Roach named pres 10-23, 959B3
TANENBAUM, Rabbi Marc
Denounces Baptist ldr's prayer remark 9-18, 811C1
TV evangelist reverses Jewish prayer stance 10-11, 811G1
TANKS—*See ARMAMENTS—Tanks*
TANNEN, Michael
One-Trick Pony released 10-3, 836D3
TANNER, Chuck
NL wins All-Star Game 7-8, 636D2
TANNER, Roscoe
Loses Richmond Classic 2-3, 607F2
Loses US Open quarterfinals 9-3, 691B2
TANZ, Mark M.
Inside Moves released 12-19, 1003A2

TANZANIA (formerly Tanganyika and Zanzibar)—*See also COMMONWEALTH of Nations, GATT, NONALIGNED Nations, OAU*
Zanzibar parlt elected 1-7, 40F1
Nyerere, Jumbe reelected 10-26; Cabt named 11-7, 888C1
Illiteracy study rptd 12-4, 953A3

Foreign Relations (misc.)
Ex-EAC leaders meet 1-2, 90E1
At regional econ unity mtg 4-1, 243D1, E1
Tito funeral held 5-8, 339B1
Uganda coup launched 5-11, 375F1-B2
Obote returns to Uganda 5-27, 446E1
Amin scores Nyerere 6-3, 446E2
China pledges Tanzam RR aid 9-2, 731B2
Salim replaced as UN Assemb pres 9-16, 736E1
PLO role at World Bank-IMF mtg vowed 9-19, 719F3
Jamal addresses World Bank-IMF mtg 9-30, 671D1
Uganda invaders ousted 10-15, 832F3
UN Namibia talks schedule agreed 11-24, 967B2
UNESCO illiteracy study rptd 12-4, 953A3
Sports
Moscow Olympic results 7-20—8-3, 588C3, 624D1, E1

U.S. Relations
Ali rebuffed 2-3, 85C1

1976

TAPIA, Col. Julio
Chile U purge rptd 1-8, 47A3
TAP Portuguese Airways (Transportes Aereos Portugueses)
Mozambique air links suspended 1-14, 52D1
TARDIF, Guy
Named munic affairs min 11-26, 903A3
TARKENTON, Fran
Named NFL MVP 1-13, 31A3
TARNOPOL, Nat
Sentenced 4-12, 316B3
TARQUINI, Jose Miguel
Assassinated 2-5, 212A2
TARSHISH (Israeli warship)
In Intl Naval Review 7-4, 488C3
TASMANIA—*See AUSTRALIA*
TATE, Allen
Gets Arts Inst award 5-19, 504D3
TATE, John
Wins Olympic medal 7-31, 574D1
TATE, Willie
Acquitted 8-12, 656B1
TATE & Lyle Ltd.
2 Iranians ousted in deal, firm denies chrg 2-10, 156D3
TAUBER, Ulrike
Wins Olympic medals 7-19, 7-24, 575A3, C3
TAUB Hummel & Schnall Inc.
Arab boycott rpts released 10-18, 10-19, 786A1, D1 ★
TAUFER, Lutz
Trial opens 5-6, 503E1
TAVERAS, Frank
NL batting ldr 10-4, 796A1
TAVGAR, Ben-Zion
Chrgd re Hebron role 10-26, 895A2
TAVIANI, Paulo-Emilio
Rptd threatened 7-12, 539C1
TAVICH Seniwongse, Gen.
Thai defense min 4-23, vs US radar pullout 4-27, 315E1
TAWAB, Air Vice Marshal Mohammed Gholam
Resigns 5-1, Rahman rift seen 5-2, 332F1
TAWIL, Raymonda
Israel ends detention 12-10, 954F1
TAWIT Seniwong
Meets Praphas 8-18, 640E1
Resigns 8-25, 677B3
Replaced as defense min 10-4, 754E1
TAX Analysts & Advocates (Wash., D.C.)
US corp tax rate data rptd 10-14, 847C2

TAXES—*See also INTERNAL Revenue Service and SOCIAL Security under U.S. GOVERNMENT*
Ford plans estate-tax change 1-5, 3B3
Sup Ct to set disclosure requiremts 1-12, 24G1
Sup Ct bars IRS emergency procedure 1-13, 23D3
Sup Ct upholds non-fed taxes on imports 1-14, 23G2
'77 budget proposals 1-21; 62C3, 63C1-A2
Ford submits Soc Sec plan 2-9, 110C1
Ford proposes estate-tax chngs 3-5, 179G3
Cong Dems vs Ford proposals 3-10, 230F2, C3
House Budget Com proposals; US budget dir scores 3-23, 231G1, F2, A3
Tax cut, Mar real pay rise linked 4-21, 306D2
'69-74 tax avoidance rptd 5-5, 480A1
Ford vetoes pub works bill 7-6, 518B2
NJ income tax bill signed 7-8, 995A2
Sen com curbs loopholes 7-23, 586B2
Ford vetoes Md congressmen tax exemptn 8-3, 636B3
Sen OKs omnibus bill 8-6, 585F3
Cong clears omnibus bill 9-16, 705D2
Ford signs tax bill 10-4, 742C3
Fscl '75 state per capita burden rptd 10-12, 959D1
Jobless benefits revisn signed 10-20, 788E1
Local govt compensatn for fed land signed 10-20, 835F1
Colo vote amendmt defeated 11-2, 824F1
Sup Ct voids NY collectn case stay 11-9, 882A3
Sup Ct rejcts Pa homeowner bias case 11-29, 900G3

1977

TAP The Airline of Portugal
Madeira crash 11-19, 928G2
TARADELLAS, Josep
Catalan Socialists ask passport 6-21, 507C1
TARAS Shevchenko (Soviet trawler)
US seizes 4-9, 269G3
US fines 5-2, frees 5-5, 363B3
TARAZI, Salah el Dine
World Ct member 4G1
TARDIF, Marc
Quebec wins WHA title 5-27, 430C1
TARHIL, Nashaat
Hanged 1-6, 2E2
TARIF, Sheik Amin
Gets plea on Israeli shelling 9-5, 697G2
TARIFF Commission, U.S.—*See U.S. GOVERNMENT—TRADE Commission*
TARKANIAN, Jerry
Las Vegas U fires 9-9, reinstated 9-30, 870D2
TARKENTON, Francis (Fran)
Raiders win Super Bowl 1-9, 24E3
Sets passing accuracy mark, injures leg 11-13, 1019C3
Vikings win in playoffs 12-26, 1020A1
TARLETON, Donald
Lance testifies 9-15, 701D1
TARRADELLAS, Josep
Generalitat restored 9-29; returns to Spain 10-23, sworn hd 10-24, 843D1
TARVER, Jack W.
Named AP chrmn 1-18, 140E2
TASCHEREAU, Pierre
Rpts Air Canada loss 4-20, 372F3
TASIC, Gradimir
Sentenced 5-16, 497A3
TATE, Sharon (d. 1969)
Polanski indicted for rape 3-24, 262D1
Manson convictn review denied 4-25, 342G2
TATUM, Earl
Traded to Pacers 12-13, 991A1
TAUB, Joseph
Vet indicted in horse-switch scandal 12-2, 971C1
TAUBE, Henry
Gets Medal of Sci 11-22, 952B1
TAUBMAN, A. Alfred
Taubman group wins Irvine 5-20, 519E1
TAUBMAN-Allen-Irvine Inc.
Irvine purchase OKd 5-20, 519B1
TAVARES, Flavio
Uruguay arrests 7-14, rptd OK 7-30, 601F1
Uruguay detentn continues 9-6, 905C2
TAVERAS, Frank
NL batting ldr 10-2, 926D3
TAWENGWA, George
Land purchase rptd 5-22, 414C1

TAXES—*See also U.S. GOVERNMENT, heads INTERNAL Revenue Service and SOCIAL Security*
Budget receipts, $ tables 32A2, E2
Sup Ct backs Calif re Forest Svc 1-25, 80G2
Carter reform plan set 2-2, 75E1
Carter plans standard credit 2-10, 110E2
Welfare cost rptd 2-19, 176C1
Carter budget revisions 2-22, 124D3
Cong sets new '77 levels 3-3, 174A1
'75 data on rich rptd 3-3, 197G2
Carter call-in on reforms 3-5, 171D1, A3
Farmland fund proposal withdrawn 3-11, 195A1
Carter town mtg on revisns 3-16, 190D3
Giaimo proposes budget 3-23, 228D3
Moon denied NY property tax exemptn 4-14, 310D1
NY mail-order mins challenged 4-15, 310B2
Tex seeks Hughes inheritance taxes 4-15, 354E3
Inmate rights rpt issued 4-26, 383E2
'76 state-local revenue mark rptd 5-4, 388D1
Stimulus bill clears Cong 5-16, 381D3-382E1; Carter signs 5-23, 417F3
Cong sets '78 budget targets, revises '77 5-17, 404A3-405E1
'76 local revenue data 7-7, 540G1
State income tax rule for Cong signed 7-19, 592A2
Carter on reform legis 7-21, 575F1
Carter rebuts black criticism 7-25, 573G1
NY Nets move to NJ set 7-26, 584E2
Carter welfare plan 8-6, 608D2-609E1
Poll rpts top econ worries 8-10, 632C2
Fscl '76 state revenue rptd 9-2, 740D1
'70-76 property tax rise rptd 9-12, 722B1
Calif phone cos ordrd to pay refunds 9-13, 839A2
Panama Canal residents exempt 9-14, 699C2
Fscl '76 state per capita burden rptd, table 10-18, 821G1
Carter delays reform proposals; asks energy, Soc Sec actn 10-27, 813A1, B3-E3
NJ income tax electn issue cited 11-8, 855A2

1978

TAPE Recordings—*See subjects*
TAPESTRIES—*See PAINTING & Sculpture*
TARAKI, Nur Mohammad (Afghan president, premier)
Heads new Afghan govt 4-30, pledges neutrality 5-4, 317C1
Denies high coup toll, Sovt links; pledges Iran, Pak, US ties 5-6, 349C2
Mtgs with Sovt amb rptd 5-19, 391E1
Ousts 2 mins 7-10, 538A1 ★
Coup attempt smashed, takes defense post 8-17, 671F1
In Moscow 12-4, signs friendship pact 12-5, 943D2
TARDIF, Marc
Nordiques win WHA All-Star game, named game MVP 1-17, 76G3
WHA scoring, assist ldr 4-11, 296G2, A3
Named WHA MVP 7-6, 656C3
TARIFFS—*See FOREIGN Trade; country names*
TARKANIAN, Jerry
House subcom probe cited 1-11—1-13, 40B2
TARKENTON, Francis (Fran)
NFL '77 passing ldr 1-1, 56E2
Breaks NFL pass completn mark 12-3, 1024C1
TAROCZY, Balazs
Wins Ocean City Intl 2-26, 419A1
TAROM (Rumanian airline)
UK jet deal signed 6-15, 515A3
TARPON Springs, Fla.—*See FLORIDA*
TARRADELLAS, Josep
Barcelona cops jeer 8-30, 706C2
TARTAGLIONE, Giraloma
Killed 10-10, 817A1
TASMANIA—*See AUSTRALIA*
TASS (Soviet press agency)
US reviews rptrs status 6-30, 7-5, 518F2
US to study San Fran bur status 7-18, 575A3
TASTE of Honey, A (singing group)
Boogie Oogie Oogie on best-seller list 9-6, 708E1; 10-11, 800E3
TATE, Rear Adm. Jackson R. (ret.)
Dies 7-19, 620G3
TATE, S(tonewall) Shepherd
Installed ABA pres 8-9, 626C3
TATE, Sharon (d. 1969)
Van Houten sentncd 8-11, 824F2
TATUM, Earl
Traded to Celtics 7-19, 655G3
TATUM, Jack
Broncos win conf title 1-1, 8G3
Stingley paralyzed 8-12, 1023G3
TAUDSHOW (play)
Opens 3-24, 887D3
TAUKE, Tom
Wins US House seat 11-7, 850C4, 854D2
TAVARES, Flavio
Uruguay frees 'provisionally' 1-5, 136F3
TAVERAS, Frank
NL stolen base ldr 10-2, 928F2

TAXES—*See also U.S. GOVERNMENT, subheads INTERNAL Revenue Service and SOCIAL Security*
'67, '77 state sales taxes rptd 1-5, 15A3
Marrieds tax law case refused 1-9, 13A2
Football TV contract value backed 1-9, 13B2
State collectns up, table 1-9, 84B2, F2
HEW proposes cigaret tax hike 1-11, 23D2
Carter budget proposals 1-23, 44G2, F3, 46E3, 47A2; table 45C2
Federal budget dollar table 63A1
Sen Banking Com rpt vs future NYC aid 2-9, 86G3
Calif, Tex dispute Hughes domicile 2-13, 3-29, 459C1
Multistate Tax Compact held constitutnl 2-21, 126F1-A2
IRS agent liability case refused by Sup Ct 3-20, 206B1
Antique gun rule declined by Sup Ct 5-22, 388B2
Hughes estate dispute interventn refused by Sup Ct 6-22, 509A1
Crane pres campaign theme 8-2, 606D1
DC funds clear Cong 8-17, 697G2, B3
Cities' power over suburbs backed by Sup Ct 11-28, 937D3
Kennedy scores Carter budget plans 12-9, 956G1
'Marriage tax' challenge refused by Sup Ct 12-11, 981C1
Cleveland mayor proposes income tax rise 12-12, city cncl OKs plan 12-22, 1008B3
Carter budget problems seen 12-14, 980D1

1979

TAPE Recordings—*See subjects*
TAPIE, Alan
2d in Napa Classic 9-23, 970E1
TARAKI, Nur Mohammad (Afghan president; ousted Sept. 16)
Rebels slay civiln backers 3-22, 232G2
Amin named premr, remains pres 3-27, 233C1
Warns Iran, Pak on aiding rebels 4-22, 368C2
Kin flees to USSR 6-7, 443A1
Sovts asks India to aid govt 6-14, 443F1
Purge rptd, USSR support doubted 6-24, 521E2
2 Cabt mins ousted 9-14, supporters attack 9-14–9-15, 695D3
Resigns 9-16, death rptd 9-18, 695C3
Amin rpts alive 9-23, 748D2
Death confirmed 10-9, 787D2
Watanjar tied to coup try 10-15–10-16, 810F3
Power shift hampers rebel defeat 10-29, 832B1
Karmal takes over in Afghan coup 12-27, 973F1
Widow released from jail 12-29, 973C2
TARGHEE National Forest (Idaho)
Fire destroys 37,000 acres 7-6–8-10, 620F1
TARIFFS—*See FOREIGN Trade; country names*
TARKANI, Taghi Haj
Assassinated 7-8, 525E1
TARKENTON, Francis (Fran)
NFL '78 passing ldr 1-6, 80E1
TARNOWER, Dr. Herman
Scarsdale Diet on best-seller list 3-4, 173E3; 4-8, 271A2; 5-6, 356C2; 6-3, 432A2; 7-1, 548B3; 8-5, 620C3; 9-2, 672B3; 10-14, 800B3; 11-4, 892B3
TAROCZY, Balazs
Loses Swedish Open 7-22, 734B2
TAROUN, Maj. Daoud
US secret cable details Dubs death 2-22, 147A2
TARTRAZINE (Yellow No. 15)—*See CHEMICALS*
TASS (Soviet press agency)
French computer deal set, '78 US ban cited 3-27, 237G2
US clears computer sale 3-29, 287F2
US false A-war alert scored 11-10, 869B3
TASTE of Honey, A (singing group)
Wins Grammy 2-16, 336E3
TATE, Allen
Dies 2-9, 176G3
TATE, John (Big John)
Decisns Coetzee for WBA heavywgt title 10-20, 838F2
TATE, Sharon (d. 1969)
NC MD gets life for '70 slayings 8-29, 817E3
Manson parole denied 11-27, 953D3
TATE, S(tonewall) Shepherd
Janofsky succeeds as ABA pres 8-15, 769B1
TATUM, Earl
Traded to Cavaliers 2-15, 526F2
TAUSTINE, Manny
Manny opens 4-18, 712C1
TAVERAS, Frank
Traded to Mets 4-19, 1002G2
NL stolen base ldr 9-30, 955F2

TAXES
Boston referendum spending case refused by Sup Ct 1-8, 14A3
Home '76-77 bills up 112% 1-11, 18D1
State fscl '78 revenues up 2-13, 152G1
Cleveland votes income tax rise 2-27, 150A1, D1
Urban fiscal standings linked 3-20, 204E1, F1, B2
State-local '78 collectns up 5-16, 386G1
Cleveland repaymt plan agreed 6-9, 580B1
Calif sales tax freeze sought 7-2, 499A3
ABA OKs state certificatn standards 8-15, 768G3
ACLU plans suit vs Phila papal altar 9-13, 760D3
IRS race bias tax power curb OKd by Cong 9-26, Carter signs 9-29, 883E2
Justice Dept cites '77 Sup Ct case errors 10-8, 848A2
'71-77 collectns rptd up 10-21, 990B3
Reagan campaign themes cited 11-14, 982C1, G1
Mil spending inequities rptd 11-18, 940E1
Rates rptd down, tax bite up 11-28, 925A1

1980

TARAKI, Nur Mohammad (d. 1979)
Sovts blame Amin for death 1-3, 1G2
USSR on Amin overthrow 1-14, 27A3
3 Amin aides face trial 1-14, 27B3
US issues rights rpt 2-5, 86B3
TARANENKO, Leonid
Wins Olympic medal 7-29, 624F2
TARIFFS—*See FOREIGN Trade*
TARNOWER, Dr. Herman
Scarsdale Diet on best-seller list 2-10, 120D3; 3-9, 200C3; 4-6, 280D3; 5-4, 359E3; 6-8, 448D3
Slain 3-10, suspect chrgd 3-11, 214E3
TAROCZY, Balasz
Wins Geneva Open 9-28, 947G1
TARRAZAS, Adm. Ramiro
Leads mil coup in Bolivia 7-17, 546A3
TARSES, Jay
Up the Academy released 6-6, 675F3
TARTAN Farms
Codex wins Preakness 5-17, 447D2
TARTIKOFF, Brandon
NBC managemt realigned 6-3, 501E2
TATAD, Francisco
Ousted as PI info min 1-17, 100B3
Chrgs electn fraud 2-4, 100B3
Quits PI ruling party 2-11, 152F2
TATE, John (Big John)
Weaver KOs for WBA heavywgt title 3-31, 320C1
TATE, Sharon (d. 1969)
Atkins denied parole 7-29, 639D2
TATUM, Jack
Stingley lawyer seeks suspensn 1-10, 175G2
TAUBER, Maurice F.
Dies 9-21, 756F2
TAUKE, Rep. Tom (R, Iowa)
Reelected 11-4, 842C4
TAUZIN, Rep. Wilbert J. (Billy) (D, La.)
Elected to US House 5-17, 404D3
Wins primary 9-13, 724A3
Reelected 11-4, 842F4
TAVARIS, Eric
Guardsman opens 1-3, 136B3
TAVOULAREAS, William P.
Saudi completes Aramco takeover, retains bd seat 9-4, 662A2
TAWIL, Irbahim
Escapes bomb blast 6-2, 417C1

TAXES
State of State messages 1-4—2-6, 268E3, 269D1-E3, 270B1, A2, A3; 1-7—1-15, 2-19, 403B2-404E1; 1-9—4-8, 482F3-484A3
RR worker compensatn liability backed by Sup Ct 2-19, 131C1
NYC revenue surplus seen 2-19, 186C3
State fscl '79 revenues rptd 2-20, 307E2-B3
Carter unveils anti-inflatn plan 3-14, 201G1
USOC tax-status review rptd 3-21, 259A1
State-local '79 collectns rptd 4-17, 307B2
PR welfare aid rate backed by Sup Ct 5-27, 453D3
DC professional tax case declined by Sup Ct 5-27, 454A1
NYC fscl '81 budget OKd 6-16, recovery plan revised 8-11, 743A1, D1
NYC '81 increases seen 7-3, 518C1
DC fiscal recovery plan proposed 7-19, 742C3, E3
Recessn impact seen 7-21, 550C2
Detroit tax revenue drop rptd 9-8, 743E2
Chicago OKs emergency borrowing 9-10, 743E3
Middle-class burden rptd 9-12, 747D1-A2
Immigratn econ impact rptd 9-22, 826E3
Canada-US treaty signed 9-26, 748B2
IRS bond exemptns rptd revoked 11-10, 989C2
Boston transit system shuts down 12-6, funding bill signed 12-7, 939G2

1976

Business Tax Issues—*See also 'Fuel & Pollution' and 'Rebate & Tax Cut Proposals' below*
Shriver stresses 1-7, 22G2
Church vs loopholes 4-19, 282D1
Dem platform text 6-15, 470C2-D2
Carter vows reform cautn 7-22, 550B3
Admin stresses incentives to spur productivity 8-2, 647B2
Sen OKs omnibus bill, anti-bribe provision 8-6, 585G3, 586F1, 669C1
Ford record cited 614F1
Options tax bill signed 9-3, 708D1
Pa VW pact signed 9-15, 988A1
Omnibus bill cleared 9-16, 705D2
Tax allowance in FPC gas hike cited 9-16—9-17, 868G1
Ford, Carter debate 9-23, 701D2-G2, 702C3
'74, '75 tax data rptd 10-2, 10-14, 847E1-G2
Ribicoff cites reform bill 10-7, 787A1
Dole, Mondale debate 10-15, 783B2
Sup Ct curbs carry-back breaks 11-2, 867C1
Treas issues boycott guidelines 11-7, Ribicoff scores 12-8, 987C2

Fuel & Pollution Issues
'77 budget proposal 1-21, 62C2
Reagan backs depletn allowance 4-6, 281F2
Dem platform text 6-15, 470C2
Mondale legis record cited 512G3
GOP platform com OKs plank 8-13, 583F1

1977

State police meal stipends taxable 11-29, 919D1
Carter plan '78-79 reforms 11-30, 913E3
NJ income tax permanent 12-15, 1008D3

Business Tax Issues—*See also 'Fuel & Pollution' below*
Ford asks $2.5 bln in cuts 1-4, 5E2
Simon vetoes housing shelter ban 1-5, 36E2
Carter plans econ stimulus pkg 1-7, 5E1
Ford backs productn incentives 1-7, 14D3
'68 NYS stock transfer tax amendmts ruled illegal 1-12, 57C2
Ford '78 budget proposals 1-17, 30A1, D1, 32A2, E2, 33A3
CEA asks cut 1-18, 35G3, 36B1
Carter plan debated 1-27—2-4, 89D2, G2
Carter on payroll credit 1-31, 89G3
Sup Ct rules on profit-sharing deductns 2-22, 150D1
ITT-Hartford suit setld 3-4, 194E3
Sup Ct broadens state tax powers 3-7, 192C2
House bars investmt credit, Blumenthal scores 3-8, 174D2
Singer, Motorola rpt paymts 3-10, 3-23, 233F2, G2
Mail-order operatns tax backed 4-4, 341E3
Carter drops credits plan 4-14, 270F2, 271B1
Carter hints credits veto 4-22, 321G2
FTC-Beneficial ad dispute review refused 4-25, 342B3
'76 state-local revenues rptd 5-4, 388F1
Employes stock plan credit cited 5-6, 409F1
Carter clarifies credits plan 5-12, 381B2
Stimulus bill clears Cong 5-16, 382A1; Carter signs 5-23, 417F3
Nader sports group planned 9-27, 820A2
Carter, steel execs discuss investmt credit hikes 10-13, 775G2
Burns asks 'bold' Admin moves 10-26, 817D2
Steel industry aid planned 12-6, 931G3
Meany urges forgn investmt credits ended 12-8, 960F3
Carter to ask $6-7 bln cut 12-20, 976B2
Ford urges tax cut by '81 12-20, 976C3

Fuel & Pollution Issues
Allied plans pollutn fund deductn 2-1, 95D1
Carter energy plan 4-20, 289D1, 290D1-G1, B2-A3; fact sheet 291C2-293D3
Cong, other reactn to Carter plan 4-20, 290C3, 293G3; 4-21—4-24, 320C1, C2, B3
Carter plan econ impact discounted 4-21, 294C2
Carter defends plan 4-22, 321D1
GOPs score Carter plan 4-25, 320F3
House OKs coal mine tax 4-29, 365B3
Carter plan scored 4-30—6-8, GOP TV rebuttal 6-2, 443E1-G2
Labor scores Carter plan 5-4, 364D3
'76 state-local revenues rptd 5-4, 388F1
Carter, Cong tussle over plan 6-9—6-14, 460F1-C2
Strip-mine bill sets coal tax 7-21, 575A3
Carter on gas-tax plan 7-22, 575B2
House OKs Carter energy pkg 8-5, 609F2-610C3
Sen com bars gas guzzler tax, backs 4¢-a-gal extensn 9-20; kills oil wellhd tax 9-26, 757E1, E2
Oil industry scores Carter progrm 10-13, 773A1
Burns links Admin policy, business fears 10-26, 817D2
Carter asks energy bill actn 10-27, 813B1
Energy bill clears Sen 10-31, 832C1-F3
Admin firm on wellhead, business tax 11-21, 917A1
Energy conf com adjourns without bill 12-22, 1002B2

1978

Business Tax Issues—*See also 'Fuel & Pollution' below*
State collections up, table 1-9, 84G2, B3
Forgn conv write-off curbs to ease 1-17, 53B3
Carter State of Union Message 1-19, 29B2, F3, 30G2
Carter Econ Message 1-20, 48C3
Carter submits plan to Cong 1-21, 48G3
Carter budget proposals 1-23, 45C2, 46E3
Federal budget dollar table 63A1
Big firms '76 nonpaymt rptd 1-27, 65D2-A3
Film industry probe rptd 2-13, Valenti denies 3-2, 251F2
Carter vs '3-martini lunch' 2-17, 123G1
AFL-CIO vs Admin plan 2-20, 141F3
Personal holding co property value tax rate affirmed 2-22, 126G2
Retroactive withholding on lunch allowances barred 2-27, 143G1
Penn Central reorganizatn plan OKd 3-9, 186C1
FRB chrmn urges payroll tax cut 3-15, 181F1
Carter unveils urban-aid plan 3-27, reactn 3-27—3-30, 217F2-218D1
Nonprofit travel agents case refused by Sup Ct 3-27, 241B2
Burns links investmt credits, $ defense 3-31, 235E2
Carter reform plan pared by House com 4-17—4-19, 305F3
Tax breaks in lease-back deals OKd by Sup Ct 4-18, 309F1-B2
Corp pol free speech backed by Sup Ct 4-26, 343G2
State stevedoring tax OKd by Sup Ct 4-26, 344B1
Carter scales back, delays reform plan 5-12, 361A1
Builders vs cuts 5-16, 362F1
Liability in bankruptcy backed by Sup Ct 5-22, 388B1
Corp takeover tax liability curbed by Sup Ct 5-22, 388F1
Corp forgn earnings case refused by Sup Ct 6-5, 431F2
Calif property-tax cut voted 6-6, 425A2
Iowa formula backed by Sup Ct 6-15, 468E2
Zenith import duty rebuffed by Sup Ct 6-21, 491A3
US Sen ratifies UK pact 6-27, 588E2
Citibank sued re forgn tax evasn 7-24, 717B3
House com OKs tax cut bill 7-27, 587C1
Regulatory overhaul asked by ABA 8-8, 626E2
House OKs tax cut bill 8-10, 604A2
TV statns protest Canadian ad law 8-29, 686A3
Goodrich chrgd with fraud 9-13, 737F1
Business spending lag linked 9-18, 716C3
Sen OKs tax-cut bill 10-10, 766B3
RR decline forecast 10-10, 812G1
Viet vets job tax-credit urged 10-10, 878G1
Tax-cut bill clears 10-15, 785D1, B3, 786B1-F1; Carter to sign 10-26, 831B2; Carter signs 11-6, 873E1
Inland Waterways authorzn signed 10-21, 897C2
Ky S&L franchise tax case refused by US Sup Ct 10-30, 832A3
Va property-tax exemptns voted 11-7, 853F1
AT&T Centrex case declined by Sup Ct 11-13, 874E2
Cleveland relief progrm cited 11-27, 916C1
Value-added tax proposed 11-30, 962B2
Job safety chngs urged 12-8, 984F3
Calif utilities refund cases refused by US Sup Ct 12-11, 981E1

Fuel & Pollution Issues
State collections up 1-9, 84F3
Oil co credits for forgn paymts revoked 1-16, 69D1
Coal tax for black lung fund signed 2-10, 125F1, C2
Carter crude oil tax passage doubted 3-7, 3-8, 220E1
Oil tax link to Soc Sec rollback proposed 4-2, 241C1
Carter energy plan tax status rptd 4-21, 305C1
Carter stresses crude oil tax legis, threatns oil import fee 6-22, 511F2
Solar energy credits backed 6-23, 493F3
Seabed mining bill clears House 6-26, 589B1
US Sen ratifies UK pact 6-27, 588D3
Crude oil import tax study rptd 6-29, 511G3
Carter vows import cuts at Bonn summit 6 7-16—7-17, 544B1
Carter energy program status cited 7-18, 550E1
Carter urges crude oil tax 7-20, 549D3
House com cuts tax deductns 7-27, 587A1
Gasoline tax hike loses in Mo 8-8, 626C1
Regulatory overhaul asked by ABA 8-8, 626E2
Carter plan clears Cong 10-15, 786B2, D2, 787D2; signed 11-9, 873A1

Proposition 13—*See 'Reform & Tax Cut Proposals' below*

1979

Business Tax Issues—*See also 'Fuel & Pollution' below*
Ill overassessmt case declined by Sup Ct 1-15, 32C1
Acctg methods limited by Sup Ct 1-16, 32G2
Amer Express files McGraw-Hill tender offer 1-16, 53D2
Carter budget proposals 1-22, 41G1, 44F1; tables 42A1, C2, 43B2
Fairchild acquitted 2-7, 88A1
State fscl '78 revenues up 2-13, 152G1
AFL-CIO urges excess profits tax 2-19, 148F2
Mont gross-receipts tax upheld by Sup Ct 2-22, 151C1
GM probe plea declined by Sup Ct 2-26, 164G2
NYC occupancy tax collectn curbed by Sup Ct 3-5, 185E1
Muffler assn denied tax break by Sup Ct 3-20, 203C3
Calif cargo container taxes voided by Sup Ct 4-30, 364A3
State-local '78 revenues up 5-16, 386C2
Cleveland repaymt plan agreed 6-9, 579F3
NJ hikes gambling tax 9-18, 851F1
Calif utilities refund challenge refused by Sup Ct 10-1, 768C1; 10-15, 848B1
Carter proposes indl innovatn 10-31, 829E3

Fuel & Pollution Issues—*See also PETROLEUM-Carter Decontrol*
Carter budget proposals 1-22, 42C1, 45A2
Dole backs excess profits tax 3-10, 186D1
Carter asks excess profits tax 4-5, 250B2, B3
NM elec tax voided by Sup Ct 4-18, 346B2
Carter proposes waste cleanup fund 6-13, 441G1
Solar heat tax credit, gasohol exemptn proposed 6-20, 498E1, F1
Metzenbaum, Moffet back oil industry reform 10-17, 831E2

Proposition 13—*See 'Reform & Tax Cut Proposals' below*

1980

Business Tax Issues—*See also 'Fuel & Pollution Issues', 'Presidential Election' below*
State of State messages 1-10, 483A1
Meal tax case refused by Sup Ct 1-14, 36F3-37A1
State fscl '79 revenues rptd 2-20, 307F2, A3
Vt tax on forgn dividends backed by Sup Ct 3-19, 249F2
Fla circus tax case refused by Sup Ct 3-24, 265A2
Idaho Asarco tax case remanded by Sup Ct 3-24, 265B2
Du Pont-IRS dispute declined by Sup Ct 4-14, 307D1
State-local '79 collectns rptd 4-17, 307C2
Small business aid proposals sent to Carter 5-15, 455B3
Wis out-of-state corp earnings tax backed by Sup Ct 6-10, 511E3
Sen Dems study plan 6-26, 480B3
Carter to aid car makers 7-8, 505B1
Iacocca asks credit for US car buyers 7-17, 541E2
'81 tax cut, recessn impact seen 7-21, 550E1, C2
Klutznick vs steel indus tax breaks 8-1, 575C3
Carter offers econ renewal plan; reactn 8-28, 663A1-D3
Carter unveils steel indus aid plan 9-30, 740A3
Inventory tax ruling impact on publishing rptd 10-5, 835F3
Inventory tax ruling amendmt discarded by House 12-13, 982F2

Fuel & Pollution Issues
Anderson backs 50 cents per gallon gas tax 1-5, 4D3
State of State messages 1-9, 1-10, 1-15, 403A3, E3, 404E1; 1-10, 2-12, 483B1, 484A3; 1-14, 1-15, 2-6, 268F3, 269A2, 270B3
Carter budget proposals 1-28, 72G3
La gas tax case fact-finder named by Sup Ct 3-3, 210G1
Windfall oil profits tax clears Cong 3-13, 3-27, Carter signs 4-2, 244B2-E3
Carter unveils anti-inflatn plan 3-14, 201E1
Vt tax on Mobil forgn dividends backed by Sup Ct 3-19, 249F2
State-local '79 collectns rptd 4-17, 307D2
Carter oil import fee blocked by Dist Ct 5-13, 366A1
Calif voters reject oil profits tax 6-3, 439D2
Oil import fee bar OKd by Cong 6-4, 6-5; Carter vetoes 6-5, veto overridden 6-5, 6-6, 436G2-437B2
Exxon out-of-state earnings tax backed by Sup Ct 6-10, 511E3
Phila refined oil dropped, co 'contributns' set 6-10, 743F3
Conn oil tax pass along ban voided 7-9, 553D3
Toxic waste clean-up funds pass House 9-19, 9-23, Sen 11-24, 898A1, F1
Gulf coast oil leasing bids set records 9-30, 785D2
Windfall profits tax suit filed 10-14, 960D2
GPU cut weighed by NRC 11-28, 961E1

1976

Presidential Election (& transition)
Reagan campaign statemts 1-5, 1-8, 4G3-5D1
Shriver proposals 1-7, 22G2
Reagan backs depletn allowance 4-6, 281F2
Carter presents health plan 4-16, 281E3
Church scores pol probes 4-19, 282C1
Carter states goals 4-23, 305B2, D2
Ford on segregated pvt schls 6-6, 410B3
Dem com OKs platform 6-15, 432B3
Dem platform text 6-15, 469D2, A3-C3, 470B1-F1, B2-E2, 473E1, 474F2
Carter vows reform 7-15, 507E1, 510G2
Carter acceptance speech 7-15, 510D2
Mondale affirms tax reform 7-15, 511D3
Mondale legis record cited 512G3
Carter defends Mondale special interest bill 7-20, 532C2
Carter vows reform cautn 7-22, 550B3
Carter outlines goals 7-28, 551A1
Mondale vows farm estate tax reform 7-31, 565A2
GOP platform com actn 8-8—8-13, 582F3, 583F1
Carter vows inequities end 8-11, 585A3
GOP platform text 8-18, 602D1, A3, D3, 603E1, B2, 604F2, C3, F3, 605A3, 606B2, 607B1, G1, 608C2
Ford acceptance speech 8-19, 611D3, 612C2
Ford record cited 614F1
Indep Party vs income tax 8-27, 666F1
Carter notes issue 8-30, 645B2
Ford vows aid re coll costs 9-15, 686B1
Carter, Ford on tax-relief proposals 9-17—9-20, 703G2-704C1
Ford, Carter debate 9-23, 701D1, F1, A2-E3, 702G1, C3
Mondale scores GOP 9-23, 725B1
Carter campaigns 9-24, 9-26, 724F1, A3
Church taxation disputed 10-2, 743C2
Baptist ldr scores Carter 10-10, 763D2
Ford: Carter big taxer 10-13, 763G2
Carter: no hike for workers 10-14, 785C2
Dole, Mondale debate 10-15, 782F2, 783B2-G2
Carter vs Ford chrgs 10-15; Ford replies 10-16, 785C1
Mondale on Carter-Cong compromise 10-17, 803C3
Ford, Carter debate 10-22, 800C1, F3, 801F3
Ford campaign issue 10-23—10-28, 802G3, 803F1, A2
Carter on conditns to tax cut 10-27—10-28, 803F2; 11-4, 819F2
Carter scores Ford proposal 10-30, 827F1
Ford pledges cut 11-1, 826A3
Burns warns vs stimulating econ 11-11; denies Carter rift 11-12, 865G1
Carter on cuts, revisn 11-15, 863E3, G3, 864A1
Lance sees cut 12-5, Carter not certain 12-6, 917B1
Carter plans program 12-9—12-14, 937E2-938A1

Rebate & Tax Cut Proposals—*See also 'Presidential Election' above*
Shriver stresses 1-7, 22G2
Ford State of Union message 1-19, 36G2, 37G2, 39F1
Mansfield sees tax-cut extensn 1-19, 40A1
'77 budget proposals 1-21, 62C3, 63C1-A2
Ford Econ Rpt 1-26, 66B3; excerpts 67A1, A3
Cong Dems ask tax cut expansn 3-10, 230B3
House Budget Com rejects Ford plan, backs '75 cuts extensn; US budget dir rebuts 3-23, 231F2, A3
'75 cuts extensn enacted 6-30, 492G1
Mondale legis record cited 512G3
Ford urges Cong action 7-19, 532C1
Sen OKs omnibus bill 8-6, 585F3
GOP platform com OKs plank 8-13, 583F1
Ford acceptance speech 8-19, 611D3
Omnibus bill clears Cong 9-16, 705D2
Ford signs tax bill, to seek more cuts 10-4, 742C3
Ford scored re Arab boycott claims 10-7, 787A1
Carter sees tax cut 11-4, 819F2
Carter clarifies stand 11-23, 881C2

Social Security—*See under U.S. GOVERNMENT*

1977

Rebate & Tax Cut Proposals—*See also 'Fuel & Pollution' above*
Ford asks $12.5 bln progrm 1-4, 5C2
Proxmire asks cut 1-6, 12D2
Carter plans econ stimulus pkg 1-7, 5D1
Carter econ plan scored 1-10, 14D1
Ford State of Union message 1-12, 13B2
Ford '78 budget proposals 1-17, 30A1, D1, 32A2, E2
CEA asks permanent cut 1-18, 35G3, 36B1
Carter revises aid plan 1-27, 51G3-52A2; submits to Cong 1-31, 75A2
Carter plan debated 1-27—2-4, 89A2
Carter budget revisions 2-22, 124D3
House OKs cuts 3-8, 174D2
Mondale urges $50 rebate 3-31, 251B1
Carter urges plan passage 4-7, 271A1
Carter drops proposals 4-14, 270F2
Carter would veto GOP plan 4-15, 299G1
Natl debt reductn planned 4-27, 407E3
Carter asks credits for working poor 5-2, 337G2
McGovern scores Carter 5-13, 381D2
Tax-cut stimulus bill clears Cong 5-16, 381D1-382E1; Carter signs 5-23, 417F3
Cong revises '77 budget levels 5-17, 405E1
Carter Miss town mtg topic 7-21, 575E1
Carter expects cut in '78 10-13, 773B1
3d ¼ GNP rpt, tax cut pressures linked 10-19, 798D1
Carter plans '78 cut 11-30, 913E3
AFL-CIO urges $13 bln cut 12-12, 961C1
Carter to ask $25-bln cut 12-20, 976A2
Ford urges $68-bln cut by '81 12-20, 976C3

1978

Reform & Tax Cut Proposals
Carter reaffirms plans 1-12, 12B2
Carter State of Union Message 1-19, 29B1, G1, B2, D2, F3, 30E2, F2
Carter Econ Message 1-20, 48A3
Carter submits $25 bln cut to Cong 1-21, 48F3
Carter budgets $25 mln cut 1-23, 44G2
Rhodes offers GOP alternatives 1-26, 63E1
Carter urges proposals kept intact 1-30, 62B3
GOP attacks Carter budget 1-31, 63C1
Carter vs '3-martini lunch' 2-17, 123G1
AFL-CIO offers plan 2-20, 141F3
Carter links to Soc Sec hikes 3-2, 141D1
Carter sees 'greater equity' 3-9, 160G3-161A1
FRB chrmn urges payroll tax cut 3-15, 181F1
Soc Sec rollback sought 4-2—4-5, 240B3-241E1
Schl tuitn credit OKd by House com, Carter vs 4-11, 260G3, 261B1
Stock mkt gain linked to Carter plan 4-14, 303C1
House com pares Carter reform plan 4-17—4-19; more chngs urged 4-20, Carter reatn rptd 4-23, 305C3
Carter plan delay boosts sagging $, weakness persists 4-19—7-14, 523B2
Tax-cut support polled 4-24, 308B1
Sen backs Carter plan, disputes starting date 4-25, 4-26, 305D2
Carter defends tax-cuts, reforms 4-25, 306C1, G3, 307B2-A3
Carter scales back, delays plan 5-12, 361A1
Cong '79 budget target cleared 5-17, 385B1, C2-G2
State tax relief measures rptd 5-25, 425D1

1979

Reform & Tax Cut Proposals
Carey asks NYS tax cut 1-3, 13G2
Brown: 'tax revolt is heard' 1-8, 13C2
Kennedy scores Carter budget approach 1-13, 70D1
Carter budget proposals 1-22, 41D2, E2, 44F1; tables 42A1, C2
Carter 'wage insurnc' credit plan opposed in Cong 1-23, 55C3
Prop 13 impact on Dec '78 CPI rptd 1-24, 73G1
Calif coll enrollmt decline, Prop 13 linked 1-29, 367E2
GOP urges indexing vs inflatn 2-4, 86B2
Carter urges 'wage insurnc' credit plan 2-12, 109F3
AFL-CIO backs 'wage insurnc', urges excess profits tax 2-19, 148E2
Calif schl aid, Prop 13 linked 3-5, 282D3, F3
Neighborhoods panel urges property tax reform 3-15, 208C3
UAW pres discounts wage insurnc 4-17, 280D1
Ullman, Long: tax cut unlikely 4-30, 327B2
Carter seeks credit expansn for 'working poor' 5-23, 384D1
Carter cites 'wage insurnc' plan defeat by House panel 5-25, 401B2
Carter doubts '80 tax cut 5-29, 402A1
Prop 13 effects reviewed 6-1—7-2, 499F2-500B2
Tax cut likelihood grows 7-9, 514B1
Volcker vs cut 9-7, 680D3
Dade Cnty (Fla) voters reject cut 9-18, 724B2
Carter sees possible cut 9-25, 723A3
Tax cut oppositn, 3d 1/4 econ rebound linked 10-19, 805F1

1980

Windfall profits item chng clears Cong 12-3, signed 12-5, 936G1
Chem clean-up bill signed 12-11, 936A1, C1

Presidential Election (& Transition)
Anderson backs 50 cents per gallon gas tax; GOP rivals debate tax cuts 1-5, 4D3
Kemp on tax cut goals 1-14, 32F1
Kennedy vs loopholes 1-28, 74G3
Kennedy for depreciatn chng 2-6, 91A1
GOP candidates debate in NH 2-20, 129C3, D3
Reagan 'basic speech' excerpts 2-29, 207E3
Kennedy 'basic speech' excerpts 3-10, 183B1, A2, 184A2
Reagan on tax-cut stand 4-8, 264G2
Carter vs tax-cut talk 6-10, 438G2
Dem platform drafted 6-24, 480A1
Reagan unveils tax-cut plan 6-25, Sen Dems reject amendmt 6-26, 480A2-B3
Sen Dems vow plan, House Dem ldrs see Admin offcls 6-26, 480F2
Sen again rejects Reagan tax amendmt 6-30, 492E3
Carter attacks GOP plan 7-3, 505C2; 7-17, 532D1
GOP drafts platform 7-10, 506A3
Reagan for car co aid 7-12, 535F1
Kemp stresses at GOP conv 7-15, 531B3
GOP platform adopted; text 7-15, 535B3, 536B1, A2
Reagan nominatn acceptance speech 7-17, 531G2, 532B2, B3-F3
Reagan rpts '79 personal data 7-31, 570D3-571A2
Anderson rpts '79 personal data 8-4, 596D3
Urban League hears pres candidates 8-5, 8-6, 597G1, B2
Reagan plans 'enterprise zones' 8-5, 597G1
Dem conv keynote speech 8-11, 612A2*, C2
Kennedy conv speech asks reform 8-12, 610D2, 614E1
Dem platform planks adopted 8-13, 611F2, 614G2, 615E1
Carter pres renominatn acceptance speech 8-14, 612E1, F3, 613G1
Carter attacks Reagan 8-22, 646F2
Carter offers econ renewal plan; Reagan scores; Carey vows support; other reactn 8-28, 663A1-D3
Anderson platform offered 8-30, 665A1, B1, E1, C2
Reagan vows tax cuts 9-1, 664C2
Bush presses GOP plans 9-1, 780B3
Reagan presents econ plan 9-9, 699A2
Reagan issues steel indus plan 9-16, 699F2
Carter vs 'quick-fix' cuts 9-18, 698C3, 699A1
Reagan, Anderson debate cuts 9-21, 721E2, D3, 722D1
Reagan farm proposal 9-30, 738B3
Reagan for savings-tax break 10-2, 738E2
Carter scores Reagan plan, backs business write-offs 10-14, 779F1
Mondale denounces Reagan cuts 10-16, 817B1
Carter scores Reagan proposals 10-24, 816G2
Reagan scores Carter policies, offers 8-pt plan 10-24, 817C2
Carter, Reagan TV debate 10-28, 813D1, E1, E2, 814D1, 815A3
Anderson answers TV debate questns 10-28, 816A1, B1
Libertarian candidate cites stance 10-28, 818G2
Reagan readies cuts 11-6, 837F2, 839B3
Reagan renews pledge 11-16, 881C2
Reagan aides stress personal, business cuts 11-23, 897D2
Reagan renews cities' plan 12-1, 914F2

Reform & Tax Cut Proposals—*See also 'Presidential Election (& Transition)' above*
Saco (Me) '79 default rptd 1-7, 54E1
Carter defers '80 cut 1-21, 43C3
Carter budget proposals 1-28, 69F2, 70A1, 72A2; tables 69G3, 70C1
Carter vs '80 cut 1-30, 74E1
Chicago City Cncl backs property tax error levy 2-14, 186G2
Roth backs cut, Proxmire vs 2-27, Cong com backs 2-28, 168G2-D3
San Fran faces budget crisis, Props 13, 9 cited 3-8, 186F3
Fla property tax cut voted 3-11, 184G1
Carter revised budget proposals 3-31, 243F2, G3
GOP budget proposed 4-1, 244F1
Alaska OKs income tax break, shares wealth 4-15, 307B3
Saco (Maine) voters repeal property tax ceiling 4-29, 744A1
Carter says cut possible 5-9, 367G1
VAT, Ullman electn linked 5-20, 404C3
Pensn changes urged 5-23, 404G1, B2
Gann wins Calif US Sen primary 6-3, 439G1
Calif voters reject income tax cut 6-3, 439C2
Dems back '81 tax cut 6-29—7-1, 492B3-493B1
US Families Conf vs marriage penalty 7-12, 601C2
McIntyre sees '81 tax cut 7-21, 550E1
Carter rejects pre-electn tax cut 8-28, 663D1
Alaska income tax break overturned 9-5, income tax repeal signed 9-24, 747A1
Election referendum results 11-4, 847C2, 848D2
Cong Dems vs action now 11-12, 866A2

1976

Tax Evasion—*See under U.S. GOVERNMENT—INTERNAL Revenue Service*

1977

School Issues
Conn funding held unconst 4-18, 302G2
Calif financing review rejctd 6-20, 517D1
NC, Tenn church coll aid backed 10-3, 760E3
Ohio s referenda results 11-8, 879D2
Ohio finance law ruled illegal 12-5, 939D3
Me funds law repealed 12-5, 939F3

Tax Evasion—*See under U.S. GOVERNMENT—INTERNAL Revenue Service*

1978

Schl tuitn credit OKd by House 6-1, Carter threatens veto 6-8, 431G2, F3
Calif voters OK Propositn 13 property-tax cut amendmt 6-6, reactn 6-7—6-8; text 425A1-426F1, 447D3
Tax-cut major issue in NJ Sen primary 6-6, 425B1, 447G3
Earned income credit expansn planned 6-7, 446G1
Carter assesses Propositn 13 impact 6-14, 446D3
Propositn 13 topic at natn-wide convs 6-17—7-6, 525F3
IRS summons power backed by Sup Ct 6-19, 492F2
Calif budget surplus aid to local govts signed 6-24, 525C3
Carter vs capital gains plans 6-26, 491A2
Kemp-Roth tax-cut theory detailed 7-3, Laffer Curve diagram 735C1
Carter plan delay cuts fscl '79 budget deficit 7-6, 506D3
Cong Budget Office rpts on Propositn 13 impact 7-6, 525E2
Propositn 13 defns spending impact rptd 7-11, 526C2
Carter cites scaled down plan at Bonn summit 7-16—7-17, 544E1
Carter vs capital-gains proposals 7-20, 549E3
NAACP dir urges relief for poor 7-21, 568B2
Tax, spending-cut amendmt drive launched 7-26, 735F3
House com OKs $16 bln cut; discards Carter 'reforms', OKs capital gains plan 7-27, 586G2-587A2
Cong study sees '79 tax hike despite cuts 8-2, 587A2
House votes $16 bln cut, capital gains plan 8-10, 604A1
July income rise, Propositn 13 linked 8-17, 643E3
Jarvis spearheads natl tax-cut movemt 8-17, new group formed 8-21, TV message aired 9-26, 735A3
Propositn 13 noted at Natl Govs mtg 8-28, 681D3, 682A1
Calif cuts income taxes $1 bln 8-30, 735E2-A3
Propositn 13, June bldg surge linked 8-31, 680G1
Conn income tax rejctd by primary voters 9-12, 716F2
Business spending lag linked 9-18, 716C3
Dems block Kemp-Roth bill in Sen com 9-18, GOP stages cross-country blitz 9-20—9-22, 734D3-735B1
Propositn 13 upheld by Calif ct 9-22, 735B2
Carter vs tax cut, tuitn credit bills 9-28, 751G3
Propositn 13, pub works veto linked 10-5, 765C1
Sen votes $29 bln tax cut, Carter scores 10-10, 766A3
Cong tax-cut actn completn cited 10-15, 784E2
Cong clears $18.7 bln cut 10-15; Roth-Kemp proposal cited; capital gains cut, other terms listed 785D1-786G1
Carter anti-inflatn plan sets rebates 10-24, 805D2
Carter to sign tax cut 10-26, 831B2
Cong 95th sessn rated 10-28, 865A3
NYS property-tax-limit case refused by US Sup Ct 10-30, 832B3
Carter signs tax-cut bill 11-6, 873E1
Boston tax referendum lobby injunctn lifted by Sup Ct 11-6, 874A1
State vote results 11-7, 847D1: Mass 847D3; Md 849A1; NJ 849B1; NY 849F1; Ala 849C3; Va 853F1; Ill 853C2; Mich 854C1; Mo 854E3; Neb 854G3; ND 855A1; SD 855C1; Ariz 855F1; Ark 855B2; Tex 855E3; Colo 855G3; Ida 856D1; Hawaii 857D1; Neb 857F1; Ore 857A2
Value-added tax proposed 11-30; reactn 12-3, 12-6, 962A2

School Issues
Wilmington busing plan ordrd 1-9, 15A3
Carter vs educ credit 2-8, 85B1
House rebuffs Carter aid plan 3-20, 202B3
Cleveland voters reject tax hike 4-6, 279D2
Tuitn tax credit OKd by House com, Carter vs 4-11, 260G3, 261B1
Northwestern U real estate dispute refused by Sup Ct 5-1, 364E1
Tuitn tax credits OKd by House 6-1, Carter threatens veto 6-8, 431G2, F3
Cleveland, Columbus, other Ohio voters rejct tax hikes 6-6, 425B1
Calif OKs property-tax cut, revenue drop seen 6-6; reactn 6-7—6-8, 425D2-426D1
NY property tax ruled illegal 6-23, 526F1
NEA conv discusses Propositn 13 7-5, 525G3
Propositn 13 upheld by Calif ct 9-22, 735C2
Carter vs tuitn credit bill 9-28, 751G3
State aid to colls rptd up 10-10, 770D2
Tuitn tax credit dies 10-15, 785G1, 807C2
Mich voucher plan defeated 11-7, 854C1

Tax Evasion (& other Irregularities)—*See also 'Business Tax Issues' above*
Abrahams sentenced on NYS probatn violatn 4-20, 283C1
'76 nonpaymt by rich rptd down 7-8, 554A2
Fairchild, chrmn indicted 9-8, 808B3
Unificatn Church abuses chrgd by House subcom 11-1, 862C3

1979

Prop 13 cited re San Fran teacher layoffs 10-23, 850F1
Municipal property tax chngs seen 10-24, 920A2
Kennedy hits oil-tax issue 11-3, 962C1
Brown offers econ plan 11-9, 962E2
Reagan seeks cuts, tax shift to states, localities 11-13, 866D2, F2
Soc Sec, Medicare chngs urged 12-7, 946B2

Tax Evasion (& other Irregularities)
ILA offcl indicted 1-17, 87B3
Fairchild acquitted 2-7, 88A1
2 Teamsters indicted 2-22, 156A1
Estes indicted 2-22, 156G1
REA vp indicted for funds misue 3-8, 239F3
Coal broker pleads guilty 3-13, 240A1
Swiss couple indicted in IRS fraud 3-16, 240E1

1980

'81 budget res clears Cong 11-20, 896A2
Boston bond rating lowered 12-2, 939D3
Budget reconciliatn signed 12-5, 936G1

Tax Evasion (& other Irregularities)
Estes '83 parole rptd 1-3, 64F3
Studio 54 owners sentenced 1-18, 64B3
Gilmour reinstated 1-30, 447C3
IRS handwriting orders upheld by Sup Ct 2-20, 170E1
Ill atty gen convicted 3-19, 215A3
IRS audit data request case refused by Sup Ct 4-28, 369E1

1978

Fruehauf Corp case refused by Sup Ct 11-6, 874D1
IRS offcl's bribery convictn review refused by Sup Ct 11-27, 937C2

1979

Fairchild IRS complaint refused by Sup Ct 3-26, 231B1
Mays chrmn convctd of IRS bribe 3-26, 239E3
IRS tap evidence backed by Sup Ct 4-2, 281D2
Ill atty gen indicted 4-9, 291B3
IRS seizure power case declined by Sup Ct 4-16, 303B1
Allied Chem indicted 4-17, 985B3
Beatles ex-mgr convicted 4-26, 392F3
Smith convicted in Calif 5-4, 5-7, sentncd 5-31, 442C2
Barry pleads guilty 6-12, 527A3; sentncd 7-10, 656D2
Studio 54 owners indicted 6-28, 647E1
Unpaid tax losses rptd 7-10, 8-31, 665E2
Beatles ex-mgr sentenced 7-10, 656E2
Firestone indicted 7-11; pleads guilty, fined 7-26, 648B3
Curran told to repay NMU benefits 7-27, 744A3
Estes sentenced 8-6, 604E3
Ex-Rep Clark sentncd 9-5, 442G2
$100, $50 bills use rptd 9-25, 727F2
SBA minority-aid abuse rptd 9-28, 947A3
Studio 54 owners plead guilty 11-2, 891G2
ILA offcl convicted 11-15, 890B1
GAO 'fraud hotline' rptd effective 12-9, 947B2
Conrad pleads guilty 12-18, 1000F1

1980

NY Deliverers Union head convicted 5-15, 370E3; sentncd 6-26, 656D1
Ala black dist judge nominee accused 5-19, Sen confirms 6-26, 744G2, B3
White House aide rptd reassigned in dispute 6-10, 638E3
Cts power to suppress evidence curbed 6-23, 554C3
NY Mafia boss indicted 6-30, 502E3, 503B1
Ill atty gen sentncd 7-29, 654F2
IRS prosecutn guidelines rptd 8-2, 601G2-D3
Sheffield probe leaked, Sen confirmatn hearings halted 8-27, 745A1

1976

TAX Foundation Inc.
Rpts '76 Cong spending 9-22, 746C1
TAXI Driver (film)
Top-grossing film 3-31, 240B3
Wins Cannes film award 5-28, 460F1
TAYLOR, Arthur R.
Fired 10-13, 892F1
TAYLOR, Capt. Cecil V.
Chrgs reduced 8-18, reprimanded 9-1, 942C2
TAYLOR, Claude
Seeks Air Canada fare hike 8-10, 587E2
Air Canada appeal rejected 9-22, 730D2
TAYLOR, Colin
Denies Angola mercenary executns 2-9, 106C1
TAYLOR, Edward
In new UK shadow Cabt 11-19, 1004A2
TAYLOR, Rep. Gene (R, Mo.)
Travel expense probe ends 10-27, 981G3
Reelected 11-2, 830B1
TAYLOR, Rep. Roy A. (D, N.C.)
Gudger elected 11-2, 822E2
TAYLOR, Judge William M.
Sets Dallas desegregatn plan 3-10, 203A3
TAZIEFF, Haroun
Injured 8-30, 643D3
Scores Guadeloupe evacuatn 9-2, 674C3
Dismissed 10-18, 905D3
TEACHERS, American Federation of (AFL-CIO)
AFSCME quits AFL-CIO unit 2-15, 154B1
Shanker endorses Carter 7-22, 551F1
Mondale addresses 8-16, 617C3
Endorses Dem ticket 8-18, 617D3
UFT scores HEW bias chrgs 11-9, 922B1
TEAGUE, Rep. Olin E. (D, Tex.)
On synfuel bill, GAO rpt 8-24, 649C2
Reelected 11-2, 830C4

1977

TAXICABS
Chicago mayor chrgd re fare hike 11-21, 944C2
TAYLOR, Audrey June
Rpts Amin phone talk 6-21, 507F3
TAYLOR, Claude
Air Canada cuts svcs 1-12, 43C2
TAYLOR, Daniel A.
Sacco, Vanzetti vindicated 7-19, 652F2
TAYLOR, David P.
Replaced as Defense asst secy 5-9, 418A2
TAYLOR, Dean P.
Dies 10-16, 872A3
TAYLOR, Rep. Gene (R, Mo.)
'76 campaign surplus rptd 5-3, 482A2
TAYLOR, James
Vs oil-price rise 4-7, 282A1
TAYLOR, John
Scores Carter B-1 cancellatn 12-7, 942B1
TAYLOR, Karen & Mickey
Seattle Slew wins Triple Crown 6-11, ownership probe rptd 6-16, 491E1
TAYLOR, Gen. Maxwell (ret.)
Testifies on Panama Canal pacts 10-10, 792G1
TAYLOR, Judge Robert L.
Mandel, 5 others convicted 8-23, 652C1
On Mandel sentence 10-7, 807E2
TAYLOR, Judge William L.
EEOC bias ruling rptd 1-20, 278F3
TEACHERS—*See under EDUCATION*
TEACHERS, American Federation of (AFL-CIO)
Detroit agency shop backed 5-23, 444D1
NY union fined $50,000 7-20, 558D2
Shanker named AFL-CIO dept head 12-7, 961F1
TEACHERS, United Federation of—*See TEACHERS, American Federation of*
TEAM Defense Project
Dawson 5 murder chrgs dropped 12-19, 991E2

1978

TAXI Tales (play)
Opens 12-29, 1031A3
TAXPAYERS, United Organization of
Calif OKs Jarvis amendmt 6-6, 425F1
TAX Reform Research Group
Tax cut bill criticism rptd 10-16, 785E2
TAYLOR, Brian
Leaves Nuggets in contract dispute 1-17, 272G2
TAYLOR, Charles Frederick
Arrested in parole payoff 12-15, 1011F1
TAYLOR, Claude
Air Canada settles with pilots 8-24, suspends svc in IAM dispute 8-25—9-5, 686D2
TAYLOR, Clavin
Denies King plot role 11-17, 938D2
TAYLOR, Don
Damien released 6-8, 619D1
TAYLOR, Dwight
Gay Divorce opens 3-9, 760C2
TAYLOR, Elizabeth
Little Night Music released 3-7, 619A3
Husband named US Sen nominee 8-12, 645B3
TAYLOR, Rep. Gene (R, Mo.)
Reelected 11-7, 851D2, 854D3
TAYLOR, Horacena J.
Nevis Mt Dew opens 12-7, 1031E2
TAYLOR, James
Wins Grammy 2-24, 315F3
Working opens 5-14, 887E3
TAYLOR, Stella
Ends Marathon swim 8-15, 653E1
TAYLOR Jr., Judge William M.
Dallas busing plan upset 4-24, 309C2
TAYLOR v. Kentucky
Presumptn-of-innocence chrg backed by Sup Ct 5-30, 430B3
TAY-Sachs—*See MEDICINE—Diseases*
TEA
Uganda smugglers sentenced 1-10, 55C3
Australia blocks UK co takeover 9-7, decisn analyzed 9-29, 754F2
Tanzania seizes Lonrho holdings 9-16, 905E2
TEACHER, Brian
Loses Tokyo Intl 11-5, 1027C2
TEACHER, The (film)
Released 5-13, 620A1
TEACHERS—*See under EDUCATION*
TEACHERS, American Federation of (AFL-CIO)
Cabt-level Educ Dept opposed 4-14, 279G1
Nurses unit formed 11-29, 961A1
Asbestos danger in schls cited 12-21, 1009G1
TEAGUE, Rep. Olin E. (D, Tex.)
A-breeder compromise proposal rptd 3-17, 3-23, 242C1
Not standing for reelectn 5-6, 363A1
Gramm wins seat 11-7, 855D3
TEAGUE, Walter W.
Named in US Teamster fund suit 2-1, 83E1

1979

TAXI (TV series)
Wins Emmy 9-9, 858E2
TAX Limitation Committee, National
Urges US spending limit amendmt 1-30, 86G2
TAXPAYERS' Union, National
Balanced budget amendmt status disputed 2-6, 86B2
TAYLOR, Brian
Joins Clippers 2-20, 291E1
TAYLOR, Charles Frederick
Indicted 3-15, 309D2
TAYLOR, Elizabeth
Wilding dies 7-8, 588F3
TAYLOR, Horacena J.
Old Phantoms opens 2-8, 292D2
TAYLOR, James
Sentncd in GSA kickback scandal 3-20, 367A3
TAYLOR, Michael
Last Embrace released 5-3, 528G2
TAYLOR, Judge Robert
Dismisses Cherokee suit 11-2, 990C1
TAYLOR, Theodore B.
Named to 3 Mile I probe 4-11, 275C1
Scores NRC licensing decision 8-23, 665C1
TAYLOR, Theodore R.
Hansen H-bomb letter published 9-16, 9-18, reactn 9-17, 714A1, C2; text of letter 714D1-717E3
TCDD (dioxin)—*See CHEMICALS*
TCHIDIMBO, Archbishop Raymond-Marie
Freed 8-6, 796A3
TEA
Kenya Jan-June '78 trade deficit rptd 1-5, 22A3
TEACHER, Brian
Wins Hall of Fame championship 7-15, 734A2
TEACHERS—*See under EDUCATION*
TEACHERS, American Federation of (AFL-CIO)
NJ colleges struck 3-20, 207E1
Educ Dept bill scored 7-11, 514F3

1980

TAXI (TV series)
Wins Emmy 9-7, 692C1
TAYLOR, A.J.P.
Quits academy re Blunt controversy 8-19, 652F1
TAYLOR, Arthur R.
Backe quits CBS post 5-8, 376E1
RCTV wins BBC rights 12-11, 1002C3
TAYLOR, Billy
NFL '79 touchdown ldr 1-5, 8E2
TAYLOR, Pvt. Cheryl
Sex harassmt convictn rptd 3-31, 348A1
TAYLOR, Don
Final Countdown released 8-1, 675E2
TAYLOR, Edward
Wins by-electn 3-13, 212A2
TAYLOR, Elizabeth
Mirror Crack'd released 12-18, 1003C2
TAYLOR, Rep. Gene (R, Mo.)
Reelected 11-4, 843D2
TAYLOR, Ila Zan
Survives parachute failure 5-11, 471E1
TAYLOR, Jeannine
Hijinks! opens 12-18, 1003B3
TAYLOR, Kenneth
Carter thanks 1-31; escape described 2-1, 88B3, E3
Honored for Iran escape role 7-25, 578A1
TAYLOR, Lee
Killed 11-13, 1002A2
TCHERVENKOV, Slavtcho
Wins Olympic medal 7-30, 624E3
TCHOUILOUYAN, Bernard
Wins Olympic medal 7-29, 623C1
TEA
Zimbabwe ends tax 4-20, 301E2
USSR drought threat rptd 8-6, 711B3
FDA issues caffeine warning 9-4, 726A2
TEACHER, Brian
Loses Kramer Open 4-20, 607B3
Loses Taipei Grand Prix 11-16, Bangkok 11-23, 947E2, F2
TEACHERS—*See EDUCATION—Teachers*
TEACHERS, American Federation of (AFT) (AFL-CIO)
Kennedy addresses conv 8-21, 629B3
Carter endorsed 8-21; addresses conv, sees clear choice 8-22, 646E2
TEALE, Edwin Way
Dies 10-18, 876D3

1976

TEAMSTERS, Chauffeurs, Warehousemen & Helpers of America, International Brotherhood of (unaffiliated)
Fitzsimmons quits Ford panel 1-8, 4A1
Calif farm labor dispute continues 1-22—2-11, 153G1
Strike, Dow avg linked 3-29, 413B2
Strike 4-1, pact agreed 4-3; Greenspan on pact 4-5, 248A3, 249A1
Anchorage Daily wins Pulitzer 5-3, 352D3
Pact ratified 5-10, 348G3
Dissidents demand reform 5-27, 398D1
Anheuser-Busch strike ends 6-6, 436A2
Las Vegas conv; Fitzsimmons reelected 6-13—6-16, 435F3
Provenzano, 3 others indicted 6-23, 460A1
US pensn fund probe, tax status rptd 6-24—7-7, 492B2
O'Brien indicted 7-7, pleads not guilty 7-11, 570D2
Calif cannery strike ends 7-31, 570D1
Parcel svc strike 9-16—12-13, 942F2
Pensn fund reorganizatn rptd 10-26, loans listed 12-28, 990E3

1977

TEAMSTERS, Chauffeurs, Warehousemen & Helpers of America, International Brotherhood of (unaffiliated)
Fitzsimmons' son, 2 others indicted 2-4, 102G3-103B1
UFW pact signed 3-10, 177D3
Pensn post revisns set 3-13, 195C1-B2
US sues Ohio pension fund 4-4, 280B2
Carter energy plan reactn 4-21, 320C2
Fitzsimmons, 3 others quit pensn posts 4-29, fiduciary named 6-17; loans to organized crime revealed 7-18, 558A2
Pre-'64 seniority bias upheld 5-31, 461C2
Lance defends bank pensn fund 7-25, 574G1
Zerilli dies 10-30, 872B3
Insurnc deal probed 10-31—11-2, 837E1
Provenzano kickback chrg dropped 11-11, 928B1
Provenzano reindicted 12-19, 991B3

1978

TEAMSTERS, Chauffeurs, Warehousemen & Helpers of America, International Brotherhood of (unaffiliated)
Ohio welfare fund bd revisd 1-3, 4E2
US sues to regain pensn funds 2-1, 83B1
'76, '77 top-paid labor ldrs rptd 2-20, 5-15, 365D1-C2
Briguglio killed 3-21, 232F2
Provenzano convicted 3-25, 232B2
Fitzsimmons' son, 2 others acquitted 4-28, 324C2
Provenzano convicted of Castellito murder 6-14, gets life term 6-21, 480B2
Hauser, 3 others indicted on union insurnc scheme 6-15, 560G2-D3
Provenzano's daughter takes over post 6-23, 560F2
Provenzano sentenced for kickbacks 7-11, 560D2
Ostrer indicted 7-18, 599D1
PROD scores pension funds 8-14, 625C1
US role in contract talks forecast 8-22, 8-23, 680F2-C3

1979

TEAMSTERS, Chauffeurs, Warehousemen & Helpers of America, International Brotherhood of (unaffiliated)
Gulf oil workers settle within US wage guidelines 1-11, 87E1
SEC role in pensn plans barred by Sup Ct 1-16, 32F1, D2
Carter warns vs strike 1-17, 251D2
Steel haulers end strike 1-18, 87D2
Fitzsimmons asks ICC chrmn firing 1-18, 111G3
N Orleans police strike 2-8—3-4, 165F3-166C1
Contract demands issued 3-6, Kahn warns 3-15; guidelines strike called, industry locks out 4-1, 251B1
Wage talks cited re Carter plan 3-13, 182C1
Hoffa link to JFK death suspected 3-16, 204C3
Pact ends strike, lockout 4-10; Carter lauds 4-11, 262C1
UAW discounts US guides 4-17, 280B1
Dissident steel haulers end strike 4-29, 384D3

1980

TEAMSTERS, Chauffeurs, Warehousemen & Helpers of America, International Brotherhood of (unaffiliated)
George Meany dies 1-10, 14E3
Lee Way settles job bias suit 1-10, 17E2
Sovt airline boycotted in NY 1-11, 55C2; 1-18, DC 1-22, 45E1
Sovt planes boycotted 1-18, 1-22, 45E1
Phila Journal strike ends 1-25, 115G2
AFL-CIO talks rptd held 2-19, 147C1
Fitzsimmons' son sentence rptd 2-19, 237F2
LIRR struck 4-1, 267F3-268B1
LIRR setlmt reached 4-11, 289E3
W Coast offcl sentenced 5-23, 482F2
Container pact ban refusal affirmed by Sup Ct 6-20, 555F2
GAO scores pension fund probe 8-25, 704C3
Reagan at Ohio conf, sees 'Carter depressn' 8-27, 664A2
Josephine Hoffa dies 9-12, 755D3
Reagan visits hq 11-18, 880D3

1976

Provenzano fed chrgs dropped 10-29, 972B1
Braniff job bias setlmt OKd 11-23, 943A3
Baron indicted 11-30, 991C1

TEAPOT Dome, Wyo.—*See WYOMING*
TEASDALE, Joseph P.
Elected 11-2, 820G2, 823A3, 831F1
TECHNOLOGY—*See SCIENCE & Technology*
TEDIASHVILI, Levan
Wins Olympic medal 7-31, 576E3
TEEM, John M.
Succeeded in ERDA post 3-23, 232E1
TEETER, Robert
Addresses GOP govs 11-29, 917B3
TEFERI Bante, Brig. Gen.
Senegal warns vs MPLA ties 1-11, 16B1 ★
Offers Eritreans peace 5-16, 364C2 ★
Accuses Somalia 9-12, 1002G1
TEISSLER, Mary
Named in Getty will 6-8, 444C2
TEIXEIRA, Paulo
Angola forgn min 11-27, 995C3
TEJCHMA, Jozef
Polish deputy premier 3-27, 268F2
TEJERINA, Col. Raul
Rptdly threatened Torres 6-8, 456G2

TELEPHONES & Telegraph—*See also company names*
Leb intl lines suspended 1-16, 33E2
Sen com cites secret NSA-telegraph co pacts 4-28, 300C1
Dem platform text 6-15, 474F2
Friis dies 6-15, 524E2
GOP platform text 8-18, 603A1, F1
AT&T reverse bias damages ordrd 8-27, 944G1
AT&T trust suit OKd 11-16, 886G3
Sup Ct bars review of '74 FCC pvt equipmt ruling 12-13, 960E2
Wiretapping & Eavesdropping—*See under 'W'*

TELEVISION—*See BROADCASTING*
TELEVISION Arts & Sciences, National Academy of (NATAS)
Emmys presented 5-17, 460A2
TELLALOV, Constantin Christov
Named Canada amb 7-7, 910E2

1977

TEAMSTERS v. U.S.
Seniority rights upheld 5-31, 461B2
TEBBIT, Donald
Refutes Sinclair strike chrgs 8-8, 632E3
TECHNOLOGY Assessment, Office of—*See under U.S. GOVERNMENT*
TEDESCO, James J.
Indicted 6-2, 520A3
TEFERI Bante, Brig. Gen.
Killed 2-3, 98C2
Mengistu to head govt 2-11, 238D2
TELECOMMUNICATIONS Industry—*See TELEPHONES & Telegraph*
TELECOMMUNICATIONS Policy, Office of—*See under U.S. GOVERNMENT*
TELEDYNE Inc.
Investors' '76 return rptd 340B3
TELEGRAPH—*See TELEPHONES & Telegraph*

TELEPHONES & Telegraph—*See also WIRETAPPING; company names*
Sup Ct refuses AT&T case 1-25, 80B2
Carter plans call-in 2-2, 75A2
Sup Ct bars AT&T-Westn Union dispute review 2-22, 150A1
FCC rules on AT&T 2-23, 217C2
Carter call-in 3-5, 171A1-G3
Appeals ct backs FCC pvt equipmt registratn order 3-22, Sup Ct refuses review 10-3, 760E3
India, USSR pacts set 4-27, 348E1
Maputo UN conf asks Rhodesia embargo 5-21, 399G2
'76 Telpak order revoked 6-1, AT&T pvt rates OKd 6-1, 6-8, 465C1
ITT sues AT&T 6-10, 520C2
Record access safeguards urged 7-12, 632C1
AT&T to maintain Telpak 7-21, FCC upheld on AT&T 'end-link' repricing 8-5, 631C3, F3
Southn Bell offcls indicted 8-2, 631A3
AT&T, CWA in 3-yr pact 8-6, 613F2
FCC acts on ads 8-26, White House backs curbs 10-21, 921A1
ESA satellite missn aborted 9-13, 736A1
2 Calif firms ordrd to refund $344 mln 9-13, 839G1
Westn Union Hawaii svc case review declined, 10-17, 798A1
Israel-Egypt link in operatn 11-19—11-22, 890A2
S Africa halts French deal 11-25, 934C2
Phone surveillnc ct orders backed 12-7, 939E1
Carter plans excise-tax end 12-20, 976G2

TELEVISION—*See BROADCASTING, ELECTRIC & Electronics Industry, PRESS*
TELEVISION Arts and Sciences, Academy of (ATAS)
Formed in Hollywood 355G3 ★
NBC cancels Emmy broadcast 4-15, 355C3
Emmy academy dispute ended 7-12, 583A3
Presents Emmys 9-11, 1021F3
TELEVISION Arts & Sciences, National Academy of (NATAS)
NBC cancels Emmy broadcast 4-15, 355C3
Emmy academy dispute ended 7-12, 583A3
Presents Emmys 11-6, 1022B1
TELEVISION Program Executives, National Association of
FCC chrmn on TV violence 2-14, 157D3, 158B1
TELLES, Godofredo
Jurists ask 'rule of law' 8-8, 633A2
TELLES, Raymond
Replaced as EEOC chrmn 5-27, 500A1

1978

Hoffa cited at JFK death hearing 9-27, 750F1
5 in NJ indicted 10-5, 770F3
US sues fund trustees 10-16, 792D1-A3
Fitzsimmons on Carter anti-inflatn plan 10-25, 806D3
US set back in fund suit 11-1, 11-7, 899C1
Steel haulers strike 11-11, 1006F1
Carter eases wage-price rules, contract talks cited 12-13, 957G2

TECHINE, Andre
Barocco released 4-7, 618B3
TECHNOLOGY Assessment Office of—*See under U.S. GOVERNMENT—CONGRESS*
TEENAGERS—*See YOUTH*
TEETERS, Nancy H.
Named to FRB 8-28, 664C1
Vs record discount rate hike 10-13, 791B2
TEIFER, Gregory
Amsterdam Kill released 3-30, 618B3
TEJCHMA, Jozef
Resigns as Mauritania culture min 1-26, 95A2
TEJERO Molina, Lt. Col. Antonio
Arrest rptd 11-21, 967F2
TELECOMMUNICATIONS—*See COMMUNICATIONS*
TELECOMMUNICATIONS & Information Agency, National—*See under U.S. GOVERNMENT—COMMERCE*
TELECOMMUNICATIONS Policy, Office of—*See under U.S. GOVERNMENT*
TELEGRAPH—*See TELEPHONES & Telegraph*

TELEPHONES & Telegraph—*See also WIRETAPPING; company names*
AT&T rate rise stay lifted 1-9, 13C2
AT&T-MCI svc case review barred 1-16, 33G1
FCC OKs Telpak rate hike 1-18, 84E1
ITT wins GTE trust suit, AT&T suit cited 3-1, 510A3
FCC to probe Western Union monopoly 3-9, 270D2
Fortune ranks '77 top 500 indls 5-8, 325E1, F1
'77 top-paid execs ranked 5-15, 364F3
AT&T-MCI svc case stay denied by Sup Ct 5-22, 388A2
Argentina phone lines commandeered for World Cup 6-1—6-25, 520G3
AT&T rate hike case declined by Sup Ct 6-5, 431D2
Viet, Thai cooperatn agreed 9-6—9-10, 696G1
LA bank robbed by phone 10-25, computer consultant arrested 11-5, 991G3-992D1
AT&T Centrex case refused by Sup Ct 11-13, 874D2
AT&T-MCI connectns case declined by Sup Ct 11-27, 937A2
SW Bell slander judgmt reversed 11-29, 963F1 ★
RCA Alaska phone unit sale set 11-30, 935B2
AT&T vows price compliance 12-1, 934B3
Conn A-sub plot wire fraud chrgd 12-6, 2 convicted 12-14, 12-19, 992E1
Calif utilities refund cases refused by US Sup Ct 12-11, 981E1

TELEPHONE Unions, Alliance of Independent
AT&T bias case declined by Sup Ct 7-3, 552A1
TELEVISION—*See under BROADCASTING; also ELECTRIC & Electronics Industry, PRESS*
TELEVISION Arts & Sciences, Academy of (ATAS)
Presents Emmys 9-17, 1030E1
TELLER, Edward
Belgian A-plant leak disputed 1-25, 69G3

1979

New pact ratified 5-18, 384A3
Apr econ indicators drop, strike linked 5-31, 463F2
Provenzano, Konigsberg '78 murder convictns upset 6-7, 491F3
Provenzano sentenced 7-10, 548E1
UPS pact rptd ratified 7-26, wage cncl OKs 7-27, 744E2
Fitzsimmons' son, 2 others indicted 8-2, 744C3
Calif lettuce settlemt cited 8-31, 698D3
Fitzsimmons on Pay Advisory Com 10-16, 829F2
Kirkland bids all unions join AFL-CIO 11-19, 885C2
Sachs to pay pension fund debt 12-10, 965C1
TEAMSTERS v. Daniel
SEC role in pensn plans barred by Sup Ct 1-16, 32F1
TEARS of Gold (book)
On best-seller list 5-6, 356E2; 6-3, 43C2
TEASDALE, Gov. Joseph P. (D, Mo.)
St Louis teachers end strike 3-12, 187B3
TECHNICON Corp.
Revlon to buy 9-6, 664A1
TECHNOLOGY Assessment, Office of—*See under U.S. GOVERNMENT-CONGRESS*
TEEKAH, Vincent
Slain 10-24, 838B2
TEENAGE Fathers (film)
Wins Oscar 4-9, 336C2
TEETH 'n' Smiles (play)
Opens 8-13, 712A3
TEHRANI, Sayed Jalaleddin
Heads Iran regency council 1-13, 25G1
In France 1-18; meets Khomeini, quits cncl 1-22, 49F2
TEIBELE and Her Demon (play)
Opens 12-16, 1007E2
TEITELBAUM, Rabbi Joel
Dies 8-19, 671F3
Nephew succeeds 9-10, 931E3
TEITELBAUM, Rabbi Moses
Appointed Satmar Hasidim ldr 9-10, 931E3
TEITELBOIM, Volodia
'75 assassinatn plot cited 1-18, 58D1, G2
TEKULVE, Kent
In World Series 10-10—10-17, 816B2
TELEGRAPH—*See TELEPHONES & Telegraph*

TELEPHONES & Telegraph
FCC OKs ITT long-distance svc 1-4, 15A2
AT&T documts order review declined by Sup Ct 1-8, 14G3
AT&T proposes speedy trust trial date, US refusal seen 1-11, 88A3
FCC ends Westn Union monopoly 1-25, 78A2
Lawyer phone waiver case declined by Sup Ct 2-26, 164F3
Washn Post TV viewing survey rptd 2-28, 3-1, 173B1
Rptrs phone bill subpoena case refused by Sup Ct 3-5, 184E3
Conn A-sub wire fraud sentences 3-15, 3-20, 240E2
Jobless pay for strikers upheld by Sup Ct 3-21, 231D1
2d LA bank wire-transfer theft 3-25, 239C2
AT&T data access case declined by Sup Ct 3-26, 231A1
LA bank computer consultant sentncd 3-26, 239G1
Jerusalem-Cairo hot-line opened 4-4, 248F3
FCC OKs local access phone pact 4-12, 350G3
Kissinger phone records case accepted by Sup Ct 4-16, 302B3
ITT offers long-distance phone svc 4-23, 350F3
Mex phone strike ends 5-2, 372F2
Japan-US sales pact signed 6-2, 416C1
FEC bills Carter com 6-4, 419A3
Canada-Saudi pact threatnd 6-19, 467E3
Warrantless surveillnc upheld by Sup Ct 6-20, 516C1
US-W Ger deal threatened 8-1, 586G1
ITT settles SEC chrgs 8-8, 648D1
Bell Canada strike 8-12, 613F1; strike ends 9-6, 685E1
UK to reform Post Office 9-12, 687B1
AT&T pvt-line rates scored 9-20, 870D1
Southn Bell pol paymts scored by FCC 9-20, 870F1
Canadian sentncd in Calif bank wire-transfer scheme 9-24, 840C3
Calif utilities refund stay refused by Sup Ct 10-1, 768C1; appeal denied 10-15, 848B1
Bell Canada, Saudi deal rptd delayed 10-18, 833A3
RCA loses satellite 12-10, 991E1
TELEVISION—*See under BROADCASTING; also ELECTRIC & Electronics Industry*
TELEVISION, National Public Affairs Center for (NPACT)
Nixon Admin moves disclosed 2-24, 194D1, B2
TELEVISION Arts & Sciences, Academy of
Presents Emmys 9-9, 858D2
TELEX Corp.
Lawyer fee case declined by Sup Ct 12-3, 964B2
TELLER, Edward
Asks US spy satellite photo release 1-31, 89F2
Hansen H-bomb letter published 9-16, 9-18, reactn 9-17, 713G2, 714B2; text of letter 714D1-717E3

1980

Presser's Reagan transitn role queried, backed 12-15, 12-18, 955E3
Donovan apptmt backed 12-16, 955B3

TEASDALE, Gov. Joseph P. (D, Mo.)
KC fire fighters end strike 3-22, 227E3
Seeks US disaster aid 5-13, 391F2
Wins Mo primary 8-5, 682F3
Loses reelectn 11-4, 847C1, 851G1
TECHNOLOGY—*See SCIENCE & Technology*
TEETERS, Nancy
Backs discount rate reductn 5-28, 400D2
TEIDE Peak
UK jet crash kills 146 4-25, 492B1
TEINOWITZ, Lois
Record divorce setlmt rptd 8-15, 639D1
TEINOWITZ, Philip
Record divorce setlmt rptd 8-15, 639D1
TEITELBAUM, Judge Hubert I.
Gypsum price fixing case settled 3-3, 557F3
TEJADA, Alfredo
In DR Emb talks 4-9, 293E3
Emb siege ends, freed in Cuba 4-27, 335G1
TEJERO Molina, Lt. Col. Antonio
Sentenced for '78 coup plot 5-7, 355G1
TEKERE, Edgar Z.
Zimbabwe dvpt min 3-11, 198D1
Chrgd with murder 8-6, 621A1
Freed 12-8, 946A2
TELECOMMUNICATIONS International Union (unaffiliated)
AT&T pact reached 8-9, 648C1
TELEGRAPH—*See TELEPHONES & Telegraph*

TELEPHONES & Telegraph
Commodity optns trader arrested in wire fraud 1-2, 94D3
Peru workers occupy Spanish Emb 2-8, 234G3
RCA to rent AT&T satellite, missing Satcom insurnc claims cited 2-20, 160C3
AT&T, ITT settle trust lawsuits 2-27, 240B1
Kissinger records access blocked by Sup Ct 3-3, 209C3
Australia labor unrest 3-7, 190G3
Fla review voted 3-11, 185B1
FCC sets phone industry deregulatn 4-7, 370E1
Japan bars NTT open bidding 5-15, 482E1
Pacific cable planned 5-19, 387E3
MCI wins $1.8 bln AT&T suit 6-13, 456B3
UK plans monopoly curbs 7-21, 563B1
Bell Canada interconnect monopoly curbed 8-5, 633A1
AT&T reaches pacts with CWA, 2 other unions 8-9, 648B1
Bell Canada gets rate hike 8-12, 632D3
AT&T, equipmt suppliers settle trust case 8-18, 917C2
AT&T begins reorgn 8-20, 648E1-A3
Bell Canada monopoly chrgd 9-23, denied 9-24, 748G2
Telecommunicatns bill tabled by Cong 9-30, 835E2
Georg Goubau dies 10-17, 876G1
Japan-US trade talks resume 10-19, 864A3
FCC OKs WATS line resales 10-21, 987B3
FCC revises phone deregulatn plan 10-28, 987G2
Marubeni, Hitachi units convicted 11-5, 957C3
Conn harassmt law challenge declined by Sup Ct 12-1, 918G2
FCC seeks small cos regulatn end 12-16, 987D3
US, Japan sign pact 12-19, 995B2

TELEPROMPTER Corp.
Showtime scores Getty Oil pay-TV film venture 4-24, 376E2
Westinghouse to acquire 10-15, 836E1
Muzak
GOP office taps suspected 6-24, 480E3
TELEVISION—*See under BROADCASTING*
TELEVISION Arts & Sciences, Academy of
Emmys presented 9-7, 692B1
TELEVISION Bureau of Advertising Inc.
'79 top 10 TV advertisers listed 4-4, 376B2
TELEVISION & Radio Artists, American Federation of (AFTRA) (AFL-CIO)
TV, film actors strike 7-21, 684A3
TV, film actors end strike 10-23, 805B3

1976

TELLI, Diallo
Chrgs CIA plot link 8-24, 1005B2
TELLO Macias, Carlos
Mexico presidency min 12-2, 906G3
TENACE, Gene
Contract rptd signed 12-5, 951D3
TENASSEE, Patrick
Cuba, China mil presence in Guyana denied 3-10, 253F1
TENDLER, Stewart
Angola ousts 6-16, 480D3
TENEKECI, Gen. Abdullah
Pleads innocent 4-7, 298G1; acquitted 4-30, 322B3

TENG Hsiao-ping
Chou En-lai dies 1-8, 8E3-G3
Eulogizes Chou 1-15, 48C1
CP split rptd 2-6, 2-8, 117F1-C2
Hua named 'acting' premr 2-7, 117E1
Attacked in pol campaign; central com split, Chiang Ching role rptd 2-10—3-9, 188C3-189G2
Attacked in press 3-10—3-28, 243F3
Pro-Chou rallies 4-1—4-5, 244A1
Ousted as premr, Hua named 4-7, 243B3
Purge backed 4-8—4-28, posters demand death 4-9, 332F3-333D1
May Day CP unity rptd 5-2, 332E3
Press attacks continue 5-7, 5-18, 439C1, E1, A2
Chu Teh buried 7-11, 521B1
Posters attack prov ldrs 7-19, 555D2
Mao dies 9-9, 657C1; announcemt text excerpt cites 659C2, B3
3 offcls rptd purged 9-11, 712C1
Hua calls for contd criticism 9-18, 711B3
Cited in Hua biog 758C1
Wan Li reinstatemt rptd 10-14, 809A3
Radical murder plot rptd 10-26, 809F2
'Gang of 4' accused 12-18, 999G3

TENG Ying-chao
At Chou rites 1-15, 48B1
Gets Standing Com post, lauds Huang appt 12-2, 904F2
TENNECO Inc.
Packaging Corp trust dvpts 2-18—10-5, 886D1; offcls sentncd 11-30, 921F2, A3
SEC lists paymts 5-12, 729C1
Newport News Shipbuilding & Dry Dock Co.
Defns Dept to pay Navy debt 4-8, 309B2
Rickover scores cost overruns 6-7, 453G3
Navy paymt talks stalled 6-10, 453F3
Tenneco Oil Co.
La refinery blast 8-12, 816A2

1977

TELLICO Dam (Tenn.)
Constructn halted 1-31, 95G2-C3
TELLMAN, Barbara
Vs Ariz water project 3-21, 210G1
TELLO Macias, Carlos
Replaced in Cabt 11-17, 966B3
'78 budget eases austerity program 12-15, 985A2
TELPAK—*See AMERICAN Telephone & Telegraph Co.*
TEMPLETON, Garry
NL wins All-Star Game 7-19, 567E2 ★
NL batting ldr 10-2, 926C3, D3
TENERIFE—*See CANARY Islands*
TENG Ah Boo
Sentenced 1-8, 223F3

TENG Hsiao-ping
Posters ask rehabilitatn 1-6, 1-7, 1G1
Wu blamed for '76 Peking riots 1-8, 1F2
Posters urge rehabilitatn 1-9—1-11, 61B2
Reinstatemt rpts 1-13, 61B2, F2; 1-20—1-24, 97F3
Radical accused of bugging 3-9, 180F1
Educators rptd rehabilitated 3-9, 180A2
Rehabilitated 7-22, 571D2
In ruling triumvirate 8-21, 645E2
Meets US Secy Vance 8-24, 645A2
Burma asks rebel aid end 779F2
Sees US ties setback, Ford vow noted 9-6; Ford denies 9-7, 686D3-687A1
Wei gets armed forces post 9-25, 743D3

TENNECO Inc.
Anaconda takeover try cited 1-12, 55C3
Newport News-Navy cost pacts set 2-11, 3-8, 232A2
Gulf of Mex gas probe set 2-17, 151F3
Channel gas diversns questnd 2-28, 3-7; FPC orders probe 3-8, 196C1
On '76 Fortune 500 list 340F1
US cancels offshore lease 6-8, 499C1
Calif land holdings breakup asked 8-22, 703G2
Buys Phila Life 8-25, 650F3

1978

TELLICO Dam (Tenn.)
TVA member links resignatn, constructn halt 5-5, 390F2
Constructn halt upheld by Sup Ct 6-15, 468A2
Endangered Species Act amended by Cong 10-15, 834C2; signed 11-10, 1003B1
TELPAK—*See AMERICAN Telephone & Telegraph*
TEMPEST Queen (race horse)
Named top 3-yr old filly 12-12, 1028C1
TEMPLETON, Garry
NL batting ldr 10-2, 928E2

TENG Hsiao-ping
Backers get key posts 1-2, 53G3
Meets French premr 1-20, 71G1
Visits Burma 1-26—1-31, Nepal 2-3—2-5, 111F2
Cleared of '76 Peking riots 2-15, 111C2
Remains 3d in hierarchy, backers get major posts 2-26—3-5, 153B1-B2
Heads Consultative Conf 3-8, 154G2
Chai named envoy to US 5-19, 384C3
Meets Brzezinski 5-21, 384G2
Asks Mao ideas reevaluated 6-3, 532E2
Urged rehabilitatn program 6-5, 435F3
Econ aid to Viet cut 6-5, 6-7, 464G1
Hosts Spain king 6-16—6-19, 576C2
US scientists visit 7-10, 564A3
Role in leng trip to Thailand rptd 7-14, 548C3
At Japan pact signing 8-12, 637D1
Foreigner contacts ban lifted 9-9, 773D2
Wu ousted as Peking mayor 10-10, 773G3
Arrives Japan 10-22, pact implemented 10-23; on US ties, Korean reunificatn, Sovt threat 10-25, 801B1-802E1
In Thailand, Malaysia, Singapore, Burma 11-5—11-14; calls USSR world threat 11-6, scores Viet pact 11-8, 894B1
OKs new poster campaign 949C1
Mao tied to 'Gang of 4' 11-19, 901F2
Posters ask '76 Peking riot probe 11-20, blame Mao for '76 purge 11-23, 949E1, F1
Chin named Peking pol head 11-22, 950G1
Hopes for US visit 11-25; invited 12-11, 974C1, D1
Calls '76 purge 'wrong' 11-26, 950B1
Lauds posters, urges caution 11-27, 949E2
Denies break with Hua 11-27, 949G2
Appears with Hua in public 12-1, 950C1
France-China trade pact signed 12-4, 986A2
US-Peking ties agreed, US visit set 12-14, 973B1, G2, 975D2, 976A2
At Peng, Tao rites 12-24, 1015A2

TENG Ying-chao
In China Politburo 12-22, 1015E1
Leads delegatn to Cambodia 1-18, 42C3
TENNA Corp.
Seatrain, Ludwig indicted 3-8, plead guilty 3-16, 184B3
SEC rebate settlemt cited 10-23, 876C3
TENNECO Atlantic Pipeline Co.—*See under TENNECO Inc.*
TENNECO Inc.
McDermott pleads guilty to payoffs 2-22, 142G2-A3
On '77 Fortune 500 list 5-8, 325F1
Albright & Wilson purchase offered 5-23, 404E1
Coal gasificatn plant financing plan submitted 6-2, 471A3
Interstate gas sales probed 6-22, 471A2
Chrmn Scott retires, Ketelsen named 6-30, 809C1
Newport News Shipbuilding and Dry Dock Co.
Navy settles Gen Dynamics, Litton contract disputes 6-9, 6-20, 469F1
Tenneco Atlantic Pipeline Co.
US rejcts Algerian gas imports 12-18, 983E3

1979

TELLICO Dam (Tenn.)
Cherokee suit dismissed 11-2, 990B1
Cong OKs 8-1, 9-10, Carter signs 9-26, 766F2
Flood gates dropped 11-29, 990B1
TELLING, Edward R.
On Sears price rollback 4-30, 363C1
Bias suit vs US dismissed 5-15, 365F3
TELTSCHER, Eliot
Wins Atlanta Open 9-17, 734E2
TEMPERLEY, Ronald
Cleared in youth's slaying 7-4, 565B1
TEMPLER, Field Marshall Sir Gerald Walter Robert
Dies 10-25, 860F3
TEMPLETON, Garry
NL batting ldr 9-30, 955D2-F2
TEMPLE University (Philadelphia, Pa.)
Wins Garden State Bowl 12-15, 1001G2
10 (film)
Released 10-5, 1008G1
Top-grossing film 10-31, 892G3
TENDER Offer—*See STOCKS*
TENEVA, Daniela
Banned from track 10-26, 912A1

TENG Hsiao-ping (Deng Xiaoping)
Photo 83D3
Toasts US-China ties 1-1, 2C1
Pinyin transliteratn set 1-1, 75F2
Meets US reps on Taiwan ties, invites Goldwater 1-2, 2F1
Hu gets top party posts, Wang demoted 1-4, 6D3, 7A1
Vs China troops to Cambodia 1-5, 1D1
Greets Sihanouk in Peking 1-6, 10D3-11A1
Meets 4 US sens; offers Taiwan autonomy, 1-9, Taiwan rejects 1-11, 26A3
Protesters barred from mtg 1-14, 58C3
Nixon invited to state dinner 1-17, 29E3
Albania CP ldr scores 1-27, 69E3
In US 1-28; meets Carter 1-29–1-30, signs pacts 1-31; communique issued 2-1, 65A1-66D2
In Atlanta, Houston, Seattle 2-1–2-5; leaves US 2-5; in Japan, meets offcls 2-6–2-7; returns to Peking 2-8, 83D2-84D1
Sovts score visit to US 2-1, 2-4, 84D1
Thai premr on China arms to Cambodia 2-7, 84D2
US warns China vs attack on Vietnam 2-9, 106B3
Sihanouk returns to Peking 2-13, 142C2
Calls Viet invasn limited 2-19, 121G1
Viet chrgs US invasn collusn 2-19, 121D2
USSR links US visit, Viet invasn 2-19–2-20, 122C2
Sees Viet war end in 10 days 2-26, 141C1
US asks Viet exit 2-27, 141C2
Compares Viet, Cuba; doubts Sovt interventn 2-27, 141D2
Warns protesters 3-16, 259A1
Meets US sens; scores Taiwan ties, offers plan to monitor SALT 4-19, 312A1
Meets Waldheim on Viet conflict 5-1, 340A2
Replies to critics rptd 5-25, 406F1
Hunan radio criticism rptd 5-29, 406B1
Meets US trade rep on textiles 5-30, 405G3
Dalai Lama rptdly backs 6-14, 445B1
New dep prmrs rptd backers 7-2, 502F2
Warns of war peril, Sovt hegemony 8-25, 644C3
Meets Mondale, signs pacts 8-27–8-28, 644B2
Nixon visits China 9-17–9-22, 751F1
Poster criticism rptd 9-22, 751E1
Politburo promotns rptd 9-28, 750D3

TENGLEMANN Group, The
A&P purchase agreed 1-16, 53C3
TENG Tuo (deceased)
Followers rehabilitated 8-3, 651B3
TENG Ying-chao
Anti-corruptn drive head 8-22, 651F3
TENNECO Inc.
On '78 Fortune 500 list 5-7, 304F1
Baltimore Canyon gas find rptd 5-23, 442F3
Baltimore Canyon oil find rptd 6-5, 518D2
Interstate gas shipmt fine imposed 7-27, 629E1
Baltimore Canyon well rptd dry 10-3, 867C2
Gulf of Mex lease bid offered 11-27, 942G3
Southwestn Life merger set 12-11, 986A3
Newport News Shipbuilding and Dry Dock Co.
NLRB to probe union vote 3-2, 187C2
Union suspends strike 4-22, 306C2
NLRB dismisses USW vote fraud chrgs 5-4, orders USW recognitn 6-26; Cambell to appeal 7-3, 560G3
Navy settles '75 A-cruiser dispute 8-29, 747C1
Tenneco Oil Co.
Ashland unit holdings sold 2-4, 560E3
Fined in La bribe case 3-17, 239B3
Gen Crude merger bid rejctd 3-28, 283A1
Hosp union organizing curbs backed by Sup Ct 6-20, 516A2
UV assets purchase set 7-23, 770B3
Tennessee Gas Pipeline Co.
Mex natural gas purchased 10-18, 814F3
TENNESSEAN, The (Nashville, Tenn. newspaper)
Gannett Co buys 7-5, 618B3

1980

TELLING, Edward R.
Backs Olympic boycott 4-3, 260A1
Named Sears pres 10-7, 959G2
TELL Me a Riddle (film)
Released 12-17, 1003E2
TELTSCHER, Eliot
Loses Birmingham WCT 1-20, 607E2
Wins Atlanta Open tennis 8-24, 691C3
Loses Canton Grand Prix 10-19, 947C1
TEMPERENCE Hill (racehorse)
Wins Belmont Stakes 6-7, 447E2
Named top 3-yr-old colt 12-17, 1002C2
TEMPLE Sr., George Francis
Dies 9-30, 756F2
TEMPLETON, Garry
NL batting ldr 10-6, 926D2
TEMPLETON Prize for Progress in Religion
Chicago theologian wins 5-13, 471D2
TEMPLE University (Philadelphia, Pa.)
Carter at town mtg 5-9, 367F1
TENA, Juan Ignacio
Strikers occupy emb 2-8, leads talks 2-11, 234G3

TENG Hsiao-ping—*See DENG Xiaoping*

TENNA Corp.
Liquidatn ordered 9-12, 985G3
TENNANT, Paula Pike
Arrested 5-27, release rptd 6-7, 444F2
TENNECO Inc.
On '79 Fortune 500 list 5-5, 290F1
10th in '79 defns contracts 5-28, 403F1
Houston Oil merger set 12-9, 985A2
Newport News Shipbuilding and Dry Dock Co.
OSHA chrgs 617 violatns 2-27, 147C3
USW pact signed 3-31, 251B2

Five-Year Index —TENNIS 867

1976

TENNESSEE
Primary date set 22B2
Hamilton bank fails 2-16, files bankruptcy 2-20, 166E3, 167E1
Primary reforms enacted 2-20, 373F1
US Sup Ct bars review of snake handling case 3-8, 219C2
Ford, Reagan visit 5-14—5-21, 374E1
Primary results 5-25, 373F1-F2, B3, 374D2
Pvtly insured S&Ls rptd OKd 6-20, 495E1
Sup Ct declines Chattanooga desegregation review 6-30, 552A3 ★
Dem conv women delegates, table 508D2
Ford OKs reactor funds 7-12, 517G1
Dem conv pres vote, table 7-14, 507D2
Sen primary results 8-5, 633G1
Ray transferred to new prison 8-13, 640D3
GOP pre-conv delegate count 8-14, 583D3
GOP conv pres, vp vote tables 8-18—8-19, 8-19, 599D1, D3
Fscl '75 per capita income, tax burden rptd 9-15, 10-12, 959D2
Carter in Nashville 10-1, 743A1
Election results 11-2; pres 818D1, 819B2; cong 819F3, 822C3, 828C3, 830B4
RC bishop grants gen absolutn 12-5, 12-12, 951E1-B2

TENNEY, Judge Charles H.
Bars NY constructn union bias 9-1, 943F3

TENNIS
Evert gets AP award 1-15, 31F3
Australia team to visit China 4-6, 249G3
Richards barred from US Open 8-27, 716E1
Godfried Von Cramm dies 11-8, 970E1
Evert named athlete of yr 12-3, 969A3

1977

TENNESSEE
Legislature schedule rptd 6F2
Indiana OKs ERA 1-18, 59C2
Fish halts Tellico Dam constructn 1-31, 95G2-C3
2 state univs ordrd merged 1-31, 112G2
Hamilton trustees sue auditors 2-11, 155A3
Nashville-Davidson busing success cited 2-15, 112G1
RC bishop '76 absolutn scored 3-25, 375D2
Storms, floods hit 4-3—4-6, 311F2
Death penalty enacted 4-11, 594E1
Biology text barred in Ind 4-14, 471E3
'76 per-capita income table 5-10, 387F2
Child porno arrest rptd 5-15—5-18, 432E2
Memphis econ data rptd; table 5-16, 384E2, B3
Ray escapes Brushy Mt prison 6-10, recaptured 6-13; plot discounted 6-14, 459A1
Maury County jail fire 6-26, 508E3
Tanzania pres visits agri projcts 8-8—8-9, 624C1
A-material rptd missing from Oak Ridge 8-8, 717A2
Elvis Presley dies 8-16, 695C3
2 Presley mourners killed 8-18, 696G1
'76 per capita income, tax burden table 9-13, 10-18, 821D2
Chuch coll student aid backed 10-3, 760E3
Ray sentncd for jail escape 10-27, 848C1
ERA rescission cited 11-14, 918E1
Memphis favored as '78 Dem conv site 12-9, 960C3
Toshiba plans Nashville TV plant 12-14, 974A2

Energy Developments
Emergency gas purchase OKd 1-20; fuel crisis spurs schl closings, job layoffs 1-22, 54C1, C2
Clinch R A-project curbed; reaction 4-7, 267E3, 268E1; 4-27, 5-2, 334C3, 335A1
Carter energy plan 4-20, 290F2, 293C2
TVA sued on air pollution 6-22, 521A3
Clinch R projct dropped from fund bill 7-25, 592A3
Clinch R A-project clears House 9-20, 758C2; Cong 10-20, 832G3; Carter vetoes 11-5, 854E2
Clinch R provisn in '78 NRC authorizatn clears Cong 11-29, 938E1; signed 12-13, 1001G2

TENNESSEE Natural Gas Lines Inc.
FPC bars emergency gas purchase 1-21, 54C1

TENNESSEE System, University of
Etnier '73 fish find cited 1-31, 95B3
Tenn State merger ordrd 1-31, 112A3
Nashville-U of Tenn merger ordrd 1-31, 112A3
Chattanooga wins NCAA basketball title 3-19, 262D2
Morgan in NFL draft 5-3, 353C3
NBA drafts 2 from Knoxville 6-10, 584A3

TENNESSEE-Tombigbee Waterway—*See RIVERS & Waterways*

TENNESSEE Valley Authority—*See under U.S. GOVERNMENT*

TENNEY, Judge Charles H.
Phone surveillnc order backed 12-7, 939F1

TENNIS
King-Va Slims dispute 3-18, 431D1
WCT, Grand Prix to merge 3-23, 353F3-354C1
USTA rejcts Richards sex test 4-12, 354C1
S Africa Davis Cup match protests 4-15—4-17, 353F2
Grand Prix Masters set for NYC 4-19, 430G3
Davis Cup rescheduling petitn rptd 5-4, 353E3
'Heavyweight championship' fee disclosures 5-7—5-20, FCC rpts probe 7-8, 548C2
WTT final standings 8-16, 787C3
Richards OKd for US Open 8-17, 787C2
US Open plagued by unrest, racial disputes; '78 move rptd 9-4—9-11, 787D1, C2
Ashe regrets S African death 9-25, 735E3
Nastase barred from '78 Davis Cup 10-3, 1020A3
'Spaghetti' racquet banned 10-19, 1020G2
House subcom probes sports coverage 11-3, 950B1
WCT settles suit vs Borg 12-6, 1020B3
Sovts quit WTT, new team announced 12-10, 1020F2

1978

TENNESSEE
'67, '77 sales-tax rates rptd 1-5, 15B3, F3
NASL '77 expansn cited 1-5, 23B1
Lance Knoxville bank loan rptd repaid 1-17, 2-13, 3-22, 204C3
Nashville prison bldg ordrd closed 1-30, 440E1
Coal shortage rptd 2-11, Carter sees gov 2-16, 104D1, D2
Waverly derailmt 2-23, propane blast 2-24; US prelim probe rptd 3-6, 196C1
Nashville Davis Cup protests 3-17—3-19, 251A1
RR safety measures ordrd 3-23, 5-9, 365A3, E3
Utility customer hearings backed by US Sup Ct 5-1, 364A1
3 arrested in Gaines kidnap 5-3, 5-4, 396A3
Amtrak Nashville route cutback proposed 5-8, 366E1
Memphis firemen strike 7-1—7-4, 513D2
Memphis on bad-air list 7-5, 513D1
Bad-air list corrected 7-19, 644B2
Memphis police, firemen strike 8-10—8-18, 644C2
Memphis blackout, looting 8-16, 644G2
Presley fans mark death 8-16, 644A3
Carter A-breeder deal rpt upsets Baker 8-24, 678A1
Maybelle Carter dies 10-23, 888G2
Memphis police rejct King death plot 11-10—11-11, 898C2
Maury Cnty '77 jail arsonist sentncd 12-20, 992A2

Clinch River Atomic Project—*See CLINCH River*

King Assassination—*See KING Jr., Rev. Martin Luther*

Politics & Government
Legislature schedule rptd 14G3
State govt tax revenue table 1-9, 84E2
Clergy pub office ban upset by US Sup Ct 4-19, 309C1
Carter in Knoxville, Oak Ridge 5-22, 386G2-B3, 390G2
Govt spending curb rptd 6-6, 425C1
Rep Allen dies 6-18, 540D2
ERA '77 rescissn cited 494D2
Primary results 8-3, 606G1
ERA rescissn amendmt rejected by US House 8-15, 661G2
ERA rescissn amendmts rejctd by US Sen 10-3, 788C1
Carter in Nashville 10-26, 831A2
Election results 11-7: cong 846A2, 848D3, 852C2, 853D1; state 845G1, 847A1, 853C1, E3
Dems meet in Memphis 12-8—12-10, 956D1
Blanton's aides arrested in parole payoff 12-15; pardons voided 12-20, defended 12-22, 12-24, 1011E1-E2

TENNESSEE, University of (Knoxville)
Wins NCAA swimming title 3-26, 780G2

TENNESSEE State University (Nashville)
Women's track team sets 640-yd relay mark 2-24, indoor sprint medley mark 6-8—6-10, 600B3, E3

TENNESSEE Valley Authority—*See under U.S. GOVERNMENT*

TENNIS
'77 USTA rankings 1-5, 22D3
AIAW chngs scholarship rules 1-7—1-11, 40B3
Navratilova sets Va Slims win record 1-8—3-5, 419E1
Wussler quits CBS Sports 3-15, FCC censures 'Heavyweight Championship' tourn 3-16, 252D1
US-S Africa Davis Cup protests 3-17—3-19, 251A3
S Africa barred from Davis, Federatn cups 4-16, 419F2
WTA ends Va Slims pact 4-21, Avon '79 sponsorship rptd 5-17, 419B2
Stars defy 'Super Grand Prix' 4-23, 418A3
Borg quits Grand Prix bonus chase 6-2, 540G1
Guthrie celebrity tourn injury rptd 6-29, 538E2
WTT final standings 8-14, 1027C1
Evert named WTT playoff MVP 9-21, 1027G1
WTT clubs fold 10-27—11-11, new franchises rptd planned 12-1, 1027A1

1979

TENNESSEE
Legislature schedule rptd 5F3
Memphis leukemia study rptd 2-9, 139A2
Tombigbee projct upheld 3-13, 188A3
Presley estate probated 3-24, 272G1
Hardware dealers shift conv to Memphis 4-4, 260B2
Regulatory bds rptd segregated 4-9, 307A2
Floods hit 5-4, 472D2
Hosp union organizing curbs backed by Sup Ct 6-20, 516A2
Truckers stage protest 6-28, 479C2
Gannett buys, sells Nashville papers 7-5, 618B3
Flash-flood warnings posted 9-14, 691F1
'78 per capita income rptd 9-16, 746F2
Memphis Rogues sale OKd 10-15, 1004B2
US sues Sears re job bias 10-22, 885D3
Chandler reelected mayor 11-15, 904E3
Midwest quake threat rptd 11-15, 954D1

Atomic Energy
Clinch R projct not budgeted 1-22, 45A3
Carter vs Clinch R projct 5-4, 346G3
Sequoyah reactor licensing delayed 5-21, 381G3
Carter scores Clinch R project 5-4, 346G3
Erwin A-fuel plant shut 9-18, FBI probes uranium loss 10-10, 809A3
Oak Ridge rpt sees A-plant cooling system hazard 11-1, NRC discounts 11-2, 849F1-C2
Sequoyah reactor licensing delay extended 11-5, 849C1

Crime & Civil Disorders
Fed parole-selling probe continues 1-4; Blanton pardons felons 1-16; Alexander replaces Blanton as gov, curbs convict releases 1-17, 36F1-B3
Ray parole deal rptd too costly 1-18, Brushy Mt escape convictn upheld 2-21, 156D2
Sen censures Blanton, pardons still in dispute 1-19–1-31; Alexander orders audits 1-22, asks prison reform 2-14, 152E2
Blanton ex-comr sentncd 1-26, 156E2
6 indicted in pardon sales 3-15, appeals ct upholds Blanton pardons 4-10; 2 murders linked 4-14, 4-17, 309C2-B3
Co-defendant confessns allowed by Sup Ct 5-29, 422A1
Power to void state convictns backed by Sup Ct 7-2, 558E3
Ray jail break fails 11-5, 891E2
Presley MD drug chrgs rptd 12-19, 1005C3

King Assassination—*See KING Jr., Rev. Martin Luther*

School Issues
Peabody, Vanderbilt colls merge 3-19, 209D1
Nashville univ merger, higher educ integratn plans upheld 4-13, 326G2-C3
Nashville univ merger stay denied by Sup Ct 6-18, 499B2

TENNESSEE Gas Pipeline Co.—*See under TENNECO Inc.*

TENNESSEE River
Tombigbee waterway upheld 3-13, 188A3

TENNESSEE State University (Nashville)
Tenn merger upheld 4-13, 326G2-C3
McLendon in basketball HOF 4-30, 526E3
Tenn U merger stay denied by Sup Ct 6-18, 499B2

TENNESSEE System, University of
Nashville campus merger upheld 4-13, 326G2-C3
Shaw in NFL draft 5-3, 335G2
Knoxville loses NCAA doubles title 5-28, 570B2
Nashville campus merger stay denied by Sup Ct 6-18, 499B2
Knoxville loses Bluebonnet Bowl 12-31, 1001C3

TENNESSEE Valley Authority (TVA)—*See under U.S. GOVERNMENT*

TENNIS
Borg, Evert named '78 top players by ITF 1-18, 103F2
Grand Prix dispute setld 2-10, 391E1
WTT demise announced 3-8, 391D3
Evert, Lloyd wed 4-17, 392B2
Ashe suffers heart attack 7-31, undergoes surgery 12-13, 1004A1

1980

TENNESSEE
House for cats rptd purchased 2-9, 200G1
Memphis hay fever study rptd 2-18, 159G3
Allis-Chalmers pact set 3-15, 308A3
TVA dam construction challenge declined by Sup Ct 3-24, 265B2
Memphis area illness probed 4-2, 331F2
Tornado hits 4-7—4-8, 391A3
Harvester strike ends 4-20, 308G2
Chattanooga papers partially join 5-12, Civiletti OKs 9-2, 732E2
N&W, Southn RR merger sought 6-2, 427E2
Tombigbee funds bill clears Cong 6-25, 9-10, Carter signs 10-1, 803C2
Scopes trial lawyer dies 6-27, 528A2
Chattanooga papers' pact gets final OK 11-6, 907E1
Levi trust case setlmt award rptd 12-2, 917A3

Atomic Energy & Safeguards
Erwin A-fuel plant reopened despite uranium loss 1-16, 54B1
Oak Ridge rpt confirms '57 Sovt mishap 2-13, 153C1
Sequoyah plant start-up license OKd 2-28, 169F2
Sequoyah plant gets operating license 9-16, 723A2

Crime & Civil Disorders
Presley MD license suspended 1-19, 199C1
Bahamas bank looting case rptd 3-3, 229B1
State legislators' immunity curbed by US Sup Ct 3-19, 249E3
KKK members arrested in Chattanooga shooting 4-19, 333E1
Presley MD indicted 5-16, 414B2
Road builders bid-rigging guilty pleas rptd 7-5, 655F1-A2
KKK members acquitted in Chattanooga shooting 7-22, racial disorders erupt 7-22—7-26, 575F3

Obituaries
Hicks, Sue Kerr 6-27, 528A1
Jenkins, Ray H 12-26, 1004B2
Phillips, D 10-23, 876C3

Politics & Government—*See also other appropriate subheads in this section*
Legislature schedule rptd 18F1
Pres primary results 5-6, 341F2, 342D1
US House primary results 8-7, 682G3
Reagan in Knoxville 9-22, 723A1
Carter campaigns in Bristol, Nashville 10-9, 778C2
Carter tours 10-31, 841B1
Election results 11-4; pres 838D1, 839B2, G3; cong 840D3, 844C2, 850G1; state 845E3
'80 census rptd, reapportmt seen 12-31, 983G1

Sports
NASL Memphis club move to Calgary set 12-8, 1001F1

TENNESSEE, University of (Knoxville)
Loses AIAW basketball title 3-23, 240A3
James in NFL draft 4-29, 336F3
2 win NCAA doubles tennis title 5-26, 607D1
Johnson in NBA draft 6-10, 447F2

TENNESSEE State University (Nashville)
Mile relay record set 2-8, 892F2
Davis in NBA draft 6-10, 447G2

TENNESSEE-Tombigbee Waterway
Appropriatn clears Cong 6-25, 9-10, signed 10-1, 803C2

TENNESSEE Valley Authority (TVA)—*See under U.S. GOVERNMENT*

TENNIS
NCAA OKs women's title tourns 1-8, 103C3
Borg, Navratilova named top '79 players 1-21, 213D2
US eliminated from Davis Cup 3-9, 607F1
Ashe retires 4-16, 607A2
Hunts' bailout loan collateral 5-28, 425E3
French Open default controversy 6-3, 606F3
Borg sets French Open win marks 6-8, 606A3
Borg sets Wimbledon match win mark 7-6, 606D2
Pros threaten US Open boycott 7-12, settle USTA rules dispute 7-16, 691D3
Ashe named Davis Cup captain 9-7, 692A1
Borg, McEnroe decline S Africa match 10-16, 947E1
Women end US Open boycott threat 11-12, 947B1

1976

Winners
Alan King Classic, Connors 5-16, 716B2
Amer clay ct, Connors 8-16, 656C2
Australian Open, Edmondson, Goolagong 1-4, 31E3
Baltimore intl indoor, Gorman 1-25, 123G2
Birmingham intl indoor, Connors 1-25, 123G2
British hardct, Fibak 5-16, 716C2
Challenge Cup, Connors 2-29, 716D2
DC Va Slims, Evert 1-25, 123A3
Federatn Cup, US 8-29, 716A2
Houston Va Slims, Navratilova 1-18, 123A3
Italian Open, Panatta 5-30, 656C2
L'eggs World Series, Evert 1-11, 31D3
Players Assn, Connors 3-14, 716C2
Rotterdam WCT, Ashe 2-29, 716D2
Sarasota Va Slims, Evert 2-29, 716C2
Tennis Wk Open, Nastase, Kruger 8-29, 716G1
US Open (doubles), Riessen, Okker, Boshoff, Kloss 9-12, 716C1
US Open (mixed doubles), King, Dent 9-12, 716D1
US Open (singles), Evert, Connors 9-11, 9-12, 716A1
US Pro, Borg 8-31, 716G1
US pro indoor, Connors 2-1, 123A2
Volvo intl Connors 8-9, 656B2
Washington Star, Connors 7-27, 716B2
WCT finals, Borg 5-9, 504G1
Wimbledon, Evert, Borg, 7-2, 7-3, 504E1

1977

Obituaries
Allison, Wilmer 4-20, 356F2
Winners
Australian Open, Tanner, Reid 1-9, 103D3
Baltimore Intl Indoor, Gottfried 1-23, 103G3
Bloomington Va Slims, Navratilova 1-30, 104A1
Bridgestone Women's Doubles, Stove, Navratilova 4-10, 430D3
Charlotte WCT, Barazzutti 4-24, 430A3
Chicago Va Slims, Evert 2-13, 431E1
Davis Cup, Australia 12-4, 970F1
DC Va Slims, Navratilova 1-9, 103G3
Denver Grand Prix, Borg 4-24, 431B1
Detroit Va Slims, Navratilova 2-27, 431F1
Family Circle Cup, Evert 4-3, 430C3
French Open, Vilas, Jausovec 6-5, 548A2
German Intl, Bertolucci 5-15, 431B1
Heavyweight championship, Connors 3-6, 548E2
Hollywood Va Slims, Evert 1-16, 103G3
Houston WCT, Panatta 4-18, 430A3
Italian Open, Gerulaitis, Newberry 5-22, 430A3
King tourn, Connors 5-1, 430F3
La Costa Intl, Gottfried 3-29, 431B1
LA Va Slims, Evert 2-20, 431E1
London WCT, Dibbs 4-3, 430G2
Mex City WCT, Nastase 2-13, 430F2
Miami Grand Prix, Dibbs 2-13, 431A1
Monte Carlo WCT, Borg 4-10, 430G2
Ocean City Intl, Gerulaitis 2-20, 430C3
Palm Springs Grand Prix, Gottfried 2-27, 431A1
Pepsi Grand Slam, Borg 1-23, 103G3
Port Wash Lionel Cup, King, Richards 4-17, 430E3
Richmond WCT, Okker 2-6, 430F2
Rotterdam WCT, Stockton 3-27, 430G2
San Fran Va Slims, Barker 3-6, 431F1
Seattle Va Slims, Evert 2-6, 431E1
Springfield Championship, Vilas 2-13, 430B3
SW Pacific Championship, Gottfried 4-3, 430D3
Toronto WCT, Stockton 2-20, 430F2
US Indoor, Borg 3-6, 430C3
US Open (doubles), Stove, Navratilova, Hewitt, McMillan 9-9, 9-11, 787A2
US Open (singles), Vilas, Evert 9-10, 9-11, 787C1
US Pro Indoor, Stockton 1-3, 103F3
Va Beach Championship, Vilas 4-23, 430F3
Va Slims title, Evert 3-27, 431B1
Volvo Classic, Gottfried 3-20, 431A1
WCT Challenge Cup, Nastase 4-10, 430E2
WCT doubles title, Stockton, Amritraj 5-8, 430D2
WCT singles title, Connors 5-15, 430C2
Wimbledon, Borg, Wade 7-1, 7-2, 548D1
Women's World Series, Evert 4-17, 430E3
World Cup, US 3-11—3-13, 431F1
WTT championship, NY Apples 8-27, 787C3

1978

Obituaries
Brugnon, Jacques 3-30, 252D2
Doeg, John Hope 4-27, 440E2
Winners
Amer Airlines Games, Tanner 2-19, 419A1
Atlanta Women's Classic, Evert 10-2, 1027B2
Australian Open, Gerulaitis, Goolagong 12-31-77, 1-1, 22F3
Australian Indoor, Connors 10-22, 1027C2
Benson & Hedges, McEnroe 11-19, 1027C2
Birmingham WCT, Borg 1-15, 418F3
Boston Va Slims, Goolagong 3-19, 419A2
Brinker tourn, Goolagong 3-12, 419A2
Canadian Open, Marsikova, Dibbs 8-19, 8-20, 1027A2
Chicago Va Slims, Navratilova 2-5, 419F1
Davis Cup N America Zone, US 3-19, 252A1
Davis Cup, US 12-10, 1026D3
Detroit Va Slims, Navratilova 2-26, 419G1
Eastbourne Intl, Navratilova 6-24, 540D1
Family Circle Cup, Evert 4-16, 419A2
Federatn Cup, US 12-3, 1026G3
Fla Va Slims, Goolagong 1-15, 419G1
Forest Hills Invitatn, Gerulaitis 7-16, 1027G1
Frankfurt Cup, Nastase 12-10, 1027D2
French Open, Borg, Ruzici 6-11, 540D1
German championships, Vilas, Jausovec, 5-21, 419D1
Grand Prix Master, Connors 1-8, 22G2
Houston Va Slims, Navratilova 1-22, 419F1
Houston WCT, Gottfried 4-23, 419C1
Italian Open, Borg, Mariskova 5-27, 5-28, 418D2
KC Va Slims, Navratilova 3-5, 419G1
Kent championships, Connors, Goolagong 6-10, 540C1
King Classic, Solomon 4-30, 419C1
LA Va Slims, Navratilova 1-29, 419F1
Louisville Intl, Solomon 7-30, 1027A2
Milan WCT, Borg 4-2, 419B1
Monte Carlo WCT, Ramirez 4-16, 419C1
Nations Cup, Spain 5-15, 419D1
NCAA doubles title, Austin, Nichols, 5-29, 419E2
NCAA singles title, McEnroe 5-29, 419D2
NCAA team title, Stanford 5-29, 419E2
Ocean City Intl, Taroczy 2-26, 419A1
Pepsi Grand Slam, Borg 1-22, 418G3
Phila Va Slims, Evert 3-26, 419A2
Player Classic, Connors 6-18, 540C1
Rotterdam WCT, Connors 4-9, 419B1
Scandinavian Cup, Borg 3-8, 419B1
Seattle Va Slims, Navratilova 2-12, 419G1
Series Championshp, Evert 11-18, 1027C2
Smash '78, Borg 10-29, 1027C2
South African Grand Prix, Gullikson 12-4, 1027D2
South African Open, Richey 4-10, 419C1
St Louis WCT, Mayer 2-12, 419A1
Stockholm Open, McEnroe 11-14, 1027C2
Suntory Cup, Borg 4-23, 418B3
Tokyo Intl, Borg 11-5, 1027C2
United Bank Classic, Connors 2-26, 419A1
US Clay Courts, Connors 8-13, 1027A2
US Natl Indoor, Connors 3-5, 419A1
US Open (doubles), Navratilova, King, Smith, Lutz 9-9, 707G1
US Open (mixed doubles), McMillan, Stove 9-10, 707G1
US Open (singles), Connors, Evert 9-10, 707A1
US Pro Indoor, Connors 1-29, 418G3
US Pro, Orantes 8-29, 1027B2
Va Slims title, Navratilova 4-2, 419E1
Va WCT, Gerulaitis 2-5, 418G3
Volvo Classic, Gottfried 3-18, 419B1
Volvo Intl, Dibbs 8-6, 1027A2
Washn Star Intl, Connors 7-23, 1027A2
Washn Va Slims, Navratilova 1-8, 419F1
WCT Challenge Cup, Nastase 12-17, 1027D2
WCT doubles title, Okker, Fibak 5-7, 418A3
WCT singles title, Gerulaitis 5-14, 418G2
WCT Tourn of Champs, Borg 3-26, 419B1
Weisman Cup, US 4-23, 419C1
Wimbledon, Borg, Navratilova 7-7, 7-8, 539E3-540C1
World Cup, US 3-9—3-12, 252C1
WTT championshp, LA Strings 9-21, 1027D1

1979

Obituaries
Ryan, Elizabeth 7-6, 570C1
Winners
Argentine Open, Vilas 11-25, 1003G3
Assn of Tennis Pros, Fleming 8-27, 734E2
Atlanta Open, Teltscher 9-17, 734E2
Australian Hard Ct, Vilas 1-7, 391F2
Australian Indoor, Gerulaitis 10-21, 1003E3
Australian Open, Vilas, O'Neill 1-3, 103C2
Austrian Grand Prix, Gerulaitis 7-29, 734B2
Avon Championship, Navratilova 3-25, 391A2
Baltimore Grand Prix, Solomon 1-21, 391F2
Berlin Intl, Stoll 5-27, 570D2
Birmingham WCT, Connors 1-21, 391F2
Bologna Grand Prix, Walts 11-25, 1003G3
Boston Avon, Fromholtz 3-18, 391D2
Canadian Open, Borg 8-20, 734D2
Carte Blanche Legends, Rosewall 8-26, 734D2
Chicago Avon, Navratilova 2-4, 391C2
Chichester, Goolagong 6-17, 570D2
Cleveland Grand Prix, Smith 8-20, 734D2
Cologne Grand Prix, Mayer 11-4, 1003F3
Davis Cup, US 12-16, 1003G2
Denver Grand Prix, Fibak 2-25, 391G2
Detroit Avon, Turnbull 2-25, 391C2
Dublin (O) Grand Prix, Gottfried 8-12, 734C2
Eastbourne Intl, Evert Lloyd 6-23, 570E2
English Women's Grand Prix, Navratilova 11-25, 1004A1
Family Circle, Austin 4-15, 391C3
Federatn Cup, US 5-6, 391D2
Forest Hills Invitatnl, Dibbs 7-17, 734A2
French Open, Borg, Evert Lloyd 6-9, 6-10, 570E1
Grand Prix doubles title, McEnroe, Fleming 1-7, 103D3
Grand Prix Masters, McEnroe 1-14, 103A3
Greater Pittsburgh Open, Barker 9-16, 734E2
Hall of Fame, Teacher 7-15, 734A2
Hong Kong Grand Prix, Connors 11-11, 1003F3
Houston WCT, Higueras 4-22, 391C3
Indian Grand Prix, Amritraj 11-25, 1003G3
Italian Open, Gerulaitis 5-27, 570D2
King Classic, Borg 4-28, 391C3
Little Rock Grand Prix, Gerulaitis 2-4, 391G2
London Grand Prix, McEnroe 11-18, 1003G3
Milan WCT, McEnroe 4-1, 391B3
Monte Carlo WCT, Borg 4-15, 391B3
Nations Cup, Australia 5-14, 570C2
NCAA doubles title, Iskersky, McKown 5-28, 570B2
NCAA singles title, Curren 5-28, 570A2
NCAA team title, UCLA 5-24, 570A2
N Orleans Grand Prix, McEnroe 3-25, 391A3
Oakland Avon, Navratilova 1-15, 391C2
Paris Open, Solomon 11-4, 1003F3
Pepsi Grand Slam, Borg 2-11, 391C2
Phila Avon, Turnbull 3-11, 391C2
Phoenix Open, Navratilova 10-14, 1003E3
Richmond Classic, Borg 2-4, 391F2
Richmond Intl, Navratilova 8-19, 734C2
Rotterdam WCT, Borg 4-8, 391B3
Stella Artois, McEnroe 6-18, 570D2
Stockholm Open, McEnroe 11-13, 1003G3
Stowe Grand Prix, Connors 8-19, 734C2
Stuttgart Grand Prix, Fibak 4-1, 391B3
Swedish Open, Borg 7-22, 734B2
Swiss Indoor, Gottfried 10-21, 1003E3
Tennis Legends, Rosewall 4-22, 391C3; 8-12, 734B2
Tokyo World Singles, Borg 11-4, 1003F3
Toray Sillock, King 9-16, 734E2
Tulsa Grand Prix, Connors 4-15, 391B3
US Clay Cts (singles), Connors, Evert Lloyd 8-12, 734C2
US Natl Indoor (doubles), Okker, Fibak 3-4, 391A3
US Natl Indoor (singles), Connors 3-4, 391A3
US Open (doubles), McEnroe, Fleming, Stove, Turnbull 9-8, 734G1
US Open (mixed doubles), Hewitt, Stevens 9-9, 734G1
US Open (singles), McEnroe, Austin 9-9, 734A1
US Pro Indoor, Connors 1-28, 391F2
US Pro Outdoor, Higueras 8-27, 734E2
Vienna Grand Prix, Smith 10-29, 1003E3
Vienna Open, Evert Lloyd 5-20, 570D2
Volvo Classic, Tanner 3-17, 391A3
Volvo Cup, Evert Lloyd 8-26, 734D2
Volvo Games, Tanner 2-18, 391G2
Washn Avon, Austin 1-7, 391C2
Washn Star Intl, Villas 7-22, 734B2
Wightman Cup, US 11-4, 1003B3
Women's Stockholm Open, King 11-6, 1003F3
WCT singles title, McEnroe 5-6, 391A1
WCT Challenge Cup, Borg 12-9, 1003C3
WCT Tourn of Champs, Connors 2-25, 391A3
West German Grand Prix, Smid 7-22, 734B2
West German Open, Higueras 5-20, 570C2

1980

Obituaries
Etchebaster, Pierre 3-24, 279E2
Winners
AIAW doubles title, Lewis, White 6-11, 607E1
AIAW singles title, White 6-11, 607E1
AIAW team title, USC 6-7, 607D1
Assn of Tennis Pros, Solomon 8-24, 691C3
Atlanta Classic, Mandlikova 9-28, 947G1
Atlanta Open, Teltscher 8-24, 691C3
Australian Indoor, McEnroe 10-19, 947B2
Australian Hard Ct, Glickstein 1-6, 607D2
Australian Open, Vilas, Jordan 1-1, 1-2, 213E1
Austrian Indoor, Graham 3-23, 607G2
Austrian Grand Prix, Vilas, Ruzici 7-27, 691A3
Avon Championship, Austin 3-23, 607B2
Baltimore Grand Prix, Solomon 1-20, 607E2
Bangkok Grand Prix, Amritraj 11-23, 947F2
Bavarian Grand Prix, Gehring 5-25, 607D3
Birmingham WCT, Connors 1-20, 607E2
BMW Championship, Austin 6-21, 607E3
Boston Avon, Austin 3-16, 607D2
Canadian Open, Lendl 8-17, 691B3
Canton Grand Prix, Connors 10-19, 947C1
Chicago Avon, Navratilova 1-27, 607D2
Chichester, Evert Lloyd 6-14, 607E3
Cincinnati Avon, Austin 1-13, 607C2
Clairol Championship, Austin 3-30, 607A3
Colgate Championship, Navratilova 1-7, 607E2
Cologne Cup, Lutz 11-2, 947C2
Davis Cup, Czech 12-7, 946C3
Davis Cup Amer Zone, Argentina 3-9, 607F1
Denver Grand Prix, G Mayer 2-24, 607F2
Detroit Avon, King 2-24, 607D2
Dubai Golden, Fibak 11-23, 947F2
English Women's Grand Prix, Evert Lloyd 10-26, 947C2
Family Circle, Austin 4-13, 607B3
Federatn Cup, US 5-25, 607B1
Florence Grand Prix, Panatta 5-18, 607D3
Florida Fed, Jaeger 11-16, 947E2
Frankfurt WCT, Smith 3-23, 607A3
French Open (men's doubles), Amaya, Pfister 6-7, 606F3
French Open (singles), Borg, Evert Lloyd 6-7, 6-8, 606A3
French Open (women's doubles), Jordan, Smith 6-6, 606E3
Geneva Open, Taroczy 9-28, 947G1
German Indoor, Smid 3-16, 607G2
Grand Prix Masters doubles title, McEnroe, Fleming 1-12, 213B2
Grand Prix Masters singles title, Borg 1-13, 213G1
Grand Prix of Tennis, Borg 4-27, 607B3
Hall of Fame, Amritraj 7-14, 691G2
Italian Indoor, Smid 11-23, 947F2
Italian Open, Vilas 5-25, 607D3
KC Avon, Navratilova 1-20, 607C2
Kramer Open, G Mayer 4-20, 607B3
LA Avon, Navratilova 2-10, 607D2
Lions Cup, Navratilova 11-23, 947F2
London Grand Prix, McEnroe 11-16, 947D2
Louisville Intl, Connors 5-18, 607D3
Melbourne Indoor, Gerulaitis 10-26, 947C2
Milan WCT, McEnroe 3-30, 607A3
Monte Carlo Grand Prix, Borg 4-6, 607A3
Naples Grand Prix, Barazzutti 10-19, 947B2
Nations Cup, Argentina 5-12, 607G1
NCAA doubles title, Purcell, Harman 5-26, 607D1
NCAA singles title, Van't Hof 5-26, 607D1
NCAA team title, Stanford 5-22, 607C1
New South Wales champ, Turnbull 12-7, 947A3
NH Grand Prix, Connors 8-3, 691A3
Nice Open, Borg 3-30, 607A3
Paris Open, Gottfried 11-2, 947D2
Pepsi Grand Slam, Borg 2-10, 607F2
Phoenix Classic, Marsikova 10-12, 947A2
Players Challenge, Navratilova 7-20, 691G2
Queen's Club Grass, McEnroe 6-15, 607E3
Richmond Intl, Navratilova 7-27, 691A3
Richmond Classic, McEnroe 2-3, 607F2
Riviera Women's Classic, Jaeger 9-21, 947G1
Rotterdam WCT, Gunthardt 3-16, 607G2
Sabra Classic, Solomon 10-12, 947A2
Seattle Avon, Austin 2-3, 607D2
Sicilian Grand Prix, Vilas 9-14, 947F1
South African Open, Warwick 12-2, 947G2
South Pacific, McEnroe 10-12, 947A2
Spanish Grand Prix, Lendl 10-12, 947A2
Stockholm Open, Borg 11-10, 947D2
Stowe Grand Prix, Lutz 8-17, 691C3
Sunbird Cup, Navratilova 5-4, 607C3
Surrey Grass Cts, Gottfried 6-21, 607E3
Swiss Indoor, Lendl 10-19, 947B2
Taipei Grand Prix, Lendl 11-16, 947E2
Tennis Legends, Rosewall 5-4, 607C3
Tokyo Invitatnl, Connors 4-13, 607B3
Tourn of Champs, Gerulaitis 5-12, 607C3
US Clay Cts (singles), Evert Lloyd, Clerc 8-9, 8-10, 691B3
US Natl Indoor (singles), McEnroe 3-2, 607F2
US Open (men's doubles) Smith, Lutz 9-6, 691F2
US Open (mixed doubles), Riessen, Turnbull 9-7, 691F2
US Open (singles), McEnroe, Evert Lloyd 9-6, 9-7, 691F1

1976

TERAN Ortuno, Sgt. Mario (ret.)
Rptdly executed Guevara 4-14, 415D3
TERMAN, Frederick E.
Gets Medal of Science 10-18, 858F3
TERNEIRO, Adm. Henrique dos Santos (ret.)
Release from prison rptd 1-23, 53A2
TERRA, Daniel
'72 campaign gift listed 4-25, 688B1
TERRE Haute, Ind.—*See INDIANA*

TERRORISM, International—*Note: Only general material listed here. For specific incidents, see AVIATION—Plane Hijackings, CRIME, 'Palestinian Developments' under MIDDLE EAST—ARAB Policies; also country names*
Ford seeks curbs on CIA spying 2-18, 127A2
US Sen curbs forgn aid 2-18, 151G3
US-Canada extradition treaty 3-22, 238D3
Ford signs arms aid bar 6-30, 533F1
Carter, Mondale score 7-15, 507G1, 510D3, 511C3
Libya world network rptd 7-15, 531D1
W Ger to propose UN accord 7-16, 530A3
FBI reforms set 8-11, 633C3
GOP platform text 8-18, 604D2, 610E3
Mondale scores Ford Admin 9-1, 665B3
TERZI, Zehdi Labib
Asks UN fact-finders to Mideast 3-4, 161G2
Vs US UN veto 3-26, 227G2
Chrgs Israel-S Africa tie 4-29, 320D3
In UN seating dispute 5-4, 320C1
Vs Israel occupatn 11-1, 842G1
TETON River (Idaho)
Dam collapses 6-5, 423B1
Ford OKs dam victims aid 7-12, 517E3; 9-7, 665C1
Dam collapse rpts 7-15, 9-25, 736C1
TETRACYCLINE—*See 'Drugs' under MEDICINE*
TEWOFLOS, Abuna (Archbishop)
Deposed 2-18, arrest rptd 3-1, 173D1
TEXACO Inc.
No Guatemala quake damage rptd 2-24, 155F3
Pending '74 NY trust case cited 3-11, 413G1
Angola '75 royalties paid 3-17, 287G2
Vows no boycott compliance 3-18, 747B2
Leftists admit Italy arson 4-21, 297D1
On '75 Fortune 500 list 437A1, D1, G1
Pays Ecuador back taxes 8-20; Ecuador to buy pipeline 9-17, Gulf assets 10-25, 872B1
Rptd vs House boycott bill 9-19, 746C3
'75 US tax paymt rptd 10-2, 847A2

1977

TENNIS Association, U.S.—*See TENNIS*
TENNIS Council, Men's International Professional—*See TENNIS*
TENNIS Federation, International—*See TENNIS*
TENORIO Sandoval, Horacio
Protests mount 2-22—3-2, new rector named 3-3, 240A2
Drops Oaxaco rectorship bid 4-24, 528F2
TERKEL, Studs
Group buys Nation mag 12-22, 1004G3
TERRE Haute, Ind.—*See INDIANA*

TERRORISM, International—*Note: Only general material listed here. For specific incidents, see AVIATION—Plane Hijackings, CRIME, MIDDLE EAST; also country names*
'76 Eur Cncl pact cited 9G2
US orders A-plant security tightened, '76 threats rptd 2-22, 197E1-B2
US issues rpt 3-2, 483F3
Breeder reactor called safe 3-26, 235A1, C1
US Sen panel dies 3-31, 252A1
US accuses Libya, Iraq, S Yemen, Somalia 5-8, 380D1-B2
US probes rptd down 6-6, 481A1
OAS assemb scores, sets study 6-21, 494A1
TERRY, Bill
Carew named AL MVP 11-16, 927D1
TETANUS—*See MEDICINE—Diseases*
TETON River (Idaho)
Dam collapse rpt published 1-6, 120B3
TETRACYCLINE—*See MEDICINE—Drugs*
TETTAMANTI, Tito
AECL agent tied to pol paymt 1-7, denies link 1-13, 43B1
TETZEL, Joan
Dies 10-31, 872A3
TEXACO Inc.
Ecuador buys Gulf assets 1-1, 8A1
To mkt extra Saudi oil 2-16, 108C1, D1
Gulf of Mex gas probe set 2-17, 151F3
Gas withholding chrgd 2-22, denied 2-23, 152E1
World Ct awards Libya natlizatn damages 3-2, 488E1
On '76 Fortune 500 list 340D1, D3
Saudi fire forces sales cut 5-19, 402C2
Lonrho sues re Rhodesia sales 5-31, 413C2
US cancels offshore lease 6-8, 499C1
FTC info order review rejctd 6-13, 517G1
FPC gas dispute resolved 7-14, 559A3
Loop license signed 8-1, 724E3
Washington state sues 8-16, 691E3
Libya compensatn agreed 9-26, 772C2
Carter attack rebuttal 10-13, 772G3
Caltex Oil Co.—*See separate listing*
Sabine Pipe Line Co.
FPC dispute resolved 7-14, 559B3

1978

TENNIS Federation, International (ITF)—*See TENNIS*
TENNIS Game, The (Play)
Opens 11-5, 1031B3
TENNIS Professionals, Association of—*See TENNIS*
TERAN, Jose Francisco
Arrested 9-4, 690B3
TERKEL, Studs
Working opens 5-14, 887E3

TERRORISM, International—*Note: Only general material listed here. For specific incidents, see AVIATION—Hijacking, CRIME, MIDDLE EAST; country names*
France, W Ger discuss controls 2-6—2-7, 122C1
US intell reorganizatn proposed 2-9, 107E1
Commonwealth regional conf sets study 2-16, 121D2
Solzhenitsyn scores West 6-8, 444F2
LNG safety measures urged 7-31, 610B1
TERZIAN Associates
CPSC chrmn quits, Justice probe cited 2-8, 185F2
TEST-Tube Babies (embryo implants)—*See CHILDBIRTH*
TETRACHLOROETHYLENE—*See CHEMICALS*
TETRACYCLINE—*See MEDICINE—Drugs*
TEXACO Inc.
In Dow Jones indl avg 66F2
US to drop trust suit 1-3, 67E2
Rebates to consumers barred 1-20, 109A1
OSHA fines for '77 Tex fire 3-2, 212F3
Tiger Shoals gas output hike vowed 4-27, 322D1
On '77 Fortune 500 list 5-8, 325E1, A2
Pipeline divestiture urged by Sen subcom 6-21, 471E1
NJ offshore gas find rptd 8-14, 8-18, 665B3
Gas rationing rptd sought 12-3, 939C1
NJ offshore wells rptd dry 12-6, 12-11, 12-27, 1010E1

1979

Wimbledon (men's doubles), Fleming, McEnroe 7-7, 570D1
Wimbledon (mixed doubles), Hewitt, Stevens 7-7, 570D1
Wimbledon (singles), Borg, Navratilova 7-6, 7-7, 569C3
Wimbledon (women's doubles), King, Navratilova 7-7, 570B1
Women's Italian Open, Austin 5-14, 570B2
World Invitatn, Navratilova, Amaya 5-20, 570C2
TENNIS Federation, International (ITF)—*See TENNIS*
Ter BEK, Relus
Testifies in Letelier case 1-16, 57G3
TERESA, Mother (India)
Leads anti-conversn bill protest 4-14, 376E3
Wins Nobel Peace Prize 10-17, 857E3
TERESA the Thief (film)
Released 5-5, 528F3
TERLESKAS, Antanas
Arrested 11-1, 856A3
TERNBACH, Joseph
To restore Poncet sculpture 5-6, 375D1
TERRANOVA, Cesare
Murdered 9-25, 793C2

TERRORISM, International—*Note: Only general material listed here. For specific incidents, see AVIATION—Hijacking, CRIME, MIDDLE EAST; country names*
US FBI informant loss rptd 3-22, 232C3
CIA seeks more armed agents 4-4, 310B2
'Backpack' A-bomb said possible 4-25, 327D2
Worldwide activity rptd up 11-15, 882E1
Amnesty Intl reviews '79 12-9, 980C2
UN outlaws hostage-taking 12-17, 957F2-958A1
Baker urges '1st Brigade' 12-19, 983C1
TERRY v. Ohio
Case cited by Sup Ct 11-28, 944A3
TERSON, Peter
Good Lads opens 3-27, 711E3
TERZI, Zehdi Labib
Sees US UN Amb Young 7-26, US briefed 8-11; backs Young rpt 8-13, 8-14; US, Israel vs mtg 8-14; Young quits UN 8-15, 605A1-606A1
Says Israel pressured Young resignatn 8-15, 606C2
Young, Admin controversy on mtg 8-18—8-20, 624E2
Meets SCLC pres, lauds PLO backing 8-21, 624B1
Vs UN Assemb com res on Palestinians 8-21, 642D2
Carter denies US Jewish pressure to oust Young 9-23, Young: Dayan aired mtg 9-24, 763F2, G2
US rep rebuts Young re mtg rpt 10-28, 823E2
TESICH, Steve
Breaking Away released 7-17, 819F3
TEST-Tube Babies (embryo implants)—*See CHILDBIRTH*
TETON River (Idaho)
Dam defects rptd 11-28, 954A3
TETRACYCLINE—*See MEDICINE-Drugs*
TEWELL, Doug
2d in Tex Open 10-7, 970F1
TEWKESBURY, Joan
Old Boyfriends released 3-21, 528C3
TEXACO Inc.
In Dow Jones indl avg 72F1
Indonesia Caltex prices raised 1-1, 52G1
Colombia exec killed 1-4, 22D2
US files overchrg suit 1-5, 17B1
UK oil tank drivers end strike 1-11, 20B3
Iran oil crisis forces sales curbs 2-6, 83A1
NY, Midwest gas statns closed 3-1, 183C3
2d NJ offshore well rptd dry 3-13, 361D3
Fined re Calif gas-switching 4-26, 301D2
1st 1/4 oil profits rptd 4-27, 301G1, B2
US overchrg claims denied 5-2, 343B2

1980

US Open (women's doubles) King, Navratalova 9-6, 691F2
US Pro Indoor, Connors 1-27, 607E2
US Pro Outdoor, Dibbs 7-20, 691G2
US Women's Indoor, Austin 10-5, 947G1
Vienna Grand Prix, Gottfried 10-26, 947B2
Volvo Cup, Mandlikova 8-24, 691D3
Washn Star Intl, Gottfried 7-27, 691A3
WCT Challenge Cup, McEnroe 12-14, 1002D2
WCT doubles, Gottfried, Ramirez 1-6, 213B2
WCT singles title, Connors 5-4, 607A1
WCT Tourn of Champs, Borg 2-24, 607F2
Western Open, G Mayer 8-17, 691C3
W Ger Grand Prix, Gerulaitis 7-20, 691G2
W Ger Open, Solomon 5-18, 607D3
Wightman Cup, US 11-1, 946F3-947A1
Wimbledon (men's doubles), McNamee, McNamara 7-5, 606G2
Wimbledon (mixed doubles), T Austin, J Austin 7-5, 606A3
Wimbledon (singles), Borg, Goolagong 7-4, 7-6, 606G1
Wimbledon (women's doubles), Jordan, Smith 7-5, 606A3
Women's Australian Open, Mandlikova 11-30, 947G2
Women's Dutch Indoor, Mandlikova 11-16, 947E2
Women's Italian Open, Evert Lloyd 5-11, 607C3
Women's Stockholm Open, Mandlikova 11-2, 947C2
World Super, Connors 11-2, 947C2
WTA Championship, Navratilova 4-20, 607B3
TENSER, Mark
Hearse released 6-7, 675G2
TERESA, Mother (Agnes Gonxha Bojaxhiu)
Ends US visit 8-7, 638F1
TERKEL, Studs (Louis)
FBI files case refused by Sup Ct 1-7, 15G3
Addresses Citizens' Party 4-11, 288D3
TERKEL v. Webster
Case refused by Sup Ct 1-7, 15G3
TERRA Gallinal, Horacio
Arrested 11-14, 888A3
TERRAZAS, Laurence J.
Citizenship revocatn backed by Sup Ct 1-15, 51C2
TERRELL, Jerry
Votes vs baseball strike 4-1, 637C2
TERRORISM, International—*Note: only general material listed here; see also country, region names*
Italian, forgn terrorist links chrgd 1-2, 20F2
US issues rights rpt 2-5, 87B3
CIA rpts '79 dvpts 5-11, 365D3
Venice summit condemns hostage-taking 6-22, 473D1
NATO condemns 6-26, 490B1
US counterterrorist unit proposed 8-23, 644E1
Carter, Reagan TV debate 10-28, 814E2, A3
TERROR Train (film)
Released 10-3, 836G3
TESICH, Steven
Wins Oscar 4-14, 296G1
Division St opens 10-8, 892B3
TESORO Petroleum Corp.
Paymts case setld 11-21, 957D3
TESS (film)
Released 12-12, 1003E2
TETERBORO (N.J.) Airport
US Customs corruptn probed 2-13, 359G2
TETRACHLORIDE—*See CHEMICALS*
TETRAHYDROCANNABINOL (THC)—*See NARCOTICS*
TEUFEL, Fritz
Sentenced on terrorist charges, released 10-13, 833B1
TEWARI, N. D.
Sworn Indian planning min 6-8, 445F1
TEWELL, Doug
Wins Phila Classic 8-3, 972E1
TEXACO Inc.
In Dow Jones indl avg 76F1
'79 profit rptd 1-24, 90F2, B3
Belridge litigatn dropped 3-6, 385C3
Hunts sell shares to cover margin calls on silver 3-27, 223C2
1st 1/4 profit rptd 4-27, 331D1, E1
On '79 Fortune 500 list 5-5, 290E1
Saudi hikes prices 8% 5-14, 365B1
Granville to quit bd 6-30, 600B3
Wholesale gas price cut rptd 8-1, 666D3
Gasoline dealer rebates revived 9-1, prices cut 9-18, 786B1, D1
Saudi completes Aramco takeover, bd members listed 9-4, 662B1, A2
OPEC pricing agrmt impact seen 9-18, 695B1
La lake 'swallowed' in oil rig accident 11-20, 970D2

1976

TEXAS
Sup Ct sets death sentnc review 1-22, 87A3
A-engineer quits NRC 2-9, 115F1
Dallas violent crime up 3-2, 336D3
Houston bank fails, rechartered 3-3, 167C2
Dallas desegregatn ordrd 3-10, 203A3
Kissinger speaks in Dallas 3-22, 214D3
Soc Sec withdrawals rptd 3-23, 994G1
NLRB rules on journalists 4-5, 249D1
Oil rig sinks 4-15, 544E3
EPA studies Dallas water 4-30, 349G1
French pres visits US 5-17—5-22, in Houston 372F1
2d Houston bank closed 6-3, 438D1 ★
Houston Anheuser-Busch strike ends 6-6, 436B2
FBI notes letter bombs 6-15, 504D1
US Sup Ct upholds death penalty 7-2, 491F1
Carrizo Springs bank fails 7-7, 940B2
Hughes legal residnc disputed 7-13, 596E3
Tullers' murder chrgs pending 7-16, 544D1
Gulf job bias setlmt rptd 7-16, 943D3
Powell stays execution 7-22, 568F2
FBI Dallas Arab cntr break-in cited 8-17, 634A2
Mex Fair opens in San Antonio 9-7, 694C3
'74-75 Dallas, Houston, Ft Worth SATs rptd 9-13, 993G1
Dallas desegregatn praised 9-14, 992G3
Fscl '75 per capita income, tax burden rptd 9-15, 10-12, 959D2
Death penalty reaffirmed 10-4, 746F1
Sup Ct bars review of juvenile evidence case 10-4, 766C1
Grain chrgs vs Houston inspectors dropped 11-2, 990D3
US sues state accountants bd 11-18, 989A1
Oil output cut backs ordrd 11-18, 12-16, 991C3
US Sup Ct vacates Austin busing plan 12-6, 920B2
US Sup Ct stays White executn 12-6, 920G2
Velsicol workers poisoning probed 12-6, 950B2
Oil stockpile plan proposed 12-15, 991D3
Flu shot paralysis rptd 12-17, 950E1
SW Bell loses tap suit 12-17, 955E1-A2
Coleman to OK superport 12-17, 992E1
Houston, Dallas-Ft Worth transatlantic air routes rejctd 12-28, 992E2

1977

TEXAS
Ford '78 budget proposal 1-17, 31D2
Austin EEOC bias ruling rptd 1-20, 278A3
Schl desegregatn reviews set 2-17, 156D3
Millionairess dies 3-10, buried in car 5-19, 532D2
Austin schl integratn plan asked 3-18, 216A3
Intra-group grand jury bias affirmed 3-23, 276C2
Drought hurts High Plains 3-24, 244F3
Jet crash victims arrive Brooke Army burn center 3-30, 244E1
Edward Marcus dies 4-4, 356D3
Houston, Dallas, San Antonio on '75 10 largest cities list; El Paso growth rptd 4-14, 388A1-D1
Biology text barred in Ind 4-14, 471E3
Hughes inheritance tax sought 4-15, 354E3
Galveston hotel burns 4-19, 508G3
'76 per-capita income table 5-10, 387F2
Houston law business boom rptd; table 5-16, 383G1, A2
Dallas-Fort Worth, Houston econ data rptd; table 5-16, 384F2, 385B1
NBA aids San Antonio Spurs 6-15, 583E3, 584D1
Rain saves wheat crop 6-16, 492A3
Laetrile legalization cited 6-23, 508E1
RC traditionalist church consecrated 7-10, 620F2
Seadock superport aid bill signed 7-27, 725A1
Archbp Lucey dies 8-1, 696B3
US asks farm holdings breakup 8-22, 703G2
'76 per capita income, tax burden table 9-13, 10-18, 821E2
Natl Women's Conf, counterrally held in Houston 11-19—11-21, 917F2, F3
Protesting farmers delay Lubbock newspaper delivery 12-21, strike support rptd atrong 12-22, 1003B1, D1
Nazi tape restraining order upheld 12-21, 1008A2
Houston bank ownershp cited 12-27, 1003G2
Galveston grain elevator blast 12-27, 1023G1-B2

Air Transport
Braniff-Concorde Dallas-Eur pact rptd 2-11, 213C1
UK air svc pact set 6-22, 500A2
Houston, Dallas landing rights for Concorde proposed 9-23, 738B2
Dallas/Ft Worth, Houston 'gateway' air svc OKd 12-21, 1006C2
Braniff awarded Dallas-London air route 12-21, 1006D2
Pan Am awarded Houston-London route 12-21, 1006A3

Crime
Jurek executn filming protested 1-3, US Sup Ct delays death 1-17, 40B3
1-judge juvenile prison ruling upheld 3-21, 230A3
US Sup Ct declines Jurek case review 3-28, 276D3
Pot decriminalizatn impact rptd 3-31, 332A3
Pot smuggling from Mex rptd 4-8, 332D2
Mex drug ring arrests 4-20, 711C3
White case review declined 4-25, 342A3

1978

TEXAS
Tyler asbestos workers get $20 mln setlmt 2-8, 326C3
Hughes ruled legal resident 2-13, 459D1
3d in US defense contracts 2-21, 127D2
Amarillo farmers pelt Bergland 2-21, 163F2
Braniff Dallas/Fort Worth-London air-fare dispute flares 2-28, 3-7, setlmt reached 3-17; svc starts 3-18, 206G1, D2
'Right-to-die' law rptd 3-18, 597F3
Dallas busing plan upset 4-24, 309B2
Austin '77 living costs rptd 4-26, 349D1
Amtrak Dallas route cutback proposed 5-8, 366E1
Construction pact signed 5-22, 429D3
Algur Meadows dies 6-10, 540C3
Union pol organizing backed by US Sup Ct 6-22, 508B3
Hughes estate dispute interventn refused by US Sup Ct 6-22, 509A1
Tourism to Mex reopens 6-29, 517G2
Houston makes bad-air list 7-5, 513D1
Bad-air list corrected 7-19, 644B2
Pan Am Houston svc OKd 9-1, 701E1
El Paso-Mex border fence set 10-24, 818B1
Measles infestatn in mil rptd 11-10, 927B3
Securities-regulatn case refused by Sup Ct 11-13, 874C3
Beaumont schl integratn case declined by US Sup Ct 12-4, 959A2
Houston, Dallas, San Antonio populatns ranked 12-6, 942E3, F3
LBJ's brother dies 12-11, 1032A3

Accidents & Disasters
Galveston '77 grain blast violatns rptd 2-23, 636E2
Texaco fined for '77 Port Arthur fire 3-2, 212F3
West central drought rptd 3-5, 207D2
Garland church roof collapses 5-21, 460F1
Tex City oil blast kills 7 5-30, 460F2
Heat wave 7-20, flash floods 8-8, 654E3
Grasshopper invasn rptd 7-31, 654B3

Crime & Civil Disorders
Ex-judge sentenced for perjury 1-27, 232A3
SW Bell '76 tap rule reversed 2-16, 142E3
Castroville marshal sentncd 2-18, 991E3
Hidalgo farmers block Mex food imports, 200 arrested 3-1, 3-3, 163F1-B2
Death sentencing bias rptd 3-6, 389A1, C1
3 Houston ex-cops sentncds in Torres case 3-28, appeal rptd 12-14, 991B3

1979

On '78 Fortune 500 list 5-7, 304E1
Baltimore Canyon '78 gas find cited 5-23, 442F3
June gas supplies cut 5-29, 395B3
Gasohol marketing test set 8-10, 649F1
Angola oil pact signed 9-4, 705G2
'79 heating oil price freeze set 9-7, 703B1
Baltimore Canyon gas finds rptd 10-22, 11-12, 867A2-C2
US overchrgs alleged 10-25, 849E3
3d 1/4 profits rptd up 10-26, 804C2, C3
US Steel chem deal set 11-14, 941D3
Baltimore Canyon gas find rptd 11-23, 943B1
Shell acquires Belridge Oil 12-10, sues 12-11, 942E1
US overchrgs alleged 12-19, 990E2

TEXAS
Big Sandy coll campus sale by Worldwide Church barred 1-3, 23B3
Concorde Dallas-DC svc begins 1-12, 35A3
Nugent divorce suit rptd 1-19, 79B2
Blue law case declined by Sup Ct 1-22, 54E1
Teng visits Houston, Simonton 2-2—2-3, 83G2-F3
Buckley, Sitco partners settle SEC chrg 2-7, 132C1
Mex record Jan crossings rptd 2-11, 127D2
Optometrists' use of corp names curbed by US Sup Ct 2-21, 128D2
Davis divorce case judge withdraws, declares mistrial 3-25, 272A1; $3 mln setlmt reached 4-20, 392D3
Mex border fence dropped, El Paso repairs set 4-26, 327F2-B3
US-French air svc pact rptd 5-12, 465C3
Fed ct welfare suits curbed by Sup Ct 5-14, 384A1
Davis divorce rptd final, remarried 5-25, 527C3
Dallas/Ft Worth on '78 world's busiest airport list 6-1, 421C1
Fed child custody fights curbed by Sup Ct 6-11, 478F3
Half-Indian child custody case refused by Sup Ct 6-18, 499A2
Houston condominium growth rptd 6-23, 482B3
Idaho takeover law challenge rejctd by Sup Ct 6-26, 540E3
Offshore port OKd 7-2, 518F2
ABA meets in Dallas 8-13, 630B3
Army recruiting fraud probed 8-19, 649G2
Amer Legion conv in Houston 8-22, 644C1
Amtrak Chicago-Houston train ordered cut 8-29, 868B1
Baker Hotel in Dallas closes 8-31, 887B2
Nugents divorced 8-31, 859B3
'78 per capita income rptd 9-16, 746F1, F2
Houston, Dallas, San Antonio bond ratings listed 9-20, 920F3
Horizon land sales scored by FTC 10-3, 903F1
Dallas museum said to get Church painting 10-25, 892B1
Freeport longshoremen boycott Iranian cargo 11-13, 879C1
Shah flown to Lackland for convalescence 12-2, 914A1
Iran consulate staff in Houston ordrd cut 12-12, 933C1
Austin '79 living costs ranked 12-28, 990F3, 991A1

Accidents & Disasters
Wichita Falls, Vernon, Harrold hit by tornadoes 4-10, 288F2
Nacogdoches floods 6-2, 472E2
Tanker collisn survivor flown to Galveston 7-22, 553F3
Tropical storm kills 7, disaster declared 7-24—7-28, 638D3
Houston townhouses burn 7-31, wooden shingles curbed 8-2, 620C2
Mex oil hits beaches 8-9, threatens tourism 8-17, 608G1; Sedco role rptd 8-21, 636B1
Mex oil damages asked, cleanup costs rptd 8-23; Lopez bars liability 8-24, 688E3, 689B1
Mex oil spill suits filed 9-13—9-18; Clements-Sedco link probed 9-22, 718G2
Mex OKs oil blowout talks 9-28—9-29, 753A2
Mex cones blown-out well 10-14, 782B1
Sedco sued for Mex oil spill cleanup 10-18, 10-23, 809D2
Liberian freighter, tanker collide in Galveston Bay; oil spill cleanup rptd 11-1, 954F3

Atomic Energy
Austin votes A-bond issue 4-7, 259D3, 261C3
Allen's Creek A-plant delay seen 5-9, 382C1
Glen Rose, Bay City protests 6-2, 416C2

Crime & Civil Disorders
Houston '78 Nazi activity cited 1-19, 102B1
Davis freed after '77 kill-for-hire mistrial 1-22, 64D3
Cuevas gets death sentnc 1-26, 400B2
Houston ex-police chief sentncd 1-29, 79C1
3 Houston ex-cops win Torres case appeal 2-6, 156B2
Estes indicted by US 2-22, 156G1

1980

TEXARKANA—*See ARKANSAS*

TEXAS
Woman gives birth to 21st child 1-12, 200F1
Braniff drops DC Concorde svc 4-14, 346F3
DES in cattle rptd 4-24, 358F1
Saudi film telecast ordrd 5-9, overturned 5-12, 375F3
Fed unincorporated business trust suits backed by US Sup Ct 5-19, 440F2
Hunts' bailout loan collateral 5-28, 425D3-G3, 426D1
MX sites chosen 11-18, 897A1

Accidents & Disasters
Mex caps blown-out well, total spill rptd 3-24, 233D3
Tornadoes hit 4-7—4-8, 391G2
Drought, heat wave hit, death toll rptd 6-23—8-15; Carter declares disaster area 7-16, 616C1, G1-D2
Hurricane Allen hits Gulf Coast 8-9; crop damage rptd 8-13, 621G1, G2, B3
Drought, heat wave damage final rpt 9-7, 857D2
Snowstorm hits 11-16, 948A1

Atomic Energy
Carter outlines A-waste storage plan 2-12, 127F3
Demonstratns mark 3 Mile I mishap 3-28—3-31, 249B1

Crime & Civil Disorders
Estes '83 parole rptd 1-3, 64G3
Jones arrested for rape 1-31, complaint dropped 2-1, 320D3
Witches' priest acquitted of '77 Dimmitt murder 2-1, 238E1
Hayes paroled 2-6, released from prison 2-27 175F2
FBI Brilab probe rptd 2-8—2-9, 111F2, E3
FBI 'Miporn' probe rptd 2-14, 136F1
Habitual-offender law upheld by Sup Ct 3-18, 226F2

1976

Politics
Primary date set 22A2
Ex-Sen Blakley dies 1-5, 56A3
Casey confrmd to US post 1-21, resigns House seat 1-22, 68C1, D3
Ford sees GOP delegation 3-24, 231C3
Ford, Reagan campaign 4-4—4-19, 280E3-281E3
Ford, Reagan end campaigns 4-30, 323G2
Carter attacks Ford 4-30, 324D1
Primary results 5-1, 322D2
'71 YSA conv surveillnc rptd 5-25, 569D3
Sex chrg vs Young rptd 6-11, 433E3
Carter at Dallas fund-raiser 6-14, 433B1
Strauss honored at Houston fund-raiser 6-18, 452E1
Reagan wins 4 at-large delegates 6-19, 450G2
Carter visits Houston 7-1, 490D2
Dem conv women delegates, table 508D2
Dem conv pres vote, table 7-14, 507D2
GOP pre-conv delegate count 8-14, 583D3
Young cleared 8-16, 636B2
GOP conv pres, vp vote tables 8-18—8-19, 8-19, 599D1, D3
Ford wins pres nominatn 8-19, 597E2
GOP conv delegates back Helms as vp 8-19, 598F2
Dole campaigns 9-10—9-11, 686F3
Carter, wife visit 9-23—9-24, 724E2
Ford in Dallas 10-9—10-10, 763B2, 787G3
Dole, Mondale debate in Houston 10-15, 782F1
Ford in Houston 10-30, 826D3
Carter for Atlantic offshore oil search 10-30, 827G1
Carter in Dallas 10-31, 826F3, 827E1, A2
Dole campaigns 10-31, 827A3
US Sup Ct affirms candidacy law 11-1, 867F3
Election results 11-2; pres 817D2, 818D1, E1 A3, 819B1; cong 820D1, D2, 822E3-823A1, 828C3, 830C4; state 825E3
Strauss to quit Dem post 11-8, 845F3
Carter contributns rptd 11-17, 938G2

1977

Executn by drugs OKd 5-11, 594G1
'73 Houston sex murders cited 5-15, 432A3
'77 death row populatn rptd 6-7, 594C1
Dallas LEAA office to close 6-20, 630E2
Braniff, Tex Intl indicted 8-16, 629C3
Southwestn Bell loses slander suit 9-12, 724B2
Castroville marshal convctd 9-29, 821C1
4 ex-Houston police indicted 10-20, 820F3
Felony probatn case review declined 11-14, 878B3
Davis acquitted of murder 11-17, 928A1
US-Mex exchng prisoners 12-9, 957C2

Energy
FPC OKs emergency gas sale 1-20, 54C1
'75 interstate gas sales cited 1-28, 76C3
Emergency natural gas bill signed 2-2, 76E2
US acts to free gas 2-5, 91A3
Carter energy plan 4-18, 294A3; reactn 4-20, 320D2
Offshore tanker port imperiled 7-12, 559A2
FPC-Texaco gas dispute resolved 7-14, 559A3
Calif oil pipe OKd 12-2, 942E3
Coastal States customer refunds ordrd 12-12, 980D1
3 utilities settle Westinghouse suit 12-26, 1003A3

Politics & Government
Legislature schedule rptd 6F2
White confrmd Agri dep secy 3-15, 211G1
Meier sets filibuster record 5-4, 532G1
Shapp fund repaymt ordrd 5-12, 482D2
Paul electn challenge refused 6-6, 479A1
US voting rights powers upheld 6-20, 517B1
LBJ '48 Sen primary fraud chrgd 7-30; denied 8-1, 8-3; '41 Sen bid fraud seen 8-6, 631G1, F2
Weddington confrmd Agri gen counsel 8-4, 626F3
State, Dallas referenda OKd 11-8, 879D2
McConn elected Houston mayor 11-22, 900B3
McCarthy lawyer fee case declined 12-5, 939B1

1978

Boy kills teacher 5-18, 396A2
4 Houston ex-cops chrgd in '77 Webster death cover-up 6-3, 991F2
Executn filming case declined by US Sup Ct 7-3, 552D2
US drops dual prosecutn of Dallas cop in '73 Rodriguez case 7-14, 991C3
SW Bell slander judgmt reversed 11-29, 963F1 ★
Houston ex-police chief Lynn convicted of extortn 12-14, 991A2
2 Houston ex-cops chrgd in '75 Joyvies cover-up 12-14, 991D2
'74 Houston sex slayer's sentnc reversed 12-20, 992B2

Energy
Exxon cited for overchrgs 1-11, 14C2
Natural gas diversn curbed by Sup Ct 5-31, 430E3-431D1
Exxon sued for overchrgs 6-8, 450A3
GAO backs W Coast oil pipe 9-12, 702F1
Natural gas price controls suit filed 11-20, 900B1

Kennedy Assassination—*See KENNEDY, John Fitzgerald*

Politics & Government—*See also 'Crime' above*
'67, '77 sales-tax rates rptd 1-5, 15F3
State tax revenue data 1-9, 84E2, G3
White installed Dem natl chrmn 1-27, 87G2
Primary results 5-6, 362D3-363B1
Primary runoff results 6-3, 426E2
Dems bar 'loophole primary' 6-9, 448A3
Carter on pol tour, in Ft Worth 6-23—6-24, 490F3, 509F3
Burger urges judgeshp bill OK 7-23, 626F3
Jarvis visits Fort Worth 8-17, 735C3
Johnson library rptdly offered Viet documts 9-13, 720B2
Election results 11-7: cong 846A2, A3, 848D3, 852D2, 855C3; state 845G1, 846B3, 847D1, E1, 853E3, 855A3
Nixon at Dallas-Ft Worth airport 11-10, 900B3

Sports
NASL adds Houston club 1-5, 23A1
NEA meets in Dallas 7-5, 525G3
Houston WHA team folds 7-6, 656G2
WTT Dallas franchise set 12-1, 1027C1

1979

Mex alien deportatn spurs protests 3-9, 3-10, 308E1
San Antonio fed judge slain 5-29, 431D2
'78 inmate totals rptd 6-21, 548C2
Identificatn law convictn voided by Sup Ct 6-25, 540D2
Burger assails Sup Ct bar admissn 6-25, 541B1
Houston sex slayer convicted again 6-27, 819C1
Seadrift fisherman slain, anti-Viet violence erupts 8-3; US seeks mediatn 8-9, 8-15, 660C1
Estes sentenced 8-6, 604E3
Chagra convicted in drug case 8-15, 818F3
Cocaine trade growth rptd 9-5, 972G2
3 Houston ex-cops resentncd 10-30, 839B3
Iranians demonstrate in Houston 11-7, 11-8, 842B3
Davis acquitted in kill-for-hire case 11-9, 890D2
Euless KKK activity cited 865B1
El Paso hijacker demands Iran flight 11-24, 898E2
Death row populatn rptd 11-25, 989F3

Energy—*See also 'Atomic' above*
Ashland unit offshore holdings sold 2-4, 560F3
Calif oil pipe canceled 3-13, 183D1
Carter asks Calif pipe resumptn 4-5, 250E3
Calif pipe cancellatn reaffirmed 5-24, 396F1
'78 per capita gas use rptd 5-27, 395F2, A3
Odd-even gas rationing set 6-19, 462F2
Mobil accused of natural gas overchrgs 6-22, 518G1
Gulf of Mex oil, gas lease bids placed 7-31, accepted 8-28, 664E3
Sedco role in Mex well blowout rptd 8-21, 636B1; liability unclear 8-23, 689C1
Odd-even gas rules lifted 9-3, 683F1
Sedco sued for Mex oil blowout role 9-13—9-18; Clements link probed 9-22, 718G2
US strategic oil reserve storage cited 9-26, 781B2
Mex OKs oil blowout talks 9-28—9-29, 753A2
NM suit refused by Sup Ct 10-9, 784D1
Mex cones blown-out well 10-14, 782B1
Supertanker port OKd 10-15, 769B3
Sedco sued for Mex oil spill cleanup 10-18, 10-23, 809D2

Kennedy Assassination—*See KENNEDY, John Fitzgerald*

Medicine & Health
Houston breast-feeding survey rptd 1-5, 64B2
Abortn record access case declined by US Sup Ct 1-22, 54A2
Blue Shield drug plan trust rule upheld by US Sup Ct 2-27, 165B1
Mental health commitmt standard tightened by US Sup Ct 4-30, 364E2
Marijuana med use rptd OKd 6-1, 492B3
Rabies cases rptd up 7-14, 620G2

Obituaries
Furey, Archbishop 4-23, 356E3
Jones, Preston 9-19, 756E2
Kleberg Jr, Richard M 5-8, 432B3
Murchison, John D 6-14, 508C3
Wood, John H 5-29, 431D2

Politics & Government—*See also other appropriate subheads in this section*
Legislature schedule rptd 5F3
Connally announces pres bid 1-24, 70F2
Fscl '78 tax revenue rptd 2-13, 152B2
Carter visits Dallas 3-25, 230E1-C2
Goodfellow AF base to close 3-29, 265F3
San Antonio, Austin electn results 4-7, 259D3, 261C3, 265B2
Bush enters pres race 5-1, 326C1
'Killer Bees' disrupt Sen, pres primary chng in doubt 5-18—5-22, 594G2-D3
Kerr quits as asst US atty 8-15, 819B1
Houston mayoral runoff set 11-6, 846D3
Houston city cncl electns 11-6, 904E3
Dems meet in San Antonio 11-9, 961D2
Baker addresses GOP govs in Austin 11-18, 983E1
McConn reelected Houston mayor 11-20, 904E3

Sports
Houston Astros sold 5-11, NL owners OK 5-16, 619D1
Dallas gets WBL team 6-12. 526G2

1980

Porno film restraints voided by Sup Ct 3-18, 226E3
Alamo occupied by radicals 3-20, 485A2
FBI Brilab probe indictmts 6-12, 454E2
Daingerfield church shooting 6-22, 5 dead 6-23, 568D2
Clayton, 2 others acquitted in Brilab case 10-23, 971B2

Energy—*See also 'Atomic Energy above*
Standard Oil settles price case 2-14, 190B1
Mex caps blown-out well, total spill rptd 3-24, 233D3
US intrastate gas sale power affirmed 6-6, 552B3

Labor & Employment
Houston port congestn rptd 1-19, 45C1
Firestone Orange plant cited for job bias 3-21, 251G2
Harvester strike ends 4-20, 308G2
ILA dock pact setld 5-27, 482B2
Firestone US contracts voided 7-15, 560B2
Chem workers cancer cases rptd 7-24, 584C2
Houston ILA workers reject pact 9-18, 826F2

Obituaries
King Jr, Richard 3-30, 279G3
McFarlane, William 2-18, 176E2
Vance, Nina 2-18, 176G3

Politics & Government—*See also other appropriate subheads in this section*
Fscl '79 tax revenue rptd 2-20, 307B3
5th judicial circuit split 10-14, 918A3
Election results 11-4; cong 837E1, 840D3, 840D2-B3, 846F1, 850G1-C2; state 845E3, 11-4, 847C3
US Sup Ct bars extended judicial immunity 11-17, 882B1
Troup to end black svcs bias 12-11, 963A2
'80 census rptd, reapportmt seen 12-31, 983G1

Presidential Election (& Transition)
Bush denies '70 campaign gift coverup 2-7, 128F3
Connally Saudi bank connectn, '78-79 fund transfers rptd 2-11, 129A2
Connally backs Reagan 3-25, 221F2
Reagan campaigns 4-9, 288F2; in Houston 4-18, 327E3
Pres primary results 5-3, 342A2
Bush ends pres race 5-26, 398E2-399B1
Bush gets vp nominatn 7-17, 529G1; for subsequent developments, see BUSH, George
Carter in Dallas 7-21, 549E3
Reagan in Dallas 8-22, 646E1, B2
Carter in Corpus Christi 9-15, 699C1
Reagan tours border towns 9-16, 699F3
Reagan in El Paso 9-24, 723A1
Mondale in Houston 10-2, 780F2
Carter in Waco 10-22, 802E3
Kennedy stumps for Carter 10-22, 817C1
Mondale stop in Laredo rptd 10-26, 816G3
Reagan hits Carter econ record 10-29, 817G1-A2, 840A1
Carter stumps 11-1, 841B1
Press endorsmts rptd 11-1, 841G3, 844F1
Election results 11-4, 838D1, 839B1, G3
Connally, Clements visit Reagan 11-15—11-16, 881A2

School Issues
Austin busing plan OKd 1-3, 5B3
Dallas busing case refused by Sup Ct 1-21, 93D2
Schl prayer law cited 2-6, 156A2
Ex-atheist apologizes in prayer dispute 5-9, 471F2
Houston desegregatn suit filed 5-15, 559C1
Aliens schooling ordered 7-21, 576G1

Sports
Dallas gets NBA team 2-2, 119C2
Dallas NBA team OKd 5-1; expansn draft held 5-28, 447D1
NASL Houston club put on notice 11-24, terminated 12-8, 1001C1

1976

TEXAS, University of (Austin)
'75 football rank rptd 1-2, 31B3
Hardesty confrmd Postal Svc gov 8-8, 808A1
Marshall named Labor secy 12-21, 956E2
TEXASGULF Inc.
'75 profit margin rptd 437D2
TEXAS Steel Co.
Fined 4-10, 988E3
TEXAS Technical University (Lubbock)
Loses Astro-Bluebonnet Bowl 12-31, 1014A3
TEXTILES
Trinidad polyester plant set 1-2, 55D3
W Ger-China plant deal rptd 1-6, 78C1
'75 Dutch productn drops 1-6, 102G2
Dec '75 output rptd up 1-16, 92C1
'75 4th ¼ profits rptd 2-3, 215A3
Group of 77 sets trade guidelines 2-10, 108C1
Cuba, Colombia sign trade pact 2-20, 251F3
AFL-CIO sets up Stevens unit 2-23, 149E1
1st ¼ profits rptd 4-29, 376C3
Angola natlizes Portugal co 5-6, 371A2
Clothing, textile unions merge 6-3, 436E1
J P Stevens bias end ordrd 6-25, 944C1
2d ¼ profits rptd 7-28, 708F3
US GOP platform text 8-18, 602B3
3 UK plants to close 10-22, 889E3
France, UK set cooperatn 11-12, 880C2
EEC-Rumania pact rptd 11-12, 907E2
Dacron price hike set 11-30, 898G1
TEXTILE Workers Union of America (AFL-CIO)
Merges with clothing union 6-3, 436E1
TEXTRON, Inc.
'75 arms sales listed 2-6, 147B2
Vows no boycott compliance 3-18, 747B2
THAI International Airlines
Qantas admits price cutting 9-23, 749E3

THAILAND—*See also ADB, ASEAN*
Kukrit asks rice price rise 1-1; protested 1-5, plan withdrawn 1-6, 30G3
Coalition expanded 1-6, cabt shift 1-8, 30E3
Kukrit quits, Parlt dissolved 1-12, 30C3
Seni scores govt re corruptn 1-12, 30D3
Listed as 'free' nation 1-19, 20C3
Socialist leader slain 2-28, 176E3
Pre-electn violence 3-3, 3-25, 4-1, 255E3
Kukrit ousted in electns, Seni to replace 4-4, 255C3
House OKs Seni Cabt 4-17; king proclaims 4-21, sworn 4-22, 315D1
New defense min dies, replaced 4-23, 315E1
Seni wins confidence vote 4-30, 335C2
8 soldiers die in rebel clash 5-2, 335C2
New Bronze Age date set 5-13, 504E3
Rebels raid army camp 5-17, 403C3
Rebels down jet fighter 6-11, 502A2
Rpt rebels kill 22 soldiers 7-9, 677F3
US sues former Eximbank offcls 8-9, 709D3
Praphas returns 8-15; riots, protests 8-17—8-21; deported 8-22, 640C1-A2
Defense Min Tawit quits 8-25, 677B3
Thanom return barred 8-31, 677C3
Wan Waithayakon dies 9-5, 970D3
Thanom returns, students riot 9-19; asked to leave 9-21, 753G3, 754A2

1977

TEXAS, University of (Austin)
Campbell wins Heisman, Downtown AC trophies 12-8, 950A2
TEXAS A & M University (College Station)
Wins Sun Bowl 1-2; '76 rank rptd 1-2, 1-3, 8E3
Jackson in NFL draft 5-3, 353B3
Loses Bluebonnet Bowl 12-31, 1020C2
TEXAS Eastern Corp.
Texas Eastern Transmission Corp.
Gulf gas withholding chrgd 2-23, 152G1
FPC splits on Alaska pipe route 5-2, 369B3
TEXAS Eastern Transmission Corp.—*See under TEXAS Eastern Corp.*
TEXAS Electric Services Co.
Westinghouse suit setld 12-26, 1003C3
TEXAS International Airlines Inc.
CAB OKs fare reductn plan 1-31, 324D3
Indicted 8-16, 629C3
TEXAS Power & Light Co.
Westinghouse suit setld 12-26, 1003C3
TEXAS Southern University (Houston)
Wins NAIA basketball title 3-12, 262F2
TEXAS System, University of
El Paso 2d in NCAA indoor track 3-12, 603B1
Clayborn in NFL draft 5-3, 353B3
Schild dies 5-24, 425E3
TEXAS Utilities Service Inc.
Westinghouse suit setld 12-26, 1003C3
TEXON Finanzanstalt
3 Swiss Credit Bank officers arrested 4-24, 350A3
Swiss Credit Bank scandal spreads 4-26—6-20, 565A1, C1
TEXTILE Manufacturers Institute, American
Tris recall cost sharing ordrd 4-28, upheld 5-19, 483B2
TEXTILES—*See also company, country names*
Gas shortage forces layoffs 1-17, 37D2
'76 4th ¼ profits rptd 2-8, 301D1
Unionists protest at Stevens mtg 3-1, 153D3
1st, 2d ¼ profit drop rptd 4-28, 7-28, 668B3, E3
UM&M closes Robert Hall 6-16, 520C1
UM&M seeks bankruptcy 7-12; losses rptd 7-28, 612F1-E2
Hong Kong scores quotas 10-4, 780D3
Stevens' fines set 10-27, union sues 11-1, 11-10, 899B1
Stevens chrgd re contract bargaining 12-21, 1005C1
Foreign Developments (including U.S. International news)
IFC loan to Ivory Coast rptd 1-5, 24A2
EC, 3 Arab natns sign pacts 1-18, 73G3
Australia import quotas kept 2-16, 158B2
Labor ldrs see Carter, asks import curbs; workers stage protests 4-13, 271D2
Australia sets NZ import quotas 4-17, extends quotas 5-2, 345G3
Australia rebuffs NZ quota plea 5-18, 410C2
France imposes import curbs 6-19, 1012D2, D3
Australia rejcts ASEAN trade criticism 7-9, 561A1
China aids Guyana plant constructn 9-2, 710B3
Canada cuts US import duties 9-12, 705F2-A3
France asks 'organized free trade' 9-15—9-16, 1012D3
Eur to cut S Kor imports 10-5, 804D3
Multifiber pact extended, protectnist clause added 12-13, 974C3-975A1
EC curbs imports 12-20, 998B1
TEXTRON Inc.
Miller to succeed Burns 12-28, 1000D1, D3

THAILAND—*See also ASEAN, SEATO*
Praphas returns 1-8, 473C3
Anti-rebel drive 1-9, 1-10, 47C3
Rebels ambush royal mil truck 2-13, 138E1
Rebels down govt copter, princess dies 2-16, 138D1
'76 govt, rebel losses rptd 2-24, 203E1
Rebels slay 30 3-4, 203D1
Coup try blocked 3-26; rightists seized 3-28—3-30, 243E1 ★
Poppy planting rptd up 4-1, 393D3
Drug peddler executed 4-14, Kirangsak leaves 4-21, 331F2
Coup ldr executed, 4 sentncd 4-21, 331E2
More plotters sentncd 5-10, 393C3
Narong ends exile 7-10, 641A3
King, queen escape bomb blast 9-22, 747G1
King's assailants seized 10-10, 827G1
Mil seizes power; const revoked 10-20, plans rptd 10-21, Revolutnary Cncl formed 10-22, 826G3
Interim charter set, '79 electns vowed 11-10; Kriangsak named premr 11-11, forms Cabt 11-13, 904C3

1978

TEXAS, University of
Loses Cotton Bowl 1-2, '77 rank rptd 1-3, 8A3
Wins NIT 3-21, 272G1
Campbell in NFL draft 5-2, 336A1, E3
Plock, Curren lose NCAA tennis title 5-29, 419E2
2d in NCAA outdoor track champ 6-1—6-4, 600F3
Hughes Mormon will ruled fake 6-8, trial costs rptd 6-12, 458G3, 459A1
Wins Sun Bowl 12-23, 1025D2
TEXAS A & M University (College Station)
Wins Hall of Fame Bowl 12-20, 1025C2
TEXAS City, Tex.—*See TEXAS*
TEXAS City Refining Inc.
Oil blast kills 7 5-30, 460F2
TEXAS Eastern Corp.
Olinkraft merger set 7-17, 700E3
Johns-Manville wins Olinkraft bidding 10-27, Morgan Stanley sued 11-8, 896A3, F3
Texas Eastern Transmission Corp.
Gulf contract compensatn challenge refused 2-21, 126B2
TEXAS Eastern Transmission Corp.—*See under TEXAS Eastern Corp.*
TEXAS Gulf Corp.
'76 tax nonpaymt rptd 1-27, 65G2
TEXAS Instruments Inc.
ICAO picks US bad-weather landing system 4-19, 319C3
Bucy vs USSR oil equipmt sale 9-6, 743D1
Trade missn arrives Japan 10-2, 797D3, 798B1
TEXAS International Airlines Inc. (TXI)
Black woman qualifies as pilot 4-19, 420C1
Natl Airlines stock purchase OKd 8-17, Pan Am-Natl merger agrmt scored 9-12, 701B1, D1
Eastn seeks Natl merger 12-11, SEC probe rptd 12-22, 1007C3
TEXAS System, University of
El Paso wins NCAA indoor track champ, Treacy sets 3-mi run mark 3-10—3-11, 692C3
TEXTILE Manufacturers Institute, American
Challenges cotton dust rules 6-19, 471F3
TEXTILES
US issues acrylonitrile rule 1-16, 85F3
Canada sets metric conversn 1-16, 89C1
Stevens contempt rule review refused, stiff fines seen 2-21, 125F3
US-Taiwan export agrmt rptd 2-27, 140B3
Stevens' head forced off bank bd 3-7, 163A1
Avon chrmn quits Stevens bd 3-21, 205D1
USSR in Nigeria deal 3-21, 248F1
Stevens union bargaining rep ordrd 3-26, 243B2
Quebec ends sales tax 4-11, 286G2
Stevens settles NLRB suit 4-28, 324E1-C2
Cotton dust rules issued, suits filed 6-19, 471C3
E Ger-Brazil deal rptd 7-13, 649D1
Australia tariff proposal scored 8-17, 646A2
Stevens loses more bd dirs 9-12, 699C2
US finalizes acrylonitrile rule 9-29, 753G3
Hollings trade amendmt OKd 10-6, Carter vetoes 11-11, GATT talks rift cited 12-22, 998D1
EC Comm orders fiber cartel modificatn 11-9, 871B3
Belgium vows indus aid 11-24, 921F1
TEXTRON Inc.
Miller queried re Iran, Nigeria paymts 1-24—2-28; CIA, Pentagon rptdly knew of Khatemi link 1-25, 2-17, 161F1, E2-B3
SEC seeks subpoena 3-2, 161A2
Miller confrmd FRB chrmn 3-3, sworn 3-8, 161E1, B3
Bribe evidence rptd destroyed 5-8, 448G3
Indicted on price fixing 11-1, 935A3
Bell denies Rhodesia copter sale 12-14, 1019G3

THAILAND—*See also ASEAN*
Egypt '76 jet crash rpt issued 5-12, 460A1
Cabt shift rptd 8-13, 691B2
Thammasat 18 freed 9-17, 841E1

1979

TEXAS A&I University (Kingsville)
Wins NAIA Div I football title 12-15, 1001G2
TEXAS Eastern Corp.
Texas Eastern Transmission Corp.
Mex natural gas purchased 10-18, 814F3
TEXAS International Airlines Inc. (TXI)
Braniff pays trust fine 2-23, 206D2
CAB OKs Natl merger bid 7-10; quits race 7-28, sells Natl stock to Pan Am 8-2, 578D3
TWA merger sought 9-13; Trans World dirs vs 9-19, bid continues 9-26, 830C1
TEXAS State Optical
Corp name use curbed by US Sup Ct 2-21, 128E2
TEXAS System, University of
Austin Campus
'78 rank rptd 1-2, 1-3, 8E2
Erxleben in NFL draft 5-3, 335F2
Curren wins NCAA tennis title 5-28, 570A2
Cholera vaccine advance rptd 8-2, 692A3
Loses Sun Bowl 12-22, 1001A3
El Paso Campus
2d in NCAA indoor track champ 3-10, wins NCAA outdoor champ 6-3, 911F2, B3
TEXAS Utilities Services Inc.
Uranium supply suit setlmt cited 5-15, 366B2
TEXTILES
US '78 trade gap rptd 1-30, 71D3
US import protectn deal set 2-15; House OKs duty waiver bill 3-1, 159E1
Bagley indicted 3-14, SEC chrgs filed 3-15, 292A1
US duty waiver bill signed 4-3, 298G3
GATT pact signed, tariff cuts seen 4-12, 273G1
'79 fashion roundup rptd 1006G1, E2
US-China exports agrmt pending 5-14, 370B1
US-China talks collapse 5-30, US sets quotas 5-31, 405C3
Carter submits trade bill to Cong 6-19, sets tariff cuts 6-21; House OKs bill 7-11, 541F1-A2
China-US pact signed 7-7, 523G2-A3
Canada tariff cuts rptd 7-12, 543E1
EC, China initial pact 7-18, 554E3
Stevens '77 union suits dismissed 7-18, 8-6, 598C3
Bagley acquitted 8-1, 578D2
French knitwear import curbs protested in Italy 8-20, 668D3
US exec flees El Salvador 8-24, 668B2
US orders China shirt embargoes 9-27, sets new quotas 10-30, 834B1
TEXTRON Inc.
Rhodesia chrgd re Bell copters 1-5, 7F3
Wage-price compliance claimed 2-6, 128B1
Pleads guilty to currency violatns 7-10, overseas payoffs admitted 7-26; Proxmire asks study 10-31, 923B2-B3
Proxmire vs Miller Treas apptmt 8-2, 627C2
Bell employes seized in Iran 11-7, 841F1
THACH, Nguyen Co
Rpts limited China air role 2-22, 122A1
Claims US talks on ties held 8-9, 8-11, 607G2
Denies US visa processing agrmt 8-11, 607E2
Meets Thai premr 10-19—10-20, 811D3
US sens visit Cambodia, aid policy questnd 10-21—10-23, 824C1

THAILAND—*See also ASEAN*
Freedom House lists as partly free 12G3
Rebel force smashed 4-9, 298E2
Electns yield no majority, Kriangsak power seen unabated 4-22, 314D2
New Cabt rptd named 5-25, 428F3
Bus, truck collisn kills 52 6-2, 639A2

1980

TEXAS A&M University (College Station)
Dana Bible dies 1-19, 104F1
Dickey wins NCAA indoor 60-yd dash 3-15; Hall sets pole vault mark 6-7, 891F3, 892A1
NCAA basketball tourn results 3-24, 240F1
Dickey, Green in NFL draft 4-29, 336E3, F3
TEXAS Capricorn (U.S. oil tanker)
Collides with Coast Guard cutter 1-28, suit rptd filed 2-3, 256D2
TEXAS Gas Transmission Corp.
Commercial Carriers Inc.
Fla deregulates trucking 7-1, 558F2
TEXAS Instruments Inc.
Haggerty dies 10-1, 876G1
TEXAS Monthly (magazine)
New West purchase rptd 8-27, 732E3
TEXAS Pacific Oil Co. Inc.—*See SEAGRAM*
TEXAS System, University of
'79 endowmt earnings rptd 3-24, 319B2
Austin Campus
Dana Bible dies 1-19, 104F1
Sterkel sets swim marks 3-20—3-22, team 2d in AIAW Championship 3-22, 835C1
George Watts dies 3-29, 280E2
2d in NCAA swim championships 3-29, 835B1
3 in NFL draft 4-29, 336E3-G3
Stellar study questns planet presence 6-29, 715D2
World illiteracy study rptd 12-4, 953A2
Loses Bluebonnet Bowl 12-31, 999E3
El Paso Campus
Wins NCAA indoor track champ 3-14—3-15; NCAA outdoor champ 6-5—6-7, 891F3-892A1
Medical Branch (Galveston)
Office machine cancer risks rptd 4-11, 357A2-A3
TEXTILE, Garment and Leather Workers' Association, International
Polish worker aid rptd 9-4, 659C3
TEXTILES
UK seeks EC curb on US fibers 2-5, 2-7, 125E1
Marcel Boussac dies 3-21, 279E1
Italy ct rules vs US fibers 4-4, 294B3
EC probes US polyester fiber dumping 5-5, sets acrylics duties 5-6, 411F3
Taiwan '79 sales rptd down 7-4, 567B3
Australia import tariffs kept 8-15, 632F2-D3
EC sets US polyester duties 9-1, 662E2
US-China pact signed 9-17; US clothing execs vs high imports 9-18, 706G3-707G1
OSHA cotton dust standard case accepted by Sup Ct 10-6, 782C1
Stevens, union come to terms 10-19, 805B1-D2
Stevens union access case refused by Sup Ct 10-20, 807A2
Deering Milliken '56 labor dispute setld 12-3, workers OK 12-14, 962D2
'80 fashion roundup rptd 998B2
TEXTRON Inc.
SEC chrgs settled, Miller knowledge of payoffs alleged 1-31, Miller denies 2-1, 92C1-A2
Miller spec prosecutor sought 2-8—2-11, 145E1-B2; rejctd 3-11, 185D2
Iran copter deliveries canceled 4-8, 282D1
THACH, Nguyen Co
Named Viet forgn min 2-7, 90G1
Denies Thai frontier breach 6-26, 508G1
Chrgs China troops mass 7-7; West sees no move 7-9, 508E2
THAI Airways
Jet crash kills 40 4-27, 527G3

THAILAND—*See also ADB, ASEAN*
Freedom House lists as partly free 87E3
Kriangsak shifts Cabt 2-11, 196F3
Kriangsak quits as premr 2-19; Prem succeeds 3-3, forms Cabt 3-12, 196D3
Jet crash kills 40 4-27, 527G3

1976

Seni quits 9-23, renamed 9-25; names new Cabt 10-5, 754E1
Anti-Thanom riots 10-4—10-6, 754C1
Sa-Ngad named defense min 10-4, 754E1
Seni ousted, mil takes power 10-6, 753F3-754C1 ★
Bangkok curfew lifted 10-7, 775D2
Reds tied to violence 10-7, 775E2
Ex-univ rector leaves 10-7, 813E3
Thanin named premier 10-8, lists aims 10-9, 775F2
Security, internal affairs heads named 10-8, 775A3
More junta curbs, press ban eased 10-8, 775B3
Pre-coup death toll rptd 10-9, 775E2
Purges ordrd, charter group formed, press curbed 10-11, 775C3
Anti-junta group forms govt-in-exile in Laos 10-12, 794F3
Leftists flee Bangkok 10-13, 794D3
Bangkok curfew reimposed 10-13, 794G3
Free electns delayed 4 yrs 10-13, 795A1
Reeducatn centers formed 10-14, 794G2
Leftists seized 10-15, 10-19, 794D2, B3
Chatichai leaves 10-16, 813D3
Gen Chalard forced to retire 10-16, becomes monk 10-19, 813D3
200 students flee 10-20, 813C3
Anti-dissident edicts 10-20, 813E3
New Cabt formed 10-22, 813D2
6 govt aides ousted 10-24, 813G2
5,287 post-coup arrests rptd 10-25, 813B3
Schls reopen 11-1, 929F2
Natl Assemb named 11-20, 929E2
20 rebels slain 11-21, 929D2
Listed as not free 12-22, 977B3
Rebels down copter, dep gov dies 12-22, 1013D3
Rebels kill 22 troops 12-25, 1013D3

Foreign Relations (misc.)

Reopens Laos border 1-1, 31F1
Australia in SE Asia talks 1-16—1-17, 46B1
Cambodia refugees rpt on exodus 1-19, 46D2
Cambodia troops slay refugees 1-26, 98E3
Laos, N Viet bolster ties 2-11, 121E1
SEATO formally disbanded 2-20, 148C1
S Viet returns bodies of 2 US marines 2-22, 157A2
Cambodia chrgs US jet raid 2-25; US, Thais deny 2-27, 172D3
S Viet airman defects to 3-8, 223A2
Laos pilot defects to 3-9, 222F1
Australia wheat deal rptd 3-11, 187D3
Indochina refugees in Australia 3-19, 237B2
Thais order US base shutdown 3-20; operatns ended 3-21, 223B2
Anti-US rally, 4 die 3-21, 223C2
US servicemen leave 3-21—3-27, 255G3
Kukrit for smooth US exit 3-22, 223G2
Hijacked PI jet lands 4-9, leaves 4-12, 260A3
Laos prisoners escape 4-26, 333F3
Defense min vs US radar pullout 4-27, 315E1
Cambodia pilot defects 4-30, asks asylum 5-2, 335E1
Bangladesh exile stops over 5-2, 332A2
Malaysian force protested 5-17, 403D3
US quits satellite statn 5-19, 502G1
At Timor assembly meeting 5-31, 423A1
Malaysians asked to quit border area 6-6, Thais replace 6-17, 502A2
S Viet refugees flee 6-7, 441D3
US closes last 2 major bases 6-20, 502F1
Libya rebel arms aid rptd 7-15, 531F1
Thais assured on US mil exit 7-19; US leaves 7-20, 541E3, G3 ★
Viet refugees protested 7-29—8-27, Viet scores rightists 8-26, 678A1
Laos border, prisoner release pact 8-3, Cambodia border reopened 8-30, 677F3
Vietnam OKs ties 8-6, 593D2
US GOP platform text cites 8-18, 610A2
Rpt rebels get Viet, China, Cambodia aid 9-3, 677D3
Cambodia asks 4 ex-offcls return 9-4, 734E3
Rpt Laos refugees arrive US 9-14, 696B3
Qantas admits price cutting 9-23, 749E3
Viet, Laos, Sovt tie US to coup 10-8, 775F3-776A1
Forgn publicatns censored 10-11, 775E3
Thai students score US 10-13, 794E3
Laos border clashes 10-14, 795C1; 10-17, 10-20, 814A1
Viet scores junta 10-17, 795D1
US base talks aide ousted 10-24, 813A3
'76 US Eximbank loan default rptd 11-11, 915A3
26 Cambodian refugees returned 11-23, UN protests 12-3, 929B2
22 Cambodians die in clashes 11-25, 929D2
Viet invasion plan chrgd 12-8, 949C3
Sovt missile silos in Laos rptd 12-27, 1013C1

Sports

Olympic results 7-18—7-31, 573F3, 574A1

1977

Foreign Relations (misc.)

UN Assemb member 4C1
Viet refugee factns clash 1-12, 47E3
Malaysia joins drive vs rebels 1-14—1-17, base rptd seized 1-29, 87F3
Intl rubber buffer stock plan rejctd 1-23, 169G2
Cambodians raid 4 villages 1-28—1-29; Thais close border 1-30, alert army 1-31, 87D3
Cambodia chrgs raids 2-4, 2-12, 138G1
Laotian troop clash 2-6—2-7, 138F1
Malaysia border pact signed 3-4, 203C1
Viet refugee rise rptd 3-25, 243F3
Taiwan bars coup plotters 3-27, 243B2
Burma rebels retreat rptd 3-27, 243C3
Laos protests rebel aid 4-9, closes border 4-11, 305A1
Intl drug conf opens 4-14, US questions peddler's executn 4-15, 331G2
Cambodia, Laos refugee exodus rptd 5-2, 5-3, 337A1, E1
Cambodia border clashes 5-6, 5-8, 5-12, 393G2
Viet refugees leave 6-12, 497D1, F1
World Food Cncl OKs rice plan 6-23, 513E3
Cambodia border clashes 7-20—7-22; Thai protest 7-25, 571G3
Cambodia clashes continue 7-23—8-8, Thanin confirms 8-6, 607A3, B2
Viets sink fishing boat 7-25, 607E3
Malaya aids drive vs rebels 8-7, 607F3
Kriangsak identifies Pol Pot as top Cambodia ldr 8-19, 741F2
Indochina refugee data rptd 8-31, 685F2
Cambodia premr cites clashes 9-28, 741E3
Cambodia hints at clashes 10-2, 779G3
Cambodia border incursns repelled 10-15—10-16, 10-31, 840D3
W Eur heroin conf 10-17—10-21, 972A1
Trade embargo vs Laos lifted 10-19, 885D1
New rulers for ties with Viet, Laos, Cambodia 10-21, 827D1
Viet refugees bar sought, UN role cited 11-25, 1018F2-A3
Cambodia border clashes 12-21—12-22, 999C3
32 Viet refugees arrive 12-23, 1018B2

1978

Foreign Relations (misc.)—*See also 'Monetary, Trade, Aid & Investment' below*

Cambodia raid, 7 die 1-23; '77 casualties 61C1
Cambodia talks, tie renewal set 1-30—2-2, 61B1
Uppadhit denies Pnompenh 'ghost city' 2-2, 61E1
Cambodians, Thai rebels abduct villagers 2-9; border clashes 2-10, 2-16, 121G1
Laos, Viet reopen air lane 2-11, 140C1
Laos refugees forced back, UN distressed 2-16; 3 rptd killed 2-24; refugee data rptd 139C3-140B1
Civlns abducted to Cambodia 3-5, 237C3
Australia to accept Indochina refugees 3-15, 187G2
Meos refugee from Laos rptd 3-24, 3-28, 237F2
Rebels, Cambodians kill 19 civlns 4-9, 301A3
CP rebels rptdly extend frontier control 4-10, 301F2
Cambodia-Viet fighting confrmd 4-12, 277D3
Cambodia rptd clearing out civlns in border area 4-19, 301A3
3 arrested in Australia emb bomb plot 4-21, 311A1
Cambodian refugees placed in camp 4-30, 341C2
Australia to admit 9,000 refugees 5-17, 369B3
Cambodia aide visits, border pact agreed 7-14—7-17, 548F2
New Cambodia refugee flights rptd 8-8, 8-10, 659F3-660B1
Viet premr visits; econ, refugee agrmts reached 9-6—9-10, 696E1-A3
UN Assemb member 713F3
Viet party problems rptd 10-18, 823B1
Viet impasse over refugees 10-29, 830G1-B2
China dep premr visits 11-5—11-9, 894B1
Viet refugee aid asked 12-12, 956B2
China-US ties lauded 12-16, 977D1
Viet refugee boat to Taiwan chngs course 12-19, 997F2

Monetary, Trade, Aid & Investment

Viet trade pact signed 1-12, 21A3
US vows refugee resetlmt, arms aid 5-4—5-5, 360E3
S Africa trade ban rptd 8-7, 670A1
Australia tariff proposals scored 8-17, 646B2
Viet econ ties agreed 9-6—9-10, 696G1

1979

Foreign Relations (misc.)—*See also 'Monetary' and 'UN' below*

Cambodia forgn offcls seek refuge 1-8, 9G2
Cambodia's Ieng rescued, denied asylum 1-11; flown to China 1-12, 9F2
USSR, Viets warned by US 1-17, 30A1
Cambodia troops get asylum 1-18, 68G2
Viet, Cambodia sign friendship pact 2-18, 123C2
Cambodia war troop spillover 3-4, 229B2
250,000 Laotian refugees rptd 3-24, 331E3
Laos peace pact signed 4-4, 298C2
Pol Pot escape from Cambodia rptd 4-5, 800 soldiers 4-12, 278E3, F3
Cambodia civilns, Pol Pot troops seek refuge; forced back, shelling chrgd 4-16—4-29, 318B1-B2
Refugee data rptd 4-25, 5-19, 379C2, F2
More Cambodians arrive 5-9—5-11, 360C2
Cambodian ousted refugees rptd killed 6-4, 436A1
Cambodian refugees returned 6-11; permit 1,430 temporary stay, ask Pol Pot stop flow 6-12, 435E3, 436B1
China asked to accept Cambodian refugees 6-12, 436C1
Cambodia chrgs refugees killed 6-22, 474G1
Cambodian refugee ousters delayed, UN conf awaited 6-25, 474F1
More refugee admissns barred 6-30; US, Japan seek aid 7-2, 495A2
Cambodian refugee expulsn halt rptd 6-30, temporary asylum OKd 7-10, 550F1
China closes anti-Thai radio statn, Viet conflict cited 7-11, 537C3
Cambodia clash near border rptd 7-19, 550A3
Viet refugee cites pirates 7-31, 626F1
Refugee Aug data rptd 8-22, 625F3
Laos refugee pact rptd 8-25, 659B3
Cambodia emergency aid rptd 8-29, 9-8, 684A2
Cambodia threatened by war, famine 8-30; refugees mass near border 9-9, 684C2
Cambodia refugee temp asylum OKd 9-26, 764A2
Indochina refugee Sept exit sets record 10-3, 764A1
70,000 Cambodian refugees enter 10-10—10-20, camps shelled 10-12, 10-14, 811B3
Sihanouk seeks Cambodian refugee ouster end 10-11, 811F2
Viets chrg Cambodia war role 10-18, talks held 10-19—10-20, 811C3
Cambodia refugee camps toured by US sens 10-21—10-23, food convoy proposal rejctd 10-27, 823C3-824E1
Refugees visited by Mrs Carter 11-8—11-10, 863G1
Cambodia refugee camp shelled 11-8, 863C2
Refugee aid airlift ordrd by US 11-13, 863E2
2 Cambodia refugee camps declared 'safe havens' 11-29, 917G2
Cambodia border relief blocked, Free Khmer blamed 12-3, 917F2

Monetary, Trade, Aid & Investment

US mil aid hiked 1-21, 84E2
USSR mil aid to Viet rptd 2-22, 122B1
China rptdly channels mil aid to Pol Pot forces in Cambodia 3-19, 229E2
US vows arms, refugee resetlmt aid 2-7, 84C2

1980

Foreign Relations (misc.)—*See also 'Monetary' below*

Cambodian refugee camp fighting rptd, 1000s cross border 1-4—1-6, 12B3
Cambodia refugee aid halted 1-10; resumed 1-20, 49F1
Pirates kill 167 Viet refugees 1-10, 49A2
Pacific orgn studied 1-20, 78C2
Cambodia-Viet clashes rage near border 1-25—1-31, US sees Viet drive threat 1-26, 68C2
Cambodia blocks intl aid convoy; US, French protest 2-6, 108B2
Cambodia aid suspended at Nong Chan 2-7, 108G1
Vietnamese escape via Cambodia rptd 2-24, 141E1
Cambodia refugee camp battle 3-19; fighting ends, residents return 3-21, 262B1
UN holds Cambodia aid conf 5-26—5-27, 397D2
Cambodia refugee repatriatn delay asked 6-15; 823 sent back 6-17—6-18, 475D3
Laotians fire on Thai craft, border closed 6-15; peace talks deadlocked 7-21—7-23, 547A3
Cambodia relief aid halted 6-17, Viet blamed 7-9; Thais, Red Cross, UN OK renewal 7-27, 591C2
Viet troops raid from Cambodia 6-23—6-24; Thailand protests 6-24, 475F2-C3
China vs Viet raids 6-25, 7-2, 508A2, D2
US asks Viet raid halt 6-25, seeks Moscow aid 6-25, 6-26, 508B2
Viets capture 4 Westn civilians 6-25, release 6-29, 508F2
100,000 Cambodians flee Viet drive 6-26, 508D1
ASEAN conf scores Viet incursn; Viets deny frontier breach 6-26, 508E1-A2
Viet artillery clashes near Cambodia border 6-28, 508C1
USSR scores US arms lift 7-5, 508B1
Viet Thai-Cambodia DMZ plan opposed at forgn min talks 7-18, 591F1
Cambodia chrgs mil raids, scores DMZ plan rejectn 7-26, 591G1-C2
ASEAN vs Viet Cambodia DMZ plan 8-1, 591E1
Waldheim visits, seeks Thai-Viet pact re Cambodia conflict 8-2—8-5, 591A1
Cambodia relief aid resumed 8-4, 644G3
Viet rptd vs US MIA proposals 10-6, 855B2
In China talks on Cambodia conflict 10-30, 952B1
Cambodian refugees return home 11-13, 951G3
Red Cross ends Cambodia food aid 12-16, 951E3

Monetary, Trade, Aid & Investment

US '79 arms orders, '80 speedup rptd 1-5, 68G2
Pacific orgn studied 1-20, 78C2
US arms lift starts 7-5, 508B1
World Bank '80 loans rptd 9-22, 720E1

1976

THALER, Seymour R.
Dies 2-5, 124F3
THAMES River
Tanker leaks oil 12-28, 1014G1
THANAT Khoman
Rpts Sovt missile silos in Laos 12-27, 1013C1
THANG, Ton Duc
Pres of united Vietnam 7-3, 502D3
THANIN Kraivichien (Thai premier)
Gets absolute power 10-2, 813D2
Named premier 10-8, lists aims 10-9, 775F2 ★
Elections delayed 4 yrs 10-13, 795A1
THANOM Kittikachorn
Praphas returns 8-15, deported 8-22, 640D1
Thais bar return 8-31, 677C3
Rpt Laos trains rebels 9-3, 677E3
Returns Thailand, students riot 9-19; asked to leave 9-21, 753G3, 754A2
Seni quits 9-23, renamed 9-25, 754F1
Students riot 10-4—10-5; mil seizes power 10-6, 753G3-754D1
THARPAR, Romesh
India journal rptd closed 7-25, 620G3
THATCHER, Margaret
Scores home-rule plan 1-13, 73B1
Shadow cabt reshuffled 1-15, 101B2
Scores detente, backs strong NATO 1-19, 101C1-A2
Scores '76-77 budget 4-6, 266A3
Govt wins ship natlzn ruling 5-27, meets Callaghan 5-28, 402B1
Tito cancels visit 9-16, 734G2
Vs lending rate hike 10-11, 773F1
Hails by-electn win 11-4, 853F1
Changes shadow Cabt 11-19, 1004G1 ★
Party vs devolutn bill 12-9, 1004F1
THAYER, Louis M.
Replaced on Transport Safety Bd 4-12, 412F1

1977

U.S. Relations
US questns drug peddler's executn 4-15, 331G2
US arms aid authorized 8-4, 668C1
Exxon admits paymts 10-25, 818A2
US rpts heroin trade down 11-7, 972B1 ★
CIA post-war plans scored 11-18, 898E1
THALER, William
Backs phone ad curbs 10-21, 921B1
THANI, Sheik Abdul Aziz Bin Khalifa al-
Saudis rejct oil price compromise 2-6, 107A3
THANIN Kraivichien (Thai premier; ousted Oct. 20)
Assures Thais after coup try 3-26, 243A2
At ASEAN summit 8-4—8-5, 607A2
Confrms Cambodia border clashes 8-6, 607A3
Ousted by mil coup 10-20, 826G3
Successor named 11-11, 904D3
THANOM Kittikachorn
Son ends exile 7-10, 641A3
THAN Sein
Rptd purged 10-8, 779B3
THATCHER, Margaret
Labor wins no-confidence vote 3-23, 239G2
Scores Healey budget 3-29, 256A3
In China 4-11, 282B2
Sees Carter 5-8, 359E2
Sees Carter 9-13, ends US visit 9-15, 883C3
Vows moderate govt 10-14, 863F3
Shifts oppositn spokesmen 11-4, 883B3
THATCHER Glass Division—*See under DART Industries*
THAVORN Udomleudej
Executed 4-14, 331F2
US rep questns executn 4-15, 331A3

1978

U.S. Relations
US info leaks cited in Viet spy chrgs 1-31, 68E3
US issues rights rpt 2-9, 101D3
US distressed re refugees 2-16, 139G3-140A1
US natl arrested in Australia emb bomb plot 4-21, 311A1
Mondale visits; vows refugee resetlmt, arms aid 5-4—5-5, 360E3
US-China ties lauded 12-16, 977D1
THAIN, Dr. Wilbur S.
Indicted on drug chrg 6-6, 459A2
Acquitted 9-21, 1011A1
THALER, Fred
Platinum opens 11-12, 1031F2
THALIDOMIDE—*See MEDICINE—Drugs*
THAM, Carl
Swedish coordinatn min 10-18, 822A3
THANH, Tran Tu
Father's '76 death rptd 7-10, 692G1
THANK God It's Friday (film)
Released 5-19, 620B1 ★
Top-grossing film 5-31, 460E3
THANOM Kittikachorn
18 jailed protesters freed 9-17, 841E1
THATCHER, Margaret
Urges immigratn cutoff 1-30, Parlt scores 1-31, 90D1
Heath warns vs immigratn bar 2-13, 167D3 ★
Tories win Ilford North by-electn 3-2, voting analyzed 3-3—3-6, 167E2, B3
House of Lords revisn proposed 3-20, 227A1
Vs govt oil revenue plans 3-21, 227F1
Scores '78-79 budget 4-11, 267A3
Hails Eur conservative coalitn 4-24, 424B3
Labor wins confidence vote 6-14, 496G2
Scores Callaghan electn delay 9-7, 704F3
Backs free mkt pay policy 10-10, 763G2
At Spain party cong, urges EC entry 10-21, 821F2
Poll rpts 40% 'satisfied' 10-28, 867F1
Scores sanctions vs Ford 11-28, 923F3
Tories score pay sanctns 12-13; Callaghan renounces, wins confidnc vote 12-14, 964B3

1979

UN Policy & Developments
Waldheim visits refugee camps 5-13, 379D2
Membership listed 695A3
U.S. Relations
Carter: USSR, Viets warned 1-17, 30A1
US mil aid hiked 1-21, 84E2
Kriangsak meets Carter; US vows arms resetlmt aid 2-6—2-7, 84A2
US vows arms, refugee resetlmt aid 2-7, 84C2
US issues rights rpt 2-10, 107E3
Student enrollmt in US rptd 167D2
US concerned re refugee ouster 6-11, 6-12, 435F3, 436C1
US seeks refugee asylum 7-2, 495D2
US reps visit Viet refugee camps 8-6, 607G1
Mondale in refugee talks 9-1, 660A3
Refugee outflow to US in Sept rptd 10-3, 764A2
Sihanouk seeks Thai aid on Cambodia refugees 10-11, 811F2
3 sens visit Cambodia refugee camps 10-21—10-23; food convoy urged 10-24, rejectd by Cambodia 10-27, 823C3-824E1
Mrs Carter visits refugees 11-8—11-10, 863G1
Refugee aid airlift ordered 11-13, 863E2
US Emb bombed 11-30, 2d threat rptd 12-2, 915C1, D1
Carter reaffirms defns commitment 12-12, 963C1
THALIDOMIDE—*See MEDICINE—Drugs*
THANK God It's Friday (film)
Jabara wins Oscar 4-9, 336B2
THANT, U (1909-74)
Israel vs UNTSO in Sinai 7-24, 551F1
THATCHER, Denis
Wife apptd UK prime min 5-4, 338E2
THATCHER, Margaret (British prime minister)
Poll rpts approval rise 2-6, 116B1
Scores govt on lending rate 2-8, 116D1
Scores TUC-govt accord 2-14, 115A3
Warns vs devolutn efforts 3-2, 169G1
Lauds Neave 3-30, 254B2
Tories set Africa policy 4-11, 285B3
Vs Natl Front rally violence 4-24, 313E1
Defends N Ireland policy 4-30, 312G2
Wins electn 5-3, apptd prime min 5-4, names Cabt 5-5; photo, facts on 337A1-338A3
Tory programs outlined 5-15, 358D2
Budget presented 6-12, 445F1
Asks UN conf on Indochina refugees 6-18; US, Viet OK 6-19, 6-20, 474A1
Confers with union ldrs 6-25, 502F3
At Tokyo energy summit 6-28—6-29, 493B1
Zimbabwe sanctns end hinted 7-1, sees Muzorewa 7-13, 546C3, E3
Salary hike rptd rejected 7-7, 543A3
Death penalty ban upheld 7-19, 543E2
Nigeria natlizes BP, Zimbabwe ties cited 7-31, 584C3
Addresses Commonwealth conf on Zimbabwe 8-3; Zimbabwe plan agreed 8-6; reactn 8-6—8-9, 589A2-E2, 590E1-C2
Deplores Mountbatten murder 8-27, sees mins on N Ireland 8-28, 641D1, C2
Visits N Ireland 8-29; attends Mountbatten funeral, sees Lynch 9-5, 669C1, D2, G2
N Sea oil assets sale barred 9-14, 707A2
N Ireland security accord set 10-5, 792F3
Addresses Tory conf, policies backed 10-10, 791G2
Greets China premr 10-28, OKs accords 11-1, 854E1-B2
Hails BL workers' vote on cutbacks 11-1, 855A3
Zambia pres visits UK re Zimbabwe 11-8—11-10, Nigeria envoy 11-15, 881E1
Immigratn curbs proposed 11-14, 873D2
On lending rate hike 11-15, 889D2
Names Blunt as 4th spy 11-15, addresses Parlt 11-21, 908C2-909B1
Contacts Zambia pres re Zimbabwe raids 11-20, 899E2
EC cost contributn reductn demands rejected 11-29—11-30, 917B3
Sees Vance on Iran 12-10, 933G2
In DC, visits Carter 12-17, sees UN offcls in NY 12-18, 968F1
Backs Churchill re security 12-17, 994G2
Protests to Brezhnev re Afghan invasn 12-29, 974C2

1980

U.S. Relations
US '79 arms orders, '80 speedup rptd 1-5, 68G2
Viet drive near Cambodia-Thai border feared 1-26, 68F2
Pan Am revives discount coupons 3-10, 346E3
US concerned re Viet attack, plans more arms aid 6-24, 475C3
US arms asked 6-25, Carter orders airlift 7-1, 491A3
US arms lift starts, Sovts score 7-5, 508B1
US Viet MIA proposals rptd rejected 10-6, 855B2
THAM, Michael Ray
Sentenced 5-23, 482F2
THANG, Ton Duc
Dies 3-30, 280D2
THATCHER, Margaret (British prime minister)
Steelworkers strike 1-2, 6F3, G3
Sets 'Quango' paring 1-16, 79E2
To seek Moscow Olympics shift 1-17, backs Carter move 1-21, 45A3
Offers UK Olympic site 1-22, 68C1
Carter Afghan support cited 2-5, 125A2
Pub housing sale sought 2-7, 149G3
Labor censure vote defeated, defends econ policies 2-28, 172G1
Lauds Zimbabwe vote 3-4, 161G2
Prior dismisses Cabt split rpts 3-9, 193B3
Admits econ problems 3-12, 212G1
Tories win Southend by-electn 3-13, 212E1
Lords reject school transport bill 3-13, 254G2
Vs EC budget contributn 3-19, 3-20, summit delay 3-24; Schmidt backs stance 3-28, 242C2
Olympic com defies Moscow boycott 3-25, 259E2
Steel strike settled 4-1, 254E2
Vows strong actn vs Iran 4-14, 282C1
EC budget impasse continues 4-27, 4-28, 327C1-G1
W Ger EC fund hike unlikely 4-30, 355G3
Lauds London Emb rescue 5-6, 337D1
At Tito funeral 5-8, 339A1
Mugabe seeks more UK mil trainers 5-9, 469B1
Meets Haughey re Ulster 5-21, 389E3
OKs EC budget compromise 6-2, 421C2, A3
Sees interest rate cut 6-6, 444F3, 445D1
Son crashes at LeMans 6-15, 637C3
June unemploymt sets mark 6-24, 498E1
Min lending rate cut 7-3, 523F1
Anderson visits 7-16—7-17, 550B1
Wins no-confidence vote 7-29, 578C1
Walls reveals Zimbabwe electn void request 8-11, 731E2, F2
Carter urges Poland aid 8-29, 659C1
TUC conf scores 9-1—9-5, 688A2
US briefs on hostages in Iran 9-19, 719C3
Labor Party conf 9-29—10-3, 768G2
Affirms policies at Tory conf 10-10, 790E2
Rejects TUC econ plan 10-14, 790C3, F3
Econ outlook grim, spending cuts considered 11-4, 859E2
Pub sector 6% pay lid affirmed 11-7, 886B3
Queen opens Parlt, charts govt programs 11-20, 900E3, 901E1
Govt spending cuts announced 11-24, 901E2
Jobless protest in Liverpool 11-29, 922D1
Meets Haughey in Dublin 12-8, 942F2
IRA hunger strike ends 12-18, 12-19, 993D3
Urges BL strike end 12-31, 994F1
THATCHER, Mark
Crashes at LeMans 6-15, 637C3
THAT Girl (TV series)
Thomas marries 5-22, 471A2
THC (tetrahydrocannabinol)—*See NARCOTICS*

1976

THEATER
Czech bars Havel Austria visit 10-9, 852A1
Broadway long runs listed 12-31, 1014G3
Awards
Tony awards presented 4-18, 460C2
Chorus Line wins Pulitzer 5-3, 352C3
Obituaries
Baddeley, Angela 2-22, 192C3
Bloomgarden, Kermit 9-20, 970C1
Cambridge, Godfrey 11-29, 932D3
Cassidy, Jack 12-12, 1015C1
Cobb, Lee J 2-11, 160C3
Dowling, Eddie 2-18, 160D3
Evans, Dame Edith 10-14, 970G1
Ford, Paul 4-12, 316A1
Hornblow, Arthur 7-17, 716B3
Lackey, Kenneth 4-16, 316A1
Leighton, Margaret 1-13, 56E3
Lowry, Judith 11-29, 932E3
McDevitt, Ruth 5-27, 524B3
Mielziner, Jo 3-15, 240E3
Miller, Ruby 4-2, 524C3
Nichols, Barbara 10-5, 970F2
Pontes, Paulo 12-28, 1015D2
Redfield, William 8-17, 892D3
Robeson, Paul 1-23, 80F3
Sim, Alastair 8-20, 892F3
Thorndike, Dame Sybil 6-9, 444G2
Play Openings (N. Y.)
Best Friend 10-19, 1014E3
Boy Meets Girl 4-13, 1014C3
Bubbling Brown Sugar 3-2, 1014B3
California Suite 6-10, 1014D3
Checking Out 9-14, 1014D3
Comedians 11-28, 1014F3
Days in the Trees 9-26, 1014E3
Des Journees Entieres Dan les Arbres
Don't Step on My Olive Branch 11-1, 1014F3
Eccentricities of a Nightingale 11-23, 1014F3
Equus 10-5, 1014E3
Fiddler on the Roof 12-28, 1014F3
For Colored Girls Who Have Considered Suicide/When the Rainbow is Enuf 9-15, 1014D3
Godspell 6-22, 1014D3
Going Up 9-19, 1014E3
Heiress 4-20,1014C3
Herzl 11-30, 1014F3
HMS Pinafore 5-16, 1014D3
Home Sweet Homer 1-4, 1014B3
I Have a Dream 9-20, 1014E3
Innocents 10-21, 1014F3
Knock, Knock 2-24, 6-6, 1014B3
Lady From the Sea 3-18, 1014C3
Last Mtg of Knights of White Magnolia 9-21, 1014E3
Legend 5-13, 1014D3
Let My People Come 8-11, 1014D3
Lu Ann Hampton Lavery Oberlander 9-22, 1014E3
Matter of Gravity 2-3, 1014B3
Mikado 5-5, 1014C3
Monty Python Live! 4-15, 1014C3
Mrs Warren's Professn 2-18, 1014B3
My Fair Lady 3-25, 1014C3
Music Is 12-20, 1014F3
Night of the Iguana 12-16, 1014F3
No Man's Land 11-9, 1014F3
Oh! Calcutta 9-24, 1014E3
Oldest Living Graduate 9-23, 1014E3
Pacific Overtures 1-11, 1014B3
Pal Joey 6-27, 1014D3
Pirates of Penzance 5-6, 1014C3
Poison Tree 1-8, 1014B3
Poor Murderer 10-20, 1014F3
Porgy and Bess 9-26, 1014E3
Rex 4-25, 1014C3
Robber Bridegroom 10-10, 1014E3
Runner Stumbles 5-18, 1014D3
Rockabye Hamlet 2-17, 1014B3
Secret Service 4-12, 1014C3
1600 Pennsylvania Avenue 5-4, 1014C3
Sly Fox 12-14, 1014F3
So Long, 174th Street 4-27, 1014C3
Something's Afoot 5-27, 1014D3
Streamers 4-21, 1014C3
They Knew What They Wanted 1-27, 1014B3
Threepenny Opera 5-2, 1014C3
27 Wagons Full of Cotton & Memory of 2 Mondays 1-26, 1014B3
Wheelbarrow Closers 10-11, 1014E3
Who's Afraid of Virginia Woolf 4-1, 1014C3
Your Arm's Too Short to Box With God 12-22, 1014F3
Zalmen or Madness of God 3-17, 1014C3

1977

THEATER
'76-77 box office record rptd 6-8, 472D3
Holzer indicted 7-12, 10-13, 848F1
Viacom-RCA satellite pact rptd 10-25, 921E1
Awards
Shadow Box wins Pulitzer 4-18, 355D2
Obituaries
Barrett, Edith 2-22, 164C2
Ben-Ami, Jacob 7-22, 604E2
Bissell, Richard 5-4, 452D2
Brooks, Geraldine 6-19, 532F2
Cabot, Sebastian 8-23, 696E2
Colt, Ethel Barrymore 5-22, 452F2
Finklehoffe, Fred 10-5, 872F1
Foy, Bryan 4-20, 356B3
Hull, Henry 3-8, 264A3
Lunt, Alfred 8-3, 696B3
Marx, Groucho 8-20, 696C3
Marx, Gummo (Milton) 4-21, 356D3
Mostel, Zero 9-8, 788G1
Patterson, Russell 3-17, 264D3
Rattigan, Terence 11-30, 952B3
Ritchard, Cyril 10-18, 1024G2
Tetzel, Joan 10-31, 872A3
Waters, Ethel 9-1, 788A3

1978

THEATER
Carter vs business tax break 2-17, 123A2
Spain ends censorship 3-3, 250B2
Actress killed in Mich auditn 4-10, 380E2
Radio City Music Hall saved 4-13, 293C1
NY newspaper strike impact rptd 11-6, 865G1
Awards
Coburn, Kerr win Pulitzers 4-17, 315C1, B2
Tonys presented 6-4, 579E2
N.Y. Openings
Ain't Misbehavin' 5-9, 760A1 ★
All's Well That Ends Well 7-5, 760B1
Amen Corner 4-22, 760B1
Andy Warhol's Last Love 6-30, 887A1
Angel 5-10, 760C1
Approaching Zero 11-30, 1030G3
Ballroom in St Patrick's 12-1, 1031A1
Beasts 2-8, 760C1
Best Little Whorehouse in Tex 4-17, 760D1
Biko Inquest 5-17, 760D1
Bistro Car on CNR 3-23, 887B1
Black Body Blues 1-24, 887B1
Blacks 5-24, 887B1
Bleacher Bums 4-24, 760E1
Bright & Golden Land 4-3, 760E1
Broadway Musical 12-21, 1031B1
Buried Child 11-6, 1031B1
Catsplay 4-16, 887C1
Cheaters 1-15, 760E1
Choices 12-10, 1031C1
City Sugar 6-5, 887C1
Company 5-7, 887D1
Contessa of Mulberry St 1-4, 887D1
Coolest Cat in Town 6-23, 760F1
Cops 3-28, 760F1
Crane's Way 7-12, 760G1
Cromwell 7-12, 887E1
Crucifer of Blood 9-28, 1031C1
Da 3-13, 887E1
Dancin' 3-27, 887F1
Dead End 5-4, 760G1
Death Trap 2-26, 760A2
Diary of Anne Frank 12-18, 1031C1
Diversns & Delights 4-12, 887F1
Do Lord Remember Me 4-4, 887F1
Do You Turn Somersaults 1-9, 760A2
Drinks Before Dinner 11-23, 1031D1
Early Dark 4-25, 760A2
Eubie 9-20, 1031E1
Family Business 4-12, 760B2
Fathers & Sons 11-16, 1031E1
Fight for Barbara 11-27, 1031F1
5th of July 4-27, 760B2
First Monday in Oct 10-3, 1031F1
Forever Yours, Marie-Lou 6-2[illegible], 887G1
Gay Divorce 3-9, 760C2
Gimme Shelter 12-10, 1031G1
Halloween Bandit 12-18, 1031G1
Hello Dolly 3-5, 887G1
Henry IV: Part 1 & II 11-27, 1031A2
History of Amer Film 3-30, 760C2
Hooters 4-30, 760D2
In Recovery Lounge 12-7, 1031B2
Inspector General 9-21, 1031A2
International Stud 5-22, 887A2
King of Hearts 11-22, 1031B2
Kingfisher 12-6, 1031B2
Living At Home 12-11, 1031C2
Lulu 2-17, 760D2
Mahalia 6-5, 887A2
Man & Superman 12-17, 1031D2
Master & Margarita 11-11, 1031D2
Mighty Gents 4-16, 760E2
Modigliani 5-17, 760E2
Moliere In Spite Of Himself 3-12, 887B2
Mr Joyce 4-23, 760E2
My Astonishing Self 1-18, 760F2
My Cup Runneth Over 6-22, 760F2
My Old Friends 12-2, 1031E2
Native Son 3-27, 760G2
Nayatt School 5-12, 887B2
Neon Woman 4-16, 760G2
Nevis Mountain Dew 12-7, 1031E2
Nongogo 12-3, 1031F2
November People 1-14, 760A3
On Twentieth Century 2-19, 887C2
Once In Lifetime 6-15, 887C2
Othello 1-30, 887D2
Patio/Porch 4-13, 887D2
Paul Robeson 1-19, 760A3
Piano Bar 6-8, 887E2
Pins & Needles 7-6, 760A3
Platinum 11-12, 1031F2
Playboy of Weekend World 11-16, 1031G2
Players 9-6, 887E2
Porch 11-14, 1031G2
Prayer For My Daughter 1-17, 760B3
Price of Genius 6-26, 887E2
Promise 3-8, 760B3
PS Your Cat Is Dead 3-22, 887F2
Rear Column 11-19, 1031A3
Rib Cage 5-28, 887F2
Run'ers' 5-3, 887A3
Runaways 3-9, 887G2
Safe House 4-13, 760C3
Scenes From Country Life 3-13, 887A3
Shay 3-7, 887A3
Show-off 5-18, 760C3
Spring Awakening 7-13, 887B3
Stages 3-19, 760D3
Starving Class 3-2, 887B3
Stop the World I Want To Get Off 8-3, 887C3
Strawberry Fields 6-4, 887C3
Taudshow 3-24, 887D3
Taxi Tales 12-29, 1031A3
Tennis Game 11-5, 1031B3
13 Rue De L'Amour 3-16, 760D3
This Room 6-15, 760E3
Thread of Scarlet 12-8, 1031B3
Timbuktu 3-1, 760E3
Tribute 6-1, 887D3
Twilight Dinner 4-18, 760F3
Unicorn in Captivity 11-15, 1031B3
Utopia Inc 12-4, 1031C3

1979

THEATER
Holzer convicted of grand larceny 3-15, 239E2; sentenced 5-3, 431A3
Brecht '43-56 FBI surveillnc rptd 3-29, 367C3
PEN Club cong ends 7-21, 553G3
USSR cancels Norway, Sweden tour; defectns cited 10-1, 775B1
'78-79 Broadway season rptd successful 11-4, 956C2
'Grease' becomes longest-running Broadway show 12-8, 956E2
Pulitzer Prizes Awarded [illegible], [illegible]C2
N.Y. Openings
Bedroom Farce 3-29, 711C1
Beggars Soap Opera 7-23, 711D1
Bent 12-2, 1007B2
Big Bad Burlesque 8-14, 711E1
Biography: A Game 4-5, 711E1
Bosoms and Neglect 5-3, 711F1
Brass Ring 7-2, 711F1
Break a Leg 4-29, 711G1
But Never Jam Today 7-31, 711G1
Candida 3-6, 711A2
Carmelina 4-8, 711A2
Chinchilla 6-4, 711B2
City Suite 4-2, 711B2
Class Enemy 6-18, 711C2
Comin' Uptown 12-20, 1007C2
Coriolanus 3-14, 292C1; 6-28 711C2
Dancing In The Dark 1-21, 292D1
Dark at the Top of the Stairs 11-29, 956G2
Deadly Delilah 7-6, 711C2
Devour the Snow opens 5-13, 711D2
Dispatches 4-18, 711D2
Don Juan Comes Back from the War 4-15, 711E2
Elephant Man 1-14, 292D1
Enchanted Pig 4-23, 711E2
Every Good Boy Deserves Favour 7-30, 711F2
Evita 9-25, 956A3
Eyes on the Harem 4-24, 711F2
Faith Healer 4-4, 711G2
Father's Day 6-21, 711G2
Festival 5-7, 711A3
Flying Blind 11-15, 956A3
Frequency 4-25, 711B3
Getting Out 5-15, 711B3
Gilda Radner Live from New York 8-2, 711B3
Glorious Monster in the Bell of the Horn 7-10, 711C3
God Bless You Mr Rosewater 5-20, 711D3
Goodbye People 4-30, 711D3
Good Lads at Heart 3-27, 711E3
Grand Tour 1-11, 292E1
GR Point 4-16, 711E3
Hitting Town 1-6, 292F2
Holeville 12-4, 956B3
Homeland 4-16, 711F3
I Love My Wife 5-15, 711F3
I Remember Mama 5-31, 711G3
Just a Little Less Than Normal 5-20, 711G3
Kid Champion 8-27, 712A1
King of Schnorrers 11-28, 956B3
Knockout 5-6, 712A1
Later 1-15, 292F2
Leave It to Beaver is Dead 4-3, 712B1
Light Shines in Darkness 1-11, 292G1
Little Eyolf 6-29, 712B1
Loose Ends 6-6, 712B1
Losing Time 9-30, 956C3
Loudspeaker 4-30, 712C1
Lovely Sunday For Creve Coeur 1-21, 292A2
Madman & the Nun 1-18, 292A2
Manny 4-18, 712C1
Marquis of Keith 3-13, 712D1
Meeting By the River 3-28, 712D1
Men in White 7-11, 712D1
Mercier & Camier 10-25, 956C3
Minnesota Moon 1-31, 292B2
Miracle Worker 1-6, 292B2
Miss Truth 7-22, 712E1
Month in the Country 12-11, 1007C2
Most Happy Fella 10-11, 956D3
Murder at the Howard Johnson's 5-17, 712E1
Nasty Rumors and Final Remarks 4-12, 712F1
Nature & Purpose Of Universe 2-23, 292C2
New Jerusalem 2-15, 712F1
Night & Day 11-27, 956E3
1940's Radio Hour 10-7, 956E3
Oklahoma! 12-13, 1007D2
Old Phantoms 2-8, 292C2
Once A Catholic 10-10, 956F3
On Golden Pond 2-28, 712G1
On Mount Chimborazo 5-21, 712G1
Othello 8-8, 712A2
Paris Was Yesterday 12-19, 1007D2
Peter Pan 9-6, 956G3
Plays From Africa 1-14, 292D2
Poet and the Rent 5-9, 712A2
Price 4-19, 712B2
Rat's Nest 2-2, 292D2
Re-Arrangements 3-9, 292E2
Richard III 6-14, 712B2
Ride A Cock Horse 3-18, 292E2
Romantic Comedy 11-8, 956G3
Sancocho 3-28, 712B2
Sarava 2-11, 292F2
Says I, Says He 2-20, 292F2
Season To Unravel 1-25, 292G2
Second Thoughts 5-4, 712C2
Seduced 2-1, 292G2
Shelley 4-14, 712D2
Simpson Street 3-5, 292A3
Sky High opens 6-28, 712D2
Songs From the City Streets 4-9, 712D2
Sorrows of Stephen 12-11, 1007E2
Southern Exposure 2-27, 292A3
Spell #7 7-15, 712E2
Spokesong 3-15, 712F2

1980

THEATER
NY transit strike impact cited 4-10, 268D2
ABC, CBS in cable-TV deals 12-2, 12-10, 1003A1
Awards & Honors
Wilson wins Pulitzer 4-14, 296C2
Tonys presented 6-8, 692G2
N. Y. Openings
Act of Kindness 9-11, 756A3
Amadeus 12-17, 1003G2
American Clock 11-20, 1003G2
Back in the Race 4-17, 392C2
Barnum 4-30, 392D2
Billy Bishop Goes to War 5-29, 756B3
Blood Wedding 6-2, 756B3
Brigadoon 10-16, 892A3
Bull Pen 6-12, 756C3
Canterbury Tales 2-12, 136A3
Charlie & Algernon 9-14, 892A3
Charlotte 2-27, 392D2
Children of a Lesser God 3-30, 392D2
Clothes for a Summer Hotel 3-26, 392E2
Coming Attractions 12-3, 1003A3
Das Lusitania Songspiel 1-10, 136B3
Day in Hollywood/Night in Ukraine 5-1, 392E2
Dead End Kids 11-18, 1003A3
Dented 8-11, 756C3
Division St 10-8, 892B3
Dona Rosita 3-20, 392F2
Fifth of July 11-6, 892C3
Filumena 2-10, 392F2
42d Street 8-25, 756D3
Front Page 12-22, 1003B3
Glass Menagerie 11-4, 892C3
Goodbye Fidel 4-23, 392G2
Guardsman 1-3, 136B3
Happy New Year 4-27, 392A3
Harold & Maude 1-7, 136B3
Heartaches of a Pussycat 3-19, 392A3
Heartbreak House 4-29, 392B3
Hide & Seek 5-4, 392B3
Hijinks! 12-18, 1003B3
Home 5-7, 392B3
Horowitz & Mrs Washington 4-2, 392C3
Incomparable Max 6-15, 756D3
Interview 4-24, 392C3
I Ought to be in Pictures 4-3, 392D3
John Gabriel Borkman 12-18, 1003C3
Ka-Boom! 11-20, 1003C3
Killings on the Last Line 6-5, 756E3
Lady From Dubuque 1-31, 136C3
Lesson From Aloes 11-17, 1003D3
Life 11-3, 892G2
Lunch Hour 11-12, 892D3
Major Barbara 2-26, 392D3
Manhattan Showboat 7-1, 756E3
Marie & Bruce 2-3, 136C3
Mecca 2-2, 136D3
Morning's at Seven 4-10, 392E3
Mother Courage 5-13, 392E3
Music Man 6-6, 756F3
My Mother, My Father & Me 1-9, 136D3
Of the Fields, Lately 5-27, 756F3
Onward Victoria 12-14, 1003E3
Paris Lights 1-24, 136E3
Passione 5-22, 756F3
Past Tense 4-24, 392E3
Perfectly Frank 11-30, 1003D3
Quick Change 10-30, 892D3
Really Rosie 10-12, 892E3
Reggae 3-27, 392F3
Roast 5-8, 392G3
Salt Lake City Skyline 1-23, 136E3
Sea Gull 11-11, 892E3
Sim 6-2, 756G3
Sunday Runners in the Rain 5-4, 392G3
Tintypes 10-23, 892F3
Tricks of the Trade 11-16, 892F3
Trouble With Europe 1-28, 136F3
True West 12-23, 1003E3
Turns 6-16, 756G3
Twelfth Night 12-16, 1003F3
Watch on the Rhine 1-3, 136F3
West Side Story 2-14, 136G3
We Won't Pay! 12-17, 1003F3
You Know Al He's A Funny Guy 11-13, 892G3
Obituaries
Adamson, Harold 8-17, 675G3
Aronson, Boris 11-16, 928B2
Buchanan, Bessie A 9-27, 755D2
Champion, Gower 8-25, 676A1
Clurman, Harold E 9-9, 755E2
Connelly, Marc 12-21, 1004B1
Durante, Jimmy 1-29, 104C2
Emery, Katherine 2-8, 176A1
Enlow, Grayson Maynard 5-18, 448E1
Fuller, Frances 12-18, 1004F1
Garcia, Sara 11-21, 1004F1
Gardiner, Reginald 7-7, 608F1
Gear, Luella 4-3, 360G1
Griffith, Hugh 5-14, 448F1
Janney, Leon 10-28, 876B2
Kaminska, Ida 5-21, 448B2
Levene, Sam 12-28, 1004D2
Loden, Barbara 9-22, 756B1
McCarty, Mary 4-5, 360D2
Medford, Kay 4-10, 360E2
Mercer, David 8-8, 676C2
Nugent, Elliott 8-9, 676D2
O'Neil, Barbara 9-3, 756D1
Sandrini, Luis 7-5, 608G2
Sands, Dorthy 9-11, 756C2
Schary, Dore 7-7, 608A3
Snow, C P 7-1, 608D3
Strong, Michael 9-17, 756E2
Tobias, George 2-27, 176F3
Travers, Ben 12-18, 1004D3
Tynan, Kenneth 7-26, 608E3
Van, Bobby 7-31, 608F3
Vance, Nina 2-18, 176G3
Vysotsky, Vladimir 7-24, 580C2
West, Mae 11-22, 928F3

1978

Verandah 5-14, 760F3
Water Engine 1-5, 760G3
Winning Isn't Everything 12-3, 1031C3
Working 5-14, 887E3
Zinnia 3-22, 760G3
Obituaries
Betz, Carl 1-18, 96C3
Boyer, Charles 8-26, 708B2
Bradford, Alex 2-15, 196D2
Brel, Jacques 10-9, 888E2
Cazale, John 3-12, 252E2
Chase, Ilka 2-15, 196E2
Compton, Fay 12-12, 1032D2
Dailey, Dan 10-16, 888A3
Daly, James 7-3, 620F2
Dauphin, Claude 11-17, 972G2
Fields, Totie 8-2, 708F2
Geer, Will 4-22, 356F2
Genn, Leo 1-26, 96B2
Gordon, Max 11-2, 972C3
Greenwood, Charlotte 1-18, 196A3
Homolka, Oscar 1-27, 96E2
McGrath, Paul 4-13, 356B3
Messel, Oliver 7-13, 620B3
Miller, Izetta Jewel 11-15, 972D3
Shaw, Robert 8-28, 708D3
Wood, Peggy 3-18, 252F3
Young, Gig 10-19, 888G3

1979

Strider 5-31, 712F2
Suicide In B Flat 3-13, 292B3
Sweeney Todd 3-1, 292B3
Table Settings 3-23, 712G2
Take It From The Top 1-19, 292C3
Taken In Marriage 2-26, 292D3
Talley's Folley 5-3, 712G2
Teeth 'n' Smiles 8-13, 712A3
Teibele & Her Demon 12-16, 1007E2
They're Playing Our Song 2-11, 292E3
Tip Toes 3-26, 712A3
Tunnel Fever 5-10, 712B3
Umbatha 4-9, 712B3
Umbrellas Of Cherbourg 2-1, 292E3
Utter Glory of Morrissey Hall 5-13, 712B3
Victim 5-3, 712C3
Voice of My Own 5-2, 712C3
Warriors from a Long Childhood 5-22, 712D3
Welfare 5-10, 712D3
What the Devil 4-16, 712E3
Whoopee! 2-14, 292F3
Whose Life Is It Anyway? 4-17, 712E3
Wild Oates 1-8, 292F3
Wine Untouched 6-22, 712F3
Wings 1-28, 292G3
Winter Signs 3-11, 712F3
Woods 4-25, 712F3
Zoot Suit 3-25, 712G3
Obituaries
Belmont, Eleanor 10-24, 860A2
Bolton, Guy R 9-5, 756B2
Brent, George 5-26, 432D2
Costello, Dolores 3-1, 272C2
Davis, Benny 12-20, 1008D2
Harper, Ethel 3-31, 272E2
Harris, Jed 11-15, 932A3
Jones, Preston 9-19, 756E2
Marques, Rene 3-22, 272B3
Perelman, S J 10-17, 860C3
Rand, Sally 8-31, 671E3
Rodgers, Richard 12-30, 1008D3
Shumlin, Herman 6-14, 508E3
Skinner, Cornelia Otis 7-9, 588D3
Vance, Vivian 8-17, 671F3
Wilding, Michael 7-8, 588F3

1976

THEBES Shpping Inc.
Nantucket oil spill liability hearing 12-28—12-31, suit delayed 12-30, 1013F3
THEIS, Paul
Named Agri dep asst secy 1-21, 40C3
THEODOLI, Giovanni
Shot by leftists 4-21, 297D1
THEOPHYLOYANAKOS, Theodoros
Sentence cut 4-22, 333A2
THERMOGRAPHY
Effectiveness held limited 7-28, 680B1
Cancer detectn use cited 7-28, 680B1
THERRIEN, Andre
Convicts ask mtg 9-27, ask resignatn 10-1, 789G2, D3
To honor prison pact 836C3
THEY Knew What They Wanted (play)
Opens 1-27, 1014B3
THI, Dinh Ba
Scores US UN veto 11-15, 862D3
THIANDOUM, Msgr. Hyacinthe
Appointed cardinal 4-27, 336B2
THIEU, Nguyen Van
Sach plot cited 176B3
Political foes warned 4-22, 367E2
N Viets surprised by '75 victory 4-24, 4-25, 315G2
THIRD World—*See DEVELOPING Countries, NONALIGNED Nations Movement*
THLOLOE, Joseph
Arrest confirmed 9-1, 662C2
THO, Le Duc
In Politburo 12-19, 967F3
THO, Nguyen Huu
Vice pres of united Vietnam 7-3, 502E3
THOENI, Gustavo
Wins Olympic medal 2-14, 158D3
THOMAI, Themie
Albania agri min 4-30, 331F3
THOMAS, Franklin A.
Declined Carter post 12-16, 937A2
THOMAS, George
Govt wins ship natlzn ruling 5-27, 401E3, G3*
THOMAS, Helen
Lewine joins Gridiron Club 3-5, 272A1
THOMAS, James T.
Dies 1-23, 80G3
THOMAS, John
Shot 5-5, 384E2
THOMAS, Karl
Atlantic balloon flight fails 7-1, 640E3
THOMAS, Michael Tilson
Wins Grammy 2-28, 460D3
THOMERSON, Bruce
Captured 5-2, freed 10-2, 1002B2
THOMPSON, Dudley
Chrgs US destabilizatn campaign 6-20, 522G1

1977

THEBEHALI, David
Resigns 6-2, 469F1
THEBERGE, James D.
On US rights pressure 3-2, 168E2
Replaced as amb to Nicaragua 7-28, 626E3
THEODOSIUS, Bishop
Named Orthodox Church head 10-25, 906F3
THERON, Erika
White paper on coloreds issued 4-19, 350A1
THEVIS, Michael G.
Young cleared in aid chrg 10-19, 861D3
THIBAULT, J. Laurents
Backs Japan econ policy criticism 9-29, 780C3
THIERIOT, Charles deYoung
Dies 3-21, 264F3
THIEU, Nguyen Van
CIA payments rptd 2-19, 124F1
THIOKOL Corp.
Govt liable in '71 blast 6-23, 604B1
THIRD Parties—*See under POLITICS*
THIRD World—*See DEVELOPING Nations*
THLOLOE, Joseph
Rptd held 3-2, 349E3
THOMAIDIS, Elias
Stamatis attack foiled 1-18, 182E2
THOMAS Jr., Dr. Charles A.
Harvard DNA resrch halted 12-15, 1022F2
THOMAS, Joe
Clark fired as 49er coach 4-6, 1020A2
THOMAS, Jerry
Replaced as Treas undersecy 3-29, 272E2
THOMAS, Joe
Signing with 49ers rptd 3-29, 263F2
THOMAS, John M.
Keeps State Dept post 1-21, 53E1
THOMAS, Dr. Lewis
Urges human laetrile tests 6-15, 508C2
THOMAS, Norman M. (1884-1968)
Biog wins Natl Book Award 4-11, 355B2
FBI surveillance rptd 6-19, 481E1
THOMAS, William
Scores Toth chrg 7-12, 564G1
THOMES, Charles
Oxygen, anesthesia mixup rptd fatal 9-10, 748B2
THOMPSON, David
Named to NBA all-star team 6-13, 584G3
THOMPSON, Dudley
Shifted to mining min 1-4, 46A1, C1

1978

THEODOULOU, Emilios
Named Cyprus labor min 3-8, 189A2
THERMAL Energy
US rpt discounts ocean use 6-7, 512B2
THEUS, Reggie
In NBA draft 6-9, 457F2
THEVIS, Michael G.
Flees jail 4-28; govt witnesses slain 10-25, arrested 11-9, 971B2
THI, Dinh Ba
Vs US remark on 'proxy war' 1-16, 43E1
US links to spy plot 1-31, 68D3
US ousts 2-3; Viet, others protest 2-3—2-9; stay issued, leaves US 2-10, 103E2
Killed 6-17, rptd slain 7-3, 549B2
THIEN Minh, Thich
Death rptd 10-26, 888F3
THIEU, Nguyen Van
Tuyen '76 death rptd 7-10, 692F1
THIRD Parties—*See under POLITICS*
THIRD World—*See DEVELOPING Nations*
THIRKIELD, Rob
Lulu opens 2-17, 760D2
13 Rue De L'Amour (play)
Opens 3-16, 760D3
THIS Room and This Gin and These Sandwiches (play)
Opens 6-15, 760E3
THOMAS, B. J.
Wins Grammy 2-24, 316A1
THOMAS, Bob
NFL '77 kicking ldr 1-1, 56F2
THOMAS, Clayton
Foiled in hijack attempt 3-13, 212B2
THOMAS, Dan
AL batting ldr 10-2, 928E3
THOMAS, Eugene
Rowe indicted for '65 slaying 7-20, 720E2
THOMAS, George
OKs questns on blacklisted cos 2-3, 131D2
THOMAS, James
Charged in hammer murder 4-10, 380F2
THOMAS, Kenneth
On pay, price statemt rejectn 10-14, 903B2
THOMAS, Kurt
At World Gym Championships 10-23—10-29, 928C3
THOMAS, Mike
NFL '77 rushing ldr 1-1, 56E3
THOMAS, Richard
'Sept 30 1955' released 3-31, 619E3
THOMAS, Sharon
Indicted 8-15, 644F3, 645A1
THOMAS, Thom
Approaching Zero opens 11-30, 1031A1
THOMAS, William
Wins US House seat 11-7, 850F1
THOMAS a Kempis (1380-1471)
Pope John Paul I dies 9-28, 746C3 *
THOMASSON, Gary
Traded to A's 3-15, 194G3
THOMAZ, Americo
Returns to Portugal 7-23, 594E1
THOMOPOULOS, Anthony D.
Named NBC Entertainment pres 2-1, 75G2
THOMPSON, David
East wins NBA All-Star game 2-5, 271D3
NBA scoring ldr 4-9, 271E1, D2
Signs Nuggets deal, becomes top-paid NBA player 4-18, 656F1
On NBA all-star team 6 13, 457C3

1979

THEBEHALI, David
Urges black land ownership 8-31, 732D3
THEIS, Judge Frank
Silkwood estate wins A-suit 5-18, 381A2-G2
Upholds Silkwood damages award 8-20, 629G3
THEME from Close Encounters of the Third Kind (recording)
Wins Grammy 2-16, 336G3
THERM-AIR Manufacturing Co. Inc.
Aladdin casino deal rejected 12-15, 965D1
THEROUX, Paul
Saint Jack released 4-26, 528E3
THEVIS, Michael G.
Convicted in murder case 10-21, 818G1
THEY Knew What They Wanted (book)
Most Happy Fella opens 10-11, 956D3
THEY'RE Playing Our Song (play)
Opens 2-11, 292E3
THIEU, Nguyen Van
Nixon '73 peace pressure rptd, coup feared 1-7, 29E1, G1
THINK of a Number (book)
Silent Partner released 5-10, 528E3
THIRD Parties—*See under POLITICS*
THIRD World—*See DEVELOPING Nations*
THIRD World War: August 1985, The (book)
On best-seller list 6-3, 432A2; 7-1, 548B3; 8-5, 620B3
13-30 Corp.
Esquire purchase rptd 5-1, 334D2
13TH Man, The (book)
Last Embrace released 5-3, 528F2
THOMAS, B. K.
Angels win WBL title 5-2, 507D1
THOMAS, Franklin A.
Named Ford Foundatn pres 1-30, 78E3
THOMAS, Gorman
AL batting ldr 9-30, 955E3
THOMAS, Jeremy
Shout released 11-9, 1008E1
THOMAS, Jessie
Undergoes spinal replacemt surgery 8-31, 736E2
THOMAS, Joe
Fired as 49ers gen mgr 1-8, 175E2
THOMAS, Kurt
2d in World Gym Championships 10-5—10-9, 1005C2
THOMAS, O. P.
Sees Kahn, wage-guide compliance urged 4-20, 344G3
THOMAS, Pat
NFL '78 interceptn ldr 1-6, 80G1
THOMAS, Sharon
Sentenced 12-6—12-7, 1000C1
THOMAS, Judge Williams K.
Fines Firestone on tax chrgs 7-26, 648B3
THOMPON, Daniele
Your Turn, My Turn released 1-27, 174G3
THOMPSON, Caroline
Abducted 7-28, parolee arrested 7-30, 604G3
THOMPSON, David
West wins NBA All-Star game, named game MVP 2-4, 175B1
NBA scoring ldr 4-8, 290E2
THOMPSON, David
Named Australia sci min 12-8, 948E1
THOMPSON, Donovan J.
Terminally ill treatmt study rptd 5-31, 471E2

1980

THEBAHALI, David
Blacks protest Koornhof Soweto citizenship 10-15, 793E1
THEISMANN, Joe
NFL '79 passing ldr 1-5, 8D2
THEISS, Adolf
Kung controversy setlmt reached 4-10, 364B2
THERA, Georgia Mahoney (d. 1979)
La Scola insulin-slaying chrgs reduced 12-29, 997B2
THEURER, Elisabeth
Wins Olympic medal 8-1, 622A3
THEVIS, Michael G.
Firearm convictn case refused by Sup Ct 4-21, 344B2
THEVIS v. U.S.
Case refused by Sup Ct 4-21, 344B2
THEY Call Me Assassin (book)
Stingley lawyer seeks Tatum suspensn 1-10, 175G2
THIGPEN, Lynne
Tintypes opens 10-23, 892F3
THIRD Parties—*See under POLITICS*
THIRD Wave, The (book)
On best-seller list 5-4, 359D3; 6-8, 448C3; 7-13, 568C3
THIRD World—*See DEVELOPING Nations*
THIRD World War: August 1985, The (book)
On best-seller list 5-4, 359F3
39 Steps, The (film)
Released 5-2, 416F3
THOMAS, Lord (William Miles Webster)
Dies 2-8, 176F3
THOMAS, Barbara S.
Sworn SEC comr 10-21, 960B1
THOMAS, Billy
Dies 10-11, 876E3
THOMAS, Bob
NFL '79 kicking ldr 1-5, 8F2
THOMAS, Gorman
AL batting ldr 10-6, 926E3
THOMAS, Janice
Stars win WBL title 4-10, 432B2
THOMAS, Jeremy
Bad Timing released 9-21, 836D2
THOMAS, Jewerl
North wins Senior Bowl 1-12, 62B2
THOMAS, John
Iran hostages' letters publshd 1-18—1-20, 47A3
THOMAS, Mario
Marries 5-22, 471A2
THOMAS, Pat
Steelers win Super Bowl 1-20, 62A1
THOMAS, Richard
Chrgs Bache loan deceptn 5-30, 425A2
THOMAS, Thom
Interview opens 4-24, 392C3
THOMAS, Tony
Dies from boxing injury 1-1, 907E3
THOMAS, Rep. William (R, Calif.)
Reelected 11-4, 842F1
THOMAS Road Baptist Church (Lynchburg, Va)
Falwell profiled, SEC '73 suit cited 9-15, 819C3, F3
THOMPSON, Daley
Wins Moscow Olympics decathlon 7-26, 589B1, 624A1

1976

THOMPSON, Edward
Hails Fla wetlands decisn 4-16, 284D3
THOMPSON Jr., Rep. Frank (D, N.J.)
Named Admin com chrmn 6-23, 551G2
Reelected 11-2, 830D1
THOMPSON, James Robert
Nominated for governor 3-16, 196G2
Elected 11-2, 820E3, 823A2, 831E1
At Daley funeral service 12-22, 969D3
THOMSON, George
Assures Greece re EC entry 11-3, 853G3
THOMSON Jr., Gov. Meldrim (R, N.H.)
Campaigns with Reagan 2-11, 109F2
Withdraws Reagan backing 7-27, 550C1
Wins renomination 9-14, 705D1
Reelected 11-2, 820F3, 831F1
NE govs meet 11-13—11-14, 864C3
THOMSON, Sue Park
S Korea payoffs probed 2-19, 171E1
THOMSON, Vernon W.
Renamed to FEC 5-17; confrmd 5-18; sworn, named chrmn 5-21, 391B3
THOMSON of Fleet, Lord (Roy Herbert Thomson)
Dies 8-4, 816G3
THOMSON Scottish Associates
N Sea oil Euroloans rptd 2-4, 2-5, 173E3
THONE, Rep. Charles A. (R, Neb.)
Chrgs grain scandal coverup 1-29, 136D1
Reelected 11-2, 830C1
THORN, Gaston
Comecon talks open 2-16, 164E1
Eur liberals meet 3-26—3-27, 260C3
Replaced as Assemb pres 9-21, 719A1
THORNBURGH, Richard L.
New Justice unit formed 1-14, 78D3
THORNDIKE, Dame Sybil
Dies 6-9, 444G2
THORNTON, Dan
Dies 1-18, 80G3
THORNTON, Rep. Ray (D, Ark.)
Reelected 11-2, 828G3
THORPE, Jeremy
Chrgs Sovt Angola bribe 1-3, 2E2
Scores home-rule plan 1-13, 73C1
Denies financial, sexual chrgs 1-29; Liberals back 1-30, 2-5, 174B2
'71 probe rptd 2-6, coverup chrgd 2-14, 174E2
Bars resignation 3-7, Liberals back 3-17, 252D2
S Africa plot rptd 3-9, 3-10, denied 3-13, 252E2-A3
Liberals ask clarificatn 5-8—5-9; releases letters 5-9, resigns 5-10, 350G3
Successor named 5-12, 364E3
'Coverup' detailed 5-12, Scott drops libel suit 5-14, 364F3
THOUSAND Islands, N.Y.
Oil spill pollutes area 6-23, 859D2
3M Co. (formerly Minnesota Mining & Manufacturing Co.)
SEC lists paymts 5-12, 725G3, 729D1
Slush fund tax chrgs dismissed 7-27, 566B2
Sex bias damages ordrd 10-26, class action filed 11-5, 943C3
THREEPENNY Opera, The (play)
Opens 5-2, 1014C3
THU, Thich Tri
Backs S Viet govt 1-10, 54A2
Rpts '75 mass Buddhist suicide 9-8, 678C3
THUEMER, Petra
Sets world swim mark 6-1—6-5, 424G3
THUMER, Petra
Wins Olympic medals 7-20, 7-25, 575B3, C3
THURMOND, Sen. Strom (R, S.C.)
200-mi fishing zone delay OKd 1-28, 94C1
Named to intelligence com 5-20, 377E1
Endorses Reagan 7-20, 531E3
THUROW, Lester
Carter econ adviser 4-23, 305F2

1977

THOMPSON, Edward G. & Catherine
Carter overnight guest 3-16, 190B3
THOMPSON Jr., Rep. Frank (D, N.J.)
'76 spec interest gifts rptd 2-4, 128G3, 129C2
Cited in Park indictmt 9-6, 688D1
THOMPSON Jr., Judge Gordon
OKs laetrile use 1-21, 376F1
THOMPSON, Judge Howard
Daughter found dead 9-20, 871F2
THOMPSON, Gov. James Robert (R, Ill.)
'70-76 Chicago pol indictmts rptd 2-10, 162D3
For Carter energy plan 4-20, 320E2
Signs death penalty bill 6-21, 594E2
Govs' panel visits DC 11-29, 960A1
THOMPSON, Leonard
2d in Hall of Fame tourn 8-28, 675D3
Wins Pensacola Open 10-30, 950F3
THOMPSON, Lynn
Found dead 9-20, 871F2
THOMPSON, William P.
Carter gets protest on S Korea govt foes 4-19, 305D3
THOMPSON, Co., J. Walter
Sup Ct declines FTC complaint 5-16, 419D2
THOMSON Jr., Gov. Meldrim (R, N.H.)
Asks aid vs A-plant protest 5-6, 410D1
Vs Carter welfare plan 9-9, 719A2
THOMSON, Suzi Park
Named KCIA agent 6-5—6-8, 442B1, C1, C2
Denies KCIA lobbying role 7-7, 556G3
Questnd by House ethics com 8-17, 8-25, 688G1
THOMSON, Vernon
Denies Kim Han Cho link 9-27, 773F3
THOREAU, Henry David (1817-62)
Fire destroys Brook Farm 3-27, 396B2
THORMAN, Donald J.
Dies 11-30, 952F3
THORN, Gaston (Luxembourg premier)
Or birthrate decline 7-21, 745C3
THORN Birds, The (book)
Paperback record sum rptd 3-1, 356A2
On best-seller list 6-4, 452A2; 7-3, 548D3; 8-14, 643F1; 9-4, 712C3; 10-2, 808C3; 11-6, 872C3; 12-4, 1021F3
THORNBURGH, Richard
'70-76 pol indictmts rptd 2-10, 162D3
Replaced as asst atty gen 3-4, 211D1
THORNE, Stanley
Scores Hong Kong ties 11-24, 936B2
THORPE, Jeremy
Scott scandal revived; bars Parlt resignatn, denies murder plot link 10-27, 883G1
THOUSAND Islands Bridge
US-Canada pact signed 2-5, 133B1
3M Co. (formerly Minnesota Mining & Manufacturing Co.)
To promote S Africa equality 3-1, 160B3
THUNDERBOLT (newspaper)
Subscriber kills 5, self 2-14, 162A3
THURMOND, Sen. Strom (R, S.C.)
Mil unionizatn ban studied 3-18, 343C1
Plans fight vs Panama Canal treaty 8-12, 621G2
In Canal Zone, campaigns vs treaty 8-19—8-20, 878F1
Questns mil support for Canal pacts, Sarbanes scores 10-4, 755E2
In TV campaign vs Canal pacts 10-29, 912C1

1978

THOMPSON, Eric (Jomo)—*See DAVIS, Cleveland*
THOMPSON Jr., Rep. Frank (D, N.J.)
Cleared by ethics com re Park gift 7-13, 527A2
Reelected 11-7, 851A3
PAC contributions rptd 12-24, 1008E1
THOMPSON, Judge Howard
Sentences Bolles killers 1-10, 24B2
THOMPSON, Gov. James Robert (R, Ill.)
Laetrile bill veto cited 1-10, 23B3
Unopposed in primary 3-21, 207A2
Reelected 11-7, 853A2, E2
Ill votes pay hike 11-29, Carter angry 12-1, Kahn asks rollback 12-4, 934G3-935A1
THOMPSON, Lee J.
Greek Tycoon released 5-12, 619C2
THOMPSON, Mychal
4th in coll basketball 3-13, 272E2
In NBA draft 6-9, 457B2, F2
THOMPSON, Robert G.
In 3-way prisoner swap 4-30, 318C2
THOMPSON, Sada
Wins Emmy 9-17, 1030F1
THOMPSON, William P.
Howard suceeds as NCC pres 11-4, 907G1
THOMSON, Lord of Monifieth (George Morgan Thomson)
Disputes Wilson on Rhodesia sanctns 9-2—9-7, 756D3
THOMSON Jr., Gov. Meldrim (R, N.H.)
Issues flag-lowering proclamatn 3-21; ct challenges 3-22, 3-23, Sup Ct stays 3-24, 221G1
Flag lowering stay extensn denied by Sup Ct 4-24, 322G2
At Manchester rally 6-25, calls Seabrook protest failure 6-26, 494F1
Scores Seabrook A-plant halt 6-30, 529D3
Lauds Seabrook A-plant OK 8-4, 609D2
Govs reject spending res 8-29, 682E1
Renominated 9-12, 736F1
Loses reelectn 11-7, 847A1, E3
THOMSON, Peter
2d in Legends of Golf tourn 4-30, 356B1
THOMSON, Suzi Park
Mitchell: '71 FBI memo linked KCIA 3-21, 203E2, F2 ★
THOMSON Organization Ltd.
Halts publicatn of London Times, Sunday Times 11-30, 924A1
THONE, Rep. Charles A. (R, Neb.)
Wins primary for gov 5-9, 363D1
Elected, seat filled 11-7, 853G2, 854F3, G3
THORN, Dr. George W.
Describes Hughes Med Inst 12-7, 1010C3-1011A1
THORN Birds, The (book)
On best-seller list 1-8, 24D3; 2-5, 116B3; 3-5, 195D3; 4-2, 272A3; 4-30, 356F1; 7-2, 579D3; 8-6, 620B2; 9-4, 708D1; 10-9, 800C3; 11-6, 888B1; 12-3, 971C1
Puzo paperback rights sale sets record 6-16, 620E2
THORNBURGH, Richard L.
Wins primary for Pa gov 5-16, 389B3
Elected 11-7, 846C3, 849B2, 853D3
Notes black vote 11-27, 916B1
THORNE, Oakleigh L.
Dies 2-15, 196F3
THORNTON, Andre
AL batting ldr 10-2, 928E3-F3
THORNTON, James
Injured in horse race 5-3, 539C3
THORNTON, Rep. Ray (D, Ark.)
Loses Sen primary 5-30, 426G1
Anthony wins seat 11-7, 855A2
THORNTON, Thomas J.
Sues Islanders owner 5-2, 656C2
THORNWELL, Al
NASL OKs Caribous sale, Atlanta move 10-3, 969A3
THORPE, Jeremy
Arrested in murder plot 8-4; sets reelectn bid, Liberals score 8-5, 614A2
Faces 2d chrg re murder 9-2, 688B2
Pretrial hearings; hired killer, Scott testify 11-20—12-4, 944G3-945C2
Panel orders trial 12-13, 987D3
THORSNESS, Leo K.
Wins US House seat 11-7, 852C2, 855C1
Loses seat on recount 12-19, 1008G1
THREAD of Scarlet, A (play)
Opens 12-8, 1031B3
THREE Graces, The (painting)
Stolen 4-21, recovered 4-23, 335A2
3M Co. (formerly Minnesota Mining & Manufacturing Co.)
In Dow Jones indl avg 66F2
THREE'S Company (TV series)
Sears withdraws ads 5-12, 599C3
THREE Times A Lady (recording)
On best-seller list 8-2, 620E1; 9-6, 708E1
THRIFT Institutions—*See BANKS—Savings and Savings Banks*
THURMOND, Sen. Strom (R, S.C.)
Votes vs Panama Canal neutrality pact 3-16, 177G2
Votes vs 2d Canal pact 4-18, 273B1
Marston cover-up rpt rejctd by Sen 5-4, 343B1
Unopposed in primary 6-13, 467C1
Backs DC voting amendmt 8-22, 661B2
Burger vs bankruptcy bill 9-28, 788E3
Reelected 11-7, 848C3, 852G3
Buzhardt dies 12-16, 1032D2
THYSSEN-Hutte AG, August
Budd bid revealed 1-12, talks OKd 1-17, 66D1

1979

THOMPSON, Ernest
On Golden Pond opens 2-28, 712G1
THOMPSON Jr., Rep. Frank (D, N.J.)
House Admin Com chrmn 1-24, 71D1
On electn financing bill defeat 5-24, 401E2
THOMPSON, Fred
Tip Toes opens 3-26, 712A3
THOMPSON, Jack (The Throwin' Samoan)
Pac-10 wins Challenge Bowl 1-14, 63B2
In NFL draft 5-3, 335E1
THOMPSON, Gov. James R. (R, Ill.)
Orders A reactor review 4-2, 261A3
Chicago schls miss payday 12-21, 991F1
THOMPSON, Jesse
NFL '78 punt return ldr 1-6, 80F2
THOMPSON, M. E.
Fortson dies 5-19, 432F2
THOMPSON, Norm
NFL '78 interceptn ldr 1-6, 80D1
THOMPSON, Ralph
On Tex tourism drop 8-17, 608A2
THOMPSON, Robert
Patrick released 9-7, 820F2
THOMPSON, William Aubrey
Indicted 3-15, 309D2
THOMPSON Co., J. Walter
FTC complaint setld 4-15, 308F3
THOMPSON-Hayward Chemical Co.
Agent Orange suit filed 11-26, 904A3
THOMPSON v. Louisville
Case cited by Sup Ct 6-28, 558E2
Case cited by Sup Ct 10-9, 784C1
THOMSON, Kenneth (Lord Thomson of Fleet)
Wins Hudson's Bay control 4-8, 284E3
THOMSON Jr., Meldrim
Announces pres bid 10-31, 829D1
THOMSON, Robert
On Antarctica DC-10 crash 11-29, 912F1
THORN, Gaston (Luxembourg premier)
Eur Parlt electns held 6-10, 434C2
Coalitn loses electn, to run for Eur Parlt pres 6-10, resigns govt 6-11, 469C2
THORNBURGH, Gov. Richard L. (R, Pa.)
Acts in 3 Mile I A-accident 3-29—4-3, 241B1-245F3
Tours 3 Mile I 4-7, lifts advisories 4-9, 259E2, 261A1, A2, F2
3 Mile I NRC transcripts released 4-12, 275G2
Cattle deaths near 3 Mile I rptd 5-20, 382F1
Gets reassurance on heating fuel supply 8-28, 703C2
THORNBURGH v. Casey
Case declined by Sup Ct 3-5, 185D1
THORNBURY, Bill
Phantasm released 6-1, 820G2
THORNWELL, James R.
Settles LSD suit 9-6, 705F1
THORPE, Jeremy
Loses Parlt seat 5-3, 337A2
Acquitted 6-22, 485D3-486C1
Liberals hold conf 9-25—9-29, 792F1
THORPE, Jim
Ties for 2d in Tucson Open 2-18, 220E3
THOR Power Tool Co. v. Commissioner of Internal Revenue
Tax acctg methods limited by Sup Ct 1-16, 32G2
THRASHER, Bruce
Urges labor law reform 4-11, 306B3
3M Co. (formerly Minnesota Mining & Manufacturing Co.)
In Dow Jones indl avg S1-1, 72F1
Dow Jones index revised 6-28, 481G2
THREE Mile Island Nuclear Station—*See PENNSYLVANIA—Atomic Energy*
THREE Troikas (race horse)
Wins Arc de Triomphe 10-7, 876B3
THRIFT Institutions—*See BANKS—Savings & Savings Banks*
THROUGH the Looking Glass (book)
But Never Jam Today opens 7-31, 711G1
THURMAN, Gary
Vitamin C anti-infectn role studied 5-5, 691D2
THURMOND, Sen. Strom (R, S.C.)
Scores Carter peanut probe limits 3-20, 203F1
Seeks ct-apptd spec prosecutor in Carter probe 3-23, 301B3
Scores SALT treaty 4-5, 258G1
Vs direct pres vote 7-10, 515C1
Backs FBI charter 7-31, 599A3
Votes vs Talmadge denunciatn 10-10, 769G1
Life of Brian denunciatn rptd 10-24, 859D2
Endorses Connally 12-27, 982F2, G2
THYSSEN, Greta
Victim opens 5-3, 712C3

1980

THOMPSON Jr., Rep. Frank (D, N.J.)
Facts on 81E1
Linked to bribery in Abscam probe 2-2, 2-3, 81C1, 82F1
Indicted in Abscam probe 6-18, 454F1-D2
Abscam judge quits case 8-7, 599E3
Abstains on Myers House expulsn 10-2, 740A2
Loses reelectn 11-4, 846A2, 848G2
Convicted in Abscam case 12-3, 919D1
THOMPSON, Gregg
USF wins NCAA soccer title 12-14, 1001D3
THOMPSON, Gov. James R. (R, Ill.)
State of State message 1-9, 483D2
Endorses Reagan 5-4, 342D3
ERA rejected by Ill house 6-18, 482D3
Names Fahner atty gen 7-29, 654G2
With Reagan in Chicago 9-8, 699C3
THOMPSON, Joe
Death rptd 4-21, 360F3
THOMPSON, John
Scores NBC early electn projectns 11-5, 866B1
THOMPSON, Lea
Wins Polk award 2-25, 692F3
THOMPSON, Leonard
2d in Bay Hill Classic 3-2, 412F2
THOMPSON, Myron H.
Nominated US dist judge 9-17, 744D3
THOMPSON, Rev. Nelson
Visits US hostages in Iran 4-6, 258D2
THOMPSON, Judge Ralph
Affirms US intrastate gas sale power 6-6, 552B3
THOMPSON v. U.S.
Case remanded by Sup Ct 1-14, 37A2
THOMS, Lothar
Wins Olympic medal 7-22, 622E2
THOMSON, Lord Kenneth
Buys FP Publicatns 1-11, 38G1
THOMSON Jr., Meldrim
Ends pres bid, backs Reagan 4-14, 288F3
Wins primary for gov 9-9, 700F2
Loses NH gov electn 11-4, 848E2
THOMSON Organization Ltd.
Thomson Newspapers buys FP publicatns 1-11, 400G1
London Times journalists strike 8-22, 652B2
Thomson Newspapers closes Ottawa Journal, makes Southam deals 8-27, 668A3
London Times journalists end strike 8-29, 670F2
London Times offered for sale 10-22, 808A3
THONE, Gov. Charles (R, Neb.)
State of State message 1-10, 403B1
Calls out Natl Guard in Grand I tornado 6-3; visits, asks US disaster aid 6-4, 527A3
THORN, Gaston
Meets Begin in peace missn 7-31—8-1, Arafat 8-4, 585E2-586C1
Uncertain on Reagan electn 11-5, 841A3
THORNBURG, Buck
Plugged Nickle wins Wood Memorial 4-19, 448A1
THORNBURGH, Gov. Richard L. (R, Pa.)
3 Mile I gas venting proposed 3-12, 248E3
3 Mile I gas venting OKd 6-10, 441A1
THORNWELL, James R.
Setlmt clears Cong 12-5, signed 12-18, 981F3
THORODDSEN, Gunnar
Forms govt 2-8, 117E3
THOR Power Tool Co. v. Commissioner of Internal Revenue
Inventory tax ruling impact on publishing rptd 10-5, 835G3
Inventory tax ruling amendmt discarded by House 12-13, 982F2
THORSON, Ralph (Papa)
Hunter released 8-1, 675A3
THOSE Lips, Those Eyes (film)
Released 9-9, 836G3
3M Co. (formerly Minnesota Mining & Manufacturing Co.)
In Dow Jones Indl avg 76F1
Lehr named chrmn 5-13, 456E2
US fines 10-30, 985G2*
Scotch tape inventor dies 12-7, 1004D1
THREE Mile Island Nuclear Station—*See PENNSYLVANIA—Atomic Energy & Safeguards*
THUNA, Leonora
How to Beat the High Cost of Living released 7-11, 675A3
THURMOND, Sen. Strom (R, S.C.)
Asks Miller-Textron spec prosecutor 2-11, 145B2
Connally ends pres bid 3-9, 183G3
B Carter probe vice-chrmn 7-24, 549A1
Chastises B Carter re Libya 8-22, 647G1
Scores Jenrette Abscam chrgs 9-12, 783A1
Brzezinski testifies in B Carter probe 9-17, 701B2
Condemns Admin in B Carter affair 10-2, 764F1
Slated to chair Judiciary Com 11-4, 837E1
Named Sen pres pro tempore 12-2, 915F2
Predicts '81 antibusing legis 12-10, 954E1
THY Neighbor's Wife (book)
On best-seller list 6-8, 448C3; 7-13, 568B3; 8-17, 640F3

1976

TIANDRAZA, Remi
Named science min 8-20, 926C1
TIANT, Luis
AL pitching ldr 10-4, 796D1
TIBERI, Jean
French food productn min 1-12, 49D2
TIBET
'74 Hua visit cited 758B1
T. I. Corp. (Ticor)
Indicted 1-14, unit chrgd 2-2, 160C1
TIDROW, Dick
Yankees win pennant 10-14, 796G1
In World Series 10-16—10-21, 815D3
TIERNAN, Robert O.
Renamed to FEC 5-17; confrmd 5-18, sworn 5-21, 391D3
TIERNO Galvan, Enrique
Scores new Cabt 7-8, 523G2
Lauds Cabt policy statemt 7-18, 541E1
Univ chair restored 8-7, 753B3
Sess Suarez 9-5, 752E3
Lauds chng of defense min 9-22, 753A1
On econ crisis 11-12, 929B1
Oppositn-govt electn talks set 12-9, 967B2
TIGER International Inc.
CAB chrgs Flying Tiger 12-29, 986D1
TIKHONOV, Nikolai A.
Named Kosygin aide 9-2, 857A2
TILLINGHAST Jr., Charles C.
Announces retiremt 9-22, 892F1
TIMBER Industry—*See LUMBER*
TIME
Australia state backs DST 5-1, 349C3
DST extensn bill defeated 9-21, 883G1
TIME (magazine)
Canada-Reader's Digest pact rptd 2-3, 116F3
Rpts W Ger co Colombia bribes 2-23, 147G2
Canada editn end set 2-25, 188G2
Sup Ct rules on Firestone libel case 3-2, 169E2
Rpts Admin gets Nixon China trip rpt 3-22, 215C1
Names 2 as Sovt spies 3-22, 559B1
Israel denies A-bomb rpt 4-5, 243D1
Guild begins strike 6-2, 398C1
Guild ends strike 6-21, 454C2
On state death penalty laws 7-12, 491C3
Mondale addresses conf 9-26, 724F3
Faces Thai censorship 10-11, 775E3
Rpts pres endorsemts 11-8, 827D3
Carter interview 12-27, 978A3, C3
TIME, Inc.
EasTex trust suit dvpts 2-18—10-5, 886C1, D2
Sup Ct bars privacy suit review 5-24, 393B2
Guild begins strike 6-2, 398B1
Guild ends strike 6-21, 454C2
Carter sees editors 7-22, 551E1
Time (magazine)—*See separate listing*
TIME-Life Books
Guild begins strike 6-2, 398C1
Guild ends Time strike 6-21, 454C2
TIMES, The (London newspaper)
Angola ousts Tendler 6-16, 480D3
TIMES Mirror Co.
US files consent decree 7-27, 989A2
Makes Booth chain bid 10-22, 901G2
TIMM, Robert D.
Succeeded at CAB 3-22, 232F1
TIMOR
Fretelin bars UN envoy, holds Australia mtg 2-2; chrgs Australia-Indonesia collusn 2-10, 122D3
Indonesian forces, casualties rptd 2-11, 123A1
Fretelin defeat claimed, death total rptd 2-11, 2-14, 192D1, F1
UN envoy sees Portugal forgn min 2-11, 192F1
Pro-Indonesian mass graves rptd 2-21, 192G1
Portugal charter OKs independnc 4-2, 367D1
UN debates 4-12, asks Indonesia exit 4-22, 334F3
Australia-Indonesia talks 4-14, 309A3
Indonesia rpts troop exit 4-17, 334G3
Assemb backs joining Indonesia 5-31, 422G3
Indonesia declares 27th prov 7-17, 543F3
Fighting rptd 8-18, Suharto rpt quoted 8-25, 679E1
Australia vows aid 10-10, 789C2
TIN
UK price gains 3-3, 175B3
Bolivia vs UN pact 4-26; gets price hike, signs 4-30, 416F1
Australia OKs UN pact, US ratification cited 4-28, 380F1
Hungary ratifies '75 pact 6-11, 543G2
TINBERGEN, Jan
Pleads for Sovt dissident 3-24, 421A3
TIN Council, International
Bolivia warns on intl pact 4-26; signs 4-30, 416F1
TINDEMANS, Leo (Belgian premier)
Rpts on European unity 1-7, 20C1
French socialists score rpt 1-29, 119C3
Europn unity rpt debated 2-5—2-8, 164A1
Lockheed bribe probe set 3-9, 220B3
EC summit held 4-1—4-2, 276E1
EC center-right party formed 4-30, 389A2
Reshuffles Cabt 12-8, 1012E2
TING, Samuel Chao Chung
Wins Nobel Prize 10-18, 840F1
TIN U
Plotters arrested 7-2, 543D2
TINUBU, Kafuru
Nigeria health min 3-15, 222A3
TIP, Karel
Acquitted 12-2, 927A2
TIRAT, Jean-Christian
USSR expels 10-21, 857E1
TIRES—*See RUBBER*

1977

TIBET (China autonomous region)
Dalai Lama invited to return 5-1, 347D1
China chrgs India rebel aid 8-6, 616E3
TIDAL Marine International Corp.
SEC sues Leidesdorf 2-16, 156C2
TIDROW, Dick
In World Series 10-11—10-18, 806C2
TIKHY, Oleska
Arrested 2-5, 117E1 *
Sentenced 7-1, 512C3
TIKKA Khan, Gen.
In Pak Cabt 4-27, 313D2
TIMAKOV, Vladimir D.
Dies 6-21, 532G3
TIMBER—*See LUMBER*
TIMBRELL, Dennis
Bares RCMP-OHIP link 11-29, 945C2
TIME (magazine)
Sees Sovt dissident crackdown 2-14, 101C2
Carter poll rptd 4-4, 251E1
Nixon disputed re Adams firing 5-5, 367D1
Carter summit diplomacy hailed 5-16, 359F1
Mafia rptd in transitn 5-16, 568C1
Lance story publishd 5-23, 719D1
Rpts Israel uranium plot 5-30, 416G2
Rpts Israel Leb role 8-22, 648D1
Rpts FBI blackmail in Sovt spy recruitmt 11-7, 866B3
On most reliable govt news source list 12-10, 1009B1
T.I.M.E.-D.C. Inc.
Pre-'64 seniority bias upheld 5-31, 461B2
T.I.M.E.-D.C. Inc. v. U.S.
Pre-'64 seniority bias upheld 5-31, 461C2
TIME, Inc.
Little, Brown buys Kissinger memoirs 2-7, 131F1
Book-of-the-Month Club purchase set 7-5, 519D2
CIA links charged 9-12, 720C3
Cable-TV purchase planned 12-22, 1004C3
Time (magazine)—*See separate listing*
TIMERMAN, Hector
Arrested 4-29, 371B2
TIMERMAN, Jacobo
Arrested 4-14, 345B3
Graiver probe protectn rptd 4-22, 371E2
Anti-Semitism linked 7-7, 614G3
Loses rights, detained indefinitely 11-10, 11-12, 922E2
Jewish ldrs see Vance 11-21, 912A3
TIMES Mirror Co.
Brown rpts net worth 2-25, 147F3
At USSR book fair 9-6—9-14, 765F3
Los Angeles Times—*See separate listing*
TIMOTHEOS, Bishop
Dies 12-14, 1024E3
TIN
Price breaks pact ceiling 1-6, buffer stock runs out 1-13, 169C2
Rpt Bolivia bars intl pact ratificatn 1-10, 169F1
Price hits record high 3-4, 169E1
London mkt dvpts 3-16—4-18; Bolivia to ratify pact 3-29, 298C1
US reserve release asked 3-16, 298G1
TIN Council, International
Bolivia bars pact ratificatn 1-10, price curbs face collapse 3-4, 169E1
Price support reviews OKd, Bolivia to ratify pact 3-29, 298C1
TINDEMANS, Leo (Belgian premier)
Mobutu in Belgium 1-17—1-24, 200A1
Mondale visits 1-24, 70C1
Ousts RW mins 3-4, calls gen electn 3-9, 199B2
Rpts Zaire advisers 4-12, 265F2
Party gains in electn 4-17, asked to form govt 4-22, 326D2
Federatn plan OKd 5-24, Cabt sworn 6-3, 465E3
New govt wins confidence vote 6-9, 561B1
TIPTON, Jennifer
Wins Tony 6-5, 452E1
TIRAN, Strait of
Israel seeks free use 10-10, 769B2
TIRES—*See RUBBER*
TIRIAC, Ion
US Open results 9-11, 787G1
TIRSO Rivilla, Luis
SEC sues 1-12, 79B3

1978

TIANT, Luis
Signs with Yankees 11-13, 1025F3
Kuhn scores free-agent system 12-5, 1026D2
TIBET (Chinese autonomous region)
Panchen Lama at China mtg 2-24—3-8, 154G2
Rebels freed 11-4, 11-15, 880F1-A2
TICKNER, Charles
Wins world figure-skating title 3-9, 316D3
TICKS
Virus studied as control agent 2-23, 334E1
TIDAL Wave
El Salvador hit 8-18, 759C1
TIDROW, Dick
In World Series 10-10—10-17, 800E1
TIEDE, Detlef Alexander
Hijacks Polish plane to W Berlin 8-30, 894G3
TIEN Pao
Asks Tibetan exiles return 11-15, 880A2
TIFFANY & Co.
Warns re diamond prices 3-17, surchrg effect assessed 4-27, 319C1
TIGERCAT (surface-to-air missile)—*See ARMAMENTS—Missiles*
TIGER International, Inc.
Flying Tiger Line Inc.
Prescott dies 3-3, 252C3
TIGHT Rope Walking
Wallenda dies in fall 3-22, 252F3
TIKHONOV, Nikolai Alexandrovich
USSR Politburo alternate 11-27, 924D3
TIKKA Khan, Gen.
Arrested 3-20, 229A1
TILLY, John
Wins Lambeth by-electn 4-27, 329D1
TIMBER—*See LUMBER*
TIMBUKTU (play)
Opens 3-1, 760E3
TIME
Swiss rejct daylight saving time 5-28, 558F2
TIME (magazine)
Parent co to buy Washn Star 2-3, 109A3
Donovan Synanon threats probed 10-15, 842A1
Alexander dies 10-30, 888D2
TIME Inc.
Washn Star purchase agreed 2-3, 109E2
Washn Star purchase completed 3-16, 270B3
'Life' revival rptd planned 403B3
Inland Container purchase planned, '77 profits cited 5-19, 403G2-C3
Allbritton resigns as Washn Star publisher 5-31, 672D2
Synanon threats probed 10-15, 842B1
Book-of-the-Month Club—*See separate listing*
Eastex Inc.
Union pol organizing backed by Sup Ct 6-22, 508B3
Time (magazine)—*See separate listing*
TIME Reference Scanning Beam (TRSB)—*See MICROWAVES*
TIMERMAN, Jacobo
US rep asks release 3-13, 208B1
Moved to house arrest 4-17, 285F3
Remains under house arrest despite ct release order 7-24, 792F3
IAPA scores detentn 10-13, 829G1
TIMES (St. Petersburg, Fla. newspaper)
Poynter dies 6-15, 540F3
TIMES, The (London newspaper)
Scores Carter econ, energy policy; links $ drop 1-4, 27B3
Publicatn suspended 11-30, 923G3-924E1
TIMES Mirror Co.
New American Library, Inc.
Puzo paperback rights bought for record sum 6-16, 620D2
TIMOFEYEV, Feodor
Guyana cult contacts rptd 11-27, 910C3
Guyana cult bequest found 12-17, 1000B2
TIMOR—*See INDONESIA*
TIMOSHUKOV, Mikhail
Seized re Moscow shootout 5-24, 416E2
TINDEMANS, Leo (Belgian premier)
On devolutn plan 1-1, dispute rptd 1-6, 34F3
Devolutn plan accepted 1-17, 69D3
Sees Caramanlis on EC entry 1-26, 149B2
Scores French re Zaire rescue 5-19, 381C2
Backs Zaire security force 5-24, 417D3
Offers resignatn in govt crisis 6-15, King rejects 6-19, 612E2-F3
Resigns in devolutn dispute 10-10, 764A2
Caretaker govt formed, Boeynants premr 10-20, 813D1
Electns indecisive 12-17, 1013F1
TIPPETT Jr., W. Paul
Named AMC pres 10-20, 809A2
TIRAN, Strait of
Camp David summit pact affirms navigatn rights 9-17, 712B2, B3
TIRANA, Bardyl R.
New civil defns plan rptd 11-12, 895F1
TIRES—*See RUBBER*

1979

TIAN Bao
Gets top Tibet post 8-6—8-14, 685D3
TIBET—*See under CHINA, People's Republic of*
TICKNER, Charles
Wins US figure-skating title 2-3, 392A1
Loses world figure-skating title 3-15, 391F3
TICOR Corp.
Southn Pacific to buy 3-28, 283D1
TIDAL Waves—*See STORMS & Floods*
TIDROW, Dick
Traded to Cubs 5-23, 1002G2
TIEDE, Detley Alexander
Freed in W Berlin 5-28, 430E2
TIERNAN, Robert O.
Elected FEC chrmn 5-17, 401C3
TIERNO Galvan, Enrique
Electn as Madrid mayor seen 4-5, 256E2
TIFFANY & Co.
Avon purchase agreed 1-18, 89E1
TIGER International Inc.
Seaboard, Flying Tiger to merge 7-18, 579D1
Justice Dept asks Seaboard merger ban 10-2, Seaboard shareholders OK deal 10-19, 830B2
TIKHONOV, Nicolai Semyonovich
Dies 2-8, 176G3
TIKHONOV, Nikolai Alexandrovich
Full Politburo member 11-27, 929B1
TIKHONOV, Viktor
Soviets win Challenge Cup 2-11, 118C3
TIKKA Khan, Gen.
Released 5-21, 430C2
TILL, Eric
All Things Bright & Beautiful released 3-8, 528B1
TILLAR, Col. Donaldson P.
West Pt hazing probe rptd 11-9, 868E3
TILLEY, Pat
NFL '78 receiving ldr 1-6, 80F1
TILLEY, Patrick
Legacy released 9-28, 820E1
TILL Marriage Do Us Part (film)
Released 7-20, 820D3
TIMBER—*See LUMBER*
TIMBRELL, Dennis
Rpts OHIP doctors leaving 3-13, 211B1
TIME (magazine)
Brezhnev interview rptd 1-9, 11A2
Teng attack on USSR rptd 2-5, 65G1
Donovan retires, Grunwald named ed-in-chief 6-21, 556E1, G1
Art show sponsorship rptd 7-19, 672C2
H-bomb letter cites '54 article 9-16, 9-18, 715E2
TIME Inc.
Inland Container trust setlmt revealed 5-1, 327E1
Larsen dies 9-10, 756F2
Time (magazine)—*See separate listing*
TIMERMAN, Jacobo
Wins Freedom Prize 6-17, 467E1
Ordrd freed 9-18, expelled 9-25, 728A1
Army rebellion crushed 9-29, 748E3
Case cited in Argentine army rift 12-7, 947G2
Cox leaves Argentina 12-16, 966F2
TIMES, The (London newspaper)
Labor negotiatns continue 4-16—4-18, 330G3-331A1
Intl wkly planned 4-20, printing halted 4-29, 330C3
Labor pact reached 10-21, 813E2
Resumes publicatn 11-13, 874B1
TIMES Mirror Co.
New American Library Inc.
Krantz paperback rights sold for record sum 9-12, 755D3
TIMOR—*See INDONESIA*
TIN
China-US pact signed 7-7, 523G2
Floor price lifted 11% 7-23, 781D3
Bolivia scores US sale plan, '78 data rptd 10-22, 824G1
TIN Council, International
Floor price raised 11% 7-23, 781D3
TING, Samuel
Backs quantum chromodynamics 9-2, 692F3
TINSLEY, Bernard S.
Sentenced in GSA scandal 7-16, 964F3
TIOMKIN, Dimitri
Dies 11-11, 932F3
TIP Toes (play)
Opens 3-26, 712A3
TIRES—*See RUBBER*

1980

TIBET—*See under CHINA*
TICHNELL, Richard D.
Md ct voids death sentence 6-10, 869F1
TICKNER, Charles
Retains US figure skating title 1-19, 470E2
Wins Olympic medal 2-19, 155F3
TICOR Mortgage Insurance Co.
Maxwell named Fannie Mae pres 9-24, 960A1
TIERI, Frank (Funzi)
Indicted 6-30, 502E3
Convicted 11-21, 971D2
TIFFANY & Co.
Hoving retires 11-17, 959D2
TIGER International Inc.
CAB OKs Seaboard merger 5-8, 516F1-A2
Ford hired as consultant 6-25, 600A3
TIGHE Jr., Lt. Gen. Eugene F.
Confirms 400 US bodies found in Hanoi 6-27, 508A3
TIKHONOV, Nikolai Alexandrovich (Soviet premier)
W Ger trade pact set 5-29, 411C2
Named Sovt premier, facts on 10-23, 797A1, G1
Press coverage rptd 10-24, 831G3
Arkhipov named 1st dep premr 10-27, 832A1
Hopeful on Reagan electn 11-6, 841C3
Meets Norway forgn min 12-22—12-23, 979B2
TIMBER—*See LUMBER*
TIME (magazine)
Iran readmits newsmen 3-7, 178C2
Reagan scores press 4-10, 288B2
Liddy book excerpts publshd 4-21, 333A3
Kronenberger dies 4-30, 360C2
Pres poll standings tighten, toss-up seen 10-26, 816G1
TIME Inc.
Us magazine sale rptd 3-7, 239B2
New mgt team named 5-15, 456E2
Getty Oil pay-TV film plan draws trust suit 8-4, 639F3
Time-Life Television
RCTV wins BBC rights 12-11, 1002D3
TIMES, The (London newspaper)
Journalists strike 8-22, 652G1; strike ends 8-29, 670F2
Offered for sale 10-22, 808A3
TIMES Mirror Co.
Conn media divestiture ordered 1-24, 120A1
Denver Post purchase set 10-22, 857C1
Communications Properties Inc.
Conn divestiture ordered 1-24, 120B1
TIMM, Barbara
In Teheran 4-19, sees son 4-21, 299E1-B2
Vs US hostage rescue try 4-26; returns to US 4-28, 323B1
TIMM, Kenneth
In Teheran 4-19, wife sees son 4-21, 299E1-B2
TIMONY, Judge James P.
Orders Beatrice to divest Tropicana 11-28, 917G3
TIN
Bolivia miners strike 7-20, 546B3
Geneva talks fail, US rejcts export quotas 12-8, 979B3
TINBERGEN, Jan
Klein wins Nobel 10-15, 890B1
TIN Drum, The (film)
Released 4-11, 416F3
Wins Oscar 4-14, 296A2
TINTYPES (play)
Opens 10-23, 892F3
TIPPING, Jeff
Named ASL title game defensive MVP 9-18, 771G1
TIRELLI, Jaime
Bull Pen opens 6-12, 756C3
TIRES—*See RUBBER (& Rubber Products)*

1976

TISCH, Harry
E Ger Politburo enlarged 5-22, 381E2
TITIANIUM
Price-fixing talks rptd 12-5, 988A2
TITIANIUM Metals Corp. of America
Price-fixing talks rptd 12-5, 98A2

TITO, Josip Broz (Yugoslav president)
US to resume arms sales 1-13, 1-14, 55C1
Sciatica rptd 1-19, confident re Yugo CP system 2-1, 223D3
Not at Sovt CP Cong 2-24—3-5, 195C3
Sees Castro in Yugo 3-6—3-7, 251B3
In Latin Amer, Portugal 3-9—3-22, 256C2
4 sentncd re emigre plot 3-12, 223C3
Sadat visits 4-8—4-9, 275D2
Scores Sonnenfeldt statemt 4-14, 277A2
9 Cominformists sentenced 4-14, 542G3
In Greece 5-10—5-13, Turkey 6-8—6-10, 543C3
Opens Adriatic-Belgrade RR 5-28, 543D3
Meets Brezhnev 6-28, 461D2
At E, W Eur CP conf 6-29—6-30, 461F1
Rptd vs Austria minorities bill 7-6, 554A3
Scores US amb 7-31, 594D1
Ill, cancels visits 9-10, 734E2
US press scored re Croat hijack demands 9-12, 685D2
US pres debate 10-22, 800A1, 802D2
Brezhnev visits, denies threat 11-14—11-17, 909D3
Giscard visits 12-6—12-7, 1012A2
TKAC, Anton
Wins Olympic medal 7-24, 574C2
TLAS, Maj. Gen. Mustafa
Damascus raiders crushed 8-26, 720G3
OKs Saudi Golan exit 10-3, 738B2

TOBACCO
UK to hike taxes 4-6, 266E2
'75 top 500 indls ranked 437E1
Latin output rptd 5-7, 466C1
Reynolds admits US, forgn paymts 5-28, 9-10, 689F2
US GOP platform com actn 8-12, 8-13, 582F3
Rhodesian subsidy cut rptd 8-25, 713A3
UK seizes Rhodesian shipmt 9-18, 713F2
Scandinavia expels N Korea envoys 10-15—10-22, 799E2
3d ¼ profits rptd down 10-28, 866F2
Smoking-Health Link
HEW rpt scores excess use 1-12, 32A1
US cncl cites cigaret pollutn 2-27, 171D2
Australia bans TV ads 3-23, 237G1
Cockpits smoking ban sought 4-20, 308G1
Sup Ct bars review of FTC fines 6-1, 414A3
Smoking survey released 6-15, 875B3
PHS issues 5-yr plan 9-7, 680G1
Tar, nicotine study rptd 9-14, 875F3
Cancer Soc announces drive 10-15, 875D3
MD urges reduced toxins 10-28, 876B1
TOBACK, Emily
Soliah acquitted 4-23; comments 4-30, 368A2
TOBEY, Mark
Dies 4-24, 368B3
TOBIAS, Andrew
Fire & Ice on best-seller list 12-5, 972D2
TOBIN, Patricia C.
Cited in Hearst trial 2-23, testifies 3-16, 201D3, 202F2
TOBOCMAN, Irwin
Arrested 5-15, 401E2
TODD, Garfield
House arrest lifted 6-5, 428D2
On Rhodesia solutn 9-19, 698B2
Rhodesia conf delegate 10-14, 781E2
Asks UK name interim govt head 12-1, 893B2
TODD, Richard W.
On Australia gas purchase plan 8-8, 650A2
TODD Jr., Webster
Natl Transport Safety Bd chrmn 1-20; confrmd 2-5, 110D2
TODD Shipyards Corp.
Ford campaigns 10-25, 802E3
TODOROV, Georgi
Wins Olympic medal 7-19, 576D2
TODOROV, Stanko
On Bulgaria Politburo 4-2, 250D1

TOGO—*See also AFRICAN Development Bank, NONALIGNED Nations Movement, OAU*
Listed as 'not free' nation 1-19, 20E3
Angola MPLA recognized 2-10, 105E2
Benin border reopened 3-27, 372C1
At France-Africa summit 5-10—5-11, 355A3

1977

TISON, Eugene
Survives bloodless surgery 6-2, 620A1
TITAN (ICBM)—*See ARMAMENTS—Missiles*

TITO, Josip Broz (Yugoslav president)
Bars Sovt mil pact 1-9, 24A1
Sadat visit canceled 1-20, 43F3
Sees Mondale, scores rights stance 5-21, 398D2
Wife in seclusn 6-15, illness denied 10-11, 786A1
Brezhnev honors 8-16, 640C2
Albania denounces 9-2, 710C1
Addresses Helsinki review conf 10-4, 752C2
Kardelj firm re nonalignmt 10-4, 785F3
Torrijos quotes Canal advice 10-6, 792C2
In France, Portugal, Algeria 10-12—10-20, 844E2
Wife accused of Serb natlism 10-25, 844A2

TITO, Marcos
Geisel fires 6-14, 523E3
TIWARI, D. N.
Quits party 2-2, 71E1
TKATCHENKO, Alexander
US tour results 1-29—2-5, 263G1
TLATELOLCO, Treaty of
Carter pledges ratificatn 4-14, 295F2; signs 5-26, 415D3
Argentina to sign 11-21, 912A3
TM—*See TRANSCENDENTAL Meditation*
TOBACCO
Philip Morris-USSR deal set 1-17, 47F2
Sovt bloc chrgd re Rhodesia sanctns 2-10, 123A1
Loews forgn paymts rptd 2-14, 233A3
Carter backs pot decriminalizatn 3-14, 332A2
'76 profit gain rptd 340A2
Cigar makers' merger blocked 6-28, 520E3
Ga drought crop damage rptd 7-28, 659F3
Rhodesia sets subsidies 8-25, 730E3
Smoking-Health Link
Finland bans ads 3-1, 182B2
Birth pill-smoking risk rptd 3-29, 287E3
Eastn to add no-smoking seats 6-14, 593G1
Bladder cancer data rptd 6-17, 530G3
Early menopause, heart disease, other illness in women linked 6-25, 620C1
Smoking among teenaged girls rptd up 6-25, 620E1
Carter drug-abuse message 8-2, 609A2
FAA rejects flight crew ban 9-1, 778F3
CAB votes airline cigar, pipe smoking ban 11-22, 900G1
TOBACCO Institute, American
CAB votes airline cigar, pipe smoking ban 11-22, 900A2
TOCCOA Falls (Ga.) Bible College
Kelly Barnes dam bursts 11-6, 888F2 ★
Dam burst laid to seepage 12-21, 1023E3
TODAY (Fla. newspaper)
Libel case review refused 11-7, 857D2
TODD, C. L.
Chrgs dropped 9-12, 724D2
TODMAN, Terence A.
In Cuba 4-24—4-28, fishing pacts signed 4-27, 390B1
Visits 4 Latin natns 5-8—5-17, 414C1
Replaced as amb to CR 5-25, 500D1
On Mrs Carter's Latin tour 5-30—6-12, 454F1
Chile loans blocked 6-28, 493B1
Nicaragua mil aid stand rptdly misrepresented 8-6, 656C3
Visits Chile 8-11—8-12, 635B2
In Argentina, rpts rights progress 8-13—8-16, 670C1
In Paraguay re rights 8-17—8-18, 803B2
Visits Uruguay 8-17—8-19, 905B1
Sees Haiti rights progress 10-21, 905F2

TOGO—*See also NONALIGNED Nations Movement, OAU*
UN Assemb member 4C1
Benin raiders flee 1-17, 48C1
At France-Africa summit 4-20—4-21, 316F3
UK foils asassinatn plot 10-13, 988F2

1978

TITANIUM
Du Pont titanium dioxide monopoly chrgd 4-10, 346A1
4 cos, 5 execs indicted 9-28; new US trust disclosure plan set 10-4, 768F1, C2
TITANIUM Dioxide—*See CHEMICALS*
TITANIUM Metals Corp. of America
Named unindicted co-conspirator 9-28, trust disclosure role cited 10-4, 768F1, D2

TITO, Josip Broz (Yugoslav president)
Visits US 3-6—3-9, 193G3-194F1
Albania-Greek trade pact signed 3-28—3-30, 374E2
US, N-S Korea talks proposal rptd 4-5, 4-19, 277A3
Perovic sentenced 4-13, 292E1
CP cong speech 6-20, 519D2
Warns nonaligned vs Cuba, USSR, West 7-25, 583B2
Hua visits Yugo 8-21—8-29, hails 8-28, 674A3, 675A2
Croat natlist killed 10-16, 805A3
US chrgs 6 in murder plot 12-1, 933C3

TITTERTON, Ernest
Denies Maralinga A-waste mass 10-5, 771B3
TJONGARERO, Daniel
Arrested 12-3, 988C3
Rptd freed 12-27, 1020A2
TLATELOLCO, Treaty of
Carter lauds signatories, Cuba avoidance cited 6-21, 489C3

TOBACCO
Agri Dept price supports scored 1-11, 23A3
Zambia hikes cigaret tax 1-27, 95D2
US pesticide sales curbed 2-15, 16B3
BAT industries US operatns cited 5-5, 345C3
Philip Morris to buy 7-Up 5-15, 364F2-B3
Reynolds settles SEC paymts chrgs 6-6, 449D2
Cigaret smoking data rptd 7-5, 727C1
Philip Morris buys Liggett forgn units 7-26, 718C1
Reynolds seeks Del Monte 8-3, bid OKd 9-25, 752B3
Carter visits Wilson (NC) 8-5, 605F3
Australia tax hike proposed 8-15, 628A2
China '77 indus data rptd 9-28, 727C2
Smoking-related fire data rptd 10-8, 972B2
Liggett to buy SC Pepsi bottler 11-16, 1005C2
Greek EC entry terms set 12-21, 1017D3
Smoking-Health Link
HEW anti-smoking crusade set; Nader, other lobbyists score 1-11, 23B2, G2
Carter budgets anti-smoking drive 1-23, 48E2
UK proposes cigaret tax hike 4-11, 267A3
Asbestos workers warned 4-26, 326B3
Women smokers risk heart attacks 6-8, 727A1
Indus-funded AMA study finds cigaret smoking harmful 8-5, 726D3
'Tolerable' cigaret rpt debated 8-9, 8-10, 726F2-D3
Chinese get 1st cigaret warning, cancer deaths noted 8-28, 727F1
Calif rejcts smoking ban 11-7, 847A3, 856G3
TOBACCO Institute, American
HEW anti-smoking plan scored 1-11, 23A3
TOBACCO Tax Council (Richmond, Va.)
'77 cigarette consumptn rptd 7-5, 727C1
TOBACCO Workers International Union (AFL-CIO)
Merges with Bakery & Confectionery Workers 8-16, 700G1-B2
TOBACK, James
Fingers released 3-2, 619G1
TOBIN, Austin J.
Dies 2-8, 196G3
TODD, Ronald
On Ford workers strike 9-21, 763E3, 764B1
TODMAN, Terence A.
On Carib trade dvpt 1-22, 100D3

TOGO—*See also GATT, NONALIGNED Nations Movement, OAU*
At W African mtg, backs ECOWAS 3-18; USSR scores 3-20, 237E1
Zaire peace troops rptd 6-19, 478A2
Kodjo named OAU secy gen 7-22, 561C2
UN Assemb member 713F3
Polisario recognitn cited 11-10, 999G2

1979

TISSOT, Ernest
On Indochina refugee drop 8-4, 626A1
TITANIUM
USSR high-speed sub rptd 5-17, 390D2
TITANIUM Dioxide—*See CHEMICALS*
TITCHBOURNE, Julie C.
Wins Scientology fraud suit 8-15, 640E2
TITIAN (Tiziano Vecellio) (1477-1576)
Church painting sold for record sum 10-25, 891G3
TITLE, Judge Julius M.
Lifts Worldwide Church receivership 3-17, 376C2

TITO, Josip Broz (Yugoslav president)
'78 divorce, remarriage rptd 2-4, 176C1
Kardelj dies 2-10, 176C3
Calls Bhutto executn 'murder' 4-4, 247G1
Djilas warned vs dissent 4-8—4-9, 334F1
Dolanc demoted 5-16, 430B3
Sees Brezhnev, backs nonalignmt 5-16—5-18, 379D3
Serbians sentncd in US 6-22, 491B3
Urges nonaligned unity 9-4, 674C2, F2

TIYENSAN, Husamettin
On Turkey truckers strike 3-29, 333F2

TOBACCO
Hungary ups prices 1-8, 101B2
Carter backs subsidies 1-17, 30C1
Tax collectn speed-up proposed 1-22, 42C1
Cigaret, ad cos ordrd to obey FTC subpoenas 1-25, 91C3
Cigaret mfr rise rptd 2-11, 218E2*
GATT pact signed 4-12, 273F2
US teenaged male smokers rptd down, female smokers up 4-27, 470C3
Fortune rpts '68-78 indus stock gain 5-7, 305A2
State-local '78 tax revenues up 5-16, 386C2
Japan-US sales pact signed 6-2, 416E1
NC PCB dumping chrgd 6-4—6-13, disposal disputed 6-5, 597C3
NZ cigaret tax plans rptd 6-22, 566A3
Dutch plan tax hike 9-18, 730C3
US use rptd down 10-16, 970A3
'78 consumptn, smoking rptd up worldwide, '70s export hikes noted 11-22, 970E2-A3
Canada cigaret price hike budgeted 12-12, defeated 12-13, 936D3
Mergers & Acquisitions
Liggett to sell US cigaret business 1-26, 283E1
Amer Brands acquires FDS 2-14, 132B2
Liggett US sale talks end 6-14, 517G1
Imperial Group to buy Howard Johnson 9-10; Calif bar seen 10-12, 942B3-E3
Smoking-Health Link
HEW rpt issued, campaign set 1-11, 23A1
Birth perils rptd 1-16, 63E3
Carter warns on perils 1-17, 30C1
Carter budgets anti-smoking drive 1-22, 44A3
Filter cigarets rptd less perilous 2-22, 218G1
Strokes rptd down 2-28, 195F2
Cancer death rate rise rptd 3-5, 195E3
Me pub mtg smoking ban vetoed 3-13, 218F2
Bulgaria hosp personnel cigaret ban rptd 3-19, 218F2
Camel cigaret sales rptd 3-20, 218G2
Miami voters rejct anti-smoking law 5-8, 350C3
Califano fired, anti-smoking policy cited 7-18, 529F2
FTC rpts on life expectancy 9-2, 970B3
Fed workers case declined by Sup Ct 10-29, 884D2
'78 smoking down in US, other indl natns 11-22, 970F2
TOBACCO Institute, American
HEW rpt called 'rehash' 1-10, 23E1
TOBAGO—*See TRINIDAD & Tobago*
TODA Jr., Benigo
Named in McDonnell Douglas paymts chrg 11-9, 886D2
TODD Jr., Michael
Bell Jar released 3-20, 528D1
TOGNAZZI, Ugo
Cage aux Folles released 5-12, 528F1
TOGO—*See also GATT, NONALIGNED Nations Movement, OAU*
US aircraft co admits paymts 1-3, 16F1
Ghana executns rptd scored 6-30, 524D2
CAE student massacre probe rptd 8-6, 601A3

1980

TISCH, Steve
Coast to Coast released 10-3, 836E2
TISHMAN, David
Dies 6-18, 528F3
TITANIUM
US defns posture, supply linked 1-25, 65G2
Australia sets Sovt export ban 1-28, 116E1; lifts 2-12, 1-28, 148A1
Va mine linked to Abscam defendant 10-30, 824D2
TITIAN (Tiziano Vecelli) (1477-1576)
Forged paintings chrgd 2-26, 472B3
TITLE Insurance and Trust Co.
Kuwait seeks 15% of Getty Oil 7-14, 542B3; bid rejctd 7-18, 557B1
TITO, Josip Broz (Yugoslavian president)
Gold prices soar 1-2—1-18, 30B3
Leg amputated 1-20, 49C2
In intl appeal for detente 2-21, Carter responds 2-25, 139A3
EC-Yugo trade pact signed 4-2, 365C3
Dies 5-4, funeral held 5-8; facts on, photo 338G1-339C2
Mijatovic installed pres 5-15, 381G3
CP leader post filled 6-12, 487G2
Carter cites funeral 8-4, 594G2

TITTEMORE, Charles
CPU strikes Abitibi mills 6-27, 497C2
TJOFLAT, Judge Gerald B.
Voids itinerants registratn 5-13, 370F2
TKACHENKO, Nadezhda
Wins Olympic medal 7-24, 624F1
TKACHYOV, Alexandr
Wins Olympic medals 7-25, 622F3

TOBACCO
Cuba '79 crop damaged by rust 1-1, 38G2
Carter tax proposal 1-28, 70B1
Fscl '79 tax revenue rptd 2-20, 307G2
Latham dies 2-21, 176B2
Ireland plans cigaret levy hike 2-27, 150G3
UK plans cigaret tax hike 3-26, 232E1
'79 US consumptn rptd down 4-7, 318C2
Rhodesia sells openly 4-8, 301E3
State-local '79 tax collectns rptd 4-17, 307D2
Zimbabwe hikes prices 4-20, 301E2
Canada plans tax hike 4-21, 310F2
US drought damage rptd 6-23—8-15, 616C2
Anderson, Reagan debate excise tax 9-21, 722E1
Norway sets tax hike 10-6, 792G3
Japan-US trade talks resume 10-19, 864A3
Japan to ease US tariffs 11-21, 902E1
Cuba '81-85 plan outlined, '80 setbacks admitted 12-17, 12-20, 992G3
Mergers & Acquisitions
Liggett bid raised, Standard Brands quits 5-14; Grand Met offer OKd 5-16, 557A3
Smoking-Health Link
Maternity smoking risks rptd 1-4, 23C3
Female lung cancer rise rptd 1-14, 40A2
Life span changes rptd 1-19, 62G3
Fewer lung cancer tests urged 3-20, 316C3
Smoking risk to nonsmokers rptd 3-26, 318F1
Iowa farm cancer study rptd 4-15, 357D3
3 Mile I health study rptd 4-17, 332B3
Calif rejcts smoking ban 11-4, 847A2, A3
TOBACCO Institute, American
US smoking rpt scored 1-14, 40E2
TOBAGI, Walter
Slain 5-28, 408A2
TOBAGO—*See TRINIDAD & Tobago*
TOBIAS, George
Dies 2-27, 176F3
TODD, Garfield
Arrested 2-9, 118F3
TODD, Dr. J. K.
Toxic-shock syndrome research cited 6-6, 584E3
TODISCO, George
Dented opens 8-11, 756C3
TOFFLER, Alvin
Third Wave on best-seller list 5-4, 359D3; 6-8, 448C3; 7-13, 568C3
TO Forget Venice (film)
Released 1-28, 216F3

TOGO—*See also GATT, NONALIGNED Nations, OAU*
Protesters occupy emb in Paris 1-12, 61D2
Eyadema proclaims 3d republic, frees prisoners; '79 reelectn cited 1-13, 61C2
Eyadema in Chad truce attempt 4-5, 311E1

1976

Olympic withdrawal rptd 7-21, 528B3
Palmer confrmd US amb 9-15, 808C1
ECOWAS rptd ratified 11-6, 974E2

TOGO, Fumihiko
Seeks US data on Lockheed 2-24, 190C2
TOIYONEN, Irma
Sworn Finnish soc affairs min 9-29, 750D3
TOKYO Rose—*See D'AQUINO, Iva Toguri*
TOLAND, John
Adolf Hitler on best-seller list 12-5, 972D2
TOLBERT Jr., William R. (Liberian president)
Kissinger in Liberia 4-30—5-1, 318A2, B3

TOLEDANO, Shmuel
On Arab grievances 5-23, 370D1
TOLEDO, O.—*See OHIO*
TOLEDO Plata, Carlos
Arrest rptd 4-19, 311F1
TOLKUNOV, Lev N.
Novesti Central Com head 3-5, 195A3
TOLPO, Carl
Dies 9-25, 892G3
TOL Saut
Named Cambodia premier 4-14, 265D1
TOLSTIKOV, Vasily S.
On Peking emb blast 4-30, 341E2
Quits China banquet 11-15, 871C3
TOLSTOY, Leo Nikolayvich (1828-1910)
Mary Tolstoy dies 11-21, 970C3
TOLSTOY, Countess Mary Koutouzow
Dies 11-21, 970C3
TOMAL, Zdzislaw
On Polish State Cncl 3-25, out as dep premr 3-27, 268C2, E2
TOMANOVA, Renata
Loses Australian Open 1-4, 31E3
TOMASSON, Thomas A.
Warns on Iceland NATO pullout 1-12, 50C3
TOMATOES—*See FRUITS & Vegetables*
TOMLIN, John
Injured 8-30, 643D3
TOMMY (film)
'75 top rental film 1-7, 32F3
TOMOV, Alexander
Wins Olympic medal 7-24, 576B3
TONELLI, Joseph P.
Addresses Canada labor cong 5-18, 401D1
TONGA—*See also ADB, COMMONWEALTH of Nations*
Listed as 'partly free' 1-19, 20D3
S Pacific Forum meets 3-8—3-9, 179B2
Commonwealth gets UN observer status 10-18, 799D2
Listed as partly free 12-22, 977B3
TONGOGARA, Josiah
Chrgd in Chitepo murder 4-21, 428G1-A2
TONGPAK Plangket
Heads govt-in-exile 10-12, 794F3
TONRY, Richard A(lvin)
Wins La House runoff spot 8-14, 633D1
Elected to US House 11-2, 822A2 * 829F3 *
TONY Awards—*See PERRY Awards*
TOON, Malcolm
Israel vs Scranton UN speech 3-26, 227B3
Chrgs Israel pressures US 4-8, Israel scores 4-9, 258E1
Israel vs US UN vote 11-12, 863B1
TOOTE, Gloria E. A.
Seconds Reagan nominatn 8-18, 598C1
TOPEKA, Kan.—*See KANSAS*
TOPEKA Capital (newspaper)
Ford endorsement rptd 10-30, 827G3
TOROCSIK, Mari
Wins Cannes film award 5-28, 460F1
TORO Hardy, Jose
Arrest ordered 7-14, 593C1
Occidental chrgs dismissed 11-16, 930E1
TOROSYAN, David
Wins Olympic medal 7-31, 574A1
TORRES, Emma Obleas de
Arrives Mex 6-7; scores Bolivia, Argentina 6-8, 456F2
TORRES, Gen. Juan Jose (ret.)
Scores Chile sea outlet plan 1-1, asks Banzer ouster 1-5, 27F1
Bolivia chrgs plot; denies 2-18—2-19, 238A1
Guevara death controversy grows 4-14—5-13, 415B3
Kidnapped 6-1, found dead 6-2, 415D2-A3
Body flown to Mex 6-7, buried 6-9, 456F2
Bolivia protests grow 6-8—6-19, 456D1

1977

TOILETRIES—*See COSMETICS*
TOKYO Rose—*See D'AQUINO, Iva Toguri*
TOKYO Shibaura Electric Co. Ltd. (Toshiba)
Nashville TV plant planned 12-14, 974A2

TOLBERT Jr., William R. (Liberian president)
Sees Young 5-13, 399A1

TOLEDO, O.—*See OHIO*
TOLKEIN, J. R. R.
Silmarillion on best-seller list 10-2, 808C3; 11-6, 872C3; 12-4, 1021F2
TOL Saut—*See POL Pot*
TOLUENE-2, 4-diamine—*See CHEMICALS*
TOMAINE, Carol J.
Fined $5,000 3-21, 520B3
TOMANOVA, Renata
Loses Italian Open 5-22, 430B3
TOMASEK, Frantisek Cardinal
'76 apptmt as cardinal disclosed 6-27, 768B3
TOMATOES—*See FRUITS & Vegetables*
TOMJANOVICH, Rudy
Injured in NBA brawl 12-9, 990B3
TOMLIN, Lily
Wins Tony 6-5, 452E1
TOMORROW Entertainment Inc.
Libel suit vs NBC dismissed 7-12, 643D1
TONER, Pauline
Wins Greensborough by-electn 11-5, 922C3
TONGA—*See also COMMONWEALTH of Nations*
NZ to set 200-mi fishing zone 9-7, 729B3
TONRY, Rep. Richard A(lvin) (D, La.)
Resigns 5-4, indicted 5-12, 418A3
Loses primary 6-25, 501E1
Sentenced 7-28, 603A3
GOP wins Cong seat 8-27, 693B1
TONY Awards—*See PERRY Awards*
TOON, Malcolm
Moscow receives as amb 1-18, 47A2
Replaced as amb to Israel 4-25, 418F1
Renamed amb to USSR 4-25, confrmd 6-7, 500C1
USSR bars Independnc Day speech 7-4, 529G3
Sees Brezhnev 7-5, 529E3
On emb fire security 8-27, 673F2
Rpts looting in emb fire 9-2, 766D1
TOONE, Bernard
Marquette wins NCAA title 3-28, 262A2
TOPEKA, Kan.—*See KANSAS*
TOPIARZ, Frantisek
Trial opens 1-10, 82F3
Sentenced 2-3, 115C1
TOPKIS, Jay
Jurek executn delayed 1-17, 40D3
TORBORG, Jeff
Replaces Robinson as Indian mgr 6-19, 644A2
TORNADOES—*See STORMS*
TORONTO Globe and Mail (newspaper)
China expels Munro 11-27, 946C2
TORRAS, Pelegrin
Signs US-Cuba pact 5-30, 455E3
TORRES, Carlos Alberto
2 arrested re FBI probe 3-21, 261E2
TORRES, Joe Campos
Found dead 5-8, 4 ex-cops indicted 10-20, 820F3
TORRES, Jorge
Kidnapers murder 11-10, 1011G1
TORREY Canyon (Liberian tanker)
'67 oil spill cited 2-24, 214B3
TORREZ, Mike
In World Series 10-11—10-18, 806F2
Signs with Red Sox 11-21, 989E3

1978

TOILETRIES—*See COSMETICS*
TOKAR, Norman
Cat From Outer Space released 6-30, 618F3
TOKAS, Norman
Candleshoe released 8-4, 969F3

TOLBERT Jr., William R. (Liberian president)
Sees Carter in Monrovia 4-3, 234D1

TOLBUTAMIDE (Orinase)—*See MEDICINE—Drugs*
TOLEDO, O.—*See OHIO*
TOLKIEN, J. R. R.
Silmarillion on best-seller list 1-8, 24C3; 2-5, 116A3; 3-5, 195D3; 4-2, 272B3
Hobbit on best-seller list 2-5, 116D3
Lord of Rings released 11-15, 970A2
TOL Saut—*See POL Pot*
TOLSTIKOV, Vasily Sergeevich
Gets China protest note 5-11, 360F2
TOMASEK, Frantisek Cardinal
Named Czech church ldr 1-10, 17C3
TOMATOES—*See FRUITS & Vegetables*
TOMBAZOS, George
Named Cyprus agri, resources min 3-8, 189A2
TOMLIN, Lily
Moment by Moment released 12-21, 1030C3
TOMLIN, Zimmerman & Parmalee Inc.
SEC censures re Equity Funding 9-4, 681B2
TOM Tom Communications Inc.
SBA loan guarantee rptd 11-16, 919E3
TOMURA, Issaku
Hails Narita airport riots 3-28, 228C1
TONDON, Yvon
Wins French legis seat 10-1, 815A2
TONELLI, Joseph P.
Indicted 7-19, 598D3
TONGA—*See COMMONWEALTH of Nations, SOUTH Pacific Forum*
TONGLET, Anne-Marie
Rapists convicted 5-3, 396C1
TONGSUN Park—*See PARK Tong Sun*
TONGTA Kiatvayupak
Cervantes KOs 4-29, 379D2
TONG Yuk-phing
Sentenced 1-23, 189E3
TONNA, Gratien
Minter wins Eur middlewgt title 7-19, 600C2
TONY Awards—*See PERRY Awards*
TOO Much Too Little Too Late (recording)
On best-seller list 5-3, 356D1; 6-7, 460F3
TOON, Malcolm
US emb personal contacts rptd curbed 1-5, 21B1
Warns re Shcharansky 4-3, 275E3
USSR gives custody of US businessman 6-26, 506F1
On rptrs slander chrg 6-30, 518A2
Pravada chrgs 'slander' 10-14, 821B1
TOP Rank Inc.
Arum reveals Spinks-CBS pact 2-17, threatens suit vs WBC 3-16, 211E3, 212C1
Spinks-Ali rematch contract signed 4-11, 378F3
TOPUZ, Ali
Named Turkey rural affairs min 1-5, 21F2
TORNADOES—*See STORMS*
TORONTO, University of
Brain tissue recovery after alcoholism rptd 6-10, 1023C2
TORONTO Sun, The (newspaper)
Secrets Act violatn chrgd 3-17, 208F3
TORPEDOES—*See ARMAMENTS—Ships*
TORRES, Antonio
Slain 6-2, 476D3
TORRES, Joe Campos (d. 1977)
3 Houston ex-cops sentncd 3-28, appeal rptd 12-14, 991B3
TORRES, Juan Jose (d. 1976)
Bolivia press freedoms guaranteed 8-18, 691E2
TORRES, Rusty
Traded to White Sox 5-17, 779A3
TORRES Garcia, Joaquin (deceased)
Paintings destroyed in Brazil museum fire 7-8, 579B2
TORREY, Bill
Islanders fscl mgr named 6-6, refinancing plan OKd 8-10, 656B2, E2
TORREY Canyon (tanker)
'67 record oil spill cited 3-17, 201D3
TORRIJOS Herrera, Hugo
Named Panama amb to Spain 3-1, 211E2

1979

Zaire troop exit rptd 8-14, 733G3
UN membership listed 695A3

TOKYO Economic Summit
US, Japan prelim talks 6-26, 494A2
7 natl ldrs meet, oil import targets set 6-28—6-29, 493A1-494C1

TOLBERT Jr., William R. (Liberian president)
On food price rioting 4-18, 279F3
Rejects price hikes 4-18; closes univs 4-21, gets emergency powers 4-27, 314F3
Suspends habeas corpus 5-2, 374G2
OAU chrmn, scores African rights policy 7-17, 552E2
Young urges Israel ties 9-6; reacts 9-7, 720B3
TOLEDANO, Mauricio Hatchwell
Vs Arafat visit to Spain 9-14, 695C1
TOLEDO, O.—*See OHIO*
TOLEDO, Judge Jose V.
Holds US welfare in PR discriminatory 10-11, 786F2
TOLEDO Plata, Carlos
Signs arsenal raid communique 1-3, 115D1
TOLKIEN, J. R. R.
Silmarillion on best-seller list 1-7, 80B3; 4-8, 271C2
TOL Saut—*See POL Pot*
TOLSTOY, Alexandra
Dies 9-26, 756E3
TOLSTOY, Leo (1828-1910)
Light Shines opens 1-11, 292G1
Strider opens 5-31, 712F2
Daughter dies 9-26, 756E3
TOMASEK, Frantisek Cardinal
Poles ask dissident support 7-5, 802E2
TOMASZEWSKI, Henry
Billy released 1-31, 174C2
TOMBIGBEE River (Ala., Miss.)
Tenn R waterway upheld 3-13, 188A3
TOMEI, Concetta
Little Eyolf opens 6-29, 712B1
TOMINOVA, Zdena
Named Charter 77 ldr 2-8, 126F3
TOMONAGA, Shinichero
Dies 7-8, 588E3
TOMSETH, Victor
Hostage status disputed 11-30—12-1, spy trial threatened 12-1, 12-4, 914D2
TOMS River, N.J.—*See NEW Jersey*
TONGA—*See COMMONWEALTH of Nations*
TONGOGARA, Josiah
Killed 12-29, 976A1
TONG Sun Park—*See PARK Tong Sun*
TONIGHT Show (TV series)
Carson won't quit 5-2, 334B3
TONKIN, David
Wins S Australia electns 9-15, takes office 9-18, 749G1
TOO Much Heaven (recording)
On best-seller list 1-10, 80E3; 2-7, 120E3
TOON, Malcolm
Protests USSR rpts on Iran 2-16, 125D3
Sovt natl kills self in emb 3-28, 237G3, 238A1
U-2 flights over Turkey rptd backed 5-29, 397F3
Cited in SALT II summit communique 6-18, 457C1
'Confident' on SALT II verificatn 6-22, 496F3
Backs SALT ratificatn 7-26, 644B1
Leaves USSR, scores Dobrynin reliance 10-16; Watson replaces 10-17, 794D3-795A1
TOP of the World Inc.
Colo land sale refunds set 5-8, 596A1
TOP Rank Inc.
Arum chrgs Benitez fight fix 1-14, 79B3
TORN, Rip
Seduced opens 2-1, 292A3
Joe Tynan released 8-17, 820C3
TORNADOES—*See STORMS*
TORONTO Sun, The (newspaper)
Secrecy trial barred 4-23, 311B2
TORPEDOES—*See ARMAMENTS—Ships*
TORRENCE, Richard
Umbatha opens 4-9, 712B3
TORRES, Ed
Aladdin casino bid rejected 12-15, 965D1
TORRES, Esteban E.
Named Carter spec asst 8-10, 608F2
TORRES, Joe Campos (d.1977)
3 Houston ex-cops win appeal 2-6, 156C2
3 Houston ex-cops resentncd 10-30, 839B3
TORRES v. Puerto Rico
Case decided by Sup Ct 6-18, 499A2

1980

CEAO mtg held 5-28, 469G1-A3
Chad peace conf fails 10-18—10-19, 810G1
Chad cease-fire agreemt completed 11-28, 965E1
Libyan Chad role opposed 12-23—12-24, 979E1
TOKUHATA, Dr. George
On 3 Mile I health study 4-2, 332A2-G2
TOLARO, Pfc. Sarah
Testifies on sex harassment 2-11, 188F3
TOLBERT, Adolphus B.
Seized at French Emb 6-14, 499C1
TOLBERT, Frank
Executed 4-22, 353A2
TOLBERT Jr., William R. (Liberian president; killed Apr. 12)
Oppositn ldr asks overthrow 3-7, arrested 3-9, 278C2
Killed in coup 4-12, buried 4-15; facts on 284A3, D3, F3
Brother executed 4-22, 353A2
Son seized at French Emb 6-14, 499C1

TOLEDO—*See OHIO*
TOLEDO Edison Co.
NRC asks Babcock fine re '77 A-plant accident 4-10, 332C1
'79 A-plant mishaps rptd 7-14, 551F2
TOL Saut—*See POL Pot*
TOMA, Sanda
Wins Olympic medal 7-26, 623A2
TOMANOVA, Renata
Australian Open results 1-1, 213F1
TOMATOES—*See FRUITS & Vegetables*
TOMBAZOS, George
Named Cyprus health min 9-9, 749F2
TOMIN, Julius
Police disrupt lectures 3-9, 3-19, 4-2, 262C2
Arrested 4-9, 4-12, 326D3
TOMLIN, Lily
Nine to Five released 12-19, 1003C2
TOMOV, Aleksandr
Wins Olympic medal 7-24, 624C3
TOM Petty & the Heartbreakers (singing group)
Damn The Torpedoes on best-seller list 2-6, 120G3; 3-5, 200F3
TOMSETH, Victor
Sought for Forghan link 3-2, 164G2
UN comm visit rptd 3-12, 178D1
Prelate visits 12-25, 974A2
TONE, Philip W.
Named B Carter probe counsel 8-11, 647E2
Rpts 2 B Carter associates under investigatn 8-21, 647A2
TONELLI, John
Islanders win Stanley Cup 5-24, 487G3
TONEY, Andrew
In NBA draft 6-10, 447F1
TONGA—*See also ADB, COMMONWEALTH of Nations*
Island trade pact rptd 7-24, 576G2
TONIGHT Show (TV series)
Carson contract signing rptd 5-6, 470G3
TOPPING, Seymour
Iran chrgs shah gave gifts 2-9, 122B3
TOPPS Chewing Gum Inc.
Baseball card trust violatn rptd 7-2, 917E3
TORMANEN, Jouko
Wins Olympic medal 2-23, 155D3
TORNADOES—*See STORMS & Floods*
TORO Enterprises
Youngstown US Steel plant suit ends 11-14, 917A1
TORONTO-Dominion Bank, The
Brazil oil loan rptd 3-5, 191F1
TORRES, Carlos Alberto
Arrested 4-4, apartmt raided 4-8, 308F3, 309D1
Convicted 7-30, 601D1
Indicted 12-10, 963F3
TORRES, Marie Hayde
Arrested 4-4, 308G3
Extraditn, sentencing rptd 8-4, 601E1 *
TORRES Rojas, Gen. Luis
Loses Madrid post 1-24, 101A2, C2

1976

TORRIJOS Herrera, Brig. Gen. Omar (Panamanian head of state)
In Cuba, signs pacts 1-10—1-15, 52C2
Javits warns on anti-US comments 1-11, 52F2
Régime exiles critics 1-21, business ldrs score 1-22, 1-26, 121E2-D3
Bars Arias return 1-29, 121F3
Warns vs canal talks failure 3-7, 291D3
On new US Canal Co treaty 3-22, 292A1
Tack quits Panama posts 4-1, 291C2
Scores US pres candidates, Reagan rebuts 4-21, 281C3, 291E2
Asks nonaligned support vs US 8-17, 621F3
Students riot, CIA role chrgd 9-10—9-20; Boyd denies econ causes 9-22, 792C1-E1, B3
Scores US pres candidates 10-7; warns US 'intruders' 10-11, 792F3
Scores US Canal Zone blast chrgs 11-29, 1008A3

TOSKA, Haki
Named finance min 10-14, 949A2
TOTAL Compagnie Francaise des Petroles
Rhodesia sanctn violatns chrgd 6-21, 621A2
TOTALITARIAN Temptation, The (book)
Publicatn rptd 1-20, 119A3
TOTAL Woman, The (book)
On best seller list 1-25, 80D3
TOTH, Laszlo
Yugo upholds arrest 3-17, 256F1
Silberman resigns 11-17, 910B2
Pardoned 6-4, freed 7-23, 559A2
TOTSCHNIG, Brigitte
Wins Olympic medal 2-8, 158E3
TOTTEN, Don
Scores Ford campaign 3-12, 197B1
TOUCHE Ross & Co.
Sup Ct bars review of class-action ruling 10-4, 807C3
TOUCH Not the Cat (book)
On best-seller list 12-15, 972F2
TOUFANIAN, Gen. Hassan
US arms purchase drop seen 2-4, 102F1
In Grumman commission feud 2-17, 140C1
TOURE, Ahmed Sekou (Guinean president)
Rpts May assassinatn try 6-9, 503A3
Plotters arrested 7-15, 8-10, 1005A2
Shuffles Cabt 12-11, 1005F1
TOURINE, Charles
Indicted 7-8, 816G2
TOURISCHEVA, Ludmila
Wins Olympic medals 7-19—7-22, 563D1, 574D3, E3
TOURISM—*See TRAVEL*
TOVARISCH (USSR sailing ship)
In Operation Sail 7-4, 488A3
TOVIN, Jack D.
Sentenced 11-30, 921A3
TOWE, Peter
Vs energy sharing 1-30—1-31, 108F1
TOWE, Thomas E.
Loses US House electn 11-2, 824B2
TOWELL, David
Wins Nev Sen primary 9-14, 705C1
Loses US Sen electn 11-2, 824C2
TOWER, Sen. John G. (R, Tex.)
Intelligence com issues rpt 4-26, 304C3
Reagan sweeps Tex vote 5-1, 322G3
Permanent intelligence com created 5-19, 377B1
Role in blocking anti-boycott bill disputed 9-30—10-7, 786C3
Lobbying disclosure bill not cleared 10-2, 883D1
TOWERING Inferno (film)
'75 top rental film 1-7, 32F3

1977

TORRIJOS Herrera, Moises
US concedes '72 drug indictmt 10-14, 792D1
Drug chrgs anger govt 11-13, Dole to get files 11-16, 912C2
TORRIJOS Herrera, Brig. Gen. Omar (Panamanian head of state)
Unions protest econ pkg 1-4, 1-14, 46D2
Sets new austerity program 1-22, 379A3
Boyd quits Canal talks 2-9, 379B1
US sen chrgs Linowitz ties 2-21, 379E1
US Canal talks end 5-11, defense role disputed 5-17—5-18, 378G2, A3
Guatemala severs ties re Belize 5-19; chrgs exchngd 5-20, 5-24, Latin mediatn asked 5-27, 414A3
Venez advice on Canal treaty rptd 7-27, 590C1
Carter clarifies Canal treaty stance 7-29, 589E2-A3
Meets regional ldrs 8-5—8-6; new Canal pact backed, Intl Coffee Fund set 8-6, 606A3-607A1, 608A3
Canal treaty compensatn rptd resolved 8-8, 607B1
Canal treaty reached 8-10, ratificatn seen 8-12, 621A1, 622E2
Sees Carter 9-6; signs Canal treaties 9-7, 677A1
Reagan sees greater Castro 'presence' 9-8, 699B1
Reagan scores rights record 9-8, 699C1
Bunker cites State Dept rights rpt 9-8, 699E1
Sets Oct plebiscite, lauds pacts 9-9, 698G1
Asks OAS rights probe, UN observe pact vote; Linowitz lauds 9-13, 699F1
US debate on treaties continue 9-14, 9-16; rpts John Wayne support 9-20, 716B3-E3
OKs return of pol exiles 9-17, 716F3
'74 US tap rptd 9-20, 716B2, E2
Begins 10-natn Canal treaty tour 9-24, 755D3; completes tour 10-14, 792B2
Panamanian treaty backing grows 9-27, 756B1
Replies to US critics 9-28, 755G3
Lopez: US misinterprets Canal defns statemt 10-4, 754G3
US mil ldrs dispute Cuba, Moscow link 10-10, 792A2
Dole chrgs drug role 10-13; US clears, concedes brother's indictmt 10-13—10-15, 792D1
Clarifies Canal treaties with Carter 10-14, 791A3
Repressn scored by law group 10-14, 809G1
Defends treaties, US 'defns umbrella' 10-20—10-21, 809C2
Lauds Canal plebiscite 10-24, 809B1
Canal plebiscite final vote rptd 10-29, 845A1
Hosts US sens; vows econ, rights reforms 11-9—11-12, 911B2
Angered by drug chrgs 11-13, Dole to get brother's files 11-16, 912C2
TOSE, Leonard
Loses Eagles financial control 8-8, 659A1
TOTENBERG, Nina
Leaks Sup Ct Watergate rule 4-21, 382B2; rpt confrmd 5-23, 406E1
TOTH, Robert
USSR detains 6-11—6-15, expels 6-17; US protests 6-14, 6-17, 474C3
USSR chrgs espionage 7-12, 564E1
Axelrod arrested 9-21, 753C1
TOUCHE Ross & Co.
Sen subcom rpt scores 1-17, 78C3
Merges with Lasser 8-22, 650E2
TOUCH Not the Cat (book)
On best-seller list 9-4, 712F3
TOUFANIAN, Gen. Hassan
Confrms purchase of 7 US AWACS 11-8, 905A3
TOUPALIK, Vlastimil
Hijacks Czech plane 10-11, 848G3

TOURE, Ahmed Sekou (Guinean president)
Amin on '76 death plot 7-4, 512A2
TOURISM—*See TRAVEL*
TOURNEUR, Jacques
Dies 12-19, 1024E3
TOURTELLOT, Arthur Brown
Dies 10-18, 872B3
TOVIN, Jack D.
Sentence cut 2-17, 504E1
TOWE, Peter Milburn
Named Canada amb to US 6-3, 525A3
TOWER, Sen. John G. (R, Tex.)
Sen ethics code adopted 4-1, 251D3
On Carter energy plan 4-20, 293G2, 320D2
Fed Reserve revisns signed 11-1, 878C2
TOWER City, Pa.—*See PENNSYLVANIA*
TOWNES, Charles H.
Laser patent, Nobel prize cited 10-11, 860B1

1978

TORRIJOS Herrera, Moises
US Sen hears Intell Com rpt, drug indictmt unsealed 2-21; denies chrgs 2-22, 120E2
Quits as amb to Spain 3-1, 211E2
TORRIJOS Herrera, Brig. Gen. Omar (Panamanian head of state)
Baker visits 1-3—1-7, 58G1
US Sen com OKs pacts, asks addenda 1-30, 58B1
Carter in TV appeal for treaty 2-1, 58A3
Drug link raised by Dole 2-10; US Sen probes 2-21—2-22, Canal votes rptd unchngd 2-22, 120B2
Moises quits as Spain amb, Hugo replaces 3-1, 211E2
US Sen amends Canal neutrality pact 3-10, 3-13, 177G3-178A1
Scores DeConcini treaty reservatn, Carter placates 3-15; Escobar buys time 3-16, 255B2
Orders Canal pact chngs studied 3-16, 178B2
Initiates diplomatic maneuvers vs DeConcini reservatn 4-6, 4-7, 4-9; Carter warns 4-7, Byrd discounts 4-8, 255E2
DeConcini OKs noninterventn 'understanding' 4-13, 255G3
OKs 2d DeConcini reservatn 4-17, hails Canal pact ratificatn 4-18, 273F1, G2
Amnesties pol exiles 4-18; Arias returns, scores govt 6-10, 463C3
Carter consults on DR electn 5-19, 414C3
Exchngs treaty instrumts with Carter 6-16; Zonian posters score Carter 6-17, 463F2, 464E1
Pol party planned 7-8, 632G1
Natl Assemb elected 8-6; lauds voters, scores Arias 8-7, 632D1
Bars presidency, to keep mil post; backs Royo as pres 9-1, 691F3
Royo elected pres 10-11, 764C3; names backers to Cabt 10-12, 884A2
Gonzalez Revilla leads party 10-12, 884C2
Natl Guard dep cmdr fired 10-16, 884C2

TOSHIBA Corp.
UK joint plant set 8-23, 667C3
TOTAL Group of France
S Africa unit role in UK sanctns-breaking detailed 9-19, 756D1
TOTH, Robert
Denies spy link re Shcharansky 7-11, 541D1
TOUCHE, Ross & Co.
'77 top-paid corp execs ranked 5-15, 364G3
TOURISM—*See TRAVEL*
TOVATT, Ellen
Show-off opens 5-18, 760D3
TOWELI, Ali
Amin ousts 5-3, 331D3
TOWER, Sen. John G. (R, Tex.)
Votes vs Panama Canal neutrality pact 3-16, 177G2
Votes vs 2d Canal pact 4-18, 273B1
Scores Carter forgn policy 5-3, 342F2
Unopposed in primary 5-6, 362F3
Reelected 11-7, 846A2, 848D3, 855C3
TOWNLEY, Mariana Callejas de (Mrs. Michael Vernon)
Scores husband's expulsn 4-10, 266G3
Rptd to be DINA agent 4-21, 371D1
Claims DINA chose husband for Letelier murder, Pinochet urged probe cooperatn 5-2; US sources confirm 5-5, 370F3-371A1
Cites DINA paychecks to husband 5-3, 371E1
Under US protectn 10-18, 795C3

TOWNLEY, Michael Vernon (alias Juan Williams Rose)
US seeks in Letelier murder probe 2-21, Chile: no record 2-24, 146E2
Identified as Letelier murder suspect 3-3—3-9, 188B3-189B1; 3-20, 209B3
Chile OKs US questioning, disputes Williams Rose identity 3-23; takes 5th 4-1, 266B3
Denies murder, scores US 4-6, 266F3
Deported to US 4-8, arraigned 4-10, 266F2
Wife chrgs junta betrayal 4-10, 266G3
Linked to Cuban exiles 4-19, 370B3
Chile friends say extraditn illegal 4-21, 371C1

1979

TORRIJOS Herrera, Brig. Gen. Omar
Canal treaty implementatn effort rptd 6-7, 481C1
Coup plot revealed 10-24, 836D3
Shah quits US for Panama 12-15, US aid motive rptd 12-18, 957C1, B2

TOUCHE Ross & Co.
Urban fiscal standings rptd 3-20, 204A2
Customer suits curbed by Sup Ct 6-18, 499C1
TOUCHE Ross & Co. v. Redington
Case decided by Sup Ct 6-18, 499C1
Case cited by Sup Ct 11-13, 902D1
TOUCHING (book)
Novelist libel case refused by Sup Ct 12-3, 964G1

TOURE, Ahmed Sekou (Guinean president)
In US, gets aid pledge 8-8—8-15, 796B3
TOURISM—*See TRAVEL*
TOVAR, Irene
Backs Brown at Dem Natl Com mtg 11-9, 961D2
TOWE, Peter
Gets US tuna protest 8-31, Atlantic fish pact threatened 9-4, 667F1, C2
TOWER, Sen. John G. (R, Tex.)
Sen GOP Policy Com chrmn 1-23, 71B2
Sees Teng 1-30, 66C1
Shuns Teng 2-2, 83C3, F3
For arms hike link to SALT 8-2, 591B1
Votes vs Hufstedler 11-30, 946G2
TOWNLEY, Mariana Callejas de (Mrs. Michael Vernon)
'75 assassinatn plot cited 1-18, 58E1
TOWNLEY, Michael Vernon (alias Juan Williams Rose)
Letelier murder trial opens 1-9—1-12, 19F2
CIA '71, '73 'interest' rptd 1-11, 19D3
Letelier trial testimony begins 1-15; testifies 1-18—1-24, 57E3, 58C1-A3
Questioning curbed by '78 US-Chile pact 1-23, 75B1
Chile press calls CIA agent 2-7, 114D3
Pinochet rptdly sought false '76 passport 2-9, 114E3-115B1
Credibility debated 2-12—2-13; 3 Cubans convicted 2-14, 114E2
Plea-bargain defended, 3 Cubans sentncd 3-23, 234G2

1980

TORRIJOS Herrera, Gen. Omar
Party wins Panama cncl electns 9-28, 752A2

TORRUELLA, Judge Juan R.
Blocks PR refugee camp 12-18, 988B2
TOSCO Corp.
Exxon buys Arco shale oil project share 5-13, 553B3
TOTAL Petroleum (North America) Ltd.
Vickers Petrol merger set 8-26, 745F2
TOTH, Istvan
Wins Olympic medal 7-22, 624A3
TOUBI, Tewfik
Meets Arafat, 3 W Bank mayors 9-25, 736E3
TOUCHE Ross & Co.
Chrysler viability questioned 2-7, 127A2

TOURE, Ahmed Sekou (Guinean president)
Escapes assassinatn attempt 5-14, 431E3
TOURISM—*See TRAVEL & Tourism*
TOUTLE River (Wash.)
Mt St Helens erupts 5-18, 382C1
TOVROV, Orin
Dies 8-16, 676D3
TOWE, Peter
Signs US acid rain pact 8-5, 603E1
TOWER, Sen. John Goodwin (R, Tex.)
Platform hearings open, chrgs Dems caused US intl decline 1-14, 32B1
FRB banking bill scored 2-4, 113B3
Study faults Iran rescue missn 6-5, 419F1
Retains Sen GOP post 12-2, 915E2
TOWLES, Dr. Jeff
On Jordan injury 5-29, 401F2

TOWNLEY, Michael Vernon (alias Juan Williams Rose)
Letelier case sentnc upheld 9-15, 704A1
Letelier, Moffitt kin awarded $5 mln 11-5, 869F3

1976

TOYO Kogyo Co. Ltd.
US ends car dumping probe 5-4, 321D2
US rates Mazda fuel econ 9-22, 766B2, 767A3

TOYOTA Motor Works, Ltd.
US car dumping chrgs end 5-4, 320F3, 321D2
Australia OKs projects 6-10, 438B3
US rates Corolla fuel econ 9-22, 766A2, 767A3, 769C1
Oct US sales rptd 11-3, 885A3

TOYS
Dem platform text 6-15, 471F2
Peter Hodgson dies 8-6, 892A3
'60-75 consumer spending rptd 11-23, 959G2

TRA, Lt. Gen. Tra Van
Replaced in Saigon city rule 1-21, 54E1

TRACK & Field
Boston Marathon 4-19, 292E3
Bell sets pole-vault mark 5-29, 424D3
Stones sets high jump mark 6-5, 444G3
Hubbard dies 6-23, 524G2
Olympic results 7-23—7-31; death threat, disqualificatns rptd 7-30, 7-31, 562E1, A3, 563B2, 575E3, 576E1

1977

TOWNS, Morris
In NFL draft 5-3, 353B2

TOWNSEND, W. Wayne
Backs ERA 1-18, 59B2

TOXAPHENE—*See PESTICIDES*

TOYE, Jeremy
Ethiopia ousts 4-25, 327C3

TOYO Kogyo Co. Ltd.
Rotary engine work cited 4-12, 409E1

TOYOTA Motor Works, Ltd.
US '76 new-car sales rptd 1-6, 38F3
US import lead cited 4-11, 463G3
Volvo, Saab agree to merge 5-6, 469D3
Toyota tops LA June car sales 9-6, 722A3
US prices hiked 11-24, 932F3

TOYS
Hasbro rpts rebates 1-19, 94E2

TRABERT, Tony
Davis Cup match protests 4-15—4-17, US beaten 4-29—5-1; scores Dibbs 5-1, 353G2, E3

TRACK & Field
Natl Invitatl indoor champ 1-14, 603A1
Milrose Games 1-28, 603A1
LA Times Indoor Games 2-4, 603A1
San Diego Indoor Games 2-19, 603B1
AAU indoor champ 2-25, 602D3
IC4A indoor champ 3-7, 603B1
NCAA indoor champ 3-12, 603B1
Boston Marathon 4-18, 602G3
Penn Relays 4-30, 603C1
IC4A outdoor champ 5-21, 603C1
NCAA outdoor champ 6-3, 603C1
AAU outdoor champ 6-9—6-11, 602A3
US-USSR meet 7-1—7-2, jr meet 7-2—7-3, 602D2

Obituaries
Dodds, Gil 2-3, 164F2

Records & Achievements, Men's
Ariz State U, 800-mtr relay 4-30, 603C1
Bayi, mi run 2-25, 602D3
Doubley, long jump 6-3, 603C1
Drayton, Boston Marathon 4-18, 602G3
Haynes, long jump, triple jump 2-25, 602F3
Kimombwa, 10000-mtr run 6-30, 603D1
Livers, triple jump 7-1—7-2, 602E2
Malley, 3000-mtr steeplechase 6-9—6-11, 602B3
Moses, 400-mtr hurdles 6-11, 602A3
Munyala, 3000-mtr steeplechase 6-9—6-11, 602B3
Piskulyn, triple jump 7-1—7-2, 602F2
Pyke, 20-km walk 7-1—7-2, 602E2
Quax, 5000-mtr run 7-5, 603D1
Scully, 2-mi walk 2-25, 602E2
Trofimenko, pole vault 7-1—7-2, 602E2
Yaschenko, high jump 7-2, 602G2

Records & Achievements, Women's
Ashford, 100-mtr dash, 200-mtr dash 6-9—6-11, 602A3, C3
Ayer, 400-mtr hurdles 6-9—6-11, 602C3
Brodock, mi walk 2-25, 602E3
Bryant, 440-yd dash 1-28, 500-mtr run 2-4, 500-yd run 2-19, 220-yd dash 2-25, 602G3, 603A1
Forde, 440-yd dash 1-14, 603A1
Frederick, 60-yd hurdles 2-25, 602F3
LaPlante, 60-yd hurdles 2-25, 602F3
Lutz, 2-mi run 2-25, 602D3
Neppel, 10000-mtr run 6-9—6-11, 602C3

1978

Wife rptd to be DINA agent 4-21, 371D1
Osorio autopsy details leaked by US 4-21, 371F1
Chrgd 4-26; probe cooperatn, plea bargaining rptd 4-27, 370A3, 371A1
Implicated in Latin bombings 4-26, 371B1
Wife claims DINA chose for Letelier murder, Pinochet urged probe cooperatn 5-2; US sources confirm 5-5, 370F3-371A1
Govt denies DINA agent, wife cites paychecks 5-3, 371E1
Pinochet 'disloyalty' seen by ex-DINA men 5-23, 452G1
US reveals Letelier murder details 6-2, 451G3
US amb recall, Chile inactn re Paraguay visa info linked 6-23, 495F3
Judge to study plea-bargain pact 8-3, 614C1
Admits placing Letelier bomb, plea-bargain OKd 8-11, 647A3
Under US protectn 10-18, 795B3
CIA cleared in Letelier murder 10-18, 795C3
Contreras hints CIA tie 10-24, 1014E3

TOWNS—*See CITIES, Suburbs & Towns*

TOWNSEND, Ray
In NBA draft 6-9, 457G2

TOYO Kohan Co.
Australia iron imports set 5-30, 411F1

TOYOTA Motor Works Ltd.
US car prices hiked 4-14, 283F2
US '78 import price hike rptd 7-17, 665E1
Aug export drop rptd 9-13, 694D2
Ford Pinto sales rptd up 9-14, 722G1
US prices hiked, $ drop linked 10-8; Nov US sales rptd down 12-6, 935F3

TOYS
Mattel offcls indicted 2-16, 116D2
CPSC OKs sharp-edge tests 3-10, 264G3
Water toy recall set 4-13, 348F1
'77 indus profit drop rptd 5-8, 325A3
CPSC proposes small size ban 10-5, 769C3
FTC children's ad probe curbed 11-3; stay denied, probe affirmed 11-17, 941A3

TR-1 (spy plane)—*See ARMAMENTS—Aircraft*

TRACK & Field
AIAW chngs scholarship rules 1-7—1-11, 40B3
Muhammad Ali Invitatl 1-7, 76F2
Natl Invitatl Indoor Champ 1-13—1-14, 76C2
Dartmouth Relays 1-15, 76A3
Millrose Games 1-27, 76A3
Jenner 2d in Sullivan vote 2-7, 780F2
AAU indoor champ 2-24, 600C3
Rono sets 4 world marks 4-8—6-27, 600E2
Boston Marathon 4-17, 692G2
AAU outdoor champ 6-8—6-10, 600A3
AAU suspends 4 stars 6-23, 692E2
US-USSR meet 7-7—7-8, jr meet 7-8—7-9, 692B3

Obituaries
Ray, Joie 5-13, 440D3

Records & Achievements, Men's
Ashford, 200-m dash 7-8, 692B3
Belger, 880-yd run 1-13, 76E2
Beyer, shot put 7-6, 692G3
Buerkle, indoor mile 1-13, Wanamaker Mile 1-27, 76D2, B3
Buerkle, Wanamaker Mile 1-27, 76B3
Carter, jr shot put 6-25, 692G3
Decker, 1000-yd run 2-4, 692E3
Edwards, 100-m dash, 200-m dash 6-1—6-4, 6-8—6-10, 600A3, F3
Frazier, indoor 500-m run 1-7, 76G2
Gardenkrans, discus 6-1—6-4, 600G3
Jacobs, indoor high jump 1-27, 76A3
Joy, indoor high jump 1-13, 76F2
Livers, triple jump 6-1—6-4, 600G3
McTear, indoor 60-yd dash 1-7, 1-27, 76G2, B3; 2-24, 600C3
Myslivsev, 20-km walk 5-12, 692F3
Nehemiah, indoor 60-yd high hurdles 1-27, 76B3; 110-m hurdles 6-8—6-10, 600B3
Ripley, pole vault 6-8—6-10, 600B3
Rono, 5000-m run 4-8, 3000-mtr steeplechase 5-13, 6-1—6-4, 10000-m run 6-11, 3000-m run 6-27, 600F2, G3
Scully, 20-km walk 6-8—6-10, 600C3
Shipp, indoor 60-yd high hurdles 1-13, 76E2
Stones, indoor high jump 2-24, 600E3
Treacy, indoor 3-mi run 3-10, 692D3
Tully, pole vault 1-7, 76G2; 3-11, 5-19, 692D3, F3; 6-1—6-4, 600G3
US, 1600-m relay 7-8, 692B3
US jr, 400-m relay 7-8, 692C3
Yaschenko, indoor high jump 3-12, 692E3

Records & Achievements, Women's
Anderson, long jump 6-8—6-10, 600C3
Brill, indoor high jump 2-24, 600E3
Brodock, indoor mile walk 2-24, 600D3
Forde, indoor 500-m run 1-15, 76A3; 400-m dash 6-8—6-10, 600B3
Huntley, indoor high jump 1-14, 76F2
Koch, 400-m dash 7-2, 692G3

1979

Sentenced 5-11, 369E2
Chile bars US extraditn request 10-1, 750A2
Contreras funds shift probed 10-9, 772E2

TOWNS—*See CITIES, Suburbs & Towns*

TOWNSEND, Peter
2d in Eur Championship 9-9, 970D1

TOWNSHEND, Peter
Kids Are Alright released 6-15, 820E1

TOYO Kogyo Co. Ltd
Ford buys share 9-7, 745D3

TOYS
Mattel to buy Westn Publishing 1-9, 16B1
Mattel recalls space toys 1-11; ACT: recall ineffective 2-27, 308A3
CPG settles FTC chrg 5-23, 596G1
CPSC adopts small toy ban 6-17, 596B2
Mattel bid accepted, rejected by Macmillan 8-30, 942B3

TOZZI, Giorgio
Most Happy Fella opens 10-11, 956E3

TRACK & Field
Nehemiah sets 5 world marks 1-20—5-6, 911A1, B1
AAU bans S Africans from Boston Marathon 4-12, 911D3
Coe sets 3 world marks 7-5—8-15, 911A1, B1, E1
7 E Eur women banned by IAAF 10-26, 911F3
Coe, Moses expense paymts probe rptd 11-12, Coe named to UK Olympic team 11-13, 956A2
Stones reinstated by AAU 11-28, 956D1
ITA stars cleared for US meets 11-29, 956F1

Events
AAU indoor champ 2-23—2-24, 911D2
AAU outdoor champ 6-15—6-17, 911G1
Boston Marathon 4-16, 911C3
IC4A indoor champ 3-3—3-4, 911F2
IC4A outdoor champ 5-20—5-21, 911A3
Millrose Games 2-9, 911C2
NCAA indoor champ 3-8—3-10, 911F2
NCAA outdoor champ 6-2—6-3, 911B3
NYC Marathon 10-21, 911E3
Pan Am Games 7-1—7-15, 798G2
Penn Relays 4-27—4-28, 911A3
Phila Track Classic 1-19, 911C1
US Olympic Invitatnl 1-20, 911C1

Records & Achievements, Men's
Coe, 800-m run 7-5, mile run 7-17, 1500-m run 8-15, 911A1, B1, E1
Mennea, 200-m dash 9-12, 799A2
Nehemiah, indoor 55-m, 60-yd high hurdles 1-20, indoor 50-yd high hurdles 2-2, indoor 50-m high hurdles 2-3, 110-m high hurdles 5-6, 911A1, B1
Phila Pioneer Club, indoor sprint medley 2-23, 911E2
Rodgers, marathon 4-16, 911C3
Villanova U, 6000-m relay 4-28, 911A3
Virgin, 10000-m run 6-17, 911A2

Records & Achievements, Women's
Ashford, 60-yd dash 2-23, 100-m dash 6-16, 911A2, E2
Benoit, marathon 4-16, 911D3
Brodock, 5000-m walk 6-16, 10000-m walk 6-17, 911C2
Cheeseborough, indoor 220-yd dash 2-23, 911E2
LaPlante, 100-m hurdles 6-17, 911B2
Makeyeva, 400-m hurdles 7-27, 799E1
Shea, 10000-m run 6-16, 911B2
Sidler, shot put 6-17, 911C2
Waitz, marathon 10-21, 911E3
Young, indoor 60-yd hurdles 2-23, 911D2

1980

TOWNS—*See CITIES*

TOWNSEND, E. Reginald
Executed 4-22, 353A2

TOWNSEND, James B.
In Okla US House primary; runoff set 8-26, 683B1

TOXIC-Shock Syndrome—*See MEDICINE--Diseases*

TOYO Kogyo Co. Ltd.
Ford-Toyota talks rptd 7-9, 556A3

TOYOTA Motor Works Ltd.
UAW pres asks US plants 1-13, 35C2
US Jan sales rptd up 2-5, 127B3
US export curb set 2-18, Fraser backs 2-19, 127E1
US prices hiked 2-20, 288A1
Ford Pinto trial evidence cited 3-13, 186C1
US raises truck import duty 5-20, 384A2
Raises prices 2.8% 5-27, 482A1
Spain investmt talks rptd 6-4, 467C3
Ford productn talks revealed 7-9; Ford rejectn rptd 7-14, 556G2-A3
Canada min in Japan 8-2—8-11, 618B2
SEAT talks rptd 10-8, 793A3*
ITC bars Japan import curbs 11-10, 866F3

TOYS
'79 Fortune 500 data rptd 5-5, 291D1
CBS unit toy gym recall set 6-2, 703G2
'Cootie' inventor dies 9-8, 756C2

TRABERT, Tony
Replaced as Davis Cup captain 9-7, 692A1

TRACINDA Corp.
Kerkorian sues Columbia 9-30, Columbia countersues 10-2, 10-20, 906E2

TRACK & Field
Decker makes comeback 1-1—7-12, 891A1
Davenport on US Olympic bobsled team 2-24, 154C3
IAAF OKs ex-pros for intl meets 3-11; TAC bans from US Olympic trials 6-16, judge voids 6-25, 891F2
USC transcript scandal rptd 3-18, 469B3
Ruiz Boston Marathon win disputed 4-21; '79 NYC run invalidated 4-25, Garreau awarded Boston title 4-29, 527D2
NCAA aid limit case declined by Sup Ct 5-12, 426B3
Boyle bars Olympic participatn 5-28, 421D1
Anderson denies steroid chrg 6-28, 891D2
TAC OKs paid amateur meets; ATFA formatn cited 6-28, 891C3
Moscow Olympic results 7-24—8-1; Australian triple jump disallowed 7-25, IAAF backs Sovts 7-31, 589B1, F1, B3, 623G3-624C2
Pac-10 punishes USC in transcript scandal 8-11, 875F1

Events
Astrodome Invitatnl 2-16, 891D1
Boston Marathon 4-21, 527A2
Cherry Blossom run 3-30, 527G2
Drake Relays 4-25—4-26, 892F2
IC4A indoor champ 3-8—3-9, 892C2
IC4A outdoor champ 5-24—5-25, 892A2
L'eggs Mini Marathon 5-31, 527A3
Millrose Games 2-8, 891D1, 892E2
Moscow Olympics 7-24—8-1, 589B1, F1, 623G3-624C2
Natl indoor champ 2-29—3-1, 892D1
Natl outdoor champ 6-13—6-16, 892B1
NCAA indoor champ 3-14—3-15, 891F3
NCAA outdoor champ 6-5—6-7, 891G3
NYC Marathon 10-26, 890E3
Penn Relays 4-24—4-25, 892D2
San Diego Invitatnl 2-23, 891E1
US Olympic Trials 6-21—6-29, 891F1

Obituaries
Owens, Jesse 3-31, 280E1
Walsh, Stella 12-4, 1004F3

Records & Achievements (Men's)
Coe, 1000-m run 7-1, 589G1
Dombrowski, long jump 7-28, 589B1
Hall, pole vault 6-7, 892A1
Kozakiewicz, pole vault 7-30, 589C1
Marsh, 3000-m steeplechase 6-28, 891B2
Nyambui, NCAA indoor double 3-15, 891F3
Ovett, 1500-m 8-27, 892G1
Ovett, mile run 7-1, 1500-m run (tie) 7-15, 589A2
Phila Pioneers, indoor sprint medley relay 2-29, 892F1
Rodgers, 10 mile run 3-30, 527G2
Salazar, NYC Marathon 10-26, 890F3
Wessig, high jump 8-1, 589D1

1976

TRADE, Foreign—*See FOREIGN Trade*
TRAFFIC International Corp.
Arab boycott rpt released 10-19, 786D1
TRAGER, Dr. William
Cultures malaria parasite 6-1, 423A3
TRAIN, Russell E.
Urges toxic chem law 2-26, 171E2
Issues fuel-econ ratings 9-22, 766G1
Gas-lead deadlines eased 9-24, 767B3
Lauds NATO air quality progrms 10-16, 934D1
Orders Chrysler recall 12-10, 942F3
Backs coyote-poison ban 12-21, 980C2
On Nantucket oil spill 12-22, 968E3
On A-blast cancer threat 12-27, 992G1
TRANSCENDENTAL Meditation (TM)
Suit seeks bar in NJ schools 2-25, 203C2
TRANS International Forwarders
Arab boycott rpt released 10-18, 786B1
TRANSIT, Union, Amalgamated (AFL-CIO)
NJ bus strike 3-9—3-22, 220B2
NY strike averted 4-1, 235E3

TRANSKEI, Xhosa Republic of the
Citizenship bill publshd 5-26, S Africa Parlt debates 6-7, 428F2
Assemb OKs independnc 7-27, 592A2
Independnc party wins electn 9-29, 813G1
Sigcau named pres, Matanzima prime min 10-19, 813A2
US bars recognitn 10-21; OAU, UN score 10-22, 813F1
2 actors expelled 10-24, 813B2
UN bars forgn contacts 10-26, 799F1
Gets independnc 10-26, 813A1
S. Africa police ousted 11-11, 927D3
Lesotho border rptd closed 11-13, 927E3
UN chrgs S Africa pressure vs Lesotho 12-22, 954B3
Listed as not free 12-22, 977B3
Rioting rptd 12-30, 1010C2
TRANSLINEAR, Inc.
Chrgs Duvalier asked bribe 3-2, 267B3
TRANSOCEANIC Shipping Co.
Arab boycott rpt released 10-20, 786B2
TRANSPORTATION—*See also specific types*
US budget proposals 1-21, 63F1, 64A3, 65F3
Dec, '75 CPI 1-21, 90D1
'74, '75 food transport costs rise linked 2-11, 216G1
Feb CPI up 3-19, 215B2
Fscl '77 US budget estimate tables 231B1, 358C2
'75 fuel use up 4-4, 285C1
ERDA stresses energy conservation 4-19, 284G3
Jan-Mar CPI up 4-21, 306C2
Ford urges regulatory reform 5-13, 346G3
Apr CPI rptd up 5-21, 375F1
Dem platform text 6-15, 470A2, 474G1, E2
1st ¼ labor costs rptd 6-18, 494G1
Cong OKs '77 funds 8-4, 646A2; Ford signs 8-14, 982F1
GOP platform text 8-18, 603A1, 605G3, 606F2, 607D1
Cong sets '77 budget levels chart 9-16, 706B2
NE govs seek plan 11-14, 864G3
Oct '75-76 CPI rptd 11-19, 885A1
Venez, UK pact signed 11-23, 929D3
Adams vs deregulatn 12-14, 936G1, G3
Nov '75-76 CPI rptd 12-21, 958A2
Mass Transit
Ford State of Union message 1-19, 37F3, 39D2
US budget proposals 1-21, 65G3
San Fran strike 3-31—5-8, 348C3
NY strike averted 4-1, 235C3
NYC fare cut rejected 4-26, 308F1
Road aid extensn curbed 5-5, 919A3
Dem platform text 6-15, 474G1
Carter lauds Eur 6-23, 451A3
Carter urges fed aid 6-29, 468E1
Cong OKs '77 funds 8-4, 646E2; Ford signed 8-14, 982F1

1977

TRACTMAN, Lawrence
Tried in absentia 2-10, 100B1
TRADE, Foreign—*See FOREIGN Trade*
TRADE Commission, U.S. International—*See under U.S. GOVERNMENT*
TRADE Unions, International Confederation of Free (ICFTU)
UK unions to boycott S Africa 1-13, 29F2
S Africa boycott fails 1-21, 67A3
Czech scored re dissidents 1-24, 82A3
TRAFALGAR House Investments Ltd.
Beaverbrook chain purchased 6-30, 526F3-527B1
TRAFFIC—*See ROADS*
TRAFFICANTE Jr., Santo
Assassinatn com questns 3-16, 228E2
TRAGLIA, Luigi Cardinal
Dies 11-22, 952F3
TRAIN, Russell E.
A-plant radiatn limits set 1-6, 95C2
Bars PCB dischrgs 1-19, 95E1
Replaced as EPA admin 3-4, 211E1
TRAINS—*See RAILROADS*
TRANQUILIZERS—*See NARCOTICS & Dangerous Drugs*
TRANS-Alaska Pipeline—*See 'Oil & Gas' under ALASKA*
TRANSAMERICA Corp.
EEOC Occidental suit time-limit barred 6-20, 517D1
TRANSCENDENTAL Meditation (TM)
US data rptd 4-26—4-29, 470D3
NJ schools ban 10-20, 845D3
TRANSCO Cos.
Transcontinental Gas Pipe Line Corp.
FPC OKs emergency gas sales 1-14, 37B1
FPC OKs gas reserve drawdown 1-20, 54D1
Asks 'nonessential' gas cutoffs 1-28, 75D3
FPC orders Westn gas transfer 2-3, 91A3
TRANSFER Payments—*See INCOMES*

TRANSKEI, Xhosa Republic of the
Refugee deaths rptd 1-11, 47E1
3 oppositn party members freed 2-25, 160C3
Party cong opens 3-8, 350E2
Assemb opens 3-9, 350E2
Mandela travel OKd 5-24, 400A1
Gabon bars reps to OAS summit 6-22, 512F2
S Africa shantytown demolitn scored 8-9, 640C1

TRANSPORTATION—*See also specific types*
DOT issues future trends rpt 1-15, 58D2
Ford '78 budget proposals 1-17, 32F2, 33C1
Weather effects rptd 1-19; CAB, ICC act 1-19, 1-24, 53C3, 54E1, C2
Carter budget revisns 2-22, 125A2, G2
'76 wage hikes rptd 3-3, 154E2
'76 energy use rptd 3-13, 196A2
Carter vows surface transit deregulatn 3-16, 190E3
Feb CPI rise rptd 3-18, 215D1
Carter energy plan 4-18, 4-20, 289F1, 290C1, 295A1; fact sheet 291C2-F3, 293F3
Mar CPI rptd 4-21, 324C2
Sup Ct remands EPA appeals cases 5-2, 406E2
'60-61, '72-73 family spending compared 5-10, 423D2
'76 deaths rptd 5-12, 412E2
Apr CPI rptd 5-22, 406B3
May CPI rptd 6-22, 482C1
June CPI rptd 7-21, 554D2
July CPI rptd 8-19, 651F1
2d ¼ wage gains rptd 8-31, 704A2
'76 cargo thefts rptd 11-17, 919C1

Mass Transit
Ford State of Union message 1-12, 13G2
Ford '78 budget proposals 1-17, 33C1, G1
Carter budget revisions 2-22, 125G2, C3
Adams asks new projects delay, backs more aid to cities 2-25, 213A3
Carter energy plan 4-18, 4-20, 291D3, 295A1; reactn 4-21, 320B2, F2
Carter defends energy plan 4-22, 321A2
Sup Ct curbs Port Auth aid 4-27, 382G3
Energy plan scored 5-19, 6-2, 443E1, B2
Detroit workers strike 7-6, 558G2

1978

LaPlante, indoor 60-yd high hurdles 2-24, 100-mtr hurdles 6-8—6-10, 600C3, D3
Lutz, indoor mile run 2-24, 600E3
Merrill, 3000-m run 6-8—6-10, 600C3
Sidler, shot put 6-8—6-10, 600C3
Tenn State U, 640-yd relay 2-24, indoor sprint medley 6-8—6-10, 600B3, E3
Webb, indoor 2-mi run 2-24, 600E3

TRACK Record (race horse)
Loses Preakness 5-20, 539E1
TRADE, Foreign—*See FOREIGN Trade*
TRADE Commission, U.S. International—*See under U.S. GOVERNMENT*
TRADE and Development, UN Conference on—*See under UNITED Nations*
TRADEMARKS—*See PATENTS & Trademarks*
TRADE Union Confederation, European—*See EUROPEAN Trade Union Confederation*
TRADE Unions, International Confederation of Free (ICFTU)
USSR dissident union backed 1-27, 180C1
Tunisia labor ldr's release asked 1-31, 170E1
Tunisia bars rep 7-16, 671E1
ORIT votes Chile trade boycott 11-24; Chile, US reactn 12-6—12-15, 1014E1
TRAFFICANTE, Santo
Cited at JFK death hearings 9-26, 9-27, testifies 9-28, 750B1-C2
TRAILS—*See PARKS & Recreation Areas; specific names*
TRAINS—*See RAILROADS*
TRANSAMERICA Corp.
Top United Artists execs quit 1-13, 1-16, Albeck named pres 1-17, 75G2-B3
TRANSCO Cos. Inc.
Coal gasificatn plant financing plan submitted 6-2, 471A3
TRANSFER Payments—*See INCOMES*

TRANSKEI, Xhosa Republic of the
Cape Town shanty demolitn begun 1-16, 39B1
Breaks S Africa ties re land claim 4-10, Vorster regrets 4-11; map 258A3
S Africa paymts for favorable press coverage alleged 4-17, 377D3
S Africa ends mil training 4-28; non-aggressn pact canceled 5-10, 617B3
S Africa Methodist church rptd banned 5-27, 617C3
Blacks denied S African passports, citizenship 6-9, 6-12, 536B3, F3
Black S African pol support polled 6-15, 6-22, 536A3
Arab loan rptd 8-22, 885G3
UN racism conf vs recognitn 8-26, 676A2
PRES Sigcau dies 12-1, 1032E3
TRANS-Mex Lines
FMC rebate chrgs rptd setld 10-1, 752G3
TRANSPLANTS—*See MEDICINE & Health-Surgery*

TRANSPORTATION—*See also specific types*
Carter budget proposals 1-23, 44F2, 47G2; table 45E2
Adams issues policy statemt 2-8, 109B1
Adams backs more Conrail aid 2-15, 224D3
Cong '79 budget target res cleared 5-17, 385F1
Carter plans budget cuts 5-25, 404A3
2d ¼ employmt cost rpt cites 8-30, 680B2
Borg-Warner, Firestone to merge 11-28, 935E1
Environmtlists urge natl policy 12-20, 1009F1

Mass Transit
Carter State of Union Message 1-19, 32A1
Carter budget proposals 1-23, 47A3
Adams issues policy statemt 2-8, 109E1
Carter unveils urban-aid plan 3-27, 217D3, 218A1, C1
S Bronx offered US aid 4-12, 285G1
Boston strike 7-6, 565A2
DC strike 7-19—7-25, 565G1-A2
Cong actn cited 10-15, 784G3
Carter signs funds 11-8, 875D2

1979

TRADE, Foreign—*See FOREIGN Trade*
TRADE and Development, UN Conference on—*See under UNITED Nations*
TRADEMARKS—*See PATENTS & Trademarks*
TRADE Unions, International Confederation of Free (ICFTU)
ORIT drops trade boycott of Chile, Nicaragua, Cuba 1-15—1-16, 28C3
TRAFELET v. Thompson
Case refused by Sup Ct 10-9, 784G1
TRAFFICANTE, Santos
House com suspects JFK death link 3-16, 204E3
House com final rpt cites 7-17, 538B1
TRAFFICANTE v. Metropolitan Life
Racial 'steering' suits allowed by Sup Ct 4-17, 325C3
TRAGEDY (recording)
On best-seller list 3-7, 174D1; 4-4, 271D2
TRAGESER v. Libbie Rehabilitation
Case refused by Sup Ct 6-18, 499E2
TRAILWAYS Inc.
Holiday Inns completes sale 8-21, 682E3
TRAIN Dispatchers Association, American (ATDA) (AFL-CIO)
Carter averts strike 5-8, contract accord reached 5-31, 598E2
TRANSAMERICA Corp.
Interway bidding won 5-29, 560B2
Investors suits vs advisers curbed by Sup Ct 11-13, 902B1
Transamerica Computer Corp.
IBM wins trust suit 10-18, 851F2
TRANSAMERICA Mortgage Advisors v. Lewis
Case decided by Sup Ct 11-13, 901G3
TRANSCO Cos. Inc.
Mex natural gas purchased 10-18, 814F3
TRANSFER Payments—*See INCOMES*
TRANSKEI, Xhosa Republic of the
Freedom House lists as partly free 12G3
Matanzima elected pres 2-19, 215D3
Venda declared independent 9-13, 732G1
TRANSPLANTS—*See MEDICINE-Surgery*

TRANSPORTATION
Carter budget proposals 1-22, 45B1; table 42E2
US, Mex sign cooperatn pact 2-16, 124D3
Carter proposes regulatory reform 3-25, 230G1
US-Taiwan relatns bill signed 4-10, 259B3
GATT pact signed, equipmt tariff cuts seen 4-12, 273A2
Transamerica to buy Interway 5-29, 560C2
Truckers strike 6-7—6-15, 462D3
A-waste rules set 6-15, 610C1
Gelco to buy CTI Intl 7-16, 560D2
NY, NJ bond issues OKd 11-6, 846B2, G3
'80 Transport Dept funds clear Cong 11-15, 11-19, Carter signs 11-30, 920C1
Goldschmidt threatens Chicago aid loss 11-20, 983F3

Mass Transit
Carter budget proposals 1-22, 45A2
Adams outlines urban-aid policy 2-13, 129B3
Carter asks oil tax fund, fuel-saving measures 4-5, 250C3, F3
Carter seeks oil tax fund 4-10, 263F2
Cong gets oil tax plan 4-26, 301D1
Calif odd-even gas rationing exemptn 5-9, 342F2
Diesel fuel shortage seen 5-18, 361B3
Diesel fuel allocatn rules adopted 5-25, 395C2

1980

Woodward, high jump 6-7, 892A1
Yifter, Olympic 'distance double' 7-27, 8-1, 589D1
Records & Achievements (Women's)
Anderson, long jump 6-28, 891D2
Bryant, indoor 440-yd dash 2-29, 892D1
Decker, outdoor mile 1-1, indoor 1500-m 2-8, indoor mile 2-16, 800-yd run 2-23, outdoor 1500-m 7-12, 891A1
Hightower, 60-yd hurdles 2-8, 892E2
LA Naturite TC, 640-yd relay 2-29, 829E1
Ottey, indoor 220-yd dash 2-29, 892E1
Sullivan, 10 mile run 3-30, 527G2
Tenn State, mile relay 2-8, 892F2
Waitz, 6.2 km run 5-31, 527A3; marathon 10-26, 890G3

TRADE, Foreign—*See FOREIGN Trade*
TRADE Commission, U.S. International—*See under U.S. GOVERNMENT*
TRADEMARKS—*See PATENTS & Trademarks*
TRAILWAYS Inc.
Fla fares cut 7-1, 558D2
TRAMMELL, Alan
AL batting ldr 10-6, 926F3
Wins Golden Glove Award 12-6, 926D1
TRAMMEL v. U.S.
Case decided by Sup Ct 2-27, 188B2
TRANQUILIZERS—*See NARCOTICS*
TRANSAMERICA Corp.
Harvey apptmt cited 12-12, 986A3
TRANSBRASIL Airlines
Jet crash kills 54 4-12, 527G3
TRANSCONTINENTAL Gas Pipeline Corp. v. FERC
Case refused by Sup Ct 3-3, 210A2
TRANSIT Union, Amalgamated (AFL-CIO)
NYC strike starts, issues detailed 4-1; fined 4-8, 267D3, 268B1-G1
NYC setlmt OKd 4-11, 289A3

TRANSKEI, Xhosa Republic of the
Econ aid need rptd 2-8, 134F2
S Africa rptd planning consolidatn, ties resumptn rptd asked 2-9, 134G2-A3
Ciskei advised vs statehood 2-12, 134B2
Port St Johns transfer cited 3-27, 278E1
TRANSOCEAN Oil Inc.
Sale to Mobil Oil rptd 8-26, 745E2

TRANSPORTATION
Copper futures trading limited 1-24, 69C1
Carter budget proposals 1-28, 72G3; table 70E1
Carter revised budget proposals 3-31, 244D1
Puget Sound ferry strike ends 4-16, 308B3
Mex-Canada ventures agreed 5-27, 409D2
GOP platform adopted 7-15, 535C3, 537C1
Brit Rail plans sales 7-15, 544E1
Pullman, Wheelabrator merger 9-25, 784G2
Islamic econ conf 11-4—11-6, 865C1

Mass Transit
State of State messages 1-2—2-6, 270C1-B3; 1-8, 1-9, 1-15, 483D3, 484F1
Carter budget proposals 1-28, 72G3; table 70E1
San Fran fare hike proposal cited 3-8, 187B1
Carter anti-inflatn plan sets fed spending cuts 3-14, 201B1
Carter revised budget proposals 3-31, 244D1

1976

GOP platform text 8-18, 607A2
Ford, Carter debate 10-22, 801E3
NE govs seek plan 11-14, 865A1

TRANSPORTATION Parts Co.
Chrgd re Arab boycott 10-20, 786F1
Chrgd re Arab boycott 11-3, 986C3
TRANSPORT of New Jersey
14-day strike ends 3-22, 220G1
TRANSPORT Workers Union of America (AFL-CIO)
NY strike averted 4-1, 235D3
TRANSSEXUALS
Richards barred from US Open 8-27, 716E1
Sup Ct bars review of teacher firing 10-18, 867B3
TRANS World Airlines Inc (TWA)
Howard Hughes dies 4-5, 336C1
Ct voids '75 route swap 6-30, CAB overrules 11-19, 992E2
Croats hijack jet in US 9-10—9-12, 685A1
Tillinghast sets retiremt, Smart named 9-22, 892F1
Sup Ct bars review of '73 liability case 10-12, 848B3
Pregnancy bias ruling rptd 10-14, 943A3
Ford rejcts transatlantic plan 12-28, 992D2
TRANS World Corp.
Trans World Airlines Inc.—*See separate listing*
TRAORE, Lt. Col. Moussa
At France-Africa summit 5-10—5-11, 355G2
Single party formed 9-21, 1013E1
TRAORE, Zoumana
Upper Volta labor min 2-9, 269D3
TRAPSHOOTING—*See SHOOTING*

TRAVEL
Argentina tourism soars 1-9, 96A3; 2-27, 212C3
US Jews cancel Brazil tours 1-15, 27G2
Clay Cong bills questnd 3-23, 247E1
Italy sets $ deposits 5-5, 365G3
USSR chrgs US visa curbs violate CSCE 5-25—5-28, 407F3
US tourism to Jamaica down 6-20, 522A2
US researcher scores Sovt visa denial 7-3, 540B3
Govs vs call for US dept 7-6, 493A1
Richard Joseph dies 9-30, 970B2
US Cong expenses probe ends 10-27, 981F3
US, Czech ease curbs 11-3, 946E1
Grenada tourism rptd down 12-7, 925F1
US rpts post-Helsinki gains 12-8, 934B2

1977

NYC blackout halts subways 7-13—7-14, 537F2
Carter on gas-tax plan 7-22, 575B2
Sen OKs fed employe van-pooling 9-13, 703F1
Chicago funds OKd 9-19, 778D3
Oil wellhead tax funding debated 9-21, 757A2
Commuter line aid bill signed 11-16, 900A1

TRANSPORTATION, Department of—*See under U.S. GOVERNMENT*
TRANSPORT Workers Union of America (AFL-CIO)
EEOC suit rptd 3-15, 279C2
TRANSSEXUALS
Richards sex test rejctd 4-12, 354C1
Ct OKs Richards US Open play 8-17, 787C2
TRANS World Airlines Inc. (TWA)
Indicted for rate-fixing 2-3, 93F2
Rpts paymts, rebates 2-8, 94A2
Sup Ct bars tour case review 3-7, 211D2
'76 Croat hijackers convctd 5-5, 1 sentncd 5-12, 451A3
CAB 'no-frills' rule review denied 5-16, 419C2
'On-time' ads curbed 6-13, 463D2
Laker 'Skytrain' svc OKd 6-13, 500G2
Employees religious rights limited 6-13, 517C3
UK air svc pact set 6-22, 500G1
'76 Croat hijackers sentncd 7-20, 642A2
US-UK fare cut sought 8-1, 593E1
CAB acts on NY-London budget fare 9-9, 9-15, Carter overrules 9-26, 860E2
CAB procedures case review refused 10-3, 760B3
TRANS World Corp.
Canteen Corp.
Paymts, rebates rptd 2-8, 94C2
Hilton International Co.
Paymts rptd 2-8, 94C2
Trans World Airlines Inc.—*See separate listing*
TRANSYLVANIAN Alps
Quake hits Rumania 3-4, 204F1
TRAORE, Zoumana
Replaced as labor min 1-14, 183B2
TRAUBE, Klaus R.
Phone tap rptd 2-27; cleared of chrgs 3-16, 259B3
Baader trial adjourned 3-17, 260D1
Dirnhofer arrested 12-1, 968E1

TRAVEL
Yugo passport rules protested 2-2, 139B3
US, other tourists airlifted from Tanzania 2-6, 2-7, 106E1
Cuba rptd ready for US tourists 2-8, 181D1
Greek '76 paymts gap narrows 2-10, 135B1
Asia '76 econ growth rptd 2-16, 147D2
Carter for eased curbs 2-23, 126C2; 3-17, 186G1
TWA tour case review barred 3-7, 211D2
US to lift bans for Americans 3-9, 172F3
Iran, Pak, Turkey sign pact 3-12, 190C2
Canada '76 paymts deficit rptd 3-16, 218D2
US eases Cuba currency curbs 3-25, 283E2
US Sen ethics code adopted 4-1, 251B3
Cuba welcomes US tourists 4-9, 283D1
Sovt unionists denied US visas 4-16, 306F2
Portugal tourism up 4-20, 331A1
US OKs Cuba tours 5-13, cruise ship sails 5-15, 390F1
US Southeast boom rptd 5-16, 384A3
US scores Sovt bloc on visas 6-6, 473D1
Peru tourism disrupted 6-15—6-17, 488A3
Mex tourism income up 6-17, 528E1
Italy lauds US open door 7-25—7-27, 581E2
Visa curbs to US eased 8-17, 667D2
E-W Ger talks set 10-5, 984E1
Medit natns reach pollutn pact 10-21, 876E2
Bulgaria, US ease limits 11-9, 989E1
ERA econ boycotts rptd 11-14, 918B1

1978

Statistics
'64-78 spending pattern chngs reflected in new CPIs 222D2
Jan, Feb CPIs 2-27, 3-28, 222E1, F1
May CPI 6-30, 507A1
June CPI hike rptd 7-28, 607G1
July CPI 8-29, 679B3
Aug CPI 9-26, 752D1
Sept CPI 10-27, 864D1
Oct CPI 11-28, 918E2
Nov '77-78 CPI 12-22, 1003A2

TRANSPORTATION, Department of—*See under U.S. GOVERNMENT*
TRANSPORTATION Safety Board, National—*See under U.S. GOVERNMENT—NATIONAL Transportation Safety Board*
TRANSPORTATION Union, United (AFL-CIO)
New RR pact set 7-21, 565D1
Conrail gets crew-size pact 9-14, 700C1
TRANSSEXUALITY
Ct awards disability pay 2-16, 327D2
TRANS World Airlines Inc. (TWA)
Ex-chrmn Pierson dies 1-12, 96C3
LA gets 2-carrier London svc 6-9, 570D1
3-class svc starts 10-15, 812D2
US, W Ger air svc pact expanded 10-25, 831G1
Va '74 crash claims setld 11-4, 908C2
3-class svc dropped 12-6, 1007E3
TRANS World Corp.
Canteen Corp.
Ford kickbacks alleged 4-25, 390A3
Hilton International Co.
Hilton withdraws Amer Medicorp bid 1-10, 66A3
Australia hotel bombed 2-12, 110E1 ★
Trans World Airlines Inc.—*See separate listing*
TRAORE, Daouda
Upper Volta interior min 7-18, 596B3
TRAORE, Col. Moussa (Mali president)
Shuffles Cabt 1-7, 75E1
TRAORE, Lt. Col. Youssouf
Named Mali educ min 1-7, 75F1
TRAPNELL, Garrett Brock
Hijacker demands release 12-21, 1029F1
TRAPPING—*See WILDLIFE*
TRAUBE, Klause
'77 tap chrgs cited 74E2
TRAUTWEIN, Judge Theodore R.
Sentences Farber, NY Times in Jascalevich press freedom case 7-24, affirms penalties 8-28, 678G2, F3
Releases Farber, lifts NY Times fine 10-24, 841F2

TRAVEL
USSR areas open, China border region closed 1-19, 39A2
Jamaica tourism revives 1-19, 94G3-95A1
Malta '77 paymts surplus rptd 2-15, 228B3
USSR curbs UK, US envoys 2-17, 230E1
USSR CP ousts physicist over protest 2-21, 275D3
Helsinki review conf ends 3-9, 179B2
Turkey eases curbs on Greeks 3-9, 216F2
ERA boycott effect on tourism rptd 3-20, 494G2
French industry rptd hurt 3-22, 201G3; 3-23—3-29, 238D1
Nonprofit agents case refused by Sup Ct 3-27, 241B2
US scores Rumania visa curbs 4-11, 291G1-A2
W Ger leftist border checks protested 5-19, 439B2
DR tourism rptd down 5-25, 414A3
E Carib tourism rptd down 6-2, 559A2
S African blacks denied passports 6-9, 6-10, 536B3
US, India in visa talks 6-13—6-15, 466F3
US urges malaria precautns 6-26, 635G3
US tourism to Mex reopens 6-29, 517G2
Air Canada shutdown strands travelers in UK 8-25—9-5, 686F2
Hungary eases curbs, rpts '77 data 10-31, 841B1
USSR bars US businessman's exit 11-7, 884B3
Hungary devalues florint 11-11, 906A3
US Cong overseas trips rptd 12-10, 958B3

1979

'78 state gas use rptd 5-27, 395F2
Calif plan proposed 5-31, 418F3
Auto role seen undiminished 6-18, 514A3
Odd-even gas rationing spreads to E Coast, Tex 6-19—6-21, 462E2
Md sues US re gas allocatn 6-26, 479B2
Carter offers 6-pt energy plan 7-15, 7-16, 532E2, D3, 534E1
Adams fired, cites commitmt 7-20, 531A2
NYC subway receipts rptd stolen 7-23, 656E1
Mondale offers more fed aid 8-22, 726B1
BART svc curtailed 8-31–11-21, 922B3
Mass transit-highway agencies merger dropped 9-17, 726F1
San Fran cable cars shut down 9-26, Goldschmidt backs funds request 10-13, 831C1
San Fran cable cars resume svc 11-5, 989E3
NYC bond issue OKd 11-6, 846G3
Chicago strike 12-17–12-20, 987C2
Mass gov takes over Boston line 12-18, 989B3
Statistics
Dec '78 CPI 1-24, 73A2
Jan CPI 2-23, 151B2
Feb CPI 3-25, 252G1
Mar CPI 4-26, 324G3
Apr CPI 5-25, 402E3
May CPI 6-26, 480C3
June CPI 7-26, 556G3
July CPI 8-25, 646C2
Aug CPI 9-25, 725D2
Sept CPI 10-26, 827G3
Oct CPI 11-27, 903G2
Nov CPI 12-21, 984D2

TRANSPORTATION, Department of—*See under U.S. GOVERNMENT*
TRANSPORTATION Safety Board, National—*See U.S. GOVERNMENT–NATIONAL Transportation Safety Board*
TRANSPORTATION Union, United (AFL-CIO)
Dues case refused by Sup Ct 1-8, 14E3
Rock Island struck 8-29, Carter orders return 9-20; takeover set, pay issue settled 9-26, 722F1-B3
Rock Island svc resumes 10-5, accord reached 10-22, 830C3, G3
TRANSPORT Workers Union of America (AFL-CIO)
Iran US Emb seizure protested 11-9, 863D1
TRANS-STERLING Inc.
Argent sale completed 12-10, 965C1
TRANS World Airlines Inc. (TWA)
London fares cut urged by CAB 1-23, 87F3
Fuel shortage forces flight cuts 3-7, 162B2
727 mid-air plunge, Detroit emergency landing 4-4; tape gap rptd 5-13, 412G1
US-French air svc pact rptd 5-12, 465C3
IAM strike vs United ends 5-24, 402F2
TXI eyes merger 9-13; Trans World dirs vs 9-19, TXI undaunted 9-26, 830C1
TRANS World Corp.
Canteen Corp.
Ford stockholders suit barred in NY 3-8, 202B3
Hilton International Co.
Conrad Hilton dies 1-3, 104A3
Trans World Airlines Inc.—*See separate listing*
TRAPNELL, Garrett Brock
Sentncd to 2d life term 2-9, 119C2
TRAUTWEIN, Judge Theodore R.
Orders Jascalevich trial costs paid by NY Times 8-14, 656F2

TRAVEL
Jamaica tourism cut by riots 1-8–1-10, 21F2
Utah A-cancer impact noted 1-13, 91C1
Carter ends US Travel Svc 1-22, 45A2
Rhodesia air svc cut 2-18, 2-22, resorts rptd closed 2-28, 170F2
CAB adopts new charter rules 3-1, 166C3
US no longer top DC area hirer 3-24, 232B2
Grenada US aid overtures rptd 3-24, 236D3
Canada '78 tourism deficit rptd 4-7, 311G3
Turkey devalues currency 4-10, 333F1, B2; 6-12, 447C1
Greece-Turkey tourism pact 6-5, 447A2
Egypt-Israel pact set 6-6, 415E2
PR search law voided by Sup Ct 6-18, 499A2
US tourism earnings, paymts surplus linked 6-21, 463C2
Spain '78 tourism rptd 505B1
Egypt to issue Israel permits 7-12, 511A3
Hungary, Czech order Rumania ban 8-1, 645F3
Tex tourism down, Mex oil blow out blamed 8-17, 608A2; suit filed 9-17, 718C3
Turkey tourism earnings up 8-21, 637B2
Amer Express travelers check TV ad chngd 8-29, 903C1
San Fran cable cars shut down 9-26, 831D1
US Iranian visa check rptd 11-23, 898F1
US sets curbs on Islamic natns 11-26, 894F1

1980

NYC strike starts 4-1, impact rptd 4-1—4-10, unions fined 4-8, 267D3, 268B1-D2
LIRR struck 4-1, 267E3-268B1; pact reached 4-11, 289C3
Windfall oil profits tax signed 4-2, 244D3
NYC strike ends 4-11, 289C2
Anderson urges urban aid 6-9, 438F3
Dem platform drafted 6-24, 480A1
NYC strike fines raised 7-2, 518E1
Detroit workers strike 7-2, 518G1; end strike 7-12, 542G1
Urban League hears pres candidates 8-4, 8-6, 597E1, C2
Carter pres renominatn acceptance speech 8-14, 612F1, 613F1
Carter offers econ renewal plan 8-28, 663B2
Anderson, Reagan TV debate 9-21, 722A1
Mondale denounces Reagan tax cuts 10-16, 817C1
Boston system broke, state takes over 11-18; ct bars move 11-28; system shuts down 12-6; funding bill signed 12-7, 939A2
Rockwell Intl NYC subway damages awarded 12-24, 985A3
Statistics
Dec '79 CPI 1-25, 75D2
Jan CPI 2-22, 144F1
Feb CPI 3-25, 222B2
Apr CPI 5-23, 400C3
May CPI 6-24, 481C1

TRANSPORTATION, Department of—*See under U.S. GOVERNMENT*
TRANSPORTATION Union, United (AFL-CIO)
LIRR pres strike bd rpts; '79 agrmt cited 1-14, 53A2
LIRR ruled exempt from Taylor Law 3-4; pact reached 4-11, 289E3
TRANSPORT Workers Union of America (AFL-CIO)
NYC strike starts, issues detailed 4-1; fined 4-8, 267D3, 268B1-G1
NYC strike ends 4-11, 289G2
TRANS Union Corp.
Marmon merger set 9-22, 746F1
TRANS World Airlines (TWA)
World Airways Boston-London svc OKd 4-10, 346D2
Coast-to-coast fares cut 6-7, hiked 7-1, 516B2, C2
TRAPPER John, M.D. (TV series)
McCarty dies 4-5, 360D2
TRASK, Willard R.
Dies 8-10, 676D3
TRAUTLEIN, Donald H.
Named Bethlehem chairman 1-31, 224F3
On Carter econ renewal plan 8-28, 663B3
TRAVEL Agents, American Society of
Pl rebels warn vs conf 10-1, 10-4, bomb parley 10-19, 809D1
4 held in Pl bombing 10-31, 874A2
TRAVEL Service, U.S.—*See under U.S. GOVERNMENT--COMMERCE*

TRAVEL & Tourism
US territories set projects 2-19—2-22, 495E1
S Africa eases money curbs 3-26, 277F3
France to build Cuban tourist complex 4-1, 253A3
Jamaican tourism rptd up 4-7, 276F1
Carter theatens Olympic boycott enforcemt 4-10, 259B1
NY transit strike impact cited 4-10, 268D2
US protests Sovt harassmt 4-11, 4-18, 431F1
US bans Iran travel, exempts rptrs 4-17, 281C1; 4-21, 299B2
NBC drops Olympic telecast, estimates loss 5-6, 379F3
Mt St Helens damage assessed 5-24—7-4, 504C3
US group defies Iran travel ban 5-30, 6-2, 419A1; Carter for prosecutn 6-10, 459A3
Portugal pilots strike 6-23—7-14, 580A2
Spain beach resorts bombed 6-25, 500G1
Ariz ex-football coach, others indicted 7-24, state probe asked 10-16, 875A3
French port blockade eased, UK tourists return home 8-19, 633F3-634A1
Pl rebels warn vs US conf 10-1, 10-4, bomb parley 10-19, 809D1
Agee passport revocatn case accepted by Sup Ct 10-6, 782C3
E Ger curbs Poland travel 10-28, 828G3; Poland scores 10-30, 860C1
Czechs curb Polish travel 11-20, 879C1
US tourism agency clears Cong 12-9, 12-11, 953E2
China sets parallel exchng rates 12-15, 975F3
US forgn tourism agency bill vetoed 12-25, 982D1

1976

TRAVELER'S Insurance Co.
Calif MDs end slowdown 2-5, 144D3
TRAVERS, Howard K.
Dies 12-25, 1015G2
TRAVESTIES (play)
Wins Tony 4-18, 460D2
TRAXLER, Rep. Bob (D, Mich.)
Reelected 11-2, 829D4
TRBOVICH, Mike
US clears top UMW aides 5-18, 379A1
TREASON—*See ESPIONAGE*
TREEN, Rep. David C. (R, La.)
Endorses Ford 7-29, 550E2
Proposes GOP platform amendmt 8-12, 582F3
GOP conv OKs platform plank 8-18, 600C3
GOP conv vp vote table 8-19, 599F3
Reelected 11-2, 829F3
TREIBER, Birgit
Sets world swim marks 6-1—6-5, 424F3
Wins Olympic medals 7-21, 7-25, 575G2
TREMBLAY, Rodrigue
Named industry min 11-26, 903G2
TRENTIN, Bruno
Scores austerity plan 10-15, 838A2
TRENTON, Mich.—*See MICHIGAN*
TRENTON, N.J.—*See NEW Jersey*
TREURNICHT, Andries
Named Bantu admin dep min 1-24, 76D1
TREWHITT, Henry L.
Pres debate panelist 10-6, 740F2
TRIANGLE Publications Inc.
Canada TV Guide sale rptd 11-27, 945F3
TRIANTAFELLU, Rockly
Swedish spy device sale rptd 9-14, 734E1
TRIBBITT, Gov. Sherman W. (D, Del.)
Loses reelection 11-2, 820E3, 821B1
TRIBLE Jr., Paul S.
Elected 11-2, 823C1, 830G4
TRIDENT Submarine—*See 'Ships & Submarines' under ARMAMENTS*
TRIMBLE, Phillip R.
US team climbs Mt Everest 10-8, 876B3
TRINH, Nguyen Duy
United Viet forgn min 7-3, 502E3
In Politburo 12-19, 967F3
Addresses party cong 12-20, 967F3-968A1

TRINIDAD & Tobago—*See also CARIBCOM, COMMONWEALTH of Nations, IDB, NONALIGNED Nations Movements, OAS, SELA*
Govt sets 8-yr indl plan 1-2, 55D3
Listed as 'free' nation 1-19, 20C3
Fay confrmd US amb 2-4, 110B2
Total IMF oil loan rptd 4-1, 340G2
New constitutn implemented 8-1, 714B3
PNM wins electns 9-13, 714E2
Cuba exiles seized 10-7; Venez offers bombing info 10-16, 779C3, G3
Venez rpts Cuba exile terrorist plan, Guyana consulate bombing 10-19, 780C2
Bombing trial set in Venez 10-21—10-22; exiles deported 10-26; 4 indicted 11-2, 843G2
Sports
Olympic results 7-18—7-31, 573E3, 575F3

TRINITY (book)
On best-seller list 12-5, 972E2
TRIPPET, Robert S.
Fined 12-22, 1016C2
TRIUMPH and Tragedy. . .the Olympic Experience (TV special)
Wins Emmy 5-17, 460C2
TRODSSON, Ingegaerd
Named to Swedish Cabt 10-8, 794C2
TROMP (Dutch warship)
In Intl Naval Review 7-4, 488B3
TRONDHEIM (Norwegian warship)
In Intl Naval Review 7-4, 488D3

1977

US agents in Bermuda 12-1—12-3, ldrs fear riot repercussns 12-6, 935F3
Kenya bans game skin sales 12-12, 976F1
US-Sovt agri visas eased 12-13, 1017A3
TRAVIS, James W.
Indicted 8-2, 631B3
TREASON—*See ESPIONAGE; also country names*
TREASURY, Department of the—*See under U.S. GOVERNMENT*
TREATY Ratification (U.S.)—*See under U.S. GOVERNMENT—SENATE*
TREHARNE, Gordon W.
Hughes '38 will sought 1-17, 120D2
TREIBLE, Kathy
Sets swim record 8-18—8-21, 828F3
TREMBLAY, Jean-Claude (J. C.)
Quebec wins WHA title 5-27, 430C1
TREMBLAY, Rodrigue
Hosts Rossi 1-11, 43D1
TREVINO, Lee
Wins Canadian Open 7-24, 676A2
TRIAL Lawyers of America, Association of
Fed no-fault auto insurnc standards opposed 7-18, 595A1
TRIB New York Inc.
IHT files trademark suit 8-24, 723F1
Trust suit vs NY Times, IHT, intl Trib filed 9-13, 723D1
TRIBUNE Publishing Co.
Secret news source case review refused 10-31, 835F2
TRIBUNE Publishing Co. v. Caldero
Sup Ct refuses review 10-31, 835F2
TRIDENT—*See ARMAMENTS, subheads 'Missiles' and 'Ships & Submarines'*
TRIEKI, Ali Abdusalam
Pl-Moslem rebel talks collapse 4-21—4-30, 468F2
Mediates Pak feud 5-4, 348E3
TRIESTE
Italy, Yugo exchng '75 pact 4-2, 309D2
TRIFA, Archbishop Valerian D.
Suspended from NCC 2-4, 119F3
TRIGO Ramirez, Col. Julio
Loses Cabt post 10-13, 902C1
TRIMBLE v. Gordon
Illegitimates' rights backed 4-26, 382G2-D3

TRINIDAD & Tobago—*See also COMMONWEALTH of Nations, IDB, NONALIGNED Nations Movement, OAU*
UN Assemb member 4C1
'75-76 trade, paymts table 3-11, 189A2 ★, C2
Belizean ties cited 5-19, 414D3
'61-75 GDP variatns table 5-30, 439C1
Australia asks trade office closed 6-2, 484E3
US amb confrmd 6-7, 499E3
Belize independnc backed 6-16, 494G2
Miss Univ crowned 7-16, 808G2
'76 oil profits rptd 7-27, forgn investors attracted 8-22, 905F3
Young visits, tech aid discussed 8-11—8-12, 646E1, 647A1
$150-mln Euro$ loan rptd 9-19, 905F3
Venez tries Cuba exiles re '76 crash 10-10, 867G1
Oil workers boycott Guyana shipmts; Guyana withdraws sugar strike breakers 11-4, 869F1
TRINITY (book)
On best-seller list 2-6, 120E3; 3-6, 184E3; 4-3, 264F1; 5-1, 356C2; 6-4, 452A2; 10-2, 808E3
TRIPOLI Meeting of Confrontation States—*See MIDDLE EAST—EGYPT-Israel Peace Moves*
TRIS (2,3 dibromopropyl phosphate)—*See under CHEMICALS*
TRISTAN, Concepcion
Freed from prison 7-17, 582B3
TROFIMENKO, Vladimir
Sets pole vault mark 7-1—7-2, 602E2
TROPIGAS International Corp.
US acts re gas transport 2-3, 76G1
TROPIGILIANI, Msgr. Bruno
Vs anti-govt stand 1-25, 99F3

1978

US SSI forgn travel rule backed by Sup Ct 12-11, 981A1
US seeks visa abuse reforms 12-20, 1010E2
TRAVEL Agents, American Society of
Nonprofit agents case refused by Sup Ct 3-27, 241B2
TRAVOLTA, John
Grease released 6-16, 619C2
You're The One on best-seller list 6-7, 460F3; 7-5, 579G3; 8-2, 620F1
Moment by Moment released 12-21, 1030C3
TRAXLER, Rep. Bob (D, Mich.)
Reelected 11-7, 851E1
TREACY, John
Sets indoor 3-mi run mark 3-10, 692D3
TREASON—*See ESPIONAGE; country names*
TREASURY, Department of the—*See under U.S. GOVERNMENT*
TREATY Ratification (U.S.)—*See under U.S. GOVERNMENT—SENATE*
TREEN, Rep. David C. (R, La.)
McDermott admits paymts 2-22, 142A3
Reelected 11-7, 850F4
TREMBLAY, Mario
Montreal wins Stanley Cup 5-25, 458F1
TREMBLAY, Michel
Forever Yours opens 6-21, 887G1
TRENCHFOOT—*See MEDICINE—Diseases*
TREPANG, U.S.S. (nuclear submarine)
Theft plot foiled 10-4, 824F1
TREU, Alexander Peter
Sentenced 5-5; secret trial scored 6-13—6-14, 451B3
TREURNICHT, Andries
Elected Transvaal ldr 11-25, 946C2
TREVINO, Lee
2d in Phoenix Open 1-16, 76D1
2d in Tourn of Champs 4-16, 355G2
2d in Byron Nelson Classic 5-7, 580D3
Wins Colonial Natl 5-14, 580D3
2d in Memphis Classic 6-11, 580F3
2d in Milwaukee Open 7-9, 672C3
Wins Lancome Trophy tourn 10-22, 990C2
PGA top money winner 10-31, 990B3
TRIACA, Enrico
Red Brigades hideout found 5-18, 393C1
Moretti sought in Moro case 5-20, 393D3
Chrgd in Moro case 6-5, 689B2
TRIANGLE PWC Inc.
Sued re price fixing 9-21, 769C1
TRIB, The (newspaper)
Debuts 1-9, Learsy elected chrmn 1-17, 75C3
Ceases publicatn 4-5, 270A2
TRIBLE Jr., Rep. Paul S. (R, Va.)
Reelected 11-7, 852C3
TRIBUNE Co.
FCC renews WPIX-TV license 6-16, 672D1
TRIBUTE (play)
Opens 6-1, 887D3
TRIDENT—*See ARMAMENTS, subheads 'Missiles' and 'Ships & Submarines'*
TRIEKI, Ali Abdusalam
Signs China pact 8-9, 691F2
TRIGANO, Gilbert
On Club Medit bombings 6-11, 473F3
TRIHALOMETHANES—*See CHEMICALS*
TRILATERAL Commission
Study faults govts on energy policy, summit urged 6-13, 450B2
TRINH, Nguyen Duy
In trade missn to Malaysia, Indonesia, Pl; Thai pact signed 1-12, 21B3

TRINIDAD & Tobago—*See also CARIBBEAN Community, COMMONWEALTH of Nations, GATT, IDB, NONALIGNED Nations Movement, OAS*
Aluminum smelter, food corp planned, shipping co rptd 1-13, 100G2
Jamaica Jan-Oct '77 exports rptd 1-13, 100C3
Jobless rate rptd 14.1% 2-10, 194F2
Strike closes intl airline 6-2, 559A2
Abstains in UN vote on PR colony status 9-13, 979E3
UN Assemb member 713F3
Dry gas reserves rptd 11-3, 886A1

TRINTIGNANT, Jean-Louis
Faces of Love released 7-7, 970C1
TRIPLE Crown—*See HORSE Racing*
TRIS (2,3 dibromopropyl phosphate)—*See under CHEMICALS*
TRISKA, Jan
Master & Margarita opens 11-11, 1031D2
TROJAN Decommissioning Alliance
Ore A-plant protested 8-6—8-7, 609C3
TROPICANA Products Inc.
Beatrice merger planned, Kellogg talks cited 3-5, 184F3
Beatrice trust challenge rejctd 8-2, cos merge 8-7, 767C2, D3

1979

N Orleans tourism stress cited 11-29, 921G1
TRAVEL Service, U.S.—*See under U.S. GOVERNMENT-COMMERCE*
TRAVIS, J. Mark
Richard Pryor Live released 2-15, 174E3
TRAVIS, Robert
Dies 11-19, 932F3
TRAVIS, Stephen
FBI suspensn rptd 10-17, 787A3
Pleads guilty to conspiracy 11-15, 906G1*
TRAVOLTA, Joey
Sunnyside released 6-1, 820D3
TREASURY, Department of the—*See under U.S. GOVERNMENT*
TREASURY Employees Union, National (NTEU) (unaffiliated)
Backs Kennedy 10-30, 847C2
TREATY Ratification (U.S.)—*See under U.S. GOVERNMENT-SENATE*
TREEN, Rep. David C. (R, La.)
Elected gov 12-8, 946C3
TREMAINE, Scott
Uranus ring theory rptd 1-11, 289G3
TREMBLAY, Rodrigue
Quits, scores Levesque 9-21, 750B1
TRENTON, N.J.—*See NEW Jersey*
TRETIAK, Vladislav
Soviets win Challenge Cup 2-11, 118C2, A3
TREU, Alexander Peter
Cleared in appeal 2-20, 189A2
TREURNICHT, Andries
S Africa pub works min 6-14, 469A3
TREVANIAN
Shibumi on best-seller list 7-1, 548A3; 8-5, 620B3
TREVINO, Lee
2d in Hope Desert Classic 1-14, 220C3
Wins Canadian Open, career earnings top $2 mln 6-24; ties for 2d in Greater Milwaukee Open 7-15 587B3, E3
Wins Canadian PGA 9-2; 2d in World Series of Golf 9-30, Lancome Trophy tourn 10-28, 969B3, 970C1, B2
PGA top money winner 11-30, 969F2
TRICHOMONIASIS—*See MEDICINE-Diseases*
TRIDENT Submarine-Launched Ballistic Missile—*See ARMAMENTS, subheads Missiles and Ships & Submarines*
TRIFFIN, Robert
On '29 Depression, '80s econ forecast 11-1, 827B2
TRILENE—*See MEDICINE-Drugs*
TRILLO, Manny
Wins Golden Glove Award 11-20, 956C1
TRINH Van-Can, Cardinal Joseph Marie
Installed cardinal 6-30, 640B2

TRINIDAD & Tobago—*See also COMMONWEALTH of Nations, GATT, IDB, NONALIGNED Nations Movement, OAS*
IAPA conf hosted 3-21, 255G3
Tankers collide off Tobago, spill oil 7-19, 553G2
UN membership listed 695A3

TRINITY College (Washington, D.C.)
Pope holds ecumenical prayer svc 10-7, 760B1
TRINITY University (San Antonio, Tex.)
Loses NCAA team tennis title 5-24, 2 win doubles title 5-28, 5-24, 570A2
TRIPLE (book)
On best-seller list 10-14, 800B3; 11-4, 892B3
TRIPLE Crown—*See HORSE Racing*
TROELL, Jan
Hurricane released 4-11, 528E2
TROJAN Nuclear Plant—*See OREGON-Atomic Energy*

1980

TRAVERS, Ben
Dies 12-18, 1004D3
TRAVKOV, Gennady
Seized as Sovt spy 2-9, leaves France 2-10, 141G2
TRAVOLTA, John
Urban Cowboy released 6-11, 675F3
TRAXLER, Rep. Bob (D, Mich.)
Reelected 11-4, 843E1
TREASURY, Department of the—*See under U.S. GOVERNMENT*
TREEN, Gov. David C. (R, La.)
Dem wins cong seat 5-17, 404D3
Addresses GOP conv 7-16, 531E3
TREIBER, Birgit
Wins Olympic medal 7-27, 623B3
TRETHOWAN, Ian
BBC announces cutbacks 2-28, 172F3
TRETIAK, Vladislav
Sovt Olympic hockey team loses to US 2-22, 155A2
TREU, Alexander Peter
Accused of passing secrets 1-11, 78B3
Legal costs compensatn denied 3-17, 211D1
TREURNICHT, Andries
Botha scores 3-7, Cabt ouster fails 3-11, 3-12; poll backs Botha 3-16, 255B2
Named S Africa civil svc min 8-26; addresses Transvaal party 9-1, 689G3, 690B1
TREVANIAN
Shibumi on best-seller list 7-13, 568D3; 8-17, 640G3
TREVES, Sir Frederick (deceased)
Elephant Man released 10-3, 836F2
TREVINO, Lee
2d in Hawaiian Open 2-10, Greater New Orleans 4-27, Houston 5-4, 412D2, E3, F3
Wins Tourn Players, career earnings at $2.2 mln 3-23, 412A3
Watson penalized for advising 4-20, 412D3
Wins Memphis Classic 6-29, 715B1
2d in Brit Open 7-20, 714A3
Clinches Vardon Trophy 9-21, 971C3
Wins Texas Open 9-21, Lancome Trophy tourn 10-19, 972B2, F2
PGA top money winner 10-12, 971E3
TRIANO, Guillermo
Released 4-6, 293B3
TRIBLE Jr., Rep. Paul S. (R, Va.)
Chrgs Navy unfit ship deploymt 6-30, 517F3
Reelected 11-4, 844D3
TRIBUTE (film)
Released 12-13, 1003F2
TRICKS of the Trade (play)
Opens 11-16, 892F3
TRIDENT (British freighter)
Supertanker crew rescued 1-17, 108E2
TRIDENT Submarine-Launched Ballistic Missile—*See ARMAMENTS--Missiles,*
TRIGON (CIA operative)
USSR-Kissinger controversy rptd 7-14—10-4, 753F3
Carter aide cleared in identity leak 12-5, 940B3
TRILLIN, Calvin
Boycotts Amer Book Awards 5-1, 692G1
TRILLO, Manny
Phillies win NL pennant 10-12, 796D1-G1
In World Series 10-14—10-21, 811D3-812C3
TRINCA, Alvaro
Soccer scandal rptd 3-6, 194F2
TRINH, Nguyen Duy
Replaced as Viet forgn min 2-7, 90G1
TRINIDAD & Tobago—*See also COMMONWEALTH of Nations, GATT, IDB, NONALIGNED Nations, OAS*
Separatists win Tobago parlt vote 11-24, 923A3

TRINITY Evangelical Divinity School (Deerfield, Conn.)
Brown on evangelical pol movemt 8-19, 819D1
TRINITY University (San Antonio, Tex.)
2 lose NCAA doubles tennis title 5-26, 607D1
TRINQUET, Pascale
Wins Olympic medal 7-24, 622C3
TRIPLE (book)
On best-seller list 1-13, 40B3; 2-10, 120C3; 12-7, 948F3
TRONSTAD, Bjorn
USF wins NCAA soccer title 12-14, 1001D3
TROPICANA Products Inc.
Beatrice merger found illegal 11-28, 917G3

1976

TROY, O.—*See OHIO*

TROY, Matthew H.
- Pleads guilty 7-1, sentncd 9-29, quits post 9-30, jailed 10-22, 860B2

TROYANOVSKY, Oleg A.
- Replaced as amb to Japan 4-17, 314B1
- Named UN amb 12-14, 967C1

TRUCCO, Manuel
- Says 1 pol prisoner left 12-18, 963C1

TRUCKING Employers Inc.
- Teamsters pact settled 4-3, 248D3

TRUCKS & Trucking—*See also country names*
- FTC proposes used-truck data rule 1-2, 7B2
- Ford rescinds price hike 1-15, 280A3
- Ford State of Union message 1-19, 37D3, 39C2
- Ford urges regulatory reform 2-5, 110A1
- Strike, Dow avg linked 3-29, 413B2
- Teamsters strike 4-1, settle 4-3; Greenspan on pact 4-5, 248B3, 249A1
- Teamsters pact ratified 5-10, 348G3
- Fruehauf offcls sentncd 6-30, 523G3
- GOP platform text 8-18, 607E1
- GM hikes price 8-25, 647E1
- Deregulatn bill not cleared 10-2, 884F1
- New potato futures contract OKd 11-2, 990B1

TRUDEAU, Margaret Sinclair (Mrs. Pierre Elliott Trudeau)
- In Latin Amer 1-24—2-2, defends protocol gaffs 2-3, 2-6, 116G2

TRUDEAU, Pierre Elliott (Canadian prime minister)
- Econ remarks scored 1-5—1-11 27A3, B3 *
- Defends econ policies 1-19, 46A3
- In Mex, Cuba, Venez 1-24—2-2; defends trip 2-3, 116C2

1977

TROTSKY, Leon (Lev Davidovich Bronstein) (1879-1940)
- USSR bars books entry 9-6, 766A1

TROTTIER, Edgar
- Killed 2-6, autopsy 2-7, 113D3
- Levesque cleared 2-21, 2-25, 159C1

TROW, Martin
- Issues campus study 1-14, 157F1

TROYANOVSKY, Oleg A.
- Bars UNEF funds 1-6, 4B2
- Meets Israel UN rep on PLO peace role 2-3, 86D3

TRUCKS (& Trucking)
- Poultry driver bargaining right upheld 1-11, 58B1
- DOT issues future trends rpt 1-15, 58C3
- ICC acts re gas shortage 1-24, 54E1
- Ford hikes prices 2-7, 155E3
- Teamsters, UFW sign pact 3-10, 177G3
- Cost data in rate-setting affirmed 4-18, 342C1
- Carter energy plan 4-20, 291C2
- Egypt OKs Ford plant agrmt 5-10, 390A2
- Pre-'64 seniority bias upheld 5-31, 461C2
- ICC suspends 2 in probe 6-8, 500C3
- O'Neal rpt scores ICC 8-3, 651A3
- EPA sets exhaust rules 9-5, 739D3
- FHWA inspections intensify 9-8, 778C3
- Grain shipping price policy curbed 10-3, 760D2
- Lee Way blacks win record back pay 10-11, 818G3
- Ford, Egypt sign pact 10-29, 863G1
- ICC sues firms over double billing 11-3, 861A1
- Ga GM franchise case review refused 12-12, 960E2

TRUDEAU, Margaret Sinclair (Mrs. Pierre Elliot)
- Denies Jagger link 3-28, separatn rpts 4-8, 4-11, 281C3
- Separatn announced 5-27, 426F1

TRUDEAU, Pierre Elliott (Canadian prime minister)
- On defns costs 1-13, 82A2
- Scores Levesque speech 1-26, 82E1
- Confrms blacklist 1-26, bars access 2-3, 97F1
- Calls for separatism vote 1-28, 113A3

1978

TROTSKY, Leon (Lev Davidovich Bronstein) (1879-1940)
- Spain book hints murder secrets 2-24, 136D2
- Assassin dies 10-18, 888B3

TROTTIER, Bryan
- NHL assist ldr 4-9, 296D2

TROW, George W.S.
- Tennis Game opens 11-5, 1031A3

TROYANOVSKY, Oleg Alexandrovich
- Meets Shevchenko 4-9, 302D2

TRSB (Time Reference Scanning Beam)—*See MICROWAVES*

TRUCCOLI, Antonio
- Detained re econ policy criticism 4-23, 611D3

TRUCKING Associations Inc., American
- Splinter group formed 11-15, 1007B2

TRUCKING Management Inc.
- Bosworth addresses, forecasts US role in Teamster talks 8-22, 680G2

TRUCKS (& Trucking)
- Carter State of Union Message 1-19, 32B1
- Adams issues policy statemt 2-8, 109F1
- Wis length limit overturned by Sup Ct 2-21, 126D1
- US OKs Ethiopia delivery 2-22, 137C2
- New fuel standards for light trucks issued 3-15, 284F1-B2
- REA bankruptcy case review refused by Sup Ct 3-20, 206A1
- AMC, Renault plan joint productn, distributn 3-31, 283G3
- Groups get 7½% freight-rate hike 3-31, 284B2
- Carter asks regulatory probe 4-11, 259F3
- '75, '76 AMC recall ordrd 5-1, 349C1
- ICC fires Kyle 6-7, 570B2
- Renault Rumania expansn rptd 6-14, 651B1
- Sup Ct '77 race bias case cited in Bakke decisn 6-28, 482F1
- LNG safety measures urged 7-31, 610A1, C1
- Chrysler sale of Turkish unit cited 8-10, 623D3
- US role in Teamster talks forecast 8-22, 8-23, 680F2-C3
- Ford transmissn hazard warned 8-29 722A2
- ICC ex-offcl indicted 9-22, 770F2; acquitted 12-21, 1007G3
- Joint rate expansn case declined by Sup Ct 10-10, 789B3
- RR decline seen, user chrg hikes urged 10-10, 812E1
- ICC proposes deregulatn; industry, cong ldrs leery 11-7—12-21, 1007C1
- Steel haulers strike 11-11, 1006F1-A2
- ICC voids freight-rate hike 11-27, 1007E2
- Freight-rate case refused by Sup Ct 12-4, 959B2
- Output record in '78 rptd 12-21, 1004G1
- **Accidents**—*See ACCIDENTS—Motor Vehicle*

TRUDEAU, Pierre Elliott (Canadian prime minister)
- Threatens force vs Quebec separatn 1-1, 6F3
- Sees Sun Life offcls on relocatn 1-12, warns Quebec 1-13, 35E3
- Basford sets retiremt 1-13, 89D1

1979

TROTTER, Desmond
- Seraphine pledges probe 6-29, 502E3

TROTTIER, Bryan
- Soviets win Challenge Cup 2-11, 118G2, E3
- NHL scoring ldr, wins Ross Trophy 4-8, 355D2, G3
- Named NHL MVP 6-12, 470B2

TROY (race horse)
- Wins English Derby 6-6, 448B3
- Wins Irish Derby, Derby double 7-1, 3d in Arc de Triompe 10-7, 876C3, D3

TROYANOVSKY, Oleg Alexandrovich
- Vetoes UN res on Viet, Cambodia conflicts 3-16, 200E1
- Vs Pol Pot govt UN seat 9-21, 741A2
- On Sovt relief aid to Cambodia 11-5, 863D3

TRT Telecommunications Corp.—*See under UNITED Brands Co.*

TRUCKING Associations Inc., American
- Cannon, Kennedy clash over deregulatn 2-7, 111C3
- Truck strike data rptd 6-21, 479G2

TRUCKING Management Inc.
- Teamsters strike lockout asked 4-1, 251C1
- Teamsters' pact set 4-10, 262C1

TRUCKS (& Trucking)
- SEC role in pensn plans barred by Sup Ct 1-16, 32F1-D2
- Steel haulers end strike 1-18, 87C2
- EPA tightens exhaust rule 2-15, 187C1
- ICC misconduct dismissals backed 3-5, 309E1
- Teamsters issue demands 3-6, Kahn warns 3-15; guidelines strike called, industry locks out 4-1, 251B1
- Retroactive seniority case declined by Sup Ct 4-2, 281C2
- Teamsters' pact set 4-10, 262C1
- Mechanics end strike 4-10, 384E3
- ICC OKs rate hikes 4-11, 262D2
- Western mechanics end strike 4-16, 384E3
- Dissident steel haulers end strike 4-29, 384C3
- Apr jobless rate, indl output, incomes linked to strike 5-4, 5-16, 5-17, 362C3, F3, 363A; 6-19, 463A31
- Diesel fuel shortage seen 5-18, 361C3
- Teamsters ratify pact 5-18, 384A3
- Diesel fuel allocatn rules adopted 5-25, 395C2
- '78 state gas use rptd 5-27, 395A3
- ICC motor carrier damage case refused by Sup Ct 5-29, 421G3
- Indep truckers strike 6-7–6-15; ICC orders surcharge 6-15, 462D3-463B1
- A-waste transport rules set 6-15, 610C1
- Strike persists, violence mounts; impact assessed 6-18–6-28, 479B2-A3
- Carter, Admin move on strike demands, task force formed 6-21–6-27, 479B3
- Diesel fuel allocatn rule canceled 6-22, 479D3
- Admin sets 6-point truckers' plan 6-29, strike ebbs 7-7, 7-9, 516D2
- Teamsters chief's son indicted 8-2, 744C3
- ICC order ruling reversed by Sup Ct 10-15, 847G3
- Sept indl output rise, truck assemblies linked 10-16, 784B2
- Nov indl output drop, truck productn linked 12-14, 964B1

Deregulation
- ACT sues ICC over vacant seats 1-4, 111D3
- 2 reps soften ICC stand 1-9, 111E3
- Fitzsimmons asks ICC chrmn firing 1-18, 111G3
- Kennedy introduces bill 1-22, clashes with Cannon 2-7, 111F2
- Carter State of Union Message 1-23, 46G3
- ICC limits trust immunity 2-28, 166E3
- Kahn threatens Teamsters 3-15, 251G1
- Kennedy, Cannon end dispute 3-21, 308G3
- O'Neal to leave ICC post 10-4, 831C1
- ICC rules bar clears Cong 11-15, 11-19, Carter signs 11-30, 920E1

Foreign Developments (including U.S. international news)
- UK strike 1-3, union sanctns 1-11; lay-offs rptd 1-11, 1-12, 20D2-A3, E3; 1-23, 59E3; strike ends 1-29, 75B3
- Mack Trucks-Renault deal rptd 3-19, 3-20, 236E2, 283A1
- Ford leads in Argentina sales 7-20, 562F1
- Mercedes US plant plan rptd 7-26, 663F3
- Uganda vowed US aid 9-19, 721F1
- US resumes spare part shipmts to Iran 10-5, 773C3
- Renault interest in Mack Trucks cited 10-12, 784G3
- USSR mil aided by US trade 11-8, 856F3
- US denies USSR plant mil use 12-17, 997F2

TRUCK Stop Operators, National Association of
- Diesel fuel supplies rptd down 5-18, 361C3

TRUDEAU, Margaret Sinclair (Mrs. Pierre Elliott)
- Rpts spouse 'abuse' 3-8, Kennedy liaison 3-20; women's group honors 3-23, 271C3

TRUDEAU, Pierre Elliott (Canadian prime minister; replaced June 4)
- Elliott dies 1-9, 104A3
- Unity Cncl rpt scores bilingualism 1-16, 57F1
- On Unity Task Force rpt 1-26, 74C3

1980

TROTT, Stephen S.
- La Scola insulin-slaying chrgs reduced 12-29, 997B2

TROTTER, John Clinton
- Coca-Cola plant labor unrest, intl protests; sale pressed 4-16—5-27, 463D3

TROTTIER, Bryan
- Islanders win Stanley Cup, named playoff MVP 5-24, 487F3, 488A1

TROUBLE With Europe, The (play)
- Opens 1-28, 136F3

TROUP—*See TEXAS*

TROYANOVSKY, Oleg Alexandrovich
- Vs UN res on Afghan pullout 1-5, 1-7, 2G1
- Defends Afghan invasn in UN debate 1-11, 25F2
- Assaulted at UN mtg 4-30, 325G1
- Scores UN Afghan res 11-20, 899G3

TRUCE Supervision Organization, UN—*See UNITED Nations--UNTSO*

TRUCKING Association, American
- Carter signs deregulatn bill 7-1, 494E1

TRUCKS (& Trucking)
- EPA sets exhaust rule 1-2, 5F2
- Ford sets plant closings 1-3, 35G1
- Hijack prosecutn disparities rptd 1-6, 24C3
- Lee Way settles job bias suit 1-10, 17C2
- Carter asks deregulatn 1-21, 43F3
- NM State of State message 1-25, 269G3
- Teamsters chief's son, 2 others rptd sentenced 2-19, 237F2
- Diesel exhaust rules set 2-21, 145G3
- Carter seeks deregulatn legis 3-14, 201F1
- Pa Mafia ldr slain 3-21, 237D2
- UPS ICC regulatn case refused by Sup Ct 4-14, 307G1-A2
- Ford productn cuts set 4-15, 287G1
- Ford transmissn hazard determined 6-11; denial issued, info suit filed 8-20, 702D1
- Deregulatn bill clears Cong 6-19, 6-20, 479A1; Carter signs 7-1, 494B1
- Ford asks parts suppliers to cut prices 6-21, 481G3
- Fla deregulates 7-1, 558D2
- Deregulatn cited in Dem conv keynote address 8-11, Kennedy speech 8-12, 612A2*, D2, 614B1
- White Motor files for bankruptcy 9-4, 985E3
- Multi-employer pensn plan reform signed 9-26, 856D3
- Sept producer prices reflect rebates 10-3, 783F1
- Itel rpts huge '79 loss 10-16, 784F1
- ITC bars Japan import curbs 11-10, 866E3
- Diesel emissns rule set 12-24, 987E2

Foreign Developments (including U.S. international news)
- Nissan US productn plan rptd 2-18, 127D1; 4-17, 288D1
- US concerned re Japan imports 5-14, 384G1-A2
- US raises import duty, Japan rues 5-20, 384A2
- Spanish-French produce dispute spurs violence, truckers block border 6-16—6-20, 525A3
- Canada June sales rptd 7-5, 520A3; July sales 8-7, 618C2

TRUDEAU, Pierre Elliott (Canadian prime minister)
- Clark scores 1-2, 37F3
- Jerome named to Fed Ct 1-4, 38E2
- Asks consultatn on Sovt Afghan crisis 38D1
- Ryan offers const reform 1-10, 19C1

1976

Turner quits Commons 2-13, 188G2
In A-talks with Bhutto 2-23—2-25, 175A1
Bars judicial interfernc probe 3-3, 187E3
Seeks BNAA return, scores Language Act 3-5, 238A3
Rejects Drury resignatn re judge's chrgs 3-12, Ouellet resigns 3-16, 220D3-221B2
Outlines charter proposals 4-1, 4-9, 265C2
In prov oil price, const talks 5-6, 380D3, F3 ★
Lockheed deal collapses 5-18, 362G3
CLC-govt mtg set 5-20, 401B1
Plumptre quits AIB 6-10, 439A1
Sees premrs on fed revenue 6-14—6-15, 456E3
Visits Ford 6-16, 481A3
On air svc strike 6-23, 6-25, 481C2
At 7-nation econ summit 6-27—6-28, 461G2, 462E1
Marchand resigns 6-28, 496E2
Pushes bilingualism 7-9, 537B2
US ties rptd strained 7-26, 587C3
Reshuffles Cabt 9-14, 692B1
Callaghan meets 9-16, 9-18, 730B2
Inflatn plan protested 9-17—10-1, 10-14, 771A1
Const talks 10-1—10-2, changes asked 10-2, 750B1
Poll: Clark backed as prime min 10-16, 808G2
On by-electns 10-19, 808F2
In Japan 10-20—10-26, 836G2
Names new mins 11-3, 851E2
On Quebec electn, separatism 11-15, 11-16, 870B2
Asks unity 11-25, Levesque scores 11-26, 903B3
Presents rebates rpt to Parlt 11-26, 904G1; defends Polysar 11-30, 924A1
On forgn business agents 12-2, 962D3
Scores prov tax demands 12-8, 945G1; 5-yr plan set 12-13—12-14, 962F1, E2

TRUJILLO, Julio Cesar
Gets amnesty 1-22, 363E3
Leads Conservative faction 3-8, 363A3
TRUMAN, Harry S. (1884-1972)—*See 1945, pp. 115P-116B; 1948, p. 229 A-C; 1972, p. 1044F1-2, for biog. data*
Mackenzie King diaries publshd 1-1, 8D1
Primary precedent cited 231G3
Ford pays homage 5-8, 342A3
Tap on ex-aide rptd 5-9, 344F2
Ford whistle-stop campaign 5-15, 357A1
Carter hails leadership 7-15, 510E1
Bill ends '50 emergency 9-14, 689B2
Carter whistlestop tour 9-20—9-21, 704A3
Robert Hale dies 11-30, 970A2
TRUMBO, Dalton
Dies 9-10, 1015G2
TRUMBULL, Neb.—*See NEBRASKA*
TRUXTON (U.S. nuclear warship)
NZ docking spurs strike 8-27—9-2, 677E2
Australia docking prompts strike 9-7, 691C3
TRYON, Thomas
Lady on best seller list 1-25, 80D3
Crowned Heads on best-seller list 12-5, 972F2
TSEDENBAL, Yumjaagiyn
Signs USSR pact 10-19, 949B3
TSEGAYE, Gebre Medhin
Artists score 4-22, 311B3
TSHAZIBANE, Wellington
Rptd hanged 12-13, 1010G2
TSONGAS, Rep. Paul E. (D, Mass.)
Reelected 11-2, 829B4
TSUKAHARA, Mitsuo
Wins Olympic medals 7-21, 7-23, 574B3, C3

1977

In Australia, US uranium collaboratn exchng 2-4—3-11, 624F3, 625A1
Polysar admits illegal rebates 2-8, 114D2
Warren dispute denied 2-17, 132E3
In US 2-21—2-23, 127E3, 132F2
Assassinatn plot rptd 2-23, 261A3
Network bias probe asked 3-4, 179A3
Leads Clark in poll 3-5, 218D3
Levesque opens Quebec Assemb 3-8, 179C2
Scores Quebec white paper 4-5, 281F2
Names 4 to Senate 4-5, 281A3
Marriage separatn rpts 4-8, 4-11, 281C3
Campaigns for unity 4-18—4-20, 346F1
Horner joins Liberals 4-20, 304A1
At wage-price curbs mtg 4-22, 327D2
Scores Quebec cos exodus 4-28, 346E2
Scores Quebec white paper 4-28, 346F2
At 7-natn econ summit 5-7—5-8, 357B1
In France, sees Giscard 5-11—5-14, 389G1
Liberals win 5 by-electns 5-24, 410A3
On '72 police break-in 5-26, 426E1
Announces separatn 5-27, 426F1
Names Towe amb to US 6-3, 525A3
At Commonwealth Conf, scores Amin 6-8—6-15, 486C3
On language freedom 6-23, 505A2
Names unity task force 7-5, 542E1
Sees Schmidt 7-6—7-12, scores US rights policy 7-14, 566G1, F2
Polysar scored re rebates 7-7, 542B1
Scores new language bill 7-14, 561F2
Bars CBC apology, repeats separatism chrg 7-21, 579B3
Scores Levesque language deal 7-28, 596G3
Asks wage, price controls end 7-29, 616A3
Sees Tanzania pres 8-2—8-3, 624C1
Natives score prov plan rejectn 8-4, 616G2
Labor rejcts wage, price plan 8-17, 634E2
At Panama Canal pact signing 9-7, 678C1
OKs Alcan gas pipe 9-8, 687B1
Levesque rejcts language amendmt 9-9, 741F3
Vows Quebec referendum bar 9-9, 742E1
Shuffles Cabt 9-16, 725E2
Begin yields women's post 9-23, 763C3
Torrijos begins intl tour 9-24, 755F3
Bars actn vs language bill 10-6, 780C1
Queen Eliz visits 10-14—10-19, 822B2
Asks intl nickel cartel 10-21, 924B1
On RCMP '73 PQ break-in 10-28, 841B1
In Alberta, BC 10-31—11-1, 882A3
Backs RCMP 11-2, 882F2
Scores PC tap chrgs 11-3, 902E2
RCMP memo urged '72 raid briefing 11-8, 903A2
RCMP file chrgd 11-15, 923A2
Discounts RCMP file 11-16; defends RCMP mail opening, bars Cabt resignatns 11-18, 923C2

TRUMAN, Harry S. (1884-1972)—*For biog. data, see 1945, pp. 115P-116B; 1948, p. 229AC; 1972, p. 1044F1-A2*
'75 radical bombing convictn reversed 4-5, 484F1
Arvey dies 8-25, 696C2
TRUNKLINE Gas Co.—*See under PANHANDLE Eastern Pipe Line Co.*
TRW Inc.
Boyce arrested as spy 1-16, 41E2
Boyce convicted as spy 4-28, 344A2
TSANAS, Andrew
Convicted 6-15, sentenced 8-5, 848A2
TSANAS, Pauline
Sentence suspended 8-5, 848B2
TSEGAYE Debalke
Killed 2-2, 98F2
TSHOMBE, Daniel
Popular support rptd 3-24, 260F3
TSHOMBE, Moise (d. 1969)
Cuba aid to foes cited 1-9, 19A1
Zaire prov invaded 3-8, 207C2
Mwant Yav treason chrgd 8-13, 641E2
TSONGAS, Rep. Paul E. (D, Mass.)
Sees Ethiopia ldr 12-13, rpts terror 12-16, 998C2
TUAN Chun-yi
Named rail chief 2-20, 134D1
TUBBS, Tony
USSR tour results 1-29—2-5, 263C2
TUBERCULOSIS—*See MEDICINE—Diseases*
TUCHMAN, Jessica
On arms-sales policy 5-19, 380E2

1978

US natural gas, tariff agrmts OKd 1-17, 53G2
Fox resigns 1-30, Cabt shuffled 2-2, 70D1, F1
On USSR spy ring 2-10, 111B1
Sees prov premrs on econ 2-13—2-15, 111D1
Bars Kitimat oil depot plan 2-23, 130F1
Backs Fox decision 2-23, 166E2
At Liberal Party conv 2-24—2-26, 145E2
Names ECC new wage-price monitor 3-11, 209D2
Addresses NY investors 3-21, 225F2
Goyer sets resignatn 4-6, 287E1
Scores Quebec tax cuts 4-13, 286B3
Admits RCMP candidate monitoring 4-27, 328C2
Delays gen electn 5-11, 350E1
Levesque scores electn delay 5-14, 370D1
Stevens retracts C$ speculatn chrg 5-24, 412G3, 413A1
Addresses UN disarmamt sessn, ends A-arms role in Eur 5-26, 421G1, 422A1
Offers const plan, rights charter 6-12, 451D1
Bars Treu case interventn 6-13—6-14, 451D3
Presents const legislatn 6-20, 472F2
Quebec labor law challenge asked 6-22, 571C3
Backs ct re airport French ban 6-30, 515E1
Chrgs Maschino kidnaped 7-1, 531F3
At 7-natn Bonn econ summit 7-16—7-17, 543C3, 544B2
Signs hijacking pact 7-17, 544A3
Offers econ stimulatn, PO reorgnzn plan 8-1, 613D1
Premiers score const plan 8-10, defends 8-16, 646G3-647A2
Budget cuts detailed 8-16, 8-24, 666C2
Accepts Munro resignation 9-8, 721D2
Cited re C$ weakness 9-11, 703F3 ★
Sup Ct to hear const plan 9-13, letter scores provs 9-18, 754E3
Sets '79 general electn 9-15, 738F3
Liberal loss seen in by-electns 10-16, 813F1, B2
In const talks, OKs power sharing 10-31—11-1; vows '79 chngs 11-2, 866E1-C3
Defends Petro-Canada purchase 11-15, 901D2
Shuffles Cabt; creates econ panel, ends urban affairs post 11-24, 921G2
Sees prov premrs on econ 11-27—11-29, 944F1
Names Schreyer gov gen 12-7, 963D3
Bars resignatn 12-14, 985D3
Admits wages lag behind prices 12-19, 1013D2

TRUESDELL Jr., Maj. Gen. Karl (ret.)
Dies 8-22, 708F3
TRUJILLO, Flor de Oro
Dies 2-15, 196G3
TRUJILLO, Julio Cesar
Arrested 1-15, freed 1-30, 112B1
TRUJILLO, Rafael Leonidas (1891-1961)
Daughter dies 2-15, 196G3
TRUMAN, Harry S (1884-1972)—*See 1945, pp. 115P-116B; 1948, p. 229AC; 1972, p. 1044F1-A2, for biog. data*
Carter State of Union Message 1-19, 30D1
Judge Youngdahl dies 6-21, 540G3
'50 Blair House guard dies 7-13, 620F2
Sister dies 11-3, 972F3
Carter urges Genocide Conv ratificatn 12-6, 934B1
Nev A-test site '47 debate rptd 12-18, 1012C1
TRUMAN, Mary Jane
Dies 11-3, 972F3
TRUONG Dinh Dzu
Son seized as Viet spy 1-31, 68B3
TRUONG Dinh Hung (David Truong)
Arrested as Viet spy 1-31, 68B3
Convicted 5-19, 389F3-390F1
Sentenced 7-7, 555A1
TSAO Ti-chiu (d. 1976)
Rehabilitated 6-23, ashes brought to Peking 6-28, 515G1
TSENG Shao-shan
Loses Liaoning post 10-23, 814B2
TSHIVEKA, Gen.
Sentncd to death 5-27, gets reprieve 6-1, 441C2
TSIANG Yen-si
Heads Kuomintang 5-20, 401G3
Doubts US would honor Taiwan pledge 12-28, 994C3
TSIRANANA, Philibert
Dies 4-16, 356E3
TSIRONIS, Vasilios
Killed 7-11, 631C2
TSONGAS, Rep. Paul E. (D, Mass.)
Rpts Egypt, Sudan aid to Somalia 1-26, 99F3
Wins US Sen primary 9-19, 736B3
Elected 11-7, 846E1, 847F2, 858C2
TSOUMAS v. Glen Ellyn Savings and Loan Assn.
Case refused by Sup Ct 10-30, 832D3
TSWAIPE, Ompatile
Cleared in death of UK student, 2 others 11-13, 906D2
TUAN Chun-yi
Gets top Honan post 10-23, 814F1
Replaced as China rail min 10-26, 837G3
TUCHMAN, Barbara W.
Distant Mirror on best-seller list 10-9, 800C3; 11-6, 887G3; 12-3, 971B1

1979

Const talks continue, minor reforms OKd 2-5–2-6, 113F2-114B1
Defends corp profit 2-7, 114E1
Sees Barre 2-8, 133E3
Sees Carter, gets Alcan pipeline vow 3-3, 168F1
Stewart joins PCs 3-7, 189C1
Wife chrgs 'abuse' 3-8, 271C3
Sets electns, Liberal strength down 3-26, 233B3, E3
Starts electn campaign 3-27–3-29, 266G2
Denies past knowledge of RCMP illegalities 3-30, 253F2
Offers US oil pipe routes 4-10, 284E2
Liberals lose last prov govt 4-23, 311B2
Backs unilateral const patriatn 5-9, 368D3
In TV debate, asks natl unity 5-13, 368C3
Liberals lose electn 5-22, 377A1, C2, 378A1
Resigns 6-4, 423D3
Unveils shadow cabt, scores Clark 7-19, 563B2
Lauds bilingual air control rule 8-22, 651B1
On crown corp sales 9-28, 749C3
Scores PC speech 10-9, 788F2
Liberals attack policies 10-12–10-14, 812G1
Scores PCs re Israel Emb issue 10-29, 833F2
Scores PQ white paper 11-1, 853C2
Resigns Liberal ldrship 11-21, 907G2
NDP holds conv 11-22–11-25, 927E1
Poll backs ldrship 12-3, 927C1
To remain Liberal ldr 12-18, 966G3

TRUFFAUT, Francois
Love On The Run released 4-5, 528A3
TRUMAN, Harry S (1884-1972)—*See 1945, pp. 115P-116B; 1948, p. 229A-C; 1972, p. 1044F1-A2, for biog. data*
Rockefeller dies 1-26, 103G3
Meany prefers to Carter 2-19, 149E1
Anna Strauss dies 2-23, 176F3
Labor ldr cites '48 polls 6-7, 419G3
Cited in Carter SALT address 6-18, 458G2
Carter poll rating compared 7-1, 497F2
PR natist's sentence commuted 9-6, 666D1
TRUNK, Anne D.
Named to 3 Mile I probe 4-11, 275C1
TRUSCOTT IV, Lucian K.
Dress Gray on best-seller list 3-4, 173D3
TRUTH, Sojourner (1797-1883)
Miss Truth opens 7-22, 712E1
TRYON, Thomas
Fedora released 4-14, 528C2
TSATSOS, Constantine (Greek president)
Orders price freeze 2-23, 154B3
TSIPIS, Kosta
Cited in H-bomb letter 9-16, 9-18, 715F2
TSONGAS, Sen. Paul E. (D, Mass.)
Finances disclosed 5-18, 383G3
TSUDENGDANDA
Dalai Lama return OKd 7-18, 563B3
TU-22M (Backfire bomber)—*See ARMAMENTS—Aircraft*
TUBERCULOSIS—*See MEDICINE–Diseases*
TUCCI, John
Fired re Sup Ct news leaks 4-20, 302G2
Govt Printing Office transfer rptd 4-27, 382B3
TUCHMAN, Barbara
Distant Mirror on best-seller list 1-7, 80B3; 2-4, 120C3; 3-4, 173E3
Elected Arts Inst pres 2-27, 176F1

1980

Makes campaign vows 1-12, 38B1
Vs PCs re US pipe decisn 1-17, 56D3
Reelected 2-18, sets policies 2-19, 121A1, D2
Sworn, names Cabt 3-3, 171D1
Names Sauve House speaker 3-3, 171D2
Party wins Quebec by-electn 3-24, 230E3
Olympic com rejcts Moscow boycott 3-30, 259A3
Parlt opens, Throne Speech vows more econ control 4-14, 292E3
Bars Quebec negotiatns 4-15, 293A2
Urges Canada Cup play 4-28, 488E3
Campaigns vs PQ referendum in Montreal, Levesque scores 5-2, 350D2-G2
On Quebec referendum defeat 5-20, vows Const talks 5-21, 377D1
Sees Mex pres, signs trade agrmt 5-25—5-27, 409A3
Agrees to const negotiatns 6-9, 443C3
Lougheed oil price mtg set 6-19, 486D1
Sees Cossiga on A-reactors 6-24, 486F1
Affirms const vow, oil policy 7-6, 543A2
Prelim const talks held 7-8—7-24, 603B1
Gets US assurances on Alcan pipe completn 7-17, 562A2
Alberta oil talks fail 7-25, prices hiked 7-31, 577A2, A3
Const talks held, proposals rejected 9-8—9-13, 705E3-706F1
Sees Liberal caucus, Cabt 9-17, 9-18; recalls Parlt for const 'patriatn' 9-18, 728E1
Natl energy plan, budget proposal spurs heated oppositn 10-29—10-30; sees ct action vs Alberta oil productn cutback 10-31, 858B1
Patriatn plan opposed in poll 12-10, 964F2

TRUDEAU, Regis
Chrgd in '76 Olympic fraud 10-2, 788F1
TRUE Romance (magazine)
Us magazine sale rptd 3-7, 239B2
TRUE West (play)
Opens 12-23, 1003E3
TRUMAN, Harry R.
Missing in volcano eruptn 5-18, 382G1
Presumed dead 6-15, 504D3
TRUMAN, Harry S (1884-1972)—*See 1945, pp. 115P-116B; 1948, p. 229A-C; 1972, p. 1044F1-A2, for biog. data*
Ewing dies 1-8, 104E2
'46 inflatn rate cited 1-25, 75B2
Rose Conway dies 3-17, 279A2
Carter veto overridden 6-5, 6-6, 437B1
Carter pres renominatn acceptance speech 8-14, 612D1, 613B1
Reagan invokes name 10-1, 738G1
Carter cites arms-control stance 10-2, 762C2
Carter cites in TV debate 10-28, 814C3
Reagan hits Carter record 10-29, 817A2
Vote turnout cited 11-4, 838B3
TRUNBULL, Wendy
Loses Atlantic Classic 9-28, Phoenix 10-12, Australia Open 11-30; wins New S Wales champ 12-7, 947G1, A2-A3
TRUST for Public Land
Land donation rptd 12-19, 987G1
TRYFOROS, Lynne
'Scarsdale Diet' MD slain, 3-10, 215B1
TSATSOS, Constantine (Greek president)
Caramanlis elected pres 5-5, 352B2
TSONGAS, Sen. Paul E. (D, Mass.)
Alaska lands bill passes 8-19, 631E2
TSOTADZE, Liana
Wins Olympic medal 7-26, 623F3
TUAN, Lt. Col. Pham
Launched into space 7-23, 547G3
Returns to Earth 7-31, 592D1
TUBERCULOSIS—*See MEDICINE—Heart & Lungs*
TUCHMAN, Barbara W.
Distant Mirror wins Amer Book Award 5-1, 692E2

1976

TUCKER, C. Delores
- Carter meets black leaders 7-12, 513D2
- Dem conv rule debated 7-13, 513D1

TUCKER, James Guy
- Elected 11-2, 821G3, 828G3

TUCKER, Sterling
- Carter meets black leaders 7-12, 513C2

TUCSON (Ariz.) Daily Star, The (newspaper)
- Ariz crime probed 10-2, 849D2

TUCUMCARI (N.M.) News
- McCarthy endorsemt rptd 10-30, 827E3

TUENI, Ghassan
- Suspends publicatn 12-30, 974D1

TUFTS University (Medford, Mass.)
- Kemp mil capability study rptd 1-25, 68F2
- Mayer becomes pres 7-1, 504D2

TUGENDHAT, Christopher
- Europn Comm meets 12-22—12-23, 977F1

TUKEY, Dr. John W.
- Panel urges aerosol curb 9-13, 691F2

TUKKALO, Helena
- Wins Olympic medals 2-7, 2-10, 159D1

TULARE (Calif.) Advance Register (newspaper)
- Carter endorsement rptd 10-30, 831G2

TULLER, Bryce
- Sentencd in '72 hijack 7-16, 544C1

TULLER, Charles
- Sentencd in '72 hijack 7-16, 544C1

TULLER, Jonathan
- Sentencd in '72 hijack 7-16, 544C1

TULLY, Jack
- Uganda releases 8-3, 581A1

TULSA, Okla.—*See OKLAHOMA*

TULSA World (newspaper)
- Ford endorsement rptd 10-30, 831F2

TUMERMAN, Leo
- On Sovt A-disaster 12-8, 948E3

TUMMERMAN, Alexis
- Sahara diplomatic efforts continue 2-1—2-6, 107A3
- USSR chrgs Israel internmt 2-4, 122C2

TUNA—*See FISH*

TUNA Boat Association, American
- To appeal porpoise ruling 5-11, 398E2

TUNCSIK, Jozsef
- Wins Olympic medal 7-30, 574G3

TUNISIA—*See also AFRICAN Development Bank, ARAB League, NONALIGNED Nations Movement, OAU*
- EC pact rptd 1-13, 84E2
- Listed as 'not free' nation 1-19, 20E3
- Sahara plea rptd 1-29, 58D2
- EC pact 'bias' protested 2-3, signing delayed 2-4, 164F2 ★
- Angola MPLA recognized 2-14, 163E2
- Shuns UN pollutn pact signing 2-16, 126B3
- UN Palestine com member 2-26, 162C1
- Aide in bombed Cambodian town 3-2—3-4, 238B2
- Mulcahy confrmd US amb 3-3, 186B2
- Egypt detains Masmoudi 3-9, 205A2
- Rpt Libya expels natls 3-21, 239F2
- 3 Libyans arrested, amb recalled in death plot; Libya denies 3-22, 239C2
- Libya accuses re Gabes oil moves 3-22, 239F2
- Qaddafi assassinatn try rptd 4-19, 334F1
- Death plot trial 4-19—4-23, Libyan gets death 4-23, 335A1
- Expulsns from Libya rptd 5-3, 335D1
- Defense min dies 5-25, 503C3
- Cabt shuffled 5-31, 503C3
- Bars Libyan hijacked jet 7-6, 539A2
- Rptd Libya terror target 7-15, 531E1
- Olympic withdrawal rptd 7-21, 528B3
- Libyan invasn plan chrgd 8-13, 629G3
- Moufida Bourguiba dies 11-14, 932C3
- **Middle East Conflict**—*See MIDDLE EAST*

TUNNELS—*See BRIDGES & Tunnels*

TUNNEY, Gene
- Ali decisns Norton 9-28, 756F2

TUNNEY, Sen. John V(arick) (D, Calif.)
- Chrgs US arms airlift to Angola 1-6, US denies 1-7, 3D2
- Aide rpts MPLA seeks US ties 1-25, 82D2
- Beats Hayden in primary 6-8, 409B2
- On tap warrants bill 9-20, 884E1
- AFL-CIO donatn rptd 10-22, 938D3
- Loses reelection 11-2, 817E1, 819D3, G3, 824F3
- Flying Tiger gifts rptd 12-29, 986E1

TURBAY Ayala, Julio Cesar
- Lopez rejects reelectn move 1-7, 31C1
- Election results 4-18, 310G3

TURCHIN, Valentin
- Tverdokhlebov sentncd 4-15, 292B2

TURESSEN, Bo
- Named to Swedish Cabt 10-8, 794C2

1977

TUCKER, Dr. Benjamin
- At Biko inquest 11-23, 934C1

TUCKER, C. DeLores
- Shapp defends ouster 9-28, 800C2

TUCSON, Ariz.—*See ARIZONA*

TUCSON Gas and Electric Co.
- Navajo ldr indicted 2-9, 162E3
- Navajo fraud case dismissed 5-17, 492A1

TUGENDHAT, Christopher Samuel
- Gets Eur Comm post 1-7, 74D2
- Labor loses by-electn 2-24, 201B1

TUG Fork River (Ky., Va.)
- Floods rptd 4-3—4-6, 311G2

TUIJNMAN, Daniel
- Named Dutch transport min 12-19, 986B1

TULANE University (New Orleans, La.)
- Schally wins Nobel 10-13, 951D3

TULLY, James
- Loses parlt seat 6-16, 475C2

TULSA, Okla.—*See OKLAHOMA*

TULSA, University of
- August in NFL draft 5-3, 353B3

TUNISIA—*See also ARAB League, NONALIGNED Nations Movement, OAU*
- UN Assemb member 4C1
- '76 EC trade pact cited 1-18, 73E3
- Wage hikes set 1-19, 140A1
- 20 students sentenced 1-24, 140B1
- EC-Arab League mtg 2-10—2-12, 146G1
- Israel boycott eased 2-18, 167F2
- Students rptd freed 3-15; gen amnesty, liberties asked 4-12, 567F1
- US oil rig in Gabes protested 5-27, 497G2
- World Ct to hear Libya Gabes disputed 6-10, 497E2
- Ben Salah, others sentncd 8-20; Swiss group scores torture 9-1, 867D2
- France guillotine Tunisian 9-10, 728C2
- Textile workers strike, police quell 10-10—10-13, union asks probe 10-26, 867C2
- Sweden lets debts stand 10-12, 904A1
- UN pollutn conf ends, Medit pact reached 10-21, 876B2
- Exxon admits paymts 10-25, 818A2
- Sadat Israel trip backed 11-19, 890B3
- Interior min ousted 12-23; 6 mins resign, pro-labor stand cited 12-25, 1019D2

TUN Lin
- Rptd purged 10-8, 779B3

TUNNEY, John V(arick)
- '76 spec interest gifts rptd 2-15, 128C2

TUPELO, Miss.—*See MISSISSIPPI*

TURBAY Ayala, Julio Cesar
- OKs '78 pres primary 3-21, 255A2
- Affirms '78 primary plan 8-17, 727E2

TURCHIN, Valentin
- Arrested 7-4, 551B3
- Leaves USSR 10-14, 812B2

TURKAWI, Rami Deeb
- Convicted 6-2, executed 6-13, 457B3

TURKES, Alparslan
- NAP violence alleged 5-3, 351C1
- Ecevit wins elections 6-5, 451E1
- Demirel wins confidence vote 8-1, 641D1

1978

TUCKER, Rep. James Guy (D, Ark.)
- Faces Sen primary runoff 5-30, 426G1
- Loses runoff 6-13, 467E1
- Bethune wins seat 11-7, 855A2

TUEART, Dennis
- Cosmos win NASL title 8-27, named playoff MVP 8-31, 707C2, E2

TUENI, Ghassan
- Asks Israelis quit Leb 3-17, 197B2

TUGWELL, Franklin
- Study faults govts on energy policy 6-13, 450G2

TUHAMI, Hassan
- Seeks Arab support for summit pact 9-24, 730A3

TULANE University
- Long proposes value-added tax 11-30, 962A2

TULLY, Mike
- Sets indoor pole vault record 1-7, 76G2
- Sets pole vault marks 3-11, 5-19, 692D3, F3; 6-1—6-4, 600G3

TULSA, Okla.—*See OKLAHOMA*

TUNE, Tommy
- Best Little Whorehouse opens 4-17, 760D1

TUNICK, Jonathan
- Wins Oscar 4-3, 315C3

TUNISIA—*See also ARAB League, NONALIGNED Nations Movement, OAU*
- Labor ldrs quit PSD posts 1-10, 1-11; gen strike provokes violence, arrests 1-26—1-28, 74A1
- Strike ldr Achour's release sought 1-31; arrest total rptd, 160 sentenced 2-5, 170E1
- Unionists denounce gen strike 2-1; UGTT suspends Achour, 10 others 2-2, 170D1
- Labor army draft plan rptd 3-3, 170A2
- UGTT members on trial 7-19, security ct to hear case 8-15, 671A1
- Amnesty Intl chrgs workers tortured 8-1, 671E1
- Worker trials rptd, Achour to face coup chrg 8-11, 671C1
- Achour, other UGTT offcls sentncd 10-10, 872E3
- **Foreign Relations (misc.)**
- Qaddafi visits, Libya agitatn chrgd 2-6, 170G1
- Arab fund poor-natn aid rise rptd 4-9, 257F2
- French identify 2 as slain Leb guerrillas 5-22, 384A1
- France UGTT trial observers barred 7-16, 7-18, 671D1
- Arab fund loan to Sudan rptd 8-17, 925F3
- UN Assemb member 713F3
- **Sports**
- World Cup soccer finals, sidelights 6-1—6-25, 519F3

TUNNELS—*See BRIDGES*

TUNNEY, Gene
- Dies 11-7, 972F3

TURBAY, Diana
- Colombia pres pvt secy 8-7, 629F3

TURBAY Ayala, Julio Cesar (Colombian president; sworn Aug 7)
- Lopez favoritism chrgd 2-20, 147A2
- Wins Liberal pres nominatn 2-26, campaign 'name-calling' rptd 2-28, 147C1
- Scores Betancur, ends pres campaign 5-28, 413A2
- Wins electn 6-4; Betancur disputes count, Conservatives protest 6-5—6-9; postpones Venez visit 6-9, recount begins 6-11, 443E1-E2
- Wins pres vote recount 6-15; Betancur concedes 6-20; Turbay scores 6-23, 629F3
- Sworn pres, vows rights respect 8-7, 629F2
- On all-male Cabt 8-7, women score 8-9, 629E3
- 'Security statute' enacted, scored 9-6, 814C2
- Balcazar elected vice pres 10-11, 815A1
- Security statute scored; probe set, dropped 10-29—11-4, 1015G2-A3
- Torture in mil jail rptd 11-8, 1015D2
- Vs House, Sup Ct pay hike 11-10, 1015G3

TURBITT, William
- Kidnaped 6-17, rptd 'executed' 6-19, 474E2
- IRA scores RC primate 7-1, 630A2

TURCOTTE, Rudy
- Injured in horse race 5-3, 539C3

1979

TUCKER, Henry
- Gets prison abuse award 1-5, 24A2

TUCKER, James Keith
- Arrested on kidnap chrgs 7-30, 604G3

TUCSON, Ariz.—*See ARIZONA*

TUENI, Ghassan
- Vs UN Palestinian film 8-28, 643E2
- Scores Israel Leb attacks 8-29, 658F2

TUFTS University (Medford, Mass.)
- Monkeys rptdly help handicapped 3-19, 219C2
- S Africa stock divestiture rptd 3-24, 271C1
- Cormack wins Nobel 10-12, 858E1

TUGGLE, Richard
- Escape from Alcatraz released 6-21, 820B1

TUGWELL, Rexford Guy
- Dies 7-21, 588E3

TUIASOSOPO, Manu
- In NFL draft 5-3, 335F1

TULANE University (New Orleans, La.)
- Loses Liberty Bowl 12-22, 1001A3

TULSA (Okla.) Tribune, The (newspaper)
- Bilingual educ oppositn rptd 1-29, 127C2
- Scores Carter energy speech 7-16, 534D3

TUNA—*See FISHING Industry*

TUNISIA—*See also ARAB League, NONALIGNED Nations Movement, OAU*
- Egypt recalls envoy 4-7, 278D1
- Egypt ties cut 4-27, 319C2
- Arab League meets, Klibi named head 6-28, 475E2
- PLO arms to Nicaragua confiscated 7-11, 512E2
- UN membership listed 695A3

TUNNEL Fever (play)
- Opens 5-10, 712B3

TUR, Juan
- PR prisoner trade denied 9-6, 666A2
- Released 9-17, 706E3

TURANO, Giuseppe
- Slain 7-12, 547B1

TURBAY Ayala, Julio Cesar (Colombian president)
- Suspends const rights 1-9, 115E1
- At Andean Group mtg; named trade rep, OKs Venez oil talks 5-26—5-28, 398A2, C2
- Roldos sworn Ecuador pres 8-10, 613F2
- Army power gain in '79 guerrilla drive rptd 11-14, 993A1

TURGENEV, Ivan Sergeyevich (1818-1883)
- Month in the Country opens 12-11, 1007C2

TURKEL, Studs
- Joins Citizens Party 8-1, 594F3

TURKES, Alparslan
- NAP hq attacked 6-30—7-1, 568F2

1980

TUCKER, Dr. Benjamin
- Biko probe squashed 6-29, 525E1

TUCKER, Carll
- Sells Saturday Review, retains editorial post 5-20, 582E3

TUCKER, Col. Charles
- Attacked in PR 3-12, 190D1

TUCKER, Jim Guy
- Families Conf opens 6-5, 442E3

TUCKNER, Howard
- Dies 8-2, 676E3

TUCSON—*See ARIZONA*

TUCSON Citizen, The (newspaper)
- Ariz U to seek athletic dept fraud probe 10-16, 875A3

TUITE, Gerard
- Escapes London jail 12-16, 994C1

TULANE University (New Orleans, La.)
- Loses Hall of Fame Bowl 12-27, 999D3

TULLY, James
- In Viet MIA missn 10-1—10-4, 855C2

TULSA—*See OKLAHOMA*

TUMER, Adm. Nejat
- In Turkey mil junta 9-21, 720C3

TUNA—*See FISHING Industry*

TUNE, Tommy
- Day in Hollywood opens 5-1, 392F2
- Wins Tony 6-8, 692C3

TUNGUSKA River
- '08 blast linked to meteorite 1-24, 160E3

TUNGUYAN, Mohammed Jawad Baqir
- Iraq captures 10-31, rptd wounded 11-6; Iran demands return 11-2, Iraq rejects 11-3, 854B3
- Iran demands release 12-15—12-16, 951F2-G2*

TUNISIA—*See also ARAB League, NONALIGNED Nations, OAU*
- Phosphate productn cited 2-25, 139F3
- Nouira ill 2-25; Mzali named interim premr 3-1, 196G3
- 13 hanged re Gafsa attack 4-17, 316G2
- Mzali confrmd premr, party ldr 4-23, 316A3
- **Foreign Relations (misc.)**
- UN Cncl seat taken 1-1, 12B2
- Gafsa attacked, Libya chrgd 1-27—1-28, 89G3-90B1
- Libyans wreck French emb 2-4, 90D1
- US closes Libya emb 2-7, 198E2
- Arab League mtg on Gafsa attack ends 2-28, comm named in Libya dispute 2-29, 197B1
- Carter vows support, heavy arms airlifted 2-29, 197C1
- Tito funeral held 5-8, 339B1
- UN Cncl scores Israel Jerusalem move 8-20, 627C2
- Libya, Syria to merge; '74 pact cited 9-2, 660G3
- Slim asks Iraq, Iran end war 9-23, 718D3
- Palestinian rights, Israel exit from Jerusalem urged 11-28, 950F2

TUNNELS—*See BRIDGES & Tunnels*

TUPPER, John (d. 1978)
- Jacobson sentenced for murder 6-3, 502B2

TURA, Eshetu
- Wins Olympic medal 7-31, 624D1

TURBAY Ayala, Julio Cesar (Colombian president)
- Amnesty Intl chrgs harrassmt 1-17, 96F2
- Receives E Ger amb 2-27, 141D1
- Party wins by-electns 3-9, 180F3
- Castro offers asylum to DR Emb captors 3-18, 211C3
- DR Emb captors ask Panama mtg 4-19, 'dialogue' rejcted 4-21, 311F2, C3
- Scores Amnesty Intl, asks OAS rights probe 4-20, 311F3
- On DR Emb siege victory 4-27, 335G2
- Condemns Bolivia coup 7-29, 577D1
- Attends Santa Marta conf 12-17, 992B3

TUREL, Vecdi
- Wounded 4-17, 316A2

TURK, Judge James C.
- Sentences Nixon impeachmt lawyer 6-10, 460C1
- Fines Pittston unit $100,000 12-4, 963A1

TURKES, Alpaslan
- Surrenders 9-14, 696E2
- Arrested 10-11, 793E3

1976

TURKEY—*See also IEA, NATO, OECD*
Student unrest, univs shut 1-8—3-8, 192D2
Listed as 'free' nation 1-19, 20C3
4 'Liberatn Army' members killed 1-22, 192A3
6 plotters sentenced 2-7, 192B3
Ergin named AF cmdr 3-5, 192D2
3 dead in univ clashes 4-8, 315A2
Film dir, nephew sentncd 7-13, 873G3
3 killed in factnl unrest 9-5, 873G3
Turkish jet hits Karakaya Mt 9-19, controller suspended 9-21, 736F1-A2
Strikes vs special cts, DISK arrests rptd 10-3; cts abolished 10-11, 873D3
Oil search shifted to E Medit 11-12, 897B2
Quake hits, toll over 4,000 11-24, 896F3; map 897A1
'70 quake casualties cited 11-27, 932A1
Sets '77 budget, defnse hike 12-1, 1011G3
Students killed 12-10, univ closed 12-13, 1012A1
Bursa auto plant to close 12-24, 1012A1
Cyprus—*See under 'C'*
European Force Reduction Issues—*See under EUROPE*
Foreign Relations (misc.)
Balkan natns meet 1-26—2-5, 213E3
Lockheed payoffs rptd 2-4, 2-6, 130E2, C3, 131B1
Lockheed probe rptd, AF cmdr quits 2-9—3-12, 192A2
Emb aide slain in Leb 2-16, amb car attacked 2-17, 125A2
OKs UN Medit pollutn pact 2-16, 126C3
Northrop paymts rptd 2-20, 362C3
US coal venture failure rptd 2-21, 167B1
UN Palestine com member 2-26, 162C1
US aid, base pact reached 3-26, 244F1
Greek protest of US pact cited 3-31, 259C2
Assemb vote on US pact set, Demirel warns US vs pact chng 4-1, 259E2
IMF OKs SDR buy 4-1, 315F1
Total IMF oil loan rptd 4-1, 339G3, 340B2
Lockheed mil trial 4-7, 298F1; gens cleared, probe quashed 4-30, 322A3
At Pak, Iran econ summit 4-21—4-22, 298A2
Islamic Conf held 5-12—5-15, 373B1
PLO office to open 5-12, 373B2
Arms sales to Ethiopia rptd 5-19, 364A3
Tito visits 6-8—6-10, 543D3
'70 Sovt hijackers refused US asylum 6-24; freed 7-10, fly to Rome 7-11, 543G3
Ship in US Bicentennial event 7-4, 488D3
US urges Aegean oil search delay 7-13, 538E1
Lets Sovt carrier enter Medit 7-18, 540F2
Israel seizes freighter 8-10, 578G1
Guerrillas land from ship at Tel Aviv 9-25, 10-13, 759E2
'77 US aid funds signed 10-1, 806E3
US base pact not cleared 10-2, 883C3
Syria border clash 10-14, 858A3
US backs Denktash UN debate role 11-9, 863E1
US offers quake aid 11-25, 11-28, 897D1
US arms embargo cited 12-1, 1011G3
Energy min in USSR, loan set 12-21, 1011B2
Renault sets plant closing 12-24, 1012A1
Yugo drug smuggling rptd 12-29, 1012A2

1977

TURKEY—*See also CENTO, IEA, NATO, OECD*
Univ reopens, student violence mounts 2-3, 138D2
Dec '75-76 inflatn rate rptd 2-7, 287B2
Lira devalued 3-2, 259A3
2 hijackers seize jet 3-19, 224F3
Izmir, Ankara bombings 3-24, 3-29, 259F2
Elazig Prov quake 3-25, 286D3
Pol violence 4-26—4-28, May Day riot 5-1; Koruturk issues plea 5-3, 350G3
Orient Express ends svc 5-22, 458F3
Ecevit's party wins electns 6-5, 451C1
Credit loss halts oil drilling 6-20, 565C2
Austerity measures imposed 9-8, 709B2
Lira devalued 10% 9-21, 730F3
Cholera outbreak suspected 9-26, 748A1
Student shot, pol deaths rptd 12-30, 1018A2
Cyprus—*See under 'C'*
Foreign Relations (misc.)—*See also 'Monetary, Trade & Aid' below*
UN Assemb member 4C1
'76 Eur Cncl pact vs terror cited 9G2
Rumania blocks dissident contact 4-2, 315F1
Vatican amb slain 6-9, 565G1-A2
UK warned re Makarios successor 8-12, 617E1
Eur Cncl to study rights abuses 9-8, 764G1-A2; rpt shelved, Greece protests 11-3, 946E3
Israel accused re '67 US ship raid 9-18, 715D1
W Ger jet hijackers seek prisoners' release 10-13, 789B1
W Ger asks more Istanbul airport security 10-23, 868D3
Government & Politics—*See also other appropriate subheads in this section*
Gen scores govt 2-10; Demirel warns vs coup 2-11, coalitn rptd weak 2-16, 138B2
Ecevit forms govt 6-21; loses confidence vote, resigns 7-3, 530A2
Demirel asked to form new govt 7-4, Erbakan backs 7-5, 530D2
Demirel forms govt 7-21, 565D1
Demirel wins confidence vote 8-1, pol violence rptd 8-2, 8-7, 641C1
Munic electns weaken govt 12-11, Demirel resigns 12-31, 1018E1

1978

TURIN, Shroud of—*See SHROUD of Turin*
TURKEY—*See also COUNCIL of Europe, GATT, IEA, NATO, OECD*
Ecevit eases curbs on Turkish Greeks 3-9, 216F2
'74 jet crash damages awarded 5-13, 460E1
Cyprus—*See CYPRUS*
Economy & Labor (domestic)
Ecevit announces priorities 1-4, 8C2
'77 inflatn rate rptd 36.6% 3-1, 170D3
Dvpt progrm, aid linked 10-12, 10-19, 840F1
European Force Reduction Talks—*See under EUROPE*
Foreign Relations (misc.)—*See also 'Monetary, Trade, Aid & Investment' below*
Ecevit announces priorities 1-4, 8C2
Bhutto death sentnc reversal plea rptd 3-22, 229B1
USSR staff chief in Ankara 4-26, 477D1
Ecevit rptd in W Eur 5-11, 378E1; 5-15—5-17, 398E2, A3
Ecevit hints USSR visit 5-29, 397D2
Wife of amb to Spain, 2 others slain 6-2, 476D3
Ecevit in Moscow; signs nonagressn, other pacts 6-21—6-23; West reassured 6-24, 6-30, 595F1
USSR lauds ties 6-25, 488D3
Kocas questns UK rptr's '71 death 7-24, 631A3
UN Assemb member 713F3
Government & Politics—*See also other appropriate subheads in this section*
Ecevit named premr 1-1; independents back 1-2, Cabt expansn seen 1-5, 8A2
Ecevit announces priorities 1-4, 8C2
Ecevit names Cabt 1-5, 21C2
Ecevit unity speech spurs parlt fistfight 1-15, 74G1
Ecevit wins confidence vote 1-17, 74E1, A2

1979

TURKEY—*See also COUNCIL of Europe, GATT, IEA, NATO, OECD*
Cyprus—*See CYPRUS*
Economy & Labor
Econ problems rptd 1-12, 40E2
Austerity measures disputed 2-7, 116G3
Austerity plan announced 3-16, 3-19, econ goals listed 3-21, 214E1-E2
Strike banned by govt 3-29, 333C2
Currency steps taken, black mkt costs seen 4-11, 333G1, C2
Union ldrs arrested 5-1, 333D1; freed 5-22, 398F1
Businessmen attack govt policies 5-15, 398C1
More currency steps, austerity measures set 6-12, 447A1
Mid '78-79 inflatn ranked worst in OECD 8-9, 627C1
European Force Reduction Talks—*See under EUROPE*
Foreign Relations (misc.)—*See also 'Monetary' and 'UN' below*
Ecevit sees forgn origins of terrorism 1-2, 8C1
Westn-natn Guadeloupe summit topic 1-5—1-6, 12G2
Kurds press Iran autonomy demands 2-22—3-1, 145E2
Turkish-Kurdish clashes in Azerbaijan 4-21, 297C3
USSR rptd vs U-2 flights 5-14—5-29, 397B3
Israel, USSR consul murder plans rptd 7-11, 568E2
Palestinian rebels raid Egypt Emb 7-13, siege ends 7-15, 536C2
Egypt Emb attack, PLO aide's murder linked 7-26, 552B1
USSR aid to Iran Kurds rptd 9-4, 688B2
Canada envoy tours Mideast 9-9—10-20, 833D2
USSR OK denied sought re U-2 use 9-12, 762E1
PLO gets full status 9-27, 740C3
Pope visits; seeks Eastn Orthodox reunificatn, Islam ties 11-28—11-30, sees Dimitrios I 11-29, 11-30, 930A3
Sovt Afghan invasn opposed 12-30, 974E2
Government & Politics—*See also other appropriate subheads in this section*
Ozaydinli quits as interior min 1-2, 8B1
Censure motion fails 1-4, 7G3
Defns min quits; new defns, interior mins named 1-14, 40F2
Cabt dispute resolved 4-17, 287D3
3 MPs quit Ecevit party 4-23, 397D2
Repub People's Party cong rptd, Ecevit reelected chrmn 5-28, 397G3-398B1
Parlt recesses after anti-Ecevit moves fail 6-28, 488F1-B2
Dep premr resigns 9-20, 775E1
Housing min resigns 9-29, 775C2
Interior min quits 10-5, 795D3
Right wins parlt electns 10-14, Demirel asks gen electns 10-15; **Ecevit govt resigns 10-16,** 795G2
Demirel forms govt 11-12, 876B1
Demirel wins confidence vote 11-25, 929G2-A3

1980

TURKEY—*See also COUNCIL of Europe, CSCE, GATT, IEA, MBFR, NATO, OECD*
Cyprus—*See CYPRUS*
Economy & Labor
Gens seek united parties 1-2, 22E3
Workers riot in Izmir 1-22, 61C1
Austerity steps rptd 1-25, 80A1
Textile workers arrested amid growing labor unrest 3-13, 197F1
Econ problems noted 3-26, 236B2
Apr inflatn decline rptd 5-28, 410E3
Gens urge unity 5-30, 445A3
Interest rate rules eased 6-6, 446B1
Coal mines rptd denatlzd 6-10, 445F3
Demirel wins confidence vote 7-2, 500F2
Labor ldr slain 7-22, workers protest 7-23, 580D3
Econ ills, coup linked 9-12; coup ldrs back Demirel plan 9-15, 696G2, B3
Ozal gets Cabt post 9-21; Ulusu to continue econ austerity plan 9-22, 720B3, E3
New budget announced 12-1, 924A1
Foreign Relations (misc.)—*See also 'Monetary', 'UN Policy' below*
El Al rep slain 1-2, suspects arrested 2-13, 135G3, 136A1
USSR Afghan invasn scored 1-4, 10D3
Sovt base monitor accord with US set 1-9, curbs laid to Iran 1-10, 22G2
EC initiative launched, assured re Greek role 2-5, membership bid seen 2-7, 102A3
Amb to Switz attacked 2-6, other envoy deaths noted 2-28, 197A2
Aegean Sea air dispute ended 2-22, 2-23 150F2
Emigre worker draft exemptn bill OKd 2-29, 197E1
Illegal workers protest in Paris 3-3, 193B1
Rome Turkish Airlines office bombed 3-10, amb to Vatican attacked 4-17, 316G1-A2
USSR May Day parade marked 5-1, 354A3
Olympic boycott backed 5-22, Olympic com OKs 5-23, 421E1
Amnesty Intl chrgs torture 6-9, 445D3
W Ger drug arrests rptd 6-13, 517E1, G1
EC assoc status renewed, membership aim reaffirmed 7-1, 526F1
USSR consultatn barred re U-2 7-4, 526C1
W Ger pol asylum rules rptd tightened 7-31, 581C2, E2
Armenians attack diplomat in Greece 7-31, France 8-5, 606A1
Jerusalem consulate to close 8-28, 660C3
2 Afghan Emb aides defect to US 9-6, 705C1
Coup reaction 9-12—9-16, 696D3
Belgium links coup, NATO maneuvers withdrawal 9-15, 696B2
Kurds bomb Iraq pipeline 9-26, Iraq rpts repair work 9-27, 735D1
Iraq, Iran airspace denied 10-8, 774E2
Kurds attack W Berlin consulate 10-8, 794A2
Armenians bomb London office 10-12, 794G1*
Islamic econ conf held 11-4—11-6, 865B1
Islamic League meets 11-10, 895B2
Iraq renews pipeline use 11-20, 894A2
Spain weighs mil coup solutn 11-22, 903A3
Israeli ties cut 12-2, 912A1
Armenians kill 2 aides in Australia 12-17, 991A2
Iraq halts pipeline deliveries 12-19, 978A2
Government & Politics—*See also other appropriate subheads in this section*
Mil warns pol ldrs, urges unity 1-2, 7A2
Ecevit backs coalitn govt 1-9, 22D3
Ecevit scores govt, coalitn in doubt 2-14, 135E2
Pres electn deferred 3-22, 236D1
Pres impasse continues 4-10, 278A2
Pres voting chng barred 5-24—5-25, 410G3-411C1
Demirel wins confidence vote 7-2, 500E2
Erim slain 7-19, interior min quits 7-21, 567B3
Ecevit urges coalitn govt 7-21, 567G3
Mil coup ousts govt 9-12, 679D2-A3
Parlt members arrested, Evren sees return to civiln rule 9-12; right-wing ldr surrenders 9-14, junta sworn 9-18, 696C2-C3
Ulusu named premr 9-20; names Cabt 9-21, sets goals 9-22, 720A3
1,700 mayors dismissed 9-26, 754B3

1976

Greek Relations—*See 'Turkish Relations' under GREECE*

1977

Greek Relations—*See GREECE—Turkish Relations*
Helsinki Agreement—*See EUROPE—Security and Cooperation*
Monetary, Trade & Aid Issues (including all foreign economic developments)
Rpt Israel sells US-made arms 1-6, denied 1-7, 28C3
US rejects air fare hike 2-1, 324E3
W Ger arms sales set 2-2, 139E2
US aid deal rptd delayed 2-13, 109B1
EC stalled entry talks cited 2-13, 109C1
US arms talks fail 2-23, 122C3
Pak, Iran pact signed, RCD revitalized 3-12, 190B2
Trade deficit up in Jan, Feb 3-30, 259A3
Carter backs arms aid agrmt 4-19, Demirel scores delays 4-29, 351E1
US vows more mil aid 5-10, 359C1
US scores on defns agrmt 5-14, 380C1
Foreign reserves crisis 5-24—7-4, 565D2
'68 Israeli uranium purchase rptd 5-30, 416E3
Forgn exchng reserves rptd depleted 6-2, debts to be rescheduled 6-5, 451B2
Iraq pipeline opened 6-11, 565B2
'77 paymts deficit forecast 7-31, 586D2
US arms aid authorized 8-4, 668C1
'Luxury car' imports banned, export credits set 9-8, 709D2
Not in UN Medit pollutn pact 10-21, 876B2

1978

Greek Relations—*See GREECE—Turkish Relations*
Helsinki Agreement—*See EUROPE—Security and Cooperation*
Monetary, Trade, Aid & Investment—*See also 'U.S. Relations' below*
'77 paymts deficit up 2-6; import paymts, loan defaults rptd 3-1, 170B3
Currency devalued 23% 3-1, 170A3
IMF $450 mln loan granted 3-24, 291G3
USSR trade accord signed 4-5, 477C1
Islamic bank poor-natn aid rise rptd 4-9, 257F2
USSR proposes arms aid 4-26, 477D1
W Ger aid pledge rptd 5-15, 398F2
USSR trade pacts signed, aid hike vowed; '54-76 credits rptd 6-21—6-23, 595F1, D2
EC, other forgn aid sought 10-12, 10-19, 840E1
Forgn investmt campaign launched, code drafted 10-19, 10-26, 840D2
Debt restructuring planned 10-24, 840A2
Ecevit warns West on aid rise 11-4, 905G2

Terrorism & Unrest (domestic)
Gaziantep unrest 1-16, 74A2
Bomb explodes at rightist rally, Jan death total at 48 1-30, 170D3
Amkara, Izmir bomb blasts 2-18—2-19; total deaths at 64 2-20, 170E3
Istanbul Univ bomb attack kills 9 3-16, 230C2
Istanbul police chief attacked 3-16, 230C2
5 right-wing workers slain, Istanbul police arrest 80 3-19, 230D2
Ankara prosecutor assassinated, Ecevit scores 3-24; death total at 100 3-25, 230G1
Ankara bombing injures 20 4-12, 291F3
Malatya mayor, family killed in bombing 4-17; riots erupt, 3 leftists killed 4-17—4-19, 291B3
Right blamed for Malatya bombing 4-19, 378C2
Erzerum univ closed, 200 arrested 4-21, 378D2
Igdir rioting 4-23, 378E2
Left-wing ldrs sentenced 4-28, 378E2
Martial-arts clubs closed 4-28, 378G2
'78 death toll rptd 5-6, 378G2
Nikip riots, student killed 5-8, 476G3
Demirci pol groups clash, burn Ecevit hq 5-27, 477A1
Gaziantep, other pol violence rptd 5-31, 6-3, 477B1
Wife of amb to Spain, 2 others slain, Armenians take credit 6-2, 476D3
Ortaklar bombing kills 3 6-5, 477C1
Ex-naval officer, aide slain 6-23, 595D3
Comert slain; univ closed, students protest 7-11, 595B3
Police assns dissolutn order rptd overturned 7-20, 595E3
Pol deaths rptd at 2 per day 7-20, 595G3
Urfa, Kirikhan killings rptd 7-25, 595G3
Right-wing, left-wing clashes 8-8—8-11; Hasatli slain 10-3, 822A3
6 Labor Party members slain 10-8, party scores deaths 10-9, 822B3
Moslem sect riots 12-22—12-29, martial law decreed 12-26, 1021A1
Eceuit says right foments riots, Demiral blames govt 12-26, 1021E1

1979

Helsinki Agreement—*See EUROPE—Security and Cooperation*
Monetary, Trade, Aid & Investment
Westn natn aid offer rptd, forgn debt cited 1-12, 40B2
OECD takes aid role 2-6; needs rptd at $10 bln, IMF dispute cited 2-7, 116D3
Econ rescue plan announced, IMF linked 3-16; goals listed 3-21, 214E1-E2
Lira devaluatn vs $, exchng rates set 4-10; black mkt costs estimated 4-11, 333F1-C2
Cabt dispute resolved 4-17, 287E3
Businessmen attack govt policies 5-15, 398C1
Westn natns set aid, US offcls hail 5-30, 397E1, F2
USSR to build A-plant, ship more oil 6-5, 488F2-A3
Lira devalued vs $ again, exchng rates set 6-12, 447A1
IMF accord announced 6-13, 447E1
Hard currency use resumed, more imports set 7-31, 637D1
1st 1/2 current acct deficit down, trade data rptd 8-21, 637F1
Africa, E Eur trade hike set 8-21, 637E2
Forgn debt restructuring pact OKd 8-29, 711A1

Terrorism & Unrest
Interior min scored, quits 1-2, 8B1
Govt censure motion fails 1-4, 7G3
Milliyet editor killed 2-1, 117A1
Martial law extended 2 mos 2-25, 214E2
PLO aide sees Islamic upheaval 2-26, 144G1
Cabt rift resolved 4-17, 287E3
Martial law renewed, extended 4-25, 333E1
Terrorist arrests rptd 4-30; May Day arrests, rallies 5-1, 333B1
Union ldrs rptd freed 5-22, 398F1
Milliyet ed's slayer arrested 6-24, 568D2
NAP hq attacked 6-30—7-1; Marxist police cell found 7-14, 568E2
Student admits consul murder plans 7-11, 568E2
Egypt Emb raided, 2 guards die 7-13; hostages freed 7-15; 536C2; PLO aide's slaying linked 7-26, 552B1
Martial law extended 8-21, 637B2
Kurdish unrest probed 8-21—8-24, 795E3-796A1
Monthly deaths estimated 8-22, 637E2
Electn day violence rptd 10-15, 795B3
Publisher killed in Istanbul 11-19, prof 11-20, 5 in cafe 12-15, 998E1
Pope gets tight security 11-28—11-30, 930B3
4 Americans killed 12-14, 998B1
Martial law extended 12-19, 998F1
Violence marks '78 sectarian clash anniv 12-24, continues 12-25, 12-26, 998F1

1980

Demirel, Ecevit, MPs freed; Turkes, backers arrested 10-11; Erbakan chrgd 10-15, 793C3-794A1
Mil junta revises const, affirms powers 10-27, 832F2
Ecevit resigns party post 10-30, 832B3
Greek Relations—*See GREECE—Turkish Relations*

Monetary, Trade, Aid & Investment
US bases pact spurs aid pkg 1-9; curbs laid to Iran oil deal 1-10, 22A3
Lira devalued vs $, forgn debt, currency shortage cited 1-24, 61A1
Export, investmt incentives, tight money policy rptd 1-25, 80A1, C1
Debt plan announced 1-28, 80D1
Forgn debt restructuring sought 2-11; W Ger takes aid role, reassures Greece 2-16—2-19, IMF OKs loan 2-21, 135B3
W Ger mil aid plans noted 2-25, 153E3
Forgn exchng shortage linked to draft exemptn bill 2-29, 197E1
$3 bln forgn aid seen 3-8, 3-26, 236C2, D2
W Ger aid plans cited 3-10, 205E2
OECD aid package deferred 3-26, 236A2
US aid accord signed 3-29, 255A3
OECD OKs $1.16 bln aid 4-15, 295A3
W Ger budgets aid 4-30, 355E3
EC dumping probe cited 5-6, 412B1
IMF econ proposals rptd 5-6, 446C1
Iran sanctns barred 5-22, 393B2
US aid, influence linked 5-30, 445B3
Revised debt plan rptd 6-6, 445G3
Lira devalued vs $ 6-10, 445E3
IMF OKs $1.6 bln loan 6-18; '79 forgn debt, rescheduling rptd 6-19, 468E1
EC aid pact set 7-1, 526F1
Debt rescheduling rptd 7-24, 568A1
US to continue aid 9-12, 696E3
World Bank '80 loans rptd 9-22, 720E1
Iran, Iraq seek more trade 10-18, 821G1
US stays debt paymts 10-24, 874E3

Terrorism & Unrest
Gens seek united parties 1-2, 22E3
Workers riot in Izmir 1-22, 61C1
Amb to Switz attacked 2-6, other envoy deaths noted 2-28, Armenian terrorist groups described 3-1, 197A2
Violence continues, 4 die 2-10—2-18, 135A2
Leftists held in murder of El Al rep, 4 Americans 2-13, 135G3
Mil asks more powers 2-15, 135A3
Martial law extended 2-20, 135G2
Death toll rptd at 2,000 2-21, 135A3
New anti-terrorist steps seen 3-22, 236A2
US soldier killed 4-16, 316C2
Martial law extended again, violence toll rptd 4-18, 316B2
Rightist killed 5-27, violence worsens 5-29, 5-30; Ecevit scores govt 5-30, 445G2
Gens warn vs violence 5-30, 445G2
Amnesty Intl chrgs torture 6-9, 445D3
Oppositn offcl killed 6-17, funeral attacked 6-18, 468C2
Martial law extended 2 mos 6-18, 468B2
Econ steps' impact feared 6-19, 468B2
Corum hit by Moslem riots 7-4—7-5, 544D3
Fatsa seized by army; curfew set, over 300 arrested 7-11, 544A3
Koksaloglu murdered, sec cncl urges new laws 7-15, 544F3
Erim slain 7-19, interior min quits 7-21, 567B3
Mil impatience rptd 7-21, 567G3
Labor leader slain 7-22, 580D3
Anti-terrorist bills set 7-24, 580A3
Armenians attack diplomat in Greece 7-31, France 8-5, 606A1
'78 rioters sentenced 8-8, 620E3
Evren links pol violence, mil coup 9-12, 696G2
Army officer, leftist killed 9-14, leftist gets death sentence 9-19, 720F3
Martial law chngs 9-21; Ulusu seeks terrorism end 9-22, 720D3
500 Kurds arrested after martial law protest 9-22, 720G3-721A1
Kurds bomb Iraq pipeline 9-26, 735D1
Mayors dismissed, firearms controls set 9-26, 754B3
Erim murder suspects rptd arrested 10-3, 794B1
2 terrorists executed 10-8, 794A1
Kurds attack W Berlin consulate 10-8, 794A2
Turkes, backers arrested 10-11, Erbakan chrgd 10-15, 793E3, G3
Armenians bomb offices in NY, Calif, London 10-12, 794D1, G1*
Moslem extremists hijack plane 10-13, commandos overcome 10-14, 794A2
Mil arrests rptd over 11,000 10-28, 832G2
Left-wing publisher arrested 11-5, dies in jail 11-7, 923F3
Left-wing newspaper banned 11-11, 874C3; ban lifted 11-20, 924F1
Right, left-wing extremists ordrd arrested 11-12, 888C3
Violence rptd down since coup 11-14, 888F1-A2
US soldier killed 11-15, 888A2
Executn sought for 30 leftists 11-18, 888B2
200 Kurdish plotters chrgd 11-19, 924D1
Torture, jail deaths chrgd 11-27, 923E3
Armenians kill 2 aides in Australia 12-17, 991A2
4 Palestinians get death for '79 Egypt Emb attack 12-23, 997A1
Mil arrests rptd at 30,000 12-27, 997A1

1976

TURKMEN Soviet Socialist Republic—*See 'Republics' under USSR*
TURNER, Henry B.
Succeeded in Commerce post 2-26, 186A2
TURNER, John M.
Quits Commons seat 2-13, 188F2
TURNER, Richmond K. (U.S. warship)
In Intl Naval Review 7-4, 488D3
TURNER, Russell
Held in Indian shooting 5-5, 384F2
TURNER Elkhorn Mining Co.
Black lung law upheld 7-1, 568G3
Ariz crime probed 10-2, 849D2
TUVALU (formerly Ellice Islands) (British colony)
Secedes from Gilberts 12-31-75, 12F3
TVERDOKHLEBOV, Andrei N.
Sentenced 4-15, 292F1
Appeal denied 5-12, 4421G2
TV Guide (magazine)
Canada editns rptd purchased 11-27, 945F3
XII Winter Olympic Games (TV special)
Wins Emmy 5-17, 460C2
27 Wagons Full of Cotton and A Memory of Two Mondays (play)
Opens 1-26, 1014B3

1977

U.S. Relations—*See also 'Monetary, Trade & Aid' above*
US envoy sees ldrs 2-20—2-22; arms, base talks fail 2-23, 122F1, B2
US Gen's view of cong actn rptd 3-27, 232A1
US consul's house fired on 3-29, 259F2
Carter meets Demiral, vows more mil aid 5-10, 359C1
Spiers confrmd amb 5-25, 500B1
Ecevit vows better ties 6-5, 451C2
US warned re Makarios successor 8-12, 617E1
Israel accused re '67 US ship raid 9-18, 715D1
TURKISH Airlines
Hijackers seize jet 3-19, 224F3
'74 Paris crash cited 3-27, 244D2
'74 Paris crash claims setld 4-14, 312C1
TURNBULL, Wendy
Loses US Open 9-11, 787C1
TURNER, Ann Sheppard
Wilmington 10 pardon sought 12-4, 943B1
TURNER, Dan
Rpts Trudeau separatn 4-8, 281C3
TURNER, Jessie
On '76 NAACP budget surplus 1-10, 59A3
TURNER, Adm. Stansfield
Named CIA dir 2-7, confrmd 2-24, 148G3
Backs criminal penalties for leaks 3-9, 212D1
On Sovt mil buildup 3-20, 211C3
CIA reorganizatn dispute 6-10, 6-12, Knoche resigns 7-13, 576B2, E2
Testifies on CIA mind-control tests 8-3, 611F1; 9-21, 721C3
Given new powers 8-4, 610F2
Denies Park pres mansn taps 8-9, 688E2
Agent cuts proposed 8-9, 11-12, 880C3
China econ outlook rptd 8-15, 635D3
Testifies on canal talks tap rpt 9-19, 716D2
Bars press intell work 11-30, 941C1 ★, A2
TURNER, Ted
Loses interim mgr dispute 5-11—5-13, suit vs Kuhn 5-19, 567D3, F3
Courageous retains America's Cup 9-18, 828G2
Fires Hawks pres 9-27, 870B3
Suspensn lifted 12-8, 990D2
TURNER Trucking
ICC sues 11-3, 861D1
TUTHILL, Samuel J.
Replaced as FEA asst admin 8-4, 626D3
TVA—*See U.S. GOVERNMENT—TENNESSEE Valley Authority*
TWA—*See TRANS World Airlines*
TWENTIETH Century-Fox Film Corp.
Rpts record profit 11-1, Star Wars sets rentals mark 11-19, 1021B3
TWENTIETH Century Fund
Rpt scores US energy programs 1-11, 170B1

1978

U.S. Relations
US troop presence rptd 1-2, 5C2
Ecevit scores US role in Greek dispute 1-4, 8C2
US alerts to USSR satellite fall 57E1
Vance visits 1-20—1-21, US peace role discouraged 1-20, 170F2
Vance links arms aid, Cyprus 3-9; Ecevit scores 3-10, 216C3
Ecevit warns US on defns ties 3-24, 230E2
US dispatches diplomatic missn 3-29, moves to lift arms embargo 4-1—4-6; Ecevit hails actn 4-4, 276G1
Greeks, Cypriots condemn US actn 4-2—4-16, 276F3-277G1
US congressmen oppose embargo end 4-5, 276E3
US House com backs arms embargo end 5-3; Sen com upholds ceiling, OKs econ aid 5-11; reactn 5-12, 378B1
Ecevit scores US arms embargo 5-30, 397D2
USSR pacts strain US ties 6-21—6-23, West reassured 6-24, 6-30, 595G1
Arms embargo end, base reopening seen 6-28, 587C3
Carter urges arms ban end 7-20, 549F3
Kocas implicates CIA in '71 Greek death 7-24, 631A3
Arms embargo end gets Cong prelim OK 8-1, reactn 8-2, 587D2-588B1
Chrysler unit sale cited 8-10, 623D3
Pan Am to end Ankara svc 9-7, 701G1
Arms embargo end signed 9-26, 734D1, G1, B2
US mil base reopening OKd 10-4, 776F1-A2
ITT paymts chrgd 11-2, 876C1
TURKINGTON, Dr. Roger W.
Rpts diabetes misdiagnoses 8-29, 947E3
TURMAN, Glynn
Marries 4-12, 420F2
TURNBLAZER, William
Boyle convicted again 2-18, 129B1
TURNBULL, Wendy
Loses Fla Va Slims 1-15, 419G1
Loses US Open doubles title 9-9, women's singles 9-10, 707F1, G1
US wins Federatn Cup 12-3, 1026G3, 1027A1
TURNER, Ann Dickinson
Sun Oil buys Becton shares 1-17, 65F3
TURNER, Ann Sheppard
Wilmington 10 denied convictn review 1-5, 24D2
TURNER, Chris
On NASL All-Star team 8-20, 707B3
TURNER, J. C.
On '77 top-paid labor ldrs list 5-15, 365F1
TURNER, Jim
Cowboys win Super Bowl 1-15, 39C3
TURNER, John
Favored as Liberal ldr in poll 12-9, 985D3
TURNER, Richard
Killed 1-8, 20D2
Angola, Ethiopia rebel aid plan rptd 5-24, 383B2
TURNER, Adm. Stansfield
Carter reorganizes intell units 1-24, 49D2, F2
Sees USSR civil defns overrated 2-17, 127A1
Clark mtg on rebel aid plan rptd, Carter denies knowledge 5-24, 383B2, 443D1
Briefs Cong on Cuba role in Zaire 6-2—6-9, 442F1-D2
At Carter mtg on security leaks 7-11, 524G2
On CIA 'mole' issue 10-22, 940F2
Security memo cited in spy trial 11-9, 940D2
Carter rptd critical of pol intellignc 11-25, 917C1
Reveals secret Harvard ties 12-1, 962F2
Retires from Navy, retains CIA post 12-31, 1009E2
TURNER, Ted
Bouton returns to major leagues 9-10, 779E3
TURNER, Thomas Wyatt
Dies 4-21, 356E3
TURNING Point (film)
Top-grossing film 2-1, 116E3
TURNIPSEED, Rhett
Cautious on new solar cell 12-1, 983C2
TUSCALOOSA, Ala.—*See ALABAMA*
TUTU, Bishop Desmond
Marks Soweto '76 riot 6-16, 535B3, C3
TUVALU (formerly Ellice Islands) (British colony)
Independence from UK effected 9-30, 1022B2
TUYEN, Tran Van
'76 death rptd 7-10, 692F1
TVA—*See U.S. GOVERNMENT—TENNESSEE Valley Authority*
TVA v. Hill
Tellico Dam constructn halt upheld by Sup Ct 6-15, 468G1
TWA—*See TRANS World Airlines*
TWAIN, Mark (Samuel Langhorne Clemens) (1835-1910)
Crossed Swords released 3-2, 619C1
TWEEDSMUIR, Baroness (Priscilla Jean Fortescue)
Dies 3-11, 252E3
TWENTIETH Century-Fox Film Corp.
New film indus probe set, Deluxe Gen fraud suit cited 7-14, 599A3
Star Wars grosses $10.1 mln 7-21—7-23, world rental mark rptd 8-2, 672B1
Fined for 'block booking' 9-12, 759B2

1979

UN Policy & Developments
Membership listed 695A3
U.S. Relations
Westn-natn Guadeloupe summit topic 1-5–1-6, aid offer rptd 1-12, 12G2, 40B2
US prisoner accord initialed 1-11, 40G2
OECD takes aid role 2-6, 116E3
US Marine landing barred 2-12, 106C1
US aid sought 3-16, 214B2
Lira devalued vs $ 4-10, 333F1; 6-12, 447A1
US base talks 5-7, 5-8, 397A3
US U-2 flights disputed 5-14–5-29, 397B3
Sen OKs mil grants 5-22, 397E2
Aid pkg agreed, hailed 5-30, 397A2, F2
Prisoner transfer accord signed 6-7, 488B3
SALT II verificatn talks rptd 6-21, U-2 substitutes sought 6-28, 497B1
Evren, Ecevit vs U-2 flights 6-24, 6-27, 488C2
US consul murder plan rptd 7-11, 568E2
U-2 plan for SALT dropped 9-12, 762E1
Lockheed bribery cover-up chrgd 9-20, 775F1
US base extensns set 10-8, 796A1
Iran bars 2 US mediators 11-7, 841D2; mediators recalled 11-14, 862G2
Anti-US protests 11-22, 894D1
4 Americans killed 12-14, 998B1
TURKI, Abdul Aziz al-
Saudi oil productn cut set 4-9, 279A1
TURKMEN Soviet Socialist Republic—*See USSR–Republics*
TURMAN, Lawrence
Walk Proud released 6-15, 820F3
TURNAGE, William
Vs US timber sales order 6-11, 441E1
TURNBULL, Perry
In NHL entry draft 8-9, 655A2
TURNBULL, Wendy
Wins Avon tourns 2-25, 3-11, 391C2
US wins Federatn Cup 5-6, 391E2
Loses French Open 6-9, Wimbledon women's doubles 7-7, 570C1, E1
Wins US Open doubles title 9-8, 734G1
TURNER, Adm. Stansfield
Carter dissatisfactn rptd 2-22, 131B1
China-Viet war info praised 3-25, 232B1
SALT missile verificatn gap rptd seen 4-16, Brown disputes 4-17, 279D2
TURNER, Ted
WTCG to expand programming 4-23, 334E3
TUSCALOOSA, Ala.—*See ALABAMA*
TUSK (recording)
On best-seller list 11-7, 892F3
TUTANKHAMUN (c. 1358 B.C.)
NYC museum benefits rptd 7-30, 672A2
TUTU, Bishop Desmond
Meets with US' Jackson, domestic black ldrs 7-30, 617B2
TUVALU—*See also COMMONWEALTH of Nations*
Freedom House lists as free 12F3
TWAIN, Mark (Samuel Longhorne Clemens) (1835-1910)
Carter visits hometown 8-23, 623A1
TWALA, George
Sentenced 5-11, 373G1
TWALA, Wilson
Sentenced 5-11, 373G1
TWENTIETH Century-Fox Film Corp.
Pres, aides resign 6-7, 587G3
Darryl F Zannuck dies 12-22, 1008G3

1980

UN Policy & Developments
Indl dvpt aid fund disputed 2-9, 124D2
U.S. Relations
Bases accord set 1-9, 22G2
Lira devalued vs $ 1-24, 61A1
Turkey offers $ debt paymt 1-28, 80F1
Leftists arrested re '79 murder of 4 2-13, 135G3
Terrorists attack cars, homes 2-18, 135C2, D2
US aid sought 2-19, 135D3
OECD aid pkg deferred, US aid vow rptd 3-26, 236A2, E2
Bases, aid accord signed 3-29, 255A3
OECD aid OKd 4-15, 295A3
US soldier killed 4-16, 316C2
'79 terrorism deaths rptd 5-11, 365E3
Iran hostage release effort vowed 5-22, 393B2
Mil takeover seen unlikely 5-30, 445A3
Lira devalued vs $ 6-10, 445E3
'79 debt, rescheduling rptd 6-19, 468F1
USSR consultatn barred re U-2 7-4, 526C1
Coup rptd nonviolent 9-12, 679A3
Coup response moderate 9-12, 696D3
US to continue aid 9-12, 696E3
Prisoner transfer accord OKd 10-8, 794B1
Armenians bomb NY, Calif offices 10-12, 794D1
US stays debt paymts 10-24, 874E3
US soldier killed 11-15, 888A2
TURKI, Abdul Aziz al-
Agrees to OPEC pricing proposal 9-18, 694C3
TURKISH Airlines
Rome office bombed 3-10, 316B2
London office bombed 10-12, 794G1*
Moslem extremists hijack jet 10-13, commandos overcome 10-14, 794A2
TURKLER, Kemal
Slain 7-22, 580D3
TURKMEN, Ilter
Named Turkey forgn min 9-21, 720C3
TURNAGE, William
Denounces Watt apptmt 12-22, 979G3
TURNBULL, Wendy
US wins Federatn Cup 5-25, 607B1
Loses BMW championship 6-21, 607E3
Wimbledon results 7-4—7-6, 606D2, A3
Wins US Open mixed doubles 9-7, 691F2
TURNBULL, William W.
Disputes aptitude test study 1-14, 36D2
TURNER, Cleveland
Sentenced 1-11, 64A2
TURNER, Adm. Stansfield
Admits CIA use of press, clergy, academics 2-21, Aspin asks details 2-25, 189A3
Backs newsmen, academics, clergy as agents 4-10, 458G3
Signed oath re leaks 7-16—7-17, 549A2
Sen subcom releases testimony 9-24, issues critical rpt in B Carter case 10-2, 763G3, 764D1
Briefs Reagan 11-19, 881E1
TURNER, Ted
Cable-TV news network debuts 6-1, 501B3
Courageous eliminated from America's Cup trials 8-25; sold 9-25, 834F1
TURNLEY, John
Killed 6-4, 619D2
TURNS (play)
Opens 6-16, 756G3
TUSCUMBIA—*See ALABAMA*
TUTI, Mario
Affatigato arrested 8-6, 620C1
TUTU, Bishop Desmond
Arrest, release rptd 6-1, 466E2
TUVALU—*See also COMMONWEALTH of Nations*
Island trade pact rptd 7-24, 576G2
TVA (Tennessee Valley Authority)—*See under U.S. GOVERNMENT*
TWA—*See TRANS World Airlines*
TWAIN, Mark (Samuel Langhorne Clemens) (1835-1910)
Harper's to cease publicatn 6-17, 501A1
TWELFTH Night (play)
Opens 12-16, 1003F3
TWENTIETH Century-Fox Film Corp.
Woman named pres 1-1, 199B1
In Getty Oil pay-TV film venture 4-22, Justice Dept to probe 4-24, 376E2
Pay-TV film plan draws trust suit 8-4, 639F3

1976

TWIN Cities Savings & Loan Association (Pascalouga, Miss.)
In receivership 6-15, 495B1
TWINE Jr., Thomas J.
Moves into Ford column 8-3, 564C2
TWIN Falls, Ida.—*See IDAHO*
TWINAM, Joseph W.
Replaced as Bahrain amb 9-30, 807F3
TWOMEY, Brig. Gen. David
On training reforms 4-27, 378E1
TWOMEY, Seamus
Replaced as IRA staff chief 2-10, 147D1
TYACKE, Eric & Jean
Banned 11-16, 927B3
TYDINGS, Joseph D.
Loses Senate primary 5-18, 357A2
TYLER, Harold R.
Ford funds probe rptd 10-1, 723E2
TYLER, Lindsay
Rptd held by Ethiopian rebels 9-7, 674A3
TYLER (Tex.) Junior College
Ford campaign appearance 4-28, 323A3
TYPHOID—*See 'Diseases' under MEDICINE*
TYPHOONS—*See STORMS*
TYPOGRAPHICAL Union, International (AFL-CIO)
Units cross picket line 2-16, 153E3

1977

TWINING Jr., Charles H.
On Cambodia death toll 7-26, 590D2
TYLER Jr., Harold
Replaced as dep atty gen 4-5, 272G2
TYLER, Lindsay
Freed 1-5, 20A2
TYLER Ecology Award, John & Alice
Odum gets award 4-15, 354F1
2, 4-diaminoanisole (4MMPD)—*See CHEMICALS*
TYPHOONS—*See STORMS*
TYRANNOSAURUS Rex (T-Rex) (musical group)
Marc Bolan killed 9-16, 787G3
TYSON, Brady
Regrets US role in Chile coup 3-8; US disavows 3-8—3-9, summons home 3-9, 218E3
Scores Uruguay rights abuse 3-8, 219G1

1978

TWILIGHT Dinner, The (play)
Opens 4-18, 760F3
TWINAM, Joseph W.
Coup cancels S Yemen mission 6-26, 499E1
TWINS (book)
On best-seller list 7-2, 579E3
TWITTY, Howard
3d in Tucson Open 1-8, 76C1
Ties for 2d in HOF Classic 8-27, 672G3
TWOMEY, Seamus
Sentenced 6-13, 474F3
TXI—*See TEXAS International Airlines*
TYCO Laboratories Inc.
Loses Leeds takeover bid 7-7, 553D1
TYE, A. Raymond
Brooke changes loan data 5-26, 406C1
TYE, Lawrence
Scores NRC A-plant safety progrm 11-25, 940E3
TYLER, Tex.—*See TEXAS*
TYLER, Bonnie
It's a Heartache on best-seller list 6-7, 460F3
TYPHOONS—*See STORMS*
TYRIE, Andrew
Asks calm after Belfast bombing 2-20, 132D2

1979

TWITTY, Howard
2d in Westchester Classic 8-19; wins BC Open 9-2, 969G3, 970C1
2,4,5-T—*See HERBICIDES*
TWO Guys—*See VORNADO Inc.*
2 Hot (recording)
On best-seller list 5-2, 356A3
TYACK, Judge George B.
Acquits Cleveland cncl pres 7-18, 580F1
TYACKE, Eric & Jean
'76 ban lifted 9-17, 732F2
TYCO Laboratories Inc.
Ludlow takeover bid 2-9, drops offer 5-3, 560C3
TYLER, Jan
Jordan cocaine probe immunity bid rptd 9-28, 767E3
TYNAN, Kathleen
Agatha released 2-8, 174C2
TYRONE Energy Park—*See WISCONSIN—Atomic Energy*
TYSON, Cicely
Concorde Airport '79 released 8-3, 820A1

1980

TWIN City Bank (North Little Rock, Ark.)
Backs Chrysler rescue plan 6-20, 481A3
TWINKLE, Twinkle Killer Kane (film)
Released 8-8, 675E3
TWITTY, Howard
2d in Great Milwaukee Open 7-13, wins Greater Hartford 7-27, 715D1
TYLER, Wendell
Steelers win Super Bowl 1-20, 61C3-62C1
TYNAN, Kenneth
Dies 7-26, 608E3
TYRER, James (Jim)
Slain 9-15, 756G2

U

1976

UCHIDA, Tsuneo
Heads LDP 9-15, 694E1
UDALCHOV, Ivan
Named Greece amb 4-2, warnd vs pol mtgs 5-16, 402F1, A2
UDALL, Rep. Morris K. (D, Ariz.)
Gets US campaign subsidy 1-2, more funds OKd 1-8, 22E3, F3
Endorsed by O'Neill 1-7, 22C3
Common Cause rpts campaign code backing 1-9, 23A1
4th in Iowa precinct vote 1-19, 41A1
2d in NH primary 2-24, 148E1, B3
2d in Mass primary 3-2, 165A1
Fed fund total listed 3-4, 180D3
Seeks liberal coalition 3-7, 179A3
5th in Fla primary 3-9, 179D2
Bond running for delegate 3-15, 214G2
Wis campaign dvpts 3-15—4-5, 233B2, 245E2
Gets 2% vote in NC 3-23, 214B1
Humphrey upstages in NY 4-1, 233D2
Wins 70 NY delegates 4-6, 244F3
2d in Wis primary 4-6, 245C1
Scores Carter 'ethnic purity' remark 4-7, 260F3
3d in delegate count 4-9, 261A1
Carter offers health plan 4-16, 282A1
Loses Sup Ct funds plea 4-23, 306C1
Pa primary results 4-27, 304F3, 305E1, F1
Sees uphill fight vs Carter 4-28, 324A3
'Down to Carter & me' 4-28, 4-30, 324B3
Delegate count 4-30, 324A3
On Jackson pullout rpt 4-30, 324B3
At black Dem caucus 5-2, 343A3
Not on Ind ballot; Ga, DC results 5-4, 323G1, B2, F2
Neb vote results 5-11, 342G1
2d in Conn voting 5-11, 342E3
Scores strip-mine rules 5-11, 359G2
In Mich, Conyers support cited 5-15, 5-17, 357B1
Fed funding resumed 5-21, 391E3
Wins 6 delegates 5-25, 373A3, 374B2-D3
Carter scores; rebuts 5-27—5-31, 390F2
2d in SD primary 6-1, 389G2, G3, 390A1, B2
Delegate strength 6-8, 408G3, 409A3
Calif, NJ, Ohio vote results 6-8, 409A1, G2, F3
Inactivates pres campaign 6-14, 432A1
Dem platform supported 6-15, 432A3
Campaign debt rptd 6-16, 491E1
FEC ends fed funds 6-23, total rptd 7-1, 490F3, 491B1
Nominated at conv, releases delegates, 2d in voting 7-14, 505G1, 506A1, 507A2
Dem conv pres vote, table 7-14, 507A3
Conv rules debated 7-15, 513F2
Scores coal-leasing bill veto 8-4, 566G2
Reelected 11-2, 824D1, 828F3
FEC certificatn total rptd 12-31, 979G2
UEKI, Shigeaki
Rpts new oilfield found 1-6, 27D2
Corruptn expose cites 8-3—8-5, 851B1
UEKI, Tadao
Arrested 6-22, 450B3
Indicted 7-13, 557B2
UEMURA, Haruki
Wins Olympic medal 7-31, 575B1
UGANDA—*See also AFRICAN Development Bank, COMMONWEALTH of Nations, NON-ALIGNED Nations Movement, OAU*
Listed as 'not free' nation 1-19, 20E3
Angola MPLA recognized 2-10, 105E2
Total IMF oil loan rptd 4-1, 340E2
IMF OKs SDR purchase 4-6, 295B1
Blocks oil to Rwanda 4-7, 502F2
Sovt mil buildup cited 4-25, 295B1
Nsubuga named cardinal 4-27, 336B2
Zaire cites Sovt arms buildup 4-30, 318A3
IBRD suspends EAC loans 5-11, 371F3
WHO cancer studies rptd 6-3, 484B3
Amin assassinatn try 6-10, purge rpts denied 6-14, 502C2
Sovt mil presence rptd 6-13, 467C1
Amin named pres for life 6-25, 523F3

1977

UAE—*See UNITED Arab Emirates*
UAL, Inc.
United Air Lines seniority rule upheld 5-31, 461G2
Early retiremt plan backed 12-12, 960G1, A2
UAW—*See UNITED Automobile, Aerospace and Agricultural Implement Workers of America*
UDALL, Rep. Morris K. (D, Ariz.)
'76 special interest gifts rptd 2-4, 128G3, 129A2-D2
Bracy confrmd to Transport post 2-10, 148C3
Backs Central Ariz Project 3-21, 210F1
Carter backs Central Ariz water projct 4-18, 299E3
Backs Carter energy plan 4-20, 294A1
Cited in Park indictmt 9-6, 688D1
UDRESCU, Dumitru
US asylum rptd granted 2-24, 315B1
UEKI, Shigeaki
Vows to continue A-progrm 3-26, 268F3
UFT (United Federation of Teachers)—*See TEACHERS, American Federation of*
UFW—*See UNITED Farm Workers of America*
UGANDA—*See also COMMONWEALTH of Nations, EAST African Community, NON-ALIGNED Nations Movement, OAU*
Amin 6th anniv fete 1-25, 102D3
Plane downed in Sudan 1-30, 20 rescued 2-1, 102C3
Purge rptd 2-13; Amin denies, warns Luwum 2-14, 138E3
Luwum, 2 mins killed 2-16, 138B3-139E1
Army unrest rptd 2-22, 139F1
Amin admits mil unrest 2-23, 141F2
Christian purge detailed 2-23, 2-25, 3-2, 141G2
Culture min ousted, arrested 2-23; indl min defects 2-28, 142D1
Anglican bishop ousted 3-4, 308C3
Atrocity rpts continue 3-9—3-29, army purge detailed 4-2, 308C1, B2

1978

U-2 (spy plane)—*See ARAMAMENTS—Aircraft*
UAE—*See UNITED Arab Emirates*
UAL, Inc.
United Airlines Inc.—*See separate listing*
UAW—*See UNITED Automobile, Aerospace and Agricultural Implement Workers of America*
UCLA—*See CALIFORNIA, University of—Los Angeles Campus*
UCLES, Jose Trinidad
Guatemala Cong speaker 7-21, 722C3 *
UDALL, Rep. Morris K. (D, Ariz.)
Cleared by ethics com re Park gift 7-13, 527A2
Coal slurry pipeline bill defeated 7-19, 550C2
House job bias proposal rptd 9-21, 720C3
Civil Svc reform enacted 10-13, 787C3
Reelected 11-7, 850C1, 855F1
UDALL, Stewart L.
Files Nev A-test claims 12-21, 1011F3
UDELL, Peter
Angel opens 5-10, 760C1
UEKI, Shigeaki
On lagging A-power progrm 10-15, 836D3
UEMURA, Banjiro
Message From Space released 11-17, 970B2
UEMURA, Nami
Reaches North Pole 5-1, 420A2
UFW—*See UNITED Farm Workers of America*
UGANDA—*See also COMMONWEALTH of Nations, GATT, NONALIGNED Nations Movement, OAU*
Tea smugglers sentenced 1-10, 55C3
Secret police disciplined for smuggling 2-1, 95B2
Vice pres rptd injured, assassinatn attempt suspected 4-19, 331B3
Amin takes Cabt posts, arrests rptd 4-28, 5-3, 331A3, C3
'77 coffee output, smuggling rptd 6-24, 616G2
Oil shortage bared 7-10, 616A3
Ali rptd dismissed 7-26, 616A3
Amin popularity rptd up 11-15, 870C2

1979

UAE—*See UNITED Arab Emirates*
UAL Inc.
United Airlines Inc.—*See separate listing*
UBATUBA (sculpture)
NYC vandals smash 5-6, 375C1
Rededicated in NYC 9-15, 892F2
UCLA—*See CALIFORNIA, University of—Los Angeles Campus*
UDALL, Rep. Morris K. (D, Ariz.)
Plans NRC A-safety hearings 1-20, 54D3
Interior Com chrmn 1-24, 71D1
Calls for A-plant safety study 4-1, 245E1
Alaska land bill OKd 5-16, 367A1
Told to repay '76 electn funds 6-18, 595E1
Suggests Mondale '80 pres race 9-5, 662B1
Scores 'Sagebrush Revolt' 9-5, 704B1
Endorses Kennedy 12-18, 962B2
UDALL, Stewart L.
Files more Nev A-test claims 2-23, 208C1
UDELL, Peter
Comin' Uptown opens 12-20, 1007C2
UFOs—*See UNIDENTIFIED Flying Objects*
UFW—*See UNITED Farm Workers*
UGANDA—*See also COMMONWEALTH of Nations, GATT, NONALIGNED Nations Movement, OAU*
Econ problems cited 5-24, 429E2
Wildlife herds threatened 8-13, 637D3
5-yr hunting ban set 8-23, 815C3
Currency exchange held 10-21—10-28, 998C2
Christian ban rescinded 11-7, 998D2

1980

UAE—*See UNITED Arab Emirates*
UBATUBA (sculpture)
Vandals smash again 3-24, 472D3
UDALL, Rep. Morris K. (D, Ariz.)
Lauds new Park Svc dir 5-1, 333E2
Open conv move forms 7-25—7-31, bars pres bid 7-28, 570D3
Gives Dem conv keynote speech 8-11, 612A2*
Reelected 11-4, 842C1, 851B3
Alaska lands bill clears House 11-12, 866B3
UDOFF, Yale
Bad Timing released 9-21, 836D2
UFW—*See UNITED Farm Workers of America*
UGANDA—*See also COMMONWEALTH of Nations, GATT, NONALIGNED Nations, OAU*

1976

Hijacked jet lands 6-28, 462C2; **for subsequent developments, see 'Entebbe' under MIDDLE EAST—AVIATION Incidents**
Chrgs US, Israel air threat 7-7, 516C2
France vs Libya Mirage transfer 7-8, 30 rptd sent 7-9, 516A3
Univ protest foiled 7-10; troops raid campus 8-3—8-5, massacres rptd 8-9; Amin denies rpts 8-9, 10-8, 874E1
Rpts US, Israel mil men in Kenya 7-12, 516D3
UK envoys ousted 7-13—7-22, ties cut 7-28, 547F3
Oil, food shortages rptd 7-16, 7-27; gas sales banned 7-22, forgn air flights suspended 7-25, 548G1, F2, A3
Chrgs US, UK, Israel mercenaries in Kenya 7-17, 548B2
Libya confrms Mirage transfer 7-18, 548C2 ★
Olympic withdrawal rptd 7-21, 528B3
Troop mutinies rptd 7-21, 4 rptd chrgd 7-22, 548E2
Rwanda oil crisis rptd 7-22, 559G3
Seizes 2 Britons; frees 1 8-3, 581A1
2 Canadian priests expelled 8-13, 874D2
Munno rptd closed, reporters arrested 8-20; ed rptd dead 10-7, 874C2
Frees 2d Briton 8-25, 874E1
4 officials freed 9-1, 874A2
Amin returns jet to Israel 9-6, 663A3
EAC ry project rptd near collapse 9-12, 974A3
Amin vows better UK ties 10-7, 874B1
Defense min quits, replaced 10-12, 874A2
Parma arrested 10-14; body rptd found 10-21, 874B2
Amin assumes AF cmdr post 11-11, 874G1
Tanzania, Kenya feud re EAC 12-7, 974E2
OKs EAC airline paymts 12-14—12-16, 974A3

Kenyan Relations
Kenya-US F-5 sale set 6-15—6-17, 467B1
Uganda chrgs air threat, Kenya scores 7-7, 516C2
Kenyans curb trade 7-8, 516D2
Kenyans slain in Uganda 7-10, 7-12; UN gets Kenya complaint 7-13, 516E2-A3, B3
US jets, ship visits Kenya 7-10, 7-12, 7-13, 516E3
Troop massing chrgs traded 7-12, 516B3
Uganda chrgs Israel, US mil men in Kenya 7-12, 516D3
Uganda chrgs Kenya oil blockade; seeks Zaire, Sudan, Rwanda aid 7-16, 548F1-A2
Uganda, Kenya trade chrgs 7-17—7-28; Amin asks UN, OAU mediatn 7-25, 548A2
Accord signed 8-7; 99 Kenyans to be freed 8-8, 580E3
72 Kenyans freed 8-10, 874B1
Oil deliveries to Uganda, Kenya elec power restoratn rptd 8-17, 8-23; Uganda border troops withdrawn 8-28, 874C1
Uganda vows better ties 10-7, 874B1

UGARTE Roman, Marta
Found strangled 9-12, 963A2

1977

Jobless round-up decreed 3-12, 308F3
Coffee smuggling rptd 3-16, 11 Kenyans arrested 4-13, 308D3
Anglicans elect new archbp 3-19, 308F2
Amin ex-min: Bloch, Luwum deaths ordrd 6-8, 487A1
Amin assassinatn plot rptd 6-18, denied 6-23, 507E3
Amin assassinatn plot purges rptd 6-20—6-23, 508A1
Defectns of 2 mins rptd 7-2, 600D3
Amin chrgd Luwum arms smuggling 7-15, 600B3
Amin chrgs army, civilns in new plot 7-30, 641G1
7 executns rptd 8-6, 8-17, 641A2
Amin in hosp, coma rumored 9-7, denied 9-11, 709G2
15 anti-Amin plotters executed 9-9, 709E2
Christian groups ousted 9-20, 805D2
Renewable energy urged for 3d World 12-11, 975E3

Foreign Relations (misc.)
UN Assemb member 4C1
UK plane passengers rescued in Sudan 2-1, 102C3
UK group enroute to Amin anniv rite rescued in Sudan 2-1, 102C3
Amnesty Intl chrgs purges, asks UN probe 2-6, 139G1
UN comm scores Israel occupatn rule 2-15, 107F2
Luwum death protests mount 2-17—2-21, 138G3-139E1
Amin claims invasn threats 2-22—3-2, 141C2
Waldheim asks Luwum death probe 2-24, 142B1
Cuba mil delegatn arrives 2-26, 141F2
UN rights comm rejcts UK probe plan 3-1, 142A1
Amin sees Sovt, Cuban envoys 3-4; Sovt aid rptd, Cuban advisers denied 4-2, 4-7, 308A2, C2
Amin denies atrocities 3-7, 3-8, 170D2
UN rights comm sessn ends 3-11, 207F1
Pilot defects to UK 3-13, 308D2
Amin warns UK natls 3-13, 308E2
Anglicans ask OAU, UN interventn 3-14, 308A3
Currency exchng banned, black mkt rptd 3-21, 308E3
NZ terms Amin 'maniac' 3-31, 258C2
Kenyans rptd arrested re coffee smuggling 4-13, 308D3
Amin in Zaire; pledges aid, scores Angola 4-22, 317B2
Forces sent to Zaire, Amin arrives 4-28, 394C1
Tanzania plot chrgd 5-3; invaders pardoned, given asylum 5-11, 429A2
ICJ blames Amin for killings, scores UN inactn 5-17, 429G1
Guatemala pres cites Amin 5-20, 414B3
Ghana closes missn 5-22, Uganda shifts Ghana missn to Nigeria 5-24, 429C2
Amin threatens to 'crash' Commonwealth conf 6-7, 486E3
Amin mtg with Zambia, Tanzania rebels rptd 6-8, 487A1
UK natls warned 6-8, 487A1
UK natls curbed, UK-born citizen arrested 6-10, 508B1
Commonwealth conf condemns Amin 6-15, 486B3
EEC bars aid 6-21, 508C1
Canada rptr arrested 6-22, sees Amin 7-10, 600A3
Curbs on UK natls lifted 7-1, 600C3
Defectns of 2 mins rptd 7-2, 600D3
Amin addresses OAU summit, confrms death plot chrgs 7-4, 512G1
Horn of Africa alliances shift 7-6, 588F1
Amin foes unite in Zambia 8-8, 641F1
USSR envoy defectn rptd 8-11, 606F2
Exiles ask UK trade boycott 9-12, 805G1
UK natl escapes jail 9-22, rptd slain 10-9, 805F1
Kenya bars traffic entry 10-4, 805C2
Amin repudiates EAC debts; scores Kenya, Tanzania 10-9, 805B2
Cuba mil advisers rptd 11-17, 896G1

U.S. Relations
Luwum death scored by Young, Carter 2-17, 2-20, 139B1
Carter scores re rights abuses 2-23, 126E2
Amin bars US natls exit, relents 2-25—3-1, 141A1
Carter call-in topic 3-5, 171E1
Amin asks US reopen emb 3-6, 308F2
Amin chrgs agressn 3-8, 170D2
Amin warns natls 3-13, 308E2
Amin chrgs CIA-church ties 3-26, 308G2
US rpts Sovt envoy defectn 8-11, 606F2
2 '71 US deaths detailed 9-2, 709A3
US forgn aid clears Cong 10-19, 815A2; Carter signs 11-1, 834D1

1978

Foreign Relations (misc.)
2 tea smugglers sentenced 1-10, 55C3
7 Kenya coffee smugglers pardoned 1-31, 95C2
Kenya improved ties sought, rail shipmt halt revealed 2-8, 3-8—3-10, 289C2
Vice pres rptd in Egypt hosp 4-24, 331C3
Kenya blames re air crash 5-26, denies chrg 5-27, 479B1
Envoy to Denmark loses libel suit re murder chrg 6-18, 688B1
Oil shortage rptd, Kenya paymts delay cited 7-10, 616B3
UN Assemb member 713F3

Tanzanian Dispute—*See TANZANIA—Ugandan Dispute*

U.S. Relations
Page gift to Amin chrgd 4-13, 449B2
US trade ban backed by House com 5-16; coffee cos set boycott 5-16—5-19, 416C3
US trade ban OKd by House 6-12, Sen votes mandatory ban 7-28, 616D2
Sen subcom gets terror rpt 6-15, 616F2
Amin warns US re trade ban 10—12, 822G3
McDonnell Douglas paymts rptd 12-15, 982F2

UGUR, Necdet
Named Turkey educ min 1-5, 21E2

UHL, Edward G.
Indicted 9-8, 808A3

1979

Foreign Relations (misc.)—*See also 'Tanzanian-Rebel Conflict' below*
New govt recognized by 4 other African natns 4-12, UK 4-15, 288A2
UK High Comm office reopens 4-21, 314D3
USSR scores Amin 4-29, forgn aid rptd 5-28, 429G1
E Ger mil aid rptd 5-23, 406A3
EC aid pledged 5-23–5-24, 429D2
Entebbe victim's body found 5-30, 429E1
Amin confirmed in Libya 6-13, 489A1
Lule flies to UK 7-8, 637F2
Sudan denies Amin residence, Uganda invasn plan 8-9, 637C3
UN membership listed 695A3
Borders closed 10-21–10-28, 998C2

Government & Politics—*See also other appropriate subheads in this section*
Amin flees Kampala 3-25, 257D1
Kampala falls, new govt formed 4-11, 257A1, C2
Lule, Cabt sworn 4-13, 288A1
Astles returned 6-8, stands trial 6-11, 488G3-489A1
Lule ousted, Binaisa replaces 6-20; Lule leaves 6-22, protests back 6-21, 6-25, 488D3
Lule detentn in Tanzania ends, strife ensues 7-8; 3 backers arrested 8-19, 637G2
Reward offered for Amin capture 8-5, 637B3
Pol prisoners freed 10-16, 998E2
Cabt shuffled 11-19, Binaisa defends actn 11-22, 998G1

Tanzanian-Rebel Conflict
Obote asks Amin ouster 1-12, 78G1
Fighting rptd 1-20; Amin chrgs village capture, seeks mediatn 1-25, 85C3
Kampala sites bombed 2-3, rebel group takes blame 2-5, 101A3
Tanzanian forces, Ugandan exiles advance on Kampala; Amin ouster vowed, casualities rptd 2-11–3-1, 146C3
OAU meets 2-21; Amin seeks mediatn, Nyerere issues demands 2-28, 146G3
Rebels advance; Libyan, Palestinian aid to Amin rptd 3-1, 257B1-C2
Exiles in Tanzania meet 3-23–3-25, 257D2
Amin flees Kampala 3-25, 257D1
Westn newsmen rptd killed 4-9, 257D2
Kampala falls, new govt formed; Amin denies defeat 4-11, 257A1, C2
Tanzania recognizes new govt 4-12, 288A2
Lule, Cabt sworn 4-13; atrocity probe vowed, police hq, Amin residence toured 4-14; Kampala calm 4-17, 288A1, F1
Tanzanians launch offense, Uganda army remnants rptd on rampage; Astles arrest rptd 4-18, 288C1
Jinja falls 4-22, 314A3
Westn newsmen bodies found 4-26, 429F1
Rebels advance 5-1, take Arua 5-27–5-29, complete conquest 6-2–6-3, 429B1
Amin locatn rpts vary 5-27, 429F1
E Ger amb, wife rptd killed 6-1, 429B2
Sudan refugees, atrocities vs northerners rptd 6-8, 489B1
Tanzania frees Lule 7-8, 637G2
Chaos, violence continues; forgn embs rptd arming, Westn aid blocked 9-1, 815B3
Tanzania troop presence cited 9-19, 721E1
Libyan prisoners returned 11-28, 998D2
Tanzania mil training pact signed, troop data rptd 12-13, 998E2

U.S. Relations
US rights rpt omits 2-10, 107A2
US to reopen emb 4-16, 288D2
US magazine prints CIA-disputed article 4-19, 309B3
US reps welcomed 4-23, 314C3
Entebbe hijack case declined by US Sup Ct 4-30, 364F3
US trade rptd 5-28, 429C2
US Emb rptd reopened 6-21, 489C1
Young, trade delegatn visit, aid pledged 9-19, 721D1

UGOLINI, Roberto
Shot 3-30, 269G1

UGUETO, Luis
Venez finance min 3-10, 192C3
Details econ plans 5-28, 429C3
On '79 inflatn rise 10-23, 838B1

UHL, Edward G.
Acquitted on tax chrgs 2-7, 88A1

1980

Foreign Relations (misc.)
Ex-EAC leaders meet 1-2, 90E1
Islamic conf boycotted 1-27—1-29, 67C2
S Africa trade cited 4-1, 243B2
Tanzania linked to coup 5-11, 375F1-B2
Olympic boycott stand reversed 5-24, 421G1
Zaire, Sudan invasn support chrgd 10-10, 794E2
Tanzania aids invaders ouster, Saudi denies role 10-15, 832G3
UN Cncl seat won 11-13, 896E1

Government & Politics—*See also other appropriate subheads in this section*
Muwanga dismissed in press conflict 2-10, 125F3
Pol parties banned 5-5, army chief ousted 5-10; mil seize power 5-11—5-14, 375D1
Obote returns 5-27, 446E1-C2
Amin desires return, scores Nyerere 6-3, 446D2
Obote party ousts Cabt rivals 9-17, 731B1
Amin backers invasn rptd 10-6—10-7; govt confirms 10-10, 794D2
Amin backers flee 10-15, 832F3
Chief justice rptd dismissed 12-2, 946F1
Electn outcome uncertain, results publicatn banned 12-10—12-11, 945E1-946F1
Electn decisn reversed 12-12; Obote wins 12-13, inaugurated 12-15, 968F2

Sports
Olympic boycott stand reversed 5-24, 421G1
Moscow Olympic results 7-20—8-3, 588C3, 622G1

U.S. Relations
US issues rights rpt 2-5, 87E2

UGRYUMOV, Viktor
Wins Olympic medal 8-1, 622A3

1976

UHLMAN, Wes
Loses Dem gov primary 9-21, 804C3
UIHLEIN Jr., Robert A.
Dies 11-12, 970C3
UK—*See GREAT Britain*
UKIL, Abu Melek
Arrested 11-29, 923E2
UKKOLA, Pertti
Wins Olympic medal 7-24, 576G2
UKRAINIANS in the United States, Congress of
Dobriansky scores Ford 10-8, 762D3
UKRAINIAN Soviet Socialist Republic—*See 'Republics' under USSR*
ULASEWICZ, Anthony T.
Convicted 12-23, 981B1
ULBRICHT, Walter
Cited re Honecker electn 10-29, 889D1
ULLMAN, Rep. Al (D, Ore.)
Reelected 11-2, 830C3
Carter meets cong ldrs 11-17, 864B2
ULLMAN, Capt. John B.
Bronson trial 6-23, 493G2
McClure prosecutions end 9-1, 942E2
ULLSTEN, Ola
Named to Swedish Cabt 10-8, 794B2
ULMER, Brig. Gen. Walter F.
Reinstates chrg vs Ringgold 5-25, 395G1
ULSTER—*See NORTHERN Ireland*
UMBRICHT, Victor
UN urges aid to Vietnam 6-1, 408C2
UMM al Quwain—*See UNITED Arab Emirates*
UNAMUNO, Miguel
Argentina labor min 2-3, 154G2
Arrested 3-24, 211G2
UNANUE Ruiz, Jose
Freed 8-4, 753G2
UNDERDEVELOPED Countries—*See DEVELOPING Countries*
UNDERWOOD, Cecil H.
Wins primary for gov 5-11, 342D3
Loses election 11-2, 820C3, 823E1
UNEMPLOYMENT—*See under LABOR*
UNGER, Leonard
Taiwan A-fuel reprocessing to end 9-14, 858D2
UNGUREANU, Teodora
Wins Olympic medals 7-19, 7-22, 574D3-F3
UNIFICATION Church
Property holdings, assessmt rptd 5-12, 6-2, 9-8, 971C1
IRS probe rptd 6-1, 971B1
Moon ends US ministry; parents score 9-18, 970E3
S Korea influence peddling in US rptd 10-24—11-14, rally vs Nixon impeachmt cited 11-7, 899B1, A2-B3
Announces NYC newspaper 12-14, 971F1
UNION Bancorp Inc.
Rptd on FRB 'problem' list 1-22, 111C2
Union Bank (Los Angeles)
Rptd on comptroller's FRB 'problem' lists 1-26, 1-29, 113B1, D1
UNION Bank of Switzerland (Zurich)
IMF gold buyer 9-15, 739E3
UNION Bank & Trust Co. (Grand Rapids, Mich.)
Ford pol acct probed 10-8, 764A2
UNIONDALE, N.Y.—*See NEW York State*
UNION of Concerned Scientists—*See SCIENTISTS, Union of Concerned*
UNION Of Orthodox Jewish Congregations of America—*See ORTHODOX Jewish Congregations of America, Union of*

1977

UHLENBECK, George E.
Gets Medal of Sci 11-22, 952C1
UHLMANN, Michael M.
Replaced as asst atty gen 3-4, 211G1
UK—*See GREAT Britain*
UKRAINIAN Soviet Socialist Republic—*See USSR—Republics*
ULANFU
In Politburo 8-21, 645F2
ULASEWICZ, Anthony T.
Sentenced 2-18, 197E2
ULCERS—*See MEDICINE—Diseases*
ULEVICH, Neal
Wins Pulitzer Prize 4-18, 355A3
ULLMAN, Rep. Al (D, Ore.)
On business tax credit plan 2-1, 89D2
'76 special interest gifts rptd 2-4, 128G3, 129G1
Backs employmt tax credit 4-14, 270F3
ULLMANN, Liv
'Changing' on best-seller list 4-3, 264A2; 6-4, 452A2
ULLOA, Manuel
Pol, econ plan issued 2-25, 241D2
ULLSTEN, Ola
Cancels 8 poor natns debts 10-12, 903G3
ULMER, Brig. Gen. Walter F.
Scores chrgs 12-28-76; transfer linked 1-5, 41E1
ULSTER—*See NORTHERN Ireland*
ULTRAMAR Co. Ltd.
Unit settles suit 8-31, 691D3
U LWIN—*See LWIN, U.*
UMBA Di Lutete
Named Zaire forgn min 8-13, 641E2
UMM al Quwain—*See UNITED Arab Emirates*
UMTA—*See U.S. GOVERNMENT—TRANSPORTATION—Urban Mass Transportation Administration*
UMW—*See UNITED Mine Workers of America*
UNCETA Barrenechea, Augusto
Assassinated 10-8, ETA claims credit 10-9, 826B2
UNCTAD—*See UNITED Nations—Trade and Development, UN Conference on*
UNDERHILL, Francis T.
Replaced as amb to Malaysia 5-25, 500A1
UNDERWOOD, Tommy
Traded to Cardinals 6-15, 644E2
UNECE—*See UNITED Nations—Europe, Economic Commission for*
UNEF—*See under MIDDLE EAST—UN DEVELOPMENTS*
UNEMPLOYMENT—*See LABOR—Employment*
UNEMPLOYMENT Insurance—*See LABOR—Employment & Unemployment*
UNESCO—*See UNITED Nations—Educational, Scientific and Cultural Organization*
UNFICYP—*See UNITED Nations—Cyprus, UN Force in*
UNIFICATION Church
5 Calif disciples in parental custody 3-24, Boonville seminars halted 3-28, 286F3
Parents lose Calif custody 4-11, 310B1
NY property tax exemptn denied 4-14, 310D1
Moon called KCIA agent 6-5, 441G3
UNIFORMED Services University of the Health Sciences—*See under U.S. GOVERNMENT—DEFENSE*
UNILEVER
Plans Natl Starch takeover 12-11, 1004D2
UNION Bank of Switzerland
Geneva dir chrgd with fraud 8-15, 658D1
UNION Carbide Corp.
To promote S Africa equality 3-1, 160B3
Egypt agrmt rptd near 5-16, 390E2
UNION College (Schenectady, N.Y.)
Hockey coach resigns 12-23, players quit 12-27, 1021G1

1978

UHNAK, Dorothy
Investigation on best-seller list 6-4, 460D3
UK (United Kingdom)—*See GREAT Britain*
UKRAINIAN Soviet Socialist Republic—*See USSR—Republics*
ULCERS—*See MEDICINE—Diseases*
ULLMAN, Rep. Al (D, Ore.)
Vs splitting energy bill 3-8, 219G2
Suggests oil tax-Soc Sec link 4-2, 241C1
Carter tax plan pared by com 4-17—4-19; sees Carter 4-20, rpts reactn 4-23, 305D3, 306B1
On vote vs Soc Sec rollback 5-17, 386E1
Welfare compromise prepared 6-7, 446B2
Backs $16 bln tax cut bill 7-27, 586C3
House votes $16 bln tax cut bill 8-10, 604C1
Reelected 11-7, 852B1
Backs VAT proposal 12-6, 962E2
PAC contributions rptd 12-24, 1008E1
ULLMAN, Liv
Serpent's Egg released 1-27, 619F3
Autumn Sonata released 10-8, 969B3
ULLSTEN, Ola (Swedish premier)
Falldin resigns 10-5, 764B3
Becomes premr 10-13, names Cabt 10-18, 822C2, F2
Hails Volvo, Sweden-Norway pacts 12-8, 965B3
ULMER, John
Show-off opens 5-18, 760C3
ULSTER—*See NORTHERN Ireland*
ULTRASONICS—*See MEDICINE—Drugs*
UMARJADI Njotowijono
Heads ASEAN 2-18, 122B2
UMM al Quwain—*See NONALIGNED Nations Movement, UNITED Arab Emirates*
UMPIRES Association, Major League
Strike 8-25—8-26, 779G1
UMW—*See UNITED Mine Workers of America*
UNCTAD—*See UNITED Nations—Trade and Development, UN Conference on*
UNDERHILL, Roger D.
Testifies vs Thevis 4-28, slain 10-25, 971D2
UNDOF (UN Disengagement Observer Force)—*See under MIDDLE EAST—UN*
UNECE—*See UNITED Nations—Europe, Economic Commission for*
UNEF—*See under MIDDLE EAST—UN*
UNEMPLOYMENT—*See LABOR—Employment*
UNESCO—*See UNITED Nations—Education, Scientific and Cultural Organization*
UNGER, Leonard
Taiwan vs US-Peking ties 12-16, 974G1
UNGER, Oliver A.
Force 10 released 12-21, 1030G2
UNICEF—*See UNITED Nations—Children's Emergency Fund*
UNICORN in Captivity, The (play)
Opens 11-15, 1031B3
UNIFICATION Church
NY denies seminary charter; '77 solicitatn bar, deportatns cited 2-22, 295G2
KCIA link probed by US House subcom 3-15, 3-22, 203D1
Helander deprogramming suit rptd 4-16, 295E3
Moon subpoenaed by House subcom, US exit rptd 6-6, 433C1
US House subcom chrgs abuses, asks interagency probe; reactn 11-1, 862C3, G3
Weiss loses deprogramming suit 12-29, 1012A2
UNIFIL—*See MIDDLE EAST, subheads LEBANON and UN*
UNION Bancorp Inc.
UK bank to buy 6-8, 553B1
UNION Bank of Switzerland
Top-ranked '77 per capita GNP natns rptd 7-18, 624D1
UNION Camp Corp.
Okefenokee Refuge land donated 3-14, 186B3
UNION Carbide Corp.
In Dow Jones indl avg 66F2
Molecular sieve announced 2-9, 293C3
UNION of Concerned Scientists—*See SCIENTISTS, Union of Concerned*
UNION of Concerned Scientists

1979

UHL, Peter
Arrested 5-29, sentncd 10-23, 802A2
UHLER, Lewis
US spending limit amendmt urged 1-30, 86B3
UK (United Kingdom)—*See GREAT Britain*
UKRAINIAN Soviet Socialist Republic—*See USSR-Republics*
ULAM, Stan
Cited in H-bomb letter 9-16, 9-18, 714G3-715D2
ULANFU
Business class rehabilitated 1-25, 75A2
ULCERS—*See MEDICINE-Diseases*
ULLMAN, Rep. Al (D, Ore.)
Vs Carter Soc Sec, 'wage insurnc' tax credit plans 1-23, 55A3
Ways & Means Com chrmn 1-24, 71F1
Backs Carter oil tax 4-26, 301D1
Says tax cut unlikely 4-30, 327B2
Sponsors new welfare plan 5-23, 384G1
House OKs oil profits tax 6-28, 541E2
ULLMANN, Liv
I Remember Mama opens 5-31, 711G3
ULLSTEN, Ola (Swedish premier; replaced Oct. 11)
To meet Norway premr 1-27, 77D2
Energy bill rptd 3-13, 213D3-214A1
A-waste plans faulted 3-14, 214D1
A-plant fueling OKd 6-25, 505G1, A2
Nonsoclsts win electn, resigns 9-20, 697F1
Falldin named premier 10-9, confrmd 10-11, 795A2
ULMER, Ralph E.
Quits Vesco jury, claims cover-up 8-29, 647E2
Resignation rejected 9-7, 725C3
UMBA Di Lutete
Zaire culture min 3-6, 215C2
UMBATHA (play)
Opens 4-9, 712B3
UMBRELLAS Of Cherbourg, The (play)
Opens 2-1, 292E3
UMM al Quwain—*See UNITED Arab Emirates*
UMPIRES Association, Major League
3-mo walkout setld, terms rptd 5-18, 569B2
UNCTAD—*See UNITED Nations-Trade and Development, UN Conference on*
UNDERHILL, Roger Dean (d. 1978)
Thevis, 2 others convicted of murder 10-21, 818A2
UNDERWOOD, Tom
Traded to Yankees 11-1, 1002C3
UNDOF (UN Disengagement Observer Force)—*See under MIDDLE EAST-U.N.*
UNECE—*See UNITED Nations-Europe, Economic Commission for*
UNEF—*See under MIDDLE EAST-U.N.*
UNEMPLOYMENT—*See LABOR-Employment*
UNESCO—*See UNITED Nations-Education, Scientific and Cultural Organization*
UNGO, Guillermo Manuel
Joins El Salvador junta 10-17, 790F2
UNICEF—*See UNITED Nations-Children's Emergency Fund*
UNIDENTIFIED Flying Objects (UFOs)
CIA probe detailed 1-12, 93A1
Grenada renounces mysticism 3-16, 236D3
UNIFICATION Church
DC bank fraud chrgd 5-1, 376D2
UNIFIED Industries Inc.
Liberia deal set 9-7, 720E3
UNIFIL—*See MIDDLE EAST, heading LEBANON and U.N.*
UNILEVER
Denmark files trust chrgs 7-2, 563F3
UNION Bancorp Inc.
FRB OKs UK bank 3-16, 205C1
UNION Bank of Switzerland
Top-ranked '78 per capita GNP natns rptd 7-24, 575D3
Pahlevi family assets identified 11-26, 897E2
UNION Carbide Corp.
In Dow Jones indl avg 72F1
UNION City, N.J.—*See NEW Jersey*
UNION Leader Corp.
Loeb settles pensn suit 7-9, 640F3
UNION of Arab Chambers of Commerce
Iran assets freeze in US scored 11-14, 862A1
UNION of Concerned Scientists (UCS)
Ford lauds NRC A-safety rule 1-20, 54B3
A-plant shutdown proposed, NRC hedges 1-26, 90G2
NRC A-plant closings scored 4-27, 322E3
NY A-plant shutdown urged 9-17, 743B2
Ford on 3 Mile I comm final rpt 10-30, 826F1

1980

UKRAINIAN Soviet Socialist Republic—*See UNION of Soviet Socialist Republics--Republics*
ULLMAN, Rep. Al (D, Ore.)
Wins primary 5-20, 404C3
Loses reelectn 11-4, 837E1, 846E1, 852F2
ULLMANN, Liv
At Cambodia border aid vigil 2-6, 108D2
ULLOA, Felix Antonio
Slain 10-29, 871G3
ULMER, Ralph E.
Vesco grand jury ends 4-1, 251E3
ULQUINAKU, Esama
Albania light industry min 5-2, 356F2
ULRICH, Donna (d. 1978)
Ford acquitted in Pinto trial 3-13, 185C3
ULRICH, Frank
Wins Olympic medals 2-16, 2-19, 155D3
ULRICH, Judy (d. 1978)
Ford acquitted in Pinto trial 3-13, 185C3, 186C1
ULRICH, Lyn (d. 1978)
Ford acquitted in Pinto trial 3-13, 185C3
ULSTER—*See NORTHERN Ireland*
ULTRAVIOLET Rays
US solar study satellite launched 2-14, 160D2
ULTSCH, Detlef
Wins Olympic medal 7-28, 623D1
ULUSU, Bulent (Turkish premier)
Named premr 9-20; names Cabt 9-21, sets goals 9-22, 720A3
UMM al Quwain—*See UAE*
UNC Resources Inc.
Westn Air merger sought 12-24, 985C1
UNDERHILL, Lord
Trotskyist rpt debated 1-7—1-17, 58B3; publicatn barred 1-23, 79C2
UNDERWOOD, Barbara Lee
Navy actn on lesbian chrgs cited 899A1
UNEMPLOYMENT—*See LABOR--Employment & Unemployment*
UNESCO—*See UNITED Nations--UNESCO*
UNGO, Guillermo Manuel
Resigns 1-3, 6B2
Junta replacemt named 1-9, 19G3
Named to new leftist govt 12-26, 993F2
UNHOLY Child (book)
On best-seller list 12-7, 948F3
UNICEF—*See UNITED Nations--UNICEF*
UNIFIL—*See UNITED Nations--UNIFIL*
UNION—*See New York*
UNION Bank of Switzerland
Purchasing power survey rptd 2-12, 125D3
UNION Carbide Corp.
In Dow Jones indl avg 76F1
Canada unit '79 profits rptd up 2-7, 116C2
Tex chem plant cancer cases rptd 7-24, 584D2, F2
UNION Corp., The
Metal Bank of America Inc.
US sues on PCB pollution 4-24, 331E3
UNION of Concerned Scientists
3 Mile I gas venting OKd 6-10, 441A1

UNION OF SOVIET SOCIALIST REPUBLICS

1976

UNION of Soviet Socialist Republics (USSR)—*See also COMECON, WARSAW Pact*
Film wins US Oscar 3-29, 240B3
Modernists exhibit 5-11, 421F3
Ilyushin 62 crash in Czech 7-28, 560G3
Aeroflot crash kills 72 11-28, 912C2
Angola Issue
UK chrgs African bribe 1-3, USSR denies 1-6, 2E2
Ford scores Sovt role, bars grain sales boycott 1-5, 2B2, 3F1
Defends MPLA aid, rebuffs US interventn chrgs 1-6, 2B2
US scores warships presence 1-7, USSR denies 1-8, 2E1

1977

UNION of Soviet Socialist Republics (USSR)—*See also COMECON, DISARMAMENT—Geneva Committee, WARSAW Pact*
Moscow Metro blast 1-8, 22A2
More Moscow blasts 1-21; Metro toll rptd 2-12, 117F1
Jan populatn total 257.9 mln 1-22, 101A3
Mid-'75 populatn rptd 1-30, 123G2
Moscow hotel blaze 2-25, 204C2
Rumania quake felt 3-4, 204F1, C2
Aeroflot jet crash in Cuba 5-27, 604D1
Sovietskaya hotel blast 6-11, suspect arrested 7-7, 564G2
Open sector cyclotron use cited 825B3
Orthodox church bars female ordinatn 9-25, 845B3

1978

UNION of Soviet Socialist Republics (USSR)—*See also COMECON, DISARMAMENT—Geneva Committee, WARSAW Pact*
Populatn rptd at 260 mln 1-4, 230F1
Moscow shootout, hostages escape 5-24, 416D2
Icebreaker Sibir opens northn Arctic path 5-25—6-12, 506A2
'77 Moscow blast arrests rptd 6-7, 499A3
Nazi collaborators rptd sentncd 6-7, 499C3
Christina Onassis weds ex-shipping offcl 8-1, 844E3

1979

UNION of Soviet Socialist Republics (USSR)—*See also COMECON, DISARMAMENT-Geneva Committee, WARSAW Pact*
'77 Moscow subway blast suspects executed 1-30, 100F2
Moscow airliner crash kills 90 3-17, 240B3
Aeroflot jet collisn kills 173 8-17, 639D1
Anti-crime drive launched 9-11, 857B2
Birth rate rise urged; populatn, male-female ratio rptd 10-10, 857D1
Amnesty for youths, mothers set 10-19, 857D2
Parade marks revolutn anniv 11-7, 856D2

1980

UNION of Soviet Socialist Republics (USSR)—*See also COMECON, CSCE, GENEVA Committee, MBFR, WARSAW Pact*
Siberia '08 blast linked to meteorite 1-24, 160D3
'79 populatn rptd 1-25, 79E3; census reveals ethnic shift 2-9, 152E3
Caspian Sea drainoff plugged 3-2, 235F3

1976

Nigeria repudiates US plea 1-7, 2B3, 3A1
Reagan scores US policy 1-8, 5E1
OAU deadlock on Sovt role 1-10—1-13, 15D3
MPLA troop support rptd 1-11, 16D3
FNLA rpts arms seizure 1-12, 16F2
Kissinger sets Moscow trip 1-14, 17A1
Zaire warns USSR 1-17, 1-19, 36A1, B1
Tanzania scores Angola role 1-18, 36D1
UK Tory leader scores USSR 1-19, 101D1
Kissinger in Moscow 1-21—1-23, 61F3
MPLA forms MiG AF 1-22, 57F1
S Africa defends Angola role 1-26, 57D2
Zambia scores Angola role 1-28, 77F3
Hints pol compromise 1-29, scores Kissinger statemts 2-1, 2-4, 82A3
Kissinger studies open Angola aid, backs Sovt confrontatn 1-29—1-30, 88B3
MPLA urges Westn support 1-30, 82B2
S Africa denounces Angola role 1-31, 103F2
US Cong aid bar scored by Kissinger 2-3, Ford 2-10, 88D2, 109G2-B3
Ships sighted off Lobito 2-5, shelling rptd 2-11, 105D1
Kissinger on Cuba interventn 2-5, 138D1
Reagan scores US policy 2-10, 109F2
Brezhnev cites aid to MPLA 2-24, 194G1
UK forgn min sees Lunkov 3-15—3-19, 229A1
US halts joint Sovt talks 3-16, 196F1
Kissinger warns Cuba anew 3-22, 3-23, 214E3
MPLA vows for S Africa rptd 3-25, 3-26, 228B1
Gromyko UK talks end 3-25, 228G3
Angola defends aid 3-26, 228E2
US UN amb scores role 3-31, 228C3
US-Zaire talks on Sovt arms buildup rptd 4-30, 318A3
Nascimento visits USSR, mil aid vow rptd 5-31, 480F3 ★
Australia scores Sovt role 6-1, 438D2
Sovt presence rptd 6-13, 467C1
US-Zaire talks re Sovt role 6-17—6-19, 467B1
US vetoes Angola UN membership 6-23, 455A2
US scores interventn 9-30, 719E1
Angola-Portugal ties restored 9-30, 812D2
Neto in USSR 10-7—10-13; signs treaty 10-8; statemt issued 10-14, 856C3
China shuns Angola UN entry vote 11-22, 879E1
Armaments—*See appropriate subheads under ARMAMENTS; also 'Weapons' under ATOMIC Energy*

1977

SST passenger svc starts 11-1; facts on 831F3
African Relations—*See also 'Monetary, Trade & Aid' below*
Angola war role rptd 1-3, 1-31, 86C1
UK sees Rhodesia interventn 1-25, 49B2
Benin coup attempt detailed 2-1, 96F1
Reps at Frelimo cong 2-3—2-7, 137D1
Africa federatn backed by Cuba 3-10—3-16, 249D2
Podgorny in Africa 3-23—4-2, backs Indian O demilitarizatn 3-24, 247G2
Egypt sees Africa threat 4-5, 245C1
Kissinger scores re Zaire invasn 4-5, 261E1 ★
Zaire chrgs denied 4-7, 4-11, 4-12, 265G2
Zaire scores invasn role 4-9, 265C2
Young on Angola role 4-11, 272A1
France notes Africa role 4-12, 265D1
Brezhnev vs Zaire meddling 4-18, 317C2
Zaire ends exchg program, chrgs Zambia raid 4-20, 317F1
Morocco scores Africa subversn 4-23, 317B2
Mozambique arms shipmts rptd 4-24, 456E3
Senegal scores Africa role 5-3, 394E1
Ethiopia's Mengistu visits, student protest rptd 5-4—5-8, 390E3
US ambs on Africa role 5-9—5-12, 398B3
Sudan-French talks stress Africa ties 5-17—5-19, 450D1
Sudan expels mil advisers 5-18, 416G3
Somalia rejcts Africa federatn 5-18, 428E2
Sudan orders emb staff cut 5-19; amb recalled 5-31, 548C1
Angola purges 2 pro-Sovts 5-21, rebelln suppressed 5-27, 424G1-A2
Seychelles coup aid chrgd 6-5, denied 6-6, 451A1
Cubans in Africa held USSR 'surrogates' 6-5, 456A1
Ethiopia rebels rejct federatn offer 6-9, 486G1
Ethiopia students score govt 6-13, 486B2
Angola rebelln detailed 6-20, 484C2
Somalia denies advisers ousted 7-18, backs ties 7-28, 588A1
Giscard evaluates Africa role 7-25, 551B1
Ethiopia rpts Sovt-made Somali jets downed 7-27, 587D3
Somalia truce request rptd 8-4, 608G1
S Africa A-capacity chrgd 8-9, 8-14, 656G3
Uganda envoy defectn rptd 8-11, 606F2
Ethiopia backed re Ogaden 8-14, 8-16; Somalia scored 8-19, 648F3
East Ger Africa role rptd 8-21, 684G3
S Africa A-test rptdly headed off 8-28—8-29, 663A3
Somali ldr visits re Ogaden 8-29—8-31, 684A3
Somalia Ogaden role scored 9-28, arms aid cut 10-19; Barre denounces 10-21, 829G2
Angola pres visits 9-28, 830D1
UK forgn secy in Rhodesia talks 10-10—10-11, 812F3
Somalia ends '74 treaty, ousts aides 11-13; Moscow scores 11-15, 874D3
Nigeria officer training set 11-13, 986A3
Cuban role rptd encouraged 11-17, 896B1, E2
Guinea halts spy flights 11-19, 989F1
Young scores Africa role 12-6, 1011A3

1978

African Policy
Ethiopian airlift halt rptd 1-5, 3C3
African role scored by US 1-12, 12E1
Eritrea rebels rpt Sovt troop capture 1-15, mil role chrgd 2-2, 100A2
Ethiopia aid total cited 1-18, 43A3
Ethiopia troops denied 1-18, 43E3
Ethiopia role discussed by US, allies 1-21, 43F2
Ethiopian counteroffensive in Ogaden gains 1-22—2-14, 99C2
Somali arms sources rptd 1-24, 44C1
US warns re Ethiopia role 1-25, 43D3
Equatorial Guinea aid rptd 1-25, 152A3
Rhodesia rebel aid cited 59B1
Morocco phosphate dvpt pact rptd 1-31, 95E1
US pledges neutrality, assured vs Somalia invasn 2-8, 2-10, 99A3
Somalia orders gen mobilizatn 2-11, 99D3
Somali pres sees Italy CP rep, denies Ogaden proposal 2-20—2-22, 138A1
US ups Ethiopia troops, arms estimates 2-24, 2-25; issues warning 2-25, 137A1; 3-2, 140E2
Mali arrests 4 mins 2-28, 3-9, 250G3
US links SALT delay, Ethiopia role 3-1; USSR scores 3-2, 178F3
Rhodesia rpts Sovt arms seized in Zambia raid 3-5—3-6, 156B1
Ethiopia exit urged by US, Yugo 3-7—3-9, 194A1
Ethiopia troop reductn, cease-fire plan rptd 3-10, 178G2
Rhodesia rebel role rptd 3-12, 210C3
Ethiopia backed vs Eritrea rebels; US on troop cut vow 3-15, 215E3, F3
Carter warns vs interventn, Tass scores 3-17, 202E1, G2
ECOWAS scored 3-20, 237E1
Nigeria trade pact signed 3-21, 248E1
Israel Sinai air base use by US for surveillnc rptd 3-26; US denies 3-27, 215F1
Arab League scores moves 3-29, 215D1
Ethiopia advisers estimated 3-31, 372D2
Angola anti-rebel drive rptd 4-4, 265C2
UK scores Africa Horn role 4-5, amb protests 4-6, 259C1
Somali pres seeks China support 4-13, 353E2
Carter scores USSR role 5-5, 342E1
US CIA propaganda in '75 Angola war chrgd 5-8, 367G2
Saudis note Ethiopia role 5-13, 358E2
Zaire chrgs Shaba rebel aid 5-14, 359A2
Kaunda on Rhodesia role 5-16, 395E2, A3
Zaire advisers rptd seen by France 5-19, 382C1
Carter scores US curbs 5-19, Young rebuts 5-21, 383A1, F1
Zaire rescue operatn scored 5-22, 382D1
E Ger role in Africa rptd 5-22, 382G1
US-China concern noted 5-22, 384B3
IISS blames US re influence 5-24, 488C1
Iraq warns vs Ethiopia rebel aid 5-25, 416D1
Zaire massacre laid to French, Belgians 5-25, 417C3
Carter chrgs Zaire role 5-25, Cuba denies 5-20, 418B1, F1
Gromyko disputes Carter on Zaire role; Powell, Vance rebut 5-27; US propaganda scored 6-4, 422E1-C2
NATO summit debates role 5-30—5-31, 397D1
Brezhnev scores NATO role in Zaire 5-31, 423G1
Rhodesia rebel arms aid rptd 6-6, 455D2
Carter chrgs Angolia, Ethiopia proxy role 6-7, 423C3
Zaire role scored by China 6-7, 441D2
Tanzania defends Africa role 6-8, 442A1
Angola denies Zaire role 6-10, 441A2
Hungary defends Africa role 6-10, 534F2
US scored re Sovt-Cuban role talk 6-17, 464G3
Vance denies SALT link 6-19, 490D3
US will not mirror activities 6-20; Tass rebuts 6-22, 487D1, B3
Ethiopia rebel ldr visit rptd 6-22, 584F2
Poor natns '77 trade rptd 6-28, 634E3
Rhodesia forgn min: US lacks 'guts' 6-30, 615E2
Nigeria warns vs role 7-18, 561G1-A2
Nonaligned warned vs influence 7-25, 583B2
Eritrea troop role rptd ended 7-29, 584B3
Seychelles warns vs Indian O mil activity, denies sub base offer 8-7, 8-20, 692C1
China, Yugo vs African role 8-25—8-27, 675G2
Ghana rptdly ousts envoys 9-8, 841A1
US amb scored by Pravda 10-14, 821C1
Rhodesia Patriotic Front backing cited 10-25, 906F3
Tanzania, Uganda MiGs cited 11-2, 860C1
Algeria pres med treatmt fails 11-14, 1012F2
US sens, Kosygin dispute Sovt mil role 11-16, 905F1
Ethiopia cooperatn pact signed 11-20, 922C3
Ethiopia role rptd 'decesive' 12-2, 1016E2
Angola pro-West trend seen 12-10, 985C1
Guinea Westn tilt noted 12-22, 1018B1
Arts & Sciences—*See also 'Human Rights' below*
Nonconformist art show opens 3-7, 180E1

1979

Afghanistan Relations—*See AFGHANISTAN--Soviet Military Intervention*
African Relations
Rhodesian dispute role cited 170B2
UK warns on Rhodesia conf failure 1-17, 39F3
Somalia hints improved ties 1-21, 85F3
Somalia scores US arms delay 2-7, 193A2
US response to Sovt surrogates urged 2-8, 89B2
Ethiopian troop presence rptd 3-2, 271D1
Zaire ends rocket tests 4-27, 411A3
Amin scored by Pravda 4-29, aid to Uganda rptd 5-28, 429G1
US fears Sovt escalatn re Rhodesia sanctns end 5-15, 359C2
E Ger role rptd 5-23, 406F2
Carter to keep Zimbabwe trade ban 6-7, 434E2
US sen scores Sovt policy 6-12, 459F2
SALT II summit topic 6-15–6-18, 449D1, 458A2
Brezhnev warned on Cuba role 6-18, 449E2, 459A3
Ethiopia govt arms cited 7-14, 638E2
SALT linkage proposed by Kissinger 7-31, 590B3
Ethiopian adviser total rptd 8-3, mil aid lauded 8-23 8-3, 791C1
US on troop presence 8-31, 657E1; 9-12, 673E2
Angola's Neto dies 9-10, lauded 9-11, 705A2
Equatorial Guinea ruler executed 9-29, 742E1
S Africa suggests sub mishap as A-blast cause 10-27, 824E3
UN abstentn on Zimbabwe sanctns vote 12-21, 976C3
Arts & Sciences—*See also 'Human Rights' below*
Sci acad ousts Levich 4-5, 272E1
Hermitage US show rptd set 7-19, 672E2

1980

Afghanistan Relations—*See AFGHANISTAN--Soviet Military Intervention*
African Relations
Ethiopia Eritrean evacuatn aid rptd 1-12, 40C1
CAR breaks ties 1-22, 336B2
Equatorial Guinea fish pact expiratn rptd 1-28, 119C1
Zambia announces arms purchase 2-7, 119E1
Zimbabwe gains indepndnc 4-18, 301F1
Chad envoy dies 6-7, body misplaced 6-17, 491C3
Ethiopia gets combat copters 6-13, 509B2
Algeria quake aid rptd 10-11, 776E1
'79 arms sales rptd up 12-10, 933A2
Arts & Sciences—*See also 'Human Rights' below*
Science acad meets 3-4—3-6, 181D2
Jewish scientists hold conf 4-13—4-15, 326D2

1976

Astronautics—*See under 'A'*
Censorship & Dissent—*See also 'Emigration' and 'Jews' below*
Plyushch, Amnesty Intl rpt pol patients 1-11, 30A3
'75 ship mutiny rptd foiled 1-22, 122G2
Plyushch details asylum stay 2-3, 122C1
Psychiatric abuses denied, West accused 2-4, 122B2
UK CP scores repressn 2-7, 174B3
Melchuk loses post re Sakharov 3-26, 314A1
UN staff asks ex-colleague freed 3-30, 421B3
Sakharovs detained at Dzhemilev trial 4-14—4-16; Dzhemilev, Tverdokhlebov sentncd 4-15, 292C1, F1
'75 ship mutineers rptd bombed 5-4, 5-5, 421A2
Tverdokhlebov appeal denied 5-12, 421G2
9 dissidents to monitor CSCE compliance 5-13, Orlov detained 5-15, 408F1
Moroz rptd in mental hosp 5-18, 421F2
Leningrad artists detained, 1 chrgd 5-31, 421E3 ★
Levich scores Ford rights stand 6-25, 540A3
Eur Parlt scores Bukovsky mistreatmt 7-9, 540B3
Chess player defects 7-27, 558F3
Olympic diver defects 7-29—7-31, 562C2
US GOP platform text cites 8-18, 610A3
Korchnoi loses Sovt honors 9-4, 857B1
MiG-25 pilot defects in Japan, asks US asylum 9-6, arrives US 9-9, US-Japan plot chrgd 9-14, 695D3-696D1
USSR Chrgs Japan re MiG pilot defectn 9-9, Japan rejects chrg 9-20; pilot bars return 9-28, 839F2
Soldier defects in W Ger 9-9, 857D1
Pilot defects to Iran, asks US asylum 9-23; Sovt protests 9-26, 773D2; Iran returns 10-25; dissidents, UN protest 10-28, 11-1, 854B2
CP member resigns 10-6, 857D1
Bukovsky, Corvalan exchngd 12-18; Bukovsky press conf 12-19; W Eur CPs vs exchng 12-22, 955D2-F3
Chinese Relations—*See 'Soviet Relations' under CHINA*
Communist Countries Relations—*See also 'Soviet Relations' under CHINA and CUBA; also COMECON, WARSAW Pact*
Oil price to Hungary up 1-15, 101D2
Polish charter cites ties 2-10, 268B1
Cuba, Rumania, Yugo at CP cong 2-24—3-5, 195B3, 196C1, E1
Yugo sentncs 4 in emigre plot 3-12, 223C3
Yugo jails 10 pro-Sovts 3-16, 256E1
US columnists rpt US backed Sovt-Eur union 3-22, Kissinger rebuts 3-29, 232G2
Brezhnev not at Bulgaria CP cong 3-29, 250E1
Hungary barter pact rptd 4-1, 543A3
Yugo holds aide as spy 4-6, 256B1
Czech CP Cong 4-12—4-16, 289E1
Yugo sentences Cominformists 4-14, 542G3
Zagladin on independent CP issue 4-20, 341A2
Albania anti-China plot, purge rptd 4-30, 331D3
Yugo paper shuts Czech bur 4-30, 341A3
Eur CPs meet, cong set 5-4—5-6, 341F1
'75 trade rptd 5-5, 340C3, F3
E Ger SED cong lauds USSR 5-18; Suslov addresses 5-19; energy projcts cited 5-21, 381D1, C2
Yugo sentences spy 5-25, 542C3
Katushev in Rumania re Eur CP mtg 5-28, Ceausescu eases stance 6-2, 420A3
US Dem platform text cites 6-15, 477F2
Brezhnev meets Tito 6-28, 461D2
Brezhnev at E, W Eur conf, Sovt ldrship role rebuffed 6-29—6-30, 461A1
Berlin bus protest rejctd 8-27, 678D3
Role in Sovt space progrm set 9-14, Soyuz 22 carries E Ger cameras 9-15, 684D1
Cuts oil to Czech 10-4, 851B3
US pres campaign debate issue 10-6, 741B3
Ford debate gaffe scored in US 10-7—10-12, 762A1, A3
Ford admits debate error 10-12, 10-14, 761E3, 762G3
US vp candidates debate 10-15, 782E3
Ford, Carter debate Yugo threat 10-22, 800A1, 802D2, 803B1-D1, 804F2
Brezhnev seeks closer Albania ties 10-25; Hoxha scores USSR 11-2, 849G3
Yugo doubts Sovt threat 10-28, 910B1
Brezhnev-Gierek talks 11-9—11-15; communique 11-16, 907D1
Brezhnev in Yugo, denies threat 11-14—11-17, 909D3
EEC discusses Yugo trade aid 11-15, 955A2
Brezhnev in Rumania 11-22—11-24, 907A2
Yugo assures US re tech secrets 11-25—11-27, 1012C1

1977

Astronautics—*See under 'A'*
Censorship & Dissent—*See 'Human Rights' below*
Communism & Communist Country Relations—*See also CHINA—Soviet Relations also COMECON, WARSAW Pact*
West scores E Ger Berlin visas 1-6, 7E2; lodges protests 1-11, 20F1
Hungary rpts oil price rise, other E Eur hikes seen 1-6, 67C3
Yugo rebuffs mil pact 1-9, 24A1
Kapitonov arrives Czech 2-8, 115B1
Eurocommunist ldrs meet 3-2—3-3, 242F3
Castro presses S Yemen-Somalia-Ethiopia alliance re Djibouti 3-10—3-16, 249D2
Rumania quake aid set 3-13, 204C2
Yugo CP ldr backs Carter on rights 3-13, 226G1
Castro visits 4-4—4-9, 249G1, F3, 282E3
NATO warns re Berlin 5-9, 358C2
NATO Berlin warning scored 5-14, E Berlin sovereignty upheld 5-15, 496A3
Cubans in Africa held USSR 'surrogates' 6-5, 456A1
Yugo ousts Jewry backers 6-15, 473A2
Brezhnev in Belgrade 6-15, 496B2
Spain Eurocommunism scored 6-23; CP, Carrillo respond 6-25, 6-27, 507F1
Hungary, Rumania back Eurocommunism 6-30, 7-5, 513E2
Sovt bloc on Eurocommunism 7-3—7-24, 590A3
Carrillo criticism renewed; Spain, Italy, France CPS exonerated 7-6, 545C3
Castro, Church discuss detente 8-10, 653G3
Tito visits, econ aid sought 8-16—8-18, joint statemt backs independnc 8-19, 640C2, 709D3
E Ger Africa role rptd 8-21, 684G3
Italian barred 9-6, bar lifted 9-7, 766C1
E Ger emb chrgs US rights violatns 9-28, 752B3
E Ger rioters score USSR 10-8, 782B1
US criticism of Czech trial scored 10-18, 812A2
Portugal CP ldr vs Eurocommunism 10-28, 886F3
Bolshevik Revolutn 60th anniv rites, Eurocommunism scored, Carrillo speech barred 11-2—11-7, 865D2; photo 11-7, 865A2
Cuban role in Africa rptd encouraged 11-17, 896E1, B2
Yugo pro-Sovt exiles rptd seized 11-22, 12-17, 1018B3
Castro ties 'decisive' 12-24, 1011C3

1978

Protein spatial structure predicted 3-16, 334F2
Wyeth elected to Sovt Acad 4-24, 335D3
2 Amers win Tchaikovsky competitn 7-4, 7-5, 844A2
Margulis wins Field Medal 8-15, 1023F2
Intl genetics conf held 8-21—8-30, 670D2
Kapitsa wins Nobel 10-17, 886C2
At intl whaling conf 12-8, 1001B3
Astronautics—*See ASTRONAUTICS*
Chinese Relations—*See CHINA—Soviet Relations*
Communism & Communist Country Relations—See also CAMBODIA—Vietnam Conflict; CHINA—Soviet Relations; COMECON, WARSAW Pact
Cuba African role scored by US 1-12, 12E1
E Ger presence increased, ties stressed; oppositn rpts cited 1-29, 1-31, 61G3
E Ger, Poland, Czech observe mil maneuvers 2-6—2-10, 103C2
US ouster of Viet UN amb protested 2-9, 103A3
Italy CP rep sees Somali pres, Ogaden proposal denied 2-20—2-22, 138A1
Spain book chrgs Eurocommunists aided Stalin purges 2-24, 136D2
Czech joins space flight, ties lauded 3-2, 157E2
Yugo backs Ethiopia exit 3-7—3-9, 194A1
Berlin demilitarized status cited 3-14, 275B1
Spy truck transit denied 3-15, 291F2
'77 trade rptd 3-28, 230B1
'68 Czech invasn cited 4-11, 333D1
Yugo sentences pro-Sovt Tito foe 4-13, 292F1
US, E Ger prisoner exchng talks rptd 4-24; 3-way swap completed 5-1, 318A2
Arms tech transfer agrmt rptd 4-25, 297C1
E Ger role in Africa rptd 5-22, 382G1
Cuba Africa role scored by US 5-25, Cuba denies 5-30, 418B1, F1
Iraq executes 14 CP members 5-26, 415G3
Brezhnev in Czech 5-30—6-2, 423A2
Poland default held unlikely 6-1, 535G2
'50 Korean war role chrgd 6-7, 423D3
Cuba role in nonaligned movemt scored by US 6-7, 423D3
Marxist-Leninist model rptd being abandoned 6-7, 423G3
Hungary backs re Africa, '56 invasn, troop role 6-10, 534F2
Sovt soldier in E Berlin shootout 6-19, 549F1
Yugo warns vs world war 6-20, 519D2
E-W Ger ties improved, Brezhnev visit cited 6-24, 622G2
E Ger maneuvers held 7-3—7-7, 648D3
Czech ousts W Ger rptr re '68 invasn rpt 7-4, 635F1
Poland plane order rptd 7-5, 650D2
Italy CP scores dissident trials 7-11, 7-12, 543A1
Viet-Sovt plot to control SE Asia chrgd 7-12, 547G3; 9-6, 696D1
Nonaligned vs Cuba alliance 7-25—7-30, 583B2
Albania details China split 7-30, 635D1
China premr scored re Rumania, Yugo trip 8-5, 8-21, 8-27; Rumania pres reassures Brezhnev 8-7, 675D3-676A1

1979

Intl Pol Sci Assn meets 8-12–8-18, 637A1
2d intl book fair held 9-4–9-10, 689F3
Computer programming breakthrough rptd 10-6, 1000D2
Astronautics—*See ASTRONAUTICS*
Atomic Energy & Safeguards
Nuclear 'doomsday clock' unchngd 1-1, 13F1
A-test rptd 1-17, 52D1
'78 A-tests set record 1-31, 109B2; record noted 3-6, 625D3
US A-accident reactn 4-4, 246B3
A-accidents disclosed 4-22, 323F1
India A-plant bid rejctd 5-2, 323F2
Turkey A-plant deal set 6-5, 488F2
Urban A-plants rptd planned 6-6, 476B3
Underground A-blast rptd 6-27, 625E3
E Ger pact signed 10-5, 761C2
A-safety doubts rptd publshd 10-14, 815B2
S Africa suggests sub mishap as A-blast cause 10-27, 824E3
Chinese Relations—*See CHINA–Soviet Relations*
Communism & Communist Country Relations—*See also CAMBODIA, CHINA and CUBA; COMECON, WARSAW Pact*
Hungary oil imports cited 1-8, 101A2
Poland defense outlay frozen 1-9, 39E2
Oil price hiked 3-21, 228B1
Bulgarian aboard Soyuz 4-10–4-12, 279B2
SS-21 deploymt in E Ger rptd 4-23, 340E1; NATO error admitted 5-23, 399E1
French CP Eurocommunism shift seen 5-10–5-15, 371A2, E2
Yugo pres visits 5-16–5-18, 379D3
E Ger African role rptd 5-23, 406F2
Kosygin in Czech, urges Sovt bloc energy conservatn 5-24, 397B1
Brezhnev in Hungary, backs econ dvpts 5-30–6-1, 416F3
Pope arrives Poland, border rptd closed 6-2; visit covered 6-3, 413B2, 414F1
Berlin violatns cited 6-28, 513C1
Oil exports promise backed 6-29, 497C2; hike seen 7-18, 568G1
Viet bases noted by Kissinger 7-31, 590D3
Laos pledge re anti-Thai rebels rptd 8-25, 659C3
Polish dissidents seek independence 9-1, 802F2
Brezhnev in E Ger 10-4–10-8; sets troop cut 10-6, reactn 10-7, 10-9, 10-6, 761C1-E3
E Eur troop deploymt rptd 761F2
Eur troop, tank, missile cuts offered 10-13–11-6, 880G2
Polish dissidents score dominatn 11-11, 939A2
Rumania Party Cong backs indep 11-19–11-23, 910G1
Mongolia troop exit sought by China 11-30, 918A1
E Ger troop pullout begun 12-5, 938C3

1980

Hann icons sold for record sum 4-17, 472A3
Stellar civilizatns discounted 4-25, 416A1
US scientific literacy lag rptd 10-22, 990C1
Astronautics—*See ASTRONAUTICS*
Atomic Energy & Safeguards
Italy plant equipmt sale rptd 1-10, 28A1
'70-79 A-tests rptd 1-17, 31F3
A-plant constructn lag rptd 1-25, 79E3
'57 A-waste mishap confrmd by US probe 2-13, 153B1
Breeder reactor started at Beloyarsk 4-8, 316C1
NATO ups A-superiority predictn 6-4, 450E2
W Ger, USSR sign pact 7-1, 489D2
A-sub crippled off Japan 8-20, no leak rptd 8-24, 653B1
A-nonproliferatn treaty review conf ends, Sri Lanka cites implementatn failure 9-7, 696C1
A-test rptd 9-14, US protests 9-15, 730F1
'79 shale oil detonatn cited 12-5, 951E3
Chinese Relations—*See CHINA--Soviet Relations*
Communism & Communist Country Relations—*See also CHINA, CUBA*
Afghan invasn reactn 1-1—1-10, 11A1
French CP ldr starts visit, rapprochemt seen 1-7, 57F2
Yugo warns re territorial claims 1-15, 1-18, 49E2
Sovt-bloc visit cancellatns re W Ger linked 1-30, 103F1
Gromyko in Rumania, urges unity 1-31—2-2, 108F3, 109A1
Sovt energy prices, E Eur econ slowdown linked 2-4, 166A3
Poland backs detente, USSR 2-11; Suslov addresses CP cong 2-12, 152B3
Yugo threat aid vowed by US 2-13, 110D1
French CP forms rights group; issues rpt, scores Sakharov 2-20, 149C3, D3, E3
'79 COMECON oil sales rptd 3-3, 166C1
Pole kills self re Katyn protest 3-20, 262F3
Hungary CP ldr cites loyalty, raw material price hikes 3-24, 274E3, G3
Italy CP rejects Paris parley 4-2, 254D3
Yugo-EC trade pact signed 4-2, 365C3
Italy CP renews China ties 4-15, clarifies USSR stance 4-22, 314F1, B2
E Ger seeks W Ger Olympics boycott bar 4-17, 303B2
E Eur trade sanctns opposed by W Ger, US role cited 4-17, 303A3
Europn CPs meet 4-28—4-29, 327C2, B3
Tito lauded 5-4, Brezhnev at funeral 5-8, 338F2, 339A1
Cambodia aid conf boycott scored by US 5-26, 397B2
Hungarian joint space flight launched 5-26, 397B3
COMECON to keep fixed prices for commodity purchases 5-29, 451F1
Oil exports to Rumania rptd 6-4, 465F3
S Yemeni activity growth rptd 6-9, 468G2
US seeks Viet Thai raid halt 6-25, 6-26, 508B2
Cambodia-India ties lauded 7-7, 547A3
Poland warns strikers re Sovt response 7-18; Tass rpts unrest, cites premr's speech 8-18, 626D1, B2
Joint Viet space flight launched 7-23, 547F3; returns 7-31, 592C1
Polish premr's resignatn, strike reactn rptd 8-24—8-27, 642B1
Poland strike setlmt scored, subversn chrgd 8-31—9-3, 658D2
Poland hard currency loan rptd 9-3, 658G2, A3
Poland reaffirms ties 9-4, 658G2, C3
Westn aid to Poland opposed, '79 debt chrgs cited 9-4, 659D2
Brezhnev lauds Polish CP promotn 9-6, 678A3

1976

N Korea envoys rptd ousted 12-8, 967D1
E Eur hails Chile prisoner exchng 12-18, 955D3, E3

Disarmament—*See DISARMAMENT*

Economy & Labor (domestic)
'75 grain, agri output drop rptd 1-31, 206D2
Brezhnev, Kosygin rpt on econ at 25th cong 2-24, 3-1; cong OKs 5-yr plan 3-5, 194E2, B3
Meatless days rptd 5-6—5-15, 420F3
Jan-Mar meat output down, livestock epidemic rptd 5-15, 421A1
Harvest measures set 5-22, 421E1
'75 oil output, consumptn rptd 5-24, 655C3
Agri-indl complexes backed 6-1, 421C1
Sausage meat content cut 6-7, 421B1
'76 grain harvest forecast 6-8, 421F1
6-mo meat output rptd down 7-23, 752E2
Indl output rptd up 7-23, US sees 5-yr growth drop 8-18, 752E2
'76 crop forecast revised 9-9, 752C2
Arms share of GNP, econ resources rptd 10-5, 960F3, 961A1
Crop estimate revised again 10-8, 839G1
Jan-Sept indl output rptd up 10-24, 856B2
Central Com hears Brezhnev on crop, '76-80 agri investmt 10-25; 5-yr plan OKd 10-26, 839F1
'74-84 growth rate estimated 10-25, 856D2
Trade union official scores econ performance 10-28, 856C2
Sup Sovt OKs 5-yr plan 10-29; plan detailed 856F1
Latvia meat price strikers sentncd 10-31, 966F3
Whale catch curb rptd 11-3, 1011C2
Wage hikes set 12-27, 1011D2

Emigration Developments
Plyushch arrives in Paris 1-12, 30E2
China scores Sovt policy 1-15, 60A1
'75 Jewish data, '45-75 total 1-22, 76B3
Westn emigre internmt chrgd 2-4, French press refutes 2-6, 122C2
Returned emigre Jews score Israel 2-6, 122B3

1977

Defense & Armed Forces—*See also 'U.S.-Soviet' below and under DISARMAMENT*
Ogarkov named army staff chief 1-9, 47B3
Kulikov, Ogarkov promoted 1-14, 88G1
Civiln defns chief promoted 2-16, 306D3
IISS warns on mil strength 4-28, 401F1
NATO warned on buildup 5-10, 358A3
West concerned re civil defns 5-11, 360A1
NATO rpts spending, strength data 5-17, 379E3
SS-20 missile deploymt rptd 6-9, 530G1
Sovt advances held costly 6-30, 673D3
W Eur observers at mil exercises 7-11, 551C1
Submarine exercise rptd 7-28, 591E1
GNP, arms ratio rptd; mil spending cuts seen 8-8, 949A1
Draftee training scored 8-20; facts on mil svc 674B1
Sub superiority rptd 8-25, 686D2
Major buildup rptd since '64 9-26, 858D1
WWII vets get limited amnesty 11-5, 866C1
Revolutn 60th anniv mil review, T-72 displayed 11-7, 866A1
Hovercraft, T-80 tank threat seen by NATO 12-8, 941D3
'78 budget set 12-14, 988A1

Economy & Labor (domestic)
Price hikes, cuts set 1-4, 22B1
Record '76 grain harvest rptd 1-5, 21G3
'76 indl output, income, productivity data rptd 1-17, 1-18, 47A3
'76 econ growth, indl wages rptd 1-22, 101D2
GNP defense share examined 2-28, 211F3
Maltsev named oil min 4-5, 306C3
Plutonium, breeder reactor use affirmed 5-9, 403A1
NATO rpts defns spending, GNP data 5-17, 379E3
Const draft publshd 6-4, 433B2, 434D2-A3
'76 oil output rptd 6-11, 513G1
Record grain crop seen 7-7, 7-29, 612A1, 619D1
Pvt farming rptd backed, productn data cited 7-10, 619E1
Consumer goods, svcs improvemt asked 7-19, 619G1
1st ½ indl output up 7-20, 619C1
'80s downturn forecast; oil, manpower decline cited 8-8, 948F3-949C1
Oil pipe constructn rptd 9-17, 949D1
Const chngs noted 10-7, 785E2, F2
Grain harvest shortfall rptd 11-2, 948D2
Poor grain harvest rptd 11-15, 916F2
'78 econ goals cut, budget set 12-14, 987D3
Harvest total revised down 12-14, 988B1
Workers rptd fired, Klebanov arrested for protests 12-20, 988A2

Emigration—*See 'Human Rights' below*

1978

Laos pressured to back Viet in China feud 8-8, 603B2
Sovt gas-export rise seen 8-13, 635A1
China premr visits Rumania, Yugo; seeks to counter Sovt influence 8-16—8-29, 674G2-675A3
Czechs mark '68 invasn 8-21, 691G2
Czech blast marks '68 invasn 9-2, 868F3
Viet aide in Moscow 11-2, friendship pact signed 11-3, 859E2
Poles protest Katyn massacre 11-11, 925D3
Cuba rptdly gets MiG-23s 11-14, Kosygin defends 11-16, 905A1; US: assured 11-20, 1016F1
Rumania independnc, China premr visit cited 11-25, 913F2
US support of Rumania stance seen 12-8—12-9, 965C3-966A1
Rumania defns stand scored at intl CP conf 12-15, 1020C1

Defense & Armed Forces—*See also 'U.S.-Soviet Defense' below and under DISARMAMENT*
Air Force buildup rptd 1-29, 81B3
Strategic, conventional arms dvpt, civil defns system rptd 2-2, 81D1
Land, air maneuvers in Byelorussia 2-6—2-10, 103A2
Civil defns rptd overrated 2-17, 127A1
Brezhnev gets Victory medal 2-20, 151C3
SS-20 deploymt rptd 2-21, 140F1
Army 60th anniv marked, Ustinov asserts strength 2-22, 140G1
SS-16 deploymt rptd 2-22, 298G1
Navy ships rptd near obsolescence; sub, bomber strength seen 2-23, 127B2
China border maneuvers staged 4-5, 237G3
Killer satellite test rptd 5-24, 488F2
Defense priorities examined 5-30, 397E2
Hungary notes troop data 6-10, 534B3
New A-bomber rptd 6-19, 518E3
'67-77 arms spending studied, '80s forecast issued 6-27, 563A3
Maneuvers held in E Ger 7-3—7-7, 648D3
Civil defns study issued 7-19, 563F3
'76 arms spending rptd 7-23, 585A2
Reconnaissance plane crashes in Norway 8-28, 820G1
A-arms, nonstrategic weapon power assessed 9-1, 676B3, D3
Barentsburg radar equipmt rptd 9-28, 820D2
Anti-cruise missile success rptd, ships rptd armed 10-23, 877C2
Pacific buildup rptd 11-9, 914G1-A2
Neutron bomb test revealed 11-17, 905D1
Radar vs low-flying aircraft rptd, cruise missile defns discounted 12-26, 1020C3

Dissidents—*See 'Human Rights' below*

Economy & Labor (domestic)
Klebanov rptd freed 1-3, workers repeat protests 1-10, 20G3-21A1
'77 indl, agri output; income growth, wages rptd 1-27, 92A3
Workers form union 2-1, Klebanov arrested 2-7, 180A1
Coffee, gas, other prices hiked 3-1, 151G2
Dissident union denied ILO recognitn 4-14, 275G2
Econ growth lag forecast 5-30, 397G2
Econ weakness detailed 6-7, 423E3
Abkhaz dvpt plan, secessn threats rptd 6-7, 6-25, 519A1
Grain crop estimated by US 6-12, 499A3
Shipbldg tech extends Arctic shipping season 6-12, 506A2
Brezhnev addresses CP com mtg on agri 7-3; '81-85 targets raised 7-4, 518G2-B3
Kosygin compares Eur, Japan, US indus growth 7-5, 518D3
'77 per capita GNP ranked 7-18, 624F1
Jan-June indl output, labor productivity rptd 7-22, 634C3
Grain crop estimated by US, record seen 8-9, 634G2
Gas reserves estimated by US 8-13, 634G3
SST fleet rptd grounded after crash 10-27, 1032B1
Record grain crop seen 11-4, 884C3
Brezhnev repts record grain harvest, scores other sectors 11-27, 966E2
'78 econ plan prelim results, record harvest rptd; '79 forecast 11-29, 1020A2
Whaling end planned 12-8, 1001A3
'78 oil output rise rptd 12-26, 1000C3

Emigration—*See 'Human Rights' below*

1979

Cuban Relations—*See CUBA-Soviet Relations*

Defense & Armed Forces—*See also "Atomic" above, 'U.S.-Soviet Defense' below and under DISARMAMENT*
'67-77, '78 mil spending, draft data 1-25, 2-2, 99E2-E3
Long-range cruise missile tests rptd 2-1, 99E3
SS-20 threat seen by NATO 2-20, 148A1
Viet-China battle zone recon rptd, E China fleet reinforced 2-21, 122B1
Indian O naval activity rptd 4-12, 313E3-314A1
SS-21 deploymt in E Ger rptd 4-23, 340E1; NATO error admitted 5-23, 399E1
High-speed sub rptd 5-17, 390B2
1st-strike ability rptd sought 5-30, 410G1
SS-18, SS-19 warhead yields estimates lowered 5-31, 410C1
IISS warns re modernztn effort 9-4, 825B2, A3
E Ger troop cut set, Eur missile freeze offered 10-6; reactn 10-7, 10-9, 761E1, A3-F3
E Eur troop deploymt rptd 761F2
T-72 tanks in E Ger parade 10-7, 761D2
'77 mil spending total rptd 10-13, 804F1
Mil parade marks revolutn anniv 11-7, 856D2
'80 budget reductn rptd 11-28, 929A1
A-powered aircraft carrier rptd built, global navy capability seen 12-17, 997G2

Dissidents—*See 'Human Rights' below*

Economy & Labor
'78 econ performance rptd 1-19, 60D1
Oil switch rptd in 3 republics 1-23, 50B2
Mil spending share of '67-77 GNP rptd 1-25, 99A3
Serbian rail link completed 6-22, 504F2
'78 oil productn lag cited 6-26-6-29, 497B2
Prices of luxuries raised 7-2, 504D2
Grain harvest estimate reduced 7-12, 573D3
1st 1/2 growth rptd weak 7-20, 568D1
Grain harvest shortfall rptd 9-28, 774E3
Male deaths, indl accidents linked 10-10, 857B2
Brezhnev scores econ performance, rpts low grain harvest 11-27, 928A3
'80 econ plan rptd 11-28, 928D3

Emigration—*See 'Human Rights' below*

Energy—*See also 'Atomic' above, 'Middle East' below*
Hungary oil imports cited 1-8, 101A2
Oil price hike rptd sought 2-27, 145B3
Oil prices raised 3-21, 228A1
Sovt bloc 1st 1/4 oil exports rptd 5-31, 397B1
Turkey oil deal set 6-5, 488A3
Oil exports promise backed 6-29, 497C2
Oil export freeze rptd 7-18, 568F1
Oil reserves called world's largest 11-19, 928G3
Oil conservatn asked 11-27, 928C3
Oil, coal productn shortfall, '80 targets rptd 11-28, 928E3
US co signs tech deal 12-14, 997E2

1980

Polish aid rptd 9-8; talks held, increase pledged 9-10—9-11, 679C1
Poland granted $670 mln US grain credit 9-12, 710B3
Yugo exports rptd up 9-18, 833E2
Poland union warned 9-25, 9-27, 752E3; 10-8, 761D1
Hungary elec grid cited 10-1, 753D3
Portugal CP support slips 10-5, 760E1
Poland interventn hinted 10-13, 831A2
E Ger hard currency rules chng backed 10-14, 789C2
Gromyko in Poland for Warsaw Pact mtg 10-19—10-20, 800E2
Poland ldrs visit: ask aid, score E Ger travel curbs 10-30, 860A1
Rights curbs scored at CSCE Madrid mtg 11-13, 863D1; Polish invasn scored 11-14—12-19, 950E1
Westn backing of Polish oppositn chrgd 11-16; Czech warning to Poland echoed 11-30, 910C2, E2
Poland reveals USSR aid 12-1, 910B1
E Ger-Polish border shut 12-1; reserves rptd active, Sovts deny 12-2, 910F2
Poland invasn preparatn rptd complete 930B1
Poland dissidents factory takeover chrgd 12-8; mil action hinted, US 'fanning war psychosis' claimed 12-11, 929A1, E2
NATO mins warn re Poland 12-10, 12-12, 949A1
Polish aides visit Moscow re aid 12-26, 12-29, 976G2
Pravda scores free trade unions 12-26, 976B3

Cuban Relations—*See CUBA-Soviet Relations*

Defense & Armed Forces—*See also 'Atomic Energy' above*
Kama R truck plant mil mfg rptd 1-21, 45F1
ABM penetratn sought by UK 1-24, 79A2
CIA estimates '79 outlays 1-27, 65D2
Naval squadron rptd in S China Sea 2-5, 84E2
Sverdlovsk biological weapons mishap suspected 3-18, 235B2
Killer satellite test rptd 4-18, 365A2
'79 anthrax cover-up chrgd by US 6-29, 500A1
Philby honored 7-15, 566G2-B3
Mil buildup, Viet bases cited by Japan 8-5, 635C3
ABM system rptd updated 9-14, 730A3
ICBMs rptd accurate 9-18, 730E3

Economy & Labor
'79 econ growth, wage lag rptd 1-25, 79G2
Kosygin scores econ policies 2-21, 153A1
Caspian Sea drainoff plugged 3-2, 236A1
Spring wheat planting delayed; 1st 1/4 meat, feed grain output rptd 4-8, 336A2
Grain embargo impact seen 4-9, 316A1
ILO scores work laws 5-12, 381E2
Transport system scored, massive improvemts ordrd 5-27, 412C1
Auto workers strike rptd 6-13, 467E1-C2
1st 1/2 dairy, meat, grain productn rptd down; grain embargo, bad weather linked 7-16—9-15, 711F2
Sugar futures hit 5 1/2-yr high 10-9, 777B2
Econ, agri problems detailed; '81 targets set 10-21—10-23, 797B1, F2, 798F1
11th 5-yr plan set, '76-80 performance scored 12-1, 945G1

Energy—*See also 'Atomic Energy' above*
Long-term oil supply cited 1-15, 60A2
Afghan gas field rptd opened 1-27, 85A3
High prices, E Eur econ slowdown linked 2-4, 166A3
Oil dvpt methods scored 2-13, 235C3
Kuwait OKs oil sales 3-2; '79 Comecon sales, '80 estimate rptd 3-3, 166B1
Urengoy gas dvpt lag noted 3-6, 235A3
Hungary oil price hikes rptd 3-24, 274E3
'79 oil exports linked to Westn trade deficit reductn 3-26, 235E3
W Ger exploratn pact set 5-29, 411C2
Oil exports to Rumania rptd 6-4, 465F3
Oil productn lead cited 9-4, 662D1
COMECON export rise pledged 10-1, 753B3
Brazil oil deal rptd 10-2, 759G1
Oil productn, '81 projectn rptd 10-22, 798C2
11th 5-yr plan sets oil, gas productn 12-1, 945A2
Huge Siberia oil find denied 12-5, 951B3

1976

Rubin, other Jews denied exit visas 2-16, 421E2
Brezhnev scores US trade curbs 2-24, 194A1, D1
Neizvestny emigrates 3-10, 206E3
Amalrik seeks to emigrate 4-8, chrgs harassmt 4-12, 313F3
'76 Israel, US emigratn data 5-26, 421C3
Rubin granted exit visa 6-3, 421D2
US Dem platform text cites 6-15, 477C3
Amalrik, wife emigrate 7-15, 540G2
Olympic diver to return 8-17, 655C2
Solzhenitsyn move to US rptd 9-9, 680B3
Jews stage sit-in 10-18—10-23; arrests rptd 10-21, 10-25; Carter sends wire 10-25, 856F3-857B1
Jewish protesters freed 11-8, 11-15, 966C3
Israel vs emigratn to US 11-10, 12-12, 966F3
US trade policy scored at US-USSR Trade Cncl 11-30, 12-1, 947C3, E3
Ford cites lower fees 12-8, 934B2
'76 Jewish emigratn data rptd 12-17, 967C1

European Force Reduction Issues—*See under EUROPE*

Foreign Economic Developments—*See also 'Angola' above; also 'Soviet Developments' under GRAIN*

EC rpt urges joint actn 1-7, 20G1
Greek oil, elec deals rptd 1-12, 1-19, 73B2
S Yemen arms aid rptd 1-14, 52A2
Oil price to Hungary up 1-15, 101D2
Italy CP denies covert aid 1-16, 74E3
Austria rptd in Iran-W Ger gas pact 1-19, 97E3
In 7-natn A-safeguards pact 1-27, 84A1
US Sen OKs 200-mi fishing zone 1-28, 94F1
US bars trade curb end 1-30, 88C3
Finland seeks more trade 2-2, 155B2
Kissinger scores Cong credit bar 2-3, 88C2, F2
Lockheed exec testifies 2-6, 131C1
Cuba trade pact agreed 2-6, 138E2
Brezhnev scores US trade curbs, urges barriers end 2-24, 194A1, D1
Chile arms sales rptd 2-25, 288E3
Cuba oil exports rptd 3-2, 252A1
Reagan scores Ford policy 3-4, 166B1
Cape Verde shipping pact rptd 3-6, 404D1
Sugar purchase data disputed 3-12—3-16, 278G1
US halts joint talks 3-16, 196G1
Gromyko assures UK on '75 credit vow 3-25, 229B1
W Ger A-plant plan dropped 3-30, 243C2
US, Japan gas pact reached 3-31, 655C3
Hungary barter pact rptd 4-1, 543A3
Argentina beef buys cited 4-9, 264D3
Uruguay trade pact rptd 4-30, 441F2
'75 trade deficit, '65-75 data rptd 5-5, 340A3-341B1
US '75 trade rank rises 5-5, 340E3
Canada fishing zone pact 5-19, 417E1
E Ger to up energy investmt 5-21, 381C2
'75 oil exports to West up 5-24, 655B3
W Ger gas turbine deal 6-1, 540D2
Wozchod IMF gold purchase rptd 6-3, 6-9, 430G2, A3
1st ¼ trade deficit, US trade data rptd 6-4, 655G2
US Dem platform text cites ties 6-15, 477A3
US' Carter scores re forgn aid 6-23, 451F3
Eur, Japan seek ship rate agrmt 6-24; US pact signed 7-19, 558D3
French aluminum plant deal set 7-3, 540E2
Banks set $250 mln loan pact 7-16, 540D2
French A-safeguards pact signed 7-16, 540E2
US, Finns to build oil drill 7-16, 540E2
Gold sales rptd 7-21, 530C2
Australia meat deal set 8-3, 587C2
Pepsi deal signed 8-18, 679E2
US indl output forecast rptd 8-18, 752E2
Peru plane deal rptd 8-19, 652C3
Italy steel sale OK rptd 8-20, 752D2
SWAPO seeks arms 8-22, 654G2
Gold sales rpts denied 8-23, 643B1
US OKs IBM sale 9-2, 752D2
Libya pact signed 9-6, 949B1
2d ¼ trade gap with West, US 6-mo data rptd 9-20, 9-29, 752F1
Kissinger hits 3d World aid 9-30, 719B2
Cuts oil to Czech 10-4, 851B3
CBS signed pact 10-6, Otis Elevator pact rptd 10-9, 907G3
Mongolia pact signed 10-19, 949B3
Seeks Atlantic shipping conf entry 10-22, 948C1
'74-84 econ growth, Westn ties linked 10-25, 856D2
'75-76 US farm imports rptd up 10-27, 856F2
US computer sale rptd 11-1, 832B3
Australia sees Sovt oil threat 11-4, 850B2
NATO sales cited 11-4, 880B1
Gierek in USSR, aid pact signed 11-9—11-15; trade rise seen 11-16, 907C1
EEC discusses Yugo trade aid 11-15, 955A2
'75 trade deficit rptd 11-18, 977D1
Hammer sees Brezhnev 11-20, 947E3
US 200-mile limit OKd 11-26, 916B2
Venez signs econ, oil pacts 11-26, 929F3
US-USSR Trade Cncl mtg 11-30—12-1, 947A3
Jan-Sept US exports, '77 forecast rptd 11-30, 947C3
3d ¼ trade gap with West, US 9-mo gap rptd 12-7, 1011D1

1977

1978

European Force Reduction Talks—*See under EUROPE*

1979

European Force Reduction Talks—*See under EUROPE*

1980

1976

US baby formula co pact 12-8, 948C2
India heavy water sale rptd 12-8, 955A2
Qaddafi meets Fiat head 12-9, Sovt benefits denied 12-10, 965D1
Sets 200-mi limit 12-10, 1011C2
US study rpts forgn paymts 12-20, 985E2
US soil research exchng canceled 12-20, 1011E1
Turkey gets loan 12-21, 1011B2
UK gas pumping deal rptd 12-24, 1011A2

Foreign Relations (misc.)—*See also 'Angola' and 'Emigration' above, 'UN Policy' below*
EC rpt urges detente 1-7, 20G1
Uruguay anti-CP drive scored 1-10, 55F3
Denmark '75 expulsn of agents rptd 1-11, 101C1
French paper named 2 as spies 1-19, 50A1
Medit anchorage sites rptd 1-19, 73A2
UK Tory ldr scores detente 1-19, rebuttal 1-22, 1-30, 101D1
Laos ICC disbands 1-21, 55E2
More Westn dailies to be available 1-21, 76F2
Sweden rpts '75 ship mutiny foiled 1-22, 122G2
Morocco summons amb re Sahara 1-28, 58B2
French CP scores 2-4—2-7, reactn rptd 2-8, 119B2
French Comoro policy scored 2-5, 118G3
UK CP scores Sovt ties 2-7, 174A3
Belgium intl conf on Jews' rights 2-17—2-19, 206F2-C3
Brezhnev 25th cong policy speech, scores Westn CPs 2-24, 194C1-D2, 195D3
Forgn delegates address 25th cong 2-24—3-5, 195A3
Brezhnev meets Italy CP ldr 3-1, 195F3
Australia, NZ score Indian O buildup 3-8—3-11, 187C3
Vs Solzhenitsyn on French TV 3-10, 424E1
Emb in Laos bombed 3-12, 222G1
UK forgn min sees Lunkov 3-15—3-19, 229A1
Gromyko ends UK visit, denies Rhodesia, Namibia roles 3-25, 228F3
W Ger A-plant plan dropped 3-30, 243C2
New amb to Greece named 4-2; warned vs pol mtgs 5-16, 402F1, A2
Mil buildup in Red Sea area rptd 4-5, 242F1
Laos sentncs emb raiders 4-16, 333G3
Kenya cites arms to Uganda, Somalia 4-25, 295B1
Radar station in Laos cited 4-27, 315F1
Nigeria, Ghana cancel US trip 4-28, 295A2
Eur CPs meet, cong set 5-4—5-6, 341F1
Sweden rpts '75 ship mutineers bombed 5-4, 5-5, 421A2
Uruguay rights abuse protested 5-10, 441A2
Sovt dissidents to monitor Helsinki compliance 5-13, 408F1
Mozambique ldr visits 5-17—5-23, 403C1
France backs strong Westn deterrent 5-18, 372C2
Suslov scores 'enemies of detente' 5-19, 381G1
NATO scores 5-21, 353A1
Pl pres visits, ties set 5-31—6-2, 440F1
Australia scores mil expansn 6-1, 438C2
Chile scores 'expansionism' 6-4, 464B3
Gandhi visits, Indian ties bolstered 6-8—6-11; Indian O bases opposed 6-13, 440A1
Rhodesia guerrilla deaths rptd 6-10, 428D1
Sovt rocket use in Mozambique attack on Rhodesia rptd 6-12, 427B2
Africa mil presence rptd 6-13, 467C1
Italy CP discounts Sovt threat 6-15, 446D1
US Dem platform text cites 6-15, 477E2, 478B3
Canada chrgs Arctic island occupatn 6-17, 456C3
Snubs Fraser in China; Australia vs Indian O role 6-20, 481C1
Kissinger on E-W ties strength 6-25, 466G1, D2
Brezhnev at E, W Eur CP conf, Sovt ldrship role rebuffed 6-29—6-30, 461A1
Eur Parlt chrgs CSCE rights violatn 7-9, 540B3
Eur Parlt chrgs Helsinki rights violatn 7-9, 540B3
Turkey frees '70 Sovt hijackers 7-10, Italy harbors 7-11, 543G1
Japan warns US vs concessns 7-12, 555E2
Aircraft carrier enters Medit 7-18, 540F2
Portugal to seek full ties 7-19, 558E1
Medit fleet strength rptd 7-22, 558B3
Backs IAAF S Africa expulsn 7-22, 562C2
UK natl drug sentnc cut 7-30, 655B2
Spain CP ldr vs forgn mil bases 7-31, 753G1
New amb arrives Zambia 8-10, 950B1
S Africa, Rhodesia on Africa role 8-13, 8-20, 661C1
Swiss expel envoy 8-16, 640B1
Nonaligned conf backs US detente 8-20, 821D3
Aid to Rhodesia ANC factn rptd 8-23, 661G3
Steps up Spain CP contacts 8-23, 753A2
Sovt drug drive rptd 8-25, 665B2
Berlin bus protest rejctd 8-27, 678D3
Swiss, Britons sentncd re drugs 9-3, 9-9, 857F1

1977

Foreign Relations (misc.)—*See also 'Communism' above, 'Monetary, Trade & Aid' and 'UN Policy' below*
Australia asks ship to leave 1-4, 17G1; USSR issues order 1-5, 42C3
US, UK, France vs E Ger Berlin visas 1-6, 7E2; 1-11, 20F1
French CP ldr scores pol repressn 1-6, 63D2
Brandt warns on W Berlin 1-24, 102A2
UK sees Rhodesia interventn 1-25, 49B2
Australia denies chrgs on US bases 1-25, 81A2
Norway expels 6 spies 1-28, 99A3
Sovt sailor defects to Canada 2-8, 117G1
Spain ties renewed 2-9, refugee return unsetld 2-14, 242C2
2 Norway diplomats expelled 2-14, 967A3
Amalrik protests French policy 2-23, 2-24, 143A1
Danes rpt Sovt radio jamming 2-23, Danish defns chiefs mocked 3-23, 426A3
ASEAN mil plans chrgd 2-24, 145B3
Canada deports scientist as spy 2-24, 159E1
Hess denied amnesty 2-24, 298C3
Eurocommunist ldrs meet 3-2—3-3, 242F3
Spain fascist groups oppose 3-2, 307G2
France, W Ger concerned re US rights stand 3-4, 226F1
Red Sea summit 3-22—3-23, 208F2
French arrest 4 as spies 3-22, 255B3
Italy CP member backs vs NATO 4-2, 284A2
France notes Africa role 4-12, 265D1
Ukraine dissident arrives Austria 4-13, 314C3
Intl A-energy conf ends 4-13, 334F2
Irish-UK torture trial cites 4-19—4-22, 315E3
UK atty to defend Helsinki monitor 4-20, 314E2
Belgian natl sentence upheld 4-25, 314B3
Gromyko in India 4-25—4-27, 348D1
Sovt student defects to Australia 4-27, 314D3
NATO warns re Berlin 5-9, 358C2
NATO warned on Sovt buildup 5-10, 358A3
Westn concern re civil defns noted 5-11, 360A1
NATO Berlin warning scored 5-14, 496F2
NATO rpts defns data 5-17, 379E3
Kosygin visits Finland 5-22—5-26, 391A2
Plane hijacked to Sweden 5-26, 429B1
Austrian defns min quits 5-30, 425B1
Const draft publshd 6-4, 433E1, 434B3
Siberian Eskimos not at intl conf 6-13—6-17, 619G2
Swiss gen convctd of spying 6-17, 489C2
Brezhnev in France 6-20—6-22, 494C3-495A2
Egypt: 'no progress' in talks 6-24, 496A2
Spain CP, Eurocommunism backed by Hungary, 6-30, Rumania 7-5, 513E2
US scores Africa arms race 7-1, 535D3
OAU scores Africa role 7-2—7-5 512D1, G1
Spain seizes Sovt agent 7-2, expels 7-4, 546A1
Sovt bloc on Eurocommunism 7-3—7-24, 590A3
Jet hijacked to Finland 7-10—7-12, 537F1-A2
W Eur observers at mil exercises 7-11, 551C1
Canada chrgs envoy as indl spy 7-20, 579F3
Giscard evaluates Africa role 7-25, 551B1
USSR sub power ranked 1st 8-25, 686D2
French Airbus barred 9-1, Concorde refueling 9-2, 736F1
UK, Italy books barred from intl fair 9-6, 765G3
Italy Communist barred 9-6, bar lifted 9-7, 766C1
NATO war games observed 9-13, 700B1
Haiti to expel Sovt-trained pol prisoners 9-21, 767E2
Maldives vs base bid 10-2, 844G3
West scored on human rights 10-4, 785A3
UK forgn secy visits, A-war pact signed 10-10—10-11, 812F3
NZ envoy assault regretted 10-18, 926C1
W Ger thanks for hijacked jet rescue aid 10-20, 790G1
Indian prime min visits 10-21—10-26, 842F2
Malta premr provokes Sovt walkout in Peking 11-3, 925E2
Finland hijackers sentncd 11-10, 988E2
Japan A-pact rptd 11-21, 988G1
Westn attys plan pub trials for dissidents 11-28, 955B2
NATO sees T-80, hovercraft threat 12-8, 941D3
NATO scores abuses 12-9, 957B1
Dutch sentence war criminal 12-14, 986D1
Iran executes gen as spy 12-25, 1019F1

1978

Foreign Relations (misc.)—*See also 'African Policy' and 'Communism' above; 'Human Rights', 'Monetary, Trade, Aid & Investment' and 'UN' below*
Japan peace talks deadlocked 1-9—1-10, 28C3
Finland relatns cited 1-16, 36E2
Dutch premr warns vs arms buildup 1-16, 90B3
Baltic, Moscow area opened to travel, China border region closed 1-19, 39A2
NATO warned vs neutron bomb deploymt 1-23, 103C2
Spy satellite falls into Canada 1-24; radiatn detected, debris found 1-25—2-1, 57A1-C2
Canada protests satellite policy 1-25, 57G2
NATO threatened by Sovt air buildup 1-29, 81B3
French sentnc 5 in spy ring 2-1, 71B2
Canada rpts satellite search cost 2-3, plans paymt claim 2-13, 103E1
Canada retrieves satellite radioactive debris, Sovt scientist admits error 2-4, 103A1
W Eur natns observe mil maneuvers 2-6—2-10, 103A2
Austria chancellor visits 2-6—2-8, 110C2
Canada accuses 13 of spying 2-9, 110D3
Canada satellite damages offered 2-14, 238A2
UK envoy barred from Baltic, Ural Mt cities 2-17, 230E1
UK scores campaign vs neutron bomb, sees SS-20 threat 2-21, 140D1
Japan rejcts peace bid, 2-22, draft publshd 2-23; Japan Cabt ignores 2-24, 121D3
India talks, joint projcts set 3-1—3-6, 169C1
Sweden protests sub patrols 3-1, 291A3
Canada spy rpt leaked 3-7, 208F3-209E1
French Airbus landings OKd 3-8, 238D2
Baltic spy trawlers rptd 3-11, 291A3
Greek film show bombed 3-11, 374E1
Canada spy frame-up chrgd 3-15, 209E1
Scandinavian spy truck transit denied 3-15, 291E2
Eur mil buildup chrgd by Carter 3-17, 202E1
Dutch neutron bomb protest 3-18—3-19, 255D1
Dutch name 3 Sovts as spies 3-30, 247E3
Canada satellite search rptd ended 4-2, 238C2
Leningrad resident sentncd as spy 4-10, 416A3
Air svc to Tbilisi canceled 4-14—4-15, 275A2
NATO backs neutron bomb delay 4-19, 298C2
S Korea passenger jet downed, 2 die 4-20; details rptd 4-21; passengers freed, 2 crewmen detained 4-23, 301G3
Marshal Ogarkov in Turkey 4-26, 477D1
S Korea crewmen freed 4-29, 318D1
Afghan coup recognized 4-30, 317C1
UK defns chief's criticism causes uproar 5-1, 329G2
Brezhnev offers mutual force cuts 5-2; visits W Ger 5-4—5-7, 417A1-B2
Afghans deny links 5-6, Sovts deny coup role 5-7, 349F2, A3
S Korea puppet regime chrgd 5-7, 349B3
Turkey discounts threat 5-15, hints visit 5-29, 397D2, 398F2
At Helsinki naval conf 5-16—5-18, 424F3
Pak fears Afghan role 5-19, 391D1
Finnair Moscow office shootout 5-24, 416E2
3 Westn rptrs detained, new film seized 5-24, 416F2
W Ger chancellor reviews Brezhnev visit 6-1, 519A2
W Ger physicist cancels trip 6-2, 504C1
'50 Korean war role chrgd 6-7, 423D3
Japan protests Kurile maneuvers 6-7, 585B3
W Ger plea to free Hess rptd rejctd 6-11, 477E3
Sovt soldier injures W Ger envoy in E Berlin shootout 6-19, 549F1
Turkey premr visits; signs nonagressn, other pacts 6-21—6-23; West reassured 6-24, 6-30, 595F1
Eur troop threat, NATO weakness conceded by US 6-23, 493E2
W Eur, Turkey ties lauded 6-25, 488C3
Cyprus policy shifted, direct talks backed 6-25, 595F2
Swedish tourists killed 6-27, 519E1
Westn observers barred from mil maneuvers 7-3—7-7, 648D3
Canada presses satellite search, total cost cited 7-5, 514C3
UK warns strengthnd China ties 7-10, 542B3
France ousts Sovt diplomat 7-15, 649F3
Nonaligned warned vs influence 7-25, 583C2
Japan defense white paper chrgs Asia threat 7-28, 585C2
Intl genetics conf held 8-21—8-30, 670D2

1979

Foreign Relations (misc.)—*See also 'Atomic' above, 'Human Rights', 'Monetary' and 'UN' below*
Westn-natn Guadeloupe summit 1-5—1-6, backs detente 1-6, 12D2, F2, C3
Westn natn warning on China ties cited 1-5, 12C3
W Eur threat seen by US mil ex-ldrs 1-12, 15C1
US warns re Thailand threat 1-17, 30A1
Japan protests A-test 1-19, 52D1
China vows to aid Pak vs 'aggressn' 1-22, 59D3
Gromyko in Italy 1-22—1-26, sees Pope 1-24, 60F2
Canada bills for satellite search 1-23, 96D1
Japan chrgs Kuriles buildup 2-5, Sovt test fire rptd 2-6, 85A3
Paks protest Bhutto death sentnc 2-12, Zia scorns clemency plea 2-14, 116B2, D2
NATO sees Sovt SS-20 threat, W Ger missile deploymt hinted 2-20, 148A1
China troops rptd near Laos 3-2, 200D1
Kosygin in India 3-9—3-15, 200G1
Pak, Iran aid to Afghan rebels chrgd 3-18, 209D2; denied 3-23, 232G3-233A1
Australia renews culture, sci ties 4-3, 253E1
Norway backed by US in Svalbard dispute 4-17, 299D2
French pres trip rptd canceled 4-18, 314C1
UK rptr abuse protested 4-20, 390F1-A2
Canada newspr avoids trial re spy rpt 4-23, 311C2
French pres visits: pacts signed; space flight, arms talks unsetld 4-26—4-28, 323A3
UK drug smugglers freed 5-6, 390B2
French CP backs 5-10—5-14, 371A2, E2
Turkey-US controversy re U-2 flights 5-14—5-29, 397B3
W Ger TV rptrs ousted 5-16, 410B2
E-W detente backed by Tito, Brezhnev; nonalignmt dispute cited 5-18, 379E3
Elton John in concert tour 5-21—5-30, 410C2
Pak warned re Afghan rebel aid 6-1, 6-11; India interventn asked 6-14, 443C1, D1
SALT II summit topic 6-15—6-18, 449D1, 458C1
E-W cable link hinted 6-27, 497D2
Turkey student admits consul murder plan 7-11, 568E2
Norway rptd scored re SALT role 7-26, 762G1
SE Asia SALT linkage proposed 7-31, 590B3
UK rptr's visa extended 8-3, 636G3
Swedish envoy '45 disappearance case reopened 8-4, 690C2
Intl pol sci mtg held 8-12—8-18, 637B1
Nonaligned tilt seen 9-3—9-9; Sovts laud conf 9-9, 674B2, 675B1, C2
Turkey denies OK sought re U-2 9-12, 762E1
Skating stars defect to Swiss 9-21, 721B3; get asylum 10-30, 939G3
Chess player gets Swiss asylum 9-24, 721D3
W Ger defense paper cites missile strength 9-24, 733E1
Japan rpts Kurile buildup 9-26, 9-27, protests 10-2, 742B1
Burma quits nonaligned movemt 9-28, 724C2
Norway, Sweden theater tour canceled 10-1, 775B1
Troop cut, Eur missile freeze offered 10-6; Westn reactn 10-7, 10-9, 761D1, A3-E3
NATO A-missiles opposed 10-13—11-6, 880F2
W Ger rpts defector kidnaped 10-15, 856C3
Japan visit by US defns secy scored 10-16, talks note Kuriles 10-20, 803C3
China premr warns vs threat in W Ger 10-22, UK 10-28, 853G3, 854E1
Newsman flies to US after Japan defectn 10-24, 856D3
UK spy ring scandal reopened 10-28, 10-29, 873F3; 4th member named, controversy ensues 11-15—11-21, 908D2-902F1
French pres visits W Berlin 10-29, 835B2
NATO missile plans seen 11-7, 856E2; 11-14, 880A2
SS col arrested in W Ger 11-14, 876C2
Sweden group rpts on oil 11-19, 928G3
Gromyko in W Ger, warns vs NATO missiles 11-21—11-24, 938A3
India consulate attacked 11-23, 894C1
Schmidt plans '80 Brezhnev mtg 12-4, 938F2
NATO pressed by US on A-missiles 12-7, 938F1
NATO OKs A-missile deploymt, 12-12; scores 12-13, 12-14, 12-16, 959D2, F2

1980

Foreign Relations (misc.)—*See also 'Atomic Energy' above, 'Human Rights', 'Monetary', 'UN Policy' below; also AFGHANISTAN—Soviet Military Intervention, PAKISTAN--Soviet-Afghan Issue, PERSIAN Gulf*
NATO A-missile talks rejctd, deploymt blamed 1-3, 4A3
French CP ldr leaves for Moscow, USSR rapprochemt seen 1-7, 57F2
Australia bars Aeroflot flights 1-9, 9E2
Turkey-US base accord set 1-9, 22G2
Aeroflot flight diverted to Montreal 1-11, 55C2
Japan arrests 3 as spies 1-18, 60A1; scandal prompts mil resignatns 1-28, 2-3, 99C3
Pacific orgn studied 1-20, 78C2
Canada ousts 3 for spying 1-21, 56F2
NZ expels rptr 1-22, amb 1-24, 100A2; NZ envoy ousted 1-29, 119D1
French Assemb pres cuts visit 1-23, 86C1
UK A-weapon plans rptd 1-24, 79A2
W Ger labor min's visit cancelled 1-30, 103F1
Canada attache expelled 1-31; Canada expels Sovt envoy 2-7, 95E3
Brezhnev backs detente, Eur-US split sought 2-4, 84E3; offcls affirm stance 2-7, 106C3
French discover spy 2-9, 141F2
Spain arrests Sovt as spy 2-14, another leaves for Moscow 2-16, 141A3
Swiss allege 200 spies 2-18, 141B3
Paris Aeroflot office bombed 2-24, 149F3
N Korea, Indochina cited by US pres candidate 2-29, 207B3
W Berlin consulate bombed, Aeroflot Frankfurt office bomb found 3-7, 236B1
Norway scored re NATO maneuvers 3-14—3-19, 285D3
Finns sentnc spy 3-18, 213C1
3d World role cited by US 3-27, 243C3
Pope names Ukranian RC ldr 3-27, 413F3
UK sees chem warfare threat 4-2, 274F1
Eur scientists at dissident conf 4-13—4-15, 326E2
Italy CP renews China ties 4-15, clarifies stance 4-22, 314F1, B2
W Ger sees war threat 4-20, 303D1
Gromyko visits France 4-24—4-25, 351E3
May Day parade boycotted 5-1, 354F2
Giscard meets Brezhnev 5-19, 378G2-379D1
W Ger, France note Muskie-Gromyko mtg 5-19, 5-21, 378D3, 379D1
China backs Japan mil buildup 5-28, 422C1
New Hebrides role chrgd 6-8, 436F2
W Ger warned vs NATO A-missiles 6-12, 451D1
W Ger vs Carter trip criticism 6-21, 473E1
Schmidt's trip plans rptd 6-23, 474E1
Viet Thai raid halt sought by US 6-25, 6-26, 508B2
France neutron bomb test rptd 6-26, 486D3
Schmidt visits, discusses A-missiles 6-30—7-1, 489A1-D2
French arrest 11 re Aeroflot bombing 7-1, 522A2
Turkey bars consultatn re U-2 7-4, 526C1
US arms lift to Thais scored 7-5, 508B1
India-Cambodia ties lauded 7-7, 547A3
Japan, China, US 'axis' chrgd 7-8, 7-10, 506F1
French Bastille Day broadcast barred, Giscard congratulated 7-14, 566B3, D3
UK double agent honored 7-15, 566G2
W Ger lifts navy curbs 7-18, 540F1
Eur concern re Reagan rptd 7-20, 550C1
Japan backs defns hike, notes Sovt mil buildup 7-29, 579D2
Japan weapons dvpt urged 8-5, 635C3
UK spy quits British Academy 8-18, 652D1
Violinist seeks W Ger asylum 8-19, 908E1
Westn radio broadcasts jammed 8-20, denial rptd 8-21, 626D2
Canada immigratn records rptd found 8-20, 651F1-C2
A-sub crippled off Japan 8-20, territorial waters entered 8-22; no A-leak rptd 8-24, 653B1
Portugal expels 4 diplomats 8-20, 'unacceptable activities' cited 8-21, 689A3
China chrgs 'aggression' 9-11, 9-14, 706F3
Gromyko meets Japan forgn min 9-24; Japan denies mil power goal 9-25, 752D1
Giscard warns re power monopoly 10-17, 829C3
French arrest NATO spy, expel 2 Sovt Emb aides 11-13, 921B3
'78 Canada satellite crash paymt set 11-21, 920C3
Swedish envoy's family at Madrid CSCE 11-28, 950D2
Sweden rpt on Siberia oil find denied 12-5, 951B3

1976

Swedish-US spy-device rptd 9-14, 734E1, G1
Tanzania: S Africa, Rhodesia rebels use arms 9-15, 681E1
Pilot defects to Iran 9-23, USSR protests 9-26, 773D2
Vs Rhodesia majority rule plan 9-25, 718B3
Gromyko, Kissinger trade chrgs re Africa 9-28, 9-30, 719B1
W Ger rpts Brezhnev visit set 10-4, 754G2
Greece sentences US rptr 10-4, 873D1
Brezhnev in French TV interview 10-5, 739F1
Kolman asks Swedish asylum 10-6, 857D1
US, UK scored re southn Africa 10-7, 856E3
Tied to Rhodesia natnlsts 10-9, 781F1
France expels diplomat 10-14, 852F2
Mongolia pact signed 10-19, 949B3
Frenchman expelled 10-21, 857E1
US warns re southn African talks 10-29, 832B1
Australia ups defns, cites Indian O buildup 11-4, 850B2
Nkomo favors Sovt ties 11-8, 843D2
Swiss gen chrgd as spy 11-10, 2 others arrested 11-24, 1011A3
Rpt S Africa students offered rebel training 11-24, 927G1
Venez pres visits 11-24—11-27, 929E3-930A1
Vows radio interference end 12-3; improvemt rptd 12-28, 1011B1
Canada ousts envoy 12-9, 963B1
Schmidt for eased tensn, confrms Brezhnev visit 12-16, 968C2
In Chile prisoner exchng 12-18; W Eur CPs score 12-22, 955D2-F3
Bukovsky scores Helsinki pact 12-19, 955A3
Missile silos in Laos rptd 12-27, 1013C1

Government & Politics—*See also other appropriate subheads in this section*
High defense spending rptd 1-2, 60F3
Listed as 'not free' nation 1-19, 20E3
25th cong 2-24—3-5; econ rpt OKd, new Politburo drops agri min, Secretariat, Central Com listed 3-5, 193G1-196E1
Membership, expulsns rptd 2-24, 194A3
Sizov vs local units fiscal methods 2-25, 195D1
Agri min ousted 3-16, 206B2
Polyansky named Japan amb 4-1, 314B1
Shtemenko dies 4-23, 368A3
Grechko dies 4-27, 315E3
Ustinov named defense min 4-29, 334F2
Brezhnev named field marshal, bust dedicated 5-8, 421G1-A2
Ustinov, Gribkov promoted 7-30, 10-30, 908G1-A2
Kosygin rptd ill 8-30; aide named 9-2; appears in public 10-18, 857A2
Civil defns plans rptd 10-11, 934B1
Central Com 10-25—10-26; 5-yr plan OKd 10-26, 839F1
Sup Sovt meets 10-27—10-29; econ performance hit 10-28; 5-yr plan detailed, OKd 10-29, 856F1

Japanese Relations—*See 'Soviet Relations' under JAPAN*

1977

Government & Politics—*See also other appropriate subheads in this section*
Katushev named min cncl vp 3-16, 306D3
Maltsev named oil min 4-5, 306C3
Podgorny, Katushev ousted from party posts; Rusakov named 5-24, 412A2
Const draft rptd completed 5-24, 412B2
'Stalinism' end vowed 5-24, 433F2
Const draft OKd by Presidium 5-27; publshd 6-4; text excerpts 434A1-436D3
Podgorny retires, Brezhnev elected pres 6-16, 469C2
Natl anthem revised; texts 9-1, 766B2
KGB founder honored 9-9, 753E1
2 named to Politburo 10-3, 785C3
Sup Sovt opens const talks 10-4; const OKd, chngs noted 10-7, 785D2
1st vp named 10-7, 785B3
Bolshevik Revolutn 60th anniv rites 11-2—11-7, 865D2; photo 11-7, 865A2

Helsinki Agreement—*See EUROPE—Security and Cooperation*

Human Rights (including emigration and Jewish issues)
French CP ldr scores Bukovsky-Corvalan exchng 1-6, 63D2
Dissident fund seized 1-10, 22B2
US bars Sovt ed; cong comm '76 bar cited 1-12, 22D1
Zavurov jailed 1-13, US sens protest 2-19, 226A2
Sakharov chrgs police Metro blast role 1-14, govt warns 1-25; US defends, controversy ensues 1-27—2-1, 83E3-84E1
US gets Sakharov plea, other dissidents seek intl support 1-28, 84E1
Barshai arrives Israel 1-30, 117G1
US speeds Jews' visas 1-30, 117A2
US newsmen harassmt renewed 2-2, 2-5, 101D1, A2
Ginzburg rpts dissident funding 2-2, arrested 2-3; US protests 2-4, 101B2
AP newsman ousted 2-4, 101C1
Orlov, 2 other Helsinki monitors arrested 2-5, 2-10; US reactn 2-11, 117B1
US rights commitmt reaffirmed 2-8, 88F2
Sailor defects in US 2-8, 117G1
Helsinki monitor crackdown seen 2-14, 101C2
Sakharov gets US reply 2-17, US-Sovt tensn mounts 2-17—2-18, 137B2
US asks UN dissident info 2-18, 137G2
Jews stage city cncl sit-ins 2-21, 226B2
Helsinki monitor exit rptd 2-22, 137C3
US rights protests explained 2-23, 126B2
Bukovsky in US, urges rights stand 2-23—3-1; USSR scores 2-24, 142G2
Amalrik protests French policy 2-23, 2-24, 143A1
US poet protests dissident arrests 2-25, 226B2
Aeroflot matzos ban protested 2-25, 226C2
Ginzburg chrgd 2-25, US atty to defend 2-28, 226C2, D2
3 Jewish dissidents detained, US protests 2-28—3-10, 226D2-A3, D3
Pravda on US stance 3-2, 3-13, 226D1
France, W Ger concerned re US rights stand 3-4, 226F1

1978

Spy plane crashes in Norway 8-28, Moscow protests probe 10-6, 10-12, 820G1-C2
UK natls detained 9-4, 947C2
Norway rpts Barentsburg radar installatn 9-28, 820D2
Austrian rptr expelled 9-30, 821E1 ★
3-natn A-test ban talks rptd delayed 10-5, 996D2
Canada ends satellite search 10-18, 1013G2
Gromyko in France, tensns rptd 10-25—10-28, 830E3-831A1
Australia chrgs emb bugged 11-14, 878C3
Finland mil link rptd pressed, defns min denies; West rptd concerned 11-15, 894B2
Afghan premr visits 12-4—12-5, 943D2
Whaling end vowed at IWC mtg 12-8, 1001B3

Government & Politics—*See also 'Republics' and other appropriate subheads in this section*
Brezhnev gets Order of Victory 2-20, 151C3
Gorbatyuk death rptd 3-5, 252G2
CP Central Com mtg 7-3—7-4, 518G2-B3
Supreme Sovt summer sessn opens 7-5, 518C3
Kulakov dies 7-16, 620G2
Politburo posts filled, alternates named 11-27, 924B3
Mazurov quits Politburo 11-27, 924D3

Guyana Cult Developments
Guyana emb, US cult talks rptd 11-27; money transfer plan claimed 11-28, 910B3
Guyana cult victims lauded by Sovt press 11-28, 911D2
Death ritual tape cites USSR emigratn plan 12-8, 955A1
Cult bequest rptd 12-17, rejctd 12-18, 1000A2

Helsinki Agreement—*See EUROPE—Security and Cooperation*

Human Rights (including Soviet dissident, emigration, Jewish issues and foreign reaction)
Klebanov rptd freed 1-3, workers repeat protests 1-10, 20G3-21A1
US emb personal contacts rptd curbed 1-5, 21A1
Georgia Helsinki monitor arrested 1-25, 180F1
Workers form union 2-1, Klebanov arrested 2-7, 180A1
Semyonov visa OK rptd 2-4, 180A2
Shcharansky wife called imposter 2-8, 180A1
Grigorenko citizenship revoked 2-13, scores actn 3-13, 179F2
CP ousts Polikanov over travel curb protest 2-21, 275D3
Shcharansky lawyer rptd named 2-24, 179G3
US rptr's notes seized 3-2, US protests 3-8, 180D1
Shcharansky roommate rptd CIA agent 3-6, 179D3
Amnesty Intl rpts 14 workers held in '77 3-6, 180D1
Art show held 3-7, 180E1
Beilin visa OK rptd 3-7, 180G1
Amnesty Intl chrgs MDs torture 3-11, 180C3
7th Day Adventist ldr arrested 3-14, 275C3
Rostropovich, wife lose citizenship 3-15; US: actn 'unacceptable' 3-16, 179B3
Shcharansky rejcts Sovt atty 3-15, 275G3
Jewish dissident jailed 3-20, 275C3
Ukrainian Helsinki monitors rptd sentncd 3-30, 275B3
US warns on Shcharansky 4-3, 275E3
Shevchenko renounces citizenshp 4-10, defects 4-26, 302A2
Naturalized US citizen rptd held 4-12, 275G2; returns to US 4-28, 360A1
Georgia, Armenia win language rights 4-14, 4-16, 275F1
Dissident union denied ILO recognitn 4-14, 275F2
Lithuanian dissident fund aide rptd sentncd 4-16, 275F2

1979

Government & Politics—*See also other appropriate subheads in this section*
Sovt electn process detailed, dissidents pick slate 2-2, 100D1
Dissident slate rejctd 2-17, electns held 3-4, 172D2
Brezhnev Sup Sovt electn speech 3-2, duties described 172E1
Podgorny pol career ends; facts on 3-4, 237D2
Ryabov moved to Planning Comm 4-17, 314D1
Brezhnev, Kosygin, Presidium reelected 4-18, 314B1
Romanov career imperiled by scandal 929D1
Tikhonov named full Politburo member, Gorbachov, alternate member 11-27, 929B1
Kosygin heart attack confrmd 11-28, 929D1

Guyana Cult Developments
Guyana gets cult money 1-1, 117C3
Jones aide commits suicide 3-13, 220E1
Jonestown tape copy rptd 3-15, 219D3

Helsinki Agreement—*See EUROPE—Security and Cooperation*

Human Rights
Authors issue rejected works, ask censorship end 1-18, 100B2
Dissidents set electn slate 2-2, 100D1; slate rejctd, 2-17, 172D2
US rights rpt omits 2-10, 107A2
US Christians rptd backing emigratn 2-26, 172E2
US scientists cut links re Shcharansky, Orlov 3-1, 172A2
Tatar activist rptd exiled 3-6, 172F2
Ukrainian dissident kills self 3-6, 238D1
'78 Jewish emigratn total rptd 3-7, 172A3
Bible smuggling rptd 3-13, 238E1
7th-day Adventist ldr sentncd 3-23, 238C1
US extends refugee paroles 3-26, 308B1
3 Volga Gers held re visa protest 3-27, 238B1
Soviet suicide in US Emb 3-28, 237E3
Metropole authors rptd banned 4-6, underground publishers warned 4-30, 317G1
US reps visit, rpt Jewish emigratn rise, see Jewish dissidents 4-13—4-22; 5 jailed in '70 hijack plot freed 4-17, 314F1
UK rptr's abuse chrg protested by US 4-20, 390F1-A2
Ginzburg, 4 other dissidents exchngd for 2 US spies 4-27, 317A1
Poland border rptd closed re Pope's visit 6-2, 413B2, 414F1
US sen scores Sovt policy 6-12, 459F2
Vins' family leaves 6-13, 476A3
SALT II summit topic 6-15—6-18, 449D1
Georgia dissident pardoned 6-29, 504B3
PEN seeks Ogourtsov release 7-21, 554A1
UK rptr's visa extended 8-3, 636G3
Swedish envoy '45 disappearance case reopened 8-4, 690C2
Jewish dissident barred from intl pol sci conf, USSR scored 8-12—8-18, 637C1
Underground author arrested 8-13, 980B3
Bolshoi dancer defects to US 8-23; US detains wife 8-24, releases 8-27, 644D3-645F1

1980

Brezhnev in India 12-8—12-11; meets Gandhi 12-8—12-9, joint declaratn 12-11; offers Persian Gulf peace plan in parlt speech 12-10, US rejects 12-11, 930D1-A3
Japan rpts Backfire bomber coastal deploymt 12-11, 953C1
Norway-US arms stockpiling plan scored, Barents Sea talks agreed 12-22—12-23, 979A2

Government & Politics—*See also other appropriate subheads in this section*
Kirillin resignatn rptd 1-22, 46E3
Suslov influence increase seen 2-12, 152C3
Kosygin reappears after illness 2-21, 153A1
Caviar scandal probe, arrests rptd 4-15, 354B3
May Day parade held 5-1, 354F2
Brezhnev addresses CP Central Com 10-21, 797E2
Gorbachov named full Politburo member; Kiselev, alternate 10-21, 798C1
Sup Sovt opens, Baibakov addresses 10-22, 798F1
Kosygin resigns as premr, Tikhonov replaces 10-23, 797A1
Brezhnev lauds Kosygin, press ignores resignatn 10-24, 831E3, G3
Arkhipov named 1st dep premr 10-27, 832A1
Kirgiz premr slain 12-4, 945C3
Bodyul, Antonov named dep premrs 12-19, 966B2
Kosygin death rptd 12-19, 951B1; confrmd 12-20, 996G1-B2

Human Rights
'79 Jewish emigratn sets record 1-11, 47A1
Poets quit union over Metropole 1-12, 46G3
Lithuanian natlst rptd arrested 1-14, Moscow priest 1-15, 46F3
Sakharov expelled, awards revoked; US, others score 1-22, 46F2
Outcry over Sakharov grows 1-22—2-5; Sakharov demands trial, statemt text 1-28, 85F3-86A2, B2
Stefanov defectn in Rome rptd 1-23, 88F1
Adventist ldr dies in prison 1-27, 87G3
Ginzburg family arrives NY 2-2, 87F3
US issues rights rpt 2-5, 87B1
Bolshoi's Messerers defect 2-6, 88D1
'79 Jewish populatn rptd down, '70-79 emigratn cited 2-9, 152G3
UN workers '79 rally protested 2-14, 221B1
Intl protests re Sakharov grow 2-18—3-11, 181F2-A3
Sakharov chrgs police brutality 2-18, Moscow apartmt blocked 3-4, 3-5, 181B3, C3
French CP scores Sakharov, issues rights rpt 2-20, 149D3, E3, F3
Pre-Olympic dissident roundup, youth curbs rptd 2-27, 3-18, 3-25, 259A2, 262D1
Sakharov protests sci acad mtg bar 3-4, keeps membershp 3-6, 181D2, B3
Orlova ousted from CP, writers' union re Sakharov 3-12, 3-15, 181C3
Landa exiled internally 3-26, 262A2
Borisov arrested, placed in mental hosp 3-29, 262G1
Stefanov returns 4-1, 262A2
Israel scores US on Jewish emigres 4-2, 262C3
Moscow Jews get new rabbi 4-12, 431D1
Jewish scientists hold conf 4-13—4-15, 326D2
US scientists seek boycott 4-16, 326A3
Aksyonov, Voinovich plan emigratn 4-16, 4-17, 326B3
Amnesty Intl rpts on '75-79 prisoners 4-29, 326A2

1976

1977

US dissident spy recruiting chrgd 3-4, 226B3
Warsaw Pact vows battle vs dissidents 3-4, 226C3
US drops UN dissident info bid 3-7, comm sessn ends 3-11, 207E1, A2
Slepak, Shcharansky press interview blocked 3-7, 226C3
Ethnic Ger emigratn protesters arrested 3-8, 226D3
Izvestia notes Carter contradictns 3-9, 219E1
Yugo CP ldr backs Carter 3-13, 226G1
Shtern freed 3-14, 226D3
Shcharansky arrested 3-15, 226E3
Carter defends rights stand 3-17, 185B1
Brezhnev scores Carter stance 3-21, 226A1
US sens back Carter stand 3-25, 226G2
Pravda, Izvestia score US 3-26, 225B2
Brezhnev scores US stand; Vance defends 3-28, denies SALT link 3-30, 225B2, C2
Carter reaffirms commitmt 3-30, 225G2
Religious persecutn rptd 3-30, 4-3, 314E2
Armenia Helsinki monitors rptd 4-6, 314D1
Georgia Helsinki monitor, 2 other natlists arrested 4-7, 314G1
Shtern arrives Vienna 4-13, lauds forgn pressure 4-21, 314C3
Jewish scientists hold seminar 4-18—4-20, 315C2
Irish-UK torture trial cites 4-19—4-22, 315E3
UK atty to defend Orlov 4-20, 314E2
2 Ukraine Helsinki monitors arrested 4-23, 314F1
Belgium natl sentence upheld 4-25, 314B3
Student defects to Australia 4-27, 314D3
US sci acad sets Orlov, Kovalev probe 4-27, 315G1
IISS scores Carter policies 4-28, 401D1
Emigre Jews ask return 4-28, 436E3
UK atty barred re Orlov defns 5-4, 436G2
Schmidt scores Carter stand 5-7—5-8, 357F2, 358E1
Nixon comments on Jews 5-12, 386D2
Germans arrested re emigratn try 5-18, 436G2
Press calls US Wilmington 10 pol prisoners 531F3
Young chrgs racism 5-25, 417F2
Shcharansky treason chrgd 6-1; US 'concerned' 6-2, denies CIA tie 6-6; Carter scored 6-7, 436E1
Jewish dissident sentncd 6-1, 436E2
US atty rpts visa denial re Ginzburg 6-1, 436F2
Const draft publshd 6-4, 433G1, 434D3, 436A2
US rpt chrgs Helsinki non-compliance 6-6; reactn 6-8, 6-13, 473C1
Solovyov, Klepikova exit rptd 6-9, 512E3
US rptr held 6-11—6-15, expelled 6-17; US protests 6-14, 6-17, 474C3
UK atty holds mock Orlov trial 6-13, 512D3
Yugo ousts Jewry backers 6-15, 473A2
US Indians to list chrgs 6-17, 473A2
Giscard stresses re detente 6-21, 495B1
Orlov rptd chrgd 6-27, 512C3
Carter affirms commitmt, denies SALT link 6-30, 515A1
Ukraine Helsinki monitors sentncd 7-1, 512B3
US amb speech barred 7-4, 530A1
Turchin arrested 7-4, 551B3
Brezhnev scores Carter stance 7-5, 529E3
Azbel arrives Vienna 7-6, 512E3
Schmidt in US, Canada talks 7-6—7-14, 566D2, F2
Oxford sci conf honors Levich 7-11—7-13, 551C2
Fein in Israel 7-11, 551A3
Carter defends policy 7-12, 533D1
US rptr chrgd as spy 7-12, 564E1
Levich questnd re Shcharansky 7-20, 551G2
Carter affirms commitment 7-21, 550F2
Giscard scores Carter policy 7-25, 551A1
Arbatov scores Carter stance 8-3, 590F1
US Cong comm scores 8-5, 606B2
Mnyukh emigratn rptd 8-8, 606G2
Press union scores US Cong comm criticism 8-17, 640A3
US photo exhibit censored 8-18, Tass explains 8-24, 657F2
Levich scored 8-24; rebuts 8-29, 683F3
Helsinki monitor arrests rptd 8-24, 684C1
Emigre psychiatrist details dissident cases 8-31, 684B1
US, UK, Italy books barred from intl fair 9-6, 765G3
Italian Communist barred 9-6, bar lifted 9-7, 766C1
Baptists, police clash in Bryansk 9-7, 753F1
US publishers host dissidents 9-8, 766B1
KGB head scores dissidents 9-9, 753E1
O Rabin arrested 9-12, 753D1
Psychologist arrested 9-21, 753B1
Ex-prisoners emigratn plea rptd 9-23, 753C1
Ukrainian writer rptd jailed 9-26, 753B1
Gromyko warns US on policy 9-27, 769F2
Jewish sit-in rptd foiled 10-3, 753A1
Brezhnev scores West 10-4, 785A3
Const chngs noted 10-7, 785E2
Jewish sit-in foiled 10-10, 956A1
Amnesty Intl head replaced 10-14, 812B2
Jewish emigratn rptd up 10-14, 956A1

1978

Grigorenko gets US asylum 4-19, 275E2
US prof's wife seized 4-20, news coverage bar protested 4-21, 360B1
UK psychiatrist rpts confined dissidents sane 4-20, 360C1
Shcharansky swap rptd discussed, US discounts 4-24, 318F2
Grigorenko leads W Ger protests 5-4—5-7, 417A2
Carter chrgs 'racism' 5-5, Tass rebuts 5-6, 342E1
Shevchenko's wife kills self 5-8, 440E3
Jewish women stage sit-ins 5-11, 5-12, 360E1
Podrabinek arrested re psychiatric abuse rpt 5-14, 504C1; sentncd 8-15, 634G1
Orlov trial opens 5-15; sentenced, US condemns 5-18; facts on Helsinki monitors 359B3
UK atty holds mock Orlov trial 5-15, 360A1
Begun arrested 5-17, sentncd 7-28, 543C1
USSR defends Orlov sentence, scores protests 5-18, 5-21, 401C2
Orlov sentence protested in West; US scientists, offcls cancel visits 5-19—5-30, 401C1
Georgia Helsinki monitors sentncd 5-19, 401D2
Carter cautns vs contd abuses 5-25, 418C1
US, W Ger scientists cancel trip re Orlov 6-2, 504B1
Yugo dissident compares 6-6, 504A3
Carter scores abuses 6-7, 423F3
Solzhenitsyn scores West 6-8, 444A2 ★, G2
Jan-May Jewish emigratn up, '75-77 data 6-8, 504D1
10 Jews jailed re visa protest 6-9, 504B1
US rpts 20 Helsinki monitors jailed 6-12, 504A1
US criticism scored 6-17, 465A1
Slepak sentenced 6-21, 503E3
Nudel sentenced 6-21, 504A1
Tatar kills self, deportatn cited 6-23, 543A2
Carter on trade 'linkage' 6-26, 491C1
Pentecostalists in US emb sit-in 6-27, 543B2
2 US rptrs chrgd re Georgia dissident trial 6-28; US warns 6-29, Vance, Dobrynin meet 7-1; rptrs statemts 7-3, 518B1-F2
Rabin citizenship revoked 6-30, 543D1
UK OKs crime equipmt sale 7-6, 10-13, 905C2
Shcharansky, Ginzburg trials set; US warns 7-7, cancels trips 7-8, 542A1
Shcharansky trial begins 7-10, link with US rptr stressed; **sentncd 7-14;** US, other protests 7-10—7-18, 541A1-543C1
Ginzburg trial starts 7-10, sentncd 7-13, dissident fund cited; US, other protests 7-10—7-18, 541A2-543C1
US congressmen link Shcharansky trial, SALT mtg 7-10—7-12; Vance vs link 7-10, 542D1, 543G2-B3
Carter condemns trials 7-12, 541G2 ★ -542A1
US Amb Young queried on Shcharansky, Ginzburg 7-12; Carter, Vance rebuke for US 'pol prisoners' remark 7-12—7-15, 7-20, 542D2, 549E2
Vance delivers Carter protest of Shcharansky trial 7-12, sees wife 7-13, 543E2
Lithuanian Helsinki monitor sentncd 7-13, 541E2
Filatov sentncd as spy 7-14, 541E2
San Marino scores dissident trials 7-18, 575B2
2 US rptrs convctd 7-18, 575D2
Carter deplores Shcharansky, Ginzburg convictns 7-20, 549C2
Carter vs US Olympics boycott 7-20, 549C3
Ukrainian Helsinki monitor sentncd 7-20, 634B2
Slepak's wife gets suspended sentnc 7-26, 634F1
2 US rptrs pay fines 8-4, new retractn deadline set 8-7, 634A1
Jan-June Jewish emigratn rptd 8-5, 634C2
Armenian woman joins US emb sit-in 8-11, 634B2
US geneticists urge intl conf boycott 8-16, sci acad sees exchngs endangered 8-22, 670D2
Psychiatrist confrms Podrabinek mental abuse chrgs 8-16, 670E3
2 US rptrs case closed 8-18, 651E1; offcl warning issued 8-24, 670C2
Tatar petitns rptd 8-22, 671A1
Kennedy sees dissidents 9-9, confident re exit 9-11, Pravda scores 9-15, 743A3
UN translator granted US asylum 9-18, 946G3
Jewish emigratn rise, 10-yr total rptd; anti-Semitism cited 9-28, 947B1
Austrian rptr expelled 9-30, 821E1 ★
Polikanov arrives Denmark 10-10, 946F3
USSR-France tensns re Orlov trial cited 10-29, 830G3
Laborer's walk to Sweden rptd 11-1, 947A1
Armenian woman ends US emb sit-in 11-1, 947A2
Pentecostalists continue US emb sit-in 11-1, 947B2
US sen's give Gromyko emigratn list 11-15, see Jewish dissidents 11-17, 905G1
Airline hijacker rptd killed 11-15, 927A1
Podrabinek sentnc upheld 11-23, 947G1

1979

Intl book fair publshrs barred 8-23–9-4, US books seized 9-4, 689F3-690A2
Pentecostal natl cncl rptd 9-5, 690F2
Orlov's prisoner total estimate rptd 9-14, 697E2
Skating stars defect to Swiss 9-18, 721B3; get asylum 10-30, 939G3
Chess player gets Swiss asylum 9-24, 721D3
US concert tour canceled, defectns cited 9-27, 774G3
Norway, Sweden theater tour canceled; defectns linked 10-1, 775B1
W Ger rpts defector kidnaped 10-15, 856B3
Underground journal rptd suppressed 10-21, 980A3
US links emigratn, trade benefits 10-23, 834A2
Newsman flies to US after Japan defectn 10-24, 856D3
Jews rptd arrested in Kiev 10-28, 856B3
Dissidents seized in Moscow, Vilnius 11-1, 856G2
2 seized near US Emb 11-6, 856B3
Helsinki monitor arrested 12-7, 939F1
Amnesty Intl scores dissident rights 12-9, 980C2
Silent protests blocked 12-10, 939G1
Metropole authors reinstatemt rejctd 12-17, Aksyonov hints union resignatn 12-19, 980E2-A3
Korchnoi's son sentncd for draft evasn 12-19, 980B3

1980

ILO scores work laws 5-12, 381E2
Emigratn of Armenians up, Jews down 5-25 5-24, 467E2
Helsinki monitors sentenced 6-13, 680B3, C3
Moscow priest recants 6-20, 500E1
Trade unionist expelled 6-22; in Austria, chrgs KGB murdered wife 7-25, 680A3
Feminist expelled 7-20, 680C2
Ukrainian youth granted asylum in US 7-21, 560C1
Olympic crackdown seen 7-21, 590F1
Aksyonov leaves Moscow for US 7-22, 566E3
Vysotsky funeral demonstrations 7-28, 580D2
Bolshoi dancer seeks US return 8-1, 638C2
French athletes deliver appeal 8-2, 590E2
Violinist seeks W Ger asylum 8-19, 908E1
Russian Orthodox priest sentncd 8-28, 680B2
Mathematician convicted, sentncd 8-29, 680B2
Grivnina arrest rptd 9-17, Bakhmin sentncd 9-24, 863D2
W Berlin Jewish immigratn curb set 9-24, 833C1
Orthodox dissidents sentncd 9-24, 10-9, 863C2
Grimm, Abramkin sentncd 10-1, 10-11, 863B2
Amalrik dies 11-11, 928G1
Kopelev, wife expelled 11-12, 863G1,A2
Brailovsky arrested 11-13, 863G1
Sovts scored by US at CSCE conf, defended by Czechs, Hungary 11-13, 863D1; scored 11-14—12-19, 950E1
Amnesty Intl scores 12-10, 978G2
Iran-Iraq War
Iran chrgs arms to Iraq, threatens to recall amb 8-8, 644E3
Iran chrgs border breach, Kurdish rebel aid 8-12, 644D3
Iran-Iraq war neutrality vowed in mtgs with Iraq offcls 9-21—9-22; Iran amb 9-23, US' Muskie 9-25, 719B1-C2
Gromyko meets Waldheim on Iran-Iraq war 9-23, 718E3
Settlement urged, US exploitatn chrgd 9-30, 758G2
Supply ships for Iraq rptd at Jordan port; arms in S Yemen, Ethiopia sent 10-6, 757C1
US notes Sovt restraint 10-7, 758E1
Arms offer to Iran denied 10-8, 774F2
Libya-Iran airlift rptdly uses airspace 10-10, 774D2
Iraq seeks more arms 11-11—11-12, 879G2

1976

Jews—*See also 'Emigration Developments' above*
UK CP scores anti-Semitism 2-7, 174B3
Sovts meet in Brussels, anti-Semitism growth chrgd, denied 2-16, 206C3
Brussels intl conf on rights 2-17—2-19, 206F2-B3
US, Sovt diplomatic harrassmt incidents 2-27—3-30, 229C2, C3★; 3-31—4-6, 259E3
US sen scores Sovt policy 3-22, 246A1
Nobel winners plead for Shtern 3-24, 421A3
Culture conf held, 45 arrested, visas denied 12-21, 966E3

Middle East—*See also MIDDLE EAST*
Egypt ends friendship treaty 3-15, 193A1, 194B2; **for subsequent developments, see 'Egypt' under MIDDLE EAST—ARAB Policies**
Hussein in USSR 6-17—6-28, 464F1
Libya terrorist training rptd 7-15, 531B2
Libya vs Cuba ties 8-18, 622A1
Backs Libya in Egypt feud 8-30, 682B3
Arms in Libya parade 9-2, 682D3
Iran returns defector 10-25; USSR explains, dissidents score 10-28; UN protest 11-1, 854B2
Libya ldr visits 12-6—12-9, 949B1

1977

US rejcts Sovt statemt on dissident mental abuses 10-28, 866A2
Shcharansky to face treason chrg 10-28, US voices concern 10-31, 11-17, 955A2
US scored re alleged ex-Nazi 10-29, 866B3
Lithuania anti-Russian riot rptd 10-30, 955D3
Dissident artist, family emigrate 10-31, 956D1
Limited amnesty set 11-5, 866B1
Dissident fund dir ousted 11-6, 956C1
Sakharov, family rpt harrassmt 11-10, 11-16; US labor union visit blocked 12-1, 955F2
Sakharov kin emigrate 11-12, 955C3
Exhibit in US opens, treatmt of Jews protested 11-12, 988D2
Sakharov, Shcharansky honored by Bnai Brith 11-20, 955G1
Westn attys plan pub trials for Shcharansky, others 11-28, 955B2
Amnesty Intl cites Gluzman detentn 11-28, 956F2
Grigorenko leaves for US visit 11-30, 956D1
Shcharansky atty expelled 12-4, 956B1
US publishers bar book pact 12-7, 955C2
NATO scores abuses 12-9, 957B1
20 barred from silent vigil 12-10, 955F3
AFL-CIO hears Sakharov appeal, Bukovsky 12-12, 961D1
US to admit more Jewish emigres 12-14, 956E1
US sci acad asks Shcharansky trial observers 12-15, 1017E1
Shcharansky detentn extended 12-15, 1017G1
Galich dies in Paris 12-15, 1024F1
Workers rptd fired, Klebanov arrested for protests 12-20, 988A2
2d dissident artist emigrates 12-20, 1017D2
Israel immgratn rptd up 12-21, 1017D2
Tatar natlst rptd freed 12-22, 1017B2

Jews—*See 'Human Rights' above*

Latin American Relations—*See also 'Communism' above, 'Monetary, Trade & Aid' below*
Chile restores Corvalon pensn 1-5, 18D3
Jamaica to set ties 1-19, 257E2
Nicaragua anti-Sovt stance cited 6-21, 656B3
On Panama Canal pacts 9-10, 699B2
Chile on Sovt Latin role 9-11, 742F3
Argentina seizes fishing boats 9-21—10-1, protested 9-23, 10-8, 944F2
Canal pact interest disputed in US 10-10, 792G1
Panama fears Canal threat 10-20, 809D2
Argentina frees ship 11-9, 982D1

Middle East—*See also 'Monetary, Trade & Aid' below*
Egypt deteriorating ties cited 1-9, 24C1
Egypt riots chrg denied 1-22, press scores 1-23, 62C2
Sadat memoirs scored 2-19, Egypt replies 2-22, 144A2
Sudan joins Egypt-Syria cmnd 2-28, 143A3
Arafat visits 4-4—4-8; Assad 4-18—4-22, 297B2, 317C2
Egypt seeks US arms vs Africa threat 4-5, 245C1
Note chrgs Egypt mil plot vs Libya 4-24; Egypt protests 4-27—4-29; note withdrawn 5-5, 361G2
Egyptian talks 6-9—6-10; joint statement 6-11, 457F2
Brezhnev sees Fahmy 6-15; Egypt visit set 6-22, Cairo denies 6-24, 496B2
Israel asks renewed ties 6-21, 474D2
US warns vs Palestine state 7-6, 509G2
Sadat ties to Libya clashes 7-22, 569F1
Plan to subvert Egypt, Sudan rptd 7-25, 569B2
Egypt-Libya conflict restraint noted 7-28, 574B3
W Bank Arabs send Geneva demands 8-10, 605C2
Arafat visits 8-30—8-31, 663C1
US scored re W Bank setlmts 9-2, 685C2
Gromyko, Vance meet 9-30; joint statemt on Geneva 10-1, 749B2-750A3; text 750A1
Israel-US Geneva plan submitted 10-5, 749D1, E1
Arab League urges measures vs Israel 11-14, 874G1
Sadat Israel visit scored 11-15, 874A1; 11-19, 894F3
Sadat reactn to Israel visit protests 11-21, 890B1
Sadat Cairo conf rejctd 11-29, scored 11-30, 910D1
Syria forgn min visits 11-29, 910E1
Carter on Sovt role 11-30, 913G2-C3
US effort re Cairo conf rptd 12-1, 910D1
Egypt recalls amb 12-4, closes Sovt-bloc consulates, culture cntrs 12-7, 929B1, C2, 930B1
Sadat peace move criticism continues 12-4—12-5; US, USSR confer 12-5—12-6, Vance scores attacks 12-6, 930D1
Sadat scores critics; cites '75 Sinai pact, '71 visit 12-6, 929C2

1978

Sakharov apartmt ransacked 11-29, KGB blamed 12-2, 947D1
Levich emigrates, Kennedy interventn cited 11-30, 946F2
Kats family emigrates 11-30, 946C3
Kondrashin defects 12-4, 946E3
Armenian Helsinki monitors rptd sentncd 12-5, 947E1
Carter cites repression 12-6, 934C1

Jews—*See 'Human Rights' above*

Latin American Relations—*See also 'Guyana Cult' above*
Cuba African role scored by US 1-12, 12E1
US Sen debates Panama Canal pact 2-8, 120F1
Peru gen ends visit, arms paymt rptd rescheduled 4-9, 353A2
Guyana ldr ends visit; communique 4-22, 301G3
DR pres-elect rejects ties 5-21, 414F2
Cuba Africa role scored by US 5-25, Cuba denies 5-30, 418B1, F1
Cuba role in nonaligned movemt scored by US 6-7, 423D3
Cuba Africa role backed by Tass 6-22, 487C3
Colombia rebels rptdly merge 8-24, 814E3
In Venez, Cuba oil pact 9-15, 822C1
Dominica independnc recognized 11-2, 861E3
Cuba rptdly gets MiGs 11-14, Kosygin defends 11-16, 905A1; US assured 11-20, 1016F1

Middle East
Syria arms deal rptd 1-11, 42B2
US urges cooperatn 1-25, 43D3
Iraq arms shipmts cited 2-14, 97F1
US defends Mideast jet sales 2-17, 123D2
Assad visits 2-21—2-22, Syria to get more arms 2-24, 139D2
Libya aide in Syria talks 2-21—2-24, 139E2
Brezhnev scores US peace stand 2-21, 139F2
Sadat scores Syria arms aid 2-25, 139G2
Arafat visits 175D3
Begin ties to PLO raid 3-13, 175F3
Begin chrgs aid to PLO 3-15, 173F2
Leb asks anti-Israel actn 3-15, 174D3
Israel Leb invasn scored, US complicity chrgd 3-15, 3-16, 175B1
UN Leb force abstentn 3-19, 197C1
Iran rpts spy ring smashed 3-27, 4-16, 288G3
Arab League scores Africa role 3-29, 215D1
Iraq rift re Israel policy cited 416B1
Israel rpts arms capture in Leb 4-12, 256D3
Arafat asks guarantees for Israel, Palestine state 5-1, 339B3
UN Leb force expansn abstentn 5-3, 340F1
Saudis see stepped-up expansn 5-13, 358E2
Iran fears Afghan role 5-19, 391D1
Iraq warns vs Ethiopia rebel aid, Baghdad emb relocated 5-25, 416D1
Brzezinski scores role 5-28, 399D1
Israel found '73 chem warfare evidence 6-5, 433G1
2 Iran army copters downed 6-21; Iran, Sovt rpts 7-17, 7-18, 573F3
S Yemen pres executed 6-26, 499D1
Saudi sees oil import hike, notes OPEC talks 6-29, 635B1
Israel vs Geneva conf role 7-1, 502G1
Leb Christn ldr asks end to Syrian attacks 7-2, 502G2
S Yemen denies Sovts dominate S Yemen force 7-2, 522C2
Syria aid vs Israel attack in Leb vowed 7-8, 522A1
China, Rumania communique scored 8-21, 675E3
Camp David summit denounced 9-6, 673F2
Camp David summit pacts scored 9-18, 712E2; 9-22, 731E1

1979

Latin American Relations—*See also 'Guyana' above; CUBA–Soviet Relations*
Chile refugee relocatn rptd 5-7, 369B3
3 envoys ousted in CR labor unrest 8-19, 667B3

Middle East Relations
Iran gas cutoff rptd, '70 import deal cited 1-23, 50B2
US response to Sovt surrogates urged 2-8, 89D2
US concerned re Iran F-14 acquisitns 2-12, 106D1; 8-10, 634F3
Iran govt recognized 2-12, 106A2
Iraq, Syria MiG-23 buildup rptd 2-13, 143A3
Iran broadcasts prompt US protests 2-14–2-16, 125D3
US warns vs Iran interventn 2-20, 123B3
Iran warns vs interference, scores gas deals 2-24, 145D1
S Yemen mil role questnd by US 2-28, 144E2
S Yemen adviser role rptd 3-8, denied 3-14, 179E1
US influence re Israel-Egypt pact feared 3-15, 178C2
Gromyko in Syria 3-24; Israel-Egypt pact scored 3-26, 222D2
PLO asks alliance vs US, Israel, Egypt 3-25, 222B2
Iran gas deliveries resumed 4-5, 279G1
Iran protests staged 5-24, 407B3; Khuzistan, Afghan policy scored 6-12, 445G3-446D1
Iran banks natlzd 6-7, compensatn vowed 6-10, 469C2
US sen scores Soviet policy 6-12, 459F2
SALT II summit topic 6-15–6-18, 449D1, 458A2
Iran insurnc cos natlzd 6-25, 486E2
UNTSO to replace UNEF in Sinai, Israel vs 7-24, 551B1
Iran cuts gas exports, drops pipe plans 7-28, 582G3-583C1
Kissinger backs SALT linkage, notes S Yemen bases 7-31, 590B3, D3
UNTSO offcr departures rptd 8-1, 574E2
Israel warns vs Palestinian state 8-2, 575A1
Israel reps allowed at pol sci mtg 8-12–8-18, 637B1
Israel pressure blamed for Young resignatn 8-16, 606F2
T-72 tank shipmt to Syria rptd 8-28, 643B2
Iran chrgs Kurd aid 8-31, 670C1
Kurdish rebel aid denied 9-4, 688B2
Israel publishers bar scored 9-4, 690A2

1980

Latin American Relations—*See also CUBA--Soviet Relations*
Colombia amb eludes DR emb raiders 2-27, 141D1
Peru fighter plane sale rptd 3-12, 213D1
Nicaragua trade missn visits, accord signed 3-19, 234F2
Argentine trade deal signed; '79, 1st 1/4 data 4-15, 336F1
Nicaragua delegatn marks Somoza downfall 7-19, 565G2
Peru vs Sovt fighter purchase 7-28, 580B1
Brazil oil deal rptd 10-2, 759G1
Chile debt rescheduled 11-26, 965G1
Reagan policy scored by US amb 12-11, 942E1

Medicine & Health
Sverdlovsk anthrax epidemic rptd 3-18, denied 3-20, 3-26, 235B2; coverup chrgd 6-29, 500A1
'71-76 infant mortality rise rptd 6-25, 525D2
Sverdlovsk anthrax outbreak convictns rptd 9-25, 754A2

Middle East Relations—*See also 'Iran-Iraq War' above; also PERSIAN Gulf*
Connally sees Iran role 1-11, 91F3
UN Iran sanctns vetoed 1-13, reactn 1-14, 28G3, 29G1
2 offcrs in Syria slain 1-15; 1 civiln wounded 1-16, 102E1
Gromyko in Syria, vows arms 1-27—1-29, 140D3
Egypt cuts emb staff, ousts experts 1-28, 69F1
Egypt: Saudi air space used for S Yemen arms aid 1-28, 69A2
Brezhnev backs detente, Mideast solutn 2-4, 84F3
Israel says PLO gets tanks 2-12, 107E3
Kuwait OKs oil sales 3-2, 166B1
Arab hardliners reaffirm support 4-14—4-15, 284E2
New Iran trade deal 4-23, 298G1
UN scores Israel on Leb 4-24, 302E3
Gromyko in French talks on Mideast, Iran 4-24—4-25, 351F3-352A1
Iran hostage rescue try scored 4-25, 4-27, 324B1
UN Palestinian state res backed, Sovt aide assaulted 4-30, 325D1, G1
Iran expels diplomat as spy 6-30; orders staff cuts, scores Iran CP role 7-2, 491B1
Emb takeover in Iran feared; Ghotbzadeh reassures 7-7, 507C2
Iran coup plot role chrgd 7-11, 539D2
Arafat tours Moscow Olympic Village 7-20, 590C1
Iran Emb shift barred, prov consulate closed 8-19, 644C3
Iran interventn to counter US moves seen 8-25, 644A2
Syria friendship pact signed 10-8, 759D2
Jordan King Hussein visit canceled 10-11, 774B3
PLO prisoner in Israel admits mil training 10-31, 912F2
Sadat warns Reagan on policy shift 11-23, 894F1
Jordan says foments Syrian troop moves 12-1, 911C3
Syrian pact implemented 12-2, 911F3
US Sen Percy backs Palestinian state 12-5, 931C1

1976

1977

Israel scores peace stance, urges positive role 12-7, 931B1
Boycotts Cairo conf 12-14, 953B1
Carter on Sovt role, cites Cairo conf boycott 12-15, 955B1
PLO chrgs US reneges on US-Sovt vow 12-16, 995A2
Vs Begin-Sadat summit 12-25, 12-26, 995E3

Monetary, Trade & Aid Issues (including all foreign economic developments)—*See also 'U.S.-Soviet Trade Developments' below*
Peru arms sales cited 1-1, 1-10, 2A3, D3
UK 200-mi fishing zone in effect 1-1, 21A1
Hungary oil prices raised, other E Eur hikes seen 1-6, 67C3
Italy trade talks 1-10—1-13, '76 data rptd 1-12, 64A3
Sweden to settle US-Sovt business disputes 1-11, 29F3
In Philippine sugar deal 1-18, 47F2
'76 trade total rptd up 1-22, 101G2
Rpt seeks OPEC oil cartel plan 1-24, rejctd 1-29, 108F1
'76 OECD trade gap rptd 1-26, 123C2
Air Canada to end svc 1-31, 43D2
'76 W Ger trade rptd 2-9, 102F2
Spain gold claim unresolved 2-9, 242E2
Rhodesia sanctn violatns chrgd 2-10, 122D3
UK gas equipmt deal set 2-11, 134E3
Western debt growth rptd 2-13—4-13, 335C3
EC grants fishing licenses 2-18, 146D3
'67, '73 Egypt arms aid admitted 2-19, 144D2
India oil-trade deal signed 2-19, 161E1
Japan protests Kurile fishing curb 2-26, rejected 3-8, 250C1
Egypt to get 50 MiG-21s 2-27, 144F1
200-mi fishing limit set, Japan agrmt rptd 3-1, 147E1
EC sells butter 3-1, curbs furture sales 3-2, 269F1-A2
'76 trade data rptd 3-8, 188F2, B3
Rumania quake aid set 3-13, 204C2
Japan fishing talks impasse 3-15—3-31, 249G3
Gold sales cited 3-18, 336C1
'76 forgn trade gap down 3-21, 285F1
Tanzania loan set 3-26, 247D3
Japan bars ships 3-31, 250A1
Uganda advisers, pilots rptd 4-2, 308A2
'66-75 Latin arms transfers rptd; table 4-8, 415A3, C3
Japan fishing demands scored 4-12, 319B2
Japan fishing talks impasse continues 4-13—4-14; Kurile dispute unresolved 4-13, 4-16, 319F1-E2
Kuwait mil aid pact signed 4-13, 394D3
Africa aid strategy rptd, Somalia cited 4-16, 328B1
Israel aid to Zaire chrgd 4-18, 317D2
'76 Ethiopia mil aid agrmt rptd 4-24, 328A1
India pacts set 4-27, 348D1
A-suppliers conf meets 4-28—4-29, 403F1-A2
Japan extends territorial waters 4-28, 5-2, 411D2
Egypt arms Zaire vs Sovt threat 5-2, 394B1
Ethiopia pact signed 5-6, 390E3
Kosygin in Finn trade talks, opens A-plant 5-22—5-26, 391A2
Japan fishing pact signed 5-27, ratified 6-10, 458F2-A3
'68 Israeli uranium purchase rptd 5-30, 416A3
Morocco phosphate pact rptd 6-6, 513B3
Seychelles ldr denies coup aid 6-8, 489C1
'76 oil sales to West rptd 6-11, 513F1
Giscard, Brezhnev sign agrmts 6-22, 495D1
IWC cuts whaling quotas 6-24, 496E3
Egypt rpts China arms aid 6-25, 496C2
NZ to import Lada auto 7-4, 638E2
Guyana tech cooperatn pact rptd 7-11, 710C3
Sadat: Egypt mil deals cut 7-16, 550B1
Somalia offered US arms aid 7-26, 587G3
Ethiopia mil aid rptd 7-26, 588B1
Somali OKs US, UK arms aid 7-28, 608A2
Australia wheat deal rptd 8-2, 596B1
Arbatov scores US policy 8-3, 590F1
Chrome productn cited 8-3, 662A2
Egypt curbs cotton trade 8-14, 636A3
China trade pact rptd 8-15, 853F2
Somalia cooperatn pact rptd 8-17, arms shipmts resume 8-18, 649A1
Sovt-backed co svcs NATO 8-19, 700G1
India drops steel plant aid 8-24, 655B2
Australia uranium ban end scored 8-25, 8-26, 693D3
Somali ldr seeks arms aid 8-29—8-31, 684A3
Peru arms buys cited 8-31, 9-1, 785A1, C1
1st, 2d, 3d ¼ Westn trade debt data rptd 8-31, 11-23, 12-9, 988B1
Ethiopia arms deal rptd 9-1, 684C3
Norway Barents Sea fishing talks rptd 9-2, Svalbard zone disputed 11-11, 967F2

1978

Unifil extensn vote abstentn 9-18, 713B1
Arab hardliners seek contact 9-24, 730A1
Libya A-power deal rptd 10-4, 821A1
US asks Leb truce role 10-5, 761B1
Assad visits; Syria to get more arms, Israel scored re Leb 10-5—10-6, 762C3
N Yemen coup role chrgd 10-21, 885F3
Arafat visits, Camp David pact scored 10-29—11-1, 828C1
Nixon backs Iran shah 11-11, 900A3
US warned vs Iran interventn 11-19, 893D3
US Iran interventn chrgs traded 12-28; US alerts naval force 12-29, 994F1

Monetary, Trade, Aid & Investment—*See also 'African Policy' and 'Middle East' above, 'U.S.-Soviet Trade' below*
Swedish fishing zones rptd set 1-1, 21B2
PI offered A-plant 1-5, 2-14, 134B3
Swiss trade pact rptd 1-17, 28G3
US oil shortage forecast disputed 1-18, 52E3
EC steel dumping probe begins 1-23, 80C2
Finland '77 trade surplus rptd 1-30, 90C1
EC-China trade pact scored 2-6, 2-9, 102B3; 4-4, 302G3
Austria trade deficit talks, '77 data cited 2-6—2-8, 110C2
Trade min cancels Canada trip 2-14, 111A1
Australia joins A-supplier group 2-24, 129C2
India joint projects set 3-1—3-6, 169C1
Unctad debt relief stand cited 3-11, 301D1
Westn '77 trade deficit down; Sovt bloc, developing natns cited 3-28; total debt estimated 3-29, 230A1
W Ger weighs uranium deal 4-2, 258C2
Turkish trade accord signed 4-5, 477C1
NZ fishing accord signed 4-5, 498G1
Peru arms paymt reset 4-9, 353A2
Arms tech transfer agrmt rptd 4-25, 297C1
Turkey arms aid proposed 4-26, Cyprus reassured 5-5, 477D1
W Ger trade pact signed 5-7, 417F1
US CIA '77 oil study assessed 5-21, 384E1
Cobalt purchases rptd up 5-23, 382D2
Patent accord takes effect 6-1, 506B3
Poland default seen unlikely 6-1, 535G2
Forgn income taxes rptd 6-2, 499G3
Carter scores mil aid 6-7, 423C3
Turkey trade pacts signed, aid hike vowed; '54-76 credits rptd 6-21—6-23, 595F1, D2
W Ger probes terrorist aid 6-22, 500F1
Comecon integratn bid 6-27, fails 6-29, 504G3
Poor natns '77 trade rptd 6-28, 634E3
US CIA oil study backed by Saudi 6-29, 635B1
Poland plane order rptd 7-5, 650D2
Shipping growth rptd, West concerned 7-11—8-24, 670G2-E3
Finland signs Australia uranium accord 7-20, 590G1
Jan-June trade total rptd 7-22, 634D3
Gas seen by US as major export in '80s 8-13, 634F3
EC scores shipping rate cuts 9-11, Moscow defends 9-11, 9-19, 820A3, D3
In Cuba, Venez, Spain oil pact 9-15, 822C1
Japan color TV deal rptd 10-5, 820F3
Trade missn rptd in Japan 10-18, 798D1
Viet econ, sci, tech pact signed 11-3, 859E2
Moscow bank rptd '77 world's largest 11-8, 914D1
Canada Lada sales rptd 11-13, 1020F3-1021A1
Cuba rptdly gets MiG-23s 11-14, Kosygin defends 11-16, 905F1
Cuba MiGs claimed 'defensive' 11-20, 1016G1
Westn debt rptd 11-21, 11-28, 999A2
Afghan pact signed 12-5, 943D2
OPEC oil price hike praised 12-18, 978A2

1979

Israel, Egypt OK Sinai patrols 9-5, 658F1
Khomeini rule scored 9-8, 688C1
PLO accepts '80 Olympics invite, IOC 'astonished' 10-2, 798G1
Syria unrest tied to Egypt-Israel treaty 10-14, 857F2
Syria pres visits, arms vowed 10-15–10-18; Syria debt rptd canceled 11-3, 857E2, G2
Yemen pres visits 10-24, signs friendship pact 10-25, 802B1
Iran cancels mil pact 11-5, 841G1
Iran broadcast criticism rejctd 11-13, 878G2
Saudis implicate in mosque raid, US confrms 12-16, 997A1

Monetary, Trade, Aid & Investment—*See also 'African', 'Atomic', 'Energy', 'Latin', and 'Middle East' above, 'U.S.-Soviet Trade' below*
'74-77 arms sales rptd 1-7, 13G1
Gromyko in Italy trade talks 1-22–1-26, 60A3
Finland '78 trade rptd 2-2, 215G2
Viet asks China invasn aid 2-17, 121G1; mil supplies rptd, China warns 2-21, 2-22, 122B1
India aid agrmts signed 3-14, 200G1
Krupp steel sale, $ paymt rptd 3-26, 237D3
French computer deal set, '78 US ban cited 3-27, 237G2
'78 Westn trade deficit, total surplus rptd 3-28, 237C3
Australia sets whaling ban 4-4, 284C2
French econ pact, cooperatn agrmts signed 4-26–4-28, 723A3
Hungary trade cited 5-30, 417C1
Whaling banned, Indian O sanctuary set 7-11, 554D2
Gold price rise, sales drop linked 8-27, 645C3
2d intl book fair held, deals set 9-4–9-10, 689E3-690C2
Gold productn ranked 2d 9-6, 684D3
Greek ship accord rptd signed 9-11, 708C1
EC ball bearing dumping probe opened 9-20, 719E2
Platinum trading OKd 9-28, price rise linked 10-4, 740G1
Cambodia relief aid rptd 9-30, 741C1; 11-5, 863D3; 12-2, 12-3, 917A2; restraints denied 12-13, 12-30, 977C3, 978G1
E Ger trade pact signed 10-5, 761C2
Rumania oil independnc seen 11-19, 910A2
Australia wheat sales detailed 11-28, 948B1
Taiwan affirms trade bar 11-28, 952B3
Gold coin sales pushed 11-29, 929E1
Viet aid end sought by China 11-30, 918A1
Japan co signs steel pact 12-17, 997C2

1980

Monetary, Trade, Aid & Investment *See also 'African Relations', 'Atomic', 'Communism & Communist Country Relations', 'Latin American', 'Middle East' above, 'U.S.-Soviet Trade' below; also GRAIN—Soviet Developments*
Australia halts fishing projct, other curbs imposed 1-9, 9D2
Gold price benefits noted 1-18, 30F2
Pacific orgn studied 1-20, 78C2
NZ cuts fishing ships 1-22, 100D2
Australia widens trade curbs, '79 trade data cited 1-29, 116C1
Westn debt estimated 2-4, 166B3
Strategic metals '78, '79 buying noted; US imports compared 2-5, 85D1
Afghan trade pact rptd 2-5, 85C3
Australia lifts trade curbs 2-12, 148A1
Japan steel deal delay OKd 2-19, 235F3
Canada grain sale, '79 data rptd 2-29, 171E2
W Ger compares US policy 3-10, 205E2
'79 total trade up, Westn debt down 3-26, 235D3
'79 Westn exports cited 4-1, 285B3
EC-Yugo trade pact signed 4-2, 365C3
Caviar export scandal rptd 4-15, 354A3
Antarctic fishing pact set 5-20, 398D1
W Eur trade blitz rptd 5-22, 430G3-431A1
US scores Cambodia aid conf boycott 5-26, 397B2
Indian aid pact signed 5-28, US concerned 5-29, 398A1
W Ger draft trade pact set, '79 data cited 5-29, 411A2
Australia wheat sale hike rptd 6-17, 460E2
W Ger vows pact adherence 6-23, 474G1
Portugal urges anti-Sovt actns 6-26, 475C1
W Ger econ pact signed, gas pipe OKd 7-1, 489B3
Canada lifts grain embargo 7-24, 577F3
Canada chrgs auto dumping 8-7, record sales rptd 8-8, 618C1-F1
Antarctic fishing pact signed 9-11, 721B1
US protests French steel deal 9-19, 728D3
US Cong fails to bar India uranium sale 9-24, 723F1
Swiss gold sales rptd resumed; Aug silver purchases rptd 9-24, 730D3
'80 sugar purchases rumored 10-9, 777B2
Canada 13-yr debt dispute rptd settled 10-22, 828B2
EC to resume barley sales 10-23, 832B1
IMF Pak loan protested 11-25, 904D3
'79 3d World arms sales rptd up 12-10, 933A2
India trade ties expanded 12-11, 930E2

1976

Obituaries
Arzumanyan, Grigory 11-28, 932C3
Brailowsky, Alexander 4-25, 524C2
Druzhinin, Vladimir 8-20, 892G2
Frumkin, Alexander 5-27, 404G1
Grechko, Andrei 4-27, 315E3
Koshevoi, Pyotr 8-30, 892A3
Lukonin, Mikhail 8-5, 892C3
Lysenko, Trofim 11-20, 970D2
Menshikov, Mikhail 7-21, 716D3
Muskhelishvili, Nikolai 7-15, 716E3
Peive, Jan 9-17, 970A3
Piatigorsky, Gregor 8-6, 892D3
Rukhin, Yevgeny 5-24, 404D2
Satyukov, Pavel 11-17, 970B3
Shtemenko, Sergei 4-23, 368A3
Vishniak, Mark 11-30, 1015A3
Yakubovsky, Ivan 11-30, 932G3

Republics
'75 ship mutineers rptd jailed in Latvia 1-22, 122A3
Plyushch details Ukraine hosp stay 2-3, 122F1
Ukraine, Byelorussia anti-Semitism chrgd 2-16, 206E3
Ukraine on UN Palestine com 2-26, 162C1
New CP Politburo named 3-5, 195D2
Georgian harvest damage rptd 3-23, 321E3
Nobel winners plead for Ukraine MD 3-24, 421A3
'75 ship mutineers rptd executed in Latvia 5-4, 421B2
Ukraine town honors Brezhnev 5-8, 421A2
Earthquake hits Uzbek 5-17, 404F2
Ukraine dissident rptd in mental hosp 5-18, 421F2
US newsman chrgd re Georgia, Estonia incitemt 5-26, 371E3
Armenian emigratn data 5-26, 421D3
Latvia meat price strikers sentncd 10-31, 966F3
Turkish quake hits Armenia 11-24, 896G3
Arzumanyan dies 11-28, 932C3
Moldavian ldr in Rumania 12-3—12-7, 1010E1

Sports
Mishap at US hockey game 1-11, Sovt tour ends 1-12, 56E1
Winter Olympics results 2-4—2-15, 158E3-159A2
Summer Olympics results 7-18—7-31, 563A1-E2, 573B3, F3-576G3
Olympic pentathlon star disqualified 7-19, 7-20, 563F1
Olympic diver defects 7-29—7-31, 562C2

1977

Intl book fair held 9-6—9-14, 765C3
Somalia scores arms-flow halt 9-7, warns vs Ethiopia aid 9-14, 715A3
US to aid Egypt repair MiG-21s 9-15, 698C1
Ethiopia seeks arms purchase 9-18, 715E2
A-suppliers conf OKs safeguards 9-21, 717D1
Barents fishing curbed 9-24, 9-27, EC bans Sovt trawlers 9-31, 771F2
Canada grain sales rptd 9-30, 948C3
Sakhalin oil find announced 10-12, 853E3
'76 arms sales, econ aid to Mideast, Latin Amer, Africa rptd 10-13, 949B2
Somalia arms aid ended 10-19, 829G2
Egypt suspends debt paymts, cotton exports 10-26, 811F3
India econ aid vowed 10-27, 842F2
Forgn co growth detailed by CIA 10-31, 949E1
Malta premr scores aid indifference 11-3, 925E2
Ethiopia aid vow worries US 11-17, 896B2
Nigeria arms purchases cited 11-23, 986A3
Whale kill quotas raised 12-6, 12-7, 936B3
US publishers bar book pact 12-7, 955C2
Ethiopia arms, aides rptd hiked 12-16, 998E1
2 US reps urge Ethiopia aid 12-16, 998E2
Peru near default on arms debt 12-16, 1015A2
US OKs Sudan jet sale 12-23, 1019C2

Obituaries
Budker, Gersh 7-6, 604F2
Eglevsky, Andre 12-4, 1024E1
Fedin, Konstantin 7-15, 604A3
Gabo, Naum 8-23, 696F2
Galich, Alexander 12-15, 1024F1
Ilyushin, Sergei 2-9, 164B3
Litvinov, Ivy 4-28, 356C3
Luria, Aleksandr 8-16, 696C3
Roslavleva, Natalia 1-2, 84E3
Shashin, Valintin D 3-22, 306C3
Skochilov, Anatoly (rptd) 7-7, 604F3
Soloviev, Yuri 1-16, 84G3
Stakhanov, Alexei 11-5, 952D3
Timakov, Vladimir 6-21, 532G3
Vasilevsky, Aleksandr 12-5, 1024F3
Vereshchagin, Leonid (rptd) 2-23, 164F3

Republics
Byelorussia, Ukraine UN Assemb membership cited 3G3, 4C1
2 Ukraine Helsinki monitors arrested 2-5, 117E1
Ukraine MD freed 3-14, 226D3
Armenia Helsinki monitors rptd 4-6, 314D1
Georgian Helsinki monitor, 2 other natlists seized 4-7, 314G1
Ukraine MD in Vienna 4-13, 314C3
Ukraine Helsinki monitors arrested 4-23, 314F1
Ukraine Helsinki monitors sentncd 7-1, 512B3
Ukraine mil exercises 7-11, 551C1
Byelorussia mil chief scores draftee training 8-20, 674A1
2 rights activists rptd arrested in Lithuania 8-24, 684C1
3 dissidents rptd in Georgia mental inst 8-31, 684C1
Siberia-Byelorussia oil pipe rptd 9-17, 949D1
Ukrainian writer rptd jailed 9-26, 753B1
KGB tries to blackmail US envoy 10-19, 866C2-B3
Lithuania anti-Russian riot rptd 10-30, 955D3
Tatar natlst freed 12-22, 1017B2

Sakhalin Island—*See SAKHALIN*
SALT—*See DISARMAMENT—U.S.-Soviet Developments*
Soviet Bloc—*See COMMUNISM and Communist Countries*

Sports
US boxing tourn results 1-29, 2-3, 2-5, 263F1
NBC gets '80 Olympics 2-1, 130G3
Czechs retain hockey title 5-8, 430A2
US track meets 7-1—7-3, 602D2
US House subcom queries NBC Olympic deal 10-4, 950C1
Soccer match, riot rptd 10-30, 955D3
Sovt tennis team quits WTT 12-10, 1020F2

1978

Obituaries
Alikhanian, Artemi I 2-25, 196B2
Bushuyev, Konstantin D 10-26, 888F2
Geidarov, Arif Nazar 6-29, 518G3
Gorbatyuk, Yevgeny M 3-5, 252F2
Karasavina, Tamara 5-26, 440G2
Keldysh, Mstislav 6-24, 540A3
Khachaturian, Aram 5-1, 440A3
Kulakov, Fyodor D 7-16, 620G2
Kyazimov, Saladin 6-29, 519A1
Mikoyan, Anastas Ivanovich 10-22, 888C3
Nabokov, Nicholas 4-6, 356C3
Nikodim, Metropolitan 9-5, 778G1
Pervukhin, Mikhail (rptd) 7-25, 620D3
Saikhanov, Aziz 6-29, 519A1
Shevchenko, Leongina I 5-8, 440E3
Vader, Artur Pavlovich 5-26, 440F3

Press & Censorship—*See 'Human Rights' above*

Republics
Baltic areas opened to foreigners, Kazakhstan, Birobidzhan closed 1-19, 39A2
Georgia dissident arrested 1-25, 180F1
Byelorussia mil maneuvers observed 2-6—2-10, 103A2
Baltic, Ural Mt cities bar US, UK envoys 2-17, 230E1
Lithuanian Nazi collaborator rptd sentncd 2-21, 151E3
Ukraine Nazi collaborators rptd executed 3-8, 416B3
Georgian dissident jailed 3-20, 275C3
Ukrainian Helsinki monitors rptd sentncd 3-30, 275B3
Georgia, Armenia get new charters, win language rights 4-14, 4-16, 275F1
Lithuanian dissident rptd sentncd 4-16, 275F2
Ukraine, Kazakhstan grain checked by US aide 5-9, 499E2
Georgia Helsinki monitor sentenced 5-19, 401D2
Kazakhstan convict held in Moscow shootout 5-24, 416E2
Estonia pres dies 5-26, 440F3
Georgia's Abkhaz region dvpt plan, secessn threats rptd 6-7, 6-25, 519A1
Byelorussia capital gets Order of Lenin 6-25, 488C3
2 US rptrs chrgd re Georgia dissident trial 6-28, 518C1-F2; convicted 7-18, 575D2; pay fines 8-4, 634A1
Azerbaijan interior min slain 6-29, 518G3
Lithuanian Helsinki monitor sentncd 7-13, 541E2
Ukrainian dissident sentenced 7-20, 634B2
Armenian woman joins US emb sit-in 8-11, 634B2
US rptrs case closed 8-18, 651E1; warned by Forgn Min 8-24, 670C2
Latvian UN aide gets US asylum 9-18, 946G3
Byelorussia, Ukraine UN Assemb members 713C3, F3
Armenian woman ends US emb sit-in 11-1, 947A2
Georgia's Gorbachev named to Politburo 11-27, 924D3
Armenian dissidents rptd sentncd 12-5, 947F1

SALT—*See DISARMAMENT—U.S.-Soviet Developments*
Soviet Bloc—*See 'Communism' above; also COMMUNISM and Communist Countries*
Space—*See ASTRONAUTICS*

Sports
Olga Korbut marries 1-7, 95G3
4 win world figure-skating titles 3-9, 3-11, 316E3
Yashchenko sets indoor high jump mark 3-12, 692E3
Coca-Cola chosen for '80 Olympics 3-14, 230C1
US wins dual swimming meet 4-15—4-16, 780E1, B3
1000-mtr speed-skating mark rptd 4-16, 316C3

1979

Obituaries
Kapler, Aleksei Y (rptd) 9-15, 756F2
Kuznetsov, Anatoly V 6-13, 508C3
Pospelov, Pyotr 4-24, 356F3
Radzievsky, Alexei 9-3, 756D3
Simonov, Konstantin 8-28, 671E3
Solovyev-Sedov, Vasily 12-2, 1008F3
Tikhonov, Nicolai S 2-8, 176G3
Tolstoy, Alexandra 9-26, 756E3

Press & Censorship—*See 'Human Rights' above*

Republics
Armenia, Azerbaijan, Georgia rptd affected by Iran gas cutoff 1-23, 50B2
Lithuania Catholicism cited 1-24, 60G2
Armenian executed re '77 Moscow subway blast 1-30, 100F2
Podgorny ends pol career 3-4, 237G2
Crimean Tatar activist exiled 3-6, 172F2
Ukrainian dissident kills self 3-6, 238D1
Iran gas deliveries resumed 4-5, 279G1
Byelorussia hit by floods 4-8, 289A1
Soyuz lands in Kazakhstan 4-12, 279C2
Uzbekistan abuse chrg by UK rptr protested 4-20, 390F1
2 Ukraine dissidents freed in spy swap 4-27, 317G2
Georgia dissident pardoned 6-29, 504B3
US rptr scored re Ukraine visit 7-10, 637A1
Aeroflot jets collide over Ukraine 8-17, 639D1
Byelorussia, Ukraine UN membership listed 695F2, A3
Populatn data rptd 10-10, 857F1*
Ukrainian Jews rptd arrested 10-28, 856B3
Lithuanian natlst arrested 11-1, 856A3

SALT—*See DISARMAMENT-U.S.-Soviet Developments*
Soviet Bloc—*See 'Communism' above and under 'C'*

Sports
Challenge Cup won 2-11, 118F1
3 win world figure-skating titles 3-15, 391E3, 392A1
World Cup wrestling results 4-1, 507G3
World ice hockey title retained 4-25, 448D1
US wins Federatn Cup 5-6, 391E2
Karpov marries 6-1, 527D2
Spartakaide hosted 7-21–8-5, 799D1
World U Game results 9-8–9-13, 799F1

1980

Obituaries
Amalrik, Andrei A 11-11, 928G1
Dimitri, Prince 7-7, 608F1
Golikov, Filipp (rptd) 7-31, 676E1
Ibraimov, Sultan 12-4, 945D3
Kosygin, Alexei N (rptd) 12-19, 951B1, 996G1-B2
Malik, Yakov 2-11, 176D2
Mandelstam, Nadezhda 12-29, 1004E2
Paleckis, Justas 1-26, 176G2
Paputin, Viktor S (rptd) 1-3, 26B2
Petrov, Boris N (rptd) 8-26, 676E2
Vodopyanov, Mikhail V (rptd) 8-14, 676E3
Vysotsky, Vladimir 7-24, 580C2
Zimin, Alexandr A. (rptd) 3-14, 280G2

Pakistan Relations—*See PAKISTAN--Soviet-Afghan Issue*

Republics
Lithuanian natlst rptd arrested 1-14, 46F3
Slavic populatn rptd down 2-9, 152F3
Byelorussia vs UN Afghan res 2-14, 123E3
Estonian dissident arrested 3-18, 262E1
Ukranian RC ldr named 3-27, 413F3
Ukraine wheat planting delayed 4-8, 336A2
Ukraine, Byelorussia work laws scored 5-12, 381E2
Ukranian youth granted asylum in US 7-21, 560C1
Georgia drought harvest threat rptd 8-6, 711B3
Iran refused Tadzhikistan consulate 8-19, 644D3
Canada immigratn records rptd found 8-20, 651C2
Ukraine grain prductn rptd off, flooding linked 9-7, 711C3
Ukraine-Hungarian electric grid cited 10-1, 753D3
2 named to Politburo 10-21, 798C1, E1
Russian named 1st dep premr 10-27, 832A1
Kirgiz premr slain 12-4, 945C3
Moldavian ldr named dep premr 12-19, 996C2

SALT—*See DISARMAMENT--U.S.-Soviet Developments*
Soviet Bloc—*See 'Communism & Communist Country Relations' above*

Sports
World speed skating title won 1-13, records set 3-27, 3-29, 470E1, A2
Carter urges Moscow Olympics shift 1-20, 45B2; for subsequent developments, see SPORTS—Olympic Games (Moscow)
Lake Placid Olympics role planned 1-20, 45F3
Eur, world figure skating titles 1-25, 3-12, 470B2, F2

1976

Olympic sprinter death threat rptd 7-31, 562A3
'80 Olympics in Moscow set 8-1, 562D1
Olympic diver to return 8-17, 655C2
Canada Cup Hockey results 9-15, 736G3

UN Policy & Developments
Council member 62F2; 720C1
'66 rights covenant in effect 1-4, 36E3
China Cncl clash on Mideast 1-15, 60A1
OKs Cncl pro-Palestine resolutn 1-26, 59G2
Ukraine on UN Palestine com 2-26, 162C1
NY delegatn incidents 2-27, 229C2; 3-15, 4-2, 259E3
At transnatl comm mtg 3-2—3-12, 297G3
China Cncl clash on Angola 3-26, 3-30, US censures USSR 3-31, 228D2
Angola rep defends aid 3-26, 228E2
UN staff asks ex-translator freed 3-30, 421B3
Disputes PLO seating 5-4, 320D1
WHO rpts no swine flu 6-3, 423F3
OKs Israel Arab land exit 6-29, 464C1
Shuns vote on anti-terror 7-14, 515G3
Gromyko addresses Assemb 9-28, 719B1, A3
A-blast inspectn OKd 10-4, 739C1
China scores at Assemb 10-5, 759F3
US accuses Waldheim on UN jobs 10-11, 760C2
S Africa arms ban vetoed 10-19, 781D3
Refugee comr vs Sovt defector return 11-1, 854D2
UNESCO shelves press plan 11-6, 842A2
US actn vs UN missn offcl rptd 11-17, 907D3
Malik removal confirmed 11-23, 908F1
Vs West on press plan 11-25, plan delayed 11-29, 895E3
UNDOF renewal link blocked 11-30, 895C2
UN votes on environmt 12-10, 955D1
Troyanovsky named amb 12-14, 967C1

U.S. Presidential Election (& Transition)
Reagan scores Ford on detente 1-5, 4C3
Muskie backs lessened tensns 1-21, 40F2
Reagan: deal from strength 2-10, 109D2
Jackson detente stand cited 3-2, 165D1
Reagan chrgs US lags in might, blames Ford 3-4, 165F3
Ford rebuts Reagan 3-5, 179E3
Reagan cites Nixon China visit 3-6, 180E1
Reagan hits defense issue 3-22, 214C1
Ford vows strong defense 3-24—3-29, 231C3-G3
Reagan stresses US mil inferiority, attacks Ford, Kissinger 3-31, 232B2, D2
Ford defends Kissinger vs Reagan 4-2, 245B2
Pravda: US threatens detente 4-2, 277C2
USSR protests anti-Sovt hysteria 4-5, 260B1
Ford, Reagan debate defense 4-9—4-21, 280F3, 281B1, C2, A3
US delays A-pact 5-12, 371F2
Carter scores A-pact 5-13, 375C1; 5-14, 390F3
Ties a US Dem platform item 6-15, 432E3
Dem platform text cites ties 6-15, 477D2, A3, 478B3
Carter on human rights 6-23, 451A3
US vetoes Angola UN membership 6-23, 455B2
Carter on A-strengths, vs 'bargaining chips' 6-24, 490F1, A2
GOP platform com OKs plank 8-13, 582C3
GOP conv platform plank OKd 8-18, 600F3; text 608F3, 610G1
Ford acceptance speech cites 8-19, 612B1
Carter on Sovt dissidents 9-8, 664B3
Scores Kissinger Africa talks 9-17, 698D1
Harriman sees Brezhnev 9-20, 752B1
US '77 defns funds signed 9-22, 706G3
Ford, Carter debate 10-6, 740C3-G3, 741A3, 742A1, D1
Ford debate gaffe scored in US 10-7—10-12, 762A1, A3
Ford admits debate error 10-12, 10-14, 761E3, 762G3
US vp candidates debate 10-15, 782E3
Ford, Carter debate Yugo threat 10-22, 10-26, 800A1, 802D2, 803B1-D1, 804F2
Brezhnev scores Ford, Carter 10-25, 839B2
Reactn to Carter electn 11-3—11-4, 826F1
Brezhnev not to 'test' Carter 12-3, 916E2
Carter sees summit mtg 12-27, Brezhnev favorable 12-29, 978G2

1977

UN Policy & Developments
Assemb, Cncl member; Morozov on World Ct 3G3, 4C1-G1
Bars UNEF funds 12-30-76; renews stand 1-6; US scores 1-7, 4G1
Israel rep meets Troyanovsky on PLO peace role 2-3, 86D3
Rhodesia sanctn violatns chrgd 2-10, 122D3
French oust UNESCO offcl as spy 2-11, 159C3
US asks rights comm dissident info 2-18, 137G2
Leb consults on troop use 3-1, 143D2
US drops rights comm dissident info bid 3-7, sessn ends 3-11, 207E1, A2
At Water Conf 3-14—3-25, 250E1
Carter defends rights stand 3-17, 185B1
Weather war pact signed 5-18, 400B3
Gromyko addresses Assemb 9-27, 769F2
Abstains on Rhodesia rep 9-29, 809G2
USSR-US Geneva plan cites 10-1, 750A2
US UNESCO envoy blackmail chrgd 10-19, 866C2-B3
Dissidents hold rights vigil 12-10, 955G3

1978

US wins Weisman Cup 4-23, 419C1
World Amateur Boxing tourn results 5-6—5-20, 600D2
Myslivsev 20-km walk mark rptd 5-12, 692F3
World hockey title won 5-14, 458B3
US OKs crime equipmt sale for '80 Olympics 7-6, 10-13, 905C2
US-USSR track meets 7-7—7-9, 692B3
'80 Olympics site opposed re Shcharansky trial 7-17, 542D1, E1
Karpov retains world chess title 7-18—10-17, honored 10-28, 843A1, C2
Carter vs Olympics boycott 7-20, 549C3
2d in World Swim Championships, US resurgnc noted 8-18—8-28, 780C1, A2
World Gym Championships 10-23—10-29, 928B3
US wins Federatn Cup 12-3, 1027A1

UN Policy & Developments
US ouster of Viet amb protested 2-9, 103A3
Canada satellite safety study vetoed 2-14, 238A2
Unctad debt relief stand cited 3-11, 301D1
Leb asks anti-Israel actn 3-15, 174D3
UN Leb force abstentn 3-19, 197C1
Shevchenko renounces citizenship 4-10, defects 4-26, 302A2
ILO bars dissident union 4-14, 275F2
UN Leb force expansn abstentn 5-3, 340F1
Leb force expansn extensn 5-3, 340F1
US arrests 2 Sovts as spies, asks 3d to leave 5-20, 409G2
Assemb disarmamt sessn opens 5-23, Gromyko sees SALT treaty, A-test ban 5-26, 421G1
Geneva aide defects to UK 678G1
Assemb disarmamt sessn ends, vows A-weapon restraint, bars total test ban 6-30, 522B3, 523C1
UK forces resignatn of ILO aide; 2d aide tied to KGB by Swiss 7-26, ousted 7-31, 676C1
Namibia plan abstentn 7-27, 562A1
Sovt aide promoted despite US, UK spy chrgs 8-29, 676E1
Kennedy addresses WHO conf 9-6, 742G3
PR called US colony 9-13, 979E3
Unifil extensn abstentn 9-18, 713B1
Latvian aide gets US asylum 9-18, 946G3
Cncl, Assemb member 713A3, C3, F3
Namibia plan abstentn 9-29, 819E2
Huang speech scored by Pravda 10-10, 796C2
US convicts 2 Sovts as spies 10-13, sentenced 10-30, 835A2; USSR demands return 11-4, 863E1
UNESCO OKs world free press, Sovt proposal barred 11-22, 931D1, E1

1979

Skating stars defect to Swiss 9-18, 721B3; get asylum 10-30, 939G3
Chess player gets Swiss asylum 9-24, 721D3
PLO accepts '80 Olympics invite, IOC 'astonished' 10-2, 798G1
World Gym Championships results 10-5–10-9, 1005B2
W Ger rpts canoeist kidnaped 10-15, 856C3
2 women banned from track 10-26, 912A1

UN Policy & Developments
Cambodia Cncl plea vs Viet unblocked 1-11, 10G1
Cncl action on Cambodia-Viet war vetoed 1-15, 28E1
Unifil extension opposed 1-19, 51D1
Cncl meets on China, Viet wars 2-23; actn stalled 2-28, 142A1
Viet-Cambodia, China-Viet res vetoed 3-16, 200D1
US swaps Sovt spies for dissidents 4-27, 317B1
Unifil renewal abstentn 6-14, 436A3
Assemb disarmamt sessn cited in SALT II communique 6-18, 457B2, 458A1, D1
US double agent rptd exposed 6-24, 521C1
UNTSO to replace UNEF, Israel vs 7-24, 551B1
UNTSO offcr departures rptd 8-1, 574E2
Membership listed 695B3
Pol Pot govt seat opposed 9-21; US, China 'tricks' chrgd 9-22, 695D2, 741G1
Gromyko Assemb address scores 'lies' re Cuba 9-25, 738B2
China cites war threat 9-27, 741B2
Intl Yr of Child cited 10-19, 857D2
Cambodia relief aid rptd 11-5, 863D3
Res re Viet exit from Cambodia opposed 11-14, 863G3
Cncl debate on Iran, US hostage release urged 12-1–12-2, 913F1
NYC missn bombed 12-12, 965C3
UNICEF denies Cambodia relief restraints 12-13, 977C3
Zimbabwe sanctns vote abstentn 12-21, 976C3
US warns vs Iran sanctns veto 12-22, abstains on res 12-31, 974F2, C3

1980

Lake Placid Winter Olympics results 2-12—2-24, 154F2, 155F2-156D1
Canada Cup hockey tourn cancelled 4-30, 488B3
Chess Olympiad won 12-7, 972A3

UN Policy & Developments
Cncl mtg sought on Afghan invasn 1-3—1-4; debate 1-5—1-6; vetoes res for pullout 1-7, 2F1
Cncl res to shift Afghan issue to Assemb opposed 1-9; Assemb res scores invasn 1-14, 1-9, 25D1
US-proposed Iran sanctns vetoed 1-13, reactn 1-14, 28G3, 29G1
Rights comm sets Sakharov debate 2-5, 85F3; postpones 3-11, 181A3
Indl dvpt aid fund disputed 2-9, 124D2
Rights comm Afghan res opposed 2-14, 123D3
UN workers '79 rights rally protested 2-14, 221B1
Swiss allege 200 spies at UN offices 2-18, 141C3
Afghan peace force rptd weighed 2-27, 165F1
US anti-Israel vote disavowal disputed 3-5, 163G3
Israel Leb incursn res abstentn 4-24, 302E3
Palestinian state res backed, Sovt aide assaulted 4-30, 325D1, G1
ILO scores work laws 5-12, 381E2
World Ct demands Iran free US hostages 5-24, 393B1
Gromyko meets Waldheim on Iran-Iraq war 9-23, 718F3
Pol Pot govt keeps Assemb seat 10-13, 775B2
Assemb again votes Sovt Afghan exit 11-20; res scored 11-20, 899F2-900A1
UNESCO illiteracy study rptd 12-4, 953F1
UNIFIL mandate extensn abstentn 12-17, 977D3

U.S. Presidential Election (& Transition)
GOP chrmn urges Moslem natn aid offer 1-1, 5C1
Iowa GOP pres debate topic 1-5, 4G2
Reagan backs US Mideast bases, vs mil confrontatn 1-9, 1-10, 13D2
Kennedy seeks firm US stand 1-14, 32D3
Connally, Reagan vs 'appeasemt' 1-17, 1-29, 91C3, E3
Kennedy scores Carter on 'Cold War II' stand, draft 1-28, 74A3
GOP vs Carter Persian Gulf doctrine 1-28, 75D1
Connally chrgs Carter appeasemt 2-14, 129F1
Reagan assails Carter policies 2-15, 128C3
GOP candidates debate in NH 2-20, 129E3
Reagan 'basic speech' scores detente 2-29, 207A3
Connally 'basic speech' excerpts 3-7, 184C2, D3, 185F1
Reagan stresses arms talks 3-17, 208G1-B2
GOP drafts platform 7-10, 506B3
Kissinger scores Carter 7-15, 534D3
GOP platform adopted; text 7-15, 535B3, 536E1, C2, F2, B3
Reagan accepts nominatn 7-17, 533A1, 534G3
Anderson scores Reagan 7-20, 550C1
Dem platform planks adopted 8-13, 611D2, 615A3
Reagan urges US strength 8-18, 8-20, 629B1, E1
Anderson platform offered 8-30, 665C1, G1, B2
Carter, Reagan remarks on Poland scored 9-2, 659E2
Carter blasts Reagan on A-arms race 9-2, 664A3
Reagan scores 'stealth' plane disclosure 9-4, 665F3
Bush scores Carter policy 9-5, 9-25, 780D3, 781E1
Muskie warns of Reagan's 'endless' wars 10-11, 776B3
Brezhnev: no pres preference 10-14, 776C3
Muskie scores Reagan 10-16, 776A2, D2
Reagan gives policy tenet 10-19, 801G2
Mondale hails grain embargo 10-26, 816E3
Carter chrgs Reagan 'flipflop' on grain embargo 10-27, 816B3
Carter, Reagan TV debate 10-28, 814B3, D3, 815A1
Anderson answers TV debate questns 10-28, 816C1
Carter defeated by Reagan 11-5; reactn 11-6, 841A3, C3
Reagan favors 'linkage' 11-6, 839D2
Sadat warns Reagan on policy shift 11-23, 894F1
Reagan Latin policy scored by US amb 12-11, 942E1

1976

U.S. Relations—*See also 'Angola', 'Foreign Economic Developments' and 'U.S. Presidential Election' above; also ARMAMENTS, DISARMAMENT, GRAIN, 'USSR' under MIDDLE EAST—INTERNATIONAL*
CIA bars data on Hughes LA office robbery 1-5, 24E2
Sovt hockey tour ends 1-12, 56E1
CIA ends sub salvage plans 1-13, 24G2
Rosenberg case dvpts 1-13, 70C2
CIA media manipulatn rptd 1-17, 92D3
'68 Czech invasn info rptd scored 1-20, 93B3
More US papers to be available 1-21, 76F2
US defns needs outlined 1-27, 68D2
US Marines reorganizatn urged 2-2, 95C3
Kissinger seeks support for detente 2-3, 2-4, 88A2, G3
US emb microwave taps rptd 2-6—2-10, 122D2
Nixon in China, scores detente 2-22, 189D3
CR forgn min lauds US 2-23, 178E1
Brezhnev lauds detente 'progress', deplores US criticism 2-24, 193G2
USSR ties microwaves to US bugging 2-26; US denies med problem 2-29, 196C2
Moscow, NY diplomatic harrassmt incidents 2-27—3-30, 229C2, C3 ★ 3-31—4-6, 259E3
Ford vs word 'detente' 3-1, 165D3
FBI intellignc penetratn rptd 3-10, 248E2
Kissinger on detente problems, cites 'reciprocity', warns US critics 3-11, 196A2, B3
CIA discounts space program 3-11, 216F2
Ford 'detente' bar scored 3-14, 196B2
US halts joint talks 3-16, 196F1
Alger Hiss book review rptd 3-18, 217E3
Nixon rpts on China trip 3-22, 215D1
US columnists rpt US backed Sovt-E Eur union 3-22, Kissinger rebuts 3-29, 4-1, 232G2, 233B1
US sen scores treatmt of Jews 3-22, 246A1
Rockefeller scores Indian O role 3-30—3-31, 249F2
Eastern bloc scores US critics 4-9—4-18, 276E3
USSR chrgs Helsinki violatn 4-18, US denies 4-19, 277B1
US study cites Sovt mil buildup 4-18, 309C1
FBI data on spies in US rptd 4-26, 304F1
Ghana cancels US trip 4-28, 295A2
Kissinger proposes Sahel aid program 5-1, 318F2
Japan chrgs Sovt newsman as spy 5-12—5-14, 356E1
Suslov scores re detente 5-19, 381G1
Japan frees alleged Sovt spy 5-22, 373B2
3 US newsmen linked to CIA 5-25, 5-26, 371G2
USSR: visa curbs violate CSCE 5-25—5-28, 407F3
USSR: visa curbs violate Helsinki 5-25—5-28, 407F3
'76 Sovt emigratn data 5-26, 421C3
Fraser on US role re Sovt Indian O buildup 6-20, 481D1
US refuses '70 hijackers asylum 6-24, 544A1
Kissinger on mil, navy weakness 6-25, 466A2
Sovt dissident scores Ford 6-25, 540A3
US emb sends 2 home 6-25, 540D3
US newsman sues journal re CIA chrg 6-25, 559B1
US researcher scores visa denial 7-3, 540B3
Ship in US Bicentennial event 7-4, 488A3
US emb microwave level rptd down 7-7, 540C3
Japan warns US vs concessns 7-12, 555E2
US cites Asian threat 7-22, 557E2
Sovt Medit strength rptd 7-22, 558D3
US indicts Aeroflot re rebates 7-27, 908B1
Nonaligned conf backs detente 8-20, 621D3
3 sentncd in drug case 8-27, 655E1-A2
Berlin bus protest rejctd 8-27, 678D3
Ships collide in Ionian 8-28, 941B3
MiG-25 pilot lands Japan, asks US asylum 9-6; arrives US 9-9; USSR chrgs plot 9-14, 695G3-696F1
Solzhenitsyn move to US rptd 9-9, 680B3
Sovt containership bombed 9-17, 908A1
Sovt pilot lands Iran, asks US asylum 9-23; Sovt protest 9-26, 777D2
Kissinger Rhodesia plan scored 9-25, 718B3
Gromyko scores US Africa role 9-28, Kissinger rebuts, scores re Mideast role, 3d World aid 9-30, 719B1
MiG pilot bars return 9-28; US experts rpt on plane 10-7, 839G2
Gromyko sees Kissinger in NY 9-29, 10-1, 719E3
Harriman: Brezhnev regrets Nixon resignatn 9-29, 752D1
Sovt scientists robbed in DC, Calif 10-2, 10-14; USSR protests 10-19; DC victim dies 10-24, 857G1
Greece sentences US rptr 10-4, 873D1
Brezhnev scores re southn Africa 10-7, 856E3
US tied to Thai coup 10-8, 775F3-776A1
US accuses Waldheim on UN jobs 10-11, 760C2
Gen Brown denies quote 10-18, 787A3

1977

U.S. Relations—*See also 'Human Rights' and 'Middle East' above, 'U.S.-Soviet' subheads below*
Ex-CIA employe arrested as spy 12-22-76, 41B2
US emb discounts microwave threat 1-4, 22F1
US vs E Ger Berlin visas 1-6, 7E2; 1-11, 20F1
US arrests 3 as spies 1-6, 1-7, 1-16, 41D2-D3
CIA mail-opening prosecutn barred 1-14, 41E3
Polluted drinking water rptd in Moscow housing 1-15, 47C2
Toon received as amb 1-18, 47A2
US emb blood, water tests ordrd, microwave link denied 1-19, 1-21, 161G1-A2
Solzhenitsyn US publishing co rptd 1-21, 140F3
Australia denies chrgs on US bases 1-25, 81A2
US boxing tourn results 1-29, 2-3, 2-5, 263F1
Carter sees Dobrynin 2-1, 84D1
NBC gets '80 Olympics 2-1, 130G3
Sovt sailor defects 2-8, 117G1
Carter asks more RFE, Radio Liberty funds 3-22, 229F3; USSR scores 3-24, 226G2
Carter poll standings 4-4, 251D1, F1
Kissinger scores re Zaire invasn 4-5, 261E1 ★
Young on Sovt role in Africa 4-5, 4-11, 271D3, 272A1, E2
US denies rift re Zaire 4-12, limits Africa role 4-13, 265B2
US bars union reps 4-16, 306F2
US rpts arms shipmts to Mozambique 4-24, 456E3
US convicts 2 as spies 4-28, 344A2; 5-15, 409C3
Ex-CIA employe convicted 5-5, 409D2
US ambs on Africa role 5-9—5-12, 398B3
CIA mail surveillance damages backed 5-12, 423B1
China sees possible war 5-13, 449E2
Cooperation pact, UN conv signed 5-18, 400A3
Carter outlines policy, stresses detente 5-22, 397E1-D2
Vows no tension after US S Korea exit 6-5, 440F3
Cubans in Africa held USSR 'surrogates' 6-5, 456A1
US rpt chrgs Helsinki non-compliance 6-6, reactn 6-8, 6-13, 473C1
Toon confrmd amb 6-7, 500C1
Carter for aggressive policy 6-10, 460D2
US gen reprimanded for speech 6-17, 482E3
Brezhnev, Giscard stress detente; Brezhnev scores US 'ideological war' 6-21—6-22, 494D3, 495C1
Vance: ties 'satisfactory' 6-24, 495A2
Microwave harm ruled out 6-27, 530D1
Carter asks Brezhnev talks 6-30, Brezhnev vs 7-5, 515D1, 529F3
Vance vs Africa arms race 7-1, 535D3
US track meets 7-1—7-3, 602D2
Toon Independnc Day speech barred 7-4, 529G3
Brezhnev sees Toon 7-5, 529E3
Sovt telephone monitoring revealed 7-10, 551E1-C2
Carter defends policy, downplays eavesdropping 7-12, 533B1, C2
Double agent's release sought 7-14, Ford '76 letter rptd 7-15, 564B2
US sentences spy to life 7-18, 576F3
Sovt study scores US Jews' policy role 7-22, 589G1
US notes Egypt-Libya conflict restraint 7-28, 574B3
Arbatov scores Carter policies 8-3, 590D1
CIA sees '80s econ problems 8-8, 948F3-949C1
Castro, Church discuss detente 8-10, 653G3
Sovt Uganda envoy defectn rptd 8-11, 606F2
Brezhnev positive on Carter Charleston speech 8-16, 640B2
CIA blamed in double agent's disappearance 8-17, 640D3
Embassy fire 8-26—8-27, 673F2
S Africa A-test rptdly headed off 8-28, 8-29, 663A3
US scored re W Bank setlmts 9-2, 685C2
Looting rptd in emb fire 9-2; Pravda scores rpts 9-6, 766D1
US publishers at book fair 9-6, 9-14, 765E3
US sentences 2d spy 9-12, 732E3
'72 drugging of Nixon staff suspected 9-21, 721A3
Improved ties seen 9-23, 750E3
Gromyko addresses UN 9-27, 769F2
US exchng scholar denied visa 10-3, 766G2
US House subcom queries NBC Olympic deal 10-4, 950C1
Panama Canal interest disputed in US 10-10, 792G1
Brzezinski sees improved ties 10-18, 866D1
KGB tries to blackmail US envoy 10-19; US protests 10-19—10-31, 866C2-B3
5-yr health pact renewed 10-28, 866A2
CIA lists USSR-owned cos 10-31, 949E1
Blackmail in US spy recruitmt chrgd 11-7, 866B3
Travel curbs cited 11-9, 989E1
Carter sees Dobrynin, gets Brezhnev note 11-18, 894E3
Young scores Africa role 12-6, 1011A3
Carter sees Brezhnev visit after SALT pact 12-28, 1002C1

1978

U.S. Relations—*See also 'Guyana Cult' and 'Human Rights' above, 'U.S.-Soviet' subheads below*
US emb personal contacts rptd curbed 1-5, 21A1
US chrgs 'proxy war' in Viet-Cambodia clashes 1-8; USSR scores 1-9, Viet 1-16, 9C2, 43E1
Carter scores Africa role 1-12, 12E1
US, USSR meet on A-satellite fall 1-12, 1-17; defend cooperatn 1-27, 1-28, 57B1, D2
US, USSR oust envoys 1-19, 39E1
US, allies meet on Ethiopia 1-21, 43F2
Carter warns vs Ethiopia role; urges Africa, Mideast cooperatn 1-25, 43D3
US A-safety team visits 2-5—2-18, protocol rptd 2-22, 202B1
US assured vs Somalia invasn, vows neutrality 2-8, 2-10, 99A3
US Sen debates Panama Canal pact 2-8, 120F1
US ouster of Viet UN amb protested 2-9, 103A3
US defends Mideast jet sales 2-17, 123D2
Envoys barred from open areas 2-17, 230E1
Brezhnev scores US Mideast peace stand 2-21, 139F2
US ups Ethiopia troops, arms estimates 2-24, 2-25; issues warning 2-25, 137A1; 3-2, 140E2
Piper's notes seized 3-2, US protests 3-8, 180D1
US urges Ethiopia exit 3-7—3-9, 194A1
Vance sees Dobrynin on Ethiopia troops 3-12; US modifies statemt on USSR vow 3-15, 215F3
Israel Leb invasn complicity chrgd 3-15, 175B1
Shevchenko renounces Sovt citizenship 4-10, defects to US 4-26; CIA, FBI links alleged 4-21, 302A2
Puka rptd held in Moscow 4-12, 275G2; returns to US 4-28, 360A1
Grigorenko gets US asylum 4-19, 275E2
Vance in Moscow 4-20—4-23, 297A1
US mediates Korean jet passengers release 4-20—4-23, 302F1
S Korea troop exit slowdown opposed 4-22, 301F3
3-way spy swap 4-23—5-1; Shcharansky, other exchngs rptd discussed 4-24, 318A2
Wyeth elected to Sovt Acad 4-24, 335D3
Carter scored by GOP sens 5-3, 342E2
Carter scores Africa role 5-5, 342E1
S Korea puppet regime chrgd 5-7, 349B3
CIA propaganda effort in '75 Angola war chrgd 5-8, 367G2
USSR sentences food tech as spy 5-15, 416G2
Carter scores Cong Africa curbs 5-19, Young rebuts 5-21, 383A1, F1
Pak seeks new US role 5-19, 391A2
Brzezinski scores China, Africa policy 5-20—5-22, 384F2, B3
U^c scientists, HEW secy cancel visits 5-20—5-30, 401C1
US arrests 2 as spies, asks 3d to leave 5-20, 409G2
Carter stresses unified Admin policy 5-23, 510A1
IISS scores US Africa policy 5-24, 488C1
Carter condemns Africa role 5-25, 418C1
Brzezinski scores Africa policy, detente 5-28; Pravda rebuts 5-30, 399B1
US emb bugging rptd 6-1, 6-2; chrgs traded 6-8, 6-9, 476B1
W Ger chancellor rpts Carter briefed on Brezhnev visit 6-1, 519A2
US scientists cancel trip 6-2, 504B1
US exhibit guides ousted 6-5, US regrets 6-6, 476A2
Solzhenitsyn commencemt address scores West 6-8, 444A2 ★ -G3
UPI Leningrad bur rptd closed 6-12, 476B2
US businessman Crawford seized, spy arrests retaliatn cited 6-12; chrgd 6-17, 476B2; Carter scores 6-26, 491E1
USSR bares Peterson expulsn as spy 6-12, 476A3
Carter warning scored by Kremlin; Cold War era cited, detente stressed 6-17, 464C3, 465C1
Vance asserts role as Carter policy rep, outlines US-Sovt course re detente, Africa 6-19, 490D2
Vance outlines US Africa policy, scores USSR 6-20; Tass rebuts 6-22, 487D1, E2, B3
Carter stresses unified US policy 6-20, 6-23, 6-26, 490D2-491F1
Yugo warns: detente 'broken down' 6-20, 519D2
Slepak sentncd, '77 spy chrg cited 6-21, 503G3
US-China ties scored by Brezhnev 6-25, 488A3; Carter replies 6-26, 491B1
2 Sovt spy suspects, Crawford freed 6-26, 506E1
Piper, Whitney chrgd re Georgia dissident trial 6-28; US warns 6-29, Vance, Dobrynin meet 7-1; statemts 7-3, 518B1-F2
US reviews Sovt rptrs status 6-30, 7-5, 518F2
Rhodesia forgn min: US lacks 'guts' re Sovt Africa role 6-30, 615F2
Dual track meets 7-7—7-9, 692B3
Intl Harvester suspends deals re Crawford 7-16, 575D3
Piper, Whitney convicted, press retractns asked, denied; US to study Tass San Fran bur status 7-18, 575C2
Carter denies 'vendetta' 7-20, 549B2

1979

U.S. Relations—*See also 'Guyana' and 'Human Rights' above, 'U.S.-Soviet' subheads below; also CUBA–Soviet Relations*
US worried re Viet-Cambodia war 1-5, 11B1; 1-17, 30A1
Westn-natn Guadeloupe summit reassures re US-China ties 1-6, 12D2
Shevchenko marriage rptd 1-8, 79D1
Vance, Brzezinski on China-US tie 1-15; Admin controversy denied 1-16, 27B2
Carter reassures re China ties 1-17, 29E3
US-China communique criticizes, US reassures 2-1, 65B2, D2
Teng visit to US scored 2-1, 2-4, 84D1
GOP sees Admin misconceptns 2-3, 86D1
US sci group in Moscow 2-5–2-7, 100C1
Sovts get plea on Asia fighting 2-9, 106C3
US rights rpt omits 2-10, 107A2
US protests role in death of US amb to Afghan 2-14, 106F2
Iran broadcasts prompt US protests 2-14–2-16, 125D3
USSR regrets death of US amb to Afghan, denies blame 2-16–2-17; US cable rebuts 2-22, 147D2
US seeks China-Sovt restraint 2-17, 122D3
US role in China-Viet invasn chrgd 2-19–2-20, 122B2
Carter warns vs Iran interventn 2-20, 123B3
Oswald KGB substitutn cited 2-23, 166A3
Gromyko: Viet invasn imperils US ties 2-26, 141G2
US questns Yemen mil role 2-28, 144E2; countered 3-8, advisers denied 3-14, 179E1
US influence re Israel-Egypt pact feared 3-15, 178C2
US drops Sterns '57 spy chrgs 3-22, 232C1
US warns vs mil aid to Afghan govt 3-23, rpts airlift increase 3-28, 232F3
US intell on China-Viet war praised 3-25, 232B1
Sovt suicide in US Emb 3-28, 237E3
US A-accident reactn 4-4, 246B3
18 reps visit, ties improvemt seen 4-13–4-22, 314G1
US backs Norway in Svalbard dispute 4-17, 299D2
US protests UK rptr's abuse chrg 4-20, 390F1-A2
2 Sovt spies exchngd for Ginzburg, 4 other dissidents 4-27, 317A1
US Emb invaded, fired on by citizen 4-27, 360F3
US defends 'new diplomacy' 5-1, 347A2
US fears African escalatn re Rhodesia sanctns end 5-15, 359C2
Jackson scores Sovt policies 6-12, 459F2
Carter, Brezhnev hold Vienna summit 6-15–6-18, 449A1; communique text 457A1-458E2
Sovts deny bases in Vietnam 6-23, 474F2
Sovt spy suspected in FBI 6-24, 521B1
US Emb constructn set 6-30, land swap OKd 7-13, 568G1
Carter energy plan assessed 7-16, 535B1
US House com issues final rpt on JFK death 7-17, 538C1
Control Data to sponsor art show 7-19, 672E2
US-USSR plan for UNTSO use set 7-24, 551B1
Watson confrmd amb 8-1; Toon leaves 10-16, Watson replaces 10-17, 794D3-795A1
USSR extends rptr's visa 8-3, 636G3
Swedish envoy '45 disappearance case reopened 8-4, 690C2
US newsman linked to KGB 8-11, 611E1
Bolshoi dancer defects 8-23; US detains wife 8-24, releases 8-27, 644D3-645F1
4 barred from book fair 8-23–9-5, US books seized 9-4, 689F3-690G1
China urges US oppose hegemony 8-25; US stresses better ties with China, USSR 8-28, 644B3
2 more Bolshoi dancers defect 9-16, 697C2
US 'tricks' chrgd re UN vote for Pol Pot govt seat 9-22, 741B2
Nixon backs US-China ties 9-22, 751C2
US rpts Kurile buildup 9-26, 742C1
Concert tour canceled, defectns cited 9-27, 774G3
US defns secy visit to Japan scored 10-16; talks note Kuriles 10-20, 803C3
Oswald KGB substitutn theory discounted 10-22, 905A3
Newsman flies to US after Japan defectn 10-24, 856D3
US denies Sovt A-sub mishap caused A-blast 10-26, 824E3
US asks calm in S Korea crisis 10-27, 822F1
Cambodia joint aid airlift urged 11-1, 863A3
2 seized near US Emb 11-6, 856B3
USSR mil aided by research exchngs 11-8, 857B1, C1
US Emb in Iran called spy cntr, US protests 11-10; Iran broadcast criticism rejctd. hostage release aid vowed 11-13, 878G2

1980

U.S. Relations—*See also 'Human Rights', 'U.S. Presidential Election (& Transition)', 'U.S.-Soviet Trade'; also AFGHANISTAN--Soviet Military Intervention, PAKISTAN--Soviet-Afghan Issue, PERSIAN Gulf*
NATO A-missile deploymt, missile talks rejectn linked 1-3, 4A3
US-China mil talks opposed 1-7, 11F2; Brown rejcts criticism 1-11, 31G1
US cuts Aeroflot flights 1-8, 9D1
Turkey-US base accord set 1-9, 22G2
US' Meany opposed detente 1-10, 14E3
Aerflot flights boycotted in NY, DC 1-11, 55C2; 1-18, 1-22, 45E1
Connally sees Iran role 1-11, 91F3
NYC Aeroflot office bombed 1-13, 55A2
Alaska gov cites visit 1-15, 268C3
US distrusts gold mkt 1-18, 30F2
Japan arrests 3 as spies 1-18, 60D1
Carter State of Union topic 1-21, 1-23, 41A1, E1-C2, 42C1, 43D3
Canada expels 3 as spies 1-21, 56F2
US spy prison escape rptd 1-22, 55F1
Tass scores Carter speech 1-24, 43A3
CIA estimates '79 outlays, ICBM spending compared 1-27, 65D2
Carter budget proposals 1-28; US-Sovt spending data cited; Carter budget called too low 70A3-F3
Pentagon sees Sovt naval threat 1-29, 65A2
Sovt-bloc visits rptd canceled, detente strains blamed 1-30, 103F1
Aeroflot radar tampering probed 1-31, USSR to end NY flights 2-4, 114F3, 115C1
Brezhnev backs detente, US-Eur split rptd sought 2-4, 84D3; offcls affirm stance 2-7, 106C3
China compares US, Sovt strength 2-5, 108B1
US pressure on France, W Ger chrgd 2-6, 84C3
US vows Yugo defns 2-13, 110D1
AFL-CIO scores Admin 2-19, 146G3
US blames re Afghan amb '79 death 2-20, 140B1
Kosygin scores US policies 2-21, 153B1
US bars scientists from 2 intl confs 2-22, 135C1
US sets ceiling for Sovt envoys, rptrs 2-22, 139G3
Soviet double agent introduced 3-3, 189F1
UN anti-Israel vote disavowal opposed 3-5, 163G3
CIA alleged agents listed 3-7, 189G2
US computer warning system rptd unreliable 3-10, 210A3
US tank detector system rptd 3-21, 267D1
Vance on US goals 3-27, 243B3
US short-range cruise missile contract set 4-2, 267B3
Tourist, envoy harassmt rptd 4-11, 4-18, 4-11, 4-18, 431F1
W Ger: US urges E Eur trade sanctns vs USSR 4-17, 303A3
US rpts killer satellite test 4-18, 365B2
W Ger sees war threat 4-20, 303D1
Italy CP vs anti-Sovt front 4-22, 314B2
Iran hostage rescue try scored 4-27, 324B1, 352A1
US MX deploymt rptd chngd 5-6, 369D2
Muskie: USSR ties top priority 5-7, 343C1
Carter on Sovt threats 5-9, 367G1
US arms outlay rise urged 5-9, 369G2-C3
Warsaw Pact backs detente 5-15, 378A1
Muskie, Gromyko meet 5-16; W Ger, France note 5-19, 5-21 378A1, D3, 379D1
US scores Cambodia aid conf boycott 5-26, 397B2
US OKs China tech sales 5-29, 398A1
US concerned re India arms pact 5-29, 398C1
Joint Chiefs score Carter defns budget 5-29, 424F2
US computer errors trigger A-alerts 6-3, 6-6, failed component blamed 6-17; valid warnings detailed 6-15, 457C3-458C2
W Ger warned vs NATO A-missiles 6-12, 451D1
Carter: detente goal 6-20, 474B2
W Ger vs Carter trip criticism 6-21, 473E1
Dem platform backs MX 6-24, 479D3
US seeks Viet Thai raid halt 6-25, 6-26, 508B2
'79 anthrax cover-up chrgd 6-29, 500A1
Carter lauds Schmidt trip 7-2, 489E1
US Independnc Day broadcast barred, Carter shunned 7-4, 566B3
US arms lift to Thais scored 7-5, 508C1
US, China, Japan 'axis' chrgd 7-8; Carter-Hua mtg scored 7-10, 506C1, F1
Trigon-Kissinger spy controversy rptd 7-14—10-4, 753F3
US revises A-war strategy 8-5, 591D3
Chem weapons use chrgd 8-7, 628C3
US reassures allies on A-strategy shift, Muskie not consulted 8-8; shift scored 8-11, 615C2-616B1
Moynihan warns of 'Soviet empire' 8-11, 612C3
Muskie regrets A-strategy ommissn, sees enhanced role 8-13, 630E2
VOA broadcasts jammd 8-20, reactn 8-21, 626D2, C3
US A-strategy outlined, ICBM vulnerability seen 8-20, 630D1
US 'stealth' fighter said to evade radar 8-20, 630B2
Canada immigratn records rptd found 8-20, 651F1-C2

1976

Brezhnev affirms detente 10-25, 839B2, C2
Drug culprits lose appeal 10-26, 857F1
US warns re southn Africa talks 10-29, 832B1
US prof denied visa 10-31, 907E3
US rpt scores NATO sales 11-4, 880B1
US cong comm barred 11-5, 880G1
Aeroflot employe arrested in US 11-10, Moscow arrests Pan Am employe 11-24, 907D3
Moscow Bicentennial show opens 11-11, bomb scare closes 11-17, 907F3
US recovers sunken F-14 11-11, 941F1
US envoy return barred; US bar of Sovt cited 11-17, 907B3
Brezhnev, Tito rptdly cite US electns re detente 11-18, 910A1
Yugo vows tech safeguards 11-25—11-27, 1012C1
Helsinki progress rpts issued 12-2, 12-8, 934E1
Scholar exchngs canceled 12-7, 12-20, 1011E1
2d Bicentennial bomb threat 12-8; show ends 12-13, 948A2
Brzezinski on detente 12-16, 936C3
US mediates Chile prisoner exchng 12-18, 955E2
FCC rpts on radio interference 12-28, 1011D1

1977

U.S.-Soviet Defense Developments—*See also DISARMAMENT—U.S.-Soviet*
US rpt on Sovt aims, power stirs controversy 12-26-76—1-18, 39E2
US defns secy sees Sovt threat, urges buildup 1-18, 39C1
Brezhnev scores US rpt 1-18, 70G1
US rpt debate continues 2-28, 3-11, CIA dir sees Sovt edge 3-20, 211C3
Carter asks Indian O restraints 3-17, 186B1
US cites '75 chem warfare push 3-21, 232G1
Ford notes Sovt buildup 3-23, 236F2
Podgorny asks Indian O demilitarizatn 3-24, 247C3
Antimissile beam rptd 5-2, US discounts 5-2, 5-3, 343D3
Carter warns NATO on buildup 5-10, 358A3
NATO Berlin warning scored 5-14, 496F2
US study discounts civil defns effort 5-16, 421E1
Defns spending, GNP data compared 5-17, 379F3
US computer sale opposed 6-5, 469G2
Indian O demilitarizatn talks 6-22—6-27, 530C1
US bars computer sale 6-23, 501D3
Carter vs B-1, backs cruise missile 6-30; Sovt reactn 7-3, 514A3, F3
Carter seeks Indian O demilitarization 6-30, 515C1
Sovt advances held more costly 6-30, tech compared 8-22, 673D3
Carter defends policy, defers neutron bomb 7-12, 533D1, F1
Carter reassures on detente, notes Indian O talks 7-21, 550E2
Somalia offered US arms aid 7-26, 587G3
Arbatov scores US cruise missile, neutron bomb dvpt 8-3, 590G2
US cruise missile, neutron bomb protests continue 8-9, 8-16, 640E2
USSR sub superiority rptd by '77-78 Jane's 8-25, 686D2
IISS assesses A-arms balance 9-2, 686B2
Brookings study sees need for focused US buildup 9-26, 858A1
Indian O ship deploymt rptd 9-26; talks end 12-10, 999A2
Gromyko backs A-test ban 9-27, 770B1
Cruise missile held ineffective 10-29, Pentagon defends 11-1, 857C3
Mil lecture exchng rptd 10-30, 866F1
US Cong clears cruise missile '78 supplemental authorizatn 11-3, 856F1

1978

Carter vs Olympics boycott 7-20, 549C3
US emb aide manhandled 7-20; US protest rptd rejctd 7-24, 575A3
US HUD trip canceled 7-25, 575C3
US emb employee barred entry; other incidents cited 7-27, 634D1
Japan warns on US-USSR confrontatn 7-28, 585E2
Piper, Whitney pay fines 8-4, new retractn deadline set 8-7, 634A1
USSR scores China policy 8-5, 675G3
Piper, Whitney case closed 8-18, 651E1; warned by Forgn Min 8-24, 670C2
Hammer sees Brezhnev, Crawford trial discussed 8-25, 670A2
Sovt UN aide promoted despite US spy chrgs 8-29, 676E1
Kennedy visits 9-4—9-10, sees Brezhnev 9-9, 742F3
7 US anti-war protesters seized 9-4, 947B2
Crawford trial opens 9-5, sentence suspended 9-7, leaves USSR 9-8, 742B3
Pan Am to end NY-Moscow svc 9-7, 701F1
PR called colony by UN panel 9-13, 979E3
JFK death com rpts surveillance of Oswald; US treatmt of defector cited 9-15, 749C3
Carter asks Leb truce role 10-5, 761B1
2 Sovts convicted as spies 10-13, sentenced 10-30, 835A2; USSR demands return 11-4, 863E1
US amb scored by Pravda 10-14, 821B1
USSR chrgs US backs China arms sales 10-26, 814C1
Dow dir refused exit 11-7, 884B3
CIA mail surveillnc damages upheld 11-9, 940D1
Nixon backs Iran shah 11-11, 900A3
US sens visit; see Brezhnev, other ldrs 11-11—11-18, 905C1
Carter on Sovt motives 11-13, 914D2
US warned vs Iran interventn, US rebuts 11-19, 893D3
US emb study discounts Sovt microwave harm 11-20, 924E3
Vance sees improved ties 11-25, 925B1
Dow dir cleared 12-1, 966E1
Blumenthal in Rumania, denies threat to USSR 12-8—12-9, 965C3-966A1
Carter links summit, SALT 12-12, 957D1
US-Peking ties agreed 12-14, 973C1
US briefs on China ties 12-15, 976G1
Eur, Asia laud US-China ties 12-15, 12-16, 977B1
Brezhnev, others 'positive' on US-China ties 12-16, 12-19, 976E1
Carter: relatns unaffected re US-China ties 12-19, 976F1
Brezhnev denies 'positive' on US-China ties 12-21, 995E1
CIA ex-aide sentncd 12-22, 1011C3
Iran interventn chrgs traded 12-28, 994F1
US House com discounts JFK murder role 12-30, 1002C2

U.S.-Soviet Defense Developments—*See also DISARMAMENT—U.S.-Soviet*
A-parity, USSR conv edge in Eur seen 1-6, 5E2
NATO warned vs neutron bomb deploymt 1-23, 103C2
Brookings study sees Sovt air threat 1-29, 81B3
Carter urges satellite safety rules, A-ban; discounts mil threat 1-30, 57E2, 62G2-A3
Pentagon urges US arms buildup; US, Sovt dvpts detailed 2-2, 81A1
US observes mil maneuvers 2-6—2-10, 103A2
Brezhnev seeks Austria aid vs neutron bomb deploymt 2-8, 110E2
US ex-aide: USSR sought '69 joint A-attack vs China 2-16, 124A2
CIA sees civil defns overrated, DIA disputes 2-17, 126G3
US affirms Asia, Pacific mil commitmt 2-20, 126C3
Sovt campaign vs neutron bomb scored, SS-20 deploymt cited 2-21, 140D1, G1
Sovt SS-16 deploymt rptd 2-22, 298G1
US Navy combat capability gains seen; Sovt sub, Backfire bomber threat 2-23, 127B2
US, Sovt arms, systems compared 3-6, 162E3-F3
Carter warns vs mil buildup, interventn; USSR scores 3-17, 202C1-A3
US shipbldg goals cut 3-24, 223A3
Carter defers neutron bomb, asks comparable Sovt restraint 4-7; USSR scores decision, calls 'maneuver' 4-7, 4-8, 253A1, 254C1
Brezhnev proposes neutron bomb restraints, Carter discounts offer 4-25, 297A2, 307A2
Haig resignatn threat rptd, cruise missile talks cited 4-25, 298F2
Carter scored by GOP sens 5-3, 342G2
US arrests 2 as spies, asks 3d to leave 5-20, 409G2
US sees anti-sub tech edge 5-24, 407B3
US rpts killer satellite test 5-24, 488F2
Cruise missile effectiveness held by US 6-1, 407F2
Chem warfare reemphasis rptd 6-5, 433E1
Carter warns re detente, scores Sovt system; Tass replies 6-7, 423D2-424F1
Killer satellite talks 6-8—6-16, 488E2
US detectn device sale bar cited 6-9, 436C2

1979

Reagan vs appeasemt 11-13, 866D2; 11-14, 982C1
US oil estimates disputed 11-19, 929A1
US backed in UN debate on Iran 12-1—12-2, 913F1
US mil 'blackmail' vs Iran chrgd, Vance scores 12-5, 913E2
UN missn in NYC bombed 12-12, US scored 12-13, 965C3
US confrms Saudi mosque raid role 12-16, 997B1
Baker compares US image 12-19, 983D1
US warns vs Iran sanctns veto 12-22, 974B2

U.S.-Soviet Defense Developments—*See also CUBA-Soviet Relations, DISARMAMENT-U.S.-Soviet Developments*
'74-77 arms sales compared 1-7, 13G1
Sovt beam-weapon threat discounted 1-10, 52F3
US mil ex-ldrs warn of Sovt challenge 1-12, 15A1
US A-target chng urged 1-13, 52A3
Carter sees no Sovt edge 1-17, 29F3
CIA rpts Iran monitor closure 1-18, 26F2
Carter budget proposals 1-22, 42F1
Microwave source rptd destroyed 1-22, 60D2
Carter State of Union Message 1-23, 47D3, 48E1
CIA ex-offcl's death probe urged 1-24, 55D1
Pentagon stresses Sovt arms threat 1-25, 52A2
GOP sees Admin misconceptns 2-3, 86D1
US civil defns spending hike favored 2-4, 89A2
China warning on USSR strength rptd 2-5, 65D2
US response to Sovt surrogates urged 2-8, 89B2
US concerned re Iran F-14 safety; intellignc monitor protectn rptd 2-12, 106D1; 8-10, 634F3
Iran bars intell posts 2-21, US personnel flee 2-24—2-28, 145F1
CIA ex-agent cleared of Sovt spy chrg 2-27, 152D3
GOP scores Carter defns policy 3-1, 165A3
US missile info leak alleged 3-1, 207E2
ESP experimts cited in '50s CIA files 3-11, 208F2
Sovts warned on Cam Ranh base use 3-28, 340F2
Trident sub launch watched 4-10, 307B3
US ex-mil ldrs chrg Sovt expansnism 4-11, 295G1
Indian O naval activity rise rptd 4-12, 4-16, 313E3-314A1
Carter concerned re US missile vulnerability 4-25, 294G2
US spy satellite data rptd compromised 4-28, 318F2
US OKs XM-1 tank productn 5-8, 386F1
'79, '72 strategic weapons compared 338E3

1980

US discounts Iran invasn plan, Sovt interventn feared 8-25, 644A2
Reagan scores 'stealth' plane disclosure; Brown, Perry testify on leaks 9-4, 665F3
US union OKs Polish worker fund 9-4; Warsaw protests 9-9—9-10, Muskie forewarning rptd 9-11, 679G1-D2
US grants Poland $670 mln grain credit 9-12, 710B3
Sovt A-test rptd 9-14, US protests 9-15, 730F1
Sovt soldr in Afghan seeks US Emb asylum 9-15; US bars release 9-16, chrgs emb pressure 9-17, 704G2
Sovt ICBMs rptd accurate, said US threat 9-18, 730E3
'81 refugee quota rptd 9-19, 883B3
Filatov rptd alive 9-23—9-24; ID controversy rptd 10-4, 753E3
Gromyko, Muskie meet on Iran-Iraq war 9-25, 719A2
Missile force data traded 9-26, 776G3
US blamed for Iran-Iraq war 9-30, US notes Sovt restraint 10-7, 758E1, A3
US MX distortn rptd 10-5, 897E1
US scientific literacy lag rptd 10-22, 990C1
Ex-CIA agent indicted on espionage 10-24, pleads guilty 10-29, 855G2
US computer error A-alert rpt issued 10-29, 986B3
Muskie: USSR seeks better ties 11-23, 915A2
Sovts vs IMF Pak loan 11-25, 904D3
USSR warned vs Poland mil interventn 12-2, 12-3, 910G2, B3
US Sen Percy support of Palestine state rptd 12-5, 931C1
Carter aide cleared in spy leak 12-5, 940B2
US rpts Poland invasn preparatn complete 12-7; US dispatches AWACS 12-7, 929F2, 930B1
Brezhnev offers Persian Gulf peace plan 12-10; US rejects 12-11, 930D1
Sovt '79 3d World arms sales rptd up 12-10, 933A2
Muskie lauds NATO warning re Poland 12-12, 949C1
Percy rpts on visit 12-12, 950A3
US warns on Polish invasn 12-19, 950E1

U.S. -Soviet Defense Developments—*See 'U.S. Relations' above; DISARMAMENT & Arms Control—U.S.-Soviet Developments*

1976

1977

US concerned re Ethiopia aid vow 11-17, 896B2
Carter B-1 cancellatn scored by Jane's 12-7, 942B1
NATO sees Sovt T-80, hovercraft threat 12-8, 941D3
Arms sale curbs discussed 12-14—12-16; US, USSR '77 sales cited 996E3

U.S.-Soviet Trade Developments
US grain imports to continue 1-5, 22A1
Sweden to settle US-Sovt business disputes 1-11, 29F3
Philip Morris deal set 1-17, 47F2
US grain shipping pact terms set 2-7, 161A1
US adopts fishing agrmt 2-21, 173D3
Bukovsky urges US trade, rights link 2-23, 142C3
US warns Sovt trawlers 3-1, 147G1
'76 Sovt trade deficit up; import, export data rptd 3-9, 3-21, 285G1
2 US execs sentncd for sales violatns 3-14, 203E2
US bars Rhodesian chrome 3-18, 191E1
US rpts fishing violatns 3-28—4-4; 2 vessels seized 4-9, 4-10, Sovts warned 4-5, 4-11, 269G3
US grain shipping pact OKd 3-30, 306C2
Carter asks US plutonium ban 4-7, 268G1
US fishing rules ordrd observed 4-14; Sovt vessels freed 4-14, 5-5, 363B3
US CIA oil import forecast 4-18, 294F1
A-suppliers conf scores Carter plans 4-28—4-29, 403F1-A2
US computer sale opposed 6-5, 469F2
US import cuts seen 6-10; trade, credit curbs cited 6-11, 530E1
US bars computer sale 6-23, 501D3
Record Sovt grain crop seen 7-7, 619D1
Carter seeks arms sales curbs 7-28, 574A3
US grain sales announced 8-9, 8-12, 640B3
1st ½ trade rptd 9-12, 766G1
US grain ceiling lifted 10-6, shipping rate pact extended 10-17, USSR purchases rptd 10-31—11-15, 948C3
CIA rpts '76 Sovt arms sales, econ aid 10-13, 949A2
Grain shortfall rptd 11-2, 948C2
USSR econ exhibit opens 11-12, 988C2
US grain sales cited 11-15, 11-30, 916F2, G2
Agri talks 12-12—12-14, pact extended 12-13; total grain purchases cited 12-14, 1017G2

1978

Hungary compares troops 6-10, 534B3
Vance pledges A-arms restraint 6-12, 445A2
US rptd worried re Sovt mil 'equality', not 'superiority' 6-17, 464E3
US civil defns reorganizatn proposed 6-19, 466A3
New Sovt A-bomber rptd 6-19, 518E3
US tests cruise missile 6-21, 493B2
US affirms mil superiority; concedes Sovt troop threat in Eur, NATO weakness 6-23, 493D2
USSR arms spending studied; SALT impact discounted, '80s forecast issued 6-27, 563A3
US surveillnc bases in Turkey seen reopening 6-28, 587C3
US Sen OKs '79 arms authrzn 7-11, 526C2
New US land-based missile plan rptd 7-12, 528G3
US arms sales policy assessed 7-16, 564A2
CIA issues civil defns study 7-19, 563F3
'76 arms spending rptd 7-23, 585B2
US pro-defns cong coalitn formed 8-8, 604C3
'79 defns funds pass US House 8-9, 604D2
Carter vetos '79 arms authorzn 8-17, 621D1, 622A1
CIA ex-employe arrested by FBI 8-17, 645D2
Brezhnev rptly wants Carter mtg 8-25, 670B2
US A-power edge seen by ACDA 8-29, 676G3
A-arms balance assessed by IISS 9-1, 676B3
Kennedy sees Brezhnev on SALT 9-9, 743A1
US reps protest MAP missile plan 9-22, 737E3
CIA ex-offcl found dead 10-1, Sovt spy link denied 10-5—10-26, 835F3
US bases in Turkey to reopen 10-4, 776G1
A-test ban talks rptd delayed, US 3-yr test-ban order cited 10-5, 995D2
2 Sovts convicted as spies 10-13, sentncd 10-30, 835A2; USSR demands return 11-4, 863E1
Shevchenko denies CIA financed gifts 10-13, 844A3
Sovt anti-cruise missile success rptd, ships rptd armed 10-23, 877C2
Carter neutron parts productn order scored 10-26, 833E2
US jt chiefs warns of Sovt buildup 10-30, 833A3
USSR Pacific buildup rptd 11-9, 914G1-A2
Carter plans civil defns spending hike 11-12, 895G1
Brezhnev rpts Sovt neutron bomb test 11-17, 905D1
CIA ex-aide convctd 11-18, satellite manual helps USSR 11-23, 940F1, G2
Carter bars arms sales 11-30, 936F2
US discounts anti-cruise missile success 12-26, 1020C3

U.S.-Soviet Trade Developments
Pepsico-vodka sales deal expanded 1-10, 20D3
US, USSR oust envoys 1-19, 39E1
Brezhnev scores trade pact delay 2-24, US links Ethiopia role 2-25, 137B1
USSR cancels grain order 2-28, probes delay 3-2; total US purchases cited 151E2
Dow signs 10-yr cooperatn pact 2-28, 151F3
Coca-Cola chosen for '80 Olympics 3-14, Fanta deal rptd 3-16, 230C1
'77 trade decline rptd 3-29, 229E3-230A1
US aide checks Sovt grain crop 5-9; USSR rpts purchases 5-22; US estimates crop 6-12, 499D2
Dresser contracts rptd 6-1, 499F3
US airborne device sale bar cited 6-9, 436C2
US warns on ship insurance 6-9, 499D3
Carter on rights 'linkage', scores Crawford arrest 6-26, 491C1
Kosygin asks trade hike 7-5, 518C3
US OKs crime equipmt sale 7-6, 10-13, 905B2
Intl Harvester suspends deals 7-16, 575D3
US cancels computer sale; to review oil sales re Shcharansky, Ginzburg sentncs 7-18, 542E1
Carter denies vendetta re computer sale cancellatn 7-20, 549D2
US issues oil equipmt sale rules 7-31, 634F2
US totals grain purchases 8-3, fears import drop 8-10, 634A3
Dresser equipmt sale OKd 8-9, 634D2; 9-6, 743D1
Occidental opens ammonia plant 8-22, 670F1
Intl Harvester resumes sales 9-11, 742F3
US Maritime Comm demands shipping data 9-13, 820F2-A3
US computer, oil equipmt sales cited re Carter 'export consequences' order 9-26, US businessmen score order 10-10, 804G2-A3
Caterpillar equipmt deal rptd 9-29, 821B1
RCA color TV plant deal set 10-5, 821A3
Control Data computer deal set 10-31, 841C1
USSR grain purchase drop seen 11-4, 884E3

1979

US studies high-speed sub 5-17, 390B2
Microwave beams rptd stopped 5-29, 410A1
Brown: USSR seeking 1st-strike ability 5-30, 410G1
Sovt warhead yields estimates lowered 5-31, 410C1
Carter OKs MX dvpt 6-8, Sovts score 6-9, 6-10, 437E3, 438D1
Jackson scores Sovt mil spending 6-12, 459F2
US gen sees Sovt mil dominance in '80s 6-15, 460C1
Carter, Brezhnev exchng chrgs 6-16, 449E1
Carter addresses Cong on SALT II 6-18, 449D2, 458F1
US seeks giant A-blast info 6-27, 625E3
Microwave beams rptd renewed 7-19, 568C2
US halts S Korea troop exit 7-20, 567F2
Kissinger sees Sovt tilt 7-31, 590C3
USSR denies 1st-strike capability, mil budget hike, scores US 8-2, 644F1
USSR steals dummy torpedo 8-9, returns 8-10, 636F3
Carter chooses 'racetrack' MX deployment plan; diagram 9-7, 677F2, 678A2
US H-bomb letter cites security 9-16, 9-18, 714D2, F3
US Defns Dept backs arms to China as counterwght 10-3, Vance reaffirms ban 10-4, 789E1
US Eur missiles scored 10-6; US vs troop cut, missile freeze offer 10-9, 761F1, A3
NATO US A-missiles opposed 10-13–11-6, 880F2
USSR mil aided by trade, research exchngs 11-8, 856E3-857D1
False US A-alert placed 11-9, USSR scores 11-10, 869F2-B3; 11-16, 882D2
NATO group backs US A-missiles 11-14, 880A2
W Ger warned re NATO A-missiles 11-21–11-24, 938A3
US presses NATO re missiles, new SS-20 deploymt detected 12-7, 938F1, A2
Carter links Soviet buildup, US spending hike 12-12, 962F3-963F1
US scored re NATO A-missiles 12-13, 12-14, 12-16, 959G2
US denies Kama truck plant mil use 12-17, 997F2

U.S.-Soviet Trade Developments
'74-77 arms sales compared 1-7, 13G1
Petro coke ship rate rptd OKd 1-25, 60A3
FMC OKs Sovt ship ban 1-29, USSR warns 2-14; Justice, State Depts sue FMC 3-6, 213G2
Sperry computer talks rptd 2-8, 237B3
'78 record trade rptd 3-6, 172E1
'78-79 corn, wheat purchases rptd 3-15, 237D3
US '78 computer sales ban cited 3-27, 237G2
Sperry computer sale OKd 3-29, 287E2
Sovt ship ban delayed 4-6, 287A3
US rep backs curbs suspensn 4-21, 314E1
Trade benefits seen in dissident-spy swap 4-27, 317F1
US rpts on grain orders, purchases 7-2–7-22, 567G3
US, China sign trade pact 7-7, 523C2
US hikes '79, '80 grain sale ceiling 8-1, 636B3
Superphosphoric acid deal rptd 8-5, 597F2
Book fair held, publishing deals set 9-4–9-10, 689F3-690B2
US bars computer parts sale 9-27, 775C1
US OKs '79-80 record grain sale limit, '78-79 sales totaled 10-3, 774B3, F3
Ammonia imports ruled disruptive 10-3, quota asked 10-5, 802B3-803B1
FMC lifts ship ban 10-16, 815F2
Carter OKs China trade benefits 10-23, 834F1
USSR mil aided by US sales 11-8, 856E3-857D1
US rpts grain purchases 11-28, 928C3
US bars ammonia import curbs 12-11, 939D2
Control Data signs energy tech deal 12-14, 997E2
Armco signs steel pact 12-17, 997C2
US denies Kama truck plant mil use 12-17, 997F2
USSR grain purchases rptd 12-20, 997F2

1980

U.S.-Soviet Trade Developments—*See also GRAIN--Soviet Developments*
Alcoa suspends smelter talks 1-3, 9G1
FX jet export OKd 1-4, 16D3
US suspends tech exports 1-4, 1D1; 1-9, 9F1; rejcts licenses 1-11, 28C2
US limits ammonia imports 1-18, 45A2
ILA shipping boycott ends 1-29, 2-1, 169B1
Illegal US tech sales probed 2-14, 135B1
Armco steel deal delay OKd 2-19, 235F3
'79 record total rptd 2-20, 134F3
Citibank office to close, Pan Am to cut staff 2-20, 134G3-135A1
US bars phosphates shipmts, '79 sales cited 2-25, 139D3
US exec sees Brezhnev re phosphate embargo 2-27, 165G1
W Ger compares US policy 3-10, 205E2
Carter asks products ban for Olympics 3-12, 206G1; issues order 3-28, 259C1
US arrests trade spy 5-18, sentenced 8-1, 598B2
Jewish emigratn drop cited 5-24, 467G2-A3
US urges anti-Sovt actns 6-26, 475C1
1st 1/2 '80 value rptd down 50% 8-20, 711B2
US protests French steel deal 9-19, 728D3

1976

UNION Oil Co. of California
Sup Ct bars review of Hartley libel suit ruling 10-4, 807D2
Tanker spills in LA harbor 12-17, 969G1
UNION Planters Corp.
Rptd on FRB 'problem' list 1-22, 111C2
Union Planters National Bank (Memphis)
Rptd on comptroller's 'problem' list 1-26, 113F1
UNIONS—*See under LABOR; specific union*
UNION Texas Petroleum—*See under ALLIED Chemical*
UNIROYAL Inc.
Rubber workers strike 4-21, 308D3
Job bias chrgs, US actn rptd 8-6, 944C2
Firestone, Goodyear strikes end 8-28, 8-29, 648B1
URW pact set 9-7, 866G3
UNITED—*For organizations not listed below, see key word*
UNITED Aircraft Corp.—*See UNITED Technologies Corp.*

UNITED Arab Emirates (Abu Dhabi, Ajman, Dubai, Fujaira, Ras al Khaima, Sharja, Umm al Quwain)—*See also ARAB League, NONALIGNED Nations Movement, OPEC*
Iran recalls amb 1-7, 12G3
Listed as 'not free' nation 1-19, 20E3
Fulbright registers as counsel 1-26, 160C2
Rpt 50,000 Pak residents 2-8, 121A2
Sadat visits, gets aid vow 2-27, 162C1
Joins Egypt aid fund 8-21, 630A1
Dickman confrmd US amb 9-23, 807F3
Oman bank buys IMF gold 10-27, 832E2
Middle East Conflict—*See MIDDLE EAST*

UNITED Automobile, Aerospace and Agricultural Implement Workers of America (UAW) (unaffiliated)
Woodcock lauds Carter 3-4, 179C3
Bargaining session 3-18—3-20, 220B1
Trade Act aid OKd 4-14, 4-26, 348E2
US ends car dumping probe 5-4, reactn 5-5, 321B2
Woodcock backs Carter 5-7, 343D2
Carter edges Udall in Mich 5-18, 357B1
Some Ford workers win Trade Act aid 6-7, 431C2
Chrysler plant strike ends 7-11, 570C2
Auto pact talks 7-19, 7-20, 570E1
Mondale addresses NC group 8-15, 617A3
Picks Ford as target co 8-24, rejects 1st offer 8-31, 669B2
Murphy on GM talks 8-25, 647B1
Strikes Ford 9-14, 689D2
Strikes Deere & Co 10-1—11-9, 847D3
Ford contract ratified 10-12, 789B1
Chrysler pacts set 11-5, 11-7, 847A3
GM strike deadline set 11-8, 847C3
Chrysler pact ratified 11-17, 887G1
GM pact set after 'mini-strike' 11-19, 887C1
Lacayo named Carter aide 11-23, 881E3
GM pact ratified 12-8, 991E1
Woodcock sees Carter 12-9, 937F3
Wins GM vote in South 12-22, 991D1

1977

UNION Oil Co. of California
TV violence curbs rptd 2-15, 157F3
Gulf of Mex gas-productn probe set 2-17, 151F3
Molycorp OKs takeover 4-14, 274F3
ICC sets Alaska pipeline rates 6-28, 498F1
Withdraws from Loop 7-29, 724D3
Washington state sues 8-16, 691E3
UNIONS—*See under LABOR; specific unions*
UNIROYAL, Inc.
Tire-grading case review denied 3-21, 230E2
UNITED—For organizations not listed below, see key word
UNITED Air Lines, Inc.—*See UAL*
UNITED Air Lines v. Evans
Sup Ct rules on seniority 5-31, 461G2
UNITED Air Lines v. McMann
Early retiremt plan backed 12-12, 960G1
UNITED American Bank (Knoxville, Tenn.)
Lance cleared in banking probe 8-18, 625B3

UNITED Arab Emirates (UAE) (Abu Dhabi, Ajman, Dubai, Fujaira, Ras al Khaima, Sharja, Umm al Quwain)—*See also ARAB League, NONALIGNED Nations Movement, OPEC*
UN Assemb member 4C1
Black Africa funds vowed 3-7, 170A2
Arab monetary fund created; hq: Abu Dhabi 4-18, 318C1
Mediates Pak feud 4-29, 348B3
Intl consortium OKs Egypt aid 5-11—5-12, 390C3
W Ger hijackers refuel in Dubai 10-15, pilot praised 10-16, 789D1, A2
State min slain, Syrian forgn min escapes, Black June takes credit 10-25; Syria blames Iraq 10-25, 10-26, 811B3
State min's slayer executed 11-16, 949B3
OPEC $ replacemt sought, $ drop cited 12-6, 933E1
Assad visits re Cairo conf 12-11, 954F2
Arab-Israeli Conflict—*See MIDDLE EAST*
Oil Developments—*See also OPEC*
Ups oil price 1-9, Abu Dhabi productn plan cited 1-10, 11F3, 12E1, G1
Saudis reject oil price compromise 2-6, 107A3
Gulf group aids Egypt 3-25, 390D3
Venez pres in Abu Dhabi 5-1, 362A1
Oil price hiked 7-1, 535D2
UNITED Artists Corp.
Charlie Chaplin dies 12-25, 1024B1
UNITED Automobile, Aerospace and Agricultural Implement Workers of America (UAW) (unaffiliated)
Woodcock scores Nader slur 1-17, 96B1
'76 cong gifts rptd 2-15, 128F1
Woodcock in Viet missn 3-16—3-20, 206B1
Warden confrmd to HEW post 3-29, 272D3
Woodcock named Peking liaison 5-12, 381A2
Conv: Carter, Kennedy address 5-16, 5-17, 381F2; Fraser elected pres 5-18, AFL-CIO reentry study OKd 5-19, 408E1-E2
House weakens '70 clean air bill 5-26, 418C2
Backs Panama Canal pacts 8-30, 679B1; Laxalt scores 9-9, 698B3
AFL-CIO reentry shelved 10-5, 762D1

1978

US bank robber arrested after Sovt diamond deal 11-5, 992C1
US bars arms sales 11-9, 901E3; 11-30, 936F2
Govt, business trade groups in talks 12-4—12-7, 966A1
Brezhnev sees Blumenthal, Kreps 12-6, 966C2

UNION Pacific Corp.
Shenandoah takeover pact lapses 5-15, 404A1
UNIONS—*See under LABOR; specific unions*
UNITAS, Johnny
Ewbank enters Pro Football HoF 7-29, 1025C1
UNITED—For organizations not listed below, see key words
UNITED Air Lines Inc.
United Air Lines hijack attempt foiled 3-13, 212A2
Maternity rule review refused by Sup Ct 3-20, 205G3
Swindler sentenced 4-10, 380D2
Boeing jets ordrd 7-14, 569F3
Pan Am, Natl merger set 9-7, 701A1
NYS maternity leave case refused by US Sup Ct 11-27, 937G1
Fined re Rhodesia pilot training 12-8, 955G3-956A1
Oregon crash kills 10 12-28, 1031D1
UNITED Air Lines v. State Human Rights Appeal Board
Case refused by Sup Ct 11-27, 937A2

UNITED Arab Emirates (UAE) (Abu Dhabi, Ajman, Dubai, Fujaira, Ras al Khaima, Sharja, Umm al Quwain)—*See also ARAB League, NONALIGNED Nations Movement, OPEC*
Dubai expenses rated 1-14, 28G2, B3
Abu Dhabi crown prince, financial adviser accused in US 2-17, 3-18; SEC suit setld 3-19, 204A2, B3
Econ dvpt plans rptd slowed 2-20, 122E1, G1
France signs AIO arms pact; US, UK deals cited 3-14, 237C1 ★
Bhutto death sentnc reversal plea rptd 3-22, 229B1
Islamic, Arab poor-natn aid rise rptd 4-9, 257C2, F2
Arab fund loan to Sudan rptd 8-17, 925F3
UN Assemb member 713F3
Leb pres visits 10-10, 761B2
U.S. Relations
Boeing chrgd re payoffs 7-28, 643B1

UNITED Artists Corp. (UA)—*See TRANSAMERICA Corp.*
UNITED Automobile, Aerospace and Agricultural Implement Workers of America (UAW) (unaffiliated)
McDonnell Douglas struck 1-13—4-16, pact OKd 4-15—4-16, 284F2
S Africa investmt ban rptd 3-6, 193B3
Striking miners get relief aid 3-9, 182E2
Anaconda strike ends 4-3, 284E3
Minn pensn funds law backed by Sup Ct 4-3, 308F3
Ldrs see Carter; rejct wage-restraint plea 5-10, 361F3
USSR trip stayed 7-14, 542B2
Fraser quits Admin labor-mgt panel 7-19, 611G1
Carter health plan scored 7-28, 586G1
10th-leading PAC fund-raiser 9-7, 753C2
GM southn plant pact set 9-11, 699B3
AMC contract signed 9-25, 737G2-C3
Pa VW plant struck 10-9—10-15, revised contract ratified 10-21—10-22, 809C3
Carter anti-inflatn plan backed 10-26, 806F3
United Tech-Carrier merger halt bid rptd 10-30, NY stay lifted 11-10, 896D2
Fraser at Dem midterm conf 12-10, 956A3

1979

UNION Oil Co. of California
Calif offshore lease bid rejctd 8-7, 649F1
US overchrg claim settled 10-18, 849D1
More overchrgs claimed 12-9, 943F1
UNION Pacific Corp.
US land grant easemt right curbed by Sup Ct 3-27, 263B2
Punitive damages vs unions barred by Sup Ct 5-29, 421C3
RR takeover of Rock Island ordered 9-26, 722C3
UNION Packing Co.
'78 beef-price suit setld 10-22, 985E3
UNIONS—*See under LABOR; specific unions*
UNIROYAL Inc.
URW contract talks, wage guides in dispute 2-2—5-9; strike begins 5-9, 344B3
Eur operatns sale set 4-17, 560F3
Ct bars wage-guide contract denial, URW sees setlmt 5-31, 399D3
URW pact reached 6-18, 480B1
Sex bias suit settled 10-23, 885F2
UNIS, Joe
Notre Dame wins Cotton Bowl 1-1, 8A3
UNITARIAN Universalist Association of North America
Carnes dies 3-17, 272C2
Pickett named pres 4-29, 376A2
UNITAS, John
Enters HOF 7-28, 1001C1
UNITED—*For organizations not listed below, see key words*
UNITED Airlines Inc.
Teng luncheon hosted 2-4, 83G3
Fuel shortage forces flight cuts 3-6, 162B2
French-US engines ordrd 3-29, 309B1
IAM strike ends, new fare plans offered 5-24, 402A2
Apr econ indicators drop, strike linked 5-31, 463F2
Allegheny Airlines name chng OKd 6-5, 465A3
DC-10s grounded, travel chaos rptd 6-6, 420G3
Half-fare plan takes effect 7-1, 579A1
Amtrak rpts record May-June record ridership, strike cited 9-8, 726B3

UNITED Arab Emirates (UAE) (Abu Dhabi, Ajman, Dubai, Fujaira, Ras al Khaima, Sharja, Umm al Quwain)/See also ARAB League, NONALIGNED Nations Movement, OPEC
Grumman admits paymts 1-3, 16F1
Abu Dhabi raises oil prices 2-15, 126D1-A2
Egypt recalls envoy 4-7, 278D1
Unifil troops to quit Leb 4-9, 341A2
Egypt ties cut 4-25, 296E1
Egypt aid group disbanded 4-27, 319D2
Arab arms plant in Egypt to close 5-14, 359E3
Abu Dhabi hikes oil prices again 5-17, 360B3
Oil prices hiked 6-28, 473C1
Libya fete attended by Arab ldrs 9-1, 688C3
UN membership listed 695B3
Khomeini envoy ouster cited 9-26, 752B3
At Persian Gulf security conf 10-14—10-16, 804A2
Oil prices hiked 12-13, per barrel price rptd 12-21, 977F1, B2
Sovt Afghan invasn opposed 12-30, 974E2
U.S. Relations
Miller tours Persian Gulf, discusses Iran crisis 11-23—11-28, 896A3
US sets evacuations, travel curbs 11-26, 894G1

UNITED Artists Inc.
Pickford dies 5-29, 432D3
UNITED Automobile, Aerospace and Agricultural Implement Workers of America (UAW) (unaffiliated)
Gulf oil workers settle within US wage guidelines 1-11, 87E1
Conv; Fraser bars US talks role 4-17, 280A1
Collective bargaining on food issues backed by Sup Ct 5-14, 383A3
Ct bars wage-guide contract denial 5-31, 399B3
Fraser warns Admin 6-30; Big 3 contract talks begin 7-16, Chrysler gets no-strike pledge 7-18, 598A1
Okla City GM organizing vote won 7-19, 598F1
Fraser vs Chrysler wage freeze plea, backs natlzn 8-3 662B3
Energy job actn held 8-22, Fraser backs oil industry protest 10-17, 831B2-B3
GM 'ministrikes' staged 8-23—8-27, 698E2
GM targeted in contract talks 8-30, 9-10; accord reached 9-14, signed 9-19, 698A1
Miller Chrysler aid pledge demand rptd 9-17, 699C1
GM pact provisn disclosed 9-18; contract rptd ratified, Kahn vs 9-30, 744F1

1980

UNION Oil Co. of California
Exxon Beaufort Sea find rptd 10-3, 785F2
UNION Pacific Corp.
Missouri Pacific merger set 1-8, 52B3
Westn Pacific purchase set 1-21, 131B2
Milwaukee Rd track deal set 4-1, 346E1
3-way merger set 9-15, 745G1
UNIONS—*See under LABOR*
UNIROYAL Inc.
Tire plant shutdowns set 1-22, 52G2-A3
Flannery elected chief exec 2-22, 225A1
Steel-belted radial recall set 3-7, 348C2
La chem-dump suit names 7-15, 558G3
UNITED—*For organizations not listed below, see key words*
UNITED Airlines Inc.
Coast-to-coast fares cut 6-7, hiked 7-1, 516B2, C2
Patterson dies 6-13, 528C3

UNITED Arab Emirates (UAE) (Abu Dhabi, Ajman, Dubai, Fujaira, Ras al Khaima, Sharja, Umm al Quwain)—*See also ARAB League, NONALIGNED Nations, OPEC*
French pres tours Arab states 3-1—3-10, 180B1
Japan oil trade seen 4-20, 299D1
Canada chrgs contractor 5-9, 406F2
OPEC base price opposed 6-9—6-10, 435E3
Syria seeks backing for Libya merger 9-10, 697G1
Gulf war prompts halt to 10% oil cut plan 9-26, 735C1
Iran chrgs Iraq ships seek shelter 9-29, warns 10-1, 735G1
Oil export hike rptd set 10-6, 758D3
US offers air defense aid 10-7, 758D1
Iran attacks ships 10-7, 758G2
Abu Dhabi lifts oil price $2 10-15, 775B1
Oil productn increase rptd 10-28, 822E2

UNITED Artists Inc.
'Cruising' opens, draws gay protests; Gen Cinema contract dispute cited 2-15, 239A3
Heaven's Gate withdrawn from theaters 11-19, 906A1
Auerbach, Albeck get new posts 12-12, 986A3
UNITED Automobile, Aerospace and Agricultural Implement Workers of America (UAW) (unaffiliated)
Canadians bar Chrysler concessns 1-3, US contract revisns set 1-5; Carter signs aid bill 1-7, council OKs pact 1-8, 14C1-A2
George Meany dies 1-10, 14E3
Fraser asks Japanese car assemb in US 1-13, 35C2
Fraser backs Kennedy 1-15, 33C1
Uniroyal to shut 2 plants 1-22, 52G2
Chrysler concessns OKd 2-1, 127C2
Fraser in Japan, asks US plants 2-11—2-14; Nissan, Toyota respond 2-18, Fraser backs 2-19, 127B1
AFL-CIO legis conf attended 2-19, 147C1
Ford contract said to violate wage-price guidelines 3-7, sanctions imposed 3-26, 225F2
Allis-Chalmers pact set 3-15, 308A3
Fraser asks Nissan US car plants 4-17, 288F1

1976

UNITED Brands Co. (formerly United Fruit Co.)
Signs Panama pact 1-8, 52B3
SEC lists paymts 5-12, 726B1, 729E1
Book links to '61 Cuba raid 10-21, 844D3
More forgn paymts, labor slush fund disclosed; Field indicted 12-10, 985C3
UNITED California Bank
Arab boycott rpt released 10-18, 786B1
UNITED Church of Christ
Accuses Mobil re Rhodesia trade 6-21, 621D1
Mobil denies chrgs; files with SEC 8-27; 698C2
Sup Ct bars equal-time review 10-12, 765E3
Moss dies 10-25, 970E2
UNITED Distillers Corp.
Margaux vineyard sold 12-18, 964F2
UNITED Farm Workers of America (UFW) (AFL-CIO)
Calif dispute continues, boycott renewal planned 1-22—2-11, 153G1
State alien job curbs upheld 2-25, 169A2
Chavez backs Carter 9-25, 724D1
Calif rejects work proposal 11-2, 825B1
UNITED Forwarders
Arab boycott rpt released 10-19, 786D1
UNITED Fruit Co.—*See UNITED Brands*
UNITED Jersey Banks
Rptd on FRB 'problem' list 1-22, 111C3
UNITED Mine Workers of America (UMW) (unaffiliated)
Sherry LaGace death rptd 1-27, 80E3
US clears top officials 5-18, 378G3
Wildcat strike spreads 7-19—7-27, 553F1
Wildcat strike ends 8-16, 669E3-670A1
Yablonski slayers sentncd 9-3, 816A3
Conventn 9-23—10-2, 748F1
Ford, Carter debate 10-22, 801B3

1977

UNITED Brands Co. (formerly United Fruit Co.)
Panama workers strike 1-4, 46C2
Calif land holdings breakup asked 8-22, 703G2
ILA offcl sentenced 12-2, 937E3
UNITED Church of Christ
Rhodesia ousts Spray 6-21, 536E2
11th synod; Christian Church merger proposed, pres elected 7-1—7-5, 642D2
UNITED Factors—*See UNITED Merchants and Manufacturers*
UNITED Farm Workers of America (UFW) (AFL-CIO)
Teamsters pact signed 3-10, 177D3
UNITED Fruit Co.—*See UNITED Brands*
UNITED Gas Pipe Line Co.
FPC OKs emergency gas sales 1-14, 37C1
UNITED Jewish Organizations of Williamsburg, N.Y. v Carey
Voter redistricting upheld 3-1, 174D3-175D1
UNITED Kingdom—*See GREAT Britain*
UNITED Merchants & Manufacturers Inc.
'75, '76 losses cited 340C2
Robert Hall divisn closed, pres fired 6-16, 520B1
Files bankruptcy 7-12, SEC asks trustee 7-20; United Factors sale OKd 7-25; losses rptd 7-28; Robt Hall sold 8-8, 612F1-E2
UNITED Mine Workers of America (UMW) (unaffiliated)
Boyle convictn upset 1-28, 95D3
Sup Ct refuses wildcat strike case 3-21, 230B3
Miller reelected pres 6-14, 462A3
Wildcat strikes 6-18—9-6, 690F2
Miller's vote certified 7-21, 691A1
Michael Widman dies 8-14, 696G3
Miller reelectn affirmed 10-11, 937E2
Stearns (Ky) strike violence 10-17, 937F2-B3
Coal strike begins 12-6, 937B1; AFL-CIO backs 12-13, 961E1
Coal talks break off 12-30, 1005F2

1978

UNITED Brands Co. (formerly United Fruit Co.)
EC '75 banana case fine upheld 2-14, 159C1
Honduras payoffs admitted 6-9, 614C3, 615A1
Pleads guilty re Honduran bribe, fined 7-19, 643F1
UNITED California Bank
Dropped from '77 world top 10 11-8, 914C1
UNITED Christian Council
Israel conversn study asked 2-1, 294B2
UNITED Church of Christ
Female clergy survey rptd 3-23, 295G1
Lobbying bill scored 4-26, 323B2
UNITED Engineers & Constructors Inc.—*See RAYTHEON Co.*
UNITED Farm Workers of America (UFW) (AFL-CIO)
Chavez ends boycotts 1-31, 83F1
UNITED Fruit Co.—*See UNITED Brands*
UNITED Jewish Appeal
Siegel booed on Saudi jet sale 176E2
UNITED Kingdom—*See GREAT Britain*
UNITED Methodist Church—*See METHODISTS*
UNITED Mine Workers of America (UMW) (unaffiliated)
Boyle gag-order case remanded 1-9, 13G1
Pensn jurisdictn case refused 1-9, 13E2
Coal strike talks resume 1-12, Carter bars interventn 1-30, 62B3; **for subsequent developments, see COAL—Strike**
Black lung bills clear Cong 1-24, 2-15; finance measure signed 2-10, 125F1
Boyle convicted again 2-18, 129A1
Constructn workers strike 3-27, tentative pact reached 3-28, 217E1
Pensn attachmt case refused by Sup Ct 4-3, 309B1
Anthracite pact ratified 4-30, 324E2
Miller recall barred by bd 7-26, 624G3

1979

Caterpillar struck 10-1–12-19, 987E1
Fraser on Pay Advisory Com 10-16, 829F2
Ford contract ratified 10-22, 805G3
Chrysler settlmt reached 10-25, 805E2
Fraser backs Chrysler rescue plan 11-1, 845F2
Kirkland bids all unions join AFL-CIO 11-19, 885C2
Cong debates Chrysler wage concessns 12-18, 12-19; aid bill OKd 12-21, 981E2-D3

UNITED Board for Christian Higher Education in Asia
China reimbursement set 3-16, 218A1
UNITED Brands Co. (formerly United Fruit Co.)
Sun Harvest Inc.
Chavez pushes banana boycott 4-26, 327A2
UFW Calif lettuce strike settled 8-31, 698A3
TRT Telecommunications Corp.
FCC unit rejects Postal Svc satellite leasing plan 10-18, 921F2
UNITED Farm Workers of America (UFW) (AFL-CIO)
Calif lettuce strike starts 1-19, worker shot 2-10; boycott set 4-26, 327A1
Ariz farm labor law restored by Sup Ct 6-5, 464B3
Lettuce strike violence 6-11, strike setld, boycott ends 8-31, 698G2
Brown vetoes Calif bill 9-7, 698E3
Field talk case refused by Sup Ct 11-5, 884C3
UNITED Financial Corp. of California
Natl Steel plans purchase 3-6, 205A2
UNITED Gas Pipe Line Co. v. McCombs
Case decided by Sup Ct 6-18, 499C2
UNITED Kingdom—*See GREAT Britain*
UNITED Merchants & Manufacturers Inc.
Fortune rpts '78 sales drop 5-7, 305C1
UNITED Methodist Church—*See METHODISTS*
UNITED Methodist Church v. Barr
Case declined by Sup Ct 11-26, 919F2
UNITED Mine Workers of America (UMW) (unaffiliated)
Boyle sentenced again 10-11, 840B1, C1*
Miller resigns as pres 11-15, Church succeeds 11-16, 885D2
Conv held 12-10–12-20; Kennedy addresses 12-13, 986D3-987D1
Wildcat strike liability limited by Sup Ct 12-10, 988D1

1980

Harvester strike ends 4-20, 308E2
Cancer probe rptd 4-22, 356G3
Fraser elected to Chrysler bd 5-13, 383C3
Fraser at White House mtg 5-14, 384F1
Truck import duty lauded 5-20, 384C2
Conv held 6-1—6-6; Fraser reelected, retiring offcls replaced 6-4, 457G1
Chrysler to keep Lynch River plant open 6-3, 457E1
Auto import curbs asked 6-12, 457E2; 7-1, 6-12, 599C1
Carter seeks auto import curb ruling, sees Fraser 7-8, 505B1
ITC blocks auto import probe speedup 7-18, 556B2
Canada workers stage sit-in 8-8—8-21, return to work 8-25, 650B3
Fraser renominates Mondale at conv 8-14, 612B1
Polish strike aid rptd 8-31, 659A3
AMC strike 9-16, pact set 9-17, 725B1
Auto import hearings held 10-8—10-10, 823E1
US funds jobless aid program 10-14, 823G2
ITC bars Japan auto import curbs 11-10, 866E3
Chrysler proposes new financial plan 12-17, pact renegotiatn OKd 12-22, 984D2
Reagan crisis mtg asked 12-20, 980E2

UNITED Brands Co. (formerly United Fruit Co.)
CR banana workers' strike ends 1-17, 117D1
UNITED Church of Canada
Intercommunion poll rptd 4-4, 413A3
UNITED Church of Christ
Protestant unity mtg ends, common ministry OKd 1-24, 156G2
Intercommunion poll rptd 4-4, 413A3
UNITED Farm Workers of America (UFW) (AFL-CIO)
Brown ends pres bid, Chavez support cited 4-1, 246D3
Chavez stumps with Mondale 10-26, 816F3
UNITED Features Syndicate
N Amer Newspaper Alliance disbanded 2-29, replaced 3-3, 239D2
UNITED Methodist Church—*See under METHODISTS*
UNITED Mine Workers of America (UMW) (unaffiliated)
Va ERA rally rptd 1-13, 54C3
Killion named vp 2-13, 147C1
AFL-CIO legis conf attended 2-19, 147C1
W Va wildcat strike 2-21—3-3, 169G3-170D1

UNITED NATIONS

1976

UNITED Nations—*Note: Only UN actions listed here. For a country's participation in UN activities and reaction to UN developments, see country names. See also WALDHEIM, Kurt*
Belize seeks indepndnc guarantee 1-8, 55B2
Bomb threat vs UN 1-12, Iraq missn 1-13, 18C2
Rpts Zambia forgn aid 1-28, 78A1
Australia aborigines to ask trade sanctns 3-11, 187A3
Carter at pvt conf 5-13, 374G3
Rights group chrgs Indian torture, asks probe 6-1; India denies 6-7, 408B3
Urges aid to Vietnam 6-2, 408C2
UN rep to chair Rhodesia govt conf 10-4, 738E2
Cuba chrgs CIA re mission bombing 10-15, 780A2
Portugal bars Azores' ldrs visit 10-23, 812B2
Agricultural Development, International Fund for—*See 'World Food Council' below*
Apartheid, Committee against
S Africa riot deaths rptd 6-23, 447C2
Cites Israel-S Africa ties 9-8, 682C2
Children's Fund, UN (UNICEF)
US '76 funds enacted 6-30, 533E2

1977

UNITED Nations—*See also country names; also WALDHEIM, Kurt*
World populatn rptd 1-30, 123F2
Afars independnc vote observed 5-8, 363B2
Southern Africa conf 5-16—5-21, 399B1
Croats raid Yugo NY missn 6-14, 497B2
Anti-apartheid conf 8-22—8-26, 661E2
Panama plebiscite observed 10-23, 809D1
Amnesty Intl faults members on rights 12-8, 956B2
Apartheid, Special Committee Against
Harriman scores Young speech 5-19, 399E2
Colonial Countries and Peoples, Special Committee on the Situation with Regard to the Implementation of the Declaration on the Granting of Independence to (Special Committee of 24)
Norfolk I pol status plea 2-9, 132A2
Rhodesia communicatns boycott asked; condemnatn passed 8-8, 662C1

1978

UNITED Nations—*See also country names; also WALDHEIM, Kurt*
Children's Emergency Fund, UN International (UNICEF)
Chile office occupied by protesters 5-22—6-9, 452D2
Colonial Countries and Peoples, Special Committee on the Situation with regard to the Implementation of the Declaration on the granting of Independence to (Special Committee of 24)
Australia announces Cocos purchase 7-2, 514G1
PR colony status voted 9-13, 979C3

1979

UNITED Nations
Apartheid, Special Committee Against
'72-78 Westn loans to S Africa rptd 4-2, 270C2
Children's Emergency Fund, UN International (UNICEF)
Cambodia missn confrms famine, torture 8-3, 600B3
Cambodia food, medicine airlifted 8-29, 9-8, 684F1
Cambodia relief agrmt set 9-26, 740G3-741A1; US backs 10-9, 767A2
Cambodia relief aid starts 10-13–10-14, 779G1
US vows Cambodia aid 10-24, 811F1; Pnompenh rejcts plan 10-27, 823D3

1980

UNITED Nations
Children's Emergency Fund, UN International—*See 'UNICEF' below*

1976

Cyprus, UN Force In (UNFICYP)
Mandate extended 6-16, 457B1
Commander resigns 11-19, 963C3
Looting, expulsn of Greeks rptd 12-13, 963G2
Sets Nicosia observatn posts 12-16, 963B3
Development Program, UN (UNDP)
Unesco literacy drive fails 2-4, 85C2
Disarmament, Conference of the Committee on—*See 'Geneva Committee' under DISARMAMENT*
Disaster Relief, Office of
Guatemala quake aid rptd 2-4—2-5, 81C1, E2
Disengagement Observer Force, UN—*See 'UNDOF' under MIDDLE EAST—UN DEVELOPMENTS*
Economic and Social Affairs, Department of
Issues world econ growth rpt 10-13, 760D1
Economic & Social Council (ECOSOC)
Racism debate 4-13—4-30, 320F2
Educational, Scientific & Cultural Organization, UN (UNESCO)
US com warns vs politics 1-5, 36B3
Postpones racism conf 1-15, 36E2
Says literacy drive fails 2-4, 85B2
Cassin dies 2-20, 192C3
Latin natns hold press parley 7-12—7-21, IAPA scores 7-23, 619C3
Argentina orders Malek arrest 8-4, Malek denies chrgs 8-5, 672A3
Meets in Nairobi 10-26; shelves Sovt press plan 11-6, 842G1
Sets '77 Israel occupied land probe 11-18, 879B1
Israel restored to Eur group 11-22, 878D3
Vs Israel policies in occupied land 11-22, 878D3
Panel OKs news plan 11-22, 879B1
Sovt vs West on press plan 11-25, plan delayed 11-29; news agency pool OKd, Israel Jerusalem digs scored 11-26; conf ends 11-30, 895E3
Kenya train crashes 11-29, 912B2
Emergency Force, UN—*See 'UNEF' under MIDDLE EAST—UN DEVELOPMENTS*
Environment Program, UN
Medit pollutn conf 2-2—2-16, 126A3
Europe, Economic Commission for (UNECE)
Energy rpt issued 2-10, 164G1
Rpts Comecon econ data 3-18, 341D3
E Eur, Sovt trade deficit rptd 11-18, 977C1

General Assembly—*Note: Only Assembly actions listed here. See also under MIDDLE EAST—UN DEVELOPMENTS; also country names*
'66 rights covenant in effect, Jamaica '75 ratificatn cited 1-4, 36D3
US Dem platform text cites 6-15, 478A1
W Ger to propose terrorism accord 7-16, 530B3
China urges US quit S Korea 8-15, 619G1
Viet entry discussn set 9-14, 682D1
31st session opens 9-21, 718C3
N Korea drops resolutn 9-21, 718D3
Gromyko addressed 9-28, Kissinger 9-30, 719B1
China scores Sovt, US 10-5, 759F3-760B1
Syria asks Israel reconsidered 10-6, 760B1
Budget Com hears US rep score Waldheim 10-11, 760A2
Panel: Chile rights abuse widened 10-14, 963E2
NZ plans curbs vs S Africa sports 10-16, 910A3
Commonwealth gets observer status 10-18, 799C2
Vs Transkei independnce 10-22, 813F1
Asks ban vs Transkei 10-26, 799F1
OKs anti-apartheid stand 11-9, 842F2
Vs Denktash in Greek-Turk debate 11-9, 863E1
Asks Turkey quit Cyprus 11-12, 863D1
Venez pres addresses 11-16, 929A3
Cncl for Angola entry 11-22, 879C1
Asks Viet entry review 11-26, 914B2
Angola voted member 12-1, 895B3
Reelects Waldheim 12-8, 914C2
Vs environmt control for mil aims 12-10, 955D1
OKs W Samoa as UN member 12-15, 955D1
Backs Namibia struggle 12-20, 955B1
'76 session recesses 12-22, 954D3
Geneva Committee—*See under DISARMAMENT*
Habitat Conference—*See 'Human Settlement, Conference on' below*
Host Country, Committee on Relations with the
US denies Sovt residence shooting role 2-27, 229E2
Human Rights, Commission on
Panel gets Chile torture testimony 1-19, 47G1
Chile rights abuse chrgd, denied 2-10—2-19; Pinochet scores probes 4-24, 310B1
Chrgs Israel 'war crimes' in Arab areas 2-13, 125D2
UK scores 4-30, 320D3
Subcom asks Rhodesia raid probe 8-30, 661F2
Human Settlement, Conference on (Habitat)
Meets; asks for land, wealth distributn 5-31—6-11, 431D2

1977

Cyprus, UN Force In (UNFICYP)
Mandate extended 6-16, 476G1
Finnish troop exit set 9-16, 764F3
Kyprianou scores Turks 11-19, 946C3
Mandate extended 12-15, 984C1
Decolonization Committee—*See 'Colonial Countries and Peoples, etc.', above*
Disarmament, Conference of the Committee on—*See DISARMAMENT—Geneva Committee*
Dues
US scores Sovt UNEF fund bar 1-6, 1-7, 4A3
Cambodia payment disputed 9-20, 713B1
Cambodia payment rptd 10-4, 770B2
Economic & Social Council (ECOSOC)
Narcotic Comm rpts Thai poppy planting rise 4-1, 396D3
PLO admitted 7-22, 572F2
Viet spec aid OKd 10-6, 770A2
Educational, Scientific and Cultural Organization, UN (UNESCO)
Athens acropolis aid urged 1-10, 63C3
George Shuster dies 1-25, 84F3
French oust Sovt envoy 2-11, 159D3
Sri Lanka energy experimt rptd 3-30, 298D3
World press role parley 4-18—4-20, 319E2
Mex names Echeverria envoy 7-8, 563A1
Young backs press controls 8-14, IAPA scores 8-16, 647G1
Israel to lift '74 ban 8-31, 663F2-A3
Rumania treatmt of offcl scored 10-8, 948D1
USSR tries to blackmail US envoy 10-19, 866D2
Kenneth Holland dies 12-9, 1024B2
Emergency Force, UN—*See MIDDLE EAST—UN—UNEF*
Environment Program, UN
Sri Lanka energy experimt rptd 3-30, 298D3
Deserts conf held, spec fund set 8-29—9-9, 770B1
Medit pollutn conf ends, pact reached 10-21, 876B2
Europe, Economic Commission for (UNECE)
Sovt-bloc Westn debt rptd 4-13, 335C3, E3
Food & Agriculture Organization (FAO)
CIA linked to Cuba swine fever 1-9, 19F2
Rpts no coffee consumptn drop 2-3, 169B1
Gambia rpts drought crisis 8-22, 660E1
New Sahel famine seen 9-19, 770F1-A2
General Assembly—*See also under MIDDLE EAST—UN*
Carter addresses 3-17, 185A1-186C2
Belize '75 independnc resolutn cited 5-20, 414C3
World Food Cncl conf to submit plans 6-24, 513F3
Resumed 31st sessn ends, N-S econ conf deadlock 9-19, 713C1
Waldheim assesses issues 9-19, 713F1
32nd sessn opens: Viet, Djibouti entry OKd; Cambodia dues disputed 9-20, 713A1
Gromyko addresses 9-27, 750G3, 769F2
Carter addresses 10-4, 749A2, 751G2-752G1
Intl pilots strike postponed 10-21, 868C3
French evacuatn of Mayotte asked 10-26, 869A1
Hijacking condemned 11-3, 852B3
S Africa occupatn of Namibia condemned 11-4, 851E1
Belize independnc backed 11-28, 969G2
S Africa anti-apartheid resolutns OKd 12-14, 1016B2
Chile rights abuse res OKd 12-16, 983D1
S Africa oil, investmt bans voted 12-16, 1016G1

Geneva Committee—*See under DISARMAMENT*

Human Rights, Commission on
Van Boven named dir 1-28, 140G3
Amnesty Intl asks Uganda probe 2-6, 139G1
33d session opens 2-7, Djilas issues plea 2-8, 139B3
US to ask Orlov probe 2-11, 117D1
Israel occupatn rule scored 2-15, 107E2
WCC asks Uganda deaths probe 2-17, 139D1
US asks Sovt dissident info 2-18, 137G2
Argentine abuses chrgd 2-21, probe barred 3-4, 198D1
Waldheim asks Uganda probe 2-24, probe barred 3-1, 142A1

1978

Decolonization Committee—*See 'Colonial Countries and Peoples, etc.' above*
Disarmament, Conference of the Committee on—*See DISARMAMENT—Geneva Committee*
Disengagement Observer Force, UN—*See MIDDLE EAST—UN—UNDOF*
Economic & Social Council (ECOSOC)
Dutch cancel 4 natns' debts 7-10, 575E1

Educational, Scientific and Cultural Organization, UN (UNESCO)
Kerr resigns Paris post 3-2, 165E1-A2
Rumanian offcl back at post 5-18, 360A2
Gen Conf opens 10-24, free press declaratn OKd 11-22, text 931C1-932F2
Israel says rpt backs occupatn policy 11-13, 931G1
Israel scored re Jerusalem digs 11-29, 931F1

Emergency Force, UN—*See MIDDLE EAST—UN—UNEF*
Europe, Economic Commission for (UNECE)
Sovt-bloc Westn debt rptd 11-21, 999G1
Food & Agriculture Organization (FAO)
Sahel relief sought 3-8, 237G1
E Africa locust plague spraying begun 6-6, spread feared 6-12, 465E2

General Assembly
Chile vote rejects rights rpt 1-4, 16A3, 17E1
Rights Comm asks Chile fund 3-6, 210G1
Ghanaian gets new econ post 3-8, 401F3
French disarmament proposal planned 4-24, 313D1
S Africa econ sanctns asked 5-3, 339C1
Disarmamt spec sessn opens 5-23; US, USSR affirm A-test ban commitmt, regional agrmts 5-24, 5-26, 421A1
France, China hint Geneva role 5-25, 5-29, 417F3, 421C2-422A1
Canada ends A-arms role in Eur 5-26, 422B1
Cuba vp addresses disarmament sessn 5-30, 418E1
Fraser urges A-arms curb 6-5, 450D3
Cambodia chrgs Viet aggressn 6-8, 6-9, 490E1
Disarmamt sessn ends; Geneva chngs OKd, A-weapon, other arms cuts urged 6-30, 522G2
Seabed res cited in UN Sea Law Conf debate 8-21—9-16, 732D3, F3
Members listed 713B3
33d sessn opens: Lievano elected pres, Solomon I admitted, 5 chosen to Cncl 9-19, 713F2, G2 ★, A3
Vance asks Palestinians join peace talks 9-29, 762E2
Pro-PLO publicity drive starts 10-7, 762G2
Cambodia for Viet pact 10-12, 794F1
Arms ban vs Israel asked 11-27, 931A3
Palestinian Rights unit marks Solidarity Day 11-29, 951E2
Carter urges US Genocide Conv ratificatn 12-6, 934B1
Nicaragua rights abuse scored 12-15, 1019D1

Geneva Committee—*See under DISARMAMENT*
Host Country Relations, Committee on
US ouster of Viet amb protested 2-9, 103A3
US sens vs Carter plea on Cambodia 10-12, 794G1
Human Rights, Commission on
Chile pres bars more rights probes 1-4, changes mind 1-5, 17E1
Israel condemned in 3 resolutns 2-14, 99G1
US scores Argentina disappearances 3-6, 208A1
Chile rights abuse resolutns, victim fund OKd 3-6, 210D1
US scores USSR re Rostropovich ouster 3-16, 179D3
Panel sets Chile repressn relief fund 6-2, 452C3 ★
Chile OKs rights probe 6-9, 452A2

1979

Cambodia relief called inadequate 11-25, 917E2
Cambodia relief rptd blocked, Sovt role denied 12-13, 977C3

Disarmament, Conference of the Committee on—*See DISARMAMENT–Geneva Committee*
Economic & Social Council (ECOSOC)
US rpts drug abuse costs 2-12, 140C2
Cyprus police force asked 9-15, 751A3

Educational, Scientific, and Cultural Organization, UN (UNESCO)
Torres named Carter spec asst 8-10, 608F2

Emergency Force, UN—*See MIDDLE EAST–U.N.–UNEF*
Europe, Economic Commission for (UNECE)
W Eur growth seen 3-13, 180A2
Sovt-bloc '78 Westn debt estimate rptd 3-20, 200C3
Pollutn pact OKd 11-13, 864B3
Food & Agriculture Organization (FAO)
Cambodia famine aid unlikely 4-22, 318D2
Hunger conf held in Rome 7-13–7-20, 554B1

General Assembly
Namibia debate opens 5-23, S Africa reps expelled 5-24, 409C3
S Africa censure voted 5-31, 428A1
Disarmament plan backed in SALT II communique 6-18, 458A1
Geneva Com '79 sessn ends 8-14, 625G2
Com OKs Palestinian rights res 8-21, Cncl delays vote 8-24, 642D1, G2
Palestinian film previewed 8-28, 643D2
34th sessn opens: Salim elected pres, St Lucia admitted 9-18; Pol Pot seat upheld 9-19, 695G1
Pol Pot rep retains seat 9-21; USSR scores US, China 'tricks' 9-22, 741F1
US urges Lebanon peace 9-24, 741C2
Hussein bars Egypt-Israel peace talks role 9-24, 741E2
Gromyko scores 'lies' re Cuba 9-25, 738B2
China cites Sovt war threat 9-27, 741B2
Mex proposes energy plan 9-27, 753C1
Burma quits nonaligned 9-28, 742C2
Nicaragua repudiates forgn debt 9-28, 753D2
Pope stresses rights 10-2, 757D1, F2
Castro scores econ disparities; blames US, asks 3d World aid 10-12, 778B2-D3
Salim asks Poland for worker detentn info 10-29, 939B2
Cambodia relief aid pledged 11-5, 863B3
Iran release of US hostages urged 11-20, 878F2
Israel-Egypt peace pact rejctd 11-29; US, Israel score vote 11-29, 12-2, 979F2
Palestinian Solidarity Day marked 11-29, 979G2
Hostage-taking outlawed 12-17, 957F2-958A1
Zimbabwe sanctns end by US, UK scored 12-18, 960F1
Geneva Committee—*See under DISARMAMENT*

Human Rights, Commission on
US envoy on Israel torture chrgs 2-11, 108D2
Israel, southn Africa white-minority govts condemned; Palestinian state backed 2-21, 148D1
Nicaragua rights abuse end sought 3-13, 255B2
Haitian 'slavery' in DR rptd 8-17, 804A3
US delegate backs anti-Israel res 9-5, US govt dissociates 9-6, 659E2
E Ger scored re prisoner ransom deals 11-28, 939B3

1980

Disarmament, Conference of the Committee on—*See GENEVA Committee*
Economic & Social Council (ECOSOC)
Narcotics Comm reclassificatn spurs US curbs 4-24, 358A2, B2

Educational, Scientific & Cultural Organization, UN—*See 'UNESCO' below*
Environment Program, UN (UNEP)
S Africa ties ended 4-28, 374G1
Medit pollutn pact signed 5-17, 381A3
US protests rejctn of Israeli bid on Nairobi hq 6-19, 476B2

Europe, Economic Commission for (UNECE)
Sovt bloc '79 Westn debt rptd 4-1, 285A3

General Assembly
4 Cncl seats filled 1-1, Mex elected 1-7, 12A2
Sovt Afghan invasn debated 1-11—1-12, res deplores, demands exit 25D1-26B1
Women's anti-bias pact signed by US, 52 others 7-17, 587C2
US walks out on Iranian speaker 7-25, 572D2
Palestine state backed, Israel asked to quit '67 lands 7-29, 572E1
11th special sessn hears Muskie, Rao on 3d World aid 8-25; Kuwait oil focus warning rptd 8-27, 642G2-643D1
11th special sessn hears MacGuigan on 3d World aid 8-26, 669B1
Waldheim gives Mideast rpt 9-12, 775G1
Econ dvpt spec sessn ends in no agrmt 9-15, 736G1
35th sessn opens; Von Wechmar elected pres, St Vincent becomes 154th member 9-16, 736E1
Members listed 9-17, 736D2-B3
Muskie addresses on Iran hostages 9-22, 719F2
Canada min addresses 9-22, 748E3-749B1
World Bank-IMF 3d World financial debate cited 9-30, 671B1
Syria asks Israel ouster 9-30, 736B2
Moslems drop plan to oust Israel 10-9, 775F1
War rules treaty endorsed 10-10, 777F1
Pol Pot govt retains seat 10-13, 775B2
Viet Cambodia exit asked 10-22, Viet rejects 10-23, 801C1
Israel for Mideast A-ban 11-13, 864A2
5 Cncl members chosen 11-13, 896C1
Sovt Afghan exit voted 11-20; res scored by USSR 11-20, Afghan 11-21, 899F2-900A1
Jordan, Israel exchng chrgs 12-8, 12-10; Israel asked to quit Arab lands; Camp David pact, E Jerusalem annexatn scored 12-15, 952F2
Geneva Committee—*See GENEVA Committee*
Headquarters & Secretariat
Libya urges hq relocatn 4-27, 324D2
US protests rejctn of Israeli bid on Nairobi hq 6-19, 476B2

Human Rights, Commission on
Sakharov debate set 2-5, 85F3
US urges anti-Sovt Afghan invasn res 2-13, res adopted 2-14, 123D3
USSR poison gas use in Afghan rptd 3-5, 205A3
Sessn opens 3-10, Sakharov debate postponed 3-11, 181A3
Cuba prison hunger strike probe asked 12-4, 965C2

1976

International Atomic Energy Agency (IAEA)
Stone confrmd US amb 2-6, 110C2
OKs French reprocessing plant for Pakistan 2-24, 175C1
Ford asks US contributn 2-26, 149G2
Signs French-Pak A-plant pact 3-18, 581C3
French A-export safeguards set 4-8, 372D3
Non-nuclear sister agency urged 5-13, 375B1
Japan ratifies A-pact 5-24, 418G3
US-USSR A-test treaty cites 5-28, 387B3
Ford backs standards 7-29, 739E2
French, S Africa plant pact signed 8-6, 631A2
Taiwan membership cited 8-29, 761A1
UK signs pact 9-6, 936A2
Conf: safeguards urged, Yugo offers plan 9-21—9-27, 760D3
USSR-India heavy water sale rptd 12-8, 955B2

International Civil Aviation Organization (ICAO)
Pak offers to drop India case 3-27, 278F2

International Court of Justice (World Court)
Greece appeals on Aegean feud 8-10, 622C3
Cncl res backs mediatn in Aegean feud, Greece vs Turk oil probe 8-25; Turks vs ct role 8-26, 643E2, G2
Greek, Turk pleas Barred 9-11, 845A1

International Labor Organization (ILO)
Rpts world jobless up 3-13, 297D3
World Employmt Conf meets 6-2—6-18; PLO seated 6-4, US, Israel boycott Mizer speech 6-8, 449D3
US GOP platform text cites 8-18, 610F3
Swiss chrg 2 as Sovt spies 11-24, 1011C3
Venez pres at Soclst Intl mtg 11-27, 930A1
Rpts Australia strike data 11-29, 896D2

Joint Inspection Unit
Bender dies 2-16, 160C3

Latin America, Economic Commission for (ECLA)
'75 Latin econ decline noted 1-13, 60C3
Rpts Uruguay '75 forgn deficit 3-12, 383C1
Chile aide found dead 7-16; UN probes 12-14, 963B2
Pemjean ouster from Chile cited 12-15, 963E2

Law of the Sea, UN Conference on the
US Sen OKs 200-mi zone 1-28, 94F1
EC backs 200-mile zone 1-30, 85D1
Conf impasse 3-15—5-7, 342C1
Sessn opens, Australian addresses 3-16, 203G3
US urges new law 4-8, 342B2
Rpts on Latin food productn 5-7, 466C1
US Dem platform text cites 6-15, 478B1
EEC OKs 200-mi limit 7-27, 563B3
Conf impasse 8-2—9-17; US urges agrmt 8-13, offers funds, 9-1, 700E1
US GOP platform text 8-18, 608C1, 610G3
US-Japan fishing talks impasse 11-8—11-12, 863C2

Membership
US vetoes Angola entry 6-23, 455E1
US to veto Viet entry 9-13; Cncl delays vote 9-14, 682B1
Seychelles 145th member, total list 9-21, 719A1, E3-720B1
China scores US role vs Viet 10-5, 760A1
Ford, Carter debate Vietnam 10-6, 742E2
Syria asks Assemb reconsider Israel 10-6, 760B1
US vetoes Viet entry 11-15, 862B3
Cncl for Angola entry 11-22, 879C1
Assemb asks Viet review, US vows 2d veto 11-26, 914B2
Angola becomes 146th 12-1, 895B3
W Samoa becomes 147th 12-15, 955D1

Middle East Actions—*See UN DEVELOPMENTS under MIDDLE EAST*

Namibia, UN Council for
Warns on Cuba, USSR role in Namibia liberatn 8-30, 660F3
Nujoma asks embargo 9-27, 793G3
S Africa plan vs Angola chrgd 12-10, 995G3

Palestinian People, UN Committee on the Exercise of the Inalienable Rights of the
Talks open, Israel boycotts 2-26; PLO, Syria in feud 3-4, 161F2
Cncl upholds Palestinian return, US vetoes resolutn 6-29, 464C1
US scores report 11-23, 878B3

1977

US backs S Africa isolatn 2-28, 145A2
US drops Sovt probe bid 3-7, sessn ends 3-11, 207E1
US aide regrets Chile coup role 3-8, US disavows, summons home 3-8—3-9, 218E3
Chile resolutn adopted 3-9, 219F1
Carter proposes monitoring chngs 3-17, 186A2
ICJ scores Uganda inactn 5-17, 429A2
Chile rptdly OKs panel visit 9-7, 743B1
Carter signs pacts 10-5, 769F2
Chile vs rights rpt 12-2, Assemb scores Chile 12-16, 983E1

Human Rights, Division of
Carter urges relocatn, other reforms 3-17, 186A2

International Atomic Energy Agency (IAEA)
Australia safeguards proposed 3-29, 253A3
US plutonium ban scored 4-17, 334A3
US proposes A-export curbs 4-27, 334E1
Salzburg intl conf 5-2—5-13, 335F1, 402E2, 403B1
Australia sets uranium export curbs 5-24, 465B3
US contribution OKd 8-2, 8-17, 689A2, C2
Vietnam, Djibouti join 9-20, 713A1
A-natns OK export safeguards 9-20, 713A1

International Civil Aviation Organization (ICAO)
Assemb condemns hijacking 11-3, 852D3

International Court of Justice (World Court)
15 members listed 4F1
Australia-PNG border talks suspended 2-7, 132E1
US cos win Libya damages 3-2, 488E1
To hear Libya-Tunisia dispute 6-10, 497E2
Libya sets US co paymt 9-26, 772C2

International Labor Organization (ILO)
ICFTU backs Czech dissidents 1-24, 82A3
Exec cncl drops Israel probe, asks depoliticizatn; US lauds 3-21, 227D2
7-natn econ summit cites jobless data 5-7—5-8, 357E1
Israel may lift ban 8-31, 663A3
US withdraws 11-1, 829A1

Korea, U.N. Command in South
N Korea sea limits opposed 8-2, 591B1, E1
Bonesteel dies 10-13, 872B1

Latin America, Economic Commission for (ECLA)
'75-76 payments, trade data; table 3-11, 189A1, D3
Hunger strikers protest Chile disappearances 6-14—6-23, 493F1
Bolivia econ data disputed 10-7, 902F1

Law of the Sea, UN Conference on the
PR statehood plan linked to oil rights 1-5, 16B3
India sets limits 1-15, 64G1
Richardson named US rep 1-25, 55G1; confrmd 2-24, 148F3
Talks adjourn 7-15, US scores rpt 7-20, 572G2

Membership
147 members listed 3E3-4D1
US backs Japan permanent Cncl seat 3-21, 209C3
Carter on Viet entry 3-24, 229B3
US to drop Viet veto 5-3—5-4, 333A1
Swiss decline entry 6-30, 565C1
Cncl OKs Viet entry 7-20, 572D2
Carter on Viet entry 7-21, 575B1
ECOSOC admits PLO 7-22, 572F2
5 nonpermanent Cncl members elected 10-24, 852E3

Middle East Actions—*See LEBANON and MIDDLE EAST, subhead UN*

Namibia, UN Council for
MacBride Dec '76 retiremt rptd, Ahtisaari named 109D3
S Africa OKs presence 10-4, 1016F3

Narcotic Drugs, Commission on—*See 'Economic & Social Council' above*

1978

Chile rights probe begun 7-12, 572F3; completed 7-27, 591C2
Cambodia denies rights breach 7-21, 660C1
Haiti abuses probed by panel 8-18—8-25, 691B3
US chrgs Cambodian cruelty 8-31, 748E1
Colombia security statute scored 10-27, 1015G2
Chile disappearances probe asked by US offcls 12-8, 1014C1

International Atomic Energy Agency (IAEA)
Canada lifts EC uranium ban; inspectn agreed, France bars 1-16, 102F3
S Africa '75 inspectn bar cited 135D1
Vance proposes A-weapons material ban 4-3, 277F2
Australia, Finland sign uranium accord 7-20, 590F1

International Civil Aviation Organization (ICAO)
US bad-weather landing system picked 4-19, 319A2-C3

International Court of Justice (World Court)
Beagle Channel ruling rejected by Argentina 1-6—2-10, 101A1
Turkey bars Aegean arbitratn 4-25, 398A3
Aegean dispute actn barred 12-19, 1000E3

International Labor Organization (ILO)
USSR dissidents to seek support 1-26, 180C1
USSR dissident union recognitn denied 4-14, 275F2
Annual conf 6-7—6-28; US urged to rejoin 6-7; anti-Israel res loses 6-27, 523D3
Deficit overcome 6-14, 524F3
Namibia entry OK rptd 6-24, 547E3
UK forces resignatn of Sovt aide; 2d aide tied to KGB by Swiss 7-26, ousted 7-31, 676C1
'77 jobless rates rptd 7-28, 677D1
June '77-78 world inflatn rates rptd 10-18, 914E1

Law of the Sea, UN Conference on the
Pres dispute delays opening 3-28, Amerasinghe elected 4-6; conf opens, deadlock continues 4-6—5-19, 401G2-D3
Ocean treaty talks resume 5-23—7-15, US seabed mining bill debated 8-21—9-16, 732C3
US House OKs seabed mining bill 7-26, 588G3
Colombia names Uribe forgn min 9-22, 815A1

Lebanon, UN Interim Force in (UNIFIL)—*See MIDDLE EAST, subheads LEBANON and UN—UNIFIL*

Membership
Gypsies ask offcl natl status 4-11, 318G2
Namibia ILO entry OK rptd 6-24, 547E3
Members listed 713B3
5 nonpermanent cncl seats filled 9-19, 713G2
Solomon I admitted 9-19, 713G2 ★
Lon Nol asks 'free Khmers' replace Cambodia 9-21, 748A2

Middle East Actions—*See MIDDLE EAST—UN*

Namibia, UN Council for
Ahtisaari arrives Namibia 8-6, 633D3; leaves, no progress seen 8-23, 669E2
Waldheim rpt issued 8-30, 741G3
Ahtisaari talks to reopen 10-19, 819E3-F3

Outer Space, Committee on Peaceful Uses of
Canada fears Sovt satellite hazard 7-5, 514C3

Palestinian People, Committee on the Exercise of the Inalienable Rights of the
UN starts pub relatns drive 10-7, 762G2-C3
Solidarity Day marked 11-29, 951E2

1979

Indochina Refugee Issue—*See INDOCHINA–Refugees*

International Atomic Energy Agency (IAEA)
Safeguards stressed in SALT II communique 6-18, 457D3
US, Australia sign uranium accord 7-5, 501E1

International Court of Justice (World Court)
US files chrgs vs Iran 11-29, 896G1
Iran vs role on US hostages 12-9, US files plea 12-10, 933D1
Iran ordrd to free US hostages 12-15, 957C2

Law of the Sea, UN Conference on the
8th session yields no accord 3-19—4-27, 360C3
US to challenge coastal sea claims 8-10, 646G1

Lebanon, UN Interim Force in (UNIFIL)—*See MIDDLE EAST, subheads LEBANON and U.N.–UNIFIL*

Membership
Dominica entry cited; St Lucia admitted 9-18, 695A2
Members listed 695D2

Middle East Actions—*See MIDDLE EAST–U.N.*

Namibia, UN Council for
Ahtisaari reopens talks 1-13; Waldheim asks truce 2-26, S Africa rejcts 3-5, 171D1
UK Tories urge rebel support end 4-11, 285D3

1980

Industrial Development Organization, UN (UNIDO)
New Delhi mtg ends in discord 2-9, 124A2

International Atomic Energy Agency (IAEA)
Iraq bars inspectn 11-7, 864B2

International Labor Organization (ILO)
US rejoins 2-18, 124F3-125A1
USSR, Czech work laws scored 5-12, 381E2
Blanchard lauds Polish workers 9-1, 659G3
Polish Sup Ct backs unions, strike averted 11-10, 862E2

Law of the Sea, UN Conference on the
9th sessn yields draft accord 7-28—8-29, 660B1
Canada min cites accord 9-22, 748G3

Lebanon, UN Interim Force in—*See 'UNIFIL' below*

Membership
4 Cncl nonpermanent members take seats 1-1, Mex elected 1-7, 12G1
Zimbabwe admitted 8-25, 643D1
St Vincent becomes 154th member 9-16, 736E1
Members listed 9-17, 736D2-B3
Cuba, CR end Cncl seat try 10-20, 11-12; 5 new nonpermanent members chosen 11-13, 896C1

Narcotic Drugs, Commission on—*See 'Economic & Social Council' above*

1976

Refugees, Office of the High Commissioner for
Chile refugees start hunger strike 1-13, 47G2
S Africa vs aid denial to Angola 2-12, 228G1
Rpts Leb civil war losses 2-21, 145E2
Argentina asylum vow rptd 4-9, 264B2
US cites re Rhodesia 4-27, 294B2
Argentina frees 25 after protest 6-12; UN seeks other refuges 6-14, 495G3
Argentina refugees stage protest 7-6—7-18, 571E2
Rpts Uruguay refugees kidnaped in Argentina 7-19, 571A3
US citizens quit Vietnam 8-1, 8-7, 593G1
Intl Angola aid progrm rptd 8-6, 862G2
Rhodesia raid on Mozambique scored 8-20, 661A2
Rpts Angola refugee total 10-2, 862C2
Vs Iran return of Sovt defector 11-1, 854D2
Vs Thai return of Cambodians 12-3, 929C2

Relief & Works Agency for Palestinian Refugees in the Near East (UNRWA)
Assemb vs Israel Gaza resetlmts 11-23, 878G2

Secretariat & Headquarters—*See also WALDHEIM, Kurt*
Geneva staff strike 2-25—3-3, 164E3
Wm Hill dies 5-18, 524F2
Spain king visits 6-4, 459B3
Waldheim 2d term seen 10-5, Echeverria sets bid 11-29, 906D3
US accuses Waldheim on jobs 10-11, 760A2
Echeverria sets secy gen bid 11-29, 906F3
Cncl backs Waldheim reelectn 12-7, 914D2
Waldheim reelected 12-8, 914C2

Security Council—*See also under MIDDLE EAST—UN DEVELOPMENTS*
'76 membership listed 62F2
Zaire protests Dilolo raid 1-16, 36A1
Asks Namibia electns, scores S Africa 1-31, 103D2
France vetoes Comoro resolutn 2-8, 118G3
Special Angola session opens 3-26; S Africa censured 3-31, 228A2
World Ct urges Aegean talks 4-11, 845B1, A2
Asks Indonesia quit Timor 4-22, 334F3
Kissinger cites African resolutns 4-27, 293F1, 294C1-D2
Extends UNFICYP 6-16, 457B1
Scores S Africa re riots, apartheid 6-19, 447F2
US vetoes Angola membership 6-23, 455E1
Sudan ties Libya to coup try 7-5, 501E3
Condemns S Africa re Zambia raid 7-30, 653E2
Greek-Turk Aegean feud debated 8-12—8-13, 622D2, D3
US rpts N Korea killings 8-19, 619D1
Namibia Cncil vs S Africa plan 8-20, 654A2
Asks Greek-Turkish talks on Aegean 8-25, 643E2
Scores S Africa Namibia plan 8-31, 653C3
US to veto Viet entry 9-13; vote delayed 9-14, 682B1
Members listed 9-21, 720C1
Rhodesia sanctn end asked 9-22, 717D1
S Africa arms ban vetoed 10-19, 781C3
US vetoes Viet entry 11-15, 862B3
For Angola membership 11-22, 879C1
US vows 2d Viet entry veto 11-26, 914C2
Echeverria sets secy gen bid 11-29, 906F3
Backs Waldheim for 2d term 12-7, 914D2
Condemns S Africa re Lesotho-Transkei pressure 12-22, 954B3

1977

Racism & Racial Discrimination, UN Decade for Action to Combat
Kurd deportatns chrgd 1-16, 257B1

Refugees, Office of the High Commissioner for
Viet refugee flow rptd up 3-25, 243E3
Westn natns to take Viet refugees 6-16, 497D1
Indochina plea studied by Japan 8-25, 685G2
Cambodia refugees get Viet asylum 10-19, 840G2

Relief & Works Agency, UN (UNRWA)
US vows more aid 7-12, 550D2

Secretariat & Headquarters—*See also WALDHEIM, Kurt*
Sovt bloc chrgd re Rhodesia sanctn violatns 2-10, 122D3
Forgn cos scored re Namibia bias 4-19, 349G2

Security Council—*See also under MIDDLE EAST—UN*
15 members listed 4E1
Botswana chrgs Rhodesia border violatns 1-12, van der Byl asks debate role 1-13, 73G1
Benin coup probe agreed 2-8, 96C3
Waldheim gets Benin probe rpt 3-8, 243A3
US backs Japan permanent seat 3-21, 209C3
Benin coup try scored 4-14, 309A2
Cyprus peace efforts rptd 5-2, 394E2
Rhodesia info offices banned 5-27, 457F1
Cyprus peace keeping mandate extended 6-16, 476G1
Mozambique aid asked 6-30, 536E1
Viet membership OKd 7-20, 572D2
US chrome imports from Rhodesia chrgd 7-26, 581G3
US to allow Rhodesia office 8-26, 699A3
Rhodesia envoy named 9-29, 809F2
S Africa arms embargo debated 10-24, 825D1
Electns held 10-24, 852E3
Rhodesia envoy tours southn Africa 10-30—11-9, 875G2
S Africa econ sanctns, permanent arms ban vetoed; apartheid res OKd 10-31, 851F2
S Africa arms ban voted; text 11-4, 851C1
Mozambique refugee aid rptd 12-13, 1000A2
Assemb urges S Africa oil, investmt embargoes 12-16, 1016G1

1978

Peace Keeping Missions in the Middle East—*See under MIDDLE EAST—UN*

Racism & Racial Discrimination, UN Decade for Action to Combat
Conf censures Israel, S Africa; Canada, Australia, NZ, 9 EC natns quit 8-26, 676G1-C2

Radio & Visual Services, Division of (Secretariat)
Israel bars filming in occupied areas 10-7, 762B3

Refugees, Office of the High Commissioner for
Hartling replaces Aga Khan 1-1, 62B1
Thai policy on Laos refugees scored 2-16, 139F3-140A1
Australia to accept Indochina refugees 3-15, 187F2
Hartling seeks more Indochina refugee funds 4-18, 341D2
Thais put Cambodian refugees in camps 4-30, 341D2
S Africa scored re Angola raid 6-16, 475D3
Viet, Cambodia, Laos refugee flow 10-11, 776C2
Honduras refugee camp aid pledged 11-6, 883D2
Indochina flow rptd high, conf planned 11-10, 870G2
Viet boat gets supplies 11-14, 871B1

Relief & Works Agency, UN (UNRWA)
Leb refugees flee Israeli invasn 3-18, 3-19, 198A2

Rhodesian Actions—*See RHODESIA—Majority Rule*

Scientific and Technical Committee, UN
Satellite safety study vetoed 3-14, 238A2

Secretariat & Headquarters—*See also WALDHEIM, Kurt*
Dadzie named econ dvpt dir gen 3-8, 401E3
USSR undersecy defects to US 4-26, 302A2
Sovt aide promoted despite US, UK spy chrgs 8-29, 676E1
Pro-Palestinian drive starts, Israel bars filming 10-7, 762G2-C3

Security Council—*See also under MIDDLE EAST—UN*
Namibia conf held by Westn members 2-11—2-12, 113A3
US bars S Africa mil, police exports 2-17, 135F1
Rhodesia internal pact rejected 3-14, 192E3
Vorster OKs western-sponsored Namibia independnc plan 4-25, 299C1
S Africa sanctns asked by Assemb 5-3, 339C1
S Africa Angola raid condemned 5-6, 339B1
Namibia plan OKd by SWAPO 7-12, 547C2
Namibia plan OKd 7-27, 561G2
Racism conf asks S Africa econ sanctns 8-26, 676A2
Waldheim presents Namibia plan 8-30, 741G3
Venez asks Nicaragua rights probe 9-2; Nicaragua scores 9-4, 9-5, 690D3
5 new nonpermanent members picked, membership noted 9-19, 713A3
Waldheim Namibia plan OKd 9-29, 819E2
Rhodesia ldrs' US visit regretted 10-10, 818F3
US asks role in Viet-Cambodia dispute 11-5, 859D3
Canada-S Africa arms deal suspected 11-6—11-7, 904E2
S Africa sanctns threatened re Namibia electns 11-13, 904A2
Assemb asks Israel arms ban 11-27, 931A3
S Africa pledges Namibia response 12-2, sanctns vote delayed 12-3, 988F3

1979

Refugees, Office of the High Commissioner for
Ethiopians rptd fleeing to Somalia 1-14, 271D1
Viets to be processed in Hong Kong 1-22, 51F2
Viet refugee exodus plan OKd 3-1, 181C1
Pl civil war refugees estimated 3-5, 193D1
Zaire refugee return data rptd 3-6, 215D2
Indonesia, Pl OK Viet refugee plan 3-30, 299G1
Viet refugee drowning scored 4-2, 299E1
Thais force Cambodia refugees back 4-20, 318D1
Indochina refugee conf held 5-15–5-16, 379E1
Viet agrmt set 6-8, 436D1
Malaysia vs plea on Viet refugees 6-15, plea renewed 6-16, 460F1, 474E1
June 1-15, total Indochina data rptd 6-21, 473G2
Japan to hike aid 7-2, 495E2
Viet vows agrmt compliance 7-20, 550G1
Geneva conf to aid Indochinese 7-21, 549C1
US-Viet visa plan talks cited 7-23, 549D2
Argentina pol refugee rights pressed 8-8, 627F1
Viet denies US visa processing agrmt 8-11, 607F2
Indochina refugees rptd down 8-22, 625E3
Cyprus rep antiquities seized 9-14, resigns 9-15 751E2
Ethiopia refugees in Somalia rptd 9-21, 791B1
Indochina refugee Sept exit from Thai rptd 10-3, 764B1

Secretariat & Headquarters—*See WALDHEIM, Kurt*

Security Council—*See also under MIDDLE EAST-U.N.*
Cambodia asks mtg on Viet invasn 1-2; US backs bid 1-3, Viet vs 1-4, 1E1
China chrgs Viet aggressn in Cambodia 1-7, 11C1
Viet invasn of Cambodia discussed 1-11–1-12, 10G1
Cambodia-Viet war debated 1-13; Sovt, Czech veto action 1-15, 28E1
Namibia plan falters 1-13–3-3, S Africa rejcts truce 3-5, 171B2, A3
Viet debate delayed 2-21, 123B1
China-Viet, Cambodia-Viet wars debated 2-23; actn stalled 2-28, 142A1
USSR vetoes res on Viet, Cambodia conflicts 3-16, 200D1
Namibia contact group, Botha meet 3-19–3-22; Pretoria vs compromise 5-7, extends assemb power 5-8, 354B2
Rhodesia electns condemned, sanctns retained 4-30, 332G1-A2
Namibia contact group abstains on S Africa censure vote 5-31, 428B1
Angola rpts S Africa '76-79 raid casualties 8-2, 617F2
Israel S Africa arms embargo compliance cited 9-7, 720D3
S Africa condemned re Angola raids 11-2, 875G1
Iran asked to free US Emb hostages 11-9, 862E1
Namibia conf held 11-12–11-16, 889D3
Iran seeks debate on US Emb takeover 11-13; US, others reject 11-14, 861B1, 862A1
US plea re Iran hostage trial rejctd 11-20, 878D2
Waldheim asks Iran debate; US, Iran agree 11-25; Iran stalls, mtg delayed 11-27, 896A1
Iran refuses to attend Cncl mtg 11-30, 913F1
Meets on Iran 12-1–12-2, asks Iran free US hostages 12-4; Waldheim contacts Iran 12-5, 913A1, G1
UK backs US re Iran 12-17, 968A2
Assemb scores Zimbabwe sanctns end by US, UK 12-18, 960F1
US seeks Iran econ sanctns 12-21, warns USSR vs veto 12-22; US-sponsored res adopted, 4 natns abstain 12-31, 974F2
Zimbabwe sanctns end voted 12-21, 976A3, C3
Iran cool to Waldheim missn 12-30; Waldheim, 2 aides depart 12-31, 974D3

1980

Refugees, Office of the High Commissioner for
Afghan war refugees in Pak rptd 1-6, 3C2
Zimbabwe refugee return begins 1-21, 49E1
Argentina ex-prisoners describe ordeal 2-4, 95B1
Zimbabwe repatriatn halted 2-25, 198A2
Cuba refugee processing aid rptd 6-9, 435A2
Thais asked to delay Cambodian repatriatn 6-15, transfer aided 6-17—6-18, 475F3
Canadian offcl freed in Kabul 6-22, 486B2
Malaysia rpts Viet refugee decline 8-10, 645D1
Viet emigratn plan seen failing 8-24, 645C1
US seeks aid re Sovt soldier asylum request 9-15, 704F3
Somalia asks aid rise 9-21, 736C1

Restricting or Banning Weapons Deemed Inhumane or Excessively Injurious, UN Conference on
Treaty produced 10-10, sessn ends 10-13, 777E1

Security Council
Waldheim in Iran on hostage missn 1-1—1-3, rpts to closed sessn 1-7, 3G2, B3
4 nonpermanent members take seats 1-1, Mex elected 1-7, 12G1
Sovt Afghan invasn mtg sought 1-3—1-4; debate 1-5—1-6; Sovts veto res for pullout 1-7, 2F1
Afghan issue shifted to Assemb 1-10, 25E1
Iran mtg 1-11—1-12; sanctns voted, Sovts veto 1-13; reactn 1-11—1-14, 28G3-29C2
Zimbabwe fair electns asked 2-2, 118C2
Syria says Israel plans attack 2-23, 140B3
Res demands Israel raze setlmts, scores E Jerusalem rule 3-1, 162E2
Israel res text 3-1, 179C1
Begin scores setlmts res, US vote reversal 3-6, 179B1-B2
US vote on Israel called mistake, US policy affirmed 3-14, 209F1
US Cong probes Israel setlmt vote, Vance defends US stand 3-20, 3-21, 218B2
Waldheim rpts Israel Leb pullout 4-13, 283G3
Israel Leb incursn scored; US, USSR, E Ger abstain 4-24, 302E3
Palestinian state res vetoed by US; US, Sovt aides assaulted 4-30, 325D1, G1
Israeli deportatn of W Bank ldrs condemned 5-8, 340D3
S Africa delays Namibia talks 5-12, 374B2
Bahamas protest Cuba air attack 5-13, 371B3
Israel censured re W Bank ousters 5-20, 381C1
PLO asks mtg on W Bank bombings 6-2, Israeli scored 6-5, 417G1, A2
Namibia talks feared imperiled 6-13, 466C3
S Africa censured for Angola raids; US, UK, France abstain 6-27, 524F3
Israel Jerusalem moves scored 6-30, 491B2
Waldheim scores Israel Leb attack 8-19, 628A1
Israel Jerusalem policies scored, US abstains 8-20, 627C2; Israel scores 8-23, 643B2; 8-28, 660A3
S Africa chrgs SWAPO support 8-29; US denies 9-9, 710D3
Iraq, Iran war end asked 9-23, 718D3

1976

Trade and Development, UN Conference on (UNCTAD)
SELA mtg ends 1-15, 60F2
PLO becomes member 1-27, 85A2
77 Group sets trade guidelines; 3 new members chosen 2-10, 107G3
Australia OKs tin pact, US ratificatn cited 4-28, 380F1
Prelim meetings 5-3, 5-4, 320D2
Nairobi conf opens, Kenyatta boycotts 5-5, 320E1
Kissinger addresses 5-6, 317A1-318G1
Conf ends, commodity fund set 5-30, 388E2
Kissinger cites Nairobi mtg 6-21, 450G1
7-natn econ summit discusses commodity fund 6-27—6-28, 462C2
Transnational Corporations, Permanent Commission on
Meeting deadlocked 3-2—3-12, 297F3
US anti-bribe plan detailed 3-5, 199F3, 200C1
US anti-bribe plan cited 8-3, 668A3
Truce Supervision Organization, UN—*See 'UNTSO' under MIDDLE EAST—UN DEVELOPMENTS*
UNCTAD—*See 'Trade & Development, UN Conference on' above*
UNDOF (UN Disengagement Force)—*See under MIDDLE EAST—UN DEVELOPMENTS*
UNEF (UN Emergency Force)—*See under MIDDLE EAST—UN DEVELOPMENTS*
UNESCO—*See 'Educational, Scientific & Cultural Organization' above*
UNICEF—*See 'Children's Fund' above*
UNRWA—*See 'Relief & Works Agency' above*
UNTSO (UN Truce Supervision Organization)—*See under MIDDLE EAST—UN DEVELOPMENTS*
U.S. Relations—*See also other appropriate subheads in this section; also UNITED Nations under U.S. GOVERNMENT*
US ties econ aid to votes 1-9, 2A1
Moynihan resigns 2-2, 89B1
No policy chng planned 2-10, 109D3
Scranton named amb 2-25, 150C1
Scranton confirmed 3-3, 186C2
White quits US delegatn 3-10, 272B1
Tin pact ratificatn cited 4-28, 380A2
US Dem platform text cites 6-15, 477C3, G3, 478E3
Young designated US amb 12-16, 936G1-C2
Vetoes
US vetoes Palestine resolutn 1-26, 59F2-G3
France vetoes Comoro resolutn 2-8, 118G3
US vetoes Israel occupatn resolutn 3-25, 211D1
US vetoes Angola entry 6-23, 455E1
US 16th on Israel exit 6-29, 464B1, D1
US, France, UK vs S Africa arms ban 10-19, 781C3
US vs Viet membership 11-15, 862B3

1977

Trade and Development, UN Conference on (UNCTAD)
Bolivia tin pact ratificatn bar rptd 1-10, 169G1
Intl rubber buffer stock plan rejctd 1-23, 169F2
Rpts '76 commodity price rise 2-14, 145F3
Commodity talks deadlocked 4-3, 297C3
Flag-of-convenience shipping study rptd 4-17, 337D2
Sugar pact talks 4-18—5-27, 457G3
North-South talks end 6-3, 437B2, F2
Common fund commodity talks fail 12-1, 974E2
Poor natn '78 debt servicing costs, '77 debts rptd 12-6, 998A1
Training and Research, UN Institute for
World oil resource rpt 4-26, 362F2
UNCTAD—*See 'Trade & Development, UN Conference on' above*
UNECE—*See 'Europe, Economic Commission for' above*
UNEF—*See under MIDDLE EAST—UN*
UNESCO—*See 'Educational, Scientific & Cultural Organization' above*
UNRWA—*See 'Relief & Works Agency, UN' above*
U.S. Policy & Developments—*See also YOUNG, Andrew*
Assemb, Cncl member; Dillard on World Ct 4C1-F1
Sovt UNEF fund bar scored 1-6, 1-7, 4A3
Young confrmd amb 1-26, 52C3
Rhodesia sanctns backed 1-31, 72F3
Rights Comm del to seek Orlov probe 2-11, 117D1
Israel occupatn rule res opposed 2-15, 107E2
Sovt dissident probe asked 2-18, 137G2; bid dropped 3-11, 207E1
Richardson confrmd sea conf rep 2-24, 148F3
Uganda mediatn role rejctd 2-27, 141F1
S Africa isolatn backed 2-28, 145A2
S Africa isolatn backed 2-28, 145A2
Tyson regrets Chile coup role 3-8; US disavows, summons home 3-8—3-9, 218E3
At Water Conf 3-14—3-25, 250E1
Carter addresses Assemb 3-17, 185A1-186B2
Rhodesian chrome ban signed 3-18, 191C1
Japan permanent Cncl seat backed 3-21, 209C3
ILO depoliticizatn moves backed 3-21, 227F2
Carter on Viet entry 3-24, 229B3
PLO Geneva conf role barred 3-29, 227B1
Plutonium ban scored 4-17, 334A3
Bennett confrmd NATO amb 4-25, 418C1
A-export curbs proposed 4-27, 334E1
Church backs IAEA powers 5-2, 335B1
Viet entry backing pledged 5-3—5-4, 333A1
At southn Africa parley 5-16—5-21, 399B1
More UNRWA aid vowed 7-12, 550D2
Sea Law Conf adjourns 7-15, US scores rpt 7-20, 572G2
Viet entry backed 7-19, Cncl OKs 7-20, 572E2; Carter comments 7-21, 575B1
ECOSOC admits PLO 7-22, 572G2
Rhodesia sanctns com accuses 7-26, 581G3
Contributn authorizatn signed 8-4, 668A2
Young backs rights comr 8-8—8-9, 646G2
Japan studies Indochina refugee plea 8-25, 685G2
Desert fund opposed 9-9, 770F1
McHenry at S Africa funeral 9-25, 735D3
Carter addresses Gen Assemb 10-4, 749A2, 751G2-752G1
Carter signs rights pacts 10-5, 769D2
Vs special Viet aid 10-6, 770B2
USSR tries to blackmail UNESCO envoy 10-19, 866C2-B3
French evacuatn of Mayotte opposed 10-26, 869A1
Abstains on anti-Israel res 10-28, 830F2
S Africa econ sanctns, permanent arms ban vetoed; apartheid res OKd 10-31, 851F2
Assemb Nambia vote abstentns 11-4, 851E1
Vs Assemb res on Israel occupatn 11-25, 910D2
Vs Palestine 'rights' drive; fund cut hinted 12-2, 931F1
Chile rights abuse res backed 12-16, 983E1
Vetoes
S Africa econ sanctns, permanent arms ban 10-31, 851F2

1978

Trade and Development, UN Conference on (UNCTAD)
Poor natn debt relief talks, '77 debt estimates cited 3-11, 301A1
Common fund commodity talks fail 11-30, 998F1
UNCTAD—*See 'Trade and Development, UN Conference on' above*
UNDOF (UN Disengagement Observer Force)—*See under MIDDLE EAST—UN*
UNECE—*See 'Europe, Economic Commission for' above*
UNEF—*See under MIDDLE EAST—UN*
UNESCO—*See 'Educational, Scientific and Cultural Organization' above*
UNICEF—*See 'Children's Emergency Fund' above*
UNIFIL (United Nations Interim Force in Lebanon)—*See MIDDLE EAST, subheads LEBANON and UN*
UNRWA—*See 'Relief & Works Agency, UN' above*
U.S. Policy & Developments—*See also YOUNG, Andrew*
US ouster of Viet amb protested 2-9, 103A3
Rights comm resolutns vs Israel opposed 2-14, 99A2
S Africa mil, police exports barred 2-17, 135F1
Argentina disappearances scored 3-6, 208A1
USSR scored re Rostropovich ouster 3-16, 179D3
Leb peace force res sponsored 3-19, 197A1
Sea Law Conf deadlock continues 4-6—5-19, 401A3
Panama circulates note on US treaty reservatn 4-7, 255E2
ICAO picks bad-weather landing system 4-19, 319A2-C3
Sun Day marked 5-3, 322A1
2 Sovts arrested as spies 5-20, 409A3
Assemb disarmamt sessn opens 5-23; affirms A-test ban committmt, regional agrmts 5-24, 421C1
Sea Law Conf talks continue 5-23—7-15, seabed mining bill debated 8-21—9-16, 732C3
ILO urges US rejoin 6-7, 523E3
Solzhenitsyn commencemt address scores 6-8, 444B2
US vows more Africa peace efforts 6-20, 487D2
McHenry in Angola 6-20—6-26, 547G2
Assemb disarmamt sessn ends; Geneva chrmn chngs OKd, total A-test ban barred 6-30, 522B3, 523B1
USSR missn picketed re Shcharansky 7-10, 542B3
Seabed mining bill clears US House 7-26, 588G3
ILO rpts '77 jobless rate 7-28, 677D1
Rhodesia sanctns conditnl end backed by Cong 8-2, 588D1
'65 papal visit cited 8-6, 601B2
Sovt aide promoted despite spy chrgs 8-29, 676E1
Cambodian cruelty chrgd 8-31, 748E1
PR called US colony 9-13, 979C3
Unifil extensn plan OKd 9-18, 713D1
Cncl, Assemb member 713A3, F3
Cncl regrets Rhodesian ldrs visit 10-10, 818F3
US sens vs Carter plea on Cambodia 10-12, 794G1
2 Sovts convicted as spies 10-13, 10-30, 835A2
Cncl role in Viet-Cambodia dispute asked 11-5, 859D3
Canada-S Africa arms sales rptd probed 11-7, 904E2
Cncl abstentn on Namibia electn warning 11-13, 904B2
UNESCO press declaratn hailed 11-22, vote on Israel scored 11-29, 931E1, G1
Assemb arms ban res vs Israel scored 11-27, 931B3
Palestinian Solidarity Day boycotted 11-29, 951G2
Carter marks Human Rights Declaration anniv, urges Genocide Conv ratificatn 12-6, 934A1

1979

Telecommunications Union, International
World Admin Radio Conf held 9-27-12-6, 1006A3
Trade and Development, UN Conference on (UNCTAD)
Commodity fund set 3-20, 200D2
Manila mtg 5-7-6-3, 417E2
Rubber accord reached 10-5, 781A3
US bars sugar price supports, ISA role 10-23, 808D2
Training and Research, UN Institute for
Canada-US oil-sands study pact signed 6-4, 444E2
UNDOF (United Nations Disengagement Observer Force)—*See under MIDDLE EAST-U.N.*
UNEF—*See under MIDDLE EAST-U.N.*
UNIFIL (United Nations Interim Force in Lebanon)—*See MIDDLE EAST, subheads LEBANON and U.N.*
UNTSO—*See under MIDDLE EAST-U.N.*
U.S. Policy & Developments—*See also YOUNG, Andrew*
Cambodia bid for mtg on Viet invasion backed 1-3, 1F1
Mezvinsky on Israel torture chrgs 2-11, 108D2
ECOSOC gets drug rpt 2-12, 140C3
Rights comm resolutns vs Israel, southn Africa, pro-Palestinian state opposed 2-21, 148E1
Cncl mtg on China, Viet asked 2-22; troop exits asked 2-23, 142B1
Namibia plan fails 3-3, S Africa rejcts proposal 3-5, 171B2, A3
Namibia compromise proposed 3-19—3-22; Pretoria bars 5-7, extends assemb powers 5-8, 354F2
UNCTAD commodity fund set 3-20, 200D2
W Bank probe res abstentn 3-22, 198E2
Bourne gets water projct post 4-25, 392G1
2 Sovt spies exchngd for dissidents 4-27, 317B1
Rhodesia electn vote abstentn 4-30, 332A2
Arabs warned on WHO actn vs Israel 5-8, 5-12, 398G2
S Africa Assemb ouster opposed 5-24, 409F3
ABA panel scores Argentine justice 5-26, 467B1
Namibia Assemb vote abstentn 5-31, 428B1
Canada oil-sands pact signed 6-4, 444E2
Unifil res called one-sided 6-14, 436B3
Assemb disarmamt sessn cited in SALT II communique 6-18, 457B2, 458A1, D1
Double agent rptd exposed by Sovt spy 6-24, 521C1
Indochina refugee conf asked 6-28, 473E2
Australia uranian accord signed 7-5, 501E1
Israel setlmt halt abstentn 7-20, 551B2
Viet USA plan talks cited 7-23, 549D2
UNTSO to replace UNEF; Israel vs, Egypt OKs 7-24; US vs Israel 7-25, 551A1
Vance sees Israel amb re UNTSO 7-27; Egypt, Israel talks asked 7-29; US force offcr departures rptd 8-1, 574E2
US, Israel meet on UNTSO 7-31; US assures on Res 242 7-31, 8-8, 591A2, F3
US denies Viet tie talks held 8-3, 8-9, Viets renew claim 8-9, 8-11, 607G2
Cambodia food aid plea issued 8-8-8-9, 600E3
Young resigns re PLO contact 8-15, hints at more contacts 8-16; US, forgn reactn 8-15, 8-16, 605A1, 606E1-F2
McHenry named amb 8-31, 660F2
Anti-Israel res backed 9-5, US govt dissociates 9-6, 659E2
Membership listed 695B3
Pol Pot govt seat upheld 9-19, 695C2
Pol Pot govt seat backed 9-21, USSR scores 9-22, 741G1, B2
Carter denies Jewish pressure to oust Young 9-23, 763E2
McHenry sworn 9-23, 763F2
Leb peace urged 9-24, 741C2
Cambodia food aid sought 10-9, 767A2
ISA participatn defeated 10-23, 808C2
Cambodia aid vowed 10-24, 811F1; 11-5 863C3
S Africa Cncl vote abstentn 11-2, 875G1

1980

Iran-Iraq war truce, mediatn asked 9-28; Iraq backs 9-29, Iran vs 10-1, 733F1, D2-734B1
Iran ends boycott, Rajai to present case vs Iraq; Iraq defends invasn 10-15, 774C1
Iran-Iraq war debate, US offers peace plan 10-17, 10-22—10-23, 798D2, 799B1
Cuba, CR end seat try 10-20, 11-12; 5 new nonpermanent members chosen 11-13, 896C1
Iran-Iraq peace missn asked 11-5; Palme named envoy 11-11, missn to Teheran, Baghdad ends 11-24, rpts to Waldheim 11-25, 894G2
Namibia talks schedule agreed 11-24, 967F1
UNIFIL mandate extended 12-17, 977D3
Israel asked to readmit 2 W Bank mayors 12-19, 952B2
Truce Supervision Organization, UN—*See 'UNTSO' below*
UNESCO (UN Educational, Scientific and Cultural Organization)
Acropolis rescue plan set 4-15, 285D2, E2
Pope addresses 6-2, 476G3
E Ger aide's arrest protested 6-6, confirmed 6-10; aide sentenced as spy 9-6, 708A1
Gen Conf in Belgrade, Israel oppositn cited 9-23—10-28; world info order backed 10-25, Arafat addresses 10-27, 821F2-F3
Afghan delegate to Belgrade conf defects 10-25, 827E2
World illiteracy study rptd 12-4, 953E1
UNICEF (UN International Children's Emergency Fund)
Cambodia backlog rptd 1-2, 12D2
Thai border statn operatn suspended 2-7, 108G1
Cambodia food disaster averted 2-10, 108D1
Cambodia famine renewal feared 3-21, rice seed airlifted 4-4, 261D3, 262A1
Cambodia relief aid halted 6-17, renewal OKd 7-12, 591D2; resumed 8-4, 644F3
S Leb dvpt plan signed 10-14, 775E2
Cambodia '81 aid end set 12-16, 951F3
UNIFIL (UN Interim Force in Lebanon)
Palestinian-Christn clashes in south 2-13, 125F2; for subsequent developments, see LEBANON—Military Developments
UNTSO (UN Truce Supervision Organization)
Christns oust 4 from Leb post 4-17, 302D3
U.S. Policy & Developments
Waldheim in Iran 1-1—1-3, briefs Carter 1-6, 3F2
Cncl seeks Afghan invasn mtg 1-3—1-4; McHenry assails USSR 1-6, pullout res vetoed 1-7, 2F1
Assemb meets on Afghan invasn 1-11—1-12; res deplores, demands exit 1-14, 25D1-26B2
Cncl meets on Iran 1-11—1-12; votes sanctns, Sovts veto 1-13; reactn 1-11—1-14, 29G3-29C2
Eichelberger dies 1-26, 104D2
Indl dvpt aid fund disputed 2-9, 124C2, F2
Kennedy, Admin exchng chrgs re Iran intl comm 2-12—2-13, 109B2-C3
Carter backs Iran intl comm 2-13, 105B1, 109C2, D3
Rights comm res on Afghan backed 2-13, res adopted 2-14, 123F3
ILO rejoined 2-18, 124F3-125A1
Israel setlmt res backed 3-1, disavowed 3-3, 162F2, 163D1
Kennedy scores Israeli setlmt vote 3-11, 183D3
Israeli setlmt vote info curbed 3-12; Cong coms open probes, Vance defends US stand 3-20, 3-21, 218B2
Carter calls Israel setlmt vote mistake, reaffirms policy 3-14, 309F1
Israeli setlmt vote a NY primary issue 3-25, 221C2, B3
Cambodia relief aid vowed 3-26, 261F3
Bush scores 'fiasco' 4-7, 264D2
Israeli Leb pullout role cited 4-13, 284A1
Israel Leb incursn res abstensn 4-24, 302E3
Darvon productn curbed 4-24, 358A2, B2
US vetoes Palestinian state res, Vanden Heuvel assaulted 4-30, 325D1
US abstains on Cncl W Bank deportatn res 5-8, 340D3
Israel W Bank ouster censure 5-20, 381D1
Cambodia aid conf opens 5-26, 397B2
Cncl vote vs W Bank bombings abstentn 6-5, 417A2
Israeli constructn bid rejctn protested 6-19, 476B2
UN Charter backed 6-25, 474B3
Cncl abstentn on S Africa raid censure 6-27, 524F3
Israel Jerusalem moves abstentn 6-30, 491C2
Women's conf attended 7-14—7-30; anti-bias pact signed 7-17, racism motion withdrawn 7-28, 5-yr plan opposed 7-30, 587E1, C2-A3
Reagan pres nominatn acceptance speech cites US vote 'mistake' 7-17, 533E1
McHenry in Nicaragua, marks Somoza downfall 7-19, 565F2
US walks out on Iranian speaker 7-25, 572D2
Assemb res backing Palestinian state opposed 7-29, 572F1

1976

Women's Year, International—*See under 'W'*
World Court—*See 'International Court of Justice' in this section above*
World Food Council
OPEC aids agri fund 5-11, 389F1
Food-stockpile plan stalled 6-14—6-16, 450B1 ★
US Dem platform text backs agri fund 6-15, 476C3
OPEC asks West aid agri fund 8-5, 643A2
World Health Organization (WHO)
Argentina rep found dead 1-21, 96A2
Guatemala quake aid rptd 2-10, 120E3
Flu alert issued 2-19, 224E2
Postwar Viet med rpt 3-20, 315D2
Israel W Bank, Gaza health data rptd 5-10, 338C2
Vs panel rpt on Israel-occupied areas 5-17; OKs anti-Israel resolutn 5-19, 355F1
Malaria parasite cultured 6-1, 423A3
Rpts no swine flu 6-3, 423E3
Cancer studies underway 6-3, 484G2
Gonorrhea strain resists penicillin 10-7, 815B1
African fever identified 10-14, 795A3
Wins Lasker award 11-17, 910D3
African fever contained 11-21, 931C3
World Meteorological Organization
UN staff asks Sovt ex-translator freed 3-30, 421B3

1977

Water Conference, UN
Parley held in Argentina 3-14—3-25, 250D1
World Food Council
Manila conf seeks hunger end 6-20—6-24, 513C3
World Food Program
Ethiopia crisis seen 8-23, 684E3
World Health Organization (WHO)
Kenya smallpox rptd 2-5, 224B1
Staff cut in goal shift 2-12, 170F3
Australia cholera strain identified 3-9, 199A2
Australia cholera danger end rptd 3-16, 280C3
Global immunizatn drive launched 4-7, 287B3
7-yr cancer study set 5-10, 431G1
Saccharin rpt finds no human risk 5-13, 531D1
Israel may lift ban 8-31, 663A3
Malaria rptd 9-4, 747D3
Syria cholera notificatn rptd 9-26, 748A1
Penicillin-resistant gonorrhea rptd 10-22, 847D2

1978

World Food Program
Ethiopia aid set 6-9, 465B3
World Health Organization (WHO)
Smallpox notificatn asked 5-26, 2 cases rptd 8-2, 636B1
S Africa scored re Angola raid 6-16, 475D3
Malaria increases rptd 8-6, 635F3
Chinese cancer deaths rptd 8-28, 727A2
Kennedy at USSR conf 9-6, 742G3
Smallpox death in UK 9-11; lab virus destructn asked 10-27, eradicatn countdown continues 11-7, 927F1-D2

1979

Namibia talks reopen 11-12–11-16, 889D3
Cncl debate on Iran hostages rejctd 11-14, 862A1
Iran hostage trial plea urged, 11-19; Waldheim issues statement, Cncl bars 11-19–11-20, 878D2
Iran Cncl debate agreed 11-25, 896C1
World Ct chrgs vs Iran filed 11-29, 896G1
Assemb vote on Egypt-Israel pact scored 11-29, 979G2
Iran hostage release asked 12-1–12-2, Cncl OKs res 12-4; US optimistic 12-5, 912A1, D2
Carter drafts hostage plan 12-8, 934C1
World Ct plea on Iran hostages filed 12-10, 933D1
UK vows Cncl support re Iran 12-17, 968A2
Zimbabwe sanctns end scored by Assemb 12-18, 960F1
Cncl sanctns vs Iran sought 12-21, USSR warned vs veto 12-22; res adopted 12-31, 974F2

WHO—*See 'World Health Organization' below*
World Food Program
Cambodia famine aid unlikely 4-22, 318D2
Cambodian refugee aid distributed in Thailand 12-18, 977G3
World Health Organization (WHO)
UK smallpox rpt released 1-3, 7B2
Alcoholism rptd on rise globally 3-9, 218B3
Assemb 5-7–5-24; Arab moves vs Israel, Egypt blocked 5-22–5-24; W Bank, Gaza health probe set 5-23, 398E2
Nicaragua announces health plan 8-9, 616A1

1980

Cncl abstentn on Israel Jerusalem policies 8-20, 627C2; Israel denounces 8-23, 643B2; 8-28, 660A3
Muskie addresses aid talks 8-25, 642G2
Richardson lauds Sea Law Conf 8-29, 660D1
Reagan scores Jerusalem abstentn 9-3, 681B3
McHenry denies S Africa chrgs 9-9, 710F3
Refugee comr aid re Sovt soldier asylum request sought 9-15, 704G3
Econ aid sessn ends in no agrmt 9-15, 736G1
Muskie addresses Assemb on Iran hostages 9-22, 719F2
Muskie sees Waldheim in Iran-Iraq war 9-23, 718E3
Carter scores move to oust Israel 9-29, 739A1
Reagan vows Israel support 10-1, 738B2
Bush scores Carter 'flipflop' 10-16, 817C3
Cncl hears Iran denunciatns 10-17, US denies chrgs 10-17—10-19, 798D2
Cncl gets Iran-Iraq peace plan 10-22—10-23, 799B1
UNESCO world info order backed 10-25, 821C3
Micronesia self-rule pacts signed 10-31, 11-17, 884D1
US votes vs Israeli exit res 12-15, 952F2
Cncl res on W Bank mayors return backed 12-19, 952C2
Reagan designates US rep 12-22, 979F2
Women, UN Decade for
Women's conf in Denmark; anti-bias pact signed, other dvpts 7-14—7-30, 587E1-D3
World Court (International Court of Justice)
Gets US plea on hostages in Iran 3-18—3-20, 203C3
Demands Iran free US hostages 5-24, 393A1
Libya ignores Malta dispute ruling 8-21, 709G1
Baxter dies 9-26, 755B2
World Food Program
Cambodia Jan aid halted 1-2, 12C2
Cambodia relief shipmts disputed 3-10, 261G3
Cambodia relief aid halted 6-17, renewal OKd 7-12, 591D2
World Health Organization (WHO)
2 TB vaccines rptd ineffective 1-20, 63E1
Brazil polio data questioned 4-16, 310B2
Malaria outbreak rptd 5-31, 478B3

1976

UNITED Parcel Service of America Inc.
Teamsters strike 9-16—12-13, 942F2-D3
UNITED Press International (UPI)
'75 coll football rankings 1-2, 31A3
Butz interview 1-4, 3A3
Ecuador ousts reporter 1-13, 28F2
Death sentnc poll results 3-30, 262C1
Reagan interview 6-28, 467B3
Developing natns OK press pool 7-13, Beaton scores 7-19, 619A3
Sees Ford nominatn 8-17, 601E3
Dobriansky interview 10-8, 762D3
Dole addresses conv 10-8, 763G3-764A1
Syrians close Beirut office 12-19, re-open 12-20, 953E2
UNITED Slaves
Cited in Sen com rpt on FBI 5-6, 344B2
U.S. CONFERENCE of Mayors—*See MAYORS, U.S.*
U.S. FINANCIAL Inc.
Walter sentenced 2-3, 124C1
U.S.-FLAG-Shipping Companies and AFL-CIO Maritime Workers
Scores USSR re grain shipmts 8-17, 655E2

1977

UNITED Nuclear Corp.
Gen Atomic uranium suit OKd 10-31, 835C3
Gulf Oil trial opens 10-31, 895D2
UNITED Press International (UPI)
'76 coll football rankings 1-2, 8E3
Carter interview 1-24, 51B3
Gas, weather layoffs rptd 2-7, 91F2
Uruguay curbs reporters 3-24, 351E2
CIA links charged 9-12, 720B3, 721C1
On most reliable govt news source list 12-10, 1009B1
UNITED Refining Co.
Dropped from Fortune 500 list 341D1
UNITED States Auto Club (USAC)—*See AUTOMOBILE Racing*
UNITED States Code—*See U.S. GOVERNMENT—LEGISLATION*
U.S.-FAR Asia Narcotics Conference
Thai sessn opens 4-14, 331G2
U.S. FILTER Corp.
On '76 Fortune 500 list 341C1

1978

UNITED Nuclear Corp.
Wins Gen Atomic uranium suit 3-2, 144C1
Gen Atomic denied damage determinatn stay by Sup Ct 3-20, 206D1
Gen Atomic rpts new evidnc 4-20, 346F2-A3
Gen Atomic documts ruling declined by Sup Ct 5-15, 387F3
Gen Atomic damages awarded 5-16, 366A3
Gen Atomic trial judge interference ruled by Sup Ct 5-30, 430A3
UNITED Presbyterian Church in the U.S.A.—*See under PRESBYTERIANS*
UNITED Press International (UPI)
'77 coll football rankings 1-3, 8F2
Gets call on PLO aide murder 1-5, 3A2
Ohio, Ind power crisis rptd 2-10, 104C1
US citizen rptd held in USSR 4-12, 275G2
Schweiker wins Pulitzer 4-17; photo mix-up rptd, resigns 4-21, 314F2
Leningrad bur rptd closed 6-12, 476B2
NY Sovt office bombed 7-10 542A3
UNITED States Auto Club (USAC)—*See AUTOMOBILE Racing*
U.S. CATHOLIC (magazine)
Laity church role surveyed 4-7, 294E3
U.S. CODE
Criminal code revisn OKd by Sen 1-30, 64F1
Carter backs criminal code revisn 5-4, 320A3

1979

UNITED Nuclear Corp.
NM A-waste spill 7-16, cleanup continues 9-5, 744C1
Gen Atomic arbitratn ruling declined by Sup Ct 10-9, 784F1
UNITED Parcel Service (UPS)
Teamster pact rptd ratified 7-26, wage cncl OKs 7-27, 744E2
UNITED Press International (UPI)
'78 coll football rankings 1-2, 8B2
FBI dir interviewed 1-7, 17A3
4 US papers to open China offices 5-30, 406B2
S Africa UPITN link confirmed 6-4, 427E3
Press partnerships sale, '74-78 revenues rptd 10-4, 859F2-A3
FALN bomb threat rptd 10-17, 786E2
UNITED Refining Co.
Crude oil operatns cut 2-14, 126A2
U.S.A.-R.O.C. Economic Council
At mtg re US-China tie 1-15, 27B3
UNITED States Auto Club (USAC)—*See AUTOMOBILE Racing*
UNITED States Bank Note Co.
Food stamp probe rptd 2-2, 93C3

1980

UNITED Parcel Service of America Inc.
ICC regulatn case refused by Sup Ct 4-14, 307G1-A2
Parcel post rate case declined by Sup Ct 5-19, 440C2
UNITED Parcel Service v. U.S.
Case refused by Sup Ct 4-14, 307A2
UNITED Press International (UPI)
'79 coll football rankings 1-2, 22G3
Financing plan fails 1-31, 120C1
Wins Polk award 2-25, 692F3
Iran readmits newsmen 3-7, 178C2
Iran photo wins Pulitzer 4-14, 317E2
Agnew interview released 4-19, 333C3
Jankowski CBS resignatn hoax 5-23, 501A2
Clark story error admitted 6-6, 507D2
Sovt Olympic press crackdown rptd 7-21, 590F1
Boston eds hear Christopher 10-7, 758C1
3d World coverage study rptd 11-29, 914D1
US (magazine)
Sale rptd 3-7, 239A2

UNITED STATES GOVERNMENT

1976

ACTION
Extension signed 5-27, 982F1
Active Corps of Executives (ACE)
Cong clears funds 5-13, 393D1; signed 5-27, 982F1

1977

ACTION
Brown confrmd dir 2-25, 148D3
King confrmd dep dir 3-4, 211E1
Lewis confrmd assoc dir 8-4, 626A3
'78 funds clear Cong 12-7, 958F3

1978

ACTION
Peace Corps
S Africa hosp use barred 5-15, 633A1
Payton resigns as dir 11-24, 915F1

1979

ACTION
Peace Corps
Tanzania OKs return 1-9, 22F3
Nicaragua volunteers recalled 2-8, 255D1

1980

ACTION
Peace Corps
Colombia volunteer freed 2-11, 117A1
El Salvador office attacked 3-30, 254B1

1976

Peace Corps
Cong authorizes fscl '77 funds 3-22, 4-27, 393B1; signed 5-7, 982F1
Kenya train crashes 11-29, 912B2
Service Corps of Retired Executives (SCORE)
Cong clears funds 5-13, 393D1; signed 5-27, 982F1
Volunteers in Service to America (VISTA)
Cong clears funds 5-13, 393D1; signed 5-27, 982F1
ACTIVE Corps of Executives—*See under ACTION in this section above*
ADVISORY Councils & Commissions
Staffing bias chrgd 9-17, 944E1
AGENCY for International Development—*See under STATE below*
AGRICULTURE, Department of—*See also BUTZ, Earl*
Rpts farms, populatn data 1-2, 1-12, 216C2
'77 budget proposals 1-21, 66G1-D2
Sen OKs rice productn bill 2-3, 135F2
Milk price bill veto upheld 2-4, 88E1
Implements new beef grading standards 2-23, 186D1
Kepone linked to Mirex program 2-26, 171D3
Raises milk price supports 3-3, 186B1
Foreign milk aid set 3-8, 186C1
Callaway chrgd 3-12, 197B2; **for subsequent developments, see CALLAWAY, Howard**
Meat grading standards upheld 3-22, 218E2
Cong OKs Beef Bd 5-3, 5-12, 358F3
Kissinger intl econ plan opposed 5-6, 317E1
Faked potato crop rpts chrgd 5-25, 397D2
Beef Board signed 5-28, 982E1
'77 funds signed 7-12, 533B3
Passman probe rptd 8-16, 633C1
Carter scores special interests 8-25, 632E1
China wheat crop rptd up 9-1, 809A3
On '76 world sugar crop, prices 9-21, 721G2-C3
Wider gene research rules urged 9-22, 860C3
Meat import quota set 10-9, 788A1
Rpts record corn, wheat crops 10-12, 787E3
Fors ups grain-support rates 10-13, 787D3
Israel agri deal delayed 10-16, 810G3
Rabbit meat inspectn vetoed 10-17, 919E2
Rpts regional farm populatn drop 10-18, 833B2
2 get Science Medals 10-18, 858F3
Resource planning bill vetoed 10-19, 919B2, D2
Grain inspection bill signed, FGIS created 10-21, 833B3
'75-76 Sovt farm imports rptd up 10-27, 856F2
Views on S Korea rice comms rptd 11-3, 899D1
Carter names transitn team 11-23, 881A3
US-Sovt wheat sale rptd 12-3, 948B1
Rpts record '76 wheat, corn crops 12-10, 983D3
USSR exchng rptd canceled 12-20, 1011E1
Appointments & Resignations
Theis named dep asst secy 1-21, 40C3
Butz resigns, Knebel named acting secy 10-4, 743F3, 744E2, E3
Bergland named secy 12-20, 956F1, 957E1
Farmers Home Administration
'77 budget proposal 1-21, 66G1
Food Price Issues—*See FOOD; commodity names*
Food Stamp Program—*See under FOOD under 'F'*
Foreign Agricultural Service
'77 funds signed 7-12, 533D3
Forest Service, U.S.
Callaway chrgd 3-12, 197A2; **for subsequent developments, see CALLAWAY, Howard**
Probes Colo gondola crash 3-29, 384F1
'77 funds signed 7-31, 623D1
GOP platform text 8-18, 608B1
Forest mgt, clear-cutting bill signed 10-22, 833F3
Smokey Bear dies 11-9, 995G2
Grain Export Probe—*See GRAIN under 'G'*
U.S.-Soviet Grain Developments—*See 'Soviet Developments' under GRAIN under 'G'*
AIR Force, Department of the (AF)
Proxmire criticisms on waste rptd 1-1, 6D3
'77 budget proposals 1-21, 63G3
Spain defns pact signed 1-24, 76E3
Marine Corps reorganizatn urged 2-2, 95D3
Aids in Guatemala quake relief 2-4—2-11, 120C3
House OKs '77 arms, manpower authorizatn 4-9, 283C2, F2
Sen OKs '77 arms, manpower authorizatn 5-26, 411D2-E2
Dem platform text cites 6-15, 477A2
Cong clears constructn bill 6-17, Ford vetoes 7-2, 518A1
'77 arms, manpower authorizatn signed 7-14, 516G2, 517A2, D2
GOP platform text cites 8-18, 609B1
Azores base talks planned 9-5, 812A2
Swedish spy device buy rptd 9-14, 734D1

1977

Peace Corps
Columbia rebels kidnap botanist 2-14, 255F1
Carter on draft options 3-5, 171G2
Tanzania pres in US talks 8-10, 624C1
Ex-CIA head scores 'cover' bar 12-27, 1006D1
Volunteers in Service to America (VISTA)
Carter on draft options 3-5, 171G2
ADMINISTRATIVE Office of the U.S. Courts—*See under JUDICIARY below*
AFFIRMATIVE Action Office—*See under HEALTH, Education & Welfare below*
AGENCY for International Development (AID)—*See under STATE below*
AGRICULTURE, Department of
'76 world coffee crop data cited 1-11, 74B3
Ford '78 budget proposals 1-17, 30B1, 32F2, A3
Rpts Fla frost damage 1-24, 54F3
Western drought continues 2-15, 152E3
Carter visits employes 2-16, 110B1
Carter keeps Ford budget 2-22, 125B2
Bergland rpts net worth 2-25, 147D3
Canada wheat-price pact set 2-25, 158F2
Coffee supply data rptd 3-10, 209D1
Sugar import license auctn asked 3-14, 189E1
No exec cooks rptd 3-24, 236F1
Thai poppy planting rptd up 4-1, 396D3
Bureaucracy scored 4-12, Bergland vows reform 4-14, 364F3
W Coast snowpack rptd down 4-19, 376C3
'77 supplemental funds signed 5-4, 339E1
Jan-Mar coffee consumptn rptd 5-19, 458B2
House votes saccharin ban delay 6-21, 531B1
'78 funds signed 8-12, 688B3
34 states, PR, VI to get drought aid 8-24, 659D3
Carter cuts wheat acreage 8-29, 666C2, A3
Farm bill target prices scored 9-24, 736G3
Farm bill signed 9-29, 736D2
Meyer personal lobbying halted 9-30, 773C1
Seeks nitrite-nitrate data 10-18, 820A1
Fscl '77 budget overspending rptd 10-27, 835F3
Schl lunch bill signed 11-10, 897F2, A3
Bumper crop forecast 11-15, 916E2
Appointments & Resignations
Bergland confrmd secy 1-20, 34B1, C3
Foreman confrmd asst secy 3-24, 272A3
Hathaway confrmd asst secy 4-6, 272A3
Meyer quits as asst secy 10-20, 814B2
Weddington confrmd gen counsel 8-4, 626F3
White confrmd dep secy 3-15, 211G1
Commodity Credit Corp.
Hathaway confrmd dir 4-6, 272A3
Farm Income—*See INCOMES*
Food Prices—*See FOOD under 'F'*
Food Stamp Program—*See FOOD under 'F'; commodity names*
Forest Service, U.S.
Sup Ct backs Calif tax power 1-25, 80G2
'78 funds signed 7-26, 592E3
'77 natl forest fire data rptd 8-23, 660F1
Rural Electrification Administration
Ford proposes energy dept 1-11, 14F3
Bureaucracy scored 4-12, 365B1
U.S.-Soviet Grain Developments—*See GRAIN—Soviet Developments*
AID—*See STATE—Agency for International Development below*
AID to Families With Dependent Children (AFDC)—*See HEALTH, Education & Welfare below*
AIR Force, Department of the
Ford '78 budget proposals 1-17, 30A3-31C1
Dummar discharge cited 1-26, 120A2
Unionizatn survey released 2-7; Jones on threat 4-5, 342G3, 343D1
Cong probes computer project 4-27—5-10, 421E2
USSR computer sale opposed 6-5, 469A3
Mark confrmd undersecy 7-21, 626A3
'78 mil constructn authorizatn signed 8-1, funds signed 8-15, 668D2
Women to be assigned to missile sites 9-23, 777C3
Clark AF Base cited in US-PI talks 9-24, 824G2
'76 desertion rate rptd 10-27, 858A2
Aircraft & Missiles—*See appropriate subheads under ARMAMENTS under 'A'*

1978

AGENCY for International Development (AID)—*See under STATE below*
AGRICULTURE, Department of
Tobacco subsidies scored by health group 1-11, 23A3
Carter budget proposals 1-23, 48E1
Sadat sees Bergland, asks food aid 2-6, 77G2
Timber sales sealed-bid repeal clears Cong 2-6, 107D3; 2-20, 218A2
Grain acreage set-aside participatn rptd small 2-8, Bergland tours farm states 2-21, 163E2
Farmers occupy hq 3-16, 219F1
Set-aside paymts in Sen farm bill 3-21, 218F2
Ky horse shipmts banned 4-3, 5-30, 539D2
Carter denies Bergland split 4-11, 260G3
Child nutritn progrms in Educ Dept proposal 4-14, 279D1
Colo sen scores Bergland 5-2, 342B2
Bergland checks Sovt grain crop 5-9; crop estimated 6-12, 499D2
Nitrite-cured bacon curbed 5-15, 728F1
Denver dam permit blocked 5-25, 409C1
House OKs fund bill 6-22, 467D2-A3
Secrecy classificatn powers cut 6-29, 508E1
US offcls' legal immunity defined by Sup Ct 6-29, 567B2
Sovt grain purchases totaled 8-3, crop estimated 8-9, 634G2, C3
Nitrite-cancer link rptd 8-11, 728A1
Rural health progrm planned 10-2, 770E1
Land purchase registratn signed 10-14, 897B2
Secy to sit on Endangered Species Com 10-15, 834E2; 11-10, 1003B1
Carter anti-inflatn plan sets crop watch 10-24, 806D1
Sovt harvest estimate revised 11-4, 884D3
Bergland ends China visit; sees grain, cotton sales rise 11-14, 901G3
USSR grain purchases rptd 12-26, 1020A3
Appointments & Resignations
Weddington named pres asst 8-31, 681C3
White installed Dem natl chrmn 1-27, 87A3
Commodity Credit Corp.
Carter budget proposals 1-23, 48E1
Borrowing ceiling hike clears Cong 5-4, 343G1; signed 5-15, 465D3
Loan redemptn cited 10-20, 864C1
Food Stamp Program—*See under FOOD under 'F'*
Statistics
Feb farm prices 2-28, 163F2
'78 food inflatn forecast revised 3-28, 5-30, 219D2, 428C2
Mar-June farm prices, June costs 6-30, 507C1
'74 black, white-owned farms 7-20, 811G2
'79 food inflatn forecast 11-14, 1003C2
July-Dec farm prices 12-29, 1003B2
AID—*See STATE—Agency for International Development below*
AID to Families With Dependent Children (AFDC)—*See HEALTH, Education & Welfare below*
AIR Force, Department of the
Carter budget proposals 1-23, 45C1-E1
Gen James dies 2-25, 196C3
Jones to chair Joint Chiefs, Allen named to staff 4-5, 281A2
Fla '76 plane collisn damages awarded 5-5, 460E1
'45 Hiroshima pilot dies 7-1, 620F2
Gen Truesdell dies 8-22, 708F3
Allen backs MAP missile 9-23, 737G3
Agent Orange health damage denied 10-11, 984A2
'57 jet wreckage identified 10-12, 843E3
Guyana cult victims removed, flown to Del air base 11-24—11-26; final death toll 911 11-30, 909D1-910C2
RCA Alaska phone unit purchase '71 cited 11-30, 935C2
Black '70-78 enlistmt rise rptd 12-6, 960B1
Matlovich dischrg held unfair, review ordrd 12-6, 960B2

1979

Celeste named dir 3-29, 310F2
El Salvador volunteer seized 12-13, 968D1; freed 12-21, 993E2
El Salvador staff cut 12-26, 993F2
ADMINISTRATIVE Office of the U.S. Courts—*See under JUDICIARY below*
AGENCY for International Development—*See under STATE below*
AGRICULTURE, Department of
Adams' rail deregulatn plan criticism rptd 1-15, 35F3
Carter budget proposals 1-22, 45G3-46D1
Borden price compensatn case declined by Sup Ct 1-22, 54B2
Farmers protest in DC 2-5–2-6, Bergland sees no price support hike 2-6, 109E2
Nutritn progrms excluded from proposed Educ Dept 2-8, 110A3
USSR grain purchases rptd 3-15, 237D3
Price guideline monitoring set 3-29, 264G1
Sovt wheat, corn orders confrmd 7-5; '79-80 purchases rptd 7-12, 7-13, 567G3
Sovt crop estimate cut 7-12, 567D3
Sovt grain sale ceiling hiked; US wheat acreage, loan rate increased, support price cut 8-1, 636E3
Nicaragua beef imports banned 8-6, 616C2
PCBs contaminate food in West 9-17, 704B3
USSR grain harvest shortfall rptd 9-28, 774E3
USSR grain sale limit hiked 10-3, 774B3
Tobacco use rptd down 10-16, 970A3
'80 funds bill clears Cong 10-26, 10-31, Carter signs 11-9, 920A1
'78 smoking rptd up worldwide, down in US; US tobacco exports cited 11-22, 970E2, G2
Sovt wheat, corn purchases rptd 11-28, 928C3
Intl sugar agrmt OKd by Sen 11-30, 987A3
Farmers Home Administration
Loan progrm transfers proposed 3-1, 164G1
Wheeling-Pittsburgh aid OKd, indl rivals score 8-28, 681G3
Food Stamp Program—*See under FOOD under 'F'*
Forest Service
Wilderness proposal scored 1-4, 16A2
Carter budgets job cuts 1-22, 46D1
Natural Resources Dept proposed 3-1, 164B1, F1
Cong gets wilderness proposal 4-16, 282E1
Wood fuel use estimated 5-20, 419F1
Carter orders timber sales 6-11, 441A1, D1
Idaho fires destroy 130,000 acres, policies questnd 7-6–8-12, 620F1
West mounts 'Sagebrush Revolt' 7-13–9-7, 703G3
Calif brush fires rptd 9-11–9-23, 799F3
'80 funds clear Cong 11-9, 883F1
4-H Club Program—*See 4-H under 'F'*
Soil Conservation Service
Natural Resources Dept proposal excludes 3-1, 164E1
Statistics
Jan farm prices, costs 1-31, 111G1
Mar farm prices, Dec '78-Feb revised 3-30, 280C3
Apr-July farm prices 7-31, 578A1
Aug-Nov farm prices 11-30, 941B2
'79, Dec farm prices, Nov revised; '79 food inflatn, '80 forecast 12-31, 985A1
'79 grain output, farm exports 12-31, 985B1
'79 farm acreage, other data 12-31, 985D1
AID—*See STATE–AGENCY for International Development below*
AID to Families With Dependent Children (AFDC)—*See HEALTH, Education & Welfare below*
AIR Force, Department of the
Female mil personnel rise seen 1-2, 53A2
300 to visit Saudi 1-10, 12B2
CIA UFO probe detailed 1-12, 93C1
Carter budget proposals 1-22, 43A1
Peoples Temple sued re body removal costs 1-22, 588 rptd unclaimed 2-1, 117E2
Saudi visit ends 1-23, 50F1
Pilot morale loss cited 2-15, 130E2
'78 4th 1/4 volunteer shortage rptd 2-15, 130G2
MD shortage rptd 2-16, 130C2
Iran bans intell posts 2-21, US personnel flee 2-24–2-28, 145F1
Base closings set 3-29, 265D3
S Africa ousts 3 as spies 4-12, 286F3
2 F-5Es lost 4-12, crewmen feared dead 5-5, 404A3
Peoples Temple bodies transfer set, 546 rptd unclaimed 4-21, 336E1

1980

ADMINISTRATIVE Office of the U.S. Courts—*See JUDICIARY in this section*
AGRICULTURE, Department of
USSR grain orders speedup, total purchases rptd 1-3, 2D1
Sovt grain contracts to be bought 1-7, 9G2
'Junk food' rules rptd 1-27, 157E3
Carter budget proposals 1-28, 73A2
Cancer-nitrite study scored 1-31, 159G1
Dietary guidelines issued 2-4, 157G2
USSR grain need seen met 4-9, 315G3
Reagan scores Foreman 4-18, 327F3
PCB rules published 5-9, 387B2
De Angelis sentncd in pork swindle 7-21, 655C1
Carter orders grain price support increase 7-28, 575E1
Nitrite ban rejected 8-19, 726D1
Forgn Svc reorgn bill clears Cong 10-1, signed 10-17, 981E2
'81 grain stockpiles seen down 11-4, 855E1
'81 funds clear Cong 12-4, 954B3; signed 12-15, 982B1
Block named secy 12-23, 980E1
Commodity Credit Corp.
Sovt grain contracts to be bought 1-7, 9E2
Poland granted $670 mln grain credit 9-12, 710F3*
Farmers Home Administration
Loan sell-off budgeted 1-28, 73A2
Food Stamp Program—*See under FOOD under 'F'*
Forest Service
Ky, W Va fire damage rptd 11-13, 971B1
Statistics
Jan farm prices 1-31, 92E2
Feb farm prices 2-29, 168C1
Mar farm prices 3-31, 263E3
'79 tobacco use rptd down 4-7, 318C2
Apr farm prices 4-30, 329G2
May farm prices 5-30, 425C1
June farm prices 6-30, 492C2
July farm prices 7-31, 575C1
Aug farm prices, July revised 8-29, 666D1
Sept farm prices 9-30, 741A2
Oct farm prices 10-31, 883B1
Nov farm prices 11-28, 938B2
AIR Force, Department of the
Quake hits Azores, rescue operatns rptd 1-1, 24G2
Lt Col Powers dies 1-1, 104E3
23 NORAD guards disciplined in drug probe 1-17, 115F3
Petitn limits upheld by Sup Ct 1-21, 93B1
DC-10 pylon study reviewed 1-23, 53C2
Carter budget proposals 1-28, 70F3, 71B1-F1
US Iran envoys at Dover base 1-30—1-31, 88D3
Playboy photo series rptd 2-21, 189C1
Boeing wins cruise missile contract 3-25, 228E1
Dow chrgs EPA spying 3-25, 387A3
Memphis area illness probed 4-2, 331A3
House OKs draft registratn funds 4-22, 349F1
Finletter dies 4-24, 360E1
Eglin base to process Cuban refugees 5-1, 326G1

1976

'77 manpower funds signed 9-22, 707C2, D3
Arms cost estimate rptd hiked 11-16, 982D3
Aircraft—*See 'Aviation' under ACCIDENTS, 'Aircraft' under ARMAMENTS*
Amnesty Issue—*See under ARMED Forces below*
Missing in Action—*See under ARMED Forces below*
Personnel
Fitzgerald legal costs award rptd 1-1, 6F3
Hughes, Knapp confrmd asst secys 3-10, 232E1, F1
Recruitmt bias cover-up chrgd 6-7, 454A2
Ct upholds homosexual firing 7-16, 944F1
Mary Josephine Shelly dies 8-6, 892E3
Keech confrmd asst secy 9-10, 808B1
Panama arrests Canal Zone employe 9-17, 792B2
Ford cites black gen 10-22, 801G3
Reserve Forces—*See under ARMED Forces below*

ALCOHOL Abuse & Alcoholism, National Institute on—*See 'Alcohol, Drug Abuse, & Mental Health Administration' under PUBLIC Health Service below*
ALCOHOL, Drug Abuse, and Mental Health Administration—*See under PUBLIC Health Service below*
ALCOHOL, Tobacco & Firearms, Bureau of—*See under TREASURY below*
AMTRAK—*See under 'A'*

ARMED Forces—*See also DEFENSE below; also specific branches of service*
House OKs '77 manpower authorizatn 238E2
Ford budget proposals 1-21, 66E2
Pentagon urges Eur troop reinforcemts 1-27, 68D2
Sup Ct rules on counsel, pol activity 3-24, 218F2, G2
Cong OKs Hatch Act repeal 3-31, 234A2
House OKs '77 manpower authorizatn 4-9, 283B2, F2
Manpower study issued 4-18, 309D1-A2
Sup Ct backs acad honor-code disclosures 4-21, 331B3
Rumsfeld sets mil training reform 5-2, 378E1
Sen OKs '77 manpower authorizatn 5-26, 411B2
Manpower study scored 6-7, 454E1
'77 manpower authorizatn signed 7-14, 517D2
GOP platform text cites 8-18, 608F3
Ford acceptnc speech cites 8-19, 612C1
Dole scores Carter on troop exit 9-1, 645G3; Ford scores 9-9, 665B2
Panama arrests Canal Zone employes 9-17, 792F1
Workers get 4.8% pay rise 9-29, 742B3
Amnesty Issue
ACLU disputes clemency bd data 1-6, 4E1
Study on deserters rptd 1-10, 43B1
Clemency bd final rpt issued, Goodell urges revival 1-15, 43F1
Dem platform OKs pardon 6-15, 432D3, G3
Dem platform text 6-15, 472A2
Efaw addresses Dem conv 7-15, 506C3
Efaw draft chrgs dropped 8-11, 680A3
Carter on amnesty-pardon stand 8-24, Amer Legion, Dole score 8-24, 8-25, 631F2, D3, 632B2
Calley favors total amnesty 9-8, 680A3
Ford, Carter debate 9-23, 701E3
Lutherans for total 10-10—10-11, 932D2
Carter to issue pardon 11-27, 898C3
Ford vows reconsideratn 12-27, 980G1
Missing in Action
McCloskey on Hanoi econ aid claim 2-1, 103D1
US proposes Hanoi talks 3-25, 255B2
US seeks N Viet data 4-14, 291F1
Return by Viet doubted 7-23, 593C2
Schrump addresses GOP conv 8-17, 615A2
GOP platform text 8-18, 606G2, 609G2
Viet names 12 pilots killed, US asks full list 9-6, 678E2
Ford demands accounting 9-7, 665B1
Ford links Viet ties to full list 9-7 ordrs UN entry veto 9-13; Viet scores 9-11, 9-13 682C1
Ford, Carter debate 10-6, 742D2
Dole, Mondale debate 10-15, 782C3
US-Viet talks open 11-12, 863B2
Reserve Forces
'77 budget proposes Navy unit cut 1-21, 63F3
Sen OKs pres call-up power 1-26, 135E1
Pentagon rpt to Cong issued 1-27, 68A2
House OKs '77 manpower authorizatn, drops Navy cut 4-9, 283B2, F2
US study opposes cuts 4-18, 309C1
Cong clears pres call-up power 5-3, 345D3
Pres call-up powers signed 5-14, 982E1
Sen OKs '77 manpower authorizatn 5-26, 411B2
Ford vetoes constructn bill 7-2, 518B1
'77 manpower authorizatn signed 7-14, 517D2
'77 manpower funds signed 9-22, 707D3
Veterans—*See VETERANS under 'V'*

ARMS Control & Disarmament Agency, U.S.
Ikle testifies on safeguards 2-23, 175C1, 243A3

1977

Air Force Academy, U.S. (Colorado Springs, Colo.)
Brown addresses 6-1, 420E3
Diego Garcia Base—*See under 'D'*
Reserve Forces—*See under ARMED Forces in this section below*
Strategic Air Command (SAC)
To get cruise missiles 4-24, 343F2
Carter visits hq in Neb 10-22, 817D1
Veterans—*See VETERANS under 'V'*
WASPs (Women's Air Force Service Pilots) (defunct)
Vet benefits bill clears Cong 11-4, 877C3

ALCOHOL, Drug Abuse & Mental Health Administration—*See under PUBLIC Health Service below*
ALCOHOL, Tobacco & Firearms, Bureau of—*See under TREASURY below*
ALLERGY and Infectious Diseases, National Institute of—*See under PUBLIC Health Service—National Institutes of Health below*
AMTRAK—*See under 'A'*

ARMED Forces—*See also DEFENSE below; also specific branches of service*
CBO rpts on manpower costs, policy 1-21, 94G3-95A1
MD malpractice review barred 3-7, 211F2
Unionizatn threat seen 3-18—4-19, 342E3
Gay rights group sees Carter aide 3-26, 278D2
Industry hiring of retirees rptd 4-12, 344C1
Pension, troop strength amendmts fail 4-25, 324C1
Pay hike funds signed 5-4, 339F1
Savannah (Ga) payroll growth rptd 5-16, 384B3
Sup Ct backs svc pensn credit 6-6, 478G2
Manpower costs panel named 6-27, 499A3
Active-duty ceiling, officer cuts clear Cong 7-14, 576G1-A2
'78 personnel, pensn funds cleared 9-9, 704B3; signed 9-21, 834D1
Unionizatn bar voted by Sen 9-16, 759D3-760C1
Pay, pensn, career length revisns urged 9-25, 777E2, A3
Strikes, organizing barred by Brown 10-6, 777E3
Desertn rates rptd 10-27, 858G1
Discharges rptd over 40% 11-15, 920E1
Amnesty Issue
Ford bars blanket amnesty, OKs some dischrg upgrades 1-19, 36A2
Draft evaders pardoned, reactn 1-21, 51A2, D2
Carter call-in topic 3-5, 171E2
Viet dischrg upgrading OKd by Carter 3-28, 231B3
Carter poll ratings low 4-4, 251C1
Dischrg upgrade response weak 5-10, 421B1
Cong bars use of funds 7-19, 667D3
Dischrg review, benefits bill clears Cong 9-23, 759C2; signed 10-8, 773A2
HUD funds OKd by House, vet benefits killed 9-28, 796B3
Dischrg upgrade data rptd 10-1, 759B3
Dischrg review phone svc ends 10-4, 759G2
Draft—*See SELECTIVE Service below*
Missing in Action (MIA)
Carter plans mission to Viet 2-11, 110B2
US sets Viet missn 2-25, 206F2
Carter on Viet missn 3-5, 171E1, C2; 3-17, 186C2
5-man comm in Viet, Laos; gets 12 bodies 3-16—3-20; Carter gets rpt, OKs talks 3-23, 206A1
Carter lauds Viet missn 3-24, 229C3
Viet vows info effort 5-3—5-4, 333B1
Viet gives new list 6-3, 441E1
Viets return 22 bodies 9-30, 795D1
Prisoners of War
POW disclosure code eased 11-3, 858E1
Reserve Forces
Sup Ct backs retiremt pay rule 4-4, 341F3
Manpower problem seen 4-6, 343G1
House bars naval reserve cut 4-25, 324F1
Army, Navy ROTC enrolmt rise, AF decline rptd 5-20, 421B2
Unionizatn bar voted by Sen 9-16, 759D3-760C1
Reenlistment bonuses set 11-15, 942C2
Veterans—*See VETERANS under 'V'*

ARMS Control & Disarmament Agency, U.S. (ACDA) (of State Department)
Warnke named dir 2-2, controversy ensues 2-3—2-8, 88F3; confrmd 3-9, 171G3

1978

592 Guyana victims identified 12-8, 1st bodies leave Dover base 12-9, 955F2
C-130 crashes in Ky 12-10, fleet grounded 12-11, 984E2
Volunteer shortage seen 12-12, 960C1
Pilot drain to commercial airlines rptd 12-13, 984B2
Aircraft & Missiles—*See ARMAMENTS under 'A'*
Air Force Academy, U.S. (Colorado Springs, Colo.)
Woodward dismissal rptd 4-21, 420C1
Drop-out rate rptd 40% 11-20, 916G3-917B1
Veterans—*See VETERANS under 'V'*

AIR Force Academy, U.S.—*See under AIR Force in this section above*
ALCOHOL, Drug Abuse & Mental Health Administration—*See under PUBLIC Health Service below*
ALCOHOL, Tobacco & Firearms, Bureau of—*See under TREASURY below*
AMTRAK—*See AMTRAK under 'A'*

ARMED Forces—*See also DEFENSE below; also specific branch of service*
Troop strength abroad rptd up; table 1-2, 5B2
CBO pension revisn optns outlined 1-11, 52F3
Carter budgets manpower 1-23, 45C1
Volunteer force cost put at $18 bln 2-6, 82C1
Basic training cuts set 2-25, 162G3
New CPIs described 222C2
Women's combat bar repeal rptd sought 3-4, 162G1
Pension overhaul urged by Pres Comm 4-10, 280E3-281F1
Double-dipping curb review declined by Sup Ct 4-17, 308C3
Hard drug use rptd, random tests backed by White House 4-25, 4-27, Pentagon opposes 4-28, 368B2-A3
Base closings, cutbacks proposed 4-26, 368C1
Drug use study rptd 5-24, E Ger heroin smuggling scored 6-1, 433D2-B3
Singlaub vs combat role for women 6-2, 433C2
Recruitmt standards lowering urged 7-2, 528E3
Abortn fund curb passes House 8-9, 604F2
'79 arms authorzn, recruitmt initiatives vetoed 8-17, 622A1
Mil constructn funds clear Cong 8-21, 662D1
Gay dischrg policy chng rptd 8-21, 683E2
'79 manpower funds, abortn curb signed 10-13, 833B1, F1
'79 revised arms authorzn signed 10-20, 833F1-A2
Measles, rubella infestatn rptd; immunizatn asked 11-10, 927A3
Moblization ability scored 12-3, 984B1
Black '70-78 enlistmt rise rptd 12-6, 960A1
Gays' dischrg held unfair 12-6, 960A2
Brown urges mil pensn reform 12-14, 1009C2
Draft—*See SELECTIVE Service below*
Prisoners of War
Nixon hosts Viet ex-POW receptn, Los Angeles conv cited 5-27, 513D2
Reserve Forces
Black officers rptd underrepresented 8-16, 683B2
Veterans—*See VETERANS under 'V'*
ARMED Forces Policy Council—*See under DEFENSE below*

ARMS Control & Disarmament Agency (ACDA) (of State Department)
A-weapons material ban rptd urged 4-3, 277B2

1979

Officers end China visit 5-15, 370C2
35-man unit lands in CR 7-8, ordrd out 7-10, 512F2-A3
Coastal sea claim challenges ordered 8-10, 646G1
Volunteer shortage rptd 8-20, 649B2, E2
Maj Gen Weyland dies 9-2, 756G3
Army guns rptd found 10-4, 852C1
Gay capt discharged 10-15, 850C3
F-15, F-16 engine trouble rptd 10-24, 852G1-A3
'79 enlistment gap rptd 10-25, 903C3
'80 mil constructn funds signed 11-30, 945A2
Aircraft & Missiles—*See ARMAMENTS under 'A'*
Air Force Academy, U.S. (Colorado Springs, Colo.)
Senior cadets confined for prank 2-21, order lifted 2-23, 207B3
'80 female grads to get pilot training 9-10, 725A1
Reserve Forces—*See under ARMED Forces below*
Strategic Air Command (SAC)
'56 UK crash rptd 11-5, 845G1
Veterans—*See VETERANS under 'V'*
AIR Force Academy, U.S.—*See under AIR Force in this section above*
ALCOHOL, Drug Abuse & Mental Health Administration—*See under PUBLIC Health Service below*
ALCOHOL, Tobacco & Firearms, Bureau of—*See under TREASURY below*
AMTRAK (National Railroad Passenger Corp.)—*See AMTRAK under 'A'*
ANTITRUST Laws and Procedures, National Commission for the Review of
Final rpt issued 1-16, 88C2
ARMED Forces
Female mil personnel rise seen 1-2, 53G1
Mil dischrg suits filed 1-19, 53B1
'Sexist' language review conducted 1-19, 89D3
Carter budgets manpower 1-22, 42A3
'78 4th 1/4 volunteer shortage rptd 2-13, 130G2
MD shortage rptd 2-16, 130C2
Women's volunteer standards eased by Army 4-9, 307E2
SALT scored by ex-offcrs 4-11, 294D3-295A2
Older soldiers rptd more productive 6-17, 519E2
Gas allocatn limit set 7-16, 557A3
Cong OKs mil pay hike funds bill 7-17, 7-20, Carter signs 7-25, 700G1
Retiremt plan proposed 7-19, 628E1
Racism in military seen 7-23, 561B3; Navy progrm launched 8-29, 664E2
ABA backs divorce pensn law chngs 8-15, 769A1
Little League semifinal lost 8-23, 797B3
Carter proposes 7% '80 pay hike 8-31, 700D2
Hawaii personnel assaults rptd up 9-21, 809F1
'79 enlistment gap rptd, pay boost seen 10-25, 11-13, 903B3-F3
Draft—*See SELECTIVE Service below*
Prisoners of War
Viet detainmt discounted 2-5, 112F2
Viet-era Marine returns to US 3-25, 266A1
Calif apptmt of ex-POW causes furor 7-13—8-8, 593B2-B3
Reserve Forces
Draft need disputed 3-13, 307A2
Veterans—*See VETERANS under 'V'*

ARMS Control & Disarmament Agency (ACDA) (of State Department)
Seignious confrmd dir 3-1, 272C1
SALT II communique, Carter Cong address cites 6-18, 457C1, 458E3

1980

Eglin hit by unrest, resetlmt delays rptd 5-24—5-25; US marshals called in 5-26, 395F3-396B1
Computer errors trigger A-alerts 6-3, 6-6, failed component blamed 6-17, 457C3-458G1
Sen com study faults Iran rescue missn 6-5, 419B2
Apr recruiting rptd 6-11, 458D2
Delta jet lands at McDill AF base 6-21, 519C2
Iran hostage arrives W Ger base 7-12, 539E1
'79 recruits mental standards down 7-31, 598E1
'Stealth' fighter rptd tested at Nellis 8-20, 630B2
Ark A-missile silo blast kills 1 9-19, warhead removed 9-22; diagram 765B2
Matlovich reinstatemt ordered 11-9, setlmt reached 11-24, 962G1
MX sites chosen 11-18, 897A1
Las Vegas hotel fire evacuatns 11-21, 893E2
Sen OKs procuremt appropriatn 11-21, 896E3
Air Force Academy, U.S. (Colorado Springs, Colo.)
12 cadets resign re pot use 1-24, 115E3
Women graduate 5-28, 428E1
Reserves—*See ARMED Forces in this section*
Strategic Air Command (SAC)
Computer errors trigger A-alerts 6-3, 6-6, failed component blamed 6-17, 457F3, 458E1
ALCOHOL, Drug Abuse & Mental Health Administration—*See under PUBLIC Health Service in this section below*

ARMED Forces
Carter State of Union hits volunteer force 1-23, 41B1, 43B1
Carter budgets manpower 1-28, 70F3-71A1
Sex harassment alleged 2-11, 188E3
Reagan 'basic speech' excerpts 2-29, 207F3
Iran returns dead US raiders, offcl mourning declared 5-6, 337A2
Carter backs compensatn bill 5-26, 403A2
GOP platform adopted; text 7-15, 535B3, 536E1, E2
Reagan pres nominatn acceptance speech 7-17, 533C1
Dem platform planks adopted 8-13, 615C1, A2
Mondale vp renominatn acceptance speech 8-14, 612C1
Anderson would upgrade 8-19, 630A1
Reagan for pay boost 8-20, 629E1
Anderson platform offered 8-30, 665A2
Mil pay authrzn signed 9-8, 764F3
Mil benefits authrzn signed 9-8, 765C1
Mil pay, benefits appropriatn OKd by House 9-16, 741F3, 742A1; excluded by Sen 11-21, 896F3; clears Cong 12-5, 935A3; signed 12-15, 982B1
Mil pensn divorce case accepted by Sup Ct 10-20, 807A3
Carter, Reagan TV debate 10-28, 815B3
Mil pay, benefits hike clears Cong 12-5, 953G2; signed 12-23, 982C1
Draft—*See under SELECTIVE Service System in this section below*
Reserves
Carter budget proposals 1-28, 70G3
Funding hike sought 5-7, 369E3
Mt St Helens rescue effort rptd 5-18—5-19, 382G1
Dem platform plank adopted 8-13, 615B2

1976

Arms spending study released 2-29, 182G3
'77 funds signed 7-14, 534D2
Ikle scores US A-aid 7-23, 739F2
Ford gives rpt to Cong 7-29, 739E1, D2
Ikle cites Sovt MIRV buildup 8-31, 739D1

ARMY, Department of the
Angola mercenary training rptd 1-2, 3C2
Fair loses command, resigns 1-5, 43C2 ★
'70 Wis bombing suspect arrested 1-7, 32D2
ELF frees Strickland 1-9, 31E1
'70-75 Peru mil training rptd 1-16, 142C3
'77 budget proposals 1-21, 63G3, 64E1
Marine Corps reorganizatn urged 2-2, 95D3
Aids in Guatemala quake relief 2-4—2-11, 120C3, F3
Callaway chrgd 3-12, 197B2; **for subsequent developments, see CALLAWAY, Howard**
House OKs '77 arms, manpower authorizatn 4-9, 283F2
Sen com cites intelligence files 4-28, 326A3, 330C1
Meat scandal chrgd 5-7—5-12, 395A2
Sen OKs '77 arms, manpower authorizatn 5-26, 411B2
Recruitmt bias cover-up chrgd 6-7, 454G1
Dem platform text cites 6-15, 477A2
Cong clears constructn bill 6-17, Ford vetoes 7-2, 518B1
Copter pilot chrgs bias, quits 6-29, 484E2
Denies role in Utah horse deaths 7-9, 587D1
Recruit deaths cited 7-10, 587B1
'77 arms, manpower authorizatn signed 7-14, 517D2
GOP platform text cites 8-18, 609A1
2 killed in Korea DMZ 8-18, 618B3
Panama arrests Canal Zone soldier 9-17, 792B2
'77 manpower funds signed 9-22, 707C2
Gen Arnold dies 9-30, 1015B1
Korean bid-rigging chrgd 10-27, 982A2-A3
Overspending rptd 11-19, 982A3
Amnesty Issue—*See under ARMED Forces in this section above*
Arms Issues—*See ARMAMENTS under 'A'*
Engineers, Corps of
Filtratn projct in Reserve Mining pollutn case ordrd 1-6, 25E2
Rejcts Fla wetlands dvpt 4-16, 284G2-D3
Cong clears '77 pub works funds 6-29, Ford signs 7-12, 517E1
GOP platform text 8-18, 603G1
'77-78 pub works projects signed 10-22, 835A2
Military Academy, U.S. (West Point, N.Y.)
50 guilty in cheating scandal 4-22, 286G3
Honor system probe asked 5-18, cheating cases mount 5-24—6-1, Hoffman sees possible review of code 6-2, 394E3
Cheating scandal dvpts 6-11—8-31; Hoffman offers readmissn plan, cadets protest 8-23; total chrgs rptd 8-31, 670D1
Missing in Action—*See under ARMED Forces above*
Panama Canal Co.—*See separate listing in this section below*
Reserve Forces—*See under ARMED Forces in this section above*

1977

Warnke in SALT talks 3-28—3-30, 225D2
'66-75 Latin arms transfers rptd; table 4-8, 415A2, D2
Warnke in Indian O demilitarizatn talks 6-22—6-27, 530C1
'78 funds signed 8-2, authorizatn signed 8-17, 689G1, D2
SALT extensn announced 9-23, 751C1

ARMY, Department of the
Espionage role in Czech rptd 1-6, 19G3
Canal Zone troops on alert 1-8—1-9, 46E1
Czech defectn denied 1-14, 82G3
Ford '78 budget proposals 1-17, 30A3-G3
Buffalo (NY) snow removal aid 1-27, 75A3
Carter call-in on karate 3-5, 171F1
Germ warfare tests revealed 3-8, 195C2
Chem warfare effort rptd 3-21, 232F1
Rogers lauds volunteers, women 4-6, 343F1
Ethiopia closes aid office 4-23, 327G2
Singlaub loses S Korea cmnd 5-21, 403G2-404G1
Carter defends Singlaub removal 5-26, Singlaub reassigned 5-27, 417A2
Starry reprimanded for speech 6-17, 482E3
Mil constructn authorizatn signed 8-1, funds signed 8-15, 668C2
Slovik convictn reversal denied 9-13, 808F1
'76 desertion rate rptd 10-27, 858A2
Journalists thoughts re Herbert protected 11-7, 920A3
Sup Ct remands tank injury suit 11-14, 878A3
Canada deserter surveillnc alleged 11-24, 923E1
Appointments
Alexander named secy 1-19, 52F3; confrmd 2-11, 148C3
Gibbs confrmd asst secy 4-25, 418D1
Goodpaster, West Pt head 4-4, 354B2
LaBerge confrmd undersecy 7-21, 626A3
Nelson confrmd asst secy 5-27, 500A1
Pierre confrmd asst secy 5-9, 418G1
Singlaub, Ft McPherson head 5-27, 417D2
Arms Issues—*See ARMAMENTS under 'A'*
Engineers, Corps of
Water projects cut 3-23, Carter explains 3-24, 210D1
Carter energy plan 4-20, 293F2
Sup Ct declines dredging case review 4-25, 342E3
'78 funds clear Cong 7-25, 592C3
Ga dam bursts 11-6, '76 inspectn denied 11-8, 888F2 ★, G2
Ga dam burst laid to seepage 12-21, 1023F3
Korea Troop Pullout—*See KOREA (South)—U.S. Troop Pullout*
Military Academy, U.S. (West Point, N.Y.)
June readmissns set; Borman rpt, code chngs cited 1-5, 40G3
Ind kidnaper link denied 2-9, 162E2
Goodpaster named head 4-4, 354B2
Bard lectures in USSR 9-26, 9-28, 866F1
Reserve Forces—*See under ARMED Forces in this section above*
Veterans—*See VETERANS under 'V'*

1978

Warnke rptd concerned re civil defns reorganizatn 6-19, 466F2
'76 worldwide arms spending rptd 7-23, 585A2
Warnke backs MAP 8-23, 747B3
US A-power edge over USSR seen 8-29, 676G3
Warnke sees Gromyko, rpts SALT progress 9-7—9-8, 747E2
Warnke resigns as dir 10-10, 766F3, 804F1
Seignious named dir, Earle SALT negotiator 10-20, 804A2

ARMY, Department of the
W Ger base job plan scored 1-11, 55B2
Carter budget proposals 1-23, 45C1
In Ohio storm-rescue missn 1-26, 105A3
Basic training cut set 2-25, 162G3
Gen Clay dies 4-16, 356D2
Singlaub scores Carter, recalled to DC 4-27; resigns 4-28, 321D2-B3
Hard drug use rptd 4-27, 368D2
Drug use study rptd 5-24, E Ger heroin smuggling scored 6-1, 433D2-B3
W Ger hotel bombed 5-31, 439A3
Carter visits Canal Zone base 6-17, 464B1
Carter visits Ft Hood 6-24, 509G3
1st woman named maj gen 7-1, 843C3
Maj Gen Lanham dies 7-20, 620A3
Black disciplinary problems rptd 8-15, 683F1
Equal opportunity study rptd 8-16, 683A2
Mil constructn funds clear Cong 8-21, 662D1
Fleming given honorable dischrg 8-31, 843F3
2 employes indicted in GSA probe 9-29, 753B3
Secy to sit on Endangered Species Com 10-15, 834E2; 11-10, 1003B1
Nerve gas productn order rptd 10-19, 833G2-A3
Marines urge draft registratn 10-29, 895D1
MD dismissed, recruiters scored 11-4, 877A3
2-yr enlistmt plan rptd, offcls deny racial aim 11-10, 895E2-A3
Troops aid Guyana cult victims removal 11-21, 891B1
Guyana cult victims removed, flown to Del air base 11-24—11-26; final death toll 911 11-30, 909F1-910C2
MD shortage rptd 11-27, 916D3
Child-care rules tightened 11-29, 960F2
Sex fraternizatn curb rptd 12-4, 960E1
Black '70-78 enlistmt rise rptd 12-6, 960A1
Westmoreland rpts Viet war med advances 12-6, 960D3
Arms Issues—*See ARMAMENTS under 'A'*
Engineers, Corps of
EPA bars Denver dam permit 5-25, 409D1
Constructn co price fixing chrgd 9-27, 769A1
Public works veto upheld 10-5, 765E1
Parks bill cleared 10-13, 834B3
Nev A-test site '47 debate rptd 12-18, 1021D1
Korea Troop Pullout—*See KOREA (South)—U.S. Troop Pullout*
Military Academy, U.S. (West Point, N.Y.)
Somoza fetes '46 grads 5-30, 593A2
Veterans—*See VETERANS under 'V'*

1979

Seignious backs SALT 6-30, 496E3; 7-10, 510E2
'77 world mil spending rptd 10-13, 804F1

ARMY, Department of the
Female mil personnel rise seen 1-2, 53G1
Haig sets resignatn 1-3, 3A2
16 GIs die in Canal Zone truck crash 1-11, 140D3
Ft Carson child abuse data rptd 1-21, 93E3
Carter budget proposals 1-22, 43D2, G2
Spanish language ban in W Ger rescinded 2-7, 89D2
'78 4th 1/4 volunteer shortage rptd 2-13, 130G2
MD shortage rptd 2-16, 130C2
Rodgers names NATO cmdr 2-28, 147C3
MacDonald murder trial challenge declined by Sup Ct 3-19, 203G2-A3
Base closings set 3-29, 265D3
Women's volunteer standards eased, recruitmt data cited 4-9, 307E2
Ex-gens score SALT 4-11, 294D3-295A2
'State of mind' libel queries backed by Sup Ct 4-18, 301G3
Peoples Temple bodies transfer set 4-21, 336E1
Meyer named staff chief 5-2, 347F2
Ga wildlife refuge protesters jailed 5-4—5-10, 368E1
Deserter surrenders in W Ger 5-7, 392F2
Officers end China visit 5-15, 370C2
Col Simons dies 5-21, 432F3
'Quick-strike' force planned 6-21, 482C3
Meyer installed 6-22, 482C3
Male recruiting standards eased 7-6, 519C2
Rowny resignatn re SALT cited 7-12, 536E1
Recruiting fraud probed 8-19, 649E2
Volunteer shortage rptd 8-20, 649B2, E2
Reserve recruiting failure rptd 8-23, 649A3
MacDonald gets life for '70 slayings 8-29, 817F2
Trainee policy relaxed 9-3, 664B3
NRA gun resale suit lost 9-4, 747F1
LSD suit settled 9-6, 705F1
San Fran '50 germ warfare test suit rptd 9-16, 727B1
Hawaii personnel assaults rptd up 9-21, 809A2
Hallucinogen tested in '64, stockpile rptd 9-24, 727F1
Maj Gen Allen dies 9-27, 756A2
Gay policy challenged 10-1, 850E3
Coast oil refinery OKd 10-4, 769G3-770F1
'Lost' M-2s rptd found 10-4, 852A1
'50 grain blight tests rptd 10-7, 770G3
Ft Dix to stay open 10-10, 809D1
Recruiting fraud probe expands 10-15, 850B2
'79 enlistment gap rptd 10-25, 903C3
Chem test subjects sought 11-2, 850E2
W Eur heroin use, seizures rptd 11-11, 972C3, E3
Maj Gen Harmon dies 11-13, 932A3
Recruiting abuses detailed 11-19, 903F3
Short dies 11-19, 932E3
Maj Gen F Allen dies 11-20, 932A2
'67 Cuba defector returns 11-21, 924F1
Iranian flight training halted 11-23, 898G1
'60s drug tests of Pa prisoners rptd 11-25, 947E1
Viet vet drug dischrgs ordrd upgraded 11-28, 992D1
'80 mil constructn funds signed 11-30, 945A2
Ft Dix sex scandal rptd 12-3, 924A1
'50s CIA NYC biological tests chrgd 12-3, 946A1
Marines to join 'quick-strike' force 12-5, 923E3
Gas raids vs Laos rebels rptd 12-12, 979C1
'67 Cuba defector charged with desertn 12-19, 965G3
Arms Issues—*See ARMAMENTS under 'A'*
Engineers, Corps of
Natural Resources Dept proposed 3-1, 164E1
Tenn-Tombigbee projct upheld 3-13, 188B3
Bonnet Carne spillway opened 3-15, 288F3
Red R flood damage rptd 4-30, 472C2
China power dvpt aid signed 8-28, 644C2
Korea Troop Pullout—*See KOREA (South)-U.S. Troop Pullout*
Military Academy, U.S. (West Point, N.Y.)
Saban named football coach, Smith recruiting chrgs cited 1-4, 175A3
Black cadet wins top post 8-11, 609D1
Female cadets assessed 10-9, 809A1
Hazing scandal rptd 11-9, 868A3
Reserve Forces—*See under ARMED Forces in this section above*
Veterans—*See VETERANS under 'V'*

1980

ARMY, Department of the
Gay activist chrgd in murder 1-2, 18C3
Carter budget proposals 1-28, 70F3, 71D2
Reagan seeks rearmamt 1-29, 91D3
'67 Cuba defector sentenced for desertn 1-30, 94E3; sentnc overturned 2-28, 189E1
Sex harassment alleged, Ft Bragg probed 2-10, 2-11; GI sentenced in W Ger 3-6, 188E3-189B1
VW to buy Pa plant 2-12, 127C3
Playboy photo series rptd 2-21, 189C1
Rumanian envoy defects at Va base 2-24, 142B3
Reagan 'basic speech' excerpts 2-29, 207F3
Rift Valley Fever vaccine shortage rptd 3-2, 318G2-A3
Gen cleared in recruiting scandal 3-6, recruiters file suit 4-11, 369C3
Infantry shortfall seen 3-10, 267D2
3 instructors attacked in PR 3-12, 190D1
Female GI rptd convicted of sex harassmt 3-31, Eur crackdown ordered 4-23, 347F3
GI chrgd in parachute death 4-1, acquitted 5-27, 460B3
Retired soldiers mobilizatn set 4-2, 267F2
Blumenfeld confrmd Panama Canal comr 4-2, 308E3
Lesbian ordered reinstated 5-20, 428C2
Ark refugee camp calm enforced 6-2, 420C1
Sen com study faults Iran rescue missn 6-5, 419A2
Overseas duty time cut 6-6, 458G2-B3
Apr recruiting rptd 6-11, 458D2
W Ger GI drug arrests rptd 6-13, total 6-23; heroin use rptd down 6-18, 517D1, B2
Col sentenced for sex harassmt 6-28, 598G1
WW II vet wins Medal of Honor 7-19, 638E1
MacDonald murder convictn voided 7-30, 654F3
'79 recruits mental standards down 7-31, 598D1
Pa refugee cntr violence quelled 8-5, 591C3
Nev casino bomb explodes 8-27, 833F3
Anderson platform offered 8-30, 665A2
High temperature superconductor rptd 9-4, 716B2
Eur, S Korea sgts recalled 9-5; combat divisns in US said unready 9-8, 683B3
House defeats chem weapons funds challenge 9-16, 741D3
Reagan, Anderson debate pay scale 9-21, 722A1
NATO mil exercise performance scored 10-11, 777C1
W Ger offcl scores 11-6, 904C1
LSD setlmt clears Cong 12-5, signed 12-18, 981F3
Arms Issues—*See ARMAMENTS under 'A'*
Engineers, Corps of
'71 hijack ransom believed found 2-12—13, 136G2
Columbia R dredging operatn rptd 6-30, 504C3
Washn flood threats rptd 10-29, 970E3
Military Academy, U.S. (West Point, N.Y.)
Women graduate 5-28, 428D1
Obituaries
Crittenberger, Willis 8-4, 676B1
Decker, George 2-6, 175F3
Macon, Robert 10-27, 876E2
Rumbough, William 12-2, 1004C3
Simpson, William 8-15, 676B3
Reserves—*See ARMED Forces in this section above*

1976

ARTS & Humanities, National Foundation on the—*See NATIONAL Foundation, etc., below*

ATOMIC Energy Commission (AEC) (defunct)—*See also NUCLEAR Regulatory Commission below*
- Exec cited re India A-plant leak 1-30, 156E2
- Tests on prisoners confrmd 2-28, 316B2
- Sup Ct upholds waste powers 6-1, 414B3
- Cited in Carter biog sketch 512A1

BEEF Board
- Cong OKs 5-3, 5-12, 358E3-359A1

BICENTENNIAL Administration, American Revolution—*See BICENTENNIAL under 'B'*

BROADCASTING, Board for International
- RFE Olympics coverage barred 2-4, 158B3
- Dubcek RFE link chrgd 3-10, 289F2
- Ford signs '77 fund bills 7-12, 7-14, 534F1 ★, D1
- GOP platform text cites 8-18, 610B3
- Ford scores Sovt bloc re RFE, Radio Liberty 12-8, 934C2

BUDGET & Other Spending Programs (including Office of Management & Budget)—*See also specific agency headings in this section*
- Ford State of Union message 1-19, 36G2, 37G2, 39E1
- Fscl '77 budget submitted, summary 1-21, 62G1-66F2
- Budget receipts, outlays table; $ table 63E1, A2
- Econ Rpt 1-26, 67D2, D3
- Dec, 1st ½ fscl '76 deficit 1-28, 91F2
- Cong panels on fscl '77 proposals 3-10, 3-15, 230D2-231D1
- Calendar '75, 4th ¼ deficit rptd 3-19, 229E3
- Lynn on business probe panel 3-21, 262F2
- House Budget Com proposals, Ford budget compared 3-23, 231A1, D1
- Fscl '77 budgets compared 231A1
- Cong coms set fscl '77 targets 4-1, 246C1
- Sen com cites '70 memo on intelligence waste 4-26, 299F3, 300E2
- US foreign intelligence chart 304A1, A2 ★
- Cong OKs NRC authorizatn 5-5, 5-10, 358F2; signed 5-22, 982E1
- US sci office re-created 5-11, 346C1
- Cong OKs '77 targets 5-12, 5-13; Ford, OMB, Cong estimates table 358B1, B2
- Revises paymt data format 5-16, 396D2, E2
- Admin revises deficit forecasts 7-16, 536C1
- Southern govs meet 9-1, 671G2
- Keech confrmd AF asst secy 9-10, 808B1
- Cong clears tax bill 9-16, 705A3
- Cong sets '77 outlay, revenue levels 9-16, Admin comparison chart 706G1
- Program reauthorizatn bill not cleared 10-2, 883E1
- Transitn ¼ spending down, fscl '76 deficit cited 10-27, 865E3-866D1

Debt, Public
- House OKs ceiling rise 2-25, 170A3
- Temporary ceiling hike signed 6-30, 534D1
- Cong sets '77 budget level chart 9-16, 706B2, G2
- Dole, Mondale debate 10-15, 783E2

Impoundment & Rescission Issues
- HEW frees food funds for aged 4-2, 249G1
- Carter stand cited 512C2
- Fed Land Fund cited 644F2

Presidential Election (& Transition)—*See also 'Revenue Sharing' below*
- Reagan queried on plan 1-5, 1-8, 4E3-5D1; 1-9—1-15, 21G3—22C2
- Ford campaigns in NH 2-7, 109D1
- Ford scores Reagan plan 2-17, 129F2; 2-23, 149C3
- Reagan scores deficits 3-31, 232C2
- Carter states goals 4-23, 305B2
- Black Dems draft plank 5-1, 343D3
- Muskie on govt spending 5-20, 357E3
- Carter states goals 6-14, 433F1
- Dem platform text 6-15, 469D2, C3, 471A1, 473B2, 474A3
- Carter vows govs' role 7-6, 492E3
- Carter stand cited 512C2
- Carter outlines goal 7-28, 551A1
- Reagan urges strong platform plank 8-8, 583C1
- GOP platform com OKs plank 8-13, 583E1, F1
- GOP platform text 8-18, 602A1, E2, D3, 603D3, 606D3, 607B1, 608C2
- Dole vp acceptance speech 8-19, 612G3, 613D1
- Carter scores Ford vetoes 8-23, 631C3
- Carter stresses balancing 9-3, 664D1
- Dole hits Dem spending 9-11, 687A1
- Carter vows $60 bln more by '81 9-14, balanced budget 9-15, 686A3, C3
- Ford, Carter debate 9-23, 701E1, B2, C3, 702F1-D2, C3
- Ford campaign theme 9-25, 9-26, 723A3
- Ford: Carter big spender 10-7—10-13, 763G1, B2, G2

1977

ARTS, National Endowment for the—*See under NATIONAL FOUNDATION on the Arts and the Humanities below*

ARTS & the Humanities, National Foundation on the—*See NATIONAL Foundation on the Arts and the Humanities below*

ATOMIC Energy Commission (AEC) (defunct)—*See NUCLEAR Regulatory Commission below*

ATOMIC Safety and Licensing Appeal Board—*See NUCLEAR Regulatory Commission below*

BIOLOGICS, Bureau of—*See under FOOD & Drug Administration below*

BONNEVILLE Power Administration—*See under INTERIOR below*

BORDER Patrol, U.S.—*See JUSTICE—Immigration & Naturalization below*

BROADCASTING, Board for International
- Alleged RFE defector espionage role rptd 1-6, 19G3
- Carter seeks more funds 3-22, 229F3; USSR scores 3-24, 226G2
- RFE Radice interview rptd 4-2, 284A2
- Sen authorizes '78 funds 6-16, 477D3
- Sovt US expert scores RFE, Radio Liberty funding 8-3, 590A2
- '78 authorizatn signed 8-17, 667A3
- Alex Galich dies 12-15, 1024G1

BUDGET & Spending Programs (including Office of Management & Budget)—*See also LANCE, Thomas Bertram; for program recipients, see agency headings in this section and subject headings elsewhere in Index (e.g., CITIES, EDUCATION).*
- Carter studies econ stimulus plan 1-7, 5G1; spending plan scored 1-10, 14D1
- Ford State of Union message 1-12, 13E1, B2, B3
- Ford '78 budget submitted, summary 1-17, 30A1-33G3
- Budget $ table 32A2; '77-82 receipts, outlays table 32D2
- CEA econ rpt to Cong 1-18, 35E3, 36C1
- Gen Dynamics wins fed loan guarantee 1-19, 55F1
- Lance confrmd dir 1-20, 34B1, 35A1; sworn 1-23, 52E2
- Carter outlines econ stimulus plan 1-27, 51G3; submits to Cong 1-31, 75A2
- Carter econ plan debated 1-27—2-4, 89A2
- CBO on Carter goals 2-15, 126E1
- Carter submits chngs 2-22, 124B3-126E1
- Carter budget revision table 125A2
- Spending lag rptd 3-2, 174A3
- Cong sets new '77 levels 3-3, 174A1
- Carter vows balanced, zero-based budget 3-16, 190E3
- Carter urges spending cuts 3-16, 210B1
- Giaimo proposes '78 budget 3-23, 228D3
- Carter drops rebates, vs fund diversn 4-14, 270B3
- Energy plan impact discounted, cost estimated 4-21, 294B2
- Fscl '77 deficit forecast revised 4-22, 407D3
- GOPs score Carter energy taxes 4-25, 320F3
- Mar, 1st ½ fscl '77 deficit rptd 4-26, 407C3
- Carter scores liberals' criticism 5-12, 380A1
- Carter reaffirms goal 5-17, 381G2
- Cong clears '78 targets, '77 revised 5-17; table 404A3-405E1
- Carter would veto spending bills 5-26, 417B1
- Econ forecast revised 7-1, 518F3
- Exec office reorganizatn clarified 7-15, 555E3
- Carter hopeful re balancing 7-21, 575E1
- Cong sets binding '78 levels 9-15, 719D2
- Lance resigns, McIntyre becomes acting dir 9-21, 718A1, 719E1
- New dir apptmt deferred 10-2, 761D2
- Fscl '77 deficit rptd 10-27, 835D3
- Fscl '75, '76 deficit rptd on accrual basis 11-7, 941G2
- McIntyre named OMB dir 12-27, 1001B3
- Carter warns on spending lag 12-28, 1000G2
- Carter calls goal difficult 12-28, 1002B1

Debt, Public
- Carter revisions 2-22, 125A2
- 3d ¼ $2 bln repaymt planned 4-27, 407D3
- House energy bill provisn 8-5, 609G3
- Ceiling rise enacted 10-4, 773E2

Impoundment & Rescission Issues
- Navy ship funds rescinded 3-15, 195C3
- Chicago funds to be freed 3-25, 279G2
- Water projct provisn clears Cong 5-3, 365C2; Carter signs 5-13, 380D3

1978

ARTS & the Humanities, National Foundation on the
- Hal Davis dies 1-11, 96F1
- Mrs Mondale named honorary dir 2-28, 335E2
- Educ Dept plan excludes 4-14, 279E1

ATOMIC Energy Commission (AEC) (defunct)—*See also NUCLEAR Regulatory Commission below*
- Bikini Islanders relocatn planned, '54 bomb test cited 4-12, 278E2
- Nev A-test site '47 debate rptd 12-18, 1012B1
- Nev A-test claims filed 12-21, 1012A1

BORDER Patrol, U.S.—*See JUSTICE—Immigration & Naturalization Service below*

BROADCASTING, Board for International
- Bulgarian RFE freelancer slain 9-11, 748G3

BUDGET & Spending Programs (including Office of Management & Budget)—*For program recipients, see agency headings in this section and subject headings elsewhere in Index (e.g., EDUCATION)*
- IRS computer project rptd dropped 1-9, 15E1
- Carter State of Union Message 1-19, 29D2, 30C3
- Carter Econ Message 1-20, 48G2
- Fscl '79 budget submitted by Carter summary 1-23, 44C2-48E2
- '77-79 receipts, outlays table 45B2
- Federal budget dollar table 63A1
- '76-83 assumptns, projectns table 1-24, 46A2
- GOP rebuts Carter proposals 1-31, 62F3-63D1
- Carter renews balanced budget hope 2-17, 123E2
- Lance role in DC bank takeover cited 3-18, 204D2
- Carter vows to meet fscl '79 deficit target 4-11, 259D3
- Cabt-level Educ Dept proposed 4-14, 279F1 ★
- Sen votes '79 budget targets 4-26, 305B2
- Zero-based budgeting assessed, fscl '80 use modified 5-2, 344E1-A2
- Carter fscl '79 deficit target cut 5-12, 361D1
- Builders back cuts 5-16, 362G1
- Cong OKs '79 target res 5-17; table 385A1-A3
- Deficit blamed for pernicious inflatn 5-22, 6-19, 427A2, D2
- OMB backs M-X missile delay 5-24, 407B1
- Carter plans fscl '80 cuts 5-25, 404F2
- Deficit spending bar amendmt proposal rptd 6-6, 425C1
- Carter vows to hold the line 6-8, 431G3
- Carter urges Cong restraint 6-14, 446B3
- Carter on restraint 6-23—6-24, 509G3
- Fscl '78, '79 deficit, shortfall forecast revised 7-6, 506F2-C3
- Balanced budget goal dropped, '81 deficit seen 7-6, 506D3
- Carter cites austerity at Bonn summit 7-16—7-17, 544E1
- Amendmt draft drive to curb spending set 7-26, 735F3
- Cash flow savings rptd 8-19, 715E3
- Govs conf urges restraint 8-28—8-29, 681D3
- Cong sets binding '79 levels 9-23, 733E3
- Export financing aid set 9-26, 804F2
- Carter: balancing still goal 10-10, 766G2
- Tax cut bill cleared 10-15, 785A2
- 3d ¼ fed spending rptd down, 2d ¼ revised 10-20, 864B1
- Carter anti-inflatn plan sets deficit, spending cuts by fscl '80 10-24; reactn 10-25, 805G2-D3, 806C3
- GE, Armco execs for budget cutting 10-25, 806C3, D3
- Cong 95th sessn rated 10-28, 865A3
- Carter plans fscl '80 'tight' budget 11-6, 862F1; 11-9—11-14, 874D3-875A2; 11-27, 914F2
- Union sues Admin re Carter wage-price plan 12-1, 934D2
- Dem midterm conf debates 12-8—12-10, anti-Carter budget res rejctd 12-10, 956D1-C3
- Carter defends '80 budget plans amid protests 12-11—12-20, 979F2-980E2
- Carter defends plans 12-12, 956G3
- Carter restores $2 bln to '80 budget 12-22, 1002C3
- '80 budget totals estimated 12-22, 1002E3

Debt, Public (or National Debt)
- Defined 50B3
- Fscl '79 budget submitted 1-23, 44E2; table 45G2
- GOP rebuts Carter proposals 1-31, 62F3
- Ceiling extensn signed 3-27, 261A3
- Ceiling increased 8-3, 625F2
- Tax-cut proponents back set-aside paymts 8-21, 735B3

Federal Procurement Policy, Office of (OFPP)
- Fettig heads purchasing cncl 5-18, 405B2

1979

ARTS & the Humanities, National Foundation on the
- Carter budget proposals 1-22, 46A3

Arts, National Endowment for the
- Artist business skills program set 7-4, 672F2

Arts & the Humanities, Federal Council on
- Artist business skills program set 7-4, 672F2

ATOMIC Energy Commission (AEC) (defunct)
- A-test cancer link rptd ignored in '65 1-8, 17F2
- Utah sheep '53 A-deaths rptd 2-14, 112F1-A2
- Justice Dept admits H-bomb documt security error 6-8, 713E1; Hansen letter cites 716E3, 717C1, B2

BORDER Patrol, U.S.—*See JUSTICE—Immigration & Naturalization Service below*

BROADCASTING, Board for International
- RFE rpts E Eur 3 Mile I media treatmt 4-11, 323B1

BUDGET & Spending Programs (including Office of Management & Budget)
- Carter restores some '80 budget cuts 1-2—1-5, 3C3
- Carter aide warns Dems on 'new realities' 1-4, 3E2
- Brown urges balanced budget ammendment 1-8, 13C2
- Kennedy, O'Neill, ADA score Carter 1-13—1-26, 70C2
- Carter vs proposed amendmt, on '80 budget deficit 1-17, 29C2
- Lance banking practices detailed 1-17, 30G3
- Urban League dir vs Carter plans 1-17, 35D1, C2
- Fscl '80 budget submitted by Carter, summary 1-22, 41A1-46B3
- Federal budget dollar table 42A1
- '79-81 receipts, outlays table 42C2
- '77-84 assumptns, projectns table 43A2
- Carter State of Union 1-23, 46D2, E3, 47G1-A2, E2, 48A1
- GOP attacks State of Union proposals 1-24, 48F1-B2
- House com opens '80 budget hearings; Miller, Rivlin testify 1-25, 48E3
- Carter defends plans 1-26, 70A1
- Friedman group urges spending limit amendmt 1-30, 86G2
- GOP vs balanced budget amendmt, backs spending limit 2-4, 86E1-A2
- Balanced budget amendmt status disputed 2-6, 86B2
- Carter urges Cong 'hold line' 2-12, 109F3
- Govs oppose budget amendmt 2-26; back balanced budget, congressmen vs 2-27, 150G1
- Admin revises deficit forecast 3-15, 183D3
- Balanced budget fight delays debt ceiling bill, default fears raised 3-27—4-2, 251G2
- Tax cut, balanced budget linked 4-30, 327B2
- Dole seeks budget cuts 5-14, 363C3
- Cong OKs 1st '80 res 5-23, 5-24, 900C1
- Carter stresses deficit cut 5-29, 402B1
- Balanced budget amendmt progress, Prop 13 linked 6-3, 500F1
- ADA scores Carter 6-24, 982E2
- Balanced budget seen threatened 7-8, 517F3
- Consumer Affairs Cncl created 9-26, 902C3
- '79 deficit at 5-yr low 10-25, 946F1
- Brown for balanced budgets 11-8, 847G2
- Brown offers econ plan 11-9, 962F2
- Connally campaign themes cited 11-15, 983B1
- Cong OKs final '80 res 11-16, 11-28, 900A1

Debt, Public (or National Debt)
- Defined 1-1, 33A3
- Fscl '80 budget submitted 1-22, 41C1, B2; table 42D2
- Debt ceiling bill stalled, default feared 3-27—4-2; House clears bill, Carter signs 4-2, 251E2

Federal Procurement Policy, Office of (OFPP)
- Fettig calls contract denial for wage-price enforcemt legal 2-5, 127C3

1980

ARTS & the Humanities, National Foundation on the

Arts, National Endowment for the
- Extensn authrzn clears Cong 11-20, 953F2; signed 12-4, 982A1

Humanities, National Endowment for the
- Extensn authrzn clears Cong 11-20; 953F2; signed 12-4, 982A1

BROADCASTING, Board for International Radio Liberty—*See RADIO Liberty under 'R'*

BUDGET & Spending Programs (including Office of Management & Budget)
- Carter State of Union proposals 1-21, 1-23, 41F2, 43C2, C3; GOP rebuttal 1-28, 75F1
- Fscl '81 budget submitted by Carter; summary 1-28, 69B2-74B1
- Federal budget dollar table 69G3
- '79-81 receipts, outlays table 70C1
- '78-85 assumptns, projectns table 71A2
- Cong asks budget cuts 2-27, 2-28, O'Neill scores 3-5, 168E2-F3
- '80, '81 deficits seen higher 3-5, 168G1
- Carter anti-inflatn plan sets fscl '81 $13 bln spending cut 3-14, 201A1
- FTC emergency funding bills signed 3-28, 5-1, 348E1, C2
- Revised fscl '81 budget submitted by Carter, summary 3-31, 243D2-244E1
- GOP budget proposed 4-1, 244F1
- Carter warns vs Sen cutbacks 4-1, 247E1
- '80, '81 jobless aid to auto workers miscalculated 4-9, 330F1
- Kirkland scores Admin 5-6, 385G1
- Oil import fee blocked by Dist Ct 5-13, 366C1
- Cong com sets fscl '81 budget res 5-22; Carter scores 5-27, Dem ldrs back 5-28, House rejects 5-29, 424C1-C3
- Cuban refugee resetlmt costs estimated 5-25, 396D1
- UAW head scores Carter 6-1, 457D2
- Cong OKs 1st '81, final '80 budget 6-12, 452A1
- Spending cut urged by pvt anti-inflan com 6-21, 481D1
- Sen subcom scores year-end spending waste 7-20, 598F2
- Admin review sees deficit hikes 7-21, 550D1-B2
- '80 deficit doubles 10-29, 824D3
- House Com OKs fscl '81 res 11-11; Carter, cong Dems set priority 11-13, 866G1
- Reagan aides on plans 11-12, 866C2
- '81 res clears Cong 11-20, 896A2; signed 12-5, 936D1
- Info Regulatory Office set 12-11, 935D3
- Stopgap funds clear Cong, signed 953B2, 982B1 12-16, 953B2
- Amer Enterprise Inst proposals rptd 12-24, 980C3

Debt, Public (or National Debt)
- Defined 34B3
- Carter budget proposals 1-28, 69F3; tables 69G3, 70D1
- Carter unveils anti-inflatn plan 3-14, 201B1
- Deficit estimate rises, new ceiling asked 12-2, 916D2
- Limit hike clears Cong 12-12, signed 12-19, 981E1

Presidential Election (& Transition)
- GOP debate topic 1-5, 4D3
- GOP candidates debate in NH 2-20, 129A3, D3
- Reagan 'basic speech' cites deficits 2-29, 207C2, E3
- Connally 'basic speech' excerpts 3-7, 184B2
- Kennedy 'basic speech' excerpts 3-10, 183B1, F1, A2
- AFSCME backs Kennedy 4-2, 247G1
- Reagan vows spending cut 4-8, 264G2
- Reagan: budget unbalanced 5-29, 424A1
- Kennedy on balanced budget 6-14, 480E1
- Dem platform drafted 6-24, 479E3
- GOP drafts platform 7-10, 506A3
- GOP platform adopted; text 7-15, 536B1, D1
- Reagan accepts nominatn 7-17, 531G2, 532A2, 533E2
- Kennedy Dem conv speech, wins platform planks 8-12, 610D3, 614C1, 615B1
- Carter accepts renominatn 8-14, 613A2
- Carter attacks Reagan 8-22, 646F2
- Carter offers econ renewal plan 8-28, 663B2
- Reagan presents econ plan 9-9, 699A2
- Carter scores Reagan plans 10-14, 779A2
- Carter, Reagan TV debate 10-28, 813A2, E2, 814D1
- Reagan says data withheld 10-30, 840A1
- Reagan readies 2% cut 11-6, 837F1, 839B3

1976

Dole, Mondale debate 10-15, 782F3-783B3
Carter vs Ford chrgs 10-15; Ford replies 10-16, 785C1
Ford, Carter debate 10-22, 800C1, E2, 801C3, 802C1
Ford issue 10-23—10-28, 802G3, 803G1
Dole scores Dems 11-1, 827B3
Mayors seek Carter commitmt 11-7—11-8, 845G2-B3
Carter on goals 11-15, 863E2, G3
Carter meets cong ldrs 11-17, 864F1
Carter sees Lynn 11-22, 881D1
Carter names transitn aide 11-23, 881G2
Lance slated as OMB dir 11-23, 898D2 ★; Carter names 12-3, 916D1
Govs, mayors see Carter 12-9, 12-14, 937A3
Lance on econ aid prgrm 12-9, 937D3

Revenue Sharing
Chicago funds ordrd stayed 1-5, 6A2
Ford State of Union message 1-19, 38F2, 39B3
Budget outlays table 63G1
Ford details plan 2-7, 109D1
Natl Govs Conf topic 2-23—2-24, 149G2
Program attacked, defended 3-2, 187A1
Chicago funds threatened 3-31, 263B2
Sen OKs counter-cyclical aid 4-13, 283E1
Black Dems draft plank 5-1, 343D3
Cong OKs fscl '77 target 5-12, 5-13; Ford, OMB, Cong estimates table 358D2
Dem platform text 6-15, 473B2, 474A3
Carter backs state by-pass 7-6, 492F3
Carter stand cited 512C2
Ford urges Cong action 7-19, 532C1
Anti-bias laxity scored 8-4, 943E3
GOP platform text 8-18, 603D3, 606D3, 607B1
Cong sets '77 budget levels, chart 9-16, 706D2
Cong OKs extension 9-30, Ford signs 10-13, 763A3, 764B3
Ford, Carter debate 10-22, 801D3-E3
NE govs urge jobless aid 11-14, 865A1

State-Local Aid—*See also 'Revenue Sharing' above; also city, state names*
Ford urges progrm consolidatn 1-19, 39E2
Ford warns pub works, counter-cyclical veto; House passes 1-29, 93C3
Ford vetoes counter-cyclical aid 2-13, 127G3 ★
Ford asks block-grant educ aid 3-1, 166F2-D3
Sen OKs counter-cyclical aid 4-13, 283C1
Ford vetoes counter-cyclical aid 7-6, 518D2, Cong overrides 7-22, 533G2
Cong authorizes land conservation funds 9-13, 745G2-B3
Cong OKs counter-cyclical funds 9-22, 727G2; signed 10-1, 982F1
Cong extends depressed area aid 9-29, 765E1; signed 10-12, 982G1
Block-grant bills not cleared 10-2, 882G3, 883B2, E3, 884A2
Ford on aid to cities 10-14, 761G3
Ford, Carter debate 10-22, 801C3
Mayors seek Carter commitmt 11-7—11-8, 845G2-B3
NE govs draft plan 11-13—11-14, 864A3
Carter sees counter-cyclical prgrms 11-15, 863G2
Govs, mayors see Carter 12-9, 12-14, 937A3

1977

Revenue Sharing & Grants-in-Aid
Carter plans countercyclical aid boost 1-7, 5A2
Ford State of Union message 1-12, 13G2, B3
'78 budget proposals 1-17, 30B1, 32G2
Carter outlines countercyclical aid plan 1-27, 52G1; submits to Cong 1-31, 75A2
Kreps, Burns on Carter econ plan 2-3, 89E2, C3
Carter revisions 2-22, 125A2, 126D1
House, Sen OK expanded pub works bills 2-24, 3-10, 174A2, B2
Cong sets new '77 levels 3-3, 174D1
HUD grant program detailed 3-7, 178B1
Chicago funds released 3-25, 279G2
Expanded pub works jobs bill cleared 5-3, 365B2; Carter signs 5-13, 380D3
Funds clear Cong 5-5, 365G2; Carter signs 5-13, 380D3
Countercyclical aid extensn clears Cong 5-16, 382D1; Carter signs 5-23, 417F1
Cong sets '78 target 5-17, 405B1
CETA extensn signed 6-15, 500G3
'76 local tax revenue data 7-7, 540B2
Urban aid bill signed, regional conflicts re allocatn formulas cited 10-12, 796A2

1978

Revenue Sharing & Grants-in-Aid
Federal budget dollar table 63A1
Carter unveils urban-aid plan 3-27, reactn 3-27—3-30, 217C2-218D1

1979

Revenue Sharing & Grants-in-Aid
Carter to resubmit countercyclical aid progrm 1-2, 3E3
Carter budget proposals 1-22, 44A1, B2, C3; tables 42A1, F2,
Govs lobby for funding 2-27, 150B2
Carter submits countercyclical aid progrm 3-6, 164A2
Baker on GOP backing 6-13; Carter mayoral support cited 6-15, 439E3, 440A1

1980

Reagan upholds pledges 11-16, 881B2
Kennedy urges 'sensitive' cuts 11-19, 881C1
Reagan aides urge cuts 11-23, 897F1-E2
Stockman named secy 12-11, 935B1
Reagan studies immediate cuts 12-17, 956C1

Revenue Sharing & Grants-in-Aid
Utah State of State message 1-14, 270C2
Carter State of Union backs extensn 1-21, 43E3
Carter budget proposals 1-28, 73E1; table 70F1
Carter unveils anti-inflatn plan 3-14, 201C1
Revised Carter budget cuts 3-31, 244C1
Carter offers econ renewal plan, revenue sharing rise proposed 8-28, 663B2
Reagan plans bloc grants to cities 12-1, 914E2
'81 funds clear Cong 12-3, 954B3; signed 12-15, 982B1
Troup (Tex) to end black svcs bias 12-11, 936B2
'81-83 extensn clears Cong 12-12, 954G3-955B1; signed 12-28, 982C1

1976

CABINET & White House—*See also specific departments in this section; also FORD, subheads APPOINTMENTS and RESIGNATIONS; personal names*
Carter stresses independnc 6-24, 490F1
Carter proposes energy dept 9-21, 704F1, E2
Carter sees members 11-19—11-22, 881C1
Carter fills posts 12-18—12-23; photo 956A1
Carter unit meets 12-27—12-29, 978B1-G2

1977

CABINET—*See also specific departments in this section; also CARTER, subheads APPOINTMENTS and RESIGNATIONS; personal names*
Conflict-of-interest code set 1-4, 4C2
Ford proposes energy dept 1-11, 14E3
Ford proposes pay increase 1-17, 33D3
Carter urges limo svc, legal staff cuts 1-24, 53D2
Carter asks inflatn watch 1-31, 89G3
Carter cuts limo svc, revises rule procedures 2-2, 75B1, F1
Pay raises in effect 2-20, 127D2
11 rpt net worth 2-25, 147A3-148F1
Carter eases paperwork 2-28, 148B3
Sen OKs reorganizatn powers 3-3, 191B3
Reorganizatn powers cleared 3-31, 228A1
Reorganizatn powers signed, plans issued 4-6, 250C3
Carter backs spec prosecutor 5-3, 338F1
Energy Dept created, Schlesinger confrmd secy 8-4, 591C2
Women's conf rejcts dept 11-19—11-21, 917G2

1978

CABINET—*See also specific departments in this section; also CARTER, subheads APPOINTMENTS and RESIGNATIONS; personal names*
Carter cites planned Educ Dept 1-19, 29F2, 31E1, 32A1
Educ Dept not budgeted 1-23, 47A2
Carter: no staff chngs planned 4-11, 260F3
Education Dept proposed 4-14, 279A1-B2

1979

CABINET—*See also specific departments in this section; also CARTER, subheads APPOINTMENTS and RESIGNATIONS; personal names*
Carter backs Educ Dept 1-22, 44D2
Carter proposes Educ Dept 2-8, 110F2
Resources Dept proposed 3-1, 164B1
Sen OKs Educ Dept 4-30, 326B2; House OKs 7-11, 514C3
Resources Dept plan dropped 5-15, 365A2
Educ Dept created, HEW renamed 10-17, 782A2

1980

CABINET—*See also specific departments in this section; personal names*
Carter aides signed oath re leaks 7-16—7-17, 549G1
Reagan fills 2 key posts 11-14, 881E1
Carter holds final sessn 12-3, 935F2
Reagan fills 8 posts 12-11, 934G3
Reagan fills 8 more posts 12-22, 979E2

1976

CANCER Institute, National—*See 'National Institutes of Health' under PUBLIC Health Service below*
CENSUS, Bureau of the—*See under COMMERCE below*

CENTRAL Intelligence Agency (CIA)—*See also BUSH, George*
China oil study rptd 1-8, 10A1
Judge to see Rosenberg papers 1-13, 70C2
Nigeria orders radio statn shut 1-16, 103B1
Helms named Iran terrorist target 365G2
Bush confrmd dir 1-27, 68B1
Cong gets US-Sovt arms spending data 2-27; data challenged 3-5, 3-7, 182A2
Laos RC link chrgd 3-29, 267F3
Cong OKs Hatch Act repeal 3-31, 234B2
S Viet links to pol foes 4-22, 367F2
Cuba blames re Portugal emb blast 4-24, 367B2

1977

CANCER Institute, National—*See PUBLIC Health Service—National Institutes of Health below*
CENSUS, Bureau of the—*See under COMMERCE below*
CENTRAL Administrative Unit
Carter proposes creatn 7-15, 556C1
CENTRAL Intelligence Agency (CIA)
Leaked rpt on Sovt mil aims stirs controversy 12-26-76—1-18, 39E2
Ex-employe arrested 12-22-76, Bush defends security 1-2, 41A2
'64 actn vs Allende, multinatl collaboratn chrgd 1-9, 1-11, 18B2
Linked to '71 Cuba swine fever 1-9, 19E2
Cuban spy missn in Rhodesia rptd 1-10, 17A3
Rhodesia rebels chrg Mugabe link 1-14, 29D1
Mail-opening prosecutns barred 1-14, 41D3
Cuba double agent rpt denied 1-16, 61D1

1978

CENSUS, Bureau of the—*See under COMMERCE below*

CENTRAL Intelligence Agency (CIA)—*See also TURNER, Stansfield*
Press use detailed in House hearings, eds seek curbs 1-4, 1-5, 14G2
Sovt-bloc oil shortage forecast disputed 1-18, 52E3
Carter reorganizes intell units, details curbs; reactn 1-24, 49D2, G2, B3
Agee Dutch residency rejctd, W Ger bar cited 1-25, 90E3
Textron Iran paymt info rptd 1-25, 2-17, 161E2
Israel A-weapons, other natns capability rptd in '74 documt 1-26, 61F1
Intell reorg, curbs introduced in Sen 2-9, 107D3

1979

CENSUS, Bureau of the—*See under COMMERCE below*

CENTRAL Intelligence Agency (CIA)
Alleged agents listed 1-4, 17B3
US, USSR '74-77 arms sales rptd 1-7, 13G1, A3
'71, '73 'interest' in Letelier killer rptd 1-11, 19D3
UFO probe detailed 1-12, 93A1
Letelier murder testimony cites 1-15, 1-18, 57F3
'50s files made public, 'disposal' problems detailed 1-22, 55G1-C2
Paisley death probe urged by Sen com 1-24, 54G3
USSR '67-77, '78 mil spending rpts issued 1-25, 2-5, 99E2-E3
Canada '71 drug tests rptd 1-29, 95F3-96B1

1980

CENTRAL Intelligence Agency (CIA)
Indian unrest linked 445C2
Afghan ex-pres linked 1-3, 1G2; 1-21, 44F1
USSR '79 defense spending estimated 1-27, 65D2; '67-77 data 1-28, 70A3
Justice seeks suit vs Agee 2-5, ct OKs 4-1, 268E2
Iran militants seize info min 2-6, Cncl forces release 2-7, 105D2
USSR '57 A-mishap confrmd 2-13, 153C1
Afghan rebel arms rpt denied 2-16, 123B1
Disclosure limits upheld by Sup Ct 2-19, 130B3
Colby damage suit geographic relevance backed by Sup Ct 2-20, 170B3

1976

US forgn intelligence chart 304C1, A2 ★
Sen com rpt cites Welch 4-26, 304D1
Nelson quits as dep dir 4-27, 412B2
US, Sovt naval spending data cited 5-9, 394D2
Greece ends Welch death probe 5-21, 402D2
On Sovt food self-sufficiency 5-24, 856G2
USSR press links 3 US newsmen 5-25, 371A3
Iran police deny anti-terrorist aid 5-26, 418G2
US newsman sues USSR press 6-25, 559B1
Carter, Mondale briefed 7-28, 551C1
GOP platform text 8-18, 604G2
Sovt indl output forecast rptd 8-18, 752E2
Rpt Guinea min chrgs link 8-24, 1005B2
Rpts Taiwan A-bomb capacity 8-29, 761A1
Panama accuses, US denies chrg 9-17—9-22, 792C1, F1-G2
Wider gene research rules urged 9-22, 860C3
Rpts higher Sovt arms spending estimate, other econ data 10-5, 960F3
Ford Portugal statemt seen as 'confessn' 10-8, 812E2
In Letelier murder probe 10-9, 10-12, 780D3
United Brands linked to '61 Cuba raid 10-21, 844D3
'74 S Korea bribe return rptd 10-29, 900B2
Hendrix chrgd re ITT-Chile probe 11-5, 869A3
Bush resigns as dir 11-24, 917C2
Welch killers, Greek slaying linked 12-18, 1004C2
Sorensen named dir 12-23, 956F2, 958B1

Angola Issue
US mercenary training rptd 1-2, 3B2
House com rpt leaked 1-20, 92E1, D3
Mercenary role denied 2-2, 82D1
Blacks chrg CORE collaboratn 2-14, 163B3
Cuba chrgs China collusn 3-29, 228G2

Intelligence Investigations & Irregularities
Refuses data on Hughes burglary 1-5, 24E2
Italy covert aid rptd 1-7, 10E2
Colby denies Italy aid 1-9, 29B3
'58 Danish CP bugging rptd 1-9, 48E3
Olson files released 1-10, 24F3
DC area police aid rptd 1-11, 1-13, 24A3
Sovt sub salvage plans abandoned 1-13, 24G2
Paris paper links 44 1-13, 1-14, denied 1-13, 49C3
Alleged agents in Spain named 1-14, 77C1 ★
Agents in London rptd 1-15, 1-22, Italy 1-16, Holland 1-21, 50B1
Washn Post rpts CIA-news media links 1-16, 1-17, 92A3
Ford State of Union message 1-19, 36G3, 38G3, 39F3
NYT, Washn Post rpt unreleased House com findings 1-20—1-28, 92D1-93B3
Muskie defends Cong probes 1-21, 40E2
House coms dispute rpt publicatn 1-23, 1-28; House curbs 1-29, 92A2
Christian Dems urge Italy aid disclosure 1-26, 74C3
Admin denounces House com rpt leaks, Field denies blame 1-26, 92F1
Italy aid recipients named 1-31, 140A3
Pope Paul '42-50 ties alleged 1-31, 140D3
Italy backs aid disclosures 2-2, 140E3
House com rpt findings, publicatn disputed 2-2, 2-3, 150C2
McClory scores House com rpt 2-3, 150C2
Kissinger scores leaks, probes 2-4, 89A1
W Ger wkly names agents 2-9, 2-10, 158C1
House panel offers reforms 2-10, 150G1, B2
Bush limits media-contacts 2-11, 150A3
Schorr admits leaking rpt 2-12; probe voted 2-19, 150D3-151A2
Vatican infiltratn rptd 2-14, 140E3
S Vietnam chrgs plot 2-15, 143F3
Ford revises command, asks law vs leaks 2-17, 2-18, 127A1
Sen panel drops request for media contacts 2-17, 150E2
House ethics com leak probe underway 3-2—3-25, 216C3
Rebuts Pike on missing papers 3-9, 3-16, 217B1
AIFLD Uruguay cover rptd 3-10, 253G1
Dubcek-RFE link chrgd 3-10, 289E2
Nixon testimony on Chile released 3-11, 183G2
Briefs AIAA on Israel A-bomb, Sovt space program 3-11; acct publshd 3-15, 216F2
Colby vs budget disclosure 3-17, 217D1
Memos on Cuba-Oswald link rptd 3-20, 3-21, 217A2
Moynihan lauds Israel A-bomb rpt 3-25, 243B2
Rptdly had '50s Lockheed bribe data 4-2, 286C2
Church scores Ford 4-19, 282C1
Sen com issues rpt, chrgs irregularities, urges tighter control 4-26; text excerpts 298D2-304E3
Sen com rpts on domestic spying, asks curbs 4-28; text 324C3, 325C2, D3-326A2, 329C2, 330C1, F2
Helms Va break-in cited 5-17, 379B2
Permanent Sen com created 5-19, 376G3

1977

Sorensen withdraws nominatn 1-17, 35B1
USSR chrgs AP newsman link 2-2, 101D1
Colombia rebels kidnap US botanist, CIA link denied 2-14, 255F1
UK sets Agee, Hosenbell expulsns 2-16, 134A2
Uganda accuses 2-16, 138E3; 2-25, 141B1
Secret paymts to Hussein, other forgn ldrs rptd 2-18—2-22; Jordan denies 2-18; Carter news conf 2-23, 123A3-124F2
Frei denies paymts 2-21, rpts Carter apology 219A2
Saudi, Egypt liaison rptd 2-22, 124G2
Bush elected bank dir 2-23, 140F2
Turner confrmd dir 2-24, 148G3
Carter, Vance defend paymts 2-24, 2-27, 151E1
Sen intell com watch rptd 2-26, 150D3, G3
Sovt mil rpt, outside panel use debate continues 2-28, 3-11, Turner sees Sovt edge 3-20, 211C3
Lawyers Guild suit rptd 3-2, 423G1
USSR chrgs dissident recruiting 3-4, 226B3
WWII germ warfare rptd 3-9, 195B3
Leak penalties debated 3-9, 212C1
House com probes Castro plot 3-16, 228F2
Agee prosecutn barred 3-18, 212A2
Amin chrgs churches used as cover 3-26, 308G2
Ethiopia ousts 2 3-30, 327D3
De Mohrenschildt link rptd 3-31, 228C3
FBI ex-official indicted 4-7, 275F2
USSR Western debt estimated 4-7, 335D3
Zaire mercenary recruitmt denied 4-17, 317D3
Oil forecast pessimistic 4-18, 294C1
CR magazine funding chrgd 4-23, 506D2
King prober chrgs press ties 4-24, 339D2
Australia union infiltratn chrgd 4-27, 326D1-A2, 326D1-A2
2 Calif men convicted as spies 4-28, 344D2; 5-15, 409C3
Australia probe calls rptd 4-29, pol party funding chrgd 5-4, 372A1
Micronesia surveillnc rptd 5-3, 386G3
Australia halts probe 5-3, allegations continue 5-17—5-24, 410F1-B2
Nixon-Frost interview 5-4, 366A2, 367D2
Australia '72 Allende coup role rptd 5-4, 372F1
Anderson surveillnc rptd 5-4, 422G3
Ex-employe convicted as spy 5-5, 409D2
Ex-employe on oversight bd 5-5, 462E2
Mail surveillnc damages backed 5-12, 423B1
Sen com issues rpt 5-18, 386D3
GAO rpts spying abuse suits 5-22, 422C3
UK chrgs 3 5-24; Hosenball, Agee expelled 5-27, 6-3, 526C3
Ex-employe sentenced 6-1, 462G2
USSR dissident tie denied 6-6, 436G1
Korean lobbying info access OKd 6-8, 442C2
Turner centralizatn bid dispute rptd 6-10, 6-12, Knoche resigns 7-13, 576B2, E2
Agee rpts 64 agents in Greece 6-11, 618B1
Newton to face '74 Calif chrgs 6-24, 532C1
Australia Labor conv observer accused 7-5, 541B1
House oversight com created 7-14, 557D1
Shadrin release from USSR sought 7-14, 564B2
Calif man gets life sentence 7-18, 576F3
Mind-control tests revealed 8-1—8-9, 610C3
Francis Gary Powers dies 8-1, 696E3
Turner given new powers 8-4, 610F2
Australia role rptdly barred 8-4, 632G3
Mondale addresses ABA conv 8-8, 630C1
USSR econ downturn seen 8-8, 948F3-949C1
Turner denies Park pres mansn taps 8-9, 688E2
800 layoffs planned 8-9, begun 11-12; greater use of tech seen 11-21, 880C3
Amin rpts Sovt defector search 8-10, 606F2
Castro, Church discuss jailed US natls 8-10, review agreed 8-12, 653G3-654A1
China econ outlook rptd 8-15, 635B3
USSR blames in Shadrin disappearance 8-17, 640D3
Agee expelled from France 8-18, chrgs US pressure 8-19, 654D2
Mind-control tests probed by Cong 9-2—9-21, 721D1
Press links held extensive 9-12, 720F2-721C1
Palestine group accuses Israel re '67 US ship raid 9-19, 715A1
Sen Panama Canal wiretap probe subpoenas dir, postpones hearings 9-30, 756D1
Castro: terrorist training continues 10-26, 896E2
Helms indictmt decisn pending 10-27, 814C1; pleads no contest 10-31, 838A3
Jamaica ldr '75-76 death plots rptd 11-2, 884E1
USSR grain harvest misjudged 11-2, 948E2
Helms fined, prison term suspended 11-4, 861E1
China '71-75 trade rptd up 11-6, 882B3
Carter backs Helms setlmt 11-10, 877F1
Ex-analyst Snepp scores '75 Viet evacuatn 11-18, 11-20, CIA chrgs secrecy breach 11-18, 897D3-898F1

1978

Ex-analyst Snepp sued 2-15, 129C1
Haldeman book chrgs Watergate role 2-16—2-17, 124B3
USSR civil defns seen overrated 2-17, 126G3
N, S Korea econ compared 2-26, 240B3
USSR dissident tie rptd 3-6, 179D3
Letelier murder suspect linked 3-6, 188D3
Black Panther surveillnc rptd 3-17, other informants disclosed 3-30, 243E2
2 ITT aides accused of perjury in '73 Chile testimony 3-20, Geneen cover-up chrgd 3-21, 206E3
Ex-offcls vs excessive curbs 4-4—4-19, 306G1
India confirms '65 US A-device loss in Himalayas 4-17, 288F2
Shevchenko ties rptd 4-21, 302G2
Cuban prisoner swap rptd discussed 4-24, 318F2
Nixon memoir excerpt cites Watergate role 4-30, 319G3-320A1
Ex-agent Stockwell details '75 Angola war, '66 Ghana coup 5-8; Colby responds 5-14, 367A2-368C1
Nazi war criminal links rptd 5-16, 410G3
Carter gets evidence on Cuba role in Zaire 5-19, 443A1
'77 Sovt-bloc oil study assessed 5-21, 384E1
Colby book publshd in US 5-22, French versn appears uncut 11-19, 917F1-C2
Angola, Ethiopia rebel aid plan rejctn rptd 5-24, 383B2, 443D1
OPEC '85 output estimate revised down 5-26, 407F3
Cuba Zaire role evidence sought 5-26, 418B2
Cuba Zaire role evidence doubted 6-2—6-9, 442E1
USSR bares Peterson expulsn 6-12, 476A3
Cambodia chrgs joint Viet plots 6-13, 6-24, 6-25, Hanoi denies 6-27, 490C2, 548C2
Guyana cult persecutn alleged 6-15, 891G3
Castro chrgs UNITA aid 6-18, 645E3
Carter: unaware of Angola rebel aid 6-26, 491G1-A2
USSR arms spending studied; SALT impact discounted, '80s forecast issued 6-27, 563A3
USSR poor natns '77 trade rptd 6-28, 634E3
Sovt oil study backed by Saudi 6-29, 635B1
Nixon urges strengthening 7-2, 513C2
Snepp loses book suit, US to get profits 7-7, 527F2
Carter on security leaks 7-11, 524G2
USSR civil defns study issued 7-19, 563F3
UK rptr's '71 death linked 7-24, 631A3
Agee, Cubans accuse 8-1—8-4, 831B1
Rumanian defector rptd questnd 8-8, 650F3; W Ger spy scandal disclosed 9-1, 725D2 ★
Cambodia collaboratn chrgd 8-8, 659G3
USSR gas export rise seen 8-13, 634F3
Ex-employe Kampiles seized on spy chrg 8-17, 645D2
Ex-dep dir Karamessines dies 9-4, 778D1
Warrantless tap curbs rptd backed 9-7, 697D1
Book links Amer's death, Chile coup role 9-12, 795D3
Viet documt possessn by ex-amb rptd probed 9-13, 720F1
JFK death hearings cite 9-15, 9-28, 749G2, E3, F3, 750A2
Sovt defector jailing noted 9-15, 749E3
Intell agencies authrzn signed 9-17, 715C3
Paisley found dead 10-1; Sen panel probe rptd 10-5, suicide suspected 10-20, 10-26, 835D3
'Mole' issue raised 10-2, 10-22; documt security questnd 11-9, 940C2, D2
Shevchenko denies gifts financed 10-13, 844A3
Letelier murder probe documts clear 10-18, 795C3
UK drops major chrgs vs 3 10-23, 838A3
Letelier murder link implied by Chile suspect 10-24, 1014F3
Warrantless tap curbs signed 10-25, 863B1
Hunt denies JFK murder role 11-3, scores 'memo' 11-4, 898D3
Mail opening damages upheld 11-9, 940C1
Kampiles convicted as spy 11-18, manual said to aid USSR 11-23, 940F1, G2
Carter rptd critical of pol intellignc 11-25, 917C1
Paisley suicide disputed 11-25, 917C2
Harvard secret ties revealed 12-1, 962F2
Iran intelligence feud rptd 12-20, 994C2
Kampiles sentenced 12-22, 1011C3
Sovts chrg Iran role 12-28, 994F1
JFK murder role ruled out 12-30, 1002D2

Appointments & Resignations
Turner retires from Navy 12-31, 1009E2
Carlucci confrmd dep dir 2-9, 83A1

1979

Letelier murder link chrgd by Chile press 2-7, 114D3
Perjury chrgs vs ITT exec dropped, natl security cited 2-8, 88C1
Chile pres, Letelier assassins rptdly linked 2-8—2-9, 115B1
Lockheed infiltratn re Japan paymts rptd 2-15, 306E1
Early retiremts, resignatns, new security measures rptd 2-22, 132G3
Auschwitz photos released 2-22, 193D1
Angleton Sovt spy chrg rejctd 2-27, 152D3
Perjury chrgs vs 2d ITT exec dropped 3-7, 188A2
Viet War era domestic spying rptd 3-9, 207B2
ESP spies considered in '50s 3-11, 208D2
USSR 14-MIRV SS-18 '78 test rptd 3-13, 258A3
China-Viet war info praised 3-25, 231A1
More armed agents sought 4-4, 310B2
Pak A-bomb plans confirmed 4-6, 277C2
Libyan '71 A-bomb bid to China rptd 4-14, 299C3
SALT missile verificatn gap seen 4-16, Brown disputes 4-17, 279D2
Paisley death probe dropped by Justice Dept 4-18, 283F3
Ore Magazine prints Uganda article 4-19, 309B3
US spy satellite data rptd compromised 4-28, 318A3
Sen panel to probe Paisley death 4-30, 368A1
Castro '63 death plot rptd confrmd 5-2, 367E3-368A1
Agent rptd ousted re rifled JFK death probe files 6-17, 6-18, 466A3
Paisley death questioned 6-27; CIA scored on probe 7-8, 520B2-G2
'60s antiwar activist spying rptd 7-16, 561A2
House com final rpt clears in JFK, King deaths 7-17, 538C1
GOP asks intell policy chng 8-6, 610E3
Recruiting drive rptd 8-10, 610F3
US newsman link to KGB denied 8-11, 611B2
Unaware of Young-PLO talks 8-20, 624D3
Cuba pardons '60s Castro plotter 8-27, 686A1
USSR troops in Cuba confrmd 8-31, 657C1
4 prisoners released from Cuba 9-17, 706E3
Czech dissidents sentncd 10-23, 802C2
UK spy scandal reopened 10-28, 10-29, 874A1
NSA upheld on withholding data 10-29, 945G3
USSR mil truck use chrgd 11-8, 856F3
'50s NYC biological tests chrgd 12-3, 946A1
Cambodia relief rptd blocked 12-12, UNICEF refutes Sovt role 12-13, 977B3
Agee passport revoked 12-22, 991D2

Iran Issues
Iran USSR monitor rptd dismantled 1-18, 26E2
Shah aides fear hint of support 1-21, 49G3
House panel blames for Iran failure 1-24, 67F2
Iran USSR monitor protectn rptd 2-12, 106E1
Khomeini aide tap rptd barred 3-11, 180B1
Iran seized newspr linked 8-7, 602C2
Oil cutoff rumored 11-6, 843A2
USSR chrgs agents in US Emb 11-10, 878B3
Ex-agent's book recalled 11-10, 886E3
US Emb hostage spy trial threatened 12-1, 12-4, 914A2
Iranian amb to Sweden seized, US ties cited 12-19, 976A1
Agee barred Iran role 12-23; CIA files-hostage exchng rejectd 12-27, 991E2
3 hostages rptd isolated 12-28, 975A2

1980

Press, clergy, academics use admitted 2-21, Aspin asks details 2-25, 189A3
Afghan arrests alleged agent 2-22, 138E2
'60 Minutes' airs Iran segmt 3-2, govt pressure rptd 3-6, 239C1
Stockwell suit opens 3-3, 268A3
Alleged agents listed 3-7, 189F2
Syria blames for antigovt riots 3-10, 212F3
US 'spy' in Afghanistan scores 3-26, 271F2
Carter, Turner back newsmen, academics, clergy use 4-10, 4-12; Sen OKs intell oversight bill 6-3, 458C3, G3
Salisbury sues US 4-10, 459F1
Snepp rehearing denied by Sup Ct 4-14, 307E1
Cuba blames for Peru Emb incident 4-16, 285C2
Paisley cleared by Sen com 4-24, 459C1
Iran arrests alleged agent 5-6, 434P
'79 terrorism rpt issued 5-11, 365D3
Afghans free alleged agent 5-16, 443D1
Cambodia '70-79 populatn drop rptd 5-24, 397D2
Snepp novel rptd submitted for CIA OK 6-13, 517A1
Stockwell settles suit 6-25, 516D3-517A1
US anti-Khomeini broadcasts rptd; US denies 6-29, 490B3
US Emb aide in Jamaica named as operative 7-2, home machine gunned 7-4, 564E3-565A1
Trigon-Kissinger controversy rptd 7-14—10-4; sens ask probe 9-10, 753F3
Turner signed oath re leaks 7-16—7-17, 549A2
Moscow Olympics anti-US TV film aired 8-9, 590B1
Iran invasn plan discounted, Sovt interventn feared 8-25, 644G1
Somali Ogaden mil involvemt testimony rptd 8-28, 661F3
Ex-amb scores Brzezinski '79 Iran policy 9-6, 694C1
NSC Africa memo probe set 9-17, 727A1
Intell oversight bill clears Cong 9-19, 9-30; signed 10-14, 804C1
'Names-of-agents' bill defeated by Sen 9-30, 982B2
Agee profits denial refused 10-2, 990G2
Agee passport revocatn case accepted by Sup Ct 10-6, 782C3
Ex-agent indicted on espionage 10-24, pleads guilty 10-29, 855G2
Turner briefs Reagan 11-19, 881E1
Carter aide cleared in spy leak 12-5, 940B3
Sovt '79 3d World arms sales rptd up 12-10, 933A2
Casey named dir 12-11, 935E1
Ex-agent's Latin trip scored by US amb 12-11, 942D1

1976

Dem platform text cites, scores assassinatns 6-15, 477C2
Carter acceptance speech cites 7-15, 507D1, 510E2
Rogovin cited in Schorr probe testimony 7-20, 748F3
Carter lauds Bush 8-13, 616E3
Castro assassinatn plot cited 791E1
Ethics com subpoenas Schorr 8-25, drops probe 9-22, 748A3
Carter cites irregularities 9-6, 664D2
Dulles-Strauss letter termed forgery 9-22, 740B1
Mondale scores Ford 10-5, 743C3
Ford, Carter debate 10-6, 741D1
Castro ties to jet crash, other terrorism 10-15; Cuban exiles use as agents rptd 10-20, 779B3, 780A1-B2
Ford, Carter debate 10-22, 800D3
UK orders Agee expulsn 11-17, 946B2

CIVIL Aeronautics Board (CAB)
Sup Ct bars review of Western Airlines case 3-8, 219B2
Johnson confrmd member 3-22, 232E1
Dismisses Callaway chrg 3-31, 745A2
Ct voids '75 route swap 6-30; CAB overrules 11-19, 992F2
Domestic fare hike OKd 8-10, 992A3
Ford rejcts transatlantic plan 12-28, 992A2
Flying Tiger paymts chrgd, 4 others cited 12-29, 986D1

CIVIL Rights, Commission on
Louisville busing hearings held 6-14—6-16, 453E1
'77 funds signed 7-14, 534D2
Rpts '75-76 local desegregatn 'peace' 9-14, 992F3

CIVIL Service System (& Commission)
Ford budget proposals 1-21, 66D2
Hampton quits 2-10, 232A2
Sheldon confrmd v chrmn 2-26, 186C2
Hatch Act repeal clears Cong 3-31, 234A2
Ford to veto Hatch Act repeal 4-3, 245G1
Hatch Act revision vetoed 4-12, 284D1
Hatch Act veto sustained 4-29, 346E1
OKs domestic, N Atlantic, Concorde fare hikes 4-30, 378D3
Cong clears wage hike funds 5-19, 411D3
Sup Ct voids alien jobs bar; extends employe job-bias suit rights 6-1, 414G1-B2, E2-G2
Dem platform text 6-15, 471D1
Dem conv OKs Hatch Act plank revisn 7-13, 509C2
GOP platform text 8-18, 606B1
Carter, Ford debate 9-23, 702C1
Ford orders 4.8% pay rise 9-29, 742B3
Sets job exam bias rules 11-17, 884C2

CLAIMS, U.S. Court of—*See under JUDICIARY below*

COAST Guard (of Transportation Department)
Sen OKs 200-mi fishing zone 1-28, 94E1
Cong clears 200-mi fishing zone 3-30, 246C2
Oil rig sinks off Tex 4-15, 544G3
Eagle in Operatn Sail, photo 7-4, 488F1, A3
Cong OKs '77 funds 8-4, 646D2; signed 8-14, 982F1
Chem barge capsizes off Va 8-18, 796F2
US cargo ship vanishes 10-15, 912E1
Probes Miss R collisn 10-23, 876A2
Oil spill off Nantucket 12-15—12-22, 968E3, 969B1
Tanker explodes in LA harbor 12-17, 969A2
Sinks Argo Merchant 12-31, 1014D1

COMMERCE, Department of—*See also MORTON, Rogers C(lark) B.*
Sen OKs 200-mi fishing zone 1-28, 94E1
Richardson on business probe panel 3-21, 262E2
Cong clears 200-mi fishing zone 3-30, 246A2
Ford bars shoe import curb 4-16, 321G3
Ct votes porpoise protectn 5-11, 398D2
Helsinki accords panel clears Cong 5-21, 392E3
Limits porpoise killing 6-11, 570G3
Richardson vs pub works bill 6-28, 493F1

1977

Ex-agent backs Snepp, Colby disputes chrgs; Sen com sets probe 11-22, 898G1
RCMP link alleged 11-23, 11-24, 923C1
Press intell work barred 11-30, 941C1 ★, A1
Agee asked to leave Holland 12-2, 986F1
Helms setlmt scored by US rep 12-8, 979G3
Cuba to free US prisoner 12-13, 1011D3
Carlucci named dep dir 12-22, 1001E3
Colby, others defend press links, ask govt agency 'covers' 12-27, 1005E3

CIVIL Aeronautics Board (CAB)
Fare actns 1-10—3-29, 324B3-325E1
Ford proposes deregulatn bill 1-13, 36A3
OKs traffic diversns re NY, O, Pa weather-related shortages 1-19, 54F1
'75-76 commuter data rptd 2-2, 324E3
3 airlines indicted 2-3, 93A3
Airline baggage liability linked 2-3, 4-15, 324F3, 325F1
TWA rebate ruling rptd sought 2-8, 94B2
Amer Airlines paymts setlmt cited 2-9, 111E3
Regulatory agency rpt issued 2-9, 131G3
Bumping signs ordrd posted 3-1, '76 data rptd 4-7, 325A1, G1
'75 local svc data rptd 3-3, 325B1
Carter call-in topic 3-5, 171C1
Conduct rules issued 3-30, 325E1
License-fee rules suspended 4-8, 325F1
SEC new acctg rules rptd 4-29, 369B1
Robson quits as chrmn 211A2
Sup Ct refuses 'no-frills' rule review 5-16, 419C2
TWA 'on-time' ads curbed 6-13, 463D2
Laker 'Skytrain' svc OKd 6-13, 500F2
Eastn to add no-smoking seats 6-14, 593G1
Pan Am, TWA seek lower US-UK fares 7-29, 8-1, 593D1
US-Israel W Bank flights barred 8-1, 589B1
Acts on NY-London budget fares 9-9, 9-15, Carter overrules 9-26, 860D2
Sup Ct refuses procedures case review 10-3, 760B3
Air cargo deregulatn bill signed 11-9, 899C3
Airline cigar, pipe smoking ban voted 11-22, 900G1
Carter expands air svc to Eur, awards Braniff Dallas-London rte 12-21, 1006C2
Charter curbs eased 12-21, 1006C3

CIVIL Rights, Commission on
Women, minorities rptd 'last hired, 1st fired' 1-18, 278E3 ★
City-suburb busing backed 2-15, 112C1
Gay rights access promised 3-26, 278E2
TV bias study issued 8-15, 642A3
Sup Ct hears Bakke case arguments 10-12, 834D3

CIVIL Service System (& Commission)
Carter sets conflict-of-interest code 1-4, 4D2, 5C1
Sup Ct voids Washn homosexual dismissal ruling 1-10, 57A1
Ford pay-rise proposal 1-17, 30B3, 33E3
Carter plans agency ceilings 2-2, 75F1
Temporary ceilings set 3-2, 148E2
Califano hirings questnd 3-23—3-26, 236B2
Gay rights access promised 3-26, 278E2
Reorganizatn powers signed, plans issued 4-6, 250C3
Carter proposes ethics law 5-3, 338B1
House eases Hatch Act 6-7, 442G2
Mandatory retiremt curb voted by House 9-23, 737C2, E2
Carter urges jobs for women 11-17, 914E2
Denies Oswald early retiremt 12-8, 1007G1

COAST Guard (of Transportation Department)
Rpts tanker sunk off Cape Cod 1-11, 104E3
Liberian tanker fails inspectn 2-7, 214E3
Sovt trawlers boarded 3-1, 147G1
Carter asks oil-spill bill 3-18, 214C2
Sovt fishing violatns rptd 3-28—4-4; 2 vessels seized 4-9—4-10, chrgs set 4-12, 269G3
March fishing violatns rptd 270C2
'78 authorizatn clears Cong 6-21, 501A1
'78 authorizatn signed 7-1, 592G1

COMMERCE, Department of
S Africa sealskin imports OKd 1-3, 21F3
Harman named undersecy 1-6, 14F1
7 firms chrgd re Arab boycott rpts 1-7, 167G1
Gen Dynamics loan guarantee OKd 1-19, 55E1-F2
Kreps confrmd secy 1-20, 34B1, A3
Kreps on Carter econ plan 2-3, 89E2
Carter visits employes 2-9, 110G2
Carter budget revisions 2-22, 125A2
House OKs pub works expansn 2-24, 174A2

1978

CHILD Development, Office of—*See under HEALTH, Education & Welfare in this section below*

CIVIL Aeronautics Board (CAB)
HEW backs proposed smoking ban 1-11, 23C2
Natl Airlines rule review denied 1-23, 65C2
Nader group scores 1-31, 68A1
UK air-fare dispute flares 2-28, 3-7, setlmt reached 3-17, 206A2
More 'Super Saver' fares OKd 3-3, 206A3
3% domestic fare hike OKd 4-6, 264E3
Air-fare deregulatn proposed 4-14, 284E1
1st-class air fare cut OKd 5-19, 366F1
'Bumping' penalty revised 6-1, 570B1
N Central, Southn airlines merger set 7-13, 684D1
ABA proposes regulatory overhaul 8-8, 626F2
Most charter curbs ended 8-17, 640D2
TXI, Pan Am purchase of Natl Airlines stock OKd 8-17, 8-28; Pan Am, Natl set merger 9-7, TXI scores 9-12, 701A1
New air fare rules OKd 8-25, 684E1
Western, Continental airlines merger set 8-31, 684B1
Pan Am Houston svc OKd 9-1, 701E1
Pan Am to end svc to Moscow, 9 other Eur cities 9-7, 701F1
Airline deregulatn compromise clears conf com 10-6, 765F2-C3; Cong 10-14, signed 10-24, 873F1
Amer, TWA begin 3-class svc 10-15, 812D2
Kahn named anti-inflatn chief, Cohen succeeds 10-25, 806C2
IATA revises structure 11-13, 894A3
Eastern seeks Natl merger 12-11, 1007C3
Jet fuel shortage feared, new routes linked 12-14, 984A1

CIVIL Rights, Commission on
Age bias in fed progrms rptd 1-10, 14C1
Carter seeks job-bias unit reorganizatn 2-23, 123G3

CIVIL Rights, Office for—*See under HEALTH, Education & Welfare below*

CIVIL Service System (& Commission)—*See also LABOR—Government Employment*
Rpt scores CPSC 1-12, 185E2-A3
Carter seeks reform, merit system 1-19, 29B1, E2, 31E1
Carter budget proposal 1-23, 45F2
Carter seeks job-bias unit reorganizatn 2-23, 123G3
Carter proposes revision 3-2, 141B2
Mandatory retiremt curb signed 4-6, 238F2
Carter asks pay hike limit, reaction 4-11, 259D2, 260G2
Carter asks revisn support 4-25, 4-26, 306D3, 307D3
LaPrade to appeal firing 7-6, 507D3
Carter vs cong proposals 7-20, 549F3
Carter defends plan in Va 8-3, 605E3
Comm chngs take effect 8-11, overall reform legis pending 8-12, 625A2-F2
Carter reforms OKd by Sen 8-24, 661C3; House 9-13, 696C2-D3
Carter asks 5.5% pay hike 8-31, 681D2
ICC ex-offcl challenges dismissal 9-25, 770A3
Reform bill enacted 10-13, 787G2-788A1

COAST Guard (of Transportation Department)
LI Sound oil spill sealed off 1-10; gas spill rptd 3-16, 524F1, A2
Carter budgets oil pollutn fund 1-23, 47E3
Cincinnati storm airlift 1-29, 105B3
Chem-spill fines set 3-3, 163E3
States curbed on oil tanker regulatn 3-6, 162A1
Boating program rptd cut from fscl '79 budget 5-2, 344G1
Miss R boat '76 collisn rpt issued 5-17, 460B1
Canada fishing dispute rptd 6-2—6-5, 435E1
'79 authrzn signed 6-30, 525B2
Cuyahoga Chesapeake Bay collisn kills 11 10-20, 908C3

COMMERCE, Department of
Minority broadcasting ownership aid proposed 1-31, 195A2
US-Taiwan textile pact rptd 2-27, 140C3
Carter unveils urban-aid plan 3-27, 217A3
Kreps to probe export expansn 4-11, 260G1-A2
Wexler joins Carter staff 4-19, 306F3
Canada fishing boats blocked 5-5, 350D2
Wis U computer research secrecy order lifted, probe vowed 6-12, 514C1
Calif residual fuel oil exports set 6-15, 470E3-471B1

1979

CHILD Development, Office of—*See under HEALTH, Education & Welfare below*

CIVIL Aeronautics Board (CAB)
Intrastate fare order case refused by Sup Ct 1-8, 14D3
Pan Am ad deceptn chrgd 1-10, 35F2
$99 cross-country fares, routes OKd 1-12, 35D2
Pan Am, TWA warned on London fares 1-23, 87F3
New charter rules adopted 3-1, 166C3
Domestic air fare rise OKd 4-12, 465E3
Canada bargain fare protested 4-18—4-20, 329F2
North Central, Southn Airways merger OKd 4-26, 465D3
US-French air svc pact rptd 5-12, 465B3
Allegheny Airlines name chng OKd 6-5, 465G2
Pan Am, TXI bids for Natl Airlines OKd 7-10, 578G3
Continental-Westn merger blocked 7-21, 579C1
Alaska Airlines stock ploy blocked 8-28, judge backs 10-4, 830F1
Canada discount fares halted 8-30, 667D2
9.5% fare hike granted 8-31, rule clarified 9-4, 725E3
IATA gets limited trust immunity 9-10, 725G3-726A1
China charter svc pact OKd 9-17, 726D1
Eastern-Natl merger rejctd 9-27, Pan Am-Natl merger OKd 10-25, Carter approval sought 10-29, 830A1
Justice Dept asks Flying Tiger-Seaboard merger ban 10-2, 830C2
Domestic air fare rise OKd 10-26, 830A3
IATA probe ended 12-5, 989C1
3.3% fare hike OKd 12-20, 989B1
Alaska NW stock sale rejctd 12-20, 989F1
Carter OKs Pan Am-Natl merger 12-22, 989C1

CIVIL Rights, Commission on
Mil conducts 'sexist' language review 1-19, 89D3
Desegregatn lag rptd 2-13, 110B2
Rpt scores housing bias 4-11, 283F2-C3
Phila police brutality hearings 4-16—4-17, 310D3

CIVIL Service System (& Commission)
Commission replaced 1-1, 5A3, 6A1
'79-81 budget outlays 1-22, 42E2
ICC misconduct dismissals backed 3-5, 309D1
Carter asks pay-scale revisn 6-6, 419C2
Carter OKs pol '80 Census hiring 8-9, 631E1

COAST Guard (of Transportation Department)
Cuyahoga collisn rpt, safety training faulted 1-20, 140E3
Great Lakes rptd unnavigable 2-20, 176C2
2 more Cuyahoga collisn rpts issued 2-26, 3-2, 240G3
Tanker inspectn progrm rptd effective 3-20, 200E3-201A1
Oil platform workers rescued 5-10, 472G3
Tankers collide off Tobago, oil spill estimated 7-21, 553B3
Miss R barge blast rescue rptd 8-30, 800E1
Freighter, tanker collide off Tex; rescue, oil spill operatns rptd 11-1, 955B1, C1
Cuyahoga cmdr convicted for collisn 11-3, sentncd 11-5, 887A3

COMMERCE, Department of
Sperry computer sale to USSR cleared 3-29, 287E2
Kreps in China, trade pact initialed 5-5—5-14, 352G3, 369G3-370F1
China trade pact signed 7-7, 523C2, F2
Carter trade reorganizatn plan set 7-19, 647A1
'80 funds bill clears Cong 8-2, 9-10, Carter signs 9-24, 766E3
Kerosene sale to Iran announced 8-21; Carter defends 8-22, 622C3
Continental Grain unit fined 8-27, 648A3

1980

CHILD Development, Office of—*See HEALTH, Education & Welfare, Department of in this section*

CIVIL Aeronautics Board (CAB)
Fare hikes OKd 1-1, 2-26, 4-28, 346G3-347A1
Aeroflot flights cut 1-8, 9D1
Minneapolis-St Paul-London svc set 1-24, 347A2
Intl airline deregulatn clears Cong 1-31, 2-4, Carter signs 2-15, 346F1
Global airfare hikes OKd 3-12, 3-24, 346E2
Pan Am Miami-London svc retentn OKd 4-7, 346G2
World Air Boston-London route OKd 4-10, 346C2
Seaboard-Tiger merger OKd 5-8, 516F1-A2
Domestic fare hikes OKd 5-13, Nader group scores 6-18, 515G3-516D1
Global fare hikes OKd 5-15, 516E1
Laker Miami-London svc OKd 5-15, 516D2
Continental-Westn merger bid renewed 9-22, 746E2
UNC Resources seeks Westn merger 12-24, 985C1

CIVIL Rights, Commission on
Rpt sees 'drift' in '79 1-14, 36G2
Rights violatns deplored 7-9, 519G1

CIVIL Service System (& Commission)
Carter budget proposals 1-28, 69E3; table 70E1
Carter anti-inflatn plan sets fed spending cuts 3-14, 201C1
Reagan plans hiring freeze 7-17, 532F2
Carter OKs pay hike 8-29, 685C2
Reagan readies hiring freeze 11-6, 837F1, 839B3

COAST Guard (of Transportation Department)
Sovt trawlers ordrd tracked 1-8, 9C1
Cutter, oil tanker collide off Fla 1-28; suit rptd filed 2-3, hearing begins 2-6, 256D2
Playboy photo series rptd 2-21, 189C1
Storms hamper Cuban exodus; rescue efforts, shooting incident rptd 4-25—5-1, 326A1
Liberia freighter rams Fla bridge 5-9; capt's safety record rptd 5-10, 391G1
Cuba MIGs buzz rescue copter 5-12, 371C3; Havana regrets 5-15, 380B2
Carter revises Cuba refugee policy 5-14, 361E1
Cuban flotillas turned back 5-17, refugee influx slows 5-21, 379G1
Women graduate from academy 5-21, 428D1
700 Cuban flotilla boats seized, 300 stalled in Mariel 5-29, 396E1
731 Cubans arrive on US freighter, capt arrested 6-3, 420D2
Flotilla end seen 6-5, blockade expanded 6-10, 435B2
Cuban flotilla boats released 7-7, 514E3
Marines alerted; mystery freighter intercepted, no refugees found 7-14, 515A1
PR harbor beacon bombed 7-14, 559F3
Haitian exodus accelerates 9-9, 685D1
Cuba flotilla ends, blockade cost rptd 9-26, 742E1
Dutch ocean liner rescue 10-4; conditn rptd 10-7, 769D2
Haitian refugees rptd stranded in Bahamas 10-9; US news copter missing 11-13, 869G2, D3

COMMERCE, Department of
Carter signs trade reorganizatn plan 1-2, 94A3
USSR tech export licenses rejected 1-11, 28C2; computer exports barred 1-21, 45F1
USSR illegal tech sales probed 2-14, 135B1
Island territories get econ plan 2-14; govs meet, set projects 2-19—2-22, 495A1
USSR scientists barred from 2 US confs 2-22, 135D1
Phosphate exports to USSR halted 2-25, 139F3

1976

'77 funds signed 7-14, 534C2
Ford submits payoff legis 8-3, 668C2, G3, 669B1
Carter vs Ford business payoff legis 8-9, 8-11, 584G3, 585D2
Standard air-quality index proposed 8-23, 671B2
Carter proposes Cabt-level energy dept 9-21, 704F2
Helsinki panel tour barred 11-1, 880A2
Carter names transitn aide 11-23, 881B3
Yugo export licenses rptd withheld 12-27, 1012D1

Appointments & Resignations
Pate quits as asst secy 1-27, Darman confrmd 2-26, 186F1, D2
Richardson sworn secy 2-2, 110E1
Kasputys confrmd asst admin 2-26, 186A2
Smith confrmd counsel 2-26, 186C2
Eden confrmd asst secy 8-3, 807F3
Pfeiffer rejected secy post 12-16, 937B1
Kreps named secy 12-20, 956F1, 957A1, B3

Arab Boycott
Fines 6 cos 4-19, 4-20, 747F1
Boycott aid chrgd 9-7, 746E3, G3★-747B1
House OKs curbs 9-22, 746B2
Rpts compliance rate 9-30, 747C1
Ford, Carter debate 10-6, 740D2, 742B1
Ford alters disclosure vow 10-7; new rptg rules set; chrgs vs 15 cited 10-8, 10-19, 10-20, 785F2
Carter scores Ford re disclosure 10-8, 762A2
Compliance rpts released, protests rptd 10-18—10-20, 785E3
Defends some cos 10-19, 786D2
Richardson testifies on rules, Ford position 10-20, 786E2-B3
More boycott requests, noncompliance rptd 10-24—11-10, 986E2-B3
5 cos chrgd with rptd violatns 11-3, 986B3
Modifies boycott rpt rules 11-18, 986C3

Census, Bureau of the
Jobless index described 21D1
Report on women issued 4-27, 379F2
Rpts '75 death rate, populatn growth 7-31, 911E1, G1
GOP platform text 8-18, 603F2
Rpts farm populatn drop 10-5, 833F1
Mid-decade census bill signed 10-17, 834F3
Male-female earnings gap rptd wider 11-28, 943F1

National Oceanic & Atmospheric Administration (NOAA)
Rpts on Colo canyon flood 8-10, 756G1
Porpoise killing curbed 10-15, 902B1
Traces Nantucket oil spill 12-31, 1014D1

Patent & Trademark Office
Sen votes patent reform 2-26, 181B3

Statistics—*See also 'Census' above*
Nov inventories, sales; Oct revised 1-15, 91G2
'46-75 GNP, inflatn revised 1-16, 89B3-90E1
Dec, '75 income; Oct, Nov, '73, '74 revised 1-19, 91A2
'75, 4th ¼ GNP; 3d ¼ revised 1-20, 89E1
Dec, '75 trade surplus 1-27, 91B1
Dec '75 indicators, Nov revised 1-28, 90E3
Dec inventories, sales 2-13, 169C1
Jan income, Dec revised 2-17, 168E3
Jan housing starts, Dec '75 revised 2-18, 153D1
Jan indicators, Dec revised 2-27, 168A3
Jan trade deficit 2-27, 168C3
Jan inventories, sales; Dec revised 3-16, 199G1
Feb starts, permits; Jan revised 3-16, 199C2
Feb income, Jan revised 3-17, 215F3
'75, 4th ¼ profits; 3d ¼ revised 3-19, 215B2
Calendar '75 deficit 3-19, 229F3
4th ¼ '75 real GNP revised 3-19, 1st ¼ GNP 4-19, 278F3-279G1
'75, 4th, 3d ¼ paymts data; other revised data 3-24, 229G3
Feb trade deficit 3-26, 230E1
Feb indicators, Jan revised 3-29, 229F2
Feb inventories, sales; Jan revised 4-14, 279G3
Mar income, Feb revised 4-15, 279A2
Mar housing starts, permits; Feb revised 4-16, 279B3
Mar, 1st ¼ trade deficit 4-26, 307B1
Mar indicators, Feb revised 4-28, 306D2, A3★

1977

DNA patent order lifted 2-24, 184A2
Kreps rpts net worth 2-25, 148B1
Carter asks energy dept 3-1, 148C2
No exec cooks rptd 3-24, 236F1
Slater on Mar WPI rise 4-7, 274D1
Fishing rules compliance monitors set 4-13, 363E3
Carter energy plan 4-20, 292C1
Pub works jobs clear Cong 5-3, 365A2; Carter signs 5-13, 380D3
Rhodesia-Mobil probe inconclusive 5-16, 413F2
More drought aid signed 5-23, 405A3
House limits porpoise kill 6-11, 443B1
Sovt computer sale barred 6-23, 501D3
Subsidized ships OKd for Alaska oil transport 6-28, 498G1
Shoe industry aid set 7-20, 587C2
'78 funds signed 8-2, 667E3
Sirica vs whaling ban 10-21; ruling reversed, Burger backs ban 10-24, 835B2
'76 crime cost to business rptd 11-17, 919B1

Census, Bureau of the
Jobless index described 37G3-38E1
CBO issues poverty rpt 1-13, 80A3
'75 10 largest cities rptd 4-14, 387B3
'76 state-local tax revenue mark rptd 5-4, 388E1
'76 death row populatn rptd 5-5, 593G3
'76 populatn data rptd 9-19, 962G2-A3
'75, '76 income, poverty data rptd 10-3, 821G3-822B1

Economic Development Administration
'78 funds signed 8-2, 667E3

Maritime Administration
'78 funds signed 8-2, 667F3
USSR grain shipmts rptd 10-17, 948E3

National Oceanic & Atmospheric Administration (NOAA)
Weather Svc rpts blizzard 1-28—1-29, 75F2
Sunspots, weather linked 2-21, 183C2
Weather Svc on Ala storms 4-4, 311F2
Marine svcs sets Sovt chrgs 4-12, 270A2
Franck confrmd admin 7-13, 626E2
'78 funds signed 8-2, 667E3
Weather Svc delays metric conversn 10-18, 820D3
Weather Svc asked to probe grain blasts 12-28, 1023B2

Patent & Trademark Office
Laser patent awarded 10-11, 860A1

Statistics—*See also 'Census' above*
Dec '76 retail sales 1-10, 38C2
'77 capital spending forecast, '76 data 1-11, 56G3-57A1
Nov '76 inventories, sales; Oct '76 revised 1-14, 56E2
'76, Dec personal income; Nov revised 1-17, 56A3
'76, 4th ¼ GNP, inflatn; 3d ¼ revised 1-18, 56G1
'76, Dec housing starts, permits 1-18, 111G1
Indicators index described 1-28, 92C3
'76, Dec trade deficit 1-28, 92E1
Dec '76 indicators, Jan-Nov revised 1-28; graph 92F2
Jan housing starts, permits; Dec '76 revised 2-16, 130G1
'76, Dec inventories, sales; Nov revised 2-16, 130F2
Jan incomes growth, Dec '76 revised 2-17, 130C2
'76 US bank overseas loans 2-17, 145E2
Jan trade deficit 2-28, 154C1
Jan indicators, Dec '76 revised 2-28, 154F1
Feb personal income, Jan revised 3-17, 194C1
Jan inventories, sales 3-17, 194F1
Feb housing starts, permits; Jan revised 3-17, 194A2
'76 color TV imports 3-18, 208E3
'76 4th ¼ profits 3-21, 301A1
'76, 4th ¼ paymts deficit, capital flow 3-23, 234C1
Feb trade deficit, '76 revised 3-28, 233E3
Feb indicators 3-30, 234A2
'75, '76 shoe imports 248E2

1978

Secrecy classificatn powers curbed 6-29, 508E1
USSR crime equipmt sale OKd 7-6, 10-13, 905B2
USSR oil sales review set 7-18, 542G1
Seabed mining bill clears House 7-26, 589A1
GAO LNG study scored 7-31, 610G1
USSR oil tech sale rules issued 7-31, 634F2
USSR oil equipmt sales OKd 8-9, 634D2; 9-6, 743D1
USSR oil equipmt sales rptd 9-29, 821B1
US trade missn arrives Japan 10-2, 797D3-798A1
USSR computer deal OKd 10-31, 841D1
IWC whale quota cut rptd 12-25, 1001B2

Census, Bureau of the
Jobless index described 51A1
State tax revenue rptd, table 1-9, 84F2, F3
'76 pres vote data 4-13, 285A2
'77 median family income, 'real' gain rptd 8-9, 680A1
'75 abortns, illegitimate births rptd 8-10, 744C1
'77 poverty level data 8-12, 684D2
FTC business data cases refused by Sup Ct 11-6, 873F3
Black urban populatn data 11-30, 943E1
'75-77 poor migratn data 12-3, 943B1
20 largest cities rptd 12-6; table 942A3, D3

Export Administration Review Board
S Africa unit fined for Rhodesia sales 1-12, 38B3

National Fire Prevention & Control Administration
Carter proposes new emergency agency 6-19, 466F2-G3
Fire victim study rptd 10-8, 972A1

National Oceanic & Atmospheric Administration (NOAA)
Weather Svc rpts drought ending 1-8, 24D1
Weather Svc rpts Midwest blizzard 1-25—1-26, 105F2
Weather Svc probes LA cloud-seeding 2-14, 106B1
Weather Svc declares drought over 3-5, 207A2
Ocean pollutn study signed 5-8, 343B2
Marine Fisheries Svc rpts '77 Canada catch 6-5, 435A2
Admin to sit on Endangered Species Com 10-15, 834E2; 11-10, 1003B1

Patent & Trademark Office
Wis U research secrecy ordr set 4-21, lifted 6-12, 513G3

Statistics—*See also 'Census' above*
State govt tax revenue table 1-9, 84F3
'78 business spending rise seen; '77, '76 data 1-12, 65B3
'77, Dec income 1-18, 52A2★
'77, Dec housing starts, permits 1-18, 52D2
'77, Dec trade deficit 1-30, 127E2-B3
Dec '77 indicators; July-Nov revised 1-30, 127F3
'76 median family income revised, '73-75 cited 2-10, 128E3
Jan, Dec '77 retail sales 2-15, 106A2
Jan housing starts, permits; Dec '77 revised 2-17, 106C2
Jan income; Nov, Dec '77 revised 2-20, 128G2
Jan indicators 2-28, 223A1
Jan trade deficit; '77, Oct-Dec revised 3-3, 221F2-B3
Feb housing starts, permits; Jan revised 3-16, 222E3
Feb income, Jan revised 3-17, 223C1
'77 4th ¼ profits 3-20, 282B3
'77, 4th ¼ record paymts deficits 3-22, 221B3
Feb trade deficit 3-31, 262E1
Feb indicators; Nov-Dec '77, Jan revised 4-6, 262D2
Mar income, Dec '77-Feb revised 4-18, 303F3
Mar housing starts, permits; Feb revised 4-18, 304C1
1st ¼ GNP, inflatn; '77, 4th ¼ revised 4-19, 303A3
Mar trade deficit 4-26, 344B2
OPEC share in '77 trade deficit; '74-77 data, investmt shift 4-28, 344F2

1979

USSR computer sale barred 9-27, 775D1
Kreps resigns 10-4, 829B2
Carter trade reorganizatn proposed 10-25, 803B1
Cameron fine rptd 11-1, 923B3
USSR mil aided by US sales 11-8, 857C1
Klutznick named secy 11-16, 883C3
Youngstown aid set 12-3, 941F3
USSR truck plant mil use denied 12-17, 997F2

Census, Bureau of the
Population data rptd 1-1, 18B3
Home '76-77 values double 1-11, 18D1
State tax collectns rptd 2-13, 152G1
Student enrollmt decline, staffing rise rptd 5-12, 367F1-C2, E2
'78 state per capita gas use rptd 5-27, 395E2
Carter OKs pol hiring in '80 8-9, 631E1
Ga black registered voter increase cited 8-14, 724F2
Info use re deportatn barred 11-26, 924F1

Economic Development Administration
Dvpt finance progrm proposed 3-1, 164G1
Auto-Train withdraws loan applicatn 8-21, 726E2
Wheeling-Pittsburgh aid OKd, suit filed 8-28, 681G3

National Oceanic and Atmospheric Administration (NOAA)
'78 flood statistics rptd 2-11, 120A2
Natural Resources Dept proposed 3-1, 164B1, F1
Weather Svc rpts Great Lakes unnavigable 2-20, 176C2
'78 tornado data rptd 4-1, 288C3
Weather Svc rpts Miami record rainfall 4-25, 472G2
Weather Svc rpts on Red R floods 4-30, 472B2
Weather Svc rpts Tex rainfall 6-2, 472E2

Statistics—*See also 'Census' above*
Income index described 34D3
'78, Dec income 1-17, 34A3
'78, Dec housing starts; Nov revised 1-17, 35B1
'78, 4th 1/4 GNP, inflatn; 3d 1/4 revised 1-18, 72A1
Dec '78 trade gap 1-30, 71B3
Dec '78 indicators, Nov revised 1-31, 111A2
Cigaret mfr rise 2-11, 218E2*
Jan income, Dec '78 revised 2-16, 151C2
Jan housing starts, permits; Dec '78 revised 2-16, 151F2
Jan trade gap; Jan, Nov, Dec '78 deficits revised; seasonal adjustmt method chngd 2-28, 159D1
Jan indicators; Dec, Nov '78 revised 3-1, 151E1
Feb housing starts, permits 3-16, 252B3
Feb income up; Oct-Dec '78, Jan revised 3-19, 252C3
'78, 4th 1/4 profits up 3-20, 201A2
'78, 4th 1/4 GNP, inflatn revised 3-20, 202F3
'78 paymts gap, '77 revised 3-21, 252D2
Feb trade gap 3-28, 252E2-A3
Feb indicators, Dec '78 revised 4-1, 252A2
Mar housing starts, permits 4-17, 281B1
Mar income; Jan, Feb revised 4-18, 281A1
1st 1/4 GNP, inflatn 4-19, 280G1-F2
Mar trade gap 4-27, 325A2
Mar indicators; Jan, Feb revised 4-30, 325E1

1980

Sovt tech export curbs tightnd 3-18, 204F3
Steel trigger price hike rejctd, dumping suits scored 3-19, 204B3
US Steel files dumping complaint, trigger price suspended 3-21, 225E1
Mex 'dumping' suit dismissed 3-24, 233F2
EC comm rejects US Steel suits 3-27, 243A1
Me farmers ask Canada potato imports ban 3-27, 368D2
Moscow Olympic products ban ordrd 3-28, 259C1
'79 forgn investmt rptd 4-8, 329A1
Steel import probe set 4-10, 367E3
Japan typewriter duties set 4-22, 368B1
Japan TV dumping case setld 4-28, ct blocks 5-9, 368C1
Steel import damage found 5-1, 456B1
Steel trigger price return suit dismissed 5-16, 455F3-456A1
W Eur soy meal sales to USSR scored 6-2, 431B1
Minority constructn grants upheld by Sup Ct 7-2, 510B1
Klutznick vs steel indus tax breaks 8-1, 575C3
Forgn investmt data disputed 8-7, 601G3
Iraq commercial jet sale barred 8-29, 662D3
Forgn Svc reorgn bill clears Cong 10-1, signed 10-17, 981E2
Japan trade talks resume 10-19, 864A3
Arab boycott data released 10-20, 800F3
Porpoise kill limit lowered 10-21, 987F2
3M fined for Arab boycott violatn 10-30, 985G2
Sen OKs '81 funds 11-17, 880G3
Steel trigger price hiked, Japan productn costs projected 11-18, 884G2
'81 funds clear Cong 12-3, Carter vetoes 12-16; stopgap funds clear Cong 12-16, 953B2, E3, 954F1
Baldrige named secy 12-11, 935B1

Census, Bureau of the
Elected officials drop rptd 1-2, 5D3
Populatn data rptd 1-2, 54G3
Illegal aliens rptd at 6 mln 2-4, census suit dismissed 2-26, 147E1, A2
Census postponemt denied by Sup Ct 3-17, 226A1
US median age at 30 yrs 6-21, 519E1
Sovt '71-76 infant mortality rates rptd 6-25, 525D2
Hispanic crime study rptd 7-28, 654F3
Census revisn ordrd for Detroit, other cities claim undercount 9-25, 741D2
Essex Cnty (NJ) data stay extended by Sup Ct 12-15, 957C2
Census revisn ordrd for NY 12-23, Detroit rule stayed 12-24; Sup Ct bars stays 12-30; '80 figures released, table 12-31, 982D3, 983C1

Economic Development Administration
Car maker aid planned 7-8, 505F1
Cong clears extensn, drops powers expansn 11-20, 982C2

National Oceanic and Atmospheric Administration (NOAA)
Weather Svc rpts on mid-Atlantic blizzards 3-1—3-2, 292C3
Weather Svc rpts Midwest tornadoes 4-7—4-8, 391G2
Mt St Helens blast measuremt rptd 5-24, 503D3
Weather Svc rpts on Hurricane Allen 8-4, 621A2
Heat wave death toll rptd 9-7, 857G1-B3
Weather Svc rpts Northeast drought 12-1, 947F3

Patent & Trademark Office
GE microbe patent upheld by Sup Ct 6-16, 453E1

Statistics
Income index described 35B1
'76-79 GNP growth chart 51C3
'79 Nov new home sales 1-9, 15E2
'79, Dec income 1-17, 35A1
'79, Dec housing starts; Nov revised 1-17, 35D1
'79, 4th 1/4 GNP, inflatn; 3d 1/4 revised 1-18, 51F3-52C1
'79, Dec trade gap 1-29, 77B2
Dec '79 indicators, Nov revised 1-30, 92D2
Jan housing starts, Dec '79 revised 2-19, 126C3
Jan income 2-19, 145D1
Jan trade gap 2-28, 3-3, new calculatn method used 2-28, 167A3
Jan indicators, Oct-Dec '79 revised 2-29, 167G3
Feb housing starts, Jan revised 3-18, 209F2
Feb income 3-18, 209G2-B3
2d 1/4 steel trigger price hike rejected 3-19, 204C3
'79, 4th 1/4 profits up 3-19, 222C1
'79 4th 1/4 GNP revised 3-19, 305G2
'79 4th 1/4 payments deficit, 3d 1/4 surplus revised 3-20, 263A3
Feb trade gap 3-27, 247A3
Feb indicators; Jan, Dec '79 revised 3-31, 247E3
Mar housing starts; Feb revised 4-16, 286A1
Mar income 4-17, 286C3
1st 1/4 GNP 4-18, 305F2
1st 1/4 inventories, '79 4th 1/4 revised 4-18, 305C3
Mar trade gap 4-29, 328D3

1976

Mar, 1st ¼ inventories, sales; Feb revised, 5-13, 376C1
1st ¼ capital flow 5-17, 396C2
Apr housing starts, permits 5-18, 375F2
1st ¼ corp profits, 4th ¼ '75 revised 5-20, 376E2
1st ¼ real GNP, inflatn revised 5-20, 396C1
Apr indicators, Mar revised 5-28, 395B3
Apr inventories, sales 6-14, 479D3
May housing starts, Apr revised 6-16, 479F3
1st ¼ current account deficit, '75 4th ¼ revised; 1st ¼ capital flow 6-18, 479E2-A3
May trade surplus 6-28, 494C3
May indicators, Apr revised 6-29, 494A3
'60-74 disposable income 7-11, 582A1
May inventories, sales rptd; Apr revised 7-14, 536F2-A3
June housing starts, permits; May revised 7-19, 568E1
2d ¼ GNP, inflatn; 1st ¼ revised 7-20, 536D1-A2
Apr-June incomes 7-20, 568A2
June trade deficit, '75 revised 7-27, 568B1
June indicators, May revised 7-28, 567E3
2d ¼ new house prices 8-16, 647G2-A3
July housing starts, permits, June revised 8-17, 647D2
2d ¼ profits, 1st ¼ revised 8-19, 708C3
July trade deficit, 1st ½ OPEC, Japan deficits 8-26, 668B1
July indicators; '75 Aug-Dec, Feb-Mar, June revisns 8-27, 708F2
'75 per capita income 9-15, 959A1
Aug starts, permits; July revised 9-17, 709F1
Aug trade deficit 9-27, 769G3
Aug indicators, Sept revised 9-28, 768A1
Sept income; July, Aug revised 10-15, 806B2
Aug inventories, sales; July revised 10-15, 806F2
3d ¼ GNP, inflatn; 2d ¼ revised 10-19, 805E1-E2
Sept housing starts, permits 10-20, 805A3
Sept trade deficit 10-28, 833C2
Sept indicators, Aug revised 10-29, 833A1
Oct housing starts, permits; Sept revised 11-16, 866A3
3d ¼ GNP, inflatn revised 11-18, 866A2
3d ¼ corp profits, 2d ¼ revised 11-18, 866C2
Oct trade deficit 11-29, 958B2
Oct indicators, July-Sept revised 12-1, 918G2
'70-76 indicators graph 918A2
Oct inventory, sales, Sept revised 12-14, 958B3
Nov housing starts fall, Oct revised 12-16, 958D2
1st ¼ '75-3d ¼ '76 mfg utilizatn rate 12-17, 958E3
3d ¼ paymts deficit, 1st, 2d ¼ surpluses revised 12-22, 958D1
Nov trade deficit 12-28, 983G2
Nov indicators up, July-Oct revised 12-29, 983C2

COMMISSION to Report on the Assassination of President John F. Kennedy—*See WARREN Commission in this section below*
COMMODITY Futures Trading Commission
Sues Pacific exchange 5-10, 348C2
To probe potato futures default 5-25, 5-26, 397D1
'77 funds signed 7-12, 533D3
Warns 5 exchanges 9-15, 990D2
Chrgs Rosenthal & Co 10-21, ct blocks London optns rule 12-22, 990B2
OKs new potato futures contract 11-2, halts trading 11-3, 990A1
COMMUNITY Services Administration
Martinez confrmd dir 4-7, 262D3
COMPTROLLER of the Currency—*See under TREASURY below*

CONGRESS—*See also HOUSE and SENATE below; also CONGRESSIONAL Relations, LEGISLATION and MESSAGES to Congress under FORD*
Burger scores re judgeships 1-3, 24C2
Gets US health rpt 1-12, 32A1
2d 94th Cong sessn convenes 1-19, 68D3 ★
Rabin addresses 1-28, 60E1, A2
Kissinger urges support 2-3, 88A2
Va Kepone poisoning probe cited 2-26, 171B3
Kissinger scores critics 3-11, 197A3
SEC rpts on NYSE '75 profit, broker fees 4-2, 348A2
31 seek Utah projct delay 4-9, 284F2
Science office re-created 5-11, 346D1

1977

Jan-Mar retail sales 4-14, 271F1
Feb inventories, sales; Jan revised 4-15, 300F3
Mar housing starts, permits; Feb revised 4-18, 300D2
Mar income, Feb revised 4-19, 300C3
1st ¼ GNP, inflatn; '76 4th ¼ revised 4-20, 299G3, 300C1
Mar trade deficit 4-27, 339A3
Mar indicators; Jan, Feb revised 4-29, 339E2
'76 per-capita income, table 5-10, 387A3, G3
Forgn investmt in US 5-11, 385C3
Mar inventories, sales; Feb revised 5-16, 384G1-A2
Apr housing starts, permits; Mar revised 5-17, 384E1
Apr income; Feb, Mar revised 5-18, 384C1
Apr trade deficit 5-26, 445C1
1st ¼ paymts deficit; '76, 4th ¼ revised 6-22, 501G3
May trade deficit 6-27, 502G1-C2
Apr, May indicators 6-29, 502C2
'76 local tax revenue data 7-7, 540G1
Apr, May inventories, sales; Mar revised 7-15, 555A2
June housing starts, permits; Mar-May revised 7-19, 554F2
May, June income; Apr revised 7-20, 555D1
2d ¼ GNP, 1st ¼ revised 7-21, 553F2
June trade deficit 7-27, 585A1
June indicators, May revised 7-29, 593E3
July housing starts, permits; June revised 8-16, 629C1
July income; May, June revised 8-17, 629E1
1st, 2d ¼ profits 8-19, 668G2
July trade deficit 8-25, 651G1
'76 US investmts abroad 8-29, 669D1
July indicators, June revised 8-30, 669A1
Fscl '76 state spending, revenue 9-2, 740C1
'76 state per-capita income data revised, table 9-13, 821E1, F3
Aug indl output 9-16, 722D1
Aug income, July revised 9-16, 722E1
Aug housing starts, permits 9-19, 721D3
2d ¼ paymts deficit 9-21, 722E2
Aug trade deficit 9-26; July '76-Aug '77 graph 761F2
Aug indicators, May-July revised 9-29, 761E3
'76 top world exporters of cars, total productn 10-11, 853G2
Sept income, Aug revised 10-18, 798B2
3d ¼ GNP, inflatn; 2d ¼ revised 10-19, 798B1
Sept housing starts, permits; Aug revised 10-19, 817G3
'76 forgn investmt in US, '75 revised 10-26, 836G3
Sept trade deficit 10-27, 818A1
Sept indicators, May-Aug revised 10-28, 836A1
Oct income 11-16, 898F3
Oct starts, permits; Sept revised 11-16, 899A1
3d ¼ profits, 2d ¼ revised 11-17, 918F1
Oct trade deficit 11-28, 933E1-B2
Oct indicators; Aug, Sept revised 11-30, 941C2
'76 forgn investmts rptd 12-5, 997C3
Nov starts, permits; Oct revised 12-16, 977F1-A2
Nov income; Aug-Oct revised 12-16, 977A2
3d ¼ paymts gap 12-21, 977B1
Nov trade deficit 12-28, 1003E1
Nov indicators, Oct revised 12-30, 1003A2

COMMISSION to Report on the Assassination of John F. Kennedy—*See WARREN Commission in this section below*
COMMODITY Credit Corp.—*See under AGRICULTURE in this section above*
COMMODITY Futures Trading Commission (CFTC)
Rainbolt on Brazil coffee prices 2-23, 169D1
Hunts sued on soybean trading 4-28, 341E1
Hunts countersue 5-4; ct lifts trading ban 5-6, backs curbs 6-7, 464B1
'78 funds signed 8-12, 688C3
Hunt soybean trading ruled illegal 9-28, 858F3
'74 law challenge declined 11-7, 857F1
COMMUNITY Relations Service—*See under JUSTICE below*
COMMUNITY Services Administration (CSA)
Rollins confrmd to FEA 8-4, 626D3
Employe to pay bias suit costs 8-23, 669G3
'78 funds clear Cong 12-7, 958F3
COMPTROLLER of the Currency—*See under TREASURY below; also HEIMANN, John G.*

CONGRESS—*See also HOUSE and SENATE below; also CONGRESSIONAL Relations under CARTER; 'Congress' under FORD*
Sex-bias suit vs Passman OKd 1-3, 59C3
95th Cong convenes; pol lineup 1-4, 5C3
Ford proposes pay rise 1-17, 30A2, 33E3
Ldrship, coms, chrmn listed 90A2-E3
Regulatory agency oversight scored 2-9, 131B3
US rights comm backs city-suburb busing 2-15, 112G1
O'Neill vs forgn speakers 2-17, 127D3
Lopez Portillo addresses 2-17, 136B3
Pay raise takes effect 2-20, 127D2
Trudeau addresses 2-22, 132F2
Carter for joint intell com 2-24, 151B2
Carter call-in on pay hike 3-5, 171D1

1978

Mar indicators 5-1, 344B3
Apr housing starts, Mar revised 5-16, 389B2
Apr income; Feb, Mar revised 5-17, 389F2
1st ¼ profits, 4th ¼ '77 revised 5-18, 403D1
Apr trade deficit, Mar revised 5-26, 429A1
Apr leading indicators; Jan, Feb revised 6-1, 429C1
May housing starts, permits; Apr revised 6-16, 470D1
May income 6-16, 470G1
1st ¼ paymts deficit; '77 revised; acctg technique chngd 6-21, 469C3
Lightning, flash flood data 6-24, 7-4, 655A1
May trade deficit 6-27, 507E1
May indicators, Apr revised 7-3, 507G1
June housing starts, permits; May revised 7-19, 607E3
June income; Apr, May revised 7-19, 607G3 ★
2d ¼ GNP, inflatn; 1st ¼ revised 7-21, 606E2
June indicators; Mar, Apr, May revised 7-31, 607E2
July housing starts, permits; June revised 8-16, 680D2
July income; June, May revised 8-17, 643E3
2d ¼ profits; '77, 1st ¼ revised 8-18, 642E2-A3
July trade deficit, US-Japan gap 8-29, 680B1-E1
July indicators, Apr-June revised 8-31, 680E1
Aug personal income 9-18, 717B2
2d ¼ paymts gap; 1st ¼ '77 data revised 9-19, 717B1
Aug housing starts, permits; July revised 9-19, 717G2-A3
Aug trade gap, US-Japan deficit 9-27, 752F1-A2
Aug indicators, July revised 10-1, 752B2
June '77-78 $ drop index 10-4, 790E1
Sept income 10-18, 790C3
Sept housing starts, permits; Aug revised 10-18, 790D3
3d ¼ GNP, inflatn; 2d ¼ revised 10-20, 863D3
Sept trade gap, US-Japan deficit 10-26, 804C3, E3
Sept indicators, June-Aug revised 10-30, 864G2
Oct income, Sept revised 11-17, 918F3
Oct housing starts, permits; Sept revised 11-17, 919A1
3d ¼ corp profits, 2d ¼ revised 11-21, 919A2
Oct trade deficit, Japan deficit 11-29, 918B3, D3
Oct indicators, Aug revised 11-29, 918E3
Nov housing starts, permits; Oct revised 12-18, 982A2
Nov income 12-18, 982B2
Nov trade deficit 12-18, 1003F2
3d ¼ paymts gap, 2d ¼ revised 12-19, 982D1
Nov indicators, Aug-Oct revised 12-28, 1003B3
Telecommunications, Office of
Reorganized 3-28, 270C2
Telecommunications & Information Agency, National
Formed, Geller named dir 3-28, 270C2

COMMODITY Credit Corp.—*See under AGRICULTURE in this section above*
COMMODITY Futures Trading Commission (CFTC)
Lloyd Carr offcls arrested 1-10, 1-24; receiver named 1-19, Abrahams arrested 1-24, 83A3
Optns trading probes cited 1-10, 83D3
London options trading ban sought 1-31, 83E3
London options sales suspended 4-5, 283A1
Gartner confrmd member 5-17, 513A3
Carter asks Gartner quit 6-26; Gartner denies interest conflict, bars resignatn 6-28, 513F2
Mail case refused by Sup Ct 6-26, 566F3
COMPTROLLER of the Currency, Office of the—*See under TREASURY below*

CONGRESS—*See also HOUSE and SENATE below; also CARTER—CONGRESSIONAL Relations*
NCAA meets, cong probe cited 1-11—1-13, 40B2
Pay-hike suit dismissal backed by Sup Ct 1-16, 33F2
Haldeman versn of Watergate rptd 2-16—2-17, 124E3
Consumer Fed ratings issued 3-4, 183B1; 11-8, 981F2
Panama Canal treaty stay denied 4-17, 308G2
Desai sees members, defends India A-stand 6-13, 466E3
16 at Panama Canal treaty rite 6-16, 463F2

1979

Apr housing starts, permits; Mar revised 5-16, 363A1
Apr income, Mar revised 5-17, 362G3
1st 1/4 profits, 4th 1/4 '78 revised 5-19, 385A1
Apr trade gap 5-30, 402F3
Apr indicators, Jan-Mar revised 5-31, 463E2
'77, '78 forgn investmt 6-13, 463F3
May housing starts, permits; Apr revised 6-18, 463C3
May income, Apr revised 6-19, 463A3
1st 1/4 paymts surplus; '78, 4th 1/4 revised 6-21, 463B2
May trade gap 6-27, 480E3
May indicators; Mar, Apr revised 6-29, 517D1
June starts, permits 7-18, 557E1
June income; Apr, May revised 7-19, 557D1
2d 1/4 GNP, inflatn; 1st 1/4, '78 4th 1/4 revised 7-20, 556E2-C3
June trade gap 7-29, 577F2
June indicators; Apr, May revised 7-30, 577E2
July income; May, June revised 8-16, 621G2-622B1
July starts, permits 8-16, 622C1
2d 1/4 profits; 1st 1/4, '78 4th 1/4 revised 8-17, 628D2
July trade gap 8-28, 646F2
July indicators, Apr-June revised 8-29, 646D3
July inventories 9-11, 701D1
'78 state per capita income 9-16, 746D1
Aug income; June, July revised 9-18, 701E1
Aug housing starts, July revised 9-19, 701A3
2d 1/4 paymts deficit, 1st 1/4 revised 9-20, 701F2
Aug trade gap 9-27, 745B2
Aug indicators, July revised 9-28, 745F2
Sept income; July, Aug revised 10-17, 784B2
Sept housing starts, permits; Aug revised 10-17, 784D2
3d 1/4 GNP, inflatn; 2d 1/4 revised 10-19, 805D1-E2
'71-77 tax collectns 10-21, 990C3
Sept trade gap 10-30, 828F1
Sept indicators 10-30, 866E3
Oct income, Sept revised 11-19, 922A2
Oct housing starts; Sept revised 11-19, 922C2
3d 1/4 profits, 2d 1/4 revised 11-20, 922E3
'78 median family income, poverty data; '60-78 income growth 11-24, 965E1-G2
Oct trade gap 11-29, 921G3
Oct indicators, July-Sept revised 11-30, 922D1
Nov income, Oct revised 12-18, 964C1
Nov housing starts, permits 12-18, 964D1
3d 1/4 paymts surplus, 2d 1/4 revised 12-20, 984A3
Nov trade gap 12-28, 984C3
Nov indicators, Oct revised 12-31, 985E1
Travel Service, U.S.
Carter budget omits funds 1-22, 45A2

COMMODITY Futures Trading Commission (CFTC)
El Salvador coffee price squeeze chrgd 3-13, 348G1
Chicago wheat trading halt ordrd 3-15, cts stay 3-18–3-19; trading ends, speculators named 3-21, 201C3
Stone confrmd chrmn 4-11, 681D2
Maine potato trading halt probed 5-9, 348D1
T-bill, notes futures trading OKd 6-19, NYSE asks OK 6-21, 681D2
Options trading resumptn barred 9-5, 681F1
COMMON Carrier Bureau—*See under FEDERAL Communications Commission in this section below*
COMMUNITY Services Administration (CSA)
Heating aid bill OKd 11-9, 883B2
COMPTROLLER of the Currency, Office of the—*See under TREASURY below*

CONGRESS—*See also HOUSE and SENATE below; also CARTER subheads CONGRESSIONAL Relations, LEGISLATION and MESSAGES to Congress*
Convenes; ldrs elected, rule chngs voted 1-15, 30E1-C2
Adams backs '85 gas mileage standard 1-19, 87C3
Farmers rally in DC 2-5–2-6, 109E2
ABA OKs white-collar crime testimony 2-13, 130B2
'In God We Trust' suit dismissed 3-2, 208D2
Carter briefs on Mideast trip 3-15, 177E2
Freedom House to rpt on Rhodesia electn 4-20, 293D2

1980

Mar indicators; Feb, Jan revised 4-30, 329E2
Apr housing starts, Mar revised 5-16, 384G2-A3
April income 5-19, 384C3
Apr trade gap 5-28, 401B1
Apr indicators, Mar revised 5-30, 424C3
May housing starts, Apr revised 6-17, 455G1
May income, Apr revised 6-17, 455C2
1st 1/4 paymts deficit; '79, 4th 1/4 revised 6-19, 455C1
May trade gap 6-27, 492E3
May indicators, Apr revised 6-30, 492B2
US '79 manufactured goods export share 7-14, 574B3
June housing starts, May revised 7-17, 542A1
June income, May revised 7-17, 542E1
2d 1/4 GNP 7-18, 555E3
2d 1/4 inventories, 1st 1/4 revised 7-18, 556B1
June trade gap 7-29, 574D2-A3
June indicators; May, Apr revised 7-30, 574E1
July housing starts, June revised 8-18, 631C1
July income, June revised 8-18, 631A2
1st 1/2 Sovt trade drop 8-20, 711C2
July trade gap 8-27, 666E1
July indicators, June revised 8-29, 666B1
Aug housing starts, July revised 9-17, 701C3
2d 1/4 paymts deficit, 1st 1/4 revised 9-18, 725G1-A2
Aug income; July, June revised 9-18, 725B2
Aug trade gap 9-26, 741D1
Aug indicators; July, June revised 9-30, 740G3
Sept income, Aug revised 10-16, 783E2
3d 1/4 GNP 10-17, 804G2
Sept housing starts, Aug revised 10-17, 804E3
'79 median family income, poverty data 10-23, 823E3, 824B1
Sept trade gap 10-29, 824D1, F1*
Sept indicators; Aug, July revised 10-30, 824B1
3d 1/4 trade gap, deficit, 2d 1/4 revised 11-6, 867E2
Oct income, Sept revised 11-18, 883C1
Oct housing starts, Sept revised 11-19, 882F3
Oct trade gap 11-28, 916E1
Oct indicators; Sept, Aug revised 12-1, 916B2
Nov housing starts, Oct revised 12-16, 957G2
3d 1/4 paymts surplus, 2d 1/4 revised 12-18, 984B2
Nov income, Oct revised 12-22, 984B1
Nov trade gap 12-30, 984E1
Nov indicators; Oct, Sept revised 12-31, 984C1
Travel Service, U.S.
Forgn tourism agency clears Cong 12-11, 953F2; vetoed 12-25, 982D1

COMMODITY Futures Trading Commission (CFTC)
Options trader arrested 1-2, 94C3
Grain trading suspended 1-6, 2B1
Comex moves to curb silver speculatn 1-10, 31D1
Chicago Bd of Trade seeks T-bill trading 3-20, 224F1
NYFE-ACE merger proposed 3-21 3-21, 224A2
Hunt silver trading probed 3-31, 245G1
Regulators debate speculatn curbs 4-14—4-15, 290A1
Emergency order case declined by Sup Ct 4-28, 369E1
Currency futures trading on NYSE unit OKd 5-28, 481B2
NYFE awarded Treasury futures trading exclusivity 7-15; Chicago ct overturns order 7-17—7-18, Field resigns 7-22, 558G2
CBT, Merc expand financial futures trading, '79 vol rptd 7-24; NYFE opens 8-7, 616G3
Tighter trading rules set 11-25, 899B1
'81 funds clear Cong 12-4, 954C3; signed 12-15, 982B1

CONGRESS—*See also HOUSE and SENATE below; also CARTER, subheads CONGRESSIONAL Relations, LEGISLATION and MESSAGES to Congress*
Pak aid approval rptd 1-3, 27B1
Prosecutn disparities study asked 1-6, 24F3
Female smoking-health study submitted 1-14, 40A2
US rights comm scores housing programs 1-15, 36B3
Mil petitn limits upheld by Sup Ct 1-21, 93C1
Burger vs judgeships creatn power 2-3, 114A3
Illegal alien census suit dismissed 2-26, 147A2

1976

French pres addresses 5-18, 372B2
Helsinki accords panel OKd 5-21, 392E3; Warsaw natns curb tour 11-5—11-21, 880F1
Gets Soc Sec trustees rpt 5-24, 398F2
Spain king addresses 6-2, 459B2
Cong veto bill defeated 9-21, 883F1
Mid-decade census findings barred re reapportnmt 10-17, 834F3
House Dems back pub conf com mtgs 12-6—12-9, 981A2, A3

Atomic Energy Committee, Joint
House Dems back legis powers end 12-6—12-9, 981A2, D2

Budget (& Office of Budget)
Fscl '77 proposals 3-15, 230D2, D3
OKs nonbinding budget targets resolution 5-13, 358B1
Dem platform text 6-15, 471A1
Sees econ recovery continuing 8-2, 647A2
'77 binding budget resolutn OKd, 9-15, 9-16, chart 706G1
Omnibus tax bill cleared 9-16, 705B3
Fiscal '76 Cong spending 9-22, 746C1
'77 funds signed 10-1, 834A2
Resource planning costs cited 10-19, 919B2
Daft named Carter adviser 11-23, 881B3
Carter sees Rivlin 12-1, 898G2

Congressional Record
US corp '75 arms sales listed 2-6, 147D3

Defense Production Committee, Joint
Currie scored re Rockwell 10-14, 983A1

Democrats
Muskie rebuts State of Union message 1-21, 40E1
Carter budget plan compared 4-23, 305C2
Gov Brown meets 5-6, 343E2
Carter visits DC 6-24, 490C2
Ford, Carter debate 9-23, 703A1
Uruguay pres scores 10-8, 814F1
Dole chrgs 'Democrat wars', Mondale rebuts 10-15, 782G2-A3, 783C3; Dole 10-25—10-27, 804A2, D2, A3, Mondale 10-26, 804B1
Carter sees leaders 11-17, 864E1
Carter meets 12-10, 938A1

Economic Committee, Joint
GAO rpt scores defns contracting 1-11, 70G3-71C1
Subcom hears Ingersoll, Proxmire on US corp payoff disclosure plan 3-5, 199G3, 200E1
Fscl '77 budget proposals 3-10, 230D2-D3
Shiskin testimony 4-2, 263B1
Shiskin on Apr joblessness 5-7, 347B2
Hears CIA analyst re Sovt grain 5-24, 856A3
Navy shipyd overrun paymts hearing 6-7, 454A1
Gets Sovt arms, econ data 10-5, 960F3
Sovt econ rpt cited 10-25, 856D2
Shiskin on Oct jobless rate 11-5, 846F1

Intelligence Issues—*See also appropriate committee subheads under HOUSE and SENATE in this section below*
Church com faults oversight 4-26, 298D2, G2; 4-28, 325A1-330C3
Sen votes permanent com 5-19, 376D3

Legislation Defeated (& not cleared)
Natural gas deregulatn (House) 2-5, 108C2
Detente resolutn (Sen) 3-22, 245F3
DC vote representatn (House) 3-23, 234F1
No-fault insurance (Sen) 3-31, 234C2
Abortn bar amendmt (Sen) 4-28, 883D3
Nonreturnable container ban (Sen) 6-30, 833B3
'75 synfuel loan guarantee (House) cited 8-23, 649D1
Med lab standards (House) 9-20, 883F3
Cong veto of fed regulatns (House) 9-21, 883F1
Daylight savings extensn (House) 9-21, 883G1
Synfuel loan backing (House) 9-23, 883A3
Offshore oil, gas leasing revisns (House) 9-28, 883E2
Export Admin Act, anti-boycott provisns not cleared 9-30, 786C3, 883B1, 884B2
Block grants not cleared 10-2, 882G3, 883A1, B2, E3, 884A2
Strip-mining not cleared 10-2, 883A1, F2
Water pollutn authorizn not cleared 10-2, 883A1, E2
Consumer protectn agency not cleared 10-2, 883A1, G1
Soc Sec tax hike not cleared 10-2, 883A1, 884C1

1977

Carter asks pub electn funding 3-22, 210D2-G2
Brown chrgs forgn policy meddling 3-27, 231F3
US-Sovt arms talks reactn 3-31, 247F1
Delegatn visits China 4-9—4-17, 298B2
Pay-raise procedures revised 4-12, 272E3, 273B1
Delegatn visits S Korea 4-12, 305D3
Sup Ct remands suit vs pay hike 5-16, 419G1
65 vs USSR computer deal 6-5, 469F2
COL hike barred 6-28, pay raise upheld 6-29, 516F1, B2; 7-11, 592G1
State income tax rule signed 7-19, 592A2
Employe bias rptd 7-31, 8-4, coalitn urges halt 8-31, 669E3
'78 funds signed 8-5, 689B1
SEC submits NYC financial rpt 8-26, 665E2
Members regret S African death 9-25, 735E3
CIA deceptn of '75 Viet fact finders chrgd 11-18, 898D1

Atomic Energy Committee, Joint
House votes legis powers end 1-4, 36C3
Senate backs abolition 2-4, 91B1

Black Caucus—*See BLACK Americans—Politics & Government under 'B'*

Budget (& Office of Budget)
Poverty study issued 1-13, 80A3
Food-stamp study issued 1-17, 81A1
CBO on Carter goals 2-15, 126E1
Costle confrmd EPA admin 3-4, 211E1
Carter energy proposals disputed 5-31, 443F2
'77 farm disaster aid ceiling lifted 10-25, 833D3

Congressional Operations, Joint Committee on
Senate backs abolition 2-4, 91B1

Defense Production, Joint Committee on
Senate backs abolition 2-4, 91B1
Sovt civil defns effort discounted 5-16, 421E1
Funding ended 8-5, 689C1
Proxmire scores contractor gifts, cites '73-75 study 10-24, 920D2

Democrats
353 in 95th Cong 1-4, 5C3
Carter econ plan rptd after mtg 1-7, 5D1
Carter concedes mistakes 2-8, 88E3
Carter energy plan reactn 4-20, 290D3
Califano urges HEW-Labor '78 funds OKd 10-11, 786D2
AFL-CIO unit OKs 'hit list' 11-30, 961A2

Economic Committee, Joint
Carter econ plan hearings 1-27, 89C2
Schlesinger backs oil price role 5-25, 443A3
USSR defns advances held costly 6-30, 673D3
Shiskin on jobless rate 8-5, 611A3
CIA forecast of Sovt econ issued 8-8, 948F3

Legislation Defeated
Common-site picketing (House) 3-23, 229C1-D2
Anti-Concorde amendmt (House) 6-8, 463B2
Water projcts amendmt (House) 6-14, 459F3
Nicaragua mil aid cutoff amendmt (House) 6-23, 656F2
Sen campaign pub finance (Sen) 8-2, 592B2
Coal, uranium acquisitn curbs (Sen) 9-8, 702F3
Korea aid cut (House) 9-8, 774A2
SALT extensn res set aside (Sen) 10-3, 751C2
Air-bag veto (Sen) 10-12, 796G3-797A1
Oil cargo prefernc 10-19, 815A1
B-1 funds revival (House) 10-20, 795E3

1978

ERA marchers seek extensn 7-9, 529D2
Coalitn scores SALT mtg, Shcharansky trial 7-10, 543G2-A3
Young rebuked for US 'pol prisoners' remark 7-12—7-15, 542G2
Indians protest in DC 7-15—7-23, 568E3, 569A1, E1
Mrs Shcharansky addresses 7-17, 542E1
Pub financing of electns rejected 7-19, 550E2-C3
Rhodesia trade support rptd 7-23, 561C1
Judgeship bill OK urged by Burger 7-23, 626D3
Pro-defns coalitn formed 8-8, 604A3
FEC fund-raising rpt issued, 'PAC democracy' feared 9-7, 753F1-G2
Burger urges study 9-21, 751A3
86 asks Nicaragua aid cutoff 10-13, 839G2
Adjourns 10-15, appraised 10-15, 10-16, 784E2
Marian Anderson receives gold medal 10-17, 844F1
ACLU notes gains 10-20, 981A3
Conservative group, Cong Watch rate 95th sessn 10-24, 10-28, 865B2-C3
China ties reactn 12-15—12-20, Taiwan defns pact suit threatened 12-15, 974B3, 975A1, 976A1
15 sue vs Taiwan defns pact end 12-22, 995B2

Black Caucus—*See BLACK Americans—Politics & Government under 'B'*

Budget Office, Congressional (CBO)
Mil pensn changes proposed 1-11, 52F3
Carter asks coms inflatn impact rpts 4-11, 259E3
Farm bill cleared, estimates questnd 5-4, 343B2
Crude oil import fee, quota, tax study rptd 6-29, 511G3
Propositn 13 impact rpt 7-6, 525E2
Coal conversn savings estimated 7-18, 550A1
US mil mobilization ability hit 12-3, 984B1
'79 econ growth estimated at 2.4% 12-14, 980C1

Conference Committee Actions—*See subjects of legislation (e.g., ENERGY)*

Democrats
O'Neill on Carter anti-inflatn plan 10-24, 806F3

Economic Committee, Joint
CIA sees USSR civil defns overrated, DIA disputes 2-17, 127A1
Kahn rpts gas shortage probe 12-6, 962F3
Blumenthal testifies 12-14, 980D1

Korean Lobbying Scandal—*See KOREA (South)—U.S.-Korea Political Payments*

Legislation Defeated (& deferred)
Consumer Agency (House) 2-8, 82F1
Educ aid (House) 3-20, 202B3
House electn pub funding (House) 3-21, 202D3
Farm bill (House) 4-12, 261C1
Coll paymt tax deferral (House) 6-1, 431B3
Labor law revisn (Sen) 6-22, 508B2
India uranium sale res (House) 7-12, 551D1
Coal slurry pipeline bill (House) 7-19, 550F1
Cong electn funds (House) 7-19, 550E2-C3
Civil Svc reorgnzn veto (House) 8-9, 625D2
ERA rescissn amendmt (House) 8-15, 661F2
Sen office-bldg funds (House) 8-17, 681G2
Aircraft noise abatemt (Sen) 10-3, 765C3
ERA rescissn amendmts (Sen) 10-3, 788C1
Criminal code revisn (House) 10-4, 785C1
Alaska lands (Sen) 10-15, 785A1
Hospital cost lid (House) 10-15, 785B1
Educ Dept (House) 10-15, 785B1
Sugar price supports (House) 10-15, 785C1
Seabed mining (Sen) 10-15, 785C1

1979

Admin office annual rpt issued 4-28, 386G3
Ohira sees members 5-3, 320F2
Taiwan defns treaty suit dismissed 6-6, 440F1
Carter sees members 7-6–7-11, 513F2
Judge's racial slur rptd 7-14, 901A3
$1 Anthony coin oppositn rptd 9-25, 727B2
5.5% pay hike limit set 10-12, 900F1
Carter loses Taiwan defns treaty suit 10-17, 777A1
Iran release of US hostages sought 11-7, Admin urges calm 11-8, 842D3-843B1
Mil spending inequities rptd 11-18, 904E1
Taiwan defns treaty abrogatn upheld 11-30, 919G1
Taiwan treaty suit refused by Sup Ct 12-13, 940B1
96th Cong 1st sessn ends 12-21, 981F1

Budget Office, Congressional (CBO)
Rivlin vs Admin '79 econ forecasts 1-25, 48E3
NATO defns capability doubted 2-17, 147F3
GATT pact impact on US rptd 4-12, 274D1

Conference Committee Actions—*See subjects of legislation*

Democrats
Teng sees ldrs 1-30, 66D1
Labor '78 campaign gifts rptd 6-13, 595C1
Brock scores re US intell policy 8-6, 610D3

Economic Committee, Joint
Subcom hears CIA re USSR mil spending 1-25, 99F2
Norwood rpts rise in women workers, 2-income families 2-2, 110D3
Jobs gain seen in solar energy use 4-21, 419A1
Bentsen vs more interest rate hikes 9-20, 745B2
Volcker sees living standard drop 10-17, 940C3
Greenspan, Galbraith address 10-29, 826C3

Korean Lobbying Scandal—*See KOREA (South)– U.S.-Korean Political Payments*

Legislation—*See subheads below; for reaction, see subject of legislation*

Legislation Defeated (& deferred)
Sex educ amendmt (Sen) 4-30, 326D2
Standby gas rationing (House) 5-10, 342A2
Turkish mil aid (House) 6-21, 488C2
Direct pres vote (Sen) 7-10, 514G3-515D1
Anti-busing amendmt (House) 7-24, 559E2
Standby gas rationing (Sen) 8-2, 595F2
Draft registratn amendmts (House) 9-12, 724G2-B3
Panama Canal treaty implementatn (House) 9-20, 723A1
Sugar price supports, ISA role (House) 10-23, 808A2
Gas price controls amendmt (House) 10-24, 848E3
Rev King holiday (House) 11-13, 12-5, 945B2, D2
Hosp cost-control (House) 11-15, 883A1

1980

'81 budget cuts asked 2-27, 168E2
'80 spending limit rptd topped, bills delayed 3-4, 168C2
Census postponemt denied by Sup Ct 3-17, 226A1
USOC boycott talks rptd 3-21, 258C3
Judges granted 12.9% pay hike 3-24, 250F1
Phone industry deregulatn set by FCC 4-7, 370E2
Chrysler loan bd sees greater losses 4-10, 286E3
Abortn funding cases argued in Sup Ct 4-21, 306A2
Oil import fee blocked by Dist Ct 5-13, 366B1
Pretrial data secrecy rule rptd OKd by Judicial Conf 6-19, takes effect 8-1, 632C1
Medicaid abortn funding limits upheld by Sup Ct; reactn 6-30, 491F2-492A2
Forgn bank takeover moratorium ends 7-1, 806G2
Govt minority constructn grants upheld by Sup Ct 7-2, 510A1
Election recess 10-2, 785A1
Judicial pay hikes backed by Sup Ct 12-15, 956C3-957D1
Lame-duck sessn adjourns 12-16, 953B2

Budget Office, Congressional (CBO)
'80 spending limit rptd topped by Cong 3-4, 168C2
'80, '81 deficits seen higher 3-5, 168G1
Dem platform plank adopted 8-13, 614C2

Democrats
GOP links Abscam to majority 2-5, 82B2
Carter anti-inflatn plan reactn 3-14, 201D2
'81 tax cut backed, task force formed 7-1, 492B3, 493A1
Carter, ldrs meet on lame-duck agenda 11-13, 866G1
Reagan sees ldrs, vows consultatn 11-18, 880G2, A3
Greater party role urged 12-4, 938B3

Economic Committee, Joint
Connally Saudi bank connectns rptd 2-11, 129C2
Budget, tax cuts, econ policy chng asked 2-28, 168G2-D3
Russell sees continued inflatn 3-25, 222D2
Kahn on May CPI 6-24, 481A1

Legislation Defeated (& deferred)
Abscam evidence request res (House) 2-27, 143G2
Female draft registratn funds res (House) 4-22, 349G1
'81 budget res (House) 5-29, 424G2
Wilson reprimand (House) 6-10, 438A2
Kassebaum female draft registratn amendmt (Sen) 6-10, 478G1
Hatfield draft registratn amendmt (Sen) 6-12, 478E1
Tax-cut amendmt (Sen) 6-26, 480F2; 6-30, 492D3
Energy Mobilizatn Bd (House) 6-27, 515G-D2
India uranium sale bar (Sen) 9-24, 723C1
Telecommunicatns bill (House) 9-30, 835D2
CIA agents bill (Sen) 9-30, 982B2
NHTSA authrzn, air bag delay (House) 10-1, 982D1
Air transport system expansn (both houses) 10-1, 982D2
Domestic violence victims program (both houses) 11-17, 982A2
EDA powers expansion (both houses) 11-20, 982C2
Med records privacy bill (House) 12-1, 982C2
Auto import curb res (Sen) 12-4, 982A3
NHTSA authrzn (House) 12-5, 982G1
HUD fair-housing powers (Sen) 12-9, 954G1

1976

Clean air amendmts not cleared 10-2, 883A1, C2
A-export safeguards not cleared 10-2, 883B1, B3
Food-stamp reforms not cleared 10-2, 883B1, 884G1
Full employmt not cleared 10-2, 883B1, G3
Lobbying disclosure not cleared 10-2, 883C1
Fed spending reauthrzn not cleared 10-2, 883E1
Voter mail registratn not cleared 10-2, 883E1
No-fault auto insurance not cleared 10-2, 883A2
Ct-ordered busing curbs not cleared 10-2, 883B2
Wider FDA food, cosmetics authority not cleared 10-2, 883B2
Oil co divestiture not cleared 10-2, 883G2
Natural gas deregulatn not cleared 10-2, 883G2
Pvt uranium enrichmt not cleared 10-2, 883A3
Turkey bases pact not cleared 10-2, 883C3
Natl health insurance not cleared 10-2, 883D3
Medicare 'catastrophic' coverage not cleared 10-2, 883E3
Medicaid, Medicare reforms not cleared 10-2, 883F3
Youth jobs not cleared 10-2, 884B1
Handgun ban not cleared 10-2, 884C1
Special prosecutor office not cleared 10-2, 884D1
Wiretap warrants not cleared 10-2, 884E1
Crime code revisn not cleared 10-2, 884F1
Airline, trucking deregulatn not cleared 10-2, 884F1
Overseas corp bribes not cleared 10-2, 884B2
Forgn bank bill not cleared 10-2, 940F2
Fed Reserve restructure not cleared 10-2, 940G2

Legislation Introduced
Letelier murder probe resolutn (both houses) 9-21, 710E2

Legislation Passed (final action)—
See also 'Veto Action' below
Reserves call-up power 1-26, 5-3, 345D3
'76 defense funds, Angola aid ban amendmt (House) 1-27, 69A1
Revised RR aid (both houses) 1-28, 68D3
Pub works-urban aid (House) 1-29, 93C3
Rice production (Sen) 2-3, 135D2
Wildlife refuges 2-4, 2-17, 152F2-A3
Rehabilitatn act extensn 2-17, 3-2, 182D1
Parole restructuring 3-2, 3-3, 181D2
Bellmon seating (Sen) 3-4, 180B2
Drug abuse office (both houses) 3-4, 233D3
Credit bias ban (both houses) 3-9, 233A3
Consumer leasing protectn (both houses) 3-9, 234A1
Magna Carta trip 3-17, 4-5, 283G2
Peace Corps funds 3-22, 4-27, 393B1
Day care cntr funds 3-23, 3-24, 234D1
Navy oil reserves 3-24, 3-31, 246G2-C3
Conrail funds (both houses) 3-25, 233G2
City bankruptcy revisn (both houses) 3-25, 246D2
200-mi fishing zone 3-29, 3-30, 246F1
Hatch Act repeal 3-30, 3-31, 234A2
Food stamp vendor rules 4-8, 6-22 534A1
Swine flu, other funds 4-12, 282G1
Health progrm authorizatns (both houses) 4-12, 282E2
Guatemala relief 4-12, 4-13, 283B3
Consumer product safety comm revisn 4-13, 4-28, 345A3
'77-78 road aid authorzn (both houses) 4-13, 919A3
Science office re-creatn 4-27, 4-29, 346B1
Foreign aid authrzn (both houses) 4-28, 344E3
FEC revisn 5-3, 5-4, 346D3
Beef Bd bill 5-3, 5-12, 358E3-359A1
ACTION funds 5-4, 5-13, 393C1
'77 NRC funds 5-5, 5-10, 358F2
'77 nonbinding budget targets resolutn 5-12, 5-13, 358B1
FDA med-device control 5-13, 377E1
Educ broadcasting funds 5-13, 5-25, 434B3
Helsinki accords panel 5-17, 5-21, 392D3
NASA funds 5-17, 5-21, 411G3-412C1
Supplemental funds 5-18, 5-19, 411D3
IDB fund authorizatn (House) 5-20, 392B3
Noise control funds 5-20, 412C1
Disease control, health funds 5-26, 6-7, 434B2
Water-conversn funds 6-3, 6-7, 434G2
Fed debt ceiling 6-14, 6-30, 534D1
Defense construction 6-16, 6-17, 518C1
Revised pub works 6-16, 6-23, 518B2
Coal-leasing revisns (both houses) 6-21, 518D1

1977

Legislation Introduced
Antiboycott bills (Sen) 166B3, 167D1
DNA research regulatn (Sen) 2-4, 184C3
Pub electn funds 3-7, 3-16, 232C3
Human rights amendmt (House) 211A1
Cuba embargo amendmt (Sen) 5-10—5-11, 389C3
Child abuse amendmt (House) 432F3
Car air-bag res (House) 6-30, 522B1

Legislation Passed (final action)
Emergency natural gas allocatn (both houses) 2-2, 76D2
W Eur, Japan, S Korea fishing rights 2-8, 2-10, 173G3
E Eur, Taiwan fishing rights (both houses) 3-1, 173C3
'77 budget levels (both houses) 3-3, 174A1
Naval ship funds rescissn 3-3, 3-15, 195C3
Rhodesian chrome ban 3-14, 3-15, 191C1
SBA loan ceiling hike 3-14, 3-17, 250F3
Reorganization powers 3-29, 3-31, 228A1
Extra jobless benefits, Cong pay-raise procedures (both houses) 4-4, 272E3, 273B1
Drought aid (both houses) 4-4, 273E1
Interest rate ceiling powers 4-4, 4-5, 273A2
'77 Portugal mil aid 4-6, 4-19, 339G1
'77 supplemental funds 4-21, 4-22, 339D1
Canada temp fishing pact 4-25, 7-12, 688D3
More '77 rent subsidies 4-26, 4-28, 339A1
Pub works jobs, water projct provisn 4-29, 5-3, 365E1
Econ stimulus, other funds 5-4, 5-5, 365D2
Drought aid 5-11, 5-17, 405A3
'78 budget target res, '77 revised 5-13, 5-17, 404A3-405E1
Stimulus tax cuts; countercyclical, welfare aid provisns (both houses) 5-16, 381D3-382E1
CETA extensn 5-25, 6-3, 500F3
Boycott, export control 6-10, 6-12, 459G3-460E1
Coast Guard '78 authorizatn 6-15, 6-21, 501A1
Helsinki rights talks resolutn (both houses) 6-15, 501C1
NASA '78 authorizatn 6-21, 7-19, 688G3
COL pay hike bar (House) 6-28, 516B2
Weapons, civil defns '78 authorizatn 7-13, 7-14, 575D3
Health progrms extensn 7-15, 7-20, 689G2-B3
Youth jobs programs 7-19, 7-21, 609A2
'78 State, Justice, Commerce other funds, '77 supplemental (both houses) 7-19, 667C3
Mil constructn authorizatn 7-19, 7-20; funds (both houses) 8-5, 668F2
Arms control '78 funds (both houses) 7-19; authorizatn 8-17, 689G1, C2
Strip-mine rules 7-20, 7-21, 575D2-D3
Water research, saline conversn (both houses), 7-20, 689E2
'78 forgn arms, security aid 7-21, 7-22, 668A1

1978

Tuitn tax credits (Sen) 10-15, 785G1, 807D1
Illegal alien plan (both houses) 10-15, 1010B3

Legislation Introduced
Intell agency reorganizatn (Sen) 2-9, 106D3
NYC loan guarantees (Sen) 4-25, 608A3
Civil Svc reform (House) 8-11, 625F2

Legislation Passed (final action)—
See also 'Veto Action' below; also CARTER—LEGISLATION—Vetoed
Black lung benefit financing 12-15-77, 1-24; eligibility 2-6, 2-15, 125E1-E2
Child porno, prostitutn curbs (House) 1-24, 82D3
Drought aid extension 1-30, 1-31, 107A3
'78 suplmtl funds, Clinch R A-reactor provisn; B-1 rescission 2-1, 2-22, 160F2
Timber sales sealed-bid repeal (House) 2-6, 107C3
A-export controls 2-7, 2-9, 82E2, 183D2
Energy research authorizatn (Sen) 2-8, 107G1
New wilderness areas 2-8, 2-9, 109C2
Ocean pollutn study 2-28, 4-24, 343B2
DC voting representatn amendmt 3-2, 8-22, 661A1-E2
Redwood Park expansn 3-14, 3-21, 218E1
Mandatory retiremt curb 3-21, 3-23, 238E2
Debt limit extension 3-21, 3-22, 261A3
Disaster fund supplemt 3-22, 3-23, 261E3
OPIC extension 4-6, 4-11, 323E2
Farm bill (Sen) 4-10, 261E2
Child abuse extensn; adoptn, foster care provisns 4-10, 4-12, 323B3
Medicare kidney progrm revisns 5-1, 5-24, 466A1
Farm bill compromise 5-2, 5-4, 343C1-A2
Investor protectn 5-2, 5-10, 386D2, E2 ★
'79 budget target res 5-12, 5-17, 385A1-A3
DC '78 funds 5-16, 5-23, 432D1
Orlov sentnc condemnatn res (House) 5-18, 359C3
Coast Guard '79 authrzn 5-19, 6-14, 525D2
State soc svc claims setlmt 5-23, 5-25, 465F3
Korea aid-warning res (House) 5-31, 432G1
Fire fighters workweek cut 6-5, 6-7, 465C3
Wildlife program authrzn 6-12, 6-26, 568B1
Solar, other renewable energy business loan aid 6-16, 6-19, 512A2
Shcharansky trial res 7-11, 7-12, 542C1
Coal conversn 7-18, 549G3-550C1; 10-15, 786B2, 787G1
Debt ceiling increase 7-19, 8-2, 625F2-A3
NYC loan guarantees 7-25, 7-27, 608D3
Consumer co-op bank 7-27, 8-9, 663E1
Conrail aid 8-1, 10-14, 875C3
Land Managemt Bur '79-82 authorizn 8-2, 8-8, 697F2
'79 arms authorztn (both houses) 8-4, 622B1

1979

Legislation Introduced
Kennedy trucking deregulatn (Sen) 1-22, 111A3
Compulsive gambling (Sen) 1-30, 152E1
Consumer trust suits (Sen) 1-31, 308B2
Merger limits (Sen) 3-8, 202D2
Natl health insurnc (Sen) 5-14, 362C1
Catastrophic health insurnc (Sen) 5-14, 362A2
Trade liberalizatn (House) 6-19, 541F1
FBI charter (Sen) 7-31, 599A3
FBI bldg name chng (House) 10-30, 886D3
Iranian deportatn res (House) 11-8, 843A1

Legislation Passed (final action)
Debt ceiling, balanced budget optn 3-27, 4-2, 251E2, G2
US-Taiwan relations 3-28, 3-29, 259C2
Duty waiver (Sen) 3-29, 298F3
Temp controls 5-2, 5-10, 342B2
Rhodesia sanctns end res (Sen) 5-15, 359G1
Iran executn res (Sen) 5-17, 388B3
3 Mile I comm subpoena power res 5-17, 5-21, 417F3
'80 budget res 5-23, 5-24, 900C1
Shipping rebate curb 6-4, 6-5, 465F3-466A1
Defns treaty terminatn res (Sen) 6-6, 440B2
'79 supplemental funds; fed pay hike, Mideast peace treaty 7-17, 7-20, 700F1
Trade liberalizatn (Sen) 7-23, 646F3
'79 emergency food stamp funds 7-27, 8-2, 700B2
'80 water funds, Tellico Dam 8-1, 9-10, 766A3
'80 State, Justice, other funds 8-2, 9-10, 766E3
Lake Placid Olympics aid (House) 8-15, 798B2
Educ Dept 9-24, 9-27, 782B2
Panama Canal treaty implementatn 9-25, 9-26, 723A1
Amtrak funding authrzn 9-25, 9-27, 867D3
'80 Treas, Postal, other funds (both houses) 9-26, 883C2
1st '80 continuing appropriatns res (both houses) 10-12, 900E1
DC '80 funds 10-16, 10-22, 870A1
Standby gas rationing 10-17, 10-23, 848A3
'80 HUD, VA, NASA, other funds (both houses) 10-24, 883G2
'80 Agri funds 10-26, 10-31, 920A1
Milwaukee Rd aid (both houses) 11-2, 867E2
'80 Interior, Energy Dept funds, synfuel dvpt (both houses) 11-9, 883E1
'80 Transport, Amtrak, Panama Canal funds 11-15, 11-19, 920C1
Final '80 budget res 11-16, 11-28, 900A1
2d '80 continuing appropriatns res (both houses) 11-16, 900A2
'80 mil construction funds 11-16, 11-19, 945F1
Stopgap banking (both houses) 12-19, 987C3
Chrysler bailout (both houses) 12-21, 981D1

1980

Sen 'spec unterest' amendmts (House) 12-13, 953C3
Cong pay raise (Sen) 12-13, 953C3
Inventory tax ruling amendmt (House) 12-13, 982F2
Zip code warning amendmt (House) 12-13, 982F2
Criminal code revisn (both houses) 12-16, 982E2
Regulatory reform (both houses) 12-16, 982G2

Legislation Introduced
India uranium sale bar (House) 6-19, 495D3

Legislation Passed (final action)
China most-favored nation status (both houses) 1-24, 46E2
Olympic boycott res 1-24, 1-29, 68A1
Canada gratitude res (both houses) 1-30, 88B3
Intl airline deregulatn 1-31, 2-4, 346F1
Refugee reform 2-25, 3-4, 349A2
Nicaragua aid authrzn 2-27, 5-19, 410A1
Windfall oil profits tax 3-13, 3-27, 244B2-E3
FTC emergency funding 3-26, 5-1, 348D1, B2
Banking deregulatn 3-27, 3-29, 245C3
Abscam ethics probe res (House) 3-27, 267A1
Draft registratn funds res amendmt (House) 4-22, 349F1
Emergency food stamp appropriatn 5-14, 5-15; authrzn (both houses) 5-15, 403B1
FTC fund authrzn 5-20, 5-21, appropriatn 5-30, 6-3, 702D3
Amtrak, Rock I RR aid (both houses) 5-22, 427F1
Nicaragua aid appropriatn (both houses) 5-31, 709F2
Debt limit; oil import fee bar res 6-4, 6-5, 437C1
Wilson censure res (House) 6-10, 438A2
NRC '80 funds authrzn, reforms 6-10, 6-16, 479E1
1st '81, final '80 budget res (both houses) 6-12, 452A1
Draft registratn funding 6-12, 6-15, 478C1
Debt limit hike 6-13, 12-12, 981E1
Mil benefits authrzn 6-17, 8-20, 765C1
Iran hostage res (Sen) 6-18, 460A1
Trucking decontrol 6-19, 6-20, 479A1
Synfuel dvpt 6-19, 6-26, 479A2
Energy, water appropriatn 6-25, 9-10, 803C2
Alcan pipe completn res 6-27, 7-3, 562C2
'80 supplemental funds, Nicaragua aid (both houses) 7-2, 515D1
Small business aid 8-6, 9-9, 784D2
Eximbank funding 8-18, 989B1
'81 arms, mil pay authrzn (both houses) 8-26, 764G3
Wildlife Conservation Act 9-9, 9-16, 915B3
IMF fund quota hike authrzn, plo rider 9-18, 9-23, 695B3, 720A1, 981D3
Higher educ authrzn 9-18, 9-25, 803B3
Multi-employer pensn plan reform 9-18, 9-19, 856C3
Intelligence oversight 9-19, 9-30, 804D1
Stopgap funds, NYC rider 9-19, 9-29, 826C2
Iran hostage relief act 9-22, 9-30, 981B2
Fusion dvpt 9-23, 9-24, 981F2
Mental health authrzn 9-24, 9-30, 803E3
Newsroom searches curb 9-24, 10-1, 835G1-C2

1976

'76, '77 arms aid authorizatn 6-22, 6-25, 533A2
'76-80 air aid authrzn 6-23, 6-30, 567A1
Railroad safety 6-24, 6-25, 919F3
'75 tax cut extensn (Sen) 6-28, 492G1
'76 arms aid funds 6-28, 6-29, 533B2
'77 ERDA, pub works funds (both houses) 6-29, 517F1
'77 State, other authorizatns; Cong travel costs, Panama Canal riders 6-29, 6-30, 534G1 *
Coastal states aid 6-29, 6-30, 566A3
'77 agri, food funds (both houses) 6-29, 633D3
'77 arms, manpower authorizatn 6-30, 7-1, 516G2
'77 housing aid 6-30, 7-20, 566D3
'77 State, Justice, Commerce, other funds (both houses) 7-1, 534C2
Day care funds 7-1, 8-24, 689D1
Interior, related agency funds (both houses) 7-20, 623C1
Members Md tax exemption (both houses) 7-20, 636C3
'77 HUD, VA, EPA, NASA, NSF funds (both houses) 7-27, 623E1
Forgn bank regulatn (House) 7-29, 940F2
3-judge ct use cut (both houses) 8-2, 646A3
'77 transport funds 8-3, 8-4, 646A2
Pesticide bill 8-3, 8-5, 646G2
Energy bill, FEA extensn 8-5, 8-10, 622G2
Land tax compensatn for local govts 8-5, 10-1, 835E1
Voter mail registratn (House) 8-9, 883E1
Fed swine flu vaccine liability (both houses) 8-10, 586C2
New River dam bar 8-10, 8-30, 689F1
Electric car bill 8-26, 8-31, 708A1
Emergency pres powers curb 8-27, 8-31, 689G1
Govt in sunshine (both houses) 8-31, 688D3
Options tax exemptn 8-31, 9-1, 708F1
Postal subsidy 8-31, 9-10, 745C3
Auto research 8-31, 9-13, 746B1
Antitrust enforcmt 9-8, 9-16, 728D1 *
'77 defense funds 9-9, 9-13, 706G3
Amer Indian health aid 9-9, 9-16, 745D3
Land conservatn funds 9-10, 9-13, 745E2-B3
Natl park mining curbs 9-14, 9-17, 834B2
'77 binding budget levels resolutn 9-15, 9-16, 706G1
'77 mil constructn authrzn 9-15, 9-16, 745C2
Police, firemen survivor benefits 9-15, 9-16, 834D2
Tax revisns (both houses) 9-16, 705D2
'77 HEW, Labor funds 9-16, 9-17, 726G3
Eased HMO aid rules 9-16, 9-23, 765B2
Pub works funds, pub svc jobs extensn 9-17, 9-22, 727F3
'77 DC funds 9-17, 9-21, 834G1
4 vet benefits bills 9-20, 9-21, 10-1, 806G3
'77 Legis funds, salary hike bar (both houses) 9-22, 834A2
Arts & Humanities Foundatn extensn 9-22, 9-27, 834F2
'65 depressed area aid extensn 9-24, 9-29, 765E1
Ind Dunes expansn 9-24, 9-29, 834B3
'77 Science Foundatn authorizn 9-24, 9-29, 835A2
Med-educ aid 9-27, 9-30, 788D2
'77 forgn aid funds 9-27, 9-28, 806B3
Solid waste authorizatns 9-27, 9-30, 833F2
Gas pipeline safety aid 9-27, 9-28, 834C3
Toxic substances (both houses) 9-28, 764E2
HEW inspector gen 9-28, 9-29, 765F2-C3
Educational aid 9-28, 9-29, 789A1
Indian Claims Comm end 9-28, 9-29, 834G3
Civil-rights-suit fees 9-29, 10-1, 788A2
Forgn natn legal immunity 9-29, 10-1, 835B1
Occidental immigratn revisn 9-29, 10-1, 835C1
Revenue sharing extension (both houses) 9-30, 764B3
Copyright revisions (both houses) 9-30, 764E3
Pub land use 9-30, 10-1, 834C1
Forest mgt, clear-cutting (both houses) 9-30, 834C1
'77, '78 RR aid 9-30, 10-1, 834D2
Spain bases treaty aid 9-30, 10-1, 834C3
Alaska gas transport study 9-30, 10-1, 834D3
Mid-decade censuses 9-30, 10-1, 834F3
LEAA extensn, FBI dir term limit (both houses) 9-30, 835F1
Rabbit meat inspectn 11-4-75, 9-30, 919G2
Jobless benefits revision (both houses) 10-1, 788C1-A2
Grain inspectn (both houses) 10-1, 833C3
Arthritis, diabetes study authorization (both houses) 10-1, 834G2
Emergency med care extensn (both houses) 10-1, 834A3
Tax for social club bias (both houses) 10-1, 835F1
'77-78 army engineer projects (both houses) 10-1, 835A2
Resource planning (both houses) 10-1, 919E2

Legislation Passed (preliminary action)

Viet refugee educ aid (House) 1-19, 69F2
Educ broadcast funds (House) 1-20, 94A1
Reserve call-up power (Sen) 1-26, 135E1

1977

'78 forgn econ aid 7-21, 7-22, 668B2
Pub works, ERDA, water projct, other funds (both houses) 7-25, 592F2-C3 *
'78 cong funds (both houses) 7-26, 689B1
Small business aid 7-26, 7-27, 689B3
'78 agri, food funds 7-27, 7-29, 688G2
State authorizatn; visa, Korea policy provisns 7-28, 8-3, 667B3
Juvenile Justice Amendmts 7-28, 9-23, 797B1
Energy Dept (both houses) 8-2, 591E2
Clean air amendmts (both houses) 8-4, 610D1-F2
NSF '78 authorizatn 8-4, 8-5, 689D1
Debt collectn rules 8-5, 9-8, 761D1
Weapons, civil defns funds 9-8, 9-9, 704E2-B3
Farm, food stamp bill 9-9, 9-16, 736D2
'78 budget levels (both houses) 9-15, 719D2
Intl lending agency authorizatn, rights curb 9-16, 9-21, 737B3
Mex, Canada prisoner exchngs 9-21, 10-25, 834E1
Vets mil disability pensn hike (both houses) 9-21, 877G3
HUD, VA, NASA, other funds 9-23, 9-28, 796G2-F3
Debt ceiling rise 9-30, 10-4, 773E2
Urban, housing aid authorizatn 10-1, 10-4, 796F2
Mine safety rules 10-6, 10-27, 855E3
Indochina refugee aid 10-10, 10-18, 834B2
Interest deposits for fed tax, loan accts 10-11, 10-14, 815A3
Medicare, Medicaid abuse curbs (both houses) 10-13, 814D1, A2
'77 farm disaster aid ceiling removal 10-17, 10-25, 833B3
Intl lending agency, other '78 forgn aid funds 10-18, 10-19, 815A2
Minimum wage 10-19, 10-20, 795E2
Energy research authorizatn (both houses) 10-20, 832G3
Rabbit meat inspectn (both houses) 10-26, 897C3
Child nutritn, schl lunch 10-27, 10-28, 897E2
Maritime subsidy authorizatn 10-31, 11-1, 856B2
Korea ethics probe aid (House) 10-31, 915C1
Drinking water authorizatn (both houses) 11-1, 856F3
Defns suplmtl authorizatn 11-2, 11-3, 856E1-A2
Alcan gas route (both houses) 11-2, 856C3
ERDA mil authorizatn 11-2, 11-3, 878A1
Rail mass transit aid 11-2, 11-3, 900D1
Vets educ benefits 11-3, 11-4, 877D2
Vets old-age, non-mil disability hike (both houses) 11-3, 877E3
Saccharin ban delay 11-3, 11-4, 878D1
NRC '78 authorizatn Clinch R provisn 11-3, 11-29, 938D1
Career guidance aid authorizatn 11-22, 11-29, 959A2
Rural health clinic aid (both houses) 11-29, 938F1
Endangered species aid 11-29, 11-30, 938B2
US forgn-trained med student transfer 12-1, 12-7, 959C2
Forgn business bribe ban 12-6, 12-7, 937G3
HEW-Labor funds, abortn curb (both houses) 12-7, 958C2
Legal aid for poor (LSC) extended 12-7, 12-15, 1002C2
Soc Sec revisns (both houses) 12-15, 957A3
Clean water revisn, local aid (both houses) 12-15, 958G3

Legislation Passed (preliminary action)

Pub works jobs authorizatn (House) 2-24, 174G1
Pres reorganizatn powers (Sen) 3-3, 191F2

1978

Forgn bank regulatn 8-15, 8-17, 663A1
Mil constructn funds 8-17, 8-21, 662C1
Offshore oil, gas leasing 8-17, 8-22, 662F2-663A1
'78 supplemental funds 8-17, 8-25, 681F2
DC '79 funds (both houses) 8-17, 697G2
Intell agencies authrzn 8-17, 8-22, 715E3
NASA '79 authorzn 8-17, 9-19, 750A3 *, D3
Diplomatic immunity revisn 8-17, 9-18, 750D3
Customs law revisn 8-25, 9-19, 751B1
'79 mil, secuity aid authorzn 9-11, 9-12, 734G2
Public works 9-14, 9-27, 765F1
HUD, VA, other funds 9-19, 9-20, 750A3
Suffragette dollar coin (both houses) 9-19, 788B2
Energy Dept security progrm authorzn, neutron parts productn 9-20, 10-11, 833D2
Budget levels res 9-21, 9-23, 733E3
Inspector Gen Act 9-22, 9-27, 899D2
Land purchase registratn 9-26, 10-2, 897C2
Natural gas compromise 9-27, 733A1; 10-15, 787B2, 787B1
Tanker safety rules 9-30, 10-3, 807B3
Aquaculture authorzn (both houses) 10-2, 807G3
Amer Samoa House del 10-3, 10-13, 1003A1
Civil Svc reform 10-4, 10-6, 787A3
'79 revised arms authorzn 10-4, 10-7, 833B2
Judgeships increase 10-4, 10-7, 873D2
Small business aid 10-4, 10-11, 897F2
Bankruptcy revisn 10-5, 10-6, 788D2
ERA extension (Sen) 10-6, 788A1
Shipping malpractice 10-6, 10-12, 897A3
Hollings textile trade rider (Sen) 10-6, 998E1
Govt ethics 10-7, 10-12, 832B2
DC pension reform 10-7, 10-14, 897F2
Utility rates 10-9, 10-15, 786B2, 787E1
Energy conservatn 10-9, 10-15, 786B2, 787B2
Natl security warrantless tap curbs 10-9, 10-12, 863B1
Grazing land laws revisn 10-10, 10-11, 807D2
Nazi deportatn 10-10, 10-13, 872D2
Inland Waterways authorzn 10-10, 10-13, 897D2
'79 defns funds, abortn curb (both houses) 10-12, 833A1
Natl parks authorzn 10-12, 10-13, 834G2
'79 forgn aid funds, IMF contributn 10-12, 10-13, 862C2, F2
Labor, HEW '79 funds 10-12, 10-14, 873F1
Tris compensatn 10-12, 10-13, 941D3
Banking reform 10-12, 10-14, 1002F3
CETA extensn 10-13, 10-14, 807C1
Humphrey-Hawkins full-employmt 10-13, 10-15, 808A1, D1
Pregnancy benefits 10-13, 10-14, 873G1
Pres Records Act 10-13, 10-14, 897E2
Coll student aid expansn 10-14, 10-15, 807G1
Amateur sports, omnibus funds 10-14, 10-15, 842C2-C3
Airline deregulation (both houses) 10-14, 873F1
Surface transit funds (both houses) 10-14, 875E2
$18.7 bln tax cut (both houses) 10-15, 785D1, B2
Natural gas compromise (House) 10-15, 786B2, 787B1
Endangered Species revisn (both houses) 10-15, 834B2

Legislation Passed (preliminary action)—*For conference committee developments, see subjects of legislation*

Criminal code revisn (Sen) 1-30, 64F1

1979

Legislation Passed (preliminary action)

Duty waiver (House) 3-1, 159C2
PLO visa bar (House) 4-24, 319C3
Educ Dept (Sen) 4-30, 326B2
Standby gas rationing (Sen) 5-9, 342C2

1980

Refugee aid to states 9-25, 10-1, 785C1
Vet educ aid 9-25, 9-26, 856F2
Household moving 9-25, 9-30, 915G2
Auto fuel standards revisns 9-26, 9-30, 981C1
RR deregulatn 9-30, 10-1, 783E3
Housing, community dvpt authrzn (both houses) 9-30, 804B2
Judicial discipline 9-30, 10-1, 918F3
'81 Transport funds (both houses) 9-30, 980E3
'81-85 coastal zone mgt authrzn 9-30, 10-1, 981A2
Forgn Svc reorgn 9-30, 10-1, 981D2
5th judicial circuit split (both houses) 10-1, 918A3
Clean water amendmts (both houses) 10-1, 981E1
Toxic dump controls 10-1, 10-2, 981F1
Agri Act 10-1, 11-17, 981G1
Alaska lands bill (House) 11-12, 866E2-C3
Gasohol Competition Act 11-17, 11-19, 953D2
Plant Variety Protectn Act amendmt 11-17, 12-8, 980G3
Pacific NW power 11-17, 11-19, 981G1
Natl Historic Preservatn Act Amendmts 11-17, 11-19, 981C2
Natl Endowmt for Arts, Humanities authrzn 11-18, 11-20, 953F2
Paperwork Reductn 11-19, 12-1, 935C3
'81 budget res (both houses) 11-20, 896A2
Patent law revision 11-20, 11-21, 915D3
EDA extensn (both houses) 11-20, 982C2
'81 State, Justice, Commerce funds; busing amendmts 11-21, 12-3, 953F3
'81 Interior, Energy funds 11-21, 12-1, 954D2
A-arms authrzn 11-25, 12-1, 981B1
Pesticide control 12-1, 12-4, 955E1
'81 Natl Science Foundatn authrzn (both houses) 12-2, 953G2
'81 HUD, VA, NASA, other funds 12-2, 12-3, 954G2
'81 forgn aid authrzn 12-2, 12-3, 981A3
Toxic waste clean-up (House) 12-3, 935E3-936B1
Budget reconciliatn (both houses) 12-3, 936D1
Fishing indus aid 12-3, 12-4, 955B1
Medicare, Medicaid changes (both houses) 12-3, 981A1
Child nutritn authrzn (both houses) 12-3, 981B1
'81 Agri, FDA, CFTC funds (both houses) 12-4, 954B3
'81 defns appropriatn (both houses) 12-5, 935G2
Wood fuel 12-5, 12-8, 953E2
Mil pay, benefits (both houses) 12-5, 953G2
Army LSD setlmt (both houses) 12-5, 981F3
Forgn tourism agency 12-9, 12-11, 953E2
Revenue sharing renewal 12-10, 12-12, 954G3-955B1
Low-level A-waste (both houses) 12-13, 981C1
Stopgap funds; forgn aid, IMF funding riders (both houses) 12-15—12-16, 953B1, 954F1, 981A3, E3

Legislation Passed (preliminary action)

Intell oversight (Sen) 6-3, 458B3
Alaska lands bill (Sen) 8-19, 631B2-A3
'81 defns appropriatn; mil pay, benefits amendmts (House) 9-16, 741A3

1976

200-mi fishing zone (Sen) 1-28, 94C1
Renegotiatn Bd restructure (House) 1-29, 134E3-135D1
Natl park mining halt (Sen) 2-4, 135G1
Natural gas regulatn extensn (House) 2-5, 108C2-109A1
Public jobs (House) 2-10, 134F2
Copyright revisn (Sen) 2-10, 152B2
Laos refugee aid (Sen) 2-16, 182C1
Library aid extensn (House) 2-17, 170D3
Indiana Dunes enlargemt (House) 2-17, 171A1
Forgn arms aid authorizatn; export curbs (Sen) 2-18, 151C3
Conrail funds (House) 2-18, 152B1
Paint poisoning (Sen) 2-19, 170F3
Marianas commonwealth status (Sen) 2-24, 170E2
Library of Cong bldg funds (House) 2-24, 171B2
Debt ceiling rise (House) 2-25, 170A3
Patent law revision (Sen) 2-26, 181B3
Black-lung benefits (House) 3-2, 181F3
Forgn arms aid authorizatn, sales (House) 3-3, 181G1-C2
Forgn aid appropriatn (House) 3-4, 181D2
Antitrust suits (House) 3-18, 246D3-247B1
House-Sen conf com OKs Chile cash arms sales 3-31, 310A2
Food-stamp reform (Sen) 4-8, 282D3
'77 arms authorizatn (House) 4-9, 283G1
Pub works, jobs aid (Sen) 4-13, 283B1
FRB restructuring (House) 5-10, 345D1
'77 arms authrzn, B-1 funds delay (Sen) 5-20, 5-26, 392F3, 411B2
Special prosecutor office (Sen) 7-21, 884D1
Tax revisions 8-6, 585F3, 669C1
Export Act extensn, Arab boycott provisn (Sen) 8-27, 746D2
Anti-bribery bill (Sen) 9-15, 708A1
Export Act extensn, Arab boycott provisns (House) 9-22, 746A2

Legislation Proposed—*See also 'Proposals & Requests' under FORD—LEGISLATION*
GAO urges defns contracting rules 1-11, 70F3
Goodell urges clemency bd revival 1-15, 43G1
EPA urges toxic chem law 2-26, 171F2
Nader rpt asks FRB disclosure 7-5, 495A3
FEA oil stockpile plan 12-15, 991D3
Puerto Rican statehood 12-31, 994F2

Legislation Signed—*See CARTER—LEGISLATION—Signed*
Legislation Vetoed—*See 'Vetoed' under FORD—LEGISLATION*
Lobbying & Lobbyists
Dem platform text 6-15, 471G1
Carter acceptnc speech cites 7-15, 510E2
GOP platform text 8-18, 604C1
Dole denies Gulf Oil chrg 9-6, 9-8, 665D3
Gulf gifts probe ends 9-15, 980B1
Sugar groups action cited 9-21, 721C3
Ford linked to US Steel lobbyist 9-21, 722G2
Carter scores GOP 9-27, 724A2
Carter on Ford favors 10-2, 743C1
Disclosure bill not cleared 10-2, 883C1
S Korean lobbying probed 10-24—12-1, 898D3-900B2

Membership—*For Black Caucus developments, see 'Politics & Government' under BLACK Americans under 'B'*
Political lineup 1-19, 68D3 ★
Peace thru Law group issues arms spending study 2-29, 182G3
Travel expense rptg set 7-12, 534G1
Ford vetoes Md tax exemption 8-3, 636B3
173 protest West Pt cheating scandal proceedings 8-11, 670C2
GOP platform text 8-18, 604A1
Justice Dept probes US Steel gifts 9-24, 722C3
Electn results 11-2, 817E1, 819B3-820E2, G3-825G2; 95th Cong listed 828A1-831A4
8-yr term limit urged 11-29, 917G2-A3
Adams named Transport secy 12-14, 936D1, E3
Presidential Election (& transition)
Carter budget plan meets Dem level 4-23, 305C2
Gov Brown meets Dems 5-6, 343E2
Ford gets GOP support 5-11, 5-12, 343F1

1977

Tax cuts (House) 3-8, 174D2
Pub works jobs, sewage authorizatn (Sen) 3-10, 174B2
COL pay hike bar (Sen) 3-10, 191E3
Water projects amendmt (Sen) 3-10, 209F3
SST research authorizatn (House) 3-17, 213G1
CETA extensn (House) 3-29, 500F3
Clean-water act 4-5, 8-4, 900B2
Boycott, export control (House) 4-20, 323C2; 5-5, 460A1
'78 arms authorizatn (House) 4-25, 323E3
Viet aid bar amendmt (House) 5-4, 333E1
Energy department (Sen) 5-18, 405E1
Clean-air bill amendmts 5-26, 418B2; 6-10, 460E3
Hatch Act revisn (House) 6-7, 442G2
Adoption subsidies (House) 6-7, 628C3
Porpoise-kill limit (House) 6-11, 442D3
Intl lending agency authorizatns (Sen) 6-14, 477F2
State, USIA, Broadcast Bd '78 authorizatn; Korea, Cuba amendmts (Sen) 6-16, 477C3
HEW, Labor '78 funds; abortn, busing, quota curbs (House) 6-17, 478B1; 6-29, 515E2
Saccharin ban delay (House) 6-21, 531B1
B-1 funds (House) 6-28, 514G1
'78 legis funds (House) 6-29, 516G1
Energy package (House) 8-5, 609E2-610C1
Coal conversion (Sen) 9-8, 702A3
Gas-guzzler ban, homeowner energy provisions (Sen) 9-13, 703C1
Minimum wage (House) 9-15, 758F3
Pregnancy benefits (Sen) 9-16, 737G3
Armed forces union ban (Sen) 9-16, 759D3-760C1
Clinch R A-breeder authorizatn 9-20, 758C2
Mandatory retiremt curb (House) 9-23, 737C2
Natural gas deregulatn (Sen) 10-4, 757B1, F2
Labor law reform (House) 10-6, 795B2
Soc Sec revisns (House) 10-27, 814D2-815A1
Energy tax bill (Sen) 10-31, 832C1-F3
S Africa apartheid res (House) 10-31, 852D1
Amtrak '78 added funds (House-Sen com) 11-3, 860E?

Legislation Proposed—*See also 'Proposals & Requests' under CARTER—LEGISLATION; also 'Congress' under FORD, Gerald*
Maine Indian land setlmt 1-14, 59C1
Redwood Park expansn 4-19, 322F3
FBI investigative guidelines 6-6, 481A1
GOP Soc Security plan 9-9, 720G1
Alaska parks plan 9-15, 739A3
Amtrak to seek '78 funds 9-19, 778E2

Legislation Signed—*See CARTER—LEGISLATION—Signed*
Legislation Vetoed—*See CARTER—LEGISLATION—Vetoed*
Library, Joint Committee on the
Sen reorganizatn OKd 2-4, 90G2, F3
Lobbying & Lobbyists—*See also KOREA (South)—U.S.-Korean Political Payments*
'76 gifts rptd 1-15, 2-4, 2-15, 128C1-129F2
Sen reorganizatn OKd 2-4, 90F2, 91A1
House adopts ethics code 3-2, 173G2
Common-site picketing defeated 3-23, 229E1
Carter proposes ethics law 5-2, 338E1
Pro-Concorde efforts cited 5-11, 368A2
Fed Reserve actns scored 5-24, 406F3
S Africa sugar lobby sued 7-20, 614A1
USSR chrgs Zionist influence strong 7-22, 589C2
Carter scores re energy plan 9-26, 757C1
Carter halts farm aide's personal lobbying 9-30, 773C1
New England Congressional Caucus
Rpts defense job loss 8-10, 629D2

1978

Redwood Park expansion 1-31, 2-9, 85D2
Bankruptcy revisn 2-1, 9-7, 788D3
Humphrey-Hawkins full employmt (House) 3-16, 182F2
Farm aid (Sen) 3-21, 218F2-219A1
Airline deregulatn 4-19, 9-21, 765E2
Natl security warrantless tap curbs 4-20, 306D1; 9-7, 696E3
Budget target res (Sen) 4-26, 305B2
Lobbying rules (House) 4-26, 323E1-C2
Alaska lands (House) 5-19, 386F1
Mil constructn authorizatn (House) 5-22, 406G3-407B1
'79 arms procuremt, research authorizatn (House) 5-24, 406B3
Tuition tax credits (House) 6-1, 431G2
NYC loan guarantees 6-8, 6-29, 608B3
Uganda trade ban res (House) 6-12, 616F2
HEW-Labor funds; abortn, quota curbs (House) 6-13, 445C2-G3
Agri funds, S Korea food aid cutoff (House), 6-22, 467B2-A3
Oil import fee bar amendmt to Treas-PO funds bill (Sen) 6-27, 511B3, 523A3
'79 arms procuremt, research authrzn (Sen) 7-11, 526A2
Natl parks bill (House) 7-12, 526B3
Endangered species extensn (Sen) 7-19, 551A2
Turkish arms embargo end 7-25, 8-1, 587D2
Rhodesia sanctns end 7-26, 8-2, 588B1
Seabed mining (House) 7-26, 588E3
Uganda trade ban amendmt to IMF funds bill (Sen) 7-28, 616D2
'79 defns funds, abortn curb (House) 8-9, 604B2, F2
$16 bln tax cut (House) 8-10, 604A1
ERA extension (House) 8-15, 661E2
Civil Svc reforms 8-24, 661C3; 9-13, 696C2-D3
Aircraft noise abatemt (House) 9-14, 765D3
'79 forgn aid authorzn, IMF contributn (Sen) 9-22, 731E2, 732B1 ★
Educ Dept (Sen) 9-28, 785B1
$29 bln tax cut (Sen) 10-10, 766B3
Hospital costs lid (Sen) 10-12, 785B1
Sugar price supports (Sen) 10-15, 785C1

Legislation Proposed—*See also CARTER—LEGISLATION—Proposals & Requests*
Drug law revision 3-16, 231C1
Amtrak route cutbacks 5-8, 366D1
GAO asks MD training progrm 5-19, 597E2
HEW asks welfare loopholes closed 7-20, 684E3
Regulatory agency pres-veto power asked by ABA 8-8, 626F2
Trucking deregulatn 11-7, 1007E1
New fed ct urged by 3 Sup Ct justices 12-4, 958D3-959A1
Press search shield 12-13, 1029B3
Fraudulent documt lab urged 12-20, 1010F2
Legislation Vetoed—*See also CARTER—LEGISLATION—Vetoed*
Sup Ct bars cong 1-house veto case review 1-9, 12G3
Lobbying & Lobbyists—*See also KOREA (South)—U.S.-Korean Political Payments*
Gun group admits false mailings 1-16, 68F2
Flood chrgd on payoffs, ex-aide's convictn cited 2-15, 240C2
Ribicoff scores pro-Israel group 3-13, 176D3
Carter scores tax lobbyists, backs legis controls 4-25, 307F2, A3
House OKs new rules 4-26, 323E1-C2
House members speaking fees rptd 5-4, 363C2
Energy Dept policy role questned 5-15, 408E2-C3
Anti-Israel remark denied by Admin 5-16, 358E1
Carter scores spec interests 8-14, 626D1
Flood indicted 9-5, 685C1
Burger defends judicial lobbying 10-25, 832D3
Govt ethics bill signed 10-26, 832F1
PAC gifts to cong com chrmn rptd 12-24, 1008A1
Membership
'53, '78 compositn compared 1-30, 107C2
McClellan immunity case refused by Sup Ct 6-26, 566D2
DC voting representatn cleared 8-22, 661A1-E2
Poll ratings rptd 8-27, 682B2
Carter anti-inflatn plan scored 10-24, 806F3
Election results 11-7, 845B1-846A3, 847C2-857C3
Travel overseas rptd 12-10, 958B3

1979

Alaska land (House) 5-16, 366E3
Turkey mil grants (Sen) 5-22, 397F2
Shipping rebate curb (Sen) 5-23, 466A1
Energy conservation (Sen) 6-5, 595C2
Zimbabwe sanctns amendmt (Sen) 6-12, 434D3, 438F1
'80 arms authrzn (Sen) 6-13, 438E1
Panama Canal treaty implementatn (House) 6-21, 481A1
Synthetic fuels (House) 6-26, 498G1
Oil profits tax (House) 6-28, 541B2
Zimbabwe sanctns res (House) 6-28, 7-11, 546B3
Educ Dept; racial quota, anti-abortn, other amendmts (House) 7-11, 514C3
Trade liberalizatn (House) 7-11, 541E1
Gas rationing veto amendmt (House) 7-25, 557A2
Standby gas rationing (House) 8-1, 595B2
Nixon Calif estate costs res (Sen) 9-5, 683B2
Energy mobilizatn bd 10-4, 11-1, 961D1
Gas price controls amendmt (House) 10-12, 848F3
'80 Energy Dept authrzn (House) 10-24, 848G3
Synthetic fuels (Sen) 11-8, 961C1
Hosp cost comm (House) 11-15, 883A1
Rev King holiday (House) 12-5, 945B2
Oil profits tax (Sen) 12-17, 961A1
Chrysler bailout 12-18, 12-19, 981F2

Legislation Proposed—*See also CARTER—LEGISLATION—Proposals & Requests*
Food-safety law revisns 3-2, 194G3
Refugee admissn hike 3-8, 307E3
Air-safety penalty revisn 3-16, 206E1
Rhodesia sanctns end 4-24, 293F2
Bank law reforms 5-22, 403B1
Kennedy-Durkin energy plan 7-25, 557B3

Lobbying & Lobbyists—*See also KOREA (South)-U.S.-Korean Political Payments*
Carter launches hosp cost bill drive 3-6, 163B2
S Africa activity rptd 3-23, 213D2
'78 PAC spending rptd up 5-10, Common Cause deplores 5-15, 363E1-C2
Mrs Javits Iran role bared 5-30, 408B2
Wayne backs Canal treaty implementatn 6-7, 481C1
Legislators' incomes studied 9-1, 701F3
Carter hosp cost bill defeated 11-15, 883C1

Membership
Com members, chrmn confrmd 1-23–1-24, 70E3 71B3; ldrship, chrmn chart 71A1
Ruled liable to sex-bias suits by Sup Ct 6-5, 463G3-464F1
Labor '78 campaign gifts rptd 6-13, 595B1
Legal immunity broadened by Sup Ct 6-18, 498C3
Libel suit rights broadened by Sup Ct 6-26, 540A3
Financial disclosure statemts studied 9-1, 701C3-702B1

1980

Toxic waste funds (House) 9-19, 9-23, 898F1
IMF fund quota hike appropriatn (House) 9-25, 981E3
NHTSA authrzn, air bag delay (Sen) 9-25, 982F1
State, Justice, Commerce appropriatn; Sovt grain embargo, busing amendmts (Sen) 11-17, 880F3
'81 budget res (Sen) 11-19, 896G2
'81 defns appropriatn (Sen) 11-21, 896A3
Toxic waste 'superfund' (Sen) 11-24, 897G3
Auto import curb res (House) 12-2, 982B3

Legislation Proposed
Homosexual entry bar repeal backed 6-20, 514D3
DC fscl recovery plan proposed 7-19, '80 budget deficit rptd 9-30, 742A3
ABA urges pub accommodatns sex bias end 8-6, 744A2
Forgn bank takeover ban 8-28, 806G2
Inventory tax ruling relief 10-5, 836D1
Lenient sentence appeal backed by Sup Ct 12-9, 936G3

Lobbying & Lobbyists
FTC funding blocked 3-15—4-30, shuts down 5-1, reopens 5-2, 348C1
Evangelical Christians profiled 7-11—9-15, 819A1, F1, B3
Pay-TV group formed 7-15, 639G3
Synfuels trade assn rptd 9-21, 725B3
Domestic violence victims bill dropped 11-17, 986A2

Membership
Cong Watch sees anticonsumerism 1-12, 53G2
ACU '79 voting survey rptd 1-18, 53B3
Election results 11-4, 837D1, 845F1-847A1, 848B1-852C3, 97th Cong listed 840B1*, 842A1*-844E4

1976

Carter: to restore pres peace 6-14, 433F1
Dem platform text 6-15, 471G1
Carter plans forgn policy consultatn 6-24, 490E1
Carter visits DC Dems 6-24, 490C2
Carter acceptnc speech 7-15, 510E2
Ford plans poll for vp choice 7-30, 7-31, 563G3
GOP platform text 8-18, 602B2, F2, 603F2, G3, 604C1, 606D1, E1, C3, 607A2, B2, 608E2, 609F2, 610C2
Ford acceptance speech cites 8-19, 611D3-E3, 612A2
Dole acceptance speech scores 8-19, 613B1, D1
Carter appraises 8-20, 632G1
Carter on pres 'wall' 8-25, 632B1
Dole denies Gulf oil chrg 9-6, 9-8, 665D3
Ford, Carter debate 9-23, 702G3-703F1
Ford scores 10-5, 742A3
2d Ford, Carter debate 10-6, 741D1, B2
Dole, Mondale debate 10-15, 782G2-A3, 783C3; rebuttals 10-25—10-27, 804B1, A2, D2, A3
Ford, Carter debate 10-22, 800G3
Carter meets Dem ldrs 11-17, 864E1
Carter visits 11-23, 881G1
Transitn aide named 11-23, 881G2
Budget Office aide named to transitn team 11-23, 881B3
Carter sees Rivlin 12-1, 898G2
Carter seeks bipartisanship 12-1, 916D3
Carter mtgs 12-9, 12-10, 937F3, 938A1
Adams named Transport secy 12-14, 936D1, E3
Sorensen on CIA ties 12-23, 958C1

Printing, Joint Committee on
Hays asked to quit temporarily 6-2, 433G2

Republicans
Ford gets support 5-11, 5-12, 343E1
Ford to poll re vp 7-30, 7-31, 563G3

Resolutions—*See 'Legislation' subheads in this section above*

Security and Cooperation in Europe, Commission on
Communist natns bar visi 11-5, 880G1
Issues Helsinki progress rpt 12-2, 934E1

Veto Action
Treas NSC membership veto overridden 1-22, 69A3
Labor-HEW funds veto overridden 1-27, 1-28, 69A2
Milk price veto upheld 2-4, 88F1
Public jobs veto sustained 2-19, 135C2
Hatch Act repeal sustained 4-29, 346E1
Day-care veto sustained 5-5, 345G3
Fuel decontrol veto bid fails 6-30, 534B1
Pub works veto overridden 7-21, 7-22, 533E2
Mil constructn veto sustained 7-22, 533A3
Coal-leasing veto overridden 8-3, 8-4, 566E2
Elec car aid overridden 9-17, 707D3
Sen backs Ford on auto research 9-29, 745G3
'77 HEW, Labor funds veto overridden 9-30, 726F1
Overrides listed 727C3

CONGRESSIONAL Record—*See under CONGRESS above*

CONRAIL—*See under 'C'*

CONSTITUTION
Ford, Carter debate amendmts 10-22, 799G3, 802C1

Abortion Amendment Issue—*See ABORTION under 'A'*

Equal Rights Amendment—*See 'Politics & Government' under WOMEN under 'W'*

CONSTRUCTION, President's Committee on Collective Bargaining in
Union members resign 1-8, 3F3

CONSUMER Product Safety Commission
Sen OKs lead paint poison bill 2-19, 170G3
Newman confrmd to HUD 2-24, 186B2
New powers bill signed 5-11, 345G2
Byington confrmd chrmn 5-26, 412D1
Lead paint poison bill cleared 6-7, 434G2; signed 6-23, 982F1
Aerosol curbs ordrd 11-22, 902A1

CORPORATE Payments Abroad, Task Force on Questionable
Ford submits legis 8-3, 668G2

CUSTOMS, Bureau of—*See under TREASURY below*

DEBT, Public—*See under BUDGET in this section above*

DEFENSE, Department of—*See also ARMED Forces and specific branch of service in this section; for war strategy and defense systems, see ARMAMENTS under 'A' and DISARMAMENT under 'D'; for U.S. foreign policy, see specific country and organization names and appropriate subheads under MIDDLE EAST*
Proxmire criticism of officials' flights rptd 1-1, 6E3

1977

Printing, Joint Committee on
Sen reorganization OKd 2-4, 90G2, F3

Priorities & Economy in Government, Subcommittee on (of Joint Economic Committee)
USSR defns advances held costly 6-30, 673D3

Reorganization
House rules chngs OKd 1-4, 36B3
Ford proposes com realignmt 1-17, 30D2
Sen com reorganizatn OKd 2-4, 90C1-91G1
House ethics com formed 3-9, 191C2

Republicans
181 in 95th Cong 1-4, 5C3
Ford sees leaders 3-25, 236C2
Carter would veto tax-cut plan 4-15, 299G1
Carter energy plan reactn 4-20, 290D3

Resolutions—*See 'Legislation' subheads in this section above*

Security & Cooperation in Europe, Commission on
US bars Sovt editor 1-12, 22E1
Bukovsky urges Sovt rights stand 2-23, 142B3
Vance denies Shcharansky, CIA link 6-6, 436G1
Sovt bloc rights record scored 8-5, 606B2
USSR press union scores 8-17, 640A3

CONRAIL—*See under 'C'*

CONSOLIDATED Rail Corp.—*See CONRAIL under 'C'*

CONSTITUTION—*See under 'C'*

CONSUMER Product Safety Commission (CPSC)
Ford patronage apptmt rptd 1-19, 36D2
Sleepwear flame-retardant banned 4-7, 302E2 ★
Fluorocarbon warning planned 4-26, 323A2
Tris recall cost sharing ordred 4-28, 5-3, upheld 5-19, 483A2
Fluorocarbon ban proposed 5-11, 387E1
SC mill win Tris ban exemptn 5-18, 483E2
Tris ban upset 6-23, recall enjoined 6-26, 560D1
McDonald's glass tests rptd, promotn halted 7-8—7-17, 560B1
Tris rule upheld 8-12; 2 chain stores sued 8-19, 8-22, sale halted 8-20, 651F3
Settles Fed Stores Tris complaint 8-31, sues Ward 10-16, 820A2, D2
'78 funds signed 10-4, 796F3
Aluminum elec wire makers sued 10-27, 900C3

CRIMINAL Justice Standards & Goals, National Advisory Committee on—*See JUSTICE—Law Enforcement Assistance Administration below*

CUSTOMS and Patents Appeals, U.S. Court of
Microbe patent granted 10-6, 847D1

CUSTOMS Service, U.S.—*See under TREASURY in this section below*

DEBT, Public—*See under BUDGET in this section above*

DEFENSE, Department of—*See also ARMED Forces and specific branch in this section; for weapons, see ARMAMENTS under 'A'; for arms control, see DISARMAMENT under 'D'; for foreign defense issues, see specific country and organization names*
Ford State of Union message 1-12, 12E2, E3, 13B2, C2, C3

1978

Republicans
Baker urges GOP agenda 11-28, 916D1

Security & Cooperation in Europe, Commission on
USSR Helsinki monitors rptd jailed 6-12, 504B1

Taxation, Joint Committee on
'79 tax hike seen despite cuts 8-2, 587B2

Technology Assessment, Office of (OTA)
Coal slurry study issued 1-18, 49A1
Ocean thermal energy use discounted 6-7, 512B2
Solar energy study issued 6-23, 493D1

Veto Action
'79 arms authrzn veto upheld 9-7, 677A2
Pub works veto upheld 10-5, 765A1-D2

CONRAIL—*See under 'C'*

CONSOLIDATED Rail Corp.—*See CONRAIL under 'C'*

CONSTITUTION—*See under 'C'*

CONSUMER Affairs, White House Office of
Carter broadens powers 4-27, 347D3
King named chairwoman 6-29, 589A2

CONSUMER Product Safety Commission (CPSC)
Civil Svc rpt scores 1-12, Byington resigns 2-8, 185E2-A3
McDonald's glasses rptd safe 1-31, 348B1
Toy sharp-edge tests OKd 3-10, 264G3
Fluorocarbon aerosols banned 3-15, 186A2
Firecracker ban review refused by Sup Ct 3-27, 241C2
Chain saw industry to set safety rules 3-31, 348E1
Water toy recall set 4-13, 348F1
Carter backs reauthorizatn 4-27, 347F3
Benzene curbs voted 4-27, 348G1
Tris garment exports banned 5-5, 347A3
Cancer agent rules adopted 6-1, 702C3
Zagoria namd 9-29, confrmd 10-10, 831C3
'79 funding signed 9-30, 750F2-A3
Aluminum wire dispute refused by Sup Ct 10-2, 751E1
Small toys ban proposed 10-5, 769C3
Pittway OKs smoke detector fine 11-6, 942E1

CONTRACT Compliance Programs, Office of Federal—*See LABOR—Employment Standards Administration below*

CUSTOMS Service, U.S.—*See under TREASURY below*

DEBT, Public—*See under BUDGET in this section above*

DEFENSE, Department of—*See also ARMED Forces and specific branch in this section; also BROWN, Harold; for weapons, see ARMAMENTS under 'A'; for arms control, see DISARMAMENT under 'D'; for foreign defense issues, see country, region and organization names*
US overseas troops rptd up; table 1-2, 5B2

1979

Republicans
GOP conf held in Md 2-3-2-4, 86C1
Ct bars wage-guide contract denial 5-31, 399F3
Carter sees ldrs 6-7, 419D3
Labor '78 campaign gifts rptd 6-13, 595C1

Security and Cooperation in Europe, Commission on
US Helsinki compliance assessed 11-7, 980G3

Technology Assessment, Office of (OTA)
Auto use study issued 3-10, 187D3
Antibiotics in animal feed rptd risky 6-25, 734G3

CONRAIL—*See CONRAIL under 'C'*

CONSOLIDATED Rail Corp.—*See CONRAIL under 'C'*

CONSTITUTION—*See CONSTITUTION under 'C'*

CONSUMER Affairs Council
Created 9-26, 902B3

CONSUMER Product Safety Commission (CPSC)
Lawn mower safety rules adopted 1-25, 91E3
Voluntary hair dryer recall sought 4-19, 308D2
Hair dryer recall praised 5-17, 595E3
Small toy ban adopted 6-17, 596B2
Sears TV repair recall set 8-31, 903E1
Corning percolator recall set 9-4, 902D3
Formaldehyde-cancer link rptd 10-18, 971D1

CREDIT Union Administration, National
Automatic funds shift voided 4-20, 303B3

CUSTOMS Service, U.S.—*See under TREASURY below*

DEBT, Public—*See under BUDGET in this section above*

DEFENSE, Department of—*See also ARMED Forces and specific branch in this section; for foreign defense issues, see country, region and organization names*
Female mil personnel rise seen 1-2, 53G1
Rand Corp rpt on S Viet '75 collapse issued 1-7, 29E1
Sovt beam-weapon threat discounted 1-10, 53B1

1980

Republicans
State of Union rebuttal 1-28, 75C1
Carter budget spending cuts scored 3-14, 201G2
Reagan tax plan backed 6-25, 480A2
Reagan sees ldrs 11-18, 11-19, 880G2, 881D1

Technology Assessment, Office of (OTA)
Carter vetoes dioxins study 1-2, 17A3
MD oversupply rptd 4-17, 318C1

Veto Action
Veto provisn imposed on FTC 5-28, 702F3, G3
Debt limit; oil import fee bar res veto overridden 6-5, 6-6, 437A1
Oil import fee proposal dropped 6-19, 551D3
VA MD pay hike veto overriden 8-26, 649C3

CONSUMER Product Safety Commission (CPSC)
Freedom of Info ct order bar backed by Sup Ct 3-19, 250B1
Tris ban damage suit filed 3-24, 348E2
Asbestos use data ordrd 5-30, 703F2

COPYRIGHT Royalty Tribunal
Cable-TV distant signal, syndicatn limits lifted 7-22, 583G1
Fees divided 7-29, 640E2-A3

DEFENSE, Department of—*See also ARMED Forces and specific branch in this section; for foreign defense issues, see country, region and organization names*
Weakened pres powers scored 1-14, 32E1
Annual posture statemt backs mil mobility 1-29, 65E1
Textron improprieties alleged 1-31, Miller denies 2-1, 92D1, G1

1976

Rpt to Cong released 1-27, 68E1
Ford revises intelligence command 2-17, 127D1, E2
Currie, Middendorf censured 3-16, 200G2
Rumsfeld on business probe panel 3-21, 262F2
Sen intellignc com issues rpts, drug testing cited 4-26, 299A3, 300D2, A3, 301A3, 302E3-303B1, 304F2; 4-28, 325C2, D3, 326E2
Ellsworth confrmd asst secy 5-3, 412G1
Helsinki accords panel clears Cong 5-21, 392E3
West Pt honor code review seen 6-2, 394E3
Rep Young claims confidential mtgs held 6-11, 434A1
Cong extends Export Admin Act in prelim votes 8-27, 9-22, 746C2
Major contractrs rptd not on Arab boycott list 9-7, 747A1
Govt in sunshine bill signed 9-13, 688E3
Nixon chrgd re '74 sale to Iran 9-26, 979F3
Marine recruit suit rptd 10-8, 942E2
Helsinki panel tour barred 11-1, 880A2
Denies Sovt laser use vs satellite 11-23, 961A2
Proposes corp favors curbs 12-9, 982F3
Brown named secy, Duncan dep secy 12-21, 956G1, 957G1, 978F3
Amnesty Issue—*See under ARMED Forces in this section above*
Defense Intelligence Agency (DIA)
House com urges abolitn 2-10, 150B2
Spending data cited 3-7, 182B2
De Poix on Rockwell guest list 3-17, 200G3
Sen intellignc com rpts cite 4-26, 299D3, 300F1, 302G3-303A1; 4-28, 325D3
US foreign intelligence chart 304C1, A2 ★
Budget estimated 4-27, 299D3
Dem platform cites 6-15, 477C2
Finances—*See also 'Presidential Election' below*
Regional defns spending rptd 1-2, 60F3
GAO rpt scores contracting 1-11, 70F3-71C1
Muskie urges efficiency 1-21, 40D2
'77 budget proposals 1-21, 62A3, E3, 63F1, A2, D3
'77 budget proposals defended 1-27, 68D1
Rpt to Cong issued 1-27, 68F1
Navy fleet expansn rptd abandoned 1-27, 68E2
House OKs '76 funds, Angola amendmt 1-27, 69A1
Kissinger warns vs SALT talks breakdown 2-3, 88A3
OMB 'padding' memo stirs controversy 2-4, 115G3
Ford signs '76 fund appropriatns 2-10, 109A3
US, Sovt spending data publshd 2-27, challenged 3-5, 3-7, 182G1-E2
Lockheed overseas payoffs chrgd 2-29, 3-1, probe set 3-2, 200D2
Adams seeks reduced '77 budget; Cong reactn 3-23, 231C2, B3
Ford scores Cong Dems 3-26, vows funds cut veto 3-29, 231E3, 232A1
House Budget Com votes spending fund 3-31, 231B3
Cong coms set fscl '77 targets 4-1, 246D1
Decisn to pay shipyds rptd 4-8, 309A2
House OKs '77 arms authorizatn 4-9, 283G1
Manpower costs study issued 4-18, 309D1
More missile money asked 4-26, 307C3
Intellignc budgets estimated 4-27, 299D3
Rumsfeld asks '77 budget hike 5-4, 394B1
Shipyd overrun paymts disputed 5-4—6-10, 453D3
Cong OKs '77 budget target 5-12, 5-13; Ford, OMB, Cong estimates table 358E1, B2
Cong clears added funds 5-19, 411E3; signed 6-1, 982F1
Sen OKs '77 arms authorzn 5-26, 411B2
Mayors Conf scores spending 7-1, 493D1
Ford vetoes constructn bill 7-2, 517F3
Ford signs '77 arms authorizatn 7-14, 516F2, G2 ★
'77 arms request, authorizatn table 517B2
Constructn bill veto sustained 7-22, 533A3
Ford legis record cited 613F2, F3
Cong sets '77 budget levels, chart 9-16, 706B2
Cong OKs '77 construction authrzn 9-16, 745C2; signed 9-30, 982F1
'77 funds signed; tables 9-22, 706F3
Transition ¼ fed spending rptd down 10-27, 866C1
Korean bid-rigging chrgd 10-27, 982E2-A3
NE govs seek projects 11-14, 865A1
Arms cost estimate rptd hiked 11-16, 982C3
Top fiscal '76 contractors rptd 12-21, 961G2
National Security Agency
Budget estimated 4-27, 299D3
Sen intellignc com rpt cites 4-28, 325C2, D3, 326A2, 330C1
Presidential Election (& transition)
Ford focuses on defns issue 3-24—3-29, 231C3-232B1
Reagan says US '2d best' 3-31, 232F2
Ford: US mil strength 'unsurpassed' 4-2, 245G1

1977

Ford '78 budget request 1-17, 30B1, F2-31D1, 32B2, F2, 33G3
Annual posture statemt, '77-82 spending proposals; Rumsfeld urges buildup 1-18, 39C1
Brown on budget cuts 1-25, 1-26, 94E2
Carter for strong, lean force 2-2, 75B2
Carter flies in wartime command plane 2-11, 110E3
Carter plans Ford budget cut 2-12, 110D3
Carter budget revisns 2-22, 124B3, 125A1, B2
Brown rpts net worth 2-25, 147F3
Carter asks energy dept 3-1, 148C2
Carter visits, plans pensn study 3-1, 148F2; 193B3
Carter call-in on war powers 3-5, 171D1
Carter vows fund cuts 3-16, 190E3
Mil unionizatn threat seen 3-18—4-19, 342F3
Solitron contracts case review denied 3-21, 230G2
Chem warfare effort rptd 3-21, 232E1-A2
Giaimo proposes '78 budget 3-23, 228G3
Cook rptd on payroll 3-24, 236F1
Gay rights access promised 3-26, 278E2
NE-Midwest base closing ban asked 4-6, 423G2
Industry hiring of retirees rptd 4-12, 344C1
House OKs '78 arms bill 4-25, 323E3
Arms dvpt, procuremt consolidatn rptd 4-25, 343A3
Brown backs cutbacks 5-10—6-1, 420C3
NATO rpts spending, GNP data 5-17, 379F3
Cong sets '78 budget target 5-17, 404D3-405C1
Pentagon backs base closings 5-26, 420C3
USSR computer deal opposed 6-5, 469A3
Weapons, civil defns '78 authorizatn, employee ceiling, contract curbs clear Cong 7-14, 575D2, 576A2; signed 7-30, 592A2
FALN bombs NYC office 8-3, 613D3
Low-cost steel purchases ordrd 8-5, 612D1
New England job loss, Sunbelt gain rptd 8-10, 629D2
Submits '57 A-test witness list to CDC 8-31, 1022D3
Weapons, civil defns funds clear Cong 9-9, 704E2-B3
Weapons, civil defns funds signed 9-21, 834D1
Brookings study on defns buildup 9-26, 858A1
Panama Canal treaty drafting role rptd 9-27, 755B2
Korea lobbying '70 knowledge rptd 10-12, 816E3
Contractor gifts scored by Proxmire 10-24, 920C2
Brown orders budget process revamped 10-26, sees '79 cuts 11-6, 857F2-C3
'78 supplemtl authorizatn clears Cong 11-3, 856E1-A2; signed 12-20, 1001E2
Minuteman vulnerability admitted 11-6, 996E2
Arms contract competitn planned 11-21, 942E1
Midwest bases cited for pollutn 11-25, 944C2
Appointments
Brown confrmd secy 1-20, 34B1, D3
Duncan, dep secy confrmatn hearing 1-13, 34D3; confrmd 1-31, 148F3 ★
Murray confrmd asst secy 4-25, 418F1
Ross, asst secy 1-19, 52G3; confrmd 3-4, 211F1
Siemer confrmd gen counsel 4-25, 418G1
White confrmd asst secy 5-9, 418A2
Defense Intelligence Agency (DIA)
USSR defns advances held costly 6-30, 673D3
Sen Panama Canal wiretap probe subpoenas dir, postpones hearings 9-30, 756E1
National Reconnaissance Office (NRO)
CIA dir seeks control 6-10, 6-12, 576F2
CIA dir given new powers 8-4, 610A3
National Security Agency (NSA)
Carter asks tap curbs 5-18, 386B3
CIA dir seeks control 6-10, 6-12, 576F2
Sovt tap security rptd studied 7-10, 551B2
CIA dir given new powers 8-4, 610A3
Callimahos dies 10-28, 872D1
National War College
Brown '76 speech rptd 3-27, 232A1
Prisoners of War—*See ARMED Forces above*
Selective Service—*See separate listing below*
Uniformed Services University of the Health Sciences (Bethesda, Md.)
Funds bill signed 5-4, 339G1

1978

'73 pay raise veto review barred 1-9, 13B1
Mil pensn revisns proposed share of defns costs cited 1-11, 52G3
Carter budget proposals 1-23, 44E2, D3, G3-46B1; table 45D2
Federal budget dollar table 63A1
'48-62 A-test exposure monitoring scored, dept begins info search 1-24—2-27, 164F1
Textron Iran paymt info rptd 1-25, 2-17, 161E2
Forgn constructn exempt from US arms sales ceiling 2-1, 106E2, F2
Annual posture statemt: Brown urges arms buildup, $50 bln 5-yr spending hike 2-2, 81A1
10 top states in defns contracts rptd 2-21, 127C2
Carter OKs copper stockpile purchase 3-13, 177B3
Gen Dynamics warns work stoppage 3-13, temporary accord reached 3-23, 224C1, B3
Top 10 fscl '77 contractors rptd 3-28, 224D2
Litton A-sub overbilling case dismissal reversed 4-5, 368F1
Overseas schls included in Educ Dept proposal 4-14, 279D1
Sen budget target res voted 4-26, 305B3
Base closings, cutbacks proposed 4-26, 368C1
Random drug-use test oppositn rptd 4-28, 368G2-A3
Nazi war criminal link rptd 5-16, 411B1
Cong '79 budget target res cleared 5-17, 385D1, E1, B2, A3
Contracts exempt from purchasing controls 5-18, 405G1
Mil constructn authorizatn clears House 5-22, 406G3
Wis U computer research secrecy order lifted 6-12, 514C1
Civil defns reorganizatn concern rptd 6-20, 466G2
Brown affirms US mil superiority 6-23, 493D2
Recruitmt standards lowering urged 7-2, 528E3
Carter on security leaks 7-11, 524G2
'79 arms authrzn clears Sen 7-11, 526B2
Efficiency studies urge Joint Chiefs, mil roles increase 7-12, 528C2
Vet wins A-test cancer claim 8-1, 703A1
'79 funds, abortn curb pass House 8-9, 604B2, F2
Carter vetoes '79 arms authorizatn 8-17, 621A1, 622A1; House upholds 9-7, 677A2
Mil constructn funds clear Cong 8-21, 662C1
Carter asks 5.5% pay hike 8-31, 681D2
Manpower cost reforms urged, base surplus seen 9-5, 683A3
'79 funds, abortn curb signed 10-13, 833B1
Carter signs '79 revised arms authorzn 10-20, 833F1-A2
Energy Dept natl security authorzn signed 10-25, 833C2
Joint chiefs urges budget hike 10-30, 833C3
Taiwan mil personnel cut rptd 11-6, 872A3
Brown in S Korea 11-6—11-8, joint cmnd set 11-7; in Japan 11-7, Japan to pay more for US forces 11-9, 872B3-E3
Brown rpts USSR Pacific buildup 11-9, 914F1
Measles, rubella immunizatn asked 11-10, 927C3
'80 budget hike seen 11-15, oppositn rptd 11-18, 895A2
'79 suplmtl budget request rptd 11-15, 916C3
Carter to study budget 11-27, 914E3
Carter budget plans, inflatn linked 11-28, 980F1
Carter discusses US policy 11-30, 916F2-B3
Mobilization ability scored 12-3, 984B1
Kennedy, Admin debate budget plans at Dem midterm conf 12-9, 12-10, 956C2-B3
Carter defends budget plans 12-12, 956G3
Carter defends budget plans, 2 cong ldrs score 12-14, 979F2-980A1
Mil pensn reform urged 12-14, 1009C2
Arms sales talks rift rptd 12-19, 996F3
Armed Forces Policy Council
Defns study urges larger role 7-12, 528A3
Defense Civil Preparedness Agency
Carter proposes new emergency agency 6-19, 466E2-B3
New natl plan disclosed 11-12, 895F1
Defense Intelligence Agency (DIA)
USSR civil defns threat seen 2-17, 127B1
New USSR A-bomber rptd 6-19, 518E3
Defense Systems Acquisition Review Council
Joint Chiefs role urged 7-12, 528F2
Joint Chiefs of Staff—*See separate listing below*
National Reconnaissance Office (NRO)
Carter reorganizes intell units 1-24, 49F2
National Security Agency (NSA)
Carter reorganizes intell units 1-24, 49F2
Intell legis introduced in Sen 2-9, 107C1
FBI '71 Korea lobbying info rptd 3-22, 203G2
House exempts from warrantless tap curbs 9-7, 696F3, 697D1
WWII documts on Ger, Japanese decoded messages issued 9-10—9-18, 744D2-G3

1979

A-target chng urged 1-13, 52A3
'Sexist' language review conducted 1-19, 89D3
Carter State of Union Message 1-23, 47B1, D2, 48A1
House panel blames for Iran failure 1-24, 67F2
Annual posture statemt stresses Sovt threat 1-25, 52C2
'57 A-test radiatn level revised 2-1, 91F1
Brown urges response to Sovt surrogates 2-8, 89B2
Kerr-McGee OKs jet fuel refund 2-8, 113B1
Cuba gets Sovt sub, torpedo boats 2-10, 109B3
'78 4th ¼ volunteer shortage rptd 2-13, 130G2
Brown sees US defns of Mideast interests 2-25; remarks clarified 2-26, 2-27, 143D3-144B1
Saudi rejcts base proposal 2-26, 143F2
Boeing missile info leak alleged 3-1, 207D2
N Yemen adviser role set 3-12, 178B3
US intell on China-Viet war praised 3-25, 231G3
Base closings announced 3-29, 265D3
USSR Indian O naval activity rise rptd 4-12, 4-16, 313E3-314A1
Brown disputes SALT missile verificatn gap 4-17, 279E2
Reverse Freedom of Info suits curbed by Sup Ct 4-18, 345E3
XM-1 tank productn OKd 5-8, 386D1
Carter orders gas allocatn cut 5-16, 361A2
Pension reforms proposed 7-19, 628E1
Duncan named Energy secy 7-20, 529D1
Racism in military seen 7-23, 561B3; Navy progrm launched 8-29, 664E2
Claytor confrmd dep secy 7-27, 577D1
Top 10 fscl '78 contractors rptd 8-1, 609A1
Coastal sea claim challenges ordered 8-10, 646G1
Army recruiting fraud probed 8-19, 649F2
Volunteer shortage rptd 8-20, 649A2
Army reserve recruiting failure rptd 8-23, 649B3
NRA gun resale suit lost 9-4, 747F1
MX missile mobility claimed 9-7, 678G2
Draft registratn defeated by House; cover-up re volunteer mil failure chrgd 9-12, 724A3
Ft Dix to stay open 10-10, 809D1
Army recruiting fraud probe expands 10-15, 850B2
'79 enlistment gap rptd; draft rejctd, pay boost seen 10-25, 11-13, 903B3-F3
Baker decries US decline 11-2, 983E1
False A-war alert placed 11-9, USSR scores 11-10, 869F2-B3
Drug abuse progrm lag rptd 11-11, 972E3
Female combat role urged 11-13, Westmoreland vs 11-14, 868D2
Reagan firm on defns 11-14, 982C1
Connally campaign themes cited 11-15, 983A1
Iran assets estimate hiked 11-19, 880B1
Viet troops Agent Orange exposure rptd 11-24, 904C2
Panama Canal comm apptmt delayed, treaties violatn chrgd 12-6, 939C1
Defense Intelligence Agency (DIA)
Viet collaborators rptd 2-5, 112E2-A3
USSR trade seen as mil aid 11-8, 856E3-857D1
Defense Systems Management College
Freeman named GSA head 3-23, 232D2
Finances
Women's unit attacks budget 1-12, 30E2
Carter vs proposed balanced budget amendmt 1-17, 29D2
Carter budget proposals 1-22, 41B2, 42C1-43G2; tables 42A1, D2
Federal budget dollar table 42A1
GOP chrmn backs budget proposal 1-24, 48A2
Jones backs budget hike 1-25, 52C2
Carter defends budget plans 1-26, 70A1
Sen OKs '80 arms authrzn 6-13, 435A1, 438E1
Jt Chiefs, Nunn, Amer Legion back budget, SALT linkage, Vance reaffirms budget hike vow 7-24—8-22, 643C3-644D1
Carter vs budget, SALT linkage 7-27; Kissinger backs 7-31, 8-2; US sens react 8-2, 8-3, 590G2-591D1
Carter seeks budget hike 9-11, 678D1
Ford scores Carter cuts 9-26, Brzezinski rebuts 9-27, 739E2, A3
E Coast oil refinery backed 10-4, 770D1
'77 mil spending total rptd 10-13, 804F1
Brown backs spending limit 11-8, 847G2
Mil spending inequities rptd 11-18, 904E1
'80 mil constructn funds signed 11-30, 945F1
'Quick-strike' force appropriatns rptd 12-5, 923G3
Joint Chiefs of Staff—*See separate listing below*
National Security Agency (NSA)
CIA UFO probe detailed 1-12, 93B1

1980

Computer warning system rptd unreliable 3-10, 210B2
USOC boycott talks rptd 3-21, 258C3
Cuban role in El Salvador chrgd 3-27, 220C2
Mobil awarded jet fuel contract 4-1, 248C2
WWII WAACs get vet status 4-2, 267A3
Pentagon A-protest held 4-28, 441G1
Iran rescue missn rpt issued 5-7, 337G2
Top 10 fscl '79 contractors rptd 5-28, 403C1
Computer errors trigger A-alerts 6-3, 6-6, failed component blamed 6-17; Brown discounts war 6-9, valid warnings detailed 6-15, 457C3-458C2
Sen com study on Iran missn scored 6-5, 419F1
Recruiters to stress unemploymt 6-11, 458C2
'79 recruits mental standards down 7-31, 598C1
A-war strategy revised 8-5, 592A1
Brown reassures allies on A-strategy shift, Muskie not consulted 8-8; Sovts score 8-11, 615D2-616B1
A-strategy outlined 8-20, 630D1
'Stealth' fighter said to evade radar 8-20, 630B2
Iran rescue missn final rpt issued, counterterrorist unit proposed 8-23, 644B1
Reagan scores 'stealth' plane disclosure; Brown, Perry testify on leaks 9-4, 665E3
Nicaragua aid released 9-12, 709G2
Ark A-missile silo blast kills 1 9-19, warhead removed 9-22, 765E1, B3
Brown scores Dutch, Danish mil spending 10-3, 737D1
Computer error A-alert rpt issued by Sen com 10-29, 986B3
O'Neill vows Dem cooperatn 12-8, 936F2
Schering settles job bias case 12-14, 962F3
Allen gets liaison role 12-23, 980B2
Bases, Military—*See also base names*
Egypt, Israel offer bases 1-4, Egypt renews offer 1-7; US refuses, to seek bases in Oman, Kenya, Somalia 1-9, 11E1-A2
Turkey accord set 1-9, 22G2; signed 3-29, 255A3
Oman talks rptd 1-22, 46E1
Kenya pres in US 2-20—2-22, 142B2
Oman, Kenya pacts set; Somalia talks snagged 4-21, 303A1
Oman pact formally agreed 6-4, 436D3
Israel constructn lags 6-12, 498B3
Diego Garcia base scored by OAU 7-1—7-4, 509G1
Somali base pact signed 8-21, 645B3
Somali pact scored by House subcom 8-28, 661B3
Somali mil pact testimony 9-16; House subcom chrmn briefed 9-30, 735E3, F3
Zimbabwe scores Somali bases 10-9, 795C1
USSR, India vs Diego Garcia base 12-11, 930D2
Defense Intelligence Agency (DIA)
Oversight bill voted by Sen 6-3, 458B3
400 US bodies rptd found in Hanoi 6-27, 508A3
'79 Sovt anthrax cover-up chrgd 6-29, 500C1
'79 A-blast off S Africa disputed 7-14, 548E2
Iran invasn plan discounted, Sovt interventn feared 8-25, 644G1
Finances
Carter State of Union proposals 1-21, 1-23, 42A3, 43F3
Urban League notes concern 1-22, 94C2
Copper futures trading limited 1-24, 69D1
Carter budget proposals 1-28, 69C3, 70B2-71E2; tables 69G3, 70D1
GOP backs Carter spending hike plans 1-28, 75E1
Black Caucus vs Carter budget 2-5, 94F2
Carter revised budget proposals 3-31, 244A1
GOP budget proposed 4-1, 244G1
'80 spending cut rptd 4-17, 330D1
Natl Guard seeks more funds 5-7, 369F3
Carter scores Cong '81 budget res 5-27, backs own proposal 5-28; Joint Chiefs assail 5-29, 424C1-G2
House rejcts '81 budget res 5-29, 424G2
'81 budget res clears Cong 6-12, 452C1
Evangelicals back spending hike 7-11—9-15, 819B1
'81 arms, mil pay authrzn signed 9-8, 764F3
Mil benefits authrzn signed 9-8, 765C1
House OKs '81 defns appropriatn; mil pay, benefits amendmts 9-16, 741A3
'81 final budget res clears Cong 11-20, 896E2
Sen OKs '81 appropriatn 11-21, 896A3
'81 appropriatn clears Cong 12-5, 935G2; signed 12-15, 982B1
National Security Agency (NSA)
Salisbury sues US 4-10, 459F1
Fonda-Hayden files case refused by Sup Ct 5-12, 426A3
Oversight bill voted by Sen 6-3, 458C3
Presidential Election (& Transition)
GOP debate in Ia 1-5, 4G2
GOP platform proposals 1-15, 32B2
Reagan seeks rearmamt 1-29, 91D3
GOP debate natl defns in NH 2-20, 129G2, D3
Connally 'basic speech' excerpts 3-7, 184C2
Kennedy 'basic speech' excerpts 3-10, 183B1, A2

1976

Ford, Reagan exchng chrgs 4-9—4-21, 280F3-281C3
Ford scores Reagan 4-28—5-2, 323G2, E3
Dem platform priority item 5-20, 357A3
Dem platform urges cuts 6-15, 432E3; text 476A1-C1, 477A1-C1
Ford's son cites budget 7-10, 513C3
Mondale legis record cited 512G3
Carter briefed 7-26, 551C1
Carter plans stockpiling review 7-28, 551A1
Reagan urges strong platform plank 8-8, 583C1
GOP platform com OKs plank 8-13, 582A3
Conv delegates' views rptd 8-17, 616A3
GOP platform text 8-18, 602E1, B2, 608D2, D3, F3, 610D2
Ford acceptance speech 8-19, 611E3
Ford legis record cited 613F2, F3
Carter addresses Amer Legion 8-24, 631F3
Ford urges as debate topic 8-24, 632G3
Connally scores Carter 8-27, 645B1
Ford, Carter TV debate set 9-1, 644B1
Ford stresses preparedness 9-1, 645G1
Dole stresses strength 9-1, 645F3
Carter, Ford exchanges 9-9, 664F3, 665B2
Carter stresses 9-13, 686E2
Ford stresses record budget 9-17, 9-22, 704C1
Ford campaign theme 9-25, 9-26, 723A3
Carter sees Schlesinger 10-3, 743E1
Dole scores Carter 10-4, 10-5, 743F1-B2
Ford, Carter debate 10-6, 740D2, C3, G3, 741C1, F1, 742F2
Ford stresses, scores Carter 10-7, 10-9, 763A2, C2
Dole, Mondale debate 10-15, 783G1
Carter vs Ford chrgs 10-15; Ford replies 10-16, 785D1
Ford, Carter debate 10-22, 800B1
Ford stresses 10-23—10-26, 802G3-803C1
Dole hits Carter stand 10-30, 827F2
Carter sees Rumsfeld 11-22, 881D1
Carter names liaison 11-23, 881A3
Carter visits Pentagon 12-10, 938A1
Brown named secy, Duncan dep secy 12-21, 956G1, 978F3
Carter, Brown on cuts 12-28, 12-29, 978D1
Reserve Forces—*See under ARMED Forces in this section above*
Selective Service—*See separate listing below*
Troop Issues—*See under ARMED Forces in this section above; also 'Force Reduction Talks' under EUROPE*
Volunteer Armed Forces—*See under ARMED Forces in this section above*

1977

1978

Warrantless tap curb exemptn signed 10-25, 863B1
Selective Service—*See separate listing below*

1979

WWII secret files released 2-3, 2-6, 93F1
Wiretap ct judges named 5-18, 442B3
Upheld on withholding data 10-29, 945C3
Selective Service—*See separate listing below*

1980

Citizens' Party seeks spending cut 4-13, 288D3
Reagan sets up panel 4-20, 304C3
Carter cites spending rise 5-29, 423E3
Reagan wants to rebuild 5-29, 424A1
Dem platform drafted 6-24, 479F3
GOP drafts platform 7-10, 506B3
Ford, Kissinger score Carter 7-14, 7-15, 534F2, E3
GOP platform adopted; text 7-15, 536D1, D2
Reagan accepts nominatn 7-17, 531D1, 532A1, 533B1
Carter accepts renominatn 8-14, 613A2
Reagan urges strength 8-18, 8-20, 629A1
Anderson presents views 8-19, 629F3
Carter vows spending growth, defends A-strategy shift 8-21, 629D2-A3
Carter attacks Reagan 8-22, 646F2
Anderson platform offered 8-30, 665A2
Carter backs gradual spending hike 9-2, 664C3
Reagan scores 'stealth' plane disclosure 9-4, 665E3
Reagan plans budget hike 9-9, 699A2
Reagan, Anderson TV debate 9-21, 721E2, 722A1
Reagan scores weakness 9-24, 723A1
Bush stresses strength 9-24, 781D1
Carter attacks Reagan 10-9—10-14, 778D2, G2, D3, 779A2
Reagan stresses peace thru strength 10-19—10-20, 801F2-802D1
Carter claims mil prepared 10-24, 816A3
Carter, Reagan TV debate 10-28, 813B1, A2, C2-814A1, B3, 815G2, D3
Anderson answered TV debate questns 10-28, 815G3
Libertarian candidate cites stance 10-28, 818G2
Weinberger named secy 12-11, 935A1

1976

DEFENSE Intelligence Agency—*See under DEFENSE, Department of, above*
DEFENSE Manpower Commission
Study issued 4-18, 309C1
DISEASE Control, Center for—*See under PUBLIC Health Service below*
DRUG Abuse, National Institute on—*See 'Alcohol, Drug Abuse & Mental Health Administration' under PUBLIC Health Service below*
DRUG Abuse Policy, Office of
Established 3-19, 233D3
DRUG Enforcement Administration—*See under JUSTICE below*
ECONOMIC Advisers, President's Council of (CEA)—*See also GREENSPAN, Alan*
'76 rpt urges moderate recovery pace 1-26, 66G2, 67E1; text excerpts 67A1
On '75 trade surplus 1-27, 91E1
Greenspan sees recovery pause 8-30, 647F1
Schultze designated chrmn 12-16, 936A3
EDUCATION, Office of—*See under HEALTH, Education & Welfare below*
ELECTORAL College
Votes 12-13, 979A1

1977

DEFENSE Intelligence Agency (DIA)—*See under DEFENSE above*
DEPARTMENTS & Agencies—*See EXECUTIVE Branch and specific department headings in this section*
DISEASE Control, Center for—*See under PUBLIC Health Service below*
DOMESTIC Council
Carter proposes abolitn 7-15, 556C1
DOMESTIC Policy Staff
Carter proposes creatn 7-15, 555F3
DROUGHT Coordinating Committee, Interagency
Loomis rpts drought impact 7-28, 659D3
DRUG Abuse, National Institute on (NIDA)—*See PUBLIC Health Service—Alcohol, Drug Abuse & Mental Health below*
DRUG Abuse Policy, Office of
Bourne on pot decriminalizatn 3-14, 332G1
Carter proposes abolitn 7-15, 556B1
DRUG Enforcement Administration—*See under JUSTICE below*
ECONOMIC Advisers, President's Council of (CEA)
Econ rpt to Cong 1-18, 35E3
Revises Dec '76 jobless rate 1-18, 37F3
Gramley, Nordhaus named 1-18, 52E3
Schultze confrmd chrmn 1-20, 34B1, 35A1; sworn 1-23, 52E2
Schultze at Carter plan hearings 1-27, 52A1, 89C2
Schultze rpts net worth 2-25, 148D1
Carter submits reorganizatn plan 7-15, 556D1
Schultze scores steel price hikes 7-21, 577B1
ECONOMIC Development Administration—*See under COMMERCE above*
ECONOMIC Opportunity Council
Carter proposes abolitn 7-15, 556C1
ECONOMIC Policy Board, President's
Carter submits reorganizatn plan 7-15, 556C1
ECONOMIC Policy Group
Schultze quits as co-chrmn 3-15, 211A2
EDUCATION, Office of—*See under HEALTH, Education and Welfare below*
EDUCATIONAL and Cultural Affairs, Bureau of—*See under STATE in this section below*
ELECTORAL College
Cong declares Carter pres 1-6, 14F2
Carter asks abolitn 3-22, 210C2, G2

1978

DEFENSE Civil Preparedness Agency—*See under DEFENSE in this section above*
DEFENSE Intelligence Agency (DIA)—*See under DEFENSE in this section above*
DEFENSE Systems Acquisition Review Council—*See under DEFENSE in this section above*
DEPARTMENTS & Agencies—*See EXECUTIVE Branch and specific department headings in this section*
DISEASE Control, Center for—*See under PUBLIC Health Service below*
DRUG Abuse, National Institute on (NIDA)—*See PUBLIC Health Service—Alcohol, Drug Abuse & Mental Health Administration below*
DRUG Enforcement Administration—*See under JUSTICE below*
DRUGS, Bureau of—*See FOOD & Drug Administration below*
ECONOMIC Advisers, Council of
Carter cites inflatn impact rpts 4-11, 259E3
Tax-cut plan scaled back 5-12, 361C1
EPA cuts back air rules 6-13, 512B3
Cotton dust rules issued 6-19, 471D3, G3
Natl health plan delay urged 6-26, 491F2
'78, '79 econ forecast revised 7-6, 506D2
Schultze named to labor-pact panel 8-7, 624D2
Chrmn to sit on Endangered Species Com 10-15, 834E2; 11-10, 1003B1
St Louis forum on Carter wage-price plan 11-1, 863G2-C3
Schultze scores VAT proposal 12-3, 962D2
Schultze on OPEC price hike impact 12-17, 978C1
EDUCATION, Office of—*See under HEALTH, Education & Welfare below*
EMPLOYMENT Standards Administration—*See under LABOR below*
ENDANGERED Species Committee
Created 10-15, 834E2

1979

DEFENSE Intelligence Agency—*See under DEFENSE in this section above*
DEFENSE Systems Management College—*See under DEFENSE in this section above*
DEPARTMENTS & Agencies—*See EXECUTIVE Branch and specific department headings in this section*
DISEASE Control, Center for—*See under PUBLIC Health Service below*
DRUG Abuse, National Institute on—*See PUBLIC Health Service–Alcohol, Drug Abuse & Mental Health Administration*
DRUG Abuse, Strategy Council on
Marijuana use rptd 5-21, 492G2
DRUG Enforcement Administration—*See under JUSTICE below*
ECONOMIC Advisers, Council of (CEA)
'79 econ activity forecast, '78 data cited 1-25, 48D2, A3
Miller, Rivlin vs '79 econ forecasts 1-25, 48E3
Productivity forecast cited 2-9, 111B1
Schultze backs hosp cost-control bill 3-9, 194B3
Schultze warns rubber industry on wage-guide compliance 4-20, 345A1
Schultze defends wage hike limit 5-10, 362D2
EDUCATION, Department of
Created 10-17, 782A2
Hufstedler named secy 10-30, 829F1; confrmd 11-30, sworn 12-6, 946F2
Libraries stressed at White House conf 11-15–11-19, 901B1, G1 905G2-A3
EDUCATION, Office of—*See under HEALTH, Education & Welfare below*
ELECTORAL College
Sen rejects bid to end 7-10, 514G3-515D1

1980

DEPOSITORY Institutions Deregulation Committee (DIDC)
Bank gift ban proposed 5-6, oppositn rptd 7-18, 560E3
New interest rates set 5-28, S&Ls challenge 6-16, 516B3
New acct gift rules tightened, finder's fees banned 9-9, 986E1
ECONOMIC Advisers, Council of (CEA)
'79 hourly productn drop cited 1-25, 75C3
Schultze on budget recessn forecast 1-28, 69C2
'80 econ activity forecast, '79 data cited 1-30, 74C1, A2
Schultze on Feb producer price rise 3-7, 182D2
Schultze on May producer price index 6-6, 437E3
Schultze sees Dems re taxes 6-26, 480C3
Dem platform plank adopted 8-13, 614C2
ECONOMIC Development Administration (EDA)—*See under COMMERCE in this section above*
ECONOMIC Revitalization Board
Created; Shapiro, Kirkland named co chrmn 8-28, 663C2
EDUCATION, Department of
Transition aides named 1-9, 18B2
$2 bln youth training progrm asked 1-10, 16B2
Carter budget proposals 1-28, 72D3
Operation begins 5-4, Hufstedler outlines policy 5-7, 369G3
Reagan deplores 'federalized' role 10-13, 780A1
Scientific literacy study issued 10-22, 990G1
Faculty sex-bias Title IX case accepted by Sup Ct 12-1, 918C2
EDUCATION, Office of—*See HEALTH, Education & Welfare, Department of in this section*
ELECTORAL College
Votes 12-15, 956F1

1976

ENERGY Research and Development Administration (ERDA)
OKs fast breeder dvpt 1-2, 115F2
'77 budget proposals 1-21, 64E2
A-plant growth down 63% 1-22, 115C2
Rpts on Chinese A-test 1-24, 83E3
Rpts A-tests 2-13—3-17, 243A1
'45-47 plutonium tests confrmd 2-22, 272B3
Confrms AEC prisoners tests 2-28, 316B2

1977

ENERGY, Department of
Created, Schlesinger confrmd secy 8-4, 591C2
Alcan-El Paso gas price estimates released 9-8, 687A2
Spent A-fuel storage by govt backed 10-18, 794C2
Loan guarantee authorizatn OKd by Cong 10-20, 833A2
Winter fuel-shortage plan announced 12-1, 942A3

1978

ENERGY, Department of
GAO oil import study warning 1-3, 6B1
Exxon cited again for overchrgs 1-10, 1-11, 14B2
Oil firm rebates to consumers barred 1-20, 108F3, 109A1
Budget proposals 1-23, 46E1
Critical coal shortage faced by 9 states 2-11, 104D1
Schlesinger sees govs on policy 2-26, 144G3

1979

ENERGY, Department of
Nev A-waste storage studied 1-5, 54D3
A-test cancer link rptd ignored in '65 1-8, 17E2
USSR, US A-tests rptd 1-17, 1-24, 52D1
Carter budget proposals 1-22, 45B2
2 unions ask HEW radiatn safety studies 1-30, 90E3
Schlesinger terms Iran oil crisis serious 2-7, 82F2-B3

1980

ENERGY, Department of
Alcan pipeline sectn OKd 1-10, 56G3
Tenn A-fuel plant reopens 1-16, 54C1
Carter budget proposals 1-28, 72B1
Standard Oil settles price case 2-14; 190C1
Island territories get econ plan 2-14; govs meet, set projects 2-19—2-22, 495A1
Canada gas sales blocked 2-19, ban delayed 2-20, 191F3

1976

Johnson named to CAB 3-22, 232E1
Hirsch confrmd asst admin 3-23, 232E1
Policy rpt focuses on conservatn 4-19, 284E3
US forgn intelligence chart 304A2 ★ , C2
Cong clears '77 authorizatn 6-29, Ford signs 7-12, 517E1
'77 funds signed 7-31, 623D1
Seamans scores GAO synfuel rpt 8-24, 649D2
Joint UK A-test 8-26, 663D3
Rpt calls A-waste cntrs major hazard 9-7, 671B1
Carter proposes Cabt-level dept 9-21, 704E2
Ford, Carter debate 9-23, 702A3
Auto research veto sustained 9-29, 745G3
Rpts China A-test fallout 10-5, 791A1
China computer sale confrmd 10-28, 832A3
Rpts on new China A-blast 11-17, 871G3

ENERGY Resources Council
Carter proposes Cabt-level dept 9-21, 704F2

ENGINEERS, Corps of—*See under ARMY above*

1977

Carter LNG policy faulted by GAO 12-12, 962C2
Exxon laser uranium enrichmt results classified 12-14, 975A2
Exxon overchrg claimed 12-27, 1008C2
Federal Energy Regulatory Commission—*See separate listing below*

ENERGY Research & Development Administration (ERDA)
Ford proposes energy dept 1-11, 14E3
Sludge-gasificatn test set 2-3, 278E1
Carter budget revisions 2-22, 125D2
Carter submits reorganizatn bill 3-1, 148G1, B2
New coal-burning process set 3-4, 278C1
Solar lab to open in Colo 3-24, 278F1
Clinch R A-projct curbed 4-7, 267F3
Coal-climate study rptd 4-30, 499A2
Sen votes energy dept 5-18, 405G1
Fire threatens Los Alamos lab 6-18, 660F3
Carter defers neutron bomb decisn 7-12, 533B2, 534A3
'78 A-funds clear Cong 7-25, 592F2; signed 8-8, 609D2
'78 non-nuclear funds signed 7-26, 592E3
Energy Dept to absorb 8-4, 591E2
A-material rptd missing 8-4, 8-8, 717E1
Reprocessed A-fuel bomb use rptd 9-14, 812D2-B3
House OKs Clinch R projct 9-20, 758D2
Spent A-fuel storage problems rptd 9-23, 794C2

ENERGY Resources Council
Carter proposes abolitn 7-15, 556C1

ENGINEERS, Corps of—*See under ARMY above*

1978

Cancer-radiatn probe bar chrgd 2-28, 164C3, D3
A-waste study backs rock storage 3-15, 183A3
Clinch R A-breeder compromise proposal rptd 3-17, 3-23, 241F3
Black-mkt uranium sale bid probed 3-19, 242F2
Coal industry study planned 3-25, 217A2
Environmtal Cncl rpt backs solar energy 4-12, 281G3
Low-fallout (RRR) bomb study rptd 4-30, 407G1
Annual rpt forecasts consumptn, imports 5-8, 366A2
Oil lobbyist's influence scored 5-15, 408E2-C3
Schlesinger sees reduced oil supplies, plans E Coast aid; renews uranium contracts, favors other measures 5-26, 407E3-408A2
Exxon sued for overchrg 6-8, 450A3
Neutron bomb stockpile urged by Sen com 6-11, 469B3
Schlesinger sets new oil rules for Calif, E Coast aid 6-15, 470B3-471B1
Standby gas ration plan offered 6-22, 511F1
Sen votes bar to oil import fees, quota option noted 6-27, 511E3
Appliance energy-cost labels OKd 6-28, 702B3
Arco, Getty, Shell price violatns chrgd 7-2, 8-4, 610A2
Ashland $52.1 mln refund sought 7-12, 610B3
'75-77 sex bias admitted 7-14, 1006A3
Coal conversn bill clears Sen 7-18, 550B1
Amoco '73-76 overchrgs alleged 7-21, 610C3
Conoco criminal pricing probe rptd 7-21, ex-offcl pleads no-contest 8-9, 610D3
Gulf settles overchrg claim 7-27, 610F2
GAO LNG study scored 7-31, 610A2
Fusn research advance rptd 8-12, 653F2
Oil reserve storage plans scored by GAO 8-16, 701A3
Japan joint energy research planned 9-6, 695B3 ★
Emergency plans faulted in internal study 9-11, 701B2-A3
Coal-fired power plant scrubber installatn proposed 9-11, 703A2
Public works veto upheld 10-5, 765E1
Energy pkg clears Cong 10-15, 787F1, A2
Natl security progrm authorzn signed 10-25, 833C2
Iran oil strike monitored 10-31, 827E2
Exxon gas overchrg suit filed 11-1, 900D1
'77 world fallout rise rptd, '76 China A-test linked 11-5, 1000G3
Energy bill signed, Schlesinger sees '79 proposals 11-9, 873C1
New fuel rules unveiled 11-15, 919F3-920B1
NM A-waste burial planned 11-15, 961E2
EPA fuel tests questioned 11-21, 939C2
2 oil cos begin gas rationing 12-1, 3 more seek OK 12-3; artificial shortage discounted 12-4, 939C1
Pa coal-gas conversn plant closed 12-1, 962G3-963A1
Analysts cautious on new solar cell 12-1, 983C2
House subcom staff rpt scores oil price fraud inactn, urges FBI probe 12-10, 983A3-E3
Carter vows actn vs oil industry abuses 12-12, 983E2
'75-76 oil pricing cost pass-on upheld 12-13, 983F2
Jet fuel shortage feared 12-14, 983G3-984B1
Chinese A-test rptd 12-14, 1001A2
Gas, fuel oil '79 price hike seen 12-18, 978B2
Algerian natural gas pipe rejctd 12-18, 983E3
Nev A-test claims filed 12-21, 1011F3
Iran oil export drop rptd 12-26, 994A1
Federal Energy Regulatory Commission—*See separate listing below*

ENGINEERS, Corps of—*See under ARMY in this section above*

1979

More Nev A-test claims filed 2-23, 208C1
Schlesinger sees US defns of Mideast interests 2-25, remarks clarified 2-26, 2-27, 143F3-144B1
Oil conservatn powers asked 2-26, 145B3
Gasoline price controls eased 3-2, 162F1
Colo radium waste sites rptd 3-5, 187F1
GAO warns on higher oil prices, scores US conservatn efforts 3-7, 182D2
Judge blocks H-bomb article 3-9, 193B3-194A1; 3-26, 230D1; 6-15, 713C1
Schlesinger on record oil use, offers to quit post; US oil stocks drop cited 3-12, 183C2
Calif-Tex pipe canceled, Alaska oil swap seen 3-13, 183G1
Business rpts rule compliance costs 3-14, 230A3
Home-oil reserve ordrd 4-25, 300E1
A-power radiatn risks reviewed 5-2, 609A3
May gas supplies seen tightening 5-7, 342G3
Geothermal drilling starts 5-14, 362A1
Carter hikes Calif gas allocatn 5-16, 361F1
Diesel fuel shortage rptd 5-18, 361A3
Wood use for fuel rptd up 5-20, 419E1
Diesel fuel allocatn rules adopted 5-25, 395C2
Sohio Calif-Tex pipe cancellatn scored 5-25, 396A2
Retail gas price rise rptd 5-26, 395F3
No-lead gas output incentives set 6-4, 418B3, E3
Canada oil-sands study pact signed 6-4, 444D2
Md sues re gas allocatn 6-26, 479G1
O'Leary on heating oil supplies 6-29, 514E2
Sup Ct declines H-bomb article hearing 7-2, 559A1
O'Leary resigns 7-9; Schlesinger resignatn forecast 514A1
Carter orders temp controls 7-10, 514B2
Geothermal drilling said disappointing 7-14, 787B1
Oil spot mkt directive rptd 7-16, 494E2
Gas price rise OKd, other rules revised 7-16, 557F2
Schlesinger fired, Duncan named 7-20, 529C1, 530E1
Duncan confrmd 7-31, sworn 8-24, 623E1, 627A2
Schlesinger sees $40-a-barrel oil by '89 8-5, 629A2
Oil firms cleared of hoarding, Feb-May gas shortage detailed; probe to go on 8-6, 628B3
Solar cell silicon productn method rptd 8-27, 649C1
China power dvpt aid signed 8-28, 644C2
Duncan reassures Northeast govs on heating fuel 8-28, 703G1-C2
GAO rpts on '79 oil shortage 9-13, Duncan plans policy review 9-14, 702B3
H-bomb letter published 9-16, 9-18, Justice Dept ends article censorship 9-17, 713A1, B2; text of letter 714D1-717D3
New England energy mailing planned 9-17, 703F2
Calif LNG projct OKd 9-27, 769C2
E Coast oil refinery backed 10-4, 770C1
Heating fuel storage goal rptd met 10-11, 786B3
House OKs '80 authrzn bill 10-24, 848G3
'80 funds, $20 bln synfuel clears Cong 11-9, 883E1
Heavy oil exploitatn evaluated 11-26, 953E1
Carter signs '80 funds bill 11-27, 920B1
Mex gas imports approved 12-29, 996B3
Federal Energy Regulatory Commission—*See separate listing below*

Price Violations
Sun Co chrgd 1-3, 17D1
8 firms sued, '78 Exxon suit added 1-5, 17A1
Kerr-McGee OKs refund 2-8, 112G3
Gas price gouging drive starts 4-16, 301C2
150 violatns found 4-27, 324C3
7 oil firms accused 5-2, 343B2
Gulf cleared re Vepco overchrg 6-12, 580A3
Overchrg actions 7-19–10-25, 849B3
Mobil OKs refund 9-18, 849F3
Cities Svcs OKs penalties 11-1, 850C1
Mobil, 8 others accused 11-6, 849F2
Shell, 4 others accused 11-8; Amerada Hess, 3 others accused 905E2-A3
Chevron, Gulf, 6 others accused 11-18–12-11; Getty OKs setlmt 12-4, 943B1-A2
Mobil action said improper 12-4, 990B3
Gulf, Socal chrgd; other suits setld for $23 mln 12-10, 990G2
Amerada Hess, Mobil chrgd with $1.1 bln 12-13, 990G2
7 cos accused, '73-76 total violatns at $10 bln 12-19, 990E2

ENGINEERS, Corps of—*See under ARMY in this section above*

1980

Duncan in Saudi oil talks 3-1—3-4, US stockpiling stalled 3-5, 165B3
2d 1/4 gas use targets set, '80 consumptn drop 3-20, 250C3
Duncan rescinds Sohio price hike order 5-1, 366F1
Gasoline price case refused by Sup Ct 5-12, 426D2
G&W elec car dvpt reactn 6-9, 541E3
Duncan scores OPEC price hike 6-11, 435D3
Standby gas rationing plan submitted by Carter 6-12, 552A1
Alcohol fuel import oppositn rptd 6-18, 461G1
Appropriatn bill clears Cong 6-25, 9-10, signed 10-1, 803A2, F2
Alaska oil refiners payment plan rptd 7-7, 553D2
Oil cos absolved in '79 shortage 7-17, 552B1
ND synfuel plant loan OKd 7-18, 553B2
Duncan sees conservatn acceptance 7-24, 553D1
W Ger-Japan synfuel pact signed 7-31, 666D2
Aug oil imports show record drop; Jan-Aug decline rptd 9-6, 785A3
Sawhill named Synfuels Corp chrmn 9-10, Sen panel OKs 9-25, 699C1, 725D2
Duncan in secret Saudi oil talks 9-18, stockpiling rptd resumed 10-27, 826E1
Fusion dvpt bill clears Cong 9-24, signed 10-7, 981A3
Phillips, Sun oil price setlmts OKd 9-25, 9-26, 960E1
Sawhill Synfuels Corp confirmatn blocked 10-1, named to interim bd 10-5; resignatn effective 10-8, 786F2-A3
Coalitn sues over oil price setlmts 10-8, 960G1
ND synfuels plant gets $1.5 bln fed loan 11-19, ct blocks projct 12-8, 961E3
A-arms authrzn clears Cong 12-1, signed 12-17, 981B1
'81 appropriatn clears Cong 12-1, 954D2; signed 12-12, 982B1
Standard Oil price setlmt OKd 12-3, 960C1
Edwards named secy 12-22, 979G2, F3

1976

ENVIRONMENTAL Protection Agency (EPA)
Urges ban vs Concorde 1-5, 5C2
'77 budget proposals 1-21, 66D1
High cancer areas rptd 2-16, 224F3
Bans mercury pesticides 2-18, 137F1
NY sued on taxi emissns 2-20, 154C1
Train urges toxic chem law 2-26, 171F2
Curb on lead in gas upheld 3-19, 219D2
Fla wetlands dvpt rejctd 4-16, 284D3
NY clean-air plan upheld 4-26, 308B1
Rpts asbestos in 5 water supplies 4-30, 349F1
Allied Chem indicted 5-7, 349B1
Backs strip-mine rules 5-11, 359G2
Cong clears noise control funds 5-20, 412C1; signed 5-31, 982F1
Lifts mercury ban 5-31, 571C1
Sup Ct curbs A-waste powers 6-1, 414B3
NY shore pollutn probe begun 6-24, 454B3
Fed ct review of state air plans barred 6-25, 552D2
Bars NYC ocean sewage-dumping 7-23, 570F3
Eased clean-air rules OKd 8-2, 570E2
'77 funds signed 8-9, 623G1
Pesticide bill vetoed 8-13, 646F2
GOP platform text 8-18, 603B1
Standard air-quality index proposed 8-23, 671B2
Fuel-econ ratings, table 9-22, 766G1-770C2
Eases gas-lead deadlines 9-24, 767B3
Chrysler sued for $91 mln 9-27, 729F3
Toxic chem bill signed 10-12, 764F2
Train lauds NATO programs 10-16, 934D1
Aerosol curbs ordrd 10-19, 902A1
Solid waste office OKd 10-21, 833F2
Air policy OKs new plants 11-10, 869A1
Rpts air quality improvemt 12-8, 943A1
Orders big Chrysler recall 12-10, 942D3
On Velsicol poisoning 12-14, 950E2
Train on Nantucket oil spill 12-22, 968E3
Coyote-poison ban kept 12-23, 980C2
Links China A-blast, thyroid cancer 12-27, 992F1

ENVIRONMENTAL Quality, Council on
Rpt to Cong, summary 2-27, 171G1
Backs strip-mine rules 5-11, 359G2
Standard air-quality index proposed 8-23, 671B2

EQUAL Employment Opportunity Commission (EEOC)
GE suit upheld, probe powers extended 1-23, 70C3
Boston schl admins quota set 2-24, 202G3
Leach confrmd member 3-3, 186A2
Merrill Lynch files consent 6-4, 414E1
Cited in Dem platform text 6-15, 470A1
'77 funds signed 7-14, 534D2
NY constructn union bias baned 9-1, 943F3
Vs new exam-bias rules 11-17, 884C2, G2
Case backlog rptd cut 11-19, 922C1
Sup Ct vs mandatory pregnancy benefits 12-7, 919A1
Sup Ct refuses racial, ethnic rptg appeal 12-13, 960C3
Sup Ct rules re complaint deadline 12-20, 959F3

1977

ENVIRONMENTAL Protection Agency (EPA)
Sets curbs on 5 toxic chems 1-3, 95A2
Ford '78 budget requests 1-17, 31C3
Bars PCB dischrg into waters 1-19, 95E1
Orders Ford halt productn 2-8, 113B1
Sup Ct upholds water pollutn curbs 2-23, 150D2
Cong sets new budget levels 3-3, 174D1
Blum confrmd dep admin 3-4, 211D1
Costle confrmd admin 3-4, 211E1
DNA research regulatn backed 3-8, 184B3
FMC plant shut 3-9, pact agreed 3-15, 196B3-E3
Scientists' rpt critical 3-21, 252B2
Cadillac recall ordrd 3-22, 252A3
Fluorocarbon ban planned 3-22, 323A2
NRC halts NH A-plant constructn 3-31, 344D3
US water rights in Calif upheld 4-4, 253D1
Admin auto, air pollutn views rptd 4-18, 322F2
Water pollutn control deadline upheld 4-18, 342B1
Sup Ct remands appeals cases 5-2, 406E2
Detroit sued on water pollutn 5-6, 422E2
Fluorocarbon ban proposed 5-11, 387F1
Free car-repair svc asked 5-13, 422G2
Carter message to Cong 5-23, 404D2
House weakens '70 Clean Air Act 5-26, 418F2
Sen amends '70 Clean Air Act 6-10, 461D1
US Steel settles 2 cases 6-16, 461E1
NH A-plant cooling system OKd 6-17, 498D2
Stresses water cleanup deadline 6-21, 483B3
Jorling confrmd asst admin 6-21, 626F2
McDonald's glass tests rptd, promotn halted 7-8—7-17, 560A1
NH A-plant constructn OKd 7-26, 702C2
Amended Clean Air Act clears Cong 8-4, Carter signs 8-8, 610E2
LA sewage dischrg suit filed 8-12, 724C1
Chrysler suit dismissed 8-22, 723E3
Bus, truck exhaust rules set 9-5, 739D3
DBCP curbed 9-8, 723F2
GM unveils diesel Olds 9-13, 722G3
Car fuel-econ ratings issued 9-19, 723B3
LI ocean dumping unheld 9-19, 723G3
Fed facility violatns rptd 9-19, EPA warns 10-20, 800A2
Sup Ct remands air quality cases 10-3, 760G2
'78 funds signed 10-4, 796F3
NYC clean-air case review declined 10-17, 797D3
Clean-water bill revised 11-10, 900E2, G2
Fed facilities cited for pollutn 11-25, 944B2
Calif-Tex oil pipe OK pending 12-2, 942F3
Proposes lead-pollutn rule 12-12, 1007G2
Velsicol indicted on data 12-12, 1007D3
Clean water bill clears Cong 12-15, 959A1; signed 12-28, 1001A3
Rpts clean-air progress 12-21, 1007E2
Orders chemicals rptd 12-22, 1007A2

ENVIRONMENTAL Quality, Council on
Speth confrmd member 4-4, 272C3
Carter submits reorganizatn plan 7-15, 556D1
A-plant licensing halt backed 9-29, 794A3
Carter nominee deferred by Sen com 10-17, 800G1

EQUAL Employment Opportunity Commission (EEOC)
Sup Ct voids homosexual dismissal ruling 1-10, 57B1
Employe '71 bias suit win rptd 1-20, 278F3
Cities Svc setlmt rptd 3-2, 279E1
Frontier Airlines suit rptd 3-15, 279B2
Coors signs antibias pact 5-9, 819D1
Norton confrmd chrmn 5-27, 500A1
Employes religious rights limited 6-13, 517D3
Time limit barred 6-20, 517D1
Reorganizatn plan rptd 7-20, 669E1
'78 funds signed 8-2, 667F3
Carter backs broader role 12-14, 960F1

EXECUTIVE Branch—*See also specific department and agency headings in this section*
Top-level pay hike in effect 2-20, 127D2
House ethics com formed 3-9, 191C2
Pay-raise procedures revised 4-12, 273D1
Carter proposes ethics law 5-3, 338B1
COL hike bar signed 7-11, 592G1

Reorganization
Ford proposes Energy Dept 1-11, 14E3
Ford State of Union message 1-12, 13D1, E1, A3, B3
Carter fireside chat outlines plans 2-2, 75D1, F1
Carter submits Energy Dept bill 3-1, 148F1
Sen OKs pres powers 3-3, 191F2
HEW chngs effected 3-9, 175E2
Carter vows 'sunset laws' 3-16, 190E3
Presidential powers cleared 3-31, 228A1
Pres powers signed, plans issued 4-6, 250B3
HEW Educ Office reorganized 4-11, 301D3
Carter Cabt-level educ dept vow cited 4-11, 302B1

1978

ENVIRONMENTAL Protection Agency (EPA)
Sup Ct backs asbestos rule curb 1-10, 13E2
Carter budget proposals 1-23, 47B2
Cancer chem water filtratn asked 1-25, 86B1
McDonald's glasses rptd safe 1-31, 348B1
Ohio, Ind pollutn curbs suspended 2-11, 2-16, 104F1
Ohio sulfur dioxide rules upheld by Ct 2-13, 109G1
Pesticide sales curbed 2-15, 163A3
103 areas violate air rules 2-23, 144C3
Chem-spill fines set 3-3, 163E3
Atlantic sludge sites OKd 3-3, 164A1
Fluorocarbon aerosols banned 3-15, 186A2
Motorcycle rules proposed 3-15, 186D2
DOT issues new fuel standards for light trucks 3-15, 284A2
Ill firm sued on PCB pollutn 3-17, 243B1
Seabrook A-plant hearings to reopen 3-22, 242A3
Sulfur, lime, paper plant rules set 3-22, 263F2
Aircraft emissn rules revised 3-27, 263C2
GM agrees to $170,000 fine 3-27, 263B3
Chlordimeform ban eased 3-30, 263D3
Chrysler pollutn remedy ordrd 4-20, 349C1
TVA pollutn setlmt disputed 5-5, 5-18, 390D2
AMC '76 cars ordrd recalled 5-10, 349A1
Phila sued on sewage 5-17, 5-24, 409B2
VW dealers sued 5-24, 409F2
Denver dam permit blocked 5-25, 409A1
PCB ban formerly proposed 6-7, 513A1
Smog regulatn eased 6-13, 512F2
New-plant air rules issued 6-13, 512A3
Asbestos rule amended 6-15, 512D3
Seabrook A-plant hearings protested 6-26, 494D1
Plans econ analysis 6-28, 512C3
Seabrook A-plant halt ordrd 6-30, 529A3
Ohio sulfur dioxide moratorium denied 7-6, 513E1
Grasshopper high-potency insecticide barred 7-13, 654C3
Seabrook cooling system OKd 8-4, 609G1
Clean-water rules to be eased 8-10, 644F1
Car gas-econ ratings rptd 9-15, 719F2
DBCP curbs asked 9-19, 719C2
Lead-pollutn rule issued 9-29, 754C1
'79 funds signed 9-30, 750F2-A3
Admin to sit on Endangered Species Com 10-15, 834E2; 11-10, 1003B1
Hazardous dump site perils warned 11-21, 899D2
Fuel tests questioned 11-21, 939C2
Microwave safety scored 12-11, 962B3
TVA OKs pollutn pact 12-14, 982A3
Toxic-waste rules proposed 12-14, 982C3
Recombinant DNA rules revised 12-16, 1023C1
Flexible air rule proposed 12-21, 1009A1
Asbestos inspectn in schools asked 12-21, 1009G1
Chinese A-test debris rptd over US 12-23, 1001A2

ENVIRONMENTAL Quality, Council on
Rpt sees solar energy potential, urges dvpt 4-12, 281E3-282B1

EQUAL Employment Opportunity Commission (EEOC)
Corporatns to be monitored 1-4, 5B1
Employers curbed on bias-case legal fees 1-23, 65A2
Carter seeks expansn 2-23, 123D3
GE complaint setld 6-15, 1006B3
AT&T bias case declined by Sup Ct 7-3, 552B1
Guidelines issued 12-12, 1006B2

EQUAL Employment Opportunity Coordinating Council
Carter proposes abolishmt 2-23, 123F3

EXECUTIVE Branch—*See also specific department and agency headings in this section*
Haldeman versn of Watergate rptd 2-16—2-17, 124E3
Carter signs 'plain English' order 3-23, 218D2
Carter freezes salaries 4-11, 259D2
Govt-purchasing controls ordrd 5-18, 405F1
Carter vs legis vetoes 6-21; cong reactn 6-21, 6-22, 466E1-C2
AMA asks fed expenses cut 6-21, 578C1
Carter signs fscl '78 added funds 9-8, 681F2
Burger urges study 9-21, 751A3
Carter signs ethics bill 10-26, 832F1-B2

Reorganization
Smoking & Health Office created 1-11, 23F2
Carter State of Union Message 1-19, 29B1, E2, 31C1, E1
Intell units reorganized 1-24, 49A2
CAB consumer office end urged by Nader group 1-31, 68B1
Carter seeks job-bias unit reorganizatn 2-23, 123D3-124B1
Civil Svc revisn urged 3-2, 141B2
Natl drug center proposed 3-16, 231F1
Interdept women's group vowed by Carter 3-22, 218C2
Urban-aid plan presented 3-27, 217A3
Natl dvpt bank proposed 3-27, 217A3
Telecommunicatns agency formed 3-28, 270B2

1979

ENVIRONMENTAL Protection Agency (EPA)
GAO rpt scores clean-air watch 1-9, 16E2
Diesel exhaust rule proposed 1-10, 16A3
Chems prior data sought 1-10, 16G3-17A1
Ohio sulphur-dioxide emissns case refused by US Sup Ct 1-15, 32B1
Anti-pollutn costs, gains rptd 1-19, 129C3
US Steel, Erie Coke sued 1-25, 2-5, 90E2
Smog standard eased 1-26, 90D1
Truck exhaust rule tightnd 2-15, 187C1
2 weed killers banned 3-1, 167E1-C2
Colo radium waste sites rptd 3-5, 187F1
Business rpts rule compliance costs 3-14, 230G2
2d Ohio sulphur-dioxide emissns case refused by Sup Ct 3-19, 203B3
New fines proposed 3-21, 206E2
Coal co sues vs air rule 3-22, 206B3
Ford Motor sued 3-22, 206C3
Hooker Chem case studied 4-11, 281F3
RR-yard noise rules proposed 4-16, 282A1
PCB rules issued 4-19, 281G3-282A1
Texaco fined in Calif gas-switching 4-26, 301D2
Clean-air amendment upheld re Ohio coal use 5-7, 351C1
Pittsburgh area cleanups set by Colt unit 5-7, US Steel 5-22, 385C2-B3
Utilities get coal-use rules 5-25, 403G2-404B1
Phila sewage suits settled 5-30, 704C2
Air-quality standards relaxed to spur no-lead gas output 6-4, 418B3
GM settles emissns dispute 6-5, 441G2
NC PCB disposal dispute rptd 6-5, 597C3
Cleveland utility air rule eased 6-6, 422D3-423C1
Waste cleanup proposed 6-13, 441A2
Hooker pollutn probe rptd 6-18, 597A2
Canada min to see Costle 7-26, 581F2
PCBs contaminate food in West 9-17, 704F3
Army OKs E Coast oil refinery 10-4, 770B1
'80 funds clears Cong 10-24, Carter signs 11-5, 883A3
NRC reorganizatn asked 10-30, 825F2
Chem dump site list issued 11-1, 886C1
Clean-air rule revised 12-3, 924D3
Love Canal suit filed 12-20, 990F1

ENVIRONMENTAL Quality, Council on
Anti-pollutn costs, gains rptd 1-19, 129D3
Cleanup gains cited 1-25, 90G1
Energy use growth rate curbs seen 2-20, 132C2

EQUAL Employment Opportunity Commission (EEOC)
Sears sues US on bias laws 1-24, 92E1
Norton on racial poll 2-20, 306F3
BN data curb upheld by Sup Ct 2-21, 128F3
Sears suit dismissed 5-15, 365E3, G3
Weber case Sup Ct ruling lauded 6-27, 477A3
Sears sued 10-22, 885C3

EXECUTIVE Branch
Secret tape data rptd 10-21, 10-29, 868G3-869F1

Reorganization
Civil Svc Comm replaced 1-1, 5A3, 6A1
Carter backs Educ Dept, Natl Dvpt Bank; ends Travel Svc, Youth Corp 1-22, 44D2, D3, 45A2, 46D1
State of Union Message 1-23, 46F3, G3
Carter proposes Educ Dept 2-8, 110F2
Resources Dept proposed 3-1, 164B1
Dvpt finance progrm proposed 3-1, 164G1
Carter plans pipeline regulatory agency 3-3, 168A2
Carter asks Energy Security Fund 4-5, 250C3
Sen OKs Educ Dept 4-30, 326B2; House OKs 7-11, 514C3
Resources Dept plan dropped 5-15, 365A2
Carter asks trade functn shift 7-19, 647A1
Mass transit-highway agencies merger dropped 9-17, 726F1
Pay Advisory Com set 9-28, 9-28, 829C2-B3
Educ Dept created, HEW renamed 10-17, 782A2
Natl Agenda Comm created 10-24, 810D2
Carter submits trade plan 10-25, 803C1

1980

ENVIRONMENTAL Protection Agency (EPA)
Truck exhaust rules set 1-2, 5F2
Carter budget proposals 1-28, 73E2
NJ dump to be capped 1-30, 93D3
Lilly Ind pesticide plant case declined by Sup Ct 2-19, 131E1
Diesel exhaust rules set 2-21, 145G3
Toxic waste rules set 2-26, 145D3
Connally cites in 'basic speech' 3-7, 184C3
Pollutn dischrg permit ct reviews backed by Sup Ct 3-17, 226F1
Sewage permit extensn power backed by Sup Ct 3-18, 226D3
Ct limits children's harvest work, pesticide study plan cited 3-20, 227E1, F1
Dow accuses of spying 3-25, 387C2
Toxic waste rules adopted 5-5, 387E1
PCB rules published 5-9, 387C2
Niagara dump study rptd 5-16, homeowners detain 2 offcls 5-19, 386G3-387D1
Air pollutn guidelines appeals ct review backed by Sup Ct 5-27, 453E3
Detergent carcinogen OKd 5-27, 526C3
Cleveland utility air rule firmed 6-17, 494B3
Cleanup costs overestimated 6-18, 494A2
3 Mile I krypton vented 6-28—7-11, 550A3
Lindane curbs sought 7-3, 519C3
Car maker aid planned 7-8, 505D1, A2
La chem-dump suit filed 7-15, 559A1
Chrysler K-car fuel ratings rptd 8-5, 883F1
PCB cleanup methods rptd 8-21, 9-11, 747B2
Shenango OKs Pa plant pollutn curbs 8-22, 825C2
Walsh disputes Reagan on auto regulatns 9-3, 664A3
Carter asks steel indus deadlines delayed 9-30, 740B3
Toxic dumping powers clear Cong 10-2, signed 10-21, 981F1
Toxic waste suits filed 10-7, 10-9, 825A1, F1
Reagan remark disputed 10-8, 779F2
US Steel OKs Utah plant pollutn controls 10-16, 825A2
Toxic waste policy scored 10-31, 869B2
FMA pleads guilty 11-10, 869G1
Sen OKs toxic waste clean-up fund 11-24, 898A1
New scenic area air rules issued 11-25, 898G1-C2
PPG accused of fuel-switching 11-25, 899C3
'76 Chrysler recall order challenge refused by Sup Ct 12-1, 918E2
Clean water enforcemt backed by Sup Ct 12-2, 918A1
'81 appropriatn clears Cong 12-3, 954B3; signed 12-15, 982B1
Cong amends pesticide program 12-4, 955F1
Airborne lead standards challenge refused by Sup Ct 12-8, 937F1
Toxic waste clean-up bill signed 12-11, 935G3, 936C1
Calif, Ky funds halted 12-11, 963B1
US Steel fined 12-22; Clairton deadline extended 12-30, 987C1, E1
Motorcycle noise rules set 12-24, 987D2
Diesel emissns rule set 12-24, 987E2

ENVIRONMENTAL Quality, Council on
Rpt details problems 2-19, 145C2
Rpt sees control benefits 4-21, 308A1
Global forecast gloomy 7-23, 573G1
Banned item export curb set 8-2, 599A3

EQUAL Employment Opportunity Commission (EEOC)
Lee Way settles job bias suit 1-10, 17D2
Sex harassmt barred, regulatns set 4-11, 441E2
Class actn process avoidance backed by Sup Ct 5-12, 426F1
Sears Ala bias suit dropped 5-22, 485E1
IBM sued re Md job bias 6-3, 485G1
Job bias suits setld vs CF&I 9-22, Motorola 9-23, Rockwell 9-26, 746D3
Ford settles job-bias case 11-25, 899B2

EXECUTIVE Branch

Reorganization
Carter signs trade plan 1-2, 94G2
Carter asks NRC reorganizatn 1-21, 43E3
Kennedy asks trade agency 2-6, 91B1
Island territories get econ plan 2-14, 495A1
Refugee Affairs office created 3-17, 249E2
Educ Dept begins operatn 5-4, 369G3
35 agencies implement consumer progrms 6-9, 703B1
Counterterrorist unit proposed 8-23, 644E1
Econ Revitalizatn Bd created 8-28, 663C2
Forgn Svc bill clears Cong 10-1, signed 10-17, 981D2
OMB Info Regulatory Office set 12-11, 935D3

1977

USDA bureaucracy scored 4-12, Bergland vows reform 4-14, 364F3
Carter urges Energy Dept 4-18, 4-20, 293D3, 295E1
Arms dvpt, procuremt offices consolidated 4-25, 343A3
Natl Neighborhoods Comm set 4-28, 339B1
Forgn Intell Bd disbanded, 3 named to oversight Bd 5-5, 462C2
Energy Dept OKd by Sen 5-18, 405E2
Carter backs consumer agency 6-1, 417E3
Mil manpower costs panel named 6-27, 499A3
Carter stresses 4 initial area 6-29, 499G2
Carter cites Cong actn 7-12, 534E1
Carter submits plan to Cong 7-15, 555C3
Carter Miss town mtg topic 7-21, 575E1
ICC chrmn urges chngs 8-3, 651E2
Energy Dept created 8-4, 591C2
Young Adult Conservation Corps authorized 8-5, 609C2
AFDC, SSI, food stamp programs end asked 8-6, 608C3
New Panama Canal agency agreed 8-10, 621G1
USIA-Educ, Cultural Bur plan offered 10-11, 797C2
Mine safety powers shifted 11-9, 855G3
Women's conf rejcts cabt-level dept 11-19—11-21, 917G2
Blacks seek civil rights agency chngs 12-14, 960E1

1978

Carter unveils anti-inflatn plan 4-11, 259E3
Educatn Dept proposed 4-14, 279A1-B2
HEW adoptn centralizatn signed 4-24, 323E3
Carter urges Civil Svc revisn 4-25, 4-26, 306D3, 307D3
Carter plans law enforcemt revisn 5-4, 320A3
Carter seeks fed bureaucracy chngs 5-25, 404F3
Carter proposes Fed Emergency Mgt Agency 6-19, 466D2-B3
Carter exempts from legis veto 6-21, 466E1
Intell classificatn unit formed 6-29, 508D1
LEAA plan proposed by Carter 7-10, 525C1
Natl Mil Advisers creatn urged 7-12, 528G2
Carter vs cong Civil Svc chngs 7-20, 549F3
GAO urges new energy agency 7-31, 610E1, A2
ABA asks regulatory overhaul 8-8, 626A2, D2
Civil Svc Comm reorgnzn takes effect 8-11; overall reform pending 8-12, 625A2-F2
Civil Svc reforms OKs by Sen 8-24, 661C3; House 9-13, 696C2-C3
Contract Compliance Office powers broadened 10-6, 811G2
Inspector Gen Act signed 10-12, 899C2
Civil Svc revisn signed 10-13, 787G3
Educ Dept bill dies 10-15, 785B1
Endangered Species Com created 10-15, 834E2; 11-10, 1003B1
Govt Ethics office created 10-26, 832A2
Cong 95th sessn rated 10-28, 865A3
SBA abolitn asked 11-20, 919C3
Fradulent documt lab asked 12-20, 1010F2

1976

EXECUTIVE Office of the President—*See also specific agencies in this section*
Dole urges veto process revisn 9-3, 665G3
EXPORT-Import Bank of the United States (Eximbank)
'76 Japan budget ups credits 1-2, 30D1
Spain credits set 1-24, 77B1
S Korea warned vs French A-plant buy 1-26, 103C3
Kobelinski confrmd to SBA 2-6, 110B2
Turkey loans agreed 3-26, 244A3
Australia loan OK rptd 4-13, 264E3
Sets new credit terms 6-9, 529C3
Gianturco confrmd vp 7-29, 807G3
Citibank sues re Zaire loan 8-9, 621B2
Kearns, Bostwick sued 8-9, 709C3
Govt in sunshine bill signed 9-13, 688E3
Citibank, Bankers Trust drop suits re Zaire; new paymt plan OKd 10-13, 890G2-C3
'76 loan defaults, income rise rptd 11-11, 915F2
Confrms Arab boycott loan bar 12-7, 986G3
FARMERS Home Administration—*See under AGRICULTURE, Department of, above*
FEDERAL Aid & Spending Programs—*See BUDGET in this section above*
FEDERAL Aviation Administration—*See under TRANSPORTATION below*

1977

EXECUTIVE, Legislative and Judicial Salaries, Commission on
Burger endorses rpt 1-1, 15A2
Sen forms ethics panel 1-18, 77A3
EXECUTIVE Office of the President—*See also specific offices and councils in this section*
Top-level pay hike takes effect 2-20, 127D2
Top advisers rpt net worth 2-25, 147G3
Pres reorganizatn powers signed, plans issued 4-6, 250B3
Pay-raise procedures revised 4-12, 273D1
COL hike bar signed 7-11, 592G1
Carter submits reorganizatn plan 7-15, 555D3
EXPORT-Import Bank of the United States (Eximbank)
Hughes Indonesia kickback rptd, '74 loan cited 1-25, 182G3
Yugo loans OKd 3-2, 309B1
Panama credits in canal pact 8-12, 621D2
OKs Mex gas-pipe loans 12-15, 985C2
FEDERAL Aviation Administration—*See under TRANSPORTATION below*

1978

EXECUTIVE Orders—*See under CARTER*
EXPORT Administration Review Board—*See under COMMERCE in this section above*
EXPORT-Import Bank of the United States (Eximbank)
S Africa loan guarantee cutoff asked 1-25, '77 credit total rptd 2-9, 135A2
Mauritania loan rptd 1-27, 95E1
House probes PI A-plant loan 2-8, 134C3
Korea loan, lobbying probe aid linked 2-22, 204B1
Brazil $1.7 bln debt cited 4-8, 311F1
S Africa credit ban backed by House com 5-1; Sen com rejects 5-3, 377B1
Argentina hydro loan blocked 7-19, OKd 9-26, 792D2
Export financing hike sought by Carter 9-26, 804E2
Anti-inflatn certificatn set 10-24, 806C2
FANNIE Mae—*See HOUSING & Urban Development—Federal National Mortgage Association below*
FEDERAL—For departments and agencies not listed below, see key word in this section
FEDERAL Aviation Administration—*See under TRANSPORTATION below*

1979

EXECUTIVE Office of the President
'80 funds clears Cong 9-26, Carter signs 9-29, 883C2
EXECUTIVE Orders—*See under CARTER*
EXPORT-Import Bank of the United States (Eximbank)
S Korea-Westinghouse A-deal set 8-3, 742C2
China credit pledged 8-28, 644A3
Ivory Coast pvt investmt rptd 9-8, 720F3
Uganda aid vowed 9-19, 721F1
Nicaragua debt paymts in doubt 9-28, 753A3
McDonnell Douglas indicted on fraud chrg 11-9, 886G1
Chile aid suspended 11-30, 927F2
USSR credit ban cited 12-17, 997D2
Iran declared in default 12-21, 976E1
FEDERAL—*For departments and agencies not listed below, see key word in this section*
FEDERAL Aviation Administration—*See under TRANSPORTATION below*

1980

EXPORT-Import Bank of the United States (Eximbank)
Loan offer to Australia co sparks probe 2-19; Sen com probes loan policies 5-10—5-13; GAO probe urged 10-1, 989C1, E1
Funding legis passed 8-18, signed 8-29, 989B1
Dividend skip rptd, '79 dividend cited; fscl '81 earnings drop, '82 loss seen 12-16, 988F3
FEDERAL—*For departments and agencies not listed below, see key word in this section*

1976

FEDERAL Bureau of Investigation (FBI) (of Department of Justice)
AIM ldr's Nov '75 indictmt cited 7A2
Ariz BIA bomb threat 1-1, 7F1
ACLU sues Kelley 1-5, 70A2
Fine arrested for '70 Wis bombing 1-7, 32C2
Judge to see Rosenberg papers 1-13, 70C2
Ticor indicted 1-14, 160C1
Bortnick kidnapers arrested 1-22—1-23, 159G3
Probe of bank 'problem' list leaks asked 1-25, 1-30, 112G1
Angola mercenary probe asked 1-30, 82E1
Hearst trial testimony 2-5, 114E1
'75 bombing data rptd 2-12, 159E3
Agents testify vs Hearst 2-12, 2-13; defns motns barred 3-1, 3-4, 201G1, B2, 202C1, A2
Handgun study backs curbs 2-17, 170D2
'63 Ala bomb probe reopened 2-18, 159E3
S Korea payoffs to 2 reps probed 2-19, 171E1
Probes Sovt NY residence shooting 2-27, 229A3
Forgn intell penetratn rptd 2-27, 3-10, disputed 2-27, 4-5, 248D2-A3
Delta grain inspector pleads guilty 3-5, 247A3
Hiss claims innocence 3-18, 217G3, 218F1
Rpts '75 crime data 3-25, 336G2
Hughes' body identified 4-5, 336B1
Sup Ct bars JDL wiretap review case 4-19, 331F1
Hijacker killed in Denver 4-19, 383E3
US forgn intelligence chart 304A2★, C2
Rpts letter bombs follow '75 extortn 6-15, 504B1
Carter vs checks on vp list 6-17, 452D1
Scored re Angola mercenaries 6-28, 480D2
Kelley testifies on SD '75 agents deaths 7-7, 2 cleared 7-16, 640F2★
'77 funds signed 7-14, 534E2
Chowchilla kidnap suspects arrested 7-29, 560B1
Restructuring, reforms set 8-11, 633A2, G2, F3
Confirms GOP delegate bribe chrgs 8-16, 616F1

1977

FEDERAL Bureau of Investigation (FBI) (of Department of Justice)
Ex-CIA employe arrested 12-22-76, 41B2
Informer guidelines set 1-5, 15D2-C3
Denver SWP burglary probe ends 1-6, 15C3
3 arrested as spies 1-6, 1-7, 1-16, 41D2-D3
King suits dismissed 1-31, 77C2
Feminist surveillance rptd 2-6, 423D1
Mafia informer slain 2-10, 568E2
2 chrgd in Ariz bomb plot 2-14, 162F1
Legis curbs proposed 2-15, 157A3
King rpt released 2-18, 149F1-C2
Sen intell com watch rptd 2-26, 150A3
Lawyers Guild suit rptd 3-2, 423G1
NY coffee thefts rptd 3-6, 169A1
King new ballistic tests ordrd 3-17, 228G2
324 'most wanted' rptd captured 3-19, 288D2
Health care probe role set 3-20, 236A1
FALN bombs NYC hq 3-21, 261A2, E2
'60s student radicals surrender 3-25, 6-21, 9-14, 839C1
Kearney indicted 4-7; pleads not guilty; lauded by Kelley 4-14, 275F1-G2
Hughes Mormon will called fake 4-15, 254B3
Nixon-Frost interview 5-4, 366A2
Ex-CIA employe convicted 5-5, 409F2
New Haven abuses charged 5-12, 422E3
Mafia membership, profit data rptd 5-16, 568D1
Indian sentncd in SD '75 deaths 6-2, 491G3
Internal security probes rptd down, investigative guidelines sought 6-6, 481A1
Ray escape role ordrd 6-10, 459A2
Natl crime data svc under review 6-16, 480B3
ACLU '20-42 surveillance rptd 6-19, 481B1
Golfer death threat rptd 6-19, 659C3
Newton to face '74 Calif chrgs 6-24, 532C1
Scientology offices raided 7-8, raids ruled illegal 7-27; church sues 7-18, 8-15, 628A2
Privacy comm scores data svc plan 7-12, 632E1
Double agent's release from USSR sought 7-14, 564C2
2 seized as spies in Fla 7-20, 576A3

1978

FEDERAL Bureau of Investigation (FBI) (of Department of Justice)
Hoover, top aides corruptn rptd 1-10, 15F1
Sullivan slayer fined 1-14, 69B2
More JFK assassinatn files released 1-18, 109E3
Webster named dir 1-19, 32C1; confrmd 2-9, 82G3
Carter order affirms curbs 1-24, 49G2
Lloyd Carr fugitive arrested 1-24, 83B2, D2
2 seized as Viet spies 1-31, 68G2
Intell legis introduced in Sen 2-9, 106G3
Haldeman book on Watergate rptd 2-16—2-17, 125A1
Fla derailmt rptd sabotage 3-3, 196A2
'77 derailmt convictns rptd 3-13, 196E1
UAL hijacker arrested 3-13, 212B2
Old criminal files to be destroyed 3-15, 186C3
Black-mkt uranium sale bid to Westinghouse probed 3-19, 242C2-A3
Scientology search warrant rule review denied by Sup Ct 3-20, 205D3
Korea scandal memos released, Mitchell testifies 3-21, 203A2, C2
Columbia Pictures ex-pres indicted 3-31, 251B2
Chile murder suspect escorted to US 4-8, 266G2
Gray, 2 other top ex-offcls indicted 4-10, 261E3-262A1
Bell asks disciplinary actn vs LaPrade, 68 agents; rpts Kearney chrgs dropped 4-10, 262A1
LaPrade transferred, chrgs pol influence 4-13, 285B1
Chile murder suspect, Cuban exiles linked 4-19, 370B3
Shevchenko ties rptd 4-21, 302A3
Chile murder suspect implicated in Latin bombings 4-26, 371B1
Nixon memoir excerpt cites Watergate role 4-30, 319G3-320A1
2 convicted as Viet spies 5-16, 390A1
Nazi war criminal links rptd 5-16, 411A1
2 Sovts arrested as spies 5-20, 409G2
Black ldr cited in '64 memo on King conspiracy 5-29; sources name Wilkins; SCLC, others deny 5-29—5-31, 410F2
Letelier murder details revealed 6-2, 451G3
22 indicted on port corruptn 6-7, 480F2

1979

FEDERAL Bureau of Investigation (FBI) (of Department of Justice)
Tenn parole-selling probe continues 1-4, 36F1-B3; **for subsequent developments, see TENNESSEE**
Webster warns of Chinese spies 1-7, 17G2
Stolen films seized in Ohio 1-8, intl probe rptd 1-10 102D2
Ex-agent's statemt in SWP trial sought 1-16, 92B2
Stabile sentncd for obstructing justice 1-17, 92B3
Jonestown documts to be probed by grand jury 1-17, 117E3
Paisley death probe urged 1-24, 55A1
Beckwith dismissal rescinded, demotn ordrd; Murphy retired 1-26, 92F2
Jonestown radio message transcripts rptd 1-29, 118B1
Informer testifies in Letelier trial 1-30, 75C1
GE worker chrgd in uranium theft 2-1, 119F3
W Ger terrorist sentncd in US 2-7, 119F2
KKK informant's extraditn OKd 2-7, 120C1
Chile pres, Letelier assassins rptdly linked 2-9, 114F3
Art theft symposium held in Del 2-12—2-14, 119B2
NYC airport theft arrests 2-17, 2-20, 155B3
Oswald '63 death threat revealed 2-18, 166D2
Carter peanut loan scheme denied 3-12, 184F1
Swiss banks block Peoples Temple funds 3-12, 250E1
Bell contempt citatn overturned 3-19, 207E1
Calif bank wire-transfer setup rptd 3-20, 239B2
Informant loss rptd, disclosures scored 3-22, 232C2
Brecht '43-56 surveillnc rptd 3-29, 367C3
3 Mile I A-accident sabotage ruled out 4-1, 245G1
Paisley death probe dropped by Justice Dept 4-18, 283F3
Covert 'bugging' entry upheld by Sup Ct 4-18, 346C1

1980

FEDERAL Bureau of Investigation (FBI) (of Department of Justice)
Commodity optns trader arrested 1-2, 94B3
Terkel files case refused by Sup Ct 1-7, 15G3
Seberg probe rptd extensive 1-9, 55C1
'58 Ala church bombing suspect extradited 1-11, 55C3
ILA offcls, businessmen sentenced for racketeering 1-11, 64B2
Tenn A-fuel plant reopened 1-16, 54C1
Carter asks charter 1-21, 43F3
Canada expels Sovt spies 1-21, 56G2
White-collar crime by women rptd up 1-21, 215E3
Boyce prison escape rptd 1-22, 55F1
Indian activist sentenced 1-23, 349D1
Coll transcript scandal spreads, probe rptd 1-23—5-23, 469C2
Kennedy airport Aeroflot data tampering probed 1-31, 115C1
Jamaica sues US grain shippers 2-4, 99E2
ABA backs charter 2-4, 114F3
Fla drug trial plot disclosed 2-4, 270G3
Ex-Black Panther denied parole, COINTELPRO cited 2-5, 215D2
'71 hijack ransom believed found 2-12—13, 136G2
'63 KKK church bombing prosecutn rptd blocked, informant cited 2-18, 272C2
NY record co indicted 2-28, 237F3
5 Sovt bloc diplomats rptd ousted as spies 2-29, 189C2
Soviet double agent introduced 3-3, 189F1
Ala A-plant probe disclosed 3-5, 3-7, 249F1-A2
11 FALN suspects arrested 4-4; houses raided, execs hit list seized 4-7, 4-8, 308F3-309E1
Wrightsville (Ga) racial violence probed 4-14, 333D1
'58 Ala church bomber sentncd 5-14, 405C1
Sovt trade spy arrested 5-18, sentenced 8-1, 598B2
EPA aides detained at Love Canal 5-19, 387E1
Jordan shot in Ft Wayne 5-29, 401E2; probe stymied 6-1—6-12, 442A2
Cuban refugee checks rptd, resetlmt lags 6-1, 6-2, 420D1, B2

1976

Cuban exile plot to kill Castro rptd 8-17, 791G1
Kelley announces marriage plans 9-4, 680F2
Questions Croat hijackers 9-12, 685C2
On Letelier death probe 9-22, 710F3
Ford funds probe rptd 9-24, 10-1, 722G3, 723G2
Letelier probe widened 10-9; Cuba exiles linked, DINA role rejected 10-12, 780C3-E3
Ruff clears Ford on funds use 10-14, 761F1
Term of dir limited 10-15, 835G1
Cuba exile contacts chrgd 10-17, confirmed 10-25, 844A2
Venez probe re Letelier rptd 10-18, 844F2
Rpt ex-informant with Venez police 11-1, 844F1
Rpt Grenada protects fraud suspects 12-7, 925G1
Sup Ct refuses Ray plea withdrawal 12-13, 960D2
Canada to extradite Indian ldr 12-17, 999C1

Intelligence Investigations & Irregularities

Equipmt purchasing irregularities rptd 1-1, 6A1
ACLU chrgs harassmt of amnesty groups 1-6, 4C2
Calif rt-wing terrorist aid rptd 1-11, 42A1
Privacy comm testimony cites 2-12, 151B2
Ford revises intelligence command 2-17, 127G2
House com rpt leak probe underway 3-2—3-25, 216D3
Investigatn guidelines issued 3-10, 217E2-E3
NY SWP suit bares FBI burglaries evidence 3-17, 5-25, 6-26, 569B2-B3★, C3-E3
Purchasing probe rptd renewed 3-20—3-23, 248D1
Thefts of NY leftist offices, other groups rptd 3-28, 3-29, 234A3
To destroy '69 files on Kraft 3-30, 235C1
Cointelpro targets notificatn set 4-1, 235A1
'56-72 Cointelpro actns rptd 4-2, 235B1
Black Cointelpro papers freed 4-5, 248B2
Church scores Ford 4-19, 282C1
Sen com rpts on CIA liason 4-26, 300A3-C3, 304E1
Sen com rpts abuses, asks curbs 4-28; text 324C3, 325E2, 327E1-328F3, 329D1-A2, D2, 330A1-C3
Levi orders new Rev King probe 4-29, 344E1
Sen com staff details abuses 5-5, 5-6, 5-9, 343F3-344G2
Kelley apologizes 5-8, 344G2
Radical harassmt, NY SWP burglaries rptd 5-25—7-29, 569E3
Probe of '70s burglaries rptd 6-24—6-30, 8-3; Kelley admits break-ins 6-30, 569G1
Denver SWP office burglarized 7-7, Justice Dept to probe 7-27, 569G2-B3★
Nixon disbarred in NY 7-8, 493D3
Baxter admits NY theft role 7-29, 569G3
'70s burglaries probe, SWP suit dvpts 7-30—8-26, 633A2-635D1
Reforms announced 8-11, 633A2, G2, F3
Mondale, Carter score Kelley 8-12, 8-13, 617B1
Dunphy resigns re property misuse 8-13, 666F3
Kelley admits favors, gifts 8-31; Justice rpt, Ford back Kelley 9-4, 666C2
Ford, Carter exchngs on Kelley favors, other irregularities 9-6—9-9, 664D2, E3, 665D1
Mondale scores Ford 10-5, 743C3
Agents cleared re Halperin wiretap 12-16, 981B1

1977

'78 funds signed 8-2, 667E3
ACLU ties revealed 8-4, 628E1
Mondale addresses ABA conv 8-8, 630C1
Johnson named dir 8-17, 626A2; withdraws name 11-29, 914C2
Cuba exiles vow more attacks 8-31, 686D1
Boxing scandal probe cited 9-3, 828E1
Carter cites check on Lance 9-21, 718G1
'76 crime data rptd 9-27, 847D3
Sen Panama Canal wiretap probe subpoenas dir, postpones hearings 9-30, 756E1
Gem hunt rptd 10-3, 871F3
Cuba aid to US radicals rptd 10-9, 896A3
Young cleared in prisoner aid chrg 10-19, 861E3
Blackmail in Sovt spy recruitmt chrgd 11-7, 866B3
GAO rpts domestic intell cutback, urges Cong guidelines 11-9, 861D2
Wm Sullivan dies 11-9, 952D3
Cointelpro papers released 11-21, 940A3
Scientology search warrant ruled valid 12-1, 940G1
JFK assassinatn files released 12-1, 12-7, 943C1
Phone surveillnc ct orders backed 12-7, 939F1
Justice attys ask removal from probe, Bell dispute cited 12-7, 940A1
Secretariat's missing mare rptd found 12-9, 971A2
Justice probe gets new team, Bell drops oppositn to indictmts 12-13, 979B3

1978

SWP informant case declined by Sup Ct 6-12, 468D1
Union insurnc scheme chrgd 6-15, 560C3
'68 Dem conv informants rptd 7-3, 507E3
Letelier murder suspects info reward offered 7-4, 614A1
Bell cited for contempt in SWP informants case 7-6, 507A2; order stayed 7-7, 524G3
LaPrade fired by Bell 7-6, 507G2
Scientology Church '77 raids upheld 7-6, 554E1
KKK informant rptd agent-provocateur 7-9, 7-11; Justice probes violence, cover-up 7-12, 527E3-528B2
Admits 4 news media informants 7-13, 554B1
Presley aid offer rptd 7-14, 553D3-554B1
Indians protest '73 Wounded Knee trials 7-18, 569B1
3 questnd re W Ger terrorist 7-22, 577D1
King murder plot alleged 7-26, 589E3
Religious cult ldr fraud probe rptd 8-3, 685G3
Conoco ex-offcl plea bargaining rptd 8-9, 610F3
King death probed by House com 8-14—8-18, 641D1, E2
CIA ex-employe seized on spy chrg 8-17, 645D2
Civil Svc reforms pass Sen 8-24, 661C3
Warrantless tap curbs rptd backed 9-7, 697D1
JFK assassinatn hearings cite 9-8, 698G1
Viet documt possessn by ex-amb rptd probed 9-13, 720G1, A2
JFK death hearings cite 9-13, 9-14, 749F2, G3
Stabile indicted 9-15, 11-6; resigns, pleads guilty 11-9, 886B3
PR '67 independnc movemt harassmt chrgd 9-15, 979D3
GSA probe frictn cited 9-18, 715B1
KKK informt indicted for '65 Liuzzo slaying 9-20, 720D2
A-sub theft foiled 10-4, 824G1
Warrantless tap curbs signed 10-25, 863B1
LA bank robbed by phone 10-25, computer consultant arrested 11-5, 991G3-992D1
Webster calls CIA ex-offcl's death suicide 10-26, 835G3
2 Sovt spies sentncd 10-30, 835A2
Files disclosure delay urged 11-8, 877F3-878A1
Thevis arrested 11-9, 971C2
Grand Coulee generator sabotage probed 11-10, 963D1
King murder plot link discounted 11-11, 11-17, 898C2, C3
Douglas probe rptd, files detailed 11-14, 877C3
King murder plot allegatns assailed 11-17, 11-20; probe defended 11-22, scored 11-27, 938C2-F2
CIA ex-employe convicted 11-18, 940G1
JFK murder film assessed 11-26, 916A2
Croatians rptd threatened 11-29, 933F3
SWP mail scrutiny held unconst 11-29, 940B1
Gray, 2 other top ex-offcls' dismissal motion denied 11-30, 939D3
6 chrgd in Tito murder plot 12-1, 933D3
Guyana cult tragedy probed, queries survivors 12-2—12-6; death ritual tape rptd found 12-8; Calif grand jury probe stayed 12-13, 955D1-A2
Va break-in case refused by Sup Ct 12-4, 959F1
4 penalized in break-ins 12-5, 939F2
House subcom staff rpt urges Energy Dept probe 12-10, 983C3
Ray seeks King tapes 12-12, 1002A3
Tenn gov's aides arrested 12-15, 1011E1
More Guyana cult survivors queried 12-21—12-29, 1000D2
JFK murder role ruled out, King surveillnc scored 12-30, 1002D2, G2

1979

Terrorist 'backpack' A-bomb said possible 4-25, 327D2
US spy satellite data rptd compromised 4-28, 318A3
Sen panel to probe Paisley death 4-30, 368A1
Carter alleged death plot probed 5-5—5-29, 404D1
Va A-plant sabotage probed 5-8, 5-10, 386D2
Silkwood death probe cited 5-18, 381B2
Wiretap ct judges named 5-18, 442A3
NJ indictmt details Mafia 5-23, 508C2
Morales phone tip rptd 5-25, 431B2
Fed judge in Tex slain, probe ordrd 5-29, 431E2
Julius Rosenberg article publshd 6-16, 466C1
Va A-plant sabotage chrgs rptd 6-18, 466E1
Truckers warned vs violence 6-21, 479D3
Serbian sentncd for '75 Chicago bombings 6-22, 491C3
Sullivan memoirs rpt Sovt spy suspected in NY office 6-24, 521A1
Files preservatn sought by activists 6-26, 520E3
'65 Liuzzo murder suit filed by ACLU 7-5, 521C1
House com final rpt clears in JFK, King deaths 7-17, 538C1
Personnel rules rptd dropped 7-22, 561E3
Charter proposed 7-31, 599G1
Teamster chief's son, 2 others indicted 8-2, 744D3
3 aides named in reorgnizatn 8-8, 611B1
3 agents slain 8-9, 727E3
Rptr seen as Sovt spy 8-11, 611E1
Bank robberies rise sharply 8-12, 619G2
Yeoman chrgd re secrets sale 8-14, 611D1
2 NYC bank robbery suspects arrested 8-22, 656B1
Audit shows informant rules compliance 8-22, 747E2
Jordan cocaine use depositn received 8-28, 647C2
Vesco jury foreman resigns, claims cover-up 8-29, 647G2
Jordan cocaine use testimony rptd 8-31, Calif use alleged, probe expanded 9-13—9-21, 767C2, G2
'70 Seberg slander admitted 9-14, 704G3
'70 Black Panther murder case probe set 9-24, 886E2
Yeoman pleads guilty 9-25, 747F3; sentncd 10-26, 831F3
US Marshals to track escaped prisoners 10-1, 771B1
Research group spying to end 10-4, 787G1
Letelier case funds transfer probed 10-9, 772A2
Bell contempt case declined by Sup Ct 10-9, 783D3
2d 1/4 crime rise rptd 10-9, 819A3
Tenn A-fuel plant probed 10-10, 809C3
Sindona reappears in NYC 10-16, 793G2
2 agents rptd removed for theft 10-17, Rotton kills self 10-18, 787B2; Travis pleads guilty 11-15, 906G1°
Oswald KGB substitutn theory discounted 10-22, 905C3
Hoover bldg name chng proposed 10-30, 886D3
Kissinger '50s link rptd 11-3, 870B2
Malcolm X neutralizatn plan rptd 11-5, 886A3
KKK NC slaying probe rptd 11-6, 865E3
Tex millionaire acquitted in kill-for-hire case 11-9, 890F2
Scotto convicted 11-15, 890G1
PR prisoner's death probe rptd 11-18, 904B3
Cuban exile's murder probed 11-28, 906D1
Jordan cocaine probe spec prosecutor named 11-29, 900E3
FDR said possible cancer victim 12-2, 925E3
U of New Mex basketball scandal detailed 12-13—12-21, 1003F1

1980

Panther Chicago shootout retrial order declined by Sup Ct 6-2, 513B1
Oversight bill voted by Sen 6-3, 458C3
Jail informant use curbed by Sup Ct 6-16, 511B3
Lloyd Carr chief sentenced 6-20, 503F1
Donated porno warrants required by Sup Ct 6-20, 555A3
Ala A-plant probe cited 6-28, 551B2
Ohio bribe plotters convicted 7-3, 655D2
PR navigatn statn bombings probed 7-14, 559F3
B Carter controversy grows 7-22—7-31, 569D2
8 FALN suspects convicted 7-30; 2 sentncd, 1 rptd extradited 8-4, 601D1
Ga prison escapees recaptured 7-30, 654G1
Tabatabai slayer flees US 8-6, 671D3
PR Navy ambush suspects murdered 8-11, 9-11, 1 rptd missing 9-8; natlsts plan probe 9-19, 786A2
Dem platform charter plank adopted 8-13, 615D1
B Carter probe hearing cites 9-4, 700E3
Intell oversight bill clears Cong 9-19, 9-30; signed 10-14, 804C1
Aaron probe re Trigon arrest rptd 9-22, 754B1
'79 US crime data rptd 9-24, 971D1
Buffalo area black slayings prompt probe 10-13, 997E1
Offshore bank fraud indictmts 10-20, 860E3
Ex-CIA agent indicted on espionage 10-24, pleads guilty 10-29, 856A1
2 ex-offcls tried 10-29, convicted 11-6, 884G1
Atlanta child slayings probe aid set 11-5, 927G3
Ga 'death row' escape extortn chrg 11-8, 928B1
'69 Weathermen fugitive surrenders 12-3, 928D1
Carter aide cleared in spy leak 12-5, 940B3
Sup Ct hears Nixon taps case 12-8, 937E2
Gray chrgs dropped 12-11, 940A2
2 ex-offcls sentenced 12-15, 963F2
Informant cleared re Ala '65 murder 12-15, 990B1

Abscam Scandal

8 congressmen, other pub offcls linked to bribery; operatn detailed 2-2, 2-3, 81A1-82G1
Facts on congressmen involved 81C1
Pressler rejected offers 2-3, 82A1, E1
ACLU, Nader, others score FBI, Justice tactics, leaks 2-3—2-8, 82E2
MacDonald quits NJ casino comm 2-4, 111B1
Civiletti urges cong ethics com probes delay 2-5, 2-6; coms move ahead 2-6, 82A2
GOP com links to Dem cong majority 2-5, 82B2
NJ casinos involved in probe 2-5; Casino Control Comm reform proposed 2-11, 110G3
Baker urges cong action 2-10, 110E3
Civiletti names leaks prosecutor 2-11, 111E1
US regrets Abscam term 2-12, 111A2
Spec counsel hired by ethics com 2-13; House bars Justice evidence request, com continues probe 2-27, 143D2-B3
Kelly quits House GOP conf 2-21, 143B3
House backs ethics panel probe 3-27, 267A1
Myers, Lederer, other pub offcls indicted 5-22, 5-27, 5-28, 402C2-B3
Jenrette, Thompson, Murphy indicted 6-13, 6-18, 454C1-D2
Jenrette wins primary runoff 6-24, 496F1
Pa rptr cited for silence 7-10, 554A2
Kelley indicted 7-15, 554F1
Judge quits cases 8-7, 599D3
Myers loses entrapmt plea 8-8, 684G2
Abscam term redefined 8-20, 684E2
Myers, co-defendants convicted 8-31, 684B2
Jenrette, Stowe trial opens 9-5, convicted 10-7, 782D3
Murphy wins NY primary 9-9, 682D2
2 Phila councilmen convicted 9-16, 740B2
Appeals ct backs Myers tapes broadcast 10-1; Sup Ct refuses stay, tapes aired 10-14, 781C2
Myers expelled from House 10-2, 740B1
Jenrette House expulsn hearings open 10-7, 783C1
Williams, 3 other indicted 10-30, 824C2
Myers entrapmt plea refused by Sup Ct 11-3, 856G1
Myers loses seat; Lederer, Murtha win 11-4, 846A2, 848F3
Thompson, Murphy, Jenrette lose seats 11-4, 846A2, 848G2, C3, 850E1
McCollum wins Kelly House seat 11-4, 849D2
Phila offcls' convictns dismissed 11-26, 919G1
Thompson, Murphy convicted 12-3, 919D1
Jenrette resigns from House 12-10, 962E1

Brilab Probe

Southwest corruptn probe, LA judge bribe plot rptd 2-8—2-9; organized crime summit rptd canceled 2-13, 111D2-112C1
Tex house speaker, 3 others indicted 6-12, 454E2
Marcello, 3 others indicted 6-17, 454D3
Tex house speaker, 2 others acquitted 10-23, 971B2

Miporn Probe

55 indicted, probe detailed 2-14, 136C1

1976

FEDERAL Communications Commission (FCC)
Cable TV curbs attached by House unit 1-26, Justice Dept 2-5, 135B3, D3
Polish joke case review denied 2-23, 169G3
Rules on 2 pol ad cases 3-4, 180E2-A3
Eases cable TV rules 4-2, 249B2
Equal-time rules upheld 4-12, 282D1
Sup Ct bars review of CPB bias-control case 4-19, 331B2
SEC suit vs Gen Tire settled 5-10, 360A2
Sup Ct lets stand license denials 5-24, 393E2
Reid quits 5-27, 412B2
Reagan protests Ford ads 6-5, 410B2
'77 funds signed 7-14, 534D2
Pres TV debate talks open 8-26, 632D3
Fogarty, White confrmd 9-8, 807G3, 808D1
Pres debate suits rejctd 9-17, 9-20, 703F2
Sup Ct bars equal-time review 10-12, 765D3
Hooks to head NAACP 11-6, 892B2
AT&T trust suit OKd 11-16, 886G3
NBC, US in programming pact 11-17, 869G1
Network probe asked 11-23, 901D1
Sup Ct refuses '74 phone equipmt rule 12-13, 960E2
On USSR radio interference 12-28, 1011D1

FEDERAL Deposit Insurance Corp. (FDIC)
Sets Tenn, NJ, Colo, Tex bank sales 1-11—3-3, 167E1, B2
Major banks 'problem' list rptd; Cong studies regulatory reform, disclosures disputed 1-12—2-9, 111E1-112F2
Proxmire scores bank mergers 2-17, 3-1, 185E2, D3
Del Farmers Bank aid offered 2-23; bailout set 6-10, 437F2
Barnett confrmd chrmn 3-17, 232C1
Housing bias chrgd 4-26, Sen panel rpts 5-31, 413E2-C3
Lloyds takes over Calif bank 5-23, 438D1
Texas bank closed 6-3, 438D1
NJ bank takeover set 6-14, Colo, Ky banks shut 6-25, 495F1
Texas' Citizen Bank fails 7-7, 940B2
Aids Boston bank takeover 9-15, Detroit bank 12-19, 984A1; Phila bank 10-22, New Orleans 12-5, 939F3-940A1, A2
Forgn bank bill not cleared 10-2, 940A3
Problem-bank list grows 11-2, 866D1, E1 ★

FEDERAL Election Commission
More US funding OKd 1-8, 22F3
Curtis scores Morton apptmt 1-14, 21C3
Curtis pacified on Morton role 1-19, Strauss seeks ruling 1-22, 41C2
Sup Ct rules unconst 1-30, 86E1, 87E1
Sup Ct stays rule 2-27, 169F3
Reagan camp scores Kissinger 3-13, 198D1
Sup Ct rejects matching fund plea 4-23, 306C1
Fund end hurt Dems in Pa 4-27, 305E1
Revisn enacted, powers curbed 5-11, 346B2
Reagan protests Kissinger speeches 5-14, 359E1
Reconstituted, matching funds resumed 5-21, 391F2
Campaign debts rptd 6-16, 491C1
9 denied subsidies 6-23, 490E3 ★
Fed funds total rptd 7-1, 490G3
OKs Dem electn funds 7-20, 565A3
OKs GOP ticket funds 8-24, 688A3
Fed funds total rptd 8-26; pres nominatn costs cited 8-28, 688D2
Rules on pres TV debate funding 8-30, 644D1
Pres debate suit rejected 9-17, 703F2
Lists major lobbyist, individual donatns 10-22, 938B3
Carter spending rptd 12-7, 938A2
Rpts certificatns, surplus 12-31, 979E1, F2

FEDERAL Energy Administration (FEA)
Christie confrmd asst admin 3-23, 232D1
Oil import-fees upheld 6-17, 452D3
Sup Ct bars oil entitlemt review 6-21, 569E1
Fuel controls end 7-1, 534B1
'77 funds signed 7-31, 623D1
Extension bill signed 8-14, 622F2
Carter proposes Cabt-level dept 9-21, 704E2
Proposes gas price decontrol 11-23, Ford backs 12-29, 991F2-A3

1977

FEDERAL Communications Commission (FCC)
TV network probe OKd 1-14, 119C1
AT&T rpts '76 record earnings 2-1, 93C3
Regulatory agency rpt issued 2-9, 131G3
Wiley on TV violence regulatn 2-14, 157D3, 158B1
AT&T practices cleared 2-23, reactn 2-24, 217B2
Cross-media ownershp barred 3-1, 216B1
NYC obscenity order voided 3-16, 215D3-216B1
Pvt phone equipmt registratn order backed 3-22, Sup Ct refuses review 10-3, 760E3
Pay-TV rules voided 3-25, Sup Ct appeal OKd 4-14, 376C2
McCarthy pres debate suit review declined 4-4, 341D3
U of Pa radio station loses license 4-4, 395A3
Gannett purchases OKd 4-14, 395D2
CB radio penalty raised 4-26, 345B1
SEC new acctg rules rptd 4-29, 369B1
Pol air time stand reversed 5-6, 376G1
'76 Telpak order revoked, 6-1, AT&T pvt rates OKd 6-1, 6-8, 465C1
TV network probe suspended 6-30, 583E2-A3
Wiley term expires 6-30, Hooks resignatn effective 7-27, 583F2-A3
Tennis tourn fee probe rptd 7-8, 548C2
AT&T to maintain Telpak 7-21, '75 'end-link' repricing order upheld 8-5, 631C3, F3
'78 funds signed 8-2, 667F3
TV bias study scores inactn 8-15, 642B3
Phone ad curbs studied 8-26, White House backs 10-21, 921A1
Cable TV obscenity rule ordrd suspended 9-1, 846B2
Gets boxing scandal rpt 9-3, 828D2
Comsat warned re escrow fund 9-11, refund order upheld 10-14, 944E1
Pay TV rule review declined 10-3, 760A3

FEDERAL Deposit Insurance Corp. (FDIC)
GAO scores bank regulatn 1-31, 154E3
Franklin collapse suit rptd 2-9, 155C3
3 failed banks aided 3-10, 3-28, 5-20, 578B1
Problem bank list rptd up 3-11, 194D2
Lance probe referred 9-7, 689F3, 690C2

FEDERAL Disaster Assistance Administration—*See under HOUSING & Urban Development in this section below*

FEDERAL Election Commission
'76 special interest gifts rptd 2-15, 128C1-129F2
Personal use fund-raising OKd 3-24, 233A1
GOP outspent Dems in '76 4-28, 842C1
'76 cong spending rptd 5-4, 482F1
Shapp ordrd to repay funds 5-12, 482B2
Lance probe asked 9-6, 689F3, 690D1 ★
Thomson denies Korea lobbying link 9-27, 773F3
Files suit vs AFL-CIO 12-16, 980A1

FEDERAL Energy Administration (FEA)
Ford proposes energy dept 1-11, 14E3
Home heating oil productn hike ordrd 1-24, 54G1
Rpts record Jan heating oil use 2-4, 92A1
New Eng oil import aid ordrd 2-10, 152A3
Gas crisis eases, workers return 2-18, 152E2
Regional power systems backed 2-23, 277G2
Carter submits reorgnzn bill 3-1, 148G1
Oil regulatn case review refused 4-25, 342D3

1978

FEDERAL Communications Commission (FCC)
Cowles Communicatns to liquidate 1-6, 76A1
AT&T rate rise stay lifted 1-9, 13C2
WJLA, KOCO-TV exchng OKd 1-12, Allbritton scored 2-13, 109A3
MCI phone svc case review denied 1-16, 33G1
Telpak rate hike OKd 1-18, 84E1
Minority broadcasting ownership aid proposed 1-31, 195A2
Cable-TV access rules voided 2-24, 195D2-C3
Western Union trust probe OKd 3-9, 270D2
WJLA-TV swap OKd again 3-9, Allbritton halts deal 3-24, 270A3
CBS 'Heavyweight Championship' tennis tourn censured 3-16, 251D1
ABC boxing tourn scored 4-25, 379D1
Comsat dispute setld 5-9, 494C3
WTOP radio sale OKd 5-11, WTOP-TV swap 5-18, 599E3
AT&T-MCI phone svc case stay denied by Sup Ct 5-22, 388A2
'Fairness doctrine' case refused by Sup Ct 5-30, 430D3
Allbritton resigns as Washn Star publisher 5-31, 672E2
Cross-media ban backed by Sup Ct 6-12, 467C3
WPIX-TV license renewed 6-16, 672C1
'Filthy Words' ban upheld by Sup Ct 7-3, 551F2
WGBH license renewed 7-20, censorship role rejctd 7-21, 599E1
Children's TV probe to reopen 7-28, 672A2
Gannett to sell TV statn 8-20, 760A1
WESH-TV license renewal voided, ct sets guidelines 9-25, 907D3
Cable-TV expansn rule dropped 9-27, 1030B2
Brown scores performance 10-11, 908D1
Cable-TV 'distant' signal importatn OKd 11-2, 1030C2
NYC, Phila TV statn studios in NJ ordrd 11-9, 1030D2
AT&T '76 rate hike cited 12-1, 934E3
More AM radio channels proposed 12-19, 1030G1

FEDERAL Deposit Insurance Corp. (FDIC)
Check-bouncing protectn OKd 5-5, 345E3
US Natl Bank paymt case declined by Sup Ct 10-16, 789C1

FEDERAL Disaster Assistance Administration—*See under HOUSING & Urban Development below*

FEDERAL Election Commission (FEC)
AFL-CIO fined $10,000 6-12, 509E3
Carter com, Ga bank fined for '76 plane use 6-26, 509A3
'Reverse check-off' by unions barred 7-21, 565F2-A3
Zagoria nominatn withdrawn 8-12, 831C3
Fund-raising rpt issued; 'PAC democracy' feared 9-7, 753G1-G2
McGarry replaces Staebler 10-25, Common Cause sues Carter 10-26, 831F2-B3
Sen races rptd won by big spenders 11-15, 898B1
PAC cong com gifts rptd 12-24, 1008B1

FEDERAL Emergency Management Agency
Carter proposes 6-19, 466D2-B3

FEDERAL Energy Administration (FEA)
Oil co rebates to consumers barred 1-20, 108F3
House subcom staff rpt scores on oil price fraud 12-10, 983D3

1979

FEDERAL Communications Commission (FCC)
ITT long-distance phone svc OKd 1-4, 15A2
ABC to cut children's TV ads 1-18, 78B3
Westn Union telegram monopoly ended 1-25, 78A2
Cable TV pub-access rule upset by Sup Ct 4-2, 281G1
Local access phone pact OKd 4-12, 350G3
Cable TV rate case declined by Sup Ct 4-16, 303A1
Panax granted Mich TV licenses 5-31, revoked 7-12, 618E2
Starr Broadcasting transfer to Shamrock OKd 6-8, 588F1
RKO Gen license fitness doubted 7-18, 618G1
Electronic mail project authority claimed 8-1, Postal Svc sues 10-18, 921D2
Radio deregulatn proposed 9-6, Nader opposes 9-11, ACLU asks pub review 11-5, 858E3
AT&T pvt-line rates scored 9-20, 870D1
Southn Bell pol paymts scored 9-20, 870F1
Staff scores children's TV 10-30, NAB reacts 11-1, 858A3-E3
Library, broadcast link-up urged 11-16, 901D1
'Family hour' power backed by ct 11-20, 1007B1
Carter TV ad bid upheld 11-20, 918G3
Western Union quits electronic mail project 12-4, 921A3*
More AM radio statns OKd 12-12, 1006E3
Children's TV plan modified 12-19, 1006G3

Common Carrier Bureau
Postal Svc satellite leasing plan rejected 10-18, 921F2

FEDERAL Deposit Insurance Corp. (FDIC)
'78 problem banks listed 1-30, 113A2

FEDERAL Election Commission (FEC)
SWP wins funds rpt exemptn 1-9, 13F3
McGarry, Friedersdorf confrmd 2-21, 130B3
Carter primary spending cleared 4-2, 265A1
PAC spending rptd up 5-10, 363E1, A2
Tiernan elected chrmn, Friedersdorf named v chrmn 5-17, 401C3
Carter com billed $50,203 6-4, 419G2
Labor '78 cong campaign gifts rptd 6-13, 595B1
Udall told to repay '76 electn funds 6-18, 595E1
GOP credit card plan blocked 6-21, 595G1
GOP, Carter pres campaign funds rptd 7-12, 593G3-594B1
Reagan pres campaign funds rptd 7-26, 594C1
Brown pres com formed 7-30, 593E1
Citizens Party formed, platform issued 8-1, 594E3-595A1
Pressler pres campaign com formed 8-2, 594E2
Conservative PAC plans Sen drive 8-16, 628A1
Rafshoon agency cleared in Carter '76 general campaign 8-21, 661G3
'76 election audits finished, Wallace repayment noted 9-5, 724A2
Draft Haig com formed 9-10, 680C2
Kennedy pres funding challenged 10-4, 783A3
LaRouche funds voted 12-18, 984A2

1980

FEDERAL Communications Commission (FCC)
CBS 'dovish' complaint case refused by Sup Ct 1-7, 16B1
3 RKO Gen licenses lifted 1-24, 119F2
Westinghouse unit TV license OKd 1-30, 119C3
Comsat direct satellite TV svc OKd 1-30, 240A1
Electronic mail plan OKd 2-22, 4-8, 347G2
FM radio channel increase sought 3-5, 239F3-240A1
Carter ad bid ruling upheld 3-14, 221G3
Phone industry deregulatn set 4-7, 370E1
Cox-GE merger approved 4-28, 386E1
CBS, US settle trust dispute 5-8, 501D3
CBS blocked from Cuba broadcasts 5-22, 397F1; cleared 6-1, 420A3
Protected AM signals limited; new statn minority ownership bias seen 5-29, 519A2
'69 telecommunicatns ruling cited 6-13, 456D3
TV prime-time rule failure seen 6-18, 501C1
Cable-broadcast ownership ban proposed 6-24, 583B2
Evangelical Christian pol actn profiled 7-11—9-15, 819E1
Pay-TV lobbying group formed 7-15, 640A1
Cable-TV distant signal, syndicatn limits lifted 7-22, 583B1
AT&T begins reorgn, Ferris lauds 8-20, 648E1
UHF, VHF TV statn expansn proposed 9-9, 9-18, 731C3
Comsat broadcast satellite TV plan advances 10-2, 906D3
Faith Center TV license revoked 10-10, 907B1
Commoner uses vulgar radio ad 10-15, 818B3
Westinghouse to acquire Teleprompter 10-15, 836A2
WATS line resales OKd 10-21, 987B3
Revises phone deregulatn plan 10-28, 987G2
Pol airtime case accepted by Sup Ct 11-3, 856D2
NYC TV statn move to NJ backed 11-6, 906E1
20 satellite launchings OKd 12-4, 990C3
CBS seeks cable ownership rule revocatn 12-8, 1003D1
Small cos regulatn end sought 12-16, 987D3

FEDERAL Deposit Insurance Corp. (FDIC)
First Penn bailout set 4-28, 329D3
DIDC sets interest rules 5-28, S&Ls file suit 6-16, 516G3

FEDERAL Election Commission (FEC)
Bush, Kennedy funds OKd 1-2, 1-4, 5B2
PR primary challenged 2-19, 130E1
Baker, Dole, Crane, Brown lose funds 3-13, 209C1
Reagan fund raising coms upheld by fed ct 8-28, 681G1
Anderson ruled eligible for funds 9-4, 665C2
Campaign rules issued 9-5, 681G2
Anderson bank loan plan fails 10-2, abandoned 10-15, 818D1
AFL-CIO funds case declined by Sup Ct 11-10, 868C3
Anderson paymt $4.1 mln 11-13, 866F1
Friedersdorf resigns 12-16, McGarry replaces 12-18, 955F3

1976

Alaska oil surplus export opposed 11-30, 991E3
Proposes oil stockpile plan 12-15, 991D3
Rpts oil consumptn peak 12-29, 991A3

FEDERAL Highway Administration—*See under TRANSPORTATION below*

FEDERAL Home Loan Bank Board
NY unit Chile aid offer rptd 1-26, 99E2
Rpts 'problem' savings & loans 2-17, 185C1
Housing bias chrgd 4-26, Sen panel rpts 5-31, 413E2-C3
Rpts Feb new-house costs 5-12, 375C3
Rpts Aug mortgage rates 9-16, 709C2
Rpts Sept house costs 10-20, 805F3

Federal Savings and Loan Insurance Corp.
Regulatory role cited 2-17, 185G1
Miss bank crisis 5-7—6-8, 438A2
Miss S&L coverage set 6-20, 495D1

FEDERAL Housing Administration—*See under HOUSING & Urban Development below*

FEDERAL Maritime Commission
Casey confrmd comr 1-21, 68C1
Sea-Land probe rptd 9-10, 9-13, 689G3, 690B1
USSR seeks shipping conf entry 10-22, Bakke asked to shun talks 11-26, 948C1, G1

FEDERAL Mediation and Conciliation Service
Usery named Labor secy 1-22, 40E3; confrmd 2-4, 110G1
Scearce confrmd dir 4-7, 262E3

FEDERAL Power Commission
Sup Ct remands gas reserves case 1-19, 43D1
House extends natural gas regulatn 2-5, 108D2-109A1
Ford gives Alaskan gas plan 2-26, 149A2
Sup Ct upholds gas-sale rule 3-3, 219D1
Va dam project upheld 3-24, 219A3
Sup Ct rules on job bias powers 5-19, 393F2
Sup Ct backs broad powers 6-7, 435F1
Sees winter gas shortage 6-18, 636D1
Hikes 'old' gas rate 7-1, 635G3
OKs gas rate hikes 7-27, modifies 8-9, 635D2-636C1
Moss scores rate hike 9-1, 10-30, 868E2, A3
To reconsider July rate ruling 9-2; hearings 9-16—9-17; ups cost estimate, reclassifies gas 10-20; July rate reaffirmed 11-3, vote rptd 11-5, 868B1
New River dams blocked 9-11, 689E1
Govt in sunshine bill signed 9-13, 688D3
Carter proposes Cabt-level dept 9-21, 704E2
Sup Ct bars price hike review 10-4, 807A3
Alaska gas transport study bill signed 10-22, 834D3
Staff rpt favors Alaska gas pipeline 12-7, 998A2

FEDERAL Railroad Administration—*See under TRANSPORTATION below*

FEDERAL Reserve System (including Federal Reserve Board)—*See also BURNS, Arthur*
'75 bank 'problem' list rptd; Cong studies regulatory reform, disclosures disputed 1-12—2-3, 111D1-112G1, G2-113F1
Cuts discount rate 1-16, OKs fed fund rate rise 2-27, 167C3
Forgn bank deposit disclosure agrmt rptd 1-18, 44A3
Italy seeks $250 mln loan 1-22, 74E2
Ford Econ Rpt 1-26, 67E1, C2
Gardner confrmd v chrmn 1-29, 110B2
Money supply growth targets changed 2-3, growth rptd 2-18, 167F3-168B1
Proxmire scores bank mergers 2-17, 3-1, 185E2, D3
Dow caution linked to money policy 2-27, 184E3
Volcker vs bank 'super agency' plan 3-9, 185F3
Credit bias ban signed 3-23, 233C3
Carter urges reform 4-23, 305D2
Housing bias chrgd 4-26, Sen panel rpts 5-31, 413E2-C3
Prime hike, tight money linked 4-30—6-4, 436C3, D3
Cuts money-growth targets, tightens credit 5-3, 347E2
House OKs restructuring bill 5-10, 345D1
1st ¼ lira acquisitns rptd 5-17, 396G3
Lilly confrmd to bd 5-28, 412F1
Fed funds rate hike 6-5, 436E3
Loan to prop UK £ OKd 6-7, 407B2
Cited in Dem platform text 6-15, 469G2

1977

SEC new acctg rules rptd 4-29, 369A1
Indl plant coal conversn proposed 5-9, 369G3
Goldman confrmd asst admin 5-12, 418E1
Energy dept OKd by Sen 5-18, 405G1
Alaska pipeline rate dispute 6-17, 477E2
'78 funds signed 7-26, 592E3
Energy Dept to absorb 8-4, 591E2
Rollins confrmd asst admin 8-4, 626D3
Sen OKs coal-conversn aid 9-8, 702E3
Calif-Tex oil pipe OK cited 12-2, 942F3

FEDERAL Energy Regulatory Commission
House OKs Carter energy pkg 8-5, 609D3

FEDERAL Highway Administration—*See under TRANSPORTATION in this section above*

FEDERAL Home Loan Bank Board
Rpts record '76 savings inflow 2-1, 155G1
Rpts Dec '76, Jan new house costs 2-14, 178D2
Anti-bias drive rptd 3-24, 279E2
Redlining curb set 11-9, 898C2

Federal Home Loan Mortgage Corp.
Carter natl energy plan 4-20, 292A1

FEDERAL Home Mortgage Corp.—*See under FEDERAL Home Loan Bank Board in this section above*

FEDERAL Housing Administration—*See under HOUSING & Urban Development below*

FEDERAL Maritime Commission
Settles Sea-Land case; rebate probe continues 1-5, 6B2
Regulatory agency rpt issued 2-9, 131F3
E Coast dock protest ends 4-18, 324G2
Sony settles chrgs 8-19, 650G3-651A1
McCloskey rebate amendmt rejctd 10-31, 856D2

FEDERAL National Mortgage Association—*See under HOUSING & Urban Development below*

FEDERAL Power Commission (FPC)
Ford proposes energy dept 1-11, 14F3
OKs emergency natural gas sales 1-14, 37A1
Rpts Jan gas reserves drop 1-15, 54A3
OKs emergency gas purchases 1-19, other actns 1-20, 53G3-54E1
Gas shortage layoffs estimated 1-22, 54C2
Carter asks eased gas-sale rules 1-26, 53E3
OKs more Canada gas imports 1-27, 76E1
Rpts '75 interstate gas reserves fall, prices cited 1-28, 76A3
Judge backs '76 Alaska gas pipe rpt 2-1, 82C2
Emergency gas bill signed 2-2, 76C2
Dunham named gas act admin 2-2, 91G2
Gas reserves drop rptd 2-2; Dec '76, Jan use up 2-9, 91E3
Mex, Algeria gas imports OKd 2-4, Canada elec exchng set 2-5, 91B3
Regulatory agency rpt issued 2-9, 131G3
Gas productn studies rptd 2-11, 151E3, G3, 152C1
Tenneco questns gas diversns 2-28, probe ordrd 3-8, 196D1
Carter submits reorgnzn bill 3-1, 148G1
Staff reprisals chrgd 3-10, 196A1
24-hr fuel watch ended 3-11, 277B2
'76, '71-76 elec power data rptd 3-23, 3-25, 277F1
Carter energy plan 4-20, 292C2
Algeria LNG imports OKd 4-29, 370B1
Trans-Canada gas pipe route rule 5-2, 369C2
Energy dept OKd by Sen 5-18, 405F1
'76 gas price hikes upheld 6-16, 464C2
Texaco dispute resolved 7-14, 559A3
Energy Dept to absorb 8-4, 591E2
Gas royalties dispute review refused 10-3, 760A2
Boston Ed rate rise let stand 11-14, 878D3

FEDERAL Property Council
Carter proposes abolitn 7-15, 556C1

FEDERAL Railroad Administration—*See under TRANSPORTATION below*

FEDERAL Reserve System (including Federal Reserve Board)—*See also BURNS, Arthur*
Gramley named to Treas post 1-18, 32E3
GAO scores bank regulatn 1-31, 154E3, 155D1
Burns vs anti-stimulus policies 2-3, 89C3
Bars bank S&L ownership 2-22, 155E1
'76 forgn exchng mkt tensns, central bank interventn rptd 3-2, 188C3
Harris scores housing controls 3-7, 178F1
Burns asks OPEC banker role 3-10, 363C1
Credit policy, Dow linked 3-17—5-25, 408B1
Carter: Burns monthly mtgs set 4-15, 299B1
Bank loans to Indonesia rptd risky 4-18, 392G2
Apr money growth, tight credit policy, prime rate hike linked 5-13, 5-30, 407G1
Reuss scores actions 5-24, 406D3
Policies linked to prime rate hike 6-1, 6-7, 577E3
Consumer credit rise analyzed 6-28, 555B1
Privacy comm scores computer plan 7-12, 632D1
Burns vs $ drop 7-26, US trade deficit-reducing strategy rptd challenged 8-8, 585D2
Prime hiked, tight money policy cited 8-1—9-13, 704B1

1978

FEDERAL Energy Regulatory Commission (of Energy Department)
Coal strike utility billing probe set 5-10, 366E3
Natural gas diversn curbed by Sup Ct 5-31, 430G3-431D1
Coal gasificatn plant financing plan submitted 6-2, 471E2
ICC Alaska pipe rates backed by Sup Ct 6-6, 447C2
Tenneco, Shell interstate gas sales probed 6-22, 471B2
Con Ed blamed in '77 NY blackout 7-6, 529F3
Farmers warned vs gas price compromise 8-31, 678B2

FEDERAL Highway Administration—*See under TRANSPORTATION below*

FEDERAL Home Loan Bank Board
Redlining curb adopted 5-18, 410D2
Mortgage rates rptd up 6-18, 470E1
Variable rate mortgages OKd 7-24, 605D2
McKinney vs restrictive money policy 8-7, 605C2
Mortgage rates, house costs rise rptd 11-2, 919C1
3 new mortgages OKd, '75 Cong actn cited 12-14, 962A1

FEDERAL Insurance Administration—*See under HOUSING & Urban Development below*

FEDERAL Maritime Commission
Rebate fine total cited 184F3
Labor contract jurisdictn enlarged 3-1, 143C3-144C1
Seatrain, others plead guilty on rebate chrg 3-16, 184D3
USSR shipping co gets show-cause order 9-13, 820F2-A3
Seatrain fined $2½ mln for rebates, other setlmts rptd 9-18, 752E3
Israeli co fined for rebates, Trans-Mex setlmt rptd 10-1, 752G3
Seatrain fine cited 10-23, 816D3
Shipping malpractice bill vetoed 11-4, 897G2
Japan shippers settle rebate chrgs 11-8, 961F3

FEDERAL Mediation and Conciliation Service
Coal talks resume 1-12, 62B3; **for subsequent developments, see COAL—Strike**
Postal talks resumed 8-28, 766C1

FEDERAL National Mortgage Association—*See under HOUSING & Urban Development below*

FEDERAL Nuclear Regulatory Commission
Seabrook A-plant hearings protested 6-26, 494D1

FEDERAL Power Commission (FPC)
Gulf gas pipe contract case refused 2-21, 126B2
'76 'new' gas rates review denied 2-27, 143C2
Power plant size, efficiency studied 6-2, 408E3

FEDERAL Preparedness Agency—*See under GENERAL Services Administration below*

FEDERAL Procurement Policy, Office of—*See under BUDGET in this section above*

FEDERAL Railroad Administration—*See under TRANSPORTATION below*

FEDERAL Reserve System (including Federal Reserve Board)
$ defense via swap network set 1-4, reactn 1-9, 27F1, C2
Hikes discount, fed funds rates to bolster $ 1-6, 1-9; Dow fall intensifies 1-6—1-11; other reactn rptd 1-23, 28A1, B2
Prime raised to 8%, Fed rate hikes cited 28D2
Carter on interest rates 1-12, 12C1
Miller confrmatn hearings 1-24—3-2; Sen confrms 3-3, sworn 3-8, 161E1-B3
Burns cites inflatn danger, asks energy plan OK 1-30, 161D3
Burns resigns as bd member 1-31, 161C3
$ defense rptd limited 2-6, 2-16, 118G2
Insurance sales by bank holding cos denied review 2-27, 143B2
Miller backs oil import curbs, anti-inflatn drive 3-15, 181C1-A2
Burns urges gold sale, other $ defns measures 3-31, 235B2
Forgn bank activity in US rptd up 4-3, 4-12, 263A2
Miller backs Carter inflatn plan 4-12, 260G2
Stock mkt reacts to credit moves 4-14, 4-27—28, 303C1, C2
Miller backs tax-cut delay 4-25, 307C2
Higher prime, fed funds rate linked 4-28, 326C2
Check-bouncing protectn OKd 5-1, 345D3
Textron bribe evidence rptd destroyed 5-8, 449A1

1979

FEDERAL Emergency Management Agency
A-emergency evacuatn program urged 10-30, 825F3

FEDERAL Energy Regulatory Commission (of Energy Department)
Rate relief power backed by Sup Ct 1-16, 32D2
NH A-plant constructn cost pass-on backed 1-26, 186G2
Gas productn power denied by Sup Ct 2-22, 150F3
Mobil gas overchrg suit filed 6-22, 518F1
Alaska, Indonesia LNG imports OKd 8-14; Calif terminal chosen 9-26, projct approved 9-27, 769D2
NM suit vs Texas refused by Sup Ct 10-9, 784E1
Mobil OKs overchrg refunds 11-5, 943B2

FEDERAL Highway Administration—*See under TRANSPORTATION below*

FEDERAL Home Loan Bank Board
Bank takeovers by industry scored 3-7, 205B2
Mar mortgage rate record rptd 4-6, 281D1
Automatic funds shift voided 4-20, 303B3
Savings interest rates hiked, 4-yr notes variable rate mortgage set 5-30, 403C2
July, Aug mortgage rates, house prices rptd 9-6, 701A3

FEDERAL Housing Administration—*See under HOUSING & Urban Development below*

FEDERAL Labor Relations Authority
Civil Svc Comm replaced 1-1, 5A3, 6B1

FEDERAL Maritime Commission
USSR ship ban OKd 1-29, USSR warns 2-14; State, Justice Depts sue 3-6, 213G2
USSR ship ban delayed 4-6, 287A3
7 shipping cos indicted 6-1, 423B2
Cong OKs anti-rebate bill 6-5, 465F3
USSR ship ban lifted 10-16, 815F2
Atlantica fine rptd 10-31, 985G2

FEDERAL Mediation & Conciliation Service
United Airlines strike ends 5-24, 402B2
Grain handlers strike ends 9-25, 722E3

FEDERAL Procurement Policy, Office of—*See under BUDGET in this section above*

FEDERAL Railroad Administration—*See under TRANSPORTATION below*

FEDERAL Register—*See GENERAL Services Administration-National Archives below*

FEDERAL Reserve System (including Federal Reserve Board)
Treas bills, notes explained 681D2
'Long float' check delays discouraged 1-10, 15E2
Miller on '79 inflatn, budget deficit forecast 1-25, 48E3
Hostile forgn bank takeovers opposed 3-13, 205F1-A2
Cleveland bank cleared 3-14, 204D2
Bank anti-inflatn guides set 3-16, 264E2
3 forgn bank takeovers OKd 3-16, 205B1
Treas gets $3 bln loan, early paymt 4-2, 251C3
Membership cost, erosion cited 4-9, Reuss abandons aid bill 4-24, 303D1
Miller on 1st ¼ GNP 4-19, 280C2
Automatic funds shift voided 4-20, 303F2
Barclays purchase of Amer Credit OKd 5-29, 440B3
Savings interest rate hiked, 4-yr notes created 5-30, 403C2
Citicorp unit applicatn case declined by Sup Ct 6-11, 479A1
CFTC OKs T-bills, notes futures trading 6-19, 681A3
Open Mkt rpt disclosure delay backed by Sup Ct 6-28, 558B3
Miller named Treas secy 7-19, 529D1, 530C1
Discount rate hiked, $ rebounds 7-20, 531E3
Volcker named chrmn; reactn 7-25, 555B2

1980

FEDERAL Energy Regulatory Commission (of Energy Department)
Gas pipeline capacity rule challenge refused by Sup Ct 3-3, 210A2
Alcan gas pipe eastn leg OKd 4-24, 331A1
Canada gas imports, US westn pipe leg OKd 7-3, 562E2
ND synfuels plant gets $1.5 bln fed loan 11-19, ct blocks projct 12-8, 962B1

FEDERAL Home Loan Bank Board
Janis money mkt funds testimony rptd 3-21, 223E3
Renegotiated-rate mortgages, funds infusn OKd 4-3, 266E2, F3
Apr mortgage rates at 16.56% 5-6, 384F3
DIDC sets interest rules 5-28, S&Ls file suit 6-16, 516G3
S&Ls wider credit powers OKd 7-3, 516E2
S&L loan plan proposed 7-31, 600A1
Janis resigns 12-15, 959A1

FEDERAL Maritime Commission
ILA Sovt ship boycott impact seen 1-9, 9F1*

FEDERAL Reserve System (including Federal Reserve Board)
Discount, prime rates explained 247E2
Volcker bars tight money policy change 1-2, 52C2
Solomon named NY Fed chief 1-21, 52B2
Membership exodus feared 1-23, 2-4; map, defectn chart 113B1-C3
Carter backs fiscal policy 1-30, 74D1
Miller FRB chrmnship cited 1-31, 92E1
New monetary supply terms set 2-7, 113C3
Connally Saudi bank connectns, '78-79 fund transfers rptd 2-11, 129B2
Discount rate hiked to 13% 2-15, prime follows, Volcker vows tight money supply 2-19, 126A1-A2
$-yen, mark exchng rates chart 2-18—3-20, 202D1
Tight money policy, bond price drop linked 2-19, 127B1
Reagan 'basic speech' scores 2-29, 207C2
Japan sets yen rescue plan 3-2, 173E2
Brazil forgn reserves used to offset debt 3-5, 191D1
Discount rate hike speculation rptd 3-13, 182G2
Carter anti-inflatn plan sets credit curbs 3-14; reactn rptd 3-15, 201D1, 202G1
Discount rate surchrg imposed 3-14, 201A2
Gold speculatn slows, T-bill sale reaps $3.3 bln, Dow plummets 3-17, 203B1, C2, G2

1976

Nader rpt scores bank diversificatn 7-5, 495C2-A3
Carter upholds independence 7-28, 551B1
House study scores dist bd make-up 8-15, Burns rebuts 8-30, 666G3
GOP platform text 8-18, 602A3
Bankers Trust acquisition barred 8-19, 667F1
Govt in sunshine bill signed 9-13, 688D3
Aids Amer Bank & Trust 9-13, 9-14, 940D1
Eased credit rules cited re Dow 9-21, 846A3, G3
Ford, Carter debate 9-23, 703D1
Forgn bank, restructuring bills not cleared 10-2, 940G2, A3
Problem-bank list grows 11-2, 866G1
Burns vs stimulative econ policies; rpts M1 target lowered, M2, M3 widened 11-11, 865D2
Carter states plans 11-15, 863F3
Dow rise, eased credit policies linked 11-18—12-31, 984D1
Discount, fed fund rates cut 11-19, reserve requiremt cut 12-17, 939E2
OKs Detroit bank acquisitn 12-19, 983F3

Statistics
Nov credit, Oct revised 1-12, 91C3
Dec, '75 indl output; Nov revised 1-16, 91E3
Dec credit; Nov revised 2-6, 168G3
Jan indl output; Nov, Dec revised 2-13, 168E2
Feb credit 3-8, 199B3
Feb indl output; Dec '75, Jan revised 3-16, 199G2
Nov '75-Feb indl output revised 3-26, 279G2
March indl output 4-15, 279E2
Feb credit 4-16, 279D3
Mar, 1st ¼ credit 5-6, 375E3
Apr indl output, Feb, Mar revised, '70-Apr '76 graph 5-14, 375A2
April credit 6-7, 436F2-A3
May indl output, Apr revised 6-16, 479B3
May credit; Jan, Mar, Apr revised 7-9, 519F1, A2
Business loans 7-29, 568F2
June, July credit 9-8, 709D2
June-Aug indl output; Jan '73-May '76 revised 9-16, 708G3; table 709A1
Aug credit 10-6, 806A3
Sept indl output, Aug revised 10-15, 806F1
Sept credit 11-5, 866E3
'75-76 US bank forgn lending, OPEC deposits 11-10, 915E1
Oct indl output, Sept revised 11-15, 866C3
Oct consumer credit 12-6, 958A3
Nov indl output, Sept, Oct revised 12-15, 958F2

FEDERAL Savings and Loan Insurance Corp.—*See under FEDERAL Home Loan Bank Board above*

FEDERAL Trade Commission (FTC)
Used-car trade rule proposed 1-2, 7B2
Dixon named acting chrmn 1-6, 68C1
Rpts '75 food profit margins 2-11, 216B2
Firestone settles on ads 2-16, 186B3
Seen vs ABA ad action 2-17, 136G3
Collier confrmd comr 3-18, 232D1
Accuses GM 3-22, Levi Strauss 5-7, Gen Foods 7-16, 989B3-E3
Rules vs Encyclopaedia Britannica 3-26, 235E3
Congs curbs vitamin regulatn 4-12, 282C3
Rpts Gen Tire probe 4-27, 360C2
Sup Ct voids drug price ad ban 5-24, 393F1
Sup Ct bars review of cigaret ad fines 6-1, 414A3
Car rental trust suit setld 7-12, 989G2
'77 funds signed 7-14, 534D2
Mrs Dole to take leave of absence 9-4, 666C1
Cong OKs antitrust bill 9-16, 728E1; signed 10-1, 982F1
Radiologists bar price-fixing, '75 MD agrmts cited 11-17, 988F3-989A1
Kennecott to sell Peabody Coal 12-14, 985D1

1977

Discount rate raised, money growth targets cited 8-29, 703D3
Prime rate rise, money supply growth rates linked 10-4, 10-10, 798G2
Admin warns re interest rate rise 10-20, 798B3
Discount rate hiked 10-25, 817B3
Carter on Burns reappointmt, policy criticism 10-27, 813C3
Carter sees no discord 11-10, 877C1
Sen confirmatn for apptmts set 11-16, 878B2
Carter unsure re Burns reapptmt 11-30, 914F1
Miller to replace Burns 12-28; $ drops 12-28, other reactn 12-28, 12-29, 997B3, 1000D1

Statistics
Nov '76 credit 1-7, 56E3
Oct indl output 1-15, 898D3
Dec '76 indl output 1-17, 92G3
Dec '76 credit 2-7, 93D1
Jan indl output 2-15, 129D3
Jan credit 3-4, 176F2
Feb indl output, Jan revised 3-15, 194A1
Feb credit rise 4-5, 274E1
March indl output; graph 4-14, 300A1, A3
March credit 5-5, 406B3
Apr indl output, Feb revised 5-16, 384A1
'76 forgn loans 6-5, 438E1
Apr, May credit rise 7-8, 554G3 ★
'74-77 indl output graph 7-15, 553G3
May, June, 1st, 2d ¼ indl output; Mar, Apr revised 7-15, 553G3
June credit; May, Mar revised 8-8, 611D3
July indl output, May revised 8-15, 628D3
Aug indl output, July revised 9-6, 722C1
July credit rise 9-7, 704B2
Aug credit 10-6, 798D2
Sept indl output, Aug revised 10-14, 798G1
Sept credit, Aug revised 11-4, 858F2
Oct credit 12-7, 961D3
Nov indl output 12-14, 961C3

FEDERAL Trade Commission (FTC)
Ct OKs Arco, Anaconda merger 1-12, 55G2
Dixon slurs Nader 1-17, apologizes 2-1, 2-2, 95G3
Great Western settles case 1-26, 156D1
Vitamin ads to children barred 2-7, 217C1
Regulatory agency rpt issued 2-9, 131F3
Abzug declines post 2-19, 140B3
Land-fraud setlmts scored 3-10, 203D3
Moves vs Tenneco bid for Monroe 3-15, 274G3
Pertschuk confrmd 4-6, 272B3
Beneficial ad dispute review refused 4-25, 342B3
Ford Motor complaint declined 5-16, 419D2
Sunkist accused of monopoly 6-6, 520E2
Peabody sale OKd 6-7, 520C2
Oil cos info rule review rejctd 6-13, 517E1
Kennecott sells Peabody coal 6-30, 520F1
Corrective ad rule upheld 8-2, 613F1-A2
'78 funds signed 8-2, 667F3
Asks Gulf-Kewanee merger stay 8-3, 612G2
HMO study publshd 8-5, 643C2
Funeral industry scored 8-16, 651D3

1978

Admin vs tight $ policy 5-9, 361E2
Carter tax-cut-plan reductn backed 5-11—5-13, 361B1, E1
Discount rate hiked 5-11, 361C2
CIT to sell bank, holding co limits cited 5-12, 364A2
Prime rate hike, tight money policy cited 5-25, 403G2
Miller pledges $ defense 6-13, 523F2
Discount rate hiked; Miller, Admin score 6-30, 679G1, D2
HUD secy cancels cong testimony 8-7, 605B2
Fed funds rate hiked, D marks sold 8-16, 622A2
Forgn bank regulatn clears Cong 8-17, 663B1
Discount, fed funds rate hiked to fight inflatn, aid $ 8-18, 679A1-B2
Teeters named bd member 8-28, 664C1
Interest rate strategy cited in C$ defns move 9-11, 704A1
Prime rate raised 9-15, 9-25, 752A1
Discount rate hiked to 8% 9-22, 731D2
Swiss score $ policy, rate strategy failure cited 9-27, 732C2
Carter scores rate hike 9-27, 9-28, 751C3
Bank auto-leasing case declined by Sup Ct 10-2, 751B2
'74-78 prime, discount, fed funds rate chart 791D1
Discount rate hiked 10-13, 791A2
Open Mkt Com debate on high rates vs slow growth rptd 10-16, 791C2
Fed funds target rate explained 10-18, 791A1
M1 rapid growth rptd 10-19, 791B3
Banks boost prime as credit tightens 10-23—11-3, 827C1
Oct credit tightening cited 10-30, 864A3
Discount, fed fund rate hike, massive interventn aids $ 11-1, 826B1, G2, 827B1
Meany scores discount rate hike 11-1, 863E2
Discount rate, NY mortgage rate ceiling linked 11-6, 919E1
Reuss Open Market Com case declined by Sup Ct 11-27, 937F2
Bank-holding co power backed by Sup Ct 12-11, 980D3
Miller on OPEC price hike impact 12-18, 978D1
Nov indicators drop, money supply shrinkage linked 12-28, 1003C3

Statistics
Indl output index described 52F1
'77, Dec indl output; Sept-Nov revised 1-17, 52D1
Nov, Dec '77 credit 2-10, 128B3
Jan indl output 2-15, 106E1
Jan credit, Dec '77 revised 3-8, 222F3
Feb indl output 3-16, 223E1
Feb credit 4-6, 262B3
Mar indl output; Jan, Feb revised 4-14, 304B1
Mar credit 5-6, 345C2
Apr indl output, Mar revised 5-16, 389A2
Feb-Apr $ defense costs 5-31, 523D2
Apr credit, Jan-Mar revised 6-6, 429F2
May indl output, Mar, Apr revised 6-15, 470C1
May credit 7-7, 552E3
June indl output; Apr, May revised 7-14, 553A1
June credit 8-4, 608B1
July indl output, June-Apr revised 8-15, 643D3
July credit growth 9-8, 717D2
Aug indl output, June, July revised 9-15, 717D1
Sept indl output, chart 10-17, 790C2
Oct indl output; July, Aug revised 11-15, 919G1-A2
Aug-Oct credit, May revised 12-6, 958B1
Nov indl output 12-15, 982B1
Nov factory capacity 12-15, 982C1

FEDERAL Trade Commission (FTC)
Steel trigger plan scored 1-7, 80G2
Safeway complaint rptd setld 1-10, 348A1
Ford cited re auto engine defect 1-13, 67F2
STP suit setld 2-9, 348C1
Ford engine flaw notificatn rptd 2-14, 348D1
Carter Hawley drops Marshall Field bid 2-22, 185A2
Children's TV ad curbs proposed 2-28, 4-28, Cong wary 4-26—5-2, 347G1, D2
Corrective ad rule review denied by Sup Ct 4-3, 280C3
Dougherty backs lid on oil, gas firm holdings of coal, uranium 4-5; Justice Dept proposal rptd 4-6, 282D2, A3
BOC Airco purchase suit cited 4-7, 403D3
Du Pont pigment monopoly chrgd 4-10, 345G3-346A1
Coke, Pepsi bottler curbs barred 4-25, 346B1
Australia land sale in US ended 5-1, 327F2-D3
Denver utility credit chrg setlmt rptd 5-3, 434G1

1979

Miller cleared re Textron payoffs 7-26; Proxmire asks study 10-31, 923D2, A3
Volcker confrmd 8-2, sworn 8-6, 8-2, 621C1, 627B2, F2
Discount rate hiked, tight money policy cited 8-16, 621A1; Canada rate increase linked 9-7, 684A3
Fla '78 bank deposit growth, drug traffic linked 9-6, 840E3
Discount rate hiked, short-term rates cited 9-18, 701C2
Bentsen asks rate rise halt 9-20, Proxmire backs Volcker moves 9-26, 745A2
$1 bill replacemt urged 9-25, 727A2
Discount rate hiked, **monetary policy set 10-6**; Carter, financial mkts react 10-6–10-12, 764C1-766B1
$ up on credit moves 10-22, 978B3
Discount, prime rates explained 621E1
Money supply errors admited 10-25, 10-30, NY bank takes blame 10-26; Reuss scores FRB 10-30, 828C2-C3
Chrmn on Chrysler loan bd 12-21, 981F3

Statistics
Indl output index described 33G3
Credit data described 34G3
Nov '78 credit, Oct revised 1-5, 34E3
'78, Dec indl output; Nov revised 1-17, 33F3
Dec '78 credit 2-6, 111B2
Jan indl output 2-15, 151E2
Nov '78-Jan '79 $ defense 3-7, 159A3
Jan credit 3-9, 182G3-183A1
Feb indl output, Jan revised 3-16, 252E3
Feb credit 4-6, 280D3
Mar indl output, Feb revised 4-13, 280F3
Mar credit 5-3, 325F1
Apr indl output; Feb, Mar revised 5-16, 362E3
Apr credit 6-6, 422E2
May indl output, Apr revised 6-15, 463B3
May credit, Apr revised 7-6, 517B1
June indl output; Apr, May revised 7-20, 557B1
June credit 8-6, 622E1
July indl output, June revised 8-16, 622D1
July credit; May, June revised 9-10, 681C1
Aug indl output; June, July revised 9-14, 701B1
Aug credit 10-5, 766D2
Sept indl output; July, Aug revised 10-16, 784G1
Sept credit 11-6, 866F3
Oct indl output 11-15, 922G1
Oct credit 12-7, 941G1
Nov indl output; Sept, Oct revised 12-14, 964A1

FEDERAL Trade Commission (FTC)
Oil co pipe ownership bar asked 1-4, 55E2
Generic drug drive stepped up 1-9, 23C2
Alcoa false ad chrgs setld 1-10, 91G2
Adams' rail deregulatn plan criticism rptd 1-15, 35F3
ABC to cut children's TV ads 1-18, 78B3
Cigaret, ad co subpoena compliance ordrd 1-25, 91D3
'Debit' insurnc scored 1-28, 91D2
Litton deceptive ads chrgd 2-1, 91F3
Clorox '76 complaint settled 2-19, 308G2
A&P milk price actn backed by Sup Ct 2-22, 150B3
Fedders OKs heat pump repairs 2-22, 308A3
Brewer competitn study rptd 3-2, 305C2
Williams Co settles PVM chrg 3-6, 308B3
Business rpts rule compliance costs 3-14, 230A3
ITT bread fiber chrg setld 3-25, 308C3
Bell & Howell to reimburse home-study students 3-26, 308D3
Data disclosure to states OKd 3-28, 308C2

1980

Money mkt reserve rule contested 3-20, 223E2, 224A1
Credit rptd tightened 3-27, 3-28, 222D2-A3
Banking deregulatn bill signed 3-31, 245D3
Credit controls modified 4-2, 263D2
Credit curbs, 1st 1/4 mergers decline linked 4-8, 386F1
Farm, small business loans increased 4-17, 286A2
Forgn exchng mkt activity rptd 4-30, 436B3
Discount rate surchrg ended 5-6, 344C2
Chrysler loan guarantees OKd 5-10, 383E2
Credit curb impact on auto sales rptd 5-14, 384F1
Credit controls eased 5-22; short-term interest rates fall 5-23, credit issuers rptd cautious 5-27, 399F3-400B2
Money mkt reserve rule plea rejctd 5-22, 400G1
Discount rate cut to 12% 5-28, 400B2
Sen com probes Hunt bank deals, weighs regulatory powers 5-29—5-30, 425E1-B3
Fla bank rules tightened 6-3, drug money probed 6-5, 502B1-A2
Mfrs Hanover, First Penn deal OKd 6-3, 557B2
Discount rate cut to 11% 6-12, 438E1
Credit controls ended 7-3, 513E1
Treasury futures trading rights disputed 7-3—7-22, 558E3
1st 1/2 merger pace slowed 7-9, 557E1
Discount rate cut to 10% 7-25, 574F3
'81 tight money targets vowed 7-31, House com backs 8-4, 616A3
Forgn bank takeover rules tightened 9-17, 806B3
Discount rate raised to 11% 9-25, 764A3
Bank sales of commercial paper OKd 9-29, 986A2
Carter scores policies 10-2, criticism deplored 10-2—10-3, 762F3-763G1
Citicorp Choice Card ordered ended 10-10, 985D3
Small bank weekly rpts reduced 10-22, 857F1
Forgn bank rules OKd 11-13, 867G2
Discount rate hiked to 12%, surchrg set 11-14, 882B3
Free-trade zones OKd 11-19, 958D1
Money growth targets lowered; fed funds rate range hiked 11-24, 897C3
Fed funds rate nears 19% 11-26, 937G3
Discount rate raised to 13%, surchrg to 3% 12-4, 937G1, 938A1

Statistics
Credit data described 15C2
Indl output index described 34A3-35A1
Nov '79 credit, Oct revised 1-8, 15A2
'79 money supply growth 1-10, 52A2
'79, Dec indl output; Oct, Nov revised 1-16, 34A2
Money supply terms described 2-7, 113C3
Dec '79 credit, Nov revised 2-7, 114A1
Money supply 2-15, 126C1
Jan indl output; Dec '79 revised 2-15, 126A3
Jan credit, Dec '79 revised 3-10, 182E3
Feb indl output 3-14, 247F3
Money supply, business loans 4-4, 263F1-B2
Feb credit, Jan revised 4-7, 263B2
Mar indl output, Feb revised 4-15, 286A3
Mar credit, Feb revised 5-7, 344D3
Apr indl output, Mar revised 5-16, 384A3
Apr credit 6-6, 437F3-438A1
May indl output, Apr revised 6-13, 455E1
May credit 7-9, 513E3
June indl output, May revised 7-16, 541G3
June credit 8-7, 684F1-B2
Money supply 8-15, 630D3
July indl output, June revised 8-15, 631F1
July, Aug credit 9-10, 10-7, 783B3
Aug indl output, July revised 9-16, 701A3
Sept indl output, Aug revised 10-16, 783D1
Sept credit 11-7, 867E1
Oct indl output; Sept, Aug revised 11-14, 957F2
Money supply 11-18, 882D3
Oct credit 12-3, 938D1
Nov indl output; Oct, Sept revised 12-16, 984D1

FEDERAL Trade Commission (FTC)
Carter upholds role 2-7, 91F1
Trust procedure case accepted by Sup Ct 2-25, 187E3
Birth control ads scored, complaint setld 2-28, 358F2
Schlumberger OKs Unitrode divestiture 3-4, 558A1
In Cong fund dispute 3-15—4-30; shuts down 5-1, reopens with temporary funds 5-2, 348A1
Britannica sales practices case refused by Sup Ct 3-17, 226E1
Chrysler to replace rusted fenders 4-11, 288F1
Amoco settles bias suit 4-29, 370B3
Beneficial credit pact complaint setld 5-12, 703F1
LaSalle Extensn U ads ruled misleading 5-12, 703G1
Used-car rule OKd 5-16, 702F2
Sears appliance performance claim order rptd 5-19, 703D2
Food ad rules OKd 5-21, 703D2
Tuna indus probe ended 5-22, 703E2
Trust offcl resigns in protest 5-27, 703A1
Carter signs funding bills 5-28, 6-4; temporary shortage shuts agency 6-2—6-3, 702C3

1976

FISH & Wildlife Service, U.S.—*See under INTERIOR below*
FLAG, American
Sup Ct bars review of Ill flag mutilatn ruling 4-26, 359C2
FOOD & Drug Administration (FDA) (of Public Health Service)
Requires labeling of oils, fats 1-5, 7C2
Asks DES ban in animal feed 1-9, 25E3
Bans Red #2 dye 1-19, 44A2
GAO critical re stocks 1-19, 44D3
Red #2 dye ban in effect 2-12, ct challenge continues 2-13, 137C1
Sequentials withdrawn 2-25, 224B3
Proposes chloroform ban 4-6, 249D2
Cong curbs vitamin rules 4-12, 282E2, A3
Gets swine flu funds 4-15, 282B2
Plastic beverage bottle challenged 4-21, 308A2
Flu vaccine test begins 4-21, 316A2
To keep cyclamate ban 5-11, 414F3
Cong OKs med-device control 5-13, 377E1
Schmidt inquiry criticized 5-23, 392D1
Extends liquor-labeling deadline 7-1, 571D1
Red dye ban upheld 7-6, 571B1
'77 funds signed 7-12, 533D3
Panel rpts on cold drugs 9-8, 680A2
Curbs Red #4, bans carbon black dyes 9-22, 729A3
Expanded powers bills not cleared 10-2, 883A2
Cyclamate ban to continue 10-4, 876F1
OKs marijuana use for glaucoma 10-5, 860F3
Rabbit meat inspectn vetoed 10-17, 919E2
Asks aerosol warning labels 11-23, 901E3

FOOD for Peace—*See 'Agency for International Development' under STATE below*
FOOD Stamp Program—*See FOOD under 'F'*
FOREIGN Agricultural Service—*See under AGRICULTURE in this section above*
FOREIGN Intelligence, Committee on
Cited in Sen intellignc com rpt 4-26, 300A2, C2, F3, 301B2
FOREIGN Intelligence Advisory Board, President's
Cherne named to intelligence bd 2-17, 127E1
Ford plans intell command revisn 2-17, 127E1
US forgn intellignc chart 304A2
FOREIGN Policy—*See under 'F'*
FOREST Service, U.S.—*See under AGRICULTURE in this section above*
FORTY Committee—*See NATIONAL Security Council below*

1977

LA Times ad policy challenged 8-17, 658C3
Cargo prefernce rpt released 9-9, 720C1
Debt collectn rules signed 9-20, 761F1

FILIBUSTERS—*See under SENATE below*
FISH & Wildlife Service—*See under INTERIOR below*
FOOD & Drug Administration (FDA) (of Public Health Service)
Ford '78 budget request 1-17, 32G1
Hearing-aid sales rules set 2-13, 217F1
Saccharin ban set 3-9, reactn 3-9—3-11, 176A3-177B2
Birth pill makers must warn MDs 4-8, 355D1
Saccharin ban modified 4-14, 280B1
Laetrile backers warned 4-14, 375E3
DES suit filed in Chicago 4-25, 431D3
Fluorocarbon warnings ordrd 4-26, 323E1
Laetrile hearings 5-2, ban contd 5-6, 375B3
DES cancer risk rptd less 5-3, 432E1
IUD labeling ordered 5-6, 431E2
Fluorocarbon ban proposed 5-11, 387F1
Gerovital OKd in Nev 5-20, Kratter drops approval bid 6-2, 508B3
Saccharin ban delayed 6-20, 530E3; 6-21, 531B1
Laetrile legalized in 10 states 6-23, 508E1
McDonald's glass tests rptd, promotn halted 7-8—7-17, 560A1
Phenformin sales barred 7-25, 603C2
Antiviral flu drug OK cited 8-10, 675C3
'78 funds signed 8-12, 688B3
New ulcer drug OKd 8-23, 748C2
Animal feed curbs proposed 8-30, 10-21; House com hearing 9-23, 847F2
Seeks nitrite-nitrate data 8-31, 820B1
DBCP curbed, survey set 9-8, 723F2, A3
Diet supplemt recall ordrd 9-22, 820D1
Cancer linked to hair dye 10-17, 12-14, 962E3, 963B1
Saccharin ban delay clears Cong 11-4, 878D1; signed 11-23, 1001F2
Liquid protein deaths rptd 11-9, diet warning proposed 12-1, 992A3
Coloring dyes banned 12-12, 980G3
Biologics, Bureau of
Pneumonia vaccine gets OK 11-21, 907A1

FOOD For Peace—*See 'Agency for International Development' under STATE below*
FOOD Stamp Program—*See FOOD under 'F'*
FOREIGN Intelligence Advisory Board, President's
Sovt mil aims, power controversy 12-26-76—1-18, 39G2
Carter disbands 5-5, 462C2
Carter submits reorganizatn plan 7-15, 556C1
FOREIGN Policy—*See under 'F'*
FOREIGN Service—*See under STATE below*
FOREST Service, U.S.—*See under AGRICULTURE in this section above*

1978

ICC rail rate rules backed by Appeals Ct 5-5, 434C1
Boone held liable for acne ads 5-11, 702F2-A3
Eyewear ad proposal adopted 5-24, 434C1
'75 Xerox license order cited 6-7, 510B2
Bede Aircraft complaint rptd setld 6-13, 702B2
Appliance energy-cost labels OKd 6-28, 702A3
HFC lending violatns chrgd 7-7, 589F1
Kaufman complaint rptd setld 7-7, 702D2
Interco settles chrgs 7-14, 768E3
Pertschuk worried re merger trend 7-27, 767D1
Children's TV probe to be renewed by FCC 7-28, 672B2
Beatrice-Tropicana trust challenge lost 8-2, merger set 8-7, 767C2, D3
Boeing, Lockheed, McDonnell Douglas settle paymt chrgs 8-18, 643C1
Grey dental ad complaint rptd setld 8-31, 702E2
Book club complaint rptd setld 9-7, 702G1
Carmakers sue to block probe 9-11, 768C1
Bridgestone Tire complaint rptd setld 9-14, 942A1
Anacin ads ruled misleading 9-16, 769F3
Egg ad case declined by Sup Ct 10-2, 751D2
Merger probes rptd 10-4, 767D1
Injunctn halts acne cure ads 10-10, 942B1
Montgomery Ward warranty violatn chrgd 10-11, 942B1
Ford settles repossessed cars complaint 10-14, 942C1
Allegheny drops Chemetron unit sale plan 10-24, 897G1
Child ad probe curbed 11-3; stay denied, probe affirmed 11-17, 941G2-C3
Business-data cases refused by Sup Ct 11-6, 873D3
Kennedy asks Lykes-LTV merger probe 11-9, rejects 11-21, 935E2
Shell trust probe rptd 11-28, 939C2
AMA ad ban voided 11-29, appeal set 11-30, 947D2
Vocational schl rules issued 12-13, 963B1

FISH & Wildlife Service, U.S.—*See under INTERIOR below*
FOOD & Drug Administration (FDA) (of Public Health Service)
Hair-dye warning proposed 1-4, 86A1
Birth pill warning for smokers ordrd 1-11, 23E2
Blood donor labeling ordrd 1-13, 231A3
McDonald's glasses rptd safe 1-31, 348B1
Cosmetic ingredient label rule upheld 2-12, 231G3-232A1
Ultrasonic standards issued 2-17, 231C3
Epilepsy drug OKd 2-28, 231B2
Laetrile risk rptd 3-6, 598C3
Hypoallergenic label rule revoked 3-14, 231E3
Vitamin A, D curbs revoked 3-14, 231F3
Fluorocarbon aerosols banned 3-15, 186A2
Drug law revisn proposed, PMA scores 3-16, 231C1-A2
DMSO OKd for cystitis 3-20, 231E2
Methoxychlor, malathion rptd non-carcinogenic 3-21, 3-24, 727D3
Drug seizure case refused by Sup Ct 3-27, 241E1
PCB contaminated animal feed recalled 4-12, 727C3
House subcom vs FTC children's TV ad curbs 5-2, 347E2
Calcium pangamate seizure upheld 6-14, 727F2
Liquid protein diet hazards rptd 6-26, 727G2
Saccharin study rptd by toxicology cntr 7-19, 727B3
Metoprolol OKd for high blood pressure 8-7, 727E3
Nitrite-cancer link rptd 8-11, phase-out planned 8-31, 728A1
Oil of wintergreen warning issued 8-[illegible] 727F3
Butorphanol tartrate OKd as pain killer 8-30, 727E3
Generic drugs backed, mislabeling abuses scored 9-8, 9-13, 727C2, F2
Drug expiratn date labeling ordrd 9-13, 727F2
Calorie labeling rules set 9-21, 770B1
Dobutrex (dobutamine hydrochloride) OK rptd 10-3, 948E2
Progestin birth-defect-risk warning ordered 10-12, 948D2
Vidarabine (Vira-A) OKd 10-24, 948G2
Sulindac OKd for arthritis 11-1, 948A3
Natamycin OKd for fungal keratitis 11-1, 948A3
Diabetes pills tied to heart attacks 11-6, 947G3
Microwave safety scored 12-11, 962B3
Recombinant DNA rules revised 12-16, 1023C1
FOOD For Peace—*See STATE—Agency for International Development below*
FOOD Stamp Program—*See FOOD under 'F'*
FOREIGN Intelligence Board, National
Created 1-24, 49E2
FOREIGN Policy—*See appropriate headings in this section (e.g., STATE); also FOREIGN Policy, U.S. under 'F'*

1979

Thompson settles Sears dishwasher ad chrg 4-15, 308F3
Dental ad accord reached 4-27, 596D1
Pertschuk sees merger dangers 5-7, 349C2
Colo land sale refunds set 5-8, 595G3
Oil firm-shortage link seen 5-15, 361E2
Nonprescriptn drug ad limits backed 5-22, 596G1
Film industry probe opened 5-23, 430C3
CPG settles toy ad chrg 5-23, 596A2
Amway told to stop price-fixing 5-23, 985F3
SAT coaching schl study issued 5-29, 785A2
Formica trademark case refused by Sup Ct 6-5, 464F2
Ocean Spray antitrust action urged 6-20, 985G3
Kroger ads ruled deceptive 6-21, 596C2
AMF agrees to bike safety ads 7-8, 595G2
Home insulatn rating rule OKd 8-23, 903A1
Hartz Mt settles complaint 8-29, 903B1
Amer Express travelers check TV ad chngd 8-29, 903D1
Du Pont pigment monopoly case dismissed 9-17, 810C1
Smoking health rpt issued 9-21, 970B3
Exxon buys Reliance, ends negotiatns 9-24, 770G1
Horizon land sales scored 10-3, 903E1
Mobile home warranty problems rptd 10-4, 903G1
Battle Creek seeks trust suit environmt statemt 10-9, 809G3
Bristol-Myers ads assailed 10-12, 902F3
Sears dishwasher ads faulted 10-16, 903A2
AMA ad ban, other curbs ordrd ended 10-24, 902F2
Harnischfeger acquisitn opposed 11-4, 942G2
Auto makers challenge declined by Sup Ct 11-5, 884E2
'80 continuing funds res clears Cong 11-16, Carter signs 11-20, 900B2
Mail-order ad case refused by Sup Ct 12-3, 964C2

FOOD & Drug Administration (FDA) (of Public Health Service)
Generic drug list released 1-9, 23E2
Darvon hearing, MD warning ordrd 2-15, 138G2
Food-safety law revisns urged, saccharin ban backed 3-2, 195A1
Laetrile shipmt recalled 3-8, 196A1
Laetrile testing delayed 3-13, 195F3
3 Mile I A-accident contaminatn rptd 4-3, 245G3
Kennedy resigns 4-17, 310G2-B3
Velsicol indicted for Mich PBB cover-up 4-26, 597F3
Sleep aid, nose spray ban asked 5-1, 354B3
Cancer, blood pressure drug linked 5-1, 354D3
Ulcer drug-sperm study rptd 5-3, 354G1
Diet aids approved 5-12, 571F3
FTC backs nonprescriptn drug ad limits 5-22, 596G1
Ulcer drug OKd by advisory com 6-1, 471C2
Food processing, storage rule chngs proposed 6-7, 572A1
Methapyrilene drugs recalled 6-8, 471G1
Long-wear contact lenses OKd 6-13, 572D1
Kennedy quits 6-16, 527E3
Laetrile ban upheld by Sup Ct 6-18, 498D2
Drug approval process scored 6-19, 572B2
Nonprescrptn daytime sedatives banned 6-22, 572G1
Antibiotics in animal feed rptd risky 6-25, 735D1
Yellow No 5 labeling ordrd 6-26, 571G3
PCB limits in food cut 6-28, 571C2
DES banned in animal feed 6-28, 571F2
Prescriptn drug leaflets urged 6-29, 571E1
Laetrile rptd lethal to rats 7-13, 571D1
Amphetamine ban for diets urged 7-16, 571C3
Lead-contaminated canned food drive rptd 8-30, 736G3
PCBs contaminate food in West 9-17, 704B3
Cancer agents found in beer, warning urged 9-19, 9-22, 735E3-736B1
NRC reorganizatn asked 10-30, 825F2

FOOD Stamp Program—*See under FOOD under 'F'*
FOREIGN Claims Settlement Commission of the United States
China church reimbursemt set 3-16, 217G3
FOREIGN Languages and International Studies, President's Commission on
Forgn-language study urged 9-15, 944E1
FOREIGN Service—*See under STATE below*
FOREST Service—*See under AGRICULTURE in this section above*

1980

Smith, Galveston-Houston merger deal fails 6-9, 557E2
Child ad probe case refused by Sup Ct 6-16, 511D3
Borg-Warner, Bosch trust violatn rptd 7-11, 917F2
Bendix, Warner & Swasey trust chrgs rptd setld 7-14, 917F2
AMA adopts ethics code 7-22, 583G2
Benton & Bowles settles bike ad chrg 7-31, 703D1
GM defect notificatn failure chrgd 8-8, 702A3
ICC curbs RR collective rate fixing 8-13, 616G2
UAW seat on AMC bd proposed 9-17, 725F1
Lynch testifies on auto imports 10-8, 823G1
Heublein, United Vintners divestiture order rptd overturned 10-15, 917C1
Du Pont monopoly case dismissal upheld 10-27, 916F3
Beatrice, Tropicana merger found illegal 11-28, 917G3
Oil cos trust complaint challenge curbed by Sup Ct 12-15, 957D1

FLAG, American
Moscow Olympics controversy 7-16—8-3, 588F1
FOOD & Drug Administration (FDA) (of Public Health Service)
Laetrile testing OKd 1-3, 23C2
DES, estrogen risks cited 1-25, 63B3
Smith Kline probe rptd 1-25, 63G3-64C1
Cancer-nitrite study scored 1-31, 159G1
Dietary guidelines issued 2-4, 157D3
THC dvpt aid rptd 2-4, 358B1
'69 cyclamate ban rptd upheld 2-7, 317D2
Anti-cholesterol drug risk rptd, warning issued 2-17, 159A3
Mex tomatoes found toxic 2-20; 3 packing plants closed, border checks stiffened 3-12; 233A3
Interferon productn talks rptd 3-5, 317D3
Saccharin cancer risks disputed 3-6, 317E1
DES in cattle rptd 4-24, 358D1
Anturane sale blocked 4-25, 526G3
PCB rules published 5-9, 387C2
Rabies vaccine OKd 6-9, 526A3
Tranquilizer warnings set 7-11, 584E1
Nitrite ban rejected 8-19, 726D1
Caffeine warning issued 9-4, 726A2
Laetrile ban challenge declined by Sup Ct 10-20, 807F1
'81 funds clear Cong 12-4, 954C3; signed 12-15, 982B1

1976

GENERAL Accounting Office (GAO)
HEW audit rptd 1-7, 128A1
Rpt scores defns contracting 1-11, 70F3-71C1
Navy plane repairs rptd scored 1-12, 43G2
Rpt scores FDA on stocks 1-19, 44D3
Patman asks bank regulatory audit 1-25, reactn 2-6, 2-9, 112C1
House com urges intellignc agency audits 2-10, 150E1
Backs fed grain inspectn 2-16, 136G1
Chrgs grain subsidy abuses 3-2, 247E2
Smith asks probe aid 3-5, 186B1
Finds overpaymts to vets 3-26, 262G2
Sen com asks intelligence agency audits 4-26, 299E3, 303C2; cites probe data 4-28, 325G2, 329F3, 331A1
Blames Navy on cost overruns 6-1, 454C1
Dem platform text 6-15, 471A1
Scores Treas bias actn 7-1, 943D3
US NATO faults rptd 7-8, 760F2
On revenue-sharing job bias, fund misuse 8-4, 943E3
Rpts missing A-fuel 8-5, 739A3
GOP platform text 8-18, 604B1
Rpt scores synfuel progrm 8-24, 649F1
Study faults Mayaguez action 10-5, 749B2
Ford, Carter debate Mayaguez rpt 10-6, 742A2
Rpts Army overspending 11-19, 982A3

GENERAL Services Administration (GSA)
Boston contracting violatns rptd 1-20, 71D1
Rousek returns 1-21, 40D3
Carter disavows Eckerd dumping memo 8-13, 616F3
Sup Ct accepts Nixon papers case 11-29, 900D2
National Archives & Records Service
Ford, others visit 7-2, 488G3, 489A2

GEOLOGICAL Survey—*See under INTERIOR below*
GOVERNMENT Reorganization—*See also REGULATORY Agencies below*
Cong studies bank regulatory reform 1-12—2-3, 111D1-113E2
New Justice unit formed 1-14, 78C3
House OKs Renegotiatn Bd restructure 1-29, 124E3-135D1
Marine Corps reorganizatn urged 2-2, 95B3
House com urges intellignc reforms 2-10, 150E1-B2
Ford revises intell structure 2-17, 2-18, 127A1, G2
Sen OKs patent system revisn 2-26, 181B3
Cong clears Parole Bd restructure 3-3, 181D2
Agri policy com formed 3-5, 180A1
White House drug office OKd 3-19, 233D3
Business probe panel named 3-21, 262C2
Ford urges drug-abuse coms 4-27, 307F2
Cong OKs Beef Bd 5-3, 5-12, 358E3-359A1
Consumer product comm revised 5-11, 345G2
Scier ce office enacted 5-11, 346A1
Cong clears health info office 6-7, 434D2
Govs vs tourism dept 7-6, 493A1
EPA Solid Waste Office formed 10-21, 833G2
Agri Fed Grain Inspectn Svc created 10-21, 833B3
Presidential Election (& transition)
Jackson urges health dept 1-22, 41A3
Carter on goals 6-14, 433F1
Dem platform text 6-15, 470E3-471E1, A2
Carter acceptnc speech cites 7-15, 510F2
GOP platform text 8-18, 603A3
Ford acceptnc speech cites 8-19, 612B2
Carter score Ford priorities 8-30, 645B2
Carter proposes Cabt-level energy dept 9-21, 704F1, E2
Ford, Carter debate 9-23, 702C1
Mondale, Dole debate 10-15, 782D3
Ford, Carter debate 10-22, 800F3
Carter reaffirms plans 11-15, seeks legis 11-17, 864A1, A2
Carter names advisor 11-23, 881G2
Lance remarks 12-5, 917C1

1977

GENERAL Accounting Office (GAO)
Fed bank regulators scored 1-31, 154E3
Study scores OSHA, HEW unit 3-23, 280G1-A2
Lockheed bribery sales impact rptd 4-28, 502E3
143 spying suits vs US rptd 5-22, 422A3
Alcoholic vets estimated 6-7, 472A2
Carter energy plan scored 6-8, 443F2
A-material rptd missing 8-4, 717G1
NY Concorde ban overturned 8-17, 627G1
Cargo preference, oil prices disputed 8-27, 8-29, final estimate issued 9-9, 719E3, G3, 720C1
Defaulted student loans rptd 9-6, 739E2
Concorde, FAA study scored 9-16, 738F3
Rpts FBI domestic intell cutback, asks legis 11-9, 861D2
Carter LNG policy faulted 12-12, 962G1
Hair dye cancer risk rptd 12-14, 963A1
New ground combat vehicle scored 12-15, 978G1
FEC sues AFL-CIO 12-16, 980C1

GENERAL Services Administration (GSA)
Griffin named acting admin 2-15, 148F3
Low-cost steel purchases ordrd 8-5, 612D1
National Archives & Records Service
FBI King tapes filed 1-31, 77E2

GEOLOGICAL Survey—*See under INTERIOR below*
GOVERNMENT National Mortgage Association—*See under HOUSING & Urban Development below*
GOVERNMENT Reorganization—*See EXECUTIVE Branch—Reorganization and JUDICIARY in this section*
HEALTH Care Financing Administration—*See under HEALTH, Education & Welfare below*

1978

GENERAL Accounting Office (GAO)
Tough US stand in oil dealings urged 1-3, 5F3
Volunteer armed force cost rptd 2-6, 82C1
Satellite radiatn hazard rpt released 2-6, 103F1
Clinch R breeder halt called illegal 3-10, 183D2
Conrail, FRA safety efforts scored, 3-15, 224E3-225A1
Medicare MDs list scored 3-15, 578B1
Mo A-plant safety review sought 3-29, 242C2
Trident cost overruns seen 4-13, 407A2
F-16 review urged 4-24, 407D2
House OKs lobbying bill 4-26, 323E1
Indian housing worsens 5-13, 569G1
CIA, FBI links to Nazi war criminals rptd 5-16, 410G3
MD specializatn study issued 5-19, 597E2
Lockheed cleared re overbilling 6-22, 493B3
LNG safety measures, other reforms urged; indus, fed agencies score 7-31, 609F3
Oil reserve storage plans scored 8-16, 701A3
'73-78 food price hikes analyzed 9-8, 717E2
Alaska oil exports to Japan opposed 9-12, 702D1
Fraud in fed aid programs rptd 9-18, 714G3
A-fuel plants, arms productn linked 10-23, 900F1
Drug cos data case refused by Sup Ct 11-6, 873G3
Fed agencies scored on microwave safety 12-11, 962A3

GENERAL Services Administration (GSA)
Smoking curbs proposed 1-11, 23C2
Broadcasters denied Nixon tapes by Sup Ct 4-18, 308D1
Info Sec Oversight Office created 6-29, 508D1
Griffin firing angers O'Neill, new post found 7-28—8-7, 605E2
Paymt probe indictmts seen 8-30, Carter backs 9-4; Washn Post details chrgs 9-3—9-5, 685E1
Kirbo to monitor probe 9-7, 715D1
Paymts probe 'rivalry' chrgd 9-8, 715C1
Sen subcom hears abuses detailed; Art Metal paymts, FBI frictn disclosed 9-18—9-19, 714B2-715C1
Lynch named to head probe 9-20; 18 indicted 9-29, 4 plead guilty 10-4, 753A3-G3
Borowski named probe dir 11-13, Alto steps down 11-14, 899E1-B2
More kickback indictmts 12-16, 12-21, 1011B1
Nixon data access upheld by Appeals Ct 12-21, 1011C3
Federal Preparedness Agency
Carter proposes new emergency agency 6-19, 466F2-B3
National Archives & Records Service
NSA issues WWII secret documts 9-10—9-18, 744D2
Burger urges fed govt study 9-21, 751G2
Ray seeks FBI King tapes 12-12, 1002B3

GEOLOGICAL Survey—*See under INTERIOR below*
GINNIE Mae—*See HOUSING & Urban Development—Government National Mortgage Association*
GOVERNMENT National Mortgage Association—*See under HOUSING & Urban Development below*
GOVERNMENT Printing Office
Damage suit immunity challenge refused by Sup Ct 4-17, 308A3
GOVERNMENT Reorganization—*See EXECUTIVE Branch—Reorganization in this section above*
HEAD Start—*See HEALTH, Education & Welfare—Child Development, Office of below*

1979

GENERAL Accounting Office (GAO)
EPA clean-air effort scored 1-9, 16E2
Illegal alien issue detailed 1-29, 127E1
Contract denial for wage-price enforcemt seen illegal 2-5, 2-12, 127B3
Higher oil prices warned; conservatn actn, oil cos scored 3-7, 182D2
Pvt debt collectn for US urged 3-10, 208E3
Cancer Inst blunders chrgd 4-24, 315G2-C3
Indochina refugee data rptd 4-25, 379F2
Defense OKs XM-1 tank productn 5-8, 386D1
Peoples Temple recovery costs rptd 5-17, 404C3
FDA drug approval process scored 6-19, 572B2
Canada gas pipe viability doubted 7-4, 7-5, 522B2
Tax loss from underground econ rptd 7-10, 665C3
Audit of FBI informant abuses asked 8-22, 747B3
Army reserve recruiting failure rptd 8-23, 649B3
'79 oil shortage study issued 9-13, 702A3
Army guns rptd found 10-4, 852A1
NYC fiscal study issued 11-2, 920E2
Viet troops Agent Orange exposure rptd 11-24, 904B2
'Fraud hotline' rptd effective 12-9, 947G1
Comptroller on Chrysler loan bd 12-21, 981F3

GENERAL Services Administration (GSA)
Kickback scandal guilty pleas rptd 1-3, 1-26, 92F3
Muellenberg named inspector gen 1-30, 92D3
Kickback scandal sentncs handed down 3-14—4-24, 367F2-B3
Freeman to replace Solomon 3-23, 232B2
Muellenberg confirmed 4-10, 965A3
Kickback scandal sentences continue 5-23—12-17; controversy 5-25—5-30, 964E2-965A1
Freeman confirmed 6-27, 965A3
Nixon Calif estate expenses disputed 9-5—9-6, 683A3
National Archives & Records Service
Mil dischrg suit cites Fed Register notificatn 1-19, 53F1
WWII secret files released 2-3, 2-6, 93F1
Auschwitz photos released 2-22, 193D1
Author wins Oswald med data access 2-23, 166B3

GEOLOGICAL Survey—*See under INTERIOR below*
GINNIE Mae—*See HOUSING & Urban Development, Department of-Government National Mortgage Association below*
GOVERNMENT National Mortgage Association—*See under HOUSING & Urban Development below*
GOVERNMENT Printing Office
Sup Ct worker rptd transfered 4-27, 382B3
GOVERNMENT Reorganization—*See EXECUTIVE Branch-Reorganization in this section above*
GRANTS-in-Aid—*See BUDGET-Revenue Sharing in this section above*

1980

GENERAL Accounting Office (GAO)
Sewer projects rptd costly 1-9, 54F1-D2
MIT cancer-nitrite study scored 1-31, 159F1
Space industry research backed 2-16, 160E2
Teamster pension fund probe scored 8-25, 704C3
Forgn bank takeover ban asked 8-28, 806F2
Eximbank probe urged 10-1, 989C1
EPA toxic waste policy scored 10-31, 869B2

GENERAL Services Administration (GSA)
11 more chrgd in kickback probe 1-15, Sen hearings 1-19 112C1
Griffin gets Chrysler post 3-13, 199B3
Kickback scandal funds recovery suits filed 3-17, 228F1
Furniture waste scored 3-18, 459E2
Kickback scandal indictmt, convictn totals rptd 5-2; ex-offcl indicted 5-9, 459A2
Ia schools buy White House uniforms 5-16, 460B3
National Archives & Records Service
MacArthur WWII 'gift' dispute rptd 1-30, 1-31, 115F1
Watergate tapes go public 5-28, 460D1
Nixon sues for records 12-17, 963A3

GOVERNMENT Printing Office
Bindery workers win bias suit 5-20, 442C1
GOVERNMENT Reorganization—*See EXECUTIVE Branch-Reorganization in this section above*

1976

HEALTH, Education & Welfare, Department of (HEW)
Programs, funds use faulted 1-7—2-16, 127G3-128C3
Shift from unemploymt to welfare benefits rptd 1-7, 128A3
US health rpt issued 1-12, 31G3-32A2
House subcom chrgs vulnerable to fraud 1-26, replies 1-28, 128A3
Cong overrides funds veto 1-27, 1-28, 69A2
Orders Chicago faculty integratn plan 2-8, 95E2
NJ suit vs TM in schls filed 2-25, 203E2
Md schl funds cutoff barred 3-8, 203D1
Drug funding programs signed 3-19, 233F3, 234A1
Ford asks flu vaccine drive 3-24, 224C2
Medicaid fraud effort set 3-26, 249E1
Rejects Chicago teacher integration plan 3-31, 263G1
Food funds for aged freed 4-2, 249G1
Flu vaccine test begins 4-21, 316G1
Cong clears added funds 5-19, 411E3; signed 6-1, 982F1
Flu vaccine error rptd 6-2, 423C3
Cong OKs health info office 6-7, 434D2
Vaccine-maker to lose insurance 6-15, 443A2
'70-75 desegregatn data rptd 6-19, 992D3
Some church-coll aid OKd 6-21, 452G3
Ford suspends father-son, mother-daughter schl events bar 7-7, 535E2-B3
Wilkins chrgs '60s anti-black strategy 8-12, 671F2
Bars MD collectn agent use 8-26, 715A3
Moss backs fraud unit, Mathews vs 8-30, 715C2
Rpts flu immunizatn delay 9-1, 656B3
Day care standards study set 9-7, 689C1
Research comm backs psychosurgery 9-10, 715F3
Gordon confrmd asst secy 9-23, 807G3
'77 funds vetoed 9-29, overridden 9-30, 726F1
Cong OKs inspector gen 9-29, 765F2-B3; signed 10-15, 982G1
Rpts states set competency standards 10-21, 993D3
Medicaid abortn fund stay barred 11-8, 848A2
NYC schl job bias chrgd 11-9, 921D3
DNA research rules urged 11-11, 892A1
Carter sees Matthews 11-22, 881D1
Coll enrolmt at standstill 11-22, 993E2-A3
Carter names liaison 11-23, 881C3
Califano named secy 12-23, 956E2 D3, 957D2

Education, Office of
Bell quits as comr 5-2, 412A2

Food & Drug Administration—*See separate listing above*

1977

HEALTH, Education & Welfare, Department of (HEW)
Ford '78 budget proposals 1-17, 30B1, 32C1-33C3
Desegregatn guidelines ordrd for 6 state colls 1-17, 112B2
NYC school bias chrgd 1-18, 112C2
Welfare study group formed 1-26, 175F3-176B1
Hospital-cost study asked 1-31, 89G3
Health care fraud probe controversy 2-4—3-23, 235F2
DNA patent order protested 2-7, 184C2
Califano: budget too low 2-14, 110C3
Asbestos worker suit rptd 2-15, 422C2
Carter visits employes 2-16, 110D2
Schl aid cutoffs considered; Ark, Tex reviews ordrd 2-17, 156C3
Carter buget revisions 2-22, 124C3, 125A2, D3, 126A1
Califano rpts net worth 2-25, 147G3
Reorganized, Soc & Rehab Svc ended, AFDC shifted 3-8, 175F2
Schl bias rpt non-compliance warning 3-15, 280A1
DNA control urged 3-16, 4-6, 451G3
Califano backs quotas 3-17, 217B3
Califano hirings disputed 3-23—3-26, 236B1
Gay rights access promised 3-26, 278E2
Califano backs down on quotas 3-31, 235B2
Guidelines for colls in states reordrd 4-1, 446C1
Handicapped stage protests 4-5—4-16, 301D2
Immunization drive set 4-6, 287E2
AFDC study issued 4-15, 302C1
Mental health unit meets 4-18, 322C2
Hosp cost controls urged 4-25, 322F1
Handicapped rules signed 4-28, 338E2
Carter outlines welfare reform goals 5-2, 337C3-338D1
'77 supplemental funds signed 5-4, 339F1
NAACP sues re Southn special schls 5-11, 446D2
Carter plan outlined, AFDC cited 5-25; spending level warning rptd 5-27, 445D2-E3
KC schl suit names 5-26, 446F1
O'Neill vs fund bill veto 6-2, Carter agrees to sign 6-15, 459A3
Califano backs coll admissn 'goals' 6-5, 445F3
Medicaid cuts for 20 states set 6-8, 460B3
House OKs '78 funds 6-17, 478B1
Medicaid fraud cases rptd 6-18, 643G2
Jobless-benefits standards law upheld 6-20, 516D3-517A1
'76 abortn figures rptd 6-20, 787B1
Medicaid child care role urged 6-22, 643E3
Sen OKs '78 funds 6-29, 515E2
NYC spec schl aid withheld 7-5, 631F1
Child adoptn subsidy proposed 7-12, 628G2
'78 family planning budget cited 7-19, 786E3
Phenformin sales barred 7-25, 603A2
Abortn funding banned 8-4, 786G1
HMO rpt published 8-5, 643C2
Carter proposes AFDC end 8-6, 608C3
Cong actn on hosp costs urged 8-17, 643A3
NYC, Chicago assign teachers by race 9-7, 10-11, 837E2-C3
Pvt groups to collect overdue loans 9-8, 739D2
Hosp cost cutbacks proposed 9-26, 869D2
Abortn issue delays funds bill 10-1, Califano urges passage 10-11, 786D2
NYC schl desegregatn plan ordrd 10-6, 838C1
TM banned from NJ schools 10-20, 845E3
Hq named after Humphrey 10-23, 817E1
DNA bills stalled 10-24, 846A3
Medicare, Medicaid abuse curbs signed 10-25, 814E1
Kaiser-Permanente HMO certified 10-26, 869G3
2d opinions on surgery urged 11-1, 869E3
'78 funds, abortn curbs clear Cong 12-7, 958C2; signed 12-9, 1001F2

Affirmative Action Office
Established 4-11, 301G3

Appointments & Resignations
Aaron, asst secy 1-19, 53B1
Berry, asst secy 1-19, 53A1
Boyer, Educ comr 1-19, 52G3
Califano confrmatn delayed 1-20, 34C1, E3; confrmd 1-24, sworn 1-25, 52F2
Champion, undersecy 1-19, 53A1; Sen com OKs 3-23, 235E3
Foege named CDC dir 4-5, 287D3
Martinez, asst secy 1-19, 53B1
Richmond confrmd undersecy 6-28, 626D3
Shanahan, asst secy 1-19, 53B1
Walsh quits as inspector 3-6, 235F3
Warden confrmd asst secy 3-29, 272D3

Education, Office of
Boyer named comr 1-19, 52G3
Student aid reorganized 3-9, 175C3
Reorganized 4-11, 301D3
Career guidance aid, anti-bias projcts clear Cong 11-29, 959B2; signed 12-13, 1001G2

Food & Drug Administration—*See separate listing above*

Health Care Financing Administration
Created 3-9, 175A3

Human Development, Office of
Reorganized 3-9, 175C3

1978

HEALTH, Education & Welfare, Department of (HEW)
Suits re rights enforcemt setld 1-4, 5C1
NCAA suit vs Title IX dismissed 1-9, 40E2
Age bias in fed progrms rptd 1-10, 14F1
Anti-smoking drive set; Nader, other lobbyists score 1-11, 23B2, G2
Handicapped anti-bias rules issued 1-13, 14G1
Abortion rules issued 1-26, 116D1
Va, Ga, NC coll integratn plans rejcted; Ark, Okla, Fla OKd 2-2, 85C1
Black lung eligibility bill clears Cong 2-15, 125B2; signed 3-1, 218B2
Carter backs abortn rules 2-17, 123A3
Ga, Va, NC coll integratn plans OKd 3-8—5-12, 368G3
Paraquat contaminated marijuana peril warned 3-10, 728B2
Medicare MDs list scored 3-15, 578B1
Medicaid errors rptd costly, new rules issued 3-31, 577G3
Carter proposes Educ Dept 4-14, 279B1-B2
Adoptn, foster care bill signed 4-24, 323E3
Asbestos workers warned 4-26, 326F2
Guaranteed income study rptd 5-19, 720E3
Califano delays USSR trip 5-30, 401A2
State soc svc claims setlmt signed 6-12, 465F3
NYS AFCD eligibility case refused by Sup Ct 6-12, 468C1
'79 funds OKd by House; abortn, quota curbs included 6-13, 445C2-G3
Hosp trust exemptn opposed 6-13, 577D2
State abortn funding rptd 6-20, 743A3
Natl health plan readied 6-26, 491E2
Secrecy classificatn powers cut 6-29, 508E1
Welfare waste limits proposed 7-10; SSI, AFDC paymt errors rptd 8-12, 684G2
'Runaway' father crackdown vowed, '77 data rptd 7-19, 685A1
Welfare loopholes asked closed 7-20, 684E3
Carter health plan outlined 7-29, 585F2
Employe abuses rptd in GSA probe 9-19, 714F2
Urban League pres addresses employes 9-21, 811C1
Carter scores budget bill 9-28, 751G3
Md bias suit refused by Sup Ct 10-2, 751F2
Rural health progrm planned 10-2, 770E1
Measles campaign announced 10-4, 927D3
'79 funds clear Cong 10-14, Carter signs 10-18, 873F1
Educ Dept bill dies 10-15, 785B1
US-China acad exchng set 10-22, 814E1
Vs new med schools, for class size cuts 10-24, 948C3
Army MD shortage rptd 11-27, 916F3
Califano on natl health plan 12-9, 956D2
SSI forgn travel rule backed by Ct 12-11, 980G3
Anti-fraud drive launched 12-13, 984B3
Employee indicted in GSA scandal 12-16, 1011D1
Recombinant DNA rules revised 12-16, DNA panel expanded 12-27, 1022F3, 1023C1
Hospital cost guide set 12-28, 1012G1

Child Development, Office for
Head Start in proposed Educ Dept 4-14, 279C1, A2

Civil Rights, Office for
NY pact ruled invalid 3-7, teacher assigmt by race ends 4-7, 264D1
Cabt-level Educ Dept proposed 4-14, 279C1

Education, Office of
Bilingual programs scored 5-9, 348F3

Food & Drug Administration—*See separate listing above*

1979

HEALTH, Education & Welfare, Department of (HEW)
A-test cancer link rptd ignored in '65, Califano orders probe 1-8, 17D2
Generic drug drive stepped up 1-9, 23C2
NCAA vows Title IX fight 1-10, 102C3
PHS rpts on smoking, Califano comments 1-11, 23A1
Carter AFDC budget proposals 1-22, 43G3
Procuremt offcr pleads guilty in GSA scandal 1-26, 92F3
'57 A-test, cancer link confrmd 1-29, 91E1
2 unions ask radiatn safety studies 1-30, 90D3
Carter proposes Educ Dept 2-8, 110F2
Carter hosp cost plan faces hurdles 2-13, 110C1
Califano backs natl health insurnc 2-13, 110E1
Schl desegregatn actn urged 2-13, 110B2, D2
Darvon ban rejctd; FDA hearing, MD warning ordrd 2-15, 138F2
Elderly share of '77 health costs rptd 2-24, 163F3
Low-level radiatn risks seen 2-27, 208A1
Carter sends hosp cost bill to Cong 3-5, 163D2
DES cancer study rptd 3-6, 196D1
Medicaid '78 abortn decline rptd 3-8, 315A1
Califano backs hosp cost-control bill 3-9, 194D3
Unneeded surgery crackdown sought, AMA scores 3-19, 218D3
Price guides monitoring set 3-29, 264G1
3 Mile I radiatn assessed, study set 4-4, 260E1
3 Mile I radiatn estimate hiked 5-3, 344C1
Carter natl health plan defended 5-14, 362G1
Mental health bill proposed 5-15, 365C1
Welfare plan presented 5-23, 384F1
Health team sent to Asia 6-5, 550E2
Pot controls backed 6-6, 492D2
Methapyrilene drugs recalled 6-8, 471F1
Guillain-Barre flu shot claims rptd stalled 6-10, 470E3
Schls right to bar disabled backed by Sup Ct 6-11, 478C2
Medicaid, welfare cuts set 6-19, 561E1
Gender-based welfare plan ruled illegal by Sup Ct 6-25, 539G3
Califano in China 6-28, 495A3
Malpractice cost rules modified 7-1, 570A3
Califano fired, Harris replaces 7-19, 529C1, F2-530A1
Carter on Califano firing 7-20, 7-25, 556C1
Harris confrmd 7-27, 577C1
Harris seeks black-Jewish reconciliatn 8-29, 661G2
Chicago compulsory busing progrm ordrd 8-31, 679A3
Immunizatn progrm rptd effective 9-11, 736D3
Math achievemt test study issued 9-13, 785D2
Chicago desegregatn funds barred 9-15, suit sought 10-29, 944B1
Carter scores welfare system 10-15, 807A3
Carter on busing 10-16, 807D3
Renamed; Educ Dept created 10-17, 782B2
Heating aid bill OKd 11-9, 883B2
'80 continuing funds res clears Cong 11-16, Carter signs 11-20, 900B2
Title IX job bias funds cutoff bar declined by Sup Ct 11-26, 919D2
NYC schl aid denial upheld by Sup Ct 11-28, 944B2
Title IX sports guidelines issued 12-4, 1000F2
Soc Sec panel urges chngs 12-7, 946A2

Child Development, Office for
Head Start excluded from proposed Educ Dept 2-8, 110G2
Carter backs Head Start expansn 10-15, 807A3

Education, Office of
Bilingual program rules proposed 6-29, 596F3

Food & Drug Administration—*See separate listing in this section above*

Museum Services, Institute of
Museums get $7 mln 9-5, 892A2

1980

HEALTH, Education & Welfare, Department of (HEW)
Carter vetoes dioxins study 1-2, 17G2
NCAA women's title tourn probe asked 1-8, 103G3
Cancer workplace rules set, '79 data cited 1-16, 36F1
Dietary guidelines issued 2-4, 157G2
Abortn aid resumptn order issued 2-19, 130B3
Fed funded group info access curbed by Sup Ct 3-3, 210C1
DES violators warned 4-15, 358G1
Abortn funding cases argued in Sup Ct 4-21, 306C2
Educ, Health & Human Svcs Depts begin operatn 5-4, 370A1
PR welfare aid rate backed by Sup Ct 5-27, 453D3

Child Development, Office of
Summer Head Start progrm rptd 6-30, 496A1

Education, Office of
Smith named educ comr 1-9, 18D2

Health Care Financing Administration
Med lab tests found faulty 3-23, 359B1

1976

Public Health Service—*See separate listing below*
Social Security Administration—*See separate listing below*

HEALTH Resources Administration—*See under PUBLIC Health Service below*
HEALTH Services Administration—*See under PUBLIC Health Service below*
HEALTH Services Research, National Center for—*See 'Health Resources Administration' under PUBLIC Health Service below*
HEALTH Statistics, National Center for—*See 'Health Resources Administration' under PUBLIC Health Service below*
HEART & Lung Institute, National—*See 'National Institutes of Health' under PUBLIC Health Service below*

HOUSE of Representatives—*See also CONGRESS above; also personal names*
Mex prisoner abuse hearing 1-15, 75G1

Agriculture, Committee on
3 grain inspectors indicted 1-19, 44G1
Accuses Agri Dept re grain inspectn 1-29, 136C1
Ct delays food-stamp cutback 6-19, 454C3
Findley urges Butz resign 10-2, 744B2

Appropriations, Committee on
Pentagon budget cuts seen 1-28, 68F1
Rumsfeld queried on budget 'padding' 2-4, 116B1
Subcom vs Uruguay mil aid 6-5, 441E1
Passman bribes rptd 8-16, 633B1
Army overspending rptd 11-19, 982A3
McFall subcom post rptd in danger 12-6, 919A2

Armed Services, Committee on
Pepitone testifies on draft rules 1-21, 68B3
Rumsfeld outlines defns needs; Downey, others query 1-27, 68D1-A2
Subcom probes Marine recruiting, training 4-1, 378B2
House OKs '77 arms authorizatn 4-9, 283G1
Marine probe continues 5-25—6-9, 435E2-D3
Navy shipyd overrun paymts hearings 6-1, 6-10, 453D3, 454C1

Assassinations, Select Committee on
Created 9-17, Downing to head 9-21, 728G3-729G2

1977

Public Health Service—*See separate listing below*
Social Security Administration—*See separate listing below*

HEALTH Statistics, National Center for—*See under PUBLIC Health Service—Health Resources Administration below*
HEART, Lung & Blood Institute, National—*See under PUBLIC Health Service—National Institutes of Health below*

HOUSE of Representatives—*See also CONGRESS in this section above; also personal names*
Sex-bias suit vs Passman OKd 1-3, 59C3
O'Neill elected speaker 1-4, 5C3
Rule changes OKd 1-4, 36B3
Vs Daoud release 1-14, 28C1
'76 special interest gifts detailed 1-15, 2-4, 2-15, 128C1-129F2
Ethics code proposed 1-31, 77B3
Ldrship, coms, chrmn listed; table 90A2
Pay raise opponents fail 2-16, 127G2
Speeches by forgn ldrs opposed 2-17, 127D3
Ethics code adopted 3-2, 173B2-C3
Ethics com formed 3-9, 191C2
Montgomery in Viet missn 3-16—3-20, 206B1
Fowler wins Ga seat 4-5, 252A1
Tonry resigns 5-4, indicted 5-12, 418A3
'76 campaign spending rptd 5-4, 482F1
Cunningham wins Washn seat 5-17, 382F1
Populatn com created 9-24, 833G3-834A1
Panama Canal pact OK held necessary 11-3, 912A2
Jordan bars 4th term 12-10, 1005B3

Administrative Review, Commission on
Ethics code proposed 1-31, 77B3
Ethics code adopted 3-2, 173A3
Cong aide male-female pay gap rptd 7-31, 669F3

Agriculture, Committee on
Foley spec interest gifts rptd 2-4, 129A2
Brazil coffee price hearings 2-22, 2-23, 169D1
Bergland on food-stamp plan 4-5, 250A2
S Africa sugar lobby sued 7-20, 614A1

Appropriations, Committee on
Sikes loses subcom post, Dems back McKay 1-26, 53E2
Mahon special interest gifts rptd 2-4, 129E2
Nicaragua scores rights probe 4-19; mil aid cutoff backed 6-14, 475D3
Cruise missiles set for SAC 4-24, 343F2
AF computer project scored 4-27, 421A3
Adds new water projects 5-25, 417E1
Carter agrees to sign HEW-Labor funds 6-15, 459C3
Passman gift from Park rptd, denied 11-2, 915D2

Armed Services, Committee on
Gets A-energy jurisdiction 1-4, 36F3
Price special interest gift rptd 2-4, 129D2
F-14 repair costs estimated 3-21, 343G2
'78 arms bill OKd by House 4-25, 323F3
Subcom hears Singlaub 5-25, 404D1

Assassinations, Select Committee on
Reestablished, Gonzalez named chrmn 2-2, 77C1
Gonzalez fires Sprague 2-10, controversy ensues 2-16—2-21, 126F3
Gonzalez quits 3-2, 149A1
King hearing proposed 3-3, 149D1
Stokes named chrmn 3-8, 228D2
Trafficante questioned 3-16, 228E2
King ballistic tests ordrd 3-17, Ray questnd 3-22, 228G2
Sprague quits 3-29, 228B2
De Mohrenschildt found dead 3-29, CIA link rptd 3-31, 228B3
Extended 3-30, 228A2
Press-CIA links chrgd 4-24, 339B2
Funds OKd 4-28, 339B2
Stokes fears Ray escape plot 6-11, 459D1

1978

Public Health Service—*See separate listing below*
Smoking & Health, Office on
Creation announced 1-11, 23F2
Social Security Administration—*See separate listing below*

HEALTH Services Administration—*See under PUBLIC Health Service below*
HEALTH Services Corps, National—*See PUBLIC Health Service—Health Services Administration below*
HEART, Lung & Blood Institute, National—*See under PUBLIC Health Service—National Institutes of Health below*
HIGHWAY Traffic Safety Administration, National—*See under TRANSPORTATION below*

HOUSE of Representatives—*See also CONGRESS in this section above; also personal names*
Panama Canal treaty challenge denied by Sup Ct 1-16, 33F2
Consumer Fed ratings issued 3-4, 183D1; 11-8, 981G2
Panama Canal treaty challenge refused by Sup Ct 5-15, 387G3
Montgomery missn in Viet, Laos 8-21—8-25, bring back bodies of 15 MIAs 8-27, 660G2
Job bias, other abuses chrgd 9-21, 720C3
51 reps protest MAP missile plan 9-22, 737D2
UN pro-Palestinian drive starts 10-7, 762B3
China ties reactn 12-15—12-20, Taiwan defns pact suit threatened 12-15, 975B3-976A1
8 join Taiwan defns pact suit 12-22, 995B2

Africa, Subcommittee on (of International Relations Committee)
Dem ethics chng threatens Diggs chair 12-6, 958C2

Agriculture, Committee on
Striking farmers testify 163C2

Agriculture & Related Agencies, Subcommittee on (of Appropriations Committee)
FTC children's TV ad curbs opposed 5-2, 347D2
PAC gifts to Foley rptd 12-24, 1008C1

Appropriations, Committee on
Subcom probes Pl A-plant 2-8, 134C3
Vance: US jets to Egypt, Saudi, Israel pkg deal 2-24, 139C1
Passman indicted 3-31, 239D1
Disaster fund supplemt signed 4-4, 261C3
Bikini I radiatn probed by subcom 4-12, 278C2-A3
Subcom vs children's TV ad curbs 5-2, 347D2
Mahon to retire 5-6, 363B1
Wilson role in Nicaragua aid resumptn rptd 5-16, 376F2
Skylab rocket funds uncertain 6-8—6-11, 445C1
Mil constructn funds Canal proviso clears Cong 8-21, 662B2
Skylab mission funding OKd 9-30, 750G2
Cederberg loses reelectn 11-7, 846F2, 854B1
Dems rejct ethics rule chng, Flood subcom chair secure 12-6, 958G2

Armed Services, Committee on
Brown urges arms buildup in defns posture statemt 2-2, 81B1
Arms authorizatn clears House 5-24, 406C3
Aspin urges lower recruitmt standards 7-2, 528E3
A-test ban, arms reliability doubts rptd 11-3, 877F1-B2
Price scores Selective Service 12-3, 984C1

Assassinations, Select Committee on
'78 funds OKd 3-13, 182G3
King murder plot alleged 7-26, 589G2
King hearings; Ray testifies, witness retracts alibi 8-14—8-18, 641A1-642C1
JFK hearings 9-6—9-11, 697D3-698C2
Added funds voted 9-7, 698B2
JFK hearings end 9-28, 749A2
Hunt denies JFK murder role before subcom 11-3, 898E3
King hearings resume: Ray testimony declined; conspiracy theory, FBI link discounted 11-9—11-17, 898D1-D3
King hearings end: Ray family plot, bounty offer alleged; FBI role denied, probes scored 11-17—12-1, 937G3-938F2
JFK murder film assessed 11-26, 916B2, E2
Ray seeks FBI King tapes 12-12, 1002B3
JFK, King plots seen likely; Justice review sought; US, forgn role discounted 12-30, 1002A1-A3

1979

Public Health Service—*See separate listing below*
Social Security Administration—*See separate listing below*

HEALTH and Human Services, Department of
Created from reorganized HEW 10-17, 782A2

HOUSE of Representatives—*See also CONGRESS in this section above; personal names*
Convenes; ldrs elected, rule chngs voted 1-15, 30E1
TV coverage begins 3-19, 208D1
Rhodesia electn monitors barred 4-9, 293F2
18 reps visit USSR 4-13—4-22, 314G1-C2
Taiwan defns treaty suit dismissed 6-6, 440F1
Closed sessn on Panama held 6-20, 481A2
9 tour SE Asia refugee camps 8-4—8-7, visit Hanoi 8-8—8-9, 607G1
Carter loses Taiwan defns treaty suit 10-17, 777A1
US-USSR airlift aid to Cambodia urged 11-1, 863A3
Iran hostage release urged 11-7, 842C3
Irish prime min meets reps 11-8, 874C2
Congresswomen in Pnompenh 11-12, 863E2
Hansen in Iran, sees hostages 11-20—11-28; O'Neill, others score 11-26, 895F2
5 see Waldheim on Iran crisis 12-1, 913E1

Africa, Subcommittee on (of Foreign Affairs Committee)
Diggs drops reelection bid 1-23, 71G2
US urged to abandon Mobutu 3-5, 215E1

Agriculture, Committee on
Foley elected chrmn 1-24, 71C1
Farmers boo Bergland testimony 2-6, 109E2
Foley vs Natural Resources Dept 3-1, 164D1

Appropriations, Committee on
Whitten elected chrmn 1-23, 71F1
Flood drops subcom chrmnship 1-25, 71A3
Defns subcom hears Brown on Sovt surrogates 2-8, 89B2
AF pilot drain, morale loss cited 2-15, 130F2
MD, nursing schl fund cuts trimmed 3-6, 163D3
Subcom OKs Nicaragua pkg aid 9-11, 731E2
Nicaragua army officers tour US bases 11-11—11-21, 910B1

Armed Services, Committee on
Stratton vs S Korea troop exit 1-3, 39C1
Draft renewal costs listed 1-4, 15D1
Price elected chrmn 1-24, 71C1
CIA rpts on USSR '78 mil outlay 2-2, 99D3
Mil MD shortage rptd 2-16, 130D2
Subcom rpt doubts NATO defns capability 2-17, 147E3
Aspin scores mil pension plan 7-19, 628C2
Female combat role discussed by subcom 11-3, 11-14, 868D2

Asian and Pacific Affairs, Subcommittee on (of Foreign Affairs Committee)
E Timor starvatn probed 12-4, 994A1
Gas raids vs Laos rebels rptd 12-12, 979C1
Cambodia aid rptd blocked 12-18, 978G1

Assassinations, Select Committee on
Justice review of JFK plots asked 1-1; King, JFK review delayed 1-2; Ruby crime link rptd probed 1-3, 3G3
Cong mandate expires 1-3, 4F1
JFK acoustics evidence disputed 1-4—1-5, 4F1-G2
Oswald 'look-alike' dies 1-14, 93C2
JFK, King findings challenged by 3 members 1-26, 91F1
New JFK murder film rptd 2-8, 166D1, F1
JFK draft rpt released: Hoffa, organized crime death role suspected; acoustics experts firm on 2d gunman 3-16—3-17, 204C3, G3
CIA agent rptd ousted re rifled JFK files 6-17, 6-18, 466A3
JFK autopsy photo forgery denied 7-9, 520G2
Final rpt: JFK, King death plots affirmed; Oswald crime links cited; findings scored 7-17, 537F2-538D2

1980

HEALTH & Human Services, Department of
Operation begins 5-4, 363A1
Medicaid abortn funding limits upheld by Sup Ct 6-30, 491G2
Nursing home rights detailed 7-9, 583G3
Medicaid abortn funding rehearing denied by Sup Ct 9-17, 703B3
Schweiker named secy 12-11, 935C1
Food & Drug Administration—*See FOOD & Drug Administration in this section above*
Health Care Financing Administration
Operation begins 5-4, 370B1
Human Development, Office of
Operation begins 5-4, 370C1
Public Health Service—*See PUBLIC Health Service in this section*
Social Security Administration—*See SOCIAL Security Administration in this section*

HOUSE of Representatives—*See also CONGRESS in this section above; personal names*
Iran parlt gets hostage plea 7-29, 571D3; replies 9-1, 671A2
Cuba to free US prisoners 10-13, 789C1

Africa, Subcommittee on (of Foreign Affairs Committee)
Somali mil base pact scored 8-28, 661B3
McHenry defends UN Namibia action 9-9, 710F3

Agriculture, Committee on
GAO scores cancer-nitrite study 1-31, 159A2

Appropriations, Committee on
El Salvador aid pkg studied, Cuba rebel role rptd 3-27, 220D2
Subcom hears Somali mil pact testimony 9-16; OKs pact 9-30, 735B3
House OKs '81 defense appropriatn 9-16, 741B3, G3
McKay loses reelectn 11-4, 846F1, 852D1

Armed Services, Committee on
Brown, Jones call for US mil mobility 1-29, 65E1
Subcom hears mil sex harassment chrgs 2-11, 188E3
Subcom rejects female draft registratn 3-6, 188B3
Subcom hears Joint Chiefs on defns budget 5-29, 424E2
Subcom hears 'stealth' plane disclosure testimony 9-4, 665G3
Beard chrgs Sovt SALT violatns, US denies 9-18, 730C3

Asian and Pacific Affairs, Subcommittee on (of Foreign Affairs Committee)
400 US bodies rptd found in Viet 6-27, 508A3
S Korea support qualified, govt reforms asked 8-28, 673F1

Assassinations, Select Committee on (defunct)
Justice to reopen JFK murder probe 1-4, 17E1

1976

Banking & Currency, Committee on
Bank regulatory agencies probed 1-20—2-3; reactn 2-6, 2-9, 111G3-112D1, E2-C3
Reuss bank reform bill split 3-30; action on 2 rptd 4-30, 5-3; House OKs FRB bill 5-10, 345D1
Nader rpt scores bank diversificatn 7-5, 495A3
Study scores Fed Reserve dist bds make-up 8-15, Burns rebuts 8-30, 666G3
Ford on Watergate coverup chrg 10-14, 761B3
Burns, Reuss meet on FRB-Carter cooperatn 11-12, 865B2
Subcom sets steel price probe 12-2, 898A2

Budget, Committee on the
Adams vs revenue sharing prgrm 2-23, 149D3
Rivlin on fscl '77 options 3-15, 230D3
Adams offers '77 proposals; reactn 3-23, 231D1, A3
'77 budget outlays table 231A1
Ford vs Adams mil budget cut 3-26, 231G3
Votes on defense budget 3-31, 231B3
Sets fscl '77 targets 4-1, 246C1
Dems OK new apptmt procedure 12-6—12-9, 981B3
Adams named Transport secy 12-14, 936D1

Commerce, Committee on Interstate & Foreign
GAO scores HEW health waste 1-7, subcom rpts 1-25, 128C1
Subcom rpt scores cable TV curbs 1-26, 135B3
Product safety comm enacted 5-11, 345C3
Torbert MacDonald dies 5-21, 404A2
Subcom scores Legion disease probe 11-23—11-24, 911C2

Commerce, Consumer & Monetary Affairs, Subcommittee on (of Government Operations Committee)
Bank regulatory agencies probed 1-12—2-3, 111D3, 112E2-B3
Votes comptroller probe 2-26; Smith bars 3-5, 185G3

Democrats
Ford scores defns cut talk 3-26, 231E3
Pushes through hiring, allowance reforms 6-28, 7-1, 551B2
Carter vows campaign aid 7-16, 532A3
Speaker, majority ldr elected 12-6, 919A1-B2
Back rules changes 12-6—12-9, 981A2
Whip, deputy named 12-8, 981D1

Education & Labor, Committee on
Ky mine rescue scored 11-19, 892C1

Energy & Power, Subcommittee on (of Interstate & Foreign Commerce Committee)
June, July Alaska pipeline probe findings rptd 9-5, 690F2-691A2

Ethics Committee—*See 'Standards of Official Conduct, Committee on' in this section below*

Finance Office
Hastings convicted 12-17, 982C1

1977

Banking, Finance & Urban Affairs, Committee on
Reuss special interest gifts rptd 2-4, 129A2
Reuss scores FRB actns 5-24, 406D3
Burns vs $ drop 7-26, 585F2
Lance probe opens in subcom 9-6, 690C1

Black Caucus—*See BLACK Americans—Politics & Government*

Budget, Committee on the
Carter econ plan outlined, Giaimo comments 1-27, 52A1, A2
Carter econ plan hearings 1-27, 89C2
Giaimo special interest gifts rptd 2-4, 129A2
New '77 levels cleared 3-3, 174C1
Giaimo proposes '78 budget 3-23, 228D3
House OKs '78 target res 5-17, 404E3
Gaiamo scores farm bill 9-24, 736G3

Civil & Constitutional Rights, Subcommittee on (of Judiciary Committee)
FBI domestic intell cutback rptd 11-9, 861A3
Wilmington 10 pardon sought 12-4, 943C1

Commerce, Committee on Interstate & Foreign
Gets A-energy jurisdictn 1-4, 36F3
Staggers special interest gifts rptd 2-4, 129B2
Texaco, Gulf accused 2-22, 2-23, 152E1, F1
TV violence hearings set 3-9, 157G3
FPC reprisals chrgd 3-10, 196B1
Costle on air pollutn stand 4-18, 322F2
Energy panel formed 4-21, 321C1
Auto industry reacts to Carter energy plan 4-22, 320C1
Subcom hears surgery excesses 5-9, 732E2
Panel OKs gas decontrol 6-9, 460E1
Adams backs fed no-fault auto insurnc standards 7-21, 594G3
Subcom probes missing A-material 8-8, 717G1
Subcom to get boxing scandal rpt 9-3, 828E2
Subcom hears Califano on health care costs 9-9, 869F2
TV sports probed by subcom 10-4, 11-2—11-3, 949C3
Vs air-bag veto vote 10-12, 797A1
Subcom dissidents score TV violence rpt 10-24, 921F1-C2

Communications, Subcommittee on (of Commerce Committee)
To get boxing scandal rpt 9-3, 828E2
TV sports hearings 10-4, 11-2—11-3, 949C3
Dissidents score TV violence rpt 10-24, 921F1-C2

Crime, Subcommittee on (of Judiciary Committee)
Child abuse hearing 5-23, 432E3

Democrats
292 in 95th Cong 1-4, 5C3
Leaders elected 1-4, 5D3
Full House OKs rule chngs 1-4, 36B3
Sikes ousted as subcom chrmn 1-26, 53E2

Education & Labor, Committee on
Perkins spec interest gifts rptd 2-4, 129E2
Admin asks $2.50 min wage 3-24, 229F2
Child porno, prostitutn hearing 5-27, 432B2
House rejcts min wage indexing 9-15, 759A1

Energy, Ad Hoc Select Committee on
Formed, Ashley named head 4-21, 321B1
Ashley scores Schlesinger 11-22, 916E3

Energy & Power, Subcommittee on (of Interstate & Foreign Commerce Committee)
Uranium rptd missing 8-8, 717G1

Environment, Energy & Natural Resources, Committee on (of Government Opeartions Committee)
Ryan vs US Concorde policy 9-8, 9-23, 738A3

Ethics, Select Committee on
Created 3-9, Preyer named chrmn 3-10, 191C2, E2

Ethics Committee—*See 'Standards of Official Conduct, Committee on' below*

Europe and the Middle East, Subcommittee on (of International Relations Committee)
Egypt air aid plea heard 9-15, 698D1

Financial Institutions Supervision, Regulation & Insurance Subcommittee (of Banking Committee)
Lance probe opens 9-6, 690C1

1978

Banking, Finance & Urban Affairs, Committee on
Reuss backs NYC aid 2-14, 608D2
NYC aid plan presented to subcom 3-2, 141B1
S Africa Eximbank credit ban OKd 5-1, 377B1
HUD secy cancels testimony, White House objectns cited 8-7, 605F1
Reuss Open Market Com case declined by Sup Ct 11-27, 937F2

Black Caucus—*See BLACK Americans—Politics & Government under 'B'*

Budget, Committee on the
Soc Sec tax cut backed, other cuts pared 4-4, 240F3
Carter reduces tax-cut plan 5-12, 361D1
Teeters named to FRB 8-28, 664D1
Dem caucus OKs rules chng 12-4—12-7, 958A3
Giaimo scores Carter 12-14, 980A1

Commerce, Committee on Interstate & Foreign
Subcom sports probe cited 1-11—1-13, 40B2
Radiatn-cancer link probed by subcom 1-24, 1-25, 2-28, 164E1, C3
Health subcom probes pregnancy x-ray risk 7-11, 598F2
Hosp cost bill OKd, lid rejected 7-18, 550D3
Subcom probes drug mislabeling 9-8, 727E2
Energy Dept emergency plans faulted 9-11, 701F2
Energy subcom staff rpt chrgs 'middleman' oil price fraud 12-10, 983B3
PAC gifts to Staggers rptd 12-24, 1008E1

Democrats
Leadership rebuffed 3-20, 3-21, 202A3
Soc Sec tax cut backed 4-5, 240B3
Soc Sec tax cut rejected by com 5-17, 386A1
Election results 11-7, 845C1, F1, 846B2, 847C2-857C3
Caucus meets; ethics issue debated, other rules chngd 12-4—12-7, 958F1-B3

District of Columbia, Committee on
Diggs indicted 3-23, 220E2
Diggs convicted 10-7, 791E3; reelected 11-7, 854B1

Economic Stabilization, Subcommittee on (of Banking Committee)
Moorhead backs NYC aid 2-14, 608E2
Blumenthal presents NYC aid plan 3-2, 141B1

Education & Labor, Committee on
PAC gifts to Perkins rptd 12-24, 1008D1

Energy & Power, Subcommittee on (of Commerce Committee)
Energy Dept emergency plans faulted 9-11, 701D2
Staff rpt chrgs 'middleman' oil price fraud, scores Energy Dept inactn 12-10, 983B3

Energy and the Environment, Subcommittee on (of Interior Committee)
Seabrook A-plant foes vow actn 8-7, 609A3

Ethics Committee—*See 'Standards of Official Conduct, Committee on' below*

1979

Banking, Finance and Urban Affairs, Committee on
Delegation in China 1-2, 2F1
Reuss elected chrmn 1-24, 71C1
Kahn rpts on wage-price compliance 2-6, 127G3
Reuss abandons FRB membership aid bill 4-24, 303D1
Subcom chrmn scores variable-rate mortgage 5-30, 403G2
Synthetic fuel bill amended 6-26, 498B2
Cleveland default tied to anti-mayor moves 7-17, 579A3
FRB admits money supply errors, Reuss scores 10-30, 828D2, A3
Chrysler aid bill OKd 12-21, 981E2

Black Caucus—*See BLACK Americans—Politics & Government under 'B'*

Budget, Committee on the
Jones wins seat over Fisher 1-23, 70G3
Giaimo elected chrmn 1-24, 71C1
Miller, Rivlin open fscl '80 hearings 1-25, 48E3
Volcker vows inflatn fight, vs tax cut 9-7, 680C3
Giaimo vs more fscl '80 mil spending 9-11, 679A1

Civil and Constitutional Rights, Subcommittee on (of Judiciary Committee)
Edwards scores FBI audit on informants, urges GAO probe 8-22, 747A3

Commerce, Committee on Interstate and Foreign
Subcom scores life insurance sales practices 1-2, 15F3
NCAA warned on reform 1-8, 1-10, 103C1
Staggers elected chrmn 1-24, 71D1
Waxman wins health subcom chair 1-30, 86C3
Eckhardt wins oversight subcom chair 1-30, 86F3
Carter hosp cost plan faces hurdles 2-13, 110B1
Waxman at hosp cost bill ceremony 3-6, 163C2
Niagara chem dump hearing 4-10, 281B3
Subcom probes Hooker pollutn 6-19, 597A2
Subcom rpts on dump sites 11-1, 886D1
Subcom holds NRC licensing hearing 11-5, 849B1

Defense, Subcommittee on (of Appropriations Committee)
Brown urges US response to Sovt surrogates 2-8, 89B2
AF pilot drain, morale loss cited 2-15, 130F2

Democrats
Rule chngs adopted, speaker elected 1-15, 30E1
Caucus selects chrmn 1-23, OKs ethics proposal 1-24, 70F3-71B3; ldrship, chrmn S1-23, chart 71A1
3 liberals win subcom chairs 1-30, 1-31, 86C3
Ethics com chrmn elected 1-31, 87A1
106 vs standby gas rationing 5-10, 342D2
4 launch draft-Kennedy move 5-23, 384B2
Caucus opposes oil decontrol 5-24, 395G1
Carter hosts 11 6-1—6-2, 418B2
Caucus s pports heating fuel price controls 9-19, 703F1

District of Columbia, Committee on the
Dellums elected chrmn 1-24, 71C1

Education and Labor, Committee on
Perkins elected chrmn 1-24, 71C1

Employment Opportunities, Subcommittee on (of Education and Labor Committee)
Hawkins backs jobs bill 5-23, 384B2

Energy and Power, Subcommittee on (of Commerce Committee)
NRC chrmn on licensing freeze 11-5, 849B1

Energy and the Environment, Subcommittee on (of Interior and Insular Affairs Committee)
3 Mile I A-accident probed 3-29, 242B3, 243C1
3 Mile I operators testify 5-7, 344A2

Environment, Energy and Natural Resources, Subcommittee on (of Government Operations Committee)
Moffett wins chair 1-31, 86G3
Heating oil supplies reviewed 6-28—6-29, 514E2

Ethics Committee—*See 'Standards of Official Conduct, Committee on' below*

Financial Institutions Supervision, Regulation and Insurance, Subcommittee on (of Banking Committee)
Cleveland default tied to anti-mayor moves 7-17, 579A3

Foreign Affairs, Committee on (formerly International Relations Committee)
Subcom hears rpt re CIA Iran statn closure 1-18, 26E2
Diggs drops subcom reelectn bid 1-23, 71G2
Zablocki elected chrmn 1-24, 71D1
Thai premr queried on Cambodia arms 2-7, 84D2

1980

Banking, Finance and Urban Affairs, Committee on
Volcker vows tight money supply 2-19, 126F1
FRB tight money goals backed 8-4, 616D3
Ashley loses reelectn 11-4, 846F1, 851D2

Budget, Committee on the
Cuban refugee resetlmt costs estimated 5-25, 396D1
'81 budget res OKd 11-11, 866B2
Giaimo on '81 budget res 11-20, 896B2

Business Opportunities, Access to Equity Capital and, Subcommittee on (of Small Business Committee)
Carter policies scored in rpt 5-29, 455E2

Commerce, Committee on Interstate and Foreign
Memphis area illness probed 4-2, 331F2
Van Deerlin cautns on AT&T reorgn 8-20, 648A3
Subcom scores SEC natl securities mkt plan failure 9-12, 806D1
Telecommunicatns bill tabled 9-30, 835D2
Staggers RR deregulatn bill signed 10-14, 783E3
Van Deerlin, Eckhardt lose reelectn 11-4, 846F1, 850A2, 852A2

Commerce, Consumer and Monetary Affairs, Subcommittee on (of Government Operations Committee)
Hunt silver trading probe opens 3-31, 245G1-A2
Commodity futures trading curbs debated 4-14—4-15, 289F3
Hunts threatened with contempt 4-29; testify, silver bailout set 5-2, 344F3, 345G1
Forgn investmt in US study rptd 8-7, 601D3

Communications, Subcommittee on (of Interstate and Foreign Commerce Committee)
Van Deerlin cautns on AT&T reorgn 8-20, 648A3
Van Deerlin loses reelectn 11-4, 846F1, 852A2

Defense, Subcommittee on (of Appropriations Committee)
House OKs '81 defense appropriatn 9-16, 741B3

Democrats
See Admin offcls re task-force 6-26, 480C3
Dissidents move for open conv 7-25, 7-28, 570F1, A2
Election results 11-4, 837D1, 846B1-847A1, 848B1-852C3; 97th Cong listed 842A1*-844E4
O'Neill sees Reagan, vows 'honeymoon' 11-18, 880G2, B3
Leadership posts filled 12-8, 936D2

Foreign Affairs, Committee on (formerly International Relations Committee)
Broomfield urges GOP platform plank 1-14, 32D1
Carter Olympic stand backed 1-23, 45F3
UN Mideast vote probed, Vance defends Admin stand 3-21, 218B2, F2
Zablocki, Broomfield protest Saudi film telecast 5-8, 375B3
Subcom hears rpt on 400 US bodies found in Viet 6-27, 508A3
Subcom scores Somali mil pact 8-28, 661B3
Subcom holds S Korea policy hearings 8-28, 673F1
Subcom hears McHenry on Namibia 9-9, 710F3
India uranium sale bar backed 9-10, 723D1

1976

Government Operations, Committee on
Subcom chrgs HEW open to fraud 1-26, 128A3
Brooks on revenue sharing 2-23, 149D3
Teton Dam flood probe rptd 9-25, 736D1
Bank boycott compliance rptd 9-29, 987A1
Scores comptroller re Franklin Bank 10-6, 940C2
Subcom hears Richardson on boycott 10-20, 786F2
House Administration, Committee on
Cuts ethics com probe budget 3-25, 216D3
Hays admits affair with aide 5-25, 392B2; **for subsequent developments, see HAYS, Wayne under 'H'**
Hays resigns chair 6-18, Thompson replaces 6-23, 551F2
OKs hiring, allowance reforms 6-28, allowance powers curbed 7-1, 551B2, A3
Intelligence, Special Subcommittee on (of Armed Services Committee)
Briefing on CIA Italy aid rptd 1-7, 10G2
Intelligence Activities, Select Committee on
FBI purchasing irregularities rptd 1-1, 6A1
NYT, Washn Post rpt unreleased findings 1-20—1-28, 92D1-93B3
Vs rpt publicatn curbs 1-23; Rules com, House vote censorship 1-28, 1-29, 92A2
Admin denounces rpt leaks, Field denies blame 1-26, 92F1
Rpt findings, publicatn disputed 2-2, 2-3, 150C2
Offers reforms 2-10, disbands 2-11, 150E1-B2
Schorr admits leaking rpt 2-12; House votes probe 2-19, CBS suspends 2-23, 150D3-151A2
Kurds on US aid vow 2-25, 146C1
Leak probe underway 3-2—3-25, 216C3
Pike scores CIA re missing documts issue 3-9, CIA rebuts 3-16, 216G3
FBI purchasing probe rptd renewed 3-20—3-23, 248E1
Ethics com hears leak probe testimony 7-19, 7-20; Schorr, others subpoenaed 8-25, refuse testimony 9-15; probe dropped 9-22, 748A3
International Relations, Committee on
Rabin meets 1-28, 60A2
Kissinger testifies 3-29, 232B3, 244B2
Hussein asks Syrian troops in Leb 3-31, 226G2
Uruguayan found dead in Argentina 5-20, 399B2
Hays asked to quit subcom 6-2, 433G2
Members see Spain king 6-2, 459C2
Kissinger on Leb policy, Vorster mtg 6-17, 425D2, 427D1 ★
Subcom hears Ryan Uruguay aid 8-4; Koch testimony rptd 9-20, 814C2
2 panels hear Admin rpt on Korea 9-1, 641D1
Atherton warns re anti-boycott legis, Saudi arms bar 9-27, 746B3
GAO study faults US '75 Mayaguez action 10-5, 749F2
Argentina scores subcom rights abuse probe 10-6; suit re Fraser rpt access rptd 12-19, 996F2
Subcom transcripts on NATO sales issued 11-4, 880B1
Carter meets 11-23, 881G1
Judiciary, Committee on
Handgun ban recommitted 3-2, 170E1
Spec prosecutor bill not cleared 10-2, 884D1
Mondale scores GOP ticket on Watergate 10-5, 743D3

1977

Government Operations, Committee on
IJC rpt vs ND dam projct 1-7, 60G3
Brooks special interest gifts rptd 2-4, 129C2
Pres reorganzn powers cleared 3-31, 228E1
143 spying suits vs US rptd 5-22, 422B3
Ryan vs US Concorde policy 9-8, 9-23, 738A3
Health and the Environment, Subcommittee on (of Commerce Committee)
Hears Califano on health care costs 9-9, 869F2
House Administration, Committee on
Thompson special interest gifts rptd 2-4, 129C2
Cong pub electn funds backed 3-16, 232G3
Tonry resigns 5-4, 418D3
Intelligence, Select Committee on
Created 7-14, 557C1
CIA ex-offcls defend press links 12-27, 1005E3
Interior & Insular Affairs, Committee on
Gets A-energy jurisdictn 1-4, 36F3
Udall special interest gifts rptd 2-4, 129A2
Water projects hearing 2-23, 209E3
Energy panel formed 4-21, 321C1
Coal slurry bill deferred 6-27, 515G3-F1
Minn wilderness area proposed 9-13, 724D1
Alaska parks plan proposed 9-15, 739A3
International Organizations, Subcommittee on (of International Relations Committee)
Korean probe OKd 2-3, 442G1
Ex-KCIA dir testifies 6-22, 556F3
El Salvador rights probe opens 7-21, 580B2
Kissinger, Haig Korea scandal cover-up rptd 9-5, 688G1
KCIA defector cooperatn rptd 9-28, 774D2
Korea '76 influence plan documt disclosed 11-29, bid to block Kim testimony chrgd 11-30, 914G2, F3
International Relations, Committee on
Releases forgn rights abuse rpts 1-1, 50D2
Gets A-energy jurisdictn 1-4, 36F3
Subcom Korea probe OKd 2-3, 442G1
Zablocki special interest gifts rptd 2-4, 129C2
Bingham visits Cuba 2-10, 110G1
El Salvador vote fraud hearing 3-9, 206B3
Vance on Zaire attack 3-16, 207D3
OKs boycott bill 3-31, 323F2
Subcom hears ex-KCIA dir 6-22, 556F3
Subcom opens El Salvador rights hearings 7-21, 580B2
Subcom gets rpt on Cambodia deaths, resolutn urges Carter act vs rights abuse 7-26, 590C2
AWACS to Iran opposed 7-28, deal dropped 8-2, 611E2
Kissinger, Haig Korea scandal cover-up rptd 9-5, 688G1
Bunker, Linowitz on Panama human rights 699D1
Kissinger, Rusk defend Canal pacts 9-14; vet score 9-16, 716A3
Subcom hears Egypt aircraft aid plea 9-15, 698D1
Dayan backs US naval base at Haifa 9-20, 714A1
Subcom rpts KCIA defector cooperatn 9-28, 774D2
Nigeria ldr confers 10-12, 797A2
Korea hearings continue in subcom 11-29, 11-30, 914G2, F3
Investigations, Subcommittee on (of Armed Services Committee)
Singlaub testifies 5-25, 404D1
Judiciary, Committee on
Rodino special interest gifts rptd 2-4, 129D2
Crime subcom child abuse hearing 5-23, 432E3
FBI domestic intell cutback rptd 11-9, 861A3
Wilmington 10 pardon sought 12-4, 943C1

1978

Fossil and Nuclear Energy Research, Development and Demonstration Subcommittee (of Science and Technology Committee)
Clinch R A-breeder compromise proposal rptd 3-17, 3-23, 242A1
Government Operations, Committee on
PAC gifts to Brooks rptd 12-24, 1008D1
Health & Environment, Subcommittee on (of Commerce Committee)
A-test site exposure, cancer link probed 1-24, 1-25, 2-28, 164E1
Pregnancy x-ray risk seen 7-11, 598F2
House Administration, Committee on
Assassinatn com added funds OKd 9-7, 698C2
PAC gifts to Thompson rptd 12-24, 1008E1
Intelligence, Select Committee on
CIA evidence on Cuba role in Zaire presented 6-5, 442A2
Carter on security leaks 7-11, 524G2
Interior, Subcommittee on (of Appropriations Committee)
Bikini I radiatn probed 4-12, 278C2-A3
Interior & Insular Affairs, Committee on
Seabrook A-plant foes vow actn 8-7, 609A3
International Organizations, Subcommittee on (of International Relations Committee)
Korea lobbying probed 3-15—3-22, 203D1-C3
Kissinger testifies re Korea 4-20, 280A1
Nixon ex-aide rpts Korea paymts 6-1, 433A1
Moon evades subpoena 6-6, 433D1
Korea lobbying detailed, Unificatn Church probe asked; reactn 11-1, 862B3, F3
International Relations, Committee on
Sadat asks US arms 2-7, 78A1
Indonesia student unrest hearing 2-8, 122B3
Rights rpts on 105 natns released 2-9, 101C3, E3
Vance: Saudi jet transfer barred 2-21, 139E1
Korea mil aid seen unlikely 2-22, 204D1
Korea lobbying probed by subcom 3-15—3-22, 203D1-C3
Begin questioned 3-21, 199F1
Vance, Brown urge Turkey arms embargo end 4-6, 276D2
Kissinger testifies to subcom re Korea 4-20, 280A1
Turkish arms ban end backed 5-3, 378F1
US-Israel agrmt on cluster bombs rptd 5-12, 358A3
Uganda boycott backed 5-16, 416C3
'77 rejctd arms bids rptd, '78 sales forecast 5-19, 386E3-387B1
Jaworski rpts Kim paymts proof 5-22, 432B3
Korean aid, lobby probe cooperatn linked 5-24, 406B2
Subcom hears Korea testomony 6-1; Moon evades supoena 6-6, 433A1, D1
CIA evidence on Cuba role in Zaire presented 6-8, 442C2
Sees forgn policy 'confusion' 6-8, Vance outlines policy 6-19, 490F2
Vance rpts on planned visit to Israel, Egypt 8-4, 602B2
Zablocki gets Israel plea on Leb Christns 8-7, 638D2
Carter briefs on Camp David summit 9-18, 710D1
Nicaragua aid cutoff asked by 16 10-13, 839G2
Subcom details Korea lobbying, asks Unificatn Church probe; reactn 11-1, 862B3, F3
Dem ethics chng threatens Diggs subcom chair 12-6, 958C2
PAC gifts to Zablocki rptd 12-24, 1008E1
Judiciary, Committee on
Carter urges ERA extensn 4-12, 529F2
Bell consults on Viet refugees 11-28, 933A1
Korean Lobbying Scandal—*See KOREA (South)—U.S.-Korean Political Payments*

1979

Rights rpt on 115 natns released 2-10, 107A2
US to speed arms to N Yemen 2-26, to send advisers 3-12, 144F2, 178C3
Begin briefs on US Mideast plan 3-5, 157D1
Subcom hears Zaire aid issue 3-5, 215E1
Egypt-Israel aid hearing, Vance testifies 5-8, 341B2
Vance vs Zimbabwe trade tie 6-12, 435B1
Morocco mil aid plea rptd 8-2, 592C2
Israel assures on US arms use vs Leb 9-17, 694B1
E Timor starvatn probed 12-4, 995A1
Gas raids vs Laos rebels rptd 12-12, 979C1
Cambodia aid rptd blocked 12-18, 977F3, 978G1
Foreign Operations, Subcommittee on (of Appropriations Committee)
Nicaragua aid pkg OKd 9-11, 731E2
Nicaragua army officers tour US bases 11-11—11-21, 910B1
Government Operations, Committee on
Brooks elected chrmn 1-24, 71D1
Moffett wins environmt subcom chair 1-31, 86G3
GAO, Admin debate contract denial legality 2-5, 127C3
Rosenthal vs FRB Cleveland bank rpt 3-14, 204F2
Educ Dept bill OKd 5-2, 326E2
Heating oil supplies reviewed 6-28—6-29, 514E2
Health, Subcommittee on (of Ways and Means Committee)
Carter hosp cost plan faces hurdles 2-13, 110C1
Rangel at hosp cost bill ceremony 3-6, 163C2
Rostenkowski financial disclosure statemt studied 9-1, 701D3
Health and Environment, Subcommittee on (of Commerce Committee)
Waxman wins chair 1-30, 86C3
Carter hosp cost plan faces hurdles 2-13, 110B1
Waxman at hosp cost bill ceremony 3-6, 163C2
House Administration, Committee on
Thompson elected chrmn 1-24, 71D1
Electn financing bill defeated 5-24, 401D2
Leach '78 electn challenge pending 11-3, 900F2
Intelligence, Select Committee on
Admin blamed for Iran intell failure 1-24, 67E2
US intell on China-Viet war praised 3-25, 231F3
CIA wants more armed agents 4-4, 310B2
Aspin on U-2 SALT verficatn 7-1, 497C1
Subcom chrmn rpts on Young-PLO mtg probe 10-28, 823E3
Interior, Subcommittee on (of Appropriations Committee)
Udall scores 'Sagebrush Revolt' 9-5, 704B1
Interior and Insular Affairs, Committee on
NRC A-safety hearings planned 1-20, 54D3
Udall elected chrmn 1-24, 71D1
Alaska lands bill OKd 3-1, 187E1
Subcom probes 3 Mile I A-accident 3-29, 242B3, 243C1
3 Mile I NRC transcripts released 4-12, 275D2
Subcom hears 3 Mile A-accident testimony 5-7, 344A2
A-plant permit moratorium OKd 5-9, 382B1
Judiciary, Committee on the
Rodino elected chrmn 1-24, 71D1
Holzman chrgs Viet refugee racket 2-26, 181A2
Refugee paroles extended 3-26, 308B1
FBI audit scored in subcom, GAO probe backed 8-22, 747A3
Korean Lobbying Scandal—*See KOREA (South)-U.S.-Korean Political Payments*

1980

Foreign Operations, Subcommittee on (of Appropriations Committee)
El Salvador aid pkg studied, Cuba rebel role rptd 3-27, 220D2
Somali mil pact testimony heard 9-16, arms sales backed 9-30, 735B3
Government Activities and Transportation, Subcommittee on (of Government Operations Committee)
FAA computer reliability probed 6-30, 666F3
Government Operations, Committee on
Subcom probes Hunt silver trading 3-31, 245G1-A2
Subcom debates commodity futures trading curbs 4-14—4-15, 289F3
Subcom hears Hunts testify, silver bailout set 5-2, 344F3, 345G1
Subcom probes FAA computer reliability 6-30, 666F3
Subcom warns on forgn investmt in US 8-7, 601D3
House Administration, Committee on
Thompson loses chrmnship 6-18, 454D2
Housing and Committee Development, Subcommittee on (of Banking, Finance and Urban Affairs Committee)
Ashley loses reelectn 11-4, 846F1, 851D2
Immigration, Refugees and International Law, Committee on
Chisholm scores US refugee policy 6-17, 484E3
Intelligence, Select Committee on
Subcom chrgs Sovt anthrax cover-up 6-29, 500A1
Intell oversight bill clears Cong 9-19, 9-30; signed 10-14, 804F1
Investigations, Subcommittee on (of Armed Services Committee)
Joint Chiefs score Carter defns budget 5-29, 424E2
Judiciary, Committee on the
Schl prayer legis studied 2-6, 156A2
Nixon impeachmt lawyer sentenced 6-10, 460B1
Subcom gets Haitian refugee plea 6-17, 484E3
Telecommunicatns bill tabled 9-30, 835D2

1976

Legislation—*See under CONGRESS in this section above*

Membership—*For Black Caucus developments, see 'Politics & Government' under BLACK Americans under 'B'*
Political lineup 1-19, 68D3
Hastings, Casey resign 1-20, 1-22, 68D3
Hinshaw convicted 1-26, 95F3
Jones pleads guilty on campaign chrg 1-29, 134D1
Addabbo, Leggett payoffs probed 2-19, 171D1
Dem wins Hastings seat 3-2, 166D2
Leak probe underway 3-2—3-25, 216C3
Wright Patman dies 3-7, 240E3
Clay travel bills questnd 3-23, 247E1
Environment group lists targets 3-25, 219E3
Sikes conflict of interest chrgd 4-7, 286F2
Barrett dies 4-12, 305B1, 315F3
Metcalfe tax probe dropped 4-15, 286E3
Ethics Com votes Sikes probe 4-28, 309D2
Madden loses Ind primary 5-4, 323A2
Hays admits affair with aide 5-25, 392B2; **for subsequent developments, see HAYS, Wayne under 'H'**
Torbert Macdonald dies 5-31, 404A2
Helstoski indicted 6-2, 414C3
Sex scandal spreads 6-2—6-14, 433E2-434B2
Albert announces retiremt 6-5, 434B3
Young accused of sexual hiring 6-11, 433E3
Howe arrested on sex chrg 6-12, 434G1-B2
Hiring, allowance reforms OKd 6-28, 7-1, 551A2
Howe convicted, appeals 7-23, 552A1
Sikes reprimanded 7-29, 551D3
Litton dies 8-3, 565C2
Passman loses primary, Hebert seat runoff set 8-14, 633A1
Young cleared 8-16, 636B2
Howe conviction upheld 8-24, 636E2
Hays resigns 9-1, 646G1
Ford upholds '68 ethics code 9-28, 9-30, 722E3, 723F1
Hinshaw expulsn blocked 10-1, 807E1
Pay increase barred 10-1, 834A2
S Korea influence peddling rptd 10-24—12-1, 898D3-900B2; 891F1
Travel expense probe closed 10-27, 981F3
Election results 11-2, 817E1, 820F1; 95th Cong listed 828F2-831A4
Meeds wins electn count 11-16, 865D1
Mikva declared winner 11-19, 882A1
Terms limit proposed 11-29, 917G2-A3
Repub ldrs elected 12-8, 981C3
Adams, Young named to Cabt 12-14, 12-16, 936D1-937D1; Bergland 12-20, 956G1

Merchant Marine & Fisheries, Committee on
Subcom probes Panama Canal talks 4-6—4-8; Bunker testimony revealed 4-13, 281D1, 291G2, B3

Missing Persons in Southeast Asia, Select Committee on
N Viet claims Nixon aid vow 2-1, 103B1
Chrgs Viet reneged on agrmt chrgd 7-21, 593C2
Viet names 12 pilots killed 9-6, 678A3

Oversight and Investigations Subcommittee (of Interstate & Foreign Commerce Committee)
US guns, Mex drugs trade rptd 4-14, 420D1
Chrgs Commerce Dept aids boycott 9-7, 746E3, G3 ★ -747B1

Republicans
Ldrs score hiring, allowance reforms 7-1, 551B3
Ldrs, com chrmn elected 12-8, 981C3

Resolutions—*See 'Legislation' under CONGRESS in this section above*

Rules, Committee on
Backs intellignc com rpt censorship 1-28, 92B2

1977

Legislation—*See under CONGRESS in this section above*

Merchant Marine & Fisheries, Committee on
Porpoise kill limit set 6-11, 443A1
Seadock pres scores overregulatn 7-26, 724G3
Ex-chrmn Garmatz indicted 8-1, 603D3
Cargo preference debated 8-1—8-29, 719F3
Panama Canal pact scored 8-17, 622A2

Military Construction, Subcommittee on (of Appropriations Committee)
Sikes loses post, Dems back McKay 1-26, 53E2

Narcotics Abuse & Control, Select Committee on
Pot decriminalizatn hearings 3-14, 3-15, 332G1, F3
Wolff at Thai drug conf 4-14, 331G2
Cocaine traffic rptd 8-29, 972F1

National Parks and Insular Affairs, Subcommittee on (of Interior and Insular Affairs Committee)
Minn wilderness area proposed 9-13, 724D1

Northeast-Midwest Economic Advancement Coalition
Asks base-closing ban, vs regionalism 4-6, 423G2

Outer Continental Shelf, Ad Hoc Select Committee on
Offshore leasing bill blocked 10-25, 833F2

Oversight and Investigations Subcommittee (of Interstate & Foreign Commerce Committee)
Hysterectomy excesses chrgd 5-9, 732E2
Gulf role in uranium cartel probed 6-9—6-17, 479B3, 480A1

Population, Select Committee on
Created 9-24, 833G3-834A1

Post Office & Civil Service, Committee on
Fed pay hikes take effect 2-20, 127G2

Public Works & Transportation, Committee on
Carter econ plan hearings 2-1—2-4, 89E2
Johnson special interest gifts rptd 2-4, 129B2
Adams backs mass-transit fund 10-12, 860C3

Republicans
143 in 95th Cong 1-4, 5C3
Rules changes scored 1-4, 36D3

Resolutions—*See CONGRESS—Legislation in this section above*

Rules, Committee on
Delaney special interest gifts rptd 2-4, 129A2
Offshore oil leasing bill blocked 10-25, 833C2

1978

Labor-Health, Education & Welfare, Subcommittee on (of Appropriations Committee)
Flood probed by ethics com 2-8, 240B1
Flood indicted 9-5, 685B1
Flood indicted again 10-12, 792C1
Dems rejct ethics rule chng, Flood chair secure 12-6, 958G2

Legislation—*See under CONGRESS in this section above*

Lobbying & Lobbyists—*See under CONGRESS in this section above; for Korean lobbying scandal, see KOREA (South)—U.S.-Korean Political Payments*

Membership—*See also other appropriate subheads in this section*
Flood, Eilberg inquiry rptd 2-8, formal probe asked 2-17, 239G3, 240F2
Green, Garcia win NY seats 2-14, 108F1-C2
Anderson wins primary 3-21, 207E1
Diggs indicted 3-23, 220C2
Richmond pleads not guilty 4-6, 265A1-B2
Personal finance rpts disclosed 5-4, 363A2
Milford loses primary, Young faces runoff, Krueger wins Sen primary 5-6, 5 Texans to retire 362G3-363B1
Thone wins gov primary 5-9, 363D1
Nix loses primary 5-16; Dent, Myers to retire 389D3
Breckinridge loses primary, Guethner wins Sen primary 5-23, 406D2
Young loses runoff 6-3, 426E2
Pressler wins Sen primary 6-6, 448A2
Cohen unopposed in Sen primary 6-13, 467B1
Clifford Allen dies 6-18, 540D2
Ketchum dies 6-24, 540B3
Michel mugged in DC 7-21, 843B3
Risenhoover loses primary 8-22, 683D1
Flood indicted 9-5, 685B1
Clark indicted 9-5, 685D1
Fraser loses Sen primary, Quie wins gubernatorial spot 9-12, 715G3, 716D1
Richmond wins renominatn; Delaney, Pike to retire 9-12, 716B2-C2
Jeffords unopposed in primary 9-12, 716E2
St Germain, Beard win renominatn 9-12, 716A3
Frey loses gov primary 9-12, 736D1
Kasten loses gov primary 9-12, 736G1
Roncalio to retire 9-12, 736D2
Eilberg chrgd by ethics com 9-13, 697F1
Waggonner to retire 9-16, 736D3
Harrington to retire 9-19, 736B3
Tsongas wins Sen primary 9-19, 736B3
Meeds to retire 9-19, 736F3
Burke pleads guilty on 2 bar chrgs, no contest on 3d 9-26, 734G2
Diggs convicted 10-7, 791D3-792A1
Metcalfe dies 10-11, 853B2, 888C3
Byron dies 10-11, 888G2
Flood indicted again 10-12, 792A1
Eilberg indicted 10-24, pleads not guilty 11-1, 835C2
Amer Samoa del bill signed 10-31, 1003A1
Election results 11-7, 845C1, F1, 846B2, 847C2-857C3
Ryan killed in Guyana 11-18, 889A1
Diggs sentenced 11-20, 900A2
Dems OK ethics chng, other rules 12-4—12-7, 958B2
Steiger dies 12-4, 1032E3
Travel overseas rptd 12-10, 958B3
Thorsness wins SD recount 12-19, 1008F1
PAC gifts to 22 com chrmn rptd 12-24, 1008A1

Merchant Marine & Fisheries, Committee on
Garmatz indictmt dropped 1-9, 16B1
Coast Guard '79 fund hike asked 3-31, 525C2
PAC gifts to Murphy rptd 12-24, 1008D1

Narcotics Abuse and Control, Select Committee on
Armed forces drug use survey released 4-25, random tests backed 4-27, 368C2-A3
Armed forces drug use survey described 5-24, E Ger heroin smuggling scored 6-1, 433D2, G2
Burke pleads guilty on 2 bar chrgs, no contest on 3d 9-26, 734B3

Oversight & Investigations, Subcommittee on (of Interstate & Foreign Commerce Committee)
Sports probe cited 1-11—1-13, 40B2
Sun Oil Becton Dickinson purchase probe asked 1-27, 66B1
Firestone tire recall sought 8-31, 835C1
Drug mislabeling rptd 9-8, 727E2

Population, Select Committee on
Illegal alien curbs sought, Carter plan scored 12-20, 1010B2-B3

Post Office & Civil Service, Committee on
Nix loses primary 5-16, 389D3

Public Works & Transportation, Committee on
Johnson asks ICC trucking deregulatn halt 12-7, O'Neal rejcts 12-21, 1007C2
PAC gifts to Johnson rptd 12-24, 1008D1

Republicans
Election results 11-7, 845C1, F1, 846B2, 847C2-857C3
Caucus meets 12-4, 958F1

Resolutions—*See CONGRESS—Legislation in this section above*

1979

Labor-Health Education and Welfare, Subcommittee on (of Appropriations Committee)
Flood drops chrmnship 1-25, 71A3

Legislation—*See under CONGRESS in this section above*

Legislation, Subcommittee on (of Intelligence Committee)
CIA wants more armed agents 4-4, 310B2

Membership
Dem caucus selects chrmn, OKs ethics proposal 1-23–1-24; com members, chrmn confrmd 1-24, 70E3-71B3; ldrship, chrmn chart 71A1
3 liberals win subcom chairs 1-30, 1-31, 86C3
Ethics com chrmn elected 1-31, 87A1
Flood mistrial declared 2-3, 102A2
Eilberg pleads guilty 2-24, 152C2
Diggs expulsn rejected 3-1, 165E2-A3
Passman acquitted 4-1, 265B3
Royer, Petri win Calif, Wis seats 4-3, 265E1-A2
Podell, Brasco disbarmt challenges declined by Sup Ct 4-16, 303C1
'78 PAC spending rptd up 5-10, Common Cause deplores 5-15, 363E1-C2
Anderson enters pres race 6-8, 439C2
Clark sentncd 6-12, 442G2
Labor '78 campaign gifts rptd 6-13, 595C1
Bolling hospitalized 6-25, 527A3
Diggs accepts censure 6-29, 515D1; expulsn defeated 7-30, censured 7-31, 578D1
Leach pleads not guilty to vote buying 7-24, 561D1
Jenrette denies drug role probe 8-8, 650B1
Diggs sued by US 8-16, 649G3-650B1
Passman settles sex bias suit 8-23, 649E3
Financial disclosure statemts studied 9-1, 701C3-702B1
'54 PR natlsts' sentncs commuted 9-6, 666E2, B3; freed 9-10, 683A1
Flood, Passman briber convctd 10-12, sentcd 10-24, 906D1
Dellums, Leland see Castro 10-13, 779D1
Leach acquitted 11-3, 900E2
Flood sets '80 resignatn 11-7, 900C2
Diggs convictn upheld 11-14, 900F2
Treen elected La gov 12-8, 946C3
Wilson rules violatns chrgd, announces candidacy 12-13, 945E2

Merchant Marine and Fisheries, Committee on
Murphy elected chrmn 1-24, 71E1
Nicaragua chrgs Panama rebel arms aid 6-6, 427D1

Military Personnel, Subcommittee on (of Armed Services Committee)
Mil MD shortage rptd 2-16, 130C2
Female combat role discussed 11-13, 11-14, 868D2

Narcotics Abuse and Control, Select Committee on
W Eur, US mil heroin use rptd 11-11, 972C3

Oversight, Subcommittee on (of Select Committee on Intelligence)
Aspin rpts on Young-PLO mtg probe 10-28, 823D2

Oversight and Investigations, Subcommittee on (of Interstate and Foreign Commerce Committee)
Life insurance sales practices scored 1-2, 15D3
Subcom warns NCAA on reform 1-8, 1-10, 103C1
Eckhardt wins chair 1-30, 86F3
Hooker pollutn probed 6-19, 597A2
Chem dump site list issued 11-1, 886B1

Panama Canal Subcommittee (of Merchant Marine and Fisheries Committee)
Nicaragua chrgs Panama rebel arms aid 6-6, 427D1

Population, Select Committee on
Illegal alien issue detailed 1-29, 127C1

Post Office and Civil Service, Committee on the
Hanley elected chrmn 1-24, 71E1

Public Works and Transportation, Committee on
Johnson elected chrmn 1-24, 71E1

Republicans
Dems win rules chngs, speaker electn 1-15, 30E1
Com members, chrmn confrmd 1-24, 70F3; ldrship chart 71B1

Rules, Committee on
Bolling elected chrmn 1-24, 71E1
Election financing bill revival sought 5-24, 401E2

1980

Membership
Cong Watch sees anticonsumerism 1-12, 53G2
ACU '79 voting survey rptd 1-18, 53B3
GOP wins Mikva III seat 1-22, 50D3
Flood resigns 1-31, pleads guilty 2-26, 190F1-B2
W Va Rep Slack dies 3-17, 280C2
Drinan drops reelectn bid 5-5, 341D2
Tauzin wins La seat 5-17, 404D3
Duncan loses Ore primary 5-20, 404B3
Diggs convictn review refused by Sup Ct 6-2, Diggs resigns 6-3, 428A1
Wilson loses primary; Adbnor, Grassley win Sen primaries, Hutchinson gets W Va seat 6-3, 439A2-D3
Wilson censured 6-10, 438F1-E2
Myers expelled 10-2, 740B1
Election results 11-4, 837D1, 846B1-847A1, 848B1-852C3; 97th Cong listed 842A1★-844E4
Jenrette resigns 12-10, 962E1
17 seats shifted by '80 census 12-31, 982D3, 983C1

Merchant Marine and Fisheries, Committee on
Murphy loses chrmnship 6-18, 454D2

Military Construction, Subcommittee on (of Appropriations Committee)
McKay loses reelectn 11-4, 846F1, 852D1

Military Personnel, Subcommittee on (of Armed Services Committee)
Mil sex harassment alleged 2-11, 188E3
Female draft registratn rejctd 3-6, 188B3

Oversight, Subcommittee on (of Select Committee on Intelligence)
Sovt anthrax cover-up chrgd 6-29, 500A1

Oversight and Investigations, Subcommittee on (of Interstate and Foreign Commerce Committee)
SEC natl securities mkt plan failure scored 9-12, 806D1
Eckhardt loses reelectn 11-4, 846F1, 850A2

Postal Operations and Services, Subcommittee on (of Post Office Committee)
Wilson removed as chrmn 6-10, 438D2

Post Office and Civil Service, Committee on the
Wilson removed as subcom chrmn 6-10, 438D2

Public Assistance and Unemployment Compensation, Subcommittee on (of Ways and Means Committee)
Corman loses reelectn 11-4, 846G1, 852A2

Public Works and Transportation, Committee on
Johnson loses reelectn 11-4, 837E1, 846E1, 852A2

Republicans
State of Union reactn 1-28, 75C1
Policy Com links Abscam, Dem majority 2-5, 82B2
Kelly quits conf re Abscam 2-21, 143B3
'81 counter-budget proposed 4-1, 244F1
Election results 11-4, 837D1, 846B1-847A1, 848B1-852C3; 97th Cong listed 842A1★-844E4
Reagan sees Rhodes 11-18, attends luncheon 11-19, 880G2, 881D1
Leadership named 12-8, 936A2

Research and Development, Subcommittee on (of Armed Services Committee)
Brown, Perry testify on 'stealth' plane disclosure 9-4, 665G3

1976

Small Business, Committee on
Subcom gets missing A-fuel rpt 8-5, 739A3
Standards of Official Conduct, Committee on (Ethics Committee)
House com leak probe voted 2-19, 151D1
Leak probe underway 3-2—3-25, 216C3
Sikes conflict of interest chrgd 4-7, 286F2
Votes Sikes inquiry 4-28, 309D2
Probe of Hays affair sought 5-25, 392F2
Votes to investigate Hays 6-2, 433B3
Asks Sikes reprimand 7-26, 551E3
GOP platform text 8-18, 604B1
Subpoenas Schorr, others 8-25, 748C3
Hays resigns, hearings cancelled 9-1, 646E1
Rejects Hinshaw expulsn 9-2, 807F1
Schorr, Latham refuse testimony 9-15, 748A3, 749B1
Schorr probe dropped 9-22, 748A3
Dems OK legis powers end; ask S Korea influence-peddling probe 12-6—12-9, 981A2, F2
Ways & Means, Committee on
Subcom chrmn electns vetoed 12-6—12-9, 981D1

1977

Science & Technology, Committee on
Gets A-energy jurisdictn 1-4, 36F3
Standards of Official Conduct, Committee on (Ethics Committee)
Loses legislative powers 1-4, 36B3
Korean inquiry OKd 2-9, 442A2
Flynt special interest gifts rptd 2-15, 128B2
Ethics com formed 3-9, 191D2
Nixon tapes on Korea paymts sought 7-7, 557A1
Korea lobbying operatn survey rptd 7-11, 557B1
Lacovara-Flynt Korea probe dispute rptd 7-12, Lacovara resigns 7-15; criticism intensifies 7-16—7-20, 556E1
Jaworski named Korea probe spec counsel 7-20, independnc guaranteed 7-21, 556E1, F2
Questns Thomson on Korea lobbying 8-17, 8-25, Park interview rptd foiled 8-20, 688G1, C2
O'Neill rent records subpoenaed rptd 10-7, 816D3
Korea lobbying detailed 10-19—10-21, 816A2
Korea cooperatn asked 10-31, 915C1
Albert, records rptd subpoenaed 12-1, 915F1
Passman records rptd subpoenaed 12-2, 915E2
Jaworski scores Park testimony deal 12-30, 1002C3
Ways & Means, Committee on
Carter econ plan debated 1-27—2-4, 89C2, D3
Spec interest gifts rptd 2-4, 129G1; 3-7, 232D2
Energy panel formed 4-21, 321C1
Carter energy plan hearings 5-18—5-19, 443C2
Andrus defends offshore oil sales delay 6-3, 499A1
Carter energy plan actn 6-9, 6-14, 460F1, C2

1978

Science and Technology, Committee on
Clinch R A-breeder compromise proposal rptd 3-17, 3-23, 242A1, C1
Standards of Official Conduct, Committee on (Ethics Committee)
Park testimony sought 1-4—1-23, OKd 1-31, 63G3
Korean scandal seen touching incumbents 1-20, 63A2
Flood, Eilberg inquiry rptd 2-8, formal probe asked 2-17, 239G3, 240F2
Park testifies 2-28—3-9; Kim, 4 other offcls testimony sought 3-9, 203C3-204A1, C1
Park gives pub testimony 4-3—4-4, Dore testimony disputes 4-5, 239G1-D3
Kim Dong Jo Cong paymts proof rptd 5-22—5-25; testimony warning voted by House 5-31, 432A2-D3
Korean-probe res scored 5-24, 406C2
US House votes food aid cutoff 6-22, 467C2-A3
Korea food aid cutoff OKd by House 6-22, 467C2-A3
4 cited for misconduct in Korea probe, O'Neill cleared 7-13, 527A1
Jaworski quits Korea probe 8-2, evaluates results 8-7, 604D3-605D1
Kim written testimony agreed 8-3, 605D1
Eilberg chrgd 9-13, 697F1
3 reprimanded in Korean scandal 10-13, 831D3-832A1
Cong reactn to Korea probe 10-13, 832A1
Eilberg indicted 10-24, pleads not guilty 11-1, 835E2
Flood reelected, Eilberg defeated 11-7, 849D2
Dems OK rule chng 12-6, 958B2
Wilson, Roybal exempted from rule chng 12-6, 958D2
Surface Transportation, Subcommittee on (of Public Works & Transportation Committee)
Howard asks ICC trucking deregulatn halt 12-7, O'Neal rejcts 12-21, 1007C2
Veterans' Affairs, Committee on
Subcom hears Viet vets claim Agent Orange disabilities 10-11, 984G1
Ways and Means, Committee on
Debt ceiling extended 3-27, 261B3
Tuition tax credit OKd 4-11, 261B1
Carter tax reform plan pared 4-17—4-19; 3 see Carter 4-20, reactn rptd 4-23, 305C3-306C1
Soc Sec rollback opposed 5-17, 385G3
Welfare compromise prepared 6-7, 446F1
$16 bln tax cut OKd; Carter 'reforms' discarded, capital gains plan OKd 7-27, 586G2-587A2
Cong study sees '79 tax hike despite cuts 8-2, 587A2
$16 bln tax cut bill passes House 8-10, 604E1
Ullman backs VAT proposal 12-6, 962E2
PAC gifts to Ullman rptd 12-24, 1008E1

1979

Science and Technology, Committee on
Fuqua elected chrmn 1-24, 71E1
FDA drug approval process scored 6-19, 572C2
Small Business, Committee on
Smith elected chrmn 1-24, 71E1
Standards of Official Conduct, Committee on (Ethics Committee)
Dems delay chrmn vote, face vacancies 1-23, 71G1
Bennett elected chrmn 1-31, 87A1
Flood mistrial declared 2-3, 102A2
Diggs case to be studied 3-1, 165F2
S Africa bribe probe barred 3-21, 213B2
Diggs admits funds misuse, accepts censure 6-29, 515D1
Diggs censured 7-31, 578G1
Galifianakis perjury chrg dropped 8-3, 630A2
Wilson chrgd with rules violatns 12-13, 945E2
Un-American Activities, Committee on (HUAC) (defunct)
'57 spy chrgs vs Sterns dropped 3-22, 232D1
Veterans Affairs, Committee on
Roberts elected chrmn 1-24, 71F1
Ways and Means, Committee on
Carter Soc Sec, 'wage insurnc' tax credit plans opposed 1-18, 55A3, C3
Fowler wins seat over Hall 1-23, 70F3
Ullman elected chrmn 1-24, 71F1
Conable vs balanced budget amendmt 2-4, 86G1
Carter hosp cost plan faces hurdles 2-13, 110C1
Duty waiver bill OKd 2-22, 159E1
Rangel at hosp cost bill ceremony 3-6, 163C2
Subcom rpt vs Japan trade policy cited 229G3
Ullman: tax cut unlikely 4-30, 327B2
Ullman backs welfare plan 5-23, 384G1
House OKs oil profits tax 6-28, 541B2
Rostenkowski financial disclosure statemt studied 9-1, 701D3

1980

Science and Technology, Committee on
Frosch on space shuttle test flight 1-29, 71F2
Small Business, Committee on
Carter policies scored in subcom rpt 5-29, 455E2
Standards of Official Conduct, Committee on (Ethics Committee)
Abscam probe to be broadened 2-3; Civiletti urges delay 2-5, 2-6; special counsel discussed 2-6, 82A2
Abscam spec counsel hired 2-13; House bars Justice evidence request, probe to continue 2-27, 143D2-B3
Abscam probe backed by House 3-27, 267A1
Wilson found guilty of financial misconduct 4-16, censure asked 4-24, 333F3
Wilson censured 6-10, 438B1
Myers expulsn recommended 9-24, 740B1
Jenrette expulsn hearings begin 10-7, 783C1
Veterans Affairs, Committee on
Roberts on VA MD pay hike veto 8-26, 649E3
Ways and Means, Committee on
Ullman wins primary 5-20, 404C3
Ullman, Corman lose reelectn 11-4, 837E1, 846E1, G1, 852A2, F2

1976

HOUSING & Urban Development, Department of (HUD)—*See also HILLS, Carla*
To offer low-interest mortgages 1-7, 25B2
Urban aid program reviewed 1-8, 25E1
Reagan scores program 1-9, 22B1
'77 budget proposals 1-21, 65B3
Newman confrmd asst secy 2-24, 186B2
Young confrmd asst secy 3-11, 232F1
Sup Ct backs city-suburb housing plan 4-20, 308D2
Cong clears added funds 5-19, 411E3; signed 6-1, 982F1
Ford signs Housing aid 8-3, 566G3
'77 funds signed 8-9, 623E1
Energy bill signed 8-14, 622G3
To offer low-interest mortgages 9-9, 709B2
Ford, Carter debate 10-22, 802B1
Thomas rejected secy post 12-16, 937A2
Harris named secy 12-21, 956G1, 957F2
Federal Housing Administration (FHA)
Lowers FHA mortgate rate 3-30, 375D3
Dem platform text 6-15, 473G2, A3
Low-interest mortgages planned 9-9, 709B2
Ford seeks home-ownership legis 9-15, 686B1
Hills: mortgage loan rate cut 10-15, 805D3
Sept housing starts pick up 10-19, 805D3
Ford, Carter debate 10-22, 802B1
Gurney acquitted 10-27, 846A1

1977

HOUSING & Urban Development, Department of (HUD)
Ford '78 budget request 1-17, 31F3
Sup Ct bars review of New Castle (NY) grant 1-17, 58D1
Carter visits employes 2-10, 110D2
Harris: budget 'starved' 2-14, 110C3
Carter budget revisns 2-22, 125E2
Hills named to IBM bd 2-22, 140G2
Harris rpts net worth 2-25, 148A1
Carter asks energy dept 3-1, 148C2
NYC aid seen 3-3, 193D3
Harris details grant progrm 3-7, Carter comments 3-9, 178B1
No exec cooks rptd 3-24, 236F1
Gay rights access promised 3-26, 278E2
'77 rent subsidy aid rise cleared 4-28, 339C1; Carter signs 4-30, 380E3
'77 supplemental funds signed 5-4, 339E1
KC schl integratn suit names 5-26, 446F1
'78 funds signed 10-4, 796G2-D3
Urban action grant program signed 10-12, 796C2
Harris at League of Cities conf 12-7, 959B3, 960A1, D1
Central cities to get housing aid 12-27, 1008B3
Appointments
Harris confrmd secy 1-20, 34B1, E2
Janis confrmd undersecy 3-23, 272B3
Medina confrmd asst secy 5-25, 500A1
Simons confrmd asst secy 3-23, 272C3
Federal Disaster Assistance Administration
'78 funds signed 10-4, 796F3
Federal Housing Administration (FHA)
Lower down paymts sought 1-17, 32C1
Insurance fund ceiling hike cleared 4-28, 339C1; Carter signs 4-30, 380E3
Federal National Mortgage Association (Fannie Mae)
Carter energy plan 4-20, 292A1
Government National Mortgage Association (Ginnie Mae)
Cited re Ford '78 budget 1-17, 31G3

1978

HOUSING & Urban Development, Department of (HUD)
State, local rules linked to segregatn 1-8, 13F3
Carter budget proposals 1-23, 48A1
Carter unveils urban-aid plan 3-27, reactn 3-27—3-30, 217D2-218D1
Coll housing progrm in Educ Dept proposal 4-14, 279D1
Housing bias rptd widespread 4-17, 285D2
USSR trip canceled re Shcharansky 7-25, 575C3
'79 funds signed 9-30, 750C2-A3
Federal Disaster Assistance Administration
Carter proposes new emergency agency 6-19, 466E2-B3
Cong OKs compromise budget 9-23, 734A1
'79 funding signed 9-30, 750F2-A3
Federal Insurance Administration
Carter proposes new emergency agency 6-19, 466F2-B3
Federal National Mortgage Association (Fannie Mae)
HUD outlines authority 8-14, 627D3
Government National Mortgage Association (Ginnie Mae)
'77 futures trading rise rptd 1-12, 84A1
Carter budget proposal 1-23, 48C1
Houston Univ ex-aide chrgd by SEC 10-5, 770D3

1979

HOUSING & Urban Development, Department of (HUD)
Carter budget proposals 1-22, 44E3
City revitalization impact on poor rptd 2-13, 132G2-C3
Mortgage bias vs women scored 3-9, 208G3-209B1
US comm vs housing bias 4-11, 283G2-C3
Harris named HEW secy 7-19, 529D1
Landrieu named secy 7-27, 577B1; confirmed 9-12, 700F2
'80 funds clear Cong 10-24, Carter signs 11-5, 883G2
Federal Housing Administration (FHA)
'Protective insurnc' proposed 1-22, 44G3
Government National Mortgage Association (Ginnie Mae)
Carter seeks $2 bln budget 1-22, 44G3
Futures trading cited 6-19, 681B3
New Community Development Corp.
Soul City support withdrawn 6-28, suit filed 8-17, injunctn denied 8-27, 665F1
Newfields (O) project ends 6-28, 665D2

1980

HOUSING & Urban Development, Department of (HUD)
Environmental impact ct reviews limited by Sup Ct 1-7, 15B3
Carter budget proposals 1-28, 73E1
Carter backs subsidized mortgages 4-17, 286F1
Landrieu on mortgage rates 4-28, 329C2
Summer jobs progrm rptd 6-30, 496A1
Rental shortage not linked to condos 7-2, 518A2
'81 funds clear Cong 12-3, 954G2; signed 12-15, 982B1
Fair-housing legis debated 12-4—12-9, dropped 12-9, 954A2
Pierce named secy 12-22, 979E2
Federal Housing Administration (FHA)
Mortgage rate hiked 2-8, 2-28, 145B1
Mortgage rates rise to 14% 4-3, 266F3
Unsold home financing set 4-17, 286G1
Mortgage rates drop to 13% 4-28, 329B2
Mortgage rate cut to 11.5% 5-15, 384E3
Multifamily mortgage rate cut to 12% 7-7, 513G3
Mortgage rates revisn set 10-8, 804F2
Mortgage rate rise delay scored 10-24, 823C3
Mortgage rate raised to 13.5% 11-24, 984A1
Federal National Mortgage Association (Fannie Mae)
2d 1/4 loss rptd 7-10, 576D2
Maxwell succeeds Hunter as pres 9-24, 959G3
Government National Mortgage Association (Ginnie Mae)
Carter budget item: $2 bln 1-28, 73F1
2 NY financial mkts to merge 3-21, 224D1
NYSE unit awaits futures trading OK 5-28, 481D2

1976

IMMIGRATION & Naturalization Service—*See under JUSTICE below*
INDIAN Affairs, Bureau of—*See under INTERIOR below*
INDIAN Claims Commission
Termination signed 10-8, 834G3
INFORMATION Agency, U.S.—*See U.S. INFORMATION Agency below*
INTELLIGENCE Agencies—*See also agency names*
Ford revises structure 2-17, 2-18, 127A1, G2

1977

IMMIGRATION & Naturalization Service—*See under JUSTICE below*
INDIAN Affairs, Bureau of—*See under INTERIOR below*
INFORMATION Agency, U.S.—*See U.S. INFORMATION Agency below*
INTELLIGENCE Agencies—*See also agency names*
Senate com issues rpt 5-18, 386D3
Turner centralizatn bid dispute 6-10, 6-12, 576E2
House oversight com created 7-14, 557C1

1978

IMMIGRATION & Naturalization Service—*See under JUSTICE below*
INFORMATION Security Oversight Office—*See GENERAL Services Administration in this section above*
INTELLIGENCE Agencies—*See also agency names*
Carter reorganizes, details curbs; reactn 1-24, 49A2
Haldeman book on Watergate rptd 2-16—2-17, 124E3
Sen com hearings on reorganizatn 4-4—4-19, 306G1

1979

IMMIGRATION & Naturalization Service—*See under JUSTICE below*
IMMIGRATION Policy, Commission on
Askew named chrmn 2-16, 127A1
INDIAN Affairs, Bureau of—*See under INTERIOR below*
INTELLIGENCE Agencies
Natl Intell Estimate sees Sovt mil superiority 1-12, 15B1
Natl sec legis rptd planned 2-8, 88G1
China-Viet info praised 3-25, 231F3
Carter urges SALT pact 4-25, 294E2
Wiretap ct judges named 5-18, 442B3

1980

IMMIGRATION & Refugee Policy, Select Commission on
Illegal aliens rptd at 6 mln 2-4, 147E1
'Guest worker' study rptd 2-13, 147A3
Immigratn econ impact rptd 9-22, 826D3
INTELLIGENCE Agencies
GOP platform proposals vs curbs 1-14, 1-15, 32E1, A2
Carter urges charter passage, restraints lifted 1-23, 41D1, 43C1
Sen OKs intell oversight bill 6-3, 458B3
GOP platform text 7-15, 536A3

1976

US forgn intellignc chart 304A1, A2 *
House sets assassinatn probe 9-17, 729F1
Carter names liaison 11-23, 881A3

INTELLIGENCE Oversight Board
Ford plans creation 2-17, 127C1
US forgn intellignc chart 304A2 *

INTER-American Affairs, Bureau of—*See under STATE below*

INTERIOR, Department of the—*See also KLEPPE, Thomas*
Sup Ct to hear 4-state coal mining case 1-12, 24A1
Ford aide shifted 1-21, 40D3
'77 energy proposals budgeted 1-21, 64E2
Sup Ct upholds coal mine penalty procedure 1-28, 87B3
Fisher confrmd asst secy 3-23, 232D1
Va dam project upheld 3-24, 219C3
Cong opens Navy oil reserves 3-31, 246C3
Utah power projct delay asked 4-9, 284F2
Fla wetlands dvpt denied 4-16, 284D3
Alaska offshore lease sale 4-26, 648E3
Adopts strip-mine rules 5-11, 359D2-B3
Cong clears added funds 5-19, 411E3; signed 6-1, 982F1
Coleman confrmd asst secy 5-21, 412E1
Rpts Alaska pipeline problems 5-21, warns Alyeska 7-21, 8-12; House panel rpt issued 9-5, 690A3-691E1
Frizzell quits as undersecy 5-27, 412B2
4-state strip-mining stay reversed 6-28, 569A1
Ford OKs '77 pub works funds 7-12, 517E1
Rpts on Teton Dam collapse 7-15, 736E1
'77 funds signed 7-31, 623C1
Atlantic offshore lease sale challenged 8-13—8-17, bids accepted 8-25, 648C2-F3
Suspends Colo oil shale leases 8-23, 648G3
New River in scenic system 9-11, 689E1
Carter names liaison 11-23, 881B3
Andrus named secy 12-18, 956E1, 957B1

Fish & Wildlife Service, U.S.
Cong OKs wildlife refuges 2-4, 2-17, 152F2-A3

Geological Survey
On USSR quake 5-17, 404B3
Confirms warning re Teton Dam 6-8, 423D1
Rpts China quakes 7-28, 545C1
Quake experts China visit rptd 7-29, 545F2
On Colorado canyon flood 7-31, 595G2
Rpts more China quakes 8-21, 8-22, 674F1
Warning cited in Teton Dam rpt 9-25, 736D1
Rpts on Turkish quake 11-24, 897E1
Rpts '76 quake death toll 11-27, 931G3

Indian Affairs, Bureau of (BIA)
Parker (Ariz) bomb threat 1-1, 7E1
Sup Ct bars review of Hopi suit 3-29, 261G3
Dem platform text 6-15, 472B2
'77 funds signed 7-31, 623D1

Land Management, Bureau of
Cong OKs wildlife refuges 2-4, 2-17, 152G2
On Utah horse deaths 7-24, 587E1
Pub lands bill signed 10-21, 834D1

Mines, Bureau of
'75 energy use data rptd 4-4, 285A1

Mining Enforcement & Safety Administration (MESA)
Seals Ky coal mine 3-13, 256B3
Bodies removed from Ky mine 11-19, 892B1
'75 injury, illness data 12-9, 950B3

National Park Service
Pratt donates estate 1-9, 80D2
Senate votes mining halt 2-4, 135G1
House OKs Indiana Dunes enlargemt 2-17, 171A1
Valley Forge made natl park 7-4, 489C2
Ford park plan scored 8-29, 644E3
Cong clears park land funding bill 9-13, 745F2; signed 9-28, 982G1
Mining curbs signed 9-28, 834B2
Local govt compensatn signed 10-20, 835F1

Reclamation, Bureau of
Teton R Dam bursts, probe set 6-5, 423B1
Cited in Teton Dam rpt 9-25, 736D1

INTERNAL Revenue Service (IRS) (of Treasury Department)
Sup Ct to set disclosure requiremts 1-12, 24G1
Sup Ct bars emergency paymt procedure 1-13, 23D3
'46-75 GNP revised 1-16, 90E1
Privacy comm testimony cites 2-11, 151C2
Sup Ct rules on assessmt cases 3-8, 219A2
Cong OKs Hatch Act repeal 3-31, 234B2
Alexander cleared re Projct Haven, chrgd re '73 Montoya audit 4-12, 283D3
Sup Ct backs use of accountants' worksheets 4-21, 331G2

1977

Turner given new powers 8-4, 610F2
Mondale addresses ABA conv 8-8, 630C1

INTELLIGENCE Oversight Board
Cited re CIA forgn paymts rpt 2-18, 2-23, 123F3, 124B1
Carter names 3 members 5-5, 462D2

INTELLIGENCE & Research, Bureau of—*See under STATE below*

INTERGOVERNMENTAL Relations, Advisory Commission on
Beame offered chrmnship 10-5, 761A1

INTERIOR, Department of the
PR statehood proposal linked to oil rights 1-5, 16A3
On Teton Dam collapse 1-6, 120B3
To get Alaska oil reserve 1-17, 31E2
Sup Ct bars review of New Castle (NY) grant 1-17, 58D1
Lifts gas productn limits 1-24, 54F1
Fish halts Tellico Dam 1-31, 95G2-C3
Andrus on Western drought 2-15, 2-20, 152E3
Andrus sets gas supply probe; '76 productn data cited 2-17, 151D3-152B1
Andrus at water projct hearing 2-23, 209E3
Andrus rpts net worth 2-25, 147C3
Carter asks energy dept 3-1, 148A2, B2
'76 energy use rptd up 3-13, 196F1-C2
Oil lease renewal tied to productn 3-15, 195F3
No exec cooks rptd 3-24, 236F1
Drought aid signed 4-7, 273E1, F1
Strip-mine curbs OKd by House 4-29, 365E3
'77 supplemental funds signed 5-4, 339F1
Offshore oil sales delayed 5-17, 498F3
Energy Dept OKd by Sen 5-18, 405G2
2 offshore leases canceled 6-8, 499C1
Coal slurry bill deferred 6-27, 516B1
Alaska pipe blast probe ordrd 7-11, 537F3
Alaska pipe flow resumptn OKd 7-18, 558A3
'78 funds clear Cong 7-25, Carter signs 7-26, 592C3, D3
Westn land holding breakup sought 8-18, 8-22, 703G1, F2
E Coast offshore lease sale OKd by ct 8-25, 658C1
Meteorite awarded to Calif 9-7, 712G2
Coal-leasing plan barred 9-27, 1007C2
Farm aide's personal lobbying halted 9-30, 773D1
Sirica vs whaling ban 10-21; ruling reversed, Burger backs ban 10-24, 835B2
Kent State ruling awaited 10-25, 820G2
Mine safety powers shifted 11-9, 855G3
Calif-Tex oil pipe OKd 12-2, 942D3

Appointments
Andrus confrmd secy 1-20, 34B1, G3
Herbst confrmd asst secy 4-1, 272A3
Martin confrmd asst secy 4-11, 272B3
Mendelsohn asst secy nominatn withdrawn 11-11, 877A2

Bonneville Power Administration (BPA)
10% power cut asked 2-11, 244C3

Fish & Wildlife Service, U.S.
Herbst confrmd asst secy 4-1, 272A3
Gabrielson dies 9-7, 788B1

Geological Survey
Rpts '76 quake death toll 1-20, 120E2
US gas productn info cited 2-22, 152B1
Calif land swell chng rptd 3-3, 288G1
River flow decline rptd 3-8, 244G2
2d Rumania quake forecast 3-9, 204B2
Andrus to review offshore oil leases 3-15, 196A1
W Coast drought breaks record 5-4, 376B3
Western drought continues 6-16, 492G2
Hawaii volcanic eruptns 9-13—9-28, 747E2

Indian Affairs, Bureau of (BIA)
Backs Maine Indian claims 1-11, 59D1
Mont coal leases revoked 1-13, 58F3

Land Management, Bureau of
Fire Center data rptd 8-23, 660G1

Mines, Bureau of
Ford proposes energy dept 1-11, 14F3

Mining Enforcement & Safety Administration (MESA)
Ky blasts laid to spark 6-13, 8-10, 901A1

Outdoor Recreation, Bureau of
Carter energy plan 4-20, 291D3

Reclamation, Bureau of
Cited in Teton Dam rpt 1-6, 120B3
IJC rpt vs ND dam projct 1-7, 60G3
Water projcts cut 3-23, Carter explains 3-24, 210D1
Calif water rights upheld 4-4, 253C1

Surface Mining Reclamation & Enforcement, Office of
Strip-mine bill creates 7-21, 575C3

Youth Conservation Corps
Youth jobs bill enacted 8-5, 609C2
3 new centers rptd open 8-31, 692E2

INTERNAL Revenue Service (IRS) (of Treasury Department)
Simon vetoes housing tax shelter ban 1-5, 36E2
Miami 'Leprechaun' effort rptd cleared 1-6, 15G3
Alexander defends intell curbs 1-6, 16F1
Sup Ct curbs tax seizures 1-12, 57G2
ITT-Hartford suits setld 3-4, 194E3
Farmland fund plan withdrawn 3-7, 195B1
Teamsters to revise pensn posts 3-13, 195A2
Cargill files forgn paymts rpt 3-18, 233D2
Ex-offcl sentenced 3-31, 288G2

1978

Fscl '79 authrzn signed 9-17, 715C3
Warrantless tap curbs signed 10-25, 863A1
Carter rptd critical of pol analysis 11-25, 917B1

INTELLIGENCE Tasking Center, National
CIA dir to head 1-24, 49D2

INTERAGENCY Task Force on Workplace Safety and Health
Changes urged 12-8, 984D3

INTERIOR, Department of the
E Coast offshore lease sale delayed 1-30, 108D2
Drought aid extensn cleared 1-31, 107B3; signed 2-7, 218A2
NJ offshore drilling challenge refused 2-21, 125G2-A3
Andrus sees govs on water policy 2-26, 144G3
Indian programs in Educ Dept proposal 4-14, 279D1
Oil cos cleared of '76-77 gas withholding 4-27, 322B1
Colo sen scores Andrus 5-2, 342B2
New TVA chrmn takes over 5-19, 390F2
Denver dam permit blocked 5-25, 409C1
Mendelsohn named asst 6-10, 446F3-447B1
Canada sets caribou study 7-6, 531C3
Coal slurry pipeline bill defeated 7-19, 550B2
Seabed mining bill clears House 7-26, 589A1
Offshore leasing chngs clear Cong 8-22, 662B3
Public works veto upheld 10-5, 765E1
Grazing land law revisn cleared 10-11, 807A3
Secy to sit on Endangered Species Com 10-15, 834E2; 11-10, 1003B1
Alaska lands protected 11-16, 12-1, 937C1

Bonneville Power Administration (BPA)
Power restoratn rptd 1-10, 24E1

Fish & Wildlife Service, U.S.
Carter budget proposal 1-23, 47E2

Geological Survey
'77 quake death toll rptd 1-29, 480G1
Offshore oil, gas reserve estimate cited 8-22, 662G2

Indian Affairs, Bureau of (BIA)
Aleuts win mistreatmt claim 6-21, 569F1
'Longest Walk' protests in DC, '72 occupatn cited 7-15—7-23, 568G3

Land Management, Bureau of (BLM)
'79-82 authorzn signed 8-20, 697C2
Grazing land law revisn cleared 10-11, 807G2

National Park Service
Carter budget proposal 1-23, 47F2
Mo historic hotel razed by fire 1-28, 212C3
Redwood Park expansn clears Cong 2-9, 85E2; 3-21, Carter signs 3-27, 218E1
Alaska lands bill clears House 5-19, 386G1
Park police rpt on DC march for ERA 7-9, 529E2
Indians camp outside DC 7-15—7-23, 568F3
Carters vacation in Wyo 8-24, 664F1
Natl parks authorzn cleared 10-13, 834G2; signed 11-10, 897A2

Territorial Affairs, Office of
Bikini islanders relocatn planned 4-12, 278D2-A3

INTERNAL Revenue Service (IRS) (of Treasury Department)
Cowles Communications to liquidate 1-6, 76A3
Computer return-monitoring project rptd dropped 1-9, 15C1
Oil co tax credits for forgn paymts revoked 1-16, 69D1
Retroactive withholding on lunch allowances barred 2-27, 143G1
Agent liability case review denied by Sup Ct 3-20, 206B1
Tax breaks in lease-back deals OKd by Sup Ct 4-18, 309G1
Summons power backed by Sup Ct 6-19, 492F2

1979

GOP asks intell overhaul 8-6, 610C3
USSR troops in Cuba confrmd 8-31, 657D1, C2

Iran Issues—*See under CENTRAL Intelligence Agency in this section above*

INTERIOR, Department of the
Carter budget proposals 1-22, 45E3
Natural Resources Dept proposed 3-1, 164B1
Water projct cost-sharing sought 5-16, 365F2
Carter orders timber sales 6-11, 441A1
Pollutn protectn for 47 areas proposed 9-7, 703B3
Army OKs E Coast oil refinery 10-4, 770A1
'80 funds clear Cong 11-9, 883E1; Carter signs 11-27, 920B1
'80 continuing funds res clears Cong 11-16, Carter signs 11-20, 900B2
Feathered artifact sale ban upheld by Sup Ct 11-27, 919G3

Geological Survey
Oil reserves estimate revised 1-5, 17F1
NJ offshore gas find rptd 1-17, 55C2
'78 quake death toll rptd 1-25, 140F2
E Coast offshore reserve estimate cited 2-28, 186D3
Mexico quake rptd 3-14, 316G3
Geothermal power supplies rptd 5-9, 361F3-362A1
Venus findings described 5-29, 692A1
Calif offshore oil, gas estimate 6-29, 518C2
Union Oil Calif lease bid rejctd 8-7, 649F1
Indonesia quake rptd 9-13, 800F2

Indian Affairs, Bureau of (BIA)
Schls excluded from proposed Educ Dept 2-8, 110G2
House com seeks progrm shift to proposed Educ Dept 5-2, 326F2

Land Management, Bureau of (BLM)
West mounts 'Sagebrush Revolt' 7-13—9-7, 703E3, G3
Wild horse rules issued 12-28, 990D1

National Park Service
Carter budget proposals 1-22, 45D3

Offshore Leases
Mass ban lifted 2-20, 187B1
E Coast bids low 2-28, 186C3
Calif bids placed 6-29, 518B2; accepted 8-7, 649E1
Gulf of Mex bids placed 7-31; accepted 8-28, 664D3
Mass sale delayed 11-6, OKd 11-9, 867G1
Gulf of Mex bids placed 11-27, 942G3, 943A1
Gulf of Mex bids accepted 12-10, 990C2
Alaska sale held 12-11, 990D2
Mass sale OKd bids placed 12-18, 990G1

Reclamation, Bureau of
China power dvpt aid signed 8-28, 644C2
Teton dam defects rptd 11-28, 954D3

Youth Conservation Corps
Carter budget eliminates 1-22, 46D1

INTERNAL Revenue Service (IRS) (of Treasury Department)
Peoples Temple pol activities probed 1-13, 117F3
Tax acctg methods limited by Sup Ct 1-16, 32G2
Church bingo exempted 1-26, 102C1
Hosp cost bill sent to Cong 3-5, 163C3
Muffler assn denied tax break by Sup Ct 3-20, 203D3
Carter tax data released 5-31, 420D2
Carter campaign com billed 6-4, 419A3
Tenneco seeks UV assets 7-23, 770C3
Auto-Train withdraws fed loan applicatn, probe cited 8-21, 726F2
Race bias tax powers curbed by Cong 9-26, Carter signs 9-29, 883E2

1980

Dem platform charter plank adopted 8-13, 615D1

INTERIOR, Department of the
Carter budget proposals 1-28, 73G3
Alaska land protectn extended 2-12, 131F2
Island territories get econ plan 2-14: govs meet, set projcts 2-19—2-22, 495B1
Oil leasing lottery suspended, scandal hinted 2-29; resumptn ordrd 4-7, 330B2
Water law compliance rptd 4-10, 308D1
Govt desert land retentn backed by Sup Ct 4-16, 328C3
Land-grant exchng ban upheld by Sup Ct 5-19, 440A2
Pre-1920 oil shale mining claims upheld by Sup Ct 6-2, 513D1
Imperial Valley water rights upheld by Sup Ct 6-16, 511F2
Water & Power Resources fund cut clears Cong 6-25, 9-10, Carter signs 10-1, 803F2
Andrus named to Synfuels Corp bd 9-13, Sen panel OKs 9-25, 725E2
Andrus omitted from interim Synfuels Corp bd 10-5, 786G2-A3
Beaufort Sea leases upheld 10-14, 960C3
Offshore leasing overhaul ordrd 10-31, 960A3
'81 funds clear Cong 12-1, 954D2; signed 12-12, 982B1
Watt designated secy; reactn 12-22, 979G2, F3

Fish & Wildlife Service, U.S.
New conservatn law enacted 9-29, 915D3

Geological Survey
Azores quake rptd 1-1, 24F2
Washn volcanic quakes rptd 3-26, 252F1, A2
Washn flood threats rptd 10-29, 970D3

Indian Affairs, Bureau of (BIA)
Constructn contract Indian preferenc barred by Sup Ct 5-27, 454B1

Land Management, Bureau of
Oil leasing lottery suspended, scandal hinted 2-29; resumptn ordrd 4-7, 330C2
Calif offshore leasing pressed, oppositn rptd 3-28, 330E3
Calif desert plan issued 12-22, 986G3-987C1

National Park Service
Carter budget proposals 1-28, 73G3
Whalen dismissed 4-24, Dickenson named new dir 5-1, 333A2-E2
Fla land donation rptd 12-19, 987A2

Offshore Leases
Georges Bank bids rptd accepted 1-7, 18A1
Calif '81-85 reoffering sale planned 3-28, 330C3
Andrus OKs leasing speedup 6-17, 552E2
Alaska curbs lifted 7-8, leases OKd 7-9, 552E3

INTERNAL Revenue Service (IRS) (of Treasury Department)
Handwriting orders upheld by Sup Ct 2-20, 170E1
Audit data request case refused by Sup Ct 4-28, 369F1
Middle-class tax burden rptd 9-12, 747D1-A2
Inventory tax ruling impact on publishing rptd 10-5, 835F3
Housing bond tax exemptns rptd revoked 11-10, 989C2
Inventory tax ruling amendmt discarded by House 12-13, 982F2
2 Scientologists sentenced 12-19, 997C3

1976

Sen intelligence com rpt cites 4-28, 325D2, 326C3-327A1, 328G1, 330D1
Rpts '69-74 tax avoidance up 5-5, 480A1
Unificatn Church probe rptd 6-1, 971B1
Cited in Dem platform text 6-15, 470E2
Ford submits forgn paymts legis 8-3, 668D2
Sen curbs bank record access 8-6, 586G1
GOP platform text 8-18, 603F2
Cong clears data access curb 9-16, 706E1
Atty fees to successful defendants signed 10-20, 788A2
Sup Ct curbs carry-back breaks 11-2, 867C1

Ford Tax Issue

Ruff gets tax info 9-30, 761E1
Carter cites audit 10-8, 762B2
IRS '73 audit probed 10-8, 764B1-B2
Ford on '73 audit 10-14, 761C3

Tax Evasion (& other irregularities)

Newman fined 1-6, 6C3
Joint Justice probe agrmt issued 1-10, 41B3
Meissner indicted 1-14, 78D2
Former agent sentncd 1-28, 124D1
Gulf paymts probe rptd 2-4, 133F3
Business paymts probe ordered expanded 2-10, 134D2
Merck, Amer Home Products repaymts rptd 3-9, 361C2, D2
Warner-Lambert added paymt set 3-18, 361A3
Montoya audit rptd 3-24, 247B1
Brunswick execs sentenced 4-12, 316D3
Metcalfe tax probe dropped 4-15, 286E3
Church scores Ford 4-19, 282C1
Sup Ct rules on warning targets 4-21, 331A3
Drive vs drug traffickers planned 4-27, 307F2
SEC rpts on corp paymts 5-12, 726D1
7 seized in El Salvador gun plot 5-15—5-17, 401B2
Compton (Calif) offcls sentncd 6-21, 860C2
Teamster probe rptd 6-29, 7-7, 492E2
Freuhauf officials get jail terms 6-30, 523G3
Illegal criminal evidence use upheld 7-6, 535B1
Foremost deductns rptd disallowed 7-7, 669G1
Cella, 3 associates sentncd 7-20, 860D2
3M tax case dismissed 7-27, 566B2
Phillips fraud chrgd 9-2, 725A3
Scott notice rptd 9-12; Sen com vs records release 9-15, 980D1, F1
Conrad quits RCA 9-16, 708G1-C2
Troy jailed 10-22, 860B2
Teamsters set reforms 10-26, 12-28, 990G3
'75 average sentncs cited 11-20, 885E3
Ulasewicz convicted 12-23, 981B1

INTERNATIONAL Economic Policy, Council on
Dunn on business probe panel 3-21, 262F2

INTERNATIONAL Trade Commission, U.S.—*See TRADE Commission, U.S. International, below*

INTERSTATE Commerce Commission
Cong clears revised RR rules bill 1-28, 68G3
Christian confrmd member 3-18, 232C1
RR spending control upheld 6-17, 552F3
GOP platform text 8-18, 607E1
Carter proposes Cabt-level energy dept 9-21, 704F2
US to OK 2 superports 12-17, 992C1

1977

Lockheed rpts expanded probe 4-8, 502F3
Nixon funds rptd seized 5-6, 482E2
Carters offer to pay $6,000 6-24, 499D2
Lance, comptroller monitoring rptd probed 8-18, 626A1
Lance probe asked 9-6, 689F3, 690D1
Calif phone cos ordrd to pay refunds 9-13, 839B2
State police meal stipends taxable 11-20, 919F1

Tax Evasion (& other irregularities)

Oppositn to intellignc curbs cited 1-6, 16F1
Duffy-Mott ex-pres sentncd 1-26, 103B2
Navajo leader indicted 2-9, 162E3
Ulasewicz sentenced 2-18, 197E2
Chemical Bank indicted 2-24, 155E2
Chem Bank, 2 ex-offcls plead guilty 3-3, 4-14, 540A3
Schlitz accused 4-7, 503G3
Nev sheriff indicted 4-13, 312B3
NY jeweler fined 4-20, 312G2-A3
Reinsurance agreemts backed 4-26, 382E3
Bahama bank tax evidence barred, probe scored 4-28, 395C3, 396A1
Navajo fraud case dismissed 5-17, 492A1
Simplot fined 5-20, 491D3
Gulf indicted 6-15, 504A1
FBI Scientology office raids ruled illegal 7-27, 628B2
Penney ex-employe sentncd 8-5, 848A2
Korean-born citizen indicted 9-27, 773B3; pleads not guilty 10-16, 816C3
ILA offcl sentncd 9-29, 937E3
Grant case review refused 10-3, 760F2
Nixon lawyer case review refused 10-3, 760C3
B Graham fund gifts rptd 10-21, 845G1
Tax penalties procedure backed 10-31, 835B3
Gulf pleads guilty, fined 11-22, 944A1
Phillips pleads no contest to '69-72 chrgs 11-22, 944C1
Park Tong Sun diary rptd sought 11-29, 915A3
Salerno mistrial declared 12-15, 992G1

INTERNATIONAL Communication, Agency for
Carter proposes 10-11, 797D2

INTERNATIONAL Economic Policy, Council on
Carter proposes abolitn 7-15, 556B1

INTERSTATE Commerce Commission (ICC)
Eases rules in gas shortage 1-24, 54E1
Regulatory agency rpt issued 2-9, 131G3
Milwaukee Rd-BN merger bid rejected 2-16, 213E2
Carter asks energy dept 3-1, 148D2
Chessie unit to contiose operatn 4-8, 325F2
Sup Ct backs cost data in truck rate-setting 4-18, 342C1
SEC new acctg rules rptd 4-29, 369A1
Intercity bus fare hike OKd 5-11, 5-13, 423B2, C2
Energy Dept OKd by Sen 5-18, 405E2
Moving agent crackdown set 5-23, 423E3
Alaska pipeline transport rates disputed 6-1—6-17, 477G1
2 suspended in trucking probe 6-8, 500B3
Alyeska rate bid rejctd 6-28, 497E3—498F1
BN purchase of Green Bay OKd 7-15, 613D1
Alaska pipe price ceiling upheld 7-29, 628C1
Rail grain-car deals curbed 8-1, 612G3
O'Neal report scores 8-3, 651E2
Conrail 2d ¼ loss rptd 8-4, 612E3
Bus riders 'bill of rights' set 8-8, 627B2
Amtrak redcap svc end blocked 9-12, 778A3
Grain shipping price policy curbed 10-3, 760E2
Sup Ct OKs Alaska pipe interim rate rise 10-20, upholds order 11-14, 878D2
Truckers sued over billing 11-3, 861A1
5% rail freight rate hike OKd 11-10, 899D3
Sup Ct accepts Alaska pipe rates case 11-28, 919E2
BN Green Bay line purchase OKd 11-30, BN drops offer 12-1, 1007B1
BN, Fresco OK merger 12-5, 1007E1
Offcl under probe fired 12-8, 1007E1

1978

Scientology ldrs indicted 8-15, 644B3
Jarvis extends tax-cut drive 8-21, 735A3
Milwaukee Rd wins BN merger appeal 10-5, 812B2
Truck joint rate expansn case declined by Sup Ct 10-10, 789B3
RR freight rate deregulatn urged 10-10, 812E1
Niederberger bribery convictn review refused by Sup Ct 11-27, 937C2
Value-added tax proposed 11-30, 962A2
Calif utilities refund cases refused by US Sup Ct 12-11, 981E1

Tax Evasion (& other irregularities)

Estes ordrd to pay back taxes 2-10, 127B3
Film industry probe rptd 2-13, Valenti denies 3-2, 251F2
Agnew case papers released 3-3, 164E3
Schlitz indicted for fraud 3-15, 223C2
GM fraud probe halt ordrd 4-5, 284B1
Ex-rep Passman indicted 4-28, 324B1
Ford admits probe 5-2, 391B1
NYC rabbi pleads guilty 5-11, 363F2
Tax liability in bankruptcy backed by Sup Ct 5-22, 388C1
Corp takeover liability curbed 5-22, 388F1
Gilmour indicted 6-5, 539B3
'76 tax nonpaymt by rich rptd down 7-8, 554A2
Talmadge repays Sen for excess claims 8-18, 644D1
Clark indicted 9-5, 685E1
Goodrich chrgd re slush fund 9-13, 737F1
Estes pleads guilty to new chrgs 10-18, 886E3
Hughes Med Inst probe noted 12-7, 1010E3-1011A1

INTERSTATE Commerce Commission (ICC)
REA bankruptcy case review refused by Sup Ct 3-20, 206A1
Truckers get 7½% freight-rate hike 3-31, 284B2
REA ex-chief sentenced 3-31, 310D1
Carter asks regulatory probe 4-11, 259F3
Rail rate rules backed by Appeals Ct 5-5, 433G3
Moving industry reweighing order issued 5-31; defamatn chrgs rebutted 6-30, 2 firms sued 7-6, 7-25, 589B2
Kyle resigns 6-5; withdraws resignatn, fired 6-7, 570F1
Alaska pipe rates backed by Sup Ct 6-6, 447B2
Rail lines fined in freight-car shortage 6-15, 7-3, 569A2
Exxon cites pipeline regulatn 6-21, 471G1
Rail freight rate cut back ordrd 6-30, 569F2-A3
Freight-car svc order revised 7-31, rail fines cut 8-11, 643E2
Ex-offcl indicted 9-22, pleads not guilty 9-20; challenges dismissal 9-25, 770E2
O'Neal proposes trucking deregulatn; indus, cong ldrs leery 11-7—12-21, 1007C1
Trucking freight-rate hike voided 11-27, 1007E2
Trucking freight-rate case refused by Sup Ct 12-4, 959B2
6½% rail rate hike OKd 12-11, 1007B3
Ex-offcl acquitted 12-21, 1007G3

1979

Carter business probe tax findings to be rptd 10-16, 782F3
Scientologists convicted as spies 10-26, 839C2; sentncd 12-6–12-7, 1000B1

Tax Evasion (& other irregularities)

Park assets seizure stay denied 1-3, 4C3
ILA offcls indicted 1-17, 87B3
2 Teamsters indicted 2-22, 156A1
Estes indicted 2-22, 156G1
GM tax probe plea declined by Sup Ct 2-26, 164G2
Coal broker pleads guilty 3-13, 240A1
Swiss couple indicted 3-16, 240E1
Fairchild complaint refused by Sup Ct 3-26, 231B1
Mays chrmn convctd of bribe 3-26, 239E3
Tap evidence backed by Sup Ct 4-2, 281D2
Ill atty gen indicted 4-9, 291B3
Seizure power case declined by Sup Ct 4-16, 303B1
Allied Chem indicted 4-17, 985B3
Beatles ex-mgr convicted 4-26, 392F3
Ex-Rep Clark sentncd 6-12, 442G2
Berry pleads guilty to '73 evasn 6-12, 527A3; sentncd 7-10, 656D2
Studio 54 owners indicted 6-28, 647E1
Unpaid tax losses rptd 7-10, 8-31, 665E2
Beatles ex-mgr sentenced 7-10, 656E2
Estes sentenced 8-6, 604E3
Studio 54 owners plead guilty 11-2, 891G2
Pauline Fathers probe rptd 11-9, 905F3
ILA offcl convicted 11-15, 890B1

INTERNATIONAL Communications Agency (formerly U.S. Information Agency)
Jones captivity in Iran confrmd 12-25, 975F1

Voice of America

USSR denies rptr visa 9-5, 690C1
Straus resigns 10-1, 771D1

INTERSTATE Commerce Commission (ICC)
ACT sues over vacant seats 1-4, 111D3
2 reps soften trucking deregulatn stand 1-9, 111F3
Adams' rail deregulatn plan rptd 1-15, 35D3
45 moving firms fined 1-15, 92A1
Fitzsimmons asks O'Neal firing 1-18, 111G3
Seaboard cleared of trust chrgs 2-22, 205G3
Truckers' trust immunity limited 2-28, 166E3
Misconduct dismissals backed 3-5, 309D1
Rail-freight fee case refused by Sup Ct 3-19, 203D2
Passthrough rate-hike policy rptd 4-4, 251F1
Trucking rate hikes OKd 4-11, 262D2
Conrail employee fund depletn rptd 5-27, 465D2
Motor carrier damage case refused by Sup Ct 5-29, 421G3
Milwaukee Rd svc cut denied 6-1, 465A2
Rail rate suspensn power backed by Sup Ct 6-11, 478D3
Trucking surcharges ordered 6-15, 463A1; 6-26, 479F3
Intercity summer bus svc expansn OKd 7-12, Greyhound sues 7-13, 579B2
Auto-Train withdraws fed loan applicatn 8-21, Seaboard extends pact 8-24, 726D2
Carter asks Rock I RR takeover 9-20, judge vs 9-21; takeover ordrd 9-26, 722A1-G2
Amtrak funding bill signed 9-29, 868A1
O'Neal to leave post 10-4, Gaskins named chrmn 10-12, 831A1
Rock I RR svc resumes 10-5, 830C3
Trucking order ruling reversed by Sup Ct 10-15, 847G3
Milwaukee Rd embargoes westn track 11-1, Carter signs aid bill 11-4, embargo lifted 11-5, 867A3
'80 rail funds, trucking deregulatn rules bar clears Cong 11-15, 11-19; Carter signs 11-30, 920E1
Rock I takeover order extended 11-28, 989B2
Auto-Train financing plan OKd 12-7, 989A3

1980

Tax Evasion (& other irregularities)

Estes '83 parole rptd 1-3, 64G3
Studio 54 owners sentenced 1-18, 64B3
'Church' founder, aide convicted of mail fraud 2-9, 157E2
Ill atty gen convicted 3-19, 215C3
Du Pont dispute declined by Sup Ct 4-14, 307D1
NY Deliverers Union head convicted 5-15, 370E3; sentncd 6-26, 656D1
Ala black dist judge nominee accused 5-19, Sen confrms 6-26, 744G2, B3
Commodities trading straddles to be curbed 5-22, 481F1
White House aide rptd reassigned in dispute 6-10, 638E3
Cts power to suppress evidence curbed 6-23, 554C3
Evangelical Christian pol actn profiled 7-11—9-15, 819E1
Ill atty gen sentncd 7-29, 654F2
Auto-Train suit filed 7-31, 958E2
Prosecutn guidelines rptd 8-2, 601G2-D3
Sheffield probe leaked, Sen confirmatn hearings halted 8-27, 745A1

INTERNATIONAL Communications Agency
FTC emergency funding bill signed 3-28, 348E1
Forgn Svc reorgn bill clears Cong 10-1, signed 10-17, 981E2

Voice of America

Moslem broadcast dissatisfactn rptd 6-29, 490G2
USSR jams broadcasts 8-20, denies 8-21; US reactn 8-21, 626E2, C3

INTERNATIONAL Trade and Investment Policy, President's Commission on (defunct)
Allen conflict-of-interest chrgd 10-28, quits Reagan post 10-30, 817G3

INTERSTATE Commerce Commission (ICC)
Burlington refund order issued 1-4, Sup Ct refuses stay 1-14, 37A3
Milwaukee Rd westn track purchase rejected in '79 1-7, 53A1
Union Pacific, MoPac set merger 1-8, 52F3
Union Pacific seeks Westn Pacific 1-24, 131D2
Rock I RR liquidatn ordrd 1-25, svc extensn asked 2-14, 131A2
Rock I service extended 2-22, 147F3
Milwaukee Rd reorganizatn plans rejected 3-19, 346B1
Rock I svc continues 3-31, judge warns on paymt 4-1, 345C3
UPS merger case refused by Sup Ct 4-14, 307G1-A2
BN, Frisco Rail merger OKd 4-17, 345D2
Santa Fe, Southn Pacific RR merger set 5-15, 427B3
Rock I aid bill clears Cong 5-22, Carter signs 5-30, 427F1
Rock I svc cutback urged 5-27; segment sale OKd 6-10, 598B3-F3
Rock I svc extended again 5-30, 427B2
Southn Railway, N&W seek merger 6-2, 427E2
Trucking decontrol bill clears Cong 6-19, 6-20, 479B1; Carter signs 7-1, 494E1
Fla trucking deregulatn study set 7-1, 558F2
RR collective rate fixing curbed 8-13, 616E2
Auto-Train suit filed 8-19; crditors svc cut conditns set 9-26, 958F2, D3
Santa Fe, Southn Pacific merger canceled 9-12, 745D2
Union Pacific, MoPac, Westn Pacific to merge 9-15, 745A2
Chessie, Seaboard merger set 9-24, 745A3
Household moving bill clears Cong 9-25, 9-30; Carter signs 10-15, 915G2
RR deregulatn clears Cong 9-30, 10-1; signed 10-14, 783E3-784B1
RR A-fuel tariffs case declined by Sup Ct 10-6, 782D2
BN-Frisco rail merger OKd by appeals ct 11-24, 937A3

1976

JOINT Chiefs of Staff
Ford revises intelligence command 2-17, 127E2
Ex-chrmn on Rockwell guest list 3-17, 200F3
Cited in Sen intellignc com rpt 4-26, 300E2, 303A1
Gen Brown criticized 10-17, 10-18, backed by Ford 10-20, 787C1
Ford, Carter debate Brown 10-22, 799F3, 801D1, C2

JUDICIARY—*See also SUPREME Court below; subjects of rulings*
Burger urges more judgeships 1-3, 24C2
Judge removed in pollutn case 1-6, 25C2
Ford State of Union message 1-19, 38C2
Fed ct case remanding curbed 1-20, 43F1
44 judges sue for higher pay 2-11, ABA reactn 2-13, 2-16, 136D2
Burger lauds fed judges, urges new judgeships 2-15, 136A3
Pres candidates vow black judges 5-2, 343B3
Oliver Carter dies 6-14, 524D2
Dem platform text 6-15, 471F1, 473F3, 474D1
Claims ct salary suit rule rejctd 6-21, 552G3
Fed ct review of state air plans barred 6-25, 552C2
Fed ct review of illegal evidence challenges curbed 7-6, 534A3
'77 funds signed 7-14, 534C2
3-judge ct curb signed 8-12, 646A3
GOP platform text 8-18, 604A2
Pay increase barred 10-1, 834A2
Ford, Carter debate 10-22, 802B2

Administrative Office of the U.S. Courts
Sup Ct backs magistrates' review of Soc Security cases 1-14, 24A2

Claims, U.S. Court of
Indian Claims Comm end signed 10-8, 835A1

Judicial Conference of the U.S.
Burger seeks more fed judgeships 1-3, 24C2
Ford State of Union message 1-19, 38C2

Military Appeals, U.S. Court of
Cadets file honor code suit 7-13, Army seeks dismissal 8-11, 670G2

JUSTICE, Department of—*See also LEVI, Edward H.*
Joint IRS probe agrmt issued 1-10, 41B3
New corruptn unit formed 1-14, 78C3
Sues Bechtel 1-16, 44D2
Fulbright registers as Emirates counsel 1-26, 160C2
Mrs Javits quits Iran post 1-27, 160B2
Backs suit vs cable TV curbs 2-5, 135D3
Privacy comm testimony cites 2-11, 151C2
Vs ABA proposals 2-16, 137B1, C1
Ford revises intelligence command 2-17, 127F2
Issues FBI guidelines 3-10, 217E2-E3
Fed prison populatn 3-14, 336F3
Sup Ct exempts some redistricting plans from review 3-30, 262C1
Cong OKs Hatch Act repeal 3-31, 234B2
FBI Cointelpro study panel formed 4-1, 235A1
Clears Alexander re tax probes 4-12, 283D3
Pocket-veto use limited 4-13, 284E1
Metcalfe probe dropped 4-15, 286D3
Church com issues rpts, backs oversight 4-26, 300C2, A3, 302D2, 304G1; 4-28, 324G3, 325F2, 326B1-329D2, D3, 330C3
New Rev King probe set 4-29, 344E1
Mil meat-purchasing probe rptd 5-8, 395A3
Helms Va break-in ruling cited 5-17, 379B2
Hays admits affair with aide 5-25, 392F2
House to cooperate in Hays probe 6-9, 433B3
Gardner sex chrg vs Young rptd 6-11, 433E3
Cited in Dem platform text 6-15, 470A1, 471D2, 474F1
Teamsters fund probed 6-29, 492E2
Nixon disbarred in NY 7-8, 493F3
'77 funds signed 7-14, 534C2, E2
Sues former Eximbank offcls 8-9, 709B3
GOP conv delegate bribes chrgd 8-16, 616F1
Passman probe rptd 8-16, 633C1
Clears Young 8-16, 636B2
Sues Chrysler 9-27, 729E3
Letelier murder probe rptd 10-9, 780E3
Ford, Carter debate 10-22, 802F1
Hays suit dismissed 10-26, 12-8, 982B1
Ends travel expense probe 10-27, 981F3
Hendrix chrgd re ITT-Chile probe 11-5, 869G2
Medicaid abortn fund stay barred 11-8, 848B2
Charges vs Agee considered 11-18, 946C3
Carter names liaison 11-23, 881A3
Cook Indus vs damages paymt 12-15, 990A3

Antitrust Division & Actions
Bechtel sued 1-16, 44E2
Seen vs ABA ad action 2-17, 136G3
Proxmire rpts on '69-74 bank mergers 2-17, 3-1, 185G2, C3
Paperbd indictmts 2-18; cos fines 9-20, stiffer penalties asked 10-5, 885F3; offcls sentncd 11-30, 921D2
Goodyr, Firestone suits dropped 3-2, 988G2
Kauper trust bill backing rptd 3-18, 247B1
9 steel firms fined 4-10, 988D3

1977

JOB Corps—*See LABOR—Manpower Administration below*

JOINT Chiefs of Staff
Rpt denies Sovt mil edge 1-30, 70E2
Brown scores Cong, backs mail surveillnc 3-27, 231F3
Rowny in SALT talks 3-28—3-30, 225D2
Singlaub loses S Korea cmnd 5-21, 403G2, 404B1
Bunker, Linowitz brief on Panama Canal pact 8-12, ratificatn drive planned 8-16, 621D1, E2, 622D1
Carter cites Canal treaty support 8-23, 649B3
Canal pact backing held forced 9-20, 10-4, denied 9-27, 755F1

JUDICIARY—*See also SUPREME Court below; also COURTS under 'C'; subjects of rulings*
Burger issues rpt; asks judgeship, pay hikes 1-1, 15F1-C2
Ford State of Union message 1-12, 13D1, B3
Ford seeks pay hikes; other budget requests 1-17, 30A2, 32G2, 33D3
Pay hikes take effect 2-20, 127D2
1-judge prison rulings 3-21, 230A3
DC ct reorganizatn upheld 3-22, 231D1-B2
Fed role in state civil actns curbed 3-22, 231B2
Pay-raise procedures revised 4-12, 273D1
Burger disputes critics 5-17, 419E2-B3
COL hike bar signed 7-11, 592G1
'78 funds signed 8-2, 667F3
Sirica retires 10-4, 927E3

Administrative Office of the U.S. Courts
Kirks dies 11-2, 952G2

JUSTICE, Department of—*See also BELL, Griffin*
Burger lauds Carter re US attys 1-1, 15C2
FBI informer guidelines issued 1-5, 15D2-C3
NAACP vs Bell confrmatn 1-10, 59B3
Callaway probe ended 1-11, 59D2
CIA mail-opening prosecutn barred 1-14, 41D3
Cong Maine Indian settmt urged 1-14, 59C1
Sup Ct expands tap use 1-18, 58F1
Levi gets King probe rpt 1-20; release delayed, accounts publshd 2-2, 77A2
Sup Ct voids Indianapolis busing plan 1-25, 79E3, 80C1
Archbp Trifa chrgs cited 2-4, 120C1
'70-76 pol indictmts rptd 2-10, 162C3
Ind kidnaper arrested 2-11, 162C2
FBI curbs proposed 2-15, 157C3
King rpt released 2-18, 149F1
Mardian reinstated to Sup Ct bar 2-28, 175C2
Maine Indian claims backed 2-28, 196E3
Sup Ct backs racial voter redistricting 3-1, 174D3
Agee prosecutn barred 3-18, 212A2
Wilmington (Del) busing backed 3-18, 216C2
Flu damage claims rptd 3-21, 224G1-C2
Solitron case review denied 3-21, 230G2
DC ct reorganizatn upheld 3-22, 231G1, B2
Austin integratn plan asked 3-23, 216A3
Cook rptd on payroll 3-24, 236F1
Gay rights access promised 3-26, 278E2
ERA rescission memo rptd 3-27, 279F3
Cook Cnty (Ill) jails scored 4-4, 288F3
Ex-FBI official indicted 4-7, 275F1-G2
CAB suspends license-fee rules 4-8, 325F1
Backs Dayton busing order 4-22, 446D1
Navy homosexual dischrg upgraded 4-27, 344G1
Detroit sued on water pollutn 5-6, 422D2
Bus fare hike appeal rejctd 5-13, 423A2
Mafia business infiltratn rptd 5-16, 6-13, 568E1, F1
Woolworth Tris suit settled 5-18, 483D2
Uniform fed death penalty procedures backed 5-18, 594D3
Lawyer fees in spy suits rptd 5-22, 422B3
Nixon-Frost interview 5-25, 419G3
ICC suspends 2 in trucking probe 6-8, 500B3
Alaska pipeline rates challenged 6-15, 477B2; ICC sets rates 6-28, 498E1
Natl crime data svc under review 6-16, 480B3
Sup Ct curbs warrantless searches 6-21, 539A1
Newton to face '74 Calif chrgs 6-24, 532B1
S Africa sugar lobby sued 7-20, 614A1
AT&T to maintain Telpak 7-21, 631E3
FBI Scientology office raids ruled illegal 7-27, 628B2
Hyde abortn amendmt opinion issued 7-27, 786C2
'78 funds signed 8-2, 667B3
Bell vs grand jury chngs 8-9, 630E1
Kan City integratn plan challenged 8-15, 631D1
Slovik case referred 8-16, 808G1

1978

JOB Corps—*See LABOR—Manpower Administration below*

JOINT Chiefs of Staff
Brown on mil pensn revisns 1-18, 53D1
Brown sees USSR mil gains 2-2, 81A3
Jones named chrmn; Allen, Hayward get AF, Navy posts 4-5, 281F1
Singlaub scores Carter 6-2, 433B2
Defense study urges upgrading 7-12, 528C2
Jones warns of Sovt buildup, urges defns budget hike 10-30, 833A3
Draft registratn urged 11-21, 895A1
CBO scores Selective Service 12-3, 984C1
Brown dies 12-5, 1032C2

JUDICIAL Conference of the U.S.—*See under JUDICIARY below*

JUDICIARY—*See also SUPREME Court below; also COURTS under 'C'; subjects of rulings*
'73 pay raise veto review rejctd 1-9, 13B1
Carter budget proposal 1-23, 44F2; table 45E2
Criminal code revisn clears Sen 1-30, 64E2
Carter backs criminal code reform; more minority, women judges 5-4, 320A3
Burger urges judgeship bill OK, notes caseload rise 7-23, 626D3
Burger urges study 9-21, 751A3
Bankruptcy revisn delay sought by Burger 9-28, Cong clears 10-6, 788E2-789B1
Carter signs judgeships bill 10-20, backs merit selectn 11-8, 873C2-C3
Burger defends judicial lobbying 10-25, 832D3
Bankruptcy revisn signed 11-6, 1003B1
3 Sup Ct justices urge new fed ct 12-4, 958D3-959A1

Judicial Conference of The U.S.
Burger urges study of fed govt 9-21, 751B3
Burger vs bankruptcy bill 9-28, 788G3

JUSTICE, Department of—*See also BELL, Griffin*
Marston dismissal controversy 1-10, 1-12, 12C2; Bell ousts 1-20, 32F1; **for subsequent developments, see MARSTON, David**
Webster named FBI dir 1-19, 32C1
Carter details intell curbs 1-24, 49G2
Timber sales sealed-bid repeal clears Cong 2-6, 107D3; 2-20, 218A2
Byington resigns as CPSC chrmn, probe cited 2-8, 185F2
Asbestos workers get $20 mln setlmt 2-8, 326D3
Bell disputes Burger on trial lawyers 2-12, 108C1
Ex-CIA analyst sued re book 2-15, 129C1
Carter defends apptmt of US attys 2-17, 123E2
Letelier murder probe suspects sought 2-21—2-24, 146C2, E2
Carter seeks job-bias unit reorganizatn 2-23, 123G3
Agnew case papers released 3-3, 164E3
Taft-Hartley invoked in coal strike 3-6, gets ct order 3-9, 159C2, 160C2; effected, slip-up cited 3-13, 181F2
Cities subject to US electn law 3-6, 162F1
Chile backs Letelier murder probe 3-6, 188G2
Taft-Hartley extensn barred 3-17, 217C1
2 ITT aides accused of perjury in '73 Chile testimony, Geneen chrgs declined 3-20; cover-up chrgd 3-21, 206C3
Vaira named Phila US atty 3-23, 243B3
GM agrees to $170,000 pollutn fine 3-27, 263B3
GM tax fraud probe halt ordrd 4-5, 284B1
Proposed lid on oil, gas co coal, uranium reserves rptd 4-6, 282A3
Gray, 2 other FBI ex-offcls indicted; disciplinary actn vs LaPrade, 68 agents, 2 attys sought; '77 chrgs vs ex-aide dropped 4-10, 261E3-262D1
LaPrade chrgs pol influence exerted on dept 4-13, 285C1
Civiletti dep atty gen confirmatn backed by Sen com 4-14, 309C3, D3; confrmd 5-9, 342D3
Warrantless taps curbed by Sen 4-20, 306F1
ICC rail rate rules backed by Appeals Ct 5-5, 434C1
Legal actn vs CIA ex-agent weighed 5-8, 367A3
Phila sued on sewage 5-24, 409G1
VW dealers sued 5-24, 409C2
W Va scaffold collapse negligence chrgd 6-8, 459F3
Rail lines fined in freight-car shortage 6-15, 7-3, 569F2
Goodwin legal immunity case declined by Sup Ct 6-19, 492D2
IRS summons power backed by Sup Ct 6-19, 492G2
Legislative vetoes scored 6-21, 466A1, F1
Zenith import duty rebuffed by Sup Ct 6-21, 491C3
Chile chrgd re Letelier probe noncooperatn 6-23, 495E3, G3
Bakke med schl admissn backed by Sup Ct 6-28, 481D2

1979

JOINT Chiefs of Staff
Jones warns of Sovt threat 1-25, 52C2
SALT II communique, Carter Cong address 6-18, 457B1, 458E3
SALT ratificatn backed 7-11, 510E2
Rowny, Moore score SALT 7-12, 7-17, 536D1, G1
SALT testimony continues 7-24, 643D3
Mil pay increase asked 11-13, 903E3

National Defense University (Washington, D.C.)
Officers end China visit 5-15, 370C2

JUDICIARY
Burger names special prosecutor panel 1-12, 56F1
ABA reassured on minority apptmts 2-12, 130F1
Judge blocks financial disclosures 5-15, 382A2
Burger names 10 to wiretap ct 5-18, 442A3
All-white club memberships assailed 7-14, 9-19, 9-25, 901E2
'80 funds clear Cong 8-2, 9-10, Carter signs 9-24, 766E3
Black woman sworn US magistrate 8-7, 901F3
Financial disclosure law upheld 11-19, 901B2

Administrative Office of the U.S. Courts
'78 wiretaps rptd 4-28, 386G3
Carter sued over pay limit 11-9, 901C2

Judicial Conference of the U.S.
All-white club memberships assailed 9-19, 901G2

JUSTICE, Department of
House com JFK, King murder plot findings review delayed 1-2, 3G3
Tenn parole-selling probe continues 1-4, 36F1-B3; **for subsequent developments, see TENNESSEE**
Gas overchrgs vs 8 firms filed, '78 Exxon suit added 1-5, 17A1
Jonestown bodies transfer refused 1-6, Peoples Temple sued 1-22, 117D2, E2
SEC role in pensn plans barred by Sup Ct 1-16, 32D2
FBI ex-agent's statemt in SWP trial sought 1-16, 92B2
CIA ex-offcl's death probe urged 1-24, 54G3
Food stamp probe rptd 2-2, 93B3
Contract denial re wage-price enforcemt OKd 2-5, 127C3
Appeals Ct rejcts Torres case appeal 2-6, 156B2
Hazardous-waste suit filed in NJ 2-7, 129G3-130B1
Perjury chrgs vs ITT exec dropped, natl sec cited 2-8, 88C1
Bell reassures ABA on minority apptmts 2-12, 130F1
GM tax probe plea declined by Sup Ct 2-26, 164A3
Boeing missile info leak alleged 3-1, 207G2
ICC misconduct dismissals backed 3-5, 309E1
USSR ship ban opposed 3-6, 213A3
Perjury chrgs vs 2d ITT exec dropped 3-7, 188G1
Kennedy merger-limit bill backed 3-8, 202F2
H-bomb article publicatn barred 3-9, 193A3-194A1; 3-26, 230A1
Firestone '72 gold trading chrgd 3-15, 202A2
House com rpt on JFK released 3-16, 204E3
Bell contempt citatn overturned 3-19, 207E1
Carter peanut probe spec counsel named, limits scored 3-20, 203A1
'57 spy chrgs vs Sterns dropped 3-22, 232C1
S Africa lobbying rptd 3-23, 213C2
Carter probe spec counsel gains new power 3-23, 301G2-C3
Wallace argues Weber case in Sup Ct 3-28, 262F3, 263A1
Viet ex-amb documt possessn prosecutn dropped 3-30, 252F3
IRS tap evidence backed by Sup Ct 4-2, 281D2
USSR ship ban delayed 4-6, 287A3
Muellenberg confirmed GSA inspector gen 4-10, 965B1
Hooker Chem case studied 4-11, 281F3
Lance grand jury dismissal motn rejctd 4-13, 327F3
B Carter Libya ties probed 4-15, 310E1
CIA ex-offcl's death probe dropped 4-18, 283F3; Sen panel to probe 4-30, 368A1
Mafia alleged chieftain indicted 4-27, 368F1
PR soclsts '78 deaths disputed 4-30–5-3, probe ordrd 5-2, 350F1-G2
Beneficial Corp credit bias chrgd 5-8, 596E1

1980

JOINT Chiefs of Staff
Jones warns of Sovt aggressn 1-29, 65E1, C2
Carter defns budget scored 5-29, 424E2
Hayward backs draft 6-19, 478F3
Iran hostage rescue rpt issued 8-23, 644B1

JUDICIARY
Burger '79 study rptd 1-3, 51F2
2 Ala blacks nominated 1-10; controversy ensues 5-19—9-17; Clemon confrmd 6-26, Gray withdraws 9-17, 744B2
Burger ABA address 2-3, 114E2
Carter nominee called 'unqualified' 3-2, Sen panel rejcts 3-4, 250E2
Va black named dist judge 4-9; tax probe leak halts Sen hearings 8-27, fight vowed 9-9, 744D3
Voting Rights Act provisn upheld by Sup Ct 4-22, 344D1
Mitchell named to Sen seat 5-8, 367B2
Burger warns vs ct systems 'merger' 6-10, 632D1
ABA OKs apptmt resolutns 8-6, 744E1, F1
5th circuit split signed 10-14, 918A3
Judicial discipline bill signed 10-15, 918F3
Ervin vs 'judicial verbicide' 10-22, 908A2
Pay hikes backed by Sup Ct 12-15, 956C3-957D1

Administrative Office of the U.S. Courts
Judges granted 12.9% pay hike 3-24, 250E1
Personal bankruptcy rise rptd 3-25, 263C3

Judicial Conference of the U.S.
Burger urges judgeships creatn power 2-3, 114B3
Affirmative actn jobs plan ordrd 3-6, 250B2
Ctroom cameras case accepted by Sup Ct 4-21, 344G1
Pretrial data secrecy rule rptd OKd 6-19, takes effect 8-1, 631G3
Judicial discipline bill signed 10-15, 919A1

JUSTICE, Department of
JFK murder probe reopened 1-4, 17E1
Prosecutn disparities rptd 1-6, 24A3
Lee Way settles job bias suit 1-10, 17D2
ILA ldrs, businessmen sentenced for racketeering 1-11, 64B2
'Petite' policy cited in Ky firearms Sup Ct case 1-14, 37G1
Nazi search deadline rptd set 1-16, 228D2
Female white-collar crime rpt disputed 1-21, 216G3
ILA Sovt boycott end asked 1-28, ct backs 1-29, 169E1
Agee suit asked 2-5, ct OKs 4-1, 268E2
FBI 'Miporn' probe rptd 2-14, 136B2
SC reapportionmt suggestd 2-14, 185A2
FBI informant probe cited 2-18, 227A3
Peoples Temple funds in Panama returned 2-28, 170C3
Stockwell suit re Angola opens 3-3, 268A3
Racketeer law cases declined by Sup Ct 3-24, 265D1
Chicago strip search suit setld 3-26, 404D2
Pres campaign spending limit upheld by Sup Ct 4-14, 306G3
SC reapportionmt suit filed 4-18, 349A2
Voting Rights Act provisn upheld by Sup Ct 4-22, 344D1
Civiletti warns vs FTC debt 4-25, 348E1
PR cops cleared in '78 killings 4-25, 348B3
Amoco settles credit bias suit 4-29, 370B3
Civiletti acts to stem Miami rioting 5-19—5-20, 382G2, D3
Nixon taps case accepted by Sup Ct 5-19, 440F1
Black ldr warns re despair 5-29, 460A2
Talmadge finances probe dropped 5-30, 427E3-428A1
Clark Iran trip probe sought 6-7, Carter for prosecutn 6-10, 6-16, 459B3
Lance case closed 6-9, 459G2
Oil cos absolved in '79 shortage 7-17, 552B1
DIDC bank gift ban oppositn rptd 7-18, 560G3
Brennan permits draft registratn 7-19, 598A1
Hispanic crime study rptd 7-28, 654F3
Sheffield tax probe leaked, Sen confirmatn hearings halted 8-27, 745A1
UAW seat on AMC bd proposed 9-17, 725F1
NSC Africa memo probe set 9-17, 727A1
Phillips, Sun oil price setlmts OKd 9-25, 9-26, 960E1
Agee profits denial refused 10-2, 990G2
5th judicial circuit split, backing cited 10-14, 918D3
Ex-CIA agent indicted on espionage 10-24, pleads guilty 10-29, 855G3
Cuba frees 30 US prisoners, 5 arrested in Miami 10-27, 828C3
Marubeni, Hitachi units convicted 11-5, 957D3
Sen OKs appropriatn bill, Civiletti scores 11-17, 880G3, 881A1
NC KKK acquittals review vowed 11-17, 898A3
LA DA ends 'Charlie's Angels' probe 12-2, 1002B3

1976

Files Mid-Amer Dairymen consent 5-28, 989B2
Indicts 7 oil cos 6-1, 412C3
Potash producers indicted 6-29, 748A1
Files consent vs 21 publishers 7-27, 989D1
Carter backs strengthnd role 8-9, 585A1
'69 drug suit ends in mistrial 8-17, 988A3
Chrgs US, Canadians re potash 8-30, 673E2
Cong clears enforcemt bill 9-16, 728D1*; signed 10-1, 982F1
Canada scores potash suit 9-21, 750B2 ★
5 paper-bag makers indicted 10-29, 11-4, 886B3
AT&T suit OKd 11-16, 886G3
Files consent decree vs 9 dye cos 11-16, 989B1
NBC OKs programming pact 11-17, 869D1
Sues Tex accountants bd 11-18, 989A1
Jail terms for price-fixing asked 11-20, 885B3
FCC network probe asked 11-23, 901D1
Bakke role in Sovt shipping conf entry talks opposed 11-26, 948G1
Titanium price-fixing talks rptd 12-5, 988A2
GE, Westinghouse suits dropped 12-10, 988C2
GE, Utah Intl merge 12-16, 985A1
Superport advice rejctd 12-17, 992B1

1977

Sugar subsidies ruled illegal 8-19, 854G3
EPA suit vs Chrysler dismissed 8-22, 723E3
SEC submits NYC financial rpt 8-26, 665E2
Letelier murder probe continues 9-7—9-8, 743E2
Amtrak redcap svc end blocked 9-12, 778A3
Carter OKs NY-London budget fares 9-26, 860A3
Va A-plant safety cover-up rptd 9-30, 838D1
Young cleared in prisoner aid chrg 10-19, 861D3
Helms indictmt decisn pending 10-27, 814C1; pleads no contest 10-31, 838B3-G3
Defends minority constructn quota 10-31, 979A1
Helms sentenced 11-4, 861B2
TVA bias-suit case review refused 12-5, 939D1
FBI probe attys clash with Bell, ask removal from case 12-7, 940A1
FBI probe gets new team, Bell drops oppositn to indictmts 12-13, 979B3

Antitrust Division & Actions

NY Mag purchase probed 1-6, 48E3
Bechtel settles Arab boycott suit 1-10, 78B2
Arco acquires Anaconda 1-12, 55B3
FCC OKs TV network probe 1-14, 119D1
NBC gets Moscow Olympics 2-1, 131C1
3 airlines indicted 2-3, 93F2

1978

FCC 'Filthy Words' ban upheld by Sup Ct 7-3, 551F3
LaPrade fired 7-6, 507G2
Bell contempt order stayed 7-7, 524G3
KKK informant rptd agent-provocateur 7-9, 7-11; violence, cover-up probed 7-12, 527E3-528B2
Dallas cop dual prosecutn dropped 7-14, 991C3
Energy Dept '75-77 sex bias admitted 7-14, 1006A3
Tonelli indictmt rptd 7-19, 598G3
Lockheed '71 claims vs Navy settled 7-28, 665G3
Townley plea-bargain pact Letelier OKd 8-11, 647B3
Scientology ldrs indicted 8-15, 644B3
3 chrgs vs ITT aide dropped 8-18, 643B3
Talmadge repays Sen for expenses 8-18, 644D1
Warrantless taps curbed by House 9-7, 697D1
Fox fined for 'block booking' 9-12, 759C2
Viet documt possessn by ex-amb probed 9-13, 720F1
Goodrich chrgd with tax fraud 9-13, 737G1
GSA probe coordinatn set 9-18, 715B1
GSA probe coordinator named 9-20, employe indicted 9-29, 753B3, G3
Bankruptcy law revisn cleared by Cong 10-6, 788G2, B3
Sup Ct ruling on FDIC case scored 10-16, 789G1
GSA probe head steps down 11-14, 899F1
SBA minority-aid abuse probe rptd 11-21, 919C3
King probe scored 11-27, 938E2
Ga schl bd pol rule struck down by Sup Ct 11-28, 937E3
Ga, Tex schl integratn cases declined by Sup Ct 12-4, 959A2
Weber reverse job-bias case accepted by Sup Ct, brief cited 12-11, 980C3
3 Houston ex-cops sentnc appealed 12-14, 991B3
Peoples Temple Swiss bank accts rptd 12-15, located frozen in Panama 12-20, 1000F1
House com scores JFK, King death probes; asks review 12-30, 1002D1, E2, A3

Antitrust Division & Actions

Texaco suit to be dropped 1-3, 67E2
Elec wiring device makers sentencd 2-3, 142F1
Film, TV industry probe rptd 2-4, Valenti denies 3-2, 251E2
Armored car firms fined 4-22, 5-4, 511D1

1979

Lance, 3 others indicted in Ga bank plot 5-23, plead not guilty 5-24, 380B2
NJ indictmt details Mafia 5-23, 508C2
Carter '76 campaign ad financing probed 5-25, 401A3
Carter peanut business documts rptd subpoenaed 5-27, 5-28, 401B2
'78 E Ger hijacker freed 5-28, 430F2
Mrs Javits Iran role detailed 5-30, 408E2
Lance witness plea bargain blocked 6-6, 500A3
H-bomb documt security error admitted 6-8, judge continues to block article publicatn 6-15, 713C1, E1
Civiletti backs eased pot laws 6-9, 492A2
Guillain-Barre flu shot claims rptd stalled 6-10, 470E3
NAB sued over TV ad limit 6-14, 618G2-A3
Hooker pollutn probe rptd 6-18, 597A2
Carter '76 campaign ad financing improprieties denied 6-22, 500C2
Textron pleads guilty to currency violatns 7-10, Proxmire asks study 10-31, 923G2-A3
Panax TV licenses revoked, McGoff probe cited 7-12, 618F2
Judge's racial slur rptd 7-14, 901A3
Bell quits, Civiletti succeeds 7-19, 529C1, D1
Firestone tax chrg plea bargain cited 7-26, 648B3
Minchew pleads guilty to fraud 7-30, 702C2
FBI charter backed 7-31, 599A3
Civiletti confrmd 8-1; sworn 8-16, 700A3
Kenny fined for Cook I '78 electn fraud role 8-2, 648C2
'80 funds clear Cong 8-2, 9-10, Carter signs 9-24, 766E3
Oil firms cleared of hoarding, Feb-May gas shortage detailed; probe to go on 8-6, 628B3
Rep Jenrette denies drug role probe 8-8, 650B1
Tex-Viet refugee mediatn sought 8-9, 8-15, 660E1
Admin denies forgn spy aid 8-9, 664D2
Phila police brutality complaint signed 8-10; chrgs filed, Rizzo calls suit political 8-13, 610E1-E2
Yeoman chrgd re secrets sale 8-14, 611E1
Guillian-Barre flu shot claim settled, fatalities cited 8-14, 771G1
Bell scores Carter 8-14, leaves office 8-16, 8-16, 608C3
Rep Diggs sued 8-16, 649G3-650B1
Jordan cocaine use probe rptd 8-24, 647E1
Vesco jury foreman resigns, claims cover-up 8-29, 647E2, A3
Vesco case perjury rptd 8-30, Heymann denies 8-31, 725F2
Vecso case cover-up chrgs denied by Carter 8-31, jury foreman resignatn rejected 9-7, 725B3-E3
Jordan cocaine probe continues 8-31–9-28, expanded 9-13, 767C2
4 PR natlsts' sentences commuted, Cuba exchng denied 9-6, 666G1
GAO rpts on '79 oil shortage 9-13, 702D3
Talmadge Sen files acquired 9-14, 702E1
H-bomb letter publicatn banned 9-15, 2 papers defy ban 9-16, 9-18; suit dropped, probe vowed 9-17, 713B1, G1, 714B2; text of letter 714D1-717E3
H-bomb article publicatn bars lifted 9-17, 713A1, F1
Cook settles grain export chrgs, Miss River Grain case cited 9-26, 727G2-C3
Ex-Mafia informant sues 9-26, 840F2
Chile extraditn rule scored, retaliatn weighed 10-1, 750B2
'77 Sup Ct tax case errors cited 10-8, 848A2
Carter loses Taiwan defns treaty suit 10-17, appeal filed 10-18, 777G1
Jordan alleged cocaine supplier indicted 10-23, NY disco owners plead guilty to tax chrgs 11-2, 891A3, E3
Sedco sued for Mex oil spill cleanup 10-23, 809D2
Scientologists convicted as spies 10-26, 839C2; sentncd 12-6–12-7, 1000B1
HEW seeks Chicago desegregatn suit 10-29, 944D1
Phila police brutality suit dismissed 10-30, 831B3
KKK probe set 11-6, 865D3
US Helsinki review com scores monitoring 11-7, 981A1
Pauline Fathers probe rptd 11-9, 905E3
Scotto convicted 11-15, 890C2
Renfrew named dep atty gen 11-20, 946A3
Census use re deportatn barred 11-26, 924F1
Jordan cocaine probe spec prosecutor named 11-29, 900E3
Civiletti quits Vesco probe 12-7, 943B3
GAO 'fraud hotline' rptd effective 12-9, 947B2
Love Canal suit filed 12-20, 990F1

Antitrust Division & Actions

Oil co pipe ownership bar asked 1-4, 55F2
AT&T proposes speedy trial date, refusal seen 1-11, 88A3
IBM case marks 10th yr 1-17, 88D3
AT&T data access case declined by Sup Ct 3-26, 231A1

1980

'81 funds clear Cong 12-3, Carter vetoes 12-16; stopgap funds clear Cong 12-16, 953B2, E3, 954F1
Standard Oil price setlmt OKd 12-3, 960C1
Boston settles job bias suit 12-5, 962B3
Army LSD setlmt clears Cong 12-5, signed 12-18, 981G3
McCree argues Nixon taps case in Sup Ct 12-8, 937C2
Lenient sentence appeal backed by Sup Ct 12-9, 936B3
Smith named atty gen 12-11, 935D1
Gray chrgs dropped 12-11, 940A2
Troup (Tex) to end black svcs bias 12-11, 963B2
2 Scientologists sentenced 12-19, 997C3

Antitrust Division & Actions

Real estate brokers subject to suits by Sup Ct 1-8, 16E1
IBM judge's ouster rejected 2-25, 266C2
Gypsum price fixing case settled 3-3, 557F3
Phone industry deregulatn set by FCC 4-7, 370D2

1976

Appointments & Resignations
Keuch, Waldman named dep asst attys gen 1-14, 78F3
Richards named fraud unit dir 1-14, 78G3
Baker confrmd asst atty gen 8-6, 807D3
Garza rejctd atty gen post 12-16, 937B1
Bell named atty gen 12-20, controversy flares 12-20—12-22, 956F1, G2
Bensinger confrmd to DEA 2-5, 110A2

Civil Rights Issues
Wins job bias suit vs Chicago police 1-5, 6C2
Backs pvt schl desegregatn 4-9, 263C2
Files home loan bias suits 4-15, 4-16, 285G1
Orders multilingual electns 4-21, 307D3
Seeks busing rule review 5-14, Ford seeks 5-18, 5-19, 377E2-D3
Levi drops Boston busing review 5-29; Ford, other reactn 5-29—6-2, 391E3
Sen com scores 4 agencies on bias 5-31, 413B3
Sup Ct rules on fed job bias suits 6-1, 414F2
Sup Ct vs pvt schl bias 6-25, 479F1
Sup Ct bars review of housing bias ruling 10-4, 766B1
Job exam bias rules set 11-17, 884C2
Sues Boston re job bias 11-26, 944E1
Sup Ct vacates Austin busing plan 12-6, 920D1

Drug Enforcement Administration (DEA)
'75 Mex drug drive rptd launched 1-2, 61E1
Bensinger confrmd admin 2-5, 110A2
Privacy comm testimony cites 2-11, 151C2
Mex officials score 3-16, 6-9, 419G3-420B1
Intl dealers arrested 5-27, 2 convicted 12-9, 971C3
Most abused drugs rptd 7-9, 524G1
'77 funds signed 7-14, 534E2
Detroit police dep probe rptd 8-20, 776D2
Marijuana OKd for glaucoma use 10-5, 860G3

Federal Bureau of Investigation—*See separate listing above*

Grain Export Probe—*See GRAIN*

Immigration & Naturalization Service
Privacy comm testimony cited 2-11, 151C2
Solzhenitsyn seeks visa 6-22, 680B3
'77 funds signed 7-14, 534E2
Sup Ct bars review of Border Patrol car search 10-18, 867E2

1977

Podiatrists sued 2-15, 156B3
FCC backs AT&T practices 2-23, 217E2
Chrgs dismissed vs Potash Co of Amer 2-25, 5 others 6-10, 483C3
6 coal cos sentenced 3-21, 520B3
Gulf uranium cartel role rptd 4-25, 479C2
Japan TV probe rptd 5-20, 416F1
3 steel firms indicted 6-6, 504B1
Brink's, Wells Fargo indicted 6-21, 520D3
Cigar cos merger blocked 6-28, 520E3
United Tech's Babcock takeover blocked 7-5, 520D1
Multinatl probes vowed 8-8, 629E3
McDermott wins Babcock bidding war 8-25, 666F3
5 indep oil cos convicted 8-30, 691G2
Westn oil cos settle suit 8-31, 691C3
Record fine levied vs Medusa unit 10-5, 918E2
NY sugar exchng chrgd 10-17, 818G2
Lykes, LTV merger probed 11-4, 943A3
Inco allowed to retain ESB 11-11, 918E3
'71 ITT divestiture order cited 11-14, 879G3-880A1
Sup Ct bars AT&T appeal 11-28, 919B2
NBC accord OKd 12-1, 918B3
UK vs uranium cartel jurisdictn claim 12-1, 1003E3
Hunt oil-suit case refused by Sup Ct 12-5, 938F3
Revere sale to Alcan opposed 12-9, 1004E3

Appointments & Resignations
Babcock confrmd asst atty gen 3-4, 211D1
Bell confrmatn hearings 1-11—1-18, confrmatn delayed 1-20, 34C1; confrmd atty gen 1-25, sworn 1-26, 52G2
Civiletti confrmd asst atty gen 3-4, 211D1; dep atty gen 12-6, 1001D3
Days confrmd asst atty gen 3-4, 211E1
Flaherty confrmd dep atty gen 4-5, 272G2
Flaherty quits as dep atty gen 11-26, 914D2
Olson confrmd asst atty gen 3-18, 211F1

Civil Rights Issues
Dual prosecutn rule modified 2-11, 821B1
FBI ex-official indicted 4-7, 275A2, G2
LA police dept bias chrgd 6-2, 819D2
La cities OK police, fire dept job quotas 6-29, 819F1
Laws to be screened for sex bias 7-18, 669D2
NYS police bias chrgd 9-8, 819B2
Bakke brief filed 9-19, McCree argues before Sup Ct 10-12, 834E3, 835F1
NJ firefighter bias chrgd 10-4, 819B2
Bias suit wins record back pay 10-11, 818G3
4 ex-Houston police indicted 10-20, 820F3, 821A1
ERA deadline extensn ruled legal 11-1, 918E1
Appraisers OKs anti-bias rule 11-11, 898A3
FBI-probe attys ask removal from case 12-7, 940B1

Community Relations Service
Chicanos end Coors boycott 4-8, 819E1

Drug Enforcement Administration
Mex-US drug ring broken by 'Operatn Wishbone' 4-20, 711C3
'78 funds signed 8-2, 667D3
Cocaine traffic estimate disputed 8-29, 972E1
Eur heroin use rptd up 10-17—10-21, 971F3
'Angel dust' health risk rptd 11-1, 972B2
Dole to get file on Torrijos brother 11-16, 912C2

Federal Bureau of Investigation (FBI)—*See separate listing in this section above*

Immigration & Naturalization Service
Speeds Sovt Jews' visas 1-30, 117B2
Carter gets illegal alien plan 4-27, 370F1
'78 funds signed 8-2, 667E3
Border Patrol hike proposed 8-4, 592D1
Haitians in Fla to be freed 11-8, 1019E1
Sovt Jews' quota raised 12-14, 956E1

1978

IBM trust suit rested 4-26, 510C2
Gulf chrgd re uranium cartel 5-9, 346D1-D2
15% lid on oil, gas co coal reserves, 10% lid on uranium backed 5-15, 471C2
CBS suit seeks Fawcett divestiture 6-1, 510E3
Nuclear Exchng exec chrgd 6-2, 449B3
FCC cross-media ban backed by Sup Ct 6-12, 467B3
Sugar refiners settle '74 chrgs 6-12, 511B1
Hosps denied cost containmt exemptn 6-13, 577C2
Mt Hood award vs Greyhound curbed by Sup Ct 6-19, 492B3
Bell backs LTV-Lykes merger 6-21, 492C3
IBM-Memorex case mistrial 7-5, 510G2
Shenefield on '71-77 big merger rise 7-28, 767D1
ITT-Hartford setlmt cited 7-28, 767G1
Occidental seeks Mead takeover 8-11, Mead rejcts 8-18, 767C2, G2
Merger notificatn asked 9-5, trust probes rptd 10-4, 767B1
Copper wire producers sued 9-21, 769B1
Elec cable makers chrgd 9-22, 768G3
Constructn cos, execs chrgd 9-27, 769A1
Elec fuse makers, execs chrgd 9-28, 769C1
Voluntary disclosure plan set, Titanium Metals role cited; '74 law prosecutns, '78 convctns cited 10-4, 768E1-C2
Occidental-Mead merger suit filed 10-11, chrgs expanded 10-25, 895A3
Rockwell, Textron indicted on Singer disclosure 11-1, 935B3
Lykes-LTV merger OK scored by Kennedy, FTC probe asked 11-9; Bell rptd angry; FTC rejcts probe 11-21; shareholders OK merger 12-5, 935C2
AT&T documts order backed by Sup Ct 11-13, 874A3
United Tech-Carrier merger suit filed 11-13, 896D1
Occidental restrained by ct 12-9, ends Mead takeover fight 12-20, 1004D3
Carter vows actn vs oil industry abuses 12-12, 983E2

Drug Enforcement Administration (DEA)
Torrijos drug link data cited by Dole 2-10; Sen discusses 2-21, 120C2
Ex-agents convicted in computer plot 3-10, 380B1
3 Hughes ex-aides indicted 3-16, 6-6, 459B2, E2

Federal Bureau of Investigation—*See separate listing in this section above*

Immigration & Naturalization Service
Unificatn Church '77 deportatns cited 2-22, 295C3
Nazi war criminal prosecutn probe rptd 5-16, 411C1
Alien deportatn trial backed by Sup Ct 6-6, 447E3
Border Patrol seizes W Ger terrorist 7-16, 577A1
Cuba OKs emigratn of dual citizens 8-17, pol prisoners 8-31, 687B1
Cuba ex-prisoners begin arriving 10-21, screening speed up urged 11-13, 880G2
Mex border fence planned 10-24, 818B1
Cuba to free all pol prisoners, terms set 11-22, 12-9; ex-prisoners fly to Miami 12-12, 1016A1
House com seeks illegal alien curbs 12-20, 1010F2

1979

United Tech-Carrier merger set 3-30, 349E3, 350A1
Cardbd mfrs acquitted 4-29, 327B3
Merger curbs rptd backed 5-7, 349F2
Oil firm-shortage link probed 5-15, 361E2
7 shipping cos indicted 6-1, 423B2; fined 6-8, 442A2
United Tech-Carrier merger faulted 6-25, 541D3
Paperbd civil suit setld 6-28, 647G3
Tex offshore port OKd 7-2, 518F2
Kerkorian case dismissed 8-14, 756D1
NBC '77 setlmt challenge refused by Sup Ct 10-1, 768C2
Flying Tiger-Seaboard merger ban asked 10-2, 830C2
'78 LA-area beef-price suit setld 10-22, 985C3
Cincinnati papers joint pact OKd 11-26, 1007G1

Drug Enforcement Administration (DEA)
CBOE raid nabs 10 cocaine traders 2-7, 119C3
Calif bank wire-transfer setup rptd 3-20, 239B2
Fla pot ring rptd broken 5-1, 492F3
Califano backs pot controls 6-6, 492D2
Hell's Angels arrested 6-14, 492B1
Amphetamine abuse detailed 7-16, 571D3
Cocaine trade growth rptd 9-5, 972E2
Cocaine seized in Fla 10-12, 10-14, 819B3

Federal Bureau of Investigation—*See separate listing in this section above*

Immigration & Naturalization Service (INS)
'64-78 illegal alien deportatn data 127A2
Forgn students surveyed, visa probe planned 1-29, 93F2
Mex record Jan crossings rptd 2-11, 127D2
Forgn student abuses detailed 3-2, visa crackdown set 3-8; enrollmt chart 167C2, E2
Refugee bill proposed 3-8; Bell extends Sovt, Indochinese paroles 3-26, 307E3-308D1
Mex deportatn spurs protests 3-9, 3-10, 308E1
Soccer players warned 4-13, rescinded 4-17, 431E3, 432A1
Mex border fence dropped 4-26, 327F2-B3
Castillo resigns 8-10, 630D3
Gay alien curb lifted 8-14, 631G1
Iranian students demonstrate 11-8, 842B3
Iranian status review set 11-13, 863F1; visa checks rptd 11-23, 898F1; 12-13, 935B3
Iranians ordrd to leave 11-16, 11-17, 879D1
Neighborhood raids curbed 11-26, 924B1
Iranian bias probes ordrd 11-27, 898C1
Iranian visa checks ruled illegal 12-11, appealed 12-12, 935F2
Gay alien curb revived 12-26, 992B1
Iranian visa check upheld; deportatns, other data rptd 12-27, 975B2

1980

Getty Oil pay-TV film venture probe set 4-24, 376F2
CBS dispute setld 5-8, 501C3
Paint-resin price setlmt reached 7-22, 917D1
Getty Oil pay-TV film plan draws suit 8-4, 639D3
ABC ties to Spelling-Goldberg rptd probed 8-7—8-8, 640B1
ICC curbs RR collective rate fixing 8-13, 616G2
AT&T begins reorgn 8-20, 648B2
ABC settles suit 8-22, 732E1
Civiletti OKs Chattanooga (Tenn) papers' joint pact 9-2, 732E2
Santa Fe, Southn Pacific RR merger canceled 9-12, 745D2
Rockwell, Serck settle 10-1, 917G1
Civiletti gives final OK to Chatanooga (Tenn) papers' pact 11-6, 907E1
Aluminum indus suit rptd dropped 11-18, 916E3
Flat-rolled steel probe dropped 12-8, 986D1
Goodrich settles suit 12-15, 986C1

Billy Carter Issue
Registers as Libyan agent 7-14, 542A2
Controversy grows 7-22—7-31, 569A1-570D1; Sen probe set 7-24, 549A1
Civiletti withheld info 8-6, probe rptd under way 8-7, 595G1, D2
Sen hears B Carter testimony 8-21, 647E1
Sen probe continues 9-4—9-17, 700D3
Sen probe concluded 9-22—9-24, critical rpt issued 10-2, 763F3
Carter faulted on Sen probe 10-29—11-1, 841F1

Drug Enforcement Administration (DEA)
Darvon to be curbed 4-24, 358A2
Airport detainmt procedure backed by Sup Ct 5-27, 453G3-454A1
Detainmt procedure curbed by Sup Ct 6-30, 511G1

Environment & Pollution
Ark chem-dump suit filed 3-4, 190E3
La chem-dump suit filed 7-15, 558G3
EPA toxic waste suits filed 10-7, 10-9, 825A1, F1
US Steel fined for Pa pollutn 12-22, 987C1

Immigration & Naturalization Service (INS)
125 Iran envoys in US rptd 'missing' 2-4, 122G2
Illegal aliens rptd at 6 mln 2-4, 147F1
N Marianas lose US citizenship 3-7, 495F1
Iranians rptd entering US 3-12, 178F1
Iranian visa extensns rejected 4-12; ouster orders challenged 4-17, 282D3
Haitians reach Fla in record numbers, status delayed by suits 4-13, 294C2
Cuban refugees warned 4-23, granted conditional entry 4-24, 300F3
Cuban refugees pour into US; 55 detained, fines imposed 5-1, 326C1
Cuban refugee processing cntr set 5-1, 326G1
Cuban refugee policy revised 5-15, 361C2
Cuban refugee checks rptd, resetlmt lags 6-2, 420D1
Cuban criminal refugees ordered expelled 6-7, 435A1
Cubans, Haitians granted 6-mo reprieve 6-20, 484F3
Homosexual entry bar repeal backed 6-20, 2000 await processing 7-7, 514A3
Nicaraguans get 3-mo extensn 6-30, 495B2
El Salvador rightist in US illegally 6-30—7-3, 521C3
Haitians win suit, deportatns ordrd halted 7-2, 514E1
Border Patrol rescues El Salvador aliens in Ariz desert 7-4—7-5; search continues 7-7, arrests rptd 7-9, 518E2-C3
Ukrainian youth granted asylum 7-21, 560D1

1976

Law Enforcement Assistance Administration (LEAA)
Violent crime rise rptd 3-2, 336C3
School violence study released 3-18, 263E1
Dem platform text 6-15, 474A1
'77 funds signed 7-14, 534E2
GOP platform text 8-18, 604F1, C2
Extension signed 10-15, 835F1
Marshals Service, U.S.
Tighter A-material security urged 2-2, 115A3
Occupational Safety & Health Administration
GOP platform text 8-18, 603C1, C3, 606C1
Parole Commission, U.S.
Cong clears parole reform 3-3, 181D2
Leary paroled 4-20, released 6-7, 424G1
Alters crime ratings 10-4, 796F3
Political Payments Issues
Defns contracting gift prosecutn rejctd 1-11, 71C1
Gulf paymts probe rptd 2-4, 133F3
Forgn payoff disclosure plans detailed 3-5, 199G3, 200F1
Lockheed data pacts 3-23, 3-30, 4-20, 286B1, E1
Dutch get Lockheed info 4-14, 322B2
Lockheed Australia payoff chrgd 4-29, 322A2
Ford submits forgn paymts legis 8-3, 668D2
Levi rpt on Kelley favors, gifts 9-4, 666D2
Probes US Steel gifts to congressmen 9-24, 722C3
Criminal probe task force named 10-14, 985B3
S Korea influence peddling probe rptd 10-24—12-1, 898D3-900B2
Gurney acquitted 10-27, 846B1
Watergate Special Prosecutor—*See also RUFF, Charles; for Watergate Issue, see under 'W'*
Permanent office not cleared 10-2, 884D1

1977

Korean Scandal
S Korea influence peddling probe cited 1-19, 55A2
Korean lobbying probe cited 6-5—6-9, 442F1, C2, F2
2 Amers in S Korea rptd subpoenaed 6-18, 556B3
S Korea pres mansn watch rptd 6-19, 556D3
Carter backs probe, Bell sees prosecutns 7-18, 556D2
Lobbying info sharing agreed 8-3, 688D2
Park indicted, extraditn sought 9-6, 687D2, F3
Rep Guyer denies Korea lobbying link 9-27, 773G3, F3★
'70 Pentagon knowledge of lobbying rptd 10-12, 816E3
Park interrogatn bid fails 10-16—10-20, 816D1
Derwinski KCIA defector tip-off rptd 10-28, 816F3
Park testimony deal OKd 12-30, 1002A3
Lance Probe
Lance probe asked 9-6, 689F3, 690D1
Lance on '76 probe end 9-15, 701G1, C2
Special panel set up 9-19, 719A1
Carter on campaign funds probe 9-21, 718G1
Law Enforcement Assistance Administration (LEAA)
Com issues terrorism rpt 3-2, 483F3
Pot decriminalizatn study rptd 3-31, 332G2
'76 death row populatn rptd 5-5, 593F3
NH A-protest costs rejctd 5-19, 410D1
LA Police Dept funds threatnd 6-2, 819D2
Regional offices to close 6-20, study urges reorganizatn 6-30, 630A2, D2
'78 funds signed 8-2, 667E3
Narcotics & Dangerous Drugs, Bureau of (defunct)
CIA mind-control tests revealed 8-1—8-9, 611C1
CIA mind-control tests probed 9-2—9-21, 721F1, B3
Prisons, Bureau of
Fire preventn study begun 6-27, 604G1

1978

Korean Scandal
House seeks Park testimony 1-4—1-23, 64A1
Park testimony deal signed 1-10, 1-11, terms rptd 1-13, 63G2, A3
Park queried in Seoul 1-13—2-1, 63F2-G3
Nixon Admin cover-up probe rptd 1-26, 63E2
Park testimony rptd 3-1, 203E3
Ex-rep Hanna pleads guilty 3-17, 203E3
Kissinger: notified dept of allegatns 4-20, 280B1
Hanna sentncd, calls offcls 'overzealous' 4-24, 323F3-324A1
Civiletti sees probe end near 6-1, 432G2
Jaworski notes prosecutns 8-7, 605A1
Sen asks perjury probe 10-16, 832C1
Law Enforcement Assistance Administration (LEAA)
Gambling legalizatn impact rptd 4-2, 434E2
Study finds arson rise 6-4, 440B2
Carter proposes revisn 7-10, 525C1
Victimless crime study issued 9-11, 842B2
Inner city crime survey rptd 10-16, 842A2
Marshals Service, U.S.
Taft-Hartley ordrd served in coal strike 3-9, 159D2; effected 3-13, 181G2
Narcotics & Dangerous Drugs, Bureau of (Defunct)
Drugs rptd supplied to McCarthy 11-19, 943C2
Parole Commission
Ehrlichman freed 4-27, 320C2
Hearst pardon petitioned 9-26, 824B1
Political Payments—*See also 'Korean Scandal' in this section above*
Shipping rebate probe delay barred 2-3, 184D3
Flood influence-selling rptd probed 2-19, 240E1
Seatrain, others plead guilty in shipping probe 3-16, 184C3
Williams, Control Data plead guilty for forgn paymts 3-26, 4-26, 448C3
Ford Indonesia bribe probe rptd 4-25, 390C3
ICC fires Kyle 6-7, 570G1
NYC rabbi sentncd in Flood case 6-22, 500E3
Vesco 'pol fix' rpt denied 9-10, 720B1
Fairchild Industries indicted 9-18, 808C3
ICC ex-offcl indicted 9-22, pleads not guilty 9-29, 770E2
Westinghouse guilty plea barred 10-24, payoff figure named 10-26, co fined 11-20, 961A3-D3
Schlitz sued, pleads no contest 11-1, 877E1
Diggs sentenced 11-20, 900B2
Prisons, Bureau of
Mexico prisoner exchng ends 3-6, 290F1
Ga slaying probe opens 4-10, 396A3
Ex-dir Bennett dies 11-19, 972E2

1979

Korean Scandal
Bayh perjury probe closed 1-5, 4A3
Connell prosecutn dropped 4-16, 283D2
Hancho Kim indictmt dismissed 6-15, 521A2
Park indictmt dropped 8-16, 630D1
Missing ex-KCIA chief's probe begun 10-25, 810D3
Law Enforcement Assistance Administration (LEAA)
'73-77 crime survey rptd 1-18, 118G3-119C1
Hartford crime-control progrm rptd 2-25, 156C3
Corp crime study funds asked 3-8, 240B1
'78 inmate totals rptd 6-21, 548A2
Trial speedup for robbers urged 7-22, 655D3
Marshals Service, U.S.
Prison escapee tracking set 10-1, 771B1
Parole Commission
Wis U '70 bomber freed 1-11, 102F2
Cianfrani granted '80 parole 1-11, 102A3
Galante release ordrd 2-27, 156F1
Galante hearing delayed, bail granted 3-23, 240G2
NJ ex-offcls subject to rejailing by Sup Ct 6-4, 439A1
Addonizio paroled 10-2, 891F1
Political Payments—*See also 'Korean Scandal' in this section above*
SEC, Justice chrgs vs Grumman overlap 1-4, 16G1
Japan probe of 2 Lockheed ex-aides dropped 2-15, 306C1
Eilberg pleads guilty 2-24, 152C2
2 oil execs chrgd re '76 Qatar bribe, Lance '78 influence role alleged 4-9, 305E3-306C1
Lockheed guilty in Japan payoffs, fined 6-1, 422A3
Seagram unit admits Pa bribery 9-27, 809E3
McDonnell Douglas indicted 11-9, 886C2
Prisons, Bureau of
Va inmate gets rape setlmt 3-17, 316D2
Lake Placid Olympic facilities stir controversy 4-24, 798E2
PR prisoner's death probe ordrd 11-23, 904A3

1980

Iranian jailed protesters deportatn sought 8-5, 586D2
Dem platform plank adopted 8-13, 615C1
Fla to get $16.8 mln for refugee relief 8-13, 617E1
Ariz alien retrial sought 8-29, 713A3
Cuban flotilla boat prosecutns set 9-18, 742A2
Ct bars House deportatn res 12-24, 989A2
Marshals Service, U.S.
EPA aides detained at Love Canal 5-19, 387E1
Eglin AF base security tightened 5-26, 396B1
Parole Commission
Estes '83 parole rptd 1-3, 64G3
Class actn 'moot' standard redefined by Sup Ct 3-19, 250E1
Political Payments
Civilleti vs Miller-Textron spec prosecutor 2-5, 92B2
Brilab probe rptd 2-8—2-9, 111C3
Flood pleads guilty 2-26, 190G1
Civiletti rejects Miller spec prosecutor 3-11, 185C2
Ford Indonesia probe rptd dropped 3-13, 224C3
GSA kickback scandal funds recovery suits filed 3-17, 228F1
Forgn paymts law guidance offered, SEC vs 3-24, 227G1-C2
Vesco grand jury ends, no indictmts brought 4-1, 251B3
Jenrette indicted 6-13, 454E1
Diggs suit dropped 7-24, 908D3
SEC pledges forgn paymts cooperatn 8-28, 958B1
School Integration & Busing
Austin busing plan set 1-3, 5C3
South Bend desegregatn plan set 2-8, 114D2
Houston schl desegregatn suit filed 5-15, 559C1
Chicago OKs integratn agrmt 9-24, 724F1
Chicago schls black quotas case dismissed by Sup Ct 10-20, 807C2
Civiletti scores antibusing rider 11-17, Reagan backs 11-18, 880F3

1976

LABOR, Department of
Cong overrides funds veto 1-27, 1-28, 69A2
House passes public jobs bill 2-10, 134C3
OKs Trade Act aid to steel, auto workers 3-1—4-26, 348E2-B3
Releases prison job training rpt 3-9, 271D2
Usery on Teamsters pact 4-2, 248D3
Ford bars shoe import curb 4-16, 321G3
Kissinger intl econ plan opposed 5-6, 317E1
Clears UMW aides re funds 5-18, 378G3
Cong clears added funds 5-19, 411E3
OKs Trade Act aid for some Ford workers, rpts total aid 6-7, 431A2-C2
Usery at Teamsters conv 6-14, 436D1
Cited in Dem platform text 6-15, 470A1
Blackman questns ILO rpt 6-18, 449F3
Teamster pensn fund probe rptd; Usery defends conv talk 6-24, 7-1, 492B2
Rpts Gulf bias setlemt 7-16; actn vs Uniroyal 8-6; 2 glass cos 9-11, 943C3, G3, 944C2
Westinghouse strike setld 7-20, 536D3
Usery calls rubber strike talks 8-5, 647C3
Contractors job-bias rules proposed 9-15, 884A3
Cong expands pub svs jobs program 9-22, 728C1; signed 10-1, 982F1
'77 funds vetoed 9-29, overridden 9-30, 726F1
Jobless benefits revisn signed 10-20, 788G1
Sets coke oven emissns curb 10-20, 847E3-848A1
Job exam bias rules set 11-17, 884C2
OKs Trade Act aid to AMC workers 11-17, 885D2
Carter names liaison 11-23, 881B3
Appointments & Resignations
Dunlop resigns as secy 1-14, 23B1
Usery confrmd secy 2-4, 110F1
Martinez confrmd to Community Svcs 4-7, 262D3
Moskow confrmd undersecy 5-12, 412G1
Read confrmd asst secy 5-12, 412A2
Marshall named secy 12-21, 956E2, 957D3

1977

LABOR, Department of
Prudential job-hiring plan rptd 1-10, 278C3
Ford budget proposals 1-17, 30B1, B2, 32F2, 33C2
Jobs effort for vets planned 1-27, 52B2
6 states get recovery fund offer 2-1, 75G3
Carter visits employes 2-9, 110G2
Hartford Fire age-bias suit rptd 2-9, 279B1
Meany lauds Marshall 2-21, 153G2
Marshall rpts net worth 2-25, 148D1
USW election role cited 2-28, 130D3
Teamsters revise pensn posts 3-13, 195C1-C2
Nev union fund suit filed 3-30, 261F3
Poverty level raised 4-1, 302A2
Ohio Teamster fund sued 4-4, 280B2
Carter energy plan 4-20, 292B1
Worker benzene exposure curbed 4-29, 345D1
'77 supplemental funds signed 5-4, 339F1
AMC sued on age bias 5-20, 422A2
O'Neill vs fund bill veto 6-2, Carter agrees to sign 6-15, 459A3
House OKs '78 funds 6-17, 478B1
Sen OKs '78 funds 6-29, 515E2
Labor law reform proposed 7-18, 555C2
Marshall says Teamsters fund sound 7-18, 558C2
Female constructn job quota urged 8-16, 819E2
Bars Phila co contract re bias 8-25, 669F2
Sen votes pregnancy benefits, cost estimate cited 9-16, 738E1
A&P overtime suit filed 9-27, 778C2
Abortn issue delays funds bill 10-1, Califano urges passage 10-11, 786D2
UMW vote probed ended 10-11, 937E2
US withdraws from ILO 11-1, 829A1
Mine safety supervisn assumed 11-9, 856A1
USW vote probe ended 11-11, 899F2
Phila contractor reinstated 11-23, 979F2
Marshall 'listening' sessns with UMW pres, coal indus rep 12-6, 937E1
'78 funds clear Cong 12-7, 958C2, E3; signed 12-9, 1001F2
Marshall chairs OECD labor mtg 12-15—12-16, 998F3
Job listing drops sexist titles, age refs 12-17, 979G2
OPEC price freeze hailed 12-21, 973A2
Appointments
Bingham confrmd asst secy 3-18, 272F2
Burkhardt confrmd asst secy 3-18, 272F2

1978

LABOR, Department of
Ohio Teamster fund bd revised 1-3, 4E2
Teamster pensn fund suit filed 2-1, 83B1
Coal strike setlmt pressed; White House talks open, deadlock continues 2-3—2-16, 104D3-105F1
Black lung eligibility bill clears Cong 2-15, 125A2; signed 3-1, 218B2
Top-paid labor ldrs rptd 2-20, 5-15, 365D1
Carter seeks job-bias unit reorganizatn 2-23, 123G3-124B1
Coal pact ratificatn urged 2-26, 3-1, strikers rejct 3-4—3-5, 159G3-160D1; new talks rptd 3-10, 181F3
Coal industry study planned 3-25, 217A2
Educ programs excluded from proposed Cabt-level dept 4-14, 279E1, B2
Legal fee liability case review denied by Sup Ct 4-17, 308D3
Constructn work for women expanded 5-7, 554G2
Southn constructn pact hailed 5-22, 429A3
Pvt-sector youth jobs progrm planned 5-23, 405A1
'79 funds OKd by House; abortn, quota curbs included 6-13, 445C2-G3
Cotton dust rules issued 6-19, 471D3-472E1
Secrecy classificatn powers cut 6-29, 508E1
Tonelli, 4 others indicted 7-19, 598G3
Teamster pensn funds scored 8-14, 625D1
Oil reserve storage sites scored 8-16, 701D3
Teamster talks role forecast 8-23, 680B3
Marshall addresses USW conv 9-18, 715E2
Marshall calls rail strike talks to DC 9-27, 809B3
Carter scores budget bill 9-28, 751G3
Employer retaliatn case declined by Sup Ct 10-2, 751C1
Rural health progrm planned 10-2, 770E1
'79 funds clear Cong 10-14, Carter signs 10-18, 873F1
Teamster fund trustees sued 10-16, 792D1-A3
Shiskin dies 10-28, 888E3
Teamster fund suit set back 11-1, 11-7, 899C1
Coal miners sex bias suit setld 12-26, 1006F2
Employment Standards Administration
Contract Compliance Office probes coal indus bias, orders affirmative actn 5-30, 565A3

1979

LABOR, Department of
SEC role in pensn plans barred by Sup Ct 1-16, 32D2
Armed svcs review 'sexist' language 1-19, 89D3
Wage-price guidelines reinterpreted 4-3, 251B2
Poverty levels raised 4-9, 283C3
Hoffmann-La Roche NJ unit hikes women's pay 5-13, 482G3
Teamster pact ratified 5-18, 384B3
State age bias filings required by Sup Ct, time limit barred 5-21, 400D2
Welfare plan presented 5-23, 384F1
Merck OKs minority jobs plan 6-26, 521F1
Weber case Sup Ct ruling lauded 6-27, 477A3
Loeb settles pensn suit 7-9, 640E3
Uniroyal bias suit setld 10-23, 885F2
Marshall at AFL-CIO conv 11-15, 885F1
'80 continuing funds res clears Cong 11-16, Carter signs 11-20, 900B2
Secy on Chrysler loan bd 12-21, 981G3
Contract Compliance, Office of Federal
Rougeau on Sears contract cutoff 4-24, 366B1

1980

LABOR, Department of
$2 bln youth training progrm asked 1-10, 16C2
Kellogg settles bias chrgs 2-6, 115A3
Youth jobless rate said higher 2-28, 228A3
Ct limits children's harvest work, pesticide study plan cited 3-20, 227C1, F1
Firestone cited for job bias 3-21, 251G2
'80, '81 jobless aid to auto workers miscalculated 4-9, 330G1
Child labor law fines upheld by Sup Ct 4-28, 369A1
Firestone US contracts voided 7-15, 560B3
Auto workers aid OKd 8-14, 647E3
GAO scores Teamster probe 8-25, 704C3
Jobless benefits extended 9-8, 684A1
UAW seat on AMC bd proposed 9-17, 725F1
UAW jobless aid progrm rptd 10-14, 823G2
Jobless aid re imports rejctd 11-5, 870B2
Schering settles bias case 12-14, 962D3
Reagan names Donovan secy 12-16, 955F2
Contract Compliance, Office of Federal
Ford settles bias case 11-25, 899B3

1976

Labor Statistics, Bureau of—*See also 'Statistics' below*
Shiskin on jobless rate 3-5, 198D3
'75 injury, illness, death rpt 12-9, 950F2
Occupational Safety & Health Administration
'75 injury, illness, death rpt 12-9, 950F2

Statistics
Jobless index described 21C1
CPI described 90E2
Dec, '75 jobless rate 1-9, 20F2-21C1
Dec '75 WPI 1-9, 21C2
Dec, '75 CPI 1-21, 90E1
'75, 1st ¼ wage gains 1-23, 4-25, 306B3
'75 strike data 1-26, 137A2
Jan jobless rate, '75 revised 2-5, 152A3
Jan WPI 2-13, CPI 2-20, 168B1, B2
Feb WPI 3-4, 199B1
Feb jobless rate 3-5, 198A3
Feb CPI 3-19, 215E1
March WPI 4-1, 262F3
March jobless rate 4-2, 263A1
March real pay 4-21, 306C2
1st ¼ productivity 4-26, 376F1
1st ¼ strike activity 4-28, 307F1-A2
Revised regional jobless list 5-5, 347D2
Apr WPI 5-6, jobless rate 5-7, 347C1-D2
Apr CPI, real pay 5-21, 375D1
May jobless rate 6-4, 412C2
May WPI 6-4, 412A3
1st ¼, 6 mo employmt costs 6-18, 494F1
Employment cost index described 6-18, 494D2
May CPI 6-22, 453G2
May real pay 6-22, 453D3
June jobless rate 7-2, 494A1
June WPI 7-9, 519B1
June 2d ¼ CPI 7-21, 536C2
June real pay 7-21, 536E2
2d ¼ wage gains, 1st ¼ revised 7-23, 567E1
2d ¼ productivity, labor costs; 1st ¼ '76 revised 7-26, 567D2
July jobless rate 8-6, 586F2
July WPI 8-12, 635A2
July CPI 8-20, 635E1
Aug WPI 9-2, 667C3
Aug jobless rate 9-3, 667C2
Aug CPI 9-21, 708D2
Sept WPI 10-7, 769B3
Sept jobless rate 10-8, 768E1
Sept CPI 10-21, 805F2-A3
3d ¼ wage gains, 2d ¼ revised 10-22, 805G3
3d ¼ productivity, labor costs; 2d ¼ revised 10-27, 918D1
Oct WPI 11-4, jobless 11-5, 846D1, B2
Oct CPI 11-19, 884F3
Male-female earnings gap 11-28, 943F1
2d, 3d ¼ employmt costs 11-30, 918C2
Nov WPI 12-3, 918F3
Nov jobless rate 12-5, 917D3
Nov CPI 12-21, 958G1

LABOR Relations Board, National—*See NATIONAL Labor Relations Board below*
LAND Management, Bureau of—*See under INTERIOR in this section above*
LAW Enforcement Assistance Administration—*See under JUSTICE in this section above*
LEGAL Services Corp.—*See under 'L'*
LEGISLATION—*See also CONGRESS above; LEGISLATION under FORD*
Dole urges veto process revisn 9-3, 665G3
LIBRARY of Congress
Chile aid rptdly continues 1-26, 99C2
Sen OKs copyright revisn 2-10, 152D2
US-Sovt arms study released 2-10, 182G2
House funds Madison Memorial 2-24, 171B1
'75 Sen subcom study rptd 4-4, 247G1-B2
Kissinger donates papers 12-20, 980F2
LOBBYING & Lobbyists—*See under CONGRESS in this section above*
MANAGEMENT & Budget, Office of—*See BUDGET in this section above*

1977

Marshall confirmatn delayed 1-20, 34C1; confrmd secy 1-26, sworn 1-27, 52D2, B3
Packer confrmd asst secy 3-18, 211F1 ★
Labor Statistics, Bureau of—*See 'Statistics' below*
Manpower Administration
Job Corps '77 budget levels set 3-3, 174D1
Carter asks Job Corps funds 3-9, 173G1
Mine Safety & Health Administration
Created 11-9, 856A1
Occupational Safety & Health Administration (OSHA)
Asbestos workers sue HEW 2-15, 422C2
Bingham confrmd asst secy 3-18, 272F2
Sup Ct backs penalties 3-23, 276F1
GAO study scores 3-23, 280G1-A2
Refocused from 'nitpicking' 5-19, 422F1
DBCP curbed 9-8, 723F2, G2
Chicago 7 defendant gets post 9-30, 808B2
RR regulatn dispute review refused 10-3, 760F2
To categorize carcinogens 10-3, 778E1
To drop 1,100 rules 12-5, 937B3
Fines curbed by Cong 12-7, 958D3
Probes grain explosns 12-28, 1023A2

Statistics
Jobless index described 37F3-38E1
CPI described 78C1
Dec '76 jobless rate 1-12, CEA revises 1-18, 37E2, F3
'76, Dec WPI 1-12, 38E2
'76, Dec CPI 1-19, 77E3-78B1
'76, ¼ '76 productivity, labor costs; 3d ¼ revised 1-26, 130A1
Jan jobless rate 2-4, 110G3
Jan WPI 2-11, 111A2
Feb state jobless claims 2-16, 176C2
Jan CPI 2-18, 129A3
Labor cost index described 154F2
'76, 4th ¼ labor costs 3-3, 154C2
Feb jobless rate 3-4, 176E1-B2
Feb WPI 3-10, 176D2
Workweek data 3-18, 194G2-A3
Feb CPI 3-18, 214F3-215D1
March jobless rate 4-1, 252C1
March WPI 4-7, 274A1
March CPI 4-21, 324G1
1st ¼ productivity, labor costs; '76, 4th ¼ revised 4-27, 339F3
April WPI 5-5, 383F2
April jobless rate 5-6, 383D3
'60-61, '72-73 family spending 5-10, 423D2
Apr CPI 5-22, 406G2
May jobless rate 6-3, 444F3
May WPI 6-3, 445G1
May CPI 6-22, 481F3
Jobless, WPI, CPI indexes released earlier 6-28, 554D2
June jobless rate 7-8, 554B1
June WPI 7-8, 554F1
June CPI 7-21, 554B2
2d ¼ productivity, labor costs; 1st ¼ revised 7-29, 704D1
July jobless rate 8-5, 611A3
July WPI, June revised 8-11, 628F3
July CPI 8-19, 651D1
July black youth jobless rate 8-31, 692C2
2d ¼ employmt costs, 1st ¼ revised 8-31, 704A2
Aug WPI 9-1, 692A1
Finished-goods index, June-Aug data 9-1, 692C1
Aug jobless rate 9-2, 692E1
Aug CPI 9-21, 722G1
Sept WPI 10-6, 776D3
Sept finished goods index 10-6, 776G3
Sept jobless rate 10-7, 776A3
Sept CPI 10-21, 817D3
3d ¼ productivity, unit labor costs; 2d ¼ revised 10-27, 836E1
3d ¼ wage, benefit hikes 10-28, 836C1
Oct WPI 11-3, 836C2
Oct finished-good index 11-3, 836D2
Oct jobless rate 11-4, 858D2
Oct CPI 11-22, 898E3
3d ¼ employmt costs 11-30, 941C3
Nov jobless rate 12-3, 961G2
Nov WPI 12-8, 961D2
Nov finished goods index 12-8, 961F2
Nov CPI 12-21, 977D1

LABOR Relations Board, National—*See NATIONAL Labor Relations Board below*
LAND Management, Bureau of—*See under INTERIOR in this section above*
LAW Enforcement Assistance Administration—*See under JUSTICE in this section above*
LEAA—*See JUSTICE—Law Enforcement Assistance Administration above*
LEGAL Services Corporation
'78 funds signed 8-2, 667F3
Extension signed 12-28, 1002C2
LEGISLATION—*See also under CONGRESS in this section above; also CARTER—LEGISLATION; FORD, Gerald—Congress*
US Code to be screened for sex bias 7-18, 669C2
LIBRARY of Congress—*See under 'L'*
LOBBYING & Lobbyists—*See under CONGRESS in this section above*
MANPOWER Administration—*See under LABOR in this section above*

1978

Contract Compliance Office powers broadened 10-6, 811F2
Labor Statistics, Bureau of—*See 'Statistics' below*
Manpower Administration
Job Corps rural health progrm role planned 10-2, 770F1
Occupational Safety & Health Administration (OSHA)
Acrylonitrile standard issued 1-16, 85F3
Benzene exposure rule issued, API scores 2-2, 85G2, D3
Tex, La '77 blast violatns rptd, fines proposed 2-23, 5-16; grain dust blamed 3-30, 636D2
Texaco fined for '77 Tex fire 3-2, 212F3
DBCP final rule set 3-15, 186F2-A3
Warrantless searches curbed by Sup Ct 5-23, 405B2
W Va scaffold collapse negligence chrgd 6-8, 459A3
Cotton dust rules issued 6-19, 472A1, E1
Grain elevator checks eased 7-18, 636C2
Acrylonitrile rule finalized 9-29, 753G3
Benzene exposure rule upset 10-5, 833G3-834A1
928 rules dropped 10-24, 833C3
Lead exposure rule set, indus challenges 11-13, 899A3, C3
Task force urges changes 12-8, 984E3
Microwave safety scored 12-11, 962B3
Statistics
Jobless index described 50G3
Dec. '77 jobless rate, Aug-Nov revised 1-11, 12B2, 50F2; benefits cut 1-26, 50F2, 51B2
'77, Dec WPI, finished-goods index 1-12, CPI 1-20, 51C2, B3, D3
'77 productivity, labor costs 1-26, 128B2
'77 labor wage, benefit gains 1-27, 128D2
Jan jobless rate 2-3, 127B3
Jan WPI, finished-goods index 2-10, 128E1, A2
New CPIs described 222A2
New CPIs released; Jan, Feb inflatn 2-27, 3-28, 222B1
Dec '77, Jan, Feb real earnings 2-27, 3-28, 222G1
Feb finished-goods index 3-9, 222B3
Feb jobless rate 3-10, 221F3-222B1
Mar finished goods index, Jan-Mar intermediate goods index, WPI 4-6, 262E2
Mar jobless rate 4-7, 262B2
1860-1978 consumer prices 427G1
Poverty level revised 4-19, 684D2
1st ¼ productivity, labor costs rptd; '77, 4th ¼ revised 4-25, 345G1
'76, '77 living costs, income per cities ranked 4-26, 349D1
1st ¼ wage, benefits; '77 revised 4-27, 389C2
Mar CPIs 4-28, 344F3
Apr finished-goods index 5-4, 344C3
Apr jobless rate 5-5, 345C1
'77 4th ¼; 1st ¼ employmt costs 5-30, 429D1
Coal indus personnel 5-30, 565B3
Apr CPIs 5-31, 428A3
May wholesale finished, intermediate, crude prices 6-2, 428E3
May jobless rate 6-2, 429C2
'77 industry productivity 6-14, 469G3-470B1
May CPIs 6-30, 506F3-507A1
Jan, May purchasing power; '72 erosn 6-30, 507B1
June jobless rate 7-7, 552E2
June producer price indexes (wholesale finished, intermediate, crude goods) 7-7, 552B3
Extended jobless aid in 9 states, PR rptd 7-10, 552A3; cut to 4 states, PR 8-4, 607D3
'70-78 2-income families 7-24, 679F3
2d ¼ productivity, labor costs; '77, 1st ¼ '78 revised 7-27, 606C3
June CPIs 7-28, 607E1
July jobless rate 8-4, 607G2-D3
July producer prices 8-10, 607B2
July CPIs 8-29, 679A3
2d ¼ employmt costs 8-30, 680A2
Aug jobless rate 9-1, 679C3
Aug producer prices 9-8, 717F1
Aug CPIs 9-26, 752C1
Aug real earnings down 9-26, 752E1
Sept producer prices 10-5, 790G1
'67-78 minority-white earnings gap 10-19, 812G2
Sept CPI, real earnings 10-27, 864C1
3d ¼ productivity, labor costs; 2d ¼ revised 10-27, 864D2
Oct producer prices 11-2, 864G1
Oct jobless rate 11-3, 864A3
Oct CPI 11-28, 918A3
3d ¼ employmt costs 11-30, 1003D2
Nov producer prices 12-7, 957E3
Nov jobless rate 12-8, 958D1
Nov CPIs 12-22, 1003F1
Nov real earnings 12-22, 1003B2

LAND Management, Bureau of—*See under INTERIOR in this section above*
LAW Enforcement Assistance Administration—*See under JUSTICE in this section above*
LEGISLATION—*See under CONGRESS in this section above; also CARTER—LEGISLATION*
LIBRARY of Congress
DC voting study cited 8-22, 661D1
'77 consumer utility bills rptd up 9-17, 718D3
LOBBYING & Lobbyists—*See under CONGRESS in this section above*
MANPOWER Administration—*See under LABOR in this section above*

1979

Occupational Safety & Health Administration (OSHA)
Business rpts rule compliance costs 3-14, 230A3
Magistrate search warrants case refused by Sup Ct 10-1, 768C1

Statistics
Producer price indexes described 32D3
Jobless index described 34G1
'78, Dec producer prices 1-11, 32B3
Dec '78 jobless index, '77-78 job gains 1-14, 34B1
Dec '78 CPI 1-24, 73E1
Dec '78 real earnings 1-24, 73C2
Jan jobless rate, '77-79 women workers, 2-income families 2-2, 110C3
'78, 4th 1/4 productivity, labor costs, 3d 1/4 revised; '48-77 data 2-9, 110G3
Jan producer prices 2-9, 111D1
Jan CPI 2-23, 151A2
'78, 4th 1/4, 3d 1/4 employmt costs 2-28, 183B1
Feb jobless rate 3-8, 182A3
Feb producer prices 3-8, 182D3
Feb CPI 3-25, 252D1
Mar producer prices 4-5, 252B1
Mar jobless rate 4-6, 280F2
Mar CPI 4-26, 324D3
1st 1/4 productivity, labor costs; '78, 4th 1/4 revised 4-30, 362F2
Apr producer prices 5-3, 325B1
Apr jobless rate 5-4, 362B3
Apr CPI, real earnings 5-25, 402D3
1st 1/4 employmt costs 5-31, 463E3
May jobless rate 6-1, 422C2
May producer prices 6-7, 422G1
May CPI 6-26, 480A3
June jobless rate 7-6, 516C3
June producer prices 7-6, 516F3-517A1
June CPI 7-26, 556D3
June spendable earnings 7-26, 557B1
1st 1/2 labor wage gains 7-29, 578B1
2d 1/4 productivity, labor costs; 1st 1/4 revised 7-30, 577B3
July jobless rate 8-3, 621E2
July producer prices 8-9, 621C2
July CPI, real earnings 8-25, 646B2
2d 1/4 employmt costs 8-30, 701A2
'76, '78 union membership 8-31, 666B1
Aug jobless rate 9-7, 680E3
Aug producer prices 9-7, 680G3
Aug CPI 9-25, 725B2
Aug gas, heating oil prices 9-25, 725D2
Sept producer prices 10-4, 766C1
Sept jobless rate 10-5, 766A2
Sept CPI 10-26, 827E3
Oct producer prices 11-1, 828B1
Oct jobless rate 11-2, 866C3
Oct CPI, real earnings 11-27, 903E2
3d 1/4 productivity, labor costs; 1st, 2d 1/4 revised 11-28, 940F2
3d 1/4 employmt costs 11-29, 922E2
Nov producer prices 12-6, 921D3
Nov jobless rate 12-7, 941D1
Nov CPI 12-21, 984B2
Nov real earnings down 12-21, 984F2
'79 city living costs 12-28, 990F3

LAND Management, Bureau—*See under INTERIOR in this section below*
LAW Enforcement Assistance Administration—*See under JUSTICE in this section above*
LEGISLATION—*See under CONGRESS in this section above; also CARTER–LEGISLATION*
LIBRARY of Congress
Contract denial re wage-price enforcemt seen illegal 2-12, 127E3
Kissinger phone records case accepted by Sup Ct 4-16, 302C3
LOBBYING & Lobbyists—*See under CONGRESS in this section above*

1980

Occupational Safety & Health Administration (OSHA)
Workplace cancer rules set 1-16, 36A1
Hazardous work refusals backed by Sup Ct 2-26, 188C1
Va shipyd abuses chrgd 2-27, 147C3
Connally cites in 'basic speech' 3-7, 184C3
Chlorine rules partial stay granted by Sup Ct 5-19, 440A3
Health data access eased 5-21, 404E3
Benzene standard rejected by Sup Ct 7-2, 510D3
Auto plant lead, arsenic curbs to ease 7-8, 505E1
Tex chem workers cancer cases rptd 7-24, 584E2
Cotton dust standard case accepted by Sup Ct 10-6, 782C1
Carter, Reagan TV debate 10-28, 815A2
Lead exposure rule stayed by Sup Ct 12-8, 937G1

Statistics
Producer price indexes described 15B1
Jobless index described 33A3-34A2
CPI described 75F3-77E1
'79, Dec producer prices 1-10, 14F3
Dec '79 jobless index, '78-79 job gains 1-11, 33F2
Dec, '79 CPI 1-25, 75B2
'71-79 CPI rise 1-25, 75D2
'79, 4th 1/4 productivity, labor costs 1-28, 77E1
Jan jobless rate 2-1, 92B2
Jan producer prices 2-15, 126B2
Jan CPI 2-22, 144E1
'79, 4th 1/4 employmt costs 2-28, 168D1
Feb producer prices 3-7, 182A2
Feb jobless rate 3-7, 182C3
Feb CPI 3-25, 222A2
Mar producer prices 4-4, 263A1
Mar jobless rate 4-4, 263D1
Mar CPI 4-22, 305A2
1st 1/4 productivity, labor costs 4-25, 329D1
1st 1/4 labor wage gains 4-25, 329G1
Apr jobless rate 5-2, 344E2
Apr producer prices 5-9, 367D2
Apr CPI 5-23, 400F2
1st 1/4 employmt costs, new calculatn method set 5-29, 400D3
May jobless rate 6-6, 437C2
May producer prices 6-6, 437B3
May CPI 6-24, 480F3
June jobless rate 7-3, 513D2
June producer prices 7-8, 513B3
June CPI 7-23, 556C1
2d 1/4 productivity, 1st 1/4 revised 7-28, 574A2
July jobless rate 8-1, 599D2
July producer prices 8-15, 630G2
July CPI 8-22, 648A3
Aug jobless rate 9-5, 683E1-684A1
Aug producer prices 9-5, 684D1
Aug CPI 9-23, 741A1
Sept producer prices 10-3, 783F1
Sept jobless rate 10-3, 783C2
Sept CPI 10-24, 823A3
Oct producer prices, jobless rate 11-7, 866G3, 867C1
Oct CPI 11-25, 897A3
2d 1/4, 3d 1/2 employmt costs, compensatn index 11-28, 938E1, A2
Nov producer prices 12-5, 937B3
Nov jobless rate 12-5, 938B1
Nov CPI 12-23, 983C3

LIBRARY Of Congress
'Guest worker' study rptd 2-13, 147C2
Kissinger records access blocked by Sup Ct 3-3, 209D3

1976

MARINE Corps
Brookings study urges reorganizatn 2-2, 95B3
Jackson on Leb role 3-30, 245B3
House OKs '77 arms, manpower authorizatn 4-9, 283F2
Sen OKs '77 arms, manpower authorizatn 5-26, 411B2
Reagan cites '58 Leb role 6-3, 410G1
'77 arms, manpower authorizatn signed 7-14, 517A2, D2
GOP platform text cites 8-18, 609B1
'77 manpower funds signed 9-22, 707D3
Blacks assault whites, KKK link probed 11-13—12-6, 983C1
Aircraft—*See under ARMAMENTS under 'A'*
Amnesty Issue—*See under ARMED Forces above*
Recruit Issues
McClure dies 3-13, Bronson, other ct-martials ordered 4-28, 378A1
House subcom probe opens 4-1, 378B2
Subcom probe continues 5-25—6-9, 435E2-D3
Rees suspensn rptd 5-28, 435E3
Recruitmt bias cover-up chrgd 6-7, 454A2
Bronson ct martial starts 6-14, 435D3
Bronson trial dvpts 6-16—6-23, acquitted 6-28, 493B2
'74-76 mistreatmt data rptd 6-27, 493A3
Recruit deaths, abuse convictns rptd 7-10—8-12, 586G3
Sgt convicted in McClure death 7-19, 586D3
Final chrgs in McClure death 8-18, 942A2
Reserve Forces—*See under ARMED Forces above*

MARINE Fisheries Service, National—*See 'National Oceanic & Atmospheric Administration' under COMMERCE in this section above*
MARITIME Commission, Federal—*See FEDERAL Maritime Commission above*
MARSHALS Service, U.S.—*See under JUSTICE in this section above*
MENTAL Health, National Institute of—*See 'Alcohol, Drug Abuse & Mental Health Administration' under PUBLIC Health Service below*
MILITARY Academy, U.S.—*See under ARMY in this section above*
MILITARY Appeals, U.S. Court of—*See under JUDICIARY in this section above*
MINES, Bureau of—*See under INTERIOR above*
MINING Enforcement & Safety Administration—*See under INTERIOR above*
NATIONAL Academy of Sciences—*See under 'N'*

NATIONAL Aeronautics & Space Administration (NASA)—*See also ASTRONAUTICS*
'77 budget proposals 1-21, 64C2
New artery x-ray device rptd 1-21, 159E2
Low quits 3-19, 232A2
Cong clears '77 funds 5-21, 411G3-412C1; signed 6-4, 982F1
Jupiter symposium 5-24, 443C3
'77 funds signed 8-9, 623G1
Nordberg dies 10-3, 970F2
Ames Research Center—*See separate listing under 'A'*
Jet Propulsion Laboratory—*See separate listing under 'J'*
Langley Research Center—*See under 'L'*

NATIONAL Archives & Records Service—*See under GENERAL Services Administration in this section above*
NATIONAL Cancer Institute—*See 'National Institutes of Health' under PUBLIC Health Service below*
NATIONAL Commission for the Protection of Human Subjects of Biomedical and Behavioral Research—*See 'National Institutes of Health' under PUBLIC Health Service below*
NATIONAL Earthquake Information Center—*See 'Geological Survey' under INTERIOR in this section above*
NATIONAL Foundation on the Arts & the Humanities
Orchestras get grants 1-12, 32E3
US Dem platform text backs 6-15, 473E1
'77 funds signed 7-31, 623D1
GOP platform text 8-18, 608G1
Sup Ct vacates product picketing 10-4, 807A2
Extension signed 10-8, 834F2
NATIONAL Guard
Trucks blasted in Boston 7-2, 796C3
'77 manpower funds signed 9-22, 707D3

1977

MARINE Corps
Women begin field training 1-8, combat training 3-24, 343C2
Ford '78 budget proposals 1-17, 30B3
Spanish freighter collisn 1-17, 104B3
Quantico germ warfare tests rptd 3-8, 195F2
Barnes HEW job questnd 3-23—3-26, 236B2
News probe wins Pulitzer 4-18, 355F2
'76 desertion rate rptd 10-27, 858A2
Reserve Forces—*See under ARMED Forces in this section above*
Veterans—*See VETERANS under 'V'*

MARITIME Administration—*See under COMMERCE above*
MENTAL Health, President's Commission on
Mrs Carter addresses 4-19, 322D2
MENTAL Retardation, President's Committee on
Mrs Carter at meeting 4-18, 322C2
METRIC Board, U.S.
Weather Svc delays conversn 10-18, 820F3
MILITARY Academy, U.S.—*See under ARMY in this section above*
MILITARY Compensation, Commission on
Carter names 6-27, 499A3
MINES, Bureau of—*See under INTERIOR in this section above*
MINE Safety & Health Administration—*See under LABOR in this section above*
MINE Safety & Health Review Commission
Created 11-9, 856B1
MINING Enforcement & Safety Administration—*See under INTERIOR in this section above*
MOTOR Carrier Safety, Bureau of—*See TRANSPORTATION—Federal Highway Administration below*
NARCOTICS & Dangerous Drugs, Bureau of—*See under JUSTICE above*
NATIONAL Academy of Sciences—*See under 'N'*

NATIONAL Aeronautics & Space Administration (NASA)—*See also ASTRONAUTICS under 'A'*
Ford '78 budget proposals 1-17, 31D1, 32F2
US-Eur space lab flight planned 2-16, 170C3
Shuttle test flight 2-18, 170A3
Carter keeps Ford budget 2-22, 125B2
House OKs SST research funds 3-17, 213G1
Uranus rings rptd 3-30, 908E2
USSR computer deal opposed 6-5, 469A3
'78 funds authorizatn signed 7-30, 688G3
Space shuttle flight test 8-12, 627B1
Voyager 2 launched 8-20, Voyager 1 delayed 8-29, 664B2
Moon stations closed 9-30, 908E3
'78 funds signed; orbital telescope, Jupiter probe funded 10-4, 796G2, E3
Sun-earth study satellites launched 10-22, 908A3
Contractors' gifts scored 10-24, 920C2
New form of life rptd 11-2, 907G3

NATIONAL Archives & Records Service—*See under GENERAL Services Administration in this section above*
NATIONAL Cancer Institute—*See PUBLIC Health Service—National Institutes of Health below*
NATIONAL Foundation on the Arts & the Humanities
'78 funds signed 7-26, 592F3
Arts, National Endowment for the
Biddle sworn chrmn 11-30, 927F3
NATIONAL Guard
Mobilized for storm rescue in NY 1-27, Pa, Minn, Ohio 1-28—1-29, 75E2, A3
Ohio disaster aid cited 2-8, 92C1
Sup Ct backs retiremt pay rule 4-4, 341F3
NH A-plant foes tried, freed 5-4—5-13; LEAA bars funds 5-19, 409D3, 410C1
Wis strike mobilizatn 7-3—7-18, 558F2
Kent State damage suit retrial ordrd 9-12, 820B3
Sen votes vs unionizatn 9-16, 759E3
Reenlistmt bonus trial set 11-15, 942C2

1978

MARINE Corps
Carter budget proposals 1-23, 45C1-G1
Basic training cut set 2-25, 162G3
1st woman gen named 5-11, 420E1
Memphis fire emergency aided 7-1—7-4, 513F2
Wilson urges draft registratn 10-29, 895C1
Black '70-78 enlistmt rise rptd 12-6, 960B1
12 at Camp David rptd relieved for suspected pot use 12-9, 960B3
Taiwan anti-US demonstratn, 2 hurt 12-16, 974D2
Arms Issues—*See ARMAMENTS under 'A'*

MARSHALS Service, U.S.—*See under JUSTICE in this section above*
MILITARY Bases—*See DEFENSE in this section above; also country, territory names*
MILITARY Compensation, Presidential Commission on
Pension revisn rpt issued 4-10, 280E3-281F1
NARCOTICS & Dangerous Drugs, Bureau of—*See under JUSTICE in this section above*
NATIONAL—For departments and agencies not listed below, see key word in this section
NATIONAL Academy of Sciences—*See NATIONAL Academy of Sciences under 'N'*

NATIONAL Aeronautics & Space Administration (NASA)—*See also ASTRONAUTICS under 'A'*
35 astronauts named for Space Shuttle program; women, minorities included 1-16, 157E3-158A1
Carter budget proposals 1-23, 46C1
Venus sulfuric acid calculated 5-6, 654B1
Goddard rpts San Andreas Fault shift 6-18, 480C1
'79 funds, Skylab signed 9-30, 750F2-A3
'79 authorzn, 5-shuttle fleet signed 9-30, 750A3 ★
20th anniv marked 10-1, 861C2
Xenon metallic conversn rptd 11-25, 1023C3

NATIONAL Archives & Records Service—*See under GENERAL Services Administration in this section above*
NATIONAL Center for Toxicological Research—*See FOOD & Drug Administration in this section above*
NATIONAL Commission on Working Women
Job status rptd 6-4, 554D3
NATIONAL Fire Prevention & Control Administration—*See under COMMERCE in this section above*
NATIONAL Gallery of Art—*See under 'N'*
NATIONAL Guard
In Ohio storm-rescue missn 1-26, 105A3
Ind coal strike call-up 2-14, govs vow unrest use 3-7, 160D2
Memphis fire emergency aided 7-1—7-4, 513F2
Memphis police, fire strike mobilizatn 8-10—8-18, 644E2, G2
Black officers rptd underrepresented 8-16, 683C2
Wichita fire statns manned 9-14, 753D1
Alaska rejcts armory 11-7, 915C2
La tornado call-up 12-3, 972B2

1979

MARINE Corps
Carter budget proposals 1-22, 42A2, 43B1
Iran evacuatn alert set 2-12, 106C1
Khomeini forces kidnap US sgt 2-14—2-21, 125A3
'78 4th 1/4 volunteer shortage rptd 2-15, 130G2
1st black brig gen named 2-23, 272C1
Viet-era Marine returns to US 3-25, plans desertn chrgs fight 3-31, 265G3
Barrow to succeed Wilson 4-18, 307G2
Officers end China visit 5-15, 370C2
3 Camp Pendleton sgts suspended 6-27, Calif beating incident probed 7-7, 520A1
Parris I sgt convicted 8-18, 868E3
Volunteer shortage rptd 8-20, 649B2, E2
Manpower reductn set 9-10, 724C3
13 moved on pot suspicion 9-12, 809A2
Hawaii personnel assaults rptd up 9-21, 809A2
Pope visits Iowa 10-4, 759C1
Guantanamo maneuvers begin 10-17, 781C2
'79 enlistment gap rptd 10-25, 903C3
El Salvador Emb attacked, 2 injured 10-30, 834A3
Nunn sees recruiting abuses 11-19, 903G3
Viet troops Agent Orange exposure rptd 11-24, 904C2
Viet-era desertn case opens 12-4, 924D1
'Quick-strike' force joined; manpower reductn barred 12-5, 923E3
Iran emb hostage interviewed 12-10, 934A3
Arms Issues—*See ARMAMENTS under 'A'*
Reserve Forces—*See under ARMED Forces in this section above*
Veterans—*See VETERANS under 'V'*
MARSHALS Service, U.S.—*See under JUSTICE in this section above*
MERIT System Protection Board
Civil Svc Comm replaced 1-1, 6A1
MILITARY Bases—*See DEFENSE in this section above; country, territory names*
NATIONAL—*For departments and agencies not listed below, see key word in this section*
NATIONAL Academy of Sciences—*See NATIONAL Academy of Sciences under 'N'*

NATIONAL Aeronautics & Space Administration (NASA)
Carter budget proposals 1-22, 46E1
China satellite pact signed 1-31, 65D1
Stratospheric ozone levels studied 6-22, 692D1
Skylab comes down 7-11, 509C1, F2
Tex storm shuts Johnson Space Cntr 7-24—7-28, 638D3
Solar cell silicon productn method rptd 8-27, 649C1
'80 funds clear Cong 10-24, Carter signs 11-5, 883G2
Space shuttle support affirmed despite delays 11-14, 883E3
Space shuttle funds included in '80 mil constructn bill 11-30, 945A2
Low to head air safety panel 12-19, 988F3

NATIONAL Agenda for the 80s, Commission for a
Created, McGill named chrmn 10-24, 810D2
NATIONAL Archives & Records Service—*See under GENERAL Services Administration in this section above*
NATIONAL Gallery of Art—*See under 'N'*
NATIONAL Guard
Kent State damage suit settled 1-4, 5E2
N Orleans police strike mobilizatn cited 2-8—3-4, 166B1
Ala NAACP parade guarded 6-9, NC anti-KKK march 11-11, 865B3, E3
Truckers' strike mobilizatn cited 6-18—6-28, 479C2
Recruiting failure rptd 8-23, 649C3
Ariz radioactive tritium factory seized 9-26, tritium moved 9-29, 806B2, E2

1980

MARINE Corps
Petitn limits upheld by Sup Ct 1-21, 93B1
Carter budget proposals 1-28, 70F3, 71C1
Viet-era Marine ct-martial asked 2-1, 115C3
Persian Gulf assault force dispatched 2-12, 106A2
Sgt dischrgd for Playboy pose 2-21, 189C1
Dow chrgs EPA spying 3-25, 387A3
El Salvador amb's home besieged 5-10—5-12, 372E3
Eglin refugee camp violence 5-24—5-25, 395F3
Sen com study faults Iran rescue missn 6-5, 419B2
Carter aide rptd reassigned in tax dispute 6-10, 638E3
May recruiting rptd 6-11, 458E2
500 at Camp Lejune alerted, Cuban refugee influx rumored 7-4, 515A1
'79 recruits mental standards down 7-31, 598D1
Reserves—*See ARMED Forces in this section above*

NATIONAL Aeronautics & Space Administration (NASA)
Carter budget proposals 1-28, 71E2
Solar study satellite launched 2-14, 160D2
GAO backs space industry research 2-16, 160G2
Venus contour map released 5-28, 477F1
Astronaut corps increased 5-29, 477E1
'81 funds clear Cong 12-3, 954B3; signed 12-15, 982B1

NATIONAL Credit Union Administration
DIDC sets interest rules 5-28, S&Ls file suit 6-16, 516G3
NATIONAL Guard
Carter budget proposals 1-28, 70G3
NM prison recaptured 2-3, 112D2
NC blizzard spurs mobilizatn 3-1—3-2, 292B3
KC fire fighters end strike 3-22, 227F3
Cuban refugee unrest at Key West quelled 5-6, 339E3
Conf in Portland; inadequate equipmt, staff chrgd 5-7, 369E3
Mo tornado call-up 5-13, 391F2
Miami riot call-up 5-18, 382B3; pullout begins 5-21, 401D3
Mt St Helens rescue efforts rptd 5-24—7-4, 504D3
Ark refugee camp reinforced 5-27, 396C1; calm enforced 6-2, 420C1
Grand I (Neb) curfew enforced 6-3, 527B3
Mobile (Ala) strike duty 7-14—7-20, 576D1
Miami alert reset 7-17, 560A1
Dem platform plank adopted 8-13, 615B2

1976

NATIONAL Heart & Lung Institute—*See 'National Institutes of Health' under PUBLIC Health Service below*
NATIONAL Highway Traffic Safety Administration—*See under TRANSPORTATION below*
NATIONAL Institute for Occupational Safety & Health—*See 'Health Services Administration' under PUBLIC Health Service below*
NATIONAL Institutes of Health—*See under PUBLIC Health Service below*

NATIONAL Labor Relations Board (NLRB)
Washn Post Guild dissidents seek own union 1-28, 153G3
Gets shopping cntr dispute authority 3-3, 219A1
Rejcts hosp interns unionizatn 3-22, 220E1
Rules on journalists 4-5, 249C1
Rules on newspr ethics code 4-8, 272C2
Cited in Dem platform text 6-15, 470B3
Guild wins Washn Post vote 7-22, 553D3
Sup Ct vacates product picketing 10-4, 807A2

NATIONAL Oceanic & Atmospheric Administration—*See under COMMERCE in this section above*
NATIONAL Park Service—*See under INTERIOR in this section above*
NATIONAL Railroad Passenger Corp.—*See AMTRAK under 'A'*
NATIONAL Science Foundation (NSF)
Rpts gas clouds in space 5-25, 443D2
'77 funds signed 8-9, 623G1
'77 authorizatn signed 10-11, 835A2
NATIONAL Security Agency—*See under DEFENSE above*

NATIONAL Security Council
Treas secy entry bill vetoed 1-1, 4D1; Sen overrides veto 1-22, 69A3
40 Com operatns rptd 1-26, 92G3
House com urges forgn operatns subcom 2-10, 150F1
Ford revises intellignc command, 40 Com renamed 2-17, 127C1, E2
Nixon tap depositn released 3-10, 184F1
FBI to destroy '69 files on Kraft 3-30, 235D1
Sen intellignc com issues rpt, faults 40 Com, urges reforms 4-26, 298E3, 300F1-C3, 301A3, E3, 303B1-G1
US forgn intelligence chart 304B1, A2 ★
Science office re-created 5-11, 346D1
GOP platform text 8-18, 608G2
Meets re Korea killings 8-18—8-19, 618G3
Brzezinski named Carter aide 12-16, 936A3, 937G1

NATIONAL Transportation Safety Board—
'74 TWA Va crash rpt issued 1-21, 80A1
Rpts '75 US airline deaths 1-24, 736B2
Todd confrmd chrmn 2-5, 110D2
Hogue confrmd 4-12, 412F1
Rpts on '75 Eastern NY crash 5-1, 736D2
On Calif school bus crash 5-21, 384C1
Reed confrmd to amb post 5-26, 412A2
Air bag project sought 12-6, 921C1
NATIONAL Weather Service—*See 'National Oceanic & Atmospheric Administration' under COMMERCE in this section above*

NAVY, Department of the
'77 budget proposals 1-21, 63G3
Spain defns pact signed 1-24, 76E3
Marine Corps reorganizatn urged 2-2, 95D3
Oil reserves dvpt legis urged 2-26, 149F2
Cong opens oil reserves 3-31, 246G2-C3
Duvalier assassinatn role rptd 4-1, 267A3
Oil reserves bill signed 4-5, 982E1
Decision to pay shipyds rptd 4-8, 309A2
House OKs '77 arms, manpower authorizatn 4-9, 283F2
Shipyd overrun paymts disputed 5-4—6-10, 453D3
Japan chrgs Sovt as spy 5-14, 356A1; frees 5-22, 373C2
Sen OKs arms, manpower authorizatn 5-26, 411B2
Dem platform plank 6-15, 432E3
Dem platform text cites 6-15, 477F1

1977

NATIONAL Health Services Corps—*See PUBLIC Health Service—Health Services Administration below*
NATIONAL Highway Traffic Safety Administration—*See under TRANSPORTATION below*
NATIONAL Institute of Occupational Safety & Health—*See PUBLIC Health Service—Disease Control, Center for below*
NATIONAL Institutes of Health—*See under PUBLIC Health Service below*
NATIONAL Intelligence Tasking Center
Created, Turner to chair 8-4, 610B3

NATIONAL Labor Relations Board (NLRB)
Sup Ct bars longshoremen loading case review 1-10, 57F1
Sup Ct upholds poultry driver bargaining right 1-11, 58A1
Sup Ct curbs secondary strikes 2-22, 149D3
Vs certificatn delay in bias cases 2-28, 153G3
NBA referees strike 4-10—4-25, 332B1
E Coast dock protest ends 4-18, 324E2
Catholic dispute case review denied 5-2, 406C2
Admin asks labor law reform 7-18, 555D2
JP Stevens found in contempt 8-31, 724G1
Reform Act clears House 10-6, 795B2
NBA 11-man rosters upheld 11-4, 870D1
Lawyer fees case refused 11-14, 878D3
'78 funds clear Cong 12-7, 958F3
Stevens chrgd by law judge 12-21, 1005C1

NATIONAL Marine Fisheries Service—*See COMMERCE—National Oceanic & Atmospheric Administration in this section above*
NATIONAL Oceanic & Atmospheric Administration—*See under COMMERCE in this section above*
NATIONAL Railroad Passenger Corp.—*See AMTRAK under 'A'*
NATIONAL Reconnaissance Office—*See under DEFENSE in this section above*
NATIONAL Science Foundation
'78 fund authorizatn signed 8-15, 689D1
'78 funds signed 10-4, 796F3
New form of life rptd 11-2, 907G3
Antarctic shelf penetrated 12-9, 971G2
NATIONAL Security Agency—*See under DEFENSE above*

NATIONAL Security Council—*See also BRZEZINSKI, Zbigniew*
Brzezinski sworn 1-23, 52E2
Arms sales curbs urged 1-24, 51E3
SALT II talks ordrd resumed 1-27, 70D1
Schecter rpts Viet initiative 2-11, 110A2
Brzezinski rpts net worth 2-25, 147G3
Intell advisory bd ended 5-5, 462E2
USSR computer deal opposed 6-5, 469A3
Ends 'blacklisting' of forgn ships re Cuba stops 6-10, 781D3
Turner given new powers, policy review comm created 8-4, 610B3
Ford, Kim Han Cho mtg bar rptd 11-11, 915B2
Cuba mil buildup in Africa rptd 11-17, 896D1
Korean influence plan documt disclosed 11-29, 914E3

NATIONAL Transportation Safety Board
Chicago train crash rpt 2-7, 104A3
'76 St Thomas crash probe rptd 3-6, 312A2
Pan Am, KLM 747s collide 3-27, 244D2
Pan Am-KLM crash probe opens 4-4, 311B3
'76 transport deaths rptd 5-12, 412E2
Chicago train crash rpt 5-16—5-18, 516E3
On NYC copter accident 5-17, 412C3
NATIONAL War College—*See under DEFENSE in this section above*
NATIONAL Weather Service—*See COMMERCE—National Oceanic & Atmospheric Administration in this section above*
NAVAL Research, Office of—*See under NAVY below*

NAVY, Department of the
Ford '78 budget proposals 1-17, 30A3-31D1
To lose Alaska oil reserve 1-17, 31E2
Carter asks energy dept 3-1, 148C2
Chem warfare effort rptd 3-21, 232F1
Shipyard indicted re overruns 4-6, 343G3
Unionization threat seen 4-19, 342E3
Ethiopia closes research cntr 4-23, 327G2
Homosexual dischrg upgraded 4-27, 344F1-A2
Dole asks Guantanamo vow re US-Cuba ties 6-3, 455G3
Lockheed overbilling chrgd 6-13, 482G2
Enlistmt bonus paymts upheld 6-13, 517E2
Bahrain ends US base pact 7-1, 511G3
Officer cuts clear Cong 7-14, 576A2

1978

NATIONAL Heart, Lung & Blood Institute—*See under PUBLIC Health Service—National Institutes of Health below*
NATIONAL Highway Traffic Safety Administration—*See under TRANSPORTATION below*
NATIONAL Institute of Mental Health—*See PUBLIC Health Service—Alcohol, Drug Abuse & Mental Health Administration*
NATIONAL Institute on Drug Abuse (NIDA)—*See PUBLIC Health Service—Alcohol, Drug Abuse & Mental Health Administration below*
NATIONAL Institutes of Health—*See under PUBLIC Health Service in this section below*

NATIONAL Labor Relations Board (NLRB)
'Prehire' union picketing curbed 1-17, 33G3
JP Stevens contempt review refused 2-21, 125G3
Stevens union bargaining rep ordrd 3-26, 243B2
Stevens settles suit 4-28, 324E1-C2
Unions held subject to trespass laws by Sup Ct 5-15, 387C2
Freedom of Info barred by Sup Ct 6-15, 468F2
Union curb on supervisor discipline upheld by Sup Ct 6-21, 509G1
Union pol organizing backed by Sup Ct 6-22, 508C3
Hosp union organizing backed by Sup Ct 6-22, 508E3
Civil Svc revisn signed 10-13, 787G3

NATIONAL Marine Fisheries Service—*See COMMERCE—National Oceanic & Atmospheric Administration in this section above*
NATIONAL Mediation Board
Conrail-UTU pact set 9-14, 700F1
NATIONAL Oceanic & Atmospheric Administration—*See under COMMERCE in this section above*
NATIONAL Park Service—*See under INTERIOR in this section above*
NATIONAL Register of Historic Places—*See INTERIOR—National Park Service below*
NATIONAL Research Council—*See NATIONAL Academy of Sciences under 'N'*
NATIONAL Science Foundation
Cabt-level Educ Dept proposed 4-14, 279D1
Wis U computer research secrecy order lifted 6-12, 513G3
'79 funding signed 9-30, 750F2-A3
US-China academic exchng set 10-22, 814E1
NATIONAL Security Agency—*See under DEFENSE in this section above*

NATIONAL Security Council—*See also BRZEZINSKI, Zbigniew*
Carter reorganizes intell agencies 1-24, 49C2, D2
US Jewish aide claims info withheld 3-9, 176F2, A3
Ex-agent says CIA acted without clearance 5-8, 368A1
Nixon ex-aide testifies on Korea paymts 6-1, 433C1
Carter on security leaks 7-11, 524G2
US-China acad exchng set 10-22, 814E1
Carter rptd critical of pol intellignc 11-25, 917C1
George Ball appointed 12-4, 929E2
Nev A-test site '47 debate rptd 12-18, 1012C1

NATIONAL Transportation Safety Board
'77 aviation deaths rptd 1-6, 24B1
Fla derailmt rptd sabotage 3-3, 196G1
Tenn derailmt probe rptd 3-6, 196E1
L Superior '75 ore ship sinkage rpt issued 4-20, 460A1
Ind team '77 charter crash blame fixed 8-18, 758C3
Natl Fla bay crash rpt issued 11-9, 908F2 ★
Va derailmt blame fixed 12-4, 972D1
NATIONAL Weather Service—*See COMMERCE—National Oceanic & Atmospheric Administration in this section above*
NAVAL Academy, U.S.—*See under NAVY below*

NAVY, Department of the
Troop strength abroad rptd; table 1-2, 5C2
Carter budget proposals 1-23, 45B1-G1, A3
USSR A-satellite falls in Canada 1-24; '64 US failure cited 57C1, D1
Portsmouth Shipyd radiatn-cancer link probed 2-19, 2-28; follow-up study opposed 2-28, 164D1, B3
Basic training cut set 2-25, 162G3
E Coast booms linked to aircraft, weather 3-3, 187A2
Hayward named to Joint Chiefs 4-5, 281A2
Hard drug use rptd 4-27, 368E2
2 Sovts arrested as spies, 3d asked to leave US 5-20, 409A3
Adm Fitch dies 5-22, 440F2

1979

NATIONAL Institute of Mental Health—*See PUBLIC Health Service-Alcohol, Drug Abuse & Mental Health Administration*
NATIONAL Institute on Drug Abuse (NIDA)—*See under PUBLIC Health Service below*
NATIONAL Institutes of Health—*See PUBLIC Health Service in this section below*

NATIONAL Labor Relations Board (NLRB)
Back-pay rule vs Amer Cyanamid upheld 2-10, 131A1
Va shipyd vote probe set 3-2, 187C2
Job-testing data disclosure reversed by Sup Ct 3-5, 184B3
Va shipyd strike suspended 4-22, 306E2
Soccer players, owners ordrd to bargain 5-3; '78 certificatn cited 5-3, 431D3, 432B3
Va shipyd vote chrgs dismissed 5-4, USW recognitn ordrd 6-26; co to appeal 7-3, 561A1
Murdock dies 9-15, 756C3

NATIONAL Oceanic & Atmospheric Administration—*See under COMMERCE in this section above*
NATIONAL Park Service—*See under INTERIOR in this section above*
NATIONAL Personnel Records Center—*See GENERAL Services Administration-National Archives and Records Service above*
NATIONAL Railroad Passenger Corp.—*See AMTRAK under 'A'*
NATIONAL Research Council—*See NATIONAL Academy of Sciences under 'N'*
NATIONAL Science Foundation
Carter budget proposals 1-22, 46B2
Magnet-synthesizing bacteria rptd 4-8, 691C2
Quasar sighting studied 8-23, 691G2
NATIONAL Security Agency—*See under DEFENSE in this section above*

NATIONAL Security Council
A-target chng urged 1-13, 52B3
Pickering cited in H-bomb letter 9-16, 9-18, 715F2

NATIONAL Transportation Safety Board
Japan Air '77 Alaska crash rpt issued 2-13, 412F1
'78 Chesapeake Bay collisn blame fixed 2-26, 240E3
Fla derailmt blame placed 4-8, 472E3
San Diego '78 air crash rpt issued 4-19, 412D2*
DC-10 safety flaws rptd 5-29, 411F3
Law judge OKs DC-10 flights 7-10, 538D3
Munson death blamed on pilot error 9-16, 1002F3
Mex City air crash probed 10-31, 912D2
Chicago DC-10 crash rpt issued 12-21, 988F2
NAVAL Academy, U.S.—*See under NAVY below*
NAVAL Observatory, U.S.—*See under NAVY below*

NAVY, Department of the
South China Sea deploymt rptd 1-2, 3E1
Female mil personnel rise seen 1-2, 53A2
'Sexist' language review conducted 1-19, 89D3
Carter budget proposals 1-22, 42A2, 43A1-B1, C2
Ship retiremt planned 1-23, 89B3
Portsmouth shipyd A-cancer study begins 1-31, 91A1
Pilot drain, morale loss cited 2-15, 130F2
'78 4th 1/4 volunteer shortage rptd 2-15, 130G2
MD shortage rptd 2-16, 130C2
Task force sent to Arabian Sea 3-5, 157E2

1980

NATIONAL Labor Relations Board (NLRB)
Pvt coll faculty unions curbed by Sup Ct 2-20, 146D1-B2
Va shipyd pact signed 3-31, 251C2
Hosp union limits case declined by Sup Ct 4-14, 307C1
Lubbers confrmd as counsel 4-23, 333E2
Container pact ban refusal affirmed by Sup Ct 6-20, 555F2
NASL order refused by Sup Ct 10-14, 1001E2
Stevens union access case refused by Sup Ct 10-20, 807A2
Deering Milliken '56 wage dispute setld 12-14, 962F2

NATIONAL Oceanic and Atmospheric Administration—*See under COMMERCE in this section above*
NATIONAL Science Foundation
JFK murder probe role set 1-4, 17A2
Carter budget proposals 1-28, 71D3
Scientific literacy study issued 10-22, 990G1
'81 authrzn clears Cong 12-2, 953G2; signed 12-12, 982B1
'81 funds clear Cong 12-3, 954B3; signed 12-15, 982B1

NATIONAL Security Council
Afghan rebel arms rpt denied 2-16, 123A1
Nicaragua aid released 9-12, 709G2
NYC media gets Africa memo 9-16, Admin calls forgery 9-17, 726E3-727B1
Reagan to downgrade role 10-19, 801C3
Reagan fills 2 key posts 11-14, 881F1, A2
Carter aide cleared in spy leak 12-5, 940B2
Allen gets Reagan post 12-23, 980A2

NATIONAL Transportation Safety Board
'79 aviatn accident rate rise rptd 2-20, 347D1
DC-10 probe ended by FAA 5-16, 518E3

NAVY, Department of the
Kennedy seeks Mideast presence 1-11, 32E3
Brown vows Pacific strength 1-12, 31G1
Persian Gulf buildup rptd 1-18—1-22, 46D1
PR maneuvers disrupted 1-19, 94D1
Petitn limits upheld by Sup Ct 1-21, 93B1
Iran scores forces deploymt 1-22, 44F1
Lt, 2 others arrested in PR bomb plot 1-25, 94A1
Carter budget proposals 1-28, 70F3, 71D1, F1
Reagan seeks rearmamt 1-29, 91D3
Point Mugu Base evacuated 2-18, 213A3
Playboy photo series rptd 2-21, 189C1
Reagan 'basic speech' excerpts 2-29, 207F3
Calif sailors rptd seeking food stamps 4-24, 428G1

1976

Ford vetoes constructn bill 7-2, 518A1
Ford OKs naval reactors 7-12, 517G2
'77 arms, manpower authorizatn signed 7-14, 517D1, B2, D2
Restricts PI test bombings 7-14, 539B2
Evacuates forgn natls from Leb 7-27, 546A1
Oil reserve dvpt funds signed 7-31, 623D1
GOP platform text cites 8-18, 609A1
'77 manpower funds signed 9-22, 707C2, D3
Aircraft—*See under ARMAMENTS under 'A'*
Amnesty Issue—*See under ARMED Forces in this section above*
Missing in Action—*See under ARMED Forces below*
Naval Academy, U.S. (Annapolis, Md.)
Carter backs honor code 8-11, 585D2
Personnel
ELF frees Bowidowicz 1-9, 31E1
Middendorf censured 3-16, 200A3
Shafer acquitted re Belknap collisn 5-12, Knull convicted 6-22, 941G2
Ingersoll dies 5-20, 404A2
Recruitmt bias cover-up chrgd 6-7, 454A2
Macdonald confrmd undersecy 9-8, 808C1
Ford cites black admiral 10-22, 801G3
Reserve Forces—*See under ARMED Forces in this section above*
Ships & Submarines—*See also under ARMAMENTS under 'A'*
Sub intellignc rptd 1-20, 93A3
Australia OKs A-ship visits 6-4, 455E3
Naval review marks Bicentennial 7-4, 488B3, 489B1, F1
A-ship in NZ spurs strike 8-27—9-2, 677E2; in Australia 9-7, 691C3

NUCLEAR Regulatory Commission
'77 budget proposals 1-21, 64E2, B3
Neutral on A-centers 1-22, 115E2
Asks tighter A-materials security 2-2, 115A3
A-engineer rpts resignatn re safety 2-9, 115E1
Rpt on '75 Ala fire issued 2-28, 171G3
Anders confrmd amb to Norway 4-1, 262B3
NJ A-plant OKd 4-9, 284G1-A2
Cong OKs '77 funds, bars OMB cut proposal 5-5, 5-10, 358F2; signed 5-22, 982E1
GE asks S Africa plant deal, uranium export license 5-10; protest suit filed 5-30, 388D1
Ct curbs plutonium use 5-26, 398G1
OKs Spain reactor 6-21, India fuel sale 7-21, 739B2
A-plant hearings ordrd 7-21, 570B3
A-plant licensing moratorium set 8-13, 671E3
Carter proposes Cabt-level energy dept 9-21, 704F2
Staff rpt urges environmt impact, licensing link 10-13, 849B1
Resumes plant licensing 11-5, 849A1
Sup Ct rejects Ind Dunes A-plant case 11-8, 882C3

1977

'78 mil constructn authorizatn signed 8-1; funds signed 8-15, 668D2
Energy Dept to control reserves 8-4, 591G2
Lockheed overbilling chrg overstated 8-22, 650D1
Manpower praised 8-25, 686F2
Subic base cited in PI talks 9-24, 824G2
Adm Long defends Panama Canal pacts 9-27, 755C2
Castro asks Guantanamo exit 9-29, 781F2★, G2
Pine Gap base accord renewed 10-19, 800E3
'77 desertn rate rptd high 10-27, 858G3
3 ex-officers acquitted re Iran contract fraud 11-24, 942E2
Carter to hike Elk Hills oil output 12-20, 997A3
Expanded sea duty for women backed 12-21, 978E2
Aircraft—*See ARMAMENTS under 'A'*
Appointments
Claytor, secy 1-19; confrmd 2-11, 148D3
Hidalgo confrmd asst secy 4-25, 418E1
Woolsey confrmd undersecy 3-4, 211A2
Diego Garcia Base—*See under 'D'*
Naval Academy, U.S. (Annapolis, Md.)
Boxing scandal rpt issued 9-3, 828F1
Naval Research, Office of
CIA mind-control tests revealed 8-1—8-9, 611E1
Reserve Forces—*See under ARMED Forces in this section above*
Ships & Submarines—*See also ARMAMENTS under 'A'*
Spain freighter, launch collide 1-17, 104B3
Kenya good-will visit ends 2-23, 141E2
Carter rides A-sub 5-27, 417C3
Veterans—*See VETERANS under 'V'*

NEIGHBORHOODS, National Commission on
Established 4-28, 339B1

NUCLEAR Regulatory Commission (NRC)
Regulatory agency rpt issued 2-9, 131G3
Carter budget revision 2-22, 124E3
A-plant security ordrd tightened, '76 threats rptd 2-22, 197E1-B2
Vepco fined 2-23, 235A2
Carter asks energy dept 3-1, 148B2
A-plant constructn delays rptd 3-18, 235G1
A-plant accident liability limit voided 3-31, 277E2
NH A-plant constructn halted 3-31, 344B3, D3
A-fuel licensing rules cited 268B2
Carter energy plan 4-20, 293D2
Carter asks A-export curbs 4-27, 334D1
'75 A-accident rpt cited 5-2—5-13, 402F3
Carter OKs forgn uranium shipmts 5-6, 403D2
EPA OKs NH A-plant 6-17, 498E2
NH A-plant constructn OKd 7-26, 702B2
A-material rptd missing 8-4, 717E1
Calif plant reopening opposed 8-5, 838C2
Va A-plant safety cover-up rptd 9-30, 838A2
Indian Pt (NY) plant ruled safe by Safety Bd 10-12, 838F2
Sen com rejects nominee 10-17, 800E1
A-plant closings, repairs asked 11-5; Mich unit shut 11-18, Sen Hart scores negligence 11-19, 917D1-C2

1978

Elk Hills oil productn cut opposed 5-26, 408F1
NIH aggressn tests rptd 6-3, 1023B2
Neutron beam cancer treatmt rptd 6-13, 598E2
Memphis fire emergency aided 7-1—7-4, 513F2
Observatory rpts Pluto moon 7-7, 623G1
Adm Tate dies 7-19, 620G3
Sea duty bar to women voided 7-27, 589C1
Adm Moreell dies 7-30, 620B3
Mil constructn funds clear Cong 8-21, 662D1
Gay dischrg policy chng rptd 8-21, 683G2
Employe indicted in GSA probe 9-29, 753B3
Ship duty for women planned 10-28, 8 rpt 11-1, 877F2-A3
Black '70-78 enlistmt rise rptd 12-6, 960B1
Berg dischrg held unfair, review ordrd 12-6, 960B2
Pilot drain to commercial airlines rptd 12-13, 984B2
Turner retires, remains CIA dir 12-31; 1009E2
Aircraft—*See ARMAMENTS—Aircraft*
Contract & Billing Issues
Gen Dynamics warns A-sub work stoppage 3-13, temp accord 3-23, 224C1
Litton A-sub overrun indictmt dismissal reversed 4-5, 368F1
Trident cost overruns seen by GAO 4-13, 407A2
Gen Dynamics, Claims Bd settle A-sub dispute 6-9, 469A1
Litton settles LHA, destroyer dispute 6-20, 469A2
Lockheed cleared on overbilling 6-22, 493B3
Proxmire scores Gen Dynamics, Litton 'bailouts' 7-6, 528B3
Lockheed '71 claims settled 7-28, 665E3
Litton A-sub overrun indictmt refused by Sup Ct 10-2, 751A2
Gen Dynamics, Litton setlmt funded 10-20, 833A2
Diego Garcia Base—*See DIEGO Garcia under 'D'*
Naval Academy, U.S. (Annapolis, Md.)
Carter commencemt speech 6-7, 423D2
Lawrence assumes command 8-16, 843D3
Ships & Submarines—*See ARMAMENTS—Ships*
Veterans—*See VETERANS under 'V'*

NAVY Claims Settlement Board—*See NAVY in this section above*

NUCLEAR Regulatory Commission (NRC)
Seabrook (NH) A-plant gets final OK 1-7, EPA to reopen hearings 3-22, 242D3
A-export controls clear Sen 2-7, 82F2, A3
A-waste study backs licensing control 3-15, 184A1
A-plant licensing chngs proposed by Admin 3-17, 205D2
Black-mkt uranium sale bid probed 3-19, 242C2
Mo A-worker firing probe set 3-29, 242F1
Ct A-plant rulings curbed 4-3, 280F2
EC uranium exports OKd 4-9, 278F3
India uranium shipmts barred 4-20, 288A3
Seabrook (NH) site review ordrd 4-28, 347A1
Power plant size, efficiency studied 6-2, 408E3
India uranium export talks 6-13—6-15, 466E3
Seabrook A-plant halt ordrd 6-30, 529F2
Oregon A-plant protested 8-6—8-7, 609C3
Seabrook constructn OKd 8-10, 609G1, E2
Seabrook constructn resumes 8-14, order upheld 8-22, 914A1, E1
NM A-waste burial planned 11-15, 961E2
'75 A-plant safety ratings released 11-25, 940B3

1979

Canada joint maneuvers off PR 5-9—5-19, fishermen protest 5-16, 5-19, 385B3
Officers end China visit 5-15, 370C2
Recruiting bias chrgd 6-14, 519C3
Ship fires probe rptd 7-5, 519F3
Rear Adm Dempsey dies 7-9, 588F2
Zumwalt scores SALT 7-17, 536G1
Claytor named Transport temp secy 7-20, 529D1
Coastal sea claim challenges ordered 8-10, 646G1
Yeoman chrgd re secrets sale 8-14, 611E1
Rear Adm Kauffman dies 8-18, 671F2
Volunteer shortage rptd 8-20, 649B2, E2
Vice Adm Austin dies 8-21, 671F1
Anti-racist policy, remedial educatn program set 8-29, 664E2
New drug to treat Gonnorhea rptd 9-6, 736C2
Recruiting probe focuses on Chicago 9-7, 904B1
Female sailors go overseas 9-11, 724F3
Hidalgo named secy 9-13, 700B3
Hawaii personnel assaults rptd up 9-21, 809A2
Yeoman pleads guilty to espionage 9-25, 747E3; sentncd 10-26, 831F3
Indian O buildup set 10-1, 739C1
Army guns rptd found 10-4, 852C1
Hispanic recruiting policy chng set 10-15, 850A3
Guantanamo maneuvers begin 10-17, 781F2
FALN bombs Ill training cntr, protests PR trial 10-18, 786B2, D2
Hidalgo confirmed 10-19, 965B1
'79 enlistmt gap rptd 10-25, 903C3
Arnheiter libel cases declined by Sup Ct 10-29, 884G1
Nunn sees recruiting abuses 11-19, 903G3
Ships personnel shortage rptd 11-22, 904C1
'80 mil constructn funds signed 11-30, 945A2
2 slain in PR ambush 12-3, 924G2
PR patrol attacked again 12-9, 947D3
Aircraft—*See ARMAMENTS—Aircraft*
Bethesda (Md.) Naval Hospital—*See separate listing under 'B'*
Contract & Billing Issues
Tenneco unit '75 A-cruiser dispute settled 8-29, 747C1
Diego Garcia Base—*See DIEGO Garcia under 'D'*
Indochina Refugees
Rescues ordrd 7-21, 19 saved 7-23, 549E1
Carriers pick up 74 7-27, 7-30, 575G1
Viet refugee picked up 7-31, rescues total 163 8-9, 626F1, B2
Viet protests task force 8-2, refugee rescues rptd down 8-4, 8-22, 625G3
Patrols sight 7 boats 8-25—8-28, warship rescues 154 9-3, 659G2
Long Beach (Calif.) Naval Hospital—*See separate listing under 'L'*
National Naval Medical Institute (Bethesda, Md.)—*See separate listing under 'N'*
Naval Academy, U.S. (Annapolis, Md.)
'Sexist' language review conducted 1-19, 89F3
Brown speech re USSR first-strike ability 5-30, 410G1
13 expelled re drug violatns 9-10, 725B1
Naval Observatory, U.S.
Van Flandern comet study rptd 1-4, 289D3
Reserve Forces—*See under ARMED Forces in this section above*
Ships & Submarines—*See under ARMAMENTS under 'A'*
Veterans—*See VETERANS under 'V'*

NEUROLOGICAL and Communicative Disorders and Stroke, National Institute of—*See PUBLIC Health Service—National Institutes of Health below*

NUCLEAR Regulatory Commission (NRC)
'75 A-safety rpt called unreliable 1-19, 54B2
UCS asks A-plant shutdown, Hendrie hedges 1-26, 90B3
GE worker chrgd in uranium theft 2-1, 120A1
5 A-plants ordrd shut, quake danger cited 3-13, 186E1-C2
A-plant communities studied 3-17, 207E3
Uranium sale to India OKd 3-23, 416F2
3 Mile Island A-accident 3-28; radiatn released; explosn, meltdown feared 3-28—4-3, 241B1-246A1
Colo A-plant dispute rptd settled 4-3, 344F2
3 Mile I errors, clean-up detailed; crisis declared over 4-4—4-9; Babcock plants ordrd inspected 4-5, reactors OKd 4-6, 259D2-261G2
A-reactor safety review set 4-10, 34 A-plants warned 4-12; advisory com proposes chngs 4-17, 275F1
3 Mile I transcripts released 4-12, 275D2
3 Mile I reactor shutdown starts 4-13—4-18, 274F2
'78 A-plant incidents, '77 shutdowns rptd 4-15; pipe leaks common 5-2, 322D2-D3
A-plant shutdown case refused by Sup Ct 4-16, 303A1

1980

Lesbian probe starts 5-15, scored 6-13, 6-15; 6 rptd chrgd 6-28, 517B3
Cuba refugee blockade expanded 6-10, 435C2
Apr recruiting rptd 6-11, 458D2
Elk Hills oil stockpiling site studied 6-16, 552D2
Sub reactor rptd lost 6-17, 458E2
Hayward backs draft 6-19, 478F3
Women-at-sea program evaluated 6-28, 517C2-A3
'79 gay dismissals rptd 6-28, 517A3
Unfit ship deploymt chrgd 6-30, 517F3
Sailor convicted of sex harassmt 7-11, 598E1
GOP platform adopted 7-15, 536F1
Midway collides with Panamanian freighter, 2 killed 7-29, 675D1
'79 recruits mental standards down 7-31, 598E1
A-war strategy revised 8-5, 591F3
PR ambush suspects murdered 8-11, 9-11, 1 rptd missing 9-8; natlsts plan probe 9-19, 786A2
Viet refugees rescued 8-21, 645F1
Lesbian chrgs vs 4 dropped 8-21; actn vs 4 others cited 898F3
PR refugee camp constructn begins 9-27, suits filed 9-30, 742E2
7 of 13 carriers rptd unready 9-30, 786E1
Kenya convicts sailor of murder 9-30, sentence rptd protested 10-13, 10-20, 859C3
PR refugee camp halted by legal battles 10-1—10-24, 825E3
Sub vulnerability distortn rptd 10-5, 897B1
Gay dismissals upheld 10-24, 898D3
Sen OKs procuremt appropriatn 11-21, 896E3
Mil pay, benefits clears Cong 12-5, 953C3; signed 12-23, 928C1
Israel settles Liberty '67 attack case 12-18, 966A2
Contract & Billing Issues
GE, Curtiss-Wright suit partial setlmt upheld by Sup Ct 4-22, 344C1
Naval Academy, U.S. (Annapolis, Md.)
2 expelled re drug violatns 1-17, 94G3
Women graduate 5-28, 428D1
Garden State Bowl lost 12-14, 999A3
Obituaries
Dennison, Robert 3-14, 279B2
Hayler, Robert 11-17, 928E2
Murray, Stuart 9-19, 756D1
Ward, Robert 4-9, 360F3
Reserves—*See ARMED Forces in this section above*
Ships & Submarines—*See under ARMAMENTS under 'A'*

NUCLEAR Regulatory Commission (NRC)
38 A-plants fail safety rules 1-2, 16F3
Reactor licensing resumptn urged 1-9, 17B1
Tenn A-fuel plant reopens despite uranium loss 1-16, 54A1
Carter asks reorganizatn 1-21, 43E3
Rogovin 3 Mile I study issued 1-24, Sen rpt released 7-2, 550G3
3 Mile I radioactive water leaks 2-11, 128F1
Oak Ridge rpt confrms '57 Sovt A-mishap 2-13, 153C1
Fla A-plant accident 2-26, Babcock plant review ordrd 3-4, 169E2
Tenn A-plant gets start-up license 2-28, 169F2
3 Mile I gas venting proposed 3-12, Middletown (Pa) residents vs 3-20, 248B3
Commonwealth Ed, 2 offcls indicted 3-26, 249E1
Ill A-plant '79 dischrg data rptd 4-7, revised 4-27, 441A2
Babcock fine asked re '77 Ohio plant accident 4-10, 332B1
Va, NJ A-plants get start-up licenses 4-10, 4-16, 332E1
PI A-reactor shipmt OKd 5-6, 440E3
Ark A-plant defies gas venting delay order 5-13, 441D1
India uranium sale blocked 5-16, 440C3

1976

OCCUPATIONAL Safety & Health, National Institute of—*See 'National Institutes of Health' under PUBLIC Health Service below*
OCCUPATIONAL Safety & Health Administration—*See under LABOR in this section above*
PANAMA Canal Co.
Employes strike 3-15—3-20; Torrijos on new pact 3-22, 291E3
Rpts '76 traffic, revenues down 7-9, 793F1
Denies Canal Zone racism 9-23, 792G2
Asks Ford OK toll hike 10-5, 793D1
PAROLE Commission, U.S.—*See under JUSTICE in this section above*
PATENT & Trademark Office—*See under COMMERCE in this section above*
PEACE Corps—*See under ACTION above*
PENTAGON—*See DEFENSE in this section above*
POSTAL Rate Commission
Cong bars mail svc cuts pending study 9-10, 745D3 ★

POSTAL Service, U.S.
Wage-Price Cncl backs competitn 1-19, 44F3
Ford budget proposal 1-21, 66D2
Ford seeks spying curbs 2-17, 2-18, 127F1, A3
Ct delays office closings 3-5, 186G3
Bailar warns on high costs 3-8, 186D3
Special fees hiked 4-9, 287A2
Sen intellignc com rpts illegal mail openings, urges PO security role 4-28, 324G3, 325D2, 327A1, 328D1, G1, 330C1
Postcard registratn urged 5-1, 343E3
Cong clears added funds 5-19, 411F3; signed 6-1, 982F1
Dem platform text 6-15, 471F2, 474F3
Hardesty confrmd gov 8-8, 808A1
GOP platform text 8-18, 604D1
FBI thefts rptd 8-22, 635D1
Cong authorizes subsidy, bars cuts 9-10, 745C3; signed 9-24, 982G1
'70 strike emergency ended 9-14, 689C2
Parcel svc strike 9-16—12-13, 942A3
McGee loses reelctn 11-2, 824D3
Posts surplus 11-15, 869C2
Sup Ct bars review of Ill legis case 12-6, 920C3
Hastings convicted 12-17, 982C1

PRESIDENCY—*See FORD, Gerald*
PRESIDENTIAL Clemency Board—*See 'Amnesty Issue' under ARMED Forces above*
PRIVACY Protection Study Commission
Hearings 2-11—2-13, 151A2

1977

'78 authorizatn clears Cong 11-29, 938D1; signed 12-13, 1001G2

OCCUPATIONAL Safety & Health Administration—*See under LABOR in this section above*
OFFICE of Strategic Services (OSS) (defunct)
WWII germ warfare use rptd 3-9, 195B3
CIA mind-control tests probed 9-2—9-21, 721G1
OLYMPIC Sports, President's Commission on
Issues study 1-13, 68B3
OUTDOOR Recreation, Bureau of—*See under INTERIOR in this section above*
OVERSEAS Private Investment Corp. (OPIC)
Anaconda settles Chile claim 3-31, 449F1
Panama loan guarantee in canal treaty 8-12, 621D2
PANAMA Canal Co.
'76 employe resignatns rise 2-1, 379E2
Parfitt on 2d Panama canal 7-21, 589F3
'76 toll collectn data 7-29, 589D3
New treaty sets replacemt 8-10, 621G1; 9-7, 677C2
PATENT & Trademark Office—*See under COMMERCE in this section above*
PEACE Corps—*See under ACTION in this section above*
PENTAGON—*See DEFENSE in this section above*

POSTAL Service, U.S.—*See also MAIL Surveillance under 'M'*
Navajo ldr, aide indicted 2-9, 162E3; chrgs dismissed 5-17, 492A1
Hiring ceiling excludes 3-2, 148E2
House ethics code adopted 3-2, 173G2
Sen ethics code adopted 4-1, 251B3
Mail-order mins challenged 4-15, 310B2
'77 supplemental funds signed 5-4, 339F1
Ia obscenity convictn upheld 5-23, 444D2
Mo House ex-speaker sentncd 8-16, 712A2
Md Gov Mandel convictd 8-23, 652A1
Mandel, 5 others sentncd 10-7, 807D2
Dec '75-Mar '76 rates backed 10-11, 774A3
Hanna indicted in Korea scandal 10-14, 815G3
Washn voters rejct postcard registratn 11-8, 879G2
Transport Dept aide sentncd 12-21, 1009F1

PRESIDENT, Executive Office of the—*See EXECUTIVE Office of the President above*
PRISONS, Bureau of—*See under JUSTICE, Department of, in this section above*
PRIVACY Protection Study Commission
Safeguards rpt submitted to Carter 7-12, 632B1

1978

A-plant safety program scored 11-25, 940E3
A-reactor safety test called success 12-9, scientists score 12-10, 961E1-B2

OCCUPATIONAL Safety & Health, National Institute for (NIOSH)—*See under PUBLIC Health Service—Disease Control, Center for below*
OCCUPATIONAL Safety & Health Administration (OSHA)—*See under LABOR in this section above*
OFFICE of Management & Budget—*See BUDGET in this section above*
OLYMPIC Sports, President's Commission on
Amateur sports bill, omnibus funds clear Cong 10-15, 843D2; signed 11-8, 1003B1
OVERSEAS Private Investment Corp. (OPIC)
Loses new-policy writing power 1-1, trade protectionism cited 1-3, 67A1
2 ITT aides accused re Chile claim 3-20, CIA cover-up rptd 3-21, 207B1
Extension bill signed 4-24, 323C2
PANAMA Canal Co.
Offcls doubt Canal revenues can cover US paymts to Panama 2-9, 120A2
US Sen ratifies Canal treaty 4-18, 273B2
PARK Service, National—*See under INTERIOR—National Park Service in this section above*
PAROLE Commission—*See under JUSTICE in this section above*
PATENT & Trademark Office—*See under COMMERCE in this section above*
PEACE Corps—*See under ACTION in this section above*

POSTAL Service, U.S.
Gun lobby group admits false mailings 1-16, 68E2
GOP attacks Carter budget 1-31, 63C1
Fscl '77 deficit rptd 2-3, 68C2
Rep Diggs indicted 3-23, 220F2
Kan competitn convictn refused by Sup Ct 3-27, 241E2
'77 mail frauds cost $1 bln 4-3, 389G1
Lobbying bill clears House 4-26, 323F1-C2
'75, '76 trucks recalled 5-10, 349C1
Rate hikes urged, Carter 'citizen rate' proposal rejctd 5-12, 389E1
Rate hikes approved 5-19, 389D1
Sen adds oil import fee bar to funds bill 6-27, 511C3
New labor pact settled 7-21; walkouts, other reactn 7-21—7-23, 564D2-565A1
Meany scores labor pact; union ldrs, White House protest 8-8—8-11, 624G2
Strike restraining order issued 8-26; talks resumed 8-28, mediator named 8-29, 766B1
Ex-rep Clark indicted 9-5, 685E1
Labor pact revised 9-15, Meany backs 9-22, 2 unions OK 10-10, 10-11, 765F3, 766E1, E2
Rep Diggs convicted 10-7, 791D3-792A1
SWP scrutiny held unconst, 'mail cover' curbed 11-29, 939G3

PRISONS, Bureau of—*See under JUSTICE in this section above*

1979

Maine A-plant unhurt by quake 4-17, 323E1
Terrorist 'backpack' A-bomb said possible 4-25, 327F2
Babcock plant closings ordrd, 3 Mile I reaches shutdown 4-27, 321D3-322B2
Denton, 3 Mile I operators testify 4-30, 5-7; blast danger, radiatn levels rptd 5-1, 5-5, 344E1-E2
2 Cong coms seek A-plant curbs 5-9, 5-10, 382B1
Reactor licensing delayed, task force established 5-21, 381D3
NJ A-plant reopening set 5-30, 610A1
A-waste transport rules set 6-15, 610B1
33 reactors ordrd inspected 6-25, 518D3
3 Mile I undamaged reactor No 1 shut 7-2, order extended 8-9, 629D3-G3
Task force asks A-plant chngs 7-19, 609B3
3 Mile I said preventable 8-2, 609E1
Uranium to India delayed 8-4, 646E1
3 Mile I water purification method urged 8-14, 629A3-D3
Reactor licensing freeze lifted 8-22, reversed 8-23, 664G3
A-plant site rules studied 9-17, 743E1
UCS urges NY A-plant shutdown 9-17, 743B2
Tenn A-fuel plant shut re uranium loss 9-18, FBI probes 10-10, 809A3
3 Mile I evacuation size, costs rptd 9-23, 743C3
A-plant license policy case declined by Sup Ct 10-1, 768D2
Ray asks A-waste rules enforcemt 10-4, 806A3
NY A-plant security probe set 10-20, 807G1
Met Ed fined $155,000 10-26, 826F1-E2
3 Mile I comm final rpt urges abolitn 10-30, 825C2
A-plant cooling system hazard rptd 11-1, discounted 11-2, 849F1-C2
Reactor licensing freeze continued 11-5, 848G3
Mich utility fined for safety violatn 11-9, 867A1
Carter on 3 Mile I comm rpt; replaces Hendrie, sets advisory com, vs reactor licensing freeze 12-7, 940F1-E2

OCCUPATIONAL Safety & Health, National Institute for (NIOSH)—*See PUBLIC Health Service—Disease Control, Center for below*
OCCUPATIONAL Safety & Labor Administration (OSHA)—*See under LABOR in this section above*
OFFICE of Management & Budget—*See BUDGET in this section above*
OVERSEAS Private Investment Corp. (OPIC)
Chile aid suspended 11-30, 927F2
PARK Service, National—*See under INTERIOR—National Park Service in this section below*
PAROLE Commission—*See under JUSTICE in this section above*
PAY Advisory Committee
Carter sets 9-28, names members 10-16; 1st mtg held 10-17, 829C2-B3
PEACE Corps—*See under ACTION in this section above*
PERSONNEL Management, Office of
Civil Svc Comm replaced 1-1, 6A1

POSTAL Service, U.S.
Pvt mail svc appeal declined by Sup Ct 1-15, 31G3
Mandel convictn upset 1-11, 17G3; reclaims office 1-15, 56D1
ILA offcls indicted 1-17, 87B3
'Cross of Lourdes' mail fraud indictmt set 1-19, 91B3
'79-81 budget outlays 1-22, 42F2
CBS rate rollback plea rptd 2-6, 128C1
Coal broker pleads guilty to mail fraud 3-13, 240A1
Detroit exec pleads guilty 5-21, 656A1*
Montgomery Ward settles FTC credit chrg 5-29, 596A2
Ex-Rep Clark sentncd 6-12, 442G2
Mandel convictn reinstated 7-20, 604D3
FCC claims electronic mail project authority 8-1, Postal Svc sues 10-18, 921D2
Park indictmt dropped 8-16, 630G1
Mail fraud crackdown set 9-19, 921B3
'80 funds clear Cong 9-26, Carter signs 9-29, 883C2
FCC unit rejects satellite leasing plan 10-18, 921F2
'79 fscl yr surplus rptd 11-27, 921B2
Western Union quits electronic mail project 12-4, 921G2, A3*

PRINTING & Engraving, Bureau of—*See under TREASURY below*
PRISONERS of War—*See under ARMED Forces in this section above*
PRISONS, Bureau of—*See under JUSTICE in this section above*

1980

3 Mile I gas venting OKd 6-10, 440F3
'80 funds authrzn bill clears Cong, reforms set 6-10, 6-16, 479E1; Carter signs 6-19, 494F1
3 Mile I gas venting danger discounted 6-18, krypton vented 6-28—7-11, 550E2-E3
Carter OKs uranium sale to India 6-19, 495F2
Ala A-plant shutdown fails 6-28; GE reactors ordered probed 7-7, 551G1-C2
Ex-member scores 7-1, 551C3
Carnesale named chrmn 7-9, 551A3
'79 A-plant mishap study rptd 7-14, 551E2
Accident rules rptd tightened 7-24, 551D1
Commonwealth Ed, 2 offcls acquitted 8-8, 649E1
Staff backs 3 Mile I cleanup 8-14, 649D2
Va A-plant conducts drill 8-16, granted operating license 8-20, 648D3
Tenn A-plant granted operating license 9-16, 723A2
Con Ed Indian Pt 2 leak controversy 10-17—10-23; NY judge backs rate surchrg 12-1, NRC staff seeks fine 12-11, 961C2
2d leak at Con Ed Indian Pt 2 11-3, 961B3
Staff lists GPU aid optns 11-28, 961A1
GPU files $4 bln damage claim 12-8, 960E3-961A1

OFFICE of Management & Budget—*See BUDGET in this section above*
PAY Advisory Committee
High raises backed 1-22, 52C1
Raise recommendatns OKd 3-13, 182A3
Carter unveils anti-inflatn plan 3-14, 201D1
Carter OKs fed pay hike 8-29, 685D2*
PEACE Corps—*See under ACTION in this section above*
PENSION Benefit Guaranty Corp.
Multi-employer pensn plan reform clears Cong 9-18, 9-19, signed 9-26, 856F3
PENSION Policy, President's Commission on
Mandatory coverage urged 5-23, 404A2
POSTAL Rate Commission
Parcel post rate case declined by Sup Ct 5-19, 440C2

POSTAL Service, U.S.
Commodity optns trader arrested in mail fraud 1-2, 94D3
Rate challenge declined by Sup Ct 1-7, 15E3
Carter budget outlays, table 1-28, 70F1
Carter seeks draft registratn 2-8, 110B3
'Church' founder, aide convicted of fraud 2-9, 157B2
Electronic mail plan OKd 2-22, 4-8, conflict of interest charge cited 4-8, 347D2-E3
AFL-CIO vs draft registratn plan 2-25, 147A1
Oil leasing lottery tainted by scandal 2-29—4-7, 330B2
Moscow Olympic stamp, postcard sale halted 3-11, 206A2
Mandel appeal refused by Sup Ct 4-14, 307A1
Rate hike proposed for '81 4-21, 347B2
Parcel post rate case declined by Sup Ct 5-19, 440C2
Illegal search protectn narrowed by Sup Ct 6-25, 541B1
Draft registratn questionaire 7-2, 493C2
Carter issues draft registratn proclamatn 7-2, 494A1
Evangelical Christan direct mail ads rptd 7-11—9-15, 819C2, E3
Zip code warning amendmt discarded by House 12-13, 982F2

1976

PUBLIC Health Service (PHS) (of Department of Health, Education & Welfare)
Identifies swine flu risk group 6-10, 443C2
5-yr health plan issued 9-7, 680E1, F1 ★
On live-virus polio vaccine 9-21, 9-23, 776B1
Flu prgrms suspended 10-12—10-17, 795F1
Missing flu vaccine enzyme rptd 10-17, 795E2
Alcohol, Drug Abuse, & Mental Health Administration
Mental illness, econ linked 1-26, 159B3
Rand study scored 6-9, 6-10, 442E3-443E1
Blue Cross studies alcohol coverage 6-9, 443F1
On Rand alcoholism study 6-10, 814G3
NIDA rpts most abused drugs 7-9, 524E1-B2
Drug Abuse Inst OKs marijuana for glaucoma 10-5, 860F3
HS drug survey rptd 11-23, 931D3
'75 heroin use, death data rptd 12-12, 972A3
Disease Control, Center for
Issues flu alert 2-19, 224D2
US flu deaths rptd 2-28, 271B3
Gets swine flu funds 4-15, 282B2
Smoking survey released 6-15, 875B3
Pa mystery disease kills 23 7-27—8-5, 573E2
Pa mystery disease probe continues 8-6—8-31, 656D2-A3
Gonorrhea strain resists penicillin 9-2, 815A1
New Legionnaire probe set 9-30, 815D1
Swine flu youth progrm limited 11-15, adult turnout rptd low 12-2, 911A1
'72-74 IUD abortn deaths rptd 11-18, 931F2
Legionnaires probe scored 11-23—11-24, 911D2
Mo swine flu case unconfirmd 11-27, 911E1
Probes Velsicol poisoning 12-6, 950C2
Swine flu program halted 12-16, 950D1
Food & Drug Administration—*See separate listing above*
Health Resources Administration
1st US health rpt issued 1-12, 32G1
Health Services Administration
'77 budget proposal 1-21, 65C1
'75 cancer data error noted 1-28, 123B3
'74 death rate rptd 2-3, 123D3
'75 birth rate rptd 3-5, 224F3
'77 funds veto overridden 9-30, 727B3
NIOSH identifies Pa plant illness 11-5, 911A2
National Institutes of Health (NIH)
'75 cancer data error noted 1-28, 123B3
Hypertensn grant rptd 1-30, 123G3 ★
NJ cancer study rptd 2-8, 224D3
Cancer-agent clearinghouse set 3-29, 384A2
FDA seeks chloroform ban 4-6, 249D2
Flu vaccine test begins 4-21, 316A2
WHO cancer studies rptd 6-3, 484B3
Pearce Bailey dies 6-23, 524C2
Issues gene research rules 6-23, 735E3
NCI urges breast X-ray curb 8-23, 679E3-680A1
Research comm backs psychosurgery 9-10, 715E3
Cancer Inst dir resigns 9-20, 876D1
Wider gene research rules urged 9-22, 860B3
'77 funds veto overridden 9-30, 727B3
Gajdusek wins Nobel 10-14, 840C1
Cancer Inst MD urges less cigaret toxins 10-28, 876B1
DNA resrch curbs urged 11-1, 11-11, 891F3, 892A1
Velsicol poisoning probed 12-6, 950B2
On Guillan-Barre paralysis 12-16, 950G1
RAILWAY Association, U.S.—*See CONRAIL under 'C'*
RECLAMATION, Bureau of—*See under INTERIOR in this section above*
REGULATORY Agencies (& Issues)—*See also agency subheads in this section; specific subjects in Index (e.g., ECONOMY, HOUSING, PETROLEUM)*
Shriver urges slackening 1-7, 22A3
Ford State of Union message 1-19, 37D3, 39C2
House extends FPC gas regulatn 2-5, 108C2-109A1
Ford signs rail reform bill 2-5, 110A1
Ford revises intellignc structure 2-17, 2-18, 127A1, G2
Issue in Pa pres primary 4-27, 305E1
House OKs FRB reform bill 5-10, 345F1
Ford urges reform 5-13, 346E3
FDA voted med-device control 5-13, 377E1
Sup Ct backs broad FPC power 6-7, 435F1
Dem platform text 6-15, 470D1, B2, G3, 471B1, F1, C2-F2
Carter on controls 7-15, 507F1, 510C3
Carter vs industry links 8-9, 584E3
Carter on appointmts 8-9, 8-11, 585G1, C2
Carter urges reform 8-16, 617F1
GOP platform text 8-18, 603B2, D2, B3, 607C1, E1, A3, 608C1
Dole scores big govt 8-19, 613B1
Reagan scores big govt 8-19, 613A3
Govt in sunshine bill signed 9-13, 688C3
Cong veto bill defeated 9-21, 883F1
Ford urges aviatn regulatn reform 10-21, 849E1
Ford vs big govt 10-25, 802G3
Adams vs transport deregulatn 12-14, 936G1, G3
RENEGOTIATION Board
House OKs strengthening 1-29, 134E3-135D1

1977

PUBLIC Health Service (PHS) (of Department of Health, Education & Welfare)
HEW reorganized 3-9, 175C3
Flu damage claims rptd 3-21, 224A2
CIA mind-control tests revealed 8-1—8-9, 611E1
Alcohol, Drug Abuse & Mental Health Administration
Homegrown pot reforms urged 2-4, 332E2
Pregnant women warned vs alcohol 6-1, 472E1
Heroin study for pain relief studied 7-1; cancer pain study cited 992G3
NIDA rpt details cocaine use 7-6, 972G1
NIDA sees 'angel dust' danger 11-10, 972E2
NIDA rpts barbiturate deaths 11-27, 972E3
Disease Control, Center for
Legionnaire bacteria rptd found 1-18, 81F1
Sencer asked to resign 2-4, 103C3
Some flu shots resumed 2-8, 103F2
2 workers die 2-27, 3-1, 288B2
Reye's syndrome cases rptd 3-11, 224E1
Measles upsurge rptd 3-19, 224C1
GAO scores occupational safety inst 3-23, 280G1-A2
Mich botulism confirmed 4-2, 288E1
Foege named dir 4-5, 287D3
Australia denies meat exports diseased 8-29, 725B2
Gets '57 A-test witness list 8-31; test link to cancer probed 12-1, 1022C3
Antibiotic-resistant pneumonia rptd 9-2, 10-21, 847F1
Legion fever cases rptd 9-23, 748D1
Liquid protein deaths probed 12-1, 992B3
Food & Drug Administration—*See separate listing in this section above*
Health Resources Administration
Life expectancy rptd 12-13, 962C3
Health Services Administration
Ford urges Health Svc Corps expansn 1-17, 32F1
NIOSH access to med data OKd 12-22, 1008F2
National Institutes of Health (NIH)
Fredrickson retained as dir 2-3, 211B1
DNA research ban ends 2-7, 103E2
DNA patent order lifted 2-24, 184A2
Gene research facility rptd 3-8, 184G2
Heart-lung unit scores bypass surgery 3-9, 907E2
Immunization conf 4-4—4-6, 287G2
Fed DNA control backed 4-6, 452B1
Sleepwear cancer agent banned 4-7, 302F2 ★
Chicago DES-cancer study rptd 4-26, 431C3
FDA renews laetrile ban 5-6, 375D3
Breast X-rays curbed 5-10, 431C2
NCI to test laetrile on humans 6-23, 508F1
Antiviral drug rptd 8-10, 675E2
Meningitis A vaccine rptd 9-28, 907G1
DNA safety debated 10-6, 846B3
Cancer linked to hair dye 10-17, 962E3, 963C1
DNA research bills stalled 10-24, 846A3
Allergy-disease unit pneumonia vaccine rptd successful 10-26, 907E1
Cancer pain study rptd 992G3
Meets on DNA rule 12-15—12-16, 1022A2
Harvard DNA resrch halted 12-15, 1022E2
RADIO Free Europe—*See BROADCASTING, Board for International in this section above*
RADIO Liberty—*See BROADCASTING, Board for International in this section above*
RAILWAY Association, U.S.—*See CONRAIL under 'C'*
RECLAMATION, Bureau of—*See under INTERIOR in this section above*
REGULATORY Agencies (& Issues)
Sen OKs legis impact resolutn 2-4, 91G1
Sen rpt scores 2-9, 131B3
Energy dept bill cites 3-1, 148D2
Sen OKs reorgnizatn powers 3-3, 191B3
Carter vows surface transport deregulatn 3-16, 190E3
Reorganizatn powers cleared 3-31, 228D1
Bank interest rate ceiling powers cleared 4-5, 273A2
Reorganizatn powers signed, plans issued 4-6, 250C3
RENEGOTIATION Board
Sen com hearing on extensn, Chase accuses Lockheed 6-13, chrgs denied 6-14, 482G2
Chase admits Lockheed chrg error 8-22, 649G3

1978

PUBLIC Health Service (PHS) (of Department of Health Education & Welfare)
Glaucoma victim wins marijuana case 5-19, 728G3
Weight loss survey rptd 7-23, 727A3
Surgeon gen vs 'tolerable' cigaret rpt 8-10, 726C3
Alcohol, Drug Abuse & Mental Health Administration
Mental Health Inst links agressn, spinal fluid 6-3, 1023B2
NIDA rpts paraquat-contaminated pot peril 8-3, 728D2
Disease Control, Center for
NIOSH urges worker chem exposure curbs 1-13, 86A1
VD '77 decline rptd 1-28, 270F1
'76 abortns, mortality rates rptd 5-24, 744C1, E1
Malaria warning issued, '77 US cases rptd up 6-26, 635G3
Teen smoking rptd up 7-5, 727E1
Measles cases rptd down 7-15, 636A1
Paraquat peril rptd exaggerated 8-3, 728B2
Legionnaires' disease bacterium isolated 8-11, 635C3
New rabies vaccine rptd 9-10, 992F2
Syphilis increase rptd 10-20, 992F2
Legionnaires' data rptd 11-10; experts meet 11-13—11-15, scientific name assigned 11-15, 927F3
Food & Drug Administration—*See separate listing in this section above*
Health Services Administration
Carter budgets health svcs corps 1-23, 48D2
National Institutes of Health (NIH)
Cancer Inst vocal cord data cited 1-9, 13E3
NJ cancer death rate studied 1-12, 23E3
Anti-viral advance rptd 4-6, 334A3
'Tolerable' cigaret rpt debated 8-9, 726F2-D3
Recombinant DNA rules revised 12-16, 1022F3
RADIO Free Europe—*See BROADCASTING, Board for International in this section above*
RAILROAD Passenger Corp., National—*See AMTRAK under 'A'*
RAILWAY Association, U.S.—*See CONRAIL under 'C'*
RECONNAISSANCE Office, National—*See under DEFENSE in this section above*
REGULATORY Agencies (& Issues)
'Plain Eng' exec order exemptns 3-23, 218E2
Cost, inflatn linked 6-12, 6-19, 427A3
Carter protests legis vetoes 6-21; cong reactn 6-21, 6-22, 466D1-C2
ABA proposes overhaul 8-8, 626A2, D2
RR decline warned 10-10, 812D1
Carter anti-inflatn plan backs cncl creatn 10-24, lauds Kahn 10-25, 805D3, 806F2
GE chrmn cites regulatn costs 10-25, 806C3
Costle to head wage-price Regulatory Cncl 10-31, 863C3
REGULATORY Council
Costle named dir 10-31, 863C3
RENEGOTIATION Board
GAO clears Lockheed re overbilling 6-22, 493B3

1979

PUBLIC Health Service (PHS) (of Department of Health, Education & Welfare)
Richmond issues smoking rpt 1-11, 23A1
Health team sent to Asia 6-5, refugees strain SF svcs 7-18, 550C2
Polio vaccinatns for Amish urged 6-9, 472D1
INS lifts gay alien curb 8-14, 631A2
Alcohol, Drug Abuse & Mental Health Administration
NIDA rpts drug abuse costs, pot use 2-12, 140C2
NIDA pot study rptd 10-14, 972B2
Disease Control, Center for (CDC)
Gonorrhea treatmt rptd 1-20, 64C3
Child abuse data rptd 1-26, 93C3
TB cases feared unrptd 2-9, 138D3
VD warning issued 2-19, 140D1
Swiss animal rabies vaccine experimt rptd 2-28, 196B2
Smallpox virus vials found 4-21, 315C3
Abortn figures rptd 4-29, 547C3
Flu vaccine progrm underutilized, '76 Guillain-Barre link cited 5-18, 471C1
Polio outbreak among Amish rptd 6-5, vaccine sent 6-9, 472E1
'78 cholera cases rptd 7-6, 620E2
Rabies cases rptd up 7-14, 620F2
Tuberculosis, parasites rptd in Viet refugees 8-25, 659D3
NIOSH study rpts 'laughing gas' peril 10-24, 971B3
Gonorrhea cases leveling off, syphilis rptd up 11-18, 971F1
National Institutes of Health (NIH)
A-test cancer link rptd ignored in '65 1-8, 17C2
Smoking tied to birth perils 1-16, 63F3
Childbirth drugs effect on babies rptd 1-16, 64C1
Carter budget proposals 1-22, 44A3
Vitamin A variant for acne rptd 2-14, 138C2
Synctial virus vaccine research rptd 2-15, 138F3
Heart Inst rpts strokes down 2-23, 195G1, G2
Cancer death rates detailed 3-5, 195A3
Cancer Inst delays laetrile tests 3-13, 195F3
GAO chrgs Cancer Inst blunders 4-24, 315G2-C3
Sleep aid, nose spray ban asked 5-1, 354C3
Cancer, blood pressure drug linked 5-1, 354D3
Virus found to cause diabetes 5-23, 471G3
Less radical breast cancer surgery backed 6-6, 471B3
Methapyrilene drugs recalled 6-8, 471G1
Diabetes, virus linked 7-5, 692D2
Estrogen use linked to uterine cancer 9-14, 735A3
Radiatn impact study urged 10-30, 825F3
Neurological Inst data cited re sex-pregnancy risk study 11-29, 971F3
RADIATION, White House Interagency Task Force on Ionizing
Low-level radiatn risks seen 2-27, 208A1
RADIO Free Europe—*See BROADCASTING, Board for International in this section above*
RAILROAD Passenger Corp., National—*See AMTRAK under 'A'*
RAILWAY Association, U.S.—*See CONRAIL under 'C'*
RECLAMATION, Bureau of—*See under INTERIOR above*
REGULATORY Agencies & Issues—*See also specific agency or department names in this section*
State of Union Message 1-23, 46G3
'78 productivity drop linked to regulatn 2-9, 111D1
Regulatory calendar issued 2-28, 164E2
Business rpts compliance costs 3-14, 3-29, 230E2-C3
Carter outlines reform plan 3-25, 230E1
Southn segregatn found 4-9, 307F1-A2
Chrysler deficit, rules cost linked 7-31, GM chrmn asks fed regulatn reform 8-2, 576B1, G3
REGULATORY Council
Regulatory calendar issued 2-28, 164E2

1980

PUBLIC Health Service (PHS) (of Department of Health & Human Services)
Richmond issues female smoking rpt 1-14, 40A2
Richmond issues dietary guidelines 2-4, 157C3
Alcohol, Drug Abuse & Mental Health Administration
New drug rptd effective vs heroin addictn 2-2, 160C2
NIDA THC dvpt aid rptd 2-4, 358B1
NIDA Darvon-related death data rptd 4-24, 358E2
Mental health authrzn clears Cong 9-24, 9-30, signed 10-7, 804B1
Disease Control, Center for (CDC)
'73 abortn data cited 1-9, 23B3
Cancer workplace rules set, '79 NIOSH data cited 1-16, 36E1
Life span, disease control changes rptd 1-19, 62E3
2 TB vaccines rptd ineffective 1-20, 63E1
Influenza deaths rptd up 2-15, 158A3
Med lab tests found 14% inaccurate 3-23, 358G3-359B1
La gonorrhea epidemic rptd 4-9, 584E3
Toxic-shock syndrome cases rptd 6-6, 584C3
Toxic-shock syndrome, tampon use linked 9-17; recall ordered 9-22, 726G2-E3
Health Resources Administration
Birth control pills rptd most effective 7-13, 584B2
National Institutes of Health (NIH)
Cancer Inst laetrile tests OKd 1-3, 23D2
New blood disease treatmt rptd 1-23, 159D3
Carter budget proposals 1-28, 72B3
DNA experiment rules eased 1-29, 416B2
Dietary guidelines issued 2-4, 157D3
Interferon test plans rptd 3-5, 317E3
Saccharin cancer risk study rptd 3-6, 317F1
Cholesterol study scored 6-1, 432C3
Tex chem workers cancer cases rptd 7-24, 584D2
REFUGEE Affairs, U.S. Coordinator for
Created 3-17, 249E2
REGULATORY Agencies & Issues
GOP pres debate topic 1-5, 4D3
Small business studies rptd 1-13, 5-15, 5-29, 455E2
Kennedy for deregulatn 2-6, 91B1
Reagan 'basic speech' urges deregulatn 2-29, 207E3
Reagan vs auto regulatn 5-15, 383B1
Legis veto provisn imposed on FTC 5-28, 702F3, G3
Reagan seeks energy deregulatn 5-29, 424B1
Trucking decontrol bill clears Cong 6-19, 6-20, 479A1; Carter signs 7-1, 494B1
GOP platform backs energy deregulatn 7-10, 506C3
GOP platform adopted; text 7-15, 535C3, 536C1, F3
Pay-TV lobbying group formed 7-15, 640A1
Vander Jagt scores big govt 7-16, 534B2
Reagan pres nominatn acceptance speech 7-17, 532C2
Dem platform plank adopted 8-13, 614C3
Bush scores 'over-regulatn' 9-18, 781A1
Bush vows fewer regulatns 10-15, 817E2
Carter, Reagan TV debate 10-28, 813D1
Libertarian pres candidate cites stance 10-28, 818G2
Reagan aide urges reform 11-23, 897E2
Reagan vows cities relief 12-1, 914F2
Reform bill dies 12-16, 982G2

1976

RESERVE Forces—*See under ARMED Forces in this section above*
REVENUE Sharing—*See under BUDGET in this section above*
SCIENCE & Technology, Office of
Re-created 5-11, 346B1
SCORE—*See under ACTION in this section above*
SECRET Service, United States—*See under TREASURY below*

SECURITIES & Exchange Commission (SEC)
Vesco, 6 others indicted 1-14, 78F2
Ticor indicted 1-14, 160C1
US Financial ex-chrmn sentncd 2-3, 124C1
Hamilton coal venture rpt cited 2-21, 167C1
Sommer quits 3-6, 232A2
Needham to quit NYSE post 4-27, 348A1
Sues Petrofunds 5-26, Geo Dynamics 6-1, 984D2
Sommer, Garrett probes cited 6-1, 6-29, 984C2
Hills on boycott rules 6-4, 747E2
Sues Milwaukee Corp, settles 6-29, 984G1
Sues Foremost-McKesson 7-7, 669D1
'77 funds signed 7-14, 534D2
Rpts on NASD boycott probe 8-11, 747D2
Govt in sunshine bill signed 9-13, 688D3
Carter proposes Cabt-level energy dept 9-21, 704F2
'74, '75 corp taxes rptd 10-2, 847G1, B2
Shipping-rebate suits cited 10-26, 948E1
Political Payments Issue
Gulf paymts detailed; probe rptd 2-4, 133G1, F3; Boeing payoff probed 2-19 138A3
Sues Boeing 2-12, ct OKs privacy 2-22; forgn paymts admitted 3-5, 362G1-C2
Drug cos rpt forgn paymts 2-17—3-26, 361A2-362G1
Northrop rpts more forgn paymts 2-20, 362B3
Japan offered Lockheed data 3-11, 199E3
ITT forgn paymts rptd 3-12, 4-16, 5-12; ct ordrs limited disclosures 5-5, 360G3-361G1
Rockwell forgn paymts rptd 4-9, 362E2
Sues Lockheed, case setld 4-13, 285F2
Sues Gen Tire, settles 5-10, 359B3-360E2, 419D3
Sues Emersons, settles 5-11, 359D3, 360F2-D3
Rpts cos chrgd, chart 5-12, 725E3-729F2
Hills testifies on forgn paymts legis 5-18, disputes Richardson re SEC role 6-11—6-17, 668C3
R J Reynolds, Sea-Land paymts rptd 5-28—9-13, 689G2
Reynolds, Kaiser admit forgn paymts 6-2, 6-10, 690D2
Butler settles suit 6-7, 986D2
Alcoa forgn paymts rptd 7-9, 7-16, 690D1
Ford submits forgn paymts legis 8-3, 668D2
Ex-Gulf exec sentenced 8-4, 566B2
Sen OKs anti-bribery bill 9-15, 708B1
Bonn to examine Lockheed files 9-17, 740F1
Probes US Steel, 22 congressmen re Ford golf trips 9-23, 9-24, 722C3
Criminal probe task force named 10-14, 985B3
Gulf shareholder suits settled 11-18, 939F1
United Brands rpts more paymts, labor slush fund 12-10, 985C3
Continental Oil fires 2 12-15, rpts paymts 12-16, 986C1
Econ cncl rpt scores guidelines 12-18, 985E1
Amer Hosp sued, setlmt agreed 12-29, 986G1

SELECTIVE Service System
'77 budget proposal 1-21, 68C3
Registratn, lottery ended 1-23, 68A3
Manpower study scores cuts 4-18, 309D1
Mondale legis record cited 512C3
Amnesty Issue—*See under ARMED Forces in this section above*

1977

RESERVE Forces—*See under ARMED Forces in this section above*
RESOLUTIONS—*See CONGRESS—Legislation in this section above*
REVENUE Sharing—*See under BUDGET in this section above*
RURAL Electrification Administration—*See under AGRICULTURE in this section above*
SCIENCE and Technology Policy, Office of
Carter submits reorganizatn plan 7-15, 556D1
SECRET Service, United States—*See under TREASURY below*

SECURITIES & Exchange Commission (SEC)
Sen subcom staff rpt scores auditors 1-17, 79B1
Stirling Homex offcls convicted 1-29, 103F1 ★, A2; sentncd 3-11, 203F2
Pertamina sued 2-2, 93G1
Regulatory agency rpt issued 2-9, 131F3
Leidesdorf sued 2-16, 156C2
Arab boycott policy rptd reversed 2-18, 167E1
Chris-Craft damage award voided 2-23, 150B2
Ct backs Boeing secrecy 2-25, 215A3
Carter asks energy dept 3-1, 148C2
Hills quits as chrmn 3-2, 211A2
Illegal investmt scheme indictmts 3-3, 204D1
Allied Chem sued re Kepone 3-4, 252E2
Options trading expanded 3-4, 521E1
Tenneco questns gas diversns 3-7, 196D1
Antifraud rules expansn barred 3-23, 276G2 ★
Williams confrmd member 4-7, 272D3
Sen accounting hearings open 4-19, tighter regulatns urged 5-10, Williams vows enforcemt 6-13, 519E2
Burlington Northern settles 4-28, 368F3
New acctg rules rptd 4-29, 369A1
Law firm settles Natl Studnt Mkting suit 5-2, 520A1
Cook disbarred 5-31, 461G3
Pertamina settles chrgs 6-1, 540C2
Negotiated fees impact rptd 6-6, 521D2
Amex asks NYSE options probe 6-13, 521C2
Du Pont-Christiana merger OKd 6-16, 518A1
IDS, brokers sued 7-19, 612A3
UM&M bankruptcy chng asked 7-20, 612B2
'78 funds signed 8-2, 667G3
Rpt chrgs NYC '74-75 financial deceptn 8-26; Beame, other reactn 8-26—8-28, 665C2, D3
Opens Lance probe 9-7, 689F3, 690D2
Merrill Lynch paymt ordrd 10-11, 859F2
Optns trading limited, probe begun 10-18, 859B3
Teamsters insurnc deal probed 10-31—11-2, 837G1
Disclosure policy backed 11-3, 859D3
ICC sues trucking firms 11-3, 861A1
Payments Issues
10 cos rpt paymts, rebates 1-3—2-8, 93G3-94E2
'76 Action, Beneficial shipping rebates cited 1-5, 6C3
Park bribery probe cited 1-19, 550B2
'70-76 total rptd 1-21, 79E1
Sues GTE, settles 1-27, 79G1
Sues Uniroyal 1-27, 93C3
Natl Distillers rpts kickbacks 1-28, 215C2
Olympia paymts rptd 2-4, 215D2
Amer Airlines settles 2-9, 111G2
Japan Boeing kickback probe cited 136F1
Voluntary disclosures continue 2-14—3-28, 233B2
'70-76 disclosures total rptd 2-28, voluntary plan end seen 3-7, 233G1
Foremost '76 setlmt cited 3-7, 215F1
Disclosures rptd 3-9—6-23, 503C1
Amer Brands rpts Beam gifts 3-10, 215C2
Canada Boeing probe pact signed 3-15, 200G1
Interstate United rpts rebates 3-16, 215F2
Sues Schlitz 4-7, Occidental 5-3, Anheuser-Busch 5-19, 503B3-504A1
Anderson Clayton disclosures 4-25, 799C2
Opens some paymts files 5-17, 502G3—503C1
Lockheed rpts '70-75 total 5-26, 502F2
BP admits overseas paymts 6-3, 526A2
US Lines settles 6-6, 651B1
Park, Diplomat Bank, others chrgd 9-28, 774B1
ITT, Lazard settle chrgs 10-13, 980B3
Seagram admits paymts 10-14, 818B2
Exxon settles chrgs 10-25, 818D1-A2
Beasley indicted, Firestone paymts cited 10-25, 818C2
Korea Research Inst, E-Systems vp probed 11-29, 915D3
Goodyr settles chrgs 12-21, 1005A1
SECURITY & Cooperation in Europe, Commission on—*See under CONGRESS in this section above*
SELECTIVE Service System
Draft revival urged 1-24, 1-25, 94E3-95A1
Carter gives views 3-1, 148G2
Carter on draft revival, women 3-5, 171F2
Peptitone quits as dir 3-9, 211A2
Army chief lauds women, vs draft revival 4-6, 343F1
Manpower costs panel named 6-27, 499B3
Canada draft dodger surveillnc alleged 11-24, 923E1

1978

RESERVE Forces—*See under ARMED Forces in this section above*
RESOLUTIONS—*See CONGRESS—Legislation in this section above*
REVENUE Sharing—*See under BUDGET in this section above*
SCIENCE and Technology Policy, Office of—*See also PRESS, Frank*
Quake disaster program ready 6-4, 480F1
US scientists visit China 7-6—7-10, 564C2-B3
SECRET Service, United States—*See under TREASURY below*

SECURITIES & Exchange Commission (SEC)
Optns trade probe cited 1-5, 4G3
Sun Oil Becton Dickinson purchase probe asked by Cong chrmn 1-27, 66A1
Film industry probe rptd 2-11, Valenti comments 3-2, 251F2
Mattel offcls indicted 2-16, 116F2
Church-bond probes rptd 2-27, 295G3
Canada asks bond sales in US 3-2, 188C1
Sun Oil sued re Becton takeover 3-9, 223E1
Lance, Arabs chrgd in bank takeover bid 3-18, suit setld 3-19, 204F1
Curtiss-Wright discloses Kennecott mtg 3-26, 402D2
Lance scores press coverage 4-12, 324F3-325A1
Trading suspensns curbed by Sup Ct 5-15, 387C1
Investor protectn bill, broker-adviser separatn delay signed 5-21, 386E2 ★
Occidental files Husky bid 6-23, withdraws 7-27, 629E1, E2
Vincent named Columbia Pictures pres 7-21, 599E2
Williams Act cited in Idaho corp takeover ruling 8-10, 700G3
Dirks, 4 cos censured re Equity Funding 9-4, 681G1
Houston Univ ex-aide chrgd 10-5, 770B3
Borowski named GSA spec counsel 11-13, 899B2
Occidental disclosures probed 11-28, 1004E3
Pan Am, TXI bids for Natl rptd probed 12-22, 1007D3
Payments Issues
McDermott paymts probe cited 2-22, 142B3
Textron paymt probe cited 2-28, subpoena sought 3-2, 161A2
Williams paymts disclosure cited 3-26, 448E3
Page Airways paymts chrgd 4-13, 449G1-C2
Lance, 2 banks sued; case setld 4-26, 324G2
Wild gives depositn 4-26, settles paymt chrgs 5-11; gift recipients rptd 6-2, 449B1
Ford admits probe 5-2, 391B1
Textron bribe evidence rptd destroyed 5-8, 449A1
Reynolds settles paymt chrgs 6-6, 449C2
Disclosure power upheld 6-8, Schlitz settles chrgs 7-9, 642C3
United Brands pleads guilty re banana bribe 7-19, 643B2
Boeing chrgd, case setld 7-28, 642F3-643C1
Parsons sued on paymts, case setld 8-4, 643C2 ★
Occidental settlemts cited 8-18, 767E2
Katy, 2 offcls chrgd; suit setld 8-20, 737B1
Vesco hearings, Admin 'pol fix' chrgd 9-1—9-15, 719G3, 720C1
Seagram sued, case settled 9-8, 961E3
Goodrich '76 rpt cited 9-13, 737F1
Ludwig, Tenna rebates setlmt cited 10-23, 876D3
Hosp Corp Saudi paymts chrgd, Amer Hosp suit cited 10-26, 876E3-877C1
ITT denied stay on sealed data by Sup Ct 10-30, 832C2, D2 ★
Schlitz paymts suit cited 11-1, 877F1
ITT paymt chrgs rptd 11-2, 816C1-B3
McDonnell Douglas sued 12-14, settles 12-15, 982D2

SECURITY & Cooperation in Europe, Commission on—*See under CONGRESS in this section above*
SELECTIVE Service System
Volunteer force cost rptd 2-6, 82C1
JCS, Marines urge draft registratn 10-29, 11-21, 895A1
Army MD shortage rptd 11-27, 916F3
Moblization ability scored 12-3, 984B1
AF volunteer shortage seen 12-12, 960C1

1979

RESERVE Forces—*See under ARMED Forces in this section above*
REVENUE Sharing—*See under BUDGET in this section above*
SECRET Service, United States—*See under TREASURY below*

SECURITIES & Exchange Commission (SEC)
O-T-C mkt explained 72C3
Parklane suit findings retrial barred by Sup Ct 1-9, 14A2
FRB discourages 'long float' check delays 1-10, 15B3
Pensn plan role barred by Sup Ct 1-16, 32F1-B2
Amer Express files McGraw-Hill tender offer 1-16, 53B2
Lance banking practices detailed 1-17, 30G3
Hughes suit settled 1-19, 88G1
Ga bank bars Lance, Carter repaymt 1-23, 55D3
Hutton censured re options trading 2-6, 349G1
Buckley, Sitco partners settle 2-7, 132A1
Options trading rpt asks overhaul 2-15, freeze end seen 2-22, 348C2-349B1
Rapid-Amer, Schenley setlmt rptd 2-16, 131E3
Bagley indicted 3-15, 291G3
Starr Broadcasting ex-execs settle 3-27, 4-9, 588G1
Niagara chem dump data released 4-10, 281D3
Moon church bank fraud chrgd, '77 complaint cited 5-1, 376D2
Occidental chem dumping rptd 6-18, 597F1
United Tech-Carrier takeover faulted 6-25, 541A3
Amer Financial settles, Lindner to repay co 7-2, 746B1
Bagley acquitted 8-1, 578D2
Gulf+Western-Dominican sugar probe rptd 8-16, 632E3
Auto-Train withdraws fed loan applicatn; probe cited 8-21, 726F2
US Steel suit settled 9-27, 941F2
Fraud powers case accepted by Sup Ct 10-15, 848B1
Pauline Fathers probe rptd 11-9, 905F3
Investor suits vs advisers curbed by Sup Ct 11-13, 902C1
Gulf+Western, execs sued 11-26, 923C1
Sun sets Becton divestiture 12-19, 985C2
Payments Issues
Grumman, Gulfstream sued; case settled 1-4, 16D1-A2
Japan probes rpt on Grumman 1-9, 98F2
Grumman discloses forgn payoffs, denies Japan bribes 2-8, 305A3
Lockheed discloses overseas bribes 2-16, 306F1-A2
ISC accused of forgn paymts 7-9, 541E3
FCC doubts RKO Gen license fitness 7-18, 618B2
Clark Oil settles Mideast chrgs 7-19, 985F2
Textron admits overseas payoffs 7-26, Proxmire asks study 10-31, 923C2, B3
Miller rptd cleared in Textron case 8-2, 627C2
ITT chrgs settled 8-8, 648D1
McDonnell Douglas indicted 11-9, 886C2

SELECTIVE Service System
Renewed draft costs listed, '78 funding cited 1-4, 15D1-A2
'78 4th 1/4 enlistee shortage rptd 2-15, 130G2
Mil ldrs dispute draft need 3-13, vet recall plan disclosed 4-10, 307C2
Carter vs draft revival 4-10, 263E3
Nunn withdraws draft amendmt 6-13, 438F1
'Catonsville 9' fugitive surrenders 6-19, 492F1
Mil volunteer shortage rptd 8-20, 649C2

1980

SECURITIES & Exchange Commission (SEC)
O-T-C mkt explained 76C3
Itel probe cited 1-16, 131E3
3 RKO Gen TV licenses lifted by FCC 1-24, 119G2
Karmel resigns 2-1, 224G3
Garrett dies 2-3, 176C1
Playboy internal audit, repayments revealed 2-12, 558B2
Dickinson damages action dropped 2-14, 558A2
Gen Dynamics settles stock suit 2-27, 558C1
United Tech settles Carrier suit 3-6, 558E1
Phila exchng censured 3-13, 224F2-B3
'Insider' trading convictn voided by Sup Ct 3-18, 226C2
Mutual fund insurance case refused by Sup Ct 3-24, 265E1
Hunt group sets silver-backed bonds issue, avoids US registratn 3-26, 223D1
Optns trading ban ended, NYSE decision deferred 3-26, 224A2
Silver prices plunge, Hunt empire totters; Bache trading halted 3-27, 223C2
Hunt silver trading, Bache ties probed 3-31—4-2, 245G1-B3
Commodity futures trading curbs backed 4-14, 289F3
Hunts chrg silver manipulatn 5-2, 345B2
Civil fraud intent proof required by Sup Ct 6-2, 512A3
ABC ties to Spelling-Goldberg rptd probed 8-7—8-8, 640B1
Auto-Train drops Swiss loan 9-8, 958E2
Natl securities mkt plan failure scored by House subcom 9-12, 806D1
Sharon Steel, UV Industries deal final 9-26, 746C2
'79 securities indus rptd strong 9-28, 806B2
FRB OKs commercial paper bank sales 9-29, 986B2
4 exchngs ban new optns issues 10-10, 986D2
Westinghouse to acquire Teleprompter 10-15, 836A2
Itel rpts huge '79 loss 10-16, 784D1
Hunts liquidate Bache stock 10-21, 867B3
Thomas sworn comr 10-21, 960B1
Parallel probe case refused by Sup Ct 11-17, 882D1
LA DA ends 'Charlie's Angels' probe 12-2, 1002B3
Payments Issues
Textron chrgs settled, Miller knowledge of paymts alleged 1-31, Miller denies 2-1, 92C1-A2
Miller-Textron spec prosecutor opposed 2-5, 92B2; rejctd 3-11, 185A3
Seatrain settles disclosure suit 2-8, 558B1
US publisher loses S Africa documt disclosure suit 3-17, 278B1
Justice Dept forgn paymts advice plan opposed 3-24, 227B2
Forgn paymts cooperatn pledged 8-28, 958B1
Tesoro Petro case setld 11-21, 957D3

SELECTIVE Service System
Kennedy vs Carter proposal, GOP backs 1-28, 74A3, 75E1
Canada warns future draft dodgers 2-7, 95G3
Reagan notes mix-up re volunteer army briefing 4-10, 288F2
GOP platform adopted 7-15, 536A1, F1
Anderson platform offered 8-30, 665A2
Draft Registration
Carter asks draft registration 1-23, 41B1, 43B1
Carter issues plan 2-8, 110F2

1976

SENATE—*See also CONGRESS above; personal names*
'75 subcom activity rptd 4-4, 247G1-B2
Rockefeller rues remarks vs Jackson aides 4-27, 305D3
Permanent intelligence com created 5-19, members named 5-20, 376D3
Ratifies Spain defns pact 6-21, 534F2
Kissinger Africa visit scored 9-9, 681A2
Aeronautical & Space Sciences, Committee on
Moss loses reelection 11-2, 819G3
Aging, Special Committee on
Subcom rpts Medicaid, Medicare scandal 2-16, 128B2
Subcom rpts Medicaid fraud, abuses 8-30; hearings 8-30—8-31, 714G3-715A3
Agriculture, Nutrition & Forestry, Committee on
Subcoms hold grain probe hearings 3-11—3-16, 247B3
Sen OKs food-stamp reform 4-8, 282F3, 283A1
Dole scores Butz 10-2, 744B2
Appropriations, Committee on
Kissinger on Syria troops in Leb, Hanoi aid 4-14, 257F2, 291E1
Permanent intelligence com created 5-19, 377A1
McGee loses reelectn 11-2, 824D3
Armed Services, Committee on
'77 defense budget hearings 5-4, 5-5, 394B1, F2
Permanent intelligence com OKd 5-19, 376F3, 377A1, B1
NATO improvemts urged 11-14, 879D3
Banking, Housing & Urban Affairs, Committee on
Proxmire asks Smith testimony 1-12, 111F2
Proxmire gets FDIC 'problem' list 1-23, 112B2
Smith on comptroller's 'problem' list 2-6, 113F1
Proxmire scores comptroller 2-17, 3-1, 185D2
Burns on money growth 5-3, 347F2
House OKs FRB reform bill 5-10, 345D2
SEC rpts on corp paymts 5-12, 725E3
Hears Hills on forgn paymts legis 5-18, OKs anti-bribery bill 6-22, 668B3
Scores fed agencies on bias 5-31, 413A3
Nader rpt scores bank diversificatn 7-5, 495A3
Burns testifies, rpts lower M1 target; Proxmire scores 11-11, 865F1, C2
Budget, Committee on the
Muskie rebuts Ford 1-21, 40F1
Muskie, Bellmon back milk price veto 2-4, 88G1
Rivlin on fscl '77 options 3-15, 230D3
Sets fscl '77 targets 4-1, 246C1
Muskie scores tax bill 8-5, 586A2
Muskie lauds Cong budget system 9-15, 706G2
Mondale cites in Dole debate 10-15, 783G1

1977

SENATE—*See also CONGRESS in this section above; also personal names*
Leaders elected 1-4, 5E3-6B2
Vs Daoud release 1-13, 28B1
'76 special interest gifts detailed 1-15, 2-4, 2-15, 128C1-129F2
Ethics panel formed, pay raise linked 1-18, 77E2
Pay raise opponents fail 2-2, 127E2
Com reorganizatn OKd 2-4, 90C1-91G1
Ldrship, coms, chrmn listed; table 90A3
36 protest Sovt Jew jailing 2-19, 226A2
Mansfield in Viet missn 3-16—3-20, 206B1
58 back Carter rights stand 3-25, 226G2
Ethics code adopted 4-1, 251A2
Mansfield confrmd amb to Japan 4-21, 418F1
'76 campaign spending rptd 5-4, 482F1
Reactn to Carter Mideast plan 6-27, 6-29, 496A1
Closed sessn debates neutron bomb 7-1, 534D3
Female aide pay bias rptd 8-4, 669F3
McClellan dies 11-27, 952A3
Aeronautical & Space Sciences, Committee on
Abolished 2-4, 91A1
Aging, Special Committee on
Calif health care fraud chrgd 3-8, 235C3
Agriculture, Nutrition & Forestry, Committee on
For Bergland confrmatn 1-11, 34C3
Talmadge special interest gifts rptd 1-15, 129E1
Admin farm plan outlined 3-23, 214C1
Antitrust & Monopoly, Subcommittee on (of Judiciary Committee)
Gas-productn study cited 2-17, 151E3
Appropriations, Committee on
Vance testifies on aid cuts 2-24, 142E1
Guatemala rejects mil aid 3-16, 187A2
AF computer projct scored 4-27, 421A3
Water project funds cut 6-15, 459E3
FCC network probe suspended 6-30, 583E2-A3
McClellan dies 11-27, 952A3
Armed Services, Committee on
For Brown, Duncan confrmatns 1-13, 34D3
Draft revival urged 1-24, 1-25, 94E3
Nunn vs Warnke appointmt 2-1, 89A1
Warnke hearings 2-22—2-28, 172D1, D2-D3
Mil unionizatn ban considered 3-18, 343B1
Sen votes vs mil union 9-16, 759G3, 760B2
Jackson vs SALT extensn 751D1
SALT leaks by subcom chrgd 11-7, 11-8, 996G2-B3
Arms Control, Subcommittee on (of Armed Services Committee)
SALT leaks chrgd 11-7, 11-8; Jackson denies 11-8, 996G2-B3
Banking, Housing & Urban Affairs, Committee on
Harris confrmatn hearings 1-10; vote 1-18, 34E2
Proxmire special interest gifts rptd 1-15, 129D1
Adams asks transit bill delay 2-25, 213B3
Vance backs Arab boycott curbs 2-28, 166B3
Problem bank list rptd up 3-11, 194D2
Antiboycott bill cited 4-20, 323C3
Renegotiatn Bd extensn hearing 6-13, 482B3
Accuses Lance, Lance vows compliance 7-15, 574A1
Renegotiatn Bd admits Lockheed chrg 'overstated' 8-22, 650E1
Lance hearings 9-26—9-27, 761G1
Black Caucus—*See BLACK Americans—Politics & Government under 'B'*
Budget, Committee on the
Muskie special interest gifts rptd 1-15, 129C1
Bennett named to State post 1-21, 53C1
Carter econ plan hearings 1-27, 89C2
Cong sets '77 levels 3-3, 174C1
Packer confrmd Labor asst secy 3-18, 211F1 ★
Burns on Carter trade policy problems 3-22, 249C1

1978

SENATE—*See also CONGRESS in this section above; also personal names*
Consumer Fed ratings issued 3-4, 183D1; 11-8, 981G2
Dayan meets 6 re US jet pkg oppositn 4-27, 299F2
Moynihan backs USSR trade halt 7-12, 542A2
Office bldg funds defeated 8-17, 681G2
Job bias bd vote blocked 9-20, cover-up chrgd 9-21—9-22, 720A3
UN pro-Palestinian drive starts 10-7, 762B3
80 urge Cambodia rights probe 10-12, 794F1
Smith sees sens, OKs all-parties conf 10-12, 819C1
12 sens visit USSR 11-11—11-18, 905C1
China ties reactn 12-15—12-20, Taiwan defns pact suit threatened 12-15, 974B3, 975A1-976C1
7 join Taiwan defns pact suit 12-22, 995B2
African Affairs, Subcommittee on (of Foreign Relations Committee)
S Africa business tax credits, guarantees end urged 1-25, 135A2
S Africa investmt rpt disputed 8-29, 669E3
Agriculture, Nutrition & Forestry, Committee on
Farmers hiss Bergland testimony 1-24, 163C2
Gartner testifies on Andreas gift, bars resignatn 6-28, 513F2, B3
Antitrust and Monopoly, Subcommittee on (of Judiciary Committee)
FTC aide backs lid on oil, gas co coal, uranium holdings 4-5, 282A3
Oil pipe ownership curb backed 6-21, 471D1
Shenefield, Pertschuk on '71-77 merger rise 7-27, 7-28, 767D1
Kennedy asks FTC probe Lykes-LTV merger 11-9, Bell rptd angry 11-16; FTC rejcts probe 11-21, 935E2
Appropriations, Committee on
Medium sized aircraft carriers backed 2-21, 127G1
Vance subcom testimony 3-9, 216C3
Weicker scores FTC children's TV ad curbs 4-26, 347F2
Mil constructn funds clear Cong, NATO dispute cited 8-21, 662G1
Skylab mission funding OKd 9-30, 750G2
Armed Services, Committee on
Holloway backs Nimitz-class carriers 2-23, 127B2
Neutron bomb stockpile urged 6-11, 469A3
Navy sets sub cost study 6-14, 469F2
New USSR A-bomber rptd 6-19, 518F3
Proxmire asks Navy contract setlmts probed 7-6, 528D3
V/STOL pkg cut by Cong 10-12, 833E1
Banking, Housing & Urban Affairs, Committee on
Key figures in NYC fscl crisis listed 86E2, A3
Proxmire, Brooke rptd vs future NYC fed aid 1-4, 87A1
Miller confirmatn hearings probe Textron Iran, Nigeria paymts 1-24—2-8; confirmatn backed, Proxmire vs 3-2, 161E1-B3
Textron Ghana paymt queried 1-24, evidence rptd destroyed 5-8, 448G3
Proxmire asks Sun Oil Becton Dickinson purchase probe 1-27, 66B1
NYC financial rpt issued; fed aid renewal, recovery plan opposed 2-9, 86E1-87A1
NY offcls score financial rpt 2-9, 87B1
Korea loan, lobbying probe aid linked 2-22, 204B1
Miller urges oil import curbs, anti-inflatn drive 3-15, 181C1-A2
Brooke on Carter urban-aid plan 3-27, 217G3
S Africa Eximbank credit ban rejctd 5-3, 377C1
NYC aid compromise reached 7-13, 608C3
Black Caucus—*See BLACK Americans—Politics & Government under 'B'*
Budget, Committee on the
Farm bill scored by Muskie 3-21, 218D3
Carter reduces tax-cut plan 5-12, 361D1
Muskie scores Carter 12-14, 979G3

1979

Draft registratn defeated by House 9-12, 724G2-B3
Army recruiting fraud probe expands 10-15, 850E2
'79 enlistment gap rptd, Defense Dept rejects draft 10-25, 903B3-E3
McCarthy backs draft registratn 11-13, 868F2
Carter reaffirms volunteer mil support 12-12, 963F1

SENATE—*See also CONGRESS in this section above; also personal names*
Convenes; ldrs elected, rule changes proposed 1-15, 30E1, A2
China's Teng meets 85 sens 1-30, 65D2
Rhodesia electn monitors barred by House 4-9, 293F2
Taiwan defns treaty suit dismissed, Carter policy rebuked 6-6, 440F1, B2
Carter loses Taiwan defns treaty suit 10-17, 777A1
Aging, Special Committee on
Chiles elected chrmn 1-23, 71C2
Agriculture, Nutrition and Forestry, Committee on
Talmadge elected chrmn 1-23, 71C2
Talmadge vs proposed Natural Resource Dept 3-1, 164D1
Subcom malnutritn hearing 4-30, 386G2
Talmadge financial disclosure statemt studied 9-1, 701E3
Appropriations, Committee on
Magnuson elected chrmn 1-23, 71C2
Subcom hears Vance on Rhodesia sanctns 4-26, 332A2
Subcom hears Blumenthal on inflatn rate 5-8, 362C2
Armed Services, Committee on
Stennis elected chrmn 1-23, 71C2
Brown, Jones warn of Sovt threat 1-25, 52A2
USSR mil spending cited in CIA rpt 1-25, 99F2
Mil ldrs dispute draft need 3-13, 307B2
SALT hearings held 7-24—8-1, 643A3
Kissinger on SALT pact 8-2, 590D3
Stennis for Canal treaty implemtatn 9-25, 723A2
Subcom hears DIA testimony re USSR trade 11-8, 856E3-857B1
Manpower subcom gets Army recruiting abuses rpt 11-19, 903F3
Brown questioned on Carter defense plan 12-13, 963B2
SALT II rejectn backed 12-20, 979D1
Aviation, Subcommittee on (of Commerce Committee)
DC-10 safety hearing held 7-12, 539D1
Banking, Housing and Urban Affairs, Committee on
Proxmire elected chrmn 1-23, 71C2
A-war survivors said to face grim future 3-23, 232D2
Proxmire praises Volcker policies 9-26, 745A2
Proxmire asks Textron study 10-31, 923A3
Proxmire scores Chrysler rescue plan 11-1, 845B3
Garn, Nader clash 11-20, 1005F3
Goldschmidt criticized 12-6, 984D1
Chrysler aid bill OKd 12-21, 981E2
Budget, Committee on the
Muskie elected chrmn 1-23, 71C2
Final '80 budget res OKd 11-16, 11-28, 900C1

1980

Kennedy vs plan 2-12, 110C2
Carter: youth overreacting 2-13, 110D1
AFL-CIO backs registratn 2-25, 147A1
Female registration rejected by House subcom 3-6, 188B3
Nunn scores Army infantry shortfall 3-10, 267E2
DC protest held 3-22, 227G3-228A1
House OKs funding amendmt, bars female funds 4-22, 349F1
Adm Hayward backs draft 6-19, 478F3
Dem platform drafted 6-24, 479E3
Carter signs funding bill 6-27, 478C1
Questionaire released 7-2, 493C2
Reagan pres nominatn acceptance speech 7-17, 533D1
Registratn blocked 7-18, Brennan OKs 7-19, 597F3
Registratn start spurs protests 7-21; evasion prosecutn seen 7-31, registratn ends 8-2, Lynn asks amnesty 8-4, 597C3
Dem platform planks adopted 8-13, 615A2, B2
Carter pres renominatn acceptance speech 8-14, 613C1
Registratn statistics disputed 8-26, 9-4, 683E2
Reagan, Anderson TV debate 9-21, 721E2, 722A1
Male-only draft case accepted by Sup Ct 12-1, 918E1

SENATE—*See also CONGRESS in this section above; personal names*
Saudi F-15 gear sale rejectn urged 7-9, 538G2
Agricultural Research and General Legislation, Subcommittee on (of Agriculture Committee)
Hunts testify, chrg SEC silver manipulatn 5-2, 345B2
Agriculture, Nutrition and Forestry, Committee on
Subcom hears Hunts testify 5-2, 345B2
Appropriations, Committee on
Vance on Persian Gulf moves 2-1, 83D2
Subcom hears Brown, Perry on MX deploymt 5-6, 369E2
Armed Services, Committee on
Nunn scores Army infantry shortfall 3-10, 267E2
Iran rescue missn hearings 5-7, 337G2
Staff study faults Iran rescue missn 6-5, 419F1
Computer error A-alert rpt issued 10-29, 986B3
Banking, Housing and Urban Affairs, Committee on
Volcker testifies re FRB membership exodus 2-4, 113F1
Miller testifies re Textron 2-8; spec prosecutor sought 2-8—2-11, 145E1-B2
Miller-Textron spec prosecutor rejctd 3-11, 185D2
Carter scored re inflatn plan 3-17, 201E2
Subcom hears Janis money mkt funds testimony 3-21, 223E3
Silver trading probe scheduled 5-2, 345C2
Eximbank hearings 5-10—5-13; Proxmire urges GAO probe 10-1, 989C1, E1
Hunt bank deals probed; Comex scored, FRB regulatn studied 5-29—5-30, 425D1-B3
Fla banks linked to drug money 6-5, 502A1-A2
Volcker vows '81 tight money targets 7-31, 616A3
Proxmire vs NYC loan guarantees 9-10, 743F1
NYC loan guarantees signed 10-1, Miller OKs funds release 10-2, 826C2
Budget, Committee on the
'81 budget cuts asked 2-27, 168F1
Muskie named secy of state 4-29, 323A3; confrmd 5-7, 343A1
Cuban refugee resetlmt costs estimated 5-25, 396D1
Hollings scores Carter budget stand 5-28, 424C2
Bellmon, Hollings debate '81 budget res 11-20, 896D2

1976

Commerce, Science & Transportation, Committee on
Concorde amendmt beaten 2-5, 94E3
Product safety comm bill signed 5-11, 345C3
Confirmation of Presidential Appointments—*See APPOINTMENTS under FORD*
Democrats
Carter endorsed 6-24, 490D2
Carter vows campaign aid 7-16, 532A3
Finance, Committee on
Kissinger testifies on Angola aid 1-30, 88C3
Long backs revenue sharing 2-23, 149D3
Tax bill study cited 5-5, 480D1
Curbs tax bill loopholes 7-23, 586B2
Subcom hears Moss on Medicare fraud 7-28, 715C3
Sen OKs tax bill 8-6, 585G3
Ford backs sugar industry probe 9-21, 721B3
Shoe import probe reopened 10-5, 976F2

Foreign Relations, Committee on
Kissinger '73 testimony cited 1-12, 184C1
Mrs Javits quits Iran Air post 1-27, 160A2
Rabin meets 1-28, 60A2
Kissinger testifies on Angola aid 1-29, 88B3
Ikle testifies 2-23, 175C1, 243A3
Detente resolutn returned 3-22, 245F3
Moynihan lauds Israel A-bomb rpt 3-25, 243A2
Hussein asks Syria troops in Leb 3-31, 226G2
Kissinger on Syrian troops in Leb 4-9, 257D1
Intellignc com rpt cites 4-26, 302F2
Permanent intelligence com created 5-19, 377A1
S Africa A-plant hearings 5-26—5-29, 388E1, G1
Members see Spain king 6-2, 459B2
US A-aid scored 7-23, 739F2
Panel rpts on US arms sales to Iran 8-1, 581E2
Subcom hears Schaufele on Ethiopia 8-7, 674E2
Admin rpt on Korean crisis 641B2
Panel asked to OK F-16s for Iran 9-16, 773G2
Vs Saudi missile sale 9-24, 746B3
Carter meets 11-23, 881G1
Carter remarks rptd 12-1, 916B3, 917A1

1977

Commerce, Science & Transportation, Committee on
Magnuson special interest gifts rptd 1-15, 129A1
For Kreps, Adams confrmatn 1-19, 34A3
Gets aeronautical, space jurisdictn 2-4, 91A1
Pertschuk confrmd to FTC 4-6, 272B3
Adams backs fed no-fault auto insurnc standards 7-15, law groups vs 7-18, 594F3, 595A1
Air-bag veto opposed 10-12, 797A1
Confirmation of Presidential Appointments—*See CARTER—APPOINTMENTS*
Democrats
61 in 95th Cong 1-4, 5C3
Byrd elected majority ldr, other ldrs elected 1-4, 5E3-6C1, E1
Humphrey gets special post 1-5, 6C1
Carter sees on water projcts 3-10, 209F3
District of Columbia, Committee on
Abolished 2-4, 91A1
Education, Arts and Humanities, Subcommittee on (of Human Resources Committee)
Biddle gets new post 11-30, 927G3
Energy & Natural Resources, Committee on
Jackson special interest gifts rptd 1-15, 129F1
Replaces Interior Com 2-4, 90F1, C3, 91C1
Schlesinger apptmt OKd 8-4, 591D2
Vs fed utility rate rules 9-14, 757D2
Vs oil wellhead tax 9-19, 757F1
Environment & Public Works, Committee on
Created 2-4, 90F1, D3, 91C1
2 Carter nominees rejctd 10-17, 800E1
Ethics, Select Committee on
Ethics code adopted 4-1, 251D3
Korean lobbying links seen 8-8, 688D2
Dole Canal documt disclosure questnd 10-6, 792C1
Korea poll response rptd 11-19, 915D3
Federal Spending Practices & Open Government, Subcommittee on (of Governmental Affairs Committee)
SBA minority aid program scored 7-6—7-8, 577A3
Filibusters
Campaign finance killed 8-2, 592B2
Gas deregulatn OKd 10-4, 757F2
Finance, Committee on
Spec interest gifts rptd 1-15, 129F1; 3-7, 232D2
For Califano, Blumenthal confrmatn 1-18, 34E3
Blumenthal backs investmt tax credit 3-8, 174F2
Health care fraud probe curb chrgd 3-17, 235A3, G3
Champion nomination OKd 3-23, 235F3
Subcom hears Califano on MD fees 6-7, 479F1
Subcom scores pensn managemt concentratn 6-28, 578C2
Vs gas-guzzler tax, backs 4¢-gal extensn 9-20, 757E2, F2 ★
Oil wellhead tax tentatively killed 9-26, 757F1
Energy tax bill clears 10-31, 832A2, C2

Foreign Relations, Committee on
Study asks US Rhodesia mission 1-10, 11A3
Ex-Chile amb on Vance 1-11, 18C2
Vance confrmatn hearings 1-11; vote 1-14, 34C3
Scores Daoud release 1-14, 28C1
Sparkman special interest gifts rptd 1-15, 129C1
Bush on Sovt mil aims rpt 1-18, 39G3
Vance testimony on Cuba released 1-27, 180C2
Sparkman backs Panama Canal talks 2-2, 379A2
Warnke testifies 2-8, 89A1, E1
Nitze testifies vs Warnke 2-9, 172C3
Warnke endorsed 2-22, 172D2
Human rights rpts issued 3-12, 187A1
Vance backs rights amendmt 3-23, 211A1
State Dept authorizatn bill cited 4-11, 283A2
For Cuba embargo ease 5-10, Carter authority re shipmts 5-11, 389C3
Young testifies 6-6, 443E3
Castro vs limited trade move 6-9, 456B2
US denies uranium cartel plans 6-29, 624E3
Atherton on Leb mil aid 6-30, 510C3
Schaufele testifies 7-12, 598F2
Vance sets SALT extensn 9-22, 750B3
SALT extensn res set 9-26, OKd without quorum 9-30, set aside 10-3, 751A2
Panama Canal hearings 9-26—10-5, 754F2, 755A2
Canal hearings continue, attendnc down 10-9—10-10, 792E1
Nigeria ldr confers 10-12, 797A2
Helms pleads no contest re '73 Chile testimony 10-31, 838A3

1978

Commerce, Science & Transportation, Committee on
Bell bars subcom ship rebate probe delay 2-3, 184E3
Subcom chrmn rptd wary re FTC children's TV ad curbs 4-27, 347A3
Seabed mining bill cited 7-26, 589A1
Communications, Subcommittee on (of Commerce Committee)
Hollings rptd wary re FTC children's TV ad curbs 4-27, 347A3
Confirmations of Presidential Appointments—*See CARTER—APPOINTMENTS*
Democrats
Carter backs Pell, Hathaway, McIntyre, Biden reelectn bids 2-17—2-20, 123E1, C3
Job bias bd vote blocked 9-20, 720A3
Election results 11-7, 845C1-846B2, 847C2-849G3, 852F1-857C3
ADA sees conservative shift 12-17, 981E2
Energy & Natural Resources, Committee on
Metcalf dies 1-12, 96A3
Subcom gets solar energy rpt 6-23, 493F3
Energy Research & Development Subcommittee (of Energy & Natural Resources Committee)
Solar energy study rptd, incentives backed 6-23, 493D3
Environment & Public Works, Committee on
PAC gifts to Randolph rptd 12-24, 1008F1
Ethics, Select Committee on
Stevenson links Korea loan, lobbying probe aid 2-22, 204B1
Weicker quits re Korea probe 4-14, 279E3
Park gift to McClellan rptd, 3 others dispute chrgs 6-19, 527D2
Talmadge says Gartner cleared 6-28, 513D3
Talmadge repays expense claims 8-18, probe to continue 8-21, 644A1
Korean probe ends 10-16, 832C1
Talmadge chrgd with rules violatns, hearing set 12-19, 981C3
Brooke probe to end 12-19, 982A1
Federal Spending Practices & Open Government, Subcommittee on (of Governmental Affairs Committee)
GSA hearings 9-18—9-19, 714B2-715C1
Filibusters
Labor law revisn blocked 5-16—6-14, 416C2, E2 ★
Labor law revisn returned to com 6-22, 508B2
FEC confrmatn bar cited 10-25, 831G2
Finance, Committee on
Long, Curtis vs Treas funding for Soc Sec; Blumenthal weighs oil tax link 4-5, 241A1, D1
'76 tax nonpaymt by rich rptd down 7-8, 554C2
Kemp-Roth proposal beaten 9-18, 734E3
Aircraft noise abatemt bill stalled 10-3, 765C3
Long proposes value-added tax 11-30, 962A2
Foreign Economic Policy, Subcommittee on (of Foreign Relations Committee)
Uganda trade ban hearings 6-15, 616F2
Foreign Operations, Subcommittee on (of Appropriations Committee)
Vance links Turkey arms aid, Cyprus 3-9, 216C3
Foreign Relations, Committee on
Subcom asks S Africa business ties end 1-25, 135A2
Panama Canal pacts OKd, addenda asked 1-30, 58A1
Sadat asks for US arms 2-7, 78A1
Rights rpts on 105 natns released 2-9, 101C3, E3
Egypt, Saudi jet sale opposed 2-14, 97E2
Admin rpts on USSR SALT compliance 2-24, 2-28, 298C1, F1
4 members urge Rhodesia pact OK 3-9, 193A2
2 ITT aides chrgd re '73 Chile subcom testimony 3-20, 206G3
Begin questnd 3-21, 199F1
Carter briefs on Begin mtg 3-23, 214F2
Vance vows more Israel F-15 sales 5-9, Brown rpts Saudi curbs 5-10, 357D1, A2
Mideast jet sale vote tied, refers issue to Sen 5-11, 357G2
Turkish arms ceiling upheld, econ aid OKd 5-11, 379B1, B2
Israel agrmt on cluster bombs rptd 5-12, 358A3
Cuba Zaire role evidence sought 5-26, 418B2
CIA evidence on Cuba role in Zaire presented 6-9, 442D2
Subcom hears Uganda terror rpt 6-15, 616F2
US aides say PLO not terror group 6-27, 503B3
Vance has no new Mideast peace plan; Egypt, Saudi hard line cited 8-1, 582D1
Sparkman gets Israel plea on Leb Christns 8-7, 638D2
McGovern asks intl force to oust Cambodia govt, US aide cautions 8-21, 659B3
Subcom S Africa investmt rpt disputed 8-29, 669E3
Carter briefs on Camp David summit 9-18, 710D1
Stone on China ties 12-17, 976B1

1979

Commerce, Science and Transportation, Committee on
Cannon elected chrmn 1-23, 71C2
Teller tells subcom US should release spy satellite photos 1-31, 89G2
Cannon, Kennedy clash over trucking deregulatn 2-7, 111G2
Cannon, Kennedy end dispute 3-21, 308G3
Rail decontrol bill scored at subcom hearing 6-6, 579D2
Aviatn subcom holds DC-10 safety hearing 7-12, 539D1
Confirmation of Presidential Appointments—*See CARTER, Pres. Jimmy—APPOINTMENTS*
Constitution, Subcommittee on (of Judiciary Committee)
Bayh disputes balanced budget amendmt status 2-6, 86D2
Democrats
Com members, chrmn confrmd 1-23, 70E3; ldrship, chrmn chart 71A1
Millionaires chart 5-18, 383C2
Conservative PAC plans drive 8-16, 627F3
Kennedy '80 pres bid rptd asked 9-11, 680A2
Heflin named Ethics Com chrmn 10-31, 945B3
Energy and Natural Resources, Committee on
Jackson elected chrmn 1-23, 71D2
Schlesinger terms Iran oil crisis serious 2-7, 82F2-B3
GAO on higher oil prices 3-7, 182E2
Schlesinger on record US oil use 3-12, 183C2
Carter agrees to energy plan modificatns 9-11, 702D2
Energy, Nuclear Proliferation and Federal Services, Subcommittee on (of Government Affairs Committee)
3 Mile I radiatn estimate hiked 5-3, 344D1
Environment and Public Works, Committee on
Randolph elected chrmn 1-23, 71D2
NRC plans A-safety review 4-10, 275F1
Subcom hears 3 Mile I A-accident testimony 4-30, 344F1
A-plant limits OKd 5-10, 382B1
Ethics, Select Committee on
Justice closes Bayh perjury probe 1-5, 4B3
Vacancy problem rptd 1-23, 71F2
Brooke cleared 3-20, 208F2
Minchew pleads guilty to fraud 7-30, 702B2
Talmadge denunciatn asked 9-14, 702B1
Talmadge denounced 10-10, 769D1
Heflin, Wallop replace Stevenson, Schmitt; Heflin named chrmn 10-31, 945A3
Filibusters
Post-cloture debate limited 2-22, 150D2
Finance, Committee on
Long elected chrmn 1-23, 71D2
Talmadge hosp cost measure cited 3-5, 163B3
Long: tax cut unlikely 4-30, 327C2
Subcom chrmn to retire 5-3, 326A2
Long backs health insurnc 5-14, 362A2; 6-12, 438A3
Miller Treas confrmatn hearing 8-2, 627C2
Long financial disclosure statemt studied 9-1, 701D3

Foreign Relations, Committee on
Church elected chrmn 1-23, 71D2
Church vs proposed Taiwan legis 1-26, 66B3
Rights rpt on 115 natns released 2-10, 107A2
Glenn fears for secret mil data in Iran 3-2, 161A3
Libya jet sales OKd 3-2, 250G1
Subcom estimates Saudi oil output cut 4-14, 279D1
Iran amb nominatn hearing 5-15, 357E2
Vance vs Zimbabwe trade tie 6-12, 435B1
SALT ratificatn hearings 7-9—7-11, 510D1-A2; 7-12, 7-17—7-18, 536D1; Kissinger testifies 7-31, 590A3
Admin denies forgn spy aid rpt, press leak probe begun 8-9, 664C2
SALT hearings stayed 9-4; pact endangered re Sovt troops in Cuba 9-5, 657F1; 9-9, 674B1
Subcom sees Nicaragua junta ldrs 9-24, 731E3
Cambodia starvatn threat rptd 9-27, 741D1
SALT verificatn rpt by Intelligence Com released 10-5, 762D1
SALT hearings end 10-10, reservatns voted 10-15—10-31, 822A2-B3
SALT II approved 11-9, 864A1
Intl sugar agrmt OKd 11-30, 987G2
Church sees Waldheim on Iran crisis 12-1, 913E1
Armed Svcs Com rejects SALT 12-20, 979E1
General Procurement, Subcommittee on (of Armed Services Committee)
DIA: Sovt trade aids mil 11-8, 856E3-857B1

1980

Confirmation of Presidential Appointments—*See APPOINTMENTS*
Defense, Subcommittee on (of Appropriations Committee)
MX deploymt chng rptd 5-6, 369E2
Democrats
Tax-cut plan vowed, econ task-force named 6-26, 480F2
Gravel loses primary 8-26, 683E1-B2
Stewart, Stone primary runoffs set 9-2, 9-2, 682F2, 700F1
Stewart, Stone lose primaries 9-23, 10-8, 745F1, 807C3
Burger stays GOP campaign aid ruling 10-17, Sup Ct continues 10-21, 856D1
Election results 11-4, 837D1, 845F1-846A1, 848B1-852C3; 97th Cong listed 840B1*
Tax-cut bill actn opposed 11-12, 866A2
Byrd sees Reagan, vows cooperatn 11-18, 880G2, C3
Leadership retained 12-4, 936G2
Energy and Natural Resources, Committee on
Synfuels Corp bd appointmts OKd 9-25, 725G2
Environment and Public Works, Committee on
3 Mile I rpt issued by subcom 7-2, 550F3
Toxic waste clean-up fund passed 11-24, 898C1, E1
Ethics, Select Committee on
Abscam probe delay urged by Civiletti 2-5, 2-6; Williams inquiry voted 2-6, 82A2
Filibusters
Labor breaks anti-Lubbers move 4-22, 333E2
Alaska lands bill debate cut off 8-18, 631D2
Finance, Committee on
Dole backs Reagan tax plan 6-25, 480C2
Dems vs tax bill now 11-12, 866A2
New debt ceiling asked 12-2, 916D2
Auto import curb res OKd 12-3, 982B3
Financial Institutions, Subcommittee on (of Banking Committee)
Janis testimony on money mkt funds rptd 3-21, 223E3

Foreign Relations, Committee on
Javits urges NATO GOP platform plank 1-14, 32B1
UN anti-Israel vote probe planned 3-5, 164A1
IMF $ support plan delay seen 3-11, 302A1
Clifford on Afghan crisis 3-18, 205F1
UN anti-Israel vote probed, Vance defends Admin stand 3-20, 218B2
Vance on forgn policy goals 3-27, 243C2
Carter consultatn on Iran mil acts asked 4-24, 297C2
Muskie named secy of state 4-29, 323A3; confrmd 5-7, 343A1
Christopher defends Iran rescue missn 5-8, 338D1
Christopher urges uranium sale to India 6-19, 495B3
India uranium sale bar backed 9-10, 723D1
Percy in Moscow, forsees SALT talks 11-26—11-28, 914G3, 915C1
Percy sees new US-Sovt arms talks 12-12, 950A3

1976

Government Operations, Committee on
A-materials export ban urged 1-19, 115C3
S Korea cancels French A-plant 1-29, 103A3
India A-plant leak rptd 1-30, 156E2
Subcom probes Army meat fraud 5-10, 395A2
US computer sale to S Africa rptd 5-26, 388B2
Rpt US India A-blast aid 8-2, 581D3
Subcom chrgs fed advisor staff bias 9-17, 944E1

Intelligence, Select Committee on
Sen creates 5-19, members named 5-20, 376D3

Intelligence Activities, Select Committee to Study Government Operations with Respect to
Briefing on CIA Italy aid rptd 1-7, 10G2
'75 ACLU study rptd 1-11, 42B1, E1
CIA media manipulatn rptd 1-16, 1-17, 92B3
Drops request for CIA-media names 2-17, 150E2
Warren knowledge of CIA plots rptd 3-1, 217E2
Nixon testimony on Chile released 3-11, 183G2
Issues rpts on US agencies 4-26; text excerpts 4-26, 298D2-304E3; 4-28, 324C3-331C1
Staff details FBI abuses 5-5, 5-6, 5-9, 343F3-344G2
ITT rpts on Chile payoffs 5-12, 361E1
Permanent intelligence com created 5-19, members named 5-20, 376D3

Intelligence Operations Subcommittee on (of Appropriations Committee)
Briefing on CIA Italy aid rptd 1-7, 10G2

Intelligence, Subcommittee on (of Armed Services Committee)
Briefing on CIA Italy aid rptd 1-7, 10G2

Interior & Insular Affairs, Committee on
Subcom majority rpt scores Callaway, Butz 10-5, 744F3

Investigations, Permanent Subcommittee on (of Government Operations Committee)
Rockefeller rues remarks vs Jackson aides 4-27, 305F3

Judiciary, Committee on
S Vietnam returns bodies of 2 US marines 2-22, 157B2
Permanent intelligence com created 5-19, 377A1
OKs oil divestiture bill 6-15, 883A3
Subcom told of US-based Cuban terrorism 8-22, 791C1

1977

Governmental Affairs, Committee on
Replaces Govt Operatns, enlarged 2-4, 91B1
Issues regulatory agency rpt 2-9, 131B3
Accounting hearings 4-19—6-13, 519G2
Subcom scores SBA minority aid progrm 7-6—7-8, 577A3
Clears Lance on finances 7-12—7-25, 573C3—574B2
Subcom holds Teamsters fund hearing 7-18, 558A2
Lance cleared in banking probe 8-18, 625A2, 626B1
Ribicoff, Percy see Carter, ask Lance resignatn 9-5; Lance probe set 9-6; Heimann testifies 9-8, 689G3-690B1
Lance hearings 9-9—9-15; Lance testifies, scores com critics 9-15, 700B3
Lance hearings 9-16—9-19, 718C2-G3
Affidavit vs Lance testimony released 9-20, 718G3

Government Operations, Committee on
Govt Affairs Com replaces 2-4, 91B1

Health, Subcommittee on (of Finance Committee)
Hears Califano on MD fees 6-7, 479F1

Health & Scientific Research, Subcommittee on (of Human Resources Committee)
Hears Califano on DNA 4-6, 452A1
Hears Califano, Gehrig on hosp costs 5-24, 479F1
Turner testifies on CIA mind-control tests 8-3, 611A2
CIA mind-control tests probed 9-2—9-21, 721D1
Kennedy withdraws DNA bill 9-27, 846F2, B3

Human Resources, Committee on
Williams special interest gifts rptd 1-15, 129A1
Created 2-4, 90F1, D3, 91D1
Army germ warfare tests rptd 3-8, 195C2
Subcom hears Califano on DNA 4-6, 452A1
Subcom hears Califano, Gehrig on hosp costs 5-24, 479F1
Subcom hears Turner on CIA mind-control 8-3, 611A2
Subcom probes CIA mind-control tests 9-2—9-21, 721F1
Kennedy withdraws DNA bill 9-27, 846F2, B3
Biddle sworn arts chrmn 11-30, 927F3

Indian Affairs, Committee on
Created in Sen reorganizatn 2-4, 90G2, F3

Intelligence, Select Committee on
Sorensen oppositn cited 1-15—1-17; nominatn withdrawn 1-17, 35B1
Cited re CIA forgn paymts rpt 2-23, 123F3
Watch on members rptd 2-26, 150A3
Micronesia surveillnc rptd 5-3, 386G3
Intell advisory bd ended 5-5, 462E2
Agencies rpt issued 5-18, 386D3
Moynihan chrgs Sovt phone monitoring 7-10, 551E1
Latin tap criticism cited 7-10, 551C2
Turner testifies on CIA mind-control tests 8-3, 611A2
US taps of canal talks probed 9-16—9-19, 716B2
Viet evacuatn probe rptd 11-22, 898B2
Curbs on CIA use of press, clergy planned 12-1, 941A2

Intelligence Activities, Select Committee to Study Government Operations With Respect to (defunct)
Korry chrgs '76 testimony on CIA-multinatl collaboratn suppressed 1-9, 18E2 ★
Castro notes plot disclosures 2-26—2-27, 180E3
Carter cites '75 Chile coup rpt 3-9, 219C1
CIA press link cover-up chrgd 9-12, 720A3

Interior & Insular Affairs, Committee on
For Andrus confrmatn 1-18, 34G3
Energy & Natural Resources Com replaces 2-4, 91C1

Internal Security, Subcommittee on (of Judiciary Committee)
Dies 3-31, 251F3

Investigations, Permanent Subcommittee on (of Government Affairs Committee)
Teamsters fund hearing 7-18, 558A2
Teamsters insurnc deal probed 10-31—11-2, 837E1

Judiciary, Committee on
Bell confrmatn hearings 1-11—1-18; vote 1-19, 34D1
Eastland special interest gifts rptd 1-15, 129D1
Subcom gas-productn study cited 2-17, 151E3
Internal Security subcom dies 3-31, 251F3
Reagan scores Panama Canal pacts in subcom testimony 9-8, 698C3-699B1
Subcom stays Panama Canal wiretap hearings 9-30, 756D1
House Panama Canal pact OK held necessary 11-3, 912B2

1978

Governmental Affairs, Committee on
Cabt-level Educ Dept proposed 4-14, 279F1 ★
McClellan immunity case refused by Sup Ct 6-26, 566E2
HEW asks welfare loopholes closed 7-20, 684D3
'77 consumer utility bills rptd up 9-17, 718D3
GSA probed by subcom 9-18—9-19, 714B2-715C1

Human Resources, Committee on
Labor law revisn returned 6-22, 508C2

Immigration, Committee on (of Judiciary Committee)
Delegatn in Viet 7-31—8-7, 603D2

Intelligence, Select Committee on
Bayh, Inouye back Carter reorganizatn 1-24, 49B2
Agency reorg, curbs introduced 2-9, 106D3
Torrijos drug link rpt read to Sen, edited versn released 2-21, 120C2
Letelier murder suspect '75 probe rptd 3-6, 188E3
CIA Black Panther surveillnc rptd 3-17, 243F2
ITT, CIA Chile probe cited 3-20, 207A1
Ex-offcls vs excessive curbs 4-4—4-19, 306G1-F2
Korea lobbying probe plans rptd 4-14, 279F3
CIA '77 Sovt-bloc oil study assessed 5-21, 384E1
Wilkins '75 denial of link to FBI anti-King effort rptd 5-31, 410F3
Carter on security leaks 7-11, 524G2
Viet documt possessn by ex-amb probed 9-13, 720B2
CIA ex-offcl's death rptd probed 10-5, 835F3

Intelligence Activities, Select Committee to Study Government Operations With Respect to (defunct)
Defns Dept intell budget share cited 9-17, 715C3

International Finance, Subcommittee on (of Banking Committee)
Korea loan, lobbying probe aid linked 2-22, 204B1

Investigations, Permanent Subcommittee on (of Government Affairs Committee)
McClellan immunity case refused by Sup Ct 6-26, 566E2

Judiciary, Committee on the
Webster hearings 1-20—1-31, 82G3
FTC aide backs lid on oil, gas co coal, uranium reserves 4-5, 282G2
Civiletti confirmatn backed 4-14, 309D3; confrmd 5-9, 342E3
No cover-up seen in Marston affair 4-24, 309A3
Marston cover-up rpt rejctd by Sen 5-4, 342G3
Oil pipe ownership curb backed by subcom 6-21, 471D1
Shenefield, Pertschuk testify re merger trend 7-27, 7-82, 767D1
Subcom delegatn in Viet 7-31—8-7, 603D2
Kennedy asks FTC probe Lykes-LTV merger 11-9, Bell rptd angry 11-16; FTC rejcts probe 11-21, 935E2

1979

Governmental Affairs, Committee on
Ribicoff elected chrmn 1-23, 71D2
Investigatns subcom food stamp probe rptd 2-2, 93B3
Ribicoff to retire 5-3, 326A2
3 Mile I radiatn estimate hiked in subcom testimony 5-3, 344D1
Resources Dept plan dropped 5-15, 365C2
Subcom urges pensn fund safeguards 11-26, 905B1

Health, Subcommittee on (of Finance Committee)
Talmadge hosp cost measure cited 3-5, 163B3

Health and Scientific Research, Subcommittee on (of Human Resources Committee)
Mrs Carter asks more mental health funds 2-7, 112B1
Cancer death rates detailed 3-5, 195B3
Kennedy at hosp cost bill ceremony 3-6, 163C2
Hosp cost-control hearings open 3-9, 194E2
3 Mile I radiatn hazards assessed 4-4, 260E1
Valium abuse detailed 9-10, 734F2

Human Resources, Committee on
Williams elected chrmn 1-23, 71E2
Mrs Carter asks more mental health funds 2-7, 112B1
Cancer death rates detailed 3-5, 195B3
Kennedy at hosp cost bill ceremony 3-6, 163C2
Subcom opens hosp cost-control hearings 3-9, 194E2
Health subcom assesses 3 Mile I radiatn hazards 4-4, 260E1
Subcom probes Valium abuse 9-10, 734F2

Indian Affairs, Committee on
Melcher elected chrmn 1-23, 71E2

Intelligence, Select Committee on
Bayh elected chrmn 1-23, 71E2
CIA ex-offcl's death probe urged 1-24, 54G3
CIA ex-offcl's death probe dropped 4-18, 283F3; new probe planned 4-30, 368A1
USSR new systems deploymt rptd allowed 7-18, 536B2
SALT verificatn assessed 10-5, 761G3
Iran bars Miller as mediator 11-7, 841D2

International Economic Policy, Subcommittee on (of Foreign Relations Committee)
Saudi oil output cut estimated 4-14, 279D1

International Trade, Subcommittee on (of Finance Committee)
Ribicoff to retire 5-3, 326A2

Investigations, Permanent Subcommittee on (of Governmental Affairs Committee)
Food stamp probe rptd 2-2, 93B3
Pensn safeguards urged 11-26, 905B1

Judiciary, Committee on the
Kennedy elected chrmn 1-23, 71E2
Kennedy, Cannon clash over trucking deregulatn 2-7, 111G2
Kennedy introduces merger-limit bill, Justice Dept backs 3-8, 202D2
Refugee bill testimony 3-14, 308A1
GOP members score Carter peanut probe limits 3-20, 203E1
Kennedy, Cannon end dispute 3-21, 308G3
FBI informant loss rptd, disclosures scored 3-22, 232C2
Refugee paroles extended 3-26, 308B1
Niagara chem dump hearing 4-11, 281E3
3 Mile I comm subpoena power OKd 5-17, 417F3
FBI charter introduced 7-31, 599B3
FBI audit shows compliance with informant rules 8-22, 747E2
Kennedy, Javits clash on Brown confirmatn; com OKs nominatn 9-25, 901E3

1980

Governmental Affairs, Committee on
Subcom hears GSA scandal testimony 1-19, 112A2
Subcom rpts govt furniture waste 3-18, 459D2
Christopher urges uranium sale to India 6-19, 495B3
Subcom rpts year-end spending waste 7-20, 598E2

Health and Scientific Research, Subcommittee on (of Human Resources Committee)
Toxic-shock syndrome cases detailed 6-6, 584A3

Human Resources, Committee on
Subcom hears toxic-shock syndrome testimony 6-6, 584A3

Intelligence, Select Committee on
Turner admits CIA use of press, clergy, academics 2-21, Aspin asks details 2-25, 189A3
CIA ex-offcl cleared 4-24, 459C1
Oversight bill OKd by Sen 6-3, 458C3
Moynihan, Wallop seek Trigon probe 9-10, 754G1
Intell oversight bill clears Cong 9-19, 9-30; signed 10-14, 804F1
Carter aide cleared in spy leak 12-5, 940B2

Judiciary, Committee on the
Carter nominee for judgeship rejctd 3-4, 250E2
Miller-Textron spec prosecutor rejected 3-11, 185D2
Kennedy visits Mex 4-28, 327G2
ABA rpts black dist judge nominees 'unqualified' 5-19; hearings end, Clemon backed 6-24, 744B3
Kennedy quits B Carter probe 7-23, panel set 7-24, 548F2, 549E1
Bayh panel plans B Carter probe 7-25—7-31, 569E1, G1
Carter issues rpt on brother 8-4, 592F1
Bayh panel opens B Carter probe 8-4, 8-6, 595F2
Watergate counsel declines B Carter probe role 8-7, 595E3
B Carter probe counsel named 8-11, 647E2
B Carter probe continues 8-19—8-22, 647A1-E2
Sheffield tax probe leak halts confirmatn hearings 8-27, 744G3
B Carter probe hearings 9-4—9-17, 700D3
'81 refugee quota cut 9-19, 883A3
B Carter probe concluded 9-22—9-24, critical rpt issued 10-2, 763B3-764F1
Justice rpt faults Carter on brother's probe 10-29—11-1, 841F1
Thurmond slated to be chrmn 11-4, 837E1

1976

Labor & Public Welfare, Committee on
Usery hearing 1-28, 110G1
Kennedy vs rpt on FDA rpt 5-23, 392A2
2 testify re Teamsters 7-1, 492B2
Subcom hearings on gene research 9-22, 860B3
Polio vaccine danger rptd 9-23, 776B1
Subcom hearing on paralysis, flu vaccine 12-17, 950A2
Legislation—*See under CONGRESS in this section above*
Manpower & Personnel, Subcommittee on (of Armed Services Committee)
Honor-code hearings 6-21, Hoffman offers ousted cadets readmissn 8-23, 670E1, C3
Membership
Political lineup 1-19, 68D3 ★
Chrgs vs Scott, others re Gulf probed 2-4, 133E3
Bellmon retains seat 3-4, 180C2
Mansfield to retire 3-4, 181D1
Montoya tax audit rptd 3-24, 247B1
Ray sex chrg vs Gravel rptd 6-12, 434B1
Mondale gets Dem vp nominatn 7-15, 506D2; **for subsequent developments, see MONDALE, Walter**
Reagan names Schweiker running mate 7-26, 549C2, 550C1
Symington to retire 8-3, 565E2
Dole gets GOP vp nominatn 8-19, 598B2-599F1; **for subsequent developments, see DOLE, Robert**
Pay increase barred 10-1, 834A2
Election results 11-2, 817E1, 819B3-820E1; 95th Congress listed 828A1-D2
Anderson seeks Mondale seat 11-10, 865B1
One 8-yr term proposed 11-29, 917G2-A3
Philip Hart dies 12-6, 1015E1
Anderson succeeds Mondale 12-30, 994C1
Multinational Corporations, Special Subcommittee on (of Foreign Relations Committee)
Forgn bank deposit disclosure agrmt rptd 1-18, 44B3
Jackson CIA contacts rptd 1-26, 93G1
Releases Lockheed bribe documents 2-4; hearing 2-6, 130E1-131D1, E3; Dutch, Japan, Bonn reactn 2-8, 2-11, 2-12, 131D2, 132E1, E2
Lockheed letters on Colombia bribes published 2-8, 147E2
Turkey opens Lockheed probe 2-9, 192B2
Northrop repays Iran agent fee 2-23, 156G2
US to free Lockheed documents 3-5, 190D2, 191D1; 3-11, 199E3
Ends Bonn payoffs probe 3-10, 200A2
Lockheed Australia payoff chrgd 4-29, 322A2
Clears Italy pres 6-15, 445D2
Told Iran seeks 300 F-16s 9-10, 773A3
Probes Nixon Grumman bid, Iran sales 9-13—9-26, 979G1-G3
Hendrix chrgd re ITT-Chile probe 11-5, 869F2
'75 hearings on OPEC bank deposits cited 11-10, 915A2
Post Office & Civil Service, Committee on
McGee loses reelectn 11-2, 819G3, 824D3
Public Works, Committee on
Sen OKs pub works bill 4-13, 283C1, F1
Resolutions—*See 'Legislation' under CONGRESS in this section above*
Rules and Administration, Committee on
Votes temporary intelligence panel 4-29, 376E3
OKs Springer nomination 5-21, 391B3
Standards & Conduct, Select Committee on
Rpts Gulf paymts probe 2-4, 133F3
Scott testimony rptd 8-31; ends Gulf gift probe 9-15, 980A1

1977

Labor & Public Welfare, Committee on
Califano hearing 1-13, 34F3
For Marshall confrmatn 1-18, 34G3
Legislation—*See under CONGRESS in this section above*
Nutrition & Human Needs, Select Committee on
Sen reorganizatn OKd 2-4, 90G2, F3
Post Office & Civil Service, Committee on
Abolished 2-4, 91B1
Private Pension Plans & Employee Fringe Benefits (of Finance Committee)
Pension mgt concentratn chrgd 6-28, 578C2
Reports, Accounting & Management, Subcommittee on (of Governmental Affairs Committee)
Staff rpt scores accountants 1-17, 78B3
Accounting hearings 4-19—6-13, 519G2
Republicans
38 in 95th Cong 1-4, 5C3
Leaders elected 1-4, 6E1-B2
Econ plan offered 2-2, 89F2
Com staff positns hiked 2-4, 90D1, 91F1
Resolutions—*See CONGRESS—Legislation in this section above*
Rules & Administration, Committee on
Cannon special interest gifts rptd 1-15, 129B1
Sen reorganizatn OKd 2-4, 90G1
Separation of Powers, Subcommittee on (of Judiciary Committee)
Panama Canal wiretap hearings stayed 9-30, 756D1
House Panama Canal pact OK held necessary 11-3, 912B2
State, Justice, Commerce, the Judiciary, Subcommittee on (of Appropriations Committee)
FCC network probe suspended 6-30, 583F2-A3
Treaty Ratification
Canada prisoner exchng 7-19, 834F1
Mex prisoner exchng 7-21, 746F2

1978

Korean Lobbying Scandal—*See KOREA (South)—U.S.-Korean Political Payments*
Legislation—*See under CONGRESS in this section above*
Lobbying & Lobbyists—*See under CONGRESS in this section above; for KOREA (South)—U.S.-Korean Political Payments*
Membership—*See also other appropriate subheads in this section*
Metcalf dies 1-12, 96A3
Humphrey dies 1-13, 32E2; wife takes seat 1-25, 52G2
Hatfield named to Metcalf seat 1-22, 52B3
Carter backs Dem reelectn bids 2-17—2-20, 123E1, C3
Percy wins primary 3-21, 207G1
Curtis to retire 5-9, 363F1
Wallace quits Ala race 5-16, 362G2
Personal finance rpts disclosed 5-19, no interest conflicts found 5-22, 385A3
Brooke admits false loan disclosure 5-26, 406B1
Allen dies 6-1, widow named to seat 6-8, 432E1
Case loses primary 6-6, 425C1, 447F3
Eastland to retire 6-6, 448C1
Hatfield loses primary 6-6, 448A2
Abourezk to retire 6-6, 448A2
Scott to retire 6-13, 467G1
Talmadge repays expense claims 8-18, denies guilt 8-18, 8-19, 643G3
Bartlett to retire 8-22, 683C1
Sparkman to retire 9-5, 699A2
Anderson wins primary 9-12, 716C1
Pell wins primary 9-12, 716G2
McIntyre wins renominatn 9-12, 736E1
Biden unopposed in primary 9-12, 736G1
Hansen to retire 9-12, 736C2
Haskell unopposed in primary 9-12, 736D2
Johnston assured reelectn 9-16, 736C3
Brooke wins renominatn 9-19, 736F2
Election results 11-7, 845C1-846B2, 847C2-849G3, 852F1-857C3
Races rptd won by big spenders 11-15, 898A1
Warner electn certified 11-27, 915A3
Travel overseas rptd 12-10, 958B3
ADA issues ratings, conservate shift seen 12-17, 981D2
Talmadge chrgd with rules violatns 12-19, 981C3
Brooke probe to end 12-19, 982A1
PAC gifts to 2 com chrmn rptd 12-24, 1008A1
Merchant Marine & Tourism, Subcommittee on (of Commerce Committee)
Bell bars rebate probe delay 2-3, 184E3
Multinational Corporations, Subcommittee on (of Foreign Relations Committee)
2 ITT aides accused re '73 Chile testimony, Geneen chrg declined 3-20, 206G3
Public Works, Committee on
Pub works veto scored by Randolph 10-7, 769B2
Republicans
Carter forgn policy scored 5-3, 342E2
McGarry, Zagoria FEC nominatns opposed 10-25, 8-12, 831G2, C3
Election results 11-7, 845C1-846B2, 847C2-849G3, 852F1-857C3
Resolutions—*See CONGRESS—Legislation in this section above*
Rules & Administration, Committee on
PAC gifts to Pell rptd 12-24, 1008E1
Securities, Subcommittee on (of Banking Committee)
Sun Oil Becton Dickinson purchase probe asked 1-27, 66B1
Small Business, Select Committee on
SBA minority-aid abuse detailed 11-21, 919B3
Social Security, Subcommittee on (of Finance Committee)
Blumenthal testifies 4-5, 241D1
Tax compensatn amendmt rejctd 8-10, 604D1
Treaty Ratification
Panama Canal debate opens 2-8—2-22, 120B1
Panama Canal neutrality pact amended 3-10, 3-13, reservatns added 3-15, 3-16; pact OKd, role call vote listed 3-16, 177C1-178A2
Panama Canal Treaty ratified 4-18, 273A1
Canada fishing rights pending 5-5, 350C2
Canal treaty challenge refused by Sup Ct 5-15, 387G3
Panama Canal pact instrumts exchngd 6-16, 463F2
Amer rights conv ratificatn vowed by Carter 6-21, 489D3
UK tax pact ratified 6-27, 588D2
Amer rights conv vote seen in '79 7-18, 829B1
Carter hopeful re SALT 9-27, 751E3; 10-10, 766G3
Carter urges UN Genocide Conv OK 12-6, 934B1

1979

Labor and Human Resources, Committee on
Hufstedler confrmatn hearing 11-27, 946G2
Legislation—*See under CONGRESS in this section above*
Lobbying & Lobbyists—*See under CONGRESS in this section above*
Manpower and Personnel, Subcommittee on (of Armed Services Committee)
Army recruiting abuses detailed 11-19, 903F3
Membership—*See also other appropriate subheads in this section*
Talmadge hospitalized for alcoholism 1-22, 176E1
Com members, chrmn confrmd 1-23, 70E3; ldrship, chrmn chart 71A1
Outside income limit delayed 3-8, 185D2
Weicker announces pres bid 3-12, 185A3
Brooke cleared of wrongdoing 3-20, 208F2
S Africa '78 campaign contributns to Jepsen chrgd, denied 3-21, 213C1
Outside income limit delayed again 3-28, 281E1
Stevenson bars reelectn bid 3-30, 265D2
Ribicoff announces retiremt 5-3, 326G1
'78 PAC spending rptd up 5-10, Common Cause deplores 5-15, 363E1-B2
Dole enters pres race 5-14, 363B3
Weicker ends pres bid 5-16, 363F3
Sens disclose worth; millionaires chart 5-18, 383C2
Labor '78 campaign gifts rptd 6-13, 595C1
Proxmire libel suit OKd by Sup Ct 6-26, 540F2
Conservative PAC plans drive 8-16, 627F3
Financial disclosure statemts studied 9-1, 701C3-702B1
Talmadge denunciatn voted 9-14, 702B1
Pressler enters pres race 9-25, 724E1
Talmadge denounced 10-10, 769B1
Baker enters pres race 11-1, 828D3
Kennedy announces pres bid 11-7, 847B1
Nuclear Regulation, Subcommittee on (of Environment and Public Works Committee)
NRC plans A-safety review 4-10, 275F1
NRC testifies on 3 Mile I A-accident 4-30, 344F1
Nutrition and Human Needs, Subcommittee on (of Agriculture Committee)
Malnutritn rptd down, fed food progrms credited 4-30, 386G2
Public Works, Committee on
Hart on 3 Mile I A-accident cleanup 4-2, 245G2
Republicans
Rule chngs proposed, ldrs elected 1-15, 30A2
Com members, chrmn confrmd 1-23, 70F3; ldrship chart 71B2
SALT treaty scored 3-4, 4-5, 258E1, G1
Carter peanut probe limits scored 3-20, 203D1
Millionaires chart 5-18, 383D2
Rules and Administration, Committee on
Pell elected chrmn 1-23, 71E2
Science, Technology and Space, Subcommittee on (of Commerce Committee)
Teller asks US spy satellite photo release 1-31, 89G2
Small Business, Committee on
Nelson elected chrmn 1-23, 71E2
Surface Transportation, Subcommittee on (of Commerce Committee)
Rail decontrol bill scored 6-6, 579D2
Treaty Ratification
SALT pact backed by UK, W Ger 1-6, 12F2
Carter State of Union Message notes SALT 1-23, 48C1
Carter sets SALT pact ratificatn as top forgn goal 1-25, 70B2
SALT reactions 2-20—4-5, 258D1
US confrms arms restraint if SALT fails, denies exec agrmt rpt 2-23, 258B2
Carter promotes SALT pact 4-25, 294A2
Carter: would uphold SALT terms despite ratificatn bar 4-30, 319A1
US sens score SALT 5-10—5-17, Jackson chrgs appeasemt 6-12, 6-17, 449F2, 459F2-460C1
Admin stresses SALT pact 5-15, 365D2
Brown cites NATO SALT support 5-16, 359B3
NATO forgn mins warn vs SALT defeat 5-31, 415D3
Schmidt backs SALT pact 6-6, 430D1
USSR warns vs SALT II chngs 6-17; pact signed, Carter asks ratificatn 6-18, 449A1, G1, C2, 458F1
Gromyko warns vs SALT II chngs 6-25, reactn 6-26—6-30, 496G2-F3
Byrd in USSR 7-1—7-5, warns vs amendmts 7-8, 511B3
SALT debated in Forgn Rel Com 7-9—7-11, 510D1-A2; 7-12, 7-17—7-18, 536D1

1980

Manpower and Personnel, Subcommittee on (of Armed Services Committee)
Nunn scores Army infantry shortfall 3-10, 267E2
Membership
Cong Watch sees anticonsumerism 1-12, 53G2
ACU '79 voting survey rptd 1-18, 53B3
Muskie named secy of state 4-29, 323A3; confrmd 5-7, 343A1
Mitchell gets Muskie seat 5-8, 367B2
Talmadge finances probe dropped 5-30, 427E3-428A1
Primaries lost by Gravel 8-26, Javits 9-9, 682D1, 683E1-B2
Primary runoffs set for Stewart 9-2, Stone 9-9, 682F2, 700F1
Primaries lost by Stewart 9-23, Stone 10-7, 745F1, 807C3
Burger stays GOP campaign aid ruling 10-17, Sup Ct continues 10-21, 856D1
Election results 11-4, 837D1, 845F1-846A1, 848B1-852C3; 97th Cong listed 840B1*
Nuclear Regulation, Subcommittee on (of Environment and Public Works Committee)
3 Mile I rpt issued 7-2, 550F3
Oversight of Government Management, Subcommittee on (of Governmental Affairs Committee)
US year-end spending scored 7-20, 598E2
Republicans
State of Union reactn 1-28, 75C1
Javits loses NY primary 9-9, 682D1
Burger stays campaign aid ruling 10-17, Sup Ct continues 10-21, 856D1
Election results 11-4, 837D1, 845F1-846A1, 848B1-852C3; 97th Cong listed 840B1*
Reagan sees Baker 11-18, attends fetes 11-19, 880G2, 881D1
Majority ldr, whip, other posts filled 12-2, 915C2
Small Business, Committee on
Business paper work costs rptd 1-3, 17D3
Treaty Ratification
Reagan 'basic speech' scores SALT 2-29, 207F2
Carter hints SALT renunciation, doubts ratification 3-14, 209E1
USSR bars SALT II talks 3-19, 219C2
Europn CPs back SALT ratificatn 4-29, 327C3
Vance urges SALT OK 6-5, 421D3
Muskie hints SALT OK 9-7, 679G3-680A1
Canada tax treaty signed 9-26, 748F2

1976

Veterans Affairs, Committee on
Hartke loses reelection 11-2, 819G3
SERVICE Corps of Retired Executives—*See under ACTION in this section above*
SMALL Business Administration (SBA)
Kobelinski confrmd admin 2-6, 110B2
Wright Patman dies 3-7, 240E3
Ex-Va official sentncd 6-25, 596G1
'77 funds signed 7-14, 534E2
GOP platform text 8-18, 603A2
MCA to aid minorities, women 8-20, 944B1
Carter scores mismanagemt 9-13, 686D2
SMITHSONIAN Institution
'77 funds signed 7-31, 623D1

SOCIAL Security Administration (& System) (of Department of Health, Education & Welfare)
Sup Ct backs review of cases by US magistrates 1-14, 24A2
Ford State of Union message 1-19, 36G2, 38D1, 39B2
SSI overpaymts, study rptd 1-20, 1-27, 128C2
'77 budget proposals 1-21, 62B3, C3, 63E1, A2, C3, 65A2
Ford Econ Rpt 1-26, 67B3
Medicare waste confirmed 2-2, 128E1
Reagan backs reforms 2-7, 130C1
Ford submits tax plan 2-9, 110C1
Ford, Reagan statemts 2-14, 2-17, 2-18, 129F2, F3, 130B1
Disability cutoff procedures upheld 2-24, 169B2
Cong econ, budget coms vs Ford tax hike 3-10, 3-23, 230B3, 231G2
NYC plans '78 withdrawal 3-22, other cities cited 3-23, 994E1
Fscl '77 US budget estimate tables 231B1, 358F1, C2
Reagan campaign position 3-31, 232C2
NY man wins bias suit 5-12, 413C3
Sup Ct affirms Utah contraceptive rule 5-24, 393D2
Trustees rpt to Cong 5-24, 398F2
Dem platform text 6-15, 470F2, 473A1
Sup Ct upholds illegitimacy rule 6-29, 568D3
Sen OKs state, local use of numbers 8-6, 586A2
GOP platform text 8-18, 604F2, 605A3, 606D2
Ford acceptance speech cites 8-19, 612C2
State, local use of numbers clears Cong 9-16, 706G1
Marion Folsom dies 9-28, 932D3
Payroll tax hike bill not cleared 10-2, 883A1, 884C1
Mondale, Dole debate 10-15, 783C1
Transitn ¼ fed spending rptd down 10-27, 866D1
Sup Ct bars divorced mother benefits 12-13, 940C3

STATE, Department of—*See also KISSINGER, Henry; for U.S. foreign policy, see specific country names and appropriate subheads under MIDDLE EAST; also subjects*
Sonnenfeldt E Eur remarks rptd 3-22, Kissinger, Reagan score 3-29, 3-31, 232G2
Cong clears 200-mi fishing zone 3-30, 246B2
Ford denies bid to Connally 4-19, 281B2
Intl buffer stock issue dispute rptd 5-6, 317E1

1977

Veterans Affairs, Committee on
Sen reorganizatn OKd 2-4, 90G2, G3
SMALL Business Administration (SBA)
Carter seeks drought aid 3-23, 210B2
Loan ceiling hike signed 3-24, 250D3
Minority aid program scored 7-6—7-8, halted 7-8, 577G2
'78 funds, '77 supplement signed 8-2, 667D3, G3
'78-79 funds authorized, disaster loans broadened 8-4, 689B3
Minority aid moratorium lifted 11-4, 859F3
SMITHSONIAN Institution
Loses bid for rare meteorite 9-7, 712G2
SOCIAL & Rehabilitation Service—*See HEALTH, Education & Welfare in this section above*

SOCIAL Security Administration (& System) (of Department of Health, Education & Welfare)
Ford asks tax rise 1-4, 5E2
Carter plans payroll tax credit 1-7, 5F1
CBO issues poverty rpt 1-13, 80C3
Ford '78 budget proposals 1-17, 32A2-F2, 33F2
Carter favors rebate 1-27, 52C1
Carter budget revisns 2-22, 124E3, 125A2, 126C1
Sup Ct voids widower benefits rule 3-2, 192C1-B2
HEW reorganized 3-9, 175B3, D3
Old-age benefits test voided 3-21, 230E1
Old-age benefits sex bias upheld 3-21, 230G1-D2
Carter drops rebate plan 4-14, 270G2
June '75 bonus cited 4-19, 300E3
Carter asks funding changes 5-9, 363F2
Carter scores liberals' criticism 5-12, 380F3
Cong sets '78 budget target 5-17, 405B1
Burger cites '69-76 cases 5-17, 419F2
Carter seeks SSI end 5-25, 445A3
State abortn curbs upheld 6-20, 516E2
HEW jobless-benefits standards law upheld 6-20, 516F3-517A1
Carter proposes illegal alien plan 8-4, 592D1
Carter proposes SSI end 8-6, 608C3
Benefits raised, July income up 8-17, 629F1
GOP offers plan to Cong 9-9, 720G1
Carter delays tax pkg, asks Soc Sec bill action 10-27, 813A1, A3, C3
Wage base, tax rate hikes, other revisns clear House 10-27, 814D2-815A1
Pa benefits seizure dispute declined 11-7, 857C2
Benefits loss on marriage upheld 11-8, 857A1
Carter hopeful on tax hikes 11-30, 914A1
Wage base, tax rate hikes, other revisns clear Cong 12-15, 957A3; signed 12-20, 1001C2
Transfer Payments—*See INCOMES*

STATE, Department of—*See also VANCE, Cyrus; for U.S. foreign policy, see specific countries, regions*
Forgn rights abuse rpts released, contd mil aid backed 1-1, 50D2
Boeing paymts secrecy backed 1-5, ct agrees 2-25, 215B3
Fishing accords approved 2-21, 3-3, 173D3
Carter addresses, backs CIA 2-24, 151F1
Arab boycott guidelines backed 2-28, 166D3

1978

SMALL Business Administration (SBA)
Minority broadcasting ownership aid proposed 1-31, 195B2
'78 disaster loan funds signed 3-7, 160F2
Solar, other renewable energy business loan aid signed 7-4, 512F1
Export financing hike sought by Carter 9-26, 804E2
Aid expansn vetoed 10-25, 897F2
Carter pocket vetoes Tris compensatn bill, asks aid 11-8, 941F3
Loan guarantee to TV host rptd 11-16, 919D3
Proxmire asks abolitn 11-20; minority-aid abuse detailed, Justice probe rptd 11-21, 919A3
SMITHSONIAN Institution—*See separate listing under 'S'*
SMOKING & Health, Office on—*See under HEALTH, Education & Welfare in this section above*

SOCIAL Security Administration (& System) (of Department of Health, Education & Welfare)
Poland lowers exchng rate for US retirees 1-1, 20E1
Carter Econ Message 1-20, 48B3
Carter budget proposals 1-23, 44E2, 46F3, 47B1; table 45C2, E2
Federal budget dollar table 63A1
AFL-CIO urges tax rollback 2-20, 141G3
PR SSI benefits exclusn upheld 2-27, 143A1
Expedited SSI benefits rule review declined 2-27, 143E1
Carter links hike, tax cuts 3-2, 141D1
Feb income drop, hike linked 3-17, 223C1
Oil tax, rollback link proposed 4-2; Blumenthal skeptical 4-5, 241C1
Tax rollback, Treas fund use backed by House Budget Com, Dem Caucus 4-4, 4-5; Admin opposes 4-5, 240B3-241B1
1st ¼ labor costs rise, tax hike linked 4-25, 345C2
CPI rise, paymts boost linked 4-28, 345B1
Trustees rpt fiscally sound, urge hosp insurnc reform 5-16, 368B3
Cong '79 budget target res cleared, rollback stand omitted 5-17, 385B2
House com bars tax rollback 5-17, 385G3
Tax hike, inflatn linked 6-19, 427D2
NYC welfare fraud crackdown rptd 7-3, 685A1
SSI recipients job tax credit OKd by House com 7-27, 587E1
SSI paymt errors rptd 8-12, 684G2
July income rise, inflatn hike linked 8-17, 643F3
Ross named comr 8-24, 664B1
SSI '74-76 overpaymt restitutn sought 8-29, 684D3
Carter bars 'substantial' chngs 11-9, 874G3
Guyana cult cache found 11-18, 890A3
Value-added tax proposed 11-30, 962A2, F2
SSI forgn travel rule backed by Sup Ct 12-11, 980G3
House com seeks illegal alien curbs 12-20, 1010F2
Transfer Payments—*See INCOMES*
SOLAR Energy Policy Committee
Draft study issued 8-25, 718A2

STATE, Department of—*See also VANCE, Cyrus; for U.S. foreign policy, see countries, regions, organizations*
GAO study re oil dealings scored 1-3, 6B1
Rights rpts on 105 natns released 2-9, 101C3
Canada fishing boats blocked 5-5, 350D2
Nazi war criminal links rptd 5-16, 411B1
'77 rejected arms bid rptd, '78 sales forecast 5-19, 386E3-387A1
Carter on security leaks 7-11, 524G2

1979

Australia Labor Party backs SALT monitoring base 7-19, 542A2
SALT debated in Armed Svcs Com 7-24–8-1, 643A3
Carter vs mil budget, SALT linkage 7-27; Kissinger backs 7-31, 8-2; US sens react 8-2, 8-3, 590G2-591D1
H Byrd vs SALT pact 7-30, 644B1
Proposed SALT additns detailed 8-30, 657F2
Canada fish pact threatened 9-4, 667C2
SALT delay seen re Cuba troop issue 9-5, 657F1; 9-6–9-11, 674B1
Panama Canal treaty implementatn clears Cong 9-26, signed 9-27, 723A1
Carter urges SALT ratification 10-1; Sen, Eur reactn 10-1–10-3, 737B1, B2, 738F1, 739F1-C2
Canal treaty implemented 10-1, 753F3
Forgn Relatns Com ends SALT hearings 10-10, reservatns voted 10-15–10-31, 822A2-B3
Byrd backs SALT pact 10-25, 822C3
Baker cites SALT debate 11-1, 828F3
SALT pact OKd by Forgn Relatns Com 11-9, 864A1
Intl sugar agrmt 11-30, 987D2
SALT debate delayed til '80 12-6, 938E3
19 sens ask SALT vote delay, Carter rejcts 12-16, 979A2
SALT opposed by Armed Svcs Com 12-20, 979D1
Veterans' Affairs, Committee on
Cranston elected chrmn 1-23, 71E2
Western Hemisphere Affairs, Subcommittee on (of Foreign Relations Committee)
Nicaragua junta ldrs meet 9-24, 731E3
SMALL Business Administration (SBA)
Loan progrm transfers proposed 3-1, 164G1
Artist business skills program set 7-4, 672F2
Minority-aid abuse rptd 9-28, 947B2-B3
SMITHSONIAN Institution—*See under 'S'*

SOCIAL Security Administration (& System) (of Department of Health, Education & Welfare)
Carter budget proposals 1-22, 41C2, F2, 43G2; tables 42A1, C2, D2
O'Neill scores Carter budget 1-22, 70E1
Carter budget cuts opposed in Cong 1-23, 55A3
Guyana rpts Peoples Temple checks 1-23, 117C3
Carter cites inflatn effects 1-25, 48G2
Carter defends budget 1-26, 70B1
Progrm chng re women urged 2-15, 132D3
Jan income slowdown, rate boost linked 2-16, 151D2
COL boost rptd 4-26, 310F1
Carter seeks SSI food stamp plan chng 5-23, 384D1
Overpaymt hearings backed by Sup Ct 6-20, 516C2
Unwed mothers denied survivors' aid by Sup Ct 6-27, 558F1
Inflatn hike, July incomes rise linked 8-16, 622A1
Alaska state workers quit system 9-10, 726F3-727B1
Heating aid bill OKd 11-9, 883B2
Tax hikes cited 11-28, 925D1
Advisory cncl urges chngs 12-7, 946A2
Transfer Payments—*See INCOMES under 'I'*

STATE, Department of—*See also VANCE, Cyrus; for U.S. foreign policy, see countries, regions and organizations*
Knoetze visa revoked 1-9, judge enjoins 1-11, Sharkey fight protested 1-13, 79F2
CIA '71 drug tests in Canada rptd 1-29, 95G3
Jonestown body transfer by Calif group OKd 2-1, 117E2
Ex-consul says fired for anti-Israel rpt 2-8, 108C1

1980

SMALL Business, White House Commission on
Small business rpt sent to Carter 5-15, 455A3
Small business aid signed 9-19, 784E2
SMALL Business Administration (SBA)
Small business defined 455D3
Business paper work costs rptd 1-3, 17C3
NY businesswoman, 2 partners indicted 1-10, 216C1
Island territories get econ plan 2-14; govs meet, set projects 2-19—2-22, 495A1
Bankruptcy rise rptd, Carter blamed 5-15, 455G2
Car dealer credit planned 7-8, 505F1
Small business aid signed 9-19, 784E2
NY businesswoman, partner convicted 12-21, 997G2

SOCIAL Security Administration (& System) (of Department of Health & Human Services)
Anderson urges tax cut 1-5, 4D3
Heating aid given despite lodging 1-9, 54D2
Meal tax case refused by Sup Ct 1-14, 36G3-37A1
Carter asks fund boost 1-21, 43F3
Carter budget proposals 1-28, 70A2, 72G1; tables 69G3, 70C1, D1
COL boost rptd set 4-22, 305E2
Pres panel urges changes 5-23, 404B2
'Son of Sam' benefits rptd 6-5, 639E2
Cubans, Haitian refugees eligible for SSI 6-20, 484F3
Rate rise deferral studied 6-26, 480A3
Reagan pres nominatn acceptance speech 7-17, 532E2
Dem platform plank adopted 8-13, 614E3
Carter pres renominatn acceptance speech 8-14, 613C2
COL boost cited 8-18, 631A2
Carter offers econ renewal plan; Reagan scores 8-28, 663F1, D2
Anderson platform offered 8-30, 665F1, C2
Carter scores Reagan stance 9-3, 699B1
Reagan vows strong system 9-7, 699A3
Mondale hits Reagan stand 9-10, 780C2
Carter backs expanded benefits 10-10, 10-14, 778B3, 779A2
Reagan assures Tampa crowd 10-10, 780B1
Carter ridicules Reagan 'secret plan' 10-22, 802E3
Mondale hits Reagan record 10-26, 816G3
Carter chrgs Reagan 'flipflop' 10-27, 816B3
Carter, Reagan TV debate 10-28, 813B2, 815A2
Libertarian pres candidate cites stance 10-28, 818G2
Rail pensn revisn backed by Sup Ct 12-9, 937A1

STATE, Department of—*For U.S. foreign policy, see country names*
Sovt aid to Cuba estimated 1-11, 38F2
Citizenship revocatn law backed by Sup Ct 1-15, 51C2
Wounded Khomeini aide treated in US 1-17, 30D1
Carter Olympic messages disclosed 1-21, 45G2
Olympic boycott list rptd 2-2, 85B1
World rights rpt issued 2-5, 86A2-87B3
Berger dies 2-12, 175E3

1976

Helsinki accords panel clears Cong 5-21, 392E3
Ford signs '77 fund bills 7-12, 7-14, 534F1 ★, C2
Black hiring scored 8-2, data issued 8-3, 922G1
Carter disavows Dominick dumping memo 8-13, 616F3
Ryan transfer rptd 9-20, 814D2
Helsinki panel tour barred 11-1, 880A2
2 win Rockefeller award 11-16, 911F3
Carter names liaison 11-23, 881A3
Agency for International Development (AID)
US econ aid tied to UN votes 1-9, 2D1
Guatemala quake aid rptd 2-10, 120D3
Parker in Guatemala 2-12—2-16; asks Cong emergency aid 2-18, 155B3
Sheldon confrmd to Civil Svc 2-26, 186C2
AIFLD Latin Amer aid rptd 3-10, 253F1
Herter, Pinkham confrmd asst admins 4-1, 262D3
Dem platform text cites Food For Peace program 6-15, 476C3
Food for Peace funds signed 7-12, 533D3
GOP platform text cites Food For Peace 8-18, 603A1
Cited re Uruguay mil aid ban 10-8, 814E1
S Korea rice sales probed 10-24, 899C1
Appointments & Resignations—*For ambassadorial developments, see 'Diplomatic' under FORD subheads APPOINTMENTS and RESIGNATIONS*
Greenwald confrmd asst secy 1-28, 186G1
Todd confrmd to Transport post 2-5, 110D2
Sisco quits as undersecy 2-23, 186E2
Sheldon confrmd to Civil Svc 2-26, 196C2
Herter, Pinkham confrmd to AID 4-1, 262D3
Robinson confrmd dep secy 4-7, 262E3
Katz confrmd asst secy 9-23, 808A1
Carter names Vance secy 12-3, 916C1
Christopher named dep secy 12-31, 978D3
Arab Boycott Issue
Justice sues Bechtel 1-16, 44A3
Atherton on US bill impact 9-27, 746A3
Foreign Service
US Sen intellignc com rpt cites 4-26, 303D1, F1
Dem platform text 6-15, 471F1
Black hiring data rptd 8-3, 922A2
Intelligence Issues—*See also under KISSINGER under 'K'*
CIA media manipulatn rptd 1-17, 92C3
Ford revises intelligence command 2-17, 127C1, E2
Sen com issues rpt 4-26, 300D2, 301A3, 303C1-G1, 304B3
US forgn intelligence chart 304A2 ★, C2
Inter-American Affairs, Bureau of
Bloomfield confrmd to Ecuador 4-1, 262C3
Political Payments Issue
Ford orders business paymts probe widened 2-10, 134C2
Lockheed data to be freed 3-5, 191D1
Data disclosure plans proposed 3-5, 199F3
Rpt CIA had '50s Lockheed data 4-2, 286E2
Ford submits forgn paymts legis 8-3, 668C2

1977

Cong gets rights abuse rpts 3-12, 186D3
No exec cook rptd 3-24, 236F1
McGovern authorizatn amendmt cited 4-11, 283G1
Forgn uranium shipmts OKd 5-6, 403D2
Arms-sales policy set 5-19, 380C3
Sen authorizes '78 funds 6-16, 477D3
'78 funds signed 8-2; authorizatn 8-17, 667B3, D3
Carter asks grain reserves 8-29, 666D2
Panama rights rpt cited 669E1
Dole chrgs harassmt 10-6, 792C1
Sirica vs whaling ban 10-21; ruling reversed, Burger backs ban 10-24, 835B2
Kissinger loses transcripts ruling 12-8, 962E2
Carter interpreter errs in Warsaw 12-29, 1001A2
Agency for International Development (AID)
Ford '78 budget proposals, Food for Peace provisn cited 1-17, 31A2
Chile loans blocked 6-28, 493B1
'78 funds authorizatn signed 8-4, 668G1
Panama housing guarantees in new Canal accord 8-12, 621D2
Jamaica aid resumed 9-12, 884C2
'78 operating funds clear Cong 10-19, 815F2; Carter signs 11-1, 834D1
Ex-CIA head scores 'cover' bar 12-27, 1006D1
Appointments—For ambassadorial appointments, see CARTER—APPOINTMENTS—Diplomatic
Bennett, asst secy 1-21, 53C1
Benson, undersecy 1-7, 14G1
Borg, exec secy 1-21, 53E1
Carter, asst secy 1-17, 53F1
Christopher confrmd dep secy 2-24, 148D3
Cooper, undersecy 1-7, 14B2
Duffey, asst secy 1-21, 53C1
Falco, narcotics aide 1-21, 53D1
Habib retained as undersecy 1-7, 14A2
Katz, asst secy 1-21, 53E1
Laise, Forgn Svc dir gen 1-21, 53E1
Lake, Policy Planning dir 1-7, 14B2
Maynes, asst secy 1-21, 53D1
Moose, dep undersecy 1-7, 14A2
Nimetz, counselor 1-7, 14C2
Nye, dep undersecy 1-21, 53D1
Read confrmd undersecy 8-3, 626D3
Saunders, intellignc bur dir 1-21, 53E1
Thomas, asst secy 1-21, 53E1
Vance confrmd secy 1-20, 34A1, C3
Vest confrmd asst secy 5-25, 500C1
Warnke, arms control agency dir 2-2, 88F3; confrmd 3-9, 171G3
Arms Control & Disarmament Agency—*See separate listing in this section above*
Education and Cultural Affairs, Bureau of
Reorgn proposed by Carter 10-11, 797C2
Foreign Service
Laise retained as dir gen 1-21, 53E1
Intelligence & Research, Bureau of
Saunders retained as dir 1-21, 53E1
STRATEGIC Air Command—*See under AIR Force in this section above*

1978

Young rebuked for US 'pol prisoners' remark 7-12, 7-13, 542D2, D3, E3
Rhodesian ldrs denied visas 10-1, granted 10-3, 818E3
Guyana cult probe neglect denied, Rep Ryan briefings cited 11-20, 891E2-A3; probes defended 11-24, 910A1
US emb study discounts Sovt microwave harm 11-20, 924E3
Carter rptd critical of pol intellignc 11-25, 917C1
Cong travel overseas rptd 12-10, 958B3
Arms sales talks rift rptd 12-19, 996F3
Iran intelligence feud rptd 12-20, 994C2
Agency for International Development (AID)
Carter budgets Food for Peace 1-23, 48F1
NYC rabbi admits bribery 5-11, 363E2
US rice dealer indicted 5-26, 432E3
S Korea Food for Peace cutoff voted by House 6-22, 467B2-A3
Arms Control & Disarmament Agency—*See separate listing in this section above*

1979

Rights rpt on 115 natns released 2-10, 107F1-108D2
Carter addresses editors' conf 2-22, 124C1
US secret cable details Dubs' death 2-22, 147F1
FMC ban on USSR ships opposed 3-6, 213A3
US intell on China-Viet war praised 3-25, 231G3
USSR ship ban delayed 4-6, 287A3
Lance '78 Qatar oil deal influence attempt alleged 4-9, 305E3, G3
Kissinger phone records case accepted by Sup Ct 4-16, 302B3
Guyana cult probe rpt issued 5-3, 335D3
Ex-employe indicted in visa fraud 6-1, 491E3
'80 funds clear Cong 8-2, 9-10, Carter signs 9-24, 766E3
Valdez named chief of protocol 9-13, 700B3
Guinea rights improvemt noted 10-6, 796B3
Carter loses Taiwan defns treaty suit 10-17, 777G1
Valdez confirmed 11-5, 965B1
Evacuatns, travels curbs ordrd for Islamic natns 11-26, 894F1
Venez tar oil dvpt assessed 11-26, 953D1
Eur missn set, Iran econ moves sought 12-5, 913C2
Iran missn in W Ger 12-6, 934A1
Panama canal comm apptmt delayed, treaties violatn chrgd 12-6, 939C1
Carter briefs Iran hostage kin 12-7, 934E1
Iran hostage list urged 12-25, 975G1
El Salvador staff cut 12-26, 993E2
Agency for International Development (AID)
Nicaragua staff cut 2-8, 255D1
Africa refugee total estimated 2-22, 201E1
Nicaragua debt paymts in doubt 9-28, 753E2
Food for Peace cigaret exports rptd 11-22, 970G2
Nicaragua loan rptd 11-27, 910A1
Arms Control & Disarmament Agency—*See separate listing in this section above*
Foreign Service
Carter proposes Taiwan inst 1-26, 66G2
Retiremt rule upheld by Sup Ct 2-22, 151B1
Cross heads Taiwan inst 4-21, 299E2
El Salvador staff cut 12-26, 993F2
STRATEGIC Air Command—*See under AIR Force in this section above*

1980

Sovt brigade in Cuba resumes maneuvers 2-29, 192D1
Kissinger records access blocked by Sup Ct 3-3, 209C3
'60 Minutes' Iran segmt pressure rptd 3-6, 239B1
Holtzman denied UN Mideast vote info 3-12, 218B3
USOC boycott talks rptd 3-21, 258C3
El Salvador Emb kin evacuated 3-25, 220G1
Cuban role in El Salvador chrgd 3-27, 220C2
Bushnel confrmd Panama Canal comr 4-2, 308E3
Vance resigns 4-28, Muskie named 4-29, 323G1-C3
FTC emergency funding bill signed 5-1, 348C2
Muskie confrmd 5-7, sworn 5-8, 343A1
Christopher defends Iran rescue missn 5-8, 338D1
Saudi film telecast protested 5-8, 375F2, A3
Carter sees 'stronger' Muskie role 5-9, 367D1
Muskie addresses employes 5-9, 367A2
Cuban personnel withdrawn, protests feared 5-14, 361C2
CBS blocked from Cuba broadcasts, previous transmissns cited 5-22; policy review rptd 5-23, 397C1; broadcasts cleared 6-1, 420G2
Pak faulted for '79 emb rescue 6-9, 477D3
Vance resumes law practice 6-11, 471G1
UN rejctn of Israeli constructn bid protested 6-19, 476B2
Christopher urges uranium sale to India 6-19, 495B3
Nicaraguan refugees get 3-mo extensn 6-30, 495C2
El Salvador rightist in US illegally 6-30—7-3, 521E3
Haitian refugee rpt scored 7-2, 514A2
Admin oaths re leaks rptd 7-16—7-17, H Carter resignatn cited 7-17, 549A2
Bowdler in Nicaragua, marks Somoza downfall 7-19, 565F2
B Carter controversy grows 7-22—7-31, 569A1-570D1
Global forecast gloomy 7-23, 573G1
B Carter releases secret cable 8-1, 595D1
Banned item export curb set 8-2, 599A3
83 Cuban interest office occupants surrender 8-7, 618E3
Muskie unaware of A-strategy shift 8-8; reactn 8-10, 8-11, 8-8, 615C2
Muskie regrets A-strategy ommissn, sees enhanced role; ex-offcl says exclusn planned 8-13, 630E2
Bolivia emb staff cut, drug enforcemt progrms halted 8-13, 667E3
Israel Leb raid weapon probe set 8-19, 627G3
B Carter rptd cautioned 8-19, 647D2
Sovt, Afghan chem weapon use disputed 8-21, 650F1-A2
Somali mil pact testimony to House subcom given 9-16, 735E3
Cuban interest office occupatn ends 9-23, 749D2
Agee passport revocatn case accepted by Sup Ct 10-6, 782C3
Japan visas tightened 10-6, 870A2
Reagan to enhance secy's role 10-19, 801C3
Japan trade talks resume 10-19, 864A3
Fla refugees plead for shelter 10-24, 825D3
PR refugee camp ban lifted 11-3, 869D2
Sen OKs appropriatn bill 11-17, 880G3
'81 funds clear Cong 12-3, Carter vetoes 12-16; stopgap funds clear Cong 12-16, 953B2, E3, 954F1
Haig apptmt seen 12-6, 12-9, 935F1
Reagan names Haig secy 12-16, 955G1
Allen gets liaison role 12-23, 980B2
Agency for International Development (AID)
Ex-offcl named in Jamaican grain fraud suit 2-4, 99A3
El Salvador pkg signed, '80 total rptd 3-28, 254A1
Foreign Service
Reorgn bill clears Cong 10-1, signed 10-17, 981D2

SUPREME Court

1976

Bars review of Conn no-fault car insurnc law 1-12, 24C1
Backs magistrates' review of Soc Security cases 1-14, 24A2
Upholds NYC Sup Ct filing fees 1-19, 43B3
Curbs fed ct case remanding 1-20, 43F1
Burger lauds fed judges 2-15, 136A3
Denies Polish joke case review 2-23, 169G3
Bars review of snake handling case 3-8, 219C2
Bars fed suits vs state officials 3-23, 218C3
Bars review of Hopi mining suit 3-29, 261F3
Bars fraud victim suits on auditor's negligence 3-30, 262E1
Bars review of JDL wiretap case 4-19, 331F1
Bars review of CPB bias-control case 4-19, 331B2
Backs auto recall fines 4-19, 331D2
Lets stand flag-burning convictions 4-26, 359C2
Sen intellignc com rpt text cites 4-28, 325G1, 329D3
Voids NJ canvasser curb 5-19, 393C3
Backs Indians' mineral rights 5-19, 394A1

1977

Burger issues annual rpt 1-1, 15F1-C2
Ind ct structure appeal refused 1-10, 57A2
Fla MD malpractice law refused 1-10, 57A2
DC Home Rule Act upheld 1-10, 57B2
Unequal food stamp prices backed 1-11, 58A1
'73 Ariz land ruling reversed 1-12, 57C3
Buckley libel case refused 1-17, 58B1
AT&T-Westn Union dispute review barred 2-22, 150A1
Ehrlichman convictn review barred 2-22, 150A1
NY prescriptn ruling voided 2-22, 150F1
Va optometry case rejected 2-22, 150G1
Chris-Craft damages voided 2-23, 150A2
Ohio attys fee upheld 2-28, 175D2
TWA tour case review barred 3-7, 211C2
NYS cnty charter amendmt system backed 3-7, 211G2
Tire-grading case refused 3-21, 230D2
Sioux ldr convictn review declined 3-21, 230F2
Solitron case review declined 3-21, 230G2
1-judge Fla, Tex prison rulings 3-21, 230A3
DC ct reorganizatn backed 3-22, 231D1-B2

1978

Burger issues annual rpt, urges jury selectn chngs 1-1, 12D3
Brennan cancer treatmt, Blackmun operatn rptd 1-9, 13D3
Burger defends trial lawyer criticism 2-12, 107F3
Burger urges improved law student skills 5-16, 388C2
Justices' voting alignmts shift noted 7-3, 565D3-566C1
Burger urges judgeship bill OK 7-23, 626D3
Burger renews trial lawyer criticism 8-9, 626A2, G2-A3
Burger urges study of fed govt 9-21, 751F2
Burger intervenes re bankruptcy bill 9-28, 788E2, D3
Judicial lobbying of Cong backed by Burger 10-25, 832D3
Burger receives Fordham award 10-25, 832D3
Ethics bill signed 10-26, 832F1
3 justices urge new fed ct 12-4, 958D3-959A1

1979

Burger names special prosecutor panel 1-12, 56F1
Burger notes bail crime rise, scores trial judges 2-11, 130D1
ABA seeks free counsel in death sentnc cases, opposes criminal procedure rule chng 2-13, 130B2
Powell surgery 3-15, tumor rptd benign 3-22, 231G2
Burger fires worker re news leaks 4-20, 302F2
8 justices disclose finances 5-15, 5-16, 382A2
Press access to ct offices curbed 5-18, 382G2
Burger names 10 to wiretap ct 5-18, 442A3
Marshall decries 2 rulings 5-27, 422C1
Workforce data rptd 6-11, 464F1
Powell reports finances 6-15, 464C3
Burger assails 2 bar admissns 6-25, 541B1
'78-79 term ends, voting alignmts rptd 7-2, 557F3
Burger, Powell comment on trial closures 8-8, 8-13, 630G2
Powell urological surgery rptd 8-31, 744G3
Brennan suffers stroke 9-4, 744E3

1980

Burger '79 judiciary study rptd 1-3, 51F2
Douglas dies 1-19, 50E3
Burger 'State of Judiciary' address 2-3, 114E2
Justices granted 12.9% pay hike 3-24, 250A2
Offcl rules revised 4-14, 307A2
Powell refutes media image 5-1, 368F2
Justices report finances 5-15, 555C3
Burger warns vs ct systems 'merger' 6-10, 632D1
'79-80 term ends, voting alignmts rptd 7-2, 540A2
Carter warns vs GOP apptmts 7-4, 515A3
Reagan: would consider female appointmts 7-15, 533E3
Reagan clarifies apptmt stand 9-30, 738C3
Reagan vows female apptmt 10-14, Carter scores 10-15, 779A1, D3
5th judicial circuit split; Burger, Powell backing cited 10-14, 918D3
Ervin vs 'judicial verbicide' 10-22, 908A2
'Mr Justice' title dropped 11-14, 882F2
Reagan sees justices 11-19, 881D1

1976

Bars Time privacy suit review 5-24, 393B2
Bars review of FTC cigaret ad fines 6-1, 414G2
'75 ruling on Emprise Corp cited 483D3
Rules on venue of suits filed vs banks 6-7, 435G1
Backs Nader suit vs airline 'bumping' 6-7, 435A2
Upholds ICC RR fund powers 6-17, 552F3
Backs local zoning referendum 6-21, 452G3
Shuns claims ct-judicial salary suit rule 6-21, 552G3
Voids Ill Serbian Church rule 6-21, 553A1
Upholds New Orleans street vendor curb 6-25, 552F1
Carter vs class actn rules 8-9, 585B1
Bars review of elec banking terminals rule 10-4, 807B2
Bars review of Ampex class-action ruling 10-4, 807B3
Bars review of TWA liability for terrorist victims 10-12, 848B3
Ford, Carter debate 10-22, 799G3, 802A2
Bars review of Quinlan case 11-1, 867F3
Refuses Ind auto suit case 11-8, 882D3
Brennan, Marshall vs summary decisns 11-8, 882E3
Burger warns vs long briefs 11-9, 882B3
Refuses Pa youth curfew case 11-15, 882F2
Accepts Nixon papers case 11-29, 900C2
Refuses '71 import surchrg challng 11-29, 901A1
FCC phone equipmt ruling review 12-13, 960E2
Refuses SC lawyer ethics case 12-13, 960D3

Abortion & Birth Control Rulings

Bishops challenge '73 rule 1-7, 32C3
Bars Mo Medicaid abortn rule review 1-26, 87B3
Ford on '73 ruling 2-3, 88B1
Bars pvt hosp abortn rule review 3-1, 170C1
Bars NY stay of Medicaid order 4-26, 359D2
Affirms Utah contraceptives for minors 5-24, 393D2
Rules on husband, parent consent 7-1, 518E2
GOP platform text cites 8-18, 605F2
Bars stay on Medicaid fund ruling 11-8, 848F1
Upholds MD office abortions 11-29, 900C3

Antitrust Actions

Lets stand NYSE svc chrg rule 1-12, 24C1
Bars review of Westn air route case 3-8, 219B2
Rules on drug sales to hosps 3-24, 218A3
Backs broad FPC powers 6-7, 435G1
Backs suits vs state-regulated elec cos 7-6, 569F1
Bars review of NC drug case 10-4, 807B3
Eases Standard Oil retrial bid 10-18, 867G2
Refuses judge removal case 11-15, 882F2

1977

Fed role in state civil actns curbed 3-22, 231B2
Antifraud security rules expansn barred 3-23, 276G2 ★
Corp double jeopardy bar upheld 3-28, 276F3
State weight-labeling rules curbed 3-29, 277A1
Calif psychotherapist rule review declined 4-4, 341E3
West fraud convictn review declined 4-4, 341F3
Sioux reservatn land laws backed 4-4, 341G3
Pay-TV rule appeal set 4-14, 376C2
Truck rate-setting rule backed 4-18, 342C1
License-plate slogans curbed 4-20, 342D2
Manson convictn review denied 4-25, 342G2
Port Auth transit aid curbed 4-27, 382G3
Inmate legal aid ordered 4-27, 383D1
Ill driver license law backed 5-16, 419F1
Cong pay hike suit remanded 5-16, 419G1
CAB power appeal refused 5-16, 419C2
Ford Motor complaint vs FTC declined 5-16, 419D2
Burger disputes critics 5-17, 419E2-B3
US fishing laws backed 5-23, 444G1
Guam Sup Ct jurisdictn curbed 5-23, 444A3
Natl Sciences Acad freed from disclosures 5-23, 444B3
Burger: Too many lawyers 5-27, 444C3
E Cleveland zoning rule upset 5-31, 461F3
Ex-Chrmn Cook disbarred 5-31, 461G3
Ill property attachmt case refused 5-31, 462A1
Customs Svc mail openings backed 6-6, 478E3
Illegal firearm rules broadened 6-6, 478F3
NYS political penalty voided 6-13, 517B2
Bank foreclosure delays upheld 6-17, 518F2
NC apple labeling rule voided 6-20, 517E1
Prison union curbs upheld 6-23, 539C2
Del stock seizure law voided 6-24, 539C3
Lawyers legal fee ads OKd 6-27, 538C3
Grain shipping price policy curbed 10-3, 760D2
FCC pay TV rule review declined 10-3, 760A3
CAB procedures case refused 10-3, 760B3
MAC legality upheld 10-3, 760C3
Pvt phone equipmt registratn case refused 10-3, 760E3
Utah State U broker dispute declined 10-11, 774A3
Dec '75-Mar '76 postal rates backed 10-11, 774A3
Conn welfare law re property sales upheld 10-17, 797F3
Paul '75 convictn case review declined 10-17, 797G3
Westn Union Hawaii svc case review declined 10-17, 798A1
Govt damage suits case declined 10-31, 835D3
Legal scholar scores rulings 10-31, 878E3
Pa Soc Sec benefits seizure dispute declined 11-7, 857C2
La judicial conduct code review refused 11-7, 857D2
Right to sue natl banks widened 11-8, 857C1
Religious mental patient drug case refused 11-28, 919B3
Police rights vs traffic violators widened 12-5, 938G3-939B1
Phone surveillnc ct orders backed 12-7, 939E1
Ga motor vehicle franchise case refused 12-12, 960D2
Oregon 'guest passenger' law review refused 12-12, 960F2

Abortion & Birth Control Rulings

Ind abortn for minors affirmed 1-25, 80F2
Conn minor abortn rule voided 5-23, 444C3
NY contraceptive curbs voided 6-9, 501G1
State abortn fund curbs upheld 6-20, 516C2
NYS, SD abortn rulings vacated; NJ case refused 6-27, 538G3
'76 Hyde Amendmt stay vacated 6-29, 557B3
Carter backs rulings 7-12, 533B1, F2
Hyde Amendmt stay lifted 8-4, 786A2

Antitrust & Merger Rulings

AT&T case review barred 1-25, 80B2
Brunswick damages voided 1-25, 80E2
US Steel credit ruling voided 2-22, 149E2
US Steel-Southn Concrete case review barred 2-22, 149B3
Double jeopardy protectn broadened 4-4, 341B3
Price-fixing suits curbed 6-9, 501E2
Du Pont-Christiana merger OKd 6-16, 518A1
'Schwinn doctrine' overturned, Sylvania rules upheld 6-23, 539E1
Vendo contract dispute award ordrd 6-29, 557D3
'74 Commodity law challenge declined 11-7, 857F1
Champion Intl convictn review declined 11-7, 857B2
AT&T appeal declined 11-28, 919B2
Hunt oil suit case declined 12-5, 938E3

1978

Abortion & Birth Control Rulings

Judicial immunity in sterilizatn case backed 3-28, 241F2
Ill control law appeal refused 10-16, 789D2
Cleveland zoning ordinance case refused 11-27, 937D2

Advertising Issues

FTC corrective ad rule review denied 4-3, 280C3
FCC 'fairness doctrine' case refused 5-30, 430C3
Commodity trader mail case refused 6-26, 566F3
FTC egg ad case declined 10-2, 751C2
Cosmetic labeling challenge refused 10-10, 789D3

Antitrust & Merger Rulings

Forgn natn suits OKd 1-11, 33A3
IBM-Greyhound trust dispute review denied 1-16, 33E2
Gen Atomic denied damage determinatn stay 3-20, 206D1
Cities ruled liable under law 3-29, 280F1-E2
Engineers fee code ruled illegal 4-25, 323A1
Gen Atomic documts ruling declined 5-15, 387E3
Ind & Mich utility suit rule refused 5-22, 388C2
Gen Atomic trial judge interference ruled 5-30, 430G2
FCC cross-media ban backed 6-12, 467B3
Poultry group denied immunity 6-12, 468A1

1979

Stevens, Blackmun comment on trial closures 9-18, 745B1
Brennan criticizes press 10-17, 848C1
Marshall injured in fall 10-17, 848G2
Brennan '80 retiremt seen 10-23, 848D2
'Brethren' publicatn stirs controversy 12-2, 988A2

Abortion & Birth Control Rulings

Pa abortn control law voided 1-9, 14A1
Tex abortn record access case declined 1-22, 54A2
'73 ruling anniv marked 1-22, 63C2
Mo abortn curb end backed 3-5, 185A1
SC MD prosecutn ban voided 3-5, 185B1
Mass Medicaid funds case refused 5-14, 383D1
Mass abortn-consent law voided 7-2, 559G1-D2
Fla trust case declined 10-29, 884D2
Fed funding cases accepted 11-26, 919A2

Advertising Issues

Professional use of corp names curbed 2-21, 128F2
Nev real estate ad rule affirmed 3-5, 184G3
Calif hearing-aid case refused 3-19, 203B3
Pa jobs-wanted case declined 6-18, 499E1
Ohio attys billbd case refused 11-5, 884B3
Utility ad ban, policy statemt cases accepted 11-26, 919A3
FTC mail-order case refused 12-3, 964C2

Antitrust & Merger Rulings

AT&T documts order review declined 1-8, 14G3
Pvt mail svc appeal declined 1-15, 31G3
Kennedy offers consumer suits bill 1-31, 308C2

1980

Abortion & Birth Control Rulings

'73 ruling cited 1-9, 23C3; 1-15, 35F3; 6-24, 479C3
Marshall stays Medicaid aid order 2-14, ct lifts stay, accepts case 2-19, 130F2-B3
Va '27 sterilizatn case cited 2-23, 158G3
Utah parental notificatn case accepted 2-25, 187G3
Medicaid funding cases argued 4-21, 306A2
Medicaid funding limits upheld; reactn 6-30, 491F2-492A2
'73 ruling cited in Dem platform 8-13, 614G3
Medicaid funding rehearing denied 9-17, 703A3
Mich contraceptive distributn case declined 10-6, 782G2

Advertising Issues

FTC TV child ad probe case refused 6-16, 511D3

Antitrust & Merger Rulings

Real estate brokers subject to suits 1-8, 16C1
Paper bag price fixing appeals declined 1-14, 37E1
Md real estate convictn appeals declined 1-21, 93B3
Berkey appeal refused 2-19, 130F3
Calif Coors case declined 2-19, 131D1
FTC procedure case accepted 2-25, 187E3
Indl Investmt vs Mitsui case declined 2-25, 188B1
Calif wine pricing law held illegal 3-3, 210E1

1976

Campaign Issues
Voids NYS campaign rules 1-12, 23D2
Upholds Calif GOP primary rule 1-19, 42G3
Upholds pub financing, disclosure rules; voids spending limits, FEC 1-30, 86C1-87A2
Bars GOP delegate rule review 2-23, 170A1
Stays FEC order 2-27, 169F3
Rejcts FEC matching funds plea 4-23, 306C1
Lets stand FCC license denials 5-24, 393E2
Bars review of Gross, Chestnut convictions 10-4, 766D1
Bars FCC equal-time rule review 10-12, 765D3
Affirms Tex pol candidacy law 11-1, 867F3

Censorship Rulings—*See also 'Press Issues' below*
Bars review of Manson film ban 4-19, 331C2
Upholds Detroit anti-porno zoning 6-24, 478G3
Bars review of art funding rules 10-18, 867A3
Bars review of Calif theater, bookstore ruling 11-1, 868A1

Defendants' Rights
Denies '72 Wilmington 10 convictn review 1-19, 43E1
Voids Pa police misconduct rule 1-21, 42D3
To review death sentnc cases 1-22, 87G2
Upholds warrantless arrests 1-26, 87A2
Bars sex 'proof' rule review 3-1, 170D1
Prosecutors granted immunity 3-2, 169C3
Curbs jury bias questioning 3-3, 219E1
Limits double jeopardy protectn 3-8, 219B2
Hears death sentnc arguments 3-30, 3-31, 261G3
Backs recess mtg with counsel 3-30, 262D1
Backs prosecutor's notes inspectn 3-30, 262E1
Rules vs convict silence in disciplinary hearings 4-20, 331E2
Backs govt access to bank records 4-21, 331C1
Strengthns '73 drug convictn rule 4-27, 349A2

1977

Campaign & Election Issues
McCarthy pres debate suit review declined 4-4, 341D3
Clark electn law challenge rejctd 6-6, 478F3
Paul electn challenge refused 6-6, 479A1
McCarthy atty-fee case refused 12-5, 939B1

Capital Punishment
Gilmore delay rejected 1-11, 1-16, 1-17, 40G1-D2
Jurek executn delayed 1-17, 40B3
Dobbs executn delayed 2-25, 174B3
Neb executns review sought 3-18, 594D1
Secret info use in sentencing curbed 3-22, 230D3
Jurek case review declined 3-28, 276D3
Darden convictn review refused 4-19, 342B2
White case review declined 4-25, 342A3
Justice Dept backs uniform fed procedures 5-18, 594D3
Mandatory sentences curbed 6-6, 478C2
Fla retroactive sentnc backed 6-17, 518F1
Executn for rape barred 6-29, 557C2
9 cases declined 10-3, 760D3

Censorship Rulings—*See also 'Press' below*
Retroactive porno prosecutns barred 3-1, 175E1
Ia obscenity convictn upheld 5-23, 444C2
Porno trial ad role upheld 6-6, 478B3
Ill obscenity law restored 6-9, 501B3
Ill Nazi rally ban upset 6-13, 517G2
Calif nightclub license revocatn case refused 10-17, 797F3
Legal scholar scores rulings 10-31, 879B1

Defendants' Rights
Burger issues annual rpt 1-1, 15C2
Ga search warrant system voided 1-10, 57E1
IRS tax seizures limited 1-12, 57G2
Govt tap use expanded 1-18, 58E1
Miranda rule limited 1-25, 80D1
SC police informant curb voided 2-22, 150B1
Juvenile ct gag order voided 3-7, 211B2
Death sentencing limited 3-22, 230D3
Miranda issue sidestepped 3-23, 275A3
Double jeopardy protectn broadened 4-4, 341B3
Plea-bargaining review backed 5-2, 406D2
Burger cites '69-76 cases 5-17, 419A3
Grand jury witness rights clarified 5-23, 444F2, G2
Indictmt delays backed 6-9, 501C3
Faulty info retrial backed 6-13, 517F2
1-man police lineups backed 6-16, 518D1
Retrial for same offense barred 6-16, 518E1

1978

Redskins liability case refused 6-12, 468E1
Md refiner-run gas statn ban upheld 6-14, 491F3
Mt Hood award vs Greyhound curbed 6-19, 492A3
Gypsum price fixing rule upheld 6-29, 567F2
Insurnc cos policyholder suits backed 6-29, 567C3
Oreck damage award case refused 10-30, 832G2
Law firm dual-rep case refused 11-6, 873G3-874A1
AT&T Centrex case refused 11-13, 874D2
AT&T documts order backed 11-13, 874A3
Calif auto franchise law upheld 12-5, 959E3

Banking Issues
Insurance sale by bank holding cos denied review 2-27, 143B2
Checking acct customer stock sale challenge denied 3-27, 241D2
Bankers Trust stock sale case refused 3-28, 241E3
Auto-leasing case declined 10-2, 751B2
Mellon Bank SC immunity case refused 10-10, 789F2
FDIC paymt case declined 10-16, 789B1
Ill redlining case refused 10-30, 832C3
Reuss Open Market Com case declined 11-27, 937F2
FRB holding co power backed 12-11, 980D3
State interest rates on credit cards backed 12-18, 981C2

Business Issues—*See also other appropriate subheads in this section*
Vesco case review denied 1-9, 13A2
AT&T rate rise stay lifted 1-9, 13C2
AT&T-MCI phone svc case review denied 1-16, 33G1
Postal competitn convictn refused 3-27, 241E2
SEC trading suspensns curbed 5-15, 387C1
AT&T-MCI phone svc case stay denied 5-22, 388A2
AT&T rate hike case declined 6-5, 431D2
Commodity trader mail case refused 6-26, 566F3
Aluminum wire dispute refused 10-2, 751E1
Litton fraud indictmt case refused 10-2, 751G1
Stirling Homex convictns review refused 10-2, 751E2
ITT denied stay on sealed data 10-30, 832B2
FTC business data cases refused 11-6, 873D3
Drug cos data case refused 11-6, 873F3
Tex securities-regulatn case refused 11-13, 874C3
AT&T-MCI connectns case declined 11-27, 937A2
Stockbroker liability case refused 12-4, 959B1

Campaign & Election Issues
Cities subject to US electn law 3-6, 162F1
Ill cnty clerk ballot case refused 3-27, 241E2
Tenn clergy pub office ban upset 4-19, 309C1
Corp free speech backed 4-26, 343D2
Cities' power over suburbs backed 11-28, 937G2
Ga schl bd pol rule struck down 11-28, 937E3

Capital Punishment
Sentencing bias found in study 3-6, 389B1
'76 rulings re 3 states cited 3-6, 389C1
Secret evidence convictn case declined 5-30, 430C3
Ohio law struck down; NY, Pa cases denied 7-3, 552D1-B2
Tex executn filming case declined 7-3, 552D2
NYS restoratn appeal declined 10-16, 789C2

Censorship Issues—*See 'Press & Censorship' below*

Defendants' Rights
Prosecutors' plea-bargaining power expanded 1-18, 64D3
Prison offcls limited immunity backed 2-22, 126C2
Scientology challenge of FBI raid ruling rejected 3-20, 205C3
Juries of less than 6 ruled illegal 3-21, 220E3
Testimony thru illegal search backed 3-21, 220G3
Indian rape retrial backed 3-22, 221D1
Judge's jury instructn on silent defendant backed 3-22, 221F1
Ark robbery, rape convictns reversed 4-3, 309B1
Hearst convictn review declined 4-24, 322F1
Va inmate parole hearings case review declined 4-24, 322E2
Ill juvenile suspects rights case review refused 4-24, 322F2
Lawyer competency case declined 5-1, 363E3

1979

A&P milk price actn backed 2-22, 150F2
Monopoly intent case refused 2-26, 164C3
Blue Shield drug plan trust rule upheld 2-27, 165A1
Auto insurnc wage rate ruling voided 3-5, 184F3
Calif fuel price law challenge declined 3-5, 185E1
AT&T data access case declined 3-26, 231A1
Kapp trust damages case declined 4-16, 302F3
Music license fee case remanded 4-17, 325G3-326A1
Consumers' right to sue protected 6-11, 478D2
Idaho takeover law challenge rejctd 6-26, 540F3
NBC '77 setlmt challenge refused 10-1, 768C2
Gypsum price fixing case refused 10-1, 768F2
Fla abortn case declined 10-29, 884D2
Telex lawyer fee case declined 12-3, 964B2
NBC '77 setlmt challenge refused again 12-10, 988A2

Banking Issues
NYC occupancy tax collectn curbed 3-5, 185E1
Citicorp unit applicatn case declined 6-11, 478G3
FRB Open Mkt rpt disclosure delay backed 6-28, 558B3
Banking svcs case declined 10-15, 847A3

Business Issues—*See also other appropriate subheads in this section*
SEC suit findings retrial barred 1-9, 14A2
Tex, NJ blue law cases declined 1-22, 54E1
Borden price compensatn case declined 1-22, 54B2
Professional use of corp names curbed 2-21, 128D2
Presley poster dispute refused 2-21, 128E3
State rent collectn bankruptcy laws backed 2-21, 128G3
Okla minnow sale ban voided 4-24, 364C2
Mutual fund dirs' power backed 5-14, 382G3
Securities law broker protectn backed 5-21, 400C3
Personal bankruptcy data collectn backed 6-4, 439B2
Customer suits vs accountants curbed 6-18, 499C1
US wage-price penalty case refused 7-2, 498C2
Mail order finance chrg case refused 10-1, 768B2
SEC fraud powers case accepted 10-15, 848B1
Franchise terminatn case refused 10-29, 884B1
Auto makers FTC challenge declined 11-5, 884E2
Investor suits vs advisers curbed 11-13, 901G3

Campaign & Election Issues
Boston referendum spending case refused 1-8, 14A3
Fla 'sunshine' amendmt review refused 1-22, 54F1
Ill 3d party electn law struck down 2-22, 150D1
Miss legis redistricting ordrd 3-26, 231C1

Capital Punishment
RI Sup Ct overturns law 2-19, 188B2
Spenkelink appeal refused 3-26, 230F3
Evans death delay refused 4-13, 400G1
Smith Va death penalty challenge declined 5-21, 400E3
Spenkelink death delay refused 5-25, 400B1
Green sentence vacated 5-29, 421E3
Bishop executn stay denied 10-21, 817D2

Defendants' Rights
NYS drug law challenge declined 1-8, 14C3
SEC suit findings retrial barred 1-9, 14E2
Mo women jury exclusn law voided 1-9, 14G2
Lawyers' interstate rights limited 1-15, 31B3
Ia criminal confessn case declined 1-22, 54G1
La juvenile trial jury ban refused 2-21, 128B3
Lawyer phone waiver case declined 2-26, 164E3
Airport luggage search case declined 2-26, 164F3
Right-to-counsel doctrine clarified 3-5, 185F1-D2
MacDonald murder trial challenge declined 3-19, 203G2-A3
Grant of immunity broadened 3-20, 203G3
Random car checks by police barred 3-27, 263D1

1980

Gypsum price fixing case settled 3-3, 557G3
UPS ICC regulatn case refused 4-14, 307G1-A2
Mandatory civil jury case refused 4-28, 369G1
Credit fixing curbed 5-27, 453F2
Unpatented key ingredient monopolies backed 6-27, 511C2
NOW Mo boycott case refused 10-6, 782F1-A2
Greyhound-Mt Hood case declined 10-6, 782C2
Beef pricing case refused 10-14, 781G3
Paperbd setlmt case dismissed 10-20, 807A3
McGraw-Hill takeover case declined 11-3, 856A2
Trust damages liability sharing case accepted 11-3, 856C2
BN rail merger stayed by Powell 11-21, stay lifted 11-25, 937G2-A3
FTC complaint challenge curbed 12-15, 957D1

Banking Issues
Franklin Bank fraud appeals refused 2-19, 131A1
Calif redlining law curbed 3-17, 226C1
Franklin Natl ex-vp fraud appeal declined 3-17, 226G1
Class actn 'moot' standard redefined 3-19, 250D1
Sindona Franklin Bank fraud suit refused 4-21, 344A2
Fla 'parochial' practices curbed 6-9, 512F2-A3

Business Issues
Postal rate challenge declined 1-7, 15E3
Control Data case refused 1-7, 16A1
State ct jurisdictn narrowed 1-21, 93F1
Customs Svc goods liability backed 1-21, 93A3
Credit clause exclusn backed 2-20, 170G2
Britannica sales practices case refused 3-17, 226D1
'Insider' stock trading convictn voided 3-18, 226A2
Mutual fund insurance case refused 3-24, 265E1
GE, Curtiss-Wright suit partial setlmt upheld 4-22, 344C1
CFTC emergency order case declined 4-28, 369D1
Parcel post rate case declined 5-19, 440C2
Fed unincorporated trust suits backed 5-19, 440E2
Credit fixing curbed 5-27, 453F2
SEC fraud intent proof required 6-2, 512A3
State sales preference backed 6-19, 554E2
Utilities' free speech upheld 6-20, 555F1-C2
Inventory tax ruling impact on publishing rptd 10-5, 835G3
Calif artist royalties case declined 11-10, 868B2
SEC parallel probe case refused 11-17, 882D1

Campaign & Election Issues
Calif lobbyist ban case refused 1-21, 93G2
Pres campaign spending limit upheld 4-14, 306E3
At-large local electns upheld 4-22, 343A2
Voting Rights Act provisn upheld 4-22, 344C1
Kennedy supporters' petitn rejctd 4-28, 369A2
'76 spending rule cited 7-1, 493C1
'76 pub financing rule cited 8-28, 681B2
PAC donatns case accepted 10-6, 782A2
Burger stays GOP campaign aid ruling 10-17, stay continued 10-21, 856D1
Pol airtime case accepted 11-3, 856D2
Trade assn PAC funds soliciting ban challege refused 11-3, 856E2
AFL-CIO funds case declined 11-10, 868C3

Capital Punishment
2 Ga appeals declined 3-24, 265C2
Ga law applicatn narrowed 5-19, 439E3
Ala death penalty struck down 6-20, 555C1; appeals Ct orders inmates retried 10-15, 869A1
Potts executn stay backed 6-30, 511E1

Census Rulings
'80 postponemt denied 3-17, 226A1
Stewart stays Detroit revisn 12-24, 982G3
'80 rpt ordrd released 12-30, 982F3

Defendants' Rights
Stoner extradited 1-11, 55B3
Ky firearms convictn case remanded 1-14, 37G1
Inmate escape justificatn curbed 1-21, 92E3
'Miranda rights' waiver proof backed 1-21, 93B3
Md real estate convictn appeals declined 1-21, 93B3
Govt damage suits geographic relevance backed 2-20, 170A3
Coerced confessn search warrant case declined 2-26, 188A2
Spouse testimony upheld 2-27, 188A2
Fed gun law prior convictn rule upheld 2-27, 188E2
Immune grand jury testimony in perjury trials backed 3-3, 210D1
Tex habitual-offender law upheld 3-18, 226F2
State legislators' immunity curbed 3-19, 249E3
Class actn 'moot' standard redefined 3-19, 250E1

1976

Rules on prisoners' trial garb 5-3, 359G1
Curbs grand jury compositn challenge 5-3, 359B2
Bars Jacobsen plea-bargaining review 5-19, 393D3
Limits grand jury witness rights 5-19, 393F3
Curbs free trial transcripts for poor 6-10, 552G2
Protects silence on arrest 6-17, 552B3
Voids ignorance guilty plea 6-17, 552C3
Backs warrantless 'doorway' arrests 6-24, 553B1
Limits defns access to prosecutn info 6-24, 553E1
Upholds hearingless prison transfers 6-25, 552A2
Upholds use of nonlawyer judges 6-28, 492E1
Upholds business record seizures 6-29, 535A2
Voids Neb press gag order, bars review of 3 other press cases 6-30, 491C3-492D1
Upholds criminal trials without juries 6-30, 552A3 ★
Upholds death penalty, OKs Tex, Fla, Ga laws, voids NC, La 7-2, 491F1
Limits fed ct review of illegal evidence challenges 7-6, 534A3
Affirms tax case use of inadmissible criminal evidence 7-6, 535B1
Upholds traffic violatn auto search 7-6, 535C1
Voids Okla death penalty law 7-6, 568B3
Mondale legis record re legal aid cited 512A3
Powell stays 3 executns 7-22, 568F2
Carter, Mondale on law enforcemt 9-13, 9-14, 686G2, 687G1
Affirms July death penalty ruling 10-4, 746E1
Bars review of juvenile evidence case 10-4, 766C1
Double jeopardy protectn curbed 10-12, 848D2
Eases retrial bid requiremts 10-18, 867F2
Civil rights suit fees bill signed, '75 rule cited 10-20, 788B2
Ford, Carter debate 10-22, 802C2
Rules re plea-bargain confessns 11-1, 867D3
Bars review of jury bias questioning rule 11-1, 867D3
Bars immediate parole-revocation hearing 11-15, 882D2
To review mandatory death for police killers 11-29, 900F2
Refuses Singer computer-evidence case 11-29, 900E3
Affirms prisoner med care right 11-30, 920E3
Stays Gilmore, White executions 12-3, 12-6, 920G2
Bars anti-death juror exclusn 12-6, 920B3
Bars review of Ill legis immunity appeal 12-6, 920C3
Vacates Gilmore stay 12-13, 952E2
Bars review of Ray plea withdrawal 12-13, 960D2
Bars Kelner convictn review 12-13, 960E3

Drug & Narcotics Rulings
Rules on drug sales to hosps 3-24, 218A3
Price ad ban voided 5-24, 393E1
Upholds traffic violatn auto search 7-6, 535C1
'74 ruling re polio vaccine liability cited 776E1

1977

Justice Dept warrantless searches curbed 6-21, 539A1
Police break-in case declined 10-3, 760B3
NJ police harassmt case refused 10-31, 835C2
Dual fed-state prosecutns curbed 11-7, 857A2
Probatn loss case review declined 11-14, 878B3
Burger blocks Scientology documt use 12-8, 940F2
Moore rape convictn reversed 12-12, 960G2

1978

Md U social-actn group case refused 5-1, 364B1
Speedy trial appeal procedure backed 5-1, 364D1
Fed tap power broadened 5-15, 387D2
Lawyer soliciting rules set 5-30, 430B2
Presumptn-of-innocence jury chrg backed 5-30, 430A3
Marshall delays Little extraditn 5-30, extraditn appeal declined 6-5, 431G1-B2
Arson probe search warrants backed 5-31, 431E1
Double jeopardy ban redefined 6-14, 468G2
Class actn suits curbed 6-19, 492G1
Murder scene search warrants backed, statemts from wounded curbed 6-21, 509D2
Class actn certificatn appeals curbed 6-21, 509F2
Ark prison reform, attys fees backed 6-23, 566D1
Cong immunity case refused 6-26, 566D2
Evidence hearing rules drawn 6-26, 566D3
Juvenile case reviews upheld 6-28, 567F1
US offcls' legal immunity defined 6-29, 567A2
Ohio death penalty law struck down; NY, Pa cases denied 7-3, 552E1-B2
Voting alignmts shift noted 7-3, 566B1
Hypnosis-related murder case refused 10-2, 751C2
Neb 'deadly force' case refused 10-16, 789C2
'Mail cover' case refused 11-6, 874C1
Ruppert retrial case refused 11-6, 874E1
Inmate suits judicial-aid case refused 11-13, 874B3
FBI break-in case refused 12-4, 959F1
Police auto search power broadened 12-5, 959C2
Mass drunk rights waiver ruling affirmed 12-11, 980G3
NJ murder sentencing system upheld 12-11, 981C1
Extraditn probes barred 12-18, 981F1

1979

IRS tap evidence backed 4-2, 281D2
Va inmate threat case refused 4-16, 302E3
Podell, Brasco disbarmt challenges declined 4-16, 303C1
6-member jury convictn rule upheld 4-17, 325F3
'State of mind' libel queries backed 4-18, reactn 4-18, 4-23, 301F3, 302B2
Covert entries for 'bugging' upheld 4-18, 346B1
Verbal rights waiver backed 4-24, 364A2
Mental hosp commitmt standard tightened 4-30, 364D2
Pretrial detectn curbs backed 5-14, 383F1
Innocence instructn refusal backed 5-21, 400E3
Guilty plea incomplete info backed 5-21, 400G3
States given parole discretn 5-29, 421D2-B3
Green death sentence vacated 5-29, 421E3
Co-defendant confessns allowed 5-29, 422A1
NY gun-in-car law upheld 6-4, 438B3
NJ ex-offcls subject to rejailing 6-4, 438F3
Lawyer's office statemts protected 6-4, 439E1
US maximum penalty prosecutn backed 6-4, 439E1
'Probable cause' backed in detentns 6-5, 464B2
Cong immunity broadened 6-18, 498C3
Helstoski indictmt rule backed 6-18, 499A1
Mont homicide convictn reversed 6-18, 499F1
PR search law voided 6-18, 499A2
Warrantless phone surveillnc upheld 6-20, 516C1
Juvenile 'Miranda rights' limited 6-20, 516B2
Luggage search warrants backed 6-20, 516C2
'Good faith' arrest backed 6-25, 540B1
Juvenile 'Miranda rights' case remanded 6-25, 540B2
Tex identificatn law convictn voided 6-25, 540D2
Libel suit rights broadened 6-26, 540D2
Rights violatn proof in false arrest suits backed 6-26, 540G3
W Va youth suspect press law voided 6-26, 541A1
Criminal evidence standard eased 6-28, 558C2
Ctroom pub access curbed; reactn 7-2, 515G1, C3
'78-79 term ends, voting alignmts rptd 7-2, 558B1, F1
Power to void state convictns backed 7-2, 558E3
Priest-penitent case declined 10-1, 767E3
Harris convictns review declined 10-1, 768B1
Neb porno case jury challenge refused 10-1, 768F1
Va men's room surveillnc case declined 10-1, 768G1
Ala legal counsel case declined 10-1, 768A2
'Exclusionary rule' case refused 10-1, 768G2
NJ ex-mayor paroled 10-2, 891G1, C2
Bell contempt case declined 10-9, 783C3
Va trial closure case accepted 10-9, 783F3
Ky manslaughter convictn vacated 10-9, 784B1
Motorist 'Miranda rights' case declined 10-9, 784D1
Neb rape bail case refused 10-15, 847E3
Mass jury approval case refused 10-29, 884A2
NYS trial closure case declined 11-5, 884E3
Arson 'dual sovereignty' case refused 11-13, 902A2
Travel Act bribery convictn upheld 11-27, 919E3
Extended searches curbed 11-28, 944E2-C3
Appointed lawyers legal immunity curbed 12-4, 987D3

1980

Racketeer law cases declined 3-24, 265C1
Car box search case refused 3-24, 265C2
Inmate mental health hearings backed 3-25, 265D2
Ctroom ID in illegal arrest backed 3-25, 265G2-C3
Va 40-yr pot case remanded 3-31, 291F2
Mandel, co-defendants appeals refused 4-14, 307A1
Warrantless home arrests curbed 4-15, 305F3
Cooperatn standard in sentencing backed 4-15, 306G1
'Good faith' municipal immunity ended 4-16, 328C2
Multiple sentencing curbed 4-16, 328B3
Ctroom cameras case accepted 4-21, 344D1
Barnes convictn review refused 4-21, 344G1
Sindona fraud suit ruling refused 4-21, 344A2
Thevis firearm convictn case refused 4-21, 344B2
Prisoners right to sue broadened 4-22, 343B3
Misdemeanor 2d offense jailing limited 4-22, 344B1
Mandatory civil jury cases refused 4-28, 369F1
Police interrogatn defined 5-12, 386B2
Atty conflict of interest probes backed 5-12, 426F2
NYS rape shield law case dismissed 5-19, 440C2
'Exclusionary rule' narrowed 5-27, 453A2
DEA detainmt procedure backed 5-27, 453G3-454A1
Pub offcl good faith defns defined 5-27, 454C1
Diggs convictn review refused 6-2, 428A1
Panther Chicago shootout retrial order declined, legal fees award voided 6-2, 512G3
Pre-arrest silence testimony backed 6-10, 512C1
Jail informant use curbed 6-16, 511A3
Ala death penalty struck down 6-20, 555C1; appeals Ct orders inmates retried 10-15, 869A1
Cts power to suppress evidence curbed 6-23, 554A3
Magistrates pretrial role upheld 6-23, 554G3
Lawyer legal fee penalty backed 6-23, 555A1
Illegal search protectn narrowed 6-25, 541A1
DEA detainmt procedure curbed 6-30, 511G1
'79-80 term ends, decisns cited 7-2, 540E2
Jail informant curbs cited 9-15, 703E3
Arrest warrant 3d party searches case accepted 10-6, 782C3
Abscam tapes broadcast stay refused 10-14, 781C2
Myers Abscam entrapmt plea refused 11-3, 856G1
Inmate cell crowding case accepted 11-3, 856E2
Inmate legal fees ruling upset 11-10, 868C1
Ctroom cameras case argued 11-12, 882A2
Extended judicial immunity barred 11-17, 882A1
Pa pretrial press exclusn case refused 11-17, 882F1
Conn phone harassmt law challenge declined 12-1, 918F2
Police interrogatn chase case declined 12-1, 918F2
Flynt Cleveland convictn case accepted 12-8, 937G1
Lenient sentence appeal backed 12-9, 936A3
Fed ct civil rights suits curbed 12-9, 937B1

1976 — Educational Issues

Educational Issues
Declines review of Denver integratn rule 1-12, 24E1
Denies review of religious class time off rule 1-19, 43C3
Bars review of sex ed suit 4-5, 262B2
Justice Dept vs pvt schl segregatn 4-9, 263C2
Justice Dept, Ford seek busing review 5-14, 5-18, 377E2-D3
Ford seeks busing review 5-26, 391E1
Levi drops Boston busing review 5-29, 391F1
Carter backs PS prayer 6-6, 411A1
Bars Boston busing review 6-14, 452G2 ★
Upholds striking teacher firings 6-17, 552D3
OKs some church-coll aid 6-21, 452D3
Rules vs private schl bias 6-25, 479B1
Vs contd schl rezoning 6-28, 468F3
Declines Chattanooga desegregatn plan review 6-30, 552A3 ★
Bars review of transsexual teacher firing 10-18, 867B3
Accepts Phila sex-segregatn case 10-18, 867C3

1977 — Education Issues

Education Issues
'75 Boston receivership review barred 1-10, 57D1
Teacher's free speech upheld 1-11, 57F3
Indianapolis busing plan voided 1-25, 79D3-80C1
Louisville busing review barred 1-25, 80D1
US rights comm backs city-suburb busing 2-15, 112F1
Colo alien voting law review declined 4-18, 342D1
Schl spankings backed 4-19, 342E1
Phila schl sex bias deadlock 4-19, 342C2
Dayton busing order backed by Justice 4-22, 446D1
RC-NLRB case refused 5-2, 406C2
Burger cites '69-76 cases 5-17, 419A3
NYS alien tuitn law voided 6-13, 517E2
Calif schl financing review rejctd 6-20, 517D1
Church schls limited state aid backed 6-24, 539F2
Dayton busing plan vacated 6-27, 538F2; US judge voids 12-15, 978B3
Detroit remedial programs upheld 6-27, 538A3

1978 — Education Issues

Education Issues
'77 Wilmington busing case cited 1-9, 15G2
SC teacher tests backed 1-16, 33D2
Mo univ Gay Lib case review refused 2-21, 125C3
Baptist schl integratn challenge refused 2-21, 126D1
Fed fund bar for ct-ordrd desegregatn denied review 2-27, 143F1
Med student ouster upheld 3-1, 143D2
VA curbs backed 3-20, 205E3
Student sex survey case review denied 3-20, 206C1
Suspended students damages curbed 3-21, 220G2
Northwestn U tax dispute review refused 5-1, 364E1
Bakke med schl admissn ordrd, race-based affirmative actn principle upheld; reactn; opinion excerpts 6-28, 481A1-487C2
NC Univ minority rep case sent back, Bakke rule cited 7-3, 552C1
LA busing stay declined by Rehnquist, Powell 9-8, 9-9, 698F3-699A1
HEW suit vs Md refused 10-2, 751F2

1979 — Education Issues

Education Issues
Pub employe free speech backed 1-9, 14G2
La schl segregatn case refused 1-15, 32E1
Okla teacher dismissal backed 2-26, 164G3
Church schl labor interventn barred 3-21, 231D2
NYS pvt schl reimbursemt bar voided 4-2, 281A3
NYS alien teacher ban backed 4-17, 325E3
'Italian Bakke case' declined 4-23, 346D2
Pvt Title IX suit allowed 5-14, 382C3
NJ pvt schl tax break ban affirmed 5-29, 421F3
Schls right to bar disabled backed 6-11, 478E1
Tenn univ merger stay denied 6-18, 499B2
Pa pvt schl transport challenge dismissed 6-25, 540C2
Ohio busing orders upheld 7-2, 539E2
Columbus busing ordr cited 8-2, 596A3

1980 — Education Issues

Education Issues
Chicago teacher firing case declined 1-7, 15D3
Ohio '79 schl segregatn rulings cited 1-14, 36E3
Dallas busing case refused 1-21, 93D2
Pvt coll faculty unions curbed 2-20, 146C1-B2
NYS pvt schl reimbursemt upheld 2-20, 146B2
Cleveland busing challenge refused 3-17, 225F3
'Good faith' schl bd immunity ended 4-16, 328C2
Wilmington (Del) busing case declined 4-28, 368E3
Atlanta schl integratn ruling upheld 5-12, 386B3
NYC parochial schl remedial aid case refused 10-6, 782F2
Detroit, Indianapolis busing challenges declined 10-6, 782G2
Chicago schls black quotas case dismissed 10-20, 807B2
SD schls religion case refused 11-10, 868G1

1976

Stays Calif U reverse bias ruling 11-15, 882C1
To review Detroit integratn plan 11-15, 882E2
Calif U to appeal 11-19, 995F2
Refuses Wilmington busing case 11-29, 900A3
Refuses La HS reverse bias case 11-29, 900F3
Vacates Austin busing plan 12-6, 920B2
Backs pub worker contract debate right 12-8, 960G1-A2
Refuses Mo tuitn aid case 12-13, 960A1

Energy Rulings
To review 4-state coal mining environment impact case 1-12, 23G3
Remands FPC gas reserves case 1-19, 43D1
Upholds FPC gas-sale rule 3-3, 219D1
Backs broad FPC powers 6-7, 435F1
Upholds oil-import fees 6-17, 452A3
Bars oil entitlemts review 6-21, 569E1
Reverses 4-state strip-mining stay 6-28, 568G3
Marshall OKs Atlantic offshore lease sale 8-17, 648C3
Bars review of gas price hike 10-4, 807A3
Refuses Lake Mich A plant case 11-8, 882C3

Environmental Rulings
To review 4-state coal mining case 1-12, 23G3
Burger rejcts Va Concorde case 5-22, 378G2
Curbs EPA A-waste powers 6-1, 414B3
Frees US bases from state permit need 6-7, 435C2
Upholds Nev water-pumping bar to save pupfish 6-7, 435D2
Upholds wild horse, burro protectn 6-17, 552F3
Bars fed ct review of state air plans 6-25, 552C2
Reverses 4-state strip-mining stay 6-28, 568G3
Declines Calif zoning rule review 6-28, 569D1
Bars review of oil-spill liability rule 10-4, 807C3
Refuses Lake Mich A plant case 11-8, 882C3
Refuses Concorde landing case 11-15, 882B2
Refuses Miss road constructn case 11-29, 901C1

Family Issues—*See also 'Abortion' above*
Bars review of rule on husband in delivery room 4-5, 262B2
Upholds illegitimacy benefits rule 6-29, 568D3
Bars Soc Sec for divorced mothers 12-13, 940C3

Food Issues
Blackmun bars stay on beef standards 1-9, 24B2
Bars Red #2 dye ban delay 2-13, 137F1
Lets stand meat grading standards 3-22, 218E2

1977

Hazelwood (Mo) teacher bias suit sent back 6-27, 538F3
Omaha, Milwaukee busing orders vacated 6-29, 557G2
Stewart, Brennan refuse to ban Kent State gym 9-3, 9-8, 820G2
Justice Dept files Bakke brief 9-19, case argued 10-12, more briefs ordrd 10-17, 834F2-835G1
Gay teacher cases refused 10-3, 760D1
Wilmington busing case declined 10-3, 760F1
NC, Tenn church coll aid backed 10-3, 760E3
Louisville busing review declined 10-31, 835A3
Legal scholar scores rulings 10-31, 878G3, 879B1
Idaho student jobless-benefit law upheld 12-5, 939C1
NYS pvt schl aid law voided 12-6, 938A3
Maternity sick-leave pay rule remanded 12-6, 938A3

Energy Issues
FEA oil regulatn case refused 4-25, 342D3
FTC oil cos info rule review refused 6-13, 517E1
Gas royalties dispute refused 10-3, 760G1
Alaska pipe interim rate rise OKd 10-20, order upheld 11-14, 878D2
Geothermal resources case review declined 10-31, 835A3
Gen Atomic uranium suit OKd 10-31, 835B3
Phillips-Ashland helium dispute case declined 10-31, 11-28, 919F2
Boston Edison retroactive rate rise let stand 11-14, 878C3
Alaska pipe rates case accepted 11-28, 919E2
Hunt oil suit case declined 12-5, 938E3

Environmental Issues
EPA water pollutn curbs upheld 2-23, 150D2
Minn logging case review barred 3-7, 211A3
Water pollutn control deadline upheld 4-18, 342A1
Corn refiners appeal refused 4-18, 342D1
Army dredging case review declined 4-25, 342D3
EPA authority cases remanded 5-2, 406E2
Air quality cases sent back 10-3, 760G2
Marshall stays Concorde landing 10-7, full ct denies stay 10-17, 797A3
Va parking ban backed 10-11, 774G2
NYC clean-air case review declined 10-17, 797C3
Burger backs bowhead whaling ban 10-24, 835G1
Calif land owners dispute declined 11-7, 857E2

Family Issues
Child custody jurisdiction review barred 1-25, 80F2
Soc Sec widower benefits rule voided 3-2, 192C1-B2
Soc Sec old-age benefits rulings 3-21, 230E1, G1-D2
Illegitimate rights backed 4-26, 382G2-C3
Illegitimate alien children ban backed 4-26, 382C3
Pa youth rights case refused 5-16, 418G3
Burger cites '69-76 cases 5-17, 419B3
NYS foster care rule upheld 6-13, 517D2
Ga racial adoptn curb review refused 6-20, 517B1
Disability benefits loss upheld 11-8, 857A1

1978

Coll sex-bias ruling voided 11-13, 874F1-C2
Ga schl bd pol rule struck down 11-28, 937E3
Ga, Tex integratn cases declined 12-4, 959G1

Energy Issues
NJ offshore oil, gas drilling review refused 2-21, 125E2
Gulf gas pipe compensatn challenge refused 2-21, 126B2
Natural gas rates review denied 2-27, 143C2
States curbed on oil tanker regulatn 3-6, 161D3
Cts curbed on A-plant rulings 4-3, 280E2
Utility customer hearings backed 5-1, 364A1
Gen Atomic documents ruling declined 5-15, 387E3
Ind & Mich utility suit rule refused 5-22, 388C2
Natural gas diversn curbed 5-31, 430E3-431D1
ICC Alaska pipe rates backed 6-6, 447A2
Md refiner-run gas statn ban upheld 6-14, 491F3
A-accident liability law backed 6-26, 567A1
Southern Calif Edison refund case refused 10-16, 789A2
Boston Edison rate limit case refused 10-30, 832G2

Environmental Issues
EPA curbed on asbestos rule 1-10, 13E2
States curbed on oil tanker regulatn 3-6, 161D3
Cts curbed on A-plant rulings 4-3, 280E2
Water-based land claims barred 5-31, 431E1
Tellico Dam constructn halt upheld re threat to snail darter 6-15, 468G1-D2
NJ waste dumping law voided 6-23, 566B2
A-accident liability law backed 6-26, 567A1
Calif, NM water rights backed 7-3, 552B2

Family Issues
Father's role in adoptns limited 1-10, 13C3
Wis remarriage law voided 1-18, 65B1
Calif jurisdictn denied in child-support case 5-15, 387F3
La 'head & master' case declined 10-10, 789D3
NYS illegitimate child inheritance law upheld 12-11, 981B1

Health & Safety Issues
No-union rule for hosp interns denied review 2-27, 143B3
FDA drug seizure case refused 3-27, 241E1
Firecracker ban review refused 3-27, 241C2
FTC corrective ad rule review denied 4-3, 280C3
Health Planning Act upheld 4-17, 308A3
NH mental health insurnc challenge denied 4-17, 308B3
NYS alien MD ruling declined 5-15, 388A1
Mine safety inspectn case remanded 6-15, 431E2
Hosp union organizing backed 6-22, 508E3
FTC egg ad case declined 10-2, 751C2
Cosmetic labeling challenge refused 10-10, 789D3
A-accident liability law backed 10-16, 789A2
Drug cos data case refused 11-6, 873F3
Swine flu law challenge refused 12-4, 959B2

1979

Title IX job bias funds cutoff bar declined 11-26, 919D2
NYC schl aid denial upheld 11-28, 944A2
Calif religious teacher firing case dismissed 12-10, 988F1

Energy Issues
Energy Comm rate relief power backed 1-16, 32D2
Cleveland bond issue ban declined 2-21, 128B3
Energy Comm gas productn power denied 2-22, 150F3
Calif fuel price law challenge declined 3-5, 185E1
A-plant shutdown case refused 4-16, 303A1
NM elec tax voided 4-18, 346B2
Forgn-flag oil tanker case refused 5-14, 383E1
Natural gas diversn curbed 6-18, 499C2
A-plant license policy case declined 10-1, 768D2
Utility ad ban, policy statemt cases accepted 10-1, 919A3
NM suit vs Tex refused 10-9, 784D1
Gen Atomic arbitratn ruling declined 10-9, 784E1
Georges Bank offshore lease sale stayed 11-6, stay lifted 11-9, 867E1-A2
Shell accident liability case refused 12-3, 964D2
Hunt-Coastal States oil suit ruling declined 12-10, 988G1
Georges Bank lease sale stayed, lifted again 12-18, 990B2

Environmental Issues
EPA Ohio sulphur-dioxide emissns case refused 1-15, 32B1
2d EPA Ohio sulphur-dioxide emissns case refused 3-19, 203B3
Okla minnow sale ban voided 4-24, 364C2
Impact statemts curbed 6-11, 478E3

Family Issues
Divorce pact excludes rail pensn 1-22, 53G3
Foster care benefits backed 2-22, 151B1
Single-sex alimony barred 3-5, 184C2
Alimony rule in NYS child custody case backed 3-19, 203F2
Unwed father adoptn consent role backed 4-24, 364A1
Unwed father damage suit bar upheld 4-24, 364A1, E1
Fed child custody fights curbed 6-11, 478F3
Half-Indian child custody case refused 6-18, 499A2
Child mental commitmt rules backed 6-20, 515E3
Unwed mothers denied survivors' aid 6-27, 558F1

Health & Safety Issues
Professional use of corp names curbed 2-21, 128D2
Blue Shield drug plan trust rule upheld 2-27, 165A1
Calif hearing-aid ad case refused 3-19, 203B3
Mental hosp commitmt standard tightened 4-30, 364D2
Coal miner pay hike case declined 4-30, 364C3
A-test radiatn liability case refused 5-21, 400A3
FDA Laetrile ban upheld 6-18, 498D2
Child mental commitmt rules backed 6-20, 515E3
Hosp union organizing curbs backed 6-20, 516A2
OSHA magistrates warrants case refused 10-1, 768C1
NJ Medicaid reimbursemt case declined 11-5, 884C3
Calif Laetrile ban challenge declined 11-13, 902E1
Onshore dockers benefits upheld 11-27, 919B3
VA malpractice ruling reversed 11-28, 944C3
Shell accident liability case refused 12-3, 964D2

1980

Ky 10 Commandmts law upset 11-17, 881B3
Faculty sex-bias Title IX case accepted 12-1, 918B2
Job bias suit filing time limit upheld 12-15, 957B2

Energy Issues
Oil tanker subsidies repaymt backed 2-20, 170E2
FTC trust procedure case accepted 2-25, 187E3
La gas tax case fact-finder named 3-3, 210G1
Gas pipeline capacity rule challenge refused 3-3, 210A2
TVA dam constructn challenge declined 3-24, 265B2
Gulf natl park drilling rights affirmed 3-31, 291A3
La oil leasing rights denied 4-28, 369C1
Gasoline price case refused 5-12, 426C2
'76 oil import fee ruling cited 5-13, 366C1
Land-grant exchng ban upheld 5-19, 440A2
Pre-1920 oil shale mining claims upheld 6-2, 513C1
Utilities' free speech upheld 6-20, 555F1-C2
Oil spill rpts backed 6-27, 511A2
RR A-fuel tarrifs case declined by Sup Ct 10-6, 782D2
FTC trust complaint curbed 12-15, 957D1

Environmental Issues
Impact ct reviews limited 1-7, 15A3
Ind pesticide plant case declined 2-19, 131D1
EPA dischrg permit ct reviews backed 3-17, 226F1
Strip-mining ruling stayed 3-17, 226G1
EPA sewage permit extensn power backed 3-18, 226D3
Gulf natl park drilling rights affirmed 3-31, 291A3
EPA guidelines appeals ct review backed 5-27, 453E3
Calif zoning ordinances backed 6-10, 512F1
Imperial Valley water rights upheld 6-16, 511E2
Oil spill rpts backed 6-27, 511A2
Strip mining cases accepted 10-6, 782D1
LA airport nuisance award case refused 10-6, 782A3
EPA Chrysler recall order challenge refused 12-1, 918E2
EPA clean water enforcemt backed 12-2, 918A1
Airborne lead standards challenge refused 12-8, 937F1

Family Issues
Calif pensn divorce case declined 1-14, 37A1
Fed worker illegitimate child aid backed 2-26, 188G1
Spouse testimony upheld 2-27, 188A2
Del 'unfit' parent case accepted 3-24, 265G1
Retarded youth surgery case refused 3-31, 291B3
Summary alimony case dismissed 5-12, 426C3
Mich contraceptive distributn case declined 10-6, 782G2
Stepfather adoptn rights case accepted 10-6, 783B3
Unwed couples child custody case refused 10-20, 807A1
Mil pensn divorce case accepted 10-20, 807A3
Stepfather adoptn right ruling vacated 11-17, 882F1

Health & Safety Issues
Pa mine inspectn case declined 1-7, 15F3
Waterway constructn injury case remanded 1-14, 37F1
Hazardous work refusals backed 2-26, 188C1
Inmate mental health hearings backed 3-25, 265D2
Retarded youth surgery case refused 3-31, 291B3
Hosp union limits case declined 4-14, 307C1
OSHA chlorine rules partial stay granted 5-19, 440A3
Nursing home aid summary cutoff backed 6-23, 554F3
Onshore docker state injury benefits backed 6-23, 555B1
OSHA benzene standard rejected 7-2, 510D3
OSHA cotton dust standard case accepted 10-6, 782C1
DES liability case declined 10-14, 781D3
Laetrile ban challenge declined 10-20, 807E1
Airborne lead standards challenge refused 12-8, 937F1
OSHA lead exposure rule stayed 12-8, 937G1

1976

Immigration & Refugee Issues
State alien job curbs upheld 2-25, 169F1
Voids civil svc jobs bar 6-1, 414G1-B2
Upholds Medicare benefits bar 6-1, 414B2
Upholds jury duty bar 6-7, 414D2
Voids PR alien engineer bar 6-17, 552E3
Upholds warrantless alien interrogatn 7-6, 534G3
Bars car search review 10-18, 867E2

Labor Rulings
'75 ruling on jobless benefit choice cited 1-7, 128A3
Declined review of Calif women's overtime rule 1-12, 24D1
Declines review of Mass police questionnaire rule 1-12, 24F1
Upholds coal mine penalty procedure 1-26, 87B3
State alien job curbs upheld 2-25, 169F1
Bars Colo race bias rule review 3-1, 170C1
Limits shopping cntr pickets 3-3, 218E3
Backs retroactive seniority 3-24, 218A2
Upholds police grooming codes 4-5, 262B2
Rules on FPC bias powers 5-19, 393F2
Civil svc job rights ruling bar 6-1, 414G1-G2
Extends job bias suit rights 6-1, 414E2-G2
Upholds police applicant test 6-7, 435A1
Backs city on withholding union dues 6-7, 435A2
Upholds NC police firing 6-10, 552D2
Upholds striking teacher firings 6-17, 552D3
Voids PR alien engineer bar 6-17, 552E3
Upholds Mo police bargaining law 6-21, 553A1
US wage laws not binding on states 6-24, 468A2
Rules rights law also protect whites 6-25, 479G1
Upholds mandatory retiremt laws 6-25, 552C1
Upholds union overtime refusal 6-25, 552B2
Bars patronage ousters 6-28, 468A3
Holds states liable for bias damages 6-28, 569C1
Upholds black-lung law 7-1, 568E3
Vs sympathy strike injunctns 7-6, 535D1
Bars review of Calif farm organizing rule 10-4, 766E1
Vs product picketing 10-4, 807G1-B2
Bars review of strikers' jobless pay 10-4, 807E2
Bars review of Washn reverse bias case 10-12, 848G2
Mass police, firemen unpaid duty upheld 10-12, 848A3
Bars review of firing of transsexual teacher 10-18, 867B3
Split vote affirms religious-day work ruling 11-2, 848B1
Refuses La HS reverse bias case 11-29, 900E3
Vs mandatory pregnancy benefits 12-7, 919G3
Backs pub worker contract debate right 12-8, 960E1-C2
Bars review of EEOC rptg rule 12-13, 960C3
Rules in EEOC complaint deadline case 12-20, 959F3

1977

Housing Rulings—*See 'Racial Bias' below*

Labor Rulings
Washn homosexual dismissal ruling voided 1-10, 57A1
NY jobs preferenc rule upheld 1-10, 57E1
Longshoremen loading case refused 1-10, 57F1
Poultry driver bargaining upheld 1-11, 58A1
Steelworker electn rule voided 1-12, 57E3
Secondary strikes curbed 2-22, 149D3
NYC minority compensatn case review denied 2-28, 175C2
Mental distress suits vs unions backed 3-7, 211F2
Arbitratn under expired contracts backed 3-7, 211B3
UMW wildcat strike case refused 3-21, 230B3
OSHA penalties backed 3-23, 276F1
RC-NLRB case refused 5-2, 406C2
Employer records cases declined 5-16, 419C1
Pregnant employe dismissal case declined 5-16, 419B2
Burger cites '69-76 case 5-17, 419A3
Govt employe agency shops backed 5-23, 444C1
Pre-'64 seniority bias upheld 5-31, 461A2
United Air Lines seniority rule upheld 5-31, 461G2
Ohio job benefits law backed 5-31, 461D3
Pensn credit for mil svc backed 6-6, 478G2
NYS jobless benefits case refused 6-6, 478G3
Employes religious rights limited 6-13, 517C3
Maritime worker compensatn law affirmed 6-17, 518E2
HEW jobless-benefits standards law backed 6-20, 516D3-517A1
EEOC time-limit barred 6-20, 517C1
Ala prison employe standards voided 6-27, 538E3
GM back-pay award case refused 6-29, 557C3
USW strike injunctn barred 7-29, 593A3
Sen votes pregnancy, disability benefits 9-16, 738A1
RR health regulatn dispute refused 10-3, 760E2
NJ jobless welfare benefits case declined 10-3, 760F2
Chicago police quota case review refused 10-3, 760A3
Vet job prefrnc law backed 10-11, 774D2
Airline employe liability case refused 10-31, 835C3
Correctns officer firing case remanded 11-14, 878C3
Lawyer fees case refused 11-14, 878D3
Test pilot age bias case refused 11-28, 919D2
State police meal stipends taxable 11-29, 919D1
Age bias filing time extended 11-29, 919A2
Idaho student jobless-benefit law upheld 12-5, 939C1
TVA bias suit refused 12-5, 939D1
Maternity leave seniority rights upheld 12-6, 938C2
Maternity sick-leave pay rule remanded 12-6, 938A3
Early retiremt plan backed 12-12, 960G1-D2

1978

Housing & Construction Issues
Arlington Hts zoning case review denied 1-9, 13D2
Hartford suburb suit ruling review denied 1-16, 33G2
Sub-subcontractors excluded from fed contructn paymt bond coverage 2-22, 126A3
Grand Central office complex barred 6-26, 566G3
Aluminum wire dispute refused 10-2, 751E1
Stirling Homex convictns review refused 10-2, 751E2
Ill redlining case refused 10-30, 832C3
Cleveland zoning ordinance case refused 11-27, 937D2

Immigration Issues
State police alien ban backed 3-22, 221A1
NYS alien MD ruling declined 5-15, 388A1
Alien deportatn trial backed 6-6, 447E3

Indian Issues
Indian ct trials of non-Indians barred 3-6, 162D1
Rape retrial backed 3-22, 221D1
Non-Indians barred from Idaho reservatn, ct trial rule cited 4-22, 327D1
Tribal authority backed 5-15, 387A3

Labor Rulings
Miners pensn jurisdictn case review denied 1-9, 13E2
'Prehire' union picketing curbed 1-17, 33F3
Employers curbed on bias-case legal fees 1-23, 65A2
JP Stevens contempt challenge refused 2-21, 125F3
NW Airline sex bias case refused 2-21, 125G3
Mgrs strike-duty overtime pay challenge refused 2-21, 126A1
Job age bias jury trials backed 2-22, 126F2
No-union rule for hosp interns denied review 2-27, 143B2
Maritime Comm contract jurisdictn enlarged 3-1, 143C3-144C1
3d party job bias case review denied 3-6, 162F1
UAL maternity rule review refused 3-20, 205G3
State police alien ban backed 3-22, 221A1
Minn pensn funds law backed 4-3, 308D3
UMW pensn attachmt case refused 4-3, 309B1
Mil pensn double-dipping rule declined 4-17, 308C3
Union legal fee liability case review denied 4-17, 308D3
Sex-based pensn plans barred 4-25, 322A3
Unions subject to trespass laws 5-15, 387A2
Rochester (NY) police hiring challenge case declined 5-22, 388B2
OSHA warrantless searches curbed 5-23, 405B2
Mine safety inspectn case remanded 6-5, 431E2
Freedom of Info in NLRB cases barred 6-15, 468F2
Unions curbed on supervisor discipline 6-21, 509D1
Union pol organizing backed 6-22, 508A3
Hosp union organizing backed 6-22, 508E3
Alaska oil job preference law voided 6-22, 508F3
Minn pensn funds law voided 6-28, 567B1
Job bias proof qualified 6-29, 567D3
AT&T bias case declined 7-3, 551F3
Calif contractors reverse bias case sent back 7-3, 552B1
Burger rejcts RR strike plea 9-26, 809A3
Employer retaliatn case declined 10-2, 751C1
Coll sex-bias ruling voided 11-13, 874F1-C2
UAL NYS maternity leave case refused 11-27, 937G1
Rail clerk strike stay renewal denied 11-27, 937E2
Ga schl bd pol rule struck down 11-28, 937E3
Weber reverse job-bias case accepted 12-11, 980E2-D3
Pub employees adultery firing case declined 12-11, 981A1

1979

Housing & Construction Issues
State rent collectn bankruptcy laws backed 2-21, 128G3
US land grant easemt right curbed 3-27, 263B2
Govt relocatn aid curbed 4-17, 325G3
Racial 'steering' suits allowed 4-17, 352G2
Govt minority grant case accepted 5-21, 400F3

Indian Issues
Child custody case refused 6-18, 499A2
State laws in land cases backed 6-20, 516G1
Washn salmon fishing treaties upheld 7-2, 559D1
Feathered artifact sale ban upheld 11-27, 919F3
Sioux Black Hills compensatn case accepted 12-10, 988F1

Labor Rulings
Religious rail worker union dues case refused 1-8, 14E3
Pub employe free speech backed 1-9, 14F2
SEC role in pensn plans barred 1-16, 32F1-D2
Divorce pact excludes rail pensn 1-22, 53G3
EEOC curb on BN data upheld 2-21, 128F3
Forgn svc retiremt rule upheld 2-22, 151A1
Engineers pensn paymts case refused 2-26, 164D3
Job-testing data disclosure reversed 3-5, 184A3
Jobless pay for strikers upheld 3-21, 231D1
NYC Transit Auth ex-addict ban backed 3-21, 231B2
Church schl interventn barred 3-21, 231D2
LA fire dept bias case found moot 3-27, 263G1
Weber reverse job-bias case argued 3-28, 262B3
Retroactive seniority case declined 4-2, 281C2
NYC union printing contract case refused 4-2, 281F2
NYS alien teacher ban backed 4-17, 325E3
Ky factory sex bias case refused 4-23, 346A3
Coal miner pay hike case declined 4-30, 364C3
Ark pub worker grievance policy backed 4-30, 364D3
Fla fed training funds challenge refused 4-30, 365A1
Collective bargaining on food issues backed 5-14, 383B2
State age bias filings required, time limit barred 5-21, 400C2
Punitive damages vs unions barred 5-29, 421B3
IAM free speech case declined 6-4, 439F1
7th-Day Adventist firing case declined 6-4, 439G1
Vets' job-prefernc law upheld; reactn 6-5, 421D1-D2
Congressmen ruled liable to sex-bias suits 6-5, 463G3-464F1
Ariz farm labor law restored 6-5, 464A3
Pa jobs-wanted case declined 6-18, 499E1
Disabled nurse firing case refused 6-18, 499D2
Union recognitn denial case declined 6-18, 499E2
Hosp union organizing curbs backed 6-20, 516A2
Meany seeks wage-price review 6-22, 480G2
Weber affirmative actn challenge rejctd, reactn; majority opinion excerpts 6-27, 477A1-478E1
Dockworker negligence suits backed 6-27, 558B2
Wage-price penalty case refused 7-2, 498C2
'78-79 Sup Ct term ends, Weber ruling cited 7-2, 558C1
OSHA magistrates warrants case refused 10-1, 768C1
Mine widows suit declined 10-1, 768F1
Ala legal counsel case declined 10-1, 768A2
Ill judge retiremt law challenge refused 10-9, 784F1
Minn pensn funds law held illegal 10-15, 847E3
Fed workers smoking case declined 10-29, 884D2
UFW field talk case refused 11-5, 884B3
Ind pregnancy jobless pay case refused 11-13, 902A2
Title IX funds cutoff bar declined 11-26, 919D2

1980

Housing & Construction Issues
Environmental impact ct reviews limited 1-7, 15A3
Real estate brokers subject to trust suits 1-8, 16C1
Black Jack (Mo) low income case refused 2-25, 188A1
NYS resident jobs preference case declined 4-21, 344C2
Mandatory civil jury case refused 4-28, 369G1
Contructn contract Indian prefernc barred 5-27, 454B1
Govt minority grants upheld 7-2, 510A1
'79-80 term ends, decisns cited 7-2, 540D2
LA airport nuisance award case refused 10-6, 782A3

Immigration Issues
Iranian student deportatn ban denied 3-31, 291G2
Iranian student immigratn case refused 5-19, 440B2
PR refugee camp blocked by legal battle 10-24, 825A3
PR refugee camp ban lifted 11-3, 869C2
Appeals ct bars House deportatn res 12-24, 989B2

Indian Issues
Indian land 'inverse condemnatn' barred 3-18, 226F3
Govt land managemt liability limited 4-15, 306F1
Constructn contract prefernc barred 5-27, 454B1
Sioux Black Hills $122.5 mln compensatn upheld 6-30, 511B1

Labor Rulings
Weber '79 affirmative actn ruling cited 1-14, 36E3
Calif divorce pensn case declined 1-14, 37B1
Conn ERISA maternity case declined 1-14, 37B1
Wis ERISA case declined by Sup Ct 1-14, 37C1
Waterway constructn injury case remanded 1-14, 37F1
Plaintiff class lawyer fees backed 2-19, 131B1
Tax liability in RR worker compensatn backed 2-19, 131C1
Pvt coll faculty unions curbed 2-20, 146C1-B2
Calif dual seniority system backed 2-20, 146F2-B3
Hazardous work refusals backed 2-26, 188C1
Fed worker illegitimate child aid backed 2-26, 188G1
Govt political firings barred 3-31, 291G1-E2
USW suit vs foundatn dissident funding refused 3-31, 291B3
Hosp union limits case declined 4-14, 307C1
NYS resident preference case declined 4-21, 344B2
Mo compensatn law voided 4-22, 344A1
Child labor law fines upheld 4-28, 369A1
Purposeful bias cases declined 4-28, 369A2
EEOC class actn process avoidance backed 5-12, 426F1
Pre-ERISA insured pensn benefits backed 5-12, 426B3
Longshoreman fatality damages ruling affirmed 5-12, 426D3
OSHA chlorine rules partial stay granted 5-19, 440A3
ILA awaits container ruling 5-27, 482B2
Ill non-labor picketing rights affirmed 6-20, 555D2
Container pact ban refusal affirmed 6-20, 555E2
Onshore docker state injury benefits backed 6-23, 555B1
Out-of-ct lawyers' fee awards backed 6-25, 540G3
OSHA benzene standard rejected 7-2, 510D3
OSHA cotton dust standard case accepted 10-6, 782C1
NASL NLRB order refused 10-14, 1001F2
Stevens union access case refused 10-20, 807A2
La itinerant registratn ruling affirmed 10-20, 807D2
Mil pensn divorce case accepted 10-20, 807A3
AFL-CIO pol funds case declined 11-10, 868C3
OSHA lead exposure rule stayed 12-8, 937G1
Rail pensn revisn backed 12-9, 936G3
Deering Milliken '56 wage dispute setld 12-14, 962F2
Judicial pay hikes backed 12-15, 956C3-957D1
Job bias suit filing time limit upheld 12-15, 957B2

1976

Military Issues
Limits right to counsel 3-24, 218F2
Upholds pol activity curbs 3-24, 218G2
Bars Calley convictn review 4-5, 262F1
Backs acad honor-code disclosures 4-21, 331B3
Personnel
Marshall has heart attack 7-5, 519D2
Ford, Carter debate 10-22, 802A2

Press Issues
Declines review of Consumer Rpts bar from Cong press gallery 1-12, 24G1
Limits 'pub figure' libel rule 3-2, 169E2
Bars review of Church libel suit 4-5, 262A2
Voids Neb gag order, bars review of 3 other press cases 6-30, 491C3-492D2
Reporter contempt chrgs left standing 6-30, 492C1
Bars review of LA Times libel rule 10-4, 807D2
Bars equal-time review 10-12, 765D3
Stays gag order in Okla murder case 11-24, 901C2
Racial Bias—*See also 'Educational Issues' above*
Bars Colo job bias rule review 3-1, 170C1
Backs retroactive seniority 3-24, 218A2
Bars review of health spa case 4-5, 262G1
Suburban low-income housing upheld 4-20, 308D2
Rules on FPC powers 5-19, 393F2
Upholds police applicant test 6-7, 435A1
Rules rights laws also protect whites 6-25, 479G1
Declines Chattanooga desegregatn plan review 6-30, 552A3 *
Bars review of Fla club case 10-4, 766A1
Bars review of housing damages ruling 10-4, 766B1
Bars review of case vs real estate cos 10-4, 807G2
Bars review of Washn reverse bias suit 10-12, 848G2
Bars review of jury questioning rule 11-1, 867D3
Declines to review homeowner tax bias rule 11-29, 900G3
Bars review of EEOC rptg rule 12-13, 960C3

1977

Military Issues
Mil MD malpractice case review barred 3-7, 211E2
Reserves retiremt pay rule backed 4-4, 341F3
Army dredging case review declined 4-25, 342D3
Pensn credit for svc backed 6-6, 478G2
Navy enlistmt bonuses upheld 6-13, 517E2
Vet job prefrnc law backed 10-11, 774D2
Army tank injury suit remanded 11-14, 878A3
Personnel
Burger urges pay increases 1-1, 15G1-B2
Ford plans pay hikes 1-17, 33D3
Pay hikes take effect 2-20, 127D2

Press Issues
Newspaper pact rule review barred 2-22, 150G1
Juvenile ct gag order voided 3-7, 211B2
Burger cites '69-76 cases 5-17, 419A3
Wyo libel jurisdictn review refused 6-20, 517C1
Media liable to performers' suits 6-28, 557F3
Ida secret news source case refused 10-31, 835E2
Fla libel case review refused 11-7, 857C2
'64 libel suit ruling cited 11-7, 920G2
Rinaldi, Glover, Fadell libel cases refused 11-28, 919A3
NY Times-Audubon libel case declined 12-12, 960E2
Racial Bias—*See also 'Education Issues' above*
Restrictive Ill suburb zoning backed, case remanded 1-11, 14G3
New Castle (NY) fed grants review refused 1-17, 58C1
Toledo housing ruling voided 1-25, 80D2
NYC minority compensatn case review denied 2-28, 175C2
Voter redistricting upheld 3-1, 174C3-175D1
Intra-group grand jury bias affirmed 3-23, 276C2
'For sale' sign ban lifted 5-2, 406G1
Burger cites '69-76 cases 5-17, 419G2-A3
Ga adoptn curb review refused 6-20, 517B1
GM back-pay award case refused 6-29, 557C3
Chicago police quota case refused 10-3, 760A3
Hinds Cnty (Miss) voter apportnmt case refused 11-28, 919F2
Toledo (O) housing suit case declined 12-5, 939C1
TVA job bias suit refused 12-5, 939D1

1978

Military Issues
Officers pensn rule review declined 4-17, 308C3
Miscellaneous Rulings
1-house cong veto case reviews denied 1-9, 12G3
Cong pay-hike suit dismissal backed 1-16, 33F2
NH gov curbed on flag lowerings 3-24, 221G1; curb extensn denied 4-24, 322G2
Sex abuse suit vs NBC OKd 4-24, 322A2
Munic legal immunity ended 6-6, 447C1-A2
Const amendmt ratificatn rule cited 10-6, 788G1
Calif United Methodist immunity case declined 10-16, 789E2
Conn legal immunity ruling vacated 11-27, 937B2
Obscenity Rulings
Ga obscenity convictn overturned 3-21, 220E3
Md rule review declined 4-24, 322F2
Children excluded from porno rule 5-23, 405G2-F3
Port of entry case declined 5-30, 430B3
FCC 'Filthy Words' ban upheld 7-3, 551F2
Patent Rulings
Miller 'Lite' trademark case review denied 1-9, 13C1
Autogiro case review denied 1-23, 65D1
Computer program patents curbed 6-22, 509B1
Roberts wins Sears suit 10-2, 844B2

Press and Censorship
Ohio, SC gag-order case review denied
Pa case remanded 1-9, 13E1
Fla tape-curb challenge refused 3-20, 206B1
Student sex-survey case review denied 3-20, 206C1
Gurney trial press-curbs case declined 4-17, 308C2
Govt Printing Office damage suit immunity challenge refused 4-17, 308A3
Broadcasters denied Nixon tapes 4-18, 308C1
Corp free speech backed, media giants warned 4-26, 343F3
Va judicial inquiry law voided 5-1, 363G2-E3
Iowa, NM info order reviews refused 5-15, 388A1, B1
Newsroom searches by police backed 5-31, 429E3
Skokie Nazi rally delay sought 6-9, stay denied 6-12, 447F2, B3
FCC cross-media ban backed 6-12, 467B3
Prison data access curbed 6-26, 566G2-D3
FCC 'Filthy Words' ban upheld 7-3, 551F2
Tex executn filming case declined 7-3, 552D2
Voting alignmt shift noted 7-3, 566C1
Chicago Nazis rally delay denied 7-7, 529B2
FCC rejcts censorship role 7-21, 599E1
White, Marshall bar Farber sentnc stay extensns 8-1, 8-4, 678B3
Farber ruling stayed by Stewart 9-26, ct lifts stay 10-6, 841E2
Skokie Nazi rally case refused 10-16, 789B2
NY Times, Farber press freedom case declined 11-27, 937E1
Racial Bias—*See also 'Education Issues' above*
Employers curbed on bias-case legal fees 1-23, 65A2
3d party job bias case review denied 3-6, 162F1
Job bias proof qualified 6-29, 567D3
AT&T bias case declined 7-3, 551F3
Weber reverse job-bias case accepted 12-11, 980E2-D3

1979

Onshore dockers injury benefits upheld 11-27, 919B3
Wildcat strike liability limited 12-10, 988C1
Libel Rulings
Arnheiter case declined 10-29, 884G1
Novelist case refused 12-3, 964F1
NM newspapers case refused 12-3, 964A2
Military Issues
'53 A-test raditn liability case refused 5-21, 400A3
Arnheiter libel cases declined 10-29, 884G1
Miscellaneous Rulings
Land appraisal reimbursemt ruling reversed 2-26, 164E3
Fair-mkt property acquisitn backed 5-14, 383B3
Taiwan defns treaty case refused 12-13, 940A1
Obscenity Rulings
'Open-ended' warrants use curbed 6-11, 478A3
Norfolk (Va) law challenge dismissed 6-25, 540A2
Neb jury challenge case refused 10-1, 768F1
Patent Rulings
Scholl-Kresge case refused 1-15, 32A1
Nonpatent royalties upheld 2-28, 165B2
'78 computer program patent curb cited 3-29, 265F2
Formica trademark case refused 6-5, 464F2
Microbe patents case accepted 10-29, 884D1
Korvettes-Shure Bros case refused 11-5, 884D3

Press and Censorship
Wichita TV rptr contempt convictn review refused 2-21, 128C3
Rptrs phone bill subpoena case refused 3-5, 184E3
Carter cites '78 newsroom search ruling 4-2, 264E3
Cable TV pub-access rule upset 4-2, 281F1
FCC cable TV rate case declined 4-16, 302G3
'State of mind' libel queries backed 4-18, reactn 4-18, 4-23, 301F3, 302B2
Ct worker fired re news leaks 4-20, 302F2
NYS pretrial press curbs affirmed 4-27, 382B3
W Va youth suspect law voided 6-26, 541A1
Ctroom pub access curbed; press reactn 7-2, 515G1, C3
'78-79 Sup Ct term ends, pretrial curbs cited 7-2, 558D1
Progressive H-bomb article hearing order denied 7-2, 559A1
Va trial closure case accepted 10-9, 783F3
Privacy Issues—*See also other appropriate subheads in this section*
Kissinger phone records case accepted 4-16, 302B3
Reverse Freedom of Info suits curbed 4-18, 345D3
Calif grand jury transcript examinatn barred 4-18, 346B2
Buian damage case declined 4-18, 346G2
Scientology documts '76 seizure upheld 5-14, 383A3
Personal bankruptcy data collectn backed 6-4, 439B2
'Open-ended' warrants use curbed 6-11, 478C3
FDA Laetrile ban upheld 6-18, 498B3
PR search law voided 6-18, 499A2
FRB Open Mkt rpt disclosure delay backed 6-28, 558B3
Extended searches curbed 11-28, 944E2-C3
Racial Bias—*See also 'Education Issues' above*
Safeway firing case declined 2-21, 128D3
LA fire dept case found moot 3-27, 263G1
Weber reverse job-bias case argued 3-28, 262B3
Retroactive seniority case declined 4-2, 281C2
Housing 'steering' suits allowed 4-17, 325G2
Govt minority constructn grant case accepted 5-21, 400F3
Weber affirmative actn challenge rejctd, reactn; majority opinion excerpts 6-27, 477A1-478E1
'78-79 term ends, voting alignmts rptd; Weber ruling cited 7-2, 557G3, 558E1
Power to void state convictns backed 7-2, 558E3
Westn Elec case refused 10-29, 884C2
Govt minority constructn grants case argued 11-27, 944F3

1980

Libel Rulings
Nader case declined 2-19, 131E1
Calif corp 'pub figures' case refused 10-6, 782E2
Del Law Schl case declined 11-10, 868B3
McCarthy TV film case refused 12-1, 918D2
Military Issues
Petitn limits upheld 1-21, 93A1
GE, Curtiss-Wright suit partial setlmt upheld 4-22, 344C1
Nixon trial order petitn rejected 5-19, 440F1
Draft registration allowed 7-19, 597F3
Divorce pensn rights case accepted 10-20, 807A3
Male-only draft case accepted 12-1, 918E1
Miscellaneous Rulings
Citizenship revocatn law backed 1-15, 51C2
Ohio boundary placemt upheld 1-21, 93F2
Charity solicitatn limit voided 2-20, 170A2
Class actn 'moot' standard redefined 3-19, 250C1
Name chng case dismissed 5-19, 440D2
Agee passport revocatn case accepted 10-6, 782C3
Obscenity Rulings
Tex porno film restraints voided 3-18, 226E3
Donated porno warrants required 6-20, 555G2
Flynt Cleveland convictn case accepted 12-8, 937G1
Patent Rulings
Upjohn microbe case remanded 1-14, 37D1
Miller 'Lite' trademark case refused 2-19, 131A1
GE microbe case cited 3-5, 318B1
'Bionic' trademark case declined 3-31, 291D3
GE microbe patent upheld; reactn 6-16, 452E3-453A2
Unpatented key ingredient monopolies backed 6-27, 511C2
Press & Censorship
CBS 'dovish' complaint case refused 1-7, 16A1
CIA disclosure limits upheld 2-19, 130B3
Des Moines Register privacy case refused 2-25, 188A1
Snepp rehearing denied 4-14, 307E1
Calif shopping cntr petitn access backed 6-9, 512A2
Snepp case cited 6-13, 517B1
Utilities' free speech upheld 6-20, 555E1-C2
Open criminal trials backed 7-2, 510C2-C3
Calif corp 'pub figures' libel case refused 10-6, 782E2
Abscam tapes broadcast stay refused 10-14, 781C2
Mass rape trial press exclusn case remanded 10-14, 782B1
Newsroom searches curb signed 10-14, 835F1-C2
Ctroom cameras case argued 11-12, 882A2
Pa pretrial press exclusn case refused 11-17, 882F1
Privacy Issues
Terkel files case refused 1-7, 15G3
IRS handwriting orders upheld 2-20, 170E1
Charity solicitatn limit voided 2-20, 170A2
Des Moines Register case refused 2-25, 188A1
Kissinger records access blocked 3-3, 209B3
Fed funded group info access curbed 3-3, 210B1
McGoff documt disclosure ordrd 3-17, 278B1
Freedom of Info ct order bar backed 3-19, 250B1
Warrantless home arrests curbed 4-15, 305F3
Fonda-Hayden NSA files case refused 5-12, 426G2-A3
Nixon taps case accepted 5-19, 440C1
DEA detainmt procedure backed 5-27, 454A1
Illegal search protectn narrowed 6-25, 541A1
'79-80 term ends, decisns cited 7-2, 540E2
Arrest warrant 3d party searches case accepted 10-6, 782C3
Newsroom searches curb signed 10-14, 835F1-C2
Laetrile ban challenge declined 10-20, 807G1
La itinerant worker registratn ruling affirmed 10-20, 807D2
Conn phone harassmt law challenge declined 12-1, 918F2
Nixon taps case argued 12-8, 937A2
Essex Cnty (NJ) census data stay extended 12-15, 957C2
Racial Bias
Calif dual seniority system backed 2-20, 146F2-B3
At-large local electns upheld 4-22, 343A2
Constructn contract Indian preferenc barred 5-27, 454B1
Pub offcl good faith dfns defined 5-27, 454C1
Ill non-labor picketing rights affirmed 6-20, 555D2
Govt minority constructn grants upheld 7-2, 510A1

1976

Sex Rulings
To review Okla beer law 1-12, 24D1
Declines review of Calif women's overtime ruling 1-12, 24D1
Backs retroactive seniority 3-24, 218B2
Bars review of NC homosexual convictn 3-29, 261E3
Upholds homosexual ban 3-30, 261B3, C3 ★
Bars review of sex educ suit 4-5, 262B2
Rules on FPC powers 5-19, 393F2
Holds states liable for bias damages 6-28, 569C1
Bars review of VFW case 10-4, 807A3
Bars review of transsexual teacher firing 10-18, 867B3
Accepts case vs Phila schools 10-18, 867C3
Refuses Va oral sex case 11-29, 901A1
Accepts physical job requiremt review 11-29, 901C1
Vs mandatory pregnancy benefits 12-7, 919G3
Refuses Ky maiden name case 12-13, 960B3
Bars Okla beer-buying bias 12-20, 960D1

Tax Rulings
Agrees to determine IRS disclosure requiremts 1-12, 24G1
Bars IRS emergency procedure 1-13, 23D3
Allows non-fed taxes on imports 1-14, 23G2
Rules on IRS assessmt cases 3-8, 219A2
Backs IRS use of accountants' worksheets 4-21, 331G2
Vs IRS warning to targets 4-21, 331A3
Backs Indians' challenge rights 4-27, 359F1
Affirms fed use of inadmissible criminal evidence 7-6, 535B1
Curbs carry-back breaks 11-2, 867C1
Bars fed ct in NY-V case 11-9, 882G2
Refuses Pa homeowner bias ruling 11-29, 900G3

1977

Sex Bias
Washn homosexual dismissal ruling voided 1-10, 57A1
Soc Sec widower benefits rule voided 3-2, 192C1-B2
Soc Sec old-age benefits test voided 3-21, 230E1
Soc Sec old-age benefits bias backed 3-21, 230G1-D2
Phila schl bias deadlock 4-19, 342C2
Miss State U gay ad case review refused 4-25, 342C3
Employer records case denied 5-16, 419C1
Pregnant employe dismissal case declined 5-16, 419B2
Burger cites '69-76 cases 5-17, 419A3
Ala prison employe standards voided 6-27, 538E3
Sen votes pregnancy, disability benefits 9-16, 738A1
Gay teacher cases refused 10-3, 760D1
Kiwanis charter withdrawal case refused 10-3, 760D3
Vet job prefrnc law backed 10-11, 774D2
Maternity leave seniority rights upheld 12-6, 938C2
Maternity sick-leave pay rule remanded 12-6, 938A3

Tax Issues
'68 NY stock transfer amendmts ruled illegal 1-12, 57C2
IRS seizures limited 1-12, 57G2
Calif Forest Svc taxatn backed 1-25, 80G2
Corp profit-sharing ruling 2-22, 150D1
State corp tax power broadened 3-7, 192C2
Mail-order operatns tax backed 4-4, 341E3
FTC-Beneficial ad dispute review refused 4-25, 342B3
Reinsurance agrmts backed 4-26, 382D3
La officeholder requiremt voided 5-16, 419B2
Calif schl financing review rejctd 6-20, 517D1
Grant case refused 10-3, 760F2
Nixon lawyer case refused 10-3, 760C3
IRS penalties procedure backed 10-31, 835B3
State police meal stipends taxable 11-29, 919D1

1978

Sex Bias
Mo univ Gay Lib case review refused 2-21, 125C3
NW Airlines pay bias case refused 2-21, 125G3
UAL maternity rule review refused 3-20, 205G3
Firestone jobless benefits challenge declined 4-17, 308B3
Sex-based pensn plans barred 4-25, 322A3
NC anti-gay ruling declined 5-15, 387E3
NH rape law case refused 6-5, 431B2
Munic legal immunity ended 6-6, 447D1-A2
Class actn certificatn appeals curbed 6-21, 509G2
AT&T bias case declined 7-3, 551F3
Coll job-bias ruling voided 11-13, 874F1-C2
UAL NYS maternity leave case refused 11-27, 937G1

Sports Rulings
Football TV contract tax value affirmed 1-9, 13B2
Montana hunting fee disparity backed 5-23, 405F3
Redskins liability case refused 6-12, 468E1
Baseball comr authority challenge refused 10-2, 751A2

Tax Issues
Marrieds tax law case review denied 1-9, 13A2
Football TV contract value affirmed 1-9, 13B2
Multistate Tax Compact upheld 2-21, 126F1-A2
Personal holding co property value affirmed 2-22, 126G2
Retroactive withholding on lunch allowances denied 2-27, 143G1
IRS agent liability case review denied 3-20, 206B1
Nonprofit travel agents case refused 3-27, 241B2
Calif brief on Hughes residence heard 3-29, 459D1
Tax breaks in lease-back deals OKd 4-18, 309F1-B2
State stevedoring tax OKd 4-26, 344B1
Northwestn U dispute refused 5-1, 364E1
Liability in bankruptcy backed 5-22, 388B1
Corp takeover tax liability curbed 5-22, 388F1
Antique gun case declined 5-22, 388B2
Corp forgn earnings case refused 6-5, 431F2
Iowa business formula backed 6-15, 468E2
IRS summons power backed 6-19, 492F2
Zenith rebuffed on import duty 6-21, 491G2
Hughes estate dispute interventn denied 6-22, 509A1
Ky franchise tax case refused 10-30, 832A3
NYS property-tax-limit case refused 10-30, 832B3
Boston referendum lobby injunctn lifted 11-6, 874A1
Fruehauf Corp convictn refused 11-6, 874D1
IRS offcl's bribery convictn review refused 11-27, 937C2
'Marriage tax' challenge refused 12-11, 981C1
Calif utilities refund case refused 12-11, 981D1

Transportation Issues
IBM-Greyhound trust dispute review denied 1-16, 33E2
CAB Natl Airlines rule review denied 1-23, 65C2
NW Airlines sex bias case refused 2-21, 125G3
Wis truck length limit overturned 2-21, 126D1
Delta Air Lines '73 Boston claim suit review denied 2-21, 126A2
States curbed on oil tanker regulatn 3-6, 161D3
UAL maternity rule review refused 3-20, 205G3
REA bankruptcy case review refused 3-20, 206A1
State stevedoring tax OKd 4-26, 344B1
Clemente family case vs FAA declined 5-1, 364C1
Mt Hood award vs Greyhound curbed 6-19, 492A3
Burger rejcts RR strike plea 9-26, 809A3
Truck joint rate expansn case declined 10-10, 789B3
Auto rental parking ticket case refused 10-30, 832F2
UAL NYS maternity leave case refused 11-27, 937G1

1979

Religious Issues
Jewish inmate rights case refused 6-4, 439F1
7th-Day Adventist firing case declined by Sup Ct 6-4, 439G1
Ga laws in church land dispute backed 7-2, 559C1
Priest-penitent case declined 10-1, 767E3
Worldwide Church receivership challenge refused 10-1, 768A2
NJ munic powers case declined 11-13, 902F1
Methodist legal immunity cases declined 11-26, 919E2
Krishna solicitatn rights case refused 11-26, 919F2
Calif teacher firing case dismissed 12-10, 988F1

Sex Bias
Mo women jury exclusn law voided 1-9, 14A3
Single-sex alimony barred 3-5, 184C2
Alimony rule in NYS child custody case backed 3-19, 203F2
Ky factory case refused 4-23, 346A3
Unwed father adoptn consent role backed 4-24, 364A1
Unwed father damage suit bar upheld 4-24, 364A1, E1
Pvt Title IX suit allowed 5-14, 382C3
Vets' job-prefernc law upheld; reactn 6-5, 421D1-D2
Congressmen ruled liable to suits 6-5, 463G3-464F1
KKK law use curbed 6-11, 479A1
Union recognitn denial case declined 6-18, 499E2
Gender-based welfare plan ruled illegal 6-25, 539C3
'78-79 term ends, voting alignmts rptd 7-2, 557G3, 558B1
'67 gay alien ruling cited 8-14, 631C2
Ex-Rep Passman settles suit 8-23, 649F3
Westn Elec case refused 10-29, 884C2
Ind pregnancy jobless pay case refused 11-13, 902A2
Title IX job bias funds cutoff bar declined 11-26, 919D2

Sports Rulings
Kapp trust damages case declined 4-16, 302F3
NYS harness-racing suspensn voided 6-25, 540E1
NFL injury suit ruling declined 10-29, 884E1

State Rights
Bi-state agency immunity curbed 3-5, 185C1
Ct immunity curbed 3-5, 185C1
Pa fed funds control case declined 3-5, 185D1
US debt collectn priority defined 4-2, 281G2
Fla fed funds challenge refused 4-30, 365A1
Fed ct welfare suits curbed 5-14, 383C3
State age bias filings required, time limit barred 5-21, 400C2
States given parole discretn 5-29, 421D2-B3
Pol party state com structure law backed 6-4, 439C1
Fed child custody fights curbed 6-11, 478F3
Indian land case laws backed 6-20, 516G1
Ga laws in church land dispute backed 7-2, 559B1

Tax Issues
Ill overassessmt case declined 1-15, 32C1
Accounting methods limited 1-16, 32G2
Mont gross-receipts tax upheld 2-22, 151C1
GM tax probe plea declined 2-26, 164G2
NYC occupancy tax collectn curbed 3-5, 185E1
Muffler assn denied tax break 3-20, 203C3
Fairchild IRS complaint refused 3-26, 231B1
IRS tap evidence backed 4-2, 281D2
IRS seizure power case declined 4-16, 303B1
NM elec tax voided 4-18, 346B2
Calif cargo container taxes voided 4-30, 364A3
NJ pvt schl tax break ban affirmed 5-29, 421F3
Calif utilities refund stay refused 10-1, 768C1; appeal denied 10-15, 848B1
Justice Dept cites '77 case errors 10-8, 848A2

Transportation Issues
CAB intrastate fare order case refused 1-8, 14D3
Religious rail worker union dues case refused 1-8, 14E3
UK airline '72 crash case refused 1-15, 32D1
'77 tire grading suit cited 2-8, 111E2
EEOC curb on BN data upheld 2-21, 128F3
GM tax probe plea declined 2-26, 164G2
ICC rail-freight fee case refused 3-19, 203D2
NYC Transit Auth ex-addict ban backed 3-21, 231B2
Random car checks by police barred 3-27, 263D1
Entebbe hijack case declined 4-30, 364F3

1980

'79-80 term ends, decisns cited 7-2, 540D2
Ala NAACP ruling cited 9-17, 744D2

Religious Issues
Chicago Jehovah's Witness firing case declined 1-7, 15D3
'63 schl prayer ruling cited 2-5, 156A2
NYS pvt schl reimbursemt upheld 2-20, 146B2
Calif Worldwide Church probe case declined 6-2, 513C1
NYC parochial schl remedial aid case refused 10-6, 782F2
SD schls case refused 11-10, 868G1
Ky 10 Commandmts schl law upset 11-17, 881B3

Sex Bias
Bank uniform case declined 3-17, 226F1
Mo workman's compensatn law voided 4-22, 344A1
Purposeful job bias case declined 4-28, 369A2
NOW Mo boycott case refused 10-6, 782F1-A2
Male-only draft case accepted 12-1, 918E1
Faculty bias Title IX case accepted 12-1, 918B2

Sports Issues
NCAA aid limit case declined 5-12, 426B3
NASL NLRB order refused 10-14, 1001F2

State Rights
Parole offcls immunity upheld 1-15, 51E1
State ct jurisdictn narrowed 1-21, 93F1
Calif wine pricing law held illegal 3-3, 210E1
Calif redlining law curbed 3-17, 226C1
Vt tax on forgn dividends backed 3-19, 249E2
State legislators' immunity curbed 3-19, 249E3
Govt desert land retentn backed 4-16, 328C3
Land-grant exchng ban upheld 5-19, 440A2
NYS civil rights suit filing limit upheld 5-19, 440F2
State ct legal immunity defined 6-2, 512E3
State sales preference backed 6-19, 554E2
Right to sue states broadened 6-25, 540C3
Calif probe of Ark prisons curbed 12-8, 937C1

Tax Issues
Meal tax case refused 1-14, 36F3-37A1
RR worker compensatn liability backed 2-19, 131C1
IRS handwriting orders upheld 2-20, 170E1
La gas tax case fact-finder named 3-3, 210G1
Vt tax on forgn dividends backed 3-19, 249E2
Fla circus tax case refused 3-24, 265A2
Idaho Asarco tax case remanded 3-24, 265B2
Du Pont-IRS dispute declined 4-14, 307D1
IRS audit data request case refused 4-28, 369E1
DC professional tax case declined 5-27, 454A1
Wis out-of-state corp earnings tax backed 6-10, 511E3
Inventory tax ruling impact on publishing rptd 10-5, 835G3

Transportation Issues
ICC Burlington shipping refund stay refused 1-14, 37A3
Oil tanker subsidies repaymt backed 2-20, 170E2
Rock I ruling refused 7-2, rail law study denied 11-10, 868E2
Greyhound-Mt Hood trust case declined 10-6, 782C2
RR A-fuel tariffs case declined 10-6, 782D2
LA airport nuisance award case refused 10-6, 782A3
BN rail merger stayed by Powell 11-21, stay lifted 11-25, 937G2-A3
EPA Chrysler recall order challenge refused 12-1, 918E2
Rail pensn revisn backed 12-9, 936G3
New Haven RR reorgn challenge refused 12-15, 957D2

1976

Voting Rights
Upholds Calif GOP primary rule 1-19, 42G3
Bars GOP delegate rule review 2-23, 170A1
Gives view on reapportionmt plans OK 3-3, 219B1
Upholds 1-member districts 3-3, 219D1
Rules on redistricting plans review 3-30, 262C1
Affirms Conn closed primary 12-6, 920D3

Welfare
'75 ruling on jobless benefit choice cited 1-7, 128A3
Disability cutoff procedures upheld 2-24, 169B2
Suburban low-income housing upheld 4-20, 308D2
Affirms Utah contraceptive rule 5-24, 393D2

1977

Voting Issues
Racial redistricting upheld 3-1, 174C3-175D1
Mich electn rules upheld 3-21, 230C3
Colo alien schl law review declined 4-18, 342D1
Miss reapportnmt rejected 5-31, 461B3
Atty Gen powers backed 6-20, 517A1
Legal scholar scores rulings 10-31, 878G3, 879B1
Hinds Cnty (Miss) apportnmt case refused 11-28, 919F2

Watergate (& other political Irregularities)
Vesco case review barred 2-22, 150E1
Mardian reinstated to bar 2-28, 175B2
Cover-up appeals rule leaked 4-21, 382B2, F2
Wild waiver declined 5-16, 419A2
Appeals denied 5-23, 406D1
Haldeman, Mitchell jail delay refused 5-31, 461F3
Haldeman, Mitchell appeals review denied 6-27, 538F3
US custody of Nixon documts upheld 6-28, 539D3
Nixon tapes OKd as civil suit evidence 10-3, 760B2
Mitchell, Ehrlichman disbarred 10-31, 835A3

1978

Rail clerk strike stay renewal denied 11-27, 937E2
Trucking freight-rate case refused 12-4, 959B2
Police auto search power broadened 12-5, 959C2
Calif auto franchise law upheld 12-5, 959C3

Treaty Rulings
Panama Canal treaty challenge refused 1-16, 33F2
Panama Canal treaty stay denied 4-17, 308G2
Panama Canal treaty challenge refused 5-15, 387G3

Watergate (& other political Irregularities)
Broadcasters denied Nixon tapes 4-18, 308C1
FBI informant case declined 6-12, 468D1
Goodwin legal immunity case declined 6-19, 492D2

Welfare Issues
PR SSI benefits exclusn upheld 2-27, 143A1
Expedited disability benefits rule review declined 2-27, 143E1
State emergency standards backed 6-6, 447D2
NYS eligibility case refused 6-12, 468C1
SSI forgn travel rule backed 12-11, 980G3

1979

Forgn-flag oil tanker case refused 5-14, 383E1
ICC motor carrier damage case refused 5-29, 421G3
ICC rail rate suspensn power backed 6-11, 478D3
Mich no-fault auto insurnc case refused 6-11, 478G3
Mass driver license suspensn rule upheld 6-25, 540G1
Burger, White back Amtrak train cuts 9-30, 10-8, 868D1
Penn Central reorganizatn challenges declined 10-1, 768E1
Motorist 'Miranda rights' case declined 10-9, 784D1
ICC trucking order ruling reversed 10-15, 847G3
Auto makers FTC challenge declined 11-5, 884E2
Pub access to waterways curbed 12-4, 987G3-988C1

Welfare & Social Services
Foster care benefits backed 2-22, 151B1
Ill overpaymts seizure curbed 3-19, 203A3
Fed welfare suits curbed 5-14, 383C3
Soc Sec overpaymt hearings backed 6-20, 516C2
Gender-based plan ruled illegal 6-25, 539C3
Unwed mothers denied survivors' aid 6-27, 558F1
Ala legal counsel case declined 10-1, 768A2

1980

Welfare & Social Services
Benefits denial hearing case declined 4-14, 307F1
PR welfare aid rate backed 5-27, 453C3
Right to sue states broadened 6-25, 540C3

1976

TARIFF Commission, U.S.—*See TRADE Commission, U.S. International, below*
TENNESSEE Valley Authority (TVA)
Rpt on '75 Ala fire issued 2-28, 172A1
Reagan scores 5-21, 374F1
TRADE Commission, U.S. International (formerly U.S. Tariff Commission)
Specialty steel import ruling rptd 1-17, 212F3
EEC vs steel policy 1-21, 85C1
Sweden protests import curbs 2-2, 104A1
Rules on shoe, flatwear imports 2-21, 3-2, 213D2-D3
Ford bars shoe import curb 4-16; eases flatware, ceramics curbs 4-30, 321F3, 322D1
Urges shrimp industry Trade Act aid 5-11; mushroom growers get aid 5-17, 431F1, D2
Ford OKs sugar industry probe 9-21, 721B3
Rules US shoe industry hurt 12-28, 976C2
TRADE Negotiations, Office of the Special Representative for
Ford threatens steel import quotas 3-16, 212E3

1977

SURFACE Mining Reclamation & Enforcement, Office of—*See under INTERIOR below*
TARIFF Commission, U.S.—*See TRADE Commission, U.S. International, below*
TECHNOLOGY Assessment, Office of (OTA)
Saccharin cancer risk affirmed 6-7, 531A1
Coal slurry bill deferred 6-27, 516D1
Oil, gas recovery prospects estimated 7-17, 559C1
TELECOMMUNICATIONS Policy, Office of
'75 warning on Sovt taps rptd 7-10, 551A2
Carter proposes abolitn 7-15, 556B1
Thaler backs phone ad curbs 10-21, 921A1
TENNESSEE Valley Authority (TVA)
Fish halts Tellico Dam 1-31, 95G2-C3
Uranium cartel hearings 6-16—6-17, 480C1, C2
Air pollutn suits filed 6-22, 521A3
Utilities suit vs Westinghouse proceeds 11-9, 895G1-B2
US, forgn uranium producers sued 11-18, 895C1
Black bias suit case review refused 12-5, 939D1
TRADE Commission, U.S. International (formerly U.S. Tariff Commission)
Shoe import injury ruled 1-6; Carter bars tariffs, quotas 4-1, 248C1
Sugar import injury ruled 3-3, quota cut asked 3-14, 189C1
TV import injury ruled 3-8, tariff hike asked 3-14, 208G2
New color TV probe voted 3-23, 318C3
Carter bars sugar quotas, OKs subsidies 5-4, 457D3
Japan OKs TV export limit 5-20, 415F3
TV probe ends, consent pact OKd 7-14, 587E1
Dumping chrgs vs Japanese steelmakers upheld 10-3, 774F3

1978

TARIFF Commission, U.S.—*See TRADE Commission below*
TECHNOLOGY Assessment, Office of—*See under CONGRESS in this section above*
TELECOMMUNICATIONS & Informations Agency, National—*See under COMMERCE in this section above*
TELECOMMUNICATIONS Policy, Office of
Minority broadcasting ownership aid proposed 1-31, 195A2
Shifted to Commerce Dept 3-28, 270B2
TENNESSEE Valley Authority (TVA)
Jenkins, Wagner quit; score EPA setlmt 5-5, 5-18; Freeman named chrmn 5-16, 390G1-G2
Wage cncl urges rate hike moderatn 5-15, increase scaled down 5-17, 362G1
Carter visits, urges broader energy role 5-22, 386G2-B3, 390G2
Tellico Dam constructn halt upheld by Sup Ct 6-15, 468G1-D2
Endangered Species Act revised, Tellico dispute cited 7-19, 551B2
EPA clean-air pact OKd 12-14, 982G2-C3
TERRITORIAL Affairs, Office of—*See under INTERIOR in this section above*
TOXICOLOGICAL Research, National Center for—*See FOOD & Drug Administration in this section above*
TRADE Commission, U.S. International (formerly U.S. Tariff Commission)
Carter bars chrome alloy duty hike 1-29, 80E3
Carter bars fastener duty hike 2-10, 181B2; cites import rise 10-31, Carter OKs hike 12-26, 998D3
Japan steel import minimum price ordrd 2-23, Carter overrules 4-24, 444B1
China glove import curbs barred 3-15, 443G3
Carter hikes CB radio tariffs 3-28, 443D3
Zinc trade relief barred 6-1, 443G2
Carter bars curbs on stainless steel utensils 7-2, clothespins 10-2, 805E1
Copper quotas urged 8-23, Carter rejcts 10-20, 804F3

1979

TECHNOLOGY Assessment, Office of—*See under CONGRESS in this section above*
TELECOMMUNICATIONS Policy, Office of (defunct)
Nixon Admin pub TV moves disclosed 2-24, 194G1
TENNESSEE Valley Authority (TVA)
Reactor flaw warning rptd 4-16, 275D1
Westinghouse settles uranium supply suit 5-15, 366F1
Tellico Dam completn clears Cong 8-1, 9-10, Carter signs 9-26, 766F2
China power dvpt aid signed 8-28, 644C2
TRADE Commission, U.S. International (formerly U.S. Tariff Commission)
Sovt ammonia imports ruled disruptive 10-3, quota asked 10-5, 802B3-803B1
Carter bars Sovt ammonia import curbs 12-11, 939E2
TRADE Negotiations, Office of the Special Representative for
Askew named spec trade rep 8-8, 647B1*
Askew sworn spec trade rep 10-2, 803E1
Carter proposes reorganizatn 10-25, 803C1

1980

SYNTHETIC Fuels Corp., U.S.
Synfuels bill clears Cong 6-19, 6-29, 479B2; Carter signs 6-30, 494G1-A2
Carter names Sawhill, 6 others 9-10, 9-13; Cary withdraws 9-24, Sen panel OKs 9-25, 699C1, 725D2
Sawhill nominatn blocked 10-1, Carter names interim bd 10-5, 786E2-A3
TENNESSEE Valley Authority (TVA)
Ala A-dump site planned 1-16, 54D1
Tenn A-plant gets start-up license 2-28, 169A3
Ala A-plant FBI probe disclosed 3-7, 249G1-A2
Freeman signs China power pact 3-15, 231B2
Dam constructn challenge declined by Sup Ct 3-24, 265B2
Tenn A-plant gets operating license 9-16, 723B2
TOXIC Substances Strategy Committee
Tighter chem controls urged 6-29, 494G2-B3
TRADE Commission, U.S. International
US Steel files dumping complaint 3-21, 225E1
Japan typewriter duties set 4-22, 368B1
Steel import damage found 5-1, 456B1
Taiwan, S Korea TV import curbs extensn asked; Japan quota end OKd 5-13, 368A2
UAW asks auto import curbs 6-12, 457E2
Carter eases Taiwan, S Korea TV quotas; lifts Japan curbs 6-30, 515E3
Japan auto import curbs asked by unions, Ford 7-1, 8-4, 599C1
Carter seeks auto ruling 7-8, 505B1
Carter auto ruling request rejected 7-18, 556G1-B2, 599F1
Japan auto import hearings held 10-8—10-10, 823E1
Japan auto import curbs barred 11-10, 866D3
TRADE Representative, Office of the Special Representative for
Nissan exec asks tariff rise delay 7-1, 599C2

1976

TRANSPORTATION, Department of
Hearing on Concorde 1-5, 5B2
Concorde test OKd 2-4, reactn 2-4—2-5, 94C2-E3
Concorde test decisn upheld 5-19, svc to US begins 5-24, 378E2
Highway funds cleared 5-19, 411F3; signed 6-1, 982F1
Alaska pipeline problems rptd 5-21, inspectn ordrd 7-6; House subcom, dept rpts issued 9-5, 9-10, 690A3-691B2
Dem platform text 6-15, 474G1
Nader at auto air bag hearing 8-3; Coleman bars mandatory requiremt seeks demonstratn projct; reactn 12-6, 920G3, 921D1
Cong OKs '77 funds 8-4, 646A2; signed 8-14, 982F1
Amtrak NE corridor buy OKd 8-29, 648G1
Aircraft noise rules set 11-18, 868B3
Carter names liaison 11-23, 881B3
Coleman to OK 2 superports 12-17, 991G3
Appointments & Resignations
Todd confrmd Safety Bd chrmn 2-5, 110D2
Gregory quits h'way safety post 2-26, 232G1
Ford cites Coleman 10-22, 801G3
Carter names Adams secy 12-14, 936C1, D3

1977

TRANSPORTATION, Department of
Issues future trends rpt 1-15, 58D2
Ford budget proposals 1-17, 32F2, 33C1
Air bag test progrm set 1-18, mandatory bags backed 3-21, 213B2
Adams confrmd secy 1-20, 34B1, B3
Bracy, Davenport confrmd asst secys, Butchman, dep secy 2-10, 148C3-E3
Coleman IBM bd membrshp cited 2-22, 140A3
Adams rpts net worth 2-25, 147B3
Adams asks transit bill delay 2-25, 213A3
On SST research authorizatn 3-18, 213B2
Oil tanker safety rules tightened 3-18, 214D2
Tire-grading case review denied 3-21, 230E2
Exec cook rptd on payroll 3-24, 236F1
Carter energy plan 4-20, 291E2; 4-22, 321B2
Amtrak 'Mountaineer' svc to end 5-3, 368E3
Adams NY Concorde ruling reactn cited 5-11, 368C2
NYC copter mishap probe set 5-16, 412C3
KC schl integratn suit names 5-26, 446F1
House Concorde amendmt fails 6-8, 463B2
UK air svc pact hailed 6-22, 500C2
Air bags on '82 cars ordrd 6-30, 521F3
Cos withdraw from Seadock 7-12, Loop expects pact 7-19, 559C2, G2
Fed no-fault auto insurnc standards backed 7-15, 7-21, 594E3-595A1
UK air svc pact signed 7-23, 593C1
Loop superport license signed 8-1, 724B3
NY Concorde ban overturned 8-17, 627A2
Concorde expanded landing rights proposed; reactn 9-23, 738A2-C3

1978

TRANSPORTATION, Department of
NE rail offcls resign 1-30; more funds allocated 2-11, projct delays rptd 2-24, 225A1
Adams issues policy statemt 2-8, 109B1
New fuel standards for light trucks issued 3-15, 284F1-B2
RR high-carbon wheels curbed 3-23, 365D3
RR roadbed, track maintenance aid hiked, '77 derailmt data cited 4-15, 365E3
Amtrak route cutbacks proposed 5-8, 366C1
Tank-car safety deadlines advanced, other safety measures planned 5-9, 365G2
'77 motorcycle deaths rptd 6-29, 636A2
'77 traffic deaths rptd 7-11, 636F1
GAO LNG study scored 7-31, 610G1
US intl air policy outlined 8-21, 640E1-B2
Adams proposes trucking, rail deregulatn 11-13, 1007F1
Adams hails RR rate hike 11-24, 1007A3

1979

TRANSPORTATION, Department of
Adams rail decontrol plan rptd 1-15, 35C3
Adams backs '85 gas mileage standard 1-19, 87C3
Coast Guard safety training faulted 1-20, 140E3
Amtrak route cutback plan revised; maps 1-31, 129A1, C1
Tire grading order upheld 2-8, 111D2
Adams outlines urban-aid policy 2-13, 129A2
Radial tire grading ordrd 3-13, 208C3
Rail decontrol bill introduced 3-23, shippers score 6-6, 579D2
'78 traffic deaths rptd 4-20, 309A2
Faulty auto repairs rptd common 5-7, 595B3
'Car of the future' plan set 5-18, 441C3
'78 state per capita gas use rptd 5-27, 395E2
Milwaukee Rd svc cut denied 6-1, 465C2
A-waste transport rules set 6-15, 610D1
Auto role seen undiminished 6-18, 514A3
Truckers' energy cntr set 6-28, 516B3
Tex offshore port OKd 7-2, 518F2
Adams fired, Claytor named temporary secy; Butchman, Bracy quit 7-20, 529D1, 530F1-B3
Goldschmidt named secy; Claytor confrmd Defense dep secy 7-27, 577B1, E3
Rock I reorganizatn plan opposed 10-10, 830F3
San Fran mass-transt request backed 10-13, 831E1
Tex supertanker port OKd 10-15, 769B3
Braniff fine sought 11-6, 868B2
'80 funds clear Cong 11-15, 11-19, Carter signs 11-30, 920C1
'80 continuing funds res clears Cong 11-16, Carter signs 11-20, 900B2

1980

TRANSPORTATION, Department of
Rock I RR assets bids rptd 2-4, svc extensn asked 2-14, 131A2
Rock I svc extended 2-22, 147F3
Rock I svc continues 3-31, 345D3
Goldschmidt sees auto execs, notes concern 5-14, 384G1
Car makers aid planned 7-8, 505E1, A2
Goldschmidt disputes Reagan on auto regulatns 9-3, 664G2
'81 funds clear Cong 9-30, signed 10-9, 980E3
Lewis named secy 12-11, 935D1

1976

Coast Guard—*See separate listing in this section above*
Federal Aviation Administration (FAA)
'74 TWA crash rpt issued 1-21, 80C1
Concorde test OKd 2-4, 94B3
Cockpit smoking ban sought 4-20, 308G1
Concorde noise monitored 5-24, 378B3
'76-80 authorizatn signed 7-12, 567C1
Cong OKs '77 funds 8-4, 646D2; signed 8-14, 982F1
Noise rule to cover old planes 10-21, 849C1
Aircraft noise rules set 11-18, 868G3
Federal Highway Administration
Dem platform text 6-15, 474A2
Cong OKs '77 funds 8-4, 646D2; signed 8-14, 982F1
Federal Railroad Administration
Ford budget proposals 1-21, 66B1
Cong OKs '77 funds 8-4, 646D2; signed 8-14, 982F1
National Highway Traffic Safety Administration
Gregory quits 2-26, 232G1
Cong OKs '77 funds 8-4, 646D2; signed 8-14, 982F1
Urban Mass Transportation Administration
Cong OKs '77 funds 8-4, 646E2; signed 8-14, 982F1

TREASURY, Department of the—*See also SIMON, William*
Secy's membership in NSC vetoed 1-1, 4D1; Sen overrides 1-22, 69A3
Pres contenders get US funds 1-2, 22C3
Simon, Yeo on Jamaica IMF monetary accord 1-8, 1-9, 13C2, 14F2
Dec '75, 1st ½ fscl '76 deficit 1-28, 91F2
Jan jobless rate rptd 2-5, 152C3
Dec inventories down 2-13, 169E1
House votes debt financing 2-25, 170C3
Dixon confrmd dep secy 3-2, 196G1
Rpts Montoya audit irregularities 4-12, 283E3
Sen intellignc com rpt cited 4-26, 302D2, 303A2
US forgn intelligence chart 304A2 ★, C2
Ends car dumping probe 5-4; VW dumping rptd 5-6, 320E3
Intl buffer stock issue dispute rptd 5-6, 317E1
US holds 7 in El Salvador plot 5-15—5-17, 401E1-E2
Cong clears added funds 5-19, 411F3; signed 6-1, 982F1
Loan to prop UK £ OKd 6-7, 407B2
Interest exempt bond bill signed 6-30, 534F1
GAO scores anit-bias actn 7-1, 943D3
Sen OKs anti-bribe tax curbs 8-6, 669D1
Eur, Canada car price hikes set 8-12, 988C1
GOP platform com OKs plank 8-13, 583F1
Macdonald confrmd Navy undersecy 9-8, 808C1
Carter proposes Cabt-level energy dept 9-21, 704F2
£ fall linked to loan curb rumor 10-25, 809E3
Rpts transitn ¼ fed spending down 10-27, 865F3
Boycott guidelines issued 11-7, Ribicoff scores 12-8, 987C2
Loan to Portugal set 11-16, another rptd pending 11-23, 966G2
New job exam bias rules signed 11-17, 884D2
Carter stresses forgn policy 11-23, 881A2
Carter names liaison 11-23, 881B3
El Salvador col sentncd 11-23, 1012C3
Carter names Blumenthal secy 12-14, 936C1, D2
Hungary pays US war debt 12-24, 1012D3

1977

Air bag, seat belt order operative 10-14, 796G3-797A1
Cong com votes '78 Amtrak funds, cuts canceled 11-3, 860G3
White cos win minority contract 12-13, 979D1, F1
Mex air svc agrmt initialed 12-19, 1006A3
Coast Guard—*See separate listing in this section above*
Federal Aviation Administration (FAA)
Disabled rules issued 4-7, 325G2
Concorde noise study backed, Dulles noise rpt issued 4-14, 368F2
Crew smoking ban rejctd 9-1, 778E3
GAO rpt scores Concorde study 9-16, 738G3
ESA satellite plan shelved 9-19, 736C1
Concorde expanded landing rights hearings proposed 9-23, 738F2
Concorde NYC operatns begin, noise data cited 10-19, 10-20, 819D3
Blasts heard off E Coast 12-2—12-22, 1008F3
Federal Highway Administration (FHWA)
Metric road signs proposed 4-27, 369D1
Metric road signs proposal dropped 6-24, 522G1-A2
Motor Carrier Bur inspectns intensify 9-8, 778C3
Weather Svc delays metric conversn 10-18, 820E3
Federal Railroad Administration (FRA)
Sullivan confrmd admin 6-23, 626F3
Milwaukee Rd stock purchase OKd 7-15, 593C2
C&NW stock purchase set 9-9, 778B3
National Highway Traffic Safety Administration (NHTSA)
Claybrook confrmd admin 4-6, 272G2
Ford sets fan hazard recalls 8-16, 651B3
Nader asks Claybrook resign, Claybrook rebuts 12-30, 1008A1
St. Lawrence Seaway Development Corporation
Canada, US set toll hikes 12-16, 982F3
Urban Mass Transportation Administration (UMTA)
Page confrmd admin 7-1, 626C3
Chicago funds OKd 9-19, 778D3
Adams backs mass-transit fund 10-12, 860B3
Ex-aide sentncd 12-21, 1009F1

TREASURY, Department of the—*See also BLUMENTHAL, W(erner) Michael*
Simon vetoes housing tax shelter ban 1-5, 36E2
Gas transport rule eased 2-2, 2-3, 76E1
Carter visits employes 2-10, 110D2
NYC loan warnings 2-27, 3-3, 3-10, funds released 3-11, 193D1, G2, E3
NY FRB forgn mkt interventn rptd 3-2, 188F3
'75 tax data on rich rptd 3-3, 197G2
Cook rptd on payroll 3-24, 236F1
Cuba currency curbs eased 3-25, 283E2
Japan TV bond requirement raised 4-7, 318G2-B3
Japan electronics import duties ordrd 4-12; opposed 4-13, 4-14, 318G1
Rpts Mar, 1st ½ fscl '77 deficit 4-26, 407C3
Natl debt to be reduced 4-27, 407D3
'77 supplemental funds signed 5-4, 339F1
Carter seeks Soc Sec chngs 5-9, 364D1-A2
Mobil-Rhodesia probe ended 5-16, 413E2
Strong $ backed 7-28; US trade deficit-reducing strategy rptd challenged 8-8, 585D2
Japan electronics duties order reversed 7-28, 586D3, 587C1
Canal demands rptd studied 7-29, 589A3
Sumitomo purchase bar sought 8-9, 669D3
Warns Chicago bank re bias 8-25, 669G2
Debt ceiling rise enacted, savings bond suspensn noted 10-4, 773G2
NYC fscl '77 budget deficit rpts vary 10-4, 881C2
Interest-bearing tax, loan accts bill clears Cong 10-14, 815A3; signed 10-28, 1001D2
Soc Sec loans clear House 10-27, 814E3
Fscl '77 budget deficit rptd 10-27, 835E3
Rpts fscl '75, '76 fed deficit on accrual basis 11-7, 941A3
Gulf fined re laundered money 11-13, 881D2
Urban plans debated 12-4, 959D3
Laurence Woodworth dies 12-4, 1024G3

1978

Coast Guard—*See separate listing in this section above*
Federal Aviation Administration (FAA)
ICAO picks TRSB bad-weather landing system 4-19, 319B3
Clemente family case declined by Sup Ct 5-1, 364C1
New air-safety rules proposed 12-27, 1006C3-1007B1
Federal Highway Administration
Carter signs fund bill 11-8, 875A3
Federal Railroad Administration (FRA)
GAO rpt scores Conrail safety efforts 3-15, 224G3-225A1
Tank-car safety deadlines advanced, other safety measures planned 5-9, 365C3
Study sees RR decline 10-10, 812E1
National Highway Traffic Safety Administration (NHTSA)
'77 motor vehicle recall record rptd 1-1, 67D3
Chevette, Pinto fail safety tests 5-4, 5-8, 365F3
Ford recalls Pintos, Bobcats 6-9, deaths rptd 7-6, 7-8, 569B3
Omnis, Horizons found safe 7-7, 569D3
Firestone tire recall sought 7-8, recall set 10-20, 834E3, 835B1; pact cited 11-28, 935A2
Pinto recall pact reached 8-21; Nader, Ford trade chrgs 8-22—8-30, 719C1
Ford transmissn hazard warned 8-29, 719A2
Carter signs fund bill 11-8, 875A3
TRANSPORTATION Safety Board, National—*See NATIONAL Transportation Safety Board in this section above*

TREASURY, Department of the—*See also BLUMENTHAL, Michael*
Blumenthal role in NYC fscl crisis 86D2
$ defense via swap network set 1-4, reactn 1-9, 27F1, C2
'77 futures trading rise rptd 1-12, 84A1
Oil co tax credits on forgn paymts revoked 1-16, 69D1
NYC fscl recovery plan issued 1-20, 87E1
AFL-CIO urges Soc Sec fund chngs 2-20, 142A1
Blumenthal presents NYC aid plan 3-2, 141B1
NYC long-term guarantees proposed 3-2, Carter signs bill 8-8, 608C2, E2
House Dems back Soc Sec funding 4-5, 240D3, 241D1
Panama Canal pact reservatn ratified 4-18, 273B2
Gold sales set 4-19, auctns held 5-23, 6-20, 523D1, C2, G2
OPEC investmt shift rptd 4-28, 344A3
Carter reduces tax-cut plan 5-12, 361E1
Soc Sec rollback opposed by House com 5-17, 386F1
Tuitn tax credits OKd by House 6-1, 431B3
Blumenthal asks exec pay curbs 6-6, 428B1
Zenith import duty rebuffed by Sup Ct 6-21, 491G2
Natl health plan delay urged 6-26, 491F2
Sen adds oil import fee bar to funds bill 6-27, 511C3
'76 tax nonpaymt by rich rptd down 7-8, 554E2
Ashland overpaymt refund sought 7-12, 610B3
Canada grant to Ford Motor scored 8-1, 613E2
Debt ceiling increased 8-3, 625A3
Treasury bill explained 10-18, 790F3, 791A1
Treas note coupon record rate posted 10-30, 827D1, F1
$ rescue plan set 11-1, 825F1-B2
IMF fund borrowed to aid $ 11-7, 998C3
Carter vows duty waiver extensn 11-11, Treas extends 12-29, 998D1
Bank interest paymt on frozen forgn assets backed 11-14, 977F1
EMS formatn backed 12-7, 952F2
Mark notes to aid $ sold 12-13, 998G2
Blumenthal forecasts '79 econ growth 12-14, 980D1

1979

Chicago aid loss warned 11-20, scored 11-20-12-6; road funds OKd 12-4, 983F3
Air safety panel formed 12-19, 988E3
Goldschmidt on Chrysler loan bd 12-21, 981G3
Coast Guard—*See separate listing in this section above*
Federal Aviation Administration (FAA)
Carter budget proposals 1-22, 45F1
NY area radar improvemt updated 3-12, 206G1
Air-safety crackdown planned 3-16, 206C1
NYC near-collisn rpt issued 4-9, 412D2
DC-10s grounded for inspectn 5-29, safety flaws rptd 5-30, 411E3-412D1
DC-10s grounded indefinitely, forgn flights banned 6-6, 420E2, F3
DC-10 legal barriers, engineering flaws discounted 7-10; flight ban lifted 7-13, 528E2
Chicago DC-10 crash rpt issued 7-10, findings disputed 7-12, 538E3-539E1
Skylab comes down 7-11, 510A1
Small airports to be upgraded 8-7, 726D3
NRC reorganizatn asked 10-30, 825F2
DC-9 inspectns ordrd 9-19, order expanded 10-9, 830C2
Prinair grounded 10-25, 830F2
Mex City air crash probed 10-31, 912D2
Amer, Continental pay fines on DC-10 11-16, 988D3
Computer system safety defended 11-20, 989A1
Air safety panel formed 12-19, 988E3
Safety Bd issues Chicago DC-10 crash rpt 12-21, 988A3
Federal Highway Administration
Urban Mass Transit Admin merger dropped 9-17, 726F1
Federal Railroad Administration (FRA)
Jan-Sept '78 derailmts rptd 4-9, 472C3
Conrail study issued 9-11, 989F2
Rock I reorganizatn plan opposed 10-10, 830F3
Urban Mass Transit Administration
Fed Highway Admin merger dropped 9-17, 726F1
TRAVEL Service, U.S.—*See under COMMERCE in this section above*

TREASURY, Department of the
T-bills, notes explained 681D2
Series E, H bond sales to end in '79 1-10, 133D1-A2
Record '78 savings bond sales rptd 1-10, 133G1
Swiss notes sold to aid $ 1-17, 84G2
Forgn debt to US rptd up 2-5, 84A3
Blumenthal questns Iran oil crisis 2-8, 82A3
Blumenthal visits China 2-24, signs assets accord 3-1, 146B2-A3
House OKs duty waiver bill 3-1, 159C1
Firestone '72 gold trading chrgd 3-15, 202B2
Duty waiver bill signed 4-3, 298E3
Color-TV dumping paymt demanded 4-13, Japan mfrs score 4-26, 298F2
Japan discount rate hike lauded 4-16, 615E3
Poland steel dumping ruled 4-18, 299A1
Gold sale cutback set 4-18, 435C3
7 oil firms accused of overchrgs 5-2, 343E2
IMF loan to Nicaragua backed 5-14, 373B1
Blumenthal at OECD mins mtg 6-14, 437B3
CFTC OKs T-bill, notes futures trading 6-19, 681A3
Blumenthal fired, Miller replaces 7-19, 529C1, D1, 530A1-D1
Fla vegetable growers withdraw Mex dumping chrgs 7-19, 553A2, F2
Carter trade reorganizatn plan set 7-19, 647B1
Miller cleared re Textron payoffs 7-26, 923D2
Chrysler aid talks rptd 7-31, 576F1
Diggs censured, paymt ordrd 7-31, 578G1
Miller confrmd 8-2, sworn 8-6, 627B2-D2
Tax collectn aid set 8-31, 665B3
'76 Wallace campaign repayment noted 9-5, 724A2
Nixon Calif estate expenses disputed 9-5-9-6, 683B2
Fla '78 FRB deposit growth, drug traffic linked 9-6, 840E3
T-bill rates cited 9-18, 701D2
$1 bill replacemt urged 9-25, 727A2
'80 funds clear Cong 9-26, Carter signs 9-29, 883C2
Bond price record drop rptd 10-10, 15-yr yields set record 10-11, 765A1
Gold sale procedures altered, record auctn price bid 10-16, 779F3
Carter trade reorganizatn proposed 10-25, 803B1
'79 budget deficit at 5-yr low 10-25, 946F1
Mex vegetable growers cleared re dumping chrgs 10-30, 831F1
Miller on Oct jobless rate 11-2, 866D3
Iran assets in US rptd 11-14, 861B2
Iran assets freeze confrmd; banks attach assets, risks detailed 11-15-11-18; estimate hiked 11-19, 879C3-880G1
Steel trigger prices hiked 11-20, 965F3

1980

Coast Guard—*See COAST Guard in this section above*
Federal Aviation Administration (FAA)
DC-10 safety system changes sought 1-12; no pylon defects found 1-23, 53B2-G2
McDonnell Douglas fine settled 1-23, 53E2
Commuter pilot safety rules stiffened 2-6, 347E1
Airline ozone standards set, studies rptd 2-12, 159C1, D1
San Diego air control zone set 3-22, 347A1
DC-10 probe ends, pylon change ordered 5-16, 518C3
Jetliner engine fails in Honolulu take-off 6-15; inspectns ordered 7-16, 667B1
Delta jet lands at wrong field 6-21, pilot suspended 6-22, 519A3
Overhaul recommended 6-26, 519A1
Computer data called reliable 6-30, 666F3
PR navigatn statns bombed, air traffic rerouted 7-14, 559F3
Hijacking security measures tightened 8-15, 631B3
Federal Railroad Administration (FRA)
Milwaukee Rd loan OKd 1-7, 52G3
Milwaukee Rd svc cut set 2-25, 346A1
National Highway Traffic Safety Administration (NHTSA)
Crash test results rptd 2-28, 225A2
Uniroyal tire recall set 3-7, 348C2
Seatbelt use decline rptd 3-26, 309A3
Firestone fined 5-13, 702D2
Ford transmissn hazard determined 6-11; denial issued, info suit filed 8-20, 702E1
Fund authrzn bills defeated by House 10-1, 12-5, 982E1, G1
TRAVEL Service, U.S.—*See under COMMERCE in this section above*

TREASURY, Department of the
Carter signs trade reorganizatn plan 1-2, 94A3
Forgery prosecutn disparities rptd 1-6, 24B3
Gold sale suspensn hinted 1-15, reserves rptd 1-18, 1-15, 30E2-A3
Solomon named NY Fed chief 1-21, 52B2
Miller knowledge of Textron payoffs alleged 1-31; Miller denies 2-1, Carter, Civiletti back 2-2, 2-5, 92D1-B2
FRB sets new monetary supply terms 2-7, 113G3
Miller-Textron spec prosecutor sought 2-8—2-11, 145E1-B2; rejctd 3-11, 185C2
Standard Oil settles price case 2-14, 190C1
Bond price drop rptd 2-19, 2-21, 126F3
NYC 'up-front' loan guarantees completed 2-21, 186E3
Miller vs wage-price controls 3-2, 168F1
T-bill prices surge after Carter anti-inflatn plan 3-17, 203A2
Mex vegetable 'dumping' suit dismissed 3-24, 233F2
USSR purchase of US soybeans in W Eur rptd 3-26, 223D1
Chrysler loan bd sees greater losses 4-10, 286E3
SEC backs govt bond trading curbs 4-14, 290A1
Miller sees mild recessn 4-15, 286C3
Bond price soars on Kaufman prime rate predictn 4-16, 286G2
Chrysler loan guarantees OKd 5-10, 383C2
Credit curb impact on auto sales rptd 5-14, 384F1
Cuba finance regulatns amended 5-15, 361A2
CBS blocked from Cuba broadcasts 5-22, 397F1; cleared 6-1, 420G2
T-bill prices drop on FRB credit moves 5-23, 400E1
NYSE unit awaits futures trading OK 5-28, 481D2
DIDC sets interest rules 5-28, S&Ls file suit 6-16, 516G3
Proxmire pays libel suit costs 5-29, 470E3
Fla bank rules tightened 6-3, drug money linked 6-5, 502A1-A2
Clark probe requested 6-7, 459C3
Miller sees Dems on tax cuts 6-26, 480C3; outlines '81 plan 6-29, 492G3-493A1
Car maker aid planned 7-7, 505A3
Chrysler loan bd OKs $250 mln guarantee 7-15, Chrysler sets cutbacks 7-16, 541A2, D2
CFTC OKs NYFE trading exclusivity 7-15; Chicago ct overturns order 7-17—7-18, enforcemt chief quits 7-22, 558G2
Year-end spending waste scored by Sen subcom 7-20, 598F2
Miller on Chrysler loss 7-31, 573F3
Chrysler loan bd OKs $300 mln guarantee 7-31, 574A1
Chile export fraud indictmt rptd 8-4, 603B3

1976

Alcohol, Tobacco & Firearms, Bureau of
Handgun study backs controls 2-17, 170C2
7 seized in El Salvador gun plot 5-15, 5-17, 401E1-E2
Comptroller of the Currency
Major banks on 'problem' lists; Cong studies regulatory reform, disclosures disputed 1-11—2-9, 110D2-113E2
FBI to probe theft 1-30, 112F1
Hamilton Natl Bank fails 2-16, Tex bank charter cited 3-3, 167E1, D2
Proxmire scores Smith 2-17, 3-1; Smith bars House probe, asks GAO aid 3-5, to reimburse office 3-7, 185C2
Housing bias chrgd 4-26, Sen panel rpts 5-31, 413E2-C3
Closes Colo bank 6-25, 495A2
Scored re Franklin Bank collapse 10-6, 940C2
Problem-bank list grows; Bloom optimistic 11-2, 866F1
Customs, Bureau of
Ford urges drug plan 4-27, 307D2, E2
Internal Revenue Service—*See separate listing above*
Revenue Sharing, Office of—*See 'Revenue Sharing' under BUDGET in this section above*
Secret Service, United States
Sen intellignc com rpt cites 4-28, 327E1
'71 watch on Young Soclsts conv rptd 5-25, 569D3
White House intruder shot 7-25, 860F1
Carter jostled in Pa 9-7, 664B1
UNITED Nations, Participation in
Cncl member 62F2; 720C1
'66 rights covenant effected 1-4, 36E3
US ties forgn econ aid to votes 1-9, 2A1
UNESCO conf postponed 1-15, 36A3
Moynihan seeks aid-vote tie support 1-23; Ford, Kissinger reaffirm backing 1-28, 67G1-68A1
Moynihan resigns 2-2, 89B1
Stone confrmd to IAEA 2-5, 110C2
No policy chng planned 2-10, 109D3
Scranton named US amb 2-25, 150C1; confirmed 3-3, 186C2
Proposes pol paymts agrmt 3-5, 199F3, 200C1
White quits delegatn 3-10, 272B1
Abstains on Timor resolutn 4-22, 334F3
Kissinger addresses UNCTAD conf 5-6, 317A1-318G1
UNCTAD rejects US bank plan 5-30, US scores 6-1, 388E2, B3
Vs World Food conf plans 6-14—6-16, 450C1
Questns ILO job rpt 6-18, 449F3
US urges seabed agrmt 8-13, offers funds 9-1, 700G1
GOP platform text cites 8-18, 610C3
Asks Greek-Turk talks on Aegean 8-25, 643F2
Mondale scores Ford on terrorism 9-1, 665B3
To veto Viet entry 9-13, 682B1
Kissinger addresses Assemb, scores USSR 9-30, 719B1
Scranton for Butz resignatn 10-3, 744C2
Ford, Carter debate Viet 10-6, 742E2
Poston scores Waldheim re jobs 10-11, 760A2
Vs Sovt UNESCO press plan 10-27, 842C2
Sovt missn offcl rptd barred 11-7, 907B3
Backs Denktash in debate 11-9, 863E1
Abstains on vote urging Turkey quit Cyprus 11-12, 863D1
Vetoes Viet membership 11-15, 862B3
USSR scores 11-25, 895G3
Vows 2d Viet entry veto 11-26, 914C2
Young designated US amb 12-16, 936G1-C2, 937C1
Scranton vows arms control 12-22, 955B1
Africa
Moynihan confrms US aid, vote link 1-23; positn backed 1-28, 67E3
Abstains in Cncl censure of S Africa 3-31, 228B2
Angola entry vetoed 6-23, 455E1
Backs Rhodesia majority rule 7-9, 523B1
Abstains on Zambia raid condemnatn 7-30, 653E2
Kissinger addresses Assemb, scores Sovt southern Africa role 9-30, 719B1
Vetoes S Africa arms ban 10-19, 781D3 *
Abstains on Transkei vote 10-26, 799F1
Asked to bar aid to S Africa 11-5, 842B3
Vs anti-apartheid stand 11-9, 842G2
Abstains on Angola entry 11-22, 879C1; 12-1, 895C3
Vs black Namibia support 12-20, 955C1
Vows majority rule role 12-22, 955B1
Middle East
Vs PLO Cncl seating 1-12, 18B1
Vetoes pro-Palestine resolutn 1-26, 59F2-G3

1977

Alcohol, Tobacco & Firearms, Bureau of
Foremost penalty cited 3-7, 215F1
Appointments
Anderson confrmd undersecy 3-29, 272E2
Axelson, dep secy 1-18, 52D3; withdraws 3-9, 191A2
Bergsten, intl affairs asst secy 1-18, 52D3
Blumenthal confrmd secy 1-20, 34A1, E3
Morton confrmd US treasurer 8-2, 626B3
Mundheim confrmd gen counsel 8-2, 626B3
Solomon, monetary affairs undersecy 1-18, 52D3
Woodworth, asst secy 1-7, 14C2; confrmd 2-21, 148G3
Comptroller of the Currency, Office of the—*See also HEIMANN, John G.*
GAO scores bank regulatn 1-31, 154F3
Problem bank list rptd up 3-11, 194E2
Women's banks OKd 7-6, 578F1
Lance probe set 7-25, 574B2
Heimann rpts on Lance banking practices, cites other probes; Lance comments 8-18, 625F1-626F1; Carter comments 8-23, 649G1
Heimann issues 2d Lance rpt 9-7, testifies 9-8, 690E1, D2
Critical FBI rpt on Lance rptd 9-12, 701D3
Lance '76 visit to Atlanta admin cited 9-15, 701C1
Lance backed as bank exec 9-26, 761A2
Koreans, DC bank, others chrgd by SEC 9-28, 774D1
Customs Service, U.S.
Pot smuggling scored 3-14, 332F3
Sup Ct backs mail openings 6-6, 478E3
Internal Revenue Service—*See separate listing in this section above*
Secret Service, United States
Maddaloni rpts plot vs Rockefeller 3-10, 261G2
Johns HEW job questnd 3-23—3-26, 236B2
Steel Issues
Countervailing duty request refused 7-10, 587D1
US Steel files Japanese dumping chrgs 9-30; Gilmore chrgs upheld 10-3, 774B3, 775A1
Carter vows dumping prosecutn 10-13, 775F2
Forgn dumping chrgs filed 10-17, 10-20, 11-3, 836B3
Japan, France, India dumping chrgs probed 10-19, 11-22, 933F2, B3
Armco chrgs UK dumping 12-5, 932C1, 933A3
US import plan rptd 12-6, 931C3, F3, 932D1
Dumping chrgs tallied 12-6, 932C1
Armco backs US plan, vows no new dumping chrgs 12-6, 932C1
TREATY Ratification—*See under SENATE in this section above*
UNITED Nations Participation—*See UNITED Nations—U.S. Relations*

1978

Alcohol, Tobacco & Firearms, Bureau of
Smoking link to cigaret tax studied 1-11, 23D2
Anheuser-Busch settles chrgs 3-31, 449F2
Comptroller of the Currency, Office of the
Lance, 2 banks sued; case setld 4-26, 324G2
FRB bank-holding co power backed by Sup Ct 12-11, 980F3
Customs Service, U.S.
New law ups duty-free allowance 9-3, 751A1
Secret Service, United States
Carter death threat hoax rptd 8-30, 664G1
JFK death hearings cite 9-13, 9-14, 749F2
Ex-chief Baugham dies 11-6, 972E2
JFK murder role ruled out 12-30, 1002D2
Steel Issues
Steel trigger price list issued 1-3, reactn 1-4, 3B2
FTC scores trigger plan 1-7, 80G2
Japan '77 dumping ruling revised 1-9, 80C2
Bethlehem scores trigger plan 2-12, 158C1
Trigger plan takes effect 2-21, 158C1
US Steel drops Japan dumping suit, trigger plan backing cited 3-1, 158B1
Carter backs Japan pricing probe 4-24, 444B1
Trigger price hikes in '78 rptd, '79 hike set 11-9, 1005F3
Trigger plan scored by US Steel pres; defended 12-28, 1005B3
Eur plate dumping probed; Natl, Armco chrgs withdrawn 12-28, 1005G3-1006C1
TREATY Ratification—*See under SENATE in this section above*
UNITED Nations Participation—*See UNITED Nations—U.S. Policy*

1979

Miller tours Persian Gulf, discusses Iran crisis 11-23–11-28, 896A3
Eur missn set, Iran econ moves sought 12-5, 913C2
Iran missn in W Ger 12-6, 934A1
Kennedy scores Miller re OPEC price hikes 12-20–12-21, 983A3
Miller on Chrysler loan bd 12-21, 981F3
'70s gold sale role cited 12-31, 978D2
Alcohol, Tobacco & Firearms, Bureau of
'78 bombing data rptd 1-1, 102G2
Alcohol ingredient labeling proposed 2-1, 91G3
5 indicted in Panama arms plot 5-14, 386C3
Hell's Angels arrested 6-14, 492B1
Comptroller of the Currency, Office of the
Banks warned re credit overextensn 9-13, 681D1
Customs Service, U.S.
Alexander's sentncd re TV rebates 3-29, 298D3
Scientology documts '76 seizure upheld by Sup Ct 5-14, 383A3
Cocaine seized in Fla 10-12, 10-14, 819C3
McDonnell Douglas indicted on paymts chrg 11-9, 886C2
Internal Revenue Service—*See separate listing in this section above*
Printing & Engraving, Bureau of
Food stamp probe rptd 2-2, 93B3
Secret Service, United States
4 arrested in White House A-protest 3-31, 261F3
3 Mile I NRC transcripts released 4-12, 276C1
Carter alleged death plot probed 5-5–5-29, 404D1
Carter orders Kennedy protectn 9-20, 723G3
Nixon San Clemente cost repaymt asked by Cong 9-26, 883G2
Pope's US visit gets record press coverage 10-1–10-7, 760E3
Castro protected in NYC 10-11–10-14, 779A1
Kennedy agents subdue woman with knife 11-28, 962D2
TREATY Ratification—*See under SENATE above*
UNITED Nations Participation—*See UNITED Nations–U.S. Policy*

1980

NYFE opens, 1st day's trading rptd 8-7, 616D3
NYC recovery plan revised 8-11, fed loan guarantees sought 9-10, 743D1
NYC pub bond sale moves rptd 9-10, 743A2
Miller scores money supply curbs 10-2, 763B1
NYC funds release OKd 10-2, 826B2
'80 budget deficit doubles 10-29, 824E3
Deficit estimate rises, new debt ceiling asked 12-2, 916D2
Regan named secy 12-11; earlier speculatn rptd 935A1, B2
Eximbank skips '80 dividend, '79 dividend rptd 12-16, 988F3, 989A1
T-bond futures gain in '80 12-31, 984G3
Alcohol, Tobacco & Firearms, Bureau of
Alcohol ingredient labeling ordrd 6-10, 485A3
Comptroller of the Currency, Office of the
Saxon dies 1-28, 104F3
Abu Dhabi bank gets DC branch OK 10-1, 806F3
Customs Service, U.S.
NY-NJ corruptn probed 1-11, offcl pleads guilty 2-13, 359C2-B3
Goods liability backed by Sup Ct 1-21, 93A3
Sears indicted on Japan TV rebates 2-26, 251G3
French wine fraud rptd 3-6, 193B2
Truck import duty raised 5-20, 384A2
700 Cuban flotilla boats seized 5-29, 396F1
Federal Financing Bank
DC fscl recovery plan proposed 7-19, 742F3
Higher educ authrzn clears Cong 9-18, 9-25, signed 10-3, 803C3
Printing & Engraving, Bureau of
Ex-dir found guilty 7-28, fined 9-15, 927B3
Secret Service, United States
Female agent slain 6-5, 503E2
Troops quell riots at Pa refugee cntr 8-6, 591B3
UNITED Nations, Participation in—*See under UNITED Nations under 'U'*

1976

Votes vs rights comm anti-Israel resolutn 2-13, 125E2
Scores Israel occupatn 3-23, 3-24, vetoes resolutn 3-25, 211E1
Backs Cncl talks on Leb 3-30, 226C2
Defends Zionism in ECOSOC racism debate 4-28, 320G2
Vs 2 WHO anti-Israel resolutns 5-17, 5-19, 355F1, D2
Vs Cncl on Israeli setlmts 5-26, 406E3
Boycotts PLO speech at ILO conf 6-8, 450A1
Vs anti-Israel resolutns at Habitat conf 6-11, 431C3
Vetoes Israel Arab land exit 6-29, 464B1, D1
Cncl vs anti-terror res 7-14, 515E3
Vs PLO in Cncl debate 11-1, 842F1
Joins Cncl stand vs Israel 11-11, 842A1
Israel vs vote re Arab areas 11-12, 863A1
UNESCO readmits Israel 11-22, 878D3
Vs UNESCO resolutn on Israel 11-22, 879A1
OKs resolutn vs Israel Gaza resettlmts 11-23, 878F2
Vs Palestinian panel rpt 11-23, 878B3
Helps soften UNDOF resolutn 11-30, 895B2
Vs assemb resolutns on Geneva conf 12-9, 914E1
Vows peace role 12-22, 955B1

U.S. INFORMATION Agency (USIA)
Nigeria USIS protests rptd 1-11, 16B2
CIA media manipulatn rptd 1-17, 92C3
2 aides freed in Beirut 2-25, 145B2
'77 funds bills signed 7-12, 7-14, 534F1 ★, E2
Voice of America
Uruguay torture rpt scored 4-21, 382G3
GOP platform text cites 8-18, 610B3
PLO contact barred 10-8, 759C3

URBAN Mass Transportation Administration—*See under TRANSPORTATION above*

VETERANS Administration (VA)
GAO rpts overpaymts 3-26, 262G2
Mortgage rate lowered 3-30, 375E3
Cong clears added funds 5-19, 411D3
Dem platform text 6-15, 473C1
Mich hosp nurses chrgd 6-16, 503E3
'77 funds signed 8-9, 623E1
Carter disavows Roudebush dumping memo 8-13, 616F3
'69 drug trust suit ends in mistrial 8-17, 988D3
GOP platform text cites 8-18, 606G2
Cong mandates pensn study 9-20, hikes med benefits 10-1, 807A1, E1
Mortgage loan rate cut rptd 10-15, 805E3
Ford at Seattle hosp 10-25, 802E3
Transitn ¼ fed spending rptd down 10-27, 866C1
Yalow wins Lasker award 11-17, 910D3
Bx hosp alcoholism test rptd 12-3, 950C3

VISTA—*See under ACTION in this section above*

VOICE of America—*See under U.S. INFORMATION Agency above*

VOLUNTEERS in Service to America—*See under ACTION in this section above*

WAGE and Price Stability, Council on
Scores Ford price hike 1-12, 280C3
Backs mail svc competitn 1-19, 44F3
Steel price hike study ordrd 8-14; revised 8-30, 646F3
'60-75 food-price rpt issued 11-9, 983E3
Steel price study set 11-24, 897G2; rpt issued 12-2, 898A1

WARREN Commission (Commission to Report on the Assassination of President John F. Kennedy)
Cited in Ford biog sketch 613F3

1977

U.S. CODE—*See LEGISLATION in this section above*

U.S. INFORMATION Agency (USIA)
Reinhardt named dir 1-7, 14G1
Carter statemt to world 1-20, 26D1, A2
Ethiopia closes office 4-23, 327G2
S Africa detains Jacobsen 6-10, 469A2
Sen authorizes '78 funds 6-16, 477C3
'78 funds signed 8-2; authorizatn 8-17, 667A3, G3
S Africa unit defends US envoy's wife 8-11, 650C1
Reorgn proposed by Carter 10-11, 797C2
Ex-CIA head scores 'cover' bar 12-27, 1006D1
Voice of America
Carter seeks fund hike 3-22 229G3
Braniff promotn rptd 5-17, 503B1
Reorgn proposed by Carter 10-11, 797D2

URBAN Mass Transportation Administration—*See under TRANSPORTATION above*

VETERANS Administration (VA)
Ford '78 budget request 1-17, 32B1, F2
Carter budget revisns 2-22, 125A2
Giaimo proposes '78 budget 3-23, 229A1
New painkiller rptd 3-31, 288C1
Hosp alcoholism problem cited 6-7, 472A2
Nurses convicted in '75 Mich hosp deaths 7-13, 568F2
Coronary bypass surgery scored 9-22, 907B2
Cong clears dischrg, benefits review bill 9-23, 759F2; signed 10-8, 773A2
Mil disability pensn hike signed 10-3, 877F3
'78 funds signed 10-4, 796G2, D3
2 hosp researchers share Nobel 10-13, 951C3, D3
Old-age, non-mil disability pensn hike clears Cong 11-3, 877E3
Educ aid bill clears Cong 11-4, 877A3; signed 11-23, 1001F2
Mich nurse convictns upset 12-19, 991G2
Transfer Payments—*See INCOMES*

VISTA—*See under ACTION in this section above*

VOICE of America—*See under U.S. INFORMATION Agency above*

VOLUNTEER Armed Forces—*See under ARMED Forces in this section above*

VOLUNTEERS in Service to America—*See under ACTION in this section above*

WAGE and Price Stability, Council on
Carter to strengthen 1-31, 89E3
Meany scores 2-24, 153G2
TV tariff hike cost cited 3-14, 208B3
Milk price support cost study rptd 3-22, 3-23, 214B1
Steel price hike opposed 5-6, 385G1
Intercity bus fare hiked 5-15, 423A2, C2
On new steel pact 6-1, 481G2
Crandall on aluminum price hike 6-14, 577A2
Carter submits reorganizatn plan 7-15, 556D1
Bosworth confirmed dir 7-22, 626D2
Steel industry study ordrd 8-5, 612C1
Steel industry analysis rptd 10-7, 776F1
Bosworth on steel price hikes 12-18, 12-22, 1003C2

WARREN Commission (Commission to Report on the Assassination of John F. Kennedy)
De Mohrenschildt testimony cited 3-29, 228B3
FBI releases JFK assassinatn files 12-7, 943F1

WASPs—*See under AIR Force in this section above*

WELFARE—*See under 'W'*

WHITE House Office
Carter cancels limo svc 1-24, 53D2
Carter reduces staff 2-2, 75F1
Energy conf 3-25, 234C2
Carter on staff cuts 4-15, 299C2
Carter submits reorganizatn plan 7-15, 555D3
Media office distributes Panama Canal 'fact sheet' 8-4, 590B1

WOMEN'S Air Force Service Pilots—*See AIR Force—WASPs in this section above*

WOMENS'S Year, 1975, National Commission on the Observance of International
Natl Women's Conf meets 11-19—11-21, 917F2

YOUNG Adult Conservation Corps
Authorized 8-5, 609C2
Operatns rptd begun 8-31, 692F2 ★

YOUTH Conservation Corps—*See under INTERIOR in this section above*

1978

U.S. INFORMATION Agency (USIA)
Taiwan sentncs 6 as spies 1-17, 38E1
Offcl chrgd as Viet spy 1-31, 68G2; witness ouster stayed 2-10, 103B3
Ex-offcl convicted as Viet spy 5-19, 389F3
Ex-offcl sentncd as Viet spy 7-7, 555B1
Voice of America
Toon interviewed 4-3, 275E3

VETERANS Administration (VA)
'75 Mich hosp death chrgs vs 2 nurses dropped 2-1, 116C2
Educ curbs backed by Sup Ct 3-20, 205E3
Educ progrms excluded from proposed Cabt-level dept 4-14, 279E1, B2
Vet wins A-test cancer claim 8-1, 702E3
'79 funds signed 9-30, 750C2-A3
Carter rpts on Viet vets; ACLU, vets cncl score 10-10, 878A1-G1
500 Viet vets claim Agent Orange disabilities 10-11, 984G1
Transfer Payments—*See INCOMES*

VOICE of America—*See under U.S. INFORMATION Agency above*

WAGE and Price Stability, Council on
Sen farm bill scored 3-22, 219B1
Steel price hike scored 3-29, lauds rollback 3-30, 262E3, 263A1
Carter cites inflatn impact rpts 4-11, 259E3
GM price hike scored 4-28, 362C2
Bosworth backs Meany wage stand 5-11, 362C1
TVA rate hike moderatn asked 5-15, increase scaled down 5-17, 362A2
Bosworth on Apr CPI, Admin inflatn plan 5-22, 428C3
Zinc trade relief barred 6-1, 443A3
Bosworth links govt regulatn cost, inflatn 6-12, 427A3
Bosworth hails steel price hike restraint 6-12, 470C2
EPA cuts back air rules 6-13, 512B3
Bosworth on steel aid-price curb tradeoff 6-19, 428G1
Bosworth links productivity, inflatn 7-27, 606D3
Meany scores Bosworth, Carter names panel 8-7, 624B2
Bosworth sees fed role in Teamster talks 8-22, 680F2, B3
'78 inflatn rate seen worsening 10-4, 789F3
$ drop, inflatn linked 10-4, 790D1
Carter anti-inflatn plan sets role 10-24; Kahn replaces Schultze as chrmn 10-25, 806A2; **for subsequent developments, see ECONOMY—Carter Anti-Inflation Plan**
US Steel hikes prices 11-14, 1006C1
Hershey bar price hike OKd 11-20, 917G3
RRs trim rate hike request to 7% 11-24, ICC OKs 6½% hike 12-11, 1007A3
Gas shortage probe rptd, rationing studied 12-6, 962E3

WARREN Commission (Commission to Report on the Assassination of John F. Kennedy)
CIA bid to discredit critics chrgd 1-4, 14C3
More FBI files on JFK released 1-18, 109G3
JFK House assassinatn com hearings 9-6—9-11, 697G3, 698E1
JFK com hears Oswald's widow, Ford 9-13, 9-14, 9-21, 749G2, F3, 750A1
JFK murder film assessed 11-26, 916F1, G1
House com finds JFK, King plots likely 12-30, 1002B1, B2

WATER Resources Council
Public works veto upheld 10-5, 765C2

WEATHER Service, National—*See COMMERCE—National Oceanic & Atmospheric Administration*

WHITE House Office—*See also CARTER, subheads APPOINTMENTS and RESIGNATIONS*
Carter: no staff chngs planned 4-11, 260F3

WOMEN, National Advisory Committee for
Cancels Carter mtg 11-22, 915E1

1979

U.S. INFORMATION Agency (USIA)—*See INTERNATIONAL Communications Agency in this section above*

VETERANS Administration (VA)
Guyana rpts Peoples Temple checks 1-23, 117C3
NJ smoking study rptd 2-22, 218A2
Amputation linked to heart deaths 2-26, 219A2
Fla sleep breathing study rptd 3-9, 196G2
WWII women pilots get benefits 3-9, 307D3
Merck OKs minority jobs plan 6-26, 521A2
Viet vet study reveals problems 9-25, 725E1
'80 funds clear Cong 10-24, Carter signs 11-5, 883G2
Viet troops Agent Orange exposure rptd 11-24, 904E2
Malpractice ruling reversed by Sup Ct 11-28, 944C3

VOICE of America—*See under INTERNATIONAL Communications Agency above*

WAGE and Price Stability, Council on
Natl trust comm rpt issued 1-16, 88G2
CBS postal rollback plea rptd 2-6, 128C1
Tough price monitors vowed 2-12, 109E3
Kahn threatens trucking deregulatn 3-15, 251G1
Price rules eased, US Steel hikes prices 6-12, 942A1
Bosworth resignatn plan rptd 6-16, 463F1
Bosworth on May CPI rise 6-26, 480B3
UPS-Teamster contract OKd 7-27, 744E2
Kahn praises UAW-GM settlemt 9-15, 698D2
Pay Advisory Com set 9-28, 829D2
Interim price rule set 9-28, unchngd 11-1, 829B3
Kahn unhappy with GM-UAW pact 9-30, 744G1
Carter Anti-Inflation Plan—*See under ECONOMY*

WARREN Commission (Commission to Report on the Assassination of John F. Kennedy)
Oswald 'look-alike' dies 1-14, 93C2
New JFK murder film rptd 2-8, 166E1
'63 death threat vs Oswald revealed 2-18, 166G2
JFK com final rpt scored 7-17, 538B2

WATER Resources Council
Natural Resources Dept proposed 3-1, 164F1

WHITE House Office—*See CARTER, subheads APPOINTMENTS, CABINET and RESIGNATIONS*
Library conf held 11-15–11-19, 901B1-A2

WOMEN, National Advisory Committee for
Carter ousts Abzug 1-12, resignatns, protests ensue 1-12–1-14, Chambers named acting head 1-16; defends 1-17, 30C2
Robb named head 5-9, 351G1-A3

YOUTH Conservation Corps—*See under INTERIOR in this section above*

1980

VETERANS Administration (VA)
Carter vetoes dioxins study 1-2, 17B3
Mortgage rate hiked 2-8, 2-28, 145B1
Mortgage rates rise to 14% 4-3, 266F3
Mortgage rate drops to 13% 4-28, 329B2
Mortgage rate cut to 11.5% 5-15, 384E3
Multifamily mortgage rate cut to 12% 7-7, 513G3
Carter vetoes MD pay hike 8-22, Cong overrides 8-26, 649C3
Mortgage rate rise delay scored 10-24, 823C3
Mortgage rate raised to 13.5% 11-24, 948A1
'81 funds clear Cong 12-3, 954G2
Schering settles job bias case 12-14, 962F3
'81 appropriatn signed 12-15, 982B1

WAGE & Price Stability, Council on
11 oil cos cited for '79 abuses, Mobil chrgd 2-25, 189C3
Kahn vs wage-price controls 3-2, 168F1
Ford-UAW contract said to violate guidelines 3-7, sanctions imposed 3-26, 225F2
Crown Central, Murphy Oil chrgd for '79 abuses 3-7, 3-25, 248E2
New pay guidelines OKd 3-13, 182A3
Carter expands staff in anti-inflatn plan 3-14, 201D1
'79 4th 1/4 price rpts sought 3-18, 209D2
Russell sees continued inflatn 3-25, 222C2
Carter scores Mobil violatns, seeks punitive measures 3-28, 4-1; formal noncompliance set 4-4, 248F1, D2
USW pact termed within guidelines 4-23, 385C1
Mobil settles price case 4-24, 309F1
Steel import damage found 5-1, 456E1
Kahn sees contd inflatn 5-23, 400A3
Kahn on May CPI 6-24, 481A1
Russell: inflatn not over 7-8, 513E3
DIDC bank gift ban opposítn rptd 7-18, 560G3
Guidelines extended 9-19, 764B3
Guidelines ended 12-16, 983A2

WATER Resources Council
Carter budgets no new projcts 1-28, 73D3
Appropriatn clears Cong 6-25, 9-10, Carter signs 10-1, 803F2

WHITE House Office
'79 A-blast mystery off S Africa unresolved 1-23, 7-14, 49A3, 548A3
Reagan fills 2 key posts 11-14, 881E1-A2
Reagan names 2 more top aides 12-17, 955C3
Reagan names Allen, 3 others 12-23, 980A2

1976

U.S. GYPSUM Co.
Vows no boycott compliance 3-18, 747B2
U.S. INDUSTRIES Inc.
'74 zero tax paymt rptd 10-2, 847G1
UNITED States-Latin American Relations, Commission on
Rpt advises Carter 12-14, 974D3
U.S. NATIONAL Bank of San Diego—*See 'Crocker National Bank' under CROCKER National Corp.*
U.S. NEWS & World Report (magazine)
Rpts Freedom House survey 1-19, 20D2-E3
Kelley interview rptd 4-5, 248F2
Enders interview publshd 6-13, 438F3
Carter visits editors 8-4, 564E3
U.S. RECORDING Co.
FBI purchasing irregularities rptd 1-1, 6C1
FBI purchasing probe rptd renewed 3-20—3-23, 248E1
U.S. STEEL Corp.
Fined 4-10, 988E3
Sets price hike 8-13, cancels 8-30, 646C3
Ford golf trips rptd 9-21; Ford, Whyte statemts 9-21—9-30; SEC probes 9-24, 722F2, 723G1
SEC probes cong entertainmt 9-24, 722C3
Mondale at Pa plant 10-25, 804A1
Hikes prices 6% 11-29, Admin, Carter reactn 11-29—12-2, 897F2, C3
U.S. TENNIS Association—*See TENNIS*
UNITED Technologies Corp. (formerly United Aircraft Corp.)
Rpts foreign payoffs 4-9, 362C2
SEC lists paymts 5-12, 729E1
Top fscl '76 defns contractor 12-21, 961B3
Pratt & Whitney Aircraft Division
'75 arms sales listed 2-6, 147C2
Pact signed with Belgium 8-24, 734D3
UNIVERSAL Federation of Christian Student Movements
Uruguay bans 1-20, 208A1
UNIVERSAL Transcontinental Corp.
Arab boycott rpts released 10-18—10-20, 786A1, D1, A2

1977

U.S. GYPSUM Co.
Convictn overturned 1-6, 156F2
UNITED States Harness Writers Association—*See HORSE Racing*
U.S. INFORMATION Agency—*See under U.S. GOVERNMENT*
U.S. LEAGUE of Savings Associations—*See SAVINGS Associations, etc.*
U.S. LINES Inc.—*See KIDDE & Co.*
U.S. METALS Refining Co.—*See AMAX Inc.*
U.S. NATIONAL Bank of San Diego—*See CROCKER National Corp.*
U.S. OLYMPIC Committee (USOC)—*See SPORTS—Olympics*
U.S. NEWS & World Report (magazine)
Rpts urban business confidence up; econ data table 5-16, 384B2, G3
Rpts Carter support of Young 6-6, 417B3
On most reliable govt news source list 12-10, 1009B1
U.S. OPEN Tennis Championships—*See TENNIS*
UNITED States Steel Corp.
Sup Ct voids credit ruling, bars concrete case review 2-22, 149E2, B3
Contract OKd, Johnston comments 4-9, 273G2, G3
On '76 Fortune 500 list 340E1, C3
Speer sees Admin on imports, price hike 5-5, 385D2
Prices hiked, Admin backs 5-9; industry follows 5-10—5-12, 385D1
2 Ind EPA cases setld 6-16, 461E1
Mahoning R clean-up planned 6-30, 521C3
Countervailing duty request refused 7-10, 587D1
Prices hiked 7-21, 577A1
1st ½ earnings drop rptd 7-26, 612E1
Layoffs, plant closings rptd 8-26—10-6, 775B3
Japanese dumping chrgs filed 9-30, Japan asks lifted 10-4, 775A1
Speer on Admin mtg on steel woes 10-13, 775F2
Homestead plant closing re anti-pollutn costs cited 10-13, 775A3
Japan dumping chrgs probed 10-19, 933F2
3d ¼ profits rptd down 10-25, 836A3
LTV, Lykes to merge 11-4, 943G2
USW ore-range strike ends 12-15, 977C3
Hikes prices, Admin reactn 12-22, 1003B2
U.S. TENNIS Association (USTA)—*See TENNIS*
UNITED States Trust Co.
Sup Ct curbs Port Auth mass transit aid 4-27, 383B1
Pensn managemt concentratn rptd 6-28, 578C2
UNITED States Trust Co. v. New Jersey
Mass transit aid barred 4-27, 382G3
U.S.-U.S.S.R. Marine Resources Co. Inc.
USSR ownership cited 10-31, 949A2
U.S. v. Donovan
Wiretap use upheld 1-18, 58F1
U.S. v. Martin Linen Supply Co.
Double-jeopardy protectn widened 4-4, 341B3
U.S. v. McGarry
Sup Ct declines review 10-31, 835D3
U.S. v. New York Telephone Co.
Phone surveillnc ct orders backed 12-7, 939F1
U.S. v. Washington
Sup Ct rules on evidence 5-23, 444G2
U.S. v. Wong
Sup Ct rules on evidence 5-23, 444F2
UNITED System Service Inc.
Pvt phone equipmt rule review refused 10-3, 760E3
UNITED Technologies Corp.
Otis to promote S Africa equality 3-1, 160B3
Babcock & Wilcox purchase planned 3-29; sued 4-4, 274B3
Revises payoffs total, Otis cited 4-28, 503C1
Sikorsky copter mishap in NYC 5-16, 412B3
Gray '76 salary rptd 5-23, 408C3
US blocks Babcock purchase 7-5, 520D1
Loses Babcock bidding war 8-25, 666E3
Bodine wins suit 9-28, 860D1
UNIVERSAL Life Church
NY min tax status challenged 4-15, 310B2

1978

U.S. GYPSUM Co.
Price fixing rule upheld by Sup Ct 6-29, 567G2
U.S. INFORMATION Agency—*See under U.S. GOVERNMENT*
U.S. LINES Inc.—*See KIDDE & Co.*
U.S. NATIONAL Bank of San Diego (defunct)
FDIC paymt case declined by Sup Ct 10-16, 789C1
U.S. NEWS & World Report (magazine)
Rpts top-paid labor ldrs 2-20, 365D1
RC schl enrollmt drop halted 3-20, 348C3
Black ldrs interviewed on voting issues 4-10, 568F2-B3
Kemp interviewed on tax cut 7-3, 735C1
Jaworski interview publshd 8-7, 604G3
Jones interviewed 10-30, 833A3
U.S. RECORDING Co.
FBI 'improper favoritism' rptd 1-10, 15B2
UNITED States Steel Corp.
In Dow Jones indl avg 66F2
Roderick cited on trigger price 1-3, 3F2
Youngstown to be closed 1-3, 4G2
'76 tax nonpaymt rptd 1-27, 65G2
Tax compact upheld by Sup Ct 2-21, 126F1
Carter sees Speer on coal strike 2-24, 122F3
Drops Japan dumping suit, backs trigger plan 3-1, 158A1
Price hike announced 3-29, Admin scores 3-29—3-30; price undercut, rolled back 3-30—4-3, 262C3
On '77 Fortune 500 list 5-8, 325F1
Speer vs Admin price restraint plea 5-24; Strauss, Bosworth scores 5-31, 6-19, 428D1
Price hike held to 3%, future price lid pledge hedged 6-13, 470F2
Black bias found at Pa plant 8-3, 811B3
RMI indicted on price fixing 9-28, 768D2
Admin price guidelines backed 11-9, prices hiked 11-14, 1006C1
Ex-pres Hood's death rptd 11-27, 972C3
China iron-ore negotiatns rptd 12-6, 986G2
Roderick scores trigger plan 12-28, 1005C3
UNITED States Steel Corp. v. Multistate Tax Commission
Sup Ct upholds tax compact 2-21, 126F1
UNITED Technologies Corp.
Carrier merger sought 9-18; Carrier vs 9-25, US sues 11-13, 896D1
McDermott takeover battles for Babcock, Otis cited 9-25, 896G1
UAW rptd vs Carrier takeover 10-30, NY lifts stay 11-10, 896D2
U.S. TENNIS Association (USTA)—*See TENNIS*
U.S.-U.S.S.R. Joint Commercial Commission
Meets 12-4—12-5, 966C1
U.S.-U.S.S.R. Trade & Economic Council
Rpts Dresser contracts 6-1, 499F3
Meets 12-5—12-7, 966C1
U.S. v. Board of Commissioners
Cities subject to US electn law 3-6, 162F1
U.S. v. Ceccolini
Testimony thru illegal search backed by Sup Ct 3-21, 221A1
U.S. v. MacDonald
Speedy trial appeal procedure backed by Sup Ct 5-1, 364E1
U.S. v. New Mexico
NM water rights backed by Sup Ct 7-3, 552C2
U.S. v. Pitcairn
Autogiro patent case review denied 1-23, 65E1
U.S. v. Scott
Double jeopardy doctrine reversed by Sup Ct 6-14, 468A3
U.S. v. Slodov
Corp takeover tax liability curbed by Sup Ct 5-22, 388F1
U.S. v. Sotelo
Tax liability in bankruptcy backed by Sup Ct 5-22, 388C1
U.S. v. United States Gypsum Co.
Price fixing rule upheld by Sup Ct 6-29, 567F2
U.S. v. Weber
Case accepted by Sup Ct 12-11, 980F2
U.S. v. Wheeler
Indian rape retrial backed by Sup Ct 3-22, 221E1
UNITED States Women's Lacrosse Association—*See LACROSSE*
UNITED Steelworkers of America v. Weber
Case accepted by Sup Ct 12-11, 980F2
UNITED Steelworkers v. Sadlowski
Union legal fee liability case refused by Sup Ct 4-17, 308D3
UNITED Technologies Corp.
In Dow Jones indl avg 66F2
Ambac purchase planned 3-2, 185C1
3d in '77 defns contracts 3-28, 224F2
Pan Am buys Lockheed jets 4-4, 264F2
Singapore Airlines to buy Boeing jets 5-9, 365F2
Pratt & Whitney Aircraft Division
UAL orders Boeing jets 7-14, 569G3
UNIVERSAL Studios—*See MCA Inc.*
UNIVERSITIES—*See EDUCATION—Colleges*

1979

U.S. GYPSUM Co.
Price fixing case refused by Sup Ct 10-1, 768F2
Gen Atomic arbitratn ruling declined by Sup Ct 10-9, 784F1
S Australia mining projct OKd 10-9, 811A1
U.S. GYPSUM Co. v. U.S.
Case refused by Sup Ct 10-1, 768G2
U.S. INFORMATION Agency—*See under U.S. GOVERNMENT*
UNITED States Lines Inc.—*See McLEAN Securities*
U.S. NATIONAL Bank of San Diego (defunct)
Smith convicted 5-4, 5-7, sentncd 5-31, 442E2
Smith damage judgemt returned 12-24, 991G3
U.S. NEWS & World Report (magazine)
Illegal alien issue detailed 1-29, 127D1
UK rptr's chrg of Sovt abuse protested 4-20, 390A2
On XM-1 tank decision 5-21, 386F1
Gen Barrow interview rptd 9-10, 724E3
UNITED States Steel Corp.
In Dow Jones indl avg 72F1
China contract signed 1-5, 7D1
Steel haulers end strike 1-18, 87D2
EPA files 2 suits 1-25, 2-5, 90E2
On '78 Fortune 500 list 5-7, 304F1
EPA Pa cleanup pact set 5-22, 385B2
US eases price rules, steel prices hiked 6-12, rolled back 7-2; raised 10-1, 11-29, 942A1
Pa cleanup suit settled 7-23, 704F2
Wheeling-Pittsburgh fed aid scored 8-28, 682A1
SEC suit settled 9-27, 941F2
Texaco chem venture set 11-14, 941D3
Plant closings, layoffs set, '78-79 earnings cited 11-27; '80s strategy rptd 12-5, 941C2-C3
U.S. v. Acres of Land
Case decided by Sup Ct 5-14, 383B3
U.S. v. Addonizio
Case decided by Sup Ct 6-4, 438G3
U.S. v. Batchelder
Case decided by Sup Ct 6-4, 439E1
U.S. v. Benmar Transportation & Leasing
Case decided by Sup Ct 10-15, 848A1
U.S. v. Bodcaw Co.
Case decided by Sup Ct 2-26, 164E3
U.S. v. Caceres
Case decided by Sup Ct 4-2, 281D2
U.S. v. Crittenden
Case decided by Sup Ct 4-2, 281G2
U.S. v. Helstoski
Case decided by Sup Ct 6-18, 498C3
U.S. v. Kimbell Foods
Case decided by Sup Ct 4-2, 281G2
U.S. v. Kubrick
Case decided by Sup Ct 11-28, 944F3
U.S. v. Naftalin
Case decided by Sup Ct 5-21, 400C3
U.S. v. Rutherford
Case decided by Sup Ct 6-18, 498F2
U.S. v. Sioux Nation
Case accepted by Sup Ct 12-10, 988F1
U.S. v. Timmreck
Case decided by Sup Ct 5-21, 400G3
U.S. v. Whelan
Case decided by Sup Ct 6-4, 438G3
U.S. v. Zbaraz
Case accepted by Sup Ct 11-26, 919A2
UNITED Steelworkers of America v. Weber
Case argued in Sup Ct 3-28, 262C3
Case decided by Sup Ct 6-27, 477B1
UNITED Technologies Corp.
In Dow Jones indl avg 72F1
Carrier takeover OKd by ct 1-31, terms set 3-30, 349E3-350A1
Gray on '78 top-paid execs list 5-14, 347F3
SEC scores Carrier merger 6-25, shareholders back 7-5, 541A3
3d in '78 defns contracts 8-1, 609C1
21% of Mostek purchased 9-17, 986G2
Haig named pres 12-26, 984F1, A2
Pratt & Whitney Aircraft Division
AF F-15, F-16 engine trouble rptd 10-24, 852A2
UNITED Van Lines Inc.
ICC fines 1-15, 92B1
UNIVERSAL Studios—*See MCA Inc.*
UNIVERSITIES—*See EDUCATION—Colleges; specific names*

1980

U.S. GYPSUM Co.
Price fixing case settled 3-3, 557F3
U.S. NATIONAL Bank of San Diego (defunct)
Smith jury award upheld 1-18, 55D2
U.S. NEWS & World Report (magazine)
Stone on pres TV debate panel 10-28, 813F1
U.S. Parole Commission v. Geraghty
Case decided by Sup Ct 3-19, 250D1
U.S. Postal Service v. United Parcel Service
Case declined by Sup Ct 5-19, 440D2
U.S. Railroad Retirement Board v. Fritz
Case decided by Sup Ct 12-9, 937A1
UNITED States Steel Corp.
In Dow Jones indl avg 76F1
Youngstown plant closings blocked 2-28, 266A2
Dumping suit re EC seen 3-14, 204D2, G2
Dumping complaint filed, trigger price suspended 3-21, US mkt withdrawals rptd 3-24, 225C1
EC comm rejects suits 3-27, 242C3
Europn steel orders resume 4-2, 262C3
EC fines French, W Ger steelmakers 4-3, 262G2
US sets steel import probe 4-10, 367E3
USW contract settled 4-15, 289B2
Nader coalitn attacks 4-17, 308B2
US finds steel import damage 5-1, 456B1, F1
On '79 Fortune 500 list 5-5, 290F1, 291E1
Steel trigger price return suit dismissed 5-16, 455F3, 456A1
Prices cut 7-10, 575F2
La chem-dump suit names unit 7-15, 558G3
Youngstown plant closings upheld 7-25, 575G1
Vance elected dir 8-7, 702C1
Dumping complaint withdrawn 9-30, 740E3
Provo emissn control plan agreed 10-16, 825A2
Arab boycott data released 10-20, 801A1
Youngstown plant suit ends 11-14, 917A1
Sohio buys coal assets 12-2, 985B2
Pa pollutn fine rptd 12-22; Clairton coke site deadline extended 12-30, 987C1, E1
U.S. v. Apfelbaum
Case decided by Sup Ct 3-3, 210D1
U.S. v. Bailey
Case decided by Sup Ct 1-21, 92E3
U.S. v. Clark
Case decided by Sup Ct 2-26, 188G1
U.S. v. Crews
Case decided by Sup Ct 3-25, 265A3
U.S. v. DiFrancesco
Case decided by Sup Ct 12-9, 936B3
U.S. v. Euge
Case decided by Sup Ct 2-20, 170E1
U.S. v. Gillock
Case decided by Sup Ct 3-19, 249E3
U.S. v. Havens
Case decided by Sup Ct 5-27, 453A2
U.S. v. Henry
Case decided by Sup Ct 6-16, 511B3
U.S. v. Hotel Conquistador Inc.
Case refused by Sup Ct 1-14, 36G3
U.S. v. Louisiana
Case decided by Sup Ct 4-28, 369C1
U.S. v. Mendenhall
Case decided by Sup Ct 5-27, 454A1
Case cited by Sup Ct 6-30, 511A2
U.S. v. Mitchell
Case decided by Sup Ct 4-15, 306F1
U.S. v. Payner
Case decided by Sup Ct 6-23, 554B3
U.S. v. Raddatz
Case decided by Sup Ct 6-23, 555A1
U.S. v. Rutherford
Case declined by Sup Ct 10-20, 807F1
U.S. v. Salvucci
Case decided by Sup Ct 6-25, 541A1
U.S. v. Sioux Nation
Case decided by Sup Ct 6-30, 511B1
U.S. v. Ward
Case decided by Sup Ct 6-27, 511A2
U.S. v. Watson
Case cited by Sup Ct 4-15, 306C1
U.S. v. Will
Case decided by Sup Ct 12-15, 956D3
U.S. v. Zbaraz
Case argued in Sup Ct 4-21, 306B2
Case decided by Sup Ct 6-30, 491G2
UNITED Technologies Corp.
In Dow Jones indl avg 76F1
Carrier SEC suit setld 3-6, 558E1
3d in '79 defns contracts 5-28, 403E1
Pratt & Whitney JT8D engine fails in Honolulu take-off 6-25, FAA orders inspectns 7-16, 667B1
Haig apptd secy of state 12-16, 955B2
UNITED Vintners Inc.
Heublein divestiture order rptd overturned 10-15, 917C1
UNITRODE Corp.
Schlumberger OKs divestiture 3-4, 558A1
UNIVERSE (TV series)
Cronkite role cited 2-15, 198E3
UNIVERSITIES—*See EDUCATION--Colleges*

1976

UNNITALO, Eino
Sworn home affairs min 9-29, 750D3
UNO, Judge Raymond S.
Sentences Howe 7-23, 552A1
UNTERMAN, Issar Yehuda
Dies 1-26, 124G3
UOP Inc.—*See under OCCIDENTAL Petroleum*
UPI—*See UNITED Press International*
UPJOHN Co.
Rpts foreign payoffs 3-26, 361D2
SEC lists paymts 5-12, 729E1
'69 trust suit ends in mistrial 8-17, 988B3
Sup Ct bars review of trust case 10-4, 807B3
Overseas unit Arab boycott rpt released 10-18, 786D1

UPPER Volta—*See also AFRICAN Development Bank, NONALIGNED Nations Movement, OAU*
Dec '75 labor unrest cited 269A3
Lamizana appeals to labor 1-17; dismisses govt 1-29, names new Cabt 2-9, 269A3
Listed as 'partly free' 1-19, 20D3
Angola MPLA recognized 2-12, 105E2
Backs UN rights comm resolutn vs Israel 2-13, 125E2
US proposes Sahel aid progrm 5-1, 318D2
At France-Africa summit 5-10—5-11, 355G2
Olympic withdrawal rptd 7-21, 528B3
Min, offcls killed 9-14, 949F3
ECOWAS rptd ratified 11-6, 974E2
UPSTAIRS, Downstairs (TV series)
Wins Emmy 5-17, 460B2
URANIUM
US exploratn budgeted 1-21, 64G2
New Australia yields rptd 1-28, govt ends role 2-1, 97A1
S Korea cancels French A-plant buy 1-29, 103C3
Westinghouse accord set 2-3, 115E3
Australia-Japan talks 2-4—2-15, 137E3
Ford seeks pvt enrichmt dvpt 2-26, 149F2
Canada, Pak talks suspended 3-2, 175A1
Australia find rptd 3-9, 187G2
Australia mine shares for sale 3-10, 187A3
Australia sets forgn investmt policy 4-1, 249A3
New Australian find rptd 4-5, 249B3
GE seeks S Africa export license 5-10; 3 US groups sue 5-30; French consortium wins pact, US to provide enrichmt 6-1, 388D1
US computer sale to S Africa rptd 5-26, 388A2
Exempt from Australia mine-investmt policy change 6-2, 415E1
US OKs reactor sale to Spain 6-21, fuel sale to India 7-21, 739C2
Australia enrichmt plant rptd 6-30, 496G1
Ford OKs ERDA funds 7-12, 517G2
Waste safeguards asked 7-12, 739A2
GAO cites missing A-fuel 8-5, 739B3
GOP platform text 8-18, 607D2, B3
Taiwan fuel reprocessing rptd 8-29, 732E1
Taiwan to end A-fuel reprocessing 9-14, 858D2
Carter assures supplies 9-25, 724C1
Yugo asks A-fuel pool 9-27, 760G3
US pvt enrichmt bill not cleared 10-2, 883A3
Australia issues rpt 10-28, 835B2
Australia lifts export ban 11-11, 888C1
French mines bombed 11-15, 1003A1
Australia blocks US antitrust actn 11-18, Westinghouse pact end cited 11-19, 997C2
Australia unions back contracts 12-8, 923C1
Utah Intl, GE merge 12-16, 985A1
Safeguards Issue—*See 'Industrial Use' under ATOMIC Energy*

1977

UNIVERSITY of California v. Bakke
Justice Dept files brief 9-19; Sup Ct hears arguments 10-12, orders more briefs 10-17, 834F2-835G1
UNIVERSITY Professors, American Association of
Davidson tenure policy chnged 5-6, 472B1
UNSER, Al
3d in Indy 500 5-29, 531G1
Wins Calif 500 9-4; final USAC standing, earnings rptd 10-31, 870F3, G3
UNTERMEYER, Louis
Dies 12-18, 1024E3
UPI—*See UNITED Press International*
UPJOHN Co.
DNA patent order lifted 2-24, 184C2
Microbe patent granted 10-6, 847D1
UPPADHIT Pajariyangkul
On Cambodia border clashes 7-22, 572C1

UPPER Volta—*See also NONALIGNED Nations Movement, OAU*
UN Assemb member 4C1
New Cabt formed 1-14, 183A2
UN comm scores Israel occupatn rule 2-15, 107F2
At France-Africa summit 4-20—4-21, 316F3
Sahel dvpt plan OKd 6-1, 458F3
New Sahel famine seen 9-19, 770A2
Civiln rule voted 11-27, 1019E2
UPSTAIRS, Downstairs (TV series)
Wins Emmy 9-11, 1021G3
URANEX
TVA sues re uranium 11-18, 859F1
URANGESELLSCHAFT G.m.b.H.
TVA sues re uranium 11-18, 895F1

URANIUM—*For atomic safeguards issue, see also ATOMIC Energy—Industrial Use*
Canada prov defends policy 1-6, 18C1
Ford urges increased enrichmt 1-7, 14C3; 1-17, 31C2
Ct OKs Arco Anaconda merger 1-12, 55F2
US, Canada, Australia in collaboratn exchng 2-4—3-11, 624E3
US sales to S Africa rptd 2-16, 160B2
Westinghouse, 3 utilities settle dispute 3-3, 177B2
Fraser rpts Carter safeguards exchng 3-23, 217G3
Westinghouse dispute formally ends 3-30, 252G1-B2
Carter proposes productn rise 4-7, 267G3
Carter energy plan 4-20, 290F2, 293C2
Canada cartel, Gulf role rptd 4-25; NYS, US cong probes 6-9—6-17; Canada blames US embargo 6-16, 6-17, 479A2-480F2
'68 high seas loss rptd 4-28—5-2, Israel denies role 4-29, 335D1-B2
France rpts new enrichmt method 5-6, 402C3
Carter OKs shipmts 5-6, 403A2
'68 loss rptd Israeli plot 5-30, 416F2
US-Canada trust com rptd set 6-18, 525A3
US denies cartel agrmt 6-29, 624C3
French plant leaks radioactive gas 7-1, 543E2
Trudeau sees Schmidt 7-6—7-12, eases export ban 7-12, 566F2, A3
FBI seizes 2 in Fla 7-20, 576D3
US rpts missing A-material 8-4, 8-8, 717D1
US vows multinatl trust probe 8-8, 629G3
US Sen bars acquisitn curbs 9-8, 702F3
Westinghouse settles Ala Power suit 9-21, utilities suit proceeds 11-9, 895G1-C2
Canada opens cartel probe 10-3, Denison scores 10-19, 895F2
Canada relaxes disclosure ban 10-14, ct lifts for MPs 11-10, 895C3
Intl fuel bank urged by Carter 10-19, 794C1
Gen Atomic suit vs United Nuclear OKd 10-31, 835B3
United Nuclear, Gulf trial opens 10-31, 895C2
US-Canada in export pact 11-15, 913D1
US sale to Brazil OKd 11-16, 895G3
TVA sues US, forgn producers 11-18, 895C1
UK bars Westinghouse Rio Tinto evidence in cartel probe 12-1, 1003C3

1978

UNIVERSITY of California Regents v. Bakke
Bakke med schl admissn ordrd, race-based affirmative actn principle upheld by Sup Ct; reactn; opinion excerpt 6-28, 481C1-483A1, E1-487C2
UNIVERSITY Women, American Association of
Women show few gains in coll jobs 4-7, 554A3
UNMARRIED Woman, An (film)
Released 3-4, 620B1
UNMISTAKABLY Lou (recording)
Rawls wins Grammy 2-24, 315G3
UNRUH, Jesse
Elected Calif treas 11-7, 856A3
UNRWA—*See UNITED Nations—Relief & Works Agency*
UNSELD, Wes
Bullets win NBA title, named playoff MVP 6-7, 457A2
UNSER, Al
Wins Indy 500 5-29, Schaefer 500 6-25, 538B2, E3
Wins Calif 500, takes USAC Triple Crown 9-3, 968F3
Sets USAC earnings record 12-24, 1028C2
UPCHURCH, Rick
NFL '77 punt return ldr 1-1, 56C3
Cowboys win Super Bowl 1-5, 39D3
UPI—*See UNITED Press International*
UP in Smoke (film)
Released 9-22, 970C3
Top-grossing film 10-11, 800G3; 11-1, 888E1
UPJOHN Co.
Sup Ct OKs forgn natn trust suit 1-11, 33E3
'77 microbe patent ruling cited 3-2, 187E1
UPPADHIT Pajariyangkul
In Cambodia talks 1-30—2-2, denies Pnompenh 'ghost city' 2-2, 61B1
Cambodia border pact reached 7-15, 548G2

UPPER Volta—*See also GATT, NONALIGNED Nations Movement, OAU*
6 W African natns back ECOWAS 3-18, USSR scores 3-20, 237E1
New parlt elected 4-30, 354D3
Lamizana elected pres 5-28, 479E2
Parlt elects pres 6-9, 479F2
Conombo elected premr 7-7; Cabt rptd 7-18, 596C3
Dutch cancel debts 7-10, 575E1
UN Assemb member 713G3

URANIUM—*For atomic safeguards issue, see ATOMIC Energy—Industrial Use*
Carter OKs sale to India 1-2, 1G2
Australia exports delayed 1-6, 16E1
Canada lifts EC ban; UK, W Ger shipmts, inspectn set 1-16, 102D3
US, Canada frictn re US trust laws cited 1-17, 53D3
Israel acquisitns cited re '74 A-rpt 1-26, 61F1
Canada, Japan initial pact 1-26, 88E3
Dutch OK Brazil sales 2-1, 169C2
Australia oxide deposit find rptd 2-3, 88A1
Chad cuts Libya ties in land dispute 2-6, 89E1
US pricing revision dropped from research bill 2-8, 107A2
Australia export contracts to be honored 2-10, 110B1
S Africa sets enrichmt expansn 2-13, 135A1
Nuclear Suppliers' Group joined by Australia 2-24, 129C2
United Nuclear wins judgmt vs Gen Atomic; impact on other Gulf suits seen 3-2, 144C1
US probes black-mkt sale bid to Westinghouse 3-19, 242C2-A3
Gen Atomic damage determinatn stay denied by Sup Ct 3-20, 206D1
Japan treaty sought by Australia 3-20, 208B3
UK OKs Windscale reprocessing plant 3-22, 227G1
Australia mining, exports protested 4-1, 243E3
Schmidt sees Giscard on Sovt deal 4-2, 258C2
US studies A-material ban 4-3, 277C2
EC disputes US export policy 4-4—4-9, 258D1
Oil, gas firms' reserves lid backed by FTC aide 4-5; Justice Dept proposal rptd 4-6, 282D2
US OKs EC exports 4-9, 278F3
W Ger scores US-EC export renegotiatns 4-12, 255B1
Gen Atomic files new evidnc 4-20, 346G2-B3
India vs US sale bar 4-23, 4-24; Carter OKs sale 4-27, 313G1
Japan sets US enrichmt paymt 5-3, 341G2
US chrgs Gulf price fixing 5-9, 346D1-D2
Gulf sues Westinghouse 5-9, 346D2
Gen Atomic documts ruling declined by Sup Ct 5-15, 387E3
Oil, gas firms' 10% lid on holdings backed by Justice Dept 5-15, 471E2

1979

UNIVERSITY Club (Memphis, Tenn.)
Brown membership disputed 9-25, 901D3
UNIVERSITY Professors, American Association of
Boston U faculty strikes 4-5—4-13, 326D3
Begin protests Hout visit 5-2, 320B1
UNIVERSITY Women, American Association of
Chambers named Carter com head 1-16, 30C3
UNSELD, Wes
NBA field-goal ldr 4-8, 290E2
Sonics win NBA title 6-1, 506F3
UNSER, Al
Forced out of Indy 500 5-27, 490A3
UNSER, Bobby
4th in Indy 500 5-27, 490B3
UNSOELD, William F.)
Killed in avalanche 3-4, 272F3
UNTSO—*See under MIDDLE EAST-U.N.*
U. of Tennessee v. Geier
Case refused by Sup Ct 6-18, 499C2
UPCHURCH, Rick
NFL '78 punt return ldr 1-6, 80C2
UPDIKE, John
Coup on best-seller list 2-4, 120B3
UPI—*See UNITED Press International*
UPJOHN Co.
'77 microbe patent rule reaffirmed 3-29, 265F2
Microbe patent case accepted by Sup Ct 10-29, 884D1
UPPADHIT Pajariyangkul
Reapptd Thai forgn min 5-25, 429B1

UPPER Volta—*See also GATT, NONALIGNED Nations Movement, OAU*
Freedom House lists as free 12F3
France debt relief vow rptd 5-4, 371C3
Ghana executns rptd scored 6-30, 524D2
UN membership listed 695B3

URANIUM—*For atomic safeguards issue, see ATOMIC Energy—Industrial Use*
Enrichmt progrm budget cut 1-22, 45G2
GE worker chrgd in uranium theft 2-1, 119F3
Westinghouse settles 3 suits 4-16, 5-5, 5-15, 366C1
NM waste spill 7-16, cleanup continues 9-5, 744A1
H-bomb letter, diagram cites 9-16, 9-18, 715C2-716G2, 717D2
Tenn A-fuel plant shut 9-18, FBI probes 10-10, 809A3
Westinghouse settles Northeast Utilities suit 9-26, 727C3
Foreign Developments (including U.S. international news)
Australia Ranger accord signed 1-9, 36C2
Canada-India '74 quarrel cited 1-11, 57A3
Urenco plans W Ger A-enrichmt plant 2-7, 101D1
Westinghouse settles 2 Swedish suits 2-9, 131C3
Australia OKs mining projct 3-1, 153D1
US OKs sale to India 3-23, 416F2
France, Mex sign agrmt; US delay cited 4-1—4-4, 372B2
Australia sees US A-accident impact 4-5, 246C3
France-Iraq deal protested by Israel 4-6, 276G1
US cuts Pak aid, chrgs A-plant threat 4-6, 277B2
Iraq A-reactor sabotaged in France 4-6, 276G1; replacemt vowed 5-9, 371G2
Libya invasn of Chad fails 4-20, 329B3
US, Australia sign accord 7-5, 501D1
Australia-UK pact OKd by EC panel 7-5, 522E1
World reserves estimated 7-20, 555A1
UK, Australia sign pact 7-24, 562F2
BP to join Australia mining project 7-27, 580G2, G3
US delays shipmt to India 8-4, 646D2
Australian govt to sell Ranger share 8-7, 600D1
Canada reserves estimate hiked 8-15, 613B2
S Australia mining dvpt seen 9-16—9-17, 749C2
Canada to sell crown co 9-28, 749G2
France freezes Iran's stake in Eurodif 10-24, 976E2
UK trust bill proposed, US targeted 10-31, 855F3
Canada NDP vs mining halt 11-22—11-25, 927F1
Australia sells Ranger 50% share 12-18, 992C2

1980

UNIVERSITY Hospital (San Diego, Calif.)
Maternity drinking risks rptd 1-4, 23G3
UNO, Commandante
On Colombia-DR emb talks 3-6, 180F2
UNSELD, Wes
NBA rebound ldr 3-30, 278E3
UNSER, Al
CART membership cited 6-30, 1002A2
UNSER, Bobby
Wins Pocono 500 6-22, 637G3
CART membership cited 6-30, 1002A2
3d in top driver vote 12-5, 1002E1
UNSER, Del
Phillies win NL pennant 10-12, 796A2
In World Series 10-14—10-21, 811F3-812B3
UNTSO—*See UNITED Nations--UNTSO*
UPCHURCH, Rick
NFL '79 receiving, punt return ldr 1-5, 8C2, C3
UPI—*See UNITED Press International*
UPJOHN Co.
GE microbe patent case remanded by Sup Ct 1-14, 37D1; upheld 6-16, 452G3
UPPADHIT Pajariyangkul
Replaced as Thai forgn min 2-11, 196F3

UPPER Volta—*See also GATT, NONALIGNED Nations, OAU*
Islamic conf boycotted 1-27—1-29, 67C2
Pope visits 5-10, 363D3
Islamic League meets 11-10, 895B2
Teachers suspend 2-mo strike 11-22, 924D2
Mil coup overthrows Lamizana, econ conditns blamed 11-25, 924G1
UPSALA College (East Orange, N.J.)
Loses NCAA Div III basketball title 3-15, 240D3
UPSIDE Down (recording)
On best-seller list 9-10, 716E3; 10-8, 796A3
UP the Academy (film)
Released 6-6, 675F3
UPTON, Gordon
Gandhi criticisms raise concern 11-6, 870G1
URANIUM
Union Pacific, MoPac set merger 1-8, 52D3
Tenn A-fuel plant reopens despite loss 1-16, 54A1
UNC Resources seeks Westn Air merger 12-24, 985C1
Foreign Developments (including U.S. international news)
UK plans enrichmt plant 1-9, 39G2
Australia mine plans rptd 1-19, 56E1
Spain '79 losses rptd 2-21, 196A3
France plans 2 more breeder reactors, US oppositn rptd 2-26, 149E2
Canada prov sets 7-yr mining ban 2-27, 148D2
US rpts Pak A-plant progrm 2-27, 165G2
France OKs Iraq enriched fuel shipmt 2-27, 192D3
Vienna conf backs plutonium fuel 2-27, 220F3
Australia plant rptd backed by France 3-3, 171A1
US delays India shipmts 3-13, 181G3
Brazil-Argentina talks open 3-18, 229D2
Italy cuts Eurodif share 5-2, 409D1
US State Dept urges sale to India 5-7, NRC blocks 5-16, 440B3
French find rptd 5-29, 407E2
France enrichmt process rptd 9-10, 707C3
US Cong fails to block sale to India 9-24, 723C1
S Africa plant capacity disclosed 9-30, 753G2
US shipmt arrives in India 10-7, 830C2
Taiwan-S Africa deal cited 10-17, 831E2
Australia dvpt rise seen 10-21, 857G3
Australia sets reprocessing terms 11-27, 919F3

1976

URANUS (planet)—*See 'Interplanetary Projects' under ASTRONAUTICS*
URBAN Development & Renewal—*See CITIES*
URBAN League, National
'75 rpt on urban aid progrm cited 25B2
Granger dies 1-9, 56D3
Carter rues remark 4-8, 261D1
Hears Kissinger on Africa 8-2, 580D3
Kissinger addresses 8-2, 922G1
Issues econ rpt 8-2, urges study panel 8-3, 922C2
Jordan named Carter aide 11-19, 881D3
San Diego offcl on black marines assault 11-29, 983D1
Jordan bars Cabt post 12-16, 937A2
URCHENKO, Vasiliy
Wins Olympic medals 7-31, 574F1
UREN, Thomas
Named dep Labor Party ldr 1-27, 71E3
URIS, Leon
Trinity on best-seller list 12-5, 972E2
URREGO, Gen. Armando
Lockheed paymts rptd 2-8, 147F2
Rpt Lockheed papers cite bribe 8-24, 740A2
URRUTIA, Carlos
Arrest warrant rptd 3-20, 499E3; amnestied 5-7 500C1
Arrested 8-17, 652D2
URSINO, Frank
2d bomb scare closes Bicen show 12-8, 948B2
URTEAGA, Jose
Killed 7-19, 571E1
URUGUAY—*See also IDB, LAFTA, OAS*
'73 defns budget, mil forces rptd 1-2, 60G2
Punta del Este bombings 1-11, 55F3
Nov vote rptd canceled 3-12, 4-11, 382E2
Bordaberry talks with mil reps end 5-7, sees mil chiefs 5-21, 6-1, 441A1
Mil ousts Bordaberry, Demicheli sworn 6-12, sees return to democracy 6-14, 440D3, 441C1
Natl Cncl formed 6-27; names Mendez pres 7-14, vows Marxist 'purge' 7-15, 7-19, 542A1
Ferreira arrest ordered 8-5, 678A2
New Cabt named, Vegh departs 8-27, 678A2
Demicheli lauds mil 8-31, 678E2
Mendez sworn pres, pol ldrs banned 9-1, 678D1
La Manana confiscated 10-10; US rep scored 10-15, 814A2, C2
Rodriquez Fabregat dies 11-21, 970B3
Economy & Labor
'73 defense budget listed 1-2, 60G2
Peso devalued 1-14, 2-9, 383D1
Price controls lifted 2-19, 383C1
Peso devalued 5-4, 441F2
Mar, 12-mo inflatn rptd 5-14, 441E2
Ban on union activities, strikes rptd 6-19, 6-21, 542D1
May, 12-month inflatn rptd 7-2, 542F1
Wage, price hikes set 7-3, 542E1
Peso devalued 7-22, 755F1
Jan-June COL data rptd 8-4, 755E1
Vegh leaks Cabt departure, peso falls 8-11, 678D2
Peso devalued 10-8, 814C3
Jan-Aug living cost wage, gas price data 10-8, 10-11, 814C3

1977

Italy suit vs Canada price policy rptd 12-13, 982B3
Laser enrichmt advncs rptd 12-14, 12-17, 975F1-G2
Canada-Italy supply pact rptd 12-15, 982A3
Canada, EC OK pact 12-20, 1010G1
Westinghouse, 3 Tex utilities settle suit 12-26, 1003A3
Australian Developments
Protest blocks shipmt 1-2, 17B2
Scientists urge mining, export ban 1-3, 7B1; dvpt defended 1-11, 17B2
Westinghouse suit rptd 1-25, '76-82 sales contracts cited 1-26, 81F2
Mine losses rptd 1-26, 81D2
US, Canada, Australia in colaboratn exchng 2-4—3-11, 624E3
Find rptd 2-16, 158C2
US, PI, EC press Australia for deals 2-24—3-16, 218B1
Mine aid set 3-5, 179D1
Fraser sees major export role, strict controls 3-23, 217G3
Australia cancels Japan contracts 3-24, 218D1
Australia asks safeguards 3-29, 253G2
Cartel role rptd 4-25, 479F2
Export guidelines set 5-24, 465B3
Comm rpt issued 5-25; reactn 5-31, 465A2-A3
Threatens EC export ban 6-1, 7-4, 595D3
US denies cartel agrmt 6-29, 624C3
Dockers protest 7-2—7-4, 523D1
Labor backs ban 7-7, 540E3
Ban lifted 8-25; output, sales forecast, reserves estimated 8-25, 8-26, 693G1-E3
Protesters surveillnc rpts unconfrmd 9-1, 923A1
Fraser rejects referendum 9-7, 705C1
Australia labor conf asks referendum 9-15, 740B2
Uren oppositn drive mounts 10-17—11-3, 901F1-A2
Dockers back boycott, demand vote 10-20, 901B2
Prelim export rules issued 11-9, 901C1
North Terr plans mining challenge 11-14, 901E1
Backs UK re US cartel probe claim 12-1, 1003F3
URBAN Areas—*See CITIES; city names*
URBAN Coalition, National
Holman at black ldrs mtg 8-29, 702E1
URBAN Development & Renewal—*See CITIES*
URBAN League, National
Bell confrmatn hearings 1-11—1-18, 34B2
Carter energy plan reactn 4-21, 320F2
Conv opens, Jordan scores Carter 7-24; Carter responds 7-25, 573C1
Black Caucus backs Carter criticism 7-29, 592F3
Jordan at black ldrs mtg 8-29, 702D1
Jordan sees Carter 12-14, 960E1
URBAN Mass Transportation Administration—*See under U.S. GOVERNMENT—TRANSPORTATION*
UREN, Thomas
Vs Whitlam uranium plan 3-29, 253D3
Scores uranium ban end 8-25, 693D2
Leads anti-uranium drive 10-17, 11-2, 901F1-A2
Loses Labor Party ldrshp post 12-22, 1009D2
URGEL, Bishop of (Spain)
Andorra asks financial review 1-5, 48A1
URIS, Leon
Trinity on best-seller list 2-6, 120E3; 3-6, 184E3; 4-3, 264F1; 5-1, 356C2; 6-4, 452A2; 10-2, 808F3
URS, Devraj
Cong Party suspends 12-26, exec com splits 12-27, 1013F3
URUGUAY—*See also IDB, OAS*
Justice Min created, independt judiciary curbed, electoral ct reorgnzd 1-27, 1-30, 351G2
Independt judiciary ended 7-1, 600F3
'81 electn plan set 8-9; party ldrs score 9-16, mil critics removed 9-23, 904E3
Economy & Labor (domestic)
Price hikes OKd 1-19; Jan-Feb living costs up 3-25, 352C1
Wage hike set 2-4, 352D1
'61-75 GDP variatns table 5-30, 439C1
Union ldrs rptd arrested 7-8, 601B1
Agrarian crisis rptd 7-8, 601B2
Elec utility rpt closes paper 9-11, 905F1
Real wages, family income down 11-18; salaries, min wage hiked; VAT cut 12-6, 970D1

1978

Gen Atomic damages awarded United Nuclear, Ind & Mich 5-16, 366G2
US lifts long-term contract curb 5-26, 408C1
Gen Atomic trial judge interference ruled by Sup Ct 5-30, 430A3
Australia mining, export rules adopted 5-31, 434B3
Schmidt reviews Carter talks 6-1, 519C2
Gulf fined in cartel case 6-2, 449G2
Nuclear Exchng exec chrgd 6-2, 449B3
Canada prov backs dvpt 6-8, 647C2
US, India in export talks 6-13—6-15, 466C3
EC seeks Australia trade talks 6-13, 495A1
US hints S Africa supply 6-25, 536G3
Dutch parlt backs Brazil sales 6-30, 575A1
India sale allowed by US House 7-12, 551D1
Australia revenue tax proposed 7-20, 570C2
Australia, Finland sign accord 7-20, 590C1
EC halts UK-Australia pact 7-27, 666E1
Australia-PI pact signed 8-7, 666G1
US-Australia pact signed 8-8, 666B2
Canada, Japan sign pact 8-22, 667B1
Australian Aborigine royalties set 8-25, 666A1
Japan import fund set 9-3, 694D1
US oil co production rptd 9-8, 700D2
Australia Aborigine compromise OKd 9-8, 9-15, new dispute delays projct 9-19, 721A1
Canada find rptd 9-13, 722A1
US energy bill clears Cong 10-15, 787B2
Brazil enrichmt progrm lags 10-15, 836D3
Australia bars Aborigine projct veto 10-16, 812C3, D3 ★
Aborigines OK mining project 11-3, 865E3
US cancels S Africa contracts 11-4, 904C2
Law firm dual-rep case refused by Sup Ct 11-6, 873G3
Carter questns oil industry acquisitns 12-12, 983E2
URBAN Areas—*See CITIES; city names*
URBAN Development & Renewal—*See CITIES*
URBAN League, National
Jordan stresses black plight 3-15, 9-21, 811C1, B2
Jordan on Carter urban-aid plan 3-27, 217F3
Jordan on Bakke ruling 6-28, 482D2
Annual conf rpts black-white econ gap widening; Jordan, Mondale, Bradley address 8-6—8-8, 810E3-811C1, F1
Martin named Carter aide 8-11, 664A1
Griffith punishmt sought 10-2, 779F2
Jordan scores Carter budget plans 12-4, 936B3
UREN, Tom
Scores Anthony uranium policy 10-16, 812F3
Arrested in Brisbane protest 10-30, 866B1
URENCO (Great Britain, Netherlands, West Germany)
Brazil uranium sales, Almelo A-plant expansn OKd 2-1; protest held 3-4, 169C2, F2
URIBE Vargas, Diego
Colombia forgn min 9-22, 815A1
Signs US drug pact 9-29, 815B1
URSINI, Raffaele
Arrest rptd 8-1, 724B2
URUGUAY—*See also GATT, IDB, OAS*
AF transport crash kills 31 2-10, 270G3
Alvarez installed as army chief 3-2, 292D1
24 leftists rptd held 3-19, 292C1
Civiln pol consultatns seen by Alvarez 3-27, 537B3
Leftist pol ldr seized 4-21, 396A1
Seregni sentncd 5-26, 537E3
Pol prisoner rpts vary 6-20, 6-29, 537F3
Intell chief fired, arrested 6-25, 6-28; mil stresses unity 6-26, 537G2
Forgn min replaced, rights victory seen 7-8, 577A2
Torres Garcia paintings destroyed in Brazil museum fire 7-8, 579B2
Poisoned wine sent to 3 ex-congressmen 9-6, 799E1-A2
Tupamaros sentncd 10-10; arrests cotinue, torture rptd down 10-16, 1022C2
Press curbs rptd by IAPA 10-13, 829A2
Economy & Labor (domestic)
Wages hiked 7% 3-1; '77 inflatn, real wages drop cited 3-10, 292E1
Dec '77 jobless rate, real incomes rptd 4-14, 395F3
Leftist labor ldr seized 4-21, 396A1
Consumptn down since '73 5-12, 395G3
Wages hiked 8%, Jan-Apr inflatn 12.3% 6-1, 537G3
Jan-July inflatn rptd 23% 8-10, 692E1
Jan-Sept COL up 32.2% 10-27, 1022E2

1979

URANUS (planet)
Ring theory rptd 1-11, 289G3
URBAN Areas—*See CITIES; city names*
URBAN Development & Renewal—*See CITIES*
URBAN League, National
Rpt details black econ plight 1-17, 35D1-C2
Bonilla elected LULAC pres 6-17, 810F1
Annual conf: Jordan scores Carter, urges black pol pressure; Admin reps, Kennedy address 7-22–7-25, 560A1
NY dir vs Carter Palestinian-US civil rights analogy 8-1, 575E1
Jordan vs black support for PLO, Baptist Conv scores 10-14; meets Jackson, 'unity' reaffirmed 10-17, 780D2, A3, B3
URCUYO Maliaños, Francisco
Succeeds Somoza, challenges power transfer 7-17; flees to Guatemala 7-18 535G1
URENCO (Great Britain, Netherlands, West Germany)
W Ger A-enrichmt plant OKd, 10-yr cooperatn agreed 2-7, 101D1
A-protesters blockade Dutch plant 10-15, 782A1
URRICARRIET, Gen. Diego
Retiremt expected 12-7, 947F3
URS, Devraj
Ousted from Cong-I Party 6-25, 503C2
URUGUAY—*See also GATT, IDB, LAFTA, OAS*
PEN scores on rights 7-21, 554B1

1980

URBAN, Matt
Awarded Medal of Honor 7-19, 638E1
URBAN Cowboy (film)
Released 6-11, 675F3
Top-grossing film 7-2, 568G3
Recording on best-seller list 7-9, 568F3
URBAN Development & Renewal—*See CITIES*
URBAN League, National
Rpt doubts '70s progress 1-22, 94B2
Jordan shot in Ft Wayne 5-29, 401D2
Carter visits Jordan 6-1; transferred to NY hosp 6-12, 442A2
Jobless study released 8-2, 597C2
Conv held; pres candidates address issues, visit Jordan 8-3—8-6; racism, apathy deplored in keynote address 8-3, 597A1-G2
Electn results evaluated 11-4, 846G3
URIBE Vargas, Diego
Rejcts DR Emb captors demands, urges more talks 3-18, 211C3
URIOSTE, Msgr. Ricardo
Chosen Romero successor; offers leftist mediatn, pleas for S Africa amb 4-8, 351G2
URQUHART, Brian E.
UN Namibia talks fail 10-20—10-24, 831B3
URS, Devraj
Gandhi wins electn 1-3, 1-6, 11D3
URSI, Corrado Cardinal
Quake relief dispute rptd 12-11, 944B1
URUGUAY—*See also GATT, IDB, OAS*
Demichelli dies 10-12, 876C1
New const published 11-2; oppositn ldrs arrested at rally 11-14, 888E2
Const proposal defeated 11-30, 924E2
Human rights record scored 12-10, 978A3

1976

Foreign Relations (misc.)—*See also 'Human Rights' below*
CP members rptd tried 1-17; '75 arrests cited 2-24, 207F3
AIFLD aid to US CIA rptd 3-10, 253G1
Bordaberry vs soclst, 3d world ties 3-12, 4-11, 382A3
'75 payments deficit up 3-12, 383B1
Stroessner, Pinochet visit 3-24—3-27, 4-21—4-24, 382D3
IMF OKs SDR sale 3-29, 383A1
Total IMF oil loan rptd 4-1, 340E2
Sovt trade pact rptd 4-20, 441F2
Liberoff kidnaped in Argentina 5-19, 399D2
Blanco ldrs seized at Gutierrez, Michelini funerals 5-25, freed 5-29, 441C2
Govt linked to Michelini, Gutierrez slayings 5-28, 441B2
US House panel bars mil aid 6-5, 441E1
Yugo dissident kills amb to Paraguay 6-8, 542D3
'75 trade deficit rptd; Kuwait, Brazil data 7-9, 542G1
IMF OKs standby credit, rpts Jan-June paymts deficit 8-4, 755D1
US House panel hearing on mil aid 8-4, 814C2
At nonaligned conf 8-16—8-20, 622C1
US bans mil aid 10-1, 806F3, 814C1
US AID funds noted 10-8, 814D1

Human Rights (including political prisoner and refugee issues)
Sovts score anti-CP drive 1-10, 55F3
Seregni rptd seized 1-11, 55G3
'75 pol arrests, torture rptd 1-13, 55E3
Russell ct scores rights abuse 1-17, 61D2
Listed as 'partly free' 1-19, 20D3
Christian youth groups banned 1-20, 208A1
Pol arrests rptdly continue 2-9—3-4, 207E3
Abstains on UN rights comm resolutn vs Israel 2-13, 125E2
Amnesty Intl chrgs rights abuse 2-18—3-11, 207E2
Venez seizes natls 3-2, 208D2
Pol refugees rptd in Mex, Colombia embs 3-3—3-12, 207G3
Jimenez vs Chile rights abuse 3-5, 310F1
'75 Bordaberry warning cited 3-12, 4-11, 382G2
Mex emb takes more refugees, 52 get safe conduct 3-16—4-9, 382A3
US officials score torture 4-21, 382F3
US amb scores VOA torture chrg 4-21, 382G3
Sovt activists protest rights abuse 5-10, 441A2
2 pol exiles kidnaped in Argentina 5-18, found dead 5-20, forgn protests 5-21, 5-24; Argentina to probe 5-24, 399E1-D2 ★
Mex, Colombia emb refugee totals rptd 5-18, 441D2
Ferreira to Argentina Austria emb 5-24, 399D2
Ferreira arrives France 5-31, 441B2
US House panel bars mil aid 6-5, 441E1
Refugee in Argentina kidnaped 6-11, freed 6-12, 495G3
106 refugees fly to Mex 6-24—7-2, 542B3
Woman seized in Venez emb 6-28—7-7, Venez suspends ties 7-6, 542B2
ICJ chrgs torture common 7-16, 542A2
Refugees rptd kidnaped in Argentina 7-19, 571A3
Ferreira aide takes Mex emb asylum 8-21, 678A2
Pol ldrs rights banned 9-1, 678E1
3 bodies found in River Plate 9-6, 814G2
Electn aide quits re pol rights ban 9-8; Bordaberry, others get back rights 10-7, 814B3
US rep, sen rpt abuses 9-20, 9-28, 814E2
US bans mil aid 10-1; reactn 10-8—10-18; AID funds noted 10-8, 806F3, 814C1
Repressn rptd up in '75-76 10-31, 975D1

1977

Foreign Relations (misc.)—*See also 'Human Rights', 'Monetary, Trade & Aid' and 'Press' below*
UN Assemb member; Jimenez World Ct pres 4D1, F1
Abstains on UN Israel occupatn rule vote 2-15, 107E2
Mendez at Panama Canal pact signing 9-7, 678D1

Human Rights (including political prisoner and refugee issues)—*See also 'Press & Censorship' below*
Prison terms cut; Amnesty Intl rpts 5000 held 1-1, 3E1
Pol refugees fly to Mexico 1-16, 352B1
Amnesty Intl chrgs Dec '76 arrests, deaths 1-27; student death rptd 2-6, 351F3
Ct bars prisoner release appeal, prisoner detentn denied 2-7, 352A1
Iguini, Perez torture rptd 2-15, 351G3
US bars mil officers 2-22, rights pressure cited 2-25, 351B3
US to cut aid re rights abuse 2-24; '78 mil credits rejctd 3-1, 142E1, B2
Brazil rejects US mil aid 3-5, 167E3
US aide scores rights abuse 3-8, UN resolutn vs Chile opposed 3-9, 219G1
US issues rights rpt 3-12, 187B1, F1
Mil officer arrests rptd, denied 3-22—4-8, debate sparked 4-22, 351B2
US stand backed by pol ldrs 4-1, 351E3
Mil dissidents to be ousted 4-20, 351F2
Massera arrest probed in US 4-27, 315A2, B2
US rights stand scored 6-1, 439D1
45 pol arrests rptd 7-8, 601B1
US delays police sales 7-17, 572F3
Colorado, Blanco parties speak out vs repression 7-17, 601A1
US ties rptd improved 8-20, 905C1
Amnesty Intl lists jailed lawmakers 9-5, 753C2

Monetary, Trade & Aid Issues (including all foreign economic developments)
Peso devalued 4 times 1-10—3-8, 352D1
US to cut aid 2-28, '78 mil credits rejectd 3-1, 142E1, B2
Brazil rejcts US mil aid 3-5, 167E3
'75-76 trade, paymts data; table 3-11, 189B1, A2 ★, C2
'66-75 arms transfers table 4-8, 415B2
Peso devalued 7-4, 7-8, 7-28, 601F2
Agrarian export crisis rptd 7-8, 601C2
'76 trade deficit $30.2 mln 7-8, 601G2
US delays police sales 7-17, 572F3
US bars mil aid credits 10-19, 815A3; 11-1, 834D1
Peso devalued for 23d time 11-25, 970E1

Press & Censorship
Argentina newspr seized, AP, UPI rptrs curbed 3-24, 351E2
3 forgn correspondents arrested, 2 freed 7-4—7-21, 601C1
Busqueda closed 8-30, reopens 10-29, 905F1
Mex newsman still held 9-6, 905C2
El Heraldo closed 9-11, 905E1
El Dia closed 9-27, editor expelled 9-29; econ sanctns imposed 10-7—10-29, 905C1
Marcha ex-editor missing 9-28; rptd in Argentina, kin fear dead 10-3, 905A2
'50-74 press, literature banned in libraries, 10-17, 905G1

U.S. Relations—*See also 'Human Rights' and 'Monetary, Trade & Aid' above*
'66-75 arms transfer table 4-8, 415B2
Pezzullo confrmd amb 7-13, 626C3
Mendez at Panama Canal pact signing 9-7, 678D1
US vet indicted in horse-switch scandal 12-2, 971B1

1978

Foreign Relations (misc.)—*See also 'Monetary, Trade, Aid & Investment' below*
Mex newsman freed 'provisionally' 1-5, 136F3
UN Chile rights abuse res opposed 3-6, 210F1
OAS unit chrgs rights abuse 3-14, 292A1
Amnesty Intl asks torture probe, rpts deaths 5-3, 395G3
Rights abuse cited at OAS mtg 6-21; Jamaica, US score; chrgs denied 6-23, 489G2, E3
Rights abuse cited by US panel 6-24, 490C1
OAS rpts rights abuses 6-28, seeks panel probe 7-1, 505B2, D2
'70 US CIA torture training chrgd 8-2—8-4, 831D1
UN Assemb member 713G3
US vet sentncd in '77 horse switch 11-3, 1028G1

Monetary, Trade, Aid & Investment
'77 export earnings up 3-10, 292F1
Peso devalued 6-1, 6-14, 6-26, 537F3; 7-10, 577B2
Peso devalued 1.1% 8-4, 692E1
Peso devalued 19th time 10-11, 1022D2

Sports
World Cup '30 title cited 6-25, 520A3

1979

Foreign Relations (misc.)
Beagle Channel papal mediatn agreed 1-8, 51C3
Brazil admits '78 kidnap 1-17, scores police probe 1-23, 95F1
Pol refugees occupy Swedish consulate in Rio, protest Argentina repressn 8-6; UN responds 8-8, 627D1, F1
UN membership listed 695B3

1980

Foreign Relations (misc.)
Colombia amb seized in DR Emb raid 2-27, 141B1; escapes 3-17, 211G2-A3
Argentine A-pact cited 3-18, 229E2
Colombian Emb attack thwarted 4-14, 293G3-294A1
Israel Emb shift rptd 8-26, 643E2
UK rptr arrested 11-7, freed 11-10, 888B3
Airliner hijacked to Argentina 11-12, hijacker surrenders 11-13, 888C3
OAS cites poor rights record 11-27, 913B3

U.S. Relations
US '76 aid cut cited 11-30, 924A3

1976

USERY Jr., W(illie) J(ulian)
Facts on 40F3
Named Labor secy 1-22, 40E3; confrmd 2-4, sworn 2-10, 110F1
Meany sees difficult role 2-17, 148E3
On Teamsters pacts 4-2, 248D3
Replaced in mediatn post 4-7, 262E3
Addresses Teamsters conv 6-14, 436D1
Defends Teamsters conv talk 7-1, 492B2
Westinghouse strike ends 7-20, 536D3
Calls rubber strike talks 8-5, 647C3
USSR—*See UNION of Soviet Socialist Republics*

1977

USERS, The (book)
On best-seller list 3-6, 184E3
On paperback best-seller list 8-14, 643A2
USES of Enchantment, The: The Meaning and Importance of Fairy Tales (book)
Wins Natl Book Award 4-11, 355A2
USHIBA, Nobuhiko
Gets new Cabt econ post 11-28, 931F2, 932G1
On US trade demands 12-8, 931G2
On Japan trade proposals to US 12-15, 973G2-974A2
USIA—*See U.S. GOVERNMENT—U.S. INFORMATION Agency*
USOC (United States Olympic Committee)—*See SPORTS—Olympics*
USSR—*See UNION of Soviet Socialist Republics*
USSURI River
USSR, China reach accord 10-7, 853D2
USTA (U.S. Tennis Association)—*See TENNIS*

1978

USAC (United States Auto Club)—*See AUTOMOBILE Racing*
USDA—*See U.S. GOVERNMENT—AGRICULTURE*
USHIBA, Nobuhiko
On Japan-US trade pact 1-13, 27B1
USIA—*See U.S. GOVERNMENT—U.S. INFORMATION Agency*
USOC (U.C. Olympic Committee)—*See SPORTS—Olympics*
USSR—*See UNION of Soviet Socialist Republics*
USSRI River
Sovt border raid 5-11, Sino-Sovt dispute cited 360C2, G2
USTA (U.S. Tennis Association)—*See TENNIS*

1979

USAC (United States Auto Club)—*See AUTOMOBILE Racing*
USHER, Jane Price
Wins parlt electn 11-21, 907B1
USHIBA, Nobuhiko
US halts trade talks 3-29, 229D3
Signs US-Japan sales pact 6-2, 416C1

1980

USAIR (formerly Allegheny Airlines)
Nader '78 'bumping' award overturned 5-16, 703C2
USHEWOKUNZE, H. S. M.
Zimbabwe health min 3-11, 198D1
USHKEMPIROV, Zaksylik
Wins Olympic medal 7-22, 624G2
USSR—*See UNION of Soviet Socialist Republics*

1976

USTINOV, Marshal Dmitri F.
Named to Politburo Secretariat 3-5, 195B2
Named Sovt defense min 4-29, 334F2
Promoted 7-30, 908A2

1977

USTINOV, Dmitri Fedorovich
Addresses Bolshevik Revolutn anniv mil review; photo 11-7, 865C3, 866A1
USV Pharmaceutical Corp.—*See under REVLON Inc.*

1978

USTINOV, Dmitri Fedorovich
Vows USSR can match weapons 2-22, 140G1
On China border tour 3-28—4-9, 238A1
Finland mil link rptd pressed 11-15, 894C2
USTINOV, Peter
Death On Nile released 9-29, 970B1
USW (United Steelworkers of America)—*See STEELWORKERS of America, United*

1979

USTINOV, Marshal Dmitri Fedorovich F.
Denounces China Viet invasn 2-23, 141G2
At SALT II summit 6-15–6-18, 449F1; communique text 457C1
Warns NATO vs A-missiles 10-25, 880B3
Marks revolutn anniv 11-7, 856E2
USW (United Steelworkers of America)—*See STEELWORKERS of America, United*

1980

USTINOV, Dmitri
Sees US Sen Percy 11-27, 915F1

1976

UTAH
Kaiparowits power projct dropped 4-14, 284B2
US files home loan bias suit 4-15, 285G1
US Sup Ct backs contraceptive rule 5-24, 393D2
Howe arrested on sex chrg 6-12, 434G1-B2
Amer Party conv in Salt Lake City 6-18, 6-19, 490C3
Horses found dead in Dugway 7-4, 587C1
Dem conv women delegates, table 508D2
Dem conv pres vote, table 7-14, 507D2
Reagan wins 20 delegates 7-17, 531E2
Howe convicted, affirms reelectn bid, 7-23, 552A1
GOP pre-conv delegate count 8-14, 583D3
GOP conv scuffle on 16-C debate 8-17, 600A2
GOP conv pres vp vote tables 8-18—8-19, 8-19, 599D1, D3
Oil shale lease suspensn sought 8-23, 649B1, E1
Howe conviction upheld 8-24, 636E2
Dole in Salt Lake City 687B1
Primary results 9-14, 705F1
Fscl '75 per capita income, tax burden rptd 9-15, 10-12, 959E2
Cong OKs land bill 9-29, 765C3; signed 10-15, 982G1
Carter in Salt Lake City 10-7, 762B1
Gilmore death sentence stirs controversy 10-7—11-22, 890E3
Election results 11-2: pres 818D1, 819B1; cong 819D3, 820E2, 824G2, 828C3, 830F3, 831D2; state 820B3, 824C3
US Sup Ct stays Gilmore executn 12-6, 920A1
Gilmore stay vacated 12-13, death rate set 12-15, 952F1
Flu shot paralysis rptd 12-17, 950E1
UTAH International Inc.
Merges with GE 12-16, 984G3

1977

UTAH
Legislature schedule rptd 6F2
Gilmore executed 1-17, 40E1
Carter cuts water projct funds 2-22, 126E1
'76 per-capita income table 5-10, 387F2
Polygamist leader slain 5-10, 6 chrgd 9-27, 847F3
Salt Lake econ data table 5-16, 384F2
Ashley Natl Forest fire kills 3 7-16—7-19, 660A3
Todman visits 8-17—8-19, ties rptd improved 8-20, 905B1
'76 per capita income, tax burden table 9-13, 10-18, 821E2
GM cuts '78 Chevette price 9-15, 722F3
Anti-abortn amendmt rptd sought 10-6, 786B3
ERA econ boycott rptd 11-14, 918E1
Death penalty law upheld 11-26, 919E3
UTAH International Inc.
GE merger cited 351A1
GE takeover cited in table 880F1
UTAH State University (Logan)
Brokerage dispute review declined 10-11, 774A3
UTE Indians—*See INDIANS, American*

1978

UTAH
Legislature schedule rptd 14G3
'67, '77 sales-tax rates rptd 1-5, 15F3
Mondale tours Westn states 1-9—1-13, 34E1, F1
State govt tax revenue table 1-9, 84E2
Wilderness area clears Cong 2-9, 109D2; 2-24, 218A2
Judge Willis dies 3-4, 252C3
Curtiss-Wright Kennecott-purchase suit filed 3-21, 402F1
Amtrak Salt Lake City route cut proposed 5-8, 366E1
'77 prison populatn rptd down 6-3, 440D1
Hughes ex-aide indicted on drug chrgs 6-6, 459A2
Mormons end ban on black priests 6-9, 480D3
Salt Lake widow, 6 children die in plunge 8-3, 685C3
Hughes ex-aide cleared on drug chrgs 9-21, 1011A1
Mormons open prayer rites to women 10-7, 907A2
Election results 11-7: cong 848D3, 852C3, 856F1; state 897C3
Carter gets Mormon award 11-27, 915C1
Nev A-test claims filed 12-21, 1011G3
UTAH Development Co.—*See under GENERAL Electric*
UTAH-Idaho Sugar Co.
Trust chrgs settled 6-12, 511C1
UTAH International Inc.—*See GENERAL Electric*
UTELY, Freda
Dies 1-21, 96F3
UTICA, N. Y.—*See NEW York State*

1979

UTAH
Legislature schedule rptd 5F3
Green River Basin oil find cited 1-5, 17G1
Mormon siege ends in shooting 1-18, 94B1
Abortn bill OKd by House 2-16, 315F1
4 acquitted in polygamist's '77 death 3-20, 240A2
'63 land mines destroyed 3-27, 307C3
US Steel vows Provo plant cleanup 5-22, 385E2
Siamese twins separated 5-30, 527F2; leave hosp 7-17, 656C2
Bundy gets death penalty in Fla 7-31, 604E2, G2
MX 'racetrack' deployment sites considered 9-7, 677G3
Ex-Rep Murdock dies 9-15, 756C3
'78 per capita income rptd 9-16, 746G2
PCBs contaminate food 9-17, 704A3, D3
Hallucinogen tested by Army in '64, stockpile rptd 9-24, 727F1
Provo bars Life of Brian action 10-26, 859D2
Ex-Rep Lloyd dies 12-15, 1008C3
Atomic Energy
A-test cancer link rptd ignored by US 1-8, 17B2
St George A-cancer apology asked 1-13, 91C1
'50s sheep A-deaths, child cancer rates rptd 2-14, 112F1-C2
Film stars' deaths tied to '53 A-test 8-4, 630C1
'50s fallout, SAT decline linked 9-17, 747C2
Sports
NBA Jazz move to Salt Lake City OKd 6-8, 527B1
UTAH, University of (Salt Lake City)
NCAA basketball tourn results 3-26, 238G2

1980

UTAH
Westn Pacific RR sale set 1-24, 131C2
Influenza outbreak rptd 2-15, 158C3
Abortn parental notificatn case accepted by Sup Ct 2-25, 187G3
MX deploymt rptd chngd 5-6, 369E2
Land-grant exchng ban upheld by US Sup Ct 5-19, 440A2
US Steel OKs Provo plant pollutn controls 10-16, 825A2
MX sites chosen 11-18, 897A1
Alton field mining OKd 12-16, 987C2
Crime & Civil Disorders
NBA player arrested for sex abuse, drug possessn 1-2; sentncd 6-4, 656G1
Polygamist convicted of murder 5-28, sentenced 6-2, 502A3
Politics & Government—*See also other appropriate subheads in this section*
Legislature schedule rptd 18F1
State of State message 1-14, 270G1
ACU '79 voting survey rptd 1-18, 53C3
GOP pres delegate picked 6-28, 506A2
Sen primary results 9-9, 700A3
Election results 11-4: pres 838D1, 839A1, G3; cong 840D3, 844C3, 845B3, 846F1, 852C1; state 845E3, 847D1, G2
'80 census rptd, reapportmt seen 12-31, 983G1
UTAH, University of (Salt Lake City)
2d in NCAA skiing 3-8, 470B1
UTAH State University (Logan)
Blake wins NCAA golf title 5-31, 714F3

1976

UTILITIES, Public—*See also ATOMIC Energy, ELECTRIC Light & Power; GAS, Natural; company names*
'77 budget tax proposal 1-21, 62C2
Ford urges regulatory reform 5-13, 346G3
Sup Ct rules on FPC bias powers 5-19, 393F2
Sup Ct backs FPC rate regulatn 6-7, 435F1
FPC gas rate hike challngd 7-28, modified 8-9, 635G2
Eased clean-air rules OKd 8-2, 570A3
Indl output index revised 9-16, 709E1
Firms effective tax rate cited 10-14, 847C2
FPC gas rate hike impact cited 10-20, 868D2

1977

UTILITIES, Public—*See also ATOMIC Energy; ELECTRIC Light & Power; GAS, Natural; company names*
Dec '76 indl output rptd 1-17, 92G3; **for subsequent data, see 'Statistics' under BUSINESS**
Stock prices hit 3-yr high 1-24, 54E3
Carter urges conservatn 2-2, 75E1
'76 wages rptd up 3-3, 154E2
Westinghouse, 3 utilities settle 3-3, 177B2; 3-20, 252G1-B2
Carter energy plan 4-20, 290A2; fact sheet 291G1, G3, 292D1, G1-C2, 293B1-A2
Carter energy plan reactn 4-24, 320A1
'75 Fed Reserve actns scored 5-24, 406G3
Sen amends '70 clean-air bill 6-10, 461D1
House OKs Carter energy pkg 8-5, 609G3
2d ¼ wage gains rptd 8-31, 704A2
Sen OKs conservatn bill 9-13, 703E1
Energy tax bill clears Sen 10-31, 832F1, C3
Ore voters rejct bond issue 11-8, 879A2
Boston Ed rate rise let stand 11-14, 878D3

1978

UTILITIES, Public—*See also ATOMIC Energy; ELECTRIC Light & Power; company names*
Coal strike threatens 9-state area 2-10—2-16; Ind, W Va order cutbacks 2-13, 104C1, E3
EPA sulfur dioxide rules for Ohio upheld 2-13, 109B2
Energy bill status rptd 4-21, 305G1, A2
1st ¼ '77, '78 profits rptd down 4-27, 403E2
Customer hearings backed by Sup Ct 5-1, 364A1
Denver utility settles FTC credit chrg 5-3, 434G1
ICC rail rate rules backed by Appeals Ct 5-5, 434B1
Coal strike billing probe set 5-10, 366E3
Dec '76-Mar '78 rate hikes rptd 5-15, 367B1
Calif residual fuel oil exports set 6-15, 470D3
EPA denies Ohio sulfur dioxide rule moratorium 7-6, 513E1
Carter energy program cited 7-18, 550C1
EPA proposes coal-fired plant scrubber installatns 9-11, 703F1
7 indicted in Fla pricing scheme 9-14, 718G2-C3
'77 consumer bills rptd up 9-17, 718C3
Productivity decline cited 10-4, 790D1
Carter energy bill clears Cong 10-15, 786B2, D2, 787E1, D2; Carter signs 11-9, 873A1
Energy Dept fuel rules unveiled 11-15, 919F3-920B1
Calif refund cases refused by US Sup Ct 12-11, 981D1
OPEC oil price hike to raise '79, '80 rates 12-19, 978D2
Industrial Production Index—*See BUSINESS—Statistics*

1979

UTILITIES, Public
Ohio EPA sulphur-dioxide emissns case refused by US Sup Ct 1-15, 32B1
Gulf States to buy Central La Energy 2-12, 132G1
Cleveland bond issue ban declined by Sup Ct 2-21, 128B3
Price guidelines revised 3-16, 264G2, B3
EPA upheld re Ohio coal use 5-7, 351C1
Coal-use rules issued 5-25, 403G2-404B1
Carter 6-pt energy plan stresses oil use cut, shift to coal 7-15, 7-16, 532D2, 534C1
Westchester rejcts Con Ed takeover 11-6, 846F3
NYS ad ban, policy statemt cases accepted by Sup Ct 11-26, 919A3
Industrial Production Index—*See BUSINESS & Industry—Statistics*

1980

UTILITIES, Public
W Va State of State message 1-9, 484D2
Carter State of Union proposal 1-21, 43D3
Kennedy urges shift to coal 2-2, 91E1; 'basic speech' excerpt 3-10, 184F2
Fscl '79 tax revenue rptd 2-20, 307A3
Carter seeks more coal use 3-6, 169A3
Connally 'basic speech' excerpts 3-7, 184F2
Free speech upheld by Sup Ct 6-20, 555F1-C2
GPU asks 3 Mile I cleanup aid, revises estimates 8-9, 649A3
New scenic area air rules issued 11-25, 898C2
GPU voluntary aid weighed 11-28, Phila Electric backs optn 12-10, 961E1
Calif desert plan issued 12-22, 987B1

1976

UTRILLA, Ricardo
Testifies re torture rpt 6-1, 501B2
UTRILLO, Maurice (1883-1955)
Works donated 1-31, 124F2
UTSONOMIYA, Tokuma
Quits parlt, LDP 10-13, 838D3
UZBEK Soviet Socialist Republic—*See 'Republics' under USSR*
UZZAN, Aharon
Abstains on Arab com formation 5-23, 370E1

1977

UTOMO, Tirto
Rptd under arrest 4-9, 304B3
UTTING, Gerald
Arrested 6-22, sees Amin 7-10, 600A3
Fails to form govt 12-8, van Agt Cabt sworn 12-19, 985A3

1978

UTOPIA, Inc. (play)
Opens 12-4, 1031C3
UV Industries Inc.
Reliance Elec to buy Fed Pacific Elec 12-18, 1005A2
UYTTERHOEVEN, Pierre
Replay released 7-10, 970F2
UZBEK Soviet Socialist Republic—*See USSR—Republics*

1979

UTILITY Workers Union of America (AFL-CIO)
Job-testing data disclosure reversed by Sup Ct 3-5, 184A3
UTTER Glory of Morrissey Hall, The (play)
Opens 5-13, 712B3
UTUKA, Lt. Gen. E. K.
Executed 6-16, 488D3
UV Industries Inc.
Bd votes to liquidate 1-18, 131F3
Tenneco seeks assets 7-23, 770B3
Sharon Steel buys assets 11-26, 986C2
UZBEK Soviet Socialist Republic—*See USSR-Republics*

1980

UUDMAE, Jaak
Olympic medal win disputed 7-25, 589E3, 623G3
UV Industries Inc.
Sharon Steel deal final; Reliance suits cited 9-26, 746B2

V

1976

VAARTEN, Michel
Wins Olympic medal 7-19, 574B2
VACCA, Roberto
Freed 12-30, 996E3

1977

VA—*See U.S. GOVERNMENT—VETERANS Adminstration*

1978

VA—*See U.S. GOVERNMENT—VETERANS Administration*
VACCA, J. Joseph
Protests Meany remarks 8-10, 624B3

1979

VA—*See U.S. GOVERNMENT-VETERANS Administration*

1980

VA (Veterans Administration)—*See under U.S. GOVERNMENT*

1976

VACCINES—*See 'Diseases' under MEDICINE*
VACULIC, Ludvic
CIA-RFE link chrgd 3-10, 289G2
VADORA, Lt. Gen. Julio
Denies rights abuse 10-12, 814B2
VAEAENAENEN, Marjatta
Sworn Finnish educ min 9-29, 750D3
VAEYRYNEN, Paavo
Sworn Finnish labor min 9-29, 750D3
VAEZ-Zaden, Parviz
Slain 12-23, 1012F3
VAIL, Colo.—*See COLORADO*
VAILLANCOURT, Michel
Wins Olympic medal 7-27, 574D2
VALDERRAMA, Nicasio
On S Africa riot deaths 6-23, 447C2
VALDEZ, Alaska—*See ALASKA*
VALDEZ, Patricio
Forced to leave Colombia, chrgs harassmt 1-28, 118A3
VALENCIA, Teodoro
Scores forgn newsmen 10-22, 855A2
VALENZI, Maurizio
Quits Naples post 5-8, 366B1
VALERIANI, Richard
Pres debate panelist 10-6, 740G2
VALERIE, Robert
Testifies at Saxe trial 9-29, 816D2
VALIUM—*See NARCOTICS & Dangerous Drugs*
VALLANCE, Jennie A.
Resigns from Army 6-29, 484E2
VALLE, Inger Louise
Norway justice min 1-12, 30A2
VALLEY Forge, Pa.—*See PENNSYLVANIA*
VALLEY Forge Military Academy
Milton Baker dies 8-7, 892F2

Van AGT, Andreas
Scored re Menten's escape 11-18, 1007D2

VANCE, Cyrus R.
Biog data 916E2
Briefs Carter on defns 7-26, 551D1
Carter campaign donatn rptd 10-22, 939B1
Confers with Carter 11-30—12-1, 898B3
Carter names secy of state 12-3, 916C1
Sees Kissinger 12-6, 916D2
Andreotti visits 12-7, 197F1
Gets rpt on Latin Amer 12-14, 974D3
Richard sees 12-21, 974C2
Names Christopher dep secy 12-31, 978E3

1977

VACCINES—*See MEDICINE—Diseases*
VACULIK, Ludvik
Austria offers asylum 1-25; refuses 1-28, 82C3
VAJIRALONGKORN, Crown Prince (Thailand)
Rebels ambush 2-13, 138E1
VAJPAYEE, Atal Behari
Indian foreign min 3-26, 240A1
VALDES, Rodrigo
Monzon decisions 7-30, 827G3
Decisns Briscoe for middleweight title 11-5, 970B3
'77 boxing champion 12-17, 970A2, A3
VALDEZ Palacio, Gen. Arturo (ret.)
Expelled to Mexico 1-8, 46A3
VALENCIA Tovar, Gen. Alvaro
Pres bid launched 9-16, 727B2
VALENTINE, Bobby
Traded to Mets 6-15, 644F2
VALENTINE 2nd, Henry L.
Elected Richmond v mayor 3-8, 252E3
VALENTINO (Valentino Garavani)
Fall fashions rptd 7-29, 1022D1
VALENZUELA Acebal, Rene
Canada expels 1-12, 42F3
VALERA, Fernando
Sees end of Spain exile govt 3-18, 242B3
Dissolves exile govt 6-21, 507F1
VALES, Cita
Capture rptd 6-19, 522E2
VALQUI, Camilo
Expulsion rptd 1-14, 46C3
VALSIC, Marc
Pleads guilty 3-2, sentncd 5-12, 451B3

Van AGT, Andreas
Refuses to form govt 7-16, 656E1
Asked to form govt 12-8; announces Cabt 12-15, sworn 12-19, 985A3, 986A1
Van ARDENNE, Gijsbert
Named Dutch econ min 12-19, 986B1
Van BOVEN, Theodoor
UN Human Rights Comm dir 1-28, 140G3

VANCE, Cyrus Roberts
Confrmatn hearings 1-11, 18D2; confrmd 1-20, 34A1, C3
Clarifies human rights policy 1-31, 105F1, 117D1
Testifies on human rights, forgn aid link 2-24; forgn reactn 2-25—3-1, 142D1, B2
Rpts personal finances 2-25, 148E1
Defends CIA paymts 2-27, 151C2
Backs forgn aid rights amendmt 3-23, 211A1
Proposes illegal alien plan 4-27, 370C2
Denies Pak plot 4-28, 349B2
Outlines human rights stand 4-30, 338C2
At N-S talks 5-30, $1 bln aid plan backed 6-30, 437E2
Turner given new powers 8-4, 610B3
Sees NZ prime min 11-9—11-10, 925E3
With Carter on world tour 12-29, 1000E3
Africa
Urges Vorster pressure Smith 1-20, 29B1
On Rhodesia setlmt, chrome sanctns 1-31, 72E3
Vs Angola forgn interventn 1-31, 105F1
Young rpts on Africa trip 2-13, 106A1
US to cut aid to Ethiopia 2-24, 142D1
Sees Carter on Amin exit bar 2-25, lauds end 3-1, 141C1, B2
On Zaire attack, US aid 3-16, 207D3
Urges S Africa apartheid end 7-1, 535B3
Sees Owen re Rhodesia 7-23, 581A3
Sees Owen, new Rhodesia plan set 8-12, 661E1
Sees Nyerere in UK 8-13, 624D1
Sees Nkomo, UK-US const plan rejctd 8-15, 624E1
Sees Obasanjo 10-11, 797A2
Sees Young on S Africa sanctns 10-24, 851D3
Rpts S Africa attache to leave 11-2, 852D1

1978

Postal pact revised 9-15, 766A2
Ousted as union pres 10-10, 766D2
VACHON, Rogatien
NHL compensatn clause ruled illegal 9-18, 990E3
VADER, Artur Pavlovich
Dies 5-26, 440F3
VADORA, Gen. Julio Cesar
Replaced as Uruguay army chief 3-2, 292D1
VAIL, Colo.—*See COLORADO*
VAIRA, Peter A.
Named Phila US atty 3-23, 243C3
VAJPAYEE, Atal Bihari
In Pak talks 2-6—2-7, 112G3
In Sovt project agrmt 3-1—3-6, 169C1
Regrets Pak-US jet deal, US denies sale 10-6; assures Pak on UK-French jet sale 10-16, 797B1
VALBERG, Birgitta
Summer Paradise released 3-11, 620A1
VALDES Hilario, Lt. Gen. Rafael
Sworn DR armed forces min, army staff chief 8-16, 648C2, E2
VALDES, Rodrigo
Corro decisns for middlewgt title 4-22, 379F1
Corro decisns 11-11, 969F1
VALDOSTA, Ga.—*See GEORGIA*
VALENCIA Tovar, Gen. Alvaro (ret.)
Pres bid rptdly worries Liberals 5-28, 413F2, G2
4th in pres vote 6-4, 443D2
VALENTI, Jack
Denies film industry probes 3-2, 251G2
VALENTINE, Ellis
Wins Golden Glove Award 11-21, 928B3
VALENTINO (Valentino Garavani)
'78 high chic fashion rptd 8-4—8-11, 10-27—11-3, 1029D2
VALENTINO, Rudolph (1895-1926)
1st wife dies 8-16, 708A2
VALERIO, Giorgio
Indicted 4-3, 330D3
VALIUM—*See NARCOTICS*
VALLARINO, Joaquin
Scores DeConcini reservatn 4-11, 255D3
VALLEJO, Jesus
Colombia econ dvpt min 8-7, 629D3
VALLI, Frankie
Grease on best-seller list 8-2, 620E1; 9-6, 708E1
VALME, Col. Jean
Haiti police chief 9-15, 777A2
VALPROATE—*See MEDICINE—Drugs*
Van AGT, Andreas (Dutch premier)
Presents policy speech to parlt 1-16, 90E2-3
Dutch OK Brazil uranium sales 2-1, 169E2
Neutron bomb policy disputed 2-24—3-8, defns min resigns 3-4, 169F1, B2
On Moluccan-held bldg assault 3-14, 192B1
Party gains in local electns 3-29, 247A3
Bomb defused in Hague 5-11, 454E3
Party gains in local electns 5-31, 454A3
Bars more Brazil uranium talks 6-28, parlt backs sale 6-30; govt crisis averted 7-1, 575A1
Backs Shcharansky 7-11, 543C1
VANCE, Charles Frederick
Engagemt to Susan Ford announced 10-17, 844C3

VANCE, Cyrus Roberts
In India with Carter 1-2, 2A1
Addresses govs on trade 2-27, 145C1
Asks A-weapons material ban 4-3, 277B2
Vows A-weapon restraint 6-12, 445F1
Outlines forgn policy, asserts role as Carter rep 6-19, 6-20; Carter stresses unified Admin stand 6-20, 6-23, 6-26, 487D1, 490E2
At Carter mtg on security leaks 7-11, 524G2
At ASEAN econ talks 8-3—8-4, 603C3
'76 Vesco bid rptd rejctd 9-11, 720A1
India warns on Pak jet sale 10-6, 797C1
US to admit Indochina refugees 11-17, 11-28, 933D1
Carter rptd critical of pol intellignc 11-25, 917C1
Africa
Rpts USSR vow vs Somalia invasn 2-10, 99A3
At Namibia mtg 2-11—2-12, sees progress 2-13, 113G3
Sees Owen, Rhodesia pact shortcomings cited 3-8, 193D1
Urges Patriotic Front joint internal pact talks 3-11, 193C1
Sees Dobrynin on USSR troops in Ethiopia 3-12; US modifies statemt on USSR vow 3-15, 215F3
Warns Liberia on oil tankers 4-3, 234E1
Seeks new Rhodesia talks 4-13—4-17, 290D2-E3
Cuba Zaire role proof rptd 5-26, 418B2
Disputes Gromyko on Zaire 5-27, 422G1-A2
On Sovt, Cuba role, US policy 6-19, 490D3
Outlines US policy 6-20, Tass rebuts 6-22, 487C1-D3
Rhodesia sanctns end barred 7-20, 561D1
Namibia plan OKd by UN 7-27, 562D1

1979

VACCINES—*See MEDICINE–Drugs*
VACHON, Rogatien
NHL reserve clause upheld 5-22, 448F1
VADNAIS, Carol
Montreal wins Stanley Cup 5-21, 447F3
VAIL, Steven A.
Scavenger Hunt released 12-25, 1008E1
VAIVE, Rick
WHA penalty minutes ldr 4-18, 355G2
VAJPAYEE, Atal Bihari
Ends China trip 2-18, rpts ties unaffected 2-21, 123D1
VAKY, Viron P.
Sees Andean natns on Nicaragua 7-4–7-5, 504B1
El Salvador visit rptd 8-2, 652C2
Urges early electns in El Salvador 9-14, 707F1
VALDARNINI, A.
Divine Nymph released 10-12, 1007C3
VALDES Hilario, Lt. Gen. Rafael Adriano
Rpts army plot foiled 9-26, 751D3
VALDEZ, Abelardo Lopez
Named chief of protocol 9-13, 700B3
Confirmed 11-5, 965B1
VALDEZ, Daniel
Zoot Suit opens 3-25, 712G3
VALDEZ, Julio
Serrano decisns 2-18, 412D3
VALDEZ, Luis
Zoot Suit opens 3-25, 712G3
VALDOSTA, Ga.—*See GEORGIA*
VALENCE, Claude
Acquitted re Marion kidnap 1-2, 6A2
VALENCE, Jeanne
Marion kidnap chrgs rptd suspended 1-2, 6C2
VALENTINE, Carl
Whitecaps win NASL title 9-8, 775A3
VALENZUELA Moreno, Col. Ojeda
Arrested 9-25, plot exposed 9-26, 751F3
VALERO, Luciano
Venez agri min 3-10, 192C3
VALIUM—*See NARCOTICS & Dangerous Drugs*
VALLE, Freddy
Simpson Street opens 3-5, 292A3
VALLE, Marc
Ties death of shah's nephew to Iran secret police 12-8, 935E1
VALLEJO, Major Arturo
On Nicaragua executns 6-21, 461B3
VALLEJO, Cesar (1895-1938)
Natl Book Awards rptd 4-23, 356B2
VALLES, Brig. Gen. Lorenzo Gonzales
Assassinated 9-23, 754G1
VALLONE, Raf
Almost Perfect Affair released 4-26, 528C1
VALOK, Marko
Quits as Fury coach 9-6, 1004E2
Van AARDENNE, Gysbert
Announces energy program 9-19, 731B1
Van AGT, Andreas (Dutch premier)
Parlt rejects NATO missile plan 12-6, 938C2
Carter sees, urges NATO missile plan OK 12-7, 938E1
Survives confidence vote on NATO missiles 12-20, 959E2
VanANDEL, Jay
Amway price-fixing end ordrd 5-23, 985F3
VANCE (U.S. warship)
Arnheiter libel cases declined by Sup Ct 10-29, 884G1
VANCE, Charles Frederick
Marries Susan Ford 2-10, 176B1
VANCE, Cyrus Roberts
At Rockefeller funeral 2-2, 104D2
Defends 'new diplomacy' 5-1, 347F1-B2
In Australia 7-4, 501A1
Urges oral Cabt resignatns 7-17, 529F1
Praises McHenry UN apptmt 8-31, 660F3
Pak A-talks held 10-17–10-18, 794B2
On A-blast mystery 10-26, 824F3
At Park funeral 11-3, 843F3
Agee passport revoked 12-22, 991D2
Africa
Rhodesia peace prospects seen dim 2-3, 98D3
Calls Rhodesia sanctns end 'premature' 4-26, 332A2
Sees Carrington re Zimbabwe Rhodesia 5-21–5-23, 393E2
Opposes Zimbabwe trade tie 6-12, 435B1
Zimbabwe recognitn terms agreed with Australia 7-4, 501A1
Muzorewa in US talks 7-10, 546E2
Meets Guinea pres 8-8, 796C3
UK protest re Zimbabwe conf rptd 9-20, 718A2
Morocco arms sale rptd opposed 10-22, 804A1
Canada
Fishing talks effort asked 1-5, 37B1
Fish pact threatened 9-4, 667C2

1980

VACCINES—*See MEDICINE--Drugs & Health-Care Products*
VACUUM Society, American
USSR barred from conf 2-20—2-22, 135G1
VADIM, Roger
Night Games released 4-11, 416C3
VAGNOZZI, Cardinal Egidio
Dies 12-26, 1004E3
VAIRA, Peter F.
Rptr cited for Abscam silence 7-10, 554B2
VAJPAYEE, Atal Bihari
Heads new Hindu party 4-6, 275D2
VALDEMAR, Carlos
Guyana released 1-25, 216F2
VALDEZ, Ruben (Cobra)
Gomez KOs 2-3, 320B3
VALENCIA, Jorge
Freed 3-30, 253E2
VALENTE, Maurice R.
Becomes RCA pres 1-1, fired 6-18, 582G1
VALENTI, Jack
Copyright royalty fee divisn praised 7-29, 640G2
VALENTINE, Alan
Dies 7-14, 608E3
VALENTINE, Carmen
Arrested 4-4, 308G3
Convicted 7-30, 601D1
Indicted 12-10, 963F3*
VALIUM—*See NARCOTICS*
VALLADARES, Ramon
Slain 10-26, 829C2
VALLANZASCA, Renato
Escapes jail, recaptured 4-28, 353D1
VALLEY Lea Dairies
Falcones indicted 7-31; Mafia, pizza indus ties probed 8-24, 714A2
VAN, Bobby (Robert King)
Dies 7-31, 608F3
VAN ITAILIE, Jean-Claude
Sea Gull opens 11-11, 892E3
VAN VLECK, John
Dies 10-27, 876E3

Van AGT, Andreas (dutch premier)
Andriessen quits Cabt 2-21, 173C3
Censure vote fails 6-27, 499F1
VANAUKEN, Sheldon
Severe Mercy wins Amer Book Award 5-1, 692F2
VAN BEVEREN, Jan
Cosmos win NASL title 9-21, 770G1, E2
VAN BOVEN, Theodoor
UN comm starts shah probe 2-21, 122E1

VANCE, Cyrus Roberts
US rejoins ILO 2-18, 124G3
On forgn policy goals 3-27, 243C2
Resigns 4-28, Muskie succeeds 4-29, 323G1
Muskie confrmd 5-7, sworn 5-8, 343D1
Carter sees 'stronger' Muskie role 5-9, 367D1
Resumes NY law practice 6-11, 471G1
Signed oaths re leaks 7-16—7-17, 549A2
Elected US Steel dir 8-7, 702C1
Afghanistan—*See 'Soviet-Afghan Issue' below*
Africa
Senghor in US 4-4—4-6, 336A3
Cambodia
Sihanouk in DC 2-22, 141E2

1976

1977

China
Backs full US-China ties 6-29, Taiwan vs stand 7-2, 513F3
Newsmen briefed on visit 8-18—8-19, 645A2
Visits, seeks normal ties 8-22—8-25, 645A1-A2
Briefs Japan on trip 8-26, returns to 8-27; briefs Carter, sees no chng in ties 664C2
Teng: visit set back ties 9-6, 686D3
Europe
Sees Kreisky in US 3-14, 425E1
Sees Schmidt, Callaghan, Giscard on arms proposals, Concorde 3-31—4-2; US reactn 3-31—4-4, 247A1, 268A3, 368B2
Giscard scores US talks with left 4-2, 255B2
At London econ summit 5-5—5-8, on paymts lending fund 5-8, 357B2, 359G2
At NATO mins closed sessn 5-11, 359G3
In Paris for OECD mtg 6-23; Giscard briefs on Brezhnev visit 6-24, 495A2
Sees UK forgn secy re Rhodesia 7-23, 581A3; 8-12, 661E1
Reassures NATO on SALT 12-8—12-9, 956F3
Latin America
Latins back Panama Canal demands 1-18, 46F1
For Cuba talks 2-3, 3-4, 180D2, 181A1
US to cut aid to Argentina, Uruguay 2-24, 142D1
Sees Cuba exiles 2-25, Castro scores 2-26—2-27, 180B3, F3
Uruguay rights pressure rptd 2-25, 351C3
Links US aid, Brazil A-safeguards 3-1, 190C1
Nicaragua aid cutoff plea rptd 3-4, 168F2
Presses Bonn on Brazil A-pact 3-31, 268A3
Wife on Latin tour 5-30—6-12, 454E1
Stresses rights, OAS reform 6-14—6-15, 494C1
Greets Venez pres 6-28, 546E1
Testifies at Sen Canal pact hearings 9-26, 754F2, B3
Brazil visit, uranium sale set 11-16, 896B1
Visits Argentina, Brazil, Venez 11-20—11-23, Latin policy examined 11-24, 912D2-913C1
Jamaica prime min visits 12-16, 1019G1
Middle East
Plans Mideast tour 1-24, 51G3
In Israel, 5 Arab states 2-15—2-21, 121A1-122C1, 124D2
PLO, Jordan OK link 2-22—2-23, 122D1
Defends Hussein CIA paymts 2-27, 151C2
Backs Arab boycott curb, vs Sen bills 2-28, 166A3
Clarifies Carter views 3-7, 3-9, 165D1, 166A1
Meets 4 Arab ambs, assures on US policy 3-12, 187C3
Carter greets PLO rep at UN fete 3-17, 185A2
Sees Israel amb on Rabin resignatn 4-8, 267F2
USSR rpts PLO eases stand on Israel 360F2
Assures Israel on US ties, doubts soft PLO stand 5-11, 360G3
On Israeli electns results 5-18, 378B1
Sees Dinitz, backs Israel on UN resolutns 5-28, 440G1
In Carter conf with US Jews 7-6, 510A1
Carter reaffirms visit 7-20, 549B2
Vs legalizatn of 3 W Bank towns 7-26, 570C1
Visits Egypt 8-1—8-2, Leb 8-3, Syria 8-3—8-4, 588G1-E3
In Jordan 8-5—8-7, Saudi 8-7—8-9, Israel 8-9—8-10; briefs Syria, Jordan, Egypt ldrs 8-11, 605A1-606A1
Briefs Carter on missn 8-14, 623C2
Arafat scores mission 8-30, 663D1

1978

OKs Rhodesia ldrs visas 10-3, sees Smith 10-9, 818E3, 819B1
Sees Botha on Namibia, delivers Carter note 10-16—10-18; asks UN delay deadline 10-19, 819B3
Sees 'cloudy future' 11-25, 925E1
Sees Botha on Namibia 11-27, 988G3
China
Forgn arms sale to China OKd 11-3, 901F3
Sees no China force vs Taiwan 12-17, 973D2
15 congressmen sue vs Taiwan tie cut 12-22; Admin defends 12-27, 995D2
Europe
Hungary gets St Stephen crown 1-6, 7G1
In Turkey 1-20—1-21, US peace role discouraged 1-20, 170F2
In Carter, Tito talks 3-8, 194C1
Links Turkey arms aid, Cyprus 3-9; Ecevit scores 3-10, 216C3
Urges Turkish arms embargo end, asks more Greek aid 4-6, 276D2
Reassures NATO on cruise missile 4-24, 297F1
Haig resignatn threat rptd 4-25, 298A3
Sees Turkey arms embargo end, US base reopening 6-28, 587C3
NATO assured re US support 12-9, 954A3
Latin America
In 4 US cities re Canal pacts 1-11—1-13, 58A2
State Dept rpt on Argentine pol prisoners cited 2-13, 207F3
Balaguer affirms DR electn pledge 5-18, 372C1
Cuba Zaire role proof rptd 5-26, 418B2
On Cuba Africa role, US Africa policy 6-19, 490D3
At DR pres inaugural 8-16, 648C1, B2
Nicaragua aid cutoff asked by 86 Congressmen 10-13, 839G2
Cuba exiles ask faster ex-prisoner screening 11-13, 880A3
Middle East
Carter airs Palestinian plan 1-6, 10F2
Delays departure for talks 1-14, leaves 1-15, 26A1
At Egypt-Israel pol talks 1-17—1-18, 25B1
Asks Sadat renew Israel talks 1-18, 25G2
Meets Begin on talks breakdown 1-19, 25D2
Sadat vs talk renewal 1-20, 41C1, G1
Meets Egypt forgn min 2-4, 77B2
Vs Sinai setlmts 2-9; Israel protests 2-12, 2-13, 97E2-98F1
Announces jet sale to Egypt, Israel, Saudi 2-14, 97C1
Meets Dayan 2-16, 139G1
Says Saudi jet transfers barred 2-21, 139E1
Says jet sale to Egypt, Saudi, Israel pkg deal 2-24, 139B1
Denies US siding in Egypt-Cyprus feud 2-26, 138A3
Rpts US-Israel impasse 3-22, 199C1
Hints Israel broke US arms law in Leb invasn, Rep Rosenthal scores 4-5, 236C2, E2
On Israel use of cluster bombs in Leb 4-6, 257A1
Meets Dayan on Egypt talks renewal 4-26—4-27, 299D2
Meets Begin 5-1, 339B2
Vows more Israel F-15 sales 5-9, 357D1
Reassures jet sale opponents 5-15—5-16, 358B1
Israel OKs forgn mins mtg 7-9, 521B1

1979

China
Taiwan arms policy cited 1-12, 27A2
Addresses businessmen on US ties impact 1-15, Admin controversy denied 1-16, 27A2, B3
Greets Teng 1-28, 66B2
Signs consulate pact 1-31, 65C1
Reaffirms US arms ban 10-3, 789E1
Europe
Sees Owen re Rhodesia 2-2–2-3, 98D3
Sees Carrington re Zimbabwe Rhodesia 5-21–5-23, 393E2
Urges common NATO policy re SALT III 5-30, 415E3
Reaffirms budget hike vow to NATO 7-30, 644A1
Swedish envoy disappearance case reopened 8-4, 690F2
Meets Suarez 8-10, 654D2
UK protest re Zimbabwe conf rptd 9-20, 718A2
Missn on Iran set, econ moves sought 12-5, 913C2
Denmark backs 6-mo NATO missile delay 12-7, 938G1
In W Eur, seeks econ sanctns vs Iran 12-10–12-11, 933B2
Indochina
Meets Sihanouk, offers US stay 1-18, 69B1
Asks ASEAN OK refugee asylum 7-2, 495D2
At ANZUS conf, backs refugee exit 7-4–7-5, 495F2
Viets: proposed talks on ties 8-11, 607G2
Iran
Says shah to form regency cncl, leave; asks Bakhtiar support 1-11, 12E1, G1
Shah asked to stay out of US 4-19, 298A1
Urges calm re emb takeover 11-8, 842E2
Meets Waldheim, UN Cncl mtg barred 11-14, 862B1
Eur missn set, econ moves sought 12-5, 913C2
Scores USSR mil 'blackmail' chrg 12-5, 913G2
Seeks Eur, Japan econ sanctns 12-10–12-11, 933B2
Warns USSR vs UN sanctns veto 12-22, 974B3
Japan
Sees Okita in Paris, seeks econ sanctns vs Iran 12-10, 933C2
Latin America
State Dept rpt finds Guyana cult probe neglect 5-3, 335D3
40 congressmen protest IMF-Nicaragua loan 5-10, 373A1
Asks OAS to mediate in Nicaragua, urges Somoza seek pol solutn 6-13, 446F3
Urges Somoza ouster, OAS peace force for Nicaragua 6-21, 460D3
Habib retiremt end rptd 7-6, 960D3
At Ecuador pres inaugural 8-10, 613D2, 354D2
USSR troops in Cuba confrmd 8-31, 657D1; Carter statemt 9-7; sees Sovt offcl 9-10, 9-12, 673D1-G2
Sees Sovt ldrs re Cuba troop issue 9-14–9-30, 738A2
Addresses OAS Assemb 10-23, 824A2
Warns Bolivia vs coup 10-23, 833E1
Middle East—*See also 'Iran' above*
Seeks peace talk renewal 1-11, 51A2
Clears Brown W Bank visit 2-13, 143A3
In Khalil, Dayan prelim pact talks 2-22–2-25; Israel Cabt, parlt briefed 2-26–2-28, 142F2, B3
Gets Egypt plan on Israel pact 3-8, 157E1
Meets Begin, Sinai oil turnover OKd 3-24, 221F2
Signs separate Israel-US agrmt 3-26, Egypt scores 3-28, 221B1, 222C1
Defends PLO offcl's visit 4-11, 319F2; Begin protests 5-2, 320B1
Scranton vs amb post 296A1
Says US-Saudi ties worsen 5-8, 341B2
US-Saudi talks on Egypt jet funding rptd 5-8, 341D2
Meets Sadat in Alexandria 5-24, Israel delegatn head in Jerusalem 5-25, 394C2
Palestinian autonomy talks open 5-25, 394E1, A2
Meets Begin, Sadat in El Arish, Beersheba 5-27, 394B3
Begin gets note re Leb raid, Syria jet clash 6-27; Begin vows contd raids 6-28, 496A2
Sees Israel amb on UNTSO, US tanks to Jordan; reassures on PLO 7-27, 574F2-A3, 575B1
Hints at Israel arms pact breach in Leb raids 8-7, 592D1
Vows contd Israel support 8-8, 591B2

1980

Iran
Sees no break in crisis 1-8, 1-9, 29B3
To press for sanctns 1-13, 29C1
Vs Kennedy on intl comm 2-13, 109A3
Ties UN comm probe to hostage release 2-27, 137A2
'60 Minutes' segmt pressure rptd 3-6, 239D1
Meets Waldheim on hostages 3-12, 178B1
Asks allied backing in crisis 4-8, 4-9, 257D2-258A1
Sen com asks consultatn on mil acts 4-24, 297C2
Resigns over Iran rescue missn 4-28, 323A2, E2
US ex-amb scores Brzezinski '79 policy 9-6, 694D1
Middle East
Asks Israel delay Hebron setlmt vote 2-17, 218D3
Briefs Israel amb on UN anti-Israel vote 3-1; takes blame, Carter exchng detailed 3-4; Sen com to probe vote 3-5, 163D2-A3, 164B1
Carter takes blame for UN vote reversal 3-8, 179B2
Defends UN vote, disavowal in Cong hearings 3-20, 3-21, 218B2
Vs French stand on PLO 3-31, 260F3
Pakistan
Offers econ, arms aid 1-12, 27A1
Discounts aid offer dismissal 3-6, 165C2
Soviet-Afghan Issue
Threatens Olympic boycott 1-14, 28C2
Vs Clark Persian Gulf warning 2-1, 83D2
France bars meeting 2-8, 106E2
Addresses IOC re boycott 2-9, 107C1
EC offers neutrality plan 2-19, 124A1
Sees Eur allies on policy coordinatn 2-20–2-21, 139G1
Sees Dobrynin 2-29, 165E1
Rebuffs allies on Olympic boycott stand 3-31, 259G3

1976

Van CLEEF & Arpels Inc.
Louis Arpels dies 3-20, 240D3
VANDAMME, Ivo
Wins Olympic medals 7-25, 7-31, 575F3, 576D1
Van DEERLIN, Rep. Lionel (D, Calif.)
Reelected 11-2, 829F1
Van den BERG, Andre
Dutch CO status rptd 2-15, 141B3
VANDENBERG, Arthur H. (1889-1951)
GOP platform text cites 8-18, 609E2
Van den BERG, Sister Maria Francis
Killed 12-5, 1009D2
Van den BERGH, Gen. Hendrik
Denies UK anti-Liberal plot 3-13, 252A3
At Kissinger-Vorster mtg 6-23—6-24, 446C3
To lead Rhodesia delegatn 11-1, 831E3
Van der BYL, Pieter
On Mozambique border closing 3-3, 175A2, 176B1
Confirms guerrilla raids from Zambia 6-10, 427G2
Asks UN inquiry re raid 8-24, 661E2
Shifted in Cabt 9-9, 713E2
On majority rule plan impasse 9-26, 718D2
Rhodesia conf delegate 10-12, 781D2
Replaces Smith at conf 11-3, 843B1
Meets Richard 11-10, 843E1
Interim govt talks open 11-29, 893E1
Vander JAGT, Rep. Guy Adrian (R, Mich.)
Reelected 11-2, 829D4
Van der MERWE, Schalk
S Africa cabt shifted 1-22, 76A2
Van der MERWE, X. P.
Wounded by gunman 7-15, 539F2
VANDERPOOL, Eugene
Identifies Socrates' jail 2-1, 124A3

1977

Sees Dayan, urges Leb restraint 9-19, 713B2, 714B3
Sees Egypt forgn min 9-21, 714D1
Vs Israel peace conditns, meets Dyan 9-26, 733E2
Meets Gromyko 9-30; joint statemt on Geneva 10-1; on Israeli reactn 10-3, 749C2, 750D2; text 750A1
Israel, US OK Geneva plan 10-5, 749C1
On Dayan airing of working paper text 10-11, 769A2
Briefs US Jews on policies 10-26, 831C1
Gets copy of Begin invitatn to Sadat 11-15, 873F1
Scores USSR re Sadat peace moves 12-6, 930E1
In Egypt, Israel, Jordan, Leb, Syria, Saudi re Cairo conf support 12-9—12-14; rpts to Carter 12-15, 953D2-954E2
Denies US backs Begin plan 12-29, 994F3

USSR
On Sakharov statemt 1-27, 1-31, 84A1
Sees Dobrynin on Krimsky, dissidents 2-4, 101G1, B2
Brezhnev on upcoming visit 3-21, 226C1
Arrives USSR 3-26; SALT talks open 3-28, issue groups set 3-29, 225G1
USSR rejcts SALT bids, Geneva talks set 3-30, 225A1
Gromyko scores arms proposals 3-31; comments 4-1, 246E2, 247B1
Sees Dobrynin on SALT 4-7, 4-15, 400C3
Labor offcls denied visas 4-16, 306A3
Plans civil defns talks 5-11, 360A1
OKs SALT framework 5-18—5-20, stresses differences 5-21, 400D2-A3
Denies Sovt dissidt-CIA link 6-6, 436G1
Gromyko mtg delayed 6-15, 530B1
Briefed on Brezhnev-Giscard talks 6-24, 495A2
Gromyko mtg delayed 8-31, cruise missile debate cited 9-11, 751C2
Sees Gromyko on SALT 9-22—9-23, extends '72 pact 9-23, 750B3, D3
Meets Gromyko on Mideast 9-30; joint statemt 10-1, 749C2, 750D2; text 750A1
Warns Dobrynin re Shcharansky 10-31, 955A2
Scores Mideast policy 12-6, 930E1
Reassures NATO on SALT 12-8—12-9, 956F3
Arms sale curbs discussed 12-14—12-16, 996E3

VANCE, Grace (Mrs. Cyrus)
On Latin tour 5-30—6-12, 454E1
VAN Cleef & Arpels Inc.
Arpels indicted 3-3, fined 4-20, 312G2
Van DAM, Philip
Sues Detroit for EPA 5-6, 422E2
Van De KAMP, John
Asks 3d Van Houten trial 9-4, 711F2
Van den BERG, Maria Francis
Confessed killer escapes 1-9, 11G2
Defends Mozambique raid 6-2, 456G2
Van der BYL, Pieter
Warns re Patriotic Front backing 1-12, 11B2
Scores Botswana 1-31, 73E1
Named info, immigratn, tourism min 9-18, 824E3
At Smith-Kaunda mtg 9-25, 810A2
Van der KLAAUW, Christoph
Named Dutch forgn min 12-19, 986A1

1978

At Egypt-Israel forgn min mtg in UK 7-18—7-19, 546C1
Dayan gave new plan on W Bank, Gaza 7-24, 563A2
To go to Israel, Egypt 7-31, to offer no US peace plan 8-1, 582B1, D1
Tells House com of Israel, Egypt visit plan 8-4, 602B2
In Israel 8-6—8-7, Egypt 8-7—8-8, 602A1
Vs new W Bank setlmts, lauds Israel plan cancelatn 8-14, 639C1
In Camp David summit talks 9-7, 673E1
Carter discloses Jordan, Saudi summit missn 9-18, 709E2
In Jordan, Saudi; seeks summit backing 9-20—9-21, 712G3-713A1
Ends summit missn to Jordan, Saudi, Syria 9-22—9-24; briefs Carter 9-25, 731B1
Asks Palestinians join peace talks 9-29, 762E2
Carter reviews Leb crisis 9-30, 745E1
Begin vows aid to Leb Christns 10-8, 762D1
In Egypt-Israel pact talks 10-12—10-18, submits draft plan 10-13, 782E2
Vs Israel setlmt expansn 10-26, 802F2
Meets Begin 11-2, 858A3
Rpts progress in Israel-Egypt pact talks 11-3, 858A3
Israelis vs Egypt pact-W Bank linkage 11-8, 858B3
Egypt seeks change in Israel pact text 11-9, 858C3
Gets new Egypt pact plan 11-9, 892C3
Meets Dayan, Israel-Egypt compromise plan set 11-12, 892G2
Meets Sadat aide on pact impasse 12-2, 930F2
To go to Egypt, Israel re pact impasse 12-5, 930A2
In Egypt, Israel; drafts new plan with Sadat; Israel vs; recalled to US 12-10—12-15, 950C2
Briefs Carter on Egypt, Israel talks; vs Israel rejectn 12-15, 978E3
Meets US Jewish ldrs on Israel-Egypt pact 12-19, 978G3
Meets Israel Egypt mins; talk revival fails 12-24, 997E3

USSR
Rpts USSR vow vs Somalia invasn 2-10, 99A3
Sees Dobrynin on USSR troops in Ethiopia 3-12; US modifies statemt on USSR vow 3-15, 215F3
In Moscow re SALT 4-20—4-23, 297A1
SALT weapon-tech transfer limit rptd 5-1, 423E1
Sees Gromyko on SALT, Zaire role disputed 5-25—5-31, 422C1-C2
Gromyko spy warning cited 6-15, 476G2
Outlines policy; on USSR Africa role, SALT, detente, 6-19, 490B3
Sees reopening of US bases in Turkey 6-28, 587C3
Sees Dobrynin re US rptrs slander chrg, other issues 7-1, 518E2
Cancels offcl trips re Shcharansky 7-8, 542B1
Defends SALT mtg 7-10, 543A3
Young rebuked for US 'pol prisoners' remark 7-12, 7-13, 542D2, D3, E3
Sees Gromyko on SALT 7-12—7-13; delivers Shcharansky trial protest 7-12, sees wife 7-13, 543D2
Warnke sees Gromyko re SALT 9-7—9-8, 747E2
Sees Gromyko on SALT 9-27—9-28, Carter mtg 9-30—10-1, 747F2
At SALT mtg with Gromyko, Brezhnev 10-22—10-23, 803C3-804E1
Rebuts USSR warning vs Iran interventn, reaffirms shah support 11-19, 893F3
Sees better ties, SALT agrmt 11-25, 925B1
Sees Gromyko, SALT pact delayed 12-21—12-23, 995F2

VANDALISM—*See CRIME; country names*
Van DAMME, Robert
Belgian A-plant leak disputed 1-25, 69G3
Van DEERLIN, Rep. Lionel (D, Calif.)
Reelected 11-7, 850C2
Van de KAMP, John
Accuses Columbia Pictures ex-pres 3-31, 251D1
Sets new film indus probe 7-14, 599F2-A3
Van den BERGH, Gen. Hendrik
Named in Info Dept press scandal 11-2, 868A2
Info Dept probers score 12-5, 946G1
Vanden HEUVEL, William
Charges Cambodian cruelty 8-31, 748F1
VANDERBILT University (Nashville, Tenn.)
US-S Africa Davis Cup protests 3-17—3-19, US wins N Amer Zone title 3-19, 251A3-252C1
Vander JAGT, Rep. Guy Adrian (R, Mich.)
Reelected 11-7, 851E1
Van der KERKHOF, Reinier
Argentina wins World Cup 6-25, 520C2
Van der KLAAUW, Christoph
Parlt neutron bomb debate 2-24, defense min resigns 3-4, 169F1
Van der MERWE, Schalk W.
Biko family sues 1-3, 20B3

1979

Scores Young for PLO contact, Israel files protest 8-14, 605B1, A2, D2
Young-PLO mtg controversy 8-18, 8-19, 624F2-A3
Strauss feud on mediator role rptd 8-22, 623D3
Lauds Dayan-PLO backers contacts 9-5, 659C1
Sees Egypt, Israel ldrs; more US aid sought 9-11, 677A2
US, Israel, Egypt Sinai pact set 9-19, 694D1
Urges Leb peace in UN speech 9-24, 741C2
Kennedy anti-shah remarks deplored 12-3, 918D3

USSR
Sees Dobrynin, discuss Viet-Cambodia war 1-5, 11B1
Addresses US businessmen on China ties impact 1-15, Admin controversy denied 1-16, 27A2, B3
Assures on US-China talks 2-1, 65D2
Dissident-spy swap talks rptd 4-27, 317D1
Defends 'new diplomacy' 5-1, 347A2
Backs SALT draft treaty, Dobrynin mtgs cited 5-9, 338D3, 339C1
Urges common NATO policy re SALT III 5-30, 415E3
At SALT II summit 6-15–6-18, 449G1; cited in communique 6-18, 457B1
Backs SALT at Sen com hearings 7-9, 7-10, 510D1, G1
Backs mil budget hike re SALT 7-30, 644A1
Swedish envoy disappearance case reopened 8-4, 690F2
Troops in Cuba confrmd 8-31; testifies 9-5, 657D1, G1; sees Dobrynin 9-10, 9-12, 673D1-G2
Sees Dobrynin, Gromyko re Cuba issue 9-14–9-30, 738A2
Sees Dobrynin, scores Iran stance 12-5, 913G2

VANCE, Vivian
Dies 8-17, 671F3
VANCE v. Bradley
Forgn svc retiremt rule upheld by Sup Ct 2-22, 151B1
VANDALISM—*See under CRIME; country names*
Van den BERGH, Gen. Hendrik
Avoids chrgs re scandal 1-25, 99D2★
Sees Rhoodie re scandal 3-7, passport seized 3-14, 190F3, 191A1, F1
Vanden HEUVEL, William
Warns re US WHO resignatn 5-12, 398A3
VANDERBILT University (Nashville, Tenn.)
Peabody Coll merger OKd 3-19, 209D1
Van der BYL, Pieter Kenyon Fleming-Voltelyn
Zimbabwe transport min 5-30, 393F1
Van der KLAAUW, Christoph
On NATO A-missiles 12-12, 959F1
VANDERMARK, George Jay
Alleged murder in CR rptd 8-20, indicted in Nev 8-23, 851D1, F1
Van der MERWE, Schalk W.
Named S Africa econ min 6-14, 469B3

1980

USSR—*See also 'Soviet-Afghan Issue' above*
On US goals 3-27, 243B3
Urges SALT OK 6-5, 421C3

VANCE v. Terrazas
Case decided by Sup Ct 1-15, 51C2
VANCE v. Universal Amusement Co.
Case decided by Sup Ct 3-18, 226F3
VANDALISM—*See under CRIME*
VAN DEERLIN, Rep. Lionel (D, Calif.)
Cautions on AT&T reorgn 8-20, 648G2
Loses reelectn 11-4, 846F1, 852B2
VAN De KAMP, John
Ends 'Charlie's Angels' fraud probe 12-2, 1002E2
VANDEN HEUVEL, William
Assaulted at UN mtg 4-30, 325G1
On US W Bank deportatn vote 5-8, 340E3
Walks out on Iranian UN speaker 7-25, 572E2
Vs UN vote on Israeli exit 7-29, 572A2
VANDERBILT, Gloria
Drops River House suit 6-12, 639G1
VAN der DUIM, Herbert
Wins world speed skating title 3-2, 470C1
VAN der ELST, Francois
Signs with Cosmos 4-3, 770B3
W Ger wins Eur Soccer Championship 6-22, 771E2
VANDEREYCKEN, Rene
W Ger wins Eur Soccer Championship 6-22, 771E2
VAN der HART, Cor
Cosmos win NASL title 9-21, 770G1
VANDER JAGT, Rep. Guy Adrian (R, Mich.)
Gives GOP conv keynote speech 7-16, 531B3, 534F1
Reelected 11-4, 843F1
Loses as House minority ldr 12-8, 936A2
VAN der LUBBE, Marinus (d. 1934)
Acquitted of Reichstag arson 12-15, 996B3

1976

Van der SPUY, Johannes
S Africa cabt shifted 1-22, 76G1
Van der STOEL, Max
Signs Canada pact 7-6, 496E3
Hails EC parlt vote accord 9-20, 722A1
Vander VEEN, Rep. Richard (D, Mich.)
Loses reelectn 11-2, 823E2
Van ELSEN, Joop
Rptd approached by Lockheed 9-1, 684B2
VANGELAKOS, George
Indicted 6-23, 460B1
Van HELDEN, Hans
Wins Olympic medals 2-11, 2-13, 2-14, 158F3-G3
Van HOLLEN, Christopher
Replaced as Sri Lanka, Maldives amb 5-26, 412A2
Van HOUTEN, Leslie
Granted new trial 8-13, 640B3
VANIDADES (magazine)
Peru renews ban 2-3, 142F3
VANIK, Rep. Charles A. (D, Ohio)
On firms '74, '75 tax paymts 10-2, 847E1-G2
Reelected 11-2, 830B3
Van KEUREN, Paul J.
Not guilty plea cited 11-30, 921D3
VANNEK, Rear Adm. Antonio
To head mil legis comm 4-2, 264B1
VAN Nuys, Calif.—*See CALIFORNIA*
Van WYCK, Col. W. P.
On Pretoria riots 6-21, 447D1
Van ZIJL, Eben
Vs Namibia independnc 8-9, 654B1
Insults conf delegate 10-19, 832G1
VARGA, Laslo
Killed 8-11, 624E3
VARGAS, Armando
On campaign vs Excelsior 7-14, 620B2
VARGAS, Gen. Raul
Chile transport min 3-8, 288F2
VARGAS, Col. Rene
In Ecuador cabt 1-14; vows oil exports hike 1-17, 49A1
Texaco pays back taxes 8-20, 872E1
VARGAS Prieto, Gen. Oscar
Retiremt set 1-2, 55B3
Quits mil, stays controller gen 1-31, 142G2
VARIETY (newspaper)
Dec '75 top-grossing films listed 32G3
'75 top rental films listed 1-7, 32F3
Top-grossing films listed 1-28, 104E3; 2-25, 208G3
Best-selling records listed 1-28, 104F3
Top-grossing films listed 3-31, 240B3
VARLEY, Eric
Leyland loan set 7-21, 556F2
Retains Cabt post 9-10, 694A1
VARON Valencia, Gen. Abraham
Renamed to Cabt post 10-19, 925B1
VASCONEZ, Gen. Gustavo
Scores Duran; loses cabt post, arrested 1-9, 28A2
Gets amnesty 1-28, 363C3
VASSILIEV, Maj. Vladimir
Canada ousts 12-9, 963B1

1977

Van der STEE, Alphons
Dutch Agri, fisheries min 12-19, 985F3, 986B1
Van der STOEL, Max
In Czechoslovakia 2-28—3-2; sees Patocka 3-1, 220G2
Van der VALK, Joop
Addresses Helsinki review conf 10-4, 752A2
Vander VEEN, Rep. Richard F. (D, Mich.)
Spec interest gifts rptd 3-7, 232C3
VANDIVER, Ernest
Bell confrmatn hearings 1-11—1-18, 34E1
Van DUNEM, Jose
Purged 5-21, rebelln backs 5-27, 424F1
Capture rptd 6-19, 522E2
Rebelln detailed 6-20, 484B2
VANE, Dr. John R.
Wins Lasker Award 11-16, 927A3
Van GRAAFEILAND, Judge Ellsworth A.
Backs JFK Concorde ban 6-14, 463F1
Backs NY Concorde ruling 9-29, 738E3
Van HOUTEN, Leslie
Mistrial declared 8-6, 3d trial to be set 9-1, 711C2
Van HOUWELING, Dr. C. D.
On FDA antibiotic ban 8-30, 847F2
Van LENNEP, Emile
Mondale visits 1-28, 69C1
VANNINI, Gen. Elivio
On upcoming electns 10-3, 784F1
Van SCHAIK, Al
Acquitted 2-8, 118E2
Van VLECK, John H.
Wins Nobel Prize 10-11, 951G2
Van VURREN, Sgt. Paul Jansen
Testifies at Biko inquest 11-14, 887C2
Van ZANT, Ronnie
Killed 10-20, 888G3
VANZETTI, Bartolomeo (d. 1927)
Vindicated 7-19, 652E2-A3
VARIETY (newspaper)
Top-grossing films listed 2-2, 120D3; 3-9, 184C3; 4-6, 264E1; 4-27, 356E2; 6-1, 452C2; 7-6, 548G3; 8-3, 643B2; 8-31, 712F3; 9-28, 808G3; 10-19, 872G3; 12-7, 1021B3
Lists TV top 10 audiences 2-9, 119C1
'76-77 theater box office records rptd 6-8, 472D3
VARLEY, Eric
On S Africa boycott 1-13, 29E2
Callaghan on indl policy 1-13, 44F2
VARMA, Ravindra
Indian labor min 3-26, 240C1
VARON Valencia, Gen. Abraham
Orders peasant abuse probe 2-23, 255D1
VARVITSIOTIS, Ioannis
Named Greek educ, religion min 11-28, 925B2
VASEV, Vladillen M.
US protests fishing violatns 4-5, 4-11, 270E1
VASILEVSKY, Marshal Aleksandr M.
Dies 12-5, 1024F3
VASILIUS, I.
Indicted 3-3, 204D1
VASQUEZ, Jerry
Ariz State wins coll baseball title 6-18, 568A1
VASSALLI, Fabil
Resigns 6-20, 565B1

1978

Vander VEEN, Richard F.
3d in Sen primary 8-8, 626A1
Van DEVERE, Trish
Movie, Movie released 11-22, 970C2
Vande WIELE, Dr. Raymond
Embryo implant trial opens 7-17, 597A2; damages awarded 8-18, 770A2
Van DYK Research Corp.
Xerox trial begins 7-12, 664E2
Van EEGHEN, Mark
NFL '77 rushing ldr 1-1, 56B3
VANEL, Charles
Calm Prevails released 4-6, 618E3
Van GOGH, Vincent (1853-90)
Paintings slashed 4-5, 4-25, 335F1
Van GOGH Museum (Amsterdam)
'Self-Portrait' slashed 4-25, 335F1
Van GREENAWAY, Peter
Medusa Touch released 4-14, 619B3
Van HOUT, Elisabeth
Arrested 5-5, jailed 8-21, 725D1
Van HOUTEN, Leslie
Sentncd 8-11, 824F2
VANIK, Rep. Charles A. (D, Ohio)
'76 business tax nonpaymt, low paymt rptd 1-27, 65D2
House votes $16 bln tax cut 8-10, 604B2
Fasteners import curb veto cited 10-31, 998G3
Reelected 11-7, 851G3
USSR scores '74 Trade Act amendmt 12-4, 966G1
Van LIER, Norm
NBA assist ldr 4-9, 271G2
Van NORMAN, Alan Stuart
In 3-way prisoner swap 5-1, 318D2
Van NOSTRAND, Maurie
Loses Sen primary in Iowa 6-6, 448F1
Van PALLANDT, Nina
Wedding released 9-29, 970D3
VARGAS, Aniceto
Gushiken KOs 1-29, 379A2
VARGAS Ramirez, Enrique
Colombia pub works min 8-7, 629D3
VARIETY (newspaper)
Top-grossing films listed 1-4, 24G3; 2-1, 116D3; 3-1, 196G3-196A1; 3-29, 272E2; 4-26, 356C1; 5-31, 460D3; 7-5, 579E3; 7-26, 620D1; 8-30, 708G1; 10-4, 800G3; 11-1, 888E1; 11-29, 970F3
Best-selling recordings listed 3-8, 196A1; 4-5, 272F3; 5-3, 356D1; 6-7, 460F3; 7-5, 579F3; 8-2, 620E1; 9-6, 708E1; 10-11, 800D3; 11-8, 888C1; 12-6, 971D1
Star Wars world rental mark rptd 8-2, 672B1
Rpts Ali-Spinks bout set TV viewing record 9-20, 726E2
VARLEY, Eric
Sets limit on shipbldg losses 7-10, 573D3
On Chrysler-Peugeot planned sale 8-10, 623B3
On Chrysler sale to Peugeot 9-28, 764F1
VARTANYAN, Igor P.
Chrgd re Canada spying 2-9, 110D3
VASECTOMIES—*See BIRTH Control*
VASQUEZ Restrepo, Alberto
Colombia mines min 8-7, 629D3
VASSALLO, Jesse
Sets 400-yd, 400-m ind medley records 4-6, 8-4, 8-21, 780B2, D2, A3

1979

Van Der VEEN, Jan
Whitecaps win NASL title 9-8, 775A3
Vander ZALM, William
Wins libel suit 1-17, 57A2
Van DRUTEN, John (1901-57)
I Remember Mama opens 5-31, 711G3
Van DYK, Hendrik
Sentences Soweto 11 5-11, 373C1
Van DYKE, Dick
Runner Stumbles released 11-16, 1008D1
Van EEGHEN, Mark
NFL '78 rushing ldr 1-6, 80B2
Van FLANDERN, T. C.
Comet study rptd 1-4, 289D3
VAN Halen (singing group)
Van Halen 11 on best-seller list 5-2, 356B3; 5-30, 448F3
VAN Halen 11 (recording)
On best-seller list 5-2, 356B3; 5-30, 448F3
VANIER, Gary
2d in West Lakes Classic 10-28, 970A2
VANIK, Rep. Charles A. (D, Ohio)
In USSR; notes improved emigratn, cites '74 Trade Act amendmt 4-13—4-22, 314E1-C2
Van LENNEP, Emile
Turkey aid package set 5-30, 397F1
VANN, Mayor David (Birmingham, Ala.)
Police slaying protest staged 7-20, 869E3
Loses reelectn bid 10-9, 829C1
VANOCUR, Sander
Nixon Admin pub TV moves disclosed 2-24, 194C1, G1
Van PATTEN, Joyce
Murder at the Howard Johnson's opens 5-17, 712F1
Van PELT, Elmer A.
Sentenced in GSA scandal 6-1, 964D3
Van RUYMBECKE, Renaud
Boulin scores in suicide note 10-31, 835G1
Van SCOTT, Glory
Miss Truth opens 7-22, 712E1
Van SLYKE, Helen
Dies 7-3, 588F3
Sisters & Strangers on best-seller list 9-2, 672D3
Van THIEL, Dr. David
Ulcer drug-sperm study rptd 5-3, 354F3
Van VALKENBURGH, Deborah
Warriors released 2-9, 174F3
Van ZYL Alberts, Josias
Passport seized 3-14, 191G1
Van ZYL Slabbert, Frederick
Named oppositn ldr 9-3, 733A1
VARGAS Garayar, Julio
Executed as spy 1-20, 51G3
VARGAS Llosa, Mario
Replaced as PEN pres 7-21, 554A1
VARIETY (newspaper)
Best-selling recordings listed 1-10, 80D3; 2-14, 120E3; 3-7, 174D1; 4-4, 271C2; 5-2, 356G2; 5-30, 448E3; 7-4, 548D3; 8-1, 620E3; 9-5, 672E3; 10-3, 800D3; 11-7, 892G3
Top-grossing films listed 1-10, 80G3; 2-7, 120G3; 2-28, 174B2; 4-4, 5-2, 356F2; 5-23, 448G3
VARIETY Stores—*See DEPARTMENT & Variety Stores*
VARISCO, Antonio
Killed 7-13, 584A1
VARNAKOV, Mikhail
Sovts win Challenge Cup 2-11, 118A3
VASARI, Giorgio (1511-74)
Da Vinci mural believed found 11-1, 892F1
VASILYEV, Valery
Sovts win Challenge Cup 2-11, 118D2
VASQUEZ, Jacinto
Gen Assemb wins Travers Stakes 8-18, 876G3
VASSALLO, Jesse
Sets 200-m ind medley record 7-6, 798A3

1980

VAN der STEE, Alphons
Dutch finance min 3-4, 276E3
Borrowing rptd at new high 3-25, 276D3
'81 budget proposed 9-6, 709D2
VANDERWYDE, James
Sentenced 1-11, 64A2
VANDER ZALM, William
Loses libel appeal 2-15, 148D3
VAN DEVERE, Trish
Changeling released 3-28, 416E2
Hearse released 6-7, 675G2
Tricks of the Trade opens 11-16, 892G3
VAN de WALLE, Robert
Wins Olympic medal 7-27, 623D1
VANDEWEGHE, Kiki
Louisville wins NCAA basketball title 3-24, 240G1, C2
In NBA draft 6-10, 447F1
VAN DYKE, Dick
Music Man opens 6-6, 756F3
VAN Dyk Research Corp.
Xerox win in trust suit rptd upheld 10-6, 917D3
VANE, Nina
Dies 2-18, 176G3
VANEK, Antonin
Apple Game released 1-16, 216B2
VAN GOGH, Vincent (1853-90)
Painting sold for record sum 5-13, 472E1
VAN Halen (singing group)
Women & Children 1st on best-seller list 4-30, 360A1; 6-4, 448F3
VAN HOOSE, Myra
2d in Corning Classic 5-26, 714G3
Named LPGA top rookie 12-9, 971D3
VANIK, Rep. Charles A. (D, Ohio)
Eckart elected to US House 11-4, 851E2
VAN LENNEP, Emile
Turkey aid pkg deferred 3-26, 236B2
Urges OECD inflatn curbs 6-4, 422F1
VAN PATTEN, Joyce
I Ought to be in Pictures opens 4-3, 392D3
VAN PEEBLES, Melvin
Reggae opens 3-27, 392F3
VAN REY, Lt. Michel
Identified as Surinam mil cncl ldr 2-29, 174G3
VAN RIJN, Michael
Hann icon bought for record sum 4-17, 472A3
VAN SLYKE, Helen
Necessary Woman on best-seller list 5-4, 359E3
No Lost Love on best-seller list 5-4, 359D3; 6-8, 448B3
VAN THIJN, Ed
Andriessen quits Cabt 2-21, 173D3
VAN'T HOF, Robert
Loses Australian Hard Ct tourn 1-6, wins NCAA singles title 5-26, 607D1, D2
VANUATU (formerly New Hebrides)
Nixon taps case accepted by Sup Ct 5-19, 440C1
Separatists seize Espiritu Santo; foreigners flee, provisional govt formed 5-28—6-3; UN gets plea 6-1, France, UK scored 6-3, 422G1
Separatist aid probed by US 6-7; Phoenix Foundatn, US exec's links detailed 6-8, 436C2-A3
Espiritu Santo hostages rptd freed 6-8, 436G1
Unrest spreads to Tanna; British, French send forces 6-11, 436E1, A2
Island trade pact rptd 7-24, 567G2
UK, French troops land on Espiritu Santo 7-24, presence backed 7-30, 580G3
Independence declared 7-30, 580E3
Papua New Guinea troops arrive 8-18; quell Espiritu Santo rebellion, arrest Stevens 8-31, 674C1
Stevens sentncd, Robert rebelln role cited 11-21, 903C3
VAN WYK, Alex
Denies surveillance chrg 1-1, 60F3
VARADI, Janos
Wins Olympic medal 8-2, 622E1
VARDANYAN, Yusik
Wins Olympic medal 7-26, 624F2
VARGA, Karoly
Wins Olympic medal 7-21, 623C2
VARGANOVA, Svetlana
Wins Olympic medal 7-23, 623C3
VARIETY (newspaper)
Best-selling recordings listed 1-2, 40E3; 2-6, 120E3; 3-5, 200D3; 4-2, 280D3; 4-30, 359G3; 6-4, 448E3; 7-9, 568D3; 8-13, 640A3; 9-10, 716E3; 10-8, 796A3; 12-3, 948A3
Top-grossing films listed 1-9, 40G3; 1-30, 120A3; 2-27, 200F3; 3-26, 280G3; 4-23, 360B1; 5-28, 448G3; 7-2, 568G3; 8-6, 640C3; 9-3, 716G3; 10-1, 769G3; 12-3, 948G3
'79 top domestic rental films listed 2-6, 120F2
US movie boxoffice slump rptd 9-10, 732B2
VARIETY Stores—*See DEPARTMENT & Variety Stores*
VARNER, Judge Robert
Dismisses US suit vs Sears 5-22, 485D1
VASILKOVA, Elvira
Wins Olympic medal 7-26, 623B3
VASQUEZ, Jacinto
Superbity wins Flamingo Stakes 3-5, 447G3
Genuine Risk wins Ky Derby 5-3; chrgs Preakness foul 5-17, 447C2
Errico convicted, Amy implicates 5-19, 447C3
VASQUEZ, Pedro
On refugee camp security 11-31, 869F2
VASSALLO, Jesse
Wins US 400-m individual medley title, beats Olympic time 7-30, 834G2

1976

VATCHARA Vethayathirang
Arrest rptd 10-19, 794D3
VATICAN—*See also ROMAN Catholic Church*
Middle East Developments—*See INTERNATIONAL Developments under MIDDLE EAST*
VAYTSEKHOVSKAIA, Elena
Wins Olympic medal 7-26, 575E3
VAZQUEZ Rana, Olegario
Bodyguards killed 5-6, 419G1
VEALEY, Claude E.
Gets life sentence 9-3, 816A3
VECERA, Bohuslav
Dismissed 9-15, 750G2
VECSEY, George
'Loretta' on best-seller list 12-5, 972D2
VEGA Rodriguez, Lt. Gen. Jose
Named Madrid mil cmdr 3-28, 314C3
VEGH Villegas, Alejandro
Vs Bordaberry pol plan 5-7, 441B1
Mil backs austerity program 6-12, 440E3
Wage, price hikes set 7-3, 542F1
Leaks departure plan 8-11, replaced in Cabt 8-27, 678B2
VEIL, Simone
Family aid plan rptd 1-2, 50G1
VELARDE, Gen. German
Peru min without portfolio 2-3, 142B3
VELASCO, Belisario
Appeals radio closing 3-22, arrested 3-24, 310A3
VELASCO Alvarado, Gen. Juan (ret.)
Fernandez named premr 1-31, 142A3
Morales scores re press 4-30, 500A1
Leftist Cabt mins ousted 7-16, 590F2
VELASCO Ibarra, Jose Maria
Nephew gets amnesty 1-22, 363F3
Rpt Ecuador vote plan scored 8-8, 693E1
Party to boycott const talks 10-11, 872F2
VELASCO Letelier, Eugenio
Exiled 8-6, 711C2
VELASQUEZ, Ramon Ignacio
On illegal Colombian immigrants 12-5, 930A2
VELCHEV, Boris
On Bulgaria Politburo 4-2, 250D1
VELSICOL Chemical Corp.—*See NORTHWEST Industries*
VENADO Air Taxi
Yopal crash 10-25, 876F2
VENEREAL Disease—*See 'Diseases' under MEDICINE*
VENERIS, James
US visit OKd 6-29, 484F2 ★

VENEZUELA—*See also ANDEAN Group, IDB, LAFTA, OAS, OPEC, SELA*
'75 mil forces rptd 1-2, 60G2
Listed as 'free' nation 1-19, 20C3
Students riot 2-14—2-25; security vowed 2-27, 208B1-A2
TV, press censured re kidnap rptg 4-6, 593A1
Guerrilla ldr's death rptd 7-2, 593A1
Floods rptd 7-18, 544B3
Torture death rptd 7-25; more tortures chrgd 7-27, admitted 7-30; dep arrests scored 8-3, defended 8-5, 592A3
Police seized re torture death 8-6, 874G2
Dep arrests re torture death stir controversy 8-12—8-26, 874D2
Univ singers die in Azores crash 9-4, 696F3
Pol prisoners on hunger strike 10-1, 874G3
Economy & Labor—*See also 'Oil' below*
Perez sees 'social democracy' 1-2, 12F2
'75 defns spending rptd 1-2, 60G2
Jan-June inflatn at 7.1% 8-6, 875B2
Airline pilots strike 9-14—9-30, 875G2-A3
World Bank lauds econ policy 10-16, 875G1

Foreign Relations (misc.)—*See also 'Oil Developments' below*
Chile presses on refugees 1-9, 47E2
Argentina econ pact signed 1-14, 96C3
French Mirage purchase cited 1-16, 36C2
Vs Cuba Angola, Guyana role 1-24, 138G1, A2
Chile emb refugees to get safe-conducts 1-25, 100C1
Canada prime min visits 1-29—2-2, 116F2
Guatemala quake aid sent 2-4, 81E1
Chile refugees leave emb 2-4, 2-16, 288D3
Envoy in China 2-7, 117D1
To buy Peru iron ore 2-10, 142F2
At intl econ conf 2-11—2-20, 148B1
More Guatemala quake aid pledged 2-11, 155B3
Perez, Kissinger meet on Cuba Angola role 2-16—2-17, 177E2
Press scores US-Brazil pact 2-23, 177D1
Guyana denies Cuba, China mil presence 2-23—3-10, 253C1

1977

VATICAN—*See ROMAN Catholic Church*
Helsinki Agreement—*See EUROPE—Security and Cooperation*
VAVURIS, Judge S. Lee
Rules parental custody for Moon disciples 3-24, 286G3; ruling upset 4-11, 310C1
VEGA Rodriguez, Lt. Gen Jose
Spain army gen staff chief 1-15, 68C2
VEGETABLES—*See FRUITS & Vegetables*
VEIL, Simone
Named health min 3-30, 239G1
VELASCO Alvarado, Gen. Juan (ret.)
Former aides expelled 1-8, 46D3
Urges civilian govt 2-3, 241G2
New pol, econ plan issued 2-6, 241B1
Dies 12-24, 1024F3
VELASCO Ibarra, Jose Maria
Party scores transitn plan 2-11, 348B1
Scores Bucaram 3-3, Bucaram challenges 3-4; asks junta revolt 3-25, 348A1
Nephew's pres bid rptd 8-26, 842G1
VELCHEV, Boris
Ousted 5-12, 451E2
VELSICOL Chemical Corp.—*See under NORTHWEST Industries*
VENDO Co.
Contract dispute award ordrd 6-29, 557D3

VENEZUELA—*See also ANDEAN Group, IDB, OAS, OPEC*
Xmas pardons granted; pol prisoner total rptd 1-1, 3F1
Students riot 5-5—5-12, 547B2
Rebels seize rural towns 9-4—10-25, 867B3

Economy & Labor (domestic)
'77 budget OKd; '74-76 spending cited 1-5, 23D1
GNP grew 11% in '76 3-11, 547D1
Tax reform vowed by Perez 3-11, 547F1
'76 agri output down 3-24, govt blamed 4-1, 6-3, 546G2
'76 budget deficit rptd 4-4, '77 estimate raised 4-14, 547E1
Food shortage protest, import curbs lifted 4-22, 546F2
Auditor scores pub admin 5-27, 546E3
'61-75 GDP variatns table 5-30, 439C1
Consumer chief quits 6-15; corruptn chrgs, business enmity cited 7-1, 565F3
Austerity measures set 7-11; business, banks score 7-15, 565F2-D3
Food shortage continues 7-11, 674F2
Jan-June inflatn 8.2% 7-22, 674E2
Copei scores inflatn, rich-poor gap 8-18, 674G1
Major bauxite deposit found 8-22, 674F2
Foreign Relations (misc.)—*See also 'Monetary, Trade & Aid' and 'Oil Developments' below*
UN Assemb, Cncl member 4D1, E1
Amnesty Intl estimates pol prisoners 1-1, 3F1
Honduras shifts mil attache 1-3, 45B2
Perez backs Panamanian Canal demands 1-18, 46G1
Brazil ties deteriorate 4-1, 547G2 ★ -B3
El Salvador prisoner haven sought 4-19, 373C2
Argentina exiles Solari 5-1, 388E3
Joint Saudi statemt on Mideast 5-6, 362D1
Videla visits; protests staged, Panama canal claim backed 5-11—5-14, 547G1-F2
Panama seeks Guatemala mediatn 5-27, 415A1
Jailed Cuba exile sued by Perez 7-4, 868B1
Uruguay release of Mex rptr demanded 7-15, 601E1
Argentine amb kidnaped 7-18, 595G1

1978

VATICAN—*See ROMAN Catholic Church*
Helsinki Agreement—*See EUROPE—Security and Cooperation*
VAUGHAN-Hughes, Gerald
Duellists released 1-14, 619F1
VAUGHN, Robert
Wins Emmy 9-17, 1030F1
VAUXHALL Motors Ltd.—*See under GENERAL Motors*
VAWTER, Ron
Nayatt School opens 5-12, 887C2
VD (venereal disease)—*See MEDICINE—Diseases*
VEECK, Bill
Vs Kuhn bar on Blue sale 3-3, 194F3
Names Doby White Sox mgr 6-30, 560F1
VEGA, Silvio
On Chamorro murder 1-13, 73E1
VEGA Gomez, Francisco
Arrested in murder case 10-21, 881F2
VEGA Uribe, Gen. Miguel
Rpts guerrilla arrests 11-4, 1015D3
Denies torture in mil jail 11-8, 1015D2
VEGETABLES—*See FRUITS & Vegetables*
VEHR, Bill
Utopic Inc opens 12-4, 1031C3
VEIL, Simone
Renamed French health min 4-5, 245F2
Press natlizatn abandoned; stock sale, ex-owner compensatn set 7-21, 692B1
VELASCO Alvaredo, Juan
Press natlizatn abandoned; stock sale, ex-owner compensatn set 7-21, 692B1
VELASCO Ibarra, Jose Maria
Asks const vote boycott 1-14, 111E3
Pres bid barred, party scores move 2-20, 148F1, B2
VELASQUEZ, Jorge
Alydar loses Triple Crown 6-10, 539C1-A2
VELIT Sabattini, Gen. Fernando
Named Peru interior min 5-15, 394E2
VELSICOL Chemical Corp.—*See under NORTHWEST Industries Inc.*
VENDING Machines
GDV acquires Servomation 8-31, 700A3
VENEMA, James A.
Loses Sen primary in Del 9-9, 736G1
VENERA (USSR interplanetary probe series)—*See ASTRONAUTICS—Interplanetary Projects*
VENERAL Disease (VD)—*See MEDICINE—Diseases*
VENETOULIS, Theodore
3d in Md primary for gov 9-12, 716E1

VENEZUELA—*See also ANDEAN Group, IDB, OAS, OPEC*
Intell cops jailed re '76 torture death 2-3, 395B2
Govt airline crash kills 47 3-3, 271A1
Guerrillas kill soldier 5-5, 395B2
Guerrilla camps dismantled 6-8, 559E2

Economy & Labor (domestic)—*See also 'Oil' below*
Budget cuts rptd 2-28, 331F3
'77 inflatn put at 8% by govt, 20% by econs 5-2, 332D1
Unemploymt falls to 5%, worker absenteeism high 5-2, 332E1
Tax reform plan OKd 5-26, 559D2
'79 budget OKd by Cong 8-23, 692E1
Jan-June inflatn 6.6% 9-1; govt to continue price controls 10-6, 799A2

Foreign Relations (misc.)—*See also 'Monetary, Trade, Aid & Investment' and 'Oil Developments' below*
Nicaragua rights abuse probe sought 2-8, 91F2
Carter, Perez back Panama Canal pacts, score Cuba Africa role 3-28, 233D1
Nicaragua rights probe sought, Somoza scores 3-28—5-8, 376A3
Chile exile returns home 4-4, 267G1
El Salvador peasants, students seize emb 4-11—4-18, 723C3 ★
Vesco leaves CR, visit set 4-30, 354E2
Colombia pres-elect postpones visit 6-9, 443C2
Cuba pressure re Africa rptd asked 6-11, 443C1
Perez at Panama Canal pact instrumts exchng 6-16, 463F2, 464A1
In 8-natn Amazon pact 7-3, 829C2
Amer rights conv enacted, ct formed 7-18, 828E3, 829C1
Nicaragua guerrillas seek asylum 8-22, plane flies guerrillas to Panama 8-24, 659A1, C1

1979

VATICAN—*See ROMAN Catholic Church*
Helsinki Agreement—*See EUROPE–Security and Cooperation*
VAUGH v. Vermillion Corp.
Case decided by Sup Ct 12-4, 988B1
VAZIRI, Yahya Sadeq
Quits as Iran justice min 1-17, 25D2
VD (veneral disease)—*See MEDICINE–Diseases*
VEBER, Francis
French Detective released 3-10
Cage aux Folles 5-12, 528F1, C2
VEGA, Evelyn
Arrested for theft, murder 4-17, 316G1
VEGETABLES—*See FRUITS & Vegetables*
VEIL, Simone
Elected EC Parlt head 7-17, 537B2
Scores Czech dissident trial 10-23, 802E2
VELA (U.S. satellite series)—*See ASTRONAUTICS–Satellites*
VELASCO Ibarra, Jose Maria
Dies 3-30, 272G3
Roldos sworn Ecuador pres 8-10, 613F2
VELAZQUEZ, Diego Rodriguez de Silva y (1599-1660)
Church painting sold for record sum 10-25, 891G3
VELIKANOVA, Tatiana
Arrested 11-1, 856G2
VELIKOVSKY, Immanuel
Dies 11-17, 932F3
VELKIN, S.
Strider opens 5-31, 712F2
VELSICOL Chemical Corp.—*See under NORTHWEST Industries*
VENDA
Independence declared 9-13, 732G1-B2
VENEREAL Disease (VD)—*See MEDICINE–Diseases*

VENEZUELA—*See also ANDEAN Group, DISARMAMENT–Geneva Committee, IDB, OAS, OPEC*

Economy & Labor—*See also 'Oil' below*
Herrera vows econ austerity, stresses agri 3-12, 192C2
Econ plans detailed; price curbs, spending, other data cited 5-28, 429C3
Unions ask wage plan, earnings cited 10-4; protest marred by violence 10-25, 837E3
'78 govt spending rptd 10-16, 837C3
Inflatn rise seen 10-23, 838B1

Foreign Relations (misc.)—*See also 'Monetary', 'Oil' and 'UN' below*
Intell offcl testifies in Letelier case 1-16, 58A1
St Lucia ties cited 2-21, 181G2
CR rifle loan rptd 3-23, 238G1
El Salvador emb seized 5-11, 371C1
12 Cubans gain asylum 5-13, 7 fail 5-25, 411C2
EL Salvador amb, aides flee emb 5-20, 387E3
Mex-CR missn on Nicaragua dispatched 5-21, 409B1
Nicaragua denounces rebel aid 5-27, 409D2
El Salvador emb seige ends 6-1, 424B3
Zambrano visits Nicaragua 6-11, 446E3
Nicaragua junta additns proposed 7-6, 504C1
Brazil pres visits 11-6–11-7, 953E1
'78 Dutch Antilles agrmt cited 11-13, 882F3

1980

VASSAR College (Poughkeepsie, N.Y.)
Buckley cancels commencemnt appearance 5-19, 471B2
VATICAN—*See CSCE*
VAUGHT, Maj. Gen. James B.
Testifies on Iran rescue missn 5-7, 338A1
Sen com study faults Iran rescue missn 6-5, 419G1
VAUXHILL Motors Ltd.—*See GENERAL Motors*
VD (venereal disease)—*See MEDICINE--Diseases*
VEBER, Francis
Coup De Tete released 1-21, 216D2
VEEE, Julie
Arrows win MISL title 3-23, 771A2
VEGETABLES—*See FRUITS & Vegetables*
VELASCO Alvadado, Gen. Juan (ret.)
Belaunde wins Peru pres electn 5-18, 390A3
VELASCO Zuazo, Maj. Jesus Maria
Assassinated 1-10, 101E2
VELAZQUEZ, Diego Rodriguez de Siva y (1599-1660)
Painting sale record cited 5-13, 472F1
VELIKANOVA, Tatyana
Sovts sentence 8-29, 680B2
VELSICOL Chemical Corp.—*See NORTHWEST Industries*
VENDA
Econ aid need rptd 2-8, 134F2
S Africa rptd planning consolidatn 2-9, 134G2-A3
VENEREAL Disease (VD)—*See MEDICINE--Diseases*

VENEZUELA—*See also ANDEAN Group, GENEVA Committee, IDB, OAS, OPEC*
Jet hijacked 12-5, 30 arrested 12-6, 968D3

Foreign Relations (misc.)—*See also 'Monetary', 'Oil & Gas', 'UN Policy' below*
Cuba emb shooting rptd 1-18, amb recalled 1-19, 103C1
Colombia amb seized in DR emb raid 2-27, 141B1
Colombia amb suffers 2d heart attack 3-17, 211A3
Colombia DR Emb siege ends; amb, envoy freed 4-27, 335F1
Surinam coup fails, mercenaries seized 5-1—5-2, 410A3
Perez in Nicaragua, marks Somoza downfall 7-19, 565F2
Emb to move from W Jerusalem to Tel Aviv 7-28, 572G3
Herrera in Peru for Belaunde inauguratn 7-28, 579E3
Bolivia coup condemned 7-29, 577D1
Herrera visits CR, sees Mex pres 8-3, 605C3
Israel Emb shift rptd 8-26, 643E2
'76 Cuba jet bombing suspects acquitted 9-26; Cuba withdraws diplomats, trades chrgs 9-29, 794G2

1976

Latin natls detained 3-2, 208D2
Tito on tour re nonaligned mtg 3-9—3-22, 256C2
Sen scores Chile rights abuse 4-23, 310G2
India natls score curbs 4-24, 313F1
Urges new world econ order 5-18, 465F3
Hosts intl soc dems mtg 5-23—5-25, 449E2-C3
Perez asks US return Panama Canal 6-22, 793C1
Uruguay woman seized in emb 6-28—7-7; Venez suspends ties 7-6, 542B2
On North-South conf impasse 7-18, 530E1
Bishop seized in Ecuador 8-12, scores junta 8-23, 693A1
At nonaligned conf 8-16—8-20, 622C1
Castro murder plot rptd 8-17—8-18, 791F1
Chile emb rptdly harbors MIR, Red Sept members 8-27, 9-8, 711D1
Intl banks set $1 bln loan 9-15, 875C1
Venez, UK, Kuwait banks form finance co 9-17, 875E1
Letelier buried, govt offers condolences 9-29, 780F3
Cuban jet bombed 10-6, Perez scores 10-8, vows info 10-16; arrests rptd 10-14, 10-15, 779A3
Cuba to honor hijack pact 10-15, 780D1
World Bank lauds econ policy 10-16, 875G1
FBI to probe Letelier murder 10-18; police deny info on exile role 10-21, 844E2, G2
Cuba exile coalitn rptd 10-19, 779E3
Cuba terrorist plan rptd 10-19, 780C2
Chrgs re Chile anti-Castro aid rptd 10-20, 780B3
Rpt Perez used Cuba exiles as Chile contacts 10-21, 780F2
Jet crash trial set 10-21—10-22; Trinidad deports 2 10-26; 4 indicted 11-2, 843F2
Rpt exiles plan Cuba emb attack 10-31, 844C1
Canada power co natlzd 11-12, 875F2
Perez at UN; tours W Eur, USSR; signs trade pacts 11-16—11-30, 929G2-930C1
S Africa trade ties cut 11-16, 929B3
Perez addresses Soclst Intl 11-28, 935D3
Columbians immigrate illegally 12-5, 930F1
North-South conf delayed 12-9, 976F3
Chile exiles Cademartori 12-11, 963E1

Oil Developments—*See also OPEC*
'75 earnings rptd 12G3
Natlizatn rite 1-1, Perez statemts 1-1, 1-2, 12D2
Daily sales to US cited 12A3
Occidental writes off investmt 1-1, 12D3
Exxon signs pact 1-6, 12B3
Dec '75 output drop rptd 1-7, 12C2
In Canada trade talks 1-29—2-2, '75 data rptd 1-30, 116F2
Japan purchase, mktg deals rptd 2-6, 2-11, 208B3
Occidental bribes rptd 2-14, 2-17, Flores offers resignatn 2-19, 147F1, F3
Perez, Kissinger talks 2-16—2-17, 177E2
Total IMF oil loan rptd 4-1, 340G2
'75 output down 4-25, 298B3
Occidental natlzatn paymt opposed 6-8, co protests 6-10, 593D1
Petrochem dvpt plan set 6-11, 875E2
Prices raised 7-1, 10-1, 875C2
Arrests ordrd in Occidental case, co denies wrongdoing 7-14, 593B1
Way to lighten 'heavy' crude found 9-9, 875E2
World Bank lauds econ policy 10-16, 874A2
Chrgs dropped in Occidental case 11-16, co asks new compensatn talks 11-17, 930C1
UK petrochem pact signed 11-23, 929D3
Sovt pact signed 11-26, 929F3
Perez on developing natns 11-28, 935D3
Portugal pact signed 11-30, 930B1

Sports
Olympic results 7-18—7-31, 573E3, 574C1

U.S. Relations—*See also 'Oil Developments' above*
Lockheed bribes rptd 2-7, AF opens probe 2-10, 147F1, E3
Kissinger visits, students riot 2-16—2-18, 177A1, A2, 208C1
Press scores US-Brazil pact 2-23, 177D1
US exec kidnaped 2-27, 208B2
US co meets exec kidnap demands, assets seized 4-6; 5 suspects seized 7-20, 8-3, 592B3

1977

Argentina newsletter scores amb's kidnap 7-26, dir disappears 8-5, 670F2
Cuba frees exile comando 8-2, 654B2
Perez sees Torrijos, regional ldrs; backs new Panama Canal pact 8-5—8-6, 606B3
Cuba exiles bomb plane in US 8-14, 868A1
Dutch Antilles independnc backed 8-19, 949G2
Perez at Panama Canal pact signing 9-7, 678D1
Spanish king visits 9-8—9-10, 804G3, 805A1
'76 Cuba jet crash mil trial rptd 10-10, 867F3-868D1
Nicaragua emb harbors rebels 10-28, 865D1
Perez in Brazil 11-16—11-20, 912D3

Government & Politics—*See also other appropriate subheads in this section*
New ministries set 1-4, Perez swears new Cabt 1-7, 23C2
Perez shuffles Cabt 7-15, 565G3
Pinerua wins AD '78 pres nominatn 7-17, 566C1
Minor pres candidates announce 7-30, 8-20, 8-26, 674C2
Herrera Campins wins Copei '78 pres nod 8-18, 674F1
CP, MEP pres candidate named 9-4, 9-25, 867F2

Monetary, Trade & Aid Issues (including all foreign economic developments)—*See also 'Oil Developments' below*
'76 import, export data rptd 1-6, 23B2
US CIA paymts to Perez rptd 2-19, denied 2-22; Carter regrets 2-23, 124F1, 151A2
'75-76 trade, paymts data; table 3-11, 189B1, A2★, C2
Intl bank loan set 3-28, 547C1
Brazil ties deteriorate re A-power 4-1, 547G2★-B3
Perez backs US on A-power spread 4-1, 547A3
'76 balance of paymts deficit rptd 4-4, 547E1
'66-75 arms transfers table 4-8, 415B2
Food imports OKd 4-22, arrivals rptd 5-13, 546F2
In 11-natn Portugal loan 6-22, 530B3
Forgn investmt welcomed 7-1, 546E2
Austerity measures set 7-11, banks score 7-15, 565G2-D3
Food import tariff suspensn contd 7-11, 674F2
Forgn reserves, paymts surplus rptd up 7-15, 565D3
Intl Coffee Fund set 8-6, 608A3
Copei chrgs forgn dependency 8-18, 674A2
Jamaica aluminum purchase set 9-2, 884E3
Spain indl, RR projcts set 9-10, 805A1
Jamaica loan rptd 9-27, 884E3
Brazil coffee policy backed 10-21, 876C3
Brazil A-policy backing rptd 11-25, 912D3

Oil Developments—*See also OPEC*
'77 budget OKd 1-5, 12C1, 23E1, F1
10% price rise in effect, no productn cut planned 1-5, 12C1
Exports rptd; Exxon to continue present level 1-6, 23G1, C2
'76 oil income rptd 1-11, 23F1
Output cut planned 4-5; 1st ¼ rise, US demand rptd 4-26, 341G2
Perez tours OPEC natns 4-21—5-5, 361G3
Peru to cut imports 5-25, 427G3
Occidental sues govt 5-27, 547B1
N-S 'dialogue' opposed 6-3, 437D2
OPEC price split ended 6-29—7-5, 535E2
Petrochem execs resign, industry reorganizatn rptd 7-8, 565E3
Exports, earnings rptd up 7-15, 565E3
Cuba oil products reach US 10-20, 896B3
Exxon admits paymts 10-25, 818A2
Vance, Perez discuss prices 11-23, 912F3-913A1

U.S. Relations—*See also 'Oil Developments' above*
'76 US imports rptd 1-6, 23C2
US CIA paymts to Perez rptd 2-19; chrgs protested, Carter regrets 2-19—2-24, 124F1, 151A2
Perez lauds US rights stand 2-27, 142F2
Perez backs US on A-power spread 4-1, 547A3
'66-75 arms transfers table 4-8, 415B2

1978

UN rights probe of Nicaragua asked 9-2, Nicaragua scores 9-4, 9-5, 690D3
Spain premier visits 9-7—9-9, 821D3
Nicaragua mediatn delayed by OAS 9-11, studied by oppositn 9-14, 705C3, D3
CR offered troops vs Nicaragua 9-13, 705E3
UN Cncl, Assemb member 713A3, G3
OAS bars Nicaragua crisis role 9-21—9-23, 757C3
OAS inactn in Nicaragua scored 10-6, 799C2
CR deports Nicaragua guerrillas 10-13, 839E3
Nicaragua denounces govt 10-14, 839B3
Nicaragua emb harbors 100 refugees 10-23, 839F3
Nicaragua rebel aid halt urged by US 12-11, 1018F3
OAS inactn on Nicaragua rights rpt scored 12-14, 1019C1
Cuba ex-prisoners arrive 12-24, 1016F1

Government & Politics—*See also other appropriate subheads in this section*
Ottolina dies in plane crash 3-16, 231A1
Pres race poll rptd 3-24, 270A1
Pres campaign opens 4-1, 269G3
AD, Copei campaign spending, media advisers rptd 5-5, 395F1
AD, Copei corruptn scandals rptd 5-5, 395A2
Arria sets pres bid; scores AD, Copei 5-21, 395E1
URD backs Herrera pres bid, Pinerua leads poll 7-15, 559C2
Pinerua, Herrera tied in pres poll 9-29, 799B2
Herrera elected 12-3, Pinerua concedes 12-5, returns incomplete 12-8, 952G2
AD, Copei even in cong vote; AD to control Sen 12-3, 952B3
Herrera declared pres-elect in final vote count 12-11, 989G3

Monetary, Trade, Aid & Investment—*See also 'Oil' below*
Forgn banks lend $1.2 bln 1-12, Arab banks $178 mln 1-17, 332F1
Jamaica aluminum deal rptd 1-13, 100F2
Trade, paymts deficits posted in '77 1-27; govt bans consumer imports 4-6, 332C1
Jamaica plans alumina deal 2-28, 194E2
Coffee exports to be withheld 3-10, 181B3
US maritime, drug pacts signed 3-28, 233D1
Colombia to press econ border projects 8-7, 629A3
Chrysler operatns cited 8-10, 623F2
Perez, Spain premr in trade talks 9-7—9-9, 821F3
Guyana cult money rptd in Venez banks 12-17, USSR rejcts bequest 12-18, 1000B2

Oil Developments—*See also OPEC*
Forgn buyers offered discounts 2-3, 332A1
Jan-Feb output drop forces budget cuts 2-28, Mar recovery rptd 4-13; US demand, forgn competitn blamed 4-16, 331F3
Brazil sales deal signed 4-28, 332B1
Nicaragua pres cites financial ills 5-8, 376D3
Jan-July oil output down 7-18, 559D2
'79 budget cuts oil reliance 8-23, 692F1
Transport pact with Spain, Cuba, USSR rptd 9-15, 822C1
Nicaragua scores prices 10-14, 839C3
Nicaragua cutoff plan rptd 11-8, 883B3
Perez revenue use scored in pres campaign 12-3, 952D3

Press & Censorship
AD, Copei media advisers rptd 5-5, 395F1; 12-3, 953A1
Press freedom rptd by IAPA 10-13, 829A2
Magazine issue seized 12-3, 953C1

Sports
World Cup soccer match televised 6-25, 520D3

U.S. Relations—*See also 'Oil' above*
Carter visits 3-28—3-29, 233B1, C1
Vesco leaves CR, visit set 4-30, 354E2
US electn consultants hired 5-5, 395G1
Carter consults on DR electn 5-19, 414C2
Bordoni extradited to US 6-2, 454C2
Cuba pressure re Africa rptd asked 6-11, 443C1
US media adviser role in electns cited 12-3, 953A1

1979

Government & Politics—*See also other appropriate subheads in this section*
'78 electn results rptd 2-2, 192A3
Herrera names Cabt 3-10; sworn pres, scores Perez 3-12, 192C2
Army chief resigns 5-22, 429B3
COPEI wins munic electns 6-3, 429G2
Perez Alfonzo dies 9-3, 756C3

Monetary, Trade, Aid & Investment—*See also 'Oil' below*
Owens-Ill takeover bid dropped 3-13, 192D3
US scored on trade curbs 3-23, 248E1
Econ plans detailed; paymts deficit, debt, other data cited 5-28, 429C3
External debt up 45%, forgn bank loans sought 10-6, 837A3
Brazil pres in trade talks 11-6—11-7, 953F1
Bolivia loan set 12-3, 926G1

Oil & Gas Developments
Exxon cuts Canada shipmts 2-15, 153B2
Fuel-oil prices hiked 2-26, 145G2
Crude oil surchrg confrmd 3-5, 162E1
Herrera vows conservatn 3-12, 192G2
Canada co ordrd to import oil 3-13, 210G2
US scored on trade curbs 3-23; Mondale-Herrera talks 3-23—3-24; productn hike OKd 3-24, 248F1, A2
Oil prices hiked 5-16, 360A3
Colombia offshore oil talks agreed 5-26—5-28, 398C2
'78 revenue rptd $5.8 bln 5-28, 429E3
Tankers collide, oil spills in Caribbean 7-19, 553C3
'78 earnings rptd 10-6, 837C3
Brazil pres in oil export talks 11-6—11-7, 953G1
Orinoco tar field reserves estimated; proven reserves, '79 productn rptd 11-21; US comments 11-26, 953A1
Price hike set 12-13, 977G1
OPEC mtg hosted, Berti elected pres 12-17—12-20; price per barrel rptd 12-21, new hike set 12-28, 977D1-C2

UN Policy & Developments
Membership listed 695B3
Energy conf gets oil rpt 11-21, 953A1

U.S. Relations—*See also 'Oil' above*
Grumman admits paymts 1-3, 16F1
Student enrollmt in US rptd 167E2
US execs' wife appeals to kidnapers 2-12, Venez closes case 3-1; Owens-Ill ends ransom effort 3-10, Venez drops takeover bid 3-13, 192D3

1980

Bolivia coup condemned by Santa Marta conf 12-17, 992A3

Government & Politics—*See also other appropriate subheads in this section*
Perez censured 5-8, 411C1-A2

Monetary, Trade, Aid & Investment—*See also 'Oil & Gas' below*
'79 forgn debt, intl bank loan talks rptd 1-14, 103B1
Argentine A-pact cited 3-18, 229E2
Shipping scandal rpt issued, Perez censured 5-8, 411C1-A2
Amazon pact signed 10-28, 865C2
US OKs Israeli jet sale 10-31, 865A2

Oil & Gas Developments
6% productn cut set, US multinatl sale curbed; '79 data, '80 estimates rptd 1-16, 102E3
Ashland unveils new refining process 3-31, 251A2
Jamaica $97 mln credit rptd 6-4, 465E1
Oil price hike set 6-11, 435G2
Latin supply guarantee set with Mex 8-3, 605C3
Gulf war prompts halt to planned 10% cut 9-26, 735C1
Brazil oil sales rptd 10-2, 759A2
OPEC mtg sought 10-22, 822B2
Fuel-oil price hiked 10-27, 822F1
Panama Canal clogged by Japan shipmts 11-24, 895D3
OPEC unity stressed 12-15, 951D2

Sports
Moscow Olympics results 7-20—8-3, 588C3, 622E1

UN Policy & Developments
Aguilar on UN comm to probe shah 2-17, 122B1
Cuba ex-offcl asks prison hunger strike probed 12-4, 965D2

U.S. Relations—*See also 'Oil & Gas' above*
Peoples Temple assets located 2-6, 170F3, G3
US OKs Israeli jet sale 10-31, 865A2

1976

'75 imports from US rptd 5-19, 466B1
OAS vs US trade curbs 6-18, 464F2
Perez asks return Panama Canal 6-22, 793C1
Ship in US Bicentennial event 7-4, 488B3
US exec kidnap arrests stir controversy 8-12—8-26; probe stalled 10-9, 874C2
US exec rptd alive 8-20, 874C3
Intl banks set $1 bln loan 9-15, 875C1
CIA linked to Cuba jet crash 10-15, 780E1
Deports US journalists 10-22, 844E1
FBI-Cuba exile contacts confrmd 10-25, 844A2
Owens-Ill natlzn talks deadlocked 11-1, 874D3
Hails Carter electn 11-3—11-4, 826D2
Perez again urges Canal return 11-16, 929C3
Perez scores arms race 11-26, 929G3-930A1

VENTO, Bruce Frank
Elected 11-2, 823A3, 829F4
VENTURA, Giovanni
Released from Rome jail 8-28, 676B3
VERA, Gen. Luis
Replaced as mines min 1-31, 142A3
VERA Institute of Justice (N.Y.)
Sturz wins Rockefeller award 11-16, 911D3
VERA Serafin, Aldo
Killed 10-25, 844C3
VERDIRAMO, Vincent L.
Indicted 6-2, 414D3
VERGOVA, Maria
Wins Olympic medal 7-29, 576A2

VERMONT
Primary date set 22A2
A-plant shut down 2-2, 115B2
Pres primary results 3-2, 165G1-B2
Dem conv women delegates, table 508D2
Dem conv pres vote, table 7-14, 507D2
US A-plant hearing ordrd 7-21, 570C3
Hurricane Belle damage rptd 8-11, 595D2
GOP pre-conv delegate count 8-14, 583E3
GOP conv pres, vp vote tables 8-18—8-19, 8-19, 599E1, E3
Solzhenitsyn move to Cavendish rptd 9-9, 680B3
Primary results 9-14, 705A2
Fscl '75 per capita income, tax burden rptd 9-15, 10-12, 959A2
Dole in Burlington, scores Butz 10-2, 744A2
Election results 11-2: pres 818D1, 819A2; cong 820D1, 821D3, 828C3, 830F4, 831D2; state 820F2, C3
US Sup Ct bars NY tax case stay 11-9, 882A3
Banks rpt Canada deposits up 11-21, 903F3

VERMONT Yankee Nuclear Power Corp.
Shut down 2-2, 115B2
VERNER, Paul
E Ger Politburo enlarged 5-22, 381F2
VERONA Corp.
US files consent decree 11-16, 989C1
VERRIER, Willy
Haiti health, populatn min 4-1, 267E2
VERSFELT, William H.
Indicted 10-29, 886D3
VESCO, Robert L.
Indicted 1-14, 78A2
CR repeals extraditn law 11-2, 1000E2, F2 ★

1977

Food imports OKd 4-22, arrivals rptd 5-13, 546F2
Todman visits 5-10—5-12, 414D1, F1
Mrs Carter visits, trade curbs discussed 6-10—6-12, 454E1, 455D2
Perez in US, sees Carter 6-27—7-2, 535F2, 546D1
Perez-Carter talks on Panama Canal rptd 7-27, 590C1
Perez lauds Panama Canal talks 8-6, 606C3
Young visits 8-12—8-13, 646E1, 647B1
Perez at Panama Canal pact signing 9-7, 678D1
Carter visit scheduled 9-23, 738F1
Exec kidnap still unsolved 9-25, 867A3
Carter visit deferred 11-7, 854A1; rescheduled 12-1, 914C2
Vance visits, sees Perez 11-23, 912F3-913A1

VENOIL (supertanker)
Collides off S Africa 12-16, 999E3
VENPET (supertanker)
Collides off S Africa 12-16, 999E3
VENTURA, Jose
Killed 1-5, 42B1
VEPCO—*See VIRGINIA Electric and Power Co.*
VERDET, Ilie
Miners hold hostage 8-2—8-3, 947F3
VEREEN, Ben
Roots makes TV history 1-23—1-30, 118G3
VERESHCHAGIN, Leonid F.
Dies 2-23, 164F3
VERIATO, Steve
2d in Atlanta Classic 5-29, 676E1
VERINGA, Gerhard
Dutch abortn rift mediated 9-2, 729F2
VERMA, Brijal
Indian industries min 3-26, 240C1
VERMILYE Jr., Rev. Claudius Ira
Arrest rptd 5-15, 432E2

VERMONT
Legislature schedule rptd 6F2
Solzhenitsyn forms publishing co 1-21, 140F3
Fed spending inequities chrgd 4-6, 423D3
'76 per-capita income table 5-10, 387C2
Vernon A-plant protest 8-6, 702E2
Drought aid OKd 8-24, 660C1
'76 per capita income, tax burden table 9-13, 10-18, 821B2
Legion fever rptd in Burlington 9-23, 748E1

VERMONT Transit Lines
Bus hijacked, 2 slain 7-4, 568D3
VERNON, Vt.—*See VERMONT*
VERSFELT, William H.
Acquitted 11-1, 918A3
VESCO, Robert L.
Sup Ct bars ICC damage case review 2-22, 150F1
CR pol financing scandal 4-23—6-13, 506A1
'73 Orfila, Graiver mtg rptd 4-26, 4-28, 371D3
Villalobos fires on home 6-2, 506A2
CR '75 gas distributor profiteering rptd 6-11, 506B2
Villalobos murder attempt chrg dropped 7-11, 710C2
Wins CR libel suit; fraud trial ordrd 9-12, 767D1
ICC settles IOS claims 12-7, 980G2
VESCO & Co.
Sup Ct bars damage case review 2-22, 150E1
VEST, George
Named State asst secy 5-5, confrmd 5-25, 500C1

1978

Nicaragua rebel aid halt urged by US 12-11, 1018F3
McDonnell Douglas paymts rptd 12-15, 982F2
Guyana cult money rptd in Venez banks 12-17, USSR rejcts bequest 12-18, 1000B2

VENGO Obregon, Maria Eugenia
Named CR educatn min 3-4, 171A1
VENIAMIN, Christodoulos
Named Cyprus interior, defns min 3-8, 189G1
VENNAMO, Veikko
Kekkonen reelected 1-16, 36G2
VENNER, Thomas
Bares RCMP tapes, break-ins 4-11, 4-18, 311F3-312B1
VENTO, Rep. Bruce Frank (D, Minn.)
Reelected 11-7, 851A2
VENTRILOQUISM
Edgar Bergen dies 9-30, 777E3
VENUS (planet)
Volcanos rptd on surface 1-26, 293F2
Sulfuric acid in atmosphere calculated 5-6, 654B1
US launches orbiter 5-20, 445D1
US launches 2d orbiter 8-8, 623B1
USSR launchings rptd 9-10, 9-15, 714D1
US orbiter arrives 12-4, probes explore atmosphere 12-9—12-11, 968C2-B3
Sovt probes land 12-21, 12-25, 1021F2
VENUTI, Joe
Dies 8-14, 708F3
VERANDAH, The (play)
Opens 5-14, 760F3
VERBLOSKY, Walter
Flood paymt chrg rptd 1-27, 240G1
VERDET, Ilie
Loses Rumania CP post, named Planning Com chrmn 3-7, 193B2
VERDI, Giuseppe (1813-1901)
Requiem wins Grammy 2-24, 316C1
VERGARA, Capt. Raul (ret.)
Exiled to UK 4-15, 287F2
VERITY Jr., C. William
Backs steel trigger prices 1-4, 3G2
Minn plant to continue 7-7, 553D3
On Carter anti-inflatn plan 10-25, 806D3

VERMONT
Legislature schedule rptd 14G3
'77 sales-tax rate rptd 1-5, 15F3
State govt tax revenue table 1-9, 84E2
Vernon A-plant ruling curbed by US Sup Ct 4-3, 280F2
Tax-relief measures rptd 5-25, 425D1
W Ger terrorist suspect seized 7-16, 577A1; 3 US citizens chrgd 8-12, 651D3; 2 plead guilty 8-28, 8-31, 725D1
Legionnaires' disease rptd in Burlington 7-21, 635E3
State judges meet in Burlington 8-3, 626A3
Primary results 9-12, 716D2
Election results 11-7: cong 848A1, D3, 852C3, state 847D1, G3, 853E3, 897C3

VERMONT Yankee Nuclear Power Co.
Ct A-plant rulings curbed 4-3, 280F2
VERMONT Yankee Nuclear Power Co. v. Natural Resources Defense Council
Ct A-plant rulings curbed 4-3, 280F2
VERNON, Vt.—*See VERMONT*
VERSAILLES, Palace of
Bombed 6-26, Breton separatists arrested 6-27, 496C1
2 more Bretons arrested for bombing 6-30, chrgd 7-4, 533E2
Breton bombers sentenced 7-25, 649F2-A3
VESCO, Robert Lee
ICC case review barred 1-9, 13A2
CR pres-elect vows expulsn 2-7, 89C3; 2-22, 152C2
Asks CR citizenship; govt, oppositn vs 2-23, 152B2
Indicted in CR 3-16, 269C3
CR fraud chrgs dismissed, begins forgn trip 4-30, 354E2
Asks CR pres study case 5-6, 478E3
Carazo hints at ouster, reentry bar rptd 5-8, 354D2
In Bahamas, plans return to CR 5-11, 478C3
CR court upholds fraud suit dismissal 6-22, Carazo bars return 7-7, 558C3
Denied CR citizenship 7-19, 617D2; ct rejects plea 8-23, 671D2
Carter aides linked to 'pol fix,' denials issued 9-1—9-15; Anderson revises article 9-11, 719D3
VESSEY Jr., John E.
Heads US-S Korea cmnd 11-7, 872C3

1979

Mondale visits; rights, drugs noted in talks 3-23—3-24, 247D3, 248E1-A2
Owens-Ill kidnaped exec rescued 6-30, 505B3
US aide confers on Nicaragua 7-4, 504B1
US bank loans rptd sought 10-6, 837D3
US Carib moves scored 10-23, 824B2
McDonnell Douglas paymts alleged 11-9, 886G1

VENNERA, Chick
Yanks released 9-19, 820G3
VENTRON Corp.
NJ Meadowlands cleanup ordrd 8-26, 704B2
VENTURA, Lino
French Detective released 3-10, 528C2
VENTURINI, Gen. Danilo
To head Figueiredo mil household 1-19, 95D1
VENUS (planet)
Carter budget cuts research 1-22, 46G1
Chasm found by Pioneer orbiter 2-7, 290A1
Surface features described 5-29, 692A1
VERDET, Ilie (Rumanian premier)
Named Rumania premr 3-30, 279D3
VEREEN, Ben
All That Jazz released 12-20, 1007F2
VERGARI, Carl A.
On Bedford Hills (NY) slayings 7-19, 548G1
VERHOEVEN, Paul
Soldier of Orange released 8-16, 820D3
VERMEIL, Dick
Named top NFL coach 1-14, 175B2

VERMONT
Legislature schedule rptd 5F3
Med malpractice arbitratn rptd 1-28, 139E3
Laetrile shipmt recalled 3-8, 196A1
A-power protests 4-1, 261G3; 4-28—4-29 322F3
Ginzburg rpts Solzhenitsyn invite 4-29, 317G2
Wood fuel use rptd 5-20, 419G1
Winter heating fuel supply promised 8-28, 703C2
'78 per capita income rptd 9-16, 746A2, C2
Carter energy mailing planned, scored 9-17, 703G2
A-power protest at Vt Yankee (Vernon) plant 9-23, 742C3
Snelling seeks Ford '80 race 10-12, 783G2

VERNIER-Palliez, Bernard
Renault to buy Volvo share 12-19, 994B1, C1
VERNON, Tex.—*See TEXAS*
VERNON, Vt.—*See VERMONT*
VERON, Judge Earl Veron
Dismisses 4 chrgs vs ex-Rep Passman 3-29, Passman acquitted 4-1, 265C3
VERONA, Stephen
Boardwalk released 11-14, 1007A3
VESCO, Robert Lee
Jury foreman resigns, claims cover-up 8-29, 647E2
Heymann, Carter deny chrgs 8-31; juror resignatn rejected 9-7, 725F2-E3
Cornfeld acquitted 10-15, 818F1
Bell testifies 12-4; Carter to videotape testimony 12-5; Civiletti quits probe 12-7, 943C2-C3
VESTOFF, Virginia
Spokesong opens 3-15, 712F2

1980

VENIAMIN, Christodoulos
Cabt shuffled 9-9, 749F2
VENICE Summit
7 natl ldrs meet 6-22—6-23, communique issued, '90 energy goal set 6-23, 473A1-474E1
US Dem platform vs A-power stand 6-24, 479B3
VENNOCHI, Joan
Wins Pulitzer 4-14, 296F2
VENTO, Rep. Bruce Frank (D, Minn.)
Reelected 11-4, 843B2
VENTURA County v. Gulf Oil
Case decided by Sup Ct 3-31, 291A3
VENUS (planet)
NASA contour map released 5-28, 477F1
Sovt missions rptd planned 11-23, 933C1
VERBANO, Valerio
Slain 2-22, 151A3
VERDAL-Austin, Robert
Sentenced 4-17, 301B3
VERGARA Campos, Lt. Col. Roger
Assassinated 7-15, 563A1
Murder laid to rightists 7-24, 603E2
Right-wing terrorists arrested 8-12, 618A3
VERITY Jr., C. William
On Carter econ renewal plan 8-28, 663B3
VERMEIL, Dick
Named top NFL coach 1-9, 175C1

VERMONT
Influenza outbreak rptd 2-15, 158C3
Tax on Mobil forgn dividends backed by Sup Ct 3-19, 249F2
S Africa arms sales admitted by US-Canada co 3-25, 278G1
A-protests mark 3 Mile I anniv 3-30, 249B1
Rockefeller's grandson arrested 8-18, denied pub defender 9-22, 908B3
Drought rptd 12-1, 947F3
Politics & Government—*See also other appropriate subheads in this section*
Legislature schedule rptd 18F1
State of State message 1-10, 270C2
Primary results 9-9, 700B3
Election results 11-4: cong 840E3, 844C3, 845A3; state 845E3, 847E1, 849D1
'80 census rptd 12-31, 983G1
Presidential Election (& Transition)
Reagan campaigns in Burlington 2-14, 128D3
Carter, Reagan win primaries 3-4, 166B2
Newspaper endorsemts rptd 11-1, 844F1
Election results 11-4, 838D1, 839A2, G3

VERMONT, University of (Burlington)
Wins NCAA skiing title 3-8, 470B1
VERNAS, Alban
Wins Olympic medal 7-26, 623F2
VERRASZTO, Zoltan
Wins Olympic medals 7-26, 7-27, 623E2, A3
VERTAC Chemical Corp.
US files Ark chem-dump suit 3-4, 190E3
VERWOERD, Hendrik Frensch (1901-66)
Son-in-law to head Broederbond 9-26, 753G2
VESCO, Robert Lee
Grand jury probe ends, no indictmts brought 4-1, 251B3
Interviewed on B Carter link 7-27, role discounted 7-30, 570D1
B Carter informant indicted in offshore bank fraud 10-20, 860C3
Allen quits Reagan post 10-30, 818C1
VESZI, Endre
Angi Vera released 1-9, 216B2

1976

VETERANS (U.S.)—*See also VETERANS Administration under U.S. GOVERNMENT*
- Angola mercenary training rptd 1-2, 3C2
- Dec, '75 transfer paymts rptd 1-19, 91D2
- '77 budget proposals 1-21, 62B3, 63F1, F3
- House Budget Com vs Ford proposals 3-23, 231E2
- Fiscal '77 Ford, House com budgets table 231B1
- VA overpaymts rptd 3-26, 262G2
- Cong OKs '77 budget target 5-12, 5-13; Ford, OMB, Cong budgets table 358F1, D2
- Cong clears added funds 5-19, 411D3; signed 6-1, 982F1
- Dem platform text 6-15, 473B1
- '77 funds signed 8-9, 623E1
- GOP platform text 8-18, 606F2-A3
- Carter cites re Viet pardons 8-24, 631D3
- Cong sets '77 budget levels, chart 9-16, 706C2
- Cong OKs 4 aid bills 9-20, 9-21, 10-1, 806G3; signed 9-30, 10-15, 10-21, 982G1
- '77 defns funds signed 9-22, 707A2, C2, D2
- Sup Ct bars review of VFW sex-bar case 10-4, 807A3
- Ford gets AMVETS award 10-19, 784D2
- Ford visits Seattle hosp 10-25, 802E3
- Dole scores Mondale 10-25, 804D2

VETERANS of Foreign Wars
- Connally addresses NYC conv 8-18, 601E2
- Sup Ct bars sex-bar case review 10-4, 807A3

VETERANS of World War II, Korea and Vietnam, American (AMVETS)
- Ford gets award 10-19, 784D2

VEVDOKIMOV, Nikolai
- Rptd USSR spy in Paris 1-19, 50B1

VIAL, Patrick
- Wins Olympic medal 7-29, 574G3

VIANA, Jose
- Car bombed 1-23, 76C1

VICKERS, D. W.
- Named to econ advisory bd 9-14, 730F1

VIDAL, Gore
- 1876 on best-seller list 12-5, 972E2

VIDELA, Lt. Gen. Jorge Rafael
- Sees mil ldrs on pol crisis 2-20, 154G1
- Escapes bomb blast 3-15, 212D1
- Leads mil coup; in junta 3-24, 211E2
- Junta gets final exec powers 3-25, 236C1
- Sworn pres, swears cabt 3-29; details plans 3-30, 236A1, E1
- On dissolutn of pol parties, unions 6-11, 520B1
- Sees church leaders 7-22, 571C2
- Plotters rptd slain 8-20, 671D3
- Nazi lit ban rptd unsigned 8-30, 672C2
- Perons buried 10-2, 12-19, 997B2
- Hard-line generals retired 12-3, 996A3

VIEIRA da Silva, Maria
- Pres bid rptd 5-12, 366D3

VIEIRA Rocha, Gen. Vasco
- Sworn Portugal army staff chief 7-19, 558G2

VIERA Trejo, Bernardo
- Perez, Bosch ties cited 10-24, 843F3

1977

VETERANS (U.S.)—*See also under U.S. GOVERNMENT*
- Ford '78 budget requests 1-17, 32B1, G2
- Ford ordrs dischrg upgrades 1-19, 36A2
- Admin plans jobs effort 1-27, 52A2
- Sen revives com 2-4, 90G2, G3
- Welfare cost rptd 2-19, 176C1
- Carter budget revisns 2-22, 125A2
- Giaimo proposes budget 3-23, 229A1
- Carter OKs Viet dischrg review 3-28, 231B3
- Dischrg program response slight 5-10, 421B1
- Cong sets '78 budget target 5-17, 405B1
- Alcoholism rptd up 6-7, 472A2
- Benefits dispute stalls HUD funds bill 6-15—9-23; House deletes curb, bill cleared 9-28, 796A3
- Nurses convicted in '75 hosp deaths 7-13, 568F2
- new trial ordrd 12-19, 991G2
- Dischrg review bill cleared 9-23, 759C2; signed 10-8, 773A2
- Dischrg upgrade data rptd 10-1, 759B3
- Mil disability pensn hike signed 10-3, 877F3
- Dischrg review phone svc ends 10-4, 759G2
- Mass job prefernc law backed 10-11, 774D2
- Pensn hike cleared by Cong 11-3, 877E3; signed 12-2, 1001F2
- Educ aid hike, revisns cleared 11-4, 877D2; signed 11-23, 1001F2
- Tex referendum OKd 11-8, 879D2

VETERANS Administration—*See under U.S. GOVERNMENT*

VETERANS of Foreign Wars (VFW)
- Scores Viet pardon action 1-21, 51E2
- Natl conv vs Panama Canal pacts 8-23, 678G1, F2
- Cong vets dischrg review bill cleared 9-23, 759E2

VETERANS of World War II, Korea and Vietnam, American (AMVETS)
- Panama Canal treaties scored 9-16, 716C3

VIACOM International Inc.

Showtime Entertainment Inc.
- RCA satellite pay-TV pact rptd 10-25, 921D1

VIDELA, Lt. Gen. Jorge Rafael (Argentine president)
- Mex asks Campora safe-conduct 1-18, 66B2
- Escapes bomb blast 2-18, 197B3
- Rights abuses chrgd 2-21, UN comm bars probe 3-4, 198D1
- Smith kidnaped 2-25, 198E3
- Visits Peru, signs A-plant pact 3-3—3-6, 259E1
- Denies rights abuses 3-15, 198C2
- Confrms Graiver-Montonero ties 4-19, 345C3
- Graiver probe deal rptd 4-22, 371E2
- At Davis Cup final 4-29—5-1, 353G2
- Visits Venez, protests staged 5-11—5-14, 547G1-F2
- Lanusee, ex-aides freed 6-13, 522E3
- On pol 'dialogue' plan 6-18, 522F2
- Army seeks new 'civic' ldrs 7-3, 615G1
- Rightist rivals cited re Venez amb's kidnap 7-18, 595A2
- Spain Soclst ldr backs Montoneros 7-23, 595C3
- Aide rptdly foiled Resnizky kidnap 8-3, 670A3
- On future govt-civilian talks 8-6, 615B2
- Sees US State Dept offcls 8-7—8-16, 670D1
- At Panama Canal pact signing 9-7, 678C1
- On rightist terror 9-9; vow to Carter rptd 9-12, 922C1
- Bravo held without ct access 9-20; 4,000 such arrests cited 9-22, 922A2
- Women protest disappearances 10-14, 922B1
- Sees Vance 11-21, 912F2
- Rights activists kidnaped 12-8, 981C3
- Plans prisoner list; says guerrilla war ending 12-10, 981C3

VIDOR, Florence
- Dies 11-3, 952F3

VIDOR, King
- Ex-wife dies 11-3, 952F3

1978

VETERANS (U.S.)
- Pensn revisns proposed by CBO 1-11, 52F3
- Carter budget proposal table 1-23, 45E2
- GOP attacks Carter budget 1-31, 63C1
- '75 Mich hosp-death chrgs vs 2 nurses dropped 2-1, 116C2
- Carter urges Civil Svc chng 3-2, 141E2
- Job priority in Humphrey-Hawkins bill 3-16, 182C3
- VA educ curbs backed by Sup Ct 3-20, 205E3
- Educ Dept plan excludes VA programs 4-14, 279B1, E2
- Cong '79 budget-target res cleared 5-17, 385F1
- Nixon hosts Viet ex-POW receptn, LA conv cited 5-27, 513D2
- Viet vet job tax credit OKd by House com 7-27, 587E1
- A-test vet wins cancer claim 8-1, 702E1
- Civil Svc legis reforms rptd 8-12, 625E2
- Civil Svc reforms pass Sen 8-24, 662A1
- Civil Svc job preference retained by House 9-11, other reforms OKd 9-13, 696C2-D3
- VA '79 funds signed 9-30, 750C2-A3
- Carter rpts on Viet vets; ACLU, vets cncl score 10-10, 878A1-G1
- 500 Viet vets claim Agent Orange disabilities 10-11, critic dies 12-4, 984D1-A2
- Civil Svc job preference kept 10-13, 788A1
- Viet vet jobs tax credit clears 10-15, 785D3
- Calif voters OK bond issue 11-7, 915D2
- Army GI bill benefits proposed 11-10, 895E2
- Nixon at Vets Day fete 11-11, 900A3
- Brown urges pensn reform 12-14, 1009C2

VETERANS Administration—*See under U.S. GOVERNMENT*

VETERANS of Foreign Wars (VFW)
- VA educ program shift opposed 4-14, 279B2

VIAL, Gonzalo
- Chile educatn min 12-26, 1014E2

VICIOUS, Sid (John Simon Ritchie)
- Chrgd with murder 10-12, attempts suicide 10-23, 842C1

VICTOR, Lucia
- Hello Dolly opens 3-5, 887A2

VICTORIA, Queen (Great Britain) (1819-1901)
- Australia announces Cocos I purchase 7-2, 514F1

VIDARABINE (Vira-A)—*See MEDICINE—Drugs*

VIDELA, Lt. Gen. Jorge Rafael (Argentine president)
- Meets Pinochet re Beagle Channel dispute 1-19, 2d mtg put off 1-24, 101B2
- US rpt on pol prisoners, '77 Vance talks cited 2-13, 207G3
- Sees Pinochet on Beagle Channel dispute 2-20, 216E1
- Church presses prisoner release 3-21, 4-10, 286B1
- Asks 'dialogue' with natl ldrs 3-29, 611C3
- Newsprs closed re pres term extensn rpt 4-21—4-23, 611F3
- Pres term extended 5-2; quits army, junta 7-31, 611F2
- Vows more dem govt 5-29, 8-1, 611G3
- Adm's daughter slain in blast 8-1, 612C1
- In Italy, leftists protest 9-5, 689D3
- Admits repressn, sees democracy 9-5, 793B1
- Sees Bolivia pres, backs sea outlet 10-25, 860C3
- Warns press 10-27, 865D3
- Shuffles Cabt 2 civilns added 11-6, 865C2
- Spain king visits 11-26—11-30, 967F3
- New Beagle Channel talks urged 12-12, 979A3
- Sees Beagle Channel mediator 12-26, 999B3

VIEIRA, Sergio
- Named Mozambique bank gov 4-22, 331E1

1979

VETERANS (U.S.)
- Mil dischrg suit filed 1-19, 53B1
- Carter budget proposals 1-22, 41C2, 43F3, 44F1; table 42E2
- Sears sues US on bias laws 1-24, 92D1
- Viet Agent Orange suit filed 2-1, 90A1
- '53 A-test radiatn liability appeal lost, notificatn suit OKd 2-9, 112C2
- WWII amputatn data rptd 2-26, 219A2
- WWII women pilots get benefits 3-9, 307D3
- Viet-era Marine returns to US 3-25, plans fight vs desertn chrgs 3-31, 265G3
- Noncombat recall plan rptd 4-10, 307C2
- Sears suit vs US dismissed 5-15, 365B3
- '53 A-test radiatn liability case refused by Sup Ct 5-21, 400A3
- Carter vows more aid 5-30, 419A2
- Nicaragua mercenary recruitmt rptd 6-2, 427F1
- Job-prefernc law upheld by Sup Ct; reactn 6-5, 421D1-D2
- Fed paymts hiked, inflatn cited 7-1, 622A1
- Pol actn comm creatn set by VFW 8-21, 628C1
- Amer Legion backs SALT 8-22, 644C1
- Army settles LSD suit 9-6, 705F1
- Viet study reveals problems 9-25, 725D1
- '80 VA funds clear Cong 10-24, Carter signs 11-5, 883G2
- Panama coup plotters arrested 10-24, 836C3
- Army seeks test subjects 11-2, 850E2
- '67 Cuba defector returns 11-21, 924F1
- Viet troops Agent Orange exposure rptd 11-24, 5 mfrs sued 11-26, 904B2-A3
- Army drug dischrgs ordrd upgraded 11-28, 992D1
- Viet-era Marine desertn case opens 12-4, 924D1
- '67 Cuba defector charged as deserter 12-19, 965G3

VETERANS, National Association of Concerned
- Mil dischrg suit filed 1-19, 53C1

VETERANS Administration—*See under U.S. GOVERNMENT*

VETERANS Education Project
- Mil dischrg suit filed 1-19, 53C1, F1

VETERANS of Foreign Wars (VFW)
- Conv: pol action com voted 8-21, Clute installed cmdr 8-24, 628C1

VETTER, Heinz
- Worker codeterminatn upheld 3-2, 172D3

VEZINA Trophy—*See HOCKEY–Awards*

VIANSSON-Ponte, Pierre
- Dies 5-7, 432G3

VIASA Airlines
- Strike averted 11-1, 874E3

VICARIO, Marco
- Wifemistress released 1-6, 174G3

VICIOUS, Sid (John Simon Ritchie)
- Dies of heroin overdose 2-2, 156B3

VICKERS, Jack E.
- Fairbanks Colo U football deal leaked 4-2, 335C2

VICKERS Energy Corp.—*See under ESMARK*

VICKS Sinex—*See MEDICINE–Drugs*

VICTIM (play)
- Opens 5-3, 712C3

VICTORIA, Queen (1819-1901) (Great Britain)
- Secret marriage, child alleged 5-22, 388F2

VICUNAS—*See WILDLIFE*

VIDELA, Lt. Gen. Jorge Rafael (Argentine president)
- Labor ldrs arrested, strike threat defused 4-23—4-27, 351F2
- Meets OAS rights comm 9-7, 683E2
- Econ aide's home bombed 9-27, 749A1
- Army rebellion crushed 9-29, 748D3
- Announces union pol ban 11-16, 887E2
- Names moderate army chief 12-7, 947F2
- Cox leaves Argentina 12-16, 966F2

VIDOR, King
- Wins Oscar 4-9, 336C2

1980

VETERANS (U.S.)
- Carter vetoes dioxins study 1-2, 17B3
- Carter budget proposal, table 1-28, 70E1
- Reagan 'basic speech' cites Viet War 2-29, 207E2
- Spanish-Amer War vet dies 3-10, 279E3
- Army sets retired soldiers mobilizatn 4-2, 267F2
- WWII WAACs get vet status 4-2, 267A3
- Reagan admits gaffe on Viet vet GI benefit eligibility 4-10, 288E2
- Mortgage rates cut 5-15, 384E3
- Carter signs Viet War mem'l bill; speech scored 7-1, 496B1-F1
- WW II Medal of Honor awarded 7-19, 638E1
- Pres candidates address VFW, Amer Legion 8-18—8-21, 629A1-A2, C2, F3-630A1, A2
- Carter vetoes VA MD pay hike 8-22, Cong overrides 8-26, 649C3
- Educ aid bill clears Cong 9-25, 9-26, signed 10-17, 856F2

VETERANS Administration—*See under U.S. GOVERNMENT*

VETERANS of Foreign Wars (VFW)
- Chicago conv hears Reagan, Anderson 8-18—8-20; pol com endorses Reagan 8-18, 629A1, G3-630A1

VEVERKA Jr., Charles R.
- Indicted 7-28, 576C1
- Acquitted 12-17, 989F3

VIACHOVA, Kristina
- Apple Game released 1-16, 216B2

VIACOM International Inc.
- Showtime scores Getty Oil pay-TV film venture 4-24, 376F2

VICEK, Oldrich
- Magicians released 12-26, 1003B2

VICKER, Raymond
- Iran chrgs shah gave gifts 2-9, 122B3

VICKERS Energy Corp.—*See under ESMARK Inc.*

VICKERS Petroleum Corp.
- Total Petroleum sale rptd 8-26, 745G2

VICTORY Carriers
- Bethlehem Steel ex-offcl pleads guilty 8-7, 600A2

VIDAL, Gore
- Caligula released 2-2, 216C2

VIDELA, Lt. Gen. Jorge Rafael (Argentine president)
- 2 ex-prisoners describe detentn 2-4, 95C1
- Sees Brazil pres, strengthens ties 5-15—5-17, 405C2
- Snubbed by Peru pres 7-28, 580C1
- Supports Bolivia mil govt 7-31, 577F1
- Junta delays naming successor, Lambruschini rift rptd 9-30, 747E2
- Viola named successor, junta rift resolved 10-3, 766E1-B2

VIDNOVIC, Martin
- Brigadoon opens 10-16, 892A3

VIEIRA, Joao Bernardo (Guinea-Bissau Premier)
- Ousts Cabral in coup 11-14, 887B1

1976

VIETNAM (North), Democratic Republic of—*See also VIETNAM, Socialist Republic of*
- Rpts mil resistance in S Viet 1-3, 1-6, 11F3
- Jamaica ties set 1-6, 51B2
- Oil pact with Algeria signed 1-17, 46A1
- Listed as 'not free' nation 1-19, 20E3
- Sahara Polisario aid rptd 1-25, 58F2
- Laotian ties bolstered 2-11, 121D1
- Le Duan addresses Sovt CP Cong 2-25, 196D1
- Aide in bombed Cambodian town 3-2—3-4, 238B2
- WHO rpts on health conditns 3-20, 315F2
- Surprised by '75 win 4-24, 4-25, 315G2
- Forgn oil co talks rptd 4-24, 352A2
- Jt S Viet assemb elected 4-26, 315C2
- Forgn aides, news svcs ordered from Saigon to Hanoi 5-2, 367E2
- Forgn oil cooperation vowed 5-7, 367A3
- Hanoi archbp named cardinal 5-24, 423G3
- UN backs postwar aid 6-2, 408C2
- Says South govt foes to be tried 6-10, 441G2
- Reunited with South 7-2, 502C3

U.S. Relations
- Nixon econ aid vow claimed 2-1; memo disclosure hinted, US comment 2-2, 103B1
- US for talks on ties 3-25, MIA info 3-26; N Viets ask econ aid 3-29, 255A2
- Hanoi answers peace bid, scores US 4-12; US calls 'negative' 4-13, 291C1
- US denies aid vow 4-14, 291E1
- US optimism scored 4-16, 291G1
- US oil co talks rptd 4-24, 352C2
- Ford vetoes aid bill 5-7, 345B1; Carter comments 5-14, 391A1
- N Viet vows oil cooperatn 5-7, 367A3
- Reagan scores US war role 5-21, 374F1
- Ford bars war role apology 5-25, 374B1
- US Dem platform text cites war 6-15, 478C2
- US aid bill signed 6-30, 533D1

VIETNAM (South)—*See also VIETNAM, Socialist Republic of*
- Mil resitance rptd 1-3, 1-6, 11E3
- Foreigners evacuated 1-3, 11G3
- Anti-corruption drive 1-3, 11G3
- Buddhists back govt 1-10, 54G1
- Saigon exodus continues 1-18, 54F1
- Listed as 'not free' nation 1-19, 20E3
- Civilians assume Saigon rule 1-21, 54D1
- '75 econ gains reviewed 1-21, 54E1
- Saigon uprising 2-12, crushed 2-13; govt statemt, other incidents 2-15, 143D3
- Aide in bombed Cambodian town 3-2—3-4, 238B2
- Airman defects to Thailand 3-8, 223A2
- Denmark OKs orphans stay 3-16, 252D1
- Refugees land in Australia 3-19, 237B2
- WHO rpts widespread disease 3-20, 315D2
- Rebels die in clashes 3-22, 4-1, 268D3
- Rebels arrested 3-27—4-8, 367G2
- Rpt Burma Reds get war arms 3-31, 265C1
- Political foes warned 4-22, 367F2
- N Viet surprised by '75 win 4-24, 4-25, 315G2
- Forgn oil co talks rptd 4-24, 352A2
- Jt N Viet assemb elected 4-26, 315C2
- Govt foes to be tried 5-25, 6-10, 441G2
- UN backs postwar aid 6-2, 408C2
- Refugees flee to Thailand 6-7, 441D3
- Reunited with North 7-2, 502C3

U.S. Relations
- Rival refugee groups split 2-20, 176F2
- Bodies of 2 US marines returned 2-22, 157A2
- Reagan scores Ford policy 3-4, 165G3
- Pol foes, CIA linked 4-22, 367F2
- US oil firm talks rptd 4-24, 352C2
- CIA-funded institute rptd 4-26, 299F1
- Ford vetoes aid bill 5-7, 345B1; Carter comments 5-14, 391A1
- Reagan scores US war role 5-21, 374F1
- Ford bars war role apology 5-25, 374B1
- US Dem platform text cites war 6-15, 478C2
- US aid bills signed 6-30, 533D1, C2

VIETNAM, Socialist Republic of—*See also ADB, NONALIGNED Nations, VIETNAM (North), VIETNAM (South)*
- Natl Assemb inaugural mtg 6-24—7-3, 502D3
- North, South formally reunite, country renamed 7-2; Hanoi ldrs get key posts 7-3, 502C3
- At COMECON summit 7-7—7-9, 722D2
- OKs ties with Pl, Thais 7-12, 8-6, 593D2
- Thai protests refugees 7-29—8-27; Viet scores 8-26, 678A1
- '70 Australia massacre denied 8-3, 571F3
- Backs econ ties with indl states 8-17, 621E3
- Australia OKs refugees entry 8-31, 672E3
- Thai rebels aid rptd 9-3, 677D3
- '75 mass Buddhist suicide rptd 9-8, 678B3
- China delegatn views Mao body 9-13, 711F3
- Joins IMF 9-15, World Bank 9-21, ADB 9-23, 721D3
- Thai junta scored 10-17, 795D1
- Thais chrg invasion plan 12-8, 949C3
- Workers Party cong, 5-yr plan OKd 12-14—12-20, 967C3-968D1
- Australia admits refugees 12-18, 997C3

1977

VIETNAM, Socialist Republic of—*See also COMECON, NONALIGNED Nations Movement; also VIETNAM War*
- Officer training progrm set 1-5, 48G2
- Unemployment, unrest admitted 1-13, 23B3
- War prisoners freed 2-18, 161F2
- Postwar conditns described 5-1, 5-2, 336D3, 337D1
- Rebel resistance admitted 6-9, 470D1
- CP Com admits agri errors 8-26, 674A3
- Saigon, Hanoi econ setbacks rptd 8-26, 8-28, 674C3
- Food shortages rptd 10-1, 988D3
- Minority resistance rptd 10-1, 989A1
- Jet hijacked to Singapore 10-29, 848C2
- Farm experts sent to south 11-11, 11-12, 988C3
- Populatn shift to south rptd 12-9, 988A3
- Singapore hijackers jailed 12-15, 991F3

1978

VIETNAM, Socialist Republic of—*See also COMECON, NONALIGNED Nations Movement*
- Business natlizatn set 3-23, ethnic Chinese flee 5-1—5-9, 340G3-341F1
- Hoarders raided, luxury items confiscated 5-5—5-6, 341F1
- Business natlizatn protests rptd 5-27, 399D3
- 10-mln populatn shift to New Econ Zones planned 5-30, 400B1
- Thi killed 6-17, rptd slain 7-3, 549B2
- Tuyen '76 death rptd 7-10, 692F1
- Party problems in south rptd 10-18, 823B1
- Thien Minh death rptd 10-26, 888F3

Cambodian Conflict—*See CAMBODIA—Vietnam Conflict*

Chinese Relations—*See CAMBODIA—Vietnam Conflict, CHINA—Vietnam Dispute*

1979

VIETNAM, Socialist Republic of—*See also COMECON, NONALIGNED Nations Movement*
- Armed resistance rptd 5-31, 547B2
- Hanoi archbp installed cardinal 6-30, 640B2
- Assemb dep chrmn defects to China 7-5; Hanoi, Peking confirm 8-6, 8-8, 604C1
- Dissident group smashed 7-17, 547A2

Cambodian Conflict—*See CAMBODIA-Vietnam Conflict*

China Conflict
- China troop mass on border rptd 1-5, 1B1
- China for expanded US naval force 1-9, 26D3
- China, Viets chrg raids, border violatns 1-15–1-18, 68C3
- US concerned 1-21, 68E3
- Teng hints at mil moves 1-30, 1-31, 65E2, F2
- Viet troop massing rptd 1-30, 68B3
- Border clashes 1-30–2-14, 107B1
- Teng: must be 'punished' 2-7, 84C1
- Sovts deploy naval force 2-7, 107A1
- USSR, US warn China on Viet attack 2-8, 2-9, 106A3
- Viets issue intl plea 2-14, 107F1
- Viets chrg war plans, China rebuffs 2-15, 122E1
- Battle zone map 121A1
- **China troops launch invasn 2-17;** hit 4 provs, take Lao Cai, advance 15 mi; Hanoi offers stiff resistance, casualties rptd high 2-17–2-22, 121D1, E2

1980

VIETNAM, Socialist Republic of—*See also ADB, COMECON, NONALIGNED Nations*
- Govt shakeup 2-7, 90G1
- Thang dies 3-30, 280D2

Cambodia Conflict—*See CAMBODIA (Democratic Kampuchea)--Vietnam Conflict*

China Conflict
- Peace talks 1-9, 1-17, 2-5; Viet rep quits 2-8, 124E1-A2
- US rights rpt scores re ethnic Chinese emigratn 2-5, 87A2
- China suspends peace talks 3-6, 181C1
- Italy CP vs China role 4-22, 314C2
- Border breaches chrgd 7-2—7-5, 508C2
- China troop mass chrgd 7-7; West sees no move 7-9, 508E2
- US MIA proposal rejectn rptd linked 10-6, 855C2

1976 | 1977 | 1978 | 1979 | 1980

1979

Viet aid plea to Sovt, others 2-17, 121G1
US asks China exit, links Cambodia invasn 2-17, 2-20, 122B3
Viet asks UN measures 2-17; Waldheim issues plea 2-18, Cncl debate delayed 2-21, 123A1
USSR warns China 2-18, accuses US 2-19–2-20, 122F1
India, PLO protest invasn; Taiwan chrgs US collusn, other natns voice concern 2-18–2-21, 123D1
Teng says operatn limited 2-19, 121G1
Viet envoy chrgs aggressn, US collusn 2-19, 121D2
Rumania splits with Sovt bloc, Albania over China condemnatn 2-19, 2-22; USSR denounces 2-21, 122E2
W Eur CPs denounce China, accuse US 2-19, 122G2
Carter bars interventn, seeks fighting end 2-20, 123E2, C3
Sovt recon jets, ships sighted 2-21; airlift to Viets rptd 2-22, 122B1
China warns Sovts vs arms aid 2-21, 122C1
Chinese cmdrs identified 2-21, 122D1
Carter defends stand 2-22, 124D1
US affirms China ties 2-23, 141D2
USSR scores China 2-23, 2-26; Teng counterchrgs, doubts interventn 2-27, 141E2, F2
UN Cncl meets, US asks China exit 2-23; actn stalled 2-28, 142A1
China retakes Viet-occupied area, demands border chng 2-24, 141F1
Viets send in regular forces 2-24, 141F1
2 US reps in war zone 2-24, 141A2
US notes concern in China talks 2-24–3-1, 146E2
China claims drive limited 2-25, Teng sees end 2-26; Hanoi chrgs 'deceptn' 2-26, 141C1
Viet, China rpt casualties 2-25, 2-27, 141E1
Chinese advance 25-40 miles, battles rage near Lang Son 2-26, 141A1
2 Viet thrusts in China rptd 2-27, 141B2
US asks China exit 2-27, 141C2
Teng likens to Cuba, doubts Sovt interventn 2-27, 141D2
Carter bars US role, defends China trade talks 2-27, 149B2, D2
Talk proposals exchngd 3-1, 3-2, China hints at pullout 3-1, 158E2
Chinese take Lang Son 3-1, Viets deny 3-4, Lang Son fighting continues 3-5, 158A3
USSR vows Viet support 3-1, 159B1
Sovt warships rptd in E China Sea 3-1, 159C1
Brezhnev warns China, affirms Viet treaty 3-2, 172A1
China rpts exit 3-5, says troops leave as victors 3-6; Viets deny pullout 3-5, chrg contd attacks 3-6, 3-7, 158F1
USSR doubts China pullout 3-5, 159A1
Attack chrgs exchngd 3-12; Viets claim Chinese units 'wiped out' 199D3
USSR doubts China pullout 3-14; USSR-India communique scores China 3-15, 3-14, 200C2
China: Viet pullout ends 3-15; talk bids exchngd 3-15, 3-17, 3-19, 199G2
Sovt air, sea lift of Viet troops, arms rptd 3-15, 199E3
USSR vetoes UN actn on China pullout 3-16, 200D1
China warns protesters 3-16, 259B1
Viet: China holds Viet border areas 3-19, 199B3
Viet admits heavy war loss 3-22, 298A2
Raid chrgs traded 3-24, 298B2
US intell praised 3-25, 231F3
US says Sovts use Cam Ranh base 3-27, 3-28, 5-9; warns USSR, Viet 3-28, 340E2
Peace talks deadlocked 4-18, 4-26, 298B1
Waldheim in Hanoi, Peking; seeks mediatn 4-26–5-1, 340G1
China raids chrgd 5-1–5-3, 340D2
China lists war losses 5-2, 340C2
French CP backs Sovt role 5-10–5-14, 371A2
Prisoner trade OKd 5-12, carried out 5-21, 379G2-A3
China: border change sought 5-13, 379C3
Viet denies ethnic Chinese forced to flee 5-16, 379F1
5th peace mtg deadlocked 5-18, 379B3
Viets chrg China troop mass 6-1, 474E2
Viets chrg prisoner abuse 6-4, 474E2
War prisoners exchngd 6-5, 474D2
China asks halt to refugee flow 6-16, 460B3
Peace talks deadlocked 6-28, 7-5, 7-18, 536G3-537C1
China '79 mil budget rise linked 6-29, 502C3
Border breaches chrgd 7-11, 7-13, 537C1
China blames for refugees 7-20, 549A2
Talks deadlock, Viet War debated 7-20, 575E2
Viet border attack 7-22, China warns 7-26, 575B3
US-China refugee actns scored 7-27, 575C2
China confrms Hoan detectn 8-8, 604E1
China chrgs raids 8-13, 8-17, border massing 9-6, 660B2
Peace talks, chrgs traded 8-14, 8-29, 660F1

1976

UN Membership Issue—*See 'Membership' under UNITED Nations*

U.S. Relations
Carter cites war 7-15, 507D1, 510E2
Mondale legis record cited 512D3
Carter LBJ remarks disclosed 7-20, 704D2
Departure plan for Americans 7-21; 39 leave 8-1, 8-7, 593G1
US cites Asian threat 7-22, 557E2
No MIA return seen 7-23, 593C2
A-aid cited 7-23, 739G2
Calley for total amnesty 8-11, 680A3
For US ties 8-17, 621E3
US GOP platform text cites 8-18, 609E2, 610A2
Ford acceptance speech cites 8-19, 612A1
Ford position cited 614A1
Dole legis record cited 614D2, F2
Nonaligned laud victory vs US 8-20, 621E3
Mondale stresses US unity 8-25, 645F2
12 MIA pilots rptd dead, US asks full list 9-6, 678E2-B3 ★
Ford asks MIA accounting 9-7, 665B1
Ford links ties to full MIA list 9-7, Viet scores 9-11, 682C2
US to veto UN entry re MIAs; Viet scores, releases notes re ties, aid 9-13, 682B1
Red Cross ends foreigner evacuatn 9-14, 696G2
US opposes in IMF 9-15, World Bank 9-21, 721E3
Carter, Ford debate 9-23, 701E3
Carter on LBJ remarks 9-27, 724F2
US forgn aid bill bars funds 10-1, 806E3
China vs US for barring Viet UN seat 10-5, 760A1
2d Ford, Carter debate 10-6, 741D1, 742D2
US tied to Thai coup 10-8, 775F3-776A1
US vp candidates debate 10-15, 783A1, D1, B2
Ford, Carter debate 10-22, 800D3, G3
Dole on Viet war 10-26, 804E2
Captured arms rptd 11-11, 961D2
Preliminary talks open 11-12, 863B2
S Korea lobbying,, troop commitmt linked 11-13, 899E3
US vetoes UN entry 11-15; Hanoi scores 11-15, 11-16, 862B3
US Army overspending rptd 11-19, 982A3
US vows 2d UN entry veto 11-26, 914C2

1977

Foreign Relations (misc.)—*See also 'UN Membership' below*
Sweden sets aid 1-10, 23B1
IMF loan OKd 1-11, 23G2
Canada '64-65 missn cover-up rptd 1-14, 97B3
'76 Swiss asylum requests rptd 1-25, 138A1
Refugee flow rptd up 3-25, 243E3
Dong visits France 4-25—4-28, oil agreemt rptd 4-28, 329A1
Postwar Cambodia ties rptd strained 5-2, 337D1
Defector rpts jailings 5-3, 470G1-A2
Cambodia border clashes rptd 5-8—8-8, 607C2-B3
Territorial water limits set 5-20, 490F2
Refugee flow increases 6-12, 6-19; UN rpts Westn asylums 6-16, Israel welcomes 66 6-26, 497B1, G1
ASEAN backs ties 7-5—7-8, 537C1
Delegatn in Laos 7-15—7-18; pacts signed, ties bolstered 7-18, 552G3
Thai fishing boat sunk 7-25, 607E3
ASEAN asks ties, Hanoi scores 8-4—8-5, 607E1
Malaysia eases refugee ban 8-31, 685D2
Amnesty Intl lists jailed lawmakers 9-5, 753C2
Lon Nol denies Cambodia border clashes 9-12, 710G1
Cambodia premr cites clashes 9-28, 741E3
E Ger chrgs US atrocities 9-28, 752B3
Cambodia hints at clashes 10-2, 779G3
Cambodia refugees get asylum 10-19, 840G2
New Thai rulers for ties 10-21, 827D1
Jet hijacked to Singapore 10-29, 848C2; hijackers jailed 12-15, 991F3
Cambodia border clashes 12-22, 12-24, 12-27; Cambodia cuts ties 12-31, 999D2

Refugees—*See IMMIGRATION & Refugees; country names*

UN Membership (& developments)
Carter on entry conditns 3-24, 229B3
US to drop veto 5-3—5-4, 333A1
US rep backs 7-19, 572E2
Council OKs 7-20, 572D2
Carter town mtg topic 7-21, 575B1
Assembly OKs 9-20, 713A1
ECOSOC OKs spec aid 10-6, 770A2

U.S. Relations
IMF loan unopposed 1-11, 23B3
Seaborn '64-65 missn cover-up rptd 1-14, 97B3
Carter plans missn to Hanoi 2-11, 110A2
CIA paymts to Diem, Thieu rptd 2-19, 124F1
US rep seeks Nixon aid pledge 2-22, 403A3
US sets mission 2-25, 206F2
Castro scores US rights pressure 2-26—2-27, 180E3
Carter on US missn 3-5, 171E1, C2; 3-17, 186C2
Carter to lift travel ban 3-9, 172F3, 173D1
US missn visits, gets 12 MIAs 3-16—3-19; Carter gets rpt, OKs talks on ties 3-23, 206A1
Carter links 'normal' ties, econ aid; lauds MIA missn 3-24, 229G2-E3
Talks on ties open; US to drop UN veto, end embargo 5-3—5-4; Hanoi asks post-war aid, US bars 5-4, 5-5, 333A1, E1
Expatriates ask US aid bar 5-4, 333E1
Kissinger vs US aid 5-4, 333G1
Nixon reminisces 5-12, 386B1
Nixon disavows aid pledge 5-14, US releases note to Hanoi 5-19, 403E2
Hanoi airs Nixon note 5-22, US claims omissns 5-23, 403E3
Talks resume, US gets new MIA list 6-2—6-3, 441E1
US to challenge USSR role 6-10, 460D2
US Sen bans loans 6-14, 477C3
US refugee asylum urged 6-19, 497G1
Viet-Laos pacts set US ties terms 7-18, 553D1
US backs UN entry 7-19, Cncl OKs 7-20, 572E2
Carter on UN entry stand 7-21, 575B1
US aid bar authorized 8-4, 668B2
E Ger chrgs atrocities 9-28, 752B3
Viets return 22 US bodies 9-30, 795D1
Nixon tapes open for civil suit 10-3, 760B2
US vs ECOSOC aid 10-6, 770B2
US yacht seized, 3 held 10-12; Viets vow release 12-20, 975G3
US forgn aid funds clear Cong 10-19, 815A2; Carter signs 11-1, 834D1
Exxon admits paymts 10-25, 818A2
US bars plea on food aid 12-16, 989B1
US-Viet talks; MIA identificatn pressed 12-19—12-20, 975F3

1978

Foreign Relations (misc.)—See also 'Monetary, Trade & Aid' below; also CAMBODIA—Vietnam Conflict
Aerial shortcut with Laos reopened 2-11, 140B1
PI occupies Spratly isle 3-11, 290G1
Troops rptd in battles vs Laos resistance groups 3-28, 237F2
China hints Sovts foment feud 6-7, 464A3
Taiwan to evacuate ethnic Chinese from Ho Chi Minh City 6-20, 464A3
Comecon joined 6-27, 504F3
China chrgs Viet-USSR plot to control SE Asia 7-12, 547G3
Romulo says stops attacks on ASEAN 8-4, 603B3
Dong in Thailand; econ, refugee agrmts reached 9-6—9-10, 696E1-A3
UN Assemb member 713G3
Fukuda corrected on China pact Korean link 10-18, 802B1
UN head OKs visit 11-1, 860A1
Le Duan in Moscow 11-2, Sovt friendship pact signed 11-3, 859E2
China scores Sovt pact 11-8, 894C1
PI signs US mil base pact, S E Asia pressure cited 12-31, 1000B3

Monetary, Trade, Aid & Investment
Trade missn to Malaysia, Indonesia, PI 21B3
China, Thai pacts 1-10, 1-12, 21G2
N, S currency unified 5-3, hoarders raided 5-5—5-6, 341D1
China to cut aid 5-12, Hanoi scores 5-30, 399A3
US wheat received 5-22, 400F1
China ends econ aid; Comecon, USSR ties cited 7-3; Hanoi discounts impact 7-4, 504B3
Laos pacts anniv marked 7-22, 603B2
World Bank loan rptd 8-8, 624F1
Thai econ ties agreed 9-6—9-10, 696G1
Canada oil exploratn pact rptd 9-7, 686G3
China oil claims cited 10-16, 871G2
USSR econ, sci, tech pact signed 11-3, 859E2
US backs interest paymts on frozen forgn assets 11-14, 977G1

Refugees—*See under INDOCHINA; country names*

U.S. Relations
3 Americans freed 1-5, 8E2
US chrgs USSR-China 'proxy war' in Viet-Cambodia clashes 1-8; scored 1-9, 1-16, 9C2, 43E1
US arrests 2 as spies, Viet denies chrg 1-31, 68G2
US ousts UN amb Thi 2-3; Viet, others protest 2-3—2-9; stay issued, Thi leaves 2-10, 103E2
US barred from air lane 2-11, 140B1
US distressed by Thai refugee policy 2-16, 140B1
US affirms Asia mil commitmt 2-20, 126D3
Viet buildup re Cambodia rptd 4-7, 277D3
Mayaguez '75 seizure cited 4-7, 278B1
Refugees ask US asylum 4-9, 265B3
US convicts 2 as spies 5-19, 389F3-390F1
US wheat received 5-22, 400G1
Solzhenitsyn scores US capitulatn 6-8, 444C3
Cambodia chrgs Viet-US plots 6-13, 6-24, 6-25, 548C2
Thi killed 6-17; US informed 6-25, rptd slain 7-3, 549B2
CIA-Viet overthrow plot chrgd by Cambodia 6-25, Hanoi denies 6-27, 490C2
US sentences 2 as spies 7-7, 555A1
US cong del arrives 7-31; takes out 29 US kin, says Viet seeks close ties 8-7, 603C2
US vs World Bank loan 8-8, 624G1
US cong missn arrives, bodies of 11 US MIAs found 8-21, returned to US 8-27; Viets drop reparatns demand 8-22, 660F2
Tie talks to resume 8-22, 660A3
US probes Viet documt possessn by ex-amb 9-13, 720F1
US vows neutral stance 10-25, 830D1
US seeks to avert major Cambodian clash 11-5, 859D3
Refugee flow data rptd; US policy review cited; Malaysia OKs provisns for 'boat people' 11-14, 870C3, 871B1
US backs interest paymts on frozen forgn assets 11-14, 977G1
Colby CIA book published uncut 11-19, 917B2
US to admit more refugees 11-28, 932G3-933D1, 934E1

1979

Huang says Sovt world strategy linked 10-18, 789A3
China gets refugee resetlmt grant 11-11, 863D3
USSR aid end sought by China 11-30, 918A1
China, Japan discuss 12-5–12-7, 939F3

Chinese Relations—*See 'China Conflict' above; also CAMBODIA-Vietnam Conflict*

Foreign Relations (misc.)—*See also 'China Conflict' above, 'UN' below; also CAMBODIA-Vietnam Conflict*
Laos confirms troop presence 3-22, 229G1
Canada expels diplomat 3-29, 267E1
Laos troop exit, China 'aggressn' end linked 7-5, 537B1
Japan trade pact rptd delayed 7-11, 550A1
Sovt bases cited by Kissinger 7-31, 590D3
Spratly I annexed by PI 9-7, 660C3
Cambodia forgn relief aid scored 9-30, 741C1

Refugees—*See under INDOCHINA; country names*

UN Policy & Developments
UN role asked 2-17; Waldheim statemt 2-18, Cncl debate delayed 2-21, 123A1
Cncl meets 2-23, actn stalled 2-28, 142A1
Pol Pot govt UN seat challenged 9-18, seat upheld 9-19, 695B2
Membership listed 695B3
Pol Pot govt seat opposed 9-21, 741G1

U.S. Relations—*See also 'China Conflict' above, also CAMBODIA-Vietnam Conflict; INDOCHINA-Refugees*
Rand Corp rpt on S Viet '75 collapse issued 1-7, 29C1-B3
Debt to US rptd past due 2-5, 84C3
US POW detainmt discounted 2-5, 112F2
US rights rpt omits 2-10, 107A2
Student enrollmt in US rptd 167D2
Viet-era Marine returns to US 3-25, 265G3
Viet ex-amb documt possessn prosecutn dropped 3-30, 252F3
Kissinger warns of Sovt bases 7-31, 590D3
US denies tie talks held 8-3, 8-9, Viets renew claim 8-9, 8-11, 607G2
US reps visit Hanoi 8-8–8-9, 607G1
US call for Cambodia relief aid scored 9-30, 741C1
Viet-era Marine desertn case opens 12-4, 924D1

1980

Economy & Labor
Econ woes admitted by govt 11-18, 952F1

Foreign Relations (misc.)—*See also CAMBODIA (Democratic Kampuchea)—Vietnam Conflict, VIETNAM—China Conflict*
Iranians hint war crimes trial for US hostage 1-4, 29G3
China claims Spratly, Paracel I 1-30, 132C3
French CP issues rights rpt 2-20, 149E3
Laos takeover cited by US pres hopeful 3-3, 208C3
China joins IMF 4-17, 302E2
US scores Cambodia aid conf boycott 5-26, 397B2
Troops in Cambodia raid Thailand 6-23—6-24; Thailand protests 6-24, 475F2-D3
4 Westn civilians captured 6-25, released 6-29, 508F2
US orders Thai arms airlift 7-1, 491A3
Thai raid, Cambodia relief aid halt linked 7-9, 591E2
Thais vs Cambodia-Thai DMZ plan at forgn min talks 7-18, 591F1
Soyuz 37 launched 7-23, 547F3
Thai DMZ plan rejection scored 7-26, 591B2
Soyuz space team lands 7-31, 592C1
ASEAN vs Cambodia-Thai DMZ plan 8-1, 591E1
Waldheim visits; seeks Thai peace pact re Cambodia conflict 8-2—8-5, 591A1
Japan cites Soviet bases 8-5, 635D3
Afghan mil role rptd 9-15, 705C1
Pol Pot govt keeps Assemb seat 10-13, 775B2
Australia bans critical book 11-9, 885E1
Cambodian refugees return home 11-13, 951G3

Refugees—*See under INDOCHINA*

U.S. Relations—*See also CAMBODIA (Democratic Kampuchea)--Vietnam Conflict, INDOCHINA--Refugees*
Iranians hint war crimes trial for US hostage 1-4, 29G3
US' Meany hawkish view cited 1-10, 14E3
Viet-era Marine ct-martial asked 2-1, 115C3
US issues rights rpt 2-5, 87A2
Reagan 'basic speech' excerpts 2-29, 207G3
Bush 'basic speech' excerpts 3-3, 208C3
Viet bias vs Viet-Amer war children rptd 3-6, 181G1
Connally cites Sovt threat 3-7, 184E3
US scores Cambodia aid conf boycott 5-26, 397B2
2 civilians captured 6-25, released 6-29, 508F2
400 US bodies rptd found in '77 6-27, 508A3
Thai arms airlift ordrd 7-1, 491A3
Chem weapons use chrgd 8-7, 628E3
Viet pressure re recognitn claimed 8-24, 645A1
US MIA missn 10-1—10-4, Hanoi rptd vs proposals 10-6, 855A2
US convicts 2 FBI ex-offcls 11-6, 884E2

1976

VIETT, Inge
Escapes from jail 7-7, 593E3
VIGLIA, William C.
Sentenced 8-4, 566A2
VIGORITO, Rep. Joseph (D, Pa.)
Loses reelectn 11-2, 821B3
VIGUERIE, Richard A.
Maddox gets Amer Indep Party nominatn 8-27, 666E1
VIKING Press Inc.
US files consent decree 7-27, 989B2
VIKING Project—*See 'Interplanetary Projects' under ASTRONAUTICS*
VIKSNINS, Victor
Scores Ford E Eur remark 10-7, 762C3
VILAS, Gen. Acdel
Rpts prof arrests, Lanusse scores 8-4, 672G2-A3 ★
VILAS, Guillermo
Loses WCT finals 5-9, 504A2
2d in Italian Open tennis 5-30, 656C2
US Open results 9-12, 716B1
VILIM, Blazej
Dies 9-23, 1015A3
VILJOEN, Marais
S Africa cabt shifted 1-22, 76G1
VILLA, Rudolfo Martin
On Oriol kidnapping 12-17, 967F2
VILLAGE Voice (newspaper)
Publishes House com rpt excerpts 2-11, 2-18; Schorr admits leak 2-12, 150D3-151C1
Schorr probe underway 3-2, 216E3
House com hearings on Schorr probe 7-19, 7-20; Schorr, others subpoenaed 8-25; probe dropped 9-22, 748B3, G3, 749G1
VILLALON, Hector
Asks Peron quit 2-23, 154D2
VILLANOVA (Pa.) University
Ford visits 10-27, 803E1
VILLAR Mir, Juan Miguel
Peseta revalued 2-9, 422B3
In US 6-15—6-17, 501F2
VILLEGAS, Daniel Cosio
Dies 3-10, 240G3
Signs Spain Concordat revisn 7-28, 753F3
VILLON, Archbishop Jean Cardinal
Signs Spain Concordat revisn 7-28, 753F3
VILLONE, Carlos
Testimony links to AAA 2-4, 212C1
Rights revoked, arrest ordrd 6-23, 520C1
Goods frozen 7-1, 520A2
VILMAIN, Jean
Loses Lorraine election 1-6, 49B3
VIMOLSIRI Chamnanvej
Gets univ min post 10-22, 813G2
VINER, Ian
Aboriginal land bill terms set 5-27, 415A2
VINNELL Corp.
'75 arms sales listed 2-6, 147A3
VINSON Jr., Fred M.
Named to Lockheed probe 2-5, 131D2
VINYL Chloride—*See CHEMICALS*
VIOLA, Gen. Roberto
Hard-line generals retired 12-3, 996C3
VIRAT Sakchirapapong
On Soclst ldr's assassinatn 2-28, 176F3
VIREN, Lasse
Wins Olympic medals 7-26, 7-30, 'blood doping' denied 7-29, 563C2; 576A1, C1

VIRGINIA
Concorde landing hearing 1-5, 5D2, A3
Southn schl assn backs '75 pvt schl bias ruling 1-5, Justice Dept disputes 4-9, 263C2
Colleges get Pratt grants 1-9, 80C2

1977

VIETNAMESE Committee for Human Rights
US Viet aid bar asked 5-4, 333D1
VIETNAM War (1954-75)
US Sen Byrd position cited 1-4, 6B1
Vance cites 'lessons' 1-11, 34C3
Viet war prisoners freed 2-18, 161F2
Bond investmt scheme indictmts 3-3, 204C1
'60s Weathermen protesters surrender 3-25—9-15, 839C1
Unificatn Church role cited 4-14, 310F1
Indochina postwar conditns rptd 5-1—5-3, 336D3—337G1
Nixon TV interview 5-19, 405F3
'70 antiwar bomber sentncd 6-8, 6-10, 492C1
Eur heroin rise linked 10-17—10-21, 971C3
US ct protects journalists' thoughts 11-7, 920A3
Ex-CIA analyst scores US evacuatn 11-18, 897D3
FBI Cointelpro papers released 11-21, 940B3
Amnesty—*See U.S. GOVERNMENT—ARMED Forces*
Missing in Action—*See U.S. GOVERNMENT—ARMED Forces*
Prisoners of War—*See Under U.S. GOVERNMENT—ARMED Forces*
VIEYRA, Gilberto
Chrgs soldiers 'executed' 500 7-5, 636B1
VIKING Press
J Onassis resigns 10-13, 927B3
VILANOVA, Jose Vicente
Vote fraud chrgd 2-21, 181B2
VILAS, Gen. Acdel
Jailed 5-27, 522B3
VILAS, Guillermo
Loses Australian Open 1-9, Baltimore Intl 1-23, 103E3, G3
Wins Springfield, Va Beach tourns 2-13, 4-23; loses Grand Prix match 2-27, 430B3, F3, 431A1
US beaten in Davis Cup 4-29—5-1, 353G2
Wins French Open 6-5, 548A2
US Open fans stage sit-in 9-5, 787D2
Wins US Open 9-11, 787C1
VILJOEN, Gerrit
Vorster bars pass-law end 1-28, 100E3
VILLA, Alessandra
Charged 5-8, 565A1
VILLAESCUSA, Lt. Gen. Emilio
Kidnaped 1-24, 68C1
Rescued 2-11, 307E1
VILLAGE of Arlington Heights v. Metropolitan Housing Development Corp.—*See ARLINGTON Heights, etc.*
VILLAGE Voice (N.Y. newspaper)
Murdoch acquires control 1-7, 48D3
VILLALOBOS, Gerardo W.
Fires on Vesco home 6-2, 506A2
Murder plot chrg dropped 7-11, 710C2
VILLALOBOS Arce, Guillermo
CR pres candidate 9-2, 710B2
VILLALPANDO, Gen. Alfonso
Anti-Banzer plot foiled 12-9, 1009E3
VILLANOVA (Pa.) University
Wins IC4A indoor track championships 3-7, 2d in outdoor 5-21, 603B1, C1
VINCENT, Roger
Frees police in '72 break-in 6-16, 485A1
VINER, Ian
Australia aboriginal affairs min 12-19, 982A2
VINSON, Elkins, Searls, Connally & Smith
On 5 largest law firms list 5-16, 383A2
VIOLA, Gen. Roberto
Smith kidnaped 2-25, 198E3
Graiver probe deal rptd 4-22, 371F2
Rpts guerrillas on run 9-30, 921E3
VIOLANTE, Robert
Shot by Son of Sam 7-31, 641D3
VIONNET, Madeleine (deceased)
'77 fall fashions rptd 7-29, 1022E1
VIPAOWADI Rangsit, Princess (Thailand)
Killed 2-16, 138D1
VIRA-A (Adenine Arabinoside)—*See MEDICINE—Drugs*

VIRGINIA
Legislature schedule rptd 6F2
FTC sues dental groups 1-14, 156A3
Coll integratn rules ordrd 1-17, 112B2
FPC OKs emergency gas purchases 1-19, 1-20, 53G3, 54C1

1978

VIETNAM Veterans, Council of
Muller scores Carter proposals 10-10, 878F1
VIETNAM Veterans Against the War
Goodwin legal immunity case declined by Sup Ct 6-19, 492D2
VIETNAM War
Humphrey stand cited 33B1
Ex-CIA analyst sued re book 2-15, 129C1
US cost, '60s inflatn linked 5-22, 427B2
Nixon hosts ex-POW receptn, LA conv cited 5-27, 513D2
Solzhenitsyn scores US capitulatn 6-8, 444C3
Carter poll standing linked 7-26, 682C3
US Army med advances rptd 12-6, 960D3
Refugees—*See under INDOCHINA; country names*
Veterans—*See VETERANS*
VIEW from the Oak: The Private Worlds of Other Creatures, The (book)
Wins Natl Book Award 4-10, 315A3
VIKING Press
Onassis joins Doubleday 2-13, 172C2
VILANCH, Bruce
Platinum opens 11-12, 1031F2
VILARO, Ricardo
Kidnapped 4-21, 396A1
VILAS, Guillermo
USTA ranks 4th 1-5, 22E3
Connors wins Grand Prix Masters 1-8, 22B3
Defies 'Super Grand Prix,' loses Suntory Cup 4-23, 418B3
Wins German championship 5-21, 419D1
Loses French Open 6-11, 540E1
VILJOEN, Gerrit
Motlana mtg rptd 8-17, interview vs apartheid 8-18, 669A3
VILLAGE People (singing group)
YMCA on best-seller list 12-6, 971E1
VILLAGE Voice (N.Y. newspaper)
Times, News strike ends 11-6, 865A2
VILLAGRA, Nelson
Last Supper released 5-5, 619G2
VILLAGRAN Kramer, Francisco
Belize talks with UK rep rptd 7-6, 538F1
VILLAMARIN, Gen. Luis
Dismissed 12-20, 1021B3
VILLANOVA (Pa.) University
Belger sets indoor 880-yd run record 1-13, 76E2
Wins IC4A track titles 3-6, 5-21, Penn Relays 4-29, 692E3, F3
3d in NCAA indoor champs 3-11, 692D3
NCAA basketball tourn results 3-27, 272C1
Arizin in basketball HOF 5-1, 457D3
VILLIERS, Sir Charles
BSC losses rptg scored 1-11, denies chrgs 1-16, 36B3, D3
VINCENT Jr., Francis T.
Hired as Columbia Pictures pres 7-21, 599C2
VINCENT, Jan-Michael
Big Wednesday released 7-27, Hooper 8-4, 969D3, 970F1
VINER, Ian
Plans Queensland Aborigine rule 3-22, 225E1
Australia employmt min 11-30, 943F3
VINH, Nguyen Trong
Vs China press rpts on Viet-Cambodia clashes 1-9, 42A3
VIOLA, Gen. Roberto
Argentina army chief, junta member 7-31, 611F2
Sees mil man as next pres 8-23, 793C1
VIOLA Sauret, Joaquin
Murdered 1-25, 136A1
VIOLETTE (film)
Released 10-9, 1030E3
VIRA-A (vidarabine)—*See MEDICINE—Drugs*

VIRGINIA
Legislature schedule rptd 14G3
'67, '77 sales-tax rates rptd 1-5, 15F3
State govt tax revenue table 1-9, 84E2
US rejcts coll integratn plan 2-2, 85C1
Coal shortage rptd 2-11, Carter sees gov 2-16, 104D1, D2

1979

VIETNAM Veterans of America
Viet study reveals problems 9-25, 725E1
VIETNAM War—*See also VETERANS*
Rand Corp rpt on S Viet '75 collapse issued 1-7, 29C1-B3
Carter cites re Iran unrest 1-17, 26D2
US-Viet collaborators rptd 2-5, 112E2-A3
US blocks H-bomb article, Pentagon Papers controversy compared 3-9, 193G3-194A1
Pol Pot document on '70 US Cambodia invasn rptd 3-18, 229G2
'State of mind' libel queries backed by US Sup Ct 4-18, 302A1
US ex-activist, alleged collaborator Calif apptmts opposed 7-13–8-8, 593B2-B3
CIA spying on antiwar activists rptd 7-16, 561A2
Viet, China debate 7-20, 575E2
Arnheiter libel cases declined by Sup Ct 10-29, 884G1
'71 protesters' award cut 12-13, 991G2-C3
Refugees—*See under INDOCHINA*
VIGLIONE, Ernesto
Arrested in Moro probe 2-7, 97F3
VIGUERIE, Richard A.
Leaves Crane for Connally campaign 8-8, 594C2
VILLANOVA (Pa.) University
Wins IC4A track titles 3-4, 5-21, NCAA indoor champ 3-10, Penn Relays 4-28, 2d in NCAA outdoor champ 6-3, 911F2-B3
VIK, Bjorg
Wine Untouched opens 6-22, 712F3
VIKING Project—*See ASTRONAUTICS–Interplanetary Projects*
VILANCH, Bruce
Festival opens 5-7, 711A3
VILAS, Guillermo
Wins Australian Open 1-3, 103C2
Wins Australian Hard Ct tourn 1-7; loses Richmond Classic 2-4, Stuttgart Grand Prix 4-1, 391F2, B3
Boycotts Grand Prix Masters 1-14, 103A3
Grand Prix dispute setld 2-10, 391F1
Loses Italian Open 5-27, 570D2
Wins Washn Star Intl 7-22, loses US Clay Cts 8-12, 734B2, C2
Loses Australian Indoor 10-21, wins Argentine Open 11-25, 10-21, 1003E3, G3
VILJOEN, Gerrit
Named Namibia head 8-1, 585A2
VILJOEN, Marais (South African president)
Named S Africa pres 6-19, 469G2
VILLA, Alessandro
Chrgd re Chiasso scandal 2-15, 137E1
Sentenced 7-3, 505E2
VILLA, Rodolfo Martin
Lauds Galicia home rule vote 11-22, 929D2
VILLAESCUSA, Lt. Gen. Emilio
Kidnapers escape jail 12-17, 997E3, G3
VILLAGE People (singing group)
YMCA on best-seller list 1-10, 80E3; 2-14, 120E3; 3-7, 174D1
Cruisin' on best-seller list 2-14, 120F3
VILLAIN, The (film)
Released 7-20, 820E3
VILLARROEL Rejas, Gen. Rene
Rocha named Bolivia army chief 11-25, 907F1
VILLAS Boas, Orlando and Claudio
Indian lands protected in Brazil 6-22, 483B2
VILLEGAS, Raimundo
Venez science min 3-10, 192D3
VILLENUEVE, Gilles
Wins S African Gr Prix 3-4, US Gr Prix West 4-8, US Gr Prix 10-7, 1005D2
VILLOT, Jean Cardinal
Dies 3-9, 272G3
VINCENTIAN Fathers
China reimbursemt set 3-16, 218A1
VINELAND, N.J.—*See NEW Jersey*
VINELAND Laboratories Inc.
DES banned in animal feed 6-28, 571B3
VINER, Robert Ian
Australia job study missn set 4-28, 351B3
VINOGRADOV, Vladimir Mikhailovich
Gets Khomeini warning 2-24, 145D1
Gets Khomeini warning re Sovt Khuzistan, Afghan actions; replies 6-12, 446A1
Iran vs Sovt Afghan invasn 12-28, 974C2
VINS, Georgi P.
Freed in spy swap 4-27, at Carter church svc 4-29; facts on 4-27, 317B1, 318A1
Family leaves USSR 6-13, 476A3
VIOLA, Gen. Roberto
Crushes army rebellion 9-29, 748G2-F3
Retiremt set 12-7, 947E2
VIRGIN, Craig
Sets 10000-m run mark, named AAU outdoor champ MVP 6-17, 911G1

VIRGINIA
Legislature schedule rptd 5F3
ERA killed by legis coms 1-17, 2-2, 128B2
Med malpractice arbitratn rptd 1-28, 139E3
Cigaret mfr rise rptd 2-11, 218E2*

1980

VIETNAM Veterans' Action Association
Australia orders Agent Orange rpt 3-26, 252F2
VIETNAM Veterans Against the War
Govt damage suit geographic relevance backed by Sup Ct 2-20, 170B3
VIETNAM Veterans of America
Carter criticized 7-1, 496E1
VIETNAM War—*See also VETERANS*
Australia defoliant study ordrd 1-8, 37F2
Snepp CIA disclosure limits upheld by US Sup Ct 2-19, 130C3
Australia orders Agent Orange rpt 3-26, 252F2
400 US bodies rptd found in '77 6-27, 508A3
Carter to press search for missing 7-1, 496E1
'70 Weatherman fugitive surrenders 7-8, 576A3
Male-only draft case accepted by Sup Ct 12-1, 918G1
U.S. Presidential Election (& Transition)
Reagan 'basic speech' excerpts 2-29, 207D2, G3
Bush 'basic speech' excerpts 3-3, 208G2
'Noble cause' says Reagan 8-18, 629C1
Mondale cites Reagan stand 9-19, 780E2
Carter, Reagan TV debate 10-28, 814A1
VIEYTEZ, Atilio
On '81 coffee crop, ICO quota 10-15, 829G1-A2
VIHARO, Robert
Hide in Plain Sight released 3-21, 216G2
VILANCH, Bruce
Divine Madness released 9-25, 836E2
VILAS, Guillermo
Wins Australian Open 1-2, 213E1
Argentina wins Davis Cup Amer Zone 3-9, 607G1
Loses Monte Carlo Grand Prix 4-6, W Ger Open 5-18; wins Italian Open 5-25, 607A3, D3
Argentina wins Nations Cup 5-12, 607A2
In French Open default controversy 6-3, 606F3
USTA, pros settle rules dispute 7-16, 691F3, G3
Wins Austrian Grand Prix 7-27, 691A3
Wins Sicilian Grand Prix 9-14; loses Spanish Grand Prix 10-12, Naples 10-19; Dubai Golden results 11-23, 947F1, A2, F2
VILJOEN, Gerrit
Named S Africa educ min 8-26, 689F3
Broederbond successor chosen 9-26, 753F2
VILLA, Pancho (Francisco) (Doroteo Arango) (d. 1923)
Gen Simpson dies 8-15, 676B3
VILLA, Rodolfo Martin
Named to Spanish Cabt 9-8, 690F2
Pledges new devolutn plan 9-17, 711G3
VILLAGE of Schaumburg v. Citizens for Better Environment
Case decided by Sup Ct 2-20, 170E2
VILLAGE Voice (newspaper)
Newfield wins Polk award 2-25, 692F3
VILLAGRAN, Adriana
Loses French Open women's doubles 6-6, 606E3
VILLAGRAN Kramer, Francisco
Resigns as Guatemala VP 9-2, 670F3
VILLALOBOS, Joaquin
Salvadoran leftists launch offensive 12-26, 993D2
VILLALON, Hector
In Iran crisis media group 4-5, 258EA1
VILLANOVA (Pa.) University
Wins IC4A indoor champ 3-8—3-9, Penn Relays 4-25, 2d in IC4A outdoor champ 5-24—5-25, 892A2-C2
Paige wins NCAA indoor 1,000-m run 3-15, 891F3
Bush campaigns on campus 4-21, 304F2
Paige in US Olympic trials 6-23, 891G1, C2
VILLANUEVA del Campo, Armando
2d in Peru pres electn 5-18, 390A2
VILLAROEL, Maj.
Krause interrogatn rptd 6-11, 443G2
VILLIERS, Charles
Sees annual 1 bln pound loss 3-6, 193B3
On steelworkers' vote 3-9, 193E2
MacGregor to succeed at Brit Steel 5-1, 352E1
VINCENT, Elmer
Reunited with brother 6-29, 638B3
VINE, Richard D.
Receives bodies of dead US raiders 5-6, 337C2
VINER, Robert Ian
Scores Labor job plan 3-23, 271C3
Sinclair takes over post 8-18, 650E2
Local worker recruitmt stressed 12-1, 940D3
VINOGRADOV, Vladimir
Meets Iran premr on Iraq war 10-4, 758C3
VIOLA, Gen. Roberto Eduardo
Junta delays naming Videla successor, Lambruschini oppositn cited 9-30, 747F2
Named Videla successor, junta rift resolved 10-3, 766E1-B2
VIRDON, Bill
Wins top mgr awards 11-1, 11-17, 926B1
VIREN, Lasse
5th in Moscow Olympics 10,000-m run 7-27, 589D1

VIRGINIA
Ct rules vs strip-mine law 1-3, 5D2
Norfolk 'test-tube baby' clinic OKd 1-8, 24E1, F1, A2
Griffin dies 1-18, 104F2
Mental hosp sterilizatn progrm rptd 2-23, 158D3

1976

CIA aid to Arlington, Fairfax police rptd 1-11, 1-13, 24C3
Norfolk Navy repair depot rptd scored 1-12, 43C3
'74 TWA crash rpt 1-21, 80A1
EEOC Lynchburg GE plant suit upheld 1-23, 70D3
Ford in Williamsburg 1-31, 88A1
Concorde tests OKd 2-4, 94C2
Ford Alexandria home rptd 2-12, 129C2
Hopewell Kepone poisoning case cited 2-26, 171G2
Southern-Delmarva talks fail 3-23, Conrail takes over tracks 4-1, 235E2-A3
New River dam project upheld 3-24, 219A3
Sup Ct upholds homosexual ban 3-30, 261B3, C3 ★
Hopewell indicted 5-7, 349D1
French pres visits US 5-17—5-22, in Yorktown, Mt Vernon 372F1
'71 photo studio break-in cited 5-17, 379B2
Carter gets 23 delegates 5-22—5-23, 373F3
Fairfax Cnty Concorde plea rejctd 5-22, 378G2
Sup Ct voids drug price ad ban 5-24, 393E1
VCU affirmative actn plan voided 5-28, 414A1
7 oil cos, trade assn indicted 6-1, 412F3
Anheuser-Busch Williamsburg strike ends 6-6, 436B2
Ford at Baptist conv in Norfolk 6-15, 433A2
Sup Ct bars pvt schl bias 6-25, 479F1
Ex-SBA official sentncd 6-25, 596G1
Alexandria builder sentncd 6-25, 860F2
Ford in Charlottesville 7-5, 488G3
Queen Eliz in Monticello 7-11, 489G2
Dem conv women delegates, table 508E2
Dem conv pres vote, table 7-14, 507E2
Ford claims delegate gains 7-20, 531E3
Miners strike spreads 7-27, 553B2
Cong tax exemption vetoed 8-3, 636C3
Ford delegate gains rptd 8-10, 583A2
GOP pre-conv delegate count 8-14, 583E3
Reagan seeks conv delegates 8-16, 601G2
GOP conv pres, vp vote tables 8-18—8-19, 8-19, 599E1, E3
Chem barge spill 8-18, 796B2
Southn govs meet in Williamsburg 9-1, 671A3
Carter visits Norfolk 9-6, 663F3
New River dams blocked 9-11, 689E1
Fiscl '75 per capita income, tax burden rptd 9-15, 10-12, 959D2
Johnson & Johnson exec jet crash 9-26, 840G2
Dole at Va Polytech 10-5, 743A2
Westn Elec bias damages, quotas ordered 10-22, 943E2
Ford in Richmond 10-23, 802D3
Carter in Alexandria 10-23, 803B2
Election results 11-2: pres 818D1, F2, 819B2; cong 820E1, E2, 823B1, 828C3, 830G4-831A1
Aeroflot employe rptd arrested 11-10, 907E3
Sup Ct bars Concorde landing review 11-15, 882B2
US Sup Ct refuses oral sex case 11-29, 901A1
Volvo delays Chesapeake plant 12-9, 987B3
Flu shot paralysis rptd 12-17, 950E1

VIRGINIA, University of (Charlottesville)
Queen Eliz visits 7-11, 489G2
Kupchan dies 10-19, 892B3
VIRGINIA Commonwealth University (VCU) (Richmond)
Affirmative actn plan voided 5-28, 414A1
VIRGINIA Polytechnic Institute (Blacksburg)
Dole addresses 10-5, 743A2
VIRGIN Islands (U.S. territory)
St Thomas air crash 4-27, 335F2
Dem conv women delegates, table 508E2
US Dem conv pres vote, table 7-14, 507E2
Ford meets delegates 7-23, 549E3
GOP pre-conv delegate count 8-14, 583E3
Reagan seeks conv delegates 8-17, 601B3
GOP conv pres, vp vote tables 8-18—8-19, 8-19, 599E1, E3
GOP platform text 8-18, 605E3
Jobless benefits bill includes 10-20, 688D1
House ldrship elected 12-6, 919C1
VIRGO, Robert
Barbados ousts 10-25, 962C1
VIRKOTYPE Corp.
Arab boycott rpt released 10-19, 786D1
VIROLAINEN, Johannes
Sworn Finnish agri min 9-29, 750D3

1977

ERA fails 1-27, 112E3
Kepone clean-up fund set 1-28, 95C1
US offers emergency job funds 2-1, 75G3
US declares emergency status 2-5, 91A2
Sup Ct bars optometry bd rule review 2-22, 150A2
Vepco fined 2-23, 235A2
Ship hits Hopewell bridge 2-24, 204F3
US Sup Ct upholds arbitratn under expired contracts 3-7, 211B3
Ft Belvoir, Quantico germ warfare tests rptd 3-8, 195F2
Richmond elects black mayor 3-8, 252C3
Vepco cancels Surry A-plants 3-18, 235E1
Death penalty bill signed 3-29, 594D1
Coll integratn rules reordrd 4-1, 446D1
Storms, floods hit 4-3—4-6, disaster areas named 4-7, 311F2-A3
Concorde noise rpt issued 4-14, 368G2
Amtrak 'Mountaineer' svc to end 5-3, 368E3
'76 per-capita income table 5-10, 387F2
Va Beach business confidence rptd 5-16, 384A3
Sup Ct backs US fishing laws 5-23, 444A2
Gov, lt gov candidates chosen 6-4, 6-14, 465A1
UMW wildcat strikes 6-18—9-6, 690F2
State abortn funding rptd 6-20, 787B1
Venez pres in Williamsburg 6-27, 546E1
Coll integratn plan issued 7-5, 630G2
Drought emergency declared 7-7, fed aid OKd 8-24, 660A1
5 indep oil cos convicted 8-30, 691A3; fined 9-16, 918F2
'76 per capita income, tax burden table 9-13, 10-18, 821D2
5 indep oil cos fined 9-16, 918F2
Carter stumps for Howell 9-24, 761C1
A-plant safety cover-up rptd 9-30, 838D1
Arlington Cnty parking ban backed 10-11, 774G2
Kepone damage suits settld 10-13, 800C1
Electn results 11-8, 855E1, G1, C2, 879C2
Econ boycott by ERA forces rptd 11-14, 918E1

VIRGINIA, University of (Charlottesville)
Meador confrmd asst atty gen 3-4, 211F1
VIRGINIA Beach, Va.—*See VIRGINIA*
VIRGINIA Commonwealth University (Richmond)
MD schl gets Kepone grant 2-1, 95D1
VIRGINIA Electric and Power Co. (Vepco)
Fined 2-23, 235A2
Surry A-plants canceled 3-18, 235E1
A-plant safety cover-up rptd 9-30, 838E1
VIRGIN Islands (U.S. territory)
'76 St Thomas air crash rpt 3-6, 312G1
Carter for Latin A-ban pact 4-14, 295F2; signs A-pact 5-26, 415D3
Drought aid OKd 8-24, 659D3

1978

6th in US defense contracts 2-21, 127D2
Coal strike emergency declared 3-7, 160D2
US OKs coll integratn plan 3-17, 368G3, 369B1
Inmate parole hearings case review declined by Sup Ct 4-24, 322E2
Judicial inquiry law voided by US Sup Ct 5-1, 363G2-E3
Coal strike utility billing probe set 5-10, 366F3
FRB head in Hot Springs 5-13, 361B2
Construction pact signed 5-22, 429D3
Primary, conv results 6-3—6-13, 467F1
Obenshain killed 8-2, Warner named GOP Sen nominee 8-12, 645A3
Carter visits Fairfax 8-3, Norfolk 8-5, 605E3
N&W strike ends 9-30, 809E2
TWA '74 crash claims setld 11-4, 908C2
Election results 11-7: cong 846D1, 848E3, 852C3, 853E1; state 847G1, 853F1
Newport News Surry A-plant rating rptd 11-25, 940D3
Warner US Sen win confrmd 11-27, 915A3
GOP govs meet in Williamsburg 11-27—11-28, 915G3
Charlottesville derailmt kills 6 12-3, 972D1
Gays' mil dischrg held unfair 12-6, 960B2
'Marriage tax' challenge refused by US Sup Ct 12-11, 981D1

VIRGINIAN-Pilot (Norfolk newspaper)
Va judicial inquiry law voided by Sup Ct 5-1, 363A3
VIRGINIA Slims (tennis circuit)—*See TENNIS*
VIRGINIA State College (Petersburg)
HEW OKs Va integratn plan 3-17, 369B1
VIRGINIA Union University (Richmond)
Med Coll monkey-cocaine study rptd 8-11, 771C1
Med Coll muscular distrophy test rptd 10-19, 948B1
VIRGIN Islands (U.S. territory)
Gov King dies 1-2, 96E2
Blair killed in air crash 9-2, 777F3
Election results 11-7, 915E3

1979

NLRB to probe Newport News shipyd vote 3-2, 187C2
Richmond fiscal status rptd 3-20, 204G1
Ft Monroe to close 3-29, 265F3
Regulatory bds rptd segregated 4-9, 307A2
Rockefeller Williamsburg estate willed to foundatn 4-13, 672E2
Newport News strike violence 4-16, 561C1
Newport News strike suspended 4-22, 306C2
Norfolk porno law challenge dismissed by Sup Ct 6-25, 540A2
Mercedes Hampton plant plan rptd 7-26, 663G3
Religious schl expulsn upheld 8-23, 650A2
Hurricane David hits 9-7, 691B1
Interior Dept seeks to protect primitive areas 9-7, 703C3
Quantico marines moved for pot suspicion 9-12, 809B2
'78 per capita income rptd 9-16, 746F2
SBA minority-aid abuse rptd 9-28, 947A3
Westn Elec bias case refused by Sup Ct 10-29, 884C2
PPA pneumonia outbreak in Charlottesville hosp cited 11-1, 971C2
Hampton Roads longshoremen boycott Iranian cargo 11-13, 879C1
Mormon feminist excommunicated 12-5, 929B3

Atomic Energy
Surry (Gravel Neck) A-plants ordrd shut 3-13, 186F1
Westinghouse settles Vepco uranium supply suit 4-16, 366D1
Surry A-plant pipe leaks rptd 5-2, 322B3
Surry plant sabotage probed 5-8, 5-10, 386D2
North Anna (Mineral) reactor licensing delayed 5-21, 381G3
North Anna protesters arrested 6-3, 416D2
Surry plant saboteurs chrgd 6-18, 466E1
North Anna A-protesters convicted 7-17, 743B1
North Anna leak 9-25, probe rptd 10-2, 786G3-787B1
North Anna coal shift studied 10-15, 807A2
Surry plant saboteurs convicted 10-16, 807D1
North Anna reactor licensing delay extended 11-5, 849C1
Surry plant saboteurs sentenced 11-27, 925B2

Crime & Civil Disorders
Convict gets prison abuse award 1-5, 24A2
Petersburg inmate gets rape setlmt 3-17, 316D2
Inmate threat case refused by US Sup Ct 4-16, 302E3
Surry A-plant sabotage probed 5-8, 5-10, 386D2
Smith death penalty challenge declined by US Sup Ct 5-21, 400E3
North Anna A-protesters arrested 6-3, 416D2; convicted 7-17, 743B1
Surry A-plant saboteurs chrgd 6-18, 466E1; convicted 10-16, 807D1; sentncd 11-27, 925B2
Criminal evidence standard eased by Sup Ct 6-28, 558D2
Trial closure ruling cited 8-4, 630E2
Men's room surveillance case declined by Sup Ct 10-1, 768G1
Trial closure case accepted by Sup Ct 10-9, 783F3

Energy—*See also 'Atomic' above*
Gulf cleared re Vepco overchrg 6-12, 580A3
Odd-even gas rationing begins 6-21, 462F2
Odd-even gas rules lifted 9-10, 683G1
Portsmouth oil refinery OKd by Army 10-4, 769G3-770F1

VIRGINIA Electric & Power Co. (VEPCO)
A-plants ordrd shut 3-13, 186F1
Westinghouse settles uranium supply suit 4-16, 366D1
Surry A-plant sabotage probed 5-8, 5-10, 386D2
Gulf cleared re overchrg 6-12, 580A3
Surry A-plant saboteurs chrgd 6-18, 466G1
North Anna leak 9-25, probe rptd 10-2, 786G3-787B1
North Anna coal shift studied 10-15, 807A2
Surry A-plant saboteurs convicted 10-16, 807D1; sentenced 11-27, 925B2
VIRGINIA Hospital, University of (Charlottesville)
PPA pneumonia outbreak cited 11-1, 971C2
VIRGINIA Polytechnic Institute & University (Blacksburg)
NCAA basketball tourn results 3-26, 238A3
VIRGINIA Union University (Richmond)
Med Coll heart transplants rptd 5-6, 355E1
VIRGIN Islands (U.S. territory)
Voters reject const 3-6, 167F3
Italian cruise ship sinks 3-30, 316B3
Forgn-flag oil tanker case refused by Sup Ct 5-14, 383E1
Prinair crash kills 8 7-24, 830G2
Army '50 grain blight tests rptd 10-7, 771A1
VIRNO, Paolo
Seized in Moro probe 6-6, 487C1

1980

Rumanian envoy defects 2-24, 142B3
OSHA cites Newport News yd 2-27, 147C3
Black conf in Richmond 2-29—3-2, 190C2
Blizzards hit, 1 killed 3-1—3-2, 292B2
Strip-mining ruling stayed by Sup Ct 3-17, 226G1
Newport News shipyd pact signed 3-31, 251B2
Nimitz returns to Norfolk 5-26, 403G1
Mormon feminist excommunicatn upheld 7-1, 638A2
McDonald's acquitted in franchise suit 9-29, 917C3
Strip mining case accepted by Sup Ct 10-6, 782E1
Zimco special labor aid OKd 11-5, 870C2
Richmond busing, housing integratn study rptd 11-16, 989E3
Drought rptd 12-1, 947F3

Atomic Energy & Safeguards
Demonstratns mark 3 Mile I mishap 3-28—3-31, 249B1
N Anna (Mineral) plant gets start-up license 4-10, 332F1
'79 A-plant mishaps rptd 7-14, 551F2
Surry (Gravel Neck) plant cleared by NRC 8-5, 649A1
N Anna plant conducts drill 8-16, gets operating license 8-20, 648D3
Vepco cancels N Anna 4 unit 11-25, 961G1

Crime & Civil Disorders
Harris chrgd in 'Scarsdale Diet' MD murder 3-11, 214E3
40-yr pot case remanded by Sup Ct 3-31, 291F2
Stowe indicted in Abscam probe 6-13, 454E1
Open criminal trials backed by Sup Ct 7-2, 510F2-C3
Road builders bid-rigging scandal rptd 7-5, 655F1, A2
Williams indicted re Piney R titanium loan 10-30, 824G2

Politics & Government—*See also other appropriate subheads in this section*
Legislature schedule rptd 18F1
State of State message 1-9, 404D1
Richmond ERA rallies held 1-13, 1-17, 54A3
Sheffield named dist judge, Byrd scores 4-9; tax probe leak halts Sen hearings 8-27, fight vowed 9-9, 744D3
State ct legal immunity defined by Sup Ct 6-2, 512F3
Reagan in Lynchburg 10-3, 763F2
Election results 11-4; pres 838D1, 839B2, G3; cong 840E3, 844D3-A4, 850D2; state 845E3
'80 census rptd 12-31, 983G1

VIRGINIA, University of (Charlottesville)
Wins NIT, Sampson named tourn MVP 3-20, 240E2
Wins Penn Relays 3,200-m Medley 4-25, 892D2
2d in NCAA lacrosse 5-31, 638B1
VIRGINIA Electric & Power Co. (Vepco)
N Anna A-plant gets start-up license 4-10, 332F1
'79 A-plant mishaps rptd 7-14, 551F2
Surry A-plant cleared by NRC 8-5, 648G3
N Anna A-plant conducts drill 8-16, gets operating license 8-20, 648D3
N Anna 4 A-plant halted 11-25, 961F1
VIRGINIA Society for Human Life
'Test-tube baby' clinic scored 1-8, 24B2
VIRGINIA Steering Committee to Stop the ERA
Anti-ERA rally held 1-17, 54D3
VIRGINIA Union University (Richmond)
Wins NCAA Div II basketball title 3-15, 240C3
VIRGIN Islands (U.S. territory)
Carter sets econ plan 2-14: govs meet, set projcts 2-19—2-22, 495A1
Reps at US Families Conf 6-5, 442B3

1976

VISALIA, Calif.—*See CALIFORNIA*
VISCONTI, Luchino
Dies 3-30, 240G3
VISHNIAK, Mark
Dies 11-30, 1015A3
VITAMINS—*See 'Drugs' under MEDICINE*
VLAMINICK, Maurice de (1876-1958)
Works donated 1-31, 124F2
VLASIC, Mark
Hijacks TWA jet 9-10, arraigned in US 9-13, 685D2
VLISMAS, Vasilios
Arrested 12-29, 1014F1
VOELKEL, Andrew J.
Sentenced 2-4, 135G3
VOGEL, Matt
Wins Olympic medal 7-21, 575D2
VOGEL, Orville Alvin
Gets Medal of Science 10-18, 858F3
VOICE of America—*See U.S. INFORMATION Agency under U.S. GOVERNMENT*
VOIGT, Angela
Wins Olympic medal 7-23, 576E1
VOLCKER, Paul A.
Vs bank regulatory merger 3-9, 185F3
VOLKMER, Harold L.
Elected 11-2, 823B3, 830B1
VOLKSWAGENWERK, A. G.
Datsun tops US '75 imports 1-11, 280G1
Nissan buys Australia plant 2-12, 137F3
US plant OKd 4-23, 321E2
US ends VW, Audi, Porsche car dumping probe; Porsche cleared 5-4, 320F3, 321B1-A2, E2
Plans US plant 5-28—10-5, 987C3
US car price hike set 8-16, 10-12, 988D1
Tops US fuel-econ ratings 9-22, 766A1-769C1
Oct US sales rptd 11-3, 885A3
VOLLEYBALL
Olympic results 7-30, 576C2
VOLLMAR, Harald
Wins Olympic medal 7-18, 575A2
VOLPE, John A.
Rptd opposed CIA Italy aid 1-7, 10B3
VOLVO, A. B.
US ends car dumping probe 5-4, 321C2
US car price hike set 8-16, 988D1
US plant delayed, '77 cutbacks set 12-9, 987A3
VOLYNOV, Col. Boris
In Salyut 5 missn 6-22, 527B2
Returns from Salyut 5 8-24, 684E1
Von ALTEN, Juergen
Suspended 5-19, 383F1
Von ALVENSLEBEN, Countess Marianne (West Germany)
Named in Getty will 6-8, 444D2
Von CRAMM, Baron Gottfried
Dies 11-8, 970E1
Von der GOLTZ, Count Bernhard
Arrested in Herstatt fraud 8-26, 679A1
Von MARBOD, Eric F.
On US-Iran air contract 11-24, 925F2
VONNEGUT, Kurt
Slapstick on best-seller list 12-5, 972G2

1977

VIRUET, Edwin
Duran decisions 9-17, 827G3
VISIONS of Terror and Wonder (musical composition)
Wins Pulitzer Prize 4-18, 355E2
VISIT Kongprasit, Maj.
Gets life sentence 4-21, 331F2
VISSER, Brig. Jan
Lauded re riot restraint 4-29, 350F1
VISTA—*See 'U.S. GOVERNMENT—ACTION—Volunteers in Service to America*
VITAMINS—*See 'MEDICINE—Drugs*
VIVAS Casanova, Jesus
Venez transport, communicatns min 1-7, 23F2
VLADIMOV, Georgi
To head USSR Amnesty Intl 10-14, 812C2
VLASIC, Marc
Pleads guilty 3-2, sentncd 5-12, 451B3
Sentncd on fed chrgs 7-20, 642C2
VLCKOVA, Ruzena
Hijacks Czech plane 10-11, 848G3
VOGEL, Hanns-Jochen
Vs terrorists' release 10-16, 791C2
VOICE of America—*See U.S. GOVERNMENT—U.S. INFORMATION Agency*
VOIGHT, Stu
Raiders win Super Bowl 1-9, 24G3
VOLCANIC Eruptions
Zaire hit 1-10, 204G2
Eruptns in Japan 8-7—8-10, Italy 8-29, Hawaii 9-19—9-28, 747B2
VOLKMAN, Ernest
Rpts CIA plots vs Jamaica ldr; CIA denies 11-2, 884F1
VOLKSWAGENWERK AG
'76 US new car sales rptd down 1-6, 38F3
Air bag test program set 1-18, 213E2
US import rank rptd down 4-11, 2d US car plant sought 6-15, 463E3
Volvo, Saab agree to merge 5-6, 469D3
US prices hiked 7-29, 585C2
EPA fuel-econ ratings issued 9-19, 723B3
E Ger barter deal set 11-30, 984F1
Currency stability asked, export harm in US mkt cited 12-7, 932D3
US prices hiked, $ drop cited 12-14, 962D1
VOLOJ, Juan Carlos
Chrgs treaty vote fraud 10-23, arrest rptd 10-24, 809D1
VOLUNTEER Armed Forces—*See U.S. GOVERNMENT—Armed Forces*
VOLUNTEERS in Service to America—*See under U.S. GOVERNMENT—ACTION*
VOLVO, A.B.
Saab merger agreed 5-6, 469B3
SAAB merger called off 8-28, 709E1
Von BRAUN, Wernher
Dies 6-16, 532G3
Von FURSTENBURG, Princess Ira
Ex-husband dies 10-27, 872F2
Von MARBOD, Erich
AWACS deal to Iran dropped 8-2, 611E2
Von NEUMANN, John
Oskar Morgenstern dies 7-26, 604D3
Von ROSEN, Count Carl Gustaf
Dies 7-13, 604G3

1978

VIRUSES—*See MEDICINE—Diseases*
VISHNEVSKAYA, Galina
Citizenship revoked 3-15, 179B3
VISIBLE Hand: The Managerial Revolution in American Business, The (book)
Chandler wins Pulitzer 4-17, 315C1
VISION—*See EYES & Eyesight*
VITALE, Dick
Named Pistons coach 5-1, 656B1
VITAMINS—*See FOOD*
VIVA Italia! (film)
Released 7-9, 970C3
VIVALDI, Antonio (1678-1741)
Four Seasons wins Grammy 2-24, 316C1
VIVES, Camilo
Last Supper released 5-5, 619G2
VOGEL, Andreas
Meyer escapes W Berlin prison 5-27, 438C3
Ct-apptd atty threatened 5-31, 439F2
VOGEL, Hans-Jochen
Retains W Ger justice post 2-3, 93A3
Asks local curbs on Nazis 2-4, 114A2
Nazi prosecutn limit rptd opposed 11-13, 872C2
VOGEL, Wolfgang
US prisoner exchng talks rptd 4-24, 3-way swap completed 5-1, 318C2
VOICE of America—*See under U.S. GOVERNMENT—U.S. INFORMATION Agency*
VOIGHT, Jon
Coming Home released 2-15, 619B1
VOLCANIC Eruptions
'77 eruptions rptd 1-29, 480A2
VOLKMER, Rep. Harold L. (D, Mo.)
Defns cuts rejctd by House 8-7, 8-8, 604D2
Reelected 11-7, 851D2
VOLKSWAGENWERK, A.G.
'Beetle' productn halted 1-19, 74D3
US car prices hiked 3-31, 283G2
Brazil factory strike rptd 5-22, 412D1
US sues VW of Amer 5-24, 409C2
Chrysler Brazil talks fail; Peugeot top ranked in Eur on Chrysler purchase 8-10, 623D2, E3
EPA rates 1st in fuel-econ 9-15, 719G2
Pa plant struck 10-9—10-15, revised contract ratified 10-21—10-22, 809C3
VOLLEYBALL
AIAW changes scholarship rules 1-7—1-11, 40B3
VOLOSHANOVICH, Alexander
Confrms Sovt psychiatric abuse 8-16, 670E3
VOLUNTEER Armed Forces—*See U.S. GOVERNMENT—ARMED Forces*
VOLVO, A.B.
Dutch rescue plant 1-5, 93G1
'77 profit down, exports up 1-27, 93E1
Norwegian deal signed 12-8, 965F2
Von BUELOW, Andreas
Questns NATO maneuvers 9-23, 748F2
Von DOHNYANI, Klaus
Greek EC entry terms set 12-21, 1017E3
Von DRENKMANN, Gunter (d. 1974)
Trail of '74 slayers opens 4-11, 353B3
Meyer escapes W Berlin prison 5-27, 438B3
Von HECKEL, Max
Loses Munich mayoral bid 3-5, 211E1
Von HIRSCH, Robert
Art Collectn auctnd 6-20—6-27, 578G2, D3
Von MANTEUFFEL, Hasso
Dies 9-24, 778B2
VONNEGUT Jr., Kurt
At pro-Shcharansky, Ginzburg rally 7-10, 542B3
Von REIBNITZ, Baroness Marie-Christine (Austria)
Married 6-30, 580F1

1979

VIRUSES—*See MEDICINE–Diseases*
VISCHER, Lukas
WCC central com votes release 1-9, 24A1
VISCONTI, Luchino (1906-76)
Innocent released 1-11, 174G2
VISENTINI, Bruno
Wage moderatn urged 4-10, 269B2
VISION—*See EYES & Eyesight*
VITALE, Stephen A.
Indicted in visa fraud 6-1, 491E3
VITAMINS—*See FOOD*
VITTI, Monica
Almost Perfect Affair released 4-26, 528B1
Teresa the Thief released 5-5, 528F3
VIZINCZEY, Stephen
In Praise of Older Women released 2-8, 174A3
VIZIRI, Yahya Sadeq
Named Iran justice min 1-6, 11G2
VIZOL, Chief Minister
On Naga attacks 1-5, 97F2
VLAD, Sanda
Banned from track 10-26, 912A1
VLASENKO, Y. M.
Kills self in US emb 3-28, 237E3
VLASOVA, Ludmila
Husband defects 8-23; US detains in NY 8-24, releases 8-27, 644D3-645F1
VOGEL, Wolfgang
Prisoner exchange rptd 7-20, 586D2
VOGEL-Heinrich, Renate
Defectn to W Ger rptd 9-18, 721E3
VOICE of America—*See under U.S. GOVERNMENT–U.S. INFORMATION Agency*
VOICE of My Own, A (play)
Opens 5-2, 712C3
VOICES (film)
Released 3-13, 528F3
VOIGHT, Jon
Champ released 4-3, 528G1
Wins Oscar 4-9, 336G1
VOINOVICH, Lt. Gov. George V. (R, O.)
Leads in Cleveland mayoral primary 10-2, 829C1
Elected mayor 11-6, 846G1, F2
VOLCANIC Eruptions
Indonesia hit 2-21, 140A3
St Vincent eruptns, residents evacuated 4-13–4-18, 399C1
Venus surface described 5-29, 692A1
Indonesia tidal wave 7-22, 638F3
Mt Etna erupts 8-4, 8-6, 639B1; kills 9 9-12, 800B2
VOLCKER, Paul Adolph
Named FRB chrmn; reactn 7-25; facts on 555B2, G2
Confrmd 8-2; sworn, FRB tight money shift seen 8-6, 621C1, 627B2, F2
Bentsen asks rate hike halt 9-20, Proxmire praises 9-26, 745A2
Meets Schmidt re $, mark rates 9-29, 779E3
IMF-World Bank mtg departure spurs $ defense rumors 10-3, 779B3, D3
Rpts FRB monetary policy move 10-6, addresses bankers mtg 10-9, 764E1, C3
Sees living standard drop 10-17, 10-28, 940B3
Galbraith scores policies 10-29, 826F3
Brazil alcohol fuel dvpt plan set 8-18, 871D2
VOLKENBORN, Arnold
Estimates Venez oil reserves 11-21, 953C1
VOLKSWAGENWERK A. G.
Steel strike affects productn 1-2, 8E1
Brazil metalworkers strike 3-13–3-27, 328C3
Chrysler purchase rumor denied 6-22, 576E2
Iran interests natlzd 7-5, 503A3
Chrysler joint venture plans in Argentina cited 7-20, 562A2
2d US car plant planned 7-26, 663D3
US Aug Rabbit sales rptd down 9-5, 663C3
Chrysler to sell Argentina operatns 9-15, 699A2
US plant, car sales cited 10-12, 784G3
Oct, Nov US car sales rptd up 11-6, 12-5, 963G2
Chrysler Argentina deal rptd set 11-19, 887F2
VOLUNTEER Armed Forces—*See U.S. GOVERNMENT–ARMED Forces*
VOLUNTEERS of the Puerto Rican Revolution
Claims credit for US, PR bombings 10-17, Navy ambush 12-3, 786D2, 924C3
VOLVO, A.B.
Stockholders block Norway deal 1-26, 77G1
'78 earnings rptd up 1-26, 77D2
Renault to buy share 12-19, 993G3-994C1
Von BAMBERG, Steffen
Spy arrest announced 6-21, 490A1
Von BULOW, Claus
Wings opens 1-28, 292G3
Von DYCK, Elisabeth
Killed 5-4, 374E2
Von HAYEK, Freidrich A.
On '29 Depression, '80s econ forecast 11-1, 827C1
Von HORVATH, Odon
Don Juan opens 4-15, 711E2
VONNEGUT, Kurt
God Bless You Mr Rosewater opens 5-20, 711D3
Jailbird on best-seller list 10-14, 800A3; 11-4, 892A3
Von SYDOW, Max
Hurricane released 4-11, 528E2

1980

VISCARDI, Michele
Arrested 10-13, 791B3
VISSER, Ria
Wins Olympic medal 2-14, 156A1
VITAMINS—*See FOOD*
VITEK v. Jones
Case decided by Sup Ct 3-25, 265D2
VITTI, Monica
Immortal Bachelor released 2-22, 216A3
VLADIMOV, Georgi
Vs Sakharov exile 1-29, 86C1
VLASOV, Viktor
Wins Olympic medal 7-23, 623C2
VLASOVA, Ludmila
Seeks US return 8-1, 638B2
VOA (Voice of America)—*See under U.S. GOVERNMENT--INTERNATIONAL Communications Agency*
VODOPYANOV, Mikhail V.
Death rptd 8-14, 676E3
VOGEL, Andreas
Sentenced 10-13, 833C1
VOGEL, Garson
Halts Cambodia Jan food aid 1-2, 12C2
VOGEL, Hans-Jochen
On RC bishops pol letter 9-13, 712G1
Sworn W Ger justice min 11-5, 925E1
VOICE of America—*See under U.S. GOVERNMENT--INTERNATIONAL Communications Agency*
VOICE of the Martyrs
Cuba to free members 10-13, 789B1
VOINOVICH, Vladimir
Plans emigratn 4-16, 326B3
VOLBRECHT, Harold
Cuevas KOs 4-6, 320D3
VOLCANIC Eruptions
Mt St Helens erupts 3-26, 252D1; 5-18, death toll, devastatn rptd 5-18—5-23, Washn declared disaster area 5-21, 382A1
Mt St Helens damage assessed 5-24—7-4, eruptns continue 5-25, 6-12; photos 503B3
Mt St Helens victim aid clears Cong 7-2, Carter signs 7-8, 515F1
Mt St Helens eruptns resume 8-7, 10-17; flood threats rptd 10-29, 970B3
VOLCKER, Paul Adolph
Bars tight money policy change 1-2, 52C2
Fears FRB membership exodus 2-4, 113F1-C3
Vows tight money policy 2-19, 126F1-A2
At IMF mtg in Hamburg 4-24, 302E1
Backs Hunt silver bailout 5-2, 344F3
Chrysler loan guarantees OKd 5-10, 383C2
Backs discount rate reductn 5-28, 400D2
DIDC sets interest rules 5-28, S&Ls file suit 6-16, 516G3
Vs FRB commodity trading regulatn 5-29, 425D1
Vows '81 tight money targets 7-31, 616A3
Carter scores FRB policies 10-2, reactn 10-3, 762G3, 763D1
VOLGER, Rudiger
Wrong Move released 1-25, 216G3
VOLKMER, Rep. Harold L. (D, Mo.)
Reelected 11-4, 843D2
VOLKOV, Konstantin
Wins Olympic medal 7-30, 624D1
VOLKSWAGENWERK A.G.
'79 US sales rptd down 1-4, 14C2
US Jan sales rptd up 2-5, 127A3
2d US plant site set 2-12, 127B3
Rabbit soot emissn cited 2-21, 146C1
Rabbit fails US crash test 2-28, 225E2
US Mar sales rptd up 4-3, 287A3
US prices hiked 4-7, 288D1
Brazil plant hit by metalworkers strike 4-19, 310C1
Research collaboratn set 4-22, 303B3
Spain investmt talks rptd 6-4, 467C3
US May sales drop rptd 6-5, 481E3
Chrysler hires US mgrs 6-9, 457E1
S Africa strike ends 6-25, 499C2
Kuwait buys 10% of Brazil unit 6-25, 542E3, 562C1
US June sales rptd up 7-6, 556D2
US Aug sales rptd up 9-4, 701G2
US Sept sales rptd up 10-6, 784G2
Oct sales rptd down 11-4, 857B1, C1
Lay-offs rptd planned 11-27, 924C3
Nissan joint productn planned 12-3, 924D3
VOLLEYBALL
NCAA OKs women's title tourns 1-8, 103C3
Moscow Olympic results 7-29, 8-1, 624C2
VOLLMER, Harald
Wins Olympic medal 7-20, 623C2
VOLVO, A.B.
Research collaboratn set 4-22, 303B3
VON BRAND, Theodor P.
Rules LaSalle Extensn U ads misleading 5-12, 703G1
VON BULOW, Andreas
Sworn W Ger research min 11-5, 925D1
VON DRENKMANN, Gunter (d. 1974)
Murder suspects acquitted 10-13, 833C1
VON HORN, Buddy
Any Which Way You Can released 12-17, 1003F1
VONNEGUT, Kurt
Jailbird on best-seller list 1-13, 40A3; 2-10, 120C3
VON SCHAMANN, Uwe
NFL '79 kicking ldr 1-5, 8B2
VON SCHLABRENDORFF, Fabian
Dies 9-3, 756G2
VON STEIN, Charlotte
Charlotte opens 2-27, 392D2
VON SYDOW, Max
Flash Gordon released 12-5, 972E3

1976

VOON, Chong Tian
Killed 6-6, 419E1
VORONEL, Alexander
Sovt anti-Semitism at high 2-16, 206D3
VORONIN, Alexander
Wins Olympic medal 7-18, 576D2
VORSTER, J. D.
On mixed marriage resolutn 8-19, 639F3

1977

VON Vet
Identified as Cambodia dep premr, CP com member 10-3, 780B1
VORHEES, Melvin B.
Dies 2-6, 164F3 *
VORONTSOV, Yuli M.
Scores US re Czech trial protest 10-18, 812A2

1978

VORONTSOV, Yuli M.
Rejects NATO Helsinki statemt 2-21, 179C2

1979

Von WEIZSAECKER, Carl-Friedrich
Carstens elected pres 5-23, 410A3
VOORHEES, Judge Donald S.
Overturns Washn anti-busing initiative 6-15, 596D3
Backs CAB order re Alaska Airlines 10-4, 830F1
VORNADO Inc.
Two Guys blue law case declined by Sup Ct 1-22, 54E1
VORNADO v. Degnan
Case declined by Sup Ct 1-22, 54E1
VORONA, Jack
Chrgs US sales aid Sovt mil 11-8, 856E3-857D1

1980

VON WECHMAR, Baron Rudiger
Elected UN Gen Assemb pres; facts on 9-16, 736E1, A2

1976

VORSTER, John (Balthazar Johannes) (South African president)
TV debuts 1-5, 11A3
Shuffles cabt 1-22, 76D1
No-confidence motn on Angola defeated 1-30, 162C3 *
On Mozambique-Rhodesia border closing 3-4, 175B3
Opens new port 4-1, 429E1
Visits Israel 4-8—4-12, 275D3
Syria scores 4-27, Israel defends visit 4-29, 320F2, C3
Mil role in Rhodesia barred 5-13, 339A1
EC asks mercy for SWAPO doomed 5-17, 386C2
OKs SWAPO const conf role 5-17, 386F2
Sees Smith 6-13—6-14, 427F1
Kissinger mtg confrmd 6-17, 6-18, 426D1 *, 427D1 *
In W Ger: sees S Africa ambs 6-21—6-22; Kissinger 6-23—6-24; Schmidt 6-25, 446E1-447A1, D3 *
Rhodesia ANC asks govt talks 6-27, 522C3
US aide begins Africa tour 7-7, 523A1
Chrgs outside agitatn re riots 8-9, 580D1
Admits problems, denies crisis 8-27; Buthelezi scores 8-29, 653B1
Vs Kissinger re white rule 9-1, 660B3
Sees Kissinger in Zurich 9-4—9-6, Rhodesia plan OK rptd 9-9, 660B2
Calls SWAPO legitimate 9-5, 660F2
SWAPO asks talks 9-6, 660D3
Bars SWAPO-govt talks 9-8, 697G2
Vows no pressure vs Rhodesia 9-13, 681E2
Sees Smith in Pretoria 9-14, 681C2
Kissinger sees Tanzania, Zambia ldrs 9-15—9-16, 681D1
Kissinger in Pretoria 9-17—9-20, 697A1
Smith accepts Rhodesia plan 9-24, pressure cited 9-25, 9-27, 717F1
Sees tribal chiefs 10-8, 793G2
On black pol role, apartheid, SWAPO talks 10-18, 793G1
Vs business race reform effort 10-18, 928B2
S Africa arms ban vetoed in UN 10-19, 781E3
Windhoek reps mtg cited 10-19, 832G1
Bars Newsweek editor 10-26, 927G2
Backs Kissinger plan 10-31, 832B1
Buthelezi asks US pressure 11-9, 928G1
Coggin protests church ldrs arrests 11-25, 927C2

1977

VORSTER, John (Balthazar Johannes Vorster) (South African prime minister)
Meets Richard 1-3, 3C2; warning re guerrillas rptd 1-16, 29C1
Meets Richard 1-19; compromise re Kissinger plan seen 1-20, 28G3
US urges pressure on Smith 1-20, 29B1
Bars Smith pressure 1-28, 72G3
Bars pass-law end 1-28, 100D3
Smith seeks support 2-9—2-10, 122F2
Withdraws press censorship bill 3-23, 349D3
Rejcts Westn compromise on Namibia 4-7, 285B1
Sees Owen, for US Rhodesia role 4-13, 296D2
Sees progress in Westn talks on Namibia 4-29, 349C2
OKs Namibia const concessns 5-9, 400D1
Sees Mondale 5-18—5-20, UK briefed 5-22, 397G2
Sees Houphouet-Boigny, scores US policy 5-22, 398F1
Rejects nonwhite govt role 5-27, 428A3
Vows Walvis Bay retentn 6-14, 457D2
Interracial sex laws debated 7-5, 7-7, 564B1
Hits US policy 8-5, 639G2
Proposes Asian, colored power-sharing plan 8-20, 657C1
Denies A-weapons program 8-23, 656G3
Sees Owen, Young on new Rhodesia plan 8-29, 661C2
On Biko death 9-16, 747C1
Dissolves Parlt, calls electns 9-20, 747B1
Scores US condemnatn 10-20, 804B2
Denies A-bomb vow 10-23, US releases letter 10-25, 825D2
Sets pass law revisn 11-3, 852E1
Wins electns 11-30, backs apartheid 12-2, 934G1

1978

VORSTER, John (Balthazar Johannes Vorster) (South African president)
Sees Ford 1-16, 39A1
Asian, colored power-sharing plan rptd shelved 1-24, 92F2
Shuffles Cabt 1-25, 55B1
Scores US re Nigeria rights abuse 3-31, 234A1
On Transkei break 4-11, 259A1
OKs Namibia plan 4-25, 299C1
Sets forgn influence-buying fund probe 5-8, 377B3
Defends influence-buying fund 5-8, abolished Info Dept 6-15, 498F2, C3
Backs Nkomo Rhodesia role 5-27, 615C2
RC bishops ask unionists release 7-4, 633F2
Delays UN Namibia plan OK re Walvis Bay 7-28, 633F3
Links Mulder, Info Dept scandal 9-1, 742F1
Resigns 9-20, named pres 9-29, 741D3
Info Dept press scandal erupts 10-29—10-30; probe judge implicates 11-2, 868D1, A2
Info Dept probe rpt clears 12-5, 946G1

1979

VORSTER, John (Balthazar Johannes) (South African president; resigned June 4)
Rhoodie scandal chrgs detailed 3-7, 3-10, 191A1, B1
Denies Rhoodie bribe chrgs 3-22, 213A2
Probe comm clears 4-2, 270C1
Natl Party expels Mulder 4-6, 270F1
Resigns re Erasmus comm rpt 6-4, 427B3
Botha shuffles Cabt 6-14, 469G2
Viljoen named pres 6-19, 469F2

1980

VORSTER, John (Balthazar Johannes)
Scores Botha re apartheid changes 3-12, 255G2

1976

VOTATOR Division of Chemetron Corp.—*See CHEMETRON*
VOTING Rights—*See under POLITICS*
VOTTERO, Tomas
Loses cabt post 1-15, 71B2
VOUEL, Raymond
European Comm meets 12-22—12-23, 977G1
VOUETO, Clement Ngai
Named interior min 9-5, 924F2
VOUGHT Corp.—*See under LTV*
VREDELING, Henk
Backs US Ger troop plan 6-11, 449G1
European Comm meets 12-22—12-23, 977G1
VUCEKOVIC, Mancilio
Croat held in 'mistaken-identity' shooting 6-8, 542E3

1977

VOTER Education Project
Lewis confrmd to ACTION 8-4, 626A3
VOTING Issues—*See under POLITICS*
VOUEL, Raymond
Gets Eur Comm post 1-7, 74D2
VOUGHT Corp.—*See LTV Corp.*
VREDELING, Henk
Gets Eur Comm post 1-7, 74E2
VYSOTSKY, Igor
US tour results 1-29—2-5, 263A2

1978

VOTAW, Carmen
Cancels Carter mtg 11-22, 915F1
VOTING Issues—*See under POLITICS*
VOYSEV, Michael
My Astonishing Self opens 1-18, 760F2
V/STOL Bombers—*See ARMAMENTS—Aircraft*
VUCKOVICH, Pete
NL pitching ldr 10-2, 928G2
VULCAN, U.S.S.
5 women rpt for duty 11-1, 877G2-A3

1979

VOTAW, Carmen Delgado
Quits Carter panel 1-12, 30A3
VOTING Issues—*See under POLITICS*
VOYAGER (U.S. interplanetary probe series)—*See ASTRONAUTICS–Interplanetary Projects*
VOZNESENSKY, Andrei Andreevich
Metropole issued 1-18, 100C2
VULCAN (U.S. repair ship)
Female sailors go overseas 9-11, 724F3
VYSOTSKY, Vladimir
Metropole issued 1-18, 100C2

1980

VOSBURGH, Dick
Day in Hollywood opens 5-1, 392E2
VSI Corp.
Fairchild merger set 8-26, 746C1
VYSOTSKY, Vladimir
Dies 7-24, honored at funeral 7-28, 580C2

W

1976

WACHTER, Michael
Cited as Carter adviser 4-23, 305F2
WADDY, Judge Joseph C.
Acquits Wild 7-27, 566A1
OKs AT&T trust suit 11-16, 886G3
WADE, Abdoulaye
Vs multiparty, pres successn amendmts 6-11, 591A3
WADE, James P.
In Moscow SALT talks 1-21—1-23, 61F3
WADE, Virginia
Loses DC Va Slims 1-25, 123A3
2d in US Open doubles 9-12, 716D1
WAGES—*See ECONOMY, LABOR*
WAGGONNER Jr., Rep. Joe D. (D, La.)
Reelected 11-2, 822B2, 829F3
WAGNER, Claude
Loses PC ldrship bid 2-23, 188D2

1977

WACKERNAGEL, Christoph
Captured by Dutch police 11-10, 887E3
Schubert kills self 11-12, 888D2
WADDY, Judge Joseph C.
Sup Ct refuses AT&T case 1-25, 80C2
WADE, Sonny
Montreal wins Grey Cup, named MVP 11-27, 950G2
WADE, Virginia
Loses Va Slims tourn 3-6, Bridgestone Doubles 4-10, 430D3, 431F1
Wins Wimbledon 7-1, 548G1
Apples win WTT title 8-27, 787E3, F3
US Open results 9-11, 787A2
WADKINS, Lanny
2d in LA Open 2-20, 311G1
2d in Houston Open 5-1, 676B1
Wins PGA championship 8-14, 659D2
Wins World Series of Golf 9-5, 950B3
US wins Ryder Cup Matches 9-17, 951A2
PGA top money winner 10-30, 950G3
WAGE & Price Stability, Council on—*See under U.S. GOVERNMENT*
WAGES—*See ECONOMY, LABOR*
WAGGONNER Jr., Rep. Joe D. (D, La.)
Spec interest gifts rptd 3-7, 232B3

1978

WACKERNAGEL, Christoph
Dutch backers stage protest 3-14, 192G1
Dutch OK extraditn 5-8, 354C1
Extradited to W Ger 10-13, 885B1
WADDILL, Jr., Dr. William
Mistrial declared in abortn death 5-5, 369C2
WADDY, Joseph C.
Dies 8-1, 708G3
WADE, Abdoulaye
Loses pres electn 2-26, 152F3
WADE, Virginia
Wimbledon results 7-7, 540A1
WADKINS, Bobby
2d in Tucson Open 1-8, 76B1
Wins Europn Open 10-22, 990B2
WADKINS, Lanny
Wins Canadian PGA 8-20, 672F3
4th in World Series of Golf 10-1, wins Garden State PGA 10-22, 990C1, B2
Brother wins Europn Open 10-22, 990B2
WAGE & Price Stability, Council on—*See under U.S. GOVERNMENT*
WAGES—*See ECONOMY, LABOR*
WAGGONNER Jr., Rep. Joe D. (D, La.)
Gas price plan clears conf com 8-17, 677C3
Not standing for reelectn 9-16, 736D3
WAGNER, Aubrey J.
Quits TVA 5-18, 390G1, A2, D2

1979

WABASHA, Minn.—*See MINNESOTA*
WADDY, Billy
Rams win in playoffs 12-30, 1001B1
WADDY-Rossow, Debra
East wins WBL All-Star game 3-14, 507F1
WADE, Rev. Thomas
Chinese chng transliteratn 1-1, 75D2
WADE, Virginia
Loses Phila Avon tourn 3-11, 391C2
US wins Wightman Cup 11-4, 1003C3
WADKIN, Sir Edward William (d. 1901)
Church painting sold for record sum 10-25, 892A1
WADKINS, Bobby
2d in Philadelphia Classic 7-29, 587F3
2d in Napa Classic 9-23, 970E1
WADKINS, Lanny
Wins LA Open 2-25, 220F3
Wins Tourn Players title 3-25, 587A2
2d in Canadian PGA 9-2; wins Japan Open 10-28, 970C1, A2
PGA top money winner 11-30, 969F2
WAGE and Price Stability, Council on—*See under U.S. GOVERNMENT*
WAGES—*See ECONOMY, LABOR*
WAGGONER, Margaret
Wilson Coll closing barred 5-26, resigns 5-27, 482E1

1980

WACCHER, William
Slain 2-7, 151C2
WACO—*See TEXAS*
WADDELL, Jean
Arrested 8-8, 671C3
WADDELL, John C.
Named Arrow chrmn, acting pres 12-8, 959F3
WADDINGTON, Sarah
On election results 11-4, 846B3
WADDY, Billy
Steelers win Super Bowl 1-20, 61F3-62C1
WADE, Earl
Elected Cairo (Ill) ward rep 11-4, 850E3
WADE, Virginia
Loses Avon tourns 2-3, 3-16, 607D2
Wimbledon results 7-4—7-6, 606E2
US wins Wightman Cup 11-1, 947A1
WAGE & Price Stability, Council on—*See under U.S. GOVERNMENT*
WAGES—*See LABOR (U.S.)--Wages, Hours & Productivity*

1976

WAGNER, Robert F.
Supports Carter 6-14, 432C1
WAINWRIGHT (U.S. warship)
In Intl Naval Review 7-4, 488B3
WAITHAYAKON, Prince Wan (Thailand)
Dies 9-5, 970D3
WAIYAKI, Munyua
Denies tie to Israel raid 7-9, scores Uganda 516A1, A3
Outlines Uganda peace terms 7-27, 548B3
On Kenya-Uganda accord 8-8, 580G3
WAKASA, Tokuji
Diet subpoenas 2-26, testifies 3-1, 190C3
Arrested 7-8, 497G2
Indicted 7-28, 624D2
WALD, David
Loses election 11-2, 824F3
WALD, Dr. George
Pleads for Sovt dissident 3-24, 421A3
Vs Harvard U DNA research 7-7, 736C1

WALDHEIM, Kurt
UN E Timor missn curbed 2-2, 122D3
Geneva staff strike setld 3-3, 164F3
Addresses UNCTAD conf 5-5, 320B2
Rights group chrgs Indian torture 6-2, 408B3
Scores S Africa rioting 7-2, 487A3
Vs Olympic boycott 7-18, 528D3
Vs S Africa plan re Namibia 8-26, 654C2
Sees Kissinger re Africa 9-2; lauds 9-16, 681A2
2d term seen 10-5, 906E3
US accuses on UN jobs 10-11, 760A2
Wins 2d term 12-7, 12-8, 914C2
Angola
Asks end to forgn interventn 1-6, 16C2
Angola vows given S Africa 3-25, 228A1
Vs UN membership veto 6-24, 455F1
Cyprus
Peace talks resumptn set 1-18, 48E2
Clerides continues as mediator 1-18, 48D2
Communal talks resume 2-17—2-21, 155C1
Kissinger asks Cyprus talks 9-30, 719F2
Asked to push peace talks 11-12, 863D1
Middle East
Backs Palestinian rights 1-9, 19A1
Meets Leb amb 1-17, urges end to strife 1-18, 34A3
Warns on Leb crisis 3-26, 3-30, 225C1, 226A2
Gets W Bank protest 5-16, 354E1
Visits Syria 5-25—5-27, Cncl renews UNDOF 5-28, 385G2
Leb vs intl silence on crisis 6-9, 406A3
Leb pres vs Libya in peace force 6-30, 487C2
Vs Israel Uganda raid, aides qualify remark 7-5, 486F2; denies anti-Israel remark 7-8, 516G1
Says Sinai front quiet 10-22, 799B2
Cncl backs peace call 11-30, 895D2
Assemb sets Geneva conf role 12-9, 914D1
Sahara
Names UN envoy 2-1, 107A3
UN envoy ends missn 2-17, 178D2
Spurns El Aiun assemb mtg 2-26, 178C2

1977

WAGNER, Gerald G.
Dies 11-22, 952F3
WAGNER, Lindsay
Wins Emmy 9-11, 1021G3
WAHLSTEN, Douglas
Chrgd 2-24, 159B1
WAIYAKI, Munyua
Sees Richard 1-8, 1-12, 11A2
Chrgs Somali invasn 6-30, 512E2
On improved Sudan ties 7-6, 588E1
WAJIMA, Koichi
Gazo TKOs 6-7, 828B1
WAKE Forest University (Winston-Salem, N.C.)
Hallberg in Walker Cup tourn 8-27, 951G1
WALD, Dr. George
Supports DNA research halt 3-7, 184F2
WALD, Patricia
Asst atty gen 2-16; confrmd 3-4, 211G1
WALDEN, Brian
On Natl Front riots 8-17, 637D1

WALDHEIM, Kurt
Sovts bar UNEF funds 12-30-76, 4A2
Kurd deportatns chrgd 1-16, 257B1
Sees Greek, Turk Cypriot ldrs 2-12, 108B3, C3
Sees Clifford 2-16, 122A2
Scores Czech press detentns 2-16, 220G3
Carter addresses UN 3-17, 185F1
El Salvador guerrilla plea 5-1, rebuked 5-2, 373E2
Rpts on Cyprus peace efforts 5-2, 394E2
Mediates hunger strike 6-14—6-23, 493G1
Scores Croat raid on Yugo missn 6-14, 497B2
Uruguay release of forgn newsmen urged 7-15, 7-21, 601E1, G1
Assesses world issues 9-19, 713F1
Vs US withdrawal from ILO 11-1, 829F1
Gets Amnesty Intl prisoner petitn 12-7, 956E2
Africa
Asks Uganda death probe 2-24, 142B1
Gets Benin coup probe rpt 3-8, 243A3
At Maputo conf on southn Africa 5-16, 399C1
Warns S Africa vs bantustans 8-22, 661F2
Smith invites Rhodesia envoy 9-28, 810B1
Names Rhodesia envoy 9-29, 809G2
Lauds S Africa arms ban vote 11-4, 851F1
Sahara rebels free French natls 12-23, 998G2
Middle East
Sees war 1-30; tours 5 Arab states, Israel 2-2—2-10, 86C2
Ends Arab-Israel missn 2-11—2-12; sees PLO moderatn 2-16, 107C1
Rpts on mission 2-28, 144B1
Begin asks aid on Syrian Jews 7-22, 570G3
Vs new W Bank setlmts 8-18, 623C1
Israel explains Leb raid 11-9, 874C3
Asks 2d pre-Geneva conf 11-29, Israel bars 11-30, 910G1
US effort to block conf rptd 12-1, 910D1
Vs UN chrmn at Cairo conf 12-13, 953C2

1978

WAGNER, Dick
Vs Kuhn bar on Blue 1-30, 194C3
WAGNER, Gustav Franz
Arrested in Brazil 5-30; W Ger, 3 other natns ask extraditn 5-31, 6-8; attempts suicide 6-14, 477G1
WAGNER, Jane
Moment by Moment released 12-21, 1030C3
WAGNER, Richard (1813-83)
Winifred Wagner released 3-23, 619C1
WAGNER, Robin
Wins Tony 6-4, 579A3
WAGNER, Rolf-Clemens
Arrested in Yugo 5-11, extraditn unresolved 5-11—5-31, 438G3
Yugo bars extraditn 11-17, release rptd 11-18, 906G1
WAHLBERG, Marianne
Swedish personnel min 10-18, 822A3
WAIGWA, Wilson
Buerkle wins Wanamaker Mile 1-27, 76B3
WAITE, Barbara
Appeal rptd lost 1-23, 114F1
WAITERS, Tony
Named NASL coach of yr 8-14, 707F2
WAJDA, Andrzej
Landscape After Battle released 2-9, 619F2
WAKE Forest University (Winston-Salem, N.C.)
Carter speech 3-17, 202C1-D2
Griffin in NBA draft 6-9, 457G3
WAKEMAN, Rick
NASL Phila club ownership cited 1-5, 23C1
WALCHER, Josef
Wins world skiing title 1-29, 316G2
WALDENSTROM, Dr. Jan G. (deceased)
Algerian pres dies 12-27, 1012F2
WALDHEIM, Kurt
Chile bars new rights probes 1-4, retracts 1-5, 17E1
Names Dadzie to new econ post 3-8, 401D3
Sees Shevchenko on resignatn 4-25, 302E2
Pleas for Moro release 4-25, 314A1
Opens UN disarmamt sessn 5-23, 421B1
Disarmamt sessn ends 6-30, 523A1
Czech dissident plea rptd 11-8, 885D2
Africa
S Africa embargo compliance lags 4-28, 377B2
Vs S Africa apartheid 8-14, 676B2
Presents Namibia plan asks 7,500 troops 8-30, 741G3
Namibia plan OKd by Cncl 9-29, 819E2
S Africa OKs Namibia rep visit 10-19, 819E3
Sees Botha 11-27, S Africa to consider Namibia plan 12-3, 988G3-989A1
S Africa OKs Namibia plan 12-22, 1020E1
Cyprus
Gets Turkish Cypriot plan 4-13, 328B3
Ecevit scores setlmt role 5-16, 398G2
Indochina
Gets copy of Viet-Cambodia peace bid 2-8, 79G3
Cambodia invites 10-13, 794D1
OKs visits to Cambodia, Viet 11-1, 859G3
Middle East
Gets Leb protest on Israel invasn 3-15, 174C3
Arab League asks actn vs Israel Leb invasn 3-15, 174G3
Leb protest cited 197C2
Sec Cncl forms Leb peace force 3-19, 197G1
Says Arafat OKs Leb truce 3-28, 213C1
Austria bars Unifil role 3-29, 214C1
Mexico vows troops for Leb 4-1, reneges 4-5, 236E1
Leb asks more Unifil troops 4-4, 236D1
Vs Israel Leb pullback plan 4-7, 256D2
To seek new peace formula 4-14, 274A3
In Leb, Israel; inspects Unifil troops, seeks peace talk 4-17—4-18; rpts to Sec Cncl 4-20, 274A2
Arafat vs Leb truce 5-11, 383A3
Aide in Leb, Israel on Leb crisis 5-20—5-22, 383E2
Israel: Unifil soft on PLO 6-13; denies, scores Israel south Leb pullout move 6-14, 462F1
Says Leb plans to send troops to south, Arafat to cooperate 6-14, 462B2
Leb to send army to south 7-28, 581E1
Gets plea on Leb army move south 8-8, 638C3
Asks Unifil extensn 9-14, 713C1
Backs French Leb peace role 10-3, 745B2
UN asks to press Leb peace 10-6, 761D1
Asks Israel, Leb Christn cooperatn 951F1
Photo removed at PLO exhibit 11-29, 951G2

1979

WAGNER, Gustov Franz
Brazil denies extradtn to 4 natns 6-20, 483A3*
Mental hosp confinemt rptd 8-8, 617C1*
WAGNER, Hans
W Gers win world 4-man bobsled title 2-25, 392F1
WAGNER, John Peter (Honus) (1874-1955)
Rose surpasses NL singles mark 8-5, 619G2
WAGNER, Robert
Concorde Airport '79 released 8-3, 820A1
WAGNER, Robert F.
Scotto indicted 11-15, 890B2
WAGNER, Rolf-Clemens
Arrest in Switz rptd 11-20, 998C3
WAHL, Ken
Wanderers released 7-13, 820F3
WAINWRIGHT, Richard
Vs Liberal growth res 9-28, 792B2
WAISBERG, Carl
Bars Toronto Sun trial 4-23, 311C2
WAITERS, Tony
Whitecaps win NASL title 9-8, 775F2
WAITZ, Grete
In NYC Marathon, sets women's world record 10-21, 911E3
WAIYAKI, Munyua
Named Kenya energy min 11-28, 969B2
WAKE Forest University (Winston-Salem, N.C.)
Hallberg wins NCAA golf title 5-26, 587G1
Loses Tangerine Bowl 12-22, 1001A3
WALCO National Corp.
Richmond stock ownership rptd 9-1, 702A1
WALD, George
On 3 Mile I radiatn 3-29, 242G3

WALDHEIM, Kurt
At Rockefeller funeral 2-2, 104D2
Africa
Urges Namibia truce 2-26, S Africa rejects 3-5, 171F1, D2-A3
Namibia conf held 11-12-11-16, 889B3
S Africa OKs Namibia plan 12-5, 969G1
Asia—*See also 'Indochina Refugees' below*
Asks China, Viet hostilities end 2-18, 123B1
Deplores Bhutto executn 4-4, 247A2
In Hanoi, Peking; seeks mediatn 4-26–5-1, 340G1
In N, S Korea to mediate feud 5-2–5-5, 341F3-342B1
Cyprus
Visits 5-17, intercommunal talks set 5-19, 387C2
Indochina Refugees
In SE Asia for talks 5-9–5-13, 379C2
Plea to Malaysia on Viets 6-15; Malaysia drops threat to shoot 6-18, 460E2
Viet OKs UN conf 6-20, 474A1
7 states ask UN conf 6-28, 473E2
Calls intl conf 6-30, held 7-20–7-21, 549A1, A3
US sens stress Cambodia aid effort 10-26, 823G3
Cambodia relief aid pledged 11-5, 863B3
Thais declare 2 Cambodia camps 'safe havens' 11-29, 917A3
Iran
Vows US hostage release aid 11-6, 841C2
Cncl mtg asked 11-13; meets Vance, Cncl rejects mtg 11-14, 862B1
Appeals for US hostages 11-19, 878E2
Asks Cncl debate 11-26, 896A1
Sees US Congressmen 12-1, 913E1
UN Cncl res asks US hostage role 12-4, contacts Iran forgn min 12-5, 913C1, G1
Assured on US hostage safety 12-9, 934F2
Iran cool to hostage missn 12-30; UN OKs res, trip starts 12-31, 974G2, D3
Latin America
Nazi fugitive loses Paraguay citizenship, extraditn pressure cited 8-8, 616C3
Middle East—*See 'Iran' above*
Scores Christn Unifil harassmt in Leb 1-16, 51E1
Gets Leb protest on Israeli shelling 1-23, 50F3
Israel denies Christian-Leb troop role 4-19, 278B1
Vs Israel, Christns, PLO role in Leb 4-21, 296D3
Asks Unifil renewal 6-11–6-12, 436D3
Israel vs UNTSO in Sinai 7-24, US disputes 7-25, 551E1, G1
Asks Leb truce observance 8-30, 658A3

1980

WAGNER, George R.
On Cuban refugee resetlmt lag 6-2, 420G1
WAGNER, Gustov Franz
Commits suicide 10-3, 810E1
WAGNER, Richard (1813-83)
Daughter-in-law dies 3-5, 280D2
WAGNER, Robert
'Charlie's Angels' fraud probe rptd 5-1, 376A3
LA DA ends 'Charlie's Angels' probe 12-2, 1002F2
WAGNER, Rolf-Clemens
Sentenced in Switzerland 9-26, 755D1
WAGNER, Winnifred
Dies 3-5, 280D2
WAITE, Ralph
On the Nickel released 5-4, 416D3
WAITZ, Grete
Wins L'eggs Mini Marathon, sets world record 5-31, 527A3
In NYC Marathon; sets women's world mark 10-26, 890G3
WAKE Island (U.S. territory)
US A-waste plan questioned 5-21, 405G2
WAKMAN, Mohammed Amin
Says Afghan rebels fight each other 9-2, 686D1
WALD, Dr. George
At anti-US conf in Iran 6-2—6-5, 418D2, 419D1

WALDHEIM, Kurt
Opens UN women's conf 7-14, 587A2
Africa
Marks Zimbabwe indepndnc 4-17—4-18, 301E1
S Africa delays Namibia talks 5-12, 374C2
US protests rejctn of Israeli bid on Kenya complex 6-19, 476B2
S Africa defends Angola raids 6-27, 524F3
At OAU summit, scores S Africa raids in Angola 7-1, 509A2
S Africa chrgs Namibia prejudice 8-29, 710D3
Namibia talks schedule agreed 11-24, 967G1
Asia
Thais protest Viet attack 6-24, 475B3
In Hanoi, Bangkok; sees Thai, Viet peace pact re Cambodia conflict 8-2—8-5, 591A1
Cyprus
Talks failure rptd 4-3, 273C2
Talks resume 8-9, 633D2
Iran—*See also 'Iran-Iraq War' below*
In Iran on hostage missn 1-1—1-3; doubts release 1-4; briefs Carter 1-6, Cncl 1-7, 3F2
Hostage compromise studied 1-11—1-12, 29D1
Presses US hostage release 1-20, 2-4, 88G2-A3
Carter backs intl probe of shah 2-13, 105B1
US OKs intl comm idea 2-13, 109A3, D3
Forms comm to probe shah 2-17; US, Iran OK 2-17—2-19, 122A1
Vance cites statemt on UN comm functns 2-27, 137B2
Says Iran reneges on hostages, bars UN comm rpt 3-10; lauds Iran govt role 3-11; meets Vance 3-12, 177G2
Carter cites US backing in hostage crisis 4-7, 257F2
To renew UN comm probe 5-17, briefs rep 5-22; Westn diplomats oppose 5-23; rep in Iran 5-26, 393D2
Role re jailed Iranians in US asked 8-5, 587D1
Iran-Iraq War
Meets Muskie, Gromyko; asks UN Cncl mtg 9-23, 718E3
Iraq backs UN truce bid 9-29, Iran vs 10-1, 733G2-734B1
Asks truce to free merchant ships 10-10; Iran replies, Iraq ignores 10-13, 774F1
Iran vows to keep Hormuz Strait open 10-22, 799F1
Iraq to free 12 Iranians 10-22, 799G1
Cncl asks peace missn 11-5; names Palme envoy 11-11, Palme rpts on trip 11-25, 894G2
Latin America
Cuba bars refugee involvmt 6-5, 435B2
Middle East—*See also 'Iran', 'Iran-Iraq War' above*
On Israeli Leb troop pullout 4-13; UNIFIL hq shelling 4-16, 283G3, 284E1
Warns of 'armed elements' in Leb 5-2, 362D3
US protests Israeli constructn bid rejctn 6-19, 476B2
Backs Palestine state 7-25, 7-28, Israel rebukes 7-28, 572F2
Scores Israel Leb attack 8-19, 628A1
Rpts to Gen Assemb 9-12, 775G1
2 deported W Bank mayors end protest 12-24, 976E3
Asked to end Syrian siege in Leb 12-26, 977C2
USSR
UN workers '79 rights rally protested 2-14, 221B1

1976

WALDIE, Jerome R.
Kim gift rptd 11-4, 900F1
WALDMAN, Jay C.
Named dep asst atty gen 1-14, 78G3
WALES—*See GREAT Britain*
WALGREN, Doug
Elected 11-2, 830F3
WALI, Sayed el-
Death confirmed 6-21, 466A3
WALKER, Gov. Daniel (D, Ill.)
Loses primary 3-16, 196F2, D3
Sees Carter, backs Howlett 7-6, 492G3
At Daley funeral service 12-22, 969D3
WALKER, John
Wins Olympic medal 7-31, 576D1
WALKER, Kathryn
Wins Emmy 5-17, 460A2
WALKER, Robert S.
Elected 11-2, 830F3
WALLACE, Douglas A.
Ordains black 4-2, barred from Mormon conf 10-3, 951C2
WALLACE, Gov. George C(orley) (D, Ala.)
Gets US campaign subsidy 1-2, 22E3
Opens Mass campaign 1-9, 22C2
Common Cause rpts code backing 1-9, 23A1
Ct orders prison reform 1-13, 25G2
Wins in Miss caucuses 1-24, 94F3
4th in Okla caucuses 2-7, 129E1
Carter sees Fla 'showdown' 2-26, rebuts 3-4, 166B2
3d in Mass primary 3-2, 165A1
Fed fund total listed 3-4, 180D3
Sees Fla win 3-7, Carter upsets 3-9, 179D1
Gallup poll results 3-15, 197E1
2d in Ill primary 3-16, 196E2, 197C1, F1
NC campaign dvpts 3-19, 3-22, Carter tops 3-23, 214A1, F1, B2
Taunted by Wis protestors 3-30, 245E3
NY primary results 4-6, 245A1
3d in Wis primary 4-6, 245D1
4th in delegate count 4-9, 261B1
Loses Sup Ct funds plea 4-23, 306C1
Pa primary results 4-27, 304F3
Tex primary results 5-1, Ind, Ga, Ala 5-4, 323A1, F1, B2, C2
Dem crossover vote to Reagan cited 5-4, 5-5, 322E3, 323C2
'Could support' Carter 5-5, 324A1
Neb, W Va primary results 5-11, 342G1, C3
Mich, Md primary results 5-18, 356G2, 357D1, G1, B2
Wins 17 delegates 5-25, 373B3, 374B2-D3
Mont, RI, SD vote results 6-1, 390B1, B2
Calif, NJ, Ohio vote results 6-8, 409B1
Primary delegates totaled 6-8, 409A3
Endorses Carter 6-9, 409F1
Carter visits 6-12, 432A2
Dem platform backed 6-15, 432A3
Campaign debt rptd 6-16; fed funds 7-1, 491B1, D1
FEC ends fed funds 6-23, 490F3
Dem conv speaker 7-13, 509C3
Dem conv pres vote, table 7-14, 507E2
Campaigns with Carter 9-13, 686C2
Pardons 'Scottsboro Boy' 10-25, 860B1
FEC certificatn total rptd 12-31, 979G2
WALLACE, Irving
R Document on best-seller list 12-5, 972G2
WALLIS, Lee
Spots kidnap suspect 7-29, 560E2
WALLOP, Malcolm
Wins Wyo Sen primary 9-14, 705D2
AMA donation rptd 10-22, 938E3
Elected to US Senate 11-2, 819E3, 824C3, 828D3
WALLRAFF, Sgt. Henry C.
Convicted 7-19, 586D3
McClure prosecutns end 9-1 942D2
WALLS, Lt. Gen. Peter
Rpts mil svc extensn 5-1, 339G1
WALL Street Journal (newspaper)
'75 4th ¼ corp profits survey rptd 2-3, 215F2
Rpts Nader car safety study 2-23, 186E2
1st ¼ corp profits survey rptd 4-29, 376G2
2d ¼ corp profits survey rptd 7-28, 708C3
Rpts Ford funds probe 9-21, 722F1
Gannon on pres debate panel 9-23, 700G3
On Ford '73 IRS audit 10-8, 764B1-B2
3d ¼ corp profits survey rptd 11-18, 866E2
WALSH, Eric
Buried 5-6, 524G3
WALSH, Ethel Bent
Rpts EEOC case backlog cut 8-20, 922D1
WALSH Jr., John J.
Ford wins pres nominatn 8-19, 597F1
WALSH, Lawrence E.
Backs judges pay raise suit 2-13, 136F2
ABA successor named 8-11, 640G3
WALSH, Rep. William F. (R, N.Y.)
Reelected 11-2, 830C2

1977

WALDOCK, Sir Humphrey
World Ct member 4G1
WALES—*See GREAT Britain*
WALI Khan, Nasim
Arrested 3-18, 223C1
WALKER, Charles M.
Replaced in Treas post 2-21, 148G3
WALKER, Bishop John T.
Installed 9-24, scores Episc fund drive 10-4, 845E2
WALKER, Margaret—*See ALEXANDER, Margaret Walker*
WALKER, Rep. Robert S. (R, Pa.)
House curbs HEW quota enforcemt 6-17, 478G1
WALL, Marvin
Bell drops oppositn to more FBI indictmts 12-13, 979D3
WALLACE, Amy
'Lists' on best-seller list 7-3, 548E3; 8-14, 643G1; 9-4, 712D3; 10-2, 808E3; 11-6, 872E3; 12-4, 1021G2
WALLACE, Cornelia (Mrs. George)
Countersues for divorce 9-15, 808C2
WALLACE, Douglas A.
Sup Ct rejcts Gilmore stay 1-11, 40G1
Loses suit vs Mormon church 3-10, 310G1
WALLACE, Gov. George C(orley) (D, Ala.)
Signs court aid bill 6-13, 464F3
Files for divorce 9-12, countersued 9-15, 808C2
WALLACE, Irving
'Lists' on best-seller list 7-3, 548E3; 8-14, 643G1; 9-4, 712D3; 10-2, 808E3; 11-6, 872E3; 12-4, 1021G2
WALLACE, Mike
Ct protects journalists' thoughts 11-7, 920B3
WALLACE, Dr. William D.
Protests AAAS Jensen honor 2-23, 183C3
WALLECHINSKY, David
'Lists' on best-seller list 7-3, 548E3; 8-14, 643G1; 9-4, 712D3; 10-2, 808E3; 11-6, 872E3; 12-4, 1021G2
WALLER, Wilfrid
Rhodesia educatn min 3-10, 223F2
WALLIS, W. Allen
Electd PBC chrmn 3-9, 396D3
WALLOP, Sen. Malcolm (R, Wyo.)
Vs Sen ethics code 4-1, 251F3
WALLS, Gen. Peter
On Mozambique raid 5-31, 413G1
WALL Street Journal (newspaper)
Says gas producers await deregulatn 2-3, 152C2
Sutowo interview publshd 2-14, 304D3
Corp paymts survey info rptd 2-28, 233C1
USDA bureaucracy scored 4-12, 364F3
Dresser boycott ad rptd 4-14, 323B3
SEC to open corp payoff files 4-27, 502G3
Rpts Australia econ trend 6-22, 504E2
Li Hsien-nien interview 10-2, 781A1
On most reliable govt news source list 12-10, 1008G3, 1009B1
WALSH, Donn
Loses electn 6-8, 466E3
WALSH, John
Resigns 3-6, 235F3
Disputes Califano on health care probe 3-17—3-23, 235G2
WALSH, Rodolfo
AP rptr questned on ties 11-10—11-11, 922C2

1978

WALDING, Mathias
Boll loses libel suit 5-30, 439E2
WALDMAN, Frank
Revenge of Pink Panther released 7-19, 970A3
WALDMAN, Honey
Family Business opens 4-12, 760B2
WALDORF-Astoria Hotel (N.Y., N.Y.)
Philippe dies 12-25, 1032D3
WALDROP, Tony
Buerkle breaks indoor mi record 1-13, 76D2
WALES—*See GREAT Britain*
WALGREN, Rep. Doug (D, Pa.)
Reelected 11-7, 852D1
WALID, Gen. Abu
Denies PLO threat vs Israel 5-1, 339D3
WALI Khan, Khan Abdul
Cleared of chrgs 1-1, 8A1
WALKEN, Christopher
Deer Hunter released 12-14, 1030F2
WALKER, Maj. Gen. Edwin A. (ret.)
Cited at JFK death hearings 9-13, 9-14, 749E2
WALKER, Margaret—*See ALEXANDER, Margaret Walker*
WALKER, Peter
My Old Friends opens 12-2, 1031E2
WALKER, Rep. Robert S. (R, Pa.)
House votes quota curb 6-13, 445G3
Reelected 11-7, 852D1
WALLACE, Amy
'Lists' on best-seller list 1-8, 24E3; 3-5, 195F3; 4-2, 272C3
WALLACE, Cornelia (Mrs. George)
Settles divorce suit 1-4, 96A1
Quits campaign for Ala gov 8-11, 699C2
WALLACE, Gov. George C(orley) (D, Ala.)
Settles divorce suit 1-4, 96A1
Quits US Sen race 5-16, 362G2
Names Sen Allen's widow to seat, weighs running 6-8, 432F1
Not standing for electn 9-5, 699B2
James elected Ala gov 11-7, 849G2
WALLACE, Irving
'Lists' on best-seller list 1-8, 24E3; 3-5, 195F3; 4-2, 272C3
WALLACH, Eli
Diary of Anne Frank revived 12-18, 1031D1
WALLACH, Roberta
Diary of Anne Frank revived 12-18, 1031D1
WALLECHINSKY, David
'Lists' on best-seller list 1-8, 24E3; 3-5, 195F3; 4-2, 272C3
WALLENDA, Karl
Dies 3-22, 252F3
WALLER, (Thomas) Fats (1904-43)
Ain't Misbehavin' opens 5-9, 760A1 ★
WALLER, William
Loses Sen primary in Miss 6-6, 448B1
WALLOP, Sen. Malcolm (R, Wyo.)
Votes vs Panama Canal neutrality pact 3-16, 177G2
Votes vs 2d Canal pact 4-18, 273B1
Civiletti confrmd, oppositn cited 5-9, 342E3
Personal finances rptd 5-19, 385D3
WALLS, Lt. Gen. Peter
Rpts USSR, Cuba rebel role 3-12, 210C3
Command reorganized 3-20, 249C1
WALL Street Journal (newspaper)
US '76-83 budget assumptns, projectns table 1-24, 46A2
Pupil competency testing rptd 5-9, 348F2
Begin interviewed 9-20, 710G1
WALSH, Paddy
Saudis sentence rptd 6-15, 516D1
WALSH, Rep. William F. (R, N.Y.)
Lee wins seat 11-7, 849B2

1979

WALDOCK, Sir Humphrey
Gets US plea on Iran hostages 12-10, 933F1
WALENTYNOWICZ, Leonard
Vs Weber case Sup Ct ruling 6-27, 477F2
WALES—*See GREAT Britain*
WALID, Gen. Abu
Iran bars US hostage mediatn role 11-8, 842C1
Ends Iran missn, leaves for Leb 11-11, 862A2
WALKEN, Christopher
Wins Oscar 4-9, 336G1
Last Embrace released 5-3, 528G2
WALKER, Lt. Col. Edward
Relieved re recruiting fraud probe 8-19, 649G2
WALKER, Jimmie
Concorde Airport '79 released 8-3, 820A1
WALKER, John
Coe breaks mile run mark 7-17, 911F1
WALKER, Peter
UK agri min 5-5, 337G2, 338F1
WALKER, Rep. Robert S. (R, Pa.)
Amends Educ Dept bill 7-11, 514D3
WALK Proud (film)
Released 6-15, 820F3
WALL Jr., Art
2d in Legends of Golf tourn 4-29, 587E2
WALL, Peter
Hired as Surf coach 5-17, 1004D2
WALLACE, George Corley
Prison policy as Ala gov cited 2-2, 112D3
'76 electn fund repaymt order cited 6-18, 595F1
Upholds integratn 8-2, 650F1
'76 pres campaign repayment noted 9-5, 724A2
WALLACE, Jackie
NFL '78 punt return ldr 1-6, 80F2
WALLACE, Lawrence G.
Argues Weber case in Sup Ct 3-28, 262F3, 263A1
WALLACE, Mike
Haldeman discloses '75 interview fee 1-27, 176C1
'State of mind' libel queries backed by Sup Ct, '73 suit cited 4-18, 302A1
WALLACE, Phyllis
On Pay Advisory Com 10-16, 829G2
WALLACH, Eli
Winter Kills released 5-17, 528G3
Every Good Boy opens 7-30, 711F2
WALLENBERG, Raoul
Disappearance case reopened 8-4, 690C2
WALLER, (Thomas) Fats (1904-43)
Wins Grammy 2-16, 336G3
WALLER, James
Slain in NC 11-3, 864D3
WALLIS, Barnes Neville
Dies 11-12, 932G3
WALLOP, Sen. Malcolm (R, Wyo.)
Scores SALT treaty 4-5, 258G1
Named to Senate Ethics Com 10-31, 945A3
WALLS, Lt. Gen. Peter
ZAPU jet downing target 2-12, 136B3
Interviewed re war 6-13, 547A1
Archbp's home attacked 7-4, 546F3
ZANU asks dismissal 7-31, 586E3
WALL Street Action (anti-nuclear group)
NYC A-protest held 10-29, 827G2
WALL Street Journal (newspaper)
Dow Jones average explained 72D1; **for trading data, see STOCKS—Dow Jones**
US '77-84 budget assumptns, projectns 1-22, 43A2
China OKs office 5-30, 406B2
Dow Jones index revisn rptd 6-28, 481E2
Carter poll rptd 7-9, 514D1
Carter energy plan reactn rptd 7-17, 534C3
Iran expels Mohan 9-26, 814B3
Connally Mideast peace plan printed 10-12, 783C2
On 3 Mile I comm final rpt 10-30, 826D1
Daily circulatn lead rptd 11-7, 1007F1
WALSH, Bill
Hired as 49ers gen mgr, coach 1-9, 175F2
WALSH, Donnie
Named interim Nuggets coach 2-1, 290C3
WALSH, Thommie
1940's Radio Hour opens 10-7, 956E3

1980

WALENTYNOWICZ, Anna
Strike staged re transfer 1-31, 88B1
WALESA, Lech
On govt recognitn of strikers 8-23, ldrshp chngs 8-24, 641C1, G1
In 3d round of strike talks, pleas for labor restraint 8-28, 657C1
Reaches prelim strike accord 8-30, formalized 8-31, 657C2, G2-658A1
Yugo lauds strike role 8-31, 659B1
Vs natl trade union federatn 9-17, 710G1
Free trade unions register; sees Jagielski 9-24, 720C2
Scores registratn conditns 10-24, 830G3
Affirms strike deadline 10-31, 860E1
E Ger, Czechs score 11-5, 860G1, A2
Sup Ct backs unions, strike averted 11-10, 862F2
Meets Kania 11-14, 878B1
Urges end to strikes 11-15, 878E1
E Ger scores 11-21—11-27, Czech criticism cited 11-27, 910F1, A2
Urges Warsaw workers' moderatn 11-27, 909A2
Urges unity at '70 riot rites 12-16, 12-17; says unions will forgo strikes 12-17, 976B2, E2
Urges Moczulki chrgs dropped 12-22, 976E1
WALESA, Stanley
At Jersey City Reagan rally 9-1, 664D2
WALGREN, Rep. Doug (D, Pa.)
Reelected 11-4, 844D1
WALI, Prince (Afghanistan)
Offers resistance ldr role 5-3, 349G2
WALK, Bob
In World Series 10-14—10-21, 811E2
WALKEN, Christopher
Sea Gull opens 11-11, 892F3
WALKER, Clarence (Foots)
NBA assist ldr 3-30, 278E3
WALKER, Fred
Music Man opens 6-6, 756F3
WALKER, Gerald
Cruising released 2-15, 216D2
WALKER, Herschel
3d in Heisman Trophy vote 12-1, 999F2
WALKER, James Dean
Calif probe of Ark prisons curbed by Sup Ct 12-8, 937D1
WALKER, Bishop John T.
At Reagan DC fete 11-18, 880E3
WALKER, Nicholas
Major Barbara opens 2-26, 392D3
WALKER, Peter
Scores French lamb curbs 2-18, 125C1
France lamb war claim dropped 10-1, 737B3
WALKER, Rep. Robert S. (R, Pa.)
Reelected 11-4, 844D1
WALKER Kay Terminal Inc.
Graivers win '76 jet crash damages 10-15, 827A1
WALL, Art
Wins Legends of Golf 4-27, 412E3
WALL, The (recording)
On best-seller list 1-2, 40F3; 2-6, 120G3; 3-5, 200F3; 4-2, 280F3; 4-30, 360A1; 6-4, 448F3
WALLACE, George Corley
'72 poll rating cited 4-1, 246G3
WALLACE, Theodore C.
US House primary results 8-5, 682A3
WALLACH, Eli
Hunter released 8-1, 675A3
WALLENBERG, Jacob
Dies 8-2, 676F3
WALLENBERG, Raoul
Family at Madrid CSCE 11-28, 950D2
WALLER, Leslie
Hide in Plain Sight released 3-21, 216G2
WALLICH, Henry C.
Vs discount rate reductn 5-28, 400D2
Absent for FRB discount rate vote 6-12, 438F1
WALLOP, Sen. Malcolm (R, Wyo.)
Seeks Trigon probe 9-10, 754G1
Carter aide cleared in spy leak 12-5, 940B3
WALLS, Lt. Gen. Peter
Meets Mugabe, sees no coup 2-25; asks calm re vote results 3-3, 162G1
To head Zimbabwe army 4-15, 301C3
Resigns army post 7-17, 568D1
Reveals electn void request 8-11, denies coup plot knowledge, racist chrgs 8-17; Mugabe urges Zimbabwe departure 8-29, formal dismissal rptd 9-17, 731D2
Mugabe vs return 9-25, bar set 9-26, 755F1
WALL Street Journal, The (newspaper)
Dow Jones average explained 76D1; for trading data, see STOCKS—Dow Jones
US '78-85 budget assumptns, projectns table 1-28, 71C3
Iran chrgs rptr took gifts from shah 2-9, 122B3
Schmidt interview 3-10, 205D2
Bartley wins Pulitzer 4-14, 296G2
Shea dies 4-27, 360E3
Jankowski CBS resignatn hoax 5-23, 501B2
Reagan aide criticized 10-28, quits post 10-30, 817F3
WALSH, Rev. John T.
Sees Iran militants 6-4, 418E3
WALSH, Mike
Disputes Reagan on auto regulatns 9-3, 664A3
WALSH, Richard
Book banned 11-9, 885D1
Book ban upheld by High Ct 12-1, 919E2
WALSH, Sharon
Loses Australian Open 1-1, 213E1
WALSH, Stella (Stanislawa Walasiewicz)
Found slain 12-4, 1004F3
WALSH, Thommie
Wins Tony 6-8, 692C3

1976

WALTER, George
Loses Antigua election 2-18, 270D1
WALTER, Robert H.
Sentenced 2-3, 124C1
WALTERS, Barbara
Signs $1 mln ABC contract 4-22, 504A2
Kissinger interview aired 5-17, 359B1
Pres debate moderator 10-22, 800A1
WAMBAUGH, Joseph
Choirboys on best seller list 1-25, 80B3; 2-29, 208E3; 12-5, 972E2
WAMPLER, Rep. William Creed (R, Va.)
Chrgs grain scandal coverup 1-29, 136D1
Reelected 11-2, 831A1
WANG Hung-wen
Chou En-lai dies 1-8, 8E3-9A1
Teng gives Chou eulogy 1-15, 48C1
Meets Australia CP delegatn 2-25, 189F1
Radical strength rptd 4-27, 333E1
Cited as possible Mao successor 9-9—9-10, 658E1
Listed in China ldrshp 9-10, 712A1
Rptd arrested 10-12, 10-13, 757G1-E2
Plot, purge confirmed 10-22, 790C2, C3
Accusatns rptd 10-24, 10-25, 10-26, 809B2
Posters detail plot role 10-30, 11-8, 871C2
Loses Shanghai post 10-30, 871A3
Tied to indl disruptn 11-2, 871G2
Blamed for Fukien, Hangchow unrest 11-23, 11-24, 904C3, F3
Drive vs backers asked, restraint urged 11-28, 904A3
Fighting rages in central provs 12-6—12-31, 1000C1-D2
Accused 12-18, faces possible executn 12-23, 999E3
Hua sees '77 natl purge 12-24, 999A3
WANG Jen-yuan
Cleared of bribery 8-6, 679D2
WANG Ming
Cited in Mao death announcemt 659B2
WANG Tung-hsing
Listed in China ldrshp 9-10, 712A1
WAN Li
Rptd purged from ldrshp 9-11, 712B1
Reinstatemt rptd 10-14, 809G2
WAQUIM, Gloria & Norma
Abductn rptd 1-17, 96G1
WAR—*See also specific war names*
Dole, Mondale debate 10-15, 782G2-A3
Dole hits Dems 10-25—10-27, 804A2, D2, A3
WARD, Charles
Watkins wins Albert's seat 11-2, 822G2
WARD, Martin J.
Quits Ford panel 1-8, 4C1
WARING, Robert O.
Slain 6-16, 425A1-C2
Body returned to US 6-19, 448F1
Americans evacuated from Leb 6-20, 447G3
WARNACO Inc.
Rpts shipping rebates, probe 9-13, 690B1
WARNECKE Electron Tubes, Inc.—*See NORTHROP Corp.*
WARNEKE, Lon
Dies 6-23, 524G3
WARNER, Carolyn
Loses Ariz Sen primary 9-7, 687B3
WARNER Jr., Roger Sherman
Dies 8-3, 716F3
WARNER Communications Inc.
Vows no boycott compliance 3-18, 747C2
WARNER-Jenkinson Co.
Red #2 dye ban in effect, ct challenge continues 1-27—2-13, 137D1
WARNER-Lambert Co.
Rpts foreign payoffs 3-18, 361F2
SEC lists paymts 5-12, 729E1
Amer Chicle factory blast 11-21, 969A2
Parke-Davis & Co.
Flu vaccine error rptd 6-2, 423D3
To lose insurance 6-15, 443G1
Flu immunizatn delay rptd 9-1, 656C3
WARNKE, Paul C.
Briefs Carter 7-26, 551D1
Carter campaign donatn rptd 10-22, 939B1

1977

WALTER, George
Arrested 3-2, 203E1
WALTER Corp., Jim
Celotex convictn overturned 1-6, 156F2
WALTERS, Barbara
Castro interview aired 6-9, 456E1
Father dies 8-15, 696G3
WALTERS, Lou
Dies 8-15, 696G3
WALTON, Bill
NBA final standings 4-10, 331C3
Portland wins NBA title, named MVP 6-5, 490G2, E3
WALTRIP, Darrell
NASCAR final standing, earnings rptd 11-20, 1020D3
WALTS, Butch
Apples win WTT title 8-27, 787E3
WAMPLER, Rep. William C. (R, Va.)
Sugar lobby gifts alleged 7-20, 614B1, E1
WANG Hung-wen
Rpt province unrest quelled 1-4, 1D1
Blamed for Fukien unrest 1-4, 1G1
Blamed for econ lag 2-1, 98G1
Heightened drive vs urged 2-5, 2-7, 98C1
Chekiang offcls disgraced 3-2, 179D3
Kweichow progress lauded 3-5, 179F3
Radical accused of bugging 3-9, 180E1
Liaoning official arrested 3-14, 220D1
Blamed for Hangchow unrest 4-11, 282B2
New leap forward rptd 5-4, 449G2
Blamed for Sept '76 riots 6-2, 449G2
Tied to Nanchang riots 6-5, 449B3
Scored at Kiangsi rally 6-6, 505D3
Cited for Hupei unrest 6-8, 505E3
Scored in Liaoning Prov 6-24, 562D1
Tied to Yunnan agents 6-29, 562C1
Rpt ousted from party 7-22, 571G2
Anti-Mao stand cited 9-8, 694B3
Mao policy distortn chrgd 9-10, 706F1
Arrest date confirmed 10-6, 780F3
'71-75 China trade rptd up 11-6, 882C3
Yu suicide rptd 11-8, 882E3
WANG Su
Named Hung Chi editor 3-7, 179G3
WANG Tung-hsing
In Politburo post 8-21, 645F2
WANI, Archbishop Silvano
Replaces Luwum 3-19, 308G2
WAN Li
Replaced as rail chief 2-20, 134D1
Named Anhwei party head 6-27, 505B3
WAR—*See specific war name*
WARD, Britt
Taiwan wins Little League title 8-27, 768C2
WARD, Chris
Wins Downtown AC Trophy 12-8, 950E2
WARD, George
Grunwick strike violence 7-11, 543B3
Strikers backed by ct 7-12; vows appeal 7-20, 617B2
WARD, Michael
On missing A-material 8-8, 717C2
WARD, Judge Robert
Haley sued 5-24, 643D1
WARDAIR International Ltd.
Not in domestic charter plan 12-7, 965G3
WARDEN, Richard D.
Named HEW asst secy 3-11, confrmd 3-29, 272D3
WARNECKE, Bishop Frederick J.
Dies 2-23, 164G3
WARNER, John
Eur heroin use rptd rising 10-17—10-21, 971F3
WARNER, Judge Joseph P.
OKs Red Sox sale 12-6, 989B3
WARNER, Marvin L.
Named amb to Switz 5-26, confrmd 6-7, 500D1
WARNER, William W.
Wins Pulitzer Prize 4-18, 355E2
WARNER Communications Inc.
Goldmark Communications Corp.
Goldmark gets Medal of Sci 11-22, 952A1
Goldmark dies 12-7, 1024A2
WARNER-Lambert Co.
Listerine corrective ad order upheld 8-2, 613F1-A2
Parke, Davis rpts antiviral drug 8-10, 675C3
WARNER National Corp.
Warner confrmd Swiss amb 6-7, 500D1
WARNKE, Paul C.
Named to disarmamt posts 2-2, controversy ensues 2-3—2-8, 88F3
Controversy continues 2-9—3-9; confrmd 171G3-172D3
Arrives USSR 3-26, in arms talks 3-28—3-30, 225D2
Admits SALT bias 4-7, sees Dobrynin 4-15, 400C3, F3
Lauds Indian O talks, doubts arms race 6-27, 530C1
'78 ACDA funds OK'd 8-2, 8-17, 689B2

1978

WALTER Corp., Jim
Celotex Corp.
Gypsum price fixing rule upheld by Sup Ct 6-29, 567G2
WALTERS, Barbara
ABC news show chngs set 4-19, 419A3
Interviews Carter 12-14, 951B1, 979G2
WALTON, Bill
Ky wins NCAA basketball title 3-27, 272E1
Named NBA MVP 5-24, 457A3
On NBA all-star team 6-13, 457C3
Trail Blazers OK trade 8-4, 1027F3
WALTON, Kathryn R.
Sues Morgan Stanley re Olinkraft merger 11-8, 896D3
WALTONS, The (TV series)
Silverman to head NBC 1-20, 75F2
WAMBAUGH, Joseph
Black Marble on best-seller list 2-5, 116B3; 3-5, 195D3
WAMPANOAG Indians—*See INDIANS, American*
WAMPLER, Rep. William Creed (R, Va.)
Reelected 11-7, 852A4
WANAMAKER, John (department store)
Carter Hawley merger planned 3-8, 185A1
WANDAWI, Mundhir Tawfik el-
Sees French pres on emb siege 7-31, 582C2
WANG, Erik B.
On Sovt satellite hazard 7-5, 514C3
WANG Chen
In China Politburo 12-22, 1015F1
WANG Feng
Becomes Sinkiang ldr 1-29, 89B2
WANG Hung-wen
Saifudin replaced as CP ldr 1-29, 89C2
Teng cleared of '76 Peking riots 2-15, 111C2
Spared executn 2-21, 130A3
Tied to Tsao persecutn 6-28, 515B2
Cited for freedom lack 7-3, 532C2
China pragmatic approach seen 532A2
Wu ousted as Peking mayor 10-10, 773G3
Mao tied to 'Gang of 4' 11-19, 901E2
WANG Jun-sheng
Signs Viet trade pact 1-10, 21A3
WANG Tung-hsing
In Cambodia, backs vs Viet 11-5—11-6, 894A2
WANG Tzu-kang
China posts min 10-26, 838A1
WAR—*See specific war name*
WARD, Chris
In NFL draft 5-2, 336E2
WARD, Douglas Turner
Black Body Blues opens 1-24, 887B1
Twilight Dinner opens 4-18, 760F3
Nevis Mountain Dew opens 12-7, 1031E2
WARD, Martin J.
On '77 top-paid labor ldrs list 5-15, 365G1
WARD, Judge Robert F.
Haley settles Courlander plagiarism suit 12-14, 1029F3
WARDEN, Jack
Stages opens 3-19, 760D3
WARD Foods Inc.
'77 equity return rptd 5-8, 325D3
WARD'S Automotive Reports
'78 record vehicle output rptd 12-21, 1004A2
WARE, Sister Ann Patrick
Clothing workers set NY Life bd bid 9-11, 699B3
WARHOL, Andy
Andy Warhol's Last Love opens 6-30, 887A1
WARNER, Jack L.
Dies 9-9, 778B2
WARNER, John W.
Loses Va US Sen nominatn 6-3, 467A2
US Sen nominee killed 8-2, gets GOP nod 8-12, 645A3
Elected 11-7, 846D1, 848E3, 853E1
Election certified 11-27, 915A3
WARNER Communications Inc.
Nixon tape access denied by Sup Ct 4-18, 308D1
Ross on '77 top-paid execs list 5-15, 364F3
Jack Warner dies 9-9, 778B2
WARNER-Lambert Co.
Amer Chicle '76 blast chrgs dismissed 2-15, 212D3
Parke, Davis drug seizure case refused by Sup Ct 3-27, 241F1
Listerine corrective ad review denied by Sup Ct 4-3, 280C3
Bobst dies 8-2, 708A2
WARNER-Lambert Co. v. FTC
Listerine corrective ad review denied by Sup Ct 4-3, 280C3
Parke Davis & Co.
Injectable Vira-A OKd by FDA 10-24, 948F2
WARNKE, Paul
Civil defns reorganizatn concern rptd 6-20, 466G2
Backs MAP 8-23, 747B3
Rpts US A-power edge over USSR 8-29, 676G3
Sees Gromyko, rpts SALT progress 9-7—9-8, 747E2
Resigns arms-control post 10-10, 766F3, 804F1
Successors named 10-20, 804A2

1979

WALSKE, Carl
On NRC A-safety rule 1-20, 54C3
WALTARI, Mika
Dies 8-26, 671G3
WALT Disney Productions
Sony video recorder copyright trial opens 1-22, 120E2
Video recorder use upheld 10-2, 858F2
WALTER Corp., Jim
Celotex Corp.
Price fixing case refused by Sup Ct 10-1, 768F2
WALTER E. Heller International Corp.
Midland Bank to acquire 7-6, 682B3
WALTERS, Barbara
Interviews shah 11-22, 897C3
WALTERS, David M.
Law firm chrgd in visa fraud 6-1, 491E3
WALTERS, Thomas
A-plant oppositn rptd 4-2, 246B2
WALTERS and Costanzo
Visa fraud chrgd 6-1, 491D3
WALTMAN, Diane
Quits Connally campaign 12-19, 983C1
WALTON, Bill
Compensatn set 9-18, injures ankle 9-28, 1003F2
WALTON, Fred
When A Stranger Calls released 10-12, 1008A2
WALTRIP, Darrell
2d in NASCAR Gr Natl, $ winnings 11-18, 1005A2
WALTS, Butch
Loses Little Rock Grand Prix 2-4, 391G2
Wins Bologna Grand Prix 11-25, 1003G3
WAMBAUGH, Joseph
Onion Field released 9-19, 820E2
WANDERERS, The (film)
Released 7-13, 820F3
WANG Chen
Says China invasn limited 2-25, 141C1
WANG Hsan-yuan
Walks out on Castro speech 9-3, 674E2
WANG Kuang-mei
Liu death confrmd by govt 1-28, 75E1
Torture reported 5-6, 353F1
WANG Tung-hsing
Loses China govt posts 1-4, 6G3-7A1
Corruptn probe target rptd 8-22, 651G3
WANSHEL, Jeff
Holeville opens 12-4, 956B3
WAR—*See specific war name*
WAR and Remembrance (book)
On best-seller list 1-7, 80A3; 2-4, 120A3; 3-4, 173C3; 4-8, 271G1; 5-6, 356C2; 6-3, 432A2
WARANEH, Maj. Gen. Mohammed Wali
Khomeini forms new militia 5-5, 353B1
WARD, Anita
Ring My Bell on best-seller list 7-4, 548E3; 8-1, 620E3
WARD, Douglas Turner
Season To Unravel opens 1-25, Old Phantoms 2-8, 292D2, G2
WARD Jr., Robert E.
Testifies on PCB dumping 6-7, acquitted 6-13, 597A3
WARD 3rd, Robert E.
PCB dump chrgs dropped 6-7, 597A3
WARD, Simon
Mtg By the River opens 3-28, 712D1
WARD, Bishop W. Ralph
Methodists uphold gay pastor 11-1, 932A1
WARDEN, Jack
Beyond the Poseidon Adventure released 5-24, 528E1
And Justice for All released 10-19, 1007G2
WARD Foods Inc.
Settles '78 beef-price suit 10-22, 985F3
WARFIELD, Donald
GR Point opens 4-16, 711E3
WARNCKE, Margaret
Knockout opens 5-6, 712A1
WARNE, Colston E.
Honored 10-19, 903A2
WARNER, Sen. John W. (R, Va.)
Scores SALT treaty 4-5, 258G1
Finances disclosed 5-18, 383E2
WARNER Communications Inc.
Panavision wins Oscar 4-9, 336C2
Fox execs join unit 7-4, 588A1
Profits down, records unit firings cited 8-10, 618E1
Life of Brian denounced, Warner Bros defends 8-27; dvpts 10-24—10-30, 859E1-D2
WARNER-Lambert Co.
Price violatn chrgd 5-17, 385A2
Gillette sued over razors 6-14, 481D3
WARNER & Swasey Co., The
Bendix wins Dominion Bridge 12-17, 986F2

1980

WALTEEUW, Ronald
Guards occupied Mex emb 2-18, 152C1
WALTER Corp., Jim
Celotex Corp.
Price fixing case settled 3-3, 557F3
WALTER Enterprises, L&M
Harrah's gets temp NJ gambling license 11-1, 988D3
WALTERS, Albert (Fernandez)
Dies 10-20, 876F3
WALTERS, Barbara
Interviews Hoffman 9-2, 713E2
Interviews Carter 10-8, 778B2
Carter, Reagan TV debate panelist 10-28, 813F1
WALTERSCHEID, Len
NFL '79 kick return ldr 1-5, 8G3
WALTER v. U.S.
Case decided by Sup Ct 6-20, 555G2
WALTKE, Trey
Loses Vienna Grand Prix 10-26, 947B2
WALTON, Todd
Inside Moves released 12-19, 1003A2
WALTON, Tony
Wins Oscar 4-14, 296A2
WAMBUZI, William
Dismissal as chief justice rptd 12-2, 946F1
WAMPLER, Rep. William Creed (R, Va.)
Reelected 11-4, 844A4
WANG Bingqain
On profits, local control 8-30, govt '79, '80 debt 9-1, 678C1, G1
WANG Chia-sheng
Gets death sentnc 7-20, 563A2
WANGERIN Jr., Walter
Book of Dun Cow wins Amer Book Award 5-1, 692G2
WANG Hongwen (Wang Hung-wen)
Gang of 4 trial set 9-27, delayed 11-1, 859B1
Indictmt aired 11-15—11-18, trial starts 11-20, 877A1, D2
Admits plot vs Deng appointmt 11-24, 975G1
WANG Jun-sheng
China propaganda chief 3-7, 231A2
WANG Kuang-mei
Liu Shao-chi memorialized 5-17, 388G3
WANG Tung-hsing
Ousted from Politburo 2-29, 171F3
WANGYAL, Phuntsog
Tibet speech spurs demonstratns 7-29, visit curbed 7-31, 603E3
WANG Zhigang
Named as Peking bomber 11-10, 878A1
WAN Li
Named China dep premr 4-16, 351E1
Tibet, Tsinghai reforms set 5-31, 6-8, 462A1, E1
WAR and Remembrance (book)
On best-seller list 6-8, 448D3
WARD, Douglas Turner
Home opens 5-7, 392C3
WARD Jr., Felker
At Wrightsville mtg 5-23, 460B2
WARD, Ken
Ka-Boom! opens 11-20, 1003D3
WARD, Rear Adm. Robert E.
Dies 4-9, 360F3
WARD Transformer Co.
Pa PCB dumping suit filed 10-9, 825B1, D1
WARNER, Bennie D.
Seeks guerrilla army 4-28, 353F2
Disavows overthrow plan 5-2, 381F3
WARNER, Sen. John W. (R, Va.)
Carter backs mil-pay bill 5-26, 403A2
Carter mil-pay bill support cited 5-28, 424C2
Addresses GOP conv 7-15, 531D3
Mil benefits authrzn signed 9-8, 765C1
House OKs mil-pay appropriatn amendmt 9-16, 742A1
WARNER, Paul
Lobbies vs MX plank 8-13, 611E2
WARNER Amex Satellite Entertainment Co.
ABC in cultural cable-TV deal 12-2, 1002G3-1003A1
WARNER-Chilcott Laboratories Inc.
US sets tranquilizer warnings 7-11, 584G1
WARNER Communications Inc.
ABC cultural cable-TV deal set 12-2, 1003A1
Franklin Mint merger set 12-24, 985B1
Warner Bros.
Ashley retires, Daly replaces 12-1, 959E1
WARNER-Lambert Co.
US sets tranquilizer warnings 7-11, 584G1
WARNER & Swasey Co.
Bendix trust chrgs rptd setld 7-14, 917E2

1976

WARRANTIES—*See CONSUMER Protection*
WARREN, Earl
Rptdly knew of US efforts vs Castro 3-1, 217E2
CIA memos on Cuba-Oswald link rptd 3-20, 3-21, 217A2
WARREN Sr., Ned
'74 Lazar murder cited 484D1
WARREN, Robert W.
Named Miss S&L conservator 6-20, 495D1
WARREN Commission—*See under U.S. GOVERNMENT*
WARRINER, Judge D. Dortch
Voids VCU affirmative actn plan 5-28, 413G3

1977

WARREN, Earl
Sup Ct rulings scored 10-31, 878G3
WARREN, Jack H.
Quits 2-14, 132D3
Towe succeeds as US amb 6-3, 525B3
WARREN Commission—*See under U.S. GOVERNMENT*
WARRENSVILLE Heights, O.—*See OHIO*
WARREN-Teed Pharmaceuticals Inc.—*See ROHM & Haas*
WARRIORS (book)
On best-seller list 5-1, 356D2; 6-4, 452B2

1978

WARNS Jr., Carl A.
Named to coal-strike bd of inquiry 3-6; hearings held 3-8, deadlock rptd 3-9, 159B2, E3
WAR and Remembrance (book)
On best-seller list 11-6, 887F3
WARREN Commission—*See under U.S. GOVERNMENT*
WAR Resisters' League
US, USSR protests 9-4, 947B2

1979

WARREN, Charles
On environmt cncl energy use rpt 2-20, 132F2
WARREN, Gertrude
Dies 9-6, 756F3
WARREN, Robert Penn
Wins Pulitzer 4-16, 336G2
WARREN, Judge Robert W.
Blocks H-bomb article 3-9, 193D2-194A1; 3-26, 230A1
Declines to lift H-bomb article injunctn 6-15, 713C1
H-bomb article hearing order denied by Sup Ct 7-2, 559B1
WARREN Commission—*See under U.S. GOVERNMENT*
WAR Resisters League
DC '78 protesters sentncd, 21 arrested 2-12, 133A3
WARRILOW, David
Southern Exposure opens 2-27, 292B3
WARRIORS, The (film)
Released 2-9, 174F3
Top-grossing film 2-28, 174B2
WARRIORS from a Long Childhood (play)
Opens 5-22, 712D3

1980

WARREN, Shields
Dies 7-1, 608G3

1976

WARSAW Pact (Warsaw Treaty of Friendship, Cooperation and Mutual Assistance) (Bulgaria, Czechoslovakia, East Germany, Hungary, Poland, Rumania, USSR)
US rep compares NATO spending data 3-7, 182B2
NATO denies study on surprise attack 3-16, 297A2
Sergei Shtemenko dies 4-23, 368A3
NATO cites mil growth 5-20—5-21, 353D1
London inst warns on NATO superiority 9-3, 760A3
NATO cites improvemts 9-25, 760E2
Sovt troop estimates rptd 10-5, NATO estimate cited 761A2
Gribkov replaces Shtemenko 10-12, 858G2
USSR, Hungary begin maneuvers 10-18, 925D2
Gribkov promoted 10-30, 908G1
US fact-finders barred 11-5—11-21, 880F1
NATO defns tactics scored 11-14, 879D3
Summit mtg urges A-war ban, sets forgn min com 11-26—11-27, 896B3
NATO mtg on mil buildup, vetoes 1st A-use ban, membership freeze proposals 12-6—12-10, 933A1-E2
Ford on Helsinki gains 12-8, 934C2
European Force Reduction Talks—*See under EUROPE*
European Force Reduction Talks—*See under EUROPE*

1977

WARSAW Pact (Warsaw Treaty of Friendship, Cooperation and Mutual Assistance) (Bulgaria, Czechoslovakia, East Germany, Hungary, Poland, Rumania, USSR)
Yugo bars Sovt mil pact 1-9, 24C1
Kulikov named cmdr 1-9, 47B3; promoted 1-14, 88G1
US rpt on manpower, arms gains issued 1-24, 70G1
Westn debt rptd mounting 2-13—4-13, 335B3
Battle vs dissidents vowed 3-4, 226B3
Danish defns budget passed 3-29, 426F2-A3
Italy CP backs vs NATO 4-2, 284B2
Carter warns NATO on buildup 5-10, 358B3
NATO sees arms threat 5-11, 359E3
Arms standardizatn rptd 5-14, 359G3
NATO rpts mil strength data 5-17, 379F3
US rpt chrgs Helsinki non-compliance 6-6, 473C1
France bars A-weapons abroad 6-23, 1012F3
IISS rpts on E-W mil balance 9-2, 686D1
NATO revises attack warning time 9-2, 700E1
UK '78-79 defns cuts scored 9-16, 957C1
NATO debates neutron bomb, cruise missile 10-11—10-12, 956B3, D3
NATO deplores mil buildup 12-9, 957B1
W Ger Defns Min spy scandal disclosed 12-12, 968D1
European Force Reduction Talks—*See under EUROPE*

1978

WARSAW Pact (Warsaw Treaty of Friendship, Cooperation and Mutual Assistance) (Bulgaria, Czechoslovakia, East Germany, Hungary, Poland, Rumania, USSR)
Conv warfare edge in Eur seen in '77 US rpt 1-6, 5B3
Air threat to NATO seen 1-29, 81E3
Dutch vs neutron bomb 2-23, 140A3
Neutron bomb deferred by US 4-7, 253B2
Czech pres visits W Ger 4-10—4-14, 333B1
Carter sees mil threat 5-30, 397E1
Hungary ldr scores arms race 6-10, 534G2
Rumanian offcl defects 7-28, US questioning rptd 8-8, 651A1, 725D2 ★
Rumanian offcl's defectn rptd 8-8, 651A1
NATO U-2 missns rptd increased 8-22, 748B3
E-W mil balance assessed by IISS 9-1, 676G2
NATO maneuvers rptd compared 9-23, 748G2
Summit 11-22—11-23, 913D2
Rumania bars defns spending rise 11-25, independnc from USSR cited 913F2
Rumania affirms defns spending stand 11-29—12-1; USSR, 3 other members score 11-30, 12-5, 929F2-930G1
US support of Rumania stance seen 12-8—12-9, 965C3-966A1
Rumania cuts defns budget 12-20, 1020A1
European Force Reduction Talks—*See under EUROPE*

1979

WARSAW Pact (Warsaw Treaty of Friendship, Cooperation and Mutual Assistance) (Bulgaria, Czechoslovakia, East Germany, Hungary, Poland, Rumania, USSR)
Westn debt '78 estimate rptd 3-20, 200D3
NATO mins note mil buildup 5-15—5-16, 359B3
NATO error re SS-21 deploymt rptd 5-23, 399G1
US confrms arms purchase 8-1, 627A1
IISS assesses mil balance 9-4, 825A3
France stresses conventional forces 9-11, 686C2
USSR E Eur troop deploymt rptd 761F2
Rumania pres skips E Ger fete 10-7, 761E2
NATO vs USSR E Ger troop cut plan 10-7, 761E3
E Berlin mtg ends; forgn mins ask arms reductn talks 12-6, 938C3
European Force Reduction Talks—*See under EUROPE*

1980

WARSAW Pact (Warsaw Treaty of Friendship, Cooperation and Mutual Assistance) (Bulgaria, Czechoslovakia, East Germany, Hungary, Poland, Rumania, USSR)
Carter cites US policy 1-23, 42G1
USSR on NATO parity 4-29, 327B3
25th anniv mtg backs detente, world summit 5-14—5-15, 377F2
France neutron bomb test rptd 6-26, 486C3
Poland plans closer ties 9-6, 678C3
E Ger maneuvers 9-8—9-11, 696D1
E Ger, Czech warn Poland 9-30, 753C1; 10-8—10-9, 761E1, F1
Poland warnings increase, interventn hinted 10-8—10-21, 831F1
Forgn mins meet in Warsaw; set CSCE strategy, reaffirm detente 10-19—10-20, 800C2
Moscow summit mtg warns Poland 12-5; mil action hinted 12-11, 929A1, E2
NATO forces imbalance cited 12-9—12-10, 949E2
US scores USSR Persian Gulf peace plan 12-11, 930C2
US: forces move in CSCE violatn 12-19, 950F1

1976

WARTENBERG, Frank
Wins Olympic medal 7-29, 576C1

1977

WARVARIV, Constantine
KGB tries to blackmail 10-19; US protests 10-26—10-31, 866C2-B3
WASAKA, Tokuji
Lockheed bribe trial opens 1-31, 83E2

1978

WASHAM, Jo Ann
2d in Bent Tree Classic 2-26, 355D3
WASHBURN, Deric
Deer Hunter released 12-14, 1030F2

1979

WARWICK, Dionne
I'll Never Love on best-seller list 9-5, 672E3
WASHAM, Jo Ann
Sets hole-in-one record, places 6th in Women's Kemper Open 4-1, 587B2
Wins Rail Charity Classic 9-3, LPGA Team tourn 9-16, 970E1, C1

1980

WARSBY, Ken
Taylor killed 11-13, 1002B2
WARTENBERG, Christine
Wins Olympic medal 8-1, 624B2
WARWICK—*See RHODE Island*
WARWICK, Dionne
Wins 2 Grammys 2-27, 296C3
WARWICK, Kim
Loses Queen's Club Grass championship 6-15, 607E3
Wins S African Open 12-2, 947G2
WASHAM, Jo Ann
2d in Women's Kemper Open 3-30, 412B3
2d in Golden Lights 6-1, Lady Keystone 6-22, 715A1, B1
LPGA top money winner 10-12, 971F3
WASHBURN, Langhorne
Auto-Train investmt plan rptd 11-26, 958A3

1976

WASHINGTON (state)
AEC tests on prisoners confrmd 2-28, 316C2
Reagan in Seattle 4-10, 281A3
Asbestos rptd in Seattle water 4-30, 349F1
GOP conv results 6-19, 450G2
Bangor Trident base funds vetoed 7-2, 518A1
Dem conv women delegates, table 508E2
Dem conv pres vote, table 7-14, 507E2
Kissinger in Seattle 7-22, 557D2
GOP pre-conv delegate count 8-14, 583E3
Mondale in Seattle 8-16, 617A3
GOP conv pres, vp vote tables 8-18—8-19, 8-19, 599E1, E3
Carter in Seattle 8-24, Dole 8-25, 631F2, C3, 632B2
Hanford A-waste cntr blast 8-30, 18 leaks rpts 9-7, 670D3, 671E1
Fscl '75 per capita income, tax burden rptd 9-15, 10-12, 959E2
Primary results 9-21, 804C3
US Sup Ct bars review of Seattle reverse bias case 10-12, 848G2
Ford visits Seattle 10-25, 802E3
Election results 11-2: pres 818D1, 819A1; cong 820D1, 825E1, 828D3, 831A1-A2; state 820F2, C3, 825D1, B2, A3, 831D2
Meeds wins US House seat 11-16, 865D1
Reagan electoral vote rptd 12-13, 979B1

1977

WASHINGTON (state)
Legislature schedule rptd 6F2
Reagan gets Electoral Coll vote 1-6, 14G2
Snowfall rptd below normal 2-1, 76G3
Drought continues, conservatn urged 2-15, 152E3
Drought hits aluminum industry 2-20, 244E3
Cloud-seeding progrm starts 2-28, 153E1
ILWU conv in Seattle 4-18—4-23, 324A3
W Coast drought sets record 5-4, 376B3
'76 per-capita income table 5-10, 387G2
Seattle econ data table 5-16, 384G2
Cunningham wins US House seat 5-17, 382F1
Drought persists 6-16, 492A3
NC apple labeling rule voided 6-20, 517E1
Seattle LEAA office to close 6-20, 630E2
UK air svc pact set 6-22, 500A2
Laetrile legalization cited 6-23, 508E1
Seattle gay rights march 6-26, 560E2
Oil cos sued on trust chrgs 8-16, 691E3
Oil cos sued by state 8-16, 691E3
Oil cos settle US suit 8-31, 691C3
'76 per capita income, tax burden table 9-13, 10-18, 821F2
GM cuts '78 Chevette price 9-15, 722F3
Seattle landing rights for Concorde proposed, offcls score 9-23, 738B2, B3
Tacoma gay teacher case review refused 10-3, 760D1
Boeing Seattle struck 10-4—11-17, 1005A2
Free abortns continued 10-12, 787A1
HMO unit certified 10-26, 870A1

1978

WASHINGTON (state)
'67, '77 sales-tax rates rptd 1-5, 15B3, F3
Mondale tours Westn states 1-9—1-13, 34E1
State govt tax revenue table 1-9, 84E2
Rain spurs aluminum productn 1-10, 24F1
Clarence Dill dies 1-14, 96F1
Marshall Field to buy Tacoma stores 1-20, 185F1
Wilderness area clears Cong 2-9, 109D2; signed 2-24, 218A2
Hanford A-plant cancer hazard disputed 2-17, 2-25, 164D1, B2
8th in US defense contracts 2-21, 127D2
Spokane meets clean-air rules 2-23, 144D3
Oil tanker regulatn curbed 3-6, 161E3
Minor quake hits NW 3-11, 480F1
Seattle-London air fare agreed 3-17, 206D2
Seattle gay rights repeal petitns rptd 4-25, 327B2
Stevedoring tax OKd by US Sup Ct 4-26, 344C1
Carter visits Spokane 5-5, 342A1, G1-A2
Canada salmon fishing blocked 5-5, 350B2
Amtrak Seattle route cutback proposed 5-8, 366E1
Seattle guaranteed income study rptd 5-19, 720F3
Canada fishing talks adjourn 5-26, 413G1
Elma A-plant protests, 156 arrested 6-25, 494G1
Spokane makes bad-air list 7-5, 513D1
2 convicted in bombings 7-11, 824A3
Bad-air list corrected 7-19, 644B2

1979

WASHINGTON (state)
Spokane air quality monitored 1-26, 90F1
Paper mill strikes end 1-30—5-9, 345D2
Seattle cancer study rptd 1-31, 139G1
Teng visits Seattle 2-4—2-5, 83G3
Seattle-Shanghai port pact rptd 2-23, 146G2
Walla Walla prison riots 548D2
Seattle terminally ill treatmt study rptd 5-31, 471E2
MD-managed insurnc plan cuts hosp costs 6-14, 570D3, E3
Anti-busing initiative overturned 6-15, 596D3
Seattle condominium growth rptd 6-23, 482B3
Indian salmon fishing treaties upheld by Sup Ct 7-2, 559D1
Bundy gets death penalty in Fla 7-31, 604E2, G2
Tuberculosis, parasites rptd in Viet refugees 8-25, 659D3
Amtrak Chicago-Seattle train ordrd cut 8-29, 868B1
Teachers' strikes rptd 9-12, 679B1
'78 per capita income rptd 9-16, 746G2
PCBs contaminate food 9-17, 704A3
Bianchi gets life for coeds' death 10-19, 818F2
Milwaukee Rd embargoes track 11-1—11-5, 867G2
Atomic Energy
HEW radiatn safety studies asked, Hanford data cited 1-30, 90F3
A-dump cited 7-24, 561B3
Hanford A-dump closed 10-4, cancer research threatened 10-23, 806G2-C3
Hanford A-dump reopened 11-19, 885D3-886A1

1980

WASHINGTON (state)
Teachers strike in 4 schl districts 9-3, 723E3
Iran hostage interview broadcast 11-11, 862B1
Fishing indus aid clears Cong 12-4, 955D1
Fishing indus aid bill signed 12-22, 982C1, 995B3
Accidents & Disasters
Mt St Helens erupts, evacuatn ordrd 3-26, 252D1
Mt St Helens erupts again 5-18, death toll, devastatn rptd 5-18—5-23, Carter declares disaster area 5-21, 382A1
Mt St Helens damage assessed 5-24—7-4, eruptns continue 5-25, 6-12; photos 503B3
Mt St Helens victim aid clears Cong 7-2, Carter signs 7-8, 515F1
Mt St Helens eruptns resume 8-7, 10-17; flood threats rptd 10-29, 970B3
Atomic Energy & Safeguards
State of State message 1-15, 484E1
Carter outlines A-waste storage plan, Hanford site studied 2-12, 127F3
A-waste restrictns OKd 11-4, 847A3
Crime & Civil Disorders
Gay chrgd in murder 1-2, 18C3
State of State message 1-15, 484A2
'71 hijack money believed found 2-10—2-13, 136G2
FBI 'Miporn' probe rptd 2-14, 136A2
Energy—See also 'Atomic' above
State of State message 1-15, 484C1
Carter OKs Alaska pipe route 1-17, 56C3
Environment & Pollution
Indian land managemt fed liability limited by Sup Ct 4-15, 306F1
DES in cattle rptd 4-24, 358F1

1976

WASHINGTON, D. C.
Primary date set 22B2
CIA aid to police rptd 1-11, 1-13, 24A3
Trucking co exec's son kidnaped 1-12—1-17, 159F3
Boston rail aid budgeted 1-21, 66A1
Cong clears revised RR aid 1-28, 68F3
Justice Dept backs cable TV suit 2-5, 135D3
Missing food stamp funds rptd 2-11, ½ found 2-12, 128G3
Cong vote representatn blocked 3-23, 234F1
Boston-DC rail funds OKd 3-30, 233F2
Amtrak to buy Boston-DC line 4-1, 235B2
Baum named cardinal 4-27, 336G1
12-mo inflatn rate cited 4-28, 340G1
Primary results 5-4, 322G2, 323E2
Off US jobless list 5-5, 347D2
French pres visits US 5-17—5-22, 372E1, D2
7 oil cos, trade assn indicted 6-1, 412F3
Sup Ct upholds police job test rule 6-7, 435A1
Dem platform text 6-15, 472G1
Bicentennial activities 7-1—7-4, protests 7-4, 488F3, 489C1, D1, A2
Air & Space Museum opens 7-1, 488F3
Dem conv women delegates, table 508E2
Dem conv pres vote, table 7-14, 507B2
Trucking co exec son's kidnappers sentenced 7-21, 544E1
White House intruder killed 7-25, 860E1
Cong tax exemption vetoed 8-3, 636C3
GOP pre-conv delegate count 8-14, 583B3
GOP conv pres, vp vote tables 8-18—8-19, 8-19, 599B1, B3
GOP platform text 8-18, 605D3
Charles Duke dies 8-21, 892G2
Amtrak Boston-DC plan set 8-29, 648G1
Carter campaign visit 8-31, 645G1
'74-75 SAT average 9-13, 993A2
Fscl '75 per capita income tax burden rptd 9-15, 10-12, 959B2
Clerics sentncd re food stamps 9-17, 776F2
Rev Moon holds final rally 9-18, 970F3
Letelier killed in bomb blast 9-21, 710C2
Letelier march, mass held 9-26, 780G3
'77 funds signed 10-1, 834G1
Dole addresses UPI conv 10-8, 763G3-764A1
Election results 11-2, 817F2, 818A1, F2, 819B2, 821C1, 829A2
Sup Ct bars Concorde landing review 11-15, 882B2
House ldrship elected 12-6, 919C1
Heroin use death data rptd 12-12, 972C3
Watergate Issue—*See WATERGATE*

1977

Seattle, Spokane mayors elected 11-8, 855C3; referenda results 11-8, 879G2
Seattle loses '78 Dem conv bid 12-9, 960C3
Striking farmers bar Seattle grain delivery 12-21, 1003B1

WASHINGTON, D.C.
US Sup Ct upholds Home Rule Act 1-10, 57B2
Rail corridor aid budgeted 1-17, 33C1
Braniff-Concorde pact rptd 2-11, 213C1
Mardian bar reinstatemt cited 2-28, 175C2
Germ warfare tests rptd 3-8, 195E2
Hanafi Muslims take 134 hostage 3-9—3-11, 192F2
Ct reorganizatn upheld 3-22, 231D1-B2
Julius Hobson dies 3-23, 264A3
Conrail line cuts set 3-31, 325F2
'75 10 largest cities list drops 4-14, 388B1
Hanafis indicted for murder 5-3, 396A1
Ex-CIA man convctd as spy 5-5, 409E2
'76 per-capita income table 5-10, 387D2
Econ data rptd; table 5-16, 384C2, D2
Australia asks envoy cuts 6-2, 484E3
Hanafis convictd 7-23, sentencd 9-6, 711D1
US bars charters to Jerusalem 8-1, 589C1
UMW striker rallies 8-5, 690B3
Baseball owners fail to agree on team 8-17, 768A1
5 indep oil cos convicted 8-30, 691A3; fined 9-16, 918F2
'76 per capita income, tax burden table 9-13, 10-18, 821F1, B2
Concorde expanded landing rights proposed 9-23, 738B2
IMF, World Bank meet 9-26—9-30, 753C2
Protesters arrested at Carter church 10-16, 797G2
'73 Hanafi massacre figure cleared 11-5, 871G2
Cong continues funding at '77 level 12-7, 958F3
Iranian protest staged 12-31, 1001B1
Watergate Issue—*See WATERGATE*

1978

Primary results 9-19, 736F3
Grand Coulee generator sabotaged 10-30, hydro projct delayed 11-10, 963C1
Election results 11-7: cong 846A3, 848E3, 852A4, 857A3; state 847A2, A3, 857C3, 897D3
WTT Cascades rptd folded 11-10, 1027B1
Pacific Power phone ownership cited 11-30, 935C2

WASHINGTON, D.C.
Canal 'truth squad' press conf 1-17, 58C2
Farmers rally 1-18—1-21, 163B2
NE rail offcls resign 1-30; more funds allocated 2-11, projct delays rptd 2-24, 225B1
UK air-fare dispute setld 3-17, 206D2
SEC chrgs Lance, Arabs re bank takeover bid 3-18, suit setld 3-19, 204F1
CIA schl informers rptd 3-30, 243A3 ★
ABC news show chngs set 4-19, 419A3
Sun Day celebrated 5-3, 321G3-322A1
Avedon imposter sentenced 5-5, 380B2
Amtrak route cutbacks proposed 5-8, 366E1
'78 funds, conv cntr provisn signed 6-5, 432B1
Redskins trust liability case refused by Sup Ct 6-12, 468F3
Refiner-run gas statn ban cited 6-14, 492B1
ADA convention site 6-17, 526B1
Abortn funding rptd 6-20, 743A3
City makes bad-air list 7-5, 513D1
FBI '77 Scientology raids upheld 7-6, 554F1
ERA marchers seek extensn 7-9, 529D2
Prison escapees win retrials 7-12, 627C3
Indians demonstrate 7-15—7-23, 568C3
Transit strike 7-19—7-25, 565G1-A2
Air quality rpt corrected 7-19, 644B2
Postal pact oppositn rptd 7-21, 565A1
Scientologists indicted 8-15, 644B3, 645C1
Fscl '79 funds clear Cong 8-17, 697G2
Voting rep amendmt clears Cong 8-22, 661A1-E2
GSA corruption alleged 9-3, 685B2
White House anti-war protesters seized 9-4, 947C2
Victimless crime study issued 9-11, 842B2
Voting rep amendmt OKd in NJ 9-11, Ohio 10-30; rejctd in Pa 11-14, 878G1, 1011F2
Senators '60 move cited 9-28, 779C2
Diplomatic immunity revised 9-30, 750E3
NASL Diplomats sale rptd 10-5, 969F2
ACLU hails voting rep amendmt 10-20, 981B3
Pension reform vetoed 11-4, 897E2
Election results 11-7: cong 848B1, 850E2
Camp David Marines rptd transferred 12-9, 960B3-C3
GSA kickback indictmts 12-21, 1011B1, E1
Watergate Issue—*See WATERGATE*

1979

Politics & Government—*See also other appropriate subheads in this section*
Legislature schedule rptd 5G3
Ex-Sen Cain dies 3-3, 272B2
Seattle fiscal status rptd 3-20, 204G1
Pol party state com structure law backed by Sup Ct 6-4, 439C1
Electn results 11-6, 846B2, E3
Sports
Seattle hosts All-Star Game 7-17, 568C3
Seattle Sounders sale OKd 10-15, 1004B2

WASHINGTON, D.C.
ITT long-distance phone svc OKd 1-12, 15E2
China dep prime min tours 1-28–2-1, 66A1
Farmers rally 2-5–2-6, 109C2
Blizzard hits 2-18–2-19, 176A2
Carter on farmer protests 2-27, 149A3
Farmers' camp permit expires 2-28, 149D3
Einstein monumt unveiled 4-22, 392E2
Minorities business contract law rptd ignored 6-13, 442E3
Condominium growth rptd 6-23, 482B3
Shrivers buy Rockefeller mansn 7-20, 656B3
Black woman wins Rhodes scholarship 9-9, 1005G2
'78 per capita income rptd 9-16, 746D1, C2
Iran Emb staff ordrd cut 12-12, 933C1
'79 living costs ranked 12-28, 991A1
Crime & Civil Disorders
3 plead guilty in GSA kickbacks 1-3, 92F3
Abortion protest held 1-22, 63D2
'78 White House anti-war protesters sentncd, 21 arrested 2-12, 133A2-B3
4 arrested in White House A-protest 3-31, 261F3
Nicaragua sympathizers protest 4-25, 332E1
Moon church bank fraud chrgd, '77 complaint cited 5-1, 376D2
Trial speedup for robbers urged 7-22, 655E3
SBA minority-aid abuse rptd 9-28, 947A3
Scientologists convctd as spies 10-26, 839F2
Iranian march permits revoked, students demonstrate 11-8, 842G2, B3
Iranians protest 11-9, parade permits barred 11-11, 863B1, F1
Anti-Teng protesters freed 11-14, 904G3
Iranian rally ban upheld by Appeals Ct 11-19, 878D3
'71 Viet-protesters' award cut 12-13, 991G2
Energy
Odd-even gas rationing begins 6-21, 462F2
Gas shortage impact rptd 6-23, 479C1
Odd-even gas rules lifted 9-10, 683G1
Labor Issues
Washn Star's labor pacts set 1-1, 5E1-C2
Teachers strike 3-6–3-29, 262G2
US no longer top area hirer 3-24, 232G1
AFL-CIO meets 11-15–11-19, 877F2, 884G3
Politics & Government—*See also other appropriate subheads in this section*
Govs meet 2-25–2-27, 150G1
Voting rep amendmt rejctd in 8 states; OKd in 3 3-7–4-26, 204G2, 367D1
'80 funds, abortn compromise bill passed 10-16, 10-22, Carter signs 10-30, 870A1
Kennedy hq opened 10-29, 847F1
Voting rep amendmt OKd in Wis 10-30, 11-1, 851C3
Religious Issues
Papal mass suit filed 9-18, case dismissed 10-3, 760B3
Pope visits, holds mass 10-6–10-7, 759B3-760C3; photo 758C1
Pope's visit cost estimated, fed aid sought 761A1, A2
Jesuit priest silenced, female ordinatn issue cited 12-1, 999F3
Sports
WBL adds new franchise 6-12, 526G2
Williams buys Baltimore Orioles 8-2, 619C1
Transportation
$99 cross-country air fares, new routes OKd 1-12, 35E2
Dallas Concorde svc begins 1-12, 35B3
Carter budgets NE rail subsidy cut 1-22, 45D1
Amtrak fare hike set 2-20, 167D1
US-French air svc pact rptd 5-12, 465C3
Eastern-Natl merger rejected 9-27, 830B1

1980

Waste disposal, water-supply bond issues OKd 11-4, 847F3
Politics & Government—*See also other appropriate subheads in this section*
Legislature schedule rptd 18F1
State of State message 1-15, 484B1
Mayors Conf in Seattle 6-8—6-10, 438E2-G3
Ray loses primary, other results 9-16, 724A2
Election results 11-4: cong 837D1, 840E3, 844A3, 845A2, 852F2; state 845F3, 847C1, A3, F3, 852F2
'80 census rptd, reapportmt seen 12-31, 983G1
Presidential Election (& Transition)
GOP platform hearing set 1-14, 32A1
Carter wins Dem caucus vote 3-11, 209B1
Carter visits Tacoma 9-23, 722G3
Carter in Seattle 11-3, 841D1
Election results 11-4, 838D1, 839A1, G3
Transportation
State of State message 1-15, 484F;
Milwaukee Rd RR svc cut set 2-25, track sale rptd 4-1, 346B1, E1
Puget Sound ferry strike ends 4-16, 308B3

WASHINGTON, D.C.
'77 abortn data rptd 1-9, 23A3
Mortgage rate rptd at 17% 3-7, 222D3
2d 1/4 gas use target set 3-20, 250F3
Home prices rptd high 3-29, 248A1
Braniff drops Dallas Concorde svc 4-14, 346F3
Earth Day celebrated 4-22, 307F3
Professional tax case declined by Sup Ct 5-27, 454A1
El Salvador rightist visits illegally 6-30—7-3, 521E3
B'nai B'rith conv held 9-3—9-4, 681A3
Korvettes closings rptd 9-8, 985C3
Auto-Train financial rescue attempt rptd 11-26, 958C2
Crime & Civil Disorders
Afghan exiles protest Sovt mil interventn 1-4, 3A1
Inmate escape justificatn curbed by Sup Ct 1-21, 92E3
Teamsters boycott Sovt plane 1-22, 45E1
GSA scandal funds recovery suits filed 3-17, 228G1
Draft protest held 3-22, 227G3-228A1
Multiple sentencing curbed by Sup Ct 4-16, 328B3
A-protests held 4-26—4-28, 441G1
GOP hq taps suspected 6-21, 6-24, 480D3
Draft registratn protested 7-21, 597E3
Iran ex-attache slain 7-22, 545A2; security chief's secret visit linked 8-14, 671F3
Iranian protesters arrested 7-27, freed 8-5; 200 stage march 8-7, 586D1, B3
Moslems march to back Palestinians, Khomeini 8-7, 8-8; deny Iranian aid 8-9, 635F1, C2
Halberstam slain 12-5; suspect chrgd 12-6, area thefts rptd linked 12-7, 939F3
Politics & Government—*See also other appropriate subheads in this section*
Voting rep amendmt rejctd in Neb 2-11, 147B3
Fscl '79 tax revenue rptd 2-20, 307G2
Voting rep amendmt OKd in Md 3-17, Hawaii 4-17, 576F1
Senghor returns Barry visit 4-4—4-6, 336D2
Amtrak aid bill signed by Carter 5-30, 427G1
Barry proposes fscl recovery plan 7-19, '80 budget deficit rptd 9-30, 742G2-G3
Election results 11-4: cong 842E2, 848F1; local 847C3, 848F1
'80 census rptd 12-31, 983D1
Presidential Election (& Transition)
Pres primary results 5-6, 341G3, 342E1
Carter visits campaign hq 5-19, 399C3
Reagan campaigns 9-13, 9-15, 699E3
Bush addresses Jewish group 10-19, 817C3
Anderson answers TV debate questns 10-28, 815F3
Election results 11-4, 837G1, 838A1, E1, 839A1, D3
Reagan fetes local ldrs 11-18, 880E3
Reagan ends visit 11-21, 897G2
Reagan visits 12-10—12-13, 956A2-F2
Religious Issues
Archbp Baum named to Vatican post 1-15, 199B2
Conservative Christians hold rally 4-29, 348C3-349B1
Sports
Rodgers wins Cherry Blossom run 3-30, 527G2
NASL club put on notice 11-24, terminated 12-8, 1001C1

1976

WASHINGTON, George (1732-99)
Mt Vernon gets French gift 1-12, 80A3
Ford State of Union message cites 1-19, 39A3
Venez pres cites 6-22, 793D1
WASHINGTON, Ned
Dies 12-20, 1015A3
WASHINGTON, University of (Seattle)
Cancer-estrogen links rptd 6-3, 460F3
WASHINGTON, Mayor Walter (Washington, D.C.)
Endorses Carter 6-10, 432F1
WASHINGTON Fringe Benefit, The (book)
Cited re Cong sex scandal 6-12, 434D1
WASHINGTON Post, The (newspaper)
Kistner interview 1-10, 32B2
Rpts on OPEC aid to poor natns 1-12, 15D1
Rpts CIA-news media links 1-16—1-23, 91D1, C2, A3
Guild dissidents seeks new union 1-28, exec bd drops chrgs 1-29, 153G3
Donnelly dies 2-10, 192D3
Craft unions cross pressmen's picket line 2-16, 2-23, 153E3
AFL-CIO urges arbitration 2-23, 149F1
Estimates US intellignc costs 4-27, 299C3
Kriegsman wins Pulitzer 5-3, 352E3
Brown visits editors 5-6, 343E2
Rpts May 25 primary votes 5-27, 374A2
Angola ousts Wright 6-9, 480B3
Napolitano interview 6-13, 445F2
15 pressmen indicted 7-14, 7-21, 553B3
Scores Mex press ousters, pres 7-14, 620F2
Guild wins bargaining vote 7-22, 553D3
GOP vp poll rptd 8-11, 583F2
Hays chrgs harassment 8-13, 636F1
GOP pre-conv delegate count table 8-14, 583D2, A3
Angola ousts Murphy 8-15, 649G2
Sees Ford nominatn 8-17, 601E3
GOP conv delegate poll rptd 8-17, 616A2, E2
Carter interview 9-4, 664C1, F1
Prints Croat hijacker demands 9-11, 685E1
Maynard on pres debate panel 10-22, 800A1, B3
Carter endorsemt rptd 10-30, 831B3
WASHINGTON Post Co.
USSR plans distributn 1-21, 76G2
Newsweek—*See separate listing*
Washington Post (newspaper)—*See separate listing*
WASHINGTON Press Club
Women rptrs cover Carter church class 8-15, 617D1
WASHINGTON Star (newspaper)
Carter visits editors 8-4, 564E3
WASHINGTON State University (Pullman)
Vogel gets Science Medal 10-18, 858F3
WASHINGTON University (Clayton, Mo.)
Davis gets Science Medal 10-18, 858D3
WASTE Disposal—*See 'Air & Water' under ENVIRONMENT*
WASTE Management Inc.
SEC lists paymts 5-12, 726B1, 729E1
WATANABE, Naoje
Testifies on Lockheed 6-16, 6-24, indicted 7-28, 624E2
Arrested 7-9, 557A2

1977

WASHINGTON, George (1732-99)
Carter visits ancestral home 5-6, 359F2
WASHINGTON, Kermit
Injures Houston player 12-9, fined 12-12, 900A3
Suspended 12-27, 1021A1
WASHINGTON, University of (Seattle)
Gibbs vs 2d Panama canal 7-25, 589F3
WASHINGTON Hospital Center (McLean, Va.)
Heart patient survives unusual surgery 6-2, 620B1
WASHINGTON Post, The (newspaper)
Canada '64-65 Viet missn cover-up rptd 1-14, 97C3
Rpts CIA forgn paymts, reactn 2-18—2-22, 2-28, 123A3-124A1, 151D2
Carter mtg rptd 2-25, 2-28, 151G2
Castro-Bradlee mtg rptd 3-6, 180C3
Boxing scandal chrgs rptd 3-24, 828D1
15 pressmen plead guilty 4-14, 345F1-A2
McPherson wins Pulitzer 4-18, 355A3
Ethiopia ousts rptr 4-25, 327C3
SEC to open corp payoff files 4-27, 502G3
Tennis tourn fee disclosures 5-8, 5-20, FCC rpts probe 7-8, 548D2
Singlaub interview publshd 5-19, 403G3
Neutron bomb disclosures rptd 6-6, 533B2
Randal held in CAE 7-14—7-21, 634E3
US-Sovt strategic weapons compared 751C3
CIA links charged 9-12, 720B3, 721A1
Trib NY sues Intl Trib 9-13, 723G1
On most reliable govt news source list 12-10, 1009B1
WASHINGTON Post Co.
Newsweek—*See separate listing*
Washington Post (newspaper)—*See separate listing*
WASHINGTON Post Writers Group, The
Wins Pulitzer Prize 4-18, 355G2
WASHINGTON Researchers
Most reliable govt news sources listed 12-10, 1009A1
WASHINGTON Star (newspaper)
Philip Love dies 8-17, 696B3
On most reliable govt news source list 12-10, 1009B1
WASHINGTON Star Communications Inc.
Nelson confrmd to Army post 5-27, 500A1
WASHINGTON State University (Pullman)
Wins NCAA indoor track championships 3-12, 603B1
WASHITA (Okla.) State Bank
1st State Bank takeover rptd 3-10, 578C1
WASPs (Women's Air Force Service Pilots)—*See under U.S. GOVERNMENT—AIR Force*
WASTE, Solid
Ford '78 budget proposal 1-17, 31D3
Sludge gasificatn test set 2-3, 278E1
Carter message to Cong 5-23, 404E2
Columbus trash-fueled elec plant voted 11-8, 879D2
WASTE Management Inc.
Sludge-gasificatn test set 2-3, 278D1
WATANABE, Naoji
Lockheed bribe trial opens 1-31, 83E2

1978

WASHINGTON, Booker T. (1856-1915)
Daughter dies 2-26, 196E3
Turner dies 4-21, 356E3
WASHINGTON, Claudell
Traded to White Sox 5-17, 779A3
WASHINGTON, Dave
Traded to Lions 4-27, 336A2
WASHINGTON, Joe
Traded to Colts 8-23, 1024B3
WASHINGTON, Kermit
Reinstated by O'Brien 2-1, 271A2
Traded to Clippers 7-7, 655A3
WASHINGTON, University of (Seattle)
Wins Rose Bowl 1-2, '77 rank rptd 1-3, 8A3, B3
Bush in NFL draft 5-2, 336F3
WASHINGTON: Behind Closed Doors (TV film)
Ehrlichman freed from jail 4-27, 320E2
WASHINGTON Office on Latin America
Paraguayan dissident seized 11-17, 989G3
WASHINGTON Pastor, Brig. Carlos (ret.)
Argentina forgn min 11-6, 865D2
WASHINGTON Post, The (newspaper)
CPSC internal rpt exposed 2-1, 185A3
Time to buy Washn Star, circulatn compared 2-3, 109F2
Film industry probe rptd 2-11, Valenti denies 3-2, 251D2
Scoops Haldeman book excerpts 2-16, upsets syndicatn plans 2-16—2-17, 124B2, C2
Pl electn coverage protested 4-11, 269C1
Greenfield wins Pulitzer 4-17, 315A2
US 'freeze' on SALT rptd, Carter denies; Bradlee stands by rpt 6-2, 422F2
Chile pres resignatn asked 6-10, 452A2
GSA corruptn allegatns rptd 9-3—9-5, 685G1, B2
Carter popularity rptd up 9-24, 736C1
Krause in Guyana 11-15, survives cult ambush 11-18, 11-19, 889G1-A2
Becker escapes Cambodia slaying 12-23, 997A2
WASHINGTON Post Co.
Time to buy Washn Star 2-3, 109G2
FCC OKs WTOP radio sale 5-11, WTOP-TV swap 5-18, 599F3
Newsweek (magazine)—*See separate listing*
Washington Post (newspaper)—*See separate listing*
WASHINGTON Star (newspaper)
Time purchase agreed, circulatn compared 2-3, 109E2
Time purchase completed 3-16, 270B3
Albritton resigns as publisher 5-31, 672D2
S Africa role in purchase bid rptd 11-1—11-2, 868D2
WASHINGTON Star Communications Inc.
WJLA, KOCO-TV exchng OKd 1-12, Time to buy Washn Star 2-3; FCC scores Allbritton 2-13, 109F2
Washington Star (newspaper)—*See separate listing*
WASHINGTON State University (Pullman)
Rono sets track marks 4-8—6-27, 600F2
Greene in NFL draft 5-2, 336F3
WASHINGTON Trollers Association
Canada fishing ban asked 5-5, 350D2
WASHINGTON University (St. Louis, Mo.)
Hamburger, cancer link rptd 5-16, 598G2
WASILEWSKI, Vincent
Vs children's TV ad curbs 4-10, 347D2
WASSERMAN, Harvey
Hails Seabrook A-plant protest 6-26, 494E1
WASSON, Craig
Go Tell Spartans released 9-23, 970E1
WASTE, Solid
Mich sues Ford Motor re pollutn 2-1, 163C3
Atlantic sludge sites OKd 3-3, 164A1
Energy source conf rptd 5-11, 367C1
Phila sued on sludge dumping 5-24, 409A2
NJ dumping law voided by US Sup Ct 6-23, 566B2
Small business energy loan aid signed 7-4, 512A2
Niagara dump site declared disaster area 8-7, 703A1
Neb, Alaska rejct mandatory container deposits 11-7, 847B3, 854G3
EPA warns on hazardous dump sites 11-21, 899D2
WATANABE, Yoshinori
Message From Space released 11-17, 970B2

1979

WASHINGTON, Edward Emmanuel (David Hill)
Denies priest's murder 7-15, 814A2
WASHINGTON, George (1732-99)
Stuart portrait goes to Natl Gallery 4-10, Boston library sale halted 4-14, 374E3, 375A1
WASHINGTON, Joe
NFL '78 kick return ldr 1-6, 80C2
WASHINGTON, Kermit
Walton compensatn set 9-18, 1003D2
WASHINGTON, Martha (1731-1802)
Boston library sale of Stuart portrait halted 4-14, 374E3
WASHINGTON, University of (Seattle)
Comet origin study rptd 289D3
Alcoholism study rptd 1-5, 289D3
Terminally ill treatmt study rptd 5-31, 471E2
Wins Sun Bowl 12-22, 1001A3
WASHINGTON Group Inc.
Bagley chrgd re stock fraud 3-14, 3-15, 292A1
Bagley acquitted 8-1, 578E2
WASHINGTON Post, The (newspaper)
Star renegotiates labor pacts 1-1, 5F1
Graham steps down as publisher, son succeeds 1-10, 78C3
Bilingual educ oppositn rptd 1-29, 127C2
US ex-consul torture chrgs vs Israel publshd 2-6; Israel denies 2-6—2-8, 2-11, 108A1-D2
US cable details Dubs' death 2-22, 147F1
TV viewing survey rptd 2-28, 3-1, 173B1
Carter peanut loan scheme alleged 3-11—3-13 183F3-184A2
US curbs on PLO offcl scored 4-12, 319A3
Block wins Pulitzer 4-16, 336B3
US, USSR strategic weapons compared 338G3
Silkwood estate wins A-suit 5-18, 381G2-A3
China OKs office 5-30, 406B2
Daily, Sunday circulatn listed 6-6, 431C1, D1
CIA agent rptd ousted re rifled JFK death probe files 6-18, 466C3
Eizenstat energy memo rptd 7-7, 513C3
Blakey interviewed 7-9, 520G2
Camp David mtg covered 7-10, 514C1
Claiborne told of Iran press curbs 7-23, 566A1
Editorial on Carter Miss R boat trip cited 8-23, 623B1
Sen com rpt on SALT leaked 10-4, 762D1
Connally Mideast peace plan printed 10-12, 783C2
Alan Barth dies 11-20, 932B2
'Brethren' publicatn stirs controversy 12-2, 988B2
WASHINGTON Post Co.
Graham retains posts 1-10, 78C3
WASHINGTON Press Club
Harris addresses 8-29, 661A3
Connally addresses 10-11, 783F1
WASHINGTON Star (newspaper)
Labor pacts renegotiated 1-1, 5E1-C2
S Africa chrgd re '74 purchase bid 3-21, 213F1
S Africa purchase bid confrmd 4-2, 270C1; 6-4 427D3
Yoder wins Pulitzer 4-16, 336B3
Connally Mideast peace plan printed 10-12, 783C2
WASHINGTON State University (Pullman)
Pac-10 wins Challenge Bowl 1-14, 63B2
Thompson in NFL draft 5-3, 335E2
WASHINGTON University (St. Louis, Mo.)
Vitamin C anti-infectn role studied 5-5, 691D2
WASHINGTON v. U.S.
Case decided by Sup Ct 7-2, 559F1
WASHINGTON v. Washington State Commercial Passenger Fishing Association
Case decided by Sup Ct 7-2, 559F1
WASSERMAN, Harvey
On China Syndrome impact 3-29, 246F3
WASTBERG, Per
Elected PEN Club pres 7-21, 553G3
WASTE, Solid
EPA wants prior data on chems 1-10, 16G3-17A1
US sues NJ cos re pollutn 2-7, 129G3-130B1
Niagara dump hearings, Hooker knew perils in '58 4-10, 4-11, 281B3
NC PCB dumping chrgd 6-4—6-13, disposal disputed 6-5, 597G2-E3
Carter proposes hazardous waste cleanup, cites Niagara dump 6-13, 441E1
Niagara dump probes rptd 6-18, 597A2
Hooker sued for Mich pollutn 6-22, 597C2
Olin convicted for mercury dumping 8-16, 704E1
NJ Meadowlands mercury cleanup ordrd 8-26, 704A2
Hooker chrgd in LI dumping 8-31, 665F3
Urban refuse collectn cutbacks seen 10-24, 920A2
Chem dump sites listed 11-1, 886B1
Eur, US, Canada pact 11-13, 864B3
Olin fined for mercury dumping 12-10, 947A1
US sues Occidental, Olin re Niagara dumps 12-20, 990F1
WATANJAR, Lt. Col. Mohammad Aslam
Out as Afghan interior min 9-14; move sparks fighting 9-14—9-15, 695D3, 696B1

1980

WASHINGTON, Harold
Elected to US House 11-4, 842D3, 846C2, D3, 850C3
WASHINGTON, Jackie
Sets indoor 640-yd relay mark 2-29, 892F1
WASHINGTON, Joe
NFL '79 receiving, rushing ldr 1-5, 8C2, B3
WASHINGTON, Richard
In NBA expansn draft 5-28, 447D1
WASHINGTON, U. L.
AL batting ldr 10-6, 926E3
In World Series 10-14—10-21, 811B3-812D3
WASHINGTON, University of (Seattle)
Gay chrgd in murder 1-2, 18C3
Mt St Helens volcanic quakes rptd 3-26, 252F1
Martin in NFL draft 4-29, 336F3
Pac-10 transcript scandal penalties avoids 8-11, 875B2
WASHINGTON Pastor, Carlos
Scores Carter rights policy 11-20, 913C3
WASHINGTON Post, The (newspaper)
Abscam probe revealed 2-2, 81B1
Jamaica sues US grain shippers 2-4, fraud detailed 2-5, 99D2
Ex-rptr named Abscam leaks prosecutor 2-11, 111G1
Rpts US arms Afghan rebels 2-14; US denies 2-16, 123B1
Randal arrives Teheran 2-25; expelled 2-28, 138A2
Iran readmits newsmen 3-7, 178D2
Waldheim interviewed 3-11, 178B1
Reagan scores press 4-10, 288B2
Anderson meets staff 4-25, 328B1
Fahd interview publshd 5-25, 395A2
Bolivia rptr detained 6-9, 443F2
Ross flees Iran 7-24, 572C1
WASHINGTON Star (newspaper)
Chappaquiddick account questioned, Kennedy rebuts 1-15, 32F3, 33B1
S Africa documt disclosure ordrd by Sup Ct 3-17, 278C1
WASHINGTON State University (Pullman)
Collins in NBA draft 6-10, 447G2
Pac-10 transcript scandal penalties avoids 8-11, 875B2
WASHINGTON University (St. Louis, Mo.)
Commoner to accept NY teaching post 3-17, 471C3
'79 endowmt earnings rptd 3-24, 319C2
Commoner heads Citizens' Party pres ticket 4-13, 288E3
WASHINGTON v. Davis
Case cited by Sup Ct 4-22, 343B2
WASILEWSKI, Vincent T.
Assails FCC cable-TV deregulatn moves 7-22, 583F1
WASLEY, Carrie
Dem platform notes A-power 6-24, 479A3
WASSBERG, Thomas
Wins Olympic medal 2-17, 155B3
WASSERMAN, Herbert
American Clock opens 11-20, 1003G2
WASSON, Craig
Outsider released 6-3, 675C3
WASTE, Solid
State of State messages 1-8, 403F3; 1-9, 483G2
GAO rpt scores sewer projects 1-9, 54F1-D2
Carter budget proposals 1-28, 73F2
NJ pollutn suit partially setld, Edison dump to be covered 1-30, 93D3
US cncl notes problems 2-19, 145D2
EPA sets toxic waste rules 2-26, 145D3
Ark dump suit filed 3-4, 190E3
Mich chem dump cleanup sought 4-17, 331D2
Eliz (NJ) chem dump burns 4-22, 331B2
Union Corp sued 4-24, 331E3
NY sues Occidental, Hooker re Niagara dumping 4-28, 331C3
EPA adopts toxic waste rules 5-5, 387E1
Niagara dump health defects rptd 5-16, US sets evacuatn 5-21, 386D3-387D1
Tighter chem controls urged 6-29, 494F2-A3
Dem platform plank adopted 8-13, 615G1
PCB cleanup methods rptd 8-21, 9-11, 747B2
House passes clean-up funds 9-19, 9-23; Sen OKs 'superfund' 11-24, 897G3-898G1
Toxic dumping controls clear Cong 10-2, signed 10-21, 981F1
EPA toxic waste suits filed 10-7, 10-9, 825A1, F1
Carter optimistic 10-12, 779D1
GAO faults EPA protectn 10-31, 869B2
Washn, NJ, Alaska waste-disposal bond issues OKd 11-4, 847F3, 848A1, A2
Clean-up bill signed 12-11, 935E3-936C1
EPA halts Calif, Ky sewer funds 12-11, 963B1
WATANABE, Michio
Japan finance min 7-17, 539A3

1976

WATER
Energy dvpt loans urged 2-26, 149E2
France-Bahrain desalinatn pact 3-2, 204G3
'75 energy use data rptd 4-4, 285C1
Seawater conversn funds cleared 6-7, 434G2; signed 6-22, 982F1
Dem platform text 6-15, 474E2
Ford OKs '77 funds 7-12, 517E1
UK, Belgian, Dutch supplies hit 8-15—8-24, 630D1-B2; stocks renewed 11-16, 12-31, 977C3
GOP platform text 8-18, 602G3, 603G1, 607D2, E3
Utah votes vs fluoridatn 11-2, 824C3
3 seized re Phila extortn try 11-3, 972D1
Drought—*See under 'D'*
Pollution—*See 'Air & Water' under ENVIRONMENT & Pollution*

WATER, Heavy—*See ATOMIC Energy*

WATERGATE Issue
Newman fined $10,000 1-6, 6B3
Nixon documts custody ruling upheld 1-7, 6E2
Kissinger, Haldeman file Halperin tap depositns 1-12, 3-11; Nixon depositn released 3-10, 183G3, 184B2
Ford State of Union message 1-19, 37A2
Muskie rebuts Ford 1-21, 40G1
Jackson, Symington CIA contacts rptd 1-28, 93B2
ABA prosecutor proposal 2-16, 137A1
Church denounces Nixon Chile testimony 3-11, 183G3
Woods wins personal items return 4-23, 316E1
Ehrlichman LA break-in verdict upheld 5-17, 379C1
Sup Ct bars Jacobsen plea-bargaining review 5-19, 393D3
Nixon disbarred in NY 7-8, 493B3
Jacobsen gets 2 yrs probatn 8-20, 1016A1
Spec prosecutor bill not cleared 10-2, 884D1
Major convictns upheld, Mardian's upset 10-12, 770E1-E2
Release of Nixon tapes OKd 10-26, 849A3
Ehrlichman enters prison 10-28, 849F2
House Dems OK rules changes 12-6—12-9, 981C2
Nixon, Mitchell, Haldeman held liable re Halperin wiretap 12-16, 980A3-981B1
Ulasewicz convicted 12-23, 981B1
Campaign Fund Issues—*See 'Political Payments' under BUSINESS, 'Campaign Finances' under POLITICS*
Presidential Election
Reagan warns GOP vs issue 3-9, 180F1
Church scores Ford re pardon 4-19, 282B1
Ford alludes to scandal 5-8, 342A3
Nixon sued re wiretap 5-10, 349E2
Strauss alludes to scandal 7-12, 509B1
Carter cites 'disgrace' 7-15, 507D1, 510E2
Mondale cites scandal, Ford pardon 7-15, 507G3, 511E2
Ford offers reform bill, backs Nixon pardon 7-19, 531G3
Carter scores Nixon pardon 7-20, 532G1
Mondale: important issue 7-31, 565C2
Connally vp selectn scored 8-5, 584E2
Carter vs condoning crimes 8-11, 585B2
Ford aides minimized refs 8-16, 615A1
Dole position cited 614A3
Carter notes 'shame' 8-30, 645B2
Mondale notes GOP 'turnover' 9-2, 665A3
Carter condemns Nixon morality 9-7, 664F2
Mondale cites 9-10, 687D1
Ruff probe of gifts to Ford rptd 9-21, 9-25; Ford, other statemts 9-21—9-30; Justice Dept referral rptd 10-1, 722E1-723G2
Ford, Carter debate 9-23, 701E3, 703D1
Carter on Ford funds chrg 9-29, 9-30, 723D1, A2
Mondale scores Ford, Dole 10-5, 743A3
2d Ford, Carter debate 10-6, 741D1
Carter links Ford, Nixon 10-9, 762C2
Ford cleared of funds misuse, comments 10-14, 761D1, F2

1977

WATCH Tower Bible and Tract Society of New York—*See JEHOVAH'S Witnesses*

WATER—*See also DAMS, FLOODS, RIVERS & Waterways*
Carter budget revisions 2-22, 124E3, 126D1
Sen backs projects 3-10, 174C2
UN conf held 3-14—3-25, 250E1
More fund cuts studied 3-23, 209D3
US rights in Calif upheld 4-4, 253B1
Carter vs tax rebates-projcts trade 4-7, 271B1
Carter backs some projects 4-18, 299E2
Cong bars funds impoundmt 5-3, 365C2; Carter signs 5-13, 380D3
Carter warns projcts bill veto 5-26, 417C1; O'Neill cautns 6-1, 459A3
Carter-Cong projct differences eased 6-15, 459E3
Coal slurry bill deferred, Westn shortages cited 6-27, 516C1
NYC blackout affects supply 7-13—7-14, 537G2
Cong OKs funds for 9 projects 7-25, 592G2; bill signed 8-8, 609D2
Research, saline conversn bill signed 8-2, 689E2
Westn land holdings breakup sought 8-18, 8-22, 703G1, F2
Carter topic in Denver 10-22, 817D1
Safe drinking water authorizatn clears Cong 11-1, 856F3; signed 11-16, 1001F2
NC, Ore voters OK projects 11-8, 879B2
Drought—*See under 'D'*
Irrigation—*See AGRICULTURE*
Pollution—*See ENVIRONMENT & Pollution—Air & Water*

WATER Conference, UN—*See under UNITED Nations*

WATERGATE Issue
Baker elected minority ldr 1-4, 6E1
Sorensen withdraws CIA nominatn 1-17, 35A2
Ulasewicz sentenced 2-18, 197E2
Sup Ct bars Ehrlichman convictn review 2-22, 150A1
4 in break-in get setlmt 2-22, 157F2
Hunt paroled 2-23, 140A3, 197F2
Castro scores US rights pressure 2-26—2-27, 180E3
Mardian reinstated to Sup Ct bar 2-28, 175B2
Liddy's term commuted 4-12, 325C3
Sup Ct cover-up appeals rule leaked 4-21, 382A2; rptd confrmd 5-23, 406D1
Carter backs spec prosecutor bill 5-3, 338F1
Nixon-Frost TV interviews 5-4, poll results, other reactn 5-4—5-9, 365G3-368A1; 5-19, 405C3; 5-25, 420F1-C2
Nixon funds rptd seized by IRS 5-6, 482E2
Carter: Nixon violated law 5-12, 381C2
Haldeman vs Nixon versn 5-26, 420B3
Haldeman, Mitchell jail delay refused 5-31, 461F3
Haldeman, Mitchell enter prison 6-21, 6-22, 483F2
Sup Ct denies Haldeman, Mitchell appeals review 6-27, 538F3
US custody of Nixon documents upheld 6-28, 539D3
Lacovara '74 resignatn cited 556G1
Nixon-Frost TV interview 9-3, 692G2
Liddy freed from prison 9-7, 725B1
Nixon tapes open for civil suit 10-3, 760B2
Mitchell, Haldeman, Ehrlichman sentences cut 10-4, 761G3
Judge Sirica retires 10-4, 927E3
Carter rpts no Liddy contact 10-27, 814D1
Canada PM rejcts RCMP comparison 10-28, 841E1
Sup Ct disbars Mitchell, Ehrlichman 10-31, 835A3

1978

WATER
Mondale tours Westn states 1-9—1-13, 34D1, F1
Carter State of Union Message 1-19, 31G3
Carter budgets water projcts 1-23, 47G2
Govs see Andrus 2-26; back state control, conservatn 2-28, 144G3, 145B1
Rural shortages rptd 4-6—4-7, 577E3
Utility customer hearings backed by Sup Ct 5-1, 364B1
Carter policy scored by Colo sen 5-2, 342B2
White House solar unit planned 5-3, 321E3
Carter plans natl policy 5-4, 320G3, 321A1
Fluoride-cancer link refuted 5-18, 598A3
EPA bars Denver dam permit 5-25, 409A1
Water-based land claims barred by Sup Ct 5-31, 431E1
Carter unveils natl policy 6-6; reactn 6-6—6-7, 426A3
Carter asks 26 projcts 6-9, threatens House bill veto 6-9, 6-14, 446E2, C3
Calif, NM rights backed by US Sup Ct 7-3, 552B2
Indians protest in DC 7-15—7-23, 568E3
Coal slurry pipe bill defeated 7-19, 550C2
Legionnaires' bacterium isolated 8-11, 635C3
Nitrites linked to cancer 8-11, 728E1
DC funds clear Cong 8-17, 697G2
Libya desalinatn projct rptd 10-4, 821A1
Pub works bill vetoed, House upholds 10-5, 765A1-D2
Environmtlists laud Carter 12-20, 1009D1
Drought—*See DROUGHT*
Irrigation—*See AGRICULTURE*
Pollution—*See ENVIRONMENT & Pollution—Air & Water*

WATERBURY, Conn.—*See CONNECTICUT*

WATER Engine, The (play)
Opens 1-5, 760G3

WATERGATE Issue
Carter compares Gandhi rule 1-2, 1G1
Segretti law practice suspensn ends 1-27, 172G2
Haldeman book excerpts scooped by Washn Post 2-16, syndicatn plans upset; Nixon accused on cover-up, break-in 2-16—2-17, 124G1-125E1
Broadcasters denied Nixon tapes by Sup Ct 4-18, 308C1
Ehrlichman freed 4-27, 320A2
Nixon memoir excerpts published 4-30, 5-1, 319D2-320A2
'72 inflatn linked 5-22, 427B2
Goodwin legal immunity case declined by Sup Ct 6-19, 492D2
Haldeman legal fees to exceed book profits 8-17, 844C1
Colson movie premieres in DC 9-24, 844D1
Hunt denies JFK murder role 11-3, 11-4, 898F3
Nixon calls break-in 'stupid', takes blame 11-28, 942C2
Fernandez says Sen com exonerated 11-29, 938C3
Buzhardt dies 12-16, 1032D2
Haldeman leaves prison 12-20, 1011G2

1979

Army coup try linked 10-15–10-16, 810F3

WATER
Carter budget proposals 1-22, 45F3
Carter asks projct cost-sharing 5-16, 365E2-A3
Carter energy goals stated 6-20, 498B1
Fluoride dental value doubted 9-1, 1000A2
Carter backs Western states control 10-10, 807E2
Irrigation—*See AGRICULTURE*
Pollution—*See ENVIRONMENT–Air & Water*

WATERBURY, Conn.—*See CONNECTICUT*
WATERFORD, Conn.—*See CONNECTICUT*

WATERGATE Issue
Haig controversy in NATO cited 1-3, 3A3
Mitchell paroled 1-19, 176D1
Connally announces pres bid 1-24, 70A3
Haldeman discloses '75 CBS-TV interview fee 1-27, 176C1
Weicker announces pres bid 3-12, 185D3
Carter peanut probe spec counsel named 3-20, 203C1
Carter probe spec counsel gains power, Bell bars comparisons 3-23, 301F2, A3
Nixon, aides ruled liable in tap suits 7-12, 611D2
Nixon tapes release OKd 7-24, 561E2
China welcomes Nixon 9-17–9-22, 751D2
'Brethren' publicatn stirs controversy 12-2, 988B2

1980

WATCHER in the Woods, The (film)
Released 4-16, 416G3
WATCH on the Rhine (play)
Opens 1-3, 136F3
WATER
State of State messages 1-7, 1-10, 404E2, D3; 1-14, 269A1
Carter budget proposals 1-28, 72A1, 73D3
Appropriatn clears Cong 6-25, 9-10, Carter signs 10-1, 803A2
Calif OKs new project 7-18, 632G1
Drought damage rpt 9-7, 857C2
Northeast shortage rptd 9-12—12-1; NJ emergency declared 10-19, comm issues warning 12-1, 947A3
Washn, NJ, Alaska water-supply bond issues OKd 11-4, 847F3, 848A1, A2
Pollution—*See ENVIRONMENT--Air & Water*

WATERGATE Issue
Ehrlichman Calif bar resignatn accepted 1-19, 199D1
Cox to head Common Cause 2-2, 115E2
Bush denies '70 campaign gift coverup 2-7, 128E3
Baker cites re Abscam probe 2-10, 110F3
Bush 'basic speech' excerpts 3-3, 208G2
Agnew death fears rptd 4-20, Liddy book excerpts reveal Anderson, Hunt plots 4-21; Dean discounts 4-23, 333G2-F3
Bennett dies 5-4, 448C1
Nixon tapes go public 5-28, 460D1
Garrison sentenced 6-10, 460B1
GOP hq taps suspected 6-21, 6-24, 480F3
Carter attacks GOP 7-17, 532E1
Neal declines Sen probe 8-7, 595E3
Ervin reveals cancer 9-12; scores 'judicial verbicide' 10-22, 908A2
Appeals ct backs Abscam tapes broadcast 10-1, 781B3
Ehrlichman parole ended 10-27, 890E1
Maguire loses reelectn bid 11-4, 848F2
Haig named secy of state 12-16, 955A2
Haig hires atty for confirmatn hearings 12-22, 980C1

1976

Ford on Dean coverup chrg 10-14, 761A3
Mondale, Dole debate 10-15, 783B1, D1, 784A1
Ford coverup probe barred 10-15, 10-20; denies chrgs 10-20, 784F3
Dole rebuts Dems 10-17—10-27, 804E1-A3
Ford denies pardon rumor 10-20, 784D3
Ford, Carter debate 10-22, 799G2, 800D3, G3, 801A1
Andreas, Dahlberg gifts to Ford rptd 10-22, 938G3
Ford confronts issue 10-27, 803E1
Mondale denounces Ford 10-29—10-31, 827B2
Dole rebuts Dems 11-1, 827B3
Rptd top electn issue 11-2, 818B3
Weicker reelected, Montoya loses 11-2, 820E1, E2
Carter on Ford voter rating 11-4, 819F2

WATERLOO, Ia.—*See IOWA*

WATER Polo
Olympic results 7-27, 576C2

WATERS, Territorial
Chile seeks compensatn for Bolivia sea outlet 1-2, 27D1
US sub intellignc rptd 1-20, 93A3
US Sen OKs 200-mi zone 1-28, 94C1
EC backs 200-mile zone 1-30, 85C1
Japan seeks 12-mi limit 2-2, 141B2
Senegal limits extended 2-5, 591F3
'75 Yugo-Albania Adriatic clash rptd 2-6, 224D1
EC extends limit, sets 200-mi zone 2-18, 164D1
Denmark decrees defense rules 2-27, 252C1
US Cong OKs 200-mi fishing zone 3-29, 3-30, 246F1
US 200-mi zone signed 4-15, 982E1
USSR signs Canada pact 5-19, Canada sets 200-mi limit 6-4, 417D1
Mex enacts 200-mi zone 6-6, 420A2
French Cabt OKs 200-mi limit draft bill 6-16, 481F3
EC OKs 200-mi limit 7-27, 563A3
UN Sea Law Conf deadlocked 8-2—9-17, 700E1
US GOP platform text cites 8-18, 611A1
US seizes Bulgaria boat 9-30, 910D2
Japan boats rptd seized off USSR 10-5, 839B3
NATO rptd concerned re UK mil cuts 10-17, 880C1
Canada-Japan accord 10-26, 836B3
Canada sets 200-mile limit 11-2, 889A1
US-Japanese fishery talks 11-8—11-12, 863B3
Canada seizes 3 Cuban boats 11-8, 888F3
USSR frees Japan fishermen 11-18, 908F1
Australia prime min tours Torres Strait re PNG seabed pact 11-22—11-24, 961C3
USSR OKs US 200-mile limit 11-26, 916B2
Greek-Turk dispute cited 11-29, 1004A3
USSR sets 200-mi limit 12-10, 1011C2
Aegean Sea—*See AEGEAN Sea*
Iceland-UK Issue—*See ICELAND*

WATERS Jr., Capt. Samuel Edwin
Vietnam rpts killed 9-6, 678B3

WATKINS, Wes
Elected 11-2, 822G2, 830C3

1977

WATERMAN, Nan
Elected Common Cause chrmn 4-23, 396C3

WATERMAN, Judge Sterry R.
Finds JP Stevens in contempt 8-31, 724B2

WATERMAN Steamship Corp.
Rebates cited 1-5, 6C3

WATERS, Ethel
Dies 9-1, 788A3

WATERS, Territorial
UK fishing zone in effect 1-1, 20G3
Canada fines Cuban boats 1-4, 7F1
PR statehood tied to oil rights 1-5, 16A3
DOT issues future trends rpt, Coleman scores Cong 1-15, 58E3
India sets sea zone limits 1-15, 64F1
Australia-Japan pact 1-17—1-18, 60B2
Denmark protests UK fishing limits 1-29, 115G2-A3
Canada, provs in mineral pact 2-1, 133B3
Australia-PNG seabed talks halted 2-7, 132C1
US-Japan fishing pact 2-10, 136G1; 173F3
EC accepts US fishing limits 2-15, 109D2
Cuba-US talks seen 2-15, 110F1
EC fish stock protectn agreed 2-15, 146F2
EC grants USSR fishing licenses 2-18, 146D3
US approves fishing agrmts 2-21, 3-3, 173C3
Canada fines Norwegian vessel 2-22, 147A2
US-Canada fishing zone agrmt rptd 2-23, 132B3
US, USSR set 200-mi limits 3-1, 147E1
Carter call-in topic 3-5, 171C2
Sovt-Japan fishing talks impasse 3-15—3-31, 249G3
US, Cuba fishing talks at impasse 3-24—3-29, Carter lauds Castro 4-11, 283F1, B2
US rpts Sovt violatns 3-28—4-4; 2 vessels seized 4-9, 4-10, Sovts warned 4-5, 4-11, 269G3
Japan plans fishing limit extensn 3-29, 250C1
US rpts Mar fishing violatns 270C2
US sets fishing rules compliance monitors 4-13, 363E3
USSR orders fishing rules observed 4-14; US frees Sovt vessels 4-14, 5-5, 363B3
US, Cuba sign fishing pacts 4-27, 390A1
Japan extends fishing limit 4-28, 5-2, 411B2
Australia-NZ defns pact rptd 5-4, 410F2
Vietnam sets limits 5-20, 490F2
Cuba-US fishing pact publshd 5-25, 456D2
Sovt-Japan fishing pact signed 5-27, ratified 6-10, 458F2-A3
Norway declares Arctic fishing zone 6-3, USSR disputes 11-11, 967F2
US Coast Guard authorizatn clears Cong 6-21, 501B1
US-Canada interim fish pact OKd 6-25, 525F2
French-UK Eng Channel dispute setld 7-18, 625C1
US-Canada interim pact signed 7-26, 688D3
N Korea sets mil, econ zones 8-1, 591A1
Norway-USSR Barents Sea talks rptd 9-2, 967G2
NZ declares 200-mi zone 9-7, 729A3
Argentina seizes USSR, Bulgaria fishing boats 9-21—10-1; USSR protests 9-23—11-4, 944F2
France rejcts Eng Channel boundary chng 9-29, UK appeals 10-12, 772F1-B2
USSR, China in river accord 10-7, 853D2
Viets seize US yacht 10-12, vow release 12-20, 975G3
UN pollutn conf ends, Medit pact reached 10-21, 876A2
Argentina-Chile Beagle Channel dispute cited 11-4, 944C3
Argentina frees Sovt ship 11-9, 982D1
US carrier oil spill liability extended 12-15, 959F1; signed 12-28, 1001A3

WATERTOWN, N.Y.—*See NEW York State*

WATERWAYS—*See RIVERS & Waterways*

1978

WATER Resources Council—*See under U.S. GOVERNMENT*

WATERS, Herb
Black-mkt uranium sale bid probed 3-19, 242D2

WATERS, Muddy
Record wins Grammy 2-24, 316A1

WATERS, Territorial
Swedish fishing zones in Baltic set 1-1, 21A2
Chile-Argentina Beagle Channel dispute dvpts 1-6—2-10; map 101D1, E1
NZ seizes Japan trawlers 1-25, 3-2; 200-mi limit in effect 4-1, fishing accord reached 5-23, 497G3
UK vetoes EC fishing policy 1-30—1-31, EC natns score 2-14, 158F3
UK fishing zone scored by France, W Ger 2-6—2-7, 122C1
Sahara rebels warn Spain on Morocco fishing pact 2-20, 278D3
Chile-Argentina Beagle Channel talks open 3-1, 216D1
Greece-Turkey seabed talks 3-10—3-11, 216G2
NZ signs fishing accords with S Korea, USSR 3-13, 4-5, 498F1
France issues tanker rules 3-23, 238G1
US, Venez set boundaries 3-28, 233E1
PNG sets 200-mi econ zone 3-31, 269E3
China boats anchor off Senkakus 4-12, Japan protests 4-14, boats rptd out 4-16, 278C1
Australia seeks 200-mi fishing zone 4-13, 286D2
US bars Canada salmon fishing 5-5, 350B2
Argentina-Chile Beagle Channel talks fail 5-22—11-2, 860E2
Canada-US talks adjourn 5-26, 413D1
Canada, US ban fishing 6-2, 6-4, 435D1
Surinam sets new limits 6-11, 559F1
Libya seizes 2 Italian fishermen 7-30, 689G3
Viet, Thai fishing agrmts reached 9-6—9-10, 696G1
Australia cautnd on Antarctic fishing zone 9-17, 900D3
USSR-Norway tensn rptd 10-12, 820C2
Bolivia Pacific outlet backed by Argentina 10-25, 860C3
Beagle Channel talks cited 10-27, 840A3
Greece protests Turkey boat sinking 11-1, 905B3
Australia panel urges whaling ban 12-18, 1012F3

WATERSHIP Down (film)
Released 11-3, 1030F3

WATERWAYS—*See RIVERS & Waterways*

WATKINS, Rep. Wesley (D, Okla.)
Reelected 11-7, 852A1

WATLINGTON, Janet
Loses VI delegate electn 11-7, 915F3

1979

WATER Heaters
2 cos acquitted re prices 10-22, 986E1

WATERS, Charlie
Cowboys win NFL conf title 1-7, 8F3

WATERS, Muddy (McKinley Morganfield)
Wins Grammy 2-16, 336G3

WATERS, Territorial
US-Canada fishing talks progress seen 1-10, '78 dispute cited 37A1
Canada, US draft pact 1-23, 95D3
Greenland-EC ties linked 4-4, 286D1
India, Bangladesh set talks 4-18, 328D2
US, Canada in tuna dispute; Atlantic fish pact threatened 8-26—9-4, 667D1
Taiwan extends offshore zones 9-6, 733F3
Australia 200-mi fishing zone takes effect 11-1, 832G1-A2

WATERWAYS—*See RIVERS & Waterways*

WATKINS, Bruce R.
Loses KC mayoral vote 3-27, 231B3

1980

WATERHOUSE, Keith
Filumena opens 2-10, 392G2

WATERLOO East High School (Iowa)
Wins Drake Relays mile 4-26, 892F2

WATERMAN, Nan
Cox succeeds 2-2, 115E2

WATER Polo
Moscow Olympic results 7-29, 624D2

WATERS, Herbert J.
Named in Jamaican grain fraud suit 2-4, 99C2

WATERS, Muddy (McKinley Morganfield)
Wins Grammy 2-27, 296G3

WATERS, Territorial
US to cut Sovt rights for Afghan invasn 1-4, 1D1
Sovt trawlers ordrd tracked by US 1-8, 9C1
Australia suspends Sovt projcts, ups surveillance 1-9, 9D2
Carter curbs Sovt fishing ships 1-23, 41B2, 42D2
USSR-Equatorial Guinea pact expiratn rptd 1-28, 119C1
Cuba sinks Bahamas patrol boat 5-10, 371A2
Iceland-Norway pact set 5-10, 398B2
Canada retaliates vs US failure to ratify Atlantic pacts 6-12, 461B2
Mex seizes US tuna boats 7-8, 7-10; US retaliates, bans tuna imports 7-14, 565B1
Bahamas convicts 8 Cubans of poaching 7-9, 563E2
Morocco attacks 2 Cuban tankers off Africa 7-12, 562C2
US fishing indus aid bill clears Cong 12-4, 955D1; signed 12-22, 982C1, 995B3
Norway orders EC ships out 12-10, 969C3
Spain recognizes Polisario; fishermen freed 12-17, 995D3
Mex ends US accords, rights dispute blamed 12-29, 995D2

WATERSTON, Sam
Lunch Hour opens 11-14, 892E3

WATERWAYS—*See RIVERS & Waterways*

WATE-TV (Pittsburgh, Pa. station)
Announcer chrgd in lottery fraud 9-19, 786B3

WATHAN, John
In World Series 10-14—10-21, 811D3

WATKINS, Rep. Wesley (D, Okla.)
Reelected 11-4, 843G4

1976

WATSON, Arthur
'72 campaign gift listed 4-25, 688B1
WATSON, Bob
NL batting ldr 10-4, 795F3
WATSON, Denise
Chrgd 2-3, pleads not guilty 2-4, 271A3
WATSON, Henry O.
Sup Ct upholds convictn 1-26, 87B2
WATSON Jr., Jack H.
Lauds transition help 11-5, 845C1
Heads Carter transitn team 11-23, 881F2
WATSON, W. Marvin
Pleads guilty, fined 9-23, 725D2
WATT, James G.
Moss threatens impeachmt 9-1, 868A3
WAUSAU, Wis.—*See WISCONSIN*
WAXMAN, Rep. Henry A. (D, Calif.)
Reelected 11-2, 829C1
WAYNE State University (Detroit, Mich.)
Sickle cell zinc treatmt rptd 2-24, 159G2
WCKT-TV (Miami TV station)
Reagan loses equal-time bid 3-4, 180G2-A3
WEAPONS—*See ARMAMENTS*

WEATHER—*See METEOROLOGY*

WEATHER Underground (formerly Weathermen) (organization)
FBI reform set 8-11; FBI ex-officials admit break-ins 8-17, 8-18, 633C2, 634A2, E2

1977

WATSON, Bob
NL batting ldr 10-2, 926C3, D3
WATSON, Henderson
Murder chrg dropped 12-19, 991F2
WATSON Jr., Jack H.
Named Carter asst, Cabt secy 1-14, 35G2
Assigned 'follow-up' role 7-15, 556A1
Assures govs of energy conf 9-8, 719B2
WATSON, Dr. James D.
DNA curbs scored 12-15—12-16, 1022B2
WATSON, Roosevelt
Murder chrg dropped 12-19, 991B2, F2
WATSON, Tom
Sets marks at Crosby, San Diego tourns 1-23, 1-30, 104A1
2d in Heritage Classic 3-27, 311B2
Wins Masters 4-10, 311C1
Wins Western Open 6-26, 676F1
Wins British Open 7-9, 659G2
PGA top money winner 10-30, 950G3
WATT, Donald B.
Dies 11-27, 952F3
WATT, James G.
Backs Alcan Alaska gas route 5-2, 369D3
WATTS, Slick
NBA final standings 4-10, 331D3
WAXMAN, Rep. Henry A. (D, Calif.)
Scores TV violence rpt 10-24, 921A2
WAYNE, John
Panama Canal pact backing rptd 9-20, 716E3
WBA (World Boxing Association)—*See BOXING*
WBC (World Boxing Council)—*See BOXING*
WCC—*See WORLD Council of Churches*
WCT (World Championship Tennis)—*See TENNIS*
WEAN United Inc.
Foreign paymts rptd 3-8, 233E2
'76 Fortune 500 list drops 341D1
India seeks plant aid 8-24, 655C2
WEAPONS—*See ARMAMENTS*

WEATHER—*See also DROUGHTS, STORMS*
Record US cold wave 1-14—1-17, 37E1, A2; 1-18—1-26, 53B3-54E3; 1-27—2-2, 75E2, 76G3, 77A1
Carter econ plan debated 1-27—2-4, 89B2
Jan, mid-Feb econ data rptd; '77 forecast revised 2-1—2-28, 129E3, 130F1, C2, 154C1, F1, B3, D3, 155G3-156A1
Emergency gas act signed 2-2, 76B2
4 states get disaster aid, 5 emergency status 2-5; record lows rptd 2-6, 91A2
Layoff rpts issued 2-7, 91E2
Ohio asks disaster status 2-8, 92C1
US gas crisis eases 2-13—2-19, record winter rptd 2-16, 152D2
Feb econ data rptd 2-16—3-17, 176E1, C2, E2, 184A2, 194B1, D1
Cloud-seeding rptd in Colo 2-21, Washn 2-28, 153C1
AAAS conv opens 2-21, St Louis METROMEX study rptd 2-23, 183C2, 184B1
Berlin aids US victims 3-2, 152E3
US cold wave eases OPEC price war 3-2, 3-24, 227G2, C3
Columbus (O) schls reopen 3-7, 196G2-A3
Wkly US oil imports rptd 3-9, 196E2
'76 energy use rptd up 3-13, 196A2
Linked to US food price rise 3-18, 215A1
Mar jobless rate rptd 4-1, 252D1
1st ¼ profits drop rptd 4-28, 668C3
Coal use impact studied 4-30, 5-31, 499C1
Low ozone concentratns linked 5-6, 369B2
US Cong vs Sovt computer sale 6-5, 469A3; US bars sale 6-23, 501F3
UN desert conf 8-29—9-9, 770E1
US delays metric conversn 10-18, 820D3
Sun-earth study satellites launched 10-22, 908B3
Winter fuel shortage plan rptd 12-1, 942A3
US to probe grain blasts 12-28, 1023B2
WEATHER Service, National—*See U.S. GOVERNMENT—COMMERCE—National Oceanic & Atmospheric Administration*
WEATHER Underground (formerly Weathermen) (organization)
Rudd, other fugitives surrender 3-25—10-13, 839C1
Ex-FBI offcl indicted 4-7, 275G1-A2
Cuba '60, '70 aid rptd 10-9, 896A3
WEAVER, A. Vernon
Halts SBA minority aid program 7-8, 577A3
SBA lifts moratorium 11-4, 859G3
WEAVER, Earl
Orioles forfeit vital game 9-14, 748B3
Named AL top mgr 10-25, 927A2
Resigns, retracts 12-8, 990E1
WEAVER, Glen (Pete)
On Okla Girl Scout murders 6-13, 492E1

1978

WATSON, Ann Hemingway
To wed Symington 4-12, 420F2
WATSON, Arthur (deceased)
Widow to wed Symington 4-12, 420F2
WATSON Jr., Jack H.
Pledges aid to S Bronx 4-12, 285F1
WATSON, Tom
Wins Tucson Open 1-8, Crosby Pro-Am 1-23; 20th in Phoenix Open 1-16, 76A1, D1
2d in Masters 4-9, 355F2
Wins Byron Nelson Classic 5-7, 2d in Atlanta 5-28, 580D3, E3
2d in PGA Championship 8-6, wins HOF Classic 8-27, 672F2, G3
3d in World Series of Golf 10-1, 2d in Lancome Trophy tourn 10-22, 990C1, C2
PGA top money winner 10-31, 990B3
WATTOO, Main Yasin
PPP acting secy gen 10-4, arrested 10-12, 818C3
WATTS, Calif.—*See CALIFORNIA*
WATTS, Glenn E.
Assails Meany criticism of Carter 12-11, 960F3
WAVERLY, Tenn.—*See TENNESSEE*
WAXMAN, Rep. Henry A. (D, Calif.)
Reelected 11-7, 850G1
WAYNE, John
Undergoes open heart surgery 4-3, marks 71st birthday 5-26, 420B1
WBA (World Boxing Association)—*See BOXING*
WBAI-FM (N.Y.C. radio station)
FCC 'Filthy Words' ban upheld by Sup Ct 7-3, 551G2
WBC (World Boxing Council)—*See BOXING*
WCC—*See WORLD Council of Churches*
WCT (World Championship Tennis)—*See TENNIS*
WEAPONS—*See ARMAMENTS*
WE Are the Champions (recording)
On best-seller list 2-4, 116F3

WEATHER—*See also DROUGHT, STORMS*
Carter agri budget proposals 1-23, 48D1
Jan econ effects rptd 2-15, 2-17, 106C1, E1, A2, C2; 2-28, 3-3, 3-8, 221G2, 222G3, 223B1
Conrail aid sought 2-15, 224B3
USSR cancels grain order 2-28, 151F2
Feb econ effects rptd 3-9, 3-10, 3-16, 221G3, 222D3, E3
Fluorocarbon aerosols banned 3-15, 186A2
'78 food inflatn forecast revised 3-28, 219E2
Feb econ effects rptd 3-31, 4-6, 262A2, E2
Mar, 1st ¼ econ effects rptd 4-14, 4-19, 303A3, 304B1
Sun/weather link studied 5-11, 654C1
1st ¼ profits drop rptd 5-18, 403E1
Record 1st ¼ RR losses rptd 5-27, 433E3
Rain damage, food inflatn linked 5-30, 428C2
India, Iran hit by heat wave 6-7, 6-12, 479D3
Rail lines fined in freight-car shortage 6-15, 7-3, 569C2
Tex heat wave 7-20, 654F3

WEATHERMEN—*See WEATHER Underground*
WEATHER Service, National—*See U.S. GOVERNMENT—COMMERCE—National Oceanic & Atmospheric Administration*
WEATHER Underground (formerly Weathermen) (organization)
3 FBI ex-offcls indicted, actn vs La Prade to start, '77 indictmt dropped 4-10, 261G3-262C1
LaPrade chrgs pol influence 4-13, 285C1
LaPrade fired 7-6, 507A3
3 FBI ex-offcl's dismissal motn denied 11-30, 939F3
FBI penalizes 4 in break-ins 12-5, 939F2
WEAVER, A. Vernon
Details minority-aid abuses; rpts Carter briefing, Justice probe 11-21, 919A3, C3
WEAVER, Fritz
'Biko Inquest' opens 5-17, 760D1

1979

WATSON, Bob
Traded to Red Sox 6-14, 1002B3
Signs with Yankees 11-8, 1001F3
WATSON, David G.
Teeth 'n' Smiles opens 8-13, 712A3
WATSON Jr., Jack H.
Named truck strike task force head; on safety precautns 6-27, 479B3, 480A1
Energy mobilizatn bd studied 7-8, 518A1
WATSON, Richard
Sentence suspended 9-28, 774E2
WATSON Jr., Thomas J.
Named amb to USSR 7-20, confrmd 8-1; arrives Moscow 10-17, 794D3-795A1
WATSON, Tom
Ties for 2d in San Diego Open 1-28, Tucson Open 2-18, 220D3, E3
2d in Tourn Players 3-25, Masters 4-15; wins Heritage 4-1, Tourn of Champs 4-22, Byron Nelson 5-13, Meml Tourn 5-27, 587B1, A2-G2
Wins Hall of Fame Classic 8-26, 970B1
PGA top money winner 11-30, 969F2
WATT, Jim
KOs Pitalua for WBC lightwgt title 4-17, 412F3
WATTS, Glen E.
Backs Carter reelectn 7-30, 593D3
WAXMAN, Rep. Henry A. (D, Calif.)
Wins health subcom chair 1-30, 86C3
On Carter hosp cost plan 2-13, 110B1
At hosp cost bill ceremony 3-6, 163C2
Sponsors mental health bill 5-15, 365G1
WAYNE, John
Undergoes abdominal surgery 1-12, 78E3
Backs Canal treaty implementatn 6-7, 481C1
Dies 6-11, 508F3
Will filed 6-20, 527C3
Nixon cancer gift rptd 7-11, 527B3
Death tied to '53 A-test 8-4, 630B1
WAYNE, Pilar
Ex-husband's will filed 6-20, 527C3
WAYNE County, Mich.—*See MICHIGAN*
WBA (World Boxing Association)—*See BOXING*
WBC (World Boxing Council)—*See BOXING*
WCT (World Championship Tennis)—*See TENNIS*
WEAPONS—*See ARMAMENTS*
WE Are Family (recording)
On best-seller list 5-30, 448E3; 7-4, 548E3

WEATHER
Australia heat wave 1-10, 18E2
Carter budgets research 1-22, 46A3
Jan CPI rise rptd 2-23, 151B2
Jan credit, weather linked 3-9, 183A1
Mar housing starts linked 4-17, 281B1
1st ¼ GNP linked 4-19, 280C2

WEATHERMAN, Dave
Cal State wins NGAA baseball title 6-8, 569B2
WEATHER Underground (formerly Weathermen) (organization)
FBI supervisor demoted 1-26, 92F2
WEAVER, Earl
In World Series 10-10—10-17, 816A2
Wins mgr awards 10-17, 10-19, 956A1
WEAVER, Fritz
The Price opens 4-19, 712B2

1980

WATSON, Bob
AL batting ldr 10-6, 926E3
WATSON, Doc
Wins Grammy 2-27, 296D3
WATSON, Gerald R.
Charged in GSA scandal 1-15, 112F1
WATSON Jr., Jack H.
Named Carter staff chief 6-11, 438G3
WATSON, Merle
Wins Grammy 2-27, 296D3
WATSON, Judge Nancy B.
Sentences 'alphabet bomber' 11-24, 927D2
WATSON Jr., Thomas J.
Recalled from Sovt post 1-2, 1C2
Independnc Day broadcast barred 7-4, 566B3
In Sovt talks with Percy 11-26—11-28, 915D1
Percy support of Palestine state rptd 12-5, 931C1
WATSON, Tom
Wins San Diego Open 1-27, LA 2-24, Tourn of Champs 4-20, Greater New Orleans 4-27, Byron Nelson 5-11; 4th in Colonial Natl 5-18, 412C2-413A1
'80 earnings at $246,525 4-27, 412E3
2d in Memorial Tourn 5-25, 714G3
3d in US Open 6-15, 714F2
Wins Brit Open 7-20, 714G2
Wins World Series of Golf 8-24, 971F3-972A1
PGA top money winner 10-12, 971E3
Named PGA top golfer 10-18, 971B3
WATT, James G.
Named Interior secy; reactn 12-22, 979G2, F3
WATT, Jim
TKOs Nash 3-15, 320B3
Decisns Davis 6-8, 1000F3
WATTS, George
Dies 3-29, 280E2
WAXMAN, Rep. Henry A. (D, Calif.)
Reelected 11-4, 842G1
WAYNE—*See MICHIGAN*
WAYNE County—*See MICHIGAN*
WAZAN, Shafiq al-(Lebanese premier)
Named Leb premr 10-22, forms Cabt 10-25, 874A1
WBA (World Boxing Association)—*See BOXING*
WBC (World Boxing Council)—*See BOXING*
WBL (Women's Basketball League)—*See BASKETBALL*
WBOL (Oberlin, Ohio radio station)
DJ fired, '79-80 'captivity' cited 2-6, 199D3
WCT (World Championship Tennis)—*See TENNIS*
WEATHER
Acid rain perils, definitn rptd 145F2, A3
Mt St Helens eruptn impact seen unlikely 5-22, 382E2
Acid rain cited re Cleveland utility air rule 6-17, 494D3, F3
Canada scores US acid rain policy 6-23, 486F2
Midwest, South hit by heat wave, death toll rptd 6-23—8-15; Carter declares disaster 7-16, 616C1-D2
US, Canada sign acid rain pact 8-5, 603E1
Midwest, South heat wave death toll final rpt 9-7, 857G1-B3
Acid rain rptd centuries old 9-18, 716E2

WEATHER Report (instrumental group)
Win Grammy 2-27, 296E3
WEATHER Underground (formerly Weathermen)
'70 bombing fugitive surrenders 7-8, 576A3
'70 bomber sentncd 10-28; '69 fugitive surrenders 12-3, 928A1, D1
2 FBI ex-offcls convicted 11-6, 884A2, E2
WEAVER, Earl
NL wins All-Star Game 7-8, 636D2

1976

WEAVER, Rep. James (D, Ore.)
Reelected 11-2, 830D3
WEBER, Ron
Rues wire re Carter church bias 11-2, 827A1
WEBER State College (Ogden, Nev.)
Hughes will forgery chrgd 12-13, 971C2
WEBSTER, Edward
Acquitted 12-2, 927A2
WEBSTER, Ronald
Party wins Anguilla electn 3-15, 270C3
WEBSTER, William
Wins Social Sec bias suit 5-12, 413D3
WEDDELL, James
Held in Indian shooting 5-5, 384E2
WEDIN, Donald H.
Sentenced 11-30, 921A3
WEECH, Patrick
Arrested 7-29, 592C1
WEED, Stephen
Testifies re Hearst kidnap 9-27, 735F2
WEEKS, Rev. James M.
Argentina arrests 8-3, expels 8-19, 672C1
Argentina calls 'subversive' 10-6, 996F2
WEGGARTEN, Rev. Possenti
Killed 12-5, 1009D2
WEGGEMAN, Peter J.
Indicted 10-29, 886C3
WEHLING, Heinz-Helmut
Wins Olympic medal 7-24, 576A3
WEHLING, Ulrich
Wins Olympic medal 2-9, 159E1
WEHNER, Herbert
2 generals dismissed 11-1, 930E3
WEIBEL, Jose
Arrested 3-29, 310A3
WEICKER Jr., Sen. Lowell P. (R, Conn.)
Rptd Ford vp prospect 8-10, 584D1
Cited in Dole biog sketch 614C3
Unopposed in primary 9-7, 687D3
Reelected 11-2, 820D1, F3, 825F2, 828C1
WEIDNER, Judge Emory
Drops UMW strike chrgs 8-16, 669F3
WEIGHT Lifting
Olympic results 7-18—7-27, 576D2
Olympics disqualify 2 7-30, 563B2
WEIGLE, Rev. Luther A.
Dies 9-2, 1015B3
WEIKERS, Walter
Arrested 11-30, 922G2
Indicted 12-28, 1016G2
WEIKUM, Edward W.
Indicted 10-29, 886D3
WEI Kuo-ching
Listed in China ldrshp 9-10, 712B1
WEIL, Simone
Named French health min 8-27, 650G3
WEILAND, Dr. Andrew
On bone cancer operatn 5-3, 384D2
WEILER Brush Co.
Boycott rpt released 10-18, 786A1
WEINBERG, Wendy
Wins Olympic medal 7-25, 575C3
WEINBERGER, Casper
'75 study group on SSI cited 1-27, 128G2
WEINGARTEN, Violet
Dies 7-17, 716G3
WEINGLASS, Leonard
Questions Hearst at hearing 5-28, 423B2
Harrises convicted 8-9, 595G3, 596F1
Scores Harris sentences 8-31, 679C3
WEINHOLD, Werner
Acquitted 12-3, 931F1-B2
WEINSTEIN, Allen
Article on Hiss rptd 3-18, 217E3
WEINSTEIN, Judge Jack B.
Sentences Hollander 5-4, 384D3
Stays Atlantic offshore lease sale 8-13, overturned 8-16, 648A3
WEINTRAUB, Sidney
Replaced as AID asst admin 4-1, 262D3
WEIRTON, W. Va.—*See WEST Virginia*
WEISBROD, Hubert
Denies Lockheed payoff role 2-10, 131A3
Dutch probe interviews end 3-5, 254A3
Cited in Bernhard probe rpt 8-26, 627G3
WEISKOPF, Tom
Runner-up in US Open Golf 6-20, 756B3
WEISS, Charles
Contacted PLO in Cyprus 759D3

1977

WEAVER, John C.
Replaced as U of Wis pres 3-11, 354A2
Rpts new pesticides developed 11-7, 945F1
WEBSTER, James
Named Australia sci min 12-19, 982A2
WEBSTER, Ronald
Loses confidence vote 2-1, replaced 2-2; backers riot 2-9, 190D2
WEDDINGTON, Sarah
Named Agri gen counsel 7-15, confrmd 8-4, 626F3
WEGENER, Federico—*See ROSCHMANN, Eduard*
WEGENER, Col. Ulrich
Anti-terrorist unit formed 11-4, 868E3
WEGGARTEN, Rev. Possenti
Killer escapes 1-9, 11G2
WEGGEMAN, Peter J.
Acquitted 11-23, 918A3
WEICK, Judge Paul
Overrules Battisti on Cleveland schl suit 11-21, 939A3
WEICKER Jr., Sen. Lowell P. (R, Conn.)
Vs Sen ethics code 4-1, 251D3, E3
Backs Panama Canal pacts 8-29, 679B1
WEIDENBACHER Jr., Dr. Richard L.
Declares Berkowitz insane 8-30, 848D3
WEIKUM, Edward W.
Acquitted 11-23, 918A3
WEI Kuo-ching
In Politburo 8-21, 645F2
Heads forces pol dept 9-25, 743D3
WEIL, Frank
Warns re paymts, trade deficits 6-21, 502B1
WEILL, Sanford I.
On Dean Witter-Reynolds merger 10-3, 799F3
WEINSTEIN, Judge Jack B.
Backs CIA mail surveillnc damages 5-12, 423B1
OKs E Coast offshore drilling 8-25, 650A1
WEISCHENBERG, Carl Lutz
Arrested by FBI 7-20, 576B3
WEISGAL, Meyer W.
Dies 9-29, 788A3
WEISKOPF, Tom
Wins Kemper Open 6-5, 676E1
3d in US Open 6-19, 659C3
3d in Westchester Classic 8-21, 675G3
2d in World Series of Golf 9-5, 950B3
PGA top money winner 10-30, 950G3
WEISS, Abraham
Replaced as Labor asst secy 3-18, 211F1 ★

1978

WEAVER, Herman
NFL '77 punting ldr 1-1, 56B3
WEAVER, Rep. James (D, Ore.)
Reelected 11-7, 852B1
WEBB, Brenda
Sets indoor 2-mi run mark 2-24, 600E3
WEBB, Kenneth
Gay Divorce opens 3-9, 760C2
WEBER, Brian F.
Reverse job-bias case accepted by Sup Ct 12-11, 980A3
WEBER, Carl
Scenes From Country Life opens 3-13, 887A3
WEBER, Judge Gerald
Fines Gulf in cartel case 6-2, 449G2-A3
WEBSTER, Donald E.
Named in Pallottine indictmt, suicide rptd 1-6, 24C3
WEBSTER, James
A-test monitoring statn declassified 3-1, 145A2
Australia environmt min 11-30, 943G3
WEBSTER, Marvin
Declared free agent 7-31, 656F1
Signed by Knicks 8-28; Seattle compensatn ordrd 10-29, 1027B3
WEBSTER, Randall (d. 1977)
4 Tex ex-cops chrgd in cover-up 6-3, 991F2
WEBSTER, William H.
Named FBI dir 1-19, 32C1; confrmd 2-9, 82G3
Vs FCC cable-TV access rules 2-24, 195E2, B3
Bell asks disciplinary probes of 68 agents 4-10, 262B1
FBI admits press informants 7-13, 554D1
Calls CIA ex-offcl's death suicide 10-26, 835G3
Urges FBI disclosure delay 11-8, 877F3-878A1
Penalizes 4 in FBI break-ins 12-5, 939F2
WECHT, Dr. Cyril H.
Disputes com findings re JFK assassinatn 9-7, 698E1
WEDDING, A (film)
Released 9-29, 970D3
On top-grossing list 11-1, 888E1
WEDDINGTON, Sarah
Named pres asst 8-31, 681C3
WEDEKIND, Frank
Lulu opens 2-17, 760D2
Spring Awakening opens 7-13, 887B3
WEDGEWORTH, Ann
Wins Tony 6-4, 579A3
WEDMAN, Scott
NBA free-throw ldr 4-9, 271F2
WEEKS, Alan
Broadway Musical opens 12-21, 1031B1
WEESE, Norris
Cowboys win Super Bowl 1-15, 39D3
WEHNER, Herbert
Nazi prosecutn limit rptd opposed 10-28, 872C2
WEICKER Jr., Sen. Lowell P(almer) (R, Conn.)
Votes for Panama Canal neutrality pact 3-16, 177F2
Quits Ethics Com over Korea probe 4-14, 279E3
Votes for 2d Canal pact 4-18, 273B1
Vs FTC children's TV ad curbs 4-26, 347F2
Uganda trade ban passed 7-28, 616E2
Father dies 11-25, 972G3
WEICKER Sr., Lowell Palmer
Dies 11-25, 972G3
WEIGEL, Judge Stanley A.
Issues postal-strike order 7-23, 564G3
WEIGHT Watchers International Inc.
Heinz purchase agreed; Pillsbury bid, '77 profit cited 5-4, 364D2
WEIL, Frank
US trade missn to Japan arrives 10-2; urges Japan policy chng 10-3, 10-5, rpts on missn 10-15, 797D3-798B1
WEILL, Claudia
Girlfriends released 8-16, 970D1
WEILL, Gus
November People opens 1-14, 760A3
WEINBERG, Steven
Unified field theory confirmatn rptd 6-12, 7-8, 654A2
WEINDLING, Dr. Howard K.
Rpts diabetes misdiagnoses 8-29, 947E3
WEINHOLD, Gunter
Rptd arrested 1-9, 36B2
WEINSTEIN, Judge Jack B.
Unseals Torrijos drug indictmt 2-21, 120F2
Rules vs schl bd pact with HEW 3-7, 264F1
CIA mail-opening damages upheld 11-9, 940C1
WEINTRAUB, Jerry
'Sept 30 1955' released 3-31, 619E3
WEIR, Peter
Last Wave released 12-18, 1030B30
WEISKOPF, Bob
Wins Emmy 9-17, 1030F1
WEISKOPF, Tom
Wins Doral Open 3-12, 355E3
Ties for 3d in US Open 6-18, 580B2
WEISS, leslie
Loses deprogramming suit 12-29, 1012A2
WEISS, Mark
Assesses JFK death shots 12-29, 1002F1, A2

1979

WEAVER, Mike (Hercules)
Holmes KOs 6-22, 838B3
WEAVER, Signourney
Alien released 5-24, 528A1
WEAVER, W. Timothy
Rpts test scores of future teachers drop 10-4, 810B2
WEBBER, Andrew Lloyd
Evita opens 9-25, 956A3
WEBBER Jr., Burt
Treasure ship find rptd 1-1, 24E1
WEBER, Brian F.
Reverse job-bias case argued in Sup Ct 3-28, 262D3
Affirmative actn challenge rejctd by Sup Ct reactn; majority opinion excerpts 6-27, 477B1-478E1
WEBER, Sigurd
Sentncd as spy 2-15, 181B1
WEBER v. U.S.
Case argued in Sup Ct 3-28, 262C3
Case decided by Sup Ct 6-27, 477B1
WEBSTER, James
Dismissed from Cabt, named high comr to NZ 12-8, 948E1
WEBSTER, Marvin
'78 compensatn set 9-18, voided 9-19 1003B2
WEBSTER, William H.
Cites danger of Chinese spies 1-7, 17G2
Rescinds Beckwith dismissal, orders demotn 1-26, 92F2
Rpts FBI informant loss, scores disclosures 3-22, 232C3
Says terrorist 'backpack' A-bomb possible 4-25, 327D2
Truckers warned vs violence 6-21, 479D3
FBI files preservatn sought by activists 6-26, 520G3
Rpts FBI drops personnel rules 7-22, 561E3
Backs FBI charter 7-31, 599A3
Names 3 aides in reorganizatn 8-8, 611B1
FBI audit shows compliance with informant rules 8-22, 747F2
Admits FBI '70 Seberg slander 9-14, 705E1
Sets '70 Black Panther murder case probe 9-24, 886E2
On FBI theft ring 10-16, 787C3
WEDDINGTON, Sarah
Named senior pres aide 8-10, 608E2
WEDEKIND, Frank
Marquis of Keith opens 3-13, 712D1
WEDEMEYER, Gen. Albert C. (ret.)
Warns Carter of Sovt challenge 1-12, 15B1
WEEMS, Dr. George
Sees 'foul play' in Paisley death 6-27, 520C2
WEGERLE, Steve
Whitecaps win NASL title 9-8, 775A3
WEHNER, Herbert
Backs statute of limitatns end for murder 1-29, 137E2
WEIANT, Ted
Miracle Worker opens 1-6, 292C2
WEIBRING, D. A.
Wins Quad Cities Open 7-22, 587E3
WEI Ching-chang
Arrest rptd 4-1, 259A2
Says pol prisoners tortured 5-6, 353E1
Sentenced 10-16, 789C2
Wall posters scored 11-3, 854C3
Denied appeal 11-6, 949F1
Sellers of trial transcript seized 11-11, 11-18, 949F1
WEICKER Jr., Sen. Lowell Palmer (R, Conn.)
Enters pres race 3-12, 185A3
Quits pres field 5-16, 363F3
Financial disclosure delay rptd 5-18, 383F2
Vs arms hike link to SALT 8-3, 591D1
WEIGAND, Richard
Sentenced 12-6—12-7, 1000D1
WEIGHELL, Sid
Scores proposed rail cuts 6-26, 486E1
WEILL, Sanford I.
Shearson, Loeb Rhoades to merge 5-14, 366C3
WEINBERG, Steven
Wins Nobel Prize 10-16, 858C1
WEINHOLD, Gunter
Prisoner exchange rptd 7-20, 586E2
WEINTRAUB, Fred
Promise released 3-7, 528D3
WEINTRAUB Gallery (N.Y., N.Y.)
Vandals smash outdoor sculpture 5-6, 375C1
WEIR, M. Brock
On Cleveland default 7-17, 579C3
WEIR, Peter
Picnic At Hanging Rock released 2-22, 174D3
WEISENBORN, Christian
I Am My Film released 4-19, 528F2
WEISKOPF, Tom
2d in Southern Open 10-14, 970G1
WEISS, Edward S.
A-test cancer link rptd ignored by US 1-8, 17C2
WEISS, Mark R.
JFK acoustics testimony reaffirmed 3-16, 205A1

1980

WEAVER, Rep. James (D, Ore.)
Joins open-conv move 7-28, 570A2
Reelected 11-4, 844B1, 852F2
WEAVER, Mike (Hercules)
KOs Tate for WBA heavywgt title 3-31, 320C1
KOs Coetzee, win spurs S Africa riots 10-25, 887E3, 1000E3
WEAVER, Robert C.
Heads new housing panel 10-8, 763B2
WEAVER, Sigourney
Lusitania Songspiel opens 1-10, 136A3
WEBB Corp., Del E.
Harrah's gets temp NJ gambling license, ties rptd severed 11-1, 988D3
WEBBER, Andrew Lloyd
Wins Tony 6-8, 692A3
WEBER, Brian F.
Govt minority constructn grants upheld by Sup Ct 7-2, 510B1
WEBER, Ed
Elected to US House 11-4, 843E4, 851D2
WEBER, Vin
Elected to US House 11-4, 843B2, 851E1
WEBSTER, James
On grain trading halt 1-6, 2C1
WEBSTER, R. Howard
Newsco bids for FP Publicatns 1-9, 1-11, Thomson wins 1-11, 38A2
WEBSTER, Ronald (Anguillan prime minister)
Elected Anguillan prime min 5-28, 469E1
WEBSTER, William H.
On V Jordan shooting 5-29, 401E2
WEDDINGTON, Sarah
Leads US UN women's conf delegatn 7-14—7-30, 587A3
WEHLING, Ulrich
Wins Olympic medal 2-19, 155B3
WEIBRING, D. A.
2d in San Diego Open 1-27, 412C2
WEICKER Jr., Sen. Lowell Palmer (R, Conn.)
Votes vs GOP tax-cut plan 6-26, 480G2
Backs Synfuels Corp bd appointments 9-25, 725A3
Leads antibusing rider oppositn 11-20—12-10, 953F3, 954D1
WEIGAND, Elizabeth
Convicted in extortn scheme 10-24, 890C1
WEIGEL, Judge Stanley
Sentences Tham 5-23, 482G2
WEIGHTLIFTING
Soviets dominate Moscow Olympics 7-20—7-30, 588F2, 624D2
WEINBERG, Irving
Sells British Guiana stamp for record sum 4-5, 472E2
WEINBERG, Melvin
Said FBI Abscam informant 5-27, 5-28, 402G2
Rep Myers, co-defendants convicted in Abscam trial 8-31, 684D2
WEINBERGER, Caspar W.
On planned '81 budget 11-13, 866D2
Urges 'severe' budget cuts 11-23, 897F1-E2
Named Defense secy 12-11, 935A1
WEINBERGER, Robert
Loses cong election 1-22, 50E3
WEINFELD, Andre
Marries Racquel Welch 7-5, 639B1
WEINGLASS, Leonard
At anti-US conf in Iran 6-2—6-5, 418D2, 419D1
WEINSTEIN, Hannah
Stir Crazy released 12-12, 1003D2
WEINTRAUB, Jerry
Cruising released 2-15, 216D2
WEINTRAUB Gallery (N.Y. N.Y.)
Poncet sculpture smashed again 3-24, 472D3
WEIR, Jim
USSR expels 1-29, 119E1
WEIR, Robert Stanley (deceased)
O Canada proclaimed natl anthem 7-1, 496G3
WEISER, Stanley
Coast to Coast released 10-3, 836D2
WEISNER, Dr. Paul
On La gonorrhea epidemic 4-9, 584F3
WEISS, Robert K.
Blues Brothers released 6-20, 675A2

1976

WEISS, Theodore S.
Elected 11-2, 821F2, 830B2
WEISS, Dr. Noel S.
Cancer-estrogen links rptd 6-3, 460F3
WELBORN, Jack
GOP conv vp vote table 8-19, 599F3
WELCH Jr., John F.
PCB pact signed with NYS 9-8, 691B3
WELCH, John J.
Loses Vt Sen primary 9-14, 705A2
WELCH, Richard (d. 1975)
Sen com cites death 4-26, 304E1
Greece ends death probe 5-21, 402D2
Killers linked to Mallios 12-18, 1004C2
WELENSKY, Roy
On Rhodesia solutn 9-19, 698A2

WELFARE
Shift from unemploymt paymts rptd 1-7, 128G2
Ford State of Union message 1-19, 38G1-A2, 39B3
HEW funds misuse chrgd 1-20, 1-27, 128A1, C2
'77 budget proposals 1-21, 65F1
HEW funds veto overridden 1-27, 1-28, 69A2
Rockefeller for federalizatn 2-24, 149G3
Cong clears added funds 5-19, 411D3
Sen OKs state, local soc security number use 8-6, 586A2; Cong clears 9-16, 706G1
Sen OKs pub svc jobs bill 9-22, 728B1
'77 HEW funds veto overridden 9-30, 727A3, B3
No reform legis cleared in '76 10-2, 884B2
Fathers must seek jobless benefits 1st 10-20, 788A2
Presidential Election (& Transition)
Reagan for state operatn 1-12, 22E1
Reagan concedes budget plan flaw 1-16, 41E1
Shapp hits Ford plan 1-20, 40B3

1977

WEISS, Ted
Asks FBI probe inquiry 12-8, scores Bell 12-9, 979F3
WEISSCREDIT Commercial and Investment Bank (Lugano, Switzerland)
Ordered closed 3-2, 489D3
WEISSMAN, Marvin
Named amb to CR 5-19, confrmd 5-25, 500D1

WEIZMAN, Ezer
Israel defense min 6-20, 474D2
Leb Christns ask mil aid 7-7, 571B2
On rights for W Bank, Gaza Arabs 8-15, 623A2
Bars Leb truce talks 10-13, sees US envoy 10-14, 793F2
Warns PLO vs shelling 11-7, 849C2
Sadat rpts Sinai clash averted 11-26, 909D1
Meets Egypt defense min, Sadat 12-20—12-21, 993G1
Heads defense com for Egypt talks 12-26, 993D1

WEIZMANN, Chaim (1874-1952)
Meyer Weisgal dies 9-29, 788A3
Cited in Begin Knesset speech 11-20, 894C1
WEIZMANN Institute of Science (Israel)
Meyer Weisgal dies 9-29, 788A3
WEKSELMAN, Judge I. Martin
Rpts Westinghouse, 3 utilities settle 3-3, 177C2
WELDON, Kenny
Chrgs tourn irregularity 3-24, 828D1

WELFARE and Poverty—*See also U.S. GOVERNMENT—HEALTH, Education & Welfare; also specific programs (e.g., FOOD—Food Stamp Program, MEDICINE—Medicaid)*
Ford asks tax chngs 1-4, 5F2
CBO issues poverty rpt 1-13, 80A3
Ford '78 budget proposal 1-17, 32A1-G1, A3, 33C3
Carter inaugural 1-20, 26B1, 27E1
Carter statemt to world 1-20, 26A3
Viet pardon bias chrgd 1-21, 51F2
Fed, state costs rptd 2-19, 176B1
Carter budget revisns 2-22, 124C3, 125A2
HEW reorganized 3-9, 175D3
Giaimo proposes budget 3-23, 229A1
Poverty level raised 4-1, 302A2
Immunization drive set 4-6, 287B3
NE-Midwest House group examines reform 423D3
HEW study issued 4-15, 302C1
GOPs score Carter energy taxes 4-25, 320F3
Fscl '78, '79 aid hike clears Cong 5-16, 382E1; Carter signs 5-23, 417F3
Cong sets '78 target 5-17, 405B1

1978

WEISS, Rep. Theodore S. (D, N.Y.)
Reelected 11-7, 851F3

WEIZMAN, Ezer
In Egypt mil talks 1-11—1-12, 10C1
Meets Sadat 1-11, 10D1
Ends Egypt mil talks, rpts Israeli Sinai plan understanding 1-13, 26F1
Halts new Sinai setlmts 1-31, 98G1
To visit US 2-15, 97A2
Setlmt policy retained 2-26, 138D3
Bars Sinai setlmt 3-1, 157E1
Bars W Bank setlmts 3-5, to quit if disobeyed 3-6, 3-7, 157D1
In US for talks 3-7, 157E1; sees US defns secy, seeks arms 3-8; meets Carter 3-10, 176E3
On Israel invasn of Leb 3-15, 173B2
US welcomes Leb pullout vow 3-15, 174B3
Says Leb villages asked Israeli invaders in 3-19, 198A2
On decisn vs Tyre capture 3-20, 198A1
In UN talks on Leb peace force, refugees 3-21, 3-22, 197E2
Issues Leb truce order 3-21, 198A1
Asks coalitn govt, Begin comments 3-24, 214C2, D3
Hints end to Leb truce 3-27, 213F1
Cairo missn announced 3-29; meets Sadat, seeks new talks 3-30—3-31; rpts to Cabt 3-31, 4-2, 235F2
W Bank settlmt work renewed 4-17, 275E1
Says Israel cluster bomb use in Leb mistake 4-20, 300G1
Penalizes W Bank officers 5-2, 340B2
Backs Eitan policy statmt 5-14, 359C1
Plans W Bank setlmt expansn 5-17, 400D2
Denies Arab land takeover plan 5-23, 400F2
Sadat cites separate peace plan rejectn 6-7, 461G2
Vs Cabt stand on W Bank, Gaza 6-18, 461D1
In Begin, Dayan policy feud, denies plan to quit 6-23, Cabt discusses feud 6-25, 489E1
Told to keep Egypt contacts 6-25, 489C1
Warns Syria vs Leb Christn attacks 7-6, 503B1
Meets Sadat, Gamasy in Austria; gets new peace plan 7-13; Cabt vs mtg 7-16, 546A2, D2
Sadat asked for El Arish, Mt Sinai return 7-23, 563E1
Jets raid PLO base in Leb 8-3, 583C1
Tells US aide of Leb crisis 8-30, 674D2
Christns OK Unifil deploymt 8-30, 713E1
In Camp David summit talks 9-6—9-7, 673C1, E1
US vows to help Israel build 2 air bases 9-28, 9-29, 746F1
Meets Carter in Egypt pact talks, recalled for consultatn 10-21, 802A3
Recalled to Jerusalem 11-2; briefs Cabt on Egypt talks 11-5—11-6; returns to DC 11-7, 858B3
Meets Vance, says Israel vs Egypt pact-W Bank linkage 11-8, 858B3
Israel halts Sinai mil gear pullout 12-20, 979C1
WELCH, Bob
Dodgers win NL pennant 10-7, 779A1
In World Series 10-10—10-17, 799E3
WELCH, Leo D.
Killed in auto crash 10-22, 888G3
WELCH, Richard (d. 1975)
CIA effort to blame Counterspy for death chrgd 1-4, 14C3
WELD, Tuesday
Who'll Stop Rain released 8-25, 1030G3

WELFARE and Poverty—*See also U.S. GOVERNMENT—HEALTH, Education & Welfare; also specific programs (e.g., FOOD—Food Stamp Program, MEDICINE—Medicaid)*
Carter State of Union Message 1-19, 30G1, F2, B3, 31B1, 32A1, B1
Carter budget proposals, reform deferred 1-23, 44C3, 46F1, F2, C3, 47A1, D1, 48C1, D2
CETA changes asked by Carter 2-22, 124F1
Unificatn Church '77 solicitatns bar cited 2-22, 295B3
PR benefits exclusn upheld by Sup Ct 2-27, 143A1
Expedited SSI benefits rule review declined 2-27, 143E1
New CPIs described 222D2
Carter urges educ aid plan 2-28, 141C3
Heating aid funds signed 3-7, 160F2
Rural MD shortage rptd 4-6—4-7, 577D3
Blacks stress reform effort as voting issue 4-10, 568F2
Black poverty data rptd by Carnegie Corp 4-10, 811F1

1979

WEISSCREDIT Commercial and Investment Bank (Lugano, Switzerland) (defunct)
4 offcls convicted 3-1, 155F2
WEIS Securities Inc.
Customer suits vs accountants curbed by Sup Ct 6-18, 499C1

WEIZMAN, Ezer
Threatns retaliatn vs Leb civilns 1-23, 50F3
Meets US defense secy 2-13, 143F2
Backs Begin talks with Carter, Khalil 2-27, 142A3
Asks US to speed arms 3-17, 198C2
In Egypt, US mil talks on Sinai pullout 3-18—3-19, 198F1
Briefs Haddad on Leb troop deploymt 4-17, 277F3
In Cairo talks on Sinai exit 4-25—4-27, 320D1
Vs Begin Palestinian autonomy plan, quits delegatn 5-17; rejoins 5-21, 394E2, A3
Says W Bank, Gaza 'parts of Israel' 5-31, 415D2
Votes vs Nablus setlmt plan 6-3, signs requisitn order 6-4, 415F1, G1
Reaffirms Elon Moreh setlmt 6-10, 436E2
Quits negotiating team 6-17, Cabt OKs 6-24, 474C3
On Arab murders 7-4, 496F2
Seeks US mil aid rise re Arab threat 9-12, sees US defns secy 9-13—9-14, 693B2
Assures US reps on US arms use vs Leb 9-17, 694B1
Disputes US aide on Leb bombing 9-18, 693E2
Nablus mayor expulsn demanded, ct delays ouster 11-8, 881G2, A3
Shaka freed 12-5, 916B3

WELDON, John
Wins Oscar 4-9, 336B2
WELFARE (play)
Opens 5-10, 712D3

WELFARE & Poverty
Kennedy scores Carter budget 1-13, 70D1
Carter vs proposed balanced budget amendmt, on '80 budget plans 1-17, 29E2, F2
Black-white gap rptd 1-17, 35G1, C2
Carter budget proposals 1-22, 43G3-44F1, 45D2; table 42E2
Carter defends budget 1-26, 70A1
'Debit' insurnc scored by FTC staff 1-28, 91D2
Illegal alien issue detailed 1-29, 127F1
Compulsive gambling bill introduced 1-30, 152E1
Drug abuse costs rptd 2-12, 140C2
HUD rpts city revitalization impact 2-13, 132G2-C3
Foster care benefits backed by Sup Ct 2-22, 151B1
Right-to-counsel doctrine clarified 3-5, 185F1-D2
Weicker sees priority 3-12, 185C3
Ill overpaymts seizure curbed by Sup Ct 3-19, 203A3
Carter urges privacy bill 4-2, 264F3
US ups poverty levels 4-9, 283C3

1980

WEISS, Rep. Theodore S. (D, N.Y.)
Reelected 11-4, 843F3
WEISSMAN, Marvin
Presents credentials to Bolivia pres, warns mil vs coup 3-26, 272B2
Anti-coup role rptd 5-31, mil scores, asks ouster 6-5—6-9, 443C2
Recalled from Bolivia 7-17, in Chile 7-20, 546D3
WEISWEILER, Hennes
Suspends Neeskens 9-11, Cosmos win NASL title 9-21, 770A2
WEISZ, Stanley
Indicted in Abscam probe 7-15, 554A2
WEITZENHOFFER, Max
Harold & Maude opens 2-7, 136C3
WEIZMAN, Ezer
OKs Sinai, land route pacts with Egypt 1-24, 68B2
Vs Hebron setlmt vote 3-24, 218C3
Orders arrest of anti-Arab plotters 5-14, 362B3
Resigns 5-25; scores Begin rule, Begin assails 5-27, 429A3
Yadin named acting defense min 6-30, 498B3
Arens vs defense min post 9-1, 712D2
With Carter campaign 10-27, 816C3
Israel vs electn tour with Carter 10-28, 830D2
Votes no-confidence vs Begin govt 11-19, 880B2
Threatens to form new party 11-22, Herut Party ousts 11-23, 901F3

WELCH Jr., Bernard Charles (alias Norm Hamilton)
Chrgd in Halberstam slaying 12-6, linked to area thefts 12-7, 940A1
WELCH, Bob
Reveals alcoholism treatmt 3-4, 637F1
NL wins All-Star Game 7-8, 636D1
WELCH Jr., John F.
Named GE chrmn, chief exec 12-19, 986G2
WELCH, Racquel
Marries 7-5, 639B1
WELCH, Richard (d. 1975)
Greek police offcl slain 1-16, 150E3
WELD, Tuesday
Serial released 3-28, 416E3
WELFARE & Poverty
Fed heating aid given despite lodging 1-9, 54D2
State of State messages 1-9, 270D1; 1-10, 1-14, 483D1, E3
Carter asks youth training progrm 1-10, 16G1-F2
Carter asks revisns 1-21, 43F3
Carter budget proposals 1-28, 69D3, 72B2; table 70E1
Black Caucus scores Carter budget 2-5, 94F2
Job project gains rptd 2-27, 228E3
Carter anti-inflatn plan sets fed spending cuts 3-14, 201C1
Carter revised budget proposals 3-31, 244B1
Benefits denial hearing case declined by Sup Ct 4-14, 307F1
DC Christian rally held 4-29, 349A1
Amoco settles bias suit 4-29, 370C3
AFL-CIO vs Admin budget 5-6, 385G1
Mass prof indicted in fraud case 5-13, 414G3
Cuban refugees rptd ineligible 5-21, 380C1

1976

Wallace upset in Fla 3-9, 179G2
Carter vs 'instant' reform 6-3, 411D1
Dem com OKs platform 6-15, 432B3
Dem platform text 6-15, 469D2, E2, 471G2, 472A1, 473A2
Govs urge natl progrm, Carter backs 7-6, 492G2, E3
Mondale acceptance speech 7-15, 507F3, 511B2
Carter acceptance speech 7-15, 510D2, G2; record cited 512C2
Carter briefed 8-16, 617F1
Conv delegates' views rptd 8-17, 616F2
GOP platform text 8-18, 604D3, 606E1
Carter scores Ford priorities 8-30, 645B2
Carter: prefers work 9-6, 664C2; 9-13, 686D2
Carter, Ford debate 9-23, 701F1, 702E3
Carter theme in NYS 9-30, 742E3
Ford, Carter debate 10-22, 801D3
NE govs urge reform 11-14, 864F3
Carter reaffirms reform 11-15, 864A1
Carter, Califano warn on reform pace 12-28, 12-29, 978G1, B2

WELLFORD, Harrison
Carter transitn advisor 11-23, 881G2
WELLMANN, Paul
Wins Olympic medal 7-31, 576D1
WELLS, Melissa F.
Guinea-Bissau, Cape Verde amb 9-9; confrmd 9-15, 808D1
WELLS Fargo & Co.
Rptd on FRB 'problem' list 1-22, 111D3
Wells Fargo Bank (San Francisco)
Rptd on comptroller's problem list 1-26, 113D1
WELSH, Rev. Walter N.
Schiess sues central NY bishop 7-8, 756A1
WENDER, Win
Wins Cannes film award 5-28, 460G1
WENDT, Rev. William A.
Cheek rejcts compromise 4-4, forms separate unit 5-9, 755D3
WENZEL, Hanni
Wins Olympic medal 2-11, 158E3
WENZEL, Peter
Wins Olympic medal 7-22, 576E2
WERNER, Ludwig
Confesses Corsican murders 9-25, 773A1
WESLEYAN University (Middletown, Conn.)
Fred Millet dies 1-1, 56F3
WEST, Frank R.
Guilty 1-21, 78B3
WEST, Harry
Scores SDLP 2-2, 146B3
WEST, Dr. Louis J.
Hearst trial testimony planned 2-4, 114C1
Testifies for Hearst 2-23—2-25, 201G3-202B1
WEST Jr., Milton H.
Elected to Summa bd 8-4, 596D3
WEST End Horror, The (book)
On best-seller list 12-5, 972A3
WESTERLUND, Sevpo
Sworn Finnish defense min 9-29, 750D3
WESTERN Air Lines Inc.
Loses case on San Diego-Denver route 3-8, 219B2

1977

Burger notes '69-76 rulings 5-17, 419A3
Ill property attachmt case refused 5-31, 462A1
HEW jobless-benefits standards law upheld 6-20, 516D3-517A1
NAACP scores Carter 6-27—6-28, Bond scores 8-15, SCLC 8-18, Meany 8-30, 702A2
Abortn alternatives proposed 7-19, 786E3
Jordan scores Carter 7-24, Carter says 'no apologies' 7-25, 7-28, 573C1, F2
Black Caucas backs Jordan vs Carter 7-29, 592G3
Carter illegal alien plan 8-4, 592A1
Pa budget passed, fscl crisis eased 8-20, 666D1
'63-77 SAT score drop rptd 8-23, 739F1
Black ldrs score Carter 8-29, 702D1
Fscl '76 state spending rptd up 9-2, 740E1
NJ jobless benefits case review declined 10-3, 760F2
'75, '76 poor family total rptd 10-3, 822B1
Conn law re property sales upheld 10-17, 797F3
Energy tax credits, 'stamp' progrm clear Sen 10-31, 832A3-C3
Legal aid for poor extended 12-28, 1002C2

Carter Reform Plan
Califano forms study group 1-26, meets 2-11, 175F3-176B1
Carter proposes rebates 1-27, 52B1
Carter Admin plans revision 2-2, 75E1
Carter call-in topic 3-5, 171D1
Admin reforms planned 3-10, 193F3
Carter outlines goals 5-2, 337C3-338A1
Labor scores Carter spending lid 5-4, 364D3
McGovern scores Carter plan 5-13, 381D2
Carter plan outlined 5-25, spending lid affirmed 5-26; Califano, Marshall urge review 5-27, 445D2-E3
Carter Miss town mtg topic 7-21, 575F1
Carter proposes new system, summary 8-6, 608C2-609E1
Govs endorse plan 9-9, 719F1
Carter cites problem 10-27, 813A3-E3
Transfer Payments—*See INCOMES*

WELLAND Canal
Carter-Trudeau toll talks 2-21—2-23, 132C3
WELLS, Sgt. Robert E.
Killed 7-13, body returned 7-16, 552F2, F3
WELLS Fargo Armored Service Corp.—*See under BAKER Industries*
WELLS Fargo Bank—*See WELLS Fargo & Co.*
WELLS Fargo & Co.
Buys Bank of Calif branches 7-6, 578E1
SF bank hikes prime 10-4, 798E2
WEN Shen-ho
Seized for Hangchow unrest 4-11, 282C2
WERNICK, Richard
Wins Pulitzer Prize 4-18, 355E2
WERTZ, Larry D.
Arrested 7-26, 627G3
WESLEY, Cynthia (d. 1963)
'63 bomber convicted 11-18, 907B3
WESSIN y Wessin, Gen. Elias (ret.)
Sets DR pres bid 9-30; Balaguer, mil chiefs vs return 10-2, 786E1
WEST, Frank R.
Sup Ct declines convictn review 4-4, 341G3
WEST, Harry
Rpts Callaghan vs Unionist devolutn plan 10-8—10-9, 783E3
WEST, John C.
Named amb to Saudi 5-24, confrmd 6-7, 500D1
WEST, Red
Presley book sets order mark 8-20, 696E1
WEST, Sandra Ilene
Dies 3-10, buried 5-19, 532D2
WEST Jr., Sol
Sister-in-law buried 5-19, 532D2
WEST, Sonny
Presley book sets order mark 8-20, 696E1
WEST Bank—*See MIDDLE EAST, subheads ARAB-Israeli Developments—Israel Occupation and EGYPT-Israel Peace Moves*
WESTCHESTER County, N.Y.—*See NEW York State*
WESTCOAST Transmission Co.
FPC splits on Alaska pipe route 5-2, 369C3
WESTERN Airlines
Airbus cancellatn spurs French boycott 2-4, 441G2

1978

Poverty level revised upward 4-19, '77 data rptd 8-12, 684D2
Carter scores attys 5-4, 320G2, D3
2 chrgd in welfare fraud 5-8, 7-25; NY crackdown rptd successful 7-3, 684F3
Cong '79 budget target res cleared 5-17, 385F2
Guaranteed income study rptd 5-19, 720G3
Female poverty data rptd 6-4, 554D3
State emergency standards backed by Sup Ct 6-6, 447D2
Reform compromise OKd by Admin, House ldrs 6-7, 446E1
State claims setlmt signed 6-12, 465F3
NYS eligibility case refused by Sup Ct 6-12, 468C1
Propositn 13 deplored 6-28, 526C1
Welfare waste limits proposed 7-10; SSI, AFDC paymt errors rptd 8-12, 684G2
Indians protest in DC, '68 'Poor Peoples Campaign' cited 7-15—7-23, 568F3
HEW vows 'runaway' father crackdown, '77 data cited 7-19, 685A1
HEW asks welfare loopholes closed 7-20, 684E3
Job tax credit OKd by House com 7-27, 587E1
Ky leads Calif refugee protest 8-2, 844E2
ABA legal aid plan rejctd 8-7, 626B2
Brown cites US commitmt 8-28, 681E3
SSI seeks '74-76 overpaymt restitutn 8-29, 684D3
World Bank poverty, income table 732A1
Jobs tax credit clears 10-15, 785D3
Admin priorities shift 11-14, 875F1
Carter cites US commitmt 11-27, 914C3
'75-77 migratn reversal rptd 12-3, 943A1
Kennedy vs Carter budget plans 12-9, 956G1
Anti-fraud drive launched 12-13, 984G2
Immigrant deportatn proposed 12-20, 1010D2
Calif woman sentncd for fraud 12-28, 1029C1
Transfer Payments—*See INCOMES*

WELLS, Jeff
2d in Boston Marathon 4-17, 692A3
WELLS Fargo Armored Service Corp.—*See under BAKER Industries Inc.*
WELLS Fargo Bank—*See WELLS Fargo & Co.*
WELLS Fargo & Co.
SF bank bars Peru loan refinancing 3-10, 353F1, B2
Chile bank loans rptd undercutting US rights policy 4-11, Reuss scores 4-12, 312G1
WENDY'S International Inc.
Earthworm rumor impact rptd 11-16, 942A2
WENGENROTH, Stow
Dies 1-22, 96G3
WENTZEL, Andreas
Wins world skiing title 2-5, 316G2
WERBLIN, David A. (Sonny)
Heads Madison Sq Garden Corp 1-1, 95F3
WERTHEIMER, Fred
On Cong electn funds rejectn 7-19, 550C3
Warns vs 'PAC democracy' 9-7, 753F2
Praises govt ethics bill 10-26, 832G1
Scores House ethics rule chng 12-6, 958E2
WERTZ, Larry D.
Convicted 5-11, 380A2
WESH-TV (Daytona Beach, Fla. TV station)
License renewal voided, ct sets guidelines 9-25, 907D3
WESLEY, Richard
Mighty Gents opens 4-16, 760E2
WESNER, Jennifer Lee
Loses primary for Pa gov 5-16, 389B3
WESSIN y Wessin, Gen. Elias (ret.)
Drops pres bid, backs Lora 3-3, 292D2
WEST, Harry
Interparty talks collapse 1-9, 18B2
Asks Protestant vigilante action 1-12, 71G2
Vs Fiaich call for end to UK Ulster rule 1-16, 37D2
WEST, John C.
US denies improper tie to Cook 3-30, 237A1
WEST Bank—*See MIDDLE EAST, subheads ARAB-Israeli Developments—Israeli Occupation Policies and EGYPT-Israel Peace Moves*
WEST Coast Schools (defunct)
Flood paymt chrg rptd, Elko convictn cited 2-15, 240C2
WESTERHOLM, Raino
Kekkonen reelected 1-16, 36G2
WESTERN Airlines Inc.
Continental Air Lines merger set 8-31, 684B1

1979

Kennedy offers natl health plan 5-14, 362D1
Fed ct welfare suits curbed by Sup Ct 5-14, 384A1
Carter proposes mental health plan 5-15, 365E1
Carter offers welfare plan 5-23, 384B1
Carter unveils natl health plan 6-12, 438D2, A3
Funding cuts set 6-19, 561E1
Gender-based plan ruled illegal by Sup Ct 6-25, 539C3
Nuns set Md hq sale 7-2, 640A3
Califano fired, reform bill role cited 7-18, 530A1
Ala legal counsel law case declined by Sup Ct 10-1, 768A2
Pope visits NY slums, scores neglect 10-2, 758G1-B2
PR allocatn held discriminatory 10-11, 786F2
Reagan seeks program shift to states, localities 11-13, 866E2
'78 US poverty data rptd 11-24, 965D2
GAO 'fraud hotline' rptd effective 12-9, 947B2
Carter Oil Profits Tax Plan—*For developments not listed here, see PETROLEUM-Carter Decontrol*
Carter seeks fund 4-5, 250C3; 4-10, 263F2
Carter scores foes 4-23, 300D2
Cong gets plan 4-26, 301D1
Carter stresses aid to poor in new energy program 7-15, 532E2, 534A2
Transfer Payments—*See INCOMES*

WELHAVEN, Sigri
Sells Matisse painting 7-3, 672B1
WELLAND, Colin
Yanks released 9-19, 820G3
WELLER, Michael
Hair released 3-13, 528D2
Loose Ends opens 6-6, 712C1
WELLES, Orson
Wins Grammy 2-16, 336F3
WELLINGTON, Duke of (1769-1852)
Funeral cited 9-5, 669C1
WELLINGTON, Harry H.
To head ITT paymts probe 8-8, 648F1
WELLS Fargo & Co.
Nicaragua operatns curbed 7-25, 574B1
Brazil '78 oil loan cited 7-28, 584C2
Wells Fargo Bank
Nicaragua debt paymts in doubt 9-28, 753F2
WELSH, Kenneth
Ride A Cock Horse opens 3-18, 292E2
WENNER, Jann
Rolling Stone, Look merge 5-7, 430E3
Fired as Look editor 7-3, 640C3
WERFEL, Franz
Grand Tour opens 1-11, 292E1
WERNER, Louis
Arrested 2-20, 155D3
WERNER, Pierre (Luxembourg premier)
Coalitn govt sworn 7-19, 568A3
WERTHEIMER, Fred
Scores PAC spending rise 5-15, 363A2
Scores Carter New England energy mailing 9-17, 703G2
WESOLOWSKA, Alicja
UN asks info re detentn 10-29, 939B2
WEST Bank—*See MIDDLE EAST-ARAB-Israeli Developments-Israel Occupation and EGYPT-Israel subheads*
WESTCHESTER County, N.Y.—*See NEW York State*
WESTERN Airlines Inc.
Continental merger blocked by CAB 7-21, 579C1
Continental ends merger bid 8-7, 830F1
Mex City crash kills 74 10-31, 912B2; rpt blames crew 12-14, 996B3

1980

Mt St Helens damage assessed 5-24—7-4, 504A3
PR aid rate backed by Sup Ct 5-27, 453C3
Cuban, Haitian refugees get eligibility; Fla curbs rptd 6-20, 484F3, 485C1
Right to sue states broadened by Sup Ct 6-25, 540C3
DC fscl recovery plan proposed 7-19, 742E3
Urban League conv 8-3—8-6, 597D1, E2
'79 family poverty data rptd 10-23, 824B1
Dorothy Day dies 11-29, 928C2
Food Stamp Program—*See under FOOD*
Presidential Election (& Transition)
Reagan assails Bush on guaranteed income 2-5, 128G2
Kennedy 'basic speech' excerpts 3-10, 183D1, 184B2
Dem platform drafted 6-24, 480A1
Reagan sees blacks 7-15, 534A1
Carter attacks GOP stands 7-17, 532E1
Dem platform planks adopted 8-12, 611B1; text excerpts 614D2, F2, G3, 615E1
Carter pres renominatn acceptance speech 8-14, 612F1, F3, 613A2
Reagan 'antipathy' scored by AFL-CIO 8-20, 647B3
Carter scores Reagan 8-22, 646F2
Carter vows fed aid to cities 10-20, 803F1

WELLER, David
Wins Olympic medal 7-22, 622E2
WELLS, Allan
Wins Olympic medals 7-25, 7-28, 623G3, 624B1
WELLS Fargo & Co.
Wells Fargo Bank
Prime rate cut to 20.5% 12-22, 983B3
Wells Fargo Interamerican Bank
Nicaragua debt rescheduled 9-5, 689G2
WELTFISH, Gene
Dies 8-2, 676F3
WELTY, Eudora
Wins Natl Medal for Lit 5-1, 692B2
WENDELL, Judge Michael J.
Clears Nev nurse of murder chrgs 5-30, 656C1
WENDERS, Wim
Wrong Move released 1-25, 216G3
Left-Handed Woman released 4-2, 416C3
WENGLER v. Druggists Mutual Insurance Co.
Case decided by Sup Ct 4-22, 344B1
WENSEL, William W.
Abortn funding cases argued in Sup Ct 4-21, 306F2
WENSINK, John
Fined over NYC brawl 1-25, 198C3
WENZEL, Andreas
Wins Olympic medal 2-19, 155F2
Wins World Cup skiing title 3-11, 469F3
WENZEL, Hanni
Wins Olympic medals 2-17, 2-21, 2-23, 155A3
Wins World Cup skiing title 3-2, 469F3
WERKER, Judge Henry
Orders census revised 12-23, Sup Ct overrules 12-30, 982E3
WERNER, Jeff
Die Laughing released 5-23, 675C2
WERNER, Pierre (Luxembourg premier)
W Ger backs NATO A-missiles 7-15, 540D1
WERSCHING, Ray
NFL '79 kicking ldr 1-5, 8F2
WERTMULLER, Lina
Blood Feud released 2-22, 216C2
WESLEYAN University (Middletown, Conn.)
Stock sold re S Africa 4-13, 374A2
WESOLOWSKA, Alicja
Sentenced as spy 3-7, 220G3
Sentence upheld 4-14, 326F3
WESSIG, Gerd
Sets high jump mark at Moscow Olympics 8-1, 589D1, 624F1
WESSINGHAGE, Thomas
Ovett breaks 1500-m mark 8-27, 892A2
WESSON, Robert
Northn Calif hit by quakes 1-24—1-27, 80B3
WEST, Howard
In God We Trust released 9-26, 836C3
WEST, Mae
Dies 11-22, 928F3
WEST African Economic Community
Liberia's Doe barred from Togo mtg 5-28, 469G1-A3
WEST Bank—*See ARAB-Israeli Developments*
WESTCHESTER Premier Theater (Tarrytown, N.Y.)
NY Mafia boss indicted 6-30, 503A1
NY Mafia boss convicted 11-21, 971G2
WESTERN Airlines Inc.
Continental merger bid renewed 9-22, 746E2

1976

WESTERN Electric Co.—*See AMERICAN Telephone & Telegraph*
WESTERN European Union (WEU) (Belgium, France, Great Britain, Italy, Luxembourg, Netherlands, West Germany)
France bars jt Eur defns 11-30, 905A3
WESTERN Growers Association
Chavez contract signed 1-31, 153B2
WESTERN Sahara—*See SAHARA, Western*
WESTERN Samoa—*See also ADB, COMMONWEALTH of Nations*
Listed as 'partly free' 1-19, 20D3
S Pacific Forum meets 3-8—3-9, 179B2
Total IMF oil loan rptd 4-1, 340E2
Commonwealth gets UN observer status 10-18, 799D2
Becomes UN member 12-15, 955D1
Gets OPEC loan 12-23, 975E3
WEST Germany—*See GERMANY, Federal Republic of*
WESTIN, Av
Quits ABC 1-26, 160E2
WEST Indies Associated States (British West Indies) (Antigua, Dominica, St. Kitts-Nevis, St. Lucia, St. Vincent)
Anguilla gets self-govt 2-10, 270A3
Antigua elections 2-18, 270D3
WESTINGHOUSE Broadcasting Co.
FCC network probe asked 11-23, 901E1
WESTINGHOUSE Electric Corp.
S Korea cancels French A-plant buy 1-29, 103C3
Uranium pact set 2-3, 115E3
SEC lists paymts 5-12, 729E1
French-W Ger A-pact OKd 5-18, 372A3
Ct curbs plutonium use 5-26, 398B2
Struck 7-12—7-20, 536B3
Australia blocks US antitrust actn 11-18, uranium pact cancelatn cited 11-19, 997D2
S Korea A-sale effort cited 12-4, 962F3
Trust suit dropped 12-10, 988C2
WESTINGHOUSE Independent Salaried Unions, Federation of
Contract settled 7-19, 536C3
WESTIN, Lynda
HEW ruling suspended 7-7, 535C3
WESTON, Michael
Held in Indian shooting 5-5, 384F2
WEST Palm Beach, Fla.—*See FLORIDA*
WEST Point, N.Y.—*See 'Military Academy' under U.S. GOVERNMENT—ARMY*
WEST Texas State University (Canyon)
Ford visits 4-10, 281B1

WEST Virginia
Primary date set 22B2
Byrd enters pres race 1-9, 21D3
Reagan in Charleston 5-4, 324C2
Moore, aide acquitted 5-5, 342E3
Weirton off US jobless list 5-5, 347E2
Primary results 5-11, 342B3
20 delegates opt for Ford 6-19, 450F3
Ford hosts GOP delegates 6-25, support slips 7-1, 467C3
Dem conv women delegates, table 508E2
Dem conv pres vote, table 7-14, 507E2
Kanawha Cnty wildcat miners strike spreads 7-19—7-27, 553F1
Reagan delegate gains rptd 8-7, 583E2
GOP pre-conv delegate count 8-14, 583E3
Wildcat miners strike ends 8-16, 669E3
Ford seeks conv delegates 8-17, 601A3
GOP conv pres, vp vote tables 8-18—8-19, 8-19, 599E1, E3
Ford wins GOP pres nominatn 8-19, 597G1
Fscl '75 per capita income, tax burden rptd 9-15, 10-12, 959D2
Election results 11-2: pres 818D1, 819B2; cong 820D1, 823E1, 828D3, 831A2-A3; state 817E2, 820F2, C3, 823D1
WEU—*See WESTERN European Union*
WEYERHAEUSER Co.
Trust suit dvpts 2-18—10-5, 886D1
'75 tax paymt rptd 10-2, 847B2

1977

WESTERN Electric Co., Inc.—*See AMERICAN Telephone & Telegraph*
WESTERN Sahara—*See SAHARA, Western*
WESTERN Samoa—*See also COMMONWEALTH of Nations*
UN Assemb member 4D1
IMF OKs trust fund loan 2-4, 87F2
NZ to set 200-mi fishing zone 9-7, 729B3
WESTERN States—*See also SUNBELT States*
Defense job gains rptd 8-10, 629E2
Drought—*See separate listing*
WESTERN Union International Inc.—*See WUI, Inc.*
WESTERN Union Telegraph Co.
Sup Ct bars AT&T dispute review 2-22, 150A1
Hawaii svc case review declined 10-17, 798A1
WEST Germany—*See GERMANY, Federal Republic of*
WEST Indies Associated States (British West Indies) (Antigua, Dominica, St. Kitts-Nevis, St. Lucia, St. Vincent)
3 Antigua ex-mins arrested 3-2, 203E1
Nevis votes to rejoin UK 8-18, Bradshaw scores 8-19, 675B2
WESTINGHOUSE Broadcasting Co.
FCC OKs TV network probe 1-14, 119D1
WESTINGHOUSE Electric Corp.
Australia uranium suit rptd 1-25, 81G2
Australia uranium find rptd 2-16, 158C2
Uranium dispute with 3 utilities setld 3-3, 177B2
Uranium dispute formally ends 3-30, 252G1-B2
Uranium cartel chrgs rptd 4-25, 479E2
Kirby vs US plutonium ban 4-27, 334B3
Sup Ct declines employer records case 5-16, 419D1
Canada scores uranium mktg 6-16, 480E2
US-Canada trust com rptd set 6-18, 525G2
Arabs drop boycott threat 6-19, 511D3
Settles Ala Power suit 9-21, bars utilities suit settlemt 11-9; 895G1 ★-C2
UK denies Rio Tinto evidence 12-1, 1003C3
3 Tex utility suits setld 12-26, 1003A3
WESTPHAL, Paul
Named to NBA all-star team 6-13, 584G3
WEST Point, N.Y.—*See U.S. GOVERNMENT—ARMY—Military Academy*
WEST Side Tennis Club (Forest Hills, N.Y.)
US Open move stirs racial dispute 9-8, 787D1, E2

WEST Virginia
Legislature schedule rptd 6G2
FPC OKs emergency gas purchase 1-19, 53G3
Gas, weather layoff total rptd 2-7, 91F2
FMC Charleston plant shut 3-9, reopened 3-15, 196B3, D3
Carter in Charleston 3-17, 190G3
Storms, floods hit 4-3—4-6, disaster areas named 4-7, 311F2-A3
'76 per-capita income table 5-10, 387F2
UMW wildcat strikes 6-18—9-6, 690F2, C3
'76 per capita income, tax burden table 9-13, 10-18, 821D2
Free abortns continued 10-12, 787A1
NIOSH wins Du Pont suit 12-22, 1008F2
WESTWEGO, La.—*See LOUISIANA*
WETLANDS—*See RESOURCES, Natural*
WEWS-TV (Cleveland, O. TV station)
Zacchini suit affirmed 6-28, 557G3

1978

WESTERN Electric Corp.—*See AMERICAN Telephone & Telegraph*
WESTERN Sahara—*See SAHARA*
WESTERN Samoa—*See also COMMONWEALTH of Nations, SOUTH Pacific Forum*
UK cancels debts 7-31, 592E1
UN Assemb member 713G3
WESTERN States—*See also state names*
Carter on 4 state tour 5-3—5-5, 320A3, G3, 321D3, 342A1, G1-D2
US Sup Ct voting alignmt shift noted 7-3, 566C1
NE migratn reversal rptd 12-3, 943D1
City populatn gains rptd 12-6, 942C3
WESTERN Union Corp.
Mgrs strike-duty overtime pay challenge refused 2-21, 126A1
Telegraph monopoly probe set 3-9, 270D2
WESTERN Union International Inc.—*See WUI Inc.*
WESTERN Union Telegraph Co.—*See WESTERN Union Corp.*
WEST Germany—*See GERMANY, Federal Republic of*
WEST Haven, Conn.—*See CONNECTICUT*
WEST Indies Associated States (British West Indies) (Antigua, St. Kitts-Nevis, St. Lucia, St. Vincent)—*See associated state names*
WESTINGHOUSE Electric Corp.
In Dow Jones indl avg 66F2
USSR offers PI A-plant 1-5, 2-14, 134B3
PI A-contract fee rptd 1-13; denies wrongdoing, PI ordrs probe 1-16, 38D2
US House, environmental group questn PI A-plant 2-8, 2-14, 134C3
Black-mkt uranium sale bid probed by FBI 3-19, 242C2-A3
US chrgs Gulf re uranium cartel 5-9, 346B2
Gulf sues 5-9, 346D2
Canada unit named re Arab boycott 6-1, 435E2
Plea bargaining pact rejctd 10-24, Egypt payoff figure named 10-26, fined 11-20, 961F2
Union gets right to job data 11-3, 899A1
Law firm dual-rep case refused by Sup Ct 11-6, 873G3
French reactor sale to China OKd 11-24, set 12-4, 986C2
Iran evacuatn set 12-8, 954D1
NJ offshore A-plant contract canceled 12-19, 1009D3
2 A-plants sold to Ill utility 12-20, 1009G3
WESTINGHOUSE Electric Corp. v. Kerr-McGee Corp.
Case refused by Sup Ct 11-6, 874A1
WEST Irian—*See INDONESIA*
WESTMINSTER Abbey (London, England)
Female canon preaches 4-2, 294D2
WESTMORELAND, Ret. Gen. William C.
Rpts Viet war med advances 12-6, 960D3
WESTON, Harold
Cuevas TKOs 3-4, 379C2
WESTON, Jack
Cheaters opens 1-15, 760F1
WESTON, Robert R.
Betsy released 2-9, 618C3
WESTPHAL, Paul
NBA scoring ldr 4-9, 271E2
WEST Point, N.Y.—*See U.S. GOVERNMENT—ARMY—Military Academy*
WEST Potomic Park (Washington, D.C.)
Indians encamp 7-15—7-23, 568F3
WESTSIDE Women's Services Inc. v. Cleveland
Case refused by Sup Ct 11-27, 937E2
WEST Virginia
Legislature schedule rptd 14G3
'67, '77 sales-tax rates rptd 1-5, 15G3
State govt tax revenue table 1-9, 84E2
Vance in Charleston re Canal pacts 1-11, 58B2
Coal shortage rptd 2-11, power cutbacks ordrd 2-13; Carter sees gov 2-16, 104D1, D2, E3
Carter sees Rockefeller on coal strike 2-23, 122E3
Willow I scaffold collapses 4-27, negligence chrgd 6-8, 459F2
Primary results 5-9, 363B1
Carter in Charleston 5-26, 404G3
'77 prison populatn rptd down 6-3, 440D1
'75 abortns rptd 8-10, 744D1
N&W Rwy strike ends 9-30, 809E2
Carter in Elkins parade 10-7, 769A2
Election results 11-7: cong 846A2, 848E3, 852B4, 854F1
Steel haulers strike 11-11, 1006G1-A2
WESTWEGO, La.—*See LOUISIANA*
WETMORE, Alexander
Dies 12-6, 1032F3
WE Will All Meet in Paradise (film)
Released 5-22, 620B1
WEXLER, Anne
Joins White House staff 4-19, 306F3
Costanza resigns 8-1, 606B1
Sees tight '80s budget 11-13, 875E1
WEYERHAEUSER Co.
Indicted for price fixing 1-25, 67B2
Pleads no contest 10-16, 1005A3

1979

WESTERN Coalition on Public Lands
'Sagebrush Revolt' mounted 9-6–9-7, 704A1
WESTERN Council of State Governments
'Sagebrush Revolt' mounted 9-6–9-7, 704A1
WESTERN Electric Co. Inc.—*See AMERICAN Telephone & Telegraph*
WESTERN Governors' Policy Office
Carter meets 10-10, 807E2
WESTERN Publishing Co.
Mattel purchase set 1-9, 16B1
WESTERN Sahara—*See SAHARA*
WESTERN Samoa—*See also COMMONWEALTH of Nations*
UN membership listed 695B3
WESTERN Union Corp.
FCC ends telegram monopoly 1-25, 78A2
FCC mailgram rate regulatn cited 10-18, 921G2
Telegraph co quits electronic mail project 12-4, 921G2, A3*
WESTERN Union Telegraph Co.—*See WESTERN Union Corp.*
WESTGATE-California Corp.
Smith convicted 5-4, 5-7, sentncd 5-31, 442E2
WEST Germany—*See GERMANY, Federal Republic of*
WESTINGHOUSE Electric Corp.
In Dow Jones indl avg 72F1
Swedish uranium supply suits setld 2-9, 131C3
NRC issues A-reactor safety warning 4-12, 275B2
Japan A-plants shut after US warnings 4-14, 323D2
Vepco uranium supply suit setld 4-16, Wis Elec 5-5, TVA 5-15, 366C1
IUE talks cited 5-31, 399D3
PI suspends A-project 6-15, 487G3-488A1
NRC orders 25 A-reactors inspected 6-25, 518D3
Electrical workers strike 7-16–9-2, 744B2
S Korea A-plant contract awarded 8-3, 742A2
Northeast Utilities uranium supply suit setld 9-26, 727C3
UK trust bill offered 10-31, 855F3
UK OKs reactor 12-18, 994C2
WESTLAND Oil Development Corp.
Fined re overchrgs 9-18, 850A1
WESTMORELAND, Earl of
To replace Wilson 11-11, 892E2
WESTMORELAND, Gen. William C. (ret.)
Vs female combat role 11-14, 868E2
WESTON, Harold
Benitez decisns 3-25, 412F3
WESTON, Jack
Break a Leg opens 4-29, 711G1
Cuba released 12-21, 1007B3
WESTPHAL, Paul
NBA scoring, assist ldr 4-8, 290E2, G2
On NBA all-league team 6-6, 526B2
WEST Point, N.Y.—*See U.S. GOVERNMENT-ARMY-Military Academy*

WEST Virginia
Legislature schedule rptd 5G3
Cyanamid sterilizatn suit threatnd 1-4, 56A3
Moore jail escape fails 2-5, 156B2
Coal broker pleads guilty to fraud 3-13, 239G3
Flood damage rptd 5-16, 472F2
Randolph '78 labor gifts rptd 6-13, 595D1
Youth suspect press law voided by Sup Ct 6-26, 541A1
'78 per capita income rptd 9-16, 746F2
SBA minority-aid abuse rptd 9-28, 947A3
Ex-Sen Revercomb dies 10-6, 860C3
Kennedy in Charleston 11-2, 962B1
WESTWEGO, La.—*See LOUISIANA*
WETZEL, Gunter
Family flees to W Ger 9-16, 697B3
WEY, Hugo
Slain in El Salvador 5-30, 406A3
WEYERHAEUSER Co.
Bodcaw takeover bid fails 3-8, 350B1
3 acquitted re price-fixing 4-29, civil trust setlmt revealed 5-1, 327C3, E3
Paper workers strike ends 5-9, 345D2
Intl Paper buys Bodcaw 8-9, 664G1

1980

UNC Resources seeks merger 12-24, 985C1
WESTERN Electric Co.—*See AMERICAN Telephone & Telegraph Co. (AT&T)*
WESTERN Ontario, University of (Canada)
Photosynthesis step rptd replicated 7-17, 715G3
WESTERN Pacific Co.
Union Pacific plans purchase 1-21, 131B2
3-way merger set 9-15, 745G1
WESTERN Sahara—*See SAHARA, Western*
WESTERN Samoa—*See also ADB, COMMONWEALTH of Nations*
Island trade pact signed 7-24, 576G2
WESTERN Union Corp.
Electronic mail plan OKd 2-22, 4-8, conflict of interest chrgd 2-27, 347F2-E3
FCC OKs satellite launchings 12-4, 990E3
WEST Frankfort—*See ILLINOIS*
WEST Germany—*See GERMANY, Federal Republic of*
WESTHEAD, Paul
Lakers win NBA title 5-16, 432E1
2d in NBA top coach vote 5-29, 656C3
WESTHEIMER, Irvin F.
Dies 12-30, 1004F3
WESTINGHOUSE Electric Corp.
In Dow Jones indl avg 76G1
NRC OKs PI A-reactor 5-6, 440E3
PI A-plant building resumes 9-25, 752C3
To acquire Teleprompter 10-15, 836E1
Northern Tier Pipeline Co.—*See NORTHERN Tier Pipeline Co.*
Westinghouse Broadcasting Co.
FCC backs San Fran license 1-30, 119C3
WESTMORELAND, James
Don't Answer the Phone released 8-9, 675C2
WESTMORELAND County—*See PENNSYLVANIA*
WEST Orange—*See NEW Jersey*
WESTPHAL, Paul
On NBA all-league team 6-2, 656D3
WEST Side Story (play)
Opens 2-14, 136G3
WESTVACO Corp.
Fine paper trust suit rptd setld 9-29, 917C2
WESTVACO Corp. v. Adams Extract Co.
Case dismissed by Sup Ct 10-20, 807A3
Case cited by Sup Ct 11-3, 856C2
WEST Valley—*See New York*

WEST Virginia
Coal miners strike 3-3, 169G3
Radical protests rptd 3-20, 485A3
Morgantown synfuel plant set 7-31, 666D2
Forest fires destroy 18,000 acres 10-31—11-13, 971A1
107-yr-old immigrant votes 11-4, 890G2
Panama Canal clogged by Japan coal shipmts 11-24, 895E3
Environment & Pollution
FMC pleads guilty re water pollutn 11-10, 869G1-C2
PPG accused of fuel-switching 11-25, 899D3
Politics & Government—*See also other appropriate subheads in this section*
Legislature schedule rptd 18G1
State of State message 1-9, 484B2
Rep Slack dies 3-17, 280C2
Primary results 6-3, 423G2, 424C1, 439C3
Anderson ballot access challenge rptd 9-27, 818C2
Carter visits 10-27, 816A3
Election results 11-4; pres 838D1, E1, 839A2, G3; cong 840F3, 844B4, 850G2; state 845F3, 847D1, C3, 850G2
'80 census rptd 12-31, 983G1
WETHERILL, Elkins
Retires from Phila Stock Exchng 12-18, 959A2
WE Won't Pay! We Won't Pay! (play)
Opens 12-17, 1003F3
WEXLER, Anne
Sears backs Olympic boycott 4-3, 260A1
WEYER, Willi
Scores IOC 5-15, 379C2
WEYERHAEUSER Co.
Fine paper trust suit acquittal rptd 12-3, 917B2

1976

WEYMANN, Ray J.
Finds gas clouds in space 5-25, 443F2
WGN-TV (Chicago TV station)
FCC rules on pol-ad case 3-4, 180E2
Lewis biog wins Pulitzer 5-3, 352C3
WHALEN Jr., Rep. Charles W. (R, O.)
Reelected 11-2, 830F2
WHALES—*See FISH*
WHARTON, Hunter P.
Quits Ford panel 1-8, 4C1
WHEAT—*See GRAIN*
WHEATON (Ill.) College
Ford addresses 3-12, 198A2
WHEELBARROW Closers (play)
Opens 10-11, 1014E3
WHEELDON, John
Quits shadow cabt post 3-25, 237A1
WHEELER, Sir Mortimer
Dies 7-23, 716G3
WHEELING-Pittsburgh Steel Corp.
Hikes prices 6% 11-26, 897E2
WHELAN, Eugene F.
Quebec dairy farmers riot 6-3, 416F2
Stays agri min 9-14, 692B2
Scores US meat quota 10-11, 837A1
Denies US beef pact agrmt 12-16, 976C2
WHIPPLE, George Hoyt
Dies 2-1, 124G3
WHITCOMB, Edgar D.
Loses Ind Sen primary 5-4, 323B2
WHITE, Barbara M.
Mills Coll pres appt rptd 3-10, 272B1
WHITE, Betty
Wins Emmy 5-17, 460B2

WHITE, Justice Byron R(aymond)—*For Supreme Court developments not listed here, see SUPREME Court under U.S. GOVERNMENT*
Upholds import tax ruling 1-14, 23D3
Rules on campaign law 1-30, 86F3, 87A2
Vs Firestone libel ruling 3-2, 169B3
Backs limited prosecutor immunity 3-2, 169E3
Backs retroactive seniority 3-24, 218E2
Vs redistricting review ruling 3-30, 262D1
Backs city-suburb housing plan 4-20, 308B3
Backs drug convictn despite govt role 4-27, 349B2
Upholds DC police job test 6-7, 435C1
Vs NC police firing rule 6-10, 552F2
Vs trial transcript rule 6-10, 552A3
Backs some church-coll aid 6-21, 452F3
Vs US wage rule re states 6-24, 468E2
Vs pvt schl bias rule 6-25, 479F1
Vs rights laws extensn 6-25, 479C2
For patronage ouster bar 6-28, 468D3
Vs press gag orders 6-30, 491F3, 492B1
Vs abortn rights extensn 7-1, 518E3
'72 vote vs death penalty cited, ct upholds penalty, voids NC, La laws 7-2, 491C2, B3
Vs fed cts illegal evidence appeals curb 7-6, 534F3
Vs car search ruling 7-6, 535C1
Backs sympathy strike ruling 7-6, 535D1
Not in Standard Oil retrial bid rule 10-18, 867A3
Backs Pa youth curfew review 11-15, 882E2
Vs MD office abortn rule 11-29, 900D3
Vs pregnancy benefits 12-7, 920E1
Vs vacating Gilmore stay 12-13, 952F2

1977

WHA (World Hockey Association)—*See HOCKEY, Ice*
WHALES & Porpoises
House curbs porpoise kills 6-11, 442D3
IWC cuts whaling quotas 6-24, 496E3
Sirica vs bowhead whaling ban 10-21; ruling reversed, Burger backs ban 10-24; bowhead data cited 835G1
Bowhead, sperm kill quotas raised 12-6, 12-7, 936G2
WHALING Commission, International (IWC)
Whaling quotas cut 6-24, 496D3
Sirica vs bowhead ban 10-21; ruling reversed, Burger backs ban 10-24, 835A2
Bowhead, sperm kill quotas raised 12-6, 12-7, 936G2
WHEALON, Archbishop John F.
Bishops OK new catechism 11-17, 906F1
WHEAT—*See GRAIN*
WHEAT Council, International
'76 world productn rptd 3-8, 179A1
WHEATLEY, Dennis
Dies 11-11, 952G3
WHEATON, Anne W.
Dies 3-23, 264G3
WHEELER Jr., Mayor Charles B. (Kansas City, Mo.)
On flood damage 9-14, 768C3
WHEELING-Pittsburgh Steel Corp.
Steelworkers OK contract 4-9, 273G2
Price hiked 5-11, 385B2 ★
Hikes prices, Admin reactn 12-18, undercut 12-22, 1003C2

WHITE, Justice Byron R(aymond)—*For Supreme Court developments not listed here, see U.S. GOVERNMENT—SUPREME Court*
Vs restrictive suburban zoning 1-11, 15E1
Rejcts Gilmore executn stay 1-16, hearing 1-17, 40B2, D2
Backs racial voter redistricting 3-1, 175C1
Vs mil MD malpractice review bar 3-7, 211F2
Death sentencing on secret info curbed 3-22, 231B1
For Miranda rule review 3-23, 276D1
Backs OSHA penalties 3-23, 276A2
Bars US antifraud rules expansn 3-23, 276C3
Vs reinsurance agrmts 4-26, 382F3
Backs price-fixing suit curbs 6-9, 501F3
Limits employe religious rights 6-13, 517E3
Vs overturning 'Schwinn doctrine' 6-23, 539B2
Backs performers' media suits 6-28, 558A1
Vs executn for rape 6-29, 557D2
Hears Bakke case arguments 10-12, 835B1
Backs NYS pvt schl aid law 12-6, 938D3
Backs phone surveillnc ct orders 12-7, 939A2
Backs mandatory early retiremt 12-12, 960B2

1978

WGBH-TV (Boston, Mass. TV station)
FCC renews license 7-20, 599G1
WHA (World Hockey Association)—*See HOCKEY, Ice*
WHALEN Jr., Rep. Charles W. (R, Ohio)
Queries Israel US arms use in Leb invasn 3-17, 236E2
Hall wins seat 11-7, 854E1
WHALEN, Robert P.
Issues Niagara chem dump site warning 8-2, 703B1
WHALES & Porpoises
Australia industry probe set 3-20, 208C3
Australia controls proposed 4-13, 286F2
IWC cuts quotas 6-30, 12-25, USSR vows halt 12-8, 1001B2-B3
Australia panel urges ban 12-18, 1012F3
Carter disregard scored 12-20, 1009E1
WHALING Commission, International (IWC)
Quotas cut 6-30, 12-25, USSR vows halt 12-8, 1001B2-B3
WHAM-O Manufacturing Co.
Water toy recall set 4-13, 348F1
WHEAT—*See GRAIN*
WHEC-TV (Rochester, N.Y. TV station)
Gannett sale set 8-20, 759F3
WHEELER, Hugh
Little Night Music released 3-7, 619A3
WHEELING-Pittsburgh Steel Corp.
Prices hiked 3-29, rolled back 4-3, 263B1
WHEELOCK, John Hall
Dies 3-22, 252F3
WHELAN, Lt. Gov. Gerald T. (D, Neb.)
Wins primary for gov 5-9, 363E1
Loses electn 11-7, 854F3
WHIPPLE, Judge Lawrence A.
Curbs FBI mail scrutiny 11-29, 939G3
WHIRLPOOL Corp.
Oreck trust damage award case refused by Sup Ct 10-30, 832A3
WHISTLE (book)
On best-seller list 4-2, 272B3
WHITAKER, Lou
Named AL top rookie 11-21, 928B2
WHITAKER, Mical
Amen Corner opens 4-22, 760B1
WHITAKER, Raymond B.
Wins US Sen primary in Wyo 9-12, 736C2
Loses election 11-7, 856F1

WHITE, Justice Byron R(aymond)—*For Supreme Court developments not listed here, see U.S. GOVERNMENT—SUPREME Court*
For SC teacher test review 1-16, 33D2
Vs 'prehire' union picketing 1-17, 34B1
Vs Multistate Tax Compact backing 2-21, 126A2
Backs limited immunity for prison offcls 2-22, 126C2
Vs med student ouster rule 3-1, 143A3
Backs Maritime Comm labor contract jurisdictn 3-1, 143F3
Backs curbs on state oil tanker regulatn 3-6, 162A1
Backs judicial immunity in sterilizatn case 3-28, 241C3
Vs cities' liability under trust law 3-29, 280D2
Backs Minn pensn funds law 4-3, 308G3
Denies broadcasters Nixon tapes 4-18, 308B2
Vs tax breaks in lease-back deals 4-18, 309B2
Vs clergy pub office ban 4-19, 309F1
Vs corp pol free speech 4-26, 343D3
Backs lawyer competency case review, scores majority 5-1, 363G3
Vs Indian tribal authority 5-15, 387D3
Backs Calif jurisdictn in child-support case 5-15, 387G3
Backs corp takeover tax liability 5-22, 388G1
Vs OSHA warrantless searches 5-23, 405D2
Vs Montana hunting fee disparity 5-23, 406A1
Backs newsroom searches by police 5-31, 430C1
Vs natural gas diversn 5-31, 431B1
Backs poultry group trust immunity 6-12, 468C1
Backs FBI informant case review 6-12, 468E1
Backs '75 double jeopardy doctrine 6-14, 468E3
Vs union supervisor discipline 6-21, 509B2
Vs Ark prison attys' fees 6-23, 566G1, A2
Vs Bakke med schl admissn, backs race-based affirmative actn principle; opinion excerpt 6-28, 481C1-F2, 486C2
Backs Minn pensn funds law 6-28, 567E1
Narrows US offcls' legal immunity 6-29, 567C2
Vs FCC 'Filthy Words' ban 7-3, 551E3
Vs Ohio death penalty law 7-3, 552F1, G1
Vs Calif, NM water rights 7-3, 552C2
Voting alignmts shift noted 7-3, 565F3-566C1
Bars Farber sentnc stay extensn 8-1, 678B3
Vs cities' power over suburbs 11-28, 937D3
Urges new fed ct 12-4, 958E3
Vs broader police auto search power 12-5, 959A3
WHITE, Daniel
Quits as SF supervisor 11-10; slays mayor, supervisor 11-27, chrgd 11-29, 920A2

1979

WEYLAND, Gen. Otto P.
Dies 9-2, 756F3
WGTQ-TV (Sault Ste. Marie, Mich. TV station)
Panax license approval revoked 7-12, 618E2
WGTU-TV (Traverse City, Mich. TV station)
Panax license approval revoked 7-12, 618E2
WHALING Commission, International (IWC)
Whaling banned, Indian O sanctuary set 7-11, 554B2
WHALES & Porpoises
Australia sets whaling ban 4-4; impact on Japan, USSR seen small 4-8, 284B2
IWC sets ban, Indian O sanctuary 7-11, 554B2
WHAT a Fool Believes (recording)
On best-seller list 4-4, 271D2; 5-2, 356A3
WHAT the Devil (play)
Opens 4-16, 712E3
WHEAT—*See GRAIN*
WHEAT Council, International
Wheat pact extended 3-23, 274G1
WHEATLEY, James B.
Sentenced in GSA scandal 5-31, 964D3
WHEELER, David
Richard III opens 6-14, 712B2
WHEELER, Hugh
Sweeney Todd opens 3-1, 292C3
WHEELER, Paul
Legacy released 9-28, 820E1
WHEELER, Dr. Ray
Rpts '67-75 malnutritn down 4-30, 386B3
WHEELING-Pittsburgh Steel Corp.
Fed aid OKd; rivals score, suit filed 8-28, 681F3
WHEELOCK, Jaime
Land expropriatn halted 12-3, 951B1
WHELAN, Thomas J.
Subject to rejailing by Sup Ct 6-4, 439A1
WHEN A Stranger Calls (film)
Released 10-12, 1008A2
Top-grossing film 10-31, 892G3
WHEN I Say God (book)
French Dominican priest censured 12-18, 999B3
WHEN You Comin' Back, Red Ryder (film)
Released 2-8, 174F3
WHITE, Lake
Hooker sued for pollutn 6-22, 597C2
Hooker settles dump suit 10-24, 808E3

WHITE, Justice Byron Raymond—*For Supreme Court developments not listed here, see U.S. GOVERNMENT—SUPREME Court*
Backs Pa abortn control law 1-9, 14F1
Vs limited lawyers' interstate rights 1-15, 31G3
Backs Energy Comm rate relief power 1-16, 32E2
Vs A&P milk price actn 2-22, 150E3
Vs Mont gross-receipts tax 2-22, 151D1
Backs job-testing data disclosure 3-5, 184D3
Backs jobless pay for strikers 3-21, 231F1
Vs NYC Transit Auth ex-addict ban 3-21, 231C2
Backs church schl labor interventn 3-21, 231G2
Vs random car checks by police 3-27, 263E1
Hears Weber case argumt 3-28, 262G3
Vs cable TV pub-access rule 4-2, 281A2
Backs 'state of mind' libel queries 4-18, 302D1
Sup Ct worker fired re news leaks 4-20, 302G2
Vs unwed father damage suit bar 4-24, 364G1
Vs pvt Title IX suit 5-14, 382F3
Backs collective bargaining on food issues 5-14, 383B2
Vs fed ct welfare suits 5-14, 384A1
Discloses finances 5-15, 382E2
Backs broader Cong legal immunity 6-18, 498G3
Backs Idaho takeover law challenge 6-26, 540F3
Backs unwed mothers survivors' aid 6-27, 558B2
Backs wage-price case review 7-2, 498D2
Vs ctroom pub access curbs 7-2, 515A3
Backs Ohio busing orders 7-2, 539A3
'78-79 Sup Ct terms ends, voting alignmt rptd 7-2, 558A1
Votes to void Rose case convictns 7-2, 558G3
Vs Ga laws in church land dispute 7-2, 559C1
Backs Mass abortn-consent law 7-2, 559D2
Backs Amtrak Chicago train cuts 10-8, 868D1
Backs Bell contempt case review 10-9, 783E3
Vs curb on investor suits vs advisers 11-13, 902C1
Not in Travel Act bribery case 11-27, 919F3
Backs Taiwan treaty case review 12-13, 940D1
WHITE, Charles
USC wins Rose Bowl, TD disputed 1-1, 8G2
Wins Heisman Trophy 12-3, 1001D2
WHITE, Charles W.
Dies 10-3, 860G3
WHITE, Daniel
Convicted in Moscone-Milk slaying, gays protest 5-22, 385G3

1980

WEYRICH, Paul M.
Political role profiled 7-11—9-15, 819G1
WGBH-TV (Boston TV station)
'Death of a Princess' protested 5-8, aired 5-12; cts rule on dispute 5-9, 5-12, 375D3
WHALEN v. U.S.
Case decided by Sup Ct 4-16, 328B3
WHALES & Porpoises
Newfoundland fishermen shoot whales 461F2
Spain impounds US vessel 6-18, escape prompts Adm's dismissal 11-15, 903A3
Porpoise kill limit lowered 10-21, 987F2
WHARTON, William
Birdy wins Amer Book Awards 5-1, 692G1, E2
WHAT a Fool Believes (recording)
Doobie Brothers win Grammy 2-27, 296A3
WHEAT—*See GRAIN*
WHEAT, Jim
Silent Scream released 2-2, 216E3
WHEAT, Ken
Silent Scream released 2-2, 216E3
WHEELABRATOR-Frye Inc.
Huyck merger set 7-30, 745E3
Pullman purchase bid offered 8-21, buys control 9-25, 784G2
WHEELER, Hugh
Nijinsky released 3-20, 216D3
WHEELING-Pittsburgh Steel Corp.
USW contract settled 4-15, 289B2
WHEELOCK, Jaime
Denies US aid pressure 5-18, 410C1
WHELAN, Eugene
Named Canada agri min 3-3, 171A2
WHELAN, Judge Roger M.
Rejects Auto-Train svc cut 9-26; OKs DC investor loan 11-26, 958B3, G2
WHELAN, Rosalie
Calls electn results 'disappointing' 11-4, 846F2
WHIP It (recording)
On best-seller list 12-3, 948B3
WHIRLPOOL Corp.
Hazardous work refusals backed by Sup Ct 2-26, 188D1
WHIRLPOOL Corp. v. Marshall
Case decided by Sup Ct 2-26, 188C1
WHITAKER, Bobby
Elected Cairo (Ill) ward rep 11-4, 850E3
WHITAKER, Frederic
Dies 3-9, 280E2
WHITE, Anne
Wins AIAW doubles tennis title 6-11, 607E1

WHITE, Justice Byron Raymond—*For Supreme Court developments not listed here, see U.S. GOVERNMENT--SUPREME Court*
Backs citizenship revocatn law 1-15, 51E2
Backs narrowed state ct jurisdictn 1-21, 93B2
Vs Ohio boundary placemt 1-21, 93F2
Backs pvt coll faculty unions 2-20, 146A2
Backs NYS pvt sch reimbursemt 2-20, 146E2
Vs charity solicitatn limit 2-20, 170C2
Not in damage suit geographic relevance cases 2-20, 170C3
Backs Tex porno film restraints 3-18, 226F3
Backs Indian land 'inverse condemnatn' 3-18, 226G3
Backs inmate mental health hearings 3-25, 265E2
Backs warrantless home arrests 4-15, 306E1
Backs Indian land managemt fed liability 4-15, 306G1
Hears abortn funding cases 4-21, 306E2
Vs at-large local electns 4-22, 343A3
Backs EEOC class actn process avoidance 5-12, 426B2
Vs pre-ERISA insured pensn benefits 5-12, 426C3
Backs Ga death penalty applicatn 5-19, 440B1
Backs narrowed 'exclusionary rule' 5-27, 453D2
Vs DEA detainmt procedure 5-27, 454A1
Backs shopping cntr petitn access 6-9, 512E2
Vs GE microbe patent 6-16, 453D1
Backs Imperial Valley water rights 6-16, 511G2
Backs use of jail informants 6-16, 511C3
Vs state sales preference 6-19, 554G2
Vs Ala death penalty rule 6-20, 555E1
Vs unpatented key ingredient monopolies 6-27, 511D2
Backs Medicaid abortn funding limits 6-30, 491G3
Backs govt minority constructn grants 7-2, 510D1
Backs OSHA benzene standard 7-2, 511A1
Vs extended judicial immunity 11-17, 882C1
'Mr Justice' title dropped 11-17, 882A3
Backs Conn phone harassmt case review 12-1, 918G2
Backs EPA clean water enforcemt 12-2, 918C1
Vs lenient sentence appeal 12-9, 936F3
WHITE, Charles
USC wins Rose Bowl, sets rushing mark 1-1, 23D1
In NFL draft 4-29, 336G2
WHITE, Bishop Dale
Urges US restraint re Iran 4-23, 324F3

1976

WHITE, F. Clifton
Seeks GOP platform compromise 8-17, 601B1
WHITE, George W.
Pallotine audit implicates 6-18, 951B1
WHITE, Kevin H.
Lauds US actn re busing review 5-15, 377D3
WHITE, Margita E.
Named to FCC 7-12; confrmd 9-8, 808D1
WHITE, Minor
Dies 6-24, 524G3
WHITE, Rep. Richard Crawford (D, Tex.)
Environmt group scores 3-25, 220B1
Reelected 11-12, 830E4
WHITE, Robert Excell
US Sup Ct stays executn 12-6, 920G2
WHITE, Roy
AL batting ldr 10-4, 796B1
In World Series 10-16—10-21, 815A3
WHITE Jr., W. S.
Named Amer Elec pres 1-27, 160E2
WHITE Consolidated Industries Inc.
SEC lists paymts 5-12, 729E1
Whitin Arab boycott rpt released 10-18, 786A1
WHITECREST Carpet Mills Inc.
Chrgd re Arab boycott 10-20, 786F1
Chrgd re Arab boycott 11-3, 986C3
WHITECROSS, Richard and Cristina
UK files habeas corpus writ 1-12, 26A2
Argentina actn sought 2-27, 220F2
Argentina frees 4-8; score police 4-11, 264A2
WHITEFORD, William K.
Gulf paymts rptd 133G2
WHITEHEAD, Donald
Named to econ advisory bd 9-14, 730F1
WHITEHURST, Rep. G. William (D, Va.)
Reelected 11-2, 830G4
WHITELAW, William
Shadow cabt home secy 1-15, 101B2
WHITELAW, William and Rosario Barreto
Found dead 5-20, 399F1
WHITE Westinghouse International Co.
Boycott rpts released 10-18, 10-20, 786A1, G1
WHITFIELD, Chester Wallace
Elected oppositn ldr 1-12, 104A2
WHITHAM, Wayne
Testifies for Concorde 1-5, 5A3
WHITIN Machine Works Inc.—*See WHITE Consolidated Industries*
WHITLAM, Gough
Natl anthem policy reversed 1-21, 46C2
Reelected Labor Party ldr 1-27, 71D3
Names shadow cabt 1-29, 116D1
Chrgs '75 ouster 'deceit' 2-9, 116E1
Fraser OKs US navigatn base 2-17, 137D2
Parlt opens, Labor boycotts, 2-17, 137B3
Garland denied contempt order 2-24, 172F2
Iraq electn fund alleged, libel suits filed 2-25—3-2, 172B2
Exchngs chrgs with Ellicott 3-4, 187D2
Censured 3-7, bars resignatn 3-7, 3-9, 187F1
Beats party ouster moves 3-17, 203C3
Reshuffles Labor shadow cabt 3-25, 237A1
Iraq fund probe rpt 3-25, 237C1
Chrgs Lockheed payoff 4-29, 322F1
Scores Fraser anti-Sovt statemt 6-1, 438A3
In China quake 7-28—7-29, 545C2
Students protest ouster 8-23, 650E1
Scores proposed budget 8-24, 672B3
Scores devaluatn 11-29, 896B2
WHITLEY, Charles
Elected 11-2, 822E2, 830E2
WHITMORE, James
Wins Grammy 2-28, 460C3
WHITTAKER Corp.
Oil rig sinks 4-15, 544G3
SEC lists paymts 5-12, 729E1
WHITTEN, Rep. Jamie L. (D, Miss.)
Unopposed in primary 6-1, 411A2
Reelected 11-2, 822C2, 829G3

1977

WHITE, E. B.
Wife dies 7-20, 604G3
WHITE, George H. (d. 1953)
CIA mind-control tests probed 9-2—9-21, 721F1, C2, B3
WHITE, John C.
Agric dep secy 3-10; confrmd 3-15, 211G1
Carter names Dem chrmn 12-28, 1005D3
WHITE, John Patrick
Named Defense asst secy 4-21, confrmd 5-9, 418A2
On volunteer force problems 11-15, 920E1
WHITE, Katherine S.
Dies 7-20, 604G3
WHITE, Lee C.
Scores Carter energy plan 5-18, 443E2
WHITE, Peter
Affirms Korean lobbying operatn 10-21, 816B3
WHITE, Robert Excell
Uruguay scores rights statemt 2-25, 351D3
Sup Ct refuses case review 4-25, 342A3
WHITE, Robert M.
Replaced as NOAA dir 7-13, 626E2
WHITE, Sammy
Raiders win Super Bowl 1-9, 24E3
WHITE & Case
Settles Natl Student Mktg suit 5-2, 520A1
WHITE Consolidated Industries Inc.
Forgn paymts rptd 4-3, 503G2
WHITEHEAD, Jerome
Marquette wins NCAA title 3-28, 262A2
WHITE House—*See CARTER—CABINET & White House Staff; also U.S. GOVERNMENT—WHITE House Office*
WHITE River National Forest (Colo.)
Fire destroys 3,800 acres 8-7, 660C3
WHITLAM, Gough
UK monarchy ties protested 3-7—3-13, 199E1
On Hayden challenge 3-13, 218G1
Asks uranium safeguards 3-29, 253G2
Fraser sets pub svc job cuts 4-4, 303A1
Morosi wins libel suit 4-22, 326B2
CIA union infiltratn probe set 4-27, 326F1
Fraser halts CIA probe 5-3, 410C2
Asks CIA probe 5-4, 372C1
Wage rise OKd 5-24, 424C3
Reelected Labor Party head 5-31, 465D3
Labor Party conv 7-4—7-11, 541A1
Kerr quits as gov gen 7-14, 541C1
Japan friendship treaty ratified 7-21, 596A1
US rptdly bars CIA role 8-4, 632G3
Cairns to retire 8-10, Ellicott resigns over probe 9-6, 693D1
Scores '77-78 budget 8-23, 671E1
Scores uranium ban end 8-26, 693D2
Vs early electn 10-27, 839D3
Cowen sworn gov-gen 12-8, 963G3
Labor Party loses electn, quits ldrship post 12-10, 963B3, D3
Replaced as Labor Party ldr 12-22, 1009D2
WHITLEY, Dr. Richard
Antiviral drug rptd 8-10, 675G2
WHITLEY, Wilson
In NFL draft 5-3, 353B2
WHITMAN, Walt (1818-92)
Emory Holloway dies 7-30, 604B3
WHITMIRE, Kathryn J.
Houston comptroller 11-22, 900B3
WHITNEY, Hassler
Gets Medal of Sci 11-22, 952C1
WHITNEY Communications Corp.
I.H.T. Corp.
Trademark suit vs Trib NY filed 8-24, 723F1
Trib NY files trust suit 9-13, 723E1
WHITTEN, Les
On Letelier death 9-8, 743F2
WHITWORTH, Kathy
Wins Colgate Winners Circle 4-3, LPGA Classic 5-22; 2d in LI Charity Classic 8-14, Colgate Far East tourn 11-13, 951B1-E1
Stacy breaks '66 LPGA record 9-5, 951D1
LPGA top money winner 11-27, 951F1
WHO—*See UNITED Nations—World Health Organization*

1978

WHITE, Danny
Cowboys win in playoffs 12-30, 1024E1
WHITE, E. B.
Wins Pulitzer citation 4-17, 315B1
WHITE, Ed
Traded to Chargers 7-29, 1024F3
WHITE, Edward E.
On Kennecott bd rival slate 3-27, 402G3
WHITE, F. Clifton
Candidate loses Venez pres electn 12-3, 953A1
WHITE, Frank
Wins Golden Glove Award 11-21, 928A3
WHITE Jr., George
Chrgd with contempt 6-2, 449B3
WHITE, James
S Australian police chief fired 1-19, 53F1
WHITE, John C.
Installed as Dem natl chrmn 1-27, 87G2
Pres conv rules chngd 6-9, 448F2
Sees Carter challenge in '80 7-26, 682A3
On vote results 11-8, 845B1
WHITE, John Patrick
Disputes volunteer force cost 2-6, 82D1
On base closings cutbacks 4-26, 368E1
Vs random drug-use tests 4-28, 368G2-A3
WHITE, John S.
Chrgd in '75 Joyvies cover-up 12-14, 991D2
WHITE, Mayor Kevin (Boston, Mass.)
Warns Carter vs budget cuts 12-20, 980C2
WHITE, R. Stuart
Early Dark opens 4-25, 760B2
WHITE, Randy
Cowboys win Super Bowl, named co-MVP 1-15, 39E3
WHITE, Rep. Richard Crawford (D, Tex.)
Reelected 11-7, 852B3
WHITE, Robert
Paraguay rights probe rptdly set 1-9, 113A2
Regrets Laino arrest, Paraguay scores 7-11, 559E1
WHITE, Roy
Yankees win AL pennant 10-7, 779C1
In World Series 10-10—10-17, 799E3
WHITE, Sammy
NFL '77 touchdown ldr 1-1, 56E2
WHITE, Stan
NFL '77 interceptn ldr 1-1, 56D2
WHITE, Theodore
In Search of History on best-seller list 9-4, 708C1; 10-9, 800B3; 11-6, 888A1
WHITEHEAD, Cmdr. Edward
Dies 4-16, 356F3
WHITEHEAD, Paxton
Crucifer of Blood opens 9-28, 1031C1
WHITE House—*See CARTER—CABINET & White House Staff*
WHITEHURST, Rep. G. William (R, Va.)
Reelected 11-7, 852D3
WHITE Motor Corp.
Minn pensn funds law backed by Sup Ct 4-3, 308F3
WHITE Sands Missile Range, N.M.—*See NEW Mexico*
WHITE Weld Holdings Inc.
Merrill Lynch plans purchase, Credit Suisse stake 4-14, 283B2
WHITLAM, Gough
Kerr resigns UNESCO post 3-2, 165E1-A2
Quits politics 7-14, 555A2
Fraser budget cuts protested 8-21, 646G1
WHITLEY, Rep. Charles (D, N.C.)
Reelected 11-7, 851B3
WHITNEY, Betsey Cushing (Mrs. John Hay)
Sister dies 11-4, 972B3
WHITNEY, Craig R.
USSR chrgs slander 6-28, issues statemt 7-3, 518C1-F2
Sovt ct convicts 7-18, 575D2
Returns USSR 7-30, pays fine 8-4, 634B1
Sovt ct closes case 8-18, 651F1
Warned by Sovt Forgn Min 8-24, 670C2
WHITNEY, Ray
Wins Wycombe by-electn 4-27, 329G1
WHITNEY, Tom
Loses primary for Iowa gov 6-6, 448E1
WHITT, Richard
Wins Pulitzer Prize 4-17, 315A2
WHITTAKER, James
Gray Lady Down released 3-10, 619B2
WHITTAKER, Robert
Wins Kan US House primary 8-1, 606F1
Elected 11-7, 850D4, 854F2
WHITTEN, Rep. Jamie J. (D, Miss.)
Reelected 11-7, 851B2
WHITWORTH, Kathy
Lopez ties tourn win mark 6-11, 580A3
Ties for 2d in Lady Stroh's Open 8-24, 672F3
WHO—*See UNITED Nations—World Health Organization*
WHO (singing group)
Who Are You on best-seller list 9-6, 708F1; 10-11, 800F3
Moon dies 9-7, 778F1
WHO Are the DeBolts? And Where Did They Get Nineteen Kids? (film)
Wins Oscar 4-3, 315D3
WHO Are You (recording)
On best-seller list 9-6, 708F1; 10-11, 800F3

1979

Sentenced in Moscone-Milk slaying 7-3, 547E3
WHITE, Danny
NFL '78 punting ldr 1-6, 80F2
WHITE, Donna Horton
2d in Women's Intl 5-6, 587E2
WHITE, Frank
Wins Golden Glove Award 11-20, 956C1
WHITE, Fred
Stabbed in Attica racial brawl 6-3, 548A3
WHITE, Gary Michael
Sees Egypt, Israel ldrs; more US aid sought 9-11, 677A2
Promise released 3-7, 528D3
WHITE, Irving S.
Magician of Lublin released 11-9, 1007G3
WHITE, John C.
Scores draft-Kennedy move 5-23, 384D2
On electn results 11-6, 846A2
Endorses Carter 11-8, 961C2
WHITE, JoJo
Traded to Warriors 1-30, 526E2
WHITE, Mayor Kevin (Boston, Mass.)
Boston library sale of Stuart portraits halted 4-14, 374G3
Reelected 11-6, 846C3
WHITE, Mark
Probes Clements-Sedco link 9-22, 718C3
Sues Sedco Permargo for oil spill cleanup 10-18, 809D2
WHITE, Randy
Steelers win Super Bowl 1-21, 63F1
WHITE, R. Stuart
Poet & Rent opens 5-9, 712A2
WHITE, Timothy
Claims new hominid species 1-18, Leakey disputes 2-17, 137F3-138D1
WHITE Consolidated Industries Inc.
Frigidaire purchased from GM 1-31, 131A3
WHITEHEAD, Clay T.
Nixon Admin pub TV moves disclosed 2-24, 194G1
WHITE House—*See CARTER—CABINET & White House Staff*
WHITEHOUSE, Alton W.
Calif-Tex pipe canceled 3-13, 183D1
Reaffirms Calif-Tex pipe cancellatn 5-24, 396A2
WHITEHURST, Rep. G. William (R, Va)
Urges Iranian deportatns 11-8, 843B1
WHITELAW, Arthur
Utter Glory opens 5-13, 712C3
WHITELAW, William
UK home secy 5-5, 338E1
WHITEMAN, Unison
Grenada aide to prime min 3-23, 237A1
WHITSON, Ed
Traded to Giants 6-28, 1002A3
WHITTEN, Rep. Jamie L. (D, Miss.)
Elected Appropriatns Com chrmn 1-23, 71F1
WHITTINGTON, Bill
Wins LeMans 6-10, 490D3
WHITTINGTON, Don
Wins LeMans 6-10, 490D3
WHITTLE, Christopher
Esquire purchase rptd 5-1, 334D2
WHITWORTH, Kathy
Ties for 2d in Lady Keystone Open 6-24, 587C3
WHO—*See UNITED Nations—World Health Organization*
WHO (singing group)
Ohio rock concert stampede 12-3, 954A2
WHO Are the Debolts and Where Did They Get 19 Kids? (TV program)
Wins Emmy 9-9, 858E2

1980

WHITE, Danny
NFL '79 punting ldr 1-5, 8F3
WHITE, Donna Horton
Wins Lady Citrus Open 4-20, Coca-Cola 5-18, 412D3, 413A1
WHITE, Frank
In World Series 10-14—10-21, 812E1-E3
Wins Golden Glove Award 12-6, 926D1
WHITE, Frank D.
Elected Ark gov 11-4, 845D2, 847B1, 849A2
WHITE, James R.
Smoking risk to nonsmokers rptd 3-26, 318B2
WHITE, John C.
Rebuts Brock Carter criticism 1-2, 5C1
Readies Carter campaign 5-2, Kennedy assails 5-5, 366E3-367A1
Anti-Reagan strategy set 7-15, 549C3
Assails Reagan Klan remark 9-2, 664A1
WHITE, Rep. Richard Crawford (D, Tex.)
Female draft registratn rejctd 3-6, 188C3
Mil recruitmt amendmt OKd by House 9-16, 741F3
Reelected 11-4, 844A3
WHITE, Robert E.
Scores El Salvador violence 3-28, 3-30, 253F3
Home besieged 5-10—5-12, US Emb machine-gunned 5-12, 372E3
Emb office hit by rocket grenades 9-16, 708C1
Scores Reagan Latin policy, reveals rightist's El Salvador presence 12-9, 941F3
WHITE, Robert L. (Rusty)
Lance mansion rptd purchased 7-9, 639B2
WHITE, Timothy Lee
Found in Calif 3-1, 3 arrested 3-2, 238D2
WHITE, Walter Thomas
Cuba to free 10-13, 789A1
WHITE, Wendy
Wins AIAW singles tennis title 6-11, 607E1
Loses Fla Fed exhibitn match 11-16, 947E2
WHITEHEAD, E. A.
Mecca opens 2-2, 136D3
WHITEHEAD, Robert
Lunch Hour opens 11-12, 892E3
WHITE House Staff—*See under CARTER*
WHITE House Years (book)
On best-seller list 1-13, 40C3
Wins Amer Book Award 5-1, 692E2
WHITEHURST, Rep. G. William (R, Va.)
Reelected 11-4, 844D3
WHITELAW, William
Blacks, cops clash in Bristol 4-2, 274C3
WHITE Motor Corp.
Moss replaces Knudsen 4-23, 456C2
Greathouse quits UAW post 6-4, 457B2
Bankruptcy filed 9-4, 985E3
WHITE River National Forest (Colo.)
Fire damage rptd 6-29, 616D2
WHITLEY, Rep. Charles (D, N.C.)
Reelected 11-4, 843B4
WHITMAN, Alden
Wins Polk award 2-25, 692G3
WHITMAN, Stuart
Guyana released 1-25, 216F2
WHITNEY, Charles (Hawkeye)
In NBA draft 6-10, 447F1
WHITTAKER, Rep. Robert (R, Kan.)
Chrgs FAA computer equipmt faulty 6-30, 666F3
Reelected 11-4, 842D4*
WHITTEN, Rep. Jamie L. (D, Miss.)
Reelected 11-4, 843B2
WHITTINGTON, Bill
Injured in Indy 500 5-25, 637F2
Drops out of LeMans 6-15, 637C3
WHITTINGTON, Don
Drops out of LeMans 6-15, 637C3
WHITWORTH, Kathy
Wins LPGA Team tourn 10-5, 972C2
WHITWORTH, William
Named Atlantic Monthly ed 9-22, 908F2
WHO—*See UNITED Nations--World Health Organization*

1976

WHOLESALE Price Index—*See 'Prices' under ECONOMY*
WHO'S Afraid of Virginia Woolf? (play)
Opens 4-1, 1014C3
WHY Not the Best? (book)
Cited in Carter biog 511G2
WHY Survive? Being Old in America (book)
Butler wins Pulitzer 5-3, 352D3
WHYTE, William G.
Ford golf trips rptd 9-21; Ford, Whyte statemts 9-21—9-30, 722G2-B3, 723F1
WICHITA, Kan.—*See KANSAS*
WICHITA Falls, Tex.—*See TEXAS*
WICHMANN, Tamas
Wins Olympic medal 7-31, 574F1
WICK, Wolfgang
Chrgd as ex-Nazi, Rotary nominatn protested 3-10, 3-11, 380E2
Rotary candidacy withdrawn 3-19, 484D2
WICKEL, Kurt
Arrested in Herstatt fraud 8-26, 679A1
WIDEMAN, Frances
Vs GOP conv platform on ERA 8-18, 601F1
WIDENER, Judge H. Emory
Vs EEOC probe powers extensn 1-23, 70F3
WIDE World of Sports (TV series)
Wins Emmy 5-17, 460C2
WIEFEL, Jurgen
Wins Olympic medal 7-23, 575A2
WIEGAN, Irving
Sentenced 4-12, 316B3
WIEGEL, Hans
Bernhard prosecutn opposed 8-30, 642E2
WIEGEL, Jurgen
Seized on spy chrgs 6-2, 441G3
WIEGHART, James
Kennedy denies pres ticket bid 5-20, 357D2
WIENER, Dr. Alexander S.
Dies 11-6, 970D3
WIESEL, Elie
At Sovt Jews rights conf 2-17—2-19, 206B3
WIESENTHAL, Simon
Rptd ending Nazi hunt 1-9, 97C3
Accuses Austrian exec, vs Rotary nominatn 3-10, 380F2
WIGGINS, Rep. Charles E. (R, Calif.)
Hinshaw expulsn blocked 10-1, 807F1
Reelected 11-2, 829E1
WIGGINS, Donald
Charged 12-15, 952D3
WIKSTROM, Jan Erik
Named to Swedish Cabt 10-8, 794C2
WILCH Jr., Paul
Sentenced 11-30, 921F2
WILCOX, Clayton E.
Sentenced 2-4, 135E3
WILD Jr., Claude C.
Gulf paymts detailed 133C2
Jones pleads guilty 1-29, 134E1
Indicted 3-12, acquitted 7-27, 566A1
Viglia sentenced 8-4, 566B2
Chrgs Dole fund abuse 9-6, retracts 9-8, 665D3
Sen com ends Scott probe 9-15, 980B1
WILDING, Michael
Margaret Leighton dies 1-13, 56E3
WILDLIFE
'75 envrionmental loss, endangered species rptd 1-18, 45B1, D1
US Cong OKs refuges 2-4, 2-17, 152F2-A3; signed 2-27, 982D1
Canada seal-hunt dvpts 3-12—3-24, 250E3
US ct orders porpoise-killing tuna fishing limited 5-11, 398B2; Commerce Dept sets quota 6-11, 570G3
Ford vs porpoise ruling 5-24, 374B1
Wild horse, burro protectn upheld 6-17, 552F3
Horses found dead in Utah 7-4, 587C1
Australia smuggling ring rptd 7-8, 537E1
GOP platform text 8-18, 608B1
Ford proposes refuges 8-29, reactn 8-29—8-31, 644C2-E3
US bans porpoise-killing tuna fishing 10-15, cts uphold 11-10, 11-12, 902B1
Smokey Bear dies 11-9, 995G2
US Sup Ct refuses Miss crane case 11-29, 901C1
Kenya sets probe 12-3, Somali killings, elephant decline rptd 12-14, 947E2
Coyote-poison ban kept 12-23, 980B2
WILDLIFE Federation, National
Environmental rpt issued 1-18, 45C1
NYC ocean sewage-dumping barred 7-23, 570G3
Sup Ct refuses Miss crane case 11-29, 901C1
Kimball visits Carter 12-16, 937C2
WILDLIFE Fund, World—*See WORLD Wildlife Fund*
WILENS, Philip
Gets new Justice Dept post 1-14, 78F3
WILES, Harry G.
Legion boos Carter 8-24, 631E3
WILEY & Sons Inc., John J.
US files consent decree 7-27, 989B2

1977

WHOLESALE Price Index (WPI)—*See ECONOMY—Prices*
WHOOPING Cough—*See MEDICINE—Diseases*
WHY Not the Best? (book)
Carter on proceeds 5-26, 417D2
WHYTEHEAD, Dr. Lawrence
On euthanasia rpt 8-17, 732A2
WICHITA, Kan.—*See KANSAS*
WIDGERY, Lord
Grunwick strikers backed 7-12, 617B2
WIDMAN Jr., Michael F.
Dies 8-14, 696G3
WIDNAR, Al
Brewers confirm firing 11-20, 990C2
WIDOWS & Widowers
Soc Sec widower benefits rule voided 3-2, 192C1; cited 3-21, 230D2
Soc Sec revisns clear House 10-27, 814D3
Soc Sec revisns clear Cong 12-15, 958B2; signed 12-20, 1001C2
WIEGEL, Hans
Named Dutch interior min, dep premr 12-19, 986A1
WIEGEL, Jurgen
Named in W Ger Defns Min spy scandal 12-12, 968E1
WIESENTHAL, Simon
Rpts Mengele in Paraguay 8-17, 803B2
WIGFORSS, Ernst
Dies 1-3, 84G3
WIGGINS, Rep. Charles E. (R, Calif.)
Vs stimulus tax bill 5-16, 381F3
WIGNER, Eugene
Endorses A-power 11-16, 936G3
WILBERFORCE, Lord
Upholds Silkin re mail boycott 7-26, 617D3
WILBORN, Andrea
Davis acquitted of murder 11-17, 928A1
WILCOX, Herbert
Dies 5-15, 452F3
WILD Jr., Claude C.
Sup Ct declines waiver case 5-16, 419A2
WILD Horse Annie—*See JOHNSTON, Velma*
WILDLIFE
US OKs S Africa sealskin imports 1-3, 22C2
Canada duck threat rptd 1-7, 60F3
Ford '78 budget proposals 1-17, 31E3
Carter budget revision 2-22, 124E3
World food loss rptd 2-22, 183E3
Canada seal hunt scored 3-15, 237E3
US drought aid signed 4-7, 273G1
North Sea oil blowout 4-23—4-30, 336E2
FPC splits on Alaska gas pipe route 5-2, 369E3
Kenya bans hunting 5-19, 470D2
House curbs porpoise kills 6-11, 442D3
Intl Inuit conf 6-13—6-17, 619G2
Velma Johnston dies 6-27, 532B3
Comanches, Utes end feud 7-24, 619A3
Ira Gabrielson dies 9-7, 788B1
Sudan canal oppositn rptd 9-7, 844C1
Alaska preserves proposed 9-15, 739A3
Ohio voters reject leg-hold trap ban 11-8, 879F2
Endangered species aid clears Cong 11-30, 938B2; signed 12-19, 1001A3
NY Times-Audubon libel case review declined 12-12, 960E2
Kenya bans game skin, sales 12-12, 976E1
WILDLIFE Management Institute
Ira Gabrielson dies 9-7, 788B1
WILDMON, Rev. Donald E.
TV boycott rptd set 2-18, 158A1
WILD Tongues (book)
Sup Ct refuses Buckley libel case 1-17, 58C1
WILDT Yates, Lt. Col. Gerardo
Named mil attache to Mex 1-3, 45A2
WILEY, Richard E.
On TV violence 2-14, 157D3, 158B1
Scores AT&T ruling 2-24, 217F2
Replaced as Defense gen counsel 4-25, 418A2
FCC suspends TV network probe, term expires 6-30, 583E2-A3
On TV bias study 8-15, 642F3

1978

WHO Is Killing the Great Chefs of Europe (film)
Released 10-6, 970D3
WHOLESALE Price Index (WPI) (producer price index)—*See ECONOMY—Prices*
WHO'LL Stop the Rain (film)
Released 8-25, 1030F3
WICHITA, Kan.—*See KANSAS*
WICKAM, Tracey
Sets 800-m freestyle mark 2-23, 780F2
WICKS, Sidney
Traded to Clippers 8-15, 655A3
WICKWIRE, James
Climbs K2 in Pakistan 9-6, 843E2
WIDENER College (Chester, Pa.)
Loses NCAA Div III basketball title game 3-18, 272B2
WIEGEL, Hans
Affirms Moluccan talks 3-16, 192D1
WIESENTHAL, Simon
Wagner arrested 5-30, 477B2
Scores W Ger Nazi trial limit 11-10, 872B2
WIGGINS, Rep. Charles E. (R, Calif.)
Scores Humphrey-Hawkins bill 3-16, 182F3
Dannemeyer wins seat 11-7, 856G3
WIKSTROM, Jan-Erik
Swedish educ min 10-18, 822A3
WILD Jr., Claude C.
Gives SEC depositn 4-26, settles Gulf paymt chrgs 5-11; gift recipients rptd 6-2, 449B1
WILD and Crazy Guy, A (recording)
On best-seller list 11-8, 888D1; 12-6, 971E1
WILDE, Jennifer
Dare to Love on best-seller list 4-2, 272D3; 4-30, 356B2
WILDE, Oscar (1854-1900)
Diversions & Delights opens 4-12, 887F1
WILDER, Thornton
Hello Dolly opens 3-4, 887A2
WILDERNESS Areas
New areas clear Cong 2-9, 109C2; signed 2-24, 218A2
Alaska lands bill clears House 5-19, 386G1
House votes $1.3 bln bill 7-12, 526B3
$1.2 bln bill cleared 10-13, 834G2
Alaska bill dies 10-15, 785A1
WILDERNESS Society
Carter gets high rating 12-20, 1009F1
WILD Geese (film)
Released 11-11, 970E3
WILDLIFE
Canada defends seal hunt 1-9; '76 earnings, '78 quotas rptd 1-12, 35F2
Canada presses Sovt satellite search 1-24, 57C2; 7-5, 514D3; to monitor radiatn 10-18, 1013B3
'77 environmental loss rptd 85A2, D2
Okefenokee Refuge expanded 3-14, 186B3
Bird kill from French coast oil spill mounts 3-23—3-29, 238E1
Idaho reservatn closed to non-Indians 4-22, 327D1
Montana hunting fee disparity backed by Sup Ct 5-23, 405F3
EPA bars Denver dam permit 5-25, 409D1
Aleuts win seal mistreatmt claim 6-21, 569F1
Canada sets caribou study 7-6, 531B3
Carter vetoes fund authrzn 7-10, 567F3-568B1
Canada settles Inuit hunting claim 7-14, 556B2
Endangered Species Act extended, revised by Sen 7-19, 551A2
NH A-plant cooling plan OKd 8-4, 609B2
Grazing land laws revisn cleared 10-11, 807G2
Endangered Species Act amended by Cong 10-15, 784F3, 834B2; signed 11-10, 1003B1
Seal kill off Scotland canceled 10-16, 816A2
Carter protects Alaska lands 12-1, 936G3
WILDLIFE Federation, National
Rpts environmental decline in '77 85G1
City air quality rated 7-5, 513C1; rpt corrected 7-19, 644B2
WILDMON, Rev. Donald E.
Sears withdraws TV ads 5-12, 599D3

1979

WHOLESALE Price Index (WPI) (producer price index)—*See ECONOMY—Prices*
WHOOPEE! (play)
Opens 2-14, 292F3
WHOSE Life Is It Anyway? (play)
Opens 4-17, 712E3
WHYMARK, Trevor
Whitecaps dethrone Cosmos 8-29, 9-1, win NASL title 9-8, 775G2-B3, E3
WHYTE, Winston
Arrested in plot 10-16, 792A3
WICHITA, Kan.—*See KANSAS*
WICHITA Falls, Tex.—*See TEXAS*
WIDENER Jr., Judge H. Emory
Mandel conviction upset 1-11, 18C1
WIEHAHN, Nicholaas
Comm backs black labor rights 5-1, 332G2
WIEN Air Alaska
CAB blocks Alaska Airlines stock ploy 8-28, judge backs 10-4, 830G1
Stock sale to HFC rptd, Alaska Air sues 11-20; CAB rejcts Alaska NW sale 12-20, 989F1
WIESENTHAL, Simon
On W Ger 'Holocaust' broadcast impact 1-29, 137E2
Heim convicted of war crimes 6-13, 490C1
Mengele extraditn pressure rptd 8-8, bounty offered 8-10, 616B3
WIFEMISTRESS (film)
Released 1-6, 174G3
WIFEY (book)
On best-seller list 8-5, 620D3; 9-2, 672D3
WIGAN, Gareth
Quits Fox Film 6-7, plans Warner unit assn 7-4, 587G3
WIGUTOW, Dan
Last Embrace released 5-3, 528G2
WILBORN, Ted
Traded to Yankees 11-1, 1002C3
WILD and Crazy Guy, A (recording)
On best-seller list 1-10, 80F3
Wins Grammy 2-16, 336F3
WILDE, Cornel
5th Musketeer released 9-7, 820B1
WILDER, Billy
Fedora released 4-14, 528B2
WILDER, Gene
Frisco Kid released 7-6, 820C1
WILDERNESS Areas
US proposal scored 1-4, 16B2
Carter proposes bill 4-16, 282E1
House OKs Alaska land bill 5-16, 366E3
Interior Dept seeks pollutn protectn 9-7, 703B3
WILDERNESS Society
US proposal scored 1-4, 16C2
Vs US timber sales order 6-11, 441D1
WILDING, Anthony F. (Tony) (d. 1916)
Borg wins Wimbledon 7-7, 569D3
WILDING, Michael
Dies 7-8, 588F3
WILDLIFE
Swiss rabies vaccine experimt rptd 2-28, 196E1
Fertilizer kills 10,000 NYS birds 3-18, 206F3
Sudan canal route rptd moved 797B1
Ga refuge protesters jailed 5-4—5-10, 368D1
House OKs Alaska land bill 5-16, 366E3
Australia hikes kangaroo kill quota 7-25, 581C1
Peru vicuna debate rptd 7-26, 584E3
Tellico Dam legis OKd 8-1, 9-10, Carter signs 9-26, 766E2
Uganda herds threatened 8-13, 637D3
Uganda sets 5-yr hunting ban 8-23, 815C3
Feathered artifact sale ban upheld by Sup Ct 11-27, 919F3
US gives rules re wild horses 12-28, 990D1
WILDLIFE Federation, National
Va oil refinery opposed 10-4, 770E1
WILD Oates (play)
Opens 1-8, 292F3
WILEY, Richard E.
FCC 'family hour' power backed 11-20, 1007C1

1980

WHOSE Life Is It Anyway? (play)
Moore wins Tony 6-8, 692D3
WICHITA—*See KANSAS*
WICKER, Judge Veronica
Orders ILA end Sovt boycott 1-29, 169C1
WICKER Man, The (film)
Released 3-26, 416G3
WICKHAM, Gen. John A.
US denies Chun pres support 8-8, 620A3
US qualifies Chun support 8-11, 645A3
WICKHAM, Tracey
Bars Olympic participatn 5-28, 421D1
WIDE-Area Telephone Service (WATS)—*See AMERICAN Telephone & Telegraph Co. (AT&T)*
WIECK, Hans
Signs Sovt econ pact 7-1, 489C2
WIEFEL, Jurgen
Wins Olympic medal 7-25, 623D2
WIERZBICKI, Miroslaw
Quits as Polish govt aide 11-17, 878A2
WIESEL, Elie
At Cambodia border aid vigil 2-6, 108C2
WIESENTHAL, Simon
Honored by Carter 8-5, 638G1
WIESER, Roland
Wins Olympic medal 7-24, 623G3
WILDE, Oscar (1854-1900)
Birthday of Infanta wins Amer Book Award 5-1, 692B2
WILDER, Alec
Dies 12-24, 1004G3
WILDER, Gene
Stir Crazy released 12-12, 1003D2
WILDER, William
Named Hiram-Consumers pres 4-8, 310F3
WILDERNESS Areas
World conf in Australia 6-10, 460F2
Alaska lands bill clears Sen 8-19, 631C2
Calif bond issue results 11-4, 847F3
Alaska lands bill clears House 11-12, 866G2-A3
Alaska lands bill signed 12-2, 915G3-916D1
Calif desert plan issued 12-22, 987A1
WILDERNESS Conference, World
Fraser addresses 6-10, 460F2
WILDERNESS Society
Whalen ousted as Park Svc dir 4-24, successor lauded 5-1, 333D2, E2
Turnage denounces Watt apptmt 12-22, 979G3
WILDLIFE
Adamson found dead 1-3, 104D1
Utah State of State message 1-14, 270C2
Acid rain defined 145B3
Adamson slaying suspect chrgd 2-2, 238B3
Africa Rift Valley Fever epidemic rptd 3-2, 318F2-D3
Australia kangeroo losses seen 4-7, 272A1
Panda finding mission begins 5-12, 398E1
Mt St Helens damage assessed 5-24—7-4, 503E3, G3
Keeton dies 8-17, 676G1
Alaska lands bill clears Sen 8-19, 631B2
Gravel loses Alaska primary 8-26, 683A2
New conservatn law enactd 9-29, 915B3
SD voters lift dove hunting ban 11-4, 847D3
Alaska lands bill clears House 11-12, 866E2
Alaska lands bill signed 12-2, 915G3-916D1
Calif desert plan issued 12-22, 987C1
WILEY, Bell I.
Dies 4-4, 360G3
WILEY, Clifford
NCAA aid limit case declined by Sup Ct 5-12, 426B3
WILEY, Peter
Wins S Africa by-electn, lauds Botha 9-3, 690C1
WILEY, Gov. Richard W. (D, S.C.)
To head A-waste advisory panel 2-12, 128D1
WILEY & Sons Inc., John
Photocopy co sued 2-5, 119G3
Photocopy suit rptd setld 3-21, 376D3

1976

WILKEY, Judge Malcolm R.
Upholds Ehrlichman verdict 5-17, 379F1
WILKIE, David
Wins Olympic medals 7-20, 7-24, 562D3, 575C2, D2
WILK Industries
Chrgd re Arab boycott 10-8, 785D3
WILKINS, Caroline
Renamed to Dem post 7-16, 532B3
WILKINS, Clarence
Resigns 9-17, 809C1
WILKINS, Mac
Wins Olympic medal 7-25, 575G3
WILKINS, Judge Philip
Orders Soliah freed on bail 1-15, 70A2
WILKINS, Roy
Resigns as NAACP dir 1-12, 80B2
Scores Ford busing bills 6-24, 452D2
Rejcts retiremt 7-1, NAACP defers decisn 7-2, 504G2
On Miss NAACP boycott ruling 8-12, 671E2
NAACP successor named 11-6, 892A2
WILKINSON, Bill
Carter church ends black ban 11-14, 864G2
WILKOMIRSKA, Wanda
Polish charter chng protest rptd 2-10, 268F1
WILKOWSKI, Jean M.
Replaced as Zambia amb 8-4, 808B1
WILLE, Frank E.
Rpts bank 'problem' list 1-23, 112G1
On GAO audit plan 2-9, 112D2
Succeeded as FDIC chrmn 3-17, 232C1
WILLIAM, Shirley
Rpts UK price curb plan 2-11, 173F1
WILLIAM and Mary, College of (Williamsburg, Va.)
Ford, Carter debate site 10-22, 800A1
WILLIAMS, Albert
On Chile, Uruguay rights abuse 4-21, 382G3
WILLIAMS, Betty
On Sinn Fein oppositn 10-9; car attacked 10-10, 773D3, F3
Ulster peace rally in London 11-27, 1008E1
WILLIAMS, David Edward
Sought in weapons case 12-13, 952F3
WILLIAMS, Dick
Named Expos mgr 10-4, 815G3
WILLIAMS, Edward Bennett
Renamed to Dem post 7-16, 532B3
WILLIAMS, Eric
PNM wins electns 9-13, 714G2-E3
WILLIAMS, Gerald P.
Indicted 5-7, 349E1
Acquitted 9-2, 767F3
WILLIAMS Jr., Sen. Harrison A. (D, N.J.)
Wins primary 6-8, 409F3, 410A1
Carter sees campaign role 6-30, 468F1
AFL-CIO donatn rptd 10-22, 938D3
Tours NJ with Mondale 10-25, 803G3
Reelected 11-2, 820D1, 821B2, 828D2
WILLIAMS, Hosea
Leads anti-Carter protest 4-13, 261D2
WILLIAMS, John
Wins Grammy 2-28, 460A3
Wins Oscar 3-29, 240B3
WILLIAMS, John Bell
Endorses Ford 9-26, 723C3
WILLIAMS, Larry E.
Gurney acquitted 10-27, 846A1, C1
WILLIAMS, Maurice
Rpt disputed poor natn aid data 1-12, 15E1
WILLIAMS, Randy
Wins Olympic medal 7-29, 576B1
WILLIAMS, Dr. Robert E.
Finds gas clouds in space 5-25, 443F2
WILLIAMS, Robert F.
Kidnap chrgs dismissed 1-16, 79A1
WILLIAMS, Sammy
Wins Tony award 4-18, 460D2
WILLIAMS, Shirley
Retains post, named paymaster gen 4-8, 266F3
Named UK educ secy 9-10, 693G3, 694A1
Loses dep ldr electn 10-21, 853A2, B2
WILLIAMS, Tennessee
Memoirs on best-seller list 12-5, 972D2
WILLIAMS, William A. H.
Sentenced 9-17, 796E3

1977

WILKENS, Lenny
Hired as Sonics coach 11-30, 991D1
WILKINSON, Bill
Ga KKK rally disrupted 7-2, 540B1
WILKINSON, Etta
Barred from S Africa diner 2-5, 101A1
WILL, George F.
Wins Pulitzer Prize 4-18, 355G2
WILL, Judge Hubert
Order FBI files on ACLU released 6-19, 481C1
WILLARD, Beatrice E.
Replaced on envirnmt cncl 4-4, 272C3
WILLIAMS, Betty
Wins Nobel Prize 10-10, 951C2
WILLIAMS, Dave
NHL season ldr 4-3, 262G3
WILLIAMS, Eddie N.
Blacks meet re govt 'neglect' 8-29, 702F1
WILLIAMS, Edward Bennett
To defend Ginzburg 2-28, 226D2
Rpts Sovt visa denied 6-1, 436F2
Helms sentenced 11-4, 861G1
WILLIAMS, Eric (Trinidad & Tobago prime minister)
Sees US envoy Young 8-11—8-12, 647B1
WILLIAMS, Harold M.
Named to SEC 3-30, confrmd 4-7, 272D3
Warns accountants 6-13, 519E2
WILLIAMS Jr., Sen. Harrison A. (D, N.J.)
'76 spec interest gifts rptd 1-15, 2-15, 128A2, C2, F3, 129A1, F1
Mass transit bill delay asked 2-25, 213B3
Vance backs boycott curbs 2-28, 167D1
'76 campaign surplus rptd 5-4, 482G1
WILLIAMS, John
On Canal Zone treaty reactn 9-7, 679A3
WILLIAMS, Judy
Protests shantytown demolitn 8-10, 640B1
WILLIAMS, Maurice
Killed 3-9, 192F2
Hanafis indicted 5-3, 396A1; sentenced 9-6, 711F1
WILLIAMS, Paul
Song wins Oscar 3-28, 264D1
WILLIAMS, Ray
In NBA draft 6-10, 584A2
WILLIAMS, Robert Anthony
Miranda rule review sidestepped 3-23, 275B3
WILLIAMS, Ronald (d. 1975)
Peltier sentncd 6-2, 492A1
WILLIAMS, Roy L.
To resign as pensn trustee 3-13, 195E1
WILLIAMS, Shirley
Grunwick strike violence 7-11, 543G3
WILLIAMS, Ted
Carew named AL MVP 11-16, 927C1
WILLIAMS, Tom
Recall asked 8-10, 640B1
WILLIAMS Brothers Concrete Co.
Sup Ct refuses US Steel case 2-22, 149C3

1978

WILHELM, Janusz
Admits censorship often excessive 2-24, 180A3
WILKENS, Lenny
Signs Sonics 5-yr contract 7-11, 656A2
WILKES, Frank
Urges Lynch, Holding corruptn probe 9-14, 771F2
WILKEY, Judge Malcolm R.
Voides WESH-TV license renewal, sets guidelines 9-25, 907G3
WILKINS, Collie Leroy
Rowe indicted for '65 slaying 7-20, 720E2
WILKINS, Roy
Linked to FBI anti-King effort, denial rptd 5-31, 410E3
WILKINSON, Charles B. (Bud)
Named Cardinals coach 3-2, 171C1
WILLENS, Doris
Piano Bar opens 6-8, 887E2
WILLIAMS, A. H. Williams
Murphy cites abductn 10-8, 824E1
WILLIAMS, Barbara
Chrgd in welfare fraud 7-25, 684F3
Convicted 11-31, sentncd 12-28, 1029C1
WILLIAMS, Betty
To quit peace movemt 4-15, disputes rptd 4-17, 373B1
WILLIAMS, Delvin
NFL '77 touchdown, rushing ldr 1-1, 56E2, E3
Traded to Dolphins 4-17, 336E1
WILLIAMS, Deniece
'Too Much' on best-seller list 5-3, 356D1; 6-7, 460F3
WILLIAMS, Doug
In NFL draft, NCAA passing record cited 5-2, 336B1, F2
WILLIAMS, Edy
Attempts strip-tease at Ali-Spinks bout 9-15, 726F1
WILLIAMS, Elmo
Caravans released 11-1, 969F3 ★
WILLIAMS, Emlyn
Playboy of Weekend World opens 11-16, 1031G2
WILLIAMS, Freeman
In NBA draft 6-9, 457F2
Traded to Clippers 7-7, 655A3
WILLIAMS Jr., Sen. Harrison A. (D, N.J.)
Asks Sun Oil Becton Dickinson purchase probe 1-27, 66B1
Votes for Panama Canal neutrality pact 3-16, 177E2
Votes for 2d Canal pact 4-18, 273B1
On labor law revisn set back 6-22, 508D2
WILLIAMS, Jay
Dies 7-12, 620G3
WILLIAMS, Jerre
Named to RR strike bd 9-28, 809C2
WILLIAMS, John
Wins Grammys 2-24, 315G3, 316B1
Wins Oscar 4-3, 315C3
WILLIAMS, Larry
Wins Mont US Sen primary 6-6, 448B2
Loses electn 11-7, 856E1
WILLIAMS, Lorraine
Caravans released 11-1, 969F3 ★
WILLIAMS, Lyle
Wins US House seat 11-7, 851F3, 854E1
WILLIAMS, Pat
Wins US House seat 11-7, 851E2, 856E1
WILLIAMS, Paul
Song wins Grammy 2-24, 315E3
Nunzio released 5-13, 619C3
WILLIAMS, Roy L.
Named in US Teamster fund suit 2-1, 83E1
'76 earnings rptd 2-20, 365B2
WILLIAMS, Samm-Art
Black Body Blues opens 1-24, 887B1
WILLIAMS, W. Dakin
Loses Dem primary for gov 3-21, 207A2

1979

WILKENS, Lenny
Sonics win NBA title 6-1, 507B1
WILKEY, Judge Malcolm Richard
Vs wage-guide contract denial 6-22, 480F2
Backs NSA withholding of data 10-29, 945F3
WILKINSON, Bill
KKK activity rptd 3-15, 7-22, 865B2
Addresses Ala KKK rally 6-9, 866A1
WILKINSON, Charles B. (Bud)
Fired 11-28, 1001D1
WILKINSON, Tom
Edmonton wins Grey Cup 11-25, 1001G1
WILL, Justice Hubert L.
Sentences Serbian natlists 6-22, 491E2
WILLARD, Mary Joan
Monkeys rptdly help handicapped 3-19, 219C2
WILLARDSON, Gregory
Sentenced 12-6–12-7, 1000D1
WILLIAMS, Anthony
Named UK amb to Argentina 11-16, 906D2
WILLIAMS, Dave
NFL '78 kick return ldr 1-6, 80G2
NHL penalty minutes ldr 4-8, 355E2
WILLIAMS, Delvin
NFL '78 rushing ldr 1-6, 80B2
WILLIAMS, Dick
Named top NL mgr 10-23, 956A1
WILLIAMS, Eddie
Plans black voter registratn drive 10-25, 808G1
WILLIAMS, Edward Bennett
Buys Baltimore Orioles 8-2, 619A1
Retained in Gulf+Western fraud suit 11-26, 923A2
WILLIAMS, Gus
Sonics win NBA title 6-1, 506E3-507B1
WILLIAMS Jr., Sen. Harrison A. (D, N.J.)
Human Resources Com chrmn 1-23, 71E2
Introduces compulsive gambling bill 1-30, 152E1
Financial disclosure statemt studied 9-1, 701F3
Votes vs Talmadge denunciatn 10-10, 769G1
Criticizes Goldschmidt 12-6, 984D1
WILLIAMS, Rev. Hosea L.
Ousted as SCLC exec dir 4-10, 283F1
WILLIAMS, John
Wins Grammys 2-16, 336G3
WILLIAMS, Justin
Yeoman pleads guilty to espionage 9-25, 747F3
WILLIAMS, Karen Hastie
Sup Ct workforce data rptd 6-11, 464A2
WILLIAMS, Kristen
Urges trial speedup for robbers 7-22, 655D3
WILLIAMS, Lionel
Convicted of Mineo murder 2-13, 119E2
Sentenced 3-15, 240D2
WILLIAMS, Nigel
Class Enemy opens 6-18, 711C2
WILLIAMS, Olivia
Season To Unravel opens 1-25, 292G2
WILLIAMS, Samm-Art
Old Phantoms opens 2-8, 292D2
WILLIAMS, Shirley
Loses Parlt seat 5-3, 337A2
WILLIAMS, Sylvester (Sly)
In NBA draft 6-25, 507B2
WILLIAMS, T. Harry
Dies 7-6, 588G3
WILLIAMS, Tennessee
Lovely Sunday opens 1-21, 292A2
WILLIAMS, Treat
Hair released 3-13, 528D2
WILLIAMS, William A. H.
'84 parole rptd set 12-18, 1005E3

1980

WILHEMINA (Wilhemina Behmenburg Cooper)
Dies 3-1, 280F2
WILKENSON, Charles B. (Bud)
Hanifan hired as Cardinals coach 1-30, 413C1
WILKERSON, Cathlyn P.
Surrenders 7-8, plea bargain rptd 7-18, 576B3
Sentenced 10-28, 928D1
WILKES, Jamaal
Lakers win NBA title 5-16, 432C1
WILKES, James
UCLA transcript scandal rptd 2-22, 469F2
WILKES-Barre—*See PENNSYLVANIA*
WILKINSON, Bill
Sees Chattanooga mayor 7-26, 576B1
Endorses Reagan 7-30, 664F1
Arrested at Conn rally 9-14, 884C3
WILKINSON, Tom
Edmonton wins Grey Cup 11-23, 999D2
WILL (book)
Excerpts publshd 4-21, 333A3, E3
On best-seller list 6-8, 448C3
WILL, George
Hosts Reagan dinner 11 20, 897F2
WILL, Judge Hubert L.
Rules Amer Airlines immune in DC-10 crash 5-23, 518F3
WILLEBRANDS, Johannes Cardinal
At Dutch bishops synod 1-14—1-31, 156G3
WILLEY, Alan
Chinaglia breaks NASL playoff scoring mark 8-31, 770G2
WILLIAM, Wendi
Navy actn on lesbian chrgs cited 899B1
WILLIAMS, Pfc. Alvin
Chrgd in parachute death 4-1, acquitted 5-27, 460B3
WILLIAMS, Aubrey
Convicted 7-19, 639B3
WILLIAMS, Doug
Rams win NFL conf title 1-6, 8G1
WILLIAMS, Edward Bennett
Scotto sentenced 1-22, 64A3
Joins open conv move 7-30, 570A2
Asks Kennedy release delegates 8-6, 596E2
Backs open conv in rules fight 8-11, 609F2
Named Reagan forgn policy advisor 11-6, 839G2
At Reagan DC fete 11-18, 880E3
WILLIAMS, Eric (Trinidad & Tobago prime minister)
Separatists win Tobago parlt vote 11-24, 923A3
WILLIAMS, Franklin
Borg, McEnroe decline S Africa match offer 10-16, 947E1
WILLIAMS, Geline
Scores Va ERA rally 1-17, 54D3
WILLIAMS, Judge Glen
Rules vs strip-mine law 1-3, 5D2
Strip-mining ruling stayed by Sup Ct 3-17, 226A2
WILLIAMS, Harold M.
Testifies on Hunt silver trading 3-31, 245G1
Backs commodity futures trading curbs 4-14, 289F3
WILLIAMS Jr., Sen. Harrison A. (D, N.J.)
Gets zero rating from ACU 1-18, 53D3
Linked to bribery in Abscam probe 2-2, 2-3, 81C1, 82F1
Facts on 81C1
Abscam probe links to NJ casino project 2-5, 110G3-111B1
Indicted in Abscam probe 10-30, 824C2
FCC backs WOR-TV move to NJ 11-6, 906G1
WILLIAMS, Hosea
Endorses Reagan 10-16, 802B2
Visits Reagan 12-9, 956A2
WILLIAMS, Jeanette (Mrs. Harrison A.)
NJ casino project, Abscam linked 2-5, 111A1
Husband indicted 10-30, 824B3
WILLIAMS, John
Named Boston Pops conductor 1-10, 199F2
Wins Grammy 2-27, 296G3
WILLIAMS, John Bell
Endorses Reagan 10-22, 802C2
WILLIAMS, Landon
Sentenced 1-11, 64A2
WILLIAMS, Rep. Lyle (R, Ohio)
Reelected 11-4, 843F4
WILLIAMS, Melvin
West wins Black Coll All-Star Game 1-5, 62B2
WILLIAMS, Nathaniel D.
Charged in GSA scandal 1-15, 112F1
WILLIAMS, Rep. Pat (D, Mont.)
Reelected 11-4, 843E2, 852A1
WILLIAMS, Paul
Wins Grammy 2-27, 296G3
WILLIAMS, Dr. R. Sanders
On blood clotting studies 5-1, 674A1, C1
WILLIAMS, Robin
Wins Grammy 2-27, 296G3
Popeye released 12-12, 972G3
WILLIAMS, Samm-Art
Home opens 5-7, 392B3
WILLIAMS, Shirley
Liberals woo Labor dissidents 9-12, 708B2
Scores Labor leftist advance 10-1, 768G2
Bars Labor candidacy, scores left 11-28, 921E3-922B1
WILLIAMS, Ted
McCovey sets retiremt 6-22, 637B1
WILLIAMS, Tennessee
Clothes for a Summer Hotel opens 3-26, 392E2
Glass Menagerie opens 11-4, 892C3
WILLIAMS, Lt. Col. Virgil H. (ret.)
On MacArthur WWII 'gift' rpt 1-30, 115A2

1976

WILLIAMSBURG, Va.—*See VIRGINIA*
WILLIAMS Companies, The
To buy Peabody Coal shares 12-14, 985C1
UK-USSR gas deal rptd 12-24, 1011A2
WILLIAMSON, Colin
Mob attacks 12-13, 965A3
WILLIAMSON, Philip G.
Carson, 5 others acquitted 2-6, 124F1
WILLIS, Eric
New S Wales premier 1-20, 46F1
Concedes electn defeat 5-10, 349A3
WILLIS, Ralph
In Australia shadow cabt 1-29, 116E1
On new wage policy 5-28, 415D1
WILLRICH, Mason
A-waste cntrs called hazard 9-7, 671B1
WILLS, Frederick
Denies Cuba, China mil presence rpts 3-3, 253D1
Backs constitutnl amendmts 10-1, 1005F2
WILLSON, Judge Joseph P.
OKs Gulf shareholder setlmt 11-18, 939E1, B2
WILMINGTON, Del.—*See DELAWARE*
WILMINGTON, N.C.—*See NORTH Carolina*
WILSON, Rep. Bob (R, Calif.)
Reelected 11-2, 829E1
WILSON, Rep. Charles (D, Tex.)
Scores Marine Corps 3-31, 378C2
Reelected 11-2, 830C4
WILSON, Rep. Charles H. (D, Calif.)
Reelected 11-2, 829D1
WILSON, Deborah
Wins Olympic medal 7-26, 575E3
WILSON Jr., E. Bright
Gets Medal of Science 10-18, 858G3
WILSON, Harold
Meets Rees 1-6, 19E2, B3
Parlt debates Scot, Wales home-rule plan 1-13—1-19, 72C3, G3
EC backs minimum oil-import price 1-16, 84G3
At Denmark socialist conf 1-18—1-19, 48G2
In Iceland fishing talks 1-24—1-27; proposals rejctd 2-4, security tightened 2-5, 155B1-E1 *
Scores Thatcher re USSR detente 1-28, 101A2
Sets Angola mercenary probe 2-10, 106A1
Sees Cosgrave 3-5, 277G3
S African anti-Liberal role alleged 3-9, 252E2
Wins no-confidence vote 3-11, 239G1
Quits as prime min 3-16, 239C1
Sees Gromyko 3-25, 228G3, 229A1
S African plot vs Hain chrgd 3-31—4-9, 351F1
Callaghan succeeds 4-5, 252A2
Callaghan names new Cabt 4-8, 266D3
Queen knights 5-19, 368B3
Thatcher ties to econ collapse 10-8, 791E3
WILSON, Jack
Withdraws Reagan backing 7-27, 550A2
WILSON, Gen. Louis H.
At Marine Corps probe 5-26, 435G2-A3
WILSON, Michael
USSR cuts sentence 7-30, 655B2
WILSON, T. A.
On Boeing forgn paymts 3-5, 362G1-B2
WILSON, William R.
Canada in Lockheed agrmt 2-29, 250A3
WINCREST Manor Nursing and Rest Home (Chicago, Ill.)
Fire kills 18 1-30, arsonist chrgd 2-3, 271A3
WINE—*See ALCOHOLIC Beverages*
WINKLER, Konrad
Wins Olympic medal 2-9, 159E1
WINKLER, Paul
Buys France-Soir 7-5, 521C2
Stays France-Soir editor 8-26, 651D1

1977

WILLIAMSBURG, Va.—*See VIRGINIA*
WILLIAMS College (Williamstown, Mass.)
Jorling confrmd to EPA 6-21, 626F2
WILLIAMS Co., Don E.
Sup Ct rules on profit-sharing tax deductns 2-22, 150E1
WILLIAMS Cos., The
Peabody Holding Co.—*See separate listing*
WILLIG, George H.
Climbs World Trade tower 5-26, 532A2
WILLINGBORO Township, N.J.—*See NEW Jersey*
WILLIS, Bill
Named to football HOF 1-17, 164C1
Inducted into HOF 7-30, 659A1
WILLS, Elliot (Bump)
Randle slugs mgr 3-28, 310F3 *
WILLS, Maury
Randle slugs mgr 3-28, 310F3
WILMINGTON, Del.—*See DELAWARE*
WILMINGTON, N.C.—*See NORTH Carolina*
WILMINGTON 10—*See NORTH Carolina*
WILNER, Meir
Loses speaker race 6-13, 474F2
WILSON, Archie
Rhodesia transport min 3-10, 223F2
WILSON, Rep. Charles H. (D, Calif.)
Pay raises take effect 2-20, 127A3
WILSON, Charles McMoran—*See MORAN, Lord*
WILSON, Edward O.
Gets Medal of Sci 11-22, 952C1
WILSON, Sir Harold
Callaghan denies secret svc bug 8-23, 745D2
WILSON, Henry
Token UAW pres candidate 5-18, 408F1
WILSON, John
Named Ireland educ min 7-5, 599A1
Tanzanian natl sentncd 10-5, 806A1
WILSON, John T.
Successor named 12-10, 1021B2
WILSON, Kenneth
Kills 2, self 9-5, 848G2
WILSON, Lt. Gen. Samuel
Rpts Sovt defns advances costly 6-30, 673D3
WILSON Food Corp.—*See LTV Corp.*
WIMBLEDON (All-England Lawn Tennis Championship)—*See TENNIS*
WINDHAM, James C.
Dies 5-11, 452F3
WINDMILLS
House OKs Carter energy pkg 8-5, 610B1
Energy tax credit bill clears Sen 10-31, 832A3
Uganda energy obstacles cited 12-11, 975E3
WINFIELD, Dave
NL wins All-Star Game 7-19, 567E2

1978

WILLIAMSBURG, Va.—*See VIRGINIA*
WILLIAMS Cos., The
Pleads guilty, fined for forgn paymts; SEC disclosure cited 3-26, 448B3
Paymts suit cited 11-20, 961D3
WILLIAMSON, David
Players opens 9-6, 887E2
WILLIAMS Rose, Juan—*See TOWNLEY, Michael Vernon*
WILLKIE, Edith Wilk
Dies 4-16, 356F3
WILLKIE, Wendell Lewis (1892-1944)
Widow dies 4-16, 356F3
WILLOW Island, W. Va.—*See WEST Virginia*
WILLRICH, Mason
Backs breeder reactor dvpt 5-10, 346D3
WILLS, Chill
Dies 12-15, 1032G3
WILLS, Elliot (Bump)
AL stolen base ldr 10-2, 928F3
WILLS & Estates—*See also personal names*
Cong sets new tax rules 10-15, 785F3
NYS illegitimate child inheritance law upheld by US Sup Ct 12-11, 981B1
WILMINGTON, Del.—*See DELAWARE*
WILMINGTON, N.C.—*See NORTH Carolina*
WILMINGTON (Del.) Evening Journal (newspaper)
Gannett buys 1-30, 109D3
WILMINGTON (Del.) Morning News (newspaper)
Gannett buys 1-30, 109D3
WILMINGTON 10—*See NORTH Carolina*
WILSON, Rep. Bob (R, Calif.)
Reelected 11-7, 850C2
WILSON, Rep. Charles (D, Tex.)
Nicaragua aid resumptn role rptd 5-16, 376E2
Nicaragua aid released 5-16, 593D2
Reelected 11-7, 852D2
WILSON, Charles Frederick
Freed from prison 12-18, 1028B3
WILSON, Rep. Charles H. (D, Calif.)
Cited for misconduct by ethics com re Park gift 7-13, 527D1
Reprimanded in Korean scandal 10-13, 831D3
Reelected 11-7, 850A2, 856C3
Exempted from House ethics rule chng 12-6, 958D2
WILSON, David Michael
Arrested 5-3, 396A3
WILSON, Edmund
This Room opens 6-15, 760E3
WILSON, Elizabeth
All's Well opens 7-5, 760B1
WILSON, Harold
Foot dies 6-18, 540F2
Rhodesia sanctn-breaking info disputed 9-2—9-7, Parlt debate set 9-28, 756D3
Callaghan urges Rhodesia sanctn violatns probed 12-15, 987D3
WILSON, Jerrel
NFL '77 punting ldr 1-1, 56B3
WILSON, Jimmy
Faces La US House runoff 9-16, 736E3
Loses electn 11-7, 855C2
WILSON, Lanford
5th of July opens 4-27, 760B2
WILSON, Larry
Enters Pro Football HoF 7-29, 1025D1
WILSON, Gen. Louis
Urges draft registratn 10-29, 895C1
WILSON, Michael
Dies 4-9, 356G3
WILSON, Neal
Elected 7th-day Adventists pres, vs Hack separatn 10-20, 907G2
WILSON, Mayor Pete (San Diego, Calif.)
4th in primary for gov 6-6, 447D3
WILSON, Robert W.
Wins Nobel Prize 10-17, 886B2
WILSON, Lt. Gen. Samuel V.
Sees USSR civil defns threat 2-17, 127B1
WILSON, Willie
AL stolen base ldr 10-2, 928F3
WILSON Sporting Goods Co.—*See under PEPSICO Inc.*
WIMBLEDON (All-England Lawn Tennis Championship)—*See TENNIS*
WINCHESTER Group—*See OLIN Corp.*
WIND Energy
Environmtal cncl rpt backs dvpt 4-12, 281F3
Carter rpts Wyo 'wind farms' 5-3, 321E3
Small business loan aid signed 7-4, 512A2
Energy bill clears Cong 10-15, 787E2
WINE—*See ALCOHOLIC Beverages*
WINFIELD, Dave
NL wins All-Star Game 7-11, 559D3, E3
NL batting ldr 10-2, 928D2
WINGS (singing group)
With a Little Luck on best-seller list 5-3, 356D1
London Town on best-seller list 5-3, 356E1; 6-7, 460G3
WINITSKY, Alex
Silver Bears released 4-20, 619G3
WINKEL, Adrian P.
On Bikini residents resetlmt 4-12, 278G2-A3
WINKLES, Bobby
Resigns as A's mgr 5-23, 560D1
WINN, Francis
Wins Synanon damage suit 9-19; atty attacked 10-10, 2 members chrgd 10-17, 841A3, D3

1979

WILLIAMSBURG, Va.—*See VIRGINIA*
WILLIAMS Co., J. B.—*See NABISCO*
WILLIAMS Cos., The
Price violatn chrgd 5-17, 385A2
WILLIAMS Rose, Juan—*See TOWNLEY, Michael Vernon*
WILLIAMS v. Zbaraz
Case accepted by Sup Ct 11-26, 919A2
WILLINGHAM, Thomas R.
Sentenced in GSA scandal 10-10, 964G3
WILLIS, Bishop Jeffery H.
Mormon feminist tried 12-1, excommunicated 12-5, 929C3
WILLIS, Ralph
Scores govt on econ 5-30, 443C2
WILLMOT, Bud
Steady Growth wins Queen's Plate 6-30, 876D3
WILLOW Run, Mich.—*See MICHIGAN*
WILLS, Elliot (Bump)
AL stolen base ldr 9-30, 955F3
WILMER, Cutler & Pickering
Cutler named Carter counsel 8-17, 623E1
WILMINGTON, Del.—*See DELAWARE*
WILMINGTON, N.C.—*See NORTH Carolina*
WILMINGTON News-Journal (newspaper)
CIA scored on Paisley death probe 7-8, 520F2
WILMINGTON Trust Co. v. Penn Central Transportation
Case refused by Sup Ct 10-1, 768E1
WILMOUTH, Robert K.
On Chicago bd wheat speculatn 3-15, 201D3
WILSON, Bruce
Named to NASL All-Star team 8-27, 776E1
WILSON, Rep. Charles (D, Tex.)
Scores Cabt, staff shake-up 7-19, 531B3
Proposed DC funds compromise bill signed 10-30, 870B1
Urges Iranian deportatns 11-8, 843A1
WILSON, Rep. Charles H. (D, Calif.)
House rules violatns chrgd; denies, announces candidacy 12-13, 945E2
WILSON, Edward O.
Wins Pulitzer 4-16, 336G2
WILSON, Elizabeth
Taken in Marriage opens 2-26, 292D3
WILSON, Harry L.
On Dade County tax cut vote 9-18, 724C2
WILSON, Sir Henry Hughes (1864-1922)
Cited re Neave murder 3-30, 254B2
WILSON, Jimmy
Leach pleads not guilty to vote buying 7-24, 561D1
WILSON, Lanford
Talley's Folley opens 5-3, 712G2
WILSON, Larry
Named Cardinals interim coach 11-28, 1001D1
WILSON, Lewis R. (Hack)
Inducted into Baseball HOF 8-5, 618D3
WILSON, Gen. Louis H.
Marine Corps successor named 4-18, 307G2
WILSON, Michael
In Canadian Cabt 6-4, 423G3
Arab deal losses rptd 10-22, 833G2
WILSON, Peter C.
Announces retirement 11-11, 892D2
WILSON, T. A.
On '78 top-paid execs list 5-14, 347F3
WILSON, Willie
AL batting, stolen base ldr 9-30, 955E3, F3
WILSON College (Chambersburg, Pa.)
Ct bars closing 5-26, Waggoner resigns 5-27, 482C1
WILSON v. Omaha Indian Tribe
Case remanded by Sup Ct 6-20, 516G1
WILT, Roger
Sentncd in GSA kickback scandal 3-24, 3-26, 367A3
WILZAK, Crissy
1940's Radio Hour opens 10-7, 956F3
WIMBLEDON (All-England Lawn Tennis Championship)—*See TENNIS*
WINBUSH, Marilynn
But Never Jam Today opens 7-31, 711A2
WIND Energy
Swedish energy bill rptd 3-13, 213F3
Calif energy plan proposed 5-31, 419A1
Carter goals stated 6-20, 198B1
Admin plans previewed 7-8, 517E3
WINDHAM College (Putney, Vt.) (defunct)
Forgn student recruitmt abuses rptd 3-2, 167B3
WINDOM, Bernie
Quits Baker campaign post 12-3, 983A2
WINE—*See ALCOHOL*
WINE Untouched (play)
Opens 6-22, 712F3
WINFIELD, Dave
NL wins All-Star Game 7-17, 569A1, B1
NL batting ldr 9-30, MVP vote rptd 11-13, wins Golden Glove Award 11-20, 955A2, E2, 956D1
WINGS (play)
Opens 1-28, 292G3
WINITSKY, Alex
Cuba released 12-21, 1007B3
WINKLER, Irwin
Rocky II released 6-15, 820C3
WINN, Rev. Albert C.
Elected Presby Church moderator 5-23, 547D2

1980

WILLIAMSBURG (oil tanker)
In Dutch ocean liner fire rescue 10-4, 769D2
WILLIAMS 3d, Henry A.
Named unindicted co-conspirator in Abscam probe 10-30, 824F2
WILLIAMSON, Nicol
Human Factor released 2-8, 216A3
WILLIAMSON County—*See ILLINOIS*
WILLIAMS v. Zbaraz
Case argued in Sup Ct 4-21, 306B2
Case decided by Sup Ct 6-30, 491F2
WILLIS, Anthony
Wins Olympic medal 8-2, 622F1
WILLIS, Gordon
Windows released 1-18, 216G3
WILLIS, Jack
Wins Polk award 2-25, 692F3
WILLS, Maury
Hired as Mariners mgr 8-4, 926A2
WILLSON, Meredith
Music Man opens 6-6, 756F3
WILMINGTON 10—*See DELAWARE, NORTH Carolina*
WILMINGTON (Ohio) College
Loses NAIA Div II football title game 12-13, 999A3
WILSON, Rep. Charles (D, Tex.)
Scores Myers expulsn proceedings 10-2, 740E1
Reelected 11-4, 844D2
WILSON, Rep. Charles H. (D, Calif.)
Found guilty of financial misconduct 4-16, censure asked 4-24, 333F3
Loses primary 6-3, 439A2
Censured by House 6-10, 438F1-E2
Dymally wins seat 11-4, 846E3
WILSON, Claire Francis
Detained in Chile 7-16—7-18, torture chrgs disputed 7-29—9-8, 749F1
WILSON, Elizabeth
Morning's at Seven opens 4-10, 392E3
WILSON, J. C.
NFL '79 interceptn ldr 1-5, 8C2
WILSON, Lanford
Wins Pulitzer 4-14, 296C2, E2
5th of July opens 11-6, 892C3
WILSON, Marc
North wins Senior Bowl 1-12, 62B2
In NFL draft 4-29, 336F2
WILSON, Otis
In NFL draft 4-29, 336F2
WILSON, Rodney
Wins IC4A 55-m hurdles 3-9, 892C2
WILSON, Willie
AL batting, stolen base ldr 10-6, 926D3-F3
In World Series 10-14—10-21, sets strikeout mark 10-12, 811B3, 812G3
Wins Golden Glove Award 12-6, 926D1
WILSON, Woodrow (1913-21)
Bryan resignatn cited 4-28, 323D2
WIMBLEDON (All-England Lawn Tennis Championship)—*See TENNIS*
WIN, Ne
U Nu returns from exile 7-29, 617D3
WINBERRY, Charles H.
ABA finds 'unqualified' for US judgeship 3-2, Sen panel rejects 3-4, 250E2
WIND Energy
Carter budget proposals 1-28, 72A1
WINDOWS (film)
Released 1-18, 216G3
WINDSOR, Duke of (Edward Albert Christian George Andrew Patrick David) (Edward VIII) (1895-1972)
Nazi contacts alleged, Flynn suit filed 8-1, 639F1
WINDSOR, Duchess of (Wallis Warfield Simpson)
Nazi contacts alleged, Flynn suit filed 8-1, 639F1
WINE—*See ALCOHOL*
WINFIELD, Dave
NL wins All-Star Game 7-8, 636A2
In free agent draft 11-13, signs record pact with Yankees 999F3-1000C1
Wins Golden Glove Award 12-6, 926E1
WINFIELD Growth Fund Inc.
Winfield & Co.
Mutual fund insurance case refused by Sup Ct 3-24, 265F1
WINGER, Debra
Urban Cowboy released 6-11, 675F3
WINGS (singing group)
McCartney deported from Japan 1-26, 200F2
Win Grammy 2-27, 296C3
WINKLER, Angela
Knife in the Head released 4-23, 416B3
WINKLER, Anton
Wins Olympic medal 2-16, 156C1
WINKLER, Irwin
Raging Bull released 11-14, 972G3
WINKLER, Konrad
Wins Olympic medal 2-19, 155B3

1976

WINN Jr., Rep. Larry (R, Kan.)
Reelected 11-2, 829D3
WINN-Dixie Stores Inc.
Davis campaign donatn rptd 10-22, 939A1
WINNING Through Intimidation (book)
On best seller list 1-25, 80C3; 2-29, 208F3; 12-5, 972C2
WINSPEARE Guicciardi, Vittorio
In E Timor, barred from Fretelin area; meets reps in Australia 2-2, 122D3
Meets Portugal forgn min 2-11, 192F1
WINSTON-Salem, N.C.—*See NORTH Carolina*
WINSTON-Salem Journal (newspaper)
Ford endorsement rptd 10-30, 831F2
WINTER, Gordon
S African anti-Liberal plot alleged 3-10, 252G2
WINTER Haven, Fla.—*See FLORIDA*
WINTER Park, Fla.—*See FLORIDA*

WIRETAPPING & Electronic Surveillance
'58 Danish CP bugging rptd 1-9, 48D3
Kissinger, Haldeman file Halperin depositns 1-12, 3-11; Nixon depositn released 3-10, 183G3, 184B2
Sovt microwave taps in US emb rptd 2-6—2-10, 122D2
Ford seeks spying curbs 2-17, 2-18, 127F1, A3
Canada seeks curbs ease 2-24, 250B3
Sovts tie microwaves to US taps 2-26, 196C2
Nixon testimony on Chile released 3-11, 183D3
Sup Ct bars JDL case review 4-19, 331F1
Sen intellignc com rpts proposals 4-28, 324G3, 328C1
Sen staff com details FBI abuses 5-5, 5-9, 344B1, E2
Times editor sues Nixon 5-10, 349E2
Dem platform text 6-15, 472G1, 474F1
PR scandal 7-30—11-27, 994E3
Illegal FBI activities rptd 8-22, 635D1
Warrant bill not cleared 10-2, 884E1
Nixon, 2 aides liable re Halperin 12-16, 980A3-981B1
SW Bell loses suit 12-17, 995E1-A2

WIROWSKI, Maciej
Named planning comm dep 12-2, 926D3
WIRTH, Rep. Timothy E. (D, Colo.)
Reelected 11-2, 824E1, 829F1
WISBEY, Thomas
Paroled 3-15, 316F3
WISCHNEWSKI, Hans-Juegen
Disputes '77 EEC budget priorities 4-5, 276F1

WISCONSIN
Primary date set 22A2
'70 bombing suspect arrested 1-7, 32C2
Reagan campaigns 1-13, 22F1
Milwaukee integratn ordrd 1-19, 42B3
Campaign dvpts 3-15—4-7, 233F1, 245F1-F3
Ex-gov Kohler dies 3-21, 316A1
Pres primary results 4-6, Ford comments 4-7, 245B1, C2
Menominee ldr convicted 4-21, 316G3
Union overtime bar upheld 6-25, 552B2
US Mayors Conf in Milwaukee 6-26—7-1, 468B1, 493C1
Dem conv women delegates, table 508E2
Dem conv pres vote, table 7-14, 507E2
Bombing suspect sentncd 8-6, 776G1
GOP pre-conv delegate count 8-14, 583E3
GOP conv pres, vp vote tables 8-18—8-19, 8-19, 599E1, E3
Sen primaries unopposed 9-14, 705C2
Milwaukee integratn praised 9-14, 993A1
Fscl '75 per capita income, tax burden rptd 9-15, 10-12, 959B2
Mondale visits 9-22, 9-29, 725A1, C1
Bahamas hangs Milwaukee man 10-19, 1012D2
Ford, Mondale in Milwaukee 10-29, 826C3, 827C2
Election results 11-2; pres 818D1, E1, 819A2; cong 820D1, 824A1, 828D3, 831A3-A4
US Sup Ct backs pub worker contract debate right 12-8, 960F1-C2

1977

WINN Jr., Rep. Larry (R, Kan.)
Aide testifies at Korea lobbying hearings 10-19—10-21, 816E2
WINPISINGER, William
Joins AFL-CIO exec cncl 12-12, 961F1
WINSLOW, Ola Elizabeth
Dies 9-27, 788B3
WINTERS v. Miller
Religious mental patient drug case refused 11-28, 919B3

WIRETAPPING & Electronic Surveillance
FBI informer guidelines set 1-5, 15G2
IRS rptd cleared in Miami probe 1-6, 16D3
Sup Ct expands govt use 1-18, 58E1
Suits vs FBI re King dismissed 1-31, 77C2
FBI curbs proposed 2-15, 157B3
King rpt scores FBI 2-18, 149B2
W Ger incidents 3-16, 3-17, 259B3, 260B1
Ex-FBI offcl indicted 4-7, 275F1
Micronesia surveillnc detailed 5-3, 387A1
New Haven abuses charged 5-12, 422D3
Carter asks curbs 5-18, 386E2
US surveillance of S Korea pres mansn rptd 6-19, 556C3
USSR rptd monitoring US phones 7-10, 551E1-A2
Carter downplays USSR eavesdropping 7-12, 533C2
Halperin awarded $5 in suit 8-5, 652B2
Mondale addresses ABA conv 8-8, 630C1
NZ prime min asks powers 9-8, 729D3
SW Bell loses slander suit, acquitted on tap chrgs 9-12, 724F2, A3
Scientology min freed 9-14, 940F2
US tap of Panama Canal talks rptd, denied, 9-16; US Sen com probes 9-16—9-19, 716A2
Sen Canal tap hearings postponed 9-30, 756D1
Defns Dept knowledge of Korea lobbying rptd 10-12, 816E3
NZ legalizatn bill protested 10-18, 926A1
Phone surveillnc ct orders backed 12-7, 939F1
FBI probe attys clash with Bell 12-7, 940A1
Canada—*See CANADA—RCMP*

WIRTH, Rep. Timothy E. (D, Colo.)
Moves vs AT&T 2-24, 217G2
Scores TV violence rpt 10-24, 921A2
WIRTZ, Willard
SAT rpt issued 8-23, 739E1
WISCHNEWSKI, Hans-Jurgen
W Ger raid frees hijacked jet 10-18, 789C2

WISCONSIN
Legislature schedule rptd 6G2
FEA orders home heating oil productn hike 1-24, 54G1
Racine teachers strike 1-25—3-17, 481C2
Sovt boxing match in Milwaukee 2-5, 263B2
Swine flu case cited 2-8, 103C3
Milwaukee schl integratn goal set 3-11, 216F3
Milk price supports hiked 3-22, 214A1
Soglin reelected Madison mayor 4-5, 252F3
Fed spending inequities chrgd 4-6, 423D3
Milwaukee teachers strike 4-7—5-10, 481E2
Milwaukee populatn rank rptd down 4-14, 388D1
'76 per-capita income table 5-10, 387D2
Lucey named amb to Mex 5-25, 499G3
AMC sets plant layoffs 6-2, 463D3
'70 Madison bomber sentncd 6-8, 6-10, 492C1
Milwaukee busing order vacated 6-29, 557G2
State workers strike 7-3—7-18, 558E2
Schreiber sworn gov 7-7, 560B3
Milwaukee ordrd to end Lake Mich pollutn 7-29, 595B1
Judge recalled re rape case 9-7, 712A1
FRA to buy C&NW stock 9-9, 778B3
'76 per capita income, tax burden table 9-13, 10-18, 821C2
Free abortns continued 10-12, 787A1
Trucking firms sued 11-3, 861A1

1978

WINN Jr., Rep. Larry (R, Kan.)
Reelected 11-7, 850D4
WINNERS and Losers: Battles, Retreats, Gains, Losses and Ruins From a Long War (book)
Wins Natl Book Award 4-10, 315D2
WINNING Isn't Everything (play)
Opens 12-3, 1031C3
WINPISINGER, William
Carter wage curb oppositn rptd 11-21, 917B3
WINSTON, Clara
Wins Natl Book Award 4-10, 315A3
WINSTON, Harry
Dies 12-8, 1032G3
WINSTON, Richard
Wins Natl Book Award 4-10, 315A3
WINTER, Catherine
Bonjour Amour released 6-11, 618D3
WINTHER, Eva
Swedish dep labor mkt min 10-18, 822A3

WIRETAPPING & Electronic Surveillance
FBI favoritism toward US Recording rptd 1-10, 15B2
W Ger tap chrgd 1-14, probe vowed 1-16; defns min quits in 2d incident 2-1, 74B2-C3; 2-3, 93D2
Carter defines intell agency curbs 1-24, 49A3; legislatn introduced in Sen 2-9, 107A1, D1
Haldeman book on Watergate rptd 2-16—2-17, 125B1
SW Bell '76 tap rule reversed 2-16, 142E3
USSR denies Scandinavian spy trucks 3-15, 291F2
Bell asks disciplinary actn vs 68 FBI agents, rpts '77 chrgs vs ex-offcl dropped 4-10, 262B1
Warrantless taps barred by Sen 4-20, 306D1
Natl security warrantless taps curbed by Sen 4-20, 306D1
Nixon memoir excerpt cites Watergate tapes 5-1, 320F1
Fed power broadened by Sup Ct 5-15, 387D2
Viet spy case raises warrantless taps issue 5-19, 390D1
US Moscow Emb bugging rptd 6-1, 6-2; chrgs traded 6-8, 6-9, 476B1
Natl security warrantless taps curbed by House 6-7, 696E3
FBI informant case declined by Sup Ct 6-12, 468D1
US surveillnc bases in Turkey seen reopening 6-28, 587C3
Bell cited for contempt in FBI informants case 7-6, 507A2; order stayed 7-7, 524G3
Turkey OKs US base reopening 10-4, 776G1
2 Brazilians chrg govt taps, Figueiredo admits 10-17, 836F2
ACLU hails warrantless tap curbs 10-20, 981B3
Natl security warrantless tap curbs signed 10-25, 863A1
US emb study discounts Sovt microwave harm 11-20, 924F3
FBI penalizes 4 12-5, 939F2
Canada—*See CANADA—RCMP*

WIRTEN, Rolf
Swedish labor mkt min 10-18, 822A3
WIRTH, Alan
Traded to A's 3-15, 194G3
WIRTH, Rep. Timothy E. (D, Colo.)
Reelected 11-7, 850C2
WISCHNEWSKI, Hans-Jurgen
Sees E Ger re ties 1-28—1-30, 61E3

WISCONSIN
Legislature schedule rptd 14G3
'67, '77 sales-tax rates rptd 1-5, 15G3
State govt tax revenue table 1-9, 84E2
FTC cites Ford re auto engine defect 1-13, 67A3
Sup Ct voids remarriage law 1-18, 65B1
Blizzard hits 1-25—1-26, 105G2
Gavin McKerrow dies 1-27, 96A3
Carter sees gov on coal strike 2-16, 104D2
Truck length limit barred 2-21, 126D1
Kenosha Anaconda strike ends 4-3, 284E3
NCR plans Appleton Paper div sale 5-5, 345C3
'77 prison populatn rptd down 6-3, 440D1
Dems bar 'open primary' 6-9, 448G2
A-plant moratorium ordrd 8-17, 665F2
Milwaukee-area diabetes misdiagnoses rptd 8-29, 947E3
Primary results 9-12, 736G1
AMC, UAW in 2-yr pact 9-25, 737C3
Election results 11-7: cong 846A3, 848F3, 852C4, 854A2; state 845G1, 846B3, 847D1, 853F3, 854G1
Black secy of state noted 11-28, 915D3
Rep Steiger dies 12-4, 1032E3
Milwaukee populatn ranked 12-6, 942F3

1979

WINPISINGER, William
Backs oil industry protest 10-17, 831C2
WINSLOW, Kellen
In NFL draft 5-3, 335F1
WINSTON, Dennis (Dirt)
Steelers win Super Bowl 1-21, 63F1
WINSTON, Hattie
I Love My Wife opens 5-15, 711F3
WINTER, William
Wins Miss Dem gov runoff 8-28, 680E2
Elected 11-6, 846E2
WINTER Kills (film)
Released 5-17, 528G3
WINTERS, Shelley
City on Fire released 9-14, 819G3
WINTERS, William R.
Acquitted re price-fixing 4-29, 327C3
WINTER Signs (play)
Opens 3-11, 712F3
WINTHROPE, Gordon
Arrested re stock fraud 1-10, 37C2

WIRETAPPING & Electronic Surveillance
FBI agent's dismissal rescinded 1-26, 92F2
Australia surveillance bill proposed 3-8, 209F2, C3
CIA wiretap of Khomeini aide rptd barred 3-11, 180B1
Bell contempt citatn overturned 3-19, 207E1
Brecht '43-56 FBI surveillnc rptd 3-29, 367C3
IRS evidence backed by Sup Ct 4-2, 281D2
Covert US entries upheld by Sup Ct 4-18, 346B1
US '78 taps rptd 4-28, 386F3
US tap ct judges named 5-18, 442A3
NJ indictmt details Mafia 5-23, 508C2
Nixon, aides ruled liable in tap suits 7-12, 611D2
FBI charter curbs taps 7-31, 599C2
Eisenhower secret tapes revealed 10-21, other Admin recording policies rptd 10-29, 868G3-869F1
Scientologists convctd as spies 10-26, 839C2; sentncd 12-6-12-7, 1000B1
US rep denies US, Israel bugged Young 10-28, 823A3
Italy anti-terrorist measures effected 12-17, 995G1
Canada—*See CANADA-RCMP*

WISCASSET, Me.—*See MAINE*

WISCONSIN
Legislature schedule rptd 5G3
Kenosha AMC-Renault plant deferred 1-10, 131F2
Blizzards hit 1-12–1-14, 1-24–1-27, 120F1
Milwaukee '78 Nazi activity cited 1-19, 102B1
Laetrile shipmt recalled 3-8, 196A1
Petri elected to Cong 4-3, 265E1, A2
Skornicka elected Madison mayor 4-3, 265C2
Milwaukee schl desegregatn case setld 5-4, 596E2
Draft-Kennedy activity rptd 5-23, 384E2
Amish polio outbreak rptd 6-5, 472F1
Emergency declared re truckers' strike 6-28, 479C2
Grain handlers strike, setlmt reached 7-6–9-25, 722D1, D3-723A1
Sens vote vs trade bill 7-23, 646G3
Ex-Rep Duffy dies 8-16, 671B2
Carter visits 8-19, 622D2
Milwaukee schl busing rptd set 9-2, 679E3
'78 per capita income rptd 9-16, 746D2
Legis OKs DC voting rep amendmt 10-30, 11-1, 851C3
Baker seeks '80 GOP primary win 11-1, 829A1
Milwaukee Rd embargoes track 11-1–11-5, 867G2
Iran interest in Milwaukee bank rptd 11-26, 898A1
Milwaukee '79 living costs ranked 12-28, 991A1
Atomic Energy
A-plant bid rejctd 2-27, 186C2
Point Beach A-plant pipe leaks rptd 5-2, 322B3
Westinghouse settles Wis Elec uranium supply suit 5-5, 366E1
Tyrone A-plant canceled 7-26, 609F3

1980

WINN Jr., Rep. Larry (R, Kan.)
Reelected 11-4, 842D4
WINN-Dixie Stores Inc.
Nader coalitn attacks 4-17, 308B2
WINNINGHAM, Mare
Wins Emmy 9-7, 692D1
WINPISINGER, William
Vs Carter endorsemt 8-20, 647A3
WINPISINGER v. Watson
Case rejected by Sup Ct 4-28, 369A2
WINTERS, Shelley
Shelley on best-seller list 8-17, 640F3; 9-14, 716B3; 10-12, 796E3
WINTOUR, Charles
London newspr merger set 10-1, 750E3

WIRETAPPING & Electronic Surveillance
FBI Seberg probe rptd extensive 1-9, 55D1
S Africa surveillance chrgd 1-15, 60F3
Italy OKs security rules 2-2, 98E3
Brilab probe use rptd 2-8—2-9, 111C3
Galante slaying probe figures indicted 3-3, 215G1
Canada '77 bugging fraud disclosed 4-28, 335A1
Nixon taps case accepted by Sup Ct 5-19, 440C1
Brilab probe indictmts 6-17, 455B1
GOP hq taps suspected 6-21, 6-24, 480D3
Bonanno convicted 9-2, 712G3
Nixon case argued in Sup Ct 12-8, 937A2

WIRNSBERGER, Peter
Wins Olympic medal 2-14, 155F2
WIROWSKI, Maciej
Ousted from Polish Cabt 11-21, 909D2
WIRTH, Rep. Timothy (D, Colo.)
Joins open-conv move 7-25, 570G1
Reelected 11-4, 842C2, 851D3
WIRTHLIN, Richard
On vote results 11-4, 838F2
WISCASSET—*See MAINE*

WISCONSIN
ERISA case declined by Sup Ct 1-14, 37C1
Allis-Chalmers pact set 3-15, 308A3
Tornadoes hit 4-7—4-8, 391G2
DES in cattle rptd 4-24, 358F1
Exxon out-of-state earnings tax backed by Sup Ct 6-10, 511E3
Racine busing, housing integratn study rptd 11-16, 989E3
Crime & Civil Disorders
Milwaukee FALN apartmt raided 4-7, 309B1
Politics & Government—*See also other appropriate subheads in this section*
Legislature schedule rptd 18G1
State of State message 2-6, 270A3
Milwaukee reelects Maier 4-1, 247B2
'79 tax collectn rptd 4-17, 307E2
Cornell drops electn bid 5-6, 341D2
Moody's lowers Milwaukee city, cnty bond ratings 6-13, 743F3
Sen primary results 9-9, 700C3
Election results 11-4: cong 837D2, 840F3, 844C4, 845A2, 851F2; state 845F3
'80 census rptd 12-31, 983G1
Presidential Election (& Transition)
Anderson strategy detailed 2-15, 129F2
Anderson in Milwaukee 3-25, 221E3
Primary results 4-1, 246E1-E3
Lucey joins Anderson ticket 8-25, 646B3
Reagan in Green Bay 10-2, 738D2
Carter in Milwaukee area 10-6, 762G2
Carter in Milwaukee 11-1, 841A1
Election results 11-4, 838D1, 839A2, G3
Refugee Issues
Ft McCoy processing camp opens 5-25, 420F1
Carter orders criminals expelled 6-7, 435D1
Ft McCoy gays await processing 7-7, 514G2
Ft McCoy riots 8-13, 27 arrested 8-14, 631F3
Ft McCoy found crime ridden 9-3; refugees riot, more troops called in 9-9—9-10, 684G3
Ft McCoy to send Ark camp 'hard-core' refugees 9-25, 725D3
Refugee aid to states clears Cong 9-25, 10-2, Carter signs 10-10, 785B1

1976

WISCONSIN, University of (Madison)
'70 bombing suspect arrested 1-7, 32C2
Bombing suspect sentncd 8-6, 776A3
Hirshfelder gets Science Medal 10-18, 858E3
WISEMAN, Michael
Angola sentences 6-28, 480B2
WISNER, Frank
Olson files made public 1-10, 25D1
Rhodesia Geneva conf opens 10-28, 797F2
WISSMANN, Matthias
Scores conservative split 11-23, 930B3
WISTAR Institute (Philadelphia, Pa.)
New rabies vaccine rptd 9-4, 972E3
WITTEVEEN, Johannes
On IMF aid to poor nations 1-9, 14A2
Addresses IMF-World Bank mtg 10-4, 777D1
WITTINGHAM, Peter
Interrogatn rptd 6-29, 522E1
WITTINGTON Imports Ltd.
Michaelson arrested 5-15, 401D2
WIZ, The (play)
Long runs listed 12-31, 1015A1
WIZ, The (record album)
Wins Grammy 2-28, 460C3
WOHLHUTER, Richard
Wins Olympic medal 7-25, 575F3
WOJTASZEK, Emil
Polish admin min 3-27, 268F2
Named forgn min 12-2, 926D3
WOLF, Edwin L.
Sentenced 2-4, 135G3
WOLFE, William (Cujo) (d. 1974)
Hearst questioned 1-7, 69E3
Cited in Hearst trial 2-9, 114B2
Hearst trial, article cites 2-17—3-18, 201D2, C3, 202E2, A3
WOLFENSTEIN, Martha
Dies 11-30, 1015B3
WOLFF, Rep. Lester L. (D, N.Y.)
Latin-US antidrug effort set 1-20, 61B1
On Mex drug traffic 3-15, 3-17, 420B1
S Korea probe rptd 10-30, 11-13, 900G1
Reelected 11-2, 830G1
Gets Sadat peace bid 11-17, 878C1
WOLFF, Paul H.
Sentenced 11-30, 921G2
WOLFGANG, Myra K.
Dies 4-12, 316D1
WOLFSON, Weiner, Ratoff & Lapin
SEC accuses Seidman 9-1, 984B3

WOMEN—*See also organization, personal names*
Anchorage anti-bias law passage rptd 1-3, 7D1
Sup Ct to hear Okla beer sale case 1-12, 24D1
US health rpt issued 1-12, 32C1
Home loan bias suits filed 4-15, 285G1
Rpt on progress issued 4-27, 379F2
Groups cited as FBI probe target 4-28, 330E1
Arts Inst admits Brooks 5-19, 504B3
Dem platform text cites housing bias 6-15, 473B3
Smoking survey released 6-15, 875B3, D3
Rights rally in Phila 7-4, 489C1
Ford cites in Bicentennial address 7-5, 489B1
Ford suspends HEW schl events rule 7-7, 535E2
Sup Ct bars review of VFW case 10-4, 807A3
Sup Ct accepts case vs Phila schools 10-18, 867C3
Yalow wins Lasker award 11-17, 910D3
Soc Sec to divorced mothers barred 12-13, 940C3
Sup Ct bars review of Ky maiden name use 12-13, 960B3
Get 1st Rhodes scholarships 12-19, 993E3
Okla beer-buying bias barred 12-20, 960D1

1977

WISCONSIN, University of Madison Campus
Young named pres 3-11, 354A2
'70 bomber sentncd 6-8, 6-10, 492C1
Suomi gets Medal of Sci 11-22, 952B1
WISE, Phil
Named Dem Party exec dir 1-21, 53C2
WITHERS, Reginald
Visits Cocos Islands 6-17—6-19, 504C3
Named Australia admin svcs min 12-19, 982A2
WITTENBERG University (Springfield, O.)
Wins NCAA basketball title 3-19, 262E2
WITTEVEEN, H. Johannes
On IMF paymts loan plan 4-29, 363G1
IMF paymts loan fund agreed 8-6, 754C2
On econ growth rates 9-11, 700E2
Retiremt plans announced 9-21, 754E2
Addresses IMF-World Bank mtgs 9-26, 9-30, 753D2, B3, 754A1
WOESES, Carl R.
New form of life rptd 11-2, 908A1
WOJTYLA, Cardinal
Backs protesters 6-9, 513C1
WOLF, Milton A.
Named amb to Austria 6-16, confrmd 6-22, 626F3
WOLF, Steve
Killed 11-21, 952G3
WOLFE, Bertram
Dies 2-22, 164G3
WOLFF, Dr. Harold
CIA mind-control tests revealed 8-1—8-9, 610G3
WOLFF, Rep. Lester L. (D, N.Y.)
Seeks Nixon Viet aid pledge letter 2-22; Nixon disavows 5-14, US releases note 5-19, 403F2
In S Korea, questns rights 4-12, 305E3
At Thai drug conf 4-14, 331A3
Revises cocaine traffic estimate 8-29, 972F1
Vs UN Palestine vote, hints fund cut 12-2, 931F1
WOLFF, Robert J.
Dies 12-29, 1024G3
WOLFF Jr., Judge William H.
Orders Dayton firemen end strike 8-10, 613C3
WOLF and Rissmiller Concerts Inc.
Steve Wolf slain 11-21, 952G3
WOLLEK, Bob
3d in Daytona endurance 2-6, 531E2
WOLPER, David L.
Roots sets TV viewing record 1-23—1-30, 118F3

WOMEN—*See also country, organization, personal names*
FBI feminist watch rptd 2-6, 423D1
AFI honors Bette Davis 3-1, 354G1
Widower benefits rule voided 3-2, 192C1-B2
Old-age benefits test for men voided 3-21, 230E1
Old-age benefits bias upheld 3-21, 230G1-D2
US drive vs home-mortgage bias rptd 3-24, 279E2
Waterman electd Common Cause chrmn 4-23, 396C3
NOW elects Smeal pres 4-24, 532F1
Burger notes '69-76 rulings 5-17, 419A3
Nationally chartered banks OKd 7-6, 578F1
Pak issues martial-law rules 7-10, 545A1
Miss Univ crowned 7-16; Miss Amer 9-10, 808G2
Kiwanis charter-withdrawal case review refused 10-3, 760D3
Natl Women's Conf meets, OKs plan of action 11-19—11-21, 917F2-918B1
DAR rpts 1st black member 12-3, 1021D2
Crime
Nurses convicted in '75 VA Hosp deaths 7-13, 568C3
Battered wife acquitted of ex-husband's murder 11-3, 928E1

1978

WISCONSIN, University of
Heiden wins speed-skating title 2-26, sets records 3-2, 3-12, 316A3
Wrestling rank rptd 3-13, Iowa wins NCAA title 3-18, 379G2-A3
Green Bay campus loses NCAA Div II basketball title game 3-18, 272B2
Madison loses NCAA hockey match 3-25, 296C3
US-imposed research secrecy order lifted after protest 4-21—6-12, 513F3
S Africa divestiture rptd 6-18, 633D1
Dreyfus wins primary for gov 9-12, 736A2
Dreyfus elected Wis gov 11-7, 846C3, 854G1
WISE, Rick
Traded to Indians 3-30, 779C3
WISNIEWSKI, Stefan
Arrested in Paris, deported 5-11; assaults W Ger judge 5-12, 439B1 ★, G1
WITH a Little Luck (recording)
On best-seller list 5-3, 356D1
WITHERS, Reginald
Fraser fires 8-7, defends actn 8-8, 612F1
Fraser denies link to scandal 8-21, no-confidence motn defeated 8-24, 703B2
Chaney replaces as admin svcs min 8-25, 703G2
WITT, Lucius Steven
Explains umbrella issue at JFK death hearing 9-25, 750C1
WITTINE, Gregory
Honored at White House 7-21, 844G1
WIZ, The (film)
Released 10-25, 970E3
On top-grossing list 11-1, 888E1; 11-29, 970G3
WJLA-TV (Washington, D.C. TV station)
FCC OKs KOCO-TV exchng 1-12, 109A3
KOCO-TV swap OKd again 3-9, Allbritton halts deal 3-24, 270A3
Allbritton resigns as Washn Star publisher 5-31, 672D2
WOJTYLA, Karol—*See JOHN Paul II, Pope*
WOLEK, Bob
2d in LeMans 6-11, 538A3
WOLF, Frank
Unopposed in Cong primary in Va 6-13, 467G1
WOLF, Fred
Mouse & His Child released 7-7, 970C2
WOLF, Jean
Indicted 4-12, 326A2
WOLFE, Gerald Bennet
Indicted 8-15, 644D3, 645A1
WOLFE, Dr. Sidney M.
Vs HEW anti-smoking plan 1-11, 23G2
WOLFE, Thomas (1900-38)
Angel opens 5-10, 760C1
WOLFF, Alan W.
Signs Japan citrus, beef pact 12-5, 988D2
WOLFF, Rep. Lester Lionel (D, N.Y.)
Reelected 11-7, 851D3
On China ties 12-20, 975C3
WOLFF, Nelson W.
Loses US House electn 11-7, 855D3
WOLFRAM
USSR, Turkey sign trade pact 4-5, 477D1
WOLFSON, Norman L.
Chrgs CR aids Nicaragua rebels 2-3, 91F1
WOLK, Andy
Rib Cage opens 5-28, 887G2
WOLLMAN, Lt. Gov. Harvey (D, S.D.)
Loses primary for gov 6-6, 448G1
Janklow elected SD gov 11-7, 855B1
WOLPE, Howard
Wins US House seat 11-7, 851E1, 854B1
WOLSTENHOLME, Guy
Wins Victorian Open 2-19, 355C3
WOMAN at Her Window, A (film)
Released 6-9, 620C1
WOMAN of Paris, A (film)
Released 4-13, 620C1
WOMEN—*See also organization, personal names*
Carter State of Union Message 1-19, 29C2, 30A3
2 elected to Arts Institute 2-7, 316E1
Black, white consumers compared 4-12, 811G3-812D1
Affirmative actn principle backed by Sup Ct 6-28, 482E1
'77 poverty level data rptd 8-12, 684F2
Suffragette $ coin bill signed 10-10, 788B2
La 'head & master' case declined by Sup Ct 10-10, 789D3
Marian Anderson honored 10-17, 844F1
Oregon man acquitted of spouse rape 12-27, 1028E3
Business—*See 'Employment' below*

1979

WISCONSIN, University of
Madison bomber paroled 1-11, 102F2
Clinard corp crime study rptd 3-8, 240B1
Green Bay campus loses NCAA Div II basketball title 3-17, 239B1
Gas cloud around galaxy rptd 6-1, 692D1
Central nerve regeneratn studied 12-14, 1000C2
WISCONSIN Electric Power Co.
Westinghouse settles uranium supply suit 5-5, 366E1
WISCONSIN Steel Corp.—*See ENVIRODYNE Industries*
WISE, John
Canada agri min 6-4, 423F3
WISE, Mike
Festival opens 5-7, 711A3
WISE, Rick
Signs with Padres 11-20, 1001G3
WISE, Robert
Star Trek released 12-8, 1008F1
WISNIEWSKI, Stefan
Chrgd re Schleyer murder 11-5, 998F3
WITCHITA, Kan.—*See KANSAS*
WITKIEWICZ, Stanislaw Ignacy
Madman and Nun opens 1-18, 292A2
WITTGREEN, Carlos
Indicted in arms plot 5-14, 386E3
WITTIG, Georg
Wins Nobel Prize 10-16, 858B1
WIZ, The (film)
Top-grossing film 1-10, 80G3
WIZAN, Joe
Voices released 3-13, 528F3
WNAC-TV (Boston, Mass. TV station)
FCC doubts RKO Gen license fitness 7-18, 618A2
WNET 13 (N.Y.C. TV station)
Nixon Admin moves disclosed 2-24, 194E1
WODEHOUSE, Sir P(elham) G(renville) (1881-1975)
Bolton dies 9-5, 756B2
WOHLFORD, Bob
Signs with Giants 12-12, 1002A1
WOJTYLA, Karol—*See JOHN Paul II, Pope*
WOLCHOK, Samuel
Dies 1-16, 104G3
WOLDIN, Judd
King of Schnorrers opens 11-28, 956C3
WOLF, David
American Game released 4-28, 528C1
WOLF, Milton A.
PLO mtg rptd 8-15, 605E1
Kreisky details PLO mtg 8-22, 625B1
WOLFE, Gerald Bennett
Sentenced 12-6–12-7, 1000D1
WOLFE, J. Richard
Indicted 8-2, 744D3
WOLFE, Tom
Right Stuff on best-seller list 11-4, 892C3
WOLFF Jr., Chuck
On Bishop executn 10-22, 817B2
WOLFSON, Louis
Affirmed pulled from Marlboro Cup 9-4, 876B3
WOLFSON, Patrice
Affirmed pulled from Marlboro Cup 9-4, 876A3
WOLSK, Eugene V.
Sarava opens 2-11, 292F2
WOLSTON, Ilya
Libel suit rights broadened by Sup Ct 6-26, 540C3
WOLSTON v. Reader's Digest Association Inc.
Case decided by Sup Ct 6-26, 540E2, B3
WOMACK v. City of Norfolk
Case dismissed by Sup Ct 6-25, 540A2
WOMAN'S National Democratic Club (Washington, D.C.)
Carter aide addresses 1-4, 3C2

WOMEN
Arts & Sciences
Tuchman elected Arts Inst pres 2-27, 176F1
Johnson named Natl Gallery trustee 5-3, 375F1

Crime & Civil Disorders
Death row populatn rptd 11-25, 989F3

1980

WISCONSIN, University of
Madison bomber rptd paroled 1-1, 24G3
Johnson on Olympic hockey team 2-24, 155B2
Snell in NFL draft 4-29, 336G3
Cholesterol rpt issued 5-27, 432G2
Matthews in NBA draft 6-10, 447D1, F2
WISE Jr., Phillip J.
B Carter probe hearing cites 9-4, 700E3
Sen subcom issues critical rpt in B Carter case 10-2, 764B1
WITCOMBE, Eleanor
My Brilliant Career released 2-1, 216C3
Getting of Wisdom released 8-5, 675F2
WITH You I'm Born Again (recording)
On best-seller list 4-2, 280E3
WITT, Elder
Sup Ct Guide wins Amer Book Award 5-1, 692E2
WITTSCHEN, Harry
Deering Milliken '56 labor dispute setlmt OKd 12-14, 962E2
WLADAR, Sandor
Wins Olympic medal 7-26, 623E2
WNAC-TV (Boston, Mass. TV station)
FCC lifts RKO Gen license, blocks sale 1-24, 119F2, B3
WOCKEL, Barbel
Wins Olympic medal 7-30, 624B2
WOHL, Ira
Wins Oscar 4-14, 296A2
WOITHE, Sergei
Wins Olympic medal 7-27, 623G2
WOJASZEK, Emil
Ousted 8-24, 641G1
WOJTYLA, Karol—*See JOHN Paul II, Pope*
WOLF, Frank
Elected to US House 11-4, 844A4, 850F2
WOLF, George
Dies 3-23, 280G2
WOLF, Louis
Names US Emb aide in Jamaica as CIA operative 7-2, 564F3-565A1
WOLF, Dr. Sidney
US to curb Darvon productn 4-24, 358E2
WOLFE, J. Richard
Sentence rptd 2-19, 237A3
WOLFE, Tom
Right Stuff wins Amer Book Award 5-1, 692A2
WOLFF, Rep. Lester L. (D, N.Y.)
Taiwan crackdown spurs concern, protests from delegatn 1-23, 1-24, 102A2, E2, F2
400 US bodies rptd found in Viet 6-27, 508A3
Loses reelectn 11-4, 848C3
WOLLARD, David A.
Denies bank, drug money links 6-5, 502E1
WOLPE, Rep. Howard (D, Mich.)
Reelected 11-4, 843E1
WOLSK, Eugene V.
Charlotte opens 2-27, 392D2
WOLSKY, Albert
Wins Oscar 4-14, 296A2
WOMAN Bathing (art print)
Sold for record sum 2-14, 472B2
WOMAN In Love (recording)
On best-seller list 10-8, 796B3; 12-3, 948B3
WOMAN of Substance, A (book)
On best-seller list 7-13, 568D3; 8-17, 640G3; 9-14, 716C3; 10-12, 796F3
WOMAN'S Democratic Club (Washington, D.C.)
Muskie addresses 10-16, 776A2

WOMEN
ABA urges pub accommodatns bias end 8-6, 744A2
Arts & Sciences
Yourcenar elected to French Acad 3-6, 471G2

Crime & Civil Disorders
NY businesswoman, 2 partners indicted 1-10, 216B1
White-collar crimes rptd up 1-21, 215E3
Chicago strip search suit setld 3-26, 404C2
Chicagoan indicted in ERA bribe probe 6-5, chrgs denied 6-6, 441C3
Secret Svc agent slain 6-5, 503E2
ERA advocate fined in Ill bribe case 11-7, 997A3
Domestic violence victims bill dropped 11-17, 982A2

1976

Employment—*See also 'Foreign Developments' below; for government and military issues, see 'Politics' below*
Quotas set for Chicago police 1-5, 6B2
Dec '75 jobless rate up 1-9, 21C1
Sup Ct declines review of Calif overtime rule 1-12, 24D1
EEOC suit vs GE affirmed 1-23, 70C3
Sotheby names 1st auctioneer 1-27, 272B1
Bennington Coll pres quits 1-29, 271F3
Jan jobless rate rptd 2-5, 152E3, G3
Feb jobless rate rptd 3-5, 198G3
Gridiron Club elects AP rptr 3-5, 272A1
ILO issues jobless rpt 3-13, 297F3
Sup Ct backs retroactive seniority 3-24, 218B2
Mar jobless data rptd 4-2, 263C1
Walters signs ABC contract 4-22, 504A2
'50-74 job, income data rptd 4-27, 379B3, 380A1
Apr jobless rate rptd 5-7, 347C2
VCU affirmative actn plan voided 5-28, 414A1
May jobless rate rptd 6-4, 412E2, G2
Merrill Lynch settles bias suits 6-4, 414D1
Bias actns rptd re: AT&T 6-9, 8-27; Gulf 7-16; Uniroyal 8-6; Owens-Ill, Kerr Glass 9-11; TWA, Amer Air 10-14; Ky coal mines 10-21; Westn Elec 10-22; 3M 10-26, 943D2-944C2
Dem platform text 6-15, 469C2, G3, 470E2, F2, A3
Conn liability in reverse bias case upheld 6-28, 569D1
Treas anti-bias actn scored 7-1, 943E3
June jobless rate rptd 7-2, 494C1
Productivity slowdown forecast 8-2, 647C2
July jobless rate rptd 8-6, 586B3
MCA to aid businesses 8-20, 944B1
Aug jobless rate, work force growth rptd 9-3, 667E2, B3
Bias rules for fed contractors scored 9-15, 884E3
Fed advisor bias chrgd 9-17, 944F1
Sept jobless rate rptd 10-8, 769A3
Sup Ct bars review of transsexual teacher firing 10-18, 867B3
Pregnancy cited re jobless benefits revision 10-20, 788G1
Oct jobless rate rptd 11-5, 846A2
NYC schl job bias chrgd 11-9, 921E3
Sandler wins Rockefeller award 11-16, 911F3
'55-74 male-female earnings gap rptd 11-28, 943E1
Sup Ct OKs physical standards review 11-29, 901B1
Nov jobless rate, work force rptd 12-5, 917F3, 918B1
Sup Ct vs pregnancy benefits 12-7, 919G3
W Ger mins named 12-15, 968A2

Foreign Developments
'75 Austria rights bill in effect 1-1, 97B3
Peru bans 3 magazines 1-10, 55C3
Mrs Javits quits disputed Iran Air post 1-27, 160G1
India equal pay law adopted 1-30, 101E3
Tito cites lack of Yugo ldrs 2-1, 223E3
Peru renews magazine ban 2-3, 142E3
Teng anti-feminism rptd 3-9, 189G2
Spain equal pay law OKd 4-6, 269B2
CAR premier dismissed 4-7, 288D2
W Ger OKs marriage reform 4-8, 4-9, 270G1
EC ct bars sex bias in pay 4-8, 276B3
French name general 4-21, 316F1
Albania names 2 mins 4-30, 331F3
Algeria OKs natl charter 6-27, 543A2
Italy labor min sowrn 7-30, 573D1
Australia sets jobs plan 9-21, 770C3
EC jobless data rptd 11-26, 935D2

1977

Education
NYC schl bias chrgd 1-18, 112C2
Schl bias data ordrd 2-17, 157A1
HEW finds schl bias rpts lacking 3-15, 279G3
Califano retracts quota stand 3-31, 235B2
HEW educ goals set 4-11, 301F3, 302A1
Phila job bias affirmd 4-19, 342C2
'63-77 SAT score drop rptd 8-23, 739F1
Women's studies urged by natl conf 11-19—11-21, 917D3
Gray named Chicago U pres 12-10, 1021B2

Employment
OECD rpts '74-75 recessn job data 1-3, 29D3
Prudential hiring plan rptd 1-10, 278C3
'76 work force growth, Dec '76 jobless rate rptd 1-12, 37G2, E3
Seniority-based layoffs scored 1-18, 278E3★
Jan jobless rate drops 2-4, 111F1
Chicago police hiring goals accepted 2-6, 279A3
NBC sex-bias suit accord rptd 2-13, 279C1
NLRB backs union certificatn 2-28, 154A1
Eastn Air weight standards OKd 3-3, 279F1
Frontier Airlines job-bias suit rptd 3-15, 279B2
Califano backs quotas 3-17, 217B3; retracts stand 3-31, 235B2
Mar jobless rate rptd 4-1, 252F1
Phila schl bias affirmed 4-19, 342C3
Apr jobless rate rptd 5-6, 383G3
Coors OKs antibias pact, EEOC drops suit 5-9, 819D1
Sup Ct declines employer records case 5-16, 419E1
Sup Ct declines pregnant employe dismissal case 5-16, 419B2
United Air Lines seniority rule upheld 5-31, 461G2
LA police bias chrgd 6-2, 819D2
May jobless rate rptd 6-3, 445B1
Ala prison employe standards voided 6-27, 538F3
La cities OK police, fire job quotas 6-29, 819F1-A2
June jobless rate rptd 7-8, 554D1
EEOC revamps case processing 7-20, 669A2
July jobless rate rptd 8-5, 611C3
AT&T pact reached 8-6, 613A3
Calif forgn bank bias chrgd 8-9, 669A3
US study chrgs TV bias 8-15, 642A3
Constructn job quota urged 8-16, 819E2
US acts on job bias 8-25, 669G2
NBC bias suit settled 8-31, 979C2
Aug jobless rate, labor force growth rptd 9-2, 692A2, C2
NYS police sued re bias 9-8, 819D2
GOP offers Soc Security plan 9-9, 720E2
Pregnancy benefits voted by Sen 9-16, 737G3
Mandatory retiremt curb voted by House 9-23, 737G2
Amer Air stewardesses win pregnancy suit 10-3, 819B1
Sept jobless rate rptd 10-7, 776D3
USSR Const seeks mothers work hours cut 10-7, 785E2
Vet job preferenc law backed 10-11, 774F2
Calif forgn bank affirmative actn agreed 10-19, 979D2
Oct jobless rate rptd 11-4, 858F2
Reader's Digest bias suit setld 11-4, 979A2
Jobs bill support cited 11-14, 877B1
Career guidance aid, anti-bias projects clear Cong 11-29, 959B2; signed 12-13, 1001G2
Nov jobless rate, '77 work force entrants rptd 12-3, 961B3
Maternity-leave seniority rights upheld 12-6, 938C2
Maternity sick-leave pay rule remanded 12-6, 938A3
TV viewing decline rptd 12-6, 1021F3

Foreign Developments—*See also 'Religion' below*
Liechtenstein vote 4-17, 567C1
Israel to ease relig mil exemptns 6-9, 474A3
Belgium FDF chrmn elected 6-15, 561D1
S Africa halts protest 8-16, 640A2
Canada min post filled 9-16, 725F2
Canada min yields women's post 9-23, 763C3
Swiss abortn reform defeated 9-25, 766C3
Swedish parlt bans titles 10-6, 904D1
USSR Const seeks mothers work hrs cut 10-7, 785E2
Greek electn results 11-20, 925E1

1978

Education
NCAA suit vs Title IX dismissed 1-9, 40E2
Davis joins SF State U faculty 1-26, 172B2
Black-white wage gap closure linked 5-8, 810B3
Coll job bias rule voided by Sup Ct 11-14, 874F1-C2

Employment & Business
Suits vs HEW rptd settled 1-4, 5C1
Dec '77 jobless rate rptd 1-11, 50G3
FCC OKs WJLA-TV swap 1-12, 109C3
6 named for astronaut spots 1-16, 157E3-158A1
Jan jobless rate 2-3, 127D3
Stewardess bias case review refused 2-21, 125G3
New CPIs described 222C2
AT&T employes profiled 2-28, 565C3
WJLA-TV swap challenged in ct 3-9, 270C3
Feb jobless rate 3-10, 222A1
UAL maternity rule review refused by Sup Ct 3-20, 205G3
Mar jobless rate rptd 4-7, 262C2
Coll job gains rptd slight 4-7, 554A3
Black, white women compared 4-12, 812B1
Firestone jobless benefits challenge declined by Sup Ct 4-17, 308B3
Black qualifies as airline pilot 4-19, 420C1
Sex-based pensn plans barred by Sup Ct 4-25, 322A3
Apr jobless rate rptd 5-5, 345F1
Constructn work rules effected 5-7, 554G2
Black-white wage gap rptd narrowed 5-8, 810G2
Redlining curb adopted 5-18, 410E2
Guaranteed income study rptd 5-19, 720F3
Mgt, professional gains rptd 5-22, 554E3
Coal indus bias probed, affirmative actn ordrd 5-30, 565B3
Legal professn gains rptd 5-31, 554E2
Law schl enrollmt rptd up 5-31, 554F2
May jobless rate rptd 6-2, 429E2
Job status rptd 6-4, 554D3
Munic legal immunity ended by Sup Ct 6-6, 447D1-A2
GE complaint setld 6-15, 1006B3
Class actn certificatn appeals curbed by Sup Ct 6-21, 509G2
AT&T bias case declined by Sup Ct 7-3, 551G3
June jobless rate rptd 7-7, 552F2
Energy Dept '75-77 bias admitted 7-14, 1006A3
'70-78 2-income families rptd 7-24, 679F3
'77 jobless rate rptd 7-28, 677F1
July jobless rate rptd 8-4, 607C3
Vet Civil Svc job preferenc clears Sen 8-24, 662B1
Aug jobless rate rptd 9-1, 679E3
Vets job preference retained by House 9-11, 696E2
Bell Canada bias ordrd ended 9-11, guidelines issued 9-21, 772F3
Pfeiffer named NBC chrmn, RCA dir 9-13, 759C3
Sen bias bd vote blocked 9-20, House abuses chrgd 9-21, 720A3
NY Times settles sex bias suit 9-28, 835F2
50.1% rptd in labor force 10-6, 790F2
Sept jobless rate rptd 10-6, 790B3
Minority-white earnings gap rptd filled 10-19, 812B3
ACLU hails pregnancy benefits law 10-20, 981B3
Pregnancy benefits bill signed 10-31, 873G1
Oct jobless rate rptd 11-3, 864C3
Unions win right to data 11-3, 899A1
Coll bias ruling voided by Sup Ct 11-13, 874F1-C2
Chicago bias suit setld 11-17, 1006G2
UAL NYS maternity leave case refused by US Sup Ct 11-27, 937A2
Nov jobless rate rptd 12-8, 958E1
EEOC issues guidelines 12-12, 1006B2
Coal miners bias suit setld 12-26, 1006F2

Foreign Developments
CR Cabt includes 4 women 3-4, 170G3
Helsinki review conf ends 3-9, 179C2
Spain ends adultery penalties 5-30, 576B3
James sails world solo 6-8, 653C2
Israel mil exempts religious 7-20, 592F1
ILO rpts '77 jobless rate 7-28, 677F1
Colombia Cabt all male 8-7, women score 8-9, 629E3
Bell Canada bias end ordrd 9-11, guidelines issued 9-21, 772F3
Swedish Cabt ⅓ women 10-18, 822F2
Italian group bombs boutiques 11-1, 1018E2

1979

Education
NCAA vows Title IX fight 1-10, 102B3
Coll 'malaise' seen 4-2, 282A3
Coll enrollmt rptd up 5-12, 367B2
Pvt Title IX suit allowed by Sup Ct 5-14, 382D3
Wilson Coll closing barred 5-26, 482C1
US black wins Rhodes scholarship 9-9, 1005F2
Title IX job bias funds cutoff bar declined by Sup Ct 11-26, 919D2

Employment & Business
Cyanamid sterilizatn suit threatnd 1-4, 56A3
Allied fluorocarbon suit setld 1-5, 56G1
Dec '78 jobless rate rptd 1-14, 34C1
AT&T cleared on '73 decree 1-17, 92F1
Sears sues US on bias laws 1-24, 92C1
Jan jobless rate, '77-79 labor force, 2-income family data rptd 2-2, 110D3
'78 productivity drop rptd 2-9, 111D1
Soc Sec chngs urged 2-15, 132D3
Feb jobless rate rptd 3-8, 182C3
HUD scores mortgage bias 3-9, 208G3-209B1
Mar jobless rate rptd 4-6, 280B3
Ky bias case refused by Sup Ct 4-23, 346A3
Sears ends fed contract work, cites suit 4-24, 366B1
Apr jobless rate rptd 5-4, 362D3
Hoffmann-La Roche NJ unit adjusts pay 5-13, 482G3
Sears suit vs US dismissed 5-15, 365B3
May jobless rate rptd 6-1, 422D2
Vets' job-preferenc law upheld by Sup Ct; reactn 6-5, 421D1-D2
Congressmen ruled liable to sex-bias suits 6-5, 463G3-464F1
Sup Ct workforce data rptd 6-11, 464G1
KKK law use curbed by Sup Ct 6-11, 479B1
Union recognitn denial case declined by Sup Ct 6-18, 499E2
Gender-based welfare plan ruled illegal by Sup Ct 6-25, 539D3
Merck OKs hiring plan 6-26, 521G1
Weber affirmative actn challenge rejctd by Sup Ct; reactn; majority opinion excerpts 6-27, 477A1-478E1
June jobless rate rptd 7-6, 516D3
Steinem cites job training as '80 electn issue 7-13–7-15, 578C3
Intl hunger conf seeks agri bias end 7-20, 554C1
July jobless rate rptd 8-3, 621F2
Ex-Rep Passman settles sex bias suit 8-23, 649E3
Carter praises workers 9-3, 661E1
Aug jobless rate rptd 9-7, 680F3
Calif lawyer survey rptd 9-17, 787G1
Sept jobless rate rptd 10-5, 766C2
Sears sued by US re bias 10-22, 885C3
Uniroyal settles bias suit 10-23, 885F2
Westn Elec bias case refused by Sup Ct 10-29, 884C2
Oct jobless rate rptd 11-2, 866D3
Ind pregnancy jobless pay case refused by Sup Ct 11-13, 902A2
'78 median income rptd 11-24, 965G2
Title IX funds cutoff bar declined by Sup Ct 11-26, 919D2
Govt constructn grants case argued before Sup Ct 11-27, 945B1
Nov jobless rate rptd 12-7, 941F1

Family Issues
Unwed couple suits rptd 2-22, 4-17, 289D2, A3
Marvin breach-of-contract suit setld 4-18, 289B1
Unwed mothers denied survivors' aid by Sup Ct 6-27, 558F1
Mass man sentncd for rape of wife 9-24, 819F3
USSR sets amnesty for mothers 10-19, 857D2
Household heads rptd 11-24, 965C2

Foreign Developments
Canada widens mil roles 1-29, 95F2
Saudi rights violatns rptd 2-10, 107B3
UK queen honored in Arab natn tour 2-12–3-2, 190C1
Greece wage growth cited 2-22, 135E3
Iran family protectn law abolished, garb curbed 3-7; mil svc exemptn set 3-8; protests staged 3-8–3-12, 179B2-A3
Mrs Trudeau honored 3-8, 271D3
Iran arrests Millet 3-17, ousts 3-19, 199B2
Paris bombings linked 5-1, 330C2
Thatcher wins UK electn 5-3, 337A1, 338A3
MacDonald gets Canada Cabt post 6-4, 423E3
Iran executes 3 7-12, 544C3
Afghan literacy rptd opposed 7-13, 521E3
Portugal caretaker premr named 7-19, 545F2
Hunger conf seeks agri bias end 7-20, 554C1
Canadian Indians protest bias 7-20, 601D2
USSR male ratio rptd 10-10, 857G1
USSR sets amnesty for mothers 10-19, 857D2

1980

Education
2 Calif coll sex harassmt cases rptd; '79 coll sex survey cited 1-9, 77D3-78C1
Coll freshmen survey rptd 1-20, 319F3
Coll enrollmt rise seen 1-22, 319C3
Math interest increase rptd 4-15, 559D2
Faculty bias Title IX case accepted by Sup Ct 12-1, 918B2
World illiteracy study rptd 12-4, 953A3

Employment & Business
Lansing named 20th Century-Fox pres 1-1, 199B1
UK nurses get 20% pay hike 1-4, 20G1
Dec '79 jobless rate rptd 1-11, 33E2
Conn, Wis ERISA maternity case declined by Sup Ct 1-14, 37B1
US rights comm scores job lag 1-15, 36C3
Washn State of State message 1-15, 484D1
Jan jobless rate rptd 2-1, 92D2
Saudi Islamic law enforcemt rptd tightened 2-5, 195B1
Kellogg settles bias chrgs 2-6, 115A3
AFL-CIO reserves cncl seat 2-21, 147A1
Canada nurses win equal-pay suit 2-25, 171F2
Feb jobless rate rptd 3-7, 182D3
Bank uniform case declined by Sup Ct 3-17, 226F1
Ia firefighter wins breast-feeding case 3-20, 441G3
Firestone cited for job bias 3-21, 251A3
Mar jobless rate rptd 4-4, 263F1
EEOC bars sex harrasmt, sets regulatns 4-11, 441E2
Canada plans jobs legis 4-14, 293C1
Mo workman's compensatn law voided by Sup Ct 4-22, 344A1
LA police purposeful bias case declined by Sup Ct 4-28, 369B2
Amoco settles credit bias suit 4-29, 370B3
Apr jobless rate rptd 5-2, 344A3
EEOC actn process avoidance backed by Sup Ct 5-12, 426G1
US bindery workers win bias suit 5-20, 442C1
May jobless rate rptd 6-6, 437E2
Mello named First Women's Bank pres 6-12, 600G2
June jobless rate rptd 7-3, 513G2
Iranians protest Islamic clothing rule 7-5; 131 fired 7-8, 507C1
Frederick rptd Paul White Award winner 7-7, 638E2
Pfeiffer resigns as NBC chrmn, RCA dir 7-10, 582C1
GOP platform text 7-15, 535F2
Firestone US contracts voided 7-15, 560B2
July jobless rate rptd 8-1, 599F2
Dem platform planks adopted 8-13, 614D2, F2
Miller named to AFL-CIO exec cncl 8-21, 647C3
Aug jobless rate rptd 9-5, 684A1
Job bias suits setld vs CF&I 9-22, Motorola 9-23, Rockwell 9-26, 746D3, E3, G3
Sept jobless rate rptd 10-3, 783E2
Oct jobless rate up 11-7, 867D1
LA settles job bias suit 11-21, 962A3
Ford settles bias case 11-25, 899B2
Natl Science Foundatn authrzn clears Cong 12-2, 953G3; signed 12-12, 982B1
Nov jobless rate rptd 12-5, 938C1
Schering settles US bias case 12-14, 962D3

Family Issues
Ia firefighter wins breast-feeding case 3-20, 441G3
Canada woman awarded 1/2 ex-spouse's stock 3-26, 273A2
India dowry murders rptd 4-9, 275D2
US Families Conf opens 6-5, 442C3
US Families Conf meets in Minn 6-19—6-21, LA 7-10—7-12, 601A2, D2
GOP platform adopted; text 7-15, 535E2, 536A1
'79 median family income rptd 10-23, 823G3
Domestic violence victims bill dropped 11-17, 982A2

Foreign Developments
UK nurses get 20% pay hike 1-4, 20G1
Saudi Islamic law enforcemt rptd tightened 2-5, 195B1
Canada nurses win equal-pay suit 2-25, 171F2
Canada House speaker, Cabt named 2-29, 3-3, 171B2, C2
Yourcenar elected to French Acad 3-6, 471G2
Nhongo gets Zimbabwe Cabt post 3-11, 198C1
Canada woman awarded 1/2 ex-spouse's stock 3-26, 273A2
UK defns white paper issued 4-2, 274A2
India dowry murders rptd 4-9, 275D2
Canada plans jobs legis 4-14, 293C1
Iran ex-min executed 5-8, 373E1
Finnbogadottir elected Iceland pres 6-30, 498F2
Iranians protest Islamic clothing rule 7-5; 131 fired 7-8, 507C1
UN, nongovt confs held in Copenhagen 7-14—7-30, anti-bias pact signed by US, 52 other natns 7-17, 587E1-D3
Sovts expel dissident feminist 7-20, 680C3
Dominica prime min named 7-21, 635G3

1976

Obituaries
Wolfenstein, Martha 11-30, 1015B3
Armstrong, Barbara 1-18, 56G2
Byron, Katharine 12-28, 1015B1
Kirchwey, Freda 1-3, 56E3
LaGace, Sherry (rptd) 1-27, 80E3
Nash, Dorothy 3-5, 484F3
Roche, Josephine 7-29, 716E3
Shelly, Mary Josephine 8-6, 892E3
Wolfgang, Myra 4-12, 316D1

Politics & Government—*See also 'Foreign Developments' above*
Armstrong confrmd UK amb 1-27, 68B1
Ohio ERA study disputed 2-13, 172G1
Ky House votes ERA rescissn 2-18, 172F1
Pro-ERA group opens DC office 2-25, 172F1
ERA loses in Ariz 3-1, 172E1
McCormack pres primary results 3-2, 165B1, A1
'72-74 electns rptd up 4-27, 379E3
Ginn confrmd Lux amb 5-20, 412E1, B2
Dem, GOP delegate selectn bias chrgd 5-27, 413F3
AFSCME sues ACTION 6-2, 414C1
Carter backs ERA, appoints women's advisory panel 6-13, 432B2
Dem platform text 6-15, 471F1, 472F1
Dems plan '80 conv rules 6-20, 451A2
Dems OK more NY delegates 6-28, 490C1
Vallance quits Army 6-29, 484E2
Carter, Dem caucus resolve conv issues 7-11—7-15, 509F3
Jordan Dem conv keynoter 7-12, 508D1
Dem conv women delegates, table 508A2
Dem conv rpt re role 7-13, 509G1
Carter seeks end to bias 7-15, 507F1, 510A3
State Dept hiring rptd 8-3, 922B2
Delegate representatn at GOP conv rptd 8-7, 8-8, 616C2, E2
GOP platform com OKs plank 8-13, 582G2, D3
Journalists cover Carter church class 8-15, 617C1
GOP conv rules com actn 8-17, 600G2
GOP conv platform adopted 8-18, 600C3, 601F1; text 605D2, 606D2
Amer Indep Party vs ERA 8-27, 666F1
White to FCC 9-8, 808D1

1977

Medicine & Health—*See also ABORTION, BIRTHS*
Birth pill-smoking risk rptd 3-29, 287E3
Birth pill warning ordrd 4-8, 355D1
Chicago DES suit filed 4-25, 431G2
DES cancer risk rptd down 5-3, 432C1
FDA orders IUD labeling 5-6, 431E2
Hysterectomy excess chrgd 5-9, 732E2
Breast X-rays curbed 5-10, 431C2
Mich '74 DES suit dismissed 5-16, 431F3-432B1
NY contraceptive curbs voided 6-9, 501C2
Smoking, early menopause linked 6-25, 620C1
Smokers' diseases, '69-75 teenaged smokers rptd up 620E1
Pregnancy proviso in new AT&T pact 8-6, 613A3
Yalow wins Nobel 10-13, 951E3
Benefits rise urged by natl conf 11-19—11-21, 917D3
Life expectancy data 12-13, 962C3

Military
Armed forces hike proposed 1-21, 95A1
Marine field, combat training begins 2-8, 3-24, 343C2
Carter call-in on draft 3-5, 171F2
Army studies draft, quota hike 4-6, 343F1
Israel to ease religious exemptns 6-9, 474A3
Missile silo assignmts set 9-23, 777C3
Vet benefits bill clears Cong 11-4, 877C3
Enlistmt rise sought 11-15, 920G1, C2
Expanded sea duty backed 12-21, 978E2

Obituaries
Bolton, Frances Payne 3-9, 264D2
Elder, Ruth 10-9, 872F1
Nin, Anais 1-14, 84D3
Paul, Alice 7-9, 604E3
Ross, Nellie Tayloe 12-10, 1024A3
Wheaton, Anne 3-23, 264G3

Politics & Government—*See also 'Foreign' above*
Bias suit vs Passman OKd 1-3, 59C3
Costanza, Mitchell named to White House staff 1-14, 35F2, C3
Indiana OKs ERA 1-18, 59A2
HEW posts filled 1-19, 1-21, 53B1-E1
Harris, Kreps confrmd to HUD, Commerce 1-20, 34B1, E2, A3
Dem natl com fills posts 1-21, 53B2
ERA fails in Va, Nev 1-27, 2-11; Idaho rescinds 2-8, 112E3
Regulatory agency apptmts scored 2-9, 131D3
Bird named Calif chief justice 2-12, 140C3; confrmd 3-11, 396B3
ERA fails in NC, total ratificatns cited 3-1, 197D2
Babcock confrmd asst atty gen 3-4, 211D1
Blum confrmd EPA dep admin 3-4, 211D1
King confrmd ACTION dep dir 3-4, 211E1
Wald confrmd asst atty gen 3-4, 211G1
Carter call-in on ERA, draft 3-5, 171E1, F2
ERA set back in 3 states 3-9—3-15, rescissn study rptd 3-27, 279B3
Bingham confrmd Labor asst secy 3-18, 272F2
Foreman confrmd Agri asst secy 3-24, 272G2
Anderson confrmd Treas undersecy 3-29, 272E2
Carter poll standing 4-4, 251G1
Claybrook confrmd to Transport post 4-6, 272G2
ERA fails in Fla 4-13, Ill 6-6, 669C2
Belgium FDF chrmn elected 6-15, 561D1
Sex bias laws to be screened 7-18, 669D2
Cong employe bias rptd 7-31, 8-4, coalitn seeks equality 8-31, 669F3

1978

Medicine & Health—*See also ABORTION, CHILDBIRTH*
Pill warning for smokers ordrd 1-11, 23E2
HEW anti-smoking drive set 1-11, 23G2
Radiatn vulnerability rptd 2-17, 164E2
Liquid protein diet risk rptd 6-26, weight loss survey 7-23, 727A3
Teen smoking rptd up 7-5, 727E1
Fire victim data rptd 10-8, 972C2
ACLU hails pregnancy benefits law 10-20, 981B3
Pregnancy benefits bill signed 10-31, 873G1
Measles infestatn in armed forced rptd 11-10, 927B3

Military
Carter budgets manpower levels 1-23, 45C1
Combat bar repeal rptd sought by Pentagon 3-4, 162G1
Marine Corps names 1st gen 5-11, 420E1
Singlaub vs combat role 6-2, 433D2
Army names 1st maj gen 7-1, 843C3
Lower recruiting standards urged 7-2, 528E3
Israel exempts religious 7-20, 592F1
Navy sea duty bar voided 7-27, 589C1
Navy plans ship duty 10-28, 8 rpt 11-1, 877F2-A3
Army 2-yr enlistmt plan bar rptd 11-10, 895F2
Measles infestatn rptd 11-10, 927B3
Army child-care rules tightened, 11-29, 960F2
Army curbs sex fraternizatn 12-4, 960E1

Obituaries
Halprin, Rose 1-8, 96B2
Jones, Blanche Calloway 12-16, 1032A3
Mead, Margaret 11-15, 972D3
Miller, Izetta Jewel 11-15, 972D3
Utely, Freda 1-21, 96F3

Politics & Government—*See also 'Foreign' above*
Mrs Humphrey named to Sen 1-25, 52G2
'53, '78 Cong membership compared 1-30, 107E2
ERA extensn backed by Carter 2-17, 123F2
ERA boycott injunctns sought by Mo, Nev 2-28, 3-3, 494F2
ERA rescinded in Ky 3-16; lt-gov vetoes 3-20, ct challenge planned 4-1, 494D2
ERA ldrs ask ratificatn extensn, see boycott losses 3-20, 5-26, 494E2, A3
Carter sees Natl Women's Conf group, vows rights effort 3-22, 218B2
'76 pres vote turnout rptd 4-13, 285B2
Carter augmts Costanza liaison role 4-19, 306F3
Carter to recruit judges 5-4, 320B3
ERA opposed by Mormons 5-5, 907D2
W Va, Neb primary results 5-9, 363B1, F1
Wesner loses Pa gov primary 5-16, 389B3
Ky, Ore primary results 5-23, 406E2, G2
ERA backed by Carter in Ill 5-26, legis rejcts 6-7, 6-22, 494A2
Tex primary results 6-3, 426E2
Carter job apptmt data rptd 6-15, 811E1
ERA '77 rescisns in Ida, Neb, Tenn cited 494D2
DC march for ERA extensn 7-9, Carter backs 7-12, 529D2
Costanza resigns as Carter asst 8-1, 605G3, 606B1
ABA rejcts ERA deadline extensn 8-8, 626B3
ERA extensn OKd by House, rescissn amendmt rejctd 8-15; poll rptd 8-16, 661E2
Shapard wins Ga primary runoff 8-22, 683E1

1979

Mecca mosque militants issue demands 11-20, 899B1
Canada NDP backs more rights enforcemt 11-22–11-25, 927B2

Medicine & Health
Estrogen, uterine cancer link rptd 1-4, 23F1-A2; 1-31, 139E1
Cyanamid sterilization suit threatened 1-4, 56A3
Allied fluorocarbon suit setld 1-5, 56G1
PHS smoking rpt warns 1-11, 23C1
Gonorrhea sterility data rptd 1-20, 64C3
VD warning issued 2-19, 140E1
Stroke study rptd 2-28, 195A3
Cancer death rates detailed 3-5, 195B3
DES cancer risk rptd less 3-6, 196C1
Exertn tests rptd inaccurate 3-8, 196D2
Sleep breathing study rptd 3-9, 196G2-B3
Teenaged smokers rptd up 4-27, 970C3
Low-level radiatn risk assessed 5-2, 609G2
Birth pill-hypertensn study rptd 5-7, 355F1
Silkwood estate wins A-suit 5-18, 381A3
Less radical breast cancer surgery backed 6-6, 471C3
DES menopause treatmt cited 6-28, 571B3
Breast cancer drug rptd effective 9-11, 736C1
Estrogen use linked to uterine cancer 9-14, 735A3
Gonorrhea rptd leveling off 11-18, 971A2
Carter abortn stand, NOW reelectn oppositn linked 12-9, 961B3

Military
Armed forces rise seen 1-2, 53G1
Armed svcs review 'sexist' language 1-19, 89D3
Canada widens roles 1-29, 95F2
Iran law exempts from svc 3-8, 179D2
WWII pilots get benefits 3-9, 307D3
Mil ldr urges registratn 3-13, 307B2
Army eases volunteer standards 4-9, 307E2
Vets job preference law upheld by Sup Ct 6-5, 421D1-D2
AF cadets to get pilot training 9-10, 725A1
Sailors go overseas 9-11, 724F3
W Point cadets assessed 10-9, 809A1; hazing scandal rptd 11-9, 868B3
Combat role discussed 11-13, 11-14, 868D2
Ft Dix sex scandal rptd 12-3, 924A1

Obituaries
Arzner, Aoris 10-1, 860G1
McClusker, Marilyn 10-2, 860G2
Payne-Gaposhkin, Cecelia 12-6, 1008D3
Strauss, Anna Lord 2-23, 176F3

Politics & Government—*See also 'Foreign' above*
Mo jury exclusn law voided by US Sup Ct 1-9, 14G2
Carter ousts Abzug from Natl Advisory Com 1-12, controversy sparked 1-12–1-17, Chambers named acting head 1-16, 30C2
ERA rejctd by Nev, Va, Mont state houses, Wyoming Sen upholds 1-15–2-13, 128A2
ERA opposed by Orthodox rabbis 1-26, 101G3
Bell reassures ABA on judicial apptmts 2-12, 130F1
Soc Sec chngs urged 2-15, 132D3
ERA conv boycott upheld 2-21, 128F1
Byrne wins Chicago mayoral primary 2-27, 149D3-150A1; elected mayor 4-3, 251G3
Cockrell reelected San Antonio mayor 4-7, 265B2
Southn regulatory bds found segregated 4-9, 307F1-A2
Robb named Natl Advisory Com head 5-9, 351G1-A3
Ky gubernatorial primary results 5-29, 420E1
Congressmen ruled liable to sex-bias suits 6-5, 463G3-464F1
Sup Ct workforce data rptd 6-11, 464G1
Mrs Carter addresses Dems 7-12, 514E1
NWPC meets, '80 electn discussed 7-13–7-15, 578G2
Alexander sworn US magistrate 8-7, 901F3
Weddington named sr pres aide 8-10, 608E2
Ex-Rep Passman settles sex bias suit 8-23, 649E3

1980

Medicine & Health
UK nurses get 20% pay hike 1-4, 20G1
Maternity smoking, drinking risks rptd 1-4, 23C3
Lung cancer rise rptd 1-14, 40A2
DES, problem pregnancies rptd linked 1-25, 63C2
VD epidemic rptd, NGU rise blamed 2-5, 157G3
Va sterilizatn progm rptd 2-23, 158E3
Canada nurses win equal-pay suit 2-25, 171F2
Saccharin warning rptd 3-6, 317C2
Fewer cancer tests urged 3-20, 316C3-317D1
Abortn funding cases argued in Sup Ct 4-21, 306B2
Toxic-shock syndrome cases rptd 6-6, 584A3
Medicaid abortn funding limits upheld by Sup Ct; reactn 6-30, 491F2-492A2
Birth control pills rptd most effective 7-13, 584A2
Toxic-shock syndrome, tampon use linked 9-17; recall ordered 9-22, 726F2-E3
DES liability case declined by Sup Ct 10-14, 781D3

Military
GOP leaders back draft 1-28, 75F1
Carter seeks draft registratn 2-8, 110E2, G2
Sex harassment alleged, Ft Bragg probed 2-10, 2-11, GI sentenced in W Germany 3-6, 188E3-189B1
Marine dischrgd for Playboy pose 2-21, 189B1
AFL-CIO backs registratn 2-25, 147A1
Draft registratn rejected by House subcom 3-6, 188B3
Female GI rptd convicted of sex harassmt 3-31, Eur crackdown ordered 4-23, 347F3
WWII WAACs get vet status 4-2, 267A3
UK white paper issued 4-2, 274A2
Draft registratn funds rejected by House 4-22, 349A2
Navy sets lesbian probe 5-15, probe scored 6-13, 6-15; 6 rptd chrgd 6-28, 517B3
1st svc academy classes graduate 5-21, 5-28, 428C1
Draft registratn amendmt defeated 6-10; ACLU sues vs registratn 6-26, 478G1, D3
Navy sea success rptd; '79 gay dismissal total 6-28, 517C2-B3
Col sentenced for sex harassmt 6-28; sailor convicted 7-11, 598E1-A2
Iranians fired re garb 7-8, 507D1
GOP platform adopted; text 7-15, 535E2, 536A1
Pa judges block male draft registratn 7-18, 597G3
Dem plank on draft adopted 8-13, 615B2
Male-only draft case accepted by Sup Ct 12-1, 918E1

Obituaries
Bernays, Doris 7-11, 608D1
Cochran, Jacqueline 8-8, 676B1
Summerskill, Edith 2-4, 176D3
Weltfish, Gene 8-2, 676F3

Politics & Government
ERA backers, foes rally 1-13, 1-17, 54A3
Carter backs ERA 1-23, 43A1, F2
Kennedy for equal rights 1-28, 75A1
Karmel resigns SEC post 2-1, 224G3
Reagan assails Bush re ERA 2-5, 128G2
State of State messages 2-19, 404C1; 4-8, 483G1
Kennedy 'basic speech' excerpts 3-10, 184A2
Harris chosen vp candidate 4-13, 288E3
DC Christian rally held 4-29, 349A1
Chicagoan indicted in ERA bribe probe 6-5, chrgs denied 6-6, 441C3
ERA spurs dispute at Families Conf 6-5—6-6, 442C3
ERA fails in Ill house 6-18, 482B3
ERA debated at US Families Conf in Minn 6-19—6-21, LA 7-10—7-12, 601A2, D2
Dem platform backs ERA 6-24, 480A1
Mormon ERA backer excommunicatn upheld 7-1, 638A2
GOP platform com debates ERA 7-7—7-10; bars support 7-9, 506G1-E2
Evangelical Christian actn profiled 7-11—9-15, 818E3, 819B1, E1, A2
Detroit pro-ERA protest held 7-14, Reagan sees GOP conv delegates 7-15, 533A3, C3
Hooks asks GOP chng re ERA 7-15, 535B1
GOP platform adopted; text 7-15, 535E2, A3, D3
Reagan pres nominatn acceptance speech 7-17, 531C1
Kennedy Dem conv speech backs rights 8-12, 610E2, 614B2
Dem platform planks OKd 8-12; Carter issues statemt, conv adopts platform 8-13, 611B1, E1; text excerpt 615B1
Mondale vp renominatn acceptance speech 8-14, 612C1

1976

Byrne confrmd Mali amb 9-15, 807E3
Wells confrmd Guinea-Bissau, Cape Verde amb 9-15, 808D1
Gordon confrmd HEW asst secy 9-23, 807G3
Carter sees feminists, backs ERA 10-2, 10-7, 762D1
Mondale addresses Ohio Dems 10-22, 803F3
Election results 11-2; cong 820C2, 825C2, 829D3, A4, C4, 830C1, E1, A2, B3, 830B4, 831E4; gov 804C3, 831D2; ERA 821G1, 825B2, G2, D3
Dole urges GOP inclusn 11-30, 917B3
Pfeiffer declined Carter post 12-14, 12-16, 936D1, 937B1
Kreps named Commerce secy, urges harder search for US posts 12-20, 956F1, 957A1

Religion
Italy feminists protest Vatican abortn policy 1-17, Pope scores 1-21, 124C2
Pope warns vs feminism 1-31, 124D2
Cheek rejcts Episc compromise 4-4, forms separate unit 5-9, 755C3
Beebe '75 convictn reversed 4-9, new trial denied 4-9, 755A3
Bittner quits Episc Church 4-9, 755E3
Schiess sues central NY bishop 7-8, 755E3
Eucharistic Cong issue 8-1—8-8, 596D2, F2
Pope, Coggin dispute ordinatn 8-20, 756A1
Episc Church OKs ordinatn 9-11—9-23, 755G1
Lutherans meet 10-10—10-11, 932D2
US Cath conf backs ordinatn 10-21—10-23, 859C1
Colo Episc parish secedes 11-28, 932F1
Canada Anglicans ordain women 11-29, 932C1
US Polish church cuts Episc ties 11-29, 932E1

WOMEN, National Organization for (NOW)
Equal-time rules upheld 4-12, 282F1
Ford suspends HEW schl events rule 7-7, 535B3
DeCrow at Dem conv rule debate 7-13, 513C1
Sup Ct bars equal-time review 10-12, 765E3
Sup Ct pregnancy benefits rule scored 12-7, 920A2
WOMEN'S Political Caucus, National
Chrgs Dem, GOP delegate selectn bias 5-27, 413F3 ★
WOMEN'S Year, International
Pope addresses com 1-31, 124D2
Harris named HUD secy 12-21, 956G1
WOOD—*See LUMBER & Lumber Products*
WOOD, Archie L.
Study vs B-1 publshd 2-8, 183B2
WOOD, George M.
Loses primary for gov 8-17, 633F1
WOOD, John
Wins Olympic medal 7-30, 574E1

1977

US employe ordrd to pay suit costs 8-23, 669G3
ERA effort launched, Carter proclaims Equality Day 8-26, 669A2
Wis judge recalled on rape case, Krueger replaces 9-7, 712A1
Pa gov defends Tucker ouster 9-28, 800C2
ERA deadline extension ruled legal 11-1, 918E1
Election results 11-8, 855F2, D3
Boycott vs non-ERA states rptd 11-14, 918B1
Carter urges US jobs 11-17, 914E2
Natl Women's Conf meets, OKs plan; 'pro-family' anti-ERA counterrally 11-19—11-21, 917F2, F3
Whitmire wins Houston race 11-22, 900B3
Carter cites campaign vow 12-28, 1002A1

Religion
1st Episc priest ordained 1-1, 119B3
Dissident Episcs unite 1-14, 119C3
RC study bans ordinatn 1-27, 119C2
Reform Jews issue new home prayer book 3-7, 471C3
US priests back ordinatn 3-23, 374G3
Anglican, Orthodox ldrs dispute ordinatn 5-1, 374D3
RC bishops uphold ordinatn ban 5-3—5-6, 375D2
Ordinatn support rptd up 5-6, 375A2
Israel to ease mil exemptns 6-9, 474B3
Dissident Episcs form schismatic church 9-14—9-16, 731C2
Russian Orthodox bar female ordinatn 9-25, 845B3
Episc ordinatn, secessn data 9-30, 845B2
Fla Episc parish secedes 10-2, 845A3
Episc bishops OK dissident clause 10-3, back Allin 10-5, 845A2, F2
US RC bishops rpt status 11-15, 906F2
Sex Crimes—*See SEX Crimes, PROSTITUTION*

Sports
Guthrie in Indy 500 5-29, 531A2
Eng Channel swim record set 9-8, 808B3

WOMEN, National Council of Negro—*See NEGRO Women, National Council of*
WOMEN, National Organization for (NOW)
Vs Bell confrmatn 1-11—1-18, 34B2
DeCrow on ERA rescissns 3-26, 279F3
Smeal elected pres 4-24, 532F1
Sup Ct declines employer records case 5-16, 419E1
ERA campaign launched 8-26, 669A2
Non-ERA state boycott rptd 11-14, 918B1
WOMEN'S Air Force Service Pilots—*See U.S. GOVERNMENT—WASPs*
WOMEN'S Bank N.A. (Denver, Colo.)
Charter OKd 7-6, 578F1
WOMEN'S Conference, National
Meets, adopts plan; conservatives rally 11-19—11-21, 917F2, F3
WOMEN'S National Bank (Washington, D.C.)
Charter OKd 7-6, 578F1
WOMEN'S Political Caucus, National
Sen employe bias rptd 8-4, 669F3
WOMEN'S Wear Daily (newspaper)
'77 fall fashion wrap-up 6-6, 7-29, 1022C1
WOMEN'S Year, International
US Natl Women's Conf meets, counterrally vs 11-19—11-21, 917F2, G3
WOMEN'S Year, 1975, National Commission on the Observance of International—*See under U.S. GOVERNMENT*
WONDER, Stevie
At pan-Africa festival 1-15—2-12, 106B1
WOOD, Daniel
Wins election 5-24, 410C3

1978

Vet Civil Svc job preferenc clears Sen 8-24, 662B1
Teeters named to FRB 8-28, 664C1
Weddington named pres asst 8-31, 681C3
NYS, Conn, Vt primary results 9-12, 716A2, C2, E2
Wyo, Mass primary results 9-12, 9-19, 736C2, A3, B3
ERA rescissn amendmts rejectd by Sen 10-3, 788C1
ERA extensn OKd by Sen, Schlafly scores 10-6, 788A1
NOW holds annual conf; ERA to be '79 priority 10-8, 788A2
ACLU hails ERA ratificatn extensn 10-20, 981A3
Election results 11-7, 845F1-F2, 847B2-849F3, 852F2-857E1, 897G3-898A1; ERA referendum 847B2, 857E1, 849F3
Carter backs judges merit selectn 11-8, 873C3
Natl Advisory Com cancels Carter mtg 11-22, 915D1
Payton quits Peace Corps 11-24, 915G1
Carter Mormon award opposed 11-27, 915B1
Carter cites repression 12-6, 934C1
Carter cites ERA support 12-8, 956E2

Religion
NCC ordinatn study issued 3-23, 295F1-B2
Mormons affirm motherhood role 4-1, 907E2
Episc canon preaches in Westminster 4-2, 294D2
Cath laity church role rptd 4-7, 294F3
Mormans oppose ERA 5-5, 907D2
Mormon priesthood ban cited 6-9, 480A3
Israel mil exempts religious 7-20, 592F1
'76 papal policy cited 8-6, 601C2
New Pope elected, views cited 8-26, 658B1
Mormon prayer rites opened 10-7, 907G1
Carter Mormon award opposed 11-27, 915B1

Sports
Caulkins leads US swimming resurgence 1-7—8-28, 780A1
NCAA suit vs Title IX dismissed 1-9, 40D2
US judge backs coed sports 1-9, 40D3
Tennis results 1-15—4-2, 419E1
Ariz State wins AIAW swimming title 3-18, 780G2
UCLA wins AIAW basketball title 3-25, 272C2
WTA ends Va Slims pact 4-21, Avon '79 sponsorship rptd 5-17, 419B2
Penn State wins lacrosse title 5-28, 540B2
Guthrie 9th in Indy 500, pre-race injury rptd 5-29, 538E2
Women rptrs gain locker room access 9-25, 1026A3
1st Amers climb Annapurna 10-15, 2 killed 10-17, 843G2
El Capitan scaled alone 10-26, 843A3
NFL ex-cheerleaders score team managemt 11-1, 1024B1
Pro basketball league begins play 12-9, 1027F2

WOMEN, Association for Intercollegiate Athletics for—*See INTERCOLLEGIATE Athletics for Women, etc.*
WOMEN, National Organization for (NOW)
ERA boycott injunctn sought by Mo, Nev 2-28, 3-3, 494F2
Annual conf held; ERA to be '79 priority 10-8, 788A2
Nev boycott suit cited 11-7, 857E1
WOMEN Lawyers, National Association of
ABA rejcts ERA deadline extensn 8-8, 626B3
WOMEN'S Conference, National
Delegatn sees Carter, rights effort pledged 3-22, 218B2
WOMEN'S Professional Basketball League—*See BASKETBALL—Professional*
WOMEN'S Room, The (book)
On best-seller list 7-2, 579C3; 8-6, 620A2; 11-6, 888A1; 12-3, 971C1
WOMEN'S Tennis Association (WTA)—*See TENNIS*
WOMEN Voters of the United States, League of—*See LEAGUE of Women Voters, etc.*
WONDERFUL (recording)
Hawkins Singers win Grammy 2-24, 316A1
WONDERFUL Wizard of Oz, The (book)
Wiz released 10-25, 970E3
WOOD, Andy
Mr Joyce opens 4-23, 760F2
WOOD, Bari
Twins on best-seller list 7-2, 579E3
WOOD, Dan
Named Caribous coach 6-27, 707E3
WOOD, John
Death Trap opens 2-26, 760A2

1979

Kreps quits Commerce post 10-4, 829B2
Hufstedler named Educ secy 10-30, 829F1
US Helsinki com lauds efforts 11-7, 981B1
Kennedy addresses activists, backs ERA 11-29, 12-4, 962F1, G1
Mormon ERA backer excommunicated 12-5, 929B3
NOW vs Carter reelectn 12-9, barred from White House mtg 12-13, 961G2, A3
Feinstein elected San Fran mayor 12-11, 946E3

Religion
'78 church attendance rptd 1-5, 24D1
Orthodox rabbis hold sexes equal, oppose ERA 1-26, 101G3
Conservative Jews OK as rabbis 1-30, 101F3
1st US rabbi resigns NY post 2-2, 176F1
Pope presents 1st encyclical 3-15, 216G3
Episc ordinatn opponents advised to stay in church 5-12, 375E3
Nuns set Md hq sale 7-2, 640A3
Anglicans bar US svcs 7-27, 640A3
Anglican ldr vs ordinatn 9-7, 755G2
Pope affirms ordinatn ban 10-4, hears plea from nun 10-7, 758D3, 759D3, 760C1
Ordinatn polls rptd 11-11, 930A2, E2-G2
RC Bishops reject prayer change 11-14, 930B1
Mecca mosque militants issue demands 11-20, 899B1
Jesuit priest silncd, ordinatn issue cited 12-1, 993F3
Mormon feminist excommunicated 12-5, 929B3

Sports
NCAA vows Title IX fight, rejcts reforms 1-8—1-10, 102B3-103G1
AIAW meets; divisn reorganizatn refined, Meyers honored, Grant elected pres 1-8—1-10, 103G1
AIAW basketball tourn results 3-25, 239A1
Lieberman named top coll basketball player 3-29, 290F3
Meyers waived by NBA team 9-9, signs with WBL Gems 11-14, 1003E2
Title IX guidelines issued 12-4, 1000F2

WOMEN, Association for Intercollegiate Athletics for—*See INTERCOLLEGIATE Athletics for Women, Association for*
WOMEN, National Advisory Committee for—*See under U.S. GOVERNMENT*
WOMEN, National Organization for (NOW)
Abortion issue conf sought 1-22, 63F2
ERA conv boycott upheld 2-21, 128F1
Smeal scores job-preferenc ruling 6-5, 421C2
Vs Carter reelectn 12-9, barred from White House mtg 12-13, 961G2, A3
WOMEN Religious, Leadership Conference of
Pope's female ordinatn stand challenged 10-7, 759E3*
WOMEN'S Basketball League (WBL)—*See BASKETBALL-Professional*
WOMEN'S Lacrosse Association (WLA)—*See LACROSSE*
WOMEN'S National Democratic Club
Mrs Carter addresses 7-12, 514E1
WOMEN'S Ordination Conference
RC Bishops prayer change rejectn scored 11-14, 930C3
WOMEN'S Political Caucus, National (NWPC)
Conv '80 electn discussed, new pres elected 7-13—7-15, 578G2
WOMEN'S Room, The (book)
On best-seller list 1-7, 80C3; 2-4, 120D3; 3-4, 173F3; 5-6, 356E2
WOMEN Voters of the United States, League of—*See LEAGUE of Women Voters*
WONG, Alfred
Sup Ct workforce data rptd 6-11, 464A2
WOOD, Charles
Cuba released 12-21, 1007B3
WOOD, Christopher
Sweeney Todd opens 3-1, 292C3
Moonraker released 6-29, 820B2
WOOD Jr., Judge John
Slain 5-29, 431D2
Chagra convicted in drug smuggling case 8-15, 819A1

1980

Carter pres renominatn acceptance speech 8-14, 612G3
Lucey scores Reagan on ERA 8-25, 646F3
Anderson platform offered 8-30, 665B2
Carter scores GOP stand 9-29, 739A1
NOW Mo boycott case refused by Sup Ct 10-6, 782F1-A2
Reagan vows Sup Ct apptmt 10-14, Carter scores 10-15, 779A1, D3
Thomas sworn SEC comr 10-21, 960B1
Carter, Reagan TV debate 10-28, 813B2, 814B2, 815C2, A3
Electn results 11-4: cong 846B2-D2, 848C2, 852E1; state 847B3
ERA advocate fined in Ill bribe case 11-7, 997A3
Carter plans to speak out 11-12, 865F2
Sup Ct drops 'Mr Justice' title 11-14, 882B3
Mrs Dole named pres asst 12-20, 980C2
Reagan makes Cabt-level apptmt 12-22, 979F2

Religion
RC bishops family life conf opens 9-26, 810C3
Pope in W Ger, ordinatn stance scored 11-19, 905F2

Sports
NCAA OKs title tourns, AIAW scores 1-8, 103C3-104C1
Lieberman named '79 top female coll athlete 1-8, 104D1; top basketball player 3-26, 240G3
NCAA wins Title IX appeal 4-19, 469D3

WOMEN, United Nations Decade for
2d world conf held in Copenhagen 7-14—7-30, 587E1-D3
WOMEN and Children First (recording)
On best-seller list 4-30, 360A1; 6-4, 448F3
WOMEN Organized Against Sexual Harassment (WOASH)
Calif sex harassmt cases rptd 1-9, 78A1
WOMEN'S Basketball League (WBL)—*See BASKETBALL*
WOMEN'S Education Fund, National
Cong election results 'disappointing' 11-4, 846F2
WOMEN'S Equal Rights Legal Defense and Education Fund
Navy lesbian probe scored 6-13, 517E3
WOMEN Voters of the United States, League of—*See LEAGUE of Women Voters*
WON Pat, Del. Antonio (D, Guam)
Backs female draft registratn 3-6, 188D3
WOOD, James
Named A&P chrmn 4-29, 456D2
WOOD, Mae C. Ryan
Dies 10-14, 876F3

1976

WOOD, Robert D.
Quits CBS 4-9, 504C2
Loses gov election 11-2, 820B3, 824B2
WOODAHL, Robert
Wins primary for gov 6-1, 411G1
WOODCOCK, Leonard
Praises Carter 3-4, 179C3
UAW bargaining mtg 3-18—3-20, 220C1
Endorses Carter 5-7, 343D2
GM contract talks open 7-19, 570F1, A2
Scores Ford UAW offer 8-31, 669C2
Ford offer rejected 9-10, 689E2
Sees Carter 12-9, 937F3
WOODMOOR, Colo.—*See COLORADO*
WOODRUFF, William
Succeeded in AF post 3-10, 232E1
WOODS, Donald
Freed 12-9, 1010B3
WOODS, Frederick Newhall
Enters Canada 7-17, arrested 7-29, 560B1
Chowchilla trial moved 11-10, 876F3
WOODS, Phil
Wins Grammy 2-28, 460B3
WOODS, Rose Mary
Wins personal items return 4-23, 316E1
WOODWARD, Bob
Final Days on best-seller list 12-5, 972A2
WOODWARD, Robert F.
Scores OAS re Chile rights abuse 3-5, 310F1
WOOL
Australia-Japan talks 2-4—2-15, 137E3
Australian strike 3-5, Japan deals hurt 4-1, 249D3
Australia packers strike 3-5—4-20, 287A3
Australia devaluatn welcomed 11-28, 896F1
WOOLBRIGHT, Donald R.
CIA bars data on Hughes burglary 1-5, 24E2
WOOLFOLK, Russell
Sentenced 6-21, 860C2
WORLD Affairs Council (Boston)
Kissinger addresses 3-11, 197A3

WORLD Bank Group
OPEC aid to poor nations cited 1-12, 14D3
Simon wage action protested 4-28, 340E1
US proposes intl resources bank 5-6, 317D2
Joint IMF mtgs in Manila 10-4—10-8; McNamara urges loan progrm expansn re poor natns, vs bank loan lid 10-4; US, others react 10-5, 777E1
Policies, ldrship questnd 11-22, 12-26, 976C1
International Bank for Reconstruction and Development (World Bank)
Deutsche mark bond issue 1-28, 158E1
Zaire copper loan rptd rejctd 2-2, 335E2
OKs Chile copper plant loan 2-3, 99F2
OKs Paraguay loan 2-27, 205B3
US rep vs Chile loan 3-19, 3-23; McNamara defends 4-12, 310E2
OKs Dutch bank loan 4-2, 366D1
Bolivia loan rptd 4-13, 416C1
Johan Beyen dies 4-29, 368E2
Suspends EAC loans 5-11, 371F3
Vietnam joins 9-21, 721D3
PI protest march thwarted 10-3, 752A1
Namibia aid offer rptd 10-8, 794B1
Venez econ policy lauded 10-16, 875G1
Ivory Coast loans OKd 12-16, 1012G3
2 Chile loans OKd 12-21, 999F1
International Development Association (IDA)
Japan vs fund hike 3-2, 191A3
US Dem platform text cites 6-15, 476F3
'77 US aid signed 10-1, 806E3
Greek loan rptd 12-10, 1004B3
Congo loan rptd 12-16, 1012A3
Mali credit OKd 12-16, 1013E1
Rwanda credit OKd 12-16, 1013C2

1977

WOOD, Orville
Awarded back pay in bias suit 10-11, 819B1
WOODALL, Howard
Bolles murder convictns 11-6, 871D2
WOODBINE, Ga.—*See GEORGIA*
WOODCOCK, Leonard
Scores Dixon anti-Nader slur 1-17, 96B1
Heads missn to Viet, Laos 3-16—3-20; Carter gets rpt 3-23, 206B1
Named to Peking liaison post 5-12, 381A2
Fraser elected UAW pres 5-18, 408E1
WOODHAM-Smith, Cecil
Dies 3-16, 264G3
WOODS, Donald
Biko death queried 9-16, 735E2
Arrested 10-19, 804A1
Appeal vs '75 jailing upheld 11-25, 935D1
WOODS, Frederick N.
Pleads guilty 7-25, 642D1
Convicted 12-15, 992D1
WOODS, M. Alan
Replaced as Defns asst secy 3-4, 211F1
WOODS, Rose Mary
Nixon-Frost TV interview 9-3, 692D3
WOOD, Struthers & Winthrop Inc.
Donaldson Lufkin buys 10-11, 800A1
WOODWARD, Bob
Final Days on best-seller list 2-6, 120G3; 3-6, 184G3
Jordan scores CIA rpt 2-18, 124E2
Carter-Post mtg rptd 2-25, 151G2
Nixon scores 5-25, 420F1, E2
WOODWORTH, Laurence N.
Named Treas asst secy 1-7, 14C2; nominated 2-17, confrmd 2-21, 148G3
Dies 12-4, 1024G3
WOOL
Record Australia exports seen 1-4, 42B2
UN rpts '76 price up 2-14, 146B1
Australia bars floor-price drop 3-15, 236E3
Australia scores EC protectionism 6-1, 595F3
Australia lowers prices 7-4, wool stock at season start rptd 652G3-653A1
Uruguay '76 export data rptd 7-8, 601G2
Australian output at 20-yr low 8-19, 652E3
Sheep disease hits Australia 11-14, 881D3
WOOLBRIGHT, Donald R.
Convicted 4-22, 396G1
WOOLRIDGE, Jim
Named dep prime min, tourism min 8-31, 969C3
WOOLSEY, R. James
Navy undersecy 2-21, confrmd 3-4, 211A2
WOOLWORTH Co., F.W.
US sues re Tris 5-17, settlemt 5-18, 483D2
Rebels set bomb at Mex co 9-14, 745F3
WORLD Affairs Council of Northern California
Mondale addresses 6-17, 473D2
WORLD Airways, Inc.
CAB 'no-frills' rule review denied 5-16, 419C2
WORLD Association of Guides and Girl Scouts
Lady Baden-Powell dies 6-25, 532E2
WORLD Bank—*See WORLD Bank Group—International Bank for Reconstruction and Development*
WORLD Bank Group
McNamara reapptd pres 4-24, 532F1
Intl consortium OKs Egypt aid 5-11—5-12, 390B3
Rich, poor natns' econ growth rptd 9-18, 717A3
Joint IMF mtgs in DC 9-26—9-30; McNamara scores '76 poor natn aid level; bank capitalizatn hike backed 9-26, 753C2, 754E1
International Bank for Reconstruction and Development (World Bank)
Chile '76 loan total rptd 3-18, 449E1
Guinea-Bissau joins 3-24, 309C2
US aid-rights compromise set 8-30, funds clear Cong 10-19, 815B2, F2; Carter signs 11-1, 834D1
Peru '70s loan rejectns cited 8-31, 785D1
US aid, rights curb voted 9-21, 737B3
Commonwealth finance mins discuss loan terms 9-21—9-24, 936D2
US aid authorizatn signed 10-3, 834D1
Uganda repudiates EAC debts 10-9, 805C2
Argentina $200 mln loan OKd 11-10, 981F2
Gaud Jr dies 12-5, 1024G1
International Development Association (IDA)
Burundi educ credit OKd 2-10, 161E2
Rumania loan OKd 2-18, 137A2
OKs Yugo agri loans 2-24, 309C1
US '78 funds clear Cong 10-19, 815F2; Carter signs 11-1, 834D1
International Finance Corp. (IFC)
Ivory Coast loan rptd 1-5, 24A2

1978

WOOD, Peggy
Dies 3-18, 252F3
WOODCOCK, Leonard
Sees better US-China ties 1-7, 17E2
US-Peking ties agreed 12-14, 973G2
WOODESON, Nicholas
Strawberry Fields opens 6-4, 887D3
WOODHEAD, Cynthia
Upset in 400-m freestyle 8-2; sets 200-m, 400-m records 8-3, 8-22, 8-26, 780C1-E2
WOODHULL, Victoria (deceased)
Thread of Scarlet opens 12-8, 1031B3
WOODRUFF, Robert
Starving Class opens 3-2, 887B3
Buried Child opens 11-6, 1031B1
WOODS, Donald
Arrives Botswana 1-3, 8E1
WOODS, Frederick N.
Sentenced for Chowchilla kidnap 2-17, 232C3
WOODS, Phil
Group wins Grammy 2-24, 315F3
WOODS, Rose Mary
Haldeman book on Watergate rptd 2-16—2-17, 124F3
WOODTHORPE, Peter
Playboy of Weekend World opens 11-16, 1031G2
WOODWARD, Bob
In Haldeman book-scoop by-line 2-16, 124F2
WOODWARD, Bronte
Grease released 6-16, 619C2
WOODWARD, Joanne
Wins Emmy 9-17, 1030G1
WOODWARD, Brig. Gen. William T.
AF Acad dismissal rptd 4-21, 420C1
WOOL
Australia stock use rptd 1-4, 6E2
US-Taiwan textile agrmt rptd 2-17, 140C3
Australian exports rptd down 4-14, 411G1
Australia sheep herds rptd down 6-14, 472A2
'77-78 Australia exports rptd 7-18, 555F1
WOOLWORTH Co., F. W.
In Dow Jones indl avg 66F2
WOOSNAM, Phil
NASL realignmt, playoff format set 1-10, 23D1
WORKING (play)
Opens 5-14, 887E3
WORLD Affairs Council
Brown affirms US commitmt to Asia Pacifc 2-20, 126C3
WORLD Bank—*See WORLD Bank Group—International Bank for Reconstruction and Development*

WORLD Bank Group
3d World '77 debt estimate cited 3-11, 301F1
Zaire emergency aid OKd 6-13—6-14, 478A1
Joint IMF mtg marked by optimism, growth rate convergence stressed 9-25—9-28, 731B2
McNamara asks trade curbs end, bank capital hike 9-25, 732F2-B3
Poverty, income table 732B3
International Bank for Reconstruction and Development (World Bank)
Mauritania ore-dvpt loan rptd 1-27, 95E1
Paraguay gets road dvpt loan 3-9, 292F3
Brazil $110 mln loan rptd 3-10, 311A2
Zambia com sets aid 6-27—6-29, 617G1
El Salvador rights situatn rptd worse 8-5, 723A3 ★
Latin loans rptd up 9-15, 828A3
Bolivia oil loan set 10-8, 840D3
International Development Association (IDA)
Viet gets irrigatn loan 8-8, 624F1
International Finance Corp. (IFC)
Latin export bank opens 9-8, 828D3

1979

WOOD, Mervyn
Corruptn chrgd, resigns 6-5, 467B2
WOOD, Natalie
Meteor released 10-19, 1008A1
WOOD, Peter
Night & Day opens 11-27, 956E3
WOODBRIDGE, N.J.—*See NEW Jersey*
WOODCOCK, George
Dies 10-30, 860G3
WOODCOCK, Leonard
Toasts US-China ties 1-1, 2C1
At Teng dinner 1-28, 66B2
With Teng in Atlanta 2-1, 83F2
Confrmd China amb 2-26, installed in Peking 3-1, 146D1
Teng vs rights complaints 3-16, 259B1
China vs US-Taiwan ties 3-16, 312D1
China-US trade pact signed 7-7, 523E2
Meets Sihanouk in Peking 10-4, 811D2
Wei sentence protested 10-17, 789E2
WOOD Energy Institute (Camden, Me.)
Wood stove use hike rptd 5-20, 419F1
WOODHEAD, Cynthia
Wins 5 gold medals at Pan Am Games 7-1—7-15, sets 200-m freestyle record 7-3, 798G2
Wins 3 gold medals at Natl Sports Festival 7-21—8-1, 799C1
WOOD-Ridge Chemical Corp.
NJ Meadowlands cleanup ordrd 8-26, 704B2
WOODRUFF, Robert W.
Gives Emory U $100 mln gift 11-8, 902C2, D2
WOODRUFF Fund Inc., Emily & Ernest
Emory U gets $100 mln gift 11-8, 902D2
WOODS, James
Onion Field released 9-19, 820E2
WOODS, The (play)
Opens 4-25, 712F3
WOODS v. Safeway Stores
Case declined by Sup Ct 2-21, 128E3
WOODWARD, Bob
'Brethren' publicatn stirs controversy 12-2, 988B2
WOODWARD, Charles
Sweeney Todd opens 3-1, 292C3
WOODWARD, Robert Burns
Dies 7-8, 588G3
WOODWARD, Wayne
Sues USAC 5-27, 491C2
WOOL
US cuts Australia tariffs 1-8, 36F2, E3
Peru vicuna debate rptd 7-26, 584E3
WOOLWORTH Co., F. W.
In Dow Jones indl avg 72F1
Brascan seeks 4-9, spurns 4-11; suits, Revco merger talks, other dvpts 4-12—4-23, 303B3-304C2
Barbara Hutton dies 5-11, 432A3
Brascan takeover delayed 5-25; bid dropped, suits setld 5-29, 440C2
WOOSNAM, Phil
Suspends Alberto 8-31, 775G3
WORCESTER, Mass.—*See MASSACHUSETTS*
WORLD According to Garp, The (book)
Natl Book Awards rptd 4-23, 356G1
On best-seller list 5-6, 356E2; 6-3, 432C2; 7-1, 548C3; 8-5, 620D3
WORLD Airways Inc.
$99 cross-country fares, new routes OKd 1-12, 35E2

WORLD Bank Group
Joint IMF mtg in Belgrade marked by $, inflatn woes 10-2—10-5; Miller vows US inflatn fight, Saudi warns re oil price rise 10-3, 779F2-F3
International Bank for Reconstruction and Development (World Bank)
St Lucia dvpt aid rptd 2-21, 181F2
Turkey aid package set 5-30, 397A2
Nicaragua $55 mln loan rptd 11-27, 909G3

1980

WOOD, Natalie
Last Married Couple released 2-8, 216B3
'Charlie's Angels' fraud probe rptd 5-1, 376A3
LA DA ends 'Charlie's Angels' probe 12-2, 1002F2
WOOD, Randall B.
Indicted in Brilab probe 6-12, 454F2
Acquitted 10-23, 971C2
WOOD, Ronald Wayne
Acquitted 11-17, 898F2
WOODARD, James
Ties Stones high jump mark 6-7, 892A1
WOODCOCK, Leonard
Shanghai consulate reopened 4-28, 351G1
Scores Reagan Taiwan remarks 8-26, 664C3
Signs US-China grain pact 10-22, 801G1
WOODEN, John
Louisville wins NCAA basketball title 3-24, 240D2
WOODHULL, Victoria (deceased)
Onward Victoria opens 12-14, 1003E3
WOODRUFF, Robert
True West opens 12-23, 1003F3
WOODSIDE Petroleum Ltd.
NW Shelf gas project rptd set 10-1, 748F1
WOODSON, Mike
In NBA draft 6-10, 447F1
WOODWARD, Bob
Brethren on best-seller list 1-13, 40B3; 2-10, 120C3; 3-9, 200B3; 4-6, 280C3
US atty named Abscam leaks prosecutor 2-11, 111C2
Powell refutes Sup Ct media image 5-1, 368A3
WOODWARD, Edward
Wicker Man released 3-26, 416G3
WOOL
Australia handler strike rptd, Japan supply needs cited 3-11, 191B1
Australia strike accord rptd 3-21, 229F2-A3
China, Australia in talks 5-7—5-11, 388A1
WOOL, Robert
All You Need to Know About the IRS on best seller list 4-6, 280B3
WOOLWORTH Co., F. W.
In Dow Jones indl avg 76G1
James Leftwich dies 7-6, 608C2
WOONSOCKET—*See RHODE Island*
WORCESTER—*See MASSACHUSETTS*
WORKING My Way Back to You (recording)
On best-seller list 4-2, 280E3
WORLD According to Garp, The (book)
Wins Amer Book Award 5-1, 692A2
WORLD Affairs Council
Carter addresses Phila group 5-9, 367G1
Bush addresses Pa groups 9-5, 9-25, 780D3, 781D1
Muskie addresses 9-18, 776E2
WORLD Airways Inc.
Coast-to-coast fares cut 4-9, 346B3
Boston-London route OKd 4-10, 346C2
Coast-to-coast fares cut 6-11, hiked 7-1, 516C2

WORLD Bank Group
International Bank for Reconstruction and Development (World Bank)
Capital doubled, outstanding loans, other data rptd 1-14, 1-15, 49G3-50B2
Afghanistan loans frozen 1-14, 50B2
UN dvpt aid fund disputed 2-9, 124C2
N-S study urges aid plan 2-12, 124D3
Turkey seeks aid 3-26, 236D2
McNamara in China 4-11—4-16, IMF to admit China 4-17, 302D2
China gains entry, Taiwan expelled 5-15, 389C1
McNamara to quit as pres 6-9, 761B2
Venice summit backs 3d World aid 6-23, 474B1
S Korea revises '80 deficit estimate 7-1, 499E3
Mex agri loan OKd, 3 other loans noted 7-10, 605D2
Guyana loan OKd, hydro project set 7-25, 791C2
Saudis, Kuwait freeze loans over PLO issue 8-2, 592A2
'80 econ forecast grim; oil price hike seen; Africa, S Asia hardest hit 8-17, 628E2
Muskie addresses UN aid talks 8-25, 642C3
Bolivia debt paymts postponed 9-3, 686B3
PLO status disputed 9-4—9-22; dirs bar observer role 9-18, agenda debate asked 9-22, 719D3-720A1
IMF oil debt role studied 9-15, 695F2
Annual rptd issued; '80 loans, disbursmts rptd 9-22, 720B1-B2
Joint IMF mtg in DC 9-30—10-3, Carter cites 'political' threat 9-30, 761A2, G3, 766A3
OPEC postpones 3d World aid mtg 10-6, 759D1
El Salvador aid rptd blocked re rights repressn 10-15, 829E1
Clausen nominated pres 10-30, 826G1
International Development Association (IDA)
China long-term credits seen 5-15, 389D1
Venice summit backs 3d World aid 6-23, 473B1
Annual rptd issued; '80 loans, disbursmts rptd 9-22, 720B1-B2
International Finance Corp. (IFC)
China long-term credits seen 5-15, 389D1

1976

WORLD Council of Churches (WCC)
Latin rights abuse denunciatn rptd 1-9, 61F2
Scores Malawi re Jehovah's Witness 6-14, 497E3
WORLD Court—*See 'International Court of Justice' under UNITED Nations*
WORLD Food Council—*See under UNITED Nations*
WORLD Health Organization—*See under UNITED Nations*
WORLD Meteorological Organization (WMO)
Limited SST fleet urged 1-17, 104A3
WORLD Offshore Exhibition (London)
Opens 10-3, 792A1
WORLD of Our Fathers (book)
On best-seller list 12-5, 972A2
WORLD Student Christian Federation
Uruguay bans 1-20, 208A1
WORLD War I (1914-18)
Dole, Mondale debate 10-15, 782A3
Hungary pays US debt 12-24, 1012D3
WORLD War II (1939-45)—*See also NAZIS*
Canada ex-prime min diaries publshd 1-1, 8C1
W Ger-Poland indemnificatn pact OKd 2-19, 3-12, 260F1
Dole, Mondale debate 10-15, 783C3
Dole scores Dems 10-25—10-27, Mondale rebuts 10-26, 804A2, D2, A3, B3
Hirohito marks 50-yr reign 11-10, 890A1
Tokyo Rose seeks pardon 11-17, 892C2
Obituaries
Cassin, Rene 2-20, 192D3
Fuchida, Mitsuo 5-30, 524E2
Gubbins, Colvin Mcvean 2-11, 160D3
Ingersoll, Royal 5-20, 404A2
Montgomery, Field Marshal 3-24, 240E3
Shimada, Shigetaro 6-7, 254E3
WORLDWATCH Institute (Washington, D.C.)
World populatn growtn down 10-28, 863G1
WORLD Wildlife Fund
Bernhard resigns post 8-26, 626G1
WORTH, Irene
Wins Tony 4-18, 460D2
WPI—*See 'Prices' under ECONOMY*

WRATHALL, John
Sworn Rhodesia pres 1-14, 53D3
WRAN, Neville
Labor wins NSW electn 5-1, 349B3
NSW plans announced 5-13, 362E3
WREN, Christopher
Sovt press chrgs CIA link 5-25, 5-26, 371B3, D3
WRESTLING
Olympic results 7-24, 7-31, 576F2, C3
WRIEDT, Kenneth
Loses shadow cabt post 3-25, 237B1
WRIGHT, Burke
On United Brands, Cuba raid link 10-23, 844G3
WRIGHT, Judge J. Skelly
EPA leaded gas curb upheld 3-19, 219F2
WRIGHT Jr., Rep. James C. (D, Tex.)
Reelected 11-2, 830D4
Elected majority ldr 12-6, 919A1
Names majority whip 12-8, 981D1
WRIGHT, Margaret
Final pres vote tally 12-18, 979C2
WRIGHT, Orville (1871-1948)
Loening dies 2-29, 192E3
WRIGHT, Robin
Angola ousts 6-9, 480B3
WRIGHT, Russell
Dies 12-22, 1015C3
WRIGHTSVILLE Beach, N.C.—*See NORTH Carolina*
WRISTON, Walter B.
Defends Citibank solvency 1-11, 110G2, 111B1

1977

WORLD Boxing Association (WBA)—*See BOXING*
WORLD Boxing Council (WBC)—*See BOXING*
WORLD Championship Tennis (WCT)—*See TENNIS*
WORLD Conference on Religion and Peace
Viet refugee boat chartered 6-12, 497C1 *
WORLD Council of Churches (WCC)
Asks Uganda deaths probe 2-17, 139C1
Coggan visits 5-3, 374F3
Mex police raid rights group 7-7, 746E1
Rhodesian army atrocities chrgd 7-8, 536A2
WORLD Court—*See UNITED Nations—International Court of Justice*
WORLD Evangelistic and Christian Education Fund
Disclosed 6-26, 731F3-732A1
WORLD Food Council—*See under UNITED Nations*
WORLD Federation, Lutherans—*See LUTHERANS*
WORLD Health Organization (WHO)—*See under UNITED Nations*
WORLD Hockey Association (WHA)—*See HOCKEY, Ice*
WORLD Jewish Congress
Carter, Kissinger address 11-2, 11-3, 830A3
WORLD Medical Assembly
Maltese doctors backed 9-9, 925B3
WORLD of Our Fathers (book)
Wins Natl Book Award 4-11, 355A2
WORLD Peace Through Law Conference
Ramsey Clark vs Manila site, PI offcl defends 8-21, 665A1
Meets in Manila, rights pressed 8-22—8-26; dels in protest 8-25, 664B3
WORLD Series—*See BASEBALL—Winners*
WORLD Team Tennis (WTT)—*See TENNIS*
WORLD Trade Center (N.Y.)
Willig climbs tower 5-26, 532A2
WORLD War II (1939-45)—*See also NAZIS*
Ford pardons Tokyo Rose 1-19, 36B2
Carter cites natl unity 2-2, 75C2
Japan rightists protest Yalta-Potsdam agrmts 3-3—3-4, 201G2
US germ warfare rptd 3-9, 195B3
USSR hears US lectures 9-26, 9-28, 866A2
WORLDWATCH Institute (Washington, D.C.)
Solar, renewable energy sources backed for 3d World 12-11, 975G2
WORLDWIDE Church of God
Workers religious rights limited 6-13, 517C3
WORTHINGTON, Peter
On Praxis document theft 5-22, 426B1
WOSIK, Judge Joseph M.
Ill Nazi rally ban upset 6-13, 517A3
WPI (wholesale price index)—*See ECONOMY—Prices*
WRAN, Neville
Rpts drug abuse, urges decriminalizatn 9-29, 944F3
WRATHALL, John James(Rhodesian president)
Opens Parlt 9-20, 824C3
WREN, Christopher
USSR renews attack 2-2, 101D1
WRESTLING
Antonino Rocca dies 3-15, 264D3
WRIGHT Jr., Rep. James C. (D, Tex.)
Carter econ plan disclosed 1-7, 5B2
Sikes loses subcom post 1-26, 53G2
'76 spec interest gifts rptd 2-15, 128B2
Vs Gonzalez resignatn 3-2, 149B1, C1
Common-site picketing defeated 3-23, 229F1
On Carter energy plan 4-20, 293G1
Backs House intell com 7-14, 557E1
Min wage indexing defeated 9-15, 759D1
WRIGLEY, Philip K.
Dies 4-12, 356G3

1978

WORLD Boxing Association (WBA)—*See BOXING*
WORLD Boxing Council (WBC)—*See BOXING*
WORLD Championship Tennis (WCT)—*See TENNIS*
WORLD Council of Churches (WCC)
S Africa church cuts Dutch ties 4-4, 269G2
Rhodesia rebel aid OKd 8-10, members protest 8-18, 8-22, 650F2
Nikodim dies 9-5, 778G1
SWAPO grant rptd 9-26, 742E2
Rhodesia, SWAPO grants protested; totals cited 10-25—11-8, 906D3, 907B1
WORLD Court—*See UNITED Nations—International Court of Justice*
WORLD Cup—*See SOCCER, TENNIS*
WORLD Food Program—*See under UNITED Nations*
WORLD Health Organization (WHO)—*See under UNITED Nations*
WORLD Hockey Association (WHA)—*See HOCKEY, Ice*
WORLD Jewish Congress
Klutznick meets Sadat 2-6, 77G2
Goldmann meets Sadat 7-10, 521A2
WORLD Peace Council
Urges Viet, Cambodia negotiate 1-2, 4A2
WORLD Series—*See BASEBALL*
WORLD War II (1939-45)—*See also NAZIS*
Carter visits Omaha Beach 1-5, 2C1
Australia hangings probe asked 5-8, 350C1
US issues secret documts on Ger, Japanese decoded messages 9-10—9-18, 744D2-G3
WORTHINGTON, Peter
Chrgd re USSR spy rpt leak 3-17, 208G3
WOUK, Herman
War & Remembrance on best-seller list 11-6, 887F3; 12-3, 971A1
WPI (wholesale price index) (producer price index)—*See ECONOMY—Price Indexes*
WPIX-FM (N.Y.C. radio station)
WPIX-TV license renewed 6-16, 672E1
WPIX-TV (N.Y.C. TV station)
FCC renews license 6-16, 672C1
WRAN, Neville
Ordrs McGeechan end inmate talks 1-10, 34C3
Dillingham to close mines 1-17, 34G2
Sets transport agency probe 12-5, 963D2

WRATHALL, John James (Rhodesian president)
Black bishop administers govt oath 3-21, 210B2
Dies 8-31, 708G3
WRATHER, Bonita Granville
Magic of Lassie released 8-3, 970B2
WRENN, Grover
On cotton dust rules 6-19, 472E1
WRESTLING
Coll rankings rptd 3-13, Iowa wins NCAA title 3-18, 379F2-A3
WRIGHT, Amy
My Cup Runneth Over opens 6-22, 760E2
WRIGHT, Frank Lloyd (1869-1959)
Son dies 5-31, 440G3
WRIGHT, Garland
Patio/Porch opens 4-13, 887D2
WRIGHT Jr., Rep. James C. (D, Tex.)
Lauds Humphrey-Hawkins bill 3-16, 182E3
House OKs abortn funding curb 6-13, 445E3
Upholds legis vetoes 6-21, 466A2
On S Korea food aid cutoff 6-22, 467D2
Turkey arms embargo end gets House prelim OK 8-1, 587G2
Reelected 11-7, 852A3
Reelected majority leader 12-4, 958A2
WRIGHT 2nd, Joe
Sentence reduced 1-23, paroled 6-1, 560B2
WRIGHT, Lloyd
Dies 5-31, 440G3
WRIGHT, Mickey
Lopez ties tourn win mark 6-11, 580A3
WRIGHT, Richard (1908-60)
Native Son opens 3-27, 760G2
WRIGHT, Robert
Timbuktu opens 3-1, 760E3
WRISTON, Henry
Dies 3-8, 252G3
WRISTON, Walter B.
Father dies 3-8, 252G3
WRITERS Guild of America Inc.
Unions curbed on supervisor discipline by Sup Ct 6-21, 509F1

1979

WORLD Boxing Association (WBA)—*See BOXING*
WORLD Boxing Council (WBC)—*See BOXING*
WORLD Championship Tennis (WTC)—*See TENNIS*
WORLD Council of Churches (WCC)
Central com votes Vischer release 1-9, 24A1
Africa grants program retained 1-10, 23E3
Baptism rites agrmt reached 3-31, 375C3
S African activist hanged 4-6, 273C3
MIT mtg ends; religion, sci rift eased 7-24, 640C1
Zimbabwe rebels get 2d grant 10-12, 778F1
N Korea bias chrgd 11-28, 928F2
WORLD Court—*See UNITED Nations–International Court of Justice*
WORLD Education
Adult literacy progrms scored 9-8, 786D1
WORLD Food Program—*See under UNITED Nations*
WORLD Health Organization (WHO)—*See under UNITED Nations*
WORLD Hockey Association—*See HOCKEY, Ice*
WORLD Series—*See BASEBALL*
WORLD War I (1914-18)
Forgn debt to US rptd 2-5, 84C3
WORLD War II (1939-45)—*See also NAZIS; VETERANS*
US secret files released 2-3, 2-6, 93F1
Iran debt to US rptd past due 2-5, 84C3
Amputatn study rptd 2-26, 219A2
US women pilots get benefits 3-9, 307D3
USSR seizes US books 9-4, 690D1
Eisenhower secret diary rptd 9-16, 9-17, 748A1
Renault seizure by French cited 10-12, 784F3
UK spy scandal reopened 10-28, 10-29, 873F3; 4th member named, controversy ensues 11-15—11-21, 908G2-909F1
WORLDWIDE Church of God
Sued, put in receivership 1-3; guards occupy offices 1-8, 23G2
Audit set 3-16, receivership lifted 3-17, 376B2
Receivership challenge refused by Sup Ct 10-1, 768A2
Calif teacher firing case dismissed by Sup Ct 12-10, 988G1
WORLDWIDE Church of God Inc. v. California
Case refused by Sup Ct 10-1, 768A2
WORLD Zionist Organization
Iran warned vs Jews mistreatmt 5-15, 357B2
WORMS
Big worm seen as new phylum 3-31, 290E1
WORTH, Marvin
Rose released 11-17, 1008C1
WORTHINGTON, Peter
Secrecy trial barred 4-23, 311C2
WOUK, Herman
War & Remembrance on best-seller list 1-7, 80A3; 2-4, 120A3; 3-4, 173C3; 4-8, 271G1; 5-6, 356C2; 6-3, 432A2
WOYZECK (film)
Released 8-24, 820F3
WOZZECK (opera)
Complete 'Lulu' debuts in Paris 2-25, 174B1
WPI (wholesale price index) (producer price index)—*See ECONOMY–Price Indexes*
WRAN, Neville
NSW police corruptn chrgd, comr quits; probe launched 6-5, 467B2
Sinclair quits Cabt post 9-27, 788A1
WRATHER, Jack
Nixon Admin pub TV moves disclosed 2-24, 194D2
WRC-TV (Washington, D.C. TV station)
Hair dryer recall sought 4-19, 308F2
WRESTLING
USSR wins World Cup over US 4-1, 507F3
Pan Am Games results 7-1–7-15, 798G2
WRIGHT, Alan
Vs US halt of arms sales to Ulster police 8-2, 602D1
WRIGHT, Garland
New Jerusalem opens 2-15, 712G1
WRIGHT, Judge J. Skelly
Backs wage-guide contract denial 6-22, 480C2
WRIGHT Jr., Rep. James C. (D, Tex.)
House majority ldr 71A1
Misses Camp David mtg 6-1, 418C2
House OKs synthetic fuel bill 6-26, 498B2
Warns Carter re Tellico veto 9-26, 766D3
WRIGHT, Cardinal John
Dies 8-10, 671G3
WRIGHT, Keith
NFL '78 kick return ldr 1-6, 80C2
WRIGHT, Larry
Sonics win NBA title 6-1, 506E3
WRIGHT, Mickey
2d in Coca Cola Classic 5-20, 587G2
WRISTON, Walter B.
Reuss vs prime rate hikes 10-31, 941A1
Lauds Iran assets freeze 11-14, 861G2
WRITERS Guild of America Inc.
FCC 'family hour' power backed 11-20, 1007C1
Novelist libel case refused by Sup Ct 12-3, 964F1

1980

WORLD Boxing Association (WBA)—*See BOXING*
WORLD Boxing Council (WBC)—*See BOXING*
WORLD Championship Tennis (WCT)—*See TENNIS*
WORLD Court—*See UNITED Nations--World Court*
WORLD Food Program—*See under UNITED Nations*
WORLD Health Organization (WHO)—*See under UNITED Nations*
WORLD Series—*See BASEBALL--Winners*
WORLD War II (1939-45)
MacArthur 'gift' dispute rptd 1-30, 1-31, 115E1
French CP ldr defends record 3-8, 193E1-A2
Katyn massacre protester kills self 3-20, 262F3
WORLDWATCH
Gasohol seen as world food threat 3-15, 251A1
WORLDWIDE Church of God
Calif probe case declined by Sup Ct 6-2, 513C1
WORLDWIDE Church of God Inc. v. California
Case declined by Sup Ct 6-2, 513C1
WORLD-Wide Volkswagen v. Woodson
Case decided by Sup Ct 1-21, 93A2
WORLD Wildlife Fund
Panda finding mission begins 5-12, 398A2
WORTH, Irene
Lady From Dubuque opens 1-31, 136C3
John Gabriel Borkman opens 12-18, 1003C3
WORTH, Marvin
Up the Academy released 6-6, 675F3
WORTH, Nicholas
Don't Answer the Phone released 8-9, 675C2
WORTLEY, George
Elected to US House 11-4, 843G3
WOR-TV (N.Y.C. station)
FCC lifts RKO Gen license 1-24, 119F2
FCC backs move to NJ 11-6, 906F1
WRANGLER—*See BLUEBELL Co.*
WRC-TV (Washington, D.C. station)
3 win Polk award 2-25, 692F3
WREBLAN, Andrezj
Ousted from Polish Politburo 12-2, 909G2
WRESTLING
Afghans defect to Pak 7-6; Olympic member denies defectn plan 7-21, 590B2
Soviets dominate Moscow Olympics 7-22—7-31, 588F2, 624G2-E3
WRIEDT, Ken
Vs Sovt rutile embargo end 2-12, 148C1
WRIGHT, Amy
5th of July opens 11-6, 892C3
Inside Moves released 12-19, 1003A2
WRIGHT, Bob
Loses Utah gov electn 11-4, 852E1
WRIGHT, Judge Craig
Cuts Penthouse publisher's libel award 4-17, 405A3
WRIGHT, Don
Wins Pulitzer 4-14, 296G2
WRIGHT, James
Dies 3-25, 280G2
WRIGHT, Rep. James C. (D, Tex.)
Scores Carter budget stand 5-28, 424B2
Meets Carter on Cuban refugees 6-4, 435B1
Asks King Hussein join peace talks 6-17, 450C1
Lauds synfuels bill 6-26, 479D2
Reelected 11-4, 844A3
Reelected House majority ldr 12-8, 936F2
WRIGHT, John
Loses US House electn 11-4, 850B2
WRIGHT, Teresa
Morning's at Seven opens 4-10, 392E3
WRIGHTSVILLE—*See GEORGIA*
WRISTON, Walter B.
Regan named Treas secy 12-11, 935B2

1976

WRONSKI, Stanislaw
Polish State Cncl member 3-25, 268D2
WRZASZCZYK, Tadeusz
Polish deputy premier 3-27, 268F2
WSZOLA, Jacek
Wins Olympic medal 7-31, 576D1
WU, Chien-Hsiung
Gets Medal of Science 10-18, 858G3
WURF, Jerry
Union quits AFL-CIO dept 2-15, 154B1
Dem conv speaker 7-13, 509E3
WURZBURGER, Rabbi Walter S.
Sworn Rabbinical Cncl pres 5-26, 932E2
WUSSLER, Robert
Named CBS pres 4-9, 504C2
WU Teh
Visits Peking riot victims 4-9, 333B1 ★
Named People's Cong chrmn 7-24, 555F1
Listed in China ldrshp 9-10, 712A1
Addresses Hua rally scores Chiang group 10-24, 809G1-B2
WYATT, Ken
Hain acquitted 4-9, 351F1
WYDLE, Edward M.
Indicted 1-19, 44E1
WYDLER, Rep. John W. (R, N.Y.)
Reelected 11-2, 830G1
WYETH Laboratories—*See AMERICAN Home Products Corp.*
WYLIE, Rep. Chalmers Pangburn (R, Ohio)
Reelected 11-2, 830A3
WYNN, Bob
Wins BC open golf 8-9, 656G1
WYNTOON, Calif.—*See CALIFORNIA*

1977

WTT (World Team Tennis)—*See TENNIS*
WUFFLI, Heinz
Resigns 5-10, 565B1
WUI, Inc.
Westn Union Hawaii svc case review declined 10-17, 798A1
WULF, Melvin
US bars Agee prosecutn 3-18, 212B2
WUNDERLE, Margaret
Vindicated of Nazi tie 5-3, 532C2
WUSSLER, Robert J.
Tennis tourn fee probe rptd 7-8, 548G2
Replaced as CBS-TV pres, named CBS Sports pres 10-17, 846F1, A2
Defends TV sports coverage 11-3, 950B1
WU Teh
Posters assail 1-8, 1F2
Chiang Ching link scored 1-9, 61C2
Anti-Teng remarks deleted 1-20, 97G3
In Politburo 8-21, 645G2
Posters assail 10-20, 823F2
WXPN-FM (Pa. radio station)
Loses license 4-4, 395A3
WYNEGAR, Butch
NL wins All-Star Game 7-19, 567E2
WYNN, William H.
Joins AFL-CIO exec cncl 12-12, 961G1
WYNNE, Lt. Patrick E.
Body misidentified 3-23, 206A2

1978

WROBEL, Brian
Chrgs Iran rights breach 2-28, 190D2
WRTV (Indianapolis, Ind. TV station)
NBC drops fall TV lineup 11-29, 1030D1
WTA (Women's Tennis Association)—*See TENNIS*
WTOP (Washington, D.C. radio station)
FCC OKs sale 5-11, 599G3
WTOP-TV (Washington, D.C. TV station)
FCC OKs WWJ-TV swap 5-18, 599F3
WUCHERER, Gerhard
McTear breaks indoor 60-yd dash record 1-7, 76G2
WUI Inc.
AT&T rate hike case declined by Sup Ct 6-5, 431D2
WUI Inc. v. FCC et al
AT&T rate hike case declined by Sup Ct 6-5, 431D2
WU Kuei-hsien
Out as China dep premier 2-26—3-5, 153F1
WULP, John
Crucifer of Blood opens 9-28, 1031C1
WURF, Jerry
Scores Carter re fed pay hike limit 4-11, 260G2 ★
On Proposition 13 6-26, 526D1
WUSSLER, Robert J.
Quits CBS Sports 3-15, FCC rpt scores 3-16, 252A2
WU Teh
'76 riot role scored 4-7, 287D3
Ousted as Peking mayor 10-10, 773F3
WWJ-TV (Detroit, Mich. TV station)
FCC OKs WTOP-TV swap 5-18, 599G3
WXIA-TV (Atlanta, Ga. TV station)
Lance becomes commentator 2-6, 172F2
WYATT, Joe
Faces US House primary runoff 5-6, 363A1
Wins runoff 6-3, 426E2
Elected 11-7, 852A3, 855E3
WYDLER, Rep. John W. (R, N.Y.)
Reelected 11-7, 851D3
WYETH, Andrew
Elected to Sovt Acad, '77 French honor cited 4-24, 335D3
WYLER, Hillary
Forever Yours opens 6-21, 887G1
WYLIE, Rep. Chalmers Pangburn (R, O.)
Reelected 11-7, 851F3
WYNEGAR, Butch
Griffith comments cause furor 9-28—10-2, 779D2
WYNN, William H.
On '77 top-paid labor ldrs list 5-15, 365F1

1979

WRYE, Donald
Ice Castles released 2-22, 174F2
WTCG (Atlanta TV station)
To expand programming 4-23, 334D3
WU Han (deceased)
Followers rehabilitated 8-3, 651B3
WUI Inc.
Xerox plans acquisitn 1-18, 89C1
WULP, John
Bosoms & Neglect opens 5-3, 711F1
WURF, Jerry
Backs oil industry protest 10-17, 831D2
WU Tai-an
Taiwan oppositn ldr arrested 1-21, 116E1
WYATT Jr., Master Sgt. Horace E.
S Africa ousts as spy 4-12, 286F3
WYETH, Andrew
SC museum gets 26 paintings 3-22, 375B2
WYLER, Leo
Jordan drug allegations rptd 9-13–9-21, 767G2
WYNN, William H.
Carter addresses new union 6-7, 419F3*
Backs Carter reelectn 7-30, 593C3

1980

WRONG Move, The (film)
Released 1-25, 216G3
WSZOLA, Jacek
Wins Olympic medal 8-1, 624F1
WU Faxien
Trial set 9-27, delayed 11-1, 859C1
Regrets Lin Liguo AF apptmt 11-23; admits all chrgs 12-18, 975G1, C2
WU Han
Cited in Gang of 4 indictmt 11-16, 877F1
WUJAK, Brigitte
Wins Olympic medal 7-31, 624B2
WURF, Jerry
AFSCME backs Kennedy 4-2, 247G1
Vs Carter platform statemt 8-13, 611A2
WURMBRANDT, Richard
Cuba to free jailed US prisoners 10-13, 789B1
WU Teh
Ousted from Politburo 2-29, 171F3
Resigns as dep premr 4-16, 351F1
WYATT, Rep. Jim (D, Texas)
Patman wins seat 11-4, 850C2
WYDEN, Ron
Wins US House primary in Ore 5-20, 404B3
Reelected 11-4, 844B1, 852F2
WYDLER, Rep. John W. (R, N.Y.)
Votes for Abscam evidence res 2-27, 143A3
WYETH Laboratories
US sets tranquilizer warnings 7-11, 584G1
WYLIE, Rep. Chalmers Pangburn (R, Ohio)
Reelected 11-4, 843E4
WYMAN, Thomas H.
Named CBS pres, chief exec 5-22; assumes posts 6-2, 501G1
Jankowski CBS resignatn hoax 5-23, 501C2
WYNDHAM-White, Eric
Dies 1-27, 104G3
WYNN, William H.
In 'Big Business Day' protest 4-17, 308C2

1976

WYOMING
US Sup Ct to hear coal mining environment impact case 1-12, 23G3
Teapot Dome reserve opened 3-31, 246A3
Reagan in Cheyenne 4-9, 281C3
Starkweather companion paroled 6-8, 442D3
Strip-mining stay reversed 6-28, 569A1
Ford delegate deal rptd 7-2, vetoes coal lease bill 7-3, 518F1
Dem conv women delegates, table 508E2
Dem conv pres vote, table 7-14, 507E2
GOP pre-conv delegate count 8-14, 583E3
Reagan, Ford seek conv delegates 8-15—8-17, 601G2, A3, B3
GOP conv pres, vp vote tables 8-18—8-19, 8-19, 599E1, E3
Colo oil shale leases suspended 8-23, 649E1
Sen primary results 9-14, 705C2
Fscl '75 per capita income, tax burden rptd 9-15, 10-12, 959E2
Election results 11-2; pres 818D1, 819A1; cong 819E3, 824C3, 828D3, 831A4
70% get swine flu shots 12-2, 911B1
WYOMING, University of (Laramie)
Kissinger addresses 2-4, 88G3
Loses Fiesta Bowl 12-25, 1014G2
WYSZYNSKI, Stefan Cardinal
Scores Polish Const amendmts 1-25, 268D1
Resigns 8-3, asked to remain 11-1, 932B3
Backs workers 9-26, 811C1
Chrgs police brutality 12-6, urges worker rebelln 12-12, 966A2

1977

WYOMING
Legislature schedule rptd 6G2
'76 per-capita income table 5-10, 387G2
Casper econ data rptd; table 5-16, 384E2, 385B1
Drought persists 6-16, 492A3
Libel jurisdictn review refused 6-20, 517C1
State abortn funding rptd 6-20, 787B1
Forest fires rptd 7-19, 660A3
'76 per capita income, tax burden table 9-13, 10-18, 821G1, E2
Nellie Tayloe Ross dies 12-10, 1024A3
WYSZYNSKI, Stefan Cardinal
Warns vs rights abuse 6-9, 513C1
Sees Gierek 10-29, 885F3
Gierek sees Pope Paul 12-1, 987D1
Mrs Carter, Brzezinski visit 12-30, 1001B2

1978

WYOMING
Legislature schedule rptd 14G3
'67, '77 sales-tax rates rptd 1-5, 15G3
State govt tax revenue table 1-9, 84E2
Wilderness area clears Cong 2-9, 109D2; signed 2-24, 218A2
Coal Policy Project issues rpt 2-9, 184F2
'Wind farms' studied 5-3, 321E3
'77 prison populatn rptd up 6-3, 440D1
Grasshopper invasn rptd 7-31, 654B3
Carters vacation 8-24, 664F1
Primary results 9-12, 736B2
Election results 11-7: cong 846G1, A3, 856F1, G1; state 847C1, 853F3, 856G1, 897C3
WYSZYNSKI, Stefan Cardinal
Bishops score censorship 9-17, 749G1

1979

WYOMING
Legislature schedule rptd 5G3
Green River Basin oil find cited 1-5, 17G1
ERA OK upheld by state Sen 1-17, 128C2
Rock Springs police chief faces murder trial 2-7, 156A1
DC voting rep amendmt rejectn rptd 3-19, 204B3
US land grant easemt right curbed by Sup Ct 3-27, 263C2
'78 per capita gas use rptd 5-27, 395A3
Forest fires rptd 8-12, 620D1
'78 per capita income rptd 9-16, 746F1, G2
PCBs contaminate food 9-17, 704A3, D3
WYOMING, University of (Laramie)
Ultraviolet study rptd 3-20, 290G1
WYSER-Pratte, Guy
Drops McGraw-Hill proxy battle 2-23, 151D3
WYSZINSKI, Stefan Cardinal
Greets Pope 6-2, 413E1

1980

WYOMING
State sales preference upheld by Sup Ct 6-19, 554G2
Energy
Oil leasing lottery suspended, scandal hinted 2-29; resumptn ordrd 4-7, 330D2
2d 1/4 gas use target set 3-20, 250F3
US intrastate gas sale power affirmed 6-6, 552B3
Politics & Government—*See also other appropriate subheads in this section*
Legislature schedule rptd 18G1
ACU '79 voting survey rptd 1-18, 53C3
State of State message 2-12, 484E2
Election results 11-4: pres 838D1, 839A1, G3, cong 840F3, 844D4, 852E1; state 845F3
'80 census rptd 12-31, 983G1
WYOMING, University of (Laramie)
State of State message 2-12, 484G2
WYRICK, Bob
Wins Polk award 2-25, 692E3
WYSOCZANSKA, Barbara
Wins Olympic medal 7-24, 622C3
WYSZYNSKI, Stefan Cardinal
Urges calm in Polish strike 8-26, 641D2, 658D2
Strike pleas rptd distorted by govt 8-28, 657F1
Ozdowski named Polish dep premr 11-21, 909C2
Polish bishops warn dissidents 12-12, 976A1

X

1976

XEROX Co.
Vows no boycott compliance 3-18, 747C2
'75 tax paymt rptd 10-2, 847B2
XIBBERAS, Maurice
Gibraltar electn results 9-29, 751D3
XIMENEZ, Miguel
Lockheed paymt rptd 11-6, 909G1
XIRINACHS, Luis Maria
Leads amnesty march 1-1, arrested 1-7, 12B1

1977

XAVIER, Prince of Borbon-Parma (Spain)
Dies 5-7, 452F3
XEROX Corp.
Egypt contract rptd sought 5-16, 390E2
Wins Canada suit vs IBM 7-5, 525B3
IBM appeals Canada ruling 8-17, seeks Xerox license 8-31, 705A3
IBM patent use rptd OKd 9-23, 764D1

1978

XENON
Metallic conversn rptd 11-25, 1023C3
XEROX Corp.
Canada unit vp named comptroller-gen 2-20, 145E3
IBM sues re patent infringemts 2-23, 510B2
McCardell heads '77 top-paid execs list 5-15, 364E3, 365B1
SCM set back in trust suit 6-7, 510E1-C2
SCM verdicts 7-10, 7-11, damages set 8-9, 8-16, 664G2
Van Dyk trial begins 7-12, 664E3
IBM patent dispute setld 8-1, 664E2
SCM trust award set aside 12-29, 1005D2

1979

XEROX Corp.
WUI acquisitn planned 1-18, 89C1

1980

XANADU (film)
Top-grossing film 9-3, 716G3
Recording on best-seller list 9-10, 716F3; 10-8, 796B3
XEROX Corp.
Office machine cancer risks rptd 4-11, 357B1-A3
McColough urges US pensn chngs 5-23, 404G1
Van Dyk trust suit win rptd upheld 10-6, 917D3
XIAO Jingguang
Rptd replaced as China navy cmdr 2-19, 132E2

1976

XM-1 Tank—*See 'Tanks' under ARMAMENTS*
X-RAYS
Artery diagnostic tech rptd 1-21, 159D2
Polanyi dies 2-22, 192F3
Breast X-ray curb urged 8-23, 679E3-680A1
Medicaid fraud chrgd 8-30, 715G1, A2

1977

XM-1 Tank—*See ARMAMENTS—Tanks*
X-RAYS
CAT scanner curbs proposed 5-2; hosp designatns 9-26, 869A3, B3
Mammography curbed 5-10, 431C2
Clilan Powell dies 9-22, 788C2

1978

XM-1 Tank—*See ARMAMENTS—Tanks*
X-Rays
Pregnancy risk seen 7-11, 598G2
Gas cloud in galaxy cluster rptd 9-16, 1023G2
US OKs USSR equipmt sale 10-13, 905B2

1979

XM-Tank—*See ARMAMENTS–Tanks*
X-RAYS
Low-level radiatn risks seen 2-27, 208B1
Hosp cost-control hearings open 3-9, 194G3
Facts on radiatn exposure 244C2
Psoriasis therapy complicatn rptd 4-12, 315C2
Blue Cross asks presurgery tests cut 5-1, 404C3
Low-level radiatn risk assessed 5-2, 609G2
Kennedy offers natl health plan 5-14, 362D1
Carter unveils natl health plan 6-12, 438B2
MD-managed insurnc plan cuts costs 6-14, 570D3
AMA chrgd in NY chiropractors suit 7-5, 570G2
Tests disprove mutatn link 7-28, 692F2
H-bomb letter cites 9-16, 9-18, 715C2-716G2
Nobel for CAT scan announced 10-12, 858E1

1980

XIE Fuzhi (Hsie Fu-chih) (d. 1972)
Ousted from CP 10-31, 859E1
Gang of 4 trial defendant 11-20—12-29, 975E2
XM-Tank—*See ARMAMENTS--Tanks*
X-RAYS
US solar study satellite launched 2-14, 160D2
Fewer cancer tests urged 3-20, 316C3
Contact binary system emissions rptd 3-20, 415E2
XU Shiyou
Promotion rptd 2-14, 132D2
XU Xiangqian
Army ldrship shuffle rptd 2-14, 132D2

Y

1976

YAACOBI, Gad
Warns hijackers 6-27, 463G1
Asks nonstop flights to Israel 7-5, 486B2
Backed Dayan mission to Uganda 7-10, 515D1
On KLM hijacker landing demand 9-5, 662C3
YABLONSKI, Joseph A. (d. 1970)
Slayers sentenced 9-3, 816A3
YADIN, Yigael
Forms new party 11-22, 949G2
YADLIN, Asher
Bank gov appointmt delayed 10-17; arrested 10-18, 810D3
Nomination withdrawn 10-24, Gafny sworn 10-31, 854E2
YAFFO (Israeli warship)
In Intl Naval Review 7-4, 488C3
YACHTING—*See BOATING*
YAGER, Paul
Hospital strike ends 7-17, 553A3
YAKER, Layachi
Vs Israel, S Africa at UNCTAD conf 5-5 320D2
YAKOVSON, Anatoly
USSR chrgs Israel internmt 2-4, 122C2
YAKUBOVSKY, Marshal Ivan
Ustinov named defense min 4-29, 334A3
Dies 11-30, 932G3
YALE University (New Haven, Conn.)
New arthritis strain rptd 7-18, 911A3
Luther Weigle dies 9-2, 1015B3
Reagan visits 10-2, 743B3
YALOW, Dr. Rosalyn S.
Wins Lasker award 11-17, 910D3
YAMAGUCHI, Toshio
In new party 6-25, 497B3
YAMANI, Sheik Ahmed Zaki
OPEC holds price freeze 5-28, 389D1
Asks OPEC price freeze 12-14; rebuffed, leaves mtg 12-16, 934G2
Iran scores OPEC price stand 12-20, 975C3
YANG K'ai-hui
Cited in Mao biog 659F1
YANG Seung Jo
Sentenced 12-15, 1013A3
YAO Wen-yuan
Radical strength rptd 4-27, 333E1
May Day CP unity rptd 5-2, 332E3
Listed in China ldrshp 9-10, 712A1
Rptd arrested 10-12, 10-13, 757A2
Radical plot, purge confirmed 10-22, 790C2, C3
Accusatns rptd 10-24, 10-25, 10-26, 809A2
Posters detail plot role 10-30, 11-8, 871C2
Loses Shanghai post 10-30, 871A3
Tied to indl disruptn 11-2, 871G2
Blamed for Fukien unrest 11-23, 904F3
Drive vs backers asked, restraint urged 11-28, 904A3
Fighting rages in central provs 12-6—12-31, 1000C1-D2
Accused 12-18, faces possible executn 12-23, 999E3
Hua sees '77 natl purge 12-24, 999A3

1977

YABLONSKI, Joseph A. (d. 1970)
Boyle convictn upset, retrial ordrd 1-28, 95D3
YADIN, Yigal
Party erodes Labor strength 5-17, 377A2
DMC joins govt 10-20, 801B3
Israeli deputy premier 10-24, 827A2
Dead Sea scroll analyzed 11-12, 1022F3
Greets Sadat, in talks 11-19, 889C1
YADLIN, Aharon
Tied to kickback chrg 2-14, 135C2
YADLIN, Asher
Trial starts 1-17; pleads guilty 2-14; sentncd 2-22, 135G1
YAFEH, Col. Yossi
Dies 2-28, 164G3
YAKUBOVSKY, Marshal Ivan I. (1912-1976)
Kulikov replaces 1-9, 47B3
YALE University (New Haven, Conn.)
Nordhaus named to US post 1-18, 52E3
Milstone dies 1-27, 164D3
Ford visits 2-6—2-8, 236B3
Rostow vs quotas 3-31, 235E2
Brewster confrmd amb to UK 4-29, 418C1
Coffin elected Riverside Church min 8-14, 808B2
Hosts Cuba-US profs mtg 11-9, 896C3
Gray named Chicago U pres 12-10, 1021A2
Giamatti named pres 12-20, 1021C2
YALOW, Rosalyn S.
Wins Nobel Prize 10-13, 951C3
YAMADA, Hisashi
Braves win Japan baseball title 10-27, 927D2
YAMANI, Sheik Ahmed Zaki
On oil productn hike 1-2, 12F1
Rpt fears CPs in France, Italy govts 1-24, 50A2
Rejcts OPEC price compromise 2-6, 107B3
On Iran, Kuwait oil exports drop 2-9, Saudi 1st ¼ output 2-16, 108A1
OPEC price plan rptd 2-14, 107D3
Denies extra oil sales plan rpt 2-15, 108D1
On May oil productn 5-10, 362A2
Sees oil scarcity in '80s 7-13, 552E2
OPEC defers price hike 12-21, 973E1
YANG Chia-lin
Econ expansn planned 9-22, 783D2
Korean lobbying role chrgd 10-19, 816B2
YANG Sen, Gen.
Dies 5-15, 452G3
YANG Yung, Gen.
Replaced as Sinkiang army chief 8-3, 616E3
YANKELOVICH, Tatyana
Emigratn rptd 11-12, 955D3
YANKELOVICH, Yefrem
Emigratn rptd 11-12, 955D3
YANKELOVICH, Skelly and White Inc.
Carter poll rptd 4-4, 251E1
YANKO, Richard
Nurses convicted in '75 VA Hosp deaths 7-13, 568B3
YANOWITCH, Harold M.
Convicted 1-29, 103F1 ★, G1
Sentenced 3-11, 203A3
YAO Wen-yuan
Rpt province unrest quelled 1-4, 1C1 ★
Blamed for Fukien unrest 1-4, 1B2
Blamed for econ lag 2-1, 98G1
Heightened drive vs urged 2-5, 2-7, 98C1
Chekiang offcls disgraced 3-2, 179D3
Kweichow progress lauded 3-5, 179F3
Radical accused of bugging 3-9, 180E1
Liaoning official arrested 3-14, 220D1
Blamed for Hangchow unrest 4-11, 282B2
New leap forward rptd 5-4, 449G2
Tied to Nanchang riots 6-5, 449B3
Scored at Kiangsi rally 6-6, 505D3
Cited for Hupei unrest 6-8, 505E3
Scored in Liaoning Prov 6-24, 562D1
Tied to Yunnan agents 6-29, 562C1
Rpt ousted from party 7-22, 571G2
Anti-Mao stand cited 9-8, 694B3
Mao policy distortn chrgd 9-10, 706F1
Arrest date confirmed 10-6, 780F3
'71-75 China trade rptd up 11-6, 882C3
Yu suicide rptd 11-8, 882E3

1978

YABLONSKI, Joseph A. (d. 1970)
Boyle convicted again 2-18, 129A1
YADIN, Yigal
Backs Weizman on setlmts, rpts Cabt rift 3-7, 157G1-A2
Vs Eitan policy statemt 5-14, 359C1
Vs Cabt on W Bank, Gaza 6-19, 461F1
Blocked com actn on W Bank setlmts 8-14, 639A1
DMC splits, stays in coalitn 8-23, 668G1
Scores Egypt pact text 11-25, 931A1
YAKOVLEV, Alexander
Gets Canada satellite protest 1-25, 57G2
YALDEN, Maxwell
Scores fed bilingual svcs, Bill 101 3-21, 225F3
YALE University (New Haven, Conn.)
Spleen regeneratn rptd 6-22, 598F1
Bork on Bakke ruling 6-28, 483A1
Pellegrino joins Cath U 9-1, 844E1
Sickle cell trait study rptd 9-28, 948F1
Multi-parent mouse created 10-14, 1023A3
YAMADA, Akiyoshi
Stockbroker liability case refused by Sup Ct 12-4, 959C1
YAMANI, Sheik Ahmed Zaki
Vs '78 oil price rise 1-12, 158G2
Sees no '78 oil price hike 5-7, 341D3
Sees '79 OPEC price rise 6-19, 465A2
Backs CIA re USSR oil imports 6-29, 635B1
On OPEC price rise 12-17, 977B3, D3
YAMASHITA, Ganri
Japan defense min 12-7, 945F2
YANG Hsi-kun
To head Taiwan office in US 12-31, 995B1
YANG Shang-kun
Rehabilitated 12-22, 1015G1
YANGTZE River
US dam aid offer to China rptd 11-6, 871C2
YANOWITCH, Harold M.
Fraud convictn review denied by Sup Ct 10-2, 751E2
YAO Wen-yuan
Saifudin replaced as CP ldr 1-29, 89C2
Teng cleared in '76 Peking riot 2-15, 111C2
Spared executn 2-21, 130A3
Tied to Tsao persecutn 6-28, 515B2
Cited for freedom lack 7-3, 532C2
China pragmatic approach seen 532A2
Wu ousted as Peking mayor 10-10, 773G3
'65 Cultural Revolutn essay scored 11-15, 901B3
Mao tied to 'Gang of 4' 11-19, 901E2

1979

YABLANS, Frank
North Dallas Forty released 8-1, 820D2
YABLANS, Irwin
Roller Boogie released 12-19, 1008C1
YABLONSKI, Joseph A. (d. 1970)
Boyle sentenced again 10-11, 840B1, C1*
YACHTING—*See BOATS & Boating*
YADIN, Yigal
Dead Sea Scroll study told 3-2, 217A3
Vs 2 new W Bank setlmts 4-22, 296A2
Votes vs Nablus setlmt plan 6-3, 415F1
Vs Carter Palestinian-US civil rights analogy 8-2, 575E1
Denies Young chrg on intransigence 8-19, 624F3
Rejects forgn min post 10-29, 856C2
YAEGER, Marshall
Umbatha opens 4-9, 712B3
YAGANEH, Nasser
Iran justice min quits 1-17, 25E2
YAGLA, Charles
USSR wins World Cup wrestling 4-1, 507G3
YAHIAOUI, Mohammed Salah
Benjedid elected pres 2-7, 94C2
YAHYAHI, Maj. Bijan
Executed 4-13, 276D3
YAKUNIN, Gleb
Arrested 11-1, 856G2
YALDEN, Maxwell
Chrgs bilingual lag, scores budget cut 2-20, 168B3
Scores bilingual bonus extensn 3-22, 234C1
YALE University (New Haven, Conn.)
'78 estrogen study cited, refuted 1-4, 23A2
Provost quits in fund dispute 5-2, May named 5-4, 392D2
Stock sold re S Africa 5-3, 332G3
4th in women's lacrosse title 5-13, 507C3
Wellington to head ITT probe 8-8, 648F1
Brown addresses 11-9, 962E2
YAMANI, Sheik Ahmed Zaki
Oil prices hiked, urges West conserve 6-28, 473E1, G1
Oil price arguments with Moinfar rptd 12-21, 977F1
YAMANI, Mohammed Abdu
New budget plans rptd 5-29, 427F2
Confirms Medina mosque attack 11-22, 898F3
Denies Saudi unrest 12-2, 916E1
YAMAOKA, Shoichi
Indicted 4-5, 389G2
YAMASHITA, Ganri
USSR Shikotan buildup protested 10-2, 742D1
Meets US defense secy 10-20, 803C3*
YAMASHITA, Toshihiko
Vs US color-TV dumping paymt 4-26, 298B3
YANG Kung-su
On China Viet war role 7-20, 575F2
YANG Shang-kun
Promotion rptd 9-28, 750E3
YANG Sung Woo
PEN seeks release 7-21, 554A1
YANG Teh-chih
Identified as Viet invasn cmdr 2-21, 122D1
YANKEE Girl, The (boat)
Spiess crosses N Atlantic 7-24, 656C3
YANKEE Nuclear Power Station—*See MASSACHUSETTS–Atomic Energy*
YANKS (film)
Released 9-19, 820G3
YAO Yi-lin
China dep premier 7-1, 502E2

1980

YACHTING—*See BOATS & Boating*
YACOUB, Patriarch Moran More Ignatius
Dies 6-25, 528G3
YADIN, Yigal
Vs Hebron setlmt vote 3-24, 218C3
Named acting prime min 6-30, 498B3
Vs deportatn of 2 W Bank mayors 12-5, 931D2
YAGI, Hirokazu
Wins Olympic medal 2-17, 155D3
YAHYA Khan, Agha Mohammad
Dies 8-8, 676G3
YAKUNIN, Gleb
Sovts sentence 8-28, 680A2
YAKUSHA, Vasily
Wins Olympic medal 7-27, 623G1
YALDEN, Maxwell
Releases bilingualism rpt 4-22, 351A1
YALE University (New Haven, Conn.)
Stuttering, genetics link rptd 1-5, 63C3
'79 endowmt earnings rptd 3-24, 319B2
Burrows dies 4-29, 360D1
Labaree dies 5-5, 448B2
Rodell dies 6-4, 528D3
Vance resumes law practice 6-11, 471A2
Forgn gene replicatn in mice rptd 9-13, 716D2
YAMAMOTO, Susumu
Picasso painting bought for record sum 5-12, 472C1
YAMANI, Sheik Ahmed Zaki
In US oil talks, bars reserve purchases 3-1—3-4, 165C3
Evaluates intl oil mkt, Saudi dvpt plans 3-5, 165F3
On OPEC pricing plan 5-8, 364C3
Vs oil price hike; links productn cut, US stockpiling 6-10, 435F2, A3
Aramco takeover completed, bd seat retained 9-4, 662G1
Quits OPEC mtg; bars price hikes, productn cuts 9-17, 694C3
In US secret talks 9-18, oil stockpiling rptd resumed 10-27, 826E1
Rpts Persian Gulf natns to hike oil exports 10-5, 758D3
Sets premium chrg on extra oil 10-28, 822C2
YAMAOKA, Shoichi
Gets suspended sentnc 7-24, 605D2
YAMBULATOV, Rustan
Wins Olympic medal 7-22, 623C2
YANG Dechi
Named China army chief 2-25, 172A1
YANG Jingren
Named deputy premier 9-10, 677F1
YANG Shouzheng
Arrives in Moscow 4-20, 354F3
YANKELOVICH, Daniel
Rpts voter discontent 6-18, 493A3
YANKOV, Ivan
Wins Olympic medal 7-31, 624D3
YAO Wenyuan (Yao Wen-yuan)
Gang of 4 trial set 9-27, delayed 11-1, 859B1
Indictmt aired 11-15—11-18; trial starts 11-20, 877A1, D2
Admits plot vs Deng appointmt 11-24, 975A2
YAO Yilin
On '79 farm, indus productn 9-1, 678D2

1976

YAR Adua, Brig. Gen. Shehu
Nigeria chief of staff 2-14, 142C1
On defense cuts 3-11, Gowon extraditn 3-12, 222E2
YARYGIN, Ivan
Wins Olpmpic medal 7-31, 576E3
YASTRZEMSKI, Carl
AL batting ldr 10-4, 796C1
YATES, Rep. Sidney R. (D, Ill.)
Reelected 11-2, 829G2
YATHOON Yasawas, Gen.
Exiled to Japan 794G3
YATRON, Rep. Gus (D, Pa.)
Reelected 11-2, 830D3
YEAR of Beauty and Health, A (book)
On best-seller list 12-5, 972B2
YEH Chien-ying
Chou En-lai dies 1-8, 8F3
Teng gives Chou eulogy 1-15, 48C1
May Day CP unity rptd 5-2, 332E3
Cited as possible Mao successor 9-9—9-10, 658F1
Listed in China ldrshp 9-10, 712A1
At Hua rally 10-24; ldrshp positn noted 10-25, 809F1
YELLOWSTONE (U.S. freighter)
Docks at Haifa 1-29, Egypt blacklists 2-21, 145A2
YELLOWSTONE National Park
Ford visits 8-29, 644E2

1977

YAQUB-Khan, Sahabzada
Mediates Hanafi surrender 3-11, 192A3
YARBOROUGH, Cale
Wins Daytona 500 2-20, 531B2
Tops in NASCAR standings, earnings 11-20; named driver of yr 12-8, 1020C3
YARMUK River (Jordan)
Israel seeks diversn bar 10-10, 769B2
YASCHENKO, Vladimir
Sets high jump mark 7-2, 602G2
YASIN, Hamid
Quits Pak ruling party 4-8, 305F2
YATRON, Rep. Gus (D, Pa.)
Sees Argentine rights progress 8-20, 670A2
YAWKEY, Jean
Fires Red Sox gen mgr 10-24, ct OKs team sale 12-6, AL owners veto 12-8, 989E2
YAWKEY, Tom (d. 1976)
AL owners veto Red Sox sale 12-8, 989F2
YAZOO City, Miss.—*See MISSISSIPPI*
YBARRA y Berge, Javier de
ETA kidnaps 5-20, 454B1
Killed 6-18, 507C3
Murder suspect detentn protested 8-18—8-24, vanishes after release 10-7, 826E2
YEAGER, Steve
In World Series 10-11—10-18, 806C2
YEGANEH, Mohammad
On Cambodia OPEC loan rejctn 3-3, 183F1
YEH Chien-ying
Army urged to stress skills 2-26, 180B1
Says forces buildup needed 5-9, 449D2
Teng 3d in line 7-22, 571F2
In ruling triumvirate 8-21, 645E2
Submits new charter 8-23, 646C1
Natl People's Cong delayed 10-23, 823F1
YELLEN, Dr. Ben
Western land holdings breakup upheld 8-18, 703A2, C2

1978

YARBOROUGH, Cale
2d in Daytona 500 2-19, 538B3
YARBROUGH, Don
Sentenced for perjury 1-27, 232A3
YARDLEY Enterprises Inc.—*See B.A.T. Industries—British-American Cosmetics*
YASHCHENKO, Vladimir
Sets indoor high jump mark 3-12, 692E3
YASIN, Ali
Slain; Iraq linked 6-15, 6-16, 489A2
2 die in Jerusalem blast, PLO takes credit 6-29, 503G2
Iraq, Nidal tied to death 7-13, 7-17, 546D3, F3
YASIN, Erol
NASL goalkeeping ldr 8-6, 655D2
YASTRZEMSKI, Carl
Misses All-Star Game 7-11, 559G2
YATES, Joy
Wyatt to oppose for Cong 6-3, 426E2
YATES, Rep. Sidney R. (D, Ill.)
House rejcts A-carrier fund bar 8-7, 604C2
Reelected 11-7, 850D3
YATES, Waverly
Scores CORE conv, Innis 9-17, 810D1
YATRON, Rep. Gus (D, Pa.)
Reelected 11-7, 852C1
YAZID, Mohammed
Mediates PLO-Iraq feud 8-23, 674B1
YEAGER, Steve
In World Series 10-10—10-17, 799B3
YEGANEH, Mohammed
On OPEC $ price base 5-7, 341G3
Sees OPEC '79 price hike 6-19, 465A2
YEH Chien-ying, Marshal
Plea to Taiwan Chinese 12-27-77, 17B3
Named China head of state 2-26—3-5, 153C1
Announces new charter 3-5, 153C2, G2
YELISEYEV, Alexei
Space indl possibilities rptd 11-3, 861D1
YELLOWSTONE National Park (Wyo., Mont., Ida.)
Carters visit 8-26, 664F1

1979

YARADUA, Shehu
Chad mediatn role rptd 2-28, 154A1
YARBOROUGH, Cale
Crashes in Daytona 500, NASCAR fines 2-20, 490F3
Crashes in Carolina 500 3-4, 491A1
YASTRZEMSKI, Carl
NL wins All-Star Game 7-17, 569A1
Hits 400th homer 7-24, 619E2
Gets 3000th hit 9-12, 1002D3
YATES, Peter
Breaking Away released 7-17, 819F3
YAZDI, Ibrahim
Named Iran dep premr 2-12, 105F2
CIA wiretap rptd barred 3-11, 180C1
Says Hoveida probe to continue 3-16, 199A2
Son-in-law's govt role scored 4-17, 277F1*
Named forgn min 4-24, 297B2
Softens criticism of US, denies Khakhali heads ct 5-21, 388G3
On Iran US amb bar 6-5, 425G2
Warns US on shah's entry 10-21, 879B2; 11-9, 862F2
Sees Brzezinski in Algiers 11-1, 842D2
Seeks Baluchi peace 12-20—12-22, 975G2-A3
YBARRA, Ventura E.
Drug convictn voided by Sup Ct 11-28, 944F2
YBARRA v. Illinois
Case decided by Sup Ct 11-28, 944E2
YEAGLEY, Dr. Miles
On military child abuse 1-21, 93E3
YEH Chien-ying, Marshal
Scores Cultural Revolutn 9-29, 750F2
YELLOW No. 5 (tartrazine)—*See CHEMICALS*

1980

YARBOROUGH, Cale
NASCAR top $ winner 11-15, 1002E1
YATES, Brock
Smokey & the Bandit II released 8-15, 675E3
YATES, Elton G.
Saudi completes Aramco takeover, retains bd seat 9-4, 662A2
YATES, Rep. Sidney R. (D, Ill.)
Reelected 11-4, 842E3
YATESVILLE—*See PENNSYLVANIA*
YATESVILLE Dam (Ky.)
Constructn funds clear Cong 6-25, 9-10, signed 10-1, 803D2
YATRON, Rep. Gus (D, Pa.)
Reelected 11-4, 844C1
YAWKEY, Thomas A. (1903-76)
Elected to Baseball HOF 8-3, 796D2
YE Fei
China navy apptmt rptd 2-19, 132E2
YE Jianying (Yeh Chian-ying)
On retiremt of top ldrs 9-10, 677G1

1976

YEMEN, People's Democratic Republic of (formerly Southern Yemen)—*See also ARAB League, NONALIGNED Nations Movement*
Oman border fighting, Sovt arms aid rptd 1-9, 1-14, 52G1
Listed as 'not free' nation 1-19, 20E3
Total IMF oil loan rptd 4-1, 339F3, 340E2
Cubans rptdly train airmen 4-5, 242A2
Hijackers seek Haithan plotter release 8-23, 629A3
Amb sought in Syria emb raid 10-11, 759F1
Downs Iran jet 11-24; chrgs spying, bans overflights 11-25—11-29, 913F2-914C1
Shuns UN Assemb Geneva conf vote 12-9, 914D1

1977

YEMEN, People's Democratic Republic of (South Yemen)—*See also ARAB League, NONALIGNED Nations Movement*
UN Assemb member 4D1
IMF OKs trust fund loan 2-4, 87F2
Castro visits, urges Djibouti federatn 3-10—3-12, return rumored 3-16—3-17, 249F1, B2, F2
At Red Sea summit 3-22—3-23, 208D2
Arab monetary fund created 4-18, 318B1
US ties to intl terror groups 5-8, 380D1, A2
Somalia rejects federatn 5-18, 428E2
Canada metric conversn rptd 9-6, 705F2
N Yemen pres slain, claim plot to bar merger 10-10, 784A1
W Ger hijacked jet lands 10-16, Sovts linked to refuge denial 10-20, 789G1, 790A2
Egypt recalls amb 12-4, cuts ties 12-5, 929A1, C2
Arab-Israeli Conflict—*See MIDDLE EAST*

1978

YEMEN, People's Democratic Republic of (South Yemen)—*See also ARAB League, NONALIGNED Nations Movement*
USSR airlift to Ethiopia rptd halted 1-5, 3D3
Eritrea mil role rptd 2-2, 100B2
Cyprus jet hijackers denied landing 2-18, 117A2
Arab fund poor-natn aid rise rptd 4-9, 257F2
Saudis stress defense needs 5-13, 358E2
Ethiopia amb exit rptd, denied 5-25, 584D3, E3
Pres Rubaya tied to N Yemen pres murder 6-24, link denied 6-25, 498E3, 499B2
Rubaya deposed, executed 6-26; pro-Sovt group takes power 6-27, 498E3
Ruling body purged CP grouping rptd 6-28, 522D2
Arab League links to N Yemen pres death, suspends ties 7-1—7-2, 522F1
N Yemen invasn chrgd 7-2, 7-3, N Yemen denies 7-4, 522B2
Sovt, Cuban dominatn of armed forces denied 7-2, 522C2
Arab fund loan rptd 8-17, 925F3
UN Assemb member 713G3
Hardliners conf ends; Egypt ties severed, USSR contacts sought 9-24, 729F2
Army troops resist disbandmt 10-20, fighting rptd 10-21, 885E3
Ismail elected pres 12-27, 1022E1
Arab-Israel Conflict—*See MIDDLE EAST*
Sports
Egypt athletes to boycott 7-24, 573C1

1979

YEMEN, People's Democratic Republic of (South Yemen)—*See also ARAB League*
N Yemen rebels rptd as main foe 158D1
US, Saudi plan mil aid to N Yemen 2-8, 89D2
N Yemen border clashes erupt 2-24; US speeds arms to North, Saudi alerts troops 2-26, 2-28; mediatn agreed 2-28, 144A2
N Yemen border clashes 3-1, 3-6, 158D1
Syria, Iraq, Jordan truce fails 3-2, Arab League plan fails 3-6, 157D2, 158B1
US sends fleet to Arabian Sea 3-5, offers Saudis jet aid 3-7, 157D2-158A1
Sovt, Cuban reinforcemts rptd 3-8; Sovts deny adviser role 3-14, 179E1
N Yemen rptd driven from border area 3-8, 179G1
US arms aid to N Yemen scored 3-10, 179E1
MiG fighters bomb N Yemen 3-12, 179A2
Cease-fire in effect 3-17, 199D2
N Yemen unificatn plan agreed 3-29, 250B1
USSR reconnaissance flights cited 4-16, 314A1
Kissinger warns of Sovt bases 7-31, 590D3
Ethiopia lauds mil aid 8-23, 791C1
Libya fete attended by Arab ldrs 9-1, 688C3
UN membership listed 695B3
Ismail in USSR 10-24, signs friendship pact 10-25, 802B1
Saudis capture mosque raiders 12-4, 916B1
Saudis implicate in mosque raid 12-16, 997A1

1980

YEMEN, People's Democratic Republic of (South Yemen)—*See also ARAB League, NONALIGNED Nations*
Ismail resigns, Hasani replaces 4-23, 315D3, E3*
Foreign Relations (misc.)
USSR Afghan invasn backed 1-8, 10C3
Saudis execute 6 mosque raiders 1-9, 22B1
Islamic conf boycotted 1-27—1-29, 67C2
Egypt chrgs Sovt arms shipmts via Saudi 1-28, 69A2
Anti-Sadat front backed 4-2, 273C3
Arab hardliners meet 4-14—4-15, 284F2
N Yemen unificatn policy rift rptd 4-23, 315E3
Iran hostage rescue try scored 4-27, 324D2
N Yemen guerrilla war escalatn rptd 6-1, 468D2
USSR, Cuba, E Ger step up activity 6-9, 468G2
Syria seeks backing for Libya merger 9-10, 697G1
Afghan mil role rptd 9-15, 705C1
Sovt arms stockpiles rptdly sent to Iraq 10-6, 757C1
Sovt '79 arms sales rptd 12-10, 933A3
U.S. Relations
Connally cites Sovt threat 3-7, 184E3
Iran hostage rescue try scored 4-27, 324D2

1976

YEMEN Arab Republic (North Yemen)—*See also NONALIGNED Nations Movement*
Listed as 'not free' nation 1-19, 20E3

1977

YEMEN Arab Republic (North Yemen)—*See also ARAB League, NONALIGNED Nations Movement*
UN Assemb member 4D1
At Red Sea summit 3-22—3-23, 208D2
Ex-premr Al-Hajari slain 4-10, 284D3
Pres, brother slain 10-10; new rulers set martial law 10-12, 783F3
More assassinatns rptd 10-12, 10-14; Ghashmi escapes death try 10-19, 824D1

1978

YEMEN Arab Republic (North Yemen)—*See also ARAB League, NONALIGNED Nations Movement*
Islamic, Arab poor-natn aid rise rptd 4-9, 257F2
Pres Ghashmi slain, S Yemen linked 6-24; Aden denies role 6-25, 498E3, 499B2
Saudis score Ghashmi murder 6-24, link defectors 6-25, 499B2
Saudis warns vs interventn after Ghashmi death 6-24, 499B2
Mil cmnd Cncl takes power 6-25, 499F1
S Yemen Pres Rubaya deposed, executed for Ghashmi death 6-26, 498E3
Arab League links S Yemen to pres death, suspends ties 7-1—7-2, 522F1
S Yemen chrgs invasn 7-2, 7-3, denies 7-4, 522B2
Saleh elected pres 7-17, 559A1
Arab fund loan rptd 8-17, 925F3
UN Assemb member 713G3
Mil coup crushed 10-15, 799B1
S Yemen fighting rptd 10-21, 885E3
Sovts tied to coup try 10-21, 885F3
12 executed for coup try 11-15, 885B3

1979

YEMEN Arab Republic (North Yemen)—*See also ARAB League*
Rebels rptd as main foe 158D1
US, Saudi mil aid plan rptd 2-8, 89D2
US vows jet sale 2-11, 143C2
S Yemen border clashes erupt 2-24; US speeds arms, Saudi alerts troops 2-26, 2-28; mediatn agreed 2-28, 144A2
S Yemen border clashes 3-1, 3-6, 158D1
Syria, Iraq, Jordan truce try fails 3-2, Arab League plan fails 3-6, 157D2, 158B1
US sends fleet to Arabian Sea 3-5, offers Saudis jet aid 3-7, 157D2-158A1
US to speed arms 3-7, send mil advisers 3-12, shun war zone 3-13; S Yemen scores aid 3-10, 178B3-179A1
Cuban, Sovts rptdly up S Yemen aid 3-8; Sovts deny 3-14, 179E1
S Yemen rptdly clears border area 3-8, 179G1
S Yemen MiG fighters bomb 3-12, 179A2
Rebel amnesty set 3-16, 199F2
Cease-fire in effect 3-17; US assures re arms 3-19, 199D2
S Yemen unificatn plan agreed 3-29, 250B1, C1*
Islamic conf suspends Egypt 5-9, 360E1
Taiwanese to pilot jets 5-29, 395F1
US mil aid rise rptd asked 6-12—6-13, 436G3
UN membership listed 695B3
US sets evacuatns, travel curbs 11-26, 894A2

1980

YEMEN Arab Republic (North Yemen)—*See also ARAB League, NONALIGNED Nations*
Guerrilla war escalatn rptd 6-1, 468D2
Foreign Relations (misc.)
Saudis execute mosque raider 1-9, 22B1
Egypt fears S Yemen threat 1-28, 69A2
S Yemen power struggle linked to unificatn plan 4-23, 315E3
Syria seeks backing for Libya merger 9-10, 697G1
Backs Iraq in Iran war 9-23, 719E2
Iraqi planes rptd stationed 10-6, 757D1

1976

YEN Ming-shen
Taiwan electn fraud rptd chrgd 1-2, 123G1
YEO, Edwin H.
On Jamaica monetary accord 1-9, 13C2
Says US plans Portugal aid 11-23, 966A3
YESHIVA University (N.Y.)
Samuel Belkin dies 4-18, 315G3
Wolfenstein dies 11-30, 1015B3
YONG Jo Gu
Wins Olympic medal 7-31, 574A1
YONKERS, N.Y.—*See NEW York State*
YONKERS Raceway (N.Y.)
Forecasts '76 losses 9-1, 680E3
YOO Sang Gon
Replaced as unificatn min 12-4, 928A3
YORK, Herbert
A-materials export ban urged 1-19, 115D3
YORK, James
Indicted 3-5, freed 4-14, 316E2
YORK, Stanley
Unopposed in Wis Sen primary 9-14, 705C2
Loses electn 11-2, 824A1
YORKTOWN, Va.—*See VIRGINIA*
YOSHIMURA, Wendy
Soliah freed on bail 1-15, 70B2
UK MD claims Hearst 'brainwashed' 1-29, 70F1
Hearst rptdly cites re bank robbery 4-16, 368D1
YOST, Ed
Breaks world ballooning records 10-10, 892E2

YOUNG, Rep. Andrew J. (D, Ga.)
On Carter's 'ethnic' remark 4-8, 261C1
Meets Carter 7-12, 513C2
Seconds Carter nominatn 7-14, 506A1
Cited in Carter biog sketch 512B2
Heads voter-registratn drive 8-23, 631F2
Reelected 11-2, 822D1, 829D2
Carter meets cong ldrs 11-17, 864B2
Named US abm to UN 12-16, 936C2, B3
Biog sketch 937C1

1977

YIPPIES—*See YOUTH International Party*
YHOMBY Opango, Brig. Gen. Joachim (Congolese president)
Named Congo pres 4-3, 282D2
YODER, Ronnie
TWA 'on-time' ad curb ordrd 6-13, 463E2
YOFRE, Ricardo
Home bombed 8-22, 670G3
YOGA
US trend rptd 4-26—4-29, 470D3
YONEZAWA, Kunio
Vs US fishing fees 2-10, 136B2
YOO Yung Soo
Confirms bid to block testimony 11-30, 914G3
YOSHIMURA, Wendy
Convicted 1-20, 59C3
Sentenced 3-17, 288A3
YOST, Charles W.
In missn to Viet, Laos 3-16—3-20; Carter gets rpt 3-23, 206C1
YOSWEIN, Judge Leonard E.
Impounds Son of Sam tapes 8-16, 642A1
YOU Light Up My Life (film)
Top-grossing film 9-28, 808G3

YOUNG, Andrew J.
Confrmd UN amb 1-26, 52C3
Runoff set for US House seat 3-15, 192A1
Carter addresses UN 3-17, 185F1
Fowler wins US House seat 4-5, 252B1
Carter gets protest on S Korea rights 4-19, 305C3
Carter reaffirms faith 5-23, 444B1
Says Sovts, Swedes racists 5-25, 417E2
Playboy interview stirs 'racism' controversy 6-3—6-7, 443B3-444A1
Cleared re prisoner aid 10-19, 861D3
Africa
On Cuba troops in Angola 1-25, 105F1
Starts Africa shuttle 2-1, 72G3
In Africa, UK 2-2—2-12, briefs Carter 2-13, 105A1
Scores Uganda deaths 2-17, Carter backs 2-20, 139B1
Sees Carter on Amin exit bar 2-25, 141C1
Rpts personal finances 2-25, 148F1
Garba sees re Zaire mediatn 3-22, 261A1
Scores UK re racism 4-5, apologizes; Carter reactn 4-7, 272D1
For S Africa sanctns 4-5, 272C2
Vs 'cold-war' policy in Africa, defends Cuba-Angola statemt 4-11, 271C3
Bars Zaire interventn 4-11, 272B1
Defends outspokenness, White House backs 4-12, 272B1
S Africa statemts scored, visit in doubt 4-14—5-11, 399D3
Tours Africa 5-10—5-24: at US ambs mtg 5-10—5-12, UN parley 5-16—5-21; sees Mondale 5-15, 398A2, G2-400C1
On Cubans in Ethiopia 5-26, 417A3
Carter backs statemts 5-26, 417B3
Sees 'race war' proliferatn 6-3, 443C3
Briefs Sen com on tour 6-6, 443E3
Carter says focus to shift 6-10, 460E2
Addresses UN apartheid conf, warns vs S Africa measures 8-25, 661G2
In southern Africa with Owen, seeks new Rhodesia plan support 8-26—8-30, 661E1-E2
Gives Smith Rhodesia plan 9-1, 699E2
Scores S Africa student ldr's death 9-13, 708B1
Smith chrgs deceptn 9-21, 735C1
Smith notes rapport 10-17, 810F1
Backs S Africa sanctns 10-24, 825C1; vetoes econ, permanent arms sanctns 10-31, 851G2
Sees Carter, others on S Africa sanctns 10-24, 851D3
Backs S Africa UN arms ban 11-4, 851F1
Scores Cuba, Sovt roles in Africa 12-6, 1011A3
Latin America
On Cuba troops in Angola 1-25, 105C1
Defends Cuba-Angola statemt 4-11, 271F3
On Cuba role in Ethiopia 5-26, 417A3
Tours Carib region 8-5—8-17, 646E1
Belize independnc backing rptd 8-12, 706G2
Haiti visit spurs civln pol ct 8-23, 707A1
Jamaica aid resumed 9-12, 11-9, 884C2
Cited re Haiti pol prisoner releases 9-21, 767F2
Scores Cuba role in Africa 12-6, 1011A3

1978

YEN Chia-kan
Chiang to replace as Taiwan pres 3-21, 251B1
YGLESIAS, John
Indicted 7-19, 598F3
YHOMBY Opango, Brig. Gen. Joachim (Congolese president)
Chrgs coup attempt foiled 8-14, 660F3
YILDIZ, Salih
Named Turkey state min 1-5, 21D2
YMCA—*See YOUNG Men's Christian Association*
Y.M.C.A. (recording)
On best-seller list 12-6, 971E1
YODA, Yoshikata
Geisha released 6-1, 619B2
YOOK In Soo
Linked to housing scandal 7-14, 594F3
YORK, Rebecca
Movie, Movie released 11-22, 970C2
YOSEMITE National Park (Calif.)
1st woman climbs El Capitan alone 10-26, 843A3
YOSHIDA, Yuki
Film wins Oscar 4-3, 315D3
YOSHIKAWA, Nayoka
2d in Amer Cancer Society tourn 2-13, 355B3
YOST, Charles
Cited in Camp David summit letter 9-22, 730E3
YOST, Robert L.
Protests DR vote count suspensn; Balaguer shuns, Nivar says situatn 'normal' 5-17, 371E3
YOS Thephasdin, Gen.
Gets Thai Cabt post 8-13, 691B2
YOU Don't Bring Me Flowers (recording)
On best-seller list 11-8, 888D1; 12-6, 971D1
YOU Light Up My Life (song)
Wins Grammy 2-24, 315E3
Wins Oscar 4-3, 315C3
YOU Make Me Feel Like Dancing (song)
Wins Grammy 2-24, 315G3
YOU Needed Me (recording)
On best-seller list 10-11, 800E3; 11-8, 888C1; 12-6, 971E1

YOUNG, Andrew J.
Speaks at Sun Day rally 5-3, 322A1
US 'pol prisoners' remark spurs controversy, Carter rebukes 7-12—7-15, 7-20, 542C2 549E2
At DR pres inaugural 8-16, 648A2
Diggs convicted 10-7, 791F3
Ravenel loses US Sen bid 11-7, 853A1
Rebuts FBI King plot allegatns 11-17, 938C2
Africa
Sees Rhodesia natlsts in Malta 1-30, 58D3
Malta mtg ends 2-1, 119G3
Scores Rhodesia internal setlmt pact 2-15, 119D3
Fears UK may 'run out' on Rhodesia, retracts 3-9, 193F1
Sees African ldrs, Patriotic Front 3-21—3-24; at front-line mtg, wins Namibia plan support 3-25—3-26, 248G2, D3
Muzorewa: Patriotic Front 'brainwashed' 3-26, 248B3
Meets Carter in Nigeria 3-31, 233F2
Rebuts Carter on aid curbs 5-21, qualifies 5-22, 383E1
Rhodesia forgn min scores 6-30, 615F2
Nigeria scores US re Rhodesia 11-24, 911G3

1979

Saudis capture mosque raiders 12-4, 916B1
YEPEZ Boscan, Guillermo
Venez culture min 3-10, 192D3
YEPREMIAN, Garo
NFL '78 kicking ldr 1-6, 80B1
NFC wins Pro Bowl 1-29, 79F3
YEROFEYEV, Viktor
Union bars reinstatemt 12-17, 980F2
YESHIVA University (N.Y., N.Y.)
Albert Einstein College of Medicine—*See separate listing*
YEVTUSHENKO, Yevgeny Alexandrovich
Shuns Metropole participatn 1-18, 100C2
YHOMBY Opango, Brig. Gen. Joachim
Resignatn rptd 1-6, 85E3
YMCA—*See YOUNG Men's Christian Association*
Y. M. C. A. (recording)
On best-seller list 1-10, 80E3; 2-14; 120E3; 3-7, 174D1
YNIGUEZ, Richard
Boulevard Nights released 3-22, 528E1
YODA, Yoshikata
My Love released 1-4, 174B3
YODER Jr., Edwin M.
Wins Pulitzer 4-16, 336B3
YOKAI, Masahiro
Kim KOs 10-4, 839C1
YOKOSHIMA, Yoshikazu
2d in Japan Open 10-28, 970A2
YORK, Pa.—*See PENNSYLVANIA*
YORK, Michael
Fedora released 4-14, 528C2
YORK, Susannah
Silent Partner released 5-10, 528F3
Shout released 11-9, 1008E1
YORKSHIRE Ripper
Kills 12th victim 9-3, 839D1
YOSHIMURA, Wendy
'77 convictn upheld 4-5, 271G2
YOU Don't Bring Me Flowers (recording)
On best-seller list 1-10, 80E3
YOU Need Me (recording)
Murray wins Grammy 2-16, 336D3

YOUNG, Andrew Jackson
For new US approach to PLO 1-16, Jewish group protests 1-17, 69E1
Lauds Khomeini 2-7; sees reps, assured re minorities 2-10, 106F1
Asks China, Cambodia conflicts end 2-23, 142B1
Chrgs Rhodesia vote fraud 5-3, 354E1
Warns UK re recognitn of Rhodesia 5-4, 338C2
Compares Spenkelink, Iran executns 5-25; Fla offcls incredulous 5-26, 400D1
At FAO hunger conf conf 7-20, 554D1
Meets PLO's Terzi 7-26, informs US 8-11, Terzi backs 8-13, 8-14; State Dept rpts 8-13; Vance, Israel score mtg 8-14; **resigns UN post 8-15,** 605A1-606A1
US black, Jewish ldrs on resignatn; PLO, other forgn reactn 8-15, 8-16, 606E1-F2
Says warned Israel of pro-PLO backlash 8-16, 606A1
US, Israel deny Terzi talks bugged 8-16, 606D1
To limit PLO contacts as Sec Cncl pres 8-17, 624F3
US denies rpt on Terzi talks, disputes US 8-18—8-20, 624E2
Jewish groups deny pressure for resignatn 8-19, 624F1
Scores US PLO policy 8-19, 624D3
Israel denies intransigence chrg 8-19, 624F3
Scores US PLO policy, Arab stand on Israel; UN delays vote on Palestinian res 8-24, 642E1-B2
Asks halt to Leb clashes 8-29, 658D2
Carter praises, denies tap 8-30, 661B2, F2
McHenry named successor 8-31, 660F2
In African tour, urges Israel ties 9-5—9-21, 720F2-721C2
NAACP reaffirms resignatn stand 9-11, 677F1
SCLC group meets Arafat, Israel rebuffs SCLC 9-20, 694D2, G2
Carter denies Jewish pressure to oust 9-23, 763E2
Rep rebuts re US rpt on Terzi talks; denies US, Israel bugging 10-28, 823D2

1980

YEO 3rd, Edwin H.
Named Chicago fscl aide 1-22, 186E2
YE Qun
Gang of 4 trial defendant 11-20—12-29, 975E2
YESHIVA University (N.Y., N.Y.)
Faculty union curbed by Sup Ct 2-20, 146D1-B2
YESHIVA University Faculty Association v. Yeshiva University
Case decided by Sup Ct 2-20, 146D1-B2
YIFTER, Miruts
Wins Olympic medals for 'distance double' 7-27, 8-1, 589D1, 624B1, E1
YIN Fa-tang
Apptmt as Tibet CP ldr rptd 5-29, 462D1
On Tibet demonstratn 7-31, 604A1
YIPPIES—*See YOUTH International Party*
YMCA—*See YOUNG Men's Christian Association*
YOCOM, David E.
Polygamist convicted of murder 5-28, sentenced 6-2, 502B3
YOHALEM, Joel
Electronic mail plan OKd, conflict of interest chrgd 4-8, 347C3
YOKICH, Stephen P.
Named UAW vp 6-4, 457C2
YORK, Susannah
Awakening released 10-31, 972C3
Falling in Love Again released 11-21, 972D3
YORKSHIRE Ripper
Kills 13th victim 11-17, 927D1
YORTY, Sam
Loses Calif US Sen primary 6-3, 439A2
YOSEMITE National Park (Calif.)
Janitor chrgd in kidnaping 3-2, 238E2
Natl Park Svc dir ousted 4-24, 333C2
Quakes hit 5-25, 5-27, 527D3
YOSHIMURA, Wendy
Paroled 8-25, 890G1
YOU Decorated My Life (recording)
Morrison, Hupp win Grammy 2-27, 296D3
YOU Know Al He's a Funny Guy (play)
Opens 11-13, 892G3

YOUNG, Andrew Jackson
Mich State U apptmt rptd 1-18, 199A1
Marks Zimbabwe indepndnc 4-17—4-18, 301F1
Reagan chrgs Klan link attempt 9-2, 664E1
Campaigns for Carter 10-10, racial remark repudiated 10-15, 803D1

1976

YOUNG, Rep. C. W. (R, Fla.)
Reelected 11-2, 829B2
YOUNG, Mayor Coleman A. (Detroit, Mich.)
Detroit fscl crisis seen 3-24, 994D2
Udall Mormon ties disputed 5-15, 5-17, 357C1
Asks juvenile law study 8-16; on emergency measures 9-16, 776B2
Declined Carter post 12-16, 937A2
YOUNG, Rep. Donald E. (R, Alaska)
Reelected 11-2, 824E3, 828G2
YOUNG, Judge George C.
Dismisses part of Gurney chrg 10-25, 846B1
YOUNG, James L.
HUD asst secy 2-23; confrmd 3-11, 232F1
YOUNG, Jimmy
Ali decisions 4-30, 424C3
YOUNG, Rep. John (D, Tex)
Gardner, Hall sex chrgs rptd 6-11, 433E3
Cleared on sex-payroll chrg 8-16, 636B2
Reelected 11-2, 820B2, 830D4
YOUNG, John Shaw
Dies 1-12, 562G3
YOUNG, Michael
In Australia shadow cabt 1-29, 116E1
YOUNG, Sen. Milton R. (R, N.D.)
Com ends Scott probe 9-15, 980B1
YOUNG, Robert A.
Elected 11-2, 823B3, 830A1
YOUNG, Samuel H.
Electn undecided 11-2, 823A2
Mikva declared winner 11-19, 882A1
YOUNG, Sheila
Wins Olympic medals, breaks 500-mtr record 2-5—2-7, 158G2, G3-159A1
YOUNG & Co., Arthur
Findley on Lockheed payoffs 2-4, 130B2
YOUNG Frankenstein (film)
'75 top rental film 1-7, 32F3
YOUNG Socialists Alliance (YSA)
'71 Secret Svc watch rptd 5-25, 569D3, E3 ★
YOUNGSTOWN, O.—*See OHIO*
YOUNGSTOWN Sheet and Rube Co.
Hikes prices 6% 11-26, 897E2
YOUR Arm's Too Short to Box With God (play)
Opens 12-22, 1014F3
YOU'RE a Good Sport, Charlie Brown (TV special)
Wins Emmy 5-17, 460C2
YOUR Erroneous Zones (book)
On best-seller list 12-5, 972C2
YOU Sexy Thing (song)
On best-selling list 1-28, 104G3

YOUTH
'75 church attendance rptd 1-3, 32B3
Dec '75 jobless rate up 1-9, 21C1
US health rpt issued 1-12, 32C1
'77 summer job program budgeted 1-21, 65A3
Jan jobless rate rptd 2-5, 152E3, G3
Feb jobless rate rptd 3-5, 198G3
ILO issues jobless rpt 3-13, 297F3
Mar jobless rate rptd 4-2, 263D1
Jobs, recreatn progrms funded 4-15, 282C2
Apr jobless rate rptd 5-7, 347C2
Cong clears ACTION funds 5-13, 393D1; Ford signs 5-27, 982F1
May jobless rate rptd 6-4, 412G2, A3
June jobless rate rptd 7-2, 494D1
Productivity slowdown forecast 8-2, 647C2
July jobless rate rptd 8-6, 586C3
Detroit gangs disrupt concert 8-15, curfew set 8-19, arrests rptd 9-16, 776F1
Aug jobless rate rptd 9-3, 667A3
Australia sets jobs plan 9-21, 770A3
Jobs bill not cleared 10-2, 884B1
Sup Ct bars review of criminal evidence case 10-4, 766C1
Sept jobless rate rptd 10-8, 769A3
Anti-smoking drive announced 10-15, 875E3
Oct jobless rate rptd 11-5, 846A2
Sup Ct bars Pa curfew review 11-15, 882E2
Swine flu shots limited 11-15, 911C1
Dole urges GOP inclusn 11-30, 917B3
Nov jobless rate rptd 12-5, 918B1
EC jobless data rptd 12-12, 935D2

1977

Middle East
UN Cncl mtg on Mideast adjourns 3-29, 227B1
Abstains on anti-Israel res 10-28, 830G2
YOUNG, Charles
Challenges NFL labor pact 4-25, 491G2
YOUNG, Mayor Coleman (Detroit, Mich.)
Police chrg reverse bias 1-4, 278B3
Dem natl vice chrmn 1-21, 53B2
Detroit sued on water pollutn 5-6, 422E2
Reelected 11-8, 855F1, G2
Scores Frostbelt-Sunbelt issue 12-7, 959E3
YOUNG, Donna
2d in LPGA Classic 5-22, Colgate Far East tourn 11-13, 951C1, E1
YOUNG, Edwin
Named U of Wis pres 3-11, 354A2
YOUNG, James L.
Replaced as HUD asst secy 3-23, 272C3
YOUNG, Jimmy
Decisns Foreman 3-17, 263B1
Norton decisions 11-5, 970C2
YOUNG, Kenneth
Scores House minimum wage bill 9-17, 758F3
YOUNG, Sen. Milton R. (R, N.D.)
Scores IJC rpt re Garrison 9-16, 726D1
YOUNG Adult Conservation Corps—*See under U.S. GOVERNMENT*
YOUNG Americans for Freedom
Sup Ct hears Bakke case arguments 10-12, 834D3
YOUNG & Co., Arthur
Sen subcom rpt scores 1-17, 78C3
Renegotiatn Bd gets Lockheed audit 8-5, 650F1
Big 8 acctg firms ranked 8-22, 650G2
YOUNGER, Evelle J.
Confirms Bird 3-11, 396B3
YOUNGSTOWN Sheet & Tube Co.—*See LYKES Corp.*
YOUR Erroneous Zones (book)
On best-seller list 2-6, 120F3; 3-6, 184F3; 4-3, 264G1; 5-1, 356C2; 6-4, 452A2; 7-3, 548E3; 8-14, 643G1; 9-4, 712D3; 10-2, 808E3; 11-6, 872E3

YOUTH—*See also organization, country names*
Ind abortn law curb upheld 1-25, 80F2
Iran, Pak, Turkey sign pact 3-12, 190C2
TV viewing decline rptd 12-6, 1021F3
Legal Svcs Corp aid ban lifted 12-28, 1002F2

Crime
Okla ct gag order voided 3-7, 211B2
1-judge Tex prison ruling upheld 3-21, 230A3
Pot use polled 4-4, 972G2-A3
3 Girl Scouts slain in Okla 6-13, 492E1
Cocaine use detailed 7-6, 972A2
San Fran Chinatown gang slayings 9-4, 9-11, 711G2
Juvenile Justice Amendmts enacted 10-3, 797B1
Eur heroin use rptd up 10-17—10-21, 971F3

Education—*See under 'E'*
Employment
Carter plans jobs effort 1-7, 5A2
Dec '76 jobless rate rptd 1-12, 37E3
Ford '78 budget proposals 1-17, 33E2
GOP sens offer jobs plan 2-2, 89G2
Jan jobless rate drops 2-4, 111F1
Feb jobless rate rptd 3-4, 176B2
Carter proposes job programs 3-9, 173E1-A2
Mar jobless rate rptd 4-1, 252F1
Job funds clear Cong 5-5, 365F2; Carter signs 5-13, 380D3
Apr jobless rate rptd 5-6, 383G3
May jobless rate rptd 6-3, 445C1
Chicago summer jobs set 6-7, 464D3
June jobless rate rptd 7-8, 554D1
Jobs bill enacted 8-5, 609A2
July jobless rate rptd 8-5, 611C3
July black jobless rate 8-31, 692C2 ★; F2

1978

YOUNG, Brigham (1801-77)
Mo Mormon ldr installed 4-5, 294A3
YOUNG, Rep. C. W. (Bill) (R, Fla.)
Reelected 11-7, 850F2
YOUNG, Mayor Coleman (Detroit, Mich.)
Diggs convicted 10-7, 791F3
Layoffs planned 12-27, 1012F1
YOUNG, Rep. Donald E. (R, Alaska)
House OKs Alaska lands bill 5-19, 386C2
Reelected 11-7, 850B1, 856C2
YOUNG, Donna Caponi
2d in Greater Baltimore Classic, 5-14, 580E2
Wins Sarah Coventry Open 9-17, Houston Exchng Clubs Classic 10-22, 990G1, C2
LPGA top money winner 11-20, 990C3
YOUNG, Edward L.
Wins primary for SC gov 6-13, 467E1
Loses electn 11-7, 853B1
YOUNG, Gig
Kills self, bride 10-19, 888G3
YOUNG, Jimmy
Norton named WBC champion 3-18, 211C3
YOUNG, Rep. John (D, Tex.)
Faces primary runoff 5-6, 363A1
Loses primary runoff 6-3, 426E2
Wyatt wins seat 11-7, 855E3
YOUNG, Sen. Milton R. (R, N.D.)
Votes vs Panama Canal neutrality pact 3-16, 177G2
Votes vs 2d Canal pact 4-18, 273B1
Gets Cong Watch low rating 10-28, 865A3
YOUNG, Rickey
Traded to Vikings 7-29, 1024G3
YOUNG, Rep. Robert A. (D, Mo.)
Reelected 11-7, 851C2
YOUNG, Wilbur
Traded to Chargers 5-3, 336B2
YOUNG Americans for Freedom
Robinson lauds Bakke ruling 6-28, 482B3
YOUNGDAHL, Judge Luther W.
Dies 6-21, 540G3
YOUNGER, Evelle J.
Wins primary for Calif gov 6-6, 447C3
Loses electn 11-7, 847B1, 856C2, G2
YOUNG Men's Christian Association (YMCA)
Amateur sports bill clears Cong 10-15, 842A3
YOUNG & Rubicam International Inc.
Ray Rubicam dies 5-8, 440D3
YOUNG Socialist Alliance
FBI informant case declined by Sup Ct 6-12, 468D1
YOUNGSTOWN, Fla.—*See FLORIDA*
YOUNGSTOWN, O.—*See OHIO*
YOUNGSTOWN Sheet and Tube Co.—*See LYKES Corp.*
YOUNT, Robin
AL batting ldr 10-2, 928E3
YOUR Erroneous Zones (book)
On best-seller list 1-8, 24F3; 2-5, 116D3; 3-5, 195F3; 4-2, 272D3, 4-30, 356B2
YOU'RE The One That I Want (recording)
On best-seller list 6-7, 460F3; 7-5, 579G3; 8-2, 620F1

YOUTH—*See also organization, country names*
'76 pres vote turnout rptd 4-13, 285A2
Intl Youth Festival in Cuba 7-28—8-5, 831B1
Draft registratn urged 10-29, 11-21, 895A1
Mich drinking age hiked 11-7, 854C1

Crime
Sex abuse suit vs NBC OKd by Sup Ct 4-24, 322B2
Ill suspects rights case refused by Sup Ct 4-24, 322G2
5 sentenced in '76 NYC racial assault 5-12, 380D3
Tex boy kills teacher 5-18, 396A2
Study finds arson rise 6-4, 440B2
Solzhenitsyn chrgs 'moral violence' 6-8, 444E2
Juvenile case reviews upheld by Sup Ct 6-28, 567F1
Sex abuse suit vs NBC dismissed 8-8, 635C2-A3
Inner city crime survey rptd 10-16, 842A2
Ill TWA hijacker seized 12-21, 1029F1

Education—*See EDUCATION*
Employment
Dec '77 jobless rate rptd 1-11, 50G3
Carter State of Union Message 1-19, 29B1, C2, 30B3
Carter budgets jobs 1-23, 46F2
Jan jobless rate 2-3, 127E3
AFL-CIO urges jobs program 2-20, 141F3
CETA revisn asked by Carter 2-22, 124E1
Feb jobless rate 3-10, 222A1
Jordan: black jobless at 60% 3-15, 811B2
EC jobs program announced 4-7, 258D2
Mar jobless rate rptd 4-7, 262C2
Educ Dept plan excludes job progrms 4-14, 279E1
Apr jobless rate rptd 5-5, 345F1
Pvt-sector initiative progrm planned 5-23, 405A1
May jobless rate rptd 6-2, 429E2
June jobless rate rptd 7-7, 552F2

1979

YOUNG, Canzetta (Candy)
Sets indoor 60-yd hurdles mark 2-23, 911D2
YOUNG, Mayor Coleman A. (Detroit, Mich.)
Announces layoffs 9-28, 921E1
Attends Carter dinner 10-24, 961F2
Wayne Cnty govt reorgnztn accord reached 11-1, 921A1, D1
YOUNG, Rep. Donald E. (R, Alaska)
Vs House Alaska land bill 5-16, 367B1
YOUNG, Donna Caponi
2d in Sahara Natl 3-25, 3d in Women's Kemper 4-1; wins LPGA Champ 6-10, 587E1, A2, B2
2d in KC Classic 9-20, 970E1
LPGA top money winner 11-30, 969G2
YOUNG, George
Hired as Giants operatns dir 2-14, 175C2
YOUNG, Judge Joseph H.
Sentncs Ellis in GSA scandal 4-24, 367B3
Sentences GSA contractor 5-29, 964C3
YOUNG, Sen. Milton R. (R, N.D.)
Financial disclosure statemt studied 9-1, 701F3
Votes vs Talmadge denunciatn 10-10, 769G1
YOUNG, Rickey
NFL '78 receiving ldr 1-6, 80F1
YOUNG, Robert M.
Rich Kids released 8-17, 820B3
YOUNG, Terence
Bloodline released 6-28, 819E3
YOUNGER, George
UK Scotland secy 5-5, 338F1
YOUNG Men's Christian Association (YMCA)
China reimbursemt set 3-16, 218B1
YOUNG & Rubicam International Inc.
Chrysler drops account 3-1, 188D1
Marsteller merger set 6-27, 560E2
Bristol-Myers ads assailed by FTC 10-12, 903A1
YOUNGSTOWN, O.—*See OHIO*
YOUNGSTOWN (O.) State University
Loses NCAA Div II football title game 12-8, 1001F2
YOUNGSVILLE, Pa.—*See PENNSYLVANIA*
YOUR Turn, My Turn (film)
Released 1-27, 174G3
YOUSSEF, Ibrahim al-
Led army cadet slayers 6-22, 488D1

YOUTH—*See also country names*
Carter Soc Sec cuts opposed in Cong 1-23, 55B3
Mass raises legal drinking age 4-16, 309E3
Bilingual program rules proposed 6-29, 597A1
Mich HS voter turnout law signed 8-14, 724D2

Crime & Civil Disorders
Cowboys quarterback robbed 1-30, 175A3
ABA asks juvenile justice reforms 2-12, 130G1
Paramount resumes 'Warriors' ads 2-22, 174G1-A2
La jury trial ban refused by Sup Ct 2-21, 128B3
Teen-age drinking linked 4-16, 309F3
Probatn officer consultatn rights limited by Sup Ct 6-20, 516B2
Norfolk (Va) porno case dismissed by Sup Ct 6-25, 540A2
'Miranda rights' case remanded by Sup Ct 6-25, 540B2
W Va press law voided by Sup Ct 6-26, 541A1
Phila police brutality chrgd 8-13, 610B2
Calif schl sniper pleads guilty 10-1, 819E2; sentncd 11-30, 953F3
Ohio rock concert stampede, 11 die 12-3, 954G1

Employment & Unemployment
Dec '78 jobless rate rptd 1-14, 34C1
Carter budget proposals 1-22, 44B1, 46D1
Jan jobless rate rptd 2-2, 110D3
'78 productivity drop rptd 2-9, 111D1
Feb jobless rate rptd 3-8, 182C3
Mar jobless rate rptd 4-6, 280B3
Apr jobless rate rptd 5-4, 362D3
May jobless rate rptd 6-1, 422D2
June jobless rate rptd 7-6, 516C3
July jobless rate rptd 8-3, 621G2
Aug jobless rate rptd 9-7, 680F3
Sept jobless rate rptd 10-5, 766C2
Oct jobless rate rptd 11-2, 866D3
Nov jobless rate rptd 12-7, 941G1

1980

YOUNG, Rep. C. W. (R, Fla.)
Reelected 11-4, 842F2
YOUNG, Candy
2d in Millrose 60-yd hurdles 2-8, 892E2
YOUNG, Mayor Coleman A. (Detroit, Mich.)
Greets GOP conv 7-14, 531B3
YOUNG, Dalene
Little Darlings released 3-28, 416C3
YOUNG, Rep. Don E. (R, Alaska)
Reelected 11-4, 842B1, 852G1
YOUNG, Donna Caponi
Wins Vegas Natl Pro-Am 3-23, Winners Circle 4-6; 2d in Amer Defender 4-13, Lady Michelob 5-11, 412B3-G3
Wins Corning Classic 5-26, 714G3
2d in Wheeling Classic 8-3; wins United Va Bank Classic 9-14, ERA Real Estate Classic 9-21, LPGA Team tourn 10-5, 972E1, B2, C2
LPGA top money winner 10-12, 971F3
YOUNG, Sen. Milton R. (R, N.D.)
ND primary results 9-2, 683C1
Andrews elected to US Sen 11-4, 845B3, 851A2
YOUNG, Rickey
NFL '79 receiving ldr 1-5, 8F2
YOUNG, Dr. Robert
A-plant defies gas venting order 5-13, 441D1
YOUNG, Rep. Robert A. (D, Mo.)
Reelected 11-4, 843C2
YOUNG, Robert M.
One-Trick Pony released 10-3, 836D3
YOUNG, Roynell
In NFL draft 4-29, 336G2
YOUNG Men's Christian Association
Chapman chrgd in Lennon slaying 12-8, 933F2
YOUNGTOWN—*See OHIO*
YOUNG v. Tennessee Valley Authority
Case declined by Sup Ct 3-24, 265C2
YOUNT, Robin
AL batting ldr 10-6, 926E3
YOURCENAR, Marguerite
Elected to French Acad 3-6, 471G2

YOUTH
State of State messages 1-15, 483D2; 2-6, 269G1

Crime
ABA tables ct jurisdictn proposal 2-4, 114E3
Mass prof indicted in fraud case 5-13, 414F3
'79 auto theft data rptd 9-24, 971A2
Mass rape trial press exclusn case remanded by Sup Ct 10-14, 782B1
Pa pretrial press exclusn case refused by Sup Ct 11-17, 882F1
Draft Registration—*See under U.S. GOVERNMENT--SELECTIVE Service System*

Employment & Unemployment
Carter asks training program 1-10, 16G1-F2
Dec '79 jobless rate rptd 1-11, 33F2
Carter State of Union proposals 1-21, 1-23, 41G2, 43D2, D3
Carter budget proposals 1-28, 69D3, 72D1
Jan jobless rate rptd 2-1, 92D2
Jobless rate rptd rising 2-28, 228A3
Feb jobless rate rptd 3-7, 182D3
Carter revised budget proposals 3-31, 244B1
Mar jobless rate rptd 4-4, 263E1
Apr jobless rate rptd 5-2, 344A3
May jobless rate rptd 6-6, 437E2
US summer jobs progrm rptd 6-30, 496A1
June jobless rate rptd 7-3, 513A3
July jobless rate rptd 8-1, 599F2

1976

Presidential Election
Carter urges US jobs 4-23, 305E2
Dem platform text 6-15, 469C2, E3, 474B1
Dems plan '80 conv rules 6-20, 451A2
Dems OK more NY delegates 6-28, 490C1
Dem conv rpt re role 7-13, 509G1
Reagan, Ford at conv rallies 8-16, 601A3
GOP platform text 8-18, 604B2, B3
Ford urges job-training prgrm 9-15, 686D1
Mondale scores GOP on jobs 9-16, 687B2
Ford, Carter debate 9-23, 701C1, A2
Ford seeks actn vs crime 9-27, 723G3
Dole attacks Carter 10-18, 804G1
Ford, Carter debate 10-22, 802B1

YOUZAITAS, Arvidas
Wins Olympic medal 7-20, 575C2

YUBA City, Calif.—*See CALIFORNIA*

YU Chan
Border talks resume 11-30, 908C1

YUGOSLAVIA—*See also COMECON, DISARMAMENT—Geneva Committee, NONALIGNED Nations Movement*
Milan Gavrilovic dies 1-1, 56C3
Croatians jailed 1-17, 224C1
Tito says system strong 2-1, 223D3
Belgrade atty sentenced 3-10, 223F3
4 sentncd for emigre plot 3-12, 223A3
10 pro-Sovts jailed 3-16, 256E1
Mihajlov ends hunger strike 3-21, 256D2
9 Cominformist sentenced 4-14, 542E3
Mihajlov transferred to hospital 4-20, 542G3
Quake injures 30 5-6, 352F2
Belgrade atty's sentnc suspended 5-26, 543B1
Adriatic-Belgrade RR opens 5-28, 543D1
Croat held in 'mistaken-identity' shooting 6-8, 542D3
5-yr plan adopted 6-20, 594F1
3 rightists sentenced 6-29, 559B3
Domestic shipbldg contract rptd 7-2, 594C2
Dapcevic sentenced 7-5, 559A3
Carlos rptd in Belgrade 9-6—9-10; Yugos deny 9-17, 722B1
Tito ill 9-10, 734F2
Tremors felt 9-11—9-16, 756F1
176 die in plane collisn 9-13, 696B3
Prince Paul Karageorgevich dies 9-14, 932E3
Slovene dissidnts sentncd 9-16, 10-15, 910D1
Slovenia econ data rptd 10-24, 910E1
CP housing bias rptd challenged 11-14, 910F1
Workers get mgt role 11-25, productivity data rptd 11-26, 1012E1
Drug use rise rptd 12-29, 1012G1

Foreign Relations (misc.)
Gens see Eastern mil threat 1-11, 55E1
Portugal trade min visits 1-13, 143B1
Listed as 'not free' nation 1-19, 20E3
Balkan natns meet 1-26—2-5, 213E3
Albanian killed in '75 Adriatic clash 2-6, 224D1
Envoy killed in W Ger 2-7, 224E1
Kosovo Albanians jailed 2-8, 2-27, 224A1
At Intl econ conf 2-11—2-20, 148B1
Backs UN rights comm resolutn vs Israel 2-13, 125E2
Shuns UN pollutn pact signing 2-16, 126B3
'75 trade deficit rptd 2-17, new measures rptd 2-25, 224F1
Total IMF oil loan rptd 2-23, 4-1, 339F3, 340B2
Tito dep at Sovt CP Cong 2-24—3-5, 195C3
UN Palestine com member 2-26, 162C1
Aide in bombed Cambodia town 3-2—3-4, 238B2
Castro visits, sees Tito 3-6—3-8, 251A3

1977

3 job corps cntrs open, young-adult program begun 8-31, 692E2
Aug jobless rate rptd 9-2, 692C2
Subminimum wage barred by House 9-15, 759A2; Sen 10-7, 795D3
Sept jobless rate rptd 10-7, 776C3
Detroit topic for Carter 10-21, 817A1
Oct jobless rate rptd 11-4, 858F2
Nov jobless rate rptd 12-3, 961C3
OECD labor mins meet 12-15—12-16, 998E3

Medicine & Health
Reye's syndrome rptd up 3-11, 224E1
Pa mental health rights case refused 5-16, 418G3
Conn abortn rule voided 5-23, 444C3
NY contraceptive curbs voided 6-9, 501A2
Female smokers rptd up in '75 620E1
Abortn alternatives urged, rates rptd high 7-19, 786E3

Religious Cults—*See under 'R'*

YOUTH Conservation Corps—*See under U.S. GOVERNMENT—INTERIOR*

YOUTH International Party (Yippies)
Protest at Carter inauguratn 1-20, 26E2

YU Chan
Reaffirms anti-Taiwan stand 10-2, 780G3

YUCHENGCO, Alfonso
SEC sues 1-12, 79A3

YU Chiu-li
In Politburo 8-21, 645G2
Discloses wage hikes 10-23, 823G1

YUGOSLAVIA—*See also COMECON, DISARMAMENT—Geneva Committee, IDB, NONALIGNED Nations Movement, WARSAW Pact*
Rumania quake felt 3-4, 204F1
Djuranovic sworn premr 3-15, 223G3
'76 econ growth, inflatn rate rptd 4-29, 513D2
Air controller sentncd in '76 crash 5-16, 497A3
Tito's wife in seclusn 6-15, illness denied 10-11, 786A1
Single party-state ldr cited 6-16, 469F2
Tito rest ordered 10-27, 844E2
Tito's wife accused of Serb natlism 12-25, 844G1

Foreign Relations (misc.)—*See also 'Human Rights' below*
UN Assemb member 4D1
Sovt mil pact barred 1-9, 24A1
Tito visit to Egypt canceled 1-20, 43F3
Spain ties rptd renewed 1-27, 242C2
'76 9-mo trade gap rptd 2-4, 309D1
Ethiopia ldr receives amb 2-11, 238A3
UN comm scores Israel occupatn rule 2-15, 107F2
New trade laws rptd 3-8, 308G3
Trieste pact rptd exchngd 4-2, 309D2
Italy begins Cavcat cargo recovery 4-4, 284B3
'76 trade data rptd 4-29, 513D2-E2
Austrian defns min quits 5-30, 424F3, 425B1
Croats invade UN mission 6-14, 487B2
Eurocommunism rptd backed, USSR scored 7-8, 590E3
Albania air link cited 595F1
Brezhnev honors Tito 8-16, 640C2
Tito in USSR, N Korea, China, Iran 8-16—9-8, 709D3

1978

Business job tax credit OKd by House com 7-27, 587E1
ILO rpts '77 jobless rates 7-28, 677F1
July jobless rate rptd 8-4, 607B3
Bradley hits black jobless 8-8, 811G1
Aug jobless rate rptd 9-1, 679E3
Sept jobless rate rptd 10-6, 790B3
Oct jobless rate rptd 11-3, 864D3
Cleveland progress re blacks cited 11-27, 916C1
Jordan distressed by Carter budget plans 12-4, 936B3
Black '70-78 mil enlistmt rise rptd 12-6, 960B1
Nov jobless rate rptd 12-8, 958F1
AF volunteer shortage tied to better job mkt 12-12, 960D1

Medicine & Health
Age bias in fed progrms rptd 1-10, 14E1
HEW anti-smoking drive set 1-11, 23C2
Epilepsy drug OKd 2-28, 231C2
Contraceptn use rptd effective 6-7, 598A2
Cigaret smoking rptd up 7-5, 727C1
Chelsea soft drink ads halted 7-22, 941G3-942A1
'75 illegitimate births rptd 8-10, 744D1

YOUTH Festival, International
Held in Cuba 7-28—8-5, 831B1

YUCELER, Mehmet
Named Turkey agri min 1-5, 21F2

YU Chan
Protests USSR border raid 5-11, 360F2

YUGOSLAVIA—*See also COMECON, DISARMAMENT—Geneva Committee, GATT, IDB, NONALIGNED Nations Movement*
Belgrade expenses rated 1-14, 28B3
Perovic sentenced 4-13, 292G1
11th CP Cong: Tito speech; Central Com, Presidium electns 6-20—6-23, 519D2-C3
'77 jobless rate cited 6-20, 519A3

Croatian Issue
4 W Ger terrorists arrested 5-11, Croatian natls exchng sought 5-11—5-31, 438E3
Croatian exiles in W Ger protest Bilandzic extraditn ruling 8-13, 706D3
2 NYC bombs defused 8-14, 706D3
2 Croatians seize W Ger emb in Chicago, ask Bilandzic release 8-17, 706E2
Croat seeks Swedish asylum 8-30, 925G3
19 Croatians rptd arrested in Australia 9-5, 706E3
W Ger rules out extraditn of Bilandzic, 2 others 9-13, 706F3
W Ger ruling on Bilandzic scored 9-13, 725F1, G1 *
US Croats killed 9-29, 11-22; threats, violence rptd; Yugo secret police blamed 11-29, 933E3
Busic killed in Paris 10-16, 805G1
Extraditn to W Ger of terrorist suspects barred 11-17, 906G1
US convicts 2 for W Ger emb seizure 12-1, 933B3
US chrgs 6 in Tito murder plot 12-1, 933C3

Foreign Relations (misc.)—*See also 'Croatian Issues' above, 'Monetary, Trade, Aid & Investment' and 'UN' below*
Pro-Sovt Tito foe kidnap chrgd 1-24, sentenced 4-13, 292G1
Middle East, Ethiopia policy talks in US 3-7—3-9, 194A1
Tito rptdly asked US, N-S Korea talks 4-5, 4-19, 277A3
Italy completes Cavcat poison cargo recovery 4-25, 330E3
Bulgaria disputes Macedonians 6-15—6-25, 531B1
Tito scores USSR-US dispute 6-20, 519D2
Cuba Eritrea role rptd opposed 6-21, 584B3
Tito warns nonaligned vs Cuba, USSR, West 7-25, 583B2
Albania details China dispute, cites '68 defns pact stand 7-30, 635E1
USSR scores China premr Hua re visit 8-5, 8-21, 8-27, 675E3

1979

Medicine & Health
PHS smoking rpt warns 1-11, 23C1
Carter budgets pregnancy preventn 1-22, 44A3
Marijuana use rptd 2-12, 140C2
Lung cancer rate rptd 3-5, 195E3
Male smokers rptd down, female smokers up 4-27, 970C3
Pot use rptd up 5-21, 492G2
Virus found to cause diabetes 5-23, 471F3
Mass abortn-consent law voided 7-2, 559G1-D2
Immunizatn progrm rptd effective, childhood diseases rptd down 9-11, 736D3
Pope warns vs drugs, sex 10-1, 757D2
Pot use risks rptd 10-14, 971F3, 972A1, C1

Military Issues
Army eases male recruiting standards 7-6, 519C2
Draft registratn defeated by House 9-12, 724G2-B3
Draft registratn backed by McCarthy 11-13, 868G2

Religion
'78 church attendance rptd 1-5, 24D1
Pope in US 10-1—10-7, 757D1, 758F2

YOUTH Conservation Corps—*See under U.S. GOVERNMENT—INTERIOR*

YUCCA Flat, Nev.—*See NEVADA*

YU Chiu-li (Yu Qiuli)
Rpts '79 econ plan 6-21, 484B3
US-China trade pact signed 7-7, 523A3

YUEHUA, Guo
Loses table tennis tourn 4-10, 527F1

YUGOSLAVIA—*See also COMECON, DISARMAMENT—Geneva Committee, GATT, IDB, NONALIGNED Nations Movement, OECD, WARSAW Pact*
'79 budget, inflatn rptd 1-5, 334G1
Tito '78 divorce, remarriage rptd 2-4, 176C1
Gas truck, Greek bus collisn kills 30 3-14, 240E3
Heart disease preventn study rptd 3-19, 219F1
Djilas warned, dissident crackdown seen 4-8—4-9, 334F1
Quake kills over 200 4-15, 316D3
Dolanc demoted 5-16, 430A3
Energy conservatn measures rptd 5-23, 397D1
Train collisn kills 60 9-13, 800C2
Djilas fined 10-15, 838D2

Foreign Relations (misc.)—*See also 'Monetary' below*
Cambodia-Viet conflict statemt 1-6, 11C2
Aides in Cambodia escape to Thailand 1-8, 10A1
Bhutto executn scored 4-4, 247G1
Tito visits USSR, reaffirms nonaligned committmt 5-16—5-18, 379D3
Pope visit to Poland gets wide coverage 6-2, 413C2
Pol Pot Cambodia forces backed 8-30, 674D3
UN membership listed 695B3
Austria fire kills tourists 9-28, 918C1

1980

Aug jobless rate rptd 9-5, 684A1
Sept jobless rate rptd 10-3, 783E2
Oct jobless rate up 11-7, 867D1
Nov jobless rate rptd 12-5, 938C1

Medicine & Health
Stuttering, genetics link rptd 1-5, 63B3
Cigarette smoking data rptd 1-14, 40G2
VD epidemic rptd, NGU rise blamed 2-5, 157G3
Utah abortn parental notificatn case accepted by Sup Ct 2-25, 187G3
Schl newspaper censorship power upheld 6-13, 582G3
Medicaid abortn funding limits upheld by Sup Ct 6-30, 492A1
Mich contraceptive distributn case declined by Sup Ct 10-6, 782G2

Military Issues—*See under U.S. GOVERNMENT*

Presidential Election (& Transition)
GOP plank scores Carter 7-10, 506A3
Dem conv keynote speech 8-11, 612A2*, A3
Kennedy Dem conv speech 8-12, 614G1
Dem platform plank adopted 8-13, 614D3
Carter, Reagan TV debate 10-28, 814G1
Reagan renews submin wage support 12-11, 956E2

Religion
'79 church attendance rptd 1-4, 7G3
Bible reading survey rptd 1-18, 157F1
W Ger RC ldrs denounce traditionalism 11-19, 905F2

YOUTH International Party (Yippies)
Rubin joins investmt firm 7-30, 638G2
Hoffman surrenders in NY 9-4, 713G1

YU, Tom
Convicted of murder 3-10, 238A2

YUGA Xona, Gregaria
Abducted 2-1, slain 2-2—2-3, 98E2

YUGOSLAVIA—*See also COMECON, CSCE, GATT, GENEVA Committee, IDB, NONALIGNED Nations, OECD*
Pvt sector growth urged 6-5, 468C3
Econ centralizatn set 9-18, 833G1

Foreign Relations (misc.)—*See also 'Monetary', 'UN Policy' below*
USSR Afghan invasn scored 1-6, 11B1
USSR, Bulgaria warned re territorial claims 1-15, 1-18, 49E2; US vows defnse 2-13, 110D1
CP boycott of Eur parley rptd 4-2, 254F3
Europn CPs meet 4-28—4-29, 327C2
Tito lauded by USSR 5-4, funeral attended by world ldrs 5-8, 338E2, B3
Iran release of US hostages sought 6-25, 474C3
Polish govt chngs rptd 8-25, 642C2
Poland strike setlmt, RC role lauded 8-31, 659B1
Afghan aide defects to W Ger 10-25, 827A3
Iraq war supplies shipped via Saudi ports 11-20, 894F2

1976

Tito in Latin Amer, Portugal 3-9—3-22, 256C2
Greek trade pact 3-16, 333C2
Sovt aide held as spy 4-6, 256B1
Sadat visits 4-8—4-9, 275D2
Reps at Czech CP Cong 4-12—4-16, 289G1
Politika shuts Prague bur 4-30, 341A3
Eur CPs meet, cong set 5-4—5-6, 341F1
Tito in Greece 5-10—5-13, Turkey 6-8—6-10, 543C3
At E Ger SED Cong 5-18—5-22, 381B2
Mil sales to Ethiopia rptd 5-19, 364A3
IMF OKs loans 5-24, 5-27, 6-1, 543E3
Sovt spy sentenced 5-25, 542C3
IDB entry set 6-3, 465D3
5-yr export plan adopted 6-20, 594G1
Tito meets Brezhnev 6-28; attends E, W Eur CP conf 6-29—6-30, 461F1, D2
6-mo export rise rptd, trade curbs eased 6-30, 594A2
Austria minorities bill opposed 7-6, 554A3
Rumania pres visits 9-8—9-10, 734G2
Tito cancels visits 9-10, 9-13, 9-16, 734F2
Addresses IAEA conf 9-27, 760F3
Czech defects to Italy 9-27, 852C1
Sovt role a US pres debate issue 10-7—10-12, 762A1-763F1; 10-26, 800A1, 800D2, 803B1-D1, 804F2; 10-27, 10-28, 910B1
French amb killed in mishap 11-6, 910G1
Brezhnev visits, denies Sovt threat 11-14—11-17, 909D3
Austrian Slovenes backed 11-14, 923F1
EEC discusses trade pacts 11-15, 955G1
Armed forces rptd ready 11-17, 910C1
US gets assurances on Sovt exports 11-25—11-27, 1012C1
Offers UN Assemb Geneva conf amendmt 12-6, 914B2
Giscard visits Tito 12-6—12-27, 1012A2
Iraq ldr ends visit 12-14, 954A1
Turk drug smuggling rptd 12-29, 1012A2

Sports

Olympic results 7-18—7-31, 573D3, 574A1, G1, 575A1, 576A3

U.S. Relations

US to resume arms sales 1-13, 1-14, 55B1
Atty for US cos sentenced 3-10, 223G3
US citizen's '75 arrest upheld 3-17, 256E1
Dow Chem oil deal OKd 3-26, 256G1
Tito scores Sonnenfeldt statemt 4-14, 277A2
US citizen pardoned 6-4, freed 7-23, 559A2
Dem platform text cites re Sovt 6-15, 477F2
Jailed US citizens rptd 7-26, 7-27, 559F2
Tito attacks amb re US citizen case 7-31, 594D1
Croats seize TWA jet 9-10—9-12, US scored 9-12, 685A1
Harriman visit canceled 9-16, 734A3
Carlos' presence denied 9-17, 722B1
Ford, Carter debate 10-6, 741C3
Ford debate gaffe scored in US 10-7—10-12, 762A1-763F1
Ford, Carter debate Sovt threat issue 10-22; rebuttals 10-26, 800A1, 802D2, 803B1-D1, 804F2; 10-27, 10-28, 910B1
US cong fact-finders visit Eur 11-5—11-21, 880F1
US amb resigns 11-17, 910B2
Richardson visits, gets assurances on US secrets 11-25—11-27, 1012C1

1977

Albania scores Tito, China dispute cited 9-2, 710C1
Albania anti-China purge rptd 9-9, 731A1
Mojsov elected UN Assemb pres 9-20, 713B1
Torrijos visits 9-30—10-1, quotes Tito advice 10-6, 792C2
Tito in France, Portugal, Algeria 10-12—10-20, 844E2
UN pollutn conf ends, Medit pact reached 10-21, 876B2
Sadat trip delayed 10-27, 844E2
Pro-Sovt exiles rptd seized 11-22, 12-17, 1018A3
Egypt amb quits 12-1, 930F2
Bauxite base price OKd 12-7, 975E1

Helsinki Agreement—*See EUROPE—Security and Cooperation*

Human Rights

Djilas, dissidents issue rights pleas; govt scores forgn coverage 2-2—2-15, 139F2
Czech scored re dissidents 2-7, 115A1
Helsinki compliance conf set 3-9, 173A1
Djilas backs US stand 3-13, 226G1
Passport petitn rejected 4-25, 315C1
Djilas cousin jailed 5-6, 437E1
Tito scores US stance 5-21, 398D2
Helsinki preparatory conf opens 6-15, 473A1
Prisoners freed; Eur protesters, newsman ousted 6-15, 473G1
Helsinki protesters ousted 6-28, 7-7, 606D2
Amnesty Intl lists jailed lawmakers 9-5, 753C2
Mihajlov freed 11-24, gen amnesty declared 11-29; Carter lauds 11-25, 956F1

Obituaries

Petrovic, Dusan 7-21, 604F3

U.S. Relations

US modifies duty-free list 2-28, 189E3
Eximbank loans OKd 3-2, 309B1
Djilas backs Carter on rights 3-13, 226G1
Croat '76 TWA hijackers convicted 5-5, 451G2
US OKs reactor parts sale 5-20, 398F2
Mondale sees Tito, rights stance scored 5-21, 398A1, D2
Eagleburger confrmd amb 6-7, 499E3
Croats invade UN missn 6-14, 497B2
2 US protesters ousted 6-28, 606D2
Croat hijackers sentncd 7-20, 7-21, 642A2
US neutron bomb ban plea 8-8, 640A3
Kardelj visits 9-28—10-4, 785D3
Mil cooperatn set 10-13, 785F3
Carter lauds Mihajlov release 11-25, 956A2

1978

Hua visits 8-21—8-29; Africa, Mideast agrmts reached 8-25—8-27; Tito hails 8-28, 674G2-C3, 675A2-A3
Albania scores Hua trip 9-3, 678B1

Helsinki Agreement—*See EUROPE—Security and Cooperation*

Monetary, Trade, Aid & Investment

US bars chrome duty hike 1-29, 80F3
'77 trade deficit rptd 2-2, 519A3
US arms deal rptd 3-8, 194C1
Albania-Greek trade pact signed 3-28—3-30, 374E2
US A-fuel export license deferral rptd 5-20, 408B2
US favored natn trade status cited 7-8, 534D2
US jet engine sale rptd, '61-79 sales cited 9-28, 758D1

Sports

Fischer plans to play Gligoric 10-20, 843D2

UN Policy & Developments

Bogicevic signs with US Cosmos 1-4, 23A2
Rights Comm condemns Israel 2-14, 99A2
Disarmament sessn ends, little progress seen 6-30, 523B1
Assemb member 713G3

U.S. Relations

US bars chrome duty hike 1-29, 80F3
US issues rights rpt 2-9, 102G1
Tito visits, joint statemt issued 3-6—3-9; ethnic emigres picket 3-7, 193G3-194F1
A-fuel export license deferral rptd 5-20, 408B2
Mihajlov in US, speaks on rights 6-6, 504G2
Tito warns vs world war 6-20, 579D2
US favored-natn trade status cited 7-8, 534D2
2 Croatian bombs defused in NYC 8-14, 706D3
2 Croatians seize W Ger emb in Chicago 8-17, 706E2
Pan Am to end Belgrade svc 9-7, 701G1
Ljubicic visits 9-24—9-29; jet engine sale rptd, '61-79 sales cited 9-28, 758D1
US Croats killed 9-29, 11-22; threats, violence rptd; Yugo secret police blamed 11-29, 933E3
2 Croatians convicted for W Ger emb seizure 12-1, 933B3
6 Serbs chrgd in Tito murder plot 12-1, 933C3

1979

Helsinki Agreement—*See EUROPE—Security and Cooperation*

Monetary, Trade, Aid & Investment

'78 paymts deficit rptd 1-5, 334A2
Uganda aid rptd 5-28, 429C2
US confrms Warsaw Pact arms shipmt 8-1, 627A1
IMF-World Bank mtgs in Belgrade 10-2—10-5, 779F2

Obituaries

Kardelj, Edvard 2-10, 176B3

Sports

UEFA Cup results 5-2, 5-16, 776B3
2 climb Everest 5-13, 392A3

U.S. Relations

US A-accident media coverage rptd 4-11, 323D1
Serbian hijacks jet 6-20, surrenders 6-21; sentncd for '75 Chicago bombings 6-22, 491E2
US confrms Warsaw Pact arms shipmt 8-1, 627A1
US denies spy aid 8-9, 664D2

1980

Government & Politics—*See also other appropriate subheads in this section*

Tito ill, leg amputated 1-5—1-20, 49C2
Tito dies, replacemts named 5-4; funeral held 5-8; facts on, photo 338G1-339C2
Mijatovic installed pres 5-15, 381G3
Doronjski named top CP ldr 6-12, 487G2
Mojsov named CP chief 10-20, 810C1

Monetary, Trade, Aid & Investment

Gold prices soar 1-2—1-18, 30B3
Mex '80 oil imports seen 1-15, 60B2
EC 5-yr trade pact signed 4-2, 365A3
China joins IMF 4-17, 302E2
Albania trade increase rptd 5-2, 356F2
OECD sees deficit reductn 6-6, 468E3
Dinar devalued 6-6, exports rptd up 9-18, 833A2, E2
Financial controls tightened 9-18; Eur, Arab loans rptd 9-20, 833G1

Obituaries

Gosnjak, Ivan 2-8, 176C1
Tito, Josip Broz 5-4, 338G1-339C2

Sports

ABC wins '84 Winter Olympic rights 1-24, 206F1
Moscow Olympic results 7-20—8-3, 588B3, D3, 622D1-624D3
Chess Olympiad results 12-7, 972B3

UN Policy & Developments

Rights comm anti-Sovt Afghan res absentn 2-14, 123E3
UN Charter backed 6-25, 474B3

U.S. Relations

Yugo independence backed 1-18, 49G2
Carter vows defns vs Sovt threat 2-13, 110D1
Tito in detente appeal 2-21, Carter responds 2-25, 139A3
Carter lauds Tito, vows Yugo support 5-4; funeral absence scored 5-8, 338E2, B3
Carter visits, backs indepndnc 6-24; joint communique issued 6-25, 474D2-C3

1976

YU Hui-yung
Praises Mao poems 1-3, 9F2
YUMIN, Vladimir
Wins Olympic medal 7-31, 576C3
YUN Po Sun
Signs anti-Park statemt 3-1, wife detained 3-4, 176F2
Faces probe, wife freed 3-10, 223B1
Sentenced 8-28, 655D1
Sentence reduced 12-29, 1013G2
YURCHENYA, Marina
Wins Olympic medal 7-21, 575A3
YURKADULER, Muzaffer
Son killed 4-8, 315B2

1977

YU Hui-yung
'76 arrest, replacemt rptd 1-29, 98C2
Suicide rptd 11-8, 882D3
YUN Po Sun
Sentence stayed 3-22, 306C1
Police raid govt foes 4-13, 305G3
Sees US offcl on rights 5-26, 441B1
Questns release of Park foes 7-19, 551E3
YUN Yat
Identified as Cambodia culture min 10-3, 780C1
YU Tai Wan
Vs Carter on rights 3-16, 203B1

1978

YUIRA, Nestor
Chuquiago released 4-18, 619A1
YUNGE, Guillermo
Arrested 1-13, banished 1-14; US protests 1-17; ct ruling rptd 1-31, 210C1
YUN Po Sun
Signs dissident document 2-24, 135F2
YUNUPINGU, Galarrwuy
Sees Fraser, OKs uranium dvpt 9-8, 721D1
YU Tai-chung
Loses Inner Mongolia post 10-23, 814B2
YZAGUIRRE, Raul
Scores House ethics com 10-12, 832A1
Scores House com illegal alien plan 12-20, 1010F2

1979

YUNESI, Ibrahim
Named Kurdish gov gen 3-25, 228F3
YUN Po Sun
On Park funeral com 11-3, 843E3
Freed from house detentn 11-6, 844D1
Vs Chung on dissidents 11-28, 928G2
YURICK, Sol
Warriors released 2-9, 174F3
YU Sok Sil
Sentncd for Park slaying 12-20, 997D1
YU Teng-fa
Arrested 1-21, 116E1

1980

YU Hak Song, Gen.
Named KCIA head 7-14, takes office 7-18, 566A2
YUNG, John
Stoner convicted, sentncd 5-14, 405C1
YUN Po Sun
Sentncd 1-25, spared 1-29, 101D1
Amnestied 2-29, 195D3
YU Yang Soo
S Korea energy min 5-21, 395D1

Z

1976

ZABLOCKI, Rep. Clement J. (D, Wis.)
Reelected 11-2, 831A3
ZACCAGNINI, Benigno
Bids Socialist cooperation 1-9, 29B2
Christian Dems reelect 3-3—3-7, 254G1
Reds bar oppositn role 6-30, 497B2
ZACHRY, Pat
NL pitching ldr 10-4, 796A1
Reds win pennant 10-12, 796F1
In World Series 10-16—10-21, 815B3
Named rookie of yr 11-23, 952F1

1977

ZABEL, Steve
NFL officiating scored 12-18, 1020F1
ZABLOCKI, Rep. Clement J. (D, Ill.)
'76 spec interest gifts rptd 2-4, 128G3, 129C2, F2
ZACCHINI, Hugo
Media suit affirmed 6-28, 557F3
ZACHRY, Pat
Traded to Mets 6-15, 644B2

1978

ZABALZAGARAY, Nibia (D. 1974)
Death cited re rights abuse 3-14, 292C1
ZABLOCKI, Rep. Clement J. (D, Wis.)
Sees Korea mil aid unlikely 2-22, 204D1
Backs CIA evidence on Cuba role in Zaire 6-8, 442D2
Gets Israel plea on Leb Christns 8-7, 638D2 *
Reelected 11-7, 852C4
PAC contributions rptd 12-24, 1008E1
ZABLOCKI v. Redhail
Wis remarriage law voided 1-18, 65D1
ZACCAGNINI, Benigno
Urges force vs terrorists 3-20, 200E2
Receives Moro letter 4-4, 246F3
Pertini elected pres 7-8, 558E1
ZACHRY, Pat
Rose gets 37th straight hit 7-24, 618F2

1979

ZABIK, Chester J.
Allied Chem indicted 4-17, 985B3
ZABLOCKI, Rep. Clement J. (D, Wis.)
Intl Relations Com chrmn 1-24, 71D1
ZACCAGNINI, Benigno
Seeks anti-terrorism steps 5-3, 331D2

1980

ZABINSKI, Andrzej
Gets Poland CP post 9-19, 720F2
ZABLOCKI, Rep. Clement J. (D, Wis.)
Protests Saudi film telecast 5-8, 375B3
Reelected 11-4, 844C4
ZACCAGNINI, Benigno
Christian Dems bar CP Cabt posts 2-21, 134D1
Piccoli made party secy 3-6, 194E2

1976

ZADEH, Hussein Ali-
Ousted re sugar deal 2-10, 156C3
ZADOK, Chaim
Rpts censorship plan deferred 1-20, 34B3
ZAFFARONI, Alejandro
'72 campaign gift listed 4-25, 688C1
ZAGALA, Maj. Gen. Rafael
Replaced as PI army cmdr 3-27, 255B3
ZAGLADIN, Vadim
On independent CPs 4-20, 341A2
ZAGORIANAKOS, Gen. Dimitri
'67 treason chrg dropped 2-28, 221F3
ZAHEDI, Ardeshir
Middendorf censured 3-16, 200C3
ZAHERI, Hamid
Asks West aid UN agri fund 8-5, 643A2
Sees OPEC price plan 8-27, 643G1
ZAHN, Tony
Edwards elected 11-2, 822B3
ZAIRE, Republic of (formerly Democratic Republic of the Congo)—*See also AFRICAN Development Bank, DISARMAMENT—Geneva Committee, NONALIGNED Nations Movement, OAU*
French, W Ger jet deliveries rptd 1-16, 36C1
French Mirage purchase cited 1-16, 36C2
Listed as 'not free' nation 1-19, 20E3
Shaba copper projct halt rptd 1-27, 335D2
Cabt, party bur shuffled; 'Mobutism' ambs named 2-4, 270B2
At intl econ conf 2-11—2-20, 148B1
Currency devalued, pegged to SDR 3-12, 270G2-A3
IMF OKs SDR purchase, standby loan 3-23, 270D2
'75 export earnings, copper data rptd 3-23, 270F2
Total IMF oil loan rptd 4-1, 340E2
At France-Africa summit 5-10—5-11, 355A3
Mercenary trial cites 6-11, 480E2
Forgn debt rescheduled 6-17, 488B1
Amb to Uganda sees Amin 7-16, 548F1
Olympic withdrawal rptd 7-21, 528B3
Viral fever hits 10-7, 795G2
Amb to France, Japan named 10-18, 949G3
Govt, forgn banks OK debt paymt plan 10-20, 11-8, 890B2
Viral fever contained 11-21, virus named 11-30, 931B3
Angola Issue
US arms airlift chrgd 1-6, denied 1-7, 3D2
MPLA northn drive rptd 1-9, 1-15, 16D2
FNLA scores US arms aid 1-11, 16F2
FNLA rpts parachute attack 1-12, 16F2
Ethiopia warned vs MPLA ties 1-13, 16A1
Chrgs Cuba aids MPLA attack 1-15, 16C3
Protests Dilolo raid to UN Cncl 1-16; warns USSR, Cuba 1-17, 1-19, 36A1
French, W Ger jet deliveries rptd 1-16, 36C2
Unita hints airlift aid 1-18, 35A3
MPLA chrgs jet attack 1-20, 36B1
Portugal resumes refugee airlift 1-22, 53F2
Unita asks Westn aid 1-29, 57C1
Troop plunder in north chrgd 1-29, 58B1
UK mercenary recruitmt rptd 2-2, 82A1
MPLA sets terms for ties 2-2, 82E2
Mercenary transit barred 2-3, 82B1
Mobutu meets Neto; MPLA recognitn, pact set 2-28, 163G1
US chrgs French covert aid 3-9, 228D3
EC aid set 4-6, 276C2
FLEC raids on Cabinda rptd 4-20, 5-12, shuts border 5-20, 480D3
US talks on Sovt arms buildup rptd 4-30, 318A3
US in talks on Sovt, Cuba roles 6-17—6-19, 467B1
Angola refugees rptd 10-2, 862D2
Rhodesian Relations—*See RHODESIA*

1977

ZACK, Albert
Union shop issue deferred 7-18, 555B3
ZADOK, Chaim
Sees Rabin on Ofer probe 1-1, 8G1
ZAEV, Petr
US tour results 1-29—2-5, 263C2
ZAGIRNYAK, Alexander
Hijacks jet 7-10, surrenders 7-12, 537F1
Sentenced 11-10, 988E2
ZAGNOLI, S. A.
On uranium cartel 6-16, 480C1
ZAHABI, Mohammed Hussein al-
Abducted 7-3, slain 7-4; body found 7-7, 525D3-526B1
Alleged slayer seized 7-8, 542A2
Moslem fanatics indicted 8-11, 636F2
ZAHEDI, Ardeshir
Mediates Hanafi surrender 3-11, 192A3

ZAIRE, Republic of (formerly Democratic Republic of the Congo)—*See also DISARMAMENT—Geneva Committee, NONALIGNED Nations Movement, OAU*
UN Assemb member 4D1
'60s Cuba role cited 1-9, 19A1
Nyiragongo volcano erupts 1-10, 204G2
Mobutu visits Belgium 1-17—1-24, 199G3
Uganda claims invasn threat 2-22, 141D2
Uganda drops US exit bar 3-1, 141B2
Shaba copper mining data 207D3
Uganda mercenary aid rptd 3-28, 308G1
Army cmdr rptd replaced 4-5, 265D2
At France-Africa summit 4-20—4-21, 316F3
Cabt dismissed, electns vowed 7-1, 583A1
Kasenga named premr 7-6, 583B1
28 army officers retired 7-11, 583B1
Natl bank gov ousted 8-11, 641F2
Umba named forgn min 8-13, 641E2 ★
Mobutu reelected 12-2, Cabt resigns 12-7, 1019F2
Monetary, Trade & Aid Issues (including all foreign economic developments)—*See also 'Shaba' below*
Cabinda rebel aid rptd 1-8, 86A2
IMF OKs trust fund loan 2-4, 87F2
CIA paymts to Mobutu rptd 2-19, 124F1 ★
Citicorp reps visit 3-17—3-26, loan effort rptd 4-28, 394C2
US copper prices rise 3-18—3-22, 209C2
IMF OKs loans 4-26, 394B2
'68 Israeli uranium purchase rptd 5-30, 416B3
Forgn debt rescheduled 7-7, 583D1
Angola chrgs UNITA aid 7-26, 675A1
US authorizes arms aid curb 8-4, 668E1
Cheap exports blamed for US copper industry woes 10-31, 859B1
In Zambia, Peru copper cutback agrmt 12-7, 975A1

Obituaries
Mobutu, Marie 10-22, 872F2
Shaba Invasion (& developments)
Shaba invaded from Angola 3-8, FLNC claims credit 3-11, 207A2; map 207A3
US sets aid, cites copper threat 3-14, 3-16; Angola role rptd 3-18, 207G2
Shaba fighting continues 3-17, Mobutu visits Kolwezi 3-19, 207D2
Belgium, France send arms 3-17, 3-18, 207G2
Castro denies invasn role 3-21, 249G2; 4-8, 283B1
US aid asked 3-21, 260G3
Angola chrgs border bombings 3-22, 260F3
China chrgs USSR role 3-23, 261E1
Rebel support, little fighting rptd 3-24, 3-25, 260E3
Nigeria mediatn OKd 3-24, 261A1
US natls leave 3-30, 261A1
Mutshatsha falls, cmdr replaced 3-31, 260B3
Rally apathy rptd 4-3, AP rptr ousted 4-4, 261B1
Cuba ties cut 4-4, US doubts Cuba adviser role 4-5, 261C1
Egypt seeks US arms vs Sovt threat 4-5, 245C1
Kissinger scores invasn 4-5, 261E1 ★
Fighting lull rptd 4-6, rebel ldr vows Mobutu overthrow 4-8, 266A1
Mobutu asks Morocco aid 4-7, Moroccan troops arrive 4-9; France defends airlift 4-10—4-12, 265A1
Forgn support, arms aid rptd 4-7—4-12; Angola scores 4-11, 265E2
USSR denies invasn role 4-7, 4-12, 265G2
US, UK mercenary bid denied 4-7, 317E3
Mobutu chrgs Sovt-Cuba invasn role, army plot 4-9, 265C2
Young bars US interventn 4-11, 271B1
US sets arms aid, bars troops 4-12, 4-13, 265E1
Zambia chrgs border bombings 4-13, 266C1
W Ger sets aid 4-14, 317F3
Fighting resumes at Kazenze 4-15, Morocco troops join offensive 4-16; Mutshatsha retaken 4-25, 316G3
French troop role rptd; planes, advisers recalled 4-15—4-21, 317F2
Morocco chrgs Cuban interventn 4-18, 317G1
USSR scores forgn meddling, chrgs Israel aid 4-18, 317D2
EC vs forgn interventn 4-18, 317E2
France-Africa summit cites 4-20—4-21, 316E3
Weapons, POWs displayed 4-20, press tour war zone 4-25, 317D1

1978

ZACK, Allen
Watts scores Meany 12-11, 961A1
ZAENTZ, Saul
Lord of Rings released 11-15, 970A2
ZAGORIA, Samuel D.
FEC nominatn withdrawn 8-12; named to CPSC 9-29, confrmd 10-10, 831C3
ZAHABI, Mohammed Hussein al- (d. 1977)
Slayers executed 3-19, 211E2
ZAHEDI, Ardeshir
US assures shah backing 12-7, 953F3
In talks on lifting march ban 12-8, 953E2
ZAHIR Shah Mohammad (Afghan ex-king)
Loses citizenship 6-14, 538B1

ZAIRE, Republic of (formerly Democratic Republic of the Congo)—*See also DISARMAMENT—Geneva Committee, GATT, NONALIGNED Nations Movement, OAU*
Uprising rptd 3-7, 13 executed in Mobutu plot 3-17, 230G2-B3
Mobutu defends govt vs corruptn chrgs 6-21, 652D2
Exiles offered amnesty 6-24, rejectd 6-26, 652E2
Nguza freed 7-14, 652E2
Cholera outbreak rptd 10-12 927E2
Cobalt productn drop rptd 11-21, 1021C2
Foreign Relations (misc.)—*See also 'Shaba Invasion' below*
Angola chrgs forgn raids 2-1, 87G3
Burundi refugees rptd by UN 3-1, 395C3
Angola rpts attack repulsed 3-24, 238B3
UN rpts S Africa arms embargo compliance lags 4-28, 377B2
W Ger satellite testing site rptd 4-29, 382G1
Mobutu in Paris for Franco-African summit 5-23, 382A3, 417E3
China forgn min ends visit 6-7, 441D2
Egypt dep forgn min visit rptd 6-13, 441G1
Paris conf OKs emergency aid 6-13—6-14, 477F3-478F1
China naval advisers rptd 6-18, 478C2
Mobutu sets exile amnesty, OAU, UN role 6-24; exiles reject 6-26, 652C2
China mil envoys arrive, arms aid review seen 6-24, 652G2
W Ger to seek EC copper aid 6-30, 584D1
Angola reconciliatn set 7-17, 562D1
W Ger telecommunicatns deal rptd 7-19, 652A3
Angola diplomatic ties OKd 7-29, 646A1
Angolan pres visits 8-19—8-21, 645G3
UN Assemb member 713G3
Belgium cholera aid rptd 10-12, 927E2
Angola RR reopened 11-4, 1021D2
Creditor natns OK aid 11-10, 1021A2
Obituaries
Adoula, Cyrille 5-24, 440D2
Shaba Invasion (& developments)
Secessionist rebels launch invasn; occupy Kolwezi, Mutshatsha 5-11; Angola, Cuban, USSR backing rptd 5-14, 359G1 ★
Shaba Prov maps 359D2, G2 ★
Mobutu seeks US, W Eur aid 5-15, 359A2
Rebel infiltratn thru Zambia chrgd 5-15, 359A3
US alerts troops 5-16, evacuates natls 5-17; Europeans rptd slain 5-18, 359B2
Cuba sees US envoy, denies role 5-17; France rpts Cuba, Sovt advisers spotted 5-19, 382A1
French, Belgium troops launch rescue operatn, occupy Kolwezi; US, UK airlift supplies 5-18—5-20, 318A1
Europn massacres rptd 5-19, death toll estimated 5-23, 381D1
French, Belgium rescue operatn rift rptd, chrgs exchngd 5-19—5-22; Mobutu scores Belgium 5-21, 381C2-382A1
Carter gets CIA evidence on Cuba role 5-19, evidnc doubted 6-2—6-9, 442A1, D1
US airlift role backed 5-20, 383E1
Belgium troops withdraw 5-22, French bar exit 5-23, 381F1
USSR scores rescue operatn 5-22, 382D1
E Ger denies rebel aid 5-22, 382F1
Franco-Africa summit backs French role 5-22—5-23, 382F2
Rebels seek econ disruptn, Mobutu downfall 5-23, 382E2
Kaunda denies Zambia role 5-23, 395B3
Mobutu sees Tindemans, Giscard; pan-African peace force backed 5-23—5-25, 417D3
US offcls dispute Cuba role evidence, seek clarificatn 5-24, 5-26, 418A2
French Legionnaires quit Kolwezi 5-25—5-28; death toll estimated 5-30, 417E2
USSR chrgs French, Belgian troops massacred whites 5-25, 417C3
Carter accuses Cuba 5-25, 5-30; Cuba denies 5-30, 418A1, E1
Gromyko disputes Carter on USSR role; Powell, Vance rebut 5-27, 422E1-A2
Casualty data rptd 5-27, 6-3, 441B2
Kolwezi gen gets death 5-27, sentnc commuted 6-1, 441C2
Brzezinski scores USSR, Cuba, E Ger 5-28; Sovts denounce 5-30, 399B1-F1
Morocco aid sought 5-29, 417G3
Mobutu chrgs rebels kill forgn hostages 5-30, 417A3
Europn mil aid rptd sought 5-31, 417A3

1979

ZADIKYAN, Stepan
Executn re '77 subway blast rptd 1-30, 100F2
ZAGARI, Mario
Defeated for EC Parlt pres 7-17, 537D2
ZAGORIA, Samuel D.
FEC vacancies filled 2-21, 130C3
ZAHEDI, Ardeshir
Emb entry bar sought 1-15, 26G2
Urges shah to stay in Morocco 1-21, 49E3
Out as Iran amb to US 2-6, 81D2
Iran urges assassinatn 5-13, 357F1
ZAHERI, Hamid
Welcomes IEA oil demand cuts 3-2, 162C2
ZAIM, Abdul Sattar
Slain 9-16, 755A1

ZAIRE, Republic of (formerly Democratic Republic of the Congo)—*See also DISARMAMENT—Geneva Committee, GATT, NONALIGNED Nations Movement, OAU*
Copper, cobalt mining recovery rptd 1-25, 2-15, 137A3
Food shortages, riots rptd 2-6, 137A3
Econ, pol status, corruptn rptdly worsens; Mobutu overthrow seen 2-11, 2-14, 3-5, 215D1-B2
Nguza reinstated in Cabt 3-6, 215C2
Currency devalued 8-28, 999C1
Kasai massacre rpt 11-8, denied 11-15, 11-8, 999G1

Foreign Relations (misc.)
CAE anti-riot aid rptd 1-20—1-21, 62A2
E Ger ties restored 1-20, 117A2
Belgium to send troops 2-6, 137F2
IMF anti-corruptn drive rptd 2-11, 215A2
Angola RR rptd unusable 2-15, 137D3
Belgian troops leave 3-15, 215D2
W Ger co rocket tests stopped 4-27, 411A3
Iran chrgs US interventn 6-5, 425F3
IMF grants loan 8-28, 999A1
UN membership listed 695B3
Creditor natns OK aid 11-29, 999D1
Forgn debt rescheduled 12-12, 999E1

Shaba Invasion (& developments)
E Ger ties restored 1-20, 117A2
Mining recovery rptd 1-25, 2-15, 137A3
Refugees total rptd 2-22, 201F1; 140,000 return 3-6, 215D2
African peace force exit rptd 8-14, 733F3

1980

ZADROZYNSKI, Edmund
2d trial rptd 4-21, 381D2
ZAEV, Pyotr
Stevenson decisns for 3d Olympic gold medal 8-2, 589E1, 622B2
ZAHIRNEZHAD, Gen. Ghassaem Ali
Named Iran army head 6-19, 464E2
ZAHIR Shah, Mohammad (Afghan ex-king)
Wali offers resistance role 5-3, 349G2
Afghan nurse rpts Sovt losses 10-8, 827D2

ZAIRE, Republic of—*See also GATT, GENEVA Committee, NONALIGNED Nations, OAU*
Currency devalued 2-22, 356B2
Kinshasa students riot vs transport prices 4-16—4-17, 356D2

Foreign Relations (misc.)
Olympic boycott movemt joined 2-1, 84G3
Debt rescheduling set 4-23, 356F1
Forgn debt at $4 bln; IMF loan blocked, new terms set 4-24, 356A2
Pope visits 5-2—5-6, 7 die in mass violence 5-4, 341B2, 363D1
Uganda chrgs invasn support 10-10, 794E2

1976

U.S. Relations—*See also 'Angola' above*
Copper projct funding rptd ended 2-2, 335D2
Kissinger visits 4-28—4-30, 293E2, 295G1, 318A3
Rumsfeld visits, pledges arms 6-17—6-19, 466F3
Paris Club defers debt 6-17, 488A2
US arms aid authorized 6-30, 532F3
A-aid cited 7-23, 739G2
Eximbank sued re loan 8-9, 621B2
Kissinger sees Mobutu 9-22, 718A1
'77 aid funds signed 10-1, 806D3
Eximbank suits dropped, new paymt plan OKd 10-13, 890G2
Banks OK debt paymt plan 10-20, 11-8, 890B2
'76 Eximbank loan default rptd 11-11, 915A3

ZAITSEV, Aleksandr
Wins Olympic medal 2-7, 159B1

ZAITSEV, Yuri
Wins Olympic medal 7-26, 576F2

ZAJICEK, Pavel
Sentenced 9-23, 851E3

ZAK, Moshe
Vs Israel censorship plan 1-18, 35A1

ZALAQUETT, Jose
Arrested 4-5, exiled 4-12; US protests 4-19, 310D2

ZALMEN or The Madness of God (play)
Opens 3-17, 1014C3

ZAMA, Alicia Escalante de
Lists Uruguay torture deaths 3-5, 207C3

ZAMBIA—*See also AFRICAN Development Bank, COMMONWEALTH of Nations, NONALIGNED Nations Movement, OAU*
Listed as 'partly free' 1-19, 20D3
Kaunda uses emergency powers 1-28, 77D3
Budget set, no copper earnings seen 1-30, 503C2
Student unrest shuts univ 2-9, arrests rptd 2-14, 503E2
Kwacha devalued 7-9, 950A1

Angola Issue
FNLA scores US arms aid 1-11, 16F2
Kaunda uses emergency powers 1-28, 77E3
Copper transit halted 1-30, 77G3
Unita guerrilla war declaratn issued 2-12, 162G2
MPLA recognitn barred 2-18, copper seizure chrged 2-20, 163E2
EC aid set 4-6, 276C2
MPLA recognized 4-15, 335E1
Kaunda sees Neto 8-21; ties, joint comm set 9-22, 862F2 ★
Angola refugees rptd 10-2, 862D2
Ousts UNITA 12-27, 995D3

Foreign Relations (misc.)
Secret Israel talks rptd leaked 35A1
Emergency powers invoked for Namibia 1-28, 77E3
'75 forgn aid rptd 1-28, deficit total 1-30, 78A1
Tanzam RR backlog rptd 1-30, 78A1
At intl econ conf 2-11—2-20, 148B1
UK lecturer rptd arrested 2-14, expelled 3-27, 503E2

1977

POWs: Cubans trained in Angola 4-20, 4-26, 317E1
Mobutu ends USSR exchng progrm, chrgs Zambia raid 4-20, 317F1
US Coca-Cola aid request denied 4-21, 317C3
Amin arrives, pledges aid, scores Angola 4-22, 317B2
US vs tank sale, doubts Cuba troop role 4-22, 317A3, 321B3
Uganda force sent, Amin arrives 4-28, 394C1
E Ger rebel support chrgd 4-30, ties cut 5-2, 394F1
Egyptian pilots arrive 5-2, 394A1
Musungi ambush rptd 5-3; Sanikosa, Kasaji retaken 5-7, 5-11, 393G3
Senegal scores forgn interventn 5-3, 394E1
Forgn newsmen ousted 5-6, 394G1
Ivory Coast scores US cautn, Young defends 5-12, 398D3
Central African Empire forces rptd 5-13, 394D1
Sudan lauds French aid 5-17, 450E1
Zaire troops retake border towns 5-20—5-26, 490C1
Moroccan troops leave 5-22, Egypt exit set 5-25, 490D1
Cuba confrms Angola pullout halted 6-9, 456G1
Mobutu thanks Giscard for aid 6-9—6-10, 490E1
Mil reorganizatn set 7-11, 583C1
French aid cited 7-18, 597G1
Saudi aid revealed 7-19, 583C1
Forgn min, tribal chief treason chrgd 8-13, 641D2
Forgn min gets death sentnc 9-13; commuted 9-15, 731C1

ZAJFRYD, Mieczyslaw
Named Poland transport min 12-17, 987G1

ZALDIVAR, Andres
'Plot' chrgd 3-11, denied 3-13, 219C3

ZAMBERLETTI, Giuseppe
Offers resignatn 9-1, govt accepts 9-8, 783B1

ZAMBIA—*See also COMMONWEALTH of Nations, NONALIGNED Nations Movement, OAU*
Price hikes set 1-28, 243F3
Cabt reshuffled, posts created 4-24, 490F1
2 escape SWAPO prison camp 5-1, 349E2
Uganda rpts Amin, rebels meet 6-8, 487A1
Bank head urges natlizatn end 6-16, 490C2
Mudenda ousted, Chona replaces 7-20, 583F1
Copper belt squatters riot 7-21, 583G1
Milner ousted 8-2, 674E3
'76 econ improvemt rptd 8-10, 674G3
Curfew set 9-3, lifted 9-20, 811A1

Foreign Relations (misc.)
UN Assemb member 4D1
Forgn exchng rules eased 1-28, 243F3
Podgorny visits 3-26—3-29, sees black natlst ldrs 3-28, 247G2, E3, 249D3
Zaire bombings chrgd 4-13, 266C1; Zaire accuses USSR 4-20, 317F1
Zaire ousts newsmen 5-6, 394A2
Cuba, Somalia aid offer OKd 7-8, 536F1
Uganda exile plot rptd 8-8, 641F1

1978

Brezhnev scores NATO role 5-31, 423G1
Saudi, Egypt aid pledges rptd 6-1, 6-7, 6-13, 441G1
Morocco vows aid 6-2; US airlifts peace force, evacuates French Legionnaires 6-4, 441A1
Mutshatsha rptd recaptured from rebels 6-4, 441B2
Cuba advisers rptd by rebels 6-5, 418A2
US rescue operatns detailed 6-5, 441D1
Westn natns meet on pan-Africa force, back short-term aid 6-5, 441E2
US extends airlift; Senegal, Gabon troops join Morocco peace force 6-6, 441C1
China pledges Mobutu support 6-7, 441D2
Tanzania vs pan-Africa force, US role; defends Cuba, USSR presence 6-8, 441G2
African natns rptd split on peace force 6-8, 442C1
Mobutu sets defns force 6-9; Belgium, French training planned 6-10, 441F1
Angola to disarm rebels; denies Cuba, USSR aid 6-10, 441A2
Castro denies Cuba role 6-13; US disputes 6-12—6-14, 442F2, 443A1
Paris conf OKs aid 6-13—6-14, 477F3-478F1
Belgium govt crisis resolved 6-15—6-19, 612F2
French end pullout 6-16, 478F1
800 Kolwezi bodies rptd 6-16, 478A2
US begins pullout 6-16, 478B2
USSR scores NATO 6-17, 464G3
Aid vs rebel buildup rptd asked 6-17, 478C2
China navy advisers rptd 6-18, 478C2
Togo, Ivory Coast troops rptd 6-19, 478A2
US seeks Angola aid 6-20, 487A3
US envoy in Angola 6-21—6-26, 487G3
Zambians rptd ousted 6-21, 652A2
Mobutu claims Cuban prisoners 6-22, US doubts 6-23, 652G1
Libya scores French role, Zaire scores Libya 7-7, 561E2
Kolwezi death toll rptd at 855 7-10, 652E1
900 rptd arrested 7-11, 652B2
Mining operatns rptd resumed 7-14, 652A3
Nigeria scores West role 7-18, 561A2
Refugees cite killings, torture by troops 7-27, 652A2
Copper indus troubles cited 10-20, 805B1
USSR-France tensns cited 10-29, 830F3
Castro scores US chrgs 12-9, 1016E1

U.S. Relations—*See also 'Shaba Invasion' above*
CIA ex-agent rpts '75 Angola war role 5-8, 367C2, G2
Vance asks econ reform, Angola border setlmt 6-20, 487F2-B3
US releases aid, Angola moves cited 8-16, 652F2
McDonnell Douglas paymts rptd 12-15, 982F2

ZAITSEV, Alexander
Wins world figure-skating title 3-9, 316E3

ZALDIVAR Cadenas, Eugenio Enrique
Flies to Miami 10-21, 880D2

ZAMBIA—*See also COMMONWEALTH of Nations, NONALIGNED Nations Movement, OAU*
Cholera outbreak rptd 1-30, 927F2
Kapwepwe, Nkumbula enter pres race 8-1, 617D1
White farmer sentncd for arms cache 11-23; others warned 11-26, 912E1
Kaunda reelected, UNIP rule chrg cited 12-12, 989D2

Economy & Labor (domestic)
Consumer subsidy end set, copper revenue fall cited 1-1, 55D3
Austerity budget set 1-27, 95C2
Wage controls, other measures planned 3-9, 333B3
Econ crisis detailed 3-20, copper output cut 3-30, 333F2, A3
Austerity measures agreed 4-26, 333E2
Crop failure feared 10-10, 783A3
Arms spending rise set, mil strength rptd 11-20, 912B1

Foreign Relations (misc.)—*See also 'Monetary, Trade, Aid & Investment' below*
Namibia torture rpt released 2-10, 114B1
Namibia rebel imprisonmt cited 113E3
Angola rpts Zaire attack 3-24, 238C3
Westn indep plan for Namibia backed 3-26, 248G2

1979

U.S. Relations—*See also 'Shaba Invasion' above*
US issues rights rpt 2-10, 107G2
US rpts econ aid mismanagemt 2-15, Mobutu support end urged 3-5, 215E1
Citibank loan rptd dropped 3-26, 999F1
McDonnell Douglas paymts alleged 11-9, 886G1, D2

ZAKES, Carle Marie
City Suite opens 4-2, 711B2

ZALMANSON, Sylvia Y.
Reunited with Kuznetsov 4-29, 317B2

ZALMANSON, Volf Y.
Release cited 4-29, 317D2

ZAMBIA—*See also COMMONWEALTH of Nations, NONALIGNED Nations Movement, OAU*
Chipanga, others freed 5-6, 374C3
Drought cited 11-5, 844A3

Foreign Relations (Misc.)
UN seeks Namibia compromise 2-26, S Africa rejcts plan 3-5, 171G1, D2
Pretoria demands SWAPO bases control 3-19–3-22, 354D2
Uganda govt recognized 4-12, 288B2
S Africa-SWAPO clashes rptd 4-27, 354A3
E Ger defense min visit rptd 5-23, 406E2

1980

U.S. Relations
Aid corruptn seen 2-28, 356C2
Debt rescheduling set 4-23, 356G1

ZAITSEV, Alexander
Regains Eur figure skating title 1-23, withdraws from world competitn 3-12, 470F2
Wins Olympic medal 2-17, 155F3

ZAMBIA—*See also COMMONWEALTH of Nations, NONALIGNED Nations, OAU*
Troops, armed men battle 10-16; curfew imposed 10-23, 833G2
Anti govt coup plot chrgd, arrests cited 10-27, 833F2
Kaunda shuffles Cabt 12-4; lifts curfew 12-8, 969E2, A3

Foreign Relations (misc.)
UN Assemb Afghan issue abstentn 1-9, 25F1
Zimbabwe air links restored 1-9, 31D3
USSR arms purchase announced 2-7, 119E1
Regional econ unity mtg hosted 4-1, 243C1, D1
Tito funeral held 5-8, 339B1

1976

Aide in bombed Cambodian town 3-2—3-4, 238B2
Total IMF oil loan rptd 4-1, 339G3, 340E2
Kissinger visits 4-26—4-27, 293A1, C2, 294D2, 295F1
Holds SWAPO members, Nujoma support cited 5-4, 386G2
Kissinger sees forgn min 5-5, 318C3
US arms aid authorized 6-30, 532F3
China turns over Tanzam RR 7-14, 560A1
S Africa border attack chrgd 7-16, 539G3
Olympic withdrawal rptd 7-21, 528B3
UN condemns S Africa raid 7-30, press rpt 8-16, 653E2, A3
IMF OKs standby loan 8-2, 949G3
Low confrmd US amb 8-4, 808B1
S Africa border clash 8-7, 653A3
New Sovt amb arrives 8-10, 950B1
Asks arms vs S Africa, Rhodesia 8-19, 622A1
Kaunda in US talks 9-9, 9-16, 681F1
US Namibia, Rhodesia rebel aid asked 9-15, 681C1
Kaunda backs gen Namibia conf 9-17, 698C1
Kissinger sees Kaunda 9-20, 717G2
US '77 aid funds signed 10-1, 806D3
Rhodesian Relations—*See 'African Relations' under RHODESIA*

ZAMYATIN, Leonid M.
Named to Central Com 3-5, 195G2
Says Egypt arms deal honored 4-6, 275C2
ZANA, Jean-Robert
Named defns min 9-5, 924F2
ZAPPIA, Joseph
Olympic fraud charged 6-30, 529B2
ZARB, Frank G.
Detained in W Bank, denies chrgs 5-7, 338F2
Ends Saudi, Iran visit 5-10, 340A1
On gas price decontrol 11-23, 991G2
Vs Alaska oil surplus export 11-30, 991E3
On US oil output 12-29, 991C3
ZARMI, Meir
Quits party post, rejoins 3-5, 253C3
ZASIMOV, Lt. Valentin E.
Defects to Iran 9-23, 773D2
Returned to USSR 10-25; protests 10-28, 11-1, 854B2
ZAUSNER, Eric Roger
Succeeded as FEA asst admin 3-23, 232D1
ZAVYALOV, Nikolai
On Moscow meatless Thursdays 5-14, 420G3
ZAWI, Mohammed Az-
Confrms Mirage transfer to Uganda 7-18, 548C2 ★
ZAYAD, Toufik
Soldiers raid home 3-30, 227C1
Israel rpt on Galilee Arabs 9-8, 683B2
On Arab Galilee strike 9-28, 738E1
ZDOVC, Edvin
Slain in W Ger 2-7, 224E1
ZECKENDORF, William
Dies 9-30, 970D3
ZEELAND (Dutch warship)
In Intl Naval Review 7-4, 488C3
ZEFERETTI, Rep. Leo C. (D, N.Y.)
Reelected 11-2, 830A2
ZEIDLER, Frank P.
Final pres vote tally 12-18, 979C2
ZEILLER, Gerard J.
Loses NH primary for gov 9-14, 705D1
ZEITLIN, Arnold
Pl ousts 11-2; protests 11-5; security cited, denies chrgs 11-6, 855D1
ZELAZNICK, Sheldon
House com subpoenas 8-25, testifies 9-15; released from subpoena 9-22, 748G3, 749A1
ZENGER, John Peter
Bolles wins press award 12-9, 971G3
ZENTENO Anaya, Joaquin
Controversy over death, Guevara executn grows 4-14—5-17, 415B3
Slain in Paris 5-11, 350D3
Torres murder scored 6-3, 415G2
ZEPPOS, Panayotis
Dropped from cabt 1-5, 73D2
ZERBO, Lt. Col. Saye
Replaced in Upper Volta Cabt 2-9, 269D3

1977

French min cuts short Africa tour 8-18, 662F2
SWAPO OKs Namibia plan 8-19, 699F3
Sweden lets debts stand 10-12, 904A1
Namibia contact group tours 11-21—12-7, 1016E3
In Peru, Zaire copper cutback agrmt 12-7, 975A1
Rhodesian Relations—*See RHODESIA*
U.S. Relations
US modifies duty-free list 2-28, 189E3
US natl seeks refuge 3-2, 144E3
Young vs US 'cold war' policy 4-11, 271D3
Young visits 5-23, 400A1
US amb sees Nkomo 5-31, 457E1
US amb sees Nkomo 7-7, 536B1
US bars arms aid 8-4, 668B1
Cheap exports blamed for US copper industry woes 10-31, 859B1
Namibia contact group in tours 11-21—12-7, 1016E3

ZAMORA, Alfonso
'77 boxing champion 12-17, 970A2
ZAMORA, Ronney
Convicted of murder 10-7, 807F2
Sentenced to life term 11-7, 907F3
ZAMORA, Ruben
Arrested 4-22, 373D3
ZANGIRA, Juma Thomas
Arrested 7-29, sentenced 10-5, 806A1
ZANZIBAR—*See TANZANIA*
ZARATE, Carlos
TKOs Rodriguez 12-2, 970D3
'77 boxing champion 12-17, 970A3
ZARATE Azuino, Manuel
Clashes force 6-mo leave 3-3, 240F1
ZARDINIDIS, Nikos
Named Greek pub works min 11-28, 925B2
ZARETSKY, Irving
On Jewish cult trend 4-18, 492F2
ZAVUROV, Amner
Jailed 1-13, US sens protest 2-19, 226A2
ZAYRE Corp.
Mass blue laws upheld 4-21, 388G1
CPSC sues 8-22, 651F3
ZEFFIRELLI, Franco
Christ TV film showings set 5-16, 395G2
ZENITH Radio Corp.
TV import quota plea rptd 3-14, 208E3
Japan electronics import duties ordrd 4-12, 318A2
Nevin backs Japan TV export limit 5-20, 416B1
Japan import duties order reversed 7-28, 587A1
Shifts TV mfr to Mex, Taiwan, ends stereo-making; layoff data rptd 9-27, 974D2
ZERILLI, Joseph
Dies 10-30, 872B3
ZERO Population Growth Inc.
Abortn alternatives proposed 7-19, 786D3

1978

Namibia rebels deny Kapuuo killing 3-28, 229D2
Zaire chrgs Shaba rebel infiltratn 5-15, 359A3
Kaunda in UK, US 5-15—5-23, 395C2
Zaire rebel retreat rptd 5-23, 381A2
Zaire rebels, troops clash 5-24, 417B3
Shipanga freed 5-25, 475G3
Namibia rebels OK talks 6-11, 475D3
Zaire rptd ousting natls 6-21, 652A2
W Ger chancellor visits 6-28—6-30; defends S Africa ties 6-30, 584B1
Westn indep plan for Namibia OKd 7-12, 547F2
Kaunda eulogizes Kenya pres 8-22, 639B3
S African troops raid 8-23—8-26, 669C2
UN Assemb member 713G3
Monetary, Trade, Aid & Investment
Copper revenue decline cited 1-1, 55D3
IMF team visits 2-14—3-7; kwacha devalued 3-17; IMF OKs loans 4-26, 333D2
Tanzania port backlog affects trade; other transport problems cited 3-8, 170A1
Tanzania port backlog rptd eased 3-30, 333G2
UN rpts S Africa arms embargo compliance lags 4-28, 377B2
UK hikes '78-79 aid 5-15, 395D2
US '78-80 econ aid set 5-18, 395G2
World Bank group sets aid 6-29, 617G1
W Ger vows EC copper aid, defends S Africa trade 6-30, 584D1
UK Rhodesia sanctns violatn scored 9-18, Callaghan meets Kaunda 9-22, 756F2-B3
US bars econ aid authorzn 9-26, 734G1
Tanzania port backlog continues 10-1, 783F2
Rhodesia rail link opposed by Mozambique, Tanzania 10-7; reopened 10-10, 783E2
Copper indus troubles cited 10-20, 805C1
UK sends arms 10-27, 10-28, 829E3-830A1
Rhodesian Relations—*See RHODESIA*
U.S. Relations—*See 'Monetary, Trade, Aid & Investment' above*

ZAMIR, Yitzhak
US Arab freed 10-18, expelled 10-20, 783D2
ZAMORA, Ricardo
Dies 9-7, 778C2
ZAMORA, Ronney
Loses suit vs TV networks 9-26, 759F2
ZANUCK, Richard D.
Jaws 2 released 6-16, 619E2
Benchley book record movie price rptd 9-1, 759E2
ZANZIBAR—*See TANZANIA*
ZARATE, Carlos
KOs Davila 2-25, 379B2
KOs Hernandez 6-9, 600G1
Gomez KOs 10-28, 969F1
ZAVALI, Michael
CIA ex-aide convicted as spy 11-18, 940G1
ZEA Hernandez, German
Colombia interior min 8-7, 629C3
ZEFERETTI, Rep. Leo C. (D, N.Y.)
Reelected 11-7, 851E3
ZEGHAR, Messaoud
Denies kidnaping sister 7-6, 531E3
ZELAYA, Fausto
Chamorro murder role chrgd; denies 1-22, 73G1
ZELAYA, Jose
Asks Somoza resign 10-5, 777F2
ZELAYA Rojas, Fernando
On Somoza unpopularity 2-27, 151A1
ZELAZ, David
Eyes of Laura Mars released 8-4, 970C1
ZELLERBACH, Harold Lionel
Dies 1-29, 96G3
ZEMECKIS, Robert
Wanna Hold Your Hand released 4-21, 619E2
ZEMSKY, Vyacheslav
Plans whaling end 12-8, 1001B3
ZENITH Radio Corp.
Import duty rebuffed by Sup Ct 6-21, 491G2
ZENITH Radio Corp. v. U.S.
Zenith import duty rebuffed by Sup Ct 6-21, 491G2

1979

Israel setlmt policy opposed in UN comm rpt 7-14, 551B2
Commonwealth conf held 8-1—8-7, 589A1
UN membership listed 695C3
Kaunda in London 11-8—11-10, 881E1
Namibia demilitarized zone OKd by UN conf 11-16, 889C3
UK bars Zimbabwe raid compensatn 11-20, high comm stormed 11-22—11-23, Allinson recalled 11-24, 899F2
Zimbabwe Relations—*See ZIMBABWE Rhodesia*

ZAMBRANO, Jose Alberto
Visits Nicaragua for Andean Group 6-11, 446E3
Scores US on Cuba naval maneuvers 10-23, 824B2
ZAMBRANO Velazco, Jose Alberto
Venez forgn min 3-10, 192C3
ZAMORA, Ruben
Named to El Salvador Cabt 10-22, 813A1
ZAMYATIN, L. M.
Cited in SALT II summit communique 6-18, 457D1
ZAND-Karami, Vali Mohammed
Executed 3-13, 179G3
ZANGGER, Claude
On Swiss probe of Pak A-sales 5-2, 342F1
ZANGWILL, Israel (1864-1926)
King of Schnorrers opens 11-28, 956B3
ZANON, Lorenzo
Decisns Evangelista for Eur heavywgt title 4-18, 412G3
ZANUCK, Darryl F.
Dies 12-22, 1008G3
ZANZIBAR—*See TANZANIA*
ZAPATA, Jose Luis
Venez informatn min 3-10, 192C3
ZAPLOTNIK, Jernej
Climbs Everest 5-13, 392A3
ZAPPOLA, George
Indicted 3-6, 220D2
ZARATE, Carlos
Pintor decisns for WBC bantamwgt title 6-3, 839A1
ZARDIS, Stephen J.
Sues 5 Agent Orange mfrs 11-26, 904G2
ZARGHANI, Maj. Gen. Sadegh Mozafar
Executed 6-17, 544B3
ZASLOVE, Arne
Biography: A Game opens 4-5, 711E1
ZEFFIRELLI, Franco
Champ released 4-3, 528F1
ZEITMAN, Jerome M.
Just You & Me Kid released 7-27, 820D1
ZELAYA Coronado, Jorge Luis
Replaced in OAS post 10-24, 824E2
ZELLER, Gen. Andre
Dies 9-18, 756G3
ZEMBRZUSKI, Rev. Michael M.
Pauline Fathers crime probe rptd 11-9, 905G3
ZEMECKIS, Robert
1941 released 12-14, 1008A1
ZERO Population Growth Inc.
Illegal alien issue detailed 1-29, 127G1

1980

S Africa delays talks re Namibia 5-12, 374D2
UN Namibia plan backed at black African summit 6-2, 466C3
China pledges Tanzam RR aid 9-2, 731B2
S Africa denies coup backing chrg 10-27, 833F2-B3
UN Cncl seat replacemt set 11-13, 896E1
UN Namibia talks schedule agreed 11-24, 967B2

ZAMBRANO, Jorge Marcos
Found dead 2-14, 335E2
ZAMBRANO, Jose Alberto
Rpts Cuban emb casualties 1-19, 103D1
ZAMBRANO Cardenas, Ramiro
Meets DR emb captors 3-2—3-13, 180C2
ZAMORA, Efrain
Murdered 5-16, 464B1
ZAMORA Rivas, Mario
Slain 2-23, 149G1
Party member quits junta 3-4, 172E1
ZAMYATIN, Leonid M.
French athletes deliver rights appeal 8-2, 590F2
Alleges West backs Polish oppositn 11-16, 910E2
ZANDAROWSKI, Zdzislaw
Ousted 8-24, 641F1
ZANON, Lorenzo
Holmes TKOs 2-3, 320F1
ZANZIBAR—*See TANZANIA*
ZAPATA, Hilario (Sugar)
Decisns Nakajima for WBC junior flywgt title 3-24, 320C3
TKOs Nakajima 9-17, 1000G3
ZAPPIA, Joseph
Chrgd re fraud 5-9, 406E2
ZAPRIANOV, Dimitar
Wins Olympic medal 7-27, 623D1
ZAPRIANOV, Petar
Wins Olympic medal 7-21, 623C2
ZAREMBA, Ota
Wins Olympic medal 7-28, 624F2
ZARGAR, Ghulam Sediq
Denies defectn plan 7-21, 590B2
ZAVALOV, Alexander
Wins Olympic medal 2-23, 155C3
ZAYAN Candal, Jorge
Murdered 9-11, 786B2
ZEA Hernandez, Herman
Bars M-19 guerrilla talks 4-21, 311D3
ZEBRO, Col. Saye
Overthrows Upper Volta pres in coup 11-25, 924A2
ZEFERETTI, Rep. Leo C. (D, N.Y.)
Reelected 11-4, 843E3
ZEITMAN, Jerome M.
How to Beat the High Cost of Living released 7-11, 675A3
ZEMAN, Jack
Past Tense opens 4-24, 392F3
ZENITH Radio Corp.
In RCA video disk pact 3-3, 239C3
ZENON, Carlos
Disrupts Navy maneuvers 1-19, 94D1
ZERDA, Lt. Alex Joseph de la
Arrested 1-25, 94A1
ZETTLER, Michael
Paris Lights opens 1-24, 136E3
ZHANG, Nikolai Petrovich
Gets 7 yrs for spying in China 7-20, 563A2
ZHANG Aiping
Named deputy premier 9-10, 677F1
ZHANG Chunqiao (Chang Chun-chiao)
Gang of 4 trial set 9-27, delayed 11-1, 859B1
Indictmt aired 11-15—11-18, trial starts 11-20, 877A1, D2
Severe penalty asked 12-29, 974A3
ZHANG Wenjin
Scores USSR at Geneva conf 2-5, 108A1
ZHAO Dan
Dies 10-10, 876G3

1976

ZHIVKOV, Todor
Sees Castro 3-8—3-12, 251C3
Reelected CP pres, 1st secy; lauds Brezhnev 3-29—4-2, 250B1, E1
Visits Greece 4-9—4-11, 333A2
ZHIVKOV, Zhivko
Bulgarian Politburo drops 4-2, 250C1
ZHOLOBOV, Lt. Col. Vitaly
In Salyut 5 missn 6-22, 527B2
Returns from Salyut 5 8-24, 684E1
ZIEGLER, Judge Donald E.
Pittsburgh teachers end strike 1-26, 95A3
ZIEGLER, Larry
Masters results 4-11, 272G1
ZIETEK, Jerzy
Polish State Cncl member 3-25, 268D2
ZIGIC, Radovan
Sentenced for emigre plot 3-12, 223B3
ZILBERMANN, Victor
Wins Olympic medal 7-31, 574C1
ZILERI Gibson, Enrique
Amnestied 5-7, returns to Peru 5-14, 500C1
ZILH, Mehti Mohammed
Seized in hijack try 8-11, 579A1
Sentenced 11-16, 861D2

ZIMBABWE—*See RHODESIA*

1977

ZHIVKOV, Todor (Bulgaria head of state)
Velchev ousted 5-12, 451F2

ZIA ul-Haq, Gen. Muhammad
Seizes power 7-5, 509B1 *
Names civil servants 7-7, 509B2
On coup plan, vs Bhutto trial 7-8, 544E3
Issues martial-law rules 7-10, 544A1
Bhutto to be freed 7-14, 545D1
States aims, electn rules 7-27, 599F1
Bhutto vs martial law 7-29, 599F1
Hints Bhutto murder link 9-6, 707G2
Ends emergency 9-15, 730B3
Ousts chief justice 9-22, 765A3
Delays electns, extends martial rule 10-1, 765B2
Meets PNA ldr, vows '78 vote 10-13, 802G3
Martial law upheld 11-10, 885D2
Extends detentn powers 11-13, 885C2
ZICARELLI, Joseph
Laetrile smugglers sentncd 5-16, 508A3
ZIEGLER Jr., John A.
Named NHL pres 6-22, 548B3
ZIELINSKI, Victoria (1942-57)
Smith confesses to murder 4-25, 396F1
ZILERI Gibson, Enrique
Govt lifts Caretas ban 1-1, 21B2

ZIMBABWE—*See RHODESIA*
Signs with Rangers 11-8, 989E3

1978

ZHIVKOV, Todor
Offers improved Yugo ties 6-15, 531C1
Markov murdered, radio rpts cited 9-11, 749A1
ZIA Rahman, Maj. Gen.—*See RAHMAN, Ziaur*

ZIA ul-Haq, Gen Muhammad (Pakistani president)
Clears Wali Khan 1-1, 8A1
UK prime min meets 1-12, 37G1
Forms advisory council 1-15, 75G1
Meets India forgn min 2-6—2-7, 113A1
Vs intl pleas for Bhutto 3-27, 229C1
Forms new Cabt 7-5, 559B1
Scores French A-contract revisn, denies China agrmt 8-23, 668A2
Sworn pres 9-16, 740C2
Backers score Bhutto 10-2, 775A2
ZIEGLER, John
On Murdoch drug suspensn 7-24, 656E3
ZIGDIS, Ioannis
DCU split rptd 3-16, 374B1

ZIMBABWE—*See RHODESIA*

1979

ZHLUKTOV, Viktor
Sovts win Challenge Cup 2-11, 118D3

ZIA ul-Haq, Gen. Muhammad (Pakistani president)
Declares Islam natl law, sets prisoner clemencies 2-10, 116E2
Scorns Bhutto clemency pleas 2-14, 116B2
Ignores Bhutto clemency plea 4-1; **Bhutto executed 4-4;** protests ensue, actn defended 4-4—4-5, 247A1-A2
Forms interim govt 4-21, 313A3
India reverses A-arms stand 8-15, 646D1
Denies A-arms plan, asks US aid resumptn 9-22, 794D2
Electn rigging chrgd 10-4, sets compromise 10-7, 794G1
Postpones electns 10-16, 794C1
Scores US Emb raid 11-21, 893E1, E2
Carter contacts in Afghan crisis 12-30, 974A2
ZIEFF, Howard
Main Event released 6-22, 820G1
ZIGLER, Judge Donald
Sentences ex-Rep Clark 6-12, 442G2

ZIMBABWE Rhodesia (formerly Rhodesia)—*See also GATT*
British Relations—*See also 'Transition' below*
All-parties conf plan abandoned 1-17, 39C3
Owen pessimistic on majority rule 2-2—2-3, 98D3
Smith chrgs betrayal 2-28, 170A1
Tories link sanctns end, fair electns 4-11, 285C3
Lusaka raid condemned 4-13, 294B1
UN Cncl electn vote abstentn 4-30, 332A2
New UK govt elected 5-3, 338D1, B2
Tories seek lasting setlmt 5-15, 358B3
UK observers back electns, Duff begins talks 5-16, 359E2
Commonwealth asks recognitn bar 5-18, 393F2
Carrington sees Vance, UK-US initiative termed dead 5-21—5-23, 393E2
London to send envoy 5-22, 393C2
Nigeria warns vs recognitn 5-31, 393G1-B2
NATO warns vs ties 5-31, 416A1
Trade decisn awaited by US 6-12, 435C1
Thatcher, Carrington hint sanctns end 7-1, 7-10, 546C3
Muzorewa in UK, sees Thatcher 7-12—7-14, 546E3
BP natlzd by Nigeria 7-31, 584C3
Commonwealth plan agreed, text 8-6; reactn 8-6—8-9, 589A1-590C2
Muzorewa, Patriotic Front accept UK setlmt conf invitatn 8-15, 8-20, 638A1
London conf opens 9-10; const change, agenda debated 9-11, 9-12, 675D2
London conf deadlocked on const 9-13, Smith-Muzorewa rift revealed 9-15—9-16, UK proposal OKd 9-21, 9-24 717F2
US Sen aides' conf role rptd 9-19; UK denies protest 9-20, 718F1
New const offered 10-3, Muzorewa OKs 10-5, Patriotic Front rejects 10-8—10-11; unilateral talks start 10-16, 777B2
Smith quits conf, seeks white support re const rejectn 10-6, returns 10-12, 778D1
UK Tories support Thatcher, Carrington 10-10, 791G2
Patriotic Front gets grant re London conf 10-12, 778G1
Front-line natns on UK talks 10-17, 778C1
Patriotic Front OKs const 10-18, 844E1
Transitn govt by UK offered, talks deadlocked 10-19; Muzorewa OKs 10-27, plan outlined 11-2, 844D1, F1
UK retains forgn exchng controls 10-24, 813B3
Transitn talks continue 11-9—11-14, Patriotic Front OKs UK plan 11-15, 880F3
UK OKs partial sanctns lapse 11-14, 881G1
UK offers cease-fire plan 11-16, Muzorewa OKs 11-26, Patriotic Front accepts gen terms 12-5, 936G3
Zambia contacted re raids 11-20, 889E2

1980

ZHAO Ziyang
Politburo promotes 2-29, 171G3
Named China dep premr 4-16, assumes power 4-17, 351E1
Succeeds Hua; photo 9-10, 677C1
Vows govt reforms; sees Viet, Sovt war threat 9-11; chrgs Sovt 'aggression' 9-14, 706C3, F3
Giscard visits China 10-15—10-22, 829B3
Meets Thai premr on Cambodia conflict 10-30, 952B1
ZHELANOV, Sergei
Wins Olympic medal 7-26, 624A1
ZHIVKOV, Todor (Bulgarian head of state)
At Moscow summit on Poland 12-5, 929E1
ZHOU Enlai (Chou En-lai) (1898-1976)
Hua '76 successn criticized 9-28, 788B3
Wang, Yao admit plot vs Deng appointmt 11-24, 975A2
Hua scored in press 12-16, 12-30, 975E3
ZHOU Yichi
Gang of 4 trial defendant 11-20—12-29, 975E2
ZIA Meng
Scores Jiang in Liu case 12-3, 975F1
ZIA ul-Haq, Gen. Muhammad (Pakistani president)
Scores USSR Afghan invasn 1-8, 10D3
Sees Sovt Afghan threat 1-12; warns vs move 1-15, 27D1
Vs call for war vs Sovts 1-13, 44B3
Asks no conditns for US aid 1-15, 27C1
Rpts Afghan army-Sovt clash 1-17, 44B1
Calls US aid package 'peanuts' 1-17; lauds new US vow 2-3, 83B1-G1
China forgn min visits 1-18—1-21, 44G2
US issues rights rpt 2-5, 87D1
US A-warning cited 2-27, 165G2
US aid offer dismissed 3-5, 165D2
Asks Afghan refugee camp inspectn 3-6, 205D3
Castro seeks to mediate Afghan feud 3-25—3-27, 271C2
Pak blocks, OKs UN vote on Iraq-Iran war 9-25, 9-28, 733F2
Says Afghan copters hit Pak border 9-26, 766A1
In Iran-Iraq peace mission 9-27—9-30; rpts failure 10-1, 734C1
ZIEGLER Jr., John A.
Suspends Bruins over NYC brawl 1-25, suspensn upheld 1-30, 198B3
Declares Stoughton free agent 10-3, 1000F2-A3

ZIMBABWE (formerly Rhodesia)—*See also COMMONWEALTH of Nations, GATT, OAU*
Press curbs announced 10-24, 833B3
British Relations—*See also ZIMBABWE—Transition*
UK jet lands in Salisbury 1-11, 31D3
UK sets aid 4-15, 301D2
Indepndnc proclaimed 4-18, 301C1
Mugabe seeks more mil trainers 5-9, 5-30, 468G3-469B1
Walls reveals electn void request 8-11, 731E2

1976

1977

1978

1979

UK High Comm in Zambia stormed re raid compensatn bar 11-22–11-23, 899F2
UK gov named 12-7, 937G1
UK ends sanctns 12-12, UN Assemb scores 12-18, 960E1
Cease-fire initialed by Muzorewa 12-15, Patriotic Front 12-17; Muzorewa asks clarificatn 12-18, 959G3
UK ends oil sanctns violatn probe 12-19, 976D3
Cease-fire, other agreemts signed 12-21, 976G2

Economy & Labor

Black-white wage gap rptd 99A1
Wankie air svc ended 2-22, resort hotels rptd closed 2-28, 170F2
'78 GDP drop, war toll cited 3-13, 3-15, 286E2
Cattle rustlers rptd active 7-8, 547C1

Emigration

'78 white data rptd 1-25, 62A3
Refugees data rptd 2-22, 201F1
Jan, Feb data rptd 3-29, 286D3
March, Apr data rptd 5-30, 435D1

Foreign Relations (misc.)—*See also 'Military', 'Monetary' and 'UN' below*

Commonwealth asks recognitn bar 5-18, 393F2
Nigeria warns US, UK vs recognitn 5-31, 393G1-B2
NATO warns US, UK vs ties 5-31, 416A1
S Africa trip by Muzorewa rptd 6-20, 490D2
Australia, US agree on recognitn terms 7-4, 501A1
Italian missionary killed 7-6, 546G3
Africa recognitn, Const chng linked 7-10, 546D3
OAU warns vs recognitn 7-21, 552F2
Commonwealth plan agreed, text 8-6; reactn 8-6–8-9, 589A1-590C2
Front-line natns linked to Patriotic Front acceptance of UK talks 8-20, 638E1
Patriotic Front admitted to nonaligned movemt 9-3, 675F1
Nigeria pres vows oppositn 10-1, 754C3
Front-line natns on UK talks 10-17, 778C1
Transitn plan sets Commonwealth natn role; rebel, refugee reentry 11-2, 844E2
Zambia pres in UK re transitn plan 11-8–11-10, Nigeria envoy 11-15, 881E1
Commonwealth natn peace force role OKd by UK 11-9, 881C1
Patriotic Front vs UK on Commonwealth force 11-19, 11-30; consults front-line natns 11-24–11-26, 937A1-E1
Forgn rptr curbs lifted 12-13; Polish newsman admitted 12-17, 960B2
Africa impact by UK accord seen 12-18, 968C2
Commonwealth peacekeeping forces arrive 12-23, 976D3

Government & Politics—*See also other appropriate subheads in this section*

Freedom House lists as partly free 12G3
Dispute personalities listed 170A2
Const draft publshd, Zimbabwe Rhodesia proposed as name 1-2, 7F2
Smith: black rule 'inevitable' 1-11, 39G3
Whites OK draft const 1-30, 76C3-77B1
Anti-bias laws enacted 2-2, 98G3
Smith to stay in politics; Sithole, others score 2-22, 170B1
Parlt ends last sessn, Smith scores UK 2-28, 169G3
Gabellah quits Sithole ZANU factn 3-5, 170F1
Electns held, black turnout praised 4-10, 4-17– 4-21; **Muzorewa wins,** asks intl recognitn, Sithole scores vote 4-24, 293A1-C2
Govt comm rules electn fair 5-3, 354F1
New Parlt convenes, Sithole factn boycotts 5-7; speaker, deputy chosen 5-8, 354C1
UANC ousts Chikerema 5-12, Muzorewa blocks 5-13, 359F2
Muzorewa defends new govt 4-29, 332D2
Senate elected 5-23, pres 5-28, 393F1
Muzorewa sworn 5-29, names Cabt 5-30, **govt installed, natn changes name 5-31, 393A1**
Chikerema, 7 MPs form party 6-20, 490F1
ZAPU detainees rptd freed 7-4, 547F1
Muzorewa bars Const chng, defends Smith role, repeats guerrilla amnesty offer 7-10, 546E2, A3
ZANU mtg; ends Assemb boycott 7-31, 586A3, E3
New flag raised 9-2, 676F1
Pol detainees freed 11-22, 937D2
Parlt dissolves, repeals '65 indepndnc act 12-11, 937A2; **for subsequent developments, see 'Transition' below**

Majority Rule—*See 'Government' above; for foreign reaction to majority rule, see other appropriate subheads in this section*

Military Developments

Salisbury home attacked 1-2, 7D3
'78, '79 death toll rptd 1-2; RC missionary found dead 1-3, 7E3
Casualties rptd 1-8, 1-27, 2-3, 99E1
Blacks, whites resist draft 1-10; men in 50s to be called 1-12, 40B1, C1
Mozambique attacks rptd increased 1-31, 99D1
ZANU frees 4 white prisoners 2-2, 99B1

1980

Economy & Labor

Mugabe assures whites 3-4, 161A2
Stock mkt reactn to Mugabe win 3-4, 162C1
Mugabe vows fast civil svc chngs 3-13, 198E1
Black worker strikes rptd 3-21, 301G2
Budget issued 4-20, 301A2
Minimum wage hike set 5-28, 412D1

Foreign Relations (misc.)—*See also 'Monetary', 'UN' below*

S African troops get transitn role 1-6, Mugabe scores 1-8, 31B3
Commonwealth peace force rpts guerrilla assemb success 1-7, 31B3
Air links restored, Zambia flight lands 1-9, 31D3
Black African natn ties improvemt seen 1-15, 48G3
Refugee return begins 1-21, 49E1
S Africa troops to leave 1-26, 88D2; exit begins 1-30, 118G3
Refugee return halted, Commonwealth force repatriatn role cited 2-25, 198G1
Commonwealth team calls vote fair 3-2; force exit starts 3-3, lauded 3-4, 162B1, F1, C2
Electn result reactn; Mugabe vows S Africa noninterference 3-4, 161C2, F2
Indepndnc marked 4-17—4-18, 301E1
Commonwealth of Nations, OAU joined 4-18, 301A2
Mozambique security vows rptd 5-30, 469B1
S Africa ties cut 6-27, OAU informed 7-4; Pretoria recalls senior staff 7-8, 509D2
Morocco war vs Polisario scored 7-1—7-4, 509E1
Mozambique pres in 1st state visit 8-4—8-9, 674C3
S Africa tie cut finalized 9-3, 690G3
Emigration rise rptd 9-30, 795E1
Somali US bases scored 10-9, 795C1

Government & Politics—*See also other appropriate subheads in this section*

Indepndnc proclaimed 4-18, 301C1
Cabt sworn 4-19, 301A2
Mugabe, Nkomo rift surfaces 6-27—7-26, 581A3
Walls resigns army post 7-17, 568D1
Tekere chrgd with murder 8-6, 621A1
Walls reveals electn void request 8-11, denies coup plot knowledge, racist chrgs 8-17; Mugabe asks Zimbabwe departure 8-29, rpts dismissal 9-17, 731D2
Smith urges whites cooperatn 8-31, 674C3
Mugabe vs Walls return 9-25, bar set 9-26, 755F1
Nkomo supporters arrested 11-21, 946E2
Munic electns early returns rptd 11-23, 946B3
Tekere freed 12-8, 946A2

Military Developments

Sinoia clash kills 7 rebels 1-1, 7A3
Govt army security role OKd 1-6, ZANU clash averted 1-7, 7E3
ZAPU, soldiers clash 1-10, 31E2
ZANU truce violatns chrgd 1-15, 1-22, 48F3, 49A1
Rival ZANU supporter slain 1-22, 80C2
13 killed in bus ambush 2-3, 118G2
Campaign-related violence 2-13—2-24; deaths rptd 2-27, 162A2, B3

1976

1977

1978

1979

Air Rhodesia flight downed 2-12; ZAPU claims credit, scores US, UK denunciatns 2-14, 136A3
Zambia, Mozambique rebel camps hit 2-17, 2-20, 136D3
Air Rhodesia, S Africa flights rptd cut 2-18, 2-22; resort hotels closed 2-28, 170F2
Plane hits mine, 4 die 2-19, 136E3
Salisbury airport shelled 2-19, 136E3
Angola ZAPU camps hit; Zambia Mozambique strikes rptd 2-23–3-1, 170G1
Botswana border train attacked 2-24, 170E3
Salisbury-S Africa traffic to get mil escort 2-27, 170E3
Econ toll rptd 3-13, 3-15, 286E2
Red Cross scores cruelty 3-20, 286B3
Mozambique rpts oil depot bombed 3-24; Red Cross plane hit 3-27, 286C3
ZAPU-Zambia tensions rptd 4-4, 294F1
Lusaka raided, Nkomo house destroyed; UK, UN condemn 4-13, 294B1
Botswana-Zambia ferry destroyed, Francistown raided 4-13, 294D1
Casualties rptd 4-14, 294E1
Oil storage depot hit 4-16, 294F1
Black electn precautns taken, 9 deaths rptd 4-17–4-21, 293G1
Salisbury bomb kills 1 4-25, 332E2
Mozambique camp raided 6-4, US scores 6-5, 435C1
Intensified war, US sanctns linked 6-13, 546G3
Nkomo rptd in E Ger re aid 6-19, 490F2
Lusaka, ZAPU camp strafed 6-26, 490E2
ZAPU-ZANU unity rptd unlikely 6-29, 547D1
Archbp Salisbury home attacked 7-4, 546F3
Italian missionary killed 7-6, 546G3
Guerrilla cattle rustling rptd 7-8, 547C1
183 ZANU troops killed 7-20, mil cmdr's dismissal sought 7-31, 586D3
New rebel amnesty offered 7-22, 638A2
RC missnaries rptd kidnaped by rebels 7-23, 638C2
Angola rpts S Africa raid refugee casualties 8-2, 617A3
Black draft increased 8-10, 638F1
ZANU-govt clash rpt issued 8-17, 638B2
Zambia rebel camps raided 8-22–8-23, 676C1
Jan-Aug death toll rptd 8-25, 676D1
School closure total rptd 9-2, 676E1
Martial law extended 9-4, 676F1
Mozambique army clash 9-5–9-7, 676A1
Abducted RC missnaries freed 9-11, 718C2
2 MPs killed by rebels 9-16, 9-21, 718B2
Mozambique ZANU camp destroyed 9-27–10-1, 778A2
Zambia camps raided 10-21–10-23, 11-1:,-11-3, 844A3
Zambia raids continue 11-18–11-19; Kaunda orders war alert 11-20, 899C2
UK High Comm in Zambia stormed re raid compensatn bar 11-22–11-23, 899F2
Zambia blames S Africa re raids 11-25, 899B3
S Africa troop exit sought by Patriotic Front; admits mil role 11-30, 937E1, B2
Zambia, Mozambique camps hit 12-9, 937D2
Soames halts raids 12-13, 960G1
Cease-fire signed 12-21, Commonwealth peacekeeping force arrives 12-23, 976G2, D3
Mozambique admits troop role 12-26, 976B1
Cease-fire in effect 12-27; rebel violatns, death toll rptd 12-28, 12-29, 976C3, F3
Tongogara killed 12-29, 976A1

Monetary, Trade, Aid & Investment

US copters ruled illegal 1-5, 7F3
WCC retains grants program 1-10, 23G3
UK Tories link sanctns end, fair electns 4-11, 285C3
US sen asks sanctns end 4-24, 293F2
US calls sanctns end 'premature' 4-26, UN votes retentn 4-30, 332G1-B2
Muzorewa asks US sanctns end, conditns S Africa aid 4-29, 332B2
US Sen votes sanctns end 5-15, action hailed 5-16, 359G1, C2
Carter keeps trade ban 6-7; Muzorewa scores, Mugabe lauds 6-8; Sen votes to end 6-12, 434D2-435C1, 438F1
US sanctns, intensified war linked 6-13, 546G3
UK hints sanctns end 7-1, 7-10, 546C3
Meat exports rptd 7-8, 547C1
Nigeria nationalizes BP 7-31, 584C3
UK sanctns cited re talks 9-16, 718C1
US sanctns end rptd seen by Sen aides 9-19, 718A2
WCC aids Patriotic Front 10-12, 778F1
UK retains forgn exchng controls 10-24, 813B3
UK sanctns end, Muzorewa OK of transitn plan linked 10-27, 844A2
Zambia corn shipmts blocked 11-5, 844E2-A3
UK OKs partial sanctns lapse 11-14, 881G1
US bars sanctns end 11-14, 881B2
UK ends sanctns 12-12, US 12-16; UN Assemb scores 12-18, 960E1

1980

ZAPU, ZANU start army training 2-25, 3-5, 198B2
Peacekeeping force exit starts 3-3, 162F1
ZANU supporters alleged slain 3-4, 161E2
2 whites sentencd in shooting spree 4-17, 301A3
Mugabe seeks more UK instructors 5-9, 5-30, 468G3-469B1

Monetary, Trade, Aid & Investment

Trade improvemt seen 1-15, 48G3
Zambia announces USSR arms purchases 2-7, 119F1
Mugabe: to honor debts 3-13, 198F1
Mugabe at regional econ unity mtg 4-1, 243D1
Tobacco sold openly 4-8, 301E3
Gold, forgn exchng reserves rptd 4-11, 301E2
UK, US set aid 4-15, 4-18, 301C2
UK amnesties sanctns violators 4-15, 301B3
Dutch bar S Africa oil embargo 6-27, 499A2
S Africa trade missn maintained 9-3, 691A1

Sports

Moscow Olympic results 7-20—8-3, 588C3, 622D2

Terrorism & Unrest

Indepndnc day violence 4-18, prisoners amnestied 4-21, 301E2
ZIPRA rebelln chrgd 6-27; ZANU, ZAPU clashes 7-9, 581D3
State of emergency extended 6-mos 7-23, 581F3
White farmer murdered 8-4, Tekere chrgd 8-6; students protest 8-8, 621A1
Guerrilla violence spreads, 4 killed 9-13—9-27; Mugabe pledges anti-violence fight 9-25, 795F1
Guerrillas clash near Bulawayo 11-10—11-11; Mugabe considers disarming 11-15, 888E3

1976

ZIMMERMAN, Augusto
Arrest rptd 7-23, 590G3
ZIMYANIN, Mikhail V.
Named to CP Secretariat 3-5, 195E2

1977

1978

1979

Zambia corn embargo lifted 12-17, 960F1
UK ends oil sanctns violatn probe 12-19, 976D3
UN votes sanctions end 12-21, 976A3, C3
Front-line states end boycott 12-23, 976D3

Transition Government (& developments)
UK gov Soames takes over, indepndnc ended 12-12, 936F3, 937A2
Soames halts executns; orders pol detainee review 12-13, 960G1, B2
Patriotic Front pol ban protested 12-13, 960B2
ZAPU office raided by police 12-14, 960A2
Thatcher on pact in US 12-17, 12-18, 968A2, C2
Patriotic Front pol ban lifted 12-21, 976G3
Mugabe home attacked, factnal tensn cited 12-22; ZANU hints separate electn role 12-30, 976B1
Peacekeeping force arrives 12-23, 976D3
Patriotic Front mil ldrs in Salisbury 12-26, 976E3
Cease-fire in effect 12-27, rebel violatns rptd 12-28, 12-29, 976C3, F3
'80 electns scheduled 12-28, 977A1
3 UK troops die in copter crash 12-29, 976A1

UN Policy & Developments
Lusaka raid condemned 4-13, 294B1
Cncl condemns electn; US, UK, France abstain 4-30, 332G1-A2
Patriotic Front for electn supervisn 8-20, 638C1
Gen Assemb pres scores on rights 9-18, 695B2
Patriotic Front seeks electn supervisn 10-26, 844B2
Assemb scores US UK sanctns end 12-18, 960F1
Cncl votes sanctns end 12-21, 976A3, C3

U.S. Relations—*See also 'Monetary' above*
US copters ruled illegal 1-5, 7F3
US backs all-parties talks end 1-17, 39F3
State of Union Message cites 1-23, 48F1
Vance pessimistic on majority rule 2-2–2-3, 96D3
US rights rpt omits 2-10, 107A2
Nkomo scores US raid denunciatns 2-14, 136C3
Freedom House: electn fair 4-20, 293C2; 5-10, 354G1
US: electn evaluatn 'premature' 4-26, 332A2
UN Cncl electn vote abstentn 4-30, 332A2
Young chrgs vote fraud 5-3, 354E1
Young warns UK on recognitn 5-4, 338B2
Vance sees Carrington, UK-US initiative called dead 5-21–5-23 393E2
Nigeria warns vs recognitn 5-31, 393G1-B2
NATO warns vs ties 5-31, 416A1
US sanctns, intensified war linked 6-13, 546G3
US unoffcl envoy named 6-25, 490C2
US, Australia agree on recognitn terms 7-4, 501A1
Muzorewa in US; sees Carter, Vance 7-9–7-11, 546B2
Commonwealth plan welcomed 8-6, 590G1-C2
US Sen aides' conf role rptd 9-19; UK denies protest 9-20, 718F1
Land compensatn fund rptd backed 10-15, 778A1
Transitn plan OK hailed 11-15, 881B1
Zambia raids scored 11-20, 899E2
UK peace force transport OKd 12-6, 937D1

ZIMMERMANN, Matilde
Named '80 SWP vp candidate 8-22, 680A3

1980

Guerrilla violence continues 11-22, 946A3
Tekere freed in murder 12-8, 946A2

Transition Government (& developments)
Freedom House lists as partly free 87E3
Rebel assemb lag rptd, deadline scored 1-4, 7F2
Soames OKs transitn role for regular, auxiliary forces, S African troops 1-6; Mugabe scores 1-8, 31B3
Guerrillas declare assembly completed, total rptd at 20,000 1-7, 31F2
Nkomo returns, asks reconciliatn 1-13, 31C2
Black parties register, ZAPU adopts Patriotic Front name; 3 party symbols rejected 1-14, 49B1
UK rpt on 1st mo issued 1-15, 48F3
Emergency state extended 1-18, 48D3
Carter cites diplomacy 1-20, 50G1
Refugee return begins 1-21, 49E1
S Africa troops to leave 1-26, 80D2; exit begins 1-30, 118G3
Mugabe returns from exile; scores UK admin, Muzorewa 1-27; ZANU dissidents freed 1-28, 80G1-C2
Smith backs Nkomo over Mugabe 1-31, 118E3
UK warned on fair electns 2-2; Carrington chrgs Mugabe voter intimidatn 2-6, 118E2
Soames assumes extra power 2-5; bars ZANU candidate 2-10, 118G2
Mugabe escapes assassinatn 2-6, 2-10, 118B3
Todd arrested, rebel support chrgd 2-9, 118G3
Soames warns re ZANU vote exclusn 2-12; sees Mugabe 2-26, 162A3
Electns held 2-14, 2-27—2-29, called fair 3-2; calm urged 3-3; Mugabe win rptd; reactn 3-4, 161A1-162E3
Mugabe photo; facts on 161C1, 162A1
Walls meets Mugabe; reassures on coup, ZANU army integratn 2-25, 162G1
Refugee return halted, torture chrgs rptd 2-25, 198G1
Mugabe sworn, names Cabt 3-11; vows fast changes 3-13, 198A1, E1
Martial law abolished 3-20, 301F3
Freedom House rpts on electn 4-11, 301D3
Walls named army head 4-15, 301C3
Indepndnc proclaimed 4-18, 301C1; for subsequent developments, see 'Government & Politics' above

UN Policy & Developments
Cncl warns UK on fair electn 2-2, 118C2
Refugees comr repatriatn role cited 2-25, 198B2
UK amnesties sanctns violators 4-15, 301C3
Waldheim marks indepndnc 4-17—4-18, 301E1
153d UN member 8-25, 643D1

U.S. Relations
Mugabe congratulated re win 3-4, 161F2
Young, Harriman mark indepndnc 4-17—4-18; emb opens, aid pact signed 4-18, 301C1, F1, C2
'79 terrorism deaths rptd 5-11, 365E3
Carter pres renominatn acceptance speech 8-14, 613D1
Mugabe visits US 8-22—8-29; asks business investmt 8-26, meets Carter, Muskie re aid 8-27, 674D2
Somali bases scored 10-9, 795C1

ZIMCO Industries
Special labor aid OKd 11-5, 870C2
ZIMIN, Aleksandr A.
Death rptd 3-14, 280G2
ZIMLIN, Sergei
New Zealand expels 1-22, 100D2
ZIMMER, Don
Fired as Red Sox mgr 10-1, named Rangers mgr 11-12, 926A3
ZIMMERMAN, Bill
Commoner uses vulgar radio ad 10-15, 818C3
ZIMMERMAN, Vernon
Fade to Black released 10-17, 836F2
ZIMYATOV, Nikolai
Wins Olympic medals 2-14, 2-23, 155A3, B3

1976

ZINC
Sickle cell treatmt rptd 2-24, 159F2
ZINN, Eifi
Wins Olympic medal 7-26, 576F1
ZINSOU, Abel
Sentenced 2-1—2-2, 404D1
ZIONISM—*See under JEWS*
ZIONIST Organization of America
Dole speech 9-9, 666A1
Rpt Sternstein seeks Gen Brown dismissal 10-20, 787C3
ZIRCON
Fraser I mining to end 11-11, 888A2
ZIRPOLI, Judge Alonso R.
Denies Hearst defns appeal 1-21, 70A1
ZIRZOW, Carola
Wins Olympic medal 7-30, 574A2
ZISK, Richie
NL batting ldr 10-4, 795G3
ZOMA, Emmanuel
Upper Volta trade min 2-9, 269D3
ZONGO, Francois-Xavier
Upper Volta justice min 2-9, 269D3
ZOOLOGY
Archbold dies 8-1, 816D3
ZOOT Suit (race horse)
3d in Hambletonian 9-4, 716F2
ZORINSKY, Edward
Elected senator 11-2, 820B1, 823C3, 828C2
ZUBIA, Gen. Eduardo
Rptdly seizes Mendez anti-US tape 10-10, 814A2
ZUDOV, Lt. Col. Vyacheslav
Soyuz 23 aborted 10-16, 839D3
ZUFRIATEGUI, Col. Carlos (ret.)
Arrest rptd 2-9, 207E3
ZUKOR, Adolph
Dies 6-10, 444A3
ZULIA (Venezuelan warship)
In Intl Naval Review 7-4, 488B3
ZUMWALT Jr., Adm. Elmo R. (ret.)
Reagan cites Kissinger quote 3-31, 232F2
Platform com testimony 5-19, 357D3
Dem conv speaker 7-13, 509E3
AFL-CIO donatn rptd 10-22, 938D3
Loses electn 11-2, 823B1
ZURBARAN, Guillermo
Oil fields opened to pvt dvpt 7-27, 554D1

1977

ZINDLER, Marvin
Nazi tape restraining order upheld 12-21 1008B2
ZINMER, Andrew J.
Charged with arson 6-27, 508F3
ZIONISM—*See JEWS*
ZIPPORI, Mordechai
New W Bank setlmts OKd 10-10, 793A2
ZISK, Richie
NL wins All-Star Game 7-19, 567D2
ZONING—*See HOUSING*
ZORINSKY, Sen. Edward (D, Neb.)
Votes vs Marshall 1-26, 52B3
ZRZAVY, Jan
Dies 10-13, 872C3
ZUCKERMAN, Lord Solly
Scores scientific research curbs 2-22, 184G1
ZUGARELLI, Antonio
Loses Italian Open 5-22, 430B3
ZUMWALT Jr., Adm. Elmo R. (ret.)
'76 spec interest gifts rptd 2-15, 128D2
Visits China 7-4, 514A2
Testifies on Panama Canal pacts 10-10, 792G1
ZUZE, Lt. Gen. Peter
Named Zambia army chief 4-24, 490A2
ZWANE, Ambrose
Scores parlt dissolutn 3-22, 394G3
ZWICK, Charles J.
Named Mil Compensatn Comm chrmn 6-27, 499D3

1978

ZINC
Mich sues Ford Motor re pollutn 2-1, 163D3
US bars trade relief, '77 imports rptd down 6-1, 443G2
Price upturn cited 10-20, 805D1
ZINI, Ivo
Killed 9-28, 817A1
ZINMER, Andrew J.
Sentence suspended 12-20, 992A2
ZINNEMANN, Tim
Straight Time released 3-18, 620A1
ZINNIA (play)
Opens 3-22, 760G3
ZINYAKIN, Vladimir
US asks exit 5-20, 409A3, D3
ZIONISM—*See JEWS*
ZIONIST Organization of America (ZOA)
Sternstein on Sadat peace plea 1-29, 60C3
Haddassah—*See separate listing*
ZIPORI, Mordechai
W Bank settlmt work renewed 4-17, 275E1
ZIPPO Manufacturing Co.
Blaisdell dies 10-3, 888D2
ZOELLER, Fuzzy
2d in N Orleans Open 4-30, 356A1
ZOETEMELK, Joop
2d in Tour de France 7-23, 692B2
ZONING—*See CONSTRUCTION, HOUSING*
ZOOLOGY
Cave salamander study rptd 1-19, 334C1
Early mammals held nocturnal, cool-blooded 3-23, 334D3
Chimps violent behavior rptd 4-19, 335A1
ZORINSKY, Sen. Edward (D, Neb.)
Mrs Carter makes Canal pact overture 3-14; votes vs pact 3-16, 177F2, D3
Votes vs 2d Canal pact 4-18, 273B1
ZOUKHAR, Vladimir
Karpov retains world chess title 10-17, 843A2
ZSIGMOND, Vilmos
Wins Oscar 4-3, 315C3
ZUKOFSKY, Louis
Dies 5-12, 440G3
ZUNIGA, Jose Leopoldo
Blamed for union ldr's death 7-23, 723E2, 723B2 *
ZURCHER v. Stanford Daily
Newsroom searches by police backed by Sup Ct 5-31, 429F3
ZWICK, Charles
Urges mil pensn overhaul 4-10, 280G3-281D1

1979

ZINDOGA, Francis
Zimbabwe law & order min 5-30, 393E1
ZINNER, Peter
Wins Oscar 4-9, 336A2
ZION, Ill.—*See ILLINOIS*
ZOELLER, Fuzzy
Wins San Diego Open 1-28, 2d in Hawaiian Open 2-11, 220D3, E3
Wins Masters 4-15, 587B1
PGA top money winner 11-30, 969F2
ZOETEMELK, Joop
2d in Tour de France 7-22, 655E2
ZOLLA, Robert R.
Convicted 2-22, sentncd 3-19, 220F2
ZONGALERO (race horse)
2d in Grand Natl 3-31, 448A3
ZOOT Suit (play)
Opens 3-25, 712G3
ZOPPI, Elvio
Convicted 3-1, 155G2
ZOPPI, Rolando
Convicted 3-1, 155G2
ZUCCOLI, Luciano
Divine Nymph released 10-12, 1007B3
ZUGARELLI, Antonio
US wins Davis Cup 12-16, 1003B3
ZUMWALT Jr., Adm. Elmo R. (ret.)
Warns Carter of Sovt challenge 1-12, 15B1
Scores SALT 7-17, 536G1
ZUNGUL, Steve
MISL top scorer 3-18, named MVP 3-22, 432C1, E1
ZUNIGA, Jose Leopoldo
Killed 3-1, 237F1
ZWEIBEL, Alan
Gilda Radner Live opens 8-2, 711C3

1980

ZINC
USSR-Argentine '79 trade rptd 4-15, 336A2
Medit pollutn pact signed 5-17, 381C3
Bolivia miners strike 7-20, 546B3
ZING, Giani Zail
Named Indian home min 1-14, 39F3
ZINK, John
In Okla US Sen primary; runoff set 8-26, 683A1
Loses runoff 9-16, 724B3
ZINNEMANN, Tim
Small Circle of Friends released 3-9, 216F3
ZION—*See ILLINOIS*
ZION Baptist Church (Philadelphia, Pa.)
Carter addresses members 9-3, 699A1
ZIONIST Organization of America
Bush scores Carter 'flip flop' 10-19, 817C3
ZIONISTS—*See JEWS & Judaism*
ZIPORI, Mordechai
Israel to build jet fighter 2-25, 180F1
Reappointment confirmed 6-1, 430A1
ZLATEV, Assen
Wins Olympic medal 7-24, 624E2
ZOETEMELK, Joop
Wins Tour de France 7-20, 835D1
ZOLOTARENKO, Vladimir
Rptd arrested as spy 11-13, 921C3
ZORN, Gen. Heinz Bernhart
Arrested in France 8-19, chrgd with spying 9-6, 707F3
ZORN, Maj. Jeffrey
Reassignmt rptd in IRS tax dispute 6-10, 638E3
ZORN, Jim
NFL '79 passing ldr 1-5, 8A2
ZOUNI, Darwich el-
Slain 12-27; front group claims credit 12-28, 996G2-A3
ZOZULYA, Vera
Wins Olympic medal 2-17, 156C1
ZUBICARAY, Jesus Maria
Slain 2-3, 101E3
ZUCKER, David
Airplane released 7-2, 675G1
ZUCKER, Jerry
Airplane released 7-2, 675G1
ZUCKERMAN, Mortimer
Atlantic Monthly purchase rptd 3-1, 239F1
Names Whitworth Atlantic Monthly ed 9-22, 908G2
ZUHAIR, Gen. Assad Abdel Aziz al-
'79 Saudi AF resignatn cited 1-1, 22E1
ZUKAV, Gary
Dancing Wu Li Masters wins Amer Book Award 5-1, 692F2
ZULPA, Robertas
Wins Olympic medal 7-26, 623F2
ZULU, Alexander Grey
Chakulya named aide 12-4, 969F2
ZUMBERGE, James H.
Named USC pres 5-21, 471A1
USC reveals faulty athletic admissns 10-13, 875D2
ZUMWALT Jr., Adm. Elmo R. (ret.)
US arms outlay increase urged 5-9, 369A3
ZUNGUL, Steve
Named MISL MVP 3-19, Arrows win MISL title 3-23, 771A2
ZUNIGA, Ricardo
Favors democracy in Honduras 7-20, 564F2
ZVOGBO, Eddison
Named Zimbabwe local govt min 3-11, to oversee tribal trust lands 3-13, 198D1, F1
ZWEIBEL, Alan
Gilda Live released 3-28, 416G2

CORRECTIONS

The following corrections should be made in the news digest (white paper) sections of Facts On File for the volumes indicated:

Vol. XXXVI-1976

Page

2D3—[See 1975, p. 993G1 (not 933G1)]
8B1—Hu (not Hou) Nim
16B1—Teferi Banti (not Benti)‡
16B3—on the eastern (not western) front
18B2—Mowaffak Allaf (not Mouaffak el-Aliaf)
20D2—Freedom House (not Foundation) report‡
27B3—[See 1975, p. 1015C1] (not 1016C1)
30F1, A2—Per (not Pea) Kleppe
32B1—fell from 29.2 (not 29.2%) . . . to 16.5 (not 16.5%)
35A3—Santo (not Sao) Antonio do Zaire
43C2—Major General (not General) Robert L. Fair
46B2—[26B3 (not 26B2)]‡
49A2, D2—Alice Saunier-Seite (not Siete)
52G1—Omani Sultan Qabus bin Said (not Said bin Qabus)
56F3—Judge John M. Murtagh (not Murtaugh)
58D2—Sheikh Sabah al-Salem al-Sabah (not Sabah Salem Sabah)
59F3—Mowaffak (not Mouffak) Allaf
62C1—. . .the capital, Malabo (formerly Santa Isabel), on the island of Macias Nguema Biyogo (not Malabo)
68D3—in the Senate . . . 38 Republicans (not Senators)
73C3—A government proposal . . . would go (not went) into effect Feb. 1.
76F1—Pieter (not Piet) Koornhof
77C1—Philip B. (not P.) Agee
82C2—Lopo do Nascimento (not Nasciemento)
84E2—Constantine Caramanlis (not Karamanlis)
116C1—George H. (not S.) Mahon
116E1—Christopher Hurford (not Furfurd)
122E2—Walter J. (not F.) Stoessel
123D1—Liechtenstein (not Lichtenstein)
123G3—National Heart and Lung Institute (not Association)
123G3—homicide increased to 10.8 (not 10.8%)
127G3—. . .the bill's "counter-cyclical" provisions, grants to states and cities of high unemployment (not "counter-cyclical" provisions, or revenue sharing grants)
136D1—Berkley (not Berkely) Bedell
143G1—Feb. (not Dec.)
150F3—Reporters' Committee for Freedom of the Press (not Reporter's Committee of the Freedom of the Press)‡
156B1-E1—Geir Hallgrimsson (not Hallgrimmsson)
157B1—. . .delete: [See p. 150G3]
162C3—[See p. 572C2] (not 576C2).
164F2—Habib Chatti (not Chatty)
176F1—African National Council (not Congress)
178C1—Peru Feb. 23 (not 20) recognized . . . Angola
187D2—Robert (not John) Ellicott
187E3—Yoshio (not Yorhio) Okawara
187F3—Jules Deschenes (not Deschaines)
191B1—Hiroshi (not Hiro) Hiyama
191D1—Robert S. (not W.) Ingersoll
193F1—Hassanien (not Hassanein) Heykal
194E1—. . .mutual and balanced force (not forced) reduction
195C2—Andrei P. Kirilenko (not Kirilinko)
199F3—Robert S. (not W.) Ingersoll
211A2—William W. (not R.) Scranton
213B2—European Economic Community's (not Commission's) executive commission
220E3—Jules Deschenes (not Deschaines)
224A3—Research in (not on) Mental Retardation
229C3—Walter J. (not F.) Stoessel Jr.
236A1, B1—Brig. Gen. (not Gen.) Horacio Liendo
236A1, C1—Maj. Gen. (not Brig.) Jose Maria Klix
236A1, B1—army Brig. Gen. (not army Gen.) Albano Harguindequy

Vol. XXXVII-1977

Page

1C1—Yao Wen (not Yen)-yuan
2B1—89.4 million barrels in 1975 (not 1976)
3D3—[See 1976, p. 1010A2] (not 1010E1)
14D2—Kenneth M. (not W.) Curtis
18E2—Senate Church (not Select) Committee
20E1—West German Permanent Mission (not Embassy)
45B3—Janata (not Janta) Congress
48G2—(federal cabinet) [not (federal parliament)]
49D3—Indiana (not Indian) ratifies
64A1—Janata (not Janta) Congress
64C2—European Economic Community (not Commission)
66D2—in April 1976 (not 1974)
71C1—Jagjivan (not Jaingvan) Ram
82C3—Zdenek Mlynar (not Mylnar)
87B1—Louis de Guiringaud (not Louis Guiringaud)
95G1—General Electric (not Electrical) Co.
98F3—Eritrean People's Liberation Front (not Forces)
103F1—Jan. 29 (not Jan. 30)
111B1—Equals (rounded off) .049 (not .0049)
111B1—Results multiplied by 100 .049 (not .0049)
112B2—Judge John H. (not A.) Pratt
114B3—Leslie Collitt (not Colitt)
116G3—Lee Chul Seung (not Chol Sung)
117E1—Oleska Tikhy (not Tykhy)
119C1—A. C. Nielsen (not Neilsen) Co.
124F1—Mobutu (not Mobuto) Sese Seko
128A1—Arlan Stangeland (not Strangeland)
144F2—Moussa (not Mousa) Sabry
148C3—Martin R. (not H.) Hoffmann
148F3—[See 1976, p. 978F3] (not 34D3)
150A1—1974 (not 1975) conviction
150A1—[See 1976, p. 379C1 (not 770E1)]
163E1—Veterans' (not Veteran) Association
164F1—World Hockey Association (not League)
164F3—[See 1954, p. 271A3 (not 271B3)]
179D2—Yao Wen (not Yen)-yuan
189A2—(all figures in millions of U.S. dollars) (not in U.S. dollars)
200E1—Canadian Pacific Air (not Airlines)
205C2—Hari R. (not M.) Gokhale
211F1—Packer. . .named assistant secretary (not secretary) of labor
213B1—would expire at midnight EDT, June 21 (not June 23), 1977
215A3—[See p. 200F1] (not 200F2)
217E1—Action for (not on) Children's Television
220B3—[See p. 114D3] (not 144D3)
243E1—Chalard Hiranyasiri (not Hiranyasari)
243F1—Sawin Hiranyasiri (not Hiranyasari)
248A1—black nationalists. (not nationalist's)
249D1—Strauss, was sworn in March 30 (not 23).
261E1— . . . Kissinger April 5 spoke out . . . .
267B2—May 17 (not 10) national elections
268A2—a 3% content (not 93% saturation) of the isotope Uranium-235.
276G2-B3—Santa (not Sante) Fe
278E3—Commission on Civil (not Human) Rights
279D1—Cities (not City) Service
283B3—Bansi (not Banai) Lal
288A3—Niederberger (not Nieder Berger)
298C2—Li Hsien-nien (not Li Hsien)
302E2—Consumer Product (not Production) Safety Commission
302F2—Tris (2,3 dibromopropyl phosphate) (not [2,3 dibromopropyl] phosphate)
305F2—Syed Fida Hassan (not Fida Hasan)
310F3, 311A1—March 28 (not 29)
324F2—Council of North Atlantic Shipping Associations (not Shippers Association)
329G1—Liam Cosgrave (not Cosgrove)

Vol. XXXVIII-1978

Page

11E2—Salyut (not Soyuz)
16D3—Leigh and Merino (not Guzman)
24E3—Jay (not Jan) Anson
37B2—Tomas O Fiaich (not O. Fiaich)
52A2—according to the Commerce Department (not Federal Reserve)
66F2—Procter (not Proctor) & Gamble
109F2—Joe (not Joel) L. Allbritton
109D3—Allbritton (not Allbriton)
110E1—Feb. 12 (not Feb. 13)
130A3—Yao Wen (not Yen)-yuan
139B3—[See 1977, p. 955E1] (not 955E2)
142F3—Gov. Alvan (not Alvin) T. Fuller
152A3—Macias Nguema Biyogo Negue Ndong (not Francisco Macias Nguema Biyogo)
157E1, G1—Nebi (not Nabi) Salah
157B2—[See 1971 (not 1977), p. 544D2]
157C2—[See 1977 (not 1971), p. 535B1]
164B2—American Assocation for (not of) the Advancement of Science
187F3—[See 1977, p. 1010C2 (not 100C2)]
191C1—Antonio Bisaglia (not Bisalgia)
192G1—Gerd (not Gert) Schneider
203F2—Thomson (not Thompson)
205A3—Natural (not National) Resources Defense Council
223G3—[See p. 127G1] (not 123G1)
226A2—Buffalo station (not stations)
232F2—Ralph Piccardo (not Picardo)
237C1—[See p. 106F2 (not 106E1)]
240B2—Head also gave $10,000 (not $10,00)
243A3—Center for National Security Studies (not Center for National Security)
260G2—American Federation of State, County and Municipal Employes (not Workers)
279F1—Senate Governmental Affairs (not Government Operations) Committee
286D2—Uniting (not United) Church
293G3—Brookhaven National (not Natural) Laboratory
310C3—Juan (not Jose) Aleman
335E3—Richard Rodgers (not Rogers)
349E2—Babrak Karamal (not Badrak Karmal)
358B2—Mohammed Ibrahim (not Ibrahim Mohammed) Kamel
359G1, G2—Mutshatsha (not Mutshalsha)
360E1—Hungarian Poet (not Post)
368G1—Judge Albert Bryan (not Bryant) Jr.
370A1—C$226 (not C$266) million
371B3, C3—Beauchamp (not Beauchamps)
371C3—May (not April) 18
372B3—Mengistu (not Mariam)
386E2—Securities Investor Protection (not Securities and Investment) Corp.
393A3—Christoforo Piancone (not Pancione)
393A3—May 17 (not May 16)
423E1—missiles (not warheads) that were MIRVed
439A1—Knut (not Kurt) Folkerts
439B1—May 11 (not May 12)
444A2—Solzhenitsyn (not Sozhenitsyn)
446E2—invoke (not involve) cloture
449E3—June 5 (not 15)
452D3—U.N. (not U.S.) Human Rights Commission
453F3—Bettino (not Bruno) Craxi
454D2—Bordoni had been indicted in 1975 (not 1976)
457G2—Winford (not Winfred) Boynes
466F3—Rep. Paul Findley (not Finley)
471B1—Rep. W. Henson Moore (R, [not D] La)
536F1—[See p. 193E2 (not 193E1)]
538A1—Premier Nur Mohammad Taraki (not Takri)
541G2—. . . condemned the trial of . . . (not the sentence given)
547G2—June 21 (not 20)—26
550G3—Joseph (not James) Califano Jr.
558G1—Bettino (not Bruno) Craxi
579F2—Barnard (Bernard) Hughes
587G1—July 26, 1978 (not July 27, 1979)
604G2—Abortion Rights Action League (not Abortion Rights League)
607G3—[See p. 470F1 (not 552E3)]
619G2—Martin Scorsese (not Scorese)

Vol. XXXIX-1979

Page

21C3—...the night of Jan. (not Nov.) 9
80B3—Rien Poortvliet (not Poorvliet)
87F3—National (not International) Aviation Club
88A2—Hughes Air West (not Corp.)
95B1—Antonio Delfim Netto (not Neto)
95D1—Murilo (not Murillo) Macedo
100E1, G1—Vladimir Sychov (not Sychyov)
105F2—Mohammed Hashem (not Mashem) Sabaghian
117A1—Abdi Ipekci (not Ipecki)
117D2—[See 1978, p. 1000E1 (not 100E1)]
125D2—Hassan Nazih (not Nasieh)
126F3—Jiri Dienstbier (not Diensbier)
130D2—Rep. Richard C. White (not Wright)
144F2—House Foreign (not International) Affairs subcommittee
174F2—Lesley (not Leslie)-Anne Down
179A3—Sadegh Ghotbzadeh (not Ghotbzabeh)
250C1—Ali Abdullah Saleh (not Salem)
265D1—Joan D. (not A.) Aikens
270A1—Cordoba . . . devalued April 6 (not 9) to 10 (not 9) to the U.S. dollar
271G3—Priscilla (not Pricilla) Davis
275B2—Combustion Engineering Inc. (not Corp.)
277F1—Deputy Ibrahim Yazdi (not Yazid)
319E2—Arab Bank (not Fund) for Economic Development in Africa
329D3—Jamie Roldos Aguilera (not Aquilera)
353B3—Sadegh Ghotbzadeh (not Ghotbzabeh)
356D2—Peter Golenbock (not Gollenbock)
376B3—Archbishop (not Bishop) Hilarian Cappucci
391F3—Jan Hoffman (not Hoffmann)
392B1—Jan Hoffman (not Hoffmann)
392E1—Erich Scharer (not Schaerer)
392B2—Lee Radziwill (not Radziwell)
392C3—Guinness (not Guiness) Book of World Records
400A3—Jaffee (not Jaffe)
407D2—Ayatollah Hasheimi (not Hashemi) Rafsanjani
409B2—Tomas Borge (not Borges)
411B2—Hans Matthoefer (not Matthofer)
412D2—September 1978 (not 1977)
419F3—William H. (not W.) Wynn
428G2—Agustin Rodriguez Sahagun (not Shagu)
432B2—Peter Golenbock (not Gollenbock)
432E2—Nikita S. Khruschev (not Krushchev)
448B1—Rich (not Rick) Preston
448F1—National Hockey League's reserve (not reverse) clause
475B1—Mayor Elias Freij (not Frej)
480F2—George E. MacKinnon (not McKinnon)
483A3—Gustov Franz (not Franz Gustov) Wagner
507B1—Denis (not John) Johnson
520G2—G. Robert (not Robert F. Blakey)
525C1—July (not June) 11
528A1—Ian (not Iam) Holm
528G1—March 16 (not 15)
528E2—Lesley-Anne (not Ann) Down
531E3—The dollar gained...July 20 (not 19)
532F2—Communications (not Communication) Workers of America
544E1—...the 538-(not 583-) member house
544E3—Adnan (not Honan) Hussein Hamdani
565B3—Sadegh Ghotbzadeh (not Ghotbzabeh)
577B2—Joseph C. Canizaro (not Canzaro) Interests Inc.
583E1—Adnan (not Abnan) Hussein Hamdani
586A1—Carlos Garaicoetxea (not Garaikoetxea)
600A2—Walter Guevera Arze (not Arce)
613E3—Masie (not Nguema)
617C1—Gustov Franz (not Franz Gustov) Wagner
629D2—[See p. 591D1 (not 00000)]
635F2—Antonio Negri (not Negro)
640B2—John Paul (not (Paul))
640D2—Tomas (not Thomas) O'Fiaich
647B1—Reubin (not Reuben) Askew
656A1—pleaded guilty May 21 to one count (not court)
656C2—five (not four) octuplets
656B3—R. Sargent (not Sargeant) Shriver

Vol. XXXX-1980

Page

21E3—Eurico de Nelo (not Melo)
81A2—Michael J. (not O.) Myers (not Meyers)
81D2—Michael J. (not 'O') 'Ozzie' Myers
114F1—Judge Thomas R. McMillen (not McMillan)
178D1—Michael Howland (not Col. Leland Holland)
192F2—Jose Antonio Morales Ehrlich (not Erhlich)
249F3—Patrizio (not Fabrizio) Peci
261C1—Tareq (not Tarel) Aziz
271C2—Isidoro (not Isodoro) Octavio Malmierca Peoli
275F3—Franco (not Massimo) Reviglio
294B3—American Cyanamid (not Cyanimid) Co.
309A3—National Highway Traffic (not Transportation) Safety Administration
315E3—Ali Nasser Mohammed al-Hasani (not Ali Nasser Mohammed)
317D3—Abbott (not Abbot) Laboratories
325D3—Rieckehoff predicted April 18
325F3—April 19 (not 14)
331F2—[See 1979, p. 808G2 (not 808E2)]
335G1, B2—Diego C. Asencio (not Ascencio)
336B1—Jeffrey (not Jeffery) Hastings
372F2—Jose Antonio Morales Ehrlich (not Erhlich)
388F1—Rudolph Kirchschlager (not Kirschschlager)
389A3—Jose Antonio Morales Ehrlich (not Erhlich)
390C1—Rafael Cordova (not Cordoba) Rivas
402D2—Michael J. (not O.) 'Ozzie' Myers (not Meyers)
409C2—On May 28 (not After their talks)
415E1—Cambridge University (not University of)
419F3—Khuzistan (not Khuzestan)
421G1—Godfrey Binaisa (not Binasa)
446F1—Paulo Muwanga (not Mwanga)
446G3—Bank for International Settlements (not Payments)
447F2—North Carolina State (not North Carolina)
472D2—$850,000 (not 850,000)
482D2—[See p. 289B2 (not 28932)]
515B1—Blue Fire (not Light)
563A3—Alvardo Piza (not Pisa)
576B3—Robert M. (not J.) Morgenthau
589F1—1,500-meter (not 1,000-meter) final
589C2—Jurgen (not Jergen) Straub
597F3—William J. (not F.) Brennan
599G1—[See p. 505B1 (not 505B2)]
599E3—Michael J. (not O.) Myers
599E3—John M. (not D.) Murphy
601A1—J. (not G.) William Middendorf 2nd, a former undersecretary (not secretary) of the Navy
601E1—Marie Hayde (not Haydee) Torres
608D3—Snow, C. P. (Charles Percy (not Piercy))
612A2—Aug. 11 (not 12)
643D3—Hurvitz (not Hurwitz)
645G1—Choi Kyu Hah (not Ha)
651G2—Hu Yoa-pang (not Yao-bang)
673B1—Kim Yong Hyu (not Huy)
684B2—Michael J. (not O.) Myers
685D2—Pay Advisory Committee (not Federal Pay Board)
688G3—parliament Sept. 10 (not Sept. 20) approved
692A1—Ashe named Sept. 7 (not 17)
703A2—Procter (not Proctor) & Gamble
710F2—Commodity Credit Corporation (not Commodity Corporation)
734D2—Iraqi (not Iranian) President Saddam Hussein
747A3—Distillery, Wine and Allied Workers International Union (not Winery, Distillery and Allied Workers Union)
751F3—Peugeot (not Peugot)
778B1—Riyadh (Saudi Arabia) Airport Aug. 19
790D1—Prince Sultan ibn (not bin) Abdul Aziz
793A3—SEAT (not Seat)
794G1—Oct (not Sept.) 12
796A1—Paul Splittorff (not Splitorff)
810G1—Goukouni Oueddei (not Oueddi)
824F1—Imports in September (not August)
840B1—97th (not 98th) Congress
842A1—97th (not 98th) Congress
842D4—Robert (not Roger) Whittaker
865D2—Surinam (not Suriname)
890G2—Nov. 4 (not 5)
951F2-G2—Mohammed Jawad Baqir Tunguyan (not Tungayan)

1976

239A2—Anthony Wedgwood (not Wedgewood) Benn‡
247D3—Mississippi River (not Mississippi) Grain Elevator Inc.
247D3—Phil McCaull (not McCall)‡
261C3—John Paul Stevens (not Stephens)
262C2—named task force March 31 (not March 21)
268F3, 269B1—Joaquin Ruiz-Gimenez (not Ruiz Jimenez)
271C3, D3—Bergman (not Bergmann)
298D1—Antonio Lefebvre (not Fefebvre)
304A2—February 18, 1976 (not 1975)‡
306A3—orders for consumer goods (not foods)
308B3—John Paul Stevens (not Stephens)
333B1—Wu Teh (not Te)
335A3—International Air Line Pilots Association (not Air Line Pilots' Union)
339A1—Rhoodie's remarks . . . on military aid for Rhodesia (not South Africa)
364C2—Teferi Banti (not Benti)‡
370D3—Lopo do (not de) Nascimento
372F3—The 18- (not 19-) nation International Energy Agency
380G3—[See p. 265C2] (not 255C2)
398A1—Peter J. Taggeres (not Taggares)‡
399D2—[See p. 264B2] (not 254B2)
401G3—Marathon Shipbuilding Co. (not Shipbuilders)
404C2, D2—[See 1965, p. 413B1 (not 41rB1)]
406D3—William W. (not R.) Scranton
410B2—. . .from Lyn Nofziger (not Hofziger).
413F3—Members of the bipartisan (not Bipartisan) National Women's Political Caucus
416C3, E3—John Keenan (not Keene)
421E3—. . .several hours May 31 (not 20)
426D1—. . .meeting June 23-24 (not 22-23)
427D1—. . .meeting. . .June 23-24 (not 22-23)
428E3—Joseph Mdluli (not Mduli)
438D1—[See p. 167C2] (not 167C3)
445A1—June 20-21 (not 21-22)
447D3—Vorster held talks in Bonn June 25 with Chancellor Helmut Schmidt
450B1—[See Vol. 1975, p. 950D1] (not 950D1)
450B1—United Nations World Food Council (not Conference)
452G2—. . .said June 14 (not 11)
458E1, A2—Yasuhiro (not Yasihiro) Nakasone
469A1—Text of Democratic Party's 1976 Platform Approved June 15 (not 16) by Committee
480F3—Lopo do (not de) Nascimento
484F2—Veneris, a Vandergrift, Pa. (not Hawthorne, Calif.) native
485C1—. . .the U.S.-born commander of a strike force unit. (not the strike force.)
485G2—Wilfried (not Wilfred) Bose
490E3, F3—Birch (not Birth) Bayh
500A2—Michael (not Michiel) C. Botha
502E1—Nimeiry (not Nimeiri)
503A2—[See p. 270G1] is incorrect
506C3—Ron Kovic (not Kovik)
511G2, 512E2—[see 1974, p. 1088F3 (not 1975)]
512E2, F3—[see 1972, p. 518G1 (not G2)]
516G2—20% higher than the fiscal 1976 (not 1975) budget
519F2—Ali Aref (not Arif) Bourhan
519F3—Gearhart's (not Gearheart's) body
520F3-Long March of 1934-35 (not 1934-36)
521B1—at demonstrations honoring Chou (not burial of Chou)
525E2—Jet Propulsion (not Propulstion) Laboratory
529C2—Note: All references to European Economic Community (EEC) should read European Community (EC)
534F1, G1—in fiscal 1977 (not 1976)
538G1—Air India (not Indian Airlines)
539A2—island of Majorca (not Palma)
540G1—in the name (not Name)
541G3—Adm. Sa-Ngad Chaloryu (not Sa-Nga Chaloyu)
543E3—Mohammed Nur Saeed (not Muhammad Nur Saad)
548C2—[See p. 516A3 (not 514E3)]
548C2—Mohammed Az-Zawi (not Az-Azwi)
552A3—In actions June 30, the court:
557D1—Hiroshi (not Hiro) Hiyama
569G2-B3—Redfearn (not Redfern)
569E3—Delete: (The YSA was a youth affiliate of the SWP)
589C3—Arnaldo Forlani (not Forlini)
593G3—Mayor Klaus Schutz (not Schultz)
595G2—1,000 (not 10,000) foot-deep canyon

1977

340F1—Western Electric Co., Inc. (not Corp.)
342F3—Navy League of the U.S. (not National Navy League)
347F1—[See p. 254A3] (not 254A1)
348F1, D2—Basppa (not Basappa) D. Jatti
355B2—Ch'en Li-li (not Li-Li Chen)
355G3—Academy of Television Arts (not Hollywood Academy)
359B3—Prince Bernhard (not Bernhardt)
369C3—Foothills (not Foothill) Pipe Lines Ltd., which comprised Westcoast Transmission
377C1—Labor Party, 32 (not 34);
378G2—Romulo Escobar Bethancourt (not Betancourt)
379C1—Escobar Bethancourt (not Betancourt)
385C2—Wheeling-Pittsburgh (not Pittsburgh-Wheeling) Steel Corp.
424B2—[See p. 86D1] (not p. 142C2)
425D3—Premiers (not Prime ministers) of the western provinces
442C1—Jhoon Rhee (not Ree)
466E2—Mark MacGuigan (not MacQuigan)
486F1—Eritrean People's (not Popular) Liberation Front
497C1—World Conference on Religion and (not in) Peace
505F3—Chi (not Chin) Teng-kuei
509B1—Gen. Mohammad Zia ul-Haq (not Huq)
525A2—Mackenzie River Delta (not delta)
526D1—[See p. 265B1] (not 503C3)
529D3—Six (not Five) former UP members
532E2—Baden-Powell, Lady Olave (not Olave, Lady Baden-Powell)
543C2—Ahmed Laraki (not Larki)
547G2—[See pp. 414G1, 268F3 (not 268F2)]
554G3—according to the Federal Reserve Board (not Commerce Department)
567E2—Garry (not Gary) Templeton
573A2—[See p. 392F3] not [329F3]
page 589B3—Romulo Escobar Bethancourt (not Betancourt)
602B2—Werner (not Walter) Maihofer
604E3—[See 1974, p. 906E2 (not 906EZ)]
607B1—Romulo Escobar Bethancourt (not Betancourt)
624D3—Joseph S. (not F.) Nye Jr.
636C2—[See p. 616G3 (not 616F2)-617B2)]
641E2—Umba Di (not De) Lutete
644E2—Rawly (not Rawley) Eastwick
645F2—Fang Yi (not Vi)
645G2—Hsu Hsiang-chien (not Heiang-chien)
652D1—transferred. . .to Lee (not Blair) June 4
652A2—Cory (not Corey)
659G3—Reuben (not Reubin) Askew
p. 678C1—Carlos Humberto (not Humerto) Romero
689F3, 690D1—Federal Election (not Elections) Commission
692F2—Young (not Youth) Adult Conservation Corps
725G2—[See p. 694B2] (not 695B2)]
728D3—Patrick Cooney (not Coony)
729A2—[See p. 658A2 (not 638A2)]
730B2—Nordli (not Nordling)
740G3—Sen. Jose (not Joao) de Magalhaes Pinto
756A3—[See. . .; 1972, p. 399C2 (not 299C2)]
757F2—on Oct. 1, 1979. (not Oct. 1.)
773F3—. . .two congressmen (not two former congressmen). . . .by former Rep. (not Reps.) Vernon Thomson
781F2—Castro acknowledged Sept. 29
804A1—. . .those place under a banning order (not arrest)
807D2—Harry (not Henry) Rodgers
816D2—Operation White Snow (not Snow White)
818G3—Metro Containers-Kraft Inc. (not Kraftco Corp.)
836F3—Keystone Consolidated (not Keystone) Industries Inc.
876D1—Marthinus (not Martinus) Steyn
888F2—Kelly (not Kelley) Barnes Dam
890C2—Mahmoud (not Mohammed Riad)
895G1—[See p. 252G1] (not 252G2)
896G2—Andres (not Angel) Figueroa Cordero
920A1—$1.19 billion (not million)
928B2—huge (not tidal)
941B1—[See p. 720F2]
970A2, D3—Cecilio (not Celio) Lastra
970C3—[See p. 970C2] (not 960C2)
972B1—Thailand (not Cambodia)
1009C2—Lionel Bowen (not Bower)

In Vol. 1976

1019 (col. 2 under ABORTION)—Sup Ct. . .11-29, 900C3 (not 899C3)
1023 (col. 2)—AMERICAN Telephone & Telegraph Co. (not Corp.)
1040 (col. 4 under BUSINESS—Statistics)—3d ¼ corp profits, 2d ¼ revised 11-18, 866C2
1056 (col. 3 under DANFORTH, John Clagett)—Wins Mo (not Mich) primary
1079 (col. 4)—GISCARD d' Estaing (not D'Estaing), Ann-Aymone
1081 (col. 2)—GRAIVER (not Gravier)
1096 (col. 4)—KEITH, Hastings (not Hasting)
1102 (col. 4)—DUAN, Le (not Le DUAN)

1978

620B1—Donna Summer (not Summers)
638D2—Clement J. (not A.) Zablocki
643C2—Ralph M. Parsons (not Parson) Co.
645D2—William P. (not T.) Kampiles
648F2—Maj. Gen. Neit Nivar Seijas (not Seixas)
681A2—Orion Capital Corp. (not Orion Corp.)
689E1—The report issued July 27 . . .
689C2—Mario Moretti (not Moretto)
695B3, D3—John Deutch (not Deutsch)
699A2—Forrest (not Forest) James
702F2—Karr Preventive (not Preventative) Medical Products Inc.
703F3—Prime Minister (not Premier) Pierre Elliot Trudeau's
708E2—Diederichs, Nicolaas (not Nicolass)
713G2—Solomon Islands was admitted as the 150th (not 105th) UN member.
716E3—Boeing Co. (not Corp.)
722B2-D3—Material beginning with 'Mujia's murder' . . . and ending with 'Gen. Kjell Laugerud' belongs on p. 723F2 instead of 'The manifesto' . . . through . . . 'Washington Post Aug. 5'.
722A3—[See p. 496G3 (not 49663)]
723F2-F3—Material beginning with 'The manifesto' . . . . and ending with 'Washington Post Aug. 5' . . . belongs on p. 722B2 instead of 'Mujia's murder' . . . . through . . . . 'Gen. Kjell Laugerud'.
725G1—[See p. 706F3 (not 706F2)]
725D2—July 28 (not Aug. 29)
725G3, 726A1—North Rhine-Westphalia (not North-Rhine Westphalia)
732C1—The delay . . . $1.83 (not $183)-billion U.S. contribution
746C3—Thomas a (not A.) Kempis
760A1—Ain't Misbehavin' (not Misbehaven)
774B2—Sept. 30 (not 3).
812D3—Anthony said Oct. 16 (not Oct. 17)
832D2—in March 1978, after the SEC said it would file (not had filed) a civil complaint
841E2—court lifted the stay (not declined to hear the case) Oct. 6.
868G2—Kurt Rebmann (not Rebman)
891D3—Deborah Layton Blakey (not Blakely)
908F2—National Transportation Safety Board (not National Transportation Board)
933G1—Heng Samrin (not Hen Somrim)
948E2—market (not marked)
963F1—T.O. (not O.T.) Gravitt
969F3—Caravans (not Caravens)
977A3, G3—Sheik Oteiba (not Manae)
984D2—Airline (not Airlines) Pilots Association
1032B3—Nikita S. Khrushchev (not Krushchev)

1979

659B2—Nicolae Ceausescu (not Ceaucescu)
665C2—Judge June (not Joyce) Green
666A2—Claudio Rodriquez Morales (not Claudio Morales)
672E3—Barbra (not Barbara) Streisand
672F3—Charlie Daniels Band (not Bank)
682G1—Lukens Steel Co. (not Corp.)
709E2—Virginio (not Virgilio) Rognoni
712E3—John Conti (not Gonti)
725F3—[See p. 721G3 (not 00000)]
750E3—Po Yi-Po (not Yibo)
759E3—Leadership Conference of Women (not Woman) Religious
763B1—Mayor (not Major) Teddy Kolleck
782G1—Premier (not Prime Minister) Dom Mintoff
790F2—Col. Jose (not Jorge) Guillermo Garcia
800G3—Monty Python's Life of Brian (not Life of Brian)
803E2—F-5F (not F-F5)
803C3—Ganri (not Gamri) Yamashita
811E1—Walter Guevara Arze (not Arce)
820C3—Edgar Rice Burroughs (not Borroughs)
820C3—Martin Bergman (not Begrman)
840C1—1970 (not 1968) murders
857F1—Tadzhikistan (not Tadjikistan)
859F3—Georgetown (not George Washington) University
882C3—Dom (not Don) Martina
885G3—Oct. 22 (not 25)
898B1—$1.65 (not $1,650,000) million
906G1—Stephen (not Steven) Travis
907F1—Nov. 1 (not No. 1)
909C3—Nov. 27 (not No. 27)
911E1—Alberto Juantorena (not Juantoreno)
918F1—Song Chen-ming (not Zhenming)
921A3—Western Union Telegraph, a subsidiary of Western Union Corp., (not Western Union Corp., a subsidiary of the telegraph company,)
927F3—Gerard (not Gerald) Fitt
930C3—Fahri Koruturk (not Koroturk)
935F2—June L. (not Joyce Hens) Green
972E3—John H. Moxley (not Moxey) 3rd
1000F1—(See 1976 [not 1977], p. 708G1)

1980

963A1—Judge James (not John) C. Turk
963C3—Pacific Homes Corp. (not Inc.)
963F3—Carmen Valentine (not Valentin)
984A1—H. F. Ahmanson (not Abrahamson)

1976	1977	1978	1979	1980

597A1—. . .Cole. . .and President Ford after their acceptance speeches Aug. (not July) 19
614D2—Haynsworth (not Haynesworth)
614C3—. . .accused Roy (not Ray)
615C2—by a 117-vote margin (not by only 57 votes)
619D1—Gen. Han Ju Kyong (not Han Kyu June)
621F1—[See 1975, p. 918B3 (not 918B2)]
623A3—Oct. 14 (not 13)
634F2—Ruckelshaus . . . acting director (not director)
640C1—Praphas Charusathien (not Charusa-thien)
640F2—Clarence M. Kelley (not Kelly)
651F2—Inflation rate up. (not down)
661E3—moderate Zimbabwe African People's (not National) Union (ZAPU) (not ZANU). . .more militant Zimbabwe African National (not People's) Union (ZANU) (not ZAPU)
672B2—Mein Kampf (not Kemph)
672G2—Gen. Acdel (not Abdel) Vilas‡
676F1, B2—Liam Cosgrave (not Cosgrove)
677D1—Yoshio (not Yoshi) Kodama
677E1, F1—Jimenez (not Sarmiento)
Page 678B3—Elwyn Rex Capling (not Elwen)
678B3—Thomas C. Kolstad (not Kilstad)
680F1—[See p. 64E3 (not 68C3)]
680F2—April 1976 (not 1975)
680C3—. . .a 78,143-seat (not 78,143) football stadium
683A1—the Aug. 23 (not 24) hijacking
687G3—Apr. (not Sept.) 25
689A3—Sea-Land Service (not Services) Inc.‡
696C2—to succeed Aref (not Arif)
722F1, 725E2—Charles F. (not R.) Ruff
728D1—powers of Justice . . . extended to probes of planned mergers as well as to mergers already completed. (not would be extended to probes of planned mergers as well as already-committed violations).
739G1—five day conference that opened in Denver, Colo. July 12
745D3—. . . a study by the Postal Rate Commission (not Commission on Postal Service)
746G3—the 1965 Export Control (not Administration) Act
750B2—Premier Allan Blakeney (not Blakeley)
754C1—Marshal Kamol Dechatungka (not Techatungka)
775F2—Justice Thanin Kraivichien (not Kravichien)
780B2—The disappearance (not abduction) of two employes
781D3—William W. (not R.) Scranton
786D1—Taub, Hummel & Schnall (not Schall) Inc.
819D3—Harrison R. (not H.) Schmitt
821D2—The vote was: Yes—1,486,880 (not 1,511,475); No—1,151,475 (not 1,511,475)
821D3—Lt. Gov. J. Joseph (not Joseph P.) Garrahy
822A2—Richard A. (not E.) Tonry
822G3—Bob (not Paul) Gammage
825F2—Barbara A. Mikulski (not Miluski)
827E3—Thomas J. (not G.) Anderson
829F3—Richard A. (not E.) Tonry
830E4—Robert Krueger (not Kruger)
831D3—. . . and Mugabe (not Magabe) headed . . .
838B3—Kenji (not Kenjo) Osano
840D2—[See p. 740C2] (not 740B1)
854C2—Andrei D. (not A.) Sakharov
857G3—Jean-Baptiste (not Baptist) Bagaza‡
860C3—See p. 735F2 (not 734)
861E2—[See p. 759C1 (not 759C2)]
862F2—after talks Aug. 21 (not 22)
864C3—James (not William) Longley
866E1—Barnett (not Coleman) declined. . .
870G3—[See pp. 806B3, 533C1 (not 533C3)]
880B2—Valery (not Valary) Giscard d'Estaing
892F3—Mohanda K. Gandhi's (not Ganhi's)
895F3—Amadou-Mahtar (not Amadou Mahta) M'Bow
898D2—The decision . . . confirmed Nov. 24 (not Nov. 14)
899A2—Pak Bo Hi (not Bo Hi Pak)
911C2—John M. (not D.) Murphy
912A1—General Assembly proclamation Nov. 23 (not 24)
912C3—Green Haven (Stormville, N. Y.) [not (N.Y.)] State Correctional Facility
951G2—[See p. 826D3 (not 826A3)]‡
951D3—Don Gullett (not Gullet)‡
952A3—Nicole Barrett (not Barret)‡
960E3—Russel (not Russell) Kelner‡
961E3—Phillip (not Philip) Lynch‡
961F3—Nov. 28 (not 29)‡
985A2—Castle & Cooke (not Cook) Inc.‡
988A2—Titanium (not Titianium) price-fixing‡

1104 (col. 3 under LITTON Industries)—Ingalls Shipbuilding Division (not Corp.)
1108 (col. 4 under MASSERA, Adm. Emilio)—On. . .2-16, 224E3 (delete entry)
1118 (col. 1 under MINORITIES)—Carter. . .4-4—4-13, 260D2(not 269D2)-261F2
1122 (col. 2)—NATIONAL (not N8IONAL) Public Radio
1128 (col. 3 under OPPENHEIMER, Harry)—10-5, 928C2 (not 924C2)
1142 (col. 2 under RHODESIA—Majority Rule)—Crosland (not Crolsland)
1146 (col. 3)—SAUD al-Faisal (not ibn Faisal), Prince
1164 (col. 3 under UNITED Nations—Educational, Scientific & Cultural Organization)—Sovt vs West. . .conf ends (not convenes) 11-30, 895E3
1179 (col. 4 under VIETNAM, Socialist Republic of—U.S. Relations)—S Korea lobbying (not lobbing)

In Vol. 1975

1039 (col. 3)—AMERICAN Telephone & Telegraph Co. (not Corp.)
1105 (col. 1)—HAMPTON, Fred (d. 1969) (not 1967)
1106 (col. 4 under HESS, Rudolph)—Denied. . .4-23, 524D3 (not 523D3)
1163 (col. 2)—POWERINE (not POWERLINE) Oil Co.

In Vol. 1974

1134 (col. 1)—CHASE, Goodwin (not Godwin)
1205 (col. 1)—MAILLIARD (not MAILLAIRD), Rep. William S.; House seat filled 6-4, 457D1 (not 357D1)
1209 (col. 1 under MEDICINE—Diseases)—US launches. . .10-10, 894B3 (not 894B2)

In Vol. 1973

446A2—Arthur S. Flemming (not Fleming)
1163 (col. 4)—FLEMMING (not Fleming), Arthur C.

In Vol. 1972

1214 (col. 2)—PELL, Sen. Claiborne (not Clairborne)
1241, col. 4 under SYMINGTON, Sen. Stuart)—Reelected 11-7, 894C1 belongs under SYMINGTON, Rep. James W. above

In Vol. 1964

492 (col. 1)—COMBS, Bert(ram) T(homas) (not COMBS, Gov. Bert T.)

In Vol. 1962

400G3—Ex-Rep. Gracie (not Grace) Pfost
614 (col. 4)—PFOST, Gracie (not Grace)

In Vol. 1955

31 (Index, col. 1)—DWINELL (not DWINNELL), Gov.
408A2—(Republican Gov. Lane Dwinell) (not Dwinnell)

In Vol. 1954

5 (Index, col. 1 under ANDERSON, Victor E.)—Elected (not reelected 11-2, 379A2
47 (Index, col. 2)—HUNT, Sen. Lester Callaway (not Gallaway)
379A2—Victor E. Anderson (R)† not (‡)

In Vol. 1952

108 (Index, col. 2 under UMSTEAD, William B.)—Elected (not reelected) 11-4, 361J
361J—★Wm. B. Umstead (not †Wm. B. Umstead)

In Vol. 1946

47 (Index, col. 2 under KILGORE, Sen. Harley M.)—Reelected (not elected) 11-5, 358H-L
50 (Index, Col. 1 under LANGER, Sen. William)—Reelected (not elected) 11-5, 358H-L

1976	1977	1978	1979	1980

991F3—Alaskan pipeline was laid (not pipeline laid)‡
994G1—Monroe, La.,. . .Sept. 17 became the first U.S. city to default‡
997F2—. . .rise in the SRD (not SDR)‡
998D1—J. J. Macdonell (not Macdonald)‡
1000F2—[See p. 78A2 (not 78A1]‡
1004G1—Reginald Maudling (not Maulding)‡
1016E3—Argonaut (not Argonault)‡

In Vol. 1975

22F3—final three quarters of 1974 (not 1973)
474A1—$36 billion (not million)
1103 (col. 4)—GRIVAS, Gen. George (1898-1974) [not 1973]
1109 (col. 3 under IDRIS Al-Mahdi as Sanusi)—10-2 entry belongs under IDRISS, Mahamat
1128 (col. 3)—LONRHO (not LONHRO) Ltd.
1135 (col. 1)—MELENDEZ, Isais (not Isaias)
1151 (col. 3 under NORTH Atlantic Treaty Organization)—'75 mil spending. . .12-12, 954G2 (not 854G2)
1156 (col. 2)—PARROTT (not PAROTT), Dr. Max
1157 (col. 4)—PERTINI, Alessandro (not Sandro)
1163 (col. 2)—POVEDA Burbanio, Rear Adm. Alfredo (not POVERA Burbano)
1166 (col. 2)—REBOZO, Charles G. (not C.)
1170 (col. 4)—SADR, Iman Mussa al- (not SADR, Imam Moussa or SADR, Musal al-)
1172 (col. 4)—SCOTT Jr., John (Jack) (not SCOTT, Jack)
1174 (col. 1 under SHERPAO, Hyat Mohammed Khan)—Govt. . . 5-7, 348G3 (not 344G3)
1179 (col. 3)—STETLER, C. Joseph (not Joseph C.)
1183 (col. 2)—TEAGUE, Rep. Olin E. (D, Tex.)
1184 (col. 4) TIERNAN, Robert O. (not C.)
1185 (col. 3)—TODMAN, Terence (not Terrence) A.
1187 (col. 2)—TURNER, John N. (not M.)
1188 (col. 2 under Communist Party & Government)—Party card . . . 2-8, 188D2 (not 188G1)
1189 (col. 3 under Obituaries subhead—Yakobson . . . 876G3 (not 876Ge)
1190 (col. 4 under UNITED Nations—International Labor Organization)—PLO gets. . .949D2★ (not 942D2★)
1190 (col. 4 under Membership subhead)—Cncl bars S Korea 8-6; US (not UN) vetoes
1195 (col. 3 under EXPORT-Import Bank)—Dubrul (not Casey) confrmd dir 12-19, 1003F2
1212 (col. 1)—WRIGHT, Judge J. Skelly (not Skelley)
1212 (col. 4)—YOUNGSTOWN Sheet (not Steel) & Tube Co.
1213 (col. 4)—ZAREV (not ZAREN), Kiril

In Vol. 1974

1124 (col. 4)—BOSTER, Davis (not David) E.
1162 (col. 1)—COPPOLA, Francis Ford (not FORD, Francis)
1234 (col. 4 under PARKINSON, Kenneth)—AMPI . . . 1-21, 266G2 (not 226G2)
1249 (col. 2)—RUBIN, Vitali: transfer 10-18 entry under 2d head to RUBIN, Vitali above
1250 (col. 4)—SAKATA, Michita (not Michi)
1256 (col. 1)—SNYDER, Rep. Marion Gene (not Gene) (R, Ky.)
1260 (col. 4)—STRINDBERG (not STRINBERG), August
1264 (col. 1)—TENNESSEE Valley Authority belongs under U.S. GOVERNMENT
1265 (col. 4)—TKACH, Dr. Walter R. (not K.)
1265 (col. 2)—THOMSON (not THOMPSON) Jr., Gov. Meldrim

In Vol. 1973

1256 (col. 1)—SHAZLI, Maj. Gen. Saad Hussein (not Eddin) al-
1263 (col. 1)—STOESSEL (not STROESSEL) Jr., Walter J.
1268 (col. 3)—TRANSCONTINENTAL Gas Pipe Line Corp. (not TRANSCO Cos. Inc.)

In Vol. 1972

1217 (col. 2)—PHILLIPS, Christopher H. (not E.)
1226 (col. 4)—ROA (not ROA Garcia), Raul
1230 (col. 2)—SALAH (not SALAM), Abdullah

1976	1977	1978	1979	1980

1230 (col. 4)—SANTOS e Castro, Augusto (not Fernando A.)
1233 (col. 2)—SHAWA, Rashid (not Rashad)
1240 (col. 3)—SUGARMAN, Jules (not Jule) M.
1244 (col. 3)—THAPPANA (not THAPANA) Nginn, Maj. Gen.
1252 (col. 3 under AGRICULTURE, Department of)—Announces . . . 1-4 (not 1-14), 128E2

In Vol. 1971

1178 (col. 4)—QADDAFLI, Col. Muammar (not Muammer) el-
1189 (col. 2)—SHAWA, Rasdhid (not Rashad)
1191 (col. 1)—SMITH Jr., Judge John Lewis (not Lewis)